The
Bedford
Introduction
to Drama

The Bedford Introduction to Drama

SIXTH EDITION

Lee A. Jacobus
University of Connecticut

BEDFORD / ST. MARTIN'S   BOSTON ◆ NEW YORK

To David Krause

For Bedford/St. Martin's

Senior Developmental Editor: Maura Shea
Production Editor: Andrea Cava
Production Supervisor: Andrew Ensor
Marketing Manager: Adrienne Petsick
Copyeditor: Constance Day
Text Design: Claire Seng-Niemoeller
Photo Research: Martha Friedman
Cover Design: Donna Lee Dennison
Cover Photo: © Donald Cooper/Photostage. Michael Matou as Theseus/Oberon and Lindsay Kemp as Puck in the 1983 Lindsay Kemp Company's production of *A Midsummer Night's Dream.*
Composition: TexTech International
Printing and Binding: Quebecor World Taunton

President: Joan E. Feinberg
Editorial Director: Denise B. Wydra
Editor in Chief: Karen S. Henry
Director of Marketing: Karen R. Soeltz
Director of Editing, Design, and Production: Marcia Cohen
Assistant Director of Editing, Design, and Production: Elise S. Kaiser
Managing Editor: Elizabeth M. Schaaf

Library of Congress Control Number: 2008925880

Manufactured in the United States of America.

3 2 1
f   e   d   c

For information, write: Bedford/St. Martin's, 75 Arlington Street, Boston, MA 02116 (617-399-4000)

ISBN-10: 0-312-47488-1
ISBN-13: 978-0-312-47488-1

Acknowledgments

Preface for Instructors

For five best-selling editions, *The Bedford Introduction to Drama* has been the most comprehensive introductory drama resource available. With an abundance of plays, commentaries, and useful editorial features, the text continues to give students a diverse overview of dramatic literature and instructors a text with enough breadth and flexibility to complement a variety of approaches. In its sixth edition, *The Bedford Introduction to Drama* remains the most complete anthology available: a collection of fifty-four important plays that have shaped dramatic literature from the time of the early Greek dramatists to the present. A number of important features distinguish this book from other introductory drama texts. Most notably, it presents three major playwrights in greater than usual depth—three plays by William Shakespeare and two each by Sophocles and August Wilson—offering students a unique opportunity to study and write about significant figures in the development of drama. The book also offers a full array of background material about the plays and playwrights, providing more resources for students than any other drama text. Accompanying all the plays are thorough biographical and critical introductions; brief performance histories; commentaries by playwrights, directors, actors, reviewers, and critics; and photographs of landmark productions. To give students a better overall view of the periods and contexts in which individual plays are written and performed, these play-specific materials are complemented by four cultural casebooks interspersed throughout the book. Each casebook presents background materials—journal entries, letters, newspaper accounts, and essays—about specific plays and dramatic periods, enabling students to think critically about a play or group of plays through a focused study of important cultural and historical contexts.

Even when it appears most timeless, all drama, like all literature, is a product of language, style, its era, and a complex range of political, social, and ethnic influences. *The Bedford Introduction to Drama* offers a succinct but thorough history of Western drama, complemented by coverage of Asian drama. A general introduction gives an overview of the great ages of drama, the major genres and elements, and the cultural value of drama. Throughout the book, introductions to significant periods of drama, the playwrights, and the plays focus on the cultural contexts of the works and on their stage history. Timelines following the introductions to each dramatic period present important developments in theater history in their appropriate cultural contexts.

The Bedford Introduction to Drama is also a complete resource for the beginning student. In the general introduction, a discussion of the elements of drama defines the important terms and concepts and demonstrates these concepts in action, drawing its examples from Lady Isabella Augusta Gregory's one-act play, *The Rising of the Moon*. Nearly every play is accompanied by one or more striking photographs, and the plays by those playwrights who are treated in depth are illustrated by photo essays that often feature more than one production to help students understand the plays as texts to be interpreted through performance.

"Writing about Drama" at the end of the book offers students possible approaches for commenting on dramatic literature and points the way for developing ideas that can result in probing critical essays. From prewriting to outlining and drafting, the process of writing about drama is illustrated by reference to *The Rising of the Moon*, and a sample essay on the play provides one example of drama criticism. Especially useful for assignments involving attendance at theater productions, the section "How to Write a Review" analyzes professional reviews and offers suggestions for students who are writing reviews.

The "Glossary of Dramatic Terms" clearly and concisely defines concepts and terms. When these terms are first introduced and defined in the text, they appear in small capital letters.

New to This Edition
New Plays and Commentaries

Sixteen plays are new to the sixth edition, most notably the inclusion of important classics, including Molière's *Tartuffe*, William Congreve's *The Way of the World*, Eugène Ionesco's *The Bald Soprano*, Samuel Beckett's *Krapp's Last Tape*, and Edward Albee's *The Zoo Story*. Also new are innovative and award-winning contemporary plays—some never before anthologized—such as Caryl Churchill's *Far Away*, Moisés Kaufman's *The Laramie Project*, Lynn Nottage's *Intimate Apparel*, Doug Wright's *I Am My Own Wife*, Conor McPherson's *Shining City*, and Sarah Ruhl's *The Clean House*. Other new plays include Harold Pinter's *The Homecoming*, Sam Shephard's *Buried Child*, Brian Friel's *Faith Healer*, August Wilson's *Ma Rainey's Black Bottom*, and selections from Suzan-Lori Parks's *365 Days/365 Plays*. Fourteen of fifty-seven commentaries are new to this edition and provide a variety of ways for students to think about a play—from the perspective of a reviewer, an actor, a director, a set designer, and a playwright.

The sixth edition continues the tradition of offering a strong representation of multicultural and women playwrights and representing them with their most significant works. The most popular, seminal works from the fifth edition have been retained, including *A Raisin in the Sun* by Lorraine Hansberry, *The Strong Breed* by Wole Soyinka, *Zoot Suit* by Luis Valdez, *Fences* by August Wilson, and *How I Learned to Drive* by Paula Vogel, but five new plays have been added, including *Far Away* by Caryl Churchill, *Intimate Apparel* by Lynn Nottage, and *Ma Rainey's Black Bottom* by August Wilson.

New Casebooks

In addition to the cultural casebook on "The 'Woman Question' in the Late Nineteenth-Century" and the "Production Casebook on *Death of a Salesman*," the sixth edition includes two new casebooks that enable students to think critically about a play or group of plays through a focused study of important cultural and historical contexts. The first new casebook invites students to explore the popular nineteenth-century genre of American Melodrama, offering excerpts and performance images from three plays along with supporting critical commentaries that contextualize the works. The second new casebook focuses on August Wilson, enhancing student understanding of the playwright and two of his most celebrated works, *Fences* and *Ma Rainey's Black Bottom*. Students are invited to explore the major influences on his writing through critical commentary, art, poetry, and blues song lyrics.

New Emphasis on Theater Design, Staging, and Performance Style

The sixth edition is committed to deepening student understanding of drama with several new features that encourage students to think critically about all aspects of a play as a work of literature and performance. New illustrated sections on "The Actor" in each historical introduction explore the development of acting styles, methods, and techniques in every major period of drama. Expanded and richly illustrated sections on staging and theater design in each historical introduction include detailed diagrams of period theaters, along with a discussion of the major technical innovations in staging. New marginal quotations, often an appreciative comment by an actor, director, or other playwright, accompany each biographical introduction and illuminate a particular playwright or work. Finally, eighty-seven new performance photographs and stage diagrams illustrate the book more richly than ever and help students visualize the plays in performance.

Companion Web Site and DVD/VHS Library

The revised and updated companion Web site at bedfordstmartins.com/jacobus helps students succeed in the course through the use of study and discussion questions; writing assignments; Web assignments; annotated research links for the plays, playwrights, and casebooks; and links to the best online drama resources (including internship opportunities). For instructors there are a selected bibliography for the major dramatic periods and playwrights, a list of audiovisual resources, an additional cultural casebook (from the fourth edition) focusing on the Abbey Theatre and the Irish Literary Renaissance, and assignment ideas.

A selection of DVDs and videotapes of plays included in the book is available from Bedford/St. Martin's for qualified adopters. Contact your sales representative for more information.

Compact Edition

The Bedford Introduction to Drama, Sixth Edition, is also available in a compact edition containing twenty-nine plays, thirty-three commentaries, and two cultural casebooks, a stylistic casebook on American Melodrama and a production casebook on *Death of a Salesman*. The compact edition retains all of the longer book's editorial features for those instructors who want a smaller, less expensive anthology.

Acknowledgments

First, I would like to thank those who offered their advice on what to include in the first edition of this book: Jeff Glauner, Park College; Susan Smith, University of Pittsburgh; and Jordan Miller, University of Rhode Island. Second, I am grateful to those who read the introductions and commentaries in the first edition and who gave me the advantage of their knowledge and wisdom. G. Jennifer Wilson, University of California, Los Angeles; William Carroll, Boston University; Ronald Bryden, Graduate Centre for the Study of Drama, University of Toronto; Robert Dial, University of Akron; Jonnie Guerra, Mount Vernon College; and John Timpane, Lafayette College, were all unhesitating in offering suggestions and improvements.

For the second edition, experts in specific historical periods examined the introductions for accuracy and comprehensiveness. Each of the introductions was revised with their suggestions in mind. These reviewers were Michael Cadden, Princeton University; Mary Coogan, University of Colorado, Boulder; Anthony Graham-White, University of Illinois, Chicago; C. Fenno Hoffman; Robert D. Hume, Pennsylvania State University; Paul G. Reeve, University of Houston, University Park; Laurence Senelick, Tufts University; and Timothy Wiles, Indiana University, Bloomington.

I am also grateful to Keith Hull of the University of Wyoming for the warmth of his response to the book. Especially helpful in preparing the second edition were Elias Abdou, Community College of Allegheny, Pittsburgh; Robert E. Aldridge, Kirkwood Community College; Katya Amato, Portland State University; Keith Appler, University of Illinois, Urbana; Nora Bicki, University of Illinois, Champaign; Reverend Doctor Nadean Bishop, Eastern Michigan University; François Bonneville, State University of New York, Albany; Michael Boudreau, University of Illinois, Urbana; David Bratt, Winona State University; Marianne Cooley, University of Houston, University Park; Walter Creed, University of Hawaii, Manoa; Mary Beth Culp, Marymount College; Merilee Cunningham, University of Houston; Joan D'Antoni, University of Louisville; Wayne G. Deahl, Eastern Wyoming College; Charlotte Doctor, Los Angeles Pierce College; Janet Dow, Western Connecticut State University; Jerry D. Eisenhour, Eastern Illinois University; Fred M. Fetrow, United States Naval Academy; Jane E. Fisher, Canisius College; Charles Frey, University of Washington; Robert W. Funk, Eastern Illinois University; Stephen R. Grecco, Pennsylvania State University; L. W. Harrison, Santa Rosa Junior College; Dave Hartley, Central Florida Community College; Andrew Jay Hoffman, Central Connecticut State University; Claudia L. Johnson, Marquette University; Ellen Redding Kaler, University of Kansas; Harvey Kassebaum, Cuyahoga Community College; Dorothy Louise, Franklin and Marshall College; Annette McGregor, Purdue University; Jack Mahoney, Vincennes University; James Marlow, Southeastern Massachusetts University; Christy Minadeo, Eastern Michigan University; Carol A. Moore, Louisiana State University; Roark Mulligan, University of Oregon; Eric Pederson, Butler County Community College; M. Bernice Pepke, Manatee Community College; Patrick Quade, Saint Olaf College; Carol Replogle, Loyola University, Chicago; William Reynolds, Hope College; Mark Rocha, California State University, Northridge; Matthew C. Roudane, Georgia State University; Dolores J. Sarafinski, Gannon University; Carol Scklenica, Marquette University; Rodney Simard, California State University, San Bernardino; James Stephens, Marquette University; Jeannie B. Thomas, University of Oregon; Gregory Ulmer, Kearney State College; Susan Vick, Worcester Polytechnic Institute; Linda Wells, Boston University; Keith Welsh, Webster University; Virginia West, Franklin and Marshall College; Paul Wood, Villanova University; and J. S. Wszalek, James Madison University.

For the third edition, Samuel Abel of Dartmouth College reviewed the historical material for accuracy and offered a number of very useful suggestions that I incorporated into the text. I am grateful for his help and for the response of those who offered suggestions and advice for improving the book, especially Cora Agatucci, Central Oregon Community College; Joan D'Antoni, University of Louisville; Harold J. Baxter, Trinity International University; Irene Blakely, Northland College; Cynthia Bowers, Loyola University, Chicago; Jody D. Brown, Ferrum College; Mark Browning, Johnson County Community College; William D. Buckley, Indiana University NW; William J. Campbell, SUNY College of Technology at Delhi; Heather S. Collins, Mott Community College; Ruth Contrell, New Mexico State University; Kenneth Cox, Oklahoma State University; Judith P. Cronk, Oklahoma State University; Marsha Cummins, Bronx Community College; James D. Cunningham, Florida Southern College; Tom DeSpain, Chemeketa Community College; Dexter Roger Dixon, University of Arkansas; Nancy Eddy, Indiana University-Purdue University at Indianapolis; Tom Empy, Casper College; Shawn Paul Evans, University of Tennessee at Chattanooga; Harry Feiner, Queens College; Monika Fischer, University of Oregon; James Fisher, Wabash College; Kay Forston, Phillips University; John E. Hallwas, Western Illinois University; Wilma Hahn Hasse, Mitchell University; David Henry, El Paso Community College; Kirsten F. Herdd, Eastern Michigan University; D. E. Jukes, Community College of Allegheny County; E. Kahn, Lehigh University; Jackson Kesler, Western Kentucky University; Lawrence Kinsman, New Hampshire College; Terry A. Klenk, Santa Fe Community College; Marcia K. Morrison, Genesee Community College; Eva Patton, Fordham University; Richard Pettergill, University of Illinois at Chicago; David Pinner, Colgate University; Joseph Rice, University of Cincinnati; Deborah A. Ring, Case Western Reserve University; Hans H. Rudnick, Southern Illinois University; Samuel Schuman, University of North Carolina; William O. Scott, University of Kansas; Rita Smilkstein, North Seattle Community College; Gerald F. Snelson, Frostburg State University; N. J. Stanley, Agnes Scott College; Catherine Stevenson, University of Hartford; John S. Terhes, Chemeketa Community College; Charles Trainor, Siena College; Anita J. Turpin, Roanoke College; Joy Walsh, Butler County Community College; Gladdy White, Notre Dame College; Celeste Wiggins, Ursuline College; Salaam Yousif, California State University; and Ruth Zielke, Concordia College.

For the fourth edition, I am grateful to those who offered suggestions and advice for improving the book, especially David Adamson, University of North Carolina, Chapel Hill; Joan Angelis, Woodbury University; Karen C. Blansfield, University of North Carolina, Chapel Hill; Stephen F. Bloom, Emmanuel College; Cathy A. Brookshire, James Madison University; Barbara Clayton, University of Wisconsin, Madison; John J. Conlon, University of Massachusetts, Boston; Heath A. Diehl, Bowling Green State University; Richard Donnelly, University of Notre Dame; Joseph Fahey, Ohio State University; John E. R. Friedenberg, Wake Forest University; Stanton B. Garner Jr., University of Tennessee; Anthony Graham-White, University of Illinois at Chicago; Leigh Harbin, Angelo State University; Jim Hauser, William Patterson University; Don Haynes, Robert Morris College; Gregory Kable, University of North Carolina, Chapel Hill; Theresa M. Kenosa, Lincoln Land Community College; Sonya Lancaster, University of Kansas; Charlotte Langford, Pima Community College;

Sandee McGlaun, Ohio State University; Deborah Montuori, Shippensburg University; Joan Navarre, Marquette University; Susan Sanders, Northern Essex Community College; Helen Scheck, University of Albany; Joel Shatzky, SUNY College at Cortland; Michelle L. Stie, University of Kansas; James Symmons, Pennsylvania State University, Media; George Wead, James Madison University; Janet S. Wolf, SUNY College at Cortland; and Tom Zimmerman, Washtenaw Community College.

For the fifth edition, I am grateful to the following reviewers for their suggestions and feedback: Alan Ackerman, University of Toronto; Sonya Alvarado, Michigan University; Dennis Black, University of North Carolina at Charlotte; Kristin Bovaird-Abbo, University of Kansas; Doug Cummins, Furman University; Merilee Cunningham, University of Houston-Downtown; J. K. Curry, Wake Forest University; Brook Davis, Wake Forest University; Marcia J. Douglas, University of Maine; James Fisher, Wabash College; Deborah Payne Fisk, American University; Christine Frezza, Southern Utah University; Jean Dobie Giebel, Hofstra University; Kellie L. Grengs, Loyola University; Mark Harvey, University of Minnesota, Duluth; Peter Hays, University of California at Davis; Helen Killoran, Ohio University at Lancaster; David Krasner, Yale University; Holly E. McDonald, University of Central Florida; Walter Metz, Montana State University-Bozeman; Kimberly A. Miller, University of Kansas; John Patton, Troy State University; Susan Proctor, St. Gregory's University; Stephen Slimp, University of West Alabama; Annette Wannamaker, Eastern Michigan University; and Craig White, University of Houston at Clear Lake.

For the sixth edition, I am grateful to the following reviewers who offered suggestions and advice for revising the book: Jerry D. Allen, Lycoming College; Matthew Andrews, Marist College; Susan Applebaum, Loyola University; Allison Cameron, Eastern Illinois University; Doug Cummins, Furman University; Brook Davis, Wake Forest University; Cara Gabriel, American University; Patrick Immel, Northwest Missouri State University; Kathleen McGeever, Georgia College and State University; Kimberly A. Miller, Fort Hays State University; Christopher J. Mitchell, Eastern Illinois University; Heather Nathans, University of Maryland; Beth Osborne, Florida State University; Jane Peterson, Montclair State University; Korey Rothman, University of Maryland; N. J. Stanley, Lycoming College; and David Wolski, Eastern Illinois University.

I am indebted to many talented people who, were they in a drama, could constitute a crowd scene, and yet each played an indispensable solo role in making this book a reality. Martha Friedman did the photo research and, as in previous editions, secured permissions for wonderful images in an outstanding fashion. Virginia Creeden cleared the text permission for the plays and commentaries in record time. Erin McGhee did a thorough job of checking controversial facts and dates throughout the book, scrutinizing the details in the new material for accuracy and consistency.

I am especially grateful to the people who worked behind the scenes at Bedford/St. Martin's to produce this book. I thank editorial assistant Erin McGhee for coordinating reviews, managing tasks large and small to prepare the manuscript for production, and overseeing the development of content for the Web site. Managing editor Elizabeth Schaaf, production editor Andrea Cava, and production supervisor Andrew Ensor managed the production of this complex project with aplomb and kept the book on schedule. Art director Donna Dennison designed the stunning cover.

As always, I owe an immense debt of gratitude to the imaginative and intelligent guidance of Joan Feinberg, president of Bedford/St. Martin's, and her predecessor, Charles Christensen. They have been friends of this book from the beginning and have helped give it special meaning. Karen Henry, my editor and muse for the first three editions of this book, is a passionate fan of theater and the values for which this book stands. Even now she remains close to this project. Mika De Roo, my editor for the fifth edition, was enthusiastic and helpful from the first. Maura Shea, my editor for the fourth edition, and now again happily for the sixth edition, sets a standard that few can match. Her taste, judgment, and editorial eye helped make this book what it is. She is my vision of the ideal editor, both talented and skilled, and aiming unerringly to help make this the best book it can be.

Lee A. Jacobus
University of Connecticut, Storrs

Contents

The
Bedford
Introduction
to Drama

Introduction: Thinking about Drama

What Is Drama?

DRAMA is the art of representing for the pleasure of others events that happened or that we imagine happening. The primary ingredients of drama are characters, represented by players; action, described by gestures and movement; thought, implied by dialogue, words, and action; spectacle, represented by scenery, music, and costume; and, finally, audiences, who respond to this complex mixture.

When we are in the theater, we see the actors, hear the lines, are aware of the setting, and sense the theatrical community of which we are a part. Even when reading a play, we should imagine actors speaking lines and visualize a setting in which those lines are spoken. Drama is an experience in which we participate on many levels simultaneously. On one level, we may believe that what we see is really happening; on another level, we know it is only make-believe. On one level we may be amused, but on another level we realize that serious statements about our society are being made. Drama both entertains and instructs.

When Aristotle wrote about drama in the *Poetics*, a work providing one of the earliest and most influential theories of drama, he began by explaining it as the imitation of an action (MIMESIS). Those analyzing his work have interpreted this statement in several ways. One interpretation is that drama imitates life. On the surface, such an observation may seem simple, even obvious. But on reflection we begin to find complex significance in his comment. The drama of the Greeks, for example, with its intense mythic structure, its formidable speeches, and its profound actions, often seems larger than life or other than life. Yet we recognize characters saying words that we ourselves are capable of saying, doing things that we ourselves might do. The great Greek tragedies are certainly lifelike and certainly offer literary mirrors in which we can examine human nature. And the same is true of Greek comedies.

The relationship between drama and life has always been subtle and complex. In some plays, such as Luigi Pirandello's *Six Characters in Search of an Author,* it is one of the central issues. We begin our reading or viewing of most plays knowing that the dramatic experience is not absolutely real in the sense that, for example, the actor playing Hamlet does not truly die or truly see a ghost or truly frighten his mother. The play imitates those imagined actions,

1

but when done properly it is realistic enough to make us fear, if only for a moment, that they could be real.

We see significance in the actions Hamlet imitates; his actions help us live our own lives more deeply, more intensely, because they give us insight into the possibilities of life. We are all restricted to living this life as ourselves; drama is one art form that helps us realize the potential of life, for both the good and the bad. In an important sense, we can share the experience of a character such as Hamlet when he soliloquizes over the question of whether it is better to die than to live in a world filled with sin and crime.

Drama and Ritual

Such imaginative participation is only a part of what we derive from drama. In its origins, drama seems to have evolved from ancient Egyptian and Greek rituals, ceremonies that were performed the same way again and again and were thought to have a propitious effect on the relationship between the people and their gods.

In ancient Egypt some religious rituals evolved into repeated passion plays, such as those celebrating Isis and Osiris at the festivals of Heb-Seb at Sakkara some three thousand years ago. Greek drama was first performed during yearly religious celebrations dedicated to the god Dionysus. The early Greek playwrights, such as Sophocles in *Oedipus Rex* and *Antigone,* emphasized the interaction between the will of the gods and the will of human beings, often pitting the truths of men and women against the truths of the gods.

In the thirteenth and fourteenth centuries drama thrived in Japan, reaching a pinnacle in the Nō drama of Zeami Motokiyo and his father, Kan'ami. Japanese Nō drama combines music and movement in intricate patterns of ritualistic formality. Nō developed in a Buddhist environment and expressed the deep religious values associated with Buddhism. Although it began as a provincial form, the beauty of Nō—its deep meditative pauses and extraordinary dance-like movement—quickly made it the major style of drama in medieval Japan.

The rebirth of Western drama in the Middle Ages—after the fall of Rome and the loss of classical artistic traditions—took place first in monasteries, then later in the cathedrals of Europe. It evolved from medieval religious ceremonies that helped the faithful understand more about their own moral predicament. *Everyman,* a late play in the medieval theater (it was written about 1500), concerns itself with the central issue of reward and punishment after this life because the soul is immortal.

Drama: The Illusion of Reality

From the beginning, drama has had the capacity to hold up an illusion of reality like the reflection in a mirror: we take the reality for granted while recognizing that it is nonetheless illusory. As we have seen, Aristotle described DRAMATIC ILLUSION as an imitation of an action. But unlike the reflection in a mirror, the action of most drama is not drawn from our actual experience of life but from our potential or imagined experience. In the great Greek drama, the illusion includes the narratives of ancient myths that were thought to offer profound illumination. The interpretation of the myths by the Greek playwrights over a two-hundred-year period helped the Greek people participate in the myths, understand them, and apply the values of those myths to their daily lives.

Different ages have had different approaches to representing reality onstage. Greek actors spoke in verse and wore masks. The staging consisted of very little setting and no special costumes except for some comedies and satyr plays. Medieval drama was sometimes acted on pushwagons and carts, but the special machinery developed to suggest hellfire and the presence of devils was said to be so realistic as to be frightening. Elizabethan audiences were accustomed to actors who spoke directly to the crowds at their feet near the apron of the stage. All Elizabethan plays were done in essentially contemporary clothing, often with no more scenery than a suggestion in the spoken descriptions of the players. The actors recited their lines in verse, except when the author had a particular reason to use prose—for example, to imply that the speaker was of low social station. Yet Elizabethans reported that their theater was much like life itself.

In Shakespeare's *A Midsummer Night's Dream,* fairies, enchantments, an ass's head on the shoulders of a man—all these are presented as illusions, and we accept them. They inform the audience—in Shakespeare's day and in modern times—not by showing us ourselves in a mirror but by demonstrating that even fantastic realities have significance for us.

Certainly *A Midsummer Night's Dream* gives us insight into the profound range of human emotions. We learn about the pains of rejection when we see Helena longing for Demetrius, who in turn longs for Hermia. We learn about jealousy and possessiveness when we see Oberon cast a spell on his wife, Titania, over a dispute concerning a changeling. And we learn, too, about the worldly ambitions of the "rude mechanicals" who themselves put on a play whose reality they fear might frighten their audience. They solve the problem by reminding their audience that it is only a play and that they need not fear that reality will spoil their pleasure.

In modern drama the dramatic illusion of reality includes not just the shape of an action, the events, and the characters but also the details of everyday life. When the action changes locale, the setting changes as well. Some contemporary playwrights make an effort to re-create a reality close to the one we live in. Some modern plays, such as August Wilson's *Fences,* make a precise representation of reality a primary purpose, shaping the tone of the language to reflect the way modern people speak, re-creating contemporary reality in the setting, language, and other elements of the drama.

But describing a play as an illusion of reality in no way means that it represents the precise reality that we take for granted in our everyday experience. Rather, drama ranges widely and explores multiple realities, some of which may seem very close to our own and some of which may seem improbably removed from our everyday experience.

Seeing a Play Onstage

For an audience, drama is one of the most powerful artistic experiences. When we speak about participating in drama, we mean that as a member of the audience we become a part of the action that unfolds. This is a mysterious phenomenon.

When we see a play today, we are usually seated in a darkened theater looking at a lighted stage. In ages past, this contrast was not the norm. Greek plays took place outdoors during the morning and the afternoon; most Elizabethan plays were staged outdoors in the afternoon; in the Renaissance, some plays began to be staged indoors with ingenious systems of lighting that involved candles and reflectors. In the early nineteenth century, most theaters used gaslight onstage; electricity took over in the later part of the century, and its use has grown increasingly complex. In most large theaters today computerized lighting boards have replaced Renaissance candles.

Sitting in the darkness has made the experience of seeing Greek and Elizabethan plays much different for us than it was for the original audiences. We do not worry about being seen by the "right people" or about studying the quality of the audience, as people did during the Restoration in the late seventeenth century. The darkness isolates us from all except those who sit adjacent to us. Yet we instantly respond when others in the audience laugh, when they gasp, when they shift restlessly. We recognize in those moments that we are part of a larger community drawn together by theater and that we are all involved in the dramatic experience.

Theaters and Their Effect

Different kinds of theaters make differing demands on actors and audiences. Despite its huge size, the open ARENA style theater of the early Greeks brought the audience into a special kind of intimacy with the actors. The players came very close to the first rows of seats, and the acoustics sometimes permitted even a whisper onstage to be audible in the far seats. The Greek theater also imparted a sense of formality to the occasion of drama. For one thing, its regularity and circularity were accompanied by a relatively rigid seating plan. The officials and nobility sat in special seats. Then each section of the theater was given over to specific families, and the less desirable edges of the seating area were devoted to travelers and strangers to the town. One knew one's place in the Greek theater. Its regularity gave the community a sense of order.

Medieval theater also gave its audiences a sense of community, both when it used playing areas called *mansions* inside and outside the churches and when it used wagons wheeled about in processions in the streets or outside the city walls. That the medieval theater repeated the same cycles of plays again and again for about two hundred years, to the delight of many European communities, tells us something about the stability of those communities. Their drama was integrated with their religion, and both helped them express their sense of belonging to the church and the community.

In some medieval performances the actors came into the audience, breaking the sense of distance or the illusion of separation. It is difficult for us to know how much participation and involvement in the action the medieval audience felt. Modern audiences have responded very well to productions of medieval plays such as *The Second Shepherds' Pageant, Noah's Flood,* and *Everyman,* and we have every reason to think that medieval audiences enjoyed their dramas immensely. The guilds that performed them took pride in making their plays as exciting and involving as possible.

The Elizabethan playhouse was a wooden structure providing an enclosed space, approximately seventy-two feet in diameter, around a courtyard open to the sky. A covered stage thrust into the courtyard. As in the Greek theater, the audience was arranged somewhat by social station. Around the stage, which was about five feet off the ground, stood the groundlings, those who paid the least for their entrance. Then in covered galleries in the building itself sat patrons who paid extra for a seat. The effect of the enclosed structure was of a small, contained world. Actors were in the habit of speaking directly to members of the audience, and the audience rarely kept a polite silence. It was a busy, humming theater that generated intimacy and involvement between actors and audience.

The proscenium stage of the nineteenth and twentieth centuries distanced the audience from the play, providing a clear frame (the PROSCENIUM) behind which the performers acted out their scenes. This detachment was especially effective for plays that demanded a high degree of realism because the effect of the proscenium is to make the audience feel that it is witnessing the action as a silent observer, looking in as if through an imaginary fourth wall on a living room or other intimate space in which the action takes place. The proscenium arch gives the illusion that the actors are in a world of their own, unaware of the audience's presence.

In the twentieth century some of the virtues of the Greek arena theater, or THEATER IN THE ROUND, were rediscovered. In an effort to close the distance between audience and players, Antonin Artaud, the French actor and director, developed in the 1920s and 1930s a concept called the *theater of cruelty*. Using theater in the round, Artaud robbed the audience of the comfort of watching a distant stage and pressed his actors into the space of the viewers. His purpose was to force theatergoers to deal with the primary issues of the drama by stripping them of the security of darkness and anonymity. Theaters in the Soviet Union and Britain developed similar spaces in the 1930s and 1940s, and since the 1950s the Arena Theater in Washington, D.C., and the Circle in the Square in New York City have continued the tradition.

Twenty-first-century theater is eclectic. It uses thrust, arena, proscenium, and every other kind of stage already described. Some contemporary theater also converts nontheatrical space, such as warehouses or city streets, into space for performance.

Reading a Play

Reading a play is a different experience from seeing it enacted. For one thing, readers do not have the benefit of the interpretations made by a director, actors, and scene designers in presenting a performance. These interpretations are all critical judgments based on a director's ideas of how the play should be presented and on actors' insights into the meaning of the play.

A reading of a play produces an interpretation that remains in our heads and is not translated to the stage. The dramatic effect of the staging is lost to us unless we make a genuine effort to visualize it and to understand its contribution to the dramatic experience. For a fuller experience of the drama when reading plays, one should keep in mind the historical period and the conventions of staging that are appropriate to the period and that are specified by the playwright.

Some plays were prepared by their authors for reading as well as for staging, as evident in plays whose stage directions supply information that would be unavailable to an audience, such as the color of the characters' eyes, characters' secret motives, and other such details. Occasionally, stage directions, such as those of Bernard Shaw and Tennessee Williams, are written in a poetic prose that can be appreciated only by a reader.

It is not a certainty that seeing a play will produce an experience more "true" to the play's meaning than reading it. Every act of reading silently or speaking the lines aloud is an act of interpretation. No one can say which is the best interpretation. Each has its own merits, and the ideal is probably to read and see any play.

The Great Ages of Drama

Certain historical periods have produced great plays and great playwrights, although why some periods generate more dramatic activity than others is still a matter of conjecture for scholars examining the social, historical, and religious conditions of the times. Each of the great ages of drama has affected the way plays have been written, acted, and staged in successive ages. In every age, drama borrows important elements from each earlier period.

Egyptian Drama

Although scholars disagree in their interpretations of archaeological evidence, the likelihood of a highly developed ancient Egyptian drama is considerable. One of the key artifacts is an incised stone stela (c. 1868 BCE) which describes the roles that an official named Ikhernofret played in a celebration that included characters and dramatic action. The Abydos Passion Play, as some modern scholars call this event, was performed annually from approximately 2500 to 500 BCE. It is the story of Osiris (the equivalent of the Greek Dionysus), who was murdered in an act of trickery by his jealous brother Seth. Osiris was dismembered (as was Dionysus in Greek myth) and his parts scattered over the land. Isis, both wife and sister of Osiris, gathered most of the parts of Osiris in order to make possible his resurrection. The celebration seems to have been timed to reflect a pattern of agricultural renewal that the rebirth myth of Osiris satisfies. In his account of his role in the event, as recorded on the stela, Ikhernofret says,

I did everything that His Person commanded, putting into effect my lord's command for his father, Osiris-Khentyamentiu, Lord of Abydos, great of power, who is in the Thinite nome. I acted as beloved son of Osiris-Khentyamentiu. I embellished his great barque of eternity; I made for it a shrine which displays the beauties of Khentyamentiu, in gold, silver, lapis-lazuli, bronze, sesnedjem-wood and cedar[?]. I fashioned the gods in his train. I made their shrines anew. I caused the temple priesthood to do their duties, I caused them to know the custom of every day, the festival of the Head-of-the-Year. I controlled work on the neshmet-barque; I fashioned the shrine and adorned the breast of the Lord of Abydos with lapis-lazuli and turquoise, electrum and every precious stone, as an adornment of the divine limbs. I changed the clothes of the god at his appearance, in the office of Master of Secrets and in my job as sem-priest. I was clean of arm in adoring the god, a sem clean of fingers.

I organized the going forth of Wepwawet when he proceeded to avenge his father; I drove away the rebels from the neshmet-barque; I overthrew the enemies of Osiris; I celebrated the great going forth. I followed the god at his going, and caused the ship to sail, Thoth steering the sailing. I equipped the barque with a chapel and affixed (Osiris's) beautiful adornments when he proceeded to the district of Peqer. I cleared the ways of the god to his tomb before Peqer. I avenged Wennefer that day of the great fight; I overthrew all his enemies upon the sandbanks of Nedyt; I caused him to proceed into the great barque. It raised up his beauties, I making glad the people/ tomb owners of the Eastern Desert, creating joy amongst the people/tomb owners of the Western Desert; they saw the beauties of the neshmet-barque when it touched land at Abydos, when it brought Osiris-Khentyamentiu to his palace; I followed the god to his house, I carried out his purification and extended his seat and solved the problems of his residence [. . . and amongst] his entourage.[1]

Parts of the celebration were public in the outdoors, but parts were also played within the walls of the temple by priests. Little if anything is known about the mysteries they performed, but Herodotus (c. 484–c. 430 BCE), who claimed to have traveled in Egypt, reported seeing public participation in mock battles associated with the celebration.

Another festival called the Heb-Seb, performed at the pyramid complex of Sakkara at the thirtieth year of a pharaoh's reign (and then every third year following), involved dance, music, and pageantry that closely resembled dramatic action. The purpose of the festival was to celebrate the longevity of the pharaoh and the resultant wellness of the land. The associated "Pyramid Texts" from Sakkara (c. 3000 BCE) also treat the resurrection of Osiris and may imply the existence of an early form of the celebration of Heb-Seb. All these festivals, supplemented by those from Busiris and Memphis in Egypt, suggest that although the Greeks believed they had invented drama, it is much more likely that the Egyptians had done so.

Greek Drama

The Greeks of the fifth century BCE are credited with the first masterful dramatic age, which lasted from the birth of Aeschylus (c. 525 BCE) to the death of Aristophanes (c. 385 BCE). Their theaters were supported by public funds, and the playwrights competed for prizes during the great festivals of Dionysus. Sometimes as many as ten to fifteen thousand people sat in the theaters and watched with a sense of delight and awe as the actors played out their tales.

Theater was extremely important to the Greeks as a way of interpreting their relationships with their gods and of reinforcing their sense of community. The fifth-century BCE audience, mostly wealthy citizens, came early in the morning and spent the entire day in the theater. Drama for the Greeks was not mere escapism or entertainment, not a frill or a luxury. Connected as it was with religious festivals, it was a cultural necessity.

Sophocles' plays *Oedipus Rex* and *Antigone* are examples of the powerful tragedies that have transfixed audiences for centuries. Euripides, slightly younger than Sophocles, was also a prize-winning tragedian. His *Trojan Women, Alcestis, Medea, Bacchae,* and *Elektra [Electra]* are still performed and still exert an influence on today's drama. The same is true of Aeschylus, who was slightly older than both and whose *Agamemnon, The Libation Bearers, The Eumenides* (known collectively as the *Oresteia*), and *Prometheus Bound* have all been among the most lasting of plays.

In addition to such great tragedians, the Greeks also produced the important comedians Aristophanes and Menander (late fourth century BCE), whose work has been plundered for plays as diverse as a Shakespeare comedy and a Broadway musical. Aristophanes' *Lysistrata,* in which the Athenian and Spartan women agree to withhold sex from their husbands until the men promise to

[1]From http://www.touregypt.net/passionplay.htm; also in Henry Breasted's *Ancient Records of Egypt,* part 2 (1906–07).

stop making war, is a powerful social comedy. Menander produced a more subtle type of comedy that made the culture laugh at itself. Both styles of comedy are the staple of popular entertainment even today. Menander's social comedies were the basis of comedy in which society's ways of behavior are criticized. Such social comedy is exemplified in William Congreve's eighteenth-century *The Way of the World* and Molière's *Tartuffe*.

Roman Drama

The Romans became aware of Greek drama in the third century BCE and began to import Greek actors and playwrights. Because of many social and cultural differences between the societies, however, drama never took a central role in the life of the average Roman. Seneca, who is now viewed as Rome's most important tragedian, almost certainly wrote his plays to be read rather than to be seen onstage.

Roman comedy produced two great playwrights, Plautus and Terence, who helped develop the STOCK (or type) CHARACTER, such as the skinflint or the prude. Plautus was the great Roman comedian in the tradition of Menander. Plautus's best-known plays are *The Braggart Warrior* and *The Twin Menaechmi;* during the Renaissance, when all European schoolchildren read Latin, his works were favorites.

Terence's work was praised during the Middle Ages and the Renaissance as being smoother, more elegant, and more polished and refined than Plautus's. In his own age Terence was less admired by the general populace but more admired by connoisseurs of drama. His best-known plays — *The Woman of Andros, Phormio,* and *The Brothers* — are rarely performed today.

Drama took its place beside many other forms of entertainment in Roman culture — sports events, gladiator battles to the death, chariot races, the slaughter of wild beasts, and sacrifices of Christians and others to animals. The Roman public, when it did attend plays, enjoyed farces and relatively coarse humor. The audiences for Plautus and Terence, aristocratic in taste, may not have represented the cross-section of the community that was typical of Greek audiences.

Medieval Drama

After the fall of Rome and the spread of the Goths and Visigoths across southern Europe in the fifth century CE, Europe experienced a total breakdown of the strong central government Rome had provided. When Rome fell, Greek and Roman culture virtually disappeared. The great classical texts went largely unread until the end of the medieval period in the fourteenth and fifteenth centuries; however, expressions of culture, including art forms such as drama, did not entirely disappear. During the medieval period the Church's power and influence grew extensively, and it tried to fill the gap left by the demise of the Roman empire. The Church became a focus of both religious and secular activity for people all over Europe.

After almost five centuries of relative inactivity, European drama was reborn in religious ceremonies in monasteries. It moved inside churches, then out of doors by the twelfth century, perhaps because its own demands outgrew its circumstances. Drama had become more than an adjunct to the religious ceremonies that had spawned it.

One reason why the medieval European communities regarded their drama so highly is that it expressed many of their concerns and values. The age was highly religious; in addition, the people who produced the plays were members of guilds whose personal pride was represented in their work. Their plays came to be called MYSTERY PLAYS because the trade that each guild represented was a special skill—a mystery to the average person. Of course, the pun on religious mystery was understood by most audiences.

Many of these plays told stories drawn from the Bible. The tales of Noah's Ark, Abraham and Isaac, and Samson and Delilah all had dramatic potential, and the mystery plays capitalized on that potential, as did plays on the life and crucifixion of Christ. Among mystery plays, *The Second Shepherds' Pageant* and *Abraham and Isaac* are still performed regularly.

Most mystery plays were gathered into groups of plays called CYCLES dramatizing incidents from the Bible, among other sources. They were usually performed outdoors, at times on movable wagons that doubled as stages. Either the audience moved from wagon to wagon to see each play in a cycle, or the wagons moved among the audience.

By the fifteenth and sixteenth centuries, a form of play developed that was not associated with cycles or with the guilds. These were the MORALITY PLAYS, and their purpose was to touch on larger contemporary issues that had a moral overtone. *Everyman,* the best known of the morality plays, was performed in many nations in various languages.

Renaissance Drama   The revival of learning in the Renaissance, beginning in Italy in the fourteenth century, had considerable effect on drama because classical Greek and Roman plays were discovered and studied. In the academies in Italy, some experiments in re-creating Greek and Roman plays introduced music into drama. New theaters, such as Teatro Olympico in Vicenza (1579), were built to produce these plays; they allow us to see how the Renaissance reconceived the classical stage. Some of these experiments developed into modern opera. The late medieval traditions of the Italian theater's COMMEDIA DELL'ARTE, a stylized improvisational slapstick comedy performed by actors' guilds, began to move outside Italy into other European nations. The commedia's stock characters, Harlequins and Pulcinellas, began to appear in many countries in Europe.

Elizabethan and Jacobean (named for King James I, who succeeded Elizabeth and reigned from 1603 to 1625) drama developed most fully during the fifty years from approximately 1590 to 1640. Audiences poured into the playhouses eager for plays about history and for the great tragedies of Christopher Marlowe, such as *Doctor Faustus,* and of Shakespeare, including *Macbeth, Hamlet, Othello, Julius Caesar,* and *King Lear.* But there were others as well: Middleton and Rowley's *The Changeling,* Cyril Tourneur's *Revenger's Tragedy,* and John Webster's *The White Devil* and his sensational *The Duchess of Malfi.*

The great comedies of the age came mostly from the pen of William Shakespeare: *A Midsummer Night's Dream, The Comedy of Errors, As You Like It, Much Ado about Nothing, The Taming of the Shrew,* and *Twelfth Night.* Many of these plays derived from Italian originals, usually novellas or popular poems and sometimes comedies. But Shakespeare, of course, elevated and vastly improved everything he borrowed.

Ben Jonson, a playwright who was significantly influenced by the classical writers, was also well represented on the Elizabethan stage, with *Volpone,*

The Alchemist, Everyman in His Humour, Bartholomew Fair, and other durable comedies. Jonson is also important for his contributions to the MASQUE, an aristocratic entertainment that featured music, dance, and fantastic costuming. His *Masque of Blackness* was performed in the royal court with the queen as a performer.

The Elizabethan stage sometimes grew bloody, with playwrights and audiences showing a passion for tragedies that, like *Hamlet,* centered on revenge and often ended with most of the characters meeting a premature death. Elizabethan plays also show considerable variety, with many plays detailing the history of English kings and, therefore, the history of England. It was a theater of powerful effect, and contemporary diaries indicate that the audiences delighted in it.

Theaters also flourished in Spain in this period, producing Lope de Vega (1562–1635), who may have written as many as seventeen hundred plays. Vega's immediate successor, Pedro Calderón de la Barca (1600–1681), is sometimes considered to be more polished in style, but also more stiffly aristocratic in appeal. He wrote fewer plays than Vega, but still produced an amazing body of work. He is said to have written at least 111 dramas and seventy or eighty *auto sacramentales,* the Spanish equivalent of religious morality plays designed for special religious ceremonies. Calderón is best known for *La vida es sueño (Life Is a Dream),* which is still performed today.

Theaters in Shakespeare's day were built outside city limits in seamy neighborhoods near brothels and bear-baiting pits, where chained bears were set upon by large dogs for the crowd's amusement. Happily, the theaters' business was good; the plays were constructed of remarkable language that seems to have fascinated all social classes, since all flocked to the theater by the thousands.

Late Seventeenth- and Eighteenth-Century Drama

After the Puritan reign in England from 1642 (when the theaters were closed) to 1660, during which dramatic productions were almost nonexistent, the theater was suddenly revived. In 1660 Prince Charles, sent to France by his father during the English Civil War, was invited back to be king, thus beginning what was known in England as the Restoration. It was a gay, exciting period in stark contrast to the gray Puritan era. During the period new indoor theaters modeled on those in France were built, and a new generation of actors and actresses (women took part in plays for the first time in England) came forth to participate in the dramatic revival.

Since the mid-1600s, French writers, interpreting Aristotle's description of Greek drama, had leaned toward development of a classical theater, which was supposed to observe the "unities" of time, place, and action: a play had one plot and one setting and covered the action of one day. In 1637 Pierre Corneille wrote *Le Cid,* using relatively modern Spanish history as his theme and following certain classical techniques. Jean-Baptiste Racine was Corneille's successor, and his plays became even more classical by focusing on classical topics. His work includes *Andromache, Britannicus,* and, possibly his best play, *Phaedra.* Racine retired from the stage at the end of the seventeenth century, but he left a powerful legacy of classicism that reached well into the eighteenth century.

Molière, an actor and producer, was the best comedian of seventeenth-century France. Among his plays, *Tartuffe, The Misanthrope,* and several others are still produced regularly in the West. Molière was classical in his way, borrowing ancient comedy's technique of using type, or stock, characters in his social satires.

Among the important playwrights of the new generation were Aphra Behn, the first professional English female writer, whose play *The Rover* was one of the most popular plays of the late seventeenth century, and William Congreve, whose best-known play, *The Way of the World*, is often still produced. The latter is a lively comedy that aimed to chasten as well as entertain Congreve's audiences.

The eighteenth century saw the tradition of social comedy continued in Richard Brinsley Sheridan's *School for Scandal* and Oliver Goldsmith's *She Stoops to Conquer*. The drama of this period focuses on social manners, and much of it is SATIRE—that is, drama that offers mild criticism of society and holds society up to comic ridicule. But underlying that ridicule is the relatively noble motive of reforming society. We can see some of that motive at work in the plays of Molière and Goldsmith.

During much of the eighteenth century, theater in France centered on the court and was controlled by a small coterie of snobbish people. The situation in England was not quite the same, although the audiences were snobbish and socially conscious. They went to the theater to be seen, and they often went in claques—groups of like-minded patrons who applauded or booed together to express their views. Theater was important, but attendance at it was like a material possession, something to be displayed for others to admire.

A wide variety of drama was extant in Japan in the late sixteenth and early seventeenth centuries. Kabuki theater, the most remarkable of popular Japanese drama, evolved in this period as a lasting form still seen today in theaters around the world. Kabuki is performed with puppets, and the resulting intensity would have surprised Western playwrights and audiences of that time. The emphasis shifted from the personality of the player to the situations and circumstances portrayed in the drama. Chikamatsu Monzaemon developed the form and was the most inventive of the Kabuki playwrights. His play *The Love Suicides at Sonezaki* was based on a genuine love suicide (*shinjū* in Japanese) and eventually created a craze for love suicide plays that ultimately resulted in an edict in 1722 that banned them entirely. Some modern writers claim that the quality of his drama was not equaled in Japan for more than two hundred years.

Nineteenth-Century Drama through the Turn of the Twentieth Century

English playwrights alone produced more than thirty thousand plays during the nineteenth century. Most of the plays were sentimental, melodramatic, and dominated by a few very powerful actors, stars who often overwhelmed the works written for them. The audiences were quite different from those of the seventeenth and eighteenth centuries. The upwardly mobile urban middle classes and the moneyed factory and mill owners who had benefited economically from the industrial revolution demanded a drama that would entertain them.

The new audiences were not especially well educated, nor were they interested in plays that were intellectually demanding. Instead, they wanted escapist and sentimental entertainment that was easy to respond to and did not challenge their basic values. Revivals of old plays and adaptations of Shakespeare were also common in the age, with great stars like Edmund Kean, Sir Henry Irving, Edwin Forrest, Edwin Booth, and William Macready using the plays as platforms for overwhelming, and sometimes overbearing, performances.

Thrillers were especially popular, as were historical plays and melodramatic plays featuring a helpless heroine.

As an antidote to such a diet, the new Realist movement in literature, marked by the achievements of French novelists Émile Zola and Gustave Flaubert, finally struck the stage in the 1870s and 1880s in plays by August Strindberg and Henrik Ibsen. Revolutionizing Western drama, these Scandinavians forced their audiences to pay attention to important issues and deeper psychological concerns than earlier audiences had done.

Strindberg's *Miss Julie,* a psychological study, challenged social complacency based on class and social differences. Ibsen's *A Doll House* was a blow struck for feminism, but it did not amuse all audiences. Some were horrified at the thought that Nora Helmer was to be taken as seriously as her husband. Such a view was heretical, but it was also thrilling for a newly awakened European conscience. Those intellectuals and writers who responded positively to Ibsen, including Bernard Shaw, acted as the new conscience and began a move that soon transformed drama. Feminism is also a theme, but perhaps less directly, of Ibsen's *Hedda Gabler,* the story of a woman whose frustration at being cast into an inferior role contributes to a destructive—and ultimately self-destructive—impulse. Both plays are acted in a physical setting that seems to be as ordinary as a nineteenth-century sitting room, with characters as small—and yet as large—as the people who watched them.

The Russian Anton Chekhov's plays *Three Sisters, Uncle Vanya,* and *The Cherry Orchard,* written at the turn of the twentieth century, are realistic as well, but they are also patient examinations of character rather than primarily problem plays—like Ibsen's successful dramas *Ghosts* and *The Master Builder.* Chekhov is aware of social change in Russia, especially the changes that revealed a hitherto repressed class of peasants evolving into landowners and merchants. *The Cherry Orchard* is suffused with an overpowering sense of inevitability through which Chekhov depicts the conflict between the necessity for change and a nostalgia for the past. The comedies of Oscar Wilde, such as *Lady Windermere's Fan* and *The Importance of Being Earnest,* poked fun at the foibles of the upper classes. Amusing as they are, their satirical quality constitutes social criticism.

These plays introduced a modern realism of a kind that was rare in earlier drama. Melodrama of the nineteenth century was especially satisfying to mass audiences because the good characters were very good, the bad characters were very bad, and justice was meted out at the end. But it is difficult in Chekhov to be sure who the heroes and villains are. Nothing is as clear-cut in these plays as it is in popular melodramas. Instead, Chekhov's plays are as complicated as life itself. Such difficulties of distinction have become the norm of the most important of contemporary drama.

Drama in the Early and Mid-Twentieth Century

The drama of the early twentieth century nurtured the seeds of late nineteenth-century realism into bloom, but sometimes this drama experimented with audience expectations. Eugene O'Neill's *Desire under the Elms* is a tragedy that features the ordinary citizen rather than the noble. This play focuses on New England farmers as tragic characters. Arthur Miller's *Death of a Salesman* invokes a sense of dreadful inevitability within the world of the commercial salesman, the ordinary man. As in many other twentieth-century tragedies, the point is that the life of the ordinary man can be as tragic as that of Oedipus.

Luigi Pirandello experiments with reality in *Six Characters in Search of an Author,* a play that has a distinctly absurd quality, since it expects us to accept the notion that the characters on the stage are waiting for an author to put them into a play. Pirandello plays with our sense of illusion and of expectation and realism to such an extent that he forces us to reexamine our concepts of reality.

Bertolt Brecht's *Mother Courage,* an example of what the playwright called EPIC DRAMA, explores war from a complex series of viewpoints. On the one hand Courage is a powerful figure who has been seen as a model of endurance, but Brecht also wanted his audience to see that Courage brings on much of her own suffering by trying to profit from war. The sole act of self-sacrifice in the play comes at the end, when Kattrin beats her drum to warn villagers of the approach of a destroying army. Brecht produced the play early in World War II as a protest. Playwrights around the world responded to events such as World War I, the Communist revolution, and the Great Depression by writing plays that no longer permitted audiences to sit comfortably and securely in darkened theaters. Brecht and other playwrights instead came out to get their audiences, to make them feel and think, to make them realize their true condition.

Samuel Beckett's dramatic career began with *Waiting for Godot,* which audiences interpreted as an examination of humans' eternal vigilance for the revelation of God or of some transcendent meaning in their lives. In the play, Godot never comes, yet the characters do not give up hope. *Endgame*'s characters seem to be awaiting the end of the world: in the 1950s the shadow of nuclear extinction cast by the cold war dominated most people's imagination.

Tennessee Williams examines a physically and psychically frail young woman's withdrawal from life in *The Glass Menagerie.* The play derives from personal experience: Williams's sister was such a woman. Personal experience may also inform his *Cat on a Hot Tin Roof,* which portrays themes of homosexuality and marital sexual tension—themes that were not openly discussed in contemporary American theater except in veiled mythic terms, in the manner, for example, of O'Neill's *Desire under the Elms.*

Nigerian playwright Wole Soyinka, who won the Nobel Prize for literature in 1986, portrays the complex intersection of a person's past and the present in his play *The Strong Breed,* set in an African village reminiscent of the Greek *polis.* Indeed, he has experimented with Greek tragic forms in *The Bacchae of Euripides,* which is also set in Africa. Soyinka's insights into the nature of culture and drama provide us with a new way of reflecting on drama's power in our lives.

Modern dramatists from the turn of the twentieth century to the Korean War explored in many different directions and developed new approaches to themes of dramatic illusion as well as to questions concerning the relationship of an audience to the stage and the players.

Contemporary Drama   The twenty-first-century stage is vibrant. The great commercial theaters of England and the United States are sometimes hampered by high production costs, but regional theaters everywhere are producing fine drama. The National Theatre in London has made inexpensive seats available for most of its plays, and other theaters are doing the same. In Latin America, Germany, Japan, China, France, and elsewhere, the theater is active and exciting. Poland's experiments in drama, led by Jerzy Grotowski's "Poor Theater," inspired experimentation that has spread throughout the world of drama. Russia, too, has produced a number of plays that have been given a worldwide currency.

The hallmark of many of these plays has been experimentalism. Caryl Churchill's *Top Girls* features characters who claim to be Pope Joan, Patient Griselda, and Lady Nijo, as well as being "themselves" — all this in the milieu of a feminist employment agency. Her newer play, *Far Away*, is a portrait of an apocalyptic world as viewed by a girl.

Sam Shepard, well known as an actor, was for many years among the most experimental playwrights living in New York's Greenwich Village. His *True West* begins as a relatively straightforward play about Austin and Lee, two brothers, but quickly reveals the drama that lies beneath the surface. Lee has arrived to steal his mother's television set but ends by stealing something of his brother's personality. *Buried Child* examines some frightening secrets in a dysfunctional family.

Luis Valdez's *Zoot Suit* explores 1940s Los Angeles when the zoot suit riots brought Chicano youth into clashes with sailors and determined police. The play is intense and filled with dynamic music, powerful language, and action.

Not all modern theater is experimental, however. August Wilson's *Fences* shows us the pain of life at the lower end of the economic ladder in a form that is recognizably realistic and plausible. The play is set in the 1950s and focuses on Troy Maxon, a black man, and his relationship with his son and his wife. Tenement life is one subject of the play, but the most important subject is the courage it takes to keep going after tasting defeat. The entire drama develops within the bounds of conventional nineteenth-century realism.

Suzan-Lori Parks has made a career of writing experimental plays, from the Brechtian *The Death of the Last Black Man in the Whole Entire World*, which structures itself in "panels" — brief, intense scenes that connect imaginatively — to *365 Days/365 Plays*, for which she wrote a play a day for a year. Tony Kushner employs similar techniques in *Angels in America*. Its brilliantly staged scenes are filled with emotional intensity, and the audience is carried on waves of imaginative speculation on America's history as well as on America's present. Moisés Kaufman and the members of the Tectonic Theater Project used highly inventive means to produce *The Laramie Project*, a play built around the murder of a young gay man, Matthew Shepherd, in Wyoming. It was a shocking crime both to the nation at large and to the local community in Laramie. The members of the project conducted many interviews with people in Laramie over a period of more than a year, and the resultant drama, largely developed from the interviews, revealed a range of surprising responses and surprising emotions. Doug Wright's *I Am My Own Wife* is an experimental play that attempts to portray the life of Charlotte von Mahlsdorf, a transvestite who survived both the Nazis and the communist regime in East Germany. One actor and one actor only is on stage throughout the play and performs thirty-five different roles. Experimentation is probably at the heart of the work of many playwrights, although it still does not please mainstream audiences to the same degree that traditional drama does.

The most celebrated of contemporary playwrights seem to mix experimental and conventional dramatic techniques. Tom Stoppard, whose work is cerebral and witty, as in his pastiche of *Hamlet* called *Rosencrantz and Guildenstern Are Dead*, continues to delve into literature for much of his work. *The Invention of Love* treats the hopeless love of the Oxford classical scholar and poet A. E. Housman for a young athlete, Moses Jackson. The play begins with Housman crossing the river Styx into the underworld. Throughout, the older Housman watches the action of himself as a young man and offers his sentiments. *Arcadia,* unlike some of Stoppard's early works, is a deeply emotional play about a thirteen-year-old girl, Lady Thomasina Coverly, gifted mathematically in an age in which such fields of study were reserved for men. The play takes place in one country house in Derbyshire, England, in both 1809 and 1989, contrasting several modes of thought and feeling—classical, romantic, and modern. Paula Vogel's plays frequently interrupt the dramatic action with asides, but they are also imaginatively structured so that time feels fluid and the action moves in emotionally significant sweeps. *The Baltimore Waltz,* derived from Vogel's experience of watching her brother die of AIDS, brings humor to a tragic situation. Similarly, *How I Learned to Drive,* which sensitively treats the subject of sexual molestation in families, also has comic moments. Recent Irish playwrights have provided us with a range of powerful plays that invoke horror, joy, and the supernatural. Conor McPherson's *Shining City* has been described in reviews as a near-perfect play. McPherson, in plays such as *The Weir* and *This Lime Tree Bower,* has experimented with long monologues and sometimes with ghosts or the threat of ghosts. *Shining City* begins slowly, but the rhythms of the speeches are powerful, punctuated by remarkable silences on stage. The dialogue seems almost casual and ordinary until the implications of what is being said begin to mount. The shocking ending of the play accounts for only some of its power. Another Irish play that ran on Broadway at the same time, Martin McDonagh's *The Lieutenant of Inishmore,* got a reputation for almost unbearable cruelty on stage, but when one reads the play carefully, it is clear that this tale of the Irish Republican Army's self-appointed "soldiers" is a farce built around a totally improbable issue revealed in the last minutes of the play. These are all careful dramatic experiments that have attained a lasting place in modern drama. The theater in our times continues with extraordinary energy to explore issues of social, historical, and psychological importance, with a wide range of techniques to which audiences respond positively.

Genres of Drama
Tragedy

Drama since the great age of the Greeks has taken several different forms. As we have seen, tragedies were one genre that pleased Greek audiences, and comedies pleased the Romans. In later ages, a blend of the comic and the tragic produced a hybrid genre: tragicomedy. In our time, unless a play is modeled on the Greek or Shakespearean tragedies, as is O'Neill's *Desire under the Elms,* it is usually considered tragicomic rather than tragic. Our age still enjoys the kind of comedy that people laugh at, although most plays that are strictly comedy are frothy, temporarily entertaining, and not lasting.

TRAGEDY demands a specific worldview. Aristotle, in his *Poetics,* points out that the tragic hero or heroine should be noble of birth, perhaps a king like Oedipus or a princess like Antigone. This has often been interpreted to mean that the tragic hero or heroine should be more magnanimous, more daring, larger in spirit than the average person.

Modern tragedies have rediscovered tragic principles, and while O'Neill and Miller rely on Aristotle's precepts, they have shown that in a modern society shorn of the distinctions between noble and peasant, it is possible for audiences to see the greatness in all classes. This has given us a new way of orienting ourselves to the concept of fate; to HAMARTIA, the wrong act that leads people to a tragic end; and to the hero's or heroine's relationship to the social order.

Aristotle suggested that plot was the heart and soul of tragedy and that character came second. But most older tragedies take the name of the tragic hero or heroine as their title; this signifies the importance that dramatists invested in their tragic characters. Yet they also heeded Aristotle's stipulation that tragic action should have one plot rather than the double or triple plots that often characterize comedies. (Shakespeare was soundly criticized in the eighteenth century for breaking this rule in his tragedies.) And they paid attention to the concept of PERIPETEIA, which specifies that the progress of the tragic characters sometimes leads them to a reversal: they get what they want, but what they want turns out to be destructive. Aristotle especially valued a plot in which the reversal takes place simultaneously with the recognition of the truth, or the shift from ignorance to awareness, as it does in Sophocles' *Oedipus Rex*.

Playwrights in the seventeenth and eighteenth centuries in France were especially interested in following classical precepts. They were certain that Greek tragedy and Roman comedy were the epitome of excellence in drama. They interpreted Aristotle's discussion of dramatic integrity to be a set of rules governing dramatic form. These became known as drama's THREE UNITIES specifying one plot, a single action that takes place in one day in a single setting. The neoclassical reinterpretation of the unities was probably much stricter than Aristotle intended.

Comedy

Two kinds of comedy developed among the ancient Greeks: OLD COMEDY, which resembles FARCE (light drama characterized by broad satirical comedy and an improbable plot) and often pokes fun at individuals with social and political power, and NEW COMEDY, which is a more refined commentary on the condition of society.

Old Comedy survives in the masterful works of Aristophanes, such as *Lysistrata*, while New Comedy hearkens back to the lost plays of Menander and resurfaces in plays such as Molière's *Tartuffe*. Molière uses humor but mixes it with a serious level of social commentary. Modern COMEDY OF MANNERS studies and sometimes ridicules modern society as in Oscar Wilde's *The Importance of Being Earnest*.

Comedy is not always funny. Chekhov thought *The Cherry Orchard* was a comedy, whereas his producer, the great Konstantin Stanislavsky, who trained actors to interpret his lines and who acted in other Chekhov plays, thought it was a tragedy. The argument may have centered on the ultimate effect of the play on its audiences, but it may also have centered on the question of laughter. There are laughs in *The Cherry Orchard*, but they usually come at the expense of a character or a social group. This is true, as well, of Samuel Beckett's *Waiting for Godot* and *Krapp's Last Tape*. We may laugh, but we also know that the play is at heart very serious.

Tragicomedy

Since the early seventeenth century, serious plays have been called TRAGICOMEDIES when they do not adhere strictly to the structure of tragedy, which emphasizes the nobility of the hero or heroine, fate, the wrong action of the hero or heroine, and a resolution that includes death, exile, or a similar end. Many serious plays have these qualities, but they also have some of the qualities of comedy: a commentary on society, raucous behavior that draws laughs, and a relatively happy ending. Yet their darkness is such that we can hardly feel comfortable regarding them as comedies.

Plays such as Sam Shepard's *Buried Child* and Lorraine Hansberry's *A Raisin in the Sun* can be considered tragicomedy. Indeed, the modern temperament has especially relied on the mixture of comic and tragic elements for its most serious plays. Eugene O'Neill, Tennessee Williams, Harold Pinter, Marsha Norman, and Caryl Churchill have all been masters of tragicomedy.

In contemporary drama, tragicomedy takes several forms. One is the play whose seriousness is relieved by comic moments; another is the play whose comic structure absorbs a tragic moment and continues to express affirmation. Yet another is the dark comedy whose sardonic humor leaves us wondering how we can laugh at something that is ultimately frightening. This is the case with some absurdist comedies, which insist that there is no meaning in events other than the meaning we invent for ourselves. Pinter's *The Homecoming* and Beckett's *Krapp's Last Tape* are such plays. They are funny yet sardonic, and when we laugh we do so uneasily.

Other genres of drama exist, although they are generally versions of tragedy, comedy, and tragicomedy. Improvisational theater, in which actors use no scripts and may switch roles at any moment, defies generic description. Musical comedies and operas are dramatic entertainments that have established their own genres related in some ways to the standard genres of drama.

Genre distinctions are useful primarily because they establish expectations in the minds of audiences with theatrical experience. Tragedies and comedies make different demands on an audience. According to Marsha Norman's explanation of the "rules" of drama, you have to know in a play just what is at stake. Understanding the principles that have developed over the centuries to create the genres of drama helps us know what is at stake.

Elements of Drama

All plays share some basic elements with which playwrights and producers work: plots, characters, settings, dialogue, movement, and themes. In addition, many modern plays pay close attention to lighting, costuming, and props. When we respond to a play, we observe the elements of drama in action together, and the total experience is rich, complex, and subtle. Occasionally, we respond primarily to an individual element—the theme or characterization, for instance—but that is rare. Our awareness of the elements of drama is most useful when we are thinking analytically about a play and the way it affects us.

For the sake of discussion, we will consider the way the basic elements of drama function in Lady Gregory's one-act play *The Rising of the Moon* (which follows this section). It has all the elements we expect from drama, and it is both a brief and a very successful play.

Plot

PLOT is a term for the action of a drama. Plot implies that the ACTION has a shape and form that will ultimately prove satisfying to the audience. Generally, a carefully plotted play begins with EXPOSITION, an explanation of what happened before the play began and of how the characters arrived at their present situation. The play then continues, using SUSPENSE to build tension in the audience and in the characters and to develop further the pattern of RISING ACTION. The audience wonders what is going to happen, sees the characters set in motion, and then watches as certain questions implied by the drama are answered one by one. The action achieves its greatest tension as it moves to a point of CLIMAX, when a revelation is experienced, usually by the chief characters. Once the climax has been reached, the plot continues, sometimes very briefly, in a pattern of FALLING ACTION as the drama reaches its conclusion and the characters understand their circumstances and themselves better than they did at the beginning of the play.

The function of plot is to give action a form that helps us understand elements of the drama in relation to one another. Plays can have several interrelated plots or only one. Lady Gregory's *The Rising of the Moon* has one very simple plot: a police sergeant is sent out with two policemen to make sure a political rebel does not escape from the area. The effect of the single plot is that the entire play focuses intensely on the interaction between the rebel, disguised as a ballad singer, and the sergeant. The sergeant meets the rebel, listens to him sing ballads, and then recognizes in him certain qualities they share. The audience wonders whether a reward of one hundred pounds will encourage the sergeant to arrest the ballad singer or, instead, the ballad singer's sense that his cause is just will convince the sergeant to let him go. The climax of the action occurs when the sergeant's two policemen return and, as the ballad singer hides behind a barrel, ask whether the sergeant has seen any signs of the rebel. Not until that moment does the audience know for sure what the sergeant will do. When he gives his answer, the falling action begins.

Plots depend on CONFLICT between characters, and in *The Rising of the Moon* the conflict is very deep. It is built into the characters themselves, but it is also part of the institution of law that the sergeant serves and the ongoing struggle for justice that the ballad singer serves. This conflict, still evident today, was a very significant national issue in Ireland when the play was first produced in Dublin in 1907.

Lady Gregory works subtly with the conflict between the sergeant and the ballad singer, showing that although they are on completely opposite sides of the law—and of the important political issues—they are more alike than they are different. The ballad singer begins to sing the "Granuaile," a revolutionary song about England's unlawful dominance over Ireland through seven centuries; when he leaves out a line, the sergeant supplies it. In that action the sergeant reveals that even though he is paid by the English to keep law and order, his roots lie with the Irish people. By his knowledge of the revolutionary songs he reveals his sympathies.

Characterization

Lady Gregory has effectively joined CHARACTER and conflict in *The Rising of the Moon:* as the conflict is revealed, the characters of the sergeant and the ballad singer are also revealed. At first the sergeant seems eager to get the reward, and he acts bossy with Policeman X and Policeman B. And when he first meets the ballad singer he seems demanding and policemanlike. It is only when he begins to sense who the ballad singer really is that he changes and reveals a deep, sympathetic streak.

Lady Gregory, in a note to the play, said that in Ireland when the play was first produced, those who wanted Ireland to become part of England were incensed to see a policeman portrayed so as to show his sympathies with rebels. Those who wished Ireland to become a separate nation from England were equally shocked to see a policeman portrayed so sympathetically.

The sergeant and the ballad singer are both major characters in the play, but it is not clear that either is the villain or the hero. When the play begins, the sergeant seems to be the hero because he represents the law, and the ballad singer appears to be the villain because he has escaped from prison. But as the action develops, those characterizations change. What replaces them is an awareness of the complications that underlie the relationship between the law and the law-breaker in some circumstances. This is part of the point of Lady Gregory's play.

Lady Gregory has given a very detailed portrait of both main characters, although in a one-act play she does not have enough space to be absolutely thorough in developing them. Yet we get an understanding of the personal ambitions of each character, and we understand both their relationship to Ireland and their particular allegiances as individuals. They speak with each other in enough detail to show that they understand each other, and when the ballad singer hides behind the barrel at the approach of the other two policemen, he indicates that he trusts the sergeant not to reveal him.

Policeman X and Policeman B are only sketched in. Yet their presence is important. It is with them that the sergeant reveals his official personality, and it is their presence at the end that represents the most important threat to the security of the ballad singer. We know, though, little or nothing about them personally. They are characters who are functionaries, a little like Rosencrantz and Guildenstern in *Hamlet,* but without the differentiating characterizations that Shakespeare was able to give minor players in his full-length play.

The plays in this collection have some of the most remarkable characters ever created in literature. Tragedy usually demands complex characters, such as Oedipus, Antigone, Medea, Hamlet, and Willy Loman. We come to know them through their own words, through their interaction with other characters, through their expression of feelings, through their decisions, and through their presence onstage depicted in movement and gesture.

Tragicomedies offer individualized and complex characters, such as Madame Ranevskaya in *The Cherry Orchard,* Miss Julie, and Nora Helmer in *A Doll House.* But just as effective in certain kinds of drama are characters drawn as types, such as Alceste, the misanthrope in Molière's play, and Everyman in medieval drama.

In many plays we see that the entire shape of the action derives from the characters, from their strengths and weaknesses. In such plays we do not feel that the action lies outside the characters and that they must live through an arbitrary sequence of events. Instead we feel that they create their own opportunities and problems.

Setting

The SETTING of a play includes many things. First, this term refers to the time and place in which the action occurs. Second, it refers to the scenery, the physical elements that appear onstage to vivify the author's stage directions. In Lady Gregory's play, we have a dock with barrels to suggest the locale, and darkness suggests night. These are important details that influence the emotional reaction of the audience.

Some plays make use of very elaborate settings, as does August Wilson's *Fences,* which is produced with a detailed tenement backyard onstage. Others make use of simple settings, such as the empty stage of Pirandello's *Six Characters in Search of an Author.*

Lady Gregory's setting derives from her inspiration for the play. She visited the quays—places where boats dock and leave with goods—as a young girl and imagined how someone might escape from the nearby prison and make his getaway "under a load of kelp" in one of the ships. The quay represents the meeting of the land and water, and it represents the getaway, the possibility of freedom. The barrel is a symbol of trade, and the sergeant and the ballad singer sit on its top and trade the words of a revolutionary song with each other.

The title of the play refers to another element of the setting: the moonlight. The night protects the ballad singer, and it permits the sergeant to bend his sworn principles a bit. The rising of the moon, as a rebel song suggests, signifies a change in society, the time when "the small shall rise up and the big shall fall down." Lady Gregory uses these elements in the play in a very effective way, interrelating them so that their significance becomes increasingly apparent as the play progresses.

Dialogue

Plays depend for their unfolding on dialogue. The DIALOGUE is the verbal exchanges between the characters. Since there is no description or commentary on the action, as there is in most novels, the dialogue must tell the whole story. Fine playwrights have developed ways of revealing character, advancing action, and introducing themes by a highly efficient use of dialogue.

Dialogue is spoken by one character to another, who then responds. But sometimes, as in Shakespeare's *Hamlet,* a character delivers a SOLILOQUY, in which he or she speaks onstage to him- or herself. Ordinarily, such speeches take on importance because they are thought to be especially true. Characters, when they speak to each other, may well wish to deceive, but generally, when they speak to themselves, they have no reason to say anything but the truth.

In *The Rising of the Moon* Lady Gregory has written an unusual form of dialogue that reveals a regional way of speech. Lady Gregory was Anglo-Irish, but she lived in the west of Ireland and was familiar with the speech patterns that the characters in this play would have used. She has been recognized for her ability to re-create the speech of the rural Irish, and passages such as the following are meant to reveal the peculiarities of the rhythms and syntax of English as it was spoken in Ireland at the turn of the century:

SERGEANT: Is he as bad as that?
MAN: He is then.
SERGEANT: Do you tell me so?

Lady Gregory makes a considerable effort to create dialogue that is rich in local color as well as in spirit. John Millington Synge, another Irish playwright, whose dialogue in *Riders to the Sea* is also an effort to re-create the sounds and rhythms of rural Irish speech, once said, "In a good play every speech should be as fully flavored as a nut or apple, and such speeches cannot be written by anyone who works among people who have shut their lips on poetry." Lady

Gregory, who produced the plays of Synge at the Abbey Theatre in Dublin, would certainly agree, as her dialogue in *The Rising of the Moon* amply shows.

Music

Lady Gregory introduces another dramatic element: music. In *The Rising of the Moon* the music is integral to the plot because it allows the ballad singer, by omitting a line of a rebel song, gradually to expose the sergeant's sympathies with the rebel cause. The sergeant is at first mindful of his duty and insists that the balladeer stop, but eventually he is captivated by the music. As the ballad singer continues, he sings a song containing the title of the play, and the audience or reader realizes that the title exposes the play's rebel sympathies.

Movement

We as readers or witnesses are energized by the movement of the characters in a play. As we read, stage directions inform us where the characters are, when they move, how they move, and perhaps even what the significance of their movement is. In modern plays, the author may give many directions for the action; in earlier plays, stage directions are few and often supplemented by those of a modern editor. In performance the movements that you see may well have been invented by the director, although the text of a play often requires certain actions, as in the ghost scene and final dueling scene in *Hamlet*. In some kinds of drama, such as musical comedy and Greek drama, part of the action may be danced.

Lady Gregory moves the ballad singer and the sergeant in telling ways. They move physically closer to one another as they become closer in their thinking. Their movement seems to pivot around the barrel, and in one of the most charming moments of the play, they meet each other's eyes when the ballad singer sits on the barrel and comments on the way the sergeant is pacing back and forth. They then both sit on the barrel, facing in opposite directions, and share a pipe between them, almost as a peace offering.

Theme

The THEME of a play is its message, its central concerns—in short, what it is about. It is by no means a simple thing to decide what the theme of a play is, and many plays contain several rather than just a single theme. Often, the search for a theme tempts us to oversimplify and to reduce a complex play to a relatively simple catchphrase.

Sophocles' *Antigone* focuses on the conflict between human law and the law of the gods when following both sets of laws seems to be impossible. Antigone wishes to honor the gods by burying her brother, but the law of Kreon decrees that he shall have no burial, since her brother is technically a traitor to the state. Similar themes are present in other Greek plays. *Hamlet* has many themes. On a very elementary level, the main theme of *Hamlet* is revenge. This is played out in the obligation of a son to avenge the murder of a father, even when the murderer is a kinsman. Another theme centers on corruption in the state of Denmark.

Lady Gregory's play has revolution as one theme. The rising of the moon is a sign for "the rising," or revolution, of the people against their English oppressors. The sergeant is an especially English emblem of oppression because the police were established by an Englishman, Robert Peele. At one point the balladeer suggests a song, "The Peeler and the Goat," but rejects it because in slang a "peeler" is a policeman.

Another important theme in *The Rising of the Moon* is that of unity among the Irish people. The sergeant seems to be at an opposite pole from the ballad singer when the play opens. He is posting signs announcing a reward that he could well use, since he is a family man. But as the play proceeds, the sergeant moves closer in thought to the Irish people, represented by the rebel, the ballad singer.

If concerned that readers and viewers will miss their thematic intentions, playwrights sometimes reveal these in one or two speeches. Usually, a careful reader or viewer has already divined the theme, and the speeches are intrusive. But Lady Gregory is able to introduce thematic material in certain moments of dialogue, as in this comment by the sergeant, revealing that the police are necessary to prevent a revolution:

> SERGEANT: Well, we have to do our duty in the force. Haven't we the whole country depending on us to keep law and order? It's those that are down would be up and those that are up would be down, if it wasn't for us.

But the thematic material in *The Rising of the Moon* is spread evenly throughout, as is the case in most good plays.

In every play, the elements of drama will work differently, sometimes giving us the feeling that character is dominant over theme, or plot over character, or setting over both. Ordinarily, critics feel that character, plot, and theme are the most important elements of drama, while setting, dialogue, music, and movement come next. But in the best of dramas each has its importance and each balances the others. The plays in this collection strive for that harmony; most achieve it memorably.

Lady Gregory

Isabella Augusta Persse (1852–1932) was born in the west of Ireland. Her family was known as "ascendancy stock"— that is, it was educated, wealthy, and Protestant living in a land that was largely uneducated, poverty-ridden, and Roman Catholic. A gulf existed between the rich ascendancy families, who lived in great houses with considerable style, partaking in lavish hunts and balls, and the impoverished Irish, who lived in one-room straw-roofed homes and worked the soil with primitive tools.

Lady Gregory took a strong interest in the Irish language, stimulated in part by a nurse who often spoke the language to her when she was a child. Her nurse was an important source of Irish folklore and a contact with the people who lived in the modest cottages around her family estate. It was extraordinary for any wealthy Protestant to pay attention to the language or the life of the poor laborers of the west of Ireland. Yet these are the very people who figure most prominently in the plays that Lady Gregory wrote in later life.

Isabella Persse met Sir William Gregory when she was on a family trip to Nice and Rome. They were actually neighbors in Ireland but only slightly acquainted. He was also of Irish ascendancy stock and had been a governor of Ceylon. They were married the following year, when she was twenty-eight and he was sixty-three. Their marriage was apparently quite successful, and in 1881 their son, Robert Gregory, was born. They used the family home, Coole Park, as a retreat for short periods, but most of their time was spent traveling and living in London, where Sir William was a trustee of the National Gallery of Art. W. B. Yeats, Bernard Shaw, and numerous other important literary figures spent time in Coole Park and its beautiful great house in the early part of the twentieth century.

Lady Gregory led a relatively conventional life until Sir William Gregory died in 1892. According to the laws of that time, the estate passed to her son, so she anticipated a life of relatively modest circumstances. In the process of finishing Sir William's memoirs, she found herself to be a gifted writer. She used some of her spare time to learn Irish well enough to talk with the old cottagers in the hills, where she went to gather folklore and old songs. Although W. B. Yeats and others had collected volumes of Irish stories and poems, they did not know Irish well enough to authenticate what they heard. Lady Gregory published her Kiltartan tales (she had dubbed her neighborhood Kiltartan) as a way of preserving the rapidly disappearing myths and stories that were still told around the hearth as a matter of course in rural Ireland.

She was already an accomplished writer when she met W. B. Yeats in 1894. Their meeting was of immense importance for the history of drama, since they decided to marshal their complementary talents and abilities to create an Irish theater. Their discussions included certain Irish neighbors, among them Edward Martyn, a Catholic whose early plays were very successful. They also talked with Dr. Douglas Hyde, a mythographer and linguist and the first president of modern Ireland. Another neighbor who took part, the flamboyant George Moore, was a well-established novelist and playwright.

The group's first plays — Yeats's *The Countess Cathleen* and Martyn's *The Heather Field* — were performed on May 8 and 9, 1899, under the auspices of the Irish Literary Theatre in Dublin at the Ancient Concert Rooms. Dedicated to producing plays by Irish playwrights on Irish themes, the Irish Literary Theatre became an immediate success. The greatest problem the founders faced was finding more plays. Lady Gregory tried her own hand and discovered herself, at age fifty, to be a playwright.

Her ear for people's speech was unusually good — good enough that she was able to give the great poet Yeats lessons in dialogue and to help him prepare his own plays for the stage. She collaborated with Yeats on *The Pot of Broth* in 1902, the year she wrote her first plays, *The Jackdaw* and *A Losing Game*. Her first produced play, *Twenty-Five*, was put on in 1903. By 1904 the group had rented the historic Abbey Theatre. Some of her plays were quite popular and were successful even in later revivals: *Spreading the News* (1904); *Kincora* and *The White Cockade* (1905); and *Hyacinth Halvey, The Doctor in Spite of Himself, The Gaol Gate,* and *The Canavans* (all 1906). In the next year, there were troubles at the Abbey over John Millington Synge's *Playboy of the Western World*. The middle-class audience resented the portrait of the Irish peasants as people who would celebrate a self-confessed father-killer, even though he had not actually done the "gallous deed." Lady Gregory faced down a rioting audience who were protesting what she felt was excellent drama.

In 1918 her son, a World War I pilot, was shot down over Italy. The years that followed were to some extent years of struggle. Lady Gregory managed the Abbey Theatre, directed its affairs, and developed new playwrights, among them Sean O'Casey. During the Irish Civil War (1920–1922), she was physically threatened, and eventually her family home, Roxborough, was burned. In 1926, after discovering that she had cancer, she made arrangements to sell Coole Park to the government with the agreement that she could remain there for life. She died in 1932, the writer of a large number of satisfying plays and the prime mover in developing one of the twentieth century's most important literary theaters.

THE RISING OF THE MOON

One of Lady Gregory's shortest but most popular plays, *The Rising of the Moon* is openly political in its themes. Lady Gregory had been writing plays only a short time, and she had been directing the Irish Literary Theatre when it became the Abbey Theatre Company and produced this play in 1907. Her interest in Irish politics developed, she said, when she was going through the papers of a distant relative of her husband. That man had been in the Castle, the offices of the English authorities given the task of ruling Ireland from Dublin. She said that the underhanded dealings revealed in those papers convinced her that Ireland should be a nation apart from England if justice were ever to be done.

In 1907 the question of union with England or separation and nationhood was on everyone's lips. Ireland was calm, and the people in Dublin were relatively prosperous and by no means readying for a fight or a revolution. Yet there had been a tradition of risings against the English dating back to the Elizabethan age and earlier. In 1907 the average Irish person believed that revolution was a thing of the past; actually, it was less than ten years in the future. Certain organizations had been developing, notably the widespread Gaelic League and the less-known Sinn Féin (We Ourselves), to promote Irish lore, language, and culture. English was the dominant language in Ireland, since it was the language of commerce, but it tended to obliterate the Irish culture. Lady Gregory's work with the Abbey Theatre, which was making one of the age's most important contributions to Irish culture, thus coincided with growing interest throughout Ireland in rediscovering its literary past.

The title *The Rising of the Moon* comes from a popular old rebel song that pointed to the rising of the moon as the signal for the rising of peoples against oppression. The main characters of the play represent the two opposing forces in Ireland: freedom and independence, personified by the ballad singer ("a Ragged Man"); and law and order, represented by the sergeant. The ballad singer is aligned with those who want to change the social structure of Ireland so that the people now on the bottom will be on top. The sergeant's job is to preserve the status quo and avoid such a turning of the tables.

In an important way, the sergeant and the ballad singer represent the two alternatives that face the modern Irish — now as in the past. One alternative is to accept the power of the English and be in their pay, like the sergeant; such a person would be well fed and capable of supporting a family. The other alternative is to follow the revolutionary path of the ballad singer and risk prison, scorn, and impoverishment. The ballad singer is a ragged man because he has been totally reduced in circumstances by his political choices.

For Lady Gregory, this play was a serious political statement. She and W. B. Yeats — both aristocratic Protestant Irish — were sympathetic to the Irish revolutionary causes. They each wrote plays that struck a revolutionary note during this period. Neither truly expected a revolution; when the Easter Uprising of 1916 was put down with considerable loss of life, Yeats lamented that his plays may have sent some young men to their deaths.

The success of *The Rising of the Moon* lies in Lady Gregory's exceptional ear for dialogue. She captures the way people speak, and she also manages to draw the characters of the sergeant and ballad singer so as to gain our sympathies for both. In a remarkably economic fashion she dramatizes the problem of politics in Ireland, characterizing the two polarities and revealing some of the complexities that face anyone who tries to understand them.

Lady Gregory (1852–1932)

THE RISING OF THE MOON

1907

Persons

SERGEANT	POLICEMAN B
POLICEMAN X	A RAGGED MAN

Scene: *Side of a quay in a seaport town. Some posts and chains. A large barrel. Enter three policemen. Moonlight.*

(*Sergeant, who is older than the others, crosses the stage to right and looks down steps. The others put down a pastepot and unroll a bundle of placards.*)

POLICEMAN B: I think this would be a good place to put up a notice. (*He points to barrel.*)

POLICEMAN X: Better ask him. (*Calls to Sergeant.*) Will this be a good place for a placard?

(*No answer.*)

POLICEMAN B: Will we put up a notice here on the barrel?

(*No answer.*)

SERGEANT: There's a flight of steps here that leads to the water. This is a place that should be minded well. If he got down here, his friends might have a boat to meet him; they might send it in here from outside.

POLICEMAN B: Would the barrel be a good place to put a notice up?

SERGEANT: It might; you can put it there.

(*They paste the notice up.*)

SERGEANT (*reading it*): Dark hair—dark eyes, smooth face, height five feet five—there's not much to take hold of in that—It's a pity I had no chance of seeing him before he broke out of jail. They say he's a wonder, that it's he makes all the plans for the whole organization. There isn't another man in Ireland would have broken jail the way he did. He must have some friends among the jailers.

POLICEMAN B: A hundred pounds is little enough for the Government to offer for him. You may be sure any man in the force that takes him will get promotion.

SERGEANT: I'll mind this place myself. I wouldn't wonder at all if he came this way. He might come slipping along there (*points to side of quay*), and his friends might be waiting for him there (*points down steps*), and once he got away it's little chance we'd have of finding him; it's maybe under a load of kelp he'd be

in a fishing boat, and not one to help a married man that wants it to the reward.

POLICEMAN X: And if we get him itself, nothing but abuse on our heads for it from the people, and maybe from our own relations.

SERGEANT: Well, we have to do our duty in the force. Haven't we the whole country depending on us to keep law and order? It's those that are down would be up and those that are up would be down, if it wasn't for us. Well, hurry on, you have plenty of other places to placard yet, and come back here then to me. You can take the lantern. Don't be too long now. It's very lonesome here with nothing but the moon.

POLICEMAN B: It's a pity we can't stop with you. The Government should have brought more police into the town, with *him* in jail, and at assize° time too. Well, good luck to your watch.

(*They go out.*)

SERGEANT (*walks up and down once or twice and looks at placard*): A hundred pounds and promotion sure. There must be a great deal of spending in a hundred pounds. It's a pity some honest man not to be better of that.

(*A Ragged Man appears at left and tries to slip past. Sergeant suddenly turns.*)

SERGEANT: Where are you going?

MAN: I'm a poor ballad-singer, your honor. I thought to sell some of these (*holds out bundle of ballads*) to the sailors.

(*He goes on.*)

SERGEANT: Stop! Didn't I tell you to stop? You can't go on there.

MAN: Oh, very well. It's a hard thing to be poor. All the world's against the poor!

SERGEANT: Who are you?

MAN: You'd be as wise as myself if I told you, but I don't mind. I'm one Jimmy Walsh, a ballad-singer.

SERGEANT: Jimmy Walsh? I don't know that name.

MAN: Ah, sure, they know it well enough in Ennis. Were you ever in Ennis, sergeant?

SERGEANT: What brought you here?

MAN: Sure, it's to the assizes I came, thinking I might make a few shillings here or there. It's in the one train with the judges I came.

---

assize: Judicial inquest.

SERGEANT: Well, if you came so far, you may as well go farther, for you'll walk out of this.

MAN: I will, I will; I'll just go on where I was going.

(Goes toward steps.)

SERGEANT: Come back from those steps; no one has leave to pass down them tonight.

MAN: I'll just sit on the top of the steps till I see will some sailor buy a ballad off me that would give me my supper. They do be late going back to the ship. It's often I saw them in Cork carried down the quay in a handcart.

SERGEANT: Move on, I tell you. I won't have anyone lingering about the quay tonight.

MAN: Well, I'll go. It's the poor have the hard life! Maybe yourself might like one, sergeant. Here's a good sheet now. (Turns one over.) "Content and a pipe"—that's not much. "The Peeler and the goat"—you wouldn't like that. "Johnny Hart"—that's a lovely song.

SERGEANT: Move on.

MAN: Ah, wait till you hear it. (Sings.)

There was a rich farmer's daughter lived near the town of Ross;
She courted a Highland soldier, his name was Johnny Hart;
Says the mother to her daughter, "I'll go distracted mad
If you marry that Highland soldier dressed up in Highland plaid."

SERGEANT: Stop that noise.

(Man wraps up his ballads and shuffles toward the steps.)

SERGEANT: Where are you going?

MAN: Sure you told me to be going, and I am going.

SERGEANT: Don't be a fool. I didn't tell you to go that way; I told you to go back to the town.

MAN: Back to the town, is it?

SERGEANT (taking him by the shoulder and shoving him before him): Here, I'll show you the way. Be off with you. What are you stopping for?

MAN (who has been keeping his eye on the notice, points to it): I think I know what you're waiting for, sergeant.

SERGEANT: What's that to you?

MAN: And I know well the man you're waiting for—I know him well—I'll be going.

(He shuffles on.)

SERGEANT: You know him? Come back here. What sort is he?

MAN: Come back is it, sergeant? Do you want to have me killed?

SERGEANT: Why do you say that?

MAN: Never mind. I'm going. I wouldn't be in your shoes if the reward was ten times as much. (Goes on off stage to left.) Not if it was ten times as much.

SERGEANT (rushing after him): Come back here, come back. (Drags him back.) What sort is he? Where did you see him?

MAN: I saw him in my own place, in the County Clare. I tell you you wouldn't like to be looking at him. You'd be afraid to be in the one place with him. There isn't a weapon he doesn't know the use of, and as to strength, his muscles are as hard as that board (slaps barrel).

SERGEANT: Is he as bad as that?

MAN: He is then.

SERGEANT: Do you tell me so?

MAN: There was a poor man in our place, a sergeant from Ballyvaughan.—It was with a lump of stone he did it.

SERGEANT: I never heard of that.

MAN: And you wouldn't, sergeant. It's not everything that happens gets into the papers. And there was a policeman in plain clothes, too. . . . It is in Limerick he was. . . . It was after the time of the attack on the police barrack at Kilmallock. . . . Moonlight . . . just like this . . . waterside. . . . Nothing was known for certain.

SERGEANT: Do you say so? It's a terrible county to belong to.

MAN: That's so, indeed! You might be standing there, looking out that way, thinking you saw him coming up this side of the quay (points), and he might be coming up this other side (points), and he'd be on you before you knew where you were.

SERGEANT: It's a whole troop of police they ought to put here to stop a man like that.

MAN: But if you'd like me to stop with you, I could be looking down this side. I could be sitting up here on this barrel.

SERGEANT: And you know him well, too?

MAN: I'd know him a mile off, sergeant.

SERGEANT: But you wouldn't want to share the reward?

MAN: Is it a poor man like me, that has to be going the roads and singing in fairs, to have the name on him that he took a reward? But you don't want me. I'll be safer in the town.

SERGEANT: Well, you can stop.

MAN (getting up on barrel): All right, sergeant. I wonder, now, you're not tired out, sergeant, walking up and down the way you are.

SERGEANT: If I'm tired I'm used to it.

MAN: You might have hard work before you tonight yet. Take it easy while you can. There's plenty of room up here on the barrel, and you see farther when you're higher up.

SERGEANT: Maybe so. (Gets up beside him on barrel, facing right. They sit back to back, looking different ways.) You made me feel a bit queer with the way you talked.

MAN: Give me a match, sergeant (he gives it and man lights pipe); take a draw yourself? It'll quiet you. Wait now till I give you a light, but you needn't turn round. Don't take your eye off the quay for the life of you.

SERGEANT: Never fear, I won't. (*Lights pipe. They both smoke.*) Indeed it's a hard thing to be in the force, out at night and no thanks for it, for all the danger we're in. And it's little we get but abuse from the people, and no choice but to obey our orders, and never asked when a man is sent into danger, if you are a married man with a family.

MAN (*sings*): As through the hills I walked to view the hills and shamrock plain,

I stood awhile where nature smiles to view the rocks and streams,

On a matron fair I fixed my eyes beneath a fertile vale,

And she sang her song it was on the wrong of poor old Granuaile.

SERGEANT: Stop that; that's no song to be singing in these times.

MAN: Ah, sergeant, I was only singing to keep my heart up. It sinks when I think of him. To think of us two sitting here, and he creeping up the quay, maybe, to get to us.

SERGEANT: Are you keeping a good lookout?

MAN: I am; and for no reward too. Amn't I the foolish man? But when I saw a man in trouble, I never could help trying to get him out of it. What's that? Did something hit me?

(*Rubs his heart.*)

SERGEANT (*patting him on the shoulder*): You will get your reward in heaven.

MAN: I know that, I know that, sergeant, but life is precious.

SERGEANT: Well, you can sing if it gives you more courage.

MAN (*sings*): Her head was bare, her hands and feet with iron bands were bound,

Her pensive strain and plaintive wail mingles with the evening gale,

And the song she sang with mournful air, I am old Granuaile.

Her lips so sweet that monarchs kissed . . .

SERGEANT: That's not it. . . . "Her gown she wore was stained with gore." . . . That's it—you missed that.

MAN: You're right, sergeant, so it is; I missed it. (*Repeats line.*) But to think of a man like you knowing a song like that.

SERGEANT: There's many a thing a man might know and might not have any wish for.

MAN: Now, I daresay, sergeant, in your youth, you used to be sitting up on a wall, the way you are sitting up on this barrel now, and the other lads beside you, and you singing "Granuaile"? . . .

SERGEANT: I did then.

MAN: And the "Shan Van Vocht"? . . .

SERGEANT: I did then.

MAN: And the "Green on the Cape"?

SERGEANT: That was one of them.

MAN: And maybe the man you are watching for tonight used to be sitting on the wall, when he was young, and singing those same songs. . . . It's a queer world. . . .

SERGEANT: Whisht! . . . I think I see something coming. . . . It's only a dog.

MAN: And isn't it a queer world? . . . Maybe it's one of the boys you used to be singing with that time you will be arresting today or tomorrow, and sending into the dock. . . .

SERGEANT: That's true indeed.

MAN: And maybe one night, after you had been singing, if the other boys had told you some plan they had, some plan to free the country, you might have joined with them . . . and maybe it is you might be in trouble now.

SERGEANT: Well, who knows but I might? I had a great spirit in those days.

MAN: It's a queer world, sergeant, and it's little any mother knows when she sees her child creeping on the floor what might happen to it before it has gone through its life, or who will be who in the end.

SERGEANT: That's a queer thought now, and a true thought. Wait now till I think it out. . . . If it wasn't for the sense I have, and for my wife and family, and for me joining the force the time I did, it might be myself now would be after breaking jail and hiding in the dark, and it might be him that's hiding in the dark and that got out of jail would be sitting up here where I am on this barrel. . . . And it might be myself would be creeping up trying to make my escape from himself, and it might be himself would be keeping the law, and myself would be breaking it, and myself would be trying to put a bullet in his head, or to take up a lump of stone the way you said he did . . . no, that myself did. . . . Oh! (*Gasps. After a pause.*) What's that? (*Grasps man's arm.*)

MAN (*jumps off barrel and listens, looking out over water*): It's nothing, sergeant.

SERGEANT: I thought it might be a boat. I had a notion there might be friends of his coming about the quays with a boat.

MAN: Sergeant, I am thinking it was with the people you were, and not with the law you were, when you were a young man.

SERGEANT: Well, if I was foolish then, that time's gone.

MAN: Maybe, sergeant, it comes into your head sometimes, in spite of your belt and your tunic, that it might have been as well for you to have followed Granuaile.

SERGEANT: It's no business of yours what I think.

MAN: Maybe, sergeant, you'll be on the side of the country yet.

SERGEANT (*gets off barrel*): Don't talk to me like that. I have my duties and I know them. (*Looks round.*) That was a boat; I hear the oars.

(*Goes to the steps and looks down.*)

MAN (*sings*): O, then, tell me, Shawn O'Farrell, Where the gathering is to be.

In the old spot by the river
  Right well known to you and me!

SERGEANT: Stop that! Stop that, I tell you!

MAN (*sings louder*): One word more, for signal token,
  Whistle up the marching tune,
With your pike upon your shoulder,
  At the Rising of the Moon.

SERGEANT: If you don't stop that, I'll arrest you.

(*A whistle from below answers, repeating the air.*)

SERGEANT: That's a signal. (*Stands between him and steps.*) You must not pass this way. . . . Step farther back. . . . Who are you? You are no ballad-singer.

MAN: You needn't ask who I am; that placard will tell you. (*Points to placard.*)

SERGEANT: You are the man I am looking for.

MAN (*takes off hat and wig. Sergeant seizes them*): I am. There's a hundred pounds on my head. There is a friend of mine below in a boat. He knows a safe place to bring me to.

SERGEANT (*looking still at hat and wig*): It's a pity! It's a pity. You deceived me. You deceived me well.

MAN: I am a friend of Granuaile. There is a hundred pounds on my head.

SERGEANT: It's a pity, it's a pity!

MAN: Will you let me pass, or must I make you let me?

SERGEANT: I am in the force. I will not let you pass.

MAN: I thought to do it with my tongue. (*Puts hand in breast.*) What is that?

VOICE OF POLICEMAN X (*outside*): Here, this is where we left him.

SERGEANT: It's my comrades coming.

MAN: You won't betray me . . . the friend of Granuaile. (*Slips behind barrel.*)

VOICE OF POLICEMAN B: That was the last of the placards.

POLICEMAN X (*as they come in*): If he makes his escape it won't be unknown he'll make it.

(*Sergeant puts hat and wig behind his back.*)

POLICEMAN B: Did anyone come this way?

SERGEANT (*after a pause*): No one.

POLICEMAN B: No one at all?

SERGEANT: No one at all.

POLICEMAN B: We had no orders to go back to the station; we can stop along with you.

SERGEANT: I don't want you. There is nothing for you to do here.

POLICEMAN B: You bade us to come back here and keep watch with you.

SERGEANT: I'd sooner be alone. Would any man come this way and you making all that talk? It is better the place to be quiet.

POLICEMAN B: Well, we'll leave you the lantern anyhow.

(*Hands it to him.*)

SERGEANT: I don't want it. Bring it with you.

POLICEMAN B: You might want it. There are clouds coming up and you have the darkness of the night before you yet. I'll leave it over here on the barrel. (*Goes to barrel.*)

SERGEANT: Bring it with you, I tell you. No more talk.

POLICEMAN B: Well, I thought it might be a comfort to you. I often think when I have it in my hand and can be flashing it about into every dark corner (*doing so*) that it's the same as being beside the fire at home, and the bits of bogwood blazing up now and again.

(*Flashes it about, now on the barrel, now on Sergeant.*)

SERGEANT (*furious*): Be off the two of you, yourselves and your lantern!

(*They go out. Man comes from behind barrel. He and Sergeant stand looking at one another.*)

SERGEANT: What are you waiting for?

MAN: For my hat, of course, and my wig. You wouldn't wish me to get my death of cold?

(*Sergeant gives them.*)

MAN (*going toward steps*): Well, good night, comrade, and thank you. You did me a good turn tonight, and I'm obliged to you. Maybe I'll be able to do as much for you when the small rise up and the big fall down . . . when we all change places at the Rising (*waves his hand and disappears*) of the Moon.

SERGEANT (*turning his back to audience and reading placard*): A hundred pounds reward! A hundred pounds! (*Turns toward audience.*) I wonder, now, am I as great a fool as I think I am?

Greek Drama

Origins of Greek Drama

Because our historical knowledge of Greek drama is limited by the available contemporary commentaries and by partial archaeological remains—in the form of ruined theaters—we do not know when Greek theater began or what its original impulses were. Our best information points to 534 BCE as the beginning of the formal competitions among playwrights for coveted prizes that continued to be awarded for several centuries. Thespis, credited as the first tragedy writer, seems to have changed the nature of the form by stepping out of the chorus and taking a solo part. But the origin of *tragedy,* which translates in Greek as "goat-song" or "song for the sacrificial goat," is obscure. One theory is that tragedy may have developed from the rites of rural cults that sacrificed a she-goat at some Dionysian festivals or from masked animal dances at certain cult celebrations.

One source that may well have influenced the Greeks was the Egyptian civilization of the first millennium BCE. Egyptian culture was fully formed, brilliant, and complex, with numerous religious festivals and a pantheon of gods who resembled, and possibly inspired, those of the Greeks. Although it is not certain that Egypt produced a fully formed dramatic literature, certain major festivals and ceremonies that were performed annually, such as the Abydos Passion Play outlining the death and resurrection of Osiris, seem to have counterparts in Greek rituals and drama. The Abydos Passion Play tells the story of the betrayal and murder of Osiris by his jealous brother Seth, the scattering of his remains, and the task of Isis to reclaim and reassemble them to permit his rebirth.

The closest Greek counterpart to Osiris was DIONYSUS, who inspired orgiastic celebrations that found their way into early Greek drama. Dionysus was an agricultural deity, the Greek god of wine and the symbol of life-giving power. In several myths he, like Osiris, was ritually killed and dismembered and his parts scattered through the land. These myths paralleled the agricultural cycle of death and disintegration during the winter, followed by cultivation and rebirth in the spring, and reinforced the Greeks' understanding of the meaning of birth, life, and death.

Drama developed in ancient Greece in close connection with the Dionysia, religious celebrations dedicated to Dionysus. Four Dionysiac celebrations were held each winter in Athens beginning at the grape harvest and culminating during the first wine tastings: the Rural Dionysia in December, the Lenaia in January, the Anthesteria in February, and the City Dionysia in March. Except for the Anthesteria, the festivals featured drama contests among playwrights, and some of the works performed in those competitions have endured through the centuries. Theories that connect the origins of drama with religion hypothesize that one function of the religious festivals within which the drama competitions took place was the ritual attempt to guarantee fertility and the growth of the crops, on which the society depended.

The CITY DIONYSIA, the most lavish of the festivals, lasted from five to seven days. It was open to non-Athenians and therefore offered Athenians the opportunity to show off their wealth, their glorious history, and their heroes, who were often honored in parades the day before the plays began. There is some question about what was presented on each day. Two days were probably taken up with dithyrambic contests among the ten tribes of Athens. Generally each tribe presented two choruses—one of men and one of boys—each singing a narrative lyric called a DITHYRAMB. A prize was awarded the best performers. Three days were devoted to contests among tragedians, most of whom worked for half the year on three tragedies and a SATYR PLAY, an erotic piece of comic relief that ended the day's performance. A tragedian's three plays sometimes shared related themes or myths, but often they did not. The tragedians wrote the plays; trained and rehearsed the actors; composed music; and created setting, dances, costumes, and masks. After 486 BCE the first comedy competition was held, when five and later three comedies were also presented during the festival. The performances were paid for by wealthy Athenians as part of their civic duty. The great Greek plays thus were not commercial enterprises but an important part of civic and religious festivals.

Judges chosen by lottery awarded prizes, usually basing their decisions on the merits of the dramas. First prize went to the tragedian whose four plays were most powerful and most beautifully conceived.

The Greeks and Their Gods

The great achievement of Greek religion was the humanizing of their gods. Apollo, Zeus, Aphrodite, Athena, and Bacchus had recognizable emotions and pleasures. The Greeks built temples to their gods and made offerings at appropriate times to avoid catastrophe and bad luck. But the Greeks had no official religious text, no system of religious belief that they all followed, and few ethical teachings derived from religion. The impression we have today is that Greeks' efforts to define and know the gods were shaped by great artists such as Phidias, who sculpted Zeus at Olympia; Homer, who portrayed the gods in *The Iliad* and *The Odyssey;* and the great Greek playwrights, who sometimes revealed the actions of the gods. Our present knowledge of Greek gods resides in the literary and artistic remains of Greek culture.

Fortunately for us, most Greek drama was associated with important celebrations designed to honor Greek gods. We would not, however, call this drama religious in nature—as we characterize the medieval drama designated to celebrate Christian holidays. What we learn from Greek drama is that the gods can favor individual humans for reasons of their own. And likewise, the gods can choose to punish individual humans. To some extent Greek drama is designed to explain the divine approach to favor and disfavor.

The Greek Stage

At the center of the Greek theater was the ORCHESTRA, where the chorus sang and danced (*orches* is derived from the Greek for "dancing place"). The audience, sometimes numbering fifteen thousand, sat in rising rows on three sides of the orchestra. The steep sides of a hill formed a natural amphitheater for Greek audiences. Eventually, on the rim of the orchestra, an oblong building called the SKENE, or scene house, developed as a space for the actors and a background for the action. The term PROSKENION was sometimes used to refer to a raised stage added in later times in front of the *skene* where the actors performed. The theater at Epidaurus (Figure 1) was a model for the Greek theater plan (Figure 2).

Greek theaters were widely dispersed from Greece to present-day Turkey, to Sicily, and even to southern France. Wherever the Greeks developed new colonies and city-states, they built theaters. In many of the surviving theaters the acoustics are so fine that a human voice onstage can be heard from any seat in the theater.

Perhaps the most spectacular theatrical device used by the Greek playwrights, the MEKANE ("machine"), was implemented onstage by means of elaborate booms or derricks. Actors were lowered onto the stage to enact the roles of Olympian gods intervening in the affairs of humans. Some commentators, such as Aristotle (384–322 BCE), felt that the *mekane* should be used only if the intercession of deities was in keeping with the character of the play. The last of the great Greek tragedians, Euripides (c. 485–c. 406 BCE), used the device in almost half of his tragedies. In *Medea* Euripides uses the *mekane* to lift Medea to the roof of the *skene* and into her dragon chariot as a means of resolving the play's conflict. At the end of the play Medea is beyond her persecutors' reach and is headed for safety in another country. Modern dramatists use a metaphorical version of this called *deus ex machina* (literally, "the god from the machine") when they rescue characters at the last moment by improbable acci-

FIGURE 1. The theater at Epidaurus, Greece, looking east. This is the best-preserved (and now restored) Greek theater. Built in the fourth century BCE by Polykleitos the Younger and approximately 124 feet in diameter, it seats twelve thousand people and remains in use today with excellent acoustics.

FIGURE 2.   The Hellenistic theater, Eretria, Greece.

dents or strokes of luck. Usually, these are unsatisfying means of solving dramatic problems.

The Greek Actor

Thespis (sixth century BCE) by legend is said to have been the first actor—the first person to step outside the choral group and assume a dramatic role. He may or may not have used a mask because we do not know by what stages of development the convention of the Greek theatrical mask evolved, but it was clear that certain requirements were soon satisfied by the use of masks. For one thing, despite the excellent acoustics in the largest of theaters, the actor had to project his voice for some distance, and certain masks were designed to amplify the voice to reach the most distant rows. For some time there was only one actor in the earliest tragedies, and the simplest way of indicating a character change was by changing masks.

We do not actually possess any of the Greek masks, but we have numerous illustrations in Greek pottery, Roman paintings, and Roman copies of Greek sculpture (Figure 3). The masks themselves were made of perishable materials (cloth, wood, and possibly plaster) and were often adorned with hair and beards. They were carved and shaped to represent a variety of dramatic types: the warrior, the philosopher, the king, the queen, an old man, an old woman, and a young man and woman. The eventual development of type characters in later drama may have been accelerated by the conventions of these masks.

FIGURE 3.   Roman rendering of Greek masks.

Even when the number of actors was increased to four, the masks permitted them to assume many roles and create a level of high dramatic complexity.

The demands on Greek actors were considerable. They were expected to be in good physical condition so as to dance with grace. Their voices had to be full and expressive, as well as flexible enough to represent different characters. The audience sitting close to the actors was often taken by the sincerity or expressiveness of the eyes seen within the mask. Often the authors themselves, such as Thespis and Aeschylus, were among the most prominent actors of their time and were celebrated for their dramatic abilities.

Genres of Greek Drama
Tragedy

Greek tragedy focused on a person of noble birth who in some cases had risen to a great height and then fell precipitately. Tragedies showed humans at the mercy of MOIRA, their fate, which they only partly understood. One objective of Greek drama was to have the audience experience a CATHARSIS, which Aristotle describes as a purging or purifying of the emotions of pity and fear. According to the Greeks, these are emotions that a person associates with the fall of someone in a high social station, such as a king or queen. A central character, or PROTAGONIST, of noble birth was therefore an essential element for the playwright striving to evoke catharsis in an audience. Twentieth-century experiments with tragic figures who are ordinary people, such as Arthur Miller's *Death of a Salesman,* as masterful as they are, would not have made sense to the Greeks. For the Greeks, tragedy could befall only the great.

The modern critic Kenneth Burke identified a pattern for Greek tragedies. The tragic figure—for whom the play is usually named—experiences three stages of development: purpose, passion, and perception. The play begins with a purpose, such as finding the source of the plague in *Oedipus Rex.* Then, as the path becomes tangled and events unfold, the tragic figure begins an extensive process of soul-searching and suffers an inner agony—the passion. The perception of the truth involves a fate that the tragic figure would rather not face. It might be death or, as in *Oedipus Rex,* exile. It always involves separation from the human community. For the Greeks, that was the greatest punishment.

According to Aristotle, the tragic hero's perception of the truth was the most intense moment in the drama. He called it ANAGNORISIS, or recognition. When it came at the same moment that the tragic figure's fortunes reversed — the PERIPETEIA — Aristotle felt that the tragedy was most fulfilling for the audience. This is the case in *Oedipus Rex*. Aristotle's comments in his *Poetics* on the structure and effect of *Oedipus Rex* remain the most significant critical observations made by a contemporary on Greek theater. (See the excerpt from the *Poetics* that begins on page 95.)

The Structure of Greek Tragedies. The earliest tragedies seem to have developed from the emotional, intense dithyrambs sung by Athenian choruses. The CHORUS in most tragedies numbered twelve or fifteen men. They usually represented the citizenry in the drama. They dressed simply, and their song was sometimes sung in unison, sometimes delivered by the chorus leader. Originally, there were no actors separate from the chorus.

According to legend, Thespis (sixth century BCE) was the first actor — the first to step from the chorus to act in dialogue with it — thus creating the AGON, or dramatic confrontation. He won the first prize for tragedy in 532 BCE. As the only actor, he took several parts, wearing MASKS to distinguish the different characters. One actor was the norm in tragedies until Aeschylus (c. 525–456 BCE), the first important Greek tragedian whose work survives, introduced a second actor, and then Sophocles (c. 496–c. 406 BCE) added a third. (Only comedy used more: four actors.)

Like the actors, the members of the chorus wore masks. At first the masks were simple, but they became more ornate, often trimmed with hair and decorated with details that established the gender, age, or station of each character. The chorus and all the actors were male.

Eventually the structure of the plays became elaborated into a series of alternations between the characters' dialogue and the choral odes, with each speaking part developing the action or responding to it. Often crucial information furthering the action came from the mouth of a messenger, as in *Oedipus Rex*. The tragedies were structured in three parts: the PROLOGUE established the conflict; the episodes or agons developed the dramatic relationships between characters; and the EXODOS concluded the action. Between these sections the chorus performed different songs: PARODOS while moving onto the stage and STASIMA while standing still. In some plays the chorus sang choral ODES called the STROPHE as it moved from right to left. It sang the ANTISTROPHE while moving back to the right. The actors' episodes consisted of dialogue with each other and with the chorus. The scholar Bernhard Zimmerman has plotted the structure of *Oedipus Rex* in this fashion:

Prologue: Dialogue with Oedipus, the Priests, and Kreon establishing that the plague afflicting Thebes will cease when Laios's murderer is found.

Parodos: The opening hymn of the Chorus appealing to the gods.

First Episode: Oedipus seeks the murderer; Teiresias says it is Oedipus.

First Stasimon: The Chorus supports Oedipus, disbelieving Teiresias.

Second Episode: Oedipus accuses Kreon of being in league with Teiresias and the real murderer. Iokaste pleads for Kreon and tells the oracle of Oedipus's birth and of the death of Laios at the fork of a road. Oedipus sends for the eyewitness of the murder.

Second Stasimon: The Chorus, in a song, grows agitated for Oedipus.

Third Episode: The messenger from Oedipus's "hometown" tells him that his adoptive father has died and is not his real father. Iokaste guesses the truth and Oedipus becomes deeply worried.

Third Stasimon: The Chorus delivers a reassuring, hopeful song.

Fourth Episode: Oedipus, the Shepherd, and the Messenger confront the facts and Oedipus experiences the turning point of the play: he realizes he is the murderer he seeks.

Fourth Stasimon: The Chorus sings of the illusion of human happiness.

Exodos: Iokaste kills herself; Oedipus puts out his eyes; the Chorus and Kreon try to decide the best future action.

As this brief structural outline of *Oedipus Rex* demonstrates, the chorus assumed an important part in the tragedies. In Aeschylus's *Agamemnon* it represents the elders of the community. In Sophocles' *Oedipus Rex* it is a group of concerned citizens who give Oedipus advice and make demands on him. In *Antigone* the chorus consists of men loyal to the state. In Euripides' *Medea* the chorus is a group of the important women of Corinth.

Satyr Plays

The drama competitions held regularly from 534 BCE consisted usually of the work of three playwrights who each produced three tragedies and one satyr play, a form of comic relief. In a satyr play, the chorus dressed as satyrs, comic half-beast, half-man figures who cavorted with a PHALLUS, a mock penis, and engaged in riotous, almost slapstick antics. The characters were not psychologically developed, as they were in tragedy; the situations were not socially instructive, as they were in comedy. Rough-hewn and lighthearted, the satyr plays may have been a necessary antidote to the intensity of the tragedies.

Only one satyr play survives, perhaps an indication that the form was not as highly valued as tragedy. In Euripides' *Cyclops,* based on Odysseus's confrontation with the one-eyed giant who dined on a number of his men, Odysseus outwits the giant with the aid of a well-filled wineskin. The powers of Bacchus (Dionysus) are often alluded to, and drunkenness is a prime ingredient. The play is witty, entertaining, and brief. It might well have been the perfect way to end an otherwise serious drama festival.

Comedy

No coherent Greek theories on comedy have come down to us. (Aristotle is said to have written a lost treatise on comedy.) In the *Poetics,* Aristotle points out that comedy shows people from a lower social order than the nobility, who are the main figures in tragedy.

The two greatest Greek comic writers were Aristophanes (c. 448–c. 385 BCE), whose *Lysistrata* appears in this collection, and Menander (c. 342–c. 291 BCE). The first was a master of OLD COMEDY (which lasted from c. 486 to c. 400 BCE), in which individuals—sometimes well known to the audience—could be attacked personally. The humor was often ribald, coarse, and brassy, but according to Aristotle, it was not vicious. Physical devices onstage, such as the erect phalluses beneath the men's garments in *Lysistrata,* accompanied ribald lines, and Athenian audiences were mightily entertained. Comedy appears to have provided release, but for entirely different emotions from those evoked by tragedy.

The Old Comedy of Aristophanes concentrated on buffoonery and farce. Although we know little about it, a form known as MIDDLE COMEDY seems to have flourished from approximately 400 to 320 BCE. Our evidence is from statuettes of players that indicate a more realistic portrayal of character and thus a less broad and grotesque form of comedy than in some of the plays of Aristophanes. The NEW COMEDY of Menander and others whose work is now lost provided a less ribald humor that centered on the shortcomings of the middle classes. Although Menander enjoyed a great reputation in his own time and was highly regarded by Roman playwrights much later, very little of his work has survived. He is said to have written a few more than one hundred plays, but only one, *The Grouch,* survives intact. Twenty-three of his plays existed in a manuscript in Constantinople in the sixteenth century, but nothing of that volume seems to have survived. We know a number of titles, such as *The Lady from Andros, The Flatterer,* and *The Suspicious Man.* And we know that the Romans pilfered liberally from his plays. Beyond that we know little.

Menander's New Comedy concentrated on social manners. Instead of attacking individuals, as Aristophanes frequently did, Menander was more likely to attack a vice, such as vanity, or to portray the foibles of a social class. He aimed at his own middle class and established the pattern of parents or guardians struggling, usually over the issue of marriage, against the wishes of their children. The children ordinarily foil their parents' wishes, frequently with the help of an acerbic slave who provides the comedy with most of its humor. This pattern has proved so durable that it is used virtually every day in modern situation comedies on television.

Both Old and New Comedy have influenced theater from the time of the Greeks to the present. The nineteenth-century comedy of Oscar Wilde (in this collection) is an example of New Comedy, and the Marx Brothers' movies are examples of Old Comedy.

The Great Age of Greek Drama

The fifth century BCE was not only the great creative age of Athenian theater but also the age of Athenian power in Greek politics. By the beginning of the century, Greece dominated trade in the Mediterranean and therefore in many of the major civilized urban centers of the world. The most important threat to Greek power came from the Persians, living to the east. After the Persians attacked in 490 BCE, Greek city-states such as Athens formed the Delian League to defend themselves, pouring their funds into the treasury at Delos. When the Persians threatened again in 483 BCE, Themistocles (525?–460? BCE), Athenian soldier and statesman, realized he could not win a battle on land. By skillful political moves he managed to create a powerful navy. When the Persians attacked Athens in 480 BCE, Themistocles left a small rear guard to defend the Acropolis, the city's religious fortress. The Persians took the fortress, burned everything, and were lured by a clever ruse to Salamis, where they thought that a puny Athenian navy was making a getaway. Once the Persians set sail for Salamis, Themistocles turned on them and unleashed a powerful fighting force that defeated the Persians once and for all.

In the years immediately following, Athens overstated its role in the Persian defeat and assumed an air of imperial importance. It appropriated the gold in the Delian League treasury, using it to rebuild the Acropolis beginning in 448 BCE. The great Greek general and leader Pericles (495?–429? BCE) chose his friend Phidias to supervise the construction of the Parthenon and the other main buildings that are on the Acropolis even today. The threat of Athenian domination seems to have triggered the Peloponnesian Wars (431–406 BCE), which pitted the Spartan alliance against the Athenian alliance. Athens eventually lost the war and its democratic government.

The events of these years—dominated by interminable wars, threats of a return to tyranny, and cultural instability—are coterminous with the great flourishing of Greek art, drama, and philosophy. The geniuses of Greek drama cluster in the period dating from the birth of Aeschylus (c. 525 BCE) to the death of the philosopher Socrates (399 BCE). Aeschylus wrote *The Persians* (472 BCE); *Seven against Thebes* (467 BCE); and the *Oresteia* (458 BCE), a trilogy centering on Orestes and consisting of *Agamemnon, The Libation Bearers,* and *The Eumenides. The Suppliants* and *Prometheus Bound* are of uncertain dates.

Aeschylus's introduction of a second actor made it possible to intensify the dramatic value of each *agon*, the confrontation between ANTAGONISTS. He is also notable for giving minor characters, such as the watchman who opens *Agamemnon*, both dimension and depth. Aeschylus's *Oresteia*, the only surviving trilogy, tells of the death of Agamemnon and the efforts of his son Orestes to avenge that death.

Sophocles (c. 496–c. 406 BCE) and Euripides (c. 485–406 BCE) learned from Aeschylus and from each other, because they were all sometimes rivals. In addition to *Oedipus Rex* (c. 429 BCE), Sophocles is known today for *Ajax* (c. 442 BCE), *Philoctetes* (c. 409 BCE), *Oedipus at Colonus* (406 BCE), and *Electra* (date uncertain).

Euripides, the last of the great tragedians, may have written as many as ninety-two plays. Of the eighteen that survive, the best known are *Alcestis* (438 BCE), *Medea* (431 BCE), *Electra* (c. 417), *The Trojan Women* (415 BCE), and *The Bacchae* (produced in 405 BCE). He is especially noteworthy for his portrayal of women and for his experimental approach to theater.

These three tragedians, along with Aristophanes, provide us with insight into the Greek dramatic imagination. They also reveal something of our common humanity, since their achievement—lost though it was for many centuries—shapes our current dramatic practice. The Greeks gave us not only the beginnings of drama but also the basis of drama. We build on it today whenever a play is written and whenever we witness a play.

Greek Drama Timeline

DATE	THEATER	POLITICAL	SOCIAL/CULTURAL
1000–800 BCE			Classic paganism is in full bloom in Greece. Temple of Hera, oldest surviving temple in Olympia, Greece, is built. **9th century:** Age of the Homeric epic; *The Iliad, The Odyssey.*
800–700		First Messenian War: Sparta gains power in Greece.	Choral and dramatic music develop. Hesiod, poet whose *Works and Days* classified the five ages of mankind: Golden (peaceful), Silver (less happy), Bronze (art and warfare), Heroic (Trojan War), and Iron (the present). **776:** First Olympian Festival (predecessor of the modern Olympic games). Only one event is featured: a footrace of approximately 200 meters.
700–600		First written laws of Athens are recorded by Draco.	Sappho of Lesbos, Greek poet. Archilochus, Greek lyricist and author of fables. Construction of the Acropolis begins in Athens.
600–500	**534:** First contest for best tragedy is held in Athens as part of the annual City Dionysia, a major religious festival. The winning playwright (and actor) is Thespis. **c. 501:** Satyr plays are added to the City Dionysia play competition. Each playwright now has to present a trilogy of tragedies and a satyr play.	**594:** Solon's law allows for the Council of Four Hundred and various reforms pertaining to land ownership and civil liberties. **c. 525–459:** Themistocles, Athenian statesman and naval commander, builds a Greek navy and fortifications. **525–405:** Persians conquer Egypt.	The influence of the oracle at Delphi and its priestess is at its height. The theater of Delphi is built. **c. 582–507:** Pythagoras, philosopher, mathematician, and musical theorist. Public libraries in Athens. **c. 563–483:** Siddartha, founder of Buddhism, begins his religious journey in 534. **c. 520–438:** Pindar, Greek musician and poet.
500–400	**487–486:** Comedy is introduced as a dramatic form in the City Dionysia. **c. 471:** Aeschylus introduces the second actor in the performance of tragedy at the City Dionysia.	**500–449:** Persian Wars **494:** King Darius of Persia annexes all of Greece. **490:** Athenians defeat the Persians in the Battle of Marathon.	**c. 460–370:** Hippocrates, Greek physician who did much to separate medicine from superstition. **485–424:** Herodotus, a Greek historian, writes the history of the Persian Wars.

Greek Drama Timeline *(continued)*

DATE	THEATER	POLITICAL	SOCIAL/CULTURAL
500–400 BCE (continued)	c. 468: Sophocles is credited with introducing the third actor in the performance of tragedies at the City Dionysia. 458: First performance of Aeschylus's trilogy the *Oresteia* at the City Dionysia. 458: *Skene,* or scene house, is introduced in Greek theater. c. 441: First performance of Sophocles' *Antigone* at the City Dionysia. c. 430–425: First performance of Sophocles' *Oedipus Rex* at the City Dionysia. 411: First performance of Aristophanes' *Lysistrata*.	480: At the Battle of Thermopylae, the Spartans defeat the Persians. 479: Xerxes, son of Darius, returns to Persia; the Persian Wars end. 462–429: Periclean Athens. 431: The Peloponnesian War begins; Athens is defeated in 404. Thucydides records the events in his history *The Peloponnesian War*.	460–370: Democritus, Greek philosopher who believed that all living things are composed of atoms. 438: **The** Parthenon is completed.
400–300	400–c. 320: Era of Middle Comedy, which concentrates on more accurately portraying daily life rather than the more fantastic plots of Old Comedy (Aristophanes). 336–300: Era of New Comedy. Menander and others move further away from Aristophanes; stock characters are common. 335–323: Aristotle writes *Poetics*.	395: The Corinthian War begins. Athens joins with Corinth, Thebes, and Argos to attack Sparta. Athens emerges from the ten-year war as a partially restored power. 332: Alexander the Great conquers Egypt. 321: Alexander the Great dies of a fever at age thirty-three. His successors divide the empire into Macedon, Egypt, and the Seleucid empire.	399: Socrates is tried and executed for corrupting the youth of Athens. 373: Plato writes *Republic*. 340–271: Epicurus, Greek philosopher who believed in pleasure, spontaneity, and freedom of will. 320–30: Hellenistic period of Greek art. 307: The museum and library of Alexandria are begun under Ptolemy Soter.
300–100	277: Artists of Dionysus, a performing artists' guild, is formed.		275–195: Eratosthenes, Greek scientist, suggests that the earth moves around the sun and makes close estimates of the earth's circumference.
100 BCE–300 CE		100 BCE–1 CE: Alexandria is the Mediterranean center of culture and commerce.	
300–400 CE			346–395: The Roman emperor Theodosius forbids the celebration of Olympic games in Greece.

Aeschylus

Very little is known for certain about the life of Aeschylus (c. 525–456 BCE) despite a first attempt at a biographical sketch in 300 BCE. What is known is that he was born in Eleusis near Athens at a time that marked Athens's beginning as an important power in Greece and as the cradle of Western art and thought. When Aeschylus was born, Athens was under the control of tyrants, a control that ended in 510 to 508 BCE; when he died, Athens was a democracy and one of the strongest states in the Greek confederation. The great threat to Athens's security came from the Persians, powerful Eastern warriors whose aim was the destruction of Greek economic power. Of the three great playwrights who lived in these times, Aeschylus is the only one who actually went to war against the Persians.

The records reveal that in 490 BCE Aeschylus fought at the battle of Marathon, in which his brother was killed. The Persians were defeated at Marathon, and their king, Darius, died shortly thereafter. For ten years the Athenians enjoyed an uneasy peace, but in 480 BCE the Persians returned under King Xerxes with a powerful fleet and army. Aeschylus fought at Salamis and probably also at a later victory in Plataea.

He seems to have been writing tragedies for fifteen years before his first victory in the drama competitions. He began competing in 499 to 496 BCE; he won his first victory in 484 BCE. Aeschylus went on to win a total of thirteen competitions with thirteen tetralogies: groups of three tragedies and a satyr play. He may have written as many as ninety plays; the titles of eighty-three have come down to us, with seven plays and many fragments surviving. *Agamemnon* is the first play in the *Oresteia*, the only surviving trilogy of Greek tragedies that we know were produced together. Sophocles' Oedipus plays, by contrast, were composed over a long period of time and were never performed as a trilogy until recent times.

Many efforts have been made to connect Aeschylus's plays to his life and times, but on the whole such efforts have been unprofitable. Clearly, though, he wrote some plays that spoke to the times, such as *The Persians* (472 BCE), undoubtedly inspired by Athenian success in the Persian Wars. He also wrote plays associated with specific places, as in *The Women of Aetna,* produced in Sicily near Mount Aetna. *The Persians* won first prize, and its expenses were paid by Athens's ruler Pericles, who, after the battle of Salamis, rebuilt the Acropolis with the Parthenon and the other important buildings, such as the Erectheum, that still stand there.

Aeschylus is sometimes credited with a rough and powerful style expressed in a language that sometimes forced him to make up new words. The power of his language is always remarked on by those who know his Greek original, and his translators have often been poets in their own right. By contrast, the younger Sophocles uses a language that is smoother, more lyrical, and more graceful. Some critics have asserted that the younger playwrights profited from Aeschylus's development of tragic style.

Aeschylus died at age sixty-eight in Gela, Sicily, where he spent time at the request of a friendly tyrant, Hieron. The story surrounding Aeschylus's death has been told many times and is probably only legend. It was said that an eagle grasping a tortoise flew high into the air and accidentally dropped the tortoise on Aeschylus's head, killing him. His death came at the height of the development of Greek tragedy.

AGAMEMNON

Agamemnon is the first play in the *Oresteia,* the only extant trilogy of Greek tragedies. The trilogy was performed in 458 BCE, winning first prize in the competition. As its name implies, it concerns the fate of Orestes, son of Agamemnon, even though Orestes does not appear in *Agamemnon.* Although he does not enter until *The Libation Bearers,* he becomes the center of the action in the third play, *The Eumenides.* As many commentators have observed, the three plays are in essence three acts of one larger play.

Underlying the action of the three plays is a memory of the horror that has befallen the House of Atreus, the family to which Agamemnon and Aegisthus and Orestes belong. Centuries before Aeschylus, Homer had told part of the story, which was a myth of significant proportions by the time Aeschylus dramatized it. It is recounted by Aegisthus near the end of *Agamemnon* (lines 1731–1766), although he omits at least one important detail. Pelops, son of Tantalus, had two sons: Atreus and Thyestes. The legend has several forms, but in essence Atreus and Thyestes have a falling out over the throne of their father. In addition, Atreus suspects that Thyestes has slept with his wife. With Atreus in control of the kingdom, Thyestes is invited to return for a reconciliation, but Atreus plans a fearful revenge. Pretending to prepare a feast of slaughtered animals, Atreus serves Thyestes his own two children chopped into a stew. Once he has eaten, Thyestes is shown the heads, hands, and feet of his children and vomits. He then flees into exile with his remaining infant son, Aegisthus.

Atreus's sons were Menelaus, who led the Greeks to Troy to regain his errant wife, Helen; and Agamemnon, who returned victorious from Troy. Agamemnon's children were Iphigenia, Electra (who figures in *The Libation Bearers*), and Orestes. The *Oresteia,* then, works out the curse on the house of Atreus.

Agamemnon reveals several forceful characters. Clytemnestra, the wife of Agamemnon, presents herself as a faithful, long-suffering wife waiting patiently for her husband's return from war. However, the Chorus, composed of older men, knows that she has taken a lover, Aegisthus. Clytemnestra faces up to the rumors of her infidelity when Agamemnon returns, daring anyone to contradict her. Secretly, though, she plans (with the help of Aegisthus) to kill Agamemnon. Her discovery that her husband is returning with a female slave, the prophetess Cassandra, as his concubine gives her further motivation. When she confesses to the murder of Agamemnon and Cassandra, she tells the Chorus that she is exacting revenge against Agamemnon for sacrificing their daughter Iphigenia in order to get a favorable wind to sail to Troy. Later, Aegisthus justifies his role in the killing as revenge against the crimes of Agamemnon's father, Atreus.

To ensnare Agamemnon, Clytemnestra has woven an intricate web—the image of the spider is invoked in the play. She is warned of his return by the pillars of fire that are set from Troy to Greece as Agamemnon returns, so she is prepared. She produces a richly woven purple cloth—the equivalent of what we call a red carpet—on which she expects Agamemnon to walk into the palace. Knowing that to do so could offend the gods, he at first refuses. Ultimately he yields to her entreaties and enters the palace, leaving Cassandra outside to prophesy his death—and hers—to the unbelieving Chorus. Inside, Clytemnestra continues the pattern by winding a regal cloak about Agamemnon as he is in the bath, disabling him so that she is able to stab him mortally.

Throughout, *Agamemnon* emphasizes issues of gender. Often the Chorus comments on Clytemnestra's speaking with the authority of a man. The invocation of the god Apollo throughout the trilogy has been taken to imply an important cultural shift that Aeschylus recognizes. Is he referring to a distant past in which female deities were dominant, later having been replaced by masculine deities? Such speculation is impossible to verify (see Lois Spatz's commentary on page 64), but it is clear that the women in the *Oresteia* are powerful in their presence, assertive in their actions, and insistent in their demand for justice. *Agamemnon* ends with Clytemnestra facing down an angry and mistrustful Chorus and with Aegisthus claiming the throne and governing as a tyrant.

Agamemnon in Performance

The first production of Aeschylus's trilogy in 458 BCE won first prize in the drama competitions. Although tragedies were not usually revived, it seems that this trilogy was played again at Greek festivals some few years after Aeschylus's death in 456 BCE. Unfortunately, after the demise of the Greek festivals, Aeschylus was not performed again until the sixteenth century. Early in the twentieth century the *Oresteia* was produced in Greek in the United States to a limited but enthusiastic audience. Harvard University produced *Agamemnon* in 1906, using all male actors, who spoke the lines in Greek. Max Reinhardt produced the trilogy in Berlin in 1915, but problems with the size of the theater and the nature of the stage resulted in an unsuccessful production. In 1968 the Minnesota Theater Company adapted the trilogy as *The House of Atreus,* directed by Tyrone Guthrie, taking it to Broadway at the Billy Rose Theater. Beginning in 1977 in New York, Andrei Serban experimented with performing *Agamemnon* in a mixture of English and Greek because, as he said, "Greek sounds have the power to catch the real emotional experience of the text." Serban produced the play at the Vivian Beaumont Theatre in Lincoln Center, New York. The high-tech staging, with exposed metal mesh floors and walls, created powerful effects. The Royal Shakespeare Company in 1980 put together an eleven-hour sequence of plays of Aeschylus, Euripides, and Sophocles on the fall of Troy, calling it *The Greeks;* it was successful both in England and abroad. The National Theatre in London produced the *Oresteia* in 1981 to considerable acclaim. Interestingly, the reviews of that production describe *Agamemnon* as having been eclipsed in dramatic importance by *The Libation Bearers,* which "becomes the great dramatic moment of the trilogy." Combining Euripides' *Iphigenia in Aulis* with the trilogy, the French Théâtre du Soleil performed *Les Atrides* in Paris, Montreal, and New York in 1992. Ariane Mnouchkine directed and conceived the production (in French with simultaneous translation), using only five actors. Paul Nadler compared *Les Atrides* with bullfights, which "deal with killers and victims acting out their fates upon fields of honor." The Royal National Theatre performed a shortened version of the *Oresteia* in January 2000 in London. The text was translated by the noted English poet Ted Hughes. *Agamemnon* was performed in its entirety to good reviews.

Aeschylus (c. 525–456 BCE)

AGAMEMNON   458 BCE

TRANSLATED BY DAVID GREENE AND WENDY DONIGER O'FLAHERTY

Dramatis Personae

SENTRY
CHORUS, *old men of Argos left behind after the Argives went to Troy*
CLYTEMNESTRA, *queen of Argos in the absence of King Agamemnon at Troy*
HERALD *from the Greek army*
KING AGAMEMNON
CASSANDRA, *princess of Troy, daughter of King Priam*
AEGISTHUS

SENTRY: You gods, release me.
    Crouched like a dog, I watch always, all year long,
    on the tower of the sons of Atreus.
    I have come to know the nightly gathering of the stars
    and those radiant dynasts of the firmament that
5   lead them.
    They bring winter and summer to men.
    Now I watch for a flaming light,
    the beacon fire, the tell-tale witness that Troy is captured.
    Such are my orders, orders from a hopeful queen
10   who thinks with the mind of a man.
    I have a bed here, soaked with dew, always shifting.
    But no dreams. Fear is my visitor, not sleep.
    I cannot close my eyes for fear.
    Sometimes I whistle or hum;
15   the tunes are my drug against my sleepiness.
    But then the sorrow comes.
    This house is in bitter trouble.
    Once it was well governed; not now.
    Still, may the fire of good news light the darkness
20   to be the lucky release from our troubles.

    The beacon! Day out of night!
    The dances everywhere in Argos!
    Thanks, good beacon!
    My lady, Agamemnon's wife, get out of bed!
    Cry aloud a blessing on this beacon,   25
    since Troy is surely captured.
    I will myself begin the dance, for I'll score to myself, too,
    the winning dice that the beacon threw for my master.
    Oh, that I could touch with this hand of mine
    the hand that I love, my lord's.   30
    As for the rest, I haven't a word;
    a great ox stands on my tongue.
    If the house itself had a voice to speak,
    it would tell the clearest story.
    I choose to speak to those who understand;   35
    for the others, I am all forgetfulness.
CHORUS: This is the tenth year
    since they launched from this land
    the Greek fleet of a thousand ships
    to help right wrongs done.   40
    They launched it, King Menelaus,
    great plaintiff against Priam,
    and Agamemnon his brother;
    twin the yoke joining them in honor and throne,
    twin their shared grace of God.   45

    From their hearts the great war cry;
    they screamed like eagles,
    that wheel and wheel high above their eyries,
    driven by the oarage of their wings,
    in lonely agony for the loss of their nestlings,   50
    and all the watchful care they had spent guarding them.

But One yet higher up, some Apollo or Pan or
    Zeus,°
hears the shrill-voiced sorrow of these settlers in
    his kingdom
and sends on the evildoers
55 the Fury that brings punishment, however late.
So a Lord greater than the kings, Zeus god of
    guest-friends,
sends the sons of Atreus on Alexander;°
in this quarrel over a woman of many men,
he would lay upon Greeks and Trojans alike
60 many wrestlings where the limbs grow heavy
and the knee is pressed into the dust
and the spear is shattered in the first rites of
    engagement.
Yet it is now as it is.
Fulfillment moves toward what is fated.
And not with burnt offerings nor with pouring on
65   of wine
nor sacrifice to the gods below
will you assuage that stubborn anger.

But we, dishonored for the ancientness of our flesh,
were left behind then when the army went;
we remain, propping on staffs a strength like a
70   child's.
For the child's marrow, too, leaps within his breast
but is only the match of an old man's;
the god of war is not there either.
And the overold, the leafage already withering,
walks his three-footed way,° no stronger than a
75   child;
wanders, a dream in the daylight.

You, daughter of Tyndareus, Queen Clytemnestra,
What's the matter? What's the news? What have
    you heard?
What message do you trust, that you order sacrifices
80 at all the altars?
Of all the gods that hold our city,
of those above and those beneath the earth,
of those at the doorpost and those at the
    marketplace,
the altars blaze with offerings.
85 Here one torch sends its flames to the sky,
and another raises its light,
charmed by the soft, guileless urgings of pure
    streams of oil
drawn from the depth of the royal store.
Tell us what you can and what may be said
90 about all these things.
Cure this care that now broods darkly on our minds.

But then hope, shining out of the sacrifice,
turns away the insatiable thoughts that might
    otherwise
eat out the heart in sorrow.

It is mine to declare the omens of victory 95
given to princely men on the journey.
For by God's grace, old age, which grows with
    life, my life,
still breathes on my lips persuasion,
the strength of song.
I tell how the princes of the Achaeans, 100
twin-throned, single-hearted
lords of the youth of Greece,
were sent against the land of Troy
with spear in hand to exact vengeance.
The furious omen-birds° sent them, 105
one black eagle, one white-tail,
the kings of birds to the kings of the ships.
Near the palace they came on the spear-striking
    side,
perched where all could see them
as they fed on the womb's gravid load of leverets,° 110
mother and all, pulled down in the hare's last
    course.
Cry sorrow, sorrow, but let the good prevail.

Yet the honest prophet of the army saw
the two sons of Atreus,
twin in military spirit, 115
and knew the princely leaders and hare-
    devourers—
knew that they were one and the same.
And so he declared in his prophecy,
"In time, this journey will capture Troy, Priam's°
    city;
and all the communal herds that graze before her
    towers 120
shall Fate give violently to plunder.
I only pray that no anger from the God will cast a
    cloud
upon this army forged from before to be
a great iron bit in the mouth of Troy.
For Queen Artemis° is full of pity out of jealousy 125
against those winged hounds of her father
who devour in sacrifice
the unhappy cowering mother with her brood
before they come to birth.
She hates the eagles' feast. 130
Cry sorrow, sorrow, but let the good prevail.

105. omen-birds: Eagles, thought to be messengers of the gods.
110. leverets: Young hares. **119. Priam:** King of Troy at the time of the Trojan War. **125. Artemis:** Greek goddess, who was the daughter of Zeus and sister of Apollo. Artemis was the protector of young animals. Angered at the slaughter of the leverets, she caused contrary winds to prevent the Greeks from sailing for Troy. Agamemnon was forced to sacrifice his daughter Iphigenia to appease Artemis and secure favorable winds.

52. Apollo or Pan or Zeus: Greek gods with the power to avenge crimes. **57. Alexander:** Also known as Paris, Alexander was the son of King Priam and Queen Hecuba of Troy. He carried off Helen, the wife of Greek commander Menelaus (Agamemnon's brother), and this action caused the Trojan War. **75. three-footed way:** Walking with a cane or staff.

Yes, she is kindly, that beautiful one,
to cubs, scarcely crawling, of savage lions,
and she finds her delight in all the breast-loving
    infants
135 of wild things of the field.
Yet she grants fulfillment of what the omens
    imply:
grant, Lady, favorable fulfillment, and void the
    other.
I call on Apollo the Healer
to keep her from setting against the Greeks
140 those contrary winds, winds that hold ships,
staying winds, winds that stop sailing altogether.
She might do this in eagerness for a different
    sacrifice,
one that is lawless and horrible,
a trueborn craftsman of quarrels,
145 that has no awe of a husband.
For full of terrors it lurks,
house keeping, crafty, long-memoried,
an anger that punishes child-slaughter."

Such were the prophecies of Calchas's° voice,
150 mingled with the good things,
and all predicted for our royal house
from omens on the way.
In harmony with these,
cry sorrow, sorrow, but let the good prevail.

155 Zeus, whoever he is,
if it is dear to him to be so called,
this is how I call him.
I have thrown all into the scale,
but cannot find his likeness—
160 there is only Zeus,
if I must cast my burden of vain care from the heart
in honest truth.

Not he that once was great,
swelling with daring, challenging all comers,
165 shall even be spoken of, for he is of the past.
And he that came after him
has had his three falls wrestling,
and is gone.
But whoever sings to Zeus
170 the victory song from a full heart,
he shall win all that his heart desires.

Zeus it is that has made man's road;
he it is who has laid down the rule
that understanding comes through suffering.
175 Instead of sleep, there drips before the heart
the recollected sorrow of past pain.
It is against our wills that we become wise.
Forced indeed upon us is the grace of our gods
that sit on their solemn thrones.

149. **Calchas:** A prophet who accompanied the Greek army to
Troy.

So on that day, the old leader of the Greek ships,   180
faulting no prophet, caught his breath at his
    sudden calamity,
when the Greek host was burdened
with ships halted and empty holds,
as they held the coast over against Chalcis,°
at Aulis° where the tides roar to and fro.   185

The hurricane that came from Strymon,°
breeding deadly delays, starvation, lost anchorages,
driving crews to aimless wanderings,
sparing neither ships nor cables,
wore down the flower of the Argives,   190
doubling their time with enforced lingering.
So when the prophet's voice rang out,
proclaiming to the princes another cure for the
    bitter storm,
a cure yet heavier to bear,
he backed his prophecies with Artemis's name,   195
and the twin sons of Atreus beat the ground with
    their staves
and could not hold back their tears.
Then the old king spoke and said,
"Heavy indeed my fate if I disobey,
but heavy, too, if I must butcher my child,   200
the glory of my house, polluting a father's hands
with streams of a virgin's blood beside the altar.
Which of these two things is without evil?
How shall I become a deserter of my fleet and fail
    my allies?
There is sacred law on their side, that they
    passionately covet   205
a virgin's blood as sacrifice to quell the winds.
May it turn out well."

When he put on the harness of Necessity,
his spirit veered in a breath of change—
to impiety, to unholiness, to desecration,   210
and from it he drew audacity for his heart
to stop at nothing.
For indeed there is a wretched distraction of the
    wits,
a primal source of ruin,
that puts recklessness in man's mind   215
and counsels ugliness.
So he dared to become his daughter's sacrificer
to aid the war waged for a woman—
first rites of deliverance for the ships.
Her prayers, and her cries of "Father," and her
    maiden life   220
they set at nothing, those military umpires.
Her father ordered his servants to lift her
carefully over the altar

184. **Chalcis:** City in Asia Minor across the straits from Aulis,
where the Greeks were detained by contrary winds.   **185.
Aulis:** City where the Greek fleet collected before sailing to
Troy.   **186. Strymon:** River in Asia Minor across from Aulis.

after the prayer, swooning, her clothes all round her,
225 like a young goat,
and with a gag on her beautiful lips
to restrain the cry that would curse his house.
Constrained to voicelessness by the violence of the
    bit,
she slipped to the ground her saffron robes,
and with darting, pitiful eyes struck each of her
230   sacrificers.
She stood out, like a figure in a picture, struggling
    to speak,
for often she had sung in her father's hospitable halls,
and with pure maiden voice lovingly honored
her beloved father's victory hymn,
235 with its triple libation to bring good luck.
What happened after that I neither saw nor tell.
But Calchas's divining art bore fruit;
the scales of justice have come down and brought,
with suffering, understanding.
240 You will learn the future when it happens.
Till then, let it be.
To do otherwise is to have sorrow before you need.
For it will come clear with the dawn's light.

(*Enter Clytemnestra.*)

But at the end of all this let there be good fortune.
245 Surely that is the wish of this (*turning to the queen*)
our sole and closest bulwark against trouble in
    Argos.
I have come, Queen Clytemnestra, to pay you my
    respects;
for it is right, in the absence of the prince,
to honor the wife of the man whose throne is empty.
250 I would be glad to know
if you are sure of good tidings or not.
Is it in the hope of happy news
that you are ordering sacrifice?
But I won't resent it if you must be silent.
255 CLYTEMNESTRA: As the proverb goes,
"May dawn be the dawn of good news
as she comes from her mother night"—
you shall learn of a joy greater than you hope.
For the Argives have captured Priam's city.
CHORUS: What? I cannot believe you; I cannot
260   understand.
CLYTEMNESTRA: Troy is the Greeks' city now. Are my
    words clear?
CHORUS: Joy steals over me, and calls out tears, too.
CLYTEMNESTRA: Your eyes proclaim you a subject
    true and loyal.
CHORUS: What makes you trust the news? Have you
    proof of it?
CLYTEMNESTRA: I have, of course—unless the gods
265   deceived me.
CHORUS: Dream visions? Do you believe in them?
CLYTEMNESTRA: No sleeping mind for me, no, nor its
    fancies.
CHORUS: Have flying rumors bloated you?
CLYTEMNESTRA: As if I were a child, you taunt me.

CHORUS: But when was it that the city was sacked?   270
CLYTEMNESTRA: In this last night that brought this
    dawn to birth.
CHORUS: What messenger can be as quick as that?
CLYTEMNESTRA: The god of fire, sending his brilliant
    glow from Mount Ida.
Beacon sent beacon here with courier fires,
Ida to the crag of Hermes in Lemnos;°   275
then from that island a third flame sent on
was welcomed by the heights of Athos that belong
    to Zeus;
and high, spanning the sea's back,
the strength of the escorting flame went joyously
    onward.
The pine fire sent its golden blaze, almost a sun,   280
to the watchtowers of Macistus.
He didn't hesitate nor carelessly succumb to sleep,
but passed his share of the message,
and from afar, over the streams of Euripus,
he gave to the sentries of Messapion   285
the sign that the beacon's light had traveled to him.
They in their turn lit up and sent the message
    farther,
firing a great heap of ancient gorse.
Still strong, the beacon's light never flagged,
but leapt over the plain of Asopus like a radiant
    moon,   290
to Mount Cithaeron, and there awakened
another relay of traveling fire.
The guard station did not refuse the far-escorted
    flame;
it kindled more than was ordered, and launched its
    light
over the Gorgon lake; and coming to   295
the goat-haunted mountain,
urged the watchman not to scant the ordinance of
    fire.
They lit a huge beard of flame that burnt
    ungrudgingly,
and sent it over the Saronic gulf, now become its
    mirror,
beyond the headland, till it struck the heights of
    Arachnus,   300
our neighboring sentry post here, and then again
struck right here on this roof of the sons of
    Atreus—
this fire that is the grandchild of that fire on
    Mount Ida.
Such were the courses of the torchbearers,
one from the other in relays,   305
and victor is he that ran first and last.
Such proof I have and such confirmation,
sent me out of Troy by my man.

273–75. **Mount Ida . . . Lemnos:** Mountain in Asia Minor
southeast of Troy from which the gods could view the battles.
The place names that follow trace the course of beacon fires set
to bring the news of the Greek victory from Troy to Greece.

CHORUS: My lady, to the gods once again
310 I shall give my prayer of thanks,
     but I would like you to tell me all this again,
     that I might hear the words and marvel at them
     from beginning to end.
CLYTEMNESTRA: Troy is captured; this is the day; the
         Greeks hold it.
315 Within that city there rings out
     a volume of cries that do not mingle.
     This is how I see it.
     Mix oil and vinegar in the same jar
     and you could not call them friends;
320 they will not be at one.
     So in Troy you might hear two sorts of crying:
     the conquered and the conquerors.
     The act is single, the meaning double.
     Here are these:
325 throwing themselves on the dead bodies
     of husbands and brothers,
     children on the bodies of their fathers,
     all sorrowing for the destiny of their dead,
     they cry from throats no longer free.
330 Then there are the others:
     roving all night after the fight
     sets them down hungry to breakfast
     on such foods as the city has;
     they all share, no rank or place assigned,
335 but as each has got the luck of the draw.
     They are already living in Troy's captured houses,
     free of the frost beneath the sky, free of the dews.
     They will sleep all night long without a guard,
     like happy men.
     If they revere the gods of that city in that captured
340   land,
     if they revere the gods' sacred places,
     they who are conquerors will not be reconquered.
     Only let no lust seize the army first,
     let no greed conquer them,
345 to make them ravish what they should not.
     They must still make the home voyage safely,
     travel the other leg of the double track.
     But even if the army came through offenseless
     in the sight of the gods,
350 the wrong done to the dead may yet awaken,
     seeking to contrive some sudden mischief.
     This is what you hear from me, a woman.
     But may the good prevail for all to see, past dispute.
     Of the many good things I might have,
355 this is what I would choose.
CHORUS: My lady, you talk wisely, like a sensible man.
     I have learned from you your convincing proofs,
     and now again I prepare to greet the gods.
     Surely we should thank them for what they have
         done for us.
360 O Zeus the king, and friendly night,
     that has endowed us with great glory,
     you that have cast upon the towers of Troy
     a close-fitting mesh so that no one young or old
     can overleap the great net of slavery,

the all-catching trap of ruin—   365
great Zeus of guest-friends I revere.
He has done all this. He has forever bent his bow
against Alexander, that no bolt should fail,
neither missing the mark nor scaling the stars.
They can say, "It is the stroke of Zeus";   370
the track of it is clear to see.
Zeus has acted as he has determined.
Someone has said,
"The gods do not deign to take heed of mortals
who trample underfoot the grace of holiness."   375
But he that said that had no piety in him.
The recklessness stands revealed
of those who breathe war beyond justice.
It is a recklessness that breeds consequences
when houses are overcrammed   380
beyond the measure of the best.
So I escape harm, let but a sufficiency be mine,
with abundance of good judgment.
For wealth gives no defense
for the man insolent with gorging,   385
who kicks the great altar of justice
to where none can see it.
Wretched persuasion,
intolerable child of forecounseling ruin,
drives him on violently.   390
And all cure is vain. It is not hidden, no—
the mischief shines, a lamp of evil light.
The black grain in Paris° shows through the test,
like base copper rubbed bare with use.
He has been like a child that chases a bird;   395
he has brought on this city an intolerable infection,
and no one of the gods will hear his prayer—
rather, pull down the unjust man
conversant with such things.
Such a one is Paris, who came   400
to the house of the sons of Atreus
and stained with shame the table of his host
by the theft of that host's wife.
She has left to her fellow citizens
the clanging of shields, the arming of sailors,
     ambushes.   405
To Ilium she has brought ruin instead of dowry.
Her daring defying all limits,
she darted quickly through the gates.
And many a groan there was
among those that spoke for the palace: 410
"Ah me, ah me, for the house, the house and the
     princes.
Ah me for the bed and the tracks of the love of
     men on it."
There one can see the silence—
dishonored, unreviling, inexorable—
of him that sits apart.   415
Through yearning for the one gone over the sea,
a ghost will seem to rule the house.

393. **Paris:** A prince of Troy, Paris abducted Helen of Greece,
thus defying Zeus's law of hospitality.

The grace of beautiful statues is hateful to the man.
Their eyes are empty, and before them
420 all passionate love falls dead.
Fancies haunt him in dreams persuasively;
theirs is a grace without substance.
Unsubstantial it is, when one sees,
and dreaming reaches to the touch,
and the phantom is gone, quickly slipping through
425   his hands,
as it follows the winged paths of sleep.
Such are the sorrows at home at the hearth;
but there are worse than these for all,
for those who joined the fleet and left the land of
        Greece.
430 In the house of every one of these
preeminent there is grief that reaches the heart.
They know whom they have sent forth, but
        instead of men
there come home urns and ashes to each house.
The war god is a money changer;
435 men's bodies are his money.
He holds the scales in the battle of the spear.
From Ilium he sends back to those who loved them
the scrapings of dust made heavy with their tears;
he loads the elegant urns with the dust that was
        once a man.
440 They mourn this man as they praise him—
how skilled he was in the fight—and another—
how gallantly he fell in his blood—
for another man's woman.
That is what they whisper and snarl;
445 and pain creeps about, full of ill will
toward the plaintiffs, the sons of Atreus.
But those others keep to their graves in all their
        beauty,
where they were, around the walls of Troy.
The enemy land that they have taken at last
450 has taken them, hidden them in itself.
The malicious speech of citizens is hard to bear;
it is the equal of a public curse.
And still I am troubled, lest I come to hear
something hidden in dark night.

455 For watchful are the gods' eyes
for those that kill by the thousands.
The black Furies reduce to dim nothingness
the man whose success has no justice in it,
wear him down, reversing his life's fortune.
460 And when he is among those we cannot see,
there is no help for him.
To be too well spoken of is heavy indeed.
For the thunderbolt is hurled from the eyes of Zeus.
May I not be a city-sacker, nor yet look upon my
        own life,
465 captured by others.
Swift is the rumor coursing through the city,
spurred by the fire of good tidings.
But whether it is true, who knows, or whether
somehow the gods deceive us.

Who is there so childish, so maimed of wit, 470
that the messages of fire should kindle his heart
only to sicken later when the news changes?
It is like the mettle of a woman's spirit
to praise the gracious gift before it is certainly there.
The limits of a woman's belief can be 475
as easily and quickly crossed
as cattle graze across a boundary.
But quickly, too, dies the report
a woman utters.
Soon we shall know about the lights from the
        beacons 480
and all the exchange of watch fires:
whether they are true or whether, like dreams,
a light of joy has stolen upon us and cheated our
        minds.
Here I see the herald coming from the shore,
shaded with twigs of olive. 485
The thirsty dust, twin sister of mud across the
        boundary,
is my witness; it witnesses to me that he has a *real*
        voice,
and so his testimony is not one of the smoky fire
of some wood on the hillside.
He will rather speak out and tell us to be glad, 490
or—God forbid it is the contrary message.
There *have* been good things that have shown
        through;
grant that this is their consummation.
Whoever prays anything else for this city,
I would he might reap the fruit of his mistaken
        thoughts. 495

(*Enter a herald.*)

HERALD: O my fathers' earth, Argos, Argos,
ten long years and I have come to you;
so many shipwrecked hopes, and one a winner.
I never dreamed that I would have for my share in
        death
a piece of dearest Argive land. 500
Now welcome earth, welcome the light of sun,
and Zeus supreme lord; and the Pythian King,°
no longer shooting his arrows against us;
you were harsh enough along Scamander's banks,
but now you are different, now you are savior and
        healer, 505
King Apollo. My greetings to all the gods in
        assembly.
My greeting to my patron god, Hermes, dear herald,
whom all heralds worship.
My greetings to the heroes that sent us out
and kindly welcome back what's left of us after
        the fight. 510
Hail, royal halls, roofs I have loved,
hail, holy seats and you divinities that face the
        sunlight.

502. **Pythian King:** The god Apollo.

Receive now with faces bright in joy—
if ever you did in days gone by—
now receive the king in glory after so long. 515
He comes and brings light after night's darkness,
a light to you and to all these—
King Agamemnon.
Give him true welcome; truly it belongs to him,
the king who dug down Troy with the spade of
        God's justice, 520
made plowland of Troy;
and the seed has perished from all their country.
Their altars and the shrines of their gods are gone.
Such a yoking chain has he cast on Troy,
the king, Atreus's son, the old and happy man. 525
And now he comes here, most worthy of all
that now live and die.
Neither Paris nor the city that supports him
can boast that they have done more than they
        have paid for.
He was condemned for rape and theft— 530
lost what he carried off.
He has reaped for harvest
the utter ruin of his father's house.
And doubly have the sons of Priam paid for their
        offenses.
CHORUS: Herald of the Argive army, joy on your
        homecoming! 535
HERALD: Joy, indeed. If the gods should end my life
        now,
I'd not deny them.
CHORUS: Has the love of your lost homeland tortured
        you so?
HERALD: Yes; the tears you see are tears of joy.
CHORUS: That disease had its pleasure for you, all the
        same. 540
HERALD: What disease? What should I understand by
        that?
CHORUS: Love's stroke. But you got love for the love
        you gave.
HERALD: You mean this land has missed the army as
        we missed you?
CHORUS: We were faint and weak and so have
        groaned for you.
HERALD: Why so uneasy? What horror was in your
        mind? 545
CHORUS: I say nothing and am safe—a long, long
        silence.
HERALD: How could that be? Your king was away;
        did you fear others?
CHORUS: As you said just now, I would have
        welcomed death.
HERALD: It *has* been a success. Of course, in the
        length of time,
one must say some things have gone well, some ill. 550
Who except the gods lives the whole span of his life
without trouble?
Yes, if I were to speak of the hard work
and the bad quarters,
the narrow gangways and the hard beds, 555

there's plenty to complain about.
Then there were the troubles on land,
disgusting things, too.
Our beds were under the enemy's walls.
Rain from the sky and dew from the grass soaked us 560
and kept rotting our clothing
and bred lice in our hair.
I could talk about the winter, which killed the birds;
Mount Ida and its snow made that intolerable.
And then there was the heat, 565
when the sea fell on its noontide bed and slept.
Not a breath of wind, not a stir on the waves—
Oh, why should I still feel pain for all this?
It's over, isn't it, all the trouble?
It's over indeed, for them, too, the dead; 570
they'll never have to trouble about getting up again.
Why should I reckon up the numbers of those
        who are gone?
Why should the living grieve because
fortune turned against us?
I'm ready to say a long goodbye to all that's
        happened. 575
For us that are left of the Greek army,
the gain certainly wins out,
and the bad side of things doesn't weigh it down.
So, those of us who have sped over land and sea
can stand facing the sunlight and make our boast: 580
"There was a day when the Argive army took Troy.
They have nailed the spoils of it
on the homes of the gods throughout Greece
to be a glory forever and ever."
When they hear this, men must praise 585
the city and its generals.
We shall also honor the grace of God
who brought it to pass.
That's my whole speech.
CHORUS: What you say wins me over; I admit it. 590
To be ready to learn is what makes a young man
out of an old one.
But it is this house and Clytemnestra
that the news most concerns,
though I, too, am the richer for it. 595
CLYTEMNESTRA: I rejoiced long ago,
and raised the cry of joy over the news,
when first the fire came as my messenger in the
        night,
telling of Troy's capture and destruction.
That was when everyone found fault with me: 600
"Is it beacon fires that convince you
that Troy has now been sacked?
How like a woman's heart to be so lifted up."
In rumors such as these I appeared
to have gone astray in my wits. 605
But yet I made the sacrifices,
and following this "woman's fashion"
they all raised the chant, now here, now there,
throughout the city,
the songs of blessing at the gods' shrines, 610
and there they lulled to sleep

the sweet-smelling sacrificial fires.
Why *now* should I depend on you to tell me more?
I shall learn the whole story from my lord himself.
615 How shall I make best haste to receive him home,
my honored husband?
What sweeter day for a wife's eye to see
than when she opens the doors to her man
coming from the army,
620 when the gods have brought him safely back to her?
Tell my husband this:
bid him come as quick as he can,
the city's darling.
And when he comes may he find his wife
625 true as he left her,
the watchdog of his house,
devoted to him, enemy to his enemies,
the same always and ever.
I never broke the seal
630 in all those years.
I know of no pleasure with another man
nor any talk or evil gossip against me,
anymore than I know how to dip this blade
to temper it.
635 Such is my boast, so full of truth
that even a well-bred wife
need not blush to utter it.

(Exit Clytemnestra.)

CHORUS: She has spoken very suitably
for those who understand her.
640 But tell me, Herald,
what of Menelaus?
Was he among the returning army?
Is he safe among you?
And will he come back home again, our dear
prince?
645 HERALD: I don't know how to put a fair face on lies:
my friends would only have good of it
for a short time anyway.
CHORUS: Why can't you tell news that is both good
and true?
When you separate them, you can't get away with it.
HERALD: Then—the man has vanished from the
650 Greek army,
he and his ship. *That* is not a lie.
CHORUS: Did you see him set forth from Ilium on his
own?
Or did some storm that struck you all together
snatch him away?
655 HERALD: You've hit it exactly;
in a few words you've covered a long, sad story.
CHORUS: What do the rest of his shipmates think?
Do they say he's alive or dead?
HERALD: No one knows how to tell the news clearly—
660 except the sun, there, that gives life to the world.
CHORUS: What do you mean? Was there a storm
that came upon the fleet by the gods' anger
and then ended?
HERALD: A day of good news—one should not
infect it

with the tongue of bad news. 665
The honor due to the two kinds of gods
is separate.
When a messenger with a gloomy face bears
cursed news
of an army's downfall,
there is one common injury which is public, 670
and then, besides, many a man is banned from his
home;
this is the double lash that the god of war loves,
a two-speared ruin, a bloody pair.
When, I say, a messenger is loaded with such
calamities,
he must sing his news as his hymn to the Furies. 675
But when the saving messenger of good news
comes to a city that rejoices in well-being
—how should I mingle good with bad
in telling you of this storm
which surely did proceed from the gods' anger 680
against the Greeks?
For fire and sea, those two oldest and deepest of
enemies,
swore a conspiracy and pledged their common
allegiance
to destroy the wretched Greek army.
In the night, waves lashed by the storm 685
arose to plague us.
For the Thracian winds battered ship on ship.
Butting one another savagely
in the hurricane and sheets of hail,
they sank from sight, as our evil shepherd 690
drove us here and there.
When the clear light of the day came back,
we saw the sea blooming,
and its flowers were dead Greeks and wrecks.
For ourselves and our boat, we went unharmed; 695
some god stole us through it or begged us off;
he must have steered us himself,
for no man touched the steering oar.
Luck chose to become our savior, and sat on our
ship,
so that we missed the driving waves when we were
at anchor, 700
nor were driven aground on the rugged land.
Afterward, when we had escaped our watery hell,
in the white light of day, we hardly dared to trust
our luck;
and in our own thoughts we were constantly
shepherds of some new calamity, 705
seeing how the fleet had been pounded and ground
to pieces.
Now, if any of them still breathes,
they speak of us as lost; of course they do.
We have much the same idea about them.
Let it turn out well. For Menelaus, 710
in all likelihood you may expect him back.
For if the beams of the sun discover him living
and seeing,
through the workings of God—

715 for surely God will not yet blot out
the whole family—
there is some hope that he'll come home again.
This is really the truth that you have heard.

(*Exit herald.*)

CHORUS: Who can have named her so,
with such truth, utterly?
720 Could it be someone we cannot see,
with foreknowledge of destiny,
that used his tongue in harmony with fortune?
She was called Helen,°
the bride won by the spear, sought in strife.
725 Helen means death, and death indeed she was,
death to ships and men and city
as she sailed out of the delicate fabrics of her
curtained room,
fanned by the breeze of giant Zephyr;°
and the man-swarm of shield-bearing hunters
730 came on the track of her,
the vanished track of the oar blades
which beached on the ever-green shores of Simoeis
on the heels of their bloody quarrel.

To Ilium it drove her,
735 the wrath that brings fulfillment,
and again the word proved true, that equates
marriage and mourning,
for the wrath exacted vengeance at the last
for the guest-table dishonored at the hearth shared
by Zeus.
740 Wrath punished as victims those men,
the new marriage kinsmen,
who on that day must celebrate,
sing out of full throats
the hymn that honored the bride.
745 Perhaps that ancient city of Priam
has learned another tune now,
a tuneful dirge that calls him
Paris the dismally bedded;
the city has endured the ruin of its life,
750 the voice of countless lamentations,
through the wretched bloodletting of its citizens.
Once on a time there was a man
who raised a lion cub in his home.
It was a little thing, starved of milk,
755 still a suckling, still in the first rituals of its life,
gentle, a friend of children,
and a delight to the old.
Many a time it lay in their arms,
like a young baby;
760 its face was bright as it fawned on the hand
at the dictates of its belly's needs.
But time passed, and it showed
what disposition it had from its breeding;

723. **Helen:** Daughter of Zeus and Leda, a mortal woman, Helen was the wife of the Greek commander Menelaus before she was abducted by Paris and brought to Troy. 728. **Zephyr:** God of the west wind.

it requited the grace of those that brought it up
by horrid slaughtering of their sheep,   765
an unbidden dinner guest.
And the house was confused and befouled with
blood;
an evil it was that the servants couldn't fight,
a very murderous mischief.
God reared the lion in the house to become   770
an additional priest of ruin.
But on that first day—as I tell the story—
she came to the city of Ilium
a spirit of windless calm,
the delicate glory of wealth,   775
the soft arrow darting from her eyes,
the flower of love that bites the heart.
Then she changed direction, and brought
a bitter ending to the marriage,
hastening to the daughters of Priam   780
to sit with them and live with them
to their ruin.
Zeus, the god of guests, brought her there,
a Fury to make wives weep.
There is an old saying among men, first spoken
long ago,   785
that a man's great prosperity, when perfected,
gives birth and doesn't die childless,
but from that good fortune in true descent
there grows an ever-greedy misery.
In this, my mind is different from others'.   790
No, I say, it is the wicked deed
that breeds more wickedness, and like to its own
kind.
For the house that is straight-dealing and just
is fated always to have good children.
The ancient deed of sacrilege always breeds a
young one,   795
full of disaster for man, now or then,
when comes the dawn appointed for its birth.
A spirit but a clansman—
one cannot war against him nor fight him—
he is a thing unholy,   800
a daring, a black ruin to the halls,
and very like his parents.
For justice shines in houses grimed with smoke,
and she honors the good man.
And those gilded palaces where hands are dirty 805
she leaves, averting her eyes;
she goes to what is clean,
for she doesn't honor power
whose coinage is misstamped by the praise of the
rich.
And she guides everything to its due end.   810

(*Enter Agamemnon and Cassandra.*)

My lord, conqueror of Troy, descendant of Atreus,
how shall I greet you, how do you reverence,
neither exceeding nor scanting due measure of
praise?
Many men, indeed, who transgress justice,

honor appearance over reality.
Everyone is ready to cry over the unfortunate,
but the bite of that sorrow doesn't reach the heart.
So, too, there are those that seem to share joy,
yet the faces that they force have no laughter in
them.
When one is a good judge of stock,
one doesn't miss the meaning of the man's eyes,
fawning in watery friendship
when they seem all loyalty.
In the days when you led the expedition from
Greece,
for Helen's sake,
I saw you painted in ugly colors—
I will not hide that from you—
as one who had an unskillful hand
on the rudder of his wits
when you tried to win back through men's dying
a willing whore.
But now from the depth of my heart, in true
friendship,
I say, May the work be kind to those who did it
so well.
In time you shall know by enquiry
which of your citizens that stayed here at home
dealt justly, and which did wrong.

AGAMEMNON: First Argos and my country's gods,
I must address you; you and I are coauthors
of my home return and the justice
I exacted from Priam's city.
The causes were not spoken aloud,
but the gods heard them
and cast their votes with no opposing voices
into the bloody urn: for Ilium's destruction
and the deaths of men.
To the other urn nothing drew near
but the shadowy hope of a hand;
there was no filling that urn.
You can still see the smoke from the city's capture.
The hot blasts of ruin live there yet,
but there is ash, too, dying
as it sends into the air its breaths fattened on rich
things.
For all of this we should pay our gods
much-remembering thanks.
We have taken vengeance for insolent robbery.
And for the sake of a woman a city has been leveled
by the biting beast of Argos, the colt,
the shield-bearing host,
that made its leap about the time of the setting
Pleiades.
A ravening lion leaped over the wall
and licked its fill of royal blood.
So far my prelude stretches; that's for the gods.
What you've said of your feelings, I've heard and
remember.
I say the same. You have me as your advocate.
In very few men is it native
to admire a successful friend without envying him.

For the poison of malice, settling on the heart,
doubles its weight in one who is stricken with envy.
He suffers under the load of his own troubles,
and groans to see the prosperity of the other man.
I know of what I speak; I very well understand
the glassy mirror of comradeship, that shadow of
a shade,
which those prove to be who seemed my truest
friends.
Only Odysseus,° who joined the fleet unwillingly,
once he was yoked was for me a ready trace horse.
Even as I speak of him, I do not know
if I speak of the dead or the living.
For other matters, we will set up public meetings
and take counsel in full assembly.
What is now well shall remain well; we shall see
to it.
But where there is need for healing medicines,
we will try by surgery or cautery°
intelligently to avert the disease.
Now I will go in, into my halls, my hearth, my
home,
and there I will first greet the gods
who sent me forth and brought me back again.
Victory has followed us;
let her be ours still, constantly!

(*Enter Clytemnestra.*)

CLYTEMNESTRA: You citizens, elders of Argos,
I will not be ashamed of speaking to you
of how I love my husband.
Modest inhibition is something
that dies away in human dealings.
I will tell of how wretched my life has been
while this man was in Troy—
at first hand I will tell it; it has been *my* life.
First, that a woman should sit in her house,
lonely without her male,
is something terrifying.
She hears so many hateful rumors;
here's one has come, and then another,
announcing a greater disaster still,
mouthing the ruin of the house.
If this man here had had as many wounds
as streams of rumor would have it,
he would have had more holes in him than a net.
If he had died, as his deaths multiplied in stories
of him,
he must have had three bodies, like Geryon;
he would have boasted of taking a triple
shroud of earth to himself.
It was because of these hateful reports
that others, not I, have loosened many a cord
as it tightened round my neck.

874. **Odysseus:** Throughout the *Iliad,* Homer's story of the Trojan war, Odysseus is a brave soldier. He gives wise, even wily, advice to the Greeks. 882. **cautery:** The process of burning with a hot iron in order to heal.

And that is why your son
915 doesn't stand beside me as he should,
the proof of our trust, mine to you, yours to me,
our Orestes.
Do not wonder at this; a loyal ally keeps him safe,
Strophius the Phocian.°
920 He spoke to me of twin troubles:
your danger at Ilium, and then that here, too,
the anarchy of the people's voices
might overturn good counsel.
Indeed, it is inbred in men
925 to kick the man that's down.
That's the advice of Strophius, and there's no deceit
in it.
For my own part, the gushing springs of my grief
have dried up;
there's not a drop left.
930 My eyes are in pain from late watching,
weeping for the beacons that should tell of you,
but never called for firing.
In my dreams, I have started up,
roused by the light strokes of the gnat's flight;
935 I have seen so much more happen to you
than could be contained within the time
with which I shared my sleep.
But now I have come through all this;
my heart is free of sorrow;
940 and so I can describe this man of mine—
a watchdog of the house,
the saving forestay of the ship,
the rooted pillar of the towering roof,
the single child of a father,
the land seen by sailors when they had given over
945 hope,
the fairest day to see after the storm,
the springwater stream for the thirsty traveler.
It is sweet indeed to escape the harsh stroke of
necessity.
Such terms of address would, I think, belong to him.
950 But let no one be jealous.
Many, indeed, were the evils we endured before.
Now, dear heart,
step from the carriage, but do not place on earth,
my king,
this foot that trod Troy to destruction.
955 Servants, to whom I have commanded the task
of strewing his path to the house with tapestries—
let his way lie straight before him strewn with purple,
that justice may guide him to the home he never
hoped for.
Everything else earned by fate
960 an unsleeping mind, with the help of the gods,
will arrange justly.
AGAMEMNON: Daughter of Leda,° guardian of my house,

your speech is a good fit for my absence:
both have stretched out long.
But to praise me in due fashion   965
is an honor that others should give.
Besides, do not make much of me in this woman's
fashion,
nor grovel and gape flatteringly, like some foreigner,
nor strew my path with garments that would make it
an object of ill will;   970
it is the gods one should honor with such things.
For one who is mortal, for me certainly,
to walk on subtly woven beauties like these
cannot be without fear.
I tell you, honor me as man, not god.   975
Footmats and embroideries—they sound
differently,
they are different.
Not to be presumptuous
is the greatest gift the gods can give you.
It's only when a life has ended, and ended well,   980
that one dare say, "Well done."
I would be cheerful if my life
were like this in everything.
CLYTEMNESTRA: Then tell me this, and let it be your
own true judgment.
AGAMEMNON: Be sure, I will not falsify that judgment.   985
CLYTEMNESTRA: Was it through fear of the gods
that you made this vow?
AGAMEMNON: I said, if any man ever did, what I
knew would happen.
CLYTEMNESTRA: And what of Priam, if he had
conquered as you have?
AGAMEMNON: He would certainly have trodden on
the tapestry.   990
CLYTEMNESTRA: Don't be ashamed, then, of human
reproach.
AGAMEMNON: Yes, but the ill repute of the people's
voices
has a great power.
CLYTEMNESTRA: He that is not envied is also not
admired.
AGAMEMNON: A woman should not long so for a fight.   995
CLYTEMNESTRA: In those that win, yielding is graceful.
AGAMEMNON: Do you set such store on victory in
this dispute?
CLYTEMNESTRA: Let me have my way. You are the victor
if you yield readily.
AGAMEMNON: Well, if you will—here, someone
undo my sandals,   1000
that are like slaves for the treading of my foot.
And as I walk upon these lovely cloths,
I pray against the envious eye of the gods
lest from afar it strike me.
It's a great shame to spoil a house's wealth,   1005
these weavings so dear in price, with the dirt of
treading feet.
Enough of this.
Bring in this stranger here, and use her kindly.
The god looks from afar with approval

919. Strophius the Phocian: A family friend with whom Orestes stayed at the time of Agamemnon's murder.   **962. Leda:** Mother of Clytemnestra by her husband, Tyndareus, and of Helen by Zeus, who approached Leda in the form of a swan.

1010 on the merciful conqueror.
No one chooses to become a slave.
This woman is the very flower, picked out
from the spoils of war;
as a gift from the army to me, she followed me.
1015 Well, since I've been subdued to listen to you,
I will go into my house, treading on purple.
CLYTEMNESTRA: There is a sea—and who shall
    drain it dry?—
nourishing a spring, always new, an abundance of
    purple
to be bought with silver for the dyeing of garments.
1020 This house, my lord, has store enough of it,
thanks be to the gods.
This house does not know poverty.
I would have vowed the treading of many garments,
had I been so ordered by the shrines of the oracles,
1025 to win the safe return of your life.
When the root is there, the leaf comes to the house,
and stretches its shade against the dog star's heat.
And when you came to this house and hearth of
    yours,
it meant what heat means in the winter time.
1030 And when Zeus makes wine from the bitter grape,
it is still cool within the house,
when its perfected lord paces through the halls.
Zeus, Zeus, that brings all to perfection,
perfect my prayer.
1035 Bring to perfection all you have to do.
CHORUS: Why this fluttering, insistent terror
that keeps guard before my heart?
Is the song prophetic
that rises unhired and unbidden?
1040 My grounded mind has no confidence to dismiss it
like an obscure nightmare.
Time has grown old since the boats,
their hawsers all thrown out along the sands,
set out to Ilium.
1045 With my eyes I am my own witness
to their homecoming.
But nonetheless, my spirit within me
drones this tune of the Furies,
accompanied by no lyre,
1050 a song taught by none but itself.
It has none of the dear confidence of hope.
Not for nothing is the boding of my entrails,
the whirling of my heart, harmonized with
eddies of my mind that will surely bring fulfillment.
1055 But I pray that what I expect may fall away,
a lie, into unfulfillment.
There is no limit in health;
it is insatiable.
For disease is its next-door neighbor;
1060 there is but a single wall between them.
A man's destiny, facing straight ahead,
often crashes on the hidden reef.
Yet, if beforehand in prudent fear,
he casts overboard part of what he owns
1065 with the derrick of good measure,

his whole house does not sink utterly,
though overloaded to overflowing,
nor does the frame of the ship sink.
Many times the generous gifts of Zeus,
and those of the furrows yearly tilled,   1070
banish the disease of hunger.
But the black blood of a man,
when once it has fallen to the earth in his death,
who shall conjure it back again with any
    incantation?
Did not Zeus, for the safety of the world,   1075
stop the wizard who would raise the dead?
If there were no fates appointed by the gods
which checked other fates from having overmuch,
my heart would have outstripped my tongue
and poured this out.   1080
But now in the dark it mutters, in heart-anguish,
with never a hope of spinning out of my burning
    mind
what is right for this moment.
CLYTEMNESTRA: In with you too, now, Cassandra,
since Zeus (you cannot be angry with Zeus)   1085
has made you a sharer in the sacrifices in our
    house,
standing near the altar with many slaves that we
    own.
Get down from that carriage;
none of your high spirit of pride.
They say that Heracles, Alcmene's son,°   1090
was sold and forced to eat the bread of slavery.
If then the necessity of fate's scales
has forced this on you,
you should be very grateful for masters anciently
    rich.
Those who have reaped a harvest they never
    expected   1095
are always excessive in harshness toward their
    slaves.
From us you will have all the usual treatment.
CHORUS: She has finished; it is to you she spoke,
and what she says is clear enough.
You are taken, a quarry in fate's net;   1100
obey her, then—
though I will understand if you don't.
CLYTEMNESTRA: If she has anything besides her
    swallow twitterings,
a barbaric speech that no one knows,
I'll try to persuade her within her understanding. 1105
CHORUS: Follow her. What she says is the best there
    is for you;
leave the carriage; obey her.
CLYTEMNESTRA: I have no time to waste here with her
    outside the palace.
The sheep stand ready for slaughter   1110
in front of the hearth at the center of the house.

1090. Heracles, Alcmene's son: Heracles was a popular Greek
hero. According to legend, he was sold into slavery to
Omphale, Queen of Lydia.

(*To Cassandra.*)

You, if you're going to do anything that I tell you,
do it quickly.
But if you disobey because you don't take in my
words—

(*To Chorus.*)

1115 Here, you!
Don't speak to her any more; use your hands;
that's all these foreigners understand.
CHORUS: I think the woman needs a good interpreter;
she looks like a wild thing newly caught.
CLYTEMNESTRA: She's crazy; she hears only her
1120   distraught mind.
Of course she does, she that has left her newly
captured city,
come here not yet knowing how to wear the curb bit,
till she's frothed out her spirit in blood.
I won't throw any more words at her to be belittled.

(*Exit Clytemnestra.*)

1125 CHORUS: I pity her, and so I won't be angry.
Come, you poor girl, desert your place in the
carriage;
yield to what must be; wear your yoke for the first
time.
CASSANDRA: Oh! Oh! Oh! Oh, the land!
Lord Apollo! Lord Apollo!
1130 CHORUS: Why do you raise such dismal cries to
Apollo?
He is no god for the singer of dirges.
CASSANDRA: Oh! Oh! Oh! Oh, the land!
Lord Apollo! Lord Apollo!
1135 CHORUS: Again she calls with her ill omens
upon the god who has no suitable place
at scenes of mourning.
CASSANDRA: Lord Apollo! Lord Apollo! God of the
streets,
god of destruction! Now again, god of my
destruction,
1140 and so easily.
CHORUS: She seems to me about to prophesy her own
misfortunes.
The gift of prophecy still sticks
even though the mind is now a slave's.
CASSANDRA: Lord Apollo! Lord Apollo!
1145 God of my destruction! God of the streets!
Through what streets have you led me now,
to what house?
CHORUS: To that of the sons of Atreus. If you don't
know that,
that I can tell you. And you won't say it's a lie.
1150 CASSANDRA: Yes, to a house the gods hate;
it has been witness of so many
murders of kin, butcheries,
bowl full of man's blood, ground soaked in shed
blood.
CHORUS: The stranger has a nose as keen as a hound;
1155   she's on the trail of a murder and will find it.

CASSANDRA: What convinces me are the witnesses—
the children, the babies screaming of their cut
throats,
of their flesh roasted and eaten by their father.
CHORUS: We have heard of your fame as a prophet;
but we need no foretellers here.   1160
CASSANDRA: Oh, what does she plan?
What is the great new grief?
It is a great evil against the house
that she is planning.
It is unbearable for its friends, uncurable.   1165
Defense stands aloof and keeps away.
CHORUS: These last foretellings are quite beyond my
understanding;
the others I know—indeed the whole city cries
them aloud.
CASSANDRA: Oh, you wretched woman,
is this what you bring to consummation?   1170
You have cleaned him in the bath
till his skin shined,
the husband to share your bed.
And how shall I tell the consummation?
It would be quick: the line of clutching hands,   1175
stretching out, one hooked to another.
CHORUS: I don't understand that yet;
you spoke riddles before,

Lilo Baur as Cassandra in the National Theatre's 2000
production of the *Oresteia*, translated by Ted Hughes and
directed by Katie Mitchell.

but now what baffles me is the dimness
1180   of what comes from the gods in words.
CASSANDRA: Oh! Oh! Oh! What is this that appears?
A net, a net of death. Can it be so?
But the meshes are the bedfellow, the accomplice
in murder.
Let the pack that ravens insatiate against the family
1185   bay for a sacrifice that merits death by stoning.
CHORUS: What Fury is this you bid raise its cries
against the house?
I find no cleaning in your words.
To my heart rush back the blood drops of
yellowing stain,
as when the eyes grow dim at the setting of a life's
1190   day,
a man falling by the point of a spear.
And destruction comes quick.
CASSANDRA: Look at that! Look at that!
Keep away the bull from the cow!
1195   She will take him in the folds of the robe
with the trick of the black horn.
She strikes! He falls! He falls
in the water of the bath.
That is his end, I tell you,
a treacherous murder in a cauldron.
1200   CHORUS: I will not boast of being a keen judge of
prophecy,
but this certainly looks like something evil.

Anyway, what good word ever came to mankind
from the prophets?
It is through evils that the wordy tricks of the
prophets   1205
bring terrors for us to understand.
CASSANDRA: Oh, the ill boding of my own sad fate!
For it is my own suffering, on top of his,
that my tongue spills out.

(*To the god.*)

Where is this you have brought me to in my
sorrow?   1210
For nothing but to share his death; what else?
CHORUS: You are someone god-possessed;
the god carries you along.
It is for yourself you cry out this tuneless tune.
Like the brown nightingale,° that can never have   1215
enough of song,
as she cries "Itys! Itys!" for her life rich in sorrows,
and her mind loves pity for herself.

1215–22. Like the brown nightingale: The chorus alludes to
the story of Philomela, who was raped by her brother-in-law,
Tereus. Although her tongue was cut out to prevent her from
telling anyone of the crime, Philomela sent her sister a piece of
embroidery that revealed all. The sisters took their revenge on
Tereus by tricking him into eating his son, Itys. According to
some accounts, the gods turned Philomela into a nightingale.

A scene from the American
Repertory Theatre's 1994
production of the *Oresteia*,
directed by François
Rochaix.

CASSANDRA: Oh! The life of the shrill-voiced
    nightingale!
1220   The gods covered *her* with a feathered body;
    I tell you, they gave her a *sweet* life,
    and her cries are not cries of sorrow.
    But what remains for me
    is the splitting of the flesh with the two-edged
    spear.
1225 CHORUS: Where do they come from, these rushes
    of useless agony carried by the god?
    You make music that is a mixture,
    ugly cries of terror and high-pitched melodies.
    Where did you get the milestones of evil words
1230   that mark your prophetic journey?
CASSANDRA: The marriage! The marriage of Paris,
    deadly to those who loved him.
    Scamander, river that my fathers drank of,
    in that time I was raised on your shores;
1235   but now around the banks of Cocytus and Acheron,°
    the rivers of death, I am likely to prophesy,
    and soon.
CHORUS: What is this word you have spoken all too
    clearly?
    A newborn child could understand.
1240   The bite of murder has pierced me
    as you whimper at your painful fortune.
    It is a heartbreak to hear you.
CASSANDRA: The agony, agony of the city utterly
    ruined.
    The sacrifices that my father made before the walls,
    the multiplied slaughter of cattle and woolly sheep.
1245   None of it helped; it was no cure.
    The city suffered as it was fated to suffer.
    And I shall soon be thrown on the ground
    in my own warm blood.
CHORUS: What you say now follows what you said
    before.
    Some malevolent god who falls on you with
1250   fearful weight
    makes you a singer of these deadly mournful things.
    But as for the end—I am at a loss.
CASSANDRA: Now my prophecy shall no longer peer
    from behind veils
    like a newly married bride.
1255   No, it will rush on, a wind brightly blowing
    into the sun's rising,
    to send disaster surging like a wave to meet the
    sunbeams,
    a disaster yet greater than this.
    I will not school you in riddles any longer.
1260   And do you be my witness that my nose is keen
    and my tracking by shortcuts
    on the path of crimes committed long ago.
    Never do they leave the house,
    that chorus that sings in ugly harmony.
1265   For their speech is of evil.

1235. **Cocytus and Acheron:** Rivers flowing together at the
entrance to the kingdom of death.

The revelers have drunk, to whet their courage
    more,
    man's blood, and so they abide in the house,
    and none shall expel them: they are the Furies,
    that attend on the murder of kin.
    The song they sing as they beleaguer the house   1270
    is the song of the primal destruction,
    when the mind is blinded.
    And each of the Furies has spat in disgust
    on the brother's bed that hates its violator.
    Hah! Am I an archer that missed,   1275
    or have I hit the mark?
    Or am I a false prophet
    that raps on doors and babbles?
    Be my witness, you, but first make your sworn oath
    that I know the story of the ancient sins   1280
    of this house.
CHORUS: How would such an oath, even plighted in
    all honesty,
    serve as any kind of cure?
    True, I do wonder at you,
    that you, reared beyond the sea and speaking a
    strange tongue   1285
    should talk of these things as if you had been there.
CASSANDRA: It was Apollo the prophet
    that charged me with the office of prophecy.
CHORUS: He fell in love with you?
    Is that possible for a god?   1290
CASSANDRA: Till now I was ashamed to speak of it.
CHORUS: As long as things go well, one has one's
    delicacy.
CASSANDRA: He was a wrestler, that breathed his
    grace into me.
CHORUS: Did you come to the breeding of children,
    like other couples?   1295
CASSANDRA: I promised the god and cheated him.
CHORUS: Had you already got your gift of prophecy?
CASSANDRA: Oh yes, I used to tell my countrymen
    all that would happen.
CHORUS: How did you escape the god's anger?   1300
CASSANDRA: Since my offense against him,
    no one believed a word of mine.
CHORUS: Ah, but to us right now, you seem to
    prophesy truly.
CASSANDRA: Oh, oh, my agony! There it is again!
    The fearful pain of true prophecy   1305
    that twists me, that drives me wild;
    and it is still only prelude.
    Look! Look! You see them! The young ones,
    sitting on the house like dream phantoms.
    They are the likenesses of those children dead and
    gone,   1310
    killed by those they loved;
    their hands are full of meat, their own flesh.
    You can see it clearly; they carry the pitiful load
    of their guts, and their father has tasted them.
    I tell you, there is punishment for this,   1315
    and someone is plotting it,
    a lion, but a coward, that wallows, a housekeeper

in the bed of the returning lord—
O mine, *my* lord—for I must bear the yoke of
   slavery.
1320 The captain of the ships, the sacker of Ilium,
he knows not what tongue is licking him,
the tongue of the hateful bitch, her ears pricked,
like a secret blind vengeance,
that will work out his evil fate.
1325 So far her daring reaches:
the woman will murder the man.
She is—what shall I call her and be right?
this monstrous, biting creature.
A snake with poison at both ends;
1330 some Scylla° living in the rocks, death to sailors;
some murderous, raging mother of hell;
some truceless god of war;
a war she has declared upon her loved ones!
So let her cry her war cry,
1335 whose daring knows no limit,
as at the moment when the battle turns.
Yet she seems to rejoice that he has come safe home.
It is all one to me, if you do not believe any of this;
what difference?
1340 It is to be and will come.
Soon you will stand here and say of me, in pity,
she was too true a prophet.
CHORUS: The feast of Thyestes, and the flesh of the
   children,
I understand and shudder; fear is on me
1345 as I hear the truth, and no mere likenesses.
But for the rest I heard from you,
I have fallen off the course and run wide.
CASSANDRA: I tell you, you will live to see
   Agamemnon's death.
CHORUS: Wretched girl, hold your tongue in piety.
CASSANDRA: No, no holy god of healing presides over
1350   this story.
CHORUS: True, if what you say is so; but God forbid
   it should be.
CASSANDRA: You are all for God forbidding;
   but their job is killing.
CHORUS: What man is he that furnishes this grief?
CASSANDRA: You have surely fallen astray of my
1355   prophecies.
CHORUS: Yes, for I do not understand how the plotter
   will make his plan work.
CASSANDRA: Yet I know Greek rather too well.
CHORUS: So does the Delphic oracle;° but it's hard to
   understand,
1360   all the same.
CASSANDRA: Oh! It attacks me like fire!
   Oh! Oh! O god! O Lycian Apollo!

There she is, the lioness, two-footed bedfellow of
   the wolf,
in the absence of the true-bred lion.
She will kill me. Like one that brews a potion,   1365
She will put my reward, too, in the drink.
She cries her glee in triumph, as she whets the knife
for a man, to pay him in murder for bringing me
   here.

(*She starts tearing off her robe and garlands.*)

Why should I have these mockeries about me,
this staff, the prophet's garlands round my neck?   1370
Before I die myself, I shall at least destroy you.
Go; you shall be no more. Lie on the ground as
   you fall.
Thus I requite you.
Enrich some other girl with blinded madness,
some other girl than me.   1375
Look, Apollo himself undoes his prophetess
of her prophetic mantle; he has watched me
laughed to scorn even in this trumpery,
laughed at by friends turned foes,
with never a quiver in the scale—what hollowness!   1380
Ill-treated like a wandering beggar priest,
in misery half-starved to death, I still endured.
But now the prophet has unmade the prophet
and brought me here to meet my chance death.
No father's altar, but a chopping block, waits for me,   1385
to be warmed with my blood as I am butchered,
the preliminary victim. Yet, all the same, I shall
   not die
dishonored by the gods.
But another will come° to take vengeance for me;
he will kill the mother in whom he was seeded,   1390
and will avenge his father.
A wanderer outcast, grown alien to this land,
who will return from exile
to put a coping stone of ruin for those he loved,
for he has sworn a great oath by the gods   1395
that his father's corpse shall bring him home again.
Why do I go on this way, crying, full of self-pity?—
now that I have seen Troy's ruin, as I saw it,
now as Troy's conquerors come off in the god's
   judgment,
as I see them now.   1400
I will go and face it; I will face my death.
These gates before me here, I call you now by name:
the gates of death.
But I pray that the stroke that reaches me
may be a mortal stroke,   1405
that without struggle, as the blood runs freely,
in easy death I may close these eyes of mine.
CHORUS: You are a woman that has suffered much,
   and have understood much; and you have said
   much.

1330. Scylla: A sea monster living in a cave opposite the
whirlpool Charybdis. Ships could not escape the double threat.
1359. Delphic oracle: The chief oracle of ancient Greece,
presided over by Apollo. The utterings of the oracle were
ambiguous and had to be interpreted.

1389. another will come: Reference to Orestes, who avenges
his father's murder in the second part of Aeschylus's trilogy.

1410 But if you truly know your fate,
why do you walk up to the altar steadfastly,
like an ox?
CASSANDRA: There is no escape, my friends; the time
is full.
CHORUS: Yet the latest moment has a special value.
CASSANDRA: This day has come; there is little I would
1415 gain by flight.
CHORUS: How courageous and steadfast!
CASSANDRA: No one who's happy hears these
compliments.
CHORUS: But death, if fame comes with it,
comes still with grace to those that must die
anyway.
CASSANDRA: I weep for you, father, and for your
1420 noble children.

(*She recoils.*)

CHORUS: What is it? What is the fear that turns you
back?

(*Cassandra shudders.*)

CHORUS: What made you shudder?
Is it something in your mind that disgusts you?
CASSANDRA: The house! It reeks of murder, of
dripping blood!
1425 CHORUS: What? It's just the blood of sacrificed animals.
CASSANDRA: No, it is just like the smell of a grave.
CHORUS: It is no delicate Syrian incense in the house
that you speak of.
CASSANDRA: Still—I will go into the house,
to mourn with cries my own and Agamemnon's
1430 deaths.
I have enough of life.
My friends, I'm not scared
like a bird startled at a bush
in empty terror.
1435 When I die, you will be my witness to this,
when a woman dies to match my woman's death,
when a man falls to match that other man,
whose wife was his assassin.
This friendly office I lay on you, as I die now.
1440 CHORUS: Poor girl, I pity you for your death,
that the god predicted.
CASSANDRA: I have one more speech to make,
or shall I call it a dirge, just for myself.
As I face this last sunlight,
1445 I call on those who shall be my avengers
to make my enemies pay for *my* murder too,
only a dead slave, such an easy victory.
Men's fortunes, when they are good,
one might say of them, "They are like shadows
only."
1450 When they're bad, a wet sponge
with one stroke wipes it all out.
The first truth has my pity, far more than the second.
(*Exit Cassandra.*)
CHORUS: To be successful is to be endlessly hungry
for more;

all men are so.
There is no one who banishes good fortune from
his house, 1455
so long as fingers point at it.
No man says, "Do not come here again, good
fortune."
Here is this king, to whom the blessed gods granted
the sacking of Priam's city;
he came home with all the honors that the gods
gave him. 1460
But now, if he shall pay for the blood of the past
and dying render the price of others' deaths,
who that hears this and must die himself
dare boast that a man may be born
to live a whole life unharmed? 1465
AGAMEMNON (*from within*): I've been hit! I am hurt
to death.
CHORUS: Hush! Who is it that cries out, hurt to
death?
AGAMEMNON: I'm hit again!
CHORUS: It is the king crying out; I think all is over.
But let us plan safety for ourselves—if we can. 1470
1. My vote is to cry, Help! to the citizens
to come to the palace.
2. Yes, and at once, I think,
to catch them red-handed with dripping sword.
3. I think you're right; at least we should do
something. 1475
It certainly isn't the moment for hesitation.
4. But we can see. This is a kind of first act;
it looks like the beginning of a tyranny.
5. Yes, it does—because we're wasting time.
Their hands don't sleep, and they trample
underfoot 1480
the good reputation of delay.
6. I really do not know what would be best.
Those who do the deed of course find it easy to
plan.
7. Yes, I am with you. Anyhow,
one cannot by talking bring the dead to life again. 1485
8. Are we then, in order to stretch our own lives,
to yield to a government that shames our royal
house?
9. No, that is awful. Death is better than that.
Death is better than subjection to a tyranny.
10. Is the evidence of the cries good enough? 1490
Are we right to predict that the man is dead?
11. Yes, one must know before one gets angry.
Knowing the truth is very far from guessing.
12. I have the support of many voices among you:
that we should be told clearly how it is with
Agamemnon. 1495

(*Enter Clytemnestra.*)

CLYTEMNESTRA: Till now I have said much to meet
the occasion,
but now I will not be ashamed to say the opposite.
How could one, rendering hate to those who hated
but looked like loved ones,

1500 hedge the trap about with sides too high to be
    leapt over?
This was my day of trial; I have thought of it
enough and long enough, a trial of an old quarrel
years and years old.
Now I stand here where I have struck him.
1505 He is dead, and the sequence ended.
This is how I managed—I will not disavow it—
that he should not escape, nor defend himself from
    death.
I threw about him an encompassing net,
as it might be for fish, all-entangling,
1510 an evil wealth of cloak.
I struck him twice. He gave two groans,
and his body went limp;
as he lay there, I gave him a third,
in honor of the Zeus that keeps the dead
1515 securely in the underworld.
This was my grace and prayer for him.
So, as he lay there, he gasped out his spirit,
choking, poured out a sharp stream of his blood
and struck me with the dark bloody shower.
1520 I rejoiced as much as the new-sown earth
rejoices in the glad rain of Zeus,
when the buds strike in earth's womb.
So it is, you old men of Argos here;
be glad, if you can. I triumph in it.
1525 If it were right to pour libations
on a dead man's body, I would have done so to
    him,
and more than justly done so.
Here's a bowl of horrors, cursed horrors,
that he filled within our house,
1530 and then he came and drank it off himself.
CHORUS: I wonder at your tongue, how boldly it wags,
that you should boast like this over a dead husband.
CLYTEMNESTRA: You try me out as if I were
a woman that cannot think.
1535 But my heart doesn't tremble,
and I speak to you who know;
whether you wish to praise or blame me is all one
    to me.
Here is Agamemnon, my husband, now a corpse—
his death the work of this right hand of mine,
1540 an efficient craftsman.
That is how *that* is.
CHORUS: Woman, what evil thing have you eaten
that grows in the earth,
what draught have you tasted that comes from the
    salt sea,
1545 that you have taken upon you so horrible a sacrifice
and the curse of the people's voice?
You have cast away, you have torn apart,
and you shall be cast and torn away from the city,
a monstrous object of hate to the citizens.
CLYTEMNESTRA: Now it's against me that you
1550   proclaim banishment,
that the hatred and curses of the citizens shall be
    mine,

but in the old days you brought nothing against
    that man,
who, with all the indifference of one whose
    pastures are full
of teeming flocks, rich in wool,
had no care for the death of a lamb.   1555
He sacrificed his own daughter,
dearest pain of my womb,
to charm the contrariness of Thracian winds.
For this, should you not have banished him,
payment for his polluting wickedness?   1560
No, you are a careful hearer and harsh judge
only of *my* acts.
Threaten away! I tell you now, if once you
    conquer me
in a fair fight, I'll be your subject;
but if God gives another outcome,   1565
you will get an education in discretion
and learn it thoroughly, though the knowledge
comes very late.
CHORUS: You think big thoughts, and you scream
    proud defiance,
as though the bloody smear of your success   1570
had maddened your mind.
The smear of blood—I can see it in your eyes.
But still you must pay stroke for stroke,
with no friend to take your part.
CLYTEMNESTRA: You may now hear the solemn
    swearing of my oath: 1575
By the justice due to my child, and now perfected,
by the Spirit of Destruction and the Fury,
in whose honor I cut this man's throat,
my hope treads not within the hall of Fear
so long as Aegisthus lights the hearth fire for me,   1580
my loyal friend, as he has always been,
shield for my daring—no small one.
There lies Agamemnon, this girl's seducer—
he was the darling of all the women of Troy—
and there she is, our prophet, prisoner of war,   1585
that shared his bed, a faithful whore
that spoke her auguries for him, and knew as well
the rubbing of the sailors' benches.
Both have suffered as they deserved.
He died as I said, and she has sung her swan song
    in death,   1590
and lies with him, her lover.
But to me she has brought an additional side dish
to *my* pleasure in bed.
CHORUS: What day of doom may I look for soon,
one with not too much pain, not too long
    bedridden,   1595
that shall bring me the sleep that has no ending,
now that my kindest of guardians has been
    overcome,
suffering so much at a woman's hands.
By a woman his life has perished.
Curse on you, crazy Helen, that were the single
    murderess   1600
of all those lives, those many lives,

lost under Troy's walls;
now you have made the fulfillment,
the fine flowering, of whatever it was,
1605 that quarrel within the house
built to bring a man to misery.
You have perfected it,
through bloodshed that cannot be washed out.
CLYTEMNESTRA: Do not pray for your end in death
1610 because of the burden of your grief in this,
nor turn your anger against Helen,
as the man-killer who destroyed
those many lives of the Greeks,
and brought into being an incurable pain.
CHORUS: Spirit that attacks the house of the sons of
1615 Atreus,
you master me to the breaking of my heart;
your power is wielded by two women of like soul.
And now you stand like an evil raven,
and croak over the dead a lawless hymn of victory.
1620 CLYTEMNESTRA: Now indeed you have made right
the judgment of your mouth,
as you name the thrice-glutted spirit of this race.
It is through him that the love of blood-licking
is nourished in the belly,
1625 and before the old wound has healed,
new pus comes.
CHORUS: Yes, the one you name is indeed great,
the spirit whose anger lies heavy on this house.
And the tale you have to tell is evil;
it has an endless appetite for the events of blind
1630 madness.
But surely these are through Zeus,
who is cause of all, who brings all to pass.
For what is there that is fulfilled for man,
except through Zeus?
1635 What is there of all this
that is not of God's accomplishment?
O my king, my king,
how shall I sorrow for you?
What shall I say from a heart that loves you?
1640 You lie there in that spider's web,
gasping out your life in an unholy death.
Oh, oh! Conquered by deadly treachery,
to fall to such an ignoble bed
by a wife's hand and a double-edged blade.
1645 CLYTEMNESTRA: You cry aloud on this as *my* work;
but do not call me Agamemnon's wife.
No, it is the old, bitter, Evil Genius
of Atreus, giver of the cruel feast,
that has likened himself to the wife of this dead man
1650 and has paid him off, sacrificing a full-grown victim
in fulfillment for those young children.
CHORUS: But who will bear you witness
that you are guiltless of the murder?
How, how so? It is true, there may be,
1655 on his father's side, the Evil Genius to help you.
And the black god of war presses on
through tides of kindred blood
to the place of his advance,

where he pays just requital
for the congealed fragments of the eaten children. 1660
O my king, my king,
how shall I sorrow for you?
What shall I say from a heart that loves you?
You lie there in that spider's web,
gasping out your life in an unholy death. 1665
Oh, oh! Conquered by deadly treachery,
to fall to such an ignoble bed
by a wife's hand and a double-edged blade.
CLYTEMNESTRA: Did *he* not also lay upon the house
a treacherous destruction? 1670
The victim, my daughter, raised from his loins,
Iphigeneia, whom I mourn for.
What he did is what he suffered for.
Let him not boast of anything in the house of death,
for he paid for what he had done 1675
with death by the mischief of the sword.
CHORUS: I am all bewildered about what road to take
as the house falls;
my wits are deserted by their skillful carefulness.
I fear the crash of the bloody torrent of rain 1680
that will shake the house to its foundation.
Now it is a shower no longer.
Fate is whetting its justice on other whetstones
for another deed of injury.
Earth, Earth, would you had received me 1685
before I lived to see him in his lowly couch
in a silver-sided bath.
Who shall bury him? Who shall keen him?
Will you dare to do this, to make lament for him,
you who killed him, your husband? 1690
Will you accomplish for his soul a grace no grace
as thanks for his great deeds?
Who shall stand at the grave and chant
a praise of the hero
with tears in the eye and truthful sorrow at heart? 1695
CLYTEMNESTRA: The care of that concerns you not at
all.
It is by our hand that he fell, that he died,
and we shall bury him
with no cries of mourning from this house.
But his daughter Iphigeneia, as is right, 1700
will welcome her father by the swift-flowing passage
over the River of Sorrows
and throw her arms around him and kiss him.
CHORUS: This is but the exchange of insult for insult;
it is hard to judge the issue of such a fight. 1705
The pirate plunders the pirate,
the killer pays for the killing.
Still there remains, as long as Zeus remains on his
throne,
the rule that he who has acted shall suffer
accordingly.
That is the divine law. 1710
Who shall expel from the house the brood of curses?
The whole race is welded to destruction.
CLYTEMNESTRA: In what you say now, the prophecy
has become truth.

For my part, I am willing to make a sworn
        compact
1715 with the evil spirit of this house
      to be satisfied with things as they are, however bad,
      on condition that he, in the days to come,
      may go from our house and wear out some other
        breed
      with murders of one another in the family.
1720 I will be utterly content with a small part of wealth,
      if I can banish from these halls
      the madness of mutual bloodletting.

(Enter Aegisthus.)

AEGISTHUS: O happy light, day of justified revenge!
      Now I will say that the gods
1725 in watchfulness so high above the earth
      still bear an eye on the sorrows of mortals to
        avenge them.
      Now I take pleasure to have seen this man
      lying here in the robes that were
      the nets of the Furies for him,
1730 paying for the plots his father's hand contrived.
      For Atreus, ruler of this land, was this man's father,
      and his brother Thyestes was my father.
      Both were Pelops's sons; this is the plain story.
      The two of them were in dispute about the throne,
1735 and Atreus banished my father from city and home.
      The unlucky Thyestes later returned,
      a suppliant at Atreus's hearth, and found safety
        there—
      I mean for his own part, for he did not die
      nor stained his fatherland with blood.
1740 But the vile Atreus, father of the dead man here,
      with show of eagerness rather than love,
      gave my father a banquet of welcome.
      He pretended to celebrate a day of feasting
      on flesh slaughtered for meat,
1745 in all hospitality,
      but the meat he gave my father was his own
        children's.
      The feet and the ends of the fingers he put apart
        and hid,
      as the guests sat man by man at separate tables.
      So Thyestes in ignorance ate the other parts,
      a meal that brought a curse, as you see, on all the
1750   race.
      Later, when he discovered what awful act he had
        committed,
      he moaned aloud, recoiled, and vomited up the
        bloody mess.
      "A doom intolerable will overtake," he said,
      "the house of Pelops."
1755 He kicked the dinner over to back the oath,
      crying, "So perish every one of all your breed."
      That is why you can see this man fallen dead here,
      and I am justly the one who stitched together his
        murder.
      I was the third son, and while I was still in
        swaddling clothes

he drove me out along with my luckless father.   1760
      But when I grew to manhood, justice brought me
        back.
      And so I laid my hand on him, though not face to
        face;
      mine was the whole contriving of the evil plot.
      So glorious the result,
      that now I would welcome death itself,   1765
      having seen him in the traps of justice.
CHORUS: Aegisthus, I do not respect insolence
      at the moment of calamity.
      Do you say that with aforethought you killed
        Agamemnon,
      that you alone planned this miserable murder?   1770
      In that case, I do not think your life will escape
      the justice of the public curse, the stoning.
      That's what I think.
AEGISTHUS: Do you talk back to me, you who sit at
        the lower oar,
      when we are in possession of the upper deck?   1775
      You will find out, despite your age,
      how uncomfortable such learning is for an old man,
      when discretion is the lesson set.
      Chains in old age and hunger's pangs
      are the very sharpest healing prophets of the mind. 1780
      Don't you see this when you see?
      Kick not against the pricks, lest your own striking
        hurt you.
CHORUS: Woman, you who were his housekeeper
      and at the same time sullied his bed,
      did you plot his death when the victors were
        newly home   1785
      and he had been their general?
AEGISTHUS: These words of yours are true
        progenitors of sorrows.
      Yours is a tongue the opposite of Orpheus's:
      he led all things his captive through the joy of his
        own voice,
      but you with silly yappings arouse others to lead
        you captive.   1790
      Once you are mastered, you'll be a tamer animal.
CHORUS: I suppose you'll be the sovereign of the
        Argives,
      you, who when you plotted this man's murder
      didn't dare to do the deed with your own hand.
AEGISTHUS: Well, no. The treachery was a woman's part, 1795
      clearly so. I would be suspected as his old enemy.
      But his wealth will give me a base to rule the
        citizens,
      and the disobedient man I will yoke in heavy chains;
      he will not be, I assure you, like a full-fed young
        trace horse.
      No, unwelcome hunger and a dark cell   1800
      will see him through into submission.
CHORUS: Why didn't you kill him yourself, with your
        cowardly soul?
      No, your partner, the woman, did the killing,
      to be the pollution of the land and of the gods of
        the land.

1805   But I tell you, Orestes still sees the light of day,
         that he may come home, and with good luck on
           his side
       be conquerer and the death of both of you.
       AEGISTHUS: Since you're resolved to act and talk like
           this,
         you'll soon know—
1810   here, my bodyguards, this is your work, right here.
       CHORUS: Here, let each one of you be ready, hand on
           sword hilt.
       AEGISTHUS: I, too, hold the hilt of my sword.
         I will face my death.
       CHORUS: You talk of death; I welcome it. But I will
1815   try my chances.
       CLYTEMNESTRA: No, dearest, no. Let us do no further
           evils.
         Those that there are, are many, a bloody harvest;
         we have a good store of calamity.
         No, no bloodletting.
1820   Good old men, off with you to your houses.
         Yield to what must be, before you suffer.
         What we did had to be done.
         If this should be all of troubles, I would gladly
           welcome it,

       though struck with misfortune
         by the heavy hoof of the evil spirit.   1825
       That is a woman's word, if anyone should think it
           worth heeding.
       AEGISTHUS: No, but to have them letting their
           tongues
         blossom in insolence, to throw their empty threats
           about—
         "That they would try their chances"—   1830
         You lack all brains, so to abuse your master.
       CHORUS: It does not fit an Argive to fawn on a villain.
       AEGISTHUS: I will get even with you in the days to
           come.
       CHORUS: Not if the Spirit brings Orestes home.
       AEGISTHUS: I know the diet of exiles is rich in hope.   1835
       CHORUS: Yes, do things, grow fat, pollute justice—
           while you can.
       AEGISTHUS: You know you will pay me for your
           foolishness.
       CHORUS: Boast, do; be bold—a cock beside your hen.
       CLYTEMNESTRA: Do not pay heed to their vain
           yappings. I
         and you together will make all things well,   1840
         for we are masters of this house.

COMMENTARY

Lois Spatz (b. 1940)
ORESTEIA: TRILOGY PRESERVED   1982

In her examination of Aeschylus, Lois Spatz discusses how he conceived of the three plays of the Oresteia *as a unified whole. She also provides some of the key background information that most of the original Greek audience would have known. Spatz connects the plays to events of the time in Athens so that we can better understand* Agamemnon *in the context of history and the other two plays to which it is linked.*

The *Oresteia* won first prize at the Great Dionysia of 458 BCE, just two years before Aeschylus's death. The three tragedies, *Agamemnon, The Libation Bearers* (*Choephoroi*), and *The Eumenides,* were presented in a sequence which concluded with a lost satyr play, *Proteus,* about the wanderings of Agamemnon's brother, Menelaus. Modern readers often study *Agamemnon* alone, although it is extremely difficult to follow and does not resolve the dramatic questions it raises, but the ancient spectators would have considered the drama as a first act in a larger whole. The trilogy is composed so that the *Agamemnon* and *The Libation Bearers* define a conflict which can only be resolved by a third and different action. *Agamemnon,* taken alone, seems an obscure play, for the extreme complexity of image, diction, and action is a dramatic device which conveys the moral, emotional, and political confusion of the initial situation. In the second play, where the next generation of characters better understand their positions and motivations, the action is clearer. In *The Eumenides*, Aeschylus illuminates the issues underlying the action and resolves them.

Because one must study the parts together to appreciate the whole, the trilogy will be treated as a single play. Although Aeschylus begins his drama *in medias res*, as Agamemnon is about to return from Troy, the audience was familiar with the stories concerning the crimes of Agamemnon's father, Atreus. Therefore, it would have suspected with increasing dread some relationship between the events of the present generation and the horrors of the past, which the poet does not mention directly until the last third of the play, when the curse on the House of Atreus becomes a central theme of the trilogy. Atreus was head of the house and ruler of Argos when Thyestes, his brother, raped his wife and attempted to steal his property and power. First Atreus exiled his brother, but judging that penalty inadequate, he invited him home and cooked and served Thyestes' children to him at a feast celebrating the reunion. When Thyestes discovered he had eaten his own sons, he cursed Atreus, promising revenge, and left Argos with his one remaining son, Aegisthus.

The curse arising from this horrible act brought misfortune to the next generation. Atreus's sons, Agamemnon and Menelaus, had married sisters, Clytemnestra and Helen, respectively. Helen, the most beautiful woman in Greece, was seduced and stolen away from the hearth of the House of Atreus by their guest, Paris (Alexander), son of King Priam of Troy. Paris's adultery was a violation of the sacred relationship between guest and host protected by Zeus Xenios ("Guest-Friend"). Therefore, the Argives considered it a serious crime demanding revenge and launched the Trojan War, subject of the *Iliad* and epic cycle.

The Greek warriors who had sworn to support Menelaus met at Aulis under the leadership of Agamemnon, elder brother of the wronged husband and most powerful king in Greece. When rough seas prevented the fleet's passage to Troy, the priest Calchas informed Agamemnon that he must sacrifice his daughter, Iphigenia, to the goddess Artemis in order to calm the winds. Agamemnon, confident of the justice of the war and fearful of his restive troops, decided to slaughter Iphigenia so that the expedition could set sail.

Aeschylus begins his drama just as the Argives receive the news that Agamemnon has defeated Troy. The audience would know, however, from such sources as the *Odyssey*, the return stories of the cycle, and the *Oresteia* by the lyric poet Stesichorus, that, during these ten years of war, Clytemnestra had sent her son Orestes away and taken Aegisthus as a lover, and that the Greek soldiers in Troy had committed crimes which were punished on the return voyages. Aeschylus's gradual and sparing presentation of this background increases the mystery surrounding the events of the play itself.

Act I and Act II are both return and revenge stories. In *Agamemnon* several characters in sequence, the watchman, citizen/chorus, Queen Clytemnestra, and the herald, express hope and anxiety about the general's experiences in the Trojan War and his safe victorious return. Tension builds because the expectation of victory as the just punishment of Troy is constantly undercut by suggestions that the general and his men have themselves committed atrocities to ensure victory. In fact, the Greek fleet has already been punished, destroyed by a god-sent storm at sea. At the midpoint in the drama, Agamemnon enters in triumph with his war prize, Cassandra, and is welcomed with Eastern pomp by his queen, Clytemnestra, who entices him to enter the palace on a luxurious tapestry. This greeting initiates the revenge story. After Agamemnon's entrance into the palace, Cassandra, the Trojan priestess of Apollo, predicts his murder and hers and relates it to the bloody history of the House of Atreus. Then Clytemnestra murders Agamemnon and his mistress and justifies her deed to the citizens as divine retribution for his sacrifice of their daughter, Iphigenia. Aegisthus, Clytemnestra's lover, later explains that history more precisely, justifying his part in Agamemnon's death as revenge for his uncle Atreus's slaughter of his brothers. Thus, the cycle of revenge as punishment which demands further revenge is clearly established by the end of the play. It is equally clear that Clytemnestra's act of revenge cannot break the cycle. She and her lover plan to replace Agamemnon as rulers of Argos, but they respond with threats of violence to the chorus's protests against their tyranny. *Agamemnon* ends with the chorus cowed for the moment, but predicting that Orestes, Agamemnon's son, sent away by Clytemnestra, will someday return to avenge the death of his father and assume his rightful place as head of the family and ruler of the state.

Act II, *The Libation Bearers,* also exhibits the return and revenge patterns, in dramatizing the murder of Agamemnon's murderers. First Orestes returns, fulfilling the hopes of his sister, Electra, and the chorus of household slaves, captives from Troy loyal to their conqueror, Agamemnon. Orestes later learns that his return has also fulfilled the nightmares of his mother, Clytemnestra. He enters, not as a conquering hero like his father, to be warmly welcomed and then duped, but as an exile in disguise, announcing his own death in order to deceive his mother and her lover. He has been spurred on by Apollo's demand that he avenge his father's death or suffer dire punishments, but he also acts from private motives as son, disinherited heir, and legitimate ruler of Argos. After praying with his sister and the chorus at the tomb of Agamemnon to invoke the aid of the gods and the powerful dead, he tricks Clytemnestra, kills Aegisthus, and then confronts his mother again. She tries to dissuade him, but he leads her into the house for the slaughter. When Orestes afterwards proclaims the justice of the matricide to the satisfied chorus, he does not gloat, as his mother before him did, for he recognizes that his deed was a crime as well as a necessity. He confesses that his pollution is a danger to himself and his community and prepares to leave Argos to be purified of blood guilt by Apollo. As he announces his plans, however, madness overtakes him; he seems to see the very Furies (Erinyes) from Hell descending on him to avenge his matricide. The chorus is puzzled that this act has not ended the chain of reciprocal revenge in the House of Atreus but sends him forward to Apollo with prayers for success.

Act III, *The Eumenides,* introduces a new story pattern, "suppliant received"; a new setting, the shrines of the gods in Delphi and Athens; and new characters, the gods themselves—Apollo, the Furies, and Athena. The play begins at the shrine of Apollo in Delphi, where Orestes has arrived as a suppliant begging asylum from the Furies and release from blood guilt. Although Apollo has temporarily drugged the Furies into sleep, he cannot permanently protect Orestes from their vengeance. The god directs the matricide to the shrine of Athena in the Acropolis of Athens, where the goddess will release him from the curse. Once Orestes has fled, the ghost of Clytemnestra angrily arouses the sleeping Furies and sends them to track their prey. Orestes arrives in Athens and clings to the goddess's shrine, but the Furies enter soon after and threaten to destroy him. Athena returns just in time, and after questioning Orestes and the chorus of Furies, she decides the conflict is too important for her to resolve alone. Instead, she establishes a homicide court (modeled on the murder trials of the Court of the Areopagus) where citizen-judges (dicasts) will hear arguments for both sides and decide between them. The two present their cases, with Apollo supporting Orestes' plea. When the jury's vote is equally split, Orestes is set free by Athena's order. Before he returns home, he thanks Apollo, Athena, and the court, promising eternal peace between Argos and Athens and wishing the city prosperity and victory forever. The Furies, incensed by the verdict, call down curses on Athens, but Athena persuades them to become honored participants in the new procedure, ever punishing injustice, but showering blessings on the good as well. When they accept her offer, they exchange their loathsome black garments for the red robes of metics (foreign residents in Athens), a visible sign of their transformation from Furies to Eumenides ("Kindly Ones"). The trilogy ends with a torchlight procession, similar to the Panathenaic Festival, in which the citizens escort the goddesses to their new home, a hallowed cave at the foot of the Acropolis.

It is a long way from the polluted House of Atreus in Argos, whose bloody Furies roost like metics on the roof (*L.B.*, 1023), to the clear bright light of Athens, with its court system, public festivals, rites of Apollo, and the patronage of Zeus's daughter, Athena. Aeschylus has chosen a primitive myth about a blood-vendetta which extends for generations and includes cannibalism and child sacrifice. But he has dramatized the saga in a way which makes it relevant to his fifth-century audience. In none of the earlier versions of the story (i.e., *Odyssey, Cypria, Nostoi,* Stesichorus's *Oresteia*) was Orestes freed by a verdict of the Court of the Areopagus in Athens. Aeschylus originated this resolution so that he could trace the development of human justice — from the blood-vendetta carried out by the family with the support of the Furies who automatically avenge kindred bloodshed, through the purification rituals performed at the shrines of Apollo, to its culmination in the state court system, established by Athena with Zeus's blessing.[1] In dramatizing the progress of justice from vendetta to trial, he is also tracing the evolution of social institutions, from family and clan united by kindred blood, through cult united by ritual and a common patron, up to its perfection in the democratic polls, exemplified by Athens, where the families were ruled by law, the gods supported the new institutions, and the citizens united into a harmonious and effective whole.[2] No Athenian could sit unmoved while Athena voted like a citizen according to the procedures established in mythic time, but still in effect in 458 BCE. Nor could he watch without pride the imitation of his great Panathenaic Festival and the respectful acceptance of the dread Furies as metics in his own state. Thus would the contemporary Athenian recognize the ideals and glory of his city in the resolution of the myth.

[1]For a different opinion of Apollo's place, see George Derwent Thomson, *Aeschylus and Athens: A Study in the Social Origins of Drama,* 2nd ed. (London: Lawrence & Wishart, 1967), pp. 259–61, and R. P. Winnington-Ingram, "The Role of Apollo in the Oresteia," *Classical Review* 47 (1933): 97–104. On the relation of purification to the laws on homicide, see D. M. MacDowell, *Athenian Homicide Law in the Age of the Orators* (Manchester: University of Manchester Press, 1963), pp. 4–5, 141–50.

[2]The family remained important, however, even in the legal prosecution for homicide, as MacDowell points out (*Athenian Homicide,* pp. 8–30). For a study of this evolution, see Richard Kuhns, *The House, the City, and the Judge: The Growth of Moral Awareness in the "Oresteia"* (Indianapolis: Bobbs-Merrill, 1962). George Thomson also traces the development from tribe to state and its influence on the form and ideas of drama, and on the *Oresteia* in particular (*Aeschylus,* pp. 229–78).

But if this resolution represents the culmination of human progress, at least two problems disturbed the polis in 458. The Court of the Areopagus (the aristocratic body of ex-archons which once functioned as supreme overseer of the laws of the land) had recently been a target of the democratic reform. In 462, Ephialtes and Pericles carried through the Assembly an act which removed the court's right to interfere with democratic legislation and reduced its jurisdiction to cases of pre-meditated murder. The aristocrats were incensed and Ephialtes himself was assassinated. Although Aeschylus's own position on this democratic reform cannot be determined with certainty, in *The Eumenides* the court's function as a tribunal for murder is given a divine validation. Ephialtes and Pericles had also favored challenging Spartan hegemony in Greece by allying with Argos, Sparta's main rival in the Peloponnese. In 461, the leader of the aristocrats, Cimon, was ostracized and the alliance with Argos approved. This change, which also produced fierce debate in the ensuing years, received attention from Aeschylus in the *Oresteia*. Orestes is clearly a political representative of Argos who allies himself with Athens, seemingly with Aeschylus's approval.[3]

It is not as important to label Aeschylus an aristocrat or radical as it is to recognize in the entire trilogy a paradigm for necessary compromise between disparate elements in the state.[4] If political vendettas are not controlled, there can be no civil order and consequently no peace and prosperity. Traditional groups like the Furies must be reconciled to the new system, treated with honor, and allowed to serve the state so that they can preserve for themselves and the community whichever of their principles remain valuable. Athena, establishing the Court of the Areopagus, defines its functions in words which echo the Furies' defense of their grim penalties:

> Here the reverence
> of citizens, their fear and kindred do-no-wrong
> shall hold by day and in the blessing of night alike
> all while the people do not muddy their own laws
> with foul infusions. But if bright water you stain
> with mud, you nevermore will find it fit to drink.
> No anarchy, no rule of a single master. Thus
> I advise my citizens to govern and to grace,
> and not to cast fear utterly from your city. What
> man who fears nothing at all is ever righteous? Such
> be your just terrors, and you may deserve and have
> salvation for your citadel, your land's defence
> such as is nowhere else found among men...
> (*The Eumenides*, 11. 690–702)[5]

Her admonitions provide not only an eternal definition of good government, but also a timely warning to a population recently embroiled in civil strife.

---

[3]The debate about Aeschylus's position on the reforms is summarized by Anthony J. Podlecki in *The Political Background of Aeschylean Tragedy* (Ann Arbor: U of Michigan P, 1966), pp. 81–92.

[4]A forceful spokesman for this view is E. R. Dodds, "Morals and Politics," from *The Ancient Concept of Progress and Other Essays* (Oxford UP, 1973), pp. 54–62.

[5]I have used the translation of Richmond Lattimore that appears in *The Complete Greek Tragedies: Aeschylus 1* (New York, n.d.).

Sophocles

Sophocles (c. 496–c. 406 BCE) won more prizes than any other tragedian in the Greek drama competitions, and he never came in lower than second place. His first victory was against the grand old master Aeschylus in 468 BCE. Sophocles' last plays, which he wrote in his eighties, were among his greatest. We have fragments of some ninety plays or poems and seven complete tragedies, and records suggest that his output numbered something over a hundred and twenty plays.

Sophocles lived in interesting times. He would have recalled the first defeat of the Persians in 490 BCE, when the news came by a messenger who had run twenty-six miles from Marathon to Athens. In his adolescence, Athens achieved its astonishing and decisive victory over the Persians at Salamis. His popularity as a tragedian and as a statesman coincided with the development of an imperial attitude in Athens. Athenian society honored the greatness of such men as Aeschylus, Sophocles, Euripides, the historian Herodotus, and all the politicians and artists that Pericles drew to Athens for its rebuilding. It was a golden age shadowed by war.

Sophocles was both sociable and religious, serving as the priest of several religious cults. He was also a man of action, popular enough to be elected as one of Athens's twelve generals; he participated with Pericles in the Samian War (440–439 BCE). His plays—especially *Antigone* (441 BCE), which preceded his election to generalship—often reflect deep political issues. One of his primary themes concerns the relation of the individual to the *polis,* the state itself. Since the Greeks valued the individual and at the same time regarded the *polis* as a sacred bulwark against a return to barbarism, conflicts between the individual and the *polis* were immensely painful.

When Sophocles began writing, he broke with an old tradition. From the time of Thespis (mid-sixth century BCE), each playwright acted in his own plays. Aeschylus probably did so, but it is on record that Sophocles' voice was not strong enough to permit him to take a part in his plays. He played the lyre well enough to appear onstage, and he participated in a game of ball in one of his plays, but he did not appear as an actor. He also introduced innovations in the structure of his plays by changing the size of the chorus to fifteen and by adding painted scenery, more props, and a third actor to the two that Aeschylus and other tragedians had used. Sophocles wrote some of his plays with specific actors in mind, much as Shakespeare, Molière, and many other first-rank playwrights have done.

Sophocles was versed in the epics of Homer. Some of his plays derive from the *Iliad* or the *Odyssey,* although Sophocles always adapted the material of others to his own purposes. His nickname was the Attic Bee because he could investigate wonderful pieces of literature and always return with a useful idea. The approach he took to the structure of the play, measuring the effect of the rising action of complication and then ensuring that the moment of recognition occurred at the same time the falling action began, was recognized as a

Bust of Sophocles. The
Capitoline Museum,
Rome.

supremely elegant skill. Nowhere is this illustrated more definitively than in *Oedipus Rex*.

The plays of Aeschylus, powerful though they are, do not have the same delicacy of construction as do Sophocles'. They are forceful but, in terms of structure, somewhat simpler. The structure of the plays of Euripides, Sophocles' successor, was never as fully worked out; and when Aristotle discussed the nature of tragedy in his *Poetics*, it was to Sophocles that he turned for a model, not to the other two master playwrights of the genre.

Besides the Oedipus plays, Sophocles' other surviving plays are *Philoctetes*, *Ajax, Trachiniae,* and *Electra.*

OEDIPUS REX

Oedipus Rex is one of three plays by Sophocles that treat the fate of Oedipus and his children. The plays were written over a period of thirty years: *Antigone* (first produced in 441 BCE), *Oedipus Rex* (produced approximately fifteen years later, between 430 and 427 BCE), and *Oedipus at Colonus* (produced in 401 BCE, after Sophocles' death). When these plays are produced together today, they are usually performed in the order that follows the events of Oedipus's and Antigone's lives—*Oedipus Rex, Oedipus at Colonus,* and *Antigone*—almost like the trilogies that Athenian audiences often viewed in the early years of the drama competitions. In fact, they were never a unified trilogy, and one of Sophocles' distinctions is that he did not present as trilogies plays that were thematically related, as poets before him had done.

The original narratives of the Oedipus plays were known to Sophocles' audience—with the possible exception of the story of Antigone—and one of the special pleasures for the audience watching the action of *Oedipus Rex* was that they knew the outcome. They watched for the steps, the choices, that led Oedipus to his fate.

Oedipus Rex is the story of a noble man who seeks knowledge that in the end destroys him. His greatness is measured in part by the fact that the gods have prophesied his fate: the gods take interest only in significant men. Before the action of the play begins, Oedipus has set out to discover whether he is truly the son of Polybos and Merope, the people who have reared him. He learns from the oracle of Apollo at Delphi, the most powerful interpreter of the voice and the will of the gods, that he will kill his father and marry his mother. His response is overwhelmingly human: he has seen his *moira,* his fate, and he cannot accept it. His reaction is to do everything he can, including leaving his homeland as quickly as possible, to avoid the possibility of killing Polybos and marrying Merope.

The Greek audience would have known that Oedipus was a descendant of Kadmos, founder of Thebes, who had sown the dragon teeth that produced the Spartoi (the sown men). Legend determined that the rulership of Thebes would be in dispute, with fraternal rivalry resembling that of the Spartoi, who fought and killed each other. This bloody legacy follows Oedipus, but it also reaches into all the plays of the trilogy. For example, in *Antigone* we learn that Antigone's brothers Polyneices and Eteocles killed each other in the shadow of the city walls. Thus, the fate Oedipus attempts to avoid actually dooms most of the characters in the three plays, including his true father, Laios, and his daughter Antigone.

Sophocles develops the drama in terms of IRONY—the disjunction between what seems to be true and what is true. Knowing the outcome of the action, the audience savors the ironic moments from the beginning of the play to the end. Oedipus flees his homeland to avoid fulfilling the prophecy, only to run headlong into the fate foretold by the oracle. He unwittingly returns to his original home, Thebes, and to his parents, murdering Laios, his true father, at a crossroads on the way and marrying Iokaste, his true mother, and becoming king of Thebes. The blind seer Teiresias warns Oedipus not to pursue the truth, but, in human fashion, Oedipus refuses to heed Teiresias's warnings. When the complete truth becomes clear to Oedipus, he physically blinds himself in horror and expiation. Like the blind Teiresias, Oedipus must now look inward for the truth, without the distractions of surface experiences.

The belief that the moral health of the ruler directly affected the security of the *polis* was widespread in Athenian Greece. Indeed, the Athenians regarded their state as fragile—like a human being whose health, physical and moral, could change suddenly. Because the Greeks were concerned for the well-being of their state, the *polis* often figures in the tragedies. The Sophoclean Oedipus trilogy is usually called the Theban plays, a nomenclature that reminds us that the story of Oedipus can be read as the story of an individual or as the story of a state.

Oedipus Rex examines the tension between and interdependence of the individual and the state. The agricultural and ritual basis of the Dionysian festivals—in which Greek drama developed—underscores the importance the Greeks attached to the individual's dependence on the state that feeds him and on the proper ways of doing things. This could be planting and harvesting or worshiping the gods or living as part of a political entity.

The underlying conflict in the play is political. The political relationship of human beings to the gods, the arbiters of their fate, is dramatized in Oedipus's relationship with the seer Teiresias. If he had his way, Oedipus might disregard Teiresias entirely. But Oedipus cannot command everything, even as ruler. His incomplete knowledge, despite his wisdom, is symptomatic of the limitations of every individual.

The contrast of Oedipus and Kreon, Iokaste's brother, is one of political style. Oedipus is a fully developed character who reveals himself as sympathetic but willful. He acts on his misunderstanding of the prophecy without reconsulting the oracle. He marries Iokaste and blinds himself without reconsulting the oracle. Kreon, who is much less complicated, never acts without consulting the oracle and thoughtfully reflecting on the oracle's message. Oedipus sometimes behaves tyrannically, and he appears eager for power. Kreon takes power only when forced to do so.

The depth of Sophocles' character development was unmatched, except by his contemporary Euripides, for almost two thousand years. Sophocles' drama is one of psychological development. His audiences saw Oedipus as a model for human greatness but also as a model for the human capacity to fall from a great height. The play is about the limits of human knowledge; it is also about the limits and frailty of human happiness.

Oedipus Rex in Performance

Oedipus Rex has enjoyed great popularity since its first performance. The Greeks, who originally restricted their plays to one performance, eventually began to revive plays of the masters. *Oedipus* was one of the most popular. In modern times, performance has been almost constant since the seventeenth century. Great dramatists have produced it in their own adaptations—Corneille (1659), John Dryden (1679), Voltaire (1718), William Butler Yeats (1923), and Jean Cocteau (1931)—proving the durability of the themes and the adaptability of the play. The early American performances (beginning in 1881) were in Greek but soon gave way to English. In his *New York Times* review of the October 2000 production in City Center, New York, Ben Brantley said, "Few productions have so hauntingly conveyed the brutal isolation of those who would be king as the National Theater of Greece's exquisitely staged *Oedipus Rex,* directed by Vassilis Papavassileiou." This production was also presented at the Roman Colosseum, the first theatrical event in that space in 1,500 years. Currently, Greek companies perform the play regularly in the theater of Dionysus in Athens as well as in Epidaurus and elsewhere.

Sophocles (c. 496–c. 406 BCE)

OEDIPUS REX

c. 430 BCE

TRANSLATED BY DUDLEY FITTS AND ROBERT FITZGERALD

Characters

OEDIPUS, *King of Thebes, supposed son of Polybos and Merope, King and Queen of Corinth*

IOKASTE, *wife of Oedipus and widow of the late King Laios*

KREON, *brother of Iokaste, a prince of Thebes*

TEIRESIAS, *a blind seer who serves Apollo*

PRIEST

MESSENGER, *from Corinth*

SHEPHERD, *former servant of Laios*

SECOND MESSENGER, *from the palace*

CHORUS OF THEBAN ELDERS

CHORAGOS, *leader of the Chorus*

ANTIGONE *and* ISMENE, *young daughters of Oedipus and Iokaste. They appear in the Exodos but do not speak.*

SUPPLIANTS, GUARDS, SERVANTS

The Scene: *Before the palace of Oedipus, King of Thebes. A central door and two lateral doors open onto a platform which runs the length of the facade. On the platform, right and left, are altars; and three steps lead down into the orchestra, or chorus-ground. At the beginning of the action these steps are crowded by suppliants who have brought branches and chaplets of olive leaves and who sit in various attitudes of despair. Oedipus enters.*

PROLOGUE°

OEDIPUS: My children, generations of the living
  In the line of Kadmos,° nursed at his ancient hearth:
  Why have you strewn yourselves before these altars
  In supplication, with your boughs and garlands?
5 The breath of incense rises from the city
  With a sound of prayer and lamentation.
                                    Children,
  I would not have you speak through messengers,
  And therefore I have come myself to hear you—
  I, Oedipus, who bear the famous name.
  (*To a Priest.*) You, there, since you are eldest in
10   the company,
  Speak for them all, tell me what preys upon you,
  Whether you come in dread, or crave some blessing:

Prologue: Portion of the play explaining the background and current action.   **2. Kadmos:** Founder of Thebes.

  Tell me, and never doubt that I will help you
  In every way I can; I should be heartless
  Were I not moved to find you suppliant here.   15
PRIEST: Great Oedipus, O powerful king of Thebes!
  You see how all the ages of our people
  Cling to your altar steps: here are boys
  Who can barely stand alone, and here are priests
  By weight of age, as I am a priest of God,   20
  And young men chosen from those yet unmarried;
  As for the others, all that multitude,
  They wait with olive chaplets in the squares,
  At the two shrines of Pallas,° and where Apollo°
  Speaks in the glowing embers.
                              Your own eyes   25
  Must tell you: Thebes is tossed on a murdering sea
  And can not lift her head from the death surge.
  A rust consumes the buds and fruits of the earth;
  The herds are sick; children die unborn,
  And labor is vain. The god of plague and pyre   30
  Raids like detestable lightning through the city,
  And all the house of Kadmos is laid waste,
  All emptied, and all darkened: Death alone
  Battens upon the misery of Thebes.

  You are not one of the immortal gods, we know;   35
  Yet we have come to you to make our prayer
  As to the man surest in mortal ways
  And wisest in the ways of God. You saved us
  From the Sphinx,° that flinty singer, and the tribute
  We paid to her so long; yet you were never   40
  Better informed than we, nor could we teach you:
  A god's touch, it seems, enabled you to help us.

  Therefore, O mighty power, we turn to you:
  Find us our safety, find us a remedy,
  Whether by counsel of the gods or of men.   45
  A king of wisdom tested in the past
  Can act in a time of troubles, and act well.
  Noblest of men, restore
  Life to your city! Think how all men call you
  Liberator for your boldness long ago;   50
  Ah, when your years of kingship are remembered,

---

24. Pallas: Pallas Athene, daughter of Zeus and goddess of wisdom.   **Apollo:** Son of Zeus and god of the sun, of light and truth.   **39. Sphinx:** A winged monster with the body of a lion and the face of a woman, the Sphinx had tormented Thebes with her riddle, killing those who could not solve it. When Oedipus solved the riddle, the Sphinx killed herself.

Let them not say *We rose, but later fell*—
Keep the State from going down in the storm!
Once, years ago, with happy augury,
55   You brought us fortune; be the same again!
No man questions your power to rule the land:
But rule over men, not over a dead city!
Ships are only hulls, high walls are nothing,
When no life moves in the empty passageways.
60   OEDIPUS: Poor children! You may be sure I know
All that you longed for in your coming here.
I know that you are deathly sick; and yet,
Sick as you are, not one is as sick as I.
Each of you suffers in himself alone
65   His anguish, not another's; but my spirit
Groans for the city, for myself, for you.

I was not sleeping, you are not waking me.
No, I have been in tears for a long while
And in my restless thought walked many ways.
70   In all my search I found one remedy,
And I have adopted it: I have sent Kreon,
Son of Menoikeus, brother of the queen,
To Delphi,° Apollo's place of revelation,
To learn there, if he can,
75   What act or pledge of mine may save the city.
I have counted the days, and now, this very day,
I am troubled, for he has overstayed his time.
What is he doing? He has been gone too long.
Yet whenever he comes back, I should do ill
80   Not to take any action the god orders.
PRIEST: It is a timely promise. At this instant
They tell me Kreon is here.
OEDIPUS: O Lord Apollo!
May his news be fair as his face is radiant!
PRIEST: Good news, I gather! he is crowned with bay,
The chaplet is thick with berries.
85   OEDIPUS: We shall soon know;
He is near enough to hear us now.   (*Enter Kreon.*)
    O prince:
Brother: son of Menoikeus:
What answer do you bring us from the god?
KREON: A strong one. I can tell you, great afflictions
90   Will turn out well, if they are taken well.
OEDIPUS: What was the oracle? These vague words
Leave me still hanging between hope and fear.
KREON: Is it your pleasure to hear me with all these
Gathered around us? I am prepared to speak,
But should we not go in?
95   OEDIPUS: Speak to them all,
It is for them I suffer, more than for myself.
KREON: Then I will tell you what I heard at Delphi.
In plain words
The god commands us to expel from the land of
    Thebes
100   An old defilement we are sheltering.

73. **Delphi:** Site of the oracle, source of religious authority and prophecy, under the protection of Apollo.

It is a deathly thing, beyond cure;
We must not let it feed upon us longer.
OEDIPUS: What defilement? How shall we rid
    ourselves of it?
KREON: By exile or death, blood for blood. It was
Murder that brought the plague-wind on the city.   105
OEDIPUS: Murder of whom? Surely the god has
    named him?
KREON: My Lord: Laios once ruled this land,
Before you came to govern us.
OEDIPUS: I know;
I learned of him from others; I never saw him.
KREON: He was murdered; and Apollo commands us
    now   110
To take revenge upon whoever killed him.
OEDIPUS: Upon whom? Where are they? Where shall
    we find a clue
To solve that crime, after so many years?
KREON: Here in this land, he said. Search reveals
Things that escape an inattentive man.   115
OEDIPUS: Tell me: Was Laios murdered in his house,
Or in the fields, or in some foreign country?
KREON: He said he planned to make a pilgrimage.
He did not come home again.
OEDIPUS: And was there no one,
No witness, no companion, to tell what happened?   120
KREON: They were all killed but one, and he got away
So frightened that he could remember one thing
    only.
OEDIPUS: What was that one thing? One may be the
    key
To everything, if we resolve to use it.
KREON: He said that a band of highwaymen attacked
    them,
Outnumbered them, and overwhelmed the king.   125
OEDIPUS: Strange, that a highwayman should be so
    daring—
Unless some faction here bribed him to do it.
KREON: We thought of that. But after Laios' death
New troubles arose and we had no avenger.   130
OEDIPUS: What troubles could prevent your hunting
    down the killers?
KREON: The riddling Sphinx's song
Made us deaf to all mysteries but her own.
OEDIPUS: Then once more I must bring what is dark
    to light.
It is most fitting that Apollo shows,   135
As you do, this compunction for the dead.
You shall see how I stand by you, as I should,
Avenging this country and the god as well,
And not as though it were for some distant friend,
But for my own sake, to be rid of evil.   140
Whoever killed King Laios might—who knows?—
Lay violent hands even on me—and soon.
I act for the murdered king in my own interest.

Come, then, my children: leave the altar steps,
Lift up your olive boughs!
                              One of you go   145

And summon the people of Kadmos to gather here.
I will do all that I can; you may tell them that.
                                (*Exit a Page.*)
So, with the help of God,
We shall be saved—or else indeed we are lost.
150 PRIEST: Let us rise, children. It was for this we came,
And now the king has promised it.
Phoibos° has sent us an oracle; may he descend
Himself to save us and drive out the plague.

(*Exeunt*° *Oedipus and Kreon into the palace by the central door. The Priest and the Suppliants disperse right and left. After a short pause the Chorus enters the orchestra.*)

PARODOS° • Strophe° 1

CHORUS: What is God singing in his profound
Delphi of gold and shadow?
What oracle for Thebes, the Sunwhipped city?
Fear unjoints me, the roots of my heart tremble.
Now I remember, O Healer, your power, and
5   wonder:
Will you send doom like a sudden cloud, or weave it
Like nightfall of the past?
Speak to me, tell me, O
Child of golden Hope, immortal Voice.

Antistrophe° 1

Let me pray to Athene, the immortal daughter of
10   Zeus,
And to Artemis° her sister
Who keeps her famous throne in the market ring,
And to Apollo, archer from distant heaven—
O gods, descend! Like three streams leap against
15 The fires of our grief, the fires of darkness;
Be swift to bring us rest!
As in the old time from the brilliant house
Of air you stepped to save us, come again!

Strophe 2

Now our afflictions have no end,
20 Now all our stricken host lies down
And no man fights off death with his mind;
The noble plowland bears no grain,
And groaning mothers can not bear—
See, how our lives like birds take wing,

152. **Phoibos:** Apollo. [S.D.] *Exeunt:* Latin for "they go out."
Parodos: The song or ode chanted by the Chorus on their entry.
Strophe: Song sung by the Chorus as they danced from stage right to stage left.   **Antistrophe:** Song sung by the Chorus following the Strophe, as they danced back from stage left to stage right.   **11. Artemis:** The huntress, daughter of Zeus, twin sister of Apollo.

Like sparks that fly when a fire soars,   25
To the shore of the god of evening.

Antistrophe 2

The plague burns on, it is pitiless,
Though pallid children laden with death
Lie unwept in the stony ways,
And old gray women by every path   30
Flock to the strand about the altars
There to strike their breasts and cry
Worship of Phoibos in wailing prayers:
Be kind, God's golden child!

Strophe 3

There are no swords in this attack by fire,   35
No shields, but we are ringed with cries.
Send the besieger plunging from our homes
Into the vast sea-room of the Atlantic
Or into the waves that foam eastward of Thrace—
For the day ravages what the night spares—   40
Destroy our enemy, lord of the thunder!
Let him be riven by lightning from heaven!

Antistrophe 3

Phoibos Apollo, stretch the sun's bowstring,
That golden cord, until it sing for us,
Flashing arrows in heaven!
                       Artemis, Huntress,   45
Race with flaring lights upon our mountains!
O scarlet god,° O golden-banded brow,
O Theban Bacchos in a storm of Maenads,°

(*Enter Oedipus, center.*)

Whirl upon Death, that all the Undying hate!
Come with blinding torches, come in joy!   50

SCENE 1

OEDIPUS: Is this your prayer? It may be answered.
   Come,
Listen to me, act as the crisis demands,
And you shall have relief from all these evils.

Until now I was a stranger to this tale,
As I had been a stranger to the crime.   5
Could I track down the murderer without a clue?
But now, friends,
As one who became a citizen after the murder,

47. **scarlet god:** Bacchus, god of wine and revelry; also called Dionysus. **48. Maenads:** Female worshipers of Bacchus (Dionysus).

I make this proclamation to all Thebans:
If any man knows by whose hand Laios, son of
10   Labdakos,
Met his death, I direct that man to tell me
      everything,
No matter what he fears for having so long
      withheld it.
Let it stand as promised that no further trouble
Will come to him, but he may leave the land in
      safety.
Moreover: If anyone knows the murderer to be
15   foreign,
Let him not keep silent: he shall have his reward
      from me.
However, if he does conceal it; if any man
Fearing for his friend or for himself disobeys this
      edict,
Hear what I propose to do:

I solemnly forbid the people of this country,
20 Where power and throne are mine, ever to receive
      that man
Or speak to him, no matter who he is, or let him
Join in sacrifice, lustration, or in prayer.
I decree that he be driven from every house,
25 Being, as he is, corruption itself to us: the Delphic
Voice of Apollo has pronounced this revelation.
Thus I associate myself with the oracle
And take the side of the murdered king.

As for the criminal, I pray to God—
30 Whether it be a lurking thief, or one of a number—
I pray that that man's life be consumed in evil and
      wretchedness.
And as for me, this curse applies no less
If it should turn out that the culprit is my guest
      here,
Sharing my hearth.
                              You have heard the penalty.
35 I lay it on you now to attend to this
For my sake, for Apollo's, for the sick
Sterile city that heaven has abandoned.
Suppose the oracle had given you no command:
Should this defilement go uncleansed for ever?
40 You should have found the murderer: your king,
A noble king, had been destroyed!
                              Now I,
Having the power that he held before me,
Having his bed, begetting children there
Upon his wife, as he would have, had he lived—
45 Their son would have been my children's brother,
If Laios had had luck in fatherhood!
(And now his bad fortune has struck him
      down)—
I say I take the son's part, just as though
I were his son, to press the fight for him
50 And see it won! I'll find the hand that brought
Death to Labdakos' and Polydoros' child,
Heir of Kadmos' and Agenor's line.°
And as for those who fail me,

May the gods deny them the fruit of the earth,
Fruit of the womb, and may they rot utterly!   55
Let them be wretched as we are wretched, and
      worse!

For you, for loyal Thebans, and for all
Who find my actions right, I pray the favor
Of justice, and of all the immortal gods.
CHORAGOS: Since I am under oath, my lord, I swear   60
I did not do the murder, I can not name
The murderer. Phoibos ordained the search;
Why did he not say who the culprit was?
OEDIPUS: An honest question. But no man in the world
Can make the gods do more than the gods will.   65
CHORAGOS: There is an alternative, I think—
OEDIPUS: Tell me.
Any or all, you must not fail to tell me.
CHORAGOS: A lord clairvoyant to the lord Apollo,
As we all know, is the skilled Teiresias.
One might learn much about this from him,
      Oedipus.   70
OEDIPUS: I am not wasting time:
Kreon spoke of this, and I have sent for him—
Twice, in fact; it is strange that he is not here.
CHORAGOS: The other matter—that old report—
      seems useless.
OEDIPUS: What was that? I am interested in all reports.   75
CHORAGOS: The king was said to have been killed by
      highwaymen.
OEDIPUS: I know. But we have no witnesses to that.
CHORAGOS: If the killer can feel a particle of dread,
Your curse will bring him out of hiding!
OEDIPUS: No.
The man who dared that act will fear no curse.   80

(*Enter the blind seer Teiresias, led by a Page.*)

CHORAGOS: But there is one man who may detect the
      criminal.
This is Teiresias, this is the holy prophet
In whom, alone of all men, truth was born.
OEDIPUS: Teiresias: seer: student of mysteries,
Of all that's taught and all that no man tells,   85
Secrets of Heaven and secrets of the earth:
Blind though you are, you know the city lies
Sick with plague; and from this plague, my lord,
We find that you alone can guard or save us.

Possibly you did not hear the messengers?   90
Apollo, when we sent to him,
Sent us back word that this great pestilence
Would lift, but only if we established clearly
The identity of those who murdered Laios.
They must be killed or exiled.
                              Can you use   95
Birdflight° or any art of divination

51–52. **Labdakos, Polydoros, Kadmos, and Agenor:** Father,
grandfather, great-grandfather, and great-great-grandfather of
Laios.   96. **Birdflight:** Prophets used the flight of birds to predict the future.

Le Clanche Du Rand as Iokaste in Donald Sutherland and Robert Loper's production of *Oedipus Rex* at the 1975 Oregon Shakespeare Festival in Ashland. (Photo by Henry S. Kranzler.)

To purify yourself, and Thebes, and me
From this contagion? We are in your hands.
There is no fairer duty
100   Than that of helping others in distress.
TEIRESIAS: How dreadful knowledge of the truth can be
    When there's no help in truth! I knew this well,
    But did not act on it; else I should not have come.
OEDIPUS: What is troubling you? Why are your eyes so cold?
105 TEIRESIAS: Let me go home. Bear your own fate, and I'll
    Bear mine. It is better so: trust what I say.
OEDIPUS: What you say is ungracious and unhelpful
    To your native country. Do not refuse to speak.
TEIRESIAS: When it comes to speech, your own is neither temperate
110   Nor opportune. I wish to be more prudent.
OEDIPUS: In God's name, we all beg you—
TEIRESIAS: You are all ignorant.
    No; I will never tell you what I know.
    Now it is my misery; then, it would be yours.
OEDIPUS: What! You do know something, and will
115   not tell us?
    You would betray us all and wreck the State?
TEIRESIAS: I do not intend to torture myself, or you.
    Why persist in asking? You will not persuade me.
OEDIPUS: What a wicked old man you are! You'd try a stone's
120   Patience! Out with it! Have you no feeling at all?
TEIRESIAS: You call me unfeeling. If you could only see
    The nature of your own feelings...
OEDIPUS: Why,
    Who would not feel as I do? Who could endure
    Your arrogance toward the city?
TEIRESIAS: What does it matter?
    Whether I speak or not, it is bound to come.
125 OEDIPUS: Then, if "it" is bound to come, you are
    bound to tell me.
TEIRESIAS: No, I will not go on. Rage as you please.
OEDIPUS: Rage? Why not!
              And I'll tell you what I think:
    You planned it, you had it done, you all but
130   Killed him with your own hands: if you had eyes,
    I'd say the crime was yours, and yours alone.
TEIRESIAS: So? I charge you, then,
    Abide by the proclamation you have made:
    From this day forth
135   Never speak again to these men or to me;
    You yourself are the pollution of this country.
OEDIPUS: You dare say that! Can you possibly think you have
    Some way of going free, after such insolence?
TEIRESIAS: I have gone free. It is the truth sustains me.
OEDIPUS: Who taught you shamelessness? It was not your craft.

TEIRESIAS: You did. You made me speak. I did not want to.
140
OEDIPUS: Speak what? Let me hear it again more clearly.
TEIRESIAS: Was it not clear before? Are you tempting me?
OEDIPUS: I did not understand it. Say it again.
TEIRESIAS: I say that you are the murderer whom you seek.
OEDIPUS: Now twice you have spat out infamy. You'll pay for it!
145
TEIRESIAS: Would you care for more? Do you wish to be really angry?
OEDIPUS: Say what you will. Whatever you say is worthless.
TEIRESIAS: I say you live in hideous shame with those Most dear to you. You can not see the evil.
OEDIPUS: Can you go on babbling like this for ever?   150
TEIRESIAS: I can, if there is power in truth.
OEDIPUS: There is:
    But not for you, not for you,   155
    You sightless, witless, senseless, mad old man!
TEIRESIAS: You are the madman. There is no one here Who will not curse you soon, as you curse me.

RIGHT: Philip L. Jones as the
Shepherd. (Photo by Henry S.
Kranzler.) BELOW: Franz Mertz's
design for a 1952 production
of *Oedipus Rex* directed by
G. R. Sellner at Darmstadt
Landestheater.

OEDIPUS: You child of total night! I would not touch
    you;
      Neither would any man who sees the sun.
TEIRESIAS: True: it is not from you my fate will come.
    That lies within Apollo's competence,
    As it is his concern.
160 OEDIPUS: Tell me, who made
    These fine discoveries? Kreon? or someone else?
TEIRESIAS: Kreon is no threat. You weave your own
    doom.
OEDIPUS: Wealth, power, craft of statemanship!
    Kingly position, everywhere admired!
165 What savage envy is stored up against these,
    If Kreon, whom I trusted, Kreon my friend,
    For this great office which the city once
    Put in my hands unsought—if for this power
    Kreon desires in secret to destroy me!

170 He has bought this decrepit fortune-teller, this
    Collector of dirty pennies, this prophet fraud—
    Why, he is no more clairvoyant than I am!
                                 Tell us:
    Has your mystic mummery ever approached the
    truth?
    When that hellcat the Sphinx was performing here,
175 What help were you to these people?
    Her magic was not for the first man who came
    along:
    It demanded a real exorcist. Your birds—
    What good were they? or the gods, for the matter
    of that?
    But I came by,
180 Oedipus, the simple man, who knows nothing—
    I thought it out for myself, no birds helped me!
    And this is the man you think you can destroy,
    That you may be close to Kreon when he's king!
    Well, you and your friend Kreon, it seems to me,
185 Will suffer most. If you were not an old man,
    You would have paid already for your plot.
CHORAGOS: We can not see that his words or yours
    Have been spoken except in anger, Oedipus,
    And of anger we have no need. How to accomplish
190 The god's will best: that is what most concerns us.
TEIRESIAS: You are a king. But where argument's
    concerned
    I am your man, as much a king as you.
    I am not your servant, but Apollo's.
    I have no need of Kreon or Kreon's name.

195 Listen to me. You mock my blindness, do you?
    But I say that you, with both your eyes, are blind:
    You can not see the wretchedness of your life,
    Nor in whose house you live, no, nor with whom.
    Who are your father and mother? Can you tell me?
200 You do not even know the blind wrongs
    That you have done them, on earth and in the
    world below.
    But the double lash of your parents' curse will
    whip you

Out of this land some day, with only night
Upon your precious eyes.
Your cries then—where will they not be heard? 205
What fastness of Kithairon° will not echo them?
And that bridal-descant of yours—you'll know it
    then,
The song they sang when you came here to Thebes
And found your misguided berthing.
All this, and more, that you can not guess at now, 210
Will bring you to yourself among your children.

Be angry, then. Curse Kreon. Curse my words.
I tell you, no man that walks upon the earth
Shall be rooted out more horribly than you.
OEDIPUS: Am I to bear this from him?—Damnation 215
    Take you! Out of this place! Out of my sight!
TEIRESIAS: I would not have come at all if you had
    not asked me.
OEDIPUS: Could I have told that you'd talk nonsense,
    that
    You'd come here to make a fool of yourself, and
    of me?
TEIRESIAS: A fool? Your parents thought me sane
    enough. 220
OEDIPUS: My parents again!—Wait: who were my
    parents?
TEIRESIAS: This day will give you a father, and break
    your heart.
OEDIPUS: Your infantile riddles! Your damned
    abracadabra!
TEIRESIAS: You were a great man once at solving
    riddles.
OEDIPUS: Mock me with that if you like; you will
    find it true. 225
TEIRESIAS: It was true enough. It brought about your
    ruin.
OEDIPUS: But if it saved this town?
TEIRESIAS (*to the Page*): Boy, give me your hand.
OEDIPUS: Yes, boy; lead him away.
                     —While you are here
    We can do nothing. Go; leave us in peace. 230
TEIRESIAS: I will go when I have said what I have to
    say.
    How can you hurt me? And I tell you again:
    The man you have been looking for all this time,
    The damned man, the murderer of Laios,
    That man is in Thebes. To your mind he is
    foreign-born,
    But it will soon be shown that he is a Theban, 235
    A revelation that will fail to please.
                         A blind man,
    Who has his eyes now; a penniless man, who is
    rich now;
    And he will go tapping the strange earth with his
    staff.
    To the children with whom he lives now he will be 240

---

206. Kithairon: The mountain where Oedipus was abandoned
as an infant.

Brother and father—the very same; to her
Who bore him, son and husband—the very same
Who came to his father's bed, wet with his father's
    blood.
Enough. Go think that over.
245   If later you find error in what I have said,
You may say that I have no skill in prophecy.

(*Exit Teiresias, led by his Page.
Oedipus goes into the palace.*)

ODE° 1 • *Strophe 1*

CHORUS: The Delphic stone of prophecies
Remembers ancient regicide
And a still bloody hand.
That killer's hour of flight has come.
5   He must be stronger than riderless
Coursers of untiring wind,
For the son of Zeus° armed with his father's
    thunder
Leaps in lightning after him;
And the Furies° hold his track, the sad Furies.

Antistrophe 1

10   Holy Parnassos'° peak of snow
Flashes and blinds that secret man,
That all shall hunt him down:
Though he may roam the forest shade
Like a bull gone wild from pasture
15   To rage through glooms of stone.
Doom comes down on him; flight will not avail
    him;
For the world's heart calls him desolate,
And the immortal voices follow, for ever follow.

Strophe 2

But now a wilder thing is heard
From the old man skilled at hearing Fate in the
20   wing-beat of a bird.
Bewildered as a blown bird, my soul hovers and
    can not find
Foothold in this debate, or any reason or rest of
    mind.
But no man ever brought—none can bring
Proof of strife between Thebes' royal house,
25   Labdakos' line, and the son of Polybos;°
And never until now has any man brought word
Of Laios' dark death staining Oedipus the King.

Ode: Song sung by the Chorus.   7. son of Zeus: Apollo.
9. Furies: Spirits called on to avenge crimes, especially against
kin.   10. Parnassos: Mountain sacred to Apollo.   25. Polybos:
King who adopted Oedipus.

Antistrophe 2

Divine Zeus and Apollo hold
Perfect intelligence alone of all tales ever told;
And well though this diviner works, he works in
    his own night;
30   No man can judge that rough unknown or trust in
    second sight,
For wisdom changes hands among the wise.
Shall I believe my great lord criminal
At a raging word that a blind old man let fall?
I saw him, when the carrion woman° faced him of
    old,
35   Prove his heroic mind. These evil words are lies.

SCENE 2

KREON: Men of Thebes:
I am told that heavy accusations
Have been brought against me by King Oedipus.

I am not the kind of man to bear this tamely.

If in these present difficulties   5
He holds me accountable for any harm to him
Through anything I have said or done—why,
    then,
I do not value life in this dishonor.
It is not as though this rumor touched upon
Some private indiscretion. The matter is grave.   10
The fact is that I am being called disloyal
To the State, to my fellow citizens, to my friends.
CHORAGOS: He may have spoken in anger, not from
    his mind.
KREON: But did you not hear him say I was the one
Who seduced the old prophet into lying?
CHORAGOS: The thing was said; I do not know how   15
    seriously.
KREON: But you were watching him! Were his eyes
    steady?
Did he look like a man in his right mind?
CHORAGOS: I do not know.
I can not judge the behavior of great men.
But here is the king himself.

(*Enter Oedipus.*)

OEDIPUS: So you dared come back.   20
Why? How brazen of you to come to my house,
You murderer!
                    Do you think I do not know
That you plotted to kill me, plotted to steal my
    throne?
Tell me, in God's name: am I coward, a fool,
That you should dream you could accomplish this?   25
A fool who could not see your slippery game?

35. woman: The Sphinx.

Josef Svoboda's stage design
for M. Machacek's 1963
production of *Oedipus Rex*
in Prague.

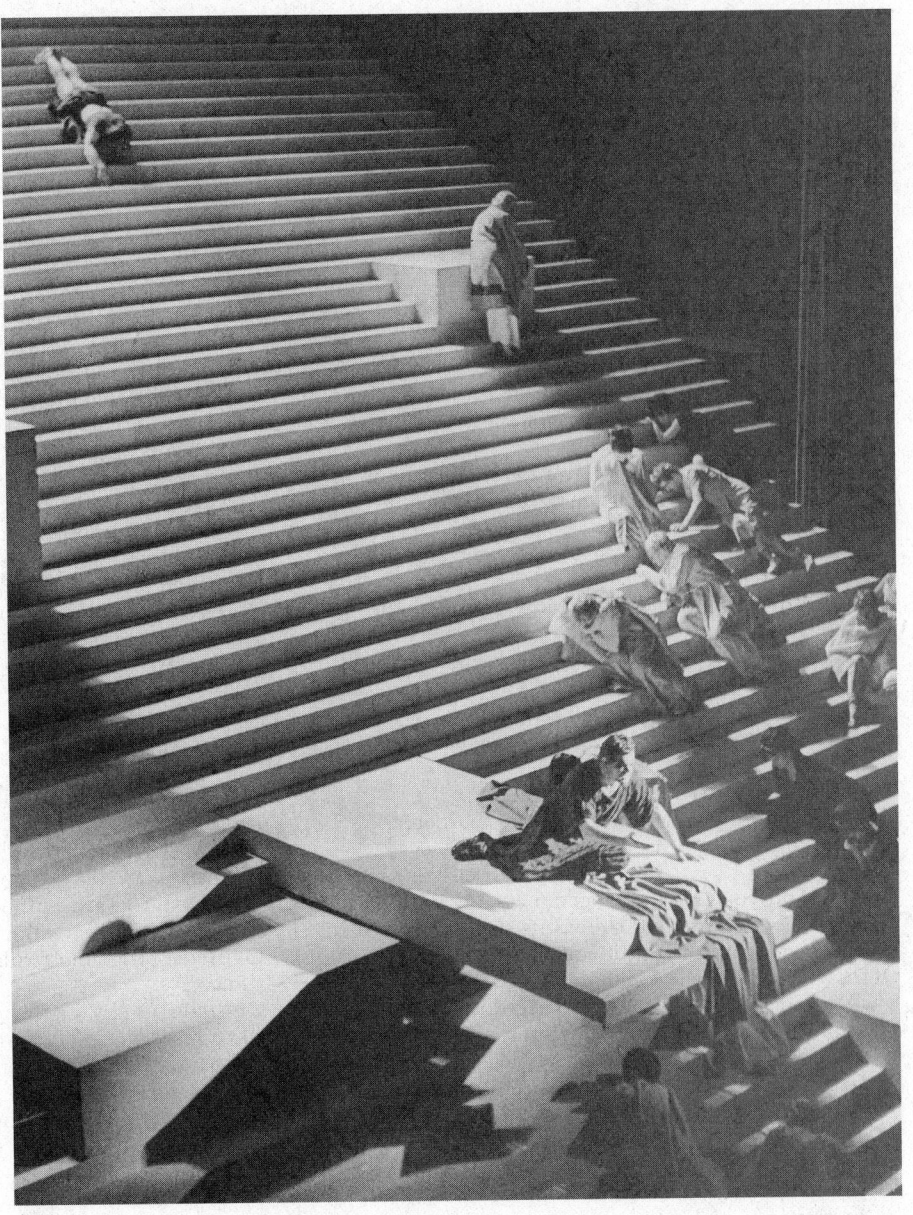

A coward, not to fight back when I saw it?
You are the fool, Kreon, are you not? hoping
Without support or friends to get a throne?
Thrones may be won or bought: you could do
30   neither.
    KREON: Now listen to me. You have talked; let me
        talk, too.
    You can not judge unless you know the facts.
    OEDIPUS: You speak well: there is one fact; but I find
        it hard
    To learn from the deadliest enemy I have.
35   KREON: That above all I must dispute with you.

OEDIPUS: That above all I will not hear you deny.
KREON: If you think there is anything good in being
    stubborn
    Against all reason, then I say you are wrong.
OEDIPUS: If you think a man can sin against his own
    kind
    And not be punished for it, I say you are mad.   40
KREON: I agree. But tell me: what have I done to
    you?
OEDIPUS: You advised me to send for that wizard,
    did you not?
KREON: I did. I should do it again.

OEDIPUS: Very well. Now tell me:
  How long has it been since Laios—
KREON: What of Laios?
45 OEDIPUS: Since he vanished in that onset by the road?
KREON: It was long ago, a long time.
OEDIPUS: And this prophet,
  Was he practicing here then?
KREON: He was; and with
    honor, as now.
OEDIPUS: Did he speak of me at that time?
KREON: He never did,
  At least, not when I was present.
OEDIPUS: But . . . the enquiry?
  I suppose you held one?
50 KREON: We did, but we learned nothing.
OEDIPUS: Why did the prophet not speak against me
    then?
KREON: I do not know; and I am the kind of man
  Who holds his tongue when he has no facts to
    go on.
OEDIPUS: There's one fact that you know, and you
    could tell it.
KREON: What fact is that? If I know it, you shall
55   have it.
OEDIPUS: If he were not involved with you, he could
    not say
  That it was I who murdered Laios.
KREON: If he says that, you are the one that knows
    it!—
  But now it is my turn to question you.
60 OEDIPUS: Put your questions. I am no murderer.
KREON: First, then: You married my sister?
OEDIPUS: I married your sister.
KREON: And you rule the kingdom equally with her?
OEDIPUS: Everything that she wants she has from me.
KREON: And I am the third, equal to both of you?
65 OEDIPUS: That is why I call you a bad friend.
KREON: No. Reason it out, as I have done.
  Think of this first: would any sane man prefer
  Power, with all a king's anxieties,
  To that same power and the grace of sleep?
70 Certainly not I.
  I have never longed for the king's power—only his
    rights.
  Would any wise man differ from me in this?
  As matters stand, I have my way in everything
  With your consent, and no responsibilities.
75 If I were king, I should be a slave to policy.
  How could I desire a scepter more
  Than what is now mine—untroubled influence?
  No, I have not gone mad; I need no honors,
  Except those with the perquisites I have now.
80 I am welcome everywhere; every man salutes me,
  And those who want your favor seek my ear,
  Since I know how to manage what they ask.
  Should I exchange this ease for that anxiety?
  Besides, no sober mind is treasonable.
85 I hate anarchy
  And never would deal with any man who likes it.

Test what I have said. Go to the priestess
At Delphi, ask if I quoted her correctly.
And as for this other thing: if I am found
Guilty of treason with Teiresias,   90
Then sentence me to death. You have my word
It is a sentence I should cast my vote for—
But not without evidence!
                        You do wrong
When you take good men for bad, bad men for
  good.
A true friend thrown aside—why, life itself   95
Is not more precious!
                      In time you will know this well:
For time, and time alone, will show the just man,
Though scoundrels are discovered in a day.
CHORAGOS: This is well said, and a prudent man
    would ponder it.
Judgments too quickly formed are dangerous.   100
OEDIPUS: But is he not quick in his duplicity?
  And shall I not be quick to parry him?
  Would you have me stand still, hold my peace,
    and let
  This man win everything, through my inaction?
KREON: And you want—what is it, then? To banish
    me?   105
OEDIPUS: No, not exile. It is your death I want,
  So that all the world may see what treason means.
KREON: You will persist, then? You will not believe
    me?
OEDIPUS: How can I believe you?
KREON: Then you are a fool.
OEDIPUS: To save myself?
KREON: In justice, think of me.   110
OEDIPUS: You are evil incarnate.
KREON: But suppose that you are wrong?
OEDIPUS: Still I must rule.
KREON: But not if you rule badly.
OEDIPUS: O city, city!
KREON: It is my city, too!
CHORAGOS: Now, my lords, be still. I see the queen,
  Iokaste, coming from her palace chambers;   115
  And it is time she came, for the sake of you both.
  This dreadful quarrel can be resolved through her.

(*Enter Iokaste.*)

IOKASTE: Poor foolish men, what wicked din is this?
  With Thebes sick to death, is it not shameful
  That you should take some private quarrel up?   120
  (*To Oedipus.*) Come into the house.
                        —And you, Kreon, go now:
  Let us have no more of this tumult over nothing.
KREON: Nothing? No, sister: what your husband
    plans for me
  Is one of two great evils: exile or death.
OEDIPUS: He is right.
                    Why, woman I have caught him squarely   125
  Plotting against my life.
KREON: No! Let me die
  Accurst if ever I have wished you harm!

IOKASTE: Ah, believe it, Oedipus!
    In the name of the gods, respect this oath of his
130   For my sake, for the sake of these people here!

Strophe 1

CHORAGOS: Open your mind to her, my lord. Be
    ruled by her, I beg you!
OEDIPUS: What would you have me do?
CHORAGOS: Respect Kreon's word. He has never
    spoken like a fool,
    And now he has sworn an oath.
OEDIPUS: You know what you ask?
CHORAGOS: I do.
OEDIPUS: Speak on, then.
CHORAGOS: A friend so sworn should not be baited
135   so,
    In blind malice, and without final proof.
OEDIPUS: You are aware, I hope, that what you say
    Means death for me, or exile at the least.

Strophe 2

CHORAGOS: No, I swear by Helios, first in heaven!
140   May I die friendless and accurst,
    The worst of deaths, if ever I meant that!
    It is the withering fields
        That hurt my sick heart:
    Must we bear all these ills,
145   And now your bad blood as well?
OEDIPUS: Then let him go. And let me die, if I must,
    Or be driven by him in shame from the land of
        Thebes.
    It is your unhappiness, and not his talk,
    That touches me.
             As for him—
150   Wherever he goes, hatred will follow him.
KREON: Ugly in yielding, as you were ugly in rage!
    Natures like yours chiefly torment themselves.
OEDIPUS: Can you not go? Can you not leave me?
KREON: I can.
    You do not know me; but the city knows me,
155   And in its eyes I am just, if not in yours.
                      (Exit Kreon.)

Antistrophe 1

CHORAGOS: Lady Iokaste, did you not ask the King
    to go to his chambers?
IOKASTE: First tell me what has happened.
CHORAGOS: There was suspicion without evidence;
    yet it rankled
    As even false charges will.
IOKASTE: On both sides?
CHORAGOS: On both.
160 IOKASTE: But what was said?

CHORAGOS: Oh let it rest, let it be done with!
    Have we not suffered enough?
OEDIPUS: You see to what your decency has brought
    you:
    You have made difficulties where my heart saw
    none.

Antistrophe 2

CHORAGOS: Oedipus, it is not once only I have told
    you—   165
    You must know I should count myself unwise
    To the point of madness, should I now forsake
    you—
        You, under whose hand,
            In the storm of another time,
            Our dear land sailed out free.   170
    But now stand fast at the helm!
IOKASTE: In God's name, Oedipus, inform your wife
    as well:
    Why are you so set in this hard anger?
OEDIPUS: I will tell you, for none of these men
    deserves
    My confidence as you do. It is Kreon's work,   175
    His treachery, his plotting against me.
IOKASTE: Go on, if you can make this clear to me.
OEDIPUS: He charges me with the murder of Laios.
IOKASTE: Has he some knowledge? Or does he speak
    from hearsay?
OEDIPUS: He would not commit himself to such a
    charge,   180
    But he has brought in that damnable soothsayer
    To tell his story.
IOKASTE: Set your mind at rest.
    If it is a question of soothsayers, I tell you
    That you will find no man whose craft gives
        knowledge
    Of the unknowable.
                 Here is my proof: 185
    An oracle was reported to Laios once
    (I will not say from Phoibos himself, but from
    His appointed ministers, at any rate)
    That his doom would be death at the hands of his
        own son—
    His son, born of his flesh and of mine!   190

    Now, you remember the story: Laios was killed
    By marauding strangers where three highways meet;
    But his child had not been three days in this world
    Before the king had pierced the baby's ankles
    And left him to die on a lonely mountainside.   195

    Thus, Apollo never caused that child
    To kill his father, and it was not Laios' fate
    To die at the hands of his son, as he had feared.
    This is what prophets and prophecies are worth!
    Have no dread of them.
                It is God himself   200

Who can show us what he wills, in his own way.
OEDIPUS: How strange a shadowy memory crossed
    my mind,
    Just now while you were speaking; it chilled my
    heart.
IOKASTE: What do you mean? What memory do you
    speak of?
205 OEDIPUS: If I understand you, Laios was killed
    At a place where three roads meet.
IOKASTE: So it was said;
    We have no later story.
OEDIPUS: Where did it happen?
IOKASTE: Phokis, it is called: at a place where the
    Theban Way
    Divides into the roads toward Delphi and Daulia.
OEDIPUS: When?
210 IOKASTE: We had the news not long before you came
    And proved the right to your succession here.
OEDIPUS: Ah, what net has God been weaving for me?
IOKASTE: Oedipus! Why does this trouble you?
OEDIPUS: Do not ask me yet.
    First, tell me how Laios looked, and tell me
    How old he was.
215 IOKASTE: He was tall, his hair just touched
    With white; his form was not unlike your own.
OEDIPUS: I think that I myself may be accurst
    By my own ignorant edict.
IOKASTE: You speak strangely.
    It makes me tremble to look at you, my king.
220 OEDIPUS: I am not sure that the blind man can not see.
    But I should know better if you were to tell me—
IOKASTE: Anything—though I dread to hear you ask
    it.
OEDIPUS: Was the king lightly escorted, or did he ride
    With a large company, as a ruler should?
IOKASTE: There were five men with him in all: one
225   was a herald;
    And a single chariot, which he was driving.
OEDIPUS: Alas, that makes it plain enough!
                                    But who—
    Who told you how it happened?
IOKASTE: A household servant,
    The only one to escape.
OEDIPUS: And is he still
    A servant of ours?
230 IOKASTE: No; for when he came back at last
    And found you enthroned in the place of the dead
    king,
    He came to me, touched my hand with his, and
    begged
    That I would send him away to the frontier district
    Where only the shepherds go—
235   As far away from the city as I could send him.
    I granted his prayer; for although the man was a
    slave,
    He had earned more than this favor at my hands.
OEDIPUS: Can he be called back quickly?
IOKASTE: Easily.
    But why?

OEDIPUS: I have taken too much upon myself   240
    Without enquiry; therefore I wish to consult him.
IOKASTE: Then he shall come.
                        But am I not one also
    To whom you might confide these fears of yours?
OEDIPUS: That is your right; it will not be denied you,
    Now least of all; for I have reached a pitch   245
    Of wild foreboding. Is there anyone
    To whom I should sooner speak?

    Polybos of Corinth is my father.
    My mother is a Dorian: Merope.
    I grew up chief among the men of Corinth   250
    Until a strange thing happened—
    Not worth my passion, it may be, but strange.
    At a feast, a drunken man maundering in his cups
    Cries out that I am not my father's son!
    I contained myself that night, though I felt anger 255
    And a sinking heart. The next day I visited
    My father and mother, and questioned them. They
    stormed,
    Calling it all the slanderous rant of a fool;
    And this relieved me. Yet the suspicion
    Remained always aching in my mind;   260
    I knew there was talk; I could not rest;
    And finally, saying nothing to my parents,
    I went to the shrine at Delphi.

    The god dismissed my question without reply;
    He spoke of other things.
                        Some were clear,   265
    Full of wretchedness, dreadful, unbearable:
    As, that I should lie with my own mother, breed
    Children from whom all men would turn their
    eyes;
    And that I should be my father's murderer.

    I heard all this, and fled. And from that day   270
    Corinth to me was only in the stars
    Descending in that quarter of the sky,
    As I wandered farther and farther on my way
    To a land where I should never see the evil
    Sung by the oracle. And I came to this country   275
    Where, so you say, King Laios was killed.

    I will tell you all that happened there, my lady.
    There were three highways
    Coming together at a place I passed;
    And there a herald came towards me, and a
    chariot
    Drawn by horses, with a man such as you describe 280
    Seated in it. The groom leading the horses
    Forced me off the road at his lord's command;
    But as this charioteer lurched over towards me
    I struck him in my rage. The old man saw me   285
    And brought his double goad down upon my head
    As I came abreast.
                    He was paid back, and more!
    Swinging my club in this right hand I knocked him

Out of his car, and he rolled on the ground.
                                        I killed him.

290 I killed them all.
Now if that stranger and Laios were—kin,
Where is a man more miserable than I?
More hated by the gods? Citizen and alien alike
Must never shelter me or speak to me—
295 I must be shunned by all.
                              And I myself
Pronounced this malediction upon myself!

Think of it: I have touched you with these hands!
These hands that killed your husband. What
      defilement!

Am I all evil, then? It must be so,
300 Since I must flee from Thebes, yet never again
See my own countrymen, my own country,
For fear of joining my mother in marriage
And killing Polybos, my father.
                                    Ah,
If I was created so, born to this fate,
305 Who could deny the savagery of God?
O holy majesty of heavenly powers!
May I never see that day! Never!
Rather let me vanish from the race of men
Than know the abomination destined me!
310 CHORAGOS: We too, my lord, have felt dismay at this.
But there is hope: you have yet to hear the
      shepherd.
OEDIPUS: Indeed, I fear no other hope is left me.
IOKASTE: What do you hope from him when he
      comes?
OEDIPUS: This much:
If his account of the murder tallies with yours,
Then I am cleared.
315 IOKASTE: What was it that I said
Of such importance?
OEDIPUS: Why, "marauders," you said,
Killed the king, according to this man's story.
If he maintains that still, if there were several,
Clearly the guilt is not mine: I was alone.
320 But if he says one man, singlehanded, did it,
Then the evidence all points to me.
IOKASTE: You may be sure that he said there were
      several;
And can he call back that story now? He can not.
The whole city heard it as plainly as I.
325 But suppose he alters some detail of it:
He can not ever show that Laios' death
Fulfilled the oracle: for Apollo said
My child was doomed to kill him; and my child—
Poor baby!—it was my child that died first.
330 No. From now on, where oracles are concerned,
I would not waste a second thought on any.
OEDIPUS: You may be right.
                              But come: let someone go

For the shepherd at once. This matter must be
      settled.
IOKASTE: I will send for him.
I would not wish to cross you in anything,   335
And surely not in this.—Let us go in.
                        (*Exeunt into the palace.*)

ODE 2 • *Strophe 1*

CHORUS: Let me be reverent in the ways of right,
Lowly the paths I journey on;
Let all my words and actions keep
The laws of the pure universe
From highest Heaven handed down.   5
For Heaven is their bright nurse,
Those generations of the realms of light;
Ah, never of mortal kind were they begot,
Nor are they slaves of memory, lost in sleep:
Their Father is greater than Time, and ages not.   10

Antistrophe 1

The tyrant is a child of Pride
Who drinks from his great sickening cup
Recklessness and vanity,
Until from his high crest headlong
He plummets to the dust of hope.   15
That strong man is not strong.
But let no fair ambition be denied;
May God protect the wrestler for the State
In government, in comely policy,
Who will fear God, and on his ordinance wait.   20

Strophe 2

Haughtiness and the high hand of disdain
Tempt and outrage God's holy law;
And any mortal who dares hold
No immortal Power in awe
Will be caught up in a net of pain: 25
The price for which his levity is sold.
Let each man take due earnings, then,
And keep his hands from holy things,
And from blasphemy stand apart—
Else the crackling blast of heaven   30
Blows on his head, and on his desperate heart.
Though fools will honor impious men,
In their cities no tragic poet sings.

Antistrophe 2

Shall we lose faith in Delphi's obscurities,
We who have heard the world's core   35
Discredited, and the sacred wood
Of Zeus at Elis praised no more?

The deeds and the strange prophecies
Must make a pattern yet to be understood.
40   Zeus, if indeed you are lord of all,
Throned in light over night and day,
Mirror this in your endless mind:
Our masters call the oracle
Words on the wind, and the Delphic vision blind!
45   Their hearts no longer know Apollo,
And reverence for the gods has died away.

SCENE 3

(*Enter Iokaste.*)

IOKASTE: Princes of Thebes, it has occurred to me
To visit the altars of the gods, bearing
These branches as a suppliant, and this incense.
Our king is not himself: his noble soul
5   Is overwrought with fantasies of dread,
Else he would consider
The new prophecies in the light of the old.
He will listen to any voice that speaks disaster,
And my advice goes for nothing. (*She approaches
the altar, right.*)
                              To you, then, Apollo,
10   Lycean lord, since you are nearest, I turn in prayer
Receive these offerings, and grant us deliverance
From defilement. Our hearts are heavy with fear
When we see our leader distracted, as helpless
sailors
Are terrified by the confusion of their helmsman.

(*Enter Messenger.*)

15   MESSENGER: Friends, no doubt you can direct me:
Where shall I find the house of Oedipus,
Or, better still, where is the king himself?
CHORAGOS: It is this very place, stranger; he is inside.
This is his wife and mother of his children.
20   MESSENGER: I wish her happiness in a happy house,
Blest in all the fulfillment of her marriage.
IOKASTE: I wish as much for you: your courtesy
Deserves a like good fortune. But now, tell me:
Why have you come? What have you to say to us?
MESSENGER: Good news, my lady, for your house and
25   your husband.
IOKASTE: What news? Who sent you here?
MESSENGER: I am from Corinth.
The news I bring ought to mean joy for you,
Though it may be you will find some grief in it.
IOKASTE: What is it? How can it touch us in both
ways?
MESSENGER: The word is that the people of the
30   Isthmus
Intend to call Oedipus to be their king.
IOKASTE: But old King Polybos—is he not reigning
still?
MESSENGER: No. Death holds him in his sepulchre.
IOKASTE: What are you saying? Polybos is dead?

MESSENGER: If I am not telling the truth, may I die
myself.   35
IOKASTE (*to a Maidservant*): Go in, go quickly; tell
this to your master.
O riddlers of God's will, where are you now!
This was the man whom Oedipus, long ago,
Feared so, fled so, in dread of destroying him—
But it was another fate by which he died.   40

(*Enter Oedipus, center.*)

OEDIPUS: Dearest Iokaste, why have you sent for me?
IOKASTE: Listen to what this man says, and then tell
me
What has become of the solemn prophecies.
OEDIPUS: Who is this man? What is his news for me?
IOKASTE: He has come from Corinth to announce
your father's death!   45
OEDIPUS: Is it true, stranger? Tell me in your own
words.
MESSENGER: I can not say it more clearly: the king is
dead.
OEDIPUS: Was it by treason? Or by an attack of
illness?
MESSENGER: A little thing brings old men to their
rest.
OEDIPUS: It was sickness, then?
MESSENGER: Yes, and his many years.   50
OEDIPUS: Ah!
Why should a man respect the Pythian hearth,° or
Give heed to the birds that jangle above his head?
They prophesied that I should kill Polybos,
Kill my own father; but he is dead and buried,   55
And I am here—I never touched him, never,
Unless he died of grief for my departure,
And thus, in a sense, through me. No. Polybos
Has packed the oracles off with him underground.
They are empty words.
IOKASTE: Had I not told you so?   60
OEDIPUS: You had; it was my faint heart that
betrayed me.
IOKASTE: From now on never think of those things
again.
OEDIPUS: And yet—must I not fear my mother's bed?
IOKASTE: Why should anyone in this world be afraid
Since Fate rules us and nothing can be foreseen?   65
A man should live only for the present day.

Have no more fear of sleeping with your mother:
How many men, in dreams, have lain with their
mothers!
No reasonable man is troubled by such things.
OEDIPUS: That is true, only—   70
If only my mother were not still alive!
But she is alive. I can not help my dread.
IOKASTE: Yet this news of your father's death is
wonderful.
OEDIPUS: Wonderful. But I fear the living woman.

52. **Pythian hearth**: Delphi.

MESSENGER: Tell me, who is this woman that you
75   fear?
OEDIPUS: It is Merope, man; the wife of King
        Polybos.
MESSENGER: Merope? Why should you be afraid of
        her?
OEDIPUS: An oracle of the gods, a dreadful saying.
MESSENGER: Can you tell me about it or are you
        sworn to silence?
80 OEDIPUS: I can tell you, and I will.
        Apollo said through his prophet that I was the
          man
        Who should marry his own mother, shed his
          father's blood
        With his own hands. And so, for all these years
        I have kept clear of Corinth, and no harm has
          come—
        Though it would have been sweet to see my
85   parents again.
MESSENGER: And is this the fear that drove you out
        of Corinth?
OEDIPUS: Would you have me kill my father?
MESSENGER: As for that
        You must be reassured by the news I gave you.
OEDIPUS: If you could reassure me, I would reward
        you.
MESSENGER: I had that in mind, I will confess: I
90   thought
        I could count on you when you returned to
          Corinth.
OEDIPUS: No: I will never go near my parents again.
MESSENGER: Ah, son, you still do not know what you
        are doing—
OEDIPUS: What do you mean? In the name of God
        tell me!
MESSENGER:—If these are your reasons for not going
95   home.
OEDIPUS: I tell you, I fear the oracle may come true.
MESSENGER: And guilt may come upon you through
        your parents?
OEDIPUS: That is the dread that is always in my heart.
MESSENGER: Can you not see that all your fears are
        groundless?
100 OEDIPUS: Groundless? Am I not my parents' son?
MESSENGER: Polybos was not your father.
OEDIPUS: Not my father?
MESSENGER: No more your father than the man
        speaking to you.
OEDIPUS: But you are nothing to me!
MESSENGER: Neither was he.
OEDIPUS: Then why did he call me son?
MESSENGER: I will tell you:
105   Long ago he had you from my hands, as a gift.
OEDIPUS: Then how could he love me so, if I was not
        his?
MESSENGER: He had no children, and his heart
        turned to you.
OEDIPUS: What of you? Did you buy me? Did you
        find me by chance?

MESSENGER: I came upon you in the woody vales of
        Kithairon.
OEDIPUS: And what were you doing there?
MESSENGER: Tending my flocks.   110
OEDIPUS: A wandering shepherd?
MESSENGER: But your savior, son, that day.
OEDIPUS: From what did you save me?
MESSENGER: Your ankles should tell you that.
OEDIPUS: Ah, stranger, why do you speak of that
        childhood pain?
MESSENGER: I pulled the skewer that pinned your feet
        together.
OEDIPUS: I have had the mark as long as I can
        remember.   115
MESSENGER: That was why you were given the name°
        you bear.
OEDIPUS: God! Was it my father or my mother who
        did it?
        Tell me!
MESSENGER: I do not know. The man who gave you
        to me
        Can tell you better than I.
OEDIPUS: It was not you that found me, but another? 120
MESSENGER: It was another shepherd gave you to me.
OEDIPUS: Who was he? Can you tell me who he was?
MESSENGER: I think he was said to be one of Laios'
        people.
OEDIPUS: You mean the Laios who was king here
        years ago?
MESSENGER: Yes; King Laios; and the man was one
        of his herdsmen.   125
OEDIPUS: Is he still alive? Can I see him?
MESSENGER: These men here
        Know best about such things.
OEDIPUS: Does anyone here
        Know this shepherd that he is talking about?
        Have you seen him in the fields, or in the town?
        If you have, tell me. It is time things were made
        plain.   130
CHORAGOS: I think the man he means is that same
        shepherd
        You have already asked to see. Iokaste perhaps
        Could tell you something.
OEDIPUS: Do you know anything
        About him, Lady? Is he the man we have
          summoned?
        Is that the man this shepherd means?
IOKASTE: Why think of him?   135
        Forget this herdsman. Forget it all.
        This talk is a waste of time.
OEDIPUS: How can you say that,
        When the clues to my true birth are in my hands?
IOKASTE: For God's love, let us have no more
        questioning!
        Is your life nothing to you?   140
        My own is pain enough for me to bear.

116. name: *Oedipus* literally means "swollen foot."

OEDIPUS: You need not worry. Suppose my mother a slave,
   And born of slaves: no baseness can touch you.
IOKASTE: Listen to me, I beg you: do not do this thing!
OEDIPUS: I will not listen; the truth must be made known.
145
IOKASTE: Everything that I say is for your own good!
OEDIPUS: My own good
   Snaps my patience, then; I want none of it.
IOKASTE: You are fatally wrong! May you never learn who you are!
OEDIPUS: Go, one of you, and bring the shepherd here.
   Let us leave this wo77man to brag of her royal
150   name.
IOKASTE: Ah, miserable!
   That is the only word I have for you now.
   That is the only word I can ever have.
                   (*Exit into the palace.*)
CHORAGOS: Why has she left us, Oedipus? Why has she gone
155   In such a passion of sorrow? I fear this silence:
   Something dreadful may come of it.
OEDIPUS: Let it come!
   However base my birth, I must know about it.
   The Queen, like a woman, is perhaps ashamed
   To think of my low origin. But I
160   Am a child of Luck, I can not be dishonored.
   Luck is my mother; the passing months, my brothers,
   Have seen me rich and poor.
                  If this is so,
   How could I wish that I were someone else?
   How could I not be glad to know my birth?

ODE 3 • *Strophe*

CHORUS: If ever the coming time were known
   To my heart's pondering,
   Kithairon, now by Heaven I see the torches
   At the festival of the next full moon
5   And see the dance, and hear the choir sing
   A grace to your gentle shade:
   Mountain where Oedipus was found,
   O mountain guard of a noble race!
   May the god° who heals us lend his aid,
10   And let that glory come to pass
   For our king's cradling-ground.

Antistrophe

   Of the nymphs that flower beyond the years,
   Who bore you,° royal child,

---

9. **god:** Apollo.   13. **Who bore you:** The Chorus is asking if Oedipus is the son of an immortal nymph and a god: Pan, Apollo, Hermes, or Dionysus.

   To Pan° of the hills or the timberline Apollo,
   Cold in delight where the upland clears,   15
   Or Hermes° for whom Kyllene's° heights are piled?
   Or flushed as evening cloud,
   Great Dionysos,° roamer of mountains,
   He—was it he who found you there,
   And caught you up in his own proud   20
   Arms from the sweet god-ravisher
   Who laughed by the Muses'° fountains?

SCENE 4

OEDIPUS: Sirs: though I do not know the man,
   I think I see him coming, this shepherd we want:
   He is old, like our friend here, and the men
   Bringing him seem to be servants of my house.
   But you can tell, if you have ever seen him.   5

(*Enter Shepherd escorted by Servants.*)

CHORAGOS: I know him, he was Laios' man. You can trust him.
OEDIPUS: Tell me first, you from Corinth: is this the shepherd
   We were discussing?
MESSENGER: This is the very man.
OEDIPUS (*to Shepherd*): Come here. No, look at me. You must answer
   Everything I ask.—You belonged to Laios?   10
SHEPHERD: Yes: born his slave, brought up in his house.
OEDIPUS: Tell me: what kind of work did you do for him?
SHEPHERD: I was a shepherd of his, most of my life.
OEDIPUS: Where mainly did you go for pasturage?
SHEPHERD: Sometimes Kithairon, sometimes the hills near-by.   15
OEDIPUS: Do you remember ever seeing this man out there?
SHEPHERD: What would he be doing there? This man?
OEDIPUS: This man standing here. Have you ever seen him before?
SHEPHERD: No. At least, not to my recollection.
MESSENGER: And that is not strange, my lord. But I'll refresh   20
   His memory: he must remember when we two
   Spent three whole seasons together, March to September,
   On Kithairon or thereabouts. He had two flocks;

---

14. **Pan:** God of nature, forests, flocks, and shepherds, depicted as half-man and half-goat.   16. **Hermes:** Son of Zeus, messenger of the gods.   **Kyllene:** Mountain reputed to be the birthplace of Hermes; also the center of a cult to Hermes. 18. **Dionysos:** (Dionysus) God of wine around whom wild, orgiastic rituals developed; also called Bacchus.   22. **Muses:** Nine sister goddesses who presided over poetry and music, art and sciences.

The Shepherd (Oliver Cliff) tells Oedipus (Kenneth Welsh) the truth about his birth in the Guthrie Theater Company's 1973 production directed by Michael Langham.

I had one. Each autumn I'd drive mine home
And he would go back with his to Laios'
25   sheepfold.—
Is this not true, just as I have described it?
SHEPHERD: True, yes; but it was all so long ago.
MESSENGER: Well, then: do you remember, back in
    those days,
That you gave me a baby boy to bring up as my
    own?
SHEPHERD: What if I did? What are you trying to
30   say?
MESSENGER: King Oedipus was once that little child.
SHEPHERD: Damn you, hold your tongue!
OEDIPUS: No more of that!
It is your tongue needs watching, not this man's.
SHEPHERD: My king, my master, what is it I have
    done wrong?
OEDIPUS: You have not answered his question about
35   the boy.
SHEPHERD: He does not know . . . He is only making
    trouble . . .
OEDIPUS: Come, speak plainly, or it will go hard with
    you.
SHEPHERD: In God's name, do not torture an old
    man!
OEDIPUS: Come here, one of you; bind his arms
    behind him.
SHEPHERD: Unhappy king! What more do you wish
40   to learn?
OEDIPUS: Did you give this man the child he speaks
    of?
SHEPHERD: I did.
And I would to God I had died that very day.
OEDIPUS: You will die now unless you speak the
    truth.
SHEPHERD: Yet if I speak the truth, I am worse than
    dead.
OEDIPUS (to Attendant): He intends to draw it out,
45   apparently—
SHEPHERD: No! I have told you already that I gave
    him the boy.
OEDIPUS: Where did you get him? From your house?
    From somewhere else?
SHEPHERD: Not from mine, no. A man gave him
    to me.
OEDIPUS: Is that man here? Whose house did he
    belong to?
SHEPHERD: For God's love, my king, do not ask me
50   any more!
OEDIPUS: You are a dead man if I have to ask you
    again.
SHEPHERD: Then . . . Then the child was from the
    palace of Laios.
OEDIPUS: A slave child? or a child of his own line?
SHEPHERD: Ah, I am on the brink of dreadful speech!
55 OEDIPUS: And I of dreadful hearing. Yet I must hear.
SHEPHERD: If you must be told, then . . .
                    They said it was Laios' child;
But it is your wife who can tell you about that.

OEDIPUS: My wife—Did she give it to you?
SHEPHERD: My lord, she did.
OEDIPUS: Do you know why?
SHEPHERD: I was told to get rid of it.
OEDIPUS: Oh heartless mother!
SHEPHERD: But in dread of prophecies . . .   60
OEDIPUS: Tell me.
SHEPHERD: It was said that the boy would kill
    his own father.
OEDIPUS: Then why did you give him over to this old
    man?
SHEPHERD: I pitied the baby, my king,
And I thought that this man would take him far
    away
To his own country.
                He saved him—but for what a fate!   65
For if you are what this man says you are,
No man living is more wretched than Oedipus.
OEDIPUS: Ah God!
It was true!
          All the prophecies!
                  —Now,
O Light, may I look on you for the last time!   70
I, Oedipus,
Oedipus, damned in his birth, in his marriage
    damned,
Damned in the blood he shed with his own hand!

(He rushes into the palace.)

ODE 4 • Strophe 1

CHORUS: Alas for the seed of men.
What measure shall I give these generations
That breathe on the void and are void
And exist and do not exist?
Who bears more weight of joy   5
Than mass of sunlight shifting in images,
Or who shall make his thought stay on
That down time drifts away?
Your splendor is all fallen.
O naked brow of wrath and tears,   10
O change of Oedipus!
I who saw your days call no man blest—
Your great days like ghosts gone.

Antistrophe 1

That mind was a strong bow.
Deep, how deep you drew it then, hard archer,   15
At a dim fearful range,
And brought dear glory down!
You overcame the stranger°—
The virgin with her hooking lion claws—
And though death sang, stood like a tower   20

18. stranger: The Sphinx.

To make pale Thebes take heart.
Fortress against our sorrow!
True king, giver of laws,
Majestic Oedipus!
25   No prince in Thebes had ever such renown,
No prince won such grace of power.

Strophe 2

And now of all men ever known
Most pitiful is this man's story:
His fortunes are most changed; his state
30   Fallen to a low slave's
Ground under bitter fate.
O Oedipus, most royal one!
The great door° that expelled you to the light
Gave at night—ah, gave night to your glory:
35   As to the father, to the fathering son.
All understood too late.
How could that queen whom Laios won,
The garden that he harrowed at his height,
Be silent when that act was done?

Antistrophe 2

40   But all eyes fail before time's eye,
All actions come to justice there.
Though never willed, though far down the deep
         past,
Your bed, your dread sirings,
Are brought to book at last.
45   Child by Laios doomed to die,
Then doomed to lose that fortunate little death,
Would God you never took breath in this air
That with my wailing lips I take to cry:
For I weep the world's outcast.
50   I was blind, and now I can tell why:
Asleep, for you had given ease of breath
To Thebes, while the false years went by.

EXODOS°

(*Enter, from the palace, Second Messenger.*)

SECOND MESSENGER: Elders of Thebes, most honored
         in this land,
What horrors are yours to see and hear, what
         weight
Of sorrow to be endured, if, true to your birth,
You venerate the line of Labdakos!
5   I think neither Istros nor Phasis, those great rivers,
Could purify this place of all the evil

33. door: Iokaste's womb.   **Exodos:** Final scene.

It shelters now, or soon must bring to light—
Evil not done unconsciously, but willed.

The greatest griefs are those we cause ourselves.
CHORAGOS: Surely, friend, we have grief enough
         already;   10
What new sorrow do you mean?
SECOND MESSENGER: The queen is dead.
CHORAGOS: O miserable queen! But at whose hand?
SECOND MESSENGER: Her own.
The full horror of what happened you can not
         know,
For you did not see it; but I, who did, will tell you   15
As clearly as I can how she met her death.

When she had left us,
In passionate silence, passing through the court,
She ran to her apartment in the house,
Her hair clutched by the fingers of both hands.   20
She closed the doors behind her; then, by that bed
Where long ago the fatal son was conceived—
That son who should bring about his father's
         death—
We heard her call upon Laios, dead so many
         years,
And heard her wail for the double fruit of her
         marriage,   25
A husband by her husband, children by her child.

Exactly how she died I do not know:
For Oedipus burst in moaning and would not let
         us
Keep vigil to the end: it was by him
As he stormed about the room that our eyes were
         caught.
From one to another of us he went, begging a
         sword,   30
Hunting the wife who was not his wife, the
         mother
Whose womb had carried his own children and
         himself.
I do not know: it was none of us aided him,
But surely one of the gods was in control!   35
For with a dreadful cry
He hurled his weight, as though wrenched out of
         himself,
At the twin doors: the bolts gave, and he rushed
         in.
And there we saw her hanging, her body swaying
From the cruel cord she had noosed about her
         neck.   40
A great sob broke from him, heartbreaking to hear,
As he loosed the rope and lowered her to the
         ground.

I would blot out from my mind what happened
         next!
For the king ripped from her gown the golden
         brooches

That were her ornament, and raised them, and
    plunged them down
45   Straight into his own eyeballs, crying, "No more,
No more shall you look on the misery about me,
The horrors of my own doing! Too long you have
    known
The faces of those whom I should never have seen,
Too long been blind to those for whom I was
    searching!
50   From this hour, go in darkness!" And as he spoke,
He struck at his eyes—not once, but many times;
And the blood spattered his beard,
Bursting from his ruined sockets like red hail.

So from the unhappiness of two this evil has sprung,
55   A curse on the man and woman alike. The old
Happiness of the house of Labdakos
Was happiness enough: where is it today?
It is all wailing and ruin, disgrace, death—all
The misery of mankind that has a name—
60   And it is wholly and for ever theirs.
CHORAGOS: Is he in agony still? Is there no rest for
    him?
SECOND MESSENGER: He is calling for someone to
    open the doors wide
So that all the children of Kadmos may look upon
His father's murderer, his mother's—no,
I can not say it!
65   And then he will leave Thebes,
Self-exiled, in order that the curse
Which he himself pronounced may depart from
    the house.
He is weak, and there is none to lead him,
So terrible is his suffering.
              But you will see:
70   Look, the doors are opening; in a moment
You will see a thing that would crush a heart of
    stone.

(*The central door is opened; Oedipus, blinded, is led in.*)

CHORAGOS: Dreadful indeed for men to see.
Never have my own eyes
Looked on a sight so full of fear.

75   Oedipus!
What madness came upon you, what demon
Leaped on your life with heavier
Punishment than a mortal man can bear?
No: I can not even
80   Look at you, poor ruined one.
And I would speak, question, ponder,
If I were able. No.
You make me shudder.
OEDIPUS: God. God.
85   Is there a sorrow greater?
Where shall I find harbor in this world?
My voice is hurled far on a dark wind.
What has God done to me?
CHORAGOS: Too terrible to think of, or to see.

Strophe 1

OEDIPUS: O cloud of night,   90
Never to be turned away: night coming on,
I can not tell how: night like a shroud!
My fair winds brought me here.
              O God. Again
The pain of the spikes where I had sight,
The flooding pain   95
Of memory, never to be gouged out.
CHORAGOS: This is not strange.
You suffer it all twice over, remorse in pain,
Pain in remorse.

Antistrophe 1

OEDIPUS: Ah dear friend   100
Are you faithful even yet, you alone?
Are you still standing near me, will you stay here,
Patient, to care for the blind?
              The blind man!
Yet even blind I know who it is attends me,
By the voice's tone—   105
Though my new darkness hide the comforter.
CHORAGOS: Oh fearful act!
What god was it drove you to rake black
Night across your eyes?

Strophe 2

OEDIPUS: Apollo. Apollo. Dear   110
Children, the god was Apollo.
He brought my sick, sick fate upon me.
But the blinding hand was my own!
How could I bear to see
When all my sight was horror everywhere?   115
CHORAGOS: Everywhere; that is true.
OEDIPUS: And now what is left?
Images? Love? A greeting even,
Sweet to the senses? Is there anything?
Ah, no, friends: lead me away.   120
Lead me away from Thebes.
              Lead the great wreck
And hell of Oedipus, whom the gods hate.
CHORAGOS: Your misery, you are not blind to that.
Would God you had never found it out!

Antistrophe 2

OEDIPUS: Death take the man who unbound   125
My feet on that hillside
And delivered me from death to life! What life?
If only I had died,
This weight of monstrous doom
Could not have dragged me and my darlings
    down.   130

CHORAGOS: I would have wished the same.
OEDIPUS: Oh never to have come here
     With my father's blood upon me! Never
     To have been the man they call his mother's
          husband!
135 Oh accurst! Oh child of evil,
     To have entered that wretched bed—
                                   the selfsame one!
     More primal than sin itself, this fell to me.
CHORAGOS: I do not know what words to offer you.
     You were better dead than alive and blind.
OEDIPUS: Do not counsel me any more. This
140   punishment
     That I have laid upon myself is just.
     If I had eyes,
     I do not know how I could bear the sight
     Of my father, when I came to the house of Death,
     Or my mother: for I have sinned against them
145   both
     So vilely that I could not make my peace
     By strangling my own life.
                              Or do you think my children,
     Born as they were born, would be sweet to my
          eyes?
     Ah never, never! Nor this town with its high walls,
     Nor the holy images of the gods.
150   For I,
     Thrice miserable!—Oedipus, noblest of all the
          line
     Of Kadmos, have condemned myself to enjoy
     These things no more, by my own malediction
     Expelling that man whom the gods declared
155 To be a defilement in the house of Laios.
     After exposing the rankness of my own guilt,
     How could I look men frankly in the eyes?
     No, I swear it,
     If I could have stifled my hearing at its source,
160 I would have done it and made all this body
     A tight cell of misery, blank to light and sound:
     So I should have been safe in my dark mind
     Beyond external evil.
                              Ah Kithairon!
     Why did you shelter me? When I was cast upon
          you,
165 Why did I not die? Then I should never
     Have shown the world my execrable birth.

     Ah Polybos! Corinth, city that I believed
     The ancient seat of my ancestors: how fair
     I seemed, your child! And all the while this evil
     Was cancerous within me!
170   For I am sick
     In my own being, sick in my origin.
     O three roads, dark ravine, woodland and way
     Where three roads met; you, drinking my father's
          blood,
     My own blood, spilled by my own hand: can you
          remember
175 The unspeakable things I did there, and the things

I went on from there to do?
                         O marriage, marriage!
The act that engendered me, and again the act
Performed by the son in the same bed—
                                   Ah, the net
Of incest, mingling fathers, brothers, sons,
With brides, wives, mothers: the last evil   180
That can be known by men: no tongue can say
How evil!
          No. For the love of God, conceal me
Somewhere far from Thebes; or kill me; or hurl me
Into the sea, away from men's eyes for ever.

Come, lead me. You need not fear to touch me.   185
Of all men, I alone can bear this guilt.

(*Enter Kreon.*)

CHORAGOS: Kreon is here now. As to what you ask,
     He may decide the course to take. He only
     Is left to protect the city in your place.
OEDIPUS: Alas, how can I speak to him? What right
     have I   190
     To beg his courtesy whom I have deeply wronged?
KREON: I have not come to mock you, Oedipus,
     Or to reproach you, either.
     (*To Attendants.*)   —You, standing there:
     If you have lost all respect for man's dignity,
     At least respect the flame of Lord Helios:°   195
     Do not allow this pollution to show itself
     Openly here, an affront to the earth
     And Heaven's rain and the light of day. No, take
          him
     Into the house as quickly as you can.
     For it is proper   200
     That only the close kindred see his grief.
OEDIPUS: I pray you in God's name, since your
          courtesy
     Ignores my dark expectation, visiting
     With mercy this man of all men most execrable:
     Give me what I ask—for your good, not for mine. 205
KREON: And what is it that you turn to me begging
          for?
OEDIPUS: Drive me out of this country as quickly as
          may be
     To a place where no human voice can ever greet
          me.
KREON: I should have done that before now—only,
     God's will had not been wholly revealed to me.   210
OEDIPUS: But his command is plain: the parricide
     Must be destroyed. I am that evil man.
KREON: That is the sense of it, yes; but as things are,
     We had best discover clearly what is to be done.
OEDIPUS: You would learn more about a man like me?   215
KREON: You are ready now to listen to the god.
OEDIPUS: I will listen. But it is to you
     That I must turn for help. I beg you, hear me.

195. Lord Helios: The sun god.

The woman is there—
220   Give her whatever funeral you think proper:
She is your sister.
                        —But let me go, Kreon!
Let me purge my father's Thebes of the pollution
Of my living here, and go out to the wild hills,
To Kithairon, that has won such fame with me,
225   The tomb my mother and father appointed for me,
And let me die there, as they willed I should.
And yet I know
Death will not ever come to me through sickness
Or in any natural way: I have been preserved
230   For some unthinkable fate. But let that be.

As for my sons, you need not care for them.
They are men, they will find some way to live.
But my poor daughters, who have shared my table,
Who never before have been parted from their
      father—
235   Take care of them, Kreon; do this for me.

And will you let me touch them with my hands
A last time, and let us weep together?
Be kind, my lord,
Great prince, be kind!
                        Could I but touch them,
240   They would be mine again, as when I had my eyes.

(*Enter Antigone and Ismene, attended.*)

Ah, God!
Is it my dearest children I hear weeping?
Has Kreon pitied me and sent my daughters?
KREON: Yes, Oedipus: I knew that they were dear
      to you
245   In the old days, and know you must love them still.
OEDIPUS: May God bless you for this—and be a
      friendlier
Guardian to you than he has been to me!

Children, where are you?
Come quickly to my hands: they are your
      brother's—
Hands that have brought your father's once clear
250   eyes
To this way of seeing—
                        Ah dearest ones,
I had neither sight nor knowledge then, your father
By the woman who was the source of his own life!
And I weep for you—having no strength to see
      you—,
255   I weep for you when I think of the bitterness
That men will visit upon you all your lives.
What homes, what festivals can you attend
Without being forced to depart again in tears?
And when you come to marriageable age,
260   Where is the man, my daughters, who would dare
Risk the bane that lies on all my children?
Is there any evil wanting? Your father killed
His father; sowed the womb of her who bore him;

Engendered you at the fount of his own existence!
That is what they will say of you.

                        Then, whom   265
Can you ever marry? There are no bridegrooms
      for you,
And your lives must wither away in sterile dreaming.

O Kreon, son of Menoikeus!
You are the only father my daughters have,
Since we, their parents, are both of us gone for ever.   270
They are your own blood: you will not let them
Fall into beggary and loneliness;
You will keep them from the miseries that are mine!
Take pity on them; see, they are only children,
Friendless except for you. Promise me this,   275
Great prince, and give me your hand in token of it.

(*Kreon clasps his right hand.*)

Children:
I could say much, if you could understand me,
But as it is, I have only this prayer for you:
Live where you can, be as happy as you can—   280
Happier, please God, than God has made your
      father.
KREON: Enough. You have wept enough. Now go
      within.
OEDIPUS: I must, but it is hard.
KREON: Time eases all things.
OEDIPUS: You know my mind, then?
KREON: Say what you desire.
OEDIPUS: Send me from Thebes!
KREON: God grant that I may!   285
OEDIPUS: But since God hates me...
KREON: No, he will grant your wish.
OEDIPUS: You promise?
KREON: I can not speak beyond my knowledge.
OEDIPUS: Then lead me in.
KREON: Come now, and leave your children.   290
OEDIPUS: No! Do not take them from me!
KREON: Think no longer
That you are in command here, but rather think
How, when you were, you served your own
      destruction.

                        (*Exeunt into the house all but
                        the Chorus; the Choragos
                        chants directly to the audience.*)

CHORAGOS: Men of Thebes: look upon Oedipus.

This is the king who solved the famous riddle   295
And towered up, most powerful of men.
No mortal eyes but looked on him with envy,
Yet in the end ruin swept over him.

Let every man in mankind's frailty
Consider his last day; and let none   300
Presume on his good fortune until he find
Life, at his death, a memory without pain.

COMMENTARIES

Critical comment on the plays of Sophocles has been rich and various and has spanned the centuries. We are especially fortunate to have a commentary from the great age of Greek thought a century after Sophocles himself flourished. In *Oedipus Rex* Sophocles gave the philosopher Aristotle a perfect drama on which to build a theory of tragedy, and Aristotle's observations have remained the most influential comments made on drama in the West. In some ways they have established the function, limits, and purposes of drama. In the twentieth century, for instance, when Bertolt Brecht tried to create a new theory of the drama, he specifically described his ideas as an alternative to Aristotelian notions.

Although not a critic, Sigmund Freud saw in the Oedipus myth as interpreted by Sophocles a basic psychological phenomenon experienced by all people in their infancy. This "Oedipus complex" is now well established in psychology and in the popular imagination.

The extraordinary range of commentary on the Oedipus story is demonstrated nowhere more amazingly than in Claude Lévi-Strauss's structural reading of the myth, both in Sophocles' version and in other versions. Lévi-Strauss shows that a pattern emerges when certain actions in the play are placed side by side. If he is correct, his theory offers a way to interpret myths and to see why they were valued so highly by the Greeks in their drama.

Aristotle (384–322 BCE)

POETICS: COMEDY AND EPIC AND TRAGEDY   *c. 334–323 BCE*

TRANSLATED BY GERALD F. ELSE

Aristotle was Plato's most brilliant student and the heir to his teaching mantle. He remained with Plato for twenty years and then began his own school, called the Lyceum. His extant work consists mainly of his lectures, which were recorded by his students and carefully preserved. Called his treatises, they greatly influenced later thought and deal with almost every branch of philosophy, science, and the arts. His Poetics *remains, more than two thousand years later, a document of immense importance for literary criticism. Although sometimes ambiguous, difficult, and unfinished, it provides insight into the theoretical basis of Greek tragedy and comedy, and it helps us see that the drama was significant enough in intellectual life to warrant an examination by the best Greek minds.*

Comedy

Comedy is, as we said it was, an imitation of persons who are inferior; not, however, going all the way to full villainy, but imitating the ugly, of which the ludicrous is one part. The ludicrous, that is, is a failing or a piece of ugliness which causes no

95

pain or destruction; thus, to go on farther, the comic mask° is something ugly and distorted but painless.

Now the stages of development of tragedy, and the men who were responsible for them, have not escaped notice but comedy did escape notice in the beginning because it was not taken seriously. (In fact it was late in its history that the presiding magistrate officially "granted a chorus" to the comic poets; until then they were volunteers.) Thus comedy already possessed certain defining characteristics when the first "comic poets," so-called, appear in the record. Who gave it masks, or prologues, or troupes of actors and all that sort of thing is not known. The composing of plots came originally from Sicily; of the Athenian poets, Crates° was the first to abandon the lampooning mode and compose arguments, that is, plots, of a general nature.

Epic and Tragedy

Well, then, epic poetry followed in the wake of tragedy up to the point of being a (1) good-sized (2) imitation (3) in verse (4) of people who are to be taken seriously; but in its having its verse unmixed with any other and being narrative in character, there they differ. Further, so far as its length is concerned, tragedy tries as hard as it can to exist during a single daylight period, or to vary but little, while the epic is not limited in its time and so differs in that respect. Yet originally they used to do this in tragedies just as much as they did in epic poems.

The constituent elements are partly identical and partly limited to tragedy. Hence anybody who knows about good and bad tragedy knows about epic also; for the elements that the epic possesses appertain to tragedy as well, but those of tragedy are not all found in the epic.

Tragedy and Its Six Constituent Elements

Our discussions of imitative poetry in hexameters,° and of comedy, will come later; at present let us deal with tragedy, recovering from what has been said so far the definition of its essential nature, as it was in development. Tragedy, then, is a process of imitating an action which has serious implications, is complete, and possesses magnitude; by means of language which has been made sensuously attractive, with each of its varieties found separately in the parts; enacted by the persons themselves and not presented through narrative; through a course of pity and fear completing the purification of tragic acts which have those emotional characteristics. By "language made sensuously attractive" I mean language that has rhythm and melody, and by "its varieties found separately" I mean the fact that certain parts of the play are carried on through spoken verses alone and others the other way around, through song.

Now first of all, since they perform the imitation through action (by acting it), the adornment of their visual appearance will perforce constitute some part of the making of tragedy; and song-composition and verbal expression also, for those are the media in which they perform the imitation. By "verbal expression" I mean the actual composition of the verses, and by "song-composition" something whose meaning is entirely clear.

---

the comic mask: Actors in Greek drama wore masks behind which they spoke their lines. The masks were made individually for each character.

Crates: Greek actor and playwright (fl. 470 BCE), credited by Aristotle with developing Greek comedy into a fully plotted, credible form. Aristophanes (c. 448–c. 385 BCE), another Greek comic playwright, says that Crates was the first to portray a drunkard onstage.

hexameters: The first known metrical form for classical verse. Each line had six metrical feet, some of which were prescribed in advance. It is the meter used for epic poetry and for poetry designed to teach a lesson. The form has sometimes been used in comparatively modern poetry but rarely with success except in French.

Next, since it is an imitation of an action and is enacted by certain people who are performing the action, and since those people must necessarily have certain traits both of character and thought (for it is thanks to these two factors that we speak of people's actions also as having a defined character, and it is in accordance with their actions that all either succeed or fail); and since the imitation of the action is the plot, for by "plot" I mean here the structuring of the events, and by the "characters" that in accordance with which we say that the persons who are acting have a defined moral character, and by "thought" all the passages in which they attempt to prove some thesis or set forth an opinion — it follows of necessity, then, that tragedy as a whole has just six constituent elements, in relation to the essence that makes it a distinct species; and they are plot, characters, verbal expression, thought, visual adornment, and song-composition. For the elements by which they imitate are two (i.e., verbal expression and song-composition), the manner in which they imitate is one (visual adornment), the things they imitate are three (plot, characters, thought), and there is nothing more beyond these. These then are the constituent forms they use.

The Relative Importance of the Six Elements

The greatest of these elements is the structuring of the incidents. For tragedy is an imitation not of men but of a life, an action, and they have moral quality in accordance with their characters but are happy or unhappy in accordance with their actions; hence they are not active in order to imitate their characters, but they include the characters along with the actions for the sake of the latter. Thus the structure of events, the plot, is the goal of tragedy, and the goal is the greatest thing of all.

Again: a tragedy cannot exist without a plot, but it can without characters: thus the tragedies of most of our modern poets are devoid of character, and in general many poets are like that; so also with the relationship between Zeuxis and Polygnotus,° among the painters: Polygnotus is a good portrayer of character, while Zeuxis's painting has no dimension of character at all.

Again: if one strings end to end speeches that are expressive of character and carefully worked in thought and expression, he still will not achieve the result which we said was the aim of tragedy; the job will be done much better by a tragedy that is more deficient in these other respects but has a plot, a structure of events. It is much the same case as with painting: the most beautiful pigments smeared on at random will not give as much pleasure as a black-and-white outline picture. Besides, the most powerful means tragedy has for swaying our feelings, namely the peripeties and recognitions,° are elements of plot.

Again: an indicative sign is that those who are beginning a poetic career manage to hit the mark in verbal expression and character portrayal sooner than they do in plot construction; and the same is true of practically all the earliest poets.

So plot is the basic principle, the heart and soul, as it were, of tragedy, and the characters come second: [. . .] it is the imitation of an action and imitates the persons primarily for the sake of their action.

Zeuxis and Polygnotus: Zeuxis (fl. 420–390 BCE) developed a method of painting in which the figures were rounded and apparently three-dimensional. Thus, he was an illusionistic painter, imitating life in a realistic style. Polygnotus (c. 470–440 BCE) was famous as a painter, and his works were on the Acropolis as well as at Delphi. His draftsmanship was especially praised.

peripeties and recognitions: The turning about of fortune and the recognition, on the part of the tragic hero, of the truth. This is, for Aristotle, a critical moment in the drama, especially if both events happen simultaneously, as they do in *Oedipus Rex*. It is quite possible for these moments to happen apart from one another.

Third in rank is thought. This is the ability to state the issues and appropriate points pertaining to a given topic, an ability which springs from the arts of politics and rhetoric; in fact the earlier poets made their characters talk "politically," the present-day poets rhetorically. But "character" is that kind of utterance which clearly reveals the bent of a man's moral choice (hence there is no character in that class of utterances in which there is nothing at all that the speaker is choosing or rejecting), while "thought" is the passages in which they try to prove that something is so or not so, or state some general principle.

Fourth is the verbal expression of the speeches. I mean by this the same thing that was said earlier, that the "verbal expression" is the conveyance of thought through language: a statement which has the same meaning whether one says "verses" or "speeches."

The song-composition of the remaining parts is the greatest of the sensuous attractions, and the visual adornment of the dramatic persons can have a strong emotional effect but is the least artistic element, the least connected with the poetic art; in fact the force of tragedy can be felt even without benefit of public performance and actors, while for the production of the visual effect the property man's art is even more decisive than that of the poets.

General Principles of the Tragic Plot

With these distinctions out of the way, let us next discuss what the structuring of the events should be like, since this is both the basic and the most important element in the tragic art. We have established, then, that tragedy is an imitation of an action which is complete and whole and has some magnitude (for there is also such a thing as a whole that has no magnitude). "Whole" is that which has beginning, middle, and end. "Beginning" is that which does not necessarily follow on something else, but after it something else naturally is or happens; "end," the other way around, is that which naturally follows on something else, either necessarily or for the most part, but nothing else after it; and "middle" that which naturally follows on something else and something else on it. So, then, well constructed plots should neither begin nor end at any chance point but follow the guidelines just laid down.

Furthermore, since the beautiful, whether a living creature or anything that is composed of parts, should not only have these in a fixed order to one another but also possess a definite size which does not depend on chance—for beauty depends on size and order; hence neither can a very tiny creature turn out to be beautiful (since our perception of it grows blurred as it approaches the period of imperceptibility) nor an excessively huge one (for then it cannot all be perceived at once and so its unity and wholeness are lost), if for example there were a creature a thousand miles long—so, just as in the case of living creatures they must have some size, but one that can be taken in a single view, so with plots: they should have length, but such that they are easy to remember. As to a limit of the length, the one is determined by the tragic competitions and the ordinary span of attention. (If they had to compete with a hundred tragedies they would compete by the water clock, as they say used to be done [?].) But the limit fixed by the very nature of the case is: the longer the plot, up to the point of still being perspicuous as a whole, the finer it is so far as size is concerned; or to put it in general terms, the length in which, with things happening in unbroken sequence, a shift takes place either probably or necessarily from bad to good fortune or from good to bad—that is an acceptable norm of length.

But a plot is not unified, as some people think, simply because it has to do with a single person. A large, indeed an indefinite number of things can happen to a given individual, some of which go to constitute no unified event; and in the same way there can be many acts of a given individual from which no single action emerges. Hence it seems clear that those poets are wrong who have composed *Heracleïds*, *Theseïds*, and the like. They think that since Heracles was a single person it follows that the plot will be single too. But Homer, superior as he is in all other respects, appears to have grasped this point well also, thanks either to art or nature, for in composing an *Odyssey* he did not incorporate into it everything that happened to the hero, for example how he was wounded on Mt. Parnassus° or how he feigned madness at the muster, neither of which events, by happening, made it at all necessary or probable that the other should happen. Instead, he composed the *Odyssey*—and the *Iliad* similarly—around a unified action of the kind we have been talking about.

A poetic imitation, then, ought to be unified in the same way as a single imitation in any other mimetic field, by having a single object: since the plot is an imitation of an action, the latter ought to be both unified and complete, and the component events ought to be so firmly compacted that if any one of them is shifted to another place, or removed, the whole is loosened up and dislocated; for an element whose addition or subtraction makes no perceptible extra difference is not really a part of the whole.

From what has been said it is also clear that the poet's job is not to report what has happened but what is likely to happen: that is, what is capable of happening according to the rule of probability or necessity. Thus the difference between the historian and the poet is not in their utterances being in verse or prose (it would be quite possible for Herodotus's work to be translated into verse, and it would not be any the less a history with verse than it is without it); the difference lies in the fact that the historian speaks of what has happened, the poet of the kind of thing that *can* happen. Hence also poetry is a more philosophical and serious business than history; for poetry speaks more of universals, history of particulars. "Universal" in this case is what kind of person is likely to do or say certain kinds of things, according to probability or necessity; that is what poetry aims at, although it gives its persons particular names afterward; while the "particular" is what Alcibiades did or what happened to him.

In the field of comedy this point has been grasped: our comic poets construct their plots on the basis of general probabilities and then assign names to the persons quite arbitrarily, instead of dealing with individuals as the old iambic poets° did. But in tragedy they still cling to the historically given names. The reason is that what is possible is persuasive; so what has not happened we are not yet ready to believe is possible, while what has happened is, we feel, obviously possible: for it would not have happened if it were impossible. Nevertheless, it is a fact that even

---

Mt. Parnassus: A mountain in central Greece traditionally sacred to Apollo. In legend, Odysseus was wounded there, but the point Aristotle is making is that the writer of epics need not include every detail of his hero's life in a given work. Homer, in writing the *Odyssey*, was working with a hero, Odysseus, whose story had been legendary long before Homer began writing.

old iambic poets: Aristotle may be referring to Archilochus (fl. 650 BCE) and the iambic style he developed. The iamb is a metrical foot of two syllables, a short and a long syllable, and was the most popular metrical style before the time of Aristotle. "Dealing with individuals" implies using figures already known to the audience rather than figures whose names can be arbitrarily assigned because no one knows who they are.

in our tragedies, in some cases only one or two of the names are traditional, the rest being invented, and in some others none at all. It is so, for example, in Agathon's *Antheus*—the names in it are as fictional as the events—and it gives no less pleasure because of that. Hence the poets ought not to cling at all costs to the traditional plots, around which our tragedies are constructed. And in fact it is absurd to go searching for this kind of authentication, since even the familiar names are familiar to only a few in the audience and yet give the same kind of pleasure to all.

So from these considerations it is evident that the poet should be a maker of his plots more than of his verses, insofar as he is a poet by virtue of his imitations and what he imitates is actions. Hence even if it happens that he puts something that has actually taken place into poetry, he is none the less a poet; for there is nothing to prevent some of the things that have happened from being the kind of things that can happen, and that is the sense in which he is their maker.

Simple and Complex Plots   Among simple plots and actions the episodic are the worst. By "episodic" plot I mean one in which there is no probability or necessity for the order in which the episodes follow one another. Such structures are composed by the bad poets because they are bad poets, but by the good poets because of the actors: in composing contest pieces for them, and stretching out the plot beyond its capacity, they are forced frequently to dislocate the sequence.

Furthermore, since the tragic imitation is not only of a complete action but also of events that are fearful and pathetic,° and these come about best when they come about contrary to one's expectation yet logically, one following from the other; that way they will be more productive of wonder than if they happen merely at random, by chance—because even among chance occurrences the ones people consider most marvelous are those that seem to have come about as if on purpose: for example the way the statue of Mitys at Argos killed the man who had been the cause of Mitys's death, by falling on him while he was attending the festival; it stands to reason, people think, that such things don't happen by chance—so plots of that sort cannot fail to be artistically superior.

Some plots are simple, others are complex; indeed the actions of which the plots are imitations already fall into these two categories. By "simple" action I mean one the development of which being continuous and unified in the manner stated above, the reversal comes without peripety or recognition, and by "complex" action one in which the reversal is continuous but with recognition or peripety or both. And these developments must grow out of the very structure of the plot itself, in such a way that on the basis of what has happened previously this particular outcome follows either by necessity or in accordance with probability; for there is a great difference in whether these events happen because of those or merely after them.

"Peripety" is a shift of what is being undertaken to the opposite in the way previously stated, and that in accordance with probability or necessity as we have just been saying; as for example in the *Oedipus* the man who has come, thinking that he will reassure Oedipus, that is, relieve him of his fear with respect to his mother,

---

fearful and pathetic: Aristotle said that tragedy should evoke two emotions: terror and pity. The terror results from our realizing that what is happening to the hero might just as easily happen to us; the pity results from our human sympathy with a fellow sufferer. Therefore, the fearful and pathetic represent significant emotions appropriate to our witnessing drama.

by revealing who he once was, brings about the opposite; and in the *Lynceus*, as he (Lynceus) is being led away with every prospect of being executed, and Danaus pursuing him with every prospect of doing the executing, it comes about as a result of the other things that have happened in the play that *he* is executed and Lynceus is saved. And "recognition" is, as indeed the name indicates, a shift from ignorance to awareness, pointing in the direction either of close blood ties or of hostility, of people who have previously been in a clearly marked state of happiness or unhappiness.

The finest recognition is one that happens at the same time as a peripety, as is the case with the one in the *Oedipus*. Naturally, there are also other kinds of recognition: it is possible for one to take place in the prescribed manner in relation to inanimate objects and chance occurrences, and it is possible to recognize whether a person has acted or not acted. But the form that is most integrally a part of the plot, the action, is the one aforesaid; for that kind of recognition combined with peripety will excite either pity or fear (and these are the kinds of action of which tragedy is an imitation according to our definition), because both good and bad fortune will also be most likely to follow that kind of event. Since, further, the recognition is a recognition of persons, some are of one person by the other one only (when it is already known who the "other one" is), but sometimes it is necessary for both persons to go through a recognition, as for example Iphigenia is recognized by her brother° through the sending of the letter, but of him by Iphigenia another recognition is required.

These then are two elements of plot: peripety and recognition; third is the *pathos*. Of these, peripety and recognition have been discussed; a *pathos* is a destructive or painful act, such as deaths on stage, paroxysms of pain, woundings, and all that sort of thing.

Sigmund Freud (1856–1939)
THE OEDIPUS COMPLEX   *1900–1930°*
TRANSLATED BY JAMES STRACHEY

Sigmund Freud was the most celebrated psychiatrist of the twentieth century and the father of psychoanalytic theory. His researches into the unconscious changed the way we think about the human mind, and his explorations into the symbolic meaning of dreams have been widely regarded as a breakthrough in connecting the meaning of world myth to personal life.

In his Interpretation of Dreams *he turned to Sophocles' drama and developed his theories of the Oedipus complex: the desire to kill one parent and marry the other may be rooted in the deepest natural psychological development of the individual. The following passage provides insight not only into a psychological state that all humans may share but also into the way in which a man of Freud's temperament read and interpreted a great piece of literature. Like Sophocles himself,*

---

her brother: Orestes is Iphigenia's brother. Aristotle may be referring to a lost play.
1900–1930: *Interpretation of Dreams* was first published in 1900 and was updated regularly by Freud through eight editions. This passage is taken from the eighth edition, published in 1930.

Freud believed that the myth underlying Oedipus Rex has a meaning and importance for all human beings.

In my experience, which is already extensive, the chief part in the mental lives of all children who later become psychoneurotics is played by their parents. Being in love with the one parent and hating the other are among the essential constituents of the stock of psychical impulses which is formed at that time and which is of such importance in determining the symptoms of the later neurosis. It is not my belief, however, that psychoneurotics differ sharply in this respect from other human beings who remain normal—that they are able, that is, to create something absolutely new and peculiar to themselves. It is far more probable—and this is confirmed by occasional observations on normal children—that they are only distinguished by exhibiting on a magnified scale feelings of love and hatred to their parents which occur less obviously and less intensely in the minds of most children.

This discovery is confirmed by a legend that has come down to us from classical antiquity: a legend whose profound and universal power to move can only be understood if the hypothesis I have put forward in regard to the psychology of children has an equally universal validity. What I have in mind is the legend of King Oedipus and Sophocles' drama which bears his name.

Oedipus, son of Laïus, King of Thebes, and of Jocasta, was exposed [to the elements and left to die] as an infant because an oracle had warned Laïus that the still unborn child would be his father's murderer. The child was rescued and grew up as a prince in an alien court, until, in doubts as to his origin, he too questioned the oracle and was warned to avoid his home since he was destined to murder his father and take his mother in marriage. On the road leading away from what he believed was his home, he met King Laïus and slew him in a sudden quarrel. He came next to Thebes and solved the riddle set him by the Sphinx who barred his way. Out of gratitude the Thebans made him their king and gave him Jocasta's hand in marriage. He reigned long in peace and honor, and she who, unknown to him, was his mother bore him two sons and two daughters. Then at last a plague broke out and the Thebans made inquiry once more of the oracle. It is at this point that Sophocles' tragedy opens. The messengers bring back the reply that the plague will cease when the murderer of Laïus has been driven from the land.

> But he, where is he? Where shall now be read
> The fading record of this ancient guilt?[1]

The action of the play consists in nothing other than the process of revealing, with cunning delays and ever-mounting excitement—a process that can be likened to the work of a psychoanalysis—that Oedipus himself is the murderer of Laïus, but further that he is the son of the murdered man and of Jocasta. Appalled at the abomination which he has unwittingly perpetrated, Oedipus blinds himself and forsakes his home. The oracle has been fulfilled.

Oedipus Rex is what is known as a tragedy of destiny. Its tragic effect is said to lie in the contrast between the supreme will of the gods and the vain attempts of mankind to escape the evil that threatens them. The lesson which, it is said, the

---

[1]Lewis Campbell's translation (1883), lines 108ff [Dudley Fitts and Robert Fitzgerald, *Sophocles: The Oedipus Cycle, an English Version* (Harcourt Brace & Company, 1949), Prologue, lines 112–13].

deeply moved spectator should learn from the tragedy is submission to the divine will and realization of his own impotence. Modern dramatists have accordingly tried to achieve a similar tragic effect by weaving the same contrast into a plot invented by themselves. But the spectators have looked on unmoved while a curse or an oracle was fulfilled in spite of all the efforts of some innocent man: later tragedies of destiny have failed in their effect.

If *Oedipus Rex* moves a modern audience no less than it did the contemporary Greek one, the explanation can only be that its effect does not lie in the contrast between destiny and human will, but is to be looked for in the particular nature of the material on which that contrast is exemplified. There must be something which makes a voice within us ready to recognize the compelling force of destiny in the *Oedipus,* while we can dismiss as merely arbitrary such dispositions as are laid down in [Grillparzer's] *Die Ahnfrau* or other modern tragedies of destiny. And a factor of this kind is in fact involved in the story of King Oedipus. His destiny moves us only because it might have been ours—because the oracle laid the same curse upon us before our birth as upon him. It is the fate of all of us, perhaps, to direct our first sexual impulse toward our mother and our first hatred and our first murderous wish against our father. Our dreams convince us that that is so. King Oedipus, who slew his father Laïus and married his mother Jocasta, merely shows us the fulfillment of our own childhood wishes. But, more fortunate than he, we have meanwhile succeeded, in so far as we have not become psychoneurotics, in detaching our sexual impulses from our mothers and in forgetting our jealousy of our fathers. Here is one in whom these primeval wishes of our childhood have been fulfilled, and we shrink back from him with the whole force of the repression by which those wishes have since that time been held down within us. While the poet, as he unravels the past, brings to light the guilt of Oedipus, he is at the same time compelling us to recognize our own inner minds, in which those same impulses, though suppressed, are still to be found. The contrast with which the closing Chorus leaves us confronted —

> . . . Fix on Oedipus your eyes,
> Who resolved the dark enigma, noblest champion and most wise.
> Like a star his envied fortune mounted beaming far and wide:
> Now he sinks in seas of anguish, whelmed beneath a raging tide . . .[2]

— strikes as a warning at ourselves and our pride, at us who since our childhood have grown so wise and so mighty in our own eyes. Like Oedipus, we live in ignorance of these wishes, repugnant to morality, which have been forced upon us by Nature, and after their revelation we may all of us well seek to close our eyes to the scenes of our childhood.[3]

---

[2]Lewis Campbell's translation, lines 1524ff [Fitts and Fitzgerald, antistrophe 2, lines 292–96].

[3][*Footnote added by Freud in 1914 edition.*] None of the findings of psychoanalytic research has provoked such embittered denials, such fierce opposition — or such amusing contortions — on the part of critics as this indication of the childhood impulses toward incest which persist in the unconscious. An attempt has even been made recently to make out, in the face of all experience, that the incest should only be taken as "symbolic."— Ferenczi (1912) has proposed an ingenious "overinterpretation" of the Oedipus myth, based on a passage in one of Schopenhauer's letters. [*Added 1919.*] Later studies have shown that the "Oedipus complex," which was touched upon for the first time in the above paragraphs in the *Interpretation of Dreams*, throws a light of undreamt-of importance on the history of the human race and the evolution of religion and morality.

There is an unmistakable indication in the text of Sophocles' tragedy itself that the legend of Oedipus sprang from some primeval dream material which had as its content the distressing disturbance of a child's relation to his parents owing to the first stirrings of sexuality. At a point when Oedipus, though he is not yet enlightened, has begun to feel troubled by his recollection of the oracle, Jocasta consoles him by referring to a dream which many people dream, though, as she thinks, it has no meaning:

> Many a man ere now in dreams hath lain
> With her who bare him. He hath least annoy
> Who with such omens troubleth not his mind.[4]

Today, just as then, many men dream of having sexual relations with their mothers, and speak of the fact with indignation and astonishment. It is clearly the key to the tragedy and the complement to the dream of the dreamer's father being dead. The story of Oedipus is the reaction of the imagination to these two typical dreams. And just as these dreams, when dreamt by adults, are accompanied by feelings of repulsion, so too the legend must include horror and self-punishment. Its further modification originates once again in a misconceived secondary revision of the material, which has sought to exploit it for theological purposes. . . . The attempt to harmonize divine omnipotence with human responsibility must naturally fail in connection with this subject matter just as with any other.

Claude Lévi-Strauss (b. 1908)
FROM *THE STRUCTURAL STUDY OF MYTH*   1955

Claude Lévi-Strauss is one of a handful of modern anthropologists whose interests span the range of thought, culture, and understanding. His work has been of immense influence on French intellectual life and, by extension, on the intellectual life of modern times. His works include Triste Tropiques *(translated as* A World on the Wane), *about his own experiences as an anthropologist;* Structural Anthropology, *about the ways in which the study of anthropology implies a study of the structure of thought; and* Mythologies, *a four-volume summation of his thought. The excerpt that follows is structuralist in scope in that it attempts to understand the myth of Oedipus by examining the patterns of repetition in the original narrative. By setting up a grid, Lévi-Strauss begins to sort out the implications of the myth and to seek a meaning that is not necessarily apparent in the chronological order of the narrative. He examines the myth diachronically—across the lines of time—and thereby sees a new range of implications, which he treats as the structural implications of the myth. His reading is complex, suggesting that the Oedipus myth is a vegetation myth explaining the origins of mankind. Lévi-Strauss gives us a new way to interpret the significance of literary myths.*

The time has come to give a concrete example of the method we propose. We will use the Oedipus myth which has the advantage of being well known to everybody

[4]Lewis Campbell's translation, lines 982ff [Fitts and Fitzgerald, scene 3, lines 67–69].

and for which no preliminary explanation is therefore needed. By doing so, I am well aware that the Oedipus myth has only reached us under late forms and through literary transfigurations concerned more with esthetic and moral preoccupations than with religious or ritual ones, whatever these may have been. But as will be shown later, this apparently unsatisfactory situation will strengthen our demonstration rather than weaken it.

The myth will be treated as would be an orchestra score perversely presented as a unilinear series and where our task is to reestablish the correct disposition. As if, for instance, we were confronted with a sequence of the type: 1,2,4,7,8,2,3,4,6,8,1,4,5,7,8,1,2,5,7,3,4,5,6,8 . . . , the assignment being to put all the 1's together, all the 2's, the 3's, etc.; the result is a chart:

```
1 2   4     7 8
    2 3 4   6   8
1       4 5   7 8
1 2       5 7
      3 4 5
              6   8
```

We will attempt to perform the same kind of operation on the Oedipus myth, trying out several dispositions. [. . .] Let us suppose, for the sake of argument, that the best arrangement is the following (although it might certainly be improved by the help of a specialist in Greek mythology):

Kadmos seeks his sister Europa ravished by Zeus.			
		Kadmos kills the dragon.	
	The Spartoi kill each other.		
			Labdacos (Laios's father) = *lame* (?).
	Oedipus kills his father Laios.		Laios (Oedipus's father) = *left-sided* (?).
		Oedipus kills the Sphinx.	
Oedipus marries his mother Jocasta.			
	Eteocles kills his brother Polyneices.		Oedipus = *swollen-foot* (?).
Antigone buries her brother Polyneices despite prohibition.			

Thus, we find ourselves confronted with four vertical columns each of which includes several relations belonging to the same bundle. Were we to *tell* the myth, we would disregard the columns and read the rows from left to right and from top to bottom. But if we want to *understand* the myth, then we will have to disregard one half of the diachronic° dimension (top to bottom) and read from left to right, column after column, each one being considered as a unit.

All the relations belonging to the same column exhibit one common feature which it is our task to unravel. For instance, all the events grouped in the first column on the left have something to do with blood relations which are overemphasized, i.e., are subject to a more intimate treatment than they should be. Let us say, then, that the first column has as its common feature the *overrating of blood relations*. It is obvious that the second column expresses the same thing, but inverted: *underrating of blood relations*. The third column refers to monsters being slain. As to the fourth, a word of clarification is needed. The remarkable connotation of the surnames in Oedipus's father-line has often been noticed. However, linguists usually disregard it, since to them the only way to define the meaning of a term is to investigate all the contexts in which it appears, and personal names, precisely because they are used as such, are not accompanied by any context. With the method we propose to follow the objection disappears since the myth itself provides its own context. The meaningful fact is no longer to be looked for in the eventual sense of each name, but in the fact that all the names have a common feature: i.e., that they may eventually mean something and that all these hypothetical meanings (which may well remain hypothetical) exhibit a common feature, namely they refer to *difficulties to walk and to behave straight*.

What is then the relationship between the two columns on the right? Column three refers to monsters. The dragon is a chthonian° being which has to be killed in order that mankind be born from the earth; the Sphinx is a monster unwilling to permit men to live. The last unit reproduces the first one which has to do with the *autochthonous*° origin of mankind. Since the monsters are overcome by men, we may thus say that the common feature of the third column is *the denial of the autochthonous origin of man*.

This immediately helps us to understand the meaning of the fourth column. In mythology it is a universal character of men born from the earth that at the moment they emerge from the depth, they either cannot walk or do it clumsily. This is the case of the chthonian beings in the mythology of the Pueblo: Masauwu, who leads the emergence, and the chthonian Shumaikoli are lame ("bleeding-foot," "sore-foot"). The same happens to the Koskimo of the Kwakiutl after they have been swallowed by the chthonian monster, Tsiakish: when they returned to the surface of the earth "they limped forward or tripped sideways." Then the common feature of the fourth column is: *the persistence of the autochthonous origin of man.* It follows that column four is to column three as column one is to column two. The inability to connect two kinds of relationships is overcome (or rather replaced) by the positive statement that contradictory relationships are identical inasmuch as they are both self-contradictory in a similar way. Although this is still a provisional formulation of the structure of mythical thought, it is sufficient at this stage.

diachronic: Not ordered linearly in time but through time.
chthonian: From the underworld.
autochthonous: Native, aboriginal; in this case, born of the earth.

Turning back to the Oedipus myth, we may now see what it means. The myth has to do with the inability, for a culture which holds the belief that mankind is autochthonous [. . .] to find a satisfactory transition between this theory and the knowledge that human beings are actually born from the union of man and woman. Although the problem obviously cannot be solved, the Oedipus myth provides a kind of logical tool which, to phrase it coarsely, replaces the original problem: born from one or born from two? born from different or born from same? By a correlation of this type, the overrating of blood relations is to the underrating of blood relations as the attempt to escape autochthony is to the impossibility to succeed in it [that escape]. Although experience contradicts theory, social life verifies the cosmology by its similarity of structure. Hence cosmology is true.

Two remarks should be made at this stage.

In order to interpret the myth, we were able to leave aside a point which has until now worried the specialists, namely, that in the earlier (Homeric) versions of the Oedipus myth, some basic elements are lacking, such as Jocasta killing herself and Oedipus piercing his own eyes. These events do not alter the substance of the myth although they can easily be integrated, the first one as a new case of autodestruction (column three) while the second is another case of crippledness (column four). At the same time there is something significant in these additions since the shift from foot to head is to be correlated with the shift from: autochthonous origin negated to: self-destruction.

Thus, our method eliminates a problem which has been so far one of the main obstacles to the progress of mythological studies, namely, the quest for the *true* version, or the *earlier* one. On the contrary, we define the myth as consisting of all its versions; to put it otherwise: a myth remains the same as long as it is felt as such. A striking example is offered by the fact that our interpretation may take into account, and is certainly applicable to, the Freudian use of the Oedipus myth. Although the Freudian problem has ceased to be that of autochthony *versus* bisexual reproduction, it is still the problem of understanding how *one* can be born from *two:* how is it that we do not have only one procreator, but a mother plus a father? Therefore, not only Sophocles, but Freud himself, should be included among the recorded versions of the Oedipus myth on a par with earlier or seemingly more "authentic" versions.

ANTIGONE

Antigone was Sophocles' thirty-second play, produced in March 441 BCE, when he was in his mid-fifties. It draws a powerful response from its audience partly because it portrays the conflict between two proud, willful people: Antigone, a daughter of Oedipus and Iokaste, and Kreon, Iokaste's brother and the king of Thebes. Its original success was due in part to its portrayal of the individual's struggle against a tyrannical king. After enjoying thirty years of peace with its archrival Sparta, Athens was moving slowly toward war; and the memory of previous tyrants—both good, like Peisistratus, and bad, like his son Hippias—remained in the minds of Sophocles' audience.

It has never been easy to determine which of the two main characters is correct. Kreon's portrayal as a tyrant content to take up the state as his private property tells us that he is not to be fully trusted. At the same time, Antigone knows that the social mores of Thebes imply that a citizen must obey the ruler. Antigone's great courage makes the audience feel sympathy and admiration for her. She is a martyr to her beliefs, an ancient Joan of Arc.

The main conflict in *Antigone* centers on a distinction between law and justice, the conflict between a human law and a higher law. Kreon, the uncle of Antigone and Ismene, has made a decree: Polyneices, the brother of Antigone and Ismene, was guilty not only of killing his brother Eteocles but also of attacking the state and, like all traitors, will be denied a proper burial. When the action of the play begins, Antigone is determined to give her brother the burial that ancient tradition and her religious beliefs demand.

The opening dialogue with Ismene clarifies the important distinction between human law and the higher law on which Antigone says she must act. Ismene declares simply that she cannot go against the law of the citizens. Kreon has been willful in establishing the law, but it is nonetheless the law. Antigone, knowing full well the consequences of defying Kreon, nonetheless acts on her principles.

The complex conflict between Antigone and Kreon occurs on the level of citizen and ruler and is affected on the personal level by the relationship between Haimon, Kreon's son, and his intended bride, Antigone. The antagonism between Kreon and Haimon begins slowly, as Haimon appears to yield to the will of his father, but culminates in Haimon's ultimate rejection of his father by choosing to join Antigone in death.

When Teiresias reveals a prophecy of death and punishment and begs Kreon, for the sake of the suffering Thebes, to rescind his decree and give Polyneices a proper burial, Kreon willfully continues to heed his own declarations rather than oracular wisdom or the pleas of others.

By the time Kreon accepts Teiresias's prophecy, it is too late: he has lost his son, and his wife has killed herself. Power not only has corrupted Kreon but also has taken from him the people about whom he cared most. He emerges as an unyielding tyrant, guilty of making some of the same mistakes that haunted Oedipus.

Antigone emerges as a heroine who presses forward in the full conviction that she is right. She must honor her dead brother at all costs. Even if she must break the law of the state, she must answer to what she regards as a higher law. As she says early in the play, she has "dared the crime of piety." Yet she has within her the complexity of all humans: she in one sense acts in the knowledge that she is right but in another dares Kreon to punish her. She challenges Kreon so boldly that her every move forces the proud Kreon to harden his position and set in motion the ultimate tragedy—the loss of all he holds dear. This is yet one more tragic irony in the Theban trilogy.

Antigone in Performance

Since the eighteenth century *Antigone* has been produced in Europe and the Western Hemisphere in more or less its original form and in various adaptations and rewritings. Jean Cocteau combined his version with music by Arthur

Honegger in 1930. It was rewritten and produced by Walter Hasenclever in 1917 as a protest against the First World War and then in 1944 by Jean Anouilh as a protest against Nazi occupation of Paris during World War II (see the excerpt on p. 128). The Royal Shakespeare Company produced *Antigone* along with all the other surviving Greek tragedies in 1980. Bertolt Brecht's production of *Antigone* in 1948 introduced a Gestapo officer and Nazi brutality. Athol Fugard's *The Island* (1973) features a remarkable production of *Antigone* as a play within a play, produced by convicts in a South African island jail as a Christmas entertainment for their jailers and specially invited white guests. Fugard found, as have so many other adapters and producers, that the political power of *Antigone* leaps out for virtually all contemporary audiences. Janusz Glowacki, a Polish playwright, produced *Antigone in New York* at the Arena Stage in Washington in March 1993. Inspired by both Sophocles and Beckett, it is set in Tompkins Square Park in New York. The action centers on a homeless Puerto Rican woman's efforts to bury a homeless man in the park. A highly regarded student production at Oxford in February 2004, directed by Zeynep Kayachin, was distinguished by the use of a new translation by a classics student, Lauren Curtiz. In recent years student productions have, like the Oxford production, used video, projections, and contemporary music to advantage. In whatever format, the play demonstrates the durability of *Antigone*'s basic concept—that a decent burial is an essential attribute of humanity.

Sophocles (c. 496–c. 406 BCE)

ANTIGONE   *441* BCE

TRANSLATED BY DUDLEY FITTS AND ROBERT FITZGERALD

Characters

ANTIGONE, } *daughters of Oedipus*
ISMENE,
EURYDICE, *wife of Kreon*
KREON, *King of Thebes*
HAIMON, *son of Kreon*
TEIRESIAS, *a blind seer*
A SENTRY
A MESSENGER
CHORUS

Scene: *Before the palace of Kreon, King of Thebes. A central double door, and two lateral doors. A platform extends the length of the facade, and from this platform three steps lead down into the orchestra, or chorus-ground.*

Time: *Dawn of the day after the repulse of the Argive army from the assault on Thebes.*

PROLOGUE°

(*Antigone and Ismene enter from the central door of the palace.*)

ANTIGONE: Ismene, dear sister,
    You would think that we had already suffered
        enough
    For the curse on Oedipus.°

Prologue: Portion of the play explaining the background and current action.   **3. curse on Oedipus:** Oedipus, king of Thebes and the father of Antigone and Ismene, was abandoned by his parents as an infant after the oracle foretold that he would one day kill his father and marry his mother. Rescued by a shepherd and raised by the king of Corinth, Oedipus returned years later to Thebes and unknowingly lived out the oracle's prophecy by killing Laios and marrying Iokaste. After his two sons, Eteocles and Polyneices, killed each other in combat, the throne went to Kreon, Iokaste's brother.

I cannot imagine any grief
5   That you and I have not gone through. And now—
Have they told you of the new decree of our King
    Kreon?

ISMENE: I have heard nothing: I know
That two sisters lost two brothers, a double death
In a single hour; and I know that the Argive army
10   Fled in the night; but beyond this, nothing.

ANTIGONE: I thought so. And that is why I wanted
    you
To come out here with me. There is something we
    must do.

ISMENE: Why do you speak so strangely?

ANTIGONE: Listen, Ismene:
15   Kreon buried our brother Eteocles
With military honors, gave him a soldier's funeral,
And it was right that he should; but Polyneices,
Who fought as bravely and died as miserably,—
They say that Kreon has sworn
20   No one shall bury him, no one mourn for him,
But his body must lie in the fields, a sweet treasure
For carrion birds to find as they search for food.
That is what they say, and our good Kreon is
    coming here
To announce it publicly; and the penalty—
Stoning to death in the public square!
25   There it is,
And now you can prove what you are:
A true sister, or a traitor to your family.

ISMENE: Antigone, you are mad! What could I
    possibly do?

ANTIGONE: You must decide whether you will help
    me or not.
30 ISMENE: I do not understand you. Help you in what?

ANTIGONE: Ismene, I am going to bury him. Will you
    come?

ISMENE: Bury him! You have just said the new law
    forbids it.

ANTIGONE: He is my brother. And he is your brother,
    too.

ISMENE: But think of the danger! Think what Kreon
    will do!

ANTIGONE: Kreon is not strong enough to stand in my
35   way.

ISMENE: Ah sister!
Oedipus died, everyone hating him
For what his own search brought to light, his eyes
Ripped out by his own hand; and Iocaste died,
His mother and wife at once: she twisted the
40   cords
That strangled her life; and our two brothers
    died,
Each killed by the other's sword. And we are left:
But oh, Antigone,
Think how much more terrible than these
Our own death would be if we should go against
45   Kreon
And do what he has forbidden! We are only
    women,

We cannot fight with men, Antigone!
The law is strong, we must give in to the law
In this thing, and in worse. I beg the Dead
To forgive me, but I am helpless: I must yield   50
To those in authority. And I think it is dangerous
    business
To be always meddling.

ANTIGONE: If that is what you think,
I should not want you, even if you asked to
    come.
You have made your choice, you can be what you
    want to be.
But I will bury him; and if I must die,   55
I say that this crime is holy: I shall lie down
With him in death, and I shall be as dear
To him as he to me.
                It is the dead,
Not the living, who make the longest demands:
We die for ever...
                        You may do as you like,   60
Since apparently the laws of the gods mean
    nothing to you.

ISMENE: They mean a great deal to me; but I have no
    strength
To break laws that were made for the public
    good.

ANTIGONE: That must be your excuse, I suppose. But
    as for me,
I will bury the brother I love.

ISMENE: Antigone,   65
I am so afraid for you!

ANTIGONE: You need not be:
You have yourself to consider, after all.

ISMENE: But no one must hear of this, you must tell
    no one!
I will keep it a secret, I promise!

ANTIGONE: O tell it! Tell everyone!
Think how they'll hate you when it all comes out   70
If they learn that you knew about it all the time!

ISMENE: So fiery! You should be cold with fear.

ANTIGONE: Perhaps. But I am doing only what I
    must.

ISMENE: But can you do it? I say that you cannot.

ANTIGONE: Very well: when my strength gives out,   75
I shall do no more.

ISMENE: Impossible things should not be tried at all.

ANTIGONE: Go away, Ismene:
I shall be hating you soon, and the dead will too,
For your words are hateful. Leave me my foolish
    plan: 80
I am not afraid of the danger; if it means death,
It will not be the worst of deaths—death without
    honor.

ISMENE: Go then, if you feel that you must.
You are unwise,
But a loyal friend indeed to those who love you.   85

(*Exit into the palace. Antigone goes off, left. Enter the
Chorus.*)

PARODOS° • *Strophe*° *1*

CHORUS: Now the long blade of the sun, lying
    Level east to west, touches with glory
    Thebes of the Seven Gates. Open, unlidded
    Eye of golden day! O marching light
5   Across the eddy and rush of Dirce's stream,°
    Striking the white shields of the enemy
    Thrown headlong backward from the blaze of
        morning!
CHORAGOS:° Polyneices their commander

Parodos: The song or ode chanted by the Chorus on its entry.
Strophe: Song sung by the Chorus as it danced from stage right
to stage left.   **5. Dirce's stream:** River near Thebes.   **8. Choragos:** Leader of the Chorus.

Roused them with windy phrases,
He the wild eagle screaming   10
Insults above our land,
    His wings their shields of snow,
    His crest their marshalled helms.

Antistrophe° *1*

CHORUS: Against our seven gates in a yawning ring
    The famished spears came onward in the night; 15
    But before his jaws were sated with our blood,
    Or pinefire took the garland of our towers,

Antistrophe: Song sung by the Chorus following the Strophe,
as they danced back from stage left to stage right.

Ismene reassures Antigone (Martha Henry) in the Repertory Theatre of Lincoln Center production of *Antigone* at the Vivian Beaumont Theatre, directed by John Hirsch in 1971.

He was thrown back, and as he turned, great
   Thebes—
No tender victim for his noisy power—
20 Rose like a dragon behind him, shouting war.
CHORAGOS: For God hates utterly
  The bray of bragging tongues;
  And when he beheld their smiling,
  Their swagger of golden helms,
25 The frown of his thunder blasted
  Their first man from our walls.

Strophe 2

CHORUS: We heard his shout of triumph high in the air
  Turn to a scream; far out in a flaming arc
  He fell with his windy torch, and the earth struck
   him.
30 And others storming in fury no less than his
  Found shock of death in the dusty joy of battle.
CHORAGOS: Seven captains at seven gates
  Yielded their clanging arms to the god
  That bends the battle-line and breaks it.
35 These two only, brothers in blood,
  Face to face in matchless rage,
  Mirroring each the other's death
  Clashed in long combat.

Antistrophe 2

CHORUS: But now in the beautiful morning of victory
40 Let Thebes of the many chariots sing for joy!
  With hearts for dancing we'll take leave of war:
  Our temples shall be sweet with hymns of praise,
  And the long nights shall echo with our chorus.

SCENE 1

CHORAGOS: But now at last our new King is coming:
  Kreon of Thebes, Menoikeus' son.
  In this auspicious dawn of his reign
  What are the new complexities
5 That shifting Fate has woven for him?
  What is his counsel? Why has he summoned
  The old men to hear him?

(*Enter Kreon from the palace, center. He addresses the Chorus from the top step.*)

KREON: Gentlemen: I have the honor to inform you that
  our Ship of State, which recent storms have threat-
10 ened to destroy, has come safely to harbor at last,
  guided by the merciful wisdom of Heaven. I have
  summoned you here this morning because I know
  that I can depend upon you: your devotion to King
  Laios was absolute; you never hesitated in your duty
15 to our late ruler Oedipus; and when Oedipus died,
  your loyalty was transferred to his children. Unfortunately, as you know, his two sons, the princes Eteocles and Polyneices, have killed each other in battle;
and I, as the next in blood, have succeeded to the full
power of the throne.
  I am aware, of course, that no Ruler can expect
complete loyalty from his subjects until he has been
tested in office. Nevertheless, I say to you at the very
outset that I have nothing but contempt for the kind
of Governor who is afraid, for whatever reason, to
follow the course that he knows is best for the State;
and as for the man who sets private friendship above
the public welfare,—I have no use for him, either. I
call God to witness that if I saw my country headed
for ruin, I should not be afraid to speak out plainly;
and I need hardly remind you that I would never
have any dealings with an enemy of the people. No
one values friendship more highly than I; but we
must remember that friends made at the risk of
wrecking our Ship are not real friends at all.
  These are my principles, at any rate, and that is
why I have made the following decision concerning
the sons of Oedipus: Eteocles, who died as a man
should die, fighting for his country, is to be buried
with full military honors, with all the ceremony that
is usual when the greatest heroes die; but his brother
Polyneices, who broke his exile to come back with
fire and sword against his native city and the shrines
of his fathers' gods, whose one idea was to spill the
blood of his blood and sell his own people into
slavery—Polyneices, I say, is to have no burial: no
man is to touch him or say the least prayer for
him; he shall lie on the plain, unburied; and the birds
and the scavenging dogs can do with him whatever
they like.
  This is my command, and you can see the wisdom
behind it. As long as I am King, no traitor is going to
be honored with the loyal man. But whoever shows
by word and deed that he is on the side of the
State,—he shall have my respect while he is living
and my reverence when he is dead.
CHORAGOS: If that is your will, Kreon son of
  Menoikeus,
You have the right to enforce it: we are yours.
KREON: That is my will. Take care that you do your
  part.
CHORAGOS: We are old men: let the younger ones
  carry it out.
KREON: I do not mean that: the sentries have been
  appointed.
CHORAGOS: Then what is it that you would have us
  do?
KREON: You will give no support to whoever breaks
  this law.
CHORAGOS: Only a crazy man is in love with death!
KREON: And death it is; yet money talks, and the wisest
  Have sometimes been known to count a few coins
  too many.

(*Enter Sentry from left.*)

Kreon (Philip Bosco), Antigone (Martha Henry), and Haimon (David Birney).

SENTRY: I'll not say that I'm out of breath from running,
King, because every time I stopped to think about
70   what I have to tell you, I felt like going back. And all
the time a voice kept saying, "You fool, don't you
know you're walking straight into trouble?"; and then
another voice: "Yes, but if you let somebody else get
the news to Kreon first, it will be even worse than that
75   for you!" But good sense won out, at least I hope it
was good sense, and here I am with a story that makes
no sense at all; but I'll tell it anyhow, because, as they
say, what's going to happen's going to happen and—
KREON: Come to the point. What have you to say?
80 SENTRY: I did not do it. I did not see who did it.
You must not punish me for what someone else
has done.
KREON: A comprehensive defense! More effective,
perhaps,
If I knew its purpose. Come: what is it?
SENTRY: A dreadful thing . . . I don't know how to
put it—

KREON: Out with it!
SENTRY: Well, then;   85
The dead man—
Polyneices—

(*Pause. The Sentry is overcome, fumbles for words.
Kreon waits impassively.*)

out there—
someone,—
New dust on the slimy flesh!

(*Pause. No sign from Kreon.*)

Someone has given it burial that way, and
Gone . . .

(*Long pause. Kreon finally speaks with deadly control.*)

KREON: And the man who dared do this?
SENTRY: I swear I
Do not know! You must believe me!
Listen: 90

The ground was dry, not a sign of digging, no,
Not a wheeltrack in the dust, no trace of anyone.
It was when they relieved us this morning: and one of them,
The corporal, pointed to it.
                              There it was,
The strangest—
95   Look:
The body, just mounded over with light dust: you see?
Not buried really, but as if they'd covered it
Just enough for the ghost's peace. And no sign
Of dogs or any wild animal that had been there.

100   And then what a scene there was! Every man of us
Accusing the other: we all proved the other man did it.
We all had proof that we could not have done it.
We were ready to take hot iron in our hands,
Walk through fire, swear by all the gods,
105   *It was not I!*
I do not know who it was, but it was not I!

(*Kreon's rage has been mounting steadily, but the Sentry is too intent upon his story to notice it.*)

And then, when this came to nothing, someone said
A thing that silenced us and made us stare
Down at the ground: you had to be told the news,
110   And one of us had to do it! We threw the dice,
And the bad luck fell to me. So here I am,
No happier to be here than you are to have me:
Nobody likes the man who brings bad news.
CHORAGOS: I have been wondering, King: can it be
that the gods have done this?
115   KREON (*furiously*): Stop!
Must you doddering wrecks
Go out of your heads entirely? "The gods"!
Intolerable!
The gods favor this corpse? Why? How had he served them?
120   Tried to loot their temples, burn their images,
Yes, and the whole State, and its laws with it!
Is it your senile opinion that the gods love to honor bad men?
A pious thought!—
                    No, from the very beginning
There have been those who have whispered together,
125   Stiff-necked anarchists, putting their heads together,
Scheming against me in alleys. These are the men,
And they have bribed my own guard to do this thing.
(*Sententiously.*) Money!
There's nothing in the world so demoralizing as money.
130   Down go your cities,
Homes gone, men gone, honest hearts corrupted,
Crookedness of all kinds, and all for money!

(*To Sentry.*)   But you—
I swear by God and by the throne of God,
The man who has done this thing shall pay for it!
Find that man, bring him here to me, or your death   135
Will be the least of your problems: I'll string you up
Alive, and there will be certain ways to make you
Discover your employer before you die;
And the process may teach you a lesson you seem to have missed:
The dearest profit is sometimes all too dear: 140
That depends on the source. Do you understand me?
A fortune won is often misfortune.
SENTRY: King, may I speak?
KREON: Your very voice distresses me.
SENTRY: Are you sure that it is my voice, and not your conscience?
KREON: By God, he wants to analyze me now!   145
SENTRY: It is not what I say, but what has been done, that hurts you.
KREON: You talk too much.
SENTRY: Maybe; but I've done nothing.
KREON: Sold your soul for some silver: that's all you've done.
SENTRY: How dreadful it is when the right judge judges wrong!
KREON: Your figures of speech   150
May entertain you now; but unless you bring me the man,
You will get little profit from them in the end.
                          (*Exit Kreon into the palace.*)
SENTRY: "Bring me the man"—!
I'd like nothing better than bringing him the man!
But bring him or not, you have seen the last of me here.   155
At any rate, I am safe!   (*Exit Sentry.*)

ODE° 1 • *Strophe 1*

CHORUS: Numberless are the world's wonders, but none
More wonderful than man; the stormgray sea
Yields to his prows, the huge crests bear him high;
Earth, holy and inexhaustible, is graven
With shining furrows where his plows have gone   5
Year after year, the timeless labor of stallions.

Antistrophe 1

The lightboned birds and beasts that cling to cover,
The lithe fish lighting their reaches of dim water,
All are taken, tamed in the net of his mind;
The lion on the hill, the wild horse windy-maned,   10

Ode: Song sung by the Chorus.

Resign to him; and his blunt yoke has broken
The sultry shoulders of the mountain bull.

Strophe 2

Words also, and thought as rapid as air,
He fashions to his good use; statecraft is his
15 And his the skill that deflects the arrows of snow,
The spears of winter rain: from every wind
He has made himself secure—from all but one:
In the late wind of death he cannot stand.

Antistrophe 2

O clear intelligence, force beyond all measure!
20 O fate of man, working both good and evil!
When the laws are kept, how proudly his city
stands!
When the laws are broken, what of his city then?
Never may the anarchic man find rest at my
hearth,
Never be it said that my thoughts are his thoughts.

SCENE 2

(*Reenter Sentry leading Antigone.*)

CHORAGOS: What does this mean? Surely this captive
woman
Is the Princess, Antigone. Why should she be
taken?
SENTRY: Here is the one who did it! We caught her
In the very act of burying him.—Where is
Kreon?
CHORAGOS: Just coming from the house.

(*Enter Kreon, center.*)

5 KREON: What has happened?
Why have you come back so soon?
SENTRY (*expansively*):   O King,
A man should never be too sure of anything:
I would have sworn
That you'd not see me here again: your anger
Frightened me so, and the things you threatened
10 me with;
But how could I tell then
That I'd be able to solve the case so soon?
No dice-throwing this time: I was only too glad to
come!
Here is this woman. She is the guilty one:
15 We found her trying to bury him.
Take her, then; question her; judge her as you will.
I am through with the whole thing now, and glad
of it.
KREON: But this is Antigone! Why have you brought
her here?
SENTRY: She was burying him, I tell you!

KREON (*severely*):   Is this the truth?   20
SENTRY: I saw her with my own eyes. Can I say more?
KREON: The details: come, tell me quickly!
SENTRY: It was like this:
After those terrible threats of yours, King,
We went back and brushed the dust away from
the body.
The flesh was soft by now, and stinking,   25
So we sat on a hill to windward and kept guard.
No napping this time! We kept each other awake.
But nothing happened until the white round sun
Whirled in the center of the round sky over us:
Then, suddenly,
A storm of dust roared up from the earth, and the
sky   30
Went out, the plain vanished with all its trees
In the stinging dark. We closed our eyes and
endured it.
The whirlwind lasted a long time, but it passed;
And then we looked, and there was Antigone!   35
I have seen
A mother bird come back to a stripped nest, heard
Her crying bitterly a broken note or two
For the young ones stolen. Just so, when this girl
Found the bare corpse, and all her love's work
wasted,   40
She wept, and cried on heaven to damn the hands
That had done this thing.
                          And then she brought more dust
And sprinkled wine three times for her brother's
ghost.
We ran and took her at once. She was not afraid,
Not even when we charged her with what she had
done.
She denied nothing.   45
                    And this was a comfort to me,
And some uneasiness: for it is a good thing
To escape from death, but it is no great pleasure
To bring death to a friend.
                          Yet I always say
There is nothing so comfortable as your own safe
skin!   50
KREON (*slowly, dangerously*): And you, Antigone,
You with your head hanging,—do you confess
this thing?
ANTIGONE: I do. I deny nothing.
KREON (*to Sentry*):   You may go.
                                    (*Exit Sentry.*)
(*To Antigone.*) Tell me, tell me briefly:
Had you heard my proclamation touching this
matter?   55
ANTIGONE: It was public. Could I help hearing it?
KREON: And yet you dared defy the law.
ANTIGONE: I dared.
It was not God's proclamation. That final Justice
That rules the world below makes no such laws.

Your edict, King, was strong,
But all your strength is weakness itself against   60

The immortal unrecorded laws of God.
They are not merely now: they were, and shall be,
Operative for ever, beyond man utterly.

I knew I must die, even without your decree:
65 I am only mortal. And if I must die
Now, before it is my time to die,
Surely this is no hardship: can anyone
Living, as I live, with evil all about me,
Think Death less than a friend? This death of mine
70 Is of no importance; but if I had left my brother
Lying in death unburied, I should have suffered.
Now I do not.
                      You smile at me. Ah Kreon,
Think me a fool, if you like; but it may well be
That a fool convicts me of folly.
CHORAGOS: Like father, like daughter: both headstrong,
75   deaf to reason!
She has never learned to yield.
KREON: She has much to learn.
The inflexible heart breaks first, the toughest iron
Cracks first, and the wildest horses bend their necks
At the pull of the smallest curb.
                              Pride? In a slave?
80 This girl is guilty of a double insolence,
Breaking the given laws and boasting of it.
Who is the man here,
She or I, if this crime goes unpunished?
Sister's child, or more than sister's child,
85 Or closer yet in blood—she and her sister
Win bitter death for this!
(To Servants.)   Go, some of you,
Arrest Ismene. I accuse her equally.
Bring her: you will find her sniffling in the house
      there.

Her mind's a traitor: crimes kept in the dark
90 Cry for light, and the guardian brain shudders;
But how much worse than this
Is brazen boasting of barefaced anarchy!
ANTIGONE: Kreon, what more do you want than my
      death?
KREON: Nothing.
That gives me everything.
ANTIGONE: Then I beg you: kill me.
95 This talking is a great weariness: your words
Are distasteful to me, and I am sure that mine
Seem so to you. And yet they should not seem so:
I should have praise and honor for what I have
      done.
All these men here would praise me
100 Were their lips not frozen shut with fear of you.
(Bitterly.) Ah the good fortune of kings,
Licensed to say and do whatever they please!
KREON: You are alone here in that opinion.
ANTIGONE: No, they are with me. But they keep their
      tongues in leash.
105 KREON: Maybe. But you are guilty, and they are not.
ANTIGONE: There is no guilt in reverence for the dead.

KREON: But Eteocles—was he not your brother too?
ANTIGONE: My brother too.
KREON: And you insult his memory?
ANTIGONE (softly): The dead man would not say that
      I insult it.
KREON: He would: for you honor a traitor as much
      as him.
ANTIGONE: His own brother, traitor or not, and equal   110
      in blood.
KREON: He made war on his country. Eteocles
      defended it.
ANTIGONE: Nevertheless, there are honors due all the
      dead.
KREON: But not the same for the wicked as for the
      just.
ANTIGONE: Ah Kreon, Kreon,   115
      Which of us can say what the gods hold wicked?
KREON: An enemy is an enemy, even dead.
ANTIGONE: It is my nature to join in love, not hate.
KREON (finally losing patience): Go join them then; if
      you must have your love,
      Find it in hell!   120
CHORAGOS: But see, Ismene comes:

(Enter Ismene, guarded.)

Those tears are sisterly, the cloud
That shadows her eyes rains down gentle sorrow.
KREON: You too, Ismene,
Snake in my ordered house, sucking my blood   125
Stealthily—and all the time I never knew
That these two sisters were aiming at my throne!
                                        Ismene,
Do you confess your share in this crime, or deny it?
Answer me.
ISMENE: Yes, if she will let me say so. I am guilty.   130
ANTIGONE (coldly): No, Ismene. You have no right to
      say so.
You would not help me, and I will not have you
      help me.
ISMENE: But now I know what you meant; and I am
      here
To join you, to take my share of punishment.
ANTIGONE: The dead man and the gods who rule the
      dead
Know whose act this was. Words are not friends.   135
ISMENE: Do you refuse me, Antigone? I want to die
      with you:
I too have a duty that I must discharge to the dead.
ANTIGONE: You shall not lessen my death by sharing it.
ISMENE: What do I care for life when you are dead?   140
ANTIGONE: Ask Kreon. You're always hanging on his
      opinions.
ISMENE: You are laughing at me. Why, Antigone?
ANTIGONE: It's a joyless laughter, Ismene.
ISMENE: But can I do nothing?
ANTIGONE: Yes. Save yourself. I shall not envy you.
There are those who will praise you; I shall have
      honor, too.   145
ISMENE: But we are equally guilty!

TOP: Kreon (F. Murray Abraham) in a scene from the 1982 New York Shakespeare Festival production directed by Joseph Chaikin. LEFT: Antigone (Lisa Banes) steadfastly admitting her guilt.

Randle Mell as Kreon and Alyssa Bresnahan as Antigone in the South Coast Repertory's 2004 production of *Antigone,* directed by Kate Whoriskey.

ANTIGONE: No more, Ismene.
   You are alive, but I belong to Death.
KREON (*to the Chorus*): Gentlemen, I beg you to
   observe these girls:
   One has just now lost her mind; the other,
150   It seems, has never had a mind at all.
ISMENE: Grief teaches the steadiest minds to waver,
   King.
KREON: Yours certainly did, when you assumed guilt
   with the guilty!
ISMENE: But how could I go on living without her?
KREON: You are.
   She is already dead.
ISMENE: But your own son's bride!
KREON: There are places enough for him to push his
155   plow.
   I want no wicked women for my sons!
ISMENE: O dearest Haimon, how your father wrongs
   you!
KREON: I've had enough of your childish talk of
   marriage!

CHORAGOS: Do you really intend to steal this girl
   from your son?
KREON: No; Death will do that for me.
CHORAGOS: Then she must die?   160
KREON (*ironically*): You dazzle me.
                 —But enough of this talk!
   (*To Guards.*) You, there, take them away and
   guard them well:
   For they are but women, and even brave men run
   When they see Death coming.
          (*Exeunt° Ismene, Antigone, and Guards.*)

ODE 2 • *Strophe 1*

CHORUS: Fortunate is the man who has never tasted
   God's vengeance!
   Where once the anger of heaven has struck, that
   house is shaken
   For ever: damnation rises behind each child
   Like a wave cresting out of the black northeast,
   When the long darkness under sea roars up   5
   And bursts drumming death upon the
   windwhipped sand.

Antistrophe 1

   I have seen this gathering sorrow from time long
   past
   Loom upon Oedipus' children: generation from
   generation
   Takes the compulsive rage of the enemy god.
   So lately this last flower of Oedipus' line   10
   Drank the sunlight! but now a passionate word
   And a handful of dust have closed up all its beauty.

Strophe 2

   What mortal arrogance
   Transcends the wrath of Zeus?
   Sleep cannot lull him nor the effortless long months   15
   Of the timeless gods: but he is young for ever,
   And his house is the shining day of high Olympos.
     All that is and shall be,
     And all the past, is his.
   No pride on earth is free of the curse of heaven.   20

Antistrophe 2

   The straying dreams of men
     May bring them ghosts of joy:
   But as they drowse, the waking embers burn them;   25
   Or they walk with fixed eyes, as blind men walk.
   But the ancient wisdom speaks for our own time:
   Fate works most for woe

165. [S.D.] *Exeunt:* Latin for "they go out."

With Folly's fairest show.
Man's little pleasure is the spring of sorrow.

SCENE 3

CHORAGOS: But here is Haimon, King, the last of all
    your sons.
Is it grief for Antigone that brings him here,
And bitterness at being robbed of his bride?

(*Enter Haimon.*)

KREON: We shall soon see, and no need of diviners.
                          —Son,
5   You have heard my final judgment on that girl:
Have you come here hating me, or have you come
With deference and with love, whatever I do?
HAIMON: I am your son, father. You are my guide.
You make things clear for me, and I obey you.
No marriage means more to me than your
10   continuing wisdom.
KREON: Good. That is the way to behave:
    subordinate
Everything else, my son, to your father's will.
This is what a man prays for, that he may get
Sons attentive and dutiful in his house,
15   Each one hating his father's enemies,
Honoring his father's friends. But if his sons
Fail him, if they turn out unprofitably,
What has he fathered but trouble for himself
And amusement for the malicious?
                       So you are right
20   Not to lose your head over this woman.
Your pleasure with her would soon grow cold,
    Haimon,
And then you'd have a hellcat in bed and
    elsewhere.
Let her find her husband in Hell!
Of all the people in this city, only she
25   Has had contempt for my law and broken it.

Do you want me to show myself weak before the
    people?
Or to break my sworn word? No, and I will not.
The woman dies.
I suppose she'll plead "family ties." Well, let her.
30   If I permit my own family to rebel,
How shall I earn the world's obedience?
Show me the man who keeps his house in hand,
He's fit for public authority.
              I'll have no dealings
With lawbreakers, critics of the government:
35   Whoever is chosen to govern should be obeyed—
Must be obeyed, in all things, great and small,
Just and unjust! O Haimon,
The man who knows how to obey, and that man
    only,
Knows how to give commands when the time
    comes.

You can depend on him, no matter how fast   40
The spears come: he's a good soldier, he'll stick it
    out.
Anarchy, anarchy! Show me a greater evil!
This is why cities tumble and the great houses rain
    down,
This is what scatters armies!
No, no: good lives are made so by discipline.   45
We keep the laws then, and the lawmakers,
And no woman shall seduce us. If we must lose,
Let's lose to a man, at least! Is a woman stronger
    than we?
CHORAGOS: Unless time has rusted my wits,
What you say, King, is said with point and dignity.   50
HAIMON (*boyishly earnest*): Father:
Reason is God's crowning gift to man, and you
    are right
To warn me against losing mine. I cannot say—
I hope that I shall never want to say!—that you
Have reasoned badly. Yet there are other men   55
Who can reason, too; and their opinions might be
    helpful.
You are not in a position to know everything
That people say or do, or what they feel:
Your temper terrifies—everyone
Will tell you only what you like to hear.   60
But I, at any rate, can listen; and I have heard
    them
Muttering and whispering in the dark about this
    girl.
They say no woman has ever, so unreasonably,
Died so shameful a death for a generous act:
"She covered her brother's body. Is this indecent?   65
She kept him from dogs and vultures. Is this a
    crime?
Death?—She should have all the honor that we
    can give her!"

This is the way they talk out there in the city.
You must believe me:
Nothing is closer to me than your happiness.   70
What could be closer? Must not any son
Value his father's fortune as his father does his?
I beg you, do not be unchangeable:
Do not believe that you alone can be right.
The man who thinks that,   75
The man who maintains that only he has the power
To reason correctly, the gift to speak, the soul—
A man like that, when you know him, turns out
    empty.
It is not reason never to yield to reason!

In flood time you can see how some trees bend,   80
And because they bend, even their twigs are safe,
While stubborn trees are torn up, roots and all.
And the same thing happens in sailing:
Make your sheet fast, never slacken,—and over
    you go,
Head over heels and under: and there's your voyage.   85

Forget you are angry! Let yourself be moved!
I know I am young; but please let me say this:
The ideal condition
Would be, I admit, that men should be right by
     instinct;
90 But since we are all too likely to go astray,
The reasonable thing is to learn from those who
     can teach.

CHORAGOS: You will do well to listen to him, King,
If what he says is sensible. And you, Haimon,
Must listen to your father.—Both speak well.

KREON: You consider it right for a man of my years
95   and experience
To go to school to a boy?

HAIMON: It is not right
If I am wrong. But if I am young, and right,
What does my age matter?

KREON: You think it right to stand up for an anarchist?
100 HAIMON: Not at all. I pay no respect to criminals.

KREON: Then she is not a criminal?

HAIMON: The City would deny it, to a man.

KREON: And the City proposes to teach me how to rule?

HAIMON: Ah. Who is it that's talking like a boy now?

KREON: My voice is the one voice giving orders in
105   this City!

HAIMON: It is no City if it takes orders from one voice.

KREON: The State is the King!

HAIMON: Yes, if the State is a desert.

(Pause.)

KREON: This boy, it seems, has sold out to a woman.

HAIMON: If you are a woman: my concern is only for
     you.

KREON: So? Your "concern"! In a public brawl with
110   your father!

HAIMON: How about you, in a public brawl with
     justice?

KREON: With justice, when all that I do is within my
     rights?

HAIMON: You have no right to trample on God's right.

KREON (completely out of control): Fool, adolescent
     fool! Taken in by a woman!
115 HAIMON: You'll never see me taken in by anything vile.

KREON: Every word you say is for her!

HAIMON (quietly, darkly):   And for you.
And for me. And for the gods under the earth.

KREON: You'll never marry her while she lives.

HAIMON: Then she must die.—But her death will
     cause another.
120 KREON: Another?
Have you lost your senses? Is this an open threat?

HAIMON: There is no threat in speaking to emptiness.

KREON: I swear you'll regret this superior tone of
     yours!
You are the empty one!

HAIMON: If you were not my father,
125 I'd say you were perverse.

KREON: You girl-struck fool, don't play at words with
     me!

HAIMON: I am sorry. You prefer silence.

KREON: Now, by God—
I swear, by all the gods in heaven above us,
You'll watch it, I swear you shall!
(To the Servants.)   Bring her out!
Bring the woman out! Let her die before his eyes!   130
Here, this instant, with her bridegroom beside her!

HAIMON: Not here, no; she will not die here, King.
And you will never see my face again.
Go on raving as long as you've a friend to endure
     you.   (Exit Haimon.)

CHORAGOS: Gone, gone.   135
Kreon, a young man in a rage is dangerous!

KREON: Let him do, or dream to do, more than a
     man can.
He shall not save these girls from death.

CHORAGOS: These girls?
You have sentenced them both?

KREON: No, you are right.
I will not kill the one whose hands are clean.   140

CHORAGOS: But Antigone?

KREON (somberly):   I will carry her far away
Out there in the wilderness, and lock her
Living in a vault of stone. She shall have food,
As the custom is, to absolve the State of her death.
And there let her pray to the gods of hell: 145
They are her only gods:
Perhaps they will show her an escape from death,
Or she may learn,
                  though late,
That piety shown the dead is pity in vain.
                              (Exit Kreon.)

ODE 3 • Strophe

CHORUS: Love, unconquerable
    Waster of rich men, keeper
    Of warm lights and all-night vigil
    In the soft face of a girl:
    Sea-wanderer, forest-visitor!   5
    Even the pure Immortals cannot escape you,
    And mortal man, in his one day's dusk,
    Trembles before your glory.

Antistrophe

    Surely you swerve upon ruin
    The just man's consenting heart,   10
    As here you have made bright anger
    Strike between father and son—
    And none has conquered but Love!
    A girl's glance working the will of heaven:
    Pleasure to her alone who mocks us,   15
    Merciless Aphrodite.°

16. Aphrodite: Goddess of love and beauty.

SCENE 4

CHORAGOS (*as Antigone enters guarded*): But I can
    no longer stand in awe of this,
  Nor, seeing what I see, keep back my tears.
  Here is Antigone, passing to that chamber
  Where all find sleep at last.

Strophe 1

5 ANTIGONE: Look upon me, friends, and pity me
    Turning back at the night's edge to say
    Good-by to the sun that shines for me no longer;
    Now sleepy Death
    Summons me down to Acheron,° that cold shore:
10   There is no bridesong there, nor any music.
  CHORUS: Yet not unpraised, not without a kind of
    honor,
    You walk at last into the underworld
    Untouched by sickness, broken by no sword.
    What woman has ever found your way to death?

Antistrophe 1

15 ANTIGONE: How often I have heard the story of Niobe,°
    Tantalos' wretched daughter, how the stone
    Clung fast about her, ivy-close: and they say
    The rain falls endlessly
    And sifting soft snow; her tears are never done.
20   I feel the loneliness of her death in mine.
  CHORUS: But she was born of heaven, and you
    Are woman, woman-born. If her death is yours,
    A mortal woman's, is this not for you
    Glory in our world and in the world beyond?

Strophe 2

25 ANTIGONE: You laugh at me. Ah, friends, friends,
    Can you not wait until I am dead? O Thebes,
    O men many-charioted, in love with Fortune,
    Dear springs of Dirce, sacred Theban grove,
    Be witnesses for me, denied all pity,
30   Unjustly judged! and think a word of love
    For her whose path turns
    Under dark earth, where there are no more tears.
  CHORUS: You have passed beyond human daring and
    come at last
    Into a place of stone where Justice sits.
35   I cannot tell
    What shape of your father's guilt appears in this.

Antistrophe 2

ANTIGONE: You have touched it at last: that bridal
    bed
  Unspeakable, horror of son and mother mingling:
  Their crime, infection of all our family!
  O Oedipus, father and brother!   40
  Your marriage strikes from the grave to murder
    mine.
  I have been a stranger here in my own land:
  All my life
  The blasphemy of my birth has followed me.
CHORUS: Reverence is a virtue, but strength   45
  Lives in established law: that must prevail.
  You have made your choice,
  Your death is the doing of your conscious
    hand.

Epode°

ANTIGONE: Then let me go, since all your words are
    bitter,
  And the very light of the sun is cold to me.   50
  Lead me to my vigil, where I must have
  Neither love nor lamentation; no song, but silence.

(*Kreon interrupts impatiently.*)

KREON: If dirges and planned lamentations could put
    off death,
  Men would be singing for ever.
  (*To the Servants.*)   Take her, go!
  You know your orders: take her to the vault   55
  And leave her alone there. And if she lives or dies,
  That's her affair, not ours: our hands are clean.
ANTIGONE: O tomb, vaulted bride-bed in eternal rock,
  Soon I shall be with my own again
  Where Persephone° welcomes the thin ghosts
    underground: 60
  And I shall see my father again, and you, mother,
  And dearest Polyneices—
                   dearest indeed
  To me, since it was my hand
  That washed him clean and poured the ritual wine:
  And my reward is death before my time!   65

  And yet, as men's hearts know, I have done no
    wrong,
  I have not sinned before God. Or if I have,
  I shall know the truth in death. But if the guilt
  Lies upon Kreon who judged me, then, I pray,
  May his punishment equal my own.
CHORAGOS: O passionate heart,   70
  Unyielding, tormented still by the same winds!

---

9. Acheron: River in Hades, domain of the dead. **15. Niobe:**
When Niobe's many children (up to twenty in some accounts)
were slain in punishment for their mother's boastfulness,
Niobe was turned into a stone on Mount Sipylus. Her tears
became the mountain's streams.

Epode: Song sung by the Chorus while standing still after
singing the strophe and antistrophe. **60. Persephone:** Abducted by Pluto, god of the underworld, to be his queen.

KREON: Her guards shall have good cause to regret
    their delaying.
ANTIGONE: Ah! That voice is like the voice of death!
KREON: I can give you no reason to think you are
    mistaken.
75 ANTIGONE: Thebes, and you my fathers' gods,
    And rulers of Thebes, you see me now, the last
    Unhappy daughter of a line of kings,
    Your kings, led away to death. You will remember
    What things I suffer, and at what men's hands,
80   Because I would not transgress the laws of heaven.
        (*To the Guards, simply.*) Come: let us wait no
    longer.   (*Exit Antigone, left, guarded.*)

ODE 4 • *Strophe 1*

CHORUS: All Danae's beauty was locked away
    In a brazen cell where the sunlight could not come:
    A small room still as any grave, enclosed her.
    Yet she was a princess too,
5   And Zeus in a rain of gold poured love upon her.°
    O child, child,
    No power in wealth or war
    Or tough sea-blackened ships
    Can prevail against untiring Destiny!

Antistrophe 1

10   And Dryas's son° also, that furious king,
    Bore the god's prisoning anger for his pride:
    Sealed up by Dionysos in deaf stone,
    His madness died among echoes.
    So at the last he learned what dreadful power
15   His tongue had mocked:
    For he had profaned the revels,
    And fired the wrath of the nine
    Implacable Sisters° that love the sound of the flute.

Strophe 2

    And old men tell a half-remembered tale
20   Of horror° where a dark ledge splits the sea
    And a double surf beats on the gray shores:
    How a king's new woman, sick

1–5. **All Danae's beauty . . . poured love upon her:** Locked away to prevent the fulfillment of a prophecy that she would bear a son who would kill her father, Danae was nonetheless impregnated by Zeus, who came to her in a shower of gold. The prophecy was fulfilled by the son that came of their union. 10. **Dryas's son:** King Lycurgus of Thrace, whom Dionysus, god of wine, caused to be stricken with madness. 18. **Sisters:** The Muses, nine sister goddesses who presided over poetry and music, arts and sciences. 19–20. **half-remembered tale of horror:** The second wife of King Phineas blinded the sons of his first wife, Cleopatra, whom Phineas had imprisoned in a cave.

    With hatred for the queen he had imprisoned,
    Ripped out his two sons' eyes with her bloody
    hands
    While grinning Ares° watched the shuttle plunge   25
    Four times: four blind wounds crying for revenge,

Antistrophe 2

    Crying, tears and blood mingled.—Piteously born,
    Those sons whose mother was of heavenly birth!
    Her father was the god of the North Wind
    And she was cradled by gales,   30
    She raced with young colts on the glittering hills
    And walked untrammeled in the open light:
    But in her marriage deathless Fate found means
    To build a tomb like yours for all her joy.

SCENE 5

(*Enter blind Teiresias, led by a boy. The opening speeches of Teiresias should be in singsong contrast to the realistic lines of Kreon.*)

TEIRESIAS: This is the way the blind man comes,
    Princes, Princes,
    Lockstep, two heads lit by the eyes of one.
KREON: What new thing have you to tell us, old
    Teiresias?
TEIRESIAS: I have much to tell you: listen to the
    prophet, Kreon.
KREON: I am not aware that I have ever failed to   5
    listen.
TEIRESIAS: Then you have done wisely, King, and
    ruled well.
KREON: I admit my debt to you. But what have you
    to say?
TEIRESIAS: This, Kreon: you stand once more on the
    edge of fate.
KREON: What do you mean? Your words are a kind
    of dread.
TEIRESIAS: Listen, Kreon: 10
    I was sitting in my chair of augury, at the place
    Where the birds gather about me. They were all a-
    chatter,
    As is their habit, when suddenly I heard
    A strange note in their jangling, a scream, a
    Whirring fury; I knew that they were fighting,   15
    Tearing each other, dying
    In a whirlwind of wings clashing. And I was
    afraid.
    I began the rites of burnt-offering at the altar
    But Hephaistos° failed me: instead of bright flame,
    There was only the sputtering slime of the fat
    thigh-flesh   20
    Melting: the entrails dissolved in gray smoke,

---

25. Ares: God of war.   **19. Hephaistos:** God of fire.

The bare bone burst from the welter. And no
  blaze!

This was a sign from heaven. My boy described it,
Seeing for me as I see for others.
25 I tell you, Kreon, you yourself have brought
This new calamity upon us. Our hearths and altars
Are stained with the corruption of dogs and
  carrion birds
That glut themselves on the corpse of Oedipus's
  son.
The gods are deaf when we pray to them, their fire
30 Recoils from our offering, their birds of omen
Have no cry of comfort, for they are gorged
With the thick blood of the dead.
                                                    O my son,
These are no trifles! Think: all men make mistakes,
But a good man yields when he knows his course
  is wrong,
35 And repairs the evil. The only crime is pride.

Give in to the dead man, then: do not fight with a
  corpse—
What glory is it to kill a man who is dead?
Think, I beg you:
It is for your own good that I speak as I do.
40 You should be able to yield for your own good.
  KREON: It seems that prophets have made me their
    especial province.
  All my life long
  I have been a kind of butt for the dull arrows
  Of doddering fortune-tellers!
                                        No, Teiresias:
45 If your birds—if the great eagles of God himself
  Should carry him stinking bit by bit to heaven,
  I would not yield. I am not afraid of pollution:
  No man can defile the gods.
                                        Do what you will,
  Go into business, make money, speculate
50 In India gold or that synthetic gold from Sardis,
  Get rich otherwise than by my consent to bury
    him.
  Teiresias, it is a sorry thing when a wise man
  Sells his wisdom, lets out his words for hire!
  TEIRESIAS: Ah Kreon! Is there no man left in the
    world—
55 KREON: To do what?—Come, let's have the aphorism!
  TEIRESIAS: No man who knows that wisdom
    outweighs any wealth?
  KREON: As surely as bribes are baser than any
    baseness.
  TEIRESIAS: You are sick, Kreon! You are deathly sick!
  KREON: As you say: it is not my place to challenge a
    prophet.
60 TEIRESIAS: Yet you have said my prophecy is for sale.
  KREON: The generation of prophets has always loved
    gold.
  TEIRESIAS: The generation of kings has always loved
    brass.

KREON: You forget yourself! You are speaking to
  your King.
TEIRESIAS: I know it. You are a king because of me.
KREON: You have a certain skill; but you have sold
  out.   65
TEIRESIAS: King, you will drive me to words that—
KREON: Say them, say them!
  Only remember: I will not pay you for them.
TEIRESIAS: No, you will find them too costly.
KREON: No doubt. Speak:
  Whatever you say, you will not change my will.
TEIRESIAS: Then take this, and take it to heart!   70
  The time is not far off when you shall pay back
  Corpse for corpse, flesh of your own flesh.
  You have thrust the child of this world into living
    night,
  You have kept from the gods below the child that
    is theirs:
  The one in a grave before her death, the other,   75
  Dead, denied the grave. This is your crime:
  And the Furies° and the dark gods of Hell
  Are swift with terrible punishment for you.

  Do you want to buy me now, Kreon?

                                        Not many days,
  And your house will be full of men and women
    weeping,   80
  And curses will be hurled at you from far
  Cities grieving for sons unburied, left to rot
  Before the walls of Thebes.

  These are my arrows, Kreon: they are all for you.

  (*To Boy.*) But come, child: lead me home.   85
  Let him waste his fine anger upon younger men.
  Maybe he will learn at last
  To control a wiser tongue in a better head.
                                        (*Exit Teiresias.*)
CHORAGOS: The old man has gone, King, but his
    words
  Remain to plague us. I am old, too,   90
  But I cannot remember that he was ever false.
KREON: That is true. . . . It troubles me.
  Oh it is hard to give in! but it is worse
  To risk everything for stubborn pride.
CHORAGOS: Kreon: take my advice.
KREON: What shall I do?   95
CHORAGOS: Go quickly: free Antigone from her vault
  And build a tomb for the body of Polyneices.
KREON: You would have me do this!
CHORAGOS: Kreon, yes!
  And it must be done at once: God moves
  Swiftly to cancel the folly of stubborn men.   100
KREON: It is hard to deny the heart! But I
  Will do it: I will not fight with destiny.

77. Furies: Spirits called on to avenge crimes, especially those
against kin.

CHORAGOS: You must go yourself, you cannot leave
    it to others.
KREON: I will go.
        —Bring axes, servants:
105 Come with me to the tomb. I buried her, I
Will set her free.
            Oh quickly!
My mind misgives—
The laws of the gods are mighty, and a man must
    serve them
To the last day of his life!   (*Exit Kreon.*)

PAEAN° • *Strophe 1*

CHORAGOS: God of many names
CHORUS: O Iacchos
                    son
of Kadmeian Semele
                O born of the Thunder!
Guardian of the West
                Regent
of Eleusis' plain
            O Prince of maenad Thebes
5   and the Dragon Field by rippling Ismenos:°

Antistrophe 1

CHORAGOS: God of many names
CHORUS: the flame of torches
    flares on our hills
                the nymphs of Iacchos
dance at the spring of Castalia:°
from the vine-close mountain
                come ah come in ivy:
10   *Evohe evohe!*° sings through the streets of Thebes

Strophe 2

CHORAGOS: God of many names
CHORUS: Iacchos of Thebes
    heavenly Child
            of Semele bride of the Thunderer!
The shadow of plague is upon us:
                come

Paean: A song of praise or prayer. 1–5. God of many
names . . . rippling Ismenos: The following is a litany of names
for Dionysus (Iacchos): he was son of Zeus ("Thunder") and
Semele; he was honored in secret rites at Eleusis; and he was
worshiped by the Maenads of Thebes. Kadmos, Semele's father,
sowed dragon's teeth in a field beside the river Ismenos from
which sprang warriors who became the first Thebans.
8. spring of Castalia: A spring on Mount Parnassus used by
priestesses of Dionysus in rites of purification. 10. *Evohe
evohe!*: Cry of the Maenads to Dionysus.

with clement feet
            oh come from Parnasos
down the long slopes
            across the lamenting water   15

Antistrophe 2

CHORAGOS: Io Fire! Chorister of the throbbing stars!
    O purest among the voices of the night!
    Thou son of God, blaze for us!
CHORUS: Come with choric rapture of circling
    Maenads
    Who cry *Io Iacche!*°
        God of many names!   20

EXODOS°

(*Enter Messenger from left.*)

MESSENGER: Men of the line of Kadmos, you who
    live
    Near Amphion's citadel,°
                I cannot say
Of any condition of human life "This is fixed,
This is clearly good, or bad." Fate raises up,
And Fate casts down the happy and unhappy
    alike: 5
No man can foretell his Fate.
                Take the case of Kreon:
Kreon was happy once, as I count happiness:
Victorious in battle, sole governor of the land,
Fortunate father of children nobly born.
And now it has all gone from him! Who can say   10
That a man is still alive when his life's joy fails?
He is a walking dead man. Grant him rich,
Let him live like a king in his great house:
If his pleasure is gone, I would not give
So much as the shadow of smoke for all he owns.   15
CHORAGOS: Your words hint at sorrow: what is your
    news for us?
MESSENGER: They are dead. The living are guilty of
    their death.
CHORAGOS: Who is guilty? Who is dead? Speak!
MESSENGER: Haimon.
    Haimon is dead; and the hand that killed him
    Is his own hand.
CHORAGOS: His father's? or his own?   20
MESSENGER: His own, driven mad by the murder his
    father had done.
CHORAGOS: Teiresias, Teiresias, how clearly you saw
    it all!
MESSENGER: This is my news: you must draw what
    conclusions you can from it.
CHORAGOS: But look: Eurydice, our Queen:

20. Io Iacche!: Ritual cry. Exodos: Final scene. 2. Amphion's citadel: A name for Thebes.

25   Has she overheard us?

(*Enter Eurydice from the palace, center.*)

EURYDICE: I have heard something, friends:
       As I was unlocking the gate of Pallas'° shrine,
       For I needed her help today, I heard a voice
       Telling of some new sorrow. And I fainted
       There at the temple with all my maidens
30   about me.
       But speak again: whatever it is, I can bear it:
       Grief and I are no strangers.
MESSENGER: Dearest Lady,
       I will tell you plainly all that I have seen.
       I shall not try to comfort you: what is the use,
35   Since comfort could lie only in what is not true?
       The truth is always best.
                              I went with Kreon
       To the outer plain where Polyneices was lying,
       No friend to pity him, his body shredded by dogs.
       We made our prayers in that place to Hecate
       And Pluto,° that they would be merciful. And we
40   bathed
       The corpse with holy water, and we brought
       Fresh-broken branches to burn what was left of it,
       And upon the urn we heaped up a towering
          barrow
       Of the earth of his own land.
                              When we were done, we ran
       To the vault where Antigone lay on her couch of
45   stone.
       One of the servants had gone ahead,
       And while he was yet far off he heard a voice
       Grieving within the chamber, and he came back
       And told Kreon. And as the King went closer,
50   The air was full of wailing, the words lost,
       And he begged us to make all haste. "Am I a
          prophet?"
       He said, weeping, "And must I walk this road,
       The saddest of all that I have gone before?
       My son's voice calls me on. Oh quickly, quickly!
55   Look through the crevice there, and tell me
       If it is Haimon, or some deception of the gods!"

       We obeyed; and in the cavern's farthest corner
       We saw her lying:
       She had made a noose of her fine linen veil
60   And hanged herself. Haimon lay beside her,
       His arms about her waist, lamenting her,
       His love lost under ground, crying out
       That his father had stolen her away from him.

       When Kreon saw him the tears rushed to his eyes
       And he called to him: "What have you done,
65   child? speak to me.

---

27. **Pallas:** Pallas Athene, goddess of wisdom.   39–40. **Hecate
and Pluto:** Goddess of witchcraft and sorcery and King of
Hades, the underworld.

       What are you thinking that makes your eyes so
          strange?
       O my son, my son, I come to you on my knees!"
       But Haimon spat in his face. He said not a word,
       Staring—
                     And suddenly drew his sword
       And lunged. Kreon shrank back, the blade missed;
          and the boy,   70
       Desperate against himself, drove it half its length
       Into his own side, and fell. And as he died
       He gathered Antigone close in his arms again,
       Choking, his blood bright red on her white cheek.
       And now he lies dead with the dead, and she is his   75
       At last, his bride in the house of the dead.
                     (*Exit Eurydice into the palace.*)
CHORAGOS: She has left us without a word. What
       can this mean?
MESSENGER: It troubles me, too; yet she knows what
       is best,
       Her grief is too great for public lamentation,
       And doubtless she has gone to her chamber to
          weep   80
       For her dead son, leading her maidens in his dirge.

(*Pause.*)

CHORAGOS: It may be so: but I fear this deep silence.
MESSENGER: I will see what she is doing. I will go in.
                     (*Exit Messenger into the palace.*)

(*Enter Kreon with attendants, bearing Haimon's body.*)

CHORAGOS: But here is the king himself: oh look at
       him,
       Bearing his own damnation in his arms.   85
KREON: Nothing you say can touch me any more.
       My own blind heart has brought me
       From darkness to final darkness. Here you see
       The father murdering, the murdered son—
       And all my civic wisdom!   90

       Haimon my son, so young, so young to die,
       I was the fool, not you; and you died for me.
CHORAGOS: That is the truth; but you were late in
       learning it.
KREON: This truth is hard to bear. Surely a god
       Has crushed me beneath the hugest weight of
          heaven,   95
       And driven me headlong a barbaric way
       To trample out the thing I held most dear.

       The pains that men will take to come to pain!

(*Enter Messenger from the palace.*)

MESSENGER: The burden you carry in your hands is
       heavy,
       But it is not all: you will find more in your house.   100
KREON: What burden worse than this shall I find
       there?
MESSENGER: The Queen is dead.
KREON: O port of death, deaf world,

Is there no pity for me? And you, Angel of evil,
105   I was dead, and your words are death again.
Is it true, boy? Can it be true?
Is my wife dead? Has death bred death?
MESSENGER: You can see for yourself.

(*The doors are opened and the body of Eurydice is disclosed within.*)

KREON: Oh pity!
110   All true, all true, and more than I can bear!
O my wife, my son!
MESSENGER: She stood before the altar, and her heart
Welcomed the knife her own hand guided,
And a great cry burst from her lips for Megareus°
dead,
And for Haimon dead, her sons; and her last
115   breath
Was a curse for their father, the murderer of her
sons.
And she fell, and the dark flowed in through her
closing eyes.
KREON: O God, I am sick with fear.
Are there no swords here? Has no one a blow for
me?
MESSENGER: Her curse is upon you for the deaths of
120   both.

114. **Megareus:** Son of Kreon and brother of Haimon, Megareus sacrificed himself in the unsuccessful attack upon Thebes, believing that his death was necessary to save Thebes.

KREON: It is right that it should be. I alone am guilty.
I know it, and I say it. Lead me in,
Quickly, friends.
I have neither life nor substance. Lead me in.
CHORAGOS: You are right, if there can be right in so
much wrong.   125
The briefest way is best in a world of sorrow.
KREON: Let it come,
Let death come quickly, and be kind to me.
I would not ever see the sun again.
CHORAGOS: All that will come when it will; but we,
meanwhile,   130
Have much to do. Leave the future to itself.
KREON: All my heart was in that prayer!
CHORAGOS: Then do not pray any more: the sky is
deaf.
KREON: Lead me away. I have been rash and foolish.
I have killed my son and my wife.   135
I look for comfort; my comfort lies here dead.
Whatever my hands have touched has come to
nothing.
Fate has brought all my pride to a thought of
dust.

(*As Kreon is being led into the house, the Choragos advances and speaks directly to the audience.*)

CHORAGOS: There is no happiness where there is no
wisdom;
No wisdom but in submission to the gods.   140
Big words are always punished,
And proud men in old age learn to be wise.

COMMENTARIES

Oliver Taplin's emphasis on the audience's emotional state during the performance of a Greek tragedy brings us back to the seminal comments of Aristotle. Tragedies were noted for their capacity to evoke pity and fear in the audience. Taplin helps us understand how an audience's emotional response can clarify our critical view of tragedy.

Jean Anouilh, a major French playwright in the mid-twentieth century, wrote a version of *Antigone* during the Nazi occupation of Paris and much of France. The political content of the play takes on interesting meaning in light of his experience. The excerpt that appears here offers a modern interpretation of the struggle between Antigone and Kreon.

Oliver Taplin (b. 1943)
EMOTION AND MEANING IN GREEK TRAGEDY   1983

Scholar Oliver Taplin focuses on one of Aristotle's concerns in his commentary on tragedy: the emotions aroused by drama. Taplin explores the argument that devalues an emotional response to tragedy, and then he considers the proposition that "tragedy is essentially the emotional experience of its audience."

It seems to me, then, that Gorgias° is right that tragedy is essentially the *emotional experience of its audience.* Whatever it tells us about the world is conveyed by means of these emotions. Plato agreed with Gorgias in this, but he disapproved of the process and regarded it as harmful. Aristotle agreed with him too, but, contrary to Plato, regarded it as beneficial and salutary. Plato's objection was that such emotions are not the province of the highest part of the soul, the intellectual part. This is the forefather of the error made by so many later critics who have not acknowledged the centrality of emotion in the communication of tragedy. They think that if tragedy is essentially an emotional experience, it must be *solely* that; and they think this because they assume that strong emotion is necessarily in opposition to thought, that the psychic activities are mutually exclusive. But is this right? Understanding, reason, learning, moral discrimination; these things are not, in my experience, incompatible with emotion (nor presumably in the experience of Gorgias and Aristotle): What is incompatible is cold insensibility. Whether or not emotion is inimical to such intellectual processes depends on the *circumstances in which it is aroused.*

The characteristic tragic emotions—pity, horror, fascination, indignation, and so forth—are felt in many other situations besides in the theater. Above all we suffer them in the face of the misfortunes of real life, of course. What distinguishes the

---

Gorgias: Greek orator and rhetorician (c. 483–376 BCE).

experience of a great tragedy? For one thing, as already remarked, we feel for the fortunes of people who have no direct personal relation to us: While this does not decrease the intensity of the emotion, it affords us some distance and perspective. We can feel and at the same time observe from outside. But does this distinguish tragedy from other "contrived" emotional experiences (most of them tending to the anti-intellectual), for example an animal hunt, a football match, an encounter group, reading a thriller, or watching a horror movie? Well, the experience of tragedy is by no means a random series of sensations. Our emotional involvement has perspective and context at the same time, and not just in retrospect. Thus the events of the tragedy are in an ordered *sequence*, a sequence which gives shape and comprehensibility to what we feel. And, most important of all, the affairs of the characters which move us are given a moral setting which is argued and explored in the play. They act and suffer within situations of moral conflict, or social, intellectual, and theological conflict. The quality of the tragedy depends *both* on its power to arouse our emotions *and* on the setting of those emotions in a sequence of moral and intellectual complications which is set out and examined. Tragedy evokes our feelings for others, like much else; but it is distinguished by the order and significance it imparts to suffering. So if the audience is not moved, then the tragedy, however intellectual, is a total failure: If its passions are aroused, but in a thoughtless, amorphous way, then it is merely a bad tragedy, sensational, melodramatic.

Thus it is that our emotions in the theater, far from driving out thought and meaning, are indivisible from them: They are simultaneous and mutually dependent. The experience of tragedy can achieve this coherence in a way that the emotional experiences of real life generally cannot because they are too close, too cluttered with detail and partiality, to be seen in perspective. Tragedy makes us feel that we understand life in its tragic aspects. We have the sense that we can better sympathize with and cope with suffering, misfortune, and waste. It is this sense of understanding (not isolated pearls of wisdom) that is the "message" of a tragedy, that the great playwright imparts. This is well put in T. S. Eliot's° essay "Shakespeare and the Stoicism of Seneca," where he argues that it is the quality of the emotional expression rather than the quality of the philosophy which makes literature great, which makes it "strong, true and informative . . . useful and beneficial in the sense in which poetry is useful and beneficial." "All great poetry," Eliot writes, "gives the illusion of a view of life . . . for every precise emotion tends towards intellectual formulation."

T. S. Eliot: Poet and critic (1888–1965).

Jean Anouilh (1910–1987)
FROM *ANTIGONE* 1942

TRANSLATED BY LEWIS GALANTIÈRE

Jean Anouilh began writing plays in 1931. Some of his best-known works, in addition to Antigone, *are* Eurydice (1941), Orestes (1942), Medea (1946), Ring Round the Moon (1947), The Waltz of the Toreadors (1951), *and* The Lark (1952), *which is about Joan of Arc. Anouilh wrote* Antigone *in 1942 in occupied Paris and produced it with his wife in the title role in February 1944, when the*

Nazis controlled most of Europe. Kreon (spelled Creon in this excerpt) is more willing to compromise in Anouilh's version of the play, and for that reason some critics saw the play as pro-Nazi. But Anouilh's sympathies were with Antigone, who represented the anti-Nazi view of the Parisian Resistance. Throughout its early run, the play was an inspiration to the patriotic French.

This excerpt begins when Ismene returns to accept some of the responsibility for Polyneices' burial and continues through the confrontation of Haimon (Haemon in this excerpt) and Kreon to the end of the play.

(*Ismene enters through arch.*)

ISMENE (*distraught*): Antigone!

ANTIGONE (*turns to Ismene*): You, too? What do you want?

ISMENE: Oh, forgive me, Antigone. I've come back. I'll be brave. I'll go with you now.

ANTIGONE: Where will you go with me?

ISMENE (*to Creon*): Creon! If you kill her, you'll have to kill me too.

ANTIGONE: Oh, no, Ismene. Not a bit of it. I die alone. You don't think I'm going to let you die with me after what I've been through? You don't deserve it.

ISMENE: If you die, I don't want to live. I don't want to be left behind, alone.

ANTIGONE: You chose life and I chose death. Now stop blubbering. You had your chance to come with me in the black night, creeping on your hands and knees. You had your chance to claw up the earth with your nails, as I did; to get yourself caught like a thief, as I did. And you refused it.

ISMENE: Not anymore. I'll do it alone tonight.

ANTIGONE (*turns round toward Creon*): You hear that, Creon? The thing is catching! Who knows but that lots of people will catch the disease from me! What are you waiting for? Call in your guards! Come on, Creon! Show a little courage! It only hurts for a minute! Come on, cook!

CREON (*turns toward arch and calls*): Guard!

(*Guards enter through arch.*)

ANTIGONE (*in a great cry of relief*): At last, Creon!

(*Chorus enters through left arch.*)

CREON (*to the Guards*): Take her away! (*Creon goes up on top step.*)

(*Guards grasp Antigone by her arms, turn and hustle her toward the arch, right, and exeunt.° Ismene mimes horror, backs away toward the arch, left, then turns and runs out through the arch. A long pause, as Creon moves slowly downstage.*)

CHORUS (*Behind Creon. Speaks in a deliberate voice*): You are out of your mind, Creon. What have you done?

CREON (*his back to Chorus*): She had to die.

CHORUS: You must not let Antigone die. We shall carry the scar of her death for centuries.

CREON: She insisted. No man on earth was strong enough to dissuade her. Death was her purpose, whether she knew it or not. Polynices was a mere pretext. When she had to give up that pretext, she found another one—that life and happiness were tawdry things and not worth possessing. She was bent upon only one thing: to reject life and to die.

CHORUS: She is a mere child, Creon.

CREON: What do you want me to do for her? Condemn her to live?

HAEMON (*calls from offstage*): Father! (*Haemon enters through arch, right. Creon turns toward him.*)

CREON: Haemon, forget Antigone. Forget her, my dearest boy.

HAEMON: How can you talk like that?

exeunt: Latin for "they go out."

CREON (*grasps Haemon by the hands*): I did everything I could to save her, Haemon. I used every argument. I swear I did. The girl doesn't love you. She could have gone on living for you; but she refused. She wanted it this way; she wanted to die.

HAEMON: Father! The guards are dragging Antigone away! You've got to stop them! (*He breaks away from Creon.*)

CREON (*looks away from Haemon*): I can't stop them. It's too late. Antigone has spoken. The story is all over Thebes. I cannot save her now.

CHORUS: Creon, you must find a way. Lock her up. Say that she has gone out of her mind.

CREON: Everybody will know it isn't so. The nation will say that I am making an exception of her because my son loves her. I cannot.

CHORUS: You can still gain time and get her out of Thebes.

CREON: The mob already knows the truth. It is howling for her blood. I can do nothing.

HAEMON: But, Father, you are master in Thebes!

CREON: I am master under the law. Not above the law.

HAEMON: You cannot let Antigone be taken from me. I am your son!

CREON: I cannot do anything else, my poor boy. She must die and you must live.

HAEMON: Live, you say! Live a life without Antigone? A life in which I am to go on admiring you as you busy yourself about your kingdom, make your persuasive speeches, strike your attitudes? Not without Antigone. I love Antigone. I will not live without Antigone!

CREON: Haemon — you will have to resign yourself to life without Antigone. (*He moves to left of Haemon.*) Sooner or later there comes a day of sorrow in each man's life when he must cease to be a child and take up the burden of manhood. That day has come for you.

HAEMON (*backs away a step*): That giant strength, that courage. That massive god who used to pick me up in his arms and shelter me from shadows and monsters — was that you, Father? Was it of you I stood in awe? Was that man you?

CREON: For God's sake, Haemon, do not judge me! Not you, too!

HAEMON (*pleading now*): This is all a bad dream, Father. You are not yourself. It isn't true that we have been backed up against a wall, forced to surrender. We don't have to say *yes* to this terrible thing. You are still king. You are still the father I revered. You have no right to desert me, to shrink into nothingness. The world will be too bare, I shall be too alone in the world, if you force me to disown you.

CREON: The world *is* bare, Haemon, and you *are* alone. You must cease to think your father all-powerful. Look straight at me. See your father as he is. That is what it means to grow up and be a man.

HAEMON (*stares at Creon for a moment*): I tell you that I will not live without Antigone. (*Turns and goes quickly out through arch.*)

CHORUS: Creon, the boy will go mad.

CREON: Poor boy! He loves her.

CHORUS: Creon, the boy is wounded to death.

CREON: We are all wounded to death.

(*First Guard enters through arch, right, followed by Second and Third Guards pulling Antigone along with them.*)

FIRST GUARD: Sir, the people are crowding into the palace!

ANTIGONE: Creon, I don't want to see their faces. I don't want to hear them howl. You are going to kill me; let that be enough. I want to be alone until it is over.

CREON: Empty the palace! Guards at the gates!

(*Creon quickly crosses toward the arch; exit. Two Guards release Antigone; exeunt behind Creon. Chorus goes out through arch, left. The lighting dims so that only the area about the table is lighted. The cyclorama° is covered with a dark blue color. The scene is intended to suggest a prison cell, filled with shadows and dimly lit. Antigone moves to stool and sits. The First Guard stands upstage. He watches Antigone, and as she sits, he begins pacing slowly downstage, then upstage. A pause.*)

cyclorama: Curved cloth or wall forming the back of many modern stage settings.

ANTIGONE (*turns and looks at the Guard*): It's you, is it?

GUARD: What do you mean, me?

ANTIGONE: The last human face that I shall see. (*A pause as they look at each other, then Guard paces upstage, turns, and crosses behind table.*) Was it you that arrested me this morning?

GUARD: Yes, that was me.

ANTIGONE: You hurt me. There was no need for you to hurt me. Did I act as if I was try-ing to escape?

GUARD: Come on now, Miss. It was my business to bring you in. I did it. (*A pause. He paces to and fro upstage. Only the sound of his boots is heard.*)

ANTIGONE: How old are you?

GUARD: Thirty-nine.

ANTIGONE: Have you any children?

GUARD: Yes. Two.

ANTIGONE: Do you love your children?

GUARD: What's that got to do with you? (*A pause. He paces upstage and downstage.*)

ANTIGONE: How long have you been in the Guard?

GUARD: Since the war. I was in the army. Sergeant. Then I joined the Guard.

ANTIGONE: Does one have to have been an army sergeant to get into the Guard?

GUARD: Supposed to be. Either that or on special detail. But when they make you a guard, you lose your stripes.

ANTIGONE (*murmurs*): I see.

GUARD: Yes. Of course, if you're a guard, everybody knows you're something special; they know you're an old N.C.O.° Take pay, for instance. When you're a guard you get your pay, and on top of that you get six months' extra pay, to make sure you don't lose anything by not being a sergeant anymore. And of course you do better than that. You get a house, coal, rations, extras for the wife and kids. If you've got two kids, like me, you draw better than a sergeant.

ANTIGONE (*barely audible*): I see.

GUARD: That's why sergeants, now, they don't like guards. Maybe you noticed they try to make out they're better than us? Promotion, that's what it is. In the army, any-body can get promoted. All you need is good conduct. Now in the Guard, it's slow, and you have to know your business—like how to make out a report and the like of that. But when you're an N.C.O. in the Guard, you've got something that even a ser-geant major ain't got. For instance—

ANTIGONE (*breaking him off*): Listen.

GUARD: Yes, Miss.

ANTIGONE: I'm going to die soon.

(*The Guard looks at her for a moment, then turns and moves away.*)

GUARD: For instance, people have a lot of respect for guards, they have. A guard may be a soldier, but he's kind of in the civil service, too.

ANTIGONE: Do you think it hurts to die?

GUARD: How would I know? Of course, if somebody sticks a saber in your guts and turns it round, it hurts.

ANTIGONE: How are they going to put me to death?

GUARD: Well, I'll tell you. I heard the proclamation all right. Wait a minute. How did it go now? (*He stares into space and recites from memory.*) "In order that our fair city shall not be pol-luted with her sinful blood, she shall be im-mured—immured." That means, they shove you in a cave and wall up the cave.

ANTIGONE: Alive?

GUARD: Yes. . . . (*He moves away a few steps.*)

ANTIGONE (*murmurs*): O tomb! O bridal bed! Alone! (*Antigone sits there, a tiny figure in the middle of the stage. You would say she felt a little chilly. She wraps her arms round herself.*)

N.C.O.: Noncommissioned officer, usually of a subordinate rank such as sergeant.

GUARD: Yes! Outside the southeast gate of the town. In the Cave of Hades. In broad daylight. Some detail, eh, for them that's on the job! First they thought maybe it was a job for the army. Now it looks like it's going to be the Guard. There's an outfit for you! Nothing the Guard can't do. No wonder the army's jealous.

ANTIGONE: A pair of animals.

GUARD: What do you mean, a pair of animals?

ANTIGONE: When the winds blow cold, all they need do is to press close against one another. I am all alone.

GUARD: Is there anything you want? I can send out for it, you know.

ANTIGONE: You are very kind. (*A pause. Antigone looks up at the Guard.*) Yes, there is something I want. I want you to give someone a letter from me, when I am dead.

GUARD: How's that again? A letter?

ANTIGONE: Yes, I want to write a letter; and I want you to give it to someone for me.

GUARD (*straightens up*): Now, wait a minute. Take it easy. It's as much as my job is worth to go handing out letters from prisoners.

ANTIGONE (*removes a ring from her finger and holds it out toward him*): I'll give you this ring if you will do it.

GUARD: Is it gold? (*He takes the ring from her.*)

ANTIGONE: Yes, it is gold.

GUARD (*shakes his head*): Uh-uh. No can do. Suppose they go through my pockets. I might get six months for a thing like that. (*He stares at the ring, then glances off right to make sure that he is not being watched.*) Listen, tell you what I'll do. You tell me what you want to say, and I'll write it down in my book. Then, afterwards, I'll tear out the pages and give them to the party, see? If it's in my handwriting, it's all right.

ANTIGONE (*winces*): In your handwriting? (*She shudders slightly.*) No. That would be awful. The poor darling! In your handwriting.

GUARD (*offers back the ring*): O.K. It's no skin off my nose.

ANTIGONE (*quickly*): Of course, of course. No, keep the ring. But hurry. Time is getting short. Where is your notebook? (*The Guard pockets the ring, takes his notebook and pencil from his pocket, puts his foot up on chair, and rests the notebook on his knee, licks his pencil.*) Ready? (*He nods.*) Write, now. "My darling . . ."

GUARD (*writes as he mutters*): The boyfriend, eh?

ANTIGONE: "My darling. I wanted to die, and perhaps you will not love me anymore..."

GUARD (*mutters as he writes*): ". . . will not love me anymore."

ANTIGONE: "Creon was right. It is terrible to die."

GUARD (*repeats as he writes*): ". . . terrible to die."

ANTIGONE: "And I don't even know what I am dying for. I am afraid . . ."

GUARD (*looks at her*): Wait a minute! How fast do you think I can write?

ANTIGONE (*takes hold of herself*): Where are you?

GUARD (*reads from his notebook*): "And I don't even know what I am dying for."

ANTIGONE: No. Scratch that out. Nobody must know that. They have no right to know. It's as if they saw me naked and touched me, after I was dead. Scratch it all out. Just write: "Forgive me."

GUARD (*looks at Antigone*): I cut out everything you said there at the end, and I put down, "Forgive me"?

ANTIGONE: Yes. "Forgive me, my darling. You would all have been so happy except for Antigone. I love you."

GUARD (*finishes the letter*): ". . . I love you." (*He looks at her.*) Is that all?

ANTIGONE: That's all.

GUARD (*straightens up, looks at notebook*): Damn funny letter.

ANTIGONE: I know.

GUARD (*looks at her*): Who is it to? (*A sudden roll of drums begins and continues until after Antigone's exit. The First Guard pockets the notebook and shouts at Antigone.*) O.K. That's enough out of you! Come on!

(*At the sound of the drum roll, Second and Third Guards enter through the arch. Antigone rises. Guards seize her and exeunt with her. The lighting moves up to suggest late afternoon. Chorus enters.*)

CHORUS: And now it is Creon's turn.

(*Messenger runs through the arch, right.*)

MESSENGER: The Queen . . . the Queen! Where is the Queen?

CHORUS: What do you want with the Queen? What have you to tell the Queen?

MESSENGER: News to break her heart. Antigone had just been thrust into the cave. They hadn't finished heaving the last block of stone into place when Creon and the rest heard a sudden moaning from the tomb. A hush fell over us all, for it was not the voice of Antigone. It was Haemon's voice that came forth from the tomb. Everybody looked at Creon; and he howled like a man demented: "Take away the stones! Take away the stones!" The slaves leaped at the wall of stones, and Creon worked with them, sweating and tearing at the blocks with his bleeding hands. Finally a narrow opening was forced, and into it slipped the smallest guard.

Antigone had hanged herself by the cord of her robe, by the red and golden twisted cord of her robe. The cord was round her neck like a child's collar. Haemon was on his knees, holding her in his arms and moaning, his face buried in her robe. More stones were removed, and Creon went into the tomb. He tried to raise Haemon to his feet. I could hear him begging Haemon to rise to his feet. Haemon was deaf to his father's voice, till suddenly he stood up of his own accord, his eyes dark and burning. Anguish was in his face, but it was the face of a little boy. He stared at his father. Then suddenly he struck him—hard; and he drew his sword. Creon leaped out of range. Haemon went on staring at him, his eyes full of contempt— a glance that was like a knife, and that Creon couldn't escape. The King stood trembling in the far corner of the tomb, and Haemon went on staring. Then, without a word, he stabbed himself and lay down beside Antigone, embracing her in a great pool of blood.

(*A pause as Creon and Page enter through arch on the Messenger's last words. Chorus and the Messenger both turn to look at Creon; then exit the Messenger through curtain.*)

CREON: I have had them laid out side by side. They are together at last, and at peace. Two lovers on the morrow of their bridal. Their work is done.

CHORUS: But not yours, Creon. You have still one thing to learn. Eurydice, the Queen, your wife—

CREON: A good woman. Always busy with her garden, her preserves, her sweaters— those sweaters she never stopped knitting for the poor. Strange, how the poor never stop needing sweaters. One would almost think that was all they needed.

CHORUS: The poor in Thebes are going to be cold this winter, Creon. When the Queen was told of her son's death, she waited carefully until she had finished her row, then put down her knitting calmly—as she did everything. She went up to her room, her lavender-scented room, with its embroidered doilies and its pictures framed in plush; and there, Creon, she cut her throat. She is laid out now in one of those two old-fashioned twin beds, exactly where you went to her one night when she was still a maiden. Her smile is still the same, scarcely a shade more melancholy. And if it were not for that great red blot on the bed linen by her neck, one might think she was asleep.

CREON (*in a dull voice*): She, too. They are all asleep. (*Pause.*) It must be good to sleep.

CHORUS: And now you are alone, Creon.

CREON: Yes, all alone. (*To Page.*) My lad.

PAGE: Sir?

CREON: Listen to me. They don't know it, but the truth is, the work is there to be done, and a man can't fold his arms and refuse to do it. They say it's dirty work. But if we didn't do it, who would?

PAGE: I don't know, sir.

CREON: Of course you don't. You'll be lucky if you never find out. In a hurry to grow up, aren't you?

PAGE: Oh, yes, sir.

CREON: I shouldn't be if I were you. Never grow up if you can help it. (*He is lost in thought as the hour chimes.*) What time is it?

PAGE: Five o clock, sir.

CREON: What have we on at five o'clock?

PAGE: Cabinet meeting, sir.

CREON: Cabinet meeting. Then we had better go along to it.

(*Exeunt Creon and Page slowly through arch, left, and Chorus moves downstage.*)

CHORUS: And there we are. It is quite true that if it had not been for Antigone they would all have been at peace. But that is over now. And they are all at peace. All those who were meant to die have died: those who believed one thing, those who believed the contrary thing, and even those who believed nothing at all, yet were caught up in the web without knowing why. All dead: stiff, useless, rotting. And those who have survived will now begin quietly to forget the dead: they won't remember who was who or which was which. It is all over. Antigone is calm tonight, and we shall never know the name of the fever that consumed her. She has played her part.

(*Three Guards enter, resume their places on steps as at the rise of the curtain, and begin to play cards.*)

A great melancholy wave of peace now settles down upon Thebes, upon the empty palace, upon Creon, who can now begin to wait for his own death. Only the guards are left, and none of this matters to them. It's no skin off their noses. They go on playing cards.

(*Chorus walks toward the arch, left, as the curtain falls.*)

Euripides

Euripides (c. 485–c. 406 BCE), last of the great Greek tragedians, did not enjoy the personal popularity accorded Aeschylus and Sophocles, possibly because his work criticized Athenian politics and society. Moreover, he was not highly regarded because he broke away from the formality of language and theme of his predecessors.

Euripides was raised in Salamis, the island from which the Greeks decisively defeated the Persians in 480 BCE. This victory heralded the Periclean Age (c. 462–404 BCE), when Athens enjoyed its greatest power. During that time, however, the Athenians spent almost three decades fighting the Peloponnesian Wars (431–404 BCE), which drained their energies and treasury. Eventually, they were forced to relinquish their dominance to Sparta. In such an environment, the officials and patriots of Athens were not happy with the work of someone who reminded them of their mistakes and questioned their values.

Euripides is especially noted for shifting the focus of dramatic events from the gods to humans. He valued individual human beings and the working of their wills. Influenced by the teaching of the Sophists, wandering professors who taught argument and philosophy, he agreed with Protagoras's principle "Man is the measure of all things." The ancients sometimes referred to Euripides as the philosopher of the stage.

One aspect of his dramatic critique of Greek culture was an unusual emphasis on women. Medea is the first thoroughly developed female character in Greek drama. She is treated as an independent woman, not just as Jason's wife or as someone's mother. She is herself. Athenians, intolerant of foreigners and women, felt both groups to be inferior to Greek aristocratic men. It is no wonder that of the twenty plays Euripides produced at the feasts of Dionysus, only five won prizes.

Of his ninety-two plays, eighteen survive — more than twice as many as survive from any other Greek tragedian: *Alcestis* (438), *Medea* (431), *The Children of Heracles* (c. 430), *Hippolytus* (428), *Andromache* (426?), *Hecuba* (c. 424), *Cyclops* (c. 423), *The Suppliants* (c. 422), *Electra* (c. 417), *Heracles* (c. 417), *The Trojan Women* (415), *Helen* (412), *Iphigenia in Taurus* (c. 412), *The Phoenician Women* (c. 412–408), *Ion* (c. 411), *Orestes* (408), *The Bacchae* (405), and *Iphigenia in Aulis* (405). Another play, *Rhesus,* long attributed to Euripides, is now thought to have been written by an anonymous fourth-century BCE playwright. Ten of Euripides' surviving plays place women at their center.

Euripides continued Aeschylus's innovations in his use of the *skene.* Instead of representing the front of a palace, the *skene* in Euripides' plays sometimes represented a peasant's hut, a rural shrine, or other common structure. He was interested in theatrical devices, especially machines that gave him the opportunity to achieve dramatic effects. He often used the *mekane*—a crane or derrick that lifted actors in or out of the play—to resolve his dramas when his characters found themselves in impossible situations. His choral odes, although beautiful, are sometimes considered detachable from the episodes of dramatic action. Moreover, his dialogue is more colloquial—closer to everyday speech—than is the dialogue found in other Greek tragedies. All these deviations from the dramatic norm emphasize the humanity in his plays and elevate human values over those of the gods.

Eighteen months before his death, Euripides left Athens for the court of King Archelaus in Macedon. His departure may have signaled his dissatisfaction with the politics of Athens, or it may have been prompted by the indifference of Athens to his talents. In any event, his works were performed long after his death, and, ironically, his posthumous popularity dwarfed that of the other tragic playwrights.

MEDEA

Although *Medea* won only last prize at the City Dionysia festival in 431 BCE, behind works by Euphorion (son of Aeschylus) and Sophocles, the play's emotional dimension and Medea's depth of feeling have made her one of the most impressive characters in dramatic fiction.

In his first play, *The Daughters of Pelias* (454 BCE), Euripides treated part of the well-known legend of Jason and Medea. On the order of his enemy, King Pelias of Iolcus, Jason sailed with the Argonauts to Colchis. There, with the help of Medea's witchcraft, he retrieved the Golden Fleece. Medea returned with Jason to Iolcus, where she convinced Pelias's daughters that they could restore their father's youth if they cut him into pieces and boiled the pieces with magic herbs, as she had done with a ram. When the daughters tried it, however, the treacherous Medea gave them impotent herbs, and Pelias died. Jason's Argonauts captured Iolcus, and Medea and Jason escaped to Corinth.

Euripides continued the tale in *Medea*. When the play opens, Jason and Medea are in exile in Corinth. Jason has decided to marry King Creon's daughter Glauke, supposedly to guarantee the safety of the children he has had with Medea. Considering all the sacrifices she has made for Jason, Medea feels betrayed and cast aside for a younger woman. Medea's situation is painful. The Chorus recognizes the legality of Jason's decision to put aside his wife in favor of a younger woman. His motives might be interpreted as plausible and perhaps noble. Medea is Asiatic, a foreigner. By marrying Glauke, Jason will confer noble status on his and Medea's children. By law he can maintain Medea as a concubine along with his wife. Medea knows this, but she rejects Jason's explanations. He assumes that she is merely sexually jealous of Glauke.

The themes of this tragedy are certainly accessible to modern audiences. As the critic G.M.A. Grube has pointed out, "The tragedy of *Medea*—of Love turning to hatred when betrayed, until the woman's whole soul is dominated by a lust for vengeance that overpowers even maternal love—is one which no modern reader should, in its essentials, find difficult to make his own." The modern audience, however, may take pause at Medea's revenge. She plans not only to rid Jason of his young bride but to kill Creon as well. And her vengeance does not stop there: she determines to kill those whom Jason most loves—their two sons.

Exploring Medea's feelings and her awareness of the gravity of her actions sets Euripides' work apart from that of other Greek tragedians. His sympathy for the many tragic heroines he created marks his work from beginning to end. Unlike other playwrights working with the Medea legend, Euripides saves Medea from the punishment of Jason and the people of Corinth. To do this, he uses the *mekane,* in the form of the dragon chariot that lifts her above the *skene* beyond Jason's reach at the end of the play. She leaves him in an agony of grief.

Medea in Performance

Medea has one of the longest and most active production histories in all of drama. Not only did Alexander the Great produce the play in the fourth century BCE, but the Roman playwright Seneca wrote his own version (60 CE), with a much less sympathetic Medea. Seneca's Jason is a reasonable man unfairly wronged by a witch. French and English productions and adaptations began in 1553 and have continued to the present. The French playwright Corneille wrote his version in 1634, and an English version of 1756 portrays Medea as insane.

Important modern productions began in the early twentieth century. The American actress Margaret Anglin was a sensation in the 1918 production, which established her as the greatest Medea up to her time. Hans Henny Jahnne adapted *Medea* for a production in Berlin in 1926. According to a review written at the time, Medea was portrayed by an older black actress whose magic potions kept Jason young while she aged. The poisoned robe Medea gave to her young rival had the power to turn the princess into an elderly woman "who gradually [grew] older and older and [decayed] into death and decomposition."

Judith Anderson made the role hers in 1947, in a version by the American poet Robinson Jeffers that played for almost a decade. In the 1982 production with John Gielgud as Jason and Zoë Caldwell as Medea, a much older Judith Anderson played the nurse and received extraordinary reviews. In 1974 Greek actress Irene Papas starred in New York in a colloquial English version. Important productions were staged in Russia in the 1960s. Countee Cullen very successfully produced the play in 1959 with a black Medea. In 1986, an all-male Kabuki version of *Medea* was presented at the Delacorte Theater in Central Park by the Japanese Toho Company under the direction of Yukio Ninagawa. A critic from the *New York Times* described the director's intentions: "Yukio

Ninagawa, known for his productions of classical theater as avant-garde spectacle, aims in his work to create a universal theater that fuses the traditions of Japanese and Western culture in an expressive style of its own" (Jennifer Dunning, *New York Times,* Aug. 31, 1986). A *Boston Globe* critic praised the power of the Kabuki production: "This was a Medea of stunning theatrical imagery. Classical Corinthian order was gradually and relentlessly replaced by savage revenge and blood-stained chaos" (Lyn Gardner, *Boston Globe,* Aug. 29, 1986). In April 1994 Diana Rigg was Medea in a production highly praised in both London and New York. She was seen as commanding and powerful in the part, played starkly and simply. The recent production at Dublin's Abbey Theatre, in 2000, used a new translation by Kenneth McLeish and Frederic Raphael and employed a modernized setting that brought the play into the early years of the twenty-first century. Directed by Deborah Warner and starring Fiona Shaw as Medea, this production and Shaw's performance received rave reviews. When the production came to the United States in 2002, a *New York Times* critic summed up the power of this new interpretation: "The miracle of this *Medea* is how completely it integrates its ideas of a latter-day culture of celebrity into a classic text . . . without ever seeming to warp the spirit of the original. . . . Ms. Shaw and Ms. Warner have created one of the most human Medeas ever, precisely because they have refused to simplify her" (see the review on pages 161 to 163).

Euripides (c. 485–406 BCE)

MEDEA   431 BCE

TRANSLATED BY PAUL ROCHE

Characters

NURSE
TUTOR *to Medea's sons*
MEDEA, *Asiatic princess*
CHORUS *of Corinthian women*
CREON, *King of Corinth*
JASON, *husband of Medea*
AEGEUS, *King of Athens*
MESSENGER
TWO BOYS, *sons of Medea*
HANDMAIDS *of Medea*
ATTENDANTS AND GUARDS *for Creon and Aegeus*

Time and Setting: *It is midmorning outside Jason's house in Corinth. Ten years have passed since the Argonauts sailed home after finding the Golden Fleece. During that time, Jason and Medea [the Asian bride he brought back with him] have been living modestly in Corinth: models of an unassailable married life of devotion to each other and their children. But the news has just broken that Jason is to marry the daughter of the*

King of Corinth. [The exit on stage left leads to the town and royal palace, that on the right to the country.]

[Enter the Nurse from the house. She is an old woman who has looked after Medea from babyhood. Her face, the only part of her showing from the dark, heavy clothes that envelop her, is puckered with age and distress.]

PROLOGUE°

NURSE: Why did the winged oars of the Argo°
    ever weave between those gnashing blue
    fjords towards the land of Colchis?
        Why did the pines in the dells of Pelion°

[**Prologue:** Portion of the play explaining the background and current action. (The editor's notes are in brackets.)]   **1. Argo:** The ship in which Jason and his companions sailed on the quest for the Golden Fleece.   **4. Pelion:** A mountain in northern Greece.

5   ever fall to the axe and fill
the rowing hands of heroes sent by Pelias°
to fetch the Golden Fleece?
     My mistress, Medea, then
never would have sailed to Iolcus° with its towers

10   or been struck to the heart with love of Jason.
     She never would have baited Pelias' daughters
to the murder of their father°
and be living here in Corinth° now
with her husband and her children . . .

15   Ah, she has merited this city's good opinion,
exile though she came,
and was in everything Jason's perfect foil,
being in marriage that saving thing:
a wife who does not go against her man.

[*With a despairing glance toward the house.*]

20   Now everything has turned to hate,
her passion to a plague.
     Jason has betrayed his sons and her,
takes to bed a royal bride
Creon's daughter—the king of Corinth's.

25   Medea, spurned and desolate,
breaks out in oaths,
invokes the solemnest vows,
calls the gods to witness
how Jason has rewarded her.

30   She does not eat,
lies prostrate, slumped in anguish,
wastes away in day-long tears.
     Ever since she heard of Jason's perfidy
she has not raised her eyes

35   or looked up from the floor.
     She might be a rock or wave of the sea,
for all she heeds of sympathy from friends,
except sometimes to tilt her pale head away
and moan to herself about her father—

40   whom she loved—
and her country and the home she sacrificed°
to journey here
with a man—oh—who so disdains her now.
     Yes, now she knows

at a terrible first hand   45
what it is to miss one's native land.

[*She pauses; almost whispers the next words.*]

     She hates her sons.
Takes no pleasure in their sight.
I dread to think
of what is hatching in her mind.   50
She is a fierce spirit:
takes no insult lying down.
I know her well. She frightens me:°
a dangerous woman, and
anyone who crosses her   55
will not easily sing a song of triumph.
     But here come the boys after their run:
suspecting nothing of a mother's tragedy . . .
     Oh, it is true—
unhappy thoughts and youth never go together.   60

[*Enter Tutor with Two Boys, aged about eight and ten. Tutor is an old man, dressed loosely in an ocher-colored cloak. The boys are squeezed into shorts and have close-fitting woolen caps on their heads. They hang about in the background, laughing and talking, while the old man advances.*]

TUTOR [*with a half-teasing familiarity*]:   Ah, Nurse!
     Faithful old appendage of my Lady's home,
what are you doing here all forlorn,
standing moaning to yourself outside the gates?
     Does Medea really want to be left alone?   65
NURSE: Ah, dogged old pedagogue of Jason's sons,
when a master's fortunes are struck down
the heart of a faithful slave is stricken too.
     I am plunged in such a depth of grief
I came out here to tell the earth and sky   70
Medea's catastrophe.
TUTOR: What! Has the poor woman not stopped her
        crying yet?
NURSE: Stopped! You amaze me.
     Her ordeal, far from halfway done,
hardly has begun.   75
TUTOR: Poor innocent fool—to be quite frank about
        our mistress—
she knows little of the latest blow.
NURSE: Latest? What's that, old man?
     Don't keep it from me.
TUTOR: Nothing, nothing . . . I'm sorry I even spoke.   80
NURSE: Come now, we're both slaves here, are we not?
     By your own gray beard, do not hold it back . . .
I can keep a secret if I must.

---

6. Pelias: When Jason came to claim the kingdom of Iolcus, from which Pelias had expelled Jason's father, Pelias sent Jason to get the Golden Fleece. **9. Iolcus:** Town from which the Argonauts sailed. **11–12. She never . . . murder of their father:** Medea, a sorceress by reputation, tricked Pelias's daughters into cutting their father into pieces and boiling them, on the pretext that this would magically restore him to youth. This was her revenge on Pelias, who had murdered Jason's father, Aeson, during Jason's absence on the quest for the Golden Fleece, which was successful. **13. be living here in Corinth:** Expelled from the kingdom [of Iolcus], Jason and Medea took refuge in Corinth, a wealthy city and rival of Athens, located on the isthmus between the Peloponnese and Attica. **41. home she sacrificed:** Medea had helped Jason take the Golden Fleece away from her own father's kingdom.

53. She frightens me: [The translator notes that he has omitted four lines bracketed by many editors as doubtful (lines 40–43 in the original Greek text).] Dramatically, they are certainly a mistake: *"I am frightened she will slip / into the palace unawares, / and in the nuptial bedroom / ram a sharp knife into Jason's side, / or even kill the King as well as bridegroom / and get herself a far worse doom."*

TUTOR: Well, I'd gone to where the old dice-players sit,
85   near Pirene's sacred fountain,
     and there I overheard (pretending not to listen)
     someone say:
          "Creon, this country's king,
     is making plans to drive these boys from Corinth—
90   their mother too"—
     I don't know if the story's true.
          I hope that it is not.
NURSE: No, surely no?
     Jason would not let his sons be treated so,
95   however far he's parted from their mother.
TUTOR [grimly]: Old loves are left behind by new.
     That man is not this house's friend.
NURSE: We're all finished, then—
     if we ship this second wave
100 before we've bailed the first.
TUTOR: Now listen—
     this is not the time to let our mistress know.
     Just keep quiet about it—not a word.
NURSE [with an anguished glance over her shoulder,
     in a whisper]: Poor little boys,
105 do you hear how much your father's worth to you?
          I wish he were . . .

[Checks herself.]

     no, not dead, he is my master still . . .
     but, oh, what an enemy he's proved
     to those he should have loved!
110 TUTOR: What human being is not?
          Is this news to you,
     that every person's dearest neighbor is himself:
     some rightly so, some out of greed and selfishness.
          This father does not love his sons, but—
115 his new wedding bed.
NURSE: Come along, boys, into the house.
     Everything is going to be all right.

[Dropping her voice.]

     Keep them away as much as you can.
     Do not let them near their mother
120 so long as she is in this deadly mood.
          Already I have caught her eyes on them:
     the eyes of a mad bull.
          There's something she is plotting
     and her fury won't lie down—this I know—
125 until the lightning strikes and someone's felled.
          Let us hope it's enemies, not friends.

[A long-drawn-out sob—Medea's—is heard from the
house.]°

MEDEA: I am so unhappy—oh!
     the misery of it! I wish I were dead.
NURSE [hustling the children toward the door]:
     Listen—there . . . poor children, your mother,

126. The next 116 lines in the Greek [to the end of the Parodos]
are cast in a different meter, which [the translator] transposed
into the nearest English equivalent.

Raking her heart up, raking her rage.   130
Quick, inside: into the house.
Don't come anywhere near her sight.
Don't approach. Beware, watch out
For her savage mood, destructive spleen:
Yes and her implacable will.   135
Off with you now; hurry inside.
Soon, I know, her fury will flare
Out from the slowly gathering cloud.
What will she perpetrate then, I fear—
Proud, importunate willful soul—   140
     So bitterly spurned.

                         [Exeunt° Tutor and Boys.]

[A long-suppressed shout is heard from inside: Medea's
voice.]

MEDEA: Oh, what misery! Oh, what pain!
     Cursed sons, and a mother for cursing!
     Death take you all—you and your father:
          The whole house wither.   145
NURSE [sobbing]: Oh, how it grieves me!
     Why make the sons
          share in their father's
     Guilt? Oh, why
          should they be hated?   150
Poor young children, your danger appals me.
Ruthless is the temper of royalty:
Often commanding, seldom commanded;
Terribly slow to forgive and forget.
How much better to live among equals.   155
I want no part of greatness and glory:
Let me decline in a safe old age.
The very name of the "middle way"
Has health in it: is best for man.
Good never comes from overreaching,   160
And when it provokes the gods, it destroys
     All the more thoroughly.

PARODOS OR ENTRY SONG

[The Chorus of Corinthian women enters, full of apprehension and concern for Medea.]

CHORUS: I heard her voice, I heard her shout,
     It was the most unhappy
Woman from Colchis—far from calm yet—
     But tell me, old Nurse.
From the porch of the house, it moaned outside.   5
     O women, I cannot delight
In the pain of Jason's house:
A house I have loved very well.
NURSE: House there is none: life of it gone.
     The master is had . . . by a princess's bed.   10
The mistress in her boudoir pines.
There are no words her friends can find
     To touch her disconsolate heart.

[141. (S.D.) Exeunt: Latin for "they go out."]

MEDEA [*in another spasm*]: Ahhh!
15 Cleave my brain with a flash from the sky.
What good is left for me in living?
Alas! Alas! Come Death, unloose
My life from a life I loathe.

[*Strophe*]°

CHORUS: Listen, O Zeus and Earth and Light
20   To the stricken tune of this plangent° wife.
And you, loveless lady,
What yearning for love on a bed of delight
Could make you hurry to death, the night?
      Pray not for that.
25   If your husband has gone to adore
A new bride in his bed, why, this
Has often happened before.
Do not harrow your soul. For Zeus
Will succor your cause. What use
30   To lessen your life with grief
For a lost lord?
MEDEA [*from inside*]: O mighty Themis,° and
      Artemis,° Queen,
For all the fine vows I bound him with,
See what my hated husband has done.
35 Grant me to watch him, at last, with his bride,
Palace and all, crumble in ruin.
How dare they do to me what they have done!
O Father, my country, the land I abandoned,
Flagrantly killing my brother.°
40 NURSE: Hear what she says
      with her cry from the heart
To Themis and Zeus:
      (goddess of rights
And he whom mankind
45   makes keeper of vows.)
Certainly soon
      in no small way
Her fury will play itself out.

[*Antistrophe*]°

CHORUS: If she would come out and, face to face,
50   Listen to what we have to say,
      She might let go
This rampant anger, spite of soul.
I hope I never fail my friends.
So go, Nurse, entice her to come:

[**Strophe**: Song sung by the Chorus as it danced from stage right
to stage left.] **20. plangent**: Lamenting. **32. Themis**: Justice.
Artemis: Guardian of women. Called Diana by the Romans.
39. killing my brother: Medea slew her brother Absyrtus when
she escaped with Jason and tossed him piecemeal over the side
of the ship, knowing that their pursuers would stop to pick the
pieces up. [**Antistrophe**: Song sung by the Chorus following
the Strophe, as it danced back from stage left to stage right.]

Say we are *with* her: we are her friends. 55
Hurry, before she does any harm
      To those inside . . .
Grief can swell to enormity.
NURSE [*walking to the door*]: I'll do my best, but am
      afraid I 60
May *not* be able to persuade My Lady; and yet
      I am glad to shoulder the burden;
Although she glares with a bull-mad gaze
(Or is it a lioness with her whelps)
When anyone comes or speaks or helps. 65

[*She turns at the door.*]

Oh, botchers and blunderers! Yes,
That's what they were, those artists of old:
Makers of music for life and joy,
For grand celebrations and groaning boards;
But, oh, nothing for sorrow and pain: 70
No music or song on hand-plucked lyre
      For the thing that brings death
And terrible endings to many a home.

Oh, what a blessing is missed
      by having no music for this! 75
What a waste of it, then
      by singing in vain,
When fullness at feasts
      is its own joy and gain.

[*Exit Nurse into the house.*]

CHORUS: Deep is her sobbing from depths of pain: 80
Shrill the news her suffering brings
Of marriage betrayed, a love gone wrong.
      Outraged, she
            importunate prays
To Themis, the daughter of Zeus:
Keeper of vows, who sailed her through 85
      Those dangerous straits and the night
To Hellas° across the salt of the sea.

FIRST EPISODE

[*Medea enters from the house, colorfully, even opu-
lently, dressed. She is wan and her eyes are red with
weeping, but she is surprisingly calm and in control.*]

MEDEA: Women of Corinth, be indulgent, please:
I have obeyed you and come out.
      The charge of aloofness—as I know too well—
is something often leveled
at both the retiring and the busy man. 5
      He who chooses a quiet life
has this alleged against him too:
laziness and lack of spirit.
      Yes, public opinion has most shallow eyes.
People hate at sight 10

87. Hellas: Greece.

a harmless human being,
knowing nothing of the real man.
    I agree, of course,
that a foreigner should conform,
15 adapt to his society . . .
and a citizen is censurable no less
when too self-centered or uncouth
to avoid offending his companions.
    Nevertheless, I . . .

[She breaks off with a pang.]

20 I . . . out of a clear sky
have been struck a blow that breaks my heart.
    My friends, it is over.
    I want to die.
    Life has lost all point.
25   The man who was my life
—and he knows it too—
has become for me beneath contempt.

[She surveys the women.]

    Of all the creatures that can feel and think,
we women are the worst-treated things alive.
30   To begin with,
we bid the highest price in dowries
just to buy some man
to be dictator of our bodies . . .
    How that compounds the wrong!
35   Then there is the terrifying risk:
Shall we get a good man or a bad?
    Divorce is a disgrace
(at least for women),
to repudiate the man, not possible.
40   So, plunged into habits new to her,
conventions she has never known at home,
she has to guess like some clairvoyant
how to handle the man who shares her bed.
    And if we learn our lesson well
45 in this exacting role,
and our husband does not kick against the
        marriage yoke,
oh, ours is an enviable life!
    Otherwise, we are better dead.
    When a man gets bored with wife and home,
50 he simply roams abroad,
relieves the tedium of his spirit:
turns to a friend or finds his cronies.
    We women, on the other hand,
turn only to a single man.
55   We live safe at home, they say.
They do battle with the spear.
    How superficial!
I had rather stand my ground three times among
        the shields
than face a childbirth once.
60   Anyway,
your case and mine are not the same.
    You have your city.
    You have your father's home.

Life offers you the sweet fellowship of friends.
    I am alone,   65
without a city, wronged by a husband,
uprooted from a foreign land.
    I have no mother, brother, cousin;
am without a haven from this storm.
    So, please, I ask you this: 70
if I can find a way to pay my husband back—
your silence.
    Woman, on the whole, is a timid thing:
the din of war, the flash of steel, unnerves her;
but, wronged in love,   75
there is no heart more murderous.
LEADER: As you wish, Medea.
    You have a score to settle with your lord.
    I do not wonder that you smart . . .
    But, look, I see Creon coming: 80
this country's king—
bristling, I dare say, with new decisions.

*[Enter Creon with attendants. He is a bearded man of
about sixty, royally but modestly dressed. His face
wears a look of troubled resolution.]*

CREON: Go, Medea. Remove yourself.
    Get packing from this land.
    I order you—   85
you with your black-faced fury
lowering against your lord.
    And take your brace of offspring with you;
no dallying either.
    I am here to see this order done,   90
and until I've pushed you out and over the border,
I'll not go home.
MEDEA: So.
    I am lost—crushed utterly.
    My enemies let out the sail,   95
while I have no place to disembark from doom.
    Nevertheless, hard-pressed as I am,
I ask you this:
    For what reason, Creon, do you drive me out?
CREON: Fear: 100
no need to camouflage the fact;
I am afraid you'll deal my child some lethal
        blow . . .
and many things conspire to make me fear.
    You are a woman of some knowledge,
versed in many an unsavory skill.   105
    Your husband's gone:
your soul is raw with loss of love . . .
and now it is reported that you threaten me:
mean to hurt the father of the bride
and of course the bride and groom.   110
    That is what I want to guard against—
an accident.
    Madam, better to be hated now by you
than soften and pay later with regrets.
MEDEA *[exchanging a look with the Chorus]*:
    Heaven help me!   115
    My reputation is a curse:

        This is not the only time it has done me lasting
            harm.
            Oh, let the perspicacious man
        keep his children from enlightenment—
120   above the general run.
            It will earn them only
        the sneer of uselessness
        and the spiteful jealousy of fellow men.
            Bring education to the dolt
125   and, far from being accounted wise,
        you will yourself be cast as dolt.
            Outshine a pundit of established fame
            and you become a byword of distaste.
            This precisely
130   is what I have to face.
            Because I have a little knowledge,
        some are filled with jealousy,
        others think me secretive, and crazy.

            In point of fact, my knowledge
135   does not amount to much.
        [*She turns upon Creon, eyes pathetic with innocence.*]
            But now I frighten *you:*
        do you think I'll strike some death-knell on your
            house?
            No, no: I am not like that.
            Creon, forget your fear:
140   I have no criminal intent against a king.
            For how have *you* wronged me?
            You simply gave your virgin child
        to a suitor of your bent.
            No, it is my husband that I hate.
145   You, I think, have acted prudently
        and even now I don't begrudge your enterprise
            success.
            Marry them both and blessings on you,
        only let me go on living in this land.
            Ill-used though I am, I shall keep quiet:
150   I am overruled.
CREON: Reassuring talk,
        but it chills me to the marrow.
            What are you really hatching in your mind?
            I trust you, Madam,
155   less even than I did before.
            The impassioned woman,
            like the impassioned man,
        is easier to watch than the crafty and the quiet.
            So, leave, I say, at once,
160   and no speeches, please.
            My mind's made up.
            You are dangerous.
            All your cleverness
        shall not keep you here.
165 MEDEA: Please, I beg you—on my knees—
        by your fresh young daughter-bride . . .
     CREON: You waste your words.
        I am adamant.
     MEDEA: Will you expel me—
170   heedless of my prayers?

CREON: I will. For I love you less
        than I love my home.
MEDEA: Ah, home! My own beloved country.
        What memories crowd upon me now!
CREON: Exactly: next to my own children,   175
        my country is *my* dearest love as well.
MEDEA: Love, did you say?
        It is a mighty curse.
CREON: In my opinion . . . that depends . . .
MEDEA: O Zeus, remember   180
        the author of this crime.
CREON: Go away—you poor deluded thing—
        rid me of my troubles.
MEDEA: The troubles are all mine:
        I have a glut of them.   185
CREON [*turning on his heel*]: I'll call the servants:
        They'll put you out by force.
MEDEA [*clinging to him*]: No, not that . . . Creon,
        I have something else . . .
CREON: You seem determined, Madam,   190
        to make a nuisance of yourself.
MEDEA: No, I'll go into banishment . . .
        That is not what I beg you now.
CREON: Then, why not *go*, and let this land be rid of
        you?
MEDEA: Just let me stay this single day   195
        to arrange my exodus from here
        and make provision for my little sons—
        whose father cannot bring himself to care.
            Be kind to them.
            You are a father too: 200
        you know what kindly feelings are.
            As for me,
        it means nothing to me
        whether I stay or go.
            It's them I shed my tears for: 205
        their lot is hard.
CREON [*after a tussle with himself*]:
        My soul is not tyrannical enough.
        My heart has often let me down . . .
        So now, Medea,
        though I know I take a false step: 210
        have it your own way.
            But let me warn you solemnly,
        if tomorrow's holy light
        sees you and your two children
        still inside the borders of this realm,   215
        you die.
            Every word of this I mean.
            Now, stay if you must; but one day only . . .
        not long enough for you to perpetrate anything I
            dread.
                          [*Exit Creon.*]
CHORUS: Ill-starred woman,   220
        Oh, what a nightmare of anguish is on you!
        Whom will you turn to? Where will you turn?
        What country, what stranger, what home for a
            haven?
            Who will receive you?

225   God has certainly steered you—
      Oh, my poor Medea—
      Into a sea-race of sorrows.
      MEDEA [*turning on them with the gleam of revenge*]:
      In the center of disasters, yes,
      but all is far from lost—make no mistake—
230   a test awaits the newlyweds,
      no little ordeal for the happy pair.

      [*With a laugh of derision.*]

      Do you think I ever would have toadied to this
          man
      if nothing could be got from it, no gain, no tool?
      No, not one syllable,
235   not a touch with my little finger.
      The fool!
      He could have scotched me with one stroke,
      flung me out;
      instead he lets me stay one extra day,
240   to make three enemies three corpses:
      ha! father, daughter, and my husband.

      [*She leans toward the Chorus.*]

      Friends,
      I can think of several ways to bring their death
          about.
      Which one shall I choose?
245   Shall I set their house of honeymoon alight,
      or creep into the nuptial bower
      and plunge a sharp knife through their vitals?
      One thing makes me pause:
      if I am caught entering the palace, or red-handed,
250   I die . . . and give my enemies the last laugh.
      No, there is a surer way,
      one more direct;
      for which I have a natural bent:
      death by poison.
255   Yes, that is it.

      [*She walks, thinking.*]

      Well, suppose they are dead:
      will any city take me in,
      will any man afford me home in a country safe for
          living
      and shield me from reprisals?
260   No, there is none.
      I must postpone it, therefore, for a while
      until some tower of strength appears for me;
      then, through trickery and stealth,
      I shall proceed with death by poison.
265   What if I'm forced to go before it's done?
      Ah, then I shall seize a sword,
      face certain death,
      and with my own hands run them through.
      I shall not shrink from such a step,
270   by Hecate,° no: the goddess who abides

270. **Hecate:** Identified with Artemis, and sometimes called Persephone (Roman name Proserpina), she was supposed to preside over magic and witchcraft.

in the shrine of my inner hearth—
the one I reverence most of all the gods
and have chosen to abet me.
      Nobody breaks my heart—
with impunity.   275
      Their wedding I'll reduce
to agony and grief:
agony for having met and married,
and grief for having banished me.
      Good!   280
      Use your magic to the hilt.
      Plot, Medea, devise your recipes:
advance to the deadly act that tests your courage.
      See your present plight:
laughed at by the seed of Sisyphus°   285
because of Jason's match?
      Never.
      Your father was a king:
his father, Helios the Sun . . .
be aware of *that*.   290
      Besides, you are a born woman:
feeble when it comes to the sublime,
marvelously inventive over crime.

FIRST CHORAL ODE°

[*The Chorus sings an ode about the topsy-turvy chang-ing standards of the world. Out of the turmoil will come a new importance for women, and a new reverence. Meanwhile, Medea is a harbinger of female indepen-dence and vitality.*]

[*Strophe 1*]

      Back to their fountains
          the sacred rivers are falling;
      The cosmos and all morality
          turning to chaos.
      The mind of a man is nothing but fraud   5
          and his faith in the gods a delusion.
      One day the story will change:
          then shall the glory
          of women resound,
And reverence will come to the race of woman,   10
      Reversing at last the sad
          reputation of ladies.

[*Antistrophe 1*]

      The ballads of ages gone by
          that harped on the falseness

[285. **seed of Sisyphus:** Sisyphus, a king of Corinth, was pun-ished in the otherworld by being made to roll a boulder up a hill. As it approached the top, the boulder would roll back down, creating a never-ending task. To be a descendant of Sisy-phus was considered a disgrace by the ancients.]   [**Ode:** Song sung by the Chorus.]

15 Of women, will cease to be sung . . .
        If only Apollo,
    Prince of the lyric, had put
        in *our* hearts the invention
    Of music and songs for the lyre
20 Wouldn't I then have raised
        up a feminine paean
    To answer the epic of men?
    Time in the roll of the ages has much to unfold
    Of the fortunes of women no less
25   than the fortunes of men.

[*Strophe 2*]

    So you, Medea, sailing away
        from your father's house,
    Threading a passage with heart on fire
        through the jowls of the Euxine
30 Cliffs° to inhabit a strange
        land where your bed is empty of man
    (The lover you lost, O heartbroken lady!)
    Now are chased from the realm,
        shamed and banned.

[*Antistrophe 2*]

35 The joy of a bond is gone;
        and wide of the world of Hellas,
    All shame has flown—
        high in the sky and away.
    Bereft of a fatherly home,
40 Where can you sail for a haven against
    The storm, unfortunate woman—
        Your bed
    Royally quelled by another
        who queens it in your home?

SECOND EPISODE

[*Jason enters from the road that leads to the palace. He is a young-looking man, dressed in the swash-buckling cloak and plumed helmet of a captain in the King's Guards.*]

JASON [*embarrassed and exasperated*]:
        So . . . this is not the first time
    I have seen irrevocable damage done
        by a barbarous rage.
        You could have stayed here,
5   in this land, in this house,
    had you submitted quietly to your ruler's plans.
        Instead, you ranted like a lunatic . . .
    so now are banished.
        To me your tirade does not mean a thing:

29–30. **Euxine Cliffs:** On the Black Sea.

go on declaiming what a monster Jason is.   10
        But when it comes to royalty,
    the princess and the king,
    count yourself lucky to be only banished.
        I have tried continuously to calm things down;
    for I should like you to remain.   15
        But you, Madam,
    obstinate in folly,
    have continuously reviled our royalty,
        And so you are banished.
        Yet, in spite of everything, I come, Medea,   20
    patient to the last with someone I am fond of,
    to do what I can to help.
        You and the children
    need not leave the country penniless
    and unprovided for . . .   25
        exile drags with it a chain of troubles.
        And hate me though you may,
    I cannot bring myself to wish you harm.
MEDEA: You criminal—
    an epithet too good for you . . . such inhumanity . . .   30
    so you come to me, do you,
    you byword of aversion both in heaven and on
        earth,°
    to me your own worst enemy?
        This is not courage.
        This is not being brave: 35
    to look a victim in the eyes whom you've betrayed—
    somebody you loved—
        This is a disease,
    and the foulest that a man can have:
    you are shameless.   40

[*With the thinnest of smiles.*]

        But you have done well to come:
    I can unload some venom from my heart
    and you can smart to hear it.
        To begin at the beginning,
    yes, first things first: 45
        I saved your life—
    as every son of Greece who stepped on board the
        Argo knows.
        You were sent to yoke
    the fire-breathing bulls
    and sow the plot of death.   50
        Yes, I saved you, lit up life for you,
    when I slew the guardian of the Golden Fleece,
    that giant snake which hugged it, sleepless,
    coil on coil.
        I deserted my own father and my home   55
    to come away with you to Iolcus by Mount Pelion,
    full of zeal and very little sense.
        King Pelias, I killed,
    a most horrid death—
    perpetrated through his daughters—   60
    and overturned their home.

32. Editors bracket this line as doubtful.

All this for you,
I even bore you sons—you most reprobate man—
just to be discarded for a new bride.
65   Had you been childless,
this craving for another bedmate
might have been forgiven.
         But no: all faith in vows is shattered.
         I am baffled:
70   Do you suppose the gods of old no longer rule?
         Or is it that mankind
now has different principles—
because your every vow to me, I'm sure you know,
is null and void.
75   Curse this right hand of mine,
so often held by yours;
and these knees of mine—
sullied to no purpose
by the grasp of a rotten man.
80   You turned my hopes to lies.
         Come now, tell me frankly—
as if we were two friends,
as if you really were prepared to help
(and I hope the question makes you feel ashamed)—
85   where do I go from here?

[*With a bitter laugh.*]

         Home to my father, perhaps,
and my native land,
both of whom I sacrificed for *you*?
         Or to the poor deprived daughters of Pelias?
90   They would be overjoyed to entertain
their father's murderer.
         Yes: this is how things stand.
         Among my own friends
I am an execrated woman.
95   There was no call for me to hurt *them*,
but now I have a death-feud on my hands—
and all for you.
         What a reward!
         What a heroine you have made me
100   among the daughters of Hellas!
         Lucky Medea, having *you*:
such a wonderful husband . . . and so loyal!
         I leave this land displaced, expelled,
deprived of friends,
105   only my children with me, and alone.
         What a charming record for our new
                bridegroom this:
"His own sons and the wife who saved him
are wayside beggars."

[*She breaks off and looks upward.*]

         O Zeus, what made you give us
110   clear signs for telling
mere glitter from true gold,
but when we need to know
the base metal of a man
no stamp upon his flesh for telling counterfeit?
115 LEADER: How frightening is resentment

how difficult to cure,
When lovers hurl past love
    at one another's hate.
JASON: I'll have to choose my words
    with no uncommon skill, it seems . . .   120
    like a good sailor riding out a storm,
    if I am to sail close-sheeted, Madam,
    through your lashing, dangerous tongue.

[*Folding his arms.*]

    So, you pile up what you did for me
    into pinnacles of grace.   125
         Well, as far as I am concerned,
    it was Aphrodite° and no one else in heaven or earth
    who saved me on my voyage.
         Your cleverness played a part, of course,
    but I could underline, if I wanted to be ungenerous, 130
    how it was infatuation, sheer shooting passion,
    that drove you to save my life.
         I shall not stress the point.
         After all, your service did no harm.
         But this I shall maintain: 135
    that what you gained by saving me
    was far more than you gave.

[*Holds up a hand to stop Medea from interrupting.*]

         In the first place,
    you have a home in Hellas
    instead of some barbarian land.   140
         You have known justice:
    the benefit of laws which never yield to might;
    have had your talents recognized all over Greece
    and won renown.
         For, were you living at the world's ends,   145
    your name would not be known . . .
         Oh, to me, houses crammed with gold,
    and a sweeter song than Orpheus sang,
    are nothing with no name.
         But, enough discussion of my dangerous voyage: 150
    an argument which *you* provoked.
         Now to your vindictive challenge
    of my royal marriage.
         I'll show you, first, it was an act of common sense,
    secondly, unselfish,   155
    and, finally, a mark of my devotion
    to you and all my family.

[*Medea gives a gasp of incredulity.*]

         No, be still.
         When I came here from the land of Iolcus,
    frustrations crowding on my trail,   160
    could I, a wretched fugitive,
    have hit upon a greater stroke of luck
    than marriage to the daughter of the king?
         It was not—which cuts you to the quick—
    that I was tired of your attractions   165
    and smitten with a longing for a new wife;

127. Aphrodite: Goddess of love, called Venus by the Romans.

still less that I was out to multiply my offspring
(I am quite satisfied with the sons we have);
no, it was simply that I wanted above all
170   to let us live in comfort, not be poor . . .
      I know too well
how the pauper is avoided by his friends.
I wanted our children to be reared
in a manner worthy of my ancestry,
175   and, begetting others, brothers for your sons,
knit them all together
into one close and happy family.
      What point was there for *you* to have more
         children?
      My intention was—and it seemed real gain—
180   to help the ones I have,
through those I hope to have.
      Was this such a wicked plan?
      You would not say so,
except through jealousy—that stinging jealousy of
         bed.
185   You women are all the same.
      If your love life goes all right,
everything is fine;
but once crossed in bed,
the liveliest and best that life can offer
190   might as well be wormwood.
      What we poor males really need
is a way of having babies on our own—
no females, please.
      Then the world would be
195   completely trouble free.
LEADER [*sternly*]: Jason, this speech of yours is
         plausible,
But say what you like, it is not right
To sacrifice your wife.
MEDEA [*with cold disdain*]:
      My outlook must be very different, then, from
         others.
200   To my mind a hypocrite who is too glib
only multiplies the danger that it puts him in:
the more he glozes° falsehood with his tongue,
the more confident and rash he grows.
      He ends by not being very clever.
205   So, you, toward me—
you'd better drop your specious pleading.
      One simple observation
lays the whole thing flat:
were you not a coward, it was your duty
210   to convince *me*; not go sneaking off to marry.
JASON: And you would have welcomed the suggestion,
         I am sure.
Why, even now you can't contain your blazing rage.
MEDEA: *That* was not what governed you:
      you felt your glory tarnished by an aging oriental
         wife.
215   JASON: Please, please believe me:
      it was nothing to do with women—

202. glozes: Glosses over.

my desire to make this match—
but as I have already said
to safeguard you and rear young princes
to be brothers to my sons . . .   220
so make our family solid.
MEDEA [*with a bitter laugh*]:
      Haha! Solid happiness on the grave of love;
      Prosperity with a secret sting . . .
      O you gods—not for me—ever.
JASON [*earnestly*]: Please change your prayer to this   225
      and make it reasonable:
         "May success not seem to me sad failure,
      nor good fortune ever a disaster."
MEDEA: You go on mocking me: *you* have roof and
         shelter.
      I am deserted, flying for my life, alone.   230
JASON: *You* chose it. Blame no one else.
MEDEA: Did I? I was the one who wed and then
         betrayed?
JASON: No: you just swore a heap of filthy curses on
         the king.
MEDEA: Yes, and you shall find that *I* am the curse
      that Fate has made to haunt you.   235
JASON: There's no point in talking any more with you.

[*Preparing to go.*]

      Anything that you or the children want in exile,
      let me know; I'd gladly furnish it,
      or send letters of introduction for you
      to friends abroad who will be kind.   240
         To turn this offer down, Medea,
      is nothing short of madness.
         Forget your feelings of resentment:
      let yourself be helped.
MEDEA [*spitting out the words*]:
      Not your friends, not your things: 245
      I would not touch anything of yours—
      how dare you offer it!
      The presents of the wicked are pure poison.
JASON [*flinging his cloak about him*]:
      In that case, heaven be my witness:
      all my design to help you and your sons   250
      is thwarted by your preference for evil.
         Your self-will cuts you off.
         Suffer then accordingly.

[*He begins to go.*]

MEDEA: Go then. Don't waste your passion here:
      go to the fresh young virgin you can't wait for . . .   255
      Have her.
               [*As Jason exits, furious and embarrassed.*]
      And God grant
      the match you make, you'll long to have unmade.

SECOND CHORAL ODE

[*The women of the Chorus, appalled by what has happened to Medea, speak of the dangers of love and the
sufferings of exile.*]

[*Strophe 1*]

    Love is a dangerous thing:
    Loving without any limit.
    Discredit and loss it can bring . . .
    But, oh, if the goddess should visit
5   A love that is modest and right,
    No god is so exquisite.
    Great lady, aim not at me
    Your gold and infallibly
    Passion-tipped, poisoned delight.

[*Antistrophe 1*]

10   Stay me with innocent living;
    Most beautiful gift of the gods.
    Never let Cypris° the fierce
    Queen of desire propel
    My heart to a dissolute lust
15   From old to a new and another
    Bed and a dissonant longing,
    But test with a sweet eye for peace
    The love-bonds of reverent women.

[*Strophe 2*]

    O my country, my home, never let
20   Me lose my state and my city—
    Living that desperate loss
    so helpless and hard, without pity.
    Death: I would bargain with death,
    To die such a day to a finish.
25   For nothing is like the sorrow
    Or supersedes the sadness
    Of losing your native land.

[*Antistrophe 2*]

    LEADER: The thing is before my eyes.
    Learned from no rumor or lies:
30   Medea without city or friends
    Nowhere where pity extends—
    Oh, how you must suffer! . . .
    Let a man rot in a charmless lot
    If he never unshutters his heart
35   To the cleansing esteem of another.
    He'll not be my friend: no, never.

THIRD EPISODE

[*Enter Aegeus from the country. He is a man in his early middle years and dressed in traveling clothes. His open*

12. **Cypris:** Aphrodite, goddess of love.

features—kindly but unimaginative—seem preoccupied. In his retinue are Noblemen and Servants.]

AEGEUS [*stretching out his hands*]:
    Medea, all health and happiness . . .
    and one can say a fairer thing when greeting friends?
MEDEA [*wanly*]: Health and happiness to you, good
    Aegeus,
    wise Pandion's son . . . But where do you stem from?
AEGEUS: I have just left Apollo's ancient oracle at
    Delphi.   5
MEDEA: What—a pilgrim there—the nub of the
    world of prophecy?
AEGEUS: I went to ask for progeny—for a fruitful seed.
MEDEA [*suddenly interested*]:
    In the name of heaven! Have you been childless all
    this time?
AEGEUS: Childless, yes—by some design of heaven.   10
MEDEA: But with a wife . . . or have you never married?
AEGEUS: I am married. Yes, I have a wife who shares
    my bed.
MEDEA: And what did Apollo say about your having
    children?
AEGEUS: Something far too deep for me, a mere mortal,
    to unravel.
MEDEA: Am I allowed to know the god's reply?   15
AEGEUS: Certainly. It would take a mind like yours to
    fathom.
MEDEA: Tell me . . . what did he say . . . since you are
    allowed?
AEGEUS: Why, just this:
    "Do not unstopper the wine-skin till . . ."°
MEDEA: Till you've done something—been
    somewhere—special?   20
AEGEUS [*baffled*]: Until I'm back at home again.
MEDEA: Then why did you sail in here?
AEGEUS: There is a man called Pittheus, king of
    Troezen . . .
MEDEA: Yes, a son of Pelops: a very pious man, they
    say.
AEGEUS: I want to ask his help about this oracle.   25
MEDEA: Yes, a clever man, and an expert in such
    things.
AEGEUS: And of all my old battle cronies, my favorite.
MEDEA: Well, I hope that all your dreams come true.
AEGEUS: Medea, you look so pale, so sad. What is it?
MEDEA: My husband, Aegeus: he is the world's most
    wicked man.   30
AEGEUS: You don't say? . . . Come, tell me all about
    your troubles.
MEDEA: He's set up a mistress to queen it in my home.
AEGEUS: Dear me! Would he really do a thing like that?
MEDEA: Yes, yes . . . And I am deposed—the one he
    loved.
AEGEUS: Did he fall in love . . . or is he just tired of *you*?   35
MEDEA: In love—Ha—head over heels . . .
    flinging all fidelity to the winds.

19. **"Do not . . . wine-skin":** Probably "Do not have sexual intercourse."

AEGEUS: Let him get on with it . . . since he's as
    wicked as you say he is.
MEDEA: But it was with royalty he fell in love:
    a king's daughter.
40 AEGEUS: Eh? What king's daughter? Please go on.
MEDEA: Creon's, king of Corinth.
AEGEUS: In that case, Madam, it *is* serious.
    You have my sympathies.
MEDEA: It is the end. What is more, I am being
    banished.
45 AEGEUS: Banished? This is indeed a crowning blow—
    but by whom?
MEDEA: Creon: he wants to banish me from Corinth.
AEGEUS: And Jason agrees? I find that monstrous.
MEDEA [*with fierce irony*]: Oh, he says he doesn't—
50   but he'll bear it bravely.

[*On her knees.*]

    Aegeus, I beg you,
by your beard,
by these knees of yours I clasp,
pity me, pity my unhappiness.
55   Do not see me banished and alone,
let me come to Athens, shelter me,
accept me in your home.
    The gods will pay you back,
give you the children you so long to have,
60 surround your death with happiness.
    You do not guess how Providence has blessed
        you, meeting me.
    I mean to end your childlessness
and make your seed bear sons.

[*Almost in a whisper.*]

    I promise it. I know the drugs.
AEGEUS [*impressed*]: Medea, many reasons make me
65   ready
to acquiesce in your request,
not least of all the gods;
then because you've given me—a promise:
promise of children . . .
70 oh, left to myself, I had all but given up.

[*Gently raising her.*]

    My proposition, then is this:
get yourself to Athens
and there, as is incumbent on me,
I shall do my utmost to protect you.
75   However, I must tell you clearly,
I cannot take you with me out of Corinth,
but if you reach my palace on your own,
there you shall have full sanctuary
and to no one shall I give you up.
80   So, by your own means you must leave this land:
I cannot risk offending the Corinthians—
who are also friends of mine.
MEDEA: As you say . . . but . . .
    if only you could promise it on oath,
85   it would make it all so . . . settled between us.

AEGEUS: Do you not trust me? What is the matter
    now?
MEDEA [*glancing nervously over her shoulders*]:
    I do trust you . . . but . . .
but I have my enemies.
    It isn't only Creon,
there is the house of Pelias too: 90
They'll want to prize me from your territories.
    If you are bound by oath
you will not give me up.
    But if you have only made a promise,
not sworn it to the gods,   95
there is always the chance that sheer diplomacy
will win you to their wishes.
    I have no weapons on my side,
on theirs is wealth and all the weight of royalty.
AEGEUS: You are very provident, Medea.   100
    However, if that is what you want,
I shall not go against it.
    In point of fact,
to swear an oath protects me too:
I can counter those who wish you ill   105
with a clear excuse;
and you of course, are well secured.
    So, name your deities.
MEDEA [*in crystal-cold syllables*]:
    Swear by the Earth on which you tread.
    Swear by the Sun, my father's father dread.   110
    Swear by every god and godhead.
AEGEUS: Yes, but what to do or not to do? Please say.
MEDEA: Never yourself to drive me from your land,
    and if an enemy of mine tries to drag me off,
    never while you live to let me go.   115
AEGEUS: I swear by the Earth and sacred light of the
    Sun
to abide by the words you have just pronounced.
MEDEA [*relentlessly*]:
    Good . . . but if you break your word—what
        penalty?
AEGEUS: The penalty for sacrilege.

[*They clasp hands in silence.*]

MEDEA: Go now and be glad. All is well.   120
    I shall come to Athens as quickly as I can,
    but first I have some work to do, to carry out a
    plan.

[*As Aegeus is leaving.*]

LEADER: We hope that Hermes, master of journeys,
    Will hasten you home safely to Athens:
    Home to the hope of your heart's desire,   125
        For, Aegeus, you are
        A most magnanimous man.
MEDEA [*wheels round and faces the Chorus*]:
    O Zeus and lady daughter, Justice,
    O resplendent Sun!
    And you my friends,   130
        At last we are on the road to vengeance
    and to our song of triumph. At last there is hope:

we shall see my enemies put down.
        At the very point my plot could founder,
135 this man opens up a port, an anchorage.
        So to Athens I shall go
and moor to her fast towers.

[*She beckons the women closer.*]

        Now I can unfold to you my whole design:
there is nothing sweet in it, as you will see.
140   I send a servant of my house to Jason
asking him to come to me.
        He arrives
I tell him in the softest accents;
how I now agree;
145 how it all seems for the best:
his royal marriage, his sacrifice of me;
everything that he has planned is for the best.
        But I ask him to let my children stay . . .
with no intention—you understand—
150 of leaving any child of mine in a hostile place
for those who hate me to maltreat.
        No, this is just a device
for murdering the daughter of the king.
        I send them there with presents in their hands,
155 presents for the bride—as a kind of plea
against their banishment—
yes, a gown of gossamer and a diadem made of
        beaten gold.
        If she takes this finery and puts it on,
the girl will die in agony
160 and anyone who touches her;
so deadly are the poisons I shall steep the presents in.
        But now my whole tone changes:
a sob of pain for the next thing I must do.
        I kill my sons—my own—
165 no one shall snatch them from me.
        And when I have desolated Jason's house beyond
        recall,
I shall escape from here:
fly from the murder of my little ones,
my mission done.
170   People that one hates, my friends,
must never have the last laugh.
        Well, so be it.
        What good is life to me?
I have no father, home, defense from danger.
175   Oh, the mistake I made was when I left his house,
trusting the word of a man from Greece . . .
but he is going to pay the price.
        Never again alive
shall he see the sons he had by me,
180 nor any child by this new bride of his—
poor girl, who has to die a wretched death,
poisoned by me.
        Let no man think me insignificant or weak:
I am no meek martyr, no—quite the contrary—
185 relentless an enemy I make;
though kind enough to friends.
        Such is the genius of my life.

LEADER [*imploringly*]:
        Though you have shared all this in confidence
                with us, Medea,
        and though I long to be of help,
        we must uphold the laws of life:
        and so I say to you: "You must not do it."   190
MEDEA: There is no other way.
        And though I understand your sentiments,
        you have not been through my agony.
LEADER: But, my lady, to kill your own two sons . . . ?   195
MEDEA: It is the supreme way to hurt my husband.
LEADER: And it makes you the most desolate of
                women.
MEDEA: Be that as it may.
        Argument is now superfluous.

[*She turns to the Nurse, who has entered during the previous dialogue.*]

        Nurse, when I need real loyalty   200
you are the one I always turn to.
        Go now and fetch Jason here.
        But as you are a woman
and a faithful servant of this house,
whisper no syllable of what I plan.   205
                [*Exit Nurse, dragging her feet.*]

THIRD CHORAL ODE

[*The Women of Corinth desperately try to move Medea from her purpose. Does she imagine Athens, that blessed land, will welcome a murderess? Surely, she herself will flinch from the cold-blooded killing of her sons?*]

[*Strophe 1*]

The people of Athens are blest through the ages,
        Seeds of the all-hallowed gods,
Born on a soil unravaged and holy,
        They feed on the wide
        Bright pastures of knowledge.   5
Lightly they walk through the crystal air
In a land where Harmonia,
        Goldenly fair,
Once gave birth, they say, to the nine
        Muses, the pure   10
        Maids of Pieria.°

[*Antistrophe 1*]

And out of the sweetly flowing currents
        Of Cephisus,° they declare,

7–11. where Harmonia . . . Maids of Pieria: Harmonia, the balance of nature, and the genius of the people resulted in the cultivation of the arts. Pieria was a holy fountain in Boetia where the nine Muses were supposed to live. 13. Cephisus: An Athenian river.

Aphrodite sprinkles the land
15   And fragrantly breathes
Delicate breezes.
Forever she sheds from the stream of her hair,
Plaited with roses,
Scented petals; and sends the Loves—the Erotes—
20   To preside with Wisdom over the heart
And together prepare
The glories of art.

[*Strophe 2*]

How then shall a glorious city,
City of sacred rivers,
25   Host of the salutary guest,
Kindly take to the killer of children,
Harbor among them a murderess?
Think of how you are stabbing your sons.
Think, too, of the blood you assume.
30   Do not, please, we beg by your knees,
By everything and every means—
Murder your children.

[*Antistrophe 2*]

Where, when, will you find the mind,
The hand or the callous heart
35   Hardened enough to strike
These, yours—oh, heartless enough?—
How then will you see through your gaze
Swollen with tears as you sight your aim?
No, no, when your little ones kneel
40   Crying for mercy, you will not
Find the nerve, never be able,
To bloody your hands.

FOURTH EPISODE

[*Jason enters with the Nurse behind him. On his face is written apprehension mixed with hope; on hers, despair.*]

JASON: I have come, Medea, because you asked me.
I put myself at your disposal
even though you are against me.
What, Madam, can I do for you?
MEDEA [*in a small, contrite voice*]:
5   Jason please forgive me for all the things I said.
Bear lightly with my outbursts, will you,
if only in remembrance of our great love together.
I have been arguing with myself,
have taxed myself severely.
10   "You raving fool," I said,
"To antagonize those who want to do you good,
setting yourself against your rulers and your husband.
His royal marriage
and his design to bring up brothers for your sons

does you the greatest service that he could.   15
Why not calm yourself?
Are *you* suffering because the gods are good?
Have you no children of your own?
And are you not aware
you came as fugitive with not too many friends?"   20
Such reflections made me realize
I have been out of my mind, hysterical.
Now I thank you.
Now I am convinced
that in securing us this benefit   25
you are the wise one, *I* the fool—
I who should have been your ally
and encouraged you.
Yes, I should have been at hand to help,
decked the bed, dressed the bride—   30
and been glad to do it . . .
But we women—
well, we are what we are: let's leave it at that!
Do not copy us in our perverseness
or try to get your own back, giving tit for tat.   35
I ask your pardon.
I admit to being wrong.
I've thought better of it now.

[*With an upsurge of put-on happiness.*]

Children, children, come out here,
out of the house.   40

[*The two Boys appear with their Tutor.*]

Come greet your father, hug him, join with me
in loving, not resenting him.
Your mother's rancor's over.
There's peace between us: the fighting's done.
Come, take his hand.   45

[*As the children run into their father's arms.*]

O God, what a presentiment!
What an image looming in the dark!
JASON: My sons, my sons,°
if only you could go on living, go on loving,
with your arms stretched out like that to me
forever . . .   50
MEDEA [*choking*]: It breaks my heart;
I am far too prone to tears, too full of tears . . .
it is the sudden ending of my quarrel with your father
which makes them flow.
A sight so touching . . .   55
it overflows.
LEADER: My eyes, too, are stinging,
but may this be the worst that is to come.
JASON [*gently releasing the Boys*]: I praise you now,
Medea,

48. To my mind there is no doubt that this line and half the next (in the Greek) go to Jason, and not Medea as the manuscripts and editors have it. Otherwise, Medea's remark in 93 [930] makes no sense. The attempt to have it correspond to Jason's wish in 72 [916] does not work. [Translator's note.]

Tokusaburo Arashi as Medea with her two sons in a Japanese version of *Medea* performed at the National Theatre in London, September 24, 1987.

60   and I did not blame you then.
          It is natural for a woman to be enraged
when her husband goes off making second marriages.
          But now
          you are in a better frame of mind
65   and, even if it took a little time,
realize the good points of this plan . . .
          the decision is a level-headed woman's.

          [*Turning to the children.*]

          As for you, my boys,
your father has been far from idle
70   and, heaven willing, he has made
good settlements for you.
          In time I shouldn't wonder
if you were not first citizens in Corinth—
along with your new brothers.

[*Laying his hands on their shoulders.*]

          Grow up now fine fellows.   75
          Your father and a kindly providence
have the rest in hand.
          How I look toward the time
when you will be two strapping grown young men,
trampling down my enemies.   80

[*Medea has averted her head and is sobbing. Her feelings, though genuine, are being used by her to further her next move.*]

          But, Medea, what is this—
these dewy eyes, these tears;
your white face turned away
as if my words struck pain, not joy?
MEDEA: It is nothing.   85
          I was just thinking of our sons.

JASON: Well, be of good heart now:
    I shall see them through.
MEDEA: I will do my best . . . it isn't that I don't
        believe you,
90   but you know how women weep.
JASON: I know, but don't be sad for *them* . . . why
        should you?
MEDEA [*watching the tender look on Jason's face*]:
    I am their mother.
    When you prayed just now
    for a long life for your sons,
95   a sudden sadness whispered: "Will this be?"
        Well, that's one item only
    of what I had to say.
        The other thing is this:
        Since the king has set his mind
100   on sending me away from Corinth,
    and since I've come to recognize that this is best
    (for I'd only be an obstacle to you,
    living with the royal family here—
    who think I am a menace to their house),
105   I shall take myself away, go into banishment.
        But the children, please, I should like *them*
    to grow up under your own hand.
        Persuade Creon to let them stay.
JASON [*taken off his guard, but flattered*]:
    I—I am not certain that I can:
110   it'll take a little trying.
MEDEA: But you could ask your wife to beg her father
    to let the two boys stay.
JASON [*reflecting*]: Why not? I think I can get her to
        agree.
MEDEA: Of course you can:
115   if she's the slightest bit like any woman.
        And here *I* can play a useful part.
        I shall send her a present
    more ravishingly beautiful, believe me,
    than anything this age has seen:
120   a gown of gossamer and a diadem of beaten gold.
        These the boys shall carry them to her.

[*She claps her hands and two Maids appear.*]

    Go quickly, one of you,
    and bring the gorgeous presents here.

[*One of the Maids hurries into the house.*]

    What a double delight
125   What a shower of happiness for her
    to have you for a hero husband
    and now these treasures which were handed down
    by my father's father—the glorious Sun.

[*The Maid comes back with two boxes. Medea turns to
the Boys.*]

    Boys, take hold of this wedding gift.
130   Carry it to the happy princess-bride.
    Place it in her hands.
    It is not the kind of present she'll despise.
JASON [*as the Boys step forward*]:

You foolish woman—why empty your hands?
Do you think a royal wardrobe is in want,
or a palace short of gold?   135
    Keep these things. Don't give them up.
    If my wife values me at all,
my mere wish will have more weight than *things*,
I'm sure of that.
MEDEA [*with an onrush of conviction*]: Do not deny me.   140
    Even the gods, they say, succumb to gifts,
and gold is stronger than the strongest wits.
    She is lucky, *she* is blessed, *she* increases.
    This exile I would barter for my babies
not just with gold but with my life.   145

[*Forcing the boxes into the Boys' hands.*]

    Go, my sons, into the halls of wealth;
down on your knees and beg her—
this new wife of your father's, and my mistress—
to let you stay in Corinth.
    Most important of all,   150
see that she takes the precious things
into her own hands.

[*Packing them off.*]

    Quick, now, go. Success be yours.
    Come and tell me the good news.
    Your mother waits with all ears.   155

[*Exeunt the Boys with their Tutor, followed by Jason.*]

FOURTH CHORAL ODE

[*The multimurders are imminent. Woe to the victims!
Woe to the murderess!*]

[*Strophe 1*]

Now has the last hope gone of the children living,
Gone and forever: they walk already to murder.
The bride is taking the golden diadem,
    Is taking the poison and doom.
Over her yellow hair her hands are fitting   5
    The decorated dying.

[*Antistrophe 1*]

The gorgeousness of the gossamer gown will win,
And the beaten gold of the diadem embrace her.
The bride is decked and ready to meet the dead.
    The trap is lethally set: 10
Doomed miserable woman, doomed to fall in—
    Ineluctably caught by Fate.

[*Strophe 2*]

And you who are groomed for a murder:
    Son-in-law of a king,

15   Jason unsuspecting—
          Are to bring on your sons a demise, and a death
          On your bride of a hideous kind.
              Unhappy man, how far
              You are falling.

   [Antistrophe 2]

20   And you the unenviable mother,
              How I weep for your pain!
              Killer of children for
          A vengeance of love that has gone, betrayed
              By your man for another
25   Bride whom he sleeps beside
              In his wrong.

FIFTH EPISODE

[The Tutor hurries in from the palace with the two Boys.]

TUTOR *[breathless with excitement]*: My lady, your
          boys—
   they won't be banished.
          And the princess, the bride—
   with her own hands—
5   she took your presents, oh, so gladly . . .
          Now the children's danger is over!

[Baffled by Medea's grim reaction.]

       Well I never! Isn't this good news?
       What so transfixes you?

[Medea draws in her breath in a muffled cry of pain.]

TUTOR: What I hear is out of tune with what I say.

[Medea sighs deeply.]

10 TUTOR: I thought I brought good news.
          What kind of news, I wonder, have I brought?
    MEDEA: What you have brought, you have brought:
          the fault is not with you.
    TUTOR: Why, my Lady, these shuttered eyes:
15   these tears falling?
    MEDEA: Oh, I am pressed, old friend—hard pressed:
          the gods and my own evil counsels.
    TUTOR: Courage, dear mistress:
          Your sons will always bring you home.
    MEDEA *[in a kind of trance]*:
20   Home? . . . First I must send others there . . . Mercy!
    TUTOR: You are not the only mother to be severed
                from her sons.
          We have to bear our own humanity—humanely.
    MEDEA *[pressing his hand]*:
          I shall try . . . Now go inside
          and see to what the children need today.
                          [Exit Tutor, worried.]
    MEDEA *[throwing out her arms toward the two
25   Boys]*: My sons, my sons,

you will have a city and a home
far from me.
       I shall be left lonely,
and you will live without your mother always.
       For I must go in exile to another land: 30
never have my joy in you,
or see your bright young progress;
never deck your brides, your marriage beds,
or light you radiant to your wedding day.

[The Boys are now in her arms.]

       Oh, what a blight my ruthlessness has been!   35
       How useless, little ones,
my nursing all your growing up!
       How useless all the cares endured:
the wearying solicitudes,
the shooting agony of giving you your lives.   40
       And now, how miserably have dwindled
my innumerable dreams of you:
your loving comfort when I'm old,
your own hands dressing me when I am dead—
a passing every person might desire.   45
       Such sweet fancy vanishes
and, wrenched from you instead,
I shall drag my sad life out alone.

[She cups their faces in her hands in turn.]

       Your own dear eyes shall miss forever
your poor mother's face—   50
your way of life and hers utterly apart.
       Oh, children
do you let those eyes now stare their fill,
and your last smiles linger to the last?

[She turns to the Chorus, panting.]

       O–h! What shall I do?   55
       My heart dissolves
when I gaze into their bright irises . . .
       No, I cannot do it.
       Goodbye to my determination.
       I shall take my boys away with me.   60
       Why damage *them* in trying to hurt their father,
and only hurt myself twice over?
       No, I cannot.
       Goodbye to my decisions.

[A pause, then she suddenly breaks away from the Boys.]

       What—what undermines me now?   65
       Do I really mean to let my enemies go,
to laugh at me?
       Steel yourself, Medea:
away with this cowardice, these arguments that melt.

[Almost pushing them.]

       Go, Boys, into the house.   70

[She turns to the Chorus grimly.]

       Anyone whose conscience will not let him stay
let him look to it: avoid my sacrifice . . .
this hand of mine shall never falter.

[*Another spasm of emotion grips her, and she runs to the Boys as they reach the door.*]

75   No, no! Stop me, my heart:
    we must not do this thing.
        Let them go, you stricken woman,
    spare your sons.
        Let them live with you in Athens:
    they will be your joy.

[*Throwing her arms round them again.*]

80   Ah! Not by all the haunting spirits of the
            underworld,
    shall I leave my children for my enemies to
        trample down.
        No, never.°

[*With a sharp realization.*]

        But—they have to die—
    the whole thing is settled anyway . . .
85   Yes . . . the diadem is on her head . . .
    the royal bride at this moment rots,
    dying in her gown—I know it.

[*She turns to the Chorus as if to explain her second impulsive embrace.*]

        You see: the path I have to tread
    is unutterably sad,
90   but the one I set these children on
    is sadder still . . .
        Therefore I desire to speak with them.

[*Seizing their hands.*]

        Give me your right hands to kiss,
    each of you, my little ones—
95   give them to your mother.

[*Covering their hands, their faces, their bodies, in kisses.*]

        How adorable—this hand—and this . . .
    These lips—how very much adored!
    And this face and form of childhood's
    ingenuous nobility . . . how I bless you both . . .
100   not here—beyond . . .
    every blessing here your father has despoiled.
        So sweet . . . the mere touch of you:
    the bloom of children's skin—so soft . . .
    their breath—a perfect balm.

[*Gently releasing them; then almost savagely turning her back.*]

105   Go, go . . . I cannot look at you.
    I am in an agony, and lost.

[*The two Boys, weeping, hurry into the house.*]

---

82. [Translator has followed] editors [who] omit lines 1062 and 1063 [of the Greek text] as a melodramatic interpolation: *"But they have to die, and since they must, / let it be by the hands of her who gave them life."*

    The evil that I do, I understand full well,
    But a passion drives me greater than my will.
        Passion is the curse of man:
    It wreaks the greatest ill.   110

FIFTH CHORAL ODE

[*If there can be a feminine philosophy of parenthood, is its honest judgment likely to be that children are worth it after all?*]

    So often before
Have I gone toward concepts far too tenuous
And come upon questions far too deep
For the race of woman to try to unravel.
Nevertheless, even we women   5
Have a muse of our own, that ushers us in.
(Though, alas, not all) to the world of wisdom.
Perhaps you might find it one in a thousand.
It serves to inspire the talent of ladies,
And makes me able now to proclaim   10
That people without the function of parent
Are happier than begetters of offspring.
The childless man has no way of telling
Whether he misses a curse or a blessing.
Nevertheless, the childless person   15
Certainly misses many a burden.
I mark how the man with children growing
Sweetly at home is worn with worrying:
How to make sure they are properly fed,
How to leave them a livelihood.   20
And then after all to be in the dark:
Were all the worries worth it or not?
Were they a worthy or worthless lot?

    But now let me tell
Of the worst and saddest trait of all.   25
Suppose the children have quite a good life,
Reach their teenhood honest and fine,
What if a fate like Death the cruel
Carries them downward body and soul?
What is the use if after all   30
(On top of all those other ones)
The gods let loose this grief as well . . .
Just for the joy of having sons?

SIXTH EPISODE

[*Medea has been sitting during the Chorus. Now she leaps up as she catches sight of a man lunging breathlessly toward them from the street: the Messenger.*]

MEDEA: Somebody with news at last, my friends,
    And from the right direction.
        Yes, I see him:
    one of Jason's men—panting as he hurries—
        With some tremendous news of bad.   5

[*The Messenger—an official of the Bride's house—bursts in: hardly able to get his words out.*]

MESSENGER: Run, Medea, run!
        What—you have done . . . is . . . too
            unthinkable . . .
    too awful . . .
        Seize whatever means you can . . .
10   sailing boat or chariot . . . Escape!
MEDEA: Run? Escape? Is it then so vital?
MESSENGER: Dead . . . They are this minute dead . . .
    the princess royal with her father—
    and through your poisons.
15 MEDEA: What a pretty word you bring—
    my benefactor, my friend forever!
MESSENGER [*recoiling*]: What are you saying, Madam?
        Are you in your right mind—not unhinged?
        A king's home a charnel house—
20   and you rejoice? . . . Are you not afraid?
MEDEA: I have my ready answer too,
    so don't be hasty, friend,
    but tell me how they perished.
        An appalling death
25   would give me double joy.
MESSENGER [*supports himself against a pillar as he
            begins to recollect an agonizing experience*]:
        We were so pleased to see your brace of boys
    come hand in hand to the bride's house with their
            father:
    for your ordeal had upset us servants greatly.
        The rumor went racing through the house
    that all was well again between your husband and
30   yourself.
        Some of us kissed the children's hands,
    kissed their golden tops;
    and I in my enthusiasm even followed them
    to the women's wing.
35   There, the mistress—
    I mean the one we have to honor now—
    had eyes so taken up with Jason
    she did not even see at first
    the two boys hand in hand.
40   But when she did,
    a veil of scorn dropped over her eyes,
    she turned her lovely face away,
    bristling at your sons' intrusion.
        Your husband then began to woo her
45 from her petulance and girlish tantrums, saying:
        "You must not hate your friends.
        Stop being hurt and turn your head around.
        Consider yours your husband's loved ones.
        Come, won't you take their presents
50   and beseech your father
    to let these boys off banishment—just for me?"

[*Pauses and sits down hopelessly on a step.*]

        When she saw how exquisite the presents were,
    far from holding out on him,
    there was nothing she withheld:

but gave in completely to her groom.   55
        And hardly had your husband and your children
    left the house
    when she took the gorgeous robe and put it on,
    and placed the golden circlet on her curls,
    arranging the ringlets in the brightness of a mirror 60
    and smiling at her own dead image there.
        Then rising from her stool
    she minced off through the halls
    on dainty milk white toes,
    wildly pleased with what she had received,   65
    over and over again
    running her eyes down the clear sweep to her heels.
        But all at once
    a hideous spectacle took place.
        Her color changed. She tottered back;   70
    shuddered in every limb; was able just in time
    to fall into a chair and not upon the floor.
        An old woman there, attending her,
    thinking that perhaps the fierce possession of Pan°
    or some other power was on her,   75
    broke into a chant of wonder,
    then saw the white froth spuming at her lips,
    her eyeballs bulging all askew,
    her skin quite leached of blood,
    and changed her chanting to a yelp: 80
    a wail of horror.
        A maid went dashing to the palace for her father,
    another went to tell the fresh-wed groom
    what was happening to his bride.
        The whole house rang with footsteps running.   85
        It took no longer than a sprinter takes
    to go the hundred yards,
    before the poor girl lay unconscious with her
            eyelids shut.
    Then suddenly she rallied
    and gave a curdling shriek,   90
    fighting off a double nightmare.

[*He pauses, gulps, takes a deep breath.*]

        The golden diadem that clasped her head
    burst into a voracious and uncanny flow of fire,
    while the robe of gossamer your children gave her
    began to eat her tender flesh away.   95
        Streaming with flame,
    she leapt up from her chair and fled,
    tossing her mane of hair from side to side,
    in a frantic bid to shake the diadem off.
        But its grip was adamant   100
    and the golden circlet held.
        The more she tossed,
    the more the fire flowed,
    till, overwhelmed with pain,
    she sank down to the floor—   105
    unrecognizable to all except her father—
    her calm regard grotesquely twisted,

---

74. Pan: The god of wild nature was supposed to be the cause of seizures and sudden madness. Hence our word *panic*.

her sweet symmetry all shattered;
and from the crown of her head in molten clots
110   fire and blood dripped down together.
         The flesh curdled off her bones
like the teardrops congealing out of pines,
inexplicably dissolved by those ravening venoms.
         It was curious and horrible to see.
115   No one dared to touch her body:
the warning was too obvious.
         But her father, unawares, poor man,
rushed headlong through the room,
flung himself lamenting on the body,
120   hugged and kissed it, sobbing out:
         "My stricken darling,
what evil power has done this to you,
who has made you dead
and left me, like some ancient tombstone, derelict?
125   O gods! . . . let me die with you, my daughter."
         But . . . but when he stopped . . .
from these outpourings—
these melancholy sobs . . .
and tried to lift his aged carcass up,
130   he found himself stuck fast—
clamped to the flimsy robe
like ivy to a laurel bole.
         A ghastly wrestling match ensued.
         He would try to raise a knee,
135   she would drag him back;
and when he took to force,
his own decrepit flesh
pulled off from the bone.
         At last, exhausted,
140   pathetically unable
to lift himself above the shambles,
he gave his spirit up.
         There they lie, corpse by corpse,
father and young daughter—
145   fit objects for our tears.

[*He rises, swaying.*]

         To you, Medea . . . from me . . .
there are no words to say.
         Retribution? You yourself will know
the best escape . . .
150   though in my esteem—and not just for today—
the whole of life is shadow,
and I would even say:
the people who know best or seem to know,
the subtlest professors,
155   are the very ones who pay the dearest price.

[*Flinging his cloak about him.*]

         A happy human being? Ha, there's no such
               thing . . .
more prosperity, more success in one maybe:
but happier? . . . It does not make one happy.
                                         [*Exit Messenger.*]
LEADER: Justice personified this day
160   has brought on Jason's head

—oh, we have seen it!—
the richest retribution.
         But it is you we weep for,
poor blighted child of Creon,
walking through the gates of death   165
because you married Jason.
MEDEA [*in clear, cold tones*]:
         Now, friends, to complete this mission with
               dispatch:
to slay my children and hurry from this land.
         I must not dawdle and betray my sons
to much more savage hands than mine to kill.   170
         There's no way out. They have to die.
         And since they must,
let me be the one to cut them down:
the very one who gave them life!

[*She begins her walk to the door, almost like a sleep-
walker, talking to herself.*]

         Yes, heart, be steel.   175
         Why vacillate?
         The act is . . .
necessary as it is cruel and hard.
         Come, reluctant hand,
grip the sword—grip it, Medea: 180
cross your borderline of lifelong pain.
         Away this flinching!
         Away this longing:
consign to oblivion the love you had for them—
the children of your flesh.   185
         Even when you kill them they are dear . . .
oh, my sons! . . . I am in despair, despair.

[*Medea, with the Nurse mutely following in tears,
passes into the house.*]

SIXTH CHORAL ODE

[*The women pray desperately for something to stop the
imminent murder.*]

[*Strophe*]

         Come Earth, come sunshafts of the Sun,
         Behold this woman and withhold her
         From her laying scarlet fingers
         On the children of her blood.
         Gold of your gold are they begotten: 5
         Heinous is to spill this holy
         Ichor in the blood of mortals.
         Curb her, stop her, godborn Light, oh,
         Keep this house from murder! Keep it
         Never haunted by the Furies.°   10

10. **Furies:** Ministers of the vengeance of the gods, employed in
punishing the guilty on earth as well as in the underworld.

[*Antistrophe*]

Were those birth pangs wasted bearing:
Children's birth pangs wasted birth?
You, my lady, after sailing
Safe between the dark blue clashing
15   Gorges, will you hug a rankling
Hatred to your heart, a loathsome
Rage for murder and revenge?
Those that spill the blood of family
Stain themselves with heaven's anger,
20   Haunt their homes with doom forever.

SEVENTH EPISODE *or* DENOUEMENT

[*Cries are heard from inside the house.*]

FIRST WOMAN: A shout—listen—a shout from the
            boys.
FIRST BOY: O–h! What can we do? . . .
    Our mother is on us!
SECOND BOY: Brother, brother! . . . We're going to be
            killed.
5   SECOND WOMAN: That murderous relentless woman!
THIRD WOMAN: Shall we break in, snatch them from
            death?
FIRST BOY: Yes, by heaven . . . save us . . . help!
SECOND BOY: We're trapped, cornered . . . now . . . by
            her sword.

[*As the Chorus beat on the barred doors, there are
groans and cries, and presently a trickle of blood oozes
from under the doors. The women watch it, fascinated.*]

CHORUS: Woman of stone, heart of iron,
10   Disconsolate woman, ready to kill
        The seed of your hands with the hand that tilled.
        One other only, one have I known
        Murderously handle the fruit of her womb:
        Ino the maniac, god-driven one,
15   Whom Zeus's wife drove out to roam—°
        Desperate woman goaded to slaughter
        The sons of her flesh, clean against nature.
        She pitched from the precipice into the sea,
        Fell where her foot fell into the ocean,
20   Dashing two infants to death with her own.
        What ghastlier thing is left to be known?

        Women, O women, in love and in pangs,
        What ruin you've brought on us human beings!

[*Jason, breathless, his face twisted with hatred, bursts in
with a troop of servants.*]

14–15. **Ino the maniac . . . out to roam:** Ino, a daughter of Cadmus and Harmonia, tried to destroy her two stepchildren so
that her own two children might ascend the throne. Pursued, in
turn, by their father, her husband Athamas, she leapt into the
sea with her two boys. [The account given here] is Euripides'
version.

JASON: You women standing here outside this house,
    is that she-ravager, Medea, still at home, or has   25
    she fled?

[*He waits for a reply, but the women cower before the
door.*]

    Deep down in the earth let that woman hide,
or wing into the highest alcoves of the sky,
before she ever saves herself from justice by this
        royal house.
    Does she think that she can kill   30
a princess and a country's king
and vanish with impunity?

[*He strides toward the door.*]

    But it is my sons, not her, I fear for.
    She, she shall be repaid
through her victims.   35
    I have come to save my children's lives
from some enormous retribution by the family of
        the dead
for those enormities their mother did.
LEADER: Jason, you poor optimistic man,
    you still don't know the evils that have come—   40
    or you would not say what you have said.
JASON: What? Does she mean to kill me too?
LEADER: Your sons are dead: murdered by their mother.
JASON [*reeling*]: What—did—you—say?
    Oh, woman—my own wife—you kill me too.   45
LEADER [*as the women form an avenue to the door,
    and Jason sees for the first time the blood
    beginning to trickle down the steps*]:
    Yes. Your children.
You cannot think of them as being alive.
JASON [*limply*]:
    Where did she kill them . . . here . . . outside,
    or was it in the house?
LEADER: Force these doors   50
    and you will see your children in their blood.
JASON [*drawing his sword in a frenzy*]: Servants, on the
            double,
    break these bolts,
    force the hinges: let me see
    the double homicide,   55
    the murdered dead . . . and the murderess to die.

[*There is a rumbling sound, and out of a cloud above
the house Medea appears in a chariot drawn by dragons. By her side are the dead bodies of the two Boys.*]

MEDEA [*in triumphant disdain*]:
    Why this battering, this beating at the doors?
    Are you looking for their bodies—
and for me who did this thing?
    Save yourself the trouble.   60
    If there's anything you want, then ask.
    But me you shall not lay a hand upon.
    This chariot, the Sun
    —my father's father—gave me
to keep me safe against my enemies.   65

Fiona Shaw as Medea with Dylan Denton and Michael Tomer as her sons in the 2002 Abbey Theatre production performed at the Brooklyn Academy of Music.

JASON [*hissing with revulsion*]:
      You miserable, mephitic° woman!
      Beyond abhorrence—
  by me, the gods, the rest of men—
  you could put your own sons to the sword,
70   the sons you bore,
  and kill me too with childlessness . . .
  Yet still look upon the sun, see the earth . . .
      Be damned! . . .
      At last I understand
75 what I never understood before,
  when I took you from your foreign home to live in
            Greece,
  the sheer wickedness of you,
  the treachery to your father and the land that
            reared you.
      You are possessed
80 and the gods have unleashed the fiend in you on *me;*
  on your own brother, too, cut down in his home

[**66. mephitic:** Foul-smelling.]

before you came aboard the sweet ship *Argo*'s hull.
      Your work already had begun.
      You married me, bore my sons,
  and murdered them through jealousy of love.   85
      No woman in the whole of Hellas
  would have dared so much;
  yet you were the one I married,
  not a girl from Greece.
      Oh, I married a tigress,   90
  not a woman, not a wife,
  and yoked myself to a hater and destroyer:
  to a viciousness more fierce than any Tuscan Scylla.°

[*Turning away from the door in a gesture of helplessness.*]

  But why go on?
  A million accusations would not make you wince: 95
  you are shameless through and through . . .
  you—you bloodstained ogress, infanticide . . .
      Hell take you!
      Leave me to mourn my destiny of pain:
  my fresh young wedding without joy,   100
  my sons begot and reared and lost—
  never to be seen alive again.
MEDEA [*with acid imperiousness from the chariot*]:
      How tediously I could rebut you point by point!
      Zeus the Father knows
  exactly what you got from me   105
  and how you then behaved.
      I would not let you or your royal princess
  set our wedded life aside,
  make me cheap,
  so that you could live in bliss;   110
  or let that match-arranger, Creon,
  dismiss me from the land without a fight.
      So, call me a tigress if you like,
  or a Scylla haunting the Tyrrhenian shore,
  I have done what I ought: 115
  broken your own heart to the core.
JASON [*wheeling round to face her*]:
  You are in agony too:
  you share my broken life.
MEDEA: It is worth the suffering
                  since *you* cannot scoff.   120
JASON: Poor children, what a monster
                  fate gave you for a mother!
MEDEA: Poor sons, what a disaster
                  your selfish father was!
JASON: It was not *his* right hand   125
                  that killed and struck them down.
MEDEA: No, it was his pride
                  the lust of his new love.
JASON: You think it right to murder
                  just for a thwarted bed.   130
MEDEA: And do you think that a thwarted bed
                  is trifling to a woman?

93. Tuscan Scylla: A monster that inhabited the straits between Italy and Sicily and snatched sailors off passing ships and devoured them.

JASON: A modest woman, yes:
        to you the world's worst crime.
MEDEA [*pointing at the dead children*]:
135   See, they are no more;
        I can hurt you too.
JASON: They'll live, I think,
        in your tormented brain.
MEDEA: The gods know who began
140   this whole calamity.
JASON: Yes, the gods know well
        your pernicious heart.
MEDEA: Hate then: I spurn
        the wormwood from your lips.
145 JASON: As I do yours; so let us
        be rid of one another.
MEDEA: Yes, but on what terms?
        That's also what *I* want.
JASON: Let me have the boys—
150   to mourn and bury them.
MEDEA: Never!
    My own hands shall bury them, they shall be carried
    to the sanctuary of Hera on the Cape,
    where no enemy shall ever do them harm
155   or violate their sepulchre.
      Here in Corinth, the land of Sisyphus,
    I shall inaugurate a solemn festival°
    with rites in perpetuity
    to exorcise this murder.
160   I myself shall go to Athens, land of Erechtheus,
    to live with Aegeus, Pandion's son . . .
    you to a paltry death that fits you well:
    your skull smashed by a fragment of the *Argo*'s hull:
    ironic ending to the saga of your love for me.

THE EXODOS°

[*As the Chorus begin to form for the exodos march, the meter changes. Jason strides into the middle of the arena.*]

JASON: Murder is punished, and you'll be destroyed
      by the avenging phantoms of your children.

---

157. solemn festival: Similar ceremonies were still performed at Corinth in Euripides' time.   [**Exodos:** Final scene.]

MEDEA: What power or divine one is ready to hear
    you:
    perjurer, liar, treacherous guest?
JASON: Vile, vile, murderess of little ones!   5
MEDEA: Go—go and bury your bride.
JASON: Broken I go: bereft of two sons.
MEDEA: You bemoan too soon: wait till you're old.
JASON: Dearest children!
MEDEA: Dear to their mother.   10
JASON: And so she slew them.
MEDEA: To get at your heart.
JASON: You did! You did! How I long to press
    my little children's lips to mine!
MEDEA: Now you are longing, now you call;   15
    you utterly turned from them before.
JASON: For the love of the gods, allow me this:
    to stroke my children's tender skin.
MEDEA: No, you shall not: you waste your words.
JASON [*flinging out his arms*]: Zeus, do you hear how
    I'm at bay,   20
    Dismissed by this ogress, odious woman,
    Tigress besmirched with the blood of her young?
    So I mourn and call on the gods while I may,
    On the powers to witness how you have slain
    My children, and now prevent my hands   25
    From touching them, dead, interring their clay.
    I'd rather they'd never been born to me
    Than have lived to see you destroy them this day.

[*Before the end of these words, Medea, with a cold, vindictive smile, has moved off in the chariot. Jason staggers out of the arena.*]

ENVOI°

CHORUS: Wide is the range of Zeus on Olympus.
    Wide the surprise which the gods can bring:
    What was expected is never perfected,
    What was not, finds a way opened up . . .
    So ended this terrible thing.   5

[**Envoi:** Concluding remarks.]

COMMENTARY

Ben Brantley (b. 1955)
REVIEW OF *MEDEA*   *2002*

Fiona Shaw's portrayal of Medea *premiered in Dublin's Abbey Theatre in the summer of 2000. Director Deborah Warner presented audiences with a powerful high-energy version in a new translation. Alan Riding described the London production as "hot" and Shaw as "quivering with passion." Ben Brantley's review of Shaw in the American production at the Brooklyn Academy of Music examines the power and timeliness of the Greek portrait of a woman used and cast aside.*

The word has gone out in Corinth that there's a celebrity in pain in the vicinity. And when the groupies who sniff for blood wounds among the incredibly famous arrive at her house, Medea doesn't disappoint.

There she is, as embodied with a harrowing lack of vanity by the brilliant Fiona Shaw, her recognizable features smudged by unhappiness, her eyes hidden by the formal shield of dark glasses, her mismatched wardrobe a thrown-on hash of running shoes, a cardigan and a little print dress. Why, she might have stepped from those pages of *The National Enquirer* devoted to stars foolish enough to leave home without makeup. The question is: Will she talk to us? Will she let us in on her truly sensational problems?

You bet she will. How satisfying, after all, can revenge be unless you have an audience to reflect it, to magnify it, to turn it into legend? Without their urging, how will you know who you really are?

In the thrilling Abbey Theatre production of Euripides' "Medea," which runs at the Harvey Theater of the Brooklyn Academy of Music through Oct. 12, Greek tragedy's most spectacularly vengeful woman has rematerialized in the dawning years of the 21st century. And it is, to tell the truth, a little frightening to see how comfortably this volcanically uncomfortable woman fits into the world of today.

What Ms. Shaw and the director, Deborah Warner, who collaborated so memorably on their staging of T. S. Eliot's "Waste Land," have achieved here seems so obvious, when you think about it, that you're amazed it hasn't been done before. For this "Medea" homes in on the parallels between the very form of Greek tragedy — with its dialogue between uncommon heroes and heroines and the common folk of the chorus — and an age in which private breakdowns, breakups and humiliations have become public rituals.

Of course if this were the only point of Ms. Warner's "Medea," it wouldn't have turned out to be the most essential ticket of this theater season. This isn't one of those stagings in which a clever concept reduces characters to glossy illustrations.

The miracle of this "Medea" is how completely it integrates its ideas on a latter-day culture of celebrity into a classic text, freshly translated by Kenneth McLeish and Frederic Raphael, without ever seeming to warp the spirit of the original. The anxious perfume that saturates this production is a compound of the passion, terror and existential ambivalence that have plagued humans for as long as they have been able to think.

Ms. Shaw's Medea has little in common with the usual majestically angry sorceress who is guided by one idée fixe: to avenge herself on her husband, Jason, for whom she betrayed her homeland and who has now left her for the young princess of Corinth. There is scant evidence of the commanding icy intellect so elegantly incarnated by Diana Rigg in Jonathan Kent's production of a proto-feminist "Medea" on Broadway in 1994.

It's not that you doubt the intelligence of Ms. Shaw's Medea. But her lacerating misfortunes have broken the circuits of that intelligence, and her responses are a toxic jumble. She seems to wear her nerves outside her skin. Numbness and excruciating pain, shrill anger and mordant, bizarre humor flit across her raw features in disjunctive parade.

Set in a half-finished courtyard littered with children's toys and cinder blocks (the designer is Tom Pye), suggesting a life interrupted, the entire production seems to occur in that heightened, instinct-addling realm that occurs during times of emergency. The evening begins in a state of breathlessness that never really lets up. And as upsetting as much of it is, the show radiates such high theatrical energy and insight that you can't help grinning through most of it.

The first image is of Medea's Nurse (Siobhan McCarthy), represented here as a student au pair type, rushing onto the stage with a handful of knives. She is also, it turns out, carrying bottles of pills. And she proceeds to hide these commonplace household objects, which in this context have suddenly turned threatening.

This interpolated scene is inspired in its banal immediacy, translating abstract terror into specific and familiar physical terms. You can't help feeling like a visitor who has showed up at just the wrong moment. Of course, you keep staring. And if you don't, there's the chorus of five townswomen who emerge from the audience and swarm onto the stage as if to act as your proxy.

They have the feverish look of fans addicted to real-life soap operas, like the kind of people who rushed to the site of Nicole Simpson's murder and stood in line for the trial of Michael C. Skakel. Their relentless talk to Medea, shaped by a sooty mix of empathy and prurience, seems perfectly natural. So, more surprisingly, does Medea's willingness to respond to them.

Then again, as a notorious exile now spurned by even the husband who brought her here, who else does she have to talk to? Besides, as Jason (Jonathan Cake) later says nastily, he and Medea have become people who would "rather be sung about than sing."

This production acutely accents the talk of reputation and fame and its rewards. And you can see that Jason and, in her more befuddled way, Medea are quite keen to put forth their respective versions of their lives together. Medea knows very well she is playing to a crowd and, by extension, to history. She accepts as her due the applause that the chorus gives after she has successfully pleaded with Kreon (Struan Rodger), the king of Crete, to postpone her exile.

If it sounds as if Ms. Shaw's Medea is a smooth spinmeister, then I'm misrepresenting her. What's so mesmerizing and truly frightening about her performance is how cogently she evokes a mind that is anything but clear. This Medea is an all too sensitive instrument played upon by overwhelming forces that come from both without and within.

Among these is simple brute lust. The superb Mr. Cake's vanity-driven Jason may not be his wife's match in ingenuity. But he knows exactly where to touch Medea to turn her into jelly. Their most rancorous arguments are punctuated by perverse sexual sparks that threaten to subdue Medea into passivity. And then the spell is broken, and she emerges all the more addled and angry.

The play's grotesque climax (mercilessly rendered here), in which Medea murders her two sons, does not seem a foregone conclusion. Ms. Shaw and Ms. Warner have created a Medea who isn't even sure herself how she will act from one moment to the next. There are stretches, as Medea rants about her diabolical plans for vengeance, when you think, "Oh, she's just playing," or to use the preferred psychobabble, "acting out."

For this Medea has a wide-ranging mind that, even in abject pain, keeps shifting perspectives on her. Suddenly, without warning, she'll do something like pick up a toy gun and simulate murder with a goofy smile. And she's funny when she's deriding her husband and his bride-to-be, finding the idea of them so unspeakable that she's reduced to making "bleah" and "ick" noises. But the noises also suggest an eloquent woman for whom words are no longer adequate.

When, toward the play's end, a messenger (Derek Hutchinson) arrives to describe the excruciating deaths of Kreon and his daughter, Jason's intended, Ms. Shaw's face goes dead white and still, showing flickers of gratification and just as often of incomprehension that her plan has come to fruition.

And therein lies the real genius of Ms. Shaw's portraiture. Real life seldom affords the tidy motives of murder mysteries or the stark psychological blueprints of novels about serial killers. And the recent spate of reality television serials have confirmed that famous people are never just the cleanly drawn cartoons we would like them to be. Witness the on-camera disintegration of Anna Nicole Smith.

Ms. Shaw and Ms. Warner have created one of the most human Medeas ever, precisely because they have refused to simplify her. Medea's acts may be monstrous, but the woman who performs them is a mass of confused impulses and thwarted drives that elude easy categorization. It is this very blurriness that makes her so vivid, so haunting and so damningly easy to identify with.

Aristophanes

"Lysistrata *is a peace play, a desperate peace play — a fantasy about how to bring war-torn nations to the peace table.*"

— ROBERT BRUSTEIN, FORMER ARTISTIC DIRECTOR, AMERICAN REPERTORY THEATRE

The best known of the Greek comic playwrights, Aristophanes (c. 448–c. 385 BCE) lived through some of the most difficult times in Athenian history. He watched Athenian democracy fade and decay as factionalism and war took their toll on the strength of the city-state. By the time he died, Athens was caught up in a fierce struggle between supporters of democracy and supporters of oligarchy, government by a small group of leaders.

Aristophanes' plays are democratic in that they appealed to sophisticated and unsophisticated theatergoers alike. Skilled at complex wordplay, he also enjoyed spirited and rowdy comedy. Since his plays were often sharply critical of Athenian policies, his ability to make people laugh was essential to conveying his message. He was a practitioner of what we now call Old Comedy, an irreverent form that ridiculed and insulted prominent people and important institutions. By Aristophanes' time, Old Comedy had become fiercely satirical, especially concerning political matters. Because Aristophanes held strong opinions, he found satire an ideal form for his talents.

Of his more than thirty known plays, only eleven survive. They come from three main periods in his life, beginning, according to legend, when he was a young man, in 427 BCE. *The Acharnians* (425 BCE), from his first period, focuses on the theme of peace. Dicaeopolis (whose name means "honest" or "good citizen") decides to make a separate peace after the Spartans have ravaged the Acharnian vineyards. The Acharnians vow revenge, but Dicaeopolis explains that peace must begin as an individual decision. Aristophanes saw war as a corporate venture; peacemaking was easier for an individual than for a group or a nation.

The Acharnians was followed by *The Peace* in 421 BCE, just before Sparta and Athens signed a treaty, and it seems clearly to have been written in support of the Athenian peace party, whose power had been growing from the time of *The Acharnians* and whose cause had been aided by that play.

His second period was also dominated by the problems of war. Athens's ill-fated expedition to Sicily in violation of the Treaty of Nicias lies thematically beneath the surface of *The Birds* (414 BCE), in which some citizens build Cloud-Cuckoo-Land to come between the world of humans and the world of the gods. *Lysistrata* (411 BCE) is also from this period; its frank antiwar theme is related to the Sicilian wars and to the ultimately devastating Peloponnesian Wars. These were wars fought by Greek city-states in the areas south of Athens, the Peloponnesus. The states had voluntarily contributed money to arm and support Athens against the Persians in 480 BCE—resulting in the Athenian victory at Salamis. The states later became angry when Pericles, the Athenian leader, demanded that they continue giving contributions, much of which he used to fund the rebuilding of the Acropolis and other civic projects in Athens.

The other Greek city-states felt that Athens was becoming imperialistic and was overreaching itself. War broke out between the city-states in 431 BCE and lasted for nearly thirty years. These struggles and the difficulties of conducting a costly, long-distance war in Sicily combined eventually to exhaust the Athenian resources of men and funds. Soundly defeated in 405 BCE, Athens surrendered to Sparta in 404. Aristophanes lived to see the Spartan ships at rest in the harbors of Athens's chief port, the Piraeus. And he saw, too, the destruction of the walls of the city, leaving it essentially defenseless.

Aristophanes' third and final period, from 393 BCE to his death, includes *The Ecclesiazusae* (c. 392 BCE) (translated as "The Women in Government"), in which women dress as men, find their way into parliament, and pass a new constitution. It is a highly topical play that points to the current situation in Athens and the people's general discontent and anxiety. The last part of *The Plutus,* written five years later, is an allegory about the god of wealth, who is eventually encouraged to make the just wealthy and the unjust poor.

Among the best known of Aristophanes' plays are several whose names refer to the disguises or costumes of the chorus, among them *The Knights, The Wasps,* and *The Frogs. The Frogs* (405 BCE) is especially interesting for its focus on literary issues. It features a contest in the underworld between Aeschylus, who had been dead more than fifty years, and Euripides, who had just died at a relatively young age. Aristophanes uses the contest to make many enlightening comments about Greek tragedy and the skills of the two authors.

Even in his last period Aristophanes was an innovative force in theater. His last surviving play virtually does away with the chorus as an important character in the action. His later plays resemble modern comedies partly because the chorus does not intrude on the action. His genius helped shape later developments in comedy.

LYSISTRATA

At the time *Lysistrata* was written (411 BCE), Athens had suffered a steady diet of war for more than twenty years. Political groups were actively trying to persuade Athenian leaders to discontinue the policies that had alienated Athens from the other city-states that were once its supporters in the Delian League, the group that had funded Athens's struggle against the Persian threat. Aristophanes opposed the imperialist attitudes that conflicted with the democratic spirit of only a generation earlier.

Lysistrata makes it clear that war is the central business of the nation at that time. No sooner is one campaign ended than another begins. The men encountered by the heroine Lysistrata (whose name means "disband the army") on the Acropolis—men who guard the national security and the national treasury—are old and decrepit. The young men are in the field. As Kalonike tells Lysistrata, her man has been away for five months. Such separations were common, and these women are fed up. Lysistrata has gathered the discontented women together to propose a scheme to bring peace and negotiate a treaty.

The scheme is preposterous, but, as is typical of Old Comedy, its very outrageousness is its source of strength. In time, the idea begins to seem almost reasonable: Lysistrata asks the women to refuse to engage in sex with their husbands until the men stop making war. The women also seize the Acropolis and hold the treasury hostage. Without the national treasury there can be no war. And because they are confident of getting the support of the larger community of women in other nations—who suffer as they do—they do not fear the consequences of their acts.

In amusing scenes generated by this situation, Aristophanes pokes fun at both sexes. We hear the gossipy conversation of the women, all of whom arrive late to Lysistrata's meeting. The men are dependent, helpless, and ineffectual, and they cannot resist the takeover. When the truth begins to settle in, the men solicit their wives' attention with enormous erections protruding beneath their gowns, one example of the exaggerated visual humor Aristophanes counted on. The double meanings in the conversations are also a great source of humor. The wonderful scene (3) between Myrrhine and her husband Kinesias is predicated on the agony of the husband whose wife constantly promises, and then reneges, to build his sexual excitement to a fever pitch. It is no wonder that Lysistrata can eventually bring the men to sign any treaties she wants.

This heterosexual hilarity is also balanced by a number of homosexual allusions. Kleisthenes, possibly a bisexual Athenian, stands ready to relieve some of the men's sexual discomfort, while Lysistrata admits that if the men do not capitulate, the women will have to satisfy their own needs. Such frankness is typical of Athenian comedy.

Women dominate the action of the play, although we must remember that male actors played women's roles. The women see the stupidity and waste of the war and devise a plan that will end it. Observing that they are the ones who suffer most from the effects of war, the women also note that they pay their taxes in babies. The suffering of women had been a major theme in the tragedies of Euripides, and everyone in Aristophanes' audience would have understood Lysistrata's motivation. The idea that a woman should keep her place is expressed by several characters. And since Athenian audiences would have agreed that women should not meddle in war or government, Aristophanes offered them a fantasy that challenged them on many levels.

Aristophanes praises Lysistrata's ingenuity and her perseverance. When the other women want to give up the plan because of their own sexual needs, she holds firm. She demands that they stand by their resolve. The picture of a strong, independent, intelligent, and capable woman obviously pleased the Athenians because they permitted this play to be performed more than once—an unusual practice. Lysistrata became a recognizable and admirable character in Athenian life.

The following translation of *Lysistrata* has several interesting features. It is composed of scenes, a division not made in the original Greek. The strophe and antistrophe are speeches given by the chorus, probably moving first in one direction and then in the opposite. Instead of having a chorus of elders, as in *Antigone*, Aristophanes uses two choruses—one of men and one of women—that are truly representative of the people: they are as divided and antagonistic as Sophocles' chorus is united and wise. The KORYPHAIOS (leader) of the men's chorus speaks alone, often in opposition to the koryphaios of the women's chorus.

The rhyming patterns of some of the songs are approximated in English, and the sense of dialect is maintained in the speech of Lampito, who represents a kind of country bumpkin. She is very muscular from the workouts that she and all other Spartans engaged in; Aristophanes reveals certain Athenian prejudices toward the Spartans in the scene where Lampito is taunted for her physique.

Lysistrata in Performance

Lysistrata has enjoyed and still enjoys numerous productions, on both college and commercial stages. Because it is a bawdy play, it has sometimes run into trouble. In 1932 the New York police shut down a performance and sent out a warrant for the arrest of "Arthur" Aristophanes. In 1959 Dudley Fitts's translation (used here) was performed at the Phoenix Theater in New York with "women . . . wearing simulated breasts, tipped with sequins, and the ruttish old men stripped down to union suits." Hunter College's 1968 production used rock music, hippie beads, and headbands. Less controversial productions include the first modern version, by Maurice Donnay in Paris (1892), in which Lysistrata takes a general as a lover. The Moscow Art Theater produced a highly acclaimed version in 1923 and brought it to the United States in 1925. That version, modified by Gilbert Seldes (published in book form with illustrations by Picasso), was produced throughout the 1930s. All-black versions of the play have been staged several times since 1938. Since 2001 this play has been produced in many countries, including France in 2006 and in the United States, in Boston with Cherry Jones as Lysistrata, in 2002. *Lysistrata* ranks among the favorites of classical drama.

Aristophanes (c. 448–c. 385 BCE)

LYSISTRATA
TRANSLATED BY DUDLEY FITTS

411 BCE

Persons Represented

LYSISTRATA,
KALONIKE, } *Athenian women*
MYRRHINE,
LAMPITO, *a Spartan woman*
CHORUS
COMMISSIONER
KINESIAS, *husband of Myrrhine*
SPARTAN HERALD
SPARTAN AMBASSADOR

A SENTRY
[BABY SON OF KENESIAS
STRATYLLIS
SPARTANS
ATHENIANS]

Scene: *Athens. First, a public square; later, beneath the walls of the Akropolis;° later, a courtyard within the Akropolis.*

Akropolis: Fortress of Athens, sacred to the goddess Athena.

PROLOGUE°

(*Athens; a public square; early morning; Lysistrata alone.*)

LYSISTRATA: If someone had invited them to a
    festival—
    of Bacchos,° say; or to Pan's° shrine, or to
    Aphrodite's°
    over at Kolias—, you couldn't get through the
    streets,
    what with the drums and the dancing. But now,
    not a woman in sight!
5   Except—oh, yes!

(*Enter Kalonike.*)

    Here's one of my neighbors, at last. Good
    morning, Kalonike.
KALONIKE: Good morning, Lysistrata.
                      Darling,
    don't frown so! You'll ruin your face!
LYSISTRATA: Never mind my face.
    Kalonike,
    the way we women behave! Really, I don't blame
10   the men
    for what they say about us.
KALONIKE: No; I imagine they're right.
LYSISTRATA: For example: I call a meeting
    to think out a most important matter—and what
    happens?
    The women all stay in bed!
KALONIKE: Oh, they'll be along.
15   It's hard to get away, you know: a husband, a cook,
    a child . . . Home life can be *so* demanding!
LYSISTRATA: What I have in mind is even more
    demanding.
KALONIKE: Tell me: what is it?
LYSISTRATA: It's big.
KALONIKE: Goodness! *How* big?
LYSISTRATA: Big enough for all of us.
KALONIKE: But we're not all here!
LYSISTRATA: We would be, if *that's* what was up!
20   No, Kalonike,
    this is something I've been turning over for nights,
    long sleepless nights.
KALONIKE: It must be getting worn down, then,
    if you've spent so much time on it.
LYSISTRATA: Worn down or not,
    it comes to this: Only we women can save Greece!
KALONIKE: Only we women? Poor Greece!
25 LYSISTRATA: Just the same,

it's up to us. First, we must liquidate
    the Peloponnesians—
KALONIKE: Fun, fun!
LYSISTRATA: —and then the Boiotians.°
KALONIKE: Oh! But not those heavenly eels!
LYSISTRATA: You needn't worry.
    I'm not talking about eels.—But here's the point:
    If we can get the women from those places—   30
    all those Boiotians and Peloponnesians—
    to join us women here, why, we can save all Greece!
KALONIKE: But dearest Lysistrata!
    How can women do a thing so austere, so
    political? We belong at home. Our only armor's   35
    our perfumes, our saffron dresses and
    our pretty little shoes!
LYSISTRATA: Exactly. Those
    transparent dresses, the saffron, the perfume, those
    pretty shoes—
KALONIKE: Oh?
LYSISTRATA: Not a single man would lift
    his spear—
KALONIKE: I'll send my dress to the dyer's tomorrow!
LYSISTRATA: —or grab a shield—
KALONIKE: The sweetest little negligee—   40
LYSISTRATA: —or haul out his sword.
KALONIKE: I know where
    I can buy the dreamiest sandals!
LYSISTRATA: Well, so you see. Now, shouldn't
    the women have come?
KALONIKE: Come? They should have *flown*!
LYSISTRATA: Athenians are always late.
                 But imagine!
    There's no one here from the South Shore, or from
    Salamis.   45
KALONIKE: Things are hard over in Salamis, I swear.
    They have to get going at dawn.
LYSISTRATA: And nobody from Acharnai.
    I thought they'd be here hours ago.
KALONIKE: Well, you'll get
    that awful Theagenes woman: she'll be
    a sheet or so in the wind.
                 But look!   50
    Someone at last! Can you see who they are?

(*Enter Myrrhine and other women.*)

LYSISTRATA: They're from Anagyros.
KALONIKE: They certainly are.
    You'd know them anywhere, by the scent.
MYRRHINE: Sorry to be late, Lysistrata.
                Oh come,
    don't scowl so. Say something!
LYSISTRATA: My dear Myrrhine,   55
    what is there to say? After all,
    you've been pretty casual about the whole thing.

Prologue: Portion of the play explaining the background and current action. **2. Bacchos:** (Bacchus) God of wine and the object of wild, orgiastic ritual and celebration; also called Dionysus. **Pan:** God of nature, forests, flocks, and shepherds, depicted as half-man and half-goat. Pan was considered playful and lecherous. **Aphrodite:** Goddess of love.

27. Boiotians: Crude-mannered inhabitants of Boiotia, which was noted for its seafood.

MYRRHINE: Couldn't find
    my girdle in the dark, that's all.
                                       But what *is*
        "the whole thing"?
KALONIKE: No, we've got to wait
60   for those Boiotians and Peloponnesians.
LYSISTRATA: That's more like it.—But, look!
    Here's Lampito!

(*Enter Lampito with women from Sparta.*)

LYSISTRATA: Darling Lampito,
    how pretty you are today! What a nice color!
    Goodness, you look as though you could strangle a
65   bull!
LAMPITO: Ah think Ah could! It's the work-out
    in the gym every day; and, of co'se that dance of ahs
    where y' kick yo' own tail.
KALONIKE: What an adorable figure!
LAMPITO: Lawdy, when y' touch me lahk that,
    Ah feel lahk a heifer at the altar!
70 LYSISTRATA: And this young lady?
    Where is she from?
LAMPITO: Boiotia. Social-Register type.
LYSISTRATA: Ah. "Boiotia of the fertile plain."
KALONIKE: And if you look,
    you'll find the fertile plain has just been mowed.
LYSISTRATA: And this lady?
LAMPITO: Hagh, wahd, handsome.
75   She comes from Korinth.
KALONIKE: High and wide's the word for it.
LAMPITO: Which one of you
    called this heah meeting, and why?
LYSISTRATA: I did.
LAMPITO: Well, then, tell us:
    What's up?
MYRRHINE: Yes, darling, what *is* on your mind, after
                                                      all?
LYSISTRATA: I'll tell you.—But first, one little question.
MYRRHINE: Well?
LYSISTRATA: It's your husbands. Fathers of your
80   children. Doesn't it bother you
    that they're always off with the Army? I'll stake my
        life,
    not one of you has a man in the house this minute!
KALONIKE: Mine's been in Thrace the last five months,
        keeping an eye
    on that General.
MYRRHINE: Mine's been in Pylos for seven.
LAMPITO: And mahn,
85   whenever he gets a *dis*charge, he goes raht back
    with that li'l ole shield of his, and enlists again!
LYSISTRATA: And not the ghost of a lover to be found!
    From the very day the war began—
                                       those Milesians!
    I could skin them alive!
                          —I've not seen so much, even,
90 as one of those leather consolation prizes.—
    But there! What's important is: If I've found a way
    to end the war, are you with me?

MYRRHINE: I should *say* so!
    Even if I have to pawn my best dress and
    drink up the proceeds.
KALONIKE: Me, too! Even if they split me
    right up the middle, like a flounder.
LAMPITO: Ah'm shorely with you.   95
    Ah'd crawl up Taygetos° on mah knees
    if that'd bring peace.
LYSISTRATA: All right, then; here it is:
    Women! Sisters!
    If we really want our men to make peace,
    we must be ready to give up—
MYRRHINE: Give up what?   100
    Quick, tell us!
LYSISTRATA: But *will* you?
MYRRHINE: We will, even if it kills us.
LYSISTRATA: Then we must give up going to bed with
        our men.

(*Long silence.*)

    Oh? So now you're sorry? Won't look at me?
    Doubtful? Pale? All teary-eyed?
                          But come: be frank with me.
    Will you do it, or not? Well? Will you do it?
MYRRHINE: I couldn't. No.   105
    Let the war go on.
KALONIKE: Nor I. Let the war go on.
LYSISTRATA: You, you little flounder,
    ready to be split up the middle?
KALONIKE: Lysistrata, no!
    I'd walk through fire for you—you *know* I
        would!—but don't
    ask us to give up *that!* Why, there's nothing like it!   110
LYSISTRATA: And you?
BOIOTIAN: No. I must say *I'd* rather walk
        through fire.
LYSISTRATA: What an utterly perverted sex we women
        are!
    No wonder poets write tragedies about us.
    There's only one thing we can think of.
                          But you from Sparta:
    if you stand by me, we may win yet! Will you?   115
    It means so much!
LAMPITO: Ah sweah, it means *too* much!
    By the Two Goddesses,° it does! Asking a girl
    to sleep—Heaven knows how long!—in a great
        big bed
    with nobody there but herself! But Ah'll stay with
        you!
    Peace comes first!
LYSISTRATA: Spoken like a true Spartan!   120

96. Taygetos: A mountain range.   **117. Two Goddesses:** A woman's oath referring to Demeter, the earth goddess, and her daughter Persephone, who was associated with seasonal cycles of fertility.

KALONIKE: But if—
                    oh dear!
                          —if we give up what you tell us to,
will there *be* any peace?
LYSISTRATA: Why, mercy, of course there will!
We'll just sit snug in our very thinnest gowns,
perfumed and powdered from top to bottom, and
    those men
125 simply won't stand still! And when we say No,
they'll go out of their minds! And there's your peace.
You can take my word for it.
LAMPITO: Ah seem to remember
that Colonel Menelaos threw his sword away
when he saw Helen's breast° all bare.
KALONIKE: But, goodness me!
What if they just get up and leave us?
130 LYSISTRATA: In that case
we'll have to fall back on ourselves, I suppose.
But they won't.
KALONIKE: I must say that's not much help. But
what if they drag us into the bedroom?
LYSISTRATA: Hang on to the door.
KALONIKE: What if they slap us?
LYSISTRATA: If they do, you'd better give in.
135 But be sulky about it. Do I have to teach you how?
You know there's no fun for men when they have
    to force you.
There are millions of ways of getting them to see
    reason.
Don't you worry: a man
doesn't like it unless the girl cooperates.
140 KALONIKE: I suppose so. Oh, all right. We'll go along.
LAMPITO: Ah imagine us Spahtans can arrange a
    peace. But you
Athenians! Why, you're just war-mongerers!
LYSISTRATA: Leave that to me.
I know how to make them listen.
LAMPITO: Ah don't see how.
After all, they've got their boats; and there's lots
    of money
    piled up in the Akropolis.
145 LYSISTRATA: The Akropolis? Darling,
we're taking over the Akropolis today!
That's the older women's job. All the rest of us
are going to the Citadel to sacrifice—you
    understand me?
And once there, we're in for good!
LAMPITO: Whee! Up the rebels!
Ah can see you're a good strate*egist*.
150 LYSISTRATA: Well, then, Lampito,
what we have to do now is take a solemn oath.
LAMPITO: Say it. We'll sweah.
LYSISTRATA: This is it.
—But where's our Inner Guard?
                    —Look. Guard: you see this shield?

Put it down here. Now bring me the victim's entrails.
KALONIKE: But the oath?
LYSISTRATA: You remember how in Aischylos'
                         Seven°   155
they killed a sheep and swore on a shield? Well,
    then?
KALONIKE: But I don't see how you can swear for
    peace on a shield.
LYSISTRATA: What else do you suggest?
KALONIKE: Why not a white horse?
We could swear by that.
LYSISTRATA: And where will you get a white horse?
KALONIKE: I never thought of that. *What* can we do?
LYSISTRATA: I have it!   160
Let's set this big black wine-bowl on the ground
and pour in a gallon or so of Thasian,° and swear
not to add one drop of water.
LAMPITO: Ah lahk *that* oath!
LYSISTRATA: Bring the bowl and the wine-jug.
KALONIKE: Oh, what a simply *huge* one!
LYSISTRATA: Set it down. Girls, place your hands on
    the gift-offering.   165
    O Goddess of Persuasion! And thou, O Loving-cup:
Look upon this our sacrifice, and
be gracious!
KALONIKE: See the blood spill out. How red and pretty
    it is!
LAMPITO: And Ah must say it smells good.
MYRRHINE: Let me swear first!   170
KALONIKE: No, by Aphrodite, we'll match for it!
LYSISTRATA: Lampito: all of you women: come, touch
    the bowl,
and repeat after me—remember, this is an oath—:
I WILL HAVE NOTHING TO DO WITH MY
    HUSBAND OR MY LOVER
KALONIKE: *I will have nothing to do with my husband
    or my lover*   175
LYSISTRATA: THOUGH HE COME TO ME IN
    PITIABLE CONDITION
KALONIKE: *Though he come to me in pitiable condition*
    (Oh Lysistrata! This is killing me!)
LYSISTRATA: IN MY HOUSE I WILL BE
    UNTOUCHABLE
KALONIKE: *In my house I will be untouchable*   180
LYSISTRATA: IN MY THINNEST SAFFRON SILK
KALONIKE: *In my thinnest saffron silk*
LYSISTRATA: AND MAKE HIM LONG FOR ME.
KALONIKE: *And make him long for me.*
LYSISTRATA: I WILL NOT GIVE MYSELF   185
KALONIKE: *I will not give myself*
LYSISTRATA: AND IF HE CONSTRAINS ME
KALONIKE: *And if he constrains me*
LYSISTRATA: I WILL BE COLD AS ICE AND NEVER
    MOVE

127–28. Colonel Menelaos . . . Helen's breast: Helen, wife of
King Menelaos of Sparta, was abducted by Paris and taken to
Troy. The incident led to the Trojan War.

155. *Seven:* Aeschylus's *Seven against Thebes*, which deals with
the war between the sons of Oedipus for the throne of Thebes.
162. Thasian: Wine from Thasos.

190   KALONIKE: *I will be cold as ice and never move*
LYSISTRATA: I WILL NOT LIFT MY SLIPPERS
            TOWARD THE CEILING
KALONIKE: *I will not lift my slippers toward the ceiling*
LYSISTRATA: OR CROUCH ON ALL FOURS LIKE
            THE LIONESS IN THE CARVING
KALONIKE: *Or crouch on all fours like the lioness in
            the carving*
LYSISTRATA: AND IF I KEEP THIS OATH LET ME
195   DRINK FROM THIS BOWL
KALONIKE: *And if I keep this oath let me drink from
            this bowl*
LYSISTRATA: IF NOT, LET MY OWN BOWL BE
            FILLED WITH WATER.
KALONIKE: *If not, let my own bowl be filled with
            water.*
LYSISTRATA: You have all sworn?
MYRRHINE: We have.
LYSISTRATA: Then thus
    I sacrifice the victim.

(*Drinks largely.*)

200   KALONIKE: Save some for us!
    Here's to you, darling, and to you, and to you!

(*Loud cries offstage.*)

LAMPITO: What's all *that* whoozy-goozy?
LYSISTRATA: Just what I told you.
    The older women have taken the Akropolis.
    Now you, Lampito,
    rush back to Sparta. We'll take care of things here.
205   Leave
    these girls here for hostages.
                        The rest of you,
    up to the Citadel: and mind you push in the bolts.
KALONIKE: But the men? Won't they be after us?
LYSISTRATA: Just you leave
    the men to me. There's not fire enough in the world,
210   or threats either, to make me open these doors
    except on my own terms.
KALONIKE: I hope not, by Aphrodite!
    After all,
    we've got a reputation for bitchiness to live up to.
                                    (*Exeunt.°*)

PARODOS:°
CHORAL EPISODE

(*The hillside just under the Akropolis. Enter Chorus of
Old Men with burning torches and braziers; much puffing and coughing.*)

---

213. [S.D.] *Exeunt:* Latin for "they go out."   **Parodos:** The
song or ode chanted by the Chorus on their entry.

KORYPHAIOS(man):° Forward march, Drakes, old friend:
    never you mind
    that damn big log banging hell down on your back.

Strophe° 1

CHORUS(men): There's this to be said for longevity:
    You see things you thought that you'd never see.
        Look, Strymodoros, who would have thought it?   5
        We've caught it—
                    the New Femininity!
    The wives of our bosom, our board, our bed—
    Now, by the gods, they've gone ahead
    And taken the Citadel (Heaven knows why!),
    Profanèd the sacred statuar-y,   10
                        And barred the doors,
                        The subversive whores!
KORYPHAIOS(m): Shake a leg there, Philurgos, man: the
    Akropolis or bust!
    Put the kindling around here. We'll build one
    almighty big
    bonfire for the whole bunch of bitches, every last one; 15
    and the first we fry will be old Lykon's woman.

Antistrophe° 1

CHORUS(m): They're not going to give me the old
    horse-laugh!
    No, by Demeter, they won't pull this off!
        Think of Kleomenes: even he
        Didn't go free
                    till he brought me his stuff.   20
    A good man he was, all stinking and shaggy,
    Bare as an eel except for the bag he
    Covered his rear with. God, what a mess!
    Never a bath in six years, I'd guess.
                        Pure Sparta, man!   25
                        He also ran.
KORYPHAIOS(m): That was a siege, friends! Seventeen
    ranks strong
    we slept at the Gate. And shall we not do as much
    against these women, whom God and Euripides hate?
    If we don't, I'll turn in my medals from Marathon.   30

Strophe 2

CHORUS(m): Onward and upward! A little push,
    And we're there.

---

1. Koryphaios: Leader of the Chorus; also called *Choragos.*
There are two Choruses and two Koryphaioi, one male and
one female.   **Strophe:** Song sung by the Chorus as it danced
from stage right to stage left.   **Antistrophe:** Song sung by the
Chorus following the Strophe, as it danced back from stage left
to stage right.

Ouch, my shoulders! I could wish
    For a pair
35 Of good strong oxen. Keep your eye
    On the fire there, it mustn't die.
        Akh! Akh!
  The smoke would make a cadaver cough!

Antistrophe 2

Holy Herakles, a hot spark
40   Bit my eye!
  Damn this hellfire, damn this work!
    So say I.
  Onward and upward just the same.
  (Laches, remember the Goddess: for shame!)
45   Akh! Akh!
  The smoke would make a cadaver cough!

KORYPHAIOS(m): At last (and let us give suitable thanks
    to God
for his infinite mercies) I have managed to bring
my personal flame to the common goal. It
    breathes, it lives.
50 Now, gentlemen, let us consider. Shall we insert
the torch, say, into the brazier, and thus extract
a kindling brand? And shall we then, do you think,
push on to the gate like valiant sheep? On the whole
    yes.
But I would have you consider this, too: if they—
55 I refer to the women—should refuse to open,
what then? Do we set the doors afire
and smoke them out? At ease, men. Meditate.
Akh, the smoke! Woof! What we really need
is the loan of a general or two from the Samos
    Command.°
60 At least we've got this lumber off our backs.
That's something. And now let's look to our fire.
O Pot, brave Brazier, touch my torch with flame!
Victory, Goddess, I invoke thy name!
Strike down these paradigms of female pride
65 And we shall hang our trophies up inside.

(*Enter Chorus of Old Women on the walls of the
Akropolis, carrying jars of water.*)

KORYPHAIOS(woman): Smoke, girls, smoke! There's smoke
    all over the place!
  Probably fire, too. Hurry, girls! Fire! Fire!

Strophe 1

CHORUS(women): Nikodike, run!
    Or Kalyke's done
70 To a turn, and poor Kritylla's
  Smoked like a ham.
          Damn

59. **Samos Command:** Headquarters of the Athenian military.

These old men! Are we too late?
I nearly died down at the place
Where we fill our jars:
  Slaves pushing and jostling—   75
  Such a hustling
I never saw in all my days.

Antistrophe 1

But here's water at last.
Haste, sisters, haste!
Slosh it on them, slosh it down,   80
The silly old wrecks!
              Sex
Almighty! What they want's
A hot bath? Good. Send one down.
Athena of Athens town,
  Trito-born!° Helm of Gold!   85
  Cripple the old
Firemen! Help us help them drown!

(*The old men capture a woman, Stratyllis.*)

STRATYLLIS: Let me go! Let me go!
KORYPHAIOS(w):   You walking corpses,
  have you no shame?
KORYPHAIOS(m):   I wouldn't have believed it!
  An army of women in the Akropolis!   90
KORYPHAIOS(w): So we scare you, do we? Grandpa,
    you've seen
  only our pickets yet!
KORYPHAIOS(m):   Hey, Phaidrias!
  Help me with the necks of these jabbering hens!
KORYPHAIOS(w): Down with your pots, girls! We'll need
    both hands
  if these antiques attack us!
KORYPHAIOS(m):   Want your face kicked in? 95
KORYPHAIOS(w): Want your balls chewed off?
KORYPHAIOS(m):   Look out! I've got a stick!
KORYPHAIOS(w): You lay a half-inch of your stick on
    Stratyllis,
  and you'll never stick again!
KORYPHAIOS(m): Fall apart!
KORYPHAIOS(w):   I'll spit up your guts!
KORYPHAIOS(m):   Euripides! Master!
  How well you knew women!
KORYPHAIOS(w):   Listen to him, Rhodippe, 100
  up with the pots!
KORYPHAIOS(m):   Demolition of God,
  what good are your pots?
KORYPHAIOS(w):   You refugee from the tomb,
  what good is your fire?
KORYPHAIOS(m):   Good enough to make a pyre
  to barbecue you!
KORYPHAIOS(w):   We'll squizzle your kindling!
KORYPHAIOS(m): You think so?

85. **Trito-born:** Athena, goddess of wisdom, was said to have
been born near Lake Tritonis in Libya.

105 KORYPHAIOS⁽ʷ⁾:   Yah! Just hang around a while!
KORYPHAIOS⁽ᵐ⁾: Want a touch of my torch?
KORYPHAIOS⁽ʷ⁾:   It needs a good soaping.
KORYPHAIOS⁽ᵐ⁾: How about you?
KORYPHAIOS⁽ʷ⁾:   Soap for a senile bridegroom!
KORYPHAIOS⁽ᵐ⁾: Senile? Hold your trap
KORYPHAIOS⁽ʷ⁾:   Just *you* try to hold it!
KORYPHAIOS⁽ᵐ⁾: The yammer of women!
KORYPHAIOS⁽ʷ⁾:   Oh is that so?
110   You're not in the jury room now, you know.
KORYPHAIOS⁽ᵐ⁾: Gentlemen, I beg you, burn off that
        woman's hair!
KORYPHAIOS⁽ʷ⁾: Let it come down!

(*They empty their pots on the men.*)

KORYPHAIOS⁽ᵐ⁾: What a way to drown!
KORYPHAIOS⁽ʷ⁾:   Hot, hey?
KORYPHAIOS⁽ᵐ⁾:   Say, enough!
KORYPHAIOS⁽ʷ⁾: Dandruff
115   needs watering. I'll make you
      nice and fresh.
KORYPHAIOS⁽ᵐ⁾: For God's sake, you,
      hold off!

SCENE 1

(*Enter a Commissioner accompanied by four constables.*)

COMMISSIONER: These degenerate women! What a
        racket of little drums,
    what a yapping for Adonis° on every house-top!
    It's like the time in the Assembly when I was listening
    to a speech—out of order, as usual—by that fool
5   Demostratos,° all about troops for Sicily,°
    that kind of nonsense—
                        and there was his wife
    trotting around in circles howling
    Alas for Adonis!—
                    and Demostratos insisting
    we must draft every last Zakynthian that can walk—
10 and his wife up there on the roof,
    drunk as an owl, yowling
    Oh weep for Adonis!—
                        and that damned ox Demostratos
    mooing away through the rumpus. That's what we
        get
    for putting up with this wretched woman-business!
KORYPHAIOS⁽ᵐ⁾: Sir, you haven't heard the half of it.
15   They laughed at us!
    Insulted us! They took pitchers of water
    and nearly drowned us! We're still wringing out our
        clothes,
    for all the world like unhousebroken brats.

---

2. Adonis: Fertility god, loved by Aphrodite. **5. Demostratos:** Athenian orator and politician. **Sicily:** Reference to the Sicilian Expedition (415–413 BCE) in which Athens was decisively defeated.

COMMISSIONER: Serves you right, by Poseidon!
    Whose fault is it if these women-folk of ours   20
    get out of hand? We coddle them,
    we teach them to be wasteful and loose. You'll see a
        husband
    go into a jeweler's. "Look," he'll say,
    "jeweler," he'll say, "you remember that gold choker
    you made for my wife? Well, she went to a dance
        last night   25
    and broke the clasp. Now, I've got to go to Salamis,
    and can't be bothered. Run over to my house tonight,
    will you, and see if you can put it together for her."
    Or another one
    goes to a cobbler—a good strong workman, too,   30
    with an awl that was never meant for child's play.
        "Here,"
    he'll tell him, "one of my wife's shoes is pinching
    her little toe. Could you come up about noon
    and stretch it out for her?"
                            Well, what do you expect?
    Look at me, for example, I'm a Public Officer,   35
    and it's one of my duties to pay off the sailors.
    And where's the money? Up there in the Akropolis!
    And those blasted women slam the door in my face!
    But what are we waiting for?
                        —Look here, constable,
    stop sniffing around for a tavern, and get us   40
    some crowbars. We'll force their gates! As a matter
        of fact,
    I'll do a little forcing myself.

(*Enter Lysistrata, above, with Myrrhine, Kalonike, and the Boiotian.*)

LYSISTRATA: No need of forcing.
    Here I am, of my own accord. And all this talk
    about locked doors—! We don't need locked doors,
    but just the least bit of common sense.   45
COMMISSIONER: Is that so, ma'am!
                        —Where's my constable?
                        —Constable,
    arrest that woman, and tie her hands behind her.
LYSISTRATA: If he touches me, I swear by Artemis
    there'll be one scamp dropped from the public
        pay-roll tomorrow!
COMMISSIONER: Well, constable? You're not afraid, I
        suppose? Grab her,   50
    two of you, around the middle!
KALONIKE: No, by Pandrosos!°
    Lay a hand on her, and I'll jump on you so hard
    your guts will come out the back door!
COMMISSIONER: That's what *you* think!
    Where's the sergeant?—Here, you: tie up that
        trollop first,
    the one with the pretty talk!

---

51. Pandrosos: A woman's oath referring to one of the daughters of the founder of Athens.

55 MYRRHINE: By the Moon-Goddess,°
        just try! They'll have to scoop you up with a spoon!
    COMMISSIONER: Another one!
                                Officer, seize that woman!
                                                    I swear
        I'll put an end to this riot!
    BOIOTIAN: By the Taurian,°
        one inch closer, you'll be one screaming bald-head!
    COMMISSIONER: Lord, what a mess! And my
60   constables seem ineffective.
        But—women get the best of us? By God, no!
                                              —Skythians!°
        Close ranks and forward march!
    LYSISTRATA: "Forward," indeed!
        By the Two Goddesses, what's the sense in *that*?
        They're up against four companies of women
        armed from top to bottom.
65 COMMISSIONER: Forward, my Skythians!
    LYSISTRATA: Forward, yourselves, dear comrades!
        You grainlettucebeanseedmarket girls!
        You garlicandonionbreadbakery girls!
        Give it to 'em! Knock 'em down! Scratch 'em!
        Tell 'em what you think of 'em!

    (*General melee, the Skythians yield.*)

70   —Ah, that's enough!
        Sound a retreat: good soldiers don't rob the dead.
    COMMISSIONER: A nice day *this* has been for the police!
    LYSISTRATA: Well, there you are.—Did you really
            think we women
        would be driven like slaves? Maybe now you'll admit
        that a woman knows something about spirit.
75 COMMISSIONER: Spirit enough,
        especially spirits in bottles! Dear Lord Apollo!
    KORYPHAIOS(m): Your Honor, there's no use talking to
            them. Words
        mean nothing whatever to wild animals like these.
        Think of the sousing they gave us! and the water
80   was not, I believe, of the purest.
    KORYPHAIOS(w): You shouldn't have come after us.
            And if you try it again,
        you'll be one eye short!—Although, as a matter of
            fact,
        what I like best is just to stay at home and read,
        like a sweet little bride: never hurting a soul, no,
85   never going out. But if you *must* shake hornets' nests,
        look out for the hornets.

Strophe

    CHORUS(m): Of all the beasts that God hath wrought
            What monster's worse than woman?

Who shall encompass with his thought
        Their guile unending? No man.   90

They've seized the Heights, the Rock, the Shrine—
        But to what end? I wot not.
Sure there's some clue to their design!
        Have you the key? I thought not.
KORYPHAIOS(m): We might question them, I suppose.   95
        But I warn you, sir,
    don't believe anything you hear! It would be un-
            Athenian
    not to get to the bottom of this plot.
COMMISSIONER: Very well.
    My first question is this: Why, so help you God,
    did you bar the gates of the Akropolis?
LYSISTRATA: Why?
    To keep the money, of course. No money, no war.   100
COMMISSIONER: You think that money's the cause of
        war?
LYSISTRATA: I do.
    Money brought about that Peisandros° business
    and all the other attacks on the State. Well and good!
    They'll not get another cent here!
COMMISSIONER: And what will you do? 105
LYSISTRATA: What a question! From now on, we intend
    to control the Treasury.
COMMISSIONER: Control the Treasury!
LYSISTRATA: Why not? Does that seem strange?
        After all,
    we control our household budgets.
COMMISSIONER: But that's different!
LYSISTRATA: "Different"? What do you mean?
COMMISSIONER: I mean simply this: 110
    it's the Treasury that pays for National Defense.
LYSISTRATA: Unnecessary. We propose to abolish war.
COMMISSIONER: Good God.—And National
        Security?
LYSISTRATA: Leave that to us.
COMMISSIONER: You?
LYSISTRATA: Us.
COMMISSIONER: We're done for, then!
LYSISTRATA: Never mind.   115
    We women will save you in spite of yourselves.
COMMISSIONER: What nonsense!
LYSISTRATA: If you like. But you must accept it, like it
    or not.
COMMISSIONER: Why, this is downright subversion!
LYSISTRATA: Maybe it is.
    But we're going to save you, Judge.
COMMISSIONER: I don't *want* to be saved.
LYSISTRATA: Tut. The death-wish. All the more reason.   120
COMMISSIONER: But the idea of women bothering
        themselves about peace and war!
LYSISTRATA: Will you listen to me?

---

55. Moon-Goddess: Artemis, goddess of the hunt and of fertility, daughter of Zeus.   **58. Taurian:** Reference to Artemis, who was said to have been worshiped in a cult at Taurica Chersonesos.   **61. Skythians:** Athenian archers.

103. Peisandros: A politician who plotted against the Athenian democracy.

COMMISSIONER: Yes. But be brief, or I'll—

LYSISTRATA: This is no time for stupid threats.

COMMISSIONER: By the gods,
  I can't stand any more!

AN OLD WOMAN: Can't stand? Well, well.

COMMISSIONER: That's enough out of you, you old
125   buzzard!
  Now, Lysistrata: tell me what you're thinking.

LYSISTRATA: Glad to.
                        Ever since this war began
  We women have been watching you men, agreeing
    with you,
  keeping our thoughts to ourselves. That doesn't mean
  we were happy: we weren't, for we saw how
130   things were going;
  but we'd listen to you at dinner
  arguing this way and that.
                        —Oh you, and your big
  Top Secrets!—
                  And then we'd grin like little patriots
  (though goodness knows we didn't feel like
    grinning) and ask you:
  "Dear, did the Armistice come up in Assembly
135   today?"
  And you'd say, "None of your business! Pipe
    down!" you'd say.
  And so we would.

AN OLD WOMAN: *I* wouldn't have, by God!

COMMISSIONER: You'd have taken a beating, then!
                        —Go on.

LYSISTRATA: Well, we'd be quiet. But then, you know,
    all at once
140   you men would think up something worse than ever.
  Even *I* could see it was fatal. And, "Darling,"
    I'd say,
  "have you gone completely mad?" And my husband
    would look at me
  and say, "Wife, you've got your weaving to attend
    to.
  Mind your tongue, if you don't want a slap.
145   'War's a man's affair!'"°

COMMISSIONER: Good words, and well pronounced.

LYSISTRATA: You're a fool if you think so.
                        It was hard enough
  to put up with all this banquet-hall strategy.
  But then we'd hear you out in the public square:
150   "Nobody left for the draft-quota here in Athens?"
  you'd say; and, "No," someone else would say, "not
    a man!"
  And so we women decided to rescue Greece.
  You might as well listen to us now: you'll have to,
    later.

COMMISSIONER: *You* rescue Greece? Absurd.

LYSISTRATA: You're the absurd one.

COMMISSIONER: You expect me to take orders from a
    woman?
                  I'd die first!   155

LYSISTRATA: Heavens, if that's what's bothering you,
    take my veil,
  here, and wrap it around your poor head.

KALONIKE: Yes
  and you can have my market-basket, too.
  Go home, tighten your girdle, do the washing, mind
  your beans! "War's   160
  a woman's affair!"

KORYPHAIOS⁽ᵂ⁾:   Ground pitchers! Close ranks!

Antistrophe

CHORUS⁽ᵂ⁾: This is a dance that I know well,
    My knees shall never yield.
  Wobble and creak I may, but still
    I'll keep the well-fought field.   165
  Valor and grace march on before,
    Love prods us from behind.
  Our slogan is EXCELSIOR,
    Our watchword SAVE MANKIND.

KORYPHAIOS⁽ᵂ⁾: Women, remember your grandmothers!
    Remember   170
  that little old mother of yours, what a stinger she
    was!
  On, on, never slacken. There's a strong wind astern!

LYSISTRATA: O Eros of delight! O Aphrodite! Kyprian!°
  If ever desire has drenched our breasts or dreamed
  in our thighs, let it work so now on the men of
    Hellas°   175
  that they shall tail us through the land, slaves, slaves
  to Woman, Breaker of Armies!

COMMISSIONER: And if we do?

LYSISTRATA: Well, for one thing, we shan't have to
    watch you
  going to market, a spear in one hand, and heaven
    knows
  what in the other.

KALONIKE: Nicely said, by Aphrodite!   180

LYSISTRATA: As things stand now, you're neither men
    nor women.
  Armor clanking with kitchen pans and pots—
  You sound like a pack of Korybantes!°

COMMISSIONER: A man must do what a man must do.

LYSISTRATA: So I'm told.
  But to see a General, complete with Gorgon-shield,   185
  jingling along the dock to buy a couple of herrings!

---

145. 'War's a man's affair!': Quoted from Homer's *Iliad,* VI,
492, Hector's farewell to his wife, Andromache.

173. Kyprian: Reference to Aphrodite's association with
Cyprus (Kyprus), a place sacred to her and a center for her
worship.   **175. Hellas:** Greece.   **183. Korybantes:** Priestesses
of Cybele, a fertility goddess, who was celebrated in frenzied
rituals accompanied by the beating of cymbals.

KALONIKE: *I saw a Captain the other day—lovely fellow he was,*
  nice curly hair—sitting on his horse; and—can you believe it?—
  he'd just bought some soup, and was pouring it into his helmet!
190 And there was a soldier from Thrace
  swishing his lance like something out of Euripides,
  and the poor fruit-store woman got so scared
  that she ran away and let him have his figs free!
COMMISSIONER: All this is beside the point.
                              Will you be so kind
  as to tell me how you mean to save Greece?
195 LYSISTRATA: Of course.
  Nothing could be simpler.
COMMISSIONER: I assure you, I'm all ears.
LYSISTRATA: Do you know anything about weaving?
  Say the yarn gets tangled: we thread it
  this way and that through the skein, up and down,
200 until it's free. And it's like that with war.
  We'll send our envoys
  up and down, this way and that, all over Greece,
  until it's finished.
COMMISSIONER: Yarn? Thread? Skein?
  Are you out of your mind? I tell you,
  war is a serious business.
205 LYSISTRATA: So serious
  that I'd like to go on talking about weaving.
COMMISSIONER: All right. Go ahead.
LYSISTRATA: The first thing we have to do
  is to wash our yarn, get the dirt out of it.
  You see? Isn't there too much dirt here in Athens?
  You must wash those men away.
210   Then our spoiled wool—
  that's like your job-hunters, out for a life
  of no work and big pay. Back to the basket,
  citizens or not, allies or not,
  or friendly immigrants.
                          And your colonies?
215 Hanks of wool lost in various places. Pull them
  together, weave them into one great whole,
  and our voters are clothed for ever.
COMMISSIONER: It would take a woman
  to reduce state questions to a matter of carding and weaving.
LYSISTRATA: You fool! Who were the mothers whose sons sailed off
  to fight for Athens in Sicily?
220 COMMISSIONER: Enough!
  I beg you, do not call back those memories.
LYSISTRATA: And then,
  instead of the love that every woman needs,
  we have only our single beds, where we can dream
  of our husbands off with the Army.
                                    Bad enough for wives!
225 But what about our girls, getting older every day,
  and older, and no kisses?
COMMISSIONER: Men get older, too.

LYSISTRATA: Not in the same sense.
                      A soldier's discharged,
  and he may be bald and toothless, yet he'll find
  a pretty young thing to go to bed with.
                                        But a woman!
  Her beauty is gone with the first gray hair.   230
  She can spend her time
  consulting the oracles and the fortune-tellers,
  but they'll never send her a husband.
COMMISSIONER: Still, if a man can rise to the occasion—
LYSISTRATA: Rise? Rise, yourself!   235
(*Furiously.*)
  Go invest in a coffin!
                        You've money enough.
                                  I'll bake you
  a cake for the Underworld.
                            And here's your funeral wreath!
(*She pours water upon him.*)
MYRRHINE: And here's another!
(*More water.*)
KALONIKE: And here's
  my contribution!
(*More water.*)
LYSISTRATA: What are you waiting for?
  All aboard Styx Ferry!
                        Charon's° calling for you!   240
  It's sailing-time: don't disrupt the schedule!
COMMISSIONER: The insolence of women! And to me!
  No, by God, I'll go back to town and show
  the rest of the Commission what might happen to them.   (*Exit Commissioner.*)
LYSISTRATA: Really, I suppose we should have laid out his corpse   245
  on the doorstep, in the usual way.
                                    But never mind.
  We'll give him the rites of the dead tomorrow morning.

    (*Exit Lysistrata with Myrrhine and Kalonike.*)

PARABASIS:°
CHORAL EPISODE • Ode° 1

KORYPHAIOS[(m)]: Sons of Liberty, awake! The day of glory is at hand.

---

240. Charon: The god who ferried the souls of the newly dead across the river Styx to Hades.   **Parabasis:** Section of the play in which the author presented his own views through the Koryphaios directly to the audience. The parabasis in *Lysistrata* is shorter than those in Aristophanes' other works and unusual in that the Koryphaios does not speak directly for the author.   **Ode:** Song sung by the Chorus.

CHORUS(m): I smell tyranny afoot, I smell it rising from
  the land.
  I scent a trace of Hippias,° I sniff upon the breeze
  A dismal Spartan hogo that suggests King
    Kleisthenes.°
5   Strip, strip for action, brothers!
    Our wives, aunts, sisters, mothers
  Have sold us out: the streets are full of godless
    female rages.
  Shall we stand by and let our women confiscate
    our wages?
                                      [Epirrhema° 1]
KORYPHAIOS(m): Gentlemen, it's a disgrace to Athens, a
    disgrace
  to all that Athens stands for, if we allow these
10   grandmas
  to jabber about spears and shields and making
    friends
  with the Spartans. What's a Spartan? Give me a
    wild wolf
  any day. No. They want the Tyranny back, I
    suppose.
  Are we going to take that? No. Let us look like
15 the innocent serpent, but be the flower under it,
  as the poet sings. And just to begin with,
  I propose to poke a number of teeth
  down the gullet of that harridan over there.

Antode° 1

KORYPHAIOS(w): Oh, is that so? When you get home,
    your own mamma won't know you!
CHORUS(w): Who do you think we are, you senile
20   bravos? Well, I'll show you.
  I bore the sacred vessels in my eighth year,° and at ten
  I was pounding out the barley for Athena Goddess;°
    then
    They made me Little Bear
    At the Brauronian Fair;°
25 I'd held the Holy Basket° by the time I was of age,
  The Blessed Dry Figs had adorned my plump
    decolletage.
                                      [Antepirrhema° 1]

3. **Hippias:** An Athenian tyrant.   4. **Kleisthenes:** A bisexual
Athenian.   **Epirrhema:** A part of the parabasis spoken by the
Koryphaios following an ode delivered by his or her half of the
Chorus.   **Antode:** Lyric song sung by half of the Chorus in
response to the Ode sung by the other half.   21. **eighth year:**
Young girls between the ages of seven and eleven served in the
temple of Athena in the Akropolis.   22. **pounding out the barley for Athena Goddess:** At age ten a girl could be chosen to
grind the sacred grain of Athena.   24. **Brauronian Fair:** A
ritual in the cult of Artemis, who is associated with wild beasts,
in which young girls dressed up as bears and danced for the
goddess.   25. **Holy Basket:** In one ritual to Athena, young
girls carried baskets of objects sacred to the goddess.   **Antepir-
rhema:** The speech delivered by the second Koryphaios after
the second half of the Chorus had sung an ode.

KORYPHAIOS(w): A "disgrace to Athens," and I, just at
    the moment
  I'm giving Athens the best advice she ever had?
  Don't I pay taxes to the State? Yes, I pay them
30 in baby boys. And what do you contribute,
  you impotent horrors? Nothing but waste: all
  our Treasury,° dating back to the Persian Wars,
  gone! rifled! And not a penny out of your pockets!
  Well, then? Can you cough up an answer to that?
35 Look out for your own gullet, or you'll get a crack
  from this old brogan that'll make your teeth see
    stars!

Ode 2

CHORUS(m): Oh insolence!
    Am I unmanned?
    Incontinence!
40   Shall my scarred hand
    Strike never a blow
    To curb this flow-
    ing female curse?

    Leipsydrion!°
45   Shall I betray
    The laurels won
    On that great day?
    Come, shake a leg,
    Shed old age, beg
50   The years reverse!
                                      [Epirrhema 2]
KORYPHAIOS(m): Give them an inch, and we're done
    for! We'll have them
  launching boats next and planning naval
    strategy,
  sailing down on us like so many Artemisias.
  Or maybe they have ideas about the cavalry.
55 That's fair enough, women are certainly good
  in the saddle. Just look at Mikon's paintings,
  all those Amazons wrestling with all those men!
  On the whole, a straitjacket's their best uniform.

Antode 2

CHORUS(w): Tangle with me,
60   And you'll get cramps.
    Ferocity
    's no use now, Gramps!
    By the Two,
    I'll get through
65   To you wrecks yet!

32. **Treasury:** Athenian politicians were raiding the funds
that were collected by Athens to finance a war against Persia.
44. **Leipsydrion:** A place where Athenian patriots had heroically fought.

I'll scramble your eggs,
I'll burn your beans,
With my two legs.
You'll see such scenes
70   As never yet
Your two eyes met.
A curse? You bet!

                                                  [Antepirrhema 2]

KORYPHAIOS⁽ʷ⁾: If Lampito stands by me, and that
        delicious Theban girl,
    Ismenia—what good are *you*? You and your
        seven
75   Resolutions! Resolutions? Rationing Boiotian eels
    and making our girls go without them at Hekate's°
        Feast!
    That was statesmanship! And we'll have to put up
        with it
    and all the rest of your decrepit legislation
    until some patriot—God give him strength!—
80   grabs you by the neck and kicks you off the Rock.

SCENE 2

(*Reenter Lysistrata and her lieutenants.*)

KORYPHAIOS⁽ʷ⁾ (*tragic tone*): Great Queen, fair
        Architect of our emprise,
    Why lookst thou on us with foreboding eyes?
LYSISTRATA: The behavior of these idiotic women!
    There's something about the female temperament
    that I can't bear!
5   KORYPHAIOS⁽ʷ⁾:   What in the world do you mean?
LYSISTRATA: Exactly what I say.
KORYPHAIOS⁽ʷ⁾: What dreadful thing has happened?
    Come, tell us: we're all your friends.
LYSISTRATA: It isn't easy
    to say it; yet, God knows, we can't hush it up.
KORYPHAIOS⁽ʷ⁾: Well, then? Out with it!
10   LYSISTRATA: To put it bluntly,
    we're dying to get laid.
KORYPHAIOS⁽ʷ⁾:   Almighty God!
LYSISTRATA: Why bring God into it?—No, it's just as
        I say.
    I can't manage them any longer: they've gone
        man-crazy,
    they're all trying to get out.
                            Why, look:
15   one of them was sneaking out the back door
    over there by Pan's cave; another
    was sliding down the walls with rope and tackle;
    another was climbing aboard a sparrow, ready to
        take off
    for the nearest brothel—I dragged *her* back by the
        hair!

---

76. **Hekate:** Patron of successful wars, object of a Boiotian cult
(later associated with sorcery).

They're all finding some reason to leave.
                            Look there!   20
    There goes another one.
                        —Just a minute, you!
    Where are you off to so fast?
FIRST WOMAN: I've got to get home.
    I've a lot of Milesian wool, and the worms are
        spoiling it.
LYSISTRATA: Oh bother you and your worms! Get back
        inside!
FIRST WOMAN: I'll be back right away, I swear I will.   25
    I just want to get it stretched out on my bed.
LYSISTRATA: You'll do no such thing. You'll stay
        right here.
FIRST WOMAN: And my wool?
    You want it ruined?
LYSISTRATA: Yes, for all I care.
SECOND WOMAN: Oh dear! My lovely new flax from
        Amorgos—
    I left it at home, all uncarded!
LYSISTRATA: Another one!   30
    And all she wants is someone to card her flax.
    Get back in there!
SECOND WOMAN: But I swear by the Moon-Goddess
    the minute I get it done, I'll be back!
LYSISTRATA: I say No.
    If you, why not all the other women as well?
THIRD WOMAN: O Lady Eileithyia!° Radiant goddess!
        Thou   35
    intercessor for women in childbirth! Stay, I pray thee,
    oh stay this parturition. Shall I pollute
    a sacred spot?°
LYSISTRATA: And what's the matter with *you*?
THIRD WOMAN: I'm having a baby—any minute now.
LYSISTRATA: But you weren't pregnant yesterday.
THIRD WOMAN: Well, I am today.   40
    Let me go home for a midwife, Lysistrata:
    there's not much time.
LYSISTRATA: I never heard such nonsense.
    What's that bulging under your cloak?
THIRD WOMAN: A little baby boy.
LYSISTRATA: It certainly isn't. But it's something hollow,
    like a basin or—Why, it's the helmet of Athena!   45
    And you said you were having a baby.
THIRD WOMAN: Well, I am! So there!
LYSISTRATA: Then why the helmet?
THIRD WOMAN: I was afraid that my pains
    might begin here in the Akropolis; and I wanted
    to drop my chick into it, just as the dear doves do.
LYSISTRATA: Lies! Evasions!—But at least one thing's
        clear: 50
    you can't leave the place before your purification.°

---

35. **Eileithyia:** Goddess of childbirth.   37–38. **pollute a sacred
spot:** Giving birth on the Akropolis was forbidden because it
was sacred ground.   51. **purification:** A ritual cleansing of a
woman after childbirth.

THIRD WOMAN: But I can't stay here in the Akropolis!
    Last night I dreamed
  of the Snake.
FIRST WOMAN: And those horrible owls, the noise they
    make!
  I can't get a bit of sleep; I'm just about dead.
LYSISTRATA: You useless girls, that's enough: Let's have
55   no more lying.
  Of course you want your men. But don't you imagine
  that they want you just as much? I'll give you my
    word,
  their nights must be pretty hard.
                    Just stick it out!
  A little patience, that's all, and our battle's won.
60 I have heard an Oracle. Should you like to hear it?
FIRST WOMAN: An Oracle? Yes, tell us!
LYSISTRATA: Here is what it says:
  WHEN SWALLOWS SHALL THE HOOPOE
    SHUN AND SPURN HIS HOT DESIRE,
  ZEUS WILL PERFECT WHAT THEY'VE BEGUN
65   AND SET THE LOWER HIGHER.
FIRST WOMAN: Does that mean we'll be on top?
LYSISTRATA: BUT IF THE SWALLOWS SHALL FALL
    OUT
      AND TAKE THE HOOPOE'S BAIT,
  A CURSE MUST MARK THEIR HOUR OF
    DOUBT,
70   INFAMY SEAL THEIR FATE.
THIRD WOMAN: I swear, *that* Oracle's all too clear.
FIRST WOMAN: Oh the dear gods!
LYSISTRATA: Let's not be downhearted, girls. Back to
  our places!
  The god has spoken. How can we possibly fail him?

      (*Exit Lysistrata with the dissident women.*)

CHORAL EPISODE • *Strophe*

CHORUS(m): I know a little story that I learned way
    back in school
  Goes like this:
  Once upon a time there was a young man—and no
    fool—
  Named Melanion; and his
  One aversion was marriage. He loathed the very
5   thought.
  So he ran off to the hills, and in a special grot
  Raised a dog, and spent his days
  Hunting rabbits. And it says
  That he never never never did come home.
10 It might be called a refuge *from* the womb.
  All right,
      all right,
         all right!
  We're as bright as young Melanion, and we hate
    the very sight
  Of you women!
A MAN: How about a kiss, old lady?
15 A WOMAN: Here's an onion for your eye!

A MAN: A kick in the guts, then?
A WOMAN: Try, old bristle-tail, just try!
A MAN: Yet they say Myronides
  On hands and knees
  Looked just as shaggy fore and aft as I!   20

Antistrophe

CHORUS(w): Well, *I* know a little story, and it's just as
  good as yours.
  Goes like this:
  Once there was a man named Timon—a rough
    diamond, of course,
  And that whiskery face of his
  Looked like murder in the shrubbery. By God, he
    was a son   25
  Of the Furies, let me tell you! And what did he do
    but run
  From the world and all its ways,
  Cursing mankind! And it says
  That his choicest execrations as of then
  Were leveled almost wholly at *old* men.   30
  All right,
      all right,
         all right!
  But there's one thing about Timon: he could
    always stand the sight
  of us women.
A WOMAN: How about a crack in the jaw, Pop?
A MAN: I can take it, Ma—no fear!   35
A WOMAN: How about a kick in the face?
A MAN: You'd reveal your old caboose?
A WOMAN: What I'd show,
  I'll have you know,
  Is an instrument you're too far gone to use.   40

SCENE 3

(*Reenter Lysistrata.*)

LYSISTRATA: Oh, quick, girls, quick! Come here!
A WOMAN: What is it?
LYSISTRATA: A man.
  A man simply bulging with love.
                O Kyprian Queen,°
  O Paphian, O Kythereian! Hear us and aid us!
A WOMAN: Where is this enemy?
LYSISTRATA: Over there, by Demeter's shrine.
A WOMAN: Damned if he isn't. But who *is* he?
MYRRHINE: My husband.   5
  Kinesias.
LYSISTRATA: Oh then, get busy! Tease him! Undermine
  him!

2. **Kyprian Queen:** Aphrodite.

Cherry Jones as Lysistrata in the American Repertory Theatre's 2002 production directed by Robert Brustein.

Geraldine James (far left) as Lysistrata in the Old Vic Theatre production in London, 1993.

The Théâtre La Licorne 2006 performance of *Lysistrata,*
adapted by Claire Dancoisne.

Wreck him! Give him everything—kissing,
   tickling, nudging,
whatever you generally torture him with—: give
   him everything
except what we swore on the wine we would not
   give.
MYRRHINE: Trust me.
10 LYSISTRATA: I do. But I'll help you get him started.
   The rest of you women, stay back.

(*Enter Kinesias.*)

KINESIAS: Oh God! Oh my God!
   I'm stiff from lack of exercise. All I can do to stand
   up.
LYSISTRATA: Halt! Who are you, approaching our lines?
KINESIAS: Me? I.
LYSISTRATA: A man?
KINESIAS: You have eyes, haven't you?
15 LYSISTRATA: Go away.
KINESIAS: Who says so?

LYSISTRATA: Officer of the Day.
KINESIAS: Officer, I beg you,
   by all the gods at once, bring Myrrhine out.
LYSISTRATA: Myrrhine? And who, my good sir, are
   you?
KINESIAS: Kinesias. Last name's Pennison. Her husband.
LYSISTRATA: Oh, of course. I beg your pardon. We're
   glad to see you.   20
   We've heard so much about you. Dearest Myrrhine
   is always talking about Kinesias—never nibbles an
      egg
   or an apple without saying
   "Here's to Kinesias!"
KINESIAS: Do you really mean it?
LYSISTRATA: I do.
   When we're discussing men, she always says   25
   "Well, after all, there's nobody like Kinesias!"
KINESIAS: Good God.—Well, then, please send her
   down here.
LYSISTRATA: And what do *I* get out of it?
KINESIAS: A standing promise.
LYSISTRATA: I'll take it up with her.
                          (*Exit Lysistrata.*)
KINESIAS: But be quick about it!
   Lord, what's life without a wife? Can't eat. Can't
   sleep.   30
   Every time I go home, the place is so empty, so
   insufferably sad. Love's killing me, Oh,
   hurry!

(*Enter Manes, a slave, with Kinesias's baby; the voice of
Myrrhine is heard offstage.*)

MYRRHINE: But of course I love him! Adore him—
                                But no,
   he hates love. No. I won't go down.

(*Enter Myrrhine, above.*)

KINESIAS: Myrrhine!
   Darlingest Myrrhinette! Come down quick!   35
MYRRHINE: Certainly not.
KINESIAS: Not? But why, Myrrhine?
MYRRHINE: Why? You don't need me.
KINESIAS: Need you? My God, *look* at me!
MYRRHINE: So long!

(*Turns to go.*)

KINESIAS: Myrrhine, Myrrhine, Myrrhine!
   If not for my sake, for our child!

(*Pinches Baby.*)

                     —All right, you: pipe up!
BABY: Mummie! Mummie! Mummie!
KINESIAS: You hear that?   40
   Pitiful, I call it. Six days now
   with never a bath; no food; enough to break your
   heart!
MYRRHINE: My darlingest child! What a father *you*
   acquired!
KINESIAS: At least come down for his sake.

MYRRHINE: I suppose I must.
45   Oh, this mother business!   (*Exit.*)
KINESIAS: How pretty she is! And younger!
     The harder she treats me, the more bothered I get.

(*Myrrhine enters, below.*)

MYRRHINE: Dearest child,
     you're as sweet as your father's horrid. Give me a kiss.
KINESIAS: Now don't you see how wrong it was to
        get involved
50   in this scheming League of women? It's bad
     for us both.
MYRRHINE: Keep your hands to yourself!
KINESIAS: But our house
     going to rack and ruin?
MYRRHINE: *I don't care.*
KINESIAS: And your knitting
     all torn to pieces by the chickens? Don't you care?
MYRRHINE: Not at all.
55   KINESIAS: And our debt to Aphrodite?
     Oh, *won't* you come back?
MYRRHINE: No.—At least, not until you men
     make a treaty and stop this war.
KINESIAS: Why, I suppose
     that might be arranged.
MYRRHINE: Oh? Well, I suppose
     I might come down then. But meanwhile,
     I've sworn not to.
60   KINESIAS: Don't worry.—Now let's have fun.
MYRRHINE: No! Stop it! I said no!
                              —Although, of course,
     I *do* love you.
KINESIAS: I know you do. Darling Myrrhine:
        come, shall we?
MYRRHINE: Are you out of your mind? In front of the
        child?
KINESIAS: Take him home, Manes.
                       (*Exit Manes with Baby.*)
                       There. He's gone.
                              Come on!
     There's nothing to stop us now.
65   MYRRHINE: You devil! But where?
KINESIAS: In Pan's cave. What could be snugger than that?
MYRRHINE: But my purification before I go back to
        the Citadel?
KINESIAS: Wash in the Klepsydra.°
MYRRHINE: And my oath?
KINESIAS: Leave the oath to me.
     After all, I'm the man.
MYRRHINE: Well . . . if you say so.
                    I'll go find a bed.
KINESIAS: Oh, bother a bed! The ground's good
70   enough for me.
MYRRHINE: No. You're a bad man, but you deserve
     something better than dirt.   (*Exit Myrrhine.*)
KINESIAS: What a love she is! And how thoughtful!

68. Klepsydra: A water clock beneath the walls of the Akropolis. Kinesias's suggestion borders on blasphemy.

(*Reenter Myrrhine.*)

MYRRHINE: Here's your bed.
     Now let me get my clothes off.
                         But, good horrors!
     We haven't a mattress.
KINESIAS: Oh, forget the mattress!
MYRRHINE: No.
     Just lying on blankets? Too sordid.
KINESIAS: Give me a kiss.   75
MYRRHINE: Just a second.   (*Exit Myrrhine.*)
KINESIAS: I swear, I'll explode!

(*Reenter Myrrhine.*)

MYRRHINE: Here's your mattress.
     I'll just take my dress off.
                         But look—
     where's our pillow?
KINESIAS: I don't *need* a pillow!
MYRRHINE: Well, *I* do.
                       (*Exit Myrrhine.*)
KINESIAS: I don't suppose even Herakles°
     would stand for this!

(*Reenter Myrrhine.*)

MYRRHINE: There we are. Ups-a-daisy!   80
KINESIAS: So we are. Well, come to bed.
MYRRHINE: But I wonder:
     is everything ready now?
KINESIAS: I can swear to that. Come, darling!
MYRRHINE: Just getting out of my girdle.
                       But remember, now,
     what you promised about the treaty.
KINESIAS: Yes, yes, yes!
MYRRHINE: But no coverlet!
KINESIAS: Damn it, I'll be your coverlet!   85
MYRRHINE: Be right back.   (*Exit Myrrhine.*)
KINESIAS: This girl and her coverlets
     will be the death of me.

(*Reenter Myrrhine.*)

MYRRHINE: Here we are. Up you go!
KINESIAS: Up? I've been up for ages.
MYRRHINE: Some perfume?
KINESIAS: No, by Apollo!
MYRRHINE: Yes, by Aphrodite!
     I don't care whether you want it or not.   90
                       (*Exit Myrrhine.*)
KINESIAS: For love's sake, hurry!

(*Reenter Myrrhine.*)

MYRRHINE: Here, in your hand. Rub it right in.
KINESIAS: Never cared for perfume.
     And this is particularly strong. Still, here goes.
MYRRHINE: What a nitwit I am! I brought you the
        Rhodian bottle.
KINESIAS: Forget it.   95

79. Herakles: Greek hero (Hercules) known for his Twelve Labors.

MYRRHINE: No trouble at all. You just wait here.
                                   (*Exit Myrrhine.*)
KINESIAS: God damn the man who invented perfume!

(*Reenter Myrrhine.*)

MYRRHINE: At last! The right bottle!
KINESIAS: I've got the rightest bottle of all,
   and it's right here waiting for you.
   Darling, forget everything else. Do come to bed.
MYRRHINE: Just let me get my shoes off.
100   —And, by the way,
   you'll vote for the treaty?
KINESIAS: I'll think about it.
                  (*Myrrhine runs away.*)
   There! That's done it! The damned woman,
   she gets me all bothered, she half kills me,
   and off she runs! What'll I do? Where
   can I get laid?
105   —And you, little prodding pal,
   who's going to take care of *you*? No, you and I
   had better get down to old Foxdog's Nursing
      Clinic.
CHORUS(m): Alas for the woes of man, alas
      Specifically for you.
110   She's brought you to a pretty pass:
      What are you going to do?
   Split, heart! Sag, flesh! Proud spirit, crack!
   Myrrhine's got you on your back.
KINESIAS: The agony, the protraction!
KORYPHAIOS(m):   Friend,
115   What woman's worth a damn?
   They bitch us all, world without end.
KINESIAS: Yet they're so damned sweet, man!
KORYPHAIOS(m): Calamitous, that's what I say.
   You should have learned that much today.
120 CHORUS(m): O blessed Zeus, roll womankind
      Up into one great ball;
   Blast them aloft on a high wind,
      And once there, let them fall.
   Down, down they'll come, the pretty dears,
125   And split themselves on our thick spears.
                  (*Exit Kinesias.*)

SCENE 4

(*Enter a Spartan Herald.*)

HERALD: Gentlemen, Ah beg you will be so kind
   as to direct me to the Central Committee.
   Ah have a communication.

(*Reenter Commissioner.*)

COMMISSIONER: Are you a man,
   or a fertility symbol?
HERALD: Ah refuse to answer that question!
5   Ah'm a certified herald from Spahta, and Ah've come
   to talk about an ahmistice.
COMMISSIONER: Then why
   that spear under your cloak?
HERALD: Ah have no speah!

COMMISSIONER: You don't walk naturally, with your tunic
   poked out so. You have a tumor, maybe,
   or a hernia?
HERALD: You lost yo' mahnd, man?
COMMISSIONER: Well,   10
   something's up, I can see that. And I don't like it.
HERALD: Colonel, Ah resent this.
COMMISSIONER: So I see. But what *is* it?
HERALD: A staff
   with a message from Spahta.
COMMISSIONER: Oh, I know about those staffs.
   Well, then, man, speak out: How are things in Sparta?
HERALD: Hahd, Colonel, hahd! We're at a standstill.   15
   Cain't seem to think of anything but women.
COMMISSIONER: How curious! Tell me, do you
      Spartans think
   that maybe Pan's to blame?
HERALD: Pan? No, Lampito and her little naked friends.
   They won't let a man come nigh them.   20
COMMISSIONER: How are you handling it?
HERALD: Losing our mahnds,
   if y' want to know, and walking around hunched over
   lahk men carrying candles in a gale.
   The women have swohn they'll have nothing to do
      with us
   until we get a treaty.
COMMISSIONER: Yes. I know.   25
   It's a general uprising, sir, in all parts of Greece.
   But as for the answer—
               Sir: go back to Sparta
   and have them send us your Armistice Commission.
   I'll arrange things in Athens.
                And I may say
   that my standing is good enough to make them listen.   30
HERALD: A man after mah own haht! Seh, Ah thank
      you.   (*Exit Herald.*)

CHORAL EPISODE • *Strophe*

CHORUS(m): Oh these women! Where will you find
   A slavering beast that's more unkind?
      Where's a hotter fire?
   Give me a panther, any day.
   He's not so merciless as they,   5
      And panthers don't conspire.

Antistrophe

CHORUS(w): We may be hard, you silly old ass,
   But who brought you to this stupid pass?
      You're the ones to blame.
   Fighting with us, your oldest friends,   10
   Simply to serve your selfish ends—
      Really, you have no shame!
KORYPHAIOS(m): No, I'm through with women for ever.
KORYPHAIOS(w):   If you say so.
   Still, you might put some clothes on. You look too
      absurd
   standing around naked. Come, get into this cloak.   15

KORYPHAIOS⁽ᵐ⁾: Thank you; you're right. I merely took it off
   because I was in such a temper.
KORYPHAIOS⁽ʷ⁾:   That's much better.
   Now you resemble a man again.
                 Why have you been so horrid?
   And look: there's some sort of insect in your eye.
   Shall I take it out?
20 KORYPHAIOS⁽ᵐ⁾:   An insect, is it? So that's
   what's been bothering me. Lord, yes: take it out!
KORYPHAIOS⁽ʷ⁾: You might be more polite.
                   —But, heavens!
   What an enormous mosquito!
KORYPHAIOS⁽ᵐ⁾:   You've saved my life.
   That mosquito was drilling an artesian well
   in my left eye.
25 KORYPHAIOS⁽ʷ⁾:   Let me wipe
   those tears away.—And now: one little kiss?
KORYPHAIOS⁽ᵐ⁾: No, no kisses.
KORYPHAIOS⁽ʷ⁾: You're so difficult.
KORYPHAIOS⁽ᵐ⁾: You impossible women! How you do get around us!
   The poet was right: Can't live with you, or without
30   you.
   But let's be friends.
   And to celebrate, you might join us in an Ode.

Strophe 1

CHORUS⁽ᵐ ᵃⁿᵈ ʷ⁾: Let it never be said
     That my tongue is malicious:
35   Both by word and by deed
   I would set an example that's noble and gracious.
   We've had sorrow and care
   Till we're sick of the tune.
   Is there anyone here
40   Who would like a small loan?
     My purse is crammed,
     As you'll soon find;
   And you needn't pay me back if the Peace gets signed.

Strophe 2

   I've invited to lunch
45   Some Karystian rips°—
   An esurient bunch,
   But I've ordered a menu to water their lips.
   I can still make soup
   And slaughter a pig.
50   You're all coming, I hope?
   But a bath first, I beg!
     Walk right up

---

45. Karystian rips: The Karystians were allies of Athens but were scorned for their primitive ways and loose morals.

     As though you owned the place,
   And you'll get the front door slammed to in your face.

SCENE 5

(*Enter Spartan Ambassador, with entourage.*)

KORYPHAIOS⁽ᵐ⁾: The Commission has arrived from
   Sparta.
             How oddly they're walking!
                  Gentlemen, welcome to Athens!
   How is life in Lakonia?
AMBASSADOR: Need we discuss that?
   Simply use your eyes.
CHORUS⁽ᵐ⁾:   The poor man's right:
            What a sight!
AMBASSADOR: Words fail me.   5
   But come, gentlemen, call in your Commissioners,
   and let's get down to a Peace.
CHORAGOS⁽ᵐ⁾:   The state we're in! Can't bear
   a stitch below the waist. It's a kind of pelvic
   paralysis.
COMMISSIONER: Won't somebody call Lysistrata?—
                      Gentlemen,
   we're no better off than you.
AMBASSADOR: So I see.   10
A SPARTAN: Seh, do y'all feel a certain strain early in the
   morning?
AN ATHENIAN: I do, sir. It's worse than a strain.
   A few more days, and there's nothing for us but
     Kleisthenes,
   that broken blossom.
CHORAGOS⁽ᵐ⁾:   But you'd better get dressed again.
   You know these people going around Athens with
     chisels   15
   looking for statues of Hermes.°
ATHENIAN: Sir, you are right.
SPARTAN: He certainly is! Ah'll put mah own clothes
   back on.

(*Enter Athenian Commissioners.*)

COMMISSIONER: Gentlemen from Sparta, welcome.
   This is a sorry business.
SPARTAN (*to one of his own group*): Colonel, we got
   dressed just in time. Ah sweah,
   if they'd seen us the way we were, there'd have been
     a new wah   20
   between the states.
COMMISSIONER: Shall we call the meeting to order?
                  Now, Lakonians,
   what's your proposal?
AMBASSADOR: We propose to consider peace.

---

16. statues of Hermes: The usual representation of Hermes was with an erect phallus. Statues of Hermes were scattered throughout Athens and were attacked by vandals just before the Sicilian Expedition.

COMMISSIONER: Good. That's on our minds, too.
                              —Summon Lysistrata.
   We'll never get anywhere without her.
25 AMBASSADOR: Lysistrata?
   Summon Lysis-*any*body! Only, summon!
   KORYPHAIOS(m):   No need to summon:
      here she is, herself.

(*Enter Lysistrata.*)

COMMISSIONER: Lysistrata! Lion of women!
   This is your hour to be
   hard and yielding, outspoken and shy, austere and
30   gentle. You see here
   the best brains of Hellas (confused, I admit,
   by your devious charming) met as one man
   to turn the future over to you.
LYSISTRATA: That's fair enough,
   unless you men take it into your heads
35 to turn to each other instead of to us. But I'd know
   soon enough if you did.
                        —Where is Reconciliation?
   Go, some of you: bring her here.
                                (*Exeunt two women.*)
                        And now, women,
   lead the Spartan delegates to me: not roughly
   or insultingly, as our men handle them, but gently,
40 politely, as ladies should. Take them by the hand,
   or by anything else if they won't give you their hands.

(*The Spartans are escorted over.*)

   There.—The Athenians next, by any convenient
      handle.

(*The Athenians are escorted.*)

   Stand there, please.—Now, all of you, listen to me.

(*During the following speech the two women reenter,
carrying an enormous statue of a naked girl; this is
Reconciliation.*)

   I'm only a woman, I know; but I've a mind,
45 and, I think, not a bad one: I owe it to my father
   and to listening to the local politicians.
   So much for that.
                     Now, gentlemen,
   since I have you here, I intend to give you a scolding.
   We are all Greeks.
50 Must I remind you of Thermopylai,° of Olympia,
   of Delphoi? names deep in all our hearts?
   Are they not a common heritage?
                          Yet you men
   go raiding through the country from both sides,
   Greek killing Greek, storming down Greek cities—
55 and all the time the Barbarian across the sea
   is waiting for his chance!
                        —That's my first point.

50. Thermopylai: A narrow pass where, in 480 BCE, an army
of three hundred Spartans held out for three days against a superior Persian force.

AN ATHENIAN: Lord! I can hardly contain myself.
LYSISTRATA: As for you Spartans:
   Was it so long ago that Perikleides°
   came here to beg our help? I can see him still,
   his gray face, his sombre gown. And what did he
      want?   60
   An army from Athens. All Messene
   was hot at your heels, and the sea-god splitting your
      land.
   Well, Kimon and his men,
   four thousand strong, marched out and saved all
      Sparta.
   And what thanks do we get? You come back to
      murder us.   65
AN ATHENIAN: They're aggressors, Lysistrata!
A SPARTAN: Ah admit it.
   When Ah look at those laigs, Ah sweah Ah'll
      aggress mahself!
LYSISTRATA: And you, Athenians: do you think you're
      blameless?
   Remember that bad time when we were helpless,
   and an army came from Sparta,   70
   and that was the end of the Thessalian menace,
   the end of Hippias and his allies.
                          And that was Sparta,
   and only Sparta; but for Sparta, we'd be
   cringing slaves today, not free Athenians.

(*From this point, the male responses are less to Lysistrata
than to the statue.*)

A SPARTAN: A well shaped speech.
AN ATHENIAN: Certainly it has its points. 75
LYSISTRATA: Why are we fighting each other? With all
      this history
   of favors given and taken, what stands in the way
   of making peace?
AMBASSADOR: Spahta is ready, ma'am,
   so long as we get that place back.
LYSISTRATA: What place, man?
AMBASSADOR: Ah refer to Pylos.
COMMISSIONER: Not a chance, by God!   80
LYSISTRATA: Give it to them, friend.
COMMISSIONER: But—what shall we have to bargain
      with?
LYSISTRATA: Demand something in exchange.
COMMISSIONER: Good idea.—Well, then:
   Cockeville first, and the Happy Hills, and the
   country between the Legs of Megara.
AMBASSADOR: Mah government objects.   85
LYSISTRATA: Overruled. Why fuss about a pair of legs?

(*General assent. The statue is removed.*)

AN ATHENIAN: I want to get out of these clothes and
      start my plowing.
A SPARTAN: Ah'll fertilize mahn first, by the Heavenly
      Twins!

58. Perikleides: Spartan ambassador to Athens who successfully urged Athenians to aid Sparta in quelling a rebellion.

LYSISTRATA: And so you shall,
90   once you've made peace. If you are serious,
    go, both of you, and talk with your allies.
COMMISSIONER: Too much talk already. No, we'll
        stand together.
    We've only one end in view. All that we want
    is our women; and I speak for our allies.
AMBASSADOR: Mah government concurs.
95 AN ATHENIAN: So does Karystos.
LYSISTRATA: Good. — But before you come inside
    to join your wives at supper, you must perform
    the usual lustration. Then we'll open
    our baskets for you, and all that we have is yours.
100   But you must promise upright good behavior
    from this day on. Then each man home with his
        woman!
AN ATHENIAN: Let's get it over with.
A SPARTAN: Lead on. Ah follow.
AN ATHENIAN: Quick as a cat can wink!
                    (*Exeunt all but the Choruses.*)

Antistrophe 1

CHORUS(w): Embroideries and
105   Twinkling ornaments and
        Pretty dresses — I hand
    Them all over to you, and with never a qualm.
        They'll be nice for your daughters
        On festival days
110   When the girls bring the Goddess
        The ritual prize.
        Come in, one and all:
        Take what you will.
    I've nothing here so tightly corked that you can't
        make it spill.

Antistrophe 2

115   You may search my house
        But you'll not find
        The least thing of use,
    Unless your two eyes are keener than mine.
        Your numberless brats
120   Are half starved? and your slaves?
        Courage, grandpa! I've lots
        Of grain left, and big loaves.
        I'll fill your guts,
        I'll go the whole hog;
    But if you come too close to me, remember: 'ware
125   the dog!   (*Exeunt Choruses.*)

EXODOS°

(*A Drunken Citizen enters, approaches the gate, and is
halted by a sentry.*)

Exodos: Final scene.

CITIZEN: Open. The. Door.
SENTRY: Now, friend, just shove along!
    —So you want to sit down. If it weren't such an old
        joke,
    I'd tickle your tail with this torch. Just the sort of
        gag
    this audience appreciates.
CITIZEN: I. Stay. Right. Here.
SENTRY: Get away from there, or I'll scalp you!   5
    The gentlemen from Sparta
    are just coming back from dinner.

(*Exit Citizen; the general company reenters; the two
Choruses now represent Spartans and Athenians.*)

A SPARTAN: Ah must say,
    Ah never tasted better grub.
AN ATHENIAN: And those Lakonians!
    They're gentlemen, by the Lord! Just goes to show,
    a drink to the wise is sufficient.
COMMISSIONER: And why not?   10
    A sober man's an ass.
    Men of Athens, mark my words: the only efficient
    Ambassador's a drunk Ambassador. Is that clear?
    Look: we go to Sparta,
    and when we get there we're dead sober. The result? 15
    Everyone cackling at everyone else. They make
        speeches;
    and even if we understand, we get it all wrong
    when we file our reports in Athens. But today—!
    Everybody's happy. Couldn't tell the difference
    between *Drink to Me Only* and   20
    The Star-Spangled Athens.
                    What's a few lies,
    washed down in good strong drink?

(*Reenter the Drunken Citizen.*)

SENTRY: God almighty,
    he's back again!
CITIZEN: I. Resume. My. Place.
A SPARTAN (*to an Athenian*): Ah beg yo', seh,
    take yo' instrument in yo' hand and play for us.   25
    Ah'm told
    yo' understand the in*tric*acies of the *floot*?
    Ah'd lahk to execute a song and dance
    in honor of Athens,
                    and, of cohse, of Spahta.
CITIZEN: Toot. On. Your. Flute.   30

(*The following song is a solo—an aria—accompanied by the flute. The Chorus of Spartans begins a slow
dance.*)

A SPARTAN: O Memory,
    Let the Muse speak once more
    In my young voice. Sing glory.
    Sing Artemision's shore,
    Where Athens fluttered the Persians. *Alalai,*°   35

35. *Alalai:* War cry.

Sing glory, that great
Victory! Sing also
Our Leonidas and his men,
Those wild boars, sweat and blood
40   Down in a red drench. Then, then
The barbarians broke, though they had stood
Numberless as the sands before!

O Artemis,
Virgin Goddess, whose darts
45   Flash in our forests: approve
This pact of peace and join our hearts,
From this day on, in love.
Huntress, descend!

LYSISTRATA: All that will come in time.
                                    But now, Lakonians,
50   take home your wives. Athenians, take yours.
Each man be kind to his woman; and you, women
be equally kind. Never again, pray God,
shall we lose our way in such madness.

KORYPHAIOS(Athenian):   And now let's dance our joy.

(*From this point the dance becomes general.*)

CHORUS(Athenian): Dance, you Graces
                                    Artemis, dance
Dance, Phoibos,° Lord of dancing
55   Dance,
In a scurry of Maenads,° Lord Dionysos
                                    Dance, Zeus Thunderer
              Dance, Lady Hera°
Queen of the sky
              Dance, dance, all you gods

---

55. Phoibos: Apollo, god of the sun.   **56. Maenads:** Female
worshipers of Bacchus (Dionysus).   **57. Hera:** Wife of Zeus.

Dance witness everlasting of our pact
Evohi Evohe°   60
Dance for the dearest
                        the Bringer of Peace
Deathless Aphrodite!

COMMISSIONER: Now let us have another song from
              Sparta.

CHORUS(Spartan): From Taygetos, from Taygetos,
Lakonian Muse, come down.   65
Sing to the Lord Apollo
              Who rules Amyklai Town.

Sing Athena of the House of Brass!°
Sing Leda's Twins,° that chivalry
              Resplendent on the shore   70
Of our Eurotas; sing the girls
              That dance along before:
Sparkling in dust their gleaming feet,
              Their hair a Bacchant fire,
And Leda's daughter, thyrsos° raised,   75
              Leads their triumphant choir.

CHORUS(S and A): *Evohe!*
              Evohai!
                        Evohe!
                                 We pass
              Dancing
                        dancing
                                 to greet
Athena of the House of Brass.

---

60. Evohi Evohe: "Come forth! Come forth!" An orgiastic cry
associated with rituals of Bacchus.   **68. *House of Brass:***
Temple to Athena on the Akropolis of Sparta.   **69. Leda's
Twins:** Leda, raped by Zeus, bore quadruplets, two daughters
(one of whom was Helen) and two sons.   **75. thyrsos:** A staff
twined with ivy and carried by Bacchus and his followers.

Roman Drama

Indigenous Sources

Roman drama has several sources, not all of them well understood. The first and most literary is Greek drama, but among the more curious are the indigenous sources, which are especially difficult to trace. One such source might be the Etruscans, members of an old and obscure civilization in northern Italy that reached its height in the sixth century BCE and that the Romans eventually absorbed. The Etruscans had developed an improvised song and dance that was very entertaining. The town of Atella provided another indigenous comic tradition known as the ATELLAN FARCE, a very broad and sometimes coarse popular comedy. Such entertainments may have been acted in open spaces or at fairs, probably not on a stage at first.

The Atellan farce is especially interesting for developments in later Roman drama and world drama. The characters in this farce seem to have been STOCK CHARACTERS, characters who are always recognizable and whose antics are predictable. The most common in the Atellan farce are Maccus the clown; Bucco the stupid, and probably fat, clown; Pappus, the foolish or stubborn old man; and the hunchbacked, wily slave Dossennus. At first these pieces of drama were improvised to a repeatable pattern, often involving a master who tries to get his slave to do his bidding but who somehow ends up being made to look the fool by the cunning slave. When the farces began to develop in Rome, they were written down and played onstage.

The concept of the stock character is associated with the masters of Roman comedy, Plautus and Terence, who often adapted Greek plays and made them their own. The braggart warrior (*miles gloriosus*), a stock character on the Roman stage, reappears in modern plays. The miser has been a mainstay in literature since Roman times and probably is best known today as Scrooge in Dickens's *A Christmas Carol* and as *The Miser* of Molière. The parasite was Roman in origin and can be seen today in numerous television situation comedies. Another Roman invention is the use of identical twins for comic effect. Because it permitted a wide range of comic misunderstandings, this device has been used by many playwrights, including Shakespeare in *The Comedy of Errors*. The Roman use of masks made the twins device much easier to employ than it would be in today's productions.

The Greek Influence

According to legend, in 240 BCE, a slave, Livius Andronicus, presented performances of his Latin translations of a Greek tragedy and a Greek comedy, giving the Romans their first real taste of Greek drama and literature. Livius soon earned his freedom, and his literary career became so firmly established that his translations from the Greek were those read in Rome for more than two hundred years. His translation of the *Odyssey* was the standard text through the time of Cicero (first century BCE).

Roman comedy derived primarily from the New Comedy of Menander, although it could, like Aristophanes' Old Comedy, sometimes be risqué. Comedy was the most well attended and the most performed of Rome's drama. That is not to say that the Romans produced no tragedies. They did, and the influence of Roman tragedy has been as long-lasting as that of comedy. Still, the Roman people preferred to laugh rather than to feel the pity and terror of tragic emotion.

Just as the Greek plays developed in connection with festivals, the Roman plays became associated with games held several times a year. During the games, performances were offered on an average of five to eleven days. The Megalesian Games took place in early April, in honor of the Great Mother, the goddess Cybele, whose temple stood on the Palatine Hill. In late April the Floral Games were held in front of the temple of Flora on the Aventine Hill. The most important were the Roman Games in September and the Plebeian Games in November.

The Greek drama competitions had no counterpart among the Romans, for whom drama was not the primary entertainment during the festivals. Roman playwrights and actors were hired to put on performances to entertain and divert the impatient audiences who could choose among a variety of spectacles, including gladiator fights, chariot races, and animal baiting. The producer had to please the audience or lose his chance to supply more entertainment.

Roman comedies were sometimes revisions or amalgamations of Greek plays. The themes and characters of Roman tragedies also derived from Greek originals. Figuring often in Roman tragedies was the Trojan War; its characters were reworked into new situations and their agonies reinterpreted.

For costumes the actors wore the Greek tunic (called a CHITON) and a long white cloak or mantle called the PALLIUM. Like the Greeks, the Romans wore a low slipper, called the SOCK, for comedy, and shoes with an elevated sole, the BUSKIN, for tragedy. For plays that had a totally Roman setting and narrative, the actors wore the Roman toga. Eventually, Roman actors used traditional Greek masks that immediately identified the characters for the audience. (The question of whether the earliest Roman actors wore masks as well has not been resolved.) The younger Roman characters wore black wigs, older characters wore white wigs, and characters representing slaves wore red wigs.

One of the most intriguing questions concerning Roman plays is the importance of music in the drama. In Greek plays the chorus took most of the responsibility for the music, but in Roman drama actors may have sung their lines, so the Roman plays may have resembled musical comedies. The dialogue in some comedies introduces an interlude of flute playing, indicating that there were times with no actor onstage, no spoken words, and no mimed action, but only a musician to entertain the audience.

The Roman Stage

In the third century BCE the Romans began building wooden stages that could be taken down quickly and moved as necessary. Eventually, they built stone theaters that followed Greek plans but varied from the Greek model in a number of important respects. They were built on flat ground, rather than on the hill-sides as were the Greek theaters. The influence of the Romans' early wooden stage remained in the permanent buildings in several ways. The Roman stage was elevated, and since there was little or no chorus, the orchestra, in which the chorus moved from place to place, was no longer needed. The SCAENA, or background, against which the action took place, was often three stories tall and was proportionally longer than the Greek *skene* (as in Figure 4). This wide but shallow stage was exploited by the playwrights, who often set their plays on a street with various houses, temples, and other buildings along it.

The space in front of the *scaena* was known as the PROSCAENA, from which the PROSCENIUM ARCH, which frames the stage and separates the actors from the audience, developed much later in the Renaissance. The action took place on the *pulpitum*, behind the *proscaena*. The potential for the proscenium arch is evident in the plan of the Theater of Marcellus (Figure 5), where the sections to the left and the right of the stage (*pulpitum*) already indicate a separation from the audience.

FIGURE 4. Roman theater at Sabratha, Libya. With the *frons scaena* still in good shape, this photograph shows how the Romans modified the basic Greek design.

FIGURE 5. Theater of
Marcellus.

As in the plan of the Theater of Marcellus, the *frons scaena* (the front wall, or façade) usually had three doors (some had only two), which were ordinarily established as doors of separate buildings, sometimes a temple and the others the homes of chief characters. These doors were active "participants" in the drama; it has been said that the most common line heard in a Roman play is a statement that the door is opening and someone is coming in. The standard Roman play takes great care to justify the entrances and exits of its characters, which may indicate that Roman audiences expected more realism in their comedies than did their Greek counterparts.

The *frons scaena,* the front of the theater, not only was several stories high but also was much more architecturally developed than the *skene* of the Greek theater. The typical Roman architectural devices of multiple arches, columns, and pilasters decorated the *scaena,* giving it a stately appearance. Like the Greek theater, the Roman theater used machinery that permitted actors to be moved through the air and to make entrances from the heavens.

The greatest of the Roman dramatists, Plautus and Terence, would have had their plays produced originally on early wooden stages or on Greek stages. The characteristic Roman theater was not created until the period of the empire, more than a hundred years after their deaths. By that time Seneca could have seen his plays produced in the Roman theater, but they may not ever have been produced in Roman times. His plays may have been closet dramas, designed only to be read.

The Roman Actor

Unlike Greek actors, who were held in high esteem even when they were not the playwrights themselves, actors in Roman times were thought to be undignified. Often they were clever slaves, and rarely were they thought worthy of the attention of nobles or people of power. Many of the theaters in which comedies

FIGURE 6.   A Roman
bas-relief depicting actors
performing a comic scene.

and tragedies were performed were haphazard, uncomfortable wooden structures with rowdy audiences. Some texts plead with the audience not to hiss
after the play; others imply that the audience had to be told what was happening onstage, as though they were incapable of following the action. The later
stone theaters (55 BCE) may have served a better audience despite the waning
of Roman drama.

Two great actors are known to us by name. Clodius Aesopus (fl. 55 BCE) was
from a good family and rose to be the most noted actor for tragedy. He was so
eloquent on stage that he tutored Cicero (106–43 BCE), one of the greatest
Roman orators and author of some of the most significant books on rhetoric,
the art of persuasion. Quintus Roscius Gallus (126–62 BCE), known as
Roscius, was born a slave but, because of his extraordinary skills as a comic
actor, rose to freedom and a high rank in Roman society. (Figure 6 shows a
scene from a comedy.) He too is said to have instructed Cicero, who wrote an
oration called *Pro Roscio comoedo* (*For Roscius the Comedian*). The connection between Roman oration and the Roman actor is not accidental. The principles of oration, as laid down by Aristotle in his *Rhetoric* and later developed
by Romans such as Quintilian and Cicero, were as useful to the actor as to the
politician. Early treatises on acting stress the skills of the orator in the training
of the actor. The Roman illustrations of actors show that an altar was often on
stage with three actors, all of whom wore masks similar to those worn by
Greek actors, which implies that the tradition had been carried on long enough
for the Romans to adopt it.

Roman Drama Timeline

DATE	THEATER	POLITICAL	SOCIAL/CULTURAL
800–600 BCE			**753:** Rome is founded.
600–500			**6th century:** The Circus Maximus is constructed for chariot races and athletic contests. **527–509:** Roman Republic
500–400			**450:** Roman law is codified in the Twelve Tables.
400–300		**390:** Rome is rebuilt after a Gallic invasion.	
300–200	**3rd century:** Atellan farce, lively improvised scenarios based on domestic life, is imported from southern Italy to Rome. **240:** Ludi Romani, a festival in honor of Jupiter, incorporates comedy and tragedy for the first time. The festival, established by the elder Tarquin, Etruscan ruler of Rome, already included chariot races, boxing matches, and other popular entertainments. The plays performed at the festival in 240 are probably translations or imitations of Greek plays. **205–184:** Titus Maccius Plautus writes his plays, including *The Twin Menaechmi.*	**272:** Rome conquers central and southern Italy. **264–241:** First Punic War with Carthage **222:** Rome conquers northern Italy. **218–201:** Second Punic War	**c. 300:** Roman consul Appius Claudius Crassus builds the Appian Way, which stretches from Rome to Capua. **287:** Full equality between plebeians and patricians in Rome
200–100	**160:** Publius Terentius Afer (Terence) writes *The Brothers.* **c. 126–c. 62:** Roscius, a popular Roman actor	**195:** Cato the Elder becomes consul and initiates many reforms in urban development and government representation. **149–146:** The Third Punic War. Rome destroys Carthage and Corinth and conquers Greece. **133:** Tiberius Gracchus, Roman reformer, is murdered at the instigation of the Senate.	**186:** Wild animals are exhibited at the Circus Maximus. Contests between wild animals and humans begin shortly thereafter. **106–43:** Cicero, Roman orator **105:** Gladiatorial contests become part of state festivals.

DATE	THEATER	POLITICAL	SOCIAL/CULTURAL
100 BCE–1 CE	**1st century:** Theaters are built throughout the Roman empire.	**69** BCE: Cleopatra born. She reigns as queen of Egypt from 51 to 49 and from 48 to her death in 30.	**87–54:** Catullus, Roman poet
	90: Vitruvius writes *De Architectura*, a treatise on Roman architecture that discusses theater architecture in Greece and Rome.	**60:** First Triumvirate (Pompey, Crassus, and Julius Caesar) rules Rome.	**70–19:** Virgil (P. Virgilius Maro), poet and author of the *Aeneid*
		47: Herod is appointed King of Judea.	**47:** The library of Ptolemy in Alexandria destroyed by fire; many valuable manuscripts and works of art are lost.
	55: The first permanent stone theater is built in Rome.	**45:** Julius Caesar is declared dictator by Roman Senate.	**46:** Julius Caesar stages the first *naumachia* (mock sea battle).
	fl. 55: Clodius Aesopus, Roman tragedian actor	**44:** On the Ides of March Caesar is assassinated.	**43** BCE–**17** CE: Ovid (Publius Ovidius Naso), poet and author of the *Metamorphoses*
		43–28: The Second Triumvirate (Antony, Lepidus, and Octavius) rules Rome.	
		27 BCE–**476** CE: Roman empire	**22:** Roman pantomime, a predecessor of modern ballet, is introduced by Pylades and Bathyllus.
	4 BCE–**65** CE: Seneca. Dates for his plays, including *Medea*, are unknown. Seneca commits suicide after suffering a decline in power and influence.	**27:** Gaius Octavius, Julius Caesar's grand-nephew, becomes the first emperor of the Roman empire, assuming the name Augustus.	**19:** Horace (65–8 BCE) writes *Ars Poetica*.
			4: Birth of Jesus
1–100		**14:** Augustus dies, and his stepson Tiberius becomes emperor.	c. **30:** Crucifixion of Jesus
		37: Tiberius's grand-nephew Gaius Caesar (Caligula) is named emperor.	
		41: Caligula is assassinated by his own guards; his wife and young daughter are also murdered. Caligula's uncle Claudius is named emperor.	
		54: Claudius is allegedly poisoned by his wife, Julia Agrippina. Claudius's stepson Nero is named emperor.	**64:** Much of Rome is destroyed by fire. Nero blames the fire on Rome's increasing Christian population and initiates the first large-scale persecution of Christians in Rome.
		68: Nero commits suicide.	**79:** Mount Vesuvius erupts, destroying Pompeii.
		69: Vespasian is named emperor. He is succeeded by his son Titus.	**80:** The Colosseum is completed.

Roman Drama Timeline (continued)

DATE	THEATER	POLITICAL	SOCIAL/CULTURAL
100–200	**197–202:** Tertullian writes *De Spectaculis*, denouncing the theater as anti-Christian.	**117:** Hadrian becomes emperor. **120:** Hadrian commissions the building of the Pantheon ("the place of all gods"). **122–126:** Hadrian's Wall is extended across Great Britain. **138:** Hadrian dies and is succeeded by Antonius Pius and then by Marcus Aurelius.	**c. 130–200:** Galen, Roman physicist and pioneer in anatomy and physiology **164–180:** A devastating plague sweeps the Roman empire.
200–300	**c. 300:** Records of earliest religious plays	Roman citizenship given to every freeborn subject in the empire. Under Roman rule, Carthage regains prominence as a center of culture and commerce. **220:** Goths invade the Balkan Peninsula and Asia Minor. **257:** Goths invade the Black Sea provinces.	
300–400		**313:** Edict of Milan. Emperor Constantine establishes toleration of Christianity. **331:** Emperor Constantine moves the Roman capital from Rome to Constantinople. **360:** Huns invade Europe.	**354–430:** St. Augustine, author of the influential *City of God* and *Confessions* **c. 360:** Scrolls begin to be replaced by books.
400–500		**401–403:** Visigoths invade Italy. **410:** Alaric, king of Visigoths, sacks Rome.	**c. 400:** In part because of the rise of Christianity, state festivals honoring pagan gods cease in Rome. **404:** Gladiatorial contests are abolished. **c. 410:** Experiments with alchemy begin. **523:** Wild animal contests are abolished.

Roman Dramatists
Plautus

All surviving Roman comedy shows the influence of Greek originals. Plautus (254–184 BCE) is among Rome's most famous playwrights and may have been a member of a troupe that performed Atellan comedy. His middle name is Maccius (a form of Maccus, the clown of the farces), possibly alluding to the role he had habitually played. Tradition has it that he was in the theater for a good while before he began writing comedies. His first plays date from 205 BCE, about thirty-five years after Livius introduced Greek drama to the Romans. No one knows how many plays he wrote, and many unauthenticated titles have been assigned to him. About twenty-one plays exist that are thought to be his, the most famous of which are *Amphitryon, The Pot of Gold, The Captives, Curculio, The Braggart Warrior, The Rope,* and *The Twin Menaechmi.*

The last play is probably the best-known Roman comedy. It features Menaechmus from Syracuse, who goes to Epidamnus searching for his lost twin. There he meets people who mistake him for his brother: a cook; a prostitute; Sponge, a typical parasite; and even his brother's wife and father-in-law. The comedy exploits all the confusions inherent in mistaken identity.

Plautus (254–184 BCE)

FROM *THE TWIN MENAECHMI*   *c. 205–184 BCE*

TRANSLATED BY LIONEL CASSON

The Twin Menaechmi was the first ancient play to be translated into a modern language and put on the stage (1486 in Italy). It has been adapted by numerous modern playwrights, including Shakespeare in *The Comedy of Errors* and, more recently, Rodgers and Hart in *The Boys from Syracuse* (1938), a musical that ran on Broadway for 235 performances. *Boys* has been revived numerous times and is still a popular summer theater play. The following scene from the beginning of Act III of *The Twin Menaechmi* shows the parasite Sponge mistaking Menaechmus of Syracuse for Sponge's friend Menaechmus of Epidamnus. They have a great go-around over a dress in a typical mixup of the kind that originated with Roman comedies and has been popular in farces and comedies ever since.

ACT III

SPONGE: I'm over thirty now, and never have I ever in all those years pulled a more damned fool stunt than the one I pulled today: There was this town meeting, and *I* had to dive in and come up right in the middle of it. While I'm standing there with my mouth open, Menaechmus sneaks off on me. I'll bet he's gone to his girlfriend. Perfectly willing to leave me behind, too!

(*Paces up and down a few times, shaking his head bitterly. Then, in a rage.*) Damn, damn, damn the fellow who first figured out town meetings! All they do is keep a busy man away from his business. Why don't people pick a panel of men of leisure for this kind of thing? Hold a roll call at each meeting and whoever doesn't answer gets fined on the spot. There are plenty of persons around who need only one meal a day; they don't have business hours to keep because they don't go after dinner invitations or give them out. They're the ones to fuss with town meetings and town elections. If that's how things were run, I wouldn't have lost my lunch today. He sure wanted me along, didn't he? I'll go in, anyway. There's still hope of leftovers to soothe my soul. (*He is about to go up to the door when it suddenly swings open and Menaechmus of Syracuse appears, standing on the threshold with a garland, a little askew, on his head; he is holding the dress and listening to Lovey who is chattering at him from inside. Sponge quickly backs off into a corner.*) What's this I see? Menaechmus—and he's leaving, garland and all! The table's been cleared! I sure came in time—in time to walk him home. Well, I'll watch what his game is, and then I'll go and have a word with him.

MENAECHMUS OF SYRACUSE (*to Lovey inside*): Take it easy, will you! I'll have it back to you today in plenty of time, altered and trimmed to perfection. (*Slyly.*) Believe me, you'll say it's not your dress; you won't know it any more.

SPONGE (*to the audience*): He's bringing the dress to the dressmaker. The dining's done, the drinks are down—and Sponge spent the lunch hour outside. God damn it I'm not the man I think I am if I don't get even with him for this, but really even. You just watch. I'll give it to him, I will.

MENAECHMUS OF SYRACUSE (*closing the door and walking downstage; to the audience, jubilantly*): Good god, no one ever expected less—and got more blessings from heaven in one day than me. I dined, I wined, I wenched, and (*holding up the dress*) made off with this to which, from this moment on, she hereby forfeits all right, title, and interest.

SPONGE (*straining his ears, to the audience*): I can't make out what he's saying from back here. Is that full-belly talking about me and my right title and interest?

MENAECHMUS OF SYRACUSE (*to the audience*): She said I stole it from my wife and gave it to her. I saw she was mistaking me for someone else, so I promptly played it as if she and I were having a hot and heavy affair and began to yes her; I agreed right down the line to everything she said. Well, to make a long story short, I never had it so good for so little.

SPONGE (*clenching his fists, to the audience*): I'm going up to him. I'm itching to give him the works. (*Leaves his corner and strides belligerently toward Menaechmus.*)

MENAECHMUS OF SYRACUSE (*to the audience*): Someone coming up to me. Wonder who it is?

SPONGE (*roaring*): Well! You featherweight, you filth, you slime, you disgrace to the human race, you double-crossing good-for-nothing! What did I ever do to you that you had to ruin my life? You sure gave me the slip downtown a little while ago! You killed off the day all right—and held the funeral feast without me. Me who was coheir under the will! Where do you come off to do a thing like that!

MENAECHMUS OF SYRACUSE (*too pleased with life to lose his temper*): Mister, will you please tell me what business you and I have that gives you the right to use language like that to a stranger here, someone you never saw in your life? You hand me that talk and I'll hand you something you won't like.

SPONGE (*dancing with rage*): God damn it, you already have! I know god damned well you have!

MENAECHMUS OF SYRACUSE (*amused and curious*): What's your name, mister?

SPONGE (*as before*): Still making jokes, eh? As if you don't know my name!

MENAECHMUS OF SYRACUSE: So help me, so far as I know, I never heard of you or saw you till this minute. But I know one thing for sure: whoever you are, you'd better behave yourself and stop bothering me.

SPONGE (*taken aback for a minute*): Menaechmus! Wake up!

MENAECHMUS OF SYRACUSE (*genially*): Believe me, to the best of my knowledge, I am awake.

SPONGE: You don't know me?

MENAECHMUS OF SYRACUSE (*as before*): If I did, I wouldn't say I didn't.

SPONGE (*incredulously*): You don't know your own parasite?

MENAECHMUS OF SYRACUSE: Mister, it looks to me as if you've got bats in your belfry.

SPONGE (*shaken, but not convinced*): Tell me this: Didn't you steal that dress there from your wife today and give it to Lovey?

MENAECHMUS OF SYRACUSE: Good god, no! I don't have a wife, I never gave anything to any Lovey, and I never stole any dress. Are you in your right mind?

SPONGE (*aside, groaning*): A dead loss, the whole affair. (*To Menaechmus.*) But you came out of your house wearing the dress! I saw you myself!

MENAECHMUS OF SYRACUSE (*exploding*): Damn you! You think everybody's a pervert just because you are? I was wearing this dress? Is that what you're telling me?

SPONGE: I most certainly am.

MENAECHMUS OF SYRACUSE: Now you go straight to the one place fit for you! No—get yourself to the lunatic asylum; you're stark-raving mad.

SPONGE (*venomously*): God damn it, there's one thing nobody in the world is going to stop me from doing: I'm telling the whole story, exactly what happened, to your wife this minute. All these insults are going to boomerang back on your own head. Believe you me, you'll pay for eating that whole lunch yourself. (*Dashes into the house of Menaechmus of Epidamnus.*)

MENAECHMUS OF SYRACUSE (*throwing his arms wide, to the audience*): What's going on here? Must everyone I lay eyes on play games with me this way? Wait—I hear the door.

(*The door of Lovey's house opens, and one of her maids comes out holding a bracelet. She walks over to Menaechmus and, as he looks on blankly, hands it to him.*)

MAID: Menaechmus, Lovey says would you please do her a big favor and drop this at the jeweler's on your way? She wants you to give him an ounce of gold and have him make the whole bracelet over.

MENAECHMUS OF SYRACUSE (*with alacrity*): Tell her I'll not only take care of this but anything else she wants taken care of. Anything at all. (*He takes the piece and examines it absorbedly.*)

MAID (*watching him curiously, in surprise*): Don't you know what bracelet it is?

MENAECHMUS OF SYRACUSE: Frankly no—except that it's gold.

MAID: It's the one you told us you stole from your wife's jewel box when nobody was looking.

MENAECHMUS OF SYRACUSE (*forgetting himself, in high dudgeon*): I never did anything of the kind!

MAID: You mean you don't remember it? Well, if that's the case, you give it right back!

MENAECHMUS OF SYRACUSE (*after a few seconds of highly histrionic deep thought*): Wait a second. No, I *do* remember it. Of course—this is the one I gave her. Oh, and there's something else: Where are the armlets I gave her at the same time?

MAID (*puzzled*): You never gave her any armlets.

MENAECHMUS OF SYRACUSE (*quickly*): Right you are. This was all I gave her.

MAID: Shall I tell her you'll take care of it?

MENAECHMUS OF SYRACUSE: By all means, tell her. I'll take care of it, all right. I'll see she gets it back the same time she gets the dress back.

MAID (*going up to him and stroking his cheek*): Menaechmus dear, will you do me a favor too? Will you have some earrings made for me? Drop earrings, please; ten grams of gold in each. (*Meaningfully.*) It'll make me *so* glad to see you every time you come to the house.

MENAECHMUS OF SYRACUSE: Sure. (*With elaborate carelessness.*) Just give me the gold. I'll pay for the labor myself.

MAID: Please, you pay for the gold too. I'll make it up to you afterward.

MENAECHMUS OF SYRACUSE: No, you pay for the gold. I'll make it up to *you* afterward. Double.

MAID: I don't have the money.

MENAECHMUS OF SYRACUSE (*with a great air of magnanimity*): Well, any time you get it, you just let me have it.

MAID (*turning to go*): I'm going in now. Anything I can do for you?

MENAECHMUS OF SYRACUSE: Yes. Tell her I'll see to both things—(*sotto voce, to the audience*) that they get sold as quickly as possible for whatever they'll bring. (*As the maid starts walking toward the door.*) Has she gone in yet? (*Hearing a slam.*) Ah, she's in, the door's closed. (*Jubilantly.*) The lord loves me! I've had a helping hand from heaven! (*Suddenly looks about warily.*) But why hang around when I have the time and chance to get away from this (*jerking his thumb at Lovey's house*) pimping parlor here? Menaechmus! Get a move on, hit the road, forward march! I'll take off this garland and toss it to the left here (*doing so*). Then, if anyone tries to follow me, he'll think I went that way. Now I'll go and see if I can find my servant. I want to let him know all the blessings from heaven I've had.

(*He races off, stage right. The stage is now empty.*)

Terence

Terence (c. 190–159 BCE) is said to have been a North African slave brought to Rome, where his master realized he was unusually intelligent and gifted. After he was freed, Terence took his place in Roman literary life and produced a body of six plays, all of which still exist: *The Woman of Andros, The Self-Tormentor, The Eunuch, Phormio, The Mother-in-Law,* and *The Brothers.* Terence's plays are notable for including a subplot or secondary action—carefully—and for avoiding the technique of addressing the audience directly.

The Romans preferred Plautus's broad farcical humor to Terence's more carefully plotted, elegantly styled plays. Terence borrowed liberally from Greek sources, often more than one for each of his plays, to develop unusually complicated plots. A manager or producer worked with him on all his plays, and the musician who worked with him was a slave, Flaccus. Terence's productive life was relatively short. He died on a trip to Greece, apparently worrying over a piece of missing luggage said to have contained new plays.

Terence's situation was unusual: he had two wealthy Roman patrons who were interested in seeing the best Greek comedy brought to the Romans. Consequently, they paid for his productions and gave him more support than the average comic playwright could have expected. Terence's dramatic skills developed considerably from the beginning to the end of his work, contrasting sharply with the repetitive nature of Plautus's work. Terence was more than a translator, but he wrote at a time when Romans were interested in emulating the Greeks, and his fidelity to Greek originals was one of his strongest recommendations.

Terence (c. 190–159 BCE)

FROM *THE BROTHERS*   *160 BCE*

TRANSLATED BY ROBERT GRAVES

The ending of *The Brothers*, generally recognized as Terence's masterpiece and certainly the most influential of his plays, has Demea planning a reversal on his brother, Micio. Micio is a good, easygoing bachelor who wishes well for others. Demea has been a stern father to one of his sons, Ctesipho, and has tried to steer him in a direction other than the one Ctesipho wants to follow. Demea has entrusted the upbringing of his second son, Aeschinus, to his lenient brother, Micio. Both sons deceive both brothers and end up with the women they want rather than the women the brothers want for them. Meanwhile, Demea gives up and turns the tables on Micio, engineering his brother's marriage to Aeschinus's mother-in-law. In the process of all this, Demea decides to adopt the gentle, easy-going ways of his brother and to forsake his former stern behavior.

This play was adapted often in the seventeenth century by Marston, Beaumont and Fletcher, and others. Molière relied on it for his *School for Wives*. At least five plays were adapted from it for the eighteenth-century English stage.

FROM ACT V

MICIO (*to Syrus, within*): My brother ordered it,° say ye! Where is he? . . . Hah, Brother, was it you who ordered this?

DEMEA: Yes, that I did! And in this and all things else I'm ready to do whatever may conduce to the uniting, serving, helping, and the joining together of both families.

AESCHINUS (*to Micio*): Pray, Sir, let it be so!

MICIO: Well, I've nothing to say against it.

DEMEA: Truth, 'tis no more than we are obliged to do. For first, she's your son's mother-in-law . . .

MICIO: What then?

DEMEA: A very virtuous and modest woman . . .

MICIO: So they say indeed.

DEMEA: Not weighed down by years . . .

MICIO: Not yet.

DEMEA: But past child-bearing: a lonesome woman whom nobody esteems . . .

MICIO (*aside*): What the Devil is he at?

DEMEA: . . . Therefore you ought to marry her; and you Aeschinus, should do what you can to bring this about.

MICIO: Who? I marry?

DEMEA: Yes, you.

MICIO: I, prithee?

DEMEA: Yes, you I say.

MICIO: Pho, you are fooling us, surely?

DEMEA (*to Aeschinus*): If thou hast any life in thee, persuade him to it.

AESCHINUS: Dear Father . . .

MICIO (*interrupting*): Blockhead! Dost thou take in earnest what he says?

DEMEA: 'Tis in vain to refuse; it can't be avoided.

MICIO: Pho, you are in your dotage!

AESCHINUS: Good Sir, let me win this one favor.

MICIO (*angrily*): Art out of thy wits, let me alone!

DEMEA: Come, come! Hearken for once to what your son says.

MICIO: Haven't ye played the fool enough yet? Shall I at threescore and five marry an old woman who's ready to drop into the grave? This is your wise counsel, is it?

AESCHINUS: Pray, Sir, do; I've promised you shall.

MICIO: You promised, with a mischief! Promise for thyself, thou chit!

DEMEA: Fie, fie! What if he had begged a greater favor from you?

MICIO: As if there were any greater favor than this!

DEMEA: Pray grant his request.

AESCHINUS: Good Sir, be not so hard-hearted.

DEMEA: Pho, promise him for once!

MICIO: Will ye never leave baiting me?

AESCHINUS: Not till I've prevailed, Sir.

MICIO: Truth, this is downright forcing a man.

DEMEA: Come, Micio, be good-natured and consent.

MICIO: Though this be the most damned, foolish, ridiculous whim, and the most averse to my nature that could possibly be, yet since you are so extremely set upon it, I'll humor ye for once.

My brother ordered it: Demea ordered the breaking down of a wall to allow the two families to communicate. In this way Demea imitates the good-naturedness of his brother, Micio, and traps him into marrying Aeschinus's mother-in-law.

AESCHINUS: That is excellent, I'm obliged to ye beyond measure.

DEMEA (*aside*): Well, what's next? . . . What shall I say next? This is as I'd have it. . . . What's more to be done?

(*To Micio.*)

Ho! There's Hegio our poor kinsman, and nearest relation; in truth, we ought in conscience to do something for him.

MICIO: What, pray?

DEMEA: There's a small plot of land in the suburbs, which you farm out — pray let's give him that to live on.

MICIO: A small one, say ye?

DEMEA: Though it were a great one, you might yet give it to him. He has been as good as a father to Pamphila; he's a very honest man, our kinsman, and you couldn't bestow it better. Besides, Brother, there's a certain proverb (none of my own, I assure you) which you so well and wisely made use of: "That age has always this ill effect of making us more worldly, as well as wiser." We should do well to avoid this scandal. 'Tis a true proverb, Brother, and ought to be held in mind.

MICIO: What's all this? . . . Well, so let it be, if he has need of it.

AESCHINUS: Brave Father, I vow!

DEMEA: Now you are my true brother, both in body and soul.

MICIO: I'm glad of it.

DEMEA (*aside, laughing*): I've stabbed him with his own weapons, i'fack!

(*Enter Syrus, with a pick-axe upon his shoulders.*)

SYRUS (*to Demea*): The job is done as ye ordered, Sir.

DEMEA: Thou art an honest lad. . . . And upon my conscience I think Syrus deserves his freedom.

MICIO: He, his freedom? For what exploit?

DEMEA: O, for a thousand.

SYRUS: O dear Mr. Demea, you are a rare gentleman, edad you are! You know I've looked after the young gentlemen from their cradles. I taught them, advised them, and instructed them all I possibly could.

DEMEA: Nothing more evident! Nay, more than that, he catered for them, pimped for them, and in the morning took care of a debauchee for them. These are no ordinary accomplishments, I can assure ye.

SYRUS: Your worship's very merry.

DEMEA: Besides, he was prime mover in buying this music-girl. It was he who managed the whole intrigue, and 'tis no more than justice to reward him, as an encouragement to others! In short, Aeschinus desires the same thing.

MICIO (*to Aeschinus*): Do you desire it too?

AESCHINUS: Yes, if you please, Sir.

MICIO: Since 'tis so, come hither, Syrus! Thou art a free man.

(*Syrus kneels down, Micio lays his hand on his head, and after that gives him a cuff on the ear.*)

SYRUS (*rising up*): Generously done! A thousand thanks to ye all, and to you, Mr. Demea.

DEMEA: I'm well satisfied.

AESCHINUS: And I too.

SYRUS: I won't question it, Sir. But I wish heartily my joy were more complete, that my poor spouse Phrygia might be made as free as I am.

DEMEA: Truth, she's a mighty good woman.

SYRUS: And your grandson's first foster-mother, too.

DEMEA: Faith, in good earnest, if for that, she deserves her freedom before any woman in the world.

MICIO: What! For that simple service?

DEMEA: Yes, indeed! In fine, I'll pay for her freedom myself.

SYRUS: God's blessing light upon your worship, and grant all your wishes.

MICIO: Syrus, thou hast made a good day's work of it.

DEMEA: Besides, Brother, it would be a deed of charity to lend him a little money to set up in business that he may face the world without fear. I undertake that he'll soon repay it.

MICIO: Not a penny-piece!

AESCHINUS: He's a very honest fellow, Sir.

SYRUS: Upon my word, I'll repay you the loan. Do but trust me!

AESCHINUS: Pray do, Sir.

MICIO: I'll consider the matter with care.

DEMEA: He shall pay ye, I'll see to that.

SYRUS (*to Demea*): Egad, you're the best man alive.

AESCHINUS: And the pleasantest in the world.

MICIO: What's the meaning of this, Brother? How comes this sudden change of humor? Why this gallant squandering and profusion?

DEMEA: I'll tell ye, Brother. These sons of yours don't reckon you a sweet-natured and pleasant man because you live as you should and do what is just and reasonable, but because you fawn upon them, cocker them up, and give them what they'll spend. Now, son Aeschinus, if you are dissatisfied with my course of life, because I wouldn't indulge you in all things, right or wrong, then I'll not trouble my head with you any further. Be free to squander, buy mistresses, and do what you will! But if you wish me to advise ye, and set ye up, and help ye too in matters of which your youth can give ye but little understanding—matters of which you are over-fond, and don't well consider—see, here I'm ready to stand by you.

AESCHINUS: Dear Sir, we commit ourselves wholly to your charge; for you know what's fitting to be done far better than we . . . But what will ye do for my brother Ctesipho?

DEMEA: Why, let him take the music-girl; and so bid adieu to general wenching.

AESCHINUS: That's very reasonable. (*To the spectators.*) Gentlemen, your favor!

(*Exeunt° all.*)

[s.d.] *Exeunt:* Latin for "they go out."

Seneca

The surviving Roman plays come from just three hands: Plautus, Terence, and Seneca (4 BCE–65 CE). The comedies of Plautus are raucous, broad, and farcical; those of Terence are polished and carefully structured. Seneca wrote tragedies that were well known to Elizabethans such as Marlowe and Shakespeare, and it is clear that the Elizabethan Age found SENECAN TRAGEDY to be peculiarly suited to its own temperament.

Senecan tragedies were based on either Greek or Roman themes and included murder, bloodthirsty actions (many of which did not occur on stage but were only described), horror of various kinds, ghosts, and long, bombastic speeches. Signs of Senecan influence can be seen in Elizabethan drama, with its taste for many of these devices; plays like *Hamlet* are notable for ending in a pool of blood, with most of the actors lying dead onstage. The theme of revenge was also prized by Seneca and, later, by the Elizabethans.

Not a professional theater person, Seneca was wealthy and learned, a philosopher active in the government of Emperor Nero's Rome. His plays, most of which were adapted from Euripides, were probably written only to be read, as was common at the time, or perhaps recited, although there is no record of their having been performed. The Roman people thirsted for mime and farce but had much less taste for serious plays.

Ten plays attributed to Seneca exist, nine of which are surely his and one of which is only possibly his. His most famous are *Mad Hercules, The Phoenician Women, Medea, Phaedra, Agamemnon, Thyestes,* and *The Trojan Women.*

Seneca (4 BCE–65 CE)
FROM THYESTES

TRANSLATED BY ELLA ISABEL HARRIS

Thyestes, probably adapted from the *Oresteia* of Aeschylus, influenced a number of Elizabethan revenge tragedies, such as Shakespeare's *Hamlet*. The story is gruesome even by modern standards. Thyestes seduces his brother Atreus's wife, and Atreus banishes him. When Atreus summons Thyestes to Atreus's home, he goes suspiciously, hoping to be able to see his children. The banquet Atreus holds for Thyestes seems to signal reconciliation between the brothers. But when it is over, Atreus brings in the heads of Thyestes' children, revealing that Thyestes has just eaten their bodies in the feast.

The second scene from act V—before Thyestes is told about the meal he has eaten—follows in its entirety. It shows Thyestes wrestling with himself in a passion of uncertainty. Thyestes' soliloquy is a psychological study of the effects of grief, care, uncertainty, and fear. Seneca's plays have many such soliloquies, and their revelations of complex emotional states deeply impressed the age of Shakespeare.

ACT V • Scene II

(Thyestes sits alone at the banquet table, half overcome with wine; he tries to sing and be gay, but some premonition of evil weighs upon him.)

THYESTES (*to himself*): By long grief dulled, put by thy cares, my heart,
    Let fear and sorrow fly and bitter need,
    Companion of thy timorous banishment,
    And shame, hard burden of afflicted souls.
    Whence thou has fallen profits more to know
    Than whither; great is he who with firm step
    Moves on the plain when fallen from the height;
    He who, oppressed by sorrows numberless
    And driven from his realm, with unbent neck
    Carries his burdens, not degenerate
    Or conquered, who stands firm beneath the weight
    Of all his burdens, he is great indeed.
    Now scatter all the clouds of bitter fate,
    Put by all signs of thy unhappy days,
    In happy fortunes show a happy face,
    Forget the old Thyestes. Ah, this vice
    Still follows misery: never to trust
    In happy days; though better fortunes come,
    Those who have borne afflictions find it hard
    To joy in better days. What holds me back,
    Forbids me celebrate the festal tide?
    What cause of grief, arising causelessly,
    Bids me to weep? What art thou that forbids
    That I should crown my head with festal wreath?
    It does forbid, forbid! Upon my head
    The roses languish, and my hair that drips
    With ointment rises as with sudden fear,
    My face is wet with showers of tears that fall

Unwillingly, and groans break off my song.
Grief loves accustomed tears, the wretched feel
That they must weep. I would be glad to make
Most bitter lamentation, and to wail,
And rend this robe with Tyrian purple dyed.
My mind gives warning of some coming grief,
Presages future ills. The storm that smites
When all the sea is calm weighs heavily
Upon the sailor. Fool! What grief, what storm,
Dost thou conceive? Believe thy brother now.
Be what it may, thou fearest now too late,
Or causelessly. I do not wish to be
Unhappy, but vague terror smites my breast.
No cause is evident and yet my eyes
O'erflow with sudden tears. What can it be,
Or grief, or fear? Or has great pleasure tears?

The surviving Roman plays offer enough variety to give us an idea of what the drama achieved. Like so much of Roman culture, Roman drama rested in the shadow of Greek accomplishments. The Romans were responsible for maintaining the Greek texts, allowing us to see a great deal of their work. Although it may be true that much of the Roman drama that was produced no longer exists, what survives shows variety and high quality.

Medieval Drama

The Role of the Church

The medieval period in Europe (476 CE–1500 CE) began with the collapse of Rome, a calamity of such magnitude that the years between then and the beginning of the Crusades in 1095 have been traditionally, if erroneously, called the Dark Ages. Historians used this term to refer to their lack of knowledge about a time in which no great central powers organized society or established patterns of behavior and standards in the arts.

Drama, or at least records of it, all but disappeared. The major Western institution to profit from the fall of the Roman empire was the Roman Catholic Church, which in the ninth and tenth centuries enjoyed considerable power and influence. Many bishops considered drama a godless activity, a distraction from the piety that the church demanded of its members. During the great age of cathedral building and the great ages of religious painting and religious music—from the seventh century to the thirteenth—drama was not officially approved. Therefore, it is a striking irony that the rebirth of drama in the Western world should have taken place in the heart of the monasteries, developing slowly and inconspicuously until it outgrew its beginnings.

The Church may well have intended nothing more than the simple dramatization of its message. Or the people may have craved drama, and the Church's response could have been an attempt to answer their needs. In either event, the Church could never have foreseen the outcome of adding a few moments of drama to the liturgy, the church services. LITURGICAL DRAMA began in the ninth century with TROPES, or embellishments, which were sung during parts of the Mass (the public celebration of the Eucharist). The earliest known example of a trope, called the QUEM QUAERITIS ("Whom seek ye?"), grew out of the Easter Mass and was sung in a monastic settlement in Switzerland called St. Gall:

ANGEL: Whom seek ye in the sepulchre, O ye Christians?
THREE MARYS: Jesus of Nazareth, who was crucified, O ye Angels.
ANGEL: He is not here; he is risen as he has foretold.
Go, announce that he is risen from the sepulchre.

Some scholars think that in its earliest form this trope was sung by four monks in a dialogue pattern, three monks representing the three Marys at Christ's tomb and the other representing the angel. Tropes like the *Quem Quaeritis* evolved over the years to include a number of participants—monks, nuns, and choirboys in different communities—as the tropes spread from church to church throughout the Continent. These dramatic interpolations never became dramas separate from the Mass itself, although their success and popularity led to experiments with other dramatic sequences centering on moments in the Mass and in the life of Christ. The actors in these pieces did not think of themselves as specialists or professionals; they were simply monks or nuns who belonged to the church. The churchgoers obviously enjoyed the tropes, and more were created, despite the Church's official position on drama.

In the tenth century a nun called Hrosvitha entertained herself and her fellow nuns with imitations of the Latin dramatist Terence. Although her own subject matter was holy in nature, she realized that Terence was an amusing comic writer with a polished style. She referred to herself as "the strong voice of Gandersheim," her community in Saxony, and said that she had "not hesitated to imitate in my writings a poet whose works are so widely read, my object being to glorify, within the limits of my poor talent, the laudable chastity of Christian virgins." Her plays are very short moral tales, often illustrating moments in the lives of Christian martyred women. As far as is known, these plays do not seem to have gone beyond the nuns' walls; therefore, they had little effect on the drama developing in the period.

Once dramatic scenes were added that took the action outside of the liturgy, it was not long before dramas were being staged outside the church. The Anglo-Norman drama *Adam*, dating from the twelfth century, has explicit stage directions establishing its setting outside the church. The play is to be staged on the west side of the church with a platform extending from the steps. The characters of Adam, Eve, God (called Figura), and the Devil and his assistants are given costumes and extensive dialogue. The dramatic detail in this play implies a considerable development of plot and action, which, despite its theological matter, is plainly too elaborate to be contained within the service of the Mass.

Miracle Plays

Once outside the church, the drama flourished and soon became independent, although its themes continued to be religious and its services were connected with religious festivals. In 1264 Pope Urban IV added to the religious calendar a new, important feast: Corpus Christi, celebrated beginning on the first Thursday after Trinity Sunday, about two months after Easter. The purpose of the feast was to celebrate the doctrine declaring that the body of Christ was real and present in the Host (consecrated bread or wafer) taken by the faithful in the sacrament of Communion.

At first the feast of Corpus Christi was localized in Liège, Belgium. But in the fourteenth and fifteenth centuries it spread through papal decree and became one of the chief feasts of the church. Among other things, it featured a procession and pageant in which the Host was displayed publicly through the streets of a town. Because of the importance and excitement of this feast, entire communities took part in the celebration.

MIRACLE PLAYS on the subject of miracles performed by saints developed late in the twelfth century in both England and on the Continent. Typically, these plays focused on the Virgin Mary and St. Nicholas, both of whom had strong followings (sometimes described as cults) during the medieval period. Mary is often portrayed as helping those in need and danger—often at the last minute. Some of those she saved may have seemed unsavory sinners to a pious audience, but the point was that the saint saved all who truly wished to be saved.

Although they quickly became public entertainments removed from the church building and were popular as Corpus Christi entertainments throughout the fifteenth century, few miracle plays survive in English because King Henry VIII banned them in the middle of the sixteenth century during his reformation of the Church. As a result, they were not performed or preserved.

The craft guilds, professional organizations of workers involved in the same trade—carpenters, wool merchants, and so on—soon began competing with each other in producing plays that could be performed during the feast of Corpus Christi. Most of their plays derived from Bible stories and the life of Christ. Religious guilds, such as the Confrèrie of the Passion, produced plays in Paris and elsewhere on the Continent. Because the Bible is silent on many details of Christ's life, some plays invented new material and illuminated dark areas, thereby satisfying the intense curiosity medieval Christians had about events the Bible omitted.

Mystery Plays

The Church did not ignore drama after it left the church buildings. Since the plays had religious subject matter and could be used to teach the Bible and to model Christian behavior, they remained of considerable value to the Church.

First performed by the clergy, these religious plays dramatized the mystery of Christ's Passion. Later the plays were produced by members of craft guilds, and they became known as CRAFT PLAYS or MYSTERY PLAYS. Beginning in the medieval period, the word *mystery* was used to describe a skill or trade known only to a few who apprenticed and mastered its special techniques; it also referred to religious mysteries.

By the fifteenth century, mystery plays and the feast of Corpus Christi were popular almost everywhere in Europe, and in England certain towns produced exceptionally elaborate cycles with unusually complex and ambitious plays. The CYCLES were groups of plays numbering from twenty-four to forty-eight. Four cycles have been preserved: the Chester, York, Towneley (Wakefield), and N-Town cycles, named for their towns of origin. N-Town plays were a generic version of plays that any town could take and use as its own, although the plays were probably written near Lincoln.

The plays were performed again and again during annual holidays and feasts, and the texts were carefully preserved. Some of the plays, such as *The Fall of Lucifer*, are very short. Others are more elaborate in length and complexity and resemble modern plays: *Noah*, from the Wakefield Cycle, which has been produced regularly in recent history; *The Slaughter of Innocents*; and *The Second Shepherds' Pageant*, one of the most entertaining mystery plays.

The producers of the plays often had a sense of appropriateness in their choice of subjects. For example, the Water-Drawers guild sponsored *Noah's Flood*, the Butchers (because they sold "flesh") *Temptation, The Woman Taken in Adultery*, and the Shipwrights *The Building of the Ark*.

Among the best-known mystery plays is the somewhat farcical *The Second Shepherds' Pageant,* which is both funny and serious. It tells of a crafty shepherd named Mak who steals a lamb from his fellow shepherds and takes it home. His wife, Gill, then places it in a cradle and pretends it is her baby. Eventually the shepherds—who suspect Mak from the first—smoke out the fraud and give Mak a blanket-tossing for their trouble. But after they do so, they see a star in the heavens and turn their attention to the birth of baby Jesus, the Lamb of God. They join the Magi and come to pay homage to the Christ Child.

The easy way in which the profane elements of everyday life coexisted with the sacred in medieval times has long interested scholars. *The Second Shepherds' Pageant* virtually breaks into two parts, the first dedicated to the wickedness of Mak and Gill and the horseplay of the shepherds. But once Mak has had his due reward, the play alters in tone and the sense of devotion to Christian teachings becomes uppermost. The fact that the mystery plays moved away from liturgical Latin and to the vernacular (local) language made such a juxtaposition of sacred and profane much more possible.

The dominance of the guilds in producing mystery plays suggests that guilds enjoyed increasing political power and authority. The guilds grew stronger and more influential—probably at the expense of the Church. Some historians have seen this development as crucial to the growing secularization of the Middle Ages.

Morality Plays

MORALITY PLAYS were never part of any cycle but developed independently as moral tales in the late fourteenth or early fifteenth century on the Continent and in England. They do not illustrate moments in the Bible, nor do they describe the life of Christ or the saints. Instead, they describe the lives of people facing the temptations of the world. The plays are careful to present a warning to the unwary that their souls are always in peril, that the devil is on constant watch, and that people must behave properly if they are to be saved.

One feature of morality plays is their reliance on ALLEGORY, a favorite medieval device. Allegory is the technique of giving abstract ideas or values a physical representation. In morality plays, abstractions such as goodness became characters in the drama. In modern times we sometimes use allegory in art, as when we represent justice as a blindfolded woman. Allegorically, justice should act impartially because she does not "see" any distinctions, such as those of rank or privilege, that characterize most people standing before a judge.

The use of allegory permitted medieval dramatists to personify abstract values such as sloth, greed, daintiness, vanity, strength, and hope by making them characters and placing them onstage in action. The dramatist specified symbols, clothing, and gestures appropriate to these abstract figures, thus helping the audience recognize the ideas the characters represented. The use of allegory was an extremely durable technique that was already established in medieval painting, printed books, and books of emblems, in which, for example, sloth would be shown as a man reclining lazily on a bed or greed would be represented as overwhelmingly fat and vanity as a figure completely absorbed in a mirror.

The central problem in the morality play was the salvation of human beings, represented by an individual's struggle to avoid sin and damnation and achieve salvation in the otherworld. As in *Everyman* (c. 1495), a late-medieval play that is the best known of the morality plays, the subjects were usually abstract battles between certain vices and specific virtues for the possession of the human soul, a theme repeated in the Elizabethan age in Marlowe's *Doctor Faustus*.

In many ways the morality play was a dramatized sermon designed to teach a moral lesson. Marked by high seriousness, it was nevertheless entertaining. Using allegory to represent abstract qualities allowed the didactic playwrights to draw clear-cut lines of moral force: Satan was always bad; angels were always good. The allegories were clear, direct, and apparent to all who witnessed the plays.

We do not have much knowledge of the origins of morality plays. Many of them are lost, but some that remain are occasionally performed: *The Pride of Life,* the earliest extant morality play; *The Castle of Perseverance*; *Wisdom*; *Mankind*; and *Everyman* are the best known. They all enjoyed a remarkable popularity in the latter part of the medieval period, all the way up to the early Renaissance.

Although Chinese and Japanese drama neither influenced nor were influenced by Western drama in the medieval period, from roughly the late twelfth to the beginning of the seventeenth centuries, they, like Western drama, were connected to temples, shrines, and religious ceremony. During this period Japanese Nō drama developed as a highly refined, deliberate, and ritualized form involving ceremonial dance and music as well as a developed narrative. Centuries later, Nō drama had an influence on Western literature, particularly on writers such as Ezra Pound and playwrights such as W. B. Yeats and Samuel Beckett.

Nō drama developed from a popular form of drama called sarugaku Nō, invented by Kan'ami (1333–1384) in the fourteenth century. The rulers of Japan at that time, shoguns (generals) of the samurai warrior class, enjoyed theater and supported performances of highly sophisticated drama. They preferred sarugaku— "monkey music"— a form that included gymnastic action, music, dance, and a story line. Kan'ami refined sarugaku into sarugaku Nō, a more deliberate and controlled form that elevated the actor and demanded more skill—the word *Nō* means "skill"—from performers. The refinement Kan'ami brought to the drama was associated with Zen Buddhism, the form of religion favored by the shogun of the period.

Nō drama, which relies on masks, ritual costume, dance, and music, is produced around the world even today. It emerged late in the fourteenth century out of Kan'ami's innovations, but it was his son, Zeami Motokiyo (1363–1443), who developed Nō into a serious form marked by the restraint and control associated with Zen Buddhism. The religious influences on Nō drama emphasized self-control, honorable behavior, and purity of action. Zeami produced a body of drama that can be seen today in the West as well as in the East. *Lady Han (Hanjo)* deals with a realistic situation in which a prostitute falls in love with a traveling captain. Before he leaves they exchange fans on which a painting of the moon will identify them. Such romances were not uncommon, and the emotions portrayed in Nō drama are derived from living experience.

The Medieval Stage

Relatively little commentary survives about the conventions of medieval staging, and some of it is contradictory. We know that in the earliest years— after the tropes developed into full-blown religious scenes acted inside the

FIGURE 7.   Pageant wagon

cathedrals—certain sections of the church were devoted to specific short plays. These areas of the church became known as MANSIONS; each mansion represented a building or physical place known to the audience. The audience moved from one mansion to another, seeing play after play, absorbing the dramatic representation of the events, characters, and locale associated with each mansion.

The tradition of moving from mansion to mansion inside the church carried over into the performances that took place later outside the church. Instead of mansions, wagons with raised stages provided the playing areas (Figure 7). Usually, the wagons remained stationary and the audience moved from one to another. During the guild cycles the pageants would move; the performers would give their plays at several locales so that many people could see them (Figure 8).

According to medieval descriptions, drawings, and reconstructions, a PAGEANT CART could also be simply a flat surface drawn on wheels that had a wagon next to it; these structures touched on their long side. In some cases a figure could descend from an upper area as if from the clouds, or actors could descend from the pageants onto the audience's level to enact a descent into an underworld. The stage was, then, a raised platform visible to the audience below.

A curtain concealed a space, usually inside or below the wagon, for changing costumes. The actors used costumes and props, sometimes very elaborate and expensive, in an effort to make the drama more impressive. Indeed, between the thirteenth and the sixteenth centuries, a number of theatrical effects were developed to please a large audience. For instance, in the morality and mystery plays the devils were often portrayed as frightening, grotesque, and sometimes even comic figures. They became crowd pleasers. A sensational element was developed in some of the plays in the craft cycles, especially those about the lives of the saints and martyrs, in which there were plenty of chances to portray horrifying tortures.

FIGURE 8.   A detail of Denis Van Alsloot's painting *Procession of the Ommeganck at Brussels in 1615* shows horse-drawn pageant wagons on the move, with several plays being performed simultaneously.

The prop that seems to have pleased the most audiences was a complex machine known as the MOUTH OF HELL or "Hell mouth," usually a large fish-shaped orifice from which smoke and explosions, fueled by gunpowder, belched constantly. The devils took great delight in stuffing their victims into these maws. According to a contemporary account, one of the machines required seventeen men to operate.

The level of realism achieved by medieval plays was at times startling. In addition to visual realism, medieval plays involved a psychological level of participation on the part of both audience and actor. Sometimes they demanded that the actors suffer in accord with the characters they played. Some records attest to characters playing Christ on the cross having to be revived after their hearts stopped, and at least one Judas apparently was hanged just a little too long and had to be resuscitated.

The Medieval Actor

In the early days of liturgical drama, the actors in the tropes were monks and choirboys, and in the mystery plays they were drawn from the guilds. At first all the actors were male, but records show that eventually women took important roles.

The demands of more sophisticated plays encouraged the development of a kind of professionalism, although it seems unlikely that players in the cycles could have supported themselves exclusively on their earnings. Special skills became essential for the design and operation of complex stage machines and for the performance of acrobatics that were expected of certain characters, such as devils. As actors developed facility in delivering lines and as writers found ways to incorporate more challenging elements in their plays, a professionalism no doubt arose, even if actors and writers had few opportunities to earn a living on the stage.

As medieval drama developed in England, France, and Germany, a few plays demanded a large number of actors—sometimes hundreds. The guilds that produced the plays could not always field enough actors from their own numbers and occasionally put out calls for auditions, usually conducted by a committee formed from the best available actors. Apparently it did not take long for guilds and other producing societies to recognize that some actors were skilled enough to demand recognition and consideration. By the sixteenth century, individual actors were noted for their skills as type characters and sometimes performed the same roles over a period of years. The costuming of actors, as illustrated in contemporary accounts, became extensive and demanding and clearly defined. The devils were attired in red with bizarre masks and performed characteristic wild movements. Military figures wore armor, and noble figures wore rich garments. Essentially, contemporary medieval dress was used in a manner that clarified the character type quickly for the convenience of the audience.

Most of the original early medieval plays were short, but in later years, up through the early sixteenth century, plays grew in length. Some took as long as twenty-four hours to produce and involved a great many actors. The early mystery plays were often produced several times during the pageant. When the stage was moved to a new location and a new audience, the actors paraded behind the pageant cart to its new location. Because the plays were in the open, the most crucial element of the actor's skill-set was the voice. It was even more important for the medieval actor than for the Greek actor that the voice be commanding and powerful enough to project into the crowd.

By the second half of the sixteenth century, the early Renaissance, groups of wandering actors were producing highly demanding and sophisticated plays, and writers such as Shakespeare were able to join them and make a living. When these professionals secured their own theaters, they had no problems filling them with good drama, with actors, and with an audience.

Dramatic techniques developed in the medieval period were put to good use in the Renaissance theater. For example, the colorful and dramatic devil characters that stalked the mystery plays were transformed into sophisticated villains in Elizabethan drama. The devil Mephistopheles (Mephistophilis) behaves like a smooth Tudor lawyer in Marlowe's *Doctor Faustus;* Iago in *Othello* is suspected of having cloven hooves. Perhaps one important difference is that the Elizabethan devil-villains are truly frightening, since they are so recognizably human in their villainy.

Medieval Drama Timeline

DATE	THEATER	POLITICAL	SOCIAL/CULTURAL
400–500		**476:** The fall of Rome and beginning of the Dark Ages **483–565:** Byzantine Emperor Justinian, author of the Code of Civil Laws	**480–524:** Boëthius, Roman scholar, philosopher, and theologian, is executed for treason.
500–600	**500–1000:** Traveling performers proliferate in Europe.		**570–632:** Muhammed, founder of Islam **590–594:** Devastating plague spreads through Europe and kills half the population.
600–700		Persians take Damascus and Jerusalem.	**636:** Anglo-Saxons are introduced to Christianity. **695:** Jews are persecuted in Spain.
700–800		**768–814:** Charlemagne reigns in France and is crowned Holy Roman Emperor in 800 by Pope Leo III in Rome on Christmas Day. **792:** Beginning of the Viking era in Britain	**c. 710:** Buddhist monasteries in Japan become centers of civilization. **787:** The Council of Nicaea officially rejects iconoclasm.
800–900	**9th century:** Beginnings of liturgical drama	**843:** Treaty of Verdun divides the Holy Roman Empire into German, French, and Italian kingdoms. **850:** Rurik, a Northman, becomes ruler of Kiev, an important Russian trading post. Trade begins with Constantinople, which remains a commercial and cultural center throughout the Dark Ages.	**c. 800–1000:** *Beowulf*, one of the first long poems written in English **855:** Earliest known attempts at polyphonic music **863:** Cyril and Methodius invent a Slavic alphabet called Cyrillic.
900–1000	**c. 900:** Farces make their first appearance since classical times. **925:** Earliest extant Easter trope **965–975:** Compilation of the *Regularis Concordia* (Monastic Agreement) by Ethelwood, bishop of Winchester, England. The *Regularis Concordia* contains the text of the earliest extant playlet in Europe, with directions for its performance.		**c. 900:** The beginnings of the famous Arabian tales called *A Thousand and One Nights*

Medieval Drama Timeline (continued)

DATE	THEATER	POLITICAL	SOCIAL/CULTURAL
900–1000 (continued)	**970:** Plays of Hrosvitha, a German nun and the first known female playwright. The six plays are modeled on the comedies of Terence but deal with serious religious matters.	**1000:** Leif Ericson, possibly the first European to venture to North America	**975:** Arabic arithmetical notation is brought to Europe by the Arabs. **980–1037:** Avicenna (Ibn Sina), Arab physician and philosopher **990:** Development of systemic musical notation.
1000–1100		**1066:** The Normans conquer Britain. **1086:** Compilation of the *Domesday Book,* a survey of the British economy, population, and land ownership at that time **1096–1099:** First Crusade. Crusaders take Jerusalem from the Arabs.	**1054:** The Great Schism separates Eastern and Western Churches in Europe. **1079–1142:** Peter Abelard, French theologian and philosopher
1100–1200	**12th century:** Religious plays are first performed outside churches.	**1109–1113:** Anglo-French War **1147–1149:** Second Crusade. Crusaders lose Jerusalem to the Arabs. **1167–1227:** Genghis Khan, founder of Mongol empire **1189–1193:** Third Crusade. Crusaders fail to recapture Jerusalem.	**c. 1125:** Beginnings of French troubadour and trouvère music **1133–1855:** St. Bartholomew's Fair, London, England **1167:** Oxford University is founded.
1200–1300	**13th century:** Beginnings of zaju drama in China **1250:** *Easter Play of Muri,* beginnings of German drama **1276–1277:** French poet Adam de la Halle writes *The Play of the Greenwood,* the oldest extant medieval secular drama.	**1202–1204:** Fourth Crusade. Crusaders seize Constantinople. **1212:** Children's Crusade. Thousands of children are sent as crusaders to Jerusalem; most die or are sold as slaves. **1215:** King John of England signs the Magna Carta, guaranteeing habeas corpus, trial by jury, and restrictions on the power of the king. **1224–1227:** Anglo-French War **1228:** Sixth Crusade **1248:** Seventh Crusade	**c. 1202:** Court jesters appear at European courts. **1225:** Guillaume de Lorris writes *Roman de la Rose,* a story of courtly wooing. **1225–1274:** Thomas Aquinas, important Scholastic philosopher **1254–1324:** Marco Polo, Venetian traveler whose accounts of life in China became famous in the West **1264:** First celebration of the feast of Corpus Christi **c. 1282:** Florence emerges as the leading European city of commerce and finance.

Medieval Drama Timeline (continued)

DATE	THEATER	POLITICAL	SOCIAL/CULTURAL
1300–1400	**14th century:** Beginnings of Nō drama in Japan **c. 1385–1450:** *The Second Shepherds' Pageant*, part of the English Wakefield Cycle **1398–1548:** Confrèrie de la Passion at Paris performs religious plays.	**1337:** Hundred Years War begins.	**c. 1302:** Dante's *Divine Comedy* **1304–1374:** Petrarch, Italian poet **1347–1351:** The Black Death kills approximately 75 million people throughout Europe. **1360–1400:** *Piers Plowman* and *Sir Gawain and the Green Knight*: achievements of Middle English literature **1387:** Chaucer's *Canterbury Tales*
1400–1500	**c. 1425:** *The Castle of Perseverance*, English morality play **1429:** Plautus's plays are rediscovered in Italy. **c. 1470:** *Pierre Patheline*, most renowned of medieval French farces **1490:** *Corpus Christi* play of Eger, Bohemia **c. 1495:** *Everyman*, best-known English morality play	**1429:** Joan of Arc's troops resist the British siege of Orléans, an important turning point in the Hundred Years War. **1431:** Joan of Arc is captured and burned as a heretic. **1453:** France wins the Hundred Years War and becomes an important continental power. England abandons the Continent to develop its naval forces. **1481:** Spanish Inquisition **1482–1485:** Reign of Richard III. Richard maintains a company of actors at court, which tours surrounding towns when not needed by His Majesty. **1485–1509:** Reign of Henry VII, first of the Tudor rulers. Like Richard III, Henry maintains a company of actors.	**1400–1455:** Fra Angelico, Italian painter **c. 1406–1469:** Fra Lippo Lippi, Italian painter best known for his frescoes **c. 1430:** Modern English develops from Middle English. **c. 1450:** Gutenberg invents movable type. **1485:** Sir Thomas Malory publishes *Le Morte Darthur*, one of the first books printed in England. **1492:** Columbus sets sail across the Atlantic.
1500–1600	**1527:** Henry VIII builds a House of Revels in which to stage court entertainments. **1548:** Production of plays is forbidden in Paris. **1558:** Elizabeth I forbids performance of all religious plays.	**1509–1547:** Reign of Henry VIII **1534:** Henry VIII breaks with the Roman Catholic Church. Drama is used as a political instrument to attack or defend opposing viewpoints. **1558–1603:** Reign of Elizabeth I	**1509:** Pope Clement V resides at Avignon, beginning the Babylonian Captivity, during which Rome is not the papal seat. **1545–1563:** The Council of Trent is convened by the Catholic Church to solidify its control over expressions of Church doctrine. Medieval religious plays are deemed provocative and controversial.

Hrosvitha

The German nun Hrosvitha (c. 935–1000) (also Hroswitha, Roswitha, Hrotsvit, and Hrotsuit) belonged to the Benedictine convent in Gandersheim, founded in 852. Her name translates to "strong voice," a term she uses to describe herself in her writing. Her voice is that of a learned woman, and today it can be heard as a feminist voice in a time and society that were unquestioningly patriarchal.

Hrosvitha is considered not only the earliest German woman poet but the first woman dramatist in Europe. A Saxon noblewoman, she entered the convent in approximately 959, living with nuns who were themselves of noble birth. The abbey was under the protection of Otto I (912–973), who united a powerful Germany and produced a long-lasting period of peace and development. Otto became the Holy Roman Emperor on February 13, 962. His rule, dubbed the Ottonian Renaissance, favored religion, learning, the arts, and music.

During this period, the abbey at Gandersheim was obligated not to the Church but to the king himself, and Otto eventually released it from his direct governance, permitting it to maintain a law court and to coin money. While such political issues may not have affected Hrosvitha, the fact that the period was one of learning and scholarship was of great importance. Hrosvitha was educated in the liberal arts, beginning with the quadrivium (geometry, arithmetic, music, and astronomy) and continuing with the trivium (grammar, rhetoric, and logic). Her studies were conducted in Latin, the language she used to write her plays. Her education was comparable to that of liberally educated men and of the nuns who lived with her.

Hrosvitha's work is deeply rooted in her religious beliefs. Her religious order meditated on the drama of the lives of Christian saints and especially on their often spectacular martyrdoms. The abbey gave its inhabitants a life of contemplation, removed from the world. But it is also clear that the nuns had the talent, education, and opportunities to write religious tracts and, in the case of Hrosvitha, religious drama. The question of whether Hrosvitha's plays were actually produced is not settled.

Hrosvitha wrote six plays and several other prose and poetic works. The plays reject the temptations of the world in the name of Christ. In *Gallicanus* the title character is promised the hand of Constantia if he wins a specific battle, but Constantia, daughter of the Christian emperor Constantine, has taken a vow of chastity. Eventually, with the aid of saints, Gallicanus converts to Christianity and becomes a martyr. The conversion of an important Roman is the theme of *Callimachus,* and the conversion theme dominates *Paphnutius* and *Abraham. Sapientia* also emphasizes martyrdom. Sapientia's three daughters, whose names translate as Faith, Hope, and Charity, offer a threat to the stability of Emperor Hadrian's rule. They are tortured brutally but survive without pain until Hadrian beheads them. Eventually Sapientia joins her daughters in heavenly bliss, inspiring the local women who have witnessed the events.

DULCITIUS

Dulcitius is probably the second of Hrosvitha's plays. It was rediscovered in 1494 in an eleventh-century manuscript along with her other dramatic works. Its first printing was in 1501 in an edition with woodcuts by Albrecht Dürer, indicating its importance at the time. The play is plainly didactic and was designed to teach a lesson rather than merely to entertain. The lesson, as in all her plays, is a moral one, urging listeners or readers to live a life of purity and virtue in order to celebrate the greatness of God. In this sense, Hrosvitha wrote in the medieval literary tradition of Europe. Her plays are fascinating to the modern reader, however, because she purposely emulated the techniques of the Roman playwright Terence.

She chose Terence as her model because his texts were used in education and were therefore widely known in Europe. Moreover, they were amusing comedies written with such great style that they were models of elocution. Hrosvitha admits to imitating Terence, but her motives were subversive. She wished to use the eloquent style of Terence not to entertain her audience with secular amusement and charming courtesans but to honor the virtue of chaste virgins who praised God and Christian virtues.

Dulcitius, a jail governor, lusts after the three virgins Agape, Chionia, and Hirena (Love, Purity, and Peace). Hrosvitha emphasizes his power, but all his worldly power comes to nothing in the face of the virgins' beliefs. In this sense, Hrosvitha celebrates how the apparent weakness of females in her own society can confound the apparent strength of males. Despite his position and power, Dulcitius's lust cannot be satisfied.

Moreover, the three virgins are problematic not only to Dulcitius but to Emperor Diocletian as well. When Agape tells Diocletian that it is dangerous to offend almighty God, Diocletian asks, "Dangerous to whom?" She responds, "To you and to the state you rule." Hrosvitha therefore establishes not only the power of the virgins but also that of the Christian religion. Astonishingly, this "new-fangled religion" threatens Rome itself, which is why Diocletian persecuted Christians so brutally during his reign.

The play's short lines, quick realistic dialogue, and carefully focused interaction are recognizably like Terence's. The present translation uses virgules (/) to indicate the end of lines as they were printed in the original Latin. The broad farcical humor of the "miraculous" scene in which Dulcitius embraces pots and pans in the kitchen, thinking they are the three virgins—a scene performed while the virgins watch through the crack in the door—is also in the tradition of Roman comedy.

Despite the three virgins' ultimate martyrdom, the play is a comedy. The soldiers and Dulcitius will end up in "Tartarus," while the virgins "will enter the heavenly bridal chamber of the Eternal King." For the devout canonness Hrosvitha, no ending could be happier.

Dulcitius in Performance

In the opinion of most scholars, the plays of Hrosvitha were not produced but instead were read as CLOSET DRAMA. On the other hand, comic scenes such as the one in which Dulcitius blackens his face against the pots and pans have led some theater historians to speculate that the plays were performed by the nuns themselves in the abbey. In any event, *Dulcitius* would not have had a public audience and may not have influenced other medieval drama. It is, however, a remarkable moment in the history of drama. As Hrosvitha tells us, "I, the strong voice of Gandersheim, have not hesitated to imitate in my writings a poet whose works are so widely read, my object being to glorify, within the limits of my poor talent, the laudable chastity of Christian virgins in that self-same form of composition which has been used to describe the shameless acts of licentious women."

Hrosvitha (c. 935–1000)

DULCITIUS   *c. 965*

THE MARTYRDOM OF THE HOLY VIRGINS AGAPE, CHIONIA, AND HIRENA

TRANSLATED BY K. M. WILSON

[Characters

DIOCLETIAN
AGAPE   WIFE (OF DULCITIUS)
CHIONIA   SISSINUS
HIRENA   SOLDIERS
DULCITIUS   GUARDS]

The martyrdom of the holy virgins° Agape, Chionia, and Hirena, whom, in the silence of the night, Governor Dulcitius secretly visited, desiring to delight in their embrace. But as soon as he entered, / he became demented / and kissed and hugged the pots and pans, mistaking them for the girls until his face and his clothes were soiled with disgusting black dirt. Afterward Count Sissinus, acting on orders, / was given the girls so he might put them to tortures. / He, too, was deluded miraculously / but finally ordered that Agape and Chionia be burnt and Hirena be slain by an arrow.

DIOCLETIAN: The renown of your free and noble descent / and the brightness of your beauty demand / that you be married to one of the foremost men of my court. This will be done according to our command if you deny Christ° and comply by bringing offerings to our gods.° ⁵

AGAPE: Be free of care, / don't trouble yourself to prepare our wedding / because we cannot be compelled under any duress / to betray Christ's holy name, which we must confess, / nor to stain our virginity. ¹⁰

DIOCLETIAN: What madness possesses you? What rage drives you three? /

AGAPE: What signs of our madness do you see? /

DIOCLETIAN: An obvious and great display. /

AGAPE: In what way? / ¹⁵

DIOCLETIAN: Chiefly in that renouncing the practices of ancient religion / you follow the useless, new-fangled ways of the Christian superstition. /

AGAPE: Heedlessly you offend the majesty of the omnipotent God. That is dangerous . . .

DIOCLETIAN: Dangerous to whom? ²⁰

AGAPE: To you and to the state you rule. /

DIOCLETIAN: She is mad; remove the fool! /

The martyrdom of the holy virgins: The martyrdom of the three virgins occurred in 290 during Diocletian's persecution of the Christians in Thessalonica.

5. deny Christ: Deny the vow of virginity they made in the name of Christ.   **6. our gods:** Gods acknowledged by the Roman empire.

CHIONIA: My sister is not mad; she rightly reprehended
25   your folly.

DIOCLETIAN: She rages even more madly; remove her
from our sight and arraign the third girl. /

HIRENA: You will find the third, too, a rebel / and resisting you forever. /

30 DIOCLETIAN: Hirena, although you are younger in birth, / be greater in worth! /

HIRENA: Show me, I pray, how?

DIOCLETIAN: Bow your neck to the gods, set an example for your sisters, and be the cause for their freedom!

35 HIRENA: Let those worship idols, Sire, / who wish to incur God's ire. / But I won't defile my head, anointed with royal unguent by debasing myself at the idols' feet.

DIOCLETIAN: The worship of gods brings no dishonor /
40   but great honor. /

HIRENA: And what dishonor is more disgraceful, / what disgrace is any more shameful / than when a slave is venerated as a master?

DIOCLETIAN: I don't ask you to worship slaves / but the
45   mighty gods of princes and greats. /

HIRENA: Is he not anyone's slave / who, for a price, is up for sale? /

DIOCLETIAN: For her speech so brazen, / to the tortures she must be taken. /

50 HIRENA: This is just what we hope for, this is what we desire, / that for the love of Christ through tortures we may expire. /

DIOCLETIAN: Let these insolent girls / who defy our decrees and words / be put in chains and kept in the
55   squalor of prison until Governor Dulcitius can examine them.

DULCITIUS: Bring forth, soldiers, the girls whom you hold sequestered. /

SOLDIERS: Here they are whom you requested. /

60 DULCITIUS: Wonderful, indeed, how beautiful, how graceful, how admirable these little girls are!

SOLDIERS: Yes, they are perfectly lovely.

DULCITIUS: I am captivated by their beauty.

SOLDIERS: That is understandable.

65 DULCITIUS: To draw them to my heart, I am eager. /

SOLDIERS: Your success will be meager. /

DULCITIUS: Why?

SOLDIERS: Because they are firm in faith.

DULCITIUS: What if I sway them by flattery? /

70 SOLDIERS: They will despise it utterly. /

DULCITIUS: What if with tortures I frighten them? /

SOLDIERS: Little will it matter to them. /

DULCITIUS: Then what should be done, I wonder? /

SOLDIERS: Carefully you should ponder. /

75 DULCITIUS: Place them under guard in the inner room of the pantry, where they keep the servants' pots. /

SOLDIERS: Why in that particular spot? /

DULCITIUS: So that I may visit them often at my leisure. /

SOLDIERS: At your pleasure. /

80 DULCITIUS: What do the captives do at this time of night? /

SOLDIERS: Hymns they recite. /

DULCITIUS: Let us go near. /

SOLDIERS: From afar we hear their tinkling little voices
clear. /   85

DULCITIUS: Stand guard before the door with your lantern / but I will enter / and satisfy myself in their longed-for embrace. /

SOLDIERS: Enter. We will guard this place. /

AGAPE: What is that noise outside the door? /   90

HIRENA: That wretched Dulcitius coming to the fore. /

CHIONIA: May God protect us!

AGAPE: Amen.

CHIONIA: What is the meaning of this clash of the pots and the pans?   95

HIRENA: I will check. / Come here, please, and look through the crack! /

AGAPE: What is going on?

HIRENA: Look, the fool, the madman base, / he thinks he is enjoying our embrace. /   100

AGAPE: What is he doing?

HIRENA: Into his lap he pulls the utensils, / he embraces the pots and the pans, giving them tender kisses. /

CHIONIA: Ridiculous!

HIRENA: His face, his hands, his clothes, are so soiled, so   105
filthy, that with all the soot that clings to him, he looks like an Ethiopian.

AGAPE: It is only right that he should appear in body the way he is in his mind: possessed by the Devil.

HIRENA: Wait! He prepares to leave. Let us watch how   110
he is greeted, / and how he is treated / by the soldiers who wait for him.

SOLDIERS: Who is coming out? / A demon without doubt. / Or rather, the Devil himself is he; / let us flee! /

DULCITIUS: Soldiers, where are you taking yourselves   115
in flight? / Stay! Wait! Escort me home with your light! /

SOLDIERS: The voice is our master's tone / but the look the Devil's own. / Let us not stay! / Let us run away; the apparition will slay us! /   120

DULCITIUS: I will go to the palace and complain, / and reveal to the whole court the insults I had to sustain. /

DULCITIUS: Guards, let me into the palace; / I must have a private audience. /

GUARDS: Who is this vile and detestable monster cov-   125
ered in torn and despicable rags? Let us beat him, / from the steps let us sweep him; / he must not be allowed to enter.

DULCITIUS: Alas, alas, what has happened? Am I not dressed in splendid garments? Don't I look neat and   130
clean? / Yet anyone who looks at my mien / loathes me as a foul monster. To my wife I shall return, / and from her learn / what has happened. But there is my spouse, / with disheveled hair she leaves the house, / and the whole household follows her in tears.   135

WIFE: Alas, alas, my Lord Dulcitius, what has happened to you? / You are not sane; the Christians have made a laughing stock out of you. /

DULCITIUS: Now I know at last. I owe this mockery to
140   their witchcraft.
WIFE: What upsets me so, what makes me more sad
    is that you were ignorant of all that happened to you.
DULCITIUS: I command that those insolent girls be led
    forth, / and that they be publicly stripped of all their
145   clothes, / so that they experience similar mockery in
    retaliation for ours.
SOLDIERS: We labor in vain; / we sweat without gain. /
    Behold, their garments stick to their virginal bodies
    like skin, / and he who urged us to strip them snores
150   in his seat, / and he cannot be awakened from his
    sleep. / Let us go to the Emperor and report what has
    happened.

DIOCLETIAN: It grieves me very much / to hear that Gover-
    nor Dulcitius has been so greatly deluded, / so greatly
155   insulted, / so utterly humiliated. / But these vile young
    women shall not boast with impunity of having made a
    mockery of our gods and those who worship them. I
    shall direct Count Sissinus to take due vengeance.

SISSINUS: Soldiers, where are those insolent girls who
160   are to be tortured?
SOLDIERS: They are kept in prison.
SISSINUS: Leave Hirena there, / bring the others here. /
SOLDIERS: Why do you except the one?
SISSINUS: Sparing her youth. Perchance, she may be con-
165   verted easier, if she is not intimidated by her sisters'
    presence. /
SOLDIERS: That makes sense. /

SOLDIERS: Here are the girls whose presence you
    requested.
170   SISSINUS: Agape and Chionia, give heed, / and to my
    council accede! /
AGAPE: We will not give heed. /
SISSINUS: Bring offerings to the gods.
AGAPE: We bring offerings of praise forever / to the true
175   Father eternal, / and to His Son co-eternal, / and also
    to the Holy Spirit.
SISSINUS: This is not what I bid, / but on pain of penalty
    prohibit. /
AGAPE: You cannot prohibit it; neither shall we ever sac-
180   rifice to demons.
SISSINUS: Cease this hardness of heart, and make your
    offerings. But if you persist, / then I shall insist / that
    you be killed according to the Emperor's orders.
CHIONIA: It is only proper that you should obey the
185   orders of your Emperor, whose decrees we disdain, as
    you know. For if you wait and try to spare us, then
    you could be rightfully killed.
SISSINUS: Soldiers, do not delay, / take these blasphem-
    ing girls away, / and throw them alive into the flames.
190   SOLDIERS: We shall instantly build the pyre you asked
    for, and we will cast these girls into the raging fire,
    and thus we'll put an end to these insults at last. /
AGAPE: O Lord, nothing is impossible for Thee; / even
    the fire forgets its nature and obeys Thee; / but we

are weary of delay; / therefore, dissolve the earthly   195
    bonds that hold our souls, we pray, / so that as our
    earthly bodies die, / our souls may sing your praise in
    Heaven.
SOLDIERS: Oh, marvel, oh stupendous miracle! Behold
    their souls are no longer bound to their bodies, / yet   200
    no traces of injury can be found; neither their hair,
    nor their clothes are burnt by the fire, / and their bod-
    ies are not at all harmed by the pyre. /
SISSINUS: Bring forth Hirena.

SOLDIERS: Here she is.   205
SISSINUS: Hirena, tremble at the deaths of your sisters
    and fear to perish according to their example.
HIRENA: I hope to follow their example and expire, / so
    with them in Heaven eternal joy I may acquire. /
SISSINUS: Give in, give in to my persuasion. /   210
HIRENA: I will never yield to evil persuasion. /
SISSINUS: If you don't yield, I shall not give you a quick
    and easy death, but multiply your sufferings.
HIRENA: The more cruelly I'll be tortured, / the more
    gloriously I'll be exalted. /   215
SISSINUS: You fear no tortures, no pain? / What you
    abhor, I shall ordain. /
HIRENA: Whatever punishment you design, / I will
    escape with help Divine. /
SISSINUS: To a brothel you will be consigned, / where   220
    your body will be shamefully defiled. /
HIRENA: It is better that the body be dirtied with any
    stain than that the soul be polluted with idolatry.
SISSINUS: If you are so polluted in the company of har-
    lots, you can no longer be counted among the vir-   225
    ginal choir.
HIRENA: Lust deserves punishment, but forced compli-
    ance the crown. With neither is one considered guilty, /
    unless the soul consents freely. /
SISSINUS: In vain have I spared her, in vain have I pitied   230
    her youth.
SOLDIERS: We knew this before; / for on no possible
    score / can she be moved to adore our gods, nor can
    she be broken by terror.
SISSINUS: I shall spare her no longer. /   235
SOLDIERS: Rightly you ponder. /
SISSINUS: Seize her without mercy, / drag her with cru-
    elty, / and take her in dishonor to the brothel. /
HIRENA: They will not do it. /
SISSINUS: Who can prohibit it? /   240
HIRENA: He whose foresight rules the world. /
SISSINUS: I shall see . . . /
HIRENA: Sooner than you wish, it will be. /
SISSINUS: Soldiers, be not afraid / of what this blasphem-
    ing girl has said. /   245
SOLDIERS: We are not afraid, / but eagerly follow what
    you bade. /

SISSINUS: Who are those approaching? How similar
    they are to the men / to whom we gave Hirena just
    then. / They are the same. Why are you returning so   250
    fast? / Why so out of breath, I ask? /

SOLDIERS: You are the one for whom we look. /

SISSINUS: Where is she whom you just took? /

SOLDIERS: On the peak of the mountain.

255 SISSINUS: Which one?

SOLDIERS: The one close by.

SISSINUS: Oh you idiots, dull and blind. / You have completely lost your mind! /

SOLDIERS: Why do you accuse us, / why do you abuse us, / why do you threaten us with menacing voice and face?

260 SISSINUS: May the gods destroy you!

SOLDIERS: What have we committed? What harm have we done? How have we transgressed against your orders?

265 SISSINUS: Have I not given the orders that you should take that rebel against the gods to a brothel?

SOLDIERS: Yes, so you did command, / and we were eager to fulfill your demand, / but two strangers intercepted us / saying that you sent them to us / to lead Hirena to the mountain's peak.

270 SISSINUS: That's new to me. /

SOLDIERS: We can see. /

SISSINUS: What were they like? /

SOLDIERS: Splendidly dressed and an awe-inspiring sight. /

275 SISSINUS: Did you follow? /

SOLDIERS: We did so. /

SISSINUS: What did they do? /

SOLDIERS: They placed themselves on Hirena's left and right, / and told us to be forthright / and not to hide

280 from you what happened.

SISSINUS: I see a sole recourse, / that I should mount my horse / and seek out those who so freely made sport with us.

SISSINUS: Hmm, I don't know what to do. I am bewildered by the witchcraft of these Christians. I keep going around the mountain and keep finding this 285 track / but I neither know how to proceed nor how to find my way back. /

SOLDIERS: We are all deluded by some intrigue; / we are afflicted with a great fatigue; / if you allow this insane person to stay alive, / then neither you nor we shall 290 survive. /

SISSINUS: Anyone among you, / I don't care which, string a bow, and shoot an arrow, and kill that witch! /

SOLDIERS: Rightly so. /

HIRENA: Wretched Sissinus, blush for shame, and pro- 295 claim your miserable defeat because without the help of weapons, you cannot overcome a tender little virgin as your foe. /

SISSINUS: Whatever the shame that may be mine, I will bear it more easily now because I know for certain 300 that you will die.

HIRENA: This is the greatest joy I can conceive, / but for you this is a cause to grieve, / because you shall be damned in Tartarus° for your cruelty, / while I shall receive the martyr's palm and the crown of virginity; / 305 thus I will enter the heavenly bridal chamber of the Eternal King, to whom are all honor and glory in all eternity. /

304. Tartarus: Hell.

COMMENTARY

Sue-Ellen Case (b. 1942)

RE-VIEWING HROTSVIT   *1983*

Sue-Ellen Case not only examines the plays of Hrosvitha but has actually produced them. She discusses the feminist issues in the plays and demonstrates the significance of the plays of Hrosvitha for a modern audience.

Performance   Hrotsvit's plays were not collected for circulation until the sixteenth century. They were not translated into modern Romance languages until the mid-nineteenth century and not into English until the twentieth century. The relative unavailability of her texts made production before the twentieth century improbable. Yet in the twentieth century, it is important to note that productions of her plays were often by women or in times in which women's issues were important to the theater world. A good example of the latter condition is the production history of Hrotsvit's work in London. The first major production of *Paphnutius* was directed by Edith Craig (daughter of Ellen Terry and sister of Gordon) in London in 1914. The production was by the Pioneer Players, a group founded and directed by Edith Craig, with Ellen Terry playing the role of the abbess in the convent in which Thais was confined. The translation was done by Christopher St. John, a *nom de plume* (indicative practice) for Christabel Marshall. Marshall had recently adapted the suffragette play *How the Vote Was Won* in 1909 and the play *The First Actress* in 1911—an indication that her interest in the text of Hrotsvit probably came from an interest in a woman playwright. Indeed, there was a movement in London theater at that time to be concerned with women's issues—particularly the vote. In 1908, actresses had formed a franchise league to support the suffrage movement, which produced plays about the vote and satires of male chauvinism.[1] The English women did not get the vote until 1928, and the decade of the 1920s was filled with the issue. Within this context, the 1920 production of *Callimachus* at the Art Theatre, the 1924 production of *Paphnutius* at the Maddermarket Theatre, the founding of the Roswitha club in 1926, the new translations by St. John, Waley and Tillyard during the decade, and the cessation of Hrotsvit productions after that decade can be easily understood.

My production of her works in 1982 came as a result of teaching a class on women and theater and becoming familiar with all of the new productions and critical studies evolving from the works of women playwrights and women's theater groups. The first problem in producing Hrotsvit is the obscurity of her name and play titles. The second is the short playing time of her texts. I decided to solve both problems by directing three plays in one evening and creating a title which might attract the Seattle women's community by identifying the plays according to the social roles of their three heroines: "The Virgin (*Dulcitius*), The Whore (*Paphnutius*), and The Desperate One" (*Callimachus*). My choice of production concept was determined by my goal of producing the first woman playwright. In order to emphasize her historical role, I decided to direct the play as a period piece. This introduces another set of difficulties, since the theater has no tradition of staging plays from the early Middle Ages and hence no concept of costumes, sets, or playing style. We took the costumes from mosaics and illuminations around the period and decided on flats, imitating the two-dimensional painting style of the time, with edifices found in Ottonian manuscript illuminations. The playing style was a combination of a classical sense of formal blocking and gestures, combined with intense, personal purpose. A projection screen rose from the back of a steeply raked stage and a processional ramp ran from the front of the stage through the center of the audience. This combination created the feeling of the space in a cathedral. The elevated ramp gave the Saints elevation and dominance. Between the plays, early medieval music was performed. All this allowed a style to emerge which was . . . an imitation of [both] classical formality and liturgical ceremony.

The context of Christianity and its trappings often created an audience response which was marked in its silent reverence. People seemed afraid to wiggle or whisper. At other times, this same sense turned into an active irreverence, manifested by

[1]Michelene Wandor, *Understudies: Theatre and Sexual Politics* (London: Eyre Methuen, 1981), p. 10.

laughter and something close to jeering. Contemporary staging of a Christian play is complicated to understand. Shakespeare productions have prepared an audience for the Elizabethan world of superstition, and Greek plays have prepared them for the world of pagan mythology, but the relative absence of medieval productions leaves the world of medieval Christianity to be understood by personal opinions about Christianity rather than the sense of it as a historical world view. Thus, for some feminists, the Christianity was seen as offensive and patriarchal. Particularly in these times of the Moral Majority, Hrotsvit's plays seemed to them to be written by an "Uncle Tom" trapped by male values. Many audience members laughed hysterically at the miracles, the voice of God, and the resurrections—seeing them not as stage conventions but as bygone beliefs. Christopher St. John records a similar reaction to the plays in their early London productions, citing a scene in *Callimachus* "Drusiana's prayer that she might die rather than yield to Callimachus was greeted with shouts of laughter" (p. 159). I think the only solution to this problem lies not in the staging concept of such scenes, but in establishing a familiarity with the playwright and her conventions through productions and an acquaintance with her texts in theater history and criticism classes.

For the actors, this problem translates into ways for them to individually understand the dilemma of their characters. The women identified instances of martyrdom and conviction which meant something to them. These ranged from pictures of concentration camp women, which some of the Jewish women brought to rehearsal, to stories of guerrillas in El Salvador or instances of rape victims who resisted. They did not focus so much on religious experiences as on sexual ones, political ones, or psychological approaches to their own fears and strengths. The men in the cast resisted identifying with the male aggression and cruelty portrayed by many of the characters. When asked to torment one of the young virgins in a flirtatious manner, they insisted they didn't know how. This identification came slowly, through memories of teasing girls in grade school, to early experiences of seduction and sexual aggression. For the men playing Saints, the problem was in giving focus to the women onstage and learning how to respond to the power of the women in a realistic fashion. This involved investigating their own fears of women's power.

For the actors, one of the most difficult aspects of Hrotsvit's work was her contiguous sense of form and her compressed, almost fragmentary sense of a scene. Characters have extremely short speeches of only one or two sentences, compressed into scenes of relatively scant dialogue and often no physical action. Fortunately, recent productions of plays by such authors as Beckett and Kroetz provided the actors with some experience in this style. The method which seemed most useful was to play the entire scene by improvising a long, literal development of its situation and then compress it moment by moment until it played in Hrotsvit's form. One fortunate consequence of this playing style is that the concentration and deliberation required by the actor made him or her oblivious to the sometimes raucous audience response.

Finally, the response of the critics illustrated an interesting aspect of viewing the plays. Almost all announcements and reviews of the plays included the words "rape" and "necrophilia" in their titles. One critic pointed out that these plays should make contemporary audiences feel less defensive about violence on TV, since it was already popular in the early Middle Ages. The titles are surprising, since neither the rapes nor the necrophilia ever occur. They are the intentions of the male characters but are foiled by heavenly intervention. The preoccupation by critics with these intentions might suggest that they were watching the male characters more than the females, even though it was not the focus of the text nor of the blocking. In fact, given the staging of resurrections and other such miracles, these dramatic intentions seemed minor parts of the staging. Yet they were the focus of critical reviews. This critical reception points out the necessity for a re-viewing of Hrotsvit from a feminist point of view and underlines the sense that her position and its implications in the world of theater [are] still long overdue.

THE SECOND SHEPHERDS' PAGEANT

The author of *The Second Shepherds' Pageant* (c. 1385–1450) has not been identified, but his style is distinct enough to permit scholars to cite him simply as the Wakefield Master. His work is so clearly superior to the other writers of mystery pageants that some critics have dubbed him a medieval literary genius. Because he used a distinctive poetic meter and rhyming style, we know that he wrote several other plays in the Wakefield Cycle, including *Noah and the Ark, The First Shepherds' Play, Herod the Great,* and *The Buffeting.* None of the thirty-two plays in the Wakefield Cycle—nor any play in other English cycles—combines the wit, cleverness, farce, and seriousness of *The Second Shepherds' Pageant.*

The Wakefield Cycle is the group of plays performed by the guilds of Wakefield during the Corpus Christi holiday, which falls eight weeks after Easter, in either late May or early June. The performances began at sunrise and continued until late in the evening, usually outdoors in good weather. The plays in all the cycles begin with the creation and continue narrating important biblical moments, such as stories of Abraham, Herod, Julius Caesar, the shepherds at the nativity, the scourging of Christ, and even the hanging of Judas. Sometimes called the Towneley Cycle because the Towneley family owned the fifteenth-century manuscripts, the Wakefield Cycle represented a highly developed tradition that was of considerable economic significance to Wakefield. Large numbers of people came from surrounding towns to see the pageants and therefore represented an important tourist traffic for local inns and businesses. The towns of York, Chester, and Coventry enjoyed the same benefits.

One of the important functions of the mystery plays was their presentation of significant and familiar biblical stories. Much of the medieval audience was illiterate or had limited access to books. Consequently, they learned or reviewed some basic Bible stories by watching these plays. The entertainment value of the plays was considered a secondary issue, although it is plain from *The Second Shepherds' Pageant* that, by the late fifteenth century, audiences were familiar enough with the material that adding a bit of farce tended to energize the drama. It is clear that the Wakefield Master, who seems to have been a minor cleric, fully understood his rural and urban audiences' need for amusement as well as their need for instruction.

In the Wakefield Cycle the same author wrote two Shepherd plays. As far as we can tell, the second play, which is presented here, followed the first. They were the twelfth and thirteenth plays in the cycle of thirty-two. Some scholars have suggested that the first play is a first draft or early version and that *The Second Shepherds' Pageant* is an improved or more fully developed play. The evidence does not support such a view, however, because Mak and Gib, the two shepherds who are at the center of the comic action, are missing from the first play. In addition, some references in the second play to characters in the first play would be meaningless to an audience who had not seen the first play. It is likely that the Wakefield Cycle was a processional cycle, in which the pageant carts carrying the guilds moved from location to location, each guild performing the same play in each locale. The audience in each location, if they stayed through the day, would have seen all the plays in succession. On the other hand, some evidence suggests that it may have been a stationary cycle, in which the plays would have been performed in succession, in a single courtyard or open space, to one audience.

If it was a processional cycle, we have no idea which guild would have sponsored *The Second Shepherds' Pageant;* nothing has come down to us to indicate a choice. However, we do know that the town of York began heavily taxing the wool industries in the early fifteenth century, and consequently those industries moved to towns like Wakefield. It may well be that the development of those industries accounts for the plural number of shepherd plays.

The Second Shepherds' Pageant joins together two well-known stories. The more important is the story of the birth of Jesus as witnessed by shepherds in Luke 2.15–20. The second narrative was also familiar from folklore: Mak's story of a shepherd who steals a lamb and tries to pass it off as his baby. The conjunction of these two stories offered the Wakefield Master a great deal of imaginative reinforcement for each narrative line. The metaphor of Jesus as a lamb was extant in Roman times in part because Jesus was offered as a sacrifice for the human race. Representing the lamb as an infant—and connecting that infant to the Christ child—thus helps intensify the concept of Christ's sacrifice. When the shepherds discover Mak's ruse—a process that not only takes some time but also involves a great deal of humor—they toss Mak in a blanket in what is essentially an act of good humor. In other words, they offer Mak the same kind of charity that Christians associate with the Christ child, and in return, they are invited to be in the presence of the Christ child.

The Second Shepherds' Pageant in Performance

In medieval times, the play was performed by amateurs, ostensibly members of the guild that produced the play. It would probably have been staged on a pageant wagon of the kind shown in Figure 7 (p. 210). Assuming that the Wakefield Cycle was extant in the early 1400s, it is remarkable to consider that one of the last known early performances of the play was in Tudor times in 1533. This means that the social issues described in the play, the hardships experienced by ordinary folk, and the complaints about taxation and rising prices were all relevant to a later generation.

Today, *The Second Shepherds' Pageant* is a favorite Christmas production at a number of universities. In addition, mystery plays have grown in popularity. The Broomhill Opera of South Africa staged an abbreviated version of the traditional cycle in 2001 and 2002. Merging African drumming and choral music with the traditional plays is intense and highly successful. The York Cycle was staged in the streets of York, England, in 1975, and a selection of nine of the plays was staged again in 1994. The Chester Cycle is staged in Chester every five years, with the most recent performance in 2008 and the next scheduled for 2013. Toronto produced the York Cycle in 1998; the

Players of St. Peter put on selections from the mystery plays each December in St. Clement, Eastcheap, London.

Mystery plays such as *The Second Shepherds' Pageant* are still emotionally resonant for a large number of people, and today's performances still attract considerable audiences.

Anonymous
THE SECOND SHEPHERDS' PAGEANT

(c. 1385–1450)

EDITED BY A. C. CAWLEY

Characters

COLL, *the First Shepherd*
GIB, *the Second Shepherd*
DAW, *the Third Shepherd*
MAK, *the Sheep-stealer*
GILL, *Mak's Wife*
ANGEL
MARY, *with the Christ-child*

Scene I.   *The open fields*

1 SHEPHERD: Lord, what these weathers are cold! And
    I am ill happed.°
  I am near-hand dold,° so long have I napped;
  My legs they fold,° my fingers are chapped.
  It is not as I would, for I am lapped°
5 In sorrow.
  In storms and tempest,
  Now in the east, now in the west,
  Woe is him has never rest
  Mid-day nor morrow!

10 But we sely husbands° that walk on the moor,
  In faith, we are near-hands out of the door.°
  No wonder, as it stands, if we be poor,
  For the tilth° of our lands lies fallow as the floor,
  As ye ken.
15 We are so hammed,°
  Fortaxed and rammed,°
  We are made hand-tamed
  With these gentlery-men.°

Thus they reave us our rest, our Lady them wary!°
These men that are lord-fast,° they cause the plough
  tarry.   20
That, men say, is for the best; we find it contrary.
Thus are husbands oppressed, in point to miscarry
On live.°
Thus hold they us under,
Thus they bring us in blunder;°   25
It were great wonder
And ever° should we thrive.

For may he get a paint sleeve or a brooch,
  nowadays,°
Woe is him that him grieve, or once again-says!°
Dare no man him repreve, what mastery he mays;°   30
And yet may no man lieve° one word that he says—
No letter.
He can make purveyance°
With boast and bragance,°
And all is through maintenance°   35
Of men that are greater.

There shall come a swain as proud as a po;°
He must borrow my wain, my plough also;
Then I am full fain to grant ere he go.
Thus live we in pain, anger, and woe   40
By night and day.
He must have, if he langed,
If I should forgang it;°

---

1. How cold this weather is! And I am poorly clad.   **2. near-hand dold:** Nearly numb.   **3. fold:** Give way.   **4. lapped:** Wrapped.   **10.** But we poor husbandmen.   **11.** We are nearly homeless.   **13. tilth:** Arable part.   **15. hammed:** Crippled.   **16. Fortaxed and rammed:** Overtaxed and crushed.   **17–18.** We are reduced to submission by these gentry.

19. They rob us of our rest, our Lady curse them!   **20. lord-fast:** Bound to a lord.   **22–3.** In danger of coming to mortal harm.   **25. Blunder:** Trouble.   **27. ever:** If.   **28.** If he is able to get an embroidered sleeve, i.e., a lord's livery.   **29. again-says:** Gainsays.   **30.** No man dare reprove him, no matter what force he uses.   **31. lieve:** Believe.   **33.** He can requisition [our belongings].   **34. bragance:** Bragging.   **35. maintenance:** Support.   **37. po:** Peacock.   **42–3.** He must have what he wants, even if I have to go without it.

Mak becomes Joseph
(Malcolm Storry) and Gill
becomes Mary (Avril Carson),
while the First Shepherd
(Philip McGough) kneels
before the manger in the 1978
Royal Shakespeare Company
production, adapted by John
Barton, titled *The Shepherds'
Play*, and directed by David
Tucker.

Philip McGough as the First
Shepherd, Malcolm Storry as
Mak, and Hilton McRae and
David Bradley as the other
two shepherds in the 1978
Royal Shakespeare Company
production.

I were better be hanged
45   Than once say him nay.

It does me good, as I walk thus by mine own,°
Of this world for to talk in manner of moan.°
To my sheep will I stalk and harken anon,
There abide on a balk,° or sit on a stone
50   Full soon;
For I trow, pardie,°
True men if they be,
We get more company
Ere it be noon.

[*Enter Second Shepherd*]

55   2 SHEP.: Benste° and Dominus, what may this bemean?°
Why fares this world thus? Oft have we not seen.°
Lord, these weathers are spitous, and the winds
     full keen,°
And the frosts so hideous they water mine een°—
No lie.
60   Now in dry, now in wet,
Now in snow, now in sleet,
When my shoon freeze to my feet
It is not all easy.

But as far as I ken, or yet as I go,
65   We sely wedmen dree mickle woe:
We have sorrow then and then; it falls oft so.°
Silly Copple, our hen, both to and fro
She cackles;
But begin she to croak,
70   To groan or to cluck,
Woe is him our cock,°
For he is in the shackles.

These men that are wed have not all their will;
When they are full hard sted, they sigh full still.°
75   God wot they are led full hard and full ill;
In bower nor in bed they say nought theretill.
This tide
My part have I fun,°
I know my lesson:
80   Woe is him that is bun,°
For he must abide.°
But now late in our lives—a marvel to me,

That I think my heart rives° such wonders to see;
What that destiny drives it should so be°—
Some men will have two wives, and some men three   85
In store;
Some are woe° that have any.
But so far can° I:
Woe is him that has many,
For he feels sore.°   90

But, young men, of wooing, for God that you
     bought,°
Be well ware° of wedding, and think in your
     thought:
'Had I wist' is a thing that serveth of nought.°
Mickle still° mourning has wedding home brought,
And griefs,   95
With many a sharp° shower;
For thou mayst catch in an hour
That shall sow thee full sour°
As long as thou lives.

For, as ever read I epistle, I have one to my fere° 100
As sharp as thistle, as rough as a briar.
She is browed like a bristle, with a sour-loten cheer;°
Had she once wet her whistle, she could sing full
     clear
Her paternoster.
She is as great as a whale,   105
She has a gallon of gall;
By him that died for us all,
I would I had run to° I had lost her!
1 SHEP.: God look over the raw! Full deafly ye stand.°
2 SHEP.: Yea, the devil in thy maw, so tariand!   110
Saw'st thou awre of Daw?
1 SHEP.:   Yea, on a lea-land
Heard I him blow.° He comes here at hand,
Not far.
Stand still.
2 SHEP.:   Why?
1 SHEP.: For he comes, hope° I.   115
2 SHEP.: He will make° us both a lie,
But if° we beware.

---

46. **mine own:** Myself.   47. **manner of moan:** Grumble.   49.
balk: A strip of rough grassland dividing two ploughed portions of a common field.   51. **pardie:** By God.   55. **Benste:**
Benedicite (bless us); **Bemean:** Mean.   56. We have not often
seen the like.   57. **keen:** Cruel.   58. **een:** Eyes.   64–6. But as
far as I know or as my experience goes, we poor married men
suffer much woe: we have sorrow time and again.   71.
Unhappy is our cock.   74. When they are hard put to it they
sigh unceasingly.   76–8. They never answer back. Now I've
found out what I have to do.   80. **bun:** Bound (in marriage).
81. **abide:** Remain so.

83. **rives:** Breaks.   84. Whatever destiny compels must come
to pass.   87. **woe:** Miserable.   88. **can:** Know.   90. **sore:**
Pain.   91. But young men, as for wooing, by God who
redeemed you.   92. **Well ware:** Very wary.   93. 'If only I had
known' is something that doesn't help you.   94. **Mickle still:**
Constant.   96. **sharp:** Pang.   98. What shall grieve you most
bitterly.   100. I have one for my mate.   102. She has bristly
brows and a sour-looking face.   108. **to:** Till.   109. God save
the audience! You stand there as deaf as a post. (The First Shepherd has evidently been trying to attract the other's attention.)
110–12. The devil in your belly for tarrying so long! Have you
seen Daw anywhere? . . . Yea, in a fallow field I heard him blow
[his horn].   115. **hope:** Think.   116. **make:** Tell.   117. **But
if:** Unless.

[*Enter Third Shepherd*]

3 SHEP.: Christ's cross me speed, and Saint Nicholas!
Thereof had I need; it° is worse than it was.
120 Whoso could take heed and let the world pass,
It is ever in dread and brickle as glass,
And slithes.
This world fared never so,°
With marvels mo° and mo—
125 Now in weal, now in woe,
And all thing writhes.°

Was never since Noah's flood such floods seen,
Winds and rains so rude, and storms so keen:
Some stammered, some stood in doubt, as I ween.°
130 Now God turn all to good! I say as I mean,
For ponder:°
These floods so they drown,
Both in fields and in town,
And bear all down;
135 And that is a wonder.

We that walk on the nights our cattle to keep,
We see sudden sights when other men sleep.
Yet methink my heart lights;° I see shrews° peep.
Ye are two all-wights°—I will give my sheep
140 A turn.
But full ill have I meant;
As I walk on this bent,
I may lightly repent,
My toes if I spurn.°

145 Ah, sir, God you save, and master mine!
A drink fain would I have, and somewhat to dine.
1 SHEP.: Christ's curse, my knave, thou art a lither
hine!°
2 SHEP.: What, the boy list rave! Abide unto syne;
We have made it.°
150 Ill thrift° on thy pate!
Though the shrew came late,
Yet is he in state°
To dine—if he had it.

3 SHEP.: Such servants as I, that sweat and swinks,°
155 Eat our bread full dry, and that me forthinks.°
We are oft wet and weary when master-men winks;°

Yet come full lately° both dinners and drinks.
But nately°
Both our dame and our sire,
When we have run in the mire,   160
They can nip at our hire,°
And pay us full lately.
But hear my truth, master: for the fare that ye make,
I shall do thereafter—work as I take.
I shall do a little, sir, and among ever lake,°   165
For yet lay my supper never on my stomach
In fields.
Whereto should I threap?°
With my staff can I leap;
And men say 'Light cheap   170
Litherly foryields.'

1 SHEP.: Thou wert an ill lad to ride on wooing
With a man that had but little of spending.°
2 SHEP.: Peace, boy, I bade. No more jangling,
Or I shall make thee full rad, by the heaven's king! 175
With thy gauds—
Where are our sheep, boy?—we scorn.°
3 SHEP.: Sir, this same day at morn
I them left in the corn,
When they rang Lauds.°   180

They have pasture good, they cannot go wrong.
1 SHEP.: That is right. By the rood,° these nights are
long!
Yet I would, ere we yode,° one gave us a song.
2 SHEP.: So I thought as I stood, to mirth us among.°
3 SHEP.: I grant.   185
1 SHEP.: Let me sing the tenory.°
2 SHEP.: And I the treble so high.
3 SHEP.: Then the mean falls to me.
Let see how ye chant.   [*They sing.*

Then Mak enters with a cloak covering his tunic.

MAK: Now, Lord, for thy names seven, that made
both moon and starns
Well more than I can neven, thy will, Lord, of me   190
tharns.
I am all uneven; that moves oft my harns.°

---

119. *it*, i.e., the world.   120–3. Anyone who could look on and
let the world go by [would see that] it is always fearful and as
brittle as glass, and slides away (i.e., is transitory). But the world
never behaved in this way before.   124. mo: More.   126.
writhes: Changes.   129. ween: Fear.   131. ponder: Consider.
138. lights: Grows light; shrews: Rogues.   139. all-wights:
Monsters.   139–44. I will turn my sheep away. But I have
been ill disposed [to the shepherds]; as I walk on this field, I
may stub my toes in easy penance.   147. lither hine: Lazy
hind.   148–9. What, the boy is pleased to rave! Wait till later;
we have finished it (i.e., our meal).   150. thrift: Luck.   152. in
state: Ready.   154. swinks: Toil.   155. forthinks: Displeases.
156. winks: Sleep.

157. lately: Tardily.   158. nately: Thoroughly.   161. They
can stint our wages.   163–5. But hear my promise, master: in
return for the food you provide, I shall do accordingly—work
as I'm paid. I shall do but little, sir, and betweenwhiles play all
the time.   168. threap: Haggle.   170–3. 'A cheap bargain
repays badly.' . . . You'd be the wrong lad for anyone that's hard
up to take a-wooing with him (cf. *Othello* III. iii. 71).   174–7.
Stop your wrangling, or I'll quickly make you, by the king of
heaven! We scorn your pranks—where are our sheep, boy?
180. Lauds: The first of the seven canonical offices, usually
sung at daybreak.   182. rood: Cross.   183. yode: Went.
184. To gladden us meanwhile.   186. tenory: Tenor.   190–2.
Now, Lord, by thy seven names, who made both moon and
stars far more than I can name, thy will concerning me, Lord, is
lacking. I am all at sixes and sevens; that often unsettles my
brain.

Now would God I were in heaven, for there weep
    no bairns
    So still.°

195 1 SHEP.: Who is that pipes so poor?°
MAK: Would God ye wist° how I foor!°
    Lo, a man that walks on the moor,
    And has not all his will.

2 SHEP.: Mak, where hast thou gone? Tell us tiding.°
200 3 SHEP.: Is he come? Then ilkone° take heed to his thing.

He takes Mak's cloak from him.

MAK: What! I be a yeoman, I tell you, of the king.
    The self and the same, sond° from a great lording,
    And sich.°
    Fie on you! Go hence
205   Out of my presence!
    I must have reverence.
    Why, who be ich?

1 SHEP.: Why make ye it so quaint?° Mak, ye do wrong.
2 SHEP.: But, Mak, list ye saint? I trow that ye long.°
210 3 SHEP.: I trow° the shrew can paint, the devil might
    him hang!°
MAK: I shall make complaint, and make you all to
    thwang
    At a word,
    And tell even how ye doth.°
1 SHEP.: But, Mak, is that sooth?
215   Now take out that Southern tooth,°
    And set° in a turd!

2 SHEP.: Mak, the devil in your eye! A stroke would I
    lene° you.
3 SHEP.: Mak, know ye not me? By God, I could
    teen° you.
MAK: God look° you all three! Methought I had seen
    you.
    Ye are a fair company.
220 1 SHEP.:   Can ye now mean you?°
2 SHEP.: Shrew, peep !°
    Thus late as thou goes,
    What will men suppose?°
    And thou hast an ill noise°
225   Of° stealing of sheep.

MAK: And I am true as steel, all men wot;
    But a sickness I feel that holds me full hot:°
    My belly fares not well, it is out of estate.°
3 SHEP.: Seldom lies the devil dead by the gate.°
MAK: Therefore   230
    Full sore am I and ill;
    If I stand stone-still,
    I eat not a needle°
    This month and more.°

1 SHEP.: How fares thy wife? By my hood, how fares
    she?   235
MAK: Lies waltering°—by the rood—by the fire, lo!
    And a house full of brood.° She drinks well, too;
    Ill speed other good that she will do!°
    But she
    Eats as fast as she can,   240
    And ilk° year that comes to man
    She brings forth a lakan°—
    And, some years, two

    But were I now more gracious,° and richer by far,
    I were eaten out of house and of harbour.°   245
    Yet is she a foul dowse,° if ye come near;
    There is none that trows nor knows a war°
    Than ken I.
    Now will ye see what I proffer?
    To give all in my coffer   250
    To-morn at next to offer°
    Her head-masspenny.

2 SHEP.: I wot so forwaked° is none in this shire;
    I would sleep if I taked less to my hire.°
3 SHEP.: I am cold and naked, and would have a fire.   255
1 SHEP.: I am weary, forraked,° and run in the mire—
    Wake thou!
2 SHEP.: Nay, I will lie down by.°
    For I must sleep, truly.
3 SHEP.: As good a man's son was I   260
    As any of you.

    But, Mak, come hither! Between° shalt thou lie down.
MAK: Then might I let you bedene of that ye would
    rown,
    No dread.°

---

194. **still:** Incessantly.   195. Who is it that cries so piteously?
196. **wist:** Knew; **foor:** Fared.   199. **tiding:** News.   200.
ilkone: Everyone.   202. **sond:** Messenger.   203. **sich:** Such
like.   208. Why are you so uppish?   209. But, Mak, do you
want to play the saint? I believe you do.   210. **trow:** Believe.
211. And have you all flogged.   213. **doth:** Do.   215. Southern speech. (Mak has been trying to talk Southern English.)
216. **set:** Put.   217. **lene:** Give.   218. **teen:** Hurt.   219. **look:**
Save.   220. Can you remember now?   221. **peep:** Pry about.
223. **suppose:** Suspect.   224. **ill noise:** Reputation.   225. **Of:**
For.

227. **full hot:** Severely.   228. **estate:** Condition.   229. Seldom
lies the devil dead by the roadside, i.e., appearances may be
deceptive.   232. **needle:** Morsel.   232–3. May I be turned to
stone if I have eaten a morsel.   236. **waltering:** Sprawling.
237. **brood:** children.   238. i.e., there is no hope of her doing
much else.   241. **ilk:** Every.   242. **lakan:** Baby.   244. **gracious:** Prosperous.   245. **harbour:** Home.   246. **dowse:**
Wench.   247. There is none who believes [he knows] or
[really] knows a worse one.   251–2. Tomorrow at the latest to
give all in my coffer as an offering for her soul.   253. **for-
waked:** Wearied with waking.   254. Even if I should get less
wages.   256. **forraked:** Worn out with walking.   257. **by:**
Nearby.   262. **between:** Between us.   263–4. Then I might
keep you from whispering what you want, no doubt.

265   From my top to my toe,   [*He recites a night-spell.*
       Manus tuas commendo,
       Pontio Pilato.
       Christ's cross me speed !

       Now were time for a man that lacks what he would
270   To stalk privily then unto a fold,
       And nimbly to work then, and be not too bold,
       For he might abuy the bargain, if it were told
       At the ending.°
       Now were time for to reel;°
275   But he needs good counsel
       That fain would fare well,
       And has but little spending.°

       But about you a circle,° as round as a moon,
       To I have done what I will, till that it be noon,
280   That ye lie stone-still to that I have done;
       And I shall say theretill of good words a fone:°
       'On height,°
       Over your heads, my hand I lift.
       Out go your eyes! Fordo your sight!'
285   But yet I must make better shift,
       And it be right.

       Lord, what they sleep hard!—that may ye all hear.°
       Was I never a shepherd, but now will I lere.°
       If the flock be scared, yet shall I nip near.°
290   How! draw hitherward! Now mends our cheer
       From sorrow
       A fat sheep, I dare say,
       A good fleece, dare I lay,
       Eft-quit° when I may,
295   But this will I borrow.

                    [*He goes home with the sheep.*

Scene II.   *Mak's cottage*

MAK: How, Gill, art thou in? Get us some light.
WIFE: Who makes such din this time of the night?
       I am set for to spin; I hope not I might
       Rise a penny to win, I shrew them on height!
300   So fares
       A housewife that has been,
       To be raised thus between.

       Here may no note be seen
       For such small chares.°
MAK: Good wife, open the heck!° See'st thou not what I
          bring?   305
WIFE: I may thole thee draw the sneck.° Ah, come in,
          my sweeting!
MAK: Yea, thou thar not reck of my long standing.°
WIFE: By the naked neck art thou like for to hang.
MAK: Do way!°
       I am worthy my meat,°   310
       For in a strait° can I get
       More than they that swink° and sweat
       All the long day.

       Thus it fell to my lot, Gill; I had such grace.
WIFE: It were a foul blot° to be hanged for the case.   315
MAK: I have scaped, Jelott, oft as hard a glase.°
WIFE: 'But so long goes the pot to the water,' men says,
          'At last
       Comes it home broken.'
MAK: Well know I the token,°   320
       But let it never be spoken!
       But come and help fast.
       I would he were flain; I list well eat.
       This twelvemonth was I not so fain of one sheep-
          meat.°
WIFE: Come they ere he be slain, and hear the sheep
          bleat—   325
MAK: Then might I be ta'en: that were a cold sweat!
       Go spar°
       The gate-door.°
WIFE: Yes, Mak,
       For° and they come at thy back—
MAK: Then might I buy, for all the pack,   330
       The devil of the war.°

WIFE: A good bourd° have I spied, since thou canst°
          none:
       Here shall we him hide, till they be gone,
       In my cradle. Abide! Let me alone,
       And I shall lie beside in childbed and groan.   335
MAK: Thou red,°
       And I shall say thou wast light°
       Of a knave-child° this night.
WIFE: Now well is me day bright
       That ever was I bred!   340
       This is a good guise and a far cast;°

272–3. For he might pay dearly for it, if it came to a final reckoning.   274. reel: Move quickly.   277. spending: Money.
278. circle: Magic circle.   281. And I shall also say a few good words.   282. height: High.   284–7. 'Lose your power of sight.' But yet I must make better efforts, if things are to come right. Lord, how soundly they sleep!   288. lere: Learn.   289. Yet I shall grab [a sheep] tightly.   290–2. Now a fat sheep shall comfort us.   294. Eft-quit: Repay.   298–304. I don't think I can earn a penny by getting up [from my spinning], curse them! Any woman who has been a housewife knows what it means to be got up from her work continually. I have no work to show because of such small chores.

305. heck: Inner door.   306. I will let you draw the latch.
307. You needn't mind about my standing [outside] so long.
309. Do way!: Enough!   310. meat: Food.   311. strait: Fix.
312. swink: Toil.   315. blot: Deed.   316. glase: Blow.   320. token: Portent.   323–4. I wish he were skinned; I am eager to eat. At no time this year have I been so glad of a meal of mutton.   327. spar: Fasten.   328. gate-door: Outer door.   329. For: If.   330–1. Then I may get the devil of a bad time from the whole pack of them.   332. bourd: Jest; canst: Knowest.
336. red: Get ready.   337. wast light: Delivered.   338. knave-child: Boy.   339–41. I'm happy when I think of the bright day I was born! This is a good method and a cunning trick.

Yet a woman's advice helps at the last.
I wot never who spies; again go thou fast.°
MAK: But I come ere they rise, else° blows a cold blast!
345 I will go sleep.
Yet sleep all this meny;°
And I shall go stalk privily,
As it had never been I
That carried their sheep.

Scene III.   *The open fields*

350 1 SHEP.: *Resurrex a mortruus!* have hold my hand!
Judas carnas dominus!° I may not well stand:
My foot sleeps, by Jesus, and I walter fastand.°
I thought that we laid us full near England.
2 SHEP.: Ah, yea?°
355 Lord, what I have slept well!°
As fresh as an eel,
As light I me feel
As leaf on a tree.

3 SHEP.: Benste° be herein! So me quakes,
360 My heart is out of skin, what-so it makes.°
Who makes all this din? So my brow blakes,°
To the door will I win.° Hark, fellows, wakes!°
We were four:
See ye awre of Mak now?°
365 1 SHEP.: We were up ere thou.
2 SHEP.: Man, I give God avow
Yet yede he nawre.°

3 SHEP.: Methought he was lapped in a wolf-skin.
1 SHEP.: So are many happed now—namely within.°
3 SHEP.: When we had long napped, methought with a
370   gin°
A fat sheep he trapped; but he made no din.
2 SHEP.: Be still!
Thy dream makes thee wood;°
It is but phantom, by the rood.
375 1 SHEP.: Now God turn all to good,
If it be his will.
2 SHEP.: Rise, Mak, for shame! Thou liest right long.
MAK: Now Christ's holy name be us among!
What is this? For Saint Jame,° I may not well gang!°
380 I trow I be the same. Ah, my neck has lain wrong

Enough.°   [*They help him to get up.*
Mickle thank! Since yester-even,
Now by Saint Stephen,
I was flayed with a sweven—
My heart out of slough.°   385

I thought Gill began to croak and travail full sad,°
Well-nigh at the first cock, of a young lad
For to mend° our flock. Then be I never glad;
I have tow on my rock more than ever I had.°
Ah, my head!   390
A house full of young tharms,°
The devil knock out their harns!°
Woe is him has many bairns,
And thereto little bread.

I must go home, by your leave, to Gill, as I
    thought.°   395
I pray you look° my sleeve, that I steal nought;
I am loath you to grieve or from you take aught.
3 SHEP.: Go forth, ill might thou chieve!° Now would
    I we sought,
This morn,
That we had all our store.°   400
1 SHEP.: But I will go before.
Let us meet.
2 SHEP.:   Where?
3 SHEP.: At the crooked thorn.

Scene IV.   *Mak's cottage*

MAK: Undo this door! Who is here? How long shall I
    stand?
WIFE: Who makes such a bere?° Now walk in the
    wenyand!   405
MAK: Ah, Gill, what cheer? It is I, Mak, your husband.
WIFE: Then may we see here the devil in a band,°
    Sir Guile!
Lo, he comes with a lote,°
As he were holden° in the throat.   410
I may not sit at my note°
A hand-long° while.

MAK: Will ye hear what fare she makes to get her a
    glose?°

---

343. Return again quickly [to the others].   344. **else:** Unless.
346. **meny:** Company. 350–1. Bad Latin for "rise from the
dead" and "Judas carnate Lord." 352. I'm tottering with
hunger. 354. **Ah, yea?:** Oh, really? 355. How well I have
slept! 359. **Benste:** Blessing. 359–60. I tremble so much, my
heart is in my mouth, whatever the reason for it. 361. **blakes:**
Darkens. 362. **win:** Go; **wakes!:** Wake up! 364. Have you
seen Mak anywhere? 366–7. I vow to God he's gone nowhere
yet. 369. Many are covered like that nowadays—especially
underneath. 370. **gin:** Snare. 373. **wood:** Mad. 379. By
Saint James; **gang:** Walk.

380–1. My neck has been lying very crookedly.   384–5. I
was terrified by a dream—I nearly jumped out of my skin.
386. **full sad:** Hard. 388. **mend:** Increase. 389. I have more
tow on my distaff (i.e., more trouble in store) than ever I had.
391. **tharms:** Bellies. 392. **harns:** Brains. 395. **thought:**
Intended. 396. **look:** Examine. 398. **chieve:** Prosper.
398–400. Now I want us this morning to see that we have all
our stock. 405. **bere:** Din; Walk in the waning moon, i.e., at
an unlucky time. 407. **band:** Noose. 409. **lote:** Noise.
410. **holden:** Held by. 411. **note:** Work. 412. **hand-long:**
Brief. 413. Will you listen to the fuss she makes in the hope of
excusing herself?

And does naught but lakes,° and claws her toes.
415 WIFE: Why, who wanders, who wakes? Who comes,
      who goes?
     Who brews, who bakes? What makes me thus hoarse?
     And then
     It is ruth° to behold—
     Now in hot, now in cold,°
420 Full woeful is the household
     That wants° a woman.

     But what end hast thou made with the herds,° Mak?
     MAK: The last word that they said when I turned my
      back.
     They would look that they had their sheep, all the
      pack.
     I hope° they will not be well paid° when they their
425   sheep lack,
     Pardie!
     But how-so° the game goes,
     To me they will suppose,°
     And make a foul noise,
430 And cry out upon me.

     But thou must do as thou hight.°
     WIFE: I accord me theretill;
     I shall swaddle him right in my cradle.
     If it were a greater sleight,° yet could I help till.
     I will lie down straight.° Come hap° me.
     MAK: I will.
435 WIFE: Behind!
     Come Coll and his marrow,°
     They will nip us full narrow.°
     MAK: But I may cry 'Out, harrow!'°
     The sheep if they find.

440 WIFE: Harken ay when they call; they will come anon.
     Come and make ready all, and sing by thine own;
     Sing lullay° thou shall, for I must groan,
     And cry out by the wall on Mary and John,
     For sore.°
445 Sing lullay on fast,°
     When thou hearest at the last;
     And but I play a false cast,°
     Trust me no more.

Scene V.   *The crooked thorn*

     3 SHEP.: Ah, Coll, good morn! Why sleepest thou not?
     1 SHEP.: Alas, that ever was I born! We have a foul
450   blot—

A fat wether have we lorn.°
3 SHEP.:   Marry, God's forbot!°
2 SHEP.: Who should do us that scorn?° That were a
  foul spot.°
1 SHEP.: Some shrew.
  I have sought with my dogs
  All Horbury° shrogs,°   455
  And, of fifteen hogs,
  Found I but one ewe.°

3 SHEP.: Now trow me, if ye will—by Saint Thomas
   of Kent,°
  Either Mak or Gill was at that assent.°
1 SHEP.: Peace, man, be still! I saw when he went.   460
  Thou slander'st him ill; thou ought to repent
  Good speed.°
2 SHEP.: Now as ever might I thee,°
  If I should even here die,
  I would say it were he   465
  That did that same deed.

3 SHEP.: Go we thither, I rede,° and run on our feet.
  Shall I never eat bread, the sooth to I wit.°
1 SHEP.: Nor drink in my head, with him till I meet.
2 SHEP.: I will rest in no stead° till that I him greet,   470
  My brother.°
  One I will hight:°
  Till I see him in sight,
  Shall I never sleep one night
  There° I do another.   475

Scene VI.   *Mak's cottage*

3 SHEP.: Will ye hear how they hack? Our sire list
   croon.°
1 SHEP.: Heard I never none crack° so clear out of tone.°
  Call on him.
2 SHEP.:   Mak, undo your door soon!°
MAK: Who is it that spake, as it were noon,
  On loft?°   480
  Who is that, I say?
3 SHEP.: Good fellows, were it day.°
MAK: As far as ye may,
  Good,° speak soft,

414. lakes: Play.   418. ruth: A pity.   419. i.e., at all times.
421. wants: Lacks.   422. herds: Shepherds.   425. hope: Think;
paid: Pleased.   427. how-so: However.   428. They will suspect me.   431. hight: Promised; I agree to that.   433. sleight:
Trick; I could still help with it.   434. straight: Straightaway;
hap: Cover.   436. marrow: Mate.   437. full narrow: Hard.
438. A cry for help.   442. lullay: Lullaby.   444. sore: Pain.
445. fast: Quickly.   447. And if I don't play a false trick.

451. lorn: Lost; God's forbot: God forbid.   452. do us that
scorn: Insult; foul spot: Disgrace.   455. Horbury, near
Wakefield; shrogs: Thickets.   456–7. Among fifteen hogs (or
young sheep) I found only one ewe, i.e., the wether was missing.   458. St. Thomas of Canterbury.   459. Either Mak or
Gill was a party to it.   462. Good speed: Quickly.   463. As I
hope to prosper.   467. rede: Advise.   468. Till I know the
truth.   470. stead: Place.   471. *My brother*, a friendly form of
address.   472. One thing I will promise.   475. There: Where.
476. Do you hear them trilling? Our gentleman is pleased to
croon.   477. crack: Bawl; tone: Tune.   478. soon: Immediately.   479–80. Who is it that spoke aloud, as though it were
noon?   482. were it: If only it were.   484. Good: Good sirs.

485   Over a sick woman's head, that is at malease;
     I had liefer be dead ere she had any disease.°
  WIFE: Go to another stead! I may not well quease;°
     Each foot that ye tread goes thorough my nose
     So high.°
490 1 SHEP.: Tell us, Mak, if ye may,
     How fare ye, I say?
  MAK: But are ye in this town to-day?
     Now how fare ye?

     Ye have run in the mire, and are wet yet;
495   I shall make you a fire, if ye will sit.
     A nurse would I hire. Think ye on yet?
     Well quit is my hire—my dream, this is it°—
     A season.
     I have bairns, if ye knew,
500   Well more than enew;°
     But we must drink as we brew,
     And that is but reason.

     I would ye dined ere ye yode.° Methink that ye sweat.
  2 SHEP.: Nay, neither mends our mood drink nor meat.
505 MAK: Why, sir, ails you aught but good?°
  3 SHEP.:   Yea, our sheep that we gete°
     Are stolen as they yode. Our loss is great.
  MAK: Sirs, drink!
     Had I been there,
     Some should have bought it full sore.°
510 1 SHEP.: Marry, some men trow that ye were,
     And that us forthinks.°

  2 SHEP.: Mak, some men trows° that it should be ye.
  3 SHEP.: Either ye or your spouse, so say we.
  MAK: Now if ye have suspouse° to Gill or to me,
515   Come and rip° our house, and then may ye see
     Who had her.
     If I any sheep fot,°
     Either cow or stot°—
     And Gill, my wife, rose not
520   Here since she laid her—

     As I am true and leal,° to God here I pray
     That this be the first meal that I shall eat this day.
  1 SHEP.: Mak, as have I sele, advise thee, I say:
     He learned timely to steal that could not say nay.°

WIFE: I swelt!°   525
     Out, thieves, from my wones!°
     Ye come to rob us for the nonce.°
  MAK: Hear ye not how she groans?
     Your hearts should melt.

WIFE: Out, thieves, from my bairn! Nigh him not there.°   530
MAK: Wist ye how she had farn, your hearts would be
     sore.°
     Ye do wrong, I you warn, that thus come before
     To a woman that has farn; but I say no more.°
WIFE: Ah, my middle!
     I pray to God so mild,   535
     If ever I you beguiled,
     That I eat° this child
     That lies in this cradle.
MAK: Peace, woman, for God's pain, and cry not so!
     Thou spillest° thy brain, and makest me full woe.   540
2 SHEP.: I trow our sheep be slain. What find ye two?
3 SHEP.: All work we in vain; as well may we go.
     But hatters!°
     I can find no flesh,
     Hard nor nesh,°   545
     Salt nor fresh,
     But two tome platters.°

     Quick cattle but this, tame nor wild,
     None, as have I bliss, as loud as he smelled.°
WIFE: No, so God me bless, and give me joy of my child!   550
1 SHEP.: We have marked amiss;° I hold us beguiled.
2 SHEP.: Sir, don.°
     Sir—our Lady him save!—
     Is your child a knave?°
MAK: Any lord might him have,   555
     This child, to his son.

     When he wakens he kips;° that joy is to see.
3 SHEP.: In good time to his hips, and in sely.°
     But who were his gossips° so soon ready?
MAK: So fair fall their lips!
1 SHEP. [Aside]:   Hark now, a lie!   560
MAK: So God them thank,°
     Parkin, and Gibbon Waller, I say,
     And gentle John Horne,° in good fay°—

485–6. Because of a sick woman who is in distress; I had rather die than she should suffer any discomfort. **487. quease:** Breathe. **488–9.** Every step you tread goes through my nose so strongly, i.e., goes right through my head. **496–8.** I would like to hire a nurse. Do you still remember [my dream about a new addition to the family]? I've been paid my wages in full for a while—this is my dream come true. **500. enew:** Enough. **503. yode:** Went. **505.** Why, sir, is anything wrong with you? **506. gete:** Tend. **509. full sore:** Paid for. **511. forthinks:** Displeases. **512. trows:** Believe. **514. suspouse:** Suspicion. **515. rip:** Ransack. **517. fot:** Fetched. **518. stot:** Heifer. **521. leal:** Honest. **523–4.** Mak, as I hope for happiness, take thought I say: he learned early to steal who could not say no [to another's property].

525. swelt: Feel faint. **526. wones:** House. **527.** You come on purpose to rob us. **530.** Do not go near him there. **531.** If you knew what she had been through. **533.** To a woman who has been in labor. **537. eat:** May eat. **540. spillest:** Injurest. **543. hatters!:** Confound it! **545. nesh:** Soft. **547. But two tome platters:** Only two empty platters. **548–9.** Live stock but this (i.e., the 'baby' in the cradle), tame or wild, none [have I found], as I hope to be happy, that smelled as loud as he (i.e., the missing sheep). **551.** Aimed wrongly, i.e., made a mistake. **552. don:** Completely. **554. knave:** Boy. **557. kips:** Snatches. **558.** A good and happy future to him. **559. gossips:** Godparents. **561.** Good luck to them. **563.** John Horne is the shepherd in the First Shepherds' Pageant who quarrels with Gyb about the pasturing of an imaginary flock of sheep; **fay:** Faith.

He made all the garray°—
565   With the great shank.°
2 SHEP.: Mak, friends will we be, for we are all one.°
MAK: We? Now I hold for me, for mends get I none.°
    Farewell all three!—all glad were ye gone.°
3 SHEP.: Fair words may there be, but love is there
        none
570   This year.   [*They leave the cottage.*
1 SHEP.: Gave ye the child anything?
2 SHEP.: I trow not one farthing.
3 SHEP.: Fast again will I fling;°
    Abide ye me there.   [*He returns to the cottage.*

575   Mak, take it to no grief,° if I come to thy bairn.
MAK: Nay, thou dost me great reprief, and foul hast
      thou farn.°
3 SHEP.: The child will it not grieve, that little day-
      starn.°
    Mak, with your leave, let me give your bairn
    But sixpence.
580 MAK: Nay, do way! He sleeps.
3 SHEP.: Methink he peeps.
MAK: When he wakens he weeps.
    I pray you go hence.

3 SHEP.: Give me leave him to kiss, and lift up the
      clout.°   [*He glimpses the sheep.*
585   What the devil is this? He has a long snout!
1 SHEP.: He is marked amiss. We wait ill about.
2 SHEP.: Ill-spun weft, iwis, ay comes foul out.°
    Aye, so!   [*He recognizes the sheep.*
    He is like to our sheep!
590 3 SHEP.: How, Gib, may I peep?
1 SHEP.: I trow kind will creep
    Where it may not go.

2 SHEP.: This was a quaint gaud and a far cast;°
    It was a high fraud.
3 SHEP.:   Yea, sirs, was't.
595   Let burn this bawd and bind her fast.
    A false scold hangs at the last;
    So shalt thou.
    Will ye see how they swaddle
    His four feet in the middle?
600   Saw I never in a cradle
    A horned lad ere now.

MAK: Peace, bid I. What, let be your fare!°
    I am he that him begat, and yond woman him bare.
1 SHEP.: What devil shall be hat,° Mak? Lo,
    God, Mak's heir!   605
2 SHEP.: Let be all that. Now God give him care,°
    I sagh.°
WIFE: A pretty child is he
    As sits on a woman's knee;
    A dillydown,° pardie,
    To gar° a man laugh.   610

3 SHEP.: I know him by the ear-mark; that is a good
      token.
MAK: I tell you, sirs, hark! his nose was broken.
    Since told me a clerk that he was forspoken.°
1 SHEP.: This is a false work; I would fain be wroken.°
    Get weapon!   615
WIFE: He was taken with° an elf,
    I saw it myself;
    When the clock struck twelve,
    Was he forshapen.°
2 SHEP.: Ye two are well feft sam in a stead.°   620
1 SHEP.: Since they maintain their theft, let do them
      to dead.°
MAK: If I trespass eft,° gird° off my head.
    With you will I be left.
3 SHEP.:   Sirs, do my rede:°
    For this trespass
    We will neither ban ne flite,°   625
    Fight nor chide,
    But have done as tite,°
    And cast him in canvas.

[*They toss Mak in a blanket.*

Scene VII.   *The open fields*

1 SHEP.: Lord, what I am sore, in point for to burst!
    In faith, I may no more; therefore will I rest.
              630
2 SHEP.: As a sheep of seven score he weighed in my fist.
    For to sleep aywhere methink that I list.°
3 SHEP.: Now I pray you
    Lie down on this green.
1 SHEP.: On these thieves yet I mean.°   635
3 SHEP.: Whereto should ye teen?°
    Do as I say you.

---

564. garray: Commotion.   565. shank: Long legs.   566. all
one: Agreed.   567. For my own part, I'm holding back, for I
get no amends.   568. [I should be] very glad if you were gone.
(Probably an aside.)   573. I will dash back.   575. Don't take
offense.   576. Nay, you do me great shame, and you have
behaved badly.   577. day-starn: Star.   584. clout: Cloth.
586–7. He is misshapen. We do wrong to pry about.... Ill-spun
weft, indeed, always comes out badly, i.e., what is bred in the
bone will come out in the flesh.   591–3. Nature will creep
where it cannot walk, i.e., assert itself in one way or another....
This was a clever dodge and a cunning trick.

602. fare: Uproar.   604. hat: Be called.   606. care: Sorrow.
sagh: Saw [the sheep myself].   609. dillydown: Darling.
610. gar: Make.   613. forspoken: Bewitched.   614. wroken:
Avenged.   616. with: By.   619. forshapen: Transformed.
620. You two are well endowed together in one place, i.e., are
as clever a pair of rascals as ever lived under one roof.   621.
dead: Death.   622. eft: Again; gird: Strike.   623. I throw
myself on your mercy.... Take my advice.   625. neither ban ne
flite: Neither curse nor quarrel.   627. as tite: At once.   632. I
think I would be glad to sleep anywhere.   635. mean: Think.
636. teen: Vex yourself.

An Angel sings 'Gloria in excelsis,' and then says:

ANGEL: Rise, herdmen hend,° for now is he born
    That shall take from the fiend that Adam had lorn;
640   That warlock° to shend,° this night is he born.
    God is made your friend now at this morn,
    He behests.°
    At Bedlem° go see
    There lies that free°
645   In a crib full poorly,
    Betwixt two beasts.

1 SHEP.: This was a quaint steven° that ever yet I heard.
    It is a marvel to neven,° thus to be scared.
2 SHEP.: Of God's son of heaven he spoke upward.°
650   All the wood on a leven methought that he gard
    Appear.°
3 SHEP.: He spake of a bairn
    In Bedlem, I you warn.
1 SHEP.: That betokens yond starn;
655   Let us seek him there.

2 SHEP.: Say, what was his song? Heard ye not how he
      cracked° it,
    Three breves to a long?
3 SHEP.:   Yea, marry, he hacked° it:
    Was no crochet wrong, nor no thing that lacked it.°
660 1 SHEP.: For to sing us among, right as he knacked° it,
    I can.
2 SHEP.: Let see how ye croon.
    Can ye bark at the moon?
3 SHEP.: Hold your tongues! Have done!
1 SHEP.: Hark after, then.   [*Sings.*

665 2 SHEP.: To Bedlem he bade that we should gang;°
    I am full adrad° that we tarry too long.
3 SHEP.: Be merry and not sad—of mirth is our song!
    Everlasting glad to meed may we fang
    Without noise.°
670 1 SHEP.: Hie we thither forthy,°
    If° we be wet and weary,
    To that child and that lady;
    We have it not to lose.°
2 SHEP.: We find by the prophecy—let be your din!—
675   Of David and Isay,° and more than I min°—
    They prophesied by clergy°—that in a virgin
    Should he light° and lie, to sloken° our sin,

    And slake° it,
    Our kind,° from woe;
    For Isay said so: 680
    Ecce virgo
    Concipiet a child that is naked.°

3 SHEP.: Full glad may we be, and abide that day
    That lovely to see, that all mights may.
    Lord, well were me for once and for ay,°   685
    Might I kneel on my knee, some word for to say
    To that child.
    But the angel said
    In a crib was he laid;
    He was poorly arrayed,   690
    Both meek and mild.

1 SHEP.: Patriarchs that have been, and prophets
      beforn,°
    They desired to have seen this child that is born.
    They are gone full clean; that have they lorn.°
    We shall see him, I ween, ere it be morn,   695
    To token.°
    When I see him and feel,
    Then wot I full well
    It is true as steel
    That prophets have spoken: 700

    To so poor as we are that he would appear
    First find, and declare by his messenger.°
2 SHEP.: Go we now, let us fare; the place is us near.

3 SHEP.: I am ready and yare;° go we in fere°
    To that bright.°   705
    Lord, if thy will be—
    We are lewd° all three—
    Thou grant us some kins glee
    To comfort thy wight.°

Scene VIII.   *The stable in Bethlehem*

1 SHEP.: Hail, comely and clean;° hail, young child!   710
    Hail, maker, as I mean, of° a maiden so mild!
    Thou hast waried,° I ween, the warlock so wild;
    The false guiler of teen, now goes he beguiled.°
    Lo, he merries,°

---

638. **hend:** Gentle.   640. **warlock:** The devil; **shend:** Destroy. 642. **behests:** Promises.   643. **Bedlem:** Bethlehem.   644. **There lies that free:** Where lies that noble one.   647. **quaint steven:** Elegant voice.   648. **neven:** Tell of.   649. **upward:** On high.   650–1. I thought he made the whole wood appear as if lit up by lightning.   656. **cracked:** Sang.   658. **hacked:** Trilled.   659. No crochet was wrong, and there was nothing it lacked.   660. **knacked:** Sang.   665. **gang:** Go.   666. **adrad:** Afraid.   668–9. We can get everlasting joy as our reward without any fuss.   670. **forthy:** Therefore.   671. **If:** Even if. 673. We must not forget it.   675. **Isay:** Isaiah; **min:** Remember. 676. **clergy:** Learning.   677. **light:** Alight; **sloken:** Quench.

678. **slake:** Relieve.   679. **kind:** Race.   681–2. Behold, a virgin shall conceive.   684–5. To see that lovely one who is almighty. Lord, I would be happy for once and all.   692. **beforn:** In the past.   694. That chance have they lost.   696. **To token:** As a sign.   702. Find [us] first of all, and make known [his birth] through his messenger.   704. **yare:** Eager; **in fere:** Together.   705. **bright:** Bright one.   707. **lewd:** Simple. 708–9. Grant us some joyful way of comforting thy child. 710. **clean:** Pure.   711. **of:** Born of.   712. **waried:** Cursed. 713. The false and malicious deceiver, i.e., the devil.   714. **merries:** Is merry.

715   Lo, he laughs, my sweeting!
       A well fare° meeting!
       I have holden my heting:°
       Have a bob° of cherries.

2 SHEP.: Hail, sovereign saviour, for thou hast us
           sought!
720   Hail, freely food and flower°, that all thing has
           wrought!
       Hail, full of favour, that made all of nought!
       Hail! I kneel and I cower. A bird have I brought
       To my bairn.
       Hail, little tiny mop!°
725   Of our creed thou art crop;
       I would drink on thy cop,°
       Little day-starn.

3 SHEP.: Hail, darling dear, full of Godhead!
       I pray thee be near when that I have need.
730   Hail, sweet is thy cheer! My heart would bleed
       To see thee sit here in so poor weed,°
       With no pennies.
       Hail! Put forth thy dall!°
       I bring thee but a ball:

716. well fare: Very fine.   717. I have kept my promise.   718.
bob: Bunch.   720. food and flower: Noble child.   724. mop:
Moppet.   725–6. You are the head of our faith; I would drink
in your cup (i.e., the cup of the Eucharist).   731. weed: Clothing.   733. dall: Hand.

       Have and play thee withal,   735
       And go to the tennis.

MARY: The Father of heaven, God omnipotent,
       That set all on seven, his Son has he sent.°
       My name could he neven, and light ere he went.
       I conceived him full even through might, as he
           meant;°   740
       And now is he born.
       He keep you from woe!—
       I shall pray him so.
       Tell forth as ye go,
       And min° on this morn.   745

1 SHEP.: Farewell, lady, so fair to behold,
       With thy child on thy knee.
2 SHEP.:   But he lies full cold.
       Lord, well is me! Now we go, thou behold.
3 SHEP.: Forsooth, already it seems to be told
       Full oft.   750
1 SHEP.: What grace we have fun!
2 SHEP.: Come forth; now are we won!°
3 SHEP.: To sing are we bun:°
       Let take on loft.°

738. That made all the world in seven days.   739–40. He
named my name and alighted in me before He went. I conceived him indeed through God's might, as His purpose was.
745. min: Remembered.   752. won: Redeemed.   753. bun:
Bound.   754. Let us begin loudly.

EVERYMAN

This late medieval play may have origins in northern Europe. A Flemish play, *Elckerlijk* ("Everyman"), dates from c. 1495, and the question of whether the English *Everyman* was translated from it or whether it is a translation of *Everyman* has not been settled. Both plays may have had a common origin in an unknown play. The English *Everyman* was produced frequently in the fifteenth and early sixteenth centuries. Its drama was largely theological, its purpose to reform the audience. One indication that entertainment was not the primary goal of this morality play is its lack of the comic moments found in other plays, such as *The Second Shepherds' Pageant*.

The author of the play may have been a priest. This assumption has long been common because the play has much theological content and offers a moral message of the kind one might expect to hear from the pulpit. The theme of the play is fundamental: the inevitability of death. And for that reason, in part, the play continues to have a universal appeal. Modern productions may not give the audience a suitable medieval chill, but the message of the play is still relevant for everyone.

The medieval reliance on allegory is apparent in the naming of the characters in *Everyman*: Death, Kindred, Cousin, Goods, Knowledge, Strength, Beauty, and Everyman himself. Each character does not just stand for a specific quality; he or she *is* that quality. The allegorical way of thinking derived from the medieval faith that everything in the world had a moral meaning. Morality plays depended on this belief and always articulated setting, characters, and circumstances in terms of their moral value. This was in keeping with the medieval belief that the soul was always in jeopardy and that life was a test of one's moral condition. When Everyman meets a character, the most important information about his or her moral value is communicated instantly in the name of the character. Characters in allegorical plays also reveal themselves through their costumes and props. The character Good Deeds is simply good deeds: there is no need for psychological development because the medieval audience had a full understanding of what good deeds meant and how Good Deeds as a character would behave.

The structure of *Everyman* resembles a journey. Everyman undertakes to see who among all his acquaintances will accompany him on his most important trip: to the grave and the judgment of God Almighty. Seeing life as a journey — or as part of a journey — was especially natural for the medieval mind, which had as models the popular and costly religious pilgrimages to holy shrines and to the Holy Land itself. If life on earth is only part of the journey of the soul, then the morality play helps to put it in clear perspective. This life is not, the play tells us, the most important part of the soul's existence.

At its core, *Everyman* has a profound commercial metaphor: Everyman is called to square accounts with God. The metaphor of accounting appears early in the play, when Everyman talks about his accounts and reckonings as if they appeared in a book that should go with him to heaven. His life will be examined; if he is found wanting, he will go into the fires of hell. If he has lived profitably from a moral viewpoint, he will enjoy life everlasting. The language of the play is heavily loaded with accounting metaphors that identify it as the product of a society quite unlike that of the Greeks or the Romans. Such metaphors suggest that *Everyman* directs its message to middle-class merchants for whom accounting was a significant concept.

Like many sermons, *Everyman* imparts a lesson that its auditors were expected to heed. Hence the key points of the play are repeated at the end by the Doctor. For moderns, didactic plays are sometimes tedious. For the medieval mind, they represented delightful ways of learning important messages.

Everyman in Performance

Very little is known about early productions of *Everyman*. It was produced in Holland and England for seventy-five years beginning in the mid-fifteenth century. The play disappeared from the stage for centuries, finally resurfacing in 1901 in a production under the auspices of the Elizabethan Stage Society in London, directed by William Poel. Poel designed the costumes and set, directed, and played at first the part of Death; when he got older, he played the part of God. Poel produced *Everyman* many times over the next fifteen years.

The 1901 production was followed by a 1902 revival in New York starring Edith Wynne Matthison and produced by Ben Greet, marking the play's first American performance. Greet continued producing *Everyman* for the next thirty-five years in both England and America.

After seeing Poel's production, Max Reinhardt, the legendary German director, decided to produce *Everyman* in Germany. The Austrian poet and playwright Hugo von Hofmannsthal wrote a new German adaptation, *Jedermann*, for Reinhardt. The adaptation features Everyman as a wealthy burgher, and central to the play is an ornate banquet scene in which Death appears. Hofmannsthal's German adaptation marked a shift in emphasis from the simpler and more personal English *Everyman* to the spectacular *Jedermann* that concentrates on a wealthy man's lustful life and his attempts to get into heaven. *Jedermann* was first produced in Berlin on December 1, 1911. In 1913 Reinhardt produced the play in Salzburg, Austria, at the Salzburg Cathedral square, and except for the years of World War II, Reinhardt's version of *Jedermann* has been performed regularly at the annual Salzburg Festival. The critic Brooks Atkinson found Reinhardt's production "nothing short of miraculous." In a review of Reinhardt's 1927 production, the critic Gilbert Gabriel found *Jedermann* "crammed with splendors for the eye, largesse of bells and uplifting voices for the ear." A reviewer at the 1936 Salzburg Festival production of *Jedermann* wrote that the play "has everything but simplicity."

The popularity of the Reinhardt productions of *Jedermann* paved the way for numerous productions of *Everyman* over the years. In 1936, during the Great Depression in the United States, the WPA (Works Progress Administration) held special Sunday church performances of *Everyman*. Other notable productions include a 1941 *Everyman* in New York performed by refugee actors from Europe, and a 1955 tour with college casts in New England and California. In 1922 a new English adaptation of the German *Jedermann* by Sir

John Martin-Harvey was presented at Stratford-on-Avon. This production toured to London and New York in 1923. In 1936 Sir John's adaptation was performed at the Hollywood Bowl in California with Peggy Wood and Lionel Braham. Long popular with college and community groups, the play continues to be performed around the world.

Anonymous

EVERYMAN

EDITED BY A. C. CAWLEY

c. 1495

Characters

GOD	KNOWLEDGE
MESSENGER	CONFESSION
DEATH	BEAUTY
EVERYMAN	STRENGTH
FELLOWSHIP	DISCRETION
KINDRED	FIVE WITS
COUSIN	ANGEL
GOODS	DOCTOR
GOOD DEEDS	

Here beginneth a treatise how the high Father of Heaven sendeth Death to summon every creature to come and give account of their lives in this world, and is in manner of a moral play.

MESSENGER: I pray you all give your audience,
　And hear this matter with reverence,
　By figure° a moral play:
　The *Summoning of Everyman* called it is,
5　That of our lives and ending shows
　How transitory we be all day.°
　This matter is wondrous precious,
　But the intent of it is more gracious,
　And sweet to bear away.
10　The story saith: Man, in the beginning
　Look well, and take good heed to the ending,
　Be you never so gay!
　Ye think sin in the beginning full sweet,
　Which in the end causeth the soul to weep,
15　When the body lieth in clay.
　Here shall you see how Fellowship and Jollity,
　Both Strength, Pleasure, and Beauty,
　Will fade from thee as flower in May;
　For ye shall hear how our Heaven King
20　Calleth Everyman to a general reckoning:
　Give audience, and hear what he doth say.
　　　　　　　　　　　　　　　　　　　(*Exit.*)

(*God speaketh.*)

GOD: I perceive, here in my majesty,
　How that all creatures be to me unkind,°
　Living without dread in worldly prosperity:
　Of ghostly sight° the people be so blind,　　25
　Drowned in sin, they know me not for their God;
　In worldly riches is all their mind,
　They fear not my righteousness, the sharp rod.
　My law that I showed, when I for them died,
　They forget clean, and shedding of my blood red;　　30
　I hanged between two, it cannot be denied;
　To get them life I suffered to be dead;
　I healed their feet, with thorns hurt was my head.
　I could do no more than I did, truly;
　And now I see the people do clean forsake me:　　35
　They use the seven deadly sins damnable,
　As pride, covetise, wrath, and lechery
　Now in the world be made commendable;
　And thus they leave of angels the heavenly
　　company.
　Every man liveth so after his own pleasure,　　40
　And yet of their life they be nothing sure:
　I see the more that I them forbear
　The worse they be from year to year.
　All that liveth appaireth° fast;
　Therefore I will, in all the haste,　　45
　Have a reckoning of every man's person;
　For, and° I leave the people thus alone
　In their life and wicked tempests,
　Verily they will become much worse than beasts;
　For now one would by envy another up eat;　　50
　Charity they do all clean forget.
　I hoped well that every man
　In my glory should make his mansion,
　And thereto I had them all elect;
　But now I see, like traitors deject,°　　55

---

23. unkind: Ungrateful.　**25. ghostly sight:** Spiritual vision.
44. appaireth: Degenerates.　**47. and:** If.　**55. deject:** Abject.

3. By figure: In form.　**6. all day:** Always.

They thank me not for the pleasure that I to them
   meant,
Nor yet for their being that I them have lent.
I proffered the people great multitude of mercy,
And few there be that asketh it heartily.
60 They be so cumbered with worldly riches
That needs on them I must do justice,
On every man living without fear.
Where art thou, Death, thou mighty messenger?

(*Enter Death*.)

DEATH: Almighty God, I am here at your will,
65   Your commandment to fulfill.
GOD: Go thou to Everyman,
And show him, in my name,
A pilgrimage he must on him take,
Which he in no wise may escape;
70 And that he bring with him a sure reckoning
Without delay or any tarrying.
                   (*God withdraws*.)
DEATH: Lord, I will in the world go run overall,
And cruelly outsearch both great and small;
Every man will I beset that liveth beastly
75 Out of God's laws, and dreadeth not folly.
He that loveth riches I will strike with my dart,
His sight to blind, and from heaven to depart°—
Except that alms be his good friend—
In hell for to dwell, world without end.
80 Lo, yonder I see Everyman walking.
Full little he thinketh on my coming;
His mind is on fleshly lusts and his treasure,
And great pain it shall cause him to endure
Before the Lord, Heaven King.

(*Enter Everyman*.)

85 Everyman, stand still! Whither art thou going
Thus gaily? Hast thou thy Maker forget?
EVERYMAN: Why askest thou?
   Wouldest thou wit?°
DEATH: Yea, sir; I will show you:
90   In great haste I am sent to thee
From God out of his majesty.
EVERYMAN: What, sent to me?
DEATH: Yea, certainly.
Though thou have forget him here,
95 He thinketh on thee in the heavenly sphere,
As, ere we depart, thou shalt know.
EVERYMAN: What desireth God of me?
DEATH: That shall I show thee:
A reckoning he will needs have
100 Without any longer respite.
EVERYMAN: To give a reckoning longer leisure I crave;
This blind matter troubleth my wit.
DEATH: On thee thou must take a long journey;
Therefore thy book of count° with thee thou
   bring,

For turn° again thou cannot by no way.   105
And look thou be sure of thy reckoning,
For before God thou shalt answer, and show
Thy many bad deeds, and good but a few;
How thou hast spent thy life, and in what wise,
Before the chief Lord of paradise.   110
Have ado that we were in that way,°
For, wit thou well, thou shalt make none attorney.°
EVERYMAN: Full unready I am such reckoning to give.
I know thee not. What messenger art thou?
DEATH: I am Death, that no man dreadeth,°   115
For every man I rest,° and no man spareth;
For it is God's commandment
That all to me should be obedient.
EVERYMAN: O Death, thou comest when I had thee
   least in mind!
In thy power it lieth me to save;   120
Yet of my good° will I give thee, if thou will be kind:
Yea, a thousand pound shalt thou have,
And defer this matter till another day.
DEATH: Everyman, it may not be, by no way.
I set not by gold, silver, nor riches,   125
Ne by pope, emperor, king, duke, ne princes;
For, and I would receive gifts great,
All the world I might get;
But my custom is clean contrary.
I give thee no respite. Come hence, and not tarry. 130
EVERYMAN: Alas, shall I have no longer respite?
I may say Death giveth no warning!
To think on thee, it maketh my heart sick,
For all unready is my book of reckoning.
But twelve year and I might have abiding,°   135
My counting-book I would make so clear
That my reckoning I should not need to fear.
Wherefore, Death, I pray thee, for God's mercy,
Spare me till I be provided of remedy.
DEATH: Thee availeth not to cry, weep, and pray;   140
But haste thee lightly that thou were gone that
   journey,°
And prove thy friends if thou can;
For, wit thou well, the tide abideth no man,
And in the world each living creature
For Adam's sin must die of nature.°   145
EVERYMAN: Death, if I should this pilgrimage take,
And my reckoning surely make,
Show me, for saint charity,°
Should I not come again shortly?
DEATH: No, Everyman; and thou be once there,   150
Thou mayst never more come here,
Trust me verily.

---

77. **depart:** Separate.   88. **wit:** Know.   104. **count:** Account.

105. **turn:** Return.   111. **Have ado . . . that way:** Let us see
about making that journey.   112. **none attorney:** No one
[your] advocate.   115. **no man dreadeth:** Fears no man.
116. **rest:** Arrest.   121. **good:** Goods.   135. **But twelve
year . . . abiding:** If I could stay for just twelve more years.
141. **But haste thee . . . that journey:** But set off quickly on
your journey.   145. **of nature:** In the course of nature.
148. **for saint charity:** In the name of holy charity.

EVERYMAN: O gracious God in the high seat celestial,
  Have mercy on me in this most need!
155 Shall I have no company from this vale terrestrial
  Of mine acquaintance, that way me to lead?
DEATH: Yea, if any be so hardy
  That would go with thee and bear thee company.
  Hie thee that thou were gone to God's magnificence,
160 Thy reckoning to give before his presence.
  What, weenest° thou thy life is given thee,
  And thy worldly goods also?
EVERYMAN: I had wend° so, verily.
DEATH: Nay, nay; it was but lent thee;
165 For as soon as thou art go,
  Another a while shall have it, and then go therefro,
  Even as thou has done.
  Everyman, thou art mad! Thou hast thy wits five,
  And here on earth will not amend thy life;
170 For suddenly I do come.
EVERYMAN: O wretched caitiff,° whither shall I flee,
  That I might scape this endless sorrow?
  Now, gentle Death, spare me till to-morrow,
  That I may amend me
175 With good advisement.
DEATH: Nay, thereto I will not consent,
  Nor no man will I respite;
  But to the heart suddenly I shall smite
  Without any advisement.
180 And now out of thy sight I will me hie;
  See thou make thee ready shortly,
  For thou mayst say this is the day
  That no man living may scape away.
              (Exit Death.)
EVERYMAN: Alas, I may well weep with sighs deep!
185 Now have I no manner of company
  To help me in my journey, and me to keep;
  And also my writing is full unready,
  How shall I do now for to excuse me?
  I would to God I had never be get!°
190 To my soul a full great profit it had be;
  For now I fear pains huge and great.
  The time passeth. Lord, help, that all wrought!
  For though I mourn it availeth nought.
  The day passeth, and is almost ago;°
195 I wot not well what for to do.
  To whom were I best my complaint to make?
  What and I to Fellowship thereof spake,
  And showed him of this sudden chance?
  For in him is all mine affiance;°
200 We have in the world so many a day
  Be good friends in sport and play.
  I see him yonder, certainly.
  I trust that he will bear me company;
  Therefore to him will I speak to ease my sorrow.
205 Well met, good Fellowship, and good morrow!

(Fellowship speaketh.)

FELLOWSHIP: Everyman, good morrow, by this day!
  Sir, why lookest thou so piteously?
  If any thing be amiss, I pray thee me say,
  That I may help to remedy.
EVERYMAN: Yea, good Fellowship, yea;   210
  I am in great jeopardy.
FELLOWSHIP: My true friend, show to me your mind;
  I will not forsake thee to my life's end,
  In the way of good company.
EVERYMAN: That was well spoken, and lovingly.   215
FELLOWSHIP: Sir, I must needs know your heaviness;°
  I have pity to see you in any distress.
  If any have you wronged, ye shall revenged be,
  Though I on the ground be slain for thee—
  Though that I know before that I should die. 220
EVERYMAN: Verily, Fellowship, gramercy.°
FELLOWSHIP: Tush! by thy thanks I set not a straw.
  Show me your grief, and say no more.
EVERYMAN: If my heart should to you break,°
  And then you to turn your mind from me,   225
  And would not me comfort when ye hear me speak,
  Then should I ten times sorrier be.
FELLOWSHIP: Sir, I say as I will do indeed.
EVERYMAN: Then be you a good friend at need:
  I have found you true herebefore.   230
FELLOWSHIP: And so ye shall evermore;
  For, in faith, and thou go to hell,
  I will not forsake thee by the way.
EVERYMAN: Ye speak like a good friend; I believe you well.
  I shall deserve° it, and I may.   235
FELLOWSHIP: I speak of no deserving, by this day!
  For he that will say, and nothing do,
  Is not worthy with good company to go;
  Therefore show me the grief of your mind,
  As to your friend most loving and kind.   240
EVERYMAN: I shall show you how it is:
  Commanded I am to go a journey,
  A long way, hard and dangerous,
  And give a strait count, without delay,
  Before the high Judge, Adonai.°   245
  Wherefore, I pray you, bear me company,
  As ye have promised, in this journey.
FELLOWSHIP: That is matter indeed.° Promise is duty;
  But, and I should take such a voyage on me,
  I know it well, it should be to my pain; 250
  Also it maketh me afeard, certain.
  But let us take counsel here as well as we can,
  For your words would fear a strong man.
EVERYMAN: Why, ye said if I had need
  Ye would me never forsake, quick ne dead, 255
  Though it were to hell, truly.

---

161. **weenest:** Suppose. 163. **wend:** Supposed. 171. **caitiff:** Captive. 189. **be get:** Been born. 194. **ago:** Gone. 199. **affiance:** Trust.

216. **heaviness:** Sorrow. 221. **gramercy:** Thanks. 224. **break:** Open. 235. **deserve:** Repay. 245. **Adonai:** Hebrew name for God. 248. **That is matter indeed:** That is a good reason indeed [for asking me].

FELLOWSHIP: So I said, certainly,
But such pleasures be set aside, the sooth to say;
And also, if we took such a journey,
260　When should we come again?
EVERYMAN: Nay, never again, till the day of doom.
FELLOWSHIP: In faith, then will not I come there!
Who hath you these tidings brought?
EVERYMAN: Indeed, Death was with me here.
265　FELLOWSHIP: Now, by God that all hath bought,°
If Death were the messenger,
For no man that is living to-day
I will not go that loath journey—
Not for the father that begat me!
270　EVERYMAN: Ye promised otherwise, pardie.°
FELLOWSHIP: I wot well I said so, truly;
And yet if thou wilt eat, and drink, and make good
　　cheer,
Or haunt to women the lusty company,°
I would not forsake you while the day is clear,°
275　Trust me verily.
EVERYMAN: Yea, thereto ye would be ready!
To go to mirth, solace, and play,
Your mind will sooner apply,
Than to bear me company in my long journey.
280　FELLOWSHIP: Now, in good faith, I will not that way.
But and thou will murder, or any man kill,
In that I will help thee with a good will.
EVERYMAN: O, that is a simple advice indeed.
Gentle fellow, help me in my necessity!
285　We have loved long, and now I need;
And now, gentle Fellowship, remember me.
FELLOWSHIP: Whether ye have loved me or no,
By Saint John, I will not with thee go.
EVERYMAN: Yet, I pray thee, take the labor, and do so
　　much for me
290　To bring me forward, for saint charity,
And comfort me till I come without the town.
FELLOWSHIP: Nay, and thou would give me a new gown,
I will not a foot with thee go;
But, and thou had tarried, I would not have left
　　thee so.
295　And as now God speed thee in thy journey,
For from thee I will depart as fast as I may.
EVERYMAN: Whither away, Fellowship? Will thou
　　forsake me?
FELLOWSHIP: Yea, by my fay!° To God I betake° thee.
EVERYMAN: Farewell, good Fellowship; for thee my
　　heart is sore.
300　Adieu for ever! I shall see thee no more.
FELLOWSHIP: In faith, Everyman, farewell now at the
　　ending;
For you I will remember that parting is mourning.
　　　　　　　　　　　　　　　　(Exit Fellowship.)

EVERYMAN: Alack! shall we thus depart° indeed—
Ah, Lady, help!—without any more comfort?
Lo, Fellowship forsaketh me in my most need.　305
For help in this world whither shall I resort?
Fellowship herebefore with me would merry make,
And now little sorrow for me doth he take.
It is said, "In prosperity men friends may find,
Which in adversity be full unkind."　310
Now whither for succor shall I flee,
Sith° that Fellowship hath forsaken me?
To my kinsmen I will, truly,
Praying them to help me in my necessity;
I believe that they will do so,　315
For kind will creep where it may not go.°
I will go say,° for yonder I see them.
Where be ye now, my friends and kinsmen?

(Enter Kindred and Cousin.)

KINDRED: Here be we now at your commandment.
Cousin, I pray you show us your intent　320
In any wise, and do not spare.
COUSIN: Yea, Everyman, and to us declare
If ye be disposed to go anywhither;
For, wit you well, we will live and die together.
KINDRED: In wealth and woe we will with you hold,　325
For over his kin a man may be bold.°
EVERYMAN: Gramercy, my friends and kinsmen kind.
Now shall I show you the grief of my mind:
I was commanded by a messenger,
That is a high king's chief officer;　330
He bade me go a pilgrimage, to my pain,
And I know well I shall never come again;
Also I must give a reckoning strait,
For I have a great enemy° that hath me in wait,°
Which intendeth me for to hinder.　335
KINDRED: What account is that which ye must render?
That would I know.
EVERYMAN: Of all my works I must show
How I have lived and my days spent;
Also of ill deeds that I have used　340
In my time, sith life was me lent;
And of all virtues that I have refused.
Therefore, I pray you, go thither with me
To help to make mine account, for saint charity.
COUSIN: What, to go thither? Is that the matter?　345
Nay, Everyman, I had liefer fast bread and water°
All this five year and more.
EVERYMAN: Alas, that ever I was bore!
For now shall I never be merry,
If that you forsake me.　350

---

265. bought: Redeemed.　270. pardie: By God.　273. haunt to women the lusty company: Frequent the lively company of women.　274. while the day is clear: Until daybreak.　298. fay: Faith.　betake: Commend.

303. depart: Part.　312. Sith: Since.　316. for kind will creep where it may not go: For kinship will creep where it cannot walk; i.e., blood is thicker than water.　317. say: Essay, try.　326. For over his kin . . . may be bold: For a man may be sure of his kinsfolk.　334. enemy: Devil.　hath me in wait: Has me under observation.　346. liefer fast bread and water: Rather fast on bread and water.

KINDRED: Ah, sir, what ye be a merry man!
    Take good heart to you, and make no moan.
    But one thing I warn you, by Saint Anne—
    As for me, ye shall go alone.
355 EVERYMAN: My Cousin, will you not with me go?
    COUSIN: No, by our Lady! I have the cramp in my toe.
    Trust not to me, for, so God me speed,
    I will deceive you in your most need.
    KINDRED: It availeth not us to tice.°
360   Ye shall have my maid with all my heart;
    She loveth to go to feasts, there to be nice,°
    And to dance, and abroad to start:
    I will give her leave to help you in that journey,
    If that you and she may agree.
    EVERYMAN: Now show me the very effect° of your
365   mind:
    Will you go with me, or abide behind?
    KINDRED: Abide behind? Yea, that will I, and I may!
    Therefore farewell till another day.
                     (*Exit Kindred.*)
    EVERYMAN: How should I be merry or glad?
370   For fair promises men to me make,
    But when I have most need they me forsake.
    I am deceived; that maketh me sad.
    COUSIN: Cousin Everyman, farewell now,
    For verily I will not go with you.
375   Also of mine own an unready reckoning
    I have to account; therefore I make tarrying.
    Now God keep thee, for now I go.
                     (*Exit Cousin.*)
    EVERYMAN: Ah, Jesus, is all come hereto?
    Lo, fair words maketh fools fain;°
380   They promise, and nothing will do, certain.
    My kinsmen promised me faithfully
    For to abide with me steadfastly,
    And now fast away do they flee:
    Even so Fellowship promised me.
385   What friend were best me of to provide?°
    I lose my time here longer to abide.
    Yet in my mind a thing there is:
    All my life I have loved riches;
    If that my Good° now help me might,
390   He would make my heart full light.
    I will speak to him in this distress—
    Where art thou, my Goods and riches?

(*Goods speaks from a corner.*)

    GOODS: Who calleth me? Everyman? What! hast thou
      haste?
    I lie here in corners, trussed and piled so high,
395   And in chests I am locked so fast,
    Also sacked in bags. Thou mayst see with thine eye
    I cannot stir; in packs low I lie.
    What would ye have? Lightly° me say.

EVERYMAN: Come hither, Good, in all the haste thou
    may,
    For of counsel I must desire thee.   400
GOODS: Sir, and ye in the world have sorrow or
    adversity,
    That can I help you to remedy shortly.
EVERYMAN: It is another disease that grieveth me;
    In this world it is not, I tell thee so.
    I am sent for, another way to go,   405
    To give a strait count general
    Before the highest Jupiter of all;
    And all my life I have had joy and pleasure in thee,
    Therefore, I pray thee, go with me;
    For, peradventure, thou mayst before God
      Almighty   410
    My reckoning help to clean and purify;
    For it is said ever among
    That money maketh all right that is wrong.
GOODS: Nay, Everyman, I sing another song.
    I follow no man in such voyages;   415
    For, and I went with thee,
    Thou shouldst fare much the worse for me;
    For because on me thou did set thy mind,
    Thy reckoning I have made blotted and blind,
    That thine account thou cannot make truly;   420
    And that hast thou for the love of me.
EVERYMAN: That would grieve me full sore,
    When I should come to that fearful answer.
    Up, let us go thither together.
GOODS: Nay, not so! I am too brittle, I may not
    endure;   425
    I will follow no man one foot, be ye sure.
EVERYMAN: Alas, I have thee loved, and had great
    pleasure
    All my life-days on good and treasure.
GOODS: That is to thy damnation, without leasing,°
    For my love is contrary to the love everlasting;   430
    But if thou had me loved moderately during,
    As to the poor to give part of me,
    Then shouldst thou not in this dolor be,
    Nor in this great sorrow and care.
EVERYMAN: Lo, now was I deceived ere I was ware, 435
    And all I may wite° misspending of time.
GOODS: What, weenest thou that I am thine?
EVERYMAN: I had wend so.
GOODS: Nay, Everyman, I say no.
    As for a while I was lent thee;   440
    A season thou hast had me in prosperity.
    My condition is man's soul to kill;
    If I save one, a thousand I do spill.°
    Weenest thou that I will follow thee?
    Nay, not from this world, verily.   445
EVERYMAN: I had wend otherwise.
GOODS: Therefore to thy soul Good is a thief;
    For when thou art dead, this is my guise—
    Another to deceive in this same wise

---

359. **tice:** Entice.   361. **nice:** Wanton.   365. **effect:** Tenor.
379. **fain:** Glad.   385. **me of to provide:** To provide myself with.
389. **Good:** Goods.   398. **Lightly:** Quickly.

429. **without leasing:** Without a lie, i.e., truly.   436. **wite:** Blame.
443. **spill:** Ruin.

450 As I have done thee, and all to his soul's reprief.°
EVERYMAN: O false Good, cursed may thou be,
Thou traitor to God, that hast deceived me
And caught me in thy snare!
GOODS: Marry, thou brought thyself in care,
455 Whereof I am glad;
I must needs laugh, I cannot be sad.
EVERYMAN: Ah, Good, thou hast had long my heartly love;
I gave thee that which should be the Lord's above.
But wilt thou not go with me indeed?
460 I pray thee truth to say.
GOODS: No, so God me speed!
Therefore farewell, and have good day.
              (Exit Goods.)
EVERYMAN: O, to whom shall I make my moan
For to go with me in that heavy journey?
465 First Fellowship said he would with me gone;
His words were very pleasant and gay,
But afterward he left me alone.
Then spake I to my kinsmen, all in despair,
And also they gave me words fair;
470 They lacked no fair speaking,
But all forsook me in the ending.
Then went I to my Goods, that I loved best,
In hope to have comfort, but there had I least;
For my Goods sharply did me tell
475 That he bringeth many into hell.
Then of myself I was ashamed,
And so I am worthy to be blamed;
Thus may I well myself hate.
Of whom shall I now counsel take?
480 I think that I shall never speed
Till that I go to my Good Deed.
But, alas, she is so weak
That she can neither go nor speak;
Yet will I venture on her now.
485 My Good Deeds, where be you?

(Good Deeds speaks from the ground.)

GOOD DEEDS: Here I lie, cold in the ground;
Thy sins hath me sore bound,
That I cannot stir.
EVERYMAN: O Good Deeds, I stand in fear!
490 I must you pray of counsel,
For help now should come right well.°
GOOD DEEDS: Everyman, I have understanding
That ye be summoned account to make
Before Messias, of Jerusalem King;
And you do by me,° that journey with you will I
495 take.
EVERYMAN: Therefore I come to you, my moan to make;
I pray you that ye will go with me.

GOOD DEEDS: I would full fain, but I cannot stand, verily.
EVERYMAN: Why, is there anything on you fall?
GOOD DEEDS: Yea, sir, I may thank you of° all;   500
If ye had perfectly cheered me,
Your book of count full ready had be.
Look, the books of your works and deeds eke!°
Behold how they lie under the feet,
To your soul's heaviness.   505
EVERYMAN: Our Lord Jesus help me!
For one letter here I cannot see.
GOOD DEEDS: There is a blind reckoning in time of distress.
EVERYMAN: Good Deeds, I pray you help me in this need,
Or else I am for ever damned indeed;   510
Therefore help me to make reckoning
Before the Redeemer of all thing,
That King is, and was, and ever shall.
GOOD DEEDS: Everyman, I am sorry of your fall,
And fain would I help you, and I were able.   515
EVERYMAN: Good Deeds, your counsel I pray you give me.
GOOD DEEDS: That shall I do verily;
Though that on my feet I may not go,
I have a sister that shall with you also,
Called Knowledge, which shall with you abide,   520
To help you to make that dreadful reckoning.

(Enter Knowledge.)

KNOWLEDGE: Everyman, I will go with thee, and be thy guide,
In thy most need to go by thy side.
EVERYMAN: In good condition I am now in every thing,
And am wholly content with this good thing,   525
Thanked be God my creator.
GOOD DEEDS: And when she hath brought you there
Where thou shalt heal thee of thy smart,
Then go you with your reckoning and your Good Deeds together,
For to make you joyful at heart   530
Before the blessed Trinity.
EVERYMAN: My Good Deeds, gramercy!
I am well content, certainly,
With your words sweet.
KNOWLEDGE: Now go we together lovingly   535
To Confession, that cleansing river.
EVERYMAN: For joy I weep; I would we were there!
But, I pray you, give me cognition
Where dwelleth that holy man, Confession.
KNOWLEDGE: In the house of salvation: 540
We shall find him in that place,
That shall us comfort, by God's grace.

(Knowledge takes Everyman to Confession.)

450. reprief: Shame. 491. should come right well: Would be very welcome. 495. by me: As I advise.

500. of: For. 503. eke: Also.

Lo, this is Confession. Kneel down and ask mercy,
For he is in good conceit° with God Almighty.
EVERYMAN: O glorious fountain, that all uncleanness
545   doth clarify,
Wash from me the spots of vice unclean,
That on me no sin may be seen.
I come with Knowledge for my redemption,
Redempt with heart° and full contrition;
550 For I am commanded a pilgrimage to take,
And great accounts before God to make.
Now I pray you, Shrift, mother of salvation,
Help my Good Deeds for my piteous exclamation.
CONFESSION: I know your sorrow well, Everyman.
555 Because with Knowledge ye come to me,
I will you comfort as well as I can,
And a precious jewel I will give thee,
Called penance, voider of adversity;
Therewith shall your body chastised be,
560 With abstinence and perseverance in God's service.
Here shall you receive that scourge of me,
Which is penance strong that ye must endure,
To remember thy Savior was scourged for thee
With sharp scourges, and suffered it patiently;
565 So must thou, ere thou scape that painful pilgrimage.
Knowledge, keep him in this voyage,
And by that time Good Deeds will be with thee.
But in any wise be siker° of mercy,
For your time draweth fast; and° ye will saved be,
570 Ask God mercy, and he will grant truly.
When with the scourge of penance man doth him
    bind,
The oil of forgiveness then shall he find.
EVERYMAN: Thanked be God for his gracious work!
For now I will my penance begin;
575 This hath rejoiced and lighted my heart,
Though the knots be painful and hard within.
KNOWLEDGE: Everyman, look your penance that ye
    fulfill,
What pain that ever it to you be;
And Knowledge shall give you counsel at will
580 How your account ye shall make clearly.
EVERYMAN: O eternal God, O heavenly figure,
O way of righteousness, O goodly vision,
Which descended down in a virgin pure
Because he would every man redeem,
585 Which Adam forfeited by his disobedience:
O blessed Godhead, elect and high divine,
Forgive my grievous offense;
Here I cry thee mercy in this presence.°
O ghostly treasure, O ransomer and redeemer,
590 Of all the world hope and conductor,
Mirror of joy, and founder of mercy,
Which enlumineth heaven and earth thereby,
Hear my clamorous complaint, though it late be;

Receive my prayers, of thy benignity;
Though I be a sinner most abominable,   595
Yet let my name be written in Moses' table.°
O Mary, pray to the Maker of all thing,
Me for to help at my ending;
And save me from the power of my enemy,
For Death assaileth me strongly.   600
And, Lady, that I may by mean of thy prayer
Of your Son's glory to be partner,
By the means of his passion, I it crave;
I beseech you help my soul to save.
Knowledge, give me the scourge of penance;   605
My flesh therewith shall give acquittance:°
I will now begin, if God give me grace.
KNOWLEDGE: Everyman, God give you time and space!
Thus I bequeath you in the hands of our Saviour;
Now may you make your reckoning sure.   610
EVERYMAN: In the name of the Holy Trinity,
My body sore punished shall be:
Take this, body, for the sin of the flesh!

(*Scourges himself.*)

Also° thou delightest to go gay and fresh,
And in the way of damnation thou did me bring,   615
Therefore suffer now strokes and punishing.
Now of penance I will wade the water clear,
To save me from purgatory, that sharp fire.

(*Good Deeds rises from the ground.*)

GOOD DEEDS: I thank God, now I can walk and go,
And am delivered of my sickness and woe.   620
Therefore with Everyman I will go, and not spare;
His good works I will help him to declare.
KNOWLEDGE: Now, Everyman, be merry and glad!
Your Good Deeds cometh now; ye may not be sad.
Now is your Good Deeds whole and sound,   625
Going upright upon the ground.
EVERYMAN: My heart is light, and shall be evermore;
Now will I smite° faster than I did before.
GOOD DEEDS: Everyman, pilgrim, my special friend,
Blessed be thou without end;   630
For thee is preparate the eternal glory.
Ye have me made whole and sound,
Therefore I will bide by thee in every stound.°
EVERYMAN: Welcome, my Good Deeds; now I hear thy
    voice,
I weep for very sweetness of love.   635
KNOWLEDGE: Be no more sad, but ever rejoice;
God seeth thy living in his throne above.
Put on this garment to thy behoof,°

---

596. Moses' table: Medieval theologians regarded the two tablets given to Moses on Mount Sinai as symbols of baptism and penance. Thus Everyman is asking to be numbered among those who have escaped damnation by doing penance for their sins. **606. acquittance:** Satisfaction (as part of the sacrament of penance). **614. Also:** As. **628. smite:** Strike. **633. stound:** Trial. **638. behoof:** Advantage.

---

544. conceit: Esteem. **549. heart:** Heartfelt. **568. siker:** Sure. **569. and:** If. **588. in this presence:** In the presence of this company.

Which is wet with your tears,
640   Or else before God you may it miss,
When ye to your journey's end come shall.
EVERYMAN: Gentle Knowledge, what do ye it call?
KNOWLEDGE: It is a garment of sorrow:
From pain it will you borrow;°
645   Contrition it is,
That geteth forgiveness;
It pleaseth God passing well.
GOOD DEEDS: Everyman, will you wear it for your heal?°
EVERYMAN: Now blessed be Jesu, Mary's Son,
650   For now have I on true contrition.
And let us go now without tarrying;
Good Deeds, have we clear our reckoning?
GOOD DEEDS: Yea, indeed, I have it here.
EVERYMAN: Then I trust we need not fear;
655   Now, friends, let us not part in twain.
KNOWLEDGE: Nay, Everyman, that will we not, certain.
GOOD DEEDS: Yet must thou lead with thee
Three persons of great might.
EVERYMAN: Who should they be?
660   GOOD DEEDS: Discretion and Strength they hight,°
And thy Beauty may not abide behind.
KNOWLEDGE: Also ye must call to mind
Your Five Wits as for your counsellors.
GOOD DEEDS: You must have them ready at all hours.
665   EVERYMAN: How shall I get them hither?
KNOWLEDGE: You must call them all together,
And they will hear you incontinent.°
EVERYMAN: My friends, come hither and be present,
Discretion, Strength, my Five Wits, and Beauty.

(*Enter Beauty, Strength, Discretion, and Five Wits.*)

670   BEAUTY: Here at your will we be all ready.
What will ye that we should do?
GOOD DEEDS: That ye would with Everyman go,
And help him in his pilgrimage.
Advise you, will ye with him or not in that voyage?
675   STRENGTH: We will bring him all thither,
To his help and comfort, ye may believe me.
DISCRETION: So will we go with him all together.
EVERYMAN: Almighty God, lofed° may thou be!
I give thee laud that I have hither brought
Strength, Discretion, Beauty, and Five Wits. Lack I
680   nought.
And my Good Deeds, with Knowledge clear,
All be in my company at my will here;
I desire no more to my business.
STRENGTH: And I, Strength, will by you stand in distress,
685   Though thou would in battle fight on the ground.
FIVE WITS: And though it were through the world round,
We will not depart for sweet ne sour.

BEAUTY: No more will I unto death's hour,
Whatsoever thereof befall.
DISCRETION: Everyman, advise you first of all;   690
Go with a good advisement and deliberation.
We all give you virtuous monition°
That all shall be well.
EVERYMAN: My friends, harken what I will tell:
I pray God reward you in his heavenly sphere.   695
Now harken, all that be here,
For I will make my testament
Here before you all present:
In alms half my good I will give with my hands twain
In the way of charity, with good intent,   700
And the other half still shall remain
In queth,° to be returned there it ought to be.°
This I do in despite of the fiend of hell,
To go quit out of his peril°
Ever after and this day.   705
KNOWLEDGE: Everyman, harken what I say:
Go to priesthood, I you advise,
And receive of him in any wise°
The holy sacrament and ointment together.
Then shortly see ye turn again hither;   710
We will all abide you here.
FIVE WITS: Yea, Everyman, hie you that ye ready were.
There is no emperor, king, duke, ne baron,
That of God hath commission
As hath the least priest in the world being;   715
For of the blessed sacraments pure and benign
He beareth the keys, and thereof hath the cure°
For man's redemption—it is ever sure—
Which God for our soul's medicine
Gave us out of his heart with great pine.°   720
Here in this transitory life, for thee and me,
The blessed sacraments seven there be:
Baptism, confirmation, with priesthood good,
And the sacrament of God's precious flesh and blood,
Marriage, the holy extreme unction, and penance;   725
These seven be good to have in remembrance,
Gracious sacraments of high divinity.
EVERYMAN: Fain would I receive that holy body,
And meekly to my ghostly father I will go.
FIVE WITS: Everyman, that is the best that ye can do.   730
God will you to salvation bring,
For priesthood exceedeth all other thing:
To us Holy Scripture they do teach,
And converteth man from sin heaven to reach;
God hath to them more power given   735
Than to any angel that is in heaven.
With five words° he may consecrate,

---

692. monition: Forewarning.   702. queth: Bequest.   returned there it ought to be: This line probably refers to restitution, that is, the restoration to its proper owner of unlawfully acquired property.   704. quit out of his peril: Free out of his power.   708. in any wise: Without fail.   717. cure: Charge.   720. pine: Suffering.   737. five words: *Hoc est enim Corpus meum* ("For this is my body," the words of the consecration of the body of Christ at Mass).

---

644. borrow: Release.   648. heal: Salvation.   660. hight: Are called.   667. incontinent: Immediately.   678. lofed: Praised.

God's body in flesh and blood to make,
And handleth his Maker between his hands.
740 The priest bindeth and unbindeth all bands,
Both in earth and in heaven.
Thou ministers all the sacraments seven;
Though we kissed thy feet, thou were worthy;
Thou art surgeon that cureth sin deadly:
745 No remedy we find under God
But all only priesthood.°
Everyman, God gave priests that dignity,
And setteth them in his stead among us to be;
Thus be they above angels in degree.

(*Everyman goes to the priest to receive the last sacraments.*)

750 KNOWLEDGE: If priests be good, it is so, surely.
But when Jesus hanged on the cross with great
       smart,
There he gave out of his blessed heart
The same sacrament in great torment:
He sold them not to us, that Lord omnipotent.
755 Therefore Saint Peter the apostle doth say
That Jesu's curse hath all they
Which God their Savior do buy or sell,
Or they for any money do take or tell.°
Sinful priests giveth the sinners example bad;
Their children sitteth by other men's fires, I have
760   heard;
And some haunteth women's company
With unclean life, as lusts of lechery:
These be with sin made blind.
FIVE WITS: I trust to God no such may we find;
765 Therefore let us priesthood honor,
And follow their doctrine for our souls' succor.
We be their sheep, and they shepherds be
By whom we all be kept in surety.
Peace, for yonder I see Everyman come,
770 Which hath made true satisfaction.
GOOD DEEDS: Methink it is he indeed.

(*Reenter Everyman.*)

EVERYMAN: Now Jesu be your alder speed!°
I have received the sacrament for my redemption,
And then mine extreme unction:
775 Blessed be all they that counselled me to take it!
And now, friends, let us go without longer respite;
I thank God that ye have tarried so long.
Now set each of you on this rood° your hand,
And shortly follow me:
780 I go before there I would be; God be our guide!
STRENGTH: Everyman, we will not from you go
Till ye have done this voyage long.
DISCRETION: I, Discretion, will bide by you also.

746. **But all only priesthood:** Except only from the priesthood. **755–58. Therefore Saint Peter . . . do take or tell:** Reference to the sin of simony, the selling of church offices or
benefits. **tell:** Count out, i.e., sell. **772. your alder speed:**
The helper of you all. **778. rood:** Cross.

Scene from the Guthrie Theater production of *Everyman,*
directed by Robert Benedetti.

KNOWLEDGE: And though this pilgrimage be never so
       strong,°
I will never part you fro.   785
STRENGTH: Everyman, I will be as sure by thee
As ever I did by Judas Maccabee.°

784. **strong:** Grievous. **787. Judas Maccabee:** Judas Macca-
beus, who overcame Syrian domination and won religious freedom for the Jews in 165 BCE, believed that his strength came not
from worldly might but from heaven (1 Maccabees 3:19).

(*Everyman comes to his grave.*)

EVERYMAN: Alas, I am so faint I may not stand;
 My limbs under me doth fold.
790 Friends, let us not turn again to this land,
 Not for all the world's gold;
 For into this cave must I creep
 And turn to earth, and there to sleep.
BEAUTY: What, into this grave? Alas!
795 EVERYMAN: Yea, there shall ye consume, more and less.
BEAUTY: And what, should I smother here?
EVERYMAN: Yea, by my faith, and never more appear.
 In this world live no more we shall,
 But in heaven before the highest Lord of all.
800 BEAUTY: I cross out all this;° adieu, by Saint John!
 I take my cap in my lap,° and am gone.
EVERYMAN: What, Beauty, whither will ye?
BEAUTY: Peace, I am deaf; I look not behind me,
 Not and thou wouldest give me all the gold in thy
  chest.   (*Exit Beauty.*)
805 EVERYMAN: Alas, whereto may I trust?
 Beauty goeth fast away from me;
 She promised with me to live and die.
STRENGTH: Everyman, I will thee also forsake and
  deny;
 Thy game liketh° me not at all.
810 EVERYMAN: Why, then, ye will forsake me all?
 Sweet Strength, tarry a little space.
STRENGTH: Nay, sir, by the rood of grace!
 I will hie me from thee fast,
 Though thou weep till thy heart to-brast.°
815 EVERYMAN: Ye would ever bide by me, ye said.
STRENGTH: Yea, I have you far enough conveyed.
 Ye be old enough, I understand,
 Your pilgrimage to take on hand;
 I repent me that I hither came.
820 EVERYMAN: Strength, you to displease I am to blame;
 Yet promise is debt, this ye well wot.
STRENGTH: In faith, I care not.
 Thou art but a fool to complain;
 You spend your speech and waste your brain.
825 Go thrust thee into the ground! (*Exit Strength.*)
EVERYMAN: I had wend surer I should you have found.
 He that trusteth in his Strength
 She him deceiveth at the length.
 Both Strength and Beauty forsaketh me;
830 Yet they promised me fair and lovingly.
DISCRETION: Everyman, I will after Strength be gone;
 As for me, I will leave you alone.
EVERYMAN: Why, Discretion, will ye forsake me?
DISCRETION: Yea, in faith, I will go from thee,
835 For when Strength goeth before
 I follow after evermore.
EVERYMAN: Yet, I pray thee, for the love of the Trinity,

Look in my grave once piteously.
DISCRETION: Nay, so nigh will I not come;
 Farewell, every one! (*Exit Discretion.*) 840
EVERYMAN: O, all thing faileth, save God alone—
 Beauty, Strength, and Discretion;
 For when Death bloweth his blast,
 They all run from me full fast.
FIVE WITS: Everyman, my leave now of thee I take; 845
 I will follow the other, for here I thee forsake.
EVERYMAN: Alas, then may I wail and weep,
 For I took you for my best friend.
FIVE WITS: I will no longer thee keep;
 Now farewell, and there an end. 850
     (*Exit Five Wits.*)
EVERYMAN: O Jesu, help! All hath forsaken me.
GOOD DEEDS: Nay, Everyman; I will bide with thee.
 I will not forsake thee indeed;
 Thou shalt find me a good friend at need.
EVERYMAN: Gramercy, Good Deeds! Now may I true
  friends see. 855
 They have forsaken me, every one;
 I loved them better than my Good Deeds alone.
 Knowledge, will ye forsake me also?
KNOWLEDGE: Yea, Everyman, when ye to Death shall
  go;
 But not yet, for no manner of danger. 860
EVERYMAN: Gramercy, Knowledge, with all my
  heart.
KNOWLEDGE: Nay, yet I will not from hence depart
 Till I see where ye shall become.
EVERYMAN: Methink, alas, that I must be gone
 To make my reckoning and my debts pay, 865
 For I see my time is nigh spent away.
 Take example, all ye that this do hear or see,
 How they that I loved best do forsake me,
 Except my Good Deeds that bideth truly.
GOOD DEEDS: All earthly things is but vanity: 870
 Beauty, Strength, and Discretion do man forsake,
 Foolish friends, and kinsmen, that fair spake—
 All fleeth save Good Deeds, and that am I.
EVERYMAN: Have mercy on me, God most mighty;
 And stand by me, thou mother and maid, holy
  Mary. 875
GOOD DEEDS: Fear not; I will speak for thee.
EVERYMAN: Here I cry God mercy.
GOOD DEEDS: Short our end, and minish our pain;
 Let us go and never come again.
EVERYMAN: Into thy hands, Lord, my soul I 880
  commend;
 Receive it, Lord, that it be not lost.
 As thou me boughtest, so me defend,
 And save me from the fiend's boast,
 That I may appear with that blessed host
 That shall be saved at the day of doom. 885
 In manus tuas, of mights most
 For ever, *commendo spiritum meum.*°

800. I cross out all this: I cancel all this, i.e., my promise to stay with you. **801. I take my cap in my lap:** Doff my cap [so low that it comes] into my lap. **809. liketh:** Pleases. **814. brast:** Break.

886–87. *In manus tuas…commendo spiritum meum:* Into your hands, most mighty One for ever, I commend my spirit.

(*He sinks into his grave.*)

KNOWLEDGE: Now hath he suffered that we all shall
        endure;
    The Good Deeds shall make all sure.
890   Now hath he made ending;
    Methinketh that I hear angels sing,
    And make great joy and melody
    Where Everyman's soul received shall be.
ANGEL: Come, excellent elect spouse, to Jesu!
895   Hereabove thou shalt go
    Because of thy singular virtue.
    Now the soul is taken the body fro,
    Thy reckoning is crystal-clear.
    Now shalt thou into the heavenly sphere,
900   Unto the which all ye shall come
    That liveth well before the day of doom.

(*Enter Doctor.*)

DOCTOR: This moral men may have in mind.
    Ye hearers, take it of worth, old and young,
    And forsake Pride, for he deceiveth you in the end;
    And remember Beauty, Five Wits, Strength, and
905   Discretion,

They all at the last do every man forsake,
Save his Good Deeds there doth he take.
But beware, for and they be small
Before God, he hath no help at all;
None excuse may be there for every man.   910
Alas, how shall he do then?
For after death amends may no man make,
For then mercy and pity doth him forsake.
If his reckoning be not clear when he doth come,
God will say: "*Ite, maledicti, in ignem eternum.*"° 915
And he that hath his account whole and sound,
High in heaven he shall be crowned;
Unto which place God bring us all thither,
That we may live body and soul together.
Thereto help the Trinity!   920
Amen, say ye, for saint charity.

Thus endeth this moral play of Everyman.

915. "*Ite, maledicti, in ignem eternum*": Depart, ye cursed,
into everlasting fire.

Renaissance Drama

Italian Drama

The period following the Middle Ages in Europe, from about the fourteenth to the seventeenth centuries, is known as the *Renaissance,* a term meaning "rebirth." In this period a shift away from medieval values and culture was motivated by a revival of classical learning; advances in physics, astronomy, and the biological sciences; exploration of the "new world" of the Americas; and political and economic developments. This shift was not abrupt, however; it was gradual, like a thaw. It began in the south, in Italy, in the late 1300s and moved northward through the activities of scholars, travelers, performers, and writers, until it reached England sometime late in the 1400s.

The Renaissance built on medieval culture and at the same time developed a secular understanding of the individual in society that eventually transformed this culture, long dominated by the Roman Catholic Church in many spheres—artistic, intellectual, political, as well as spiritual. The transformation was influenced by the work of great writers, scholars, philosophers, and scientists such as Desiderius Erasmus (1466?–1536), Niccolò Machiavelli (1469–1527), Nicolaus Copernicus (1473–1543), Francis Bacon (1561–1626), and Galileo Galilei (1564–1642). In addition, the rise in power of the guilds and the increase in wealth of the successful Italian trading states, which produced large and influential families in cities such as Florence, Venice, Milan, and Genoa, contributed to the erosion of the Church's power.

Italian scholars, following classical models, had begun in the last decades of the fourteenth century to center their studies on human achievements. Such studies, known as the humanities, became the chief concern of the most innovative thinkers of the day. Their interests were well served by the rediscovery of ancient Greek philosophical and scientific texts. Although ancient texts had been preserved in monasteries for centuries, knowledge of them was restricted. A new demand for classical texts, fed by the humanists' focus on ancient models as the source of wisdom and by their return to a liberal arts curriculum established by the Greeks, led to the wide dissemination of the works of Plato, Aristotle, Cicero, and important Greek dramatists during the Renaissance. The achievement of the ancients was an inspiration to Renaissance writers and reaffirmed their conviction that a study of the humanities was the key to transforming the old medieval attitudes into a new, dynamic worldview.

The Italian Theater   Most medieval Italian theater depended on portable stages, but it was clear in the last decades of the fourteenth century that to present the newly rediscovered Roman or Greek plays, something more closely resembling the original Greek theater would be necessary. Fortunately, *The Ten Books of Architecture* (written c. 16–13 BCE) of the great Roman architect Vitruvius (first century BCE) was rediscovered in a manuscript in the monastery of St. Gall in Switzerland. It included detailed plans for the Greek-inspired Roman theater.

Using Vitruvius's designs, the Italians began building stages that were raised platforms with a FRONS SCAENA, the flat front wall used in the Roman theater. The earliest Italian woodcuts show the stages to be relatively simple with pillars supporting a roof or cover. Curtains stretched between the pillars permitted the actors to enter and exit. Usually, three "doors" with names over each indicated the houses of specific characters.

The study of Roman architecture eventually produced, in 1584, one of the wonders of the Renaissance, the Olympic Theater (Teatro Olimpico) in Vicenza, designed by the great Renaissance architect Andrea Palladio (1508–1580), whose interpretation of Roman architecture was so compelling that it influenced architecture all over the world (Figure 9). The Olympic Theater, which has been preserved and is still used for performances, has an orchestra, a semicircular seating area, and a multistory frons scaena. But it also has several vistas of streets constructed in three-dimensional forced perspective running backward from the frons scaena.

The Olympic Theater was built with an essentially conservative design that worked well for Roman plays but not for Renaissance plays. It did not inspire new theater designs. In newer theaters, Italian plays had begun to use scenery and painted backdrops that could be changed to suggest a change in location of the action. Carefully painted backdrops were also effective in increasing illusion: one backdrop could immediately locate an action on a city street, and another could help shift the audience imaginatively to a woodland scene. These innovations proved difficult in the Olympic Theater.

The theory of vanishing-point perspective developed by the architect Filippo Brunelleschi (1377–1446) and published by Leon Battista Alberti in *On Painting* in 1435 helped revolutionize the design of flat theatrical backdrops. Earlier Renaissance painters had had no way to establish a firm sense of perspective on a flat surface, so all three-dimensional objects appeared flat; all space in a landscape or cityscape seemed shortened and unreal. The use of a single vanishing point — in which lines were lightly drawn from the edges of the canvas (or theatrical backdrop) so that they met in a single point in the center — made it possible to show buildings, trees, and figures in their proper proportion to one another (Figure 10). For the first time, Renaissance painters could achieve lifelike illusions on a flat surface. On the other hand, three-dimensional scenery was possible in the Olympic Theater — as well as some others — at this time, and the illusion of reality was thus intensified.

The designer Sebastiano Serlio (1475–1554) used the vanishing-point technique, intensified by receding lines of tiles in the floor and on the painted

ABOVE: FIGURE 9. Designed by Andrea Palladio, the Teatro Olimpico (begun 1579) in Vicenza, Italy, was the first indoor theater of the Renaissance. The scaena's openings produced an illusion of depth. RIGHT: Figure 10. Perspective setting designed by Baldassare Peruzzi (1481–1536).

backdrop. Serlio established all-purpose settings for comedy, tragedy, and satire. The rigidity of the backdrops for comedy and tragedy—both used a piazza, a small town square, ringed by stone buildings—restricted their use. But the setting for satire was rustic: trees, bushes, a couple of cottages. Until the nineteenth century, European theaters were equipped with sets of backdrops and wingpieces derived from his designs.

The most important and long-lasting development of Italian theater design in the mid-1500s was the PROSCENIUM ARCH, a "frame" that surrounds the stage, permitting the audience to look in on the scene, whether in a room or in a town square. The arch lent a finished touch to the theater, separating the action from the audience and distancing the actors. The proscenium arch is common in most theaters today.

Commedia dell'Arte

Renaissance Italy had two traditions of theater. *Commedia erudita* was learned, almost scholarly, in its interests in Roman staging and Roman plays. COMMEDIA DELL'ARTE was less reverent, more slapstick, and generally more popular. It is difficult, however, to say which was more influential on literature over the years. Each made its contribution.

In terms of acting and storytelling, the influence of the commedia dell'arte is almost unparalleled. The term means "comedy performed by professionals." The actors usually had grown up in performing families that made their living touring the countryside, performing at fairs and on feast days. From the early Renaissance through the eighteenth century, the commedia dell'arte entertained all of Europe and influenced comic theater in every nation.

The essence of commedia dell'arte was improvised scripts. A general narrative outline served as a basis, but the speeches were improvised to a degree (with some reliance on set elements and on experience with performing the same role many times). The principal characters were types who soon became familiar all over Europe: Pantalone, the often magisterial but miserly old man; Arlecchino (Harlequin), the cunning clown. Pulcinella, the Punch of Punch and Judy, and Columbina, the innocent *zanni* (servant characters), began as clowns. They joined a host of other STOCK CHARACTERS such as pedantic lawyers, a braggart captain, and a serving maid. Certain versions of general characters—such as Arlecchino, who began as a simple *zanno*—became famous and were copied in many countries. When Volpone calls Mosca a "zany" near the end of Ben Jonson's *Volpone,* he reminds his audience that his characters are indebted to the *zanni* in commedia dell'arte. Knowing who the characters were even before the play began was a convenience that Renaissance audiences enjoyed.

The youthful lovers in the commedia did not require masks, but the old men, the *zanni,* and other characters all had masks that identified them and made them look, to modern eyes, rather grotesque. These masks survive today in the carnival, in Venice, where the commedia began. Stock characters thrive in popular comedies everywhere. Molière and, much later, Bernard Shaw depended on them. One of comedy's greatest sources of energy lies in the delight that audiences have always taken in stock characters. Today hardly a situation comedy on television could survive without them.

The staging of commedia dell'arte was simple. It often took place in open air, but sometimes indoors in a more formal theatrical setting. Sometimes performers dispensed with the stage altogether and worked in marketplaces. Their scenarios were farcical crowd pleasers filled with buffoonery. They were based on the LAZZO and the BURLA. The *burla* was the general plot for any given performance. *Lazzi* were comic routines something like Abbott and Costello's "Who's on First?" skit. Abbott and Costello developed their routine for burlesque, a form of comedy popular in the first half of the twentieth century centering on broad gags, routines, and running jokes. *Lazzi* were carefully planned to seem to be spontaneous interruptions of the action. Actor Chevy Chase's trademark pratfall as he enters a scene is a descendant of the sixteenth-century *lazzo.*

Elizabethan Drama

The reign of Queen Elizabeth I (1558–1603) is known as the Elizabethan age in England—a period of discovery and prosperity as well as a period of great achievement in the arts, especially drama. Sir Francis Drake and Sir Walter Raleigh ventured across the Atlantic Ocean to the "New World," and England secured its economic future by defeating the invasion attempt of the Spanish Armada in 1588. England had become Protestant in the 1530s—one reason Catholic Spain felt it needed to subdue the nation.

Elizabethan England, especially after the defeat of the Armada, produced one of the great ages of drama, rivaling the great age of Greece. During this period, playwrights such as Thomas Kyd (1558–1594), Christopher Marlowe (1564–1593), William Shakespeare (1564–1616), Ben Jonson (1572–1637), John Marston (1576–1634), John Fletcher (1579–1625), John Webster (1580?–1625?), Thomas Middleton (1580?–1627), and John Ford (1586–1639) drew crowds by the thousands.

That the Elizabethans enjoyed plays with a moral basis is plain from the fact that so much of the great drama of the late 1500s and early 1600s is moral in character. Still, early Elizabethan plays were less obviously moralistic than the then-popular morality plays. They did not aim specifically to teach a moral lesson, although there are many lessons to be learned from Shakespeare and his contemporaries.

During Shakespeare's youth, wandering players put on a number of plays from REPERTORY, their stock of perhaps a dozen current plays they could perform. How many players there were or what their source of plays was we do not know. Much of what we know comes directly from *Hamlet* and the appearance of the players who perform Hamlet's "Mouse-trap." What we learn there tells us that dramatic styles had developed in the English country-side and that theater was thriving.

The Elizabethan Theater

The design of the Elizabethan theater is a matter of some speculation. Many of the plays popular before the theaters were built were performed in a square inn yard, with a balcony above. The audience looked out their windows or stood in the yard. One location of the earliest English drama is the Inns of Court, essentially a college for law students in London, where students staged plays. The audience there would have been learned, bright, and imaginative. Indeed, the first English tragedy, *Gorboduc,* by Thomas Sackville and Thomas Norton, was played indoors at the Inner Temple, one of the Inns of Court, in 1562, before Marlowe and Shakespeare were born.

The shape of the early theaters was often octagonal or circular, like the bear pits in which bears, tied to stakes, were baited by dogs for the amusement of the audience. The stage was raised about five feet from the ground with levels of seating in several galleries. Approximately half the area over the stage was roofed and contained machinery to lower actors from the "heavens"; it was painted blue with stars to simulate the sky. Some stages were approximately twenty-five by forty feet. Doors or curtained openings at the back of the stage served for entrances and exits, and at the back of the stage was a special room for costume changes. The stage may have contained a section that was normally curtained but that opened to reveal an interior, such as a bedroom. The existence of this feature is, however, in considerable dispute.

Although professional players' groups had long been licensed to perform in France and Italy, until the 1570s professional actors—those who had no other trade—did not enjoy favor in England. Such people could be arrested for vagrancy. The law, however, changed, and actors with royal patronage were permitted to perform. The history of theater changed, too. In 1576 James Burbage (father of the famous star of Shakespeare's plays, Richard Burbage) built the first building made specially for plays in England.

Soon there were other theaters: the Swan, the Globe (Figure 11), the Rose, the Fortune, the Hope. The Globe was large enough to accommodate two to three thousand people. Because these theaters were open-air, they could not be used in winter, but all were extraordinarily successful. Shakespeare, who was part owner of the Globe and, later, of the second indoor Blackfriars Theatre, received money from admission fees and from his role as chief playwright. He became rich enough to retire in splendid style to Stratford, his hometown. Few other Elizabethan actors and playwrights had as much of a financial stake in their work as did Shakespeare.

The Elizabethan Actor

In the early 1500s professional companies roamed the countryside with, usually, four actors and a boy who could play the female roles. They may also have been accompanied by musicians. They found work where they could, and sometimes they stirred up controversy and were prevented from performing. Numerous laws enacted to restrict them were rarely enforced. Queen Elizabeth issued a license for a professional company to James Burbage (d. 1597) in

FIGURE 11. A conjectural reconstruction of the (second) Globe Theatre, 1614–1644.

AA   Main entrances to auditorium
B   Yard for standing spectators
CC   Entrances to lowest gallery
DD   Entrances to staircase leading to upper galleries
EE   "Gentlemen's Rooms"
F   The stage
G   The stage trap (leading from the "Hell" beneath the stage)
H   Curtained space for "discovery" scenes
J   Upper stage
K   The "Heavens." (This area was probably covered with a stretched canopy that was painted to represent the sky.)

L   Backing painted with clouds. A shutter is here shown open to allow a god's throne to travel forward. (c.f. "Cymbeline," Act V sc. IV)
M   The throne about to descend to the stage
N   Backstage area (or "Tiring-house")
O   Wardrobe and dressing-rooms
P   Spectator galleries
Q   "Fly" gallery in the Heavens
R   Playhouse flag (reached from top landing of staircase, and raised to denote performance days)

FIGURE 12. William Kempe, a principal comic actor in Shakespeare's earlier plays, is shown playing a pipe and tabour.

1576, the year he built the first theater in England, called simply The Theatre. Burbage's son, Richard Burbage (1567–1619), who was born in Stratford-on-Avon (like Shakespeare, his partner in the theater), became one of the most distinguished actors of the age. He played all the important tragic roles in Shakespeare's plays. By the time the Globe Theatre was built in 1599, their company, The Chamberlain's Men, included some of the most acclaimed actors of the day. One of them, Will Kempe (fl. 1600), was the most noted comic actor of the age (Figure 12). He was both a gifted clown and a brilliant dancer. However, as popular as he was with the audience, he left the company suddenly for reasons still unknown and acted elsewhere. His great roles, the Fool in *King Lear*, the first grave digger in *Hamlet*, and Dogberry in *Much Ado About Nothing*, were filled by another actor, Robert Armin (1568–1615), whose reputation grew as large as Kempe's.

The popularity of actors such as Burbage, Kempe, and Armin indicates how powerful and far-reaching the stage was in Elizabethan England. Despite their successes, actors were still regarded as somewhat disreputable, and stories were told of actors disguised as royalty stopping in a tavern for a drink and fooling the populace, who grew surly at such tricks.

The contemporary styles of acting were probably developed by wandering players throughout the early and mid-1500s—and perhaps even earlier. In *Hamlet* Shakespeare introduces a group of roaming players and offers us a sample of their high-style formal dialogue, which contrasts sharply with Shakespeare's dialogue. Hamlet critiques and instructs the players, whose style is high-flown and overdone. In the open-air theaters, this style of acting seems to have evolved into a declamatory mode, in which the actor stands and makes his voice heard throughout the large and sometimes noisy audience. The style Hamlet critiques is probably one that he saw on stages in London. Many of the Elizabethan actors played to the audience as much as they related to each other, a trait that seems to have developed in response to the structure of the stage, with an audience on three sides and with some notables actually sitting on the stage itself. On the other hand, the Globe Theatre reportedly permitted actors to speak more naturally to one another and thus to render a more realistic performance.

The Elizabethan Audience

The entrance fee to the theaters was a penny, probably the equivalent of five to ten dollars in today's money. For another penny one could take a seat, probably on a bench, in one of the upper galleries. In some theaters more private spaces were available as well. A great many playgoers were satisfied to stand around the stage and were thus nicknamed "groundlings." Hamlet calls them the "understanding gentlemen of the ground." The more academic playwrights, Marlowe and Jonson, used the term to mean those who would not perfectly understand the significance of the plays.

Shakespeare and other Elizabethan playwrights expected a widely diverse audience—from coarse to extraordinarily polished. Shakespeare had the gift, as did Marlowe and even Jonson in his comedies, to appeal to them all. Shakespeare's plays were given in public playhouses open to everyone. They were also given in university theaters, as in the case of *Macbeth;* in indoor private theaters; and in royal command performances. Shakespeare's universality reveals itself in his appeal to many different kinds of people.

Female Characters on the English Stage

Because the theater was considered morally questionable, women were not allowed to act on English stages. Boys and young men played the parts of young female characters such as Juliet, Desdemona, and Ophelia. No contemporary commentator makes any complaint about having to put up with a boy playing the part of Juliet or any of Shakespeare's other love interests, such as Desdemona in *Othello,* Ophelia in *Hamlet,* or even Queen Cleopatra. Older women, such as the Nurse in *Romeo and Juliet,* were played by some of the gifted male character actors of the company.

The Masque

The Elizabethan MASQUE was a special entertainment of royalty. It was a celebration that included a rudimentary plot, a great deal of singing and dancing, and magnificent costumes and lighting. Masques were usually performed only once, often to celebrate a royal marriage. Masque audiences participated in the dances and were usually delighted by complex machinery that lifted or lowered characters from the skies. The masque was devised in Italy in the 1570s by Count Giovanni Bardi, founder of the Florentine Camerata, a Renaissance group of theatergoers sponsored by Lorenzo de' Medici.

The geniuses of the masque are generally considered to have been Ben Jonson and Inigo Jones. Jones was the architect whose Banqueting Hall at Whitehall in London, which still stands, provided the setting for most of the great masques of the seventeenth century. Jonson and Jones worked together from 1605 to 1631 to produce a remarkable body of masques that today resemble the bones of a dinosaur: what we read on the page suggests in only the vaguest way what the presentation must have been like when the masques were mounted.

Because of the expenses of costuming and staging, most masques were too costly to be produced more than once. The royal exchequer was often burdened in Queen Elizabeth's time, and more so after King James took the throne in 1603. Masque costumes were impressive, the scenery astounding, and the effects amazing. In all of this, the words—which are, after all, at the center of Shakespeare's plays as well as other plays of the period—were of least account. As a result of the emphasis on the machinery and designs—the work of Inigo Jones—Jonson abandoned their partnership in a huff, complaining that he could not compete with the scene painters and carpenters.

The value placed on spectacle in the masques tells us something about the taste of the aristocrats, who enjoyed sumptuous foods, clothes, and amusements. Eventually, audiences of the public theaters hungered for spectacle, too. Their appetite was satisfied by masques inserted in the plays of Marston, Webster, and Shakespeare, whose masque in *The Tempest* is a delightful short tribute to the genre. An added device for achieving spectacular effects onstage was huge storm machines installed in the Globe. Some say that one reason Shakespeare wrote *The Tempest* was to take advantage of the new equipment. Foreign visitors described London theaters as gorgeous places of entertainment far surpassing their own. The quest for more intense spectacle eventually led to disaster in one theater. The Globe actually burned down in 1613 because a cannon in the roof above the stage misfired and brought the house down in real flames.

The royal demand for masques was unaffected. As Francis Bacon said in his essay "On Masques" (1625), "These things are but toys to come amongst such serious observations. But yet, since princes will have such things, it is better they should be graced with elegancy than daubed with cost. Dancing to song is a thing of great state and pleasure."

Spanish Drama

The Spanish independently developed a corral, or open theatrical space, resembling the Elizabethan inn yard, in which they produced plays. This development may have been an accident of architecture—because of the widespread need for inns and for places to store horses—that permitted the symmetry of growth of the English Elizabethan and the Spanish Golden Age theaters.

The most important playwright of the Spanish theater was Lope de Vega (1562–1635), who is said to have written twelve hundred plays (seven hundred fifty survive). Many of them are relatively brief, and some resemble the scenarios for the commedia dell'arte. A good number, though, are full-length and impressive works, such as *The Sheep Well, The King, The Greatest Alcalde*, and *The Gardener's Dog*. Pedro Calderón de la Barca (1600–1681) became, on Lope de Vega's death, the reigning Spanish playwright. His *Life Is a Dream* is performed regularly throughout the world. Calderón became a priest in 1651 and wrote religious plays that on rare occasions got him into trouble with the Inquisition, an agency of the Catholic Church that searched out and punished heresy. He was especially imaginative in his use of stage machinery and especially gifted in producing philosophical and poetic dialogue.

Renaissance Drama Timeline

DATE	THEATER	POLITICAL	SOCIAL/CULTURAL
1300–1400	**1377–1446:** Filippo Brunelleschi, an Italian architect, develops vanishing-point perspective, which allows theatrical scenery to be drawn in realistic proportions.		**1348–1353:** Boccaccio's *Decameron* becomes a model for Italian prose. **c. 1386–1466:** Donatello, Italian painter and major innovator in Renaissance sculpture
1400–1500	**1414:** Rediscovery of Vitruvius's *De Architectura* (90 BCE). After its publication in 1486, the treatise significantly influences the development of staging practices.		**1450:** Florence under the Medici family becomes the center of the Renaissance and humanism. **1452–1519:** Leonardo da Vinci, brilliant inventor, architect, musician, and artist **1469–1527:** Niccolò Machiavelli, who writes the political treatise *The Prince* in 1513 and the comedy *Mandragola* between 1513 and 1520 **1473–1543:** Nicolaus Copernicus, founder of modern astronomy
	1495: The Dutch morality play *Elckerlijk* by Peter Dorland van Diest: possibly the prototype for the English *Everyman*.	**1494:** The Parliament of Drogheda marks the subservience of Ireland to England.	**1496:** Henry VII commissions Venetian navigator John Cabot (1450–1498) to discover a new trade route to Asia. **1497:** Cabot reaches the east coast of North America. **1497:** Vasco da Gama (c. 1469–1524) rounds the Cape of Good Hope.
1500–1600	**1508:** Vernacular drama begins in Italy with Ludovico Ariosto's *The Casket*. **1508:** The Hôtel de Bourgogne, a permanent theater building, opens in Paris.	**1503:** James IV of Scotland marries Margaret Tudor, daughter of Henry VII.	**1507:** Pope Julius II announces the sale of indulgences to finance the rebuilding of St. Peter's Basilica in Rome. **1509–1564:** John Calvin, Swiss reformer **c. 1509:** A massive slave trade begins in the New World. **1512:** Copernicus's *Commentariolus* states that the earth and other planets turn around the sun. **1514–1564:** Andreas Vesalius, Dutch physician, founder of modern anatomy **1516–1547:** Henry Howard, Earl of Surrey, English poet
	1512: The word *masque* is first used to denote a poetic drama.	**1517:** Martin Luther protests the sale of indulgences by posting his 95 theses on a church door in Wittenberg, Germany, thus launching the Protestant Reformation in Germany.	**1519:** Hernando Cortés enters Tenochtitlán, capital of Mexico; is received by Montezuma, the Aztec ruler; and assumes control of Mexico in 1521.

Renaissance Drama Timeline (continued)

DATE	THEATER	POLITICAL	SOCIAL/CULTURAL
1500–1600 (continued)	**1550–1650:** Golden Age of Spanish drama. The two principal playwrights are Lope de Vega (1562–1635) and Pedro Calderón de la Barca (1600–1681).	**1534:** Henry VIII (reigned 1509–1547) breaks with the Roman Catholic Church.	**1522:** Luther translates the New Testament into German and translates the Old Testament in 1534.
	1558–1594: Playwright Thomas Kyd, author of *The Spanish Tragedy* (c. 1587)	**1535:** Henry VIII's Act of Supremacy names him head of the Church of England. Sir Thomas More is executed after refusing to comply with the Act.	**1547–1616:** Miguel de Cervantes, author of the novel *Don Quixote* and many plays
	1562: The First English tragedy, *Gorboduc*, is performed at the Inns of Court.	**1547:** Ivan IV (the Terrible) becomes czar of Russia. Moscow is destroyed by fire in the same year.	**c. 1552–1599:** Edmund Spenser, English poet, author of *Faerie Queene*
	1564–1593: Christopher Marlowe, author of *Doctor Faustus* (c. 1588), *Tamburlaine* (1590), and *Edward the Second* (c. 1592)	**1553–1558:** Reign of Mary I of England. The country returns temporarily to Catholicism.	**1554–1586:** Sir Philip Sidney, poet and soldier, author of *An Apology for Poetry*
	1564–1616: William Shakespeare	**1558–1603:** Reign of Elizabeth I in England. Protestantism becomes the religion of the realm. England emerges as a world power.	**1561–1626:** Francis Bacon, English philosopher and statesman
	c. 1568: Formation of the Italian commedia dell'arte company I Gelosi		**1564–1642:** Galileo Galilei, Italian astronomer
	1572–1637: Playwright Ben Jonson, author of *Volpone* (1605) and *Bartholomew Fair* (1614)	**1570:** Japan opens the port of Nagasaki to trade with the West.	**1571–1630:** Johannes Kepler, German astronomer. His laws accurately describe the revolutions of the planets around the sun.
	1574: The Earl of Leicester's Men, the first important acting troupe in London, is licensed.	**1572:** At the Saint Bartholomew's Day Massacre in France, thousands of Protestants are killed.	**1572–1631:** John Donne, English metaphysical poet
	1575: *Gammer Gurton's Needle*, early English farce, author unknown		
	1576: James Burbage builds The Theatre for the public performance of plays. Blackfriars, London's first private theater, is also built.		
	1577: John Northbrooke publishes *A Treatise against Dicing, Dancing, Plays, and Interludes*, one of several tracts attacking the growing professional theater.		**1577:** *Chronicles of England, Scotland and Ireland* is published by Raphael Holinshed and provides Shakespeare with information for his historical plays.
	1580–1627: Playwright Thomas Middleton, author of *A Chaste Maid in Cheapside* (1630) and *The Changeling* (with William Rowley, 1622)		**1580:** Sir Francis Drake, first Englishman to circumnavigate the globe

263

Renaissance Drama Timeline (continued)

DATE	THEATER	POLITICAL	SOCIAL/CULTURAL
1500–1600 (continued)	**1584:** Completion of the Teatro Olimpico in Vicenza, Italy, designed by architect Andrea Palladio (1508–1580). **1586?–c. 1640:** Playwright John Ford, author of *'Tis Pity She's a Whore* (1633) **1593:** London theaters are closed because of a plague and open again in 1594. **1595–1596:** Shakespeare's comedy *A Midsummer Night's Dream* **1599:** The Globe Theatre is built in London.	**1587:** The Catholic Mary Stuart, queen of Scotland, is executed in England. **1587–1649:** John Winthrop, first governor of the Massachusetts Bay Colony **1588:** The English fleet defeats the Spanish Armada. **1589:** Henry IV of France, first of the Bourbon line **1589:** Russian czar Boris Godunov separates Moscow's church from that in Constantinople. **1595:** The Dutch begin to colonize the East Indies. **1598:** The Edict of Nantes grants French Huguenots freedom of worship but is revoked in 1685.	**1583:** Sir Philip Sidney's *Defence of Poesy* argues for literature's importance in teaching morality and virtue. **1596–1650:** René Descartes, French philosopher, mathematician, and scientist
1600–1700	**1600–1601:** Shakespeare's *Hamlet* **1611–1612:** Shakespeare's *The Tempest* **1613:** Fire destroys the Globe Theatre. **1633:** The Oberammergau Passion play is first performed in Germany. **1642:** The English Parliament closes the theaters.	**1603:** Death of Elizabeth I. James VI of Scotland, son of Mary Stuart, becomes James I of England. **1605:** The Gunpowder Plot, an attempt to blow up the English Parliament and James I, is uncovered. **1618–1648:** The Thirty Years War is initiated by a Protestant revolt in Bohemia against the authority of the Holy Roman emperor. **1625:** Death of James I. His son becomes Charles I of England. **1630:** John Winthrop founds Boston. **1642:** Civil war begins in England. **1643:** Louis XIV becomes king of France at age four. **1649:** Charles I is beheaded in England, beginning the Commonwealth and Protectorate. **1648:** The Treaty of Westphalia ends the Thirty Years War.	**1600:** Dutch opticians invent the telescope. **1602:** The Dutch East India Company is established to trade with the Far East. **1606–1669:** Rembrandt van Rijn, greatest master of the Dutch school of painting **1607:** Jamestown, Virginia, the first permanent settlement across the Atlantic, is founded. **1608–1674:** John Milton, English poet, author of *Paradise Lost* **1611:** The King James Bible is published. **1619:** The first slaves from Africa arrive in Virginia. **1620:** The Pilgrims land at Plymouth Rock, Massachusetts. **1626:** Peter Minuit purchases Manhattan Island from native Indian chiefs. **1632–1704:** John Locke, English philosopher, founder of empiricism

Christopher Marlowe

Christopher Marlowe (1564–1593) was born two months before William Shakespeare and in somewhat similar social circumstances. Marlowe's father was a shoemaker, Shakespeare's a glovemaker. But unlike Shakespeare, Marlowe won a scholarship to Cambridge, where he remained six years and began his career as a playwright. His first play, *Tamburlaine,* was finished before he left the university. When it was performed in London, it had the benefit of Edward Alleyn, the finest actor of his time, playing the title role.

The son-in-law of Philip Henslowe, who owned the Rose, the Fortune, and the Hope theaters in London, Alleyn was a rhetorical actor with a commanding voice and gestures. His style was perfect for declaiming what Ben Jonson called Marlowe's "Mighty line": his IAMBIC PENTAMETER BLANK VERSE, which moves in stately rhythms and dominated the Elizabethan stage. Marlowe's blank verse, especially in the emotional moments of Faustus's career—as in his invocation of the devils in act I, scene iii—resonates and rolls from the tongue in mighty billows. It has a virtually incantatory effect on the listener, and in a London theater of the time, as spoken by Edward Alleyn, it must have been mesmerizing.

Marlowe also had considerable success as a poet and as a translator of the classics. His version of Ovid's *Amores* is very lively, and his long poem *Hero and Leander* is a dynamic contribution to the poetry of Renaissance humanism. It shows his affection for the classics in a form that Shakespeare also employed: the longer narrative poem.

Marlowe's university scholarship was intended for those studying for the ministry, but instead of entering the ministry, he went up to London in 1587. Some of his friends revealed that his beliefs were close to those of atheism, a charge that in his time could have resulted in death. Fortunately, when he applied for his master's degree and was on the verge of having it denied, Queen Elizabeth intervened on his behalf. Her involvement has made subsequent generations think that he must have been a spy on her behalf during at least some of the time he was in Catholic sections of France.

Partly as a result of his connection with Elizabeth, Marlowe has often been portrayed as a romantic swashbuckler in the heart of complex intrigues. He was also well known to most of the literary people of London: Shakespeare, Sir Walter Raleigh, Francis Bacon, Thomas Kyd, and Thomas Harriot (an astronomer and writer) were all close associates. They and Marlowe were also acquainted with the remarkable magician Dr. John Dee. As members of a group dubbed the School of Night, they met privately to discuss ideas of the occult, alchemy, and skeptic philosophy—subjects that could not easily be talked about in the open.

Marlowe's first play was *Tamburlaine* (1587; in two parts), followed by *The Jew of Malta* (1589) and *Edward the Second* (1592). They are all powerful plays that feature a great tragic character. *The Massacre at Paris* (1593) is based on the St. Bartholomew Day's Massacre in 1573, when some thirty thousand Huguenots—French Protestants—were killed by Catholics in Paris. Marlowe's knowledge of the details of the events seems to have been considerable, although the play itself is not as powerful as his earlier tragedies. *Dido, Queen of Carthage* (1593; with Thomas Nashe) is a typical kind of collaboration of the period. None of these plays, good as they are, come to the level of *Doctor Faustus,* which stands as one of the greatest plays of the Elizabethan age.

Apparently quick to anger, Marlowe was involved in one murder before he himself was murdered over a bar bill at the inn of the Widow Bull in Deptford. He was drinking with an acquaintance, Ingram Frizer, who worked for the great Walsingham family, a patron of Marlowe's. During an argument Marlowe grabbed Frizer from behind, but Frizer broke free and stabbed Marlowe, who died instantly. At the time of Marlowe's death Shakespeare was just beginning his career as a playwright.

DOCTOR FAUSTUS

Doctor Faustus was probably written between 1588 and 1593, shortly before Marlowe died. There is a record of its being readied for the press in 1601, but if that version was printed, no copies survive. The first printed version, now called the A-text, is from 1604; an amplified version, called the B-text, came out in 1616. Neither had been supervised by Marlowe, and to make things more complicated, records indicate that Alleyn's father-in-law Philip Henslowe paid two writers a substantial sum to add to the original text. What the additions were or what the original text was, we probably will never know.

Current scholarship leads us to believe that the 1616 text, printed here, is actually closer to the original acting version than the 1604 text was. The breaking of the text into five acts and their scenes is a modern convention, as is the supplying of most of the stage directions. The five-act pattern common in classical plays is natural to Elizabethan plays as well.

The influence of the medieval stage is readily apparent in *Doctor Faustus.* The emphasis on the devils, the seven deadly sins, and the terrifying vision of hell in act V is reminiscent of the devils of the mystery plays and their reliance on frightening hell's mouth props. The allusion to medieval theater's tradition of the mansion in Mephistophilis's speech in act V also echoes the basic message of the morality plays:

> Ay, Faustus, now thou hast no hope of heaven;
> Therefore despair. Think only upon hell,
> For that must be thy mansion, there to dwell.

Doctor Faustus differs from the morality plays in one very important way, though. We are never led to think that Faustus would have lived a better or more interesting life if he had restrained his ambition. Faustus is a hero, especially of the romantic sort that strove to achieve great things and challenge the gods. The Elizabethans admired Faustus much more than they condemned him, no matter what moral tags Marlowe might have put in the play to satisfy society's official view of itself.

Among the sources of the play are a medieval folklore tradition connected with the wizard who sold his soul to the devil for greater powers and a German book called *Historia von D. Johan Fausten,* published in 1587. Marlowe may have seen the book or, more likely, may have seen an English translation of 1592 called *The History of the damnable life, and deserved death of Doctor John Faustus.* In either event, the Faust legend goes back to the early medieval period and could have reached Marlowe in any number of ways.

Doctor Faustus is one of the earliest English tragedies. Its hero is in many ways larger than life, and though not a member of the nobility, he is at ease with royalty and clearly superior in intellectual abilities. The richness of the psychological portrayal of Faustus—as well as of Wagner and Mephistophilis—elevates the play above the best earlier efforts of English and European dramatists. Faustus represents an interesting tradition: the University of Wittenberg produced the most important Protestant of the sixteenth century, Martin Luther. His daring—comparable in some ways to Faustus's overreaching—led to the Reformation, one of the most cataclysmic changes in European thought in the Renaissance. Hamlet is also a student at Wittenberg, a fact that gives us insight into the Elizabethan imagination. Wittenberg to the Elizabethans meant fierce intellectual energy and daring.

As in the case of many of Shakespeare's tragedies, *Doctor Faustus* has interludes of comic relief, with the horse coursers who are bilked by Faustus and with other clowns and mechanicals who wonder openly about the terrifying skills of the magician. This linking of magic and comic has annoyed some critics who have agreed with Aristotle that such a mixture is problematic and tends to diffuse the effect of the drama. Actually, in performance the comic scenes are in no way a dilution of effect. They tend to buoy the energy of the play and help us focus anew on the insatiable Faustus.

But *Doctor Faustus* has a modern twist that takes it out of the medieval mold. The Renaissance was a period of expansion, especially the expansion of knowledge. Astronomy was symbolic of the new age: telescopes were beginning to give Europeans a sense of the vastness and complexity of the universe. When Faustus asks information of Mephistophilis, he begins with questions about the planets and the universe, knowledge of which had long been thought to be somehow secret. Mastering that knowledge was symbolic of mastering the knowledge of the innermost workings of science.

Faustus's quest for knowledge became for some people a Renaissance theme. The magicians referred to in the text, such as Roger Bacon and Cornelius Agrippa, were genuine. Their work was read throughout Europe, and the kinds of magic actions that Faustus aspires to were thought possible. The Elizabethans definitely believed in the presence of spirits, of ghosts, of intervention through witches of the otherworld. *Doctor Faustus* fed the contemporary interest in the occult. Faustus quests for forbidden knowledge; he must sell his soul to the devil to acquire it. His lust for knowledge—he says at the outset that he has dominated all the world of learning available to him—is without bounds.

Many of Marlowe's audience would have seen in Doctor Faustus an allusion to the magus John Dee, who cast the horoscope of Queen Elizabeth. Marlowe knew Dee, on whom the description of Faustus is based. Known throughout Europe for his almost supernormal intellectual capacity, Dee was learned in many sciences. His introduction to the first English edition of Euclid's *Geometry* made him not only respected in Europe but eventually known throughout the New World. Dee's version of Euclid was used at Harvard University until the late 1700s. Because Dee was a wizard, his house at Mortlake was attacked and burned to the ground by frightened peasants while he was abroad. With his house went one of the most impressive personal libraries in Europe.

Faustus was willing to seek forbidden knowledge—in the way Adam and Eve did—at all costs, in full awareness that he risked the loss of his soul. And while Marlowe condemns Faustus to hell and does not save him at the end, we have the feeling—as did Elizabethans—that there is something grand and heroic about Faustus's risk taking. He fails, yes, but he does so in a way that makes mediocre citizens who would never have had his imagination or daring seem pallid and weak. We find ourselves involved in Faustus's struggle.

Doctor Faustus in Performance

Marlowe may not have seen *Doctor Faustus* performed. There are no performance records until 1594, when Philip Henslowe and the Royal Admiral's Men produced the play. Productions were frequent until 1598, and Henslowe's records indicate that the play was extremely popular. The great actor Edward Alleyn portrayed Faustus. Along with several reissuings of printed versions of the play, productions seem to have continued into the early part of the 1600s, when a number of writers were hired at different times to add lines to the original text. After the Restoration in 1660 and the reopening of the theaters, *Doctor Faustus* was again played frequently, with Thomas Betterton in the title role. In the eighteenth century the play was sometimes staged as a farce and in some cases reduced to a puppet show. In the nineteenth century, however, audiences were given the chance to see the play as a serious tragedy, with Sir Henry Irving, one of the greatest of the nineteenth-century actors, performing in London at the Lyceum Theatre in 1885. Twentieth-century performances included a number of amateur productions, including one during wartime by the great director Peter Brook in 1942.

Orson Welles performed the title role in a Works Progress Administration (WPA) production in New York; reviews were mixed. Welles, himself a magician, emphasized the magical elements so that trapdoors and special effects became great moments of entertainment. The Phoenix Theatre's 1964 production in New York continued that tradition, with fireworks accompanying the entrance of the "hot whore." That production emphasized the blackness of the play, with dark sets and glittering dark costumes. At the end of the play, Faustus was faced with the yawning pit of hellfire. Productions of the play were also popular in Germany in the first half of the twentieth century. In his novel *Doctor Faustus*, Thomas Mann saw in the play a metaphor for Germany's having sold its soul to Hitler.

Christopher Marlowe (1564–1593)

THE TRAGICAL HISTORY OF THE LIFE AND DEATH OF DOCTOR FAUSTUS

c. 1593

EDITED BY IRVING RIBNER

The Players

THE CHORUS
DOCTOR FAUSTUS
WAGNER, *his student and servant*
VALDES
CORNELIUS
THREE SCHOLARS
AN OLD MAN

POPE ADRIAN
RAYMOND, *King of Hungary*
BRUNO, *the rival Pope*
TWO CARDINALS
THE ARCHBISHOP OF RHEIMS
CHARLES V, *Emperor of Germany*
MARTINO
FREDERICK } *Gentlemen of the Emperor's court*
BENVOLIO
BEELZEBUB
DUKE OF SAXONY
DUKE OF ANHOLT
DUCHESS OF ANHOLT
ROBIN, *the clown, a hostler*
DICK
A VINTNER
A HORSE-COURSER
A CARTER
HOSTESS

GOOD ANGEL
BAD ANGEL
LUCIFER
MEPHISTOPHILIS
PRIDE
COVETOUSNESS
ENVY
WRATH } *The Seven Deadly Sins*
GLUTTONY
SLOTH
LECHERY
ALEXANDER, THE GREAT
HIS PARAMOUR
DARIUS, *King of Persia*
HELEN OF TROY
TWO CUPIDS
DEVILS, BISHOPS, MONKS, FRIARS, SOLDIERS

Note: Material in brackets has been added by the editor.

The Scene: *Wittenberg, Rome, the Emperor's court at Innsbruck, court of the Duke of Anholt, and the neighboring countryside.*

PROLOGUE

(*Enter Chorus.*)

CHORUS: Not marching in the fields of Trasimene
    Where Mars° did mate° the warlike Carthagens,°
    Nor sporting in the dalliance of love
    In courts of kings where state° is overturned,
    Nor in the pomp of proud audacious deeds   5
    Intends our muse to vaunt his heavenly verse.
    Only this, gentles: we must now perform
    The form of Faustus' fortunes, good or bad.
    And now to patient judgments we appeal,
    And speak for Faustus in his infancy.   10
    Now is he born, of parents base of stock,
    In Germany, within a town called Rhode.
    At riper years to Wittenberg he went,
    Whereas his kinsmen chiefly brought him up.
    So much he profits in divinity,   15
    The fruitful plot of scholarism graced,°
    That shortly he was graced with doctor's name,
    Excelling all whose sweet delight disputes°
    In th'heavenly matters of theology,
    Till swoll'n with cunning of a self-conceit,   20
    His waxen wings did mount above his reach,
    And melting,° heavens conspired his overthrow;
    For, falling to a devilish exercise
    And glutted now with learning's golden gifts,
    He surfeits upon cursèd necromancy.   25
    Nothing so sweet as magic is to him,
    Which he prefers before his chiefest bliss;
    And this the man that in his study sits.

Prologue. 1–2. Trasimene . . . Carthagens: Perhaps an allusion to a lost play about the Carthaginian Hannibal, who achieved one of his greatest victories at Lake Trasimene in 217 BCE. **2. Mars:** Roman god of war. **mate:** Rival, meet in battle. **4. state:** Government. **16. fruitful plot . . . graced:** Adorned the university. **18. whose sweet delight disputes:** Who takes pleasure in disputing. **21–22. waxen wings . . . melting:** Metaphor referring to Icarus's attempt to fly with waxen wings, which melted when he ignored his father's warning and flew too near the sun.

269

ACT I • *Scene I*

(*Faustus in his study.*)

FAUSTUS: Settle thy studies, Faustus, and begin
    To sound the depth of that thou wilt profess.
    Having commenced,° be a divine in show;
    Yet level° at the end of every art,
5   And live and die in Aristotle's works.
    Sweet Analytics, 'tis thou hast ravished me!
    Bene' disserere est finis logices.°
    Is to dispute well logic's chiefest end?
    Affords this art no greater miracle?
10   Then read no more; thou hast attained that end.
    A greater subject fitteth Faustus' wit!
    Bid *On cay mae on*° farewell, Galen° come.
    Seeing *ubi desinit philosophus ibi incipit medicus,*°
    Be a physician, Faustus; heap up gold,
15   And be eternized for some wondrous cure.
    Summum bonum medicinae sanitas.°
    The end of physic is our body's health.
    Why, Faustus, hast thou not attained that end?
    Is not thy common talk sound aphorisms?
20   Are not thy bills° hung up as monuments,
    Whereby whole cities have escaped the plague,
    And divers desperate maladies been cured?
    Yet art thou still but Faustus and a man.
    Couldst thou make men to live eternally,
25   Or, being dead, raise them to life again,
    Then this profession were to be esteemed.
    Physic, farewell! Where is Justinian?°
    Si una eademque res legatus duobus,   [*He reads.*]
    Alter rem, alter valorem rei, etc.°
30   A petty case of paltry legacies!
    Exhaereditare filium non potest pater nisi° —
                         [*He reads.*]
    Such is the subject of the Institute
    And universal body of the law.
    This study fits a mercenary drudge
35   Who aims at nothing but external trash,
    Too servile and illiberal for me.

When all is done, divinity is best.
Jerome's Bible,° Faustus, view it well:
Stipendium peccati mors est.° Ha! *Stipendium, etc.*
                         [*He reads.*]
The reward of sin is death. That's hard.   40
Si pecasse negamus, fallimur   [*He reads.*]
Et nulla est in nobis veritas.°
If we say that we have no sin,
We deceive ourselves, and there's no truth in us.
Why then belike we must sin,   45
And so consequently die.
Ay, we must die an everlasting death.
What doctrine call you this? *Che serà, serà:*
What will be, shall be! Divinity, adieu!
These metaphysics of magicians,   50
And necromantic books are heavenly.
Lines, circles, signs, letters, and characters—
Ay, these are those that Faustus most desires.
O, what a world of profit and delight,
Of power, of honor, of omnipotence   55
Is promised to the studious artisan!
All things that move between the quiet poles
Shall be at my command. Emperors and kings
Are but obeyed in their several provinces,
Nor can they raise the wind or rend the clouds,   60
But his dominion that exceeds in this
Stretcheth as far as doth the mind of man.
A sound magician is a demi-god.
Here try thy brains to get a deity!
Wagner!

(*Enter Wagner.*)

        Commend me to my dearest friends,   65
    The German Valdes and Cornelius;
    Request them earnestly to visit me.
WAGNER: I will sir.
                        (*Exit.*)
FAUSTUS: Their conference will be a greater help to me
    Than all my labors, plod I ne'er so fast.   70

(*Enter the Good Angel and the Evil Angel.*)

GOOD ANGEL: O, Faustus, lay that damnèd book aside,
    And gaze not on it, lest it tempt thy soul
    And heap God's heavy wrath upon thy head.
    Read, read the Scriptures. That is blasphemy.
BAD ANGEL: Go forward, Faustus, in that famous art   75
    Wherein all nature's treasury is contained.
    Be thou on earth as Jove is in the sky,
    Lord and commander of these elements.
                      (*Exeunt*° *Angels.*)
FAUSTUS: How am I glutted with conceit° of this!
    Shall I make spirits fetch me what I please,   80

I, I. **3. commenced:** Taken a degree. **4. level:** Aim. **7. Bene'** *disserere est finis logices:* The end of logic is to dispute well. A tenet of the anti-Aristotelian system introduced at Cambridge when Marlowe was a student there. **12. On cay mae on:** From Aristotle, being or not being. **Galen:** Greek physician regarded throughout the Middle Ages as a medical authority. **13.** *ubi desinit philosophus ibi incipit medicus:* Where the philosopher stops, the doctor begins. **16. Summum . . . sanitas:** Health is the highest good of the practice of medicine. **20. bills:** Medical prescriptions. **27. Justinian:** Roman emperor of Constantinople (527–565), responsible for assembling the Roman law and renowned throughout the Middle Ages as a jurist. **28–29. Si . . . rei, etc.:** If the same object is willed to two persons, let one have the thing itself and the other its value, etc. This is an incorrect version of one of Justinian's rules. **31. Exhaereditare . . . nisi—:** The father cannot disinherit the son except—; another of Justinian's rules roughly paraphrased.

38. Jerome's Bible: St. Jerome's Vulgate [Latin] translation of the Bible. **39.** *Stipendium . . . est:* Translated in line 40 (Rom. 6:23). **41–42. Si . . . veritas:** Translated in lines 43–44 (1 John 1:8). **78. [S.D.]** *Exeunt:* Latin for "they go out." **79. conceit:** The conception of attaining.

Resolve me of° all ambiguities,
Perform what desperate enterprise I will?
I'll have them fly to India for gold,
Ransack the ocean for orient pearl,
85 And search all corners of the new-found world
For pleasant fruits and princely delicates.
I'll have them read me strange philosophy
And tell the secrets of all foreign kings;
I'll have them wall all Germany with brass
90 And make swift Rhine circle fair Wittenberg.°
I'll have them fill the public schools with silk
Wherewith the students shall be bravely clad.
I'll levy soldiers with the coin they bring
And chase the Prince of Parma from our land
95 And reign sole king of all the provinces.°
Yea, stranger engines for the brunt of war
Than was the fiery keel at Antwerp's bridge°
I'll make my servile spirits to invent.
Come, German Valdes and Cornelius,
                                   [*He calls within.*]
100 And make me blessed with your sage conference!

(*Enter Valdes and Cornelius.*)

Valdes, sweet Valdes, and Cornelius,
Know that your words have won me at the last
To practice magic and concealed arts;
Yet not your words only, but mine own fantasy
105 That will receive no object, for my head
But ruminates on necromantic skill.
Philosophy is odious and obscure;
Both law and physic are for petty wits;
Divinity is basest of the three,
110 Unpleasant, harsh, contemptible and vile.
'Tis, magic, magic, that hath ravished me.
Then, gentle friends, aid me in this attempt,
And I, that have with subtle syllogisms
Gravelled° the pastors of the German church,
115 And made the flowering pride of Wittenberg
Swarm to my problems° as th'infernal spirits
On sweet Musaeus° when he came to hell,
Will be as cunning as Agrippa was,
Whose shadows° made all Europe honor him.
VALDES: Faustus, these books, thy wit, and our
120   experience
Shall make all nations to canonize us.
As Indian Moors° obey their Spanish lords,

So shall the spirits of every element
Be always serviceable to us three.
Like lions shall they guard us when we please,   125
Like Almain rutters° with their horsemen's staves
Or Lapland giants trotting by our sides,
Sometimes like women or unwedded maids,
Shadowing° more beauty in their airy brows
Than in the white breasts of the queen of love.   130
From Venice shall they drag huge argosies,
And from America the golden fleece
That yearly stuffs old Philip's treasury,
If learnèd Faustus will be resolute.
FAUSTUS: Valdes, as resolute am I in this   135
As thou to live; therefore object it not.
CORNELIUS: The miracles that magic will perform
Will make thee vow to study nothing else.
He that is grounded in astrology,
Enriched with tongues,° well seen in minerals,   140
Hath all the principles magic doth require.
Then doubt not, Faustus, but to be renowned
And more frequented for this mystery
Than heretofore the Delphian oracle.°
The spirits tell me they can dry the sea   145
And fetch the treasure of all foreign wracks,
Yea, all the wealth that our forefathers hid
Within the massy entrails of the earth.
Then tell me, Faustus, what shall we three want?
FAUSTUS: Nothing, Cornelius. O, this cheers my soul! 150
Come, show me some demonstrations magical,
That I may conjure in some lusty grove
And have these joys in full possession.
VALDES: Then haste thee to some solitary grove,
And bear wise Bacon's and Abanus' works,°   155
The Hebrew Psalter, and New Testament;
And whatsoever else is requisite
We will inform thee ere our conference cease.
CORNELIUS: Valdes, first let him know the words of
       art,
And then, all other ceremonies learned,   160
Faustus may try his cunning by himself.
VALDES: First I'll instruct thee in the rudiments,
And then wilt thou be perfecter than I.
FAUSTUS: Then come and dine with me, and after meat
We'll canvass every quiddity° thereof,   165
For ere I sleep I'll try what I can do.
This night I'll conjure, though I die therefore.
                                       (*Exeunt.*)

---

81. Resolve me of: Explain to me.   **90. Rhine . . . Wittenberg:** Wittenberg is actually on the Elbe River, not the Rhine. **95. provinces:** The Netherlands.   **97. fiery . . . bridge:** In April 1584 the Dutch used a fireship to destroy a bridge built across a river by the Prince of Parma in an attempt to blockade Antwerp.   **114. Gravelled:** Puzzled and amazed.   **116. problems:** Public disputations.   **117. Musaeus:** A semimythical Greek poet. Following Virgil, Marlowe has him visit hell like the mythical Orpheus.   **118–19. Agrippa . . . shadows:** Cornelius Agrippa (1486?–1535), a German physician and student of the occult, was said to have power to raise spirits (shadows) from the dead.   **122. Indian Moors:** American Indians.

126. Almain rutters: German cavalry.   **129. Shadowing:** Harboring, sheltering.   **140. Enriched with tongues:** Fluent in Latin, the language used for communicating with spirits. **144. Delphian oracle:** The high priest of Apollo at Delphi who had power to foretell the future. [An oracle is the response of a god to a question asked by one who worships the god. The Delphic Oracle was the chief oracle of Greece, presided over by Apollo.]   **155. Bacon's . . . works:** Roger Bacon (1214?–1294) and Pietro D'Abano (1250–1316) were famous in the Middle Ages for their feats of magic.   **165. quiddity:** Essential element (a term from scholastic logic).

Scene II

(*Enter two Scholars.*)

FIRST SCHOLAR: I wonder what's become of Faustus, that
    was wont to make our schools ring with *sic probo.*°

(*Enter Wagner.*)

SECOND SCHOLAR: That shall we presently know; here
    comes his boy.

5 FIRST SCHOLAR: How now sirrah! Where's thy master?
WAGNER: God in heaven knows.
SECOND SCHOLAR: Why, dost not thou know then?
WAGNER: Yes, I know, but that follows not.
FIRST SCHOLAR: Go to, sirrah! Leave your jesting and
10   tell us where he is.
WAGNER: That follows not by force of argument, which
    you, being licentiates,° should stand upon; therefore
    acknowledge your error and be attentive.
SECOND SCHOLAR: Then you will not tell us?
15 WAGNER: You are deceived, for I will tell you. Yet if you
    were not dunces, you would never ask me such a
    question. For is he not *corpus naturale,* and is not
    that *mobile?*° Then wherefore should you ask such a
    question? But that I am by nature phlegmatic, slow
20   to wrath, and prone to lechery—to love, I would
    say—it were not for you to come within forty foot
    of the place of execution, although I do not doubt
    but to see you both hanged the next sessions. Thus
    having triumphed over you, I will set my counte-
25   nance like a precisian° and begin to speak thus:
    Truly, my dear brethren, my master is within at din-
    ner with Valdes and Cornelius, as this wine, if it
    could speak, would inform your worships. And so,
    the Lord bless you, preserve you, and keep you, my
30   dear brethren.
                                                        (*Exit.*)
FIRST SCHOLAR: O Faustus, then I fear that which I
    have long suspected.
    That thou art fall'n into that damnèd art
    For which they two are infamous through the
        world.
SECOND SCHOLAR: Were he a stranger, not allied
    to me,
35   The danger of his soul would make me mourn.
    But come, let us go and inform the rector.°
    It may be his grave counsel may reclaim him.
FIRST SCHOLAR: I fear me nothing will reclaim
    him now.
SECOND SCHOLAR: Yet let us see what we
    can do.
                                                    (*Exeunt.*)

I, II. 2. *sic probo:* Thus I prove (used in scholastic argument).
12. licentiates: Holders of university degrees.   17–18. *corpus
naturale . . . mobile:* The subject matter of physics, in scholastic
terms, was *corpus naturale seu mobile* (natural body in
motion).   25. precisian: Puritan.   36. rector: Head of the university.

Scene III

(*Thunder. Enter [above] Lucifer and four Devils. Enter
Faustus to conjure.*)

FAUSTUS: Now that the gloomy shadow of the night,
    Longing to view Orion's drizzling look,
    Leaps from th'Antarctic world unto the sky
    And dims the welkin° with her pitchy breath,
    Faustus begin thine incantations,   5
    And try if devils will obey thy hest,
    Seeing thou hast prayed and sacrificed to them.
    Within this circle is Jehovah's name,
    Forward and backward anagrammatized,
    Th'abbreviated names of holy saints,   10
    Figures of every adjunct to the heavens,
    And characters of signs and erring° stars,
    By which the spirits are enforced to rise.
    Then fear not, Faustus, to be resolute,
    And try the utmost magic can perform.   15
                                                     (*Thunder.*)
*Sint mihi Dei Acherontis propitii! Valeat numen tri-
plex Jehovae. Ignei, aerii, aquatani spiritus, salvete!
Orientis princeps, Beelzebub, inferni ardentis monar-
cha, et Demogorgon, propitiamus vos, ut appareat et
surgat Mephistophilis. Quid tu moraris? Per Jehovam*   20
*Gehennam, et consecratam aquam quam nunc spargo,
signumque crucis quod nunc facto, et per vota nostra,
ipse nunc surgat nobis dicatus Mephistophilis.°*

(*Enter [Mephistophilis,] a Devil.*)

    I charge thee to return and change thy shape;
    Thou art too ugly to attend on me.   25
    Go, and return an old Franciscan friar;
    That holy shape becomes a devil best.
                                                   (*Exit Devil.*)
    I see there's virtue in my heavenly words.
    Who would not be proficient in this art?
    How pliant is this Mephistophilis,   30
    Full of obedience and humility.
    Such is the force of magic and my spells.
    Now Faustus, thou art conjurer laureate,
    That canst command great Mephistophilis.
    Quin redis Mephistophilis fratris imagine.°   35

(*Enter Mephistophilis [dressed like a Franciscan friar].*)

MEPHISTOPHILIS: Now Faustus, what wouldst thou
    have me do?

I, III. 4. welkin: Sky.   12. erring: Wandering.   16–23. *Sint . . .
Mephistophilis:* May the gods of Aceron be propitious to me.
Let the triple name of Jehova [the trinity] be gone. Hail spirits
of fire, air, and water. Prince of the East, Beelzebub, monarch of
burning hell, and Demogorgon, we petition you that Mephistophilis may appear and rise. Why do you linger? By Jehova,
Gehenna, and the holy water which I now sprinkle and the sign
of the cross which I now make and by our vows, let Mephistophilis himself now rise to serve us.   35. *Quin . . . imagine:* Return, Mephistophilis, in the shape of a friar.

FAUSTUS: I charge thee wait upon me whilst I live,
　　To do whatever Faustus shall command,
　　Be it to make the moon drop from her sphere
40　Or the ocean to overwhelm the world.
MEPHISTOPHILIS: I am a servant to great Lucifer
　　And may not follow thee without his leave.
　　No more than he commands must we perform.
FAUSTUS: Did not he charge thee to appear to me?
MEPHISTOPHILIS: No, I came hither of mine own
45　accord.
FAUSTUS: Did not my conjuring speeches raise thee?
　　Speak.
MEPHISTOPHILIS: That was the cause, but yet *per accidens,*°
　　For when we hear one rack the name of God,
　　Abjure the Scriptures and his Savior Christ,
50　We fly in hope to get his glorious soul;
　　Nor will we come unless he use such means
　　Whereby he is in danger to be damned.
　　Therefore the shortest cut for conjuring
　　Is stoutly to abjure the Trinity
55　And pray devoutly to the prince of hell.
FAUSTUS: So Faustus hath
　　Already done, and holds this principle:
　　There is no chief but only Beelzebub,
　　To whom Faustus doth dedicate himself.
60　This word "damnation" terrifies not me,
　　For I confound hell in Elysium.
　　My ghost° be with the old philosophers!
　　But leaving these vain trifles of men's souls,
　　Tell me what is that Lucifer thy lord?
MEPHISTOPHILIS: Arch-regent and commander of all
65　spirits.
FAUSTUS: Was not that Lucifer an angel once?
MEPHISTOPHILIS: Yes Faustus, and most dearly loved
　　of God.
FAUSTUS: How comes it then that he is prince of devils?
MEPHISTOPHILIS: O, by aspiring pride and insolence,
70　For which God threw him from the face of heaven.
FAUSTUS: And what are you that live with Lucifer?
MEPHISTOPHILIS: Unhappy spirits that fell with Lucifer,
　　Conspired against our God with Lucifer,
　　And are for ever damned with Lucifer.
FAUSTUS: Where are you damned?
75　MEPHISTOPHILIS:　　　　In hell.
FAUSTUS: How comes it then that thou art out of hell?
MEPHISTOPHILIS: Why this is hell, nor am I out of it.
　　Think'st thou that I who saw the face of God
　　And tasted the eternal joys of heaven
80　Am not tormented with ten thousand hells
　　In being deprived of everlasting bliss?
　　O Faustus, leave these frivolous demands
　　Which strike a terror to my fainting soul.
FAUSTUS: What, is great Mephistophilis so passionate
85　For being deprivèd of the joys of heaven?

Learn thou of Faustus' manly fortitude,
And scorn those joys thou never shalt possess.
Go bear these tidings to great Lucifer:
Seeing Faustus hath incurred eternal death
By desperate thoughts against Jove's deity,　90
Say he surrenders up to him his soul,
So he will spare him four and twenty years,
Letting him live in all voluptuousness,
Having thee ever to attend on me,
To give me whatsoever I shall ask,　95
To tell me whatsoever I demand,
To slay mine enemies, and aid my friends,
And always be obedient to my will.
Go, and return to mighty Lucifer,
And meet me in my study at midnight,　100
And then resolve me of thy master's mind.
MEPHISTOPHILIS: I will, Faustus.
　　　　　　　　　　　　　(*Exit.*)
FAUSTUS: Had I as many souls as there be stars,
　　I'd give them all for Mephistophilis.
　　By him I'll be great emperor of the world,　105
　　And make a bridge thorough the moving air,
　　To pass the ocean with a band of men.
　　I'll join the hills that bind° the Afric shore,
　　And make that country continent to Spain,
　　And both contributory to my crown.　110
　　The Emperor shall not live but by my leave,
　　Nor any potentate of Germany.
　　Now that I have obtained what I desire,
　　I'll live in speculation of this art
　　Till Mephistophilis return again.　115
　　　　　　　　　　　　　(*Exit.*)

Scene IV

(*Enter Wagner and [Robin,] the Clown.*)

WAGNER: Come hither, sirrah boy.
ROBIN: Boy! O disgrace to my person. Zounds, boy in your face! You have seen many boys with such pickedevants,° I am sure.
WAGNER: Sirrah, hast thou no comings in?°　5
ROBIN: Yes, and goings out too, you may see, sir.
WAGNER: Alas, poor slave! See how poverty jests in his nakedness. I know the villain's out of service, and so hungry that I know he would give his soul to the devil for a shoulder of mutton, though it were blood-raw.　10
ROBIN: Not so neither. I had need to have it well roasted, and good sauce to it, if I pay so dear, I can tell you.
WAGNER: Sirrah, wilt thou be my man and wait on me,　15
　　and I will make thee go like *Qui mihi discipulus?*°

47. *cause . . . per accidens:* The terms are from scholastic logic.
62. *ghost:* Spirit.

108. **bind:** Enclose.　I, IV. 4. **pickedevants:** Pointed beards.
5. **comings in:** Earnings.　16. *Qui mihi discipulus?:* Who is my disciple? (the opening words of a Latin poem by William Lyly, well known to Elizabethan schoolboys).

ROBIN: What, in verse?

WAGNER: No slave; in beaten° silk and staves-acre.°

ROBIN: Staves-acre? That's good to kill vermin. Then,
20   belike, if I serve you I shall be lousy.

WAGNER: Why, so thou shalt be, whether thou dost it or
no; for, sirrah, if thou dost not presently bind thyself
to me for seven years, I'll turn all the lice about thee
into familiars° and make them tear thee in pieces.

25 ROBIN: Nay sir, you may save yourself a labor, for they
are as familiar with me as if they paid for their meat
and drink, I can tell you.

WAGNER: Well, sirrah, leave your jesting and take these
guilders.

30 ROBIN: Yes, marry sir, and I thank you too.

WAGNER: So, now thou art to be at an hour's warning,
whensoever and wheresoever the devil shall fetch
thee.

ROBIN: Here, take your guilders again. I'll none of 'em.

35 WAGNER: Not I. Thou art pressed.° Prepare thyself, for I
will presently raise up two devils to carry thee away.
Banio! Belcher!

ROBIN: Belcher? And Belcher come here, I'll belch him. I
am not afraid of a devil.

(*Enter two Devils.*)

40 WAGNER: How now, sir? Will you serve me now?

ROBIN: Ay, good Wagner; take away the devil then.

WAGNER: Spirits away! Now, sirrah, follow me.

[*Exeunt Devils.*]

ROBIN: I will sir. But hark you, master, will you teach me
this conjuring occupation?

45 WAGNER: Ay, sirrah. I'll teach thee to turn thyself to a
dog, or a cat, or a mouse, or a rat, or any thing.

ROBIN: A dog, or a cat, or a mouse, or a rat! O brave
Wagner!

WAGNER: Villain, call me Master Wagner, and see that
50   you walk attentively, and let your right eye be always
diametrally° fixed upon my left heel, that thou may'st
quasi vestigial nostras insistere.°

ROBIN: Well, sir, I warrant you.

(*Exeunt.*)

ACT II • Scene I

(*Enter Faustus in his Study.*)

FAUSTUS: Now Faustus must thou needs be damned,
And canst thou not be saved.
What boots° it then to think on God or heaven?
Away with such vain fancies, and despair;
5   Despair in God, and trust in Beelzebub.
Now go not backward; Faustus, be resolute.

Why waver'st thou? O, something soundeth in mine
ear:
"Abjure this magic; turn to God again."
Ay, and Faustus will turn to God again!
To God? He loves thee not.   10
The God thou serv'st is thine own appetite,
Wherein is fixed the love of Beelzebub.
To him I'll build an altar and a church,
And offer lukewarm blood of new-born babes.

(*Enter the two Angels.*)

BAD ANGEL: Go forward, Faustus, in that famous art.   15

GOOD ANGEL: Sweet Faustus, leave that execrable art.

FAUSTUS: Contrition, prayer, repentance—what of
these?

GOOD ANGEL: O, they are means to bring thee unto
heaven.

BAD ANGEL: Rather illusions, fruits of lunacy,
That make men foolish that do use them most.   20

GOOD ANGEL: Sweet Faustus, think of heaven and
heavenly things.

BAD ANGEL: No Faustus, think of honor and wealth.

(*Exeunt Angels.*)

FAUSTUS: Wealth? Why, the signory of Emden° shall be
mine.
When Mephistophilis shall stand by me,
What power can hurt me? Faustus thou art safe.   25
Cast no more doubts. Mephistophilis, come
And bring glad tidings from great Lucifer.
Is't not midnight? Come, Mephistophilis.
Veni,° *veni, Mephistophile.*

(*Enter Mephistophilis.*)

Now tell me what saith Lucifer, thy lord?   30

MEPHISTOPHILIS: That I shall wait on Faustus whilst
he lives,
So he will buy my service with his soul.

FAUSTUS: Already Faustus hath hazarded that for thee.

MEPHISTOPHILIS: But now thou must bequeath it
solemnly
And write a deed of gift with thine own blood,   35
For that security craves great Lucifer.
If thou deny it, I must back to hell.

FAUSTUS: Stay, Mephistophilis! Tell me what good
Will my soul do thy lord.

MEPHISTOPHILIS: Enlarge his kingdom.

FAUSTUS: Is that the reason why he tempts us thus?   40

MEPHISTOPHILIS: *Solamen miseris socios habuisse
doloris.*°

FAUSTUS: Why, have you any pain that torture others?

MEPHISTOPHILIS: As great as have the human souls of
men.
But tell me, Faustus, shall I have thy soul?

---

18. **beaten:** Embroidered with metal. **staves-acre:** A plant
used for killing vermin. 24. **familiars:** Attendant evil spirits.
35. **pressed:** Enlisted into service in exchange for money.
51. **diametrally:** In a straight line. 52. *quasi . . . insistere:* As
if to walk in our tracks. II, I. 3. **boots:** Avails.

23. **Emden:** The chief city of East Friesland near the mouth
of the river Ems, which had considerable trade relations with
Elizabethan England. 29. *Veni:* Come. 41. *Solamen . . .
doloris:* It is a consolation in misery to have a fellow sufferer.

45   And I will be thy slave and wait on thee
     And give thee more than thou hast wit to ask.
FAUSTUS: Ay, Mephistophilis, I'll give it him.
MEPHISTOPHILIS: Then Faustus, stab thy arm
        courageously,
     And bind thy soul that at some certain day
50   Great Lucifer may claim it as his own,
     And then be thou as great as Lucifer.
FAUSTUS: [*stabbing his arm*] Lo, Mephistophilis, for
        love of thee,
     I cut mine arm, and with my proper° blood
     Assure my soul to be great Lucifer's,
55   Chief lord and regent of perpetual night.
     View here this blood that trickles from mine arm,
     And let it be propitious for my wish.
MEPHISTOPHILIS: But Faustus,
     Write it in manner of a deed of gift.
60   FAUSTUS: Ay, so I do. [*He writes.*] But Mephistophilis,
     My blood congeals, and I can write no more.
MEPHISTOPHILIS: I'll fetch thee fire to dissolve it
        straight.
                                               (*Exit.*)
FAUSTUS: What might the staying of my blood portend?
     Is it unwilling I should write this bill?
65   Why streams it not that I may write afresh?
     "Faustus gives to thee his soul." Ah, there it stayed.
     Why shouldst thou not? Is not thy soul thine own?
     Then write again: "Faustus gives to thee his soul."

(*Enter Mephistophilis with the chafer of fire.*)

MEPHISTOPHILIS: See Faustus, here is fire. Set it on.°
70   FAUSTUS: So. Now the blood begins to clear again.
     Now will I make an end immediately.
                                           [*He writes.*]
MEPHISTOPHILIS: [*Aside.*] What will not I do to obtain
        his soul?
FAUSTUS: *Consummatum est;*° this bill is ended,
     And Faustus hath bequeathed his soul to Lucifer.
75   But what is this inscription on mine arm?
     Homo fuge!° Whither should I fly?
     If unto God, he'll throw me down to hell.
     My senses are deceived; here's nothing writ.
     O yes, I see it plain. Even here is writ
80   *Homo fuge!* Yet shall not Faustus fly.
MEPHISTOPHILIS: [*Aside.*] I'll fetch him somewhat to
        delight his mind.
                                               (*Exit.*)

(*Enter Devils, giving crowns and rich apparel to Faustus. They dance and then depart. Enter Mephistophilis.*)

FAUSTUS: What means this show? Speak Mephistophilis.
MEPHISTOPHILIS: Nothing, Faustus, but to delight thy
        mind
     And let thee see what magic can perform.

FAUSTUS: But may I raise such spirits when I please?   85
MEPHISTOPHILIS: Ay Faustus, and do greater things
        than these.
FAUSTUS: Then, Mephistophilis, receive this scroll,
     A deed of gift of body and of soul,
     But yet conditionally that thou perform
     All covenants and articles between us both.   90
MEPHISTOPHILIS: Faustus, I swear by hell and Lucifer
     To effect all promises between us made.
FAUSTUS: Then hear me read it Mephistophilis.
     On these conditions following:
     First, that Faustus may be a spirit in form and sub-   95
     stance;
     Secondly, that Mephistophilis shall be his servant and
     be at his command;
     Thirdly, that Mephistophilis shall do for him and
     bring him whatsoever;   100
     Fourthly, that he shall be in his chamber or house
     invisible;
     Lastly, that he shall appear to the said John Faustus
     at all times, in what form or shape soever he please: I,
     John Faustus, of Wittenberg, doctor, by these pres-   105
     ents, do give both body and soul to Lucifer, Prince of
     the East, and his minister, Mephistophilis; and fur-
     thermore grant unto them that four and twenty years
     being expired, the articles above written inviolate,
     full power to fetch or carry the said John Faustus,   110
     body and soul, flesh, blood, or goods, into their habi-
     tation wheresoever.
                                   By me, John Faustus.
MEPHISTOPHILIS: Speak Faustus. Do you deliver this as
        your deed?
FAUSTUS: Ay, take it, and the devil give thee good of it.   115
MEPHISTOPHILIS: So now, Faustus, ask me what thou
        wilt.
FAUSTUS: First will I question with thee about hell.
     Tell me, where is the place that men call hell?
MEPHISTOPHILIS: Under the heavens.
FAUSTUS: Ay, so are all things else. But whereabouts?   120
MEPHISTOPHILIS: Within the bowels of these elements,
     Where we are tortured and remain for ever.
     Hell hath no limits, nor is circumscribed
     In one self place, but where we are is hell,
     And where hell is, there must we ever be.   125
     And, to be short, when all the world dissolves
     And every creature shall be purified,
     All places shall be hell that is not heaven.
FAUSTUS: I think hell's a fable.
MEPHISTOPHILIS: Ay, think so still, till experience
        change thy mind.   130
FAUSTUS: Why, dost thou think that Faustus shall be
        damned?
MEPHISTOPHILIS: Ay, of necessity, for here's the scroll
     In which thou hast given thy soul to Lucifer.
FAUSTUS: Ay, and body too. But what of that?
     Think'st thou that Faustus is so fond° to imagine   135

---

53. **proper:** Own.   69. **Set it on:** Set the dish of blood on the fire.   73. ***Consummatum est:*** It is completed (the words of Jesus at his Crucifixion; John 19:30).   76. ***Homo fuge:*** Fly, man.

135. **fond:** Foolish.

That after this life there is any pain?
No, these are trifles and mere old wives' tales.
MEPHISTOPHILIS: But I am an instance to prove the contrary,
For I tell thee I am damned and now in hell.
FAUSTUS: Nay, and this be hell, I'll willingly be
140　　damned.
What? Sleeping, eating, walking and disputing?
But, leaving off this, let me have a wife,
The fairest maid in Germany,
For I am wanton and lascivious,
145　　And cannot live without a wife.
MEPHISTOPHILIS: I prithee, Faustus, talk not of a wife.
FAUSTUS: Nay, sweet Mephistophilis, fetch me one, for
I will have one.
MEPHISTOPHILIS: Well, Faustus, thou shalt have a
wife.
Sit there till I come.　　　　　　　　　　[*Exit.*]

(*Enter* [*Mephistophilis*] *with a Devil dressed like a woman, with fireworks.*)

150　FAUSTUS: What sight is this?
MEPHISTOPHILIS: Now Faustus, how dost thou like thy
wife?
FAUSTUS: Here's a hot whore indeed! No, I'll no wife.
MEPHISTOPHILIS: Marriage is but a ceremonial toy,
And if thou lovest me, think no more of it.
155　I'll cull thee out the fairest courtesans
And bring them every morning to thy bed.
She whom thine eye shall like, thy heart shall have,
Were she as chaste as was Penelope,°
As wise as Saba,° or as beautiful
160　As was bright Lucifer before his fall.
Hold; take this book; peruse it thoroughly.
The iterating of these lines brings gold;
The framing of this circle on the ground
Brings thunder, whirlwinds, storm and lightning.
165　Pronounce this thrice devoutly to thyself,
And men in harness° shall appear to thee,
Ready to execute what thou command'st.
FAUSTUS: Thanks, Mephistophilis, for this sweet book.
This will I keep as chary as my life.

(*Exeunt.*)

Scene II

(*Enter Faustus in his study and Mephistophilis.*)

FAUSTUS: When I behold the heavens, then I repent
And curse thee, wicked Mephistophilis,
Because thou hast deprived me of those joys.
MEPHISTOPHILIS: 'Twas thine own seeking, Faustus;
thank thyself.
5　But think'st thou heaven is such a glorious thing?

I tell thee, Faustus, 'tis not half so fair
As thou, or any man that breathes on earth.
FAUSTUS: How prov'st thou that?
MEPHISTOPHILIS: 'Twas made for man; then he's more
excellent.
FAUSTUS: If heaven was made for man, 'twas made for
me.　　　　　　　　　　　　　　　　　　　　10
I will renounce this magic and repent.

(*Enter the two Angels.*)

GOOD ANGEL: Faustus repent; yet God will pity thee.
BAD ANGEL: Thou art a spirit;° God cannot pity thee.
FAUSTUS: Who buzzeth in mine ears I am a spirit?
Be I a devil, yet God may pity me;　　　　　　　15
Yea, God will pity me if I repent.
BAD ANGEL: Ay, but Faustus never shall repent.
　　　　　　　　　　　　　　　(*Exeunt angels.*)
FAUSTUS: My heart is hardened; I cannot repent.
Scarce can I name salvation, faith, or heaven,
But fearful echoes thunder in mine ears:　　　　20
"Faustus, thou art damned!" Then swords and
knives,
Poison, guns, halters, and envenomed steel
Are laid before me to dispatch myself;
And long ere this I should have done the deed,
Had not sweet pleasure conquered deep despair.　25
Have not I made blind Homer sing to me
Of Alexander's love and Oenone's death?°
And hath not he, that built the walls of Thebes
With ravishing sound of his melodious harp,°
Made music with my Mephistophilis?　　　　　30
Why should I die then, or basely despair?
I am resolved; Faustus shall not repent.
Come, Mephistophilis, let us dispute again
And reason of divine astrology.
Speak; are there many spheres above the moon?　35
Are all celestial bodies but one globe,
As is the substance of this centric earth?
MEPHISTOPHILIS: As are the elements, such are the
heavens,
Even from the moon unto the empyreal orb,
Mutually folded in each others' spheres,　　　　40
And jointly move upon one axle-tree.
Whose terminè° is termed the world's wide pole;
Nor are the names of Saturn, Mars, or Jupiter
Feigned, but are erring stars.°
FAUSTUS:　　　　　　　　　But have they all
One motion, both *situ et tempore?*°　　　　　　45

II, II. 13. spirit: Devil. 27. Alexander's . . . death: Paris (also called Alexander) loved the nymph Oenone when he lived as a shepherd on Mt. Ida. Oenone died of a broken heart when he left her. 28–29. he . . . harp: Amphion, son of Zeus and Antiope, caused stones to move and the walls of Thebes to be built simply by playing on the lyre given to him by Hermes. 42. terminè: Limit. 44. erring stars: Planets. 45. *situ et tempore*: In position (direction of movement) and in the time they take to revolve about the earth.

MEPHISTOPHILIS: All move from east to west in four
   and twenty hours upon the poles of the world, but
   differ in their motions upon the poles of the zodiac.
FAUSTUS: These slender questions Wagner can decide.
50   Hath Mephistophilis no greater skill?
   Who knows not the double motion of the planets?
   That the first is finished in a natural day?
   The second thus? Saturn in thirty years?
   Jupiter in twelve; Mars in four; the sun, Venus and
55   Mercury in a year, the moon in twenty eight days.
   These are freshmen's suppositions. But tell me hath
   every sphere a dominion or *intelligentia?*°
MEPHISTOPHILIS: Ay.
FAUSTUS: How many heavens or spheres are there?
60 MEPHISTOPHILIS: Nine—the seven planets, the firma-
   ment, and the empyreal heaven.
FAUSTUS: But is there not *coelum igneum, et crystalli-
   num?*°
MEPHISTOPHILIS: No, Faustus, they be but fables.
65 FAUSTUS: Resolve me then in this one question: why are
   not conjunctions, oppositions, aspects, eclipses° all at
   one time, but in some years we have more, in some
   less?
MEPHISTOPHILIS: *Per inaequalem motum respectu*
70   *totius.*°
FAUSTUS: Well, I am answered. Now tell me who made
   the world.
MEPHISTOPHILIS: I will not.
FAUSTUS: Sweet Mephistophilis, tell me.
75 MEPHISTOPHILIS: Move me not, Faustus.
FAUSTUS: Villain, have not I bound thee to tell me any
   thing?
MEPHISTOPHILIS: Ay, that is not against our kingdom.
   This is. Thou art damned. Think thou of hell.
FAUSTUS: Think, Faustus, upon God that made the
80   world.
MEPHISTOPHILIS: Remember this.
                                        (*Exit.*)
FAUSTUS: Ay, go accursèd spirit to ugly hell.
   'Tis thou hast damned distressèd Faustus' soul.
   Is't not too late?

(*Enter the two Angels.*)

85 BAD ANGEL: Too late.
GOOD ANGEL: Never too late, if Faustus will repent.
BAD ANGEL: If thou repent, devils will tear thee in
   pieces.
GOOD ANGEL: Repent, and they shall never raze thy skin.
                                 (*Exeunt Angels.*)

57. dominion or *intelligentia:* Governing angel.   62–63. *coelum...crystallinum:* The fiery heaven and crystalline sphere of
Ptolemaic astronomy.   66. conjunctions: Seeming proximities
of heavenly bodies.   oppositions: Divergences of heavenly
bodies.   aspects: Any other relations of such bodies to one
another.   eclipses: The blottings out of one heavenly body by
another.   69–70. *Per...totius:* By their unequal movements in
respect to the whole (i.e., the different speeds of the various
planets within the total cosmos).

FAUSTUS: O Christ, my Savior, my Savior,
   Help to save distressèd Faustus' soul.   90

(*Enter Lucifer, Beelzebub, and Mephistophilis.*)

LUCIFER: Christ cannot save thy soul, for he is just.
   There's none but I have interest in the same.
FAUSTUS: O, what art thou that look'st so terribly?
LUCIFER: I am Lucifer,
   And this is my companion prince in hell.   95
FAUSTUS: O, Faustus, they are come to fetch thy soul.
BEELZEBUB: We are come to tell thee thou dost injure us.
LUCIFER: Thou call'st on Christ, contrary to thy
   promise.
BEELZEBUB: Thou shouldst not think on God.
LUCIFER: Think on the devil.   100
BEELZEBUB: And his dam too.
FAUSTUS: Nor will I henceforth. Pardon me in this,
   And Faustus vows never to look to heaven,
   Never to name God, or to pray to him,
   To burn his Scriptures, slay his ministers,   105
   And make my spirits pull his churches down.
LUCIFER: So shalt thou show thyself an obedient
   servant,
   And we will highly gratify thee for it.
BEELZEBUB: Faustus, we are come from hell in person to
   show thee some pastime. Sit down, and thou shalt   110
   behold the Seven Deadly Sins appear to thee in their
   own proper shapes and likeness.
FAUSTUS: That sight will be as pleasant to me as Paradise
   was to Adam the first day of his creation.
LUCIFER: Talk not of Paradise or creation, but mark the   115
   show. Go, Mephistophilis, fetch them in.
                           [*Exit Mephistophilis.*]

(*Enter the Seven Deadly Sins, [with Mephistophilis, led
by a Piper].*)

BEELZEBUB: Now Faustus, question them of their names
   and dispositions.
FAUSTUS: That shall I soon. What art thou, the first?
PRIDE: I am Pride. I disdain to have any parents. I am   120
   like to Ovid's flea:° I can creep into every corner of a
   wench. Sometimes, like a periwig, I sit upon her
   brow. Next, like a necklace, I hang about her neck.
   Then, like a fan of feathers, I kiss her lips, and then,
   turning myself to a wrought smock, do what I list.   125
   But fie, what a smell is here! I'll not speak another
   word unless the ground be perfumed and covered
   with cloth of Arras.°
FAUSTUS: Thou art a proud knave indeed. What art
   thou, the second?   130
COVETOUSNESS: I am Covetousness, begotten of an old
   churl in a leather bag, and might I now obtain my
   wish, this house, you and all, should turn to gold, that
   I might lock you safe into my chest. O my sweet gold!

121. Ovid's flea: The medieval poem *Carmine de Pulice* (Poem
of the Flea) was generally attributed to Ovid.   128. cloth of
Arras: Flemish cloth used generally for tapestries.

Emrys James (l.) as Mephistophilis and Ian McKellen as Doctor Faustus in the 1974 Royal Shakespeare Company's production of Marlowe's play.

135   FAUSTUS: And what art thou, the third?
ENVY: I am Envy, begotten of a chimney-sweeper and an oyster-wife. I cannot read and therefore wish all books burned. I am lean with seeing others eat. O, that there would come a famine over all the world,
140   that all might die, and I live alone; then thou shouldst see how fat I'd be. But must thou sit and I stand? Come down, with a vengeance.
FAUSTUS: Out envious wretch! But what are thou, the fourth?
145   WRATH: I am Wrath. I had neither father nor mother. I leaped out of a lion's mouth when I was scarce an hour old, and ever since have run up and down the world with this case of rapiers, wounding myself when I could get none to fight withal. I was born in
150   hell, and look to it, for some of you shall be my father.
FAUSTUS: And what are you, the fifth?
GLUTTONY: I am Gluttony. My parents are all dead, and the devil a penny they have left me but a small pen-
155   sion, and that buys me thirty meals a day and ten bevers°—a small trifle to suffice nature. I come of a royal pedigree. My father was a gammon of bacon, and my mother was a hogshead of claret wine. My godfathers were these: Peter Pickled-herring and
160   Martin Martlemas-beef.° But my godmother, O, she

was a jolly gentlewoman, and well beloved in every good town and city; her name was Mistress Margery March-beer.° Now Faustus, thou hast heard all my progeny; wilt thou bid me to a supper?
FAUSTUS: Not I. Thou wilt eat up all my victuals.   165
GLUTTONY: Then the devil choke thee.
FAUSTUS: Choke thyself, glutton. What art thou, the sixth?
SLOTH: Heigh ho! I am Sloth. I was begotten on a sunny bank, where I have lain ever since, and you have done   170
me great injury to bring me from thence. Let me be carried thither again by Gluttony and Lechery. Heigh ho! I'll not speak a word more for a king's ransom.
FAUSTUS: And what are you Mistress Minx, the seventh and last?   175
LECHERY: Who, I, sir? I am one that loves an inch of raw mutton° better than an ell of fried stockfish,° and the first letter of my name begins with lechery.
LUCIFER: Away to hell! Away! On piper!
                    (*Exeunt the seven Sins [and the Piper]*.)
FAUSTUS: O, how this sight doth delight my soul!   180
LUCIFER: But Faustus, in hell is all manner of delight.
FAUSTUS: O, might I see hell and return again safe, how happy were I then!
LUCIFER: Faustus, thou shalt. At midnight I will send for thee. Meanwhile peruse this book and view it   185

156. **bevers:** Light snacks taken between regular meals.
160. **Martlemas-beef:** Salted meat hung for the winter on Martinmas, November 11.

163. **March-beer:** A fine ale made in the springtime and aged for two years before being drunk.   176–177. **raw mutton:** Common slang for "whore."   177. **stockfish:** Dried codfish.

thoroughly, and thou shalt turn thyself into what
shape thou wilt.

FAUSTUS: Thanks, mighty Lucifer.
    This will I keep as chary as my life.

190 LUCIFER: Now Faustus, farewell.

FAUSTUS: Farewell, great Lucifer. Come, Mephistophilis.
                                        (*Exeunt, several ways.*)

Scene III

(*Enter the Clown, [Robin, holding a book].*)

ROBIN: What, Dick, look to the horses there till I come
    again. I have gotten one of Doctor Faustus' conjuring
    books, and now we'll have such knavery as't passes.

(*Enter Dick.*)

DICK: What, Robin, you must come away and walk the
5   horses.

ROBIN: I walk the horses? I scorn't, 'faith. I have other
    matters in hand. Let the horses walk themselves and
    they will. [*He reads.*] *A per se a; t, h, e, the; o per se o;
    deny orgon, gorgon.* Keep further from me, O thou
10   illiterate and unlearned hostler.

DICK: 'Snails,° what hast thou got there? A book? Why,
    thou canst not tell ne'er a word on't.

ROBIN: That thou shalt see presently. Keep out of the
    circle, I say, lest I send you into the hostry with a
15   vengeance.

DICK: That's like, 'faith. You had best leave your fool-
    ery, for an my master come, he'll conjure you, 'faith.

ROBIN: My master conjure me? I'll tell thee what: an my
    master come here, I'll clap as fair a pair of horns°
20   on's head as e'er thou sawest in thy life.

DICK: Thou needst not do that, for my mistress hath
    done it.

ROBIN: Ay, there be of us here that have waded as deep
    into matters as other men, if they were disposed to
25   talk.

DICK: A plague take you! I thought you did not sneak up
    and down after her for nothing. But I prithee, tell me
    in good sadness,° Robin, is that a conjuring book?

ROBIN: Do but speak what thou'lt have me to do, and
30   I'll do't. If thou'lt dance naked, put off thy clothes
    and I'll conjure thee about presently. Or if thou'lt go
    but to the tavern with me, I'll give thee white wine,
    red wine, claret wine, sack, muscadine, malmesey
    and whippincrust.° Hold belly, hold, and we'll not
35   pay one penny for it.

DICK: O brave! Prithee let's to it presently, for I am as
    dry as a dog.

ROBIN: Come then, let's away.

                                        (*Exeunt.*)

ACT III • *Prologue*

(*Enter the Chorus.*)

CHORUS: Learnèd Faustus,
    To find the secrets of astronomy
    Graven in the book of Jove's high firmament,
    Did mount him up to scale Olympus' top,
    Where, sitting in a chariot burning bright   5
    Drawn by the strength of yokèd dragons' necks,
    He views the clouds, the planets, and the stars,
    The tropics, zones, and quarters of the sky,
    From the bright circle of the hornèd moon
    Even to the height of *Primum Mobile.*°   10
    And whirling round with this circumference,
    Within the concave compass of the pole,
    From east to west his dragons swiftly glide
    And in eight days did bring him home again.
    Not long he stayed within his quiet house   15
    To rest his bones after his weary toil,
    But new exploits do hale him out again,
    And mounted then upon a dragon's back,
    That with his wings did part the subtle air,
    He now is gone to prove cosmography,°   20
    That measures coasts and kingdoms of the earth,
    And, as I guess, will first arrive at Rome
    To see the Pope and manner of his court
    And take some part of holy Peter's feast,
    The which this day is highly solemnized.   25

                                        (*Exit.*)

Scene I

(*Enter Faustus and Mephistophilis.*)

FAUSTUS: Having now, my good Mephistophilis,
    Passed with delight the stately town of Trier,
    Environed round with airy mountain tops,
    With walls of flint, and deep entrenchèd lakes,°
    Not to be won by any conquering prince;   5
    From Paris next, coasting the realm of France,
    We saw the river Main fall into Rhine,
    Whose banks are set with groves of fruitful vines;
    Then up to Naples, rich Campania,
    Whose buildings fair and gorgeous to the eye,   10
    The streets straight forth and paved with finest brick,
    Quarters the town in four equivalents.
    There saw we learnèd Maro's° golden tomb,
    The way he cut, an English mile in length,
    Through a rock of stone in one night's space.°   15

II, III. 11. 'Snails: By God's nails.   **19. horns:** The common sign
of a cuckold.   **28. sadness:** Seriousness.   **34. whippincrust:**
Possibly a corruption of "hippocras," a highly spiced and
sugared wine.

III, Prologue. 10. *Primum Mobile*: In Ptolemaic astronomy
the outermost sphere of creation, which moves the other
nine spheres.   **20. prove cosmography:** Explore the universe.
III, I. 4. entrenchèd lakes: Castle moats.   **13. Maro:** Virgil.
14–15. way . . . space: A tunnel between the bays of Naples and
Baiae, through Mt. Posilipo, was said to have been cut by Virgil
(regarded as a magician in the Middle Ages) by supernatural
art.

From thence to Venice, Padua, and the rest,
In midst of which a sumptuous temple stands,
That threats the stars with her aspiring top,
Whose frame is paved with sundry colored stones,
20   And roofed aloft with curious work in gold.°
Thus hitherto hath Faustus spent his time.
But tell me now, what resting-place is this?
Hast thou, as erst I did command,
Conducted me within the walls of Rome?
MEPHISTOPHILIS: I have, my Faustus, and for proof
25   thereof
This is the goodly palace of the Pope;
And 'cause we are no common guests,
I choose his privy chamber for our use.
FAUSTUS: I hope his holiness will bid us welcome.
MEPHISTOPHILIS: All's one, for we'll be bold with his
30   venison.
But now, my Faustus, that thou may'st perceive
What Rome contains for to delight thine eyes,
Know that this city stands upon seven hills
That underprop the groundwork of the same.
35   Just through the midst runs flowing Tiber's stream,
With winding banks that cut it in two parts,
Over the which four stately bridges lean,
That make safe passage to each part of Rome.
Upon the bridge called Ponte Angelo
40   Erected is a castle passing strong,
Where thou shalt see such store of ordinance
As that the double cannons, forged of brass,
Do match the number of the days contained
Within the compass of one complete year;
45   Beside the gates and high pyramidès
That Julius Caesar brought from Africa.°
FAUSTUS: Now, by the kingdoms of infernal rule,
Of Styx, of Acheron, and the fiery lake
Of ever-burning Phlegethon, I swear
50   That I do long to see the monuments
And situation of bright-splendent Rome.
Come, therefore, let's away.
MEPHISTOPHILIS: Nay, stay my Faustus. I know you'd
see the Pope
And take some part of holy Peter's feast,
55   The which, in state and high solemnity,
This day is held through Rome and Italy
In honor of the Pope's triumphant victory.
FAUSTUS: Sweet Mephistophilis, thou pleasest me.
Whilst I am here on earth, let me be cloyed
60   With all things that delight the heart of man.
My four and twenty years of liberty
I'll spend in pleasure and in dalliance,
That Faustus' name, whilst this bright frame doth
stand,
May be admirèd through the furthest land.

MEPHISTOPHILIS: 'Tis well said, Faustus. Come then,
stand by me   65
And thou shalt see them come immediately.
FAUSTUS: Nay, stay, my gentle Mephistophilis,
And grant me my request, and then I go.
Thou know'st within the compass of eight days
We viewed the face of heaven, of earth, and hell.   70
So high our dragons soared into the air,
That looking down, the earth appeared to me
No bigger than my hand in quantity.
There did we view the kingdoms of the world,
And what might please mine eye I there beheld.   75
Then in this show let me an actor be,
That this proud Pope may Faustus' cunning see.
MEPHISTOPHILIS: Let it be so, my Faustus. But, first stay
And view their triumphs° as they pass this way,
And then devise what best contents thy mind   80
By cunning in thine art to cross the Pope
Or dash the pride of this solemnity,
To make his monks and abbots stand like apes
And point like antics at his triple crown,
To beat the beads about the friars' pates   85
Or clap huge horns upon the cardinals' heads,
Or any villainy thou canst devise,
And I'll perform it, Faustus. Hark, they come.
This day shall make thee be admired in Rome.

(*Enter the Cardinals and Bishops, some bearing crosiers,
some the pillars; Monks and Friars singing their procession. Then the Pope, and Raymond, King of Hungary,
with Bruno, led in chains.*)

POPE: Cast down our footstool.
RAYMOND: Saxon Bruno, stoop,   90
Whilst on thy back his holiness ascends
Saint Peter's chair and state pontifical.
BRUNO: Proud Lucifer, that state belongs to me,
But thus I fall to Peter, not to thee.
POPE: To me and Peter shalt thou groveling lie   95
And crouch before the papal dignity.
Sound trumpets then, for thus Saint Peter's heir
From Bruno's back ascends Saint Peter's chair.

(*A flourish while he ascends.*)

Thus, as the gods creep on with feet of wool
Long ere with iron hands they punish men,   100
So shall our sleeping vengeance now arise
And smite with death thy hated enterprise.
Lord Cardinals of France and Padua,
Go forthwith to our holy consistory,
And read amongst the Statutes Decretal°   105
What, by the holy council held at Trent,°
The sacred synod hath decreed for him
That doth assume the papal government

17–20. In midst . . . gold: St. Mark's cathedral in Venice.
45–46. gates . . . Africa: Before the gates of St. Peter's there still
stands the obelisk that was brought to Rome from Heliopolis
by the Emperor Caligula in the first century CE.

79. triumphs: Spectacular displays.   **105. Statutes Decretal:**
Papal decrees concerning religious doctrine or ecclesiastical
law.   **106. council . . . Trent:** The Council of Trent, held by
the Church from 1545 to 1563.

Without election and a true consent.
110   Away, and bring us word with speed.
FIRST CARDINAL: We go my Lord.
                                    (*Exeunt Cardinals.*)
POPE: Lord Raymond.   [*They talk apart.*]
FAUSTUS: Go, haste thee, gentle Mephistophilis,
      Follow the cardinals to the consistory,
115   And as they turn their superstitious books,
      Strike them with sloth and drowsy idleness,
      And make them sleep so sound that in their shapes
      Thyself and I may parley with this Pope,
      This proud confronter of the Emperor,
120   And in despite of all his holiness
      Restore this Bruno to his liberty
      And bear him to the states of Germany.
MEPHISTOPHILIS: Faustus, I go.
FAUSTUS: Dispatch it soon.
125   The Pope shall curse that Faustus came to Rome.
                  (*Exeunt Faustus and Mephistophilis.*)
BRUNO: Pope Adrian,° let me have some right of law.
      I was elected by the Emperor.
POPE: We will depose the Emperor for that deed
      And curse the people that submit to him.
130   Both he and thou shalt stand excommunicate
      And interdict from church's privilege
      And all society of holy men.
      He grows too proud in his authority,
      Lifting his lofty head above the clouds,
135   And like a steeple overpeers the church.
      But we'll pull down his haughty insolence,
      And as Pope Alexander, our progenitor,
      Trod on the neck of German Frederick,°
      Adding this golden sentence to our praise,
140   "That Peter's heirs should tread on emperors
      And walk upon the dreadful adder's back,
      Treading the lion and the dragon down
      And fearless spurn the killing basilisk,"°
      So will we quell that haughty schismatic,
145   And by authority apostolical
      Depose him from his regal government.
BRUNO: Pope Julius swore to princely Sigismond,°
      For him and the succeeding popes of Rome,
      To hold the emperors their lawful lords.
150   POPE: Pope Julius did abuse the church's rites,
      And therefore none of his decrees can stand.

126. Pope Adrian: Marlowe perhaps means Pope Hadrian IV (1154–1159), who tried to assert his authority over Frederick Barbarossa, the Holy Roman Emperor. What historicity there may be in these scenes at the papal court is badly confused. **137–138. Pope Alexander . . . Frederick:** Pope Alexander III (1159–1181), successor to Hadrian IV, continued the struggle against Barbarossa, forcing him to acknowledge the papal supremacy at Canossa.   **143. basilisk:** A mythical monster with power to kill by its looks.   **147. Pope Julius . . . Sigismond:** None of the three popes named Julius was contemporary with the Emperor Sigismund (1368–1437). Sigismund did, however, in 1414 summon the Council of Constance, which sought to end the Great Schism (1378–1417), during which the papacy in Rome was challenged by a line of popes in Avignon.

Is not all power on earth bestowed on us?
      And therefore, though we would, we cannot err.
      Behold this silver belt, whereto is fixed
      Seven golden keys fast sealed with seven seals   155
      In token of our sevenfold power from heaven,
      To bind or loose, lock fast, condemn or judge,
      Resign, or seal, or whatso pleaseth us.
      Then he and thou and all the world shall stoop,
      Or be assurèd of our dreadful curse   160
      To light as heavy as the pains of hell.
(*Enter Faustus and Mephistophilis, like the Cardinals.*)
MEPHISTOPHILIS: Now tell me, Faustus, are we not
      fitted well?
FAUSTUS: Yes, Mephistophilis, and two such cardinals
      Ne'er served a holy pope as we shall do.
      But whilst they sleep within the consistory,   165
      Let us salute his reverend fatherhood.
RAYMOND: Behold, my lord, the cardinals are
      returned.
POPE: Welcome, grave fathers. Answer presently:
      What have our holy council there decreed
      Concerning Bruno and the Emperor,   170
      In quittance of their late conspiracy
      Against our state and papal dignity?
FAUSTUS: Most sacred patron of the church of Rome,
      By full consent of all the synod
      Of priests and prelates it is thus decreed: 175
      That Bruno and the German Emperor
      Be held as Lollards° and bold schismatics
      And proud disturbers of the church's peace.
      And if that Bruno by his own assent,
      Without enforcement of the German peers,   180
      Did seek to wear the triple diadem
      And by your death to climb Saint Peter's chair,
      The Statutes Decretal have thus decreed:
      He shall be straight condemned of heresy
      And on a pile of fagots burned to death.   185
POPE: It is enough. Here, take him to your charge,
      And bear him straight to Ponte Angelo,
      And in the strongest tower enclose him fast.
      Tomorrow, sitting in our consistory
      With all our college of grave cardinals,   190
      We will determine of his life or death.
      Here, take his triple crown along with you,
      And leave it in the church's treasury.
      Make haste again, my good lord cardinals,
      And take our blessing apostolical.   195
MEPHISTOPHILIS: So, so. Was never devil thus blessed
      before.
FAUSTUS: Away, sweet Mephistophilis, be gone.
      The cardinals will be plagued for this anon.
(*Exeunt Faustus and Mephistophilis* [*with Bruno*].)
POPE: Go presently and bring a banquet forth,
      That we may solemnize Saint Peter's feast,   200

177. Lollards: Followers of John Wyclif (1320?–1384), the English reformer.

And with Lord Raymond, King of Hungary,
Drink to our late and happy victory.   (*Exeunt.*)

Scene II

(*A sennet* [*is sounded*] *while the banquet is brought in;
and then enter Faustus and Mephistophilis in their own
shapes.*)

MEPHISTOPHILIS: Now, Faustus, come, prepare thyself
   for mirth.
   The sleepy cardinals are hard at hand
   To censure Bruno, that is posted hence,
   And on a proud-paced steed, as swift as thought,
5   Flies o'er the Alps to fruitful Germany,
   There to salute the woeful Emperor.
FAUSTUS: The Pope will curse them for their sloth
   today,
   That slept both Bruno and his crown away.
   But now, that Faustus may delight his mind
10   And by their folly make some merriment,
   Sweet Mephistophilis, so charm me here
   That I may walk invisible to all
   And do whate'er I please unseen of any.
MEPHISTOPHILIS: Faustus, thou shalt. Then kneel down
   presently:
15   *Whilst on thy head I lay my hand*
   And charm thee with this magic wand.
   First wear this girdle; then appear
   Invisible to all are here.
   The planets seven, the gloomy air,
20   *Hell and the Furies'° forkèd hair,*
   Pluto's blue fire, and Hecate's tree,°
   With magic spells so compass thee
   That no eye may thy body see.
   So Faustus. Now, for all their holiness,
25   Do what thou wilt, thou shalt not be discerned.
FAUSTUS: Thanks, Mephistophilis. Now friars take heed
   Lest Faustus make your shaven crowns to bleed.
MEPHISTOPHILIS: Faustus, no more. See where the
   cardinals come.

(*Enter Pope and all the Lords. Enter the Cardinals with
a book.*)

POPE: Welcome, lord cardinals. Come, sit down.
30   Lord Raymond, take your seat. Friars attend,
   And see that all things be in readiness,
   As best beseems this solemn festival.
FIRST CARDINAL: First, may it please your sacred
   holiness
   To view the sentence of the reverend synod
35   Concerning Bruno and the Emperor?
POPE: What needs this question? Did I not tell you
   Tomorrow we would sit i' th' consistory

And there determine of his punishment?
You brought us word even now; it was decreed
That Bruno and the cursèd Emperor   40
Were by the holy council both condemned
For loathèd Lollards and base schismatics.
Then wherefore would you have me view that
   book?
FIRST CARDINAL: Your grace mistakes. You gave us no
   such charge.
RAYMOND: Deny it not. We all are witnesses   45
   That Bruno here was late delivered you,
   With his rich triple crown to be reserved
   And put into the church's treasury.
BOTH CARDINALS: By holy Paul, we saw them not.
POPE: By Peter, you shall die   50
   Unless you bring them forth immediately.
   Hale them to prison. Lade their limbs with
    gyves.°
   False prelates, for this hateful treachery
   Cursed be your souls to hellish misery.

     [*Exeunt the two Cardinals with Attendants.*]

FAUSTUS: So, they are safe. Now, Faustus, to the
   feast.   55
   The Pope had never such a frolic guest.
POPE: Lord Archbishop of Rheims, sit down with us.
ARCHBISHOP: I thank your holiness.
FAUSTUS: Fall to. The devil choke you an you spare.°
POPE: Who's that spoke? Friars look about.   60
FRIAR: Here's nobody, if it like your holiness.
POPE: Lord Raymond, pray fall to. I am beholding
   To the Bishop of Milan for this so rare a present.
FAUSTUS: I thank you, sir.   [*He snatches the dish.*]
POPE: How now? Who snatched the meat from me?   65
   Villains, why speak you not?
   My good Lord Archbishop, here's a most dainty
    dish
   Was sent me from a cardinal in France.
FAUSTUS: I'll have that too.   [*He snatches the dish.*]
POPE: What Lollards do attend our holiness,   70
   That we receive such great indignity?
   Fetch me some wine.
FAUSTUS: Ay, pray do, for Faustus is a-dry.
POPE: Lord Raymond, I drink unto your grace.
FAUSTUS: I pledge your grace.   [*He snatches the cup.*]   75
POPE: My wine gone too? Ye lubbers, look about
   And find the man that doth this villainy,
   Or by our sanctitude, you all shall die.
   I pray, my lords, have patience at this
   Troublesome banquet.   80
ARCHBISHOP: Please it your holiness, I think it be some
   ghost crept out of purgatory, and now is come unto
   your holiness for his pardon.
POPE: It may be so.
   Go then, command our priests to sing a dirge   85

III, II. 20. *Furies:* Spirits called on to avenge crimes, especially
crimes against kin.   21. *Hecate's tree:* Hecate is the goddess of
witchcraft.

52. Lade . . . gyves: Shackle their limbs.   59. an you spare: If
you hold back.

To lay the fury of this same troublesome ghost.
                                [*Exit an attendant.*]
Once again, my lord, fall to.
                        (*The Pope crosseth himself.*)
FAUSTUS: How now?
    Must every bit be spicèd with a cross?
90 Nay then, take that.   [*He strikes the Pope.*]
POPE: O I am slain. Help me, my lords.
    O come and help to bear my body hence.
    Damned be this soul for ever for this deed.

                (*Exeunt the Pope and his train.*)

MEPHISTOPHILIS: Now, Faustus, what will you do now?
95 For I can tell you you'll be cursed with bell, book,
    and candle.°
FAUSTUS: Bell, book, and candle; candle, book, and bell,
    Forward and backward, to curse Faustus to hell.

(*Enter the Friars with bell, book, and candle for the
dirge.*)

FIRST FRIAR: Come, brethren, let's about our business
100   with good devotion.   [*They chant.*]
        *Cursed be he that stole his holiness' meat from
        the table.*
            Maledicat Dominus!°
        *Cursed be he that struck his holiness a blow on
        the face.*
            Maledicat Dominus!
        *Cursed be he that struck Friar Sandelo a blow on
105   the pate.*
            Maledicat Dominus!
        Cursed be he that disturbeth our holy dirge.
            Maledicat Dominus!
        Cursed be he that took away his holiness's wine.
110   *Maledicat Dominus! Et omnes sancti.*°
        Amen.

([*Faustus and Mephistophilis*] *beat the Friars, fling fireworks among them, and exeunt.*)

Scene III

(*Enter* [*Robin,*] *the clown, and Dick, with a cup.*)

DICK: Sirrah Robin, we were best look that your devil
    can answer the stealing of this same cup, for the vint-
    ner's boy follows us at the hard heels.
ROBIN: 'Tis no matter. Let him come. An he follow us,
5   I'll so conjure him as he was never conjured in his
    life, I warrant him. Let me see the cup.

(*Enter Vintner.*)

DICK: Here 'tis. Yonder he comes. Now, Robin, now or
    never show thy cunning.

95–96. **bell, book, and candle:** Used traditionally in the rite of
excommunication. 102. *Maledicat Dominus:* May the Lord
curse him. 110. *Et omnes sancti:* And all the saints.

VINTNER: O, are you here? I am glad I have found you.
    You are a couple of fine companions. Pray, where's   10
    the cup you stole from the tavern?
ROBIN: How, how? We steal a cup? Take heed what you
    say. We look not like cup stealers, I can tell you.
VINTNER: Never deny's, for I know you have it, and I'll
    search you.   15
ROBIN: Search me? Ay, and spare not. Hold the cup, Dick.
    [*Aside to Dick.*] Come, come, search me, search me.

[*The Vintner searches Robin.*]

VINTNER: [*to Dick*] Come on, sirrah, let me search you
    now.
DICK: Ay, ay, do, do. Hold the cup, Robin. [*Aside to   20
    Robin.*] I fear not your searching. We scorn to steal
    your cups, I can tell you.

[*The Vintner searches Dick.*]

VINTNER: Never outface me for the matter, for sure the
    cup is between you two.
ROBIN: Nay, there you lie. 'Tis beyond us both.   25
VINTNER: A plague take you! I thought 'twas your knav-
    ery to take it away. Come, give it me again.
ROBIN: Ay, much. When? Can you tell? Dick, make me
    a circle, and stand close at my back, and stir not for
    thy life. Vintner, you shall have your cup anon. Say   30
    nothing, Dick, *O per se, O Demogorgon, Belcher
    and Mephistophilis.*

(*Enter Mephistophilis.* [*Exit the Vintner, in fright.*])

MEPHISTOPHILIS: Monarch of hell, under whose black
        survey
    Great potentates do kneel with awful fear,
    Upon whose altars thousand souls do lie,   35
    How am I vexèd by these villains' charms!
    From Constantinople have they brought me now,
    Only for pleasure of these damnèd slaves.
ROBIN: By Lady, sir, you have had a shrewd journey of
    it. Will it please you to take a shoulder of mutton to 40
    supper and a tester° in your purse, and go back again?
DICK: Ay, I pray you heartily, sir, for we called you but in
    jest, I promise you.
MEPHISTOPHILIS: To purge the rashness of this cursèd
        deed,
    First be thou turnèd to this ugly shape,   45
    For apish deeds transformèd to an ape.
ROBIN: O brave, an ape! I pray sir, let me have the carry-
    ing of him about to show some tricks.
MEPHISTOPHILIS: And so thou shalt. Be thou trans-
    formed to a dog, and carry him upon thy back. Away, 50
    be gone!
ROBIN: A dog? That's excellent. Let the maids look well
    to their porridge pots, for I'll into the kitchen pres-
    ently. Come, Dick, come.

                (*Exeunt* [*Robin and Dick,*] *the two clowns.*)

III, III. 41. **tester:** Sixpence.

55 MEPHISTOPHILIS: Now with the flames of everburning
        fire,
      I'll wing myself and forthwith fly amain
      Unto my Faustus, to the great Turk's court.
                                              (*Exit.*)

ACT IV • *Prologue*

(*Enter Chorus.*)

CHORUS: When Faustus had with pleasure ta'en the
        view
      Of rarest things and royal courts of kings,
      He stayed his course and so returnèd home;
      Where such as bare his absence but with grief—
5   I mean his friends and nearest companions—
      Did gratulate his safety with kind words,
      And in their conference of what befell,
      Touching his journey through the world and air,
      They put forth questions of astrology,
10   Which Faustus answered with such learnèd skill
      As they admired and wondered at his wit.
      Now is his fame spread forth in every land.
      Amongst the rest, the Emperor is one—
      Carolus the fifth°—at whose palace now
15   Faustus is feasted 'mongst his noblemen.
      What there he did in trial of his art
      I leave untold, your eyes shall see performed.
                                              (*Exit.*)

Scene I

(*Enter Martino and Frederick, at several doors.*)

MARTINO: What ho, officers, gentlemen,
      Hie to the presences° to attend the Emperor.
      Good Frederick, see the rooms be voided
        straight;
      His majesty is coming to the hall.
5   Go back, and see the state° in readiness.
FREDERICK: But where is Bruno, our elected Pope,
      That on a fury's back came post from Rome?
      Will not his grace consort the Emperor?
MARTINO: O yes, and with him comes the German
        conjurer,
10   The learnèd Faustus, fame of Wittenberg,
      The wonder of the world for magic art;
      And he intends to show great Carolus
      The race of all his stout progenitors,
      And bring in presence of his majesty
15   The royal shapes and warlike semblances
      Of Alexander° and his beauteous paramour.

IV, Prologue. 14. Carolus the fifth: Charles V, King of Spain
(as Charles I from 1516 to 1556) and Holy Roman Emperor
from 1519 to 1556.   IV, I. 2. presences: Emperor's chamber.
5. state: Throne.   16. Alexander: Alexander the Great.

FREDERICK: Where is Benvolio?
MARTINO: Fast asleep, I warrant you.
      He took his rouse with stoups° of Rhenish wine
      So kindly yesternight to Bruno's health   20
      That all this day the sluggard keeps his bed.
FREDERICK: See, see, his window's ope. We'll call to
        him.
MARTINO: What ho, Benvolio!

(*Enter Benvolio above at a window, in his nightcap, buttoning.*)

BENVOLIO: What a devil ail you two?
MARTINO: Speak softly, sir, lest the devil hear you,   25
      For Faustus at the court is late arrived,
      And at his heels a thousand furies wait
      To accomplish whatsoever the doctor please.
BENVOLIO: What of this?
MARTINO: Come, leave thy chamber first, and thou
        shalt see   30
      This conjurer perform such rare exploits
      Before the Pope° and royal Emperor
      As never yet was seen in Germany.
BENVOLIO: Has not the Pope enough of conjuring yet?
      He was upon the devil's back late enough,   35
      And if he be so far in love with him,
      I would he would post with him to Rome again.
FREDERICK: Speak, wilt thou come and see this sport?
BENVOLIO: Not I.
MARTINO: Wilt thou stand in thy window and see it
        then?   40
BENVOLIO: Ay, and I fall not asleep i' th' meantime.
MARTINO: The Emperor is at hand, who comes to see
      What wonders by black spells may compassed be.
BENVOLIO: Well, go you attend the Emperor. I am con-
      tent for this once to thrust my head out at a window, 45
      for they say if a man be drunk overnight the devil
      cannot hurt him in the morning. If that be true, I
      have a charm in my head shall control him as well as
      the conjurer, I warrant you.

(*Exit [Frederick, with Martino. Benvolio remains at the
window above].*)

Scene II

(*A sennet [is sounded. Enter] Charles, the German Emperor, Bruno, [the Duke of] Saxony, Faustus, Mephistophilis, Frederick, Martino, and Attendants.*)

EMPEROR: Wonder of men, renowned magician,
      Thrice-learnèd Faustus, welcome to our court.
      This deed of thine, in setting Bruno free
      From his and our professèd enemy,
      Shall add more excellence unto thine art   5

---

19. took . . . stoups: Had a drinking bout with brimming gob-
lets.   32. the Pope: Bruno.

Than if by powerful necromantic spells
Thou couldst command the world's obedience.
Forever be beloved of Carolus,
And if this Bruno thou hast late redeemed°
10   In peace possess the triple diadem
And sit in Peter's chair despite of chance,
Thou shalt be famous through all Italy
And honored of the German Emperor.
FAUSTUS: These gracious words, most royal Carolus,
15   Shall make poor Faustus to his utmost power
Both love and serve the German Emperor
And lay his life at holy Bruno's feet.
For proof whereof, if so your grace be pleased,
The doctor stands prepared by power of art
20   To cast his magic charms that shall pierce through
The ebon gates of ever-burning hell,
And hale the stubborn Furies from their caves
To compass whatsoe'er your grace commands.
BENVOLIO: [above] Blood, he speaks terribly, but for all
25   that, I do not greatly believe him. He looks as like a
conjurer as the Pope° to a costermonger.°
EMPEROR: Then, Faustus, as thou late did'st promise us,
We would behold that famous conqueror,
Great Alexander, and his paramour
30   In their true shapes and state majestical,
That we may wonder at their excellence.
FAUSTUS: Your majesty shall see them presently.
Mephistophilis, away,
And with a solemn noise of trumpets' sound
35   Present before this royal Emperor,
Great Alexander and his beauteous paramour.
MEPHISTOPHILIS: Faustus, I will.

                                              [Exit.]

BENVOLIO: Well, master doctor, an your devils come not
away quickly, you shall have me asleep presently.
40   Zounds, I could eat myself for anger to think I have
been such an ass all this while, to stand gaping after
the devil's governor and can see nothing.
FAUSTUS: I'll make you feel something anon, if my art
fail me not
My lord, I must forewarn your majesty
45   That when my spirits present the royal shapes
Of Alexander and his paramour,
Your grace demand no questions of the king,
But in dumb silence let them come and go.
EMPEROR: Be it as Faustus please; we are content.
50   BENVOLIO: Ay, ay, and I am content too. And thou bring
Alexander and his paramour before the Emperor, I'll
be Actaeon and turn myself to a stag.
FAUSTUS: And I'll play Diana and send you the horns
presently.

([A] sennet [is sounded]. Enter at one [door] the Emperor Alexander, at the other Darius.° They meet [in

combat]. Darius is thrown down; Alexander kills him,
takes off his crown, and, offering to go out, his paramour meets him. He embraceth her and sets Darius'
crown upon her head; and coming back, both salute the
Emperor, who, leaving his state, offers to embrace them,
which Faustus seeing, suddenly stays him. Then trumpets cease and music sounds.)

My gracious lord, you do forget yourself.
These are but shadows, not substantial.   55
EMPEROR: O pardon me. My thoughts are so ravishèd
With sight of this renownèd emperor,
That in mine arms I would have compassed him.
But, Faustus, since I may not speak to them,
To satisfy my longing thoughts at full,   60
Let me this tell thee: I have heard it said
That this fair lady, whilst she lived on earth,
Had on her neck a little wart or mole;
How may I prove that saying to be true?
FAUSTUS: Your majesty may boldly go and see.   65
EMPEROR: Faustus, I see it plain,
And in this sight thou better pleasest me
Than if I gained another monarchy.
FAUSTUS: Away! Be gone!

                                              (Exit show.)

See, see, my gracious lord, what strange beast is yon,   70
that thrusts his head out at window?
EMPEROR: O wondrous sight! See, Duke of Saxony,
Two spreading horns most strangely fastenèd
Upon the head of young Benvolio.
SAXONY: What? Is he asleep or dead?   75
FAUSTUS: He sleeps, my lord, but dreams not of his
horns.
EMPEROR: This sport is excellent. We'll call and wake
him.
What ho, Benvolio!
BENVOLIO: A plague upon you! Let me sleep a while.
EMPEROR: I blame thee not to sleep much, having such a   80
head of thine own.
SAXONY: Look up, Benvolio; 'tis the Emperor calls.
BENVOLIO: The Emperor? Where? O zounds, my head!
EMPEROR: Nay, and thy horns hold, 'tis no matter for
thy head, for that's armed sufficiently.   85
FAUSTUS: Why, how now, sir knight! What, hanged by the
horns? This is most horrible. Fie, fie, pull in your head
for shame. Let not all the world wonder at you.
BENVOLIO: Zounds, doctor, is this your villainy?
FAUSTUS: O say not so, sir. The doctor has no skill,   90
No art, no cunning, to present these lords
Or bring before this royal Emperor
The mighty monarch, warlike Alexander.
If Faustus do it, you are straight resolved
In bold Actaeon's shape to turn a stag.   95
And therefore, my lord, so please your majesty,
I'll raise a kennel of hounds shall hunt him so
As all his footmanship shall scarce prevail
To keep his carcass from their bloody fangs
Ho, Belimote, Argiron, Asterote!   100
BENVOLIO: Hold, hold! Zounds, he'll raise up a kennel of

IV, II. 9. **redeemed:** Rescued. **26. the Pope:** Bruno. **Coster-**
monger: Fruit vendor; a term of contempt. **53.** [S.D.] ***Darius:***
King Darius III of Persia (336–330 BCE), defeated at Granicus
in 334 BCE by the Greeks under Alexander the Great.

devils, I think, anon. Good, my lord, entreat for me.
'Sblood, I am never able to endure these torments.

EMPEROR: Then, good master doctor,
105 Let me entreat you to remove his horns.
He has done penance now sufficiently.

FAUSTUS: My gracious lord, not so much for injury done
to me, as to delight your majesty with some mirth,
hath Faustus justly requited this injurious° knight;
110 which being all I desire, I am content to remove his
horns. Mephistophilis, transform him.

[*Mephistophilis removes the horns.*]

And hereafter, sir, look you speak well of scholars.

BENVOLIO: [*aside.*] Speak well of ye? 'Sblood, and scholars be such cuckold makers to clap horns of honest
115 men's heads o' this order, I'll ne'er trust smooth faces
and small ruffs° more. But an I be not revenged for
this, would I might be turned to a gaping oyster and
drink nothing but salt water.

[*Exit Benvolio above.*]

EMPEROR: Come, Faustus. While the Emperor lives,
120 In recompense of this thy high desert,
Thou shalt command the state of Germany
And live beloved of mighty Carolus.

(*Exeunt.*)

Scene III

(*Enter Benvolio, Martino, Frederick, and Soldiers.*)

MARTINO: Nay, sweet Benvolio, let us sway thy
thoughts
From this attempt against the conjurer.

BENVOLIO: Away! You love me not to urge me thus.
Shall I let slip so great an injury,
5 When every servile groom jests at my wrongs
And in their rustic gambols proudly say,
"Benvolio's head was graced with horns today"?
O, may these eyelids never close again
Till with my sword I have that conjurer slain.
10 If you will aid me in this enterprise,
Then draw your weapons and be resolute.
If not, depart. Here will Benvolio die,
But Faustus' death shall quit° my infamy.

FREDERICK: Nay, we will stay with thee, betide what
may,
15 And kill that doctor if he come this way.

BENVOLIO: Then, gentle Frederick, hie thee to the grove,
And place our servants and our followers
Close in an ambush there behind the trees.
By this, I know, the conjurer is near.
20 I saw him kneel and kiss the Emperor's hand
And take his leave, laden with rich rewards.
Then, soldiers, boldly fight. If Faustus die,
Take you the wealth; leave us the victory.

FREDERICK: Come, soldiers. Follow me unto the grove.
Who kills him shall have gold and endless love.   25

(*Exit Frederick with the Soldiers.*)

BENVOLIO: My head is lighter than it was by th'horns,
But yet my heart's more ponderous than my head
And pants until I see that conjurer dead.

MARTINO: Where shall we place ourselves, Benvolio?

BENVOLIO: Here will we stay to bide the first assault.   30
O, were that damnèd hell-hound but in place,
Thou soon shouldst see me quit my foul disgrace.

(*Enter Frederick.*)

FREDERICK: Close, close, the conjurer is at hand
And all alone comes walking in his gown.
Be ready then, and strike the peasant down.   35

BENVOLIO: Mine be that honor then. Now, sword,
strike home.
For horns he gave I'll have his head anon.

(*Enter Faustus with the false head.*)

MARTINO: See, see, he comes.

BENVOLIO: No words! This blow ends all.
Hell take his soul; his body thus must fall.

[*He stabs Faustus.*]

FAUSTUS: [*falling*] Oh!   40

FREDERICK: Groan you, master doctor?

BENVOLIO: Break may his heart with groans! Dear
Frederick, see,
Thus will I end his griefs immediately.

MARTINO: Strike with a willing hand. His head is off.

[*Benvolio strikes off Faustus' false head.*]

BENVOLIO: The devil's dead. The Furies now may
laugh.   45

FREDERICK: Was this that stern aspèct, that awful
frown,
Made the grim monarch of infernal spirits
Tremble and quake at his commanding charms?

MARTINO: Was this that damnèd head whose heart
conspired
Benvolio's shame before the Emperor?   50

BENVOLIO: Ay, that's the head, and here the body lies,
Justly rewarded for his villainies.

FREDERICK: Come, let's devise how we may add more
shame
To the black scandal of his hated name.

BENVOLIO: First, on his head, in quittance of my
wrongs,   55
I'll nail huge forkèd horns and let them hang
Within the window where he yoked° me first,
That all the world may see my just revenge.

MARTINO: What use shall we put his beard to?

BENVOLIO: We'll sell it to a chimney-sweeper. It will   60
wear out ten birchen brooms, I warrant you.

FREDERICK: What shall eyes do?

109. injurious: Insulting.   **116. small ruffs:** Academic gowns.
IV, III. 13. quit: Pay for.

57. yoked: Placed the horns on.

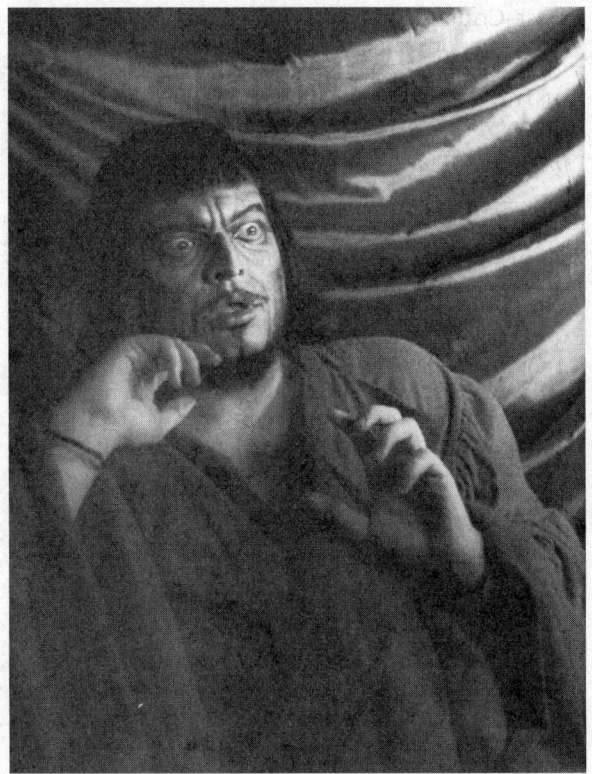

Orson Welles as Faustus in the 1937 Broadway production of *The Tragical History of Dr. Faustus*, which Welles also directed.

BENVOLIO: We'll put out his eyes, and they shall serve
    for buttons to his lips to keep his tongue from catch-
65   ing cold.
MARTINO: An excellent policy! And now, sirs, having
    divided him, what shall the body do?

[*Faustus rises.*]

BENVOLIO: Zounds, the devil's alive again.
FREDERICK: Give him his head, for God's sake.
FAUSTUS: Nay, keep it. Faustus will have heads and
70   hands,
    Ay, all your hearts, to recompense this deed.
    Knew you not, traitors, I was limited
    For four-and-twenty years to breathe on earth?
    And had you cut my body with your swords,
75   Or hewed this flesh and bones as small as sand,
    Yet in a minute had my spirit returned,
    And I had breathed a man made free from harm.
    But wherefore do I dally my revenge?
    Asteroth, Belimoth, Mephistophilis!

(*Enter Mephistophilis and other Devils.*)

80   Go, horse these traitors on your fiery backs,
    And mount aloft with them as high as heaven;

Thence pitch them headlong to the lowest hell.
Yet stay. The world shall see their misery,
And hell shall after plague their treachery.
Go, Belimoth, and take this caitiff° hence   85
And hurl him in some lake of mud and dirt.
Take thou this other; drag him through the woods
Amongst the pricking thorns and sharpest briars,
Whilst with my gentle Mephistophilis
This traitor flies unto some steepy rock   90
That, rolling down, may break the villain's bones
As he intended to dismember me.
Fly hence. Dispatch my charge immediately.
FREDERICK: Pity us, gentle Faustus. Save our lives.
FAUSTUS: Away!
FREDERICK: He must needs go that the devil drives.   95

(*Exeunt Spirits with the Knights.*)

(*Enter the ambushed Soldiers.*)

FIRST SOLDIER: Come, sirs, prepare yourselves in
    readiness.
    Make haste to help these noble gentlemen;
    I heard them parley with the conjurer.
SECOND SOLDIER: See where he comes. Dispatch and
    kill the slave.
FAUSTUS: What's here? An ambush to betray my life?   100
    Then, Faustus, try thy skill. Base peasants, stand,
    For lo, these trees remove at my command
    And stand as bulwarks 'twixt yourselves and me,
    To shield me from your hated treachery.
    Yet to encounter this your weak attempt,   105
    Behold an army comes incontinent.°

(*Faustus strikes the door, and enter a Devil playing on a drum, after him another bearing an ensign, and divers with weapons, Mephistophilis with fireworks. They set upon the Soldiers and drive them out. [Exit Faustus.]*)

Scene IV

(*Enter at several doors Benvolio, Frederick, and Martino, their heads and faces bloody and besmeared with mud and dirt, all having horns on their heads.*)

MARTINO: What ho, Benvolio!
BENVOLIO: Here! What, Frederick, ho!
FREDERICK: O help me, gentle friend. Where is Martino?
MARTINO: Dear Frederick, here,
    Half smothered in a lake of mud and dirt,   5
    Through which the Furies dragged me by the heels.
FREDERICK: Martino, see! Benvolio's horns again.
MARTINO: O misery! How now, Benvolio?
BENVOLIO: Defend me, heaven. Shall I be haunted° still?
MARTINO: Nay, fear not man; we have not power to
    kill.   10

85. caitiff: Despicable wretch. **106. incontinent:** At once. **IV, IV. 9. haunted:** (1) Bewitched; (2) hunted, pursued (since he is a stag).

BENVOLIO: My friends transformèd thus! O hellish
    spite!
  Your heads are all set with horns.
FREDERICK: You hit it right.
  It is your own you mean. Feel on your head.
BENVOLIO: Zounds, horns again!
15 MARTINO: Nay, chafe not man. We all are sped.°
BENVOLIO: What devil attends this damned magician,
  That, spite of spite, our wrongs are doublèd?
FREDERICK: What may we do, that we may hide our
  shames?
BENVOLIO: If we should follow him to work revenge,
20   He'd join long asses' ears to these huge horns,
  And make us laughing-stocks to all the world.
MARTINO: What shall we then do, dear Benvolio?
BENVOLIO: I have a castle joining near these woods,
  And thither we'll repair and live obscure
25   Till time shall alter these our brutish shapes.
  Sith black disgrace hath thus eclipsed our fame,
  We'll rather die with grief than live with shame.
                         (*Exeunt omnes.*°)

Scene V°

(*Enter Faustus and Mephistophilis.*)

FAUSTUS: Now, Mephistophilis, the restless course
  That time doth run with calm and silent foot,
  Shortening my days and thread of vital life,
  Calls for the payment of my latest years.
5   Therefore, sweet Mephistophilis, let us
  Make haste to Wittenberg.
MEPHISTOPHILIS: What, will you go on horseback, or
  on foot?
FAUSTUS: Nay, till I am past this fair and pleasant
  green,
  I'll walk on foot.
                    [*Exit Mephistophilis.*]

(*Enter a Horse-Courser.*°)

10 HORSE-COURSER: I have been all this day seeking one
  Master Fustian.° Mass, see where he is. God save you,
  master doctor.
FAUSTUS: What, horse-courser! You are well met.
HORSE-COURSER: I beseech your worship, accept of
15   these forty dollars.
FAUSTUS: Friend, thou canst not buy so good a horse for
  so small a price. I have no great need to sell him, but
  if thou likest him for ten dollars more, take him,
  because I see thou hast a good mind to him.

HORSE-COURSER: I beseech you, sir, accept of this. I am   20
  a very poor man and have lost very much of late by
  horse-flesh, and this bargain will set me up again.
FAUSTUS: Well, I will not stand with thee.° Give me the
  money.

[*The Horse-Courser gives Faustus money.*]

  Now, sirrah, I must tell you that you may ride him   25
  o'er hedge and ditch, and spare him not. But, do you
  hear? In any case, ride him not into the water.
HORSE-COURSER: How sir? Not into the water? Why,
  will he not drink of all waters?°
FAUSTUS: Yes, he will drink of all waters, but ride him   30
  not into the water—o'er hedge and ditch, or where
  thou wilt, but not into the water. Go, bid the hostler
  deliver him unto you, and remember what I say.
HORSE-COURSER: I warrant you, sir. O joyful day!
  Now am I a man made forever.   35
                      (*Exit.*)
FAUSTUS: What art thou, Faustus, but a man
  condemned to die?
  Thy fatal time draws to a final end.
  Despair doth drive distrust into my thoughts.
  Confound these passions with a quiet sleep.
  Tush! Christ did call the thief upon the cross;   40
  Then rest thee, Faustus, quiet in conceit.°

(*He sits to sleep [in his chair].*)

(*Enter the Horse-Courser, wet.*)

HORSE-COURSER: O what a cozening doctor was this? I
  riding my horse into the water, thinking some hidden
  mystery° had been in the horse, I had nothing under
  me but a little straw and had much ado to escape   45
  drowning. Well, I'll go rouse him and make him give
  me my forty dollars again. Ho, sirrah doctor, you
  cozening scab!° Master doctor, awake and rise, and
  give me my money again, for your horse is turned to
  a bottle° of hay. Master doctor!   50

(*He [tries to wake Faustus, and in doing so] pulls off
his leg.*)

  Alas, I am undone! What shall I do? I have pulled off
  his leg.

[*Faustus awakes.*]

FAUSTUS: O, help, help! The villain hath murdered me.
HORSE-COURSER: Murder or not murder, now he has
  but one leg, I'll outrun him and cast this leg into   55
  some ditch or other.
FAUSTUS: Stop him, stop him, stop him! Ha, ha, ha,
  Faustus hath his leg again, and the horse-courser a
  bundle of hay for his forty dollars.

15. sped: Provided (with horns).   **27.** [S.D.] *Exeunt omnes:*
Latin for "All go out."   IV, v. The first eleven lines of this
scene do not appear in all versions of the play, but they provide
a transition to the Horse-Courser episode and remind readers
of Faustus's impending tragedy.   **9.** [S.D.] *Horse-Courser:* One
who deals in horses.   **11. Fustian:** The perversion of Faustus's
name is a deliberate attempt at humor.

23. stand with thee: Bargain.   **29. drink . . . waters:** Be ready
for anything (a common proverb of the time).   **41. conceit:**
Thoughts.   **44. mystery:** Quality.   **48. cozening scab:** Deceitful, contemptible rascal.   **50. bottle:** Bundle.

(*Enter Wagner.*)

60   How now, Wagner, what news with thee?

WAGNER: If it please you, the Duke of Anholt doth earnestly entreat your company and hath sent some of his men to attend you with provision fit for your journey.

65   FAUSTUS: The Duke of Anholt's an honorable gentleman, and one to whom I must be no niggard of my cunning. Come away.

(*Exeunt.*)

Scene VI

(*Enter [Robin, the] Clown, Dick, [the] Horse-Courser, and a Carter.°*)

CARTER: Come, my masters, I'll bring you to the best beer in Europe. What ho, hostess! Where be these whores?

(*Enter Hostess.*)

HOSTESS: How now, what lack you? What, my old
5   guests, welcome.

ROBIN: Sirrah, Dick, dost thou know why I stand so mute?

DICK: No, Robin; why is't?

ROBIN: I am eighteen pence on the score.° But say noth-
10   ing, see if she have forgotten me.

HOSTESS: Who's this that stands so solemnly by himself? What, my old guest?

ROBIN: O hostess, how do you? I hope my score stands still.°

15   HOSTESS: Ay, there's no doubt of that, for methinks you make no haste to wipe it out.

DICK: Why, hostess, I say, fetch us some beer.

HOSTESS: You shall presently. Look up into th'hall there, ho!

(*Exit.*)

20   DICK: Come, sirs, what shall we do now till mine hostess come?

CARTER: Marry, sir, I'll tell you the bravest tale how a conjurer served me. You know Doctor Fauster?

HORSE-COURSER: Ay, a plague take him. Here's some
25   on's have cause to know him. Did he conjure thee too?

CARTER: I'll tell you how he served me. As I was going to Wittenberg t'other day with a load of hay, he met me and asked me what he should give me for as much
30   hay as he could eat. Now, sir, I thinking that a little would serve his turn, bade him take as much as he would for three farthings. So he presently gave me my money and fell to eating; and as I am a cursen°

man, he never left eating till he had eat up all my load
of hay.   35

ALL: O monstrous! Eat a whole load of hay!

ROBIN: Yes, yes, that may be, for I have heard of one that has eat a load of logs.

HORSE-COURSER: Now, sirs, you shall hear how villainously he served me. I went to him yesterday to buy a   40
horse of him, and he would by no means sell him under forty dollars. So, sir, because I knew him to be such a horse as would run over hedge and ditch and never tire, I gave him his money. So when I had my horse, Doctor Fauster bade me ride him night and   45
day and spare him no time; but, quoth he, in any case ride him not into the water. Now sir, I thinking the horse had had some rare quality that he would not have me know of, what did I but rid him into a great river, and when I came just in the midst, my   50
horse vanished away, and I sat straddling upon a bottle of hay.

ALL: O brave doctor!

HORSE-COURSER: But you shall hear how bravely I served him for it. I went me home to his house, and   55
there I found him asleep. I kept a hallooing and whooping in his ears, but all could not wake him. I seeing that took him by the leg and never rested pulling till I had pulled me his leg quite off, and now 'tis at home in mine hostry.   60

ROBIN: And has the doctor but one leg then? That's excellent, for one of his devils turned me into the likeness of an ape's face.

CARTER: Some more drink, hostess.

ROBIN: Hark you, we'll into another room and drink a   65
while, and then we'll go seek out the doctor.

(*Exeunt.*)

Scene VII

(*Enter the Duke of Anholt, his Duchess, Faustus, and Mephistophilis, [Servants and Attendants].*)

DUKE: Thanks, master doctor, for these pleasant sights. Nor know I how sufficiently to recompense your great deserts° in erecting that enchanted castle in the air, the sight whereof so delighted me, as nothing in the world could please me more.   5

FAUSTUS: I do think myself, my good lord, highly recompensed in that it pleaseth your grace to think but well of that which Faustus hath performed. But, gracious lady, it may be that you have taken no pleasure in those sights. Therefore, I pray you, tell me what is the   10
thing you most desire to have; be it in the world, it shall be yours. I have heard that great-bellied women do long for things are rare and dainty.

DUCHESS: True, master doctor, and since I find you so kind, I will make known unto you what my heart   15

IV, VI. [S.D.] *Carter:* A person who drives a cart.   **9. on the score:** In debt.   **13–14. stands still:** Does not go higher.   **33. cursen:** Christened.

IV, VII. **3. deserts:** Good deeds.

desires to have. And were it now summer, as it is January, a dead time of the winter, I would request no better meat than a dish of ripe grapes.

FAUSTUS: This is but a small matter. Go, Mephistophilis,
20 away!

(*Exit Mephistophilis.*)

Madam I will do more than this for your content.

(*Enter Mephistophilis again with the grapes.*)

Here; now taste ye these. They should be good, for they come from a far country, I can tell you.

DUKE: This makes me wonder more than all the rest,
25 that at this time of year, when every tree is barren of his fruit, from whence you had these ripe grapes.

FAUSTUS: Please it, your grace, the year is divided into two circles over the whole world, so that when it is winter with us, in the contrary circle it is like-
30 wise summer with them, as in India, Saba,° and such countries that lie far east, where they have fruit twice a year. From whence, by means of a swift spirit that I have, I had these grapes brought, as you see.

DUCHESS: And trust me, they are the sweetest grapes
35 that e'er I tasted.

(*The Clown[s, Robin, Dick, the Carter, and the Horse-Courser,] bounce at the gate within.*)

DUKE: What rude disturbers have we at the gate?
Go, pacify their fury. Set it ope,
And then demand of them what they would have.

[*Exit a Servant.*]

(*They knock again and call out to talk with Faustus.*)

[*Enter Servant to them.*]

SERVANT: Why, how now, masters, what a coil° is there?
40 What is the reason you disturb the duke.

DICK: We have no reason for it; therefore a fig for him.

SERVANT: What, saucy varlets,° dare you be so bold?

HORSE-COURSER: I hope, sir, we have wit enough to be more bold than welcome.

45 SERVANT: It appears so. Pray be bold elsewhere,
And trouble not the duke.

DUKE: What would they have?

SERVANT: They all cry out to speak with Doctor Faustus.

CARTER: Ay, and we will speak with him.

DUKE: Will you, sir? Commit the rascals.

50 DICK: Commit with us! He were as good commit with his father as commit with us.

FAUSTUS: I do beseech your grace, let them come in;
They are good subject for a merriment.

DUKE: Do as thou wilt, Faustus. I give thee leave.

FAUSTUS: I thank your grace.

(*Enter Robin, Dick, Carter, and Horse-Courser.*)

55   Why, how now, my good friends?
'Faith you are too outrageous,° but come near;

---

30. **Saba:** Sheba.   39. **coil:** Disturbance.   42. **varlets:** Knaves, rascals.   56. **outrageous:** Violent.

I have procured your pardons. Welcome all!

ROBIN: Nay, sir, we will be welcome for our money, and we will pay for what we take. What ho! Give's half a dozen of beer here, and be hanged.   60

FAUSTUS: Nay, hark you; can you tell me where you are?

CARTER: Ay, marry can I: we are under heaven.

SERVANT: Ay, but sir sauce-box, know you in what place?

HORSE-COURSER: Ay, ay, the house is good enough to drink in. Zounds, fill us some beer, or we'll break all   65 the barrels in the house and dash out all your brains with your bottles.

FAUSTUS: Be not so furious. Come, you shall have beer.
My lord, beseech you give me leave a while:
I'll gage my credit, 'twill content your grace.   70

DUKE: With all my heart, kind doctor. Please thyself;
Our servants and our court's at thy command.

FAUSTUS: I humbly thank your grace. Then fetch some beer.

HORSE-COURSER: Ay, marry, there spake a doctor indeed, and 'faith,
I'll drink a health to thy wooden leg for that word.   75

FAUSTUS: My wooden leg? What dost thou mean by that?

CARTER: Ha, ha, ha! Dost hear him, Dick? He has forgot his leg.

HORSE-COURSER: Ay, ay, he does not stand much° upon that.

FAUSTUS: No, faith; not much upon a wooden leg.

CARTER: Good lord, that flesh and blood should be so   80 frail with your worship! Do not you remember a horse-courser you sold a horse to?

FAUSTUS: Yes, I remember I sold one a horse.

CARTER: And do you remember you bid he should not ride into the water?   85

FAUSTUS: Yes, I do very well remember that.

CARTER: And do you remember nothing of your leg?

FAUSTUS: No, in good sooth.

CARTER: Then, I pray, remember your courtesy.°

FAUSTUS: I thank you, sir.   90

CARTER: 'Tis not so much worth. I pray you, tell me one thing.

FAUSTUS: What's that?

CARTER: Be both your legs bedfellows every night together?   95

FAUSTUS: Wouldst thou make a Colossus° of me, that thou askest me such questions?

CARTER: No, truly, sir. I would make nothing of you, but I would fain know that.

(*Enter Hostess with drink.*)

FAUSTUS: Then, I assure thee, certainly they are.   100

CARTER: I thank you; I am fully satisfied.

---

78. **stand much:** Make much of (with a quibble).   89. **courtesy:** Curtsy, or leg.   96. **Colossus:** A giant statue said to have stood with its legs astride at the entrance to the ancient harbor of Rhodes.

FAUSTUS: But wherefore dost thou ask?

CARTER: For nothing, sir. But methinks you should have a wooden bedfellow of one of 'em.

105 HORSE-COURSER: Why, do you hear, sir; did not I pull off one of your legs when you were asleep?

FAUSTUS: But I have it again, now I am awake. Look you here, sir.

ALL: O horrible! Had the doctor three legs?

110 CARTER: Do you remember, sir, how you cozened me and ate up my load of—

(*Faustus charms him dumb.*)

DICK: Do you remember how you made me wear an ape's—

[*Faustus charms him dumb.*]

HORSE-COURSER: You whoreson conjuring scab, do you
115   remember how you cozened me with a ho—

[*Faustus charms him dumb.*]

ROBIN: Ha' you forgotten me? You think to carry it away° with your *hey-pass* and *re-pass;* do you remember the dog's fa—

[*Faustus charms him dumb.*]   (*Exeunt Clowns.*)

HOSTESS: Who pays for the ale? Hear you, master doc-
120   tor, now you have sent away my guests, I pray who shall pay me for my a—

[*Faustus charms her dumb.*]   (*Exit Hostess.*)

DUCHESS: My lord,
     We are much beholding to this learnèd man.

DUKE: So are we, madam, which we will recompense
125   With all the love and kindness that we may.
     His artful sport drives all sad thoughts away.

                                        (*Exeunt.*)

ACT V • *Scene I*

(*Thunder and lightning. Enter Devils with covered dishes. Mephistophilis leads them into Faustus' study. Then enter Wagner.*)

WAGNER: I think my master means to die shortly.
     He has made his will and given me his wealth,
     His house, his goods, and store of golden plate,
     Besides two thousand ducats ready coined.
5   I wonder what he means. If death were nigh,
     He would not frolic thus. He's now at supper
     With the scholars, where there's such belly-cheer
     As Wagner in his life ne'er saw the like.
     And see where they come; belike the feast is done.

                                        (*Exit.*)

(*Enter Faustus, Mephistophilis, and two or three Scholars.*)

FIRST SCHOLAR: Master Doctor Faustus, since our con- 10
ference about fair ladies, which was the beautifulest in all the world, we have determined with ourselves that Helen of Greece was the admirablest lady that ever lived. Therefore, master doctor, if you will do us so much favor as to let us see that peerless dame of 15
Greece, whom all the world admires for majesty, we should think ourselves much beholding unto you.

FAUSTUS: Gentlemen,
     For that I know your friendship is unfeigned,
     And Faustus' custom is not to deny
     The just requests of those that wish him well,   20
     You shall behold that peerless dame of Greece,
     No otherwise for pomp and majesty
     Than when Sir Paris crossed the seas with her
     And brought the spoils to rich Dardania.°   25
     Be silent then, for danger is in words.

(*Music sounds. Mephistophilis brings in Helen; she passeth over the stage.*)

SECOND SCHOLAR: Was this fair Helen, whose admirèd worth
     Made Greece with ten years' war afflict poor Troy?
     Too simple is my wit to tell her praise,
     Whom all the world admires for majesty.   30

THIRD SCHOLAR: No marvel though the angry Greeks pursued
     With ten years' war the rape of such a queen,
     Whose heavenly beauty passeth all compare.

FIRST SCHOLAR: Since we have seen the pride of nature's works
     And only paragon of excellence,   35
     We'll take our leaves and for this blessèd sight
     Happy and blest be Faustus evermore.

FAUSTUS: Gentlemen, farewell; the same wish I to you.

                                   (*Exeunt Scholars.*)

(*Enter an Old Man.*)

OLD MAN: O gentle Faustus, leave this damnèd art,
     This magic that will charm thy soul to hell   40
     And quite bereave thee of salvation.
     Though thou hast now offended like a man,
     Do not persevere in it like a devil.
     Yet, yet, thou hast an amiable° soul,
     If sin by custom grow not into nature.   45
     Then, Faustus, will repentance come too late;
     Then thou art banished from the sight of heaven.
     No mortal can express the pains of hell.
     It may be this my exhortation
     Seems harsh and all unpleasant; let it not,   50
     For, gentle son, I speak it not in wrath
     Or envy of° thee, but in tender love
     And pity of thy future misery.

V, I. 22–25. peerless dame . . . Dardania: The Greek Helen (the "peerless dame"), wife of Menelaus, was carried off to Troy (Dardania) by Paris, sparking the Trojan War.   **44. amiable:** Worthy of divine love or grace.   **52. envy of:** Ill will toward.

116–17. carry it away: Come off best.

And so have hope that this my kind rebuke,
55   Checking° thy body, may amend thy soul.
FAUSTUS: Where art thou, Faustus? Wretch, what hast
         thou done?
      Damned art thou, Faustus, damned; despair and die!
      Hell claims his right, and with a roaring voice
      Says, "Faustus, come; thine hour is almost come";
60   And Faustus now will come to do thee right.

(*Mephistophilis gives him a dagger.*)

OLD MAN: O stay, good Faustus, stay thy desperate
         steps.
      I see an angel hovers o'er thy head,
      And with a vial full of precious grace
      Offers to pour the same into thy soul.
65   Then call for mercy and avoid despair.
FAUSTUS: Ah, my sweet friend, I feel thy words
      To comfort my distressèd soul.
      Leave me a while to ponder on my sins.
OLD MAN: Faustus, I leave thee, but with grief of heart,
70   Fearing the enemy of thy hapless soul.
                                          (*Exit.*)
FAUSTUS: Accursèd Faustus, where is mercy now?
      I do repent, and yet I do despair.
      Hell strives with grace for conquest in my breast.
      What shall I do to shun the snares of death?
MEPHISTOPHILIS: Thou traitor, Faustus, I arrest thy
75   soul
      For disobedience to my sovereign lord.
      Revolt, or I'll in piecemeal tear thy flesh.
FAUSTUS: I do repent I e'er offended him.
      Sweet Mephistophilis, entreat thy lord
80   To pardon my unjust presumption,
      And with my blood again I will confirm
      The former vow I made to Lucifer.
MEPHISTOPHILIS: Do it then, Faustus, with unfeignèd°
         heart,
      Lest greater dangers do attend thy drift.°

[*Faustus stabs his arm and writes on a paper with his
blood.*]

FAUSTUS: Torment, sweet friend, that base and agèd
85   man
      That durst dissuade me from thy Lucifer,
      With greatest torment that our hell affords.
MEPHISTOPHILIS: His faith is great; I cannot touch his
         soul,
      But what I may afflict his body with
90   I will attempt, which is but little worth.
FAUSTUS: One thing, good servant, let me crave of
         thee
      To glut the longing of my heart's desire—
      That I may have unto my paramour
      That heavenly Helen which I saw of late,
95   Whose sweet embracings may extinguish clear

Those thoughts that do dissuade me from my vow,
      And keep mine oath I made to Lucifer.
MEPHISTOPHILIS: This, or what else my Faustus shall
         desire,
      Shall be performed in twinkling of an eye.

(*Enter Helen again, passing over* [*the stage*] *between two
Cupids.*)

FAUSTUS: Was this the face that launched a thousand
         ships
      And burnt the topless towers of Ilium?   100
      Sweet Helen, make me immortal with a kiss.

[*She kisses him.*]

      Her lips suck forth my soul. See where it flies!
      Come, Helen, come, give me my soul again.
      Here will I dwell, for heaven is in these lips,
      And all is dross that is not Helena.   105

[*Enter the Old Man.*]

      I will be Paris, and for love of thee
      Instead of Troy shall Wittenberg be sacked;
      And I will combat with weak Menelaus°
      And wear thy colors on my plumèd crest.   110
      Yea, I will wound Achilles° in the heel
      And then return to Helen for a kiss.
      O, thou art fairer than the evening's air,
      Clad in the beauty of a thousand stars.
      Brighter art thou than flaming Jupiter°   115
      When he appeared to hapless Semele,°
      More lovely than the monarch of the sky
      In wanton Arethusa's azured arms,°
      And none but thou shalt be my paramour.

                     (*Exeunt* [*all but the Old Man*].)

OLD MAN: Accursèd Faustus, miserable man,   120
      That from thy soul exclud'st the grace of heaven
      And fliest the throne of his tribunal seat!

(*Enter the Devils.*)

      Satan begins to sift me with his pride.
      As in this furnace God shall try my faith,
      My faith, vile hell, shall triumph over thee.   125
      Ambitious fiends, see how the heavens smiles
      At your repulse and laughs your state° to scorn.
      Hence hell, for hence I fly unto my God.

                                          (*Exeunt.*)

---

55. **Checking:** Admonishing.   83. **unfeignèd:** Honest.
84. **drift:** Purpose.

109. **Menelaus:** The husband of Helen of Troy.   111. **Achilles:**
The Greek hero of the Trojan war, wounded in the heel by
Paris.   115. **Jupiter:** Zeus.   116. **Semele:** The daughter of
Cadmus and Harmonia who bore Zeus the child, Dionysus.
117–18. **monarch . . . arms:** Arethusa was a nymph, one of the
Nereids, who governed a fountain on the isle of Ortygia near
Syracuse.   127. **state:** Royal power.

Scene II

(*Thunder. Enter [above] Lucifer, Beelzebub, and Mephi-stophilis.*)

LUCIFER: Thus from infernal Dis° do we ascend
　　To view the subjects of our monarchy,
　　Those souls which sin seals the black sons of hell,
　　'Mong which as chief, Faustus, we come to thee,
5　　Bringing with us lasting damnation
　　To wait upon thy soul. The time is come
　　Which makes it forfeit.
MEPHISTOPHILIS:　　　　　And this gloomy night,
　　Here in this room will wretched Faustus be.
BEELZEBUB: And here we'll stay
10　　To mark him how he doth demean himself.
MEPHISTOPHILIS: How should he, but in desperate
　　　　lunacy?
　　Fond worldling, now his heart-blood dries with
　　　　grief;
　　His conscience kills it, and his laboring brain
　　Begets a world of idle fantasies
15　　To over-reach the devil. But all in vain;
　　His store of pleasures must be sauced° with pain.
　　He and his servant, Wagner, are at hand.
　　Both come from drawing Faustus' latest will.
　　See where they come.

(*Enter Faustus and Wagner.*)

20 FAUSTUS: Say, Wagner, thou has perused my will;
　　How dost thou like it?
WAGNER:　　　　　　　Sir, so wondrous well
　　As in all humble duty I do yield
　　My life and lasting service for your love.

(*Enter the Scholars.*)

FAUSTUS: Gramercies,° Wagner. Welcome, gentlemen.
　　　　　　　　　　　　　　　[*Exit Wagner.*]
25 FIRST SCHOLAR: Now, worthy Faustus, methinks your
　　looks are changed.
FAUSTUS: Ah, gentlemen!
SECOND SCHOLAR: What ails Faustus?
FAUSTUS: Ah, my sweet chamber-fellow, had I lived with
30　　thee, then had I lived still, but now must die eternally.
　　Look, sirs; comes he not? Comes he not?
FIRST SCHOLAR: O my dear Faustus, what imports this
　　fear?
SECOND SCHOLAR: Is all our pleasure turned to melan-
35　　choly?
THIRD SCHOLAR: He is not well with being over-solitary.
SECOND SCHOLAR: If it be so, we'll have physicians, and
　　Faustus shall be cured.
THIRD SCHOLAR: 'Tis but a surfeit sir; fear nothing.
40 FAUSTUS: A surfeit of deadly sin that hath damned both
　　body and soul.

V, II. **1. Dis:** Hades, or hell. **16. sauced:** Paid for.
24. Gramercies: Thanks.

SECOND SCHOLAR: Yet Faustus, look up to heaven, and
　　remember mercy is infinite.
FAUSTUS: But Faustus' offence can ne'er be pardoned.
　　The serpent that tempted Eve may be saved, but not　45
　　Faustus. Ah gentlemen, hear me with patience and
　　tremble not at my speeches. Though my heart pants
　　and quivers to remember that I have been a student
　　here these thirty years, O, would I had never seen
　　Wittenberg, never read book. And what wonders I　50
　　have done, all Germany can witness—yea, all the
　　world—for which Faustus hath lost both Germany
　　and the world, yea heaven itself, heaven the seat of
　　God, the throne of the blessed, the kingdom of joy,
　　and must remain in hell for ever. Hell, ah hell for　55
　　ever! Sweet friends, what shall become of Faustus,
　　being in hell for ever?
SECOND SCHOLAR: Yet Faustus, call on God.
FAUSTUS: On God, whom Faustus hath abjured? On
　　God, whom Faustus hath blasphemed? Ah, my God,　60
　　I would weep, but the devil draws in my tears. Gush
　　forth blood instead of tears, yea life and soul. O, he
　　stays my tongue! I would lift up my hands, but see,
　　they hold 'em; they hold 'em.
ALL: Who, Faustus?　　　　　　　　　　　　　　65
FAUSTUS: Why, Lucifer and Mephistophilis. Ah, gentle-
　　men, I gave them my soul for my cunning.
ALL: God forbid!
FAUSTUS: God forbade it indeed, but Faustus hath done
　　it. For the vain pleasure of four and twenty years　70
　　hath Faustus lost eternal joy and felicity. I writ them
　　a bill with mine own blood. The date is expired. This
　　is the time, and he will fetch me.
FIRST SCHOLAR: Why did not Faustus tell us of this
　　before, that divines might have prayed for thee?　75
FAUSTUS: Oft have I thought to have done so, but the
　　devil threatened to tear me in pieces if I named God,
　　to fetch me, body and soul, if I once gave ear to divin-
　　ity. And now 'tis too late. Gentlemen away, lest you
　　perish with me.　　　　　　　　　　　　　　80
SECOND SCHOLAR: O, what may we do to save Faustus?
FAUSTUS: Talk not of me, but save yourselves and de-
　　part.
THIRD SCHOLAR: God will strengthen me; I will stay
　　with Faustus.　　　　　　　　　　　　　　85
FIRST SCHOLAR: Tempt not God, sweet friend, but let us
　　into the next room and there pray for him.
FAUSTUS: Ay, pray for me, pray for me; and what noise
　　soever you hear, come not unto me, for nothing can
　　rescue me.　　　　　　　　　　　　　　　　90
SECOND SCHOLAR: Pray thou, and we will pray that God
　　may have mercy upon thee.
FAUSTUS: Gentlemen, farewell. If I live till morning, I'll
　　visit you; if not, Faustus is gone to hell.
ALL: Faustus, farewell.　　　　　　　　　　　　95
　　　　　　　　　　　　　　(*Exeunt Scholars.*)
MEPHISTOPHILIS: [*above*] Ay, Faustus, now thou hast
　　no hope of heaven;
　　Therefore despair. Think only upon hell,
　　For that must be thy mansion, there to dwell.

FAUSTUS: O thou bewitching fiend, 'twas thy
    temptation
100   Hath robbed me of eternal happiness.
MEPHISTOPHILIS: I do confess it, Faustus, and rejoice.
    'Twas I, that when thou wert i' the way to heaven,
    Damned up thy passage. When thou took'st the book
    To view the Scriptures, then I turned the leaves
105   And led thine eye.
    What, weep'st thou? 'Tis too late. Despair!
      Farewell!
    Fools that will laugh on earth must weep in hell.
                                (*Exit.*)

(*Enter the Good Angel and the Bad Angel at several
doors.*)

GOOD ANGEL: Ah, Faustus, if thou hadst given ear to
    me,
    Innumerable joys had followed thee;
    But thou didst love the world.
110 BAD ANGEL: Gave ear to me,
    And now must taste hell's pains perpetually.
GOOD ANGEL: O what will all thy riches, pleasures,
      pomps
    Avail thee now?
BAD ANGEL: Nothing but vex thee more,
    To want in hell, that had on earth such store.

(*Music while the throne descends.*)

115 GOOD ANGEL: O, thou hast lost celestial happiness,
    Pleasures unspeakable, bliss without end.
    Hadst thou affected sweet divinity,
    Hell or the devil had had no power on thee.
    Hadst thou kept on that way, Faustus, behold
120   In what resplendent glory thou hadst sat
    In yonder throne, like those bright shining saints,
    And triumphed over hell. That hast thou lost,
    And now, poor soul, must thy good angel leave thee.

[*The throne ascends.*]

    The jaws of hell are open to receive thee.
                                   (*Exit.*)

(*Hell is discovered.*)

BAD ANGEL: Now, Faustus, let thine eyes with horror
125   stare
    Into that vast perpetual torture-house.
    There are the Furies tossing damnèd souls
    On burning forks; their bodies boil in lead.
    There are live quarters broiling on the coals,
130   That ne'er can die. This ever-burning chair
    Is for o'er-tortured souls to rest them in.
    These that are fed with sops of flaming fire
    Were gluttons and loved only delicates
    And laughed to see the poor starve at their gates.
135   But yet all these are nothing; thou shalt see
    Ten thousand tortures that more horrid be.
FAUSTUS: O, I have seen enough to torture me.
BAD ANGEL: Nay, thou must feel them, taste the smart
    of all.

He that loves pleasure must for pleasure fall.
    And so I leave thee, Faustus, till anon;   140
    Then wilt thou tumble in confusion.

([*Hell disappears.*] *The clock strikes eleven.*)

FAUSTUS: Ah Faustus,
    Now hast thou but one bare hour to live,
    And then thou must be damned perpetually.
    Stand still, you ever-moving spheres of heaven,   145
    That time may cease and midnight never come.
    Fair nature's eye, rise, rise again, and make
    Perpetual day; or let this hour be but
    A year, a month, a week, a natural day,
    That Faustus may repent and save his soul.   150
    O lente, lente currite noctis equi!°
    The stars move still; time runs; the clock will strike;
    The devil will come, and Faustus must be damned.
    O, I'll leap up to my God! Who pulls me down?
    See, see, where Christ's blood streams in the
      firmament!   155
    One drop would save my soul, half a drop! Ah, my
      Christ!
    Rend not my heart for naming of my Christ!
    Yet will I call on him. O, spare me, Lucifer!
    Where is it now? 'Tis gone. And see where God
    Stretcheth out his arm and bends his ireful brows.   160
    Mountains and hills, come, come, and fall on me,
    And hide me from the heavy wrath of God.
    No, no!
    Then will I headlong run into the earth.
    Earth, gape! O no, it will not harbor me!   165
    You stars that reigned at my nativity,
    Whose influence hath allotted death and hell.
    Now draw up Faustus like a foggy mist
    Into the entrails of yon laboring cloud,
    That when you vomit forth into the air,   170
    My limbs may issue from your smoky mouths,
    So that my soul may but ascend to heaven.

(*The watch strikes.*)

    Ah, half the hour is past; 'twill all be past anon.
    O God,
    If thou wilt not have mercy on my soul,   175
    Yet for Christ's sake, whose blood hath ransomed
      me,
    Impose some end to my incessant pain.
    Let Faustus live in hell a thousand years,
    A hundred thousand, and at last be saved.
    O, no end is limited to damnèd souls.   180
    Why wert thou not a creature wanting soul?
    Or why is this immortal that thou hast?
    Ah, Pythagoras' *metempsychosis,*° were that true,
    This soul should fly from me and I be changed
    Into some brutish beast. All beasts are happy,   185

151. *O . . . equi:* O slowly, slowly; run you horses of night
(adapted from Ovid's *Amores*).   183. *metempsychosis:* Belief
in the transmigration of souls, associated with the Greek philosopher Pythagoras of Samos.

For, when they die
  Their souls are soon dissolved in elements,
  But mine must live still to be plagued in hell.
  Cursed be the parents that engendered me!
190 No, Faustus, curse thyself, curse Lucifer
  That hath deprived thee of the joys of heaven.

(*The clock strikes twelve.*)

  O, it strikes, it strikes! Now, body, turn to air,
  Or Lucifer will bear thee quick° to hell.
  O soul, be changed to little water-drops,
195 And fall into the ocean, ne'er be found!

(*Thunder, and enter the Devils.*)

  My God, my God, look not so fierce on me!
  Adders and serpents, let me breathe a while!
  Ugly hell, gape not! Come not, Lucifer!
  I'll burn my books! Ah, Mephistophilis!
                  (*Exeunt [Faustus and Devils].*)

Scene III

(*Enter the Scholars.*)

FIRST SCHOLAR: Come, gentlemen, let us go visit Faustus,
  For such a dreadful night was never seen
  Since first the world's creation did begin.
  Such fearful shrieks and cries were never heard.
5 Pray heaven the doctor have escaped the danger.
SECOND SCHOLAR: O help us, heaven! See, here are Faustus' limbs,
  All torn asunder by the hand of death.

193. quick: Alive.

THIRD SCHOLAR: The devils whom Faustus served have torn him thus;
  For 'twixt the hours of twelve and one, methought
  I heard him shriek and call aloud for help,   10
  At which self time the house seemed all on fire
  With dreadful horror of these damnèd fiends.
SECOND SCHOLAR: Well, gentlemen, though Faustus' end be such
  As every Christian heart laments to think on,
  Yet for he was a scholar, once admired   15
  For wondrous knowledge in our German schools,
  We'll give his mangled limbs due burial;
  And all the students clothed in mourning black,
  Shall wait upon° his heavy° funeral.
                  (*Exeunt.*)

EPILOGUE

(*Enter Chorus.*)

CHORUS: Cut is the branch that might have grown full straight,
  And burnèd is Apollo's laurel bough
  That sometime grew within this learnèd man.
  Faustus is gone. Regard his hellish fall,
  Whose fiendful fortune may exhort the wise   5
  Only to wonder at unlawful things,
  Whose deepness doth entice such forward wits
  To practice more than heavenly power permits.
                  [*Exit.*]

  Terminat hora diem; terminat author opus.°

V, III. 19. wait upon: Be present at. heavy: Sorrowful. Epilogue. 9. *Terminat . . . opus:* The hour ends the day; the author ends his work.

William Shakespeare

Despite the fact that Shakespeare wrote some thirty-seven plays, owned part of his theatrical company, acted in plays, and retired a relatively wealthy man in the city of his birth, there is much we do not know about him. His father was a glovemaker with pretensions to being a gentleman; Shakespeare himself had his coat of arms placed on his home, New Place, purchased in part because it was one of the grandest buildings in Stratford. Church records indicate that he was born in April 1564 and died in April 1616, after having been retired from the stage for two or three years. We know that he married Anne Hathaway in 1582, when he was eighteen and she twenty-six; that he had a daughter Susanna and twins, Judith and Hamnet; and that Hamnet, his only son, died at age eleven. Shakespeare has no direct descendants today.

We know very little about his education. We assume that he went to the local grammar school, since as the son of a burgess he was eligible to attend at no cost. If he did so, he would have received a very strong education based on

This engraving of William Shakespeare by Martin Droeshout appeared in the First Folio Edition, published in 1623.

rhetoric, logic, and classical literature. He would have been exposed to the comedies of Plautus, the tragedies of Seneca, and the poetry of Virgil, Ovid, and a host of other, lesser writers.

A rumor has persisted that he spent some time as a Latin teacher. No evidence exists to suggest that Shakespeare went to a university, although his general learning and knowledge are so extraordinary and broad that generations of scholars have assumed that he may have also gone to the Inns of Court to study law. This cannot be proved, though; thus, some people claim that another person, with considerable university education, must have written his plays. However, no one in the Elizabethan theater had an education of the sort often proposed for Shakespeare. Marlowe and Ben Jonson were the most learned of Elizabethan playwrights, but their work is quite different in character and feeling from that of Shakespeare.

One recent theory about Shakespeare's early years suggests that before going to London to work in theater, he belonged to a wandering company of actors much like those who appear in *Hamlet*. It is an ingenious theory and has much to recommend it, including the fact that it would explain how Shakespeare could take the spotlight so quickly as to arouse the anger of more experienced London writers.

Shakespeare did not begin his career writing for the stage but, in the more conventional approach for the age, as a poet. He sought the support of an aristocratic patron, the earl of Southampton. Like many wealthy and polished young courtiers, Southampton felt it a pleasant ornament to sponsor a poet whose works would be dedicated to him. Shakespeare wrote sonnets apparently with Southampton in mind, and, hoping for preferment, the long narrative poems *Venus and Adonis, The Rape of Lucrece,* and *The Phoenix and the Turtle.* However, Southampton eventually decided to become the patron of another poet, John Florio, an Italian who had translated Michel de Montaigne's *Essays.*

Shakespeare's response was to turn to the stage. His first plays were a considerable success: *King Henry VI* in three parts — three full-length plays. Satisfying London's taste for plays that told the history of England's tangled political past, Shakespeare won considerable renown with a lengthy series of plays ranging from *Richard II* through the two parts of *King Henry IV* to *Henry V.* Audiences were delighted; competing playwrights envied him his triumphs. Francis Meres's famous book of the period, *Palladis Tamia: Wit's Treasury,* cites Shakespeare as modern Plautus and Seneca, the best in both comedy and tragedy. Meres says that by 1598 Shakespeare was known for a dozen plays. That his success was firm by this time is demonstrated by his having purchased his large house, New Place, in Stratford in 1597. He could not have done this without financial security.

In the next few years Shakespeare made a number of interesting purchases of property in Stratford; he also made deals with his own theater company to secure the rights to perform in London. These arrangements produced legal records that give us some of the clearest information we have concerning Shakespeare's activities during this period. His company was called the Lord Chamberlain's Men while Queen Elizabeth was alive but was renamed the King's Men by King James in the spring of 1603, less than two months after Elizabeth died. As the King's Men, Shakespeare's company had considerable

"He was not of an age, but for all time."
— BEN JONSON

power and success. Its audience sometimes included King James, as in the first performance of *Macbeth*.

Shakespeare was successful as a writer of histories, comedies, and tragedies. He also wrote in another genre, known as romance. These plays share elements with both comedies and tragedies, and they often depend on supernatural or improbable elements. *Cymbeline, The Winter's Tale,* and *The Tempest* are the best known of Shakespeare's romances. They are late works and have a fascinating complexity.

When Shakespeare died on April 23, 1616, he was buried as a gentleman in the church in which he had been baptized in Stratford-upon-Avon. His will left most of his money and possessions to his two daughters, Judith and Susanna.

A MIDSUMMER NIGHT'S DREAM

A Midsummer Night's Dream (1595–1596) is an early comedy and one of Shakespeare's most beloved works. It is also one of his most imaginative plays, introducing us to the world of fairies and the realm of dreams. Romantic painters, such as Fuseli, have long found in this play a rich store of images that stretch far beyond the limits of the real world of everyday experience.

For Shakespeare the fun of the play is in showing how the world of the fairies intersects with the world of real people, and we can interpret the play as a hint of what would happen if the world of dreams were to cross the world of real experience. The fact that these worlds are more alike than they are different gives Shakespeare the comic basis on which to work. He also finds some new and amusing ways to interpret the device of mistaken identities.

The play is set in Athens, with Duke Theseus about to wed Hippolyta, the queen of the Amazons. Helena and Hermia are young women in love with Demetrius and Lysander, respectively. Demetrius, however, wants to marry Hermia and has the blessing of Hermia's father. Hermia's refusal to follow her father's wishes drives her into the woods, where she is followed by both young men and by Helena, who does not want to lose Demetrius.

The four young people find themselves in the world of the fairies, although the humans cannot see the fairies. Puck, an impish sprite, is ordered by Oberon, king of the fairies, to put the juice of a certain flower in Demetrius's eyes so that he will fall in love with Helena. When Puck puts it in Lysander's eyes instead, the plot backfires: Lysander is suddenly in love with Helena, and Hermia is confounded. Oberon has Puck place the same juice in the eyes of Titania, the queen of the fairies, causing her to fall in love with the first creature she sees when she awakes.

That creature is Bottom, the "rude mechanical" (ignorant artisan) whose head has been transformed into an ass's head. Such a trick opens up possibilities for wonderful comic elements. The richness of the illusions that operate onstage constantly draws us to the question of how we ever can know the truth of our own experiences, especially when some of them are dreams whose imaginative power is occasionally overwhelming.

Shakespeare plays here with some of the Aristotelian conventions of the drama, especially Aristotle's view that drama imitates life. One of the great comic devices in *A Midsummer Night's Dream* is the play within a play that Bottom, Quince, Snug, Flute, and Starveling are to put on before Theseus and Hippolyta. They tell the story of Pyramus and Thisby, lovers who lose each other because they misinterpret signs. It is "Merry and tragical! Tedious and brief!" But it is also a wonderful parody of what playwrights—including Shakespeare—often do when operating in the Aristotelian mode. The aim of the play is realism, yet the players are naive and inexperienced in drama; they do their best constantly to remind the audience that it is only a play.

The comic ineptness of the rude mechanicals' play needs no disclaimers of this sort, and the immediate audience—Theseus, Hippolyta, Demetrius, Helena, Lysander, and Hermia—is amused by the ardor of the players. The audience in the theater is also mightily amused at the antics of the mechanicals, which on the surface are simply funny and a wonderful pastiche of artless playacting.

Beneath the surface, something more serious is going on. Shakespeare is commenting on the entire function of drama in our lives. He constantly reminds us in this play that we are watching an illusion, even an illusion within an illusion, but he also convinces us that illusions teach us a great deal about reality. The real-world setting of *A Midsummer Night's Dream*—Athens—is quite improbable. The mechanicals all have obviously English names and are out of place in an Athenian pastoral setting. The play on the level of Athens is pure fantasy, with even more fantastic goings-on at the level of the fairy world. But fantasy nourishes us. It helps us interpret our own experiences by permitting us to distance ourselves from them and reflect on how they affect others, one of the deepest functions of drama.

As in most comedies, everything turns out exceptionally well. A multiple marriage, one of the delightful conventions of many comedies, ends the drama, and virtually everyone receives what she or he wanted. We are left with a sense of satisfaction because we, too, get our wish about how things should turn out. Puck, one of the greatest of Shakespeare's characters, turns out to be sympathetic and human in his feelings about people. And Bottom, a clown whose origins are certainly Greek and Roman, endears himself to us with his generosity and caring toward others. Shakespeare promotes a remarkably warm view of humanity in this play, leaving us with a sense of delight and a glow that is rare even in comedy.

A Midsummer Night's Dream in Performance

A Midsummer Night's Dream has attracted many great directors in modern times, although in the late seventeenth and eighteenth centuries the play was adapted essentially as a vehicle for presenting the world of the fairies. It even became an opera in 1692. Ludwig Tieck engaged Mendelssohn to write incidental music for the play in Berlin in 1843; their production was for many years the most influential post-Shakespearean adaptation. Beerbohm Tree's 1900 production in London's Savoy Theatre included real rabbits and many other highly realistic details; eventually it played to more than 220,000 patrons. After numerous adaptations it was produced by Granville Barker in London from 1912 to 1914 in its original text, and in New York in 1915. The Old Vic's 1954 production was so lavish that it was staged at the Metropolitan Opera House in New York. Peter Brook played down the fairies and explored the play as a study of love. His 1970 production is well remembered for his having placed Oberon and Puck on trapezes set against a stark white background. He also used some costumes and other elements of commedia dell'arte to spark the comedy. (See Barnes's review of the Brook production on p. 335.) The American Repertory Theatre's 1986 Boston production (see photos on pp. 308–309) reflects the approach to staging that the Royal Shakespeare Company has taken in recent years. The themes of love and transformation inspire the players in a way that shows off the brilliance of the play.

A Midsummer's Night Dream has been filmed several times. In 1935 both James Cagney and Mickey Rooney starred in a version that has some charm. In 1968 the Royal Shakespeare Company with Diana Rigg produced a somewhat less interesting film. The most recent version with Kevin Kline, Michelle Pfeiffer, and Stanley Tucci received generally good reviews in 1999.

William Shakespeare (1564–1616)

A MIDSUMMER NIGHT'S DREAM   c. 1596

[Dramatis Personae

THESEUS, *Duke of Athens*
EGEUS, *father to Hermia*
LYSANDER, }
DEMETRIUS, } *in love with Hermia*
PHILOSTRATE, *Master of the Revels to Theseus*

QUINCE, *a carpenter*
SNUG, *a joiner*
BOTTOM, *a weaver*
FLUTE, *a bellows-mender*
SNOUT, *a tinker*
STARVELING, *a tailor*

HIPPOLYTA, *Queen of the Amazons, betrothed to Theseus*
HERMIA, *daughter to Egeus, in love with Lysander*

HELENA, *in love with Demetrius*
OBERON, *King of the Fairies*
TITANIA, *Queen of the Fairies*
PUCK, *or Robin Goodfellow*
PEASEBLOSSOM,
COBWEB,
MOTH, } *fairies*
MUSTARDSEED,
Other FAIRIES *attending their king and queen*
ATTENDANTS *on Theseus and Hippolyta*

Scene: *Athens, and a wood near it.*]

{ACT I • Scene 1}°

(*Enter Theseus, Hippolyta, [Philostrate,] with others.*)

THESEUS: Now, fair Hippolyta, our nuptial hour
   Draws on apace. Four happy days bring in
   Another moon; but, O, methinks, how slow

Note: The text of *A Midsummer Night's Dream* has come down to us in different versions — such as the first quarto, the second quarto, and the first Folio. The copy of the text used here is largely drawn from the first quarto. Passages enclosed in square brackets are taken from one of the other versions.

I, I. **Location:** The palace of Theseus.

This old moon wanes! She lingers° my desires
5 Like to a step-dame° or a dowager°
 Long withering out a young man's revenue.
HIPPOLYTA: Four days will quickly steep themselves in
  night,
 Four nights will quickly dream away the time;
 And then the moon, like to a silver bow
10 New-bent in heaven, shall behold the night
 Of our solemnities.
THESEUS: Go, Philostrate,
 Stir up the Athenian youth to merriments,
 Awake the pert and nimble spirit of mirth,
 Turn melancholy forth to funerals;
15 The pale companion° is not for our pomp.°
        [Exit Philostrate.]
 Hippolyta, I woo'd thee with my sword,°
 And won thy love doing thee injuries;
 But I will wed thee in another key,
 With pomp, with triumph,° and with reveling.

(Enter Egeus and his daughter Hermia, and Lysander, and Demetrius.)

20 EGEUS: Happy be Theseus, our renowned Duke!
 THESEUS: Thanks, good Egeus. What's the news with
  thee?
 EGEUS: Full of vexation come I, with complaint
 Against my child, my daughter Hermia.
 Stand forth, Demetrius. My noble lord,
25 This man hath my consent to marry her.
 Stand forth, Lysander. And, my gracious Duke,
 This man hath bewitch'd the bosom of my child.
 Thou, thou, Lysander, thou hast given her rhymes
 And interchang'd love tokens with my child.
30 Thou hast by moonlight at her window sung
 With feigning voice verses of feigning° love,
 And stol'n the impression of her fantasy,°
 With bracelets of thy hair, rings, gauds,° conceits,°
 Knacks,° trifles, nosegays, sweetmeats—
  messengers
35 Of strong prevailment in unhardened youth.
 With cunning hast thou filch'd my daughter's heart,
 Turn'd her obedience, which is due to me,
 To stubborn harshness. And, my gracious Duke,
 Be it so she will not here before your Grace
40 Consent to marry with Demetrius,
 I beg the ancient privilege of Athens:
 As she is mine, I may dispose of her,

Which shall be either to this gentleman
 Or to her death, according to our law
 Immediately° provided in that case.   45
THESEUS: What say you, Hermia? Be advis'd, fair maid.
 To you your father should be as a god—
 One that compos'd your beauties, yea, and one
 To whom you are but as a form in wax
 By him imprinted and within his power   50
 To leave° the figure or disfigure° it.
 Demetrius is a worthy gentleman.
HERMIA: So is Lysander.
THESEUS: In himself he is;
 But in this kind,° wanting° your father's voice,°
 The other must be held the worthier.   55
HERMIA: I would my father look'd but with my eyes.
THESEUS: Rather your eyes must with his judgment look.
HERMIA: I do entreat your Grace to pardon me.
 I know not by what power I am made bold,
 Nor how it may concern° my modesty,   60
 In such a presence here to plead my thoughts;
 But I beseech your Grace that I may know
 The worst that may befall me in this case,
 If I refuse to wed Demetrius.
THESEUS: Either to die the death, or to abjure 65
 Forever the society of men.
 Therefore, fair Hermia, question your desires,
 Know of your youth, examine well your blood,°
 Whether, if you yield not to your father's choice,
 You can endure the livery° of a nun,   70
 For aye° to be in shady cloister mew'd,°
 To live a barren sister all your life,
 Chanting faint hymns to the cold fruitless moon.
 Thrice blessed they that master so their blood
 To undergo such maiden pilgrimage,   75
 But earthlier happy° is the rose distill'd,
 Than that which withering on the virgin thorn
 Grows, lives, and dies in single blessedness.
HERMIA: So will I grow, so live, so die, my lord,
 Ere I will yield my virgin patent° up   80
 Unto his lordship, whose unwished yoke
 My soul consents not to give sovereignty.
THESEUS: Take time to pause; and, by the next new
  moon—
 The sealing-day betwixt my love and me
 For everlasting bond of fellowship—   85
 Upon that day either prepare to die
 For disobedience to your father's will,
 Or° else to wed Demetrius, as he would,
 Or on Diana's altar° to protest°
 For aye austerity and single life.   90

---

4. lingers: Lengthens, protects. **5. step-dame:** Stepmother. **dowager:** Widow with a jointure or dower [an estate or title from her deceased husband]. **15. companion:** Fellow. **pomp:** Ceremonial magnificence. **16. with my sword:** In a military engagement against the Amazons, when Hippolyta was taken captive. **19. triumph:** Public festivity. **31. feigning:** (1) Counterfeiting, (2) faining, desirous. **32. And . . . fantasy:** And made her fall in love with you (imprinting your image on her imagination) by stealthy and dishonest means. **33. gauds:** Playthings. **conceits:** Fanciful trifles. **34. Knacks:** Knickknacks.

---

45. Immediately: Expressly. **51. leave:** Leave unaltered. **disfigure:** Obliterate. **54. kind:** Respect. **wanting voice:** Lacking Approval. **60. concern:** Befit. **68. blood:** Passions. **70. livery:** Habit. **71. aye:** Ever. **mew'd:** Shut in (said of a hawk, poultry, etc.). **76. earthlier happy:** Happier as respects this world. **80. patent:** Privilege. **88. Or:** Either. **89. Diana's altar:** Diana was a virgin goddess. **protest:** Vow.

DEMETRIUS: Relent, sweet Hermia, and, Lysander, yield
  Thy crazed° title to my certain right.
LYSANDER: You have her father's love, Demetrius;
  Let me have Hermia's. Do you marry him.
95 EGEUS: Scornful Lysander! True, he hath my love,
  And what is mine my love shall render him.
  And she is mine, and all my right of her
  I do estate unto° Demetrius.
LYSANDER: I am, my lord, as well deriv'd° as he,
100   As well possess'd;° my love is more than his;
  My fortunes every way as fairly° rank'd,
  If not with vantage,° as Demetrius';
  And, which is more than all these boasts can be,
  I am belov'd of beauteous Hermia.
105   Why should not I then prosecute my right?
  Demetrius, I'll avouch it to his head,°
  Made love to Nedar's daughter, Helena,
  And won her soul; and she, sweet lady, dotes,
  Devoutly dotes, dotes in idolatry,
110   Upon this spotted° and inconstant man.
THESEUS: I must confess that I have heard so much,
  And with Demetrius thought to have spoke thereof;
  But, being over-full of self-affairs,
  My mind did lose it. But, Demetrius, come,
115   And come, Egeus, you shall go with me;
  I have some private schooling for you both.
  For you, fair Hermia, look you arm° yourself
  To fit your fancies° to your father's will;
  Or else the law of Athens yields you up—
120   Which by no means we may extenuate°—
  To death, or to a vow of single life.
  Come, my Hippolyta. What cheer, my love?
  Demetrius and Egeus, go° along.
  I must employ you in some business
125   Against° our nuptial, and confer with you
  Of something nearly that° concerns yourselves.
EGEUS: With duty and desire we follow you.

    (*Exeunt°* [*all but Lysander and Hermia*].)

LYSANDER: How now, my love, why is your cheek so
  pale?
  How chance the roses there do fade so fast?
130 HERMIA: Belike° for want of rain, which I could well
  Beteem° them from the tempest of my eyes.
LYSANDER: Ay me! For aught that I could ever read,
  Could ever hear by tale or history,
  The course of true love never did run smooth;
135   But either it was different in blood°—

HERMIA: O cross,° too high to be enthrall'd to low!
LYSANDER: Or else misgraffed° in respect of years—
HERMIA: O spite, too old to be engag'd to young!
LYSANDER: Or else it stood upon the choice of
  friends°—
HERMIA: O hell, to choose love by another's eyes!   140
LYSANDER: Or, if there were a sympathy in choice,
  War, death, or sickness did lay siege to it,
  Making it momentany° as a sound,
  Swift as a shadow, short as any dream,
  Brief as the lightning in the collied° night,   145
  That, in a spleen,° unfolds° both heaven and earth,
  And ere a man hath power to say "Behold!"
  The jaws of darkness do devour it up.
  So quick° bright things come to confusion.°
HERMIA: If then true lovers have been ever cross'd,°   150
  It stands as an edict in destiny.
  Then let us teach our trial patience,°
  Because it is a customary cross,
  As due to love as thoughts and dreams and sighs,
  Wishes and tears, poor fancy's° followers.   155
LYSANDER: A good persuasion. Therefore, hear me,
  Hermia.
  I have a widow aunt, a dowager
  Of great revenue, and she hath no child.
  From Athens is her house remote seven leagues;
  And she respects° me as her only son.   160
  There, gentle Hermia, may I marry thee,
  And to that place the sharp Athenian law
  Cannot pursue us. If thou lovest me, then,
  Steal forth thy father's house tomorrow night;
  And in the wood, a league without the town,   165
  Where I did meet thee once with Helena
  To do observance to a morn of May,°
  There will I stay for thee.
HERMIA: My good Lysander!
  I swear to thee, by Cupid's strongest bow,
  By his best arrow with the golden head,°   170
  By the simplicity° of Venus' doves,°
  By that which knitteth souls and prospers loves,
  And by that fire which burn'd the Carthage queen,
  When the false Troyan° under sail was seen,

---

92. **crazed:** Cracked, unsound.   98. **estate unto:** Settle or bestow upon.   99. **deriv'd:** Descended, i.e., "as well born."   100. **possess'd:** Endowed with wealth.   101. **fairly:** Handsomely. 102. **vantage:** Superiority.   106. **head:** Face.   110. **spotted:** Morally stained.   117. **look you arm:** Take care you prepare. 118. **fancies:** Likings, thoughts of love.   120. **extenuate:** Mitigate.   123. **go:** Come.   125. **Against:** In preparation for. 126. **nearly that:** That closely.   127. [S.D.] *Exeunt:* Latin for "they go out."   130. **Belike:** Very likely.   131. **Beteem:** Grant, afford.   135. **blood:** Hereditary station.

136. **cross:** Vexation.   137. **misgraffed:** Ill grafted, badly matched.   139. **friends:** Relatives.   143. **momentany:** Lasting but a moment.   145. **collied:** Blackened (as with coal dust), darkened.   146. **in a spleen:** In a swift impulse in a violent flash.   **unfolds:** Discloses.   149. **quick:** Quickly; or, perhaps, living, alive.   **confusion:** Ruin.   150. **ever cross'd:** Always thwarted.   152. **teach . . . patience:** Teach ourselves patience in this trial.   155. **fancy's:** Amorous passion's.   160. **respects:** Regards.   167. **do . . . May:** Perform the ceremonies of May Day.   170. **best arrow . . . golden head:** Cupid's best gold-pointed arrows were supposed to induce love, his blunt leaden arrows aversion.   171. **simplicity:** Innocence.   **doves:** Those that drew Venus's chariot.   173–74. **by that fire . . . false Troyan:** Dido, Queen of Carthage, immolated herself on a funeral pyre after having been deserted by the Trojan hero Aeneas.

175 By all the vows that ever men have broke,
In number more than ever women spoke,
In that same place thou hast appointed me
Tomorrow truly will I meet with thee.
LYSANDER: Keep promise, love. Look, here comes
Helena.

(*Enter Helena.*)

180 HERMIA: God speed fair° Helena, whither away?
HELENA: Call you me fair? That fair again unsay.
Demetrius loves your fair.° O happy fair!°
Your eyes are lodestars,° and your tongue's sweet air°
More tuneable° than lark to shepherd's ear
185 When wheat is green, when hawthorn buds appear.
Sickness is catching. O, were favor° so,
Yours would I catch, fair Hermia, ere I go;
My ear should catch your voice, my eye your eye,
My tongue should catch your tongue's sweet melody.
190 Were the world mine, Demetrius being bated,°
The rest I'd give to be to you translated.°
O, teach me how you look, and with what art
You sway the motion° of Demetrius' heart.
HERMIA: I frown upon him, yet he loves me still.
HELENA: O that your frowns would teach my smiles
195   such skill!
HERMIA: I give him curses, yet he gives me love.
HELENA: O that my prayers could such affection°
    move!°
HERMIA: The more I hate, the more he follows me.
HELENA: The more I love, the more he hateth me.
200 HERMIA: His folly, Helena, is no fault of mine.
HELENA: None, but your beauty. Would that fault were
    mine!
HERMIA: Take comfort. He no more shall see my face.
Lysander and myself will fly this place.
Before the time I did Lysander see,
205 Seem'd Athens as a paradise to me.
O, then, what graces in my love do dwell,
That he hath turn'd a heaven unto a hell!
LYSANDER: Helen, to you our minds we will unfold.
Tomorrow night, when Phoebe° doth behold
210 Her silver visage in the wat'ry glass,°
Decking with liquid pearl the bladed grass,
A time that lovers' flights doth still° conceal,
Through Athens' gates have we devis'd to steal.
HERMIA: And in the wood, where often you and I
215 Upon faint° primrose beds were wont to lie,
Emptying our bosoms of their counsel° sweet,

There my Lysander and myself shall meet;
And thence from Athens turn away our eyes,
To seek new friends and stranger companies.
Farewell, sweet playfellow. Pray thou for us,   220
And good luck grant thee thy Demetrius!
Keep word, Lysander. We must starve our sight
From lovers' food till morrow deep midnight.
LYSANDER: I will, my Hermia.   (*Exit Hermia.*)
                    Helena, adieu.
As you on him, Demetrius dote on you!   225
                    (*Exit Lysander.*)
HELENA: How happy some o'er other some can be!°
Through Athens I am thought as fair as she.
But what of that? Demetrius thinks not so;
He will not know what all but he do know.
And as he errs, doting on Hermia's eyes,   230
So I, admiring of° his qualities.
Things base and vile, holding no quantity,°
Love can transpose to form and dignity.
Love looks not with the eyes, but with the mind,
And therefore is wing'd Cupid painted blind.   235
Nor hath Love's mind of any judgment taste;°
Wings, and no eyes, figure° unheedy haste.
And therefore is Love said to be a child,
Because in choice he is so oft beguil'd.
As waggish boys in game° themselves forswear,   240
So the boy Love is perjur'd everywhere.
For ere Demetrius look'd on Hermia's eyne,°
He hail'd down oaths that he was only mine;
And when this hail some heat from Hermia felt,
So he dissolv'd, and show'rs of oaths did melt.   245
I will go tell him of fair Hermia's flight.
Then to the wood will he tomorrow night
Pursue her; and for this intelligence°
If I have thanks, it is a dear° expense.°
But herein mean I to enrich my pain,   250
To have his sight thither and back again.   (*Exit.*)

{*Scene II*}°

(*Enter Quince the Carpenter, and Snug the Joiner, and
Bottom the Weaver, and Flute the Bellows-Mender, and
Snout the Tinker, and Starveling the Tailor.*)

QUINCE: Is all our company here?
BOTTOM: You were best to call them generally,° man by
    man, according to the scrip.°

---

180. **fair:** Fair-complexioned (generally regarded by the Elizabethans as more beautiful than dark-complexioned).   182. **your
fair:** Your beauty (even though Hermia is dark-complexioned)
happy fair: Lucky fair one.   183. **lodestars:** Guiding stars.
air: Music.   184. **tuneable:** Tuneful, melodious.   186. **favor:**
Appearance, looks.   190. **bated:** Excepted.   191. **translated:**
Transformed.   193. **motion:** Impulse.   197. **affection:** Passion.
move: Arouse.   209. **Phoebe:** Diana, the moon.   210. **glass:**
Mirror.   212. **still:** Always.   215. **faint:** Pale.   216. **counsel:**
Secret thought.

226. **o'er . . . can be:** Can be in comparison to some others.
231. **admiring of:** Wondering at.   232. **holding no quantity:**
Unsubstantial, unshapely.   236. **Nor . . . taste:** Nor has Love,
which dwells in the fancy or imagination, any *taste* or least
bit of judgment or reason.   237. **figure:** Are a symbol of.
240. **game:** Sport, jest.   242. **eyne:** Eyes (old form of plural).
248. **intelligence:** Information.   249. **dear:** Costly.   **a dear
expense:** A trouble worth taking.   I, II. Location: Athens.
Quince's house(?).   2. **generally:** Bottom's blunder for *individually.*   3. **scrip:** Script, written list.

QUINCE: Here is the scroll of every man's name which
5   is thought fit, through all Athens, to play in our
     interlude before the Duke and the Duchess on his
     wedding-day at night.
BOTTOM: First, good Peter Quince, say what the play
     treats on, then read the names of the actors, and so
10   grow to° a point.
QUINCE: Marry,° our play is "The most lamentable com-
     edy and most cruel death of Pyramus and Thisby."
BOTTOM: A very good piece of work, I assure you, and a
     merry. Now, good Peter Quince, call forth your
15   actors by the scroll. Masters, spread yourselves.
QUINCE: Answer as I call you. Nick Bottom, the weaver.
BOTTOM: Ready. Name what part I am for, and proceed.
QUINCE: You, Nick Bottom, are set down for Pyramus.
BOTTOM: What is Pyramus? A lover, or a tyrant?
20   QUINCE: A lover, that kills himself most gallant for love.
BOTTOM: That will ask some tears in the true performing
     of it. If I do it, let the audience look to their eyes. I
     will move storms; I will condole° in some measure.
     To the rest—yet my chief humor° is for a tyrant. I
25   could play Ercles° rarely, or a part to tear a cat° in, to
     make all split.°
          "The raging rocks
          And shivering shocks
          Shall break the locks
30   Of prison gates;
          And Phibbus' car°
          Shall shine from far
          And make and mar
               The foolish Fates."
35   This was lofty! Now name the rest of the players.
     This is Ercles' vein, a tyrant's vein. A lover is more
     condoling.
QUINCE: Francis Flute, the bellows-mender.
FLUTE: Here, Peter Quince.
40   QUINCE: Flute, you must take Thisby on you.
FLUTE: What is Thisby? A wand'ring knight?
QUINCE: It is the lady that Pyramus must love.
FLUTE: Nay, faith, let not me play a woman. I have a
     beard coming.
45   QUINCE: That's all one.° You shall play it in a mask, and
     you may speak as small° as you will.
BOTTOM: An° I may hide my face, let me play Thisby
     too. I'll speak in a monstrous little voice, "Thisne,
     Thisne!" "Ah Pyramus, my lover dear! Thy Thisby
50   dear, and lady dear!"
QUINCE: No, no; you must play Pyramus; and, Flute,
     you Thisby.
BOTTOM: Well, proceed.

QUINCE: Robin Starveling, the tailor.
STARVELING: Here, Peter Quince.   55
QUINCE: Robin Starveling, you must play Thisby's
     mother. Tom Snout, the tinker.
SNOUT: Here, Peter Quince.
QUINCE: You, Pyramus' father; myself, Thisby's father;
     Snug, the joiner, you, the lion's part; and I hope here   60
     is a play fitted.
SNUG: Have you the lion's part written? Pray you, if it
     be, give it me, for I am slow of study.
QUINCE: You may do it extempore, for it is nothing but
     roaring.   65
BOTTOM: Let me play the lion too. I will roar that I will
     do any man's heart good to hear me. I will roar that I
     will make the Duke say, "Let him roar again, let him
     roar again."
QUINCE: An you should do it too terribly, you would   70
     fright the Duchess and the ladies, that they would
     shriek; and that were enough to hang us all.
ALL: That would hang us, every mother's son.
BOTTOM: I grant you, friends, if you should fright the
     ladies out of their wits, they would have no more dis-   75
     cretion but to hang us; but I will aggravate° my voice
     so that I will roar you° as gently as any sucking dove;
     I will roar you an 'twere any nightingale.
QUINCE: You can play no part but Pyramus; for Pyra-
     mus is a sweet-fac'd man, a proper° man as one shall   80
     see in a summer's day, a most lovely gentleman-like
     man. Therefore you must needs play Pyramus.
BOTTOM: Well, I will undertake it. What beard were I
     best to play it in?
QUINCE: Why, what you will.   85
BOTTOM: I will discharge° it in either your° straw-color
     beard, your orange-tawny beard, your purple-in-
     grain° beard, or your French-crown-color° beard,
     your perfect yellow.
QUINCE: Some of your French crowns° have no hair at   90
     all, and then you will play barefac'd. But, masters,
     here are your parts. [He distributes parts.] And I am
     to entreat you, request you, and desire you, to con°
     them by tomorrow night; and meet me in the palace
     wood, a mile without the town, by moonlight. There   95
     will we rehearse; for if we meet in the city, we shall be
     dogg'd with company, and our devices° known. In
     the meantime I will draw a bill° of properties, such as
     our play wants. I pray you, fail me not.
BOTTOM: We will meet, and there we may rehearse most   100
     obscenely° and courageously. Take pains, be perfect;°
     adieu.

---

10. **grow to:** Come to.   11. **Marry:** A mild oath, originally the
name of the Virgin Mary.   23. **condole:** Lament, arouse pity.
24. **humor:** Inclination, whim.   25. **Ercles:** Hercules (the tradition of ranting came from Seneca's *Hercules Furens*).   **tear a
cat:** Rant.   26. **make all split:** Cause a stir, bring the house
down.   31. **Phibbus' car:** Phoebus's, the sun-god's, chariot.
45. **That's all one:** It makes no difference.   46. **small:** High-
pitched.   47. **An:** If.

76. **aggravate:** Bottom's blunder for *diminish*.   77. **roar you:**
Roar for you.   80. **proper:** Handsome.   86. **discharge:** Perform.   **your:** I.e., you know the kind I mean.   87–88. **purple-
in-grain:** Dyed a very deep red (from *grain*, the name applied to
the dried insect used to make the dye).   88. **French-crown-
color:** Color of a French crown, a gold coin.   90. **crowns:** Heads
bald from syphilis, the "French disease."   93. **con:** Learn by
heart.   97. **devices:** Plans.   98. **bill:** List.   101. **obscenely:** An
unintentionally funny blunder, whatever Bottom meant to say.
perfect: Letter-perfect in memorizing your parts.

QUINCE: At the Duke's oak we meet.
BOTTOM: Enough. Hold, or cut bow-strings.°

(*Exeunt.*)

{*ACT II • Scene 1*}°

(*Enter a Fairy at one door, and Robin Goodfellow [Puck] at another.*)

PUCK: How now, spirit! Whither wander you?
FAIRY: Over hill, over dale,
    Thorough° bush, thorough brier,
    Over park, over pale,°
5   Thorough flood, thorough fire,
    I do wander every where,
    Swifter than the moon's sphere;
    And I serve the Fairy Queen,
    To dew her orbs° upon the green.
10   The cowslips tall her pensioners° be.
    In their gold coats spots you see;
    Those be rubies, fairy favors,°
    In those freckles live their savors.°
    I must go seek some dewdrops here
15   And hang a pearl in every cowslip's ear.
    Farewell, thou lob° of spirits; I'll be gone.
    Our Queen and all her elves come here anon.°
PUCK: The King doth keep his revels here tonight.
    Take heed the Queen come not within his sight.
20   For Oberon is passing fell° and wrath,°
    Because that she as her attendant hath
    A lovely boy, stolen from an Indian king;
    She never had so sweet a changeling.°
    And jealous Oberon would have the child
25   Knight of his train, to trace° the forests wild.
    But she perforce° withholds the loved boy,
    Crowns him with flowers and makes him all her joy.
    And now they never meet in grove or green,
    By fountain° clear, or spangled starlight sheen,
30   But they do square,° that all their elves for fear
    Creep into acorn-cups and hide them there.
FAIRY: Either I mistake your shape and making quite,
    Or else you are that shrewd° and knavish sprite°
    Call'd Robin Goodfellow. Are not you he
35   That frights the maidens of the villagery,
    Skim milk, and sometimes labor in the quern,°
    And bootless° make the breathless huswife churn,

And sometime make the drink to bear no barm,°
Mislead night-wanderers, laughing at their harm?
Those that Hobgoblin call you and sweet Puck,   40
You do their work, and they shall have good luck.
Are you not he?
PUCK: Thou speakest aright;
    I am that merry wanderer of the night.
    I jest to Oberon and make him smile
    When I a fat and bean-fed horse beguile,   45
    Neighing in likeness of a filly foal;
    And sometime lurk I in a gossip's° bowl,
    In very likeness of a roasted crab,°
    And when she drinks, against her lips I bob
    And on her withered dewlap° pour the ale.   50
    The wisest aunt,° telling the saddest° tale,
    Sometime for three-foot stool mistaketh me;
    Then slip I from her bum, down topples she,
    And "tailor"° cries, and falls into a cough;
    And then the whole quire° hold their hips and
        laugh,   55
    And waxen° in their mirth and neeze° and swear
    A merrier hour was never wasted there.
    But, room, fairy! Here comes Oberon.
FAIRY: And here my mistress. Would that he were
        gone!

(*Enter [Oberon] the King of Fairies at one door, with his train; and [Titania] the Queen at another, with hers.*)

OBERON: Ill met by moonlight, proud Titania.   60
TITANIA: What, jealous Oberon? Fairies, skip hence.
    I have forsworn his bed and company.
OBERON: Tarry, rash wanton.° Am not I thy lord?
TITANIA: Then I must be thy lady; but I know
    When thou hast stolen away from fairy land,   65
    And in the shape of Corin° sat all day,
    Playing on pipes of corn° and versing love
    To amorous Phillida.° Why art thou here,
    Come from the farthest steep° of India,
    But that, forsooth, the bouncing Amazon,   70
    Your buskin'd° mistress and your warrior love,
    To Theseus must be wedded, and you come
    To give their bed joy and prosperity.
OBERON: How canst thou thus for shame, Titania,
    Glance at my credit with Hippolyta,°   75
    Knowing I know thy love to Theseus?
    Didst not thou lead him through the glimmering
        night

104. Hold . . . bow-strings: An archer's expression not definitely explained, but probably meaning here "keep your promises, or give up the play." **II, 1. Location:** A wood near Athens. **3. Thorough:** Through. **4. pale:** Enclosure. **9. orbs:** Circles, i.e., fairy rings. **10. pensioners:** Retainers, members of the royal bodyguard. **12. favors:** Love tokens. **13. savors:** Sweet smells. **16. lob:** Country bumpkin. **17. anon:** At once. **20. passing fell:** Exceedingly angry. **wrath:** Wrathful. **23. changeling:** Child exchanged for another by the fairies. **25. trace:** Range through. **26. perforce:** Forcibly. **29. fountain:** Spring. **30. square:** Quarrel. **33. shrewd:** Mischievous. **sprite:** Spirit. **36. quern:** Handmill. **37. bootless:** In vain.

38. barm: Yeast, head on the ale. **47. gossip's:** Old woman's. **48. crab:** Crab apple. **50. dewlap:** Loose skin on neck. **51. aunt:** Old woman. **saddest:** Most serious. **54. tailor:** Possibly because she ends up sitting cross-legged on the floor, looking like a tailor. **55. quire:** Company. **56. waxen:** Increase. **neeze:** Sneeze. **63. wanton:** Headstrong creature. **66, 68. Corin, Phillida:** Conventional names of pastoral lovers. **67. corn:** Here, oat stalks. **69. steep:** Mountain range. **71. buskin'd:** Wearing half-boots called buskins. **75. Glance . . . Hippolyta:** Make insinuations about my favored relationship with Hippolyta.

From Perigenia,° whom he ravished?
And make him with fair Aegles° break his faith,
80   With Ariadne° and Antiopa?°
TITANIA: These are the forgeries of jealousy;
     And never, since the middle summer's spring,°
     Met we on hill, in dale, forest, or mead,
     By paved° fountain or by rushy° brook,
85   Or in° the beached margent° of the sea,
     To dance our ringlets° to the whistling wind,
     But with thy brawls thou hast disturb'd our sport.
     Therefore the winds, piping to us in vain,
     As in revenge, have suck'd up from the sea
90   Contagious° fogs; which falling in the land
     Hath every pelting° river made so proud
     That they have overborne their continents.°
     The ox hath therefore stretch'd his yoke in vain,
     The ploughman lost his sweat, and the green corn°
95   Hath rotted ere his youth attain'd a beard;
     The fold° stands empty in the drowned field,
     And crows are fatted with the murrion° flock;
     The nine men's morris° is fill'd up with mud,
     And the quaint mazes° in the wanton° green
100 For lack of tread are undistinguishable.
     The human mortals want° their winter° here;
     No night is now with hymn or carol bless'd.
     Therefore° the moon, the governess of floods,
     Pale in her anger, washes all the air,
105 That rheumatic diseases° do abound.
     And thorough this distemperature° we see
     The seasons alter: hoary-headed frosts
     Fall in the fresh lap of the crimson rose,
     And on old Hiems'° thin and icy crown
110 An odorous chaplet of sweet summer buds
     Is, as in mockery, set. The spring, the summer,

     The childing° autumn, angry winter, change
     Their wonted liveries,° and the mazed° world,
     By their increase,° now knows not which is which.
     And this same progeny of evils comes   115
     From our debate,° from our dissension;
     We are their parents and original.°
OBERON: Do you amend it then; it lies in you.
     Why should Titania cross her Oberon?
     I do but beg a little changeling boy,   120
     To be my henchman.°
TITANIA: Set your heart at rest.
     The fairy land buys not the child of me.
     His mother was a vot'ress° of my order,
     And, in the spiced Indian air, by night,
     Full often hath she gossip'd by my side,   125
     And sat with me on Neptune's yellow sands,
     Marking th' embarked traders° on the flood,°
     When we have laugh'd to see the sails conceive
     And grow big-bellied with the wanton° wind;
     Which she, with pretty and with swimming gait,   130
     Following—her womb then rich with my young
        squire—
     Would imitate, and sail upon the land
     To fetch me trifles, and return again,
     As from a voyage, rich with merchandise.
     But she, being mortal, of that boy did die;   135
     And for her sake do I rear up her boy,
     And for her sake I will not part with him.
OBERON: How long within this wood intend you stay?
TITANIA: Perchance till after Theseus' wedding-day.
     If you will patiently dance in our round°   140
     And see our moonlight revels, go with us;
     If not, shun me, and I will spare° your haunts.
OBERON: Give me that boy, and I will go with thee.
TITANIA: Not for thy fairy kingdom. Fairies, away!
     We shall chide downright, if I longer stay.   145

     (*Exeunt* [*Titania with her train*].)

OBERON: Well, go thy way. Thou shalt not from° this
        grove
     Till I torment thee for this injury.
     My gentle Puck, come hither. Thou rememb'rest
     Since° once I sat upon a promontory,
     And heard a mermaid on a dolphin's back   150
     Uttering such dulcet and harmonious breath°
     That the rude sea grew civil at her song
     And certain stars shot madly from their spheres,
     To hear the sea-maid's music.
PUCK: I remember.
OBERON: That very time I saw, but thou couldst not,   155

78. **Perigenia:** Perigouna, one of Theseus's conquests. (This and the following women are named in Thomas North's translation of Plutarch's *Life of Theseus*.)   79. **Aegles:** Aegle, for whom Theseus deserted Ariadne according to some accounts. 80. **Ariadne:** The daughter of Minos, King of Crete, who helped Theseus escape the labyrinth after killing the Minotaur; later she was abandoned by Theseus.   **Antiopa:** Queen of the Amazons and wife of Theseus; elsewhere identified with Hippolyta, but here thought of as a separate woman.   82. **middle summer's spring:** Beginning of midsummer.   84. **paved:** With pebbled bottom.   **rushy:** Bordered with rushes.   85. **in:** On. **margent:** Edge, border.   86. **ringlets:** Dances in a ring. (See *orbs* in line 9.)   90. **Contagious:** Noxious.   91. **pelting:** Paltry; or striking, moving forcefully.   92. **continents:** Banks that contain them.   94. **corn:** Grain of any kind.   96. **fold:** Pen for sheep or cattle.   97. **murrion:** Having died of the murrain, plague.   98. **nine men's morris:** Portion of the village green marked out in a square for a game played with nine pebbles or pegs.   99. **quaint mazes:** Intricate paths marked out on the village green to be followed rapidly on foot as a kind of contest. **wanton:** Luxuriant.   101. **want:** Lack.   **winter:** Regular winter season; or proper observances of winter, such as the *hymn or carol* in the next line (?).   103. **Therefore:** I.e., as a result of our quarrel.   105. **rheumatic diseases:** Colds, flu, and other respiratory infections.   106. **distemperature:** Disturbance in nature.   109. **Hiems:** The winter god.

112. **childing:** Fruitful, pregnant.   113. **wonted liveries:** Usual apparel.   **mazed:** Bewildered.   114. **their increase:** Their yield, what they produce.   116. **debate:** Quarrel.   117. **original:** Origin.   121. **henchman:** Attendant, page.   123. **vot'ress:** Female votary; devotee, worshiper.   127. **traders:** Trading vessels.   **flood:** Flood tide.   129. **wanton:** Sportive.   140. **round:** Circular dance.   142. **spare:** Shun.   146. **from:** Go from. 149. **Since:** When.   151. **breath:** Voice, song.

Flying between the cold moon and the earth,
Cupid all° arm'd. A certain aim he took
At a fair vestal° throned by the west,
And loos'd his love-shaft smartly from his bow,
160 As° it should pierce a hundred thousand hearts;
But I might° see young Cupid's fiery shaft
Quench'd in the chaste beams of the wat'ry moon,
And the imperial vot'ress passed on,
In maiden meditation, fancy-free.°
165 Yet mark'd I where the bolt of Cupid fell:
It fell upon a little western flower,
Before milk-white, now purple with love's wound,
And maidens call it love-in-idleness.°
Fetch me that flow'r; the herb I showed thee once.
170 The juice of it on sleeping eyelids laid
Will make or man or° woman madly dote
Upon the next live creature that it sees.
Fetch me this herb, and be thou here again
Ere the leviathan° can swim a league.
175 PUCK: I'll put a girdle round about the earth
In forty° minutes.   [*Exit.*]
OBERON: Having once this juice,
I'll watch Titania when she is asleep,
And drop the liquor of it in her eyes.
The next thing then she waking looks upon,
180 Be it on lion, bear, or wolf, or bull,
On meddling monkey, or on busy ape,
She shall pursue it with the soul of love.
And ere I take this charm from off her sight,
As I can take it with another herb,
185 I'll make her render up her page to me.
But who comes here? I am invisible,
And I will overhear their conference.

(*Enter Demetrius, Helena following him.*)

DEMETRIUS: I love thee not, therefore pursue me not.
Where is Lysander and fair Hermia?
190 The one I'll slay, the other slayeth me.
Thou told'st me they were stol'n unto this wood;
And here am I, and wode° within this wood,
Because I cannot meet my Hermia.
Hence, get thee gone, and follow me no more.
195 HELENA: You draw me, you hard-hearted adamant;°
But yet you draw not iron, for my heart
Is true as steel. Leave° you your power to draw,
And I shall have no power to follow you.

DEMETRIUS: Do I entice you? Do I speak you fair?°
Or, rather, do I not in plainest truth   200
Tell you I do not nor I cannot love you?
HELENA: And even for that do I love you the more.
I am your spaniel; and, Demetrius,
The more you beat me, I will fawn on you.
Use me but as your spaniel, spurn me, strike me,   205
Neglect me, lose me; only give me leave,
Unworthy as I am, to follow you.
What worser place can I beg in your love—
And yet a place of high respect with me—
Than to be used as you use your dog?   210
DEMETRIUS: Tempt not too much the hatred of my
spirit,
For I am sick when I do look on thee.
HELENA: And I am sick when I look not on you.
DEMETRIUS: You do impeach° your modesty too much
To leave the city and commit yourself   215
Into the hands of one that loves you not,
To trust the opportunity of night
And the ill counsel of a desert° place
With the rich worth of your virginity.
HELENA: Your virtue° is my privilege.° For that°   220
It is not night when I do see your face,
Therefore I think I am not in the night;
Nor doth this wood lack worlds of company,
For you in my respect° are all the world.
Then how can it be said I am alone,   225
When all the world is here to look on me?
DEMETRIUS: I'll run from thee and hide me in the
brakes,°
And leave thee to the mercy of wild beasts.
HELENA: The wildest hath not such a heart as you.
Run when you will, the story shall be chang'd: 230
Apollo flies and Daphne holds the chase,°
The dove pursues the griffin,° the mild hind°
Makes speed to catch the tiger—bootless° speed,
When cowardice pursues and valor flies.
DEMETRIUS: I will not stay° thy questions.° Let me go!   235
Or if thou follow me, do not believe
But I shall do thee mischief in the wood.
HELENA: Ay, in the temple, in the town, the field,
You do me mischief. Fie, Demetrius!
Your wrongs do set a scandal on my sex.   240
We cannot fight for love, as men may do;
We should be woo'd and were not made to woo.
[*Exit Demetrius.*]

---

157. **all:** Fully. 158. **vestal:** Vestal virgin (contains a complimentary allusion to Queen Elizabeth as a votaress of Diana and probably refers to an actual entertainment in her honor at Elvetham in 1591). 160. **As:** As if. 161. **might:** Could. 164. **fancy-free:** Free of love's spell. 168. **love-in-idleness:** Pansy, heartsease. 171. **or . . . or:** Either . . . or. 174. **leviathan:** Sea monster, whale. 176. **forty:** Used indefinitely. 192. **wode:** Mad (pronounced "wood" and often spelled so). 195. **adamant:** Lodestone, magnet (with pun on *hard-hearted,* since adamant was also thought to be the hardest of all stones and was confused with the diamond). 197. **Leave:** Give up.

199. **fair:** Courteously. 214. **impeach:** Call into question. 218. **desert:** Deserted. 220. **virtue:** Goodness or power to attract. **privilege:** Safeguard, warrant. **For that:** Because. 224. **in my respect:** As far as I am concerned. 227. **brakes:** Thickets. 231. **Apollo . . . chase:** In the ancient myth, Daphne fled from Apollo and was saved from rape by being transformed into a laurel tree; here it is the female who *holds the chase,* or pursues, instead of the male. 232. **griffin:** A fabulous monster with the head of an eagle and the body of a lion. **hind:** Female deer. 233. **bootless:** Fruitless. 235. **stay:** Wait for. **questions:** Talk or argument.

NEAR RIGHT: Oberon instructing Puck in the power of the "little western flower" in the American Repertory Theatre's 1986 production. CENTER: Oberon with Titania upon his shoulder. FAR RIGHT: The rude mechanicals: Moonshine with Lion. BELOW: Kevin Kline as Bottom, and Michelle Pfeiffer as Titania, in a touching moment from the 1999 film, *William Shakespeare's A Midsummer Night's Dream*, directed by Michael Hoffman.

I'll follow thee and make a heaven of hell,
To die upon° the hand I love so well.　　　[Exit.]
OBERON: Fare thee well, nymph. Ere he do leave this
245　　grove,
Thou shalt fly him and he shall seek thy love.

(Enter Puck.)

Hast thou the flower there? Welcome, wanderer.
PUCK: Ay, there it is.　　　　　　　[Offers the flower.]
OBERON:　　　　　　I pray thee, give it me.
I know a bank where the wild thyme blows,°
250　Where oxlips° and the nodding violet grows,
Quite over-canopied with luscious woodbine,°
With sweet musk-roses° and with eglantine.°
There sleeps Titania sometime of the night
Lull'd in these flowers with dances and delight;

And there the snake throws° her enamel'd skin,　255
Weed° wide enough to wrap a fairy in.
And with the juice of this I'll streak° her eyes,
And make her full of hateful fantasies.
Take thou some of it, and seek through this grove.
　　　　　　　　　[Gives some love-juice.]
A sweet Athenian lady is in love　　　　　　260
With a disdainful youth. Anoint his eyes,
But do it when the next thing he espies
May be the lady. Thou shalt know the man
By the Athenian garments he hath on.
Effect it with some care, that he may prove　265
More fond on° her than she upon her love;
And look thou meet me ere the first cock crow.
PUCK: Fear not, my lord, your servant shall do so.
　　　　　　　　　　　　　(Exeunt.)

244. upon: By.　249. blows: Blooms.　250. oxlips: Flowers
resembling cow-slip and primrose.　251. woodbine: Honeysuckle.　252. musk-roses: A kind of large, sweet-scented rose.
eglantine: Sweetbriar, another kind of rose.

255. throws: Sloughs off, sheds.　256. Weed: Garment.
257. streak: Anoint, touch gently.　266. fond on: Doting on.

309

{*Scene II*}°

(*Enter Titania, Queen of Fairies, with her train.*)

TITANIA: Come, now a roundel° and a fairy song;
  Then, for the third part of a minute, hence—
  Some to kill cankers° in the musk-rose buds,
  Some war with rere-mice° for their leathern wings,
5 To make my small elves coats, and some keep back
  The clamorous owl, that nightly hoots and wonders
  At our quaint° spirits. Sing me now asleep.
  Then to your offices and let me rest.

(*Fairies sing.*)

FIRST FAIRY: You spotted snakes with double° tongue,
10   Thorny hedgehogs, be not seen;
  Newts° and blindworms, do no wrong,
    Come not near our fairy queen.
  [*Chorus.*] Philomel,° with melody
    Sing in our sweet lullaby;
15 Lulla, lulla, lullaby, lulla, lulla, lullaby.
    Never harm,
    Nor spell nor charm,
  Come our lovely lady nigh.
  So, good night, with lullaby.
20 FIRST FAIRY: Weaving spiders, come not here;
    Hence, you long-legg'd spinners, hence!
  Beetles black, approach not near;
    Worm nor snail, do no offense.
  [*Chorus.*] Philomel, with melody, etc.
25 SECOND FAIRY: Hence, away! Now all is well.
  One aloof stand sentinel.

                        [*Exeunt Fairies. Titania sleeps.*]

(*Enter Oberon [and squeezes the flower on Titania's eyelids].*)

OBERON: What thou seest when thou dost wake,
  Do it for thy true-love take;
  Love and languish for his sake.
30 Be it ounce,° or cat, or bear,
  Pard,° or boar with bristled hair,
  In thy eye that shall appear
  When thou wak'st, it is thy dear
  Wake when some vile thing is near.   [*Exit.*]

(*Enter Lysander and Hermia.*)

LYSANDER: Fair love, you faint with wand'ring in the
35   wood;
  And to speak troth,° I have forgot our way.
  We'll rest us, Hermia, if you think it good,
  And tarry for the comfort of the day.
HERMIA: Be 't so, Lysander. Find you out a bed,
  For I upon this bank will rest my head.   40
LYSANDER: One turf shall serve as pillow for us both,
  One heart, one bed, two bosoms, and one troth.°
HERMIA: Nay, good Lysander; for my sake, my dear,
  Lie further off yet, do not lie so near.
LYSANDER: O, take the sense, sweet, of my
    innocence!°   45
  Love takes the meaning in love's conference.°
  I mean, that my heart unto yours is knit
  So that but one heart we can make of it;
  Two bosoms interchained with an oath—
  So then two bosoms and a single troth.   50
  Then by your side no bed-room me deny,
  For lying so, Hermia, I do not lie.°
HERMIA: Lysander riddles very prettily.
  Now much beshrew° my manners and my pride
  If Hermia meant to say Lysander lied.   55
  But, gentle friend, for love and courtesy
  Lie further off, in human° modesty;
  Such separation as may well be said
  Becomes a virtuous bachelor and a maid,
  So far be distant; and, good night, sweet friend. 60
  Thy love ne'er alter till thy sweet life end!
LYSANDER: Amen, amen, to that fair prayer, say I,
  And then end life when I end loyalty!
  Here is my bed. Sleep give thee all his rest!
HERMIA: With half that wish the wisher's eyes be
    press'd!°   65
  [*They sleep, separated by a short distance.*]

(*Enter Puck.*)

PUCK: Through the forest have I gone,
  But Athenian found I none
  On whose eyes I might approve°
  This flower's force in stirring love.
  Night and silence.—Who is here?   70
  Weeds of Athens he doth wear.
  This is he, my master said,
  Despised the Athenian maid;
  And here the maiden, sleeping sound,
  On the dank and dirty ground.   75
  Pretty soul! She durst not lie
  Near this lack-love, this kill-courtesy.
  Churl, upon thy eyes I throw
  All the power this charm doth owe.°
                        [*Applies the love-juice.*]
  When thou wak'st, let love forbid   80
  Sleep his seat on thy eyelid.

II, I. **Location:** The wood.   **1. roundel:** Dance in a ring.
3. cankers: Cankerworms.   **4. rere-mice:** Bats.   **7. quaint:**
Dainty.   **9. double:** Forked.   **11. Newts:** water lizards (considered poisonous, as were blindworms—small snakes with
tiny eyes—and spiders).   **13. Philomel:** The nightingale.
(Philomela, daughter of King Pandion, was transformed into a
nightingale, according to Ovid's *Metamorphoses*, after she
had been raped by her sister Procne's husband, Tereus.)
30. ounce: Lynx.   **31. Pard:** Leopard.   **36. troth:** Truth.

42. troth: Faith, troth-plight.   **45. take . . . innocence:** Interpret my intention as innocent.   **46. Love . . . conference:** When
lovers confer, love teaches each lover to interpret the other's
meaning lovingly.   **52. lie:** Tell a falsehood (with a riddling
pun on *lie*, recline).   **54. beshrew:** Curse (but mildly meant).
57. human: Courteous.   **65. With . . . press'd:** May we share
your wish, so that your eyes too are *press'd*, closed, in sleep.
68. approve: Test.   **79. owe:** Own.

So awake when I am gone,
For I must now to Oberon.　　　　　　　(*Exit.*)

(*Enter Demetrius and Helena, running.*)

HELENA: Stay, though thou kill me, sweet Demetrius.
DEMETRIUS: I charge thee, hence, and do not haunt
85　　　me thus.
HELENA: O, wilt thou darkling° leave me? Do not so.
DEMETRIUS: Stay, on thy peril!° I alone will go.
　　　　　　　　　　　　　　　　　　　　[*Exit.*]
HELENA: O, I am out of breath in this fond° chase!
　　The more my prayer, the lesser is my grace.°
90　　Happy is Hermia, wheresoe'er she lies,°
　　For she hath blessed and attractive eyes.
　　How came her eyes so bright? Not with salt tears;
　　If so, my eyes are oft'ner wash'd than hers.
　　No, no, I am as ugly as a bear;
95　　For beasts that meet me run away for fear.
　　Therefore no marvel though Demetrius
　　Do, as a monster, fly my presence thus.
　　What wicked and dissembling glass of mine
　　Made me compare with Hermia's sphery eyne?°
100　But who is here? Lysander, on the ground?
　　Dead, or asleep? I see no blood, no wound.
　　Lysander, if you live, good sir, awake.
LYSANDER [*awaking*]: And run through fire I will for
　　thy sweet sake.
　　Transparent° Helena! Nature shows art,
105　That through thy bosom makes me see thy heart.
　　Where is Demetrius? O, how fit a word
　　Is that vile name to perish on my sword!
HELENA: Do not say so, Lysander, say not so.
　　What though he love your Hermia? Lord, what
　　　though?
110　Yet Hermia still loves you. Then be content.
LYSANDER: Content with Hermia? No! I do repent
　　The tedious minutes I with her have spent.
　　Not Hermia but Helena I love.
　　Who will not change a raven for a dove?
115　The will of man is by his reason sway'd;
　　And reason says you are the worthier maid.
　　Things growing are not ripe until their season;
　　So I, being young, till now ripe not° to reason.
　　And touching° now the point° of human skill,°
120　Reason becomes the marshal to my will
　　And leads me to your eyes, where I o'erlook°
　　Love's stories written in love's richest book.
HELENA: Wherefore was I to this keen mockery born?
　　When at your hands did I deserve this scorn?
125　Is 't not enough, is 't not enough, young man,
　　That I did never, no, nor never can,

Deserve a sweet look from Demetrius' eye,
But you must flout my insufficiency?
Good troth,° you do me wrong, good sooth,° you do,
In such disdainful manner me to woo.　　　　130
But fare you well. Perforce I must confess
I thought you lord of° more true gentleness.
O, that a lady, of° one man refus'd,
Should of another therefore be abus'd!°　　(*Exit.*)
LYSANDER: She sees not Hermia. Hermia, sleep thou
　　there,　　　　　　　　　　　　　　　　135
And never mayst thou come Lysander near!
For as a surfeit of the sweetest things
The deepest loathing to the stomach brings,
Or as the heresies that men do leave
Are hated most of those they did deceive,　　140
So thou, my surfeit and my heresy,
Of all be hated, but the most of me!
And, all my powers, address your love and might
To honor Helen and to be her knight!　　(*Exit.*)
HERMIA [*awaking*]: Help me, Lysander, help me! Do
　　thy best　　　　　　　　　　　　　　　145
To pluck this crawling serpent from my breast!
Ay me, for pity! What a dream was here!
Lysander, look how I do quake with fear.
Methought a serpent eat° my heart away,
And you sat smiling at his cruel prey.°　　　150
Lysander! What, remov'd? Lysander! Lord!
What, out of hearing? Gone? No sound, no word?
Alack, where are you? Speak, an if you hear,
Speak, of all loves!° I swoon almost with fear.
No? Then I well perceive you are not nigh.　　155
Either death, or you, I'll find immediately.
　　　　　(*Exit.* [*Manet*° *Titania lying asleep.*])

{*ACT III* • *Scene 1*}°

(*Enter the Clowns* [*Quince, Snug, Bottom, Flute, Snout,
and Starveling*].)

BOTTOM: Are we all met?
QUINCE: Pat, pat; and here's a marvailes° convenient
　　place for our rehearsal. This green plot shall be our
　　stage, this hawthorn brake° our tiring-house,° and
　　we will do it in action as we will do it before the　5
　　Duke.
BOTTOM: Peter Quince?
QUINCE: What sayest thou, bully° Bottom?
BOTTOM: There are things in this comedy of Pyramus
　　and Thisby that will never please. First, Pyramus　10
　　must draw a sword to kill himself, which the ladies
　　cannot abide. How answer you that?

---

86. **darkling:** In the dark.　87. **on thy peril:** On pain of danger
to you if you don't obey me and stay.　88. **fond:** Doting.
89. **my grace:** The favor I obtain.　90. **lies:** Dwells.
99. **sphery eyne:** Eyes as bright as stars in their spheres.
104. **Transparent:** (1) Radiant; (2) able to be seen through.
118. **ripe not:** (Am) not ripened.　119. **touching:** Reaching.
point: Summit.　**skill:** Judgment.　121. **o'erlook:** Read.

129. **Good troth, good sooth:** Indeed, truly.　132. **lord of:** Possessor of.　**gentleness:** Courtesy.　133. **of:** By.　134. **abus'd:**
Ill treated.　149. **eat:** Ate (pronounced "et").　150. **prey:** Act of
preying.　154. **of all loves:** For all love's sake.　156. [S.D.] **Manet:**
Latin for "she remains."　III, I. **Location:** Scene continues.　2.
marvailes: Marvelous.　4. **brake:** Thicket.　**tiring-house:** Attiring area, hence backstage.　8. **bully:** Worthy, jolly, fine fellow.

SNOUT: By 'r lakin,° a parlous° fear.

STARVELING: I believe we must leave the killing out, when all is done.°

15

BOTTOM: Not a whit. I have a device to make all well. Write me° a prologue; and let the prologue seem to say, we will do no harm with our swords and that Pyramus is not kill'd indeed; and, for the more better assurance, tell them that I Pyramus am not Pyramus, but Bottom the weaver. This will put them out of fear.

20

QUINCE: Well, we will have such a prologue, and it shall be written in eight and six.°

BOTTOM: No, make it two more; let it be written in eight and eight.

25

SNOUT: Will not the ladies be afeard of the lion?

STARVELING: I fear it, I promise you.

BOTTOM: Masters, you ought to consider with yourselves, to bring in—God shield us!—a lion among ladies,° is a most dreadful thing. For there is not a more fearful° wild-fowl than your lion living; and we ought to look to 't.

30

SNOUT: Therefore another prologue must tell he is not a lion.

35

BOTTOM: Nay, you must name his name, and half his face must be seen through the lion's neck, and he himself must speak through, saying thus, or to the same defect:° "Ladies"—or "Fair ladies—I would wish you"—or "I would request you"—or "I would entreat you—not to fear, not to tremble; my life for yours.° If you think I come hither as a lion, it were pity of my life.° No, I am no such thing, I am a man as other men are." And there indeed let him name his name, and tell them plainly he is Snug the joiner.

40

45

QUINCE: Well, it shall be so. But there is two hard things: that is, to bring the moonlight into a chamber; for, you know, Pyramus and Thisby meet by moonlight.

50

SNOUT: Doth the moon shine that night we play our play?

BOTTOM: A calendar, a calendar! Look in the almanac. Find out moonshine, find out moonshine.

[They consult an almanac.]

QUINCE: Yes, it doth shine that night.

55

BOTTOM: Why then may you leave a casement of the great chamber window, where we play, open, and the moon may shine in at the casement.

QUINCE: Ay; or else one must come in with a bush of thorns° and a lantern, and say he comes to disfigure,° or to present,° the person of Moonshine. Then there is another thing: we must have a wall in the great chamber; for Pyramus and Thisby, says the story, did talk through the chink of a wall.

60

SNOUT: You can never bring in a wall. What say you, Bottom?

65

BOTTOM: Some man or other must present Wall. And let him have some plaster, or some loam, or some rough-cast° about him, to signify wall; and let him hold his fingers thus, and through that cranny shall Pyramus and Thisby whisper.

70

QUINCE: If that may be, then all is well. Come, sit down, every mother's son, and rehearse your parts. Pyramus, you begin. When you have spoken your speech, enter into that brake, and so every one according to his cue.

75

(Enter Robin [Puck].)

PUCK: What hempen° home-spuns have we swagg'ring here,
So near the cradle of the Fairy Queen?
What, a play toward?° I'll be an auditor;°
An actor too perhaps, if I see cause.

QUINCE: Speak, Pyramus. Thisby, stand forth.

80

BOTTOM: "Thisby, the flowers of odious savors sweet,"—

QUINCE: Odors, odors.

BOTTOM: —"Odors savors sweet;
So hath thy breath, my dearest Thisby dear.
But hark, a voice! Stay thou but here awhile,
And by and by I will to thee appear."   (Exit.)

85

PUCK: A stranger Pyramus than e'er played here.°
[Exit.]

FLUTE: Must I speak now?

QUINCE: Ay, marry, must you; for you must understand he goes but to see a noise that he heard, and is to come again.

90

FLUTE: "Most radiant Pyramus, most lily-white of hue,
Of color like the red rose on triumphant brier,
Most brisky juvenal° and eke° most lovely Jew,°
As true as truest horse that yet would never tire.
I'll meet thee, Pyramus, at Ninny's tomb."

95

QUINCE: "Ninus'° tomb," man. Why, you must not speak that yet. That you answer to Pyramus. You speak all

13. By 'r lakin: By our ladykin, the Virgin Mary.   parlous: Perilous.   15. when all is done: When all is said and done.   17. Write me: Write at my suggestion.   24. eight and six: Alternate lines of eight and six syllables, a common ballad measure.   30–31. lion among ladies: A contemporary pamphlet tells how at the christening in 1594 of Prince Henry, eldest son of King James VI of Scotland, later James I of England, a "blackmoor" instead of a lion drew the triumphal chariot, since the lion's presence might have "brought some fear to the nearest."   32. fearful: Fear-inspiring.   39. defect: Bottom's blunder for effect.   42. my life for yours: I pledge my life to make your lives safe.   43. it were . . . life: My life would be endangered.

58–59. bush of thorns: Bundle of thornbush faggots (part of the accoutrements of the man in the moon, according to the popular notions of the time, along with his lantern and his dog).   59. disfigure: Quince's blunder for prefigure.   60. present: Represent.   68. rough-cast: A mixture of lime and gravel used to plaster the outside of buildings.   76. hempen: Made of hemp, a rough fiber.   78. toward: About to take place.   auditor: One who listens, i.e., part of the audience.   87. here: In this theater (?).   94. brisky juvenal: Brisk youth.   eke: Also. Jew: Probably an absurd repetition of the first syllable of juvenal.   97. Ninus: Mythical founder of Nineveh (whose wife, Semiramis, was supposed to have built the walls of Babylon where the story of Pyramus and Thisby takes place).

100 your part at once, cues and all. Pyramus enter. Your
cue is past; it is, "never tire."
FLUTE: O—"As true as truest horse, that yet would
never tire."

[*Enter Puck, and Bottom as Pyramus with the ass head.*]°

BOTTOM: "If I were fair,° Thisby, I were° only thine."
QUINCE: O monstrous! O strange! We are haunted.
Pray, masters! Fly, masters! Help!

[*Exeunt Quince, Snug, Flute, Snout, and Starveling.*]

105 PUCK: I'll follow you, I'll lead you about a round,°
Through bog, through bush, through brake,
through brier.
Sometime a horse I'll be, sometime a hound,
A hog, a headless bear, sometime a fire,°
And neigh, and bark, and grunt, and roar, and burn,
110 Like horse, hound, hog, bear, fire, at every turn.
(*Exit.*)

BOTTOM: Why do they run away? This is a knavery of
them to make me afeard.

(*Enter Snout.*)

SNOUT: O Bottom, thou art chang'd! What do I see on
thee?
115 BOTTOM: What do you see? You see an ass-head of your
own, do you?   [*Exit Snout.*]

(*Enter Quince.*)

QUINCE: Bless thee, Bottom, bless thee! Thou art translated.°   (*Exit.*)
BOTTOM: I see their knavery. This is to make an ass of
120 me, to fright me, if they could. But I will not stir from
this place, do what they can. I will walk up and down
here, and I will sing, that they shall hear I am not
afraid.   [*Sings.*]
The woosel cock° so black of hue,
125 With orange-tawny bill,
The throstle° with his note so true,
The wren with little quill°—
TITANIA [*awaking*]: What angel wakes me from my
flow'ry bed?
BOTTOM [*sings*]: The finch, the sparrow, and the lark,
130 The plain-song° cuckoo grey,
Whose note full many a man doth mark,
And dares not answer nay°—
For, indeed, who would set his wit to so foolish a
bird? Who would give a bird the lie,° though he cry
135 "cuckoo" never so?°

TITANIA: I pray thee, gentle mortal, sing again.
Mine ear is much enamored of thy note;
So is mine eye enthralled to thy shape;
And thy fair virtue's force° perforce doth move me
On the first view to say, to swear, I love thee.   140
BOTTOM: Methinks, mistress, you should have little rea-
son for that. And yet, to say the truth, reason and
love keep little company together nowadays. The
more the pity that some honest neighbors will not
make them friends. Nay, I can gleek° upon occasion.   145
TITANIA: Thou art as wise as thou art beautiful.
BOTTOM: Not so, neither. But if I had wit enough to get
out of this wood, I have enough to serve mine own
turn.°
TITANIA: Out of this wood do not desire to go.   150
Thou shalt remain here, whether thou wilt or no.
I am a spirit of no common rate.°
The summer still° doth tend upon my state;°
And I do love thee. Therefore, go with me.
I'll give thee fairies to attend on thee,   155
And they shall fetch thee jewels from the deep,
And sing while thou on pressed flowers dost sleep.
And I will purge thy mortal grossness so
That thou shalt like an airy spirit go.
Peaseblossom, Cobweb, Moth,° and
Mustardseed!   160

(*Enter four Fairies [Peaseblossom, Cobweb, Moth, and
Mustardseed].*)

PEASEBLOSSOM: Ready.
COBWEB: And I.
MOTH: And I
MUSTARDSEED: And I.
ALL: Where shall we go?
TITANIA: Be kind and courteous to this gentleman.
Hop in his walks and gambol in his eyes;
Feed him with apricocks and dewberries,   165
With purple grapes, green figs, and mulberries;
The honey-bags steal from the humble-bees,
And for night-tapers crop their waxen thighs
And light them at the fiery glow-worm's eyes,
To have my love to bed and to arise;   170
And pluck the wings from painted butterflies
To fan the moonbeams from his sleeping eyes.
Nod to him, elves, and do him courtesies.
PEASEBLOSSOM: Hail, mortal!
COBWEB: Hail!   175
MOTH: Hail!
MUSTARDSEED: Hail!
BOTTOM: I cry your worship's mercy, heartily. I beseech
your worship's name.

---

101. [S.D.] **with the ass head:** This stage direction, taken from
the Folio, presumably refers to a standard stage property.
102. **fair:** Handsome. **were:** Would be. 105. **about a round:**
Roundabout. 108. **fire:** Will-o'-the-wisp. 117–18. **translated:** Transformed. 124. **woosel cock:** Male ousel or ouzel,
blackbird. 126. **throstle:** Song thrush. 127. **quill:** Literally,
a reed pipe; hence, the bird's piping song. 130. **plain-song:**
Singing a melody without variations. 132. **dares . . . nay:**
Cannot deny that he is a cuckold. 134. **give . . . lie:** Call the
bird a liar. 135. **never so:** Ever so much.

139. **thy . . . force:** The power of your beauty. 145. **gleek:**
Scoff, jest. 148–49. **serve . . . turn:** Answer my purpose.
152. **rate:** Rank, value. 153. **still:** Ever always. **doth . . .
state:** Waits upon me as part of my royal retinue. 160. **Moth:**
Mote, speck. (The two words *moth* and *mote* were pronounced
alike.)

180 COBWEB: Cobweb.
BOTTOM: I shall desire you of more acquaintance, good
Master Cobweb. If I cut my finger, I shall make bold
with you.° Your name, honest gentleman?
PEASEBLOSSOM: Peaseblossom.
185 BOTTOM: I pray you, commend me to Mistress Squash,°
your mother, and to Master Peascod,° your father.
Good Master Peaseblossom, I shall desire you of more
acquaintance too. Your name, I beseech you, sir?
MUSTARDSEED: Mustardseed.
190 BOTTOM: Good Master Mustardseed, I know your
patience° well. That same cowardly, giant-like ox-
beef hath devour'd many a gentleman of your house.
I promise you your kindred hath made my eyes water
ere now. I desire you of more acquaintance, good
195 Master Mustardseed.
TITANIA: Come wait upon him; lead him to my bower.
The moon methinks looks with a wat'ry eye;
And when she weeps,° weeps every little flower,
Lamenting some enforced° chastity.
200 Tie up my lover's tongue, bring him silently.

(*Exeunt.*)

{*Scene II*}°

(*Enter [Oberon,] King of Fairies.*)

OBERON: I wonder if Titania be awak'd;
Then, what it was that next came in her eye,
Which she must dote on in extremity.

([*Enter*] *Robin Goodfellow* [*Puck*].)

Here comes my messenger. How now, mad spirit?
5 What night-rule° now about this haunted° grove?
PUCK: My mistress with a monster is in love.
Near to her close° and consecrated bower,
While she was in her dull° and sleeping hour,
A crew of patches,° rude mechanicals,°
10 That work for bread upon Athenian stalls,
Were met together to rehearse a play
Intended for great Theseus' nuptial day.
The shallowest thick-skin of that barren sort,°
Who Pyramus presented,° in their sport
15 Forsook his scene° and ent'red in a brake.
When I did him at this advantage take,
An ass's nole° I fixed on his head.

Anon his Thisby must be answered,
And forth my mimic° comes. When they him spy,
As wild geese that the creeping fowler eye, 20
Or russet-pated choughs,° many in sort,°
Rising and cawing at the gun's report,
Sever° themselves and madly sweep the sky,
So, at his sight, away his fellows fly;
And, at our stamp, here o'er and o'er one falls; 25
He murder cries and help from Athens calls.
Their sense thus weak, lost with their fears thus
strong,
Made senseless things begin to do them wrong,
For briers and thorns at their apparel snatch;
Some, sleeves—some, hats; from yielders all things
catch. 30
I led them on in this distracted fear
And left sweet Pyramus translated there,
When in that moment, so it came to pass,
Titania wak'd and straightway lov'd an ass.
OBERON: This falls out better than I could devise. 35
But hast thou yet latch'd° the Athenian's eyes
With the love-juice, as I did bid thee do?
PUCK: I took him sleeping—that is finish'd too—
And the Athenian woman by his side,
That, when he wak'd, of force° she must be ey'd. 40

(*Enter Demetrius and Hermia.*)

OBERON: Stand close. This is the same Athenian.
PUCK: This is the woman, but not this the man.
[*They stand aside.*]
DEMETRIUS: O, why rebuke you him that loves you so?
Lay breath so bitter on your bitter foe.
HERMIA: Now I but chide; but I should use thee worse, 45
For thou, I fear, hast given me cause to curse.
If thou hast slain Lysander in his sleep,
Being o'er shoes in blood, plunge in the deep,
And kill me too.
The sun was not so true unto the day 50
As he to me. Would he have stolen away
From sleeping Hermia? I'll believe as soon
This whole° earth may be bor'd and that the moon
May through the center creep and so displease
Her brother's° noontide with th' Antipodes.° 55
It cannot be but thou has murd'red him;
So should a murderer look, so dead,° so grim.
DEMETRIUS: So should the murdered look, and so
should I,
Pierc'd through the heart with your stern cruelty.
Yet you, the murderer, look as bright, as clear, 60
As yonder Venus in her glimmering sphere.
HERMIA: What's this to my Lysander? Where is he?
Ah, good Demetrius, wilt thou give him me?

182–83. If . . . you: Cobwebs were used to stanch bleeding.
185. Squash: Unripe pea pod. **186. Peascod:** Ripe pea pod.
190–91. your patience: What you have endured. **198. she
weeps:** I.e., she causes dew. **199. enforced:** Forced, violated;
or, possibly, constrained (since Titania at this moment is hardly
concerned about chastity). **III, II. Location:** The wood.
5. night-rule: Diversion for the night. **haunted:** Much frequented. **7. close:** Secret, private. **8. dull:** Drowsy.
9. patches: Clowns, fools. **rude mechanicals:** Ignorant artisans. **13. barren sort:** Stupid company or crew. **14. presented:** Acted. **15. scene:** Playing area. **17. nole:** Noddle,
head.

19. mimic: Burlesque actor. **21. russet-pated choughs:** Gray-
headed jackdaws. **in sort:** In a flock. **23. Sever:** Scatter.
36. latch'd: Moistened, anointed. **40. of force:** Perforce.
53. whole: Solid. **55. Her brother's:** I.e., the sun's. **th' Antipodes:** The people on the opposite side of the earth. **57. dead:**
Deadly, or deathly pale.

DEMETRIUS: I had rather give his carcass to my hounds.
HERMIA: Out dog! Out cur! Thou driv'st me past the
65   bounds
     Of maiden's patience. Hast thou slain him, then?
     Henceforth be never numb'red among men!
     O, once tell true, tell true, even for my sake!
     Durst thou have look'd upon him being awake,
70   And hast thou kill'd him sleeping? O brave touch!°
     Could not a worm,° an adder, do so much?
     An adder did it, for with doubler tongue
     Than thine, thou serpent, never adder stung.
DEMETRIUS: You spend your passion° on a mispris'd
     mood.°
75 I am not guilty of Lysander's blood,
     Nor is he dead, for aught that I can tell.
HERMIA: I pray thee, tell me then that he is well.
DEMETRIUS: An if I could, what should I get
     therefore?
HERMIA: A privilege never to see me more.
80   And from thy hated presence part I so.
     See me no more, whether he be dead or no.
                      (*Exit.*)
DEMETRIUS: There is no following her in this fierce
     vein.
     Here therefore for a while I will remain.
     So sorrow's heaviness doth heavier° grow
85   For debt that bankrupt° sleep doth sorrow owe;
     Which now in some slight measure it will pay,
     If for his tender here I make some stay.
                (*Lie down [and sleep].*)
OBERON: What hast thou done? Thou hast mistaken
     quite
     And laid the love-juice on some true-love's sight.
90   Of thy misprision° must perforce ensue
     Some true love turn'd and not a false turn'd true.
PUCK: Then fate o'er-rules, that, one man holding
     troth,°
     A million fail, confounding oath on oath.°
OBERON: About the wood go swifter than the wind,
95   And Helena of Athens look thou find.
     All fancy-sick° she is and pale of cheer°
     With sighs of love, that cost the fresh blood° dear.
     By some illusion see thou bring her here.
     I'll charm his eyes against she do appear.°

70. brave touch: Noble exploit (said ironically). **71. worm:**
Serpent. **74. passion:** Violent feelings. **mispris'd mood:**
Anger based on misconception. **84. heavier:** (1) Harder to
bear, (2) drowsier. **85. bankrupt:** Demetrius is saying that his
sleepiness adds to the weariness caused by sorrow. **86–87.**
Which . . . stay: To a small extent I will be able to "pay back"
and hence find some relief from sorrow, if I pause here a while
(*make some stay*) while sleep "tenders" or offers itself by
way of paying the debt owed to sorrow. **90. misprision:**
Mistake. **92. troth:** Faith. **93. confounding . . . oath:**
Invalidating one oath with another. **96. fancy-sick:** Lovesick.
cheer: Face. **97. sighs . . . blood:** An allusion to the physio-
logical theory that each sigh costs the heart a drop of blood.
99. against . . . appear: In anticipation of her coming.

PUCK: I go, I go; look how I go   100
     Swifter than arrow from the Tartar's bow.°
                     [*Exit.*]
OBERON: Flower of this purple dye,
     Hit with Cupid's archery.
     Sink in angle of his eye.
        [*Applies love-juice to Demetrius' eyes.*]
     When his love he doth espy,   105
     Let her shine as gloriously
     As the Venus of the sky.
     When thou wak'st, if she be by,
     Beg of her for remedy.

(*Enter Puck.*)

PUCK: Captain of our fairy band,   110
     Helena is here at hand,
     And the youth, mistook by me,
     Pleading for a lover's fee.°
     Shall we their fond pageant° see?
     Lord, what fools these mortals be!   115
OBERON: Stand aside. The noise they make
     Will cause Demetrius to awake.
PUCK: Then will two at once woo one;
     That must needs be sport alone;°
     And those things do best please me   120
     That befall prepost'rously.°
               [*They stand aside.*]

(*Enter Lysander and Helena.*)

LYSANDER: Why should you think that I should woo in
     scorn?
     Scorn and derision never come in tears.
     Look when° I vow, I weep; and vows so born,
     In their nativity all truth appears.°   125
     How can these things in me seem scorn to you,
     Bearing the badge° of faith, to prove them true?
HELENA: You do advance° your cunning more and
     more.
     When truth kills truth,° O devilish-holy fray!
     These vows are Hermia's. Will you give her o'er?   130
     Weigh oath with oath, and you will nothing weigh.
     Your vows to her and me, put in two scales
     Will even weigh, and both as light as tales.°
LYSANDER: I had no judgment when to her I swore.
HELENA: Nor none, in my mind, now you give her o'er.   135
LYSANDER: Demetrius loves her, and he loves not you.
DEMETRIUS [*awaking*]: O Helen, goddess, nymph,
     perfect, divine!
     To what, my love, shall I compare thine eyne?

101. Tartar's bow: Tartars were famed for their skill with the
bow. **113. fee:** Privilege, reward. **114. fond pageant:** Foolish exhibition. **119. alone:** Unequaled. **121. prepost'rously:**
Out of the natural order. **124. Look when:** Whenever.
124–25. vows . . . appears: Vows made by one who is weeping give evidence thereby of their sincerity. **127. badge:** Identifying device such as that worn on servants' livery. **128 advance:**
Carry forward, display. **129. truth kills truth:** One of
Lysander's vows must invalidate the other. **133. tales:** Lies.

Crystal is muddy. O, how ripe in show°
140   Thy lips, those kissing cherries, tempting grow!
That pure congealed white, high Taurus'° snow,
Fann'd with the eastern wind, turns to a crow°
When thou hold'st up thy hand. O, let me kiss
This princess of pure white, this seal° of bliss!
145 HELENA: O spite! O hell! I see you all are bent
To set against me for your merriment.
If you were civil and knew courtesy,
You would not do me thus much injury.
Can you not hate me, as I know you do,
150   But you must join in souls to mock me too?
If you were men, as men you are in show,
You would not use a gentle lady so—
To vow, and swear, and superpraise° my parts,°
When I am sure you hate me with your hearts.
155   You both are rivals, and love Hermia;
And now both rivals, to mock Helena.
A trim° exploit, a manly enterprise,
To conjure tears up in a poor maid's eyes
With your derision! None of noble sort
160   Would so offend a virgin and extort°
A poor soul's patience, all to make you sport.
LYSANDER: You are unkind, Demetrius. Be not so;
For you love Hermia; this you know I know.
And here, with all good will, with all my heart,
165   In Hermia's love I yield you up my part;
And yours of Helena to me bequeath,
Whom I do love and will do till my death.
HELENA: Never did mockers waste more idle breath.
DEMETRIUS: Lysander, keep thy Hermia; I will none.°
170   If e'er I lov'd her, all that love is gone.
My heart to her but as guest-wise sojourn'd,
And now to Helen is it home return'd.
There to remain.
LYSANDER: Helen, it is not so.
DEMETRIUS: Disparage not the faith thou dost not know,
175   Lest, to thy peril, thou aby° it dear.
Look where thy love comes; yonder is thy dear.

(*Enter Hermia.*)

HERMIA: Dark night, that from the eye his° function
takes,
The ear more quick of apprehension makes;
Wherein it doth impair the seeing sense,
180   It pays the hearing double recompense.
Thou art not by mine eye, Lysander, found;
Mine ear, I thank it, brought me to thy sound.
But why unkindly didst thou leave me so?
LYSANDER: Why should he stay, whom love doth press
to go?

HERMIA: What love could press Lysander from my
side?   185
LYSANDER: Lysander's love, that would not let him
bide,
Fair Helena, who more engilds the night
Than all yon fiery oes° and eyes of light.
Why seek'st thou me? Could not this make thee
know,
The hate I bear thee made me leave thee so?   190
HERMIA: You speak not as you think. It cannot be.
HELENA: Lo, she is one of this confederacy!
Now I perceive they have conjoin'd all three
To fashion this false sport, in spite of me.°
Injurious Hermia, most ungrateful maid!   195
Have you conspir'd, have you with these contriv'd°
To bait° me with this foul derision?
Is all the counsel° that we two have shar'd,
The sisters' vows, the hours that we have spent,
When we have chid the hasty-footed time   200
For parting us—O, is all forgot?
All school-days friendship, childhood innocence?
We, Hermia, like two artificial° gods,
Have with our needles created both one flower,
Both on one sampler, sitting on one cushion,   205
Both warbling of one song, both in one key,
As if our hands, our sides, voices, and minds
Had been incorporate. So we grew together,
Like to a double cherry, seeming parted,
But yet an union in partition;   210
Two lovely° berries molded on one stem;
So, with two seeming bodies, but one heart;
Two of the first, like coats in heraldry,
Due but to one and crowned with one crest.°
And will you rent° our ancient love asunder,   215
To join with men in scorning your poor friend?
It is not friendly, 'tis not maidenly.
Our sex, as well as I, may chide you for it,
Though I alone do feel the injury.
HERMIA: I am amazed at your passionate words.   220
I scorn you not. It seems that you scorn me.
HELENA: Have you not set Lysander, as in scorn,
To follow me and praise my eyes and face?
And made your other love, Demetrius,
Who even but now did spurn me with his foot,   225
To call me goddess, nymph, divine and rare,
Precious, celestial? Wherefore speaks he this
To her he hates? And wherefore doth Lysander
Deny your love, so rich within his soul,
And tender° me, forsooth, affection,   230
But by your setting on, by your consent?

---

139. show: Appearance.   **141. Taurus:** A lofty mountain range in Asia Minor.   **142. turns to a crow:** Seems black by contrast.   **144. seal:** Pledge.   **153. superpraise:** Overpraise. **parts:** Qualities.   **157. trim:** Pretty, fine (said ironically). **160. extort:** Twist, torture.   **169. will none:** Wish none of her. **175. aby:** Pay for.   **177. his:** Its.

188. oes: Circles, orbs, stars.   **194. in spite of me:** To vex me. **196. contriv'd:** Plotted.   **197. bait:** Torment, as one sets on dogs to bait a bear.   **198. counsel:** Confidential talk. **203. artificial:** Skilled in art or creation.   **211. lovely:** Loving. **213–14. Two . . . crest:** We have two separate bodies, just as a coat of arms in heraldry can be represented twice on a shield but surmounted by a single crest.   **215. rent:** Rend.   **230. tender:** Offer.

What though I be not so in grace° as you,
So hung upon with love, so fortunate,
But miserable most, to love unlov'd?
235   This you should pity rather than despise.
HERMIA: I understand not what you mean by this.
HELENA: Ay, do! Persever, counterfeit sad° looks,
   Make mouths° upon° me when I turn my back,
   Wink each at other, hold the sweet jest up.
240   This sport, well carried,° shall be chronicled.
   If you have any pity, grace, or manners,
   You would not make me such an argument.°
   But fare ye well. 'Tis partly my own fault,
   Which death, or absence, soon shall remedy.
245 LYSANDER: Stay, gentle Helena; hear my excuse,
   My love, my life, my soul, fair Helena!
HELENA: O excellent!
HERMIA: Sweet, do not scorn her so.
DEMETRIUS: If she cannot entreat,° I can compel.
LYSANDER: Thou canst compel no more than she
   entreat.
   Thy threats have no more strength than her weak
250   prayers.
   Helen, I love thee, by my life, I do!
   I swear by that which I will lose for thee,
   To prove him false that says I love thee not.
DEMETRIUS: I say I love thee more than he can do.
255 LYSANDER: If thou say so, withdraw, and prove it too.
DEMETRIUS: Quick, come!
HERMIA   Lysander, whereto tends all this?
LYSANDER: Away, you Ethiope!°
        [*He tries to break away from Hermia.*]
DEMETRIUS: No, no; he'll
   Seem to break loose; take on as you would follow,
   But yet come not. You are a tame man, go!
LYSANDER: Hang off,° thou cat, thou burr! Vile thing,
260   let loose,
   Or I will shake thee from me like a serpent!
HERMIA: Why are you grown so rude? What change is
   this,
   Sweet love?
LYSANDER: Thy love? Out, tawny Tartar, out!
   Out, loathed med'cine!° O hated potion, hence!
HERMIA: Do you not jest?
265 HELENA: Yes, sooth,° and so do you.
LYSANDER: Demetrius, I will keep my word with thee.
DEMETRIUS: I would I had your bond, for I perceive
   A weak bond° holds you. I'll not trust your word.
LYSANDER: What, should I hurt her, strike her, kill her
   dead?
270   Although I hate her, I'll not harm her so.

HERMIA: What, can you do me greater harm than hate?
   Hate me? Wherefore? O me, what news,° my love?
   Am not I Hermia? Are not you Lysander?
   I am as fair now as I was erewhile.°
   Since night you lov'd me; yet since night you left me. 275
   Why, then you left me—O, the gods forbid!—
   In earnest, shall I say?
LYSANDER: Ay, by my life!
   And never did desire to see thee more.
   Therefore be out of hope, of question, of doubt;
   Be certain, nothing truer. 'Tis no jest   280
   That I do hate thee and love Helena.
HERMIA: O me! You juggler! You cankerblossom!°
   You thief of love! What, have you come by night
   And stol'n my love's heart from him?
HELENA: Fine, i' faith!
   Have you no modesty, no maiden shame,   285
   No touch of bashfulness? What, will you tear
   Impatient answers from my gentle tongue?
   Fie, fie! You counterfeit, you puppet,° you!
HERMIA: Puppet? Why so? Ay, that way goes the game.
   Now I perceive that she hath made compare   290
   Between our statures; she hath urg'd her height,
   And with her personage, her tall personage,
   Her height, forsooth, she hath prevail'd with him.
   And are you grown so high in his esteem,
   Because I am so dwarfish and so low?   295
   How low am I, thou painted maypole? Speak!
   How low am I? I am not yet so low
   But that my nails can reach unto thine eyes.
        [*She flails at Helena but is restrained.*]
HELENA: I pray you, though you mock me, gentlemen,
   Let her not hurt me. I was never curst;°   300
   I have no gift at all in shrewishness;
   I am a right° maid for my cowardice.
   Let her not strike me. You perhaps may think,
   Because she is something° lower than myself,
   That I can match her.
HERMIA: Lower! Hark, again!   305
HELENA: Good Hermia, do not be so bitter with me.
   I evermore did love you, Hermia,
   Did ever keep your counsels, never wrong'd you;
   Save that, in love unto Demetrius,
   I told him of your stealth° unto this wood.   310
   He followed you; for love I followed him.
   But he hath chid me hence and threat'ned me
   To strike me, spurn me, nay, to kill me too.
   And now, so° you will let me quiet go,
   To Athens will I bear my folly back   315
   And follow you no further. Let me go.
   You see how simple and how fond° I am.
HERMIA: Why, get you gone. Who is 't that hinders you?

---

232. **grace:** Favor.   237. **sad:** Grave, serious.   238. **mouths:** Maws, faces, grimaces.   **upon:** At.   240. **carried:** Managed. 242. **argument:** Subject for a jest.   248. **entreat:** Succeed by entreaty.   257. **Ethiope:** Referring to Hermia's relatively dark hair and complexion; see also *tawny Tartar* six lines later. 260. **Hang off:** Let go.   264. **med'cine:** Poison.   265. **sooth:** Truly.   268. **weak bond:** Hermia's arm (with a pun on *bond*, oath, in the previous line).

272. **what news:** What is the matter.   274. **erewhile:** Just now. 282. **cankerblossom:** Worm that destroys the flower bud (?). 288. **puppet:** (1) Counterfeit, (2) dwarfish woman (in reference to Hermia's smaller stature).   300. **curst:** Shrewish. 302. **right:** True.   304. **something:** Somewhat.   310. **stealth:** Stealing away.   314. **so:** If only.   317. **fond:** Foolish.

HELENA: A foolish heart, that I leave here behind.
HERMIA: What, with Lysander?
320 HELENA: With Demetrius.
LYSANDER: Be not afraid; she shall not harm thee,
    Helena.
DEMETRIUS: No, sir, she shall not, though you take
    her part.
HELENA: O, when she is angry, she is keen and
    shrewd!°
    She was a vixen when she went to school;
325   And though she be but little, she is fierce.
HERMIA: "Little" again! Nothing but "low" and
    "little"!
    Why will you suffer her to flout me thus?
    Let me come to her.
LYSANDER: Get you gone, you dwarf!
    You minimus,° of hind'ring knot-grass° made!

You bead, you acorn!
DEMETRIUS: You are too officious   330
    In her behalf that scorns your services.
    Let her alone. Speak not of Helena;
    Take not her part. For, if thou dost intend°
    Never so little show of love to her,
    Thou shalt aby° it.
LYSANDER: Now she holds me not;   335
    Now follow, if thou dar'st, to try whose right,
    Of thine or mine, is most in Helena.   [*Exit.*]
DEMETRIUS: Follow? Nay, I'll go with thee, cheek by
    jowl.°

            [*Exit, following Lysander.*]

HERMIA: You, mistress, all this coil° is 'long of° you.
    Nay, go not back.°

---

323. shrewd: Shrewish.   **329. minimus:** Diminutive creature.
knot-grass: A weed, an infusion of which was thought to stunt
the growth.

333. intend: Give sign of.   **335. aby:** Pay for.   **338. cheek by
jowl:** Side by side.   **339. coil:** Turmoil, dissension.   **'long of:**
On account of.   **340. go not back:** Don't retreat. (Hermia is
again proposing a fight.)

NEAR LEFT: Elizabeth McGovern as Helena in the 1987 New York Shakespeare festival production of *A Midsummer Night's Dream,* directed by A. J. Antoon. FAR LEFT: F. Murray Abraham (left) as Bottom, playing Pyramus.

340 HELENA: I will not trust you, I,
    Nor longer stay in your curst company.
    Your hands than mine are quicker for a fray;
    My legs are longer, though, to run away.   [*Exit.*]
   HERMIA: I am amaz'd, and know not what to say.
                            (*Exit.*)
345 OBERON: This is thy negligence. Still thou mistak'st,
    Or else committ'st thy knaveries willfully.
   PUCK: Believe me, king of shadows, I mistook.
    Did not you tell me I should know the man
    By the Athenian garments he had on?
350   And so far blameless proves my enterprise
    That I have 'nointed an Athenian's eyes;
    And so far am I glad it so did sort°
    As this their jangling I esteem a sport.
   OBERON: Thou see'st these lovers seek a place to fight.
355   Hie therefore, Robin, overcast the night;
    The starry welkin° cover thou anon
    With drooping fog as black as Acheron,°
    And lead these testy rivals so astray
    As° one come not within another's way.
360   Like to Lysander sometime frame thy tongue,
    Then stir Demetrius up with bitter wrong;°

   And sometime rail thou like Demetrius.
   And from each other look thou lead them thus,
   Till o'er their brows death-counterfeiting sleep
   With leaden legs and batty° wings doth creep.   365
   Then crush this herb° into Lysander's eye,
                         [*Gives herb.*]
   Whose liquor hath this virtuous° property,
   To take from thence all error with his° might
   And make his eyeballs roll with wonted° sight.
   When they next wake, all this derision°   370
   Shall seem a dream and fruitless vision,
   And back to Athens shall the lovers wend
   With league whose date° till death shall never end.
   Whiles I in this affair do thee employ,
   I'll to my queen and beg her Indian boy;   375
   And then I will her charmed eye release
   From monster's view, and all things shall be peace.
PUCK: My fairy lord, this must be done with haste,
   For night's swift dragons° cut the clouds full fast,
   And yonder shines Aurora's harbinger,°   380

352. **sort:** Turn out.   356. **welkin:** Sky.   357. **Acheron:** River of Hades (here representing Hades itself).   359. **As:** That.   361. **wrong:** Insults.

365. **batty:** Batlike.   366. **this herb:** The antidote (mentioned in II, 1, 184) to love-in-idleness.   367. **virtuous:** Efficacious. 368. **his:** Its.   369. **wonted:** Accustomed.   370. **derision:** Laughable business.   373. **date:** Term of existence.   379. **dragons:** Supposed to be yoked to the car of the goddess of night. 380. **Aurora's harbinger:** The morning star, precursor of dawn.

At whose approach, ghosts, wand'ring here and
    there,
Troop home to churchyards. Damned spirits all,
That in crossways and floods have burial,°
Already to their wormy beds are gone.
385 For fear lest day should look their shames upon,
They willfully themselves exile from light
And must for aye° consort with black-brow'd night.
OBERON: But we are spirits of another sort.
    I with the Morning's love° have oft made sport,
390 And, like a forester,° the groves may tread
Even till the eastern gate, all fiery-red,
Opening on Neptune with fair blessed beams,
Turns into yellow gold his salt green streams.
But, notwithstanding, haste; make no delay.
395 We may effect this business yet ere day.   [Exit.]
PUCK: Up and down, up and down,
    I will lead them up and down.
I am fear'd in field and town.
Goblin, lead them up and down.
400 Here comes one.

(Enter Lysander.)

LYSANDER: Where art thou, proud Demetrius? Speak
    thou now.
PUCK [mimicking Demetrius]: Here, villain, drawn°
    and ready. Where art thou?
LYSANDER: I will be with thee straight.°
PUCK: Follow me, then,
    To plainer° ground.
        [Lysander wanders about, following the voice.]°

(Enter Demetrius.)

DEMETRIUS: Lysander! Speak again!
405 Thou runaway, thou coward, art thou fled?
Speak! In some bush? Where dost thou hide thy
    head?
PUCK: [mimicking Lysander]: Thou coward, art thou
    bragging to the stars,
Telling the bushes that thou look'st for wars,
And wilt not come? Come, recreant;° come, thou
    child,
410 I'll whip thee with a rod. He is defil'd
That draws a sword on thee.
DEMETRIUS: Yea, art thou there?
PUCK: Follow my voice. We'll try° no manhood here.
                                (Exeunt.)

383. crossways . . . burial: Those who had committed suicide
were buried at crossways, with a stake driven through them;
those drowned, i.e., buried in floods or great waters, were condemned to wander disconsolate for want of burial rites.
387. for aye: Forever.   389. Morning's love: Cephalus, a beautiful youth beloved by Aurora; or perhaps the goddess of
the dawn herself.   390. forester: Keeper of a royal forest.
402. drawn: With drawn sword.   403. straight: Immediately.
404. plainer: Smoother.   404. [S.D.] Lysander wanders about:
It is not clearly necessary that Lysander exit at this point;
neither exit nor reentrance is indicated in the early texts.
409. recreant: Cowardly wretch.   412. try: Test.

[Lysander returns.]

LYSANDER: He goes before me and still dares me on.
    When I come where he calls, then he is gone.
The villain is much lighter-heel'd than I.   415
I followed fast, but faster he did fly,
That fallen am I in dark uneven way,
And here will rest me. [Lies down.] Come, thou
    gentle day!
For if but once thou show me thy gray light,
I'll find Demetrius and revenge this spite.   [Sleeps.]   420

([Enter] Robin [Puck] and Demetrius.)

PUCK: Ho, ho, ho! Coward, why com'st thou not?
DEMETRIUS: Abide me, if thou dar'st; for well I wot°
    Thou runn'st before me, shifting every place,
And dar'st not stand nor look me in the face.
Where art thou now?
PUCK: Come hither. I am here.   425
DEMETRIUS: Nay, then, thou mock'st me. Thou shalt
    buy° this dear,°
If ever I thy face by daylight see.
Now, go thy way. Faintness constraineth me
To measure out my length on this cold bed.
By day's approach look to be visited.   430
                      [Lies down and sleeps.]

(Enter Helena.)

HELENA: O weary night, O long and tedious night,
    Abate° thy hours! Shine, comforts, from the east,
That I may back to Athens by daylight,
From these that my poor company detest;
And sleep, that sometimes shuts up sorrow's eye,   435
Steal me awhile from mine own company.
                [Lies down and] sleep[s].
PUCK: Yet but three? Come one more;
    Two of both kinds makes up four.
Here she comes, curst and sad.
Cupid is a knavish lad,   440
Thus to make poor females mad.

[Enter Hermia.]

HERMIA: Never so weary, never so in woe,
    Bedabbled with the dew and torn with briers,
I can no further crawl, no further go;
My legs can keep no pace with my desires.
Here will I rest me till the break of day.   445
Heavens shield Lysander, if they mean a fray!
                [Lies down and sleeps.]
PUCK: On the ground
    Sleep sound.
    I'll apply   450
    To your eye,
Gentle lover, remedy.
        [Squeezing the juice on Lysander's eyes.]
    When thou wak'st,
    Thou tak'st

422. wot: Know.   426. buy: Pay for. dear: Dearly.
432. Abate: Lessen, shorten.

455   True delight
     In the sight
    Of thy former lady's eye;
    And the country proverb known,
    That every man should take his own,
460   In your waking shall be shown:
     Jack shall have Jill;
     Nought shall go ill;
    The man shall have his mare again, and all shall
     be well.   [*Exit. Manent the four lovers.*]

{*ACT IV • Scene 1*}°

(*Enter* [*Titania,*] *Queen of Fairies, and* [*Bottom the*]
Clown, and Fairies; and [*Oberon,*] *the King, behind
them.*)

TITANIA: Come, sit thee down upon this flow'ry bed,
  While I thy amiable° cheeks do coy,°
  And stick musk-roses in thy sleek smooth head,
  And kiss thy fair large ears, my gentle joy.
                  [*They recline.*]
5 BOTTOM: Where's Peaseblossom?
PEASEBLOSSOM: Ready.
BOTTOM: Scratch my head, Peaseblossom. Where's
  Mounsieur Cobweb?
COBWEB: Ready.
10 BOTTOM: Mounsieur Cobweb, good mounsieur, get you
  your weapons in your hand, and kill me a red-hipp'd
  humble-bee on the top of a thistle; and, good mounsieur, bring me the honey-bag. Do not fret yourself
  too much in the action, mounsieur; and, good moun-
15 sieur, have a care the honey-bag break not; I would
  be loath to have you overflown with a honey-bag,
  signior. Where's Mounsieur Mustardseed?
MUSTARDSEED: Ready.
BOTTOM: Give me your neaf,° Mounsieur Mustardseed.
20 Pray you, leave your curtsy,° good mounsieur.
MUSTARDSEED: What's your will?
BOTTOM: Nothing, good mounsieur, but to help Cav-
  alery° Cobweb° to scratch. I must to the barber's,
  mounsieur; for methinks I am marvailes hairy about
25 the face; and I am such a tender ass, if my hair do but
  tickle me, I must scratch.
TITANIA: What, wilt thou hear some music, my sweet
  love?
BOTTOM: I have a reasonable good ear in music. Let's
30 have the tongs and the bones.°

[*Music: tongs, rural music.*]°
TITANIA: Or say, sweet love, what thou desirest to eat.
BOTTOM: Truly, a peck of provender. I could munch
  your good dry oats. Methinks I have a great desire to
  a bottle° of hay. Good hay, sweet hay, hath no fellow.°
TITANIA: I have a venturous fairy that shall seek   35
  The squirrel's hoard, and fetch thee new nuts.
BOTTOM: I had rather have a handful or two of dried
  peas. But, I pray you, let none of your people stir me.
  I have an exposition° of sleep come upon me.
TITANIA: Sleep thou, and I will wind thee in my arms.   40
  Fairies, be gone, and be all ways° away.
               [*Exeunt fairies.*]
  So doth the woodbine the sweet honeysuckle
  Gently entwist; the female ivy so
  Enrings the barky fingers of the elm.
  Oh, how I love thee! How I dote on thee!   45
               [*They sleep.*]

(*Enter Robin Goodfellow* [*Puck*].)

OBERON [*advancing*]: Welcome, good Robin. See'st
  thou this sweet sight?
  Her dotage now I do begin to pity.
  For, meeting her of late behind the wood,
  Seeking sweet favors° for this hateful fool,
  I did upbraid her and fall out with her.   50
  For she his hairy temples then had rounded
  With coronet of fresh and fragrant flowers;
  And that same dew, which sometime° on the buds
  Was wont to swell like round and orient pearls,°
  Stood now within the pretty flouriets'° eyes   55
  Like tears that did their own disgrace bewail.
  When I had at my pleasure taunted her,
  And she in mild terms begg'd my patience,
  I then did ask of her her changeling child;
  Which straight she gave me, and her fairy sent   60
  To bear him to my bower in fairy land.
  And, now I have the boy, I will undo
  This hateful imperfection of her eyes.
  And, gentle Puck, take this transformed scalp
  From off the head of this Athenian swain,   65
  That, he awaking when the other° do,
  May all to Athens back again repair,
  And think no more of this night's accidents
  But as the fierce vexation of a dream.
  But first I will release the Fairy Queen.   70
  [*Squeezes juice in her eyes.*]
  Be as thou wast wont to be;
  See as thou wast wont to see.
  Dian's bud° o'er Cupid's flower

IV, I. **Location:** Scene continues. The four lovers are still asleep
onstage. **2. amiable:** Lovely. **coy:** Caress. **19. neaf:** Fist.
20. leave your curtsy: Put on your hat. **22–23. Cavalery:** Cavalier. Form of address for a gentleman. **23. Cobweb:** Seemingly an error, since Cobweb has been sent to bring honey,
whereas Peaseblossom has been asked to scratch. **30. tongs . . .
bones:** Instruments for rustic music. (The tongs were played
like a triangle, whereas the bones were held between the fingers
and used as clappers.) [S.D.] *Music . . . music:* This stage
direction is added from the Folio.

34. bottle: Bundle. **fellow:** Equal. **39. exposition:** Bottom's word for *disposition.* **41. all ways:** In all directions.
49. favors: I.e., gifts of flowers. **53. sometime:** Formerly.
54. orient pearls: The most beautiful of all pearls, those
coming from the Orient. **55. flouriets':** Flowerets'. **66.
other:** Others. **73. Dian's bud:** Perhaps the flower of the *agnus
castus* or chaste-tree, supposed to preserve chastity; or perhaps
referring simply to Oberon's herb by which he can undo the
effects of "Cupid's flower," the love-in-idleness of II, 1, 165–68.

Hath such force and blessed power.

75 Now, my Titania, wake you, my sweet queen.
TITANIA [*waking*]: My Oberon! What visions have I
        seen!
    Methought I was enamor'd of an ass.
OBERON: There lies your love.
TITANIA: How came these things to pass?
    O, how mine eyes do loathe his visage now!
80 OBERON: Silence awhile. Robin, take off this head.
    Titania, music call, and strike more dead
    Than common sleep of all these five° the sense.
TITANIA: Music, ho! Music, such as charmeth sleep!
                                        [*Music.*]
PUCK [*removing the ass's head*]: Now, when thou
    wak'st, with thine own fool's eyes peep.
OBERON: Sound, music! Come, my queen, take hands
85 with me,
    And rock the ground whereon these sleepers be.
                                        [*Dance.*]
    Now thou and I are new in amity,
    And will tomorrow midnight solemnly°
    Dance in Duke Theseus' house triumphantly
90 And bless it to all fair prosperity.
    There shall the pairs of faithful lovers be
    Wedded, with Theseus, all in jollity.
PUCK: Fairy King, attend, and mark:
    I do hear the morning lark.
95 OBERON: Then, my queen, in silence sad,°
    Trip we after night's shade.
    We the globe can compass soon,
    Swifter than the wand'ring moon.
TITANIA: Come, my lord, and in our flight
100 Tell me how it came this night
    That I sleeping here was found
    With these mortals on the ground.   (*Exeunt.*)
                                        (*Wind horn* [*within*].)

(*Enter Theseus and all his train;* [*Hippolyta, Egeus*].)

THESEUS: Go, one of you, find out the forester,
    For now our observation° is perform'd;
105 And since we have the vaward° of the day,
    My love shall hear the music of my hounds.
    Uncouple in the western valley; let them go.
    Dispatch, I say, and find the forester.
                                [*Exit an Attendant.*]
    We will, fair queen, up to the mountain's top
110 And mark the musical confusion
    Of hounds and echo in conjunction.
HIPPOLYTA: I was with Hercules and Cadmus° once,
    When in a wood of Crete they bay'd° the bear
    With hounds of Sparta.° Never did I hear

Such gallant chiding; for, besides the groves,   115
The skies, the fountains, every region near
Seem'd all one mutual cry. I never heard
So musical a discord, such sweet thunder.
THESEUS: My hounds are bred out of the Spartan kind,
    So flew'd,° so sanded;° and their heads are hung   120
    With ears that sweep away the morning dew;
    Crook-knee'd, and dewlapp'd° like Thessalian bulls;
    Slow in pursuit, but match'd in mouth like bells,
    Each under each.° A cry° more tuneable°
    Was never holla'd to, nor cheer'd with horn,   125
    In Crete, in Sparta, nor in Thessaly.
    Judge when you hear. [*Sees the sleepers.*] But, soft!
        What nymphs are these?
EGEUS: My lord, this' my daughter here asleep;
    And this, Lysander; this Demetrius is;
    This Helena, old Nedar's Helena.   130
    I wonder of their being here together.
THESEUS: No doubt they rose up early to observe
    The rite of May, and, hearing our intent,
    Came here in grace of our solemnity.°
    But speak, Egeus. Is not this the day   135
    That Hermia should give answer of her choice?
EGEUS: It is, my lord.
THESEUS: Go, bid the huntsmen wake them with their
    horns.
                                [*Exit an Attendant.*]

(*Shout within. Wind horns. They all start up.*)

    Good morrow, friends. Saint Valentine° is past.
    Begin these wood-birds but to couple now?   140
LYSANDER: Pardon, my lord.   [*They kneel.*]
THESEUS: I pray you all, stand up.
    I know you two are rival enemies;
    How comes this gentle concord in the world,
    That hatred is so far from jealousy
    To sleep by hate and fear no enmity?   145
LYSANDER: My lord, I shall reply amazedly,
    Half sleep, half waking; but as yet, I swear,
    I cannot truly say how I came here.
    But, as I think—for truly would I speak,
    And now I do bethink me, so it is—   150
    I came with Hermia hither. Our intent
    Was to be gone from Athens, where° we might,
    Without° the peril of the Athenian law—
EGEUS: Enough, enough, my lord; you have enough.
    I beg the law, the law, upon his head.   155
    They would have stol'n away; they would, Demetrius,

---

82. **these five:** I.e., the four lovers and Bottom. 88. **solemnly:** Ceremoniously. 95. **sad:** Sober. 104. **observation:** Observance to a morn of May (I, i, 167). 105. **vaward:** Vanguard, i.e., earliest part. 112. **Cadmus:** Mythical founder of Thebes. (This story about him is unknown.) 113. **bay'd:** Brought to bay. 114. **hounds of Sparta:** Breed famous in antiquity for their hunting skill.

120. **So flew'd:** Similarly having large hanging chaps or fleshy covering of the jaw. **sanded:** Of sandy color. 122. **dewlapp'd:** Having pendulous folds of skin under the neck. 123–24. **match'd . . . under each:** Harmoniously matched in their various cries like a set of bells, from treble down to bass. 124. **cry:** Pack of hounds. **tuneable:** Well tuned, melodious. 134. **solemnity:** Observance of these same rites of May. 139. **Saint Valentine:** Birds were supposed to choose their mates on St. Valentine's Day. 152. **where:** Wherever; or to where. 153. **Without:** Outside of, beyond.

Thereby to have defeated you and me,
You of your wife and me of my consent,
Of my consent that she should be your wife.

DEMETRIUS: My lord, fair Helen told me of their
160   stealth,
Of this their purpose hither to this wood,
And I in fury hither followed them,
Fair Helena in fancy following me.
But, my good lord, I wot not by what power—
165 But by some power it is—my love to Hermia,
Melted as the snow, seems to me now
As the remembrance of an idle gaud.°
Which in my childhood I did dote upon;
And all the faith, the virtue of my heart,
170 The object and the pleasure of mine eye,
Is only Helena. To her, my lord,
Was I betroth'd ere I saw Hermia,
But like a sickness did I loathe this food;
But, as in health, come to my natural taste,
175 Now I do wish it, love it, long for it,
And will for evermore be true to it.

THESEUS: Fair lovers, you are fortunately met.
Of this discourse we more will hear anon.
Egeus, I will overbear your will;
180 For in the temple, by and by, with us
These couples shall eternally be knit.
And, for° the morning now is something° worn,
Our purpos'd hunting shall be set aside.
Away with us to Athens. Three and three,
185 We'll hold a feast in great solemnity.
Come, Hippolyta.

        [*Exeunt Theseus, Hippolyta, Egeus, and train.*]

DEMETRIUS: These things seem small and
    undistinguishable,
Like far-off mountains turned into clouds.

HERMIA: Methinks I see these things with parted° eye,
When every thing seems double.

190 HELENA: So methinks;
And I have found Demetrius like a jewel,
Mine own, and not mine own.°

DEMETRIUS: Are you sure
That we are awake? It seems to me
That yet we sleep, we dream. Do not you think
195 The Duke was here, and bid us follow him?

HERMIA: Yea, and my father.

HELENA: And Hippolyta.

LYSANDER: And he did bid us follow to the temple.

DEMETRIUS: Why, then, we are awake. Let's follow
    him,
And by the way let us recount our dreams.

                      [*Exeunt.*]

BOTTOM [*awaking*]: When my cue comes, call me, and I 200
will answer. My next is, "Most fair Pyramus."
Heigh-ho! Peter Quince! Flute, the bellows-mender!
Snout, the tinker! Starveling! God's my life, stol'n
hence, and left me asleep! I have had a most rare
vision. I have had a dream, past the wit of man to say 205
what dream it was. Man is but an ass, if he go about°
to expound this dream. Methought I was—there is
no man can tell what. Methought I was—and me
thought I had—but man is but a patch'd° fool, if he
will offer° to say what me-thought I had. The eye of 210
man hath not heard, the ear of man hath not seen,
man's hand is not able to taste, his tongue to conceive, nor his heart to report, what my dream was. I
will get Peter Quince to write a ballad of this dream.
It shall be call'd "Bottom's Dream," because it hath 215
no bottom; and I will sing it in the latter end of a
play, before the Duke. Peradventure, to make it the
more gracious, I shall sing it at her° death.   [*Exit.*]

{*Scene II*}°

(*Enter Quince, Flute, [Snout, and Starveling].*)

QUINCE: Have you sent to Bottom's house? Is he come
home yet?

STARVELING: He cannot be heard of. Out of doubt he is
transported.°

FLUTE: If he come not, then the play is marr'd. It goes 5
not forward, doth it?

QUINCE: It is not possible. You have not a man in all
Athens able to discharge° Pyramus but he.

FLUTE: No, he hath simply the best wit of any handicraft
man in Athens. 10

QUINCE: Yea, and the best person too; and he is a very
paramour for a sweet voice.

FLUTE: You must say "paragon." A paramour is, God
bless us, a thing of naught.

(*Enter Snug the Joiner.*)

SNUG: Masters, the Duke is coming from the temple, 15
and there is two or three lords and ladies more married. If our sport had gone forward, we had all been
made men.

FLUTE: O sweet bully Bottom! Thus hath he lost sixpence a day° during his life; he could not have scap'd 20
sixpence a day. An the Duke had not given him sixpence a day for playing Pyramus, I'll be hang'd. He
would have deserv'd it. Sixpence a day in Pyramus,
or nothing.

(*Enter Bottom.*)

---

167. **idle gaud:** Worthless trinket.   182. **for:** Since. **something:** Somewhat.   189. **parted:** Improperly focused.   **191–92. like . . . not mine own:** Like a jewel that one finds by chance and therefore possesses but cannot certainly consider one's own property.

206. **go about:** Attempt.   209. **patch'd:** Wearing motley, i.e., a dress of various colors.   210. **offer:** Venture.   218. **her:** Thisby's (?).   **IV, II. Location:** Athens, Quince's house (?). 4. **transported:** Carried off by fairies; or, possibly, transformed. 8. **discharge:** Perform.   **19–20. sixpence a day:** As a royal pension.

Stage model of the set for Max Reinhardt's 1913 production of *A Midsummer Night's Dream* at the Deutsches Theater in Berlin. The design called for an entire forest to be built on a stage that revolved as the action shifted.

25 BOTTOM: Where are these lads? Where are these hearts?°
QUINCE: Bottom! O most courageous day! O most happy hour!
BOTTOM: Masters, I am to discourse wonders.° But ask me not what; for if I tell you, I am no true Athenian. I
30 will tell you everything, right as it fell out.
QUINCE: Let us hear, sweet Bottom.
BOTTOM: Not a word of° me. All that I will tell you is, that the Duke hath din'd. Get your apparel together, good strings° to your beards, new ribands° to your
35 pumps, meet presently° at the palace, every man look o'er his part; for the short and the long is, our play is preferr'd.° In any case, let Thisby have clean linen; and let not him that plays the lion pare his nails, for they shall hang out for the lion's claws. And, most
40 dear actors, eat no onions nor garlic, for we are to utter sweet breath; and I do not doubt but to hear them say, it is a sweet comedy. No more words. Away! go, away!   [*Exeunt.*]

25. **hearts:** Good fellows.   28. **am . . . wonders:** Have wonders to relate.   32. **of:** Out of.   34. **strings:** To attach the beards. **ribands:** Ribbons.   35. **presently:** Immediately.   37. **preferr'd:** Selected for consideration.

{*ACT V • Scene 1*}°

(*Enter Theseus, Hippolyta, and Philostrate, [Lords, and Attendants].*)

HIPPOLYTA: 'Tis strange, my Theseus, that° these lovers speak of.
THESEUS: More strange than true. I never may° believe These antic° fables, nor these fairy toys.°
Lovers and madmen have such seething brains
Such shaping fantasies,° that apprehend   5
More than cool reason ever comprehends.
The lunatic, the lover, and the poet
Are of imagination all compact.°
One sees more devils than vast hell can hold;
That is the madman. The lover, all as frantic,   10
Sees Helen's° beauty in a brow of Egypt.°
The poet's eye, in a fine frenzy rolling,

V, I. Location: Athens. The palace of Theseus.   **1. that:** That which.   **2. may:** Can.   **3. antic:** Strange, grotesque (with additional punning sense of *antique,* ancient).   **fairy toys:** Trifling stories about fairies.   **5. fantasies:** Imaginations.   **8. compact:** Formed, composed.   **11. Helen's:** Of Helen of Troy, pattern of beauty.   **brow of Egypt:** Face of a gypsy.

Doth glance from heaven to earth, from earth to
    heaven;
And as imagination bodies forth
15 The forms of things unknown, the poet's pen
Turns them to shapes and gives to airy nothing
A local habitation and a name.
Such tricks hath strong imagination
That, if it would but apprehend some joy,
20 It comprehends some bringer° of that joy;
Or in the night, imagining some fear,°
How easy is a bush suppos'd a bear!
HIPPOLYTA: But all the story of the night told over,
And all their minds transfigur'd so together,
25 More witnesseth than fancy's images°
And grows to something of great constancy;°
But, howsoever,° strange and admirable.°

(*Enter lovers: Lysander, Demetrius, Hermia, and Helena.*)

THESEUS: Here come the lovers, full of joy and mirth.
Joy, gentle friends! Joy and fresh days of love
Accompany your hearts!
30 LYSANDER: More than to us
Wait in your royal walks, your board, your bed!
THESEUS: Come now, what masques, what dances
    shall we have,
To wear away this long age of three hours
Between our after-supper and bed-time?
35 Where is our usual manager of mirth?
What revels are in hand? Is there no play,
To ease the anguish of a torturing hour?
Call Philostrate.
PHILOSTRATE: Here, mighty Theseus.
THESEUS: Say, what abridgement° have you for this
    evening?
40 What masque? What music? How shall we beguile
The lazy time, if not with some delight?
PHILOSTRATE: There is a brief° how many sports are
    ripe.
Make choice of which your Highness will see first.
                  [*Giving a paper.*]
THESEUS [*reads*]: "The battle with the Centaurs,° to be
    sung
45 By an Athenian eunuch to the harp."
We'll none of that. That have I told my love,
In glory of my kinsman° Hercules.

[*Reads.*] "The riot of the tipsy Bacchanals,
Tearing the Thracian singer in their rage."°
That is an old device; and it was play'd   50
When I from Thebes came last a conqueror.
[*Reads.*] "The thrice three Muses mourning for the
    death
Of Learning, late deceas'd in beggary."°
That is some satire, keen and critical,
Not sorting with° a nuptial ceremony.   55
[*Reads.*] "A tedious brief scene of young Pyramus
And his love Thisby; very tragical mirth."
Merry and tragical? Tedious and brief?
That is, hot ice and wondrous strange° snow.
How shall we find the concord of this discord?   60
PHILOSTRATE: A play there is, my lord, some ten
    words long,
Which is as brief as I have known a play;
But by ten words, my lord, it is too long,
Which makes it tedious. For in all the play
There is not one word apt, one player fitted.   65
And tragical, my noble lord, it is,
For Pyramus therein doth kill himself.
Which, when I saw rehears'd, I must confess,
Made mine eyes water, but more merry tears
The passion of loud laughter never shed.   70
THESEUS: What are they that do play it?
PHILOSTRATE: Hard-handed men that work in Athens
    here,
Which never labor'd in their minds till now,
And now have toil'd° their unbreathed° memories
With this same play, against° your nuptial.   75
THESEUS: And we will hear it.
PHILOSTRATE: No, my noble lord,
It is not for you. I have heard it over,
And it is nothing, nothing in the world;
Unless you can find sport in their intents,
Extremely stretch'd° and conn'd° with cruel pain,   80
To do you service.
THESEUS: I will hear that play;
For never anything can be amiss'
When simpleness and duty tender it.
Go, bring them in; and take your places, ladies.

[*Philostrate goes to summon the players.*]

HIPPOLYTA: I love not to see wretchedness o'ercharg'd°   85
And duty in his service° perishing.
THESEUS: Why, gentle sweet, you shall see no such thing.

---

20. **bringer:** Source.   **21. fear:** Object of fear.   **25. More . . . images:** Testifies to something more substantial than mere imaginings.   **26. constancy:** Certainty.   **27. howsoever:** In any case.   **admirable:** A source of wonder.   **39. abridgement:** Pastime (to abridge or shorten the evening).   **42. brief:** Short written statement, list.   **44. "battle . . . Centaurs":** Probably refers to the battle of the Centaurs and the Lapithae, when the Centaurs attempted to carry off Hippodamia, bride of Theseus's friend Pirothous.   **47. kinsman:** Plutarch's *Life of Theseus* states that Hercules and Theseus were near-kinsmen. Theseus is referring to a version of the battle of the Centaurs in which Hercules was said to be present.

48–49. **"The riot . . . rage":** This was the story of the death of Orpheus, as told in *Metamorphoses.*   **52–53. "The thrice . . . beggary":** Possibly an allusion to Spenser's *Teares of the Muses* (1591), though "satires" deploring the neglect of learning and the creative arts were common-place.   **55. sorting with:** Befitting.   **59. strange:** Seemingly an error for some adjective that would contrast with *snow,* just as *hot* contrasts with *ice.*   **74. toil'd:** Taxed.   **unbreathed:** Unexercised.   **75. against:** In preparation for.   **80. stretch'd:** Strained.   **conn'd:** Memorized.   **85. wretchedness o'ercharg'd:** Incompetence overburdened.   **86. his service:** Its attempt to serve.

HIPPOLYTA: He says they can do nothing in this kind.°
THESEUS: The kinder we, to give them thanks for
    nothing.
90   Our sport shall be to take what they mistake;
    And what poor duty cannot do, noble respect
    Takes it in might, not merit.°
    Where I have come, great clerks° have purposed
    To greet me with premeditated welcomes;
95   Where I have seen them shiver and look pale,
    Make periods in the midst of sentences,
    Throttle their practic'd accent° in their fears,
    And in conclusion dumbly have broke off,
    Not paying me a welcome. Trust me, sweet,
100   Out of this silence yet I pick'd a welcome;
    And in the modesty of fearful duty
    I read as much as from the rattling tongue
    Of saucy and audacious eloquence.
    Love, therefore, and tongue-tied simplicity
105   In least° speak most, to my capacity.°

[*Philostrate returns.*]

PHILOSTRATE: So please your Grace, the Prologue° is
    address'd.°
THESEUS: Let him approach.   [*Flourish of trumpets.*]

(*Enter the Prologue [Quince].*)

PROLOGUE: If we offend, it is with our good will.
    That you should think, we come not to offend,
110   But with good will. To show our simple skill,
    That is the true beginning of our end.
    Consider, then, we come but in despite.
    We do not come, as minding° to content you,
    Our true intent is. All for your delight
115   We are not here. That you should here repent you,
    The actors are at hand; and, by their show,
    You shall know all that you are like to know.
THESEUS: This fellow doth not stand upon points.°
LYSANDER: He hath rid his prologue like a rough° colt;
120   he knows not the stop.° A good moral, my lord: it is
    not enough to speak, but to speak true.
HIPPOLYTA: Indeed he hath play'd on his prologue
    like a child on a recorder;° a sound, but not in
    government.°
125 THESEUS: His speech was like a tangled chain, nothing°
    impair'd, but all disorder'd. Who is next?

---

88. **kind:** Kind of thing. 92. **Takes . . . merit:** Values it for the effort made rather than for the excellence achieved. 93. **clerks:** Learned men. 97. **practic'd accent:** Rehearsed speech; or usual way of speaking. 105. **least:** Saying least. **to my capacity:** In my judgment and understanding. 106. **Prologue:** Speaker of the prologue. **address'd:** Ready. 113. **minding:** Intending. 118. **stand upon points:** (1) Heed niceties or small points, (2) pay attention to punctuation in his reading. (The humor of Quince's speech is in the blunders of its punctuation.) 119. **rough:** Unbroken. 120. **stop:** (1) The stopping of a colt by reining it in, (2) punctuation mark. 123. **recorder:** A wind instrument like a flute. 123–24. **government:** Control. 125. **nothing:** Not at all.

(*Enter Pyramus and Thisby, and Wall, and Moonshine, and Lion.*)

PROLOGUE: Gentles, perchance you wonder at this
    show;
    But wonder on, till truth make all things plain.
    This man is Pyramus, if you would know;
    This beauteous lady Thisby is certain.   130
    This man, with lime and rough-cast, doth present
    Wall, that vile Wall which did these lovers sunder;
    And through Wall's chink, poor souls, they are
        content
    To whisper. At the which let no man wonder.
    This man, with lantern, dog, and bush of thorn, 135
    Presenteth Moonshine; for, if you will know,
    By moonshine did these lovers think no scorn°
    To meet at Ninus' tomb, there, there to woo.
    This grisly beast, which Lion hight° by name,
    The trusty Thisby, coming first by night, 140
    Did scare away, or rather did affright;
    And, as she fled, her mantle she did fall,°
    Which Lion vile with bloody mouth did stain.
    Anon comes Pyramus, sweet youth and tall,°
    And finds his trusty Thisby's mantle slain; 145
    Whereat, with blade, with bloody blameful blade,
    He bravely broach'd° his boiling bloody breast.
    And Thisby, tarrying in mulberry shade,
    His dagger drew, and died. For all the rest,
    Let Lion, Moonshine, Wall, and lovers twain 150
    At large° discourse, while here they do remain.

(*Exeunt Lion, Thisby, and Moonshine.*)

THESEUS: I wonder if the lion be to speak.
DEMETRIUS: No wonder, my lord. One lion may, when
    many asses do.
WALL: In this same interlude it doth befall 155
    That I, one Snout by name, present a wall;
    And such a wall, as I would have you think,
    That had in it a crannied hole or chink,
    Through which the lovers, Pyramus and Thisby,
    Did whisper often very secretly. 160
    This loam, this rough-cast, and this stone doth show
    That I am that same wall; the truth is so.
    And this the cranny is, right and sinister,°
    Through which the fearful lovers are to whisper.
THESEUS: Would you desire lime and hair to speak better? 165
DEMETRIUS: It is the wittiest partition° that ever I heard
    discourse, my lord.

[*Pyramus comes forward.*]

THESEUS: Pyramus draws near the wall. Silence!

---

137. **think no scorn:** Think it no disgraceful matter. 139. **hight:** Is called. 142. **fall:** Let fall. 144. **tall:** Courageous. 147. **broach'd:** Stabbed. 151. **At large:** In full, at length. 163. **right and sinister:** The right side of it and the left (sinister); or running from right to left, horizontally. 166. **partition:** (1) Wall, (2) section of a learned treatise or oration.

PYRAMUS: O grim-look'd° night! O night with hue so
        black!
170   O night, which ever art when day is not!
        O night, O night! Alack, alack, alack,
        I fear my Thisby's promise is forgot.
        And thou, O wall, O sweet, O lovely wall,
        That stand'st between her father's ground and mine,
175   Thou wall, O wall, O sweet and lovely wall,
        Show me thy chink, to blink through with mine eyne!

                                [*Wall holds up his fingers.*]

        Thanks, courteous wall. Jove shield thee well for
        this!
        But what see I? No Thisby do I see.
        O wicked wall, through whom I see no bliss!
180   Curs'd be thy stones for thus deceiving me!
THESEUS: The wall, methinks, being sensible,° should
        curse again.
PYRAMUS: No, in truth, sir, he should not. "Deceiving
        me" is Thisby's cue: she is to enter now, and I am to
185   spy her through the wall. You shall see, it will fall pat
        as I told you. Yonder she comes.

(*Enter Thisby.*)

THISBY: O wall, full often hast thou heard my moans,
        For parting my fair Pyramus and me.
        My cherry lips have often kiss'd thy stones,
190   Thy stones with lime and hair knit up in thee.
PYRAMUS: I see a voice. Now will I to the chink,
        To spy an° I can hear my Thisby's face.
        Thisby!
THISBY: My love! Thou art my love, I think.
PYRAMUS: Think what thou wilt, I am thy lover's
195   grace;°
        And, like Limander° am I trusty still.
THISBY: And I like Helen,° till the Fates me kill.
PYRAMUS: Not Shafalus° to Procrus° was so true.
THISBY: As Shafalus to Procrus, I to you.
200 PYRAMUS: O, kiss me through the hole of this vile wall!
THISBY: I kiss the wall's hole, not your lips at all.
PYRAMUS: Wilt thou at Ninny's tomb meet me
        straightway?
THISBY: 'Tide° life, 'tide death, I come without delay.

                        [*Exeunt Pyramus and Thisby.*]

WALL: Thus have I, Wall, my part discharged so;
205   And, being done, thus Wall away doth go.   [*Exit.*]
THESEUS: Now is the mural down between the two
        neighbors.
DEMETRIUS: No remedy, my lord, when walls are so
        willful to hear° without warning.°
210 HIPPOLYTA: This is the silliest stuff that ever I heard.

THESEUS: The best in this kind° are but shadows;° and
        the worst are no worse, if imagination amend them.
HIPPOLYTA: It must be your imagination then, and not
        theirs.
THESEUS: If we imagine no worse of them than they of   215
        themselves, they may pass for excellent men. Here
        come two noble beasts in, a man and a lion.

(*Enter Lion and Moonshine.*)

LION: You, ladies, you, whose gentle hearts do fear
        The smallest monstrous mouse that creeps on floor,
        May now perchance both quake and tremble here,   220
        When lion rough in wildest rage doth roar.
        Then know that I, as Snug the joiner, am
        A lion fell,° nor else no lion's dam;
        For, if I should as lion come in strife
        Into this place, 'twere pity on my life.   225
THESEUS: A very gentle beast, and of a good conscience.
DEMETRIUS: The very best at a beast, my lord, that e'er I
        saw.
LYSANDER: This lion is a very fox for his valor.°
THESEUS: True; and a goose for his discretion.°   230
DEMETRIUS: Not so, my lord; for his valor cannot carry
        his discretion; and the fox carries the goose.
THESEUS: His discretion, I am sure, cannot carry his
        valor, for the goose carries not the fox. It is well.
        Leave it to his discretion, and let us listen to the   235
        moon.
MOON: This lanthorn° doth the horned moon present—
DEMETRIUS: He should have worn the horns on his
        head.°
THESEUS: He is no crescent, and his horns are invisible   240
        within the circumference.
MOON: This lanthorn doth the horned moon present;
        Myself the man i' th' moon do seem to be.
THESEUS: This is the greatest error of all the rest. The
        man should be put into the lanthorn. How is it else   245
        the man i' th' moon?
DEMETRIUS: He dares not come there for the° candle;
        for, you see, it is already in snuff.°
HIPPOLYTA: I am aweary of this moon. Would he would
        change!   250
THESEUS: It appears, by his small light of discretion, that
        he is in the wane; but yet, in courtesy, in all reason,
        we must stay the time.
LYSANDER: Proceed, Moon.

---

169. grim-look'd: Grim-looking.   181. sensible: Capable of feeling.   192. an: If.   195. lover's grace: Gracious lover.   196. Limander: Blunder for *Leander.*   197. Helen: Blunder for *Hero.*   198. Shafalus, Procrus: Blunders for *Cephalus* and *Procris,* also famous lovers.   203. 'Tide: Betide, come.   209. to hear: As to hear.   without warning: Without warning the parents.

211. in this kind: Of this sort.   shadows: Likenesses, representations.   223. lion fell: Fierce lion (with a play on the idea of *lion skin*).   229. is . . . valor: His valor consists of craftiness and discretion.   230. goose . . . discretion: As discreet as a goose, that is, more foolish than discreet.   237. lanthorn: This original spelling may suggest a play on the *horn* of which lanterns were made and also on a cuckold's horns; but the spelling *lanthorn* is not used consistently for comic effect in this play or elsewhere. In V, i, 135, for example, the word is *lantern* in the original.   238–39. on his head: As a sign of cuckoldry.   247. for the: Because of the.   248. in snuff: (1) Offended, (2) in need of snuffing.

255 MOON: All that I have to say is to tell you that the lanthorn is the moon, I, the man in the moon, this thorn-
bush my thorn-bush, and this dog my dog.
DEMETRIUS: Why, all these should be in the lanthorn; for
all these are in the moon. But silence! Here comes
260 Thisby.

(*Enter Thisby.*)

THISBY: This is old Ninny's tomb. Where is my love?
LION [*roaring*]: *Oh*— [*Thisby runs off.*]
DEMETRIUS: Well roar'd, Lion.
THESEUS: Well run, Thisby.
265 HIPPOLYTA: Well shone, Moon. Truly, the moon shines
with a good grace.

[*The Lion shakes Thisby's mantle, and exit.*]

THESEUS: Well mous'd,° Lion.
DEMETRIUS: And then came Pyramus.
LYSANDER: And so the lion vanish'd.

(*Enter Pyramus.*)

PYRAMUS: Sweet Moon, I thank thee for thy sunny
270 beams;
I thank thee, Moon, for shining now so bright;
For, by thy gracious, golden, glittering gleams,
I trust to take of truest Thisby sight.
But stay, O spite!
275 But mark, poor knight,
What dreadful dole° is here!
Eyes, do you see?
How can it be?
O dainty duck! O dear!
280 Thy mantle good,
What, stain'd with blood!
Approach, ye Furies fell!°
O Fates, come, come,
Cut thread and thrum;°
285 Quail,° crush, conclude, and quell!°
THESEUS: This passion, and the death of a dear friend,
would go near to make a man look sad.°
HIPPOLYTA: Beshrew my heart, but I pity the man.
PYRAMUS: O wherefore, Nature, didst thou lions frame?
290 Since lion vile hath here deflow'r'd my dear,
Which is—no, no—which was the fairest dame
That liv'd, that lov'd, that lik'd, that look'd with
cheer.°
Come, tears, confound,
Out, sword, and wound
295 The pap of Pyramus;
Ay, that left pap,
Where heart doth hop. [*Stabs himself.*]
Thus die I, thus, thus, thus.

Now am I dead,
Now am I fled; 300
My soul is in the sky.
Tongue, lose thy light;
Moon, take thy flight. [*Exit Moonshine.*]
Now die, die, die, die, die. [*Dies.*]
DEMETRIUS: No die, but an ace,° for him; for he is but 305
one.°
LYSANDER: Less than an ace, man; for he is dead, he is
nothing.
THESEUS: With the help of a surgeon he might yet
recover, and yet prove an ass.° 310
HIPPOLYTA: How chance Moonshine is gone before
Thisby comes back and finds her lover?
THESEUS: She will find him by starlight. Here she comes;
and her passion ends the play.

[*Enter Thisby.*]

HIPPOLYTA: Methinks she should not use a long one for 315
such a Pyramus. I hope she will be brief.
DEMETRIUS: A mote will turn the balance, which Pyra-
mus, which° Thisby, is the better: he for a man God
warr'nt us; she for a woman, God bless us.
LYSANDER: She hath spied him already with those sweet 320
eyes.
DEMETRIUS: And thus she means,° videlicet:°
THISBY: Asleep, my love?
What, dead, my dove?
O Pyramus, arise! 325
Speak, speak. Quite dumb?
Dead, dead? A tomb
Must cover thy sweet eyes.
These lily lips,
This cherry nose, 330
These yellow cowslip cheeks,
Are gone, are gone!
Lovers, make moan.
His eyes were green as leeks.
O Sisters Three,° 335
Come, come to me,
With hands as pale as milk;
Lay them in gore,
Since you have shore°
With shears his thread of silk. 340
Tongue, not a word.
Come, trusty sword,
Come, blade, my breast imbrue!° [*Stabs herself.*]
And farewell, friends.
Thus Thisby ends. 345
Adieu, adieu, adieu. [*Dies.*]

---

267. **mous'd:** Shaken. 276. **dole:** Grievous event. 282. **fell:**
Fierce. 284. **thread and thrum:** The warp in weaving and the
loose end of the warp. 285. **Quail:** Overpower. **quell:** Kill,
destroy. 286–87. **This . . . sad:** If one had other reason to
grieve, one might be sad, but not from this absurd portrayal of
passion. 292. **cheer:** Countenance.

305. **ace:** The side of the die featuring the single pip, or spot.
(The pun is on *die* as a singular of *dice;* Bottom's performance
is not worth a whole *die* but rather one single face of it,
one small portion.) 306. **one:** (1) An individual person,
(2) unique. 310. **ass:** With a pun on *ace.* 317–18.
which . . . which: Whether . . . or. 322. **means:** Moans, laments.
videlicet: To wit. 335. **Sisters Three:** The Fates. 339. **shore:**
Shorn. 343. **imbrue:** Stain with blood.

THESEUS: Moonshine and Lion are left to bury the dead.
DEMETRIUS: Ay, and Wall too.
BOTTOM [*starting up*]: No, I assure you; the wall is
350   down that parted their fathers. Will it please you to
       see the epilogue, or to hear a Bergomask dance°
       between two of our company?
THESEUS: No epilogue, I pray you; for your play needs
       no excuse. Never excuse; for when the players are all
355   dead, there need none to be blam'd. Marry, if he that
       writ it had play'd Pyramus and hang'd himself in
       Thisby's garter, it would have been a fine tragedy;
       and so it is, truly, and very notably discharg'd. But,
       come, your Bergomask. Let your epilogue alone.
                                             [*A dance.*]
360   The iron tongue of midnight hath told° twelve.
       Lovers, to bed; 'tis almost fairy time.
       I fear we shall outsleep the coming morn
       As much as we this night have overwatch'd.°
       This palpable-gross° play hath well beguil'd
365   The heavy° gait of night. Sweet friends, to bed.
       A fortnight hold we this solemnity,
       In nightly revels and new jollity.   (*Exeunt.*)

(*Enter Puck*)

PUCK: Now the hungry lion roars,
          And the wolf behowls the moon;
370   Whilst the heavy ploughman snores,
          All with weary task fordone.°
       Now the wasted brands° do glow,
          Whilst the screech-owl, screeching loud,
       Puts the wretch that lies in woe
375   In remembrance of a shroud.
       Now it is the time of night
          That the graves, all gaping wide,
       Every one lets forth his sprite,°
          In the churchway paths to glide.
380   And we fairies, that do run
          By the triple Hecate's° team
       From the presence of the sun,
          Following darkness like a dream,
       Now are frolic.° Not a mouse
385   Shall disturb this hallowed house.
       I am sent with broom before,
       To sweep the dust behind° the door.

(*Enter [Oberon and Titania,] King and Queen of Fairies,
with all their train.*)

---

351. Bergomask dance: A rustic dance named for Bergamo,
a province in the state of Venice. **360. told:** Counted,
struck ("tolled"). **363. overwatch'd:** Stayed up too late.
364. palpable-gross: Obviously crude. **365. heavy:** Drowsy,
dull. **371. fordone:** Exhausted. **372. wasted brands:**
Burned-out logs. **378. Every . . . sprite:** Every grave lets forth
its ghost. **381. triple Hecate's:** Hecate ruled in three capacities: as Luna or Cynthia in heaven, as Diana on earth, and as
Proserpina in hell. **384. frolic:** Merry. **387. behind:** From
behind. (Robin Goodfellow was a household spirit who helped
good housemaids and punished lazy ones.)

OBERON: Through the house give glimmering light,
          By the dead and drowsy fire;
       Every elf and fairy sprite   390
          Hop as light as bird from brier;
       And this ditty, after me,
       Sing, and dance it trippingly.
TITANIA: First, rehearse your song by rote,
       To each word a warbling note.   395
       Hand in hand, with fairy grace,
       Will we sing, and bless this place.

                              [*Song and dance.*]
OBERON: Now, until the break of day,
       Through this house each fairy stray.
       To the best bride-bed will we,   400
       Which by us shall blessed be;
       And the issue there create°
       Ever shall be fortunate.
       So shall all the couples three
       Ever true in loving be;   405
       And the blots of Nature's hand
       Shall not in their issue stand;
       Never mole, hare lip, nor scar,
       Nor mark prodigious,° such as are
       Despised in nativity,   410
       Shall upon their children be.
       With this field-dew consecrate,°
       Every fairy take his gait,°
       And each several° chamber bless,
       Through this palace, with sweet peace;   415
       And the owner of it blest
       Ever shall in safety rest.
       Trip away; make no stay;
       Meet me all by break of day.

                   (*Exeunt [Oberon, Titania, and train].*)

PUCK: If we shadows have offended,   420
       Think but this, and all is mended,
       That you have but slumb'red here°
       While these visions did appear.
       And this weak and idle theme,
       No more yielding but° a dream,   425
       Gentles, do not reprehend.
       If you pardon, we will mend.
       And, as I am an honest Puck,
       If we have unearned luck
       Now to scape the serpent's tongue,°   430
       We will make amends ere long;
       Else the Puck a liar call.
       So, good night unto you all.
       Give me your hands,° if we be friends,
       And Robin shall restore amends.   [*Exit.*]   435

---

402. create: Created. **409. prodigious:** Monstrous, unnatural.
412. consecrate: Consecrated. **413. take his gait:** Go his way.
414. several: Separate. **422. That . . . here:** That it is a "midsummer night's dream." **425. No . . . but:** Yielding no more
than. **430. serpent's tongue:** Hissing. **434. Give . . . hands:**
Applaud.

COMMENTARIES

Some of the finest critical commentary ever written has been devoted to the works of Shakespeare. From the seventeenth century to the present, critics have taken a considerable interest in the nuances of his work.

In the commentary on *A Midsummer Night's Dream* we find a wide range of responses. In a specifically feminist observation, critic Linda Bamber shows how assumptions regarding power in a male-female relationship affect our interpretation of the play.

Peter Brook, one of the most notable contemporary directors of Shakespeare and the producer of a landmark production of *A Midsummer Night's Dream* (1970), gives us a director's view of the play. He centers the discussion on love, which in many forms is at the heart of the play. See his review of the production on page 332.

Clive Barnes's review gives us a clear sense of the visual and kinetic details that made Peter Brook's *A Midsummer Night's Dream* one of the most memorable modern stagings of Shakespeare. The use of juggling, acrobats, and trapezes energized the production and underscored the youthful vitality of the characters.

Contemporary reviews of Shakespeare's plays take a very different approach to the plays than do critical studies. The reviewers are concerned first with the actors and their interpretation of the drama. They are then concerned with the director's insights and sense of pacing. In addition to focusing on the title roles, critics also aim to communicate a sense of the dynamics of the production as a whole. Peter Brook's production of *A Midsummer Night's Dream*, for example, was perhaps most startling for its all-white set and backdrop, and for the marvelous scenes staged with principal actors lolling on simple white swings. Critics can give us insight into the staging of the work and the ways in which the staging imparts meaning to the drama.

Linda Bamber (b. 1945)
ON *A MIDSUMMER NIGHT'S DREAM*   1982

The question of masculine and feminine is central to A Midsummer Night's Dream. *Much of the action is precipitated by a power struggle between Titania and Oberon, and the young Athenians who rush off to the woods are there because a father has decided to oppose the will of his daughter regarding her marriage. Linda Bamber is a feminist critic interested in examining the centers of power in the play, particularly with an eye for what we accept as the natural order of relationships. She shows that the action of the comedy is essentially tied into questions of gender, which begin to become questions of genre.*

The best example [in Shakespeare] of the relationship between male dominance and the status quo comes in *A Midsummer Night's Dream,* which begins with a rebellion of the feminine against the power of masculine authority. Hermia refuses the man both Aegeus and Theseus order her to marry; her refusal sends us off into the forest, beyond the power of the father and the masculine state. Once in the forest, of course, we find the social situation metaphorically repeated in this world of imagination and nature. The fairy king, Oberon, rules the forest. His rule, too, is troubled by the rebellion of the feminine. Titania has refused to give him her page, the child of a human friend who died in childbirth. But by the end of the story Titania is conquered, the child relinquished, and order restored. Even here the comic upheavals, whether we see them as May games or bad dreams, are associated with an uprising of women. David P. Young has pointed out how firmly this play connects order with masculine dominance and the disruption of order with the rebellion of the feminine:

> It is appropriate that Theseus, as representative of daylight and right reason, should have subdued his bride-to-be to the rule of his masculine will. That is the natural order of things. It is equally appropriate that Oberon, as king of darkness and fantasy, should have lost control of his wife, and that the corresponding natural disorder described by Titania should ensue.[1]

The natural order, the status quo, is for men to rule women. When they fail to do so, we have the exceptional situation, the festive, disruptive, disorderly moment of comedy.

A Midsummer Night's Dream is actually an anomaly among the festive comedies. It is unusual for the forces of the green world to be directed, as they are here, by a masculine figure. Because the green world here is a partial reproduction of the social world, the feminine is reduced to a kind of first cause of the action while a masculine power directs it. In the other festive comedies the feminine Other presides. She does not *command* the forces of the alternative world, as Oberon does, but since she acts in harmony with these forces her will and desire often prevail.

Where are we to bestow our sympathies? On the forces that make for the disruption of the status quo and therefore for the plot? Or on the force that asserts itself against the disruption and reestablishes a workable social order? Of course we cannot choose. We can only say that in comedy we owe our holiday to such forces as the tendency of the feminine to rebel, whereas to the successful reassertion of masculine power we owe our everyday order. Shakespearean comedy endorses both sides. Holiday is, of course, the subject and the analogue of each play; but the plays always end in a return to everyday life. The optimistic reading of Shakespearean comedy says that everyday life is clarified and enriched by our holiday from it; according to the pessimistic reading the temporary subversion of the social order has revealed how much that order excludes, how high a price we pay for it. But whether our return to everyday life is a comfortable one or not, the return itself is the inevitable conclusion to the journey out.

Does this make the comedies sexist? Is the association of women with the disruption of the social order an unconscious and insulting projection? It seems to

---

[1]David P. Young, *Something of Great Constancy* (New Haven, CT: Yale UP, 1966), 183.

begin as such; but as the form of Shakespearean comedy develops, the Otherness of the feminine develops into as powerful a force in the drama as the social authority of the masculine Self. For the feminine in Shakespearean comedy begins as a shrew but develops into a comic heroine. The shrew's rebellion directly challenges masculine authority, whereas the comic heroine merely presides over areas of experience to which masculine authority is irrelevant. But the shrew is essentially powerless against the social system, whereas the comic heroine is in alliance with forces that can never be finally overcome. The shrew is defeated by the superior strength, physical and social, of a man, or by women who support the status quo. She provokes a battle of the sexes, and the outcome of this battle, from Shakespeare's point of view, is inevitable. The comic heroine, on the other hand, does not fight the system but merely surfaces, again and again, when and where the social system is temporarily subverted. The comic heroine does not actively resist the social and political hegemony° of the men, but as an irresistible version of the Other she successfully competes for our favor with the (masculine) representatives of the social Self. The development of the feminine from the shrew to the comic heroine indicates a certain consciousness on the author's part of sexual politics; and it indicates a desire, at least, to create conditions of sexual equality within the drama even while reflecting the unequal conditions of men and women in the society at large.

Peter Brook (b. 1925)
THE PLAY IS THE MESSAGE . . .   *1987*

When a distinguished director becomes a critic, we have the opportunity to understand a play from the point of view of one who has to make the play work in front of an audience. Brook's production of A Midsummer Night's Dream *was a sensation in England and the United States in 1970. It featured absolutely white lighting, white sets, and actors in swings. Brook had analyzed the play in such a fashion that he saw love as its constant concern, "constantly repeated." He concluded that to present the play, the players must embody the concept of love. They must bring to the play their own realization of the play's themes — even to the point of seeing theater anew, like the mechanicals "who are touching an extraordinary world with the tips of their fingers, a world which transcends their daily experience and which fills them with wonder"— the effect of the love they bring to their task.*

People have often asked me: "What is the theme of *A Midsummer Night's Dream?*" There is only one answer to that question, the same as one would give regarding a cup. The quality of a cup is its cupness. I say this by way of introduction, to show that if I lay so much stress on the dangers involved in trying to define the themes of the *Dream* it is because too many productions, too many attempts at visual interpretation are based on preconceived ideas, as if these had to be illustrated in some way. In my opinion we should first of all try to rediscover the play as a living thing; then we shall be able to analyze our discoveries. Once I have finished working on

---

hegemony: Overriding authority.

the play, I can begin to produce my theories. It was fortunate that I did not attempt to do so earlier because the play would not have yielded up its secrets.

At the center of the *Dream,* constantly repeated, we find the word "love." Everything comes back to this, even the structure of the play, even its music. The quality the play demands from its performers is to build up an atmosphere of love during the performance itself, so that this abstract idea—for the word "love" is in itself a complete abstraction—may become palpable. The play presents us with forms of love which become less and less blurred as it goes on. "Love" soon begins to resound like a musical scale, and little by little we are introduced to its various modes and tones.

Love is, of course, a theme which touches all men. No one, not even the most hardened, the coldest, or the most despairing, is insensitive to it, even if he does not know what love is. Either his practical experience confirms its existence or he suffers from its absence, which is another way of recognizing that it exists. At every moment the play touches something which concerns everyone.

As this is theater, there must be conflicts, so this play about love is also a play about the opposite of love, love and its opposite force. We are brought to realize that love, liberty, and imagination are closely connected. Right at the beginning of the play, for example, the father in a long speech tries to obstruct his daughter's love and we are surprised that such a character, apparently a secondary role, should have so long a speech—until we discover the real importance of his words. What he says not only reflects a generation gap (a father opposing his daughter's love because he had intended her for someone else), it also explains the reasons for his feeling of suspicion toward the young man whom his daughter loves. He describes him as an individual prone to fantasy, led by his imagination—an unpardonable weakness in the father's eyes.

From this starting point we see, as in any of Shakespeare's plays, a confrontation. Here it is between love and its opposing qualities, between fantasy and solid common sense—caught in an endless series of mirrors. As usual, Shakespeare confuses the issue. If we asked someone's opinion on the father's point of view, he might say, for example, that "The father is in the wrong because he is against freedom of the imagination," a very widespread attitude today.

In this way, for most present-day audiences, the girl's father comes over as the classical father figure who misunderstands young people and their flights of fancy. But later on, we discover surprisingly that he is right, because the imaginative world in which this lover lives causes him to behave in a quite disgusting way toward the very same daughter: as soon as a drop of liquid falls into his eyes, acting as a drug which liberates natural tendencies, he not only jilts her but his love is transformed into violent hate. He uses words which might well be borrowed from *Measure for Measure,* denouncing the girl with the kind of vehemence that, in the Middle Ages, led people to burn one another at the stake. Yet at the end of the play we are once more in agreement with the Duke, who rejects the father in the name of love. The young man has now been transformed.

So we observe this game of love in a psychological and metaphysical context; we hear Titania's assertion that the opposition between herself and Oberon is fundamental, primordial. But Oberon's acts deny this, for he perceives that within their opposition a reconciliation is possible.

The play covers an extraordinarily broad range of universal forces and feelings in a mythical world, which suddenly changes, in the last part, into high society. We find ourselves back in the very real palace. And the same Shakespeare who, a few pages earlier, offered us a scene of pure fantasy between Titania and Oberon, where it would be absurd to ask prosaic questions like "Where does Oberon live?" or "When describing a queen like Titania did Shakespeare wish to express political ideas?," now takes us into a precise social environment. We are present at the meeting point of two worlds, that of the workmen and the court, the world of wealth and elegance, and alleged sensitivity, the world of people who have had the leisure to cultivate fine sentiments and are now shown as insensitive and even disgusting in their superior attitude toward the poor.

At the beginning of the court scene we see our former heroes, who have spent the entire play involved in the theme of love, and would no doubt be quite capable of giving academic lectures on the subject, suddenly finding themselves plunged into a context which has apparently nothing to do with love (with their own love, since all their problems have been solved). Now they are in the context of a relationship with each other and with another social class, and they are at a loss. They do not realize that here too scorn eliminates love.

We see how well Shakespeare has situated everything. Athens in the *Dream* resembles our Athens in the sixties: the workmen, as they state in the first scene, are very much afraid of the authorities; if they commit the slightest error they will be hanged, and there is nothing comical about that. Indeed, they risk hanging as soon as they shed their anonymity. At the same time they are irresistibly attracted by the carrot of "sixpence a day" which will enable them to escape poverty. Yet their real motive is neither glory nor adventure nor money (that is made very clear and should guide the actors who perform this scene). Those simple men who have only ever worked with their hands apply to the use of the imagination exactly the same quality of love which traditionally underlies the relationship between a craftsman and his tools. That is what gives these scenes both their strength and their comic quality. These craftsmen make efforts which are grotesque in one sense because they push awkwardness to its limit, but at another level they set themselves to their task with such love that the meaning of their clumsy efforts changes before our eyes.

The spectators can easily decide to adopt the same attitude as the courtiers: to find all this quite simply ridiculous and laugh with the complacency of people who quite confidently mock the efforts of others. Yet the audience is invited to take a step back: to feel it cannot quite identify with the court, with people who are too grand and too unkind. Little by little, we come to see that the craftsmen, who behave with little understanding but who approach their new job with love, are discovering theater—an imaginary world for them, toward which they instinctively feel great respect. In fact, the "mechanicals" scene is often misinterpreted because the actors forget to look at theater through innocent eyes, they take a professional actor's views of good or bad acting, and in so doing they diminish the mystery and the sense of magic felt by these amateurs, who are touching an extraordinary world with the tips of their fingers, a world which transcends their daily experience and which fills them with wonder.

We see this quite clearly in the part of the boy who plays the girl, Thisby. At first sight this tough lad is irresistibly absurd, but by degrees, through his love for what he is doing, we discover what more is involved. In our production, the actor playing the part is a professional plumber, who took to acting only a short while ago. He well understands what is involved, what it means to feel this nameless and shapeless kind of love. This boy, himself new to theater, acts the part of someone who is new to theater. Through his conviction and his identification we discover that these awkward craftsmen, without knowing it, are teaching us a lesson—or it might be preferable to say that a lesson is being taught us through them. These craftsmen are able to make the connection between love for their trade and for a completely different task, whereas the courtiers are not capable of linking the love about which they talk so well with their simple role as spectators.

Nonetheless, little by little the courtiers become involved, even touched by the play within the play, and if we follow very closely what is there in the text, we see that for a moment the situation is completely transformed. One of the central images of the play is a wall, which, at a given moment, vanishes. Its disappearance, to which Bottom draws our attention, is caused by an act of love. Shakespeare is showing us how love can pervade a situation and act as a transforming force.

The *Dream* touches lightly on the fundamental question of the transformations which may occur if certain things are better understood. It requires us to reflect on the nature of love. All the landscapes of love are thrown into relief, and we are given a particular social context through which the other situations can be measured. Through the subtlety of its language the play removes all kinds of barriers. It is therefore not a play which provokes resistance or creates disturbance in the usual sense. Rival politicians could sit side by side at a performance of *A Midsummer Night's Dream* and each leave with the impression that the play fits his point of view perfectly. But if they give it a fine, sensitive attention they cannot fail to perceive a world just like their own, more and more riddled with contradictions and, like their own, waiting for that mysterious force, love, without which harmony will never return.

Clive Barnes (b. 1927)
REVIEW OF *A MIDSUMMER NIGHT'S DREAM*   1970

Clive Barnes's review credits the Peter Brook production of A Midsummer Night's Dream *as a landmark. Audiences in Stratford, London, New York, and elsewhere agreed. Brook (b. 1925) emphasized the dramatic spectacle—the sets, costumes, and action—in such a way as to reveal new depths of emotion. The playfulness of the jugglers, acrobats, and those on the trapezes emphasized the joy and youth of the main characters.*

Once in a while, once in a very rare while, a theatrical production arrives that is going to be talked about as long as there is a theater, a production that, for good or ill, is going to exert a major influence on the contemporary stage. Such a production is Peter Brook's staging of Shakespeare's *A Midsummer Night's Dream*, which the Royal Shakespeare Company introduced here tonight.

It is a magnificent production, the most important work yet of the world's most imaginative and inventive director. If Peter Brook had done nothing else but this "Dream," he would have deserved a place in theater history,

Brook has approached the play with a radiant innocence. He has treated the script as if it had just been written and sent to him through the mail. He has staged it with no reference to the past, no reverence for tradition.

He has stripped the play down, asked exactly what it is about. He has forgotten gossamer fairies, sequined eyelids, gauzy veils, and whole forests of Beerbohm-trees.

He sees the play for what it is—an allegory of sensual love, and a magic playground of lost innocence and hidden fears. Love in Shakespeare comes as suddenly as death, and when Shakespeare's people love they are all but consumed with sexual passion.

Brook's first concern is to enchant us—to reveal this magic playground. He has conceived the production as a box of theatrical miracles. It takes place in a pure-white setting. The stage is walled in on three sides and the floor is also white. Ladders lead up the walls, and on the top are scaffolds and rostrums from which actors can look down on the playing area like spectators at a bullfight.

The fairy characters—Oberon, Titania, and Puck—are made into acrobats and jugglers. They swing in on trapezes, they amaze us with juggling tricks, Tarzan-like swings across the stage, all the sad deftness of clowns.

Shakespeare's quartet of mingled lovers, now mod kids humming love songs to loosely strummed guitars, are lost in the Venetian woods. The trees are vast metal coils thrown down from the walls on fishing rods, and moving in on unwary lovers like spiraling metallic tendrils. And in this wood of animal desire the noises are not the friendly warblings of fairyland but the grunts and groans of some primeval jungle.

Sex and sexuality are vital in the play. Oberon and Titania, even when quarreling, kiss with hasty, hungry passion—no shining moon for them—and the lovers seem to be journeying through some inner landscape of their own desires toward maturity.

The sexual relationships—with the wittiest use of phallic symbolism the stage can have ever seen—is stressed between Titania and her Bottom. Yet the carnality of the piece is seen with affectionate tolerance rather than the bitterness the playwright shows in *Troilus and Cressida,* and this tolerance, even playfulness, suffuses the production.

Brook is a magician and he gives us new eyes. Here, for reasons admirably supported by the text, he has Theseus and Hippolyta (that previously rather dull royal couple whose wedding provides the framework for the play) played by the same actors as play Oberon and Titania. At once the play takes on a new and personal dimension. The fairies take on a new humanity, and these human princelings, once so uninteresting, are now endowed with a different mystery, and the gentle, almost sad note on which the play ends has a feeling of human comprehension and godlike compassion to it. It is most moving.

Two other characters take on dual assignments. Philostrate, that court master of ceremonies for Theseus, is also, naturally enough, Puck. And rather more puzzlingly, Egeus, the angry father of Hermia, whose opposition to her marriage sets off the action, is also Peter Quince, one of the mechanicals. Presumably the purpose is to bring the play within the play more closely into the main structure, for just as Egeus initiates the real action, so Quince initiates the inner play. But it savors of a literary rather than dramatic device.

Puck is the key figure in this version. Looking like a more than usually perky Picasso clown, he bounces through the action with happy amiability, the model of toleration. John Kane plays him delightfully, performing his tricks with a true circus expertise and acting with unaffected delight.

The Theseus/Oberon and Hippolyta/Titania of Alan Howard and Sara Kestelman are special pleasures, and the mechanicals with the terrible tragedy of *Pyramus and*

Thisbe are the best I have ever seen, with David Waller's virile Bottom particularly splendid.

But the star of this dream is Peter Brook himself, with his ideas, his theories, and above all his practices. Of course he is helped—first by the samite-white pleasure palace devised by his Los Angeles–based designer, Sally Jacobs, and the richly evocative music and sound score provided by Richard Peaslee. But Mr. Brook is the genius architect of our most substantial pleasure.

He makes it all so fresh and so much fun. After a riotously funny and bawdy courtship of Titania by Bottom, the two leave the stage to, of all wonderful things, Mendelssohn's Wedding March, and all hell breaks loose, with confetti, paper streamers, and Oberon himself flying in urbane mockery across the stage.

And Brook uses everything to hand—he is defiantly eclectic. It is as though he is challenging the world by saying that there is no such thing as Shakespearean style. If it suits his purpose he will use a little kathakali, a pop song, sparklers borrowed from a toyshop, dramatic candles borrowed from Grotowski. It is all splendid grist to his splendid mill. Shakespeare can be fun, Shakespeare can be immediate, Shakespeare can most richly live.

HAMLET

Hamlet (1600–1601), Shakespeare's boldest, most profound play, is a landmark in the poet's work. It coincides with the new century and the uncertainties of the last years of the old regime, brought to an end by the death of Queen Elizabeth in 1603. Until the very moment of her death, the succession was in doubt, but at her death she indicated that her cousin James of Scotland would take the throne. The new age was in many ways more complicated, more ambiguous, and more democratic than the old. It was also more dangerous because it was more uncertain.

Hamlet returns to a Denmark and a court that he hardly recognizes, to a mother newly wed to his uncle and in many ways not the woman he remembers, and, finally, to a ghostly father who will not rest until the crimes against him are avenged. Like Marlowe's Faustus, Hamlet was a scholar at the University of Wittenberg, where he presumably had studied theology and therefore had a special knowledge of the world of the spirits. Perhaps he studied medicine and law as well. He gives evidence of knowing literature and having a taste for theater, and he is a ready hand with weapons when necessary.

Hamlet is also a melancholic. To the Elizabethan, *melancholic* did not mean depressed, although Hamlet dresses in black and still mourns for his father, even against the wishes of his uncle. The melancholic, rather, was introspective, thoughtful, perhaps world-weary, and possibly a touch sardonic. Above all things, he was an intellectual, a person of wide-ranging knowledge and intelligence, a reliable commentator with a probing mind.

Hamlet's broad intelligence and the penetrating introspection revealed in his soliloquies, such as his famous "To be, or not to be" meditation on suicide, make him a character with more psychological dimension, more "soul," than many people we know in life. In this sense the play is thoroughly modern; it satisfies our modern need to know the interior lives of characters who engage us onstage. Hamlet's range of feeling, his range of felt and expressed emotion, is impressive to any audience.

Hamlet is a revenge tragedy, a type of play that was especially appealing to the Elizabethans. Thomas Kyd's *The Spanish Tragedy* and John Marston's *Antonio's Revenge* are two examples of successful Elizabethan revenge tragedies. Shakespeare had written an earlier play that could be termed a revenge tragedy, *Titus Andronicus*, in 1594. Below are some characteristics of the revenge tragedy.

The revenge of a relative's murder or rape

The revenge of a father by a son, or vice versa

The appearance of a ghost

The hesitancy or delay of the hero

Tricks or devices to achieve revenge

The use of real or pretended insanity

Suicide

Political intrigue in a court

An able, scheming villain who is a ruler above the law

Philosophical soliloquies

Sensational use of horror (murder and gore onstage)

All these elements are present in *Hamlet*. But the play has other important qualities as well. The minor characters are developed in unexpected ways. Ophelia, the innocent, loving woman, becomes a touching figure in her own right. Unable to understand the nature of evil in the Danish court and driven to insanity by Hamlet's rejection of her and by her father's murder, she permits herself to sink to a watery death in a stream. Audiences are moved by her songs, her insane ramblings, and her devotion to her father as well as to Hamlet.

Characters such as Gertrude, Hamlet's mother, reveal a richness of psychology that sometimes startles us. Polonius, Ophelia's father, is virtually a stock character—the old, foolish philosopher—but he takes on special significance when he urges Ophelia to spy for him and when he ultimately dies at the hand of Hamlet. As Hamlet says, it was an unnecessary death for a "wretched, rash, intruding fool." But Polonius's son, Laertes, loved his father, and when Laertes returns grief-stricken, he does not hesitate a moment to get his revenge.

Hamlet's hesitancy is linked with his reputation as a melancholic. Because he thinks things through so deeply, he does not act instantly, as does Laertes. Even when the ghost reveals himself as his father and tells him that he has been murdered and must be avenged, Hamlet fears that the apparition might be a dangerous fakery of the devil to lure him to murder.

But Hamlet shows that he can act swiftly—indeed, rashly. His killing of Polonius is a rash act. He thinks the man behind the tapestry in his mother's bedroom is his uncle, since no other man but her husband has any right to be there. When Hamlet is sent to England with Rosencrantz and Guildenstern, he quickly senses a plot, undoes it, leaps aboard a pirate ship, and negotiates his way home with alacrity. This is not the work of a man who cannot act. In the graveyard scene he acts just as impulsively as Laertes would when he leaps into Ophelia's grave.

Hamlet's talents exhibited in his welcoming of the players in act II show him to be an experienced theatergoer, one with some skills onstage. He is also an expert writer; his additions to *The Murder of Gonzago* convert that imaginary play into a "mousetrap" baited to catch the murderer of his father. In early Renaissance paintings the mousetrap is a symbol for Jesus Christ, who catches the devil. The allusion would not have been lost on the Elizabethan audience, who would have seen Hamlet's psychological approach as quite reasonable.

Emotions are of great importance to Hamlet. He feels deeply and he watches others to see what their feelings are. He knows that their demeanor may not reveal them as they are, so he must learn to be a careful student of behavior. As he tells his mother, "I know not 'seems.'" What seems is only what is apparent; his procedure is always to penetrate the surfaces of things to know their reality, which is why he uses drama as an instrument to penetrate psychological surfaces.

Hamlet in Performance

Richard Burbage played Hamlet in its original production, which was probably in 1601 but may have been in 1600. He continued playing the part into advanced age. *Hamlet* was staged on an English ship off the coast of Africa in 1607. The first American production was in 1759. When one thinks of productions of the play, one thinks of the great actors who played the role. Their names read like a *Who's Who* of acting: David Garrick (1717–1779), Edmund Kean (1789–1833), William Charles Macready (1793–1873), and Sir Henry Irving (1838–1905) were all identified with the role.

In the twentieth century the two towering Hamlets were John Gielgud and Laurence Olivier, who both acted for the Old Vic Theatre. To interpret the part, Olivier studied psychoanalyst Ernest Jones's essay on Hamlet's Oedipus complex. Jones was a disciple of Freud, who discussed Hamlet in his *Interpretation of Dreams* (see Freud's commentary on p. 396). Paul Scofield, in Peter Brook's 1955 production, found the part so challenging that he said playing it "feels like trespassing." Christopher Plummer, Derek Jacobi, and Jonathan Pryce have played the part to acclaim from the 1950s to recent times. Richard Burton also played Hamlet in New York in 1964. Michael Pennington's version for the Royal Shakespeare Company's 1980 production (see photos on p. 370) was well received by both critics and audiences. Pennington felt that the part tested not only one's skill but also one's character. He said, "When things go well you could do three performances a day and still be the last to leave the party, and at other times the part shakes you like a rat."

The major productions in the 1980s alone were astonishingly numerous: Christopher Walken for the American Shakespeare Festival in Stratford, Connecticut (1982); Roger Rees for the Royal Shakespeare Company in Stratford, England (1984); Kevin Kline for the New York Shakespeare Festival (1986); Ingmar Bergman's acclaimed production in Swedish (1988) in Sweden and New York; Daniel Day-Lewis for the National Theatre in London (1989); and Austin Pendleton for the Riverside Shakespeare Company in New York (1989).

Franco Zeffirelli cast Mel Gibson in his 1990 film, which presents a credible Hamlet capable of deep emotional outburst. The setting of the film is lavish, and the interaction between Hamlet and Gertrude has a special psychological valence. *Hamlet* had a banner year in 1995 when Liam Neeson played the Danish prince in London and New York to considerable acclaim. That production was marked by a careful deemphasis of the great soliloquies. Ralph Fiennes, in the wake of a film success in *Schindler's List,* played in Edwardian clothes on Broadway, using madness as "a way of acting out." Keanu Reeves, another film actor, performed the part at the Manitoba Theater Center in Winnipeg, Canada. One critic said of Reeves's performance, "His hairstyle changed with his moods." Robert Wilson, known for massive semioperatic productions, played entirely alone, in a production premiered in Houston called *Hamlet: A Monologue.* On his deathbed Hamlet relives his story in flashbacks; he provides critical speeches of other characters himself. Among his efforts at Shakespeare, Kenneth Branagh took the title role in a lavish production of *Hamlet* in 1996. His richly produced Shakespeare films continue to be box office and critical successes. There is no end in sight for creative interpretations of this great play.

Hamlet has been the dream role not only of great actors but of great actresses as well. Sarah Bernhardt played Hamlet in the late nineteenth century, and Eva Le Gallienne, Siobhan McKenna, and Judith Anderson took on the part in the twentieth century. *Hamlet* has also given rise to numerous spin-offs, the best of which is Tom Stoppard's *Rosencrantz and Guildenstern Are Dead* (1967). Heiner Müller's *Hamlet-machine* (1977) is a respected avant-garde version of the play. Lee Blessing's *Fortinbras* (1991) is also an innovative retelling of the play from the point of view of a minor character—except that this character becomes the king. Blessing's success suggests that *Hamlet* is rich enough and inspiring enough to generate numerous further redactions and interpretations. Michael Almereyda's 2000 film version of *Hamlet* starred Ethan Hawke as Hamlet, Sam Shepard as the Ghost, Kyle MacLachlan as Claudius, and Bill Murray as Polonius. It is the most recent of many filmed versions of the play.

William Shakespeare (1564–1616)

HAMLET, PRINCE OF DENMARK

c. 1600

[Dramatis Personae

CLAUDIUS, *King of Denmark*
HAMLET, *son to the late King Hamlet, and nephew to the present King*
POLONIUS, *Lord Chamberlain*
HORATIO, *friend to Hamlet*
LAERTES, *son to Polonius*

VOLTIMAND,
CORNELIUS,
ROSENCRANTZ,
GUILDENSTERN,   } *courtiers*
OSRIC,
GENTLEMAN,
PRIEST, OR DOCTOR OF DIVINITY

MARCELLUS,   } *officers*
BERNARDO,   }
FRANCISCO, *a solider*
REYNALDO, *servant to Polonius*
PLAYERS
TWO CLOWNS, *grave-diggers*
FORTINBRAS, *Prince of Norway*
CAPTAIN
ENGLISH AMBASSADORS

GERTRUDE, *Queen of Denmark, mother to Hamlet*
OPHELIA, *daughter to Polonius*

LORDS, LADIES, OFFICERS, SOLDIERS, SAILORS,
    MESSENGERS, and other ATTENDANTS
GHOST *of Hamlet's father*

Scene: Denmark.]

{*ACT I • Scene 1*}°

(*Enter Bernardo and Francisco, two sentinels,* [*meeting*].)

BERNARDO: Who's there?
FRANCISCO: Nay, answer me.° Stand and unfold
    yourself.
BERNARDO: Long live the King!
FRANCISCO: Bernardo?
5 BERNARDO: He.
FRANCISCO: You come most carefully upon your hour.
BERNARDO: 'Tis now struck twelve. Get thee to bed,
    Francisco.
FRANCISCO: For this relief much thanks. 'Tis bitter
    cold,
    And I am sick at heart.
BERNARDO: Have you had quiet guard?
10 FRANCISCO: Not a mouse stirring.
BERNARDO: Well, good night.
    If you do meet Horatio and Marcellus,
    The rivals° of my watch, bid them make haste.

(*Enter Horatio and Marcellus.*)

FRANCISCO: I think I hear them. Stand, ho! Who is there?
HORATIO: Friends to this ground.
15 MARCELLUS: And liegemen to the Dane.°
FRANCISCO: Give you° good night.
MARCELLUS: O, farewell, honest soldier.
    Who hath relieved you?
FRANCISCO: Bernardo hath my place.
    Give you good night.   (*Exit Francisco.*)

Note: The text of *Hamlet* has come down to us in different
versions — such as the first quarto, the second quarto, and the
first Folio. The copy of the text used here is largely drawn from
the second quarto. Passages enclosed in square brackets are
taken from one of the other versions, in most cases the first Folio.
I. I. Location: Elsinore castle. A guard platform.   **2. me:** Francisco emphasizes that *he* is the sentry currently on watch.   **13.
rivals:** Partners.   **15. liegemen to the Dane:** Men sworn to
serve the Danish king.   **16. Give you:** God give you.

MARCELLUS: Holla, Bernardo!
BERNARDO: Say,
    What, is Horatio there?
HORATIO: A piece of him.
BERNARDO: Welcome, Horatio. Welcome, good
    Marcellus.   20
HORATIO: What, has this thing appear'd again tonight?
BERNARDO: I have seen nothing.
MARCELLUS: Horatio says 'tis but our fantasy,
    And will not let belief take hold of him
    Touching this dreaded sight, twice seen of us.   25
    Therefore I have entreated him along
    With us to watch the minutes of this night,
    That if again this apparition come
    He may approve° our eyes and speak to it.
HORATIO: Tush, tush, 'twill not appear.
BERNARDO: Sit down awhile,   30
    And let us once again assail your ears,
    That are so fortified against our story,
    What we have two nights seen.
HORATIO: Well, sit we down,
    And let us hear Bernardo speak of this.
BERNARDO: Last night of all,   35
    When yond same star that's westward from the pole°
    Had made his° course t' illume that part of heaven
    Where now it burns, Marcellus and myself,
    The bell then beating one—

(*Enter Ghost.*)

MARCELLUS: Peace, break thee off! Look where it
    comes again!   40
BERNARDO: In the same figure, like the King that's dead.
MARCELLUS: Thou art a scholar.° Speak to it, Horatio.
BERNARDO: Looks 'a° not like the King? Mark it,
    Horatio.
HORATIO: Most like. It harrows me with fear and
    wonder.
BERNARDO: It would be spoke to.
MARCELLUS: Speak to it,° Horatio.   45
HORATIO: What art thou that usurp'st this time of
    night,
    Together with that fair and warlike form
    In which the majesty of buried Denmark°
    Did sometimes° march? By heaven I charge thee
    speak!
MARCELLUS: It is offended.
BERNARDO: See, it stalks away.   50
HORATIO: Stay! Speak, speak. I charge thee, speak.
                        (*Exit Ghost.*)
MARCELLUS: 'Tis gone, and will not answer.
BERNARDO: How now, Horatio? You tremble and
    look pale.
    Is not this something more than fantasy?
    What think you on 't?   55

29. approve: Corroborate.   **36. pole:** Polestar.   **37. his:** Its.
42. scholar: One learned in Latin and able to address spirits.
43. 'a: He.   **45. It . . . it:** A ghost could not speak until spoken to.   **48. buried Denmark:** The buried king of Denmark.
49. sometimes: Formerly.

HORATIO: Before my God, I might not this believe
  Without the sensible° and true avouch
  Of mine own eyes.
MARCELLUS: Is it not like the King?
HORATIO: As thou art to thyself.
60 Such was the very armor he had on
  When he the ambitious Norway° combated.
  So frown'd he once when, in an angry parle,°
  He smote the sledded° Polacks° on the ice.
  'Tis strange.
MARCELLUS: Thus twice before, and jump° at this
65   dead hour,
  With martial stalk hath he gone by our watch.
HORATIO: In what particular thought to work I know
      not,
  But, in the gross and scope° of mine opinion,
  This bodes some strange eruption to our state.
MARCELLUS: Good now,° sit down, and tell me, he
70   that knows,
  Why this same strict and most observant watch
  So nightly toils° the subject° of the land,
  And why such daily cast° of brazen cannon,
  And foreign mart° for implements of war,
75 Why such impress° of shipwrights, whose sore task
  Does not divide the Sunday from the week.
  What might be toward,° that this sweaty haste
  Doth make the night joint-laborer with the day?
  Who is 't that can inform me?
HORATIO: That can I,
80 At least, the whisper goes so. Our last king,
  Whose image even but now appear'd to us,
  Was, as you know, by Fortinbras of Norway,
  Thereto prick'd on° by a most emulate° pride,
  Dar'd to the combat; in which our valiant
      Hamlet—
  For so this side of our known world esteem'd
85   him—
  Did slay this Fortinbras; who, by a seal'd compact,
  Well ratified by law and heraldry,
  Did forfeit, with his life, all those his lands
  Which he stood seiz'd° of, to the conqueror;
90 Against the° which a moi'ty competent°
  Was gaged° by our king, which had return'd
  To the inheritance of Fortinbras
  Had he been vanquisher, as, by the same comart°
  And carriage° of the article design'd,

His fell to Hamlet. Now, sir, young Fortinbras,   95
  Of unimproved° mettle hot and full,
  Hath in the skirts° of Norway here and there
  Shark'd up° a list of lawless resolutes°
  For food and diet° to some enterprise
  That hath a stomach° in 't, which is no other—   100
  As it doth well appear unto our state—
  But to recover of us, by strong hand
  And terms compulsatory, those foresaid lands
  So by his father lost. And this, I take it,
  Is the main motive of our preparations,   105
  The source of this our watch, and the chief head°
  Of this post-haste and romage° in the land.
BERNARDO: I think it be no other but e'en so.
  Well may it sort° that this portentous figure
  Comes armed through our watch so like the King   110
  That was and is the question of these wars.
HORATIO: A mote° it is to trouble the mind's eye.
  In the most high and palmy° state of Rome,
  A little ere the mightiest Julius fell,
  The graves stood tenantless and the sheeted° dead   115
  Did squeak and gibber in the Roman streets;
  As° stars with trains of fire and dews of blood,
  Disasters° in the sun; and the moist star°
  Upon whose influence Neptune's° empire stands°
  Was sick almost to doomsday° with eclipse.   120
  And even the like precurse° of fear'd events,
  As harbingers° preceding still° the fates
  And prologue to the omen° coming on,
  Have heaven and earth together demonstrated
  Unto our climatures° and countrymen.   125

(*Enter Ghost.*)

  But soft, behold! Lo where it comes again!
  I'll cross° it, though it blast me. Stay, illusion!
  If thou hast any sound, or use of voice,
  Speak to me!   (*It spreads his arms.*)
  If there be any good thing to be done   130
  That may to thee do ease and grace to me,
  Speak to me!
  If thou art privy to thy country's fate,
  Which, happily,° foreknowing may avoid,

57. sensible: Confirmed by the senses. 61. Norway: King of Norway. 62. parle: Parley. 63. sledded: Traveling on sleds. Polacks: Poles. 65. jump: Exactly. 68. gross and scope: General view. 70. Good now: An expression denoting entreaty or expostulation. 72. toils: Causes to toil. subject: Subjects. 73. cast: Casting. 74. mart: Buying and selling. 75. impress: Impressment, conscription. 77. toward: In preparation. 83. prick'd on: Incited. emulate: Ambitious. 89. seiz'd: Possessed. 90. Against the: In return for.... moi'ty competent: Sufficient portion. 91. gaged: Engaged, pledged. 93. comart: Joint bargain (?). 94. carriage: Import, bearing.

96. unimproved: Not turned to account (?) or untested (?). 97. skirts: Outlying regions, outskirts. 98. Shark'd up: Got together in haphazard fashion. resolutes: Desperadoes. 99. food and diet: No pay but their keep. 100. stomach: Relish of danger. 106. head: Source. 107. romage: Bustle, commotion. 109. sort: Suit. 112. mote: Speck of dust. 113. palmy: Flourishing. 115. sheeted: Shrouded. 117. As: This abrupt transition suggests that matter is possibly omitted between lines 116 and 117. 118. Disasters: Unfavorable signs of aspects. moist star: Moon, governing tides. 119. Neptune: God of the sea. stands: Depends. 120. sick . . . doomsday: See Matt. 24.29 and Rev. 6:12. 121. precurse: Heralding, foreshadowing. 122. harbingers: Forerunners. still: Continually. 123. omen: Calamitous event. 125. climatures: Regions. 127. cross: Meet, face directly. 134. happily: Haply, perchance.

135   O, speak!
          Or if thou hast uphoarded in thy life
          Extorted treasure in the womb of earth,
          For which, they say, you spirits oft walk in death,
                                                      (*The cock crows.*)
          Speak of it. Stay, and speak! Stop it, Marcellus.
140   MARCELLUS: Shall I strike at it with my partisan?°
      HORATIO: Do, if it will not stand.   [*They strike at it.*]
      BERNARDO: 'Tis here!
      HORATIO: 'Tis here!
      MARCELLUS: 'Tis gone.   [*Exit Ghost.*]
          We do it wrong, being so majestical,
          To offer it the show of violence;
145   For it is, as the air, invulnerable,
          And our vain blows malicious mockery.
      BERNARDO: It was about to speak when the cock
                  crew.
      HORATIO: And then it started like a guilty thing
          Upon a fearful summons. I have heard,
150   The cock, that is the trumpet to the morn,
          Doth with his lofty and shrill-sounding throat
          Awake the god of day, and, at his warning,
          Whether in sea or fire, in earth or air,
          Th' extravagant and erring° spirit hies
155   To his confine; and of the truth herein
          This present object made probation.°
      MARCELLUS: It faded on the crowing of the cock.
          Some say that ever 'gainst° that season comes
          Wherein our Savior's birth is celebrated,
160   The bird of dawning singeth all night long,
          And then, they say, no spirit dare stir abroad;
          The nights are wholesome, then no planets strike,°
          No fairy takes,° nor witch hath power to charm,
          So hallowed and so gracious° is that time.
165   HORATIO: So have I heard and do in part believe it.
          But, look, the morn, in russet mantle clad,
          Walks o'er the dew of yon high eastward hill.
          Break we our watch up, and by my advice
          Let us impart what we have seen tonight
170   Unto young Hamlet; for, upon my life,
          This spirit, dumb to us, will speak to him.
          Do you consent we shall acquaint him with it,
          As needful in our loves, fitting our duty?
      MARCELLUS: Let's do 't, I pray, and I this morning know
175   Where we shall find him most conveniently.
                                                  (*Exeunt.*)°

{*Scene II*}°

(*Flourish. Enter Claudius, King of Denmark, Gertrude the Queen, Councilors, Polonius and his son Laertes, Hamlet, cum aliis*° [*including Voltimand and Cornelius*].)

---

140. **partisan:** Long-handled spear.   154. **extravagant and erring:** Wandering. (The words have similar meanings.)   156. **probation:** Proof.   158. **'gainst:** Just before.   162. **strike:** Exert evil influence.   163. **takes:** Bewitches.   164. **gracious:** Full of goodness.   175. [S.D.] ***Exeunt:*** Latin for "they go out." I, II. **Location:** The castle.   [S.D.] *cum aliis:* With others.

KING: Though yet of Hamlet our dear brother's death
      The memory be green, and that it us befitted
      To bear our hearts in grief and our whole kingdom
      To be contracted in one brow of woe,
      Yet so far hath discretion fought with nature   5
      That we with wisest sorrow think on him,
      Together with remembrance of ourselves.
      Therefore our sometime sister, now our queen,
      Th' imperial jointress° to this warlike state,
      Have we, as 'twere with a defeated joy—   10
      With an auspicious and a dropping eye,
      With mirth in funeral and with dirge in marriage,
      In equal scale weighing delight and dole—
      Taken to wife. Nor have we herein barr'd
      Your better wisdoms, which have freely gone   15
      With this affair along. For all, our thanks.
      Now follows that you know° young Fortinbras,
      Holding a weak supposal° of our worth,
      Or thinking by our late dear brother's death
      Our state to be disjoint and out of frame,   20
      Colleagued with° this dream of his advantage,°
      He hath not fail'd to pester us with message
      Importing° the surrender of those lands
      Lost by his father, with all bands° of law,
      To our most valiant brother. So much for him.   25
      Now for ourself and for this time of meeting.
      Thus much the business is: we have here writ
      To Norway, uncle of young Fortinbras—
      Who, impotent and bed-rid, scarcely hears
      Of this his nephew's purpose—to suppress   30
      His° further gait° herein, in that the levies,
      The lists, and full proportions are all made
      Out of his subject;° and we here dispatch
      You, good Cornelius, and you, Voltimand,
      For bearers of this greeting to old Norway,   35
      Giving to you no further personal power
      To business with the King, more than the scope
      Of these delated° articles allow.   [*Gives a paper.*]
      Farewell, and let your haste commend your duty.
CORNELIUS, VOLTIMAND: In that, and all things, will
      we show our duty.   40
KING: We doubt it nothing. Heartily farewell.

                  [*Exit Voltimand and Cornelius.*]

      And now, Laertes, what's the news with you?
      You told us of some suit; what is 't, Laertes?
      You cannot speak of reason to the Dane°
      And lose your voice.° What wouldst thou beg,
            Laertes,   45

---

9. **jointress:** Woman possessed of a joint tenancy of an estate. 17. **know:** Be informed (that).   18. **weak supposal:** Low estimate. 21. **Colleagued with:** Joined to, allied with.   **dream . . . advantage:** Illusory hope of success.   23. **Importing:** Pertaining to. 24. **bands:** Contracts.   31. **His:** Fortinbras's.   **gait:** Proceeding. 31–33. **in that . . . subject:** Since the levying of troops and supplies is drawn entirely from the King of Norway's own subjects.   38. **delated:** Detailed. (Variant of *dilated*.)   44. **the Dane:** The Danish king.   45. **lose your voice:** Waste your speech.

That shall not be my offer, not thy asking?
The head is not more native° to the heart,
The hand more instrumental° to the mouth,
Than is the throne of Denmark to thy father.
What wouldst thou have, Laertes?

50 LAERTES: My dread lord,
Your leave and favor to return to France,
From whence though willingly I came to Denmark
To show my duty in your coronation,
Yet now I must confess, that duty done,
55 My thoughts and wishes bend again toward France
And bow them to your gracious leave and pardon.°

KING: Have you your father's leave? What says
    Polonius?

POLONIUS: H'ath, my lord, wrung from me my slow
    leave
By laborsome petition, and at last
60 Upon his will I seal'd my hard° consent.
I do beseech you, give him leave to go.

KING: Take thy fair hour, Laertes. Time be thine,
And thy best graces spend it at thy will!
But now, my cousin° Hamlet, and my son—

65 HAMLET: A little more than kin, and less than kind.°

KING: How is it that the clouds still hang on you?

HAMLET: Not so, my lord. I am too much in the sun.°

QUEEN: Good Hamlet, cast thy nighted color off,
And let thine eye look like a friend on Denmark.
70 Do not forever with thy veiled° lids
Seek for thy noble father in the dust.
Thou know'st 'tis common,° all that lives must die,
Passing through nature to eternity.

HAMLET: Ay, madam, it is common.

QUEEN: If it be,
75 Why seems it so particular with thee?

HAMLET: Seems, madam! Nay, it is. I know not "seems."
'Tis not alone my inky cloak, good mother,
Nor customary suits of solemn black,
Nor windy suspiration of forc'd breath,
80 No, nor the fruitful° river in the eye,
Nor the dejected havior of the visage,
Together with all forms, moods, shapes of grief,
That can denote me truly. These indeed seem,
For they are actions that a man might play.
85 But I have that within which passes show;
These but the trappings and the suits of woe.

KING: 'Tis sweet and commendable in your nature,
    Hamlet,
To give these mourning duties to your father.

But you must know your father lost a father,
That father lost, lost his, and the survivor bound 90
In filial obligation for some term
To do obsequious° sorrow. But to persever°
In obstinate condolement° is a course
Of impious stubbornness. 'Tis unmanly grief.
It shows a will most incorrect to heaven, 95
A heart unfortified, a mind impatient,
An understanding simple and unschool'd.
For what we know must be and is as common
As any the most vulgar thing to sense,°
Why should we in our peevish opposition 100
Take it to heart? Fie, 'tis a fault to heaven,
A fault against the dead, a fault to nature,
To reason most absurd, whose common theme
Is death of fathers, and who still hath cried,
From the first corse° till he that died today, 105
"This must be so." We pray you, throw to earth
This unprevailing° woe, and think of us
As of a father; for let the world take note,
You are the most immediate° to our throne,
And with no less nobility of love 110
Than that which dearest father bears his son
Do I impart toward you. For your intent
In going back to school in Wittenberg,°
It is most retrograde° to our desire,
And we beseech you, bend you° to remain 115
Here in the cheer and comfort of our eye,
Our chiefest courtier, cousin, and our son.

QUEEN: Let not thy mother lose her prayers, Hamlet.
I pray thee stay with us, go not to Wittenberg.

HAMLET: I shall in all my best obey you, madam. 120

KING: Why, 'tis a loving and a fair reply.
Be as ourself in Denmark. Madam, come.
This gentle and unforc'd accord of Hamlet
Sits smiling to my heart, in grace whereof
No jocund° health that Denmark drinks today 125
But the great cannon to the clouds shall tell,
And the King's rouse° the heaven shall bruit again,°
Respeaking earthly thunder.° Come away.

(Flourish. Exeunt all but Hamlet.)

HAMLET: O, that this too too sullied° flesh would melt,
Thaw, and resolve itself into a dew! 130
Or that the Everlasting had not fix'd
His canon° 'gainst self-slaughter! O God, God,
How weary, stale, flat, and unprofitable

---

47. **native:** Closely connected, related. 48. **instrumental:** Serviceable. 56. **leave and pardon:** Permission to depart. 60. **hard:** Reluctant. 64. **cousin:** Any kin not of the immediate family. 65. **A little . . . kind:** Closer than an ordinary nephew (since I am stepson), and yet more separated in natural feeling (with pun on *kind,* meaning affectionate and natural, lawful). This line is often read as an aside, but it need not be. 67. **sun:** The sunshine of the King's royal favor (with pun on *son*). 70. **veiled:** Downcast. 72. **common:** Of universal occurrence. (But Hamlet plays on the sense of *vulgar* in line 74.) 80. **fruitful:** Abundant.

92. **obsequious:** Suited to obsequies or funerals. **persever:** Persevere. 93. **condolement:** Sorrowing. 99. **As . . . sense:** As the most ordinary experience. 105. **corse:** Corpse. 107. **unprevailing:** Unavailing. 109. **most immediate:** Next in succession. 113. **Wittenberg:** Famous German university founded in 1502. 114. **retrograde:** Contrary. 115. **bend you:** Incline yourself. 125. **jocund:** Merry. 127. **rouse:** Draft of liquor. **bruit again:** Loudly echo. 128. **thunder:** Of trumpet and kettledrum sounded when the King drinks; see I, IV, 8–12. 129. **sullied:** Defiled. (The early quartos read *sallied,* the Folio *solid.*) 132. **canon:** Law.

Seem to me all the uses of this world!
135 Fie on 't, ah, fie! 'Tis an unweeded garden
That grows to seed. Things rank and gross in
    nature
Possess it merely.° That it should come to this!
But two months dead—nay, not so much, not two.
So excellent a king, that was to° this
140 Hyperion° to a satyr; so loving to my mother
That he might not beteem° the winds of heaven
Visit her face too roughly. Heaven and earth,
Must I remember? Why, she would hang on him
As if increase of appetite had grown
145 By what it fed on, and yet, within a month—
Let me not think on 't. Frailty, thy name is
    woman!—
A little month, or ere those shoes were old
With which she followed my poor father's body,
Like Niobe,° all tears, why she, even she—
150 O God, a beast, that wants discourse of reason,°
Would have mourn'd longer—married with my
    uncle,
My father's brother, but no more like my father
Than I to Hercules. Within a month,
Ere yet the salt of most unrighteous tears
155 Had left the flushing in her galled° eyes,
She married. O, most wicked speed, to post
With such dexterity to incestuous° sheets!
It is not nor it cannot come to good.
But break, my heart, for I must hold my tongue.

(*Enter Horatio, Marcellus, and Bernardo.*)

HORATIO: Hail to your lordship!
160 HAMLET: I am glad to see you well.
    Horatio!—or I do forget myself.
HORATIO: The same, my lord, and your poor servant
    ever.
HAMLET: Sir, my good friend; I'll change° that name
    with you.
    And what make° you from Wittenberg, Horatio?
165   Marcellus?
MARCELLUS: My good lord.
HAMLET: I am very glad to see you. [*To Bernardo.*]
    Good even, sir.—
    But what, in faith, make you from Wittenberg?
HORATIO: A truant disposition, good my lord.
170 HAMLET: I would not hear your enemy say so,
    Nor shall you do my ear that violence

To make it truster of your own report
Against yourself. I know you are no truant.
But what is your affair in Elsinore?
We'll teach you to drink deep ere you depart.   175
HORATIO: My lord, I came to see your father's
    funeral.
HAMLET: I prithee do not mock me, fellow student;
    I think it was to see my mother's wedding.
HORATIO: Indeed, my lord, it followed hard° upon.
HAMLET: Thrift, thrift, Horatio! The funeral bak'd
    meats   180
    Did coldly furnish forth the marriage tables.
    Would I had met my dearest° foe in heaven
    Or° ever I had seen that day, Horatio!
    My father!—Methinks I see my father.
HORATIO: Where, my lord?
HAMLET: In my mind's eye, Horatio.   185
HORATIO: I saw him once. 'A° was a goodly king.
HAMLET: 'A was a man, take him for all in all,
    I shall not look upon his like again.
HORATIO: My lord, I think I saw him yesternight.
HAMLET: Saw? Who?   190
HORATIO: My lord, the King your father.
HAMLET: The King my father?
HORATIO: Season your admiration° for a while
    With an attent° ear, till I may deliver,
    Upon the witness of these gentlemen,
    This marvel to you.
HAMLET: For God's love, let me hear!   195
HORATIO: Two nights together had these gentlemen,
    Marcellus and Bernardo, on their watch,
    In the dead waste and middle of the night,
    Been thus encount'red. A figure like your father,
    Armed at point° exactly, cap-a-pe,°   200
    Appears before them, and with solemn march
    Goes slow and stately by them. Thrice he walk'd
    By their oppress'd and fear-surprised eyes
    Within his truncheon's° length, whilst they, distill'd
    Almost to jelly with the act° of fear,   205
    Stand dumb and speak not to him. This to me
    In dreadful secrecy impart they did,
    And I with them the third night kept the watch,
    Where, as they had delivered, both in time,
    Form of the thing, each word made true and good,   210
    The apparition comes. I knew your father;
    These hands are not more like.
HAMLET: But where was this?
MARCELLUS: My lord, upon the platform where we
    watch.
HAMLET: Did you not speak to it?
HORATIO: My lord, I did,
    But answer made it none. Yet once methought   215
    It lifted up it° head and did address

---

137. **merely:** Completely. 139. **to:** In comparison to. 140. **Hyperion:** Titan sun-god, father of Helios. 141. **beteem:** Allow. 149. **Niobe:** Tantalus's daughter, Queen of Thebes, who boasted that she had more sons and daughters than Leto; for this, Apollo and Artemis, children of Leto, slew her fourteen children. She was turned by Zeus into a stone that continually dropped tears. 150. **wants . . . reason:** Lacks the faculty of reason. 155. **galled:** Irritated, inflamed. 157. **incestuous:** In Shakespeare's day, the marriage of a man like Claudius to his deceased brother's wife was considered incestuous. 163. **change:** Exchange (i.e., the name of friend). 164. **make:** Do.

179. **hard:** Close. 182. **dearest:** Direst. 183. **Or:** Ere, before. 186. **'A:** He. 192. **Season your admiration:** Restrain your astonishment. 193. **attent:** Attentive. 200. **at point:** Completely. **cap-a-pe:** From head to foot. 204. **truncheon:** Officer's staff. 205. **act:** Action, operation. 216. **it:** Its.

Itself to motion, like as it would speak;
But even then the morning cock crew loud,
And at the sound it shrunk in haste away,
And vanish'd from our sight.

220 HAMLET: 'Tis very strange.
HORATIO: As I do live, my honor'd lord, 'tis true,
And we did think it writ down in our duty
To let you know of it.
HAMLET: Indeed, indeed, sirs. But this troubles me.
Hold you the watch tonight?
225 ALL: We do, my lord.
HAMLET: Arm'd, say you?
ALL: Arm'd, my lord.
HAMLET: From top to toe?
ALL: My lord, from head to foot.
HAMLET: Then saw you not his face?
230 HORATIO: O, yes, my lord. He wore his beaver° up.
HAMLET: What, looked he frowningly?
HORATIO: A countenance more
In sorrow than in anger.
HAMLET: Pale or red?
HORATIO: Nay, very pale.
HAMLET: And fix'd his eyes upon you?
HORATIO: Most constantly.
HAMLET: I would I had been there.
235 HORATIO: It would have much amaz'd you.
HAMLET: Very like, very like. Stay'd it long?
HORATIO: While one with moderate haste might tell°
    a hundred.
MARCELLUS, BERNARDO: Longer, longer.
HORATIO: Not when I saw 't.
HAMLET: His beard was grizzl'd,—no?
240 HORATIO: It was, as I have seen it in his life,
A sable silver'd.°
HAMLET: I will watch tonight.
Perchance 'twill walk again.
HORATIO: I warr'nt it will.
HAMLET: If it assume my noble father's person,
I'll speak to it, though hell itself should gape
245 And bid me hold my peace. I pray you all,
If you have hitherto conceal'd this sight,
Let it be tenable° in your silence still,
And whatsomever else shall hap tonight,
Give it an understanding, but no tongue.
250 I will requite your loves. So, fare you well.
Upon the platform, 'twixt eleven and twelve,
I'll visit you.
ALL: Our duty to your honor.
HAMLET: Your loves, as mine to you. Farewell.
                              (Exeunt [all but Hamlet].)
My father's spirit in arms! All is not well.
I doubt° some foul play. Would the night were
255   come!

Till then sit still, my soul. Foul deeds will rise,
Though all the earth o'erwhelm them, to men's eyes.
                              (Exit.)

{Scene III}°

(Enter Laertes and Ophelia, his sister.)

LAERTES: My necessaries are embark'd. Farewell.
And, sister, as the winds give benefit
And convoy is assistant,° do not sleep
But let me hear from you.
OPHELIA: Do you doubt that?
LAERTES: For Hamlet, and the trifling of his favor,   5
Hold it a fashion and a toy in blood,°
A violet in the youth of primy° nature,
Forward,° not permanent, sweet, not lasting,
The perfume and suppliance° of a minute—
No more.
OPHELIA: No more but so?
LAERTES: Think it no more.   10
For nature crescent° does not grow alone
In thews° and bulk, but, as this temple° waxes,
The inward service of the mind and soul
Grows wide withal.° Perhaps he loves you now,
And now no soil° nor cautel° doth besmirch   15
The virtue of his will;° but you must fear,
His greatness weigh'd,° his will is not his own.
[For he himself is subject to his birth.]
He may not, as unvalued persons do,
Carve° for himself; for on his choice depends   20
The safety and health of this whole state,
And therefore must his choice be circumscrib'd
Unto the voice and yielding° of that body
Whereof he is the head. Then if he says he loves
    you,
It fits your wisdom so far to believe it   25
As he in his particular act and place
May give his saying deed,° which is no further
Than the main voice of Denmark goes withal.
Then weigh what loss your honor may sustain
If with too credent° ear you list° his songs,   30
Or lose your heart, or your chaste treasure open
To his unmaster'd importunity.
Fear it, Ophelia, fear it, my dear sister,
And keep you in the rear of your affection,
Out of the shot° and danger of desire.   35

I, III. Location: Polonius's chambers.   3. convoy is assistant:
Means of conveyance are available.   6. toy in blood: Passing
amorous fancy.   7. primy: In its prime, springtime.   8. Forward: Precocious.   9. suppliance: Supply, filler.   11. crescent:
Growing, waxing.   12. thews: Bodily strength.   temple:
Body.   14. Grows wide withal: Grows along with it.   15.
soil: Blemish.   cautel: Deceit.   16. will: Desire.   17. greatness weigh'd: High position considered.   20. Carve: Choose
pleasure.   23. voice and yielding: Assent, approval.   27.
deed: Effect.   30. credent: Credulous.   list: Listen to.   35.
shot: Range.

230. beaver: Visor on the helmet.   237. tell: Count.   241.
sable silver'd: Black mixed with white.   247. tenable: Held
tightly.   255. doubt: Suspect.

The chariest° maid is prodigal enough
If she unmask her beauty to the moon.
Virtue itself scapes not calumnious strokes.
The canker galls° the infants of the spring
40   Too oft before their buttons° be disclos'd,°
And in the morn and liquid dew° of youth
Contagious blastments° are most imminent.
Be wary then; best safety lies in fear.
Youth to itself rebels, though none else near.
45 OPHELIA: I shall the effect of this good lesson keep
As watchman to my heart. But, good my brother,
Do not, as some ungracious pastors do,
Show me the steep and thorny way to heaven,
Whiles, like a puff'd° and reckless libertine,
50   Himself the primrose path of dalliance treads,
And recks° not his own rede.°

(Enter Polonius.)

LAERTES: O, fear me not.
I stay too long. But here my father comes.
A double blessing is a double° grace;
Occasion° smiles upon a second leave.
POLONIUS: Yet here, Laertes? Aboard, aboard, for
55   shame!
The wind sits in the shoulder of your sail,
And you are stay'd for. There—my blessing with
    thee!
And these few precepts in thy memory
Look thou character.° Give thy thoughts no tongue
60   Nor any unproportion'd thought his° act.
Be thou familiar,° but by no means vulgar.°
Those friends thou hast, and their adoption tried,°
Grapple them to thy soul with hoops of steel,
But do not dull thy palm with entertainment
65   Of each new-hatch'd, unfledg'd courage.° Beware
Of entrance to a quarrel, but, being in,
Bear't that° th' opposed may beware of thee.
Give every man thy ear, but few thy voice;
Take each man's censure,° but reserve thy judgment.
70   Costly thy habit as thy purse can buy,
But not express'd in fancy; rich, not gaudy,
For the apparel oft proclaims the man,
And they in France of the best rank and station
Are of a most select and generous chief° in that.
75   Neither a borrower nor a lender be,
For loan oft loses both itself and friend,
And borrowing dulleth edge of husbandry.°

This above all: to thine own self be true,
And it must follow, as the night the day,
Thou canst not then be false to any man.   80
Farewell. My blessing season° this in thee!
LAERTES: Most humbly do I take my leave, my lord.
POLONIUS: The time invests° you. Go, your servants
   tend.°
LAERTES: Farewell, Ophelia, and remember well
What I have said to you.   85
OPHELIA: 'Tis in my memory lock'd,
And you yourself shall keep the key of it.
LAERTES: Farewell.   (Exit Laertes.)
POLONIUS: What is 't, Ophelia, he hath said to you?
OPHELIA: So please you, something touching the Lord
   Hamlet.   90
POLONIUS: Marry,° well bethought.
'Tis told me he hath very oft of late
Given private time to you, and you yourself
Have of your audience been most free and
   bounteous.
If it be so—as so 'tis put on° me,   95
And that in way of caution—I must tell you
You do not understand yourself so clearly
As it behooves my daughter and your honor.
What is between you? Give me up the truth.
OPHELIA: He hath, my lord, of late made many
   tenders°   100
Of his affection to me.
POLONIUS: Affection? Pooh! You speak like a green
   girl,
Unsifted° in such perilous circumstance.
Do you believe his tenders, as you call them?
OPHELIA: I do not know, my lord, what I should
   think.   105
POLONIUS: Marry, I will teach you. Think yourself a
   baby
That you have ta'en these tenders° for true pay,
Which are not sterling.° Tender° yourself more
   dearly,
Or—not to crack the wind° of the poor phrase,
Running it thus—you'll tender me a fool.°   110
OPHELIA: My lord, he hath importun'd me with love
In honorable fashion.
POLONIUS: Ay, fashion° you may call it. Go to, go to.
OPHELIA: And hath given countenance° to his speech,
   my lord,
With almost all the holy vows of heaven.   115

---

36. chariest: Most scrupulously modest. **39. canker galls:** Cankerworm destroys. **40. buttons:** Buds. **disclos'd:** Opened. **41. liquid dew:** Time when dew is fresh. **42. blastments:** Blights. **49. puff'd:** Bloated. **51. recks:** Heeds. **rede:** Counsel. **53. double:** I.e., Laertes has already bidden his father good-bye. **54. Occasion:** Opportunity. **59. character:** Inscribe. **60. his:** Its. **61. familiar:** Sociable. **vulgar:** Common. **62. tried:** Tested. **65. courage:** Young man of spirit. **67. Bear't that:** Manage it so that. **69. censure:** Opinion, judgment. **74. generous chief:** Noble eminence (?). **77. husbandry:** Thrift.

81. season: Mature. **83. invests:** Besieges.... **tend:** Attend, wait. **91. Marry:** By the Virgin Mary (a mild oath). **95. put on:** Impressed on, told to. **100. tenders:** Offers. **103. Unsifted:** Untried. **107. tenders:** With added meaning here of *promises to pay*. **108. sterling:** Legal currency. **Tender:** Hold. **109. crack the wind:** Run it until it is broken, winded. **110. tender me a fool:** (1) Show yourself to me as a fool, (2) show me up as a fool, (3) present me with a grandchild (*fool* was a term of endearment for a child). **113. fashion:** Mere form, pretense. **114. countenance:** Credit, support.

POLONIUS: Ay, springes° to catch woodcocks.° I do
   know,
   When the blood burns, how prodigal the soul
   Lends the tongue vows. These blazes, daughter,
   Giving more light than heat, extinct in both
120   Even in their promise, as it is a-making,
   You must not take for fire. From this time
   Be something scanter of your maiden presence.
   Set your entreatments° at a higher rate
   Than a command to parle.° For Lord Hamlet,
125   Believe so much in him° that he is young,
   And with a larger tether may he walk
   Than may be given you. In few,° Ophelia,
   Do not believe his vows, for they are brokers,°
   Not of that dye° which their investments° show,
130   But mere implorators° of unholy suits,
   Breathing° like sanctified and pious bawds,
   The better to beguile. This is for all:
   I would not, in plain terms, from this time forth
   Have you so slander° any moment leisure
135   As to give words or talk with the Lord Hamlet.
   Look to 't, I charge you. Come your ways.
OPHELIA: I shall obey, my lord.   (*Exeunt.*)

{*Scene IV*}°

(*Enter Hamlet, Horatio, and Marcellus.*)

HAMLET: The air bites shrewdly; it is very cold.
HORATIO: It is a nipping and an eager air.
HAMLET: What hour now?
HORATIO: I think it lacks of twelve.
MARCELLUS: No, it is struck.
HORATIO: Indeed? I heard it not.
5   It then draws near the season
   Wherein the spirit held his wont to walk.

      (*A flourish of trumpets, and two pieces° go off
                                                [within].*)

   What does this mean, my lord?
HAMLET: The King doth wake° tonight and takes his
   rouse,°
   Keeps wassail,° and the swagg'ring up-spring° reels;

And as he drains his draughts of Rhenish° down,   10
The kettle-drum and trumpet thus bray out
The triumph of his pledge.°
HORATIO: Is it a custom?
HAMLET: Ay, marry, is 't,
   But to my mind, though I am native here
   And to the manner° born, it is a custom   15
   More honor'd in the breach than the observance.°
   This heavy-headed revel east and west°
   Makes us traduc'd and tax'd of° other nations.
   They clepe° us drunkards, and with swinish phrase°
   Soil our addition;° and indeed it takes   20
   From our achievements, though perform'd at
      height,°
   The pith and marrow of our attribute.
   So, oft it chances in particular men,
   That for some vicious mole of nature° in them,
   As in their birth—wherein they are not guilty,   25
   Since nature cannot choose his° origin—
   By the o'ergrowth of some complexion,°
   Oft breaking down the pales° and forts of reason,
   Or by some habit that too much o'er-leavens°
   The form of plausive° manners, that these men,   30
   Carrying, I say, the stamp of one defect,
   Being nature's livery,° or fortune's star,°
   Their virtues else, be they as pure as grace,
   As infinite as man may undergo,
   Shall in the general censure take corruption   35
   From that particular fault. The dram of eale°
   Doth all the noble substance of a doubt°
   To his own scandal.°

(*Enter Ghost.*)

HORATIO: Look, my lord, it comes!
HAMLET: Angels and ministers of grace defend us!
   Be thou a spirit of health° or goblin damn'd,   40
   Bring with thee airs from heaven or blasts from
      hell,
   Be thy intents wicked or charitable,
   Thou com'st in such a questionable° shape

---

116. **springes:** Snares. **woodcocks:** Birds easily caught; here used to connote gullibility. **123. entreatments:** Negotiations for surrender (a military term). **124. parle:** Discuss terms with the enemy. (Polonius urges his daughter, in the metaphor of military language, not to meet with Hamlet and consider giving in to him merely because he requests an interview.) **125. so . . . him:** This much concerning him. **127. In few:** Briefly. **128. brokers:** Go-betweens, procurers. **129. dye:** Color or sort. **investments:** Clothes (i.e., they are not what they seem). **130. mere implorators:** Out-and-out solicitors. **131. Breathing:** Speaking. **134. slander:** Bring disgrace or reproach upon. **I, IV. Location:** The guard platform. **6. [S.D.] pieces:** I.e., of ordnance, cannon. **8. wake:** Stay awake and hold revel. **rouse:** Carouse, drinking bout. **9. wassail:** Carousal. **upspring:** Wild German dance.

10. **Rhenish:** Rhine wine. **12. triumph . . . pledge:** His feat in draining the wine in a single draft. **15. manner:** Custom (of drinking). **16. More . . . observance:** Better neglected than followed. **17. east and west:** I.e., everywhere. **18. tax'd of:** Censured by. **19. clepe:** Call. **with swinish phrase:** By calling us swine. **20. addition:** Reputation. **21. at height:** Outstandingly. **24. mole of nature:** Natural blemish in one's constitution. **26. his:** Its. **27. complexion:** Humor (i.e., one of the four humors or fluids thought to determine temperament). **28. pales:** Palings, fences (as of a fortification). **29. o'er-leavens:** Induces a change throughout (as yeast works in dough). **30. plausive:** Pleasing. **32. nature's livery:** Endowment from nature. **fortune's star:** Mark placed by fortune. **36. dram of eale:** Small amount of evil (?). **37. of a doubt:** A famous crux, sometimes emended to *oft about or often dout,* i.e., often erase or do out, or to *antidote,* counteract. **38. To . . . scandal:** To the disgrace of the whole enterprise. **40. of health:** Of spiritual good. **43. questionable:** Inviting question or conversation.

That I will speak to thee. I'll call thee Hamlet,
45 King, father, royal Dane. O, answer me!
Let me not burst in ignorance, but tell
Why thy canoniz'd° bones, hearsed° in death,
Have burst their cerements;° why the sepulcher
Wherein we saw thee quietly interr'd
50 Hath op'd his ponderous and marble jaws
To cast thee up again. What may this mean,
That thou, dead corse, again in complete steel
Revisits thus the glimpses of the moon,°
Making night hideous, and we fools of nature°
55 So horridly to shake our disposition
With thoughts beyond the reaches of our souls?
Say, why is this? Wherefore? What should we do?
([*Ghost*] *beckons* [*Hamlet*].)
HORATIO: It beckons you to go away with it,
As if it some impartment° did desire
To you alone.
60 MARCELLUS: Look with what courteous action
It waves you to a more removed ground.
But do not go with it.
HORATIO: No, by no means.
HAMLET: It will not speak. Then I will follow it.
HORATIO: Do not, my lord.
HAMLET: Why, what should be the fear?
65 I do not set my life at a pin's fee,°
And for my soul, what can it do to that,
Being a thing immortal as itself?
It waves me forth again. I'll follow it.
HORATIO: What if it tempt you toward the flood, my
lord
70 Or to the dreadful summit of the cliff
That beetles o'er° his° base into the sea,
And there assume some other horrible form
Which might deprive your sovereignty of reason,°
And draw you into madness? Think of it.
75 The very place puts toys of desperation,°
Without more motive, into every brain
That looks so many fathoms to the sea
And hears it roar beneath.
HAMLET: It waves me still.
Go on, I'll follow thee.
MARCELLUS: You shall not go, my lord.
[*They try to stop him.*]
80 HAMLET: Hold off your hands!
HORATIO: Be rul'd, you shall not go.
HAMLET: My fate cries out,
And makes each petty artery° in this body
As hardy as the Nemean lion's° nerve.°

Still am I call'd. Unhand me, gentlemen.
By heaven, I'll make a ghost of him that lets° me!   85
I say, away! Go on. I'll follow thee.
(*Exeunt Ghost and Hamlet.*)
HORATIO: He waxes desperate with imagination.
MARCELLUS: Let's follow. 'Tis not fit thus to obey him.
HORATIO: Have after. To what issue° will this come?
MARCELLUS: Something is rotten in the state of
Denmark.   90
HORATIO: Heaven will direct it.°
MARCELLUS: Nay, let's follow him. (*Exeunt.*)

{*Scene V*}°

(*Enter Ghost and Hamlet.*)

HAMLET: Whither wilt thou lead me? Speak. I'll go
no further.
GHOST: Mark me.
HAMLET: I will.
GHOST: My hour is almost come,
When I to sulph'rous and tormenting flames
Must render up myself.
HAMLET: Alas, poor ghost!
GHOST: Pity me not, but lend thy serious hearing   5
To what I shall unfold.
HAMLET: Speak. I am bound to hear.
GHOST: So art thou to revenge, when thou shalt hear.
HAMLET: What?
GHOST: I am thy father's spirit,   10
Doom'd for a certain term to walk the night,
And for the day confin'd to fast° in fires,
Till the foul crimes° done in my days of nature
Are burnt and purg'd away. But that° I am forbid
To tell the secrets of my prison-house,   15
I could a tale unfold whose lightest word
Would harrow up thy soul, freeze thy young blood,
Make thy two eyes, like stars, start from their
spheres,°
Thy knotted and combined locks° to part,
And each particular hair to stand an end,°   20
Like quills upon the fearful porpentine.°
But this eternal blazon° must not be
To ears of flesh and blood. List, list, O, list!
If thou didst ever thy dear father love—
HAMLET: O God!   25
GHOST: Revenge his foul and most unnatural murder.
HAMLET: Murder?

47. canoniz'd: Buried according to the canons of the church. **hearsed:** Coffined. **48. cerements:** Grave-clothes. **53. glimpses of the moon:** Earth by night. **54. fools of nature:** Mere men, limited to natural knowledge. **59. impartment:** Communication. **65. fee:** Value. **71. beetles o'er:** Overhangs threateningly. **his:** Its. **73. deprive . . . reason:** Take away the rule of reason over your mind. **75. toys of desperation:** Fancies of desperate acts, i.e., suicide. **82. artery:** Sinew. **83. Nemean lion:** One of the monsters slain by Hercules in his twelve labors. **nerve:** Sinew

85. lets: Hinders. **89. issue:** Outcome. **91. it:** The outcome. **I, v. Location:** The battlements of the castle. **12. fast:** Do penance. **13. crimes:** Sins. **14. But that:** Were it not that. **18. spheres:** Eye sockets, here compared to the orbits or transparent revolving spheres in which, according to Ptolemaic astronomy, the heavenly bodies were fixed. **19. knotted . . . locks:** Hair neatly arranged and confined. **20. an end:** On end. **21. fearful porpentine:** Frightened porcupine. **22. eternal blazon:** Revelation of the secrets of eternity.

GHOST: Murder most foul, as in the best it is,
But this most foul, strange, and unnatural.
HAMLET: Haste me to know 't, that I, with wings as
30   swift
As meditation or the thoughts of love,
May sweep to my revenge.
GHOST: I find thee apt;
And duller shouldst thou be than the fat weed
That roots itself in ease on Lethe° wharf,°
35 Wouldst thou not stir in this. Now, Hamlet, hear.
'Tis given out that, sleeping in my orchard,
A serpent stung me. So the whole ear of Denmark
Is by a forged process° of my death
Rankly abus'd.° But know, thou noble youth,
40 The serpent that did sting thy father's life
Now wears his crown.
HAMLET: O my prophetic soul!
My uncle!
GHOST: Ay, that incestuous, that adulterate° beast,
With witchcraft of his wits, with traitorous gifts—
45 O wicked wit and gifts, that have the power
So to seduce!—won to his shameful lust
The will of my most seeming-virtuous queen.
O Hamlet, what a falling-off was there!
From me, whose love was of that dignity
50 That it went hand in hand even with the vow
I made to her in marriage, and to decline
Upon a wretch whose natural gifts were poor
To those of mine!
But virtue, as it never will be moved,
55 Though lewdness court it in a shape of heaven,°
So lust, though to a radiant angel link'd,
Will sate itself in a celestial bed,
And prey on garbage.
But, soft, methinks I scent the morning air.
60 Brief let me be. Sleeping within my orchard,
My custom always of the afternoon,
Upon my secure° hour thy uncle stole,
With juice of cursed hebona° in a vial,
And in the porches of my ears did pour
65 The leprous° distillment, whose effect
Holds such an enmity with blood of man
That swift as quicksilver it courses through
The natural gates and alleys of the body,
And with a sudden vigor it doth posset°
70 And curd, like eager° droppings into milk,
The thin and wholesome blood. So did it mine,
And a most instant tetter° bark'd° about,

Most lazar-like,° with vile and loathsome crust,
All my smooth body.
Thus was I, sleeping, by a brother's hand   75
Of life, of crown, of queen, at once dispatch'd,°
Cut off even in the blossoms of my sin,
Unhous'led,° disappointed,° unanel'd,°
No reck'ning made, but sent to my account
With all my imperfections on my head.   80
O, horrible! O, horrible, most horrible!
If thou hast nature° in thee, bear it not.
Let not the royal bed of Denmark be
A couch for luxury° and damned incest.
But, howsomever thou pursues this act,   85
Taint not thy mind, nor let thy soul contrive
Against thy mother aught. Leave her to heaven
And to those thorns that in her bosom lodge,
To prick and sting her. Fare thee well at once.
The glow-worm shows the matin° to be near,   90
And 'gins to pale his uneffectual fire.°
Adieu, adieu, adieu! Remember me.   [*Exit.*]
HAMLET: O all you host of heaven! O earth! What
    else?
And shall I couple° hell? O fie! Hold, hold, my
    heart,
And you, my sinews, grow not instant old,   95
But bear me stiffly up. Remember thee!
Ay, thou poor ghost, whiles memory holds a seat
In this distracted globe.° Remember thee!
Yea, from the table° of my memory
I'll wipe away all trivial fond° records,   100
All saws° of books, all forms,° all pressures° past
That youth and observation copied there,
And thy commandment all alone shall live
Within the book and volume of my brain,
Unmix'd with baser matter. Yes, by heaven!   105
O most pernicious woman!
O villain, villain, smiling, damned villain!
My tables—meet it is I set it down,
That one may smile, and smile, and be a villain.
At least I am sure it may be so in Denmark.   110
                           [*Writing.*]
So, uncle, there you are. Now to my word;
It is "Adieu, adieu! Remember me."
I have sworn 't.

(*Enter Horatio and Marcellus.*)

HORATIO: My lord, my lord!
MARCELLUS: Lord Hamlet!
HORATIO: Heavens secure him!

---

34. Lethe: The river of forgetfulness in Hades.   **wharf:** Bank.
38. forged process: Falsified account.   **39. abus'd:** Deceived.
43. adulterate: Adulterous.   **55. shape of heaven:** Heavenly
form.   **62. secure:** Confident, unsuspicious.   **63. hebona:** Poison. (The word seems to be a form of *ebony*, though it is
thought perhaps to be related to *henbane*, a poison, or to *ebenus*, yew.)   **65. leprous:** Causing leprosy-like disfigurement.
69. posset: Coagulate, curdle.   **70. eager:** Sour, acid.   **72. tetter:** Eruption of scabs.   **bark'd:** Covered with a rough covering,
like bark on a tree.

73. lazar-like: Leper-like.   **76. dispatch'd:** Suddenly deprived.
78. Unhous'led: Without having received the sacrament [of
Holy Communion].   **disappointed:** Unready (spiritually) for
the last journey.   **unanel'd:** Without having received extreme
unction.   **82. nature:** The promptings of a son.   **84. luxury:**
Lechery.   **90. matin:** Morning.   **91. uneffectual fire:** Cold
light.   **94. couple:** Add.   **98. globe:** Head.   **99. table:** Writing
tablet.   **100. fond:** Foolish.   **101. saws:** Wise sayings.   **forms:**
Images.   **pressures:** Impressions stamped.

115 HAMLET: So be it!
MARCELLUS: Illo, ho, ho, my lord!
HAMLET: Hillo, ho, ho,° boy! Come, bird, come.
MARCELLUS: How is 't, my noble lord?
HORATIO: What news, my lord?
HAMLET: O, wonderful!
HORATIO: Good my lord, tell it.
120 HAMLET: No, you will reveal it.
HORATIO: Not I, my lord, by heaven.
MARCELLUS: Nor I, my lord.
HAMLET: How say you, then, would heart of man
    once think it?
    But you'll be secret?
HORATIO, MARCELLUS: Ay, by heaven, my lord.
HAMLET: There's never a villain dwelling in all
    Denmark
125   But he's an arrant° knave.
HORATIO: There needs no ghost, my lord, come from
    the grave
    To tell us this.
HAMLET: Why, right, you are in the right.
    And so, without more circumstance° at all,
    I hold it fit that we shake hands and part,
130   You, as your business and desire shall point you—
    For every man hath business and desire,
    Such as it is—and for my own poor part,
    Look you, I'll go pray.
HORATIO: These are but wild and whirling words, my
    lord.
135 HAMLET: I am sorry they offend you, heartily;
    Yes, faith, heartily.
HORATIO: There's no offense, my lord.
HAMLET: Yes, by Saint Patrick,° but there is, Horatio,
    And much offense too. Touching this vision here,
    It is an honest° ghost, that let me tell you.
140   For your desire to know what is between us,
    O'ermaster 't as you may. And now, good friends
    As you are friends, scholars, and soldiers,
    Give me one poor request.
HORATIO: What is 't, my lord? We will.
HAMLET: Never make known what you have seen
145   tonight.
HORATIO, MARCELLUS: My lord, we will not.
HAMLET: Nay, but swear 't.
HORATIO: In faith,
    My lord, not I.
MARCELLUS: Nor I, my lord, in faith.
HAMLET: Upon my sword.°   [Holds out his sword.]
MARCELLUS: We have sworn, my lord, already.
HAMLET: Indeed, upon my sword, indeed.
                    (Ghost cries under the stage.)

GHOST: Swear.   150
HAMLET: Ha, ha, boy, say'st thou so? Art thou there,
    truepenny?°
    Come on, you hear this fellow in the cellarage.
    Consent to swear.
HORATIO: Propose the oath, my lord.
HAMLET: Never to speak of this that you have seen,
    Swear by my sword.   155
GHOST [beneath]: Swear.
HAMLET: Hic et ubique?° Then we'll shift our ground.
            [He moves to another spot.]
    Come hither, gentlemen,
    And lay your hands again upon my sword.
    Swear by my sword   160
    Never to speak of this that you have heard.
GHOST [beneath]: Swear by his sword.
HAMLET: Well said, old mole! Canst work i' th' earth
    so fast?
    A worthy pioner!° Once more remove, good friends.
                    [Moves again.]
HORATIO: O day and night, but this is wondrous
    strange!   165
HAMLET: And therefore as a stranger give it welcome.
    There are more things in heaven and earth, Horatio,
    Than are dreamt of in your philosophy.°
    But come;
    Here, as before, never, so help you mercy,   170
    How strange or odd soe'er I bear myself—
    As I perchance hereafter shall think meet
    To put an antic° disposition on—
    That you, at such times seeing me, never shall,
    With arms encumb'red° thus, or this headshake,   175
    Or by pronouncing of some doubtful phrase,
    As "Well, well, we know," or "We could, an if°
    we would,"
    Or "If we list° to speak," or "There be, an if they
    might,"
    Or such ambiguous giving out,° to note°
    That you know aught of me—this do swear,   180
    So grace and mercy at your most need help you.
GHOST [beneath]: Swear.   [They swear.]
HAMLET: Rest, rest, perturbed spirit! So, gentlemen,
    With all my love I do commend me to you;
    And what so poor a man as Hamlet is   185
    May do, t' express his love and friending to you,
    God willing, shall not lack. Let us go in together,
    And still° your fingers on your lips, I pray.
    The time is out of joint. O cursed spite,
    That ever I was born to set it right!   190
            [They wait for him to leave first.]
    Nay, come, let's go together.   (Exeunt.)

117. **Hillo, ho, ho:** A falconer's call to a hawk in air. Hamlet is playing upon Marcellus's *Illo*, i.e., *halloo*. 125. **arrant:** Thoroughgoing. 128. **circumstance:** Ceremony. 137. **Saint Patrick:** The keeper of purgatory and patron saint of all blunders and confusion. 139. **honest:** I.e., a real ghost and not an evil spirit. 148. **sword:** The hilt in the form of a cross.

151. **truepenny:** Honest old fellow. 157. **Hic et ubique:** Here and everywhere (Latin). 164. **pioner:** Pioneer, digger, miner. 168. **your philosophy:** This subject called "natural philosophy" or "science" that people talk about. 173. **antic:** Fantastic. 175. **encumb'red:** Folded or entwined. 177. **an if:** If. 178. **list:** Were inclined. 179. **giving out:** Profession of knowledge. **note:** Give a sign, indicate. 188. **still:** Always.

{*Act II • Scene I*}°

(*Enter old Polonius, with his man* [*Reynaldo*].)

POLONIUS: Give him this money and these notes,
  Reynaldo.
REYNALDO: I will, my lord.
POLONIUS: You shall do marvel's° wisely, good
  Reynaldo,
  Before you visit him, to make inquire
  Of his behavior.
5 REYNALDO: My lord, I did intend it.
POLONIUS: Marry, well said, very well said. Look you,
  sir,
  Inquire me first what Danskers° are in Paris,
  And how, and who, what means,° and where they
  keep,°
  What company, at what expense; and finding
10 By this encompassment° and drift° of question
  That they do know my son, come you more nearer
  Than your particular demands will touch it.°
  Take° you, as 'twere, some distant knowledge of him,
  As thus, "I know his father and his friends,
15 And in part him." Do you mark this, Reynaldo?
REYNALDO: Ay, very well, my lord.
POLONIUS: "And in part him, but," you may say, "not
  well.
  But, if 't be he I mean, he's very wild,
  Addicted so and so," and there put on° him
20 What forgeries° you please—marry, none so rank
  As may dishonor him, take heed of that,
  But, sir, such wanton,° wild, and usual slips,
  As are companions noted and most known
  To youth and liberty.
REYNALDO: As gaming, my lord.
25 POLONIUS: Ay, or drinking, fencing, swearing,
  Quarreling, drabbing°—you may go so far.
REYNALDO: My lord, that would dishonor him.
POLONIUS: Faith, no, as you may season° it in the
  charge.
  You must not put another scandal on him
30 That he is open to incontinency;°
  That's not my meaning. But breathe his faults so
  quaintly°
  That they may seem the taints of liberty,°
  The flash and outbreak of a fiery mind,

A savageness in unreclaimed° blood,
  Of general assault.°
REYNALDO: But, my good lord—   35
POLONIUS: Wherefore should you do this?
REYNALDO: Ay, my lord,
  I would know that.
POLONIUS: Marry, sir, here's my drift,
  And, I believe, it is a fetch of wit.°
  You laying these slight sullies on my son,
  As 'twere a thing a little soil'd i' th' working,°   40
  Mark you,
  Your party in converse,° him you would
  sound,°
  Having ever° seen in the prenominate crimes°
  The youth you breathe° of guilty, be assur'd
  He closes with you in this consequence:°   45
  "Good sir," or so, or "friend," or "gentleman,"
  According to the phrase or the addition°
  Of man and country.
REYNALDO: Very good, my lord.
POLONIUS: And then, sir, does 'a this—'a does—
  what was I about to say?
  By the mass, I was about to say something.   50
  Where did I leave?
REYNALDO: At "closes in the consequence."
POLONIUS: At "closes in the consequence," ay, marry.
  He closes thus: "I know the gentleman;
  I saw him yesterday, or th' other day,
  Or then, or then, with such, or such, and, as you
  say,   55
  There was 'a gaming, there o'ertook in 's rouse,°
  There falling out° at tennis," or perchance,
  "I saw him enter such a house of sale,"
  Videlicet,° a brothel, or so forth. See you now,
  Your bait of falsehood takes this carp° of truth;   60
  And thus do we of wisdom and of reach,°
  With windlasses° and with assays of bias,°
  By indirections find directions° out.
  So by my former lecture and advice
  Shall you my son. You have me, have you not?   65
REYNALDO: My lord, I have.
POLONIUS: God buy ye; fare ye well.
REYNALDO: Good my lord.
POLONIUS: Observe his inclination in yourself.°

---

34. unreclaimed: Untamed. **35. general assault:** Tendency that assails all unrestrained youth. **38. fetch of wit:** Clever trick. **40. soil'd i' th' working:** Shopworn. **42. converse:** Conversation. **sound:** Sound out. **43. Having ever:** If he has ever. **prenominate crimes:** Before-mentioned offenses. **44. breathe:** Speak. **45. closes . . . consequence:** Follows your lead in some fashion as follows. **47. addition:** Title. **56. o'ertook in 's rouse:** Overcome by drink. **57. falling out:** Quarreling. **59. Videlicet:** Namely. **60. carp:** A fish. **61. reach:** Capacity, ability. **62. windlasses:** Circuitous paths (literally, circuits made to head off the game in hunting). **assays of bias:** Attempts through indirection (like the curving path of the bowling ball, which is biased or weighted to one side). **63. directions:** The way things really are. **68. in yourself:** In your own person (as well as by asking questions).

II, I. Location: Polonius's chambers. **3. marvel's:** Marvelous(ly). **7. Danskers:** Danes. **8. what means:** What wealth (they have). **keep:** Dwell. **10. encompassment:** Roundabout talking. **drift:** Gradual approach or course. **11–12. come . . . it:** You will find out more this way than by asking pointed questions (particular demands). **13. Take:** Assume, pretend. **19. put on:** Impute to. **20. forgeries:** Invented tales. **22. wanton:** Sportive, unrestrained. **26. drabbing:** Whoring. **28. season:** Temper, soften. **30. incontinency:** Habitual loose behavior. **31. quaintly:** Delicately, ingeniously. **32. taints of liberty:** Faults resulting from freedom.

REYNALDO: I shall, my lord.
POLONIUS: And let him ply° his music.
70 REYNALDO: Well, my lord.
POLONIUS: Farewell.   (*Exit Reynaldo.*)

(*Enter Ophelia.*)

              How now, Ophelia, what's the matter?
OPHELIA: O, my lord, my lord, I have been so
    affrighted!
POLONIUS: With what, i' th' name of God?
OPHELIA: My lord, as I was sewing in my closet,°
75   Lord Hamlet, with his doublet° all unbrac'd,°
    No hat upon his head, his stockings fouled,
    Ungart'red, and down-gyved to his ankle,°
    Pale as his shirt, his knees knocking each other,
    And with a look so piteous in purport
80   As if he had been loosed out of hell
    To speak of horrors—he comes before me.
POLONIUS: Mad for thy love?
OPHELIA: My lord, I do not know,
    But truly I do fear it.
POLONIUS: What said he?
OPHELIA: He took me by the wrist and held me hard.
85   Then goes he to the length of all his arm,
    And, with his other hand thus o'er his brow
    He falls to such perusal of my face
    As 'a would draw it. Long stay'd he so.
    At last, a little shaking of mine arm
90   And thrice his head thus waving up and down,
    He rais'd a sigh so piteous and profound
    As it did seem to shatter all his bulk°
    And end his being. That done, he lets me go,
    And, with his head over his shoulder turn'd,
95   He seem'd to find his way without his eyes,
    For out o' doors he went without their helps,
    And, to the last, bended their light on me.
POLONIUS: Come, go with me. I will go seek the King.
    This is the very ecstasy° of love
100   Whose violent property° fordoes° itself
    And leads the will to desperate undertakings
    As oft as any passion under heaven
    That does afflict our natures. I am sorry.
    What, have you given him any hard words of late?
105 OPHELIA: No, my good lord, but, as you did command,
    I did repel his letters and denied
    His access to me.
POLONIUS: That hath made him mad.
    I am sorry that with better heed and judgment
    I had not quoted° him. I fear'd he did but trifle
    And meant to wrack thee; but, beshrew my
110   jealousy!°

By heaven, it is as proper to our age°
To cast beyond° ourselves in our opinions
As it is common for the younger sort
To lack discretion. Come, go we to the King.
This must be known, which, being kept close,°
    might move   115
More grief to hide than hate to utter love.°
Come.   (*Exeunt.*)

{*Scene II*}°

(*Flourish. Enter King and Queen, Rosencrantz, and
Guildenstern [with others].*)

KING: Welcome, dear Rosencrantz and Guildenstern.
    Moreover that° we much did long to see you,
    The need we have to use you did provoke
    Our hasty sending. Something have you heard
    Of Hamlet's transformation—so call it,   5
    Sith° nor th' exterior nor° the inward man
    Resembles that° it was. What it should be,
    More than his father's death, that thus hath put him
    So much from th' understanding of himself,
    I cannot dream of. I entreat you both   10
    That, being of so young days° brought up with him,
    And sith so neighbor'd to his youth and havior,
    That you vouchsafe your rest° here in our court
    Some little time, so by your companies
    To draw him on to pleasures, and to gather   15
    So much as from occasion you may glean,
    Whether aught to us unknown afflicts him thus,
    That, open'd,° lies within our remedy.
QUEEN: Good gentlemen, he hath much talk'd of you
    And sure I am two men there is not living   20
    To whom he more adheres. If it will please you
    To show us so much gentry° and good will
    As to expend your time with us awhile
    For the supply and profit° of our hope,
    Your visitation shall receive such thanks   25
    As fits a king's remembrance.
ROSENCRANTZ: Both your Majesties
    Might, by the sovereign power you have of us,
    Put your dread pleasures more into command
    Than to entreaty.

---

70. **let him ply:** See that he continues to study.   74. **closet:** Private chamber.   75. **doublet:** Close-fitting jacket. **unbrac'd:** Unfastened.   77. **down-gyved to his ankle:** Fallen to the ankles (like gyves or fetters).   92. **bulk:** Body.   99. **ecstasy:** Madness.   100. **property:** Nature. **fordoes:** Destroys.   109. **quoted:** Observed.   110. **beshrew my jealousy:** A plague upon my suspicious nature.

111. **proper . . . age:** Characteristic of us (old) men.   112. **cast beyond:** Overshoot, miscalculate.   115. **close:** Secret.   115–16. **might . . . love:** Might cause more grief (to others) by hiding the knowledge of Hamlet's strange behavior to Ophelia than hatred by telling it. **II, II. Location:** The castle.   2. **Moreover that:** Besides the fact that.   6. **Sith:** Since. **nor . . . nor:** Neither . . . nor.   7. **that:** What.   11. **of . . . days:** From such early youth.   13. **vouchsafe your rest:** Please to stay.   18. **open'd:** Revealed.   22. **gentry:** Courtesy.   24. **supply and profit:** Aid and successful outcome.

GUILDENSTERN: But we both obey,
30   And here give up ourselves in the full bent°
      To lay our service freely at your feet,
      To be commanded.
KING: Thanks, Rosencrantz and gentle Guildenstern.
QUEEN: Thanks, Guildenstern and gentle Rosencrantz.
35   And I beseech you instantly to visit
      My too much changed son. Go, some of you,
      And bring these gentlemen where Hamlet is.
GUILDENSTERN: Heavens make our presence and our
          practices
      Pleasant and helpful to him!
QUEEN: Ay, amen!
                        (Exeunt Rosencrantz
                        and Guildenstern [with
                            some Attendants].)

(Enter Polonius.)

POLONIUS: Th' ambassadors from Norway, my good
40   lord,
      Are joyfully return'd.
KING: Thou still° hast been the father of good news.
POLONIUS: Have I, my lord? I assure my good liege
      I hold my duty, as I hold my soul,
45   Both to my God and to my gracious king;
      And I do think, or else this brain of mine
      Hunts not the trail of policy so sure
      As it hath us'd to do, that I have found
      The very cause of Hamlet's lunacy.
50 KING: O, speak of that! That do I long to hear.
POLONIUS: Give first admittance to th' ambassadors.
      My news shall be the fruit° to that great feast.
KING: Thyself do grace to them, and bring them in.
                            (Exit Polonius.)
      He tells me, my dear Gertrude, he hath found
55   The head and source of all your son's distemper.
QUEEN: I doubt° it is no other but the main,°
      His father's death, and our o'erhasty marriage.

(Enter Ambassadors [Voltimand and Cornelius, with
Polonius].)

KING: Well, we shall sift him.—Welcome, my good
          friends!
      Say, Voltimand, what from our brother Norway?
60 VOLTIMAND: Most fair return of greetings and
          desires.
      Upon our first,° he sent out to suppress
      His nephew's levies, which to him appear'd
      To be a preparation 'gainst the Polack,
      But, better look'd into, he truly found
65   It was against your Highness. Whereat griev'd
      That so his sickness, age, and impotence
      Was falsely borne in hand,° sends out arrests

On Fortinbras, which he, in brief, obeys,
Receives rebuke from Norway, and in fine°
Makes vow before his uncle never more   70
To give th' assay° of arms against your Majesty.
Whereon old Norway, overcome with joy,
Gives him three score thousand crowns in annual
      fee,
And his commission to employ those soldiers,
So levied as before, against the Polack,   75
With an entreaty, herein further shown,
                            [Giving a paper.]
That it might please you to give quiet pass
Through your dominions for this enterprise,
On such regards of safety and allowance°
As therein are set down.
KING: It likes° us well;   80
And at our more consider'd° time we'll read,
Answer, and think upon this business.
Meantime we thank you for your well-took labor.
Go to your rest; at night we'll feast together.
Most welcome home!   (Exeunt Ambassadors.)
POLONIUS: This business is well ended. 85
My liege, and madam, to expostulate°
What majesty should be, what duty is,
Why day is day, night night, and time is time,
Were nothing but to waste night, day, and time.
Therefore, since brevity is the soul of wit,°   90
And tediousness the limbs and outward flourishes,
I will be brief. Your noble son is mad.
Mad call I it, for, to define true madness,
What is 't but to be nothing else but mad?
But let that go.
QUEEN: More matter, with less art.   95
POLONIUS: Madam, I swear I use no art at all.
That he is mad, 'tis true; 'tis true 'tis pity,
And pity 'tis 'tis true—a foolish figure,°
But farewell it, for I will use no art.
Mad let us grant him, then, and now remains   100
That we find out the cause of this effect,
Or rather say, the cause of this defect,
For this effect defective comes by cause.°
Thus it remains, and the remainder thus.
Perpend.°   105
I have a daughter—have while she is mine—
Who, in her duty and obedience, mark,
Hath given me this. Now gather, and surmise.
[Reads the letter.] "To the celestial and my soul's
      idol,
the most beautified Ophelia"—   110
That's an ill phrase, a vile phrase; "beautified" is a
      vile

---

30. in . . . bent: To the utmost degree of our capacity.
42. still: Always. 52. fruit: Dessert. 56. doubt: Fear, suspect. main: Chief point, principal concern. 61. Upon our
first: At our first words on the business. 67. borne in hand:
Deluded, taken advantage of.

69. in fine: In the end. 71. assay: Trial. 79. On . . . allowance:
With such pledges of safety and provisos. 80. likes: Pleases.
81. consider'd: Suitable for deliberation. 86. expostulate:
Expound. 90. wit: Sound sense or judgment. 98. figure: Figure of speech. 103. For . . . cause: I.e., for this defective
behavior, this madness has a cause. 105. Perpend: Consider.

phrase. But you shall hear. Thus: [*Reads.*]
"In her excellent white bosom, these, etc."
QUEEN: Came this from Hamlet to her?
POLONIUS: Good madam, stay awhile; I will be
115   faithful.

                                             [*Reads.*]
    "Doubt° thou the stars are fire,
        Doubt that the sun doth move,
    Doubt truth to be a liar,
        But never doubt I love.
120   O dear Ophelia, I am ill at these numbers.° I have
    not art to reckon° my groans. But that I love thee
    best, O most best, believe it. Adieu.
              Thine evermore, most dear lady, whilst this
                  machine° is to him, Hamlet."
125   This in obedience hath my daughter shown me,
    And, more above,° hath his solicitings,
    As they fell out° by time, by means, and place,
    All given to mine ear.
KING: But how hath she
    Receiv'd his love?
POLONIUS: What do you think of me?
130 KING: As of a man faithful and honorable.
POLONIUS: I would fain prove so. But what might you
        think,
    When I had seen this hot love on the wing—
    As I perceiv'd it, I must tell you that,
    Before my daughter told me—what might you,
135   Or my dear Majesty your Queen here, think,
    If I had play'd the desk or table-book,°
    Or given my heart a winking,° mute and dumb,
    Or look'd upon this love with idle sight?°
    What might you think? No, I went round° to work,
140   And my young mistress thus I did bespeak:°
    "Lord Hamlet is a prince, out of thy star;°
    This must not be." And then I prescripts gave her,
    That she should lock herself from his resort,
    Admit no messengers, receive no tokens.
145   Which done, she took the fruits of my advice;
    And he, repelled—a short tale to make—
    Fell into a sadness, then into a fast,
    Thence into a watch,° thence into a weakness,
    Thence to a lightness,° and, by this declension,°
150   Into the madness wherein now he raves,
    And all we mourn for.
KING: Do you think this?
QUEEN: It may be, very like.

POLONIUS: Hath there been such a time—I would
        fain know that—
    That I have positively said "'Tis so,"
    When it prov'd otherwise?
KING: Not that I know.   155
POLONIUS [*pointing to his head and shoulder*]: Take
        this from this, if this be otherwise.
    If circumstances lead me, I will find
    Where truth is hid, though it were hid indeed
    Within the center.°
KING: How may we try it further?
POLONIUS: You know, sometimes he walks four hours
        together   160
    Here in the lobby.
QUEEN: So he does indeed.
POLONIUS: At such a time I'll loose my daughter to
        him.
    Be you and I behind an arras° then.
    Mark the encounter. If he love her not
    And be not from his reason fall'n thereon,°   165
    Let me be no assistant for a state,
    But keep a farm and carters.
KING: We will try it.

(*Enter Hamlet [reading on a book].*)

QUEEN: But look where sadly the poor wretch comes
        reading.
POLONIUS: Away, I do beseech you both, away.
    I'll board° him presently.

        (*Exeunt King and Queen [with Attendants].*)

                  O, give me leave.   170
    How does my good Lord Hamlet?
HAMLET: Well, God-a-mercy.°
POLONIUS: Do you know me, my lord?
HAMLET: Excellent well. You are a fishmonger.°
POLONIUS: Not I, my lord.   175
HAMLET: Then I would you were so honest a man.
POLONIUS: Honest, my lord?
HAMLET: Ay, sir. To be honest, as this world goes, is
    to be one man pick'd out of ten thousand.
POLONIUS: That's very true, my lord.   180
HAMLET: For if the sun breed maggots in a dead dog,
    being a good kissing carrion°—Have you a
    daughter?
POLONIUS: I have, my lord.
HAMLET: Let her not walk i' th' sun.° Conception° is a
    blessing, but as your daughter may conceive, friend, 185
    look to 't.

---

116. **Doubt:** Suspect, question.   120. **ill . . . numbers:** Unskilled at writing verses.   121. **reckon:** (1) Count, (2) number metrically, scan.   124. **machine:** Body.   126. **more above:** Moreover.   127. **fell out:** Occurred.   136. **play'd . . . table-book:** Remained shut up, concealing the information.   137. **winking:** Closing of the eyes.   138. **with idle sight:** Complacently or uncomprehendingly.   139. **round:** Roundly, plainly.   140. **bespeak:** Address.   141. **out of thy star:** Above your sphere, position.   148. **watch:** State of sleeplessness.   149. **lightness:** Light-headedness. **declension:** Decline, deterioration.

---

159. **center:** Middle point of the earth (which is also the center of the Ptolemaic universe).   163. **arras:** Hanging, tapestry.   165. **thereon:** On that account.   170. **board:** Accost.   172. **God-a-mercy:** Thank you.   174. **fishmonger:** Fish merchant (with connotation of *bawd, procurer*[?]).   182. **good kissing carrion:** A good piece of flesh for kissing, or for the sun to kiss.   184. **i' th' sun:** With additional implication of the sunshine of princely favors.   **Conception:** (1) Understanding, (2) pregnancy.

POLONIUS [*aside*]: How say you by that? Still harping on my daughter. Yet he knew me not at first; 'a said I was a fishmonger. 'A is far gone. And truly in my
190 youth I suff'red much extremity for love, very near this. I'll speak to him again.—What do you read, my lord?

HAMLET: Words, words, words.

POLONIUS: What is the matter,° my lord?

195 HAMLET: Between who?

POLONIUS: I mean, the matter that you read, my lord.

HAMLET: Slanders, sir, for the satirical rogue says here that old men have gray beards, that their faces are wrinkled, their eyes purging° thick amber and plum-
200 tree gum, and that they have a plentiful lack of wit, together with most weak hams. All which, sir, though I most powerfully and potently believe, yet I hold it not honesty° to have it thus set down, for you yourself, sir, shall grow old as I am, if like a crab you
205 could go backward.

POLONIUS [*aside*]: Though this be madness, yet there is method in 't.—Will you walk out of the air, my lord?

HAMLET: Into my grave.

POLONIUS: Indeed, that's out of the air. [*Aside.*] How
210 pregnant° sometimes his replies are! A happiness° that often madness hits on, which reason and sanity could not so prosperously° be deliver'd of. I will leave him, [and suddenly contrive the means of meeting between him] and my daughter.—My honorable
215 lord, I will most humbly take my leave of you.

HAMLET: You cannot, sir, take from me any thing that I will more willingly part withal—except my life, except my life, except my life.

(*Enter Guildenstern and Rosencrantz.*)

POLONIUS: Fare you well, my lord.

220 HAMLET: These tedious old fools!°

POLONIUS: You go to seek the Lord Hamlet; there he is.

ROSENCRANTZ [*to Polonius*]: God save you, sir!
                                    [*Exit Polonius.*]

GUILDENSTERN: My honor'd lord!

ROSENCRANTZ: My most dear lord!

225 HAMLET: My excellent good friends! How dost thou, Guildenstern? Ah, Rosencrantz! Good lads, how do you both?

---

194. **matter:** Substance (but Hamlet plays on the sense of *basis for a dispute*). 199. **purging:** Discharging. 203. **honesty:** Decency.

210. **pregnant:** Full of meaning. **happiness:** Felicity of expression. 212. **prosperously:** Successfully. 220. **old fools:** I.e., old men like Polonius.

LEFT: Hamlet returns to Denmark. Left to right, Voltemand (Jeremy Geidt), Gertrude (Christine Estabrook), Claudius (Mark Metcalf), Hamlet (Mark Rylance), and Laertes (Derek Smith) in the 1991 American Repertory Theatre production of *Hamlet*, directed by Ron Daniels. RIGHT: The dumb-show sequence with Candy Buckley as the Player Queen.

ROSENCRANTZ: As the indifferent° children of the earth.
GUILDENSTERN: Happy in that we are not over-happy.
230   On Fortune's cap we are not the very button.
HAMLET: Nor the soles of her shoe?
ROSENCRANTZ: Neither, my lord.
HAMLET: Then you live about her waist, or in the middle of her favors?
235 GUILDENSTERN: Faith, her privates° we.
HAMLET: In the secret parts of Fortune? O, most true; she is a strumpet.° What news?
ROSENCRANTZ: None, my lord, but the world's grown honest.
240 HAMLET: Then is doomsday near. But your news is not true. [Let me question more in particular. What have you, my good friends, deserv'd at the hands of Fortune that she sends you to prison hither?
GUILDENSTERN: Prison, my lord?
245 HAMLET: Denmark's a prison.
ROSENCRANTZ: Then is the world one.
HAMLET: A goodly one, in which there are many confines,° wards,° and dungeons, Denmark being one o' th' worst.
250 ROSENCRANTZ: We think not so, my lord.
HAMLET: Why then 'tis none to you, for there is nothing either good or bad but thinking makes it so. To me it is a prison.
ROSENCRANTZ: Why then, your ambition makes it one.
255   'Tis too narrow for your mind.

HAMLET: O God, I could be bounded in a nutshell and count myself a king of infinite space, were it not that I have bad dreams.
GUILDENSTERN: Which dreams indeed are ambition, for the very substance of the ambitious° is merely the   260
shadow of a dream.
HAMLET: A dream itself is but a shadow.
ROSENCRANTZ: Truly, and I hold ambition of so airy and light a quality that it is but a shadow's shadow.
HAMLET: Then are our beggars bodies,° and our mon-   265
archs and outstretch'd° heroes the beggars' shadows. Shall we to th' court? For, by my fay,° I cannot reason.
ROSENCRANTZ, GUILDENSTERN: We'll wait upon° you.
HAMLET: No such matter. I will not sort° you with the   270
rest of my servants, for, to speak to you like an honest man, I am most dreadfully attended.°] But, in the beaten way° of friendship, what make° you at Elsinore?
ROSENCRANTZ: To visit you, my lord, no other occasion.   275
HAMLET: Beggar that I am, I am even poor in thanks; but I thank you, and sure, dear friends, my thanks are too dear a halfpenny.° Were you not sent for? Is it your own inclining? Is it a free visitation? Come, come, deal justly with me. Come, come; nay, speak.   280

228. indifferent: Ordinary. 235. privates: Close acquaintances (with sexual pun on *private parts*). 237. strumpet: Prostitute (a common epithet for indiscriminate Fortune, see line 497 p. 360). 247–48. confines: Places of confinement. 248. wards: Cells.

260. the very . . . ambitious: That seemingly very substantial thing which the ambitious pursue. 265. bodies: Solid substances rather than shadows (since beggars are not ambitious). 266. outstretch'd: (1) Far-reaching in their ambition, (2) elongated as shadows. 267. fay: Faith. 269. wait upon: Accompany, attend. 270. sort: Class, associate. 272. dreadfully attended: Waited upon in slovenly fashion. 273. beaten way: Familiar path. make: Do. 278. dear a halfpenny: Expensive at the price of a halfpenny, i.e., of little worth.

GUILDENSTERN: What should we say, my lord?

HAMLET: Why, anything, but to th' purpose. You were sent for; and there is a kind of confession in your looks which your modesties have not craft enough to color. I know the good King and Queen have sent for you.

285

ROSENCRANTZ: To what end, my lord?

HAMLET: That you must teach me. But let me conjure° you, by the rights of our fellowship, by the consonancy of our youth,° by the obligation of our ever-preserv'd love, and by what more dear a better proposer° could charge° you withal, be even° and direct with me, whether you were sent for, or no?

290

ROSENCRANTZ [aside to Guildenstern]: What say you?

HAMLET [aside]: Nay then, I have an eye of° you.—If you love me, hold not off.

295

GUILDENSTERN: My lord, we were sent for.

HAMLET: I will tell you why; so shall my anticipation prevent your discovery,° and your secrecy to the King and Queen molt no feather.° I have of late—but wherefore I know not—lost all my mirth, forgone all custom of exercises; and indeed it goes so heavily with my disposition that this goodly frame, the earth, seems to me a sterile promontory; this most excellent canopy, the air, look you, this brave° o'erhanging firmament, this majestical roof fretted° with golden fire, why, it appeareth nothing to me but a foul and pestilent congregation of vapors. What a piece of work is a man! How noble in reason, how infinite in faculties, in form and moving how express° and admirable, in action how like an angel, in apprehension how like a god! The beauty of the world, the paragon of animals! And yet, to me, what is this quintessence° of dust? Man delights not me—no, nor woman neither, though by your smiling you seem to say so.

300

305

310

315

ROSENCRANTZ: My lord, there was no such stuff in my thoughts.

HAMLET: Why did you laugh then, when I said "man delights not me"?

320

ROSENCRANTZ: To think, my lord, if you delight not in man, what lenten entertainment° the players shall receive from you. We coted° them on the way, and hither are they coming, to offer you service.

HAMLET: He that plays the king shall be welcome; his Majesty shall have tribute of me. The adventurous

325

knight shall use his foil and target,° the lover shall not sigh gratis, the humorous man° shall end his part in peace, [the clown shall make those laugh whose lungs are tickle o' th' sere°], and the lady shall say her mind freely, or the blank verse shall halt° for 't. What players are they?

330

ROSENCRANTZ: Even those you were wont to take such delight in, the tragedians of the city.

HAMLET: How chances it they travel? Their residence,° both in reputation and profit, was better both ways.

335

ROSENCRANTZ: I think their inhibition° comes by the means of the innovation.°

HAMLET: Do they hold the same estimation they did when I was in the city? Are they so follow'd?

ROSENCRANTZ: No, indeed, are they not.

340

[HAMLET: How comes it? Do they grow rusty?

ROSENCRANTZ: Nay, their endeavor keeps in the wonted° pace. But there is, sir, an aery° of children, little eyases,° that cry out on the top of question,° and are most tyrannically° clapp'd for 't. These are now the fashion, and so berattle° the common stages°—so they call them—that many wearing rapiers° are afraid of goose-quills° and dare scarce come thither.

345

HAMLET: What, are they children? Who maintains 'em? How are they escoted?° Will they pursue the quality° no longer than they can sing?° Will they not say afterwards, if they should grow themselves to common° players—as it is most like, if their means are no better—their writers do them wrong, to make them exclaim against their own succession?°

350

355

ROSENCRANTZ: Faith, there has been much to do° on both sides, and the nation holds it no sin to tarre° them to controversy. There was, for a while, no money bid for argument° unless the poet and the player went to cuffs in the question.°

360

HAMLET: Is 't possible?

---

288. conjure: Adjure, entreat.   289–90. consonancy of our youth: The fact that we are of the same age.   291–92. better proposer: More skillful propounder.   292. charge: Urge.   even: Straight, honest.   295. of: On.   299. prevent your discovery: Forestall your disclosure.   300. molt no feather: Not diminish in the least.   305. brave: Splendid.   306. fretted: Adorned (with fret-work, as in a vaulted ceiling).   310. express: Well-framed (?), exact (?).   313. quintessence: The fifth essence of ancient philosophy, beyond earth, water, air, and fire, supposed to be the substance of the heavenly bodies and to be latent in all things.   321. lenten entertainment: Meager reception (appropriate to Lent).   322. coted: Overtook and passed beyond.

326. foil and target: Sword and shield.   327. humorous man: Eccentric character, dominated by one trait or "humor."   329. tickle o' th' sere: Easy on the trigger, ready to laugh easily. (Sere is part of a gunlock.)   330. halt: Limp.   334. residence: Remaining in one place, i.e., in the city.   336. inhibition: Formal prohibition (from acting plays in the city).   337. innovation: I.e., the new fashion in satirical plays performed by boy actors in the "private" theaters; or possibly a political uprising; or the strict limitations set on the theater in London in 1600.   343. wonted: Usual.   aery: Nest.   344. eyases: Young hawks.   cry . . . question: Speak shrilly, dominating the controversy (in decrying the public theaters).   345. tyrannically: Outrageous.   346. berattle: Berate.   346–47. common stages: Public theaters.   347–48. many wearing rapiers: Many men of fashion, who were afraid to patronize the common players for fear of being satirized by the poets who wrote for the children.   348. goose-quills: Pens of satirists.   351. escoted: Maintained.   quality: (Acting) profession.   352. no longer . . . sing: Only until their voices change.   353–54. common: Regular, adult.   356. succession: Future careers.   357. to do: Ado.   358. tarre: Set on (as dogs).   360. argument: Plot for a play.   361. went . . . question: Came to blows in the play itself.

GUILDENSTERN: O, there has been much throwing about of brains.

365 HAMLET: Do the boys carry it away?°

ROSENCRANTZ: Ay, that they do, my lord—Hercules and his load° too.°]

HAMLET: It is not very strange, for my uncle is King of Denmark, and those that would make mouths° at
370 him while my father liv'd, give twenty, forty, fifty, a hundred ducats° apiece for his picture in little.° 'Sblood,° there is something in this more than natural, if philosophy could find it out.

(*A flourish [of trumpets within].*)

GUILDENSTERN: There are the players.

375 HAMLET: Gentlemen, you are welcome to Elsinore. Your hands, come then. Th' appurtenance of welcome is fashion and ceremony. Let me comply° with you in this garb,° lest my extent° to the players, which, I tell you, must show fairly outwards,° should more appear
380 like entertainment° than yours. You are welcome. But my uncle-father and aunt-mother are deceiv'd.

GUILDENSTERN: In what, my dear lord?

HAMLET: I am but mad north-north-west.° When the wind is southerly I know a hawk from a handsaw.°

(*Enter Polonius.*)

385 POLONIUS: Well be with you, gentlemen!

HAMLET: Hark you, Guildenstern, and you too; at each ear a hearer. That great baby you see there is not yet out of his swaddling-clouts.°

ROSENCRANTZ: Happily° he is the second time come to
390 them; for they say an old man is twice a child.

HAMLET: I will prophesy he comes to tell me of the players; mark it.—You say right, sir, o' Monday morning, 'twas then indeed.

POLONIUS: My lord, I have news to tell you.

395 HAMLET: My lord, I have news to tell you. When Roscius° was an actor in Rome—

POLONIUS: The actors are come hither, my lord.

HAMLET: Buzz,° buzz!

POLONIUS: Upon my honor—

HAMLET: Then came each actor on his ass— 400

POLONIUS: The best actors in the world, either for tragedy, comedy, history, pastoral, pastoral-comical, historical-pastoral, tragical-historical, tragical-comical-historical-pastoral, scene individable,° or poem
405 unlimited.° Seneca° cannot be too heavy, nor Plautus° too light. For the law of writ and the liberty,° these are the only men.

HAMLET: O Jephthah, judge of Israel,° what a treasure hadst thou!

POLONIUS: What a treasure had he, my lord? 410

HAMLET: Why,

"One fair daughter, and no more,

The which he loved passing° well."

POLONIUS [*aside*]: Still on my daughter.

HAMLET: Am I not i' th' right, old Jephthah? 415

POLONIUS: If you call me Jephthah, my lord, I have a daughter that I love passing well.

HAMLET: Nay, that follows not.

POLONIUS: What follows, then, my lord?

HAMLET: Why, 420

"As by lot, God wot,"°

and then, you know,

"It came to pass, as most like° it was."

The first row° of the pious chanson° will show you more, for look where my abridgement° comes. 425

(*Enter the Players.*)

You are welcome, masters; welcome, all. I am glad to see thee well. Welcome, good friends. O, old friend! Why, thy face is valanc'd° since I saw thee last. Com'st thou to beard° me in Denmark? What,
my young lady° and mistress? By 'r lady, your 430
ladyship is nearer to heaven than when I saw you last, by the altitude of a chopine.° Pray God your voice, like a piece of uncurrent° gold, be not crack'd within the ring.° Masters, you are all welcome. We'll e'en to 't like French falconers, fly at anything 435
we see. We'll have a speech straight.° Come, give us a taste of your quality; come, a passionate speech.

---

365. carry it away: Win the day. **366–67. Hercules . . . load:** Thought to be an allusion to the sign of the Globe Theatre, which was Hercules bearing the world on his shoulder. **341–67. How . . . load too:** The passage, omitted from the early quartos, alludes to the so-called War of the Theatres, 1599–1602, the rivalry between the children companies and the adult actors. **369. mouths:** Faces. **371. ducats:** Gold coins. **in little:** In miniature. **372. 'Sblood:** By His (God's, Christ's) blood. **377. comply:** Observe the formalities of courtesy. **378. garb:** Manner. **my extent:** The extent of my showing courtesy. **379. show fairly outwards:** Look cordial to outward appearances. **380. entertainment:** A (warm) reception. **383. north-north-west:** Only partly, at times. **384. hawk, handsaw:** Mattock (or *hack*) and a carpenter's cutting tool, respectively; also birds, with a play on *hernshaw* or heron. **388. swaddling-clouts:** Cloths in which to wrap a newborn baby. **389. Happily:** Haply, perhaps. **396. Roscius:** A famous Roman actor who died in 62 BCE. **398. Buzz:** An interjection used to denote stale news.

404. scene individable: A play observing the unity of place. **404–05. poem unlimited:** A play disregarding the unities of time and place. **405. Seneca:** Writer of Latin tragedies. **405–06. Plautus:** Writer of Latin comedy. **406. law . . . liberty:** Dramatic composition both according to rules and without rules, i.e., "classical" and "romantic" dramas. **408. Jephthah . . . Israel:** Jephthah had to sacrifice his daughter; see Judges 11. Hamlet goes on to quote from a ballad on the theme. **413. passing:** Surpassingly. **421. wot:** Knows. **423. like:** Likely, probable. **424. row:** Stanza. **chanson:** Ballad, song. **425. my abridgement:** Something that cuts short my conversation; also, a diversion. **428. valanc'd:** Fringed (with a beard). **429. beard:** Confront (with obvious pun). **430. young lady:** Boy playing women's parts. **432. chopine:** Thick-soled shoe of Italian fashion. **433. uncurrent:** Not passable as lawful coinage. **433–34. crack'd . . . ring:** Changed from adolescent to male voice, no longer suitable for women's roles. (Coins featured rings enclosing the sovereign's head; if the coin was cracked within this ring, it was unfit for currency.) **436. straight:** At once.

FIRST PLAYER: What speech, my good lord?

HAMLET: I heard thee speak me a speech once, but it
440 was never acted, or, if it was, not above once, for the
     play, I remember, pleas'd not the million; 'twas
     caviary to the general.° But it was—as I receiv'd it,
     and others, whose judgments in such matters cried in
     the top of° mine—an excellent play, well digested
445 in the scenes, set down with as much modesty as
     cunning.° I remember one said there were no sallets°
     in the lines to make the matter savory, nor no matter
     in the phrase that might indict° the author of affecta-
     tion, but call'd it an honest method, as wholesome as
450 sweet, and by very much more handsome than fine.°
     One speech in 't I chiefly lov'd: 'twas Aeneas' tale to
     Dido, and thereabout of it especially when he speaks
     of Priam's slaughter.° If it live in your memory, begin
     at this line: let me see, let me see—
455 "The rugged Pyrrhus,° like th' Hyrcanian beast"°—
     'Tis not so. It begins with Pyrrhus:
     "The rugged Pyrrhus, he whose sable° arms,
     Black as his purpose, did the night resemble
     When he lay couched in the ominous horse,°
460 Hath now this dread and black complexion
        smear'd
     With heraldry more dismal.° Head to foot
     Now is he total gules,° horridly trick'd°
     With blood of fathers, mothers, daughters, sons,
     Bak'd and impasted° with the parching streets,°
465 That lend a tyrannous and a damned light
     To their lord's° murder. Roasted in wrath and fire,
     And thus o'er-sized° with coagulate gore,
     With eyes like carbuncles, the hellish Pyrrhus
     Old grandsire Priam seeks."
470 So proceed you.

POLONIUS: 'Fore God, my lord, well spoken, with good
     accent and good discretion.

FIRST PLAYER: "Anon he finds him
     Striking too short at Greeks. His antique sword,
     Rebellious to his arm, lies where it falls,
475 Repugnant° to command. Unequal match'd,

Pyrrhus at Priam drives, in rage strikes wide,
But with the whiff and wind of his fell° sword
Th' unnerved father falls. [Then senseless Ilium,°]
Seeming to feel this blow, with flaming top
Stoops to his° base, and with a hideous crash   480
Takes prisoner Pyrrhus' ear. For, lo! His sword,
Which was declining on the milky head
Of reverend Priam, seem'd i' th' air to stick.
So as a painted° tyrant Pyrrhus stood,
And, like a neutral to his will and matter,°   485
Did nothing.
But, as we often see, against° some storm,
A silence in the heavens, the rack° stand still,
The bold winds speechless, and the orb below
As hush as death, anon the dreadful thunder   490
Doth rend the region,° so, after Pyrrhus' pause,
Aroused vengeance sets him new a-work,
And never did the Cyclops'° hammers fall
On Mars's armor forg'd for proof eterne°
With less remorse than Pyrrhus' bleeding sword   495
Now falls on Priam.
Out, out, thou strumpet Fortune! All you gods,
In general synod,° take away her power!
Break all the spokes and fellies° from her wheel,
And bowl the round nave° down the hill of
   heaven,   500
As low as to the fiends!"

POLONIUS: This is too long.

HAMLET: It shall to the barber's with your beard.—
     Prithee say on. He's for a jig° or a tale of bawdry, or
     he sleeps. Say on, come to Hecuba.°   505

FIRST PLAYER: "But who, ah woe! had seen the
        mobled° queen"—

HAMLET: "The mobled queen?"

POLONIUS: That's good. "Mobled queen" is good.

FIRST PLAYER: "Run barefoot up and down, threat'ning
        the flames
     With bisson rheum,° a clout° upon that head   510
     Where late the diadem stood, and for a robe,
     About her lank and all o'er-teemed° loins,
     A blanket, in the alarm of fear caught up—
     Who this had seen, with tongue in venom steep'd,
     'Gainst Fortune's state° would treason have
        pronounc'd.°   515
     But if the gods themselves did see her then

---

442. **caviary to the general:** Caviar to the multitude, i.e., a choice dish too elegant for coarse tastes. 443–44. **cried in the top of:** Spoke with greater authority than. 446. **cunning:** Skill. **sallets:** Salad, i.e., spicy improprieties. 448. **indict:** Convict. 450. **fine:** Elaborately ornamented, showy. 453. **Priam's slaughter:** The slaying of the ruler of Troy, when the Greeks finally took the city. 455. **Pyrrhus:** A Greek hero in the Trojan War, also known as Neoptolemus, son of Achilles. **Hyrcanian beast:** I.e., the tiger. (See Virgil, *Aeneid*, IV, 266; compare the whole speech with Marlowe's *Dido Queen of Carthage*, II, I, 214 ff.) 457. **sable:** Black (for reasons of camouflage during the episode of the Trojan horse). 459. **ominous horse:** Trojan horse, by which the Greeks gained access to Troy. 461. **dismal:** Ill-omened. 462. **gules:** Red (a heraldic term). **trick'd:** Adorned, decorated. 464. **impasted:** Crusted, like a thick paste. **with . . . streets:** By the parching heat of the streets (because of the fires everywhere). 466. **their lord's:** Priam's. 467. **o'er-sized:** Covered as with size or glue. 475. **Repugnant:** Disobedient, resistant.

477. **fell:** Cruel. 478. **senseless Ilium:** Insensate Troy. 480. **his:** Its. 484. **painted:** Painted in a picture. 485. **like . . . matter:** As though poised indecisively between his intention and its fulfillment. 487. **against:** Just before. 488. **rack:** Mass of clouds. 491. **region:** Sky. 493. **Cyclops:** Giant armor makers in the smithy of Vulcan. 494. **proof eterne:** Eternal resistance to assault. 498. **synod:** Assembly. 499. **fellies:** Pieces of wood forming the rim of a wheel. 500. **nave:** Hub. 504. **jig:** Comic song and dance often given at the end of a play. 505. **Hecuba:** Wife of Priam. 506. **mobled:** Muffled. 510. **bisson rheum:** Blinding tears. **clout:** Cloth. 512. **o'er-teemed:** Worn out with bearing children. 515. **state:** Rule, managing. **pronounc'd:** Proclaimed.

When she saw Pyrrhus make malicious sport
In mincing with his sword her husband's limbs,
The instant burst of clamor that she made,
520   Unless things mortal move them not at all,
Would have made milch° the burning eyes of
        heaven,
And passion in the gods."
POLONIUS: Look whe'er° he has not turn'd his color and
has tears in 's eyes. Prithee, no more.
525   HAMLET: 'Tis well; I'll have thee speak out the rest of
this soon. Good my lord, will you see the players well
bestow'd?° Do you hear, let them be well us'd, for
they are the abstract° and brief chronicles of the
time. After your death you were better have a bad
530   epitaph than their ill report while you live.
POLONIUS: My lord, I will use them according to their
desert.
HAMLET: God's bodkin,° man, much better! Use every
man after his desert, and who shall scape whipping?
535   Use them after your own honor and dignity. The less
they deserve, the more merit is in your bounty. Take
them in.
POLONIUS: Come, sirs.
HAMLET: Follow him, friends. We'll hear a play tomor-
540   row. [*As they start to leave, Hamlet detains the First
Player.*] Dost thou hear me, old friend? Can you play
the Murder of Gonzago?
FIRST PLAYER: Ay, my lord.
HAMLET: We'll ha 't tomorrow night. You could, for
545   need, study a speech of some dozen or sixteen lines,
which I would set down and insert in 't, could you
not?
FIRST PLAYER: Ay, my lord.
HAMLET: Very well. Follow that lord, and look you
550   mock him not.—My good friends, I'll leave you till
night. You are welcome to Elsinore.
                        (*Exeunt Polonius and Players.*)
ROSENCRANTZ: Good my lord!
                  (*Exeunt [Rosencrantz and Guildenstern].*)
HAMLET: Ay, so, God buy you.—Now I am alone.
O, what a rogue and peasant slave am I!
555   Is it not monstrous that this player here,
But in a fiction, in a dream of passion,
Could force his soul so to his own conceit°
That from her working all his visage wann'd,°
Tears in his eyes, distraction in his aspect,
560   A broken voice, and his whole function suiting
With forms to his conceit?° And all for nothing!
For Hecuba!
What's Hecuba to him, or he to Hecuba,

That he should weep for her? What would he do,
Had he the motive and the cue for passion   565
That I have? He would drown the stage with tears
And cleave the general ear with horrid speech,
Make mad the guilty and appall the free,°
Confound the ignorant, and amaze indeed
The very faculties of eyes and ears. Yet I,   570
A dull and muddy-mettled° rascal, peak,°
Like John-a-dreams,° unpregnant of° my cause,
And can say nothing—no, not for a king
Upon whose property° and most dear life
A damn'd defeat was made. Am I a coward?   575
Who calls me villain? Breaks my pate across?
Plucks off my beard, and blows it in my face?
Tweaks me by the nose? Gives me the lie° i' th'
        throat,
As deep as to the lungs? Who does me this?
Ha, 'swounds, I should take it; for it cannot be   580
But I am pigeon-liver'd,° and lack gall
To make oppression bitter, or ere this
I should have fatted all the region kites°
With this slave's offal. Bloody, bawdy villain!
Remorseless, treacherous, lecherous, kindless° villain!   585
[O, vengeance!]
Why, what an ass am I! This is most brave,
That I, the son of a dear father murder'd,
Prompted to my revenge by heaven and hell,
Must, like a whore, unpack my heart with words,   590
And fall a-cursing, like a very drab,°
A stallion!° Fie upon 't, foh! About,° my brains!
Hum, I have heard
That guilty creatures sitting at a play
Have by the very cunning of the scene   595
Been struck so to the soul that presently°
They have proclaim'd their malefactions;
For murder, though it have no tongue, will speak
With most miraculous organ. I'll have these
        players
Play something like the murder of my father   600
Before mine uncle. I'll observe his looks;
I'll tent° him to the quick. If 'a do blench,°
I know my course. The spirit that I have seen
May be the devil, and the devil hath power
T' assume a pleasing shape; yea, and perhaps   605
Out of my weakness and my melancholy,
As he is very potent with such spirits,°

520. **milch:** Milky moist with tears.   523. **whe'er:** Whether.
527. **bestow'd:** Lodged.   528. **abstract:** Summary account.
533. **God's bodkin:** By God's (Christ's) little body, *bodykin* (not
to be confused with *bodkin,* dagger).   557. **conceit:** Conception.   558. **wann'd:** Grew pale.   560–61. **his whole . . . conceit:** His whole being responded with actions to suit his thought.

568. **free:** Innocent.   571. **muddy-mettled:** Dull-spirited.
peak: Mope, pine.   572. **John-a-dreams:** Sleepy dreaming
idler.   **unpregnant of:** Not quickened by.   574. **property:** The
crown; perhaps also character, quality.   578. **Gives me the lie:**
Calls me a liar.   581. **pigeon-liver'd:** The pigeon or dove was
popularly supposed to be mild because it secreted no gall.
583. **region kites:** Kites (birds of prey) of the air, from the vicinity.   585. **kindless:** Unnatural.   591. **drab:** Prostitute.
592. **stallion:** Prostitute (male or female). (Many editors follow
the Folio reading of *scullion.*)   **About:** About it, to work.
596. **presently:** At once.   602. **tent:** Probe.   **blench:** Quail,
flinch.   607. **spirits:** Humors (of melancholy).

Abuses° me to damn me. I'll have grounds
More relative° than this. The play's the thing
610 Wherein I'll catch the conscience of the King.
                                              (*Exit.*)

{*ACT III • Scene 1*}°

(*Enter King, Queen, Polonius, Ophelia, Rosencrantz,
Guildenstern, Lords.*)

KING: And can you, by no drift of conference,°
    Get from him why he puts on this confusion,
    Grating so harshly all his days of quiet
    With turbulent and dangerous lunacy?
ROSENCRANTZ: He does confess he feels himself
5   distracted,
    But from what cause 'a will by no means speak.
GUILDENSTERN: Nor do we find him forward° to be
        sounded,°
    But with a crafty madness keeps aloof
    When we would bring him on to some confession
    Of his true state.
10 QUEEN: Did he receive you well?
ROSENCRANTZ: Most like a gentleman.
GUILDENSTERN: But with much forcing of his
        disposition.°
ROSENCRANTZ: Niggard of question,° but of our
        demands
    Most free in his reply.
QUEEN: Did you assay° him
15   To any pastime?
ROSENCRANTZ: Madam, it so fell out that certain
        players
    We o'er-raught° on the way. Of these we told him,
    And there did seem in him a kind of joy
    To hear of it. They are here about the court,
20   And, as I think, they have already order
    This night to play before him.
POLONIUS: 'Tis most true,
    And he beseech'd me to entreat your Majesties
    To hear and see the matter.
KING: With all my heart, and it doth much content me
25   To hear him so inclin'd.
    Good gentlemen, give him a further edge,°
    And drive his purpose into these delights.
ROSENCRANTZ: We shall, my lord.
                    (*Exeunt Rosencrantz and Guildenstern.*)
KING: Sweet Gertrude, leave us too,
    For we have closely° sent for Hamlet hither,
30   That he, as 'twere by accident, may here

Affront° Ophelia.
    Her father and myself, [lawful espials,°]
    Will so bestow ourselves that seeing, unseen,
    We may of their encounter frankly judge,
    And gather by him, as he is behav'd,   35
    If 't be th' affliction of his love or no
    That thus he suffers for.
QUEEN: I shall obey you.
    And for your part, Ophelia, I do wish
    That your good beauties be the happy cause
    Of Hamlet's wildness. So shall I hope your virtues   40
    Will bring him to his wonted way again,
    To both your honors.
OPHELIA: Madam, I wish it may.
                                        [*Exit Queen.*]
POLONIUS: Ophelia, walk you here.—Gracious,° so
        please you,
    We will bestow ourselves. [*To Ophelia.*] Read on
        this book,   [*Gives her a book.*]
    That show of such an exercise° may color°   45
    Your loneliness. We are oft to blame in this—
    'Tis too much prov'd°—that with devotion's visage
    And pious action we do sugar o'er
    The devil himself.
KING [*aside*]: O, 'tis too true!   50
    How smart a lash that speech doth give my
        conscience!
    The harlot's cheek, beautied with plast'ring art,
    Is not more ugly to° the thing° that helps it
    Than is my deed to my most painted word.
    O heavy burden!   55
POLONIUS: I hear him coming. Let's withdraw, my lord.
                        [*King and Polonius withdraw.°*]

(*Enter Hamlet.* [*Ophelia pretends to read a book.*])

HAMLET: To be, or not to be, that is the question:
    Whether 'tis nobler in the mind to suffer
    The slings and arrows of outrageous fortune,
    Or to take arms against a sea of troubles,   60
    And by opposing end them. To die, to sleep—
    No more—and by a sleep to say we end
    The heart-ache and the thousand natural shocks
    That flesh is heir to. 'Tis a consummation
    Devoutly to be wish'd. To die, to sleep;   65
    To sleep, perchance to dream. Ay, there's the rub,°
    For in that sleep of death what dreams may come
    When we have shuffled° off this mortal coil,°

608. **Abuses:** Deludes. 609. **relative:** Closely related, pertinent. III, I. **Location:** The castle. 1. **drift of conference:** Direction of conversation. 7. **forward:** Willing. **sounded:** Tested deeply. 12. **disposition:** Inclination. 13. **question:** Conversation. 14. **assay:** Try to win. 17. **o'er-raught:** Overtook and passed. 26. **edge:** Incitement. 29. **closely:** Privately.

31. **Affront:** Confront, meet. 32. **espials:** Spies. 43. **Gracious:** Your Grace (i.e., the King). 45. **exercise:** Act of devotion. (The book she reads is one of devotion.) **color:** Give a plausible appearance to. 47. **too much prov'd:** Too often shown to be true, too often practiced. 53. **to:** Compared to. **thing:** I.e., the cosmetic. 56. [S.D.] *withdraw:* The King and Polonius may retire behind an arras. The stage directions specify that they "enter" again near the end of the scene. 66. **rub:** Literally, an obstacle in the game of bowls. 68. **shuffled:** Sloughed, cast. **coil:** Turmoil.

70
Must give us pause. There's the respect°
That makes calamity of so long life.°
For who would bear the whips and scorns of time,
Th' oppressor's wrong, the proud man's contumely,°
The pangs of despis'd° love, the law's delay,
The insolence of office,° and the spurns°

75
That patient merit of th' unworthy takes,
When he himself might his quietus° make
With a bare bodkin?° Who would fardels° bear,
To grunt and sweat under a weary life,
But that the dread of something after death,

80
The undiscover'd country from whose bourn°
No traveler returns, puzzles the will,
And makes us rather bear those ills we have
Than fly to others that we know not of?
Thus conscience does make cowards of us all

85
And thus the native hue° of resolution
Is sicklied o'er with the pale cast° of thought,
And enterprises of great pitch° and moment°
With this regard° their currents° turn awry,
And lose the name of action.—Soft you now,

90
The fair Ophelia. Nymph, in thy orisons°
Be all my sins rememb'red.

OPHELIA: Good my lord,
How does your honor for this many a day?
HAMLET: I humbly thank you; well, well, well.
OPHELIA: My lord, I have remembrances of yours,

95
That I have longed long to re-deliver.
I pray you, now receive them.   [Offers tokens.]
HAMLET: No, not I, I never gave you aught.
OPHELIA: My honor'd lord, you know right well you did,
And with them words of so sweet breath compos'd

100
As made these things more rich. Their perfume lost,
Take these again, for to the noble mind
Rich gifts wax poor when givers prove unkind.
There, my lord.   [Gives tokens.]
HAMLET: Ha, ha! Are you honest?°

105
OPHELIA: My lord?
HAMLET: Are you fair?°
OPHELIA: What means your lordship?
HAMLET: That if you be honest and fair, your honesty°
should admit no discourse° to your beauty.

110
OPHELIA: Could beauty, my lord, have better commerce° than with honesty?

HAMLET: Ay, truly, for the power of beauty will sooner transform honesty from what it is to a bawd than the force of honesty can translate beauty into his likeness. This was sometime° a paradox,° but now the time° gives it proof. I did love you once. 115
OPHELIA: Indeed, my lord, you made me believe so.
HAMLET: You should not have believ'd me, for virtue cannot so inoculate° our old stock but we shall relish of it.° I lov'd you not. 120
OPHELIA: I was the more deceiv'd.
HAMLET: Get thee to a nunn'ry.° Why wouldst thou be a breeder of sinners? I am myself indifferent honest;° but yet I could accuse me of such things that it were better my mother had not borne me: I am very proud, 125 revengeful, ambitious, with more offenses at my beck° than I have thoughts to put them in, imagination to give them shape, or time to act them in. What should such fellows as I do crawling between earth and heaven? We are arrant knaves, all; believe none 130 of us. Go thy ways to a nunn'ry. Where's your father?
OPHELIA: At home, my lord.
HAMLET: Let the doors be shut upon him, that he may play the fool nowhere but in 's own house. Farewell. 135
OPHELIA: O, help him, you sweet heavens!
HAMLET: If thou dost marry, I'll give thee this plague for thy dowry: be thou as chaste as ice, as pure as snow, thou shalt not escape calumny. Get thee to a nunn'ry, farewell. Or, if thou wilt needs marry, marry a fool, 140 for wise men know well enough what monsters° you° make of them. To a nunn'ry, go, and quickly too. Farewell.
OPHELIA: Heavenly powers, restore him!
HAMLET: I have heard of your paintings too, well 145 enough. God hath given you one face, and you make yourselves another. You jig,° and amble, and you lisp, you nickname God's creatures, and make your wantonness your ignorance.° Go to, I'll no more on 't; it hath made me mad. I say, we will have no moe 150 marriage. Those that are married already—all but one—shall live. The rest shall keep as they are. To a nunn'ry, go.   (Exit.)
OPHELIA: O, what a noble mind is here o'erthrown!
The courtier's, soldier's, scholar's, eye, tongue, sword, 155
Th' expectancy and rose of the fair state,°

The glass of fashion and the mold of form,°
Th' observ'd of all observers,° quite, quite down!
And I, of ladies most deject and wretched,
160   That suck'd the honey of his music vows,
Now see that noble and most sovereign reason,
Like sweet bells jangled, out of time and harsh,
That unmatch'd form and feature of blown° youth
Blasted with ecstasy.° O, woe is me,
165   T' have seen what I have seen, see what I see!

(Enter King and Polonius.)

KING: Love? His affections do not that way tend;
Nor what he spake, though it lack'd form a little,
Was not like madness. There's something in his soul,
O'er which his melancholy sits on brood,
170   And I do doubt° the hatch and the disclose°
Will be some danger; which for to prevent,
I have in quick determination
Thus set it down: he shall with speed to England,
For the demand of° our neglected tribute.
175   Haply the seas and countries different
With variable° objects shall expel
This something-settled° matter in his heart,
Whereon his brains still beating puts him thus
From fashion of himself.° What think you on 't?
180   POLONIUS: It shall do well. But yet do I believe
The origin and commencement of his grief
Sprung from neglected love.—How now,
   Ophelia?
You need not tell us what Lord Hamlet said;
We heard it all.—My lord, do as you please,
185   But, if you hold it fit, after the play
Let his queen mother all alone entreat him
To show his grief. Let her be round° with him;
And I'll be plac'd, so please you, in the ear
Of all their conference. If she find him not,
190   To England send him, or confine him where
Your wisdom best shall think.
KING: It shall be so.
Madness in great ones must not unwatch'd go.
                                        (Exeunt.)

{Scene II}°

(Enter Hamlet and three of the Players.)

HAMLET: Speak the speech, I pray you, as I pronounc'd
   it to you, trippingly on the tongue. But if you mouth
it, as many of our players° do, I had as lief the town-
crier spoke my lines. Nor do not saw the air too
much with your hand, thus, but use all gently; for in   5
the very torrent, tempest, and, as I may say, whirlwind of your passion, you must acquire and beget a
temperance that may give it smoothness. O, it
offends me to the soul to hear a robustious° periwig-
pated° fellow tear a passion to tatters, to very rags, to   10
split the ears of the groundlings,° who for the most
part are capable of° nothing but inexplicable dumb-
shows and noise. I would have such a fellow whipp'd
for o'er-doing Termagant.° It out-herods Herod.°
Pray you, avoid it.   15
FIRST PLAYER: I warrant your honor.
HAMLET: Be not too tame neither, but let your own discretion be your tutor. Suit the action to the word, the
word to the action, with this special observance, that
you o'erstep not the modesty of nature. For anything   20
so o'erdone is from° the purpose of playing, whose
end, both at the first and now, was and is, to hold, as
't were, the mirror up to nature, to show virtue her
feature, scorn her own image, and the very age and
body of the time his° form and pressure.° Now this   25
overdone, or come tardy off,° though it makes the
unskillful laugh, cannot but make the judicious
grieve, the censure of which one° must in your
allowance o'erweigh a whole theater of others. O,
there be players that I have seen play, and heard others   30
praise, and that highly, not to speak it profanely,
that, neither having th' accent of Christians nor the
gait of Christian, pagan, nor man, have so strutted
and bellow'd that I have thought some of nature's
journeymen° had made men and not made them   35
well, they imitated humanity so abominably.
FIRST PLAYER: I hope we have reform'd that indiffer-
ently° with us, sir.
HAMLET: O, reform it altogether. And let those that play
your clowns speak no more than is set down for   40
them; for there be of them° that will themselves
laugh, to set on some quantity of barren° spectators
to laugh too, though in the mean time some necessary question of the play be then to be consider'd.

---

157. **The glass . . . form:** The mirror of fashion and the pattern of courtly behavior.   158. **observ'd . . . observers:** The center of attention and honor in the court.   163. **blown:** Blooming.   164. **ecstasy:** Madness.   170. **doubt:** Fear.   **disclose:** Disclosure.   174. **For . . . of:** To demand.   176. **variable:** Various.   177. **something-settled:** Somewhat settled.   179. **From . . . himself:** Out of his natural manner.   187. **round:** Blunt.   III, II. **Location:** The castle.

3. **our players:** Indefinite use; i.e., *players nowadays.*   9. **robustious:** Violent, boisterous.   9–10. **periwig-pated:** Wearing a wig.   11. **groundlings:** Spectators who paid least and stood in the yard of the theater.   12. **capable of:** Susceptible of being influenced by.   14. **Termagant:** A god of the Saracens; a character in the St. Nicholas play, where one of his worshipers, leaving him in charge of goods, returns to find them stolen; whereupon he beats the god or idol, which howls vociferously.   **Herod:** Herod of Jewry. (A character in *The Slaughter of the Innocents* and other cycle plays. The part was played with great noise and fury.)   21. **from:** Contrary to.   25. **his:** Its.   **pressure:** Stamp, impressed character.   26. **come tardy off:** Inadequately done.   28. **the censure . . . one:** The judgment of even one of whom.   35. **journeymen:** Laborers not yet masters in their trade.   37–38. **indifferently:** Tolerably.   41. **of them:** Some among them.   42. **barren:** I.e., of wit.

45   That's villainous, and shows a most pitiful ambition
      in the fool that uses it. Go, make you ready.
                                          [*Exeunt Players.*]

(*Enter Polonius, Guildenstern, and Rosencrantz.*)

      How now, my lord? Will the King hear this piece
      of work?
POLONIUS: And the Queen too, and that presently.°
50 HAMLET: Bid the players make haste.
                                          [*Exit Polonius.*]
      Will you two help to hasten them?
ROSENCRANTZ: Ay, my lord.   (*Exeunt they two.*)
HAMLET: What ho, Horatio!

(*Enter Horatio.*)

HORATIO: Here, sweet lord, at your service.
HAMLET: Horatio, thou art e'en as just a man
55   As e'er my conversation cop'd withal.°
HORATIO: O, my dear lord—
HAMLET: Nay, do not think I flatter;
      For what advancement may I hope from thee
      That no revenue hast but thy good spirits,
      To feed and clothe thee? Why should the poor be
         flatter'd?
60   No, let the candied° tongue lick absurd pomp,
      And crook the pregnant° hinges of the knee
      Where thrift° may follow fawning. Dost thou hear?
      Since my dear soul was mistress of her choice
      And could of men distinguish her election,
65   Sh' hath seal'd thee for herself, for thou hast been
      As one, in suff'ring all, that suffers nothing,
      A man that Fortune's buffets and rewards
      Hast ta'en with equal thanks; and blest are those
      Whose blood° and judgment are so well
         commeddled°
70   That they are not a pipe for Fortune's finger
      To sound what stop° she please. Give me that man
      That is not passion's slave, and I will wear him
      In my heart's core, ay, in my heart of heart,
      As I do thee.—Something too much of this.—
75   There is a play tonight before the King.
      One scene of it comes near the circumstance
      Which I have told thee of my father's death.
      I prithee, when thou seest that act afoot,
      Even with the very comment of thy soul°
80   Observe my uncle. If his occulted° guilt
      Do not itself unkennel in one speech,
      It is a damned° ghost that we have seen,
      And my imaginations are as foul
      As Vulcan's stithy.° Give him heedful note,

      For I mine eyes will rivet to his face,   85
      And after we will both our judgments join
      In censure of his seeming.°
HORATIO: Well, my lord.
      If 'a steal aught the whilst this play is playing,
      And scape detecting, I will pay the theft.

([*Flourish.*] *Enter trumpets and kettledrums, King,
Queen, Polonius, Ophelia, [Rosencrantz, Guildenstern,
and other Lords, with Guards carrying torches*].)

HAMLET: They are coming to the play. I must be idle. Get   90
      you a place.   [*The King, Queen, and courtiers sit.*]
KING: How fares our cousin Hamlet?
HAMLET: Excellent, i' faith, of the chameleon's dish:°
      I eat the air, promise-cramm'd. You cannot feed
      capons so.   95
KING: I have nothing with° this answer, Hamlet. These
      words are not mine.°
HAMLET: No, nor mine now. [*To Polonius.*] My lord,
      you played once i' th' university, you say?
POLONIUS: That did I, my lord; and was accounted a   100
      good actor.
HAMLET: What did you enact?
POLONIUS: I did enact Julius Caesar. I was killed i' th'
      Capitol; Brutus kill'd me.
HAMLET: It was a brute part of him to kill so capital a   105
      calf there. Be the players ready?
ROSENCRANTZ: Ay, my lord; they stay upon your
      patience.
QUEEN: Come hither, my dear Hamlet, sit by me.
HAMLET: No, good mother, here's metal more attractive.   110
POLONIUS [*to the King*]: O, ho, do you mark that?
HAMLET: Lady, shall I lie in your lap?
                                  [*Lying down at Ophelia's feet.*]
OPHELIA: No, my lord.
[HAMLET: I mean, my head upon your lap?
OPHELIA: Ay, my lord.]   115
HAMLET: Do you think I meant country° matters?
OPHELIA: I think nothing, my lord.
HAMLET: That's a fair thought to lie between maids' legs.
OPHELIA: What is, my lord?
HAMLET: Nothing.   120
OPHELIA: You are merry, my lord.
HAMLET: Who, I?
OPHELIA: Ay, my lord.
HAMLET: O God, your only jig-maker.° What should a
      man do but be merry? For look you how cheerfully   125
      my mother looks, and my father died within 's° two
      hours.

---

49. presently: At once. **55. my . . . withal:** My contact
with people provided opportunity for encounter with.
60. candied: Sugared, flattering. **61. pregnant:** Compliant.
62. thrift: Profit. **69. blood:** Passion. **commeddled:** Com-
mingled. **71. stop:** Hole in a wind instrument for controlling
the sound. **79. very . . . soul:** Inward and sagacious criticism.
80. occulted: Hidden. **82. damned:** In league with Satan.
84. stithy: Smithy, place of stiths (anvils).

87. censure of his seeming: Judgment of his appearance or
behavior. **93. chameleon's dish:** Chameleons were supposed
to feed on air. Hamlet deliberately misinterprets the King's *fares*
as *feeds*. By his phrase *eat the air* he also plays on the idea of
feeding himself with the promise of succession, of being the
heir. **96. have . . . with:** Make nothing of. **97. are not mine:**
Do not respond to what I asked. **116. country:** With a bawdy
pun. **124. only jig-maker:** Very best composer of jigs (song
and dance). **126. within 's:** Within this.

OPHELIA: Nay, 'tis twice two months, my lord.

HAMLET: So long? Nay then, let the devil wear black for
130   I'll have a suit of sables.° O heavens! Die two months
ago, and not forgotten yet? Then there's hope a great
man's memory may outlive his life half a year. But,
by 'r lady, 'a must build churches, then, or else shall
'a suffer not thinking on,° with the hobby-horse,
135   whose epitaph is "For, O, for, O, the hobby-horse is
forgot."°

(*The trumpets sound. Dumb show follows.*)

(*Enter a King and a Queen [very lovingly]; the Queen
embracing him, and he her. [She kneels and makes show
of protestation unto him.] He takes her up, and declines
his head upon her neck. He lies him down upon a bank
of flowers. She, seeing him asleep, leaves him. Anon
comes in another man, takes off his crown, kisses it,
pours poison in the sleeper's ears, and leaves him. The
Queen returns; finds the King dead, makes passionate
action. The Poisoner, with some three or four, come in
again, seem to condole with her. The dead body is carried away. The Poisoner woos the Queen with gifts; she
seems harsh awhile but in the end accepts love.*)

[*Exeunt.*]

OPHELIA: What means this, my lord?

HAMLET: Marry, this' miching mallecho;° it means
mischief.

140   OPHELIA: Belike° this show imports the argument° of
the play.

(*Enter Prologue.*)

HAMLET: We shall know by this fellow. The players cannot keep counsel;° they'll tell all.

OPHELIA: Will 'a tell us what this show meant?

145   HAMLET: Ay, or any show that you will show him. Be
not you° asham'd to show, he'll not shame to tell you
what it means.

OPHELIA: You are naught, you are naught.° I'll mark the
play.

150   PROLOGUE: For us, and for our tragedy,
    Here stooping° to your clemency,
    We beg your hearing patiently.   [*Exit.*]

HAMLET: Is this a prologue, or the posy of a ring?°

OPHELIA: 'Tis brief, my lord.

155   HAMLET: As woman's love.

(*Enter [two Players as] King and Queen.*)

PLAYER KING: Full thirty times hath Phoebus' cart°
    gone round
    Neptune's salt wash° and Tellus'° orbed ground,
    And thirty dozen moons with borrowed° sheen
    About the world have times twelve thirties been,
    Since love our hearts and Hymen° did our hands   160
    Unite commutual° in most sacred bands.

PLAYER QUEEN: So many journeys may the sun and
    moon
    Make us again count o'er ere love be done!
    But, woe is me, you are so sick of late,
    So far from cheer and from your former state,   165
    That I distrust you. Yet, though I distrust,°
    Discomfort you, my lord, it nothing° must.
    For women's fear and love hold quantity;°
    In neither aught, or in extremity.
    Now, what my love is, proof° hath made you know,   170
    And as my love is siz'd, my fear is so.
    Where love is great, the littlest doubts are fear;
    Where little fears grow great, great love grows
    there.

PLAYER KING: Faith, I must leave thee, love, and
    shortly too;
    My operant° powers their functions leave to do.°   175
    And thou shalt live in this fair world behind,
    Honor'd, belov'd; and haply one as kind
    For husband shalt thou—

PLAYER QUEEN: O, confound the rest!
    Such love must needs be treason in my breast.
    In second husband let me be accurst!   180
    None wed the second but who kill'd the first.

HAMLET: Wormwood, wormwood.

PLAYER QUEEN: The instances° that second marriage
    move°
    Are base respects of thrift,° but none of love.
    A second time I kill my husband dead,   185
    When second husband kisses me in bed.

PLAYER KING: I do believe you think what now you
    speak,
    But what we do determine oft we break.
    Purpose is but the slave to memory,°
    Of violent birth, but poor validity,°   190
    Which now, like fruit unripe, sticks on the tree,
    But fall unshaken when they mellow be.

130. **suit of sables:** Garments trimmed with the fur of the sable and hence suited for a wealthy person, not a mourner (with a pun on *sable* black).   134. **suffer . . . on:** Undergo oblivion. 135–36. **"For . . . forgot":** Verse of a song occurring also in *Love's Labor's Lost,* III, I, 30. The hobby-horse was a character made up to resemble a horse, appearing in the Morris dance and such May-game sports. This song laments the disappearance of such customs under pressure from the Puritans. 138. **this' miching mallecho:** This is sneaking mischief. 140. **Belike:** Probably.   **argument:** Plot.   143. **counsel:** Secret. 145–46. **Be not you:** If you are not.   148. **naught:** Indecent. 151. **stooping:** Bowing.   153. **posy . . . ring:** Brief motto in verse inscribed in a ring.

156. **Phoebus' cart:** The sun god's chariot.   157. **salt wash:** The sea.   **Tellus:** Goddess of the earth, of the *orbed ground.* 158. **borrowed:** Reflected.   160. **Hymen:** God of matrimony. 161. **commutual:** Mutually.   166. **distrust:** Am anxious about. 167. **nothing:** Not at all.   168. **hold quantity:** Keep proportion with one another.   170. **proof:** Experience.   175. **oper-
ant:** Active.   **leave to do:** Cease to perform.   183. **instances:** Motives.   **move:** Motivate.   184. **base . . . thrift:** Ignoble considerations of material prosperity.   189. **Purpose . . . memory:** Our good intentions are subject to forgetfulness.   190. **validity:** Strength, durability.

Most necessary 'tis that we forget
To pay ourselves what to ourselves is debt.°
195 What to ourselves in passion we propose,
The passion ending, doth the purpose lose.
The violence of either grief or joy
Their own enactures° with themselves destroy.
Where joy most revels, grief doth most lament;
200 Grief joys, joy grieves, on slender accident.
This world is not for aye,° nor 'tis not strange
That even our loves should with our fortunes
     change;
For 'tis a question left us yet to prove,
Whether love lead fortune, or else fortune love.
205 The great man down, you mark his favorite flies;
The poor advanc'd makes friends of enemies.
And hitherto doth love on fortune tend;
For who not needs° shall never lack a friend,
And who in want° a hollow friend doth try,°
210 Directly seasons him° his enemy.
But, orderly to end where I begun,
Our wills and fates do so contrary run
That our devices still° are overthrown;
Our thoughts are ours, their ends° none of our own.
215 So think thou wilt no second husband wed,
But die thy thoughts when thy first lord is dead.
PLAYER QUEEN: Nor earth to me give food, nor
     heaven light,
Sport and repose lock from me day and night,
To desperation turn my trust and hope,
220 An anchor's cheer° in prison be my scope!°
Each opposite° that blanks° the face of joy
Meet what I would have well and it destroy!
Both here and hence° pursue me lasting strife,
If, once a widow, ever I be wife!
225 HAMLET: If she should break it now!
PLAYER KING: 'Tis deeply sworn. Sweet, leave me here
     awhile;
My spirits grow dull, and fain I would beguile
The tedious day with sleep.   [Sleeps.]
PLAYER QUEEN: Sleep rock thy brain,
230 And never come mischance between us twain!
                                          [Exit.]
HAMLET: Madam, how like you this play?
QUEEN: The lady doth protest too much, methinks.
HAMLET: O, but she'll keep her word.
KING: Have you heard the argument?° Is there no
235   offense in 't?

HAMLET: No, no, they do but jest, poison in jest; no
     offense i' th' world.
KING: What do you call the play?
HAMLET: "The Mouse-trap." Marry, how? Tropically.°
     This play is the image of a murder done in Vienna. 240
     Gonzago is the Duke's name; his wife, Baptista. You
     shall see anon. 'Tis a knavish piece of work, but what
     of that? Your Majesty, and we that have free° souls, it
     touches us not. Let the gall'd jade° winch,° our with-
     ers° are unwrung.°   245

(Enter Lucianus.)

     This is one Lucianus, nephew to the King.
OPHELIA: You are as good as a chorus,° my lord.
HAMLET: I could interpret between you and your love, if
     I could see the puppets dallying.°
OPHELIA: You are keen, my lord, you are keen.   250
HAMLET: It would cost you a groaning to take off mine
     edge.
OPHELIA: Still better, and worse.°
HAMLET: So° you mistake° your husbands. Begin, mur-
     derer, leave thy damnable faces, and begin. Come,   255
     the croaking raven doth bellow for revenge.
LUCIANUS: Thoughts black, hands apt, drugs fit, and
     time agreeing,
Confederate season,° else no creature seeing,
Thou mixture rank, of midnight weeds collected,
With Hecate's ban° thrice blasted, thrice infected,   260
Thy natural magic and dire property
On wholesome life usurp immediately.
          [Pours the poison into the sleeper's ears.]
HAMLET: 'A poisons him i' th' garden for his estate. His
     name's Gonzago. The story is extant, and written in   265
     very choice Italian. You shall see anon how the mur-
     derer gets the love of Gonzago's wife.
                                   [Claudius rises.]
OPHELIA: The King rises.
[HAMLET: What, frighted with false fire?°]
QUEEN: How fares my lord?   270
POLONIUS: Give o'er the play.

193–94. Most . . . debt: It's inevitable that in time we forget the
obligations we have imposed on ourselves. **198. enactures:** Ful-
fillments. **201. aye:** Ever. **208. who not needs:** He who is not
in need (of wealth). **209. who in want:** He who is in need.
try: Test (his generosity). **210. seasons him:** Ripens him into.
213. devices still: Intentions continually. **214. ends:** Results.
220. anchor's cheer: Anchorite's or hermit's fare. **my scope:**
The extent of my happiness. **222. opposite:** Adverse thing.
blanks: Causes to blanch or grow pale. **223. hence:** In the life
hereafter. **234. argument:** Plot.

239. Tropically: Figuratively. (The first quarto reading, *trapi-
cally,* suggests a pun on *trap* in *Mouse-trap.*) **243. free:** Guiltless. **244. gall'd jade:** Horse whose hide is rubbed by saddle
or harness. **winch:** Wince. **244–45. withers:** The part
between the horse's shoulder blades. **245. unwrung:** Not
rubbed sore. **247. chorus:** In many Elizabethan plays the
forthcoming action was explained by an actor known as the
"chorus"; at a puppet show the actor who spoke the dialogue
was known as an "interpreter," as indicated by the lines following. **249. dallying:** With sexual suggestion, continued in *keen,*
i.e., sexually aroused, *groaning,* i.e., moaning in pregnancy, and
edge, i.e., sexual desire or impetuosity. **253. Still . . . worse:**
More keen-witted and less decorous. **254. So:** Even thus (in
marriage). **mistake:** Mistake, take erringly, falseheartedly.
259. Confederate season: The time and occasion conspiring (to
assist the murderer). **261. Hecate's ban:** The curse of Hecate,
the goddess of witchcraft. **269. false fire:** The blank discharge
of a gun loaded with powder but not shot.

KING: Give me some light. Away!
POLONIUS: Lights, lights, lights!

(Exeunt all but Hamlet and Horatio.)

HAMLET: "Why, let the strucken deer go weep,
275   The hart ungalled° play.
For some must watch,° while some must sleep;
    Thus runs the world away."°
Would not this,° sir, and a forest of feathers°—if the
rest of my fortunes turn Turk with° me—with two
280 Provincial roses° on my raz'd° shoes, get me a fellow-
ship in a cry of players?°
HORATIO: Half a share.
HAMLET: A whole one, I.
"For thou dost know, O Damon dear,
285   This realm dismantled° was
Of Jove himself, and now reigns here
    A very, very—pajock."°
HORATIO: You might have rhym'd.
HAMLET: O good Horatio, I'll take the ghost's word for
290 a thousand pound. Didst perceive?
HORATIO: Very well, my lord.
HAMLET: Upon the talk of pois'ning?
HORATIO: I did very well note him.
HAMLET: Ah, ha! Come, some music! Come, the re-
295 corders!°
"For if the King like not the comedy,
Why then, belike, he likes it not, perdy"°
Come, some music!

(Enter Rosencrantz and Guildenstern.)

GUILDENSTERN: Good my lord, vouchsafe me a word
300 with you.
HAMLET: Sir, a whole history.
GUILDENSTERN: The King, sir—
HAMLET: Ay, sir, what of him?
GUILDENSTERN: Is in his retirement marvelous dis-
305 temp'red.
HAMLET: With drink, sir?
GUILDENSTERN: No, my lord, with choler.°
HAMLET: Your wisdom should show itself more richer
to signify this to the doctor, for for me to put him to
310 his purgation would perhaps plunge him into more
choler.

GUILDENSTERN: Good my lord, put your discourse into
some frame° and start not so wildly from my affair.
HAMLET: I am tame, sir. Pronounce.
GUILDENSTERN: The Queen, your mother, in most great   315
affliction of spirit, hath sent me to you.
HAMLET: You are welcome.
GUILDENSTERN: Nay, good my lord, this courtesy is not
of the right breed. If it shall please you to make me a
wholesome answer, I will do your mother's com-   320
mandment; if not, your pardon° and my return shall
be the end of my business.
HAMLET: Sir, I cannot.
ROSENCRANTZ: What, my lord?
HAMLET: Make you a wholesome answer; my wit's dis-   325
eas'd. But, sir, such answer as I can make, you shall
command, or rather, as you say, my mother. Therefore no more, but to the matter. My mother, you
say—
ROSENCRANTZ: Then thus she says: your behavior hath   330
struck her into amazement and admiration.°
HAMLET: O wonderful son, that can so stonish a
mother! But is there no sequel at the heels of this
mother's admiration? Impart.
ROSENCRANTZ: She desires to speak with you in her   335
closet,° ere you go to bed.
HAMLET: We shall obey, were she ten times our mother.
Have you any further trade with us?
ROSENCRANTZ: My lord, you once did love me.
HAMLET: And do still, by these pickers and stealers.°   340
ROSENCRANTZ: Good my lord, what is your cause of
distemper? You do surely bar the door upon your
own liberty, if you deny your griefs to your friend.
HAMLET: Sir, I lack advancement.
ROSENCRANTZ: How can that be, when you have the   345
voice of the King himself for your succession in
Denmark?
HAMLET: Ay, sir, but "While the grass grows"°—the
proverb is something° musty.

(Enter the Players with recorders.)

O, the recorders! Let me see one. [*He takes a recorder.*]   350
To withdraw° with you: why do you go about to
recover the wind° of me, as if you would drive me
into a toil?°
GUILDENSTERN: O, my lord, if my duty be too bold, my
love is too unmannerly.°   355
HAMLET: I do not well understand that. Will you play
upon this pipe?

275. **ungalled:** Unafflicted.   276. **watch:** Remain awake.
274–77. **Why . . . away:** Probably from an old ballad, with allusion to the popular belief that a wounded deer retires to weep
and die; cf. *As You Like It,* II, i, 66.   278. **this:** The play.
feathers: Allusion to the plumes that Elizabethan actors were
fond of wearing.   279. **turn Turk with:** Turn renegade against,
go back on.   280. **Provincial roses:** Rosettes of ribbon like the
roses of a part of France.   **raz'd:** With ornamental slashing.
280–81. **fellowship . . . players:** Partnership in a theatrical company.   285. **dismantled:** Stripped, divested.   287. **pajock:**
Peacock, a bird with a bad reputation (here substituted for the
obvious rhyme-word *ass*).   295. **recorders:** Wind instruments
like the flute.   297. **perdy:** A corruption of the French *par
dieu,* by God.   307. **choler:** Anger. (But Hamlet takes the word
in its more basic humors sense of *bilious disorder.*)

313. **frame:** Order.   321. **pardon:** Permission to depart.
331. **admiration:** Wonder.   336. **closet:** Private chamber.
340. **pickers and stealers:** Hands (so called from the catechism,
"to keep my hands from picking and stealing").   348.
While . . . grows: The rest of the proverb is "the silly horse
starves"; Hamlet may not live long enough to succeed to the
kingdom.   349. **something:** Somewhat.   351. **withdraw:**
Speak privately.   352. **recover the wind:** Get the windward
side.   353. **toil:** Snare.   354–55. **if . . . unmannerly:** If I am
using an unmannerly boldness, it is my love that occasions it.

GUILDENSTERN: My lord, I cannot.

HAMLET: I pray you.

360 GUILDENSTERN: Believe me, I cannot.

HAMLET: I do beseech you.

GUILDENSTERN: I know no touch of it, my lord.

HAMLET: It is as easy as lying. Govern these ventages°
with your fingers and thumb, give it breath with your
365 mouth, and it will discourse most eloquent music.
Look you, these are the stops.

GUILDENSTERN: But these cannot I command to any
utt'rance of harmony; I have not the skill.

HAMLET: Why, look you now, how unworthy a thing
370 you make of me! You would play upon me, you
would seem to know my stops, you would pluck out
the heart of my mystery, you would sound me from
my lowest note to the top of my compass,° and there
is much music, excellent voice, in this little organ,°
375 yet cannot you make it speak. 'Sblood, do you think I
am easier to be play'd on than a pipe? Call me what
instrument you will, though you can fret° me, you
cannot play upon me.

(Enter Polonius.)

God bless you, sir!

380 POLONIUS: My lord, the Queen would speak with you,
and presently.°

HAMLET: Do you see yonder cloud that's almost in
shape of a camel?

POLONIUS: By th' mass, and 'tis like a camel, indeed.

385 HAMLET: Methinks it is like a weasel.

POLONIUS: It is back'd like a weasel.

HAMLET: Or like a whale?

POLONIUS: Very like a whale.

HAMLET: Then I will come to my mother by and by.°

390 [*Aside.*] They fool me° to the top of my bent.°—I
will come by and by.

POLONIUS: I will say so.   [*Exit.*]

HAMLET: "By and by" is easily said. Leave me, friends.

[*Exeunt all but Hamlet.*]

'Tis now the very witching time° of night,
395 When churchyards yawn and hell itself breathes out
Contagion to this world. Now could I drink hot
blood,
And do such bitter business as the day
Would quake to look on. Soft, now to my mother.
O heart, lose not thy nature! Let not ever
400 The soul of Nero° enter this firm bosom.

Let me be cruel, not unnatural;
I will speak daggers to her, but use none.
My tongue and soul in this be hypocrites:
How in my words somever° she be shent,°
To give them seals° never, my soul, consent!   405

(Exit.)

{*Scene III*}°

(Enter King, Rosencrantz, and Guildenstern.)

KING: I like him not, nor stands it safe with us
To let his madness range. Therefore prepare you.
I your commission will forthwith dispatch,°
And he to England shall along with you.
The terms° of our estate° may not endure   5
Hazard so near 's as doth hourly grow
Out of his brows.°

GUILDENSTERN: We will ourselves provide.
Most holy and religious fear it is
To keep those many many bodies safe
That live and feed upon your Majesty.   10

ROSENCRANTZ: The single and peculiar° life is bound
With all the strength and armor of the mind
To keep itself from noyance,° but much more
That spirit upon whose weal depends and rests
The lives of many. The cess° of majesty   15
Dies not alone, but like a gulf° doth draw
What's near it with it; or it is a messy wheel
Fix'd on the summit of the highest mount,
To whose huge spokes ten thousand lesser things
Are mortis'd and adjoin'd, which, when it falls,   20
Each small annexment, petty consequence,
Attends° the boist'rous ruin. Never alone
Did the King sigh, but with a general groan.

KING: Arm° you, I pray you, to this speedy voyage,
For we will fetters put about this fear,   25
Which now goes too free-footed.

ROSENCRANTZ: We will haste us.

*(Exeunt Gentlemen [Rosencrantz
and Guildenstern].)*

(Enter Polonius.)

POLONIUS: My lord, he's going to his mother's closet.
Behind the arras° I'll convey myself

---

363. **ventages:** Stops of the recorder.   373. **compass:** Range
(of voice).   374. **organ:** Musical instrument.   377. **fret:** *Irri-*
tate (with a quibble on *fret* meaning the piece of wood, gut,
or metal that regulates the fingering on an instrument).
381. **presently:** At once.   389. **by and by:** Immediately.
390. **fool me:** Make me play the fool.   **top of my bent:** Limit of
my ability or endurance (literally, the extent to which a bow may
be bent).   394. **witching time:** Time when spells are cast and
evil is abroad.   400. **Nero:** Murderer of his mother, Agrippina.

404. **How . . . somever:** However much by my words.   **shent:**
Rebuked.   405. **give them seals:** Confirm them with deeds.
III, III. Location: The castle.   3. **dispatch:** Prepare, cause to be
drawn up.   5. **terms:** Condition, circumstances.   **our estate:**
My royal position.   7. **brows:** Effronteries, threatening frowns
(?), brain (?).   11. **single and peculiar:** Individual and private.
13. **noyance:** Harm.   15. **cess:** Decease.   16. **gulf:** Whirlpool.
22. **Attends:** Participates in.   24. **Arm:** Prepare.   28. **arras:**
Screen of tapestry placed around the walls of household
apartments. (On the Elizabethan stage, the arras was presumably
over a door or discovery space in the tiring-house façade.)

FAR LEFT: Michael Pennington as Hamlet. NEAR LEFT: A scene from the Royal Shakespeare Company's 1980 production. BELOW LEFT: Hamlet, played by Kenneth Branagh, duels Laertes, played by Michael Maloney. Branagh directed this 1996 film. RIGHT: The grave-digger holds up Yorick's skull as Hamlet and Horatio (Tom Wilkinson) look on. BELOW RIGHT: Carol Royle as Ophelia with Hamlet in the nunnery scene.

To hear the process.° I'll warrant she'll tax him
   home,°
30 And, as you said, and wisely was it said,
'Tis meet that some more audience than a mother,
Since nature makes them partial, should o'erhear
The speech, of vantage.° Fare you well, my liege.
I'll call upon you ere you go to bed,
And tell you what I know.
35 KING: Thanks, dear my lord.
                    (*Exit* [*Polonius*].)
O, my offense is rank, it smells to heaven;
It hath the primal eldest curse° upon 't,
A brother's murder. Pray can I not,
Though inclination be as sharp as will.°
40 My stronger guilt defeats my strong intent,
And, like a man to double business bound,
I stand in pause where I shall first begin,
And both neglect. What if this cursed hand
Were thicker than itself with brother's blood,
45 Is there not rain enough in the sweet heavens
To wash it white as snow? Whereto serves mercy
But to confront the visage of offense?°
And what's in prayer but this twofold force,
To be forestalled° ere we come to fall,
50 Or pardon'd being down? Then I'll look up;
My fault is past. But, O, what form of prayer
Can serve my turn? "Forgive me my foul
   murder"?
That cannot be, since I am still possess'd
Of those effects for which I did the murder,
55 My crown, mine own ambition, and my queen.
May one be pardon'd and retain th' offense?
In the corrupted currents° of this world
Offense's gilded hand° may shove by justice,
And oft 'tis seen the wicked prize° itself
60 Buys out the law. But 'tis not so above.
There is no shuffling,° there the action lies°
In his° true nature, and we ourselves compell'd,
Even to the teeth and forehead° of our faults,
To give in evidence. What then? What rests?°
65 Try what repentance can. What can it not?
Yet what can it, when one cannot repent?
O wretched state! O bosom black as death!
O limed° soul, that, struggling to be free,

Art more engag'd!° Help, angels! Make assay.°
Bow, stubborn knees, and heart with strings of steel,   70
Be soft as sinews of the new-born babe!
All may be well.
                      [*He kneels.*]
(*Enter Hamlet* [*with sword drawn*].)
HAMLET: Now might I do it pat,° now 'a is a-praying;
And now I'll do 't. And so 'a goes to heaven;
And so am I reveng'd. That would be scann'd:°   75
A villain kills my father, and for that,
I, his sole son, do this same villain send
To heaven.
Why, this is hire and salary, not revenge.
'A took my father grossly,° full of bread,°   80
With all his crimes broad blown,° as flush° as
   May;
And how his audit° stands who knows save
   heaven?
But in our circumstance and course° of thought,
'Tis heavy with him. And am I then reveng'd,
To take him in the purging of his soul,   85
When he is fit and season'd for his passage?
No!
Up, sword, and know thou a more horrid hent.°
                    [*Puts up his sword.*]
When he is drunk asleep, or in his rage,
Or in th' incestuous pleasure of his bed,   90
At game a-swearing, or about some act
That has no relish of salvation in 't—
Then trip him, that his heels may kick at heaven,
And that his soul may be as damn'd and black
As hell, whereto it goes. My mother stays.   95
This physic° but prolongs thy sickly days.   (*Exit.*)
KING: My words fly up, my thoughts remain
   below.
Words without thoughts never to heaven go.
                    (*Exit.*)

{*Scene IV*}°

(*Enter* [*Queen*] *Gertrude and Polonius.*)

POLONIUS: 'A will come straight. Look you lay° home
   to him.
Tell him his pranks have been too broad° to bear
   with,

---

29. process: Proceedings. **tax him home:** Reprove him severely. **33. of vantage:** From an advantageous place. **37. primal eldest curse:** The curse of Cain, the first murderer; he killed his brother Abel. **39. Though . . . will:** Though my desire is as strong as my determination. **46–47. Whereto . . . offense:** For what function does mercy serve other than to undo the effects of sin? **49. forestalled:** Prevented (from sinning). **57. currents:** Courses. **58. gilded hand:** Hand offering gold as a bribe. **59. wicked prize:** Prize won by wickedness. **61. shuffling:** Escape by trickery. **the action lies:** The accusation is made manifest, comes up for consideration (a legal metaphor). **62. his:** Its. **63. teeth and forehead:** Face to face, concealing nothing. **64. rests:** Remains. **68. limed:** Caught as with birdlime, a sticky substance used to ensnare birds.

69. engag'd: Embedded. **assay:** Trial. **73. pat:** Opportunely. **75. would be scann'd:** Needs to be looked into. **80. grossly:** Not spiritually prepared. **full of bread:** Enjoying his worldly pleasures. (See Ezek. 16:49.) **81. crimes broad blown:** Sins in full bloom. **flush:** Lusty. **82. audit:** Account. **83. in . . . course:** As we see it in our mortal situation. **88. know . . . hent:** Await to be grasped by me on a more horrid occasion. **96. physic:** Purging (by prayer). **III, IV. Location:** The queen's private chamber. **1. lay:** Thrust (i.e., reprove him soundly). **2. broad:** Unrestrained.

And that your Grace hath screen'd and stood between
   Much heat° and him. I'll sconce° me even here.
5 Pray you, be round° [with him.
   HAMLET (*within*): Mother, mother, mother!]
   QUEEN: I'll warrant you, fear me not.
      Withdraw, I hear him coming.
                  [*Polonius hides behind the arras.*]

(*Enter Hamlet.*)

   HAMLET: Now, mother, what's the matter?
10 QUEEN: Hamlet, thou hast thy father° much offended.
   HAMLET: Mother, you have my father much offended.
   QUEEN: Come, come, you answer with an idle°
      tongue.
   HAMLET: Go, go, you question with a wicked tongue.
   QUEEN: Why, how now, Hamlet?
   HAMLET: What's the matter now?
   QUEEN: Have you forgot me?
15 HAMLET: No, by the rood,° not so:
      You are the Queen, your husband's brother's wife
      And—would it were not so!—you are my
         mother.
   QUEEN: Nay, then, I'll set those to you that can speak.
   HAMLET: Come, come, and sit you down; you shall
      not budge.
20   You go not till I set you up a glass
      Where you may see the inmost part of you.
   QUEEN: What wilt thou do? Thou wilt not murder me?
      Help, ho!
   POLONIUS [*behind*]: What, ho! Help!
   HAMLET [*drawing*]: How now? A rat? Dead, for a
25   ducat, dead!
                  [*Makes a pass through the arras.*]
   POLONIUS [*behind*]: O, I am slain! [*Falls and dies.*]
   QUEEN: O me, what hast thou done?
   HAMLET: Nay, I know not. Is it the King?
   QUEEN: O, what a rash and bloody deed is this!
   HAMLET: A bloody deed—almost as bad, good mother,
30   As kill a king, and marry with his brother.
   QUEEN: As kill a king!
   HAMLET: Ay, lady, it was my word.
         [*Parts the arras and discovers Polonius.*]
      Thou wretched, rash, intruding fool, farewell!
      I took thee for thy better. Take thy fortune.
      Thou find'st to be too busy is some danger.—
35   Leave wringing of your hands. Peace, sit you down,
      And let me wring your heart, for so I shall,
      If it be made of penetrable stuff,
      If damned custom° have not braz'd° it so
      That it be proof° and bulwark against sense.°

QUEEN: What have I done, that thou dar'st wag thy
      tongue   40
   In noise so rude against me?
HAMLET: Such an art
   That blurs the grace and blush of modesty,
   Calls virtue hypocrite, takes off the rose
   From the fair forehead of an innocent love
   And sets a blister° there, makes marriage-vows   45
   As false as dicers' oaths. O, such a deed
   As from the body of contraction° plucks
   The very soul, and sweet religion° makes
   A rhapsody° of words. Heaven's face does glow
   O'er this solidity and compound mass   50
   With heated visage, as against the doom,
   Is thought-sick at the act.°
QUEEN: Ay me, what act,
   That roars so loud and thunders in the index?°
HAMLET: Look here, upon this picture, and on this,
   The counterfeit presentment° of two brothers.   55
               [*Shows her two likenesses.*]
   See, what a grace was seated on this brow:
   Hyperion's° curls, the front° of Jove himself,
   An eye like Mars, to threaten and command,
   A station° like the herald Mercury
   New-lighted on a heaven-kissing hill—   60
   A combination and a form indeed,
   Where every god did seem to set his seal,
   To give the world assurance of a man.
   This was your husband. Look you now, what
      follows:
   Here is your husband, like a mildew'd ear,°   65
   Blasting his wholesome brother. Have you eyes?
   Could you on this fair mountain leave to feed,
   And batten° on this moor?° Ha, have you eyes?
   You cannot call it love, for at your age
   The heyday° in the blood is tame, it's humble,   70
   And waits upon the judgment, and what judgment
   Would step from this to this? Sense,° sure, you
      have,
   Else could you not have motion, but sure that sense
   Is apoplex'd,° for madness would not err,

---

4. **Much heat:** The king's anger. **sconce:** Ensconce, hide.
5. **round:** Blunt. 10. **thy father:** Your stepfather, Claudius.
12. **idle:** Foolish. 15. **rood:** Cross. 38. **damned custom:**
Habitual wickedness. **braz'd:** Brazened, hardened. 39. **proof:**
Armor. **sense:** Feeling.

45. **sets a blister:** Brands as a harlot. 47. **contraction:** The
marriage contract. 48. **religion:** Religious vows. 49. **rhapsody:** Senseless string. 49–52. **Heaven's . . . act:** Heaven's face
flushes with anger to look down upon this solid world, this
compound mass, with hot face as though the day of doom were
near, and is thought-sick at the deed (i.e., Gertrude's marriage).
53. **index:** Table of contents, prelude, or preface. 55. **counterfeit presentment:** Portrayed representation. 57. **Hyperion:**
The sun god. **front:** Brow. 59. **station:** Manner of standing.
65. **ear:** I.e., of grain. 68. **batten:** Gorge. **moor:** Barren
upland. 70. **heyday:** State of excitement. 72. **Sense:** Perception through the five senses (the functions of the middle or sensible soul). 74. **apoplex'd:** Paralyzed. (Hamlet goes on to
explain that without such a paralysis of will, mere madness
would not so err, nor would the five senses so enthrall themselves to *ecstasy* or lunacy; even such deranged states of mind
would be able to make the obvious choice between Hamlet
Senior and Claudius.)

75 Nor sense to ecstasy was ne'er so thrall'd
    But it reserv'd some quantity of choice
    To serve in such a difference. What devil was 't
    That thus hath cozen'd° you at hoodman-blind?°
    Eyes without feeling, feeling without sight,
80 Ears without hands or eyes, smelling sans° all,
    Or but a sickly part of one true sense
    Could not so mope.°
    O shame, where is thy blush? Rebellious hell,
    If thou canst mutine° in a matron's bones,
85 To flaming youth let virtue be as wax,
    And melt in her own fire. Proclaim no shame
    When the compulsive ardor gives the charge,
    Since frost itself as actively doth burn,
    And reason panders will.°
90 QUEEN: O Hamlet, speak no more!
    Thou turn'st mine eyes into my very soul,
    And there I see such black and grained° spots
    As will not leave their tinct.°
HAMLET: Nay, but to live
    In the rank sweat of an enseamed° bed,
95 Stew'd in corruption, honeying and making love
    Over the nasty sty—
QUEEN: O, speak to me no more.
    These words, like daggers, enter in my ears.
    No more, sweet Hamlet!
HAMLET: A murderer and a villain,
100 A slave that is not twentieth part the tithe°
    Of your precedent° lord, a vice° of kings,
    A cutpurse of the empire and the rule,
    That from a shelf the precious diadem stole,
    And put it in his pocket!
105 QUEEN: No more!

(Enter Ghost [in his nightgown].)

HAMLET: A king of shreds and patches°—
    Save me, and hover o'er me with your wings,
    You heavenly guards! What would your gracious
      figure?
QUEEN: Alas, he's mad!
110 HAMLET: Do you not come your tardy son to chide,
    That, laps'd in time and passion,° lets go by
    Th' important° acting of your dread command?
    O, say!

GHOST: Do not forget. This visitation
    Is but to whet thy almost blunted purpose.   115
    But, look, amazement° on thy mother sits.
    O, step between her and her fighting soul!
    Conceit° in weakest bodies strongest works.
    Speak to her, Hamlet.
HAMLET: How is it with you, lady?
QUEEN: Alas, how is 't with you,   120
    That you do bend your eye on vacancy,
    And with th' incorporal° air do hold discourse?
    Forth at your eyes your spirits wildly peep,
    And, as the sleeping soldiers in th' alarm,
    Your bedded° hair, like life in excrements,°   125
    Start up and stand an° end. O gentle son,
    Upon the heat and flame of thy distemper
    Sprinkle cool patience. Whereon do you look?
HAMLET: On him, on him! Look you how pale he
      glares!
    His form and cause conjoin'd,° preaching to stones, 130
    Would make them capable.°—Do not look upon
      me,
    Lest with this piteous action you convert
    My stern effects.° Then what I have to do
    Will want true color°—tears perchance for blood.
QUEEN: To whom do you speak this?   135
HAMLET: Do you see nothing there?
QUEEN: Nothing at all, yet all that is I see.
HAMLET: Nor did you nothing hear?
QUEEN: No, nothing but ourselves.
HAMLET: Why, look you there, look how it steals away! 140
    My father, in his habit° as he lived!
    Look, where he goes, even now, out at the portal!
                              (Exit Ghost.)
QUEEN: This is the very coinage of your brain.
    This bodiless creation ecstasy°
    Is very cunning in.   145
HAMLET: Ecstasy?
    My pulse, as yours, doth temperately keep time,
    And makes as healthful music. It is not madness
    That I have utter'd. Bring me to the test,
    And I the matter will reword, which madness   150
    Would gambol° from. Mother, for love of grace,
    Lay not that flattering unction° to your soul
    That not your trespass but my madness speaks.
    It will but skin and film the ulcerous place,
    Whiles rank corruption, mining° all within,   155

---

78. **cozen'd:** Cheated. **hoodman-blind:** Blindman's bluff.
80. **sans:** Without. 82. **mope:** Be dazed, act aimlessly.
84. **mutine:** Mutiny. 86–89. **Proclaim . . . will:** Call it no shameful business when the compelling ardor of youth delivers the attack, i.e., commits lechery, since the frost of advanced age burns with as active a fire of lust and reason perverts itself by fomenting lust rather than restraining it. 92. **grained:** Dyed in grain, indelible. 93. **tinct:** Color. 94. **enseamed:** Laden with grease. 100. **tithe:** Tenth part. 101. **precedent:** Former (i.e., the elder Hamlet). **vice:** Buffoon (a reference to the vice of the morality plays). 106. **shreds and patches:** Motley, the traditional costume of the clown or fool. 111. **laps'd . . . passion:** Having allowed time to lapse and passion to cool. 112. **important:** Importunate, urgent.

116. **amazement:** Distraction. 118. **Conceit:** Imagination. 122. **incorporal:** Immaterial. 125. **bedded:** Laid in smooth layers. **excrements:** Outgrowths. 126. **an:** On. 130. **His . . . conjoin'd:** His appearance joined to his cause for speaking. 131. **capable:** Receptive. 132–33. **convert . . . effects:** Divert me from my stern duty. 134. **want true color:** Lack plausibility so that (with a play on the normal sense of *color*) I shall shed tears instead of blood. 141. **habit:** Dress. 144. **ecstasy:** Madness. 151. **gambol:** Skip away. 152. **unction:** Ointment. 155. **mining:** Working under the surface.

Bill Murray as Polonius and Julia Stiles as Ophelia in Michael Almereyda's 2000 film adaptation of *Hamlet,* which also starred Ethan Hawke as Hamlet, Sam Shepard as the Ghost of Hamlet's father, and Kyle MacLachlan as Claudius.

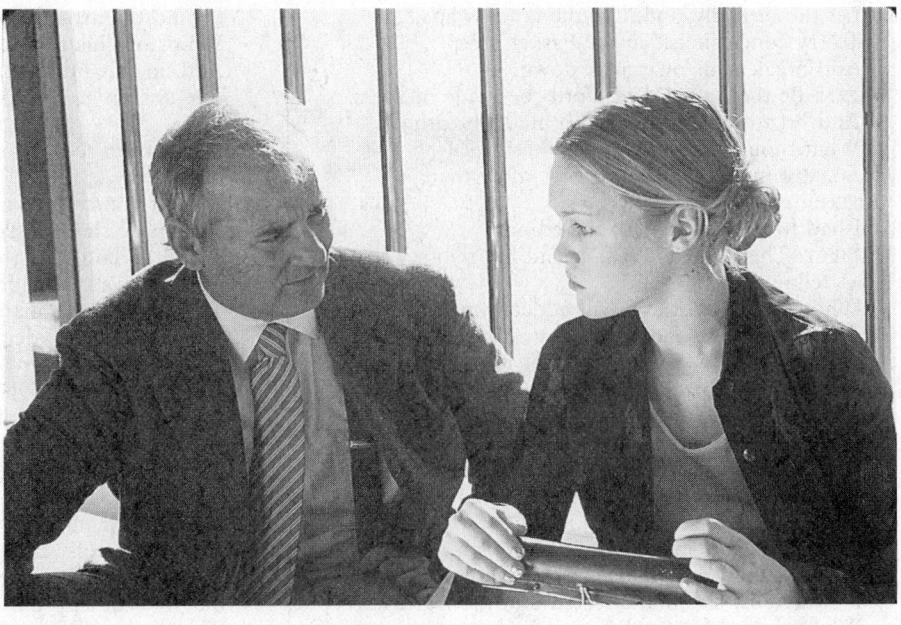

Infects unseen. Confess yourself to heaven,
Repent what's past, avoid what is to come,
And do not spread the compost° on the weeds
To make them ranker. Forgive me this my virtue;°
160   For in the fatness° of these pursy° times
Virtue itself of vice must pardon beg,
Yea, curb° and woo for leave° to do him good.
QUEEN: O Hamlet, thou hast cleft my heart in twain.
HAMLET: O, throw away the worser part of it,
165   And live the purer with the other half.
Good night. But go not to my uncle's bed;
Assume a virtue, if you have it not.
That monster, custom, who all sense doth eat,°
Of habits devil,° is angel yet in this,
170   That to the use of actions fair and good
He likewise gives a frock or livery°
That aptly is put on. Refrain tonight,
And that shall lend a kind of easiness
To the next abstinence; the next more easy;
175   For use° almost can change the stamp of nature,
And either° . . . the devil, or throw him out
With wondrous potency. Once more, good night;
And when you are desirous to be bless'd,°

I'll blessing beg of you. For this same lord,
                                    [*Pointing to Polonius.*]
I do repent; but heaven hath pleas'd it so   180
To punish me with this, and this with me,
That I must be their scourge and minister.°
I will bestow° him, and will answer well
The death I gave him. So, again, good night.
I must be cruel only to be kind.   185
Thus bad begins and worse remains behind.°
One word more, good lady.
QUEEN: What shall I do?
HAMLET: Not this, by no means, that I bid you do:
Let the bloat° king tempt you again to bed,
Pinch wanton on your cheek, call you his mouse,   190
And let him, for a pair of reechy° kisses,
Or paddling in your neck with his damn'd fingers,
Make you to ravel all this matter out,
That I essentially am not in madness,
But mad in craft. 'Twere good° you let him know,   195
For who that's but a queen, fair, sober, wise,
Would from a paddock,° from a bat, a gib,°
Such dear concernings° hide? Who would do so?
No, in despite of sense and secrecy,
Unpeg the basket° on the house's top,   200

158. **compost:** Manure.   159. **this my virtue:** My virtuous talk in reproving you.   160. **fatness:** Grossness.   **pursy:** Short-winded, corpulent.   162. **curb:** Bow, bend the knee.   **leave:** Permission.   168. **who . . . eat:** Who consumes all proper or natural feeling.   169. **Of habits devil:** Devil-like in prompting evil habits.   171. **livery:** An outer appearance, a customary garb (and hence a predisposition easily assumed in time of stress).   175. **use:** Habit.   176. **And either:** A defective line usually emended by inserting the word *master* after *either,* following the fourth quarto and early editors.   178. **be bless'd:** Become blessed, i.e., repentant.

182. **their scourge and minister:** Agent of heavenly retribution. (By *scourge,* Hamlet also suggests that he himself will eventually suffer punishment in the process of fulfilling heaven's will.)   183. **bestow:** Stow, dispose of.   186. **behind:** To come.   189. **bloat:** Bloated.   191. **reechy:** Dirty, filthy.   195. **good:** Said ironically; also the following eight lines.   197. **paddock:** Toad.   **gib:** Tomcat.   198. **dear concernings:** Important affairs.   200. **Unpeg the basket:** Open the cage, i.e., let out the secret.

Let the birds fly, and, like the famous ape,°
To try conclusions,° in the basket creep
And break your own neck down.
QUEEN: Be thou assur'd, if words be made of breath,
205 And breath of life, I have no life to breathe
What thou hast said to me.
HAMLET: I must to England; you know that?
QUEEN: Alack,
I had forgot. 'Tis so concluded on.
HAMLET: There's letters seal'd, and my two school-
fellows,
210 Whom I will trust as I will adders fang'd,
They bear the mandate; they must sweep my way,°
And marshal me to knavery. Let it work.
For 'tis the sport to have the enginer°
Hoist with° his own petar,° and 't shall go hard
215 But I will delve one yard below their mines,°
And blow them at the moon. O, 'tis most sweet,
When in one line two crafts° directly meet.
This man shall set me packing.°
I'll lug the guts into the neighbor room.
220 Mother, good night indeed. This counselor
Is now most still, most secret, and most grave,
Who was in life a foolish prating knave.
Come, sir, to draw toward an end° with you.
Good night, mother.

(Exeunt [severally, Hamlet dragging in Polonius].)

{ACT IV • Scene 1}°

(Enter King and Queen, with Rosencrantz and Guildenstern.)

KING: There's matter in these sighs, these profound
heaves
You must translate; 'tis fit we understand them.
Where is your son?
QUEEN: Bestow this place on us a little while.

[Exeunt Rosencrantz and Guildenstern.]

5 Ah, mine own lord, what have I seen tonight!
KING: What, Gertrude? How does Hamlet?
QUEEN: Mad as the sea and wind when both contend
Which is the mightier. In his lawless fit,

Behind the arras hearing something stir,
Whips out his rapier, cries, "A rat, a rat!"   10
And, in this brainish apprehension,° kills
The unseen good old man.
KING: O heavy deed!
It had been so with us, had we been there.
His liberty is full of threats to all—
To you yourself, to us, to everyone.   15
Alas, how shall this bloody deed be answer'd?
It will be laid to us, whose providence°
Should have kept short,° restrain'd, and out of haunt°
This mad young man. But so much was our love
We would not understand what was most fit,   20
But, like the owner of a foul disease,
To keep it from divulging,° let it feed
Even on the pith of life. Where is he gone?
QUEEN: To draw apart the body he hath kill'd,
O'er whom his very madness, like some ore°   25
Among a mineral° of metals base,
Shows itself pure: 'a weeps for what is done.
KING: O Gertrude, come away!
The sun no sooner shall the mountains touch
But we will ship him hence, and this vile deed 30
We must, with all our majesty and skill,
Both countenance and excuse. Ho, Guildenstern!

(Enter Rosencrantz and Guildenstern.)

Friends both, go join you with some further aid.
Hamlet in madness hath Polonius slain,
And from his mother's closet hath he dragg'd him. 35
Go seek him out; speak fair, and bring the body
Into the chapel. I pray you, haste in this.

[Exeunt Rosencrantz and Guildenstern.]

Come, Gertrude, we'll call up our wisest friends
And let them know both what we mean to do
And what's untimely done°   40
Whose whisper o'er the world's diameter,°
As level° as the cannon to his blank,°
Transports his pois'ned shot, may miss our name,
And hit the woundless° air. O, come away!
My soul is full of discord and dismay.   (Exeunt.) 45

{Scene II}°

(Enter Hamlet.)

HAMLET: Safely stow'd.
[ROSENCRANTZ, GUILDENSTERN (within): Hamlet! Lord
Hamlet!]

---

201. **famous ape:** In a story now lost. 202. **conclusions:** Experiments (in which the ape apparently enters a cage from which birds have been released and then tries to fly out of the cage as they have done, falling to his death). 211. **sweep my way:** Go before me. 213. **enginer:** Constructor of military contrivances. 214. **Hoist with:** Blown up by. **petar:** Petard, an explosive used to blow in a door or make a breach. 215. **mines:** Tunnels used in warfare to undermine the enemy's emplacements; Hamlet will countermine by going under their mines. 217. **crafts:** Acts of guile, plots. 218. **set me packing:** Set me to making schemes, and set me to lugging (him) and, also, send me off in a hurry. 223. **draw . . . end:** Finish up (with a pun on *draw*, pull). **IV, I. Location:** The castle.

11. **brainish apprehension:** Headstrong conception. 17. **providence:** Foresight. 18. **short:** On a short tether. **out of haunt:** Secluded. 22. **divulging:** Becoming evident. 25. **ore:** Vein of gold. 26. **mineral:** Mine. 40. **And . . . done:** A defective line; conjectures as to the missing words include *so, haply, slander* (Capell and others); *for, haply, slander* (Theobald and others). 41. **diameter:** Extent from side to side. 42. **As level:** With as direct aim. **blank:** White spot in the center of a target. 44. **woundless:** Invulnerable. **IV, II. Location:** The castle.

HAMLET: But soft, what noise? Who calls on Hamlet?
5   O, here they come.

(Enter Rosencrantz and Guildenstern.)

ROSENCRANTZ: What have you done, my lord, with
the dead body?
HAMLET: Compounded it with dust, whereto 'tis kin.
ROSENCRANTZ: Tell us where 'tis, that we may take it
thence
And bear it to the chapel.
10 HAMLET: Do not believe it.
ROSENCRANTZ: Believe what?
HAMLET: That I can keep your counsel and not mine
own. Besides, to be demanded of° a sponge, what
replication° should be made by the son of a king?
15 ROSENCRANTZ: Take you me for a sponge, my lord?
HAMLET: Ay, sir, that soaks up the King's countenance,°
his rewards, his authorities. But such officers do the
King best service in the end. He keeps them, like an
ape an apple, in the corner of his jaw, first mouth'd,
20 to be last swallow'd. When he needs what you have
glean'd, it is but squeezing you, and, sponge, you
shall be dry again.
ROSENCRANTZ: I understand you not, my lord.
HAMLET: I am glad of it. A knavish speech sleeps in° a
25 foolish ear.
ROSENCRANTZ: My lord, you must tell us where the
body is, and go with us to the King.
HAMLET: The body is with the King, but the King is not
with the body.° The King is a thing—
30 GUILDENSTERN: A thing, my lord?
HAMLET: Of nothing.° Bring me to him. [Hide fox, and
all after.°]   *(Exeunt.)*

{*Scene III*}°

(Enter King, and two or three.)

KING: I have sent to seek him, and to find the body.
How dangerous is it that this man goes loose!
Yet must not we put the strong law on him.
He's lov'd of the distracted° multitude,
5   Who like not in their judgment, but their eyes,
And where 'tis so, th' offender's scourge° is weigh'd,°
But never the offense. To bear° all smooth and even,
This sudden sending him away must seem

Deliberate pause.° Diseases desperate grown
By desperate appliance are reliev'd,   10
Or not at all.

(Enter Rosencrantz, [Guildenstern,] and all the rest.)

How now? What hath befall'n?
ROSENCRANTZ: Where the dead body is bestow'd, my
lord,
We cannot get from him.
KING: But where is he?
ROSENCRANTZ: Without, my lord; guarded, to know
your pleasure.
KING: Bring him before us.
ROSENCRANTZ: Ho! Bring in the lord.   15

(They enter [with Hamlet].)

KING: Now, Hamlet, where's Polonius?
HAMLET: At supper.
KING: At supper? Where?
HAMLET: Not where he eats, but where 'a is eaten. A
certain convocation of politic worms° are e'en at   20
him. Your worm is your only emperor for diet.° We
fat all creatures else to fat us, and we fat ourselves for
maggots. Your fat king and your lean beggar is but
variable service,° two dishes, but to one table—
that's the end.   25
KING: Alas, alas!
HAMLET: A man may fish with the worm that hath eat°
of a king, and eat of the fish that hath fed of that
worm.
KING: What dost thou mean by this?   30
HAMLET: Nothing but to show you how a king may go a
progress° through the guts of a beggar.
KING: Where is Polonius?
HAMLET: In heaven. Send thither to see. If your messen-
ger find him not there, seek him i' th' other place   35
yourself. But if indeed you find him not within this
month, you shall nose him as you go up the stairs
into the lobby.
KING [*to some Attendants*]: Go seek him there.
HAMLET: 'A will stay till you come.
                              [*Exit Attendants.*]
KING: Hamlet, this deed, for thine especial safety.—   40
Which we do tender,° as we dearly° grieve
For that which thou hast done—must send thee
hence
[With fiery quickness.] Therefore prepare thyself.
The bark° is ready, and the wind at help,   45
Th' associates tend,° and everything is bent°
For England.

---

13. **demanded of:** Questioned by. 14. **replication:** Reply.
16. **countenance:** Favor. 24. **sleeps in:** Has no meaning to.
29. **The . . . body:** Perhaps alludes to the legal commonplace of
"the king's two bodies," which drew a distinction between the
sacred office of kingship and the particular mortal who possessed it at any given time. 31. **Of nothing:** Of no account.
31–32. **Hide . . . after:** An old signal cry in the game of hide-
and-seek, suggesting that Hamlet now runs away from them.
IV, III. **Location:** The castle. 4. **distracted:** Fickle, unstable.
6. **scourge:** Punishment. **weigh'd:** Taken into consideration.
7. **bear:** Manage.

9. **Deliberate pause:** Carefully considered action. 20. **politic
worms:** Crafty worms (suited to a master spy like Polonius).
21. **diet:** Food, eating (with perhaps a punning reference to the
Diet of Worms, a famous convocation held in 1521).
24. **variable service:** Different courses of a single meal.
27. **eat:** Eaten (pronounced "et"). 32. **progress:** Royal journey of state. 42. **tender:** Regard, hold dear. **dearly:** Intensely.
45. **bark:** Sailing vessel. 46. **tend:** Wait. **bent:** In readiness.

HAMLET: For England!

KING: Ay, Hamlet.

50 HAMLET: Good.

KING: So is it, if thou knew'st our purposes.

HAMLET: I see a cherub° that sees them. But, come, for
England! Farewell, dear mother.

KING: Thy loving father, Hamlet.

55 HAMLET: My mother. Father and mother is man and
wife, man and wife is one flesh, and so, my mother.
Come, for England! *(Exit.)*

KING: Follow him at foot;° tempt him with speed
aboard.

Delay it not; I'll have him hence tonight.

60 Away! For everything is seal'd and done
That else leans on° th' affair. Pray you, make haste.

[Exeunt all but the King.]

And, England,° if my love thou hold'st at aught—
As my great power thereof may give thee sense,
Since yet thy cicatrice° looks raw and red

65 After the Danish sword, and thy free awe°
Pays homage to us—thou mayst not coldly set°
Our sovereign process,° which imports at full,
By letters congruing° to that effect,
The present° death of Hamlet. Do it, England,

70 For like the hectic° in my blood he rages,
And thou must cure me. Till I know 'tis done,
Howe'er my haps,° my joys were ne'er begun.

(Exit.)

{Scene IV}°

(Enter Fortinbras with his Army over the stage.)

FORTINBRAS: Go, captain, from me greet the Danish
king.

Tell him that, by his license,° Fortinbras
Craves the conveyance° of a promis'd march
Over his kingdom. You know the rendezvous.

5 If that his Majesty would aught with us,
We shall express our duty in his eye;°
And let him know so.

CAPTAIN: I will do 't, my lord.

FORTINBRAS: Go softly° on. *[Exeunt all but the
Captain.]*

(Enter Hamlet, Rosencrantz, [Guildenstern,] etc.)

HAMLET: Good sir, whose powers° are these?

10 CAPTAIN: They are of Norway, sir.

HAMLET: How purposed, sir, I pray you?

CAPTAIN: Against some part of Poland.

HAMLET: Who commands them, sir?

CAPTAIN: The nephew to old Norway, Fortinbras.

HAMLET: Goes it against the main° of Poland, sir,   15
Or for some frontier?

CAPTAIN: Truly to speak, and with no addition,°
We go to gain a little patch of ground
That hath in it no profit but the name.
To pay° five ducats, five, I would not farm it;°   20
Nor will it yield to Norway or the Pole
A ranker° rate, should it be sold in fee.°

HAMLET: Why, then the Polack never will defend it.

CAPTAIN: Yes, it is already garrison'd.

HAMLET: Two thousand souls and twenty thousand
ducats   25
Will not debate the question of this straw.°
This is th' imposthume° of much wealth and
peace,
That inward breaks, and shows no cause without
Why the man dies. I humbly thank you, sir.

CAPTAIN: God buy you, sir.   *[Exit.]*

ROSENCRANTZ: Will 't please you go, my lord?   30

HAMLET: I'll be with you straight. Go a little before.

[Exit all except Hamlet.]

How all occasions do inform against° me,
And spur my dull revenge! What is a man,
If his chief good and market of° his time
Be but to sleep and feed? A beast, no more.   35
Sure he that made us with such large discourse,°
Looking before and after, gave us not
That capability and god-like reason
To fust° in us unus'd. Now, whether it be
Bestial oblivion,° or some craven scruple   40
Of thinking too precisely on th' event°—
A thought which, quarter'd, hath but one part
wisdom
And ever three parts coward—I do not know
Why yet I live to say "This thing's to do,"
Sith° I have cause and will and strength and means   45
To do 't. Examples gross° as earth exhort me:
Witness this army of such mass and charge°
Led by a delicate and tender prince,
Whose spirit, with divine ambition puff'd
Makes mouths° at the invisible event,   50
Exposing what is mortal and unsure
To all that fortune, death, and danger dare,

---

52. **cherub:** Cherubim are angels of knowledge. 58. **at foot:** Close behind, at heel. 61. **leans on:** Bears upon, is related to. 62. **England:** King of England. 64. **cicatrice:** Scar. 65. **free awe:** Voluntary show of respect. 66. **set:** Esteem. 67. **process:** Command. 68. **congruing:** Agreeing. 69. **present:** Immediate. 70. **hectic:** Persistent fever. 72. **haps:** Fortunes. IV, IV. **Location:** The coast of Denmark. 2. **license:** Permission. 3. **conveyance:** Escort, convoy. 6. **eye:** Presence. 8. **softly:** Slowly. 9. **powers:** Forces.

15. **main:** Main part. 17. **addition:** Exaggeration. 20. **To pay:** I.e., for a yearly rental of. **farm it:** Take a lease of it. 22. **ranker:** Higher. **in fee:** Fee simple, outright. 26. **debate . . . straw:** Settle this trifling matter. 27. **imposthume:** Abscess. 32. **inform against:** Denounce, betray; take shape against. 34. **market of:** Profit of compensation for. 36. **discourse:** Power of reasoning. 39. **fust:** Grow moldy. 40. **oblivion:** Forgetfulness. 41. **event:** Outcome. 45. **Sith:** Since. 46. **gross:** Obvious. 47. **charge:** Expense. 50. **Makes mouths:** Makes scornful faces.

Even for an egg-shell. Rightly to be great
Is not to stir without great argument,
55 But greatly to find quarrel in a straw
When honor's at the stake. How stand I then,
That have a father kill'd, a mother stain'd,
Excitements of° my reason and my blood,
And let all sleep, while, to my shame, I see
60 The imminent death of twenty thousand men,
That, for a fantasy° and trick° of fame,
Go to their graves like beds, fight for a plot°
Whereon the numbers cannot try the cause,°
Which is not tomb enough and continent°
65 To hide the slain? O, from this time forth,
My thoughts be bloody, or be nothing worth!

                                                    (*Exit.*)

{*Scene V*}°

(*Enter Horatio, [Queen] Gertrude, and a Gentleman.*)

QUEEN: I will not speak with her.
GENTLEMAN: She is importunate, indeed distract.
   Her mood will needs be pitied.
QUEEN: What would she have?
GENTLEMAN: She speaks much of her father, says she
      hears
   There's tricks° i' th' world, and hems, and beats
      her heart,°
5 Spurns enviously at straws,° speaks things in doubt°
   That carry but half sense. Her speech is nothing,
   Yet the unshaped use° of it doth move
   The hearers to collection;° they yawn° at it,
10 And botch° the words up fit to their own thoughts,
   Which, as her winks and nods and gestures yield°
      them,
   Indeed would make one think there might be
      thought,°
   Though nothing sure, yet much unhappily.
HORATIO: 'twere good she were spoken with, for she
      may strew
15 Dangerous conjectures in ill-breeding° minds.
QUEEN: Let her come in.   [*Exit Gentlemen.*]
   [*Aside.*] To my sick soul, as sin's true nature is,
   Each toy° seems prologue to some great amiss.°

So full of artless jealousy is guilt,
It spills itself in fearing to be spilt.°   20

(*Enter Ophelia [distracted].*)

OPHELIA: Where is the beauteous majesty of Denmark?
QUEEN: How now, Ophelia?
OPHELIA (*she sings*): "How should I your true love
      know
   From another one?
   By his cockle hat° and staff,   25
   And his sandal shoon."°
QUEEN: Alas, sweet lady, what imports this song?
OPHELIA: Say you? Nay, pray you, mark.
   "He is dead and gone, lady,   (*Song.*)
   He is dead and gone;°   30
   At his head a grass-green turf,
   At his heels a stone."
   O, ho!
QUEEN: Nay, but Ophelia—
OPHELIA: Pray you mark.   35
   [*Sings.*] "White his shroud as the mountain
      snow"—

(*Enter King.*)

QUEEN: Alas, look here, my lord.
OPHELIA: "Larded° all with flowers   (*Song.*)
   Which bewept to the ground did not go
   With true-love showers."   40
KING: How do you, pretty lady?
OPHELIA: Well, God 'ild° you! They say the owl° was a
   baker's daughter. Lord, we know what we are, but
   know not what we may be. God be at your table!
KING: Conceit° upon her father.   45
OPHELIA: Pray let's have no words of this; but when they
   ask you what it means, say you this:
   "Tomorrow is Saint Valentine's° day.   (*Song.*)
   All in the morning betime,
   And I a maid at your window,   50
   To be your Valentine.
   Then up he rose, and donn'd his clo'es,
   And dupp'd° the chamber-door,
   Let in the maid, that out a maid
   Never departed more."   55
KING: Pretty Ophelia!
OPHELIA: Indeed, la, without an oath, I'll make an end
   on 't:
   [*Sings.*] "By Gis° and by Saint Charity,

---

58. Excitements of: Promptings by. **61. fantasy:** Fanciful caprice. **trick:** Trifle. **62. plot:** I.e., of ground. **63. Whereon . . . cause:** On which there is insufficient room for the soldiers needed to engage in a military contest. **64. continent:** Receptacle, container. **IV, v. Location:** The castle. **5. tricks:** Deceptions. **heart:** Breast. **6. Spurns . . . straws:** Kicks spitefully, takes offense at trifles. **in doubt:** Obscurely. **8. unshaped use:** Distracted manner. **9. collection:** Inference, a guess at some sort of meaning. **yawn:** Wonder, grasp. **10. botch:** Patch. **11. yield:** Delivery, bring forth (her words). **12. thought:** Conjectured. **15. ill-breeding:** Prone to suspect the worst. **18. toy:** Trifle. **amiss:** Calamity.

19–20. So . . . spilt: Guilt is so full of suspicion that it unskillfully betrays itself in fearing betrayal. **25. cockle hat:** Hat with cockleshell stuck in it as a sign that the wearer had been a pilgrim to the shrine of St. James of Compostella in Spain. **26. shoon:** Shoes. **38. Larded:** Decorated. **42. God 'ild:** God yield or reward. **owl:** Refers to a legend about a baker's daughter who was turned into an owl for refusing Jesus bread. **45. Conceit:** Brooding. **48. Valentine's:** This song alludes to the belief that the first girl seen by a man on the morning of this day was his valentine or true love. **53. dupp'd:** Opened. **59. Gis:** Jesus.

Alack, and fie for shame!
60 Young men will do 't, if they come to 't;
        By Cock,° they are to blame.
    Quoth she, 'Before you tumbled me,
        You promised me to wed.'"
    He answers:
65 "'So would I ha' done, by yonder sun,
        An thou hadst not come to my bed.'"
KING: How long hath she been thus?
OPHELIA: I hope all will be well. We must be patient, but
    I cannot choose but weep, to think they would lay
70 him i' th' cold ground. My brother shall know of it;
    and so I thank you for your good counsel. Come, my
    coach! Good night, ladies; good night, sweet ladies;
    good night, good night.
                                                    [Exit.]
KING: Follow her close; give her good watch, I pray
75   you.   [Exit Horatio.]
    O, this is the poison of deep grief; it springs
    All from her father's death—and now behold!
    O Gertrude, Gertrude,
    When sorrows come, they come not single spies,°
80 But in battalions. First, her father slain;
    Next, your son gone, and he most violent author
    Of his own just remove; the people muddied,°
    Thick and unwholesome in their thoughts and
        whispers,
    For good Polonius' death; and we have done but
        greenly,°
85 In hugger-mugger° to inter him; poor Ophelia
    Divided from herself and her fair judgment,
    Without the which we are pictures, or mere beasts;
    Last, and as much containing as all these,
    Her brother is in secret come from France,
90 Feeds on his wonder, keeps himself in clouds,°
    And wants° not buzzers° to infect his ear
    With pestilent speeches of his father's death,
    Wherein necessity, of matter beggar'd,°
    Will nothing stick our person to arraign
95 In ear and ear.° O my dear Gertrude, this,
    Like to a murd'ring-piece,° in many places
    Gives me superfluous death.   (A noise within.)
[QUEEN: Alack, what noise is this?]
KING: Attend!
100 Where are my Switzers?° Let them guard the door.

(Enter a Messenger.)

    What is the matter?
MESSENGER: Save yourself, my lord!

The ocean, overpeering of his list,°
    Eats not the flats° with more impiteous° haste
    Than young Laertes, in a riotous head,°
    O'erbears your officers. The rabble call him lord,   105
    And, as° the world were now but to begin,
    Antiquity forgot, custom not known,
    The ratifiers and props° of every word,°
    They cry, "Choose we! Laertes shall be king!"
    Caps, hands, and tongues applaud it to the clouds, 110
    "Laertes shall be king, Laertes king!"
                                        (A noise within.)
QUEEN: How cheerfully on the false trail they cry!
    O, this is counter,° you false Danish dogs!

(Enter Laertes with others.)

KING: The doors are broke.
LAERTES: Where is this King? Sirs, stand you all
        without.   115
ALL: No, let's come in.
LAERTES: I pray you, give me leave.
ALL: We will, we will.
                          [They retire without the door.]
LAERTES: I thank you. Keep the door. O thou vile king,
    Give me my father!
QUEEN: Calmly, good Laertes.
                            [She tries to hold him back.]
LAERTES: That drop of blood that's calm proclaims
        me bastard,   120
    Cries cuckold to my father, brands the harlot
    Even here, between the chaste unsmirched brow
    Of my true mother.
KING: What is the cause, Laertes,
    That thy rebellion looks so giant-like?
    Let him go, Gertrude. Do not fear our° person.   125
    There's such divinity doth hedge a king
    That treason can but peep to what it would,°
    Acts little of his will.° Tell me, Laertes,
    Why thou art thus incens'd. Let him go, Gertrude.
    Speak, man.
LAERTES: Where is my father?
KING: Dead.   130
QUEEN: But not by him.
KING: Let him demand his fill.
LAERTES: How came he dead? I'll not be juggled with.
    To hell, allegiance! Vows, to the blackest devil!
    Conscience and grace, to the profoundest pit!
    I dare damnation. To this point I stand,   135
    That both the worlds I give to negligence,°

---

62. Cock: A perversion of *God* in oaths.   79. spies: Scouts
sent in advance of the main force.   82. muddied: Stirred
up, confused.   84. greenly: Imprudently, foolishly.   85. hug-
ger-mugger: Secret haste.   90. in clouds: I.e., of suspicion and rumor.   91. wants: Lacks.   buzzers: Gossipers,
informers.   93. of matter beggar'd: Unprovided with facts.
95. Will . . . and ear: Will not hesitate to accuse my (royal)
person in everybody's ears.   96. murd'ring-piece: Cannon
loaded so as to scatter its shot.   100. Switzers: Swiss guards,
mercenaries.

102. overpeering of his list: Overflowing its shore.   103. flats:
Flatlands near shore.   impiteous: Pitiless.   104. head: Armed
force.   106. as: As if.   108. ratifiers and props: Refer to
antiquity and *custom*.   word: Promise.   113. counter: A
hunting term meaning to follow the trail in a direction opposite
to that which the game has taken.   125. fear our: Fear for my.
127. can . . . would: Can only glance; as from far off or through
a barrier, at what it would intend.   128. Acts . . . will: (But)
performs little of what it intends.   136. both . . . negligence:
Both this world and the next are of no consequence to me.

Let come what comes, only I'll be reveng'd
Most throughly° for my father.
KING: Who shall stay you?
LAERTES: My will, not all the world's.°
140   And for my means, I'll husband them so well,
They shall go far with little.
KING: Good Laertes,
If you desire to know the certainty
Of your dear father, is 't writ in your revenge
That, swoopstake,° you will draw both friend and
foe,
145   Winner and loser?
LAERTES: None but his enemies.
KING: Will you know them then?
LAERTES: To his good friends thus wide I'll ope my arms,
And, like the kind life-rend'ring pelican,°
Repast° them with my blood.
KING: Why, now you speak
150   Like a good child and a true gentleman.
That I am guiltless of your father's death,
And am most sensibly° in grief for it,
It shall as level° to your judgment 'pear
As day does to your eye.
                             (*A noise within:*) "Let her come in."
155   LAERTES: How now? What noise is that?

(*Enter Ophelia.*)

O heat, dry up my brains! Tears seven times salt
Burn out the sense and virtue° of mine eye!
By heaven, thy madness shall be paid with weight°
Till our scale turn the beam.° O rose of May!
160   Dear maid, kind sister, sweet Ophelia!
O heavens, is 't possible a young maid's wits
Should be as mortal as an old man's life?
[Nature is fine in° love, and where 'tis fine,
It sends some precious instance° of itself
165   After the thing it loves.°]
OPHELIA: "They bore him barefac'd on the bier;
                                              (*Song.*)
[Hey non nonny, nonny, hey nonny,]
And in his grave rain'd many a tear"—
Fare you well, my dove!
LAERTES: Hadst thou thy wits, and didst persuade°
170   revenge,
It could not move thus.
OPHELIA: You must sing "A-down a-down,
And you call him a-down-a."

O, how the wheel° becomes it! It is the false steward°
that stole his master's daughter.   175
LAERTES: This nothing's more than matter.°
OPHELIA: There's rosemary,° that's for remembrance;
pray you, love, remember. And there is pansies,° that's
for thoughts.
LAERTES: A document° in madness, thoughts and remem-   180
brance fitted.
OPHELIA: There's fennel° for you, and columbines.°
There's rue° for you, and here's some for me; we may
call it herb of grace o' Sundays. You may wear your
rue with a difference.° There's a daisy.° I would give   185
you some violets,° but they wither'd all when my
father died. They say 'e made a good end—
[*Sings.*] "For bonny sweet Robin is all my joy."
LAERTES: Thought° and affliction, passion, hell itself,
She turns to favor° and to prettiness.   190
OPHELIA: "And will 'a not come again?   (*Song.*)
And will 'a not come again?
      No, no, he is dead,
      Go to thy death-bed,
He never will come again.   195

"His beard was as white as snow,
All flaxen was his poll.°
      He is gone, he is gone,
      And we cast away moan.
God 'a' mercy on his soul!   200
And of all Christians' souls, I pray God. God buy you.
                                                    [*Exit.*]
LAERTES: Do you see this, O God?
KING: Laertes, I must commune with your grief,
Or you deny me right. Go but apart,
Make choice of whom your wisest friends you will,   205
And they shall hear and judge 'twixt you and me.
If by direct or by collateral° hand
They find us touch'd,° we will our kingdom give,
Our crown, our life, and all that we call ours,
To you in satisfaction; but if not,   210
Be you content to lend your patience to us,
And we shall jointly labor with your soul
To give it due content.

138. **throughly:** Thoroughly.   139. **My will . . . world's:** I'll stop (*stay*) when my will is accomplished, not for anyone else's. 144. **swoopstake:** Literally, taking all stakes on the gambling table at once, i.e., indiscriminately; *draw* is also a gambling term.   148. **pelican:** Refers to the belief that the female pelican fed its young with its own blood.   149. **Repast:** Feed. 152. **sensibly:** Feelingly.   153. **level:** Plain.   157. **virtue:** Faculty, power.   158. **paid with weight:** Repaid, avenged equally or more.   159. **beam:** Crossbar of a balance.   163. **fine in:** Refined by.   164. **instance:** Token.   165. **After . . . loves:** Into the grave, along with Polonius. 170. **persuade:** Argue cogently for.

174. **wheel:** Spinning wheel as accompaniment to the song, or refrain.   **false steward:** The story is unknown. 176. **This . . . matter:** This seeming nonsense is more meaningful than sane utterance.   177. **rosemary:** Used as a symbol of remembrance both at weddings and at funerals.   178. **pansies:** Emblems of love and courtship; perhaps from French *pensées*, thoughts.   180. **document:** Instruction, lesson.   182. **fennel:** Emblem of flattery.   **columbines:** Emblems of unchastity (?) or ingratitude (?).   183. **rue:** Emblem of repentance; when mingled with holy water, it was known as *herb of grace*. 185. **with a difference:** Suggests that Ophelia and the queen have different causes of sorrow and repentance; perhaps with a play on *rue* in the sense of ruth, pity.   **daisy:** Emblem of dissembling, faithlessness.   186. **violets:** Emblems of faithfulness.   189. **Thought:** Melancholy.   190. **favor:** Grace. 197. **poll:** Head.   207. **collateral:** Indirect.   208. **us touch'd:** Me implicated.

LAERTES: Let this be so.
His means of death, his obscure funeral—
215   No trophy,° sword, nor hatchment° o'er his bones,
No noble rite nor formal ostentation°—
Cry to be heard, as 'twere from heaven to earth,
That I must call 't in question.
KING: So you shall;
And where th' offense is, let the great ax fall.
220   I pray you go with me.   (Exeunt.)

{Scene VI}°

(Enter Horatio and others.)

HORATIO: What are they that would speak with me?
GENTLEMAN: Seafaring men, sir. They say they have let-
ters for you.
HORATIO: Let them come in.   [Exit Gentleman.]
5   I do not know from what part of the world
I should be greeted, if not from lord Hamlet.

(Enter Sailors.)

FIRST SAILOR: God bless you sir.
HORATIO: Let him bless thee too.
FIRST SAILOR: 'A shall, sir, an 't please him. There's a let-
10   ter for you, sir—it came from th' ambassador that
was bound for England—if your name be Horatio,
as I am let to know it is.   [Gives letter.]
HORATIO [reads]: "Horatio, when thou shalt have overlook'd this, give these fellows some means° to the
15   King; they have letters for him. Ere we were two days
old at sea, a pirate of very warlike appointment° gave
us chase. Finding ourselves too slow of sail, we put
on a compell'd valor, and in the grapple I boarded
them. On the instant they got clear of our ship, so I
20   alone became their prisoner. They have dealt with me
like thieves of mercy,° but they knew what they did: I
am to do a good turn for them. Let the King have the
letters I have sent, and repair thou to me with as
much speed as thou wouldest fly death. I have words
25   to speak in thine ear will make thee dumb; yet are
they much too light for the bore° of the matter. These
good fellows will bring thee where I am. Rosencrantz
and Guildenstern hold their course for England. Of
them I have much to tell thee. Farewell.
30   He that thou knowest thine, Hamlet."
Come, I will give you way for these your letters,
And do 't the speedier that you may direct me
To him from whom you brought them.   (Exeunt.)

{Scene VII}°

(Enter King and Laertes.)

KING: Now must your conscience my acquittance seal,°
And you must put me in your heart for friend,
Sith you have heard, and with a knowing ear,
That he which hath your noble father slain
Pursued my life.
LAERTES: It well appears. But tell me   5
Why you proceeded not against these feats°
So criminal and so capital° in nature,
As by your safety, greatness, wisdom, all things else,
You mainly° were stirr'd up.
KING: O, for two special reasons,
Which may to you, perhaps, seem much unsinew'd,°   10
But yet to me th' are strong. The Queen his mother
Lives almost by his looks, and for myself—
My virtue or my plague, be it either which—
She's so conjunctive° to my life and soul
That, as the star moves not but in his sphere,°   15
I could not but by her. The other motive,
Why to a public count° I might not go,
Is the great love the general gender° bear him,
Who, dipping all his faults in their affection,
Would, like the spring° that turneth wood to stone,   20
Convert his gyves° to graces, so that my arrows,
Too slightly timber'd° for so loud° a wind,
Would have reverted to my bow again
And not where I had aim'd them.
LAERTES: And so have I a noble father lost,   25
A sister driven into desp'rate terms,°
Whose worth, if praises may go back° again,
Stood challenger on mount° of all the age
For her perfections. But my revenge will come.
KING: Break not your sleeps for that. You must not
think   30
That we are made of stuff so flat and dull
That we can let our beard be shook with danger
And think it pastime. You shortly shall hear more.
I lov'd your father, and we love ourself;
And that, I hope, will teach you to imagine—   35

(Enter a Messenger with letters.)

[How now? What news?]
MESSENGER: [Letters, my lord, from Hamlet:]

---

215. **trophy:** Memorial. **hatchment:** Tablet displaying the armorial bearings of a deceased person. 216. **ostentation:** Ceremony. IV, VI. **Location:** The castle. 14. **means:** Means of access. 16. **appointment:** Equipage. 21. **thieves of mercy:** Merciful thieves. 26. **bore:** Caliber, i.e., importance.

IV, VII. **Location:** The castle. 1. **my acquittance seal:** Confirm or acknowledge my innocence. 6. **feats:** Acts. 7. **capital:** Punishable by death. 9. **mainly:** Greatly. 10. **unsinew'd:** Weak. 14. **conjunctive:** Closely united. 15. **sphere:** The hollow sphere in which, according to Ptolemaic astronomy, the planets moved. 17. **count:** Account, reckoning. 18. **general gender:** Common people. 20. **spring:** A spring with such a concentration of lime that it coats a piece of wood with limestone, in effect gilding it. 21. **gyves:** Fetters (which, gilded by the people's praise, would look like badges of honor). 22. **slightly timber'd:** Light. **loud:** Strong. 26. **terms:** State, condition. 27. **go back:** Recall Ophelia's former virtues. 28. **on mount:** On high.

These to your Majesty, this to the Queen.
                                                      [*Gives letters.*]
KING: From Hamlet? Who brought them?
MESSENGER: Sailors, my lord, they say; I saw them not.
40   They were given me by Claudio. He receiv'd them
      Of him that brought them.
KING: Laertes, you shall hear them.
      Leave us.   [*Exit Messenger.*]
      [*Reads.*] "High and mighty, you shall know I am set
      naked° on your kingdom. Tomorrow shall I beg leave
45   to see your kingly eyes, when I shall, first asking your
      pardon° thereunto, recount the occasion of my sud-
      den and more strange return.   Hamlet."
      What should this mean? Are all the rest come back?
      Or is it some abuse,° and no such thing?
LAERTES: Know you the hand?
50 KING: 'Tis Hamlet's character.° "Naked!"
      And in a postscript here, he says "alone."
      Can you devise° me?
LAERTES: I am lost in it, my lord. But let him come.
      It warms the very sickness in my heart
55   That I shall live and tell him to his teeth,
      "Thus didst thou."
KING: If it be so, Laertes—
      As how should it be so? How otherwise?°—
      Will you be ruled by me?
LAERTES: Ay, my lord,
      So° you will not o'errule me to a peace.
60 KING: To thine own peace. If he be now returned,
      As checking at° his voyage, and that he means
      No more to undertake it, I will work him
      To an exploit, now ripe in my device,
      Under the which he shall not choose but fall;
65   And for his death no wind of blame shall breathe,
      But even his mother shall uncharge the practice°
      And call it accident.
LAERTES: My lord, I will be rul'd,
      The rather if you could devise it so
      That I might be the organ.°
KING: It falls right.
70   You have been talk'd of since your travel much,
      And that in Hamlet's hearing, for a quality
      Wherein, they say, you shine. Your sum of parts°
      Did not together pluck such envy from him
      As did that one, and that, in my regard,
75   Of the unworthiest siege.°
LAERTES: What part is that, my lord?
KING: A very riband in the cap of youth,
      Yet needful too, for youth no less becomes

The light and careless livery that it wears
Than settled age his sables° and his weeds,°   80
Importing health° and graveness. Two months since
Here was a gentleman of Normandy.
I have seen myself, and serv'd against, the French,
And they can well° on horseback, but this gallant
Had witchcraft in 't; he grew unto his seat,   85
And to such wondrous doing brought his horse
As had he been incorps'd and demi-natured°
With the brave beast. So far he topp'd° my thought
That I, in forgery° of shapes and tricks,
Come short of what he did.
LAERTES: A Norman was 't?   90
KING: A Norman.
LAERTES: Upon my life, Lamord.
KING: The very same.
LAERTES: I know him well. He is the brooch° indeed
And gem of all the nation.
KING: He made confession° of you,   95
And gave you such a masterly report
For art and exercise in your defense,
And for your rapier most especial,
That he cried out, 'twould be a sight indeed,
If one could match you. The scrimers° of their
      nation,   100
He swore, had neither motion, guard, nor eye,
If you oppos'd them. Sir, this report of his
Did Hamlet so envenom with his envy
That he could nothing do but wish and beg
Your sudden coming o'er to play° with you.   105
Now, out of this—
LAERTES: What out of this, my lord?
KING: Laertes, was your father dear to you?
Or are you like the painting of a sorrow,
A face without a heart?
LAERTES: Why ask you this?
KING: Not that I think you did not love your father,   110
But that I know love is begun by time,°
And that I see, in passages of proof,°
Time qualifies° the spark and fire of it.
There lives within the very flame of love
A kind of wick or snuff° that will abate it,   115
And nothing is at a like goodness still,°
For goodness, growing to a plurisy,°
Dies in his own too much.° That° we would do,
We should do when we would; for this "would"
      changes

44. **naked:** Destitute, unarmed, without following.   46. **pardon:** Permission.   49. **abuse:** Deceit.   50. **character:** Handwriting.   52. **devise:** Explain to.   57. **As . . . otherwise:** How
can this (Hamlet's return) be true? Yet how otherwise than true
(since we have the evidence of his letter).   59. **So:** Provided
that.   61. **checking at:** Turning aside from (like a falcon leaving the quarry to fly at a chance bird).   66. **uncharge the practice:** Acquit the stratagem of being a plot.   69. **organ:** Agent,
instrument.   72. **Your . . . parts:** All your other virtues.
75. **unworthiest siege:** Least important rank.

80. **sables:** Rich robes furred with sable.   **weeds:** Garments.
81. **Importing health:** Indicating prosperity.   84. **can well:** Are
skilled.   87. **incorps'd and demi-natur'd:** Of one body and
nearly of one nature (like the centaur).   88. **topp'd:** Surpassed.
89. **forgery:** Invention.   93. **brooch:** Ornament.   95. **confession:** Admission of superiority.   100. **scrimers:** Fencers.
105. **play:** Fence.   111. **begun by time:** Subject to change.
112. **passages of proof:** Actual instances.   113. **qualifies:**
Weakens.   115. **snuff:** The charred part of a candlewick.
116. **nothing . . . still:** Nothing remains at a constant level
of perfection.   117. **plurisy:** Excess, plethora.   118. **in . . .
much:** Of its own excess.   **That:** That which.

120   And hath abatements° and delays as many
      As there are tongues, are hands, are accidents,°
      And then this "should" is like a spendthrift's sigh,°
      That hurts by easing.° But, to the quick o' th' ulcer;
      Hamlet comes back. What would you undertake
125   To show yourself your father's son in deed
      More than in words?
LAERTES: To cut his throat i' th' church!
KING: No place, indeed, should murder sanctuarize;°
      Revenge should have no bounds. But, good Laertes,
      Will you do this,° keep close within your chamber.
130   Hamlet return'd shall know you are come home.
      We'll put on those° shall praise your excellence
      And set a double varnish on the fame
      The Frenchman gave you, bring you in fine°
         together,
      And wager on your heads. He, being remiss,°
135   Most generous,° and free from all contriving,
      Will not peruse the foils, so that, with ease,
      Or with a little shuffling, you may choose
      A sword unbated,° and in a pass of practice°
      Requite him for your father.
LAERTES: I will do 't.
140   And for that purpose I'll anoint my sword.
      I bought an unction° of a mountebank°
      So mortal that, but dip a knife in it,
      Where it draws blood no cataplasm° so rare,
      Collected from all simples° that have virtue
145   Under the moon, can save the thing from death
      That is but scratch'd withal. I'll touch my point
      With this contagion, that, if I gall° him slightly,
      It may be death.
KING: Let's further think of this,
      Weigh what convenience both of time and means
150   May fit us to our shape.° If this should fail,
      And that our drift look through our bad
         performance,°
      'Twere better not assay'd. Therefore this project
      Should have a back or second, that might hold
      If this did blast in proof.° Soft, let me see.
155   We'll make a solemn wager on your cunnings—

120. **abatements:** Diminutions.   121. **accidents:** Occurrences, incidents.   122. **spendthrift's sigh:** An allusion to the belief that each sigh cost the heart a drop of blood.   123. **hurts by easing:** Costs the heart blood even while it affords emotional relief.   127. **sanctuarize:** Protect from punishment (alludes to the right of sanctuary with which certain religious places were invested).   129. **Will you do this:** If you wish to do this. 131. **put on those:** Instigate those who.   133. **in fine:** Finally. 134. **remiss:** Negligently unsuspicious.   135. **generous:** Noble-minded.   138. **unbated:** Not blunted, having no button. **pass of practice:** Treacherous thrust.   141. **unction:** Ointment. **mountebank:** Quack doctor.   143. **cataplasm:** Plaster or poultice.   144. **simples:** Herbs.   147. **gall:** Graze, wound. 150. **shape:** Part that we propose to act.   151. **drift . . . performance:** i.e., intention be disclosed by our bungling.   154. **blast in proof:** Burst in the test (like a cannon).

      I ha 't!
      When in your motion you are hot and dry—
      As° make your bouts more violent to that end—
      And that he calls for drink, I'll have prepar'd him
      A chalice for the nonce,° whereon but sipping,   160
      If he by chance escape your venom'd stuck,°
      Our purpose may hold there. [*A cry within.*] But
         stay, what noise?

(*Enter Queen.*)

QUEEN: One woe doth tread upon another's heel,
      So fast they follow. Your sister's drowned, Laertes.
LAERTES: Drown'd! O, where?   165
QUEEN: There is a willow grows askant° the brook
      That shows his hoar° leaves in the glassy stream;
      Therewith fantastic garlands did she make
      Of crow-flowers, nettles, daisies, and long purples°
      That liberal° shepherds give a grosser name,   170
      But our cold° maids do dead men's fingers call them.
      There on the pendent boughs her crownet° weeds
      Clamb'ring to hang, an envious sliver° broke,
      When down her weedy° trophies and herself
      Fell in the weeping brook. Her clothes spread wide,   175
      And mermaid-like awhile they bore her up,
      Which time she chanted snatches of old lauds,°
      As one incapable° of her own distress,
      Or like a creature native and indued°
      Unto that element. But long it could not be   180
      Till that her garments, heavy with their drink,
      Pull'd the poor wretch from her melodious lay
      To muddy death.
LAERTES: Alas, then she is drown'd?
QUEEN: Drown'd, drown'd.
LAERTES: Too much of water hast thou, poor Ophelia,   185
      And therefore I forbid my tears. But yet
      It is our trick;° nature her custom holds,
      Let shame say what it will. [*He weeps.*] When
         these are gone,
      The woman will be out.° Adieu, my lord.
      I have a speech of fire, that fain would blaze,   190
      But that this folly drowns it.   (*Exit.*)
KING: Let's follow, Gertrude.
      How much I had to do to calm his rage!
      Now fear I this will give it start again;
      Therefore let's follow.   (*Exeunt.*)

158. **As:** And you should.   160. **nonce:** Occasion. 161. **stuck:** Thrust (from *stoccado*, a fencing term). 166. **askant:** Aslant.   167. **hoar:** White or gray.   169. **long purples:** Early purple orchids.   170. **liberal:** Free-spoken. 171. **cold:** Chaste.   172. **crownet:** Made into a chaplet or coronet.   173. **envious sliver:** Malicious branch. 174. **weedy:** I.e., of plants.   177. **lauds:** Hymns.   178. **incapable:** Lacking capacity to apprehend.   179. **indued:** Adapted by nature.   187. **It is our trick:** Weeping is our natural way (when sad).   188–89. **When . . . out:** When my tears are all shed, the woman in me will be expended, satisfied.

{*ACT V • Scene 1*}°

(*Enter two Clowns*° [*with spades, etc.*])

FIRST CLOWN: Is she to be buried in Christian burial when she willfully seeks her own salvation?

SECOND CLOWN: I tell thee she is; therefore make her grave straight.° The crowner° hath sat on her, and finds it Christian burial.

FIRST CLOWN: How can that be, unless she drown'd herself in her own defense?

SECOND CLOWN: Why, 'tis found so.

FIRST CLOWN: It must be "se offendendo";° it cannot be else. For here lies the point: if I drown myself wittingly, it argues an act, and an act hath three branches—it is to act, to do, and to perform. Argal,° she drown'd herself wittingly.

SECOND CLOWN: Nay, but hear you, goodman delver—

FIRST CLOWN: Give me leave. Here lies the water; good. Here stands the man; good. If the man go to this water, and drown himself, it is, will he,° nill he, he goes, mark you that. But if the water come to him and drown him, he drowns not himself. Argal, he that is not guilty of his own death shortens not his own life.

SECOND CLOWN: But is this law?

FIRST CLOWN: Ay, marry, is 't—crowner's quest° law.

SECOND CLOWN: Will you ha' the truth on 't? If this had not been a gentlewoman, she should have been buried out o' Christian burial.

FIRST CLOWN: Why, there thou say'st.° And the more pity that great folk should have count'nance° in this world to drown or hang themselves, more than their even-Christen.° Come, my spade. There is no ancient gentlemen but gard'ners, ditchers, and grave-makers. They hold up Adam's profession.

SECOND CLOWN: Was he a gentleman?

FIRST CLOWN: 'A was the first that ever bore arms.

[SECOND CLOWN: Why, he had none.

FIRST CLOWN: What, art a heathen? How dost thou understand the Scripture? The Scripture says "Adam digg'd." Could he dig without arms?] I'll put another question to thee. If thou answerest me not to the purpose, confess thyself°—

SECOND CLOWN: Go to.

FIRST CLOWN: What is he that builds stronger than either the mason, the shipwright, or the carpenter?

SECOND CLOWN: The gallows-maker, for that frame outlives a thousand tenants.

FIRST CLOWN: I like thy wit well, in good faith. The gallows does well, but how does it well? It does well to those that do ill. Now thou dost ill to say the gallows is built stronger than the church. Argal, the gallows may do well to thee. To 't again, come.

SECOND CLOWN: "Who builds stronger than a mason, a shipwright, or a carpenter?"

FIRST CLOWN: Ay, tell me that, and unyoke.°

SECOND CLOWN: Marry, now I can tell.

FIRST CLOWN: To 't.

SECOND CLOWN: Mass,° I cannot tell.

(*Enter Hamlet and Horatio* [*at a distance*].)

FIRST CLOWN: Cudgel thy brains no more about it, for your dull ass will not mend his pace with beating; and, when you are ask'd this question next, say "a grave-maker." The houses he makes lasts till doomsday. Go, get thee in, and fetch me a stoup° of liquor.

        [*Exit Second Clown. First Clown digs.*]
                (*Song.*)

"In youth, when I did love, did love,°
   Methought it was very sweet,
To contract—O—the time for—a—my behove,°
   O, methought there—a—was nothing—a—
     meet."°

HAMLET: Has this fellow no feeling of his business, that 'a sings at grave-making?

HORATIO: Custom hath made it in him a property of easiness.°

HAMLET: 'Tis e'en so. The hand of little employment hath the daintier sense.°

                (*Song.*)

FIRST CLOWN: "But age, with his stealing steps,
   Hath claw'd me in his clutch,
And hath shipped me into the land,°
   As if I had never been such."

           [*Throws up a skull.*]

HAMLET: That skull had a tongue in it, and could sing once. How the knave jowls° it to the ground, as if 'twere Cain's jaw-bone, that did the first murder! This might be the pate of a politician,° which this ass now o'erreaches,° one that would circumvent God, might it not?

HORATIO: It might, my lord.

V, I. **Location:** A churchyard. [S.D.] *Clowns:* Rustics. 4. **straight:** Straightway, immediately. **crowner:** Coroner. 9. **se offendendo:** A comic mistake for *se defendendo,* term used in verdicts of justifiable homicide. 13. **Argal:** Corruption of *ergo,* therefore. 17. **will he:** Will he not. 23. **quest:** Inquest. 27. **there thou say'st:** That's right. 28. **count'nance:** Privilege. 30. **even-Christen:** Fellow Christian. 40. **confess thyself:** The saying continues, "and be hanged."

53. **unyoke:** After this great effort you may unharness the team of your wits. 56. **Mass:** By the Mass. 61. **stoup:** Two-quart measure. 62. **In . . . love:** This and the two following stanzas, with nonsensical variations, are from a poem attributed to Lord Vaux and printed in *Tottel's Miscellany* (1557). The *O* and *a* (for "ah") seemingly are the grunts of the digger. 64. **To contract . . . behove:** To make a betrothal agreement for my benefit (?). 65. **meet:** Suitable, i.e., more suitable. 68–69. **property of easiness:** Something he can do easily and without thinking. 71. **daintier sense:** More delicate sense of feeling. 74. **into the land:** Toward my grave (?) (but note the lack of rhyme in *steps, land*). 77. **jowls:** Dashes. 79. **politician:** Schemer, plotter. 80. **o'erreaches:** Circumvents, gets the better of (with a quibble on the literal sense).

HAMLET: Or of a courtier, which could say "Good morrow, sweet lord! How dost thou, sweet lord?" This
85 might be my Lord Such-a-one, that prais'd my Lord
Such-a-one's horse when 'a meant to beg it, might it
not?
HORATIO: Ay, my lord.
HAMLET: Why, e'en so, and now my Lady Worm's,
90 chapless,° and knock'd about the mazzard° with a
sexton's spade. Here's fine revolution,° an° we had
the trick to see 't. Did these bones cost no more the
breeding,° but to play at loggats° with them? Mine
ache to think on 't.

(Song.)

95 FIRST CLOWN: "A pick-axe, and a spade, a spade,
    For and° a shrouding sheet;
    O, a pit of clay for to be made
    For such a guest is meet."

[Throws up another skull.]

HAMLET: There's another. Why may not that be the
100 skull of a lawyer? Where be his quiddities° now, his
quillities,° his cases, his tenures,° and his tricks? Why
does he suffer this mad knave now to knock him
about the sconce° with a dirty shovel, and will not
tell him of his action of battery? Hum! This fellow
105 might be in 's time a great buyer of land, with his
statutes, his recognizances,° his fines, his double°
vouchers,° his recoveries.° [Is this the fine of his fines,
and the recovery of his recoveries,] to have his fine
pate full of fine dirt?° Will his vouchers vouch him
110 no more of his purchases, and double [ones too],
than the length and breadth of a pair of indentures?°
The very conveyances° of his lands will scarcely lie in
this box,° and must th' inheritor° himself have no
more, ha?
115 HORATIO: Not a jot more, my lord.
HAMLET: Is not parchment made of sheep-skins?
HORATIO: Ay, my lord, and of calf-skins too.

HAMLET: They are sheep and calves which seek out
assurance in that.° I will speak to this fellow.—
Whose grave's this, sirrah?°   120
FIRST CLOWN: Mine, sir.
    [Sings.] "O, a pit of clay for to be made
    [For such a guest is meet]."
HAMLET: I think it be thine, indeed, for thou liest in 't.
FIRST CLOWN: You lie out on 't, sir, and therefore 'tis not   125
yours. For my part, I do not lie in 't, yet it is mine.
HAMLET: Thou dost lie in 't, to be in 't and say it is thine.
'Tis for the dead, not for the quick;° therefore thou
liest.
FIRST CLOWN: 'Tis a quick lie, sir; 'twill away again   130
from me to you.
HAMLET: What man dost thou dig it for?
FIRST CLOWN: For no man, sir.
HAMLET: What woman, then?
FIRST CLOWN: For none, neither.   135
HAMLET: Who is to be buried in 't?
FIRST CLOWN: One that was a woman, sir, but, rest her
soul, she's dead.
HAMLET: How absolute° the knave is! We must speak
by the card,° or equivocation° will undo us. By the   140
Lord, Horatio, this three years I have taken note of it:
the age is grown so pick'd° that the toe of the peasant
comes so near the heel of the courtier, he galls his
kibe.° How long hast thou been a grave-maker?
FIRST CLOWN: Of all the days i' th' year, I came to 't that   145
day that our last king Hamlet overcame Fortinbras.
HAMLET: How long is that since?
FIRST CLOWN: Cannot you tell that? Every fool can tell
that. It was that very day that young Hamlet was
born—he that is mad, and sent into England.   150
HAMLET: Ay, marry, why was he sent into England?
FIRST CLOWN: Why, because 'a was mad. 'A shall
recover his wits there, or, if 'a do not, 'tis no great
matter there.
HAMLET: Why?
FIRST CLOWN: 'Twill not be seen in him there. There the 155
men are as mad as he.
HAMLET: How came he mad?
FIRST CLOWN: Very strangely, they say.
HAMLET: How strangely?
FIRST CLOWN: Faith, e'en with losing his wits.   160
HAMLET: Upon what ground?
FIRST CLOWN: Why, here in Denmark. I have been sex-
ton here, man and boy, thirty years.
HAMLET: How long will a man lie i' th' earth ere he rot?
FIRST CLOWN: Faith, if 'a be not rotten before 'a die— 165
as we have many pocky° corses [now-a-days], that

90. **chapless:** Having no lower jaw. **mazzard:** Head (literally,
a drinking vessel). **91. revolution:** Change. **an:** If. **93. the
breeding:** In the breeding, raising. **loggats:** A game in which
pieces of hardwood are thrown to lie as near as possible to a
stake. **96. For and:** And moreover. **100. quiddities:** Subtleties, quibbles (from Latin *quid,* a thing). **100–01. quillities:**
Verbal niceties, subtle distinctions (variation of *quiddities*).
101. tenures: The holding of a piece of property or office, or the
conditions or period of such holding. **103. sconce:** Head.
106. statutes, recognizances: Legal documents guaranteeing a
debt by attaching land and property. **106–07. fines, recoveries:** Ways of converting entailed estates into "fee simple"
or freehold. **106. double:** Signed by two signatories.
107. vouchers: Guarantees of the legality of a title to real estate.
107–09. fine of his fines . . . fine pate . . . fine dirt: End of his
legal maneuvers . . . elegant head . . . minutely sifted dirt.
111. pair of indentures: Legal document drawn up in duplicate
on a single sheet and then cut apart on a zigzag line so that each
pair was uniquely matched. (Hamlet may refer to two rows of
teeth, or dentures.) **112. conveyances:** Deeds. **113. this box:**
The skull. **inheritor:** Possessor, owner.

119. **assurance in that:** Safety in legal parchments. **120. sirrah:** Term of address to inferiors. **128. quick:** Living.
139. absolute: Positive, decided. **140. by the card:** By
the mariner's card on which the points of the compass were
marked, i.e., with precision. **equivocation:** Ambiguity in the
use of terms. **142. pick'd:** Refined, fastidious. **143–44. galls
his kibe:** Chafes the courtier's chilblain (a swelling or sore
caused by cold). **166. pocky:** Rotten, diseased (literally, with
the pox, or syphilis).

will scarce hold the laying in—'a will last you some
eight year or nine year. A tanner will last you nine
year.
170 HAMLET: Why he more than another?
FIRST CLOWN: Why, sir, his hide is so tann'd with his
trade that 'a will keep out water a great while, and
your water is a sore decayer of your whoreson dead
body. [*Picks up a skull.*] Here's a skull now hath lain
175 you° i' th' earth three and twenty years.
HAMLET: Whose was it?
FIRST CLOWN: A whoreson mad fellow's it was. Whose
do you think it was?
HAMLET: Nay, I know not.
180 FIRST CLOWN: A pestilence on him for a mad rogue! 'A
pour'd a flagon of Rhenish° on my head once. This
same skull, sir, was Yorick's skull, the King's jester.
HAMLET: This?
FIRST CLOWN: E'en that.
185 HAMLET: [Let me see.] [*Takes the skull.*] Alas, poor
Yorick! I knew him, Horatio, a fellow of infinite jest,
of most excellent fancy. He hath borne me on his
back a thousand times; and now, how abhorr'd in my
imagination it is! My gorge rises at it. Here hung
190 those lips that I have kiss'd I know not how oft.
Where be your gibes now? Your gambols, your
songs, your flashes of merriment that were wont to
set the table on a roar? Not one now, to mock your
own grinning? Quite chap-fall'n?° Now get you to
195 my lady's chamber, and tell her, let her paint an inch
thick, to this favor° she must come; make her laugh
at that. Prithee, Horatio, tell me one thing.
HORATIO: What's that, my lord?
HAMLET: Dost thou think Alexander look'd o' this fash-
200 ion i' th' earth?
HORATIO: E'en so.
HAMLET: And smelt so? Pah! [*Puts down the skull.*]
HORATIO: E'en so, my lord.
HAMLET: To what base uses we may return, Horatio!
205 Why may not imagination trace the noble dust of
Alexander, till 'a find it stopping a bung-hole?
HORATIO: 'twere to consider too curiously,° to consider
so.
HAMLET: No, faith, not a jot, but to follow him thither
210 with modesty° enough, and likelihood to lead it.
[As thus]: Alexander died, Alexander was buried,
Alexander returneth to dust; the dust is earth; of
earth we make loam;° and why of that loam, whereto
he was converted, might they not stop a beer-barrel?
215 Imperious° Caesar, dead and turn'd to clay,
Might stop a hole to keep the wind away.
O, that that earth which kept the world in awe

Should patch a wall t' expel the winter's flaw!°
But soft, but soft awhile! Here comes the King.

(*Enter King, Queen, Laertes, and the Corse* [*of Ophelia,
in procession, with Priest, Lords etc.*].)

The Queen, the courtiers. Who is this they follow?   220
And with such maimed rites? This doth betoken
The corse they follow did with desp'rate hand
Fordo it° own life. 'Twas of some estate.°
Couch° we awhile, and mark.
                    [*He and Horatio conceal themselves.
                    Ophelia's body is taken to the grave.*]
LAERTES: What ceremony else?   225
HAMLET [*to Horatio*]: That is Laertes, a very noble
youth. Mark.
LAERTES: What ceremony else?
PRIEST: Her obsequies have been as far enlarg'd
As we have warranty. Her death was doubtful,
And, but that great command o'ersways the order,   230
She should in ground unsanctified been lodg'd
Till the last trumpet. For° charitable prayers,
Shards,° flints, and pebbles should be thrown on her.
Yet here she is allow'd her virgin crants,°
Her maiden strewments,° and the bringing home   235
Of bell and burial.°
LAERTES: Must there no more be done?
PRIEST: No more be done.
We should profane the service of the dead
To sing a requiem and such rest to her
As to peace-parted souls.
LAERTES: Lay her i' th' earth,   240
And from her fair and unpolluted flesh
May violets° spring! I tell thee, churlish priest,
A minist'ring angel shall my sister be
When thou liest howling!
HAMLET [*to Horatio*]:   What, the fair Ophelia!
QUEEN [*scattering flowers*]: Sweets to the sweet!
Farewell.   245
I hoped thou shouldst have been my Hamlet's wife.
I thought thy bride-bed to have deck'd, sweet maid,
And not have strew'd thy grave.
LAERTES: O, treble woe
Fall ten times treble on that cursed head
Whose wicked deed thy most ingenious sense°   250
Depriv'd thee of! Hold off the earth awhile,
Till I have caught her once more in mine arms.
        [*Leaps into the grave and embraces Ophelia.*]
Now pile your dust upon the quick and dead,
Till of this flat a mountain you have made

174–75. **lain you:** Lain. 181. **Rhenish:** Rhine wine.
194. **chap-fall'n:** (1) Lacking the lower jaw; (2) dejected.
196. **favor:** Aspect, appearance. 207. **curiously:** Minutely.
210. **modesty:** Moderation. 213. **loam:** Clay mixture for
brickmaking or other clay use. 215. **Imperious:** Imperial.

218. **flaw:** Gust of wind. 223. **Fordo it:** Destroy its. **estate:**
Rank. 224. **Couch:** Hide, lurk. 232. **For:** In place of.
233. **Shards:** Broken bits of pottery. 234. **crants:** Garland.
235. **strewments:** Traditional strewing of flowers.
235–36. **bringing . . . burial:** Laying to rest of the body in consecrated ground, to the sound of the bell. 242. **violets:** See IV,
v, 186 and note. 250. **ingenious sense:** Mind endowed with
finest qualities.

255   T 'o'ertop old Pelion,° or the skyish head
        Of blue Olympus.°
    HAMLET [coming forward]: What is he whose grief
        Bears such an emphasis, whose phrase of sorrow
        Conjures the wand'ring stars,° and makes them stand
260   Like wonder-wounded hearers? This is I,
        Hamlet the Dane.°
    LAERTES: The devil take thy soul!
                                [Grappling with him.]
    HAMLET: Thou pray'st not well.
        I prithee, take thy fingers from my throat;
        For, though I am not splenitive° and rash,
265   Yet have I in me something dangerous,
        Which let thy wisdom fear. Hold off thy hand.
    KING: Pluck them asunder.
    QUEEN: Hamlet, Hamlet!
    ALL: Gentlemen!
    HORATIO: Good my lord, be quiet.
                    [Hamlet and Horatio are parted.]
    HAMLET: Why, I will fight with him upon this theme
270   Until my eyelids will no longer wag.
    QUEEN: O my son, what theme?
    HAMLET: I lov'd Ophelia. Forty thousand brothers
        Could not with all their quantity of love
        Make up my sum. What wilt thou do for her?
275 KING: O, he is mad, Laertes.
    QUEEN: For love of God, forbear him.
    HAMLET: 'Swounds,° show me what thou' do.
        Woo 't° weep? Woo 't fight? Woo 't fast? Woo 't
          tear thyself?
        Woo 't drink up eisel?° Eat a crocodile?
280   I'll do 't. Dost thou come here to whine?
        To outface me with leaping in her grave?
        Be buried quick° with her, and so will I.
        And, if thou prate of mountains, let them throw
        Millions of acres on us, till our ground,
285   Singeing his pate° against the burning zone,°
        Make Ossa° like a wart! Nay, an thou 'lt mouth,°
        I'll rant as well as thou.
    QUEEN: This is mere° madness,
        And thus a while the fit will work on him;
        Anon, as patient as the female dove
290   When that her golden couplets° are disclos'd,°
        His silence will sit drooping.
    HAMLET: Hear you, sir.
        What is the reason that you use me thus?

        I lov'd you ever. But it is no matter.
        Let Hercules himself do what he may,
        The cat will mew, and dog will have his day.°   295
    KING: I pray thee, good Horatio, wait upon him.

                    (Exit Hamlet and Horatio.)

    [To Laertes.] Strengthen your patience in° our last
        night's speech;
        We'll put the matter to the present push.°—
        Good Gertrude, set some watch over your son.—
        This grave shall have a living° monument.   300
        An hour of quiet shortly shall we see;
        Till then, in patience our proceeding be.   (Exeunt.)

{Scene II}°

(Enter Hamlet and Horatio.)

    HAMLET: So much for this, sir; now shall you see the
        other.°
        You do remember all the circumstance?
    HORATIO: Remember it, my lord!
    HAMLET: Sir, in my heart there was a kind of
        fighting
        That would not let me sleep. Methought I lay   5
        Worse than the mutines° in the bilboes.° Rashly,°
        And prais'd be rashness for it—let us know,°
        Our indiscretion sometime serves us well
        When our deep plots do pall,° and that should
          learn° us
        There's a divinity that shapes our ends,   10
        Rough-hew° them how we will—
    HORATIO: That is most certain.
    HAMLET: Up from my cabin,
        My sea-gown scarf'd about me, in the dark
        Grop'd I to find out them, had my desire,
        Finger'd° their packet, and in fine° withdrew   15
        To mine own room again, making so bold,
        My fears forgetting manners, to unseal
        Their grand commission; where I found, Horatio—
        Ah, royal knavery!—an exact command,
        Larded° with many several sorts of reasons   20
        Importing° Denmark's health and England's too,
        With, ho, such bugs° and goblins in my life,°
        That, on the supervise,° no leisure bated,°

No, not to stay the grinding of the axe,
My head should be struck off.
25 HORATIO: Is 't possible?
HAMLET: Here's the commission; read it at more
        leisure.   [*Gives document.*]
But wilt thou hear now how I did proceed?
HORATIO: I beseech you.
HAMLET: Being thus benetted round with villainies,
30   Or I could make a prologue to my brains,
They had begun the play.° I sat me down,
Devis'd a new commission, wrote it fair.°
I once did hold it, as our statists° do,
A baseness° to write fair, and labor'd much
35   How to forget that learning, but, sir, now
It did me yeoman's° service. Wilt thou know
Th' effect° of what I wrote?
HORATIO: Ay, good my lord.
HAMLET: An earnest conjuration from the King,
As England was his faithful tributary,
40   As love between them like the palm might flourish,
As peace should still her wheaten garland° wear
And stand a comma° 'tween their amities,
And many such-like as's° of great charge,°
That, on the view and knowing of these contents,
45   Without debasement further, more or less,
He should those bearers put to sudden death,
Not shriving time° allow'd.
HORATIO: How was this seal'd?
HAMLET: Why, even in that was heaven ordinant.°
I had my father's signet° in my purse,
50   Which was the model of that Danish seal;
Folded the writ up in the form of th' other,
Subscrib'd° it, gave 't th' impression,° plac'd it safely,
The changeling° never known. Now, the next day
Was our sea-fight, and what to this was sequent
55   Thou knowest already.
HORATIO: So Guildenstern and Rosencrantz go to 't.
HAMLET: [Why, man, they did make love to this
        employment.]
They are not near my conscience. Their defeat
Does by their own insinuation° grow.
60   'Tis dangerous when the baser nature comes
Between the pass° and fell° incensed points
Of mighty opposites.
HORATIO: Why, what a king is this!

HAMLET: Does it not, think thee, stand° me now
        upon—
He that hath killed my king and whor'd my mother,
Popp'd in between th' election° and my hopes,   65
Thrown out his angle° for my proper° life,
And with such coz'nage°—is 't not perfect
        conscience
[To quit° him with this arm? And is 't not to be
        damn'd
To let this canker° of our nature come
In further evil?   70
HORATIO: It must be shortly known to him from
        England
What is the issue of the business there.
HAMLET: It will be short. The interim is mine,
And a man's life 's no more than to say "One."°
But I am very sorry, good Horatio,   75
That to Laertes I forgot myself,
For by the image of my cause I see
The portraiture of his. I'll court his favors.
But, sure, the bravery° of his grief did put me
Into a tow'ring passion.
HORATIO: Peace, who comes here?] 80

(*Enter a Courtier [Osric].*)

OSRIC: Your lordship is right welcome back to Denmark.
HAMLET: I humbly thank you, sir. [*To Horatio.*] Dost
        know this water-fly?
HORATIO: No, my good lord.
HAMLET: Thy state is the more gracious, for 'tis a vice to   85
        know him. He hath much land, and fertile. Let a
        beast be lord of beasts, and his crib shall stand at the
        King's mess.° 'Tis a chough,° but, as I say, spacious in
        the possession of dirt.
OSRIC: Sweet lord, if your lordship were at leisure, I   90
        should impart a thing to you from his Majesty.
HAMLET: I will receive it, sir, with all diligence of spirit.
        Put your bonnet to his right use; 'tis for the head.
OSRIC: I thank your lordship, it is very hot.
HAMLET: No, believe me, 'tis very cold; the wind is   95
        northerly.
OSRIC: It is indifferent° cold, my lord, indeed.
HAMLET: But yet methinks it is very sultry and hot for
        my complexion.°
OSRIC: Exceedingly, my lord; it is very sultry, as   100
        'twere—I cannot tell how. My lord, his Majesty bade
        me signify to you that 'a has laid a great wager on
        your head. Sir, this is the matter—

30–31. Or . . . play: Before I could consciously turn my brain to the matter, it had started working on a plan. (*Or* means *ere.*) **32. fair:** In a clear hand. **33. statists:** Statesmen. **34. baseness:** Lower-class trait. **36. yeoman's:** Substantial, workmanlike. **37. effect:** Purport. **41. wheaten garland:** Symbolic of fruitful agriculture, of peace. **42. comma:** Indicating continuity, link. **43. as's:** (1) The "whereases" of formal document, (2) asses. **charge:** (1) Import, (2) burden. **47. shriving time:** Time for confession and absolution. **48. ordinant:** Directing. **49. signet:** Small seal. **52. Subscrib'd:** Signed. **impression:** With a wax seal. **53. changeling:** The substituted letter (literally, a fairy child substituted for a human one). **59. insinuation:** Interference. **61. pass:** Thrust. **fell:** Fierce.

63. stand: Become incumbent. **65. election:** The Danish monarch was "elected" by a small number of high-ranking electors. **66. angle:** Fishing line. **proper:** Very. **67. coz'nage:** Trickery. **68. quit:** Repay. **69. canker:** Ulcer. **74. a man's . . . "One":** To take a man's life requires no more than to count to one as one duels. **79. bravery:** Bravado. **86–88. Let . . . mess:** If a man, no matter how beastlike, is as rich in possessions as Osric, he may eat at the king's table. **88. chough:** Chattering jackdaw. **97. indifferent:** Somewhat. **99. complexion:** Temperament.

HAMLET: I beseech you, remember—

[*Hamlet moves him to put on his hat.*]

105 OSRIC: Nay, good my lord; for my ease,° in good faith. Sir, here is newly come to court Laertes—believe me, an absolute gentleman, full of most excellent differences,° of very soft society° and great showing.° Indeed, to speak feelingly° of him, he is the card° or

110 calendar° of gentry,° for you shall find in him the continent of what part° a gentleman would see.

HAMLET: Sir, his definement° suffers no perdition° in you, though, I know, to divide him inventorially° would dozy° th' arithmetic of memory, and yet

115 but yaw° neither° in respect of° his quick sail. But, in the verity of extolment,° I take him to be a soul of great article,° and his infusion° of such dearth and rareness,° as, to make true diction° of him, his semblable° is his mirror, and who else would trace°

120 him, his umbrage,° nothing more.

OSRIC: Your lordship speaks most infallibly of him.

HAMLET: The concernancy,° sir? Why do we wrap the gentleman in our more rawer breath?°

OSRIC: Sir?

125 HORATIO: Is 't not possible to understand in another tongue?° You will do 't,° sir, really.

HAMLET: What imports the nomination° of this gentleman?

OSRIC: Of Laertes?

130 HORATIO [*to Hamlet*]: His purse is empty already; all 's golden words are spent.

HAMLET: Of him, sir.

OSRIC: I know you are not ignorant—

HAMLET: I would you did, sir; yet, in faith, if you did, it

135 would not much approve° me. Well, sir?

OSRIC: You are not ignorant of what excellence Laertes is—

HAMLET: I dare not confess that, lest I should compare° with him in excellence; but to know a man well were to know himself.° 140

OSRIC: I mean, sir, for his weapon; but in the imputation laid on him by them,° in his meed° he's unfellow'd.°

HAMLET: What's his weapon?

OSRIC: Rapier and dagger.

HAMLET: That's two of his weapons—but well. 145

OSRIC: The King, sir, hath wager'd with him six Barbary horses, against the which he has impawn'd,° as I take it, six French rapiers and poniards, with their assigns,° as girdle, hangers,° and so. Three of the carriages,° in faith, are very dear to fancy,° very responsive° to the hilts, most delicate° carriages, and of very liberal conceit.° 150

HAMLET: What call you the carriages?

HORATIO [*to Hamlet*]: I knew you must be edified by the margent° ere you had done. 155

OSRIC: The carriages, sir, are the hangers.

HAMLET: The phrase would be more germane to the matter if we could carry a cannon by our sides; I would it might be hangers till then. But, on: six Barb'ry horses against six French swords, their 160 assigns, and three liberal-conceited carriages; that's the French bet against the Danish. Why is this impawn'd, as you call it?

OSRIC: The King, sir, hath laid,° sir, that in a dozen passes° between yourself and him, he shall not 165 exceed you three hits. He hath laid on twelve for nine, and it would come to immediate trial, if your lordship would vouchsafe the answer.

HAMLET: How if I answer no?

OSRIC: I mean, my lord, the opposition of your person 170 in trial.

HAMLET: Sir, I will walk here in the hall. If it please his Majesty, it is the breathing time° of day with me. Let the foils be brought, the gentleman willing, and the King hold his purpose, I will win for him an I can; if 175 not, I will gain nothing but my shame and the odd hits.

105. for my ease: A conventional reply declining the invitation to put his hat back on. **108. differences:** Special qualities. **soft society:** Agreeable manners. **108–09. great showing:** Distinguished appearance. **109. feelingly:** With just perception. **card:** Chart, map. **110. calendar:** Guide. **gentry:** Good breeding. **111. the continent . . . part:** One who contains in him all the qualities (a *continent* is that which contains). **112. definement:** Definition. (Hamlet proceeds to mock Osric by using his lofty diction back at him.) **perdition:** Loss, diminution. **113. divide him inventorially:** Enumerate his graces. **114. dozy:** Dizzy. **115. yaw:** To move unsteadily (said of a ship). **neither:** For all that. **in respect of:** In comparison with. **116. in . . . extolment:** In true praise (of him). **117. article:** Moment or importance. **infusion:** Essence, character imparted by nature. **117–18. dearth and rareness:** Rarity. **118. make true diction:** Speak truly. **119. semblable:** Only true likeness. **who . . . trace:** Any other person who would wish to follow. **120. umbrage:** Shadow. **122. concernancy:** Import, relevance. **123. breath:** Speech. **125–26. to understand . . . tongue:** For Osric to understand when someone else speaks in his manner. (Horatio twits Osric for not being able to understand the kind of flowery speech he himself uses when Hamlet speaks in such a vein.) **126. You will do't:** You can if you try. **127. nomination:** Naming. **135. approve:** Commend.

138. compare: Seem to compete. **139–40. but . . . himself:** For, to recognize excellence in another man, one must know oneself. **141–42. imputation . . . them:** Reputation given him by others. **142. meed:** Merit. **unfellow'd:** Unmatched. **147. impawn'd:** Staked, wagered. **149. assigns:** Appurtenances. **hangers:** Straps on the sword belt (*girdle*) from which the sword hung. **149–50. carriages:** An affected way of saying *hangers;* literally, gun-carriages. **150. dear to fancy:** Fancifully designed, tasteful. **150–51. responsive:** Corresponding closely, matching. **151. delicate:** I.e., in workmanship. **152. liberal conceit:** Elaborate design. **155. margent:** Margin of a book, place for explanatory notes. **164. laid:** Wagered. **165. passes:** Bouts. (The odds of the betting are hard to explain. Possibly the king bets that Hamlet will win at least five out of twelve, at which point Laertes raises the odds against himself by betting he will win nine.) **173. breathing time:** Exercise period.

OSRIC: Shall I deliver you so?

HAMLET: To this effect, sir—after what flourish your
180   nature will.

OSRIC: I commend my duty to your lordship.

HAMLET: Yours, yours. [*Exit Osric.*] He does well to
    commend it himself; there are no tongues else for 's
    turn.

185 HORATIO: This lapwing° runs away with the shell on his
    head.

HAMLET: 'A did comply, sir, with his dug,° before 'a
    suck'd it. Thus has he—and many more of the same
    breed that I know the drossy° age dotes on—only
190   got the tune° of the time and, out of an habit of
    encounter,° a kind of yesty° collection,° which carries
    them through and through the most fann'd and win-
    now'd° opinions; and do but blow them to their trial,
    the bubbles are out.°

(*Enter a Lord.*)

195 LORD: My lord, his Majesty commended him to you by
    young Osric, who brings back to him that you attend
    him in the hall. He sends to know if your pleasure
    hold to play with Laertes, or that you will take longer
    time.

200 HAMLET: I am constant to my purposes; they follow the
    King's pleasure. If his fitness speaks,° mine is ready;
    now or whensoever, provided I be so able as now.

LORD: The King and Queen and all are coming down.

HAMLET: In happy time.°

205 LORD: The Queen desires you to use some gentle enter-
    tainment° to Laertes before you fall to play.

HAMLET: She well instructs me.   [*Exit Lord.*]

HORATIO: You will lose, my lord.

HAMLET: I do not think so. Since he went into France, I
210   have been in continual practice; I shall win at the
    odds. But thou wouldst not think how ill all's here
    about my heart; but it is no matter.

HORATIO: Nay, good my lord—

HAMLET: It is but foolery, but it is such a kind of gain-
215   giving,° as would perhaps trouble a woman.

HORATIO: If your mind dislike anything, obey it. I will
    forestall their repair hither, and say you are not fit.

HAMLET: Not a whit, we defy augury. There is special
    providence in the fall of a sparrow. If it be now, 'tis
220   not to come; if it be not to come, it will be now, if it

---

185. **lapwing:** A bird that draws intruders away from its nest
and was thought to run about when newly hatched with its
head in the shell; a seeming reference to Osric's hat.
187. **comply . . . dug:** Observe ceremonious formality toward
his mother's teat.   189. **drossy:** Frivolous.   190. **tune:** Temper, mood, manner of speech.   190–91. **habit of encounter:**
Demeanor of social intercourse.   191. **yesty:** Yeasty, frothy.
collection: I.e., of current phrases.   192–93. **fann'd and win-
now'd:** Select and refined.   193–94. **blow . . . out:** Put them to
the test, and their ignorance is exposed.   201. **If . . . speaks:** If
his readiness answers to the time.   204. **In happy time:** A
phrase of courtesy indicating acceptance.   206. **entertainment:**
Greeting.   214–15. **gain-giving:** Misgiving.

be not now, yet it will come. The readiness is all.
Since no man of aught he leaves knows what is 't to
leave betimes,° let be.

(*A table prepar'd.* [*Enter*] *trumpets, drums, and Officers
with cushions; King, Queen,* [*Osric,*] *and all the State;
foils, daggers,* [*and wine borne in;*] *and Laertes.*)

KING: Come, Hamlet, come, and take this hand from
    me.
              [*The King puts Laertes' hand into Hamlet's.*]

HAMLET: Give me your pardon, sir. I have done you
    wrong,   225
    But pardon 't, as you are a gentleman.
    This presence° knows,
    And you must needs have heard, how I am punish'd
    With a sore distraction. What I have done
    That might your nature, honor, and exception°   230
    Roughly awake, I here proclaim was madness.
    Was 't Hamlet wrong'd Laertes? Never Hamlet.
    If Hamlet from himself be ta'en away,
    And when he's not himself does wrong Laertes,
    Then Hamlet does it not, Hamlet denies it.   235
    Who does it, then? His madness. If 't be so,
    Hamlet is of the faction that is wrong'd;
    His madness is poor Hamlet's enemy.
    [Sir, in this audience,]
    Let my disclaiming from a purpos'd evil   240
    Free me so far in your most generous thoughts
    That I have shot my arrow o'er the house
    And hurt my brother.

LAERTES: I am satisfied in nature,°
    Whose motive in this case should stir me most
    To my revenge. But in my terms of honor   245
    I stand aloof, and will no reconcilement
    Till by some elder masters of known honor
    I have a voice° and precedent of peace
    To keep my name ungor'd. But till that time,
    I do receive your offer'd love like love,   250
    And will not wrong it.

HAMLET: I embrace it freely,
    And will this brothers' wager frankly play.
    Give us the foils. Come on.

LAERTES: Come, one for me.

HAMLET: I'll be your foil,° Laertes. In mine ignorance
    Your skill shall, like a star i' th' darkest night,   255
    Stick fiery off° indeed.

LAERTES: You mock me, sir.

HAMLET: No, by this hand.

KING: Give them the foils, young Osric. Cousin Hamlet,
    You know the wager?

HAMLET: Very well, my lord.
    Your Grace has laid the odds o' th' weaker side.   260

222–23. **what . . . betimes:** What is the best time to leave it.
227. **presence:** Royal assembly.   230. **exception:** Disapproval.
243. **in nature:** As to my personal feelings.   248. **voice:**
Authoritative pronouncement.   254. **foil:** Thin metal background which sets a jewel off (with pun on the blunted rapier
for fencing).   256. **Stick fiery off:** Stand out brilliantly.

KING: I do not fear it; I have seen you both.
But since he is better'd,° we have therefore odds.
LAERTES: This is too heavy, let me see another.

[*Exchanges his foil for another.*]

HAMLET: This likes me well. These foils have all a length?

[*They prepare to play.*]

265 OSRIC: Ay, my good lord.
KING: Set me the stoups of wine upon that table.
If Hamlet give the first or second hit,
Or quit° in answer of the third exchange,
Let all the battlements their ordnance fire.
270 The King shall drink to Hamlet's better breath,
And in the cup an union° shall he throw,
Richer than that which four successive kings
In Denmark's crown have worn. Give me the cups,
And let the kettle° to the trumpet speak,
275 The trumpet to the cannoneer without,
The cannons to the heavens, the heaven to earth,
"Now the King drinks to Hamlet." Come, begin.

(*Trumpets the while.*)

And you, the judges, bear a wary eye.
HAMLET: Come on sir.
280 LAERTES: Come, my lord.   [*They play. Hamlet scores a hit.*]
HAMLET: One.
LAERTES: No.
HAMLET: Judgment.
OSRIC: A hit, a very palpable hit.

(*Drum, trumpets, and shot. Flourish. A piece goes off.*)

LAERTES: Well, again.
285 KING: Stay, give me drink. Hamlet, this pearl is thine.

[*He throws a pearl in Hamlet's cup and drinks.*]

Here's to thy health. Give him the cup.
HAMLET: I'll play this bout first set it by awhile.
Come. [*They play.*] Another hit; what say you?
LAERTES: A touch, a touch. I do confess 't.
KING: Our son shall win.
290 QUEEN: He's fat,° and scant of breath.
Here, Hamlet, take my napkin,° rub thy brows.
The Queen carouses° to thy fortune, Hamlet.
HAMLET: Good madam!
KING: Gertrude, do not drink.
295 QUEEN: I will, my lord; I pray you pardon me.

[*Drinks.*]

KING [*aside*]: It is the pois'ned cup. It is too late.
HAMLET: I dare not drink yet, madam; by and by.
QUEEN: Come, let me wipe thy face.
LAERTES [*to King*]: My lord, I'll hit him now.
KING: I do not think 't.
LAERTES [*aside*]: And yet it is almost against my
300   conscience.

---

262. is better'd: Has improved; is the odds-on favorite. **268. quit:** Repay (with a hit). **271. union:** Pearl (so called, according to Pliny's *Natural History,* IX, because pearls are *unique,* never identical). **274. kettle:** Kettledrum. **290. fat:** Not physically fit, out of training. **291. napkin:** Handkerchief. **292. carouses:** Drinks a toast.

HAMLET: Come, for the third Laertes. You do but dally.
I pray you, pass with your best violence;
I am afeard you make a wanton of me.°
LAERTES: Say you so? Come on.   [*They play.*]
OSRIC: Nothing, neither way.   305
LAERTES: Have at you now!

[*Laertes wounds Hamlet; then, in scuffling, they change rapiers,° and Hamlet wounds Laertes.*]

KING: Part them! They are incens'd.
HAMLET: Nay, come, again.   [*The Queen falls.*]
OSRIC: Look to the Queen there, ho!
HORATIO: They bleed on both sides. How is it, my lord?
OSRIC: How is 't, Laertes?
LAERTES: Why, as a woodcock° to mine own springe,°
   Osric;   310
I am justly kill'd with mine own treachery.
HAMLET: How does the Queen?
KING: She swoons to see them bleed.
QUEEN: No, no, the drink, the drink—O my dear
   Hamlet—
The drink, the drink! I am pois'ned.   [*Dies.*]
HAMLET: O villainy! Ho, let the door be lock'd!   315
Treachery! Seek it out.   [*Laertes falls.*]
LAERTES: It is here, Hamlet. Hamlet, thou art slain.
No med'cine in the world can do thee good;
In thee there is not half an hour's life.
The treacherous instrument is in thy hand,   320
Unbated° and envenom'd. The foul practice
Hath turn'd itself on me. Lo, here I lie,
Never to rise again. Thy mother's pois'ned.
I can no more. The King, the King's to blame.
HAMLET: The point envenom'd too? Then, venom, to
   thy work.   [*Stabs the King.*]   325
ALL: Treason! Treason!
KING: O, yet defend me, friends; I am but hurt.
HAMLET: Here, thou incestuous, murd'rous, damned
   Dane,

[*He forces the King to drink the poisoned cup.*]

Drink off this potion. Is thy union° here?
Follow my mother.   [*King dies.*]
LAERTES: He is justly serv'd.   330
It is a poison temper'd° by himself.
Exchange forgiveness with me, noble Hamlet.
Mine and my father's death come not upon thee,
Nor thine on me!   [*Dies.*]

---

303. make . . . me: Treat me like a spoiled child, holding back to give me an advantage.   **306. [S.D.]** *in scuffling, they change rapiers:* This stage direction occurs in the Folio. According to a widespread stage tradition, Hamlet receives a scratch, realizes that Laertes' sword is unbated, and accordingly forces an exchange.   **310. woodcock:** A bird, a type of stupidity or as a decoy.   **springe:** Trap, snare.   **321. Unbated:** Not blunted with a button.   **329. union:** Pearl (see line 271; with grim puns on the word's other meanings: marriage, shared death[?]).   **331. temper'd:** Mixed.

335　HAMLET: Heaven make thee free of it! I follow thee.
　　　I am dead, Horatio. Wretched Queen, adieu!
　　　You that look pale and tremble at this chance,
　　　That are but mutes° or audience to this act,
　　　Had I but time—as this fell° sergeant,° Death,
340　Is strict in his arrest—O, I could tell you—
　　　But let it be. Horatio, I am dead;
　　　Thou livest. Report me and my cause aright
　　　To the unsatisfied.
　　HORATIO:　　　　　　Never believe it.
　　　I am more an antique Roman° than a Dane.
　　　Here's yet some liquor left.
　　　　　　[*He attempts to drink from the poisoned cup.*
　　　　　　　　　　　　　　Hamlet prevents him.]
345　HAMLET:　　　　　　As th' art a man,
　　　Give me the cup! Let go! By heaven, I'll ha 't.
　　　O God, Horatio, what a wounded name,
　　　Things standing thus unknown, shall I leave
　　　　　behind me!
　　　If thou didst ever hold me in thy heart,
350　Absent thee from felicity awhile,
　　　And in this harsh world draw thy breath in pain
　　　To tell my story.
　　　　　　(*A march afar off* [*and a volley within*].)
　　　　　　　　What warlike noise is this?
　　OSRIC: Young Fortinbras, with conquest come from
　　　　Poland,
　　　To the ambassadors of England gives
　　　This warlike volley.
355　HAMLET:　　　　　　O, I die, Horatio!
　　　The potent poison quite o'ercrows° my spirit.
　　　I cannot live to hear the news from England,
　　　But I do prophesy th' election lights
　　　On Fortinbras. He has my dying voice.°
360　So tell him, with th' occurrents° more and less
　　　Which have solicited°—the rest is silence.　[*Dies.*]
　　HORATIO: Now cracks a noble heart. Good night,
　　　　sweet prince;
　　　And flights of angels sing thee to thy rest!
　　　　　　　　　　　　　　　[*March within.*]
　　　Why does the drum come hither?

　　(*Enter Fortinbras, with the* [*English*] *Ambassadors*
　　[*with drum, colors, and attendants*].)

　　FORTINBRAS: Where is this sight?
365　HORATIO:　　　　　　What is it you would see?
　　　If aught of woe or wonder, cease your search.
　　FORTINBRAS: This quarry° cries on havoc.° O proud
　　　　Death.
　　　What feast is toward° in thine eternal cell,

　　　That thou so many princes at a shot
　　　So bloodily hast struck?
　　FIRST AMBASSADOR:　　　The sight is dismal;　　　370
　　　And our affairs from England come too late.
　　　The ears are senseless that should give us hearing,
　　　To tell him his commandment is fulfill'd,
　　　That Rosencrantz and Guildenstern are dead.
　　　Where should we have our thanks?
　　HORATIO:　　　　　　Not from his° mouth,　　375
　　　Had it th' ability of life to thank you.
　　　He never gave commandment for their death.
　　　But since, so jump° upon this bloody question,°
　　　You from the Polack wars, and you from England,
　　　Are here arriv'd, give order that these bodies　380
　　　High on a stage° be placed to the view,
　　　And let me speak to th' yet unknowing world
　　　How these things came about. So shall you hear
　　　Of carnal, bloody, and unnatural acts,
　　　Of accidental judgments,° casual° slaughters,　385
　　　Of deaths put on° by cunning and forc'd cause,
　　　And, in this upshot, purposes mistook
　　　Fall'n on th' inventors' heads. All this can I
　　　Truly deliver.
　　FORTINBRAS:　　Let us haste to hear it,
　　　And call the noblest to the audience.　　　390
　　　For me, with sorrow I embrace my fortune.
　　　I have some rights of memory° in this kingdom,
　　　Which now to claim my vantage° doth invite me.
　　HORATIO: Of that I shall have also cause to speak,
　　　And from his mouth whose voice will draw on
　　　　more.°　　　　　　　　　　　　　395
　　　But let this same be presently° perform'd,
　　　Even while men's minds are wild, lest more
　　　　mischance
　　　On° plots and errors happen.
　　FORTINBRAS:　　　　　Let four captains
　　　Bear Hamlet, like a soldier, to the stage,
　　　For he was likely, had he been put on,°　　　400
　　　To have prov'd most royal; and, for his passage,°
　　　The soldiers' music and the rite of war
　　　Speak loudly for him.
　　　Take up the bodies. Such a sight as this
　　　Becomes the field,° but here shows much amiss.　405
　　　Go, bid the soldiers shoot.
　　　　　　(*Exeunt* [*marching, bearing off the dead bodies;*
　　　　　　　　　a peal of ordnance is shot off].)

---

338. **mutes:** Silent observers.　339. **fell:** Cruel.　**sergeant:** Sheriff's officer.　344. **Roman:** It was the Roman custom to follow masters in death.　356. **o'ercrows:** Triumphs over.　359. **voice:** Vote.　360. **occurrents:** Events, incidents.　361. **solicited:** Moved, urged.　367. **quarry:** Heap of dead. **cries on havoc:** Proclaims a general slaughter.　368. **toward:** In preparation.

375. **his:** Claudius's.　378. **jump:** Precisely. **question:** Dispute.　381. **stage:** Platform.　385. **judgments:** Retributions. **casual:** Occurring by chance.　386. **put on:** Instigated.　392. **of memory:** Traditional, remembered.　393. **vantage:** Presence at this opportune moment.　395. **voice . . . more:** Vote will influence still others.　396. **presently:** Immediately.　398. **On:** On the basis of.　400. **put on:** Invested in royal office and so put to the test.　401. **passage:** Death.　405. **field:** I.e., of battle.

COMMENTARIES

The great Shakespearean E. K. Chambers provides an introduction to *Hamlet* that examines the question of Hamlet's madness, something that has bedeviled audiences almost from the first performance. His focus is on the complexities of Hamlet's psychology.

Sigmund Freud sees in *Hamlet* the seeds of the Oedipus complex that he had already identified in Sophocles' *Oedipus Rex*. The question of how one psychoanalyzes a literary character is perhaps best raised in Freud's essay. Later, a follower of Freud, Ernest Jones, wrote an entire book on Hamlet, analyzing him from the psychoanalytic perspective.

T. S. Eliot, speaking as a careful and noted student of Elizabethan and Jacobean drama, begins to point out some of the difficulties he sees with *Hamlet*.

E. K. Chambers (1866–1954)
On Hamlet's Madness   1925

Chambers, a distinguished scholar of the works of Shakespeare, considers the question that has plagued a number of commentators, actors, and directors of Hamlet. *Is Hamlet's madness a genuine disorder or is it a dramatic camouflage designed to set him apart and thus protect him? Chambers considers the question from the point of view of a contemporary psychologist.*

Criticism of the play is apt to center round the question "Was Hamlet, at any time and in any sense, really mad?" Admittedly he set out to put an antic disposition on; but it has been held, sometimes with much learning of the alienist,° that in course of time, under the strain of the situation, the pretense adopted as a mask passed into a reality. I do not think that the text, fairly read, supports this theory, and in the abstract it is surely untenable. Psychology, indeed, is hard put to it to establish a rigid dividing-line between the sane and the insane. The pathologist may distinguish certain abnormal conditions of brain-areas and call them diseased; or the lawyer may apply working tests to determine the point at which restraint of the individual liberty becomes necessary in the public interest. But beyond that you cannot go. No one, from any wider point of view, can lay his finger upon one manifestation here or there of the infinite variety of human character, and say with assurance, "This way madness lies." Only of one thing we may be sure. Shakespeare did not mean Hamlet to be mad in any sense which would put his actions in a quite different category from those of other men. How could it be so, since the responsibility of the free agent is of the essence of psychological tragedy, and to have eliminated Hamlet's responsibility would have been to divest his story of humanity and leave it meaningless?

alienist: Psychologist.

Consideration, however, cannot make Hamlet's position other than a disconcerting one. In the first place, he is absolutely alone. The court at Elsinore is filled with quite ordinary people, none of whom can understand him, to none of whom he can look for help. This note of contrast between Hamlet and his surroundings is struck again and again. They are of another world than his, limited, commonplace, incapable of ideals. His motives and feelings, his scruples and hesitations, are hopelessly beyond their comprehension. And therefore—this is the irony of it—most of them are far more fitted to deal with a practical crisis in life than this cultured idealist of a prince. There are "the good king and queen"; Claudius, shrewd and ready for an emergency, one who has set foot in the paths of villainy and will not turn back, for all the dim visitings of momentary remorse; Gertrude, a slave to the stronger nature, living in the present, unable to realize her own moral degradation. There is Horatio, a straightforward upright soldier, one whom Hamlet intensely respects, comes even to envy, but who is not subtle enough to be of much use to him. There is Polonius, a played-out state official, vain and slow-witted, pattering words of wisdom which he does not understand and cannot put into practice. There are his son and daughter, Laertes and Ophelia; Laertes, a shallow, vigorous young noble, quick with a word, and quick with a blow, but of less than average temper in brain and ethics; Ophelia, a timid conventional girl, too fragile a reed for a man to lean upon. Hamlet loves her, and she loves Hamlet, but it is not a love that will bear him through the deep waters of affliction. The rest of the court are typified by Osric the waterfly, and by Guildenstern and Rosencrantz, of whom if you say Rosencrantz and Guildenstern it makes no difference; echoes, nonentities. With Hamlet on one side and these on the other, the elements of a tragedy are complete; the problem can work out to no satisfactory conclusion.

Once Hamlet has shrunk from immediate action, the possibilities of delay exercise an irresistible fascination over him. The ingenuity of his intellect exhausts itself in the discovery of obstacles; he takes every turn and twist to avoid the fatal necessity for action. At first he looks to Ophelia, the well-beloved. She will give him strength to accomplish his mission; but the scene in her closet, and still more the lie which she tells when her father is behind the arras, confess her weakness and compel him to renunciation. In the meantime he continues the assumption of madness. It serves a double purpose; he is free from the intolerable burden of keeping on good terms with Claudius and the rest; he can fight out the battle with himself in peace, while he mocks them with the ironies congenial to his mood. And what is more, he can let himself go; the strain of his overwrought mind relieves itself in bursts of an extravagance only half affected. He plays the madman to prevent himself from becoming one. But all the while he is no nearer the end. He has turned the whole matter over and cannot decide. His thoughts slip away from the plain issue and lose themselves in a bitter criticism of all created things. In this the speculative temper infallibly betrays itself; the interest of the universal, not of the particular, is always dominant with Hamlet; not his mother's sin, but the frailty of women, is his natural theme. And so it is with a pang that he constantly recalls himself to the insistent actual life, from the world in which he is a past-master to that wherein he gropes ineffectively. Of course he is fully aware of his own weakness; a deficiency of self-analysis is not likely to be one of his failings; but this does not give him power to throw it off, or help him from his maze of recurring dilemmas. More than once he is on the point of cutting the knot by death, but even for that he has not sufficient conviction.

At last the crisis comes. Hamlet has resolved that the play-scene shall decide once for all the question of the king's guilt. That guilt is made most manifest, and the opportunity for revenge is offered him. He does not take it. Covering his weakness with unreal reasons, he passes into the queen's chamber. After that it is too late. The impetuous murder of Polonius is the first link in a chain of calamities. Moreover it gives Claudius his chance. The king has never been wholly deceived by Hamlet's madness; he is sent to England, and only escapes that trap to fall into another. True, in the end the king dies by one impulsive stroke; but that cannot repair the ruin which Hamlet's want of purpose has caused. The infinitely sad fate of Ophelia; the deaths of Polonius, Laertes, Gertrude, Rosencrantz, Guildenstern; for all their faults, all these are a sacrifice on the altar of his infirmity. Only for Hamlet himself is the fatal blow, opening to him the doors of forgotten felicity, "a consummation devoutly to be wished."

Sigmund Freud (1856–1939)
HAMLET'S SCRUPLES   *1900–1930°*

Sigmund Freud was the most celebrated psychiatrist of the twentieth century. He was especially interested in Greek myth, as his comments on Oedipus Rex *suggest.* Hamlet *was another play that took on mythic proportions for him, in part because Freud saw in Hamlet the operation of his famous theory of the Oedipus complex. In the following excerpt Freud examines the events of the play that bear on his theory.*

Another of the great creations of tragic poetry, Shakespeare's *Hamlet,* has its roots in the same soil as *Oedipus Rex.* But the changed treatment of the same material reveals the whole difference in the mental life of these two widely separated epochs of civilization: the secular advance of repression in the emotional life of mankind. In the *Oedipus* the child's wishful fantasy that underlies it is brought into the open and realized as it would be in a dream. In *Hamlet* it remains repressed; and—just as in the case of a neurosis—we learn of its existence only from its inhibiting consequences. Strangely enough, the overwhelming effect produced by the more modern tragedy has turned out to be compatible with the fact that people have remained completely in the dark as to the hero's character. The play is built up on Hamlet's hesitations over fulfilling the task of revenge that is assigned to him; but its text offers no reasons or motives for these hesitations and an immense variety of attempts at interpreting them have failed to produce a result. According to the view which was originated by Goethe and is still the prevailing one today, Hamlet represents the type of man whose power of direct action is paralyzed by an excessive development of his intellect. (He is "sicklied o'er with the pale cast of thought.") According to another view, the dramatist has tried to portray a pathologically irresolute character which might be classed as neurasthenic.° The plot of the drama shows us, however, that Hamlet is far from being represented as a person incapable of taking any action. We see him doing so on two occasions: first in a sudden outburst of temper, when he runs his sword through the eavesdropper behind the arras, and secondly in a premeditated and even crafty fashion, when, with all the callousness of a Renaissance prince, he sends the two courtiers to the death that

---

   1900–1930: Freud's *Interpretation of Dreams* was first published in 1900 and was updated regularly by Freud through eight editions. This passage is taken from the eighth edition, published in 1930.
   neurasthenic: One who suffers from fatigue, loss of energy, and feelings of inadequacy.

had been planned for himself. What is it, then, that inhibits him in fulfilling the task set him by his father's ghost? The answer, once again, is that it is the peculiar nature of the task. Hamlet is able to do anything—except take vengeance on the man who did away with his father and took that father's place with his mother, the man who shows him the repressed wishes of his own childhood realized. Thus the loathing which should drive him on to revenge is replaced in him by self-reproaches, by scruples of conscience, which remind him that he himself is literally no better than the sinner whom he is to punish. Here I have translated into conscious terms what was bound to remain unconscious in Hamlet's mind; and if anyone is inclined to call him a hysteric, I can only accept the fact as one that is implied by my interpretation. The distaste for sexuality expressed by Hamlet in his conversation with Ophelia fits in very well with this: the same distaste which was destined to take possession of the poet's mind more and more during the years that followed, and which reached its extreme expression in *Timon of Athens*. For it can of course only be the poet's own mind which confronts us in Hamlet. I observe in a book on Shakespeare by Georg Brandes (1896) a statement that *Hamlet* was written immediately after the death of Shakespeare's father (in 1601), that is, under the immediate impact of his bereavement and, as we may well assume, while his childhood feelings about his father had been freshly revived. It is known, too, that Shakespeare's own son who died at an early age bore the name of "Hamnet," which is identical with "Hamlet." Just as *Hamlet* deals with the relation of a son to his parents, so *Macbeth* (written approximately the same period) is concerned with the subject of childlessness. But just as all neurotic symptoms, and, for that matter, dreams, are capable of being "overinterpreted" and indeed need to be if they are to be fully understood, so all genuinely creative writings are the product of more than a single motive and more than a single impulse in the poet's mind, and are open to more than a single interpretation. In what I have written I have only attempted to interpret the deepest layer of impulses in the mind of the creative writer.

T. S. Eliot (1888–1965)
HAMLET AND HIS PROBLEMS   *1934*

Not only a leading poet of the twentieth-century modernist period, T. S. Eliot also produced extremely interesting criticism of Elizabethan literature. His several collections of essays have in some cases defined important critical terms that later readers have used to gain insight into great writers. One of those terms is developed here: the objective correlative, which Eliot feels is missing in Hamlet. *His argument is provocative and revealing.*

Few critics have ever admitted that *Hamlet* the play is the primary problem, and Hamlet the character only secondary. And Hamlet the character has had an especial temptation for that most dangerous type of critic: the critic with a mind which is naturally of the creative order, but which through some weakness in creative power exercises itself in criticism instead. These minds often find in Hamlet a vicarious existence for their own artistic realization. Such a mind had Goethe, who made of Hamlet a Werther; and such had Coleridge, who made of Hamlet a Coleridge; and probably neither of these men in writing about Hamlet remembered that his first business was to study a work of art. The kind of criticism that Goethe and Coleridge produced, in writing of Hamlet, is the most misleading kind possible. For they both possessed unquestionable critical insight, and both make their critical aberrations the more plausible by the substitution—of their own Hamlet for Shakespeare's—which their creative gift effects. We should be thankful that Walter Pater° did not fix his attention on this play.

Two writers of our time, Mr. J. M. Robertson and Professor Stoll of the University of Minnesota, have issued small books which can be praised for moving in the other direction. Mr. Stoll performs a service in recalling to our attention the labors of the critics of the seventeenth and eighteenth centuries, observing that

> they knew less about psychology than more recent Hamlet critics, but they were nearer in spirit to Shakespeare's art; and as they insisted on the importance of the effect of the whole rather than on the importance of the leading character, they were nearer, in their old-fashioned way, to the secret of dramatic art in general.

Qua work of art, the work of art cannot be interpreted; there is nothing to interpret; we can only criticize it according to standards, in comparison to other works of art; and for "interpretation" the chief task is the presentation of relevant historical facts which the reader is not assumed to know. Mr. Robertson points out, very pertinently, how critics have failed in their "interpretation" of *Hamlet* by ignoring what ought to be very obvious: that *Hamlet* is a stratification, that it represents the efforts of a series of men, each making what he could out of the work of his predecessors. The *Hamlet* of Shakespeare will appear to us very differently if, instead of treating the whole action of the play as due to Shakespeare's design, we perceive his *Hamlet* to be superposed upon much cruder material which persists even in the final form.

We know that there was an older play by Thomas Kyd, that extraordinary dramatic (if not poetic) genius who was in all probability the author of two plays so dissimilar as the *Spanish Tragedy* and *Arden of Feversham;* and what this play was like we can guess from three clues: from the *Spanish Tragedy* itself, from the tale of Belleforest upon which Kyd's *Hamlet* must have been based, and from a version acted in Germany in Shakespeare's lifetime which bears strong evidence of having been adapted from the earlier, not from the later, play. From these three sources it is clear that in the earlier play the motive was a revenge motive simply; that the action or delay is caused, as in the *Spanish Tragedy,* solely by the difficulty of assassinating a monarch surrounded by guards; and that the "madness" of Hamlet was feigned in order to escape suspicion, and successfully. In the final play of Shakespeare, on the other hand, there is a motive which is more important than that of revenge, and which explicitly "blunts" the latter; the delay in revenge is unexplained on grounds of necessity or expediency; and the effect of the "madness" is not to lull but to arouse the king's suspicion. The alteration is not complete enough, however, to be convincing. Furthermore, there are verbal parallels so close to the *Spanish Tragedy* as to leave no doubt that in places Shakespeare was merely *revising* the text of Kyd. And finally there are unexplained scenes—the Polonius-Laertes and the Polonius-Reynaldo scenes—for which there is little excuse; these scenes are not in the verse style of Kyd, and not beyond doubt in the style of Shakespeare. These Mr. Robertson believes to be scenes in the original play of Kyd reworked by a third hand, perhaps Chapman,° before Shakespeare touched the play. And he concludes, with very strong show of reason, that the original play of Kyd was, like certain other revenge plays, in two parts of five acts. The upshot of Mr. Robertson's examination is, we believe, irrefragable: that Shakespeare's *Hamlet,* so far as it is Shakespeare's, is a play dealing with the effect of a mother's guilt upon her son, and that Shakespeare was unable to impose this motive successfully upon the "intractable" material of the old play.

Of the intractability there can be no doubt. So far from being Shakespeare's masterpiece, the play is most certainly an artistic failure. In several ways the play is puzzling, and disquieting as is none of the others. Of all the plays it is the longest and is possibly the one on which Shakespeare spent most pains; and yet he has left in it superfluous and inconsistent scenes which even hasty revision should have noticed. The versification is variable. Lines like

> Look, the morn, in russet mantle clad,
> Walks o'er the dew of yon high eastern hill,

are of the Shakespeare of *Romeo and Juliet.* The lines in act V, scene ii,

> Sir, in my heart there was a kind of fighting
> That would not let me sleep...
> Up from my cabin,
> My sea-gown scarf'd about me, in the dark
> Grop'd I to find out them: had my desire;
> Finger'd their packet;

are of his quite mature. Both workmanship and thought are in an unstable position. We are surely justified in attributing the play, with that other profoundly interesting play of "intractable" material and astonishing versification, *Measure for Measure,* to a period of crisis, after which follow the tragic successes which culminate in *Coriolanus. Coriolanus* may be not as "interesting" as *Hamlet,* but it is, with *Antony and Cleopatra,* Shakespeare's most assured artistic success. And probably more people have thought *Hamlet* a work of art because they found it interesting than have found it interesting because it is a work of art. It is the *Mona Lisa* of literature.

The grounds of *Hamlet*'s failure are not immediately obvious. Mr. Robertson is undoubtedly correct in concluding that the essential emotion of the play is the feeling of a son toward a guilty mother:

> [Hamlet's] tone is that of one who has suffered tortures on the score of his mother's degradation. . . . The guilt of a mother is an almost intolerable motive for drama, but it had to be maintained and emphasized to supply a psychological solution, or rather a hint of one.

This, however, is by no means the whole story. It is not merely the "guilt of a mother" that cannot be handled as Shakespeare handled the suspicion of Othello, the infatuation of Antony, or the pride of Coriolanus. The subject might conceivably have expanded into a tragedy like these, intelligible, self-complete, in the sunlight. *Hamlet,* like the sonnets, is full of some stuff that the writer could not drag to light, contemplate, or manipulate into art. And when we search for this feeling, we find it, as in the sonnets, very difficult to localize. You cannot point to it in the speeches; indeed, if you examine the two famous soliloquies, you see the versification of Shakespeare but a content which might be claimed by another, perhaps by the author of the *Revenge of Bussy d'Ambois,*° act V, scene i. We find Shakespeare's

Revenge of Bussy d'Ambois: Tragedy (1610–1611) by George Chapman, dealing with the reluctance of Clement d'Ambois to avenge his brother's death.

Hamlet not in the action, not in any quotations that we might select, so much as in an unmistakable tone which is unmistakably not in the earlier play.

The only way of expressing emotion in the form of art is by finding an "objective correlative"; in other words, a set of objects, a situation, a chain of events which shall be the formula of that *particular* emotion; such that when the external facts, which must terminate in sensory experience, are given, the emotion is immediately evoked. If you examine any of Shakespeare's more successful tragedies, you will find this exact equivalence; you will find that the state of mind of Lady Macbeth walking in her sleep has been communicated to you by a skillful accumulation of imagined sensory impressions; the words of Macbeth on hearing of his wife's death strike us as if, given the sequence of events, these words were automatically released by the last event in the series. The artistic "inevitability" lies in this complete adequacy of the external to the emotion; and this is precisely what is deficient in *Hamlet*. Hamlet (the man) is dominated by an emotion which is inexpressible, because it is in *excess* of the facts as they appear. And the supposed identity of Hamlet with his author is genuine to this point: that Hamlet's bafflement at the absence of objective equivalent to his feelings is a prolongation of the bafflement of his creator in the face of his artistic problem. Hamlet is up against the difficulty that his disgust is occasioned by his mother, but that his mother is not an adequate equivalent for it; his disgust envelops and exceeds her. It is thus a feeling which he cannot understand; he cannot objectify it, and it therefore remains to poison life and obstruct action. None of the possible actions can satisfy it; and nothing that Shakespeare can do with the plot can express Hamlet for him. And it must be noticed that the very nature of the *données* of the problem precludes objective equivalence. To have heightened the criminality of Gertrude would have been to provide the formula for a totally different emotion in Hamlet; it is just *because* her character is so negative and insignificant that she arouses in Hamlet the feeling which she is incapable of representing.

The "madness" of Hamlet lay to Shakespeare's hand; in the earlier play a simple ruse, and to the end, we may presume, understood as a ruse by the audience. For Shakespeare it is less than madness and more than feigned. The levity of Hamlet, his repetition of phrase, his puns, are not part of a deliberate plan of dissimulation, but a form of emotional relief. In the character Hamlet it is the buffoonery of an emotion which can find no outlet in action; in the dramatist it is the buffoonery of an emotion which he cannot express in art. The intense feeling, ecstatic or terrible, without an object or exceeding its object, is something which every person of sensibility has known; it is doubtless a subject of study for pathologists. It often occurs in adolescence: the ordinary person puts these feelings to sleep, or trims down his feelings to fit the business world; the artist keeps them alive by his ability to intensify the world to his emotions. The Hamlet of Laforgue° is an adolescent; the Hamlet of Shakespeare is not, he has not that explanation and excuse. We must simply admit that here Shakespeare tackled a problem which proved too much for him. Why he attempted it at all is an insoluble puzzle; under compulsion of what experience he attempted to express the inexpressibly horrible, we cannot ever know. We need a great many facts in his biography; and we should like to know whether, and when, and after or at the same time as what personal experience, he read Montaigne's *Apologie de Raimond Sebond*. We should have, finally, to know something which is by hypothesis unknowable, for we assume it to be an experience which, in the manner indicated, exceeded the facts. We should have to understand things which Shakespeare did not understand himself.

Laforgue: Jules Laforgue (1860–1887), French poet who was an important influence on Eliot.

OTHELLO

Othello was one of Shakespeare's most popular plays, produced frequently in his lifetime and throughout the seventeenth century. Although the date of composition is uncertain, we do know that the earliest recorded production was November 1, 1604, in the old Banqueting Hall at the court of King James I and his wife, Anne of Denmark. This detail is interesting because it coincides with the later production—during the same winter season and at the same theater—of Ben Jonson's *Masque of Blackness*, which was specifically commissioned by Queen Anne so that she could "paint herself black" along with the ladies in her retinue.

There seems to have been a vogue for blackness in England at the time. A great many Moors—the term, as Shakespeare and others of his time use it, means a dark-skinned person from Africa—were living in England at the end of Queen Elizabeth's reign and the beginning of King James's, the period of both performances. Her government had given Moors "full diplomatic recognition" as a gesture of thanks for their conquest of England's enemy, Spain, but in 1601 Queen Elizabeth was so alarmed by the number of blacks in England that she appointed a foreign merchant to transport them from the kingdom. In 1604 a delegation of Arabs visited London, and their customs and style caused some stir, of both admiration and concern. Although the color black was symbolically associated by white people with the devil and moral turpitude, and the practice of slavery was already advanced, a number of black African noblemen had traveled to England, and some had returned to Africa as translators and intermediaries in trading expeditions.

Aaron, a Moor in Shakespeare's *Titus Andronicus* (1594), was dark-skinned and a villain. Early on, however, Shakespeare represents black characters in other entertainments as noble. He establishes the noble birth and character of Othello, for instance, who tells us, "I am black" (III, iii, 263). The character of Othello, a general of the Venetian forces, derives from an early Italian story by Geraldi Cinthio, published in 1566 in Italian and 1584 in French. Shakespeare might have read either one. He adapted the story, adding new characters, reinterpreting the action, and completely reimagining Othello, Desdemona, and Iago.

The setting, Venice, was exotic for Elizabethan audiences, but it was appropriate for establishing a character who was unusual and something of "the other," as, for example, Shylock was in the earlier *Merchant of Venice* (1596–1597). It was especially felicitous a choice of setting for Othello's generalship because the Venetian republic, by law, had to have a foreigner as general of the armies. No one in the play disputes Othello's leadership and soldiership—not even Iago.

While the play makes great use of the contrasts of black and white, light and dark, evening and day, both to establish mood and to imply moral values, the central action is not devoted to issues related to Othello's race. The opening scenes reveal that Brabantio, Desdemona's father, and Iago, Othello's ensign, are capable of racial slurs. But each speaks out of anger and disappointment. The official governors of Venice never once imply racial inequity, nor do they condone any disrespect for Othello. Indeed, they support him in his marriage once they hear Desdemona indicate her willing choice of Othello as her mate.

The dramatic action centers on Iago's bitter disappointment at having been passed over for promotion in favor of Cassio, whom he regards as an inexperienced boy. Cassio is well enough regarded by Othello and others to end the play as governor of Mauritania, the country in northwest Africa that was settled by Berbers and from which the name "Moors" is derived. Even if Cassio was preferred because he was the intermediary between Othello and Desdemona, and even though he has the weakness of sometimes being an unsoldierly drunk, he proves more worthy than the villainous Iago, who virtually personifies the devil. At the end of the play, Othello, understanding how terribly he has been betrayed, wishes to look at Iago's foot to see if, like the devil's, it is cleft.

In some productions of the play, Iago almost steals the show. His soliloquies indicating how he will manipulate the characters to achieve his evil ends are so powerful as to chill an audience. He seems to be the force driving the action, while Othello struggles like a fly in the web of his deceit. Yet Othello is the great character in the drama. He rises majestically to deliver some of the greatest speeches Shakespeare ever wrote. Eventually, his initial innocence is replaced by rage and anger. Iago purposely infects Othello with jealousy, implying that his young, new wife Desdemona is dallying with Cassio. He offers "ocular proof" but proof that would not be convincing if Othello were not so eager to be convinced. Iago moves Othello from a contented man—a soldier at peace with himself—to a deracinated jealous husband.

Watching the progress of that action rivets the audience. Seeing how the villain Iago improvises at every turn to take advantage of each opportunity to present false "evidence" fascinates audience and reader alike. Ironically, the symbolism of blackness is reversed in Iago, whose inner soul is dark and hell bound, while Othello is led to commit a heinous crime whose horror he ultimately recognizes. He pays with his own death by his own hand. Our sympathy is with him at the end of the play, despite his moments of frightening anger and horror. He has been used by a lesser man, and what has permitted him to be deceived—as interpreted by some critics—is his essential innocence and goodness.

Among the patterns of imagery in the play, those connected with animals—such as the pig, the barbary horse, and the black ram—support Iago's efforts to emphasize Othello's bestiality. When he claims that Othello and Desdemona are "making the beast with two backs," he wishes to enlist Brabantio's aid in humiliating Othello and perhaps damaging his reputation with the Duke of Venice. The careful manipulation of this imagery helps Iago advance his plan even before he knows what it is.

Othello himself stands as one of the towering figures in Shakespeare's works, challenging actors in his own day and in ours. Desdemona may be faulted for her willfulness in marrying without her father's knowledge or permission—at the time a grave infraction. But the audience forgives her, if only because it is obvious that nothing she could have said would have convinced her father to look kindly on Othello as a son-in-law. And while passion is at the core of the play, it may not have been passion alone that caused her to act as she did.

Othello in Performance

The first recorded production of *Othello* was November 1604 at the court of King James. But public performances probably were held at the Globe Theatre sometime that year or the following. Although no reliable performance records are available, we know that the play was produced by Shakespeare's company, The King's Men, both at the Globe in April 1610 and in Oxford in September of the same year. It was performed again in 1629, 1635, and 1636. It was popular in the eighteenth and nineteenth centuries as well as in the twentieth century and is among Shakespeare's most often produced plays.

The first Othello was Richard Burbage, Shakespeare's finest actor in one of his finest roles. He wore Elizabethan clothes with no special effort to adopt a Moorish costume. We have no record of his makeup, and the only eyewitness account describes him as a "grieved Moor." However, judging from the tradition maintained up to 1709, when we have a portrait of Othello, we can assume he was played as a black man. The play enjoyed such popularity that it constantly attracted the most gifted actors of the day.

The nineteenth century produced several notable Othellos, but it also saw the beginning of a trend in which Othello became "tawny" rather than black. He became what was then known as a "white Moor." Edmund Kean, the greatest actor of his day, portrayed Othello in this fashion to extraordinary acclaim. The first black actor to play Othello was Ira Aldridge, an American on the London stage in the nineteenth century.

In modern times, two productions stand out as milestones: Paul Robeson's in New York in 1943–1944 and Laurence Olivier's in London in 1964. Robeson was known as a great singer but had performed onstage in Eugene O'Neill's *The Emperor Jones* prior to *Othello*. His physical presence on stage was striking in every way, especially when linked with his commanding voice. Martin Wine describes him as the "outstanding 'romantic' Othello of our time," by which he means a sympathetic and moving Othello. The Broadway production played for more performances than nearly any American production of Shakespeare up to that time. James Earl Jones, who played the role many years later, was in the audience and felt that Robeson's command of the concept of honor was singular and has never been approached since.

Laurence Olivier had himself made up not just as a black man but as a black African. Some critics were impressed by the achievement, but others felt it was still difficult to accept the idea of a white actor in the part. Yet Olivier's version was taut, powerful, and one of his greatest achievements. He took comfort in the fact that Shakespeare wrote the role for a white actor and did not worry over the shift in tradition. Martin Wine described his performance as "the most controversial" performance of our time. Olivier's interpretation was of an egotistical Othello, one who was tormented by neurotic tendencies and even a touch of paranoia. Olivier's Othello was less a man of the Renaissance than a man of modern times.

Most modern productions have made use of effective lighting, emphasizing the opening darkness of the drama. They also make use of simple staging, using archways effectively and suggestions of buildings, ships and sails, and sometimes Moorish architectural details.

William Shakespeare (1564–1616)

OTHELLO THE MOOR OF VENICE

The Names of the Actors

OTHELLO, THE MOOR
BRABANTIO, [a Venetian senator,] father to Desdemona
CASSIO, an honorable lieutenant [to Othello]
IAGO, [Othello's ancient,] a villain
RODERIGO, a gulled gentleman
DUKE OF VENICE
SENATORS [of Venice]
MONTANO, governor of Cyprus
LODOVICO AND GRATIANO, [kinsmen to Brabantio,]
    two noble Venetians
SAILORS
CLOWNS
DESDEMONA, wife to Othello
EMILIA, wife to Iago
BIANCA, a courtesan
[MESSENGER, HERALD, OFFICERS, VENETIAN GENTLEMEN,
    MUSICIANS, ATTENDANTS

Scene: Venice and Cyprus]

ACT I • Scene 1

A street in Venice.

Enter Roderigo and Iago.

RODERIGO: Tush, never tell me! I take it much
        unkindly
    That thou, Iago, who hast had my purse
    As if the strings were thine, shouldst know of this.°
IAGO: 'Sblood,° but you'll not hear me!
5   If ever I did dream of such a matter,
    Abhor me.
RODERIGO: Thou told'st me thou didst hold him in
        thy hate.
IAGO: Despise me if I do not. Three great ones of the
        city,
    In personal suit to make me his lieutenant,
10 Off-capped to him;° and, by the faith of man,
    I know my price; I am worth no worse a place.
    But he, as loving his own pride and purposes,
    Evades them with a bombast circumstance.°
    Horribly stuffed with epithets of war;
15 [And, in conclusion,]
    Nonsuits° my mediators; for, "Certes," says he,

"I have already chose my officer."
And what was he?
Forsooth, a great arithmetician,°
One Michael Cassio, a Florentine   20
(A fellow almost damned in a fair wife°)
That never set a squadron in the field,
Nor the division of a battle knows
More than a spinster; unless the bookish theoric,
Wherein the togèd consuls can propose   25
As masterly as he. Mere prattle without practice
Is all his soldiership. But he, sir, had th' election;
And I (of whom his eyes had seen the proof
At Rhodes, at Cyprus, and on other grounds
Christian and heathen) must be belee'd and calmed°   30
By debitor and creditor; this counter-caster,°
He, in good time, must his lieutenant be,
And I—God bless the mark!—his Moorship's
    ancient.°
RODERIGO: By heaven, I rather would have been his
    hangman.
IAGO: Why, there's no remedy; 'tis the curse of service. 35
    Preferment goes by letter and affection,°
    And not by old gradation, where each second
    Stood heir to th' first. Now, sir, be judge yourself,
    Whether I in any just term am affined°
    To love the Moor.
RODERIGO: I would not follow him then. 40
IAGO: O, sir, content you;
    I follow him to serve my turn upon him.
    We cannot all be masters, nor all masters
    Cannot be truly followed. You shall mark
    Many a duteous and knee-crooking knave   45
    That, doting on his own obsequious bondage,
    Wears out his time, much like his master's ass,
    For naught but provender; and when he's old,
        cashiered.°
    Whip me such honest knaves! Others there are
    Who, trimmed° in forms and visages of duty,   50
    Keep yet their hearts attending on themselves;
    And, throwing but shows of service on their lords,
    Do well thrive by them, and when they have lined
        their coats,
    Do themselves homage. These fellows have some
        soul;

---

19. **arithmetician:** Theoretician. 21. **almost . . . wife:** (An obscure allusion; Cassio is unmarried, but see IV, I, 115–16). 30. **belee'd and calmed:** Left in the lurch. 31. **counter-caster:** Bookkeeper. 33. **ancient:** Ensign. 36. **affection:** Favoritism. 39. **affined:** Obliged. 48. **cashiered:** Turned off. 50. **trimmed:** Dressed up.

I, I. 3. **this:** I.e., Desdemona's elopement. 5. **'Sblood:** By God's blood. 10. **him:** I.e., Othello. 13. **a bombast circumstance:** Pompous circumlocution. 16. **Nonsuits:** Rejects.

55   And such a one do I profess myself. For, sir,
     It is as sure as you are Roderigo,
     Were I the Moor, I would not be Iago.
     In following him, I follow but myself;
     Heaven is my judge, not I for love and duty,
60   But seeming so, for my peculiar end;
     For when my outward action doth demonstrate
     The native act and figure of my heart°
     In compliment extern,° 'tis not long after
     But I will wear my heart upon my sleeve
65   For daws to peck at; I am not what I am.
       RODERIGO: What a full fortune does the thick-lips°
             owe°
       If he can carry't thus!
     IAGO: Call up her father,
       Rouse him. Make after him, poison his delight,
       Proclaim him in the streets. Incense her kinsmen,
70   And though he in a fertile climate dwell,
       Plague him with flies; though that his joy be joy,
       Yet throw such changes of vexation on't
       As it may lose some color.
       RODERIGO: Here is her father's house. I'll call aloud.
75   IAGO: Do, with like timorous° accent and dire yell
       As when, by night and negligence, the fire
       Is spied in populous cities.
       RODERIGO: What, ho, Brabantio! Signior Brabantio,
             ho!
       IAGO: Awake! What, ho, Brabantio! Thieves! thieves!
             thieves!
80   Look to your house, your daughter, and your bags!
       Thieves! thieves!

Brabantio at a window.°

       BRABANTIO (*above*): What is the reason of this
             terrible summons?
         What is the matter there?
       RODERIGO: Signior, is all your family within?
       IAGO: Are your doors locked?
85   BRABANTIO: Why, wherefore ask you this?
       IAGO: Zounds, sir, y' are robbed! For shame, put on
             your gown!
         Your heart is burst; you have lost half your soul.
         Even now, now, very now, an old black ram
         Is tupping your white ewe. Arise, arise!
90   Awake the snorting° citizens with the bell.
         Or else the devil will make a grandsire of you.
         Arise, I say!
       BRABANTIO: What, have you lost your wits?
       RODERIGO: Most reverend signior, do you know my
             voice?
95   BRABANTIO: Not I. What are you?
       RODERIGO: My name is Roderigo.

       BRABANTIO: The worser welcome!
         I have charged thee not to haunt about my doors.
         In honest plainness thou hast heard me say
         My daughter is not for thee; and now, in madness,
         Being full of supper and distemp'ring draughts,   100
         Upon malicious knavery dost thou come
         To start my quiet.
       RODERIGO: Sir, sir, sir—
       BRABANTIO: But thou must needs be sure
         My spirit and my place have in them power   105
         To make this bitter to thee.
       RODERIGO: Patience, good sir.
       BRABANTIO: What tell'st thou me of robbing? This is
             Venice;
         My house is not a grange.°
       RODERIGO: Most grave Brabantio,
         In simple and pure soul I come to you.
       IAGO: Zounds, sir, you are one of those that will not 110
         serve God if the devil bid you. Because we come to do
         you service, and you think we are ruffians, you'll
         have your daughter covered with a Barbary horse;
         you'll have your nephews° neigh to you; you'll have
         coursers for cousins, and gennets for germans.°   115
       BRABANTIO: What profane wretch art thou?
       IAGO: I am one, sir, that comes to tell you your daughter
         and the Moor are now making the beast with two
         backs.
       BRABANTIO: Thou are a villain.
       IAGO: You are—a senator.   120
       BRABANTIO: This thou shalt answer. I know thee,
             Roderigo.
       RODERIGO: Sir, I will answer anything. But I beseech
             you,
         If't be your pleasure and most wise consent,
         As partly I find it is, that your fair daughter,
         At this odd-even° and dull watch o' th' night,   125
         Transported, with no worse nor better guard
         But with a knave of common hire, a gondolier,
         To the gross clasps of a lascivious Moor—
         If this be known to you, and your allowance,°
         We then have done you bold and saucy wrongs;   130
         But if you know not this, my manners tell me
         We have your wrong rebuke. Do not believe
         That, from the sense° of all civility,
         I thus would play and trifle with your reverence.
         Your daughter, if you have not given her leave,   135
         I say again, hath made a gross revolt,
         Tying her duty, beauty, wit, and fortunes
         In an extravagant and wheeling° stranger
         Of here and everywhere. Straight satisfy yourself.
         If she be in her chamber, or your house,   140
         Let loose on me the justice of the state
         For thus deluding you.

---

62. The . . . heart: What I really believe and intend.   **63. compliment extern:** Outward appearance.   **66. thick-lips:** An Elizabethan epithet for blacks, including Moors.   **owe:** Own.   **75. timorous:** Terrifying.   [S.D.] *Brabantio at a window:* (Added from quarto).   **90. snorting:** Snoring.

108. grange: Isolated farmhouse.   **114. nephews:** I.e., grandsons.   **115. gennets for germans:** Spanish horses for near kinsmen.   **125. odd-even:** Between night and morning.   **129. allowance:** Approval.   **133. from the sense:** In violation.   **138. extravagant and wheeling:** Expatriate and roving.

BRABANTIO: Strike on the tinder, ho!
  Give me a taper! Call up all my people!
  This accident° is not unlike my dream.
145   Belief of it oppresses me already.
  Light, I say! light!   *Exit [above].*
IAGO: Farewell, for I must leave you.
  It seems not meet, nor wholesome to my place,
  To be produced—as, if I stay, I shall—
  Against the Moor. For I do know the state,
150   However this may gall him with some check,°
  Cannot with safety cast° him; for he's embarked
  With such loud reason to the Cyprus wars,
  Which even now stand in act,° that for their souls
  Another of his fathom° they have none
155   To lead their business; in which regard,
  Though I do hate him as I do hell-pains,
  Yet, for necessity of present life,
  I must show out a flag and sign of love,
  Which is indeed but sign. That you shall surely
    find him,
160   Lead to the Sagittary° the raisèd search;
  And there will I be with him. So farewell.   *Exit.*

*Enter [below] Brabantio in his nightgown,° and Servants
with torches.*

BRABANTIO: It is too true an evil. Gone she is;
  And what's to come of my despisèd time
  Is naught but bitterness. Now, Roderigo,
165   Where didst thou see her?—O unhappy girl!—
  With the Moor, say'st thou?—Who would be a
    father?—
  How didst thou know 'twas she!—O, she deceives
    me
  Past thought!—What said she to you?—Get moe°
    tapers!
  Raise all my kindred!—Are they married, think
    you?
170 RODERIGO: Truly I think they are.
BRABANTIO: O heaven! How got she out? O treason
    of the blood!
  Fathers, from hence trust not your daughters'
    minds
  By what you see them act. Is there not charms
  By which the property° of youth and maidhood
175   May be abused? Have you not read, Roderigo,
  Of some such thing?
RODERIGO: Yes, sir, I have indeed.
BRABANTIO: Call up my brother.—O, would you had
    had her!—
  Some one way, some another.—Do you know
  Where we may apprehend her and the Moor?
180 RODERIGO: I think I can discover him, if you please
  To get good guard and go along with me.
BRABANTIO: I pray you lead on. At every house I'll call;

I may command at most.—Get weapons, ho!
  And raise some special officers of night.—
  On, good Roderigo; I'll deserve° your pains.   185
                      Exeunt.

Scene II

Before the lodgings of Othello.

Enter Othello, Iago, and Attendants with torches.

IAGO: Though in the trade of war I have slain men,
  Yet do I hold it very stuff o' th' conscience
  To do no contrived murther. I lack iniquity
  Sometimes to do me service. Nine or ten times
  I had thought t' have yerked° him here under the
    ribs.   5
OTHELLO: 'Tis better as it is.
IAGO: Nay, but he prated,
  And spoke such scurvy and provoking terms
  Against your honor
  That with the little godliness I have
  I did full hard forbear him. But I pray you, sir,   10
  Are you fast° married? Be assured of this,
  That the magnifico° is much beloved,
  And hath in his effect a voice potential°
  As double° as the Duke's. He will divorce you,
  Or put upon you what restraint and grievance   15
  The law, with all his might to enforce it on,
  Will give him cable.
OTHELLO: Let him do his spite.
  My services which I have done the signiory°
  Shall out-tongue his complaints. 'Tis yet to
    know°—
  Which, when I know that boasting is an honor,   20
  I shall promulgate—I fetch my life and being
  From men of royal siege;° and my demerits°
  May speak unbonneted to as proud a fortune
  As this that I have reached.° For know, Iago,
  But that I love the gentle Desdemona,   25
  I would not my unhousèd° free condition
  Put into circumscription and confine
  For the sea's worth. But look what lights come
    yond?
IAGO: Those are the raisèd father and his friends.
  You were best go in.
OTHELLO: Not I; I must be found.   30
  My parts, my title, and my perfect soul°
  Shall manifest me rightly. Is it they?
IAGO: By Janus, I think no.

185. **deserve:** Show gratitude for. I, II. 5. **yerked:** Stabbed.
11. **fast:** Securely. 12. **magnifico:** Grandee (Brabantio).
13. **potential:** Powerful. 14. **double:** Doubly influential.
18. **signiory:** Venetian government. 19. **yet to know:** Still
not generally known. 22. **siege:** Rank. **demerits:** Deserts.
24. **May speak . . . reached:** Are equal, I modestly assert, to
those of Desdemona's family. 26. **unhousèd:** Unrestrained.
31. **perfect soul:** Stainless conscience.

144. **accident:** Occurrence. 150. **check:** Reprimand. 151. **cast:**
Discharge. 153. **stand in act:** Are going on. 154. **fathom:**
Capacity. 160. **Sagittary:** An inn. [S.D.] *nightgown:* Dress-
ing gown. 168. **moe:** More. 174. **property:** Nature.

Enter Cassio, with torches, Officers.

OTHELLO: The servants of the Duke, and my
    lieutenant.
35   The goodness of the night upon you, friends!
    What is the news?
CASSIO: The Duke does greet you, general;
    And he requires your haste-post-haste appearance
    Even on the instant.
OTHELLO: What's the matter, think you?
CASSIO: Something from Cyprus, as I may divine.
40   It is a business of some heat. The galleys
    Have sent a dozen sequent° messengers
    This very night at one another's heels,
    And many of the consuls, raised and met,
    Are at the Duke's already. You have been hotly
      called for;
45   When, being not at your lodging to be found,
    The Senate hath sent about three several quests
    To search you out.
OTHELLO: 'Tis well I am found by you.
    I will but spend a word here in the house,
    And go with you.   [*Exit*]
CASSIO: Ancient, what makes he here?
50 IAGO: Faith, he to-night hath boarded a land carack.°
    If it prove lawful prize, he's made for ever.
CASSIO: I do not understand.
IAGO: He's married.
CASSIO: To who?

[*Enter Othello.*]

IAGO: Marry, to—Come, captain, will you go?
OTHELLO: Have
    with you.
CASSIO: Here comes another troop to seek for you.

*Enter Brabantio, Roderigo, and others with lights and
weapons.*

55 IAGO: It is Brabantio. General, be advised.
    He comes to bad intent.
OTHELLO: Holla! stand there!
RODERIGO: Signior, it is the Moor.
BRABANTIO: Down with him, thief!

[*They draw on both sides.*]

IAGO: You, Roderigo! Come, sir, I am for you.
OTHELLO: Keep up° your bright swords, for the dew
    will rust them.
60   Good signior, you shall more command with years
    Than with your weapons.
BRABANTIO: O thou foul thief, where hast thou
      stowed my daughter?
    Damned as thou art, thou hast enchanted her!
    For I'll refer me to all things of sense,
65   If she in chains of magic were not bound,
    Whether a maid so tender, fair, and happy,

So opposite to marriage that she shunned
The wealthy curlèd darlings of our nation,
Would ever have, t' incur a general mock,
Run from her guardage to the sooty bosom   70
Of such a thing as thou—to fear, not to delight.
Judge me the world if 'tis not gross in sense°
That thou hast practiced on her with foul charms,
Abused her delicate youth with drugs or minerals
That weaken motion.° I'll have't disputed on;   75
'Tis probable, and palpable to thinking.
I therefore apprehend and do attach° thee
For an abuser of the world, a practicer
Of arts inhibited and out of warrant.
Lay hold upon him. If he do resist,   80
Subdue him at his peril.
OTHELLO: Hold your hands,
Both you of my inclining and the rest.
Were it my cue to fight, I should have known it
Without a prompter. Where will you that I go
To answer this your charge?
BRABANTIO: To prison, till fit time   85
Of law and course of direct session°
Call thee to answer.
OTHELLO: What if I do obey?
How may the Duke be therewith satisfied,
Whose messengers are here about my side
Upon some present business of the state   90
To bring me to him?
OFFICER: 'Tis true, most worthy signior.
The Duke's in council, and your noble self
I am sure is sent for.
BRABANTIO: How? The Duke in council?
In this time of the night? Bring him away.
Mine's not an idle° cause. The Duke himself,   95
Or any of my brothers of the state,
Cannot but feel this wrong as 'twere their own;
For if such actions may have passage free,
Bondslaves and pagans shall our statesmen be.
                          Exeunt.

Scene III

The Venetian Senate Chamber.

*Enter Duke and Senators, set at a table, with lights and
Attendants.*

DUKE: There is no composition° in these news
    That gives them credit.
1. SENATOR: Indeed they are disproportioned.
    My letters say a hundred and seven galleys.
DUKE: And mine a hundred forty.
2. SENATOR: And mine two hundred.
    But though they jump° not on a just account—   5

---

41. sequent: Consecutive. **50. carack:** Treasure ship. **59. Keep
up:** I.e., sheath.

72. gross in sense: Obvious. **75. motion:** Perception. **77. attach:** Arrest. **86. direct session:** Regular trial. **95. idle:** Trifling. **I, III. 1. composition:** Consistency. **5. jump:** Agree.

As in these cases where the aim° reports
'Tis oft with difference—yet do they all confirm
A Turkish fleet, and bearing up to Cyprus.
DUKE: Nay, it is possible enough to judgment.
10　I do not so secure me° in the error
But the main article° I do approve°
In fearful sense.
SAILOR (*within*):　What, ho! what, ho! what, ho!
OFFICER: A messenger from the galleys.

Enter Sailor.

DUKE:　　　　　　　　　　Now, what's the business?
SAILOR: The Turkish preparation makes for Rhodes.
15　So was I bid report here to the state
By Signior Angelo.
DUKE: How say you by this change?
1. SENATOR:　　　　　　　　This cannot be
By no assay° of reason. 'Tis a pageant
To keep us in false gaze.° When we consider
20　Th' importancy of Cyprus to the Turk,
And let ourselves again but understand
That, as it more concerns the Turk than Rhodes,
So may he with more facile question bear° it,
For that it stands not in such warlike brace,°
25　But altogether lacks th' abilities
That Rhodes is dressed in—if we make thought of
　this,
We must not think the Turk is so unskillful
To leave that latest which concerns him first,
Neglecting an attempt of ease and gain
30　To wake and wage° a danger profitless.
DUKE: Nay, in all confidence, he's not for Rhodes.
OFFICER: Here is more news.

Enter a Messenger.

MESSENGER: The Ottomites, reverend and gracious,
Steering with due course toward the isle of Rhodes,
35　Have there injointed them with an after fleet.
1. SENATOR: Ay, so I thought. How many, as you guess?
MESSENGER: Of thirty sail; and now they do restem°
Their backward course, bearing with frank
　appearance
Their purposes toward Cyprus, Signior Montano,
40　Your trusty and most valiant servitor,
With his free duty recommends you thus,
And prays you to believe him.
DUKE: 'Tis certain then for Cyprus.
Marcus Luccicos,° is not he in town?
45　1. SENATOR: He's now in Florence.
DUKE: Write from us to him; post, post-haste dispatch.
1. SENATOR: Here comes Brabantio and the valiant
　Moor.

*Enter Brabantio, Othello, Cassio, Iago, Roderigo, and
Officers.*

DUKE: Valiant Othello, we must straight employ you
Against the general enemy Ottoman.

[*To Brabantio.*]

I did not see you. Welcome, gentle signior.　　　50
We lacked your counsel and your help to-night.
BRABANTIO: So did I yours. Good your grace, pardon
　me.
Neither my place, nor aught I heard of business,
Hath raised me from my bed; nor doth the general
　care
Take hold on me; for my particular grief　　　55
Is of so floodgate° and o'erbearing nature
That it englutts° and swallows other sorrows,
And it is still itself.
DUKE:　　　　　　　Why, what's the matter?
BRABANTIO: My daughter! O, my daughter!
ALL:　　　　　　　　　　Dead?
BRABANTIO:　　　　　　　Ay, to me.
She is abused, stol'n from me, and corrupted　　60
By spells and medicines bought of mountebanks;
For nature so prepost'rously to err,
Being not deficient,° blind, or lame of sense,
Sans witchcraft could not.
DUKE: Whoe'er he be that in this foul proceeding　　65
Hath thus beguiled your daughter of herself,
And you of her, the bloody book of law
You shall yourself read in the bitter letter
After your own sense; yea, though our proper° son
Stood in your action.°
BRABANTIO:　　　　　Humbly I thank your grace.　70
Here is the man—this Moor, whom now, it seems,
Your special mandate for the state affairs
Hath hither brought.
ALL:　　　　　　　We are very sorry for't.
DUKE [*to Othello*]: What, in your own part, can you
　say to this?
BRABANTIO: Nothing, but this is so.　　　　　　75
OTHELLO: Most potent, grave, and reverend signiors,
My very noble, and approved° good masters,
That I have ta'en away this old man's daughter,
It is most true; true I have married her.
The very head and front of my offending　　　80
Hath this extent, no more. Rude° am I in my
　speech,
And little blessed with the soft phrase of peace;
For since these arms of mine had seven years' pith°
Till now some nine moons wasted, they have used
Their dearest action in the tented field;　　　85
And little of this great world can I speak
More than pertains to feats of broil and battle;

---

6. **aim:** Conjecture.　**10. so secure me:** Take such comfort.
11. article: Substance. **approve:** Accept.　**18. assay:** Test.
19. in false gaze: Looking the wrong way.　**23. with . . .
bear:** More easily capture.　**24. brace:** Posture of defense.
30. wake and wage: Rouse and risk.　**37. restem:** Steer again.
44. Marcus Luccicos: (Presumably a Venetian envoy).

56. **floodgate:** Torrential.　57. **englutts:** Devours.　63. **deficient:** Feeble-minded.　69. **our proper:** My own.　70. **Stood in your action:** Were accused by you.　77. **approved:** Tested by experience.　81. **Rude:** Unpolished.　83. **pith:** Strength.

And therefore little shall I grace my cause
In speaking for myself. Yet, by your gracious
   patience,
90 I will a round° unvarnished tale deliver
Of my whole course of love—what drugs, what
   charms,
What conjuration, and what mighty magic
(For such proceeding am I charged withal)
I won his daughter.
BRABANTIO: A maiden never bold;
95 Of spirit so still and quiet that her motion
Blushed° at herself; and she—in spite of nature,
Of years, of country, credit, everything—
To fall in love with what she feared to look on!
It is a judgment maimed and most imperfect
100 That will confess perfection so could err
Against all rules of nature, and must be driven
To find out practices° of cunning hell
Why this should be. I therefore vouch° again
That with some mixtures pow'rful o'er the blood,°
105 Or with some dram, conjured to this effect,
He wrought upon her.
DUKE: To vouch this is no proof,
Without more certain and more overt test
Than these thin habits° and poor likelihoods
Of modern seeming° do prefer against him.
110 1. SENATOR: But, Othello, speak.
Did you by indirect and forcèd° courses
Subdue and poison this young maid's affections?
Or came it by request, and such fair question°
As soul to soul affordeth?
OTHELLO: I do beseech you,
115 Send for the lady to the Sagittary
And let her speak of me before her father.
If you do find me foul in her report,
The trust, the office, I do hold of you
Not only take away, but let your sentence
Even fall upon my life.
120 DUKE: Fetch Desdemona hither.
OTHELLO: Ancient, conduct them; you best know the
   place.

Exit [Iago, with] two or three [Attendants].

And till she come, as truly as to heaven
I do confess the vices of my blood,
So justly to your grave ears I'll present
125 How I did thrive in this fair lady's love,
And she in mine.
DUKE: Say it, Othello.
OTHELLO: Her father loved me, oft invited me;
Still° questioned me the story of my life
130 From year to year—the battles, sieges, fortunes

That I have passed.
I ran it through, even from my boyish days
To th' very moment that he bade me tell it.
Wherein I spoke of most disastrous chances,
Of moving accidents by flood and field;   135
Of hairbreadth scapes i' th' imminent deadly
   breach;
Of being taken by the insolent foe
And sold to slavery; of my redemption thence
And portance° in my travels' history;
Wherein of anters° vast and deserts idle,   140
Rough quarries, rocks, and hills whose heads
   touch heaven,
It was my hint° to speak—such was the process;
And of the Cannibals that each other eat,
The Anthropophagi,° and men whose heads
Do grow beneath their shoulders. This to hear 145
Would Desdemona seriously incline;
But still the house affairs would draw her thence;
Which ever as she could with haste dispatch,
She'ld come again, and with a greedy ear
Devour up my discourse. Which I observing,   150
Took once a pliant° hour, and found good means
To draw from her a prayer of earnest heart
That I would all my pilgrimage dilate,°
Whereof by parcels° she had something heard,
But not intentively.° I did consent,   155
And often did beguile her of her tears
When I did speak of some distressful stroke
That my youth suffered. My story being done,
She gave me for my pains a world of sighs.
She swore, i' faith, 'twas strange, 'twas passing
   strange;   160
'Twas pitiful, 'twas wondrous pitiful.
She wished she had not heard it; yet she wished
That heaven had made her such a man. She
   thanked me;
And bade me, if I had a friend that loved her,
I should but teach him how to tell my story, 165
And that would woo her. Upon this hint° I spake.
She loved me for the dangers I had passed,
And I loved her that she did pity them.
This only is the witchcraft I have used.
Here comes the lady. Let her witness it.   170

Enter Desdemona, Iago, Attendants.

DUKE: I think this tale would win my daughter too.
  Good Brabantio,
Take up this mangled matter at the best.
Men do their broken weapons rather use
Than their bare hands.
BRABANTIO: I pray you hear her speak. 175

---

90. **round:** Plain. 95–96. **her motion Blushed:** Her own emotions caused her to blush. 102. **practices:** Plots. 103. **vouch:** Assert. 104. **blood:** Passions. 108. **thin habits:** Slight appearances. 109. **modern seeming:** Everyday supposition. 111. **forcèd:** Violent. 113. **question:** Conversation. 129. **Still:** Continually.

139. **portance:** Behavior. 140. **anters:** Caves. 142. **hint:** Occasion. 144. **Anthropophagi:** Man-eaters. 151. **pliant:** Propitious. 153. **dilate:** Recount in full. 154. **parcels:** Portions. 155. **intentively:** With full attention. 166. **hint:** Opportunity.

If she confess that she was half the wooer,
Destruction on my head if my bad blame
Light on the man! Come hither, gentle mistress.
Do you perceive in all this noble company
Where most you owe obedience?
180 DESDEMONA: My noble father,
I do perceive here a divided duty.
To you I am bound for life and education;°
My life and education both do learn me
How to respect you: you are the lord of duty;
185 I am hitherto your daughter. But here's my husband;
And so much duty as my mother showed
To you, preferring you before her father,
So much I challenge° that I may profess
Due to the Moor my lord.
BRABANTIO: God be with you! I have done.
190 Please it your grace, on to the state affairs.
I had rather to adopt a child than get° it.
Come hither, Moor.
I here do give thee that with all my heart
Which, but thou hast already, with all my heart
195 I would keep from thee. For your sake,° jewel,
I am glad at soul I have no other child;
For thy escape° would teach me tyranny,
To hang clogs on them. I have done, my lord.
DUKE: Let me speak like yourself° and lay a sentence°
200 Which, as a grise° or step, may help these lovers
[Into your favor.]
When remedies are past, the griefs are ended
By seeing the worst, which late on hopes depended.
To mourn a mischief that is past and gone
205 Is the next way to draw new mischief on.
What cannot be preserved when fortune takes,
Patience her injury a mock'ry makes.
The robbed that smiles steals something from the
    thief;
He robs himself that spends a bootless grief.
210 BRABANTIO: So let the Turk of Cyprus us beguile:
We lose it not so long as we can smile.
He bears the sentence well that nothing bears
But the free comfort which from thence he hears;
But he bears both the sentence and the sorrow
215 That to pay grief must of poor patience borrow.
These sentences, to sugar, or to gall,
Being strong on both sides, are equivocal.
But words are words. I never yet did hear
That the bruisèd heart was piercèd through the ear.
220 Beseech you, now to the affairs of state.
DUKE: The Turk with a most mighty preparation makes
for Cyprus. Othello, the fortitude° of the place is best
known to you; and though we have there a substi-
tute of most allowed° sufficiency, yet opinion,° a more

sovereign mistress of effects, throws a more safer 225
voice on you. You must therefore be content to slub-
ber° the gloss of your new fortunes with this more
stubborn and boist'rous expedition.
OTHELLO: The tyrant custom, most grave senators,
Hath made the flinty and steel couch of war 230
My thrice-driven bed of down. I do agnize
A natural and prompt alacrity
I find in hardness;° and do undertake
These present wars against the Ottomites.
Most humbly, therefore, bending to your state, 235
I crave fit disposition for my wife,
Due reference of place, and exhibition,°
With such accommodation and besort°
As levels° with her breeding.
DUKE: If you please,
Be't at her father's.
BRABANTIO: I will not have it so. 240
OTHELLO: Nor I.
DESDEMONA: Nor I. I would not there reside,
To put my father in impatient thoughts
By being in his eye. Most gracious Duke,
To my unfolding lend your prosperous° ear, 245
And let me find a charter in your voice,
T' assist my simpleness.°
DUKE: What would you, Desdemona?
DESDEMONA: That I did love the Moor to live with him,
My downright violence, and storm of fortunes, 250
May trumpet to the world. My heart's subdued
Even to the very quality of my lord.
I saw Othello's visage in his mind,
And to his honors and his valiant parts
Did I my soul and fortunes consecrate. 255
So that, dear lords, if I be left behind,
A moth of peace, and he go to the war,
The rites for which I love him are bereft me,
And I a heavy interim shall support
By his dear absence. Let me go with him. 260
OTHELLO: Let her have your voice.
Vouch with me, heaven, I therefore beg it not
To please the palate of my appetite,
Not to comply with heat°—the young affects°
In me defunct—and proper satisfaction; 265
But to be free and bounteous to her mind;
And heaven defend your good souls that you think
I will your serious and great business scant
When she is with me. No, when light-winged toys
Of feathered Cupid seel° with wanton dullness 270
My speculative and officed instruments,°

182. education: Upbringing.   189. challenge: Claim the right.
191. get: Beget.   195. For your sake: Because of you.   197. escape: Escapade.   199. like yourself: As you should.   sentence:
Maxim.   200. grise: Step.   222. fortitude: Fortification.
224. allowed: Acknowledged.   opinion: Public opinion.

227. slubber: Sully.   231–33. agnize...hardness: Recognize
in myself a natural and easy response to hardship.   237. exhibition: Allowance of money.   238. besort: Suitable company.   239. levels: Corresponds.   245. prosperous: Favorable.
247. simpleness: Lack of skill.   264. heat: Passions.   young
affects: Tendencies of youth.   270. seel: Blind.   271. My...
instruments: My perceptive and responsible faculties.

That° my disports corrupt and taint my business,
Let housewives make a skillet of my helm,
And all indign° and base adversities
275 Make head against my estimation!°
DUKE: Be it as you shall privately determine,
Either for her stay or going. Th' affair cries haste,
And speed must answer it.
1. SENATOR: You must away to-night.
OTHELLO: With all my heart.
280 DUKE: At nine i' th' morning here we'll meet again.
Othello, leave some officer behind,
And he shall our commission bring to you,
With such things else of quality and respect
As doth import° you.
OTHELLO: So please your grace, my ancient;
285 A man he is of honesty and trust
To his conveyance I assign my wife,
With what else needful your good grace shall
        think
To be sent after me.
DUKE: Let it be so.
Good night to every one.
        [To Brabantio.]   And, noble signior,
290 If virtue no delighted° beauty lack,
Your son-in-law is far more fair than black.
1. SENATOR: Adieu, brave Moor. Use Desdemona well.
BRABANTIO: Look to her, Moor, if thou hast eyes to see:
She has deceived her father, and may thee.

Exeunt [*Duke, Senators, Officers, etc.*].

295 OTHELLO: My life upon her faith!—Honest Iago,
My Desdemona must I leave to thee.
I prithee let thy wife attend on her,
And bring them after in the best advantage.°
Come, Desdemona. I have but an hour
300 Of love, of worldly matters and direction,
To spend with thee. We must obey the time.

Exit Moor and Desdemona.

RODERIGO: Iago,—
IAGO: What say'st thou, noble heart?
RODERIGO: What will I do, think'st thou?
305 IAGO: Why, go to bed and sleep.
RODERIGO: I will incontinently° drown myself.
IAGO: If thou dost, I shall never love thee after. Why,
thou silly gentleman!
RODERIGO: It is silliness to live when to live is torment;
310 and then have we a prescription to die when death is
our physician.
IAGO: O villainous! I have looked upon the world for
four times seven years; and since I could distinguish
betwixt a benefit and an injury, I never found man
315 that knew how to love himself. Ere I would say I

would drown myself for the love of a guinea hen, I
would change my humanity with a baboon.
RODERIGO: What should I do? I confess it is my shame
to be so fond, but it is not in my virtue to amend it.
IAGO: Virtue? a fig! 'Tis in ourselves that we are thus or   320
thus. Our bodies are our gardens, to which our wills
are gardeners; so that if we will plant nettles or sow
lettuce, set hyssop and weed up thyme, supply it with
one gender° of herbs or distract it with many—
either to have it sterile with idleness or manured with   325
industry—why, the power and corrigible authority°
of this lies in our wills. If the balance of our lives had
not one scale of reason to poise° another of sensuality, the blood and baseness° of our natures would
conduct us to most preposterous conclusions. But we   330
have reason to cool our raging motions,° our carnal
strings, our unbitted° lusts; whereof I take this that
you call love to be a sect or scion.°
RODERIGO: It cannot be.
IAGO: It is merely a lust of the blood and a permission of   335
the will. Come, be a man! Drown thyself? Drown
cats and blind puppies! I have professed me thy
friend, and I confess me knit to thy deserving with
cables of perdurable toughness. I could never better
stead thee than now. Put money in thy purse. Follow   340
thou the wars; defeat thy favor° with an usurped
beard. I say, put money in thy purse. It cannot be that
Desdemona should long continue her love to the
Moor—put money in thy purse—nor he his to her.
It was a violent commencement in her, and thou shalt   345
see an answerable sequestration°—put but money in
thy purse. These Moors are changeable in their
wills—fill thy purse with money. The food that to
him now is as luscious as locusts shall be to him
shortly as bitter as coloquintida.° She must change   350
for youth: when she is sated with his body, she will
find the error of her choice. [She must have change,
she must.] Therefore put money in thy purse. If thou
wilt needs damn thyself, do it a more delicate way
than drowning. Make° all the money thou canst. If   355
sanctimony and a frail vow betwixt an erring° barbarian and a supersubtle Venetian be not too hard
for my wits and all the tribe of hell, thou shalt enjoy
her. Therefore make money. A pox of drowning thyself! 'Tis clean out of the way. Seek thou rather to   360
be hanged in compassing thy joy than to be drowned
and go without her.
RODERIGO: Wilt thou be fast to my hopes, if I depend on
the issue?
IAGO: Thou art sure of me. Go, make money. I have told   365
thee often, and I retell thee again and again, I hate the

Moor. My cause is hearted;° thine hath no less rea-
son. Let us be conjunctive in our revenge against him.
If thou canst cuckold him, thou dost thyself a plea-
370 sure, me a sport. There are many events in the womb
of time, which will be delivered. Traverse,° go, pro-
vide thy money! We will have more of this tomorrow.
Adieu.
RODERIGO: Where shall we meet i' th' morning?
375 IAGO: At my lodging.
RODERIGO: I'll be with thee betimes.
IAGO: Go to, farewell—Do you hear, Roderigo?
[RODERIGO: What say you?
IAGO: No more of drowning, do you hear?
380 RODERIGO: I am changed.
IAGO: Go to, farewell. Put money enough in your
purse.]
RODERIGO: I'll sell all my land.   *Exit.*
IAGO: Thus do I ever make my fool my purse;
For I mine own gained knowledge should profane
385 If I would time expend with such a snipe°
But for my sport and profit. I hate the Moor;
And it is thought abroad that 'twixt my sheets
H'as done my office. I know not if't be true;
But I, for mere suspicion in that kind,
390 Will do as if for surety. He holds me well;°
The better shall my purpose work on him.
Cassio's a proper man. Let me see now:
To get his place, and to plume up° my will
In double knavery—How, how?—Let's see:—
395 After some time, to abuse Othello's ears
That he is too familiar with his wife.
He hath a person and a smooth dispose°
To be suspected—framed to make women false.
The Moor is of a free° and open nature
400 That thinks men honest that but seem to be so;
And will as tenderly be led by th' nose
As asses are.
I have't! It is engend'red! Hell and night
Must bring this monstrous birth to the world's light.
                                                Exit.

ACT II • *Scene 1*

An open place in Cyprus, near the harbor.

Enter Montano and two Gentlemen.

MONTANO: What from the cape can you discern at sea?
1. GENTLEMAN: Nothing at all: it is a high-wrought
flood.
I cannot 'twixt the heaven and the main
Descry a sail.
5 MONTANO: Methinks the wind hath spoke aloud at land;

A fuller blast ne'er shook our battlements.
If it hath ruffianed so upon the sea,
What ribs of oak, when mountains melt on them,
Can hold the mortise?° What shall we hear of this?
2. GENTLEMAN: A segregation° of the Turkish fleet.   10
For do but stand upon the foaming shore,
The chidden billow seems to pelt the clouds;
The wind-shaked surge, with high and monstrous
mane,
Seems to cast water on the burning Bear
And quench the Guards° of th' ever-fixèd pole.°   15
I never did like molestation° view
On the enchafèd flood.
MONTANO: If that the Turkish fleet
Be not ensheltered and embayed, they are drowned;
It is impossible to bear it out.

Enter a third Gentleman.

3. GENTLEMAN: News, lads! Our wars are done.   20
The desperate tempest hath so banged the Turks
That their designment halts.° A noble ship of Venice
Hath seen a grievous wrack and sufferance°
On most part of their fleet.
MONTANO: How? Is this true?
3. GENTLEMAN: The ship is here put in,   25
A Veronesa;° Michael Cassio,
Lieutenant to the warlike Moor Othello,
Is come on shore; the Moor himself at sea,
And is in full commission here for Cyprus.
MONTANO: I am glad on't. 'Tis a worthy governor.   30
3. GENTLEMAN: But his same Cassio, though he speak
of comfort
Touching the Turkish loss, yet he looks sadly
And prays the Moor be safe, for they were parted
With foul and violent tempest.
MONTANO: Pray heaven he be;
For I have served him, and the man commands   35
Like a full soldier. Let's to the seaside, ho!
As well to see the vessel that's come in
As to throw out our eyes for brave Othello,
Even till we make the main and th' aerial blue
An indistinct regard.°
3. GENTLEMAN: Come, let's do so;   40
For every minute is expectancy
Of more arrivance.

Enter Cassio.

CASSIO: Thanks, you the valiant of this warlike isle,
That so approve the Moor! O, let the heavens
Give him defense against the elements,   45
For I have lost him on a dangerous sea!
MONTANO: Is he well shipped?

---

367. **My cause is hearted:** My heart is in it.   371. **Traverse:** Forward march.   385. **snipe:** Fool.   390. **well:** In high regard.
393. **plume up:** Gratify.   397. **dispose:** Manner.   399. **free:**
Frank.

II, I. 9. **hold the mortise:** Hold their joints together.   10. **segre-
gation:** Scattering.   15. **Guards:** Stars near the North Star.
pole: Polestar.   16. **molestation:** Tumult.   22. **designment halts:**
Plan is crippled.   23. **sufferance:** Disaster.   26. **Veronesa:**
Ship furnished by Verona.   40. **An indistinct regard:** Indistinguishable.

CASSIO: His bark is stoutly timbered, and his pilot
    Of very expert and approved allowance;
50   Therefore my hopes, not surfeited to death,°
    Stand in bold cure.°
        (*Within.*)   A sail, a sail, a sail!

Enter a messenger.

CASSIO: What noise?
MESSENGER: The town is empty; on the brow o' th' sea
    Stand ranks of people, and they cry "A sail!"
55 CASSIO: My hopes do shape him for the governor.

A shot.

2. GENTLEMAN: They do discharge their shot of courtesy:
    Our friends at least.
CASSIO: I pray you, sir, go forth
    And give us truth who 'tis that is arrived.
2. GENTLEMAN: I shall.   *Exit.*
MONTANO: But, good lieutenant, is your general
60   wived?
CASSIO: Most fortunately. He hath achieved a maid
    That paragons° description and wild fame;
    One that excels the quirks° of blazoning° pens,
    And in th' essential vesture of creation
    Does tire the ingener.°

Enter Second Gentleman.

65   How now? Who has put in?
2. GENTLEMAN: 'Tis one Iago, ancient to the general.
CASSIO: H'as had most favorable and happy speed:
    Tempests themselves, high seas, and howling winds,
    The guttered° rocks and congregated sands,
70   Traitors ensteeped° to clog the guiltless keel,
    As having sense of beauty, do omit
    Their mortal° natures, letting go safely by
    The divine Desdemona.
MONTANO: What is she?
CASSIO: She that I spake of, our great captain's captain,
75   Left in the conduct of the bold Iago,
    Whose footing° here anticipates our thoughts
    A se'nnight's° speed. Great Jove, Othello guard,
    And swell his sail with thine own pow'rful breath,
    That he may bless this bay with his tall ship,
80   Make love's quick pants in Desdemona's arms,
    Give renewed fire to our extinct spirits,
    [And bring all Cyprus comfort!]

Enter Desdemona, Iago, Roderigo, and Emilia [with Attendants].

                    O, behold!

The riches of the ship is come on shore!
    You men of Cyprus, let her have your knees.°
    Hail to thee, lady! and the grace of heaven,   85
    Before, behind thee, and on every hand,
    Enwheel thee round!
DESDEMONA: I thank you, valiant Cassio.
    What tidings can you tell me of my lord?
CASSIO: He is not yet arrived; nor know I aught
    But that he's well and will be shortly here.   90
DESDEMONA: O but I fear! How lost you company?
CASSIO: The great contention of the sea and skies
    Parted our fellowship.
        (*Within.*)   A sail, a sail! [*A shot.*]
                    But hark. A sail!
2. GENTLEMAN: They give their greeting to the citadel;
    This likewise is a friend.
CASSIO: See for the news.   95

        [*Exit Gentleman.*]

Good ancient, you are welcome.
    [*To Emilia.*]   Welcome, mistress.—
Let it not gall your patience, good Iago,
That I extend my manners. 'Tis my breeding
That gives me this bold show of courtesy.

[*Kisses Emilia.°*]

IAGO: Sir, would she give you so much of her lips   100
    As of her tongue she oft bestows on me,
    You would have enough.
DESDEMONA: Alas, she has no speech!
IAGO: In faith, too much.
    I find it still when I have list to sleep.
    Marry, before your ladyship, I grant,   105
    She puts her tongue a little in her heart
    And chides with thinking.
EMILIA: You have little cause to say so.
IAGO: Come on, come on! You are pictures out of
        doors,
    Bells in your parlors, wildcats in your kitchens,   110
    Saints in your injuries, devils being offended,
    Players in your housewifery,° and housewives° in
        your beds.
DESDEMONA: O, fie upon thee, slanderer!
IAGO: Nay, it is true, or else I am a Turk:
    You rise to play, and go to bed to work.   115
EMILIA: You shall not write my praise.
IAGO: No, let me out.
DESDEMONA: What wouldst thou write of me, if thou
        shouldst praise me?
IAGO: O gentle lady, do not put me to't,
    For I am nothing if not critical.
DESDEMONA: Come on, assay.°—There's one gone to
        the harbor?   120

---

50. surfeited to death: Overindulged. **51. in bold cure:** A good chance of fulfillment. **62. paragons:** Surpasses. **63. quirks:** Ingenuities. **blazoning:** Describing. **64–65. And . . . ingener:** Merely to describe her as God made her exhausts her praiser. **69. guttered:** Jagged. **70. ensteeped:** Submerged. **72. mortal:** Deadly. **76. footing:** Landing. **77. se'nnight's:** Week's.

84. knees: I.e., kneeling. **[s.d.]** *Kisses Emilia:* (Kissing was a common Elizabethan form of social courtesy). **112. housewifery:** Housekeeping. **housewives:** Hussies. **120. assay:** Try.

IAGO: Ay, madam.

DESDEMONA: I am not merry; but I do beguile
The thing I am by seeming otherwise.—
Come, how wouldst thou praise me?

125 IAGO: I am about it; but indeed my invention
Comes from my pate as birdlime° does from
frieze°—
It plucks out brains and all. But my Muse labors,
And thus she is delivered:
If she be fair and wise, fairness and wit—
130 The one's for use, the other useth it.

DESDEMONA: Well praised! How if she be black° and
witty?

IAGO: If she be black, and thereto have a wit,
She'll find a white that shall her blackness fit.

DESDEMONA: Worse and worse!

135 EMILIA: How if fair and foolish?

IAGO: She never yet was foolish that was fair,
For even her folly° helped her to an heir.

DESDEMONA: These are old fond° paradoxes to make
fools laugh i' th' alehouse. What miserable praise
140 hast thou for her that's foul° and foolish?

IAGO: There's none so foul, and foolish thereunto,
But does foul pranks which fair and wise ones do.

DESDEMONA: O heavy ignorance! Thou praisest the
worst best. But what praise couldst thou bestow on a
145 deserving woman indeed—one that in the authority
of her merit did justly put on the vouch° of very malice itself?

IAGO: She that was ever fair, and never proud;
Had tongue at will, and yet was never loud;
150 Never lacked gold, and yet went never gay;
Fled from her wish, and yet said "Now I may";
She that, being ang'red, her revenge being nigh,
Bade her wrong stay, and her displeasure fly;
She that in wisdom never was so frail
155 To change the cod's head for the salmon's tail;°
She that could think, and ne'er disclose her mind;
See suitors following, and not look behind:
She was a wight (if ever such wight were)—

DESDEMONA: To do what?

160 IAGO: To suckle fools and chronicle small beer.°

DESDEMONA: O most lame and impotent conclusion!
Do not learn of him, Emilia, though he be thy husband. How say you, Cassio? Is he not a most profane
and liberal° counsellor?

165 CASSIO: He speaks home,° madam. You may relish him
more in the soldier than in the scholar.

IAGO [aside]: He takes her by the palm. Ay, well said,
whisper! With as little a web as this will I ensnare as
great a fly as Cassio. Ay, smile upon her, do! I will
gyve thee in thine own courtship.°—You say true; 170
'tis so, indeed!—If such tricks as these strip you out
of your lieutenantry, it had been better you had not
kissed your three fingers so oft—which now again
you are most apt to play the sir° in. Very good! well
kissed! an excellent courtesy! 'Tis so, indeed. Yet 175
again your fingers to your lips? Would they were
clyster pipes° for your sake! (Trumpet within.) The
Moor! I know his trumpet.

CASSIO: 'Tis truly so.

DESDEMONA: Let's meet him and receive him. 180

CASSIO: Lo, where he comes.

Enter Othello and Attendants.

OTHELLO: O my fair warrior!

DESDEMONA: My dear Othello!

OTHELLO: It gives me wonder great as my content
To see you here before me. O my soul's joy!
If after every tempest come such calms, 185
May the winds blow till they have wakened death!
And let the laboring bark climb hills of seas
Olympus-high, and duck again as low
As hell's from heaven! If it were now to die,
'Twere now to be most happy;° for I fear 190
My soul hath her content so absolute
That not another comfort like to this
Succeeds in unknown fate.

DESDEMONA: The heavens forbid
But that our loves and comforts should increase
Even as our days do grow.

OTHELLO: Amen to that, sweet powers! 195
I cannot speak enough of this content;
It stops me here; it is too much of joy.
And this, and this, the greatest discords be

They kiss.

That e'er our hearts shall make!

IAGO [aside]:   O, you are well
tuned now!
But I'll set down° the pegs that make this music, 200
As honest as I am.

OTHELLO: Come, let us to the castle.
News, friends! Our wars are done; the Turks are
drowned.
How does my old acquaintance of this isle?—
Honey, you shall be well desired° in Cyprus;
I have found great love amongst them. O my
sweet, 205
I prattle out of fashion, and I dote
In mine own comforts. I prithee, good Iago,
Go to the bay and disembark my coffers.
Bring thou the master° to the citadel;

---

126. **birdlime:** A sticky paste. **frieze:** Rough cloth.
131. **black:** Brunette. 137. **folly:** Wantonness. 138. **fond:**
Foolish. 140. **foul:** Ugly. 146. **put on the vouch:** Compel
the approval. 155. **To . . . tail:** I.e., to exchange the good for
the poor but expensive. 160. **chronicle small beer:** Keep petty
household accounts. 164. **profane and liberal:** Worldly and
licentious. 165. **home:** Bluntly.

170. **gyve . . . courtship:** Manacle you by means of your
courtly manners. 174. **sir:** Courtly gentleman. 177. **clyster
pipes:** Syringes. 190. **happy:** Fortunate. 200. **set down:**
Loosen. 204. **well desired:** Warmly welcomed. 209. **master:**
Ship captain.

Sir Laurence Olivier as Othello and
Maggie Smith as Desdemona in a tense
moment in his National Theatre
production of *Othello* in London, 1964.
(Angus McBean Photograph, copyright ©
Harvard Theatre Collection.)

John Douglas Thomas as Othello and
Jennifer Mudge Tucker as Desdemona in
the Trinity Repertory production of
Othello, Providence, Rhode Island, 1998.

He is a good one, and his worthiness
Does challenge° much respect.—Come, Desdemona,
Once more well met at Cyprus.

Exit Othello [with all but Iago and Roderigo].

IAGO: [*to an Attendant, who goes out*]: Do thou meet me presently at the harbor. [*To Roderigo.*] Come hither. If thou be'st valiant (as they say base men being in love have then a nobility in their natures more than is native to them), list me. The lieutenant to-night watches on the court of guard.° First, I must tell thee this: Desdemona is directly in love with him.

RODERIGO: With him? Why, 'tis not possible.

IAGO: Lay thy finger thus,° and let thy soul be instructed. Mark me with what violence she first loved the Moor, but for bragging and telling her fantastical lies; and will she love him still for prating? Let not thy discreet heart think it. Her eye must be fed; and what delight shall she have to look on the devil? When the blood is made dull with the act of sport, there should be, again to inflame it, and to give satiety a fresh appetite, loveliness in favor, sympathy in years, manners, and beauties; all which the Moor is defective in. Now for want of these required conveniences,° her delicate tenderness will find itself abused, begin to heave the gorge,° disrelish and abhor the Moor. Very nature will instruct her in it and compel her to some second choice. Now, sir, this granted—as it is a most pregnant° and unforced position—who stands so eminent in the degree of this fortune as Cassio does? A knave very voluble; no further conscionable° than in putting on the mere form of civil and humane° seeming for the better compassing of his salt° and most hidden loose affection? Why, none! why, none! A slipper° and subtle knave; a finder-out of occasions; that has an eye can stamp and counterfeit advantages, though true advantage never present itself; a devilish knave! Besides, the knave is handsome, young, and hath all those requisites in him that folly and green minds look after. A pestilent complete knave! and the woman hath found him already.

RODERIGO: I cannot believe that in her; she's full of most blessed condition.°

IAGO: Blessed fig's-end! The wine she drinks is made of grapes. If she had been blessed, she would never have loved the Moor. Blessed pudding! Didst thou not see her paddle with the palm of his hand? Didst not mark that?

RODERIGO: Yes, that I did; but that was but courtesy.

IAGO: Lechery, by this hand! an index and obscure prologue to the history of lust and foul thoughts. They met so near with their lips that their breaths embraced together. Villainous thoughts, Roderigo! When these mutualities° so marshal the way, hard at hand comes the master and main exercise, th' incorporate° conclusion. Pish! But, sir, be you ruled by me: I have brought you from Venice. Watch you to-night; for the command, I'll lay't upon you. Cassio knows you not. I'll not be far from you: do you find some occasion to anger Cassio, either by speaking too loud, or tainting° his discipline, or from what other course you please which the time shall more favorably minister.

RODERIGO: Well.

IAGO: Sir, he's rash and very sudden in choler,° and haply with his truncheon may strike at you. Provoke him that he may; for even out of that will I cause these of Cyprus to mutiny; whose qualification° shall come into no true taste° again but by the displanting of Cassio. So shall you have a shorter journey to your desires by the means I shall then have to prefer° them; and the impediment most profitably removed without the which there were no expectation of our prosperity.

RODERIGO: I will do this if you can bring it to any opportunity.

IAGO: I warrant thee. Meet me by and by at the citadel; I must fetch his necessaries ashore. Farewell.

RODERIGO: Adieu.   *Exit.*

IAGO: That Cassio loves her, I do well believe't;
That she loves him, 'tis apt° and of great credit.
The Moor, howbeit that I endure him not,
Is of a constant, loving, noble nature,
And I dare think he'll prove to Desdemona
A most dear husband. Now I do love her too;
Not out of absolute lust, though peradventure
I stand accountant° for as great a sin,
But partly led to diet° my revenge,
For that I do suspect the lusty Moor
Hath leaped into my seat; the thought whereof
Doth, like a poisonous mineral, gnaw my inwards;
And nothing can or shall content my soul
Till I am evened with him, wife for wife;
Or failing so, yet that I put the Moor
At least into a jealousy so strong
That judgment cannot cure. Which thing to do,
If this poor trash of Venice, whom I trash°
For° his quick hunting, stand the putting on,°
I'll have our Michael Cassio on the hip,°

211. challenge: Deserve.   **218. court of guard:** Headquarters.   **221. thus:** I.e., on your lips.   **231–32. conveniences:** Compatibilities.   **233. heave the gorge:** Be nauseated.   **236. pregnant:** Evident.   **239. conscionable:** Conscientious.   **240. humane:** Polite.   **241. salt:** Lecherous.   **242. slipper:** Slippery.   **251. condition:** Character.

262. mutualities: Exchanges.   **263–64. incorporate:** Carnal.   **269. tainting:** Discrediting.   **273. sudden in choler:** Violent in anger.   **276. qualification:** Appeasement.   **277. true taste:** Satisfactory state.   **279. prefer:** Advance.   **289. apt:** Probable.   **295. accountant:** Accountable.   **296. diet:** Feed.   **305. I trash:** I weight down (in order to keep under control).   **306. For:** In order to develop.   **stand the putting on:** Responds to my inciting.   **307. on the hip:** At my mercy.

Abuse him to the Moor in the rank garb°
(For I fear Cassio with my nightcap too),
310 Make the Moor thank me, love me, and reward me
For making him egregiously an ass
And practicing upon° his peace and quiet
Even to madness. 'Tis here, but yet confused:
Knavery's plain face is never seen till used.   *Exit.*

Scene II

A street in Cyprus.

Enter Othello's Herald, with a proclamation.

HERALD: It is Othello's pleasure, our noble and valiant
general, that, upon certain tidings now arrived,
importing the mere perdition° of the Turkish fleet,
every man put himself into triumph; some to dance,
5 some to make bonfires, each man to what sport and
revels his addiction leads him. For, besides these beneficial news, it is the celebration of his nuptial. So
much was his pleasure should be proclaimed. All
offices° are open, and there is full liberty of feasting
10 from the present hour of five till the bell have told
eleven. Heaven bless the isle of Cyprus and our noble
general Othello!   *Exit.*

Scene III

The Cyprian Castle.

Enter Othello, Desdemona, Cassio, and Attendants.

OTHELLO: Good Michael, look you to the guard to-
     night.
     Let's teach ourselves that honorable stop,
     Not to outsport discretion.
CASSIO: Iago hath direction what to do;
5   But not withstanding, with my personal eye
     Will I look to't.
OTHELLO: Iago is most honest.
     Michael, good night. To-morrow with your earliest
     Let me have speech with you.
     [*To Desdemona.*]   Come, my dear love.
     The purchase made, the fruits are to ensue;
10   That profit's yet to come 'tween me and you.—
     Good night.

          Exit [Othello with Desdemona and Attendants].

Enter Iago.

CASSIO: Welcome, Iago. We must to the watch.
IAGO: Not this hour, lieutenant; 'tis not yet ten o' th'
     clock. Our general cast° us thus early for the love of

his Desdemona; who let us not therefore blame. He   15
hath not yet made wanton the night with her, and she
is sport for Jove.
CASSIO: She's a most exquisite lady.
IAGO: And, I'll warrant her, full of game.
CASSIO: Indeed, she's a most fresh and delicate creature.   20
IAGO: What an eye she has! Methinks it sounds a parley
     to provocation.
CASSIO: An inviting eye; and yet methinks right modest.
IAGO: And when she speaks, is it not an alarum to love?
CASSIO: She is indeed perfection.   25
IAGO: Well, happiness to their sheets! Come, lieutenant,
     I have a stoup° of wine, and here without are a brace
     of Cyprus gallants that would fain have a measure to
     the health of black Othello.
CASSIO: Not to-night, good Iago. I have very poor and   30
     unhappy brains for drinking; I could well wish cour-
     tesy would invent some other custom of entertain-
     ment.
IAGO: O, they are our friends. But one cup! I'll drink for
     you.   35
CASSIO: I have drunk but one cup to-night, and that was
     craftily qualified° too; and behold what innovation°
     it makes here. I am unfortunate in the infirmity and
     dare not task my weakness with any more.
IAGO: What, man! 'Tis a night of revels: the gallants de-   40
     sire it.
CASSIO: Where are they?
IAGO: Here at the door; I pray you call them in.
CASSIO: I'll do't, but it dislikes me.   *Exit.*
IAGO: If I can fasten but one cup upon him   45
     With that which he hath drunk to-night already,
     He'll be as full of quarrel and offense
     As my young mistress' dog. Now my sick fool
          Roderigo,
     Whom love hath turned almost the wrong side out,
     To Desdemona hath to-night caroused   50
     Potations pottle-deep;° and he's to watch.
     Three lads of Cyprus—noble swelling spirits,
     That hold their honors in a wary distance,°
     The very elements° of this warlike isle—
     Have I to-night flustered with flowing cups,   55
     And they watch too. Now, 'mongst this flock of
          drunkards
     Am I to put our Cassio in some action
     That may offend the isle.

*Enter Cassio, Montano, and Gentlemen [; Servants fol-
lowing with wine].*

                              But here they come.
     If consequence do but approve my dream,
     My boat sails freely, both with wind and stream.   60
CASSIO: 'Fore God, they have given me a rouse° already.

---

308. **rank garb:** Gross manner.   312. **practicing upon:** Plotting against.   **II, II. 3. mere perdition:** Complete destruction.
9. **offices:** Kitchens and storerooms.   **II, III. 14. cast:** Dismissed.

27. **stoup:** Two-quart tankard.   37. **qualified:** Diluted.   **innovation:** Disturbance.   51. **pottle-deep:** Bottoms up.   53. **That . . .
distance:** Very sensitive about their honor.   54. **very elements:**
True representatives.   61. **rouse:** Bumper.

MONTANO: Good faith, a little one; not past a pint, as I
  am a soldier.
IAGO: Some wine, ho!
  [*Sings.*]
65   And let me the canakin clink, clink;
    And let me the canakin clink
       A soldier's a man;
       A life's but a span,
    Why then, let a soldier drink.
70   Some wine, boys!
CASSIO: 'Fore God, an excellent song!
IAGO: I learned it in England, where indeed they are most
  potent in potting. Your Dane, your German, and your
  swag-bellied Hollander—Drink, ho!—are nothing
75   to your English.
CASSIO: Is your Englishman so expert in his drinking?
IAGO: Why, he drinks you with facility your Dane dead
  drunk; he sweats not to overthrow your Almain; he
  gives your Hollander a vomit ere the next pottle can
80   be filled.
CASSIO: To the health of our general!
MONTANO: I am for it, lieutenant, and I'll do you
  justice.
IAGO: O sweet England!
  [*Sings.*]
85   King Stephen was a worthy peer;
       His breeches cost him but a crown;
    He held 'em sixpence all too dear,
       With that he called the tailor lown.°
    He was a wight of high renown,
90   And thou art but of low degree.
    'Tis pride that pulls the country down;
       Then take thine auld cloak about thee.
    Some wine, ho!
CASSIO: 'Fore God, this is a more exquisite song than
95   the other.
IAGO: Will you hear't again?
CASSIO: No, for I hold him to be unworthy of his place
  that does those things.° Well, God's above all; and
  there be souls must be saved, and there be souls must
100   not be saved.
IAGO: It's true, good lieutenant.
CASSIO: For mine own part—no offense to the general,
  nor any man of quality—I hope to be saved.
IAGO: And so do I too, lieutenant.
105 CASSIO: Ay but, by your leave, not before me. The lieutenant is to be saved before the ancient. Let's have no
  more of this; let's to our affairs.—God forgive us our
  sins!—Gentlemen, let's look to our business. Do not
  think, gentlemen, I am drunk. This is my ancient; this
110   is my right hand, and this is my left. I am not drunk
  now. I can stand well enough, and I speak well
  enough.
ALL: Excellent well!
CASSIO: Why, very well then. You must not think then
115   that I am drunk.   *Exit.*

---

88. lown: Rascal.   **98. does . . . things:** I.e., behaves in this
fashion.

MONTANO: To th' platform, masters. Come, let's set
  the watch.
IAGO: You see this fellow that is gone before.
  He's a soldier fit to stand by Caesar
  And give direction; and do but see his vice.
  'Tis to his virtue a just equinox,°   120
  The one as long as th' other. 'Tis pity of him.
  I fear the trust Othello puts him in,
  On some odd time of his infirmity,
  Will shake this island.
MONTANO: But is he often thus?
IAGO: 'Tis evermore his prologue to his sleep: 125
  He'll watch the horologe a double set°
  If drink rock not his cradle.
MONTANO: It were well
  The general were put in mind of it.
  Perhaps he sees it not, or his good nature
  Prizes the virtue that appears in Cassio   130
  And looks not on his evils. Is not this true?

Enter Roderigo.

IAGO [*aside to him*]: How now, Roderigo?
  I pray you after the lieutenant, go!   *Exit Roderigo.*
MONTANO: And 'tis great pity that the noble Moor
  Should hazard such a place as his own second   135
  With one of an ingraft° infirmity.
  It were an honest action to say
  So to the Moor.
IAGO: Not I, for this fair island!
  I do love Cassio well and would do much
  To cure him of this evil.
    (*Within:* Help! Help!)
MONTANO: But hark! What noise?   140

Enter Cassio, driving in Roderigo.

CASSIO: Zounds, you rogue! you rascal!
MONTANO: What's the matter, lieutenant?
CASSIO: A knave to
  teach me my duty?
  I'll beat the knave into a twiggen° bottle.
RODERIGO: Beat me?
CASSIO: Dost thou prate, rogue?

[*Strikes him.*]

MONTANO: Nay, good lieutenant!

[*Stays him.*]

  I pray you, sir, hold your hand.
CASSIO: Let me go, sir,   145
  Or I'll knock you o'er the mazzard.°
MONTANO: Come, come,
  you're drunk!
CASSIO: Drunk?

They fight.

---

120. just equinox: Exact equivalent.   **126. watch . . . set:** Stay
awake twice around the clock.   **136. ingraft:** I.e., ingrained.
143. twiggen: Wicker-covered.   **146. mazzard:** Head.

IAGO [*aside to Roderigo*]: Away, I say! Go out and
        cry a mutiny!   *Exit Roderigo.*
        Nay, good lieutenant. God's will, gentlemen!
        Help, ho!—lieutenant—sir—Montano—sir—
150   Help, masters!—Here's a goodly watch indeed!

A bell rung.

        Who's that which rings the bell? Diablo, ho!
        The town will rise.° God's will, lieutenant, hold!
        You'll be shamed for ever.

Enter Othello and Gentlemen with weapons.

OTHELLO: What is the matter here?
MONTANO: Zounds, I bleed still. I am hurt to th' death.
        He dies.
155 OTHELLO: Hold for your lives!
IAGO: Hold, hold! Lieutenant—sir—Montano—
        gentlemen!
        Have you forgot all sense of place and duty?
        Hold! The general speaks to you. Hold, for shame!
OTHELLO: Why, how now ho? From whence ariseth
        this?
160   Are we turned Turks, and to ourselves do that
        Which heaven hath forbid the Ottomites?
        For Christian shame put by this barbarous brawl!
        He that stirs next to carve for° his own rage
        Holds his soul light; he dies upon his motion.
165   Silence that dreadful bell! It frights the isle
        From her propriety.° What is the matter, masters?
        Honest Iago, that looks dead with grieving,
        Speak. Who began this? On thy love, I charge thee.
IAGO: I do not know. Friends all, but now, even now,
170   In quarter,° and in terms like bride and groom
        Devesting them for bed; and then, but now—
        As if some planet had unwitted men—
        Swords out, and tilting one at other's breast
        In opposition bloody. I cannot speak
175   Any beginning to this peevish odds,°
        And would in action glorious I had lost
        Those legs that brought me to a part of it!
OTHELLO: How comes it, Michael, you are thus
        forgot?
CASSIO: I pray you pardon me; I cannot speak.
OTHELLO: Worthy Montano, you were wont to be
180   civil;
        The gravity and stillness of your youth
        The world hath noted, and your name is great
        In months of wisest censure.° What's the matter
        That you unlace° your reputation thus
185   And spend your rich opinion° for the name
        Of a night-brawler? Give me answer to it.
MONTANO: Worthy Othello, I am hurt to danger.
        Your officer, Iago, can inform you,

        While I spare speech, which something now
            offends° me,
        Of all that I do know; nor know I aught   190
        By me that's said or done amiss this night,
        Unless self-charity be sometimes a vice,
        And to defend ourselves it be a sin
        When violence assails us.
OTHELLO: Now, by heaven,
        My blood° begins my safer guides to rule,   195
        And passion, having my best judgment collied,°
        Assays° to lead the way. If I once stir
        Or do but lift this arm, the best of you
        Shall sink in my rebuke. Give me to know
        How this foul rout began, who set it on;   200
        And he that is approved in° this offense,
        Though he had twinned with me, both at a birth,
        Shall lose me. What! in a town of war,
        Yet wild, the people's hearts brimful of fear,
        To manage° private and domestic quarrel?   205
        In night, and on the court and guard of safety?
        'Tis monstrous. Iago, who began't?
MONTANO: If partially affined, or leagued in office,°
        Thou dost deliver more or less than truth,
        Thou art no soldier.
IAGO: Touch me not so near.   210
        I had rather have this tongue cut from my mouth
        Than it should do offense to Michael Cassio;
        Yet I persuade myself, to speak the truth
        Shall nothing wrong him. This it is, general.
        Montano and myself being in speech,   215
        There comes a fellow crying out for help,
        And Cassio following him with determined sword
        To execute° upon him. Sir, this gentleman
        Steps in to Cassio and entreats his pause.
        Myself the crying fellow did pursue,   220
        Lest by his clamor—as it so fell out—
        The town might fall in fright. He, swift of foot,
        Outran my purpose; and I returned then rather
        For that I heard the clink and fall of swords,
        And Cassio high in oath;° which till to-night   225
        I ne'er might say before. When I came back—
        For this was brief—I found them close together
        At blow and thrust, even as again they were
        When you yourself did part them.
        More of this matter cannot I report;   230
        But men are men; the best sometimes forget.
        Though Cassio did some little wrong to him,
        As men in rage strike those that wish them best,
        Yet surely Cassio I believe received
        From him that fled some strange indignity,   235
        Which patience could not pass.°

---

189. **offends:** Pains. 195. **blood:** Passion. 196. **collied:**
Darkened. 197. **Assays:** Tries. 201. **approved in:** Proved
guilty of. 205. **manage:** Carry on. 208. **partially . . . office:**
Prejudiced by comradeship or official relations. 218. **execute:**
Work his will. 225. **high in oath:** Cursing. 236. **pass:** Pass
over, ignore.

---

152. **rise:** Grow riotous. 163. **carve for:** Indulge. 166. **propriety:** Proper self. 170. **quarter:** Friendliness. 175. **peevish
odds:** Childish quarrel. 183. **censure:** Judgment. 184. **un-
lace:** Undo. 185. **rich opinion:** High reputation.

OTHELLO: I know, Iago,
Thy honesty and love doth mince this matter,
Making it light to Cassio. Cassio, I love thee;
But never more be officer of mine.

Enter Desdemona, attended.

240 Look if my gentle love be not raised up!
I'll make thee an example.
DESDEMONA: What's the matter?
OTHELLO: All's well now, sweeting; come away to bed.

[*To Montano.*]

Sir, for your hurts, myself will be your surgeon.
Lead him off.

[*Montano is led off.*]

245 Iago, look with care about the town
And silence those whom this vile brawl distracted.°
Come, Desdemona; 'tis the soldiers' life
To have their balmy slumbers waked with strife.

Exit [with all but Iago and Cassio].

IAGO: What, are you hurt, lieutenant?
250 CASSIO: Ay, past all surgery.
IAGO: Marry, God forbid!
CASSIO: Reputation, reputation, reputation! O, I have
lost my reputation! I have lost the immortal part of
myself, and what remains is bestial. My reputation,
255 Iago, my reputation!
IAGO: As I am an honest man, I thought you had received some bodily wound. There is more sense in
that than in reputation. Reputation is an idle and
most false imposition; oft got without merit and lost
260 without deserving. You have lost no reputation at all
unless you repute yourself such a loser. What, man!
there are ways to recover° the general again. You are
but now cast in his mood°—a punishment more in
policy than in malice, even so as one would beat his
265 offenseless dog to affright an imperious lion. Sue to
him again, and he's yours.
CASSIO: I will rather sue to be despised than to deceive
so good a commander with so slight, so drunken,
and so indiscreet an officer. Drunk! and speak par-
270 rot!° and squabble! swagger! swear! and discourse
fustian° with one's own shadow! O thou invisible
spirit of wine, if thou hast no name to be known by,
let us call thee devil!
IAGO: What was he that you followed with your sword?
275 What had he done to you?
CASSIO: I know not.
IAGO: Is't possible?
CASSIO: I remember a mass of things, but nothing distinctly; a quarrel, but nothing wherefore. O God, that
280 men should put an enemy in their mouths to steal
away their brains! that we should with joy, pleas-
ance, revel, and applause° transform ourselves into
beasts!
IAGO: Why, but you are now well enough. How came
you thus recovered? 285
CASSIO: It hath pleased the devil drunkenness to give
place to the devil wrath. One unperfectness shows
me another, to make me frankly despise myself.
IAGO: Come, you are too severe a moraler. As the time,
the place, and the condition of this country stands, I 290
could heartily wish this had not so befall'n; but since
it is as it is, mend it for your own good.
CASSIO: I will ask him for my place again: he shall tell
me I am a drunkard! Had I as many mouths as
Hydra,° such an answer would stop them all. To be 295
now a sensible man, by and by a fool, and presently a
beast! O strange! Every inordinate cup is unblest,
and the ingredient° is a devil.
IAGO: Come, come, good wine is a good familiar creature if it be well used. Exclaim no more against it. 300
And, good lieutenant, I think you think I love you.
CASSIO: I have well approved° it, sir. I drunk!
IAGO: You or any man living may be drunk at some
time, man. I'll tell you what you shall do. Our general's wife is now the general. I may say so in this 305
respect, for that he hath devoted and given up himself to the contemplation, mark, and denotement of
her parts and graces. Confess yourself freely to her;
importune her help to put you in your place again.
She is of so free,° so kind, so apt, so blessed a disposi- 310
tion she holds it a vice in her goodness not to do
more than she is requested. This broken joint between you and her husband entreat her to splinter;°
and my fortunes against any lay° worth naming, this
crack of your love shall grow stronger than it was 315
before.
CASSIO: You advise me well.
IAGO: I protest, in the sincerity of love and honest kind-
ness.
CASSIO: I think it freely; and betimes in the morning will 320
I beseech the virtuous Desdemona to undertake for
me. I am desperate of my fortunes if they check me
here.
IAGO: You are in the right. Good night, lieutenant; I must
to the watch. 325
CASSIO: Good night, honest Iago. *Exit Cassio.*
IAGO: And what's he then that says I play the villain,
When this advice is free I give and honest,
Probal° to thinking, and indeed the course
To win the Moor again? For 'tis most easy 330
Th' inclining Desdemona to subdue°
In an honest suit; she's framed as fruitful

---

246. **distracted:** Excited.   262. **recover:** Regain favor with.
263. **in his mood:** Dismissed because of his anger.   269–70. **par-
rot:** Meaningless phrases.   271. **fustian:** Bombastic nonsense.   282. **applause:** Desire to please.   295. **Hydra:** Monster with
many heads.   298. **ingredient:** Contents.   302. **approved:**
Proved.   310. **free:** Bounteous.   313. **splinter:** Bind up with
splints.   314. **lay:** Wager.   329. **Probal:** Probable.   331. **subdue:** Persuade.

As the free elements. And then for her
To win the Moor—were't to renounce his baptism,
335 All seals and symbols of redeemèd sin—
His soul is so enfettered to her love
That she may make, unmake, do what she list,
Even as her appetite shall play the god
With his weak function. How am I then a villain
340 To counsel Cassio to this parallel° course,
Directly to his good? Divinity° of hell!
When devils will the blackest sins put on,°
They do suggest at first with heavenly shows,
As I do now. For whiles this honest fool
345 Plies Desdemona to repair his fortunes,
And she for him pleads strongly to the Moor,
I'll pour this pestilence into his ear,
That she repeals him° for her body's lust;
And by how much she strives to do him good,
350 She shall undo her credit with the Moor.
So will I turn her virtue into pitch,
And out of her own goodness make the net
That shall enmesh them all.

Enter Roderigo.

                              How, now, Roderigo?
RODERIGO: I do follow here in the chase, not like a
355 hound that hunts, but one that fills up the cry.° My
money is almost spent; I have been to-night exceedingly well cudgelled; and I think the issue will be—I
shall have so much experience for my pains; and so,
with no money at all, and a little more wit, return
360 again to Venice.
IAGO: How poor are they that have not patience!
What wound did ever heal but by degrees?
Thou know'st we work by wit, and not by
    witchcraft;
And wit depends on dilatory time.
365 Does't not go well? Cassio hath beaten thee,
And thou by that small hurt hast cashiered Cassio.°
Though other things grow fair against the sun,
Yet fruits that blossom first will first be ripe.
Content thyself awhile. By the mass, 'tis morning!
370 Pleasure and action make the hours seem short.
Retire thee; go where thou art billeted.
Away, I say! Thou shalt know more hereafter.
Nay, get thee gone!   *Exit Roderigo.*
          Two things are to be done:
My wife must move for Cassio to her mistress;
375 I'll set her on;
Myself the while to draw the Moor apart
And bring him jump° when he may Cassio find
Soliciting his wife. Ay, that's the way!
Dull not device by coldness and delay.   *Exit.*

---

340. parallel: Corresponding. **341. Divinity:** Theology.
342. put on: Incite. **348. repeals him:** Seeks his recall.
355. cry: Pack. **366. cashiered Cassio:** Maneuvered Cassio's
discharge. **377. jump:** At the exact moment.

ACT III • *Scene 1*

Before the chamber of Othello and Desdemona.

Enter Cassio, with Musicians and the Clown.

CASSIO: Masters, play here, I will content° your pains:
    Something that's brief; and bid "Good morrow,
    general."

[*They play.*]

CLOWN: Why, masters, ha' your instruments been in
    Naples,° that they speak i' th' nose thus?
MUSICIAN: How, sir, how?   5
CLOWN: Are these, I pray you, called wind instruments?
MUSICIAN: Ay, marry, are they, sir.
CLOWN: O, thereby hangs a tail.
MUSICIAN: Whereby hangs a tail, sir?
CLOWN: Marry, sir, by many a wind instrument that I   10
    know. But, masters, here's money for you; and the
    general so likes your music that he desires you, for
    love's sake, to make no more noise with it.
MUSICIAN: Well, sir, we will not.
CLOWN: If you have any music that may not be heard,   15
    to't again: but, as they say, to hear music the general
    does not greatly care.
MUSICIAN: We have none such, sir.
CLOWN: Then put up your pipes in your bag, for I'll
    away. Go, vanish into air, away!   20

                    Exit Musician [*with his fellows*].

CASSIO: Dost thou hear, my honest friend?
CLOWN: No, I hear not your honest friend. I hear you.
CASSIO: Prithee keep up thy quillets.° There's a poor
    piece of gold for thee. If the gentlewoman that at-
    tends the general's wife be stirring, tell her there's one   25
    Cassio entreats her a little favor of speech. Wilt thou
    do this?
CLOWN: She is stirring sir. If she will stir hither, I shall
    seem to notify unto her.
CASSIO: [Do, good my friend.]   *Exit Clown.*

Enter Iago.

                    In happy time,° Iago.   30
IAGO: You have not been abed then?
CASSIO: Why, no; the day had broke
    Before we parted. I have made bold, Iago,
    To send in to your wife: my suit to her
    Is that she will to virtuous Desdemona   35
    Procure me some access.
IAGO: I'll send her to you presently;
    And I'll devise a mean to draw the Moor
    Out of the way, that your converse and
        business
    May be more free.

III, I. 1. **content:** Reward.   4. **Naples:** (Notorious for its association with venereal disease).   23. **quillets:** Quips.   30. **In
happy time:** Well met.

CASSIO: I humbly thank you for't.   *Exit [Iago].*
40   I never knew
A Florentine° more kind and honest.

Enter Emilia.

EMILIA: Good morrow, good lieutenant. I am sorry
For your displeasure: but all will sure be well.
The general and his wife are talking of it,
45   And she speaks for you stoutly. The Moor replied
That he you hurt is of great fame in Cyprus
And great affinity,° and that in wholesome wisdom
He might not but refuse you; but he protests he
loves you,
And needs no other suitor but his likings
50   [To take the safest occasion° by the front°]
To bring you in again.
CASSIO: Yet I beseech you,
If you think fit, or that it may be done,
Give me advantage of some brief discourse
With Desdemona alone.
EMILIA: Pray you come in.
55   I will bestow you where you shall have time
To speak your bosom° freely.
CASSIO: I am much bound to you.

                                        Exeunt.

Scene II

The castle.

Enter Othello, Iago, and Gentlemen.

OTHELLO: These letters give, Iago, to the pilot
And by him do my duties to the Senate.
That done, I will be walking on the works;°
Repair there to me.
IAGO: Well, my good lord, I'll do't.
5   OTHELLO: This fortification, gentlemen, shall we see't?
GENTLEMEN: We'll wait upon your lordship.   *Exeunt.*

Scene III

The castle grounds.

Enter Desdemona, Cassio, and Emilia.

DESDEMONA: Be thou assured, good Cassio, I will do
All my abilities in thy behalf.
EMILIA: Good madam, do. I warrant it grieves my
husband
As if the cause were his.
DESDEMONA: O, that's an honest fellow. Do not doubt,
5   Cassio,

But I will have my lord and you again
As friendly as you were.
CASSIO: Bounteous madam,
Whatever shall become of Michael Cassio,
He's never anything but your true servant.
DESDEMONA: I know't; I thank you. You do love my
lord;   10
You have known him long; and be you well
assured
He shall in strangeness° stand no farther off
Than in a politic distance.°
CASSIO: Ay, but, lady,
That policy may either last so long,
Or feed upon such nice and waterish diet,°   15
Or breed itself so out of circumstance,
That, I being absent, and my place supplied,
My general will forget my love and service.
DESDEMONA: Do not doubt° that; before Emilia here
I give thee warrant of thy place. Assure thee,   20
If I do vow a friendship, I'll perform it
To the last article. My lord shall never rest;
I'll watch him tame° and talk him out of patience;
His bed shall seem a school, his board a shrift;°
I'll intermingle everything he does   25
With Cassio's suit. Therefore be merry, Cassio,
For thy solicitor shall rather die
Than give thy cause away.

Enter Othello and Iago [at a distance].

EMILIA: Madam, here comes my lord.
CASSIO: Madam, I'll take my leave.   30
DESDEMONA: Why, stay, and hear me speak.
CASSIO: Madam, not now: I am very ill at ease,
Unfit for mine own purposes.
DESDEMONA: Well, do your discretion.   *Exit Cassio.*
IAGO: Ha! I like not that.
OTHELLO: What dost thou say?   35
IAGO: Nothing, my lord; or if—I know not what.
OTHELLO: Was not that Cassio parted from my wife?
IAGO: Cassio, my lord? No, sure, I cannot think it,
That he would steal away so guilty-like,
Seeing your coming.
OTHELLO: I do believe 'twas he.   40
DESDEMONA: How now, my lord?
I have been talking with a suitor here,
A man that languishes in your displeasure.
OTHELLO: What is't you mean?
DESDEMONA: Why, your lieutenant, Cassio. Good my
lord,   45
If I have any grace or power to move you,
His present° reconciliation take;
For if he be not one that truly loves you,
That errs in ignorance, and not in cunning,

---

41. Florentine: I.e., even a Florentine (like Cassio; Iago was
a Venetian).   **47. affinity:** Family connections.   **50. occasion:**
Opportunity. **front:** Forelock.   **56. your bosom:** Your
inmost thoughts.   **III, II. 3. works:** Fortifications.

III, III. 12. strangeness: Aloofness.   **13. Than . . . distance:**
Than wise policy requires.   **15. Or . . . diet:** Or be continued for
such slight reasons.   **19. doubt:** Fear.   **23. watch him tame:**
Keep him awake until he gives in.   **24. shrift:** Confessional.
47. present: Immediate.

50   I have no judgment in an honest face,
         I prithee call him back.
      OTHELLO: Went he hence now?
      DESDEMONA: Yes, faith; so humbled
         That he hath left part of his grief with me
         To suffer with him. Good love, call him back.
      OTHELLO: Not now, sweet Desdemon; some other
55   time.
      DESDEMONA: But shall't be shortly?
      OTHELLO: The sooner, sweet, for you.
      DESDEMONA: Shall't be to-night at supper?
      OTHELLO: No, not to-night.
      DESDEMONA: To-morrow dinner then?
      OTHELLO: I shall not dine at home;
         I meet the captains at the citadel.
      DESDEMONA: Why then, to-morrow night, or Tuesday
60   morn,
         On Tuesday noon or night, or Wednesday morn.
         I prithee name the time, but let it not
         Exceed three days. I' faith, he's penitent;
         And yet his trespass, in our common reason
65   (Save that, they say, the wars must make examples
         Out of their best), is not almost° a fault
         T' incur a private check.° When shall he come?
         Tell me, Othello. I wonder in my soul
         What you could ask me that I should deny
         Or stand so mamm'ring on.° What? Michael
70   Cassio,
         That came a-wooing with you, and so many a
         time,
         When I have spoke of you dispraisingly,
         Hath ta'en your part—to have so much to do
         To bring him in? By'r Lady, I could do much—
      OTHELLO: Prithee no more. Let him come when he
75   will!
         I will deny thee nothing.
      DESDEMONA: Why, this is not a boon;
         'Tis as I should entreat you wear your gloves,
         Or feed on nourishing dishes, or keep you warm,
         Or sue to you to do a peculiar profit
80   To your own person. Nay, when I have a suit
         Wherein I mean to touch your love indeed,
         It shall be full of poise and difficult weight,
         And fearful° to be granted.
      OTHELLO: I will deny thee nothing!
         Whereon I do beseech thee grant me this,
85   To leave me but a little to myself.
      DESDEMONA: Shall I deny you? No. Farewell, my lord.
      OTHELLO: Farewell, my Desdemon: I'll come to thee
         straight.
      DESDEMONA: Emilia, come.—Be as your fancies teach
         you;
         Whate'er you be, I am obedient.   *Exit [with Emilia].*
90   OTHELLO: Excellent wretch!° Perdition catch my soul

But I do love thee! and when I love thee not,
   Chaos is come again.
IAGO: My noble lord—
OTHELLO: What dost thou say, Iago?
IAGO: Did Michael Cassio, when you wooed my lady,
   Know of your love?   95
OTHELLO: He did, from first to last. Why dost thou
   ask?
IAGO: But for a satisfaction of my thought;
   No further harm.
OTHELLO: Why of thy thought, Iago?
IAGO: I did not think he had been acquainted with her.
OTHELLO: O, yes, and went between us° very oft.   100
IAGO: Indeed?
OTHELLO: Indeed? Ay, indeed! Discern'st thou aught in
   that?
   Is he not honest?
IAGO: Honest, my lord?
OTHELLO: Honest. Ay, honest.
IAGO: My lord, for aught I know.
OTHELLO: What dost thou think?
IAGO: Think, my lord?
OTHELLO: Think, my lord?   105
   By heaven, he echoes me,
   As if there were some monster in his thought
   Too hideous to be shown. Thou dost mean
   something:
   I heard thee say even now, thou lik'st not that,
   When Cassio left my wife. What didst not like?   110
   And when I told thee he was of my counsel
   In my whole course of wooing, thou cried'st
   "Indeed?"
   And didst contract and purse thy brow together,
   As if thou then hadst shut up in thy brain
   Some horrible conceit.° If thou dost love me,   115
   Show me thy thought.
IAGO: My lord, you know I love you.
OTHELLO: I think thou dost;
   And, for I know thou'rt full of love and honesty
   And weigh'st thy words before thou giv'st them
   breath,
   Therefore these stops of thine fright me the more;   120
   For such things in a false disloyal knave
   Are tricks of custom; but in a man that's just
   They are close dilations, working from the heart
   That passion cannot rule.°
IAGO: For Michael Cassio,
   I dare be sworn I think that he is honest.   125
OTHELLO: I think so too.
IAGO: Men should be what they seem;
   Or those that be not, would they might seem
   none!°
OTHELLO: Certain, men should be what they seem.
IAGO: Why then, I think Cassio's an honest man.

---

66. **not almost:** Hardly.   67. **a private check:** Even a private reprimand.   70. **mamm'ring on:** Hesitating about.   83. **fearful:** Dangerous.   90. **wretch:** (A term of endearment).

100. **went . . . us:** (I.e., as messenger).   115. **conceit:** Fancy. 123–24. **close dilations . . . rule:** Secret emotions which well up in spite of restraint.   127. **seem none:** I.e., not pretend to be men when they are really monsters.

130 OTHELLO: Nay, yet there's more in this.
    I prithee speak to me as to thy thinkings,
    As thou dost ruminate, and give thy worst of
       thoughts
    The worst of words.
    IAGO: Good my lord, pardon me:
    Though I am bound to every act of duty,
135 I am not bound to that all slaves are free to.°
    Utter my thoughts? Why, say they are vile and false,
    As where's that palace whereinto foul things
    Sometimes intrude not? Who has a breast so pure
    But some uncleanly apprehensions
140 Keep leets and law days,° and in Sessions sit
    With meditations lawful?
    OTHELLO: Thou dost conspire against thy friend, Iago,
    If thou but think'st him wronged, and mak'st his ear
    A stranger to thy thoughts.
    IAGO: I do beseech you—
145 Though I perchance am vicious in my guess
    (As I confess it is my nature's plague
    To spy into abuses, and oft my jealousy°
    Shapes faults that are not), that your wisdom yet
    From one that so imperfectly conjects°
150 Would take no notice, nor build yourself a trouble
    Out of his scattering and unsure observance.
    It were not for your quiet nor your good,
    Nor for my manhood, honesty, and wisdom,
    To let you know my thoughts.
    OTHELLO: What dost thou mean?
155 IAGO: Good name in man and woman, dear my lord,
    Is the immediate° jewel of their souls.
    Who steals my purse steals trash; 'tis something,
       nothing;
    'Twas mine, 'tis his, and has been slave to
       thousands;
    But he that filches from me my good name
160 Robs me of that which not enriches him
    And makes me poor indeed.
    OTHELLO: By heaven, I'll know thy thoughts!
    IAGO: You cannot, if my heart were in your hand;
    Nor shall not whilst 'tis in my custody.
    OTHELLO: Ha!
165 IAGO: O, beware, my lord, of jealousy!
    It is the green-eyed monster, which doth mock°
    The meat it feeds on. That cuckold lives in bliss
    Who, certain of his fate, loves not his wronger;
    But O, what damnèd minutes tells he o'er
170 Who dotes, yet doubts—suspects, yet strongly loves!
    OTHELLO: O misery!
    IAGO: Poor and content is rich, and rich enough;
    But riches fineless° is as poor as winter
    To him that ever fears he shall be poor.

    Good God, the souls of all my tribe defend   175
From jealousy!
OTHELLO: Why, why is this?
    Think'st thou I'ld make a life of jealousy,
    To follow still the changes of the moon
    With fresh suspicions? No! To be once in doubt
    Is once to be resolved. Exchange me for a goat   180
    When I shall turn the business of my soul
    To such exsufflicate and blown° surmises,
    Matching this inference. 'Tis not to make me jealous
    To say my wife is fair, feeds well, loves company,
    Is free of speech, sings, plays, and dances;   185
    Where virtue is, these are more virtuous.
    Nor from mine own weak merits will I draw
    The smallest fear or doubt of her revolt,°
    For she had eyes, and chose me. No, Iago;
    I'll see before I doubt; when I doubt, prove;   190
    And on the proof there is no more but this—
    Away at once with love or jealousy!
IAGO: I am glad of this; for now I shall have reason
    To show the love and duty that I bear you
    With franker spirit. Therefore, as I am bound,   195
    Receive it from me. I speak not yet of proof.
    Look at your wife; observe her well with Cassio;
    Wear your eyes thus, not jealous nor secure:°
    I would not have your free and noble nature,
    Out of self-bounty,° be abused. Look to't.   200
    I know our country disposition well:
    In Venice they do let God see the pranks
    They dare not show their husbands; their best
       conscience
    Is not to leave't undone, but keep't unknown.
OTHELLO: Dost thou say so?   205
IAGO: She did deceive her father, marrying you;
    And when she seemed to shake and fear your looks,
    She loved them most.
OTHELLO: And so she did.
IAGO: Why, go to then!
    She that, so young, could give out such a seeming
    To seel° her father's eyes up close as oak°—   210
    He thought 'twas witchcraft—but I am much to
       blame.
    I humbly do beseech you of your pardon
    For too much loving you.
OTHELLO: I am bound to thee for ever.
IAGO: I see this hath a little dashed your spirits.
OTHELLO: Not a jot, not a jot.
IAGO: I' faith, I fear it has.   215
    I hope you will consider what is spoke
    Comes from my love. But I do see y' are moved.
    I am to pray you not to strain my speech
    To grosser issues° nor to larger reach
    Than to suspicion.   220

---

135. bound . . . free to: Bound to tell that which even slaves are allowed to keep to themselves. **140. leets and law days:** Sittings of the courts. **147. jealousy:** Suspicion. **149. conjects:** Conjectures. **156. immediate:** Nearest the heart. **166. mock:** Play with, like a cat with mouse. **173. fineless:** Unlimited.

182. exsufflicate and blown: Spat out and flyblown. **188. revolt:** Unfaithfulness. **198. secure:** Overconfident. **200. self-bounty:** Natural goodness. **210. seel:** Close. **oak:** Oak grain. **219. To grosser issues:** To mean something more monstrous.

Laurence Fishburne, Othello,
and Kenneth Branagh, Iago,
in Oliver Parker's 1995 film
version of Othello.

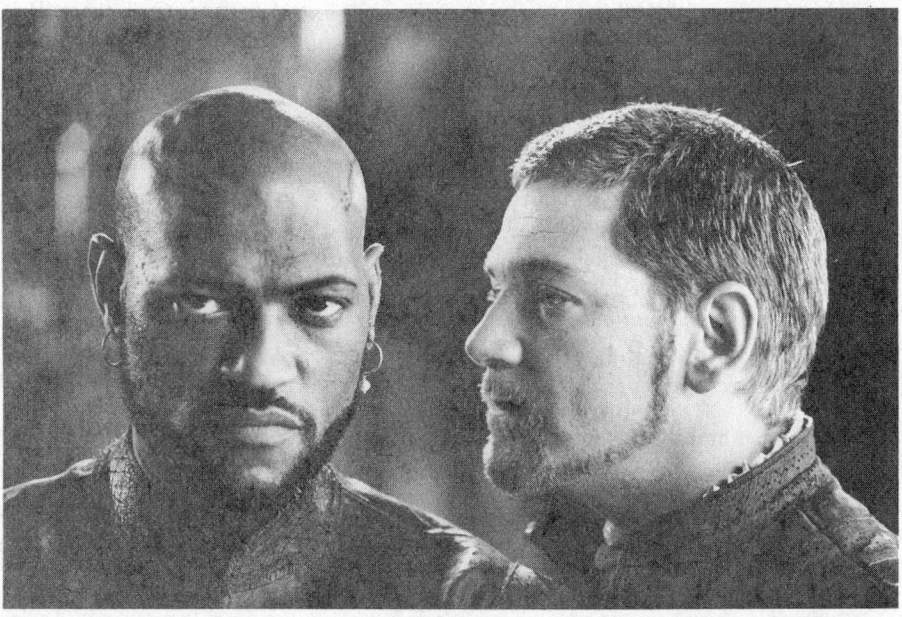

OTHELLO: I will not.
IAGO: Should you do so, my lord,
    My speech should fall into such vile success°
    As my thoughts aim not at. Cassio's my worthy
        friend—
    My lord, I see y' are moved.
OTHELLO: No, not much moved:
225 I do not think but Desdemona's honest.°
IAGO: Long live she so! and long live you to think so!
OTHELLO: And yet, how nature erring from itself—
IAGO: Ay, there's the point! as (to be bold with you)
    Not to affect many proposèd matches
230 Of her own clime, complexion, and degree,
    Whereto we see in all things nature tends—
    Foh! one may smell in such a will most rank,
    Foul disproportions, thought unnatural—
    But pardon me—I do not in position°
235 Distinctly speak of her; though I may fear
    Her will, recoiling° to her better judgment,
    May fall to match° you with her country forms,
    And happily° repent.
OTHELLO: Farewell, farewell!
    If more thou dost perceive, let me know more.
240 Set on thy wife to observe. Leave me, Iago.
IAGO: My lord, I take my leave.   [Going.]
OTHELLO: Why did I marry? This honest creature
        doubtless
    Sees and knows more, much more, than he unfolds.

IAGO [returns]: My lord, I would I might entreat your
        honor
    To scan this thing no further: leave it to time.   245
    Although 'tis fit that Cassio have his place,
    For sure he fills it up with great ability,
    Yet, if you please to hold off a while,
    You shall by that perceive him and his means.
    Note if your lady strain his entertainment°   250
    With any strong or vehement importunity;
    Much will be seen in that. In the mean time
    Let me be thought too busy° in my fears
    (As worthy cause I have to fear I am)
    And hold her free,° I do beseech your honor.   255
OTHELLO: Fear not my government.°
IAGO: I once more take my leave.   *Exit.*
OTHELLO: This fellow's of exceeding honesty,
    And knows all qualities,° with a learned spirit
    Of° human dealings. If I do prove her haggard,°   260
    Though that her jesses° were my dear heartstrings,
    I'd whistle her off and let her down the wind
    To prey at fortune.° Haply, for I am black
    And have not those soft parts of conversation°
    That chamberers° have, or for I am declined   265
    Into the vale of years—yet that's not much—

222. vile success: Evil outcome.   225. honest: Chaste.
234. position: Definite assertion.   236. recoiling: Reverting.
237. fall to match: Happen to compare.   238. happily: Haply,
perhaps.

250. strain his entertainment: Urge his recall.   253. busy:
Meddlesome.   255. hold her free: Consider her guiltless.
256. government: Self-control.   259. qualities: Natures.
259–60. learned spirit Of: Mind informed about.   260. hag-
gard: A wild hawk.   261. jesses: Thongs for controlling a
hawk.   262–63. whistle . . . fortune: Turn her out and let her
take care of herself.   264. soft . . . conversation: Ingratiating
manners.   265. chamberers: Courtiers.

She's gone. I am abused, and my relief
Must be to loathe her. O curse of marriage,
That we can call these delicate creatures ours,
270 And not their appetites! I had rather be a toad
And live upon the vapor of a dungeon
Than keep a corner in the thing I love
For others' uses. Yet 'tis the plague of great ones;°
Prerogatived° are they less than the base.
275 'Tis destiny unshunnable, like death.
Even then this forkèd plague° is fated to us
When we do quicken.° Look where she comes.

Enter Desdemona and Emilia.

If she be false, O, then heaven mocks itself!
I'll not believe't.
DESDEMONA: How now, my dear Othello?
280 Your dinner, and the generous° islanders
By you invited, do attend your presence.
OTHELLO: I am to blame.
DESDEMONA: Why do you speak so faintly?
Are you not well?
OTHELLO: I have a pain upon my forehead, here.
DESDEMONA: Faith, that's with watching;° 'twill away
285   again.
Let me but bind it hard, within this hour
It will be well.
OTHELLO: Your napkin° is too little;

[*He pushes the handkerchief from him, and it falls unnoticed.*]

Let it° alone. Come, I'll go in with you.
DESDEMONA: I am very sorry that you are not well.

                    Exit [with Othello].

290 EMILIA: I am glad I have found this napkin;
This was her first remembrance from the Moor,
My wayward husband hath a hundred times
Wooed me to steal it; but she so loves the token
(For he conjured her she should ever keep it)
295 That she reserves it evermore about her
To kiss and talk to. I'll have the work ta'en out°
And give't Iago.
What he will do with it heaven knows, not I;
I nothing but to please his fantasy.°

Enter Iago.

300 IAGO: How now? What do you here alone?
EMILIA: Do not you chide; I have a thing for you.
IAGO: A thing for me? It is a common thing—
EMILIA: Ha?
IAGO: To have a foolish wife.

EMILIA: O, is that all? What will you give me now   305
For that same handkerchief?
IAGO: What handkerchief?
EMILIA: What handkerchief!
Why, that the Moor first gave to Desdemona;
That which so often you did bid me steal.
IAGO: Hast stol'n it from her?   310
EMILIA: No, faith; she let it drop by negligence,
And to th' advantage,° I, being here, took't up.
Look, here it is.
IAGO: A good wench! Give it me.
EMILIA: What will you do with't, that you have been
so earnest
To have me filch it?
IAGO: Why, what is that to you?   315

[*Snatches it.*]

EMILIA: If it be not for some purpose of import,°
Give't me again. Poor lady, she'll run mad
When she shall lack it.
IAGO: Be not acknown on't;° I have use for it.
Go, leave me.   *Exit Emilia.*   320
I will in Cassio's lodgings lose this napkin
And let him find it. Trifles light as air
Are to the jealous confirmations strong
As proofs of holy writ. This may do something.
The Moor already changes with my poison: 325
Dangerous conceits° are in their nature poisons,
Which at the first are scarce found to distaste,
But with a little act upon the blood
Burn like the mines of sulphur.

Enter Othello.

                        I did say so.
Look where he comes! Not poppy nor mandragora,° 330
Nor all the drowsy syrups of the world,
Shall ever med'cine thee to that sweet sleep
Which thou owedst yesterday.
OTHELLO: Ha! ha! false to me?
IAGO: Why, how now, general? No more of that!
OTHELLO: Avaunt! be gone! Thou hast set me on the
rack.   335
I swear 'tis better to be much abused
Than but to know't a little.
IAGO: How now, my lord?
OTHELLO: What sense had I of her stol'n hours of lust?
I saw't not, thought it not, it harmed not me;
I slept the next night well, fed well, was free° and
merry;   340
I found not Cassio's kisses on her lips
He that is robbed, not wanting° what is stol'n,
Let him not know't, and he's not robbed at all.
IAGO: I am sorry to hear this.

273. **great ones:** Prominent men. 274. **Prerogatived:** Privileged. 276. **forkèd plague:** I.e., horns of a cuckold. 277. **do quicken:** Are born. 280. **generous:** Noble. 285. **watching:** Working late. 287. **napkin:** Handkerchief. 288. **it:** I.e., his forehead. 296. **work ta'en out:** Pattern copied. 299. **fantasy:** Whim.

312. **to th' advantage:** Opportunely. 316. **import:** Importance. 319. **Be . . . on't:** Do not acknowledge it. 326. **conceits:** Ideas. 330. **mandragora:** A narcotic. 340. **free:** Carefree. 342. **wanting:** Missing.

345 OTHELLO: I had been happy if the general camp,
    Pioneers° and all, had tasted her sweet body,
    So I had nothing known. O, now for ever
    Farewell the tranquil mind! farewell content!
    Farewell the plumèd troop, and the big° wars
350 That make ambition virtue! O, farewell!
    Farewell the neighing steed and the shrill trump,
    The spirit-stirring drum, th' ear-piercing fife,
    The royal banner, and all quality,
    Pride, pomp, and circumstance° of glorious war!
355 And O you mortal engines° whose rude throats
    Th' immortal Jove's dread clamors counterfeit,°
    Farewell! Othello's occupation's gone!
    IAGO: Is't possible, my lord?
    OTHELLO: Villain, be sure thou prove my love a
        whore!
360 Be sure of it; give me the ocular proof;
    Or, by the worth of mine eternal soul,
    Thou hadst been better have been born a dog
    Than answer my waked wrath!
    IAGO: Is't come to this?
    OTHELLO: Make me to see't; or at the least so prove it
365 That the probation° bear no hinge nor loop
    To hang a doubt on—or woe upon thy life!
    IAGO: My noble lord—
    OTHELLO: If thou dost slander her and torture me,
    Never pray more; abandon all remorse;
370 On horror's head horrors accumulate;
    Do deeds to make heaven weep, all earth amazed;
    For nothing canst thou to damnation add
    Greater than that.
    IAGO: O grace! O heaven forgive me!
    Are you a man? Have you a soul or sense?—
375 God b' wi' you! take mine office. O wretched fool,
    That liv'st to make thine honesty a vice!
    O monstrous world! Take note, take note, O world,
    To be direct and honest is not safe.
    I thank you for this profit;° and from hence
380 I'll love no friend, sith love breeds such offense.
    OTHELLO: Nay, stay. Thou shouldst be honest.
    IAGO: I should be wise; for honesty's a fool
    And loses that it works for.
    OTHELLO: By the world,
    I think my wife be honest, and think she is not;
385 I think that thou art just, and think thou art not.
    I'll have some proof. Her name, that was as fresh
    As Dian's visage, is now begrimed and black
    As mine own face. If there be cords, or knives,
    Poison, or fire, or suffocating streams,
390 I'll not endure it. Would I were satisfied!°
    IAGO: I see, sir, you are eaten up with passion:
    I do repent me that I put it to you.
    You would be satisfied?

OTHELLO: Would? Nay, I will.
IAGO: And may; but how? how satisfied, my lord?
    Would you, the supervisor,° grossly gape on?   395
    Behold her topped?
OTHELLO: Death and damnation! O!
IAGO: It were a tedious difficulty, I think,
    To bring them to that prospect. Damn them then,
    If ever mortal eyes do see them bolster°
    More than their own! What then? How then?   400
    What shall I say? Where's satisfaction?
    It is impossible you should see this,
    Were they as prime° as goats, as hot as monkeys,
    As salt° as wolves in pride,° and fools as gross
    As ignorance made drunk. But yet, I say,   405
    If imputation and strong circumstances
    Which lead directly to the door of truth
    Will give you satisfaction, you may have't.
OTHELLO: Give me a living reason she's disloyal.
IAGO: I do not like the office.   410
    But sith I am ent'red in this cause so far,
    Pricked to't by foolish honesty and love,
    I will go on. I lay with Cassio lately,
    And being troubled with a raging tooth,
    I could not sleep.   415
    There are a kind of men so loose of soul
    That in their sleeps will mutter their affairs.
    One of this kind is Cassio.
    In sleep I heard him say, "Sweet Desdemona,
    Let us be wary, let us hide our loves!"   420
    And then, sir, would he gripe and wring my
        hand,
    Cry "O sweet creature!" and then kiss me hard,
    As if he plucked up kisses by the roots
    That grew upon my lips; then laid his leg
    Over my thigh, and sighed, and kissed, and then   425
    Cried "Cursèd fate that gave thee to the Moor!"
OTHELLO: O monstrous! monstrous!
IAGO: Nay, this was but
    his dream.
OTHELLO: But this denoted a foregone conclusion;°
    'Tis a shrewd doubt,° though it be but a dream.
    IAGO: And this may help to thicken other proofs   430
    That do demonstrate thinly.
OTHELLO: I'll tear her all to pieces!
IAGO: Nay, but be wise. Yet we see nothing done;
    She may be honest yet. Tell me but this—
    Have you not sometimes seen a handkerchief
    Spotted with strawberries in your wife's hand?   435
OTHELLO: I gave her such a one; 'twas my first gift.
IAGO: I know not that; but such a handkerchief—
    I am sure it was your wife's—did I to-day
    See Cassio wipe his beard with.
OTHELLO: If it be that—

---

346. **Pioneers:** Sappers, laborers. 349. **big:** Stately. 354. **circumstance:** Pageantry. 355. **mortal engines:** Deadly artillery.
356. **counterfeit:** Imitate. 365. **probation:** Proof. 379. **profit:** Profitable lesson. 390. **satisfied:** Completely informed.

395. **supervisor:** Spectator. 399. **bolster:** Lie together.
403. **prime:** Lustful. 404. **salt:** Lecherous. **pride:** Heat.
428. **foregone conclusion:** Previous experience. 429. **a shrewd doubt:** Cursedly suspicious.

440 IAGO: If it be that, or any that was hers,
    It speaks against her with the other proofs.
    OTHELLO: O, that the slave had forty thousand lives!
    One is too poor, too weak for my revenge.
    Now do I see 'tis true. Look here, Iago:
445 All my fond love thus do I blow to heaven.
    'Tis gone.
    Arise, black vengeance, from the hollow hell!
    Yield up, O love, thy crown and hearted throne
    To tyrannous hate! Swell, bosom, with thy
        fraught,°
    For 'tis of aspics'° tongues!
450 IAGO: Yet be content.
    OTHELLO: O, blood, blood, blood!
    IAGO: Patience, I say. Your mind perhaps may
        change.
    OTHELLO: Never, Iago. Like to the Pontic sea,°
    Whose icy current and compulsive course
455 Ne'er feels retiring ebb, but keeps due on
    To the Propontic and the Hellespont,
    Even so my bloody thoughts, with violent pace,
    Shall ne'er look back, ne'er ebb to humble love,
    Till that a capable° and wide revenge
    Swallow them up.
460 (He kneels.)   Now, by yond marble heaven,
    In the due reverence of a sacred vow
    I here engage my words.
    IAGO: Do not rise yet.

    (Iago kneels.)

    Witness, you ever-burning lights above,
    You elements that clip° us round about,
465 Witness that here Iago doth give up
    The execution° of his wit,° hands, heart
    To wronged Othello's service! Let him command,
    And to obey shall be in me remorse,°
    What bloody business ever.

    [They rise.]

    OTHELLO: I greet thy love,
    Not with vain thanks but with acceptance
470   bounteous,
    And will upon the instant put thee to't.
    Within these three days let me hear thee say
    That Cassio's not alive.
    IAGO: My friend is dead; 'tis done at your request.
475 But let her live.
    OTHELLO: Damn her, lewd minx! O, damn her! damn
        her!
    Come, go with me apart. I will withdraw
    To furnish me with some swift means of death
    For the fair devil. Now art thou my lieutenant.
480 IAGO: I am your own forever.   Exeunt.

---

449. fraught: Burden.   450. aspics: Deadly poisonous snakes.
453. Pontic sea: Black Sea.   459. capable: All-embracing.
464. clip: Encompass.   466. execution: Activities. wit:
Mind.   468. remorse: Pity.

Scene IV

The environs of the castle.

Enter Desdemona, Emilia, and Clown.

DESDEMONA: Do you know, sirrah, where Lieutenant
    Cassio lies?°
CLOWN: I dare not say he lies anywhere.
DESDEMONA: Why, man?
CLOWN: He's a soldier, and for me to say a soldier lies is   5
    stabbing.
DESDEMONA: Go to. Where lodges he?
CLOWN: To tell you where he lodges is to tell you where
    I lie.
DESDEMONA: Can anything be made of this?   10
CLOWN: I know not where he lodges; and for me to
    devise a lodging, and say he lies here or he lies there,
    were to lie in mine own throat.
DESDEMONA: Can you enquire him out, and be edified
    by report?   15
CLOWN: I will catechize the world for him; that is, make
    questions, and by them answer.
DESDEMONA: Seek him, bid him come hither. Tell him I
    have moved° my lord on his behalf and hope all will
    be well.   20
  CLOWN: To do this is within the compass of man's wit,
    and therefore I'll attempt the doing of it.   *Exit.*
DESDEMONA: Where should I lose that handkerchief,
    Emilia?
EMILIA: I know not, madam.   25
DESDEMONA: Believe me, I had rather have lost my
    purse
    Full of crusadoes,° and but my noble Moor
    Is true of mind, and made of no such baseness
    As jealous creatures are, it were enough
    To put him to ill thinking.
EMILIA: Is he not jealous?   30
DESDEMONA: Who? he? I think the sun where he was
    born
    Drew all such humors° from him.

Enter Othello.

EMILIA: Look where he comes.
DESDEMONA: I will not leave him now till Cassio
    Be called to him—How is't with you, my lord?
OTHELLO: Well, my good lady. [Aside.] O, hardness to
    dissemble!—   35
    How do you, Desdemona?
DESDEMONA: Well, my good lord.
OTHELLO: Give me your hand. This hand is moist,
    my lady.
DESDEMONA: It yet hath felt no age nor known no
    sorrow.
OTHELLO: This argues fruitfulness and liberal heart.

III, IV. 2. lies: Lives, lodges.   19. moved: Made proposals to.
27. crusadoes: Portuguese gold coins.   32. humors: Inclinations.

40   Hot, hot, and moist. This hand of yours requires
    A sequester° from liberty, fasting and prayer,
    Much castigation, exercise devout;
    For here's a young and sweating devil here
    That commonly rebels. 'Tis a good hand,
    A frank one.
45 DESDEMONA: You may, indeed, say so;
    For 'twas that hand that gave away my heart.
    OTHELLO: A liberal hand! The hearts of old gave
      hands;
    But our new heraldry° is hands, not hearts.
    DESDEMONA: I cannot speak of this. Come now, your
      promise!
50 OTHELLO: What promise, chuck?
    DESDEMONA: I have sent to bid Cassio come speak
      with you.
    OTHELLO: I have a salt and sorry rheum° offends me.
    Lend me thy handkerchief.
    DESDEMONA: Here, my lord.
    OTHELLO: That which I gave you.
    DESDEMONA: I have it not about me.
    OTHELLO: Not?
    DESDEMONA: No, faith, my lord.
55 OTHELLO: That's a fault.
    That handkerchief
    Did an Egyptian° to my mother give.
    She was a charmer,° and could almost read
    The thoughts of people. She told her, while she kept
      it,
60   'Twould make her amiable° and subdue my father
    Entirely to her love; but if she lost it
    Or made a gift of it, my father's eye
    Should hold her loathèd, and his spirits should hunt
    After new fancies. She, dying, gave it me,
65   And bid me, when my fate would have me wive;
    To give it her. I did so; and take heed on't;
    Make it a darling like your precious eye.
    To lose't or give't away were such perdition°
    As nothing else could match.
    DESDEMONA: Is't possible?
70 OTHELLO: 'Tis true. There's magic in the web of it.
    A sibyl that had numb'red in the world
    The sun to course two hundred compasses,°
    In her prophetic fury sewed the work;
    The worms were hallowed that did breed the silk;
75   And it was dyed in mummy° which the skillful
    Conserved of maidens' hearts.
    DESDEMONA: I' faith? Is't true?
    OTHELLO: Most veritable. Therefore look to't well.
    DESDEMONA: Then would to God that I had never
      seen't!

OTHELLO: Ha! Wherefore?
DESDEMONA: Why do you speak so startingly and
    rash?   80
OTHELLO: Is't lost? Is't gone? Speak, is it out o' th'
    way?
DESDEMONA: Heaven bless us!
OTHELLO: Say you?
DESDEMONA: It is not lost. But what an if it were?
OTHELLO: How?   85
DESDEMONA: I say it is not lost.
OTHELLO: Fetch't, let me see't!
DESDEMONA: Why, so I can, sir; but I will not now.
    This is a trick to put° me from my suit:
    Pray you let Cassio be received again.
OTHELLO: Fetch me the handkerchief! My mind
    misgives.   90
DESDEMONA: Come, come!
    You'll never meet a more sufficient man.
OTHELLO: The handkerchief!
[DESDEMONA: I pray talk me of Cassio.
OTHELLO: The handkerchief!]
DESDEMONA: A man that all his time°
    Hath founded his good fortunes on your love,   95
    Shared dangers with you—
OTHELLO: The handkerchief!
DESDEMONA: I' faith, you are to blame.
OTHELLO: Zounds!   *Exit Othello.*
EMILIA: Is not this man jealous?   100
DESDEMONA: I ne'er saw this before.
    Sure there's some wonder in this
      handkerchief;
    I am most unhappy in the loss of it.
EMILIA: 'Tis not a year or two shows us a man.
    They are all but stomachs, and we all but food;   105
    They eat us hungerly, and when they are full,
    They belch us.

Enter Iago and Cassio.

                    Look you—Cassio and my husband!
IAGO: There is no other way; 'tis she must do't.
    And lo the happiness!° Go and importune her.
DESDEMONA: How now, good Cassio? What's the news
    with you?   110
CASSIO: Madam, my former suit. I do beseech you
    That by your virtuous means I may again
    Exist, and be a member of his love
    Whom I with all the office of my heart
    Entirely honor. I would not be delayed.   115
    If my offense be of such mortal kind
    That neither service past, nor present sorrows,
    Nor purposed merit in futurity,
    Can ransom me into his love again,
    But to know so must be my benefit.   120
    So shall I clothe me in a forced content,

---

41. **sequester:** Removal.   48. **heraldry:** Heraldic symbolism.
52. **salt . . . rheum:** Distressing head cold.   57. **Egyptian:** Gypsy.
58. **charmer:** Sorceress.   60. **amiable:** Lovable.   68. **perdition:** Disaster.   72. **compasses:** Annual rounds.   75. **mummy:**
A drug made from mummies.

88. **put:** Divert.   94. **all . . . time:** During his whole career.
109. **happiness:** Good luck.

And shut myself up in° some other course,
To fortune's alms.
DESDEMONA: Alas, thrice-gentle Cassio!
My advocation° is not now in tune.
125 My lord is not my lord; nor should I know him,
Were he in favor° as in humor altered.
So help me every spirit sanctified
As I have spoken for you all my best
And stood within the blank° of his displeasure
130 For my free speech! You must a while be patient.
What I can do I will; and more I will
Than for myself I dare. Let that suffice you.
IAGO: Is my lord angry?
EMILIA: He went hence but now,
And certainly in strange unquietness.
135 IAGO: Can he be angry? I have seen the cannon
When it hath blown his ranks into the air
And, like the devil, from his very arm
Puffed his own brother—and is he angry?
Something of moment then. I will go meet him.
140 There's matter in't indeed if he be angry.
DESDEMONA: I prithee do so.   Exit [Iago].
      Something sure of state,°
Either from Venice or some unhatched practice°
Made demonstrable here in Cyprus to him,
Hath puddled° his clear spirit; and in such cases
145 Men's natures wrangle with inferior things,
Though great ones are their object. 'Tis even so;
For let our finger ache, and it endues°
Our other, healthful members even to a sense
Of pain. Nay, we must think men are not gods,
150 Nor of them look for such observancy
As fits the bridal. Beshrew me much, Emilia,
I was, unhandsome warrior° as I am,
Arraigning his unkindness with my soul;°
But now I find I had suborned the witness,
155 And he's indicted falsely.
EMILIA: Pray heaven it be state matters, as you
      think,
And no conception nor no jealous toy°
Concerning you.
DESDEMONA: Alas the day! I never gave him cause.
160 EMILIA: But jealous souls will not be answered so;
They are not ever jealous for the cause,
But jealous for they're jealous. 'Tis a monster
Begot upon itself,° born on itself.
DESDEMONA: Heaven keep that monster from Othello's
      mind!

EMILIA: Lady, amen.   165
DESDEMONA: I will go seek him. Cassio, walk here
      about:
If I do find him fit, I'll move your suit
And seek to effect it to my uttermost.
CASSIO: I humbly thank your ladyship.

            Exeunt Desdemona and Emilia.
Enter Bianca.

BIANCA: Save you, friend Cassio!
CASSIO: What make you from home?   170
How is't with you, my most fair Bianca?
I' faith, sweet love, I was coming to your house.
BIANCA: And I was going to your lodging, Cassio.
What, keep a week away? seven days and nights?
Eightscore eight hours? and lovers' absent hours,   175
More tedious than the dial° eightscore times?
O weary reck'ning!
CASSIO: Pardon me, Bianca:
I have this while with leaden thoughts been pressed;
But I shall in a more continuate° time
Strike off this score of absence. Sweet Bianca,   180

[*Gives her Desdemona's handkerchief.*]

Take me this work out.°
BIANCA: O Cassio, whence came this?
This is some token from a newer friend.
To the felt absence now I feel a cause.
Is't come to this? Well, well.
CASSIO: Go to, woman!
Throw your vile guesses in the devil's teeth,   185
From whence you have them. You are jealous now
That this is from some mistress, some
      remembrance.
No, by my faith, Bianca.
BIANCA: Why, whose is it?
CASSIO: I know not, sweet; I found it in my chamber.
I like the work° well; ere it be demanded,   190
As like enough it will, I'd have it copied.
Take it and do't, and leave me for this time.
BIANCA: Leave you? Wherefore?
CASSIO: I do attend here on the general
And think it no addition, nor my wish,   195
To have him see me womaned.
BIANCA: Why, I pray you?
CASSIO: Not that I love you not.
BIANCA: But that you do not love me!
I pray you bring me on the way a little,
And say if I shall see you soon at night.
CASSIO: 'Tis but a little way that I can bring you,   200
For I attend here; but I'll see you soon.
BIANCA: 'Tis very good. I must be circumstanced.°
            Exeunt.

122. **shut myself up in:** Confine myself to. 124. **advocation:** Advocacy. 126. **favor:** Appearance. 129. **blank:** Bull's-eye of the target. 141. **state:** Public affairs. 142. **unhatched practice:** Budding plot. 144. **puddled:** Muddied. 147. **endues:** Brings. 152. **unhandsome warrior:** Inadequate soldier. 153. **Arraigning . . . soul:** Indicting his unkindness before the bar of my soul. 157. **toy:** Fancy. 163. **Begot . . . itself:** Self-engendered.

176. **dial:** Clock. 179. **continuate:** Uninterrupted. 181. **Take . . . out:** Copy this embroidery for me. 190. **work:** Needlework. 202. **circumstanced:** Governed by circumstances.

ACT IV • *Scene I*

The environs of the castle.

Enter Othello and Iago.

IAGO: Will you think so?
OTHELLO: Think so, Iago?
IAGO: What,
  To kiss in private?
OTHELLO: An unauthorized kiss.
IAGO: Or to be naked with her friend in bed
  An hour or more, not meaning any harm?
5 OTHELLO: Naked in bed, Iago, and not mean harm?
  It is hypocrisy against the devil.°
  They that mean virtuously, and yet do so,
  The devil their virtue tempts, and they tempt
    heaven.
IAGO: So they do nothing, 'tis a venial slip.
10 But if I give my wife a handkerchief—
OTHELLO: What then?
IAGO: Why, then 'tis hers, my lord; and being hers,
  She may, I think, bestow't on any man.
OTHELLO: She is protectress of her honor too;
15 May she give that?
IAGO: Her honor is an essence that's not seen;
  They have it very oft that have it not.
  But for the handkerchief—
OTHELLO: By heaven, I would most gladly have forgot
  it!
20 Thou said'st—O, it comes o'er my memory
  As doth the raven o'er the infected° house,
  Boding to all!—he had my handkerchief.
IAGO: Ay, what of that?
OTHELLO: That's not so good now.
IAGO: What
  If I had said I had seen him do you wrong?
25 Or heard him say—as knaves be such abroad
  Who having, by their own importunate suit,
  Or voluntary dotage of some mistress,
  Convincèd or supplied° them, cannot choose
  But they must blab—
OTHELLO: Hath he said anything?
30 IAGO: He hath, my lord; but be you well assured,
  No more than he'll unswear.
OTHELLO: What hath he said?
IAGO: Faith, that he did—I know not what he did.
OTHELLO: What? what?
IAGO: Lie—
OTHELLO: With her?
35 IAGO: With her, on her; what you will.
OTHELLO: Lie with her? lie on her?—We say lie on
  her when they belie her.—Lie with her! Zounds,
  that's fulsome.—Handkerchief—confessions—
  handkerchief!—To confess, and be hanged for his

labor—first to be hanged, and then to confess! 40
I tremble at it. Nature would not invest herself in
such shadowing passion without some instruction.°
It is not words that shakes me thus.—Pish! Noses,
ears, and lips? Is't possible?—Confess?—Handkerchief?—O devil!   45

(Falls in a trance.)

IAGO: Work on,
  My med'cine, work! Thus credulous fools are
    caught,
  And many worthy and chaste dames even thus,
  All guiltless, meet reproach.—What, ho! my lord!
  My lord, I say! Othello!

Enter Cassio.

               How now, Cassio?   50
CASSIO: What's the matter?
IAGO: My lord is fall'n into an epilepsy.
  This is his second fit; he had one yesterday.
CASSIO: Rub him about the temples.
IAGO: No, forbear.
  The lethargy° must have his quiet course.   55
  If not, he foams at mouth, and by and by
  Breaks out to savage madness. Look, he stirs.
  Do you withdraw yourself a little while.
  He will recover straight. When he is gone,
  I would on great occasion speak with you.   60
                  [Exit Cassio.]
  How is it, general? Have you not hurt your head?
OTHELLO: Dost thou mock me?
IAGO: I mock you? No, by heaven.
  Would you would bear your fortune like a man!
OTHELLO: A hornèd man's° a monster and a beast.
IAGO: There's many a beast then in a populous city,   65
  And many a civil monster.
OTHELLO: Did he confess it?
IAGO: Good sir, be a man.
  Think every bearded fellow that's but yoked
  May draw with you. There's millions now alive
  That nightly lie in those unproper° beds   70
  Which they dare swear peculiar:° your case is better.
  O, 'tis the spite of hell, the fiend's arch-mock,
  To lip a wanton in a secure° couch,
  And to suppose her chaste! No, let me know;
  And knowing what I am, I know what she shall be.   75
OTHELLO: O, thou art wise! 'Tis certain.
IAGO: Stand you
    awhile apart;
  Confine yourself but in a patient list.°
  Whilst you were here, o'erwhelmèd with your
    grief—

IV, I. **6. hypocrisy . . . devil:** I.e., feigned sin instead of feigned virtue. **21. infected:** Plague-stricken. **28. Convincèd or supplied:** Overcome or gratified.

41–42. Nature . . . instruction: My natural faculties would not be so overcome by passion without reason. **55. lethargy:** Coma. **64. hornèd man:** Cuckold. **70. unproper:** Not exclusively their own. **71. peculiar:** Exclusively their own. **73. secure:** Free from fear of rivalry. **77. in a patient list:** Within the limits of self-control.

A passion most unsuiting such a man—
80 Cassio came hither. I shifted him away
And laid good 'scuse upon your ecstasy,°
Bade him anon return, and here speak with me;
The which he promised. Do but encave° yourself
And mark the fleers, the gibes, and notable scorns
85 That dwell in every region of his face;
For I will make him tell the tale anew—
Where, how, how oft, how long ago, and when
He hath, and is again to cope° your wife.
I say, but mark his gesture. Marry, patience!
90 Or I shall say y'are all in all in spleen,°
And nothing of a man.
OTHELLO: Dost thou hear, Iago?
I will be found most cunning in my patience;
But—dost thou hear?—most bloody.
IAGO: That's not amiss:
But yet keep time in all. Will you withdraw?

[*Othello retires.*]

95 Now will I question Cassio of Bianca,
A huswife° that by selling her desires
Buys herself bread and clothes. It is a creature
That dotes on Cassio, as 'tis the strumpet's plague
To beguile many and be beguiled by one.
100 He, when he hears of her, cannot refrain
From the excess of laughter. Here he comes.

Enter Cassio.

As he shall smile, Othello shall go mad;
And his unbookish° jealousy must conster°
Poor Cassio's smiles, gestures, and light behavior
105 Quite in the wrong. How do you now, lieutenant?
CASSIO: The worser that you give me the addition°
Whose want even kills me.
IAGO: Ply Desdemona well, and you are sure on't.
Now, if this suit lay in Bianca's power,
How quickly should you speed!
110 CASSIO: Alas, poor caitiff!°
OTHELLO: Look how he laughs already!
IAGO: I never knew a woman love man so.
CASSIO: Alas, poor rogue! I think, i' faith, she loves me.
OTHELLO: Now he denies it faintly, and laughs it out.
IAGO: Do you hear, Cassio?
115 OTHELLO: Now he importunes him
To tell it o'er. Go to! Well said, well said!
IAGO: She gives out that you shall marry her.
Do you intend it?
CASSIO: Ha, ha, ha!
120 OTHELLO: Do you triumph, Roman? Do you triumph?
CASSIO: I marry her? What, a customer?° Prithee bear
some charity to my wit; do not think it so unwhole-
some. Ha, ha, ha!

OTHELLO: So, so, so, so! They laugh that win!
IAGO: Faith, the cry goes that you shall marry her.   125
CASSIO: Prithee say true.
IAGO: I am a very villain else.
OTHELLO: Have you scored me?° Well.
CASSIO: This is the monkey's own giving out. She is per-
suaded I will marry her out of her own love and flat-   130
tery, not out of my promise.
OTHELLO: Iago beckons° me; now he begins the story.
CASSIO: She was here even now; she haunts me in every
place. I was t' other day talking on the sea bank with
certain Venetians, and thither comes the bauble,°   135
and, by this hand, she falls me thus about my neck—
OTHELLO: Crying "O dear Cassio!" as it were. His gesture imports it.
CASSIO: So hangs, and lolls, and weeps upon me; so
shakes and pulls me! Ha, ha, ha!   140
OTHELLO: Now he tells how she plucked him to my
chamber. O, I see that nose of yours, but not that dog
I shall throw it to.
CASSIO: Well, I must leave her company.

Enter Bianca.

IAGO: Before me! Look where she comes.   145
CASSIO: 'Tis such another fitchew!° marry, a perfumed
one. What do you mean by this haunting of me?
BIANCA: Let the devil and his dam haunt you! What did
you mean by that same handkerchief you gave me
even now? I was a fine fool to take it. I must take out 150
the whole work? A likely piece of work that you
should find it in your chamber and know not who
left it there! This is some minx's token, and I must
take out the work? There! Give it your hobby-horse.°
Wheresoever you had it, I'll take out no work on't.   155
CASSIO: How now, my sweet Bianca? How now? how
now?
OTHELLO: By heaven, that should be my handkerchief!
BIANCA: An you'll come to supper to-night, you may; an
you will not, come when you are next prepared for.   160
                                             Exit.
IAGO: After her, after her!
CASSIO: Faith, I must; she'll rail in the street else.
IAGO: Will you sup there?
CASSIO: Yes, I intend so.
IAGO: Well, I may chance to see you; for I would very   165
fain speak with you.
CASSIO: Prithee come. Will you?
IAGO: Go to! say no more.   *Exit Cassio.*
OTHELLO [*comes forward*]: How shall I murder him,
Iago?   170
IAGO: Did you perceive how he laughed at his vice?°
OTHELLO: O Iago!
IAGO: And did you see the handkerchief?
OTHELLO: Was that mine?

---

81. ecstasy: Trance.   83. encave: Conceal.   88. cope: Meet.
90. all in all in spleen: Wholly overcome by your passion.
96. huswife: Hussy.   103. unbookish: Uninstructed.   conster:
Construe, interpret.   106. addition: Title.   110. caitiff: Wretch.
121. customer: Prostitute.

128. scored me: Settled my account (?).   132. beckons: Signals.   135. bauble: Plaything.   146. fitchew: Polecat (slang for
whore).   154. hobby-horse: Harlot.   171. vice: I.e., vicious
conduct.

175 IAGO: Yours, by this hand! And to see how he prizes° the
      foolish woman your wife! She gave it him, and he
      hath giv'n it his whore.
     OTHELLO: I would have him nine years a-killing—A
      fine woman! a fair woman! a sweet woman!
180 IAGO: Nay, you must forget that.
     OTHELLO: Ay, let her rot, and perish, and be damned to-
      night; for she shall not live. No, my heart is turned to
      stone; I strike it, and it hurts my hand. O, the world
      hath not a sweeter creature! She might lie by an
185   emperor's side and command him tasks.
     IAGO: Nay, that's not your way.
     OTHELLO: Hang her! I do but say what she is. So deli-
      cate with her needle! an admirable musician! O, she
      will sing the savageness out of a bear! Of so high and
190   plenteous wit and invention°—
     IAGO: She's the worse for all this.
     OTHELLO: O, a thousand thousand times! And then, of
      so gentle a condition!°
     IAGO: Ay, too gentle.
195 OTHELLO: Nay, that's certain. But yet the pity of it, Iago!
      O Iago, the pity of it, Iago!
     IAGO: If you are so fond over her iniquity, give her
      patent° to offend; for if it touch not you, it comes
      near nobody.
200 OTHELLO: I will chop her into messes! Cuckold me!
     IAGO: O, 'tis foul in her.
     OTHELLO: With mine officer!
     IAGO: That's fouler.
     OTHELLO: Get me some poison, Iago, this night. I'll not
205   expostulate with her, lest her body and beauty
      unprovide° my mind again. This night, Iago!
     IAGO: Do it not with poison. Strangle her in her bed,
      even the bed she hath contaminated.
     OTHELLO: Good, good! The justice of it pleases. Very
210   good!
     IAGO: And for Cassio, let me be his undertaker,° you
      shall hear more by midnight.
     OTHELLO: Excellent good!

     A trumpet.

      What trumpet is that same?
     IAGO: I warrant something from Venice.

     Enter Lodovico, Desdemona, and Attendants.

215   'Tis Lodovico.
      This comes from the Duke; and see, your wife is
      with him.
     LODOVICO: God save you, worthy general!
     OTHELLO: With all my
      heart, sir.
     LODOVICO: The Duke and senators of Venice greet you.

     [*Gives him a letter.*]

OTHELLO: I kiss the instrument of their pleasures.

[*Opens the letter and reads.*]

DESDEMONA: And what's the news, good cousin
  Lodovico?   220
IAGO: I am very glad to see you, signior.
  Welcome to Cyprus.
LODOVICO: I thank you. How does Lieutenant
  Cassio?
IAGO: Lives, sir.
DESDEMONA: Cousin, there's fall'n between him and
  my lord
  An unkind breach; but you shall make all well.   225
OTHELLO: Are you sure of that?
DESDEMONA: My lord?
OTHELLO [*reads*]: "This fail you not to do, as you
  will—"
LODOVICO: He did not call; he's busy in the paper.
  Is there division 'twixt thy lord and Cassio?   230
DESDEMONA: A most unhappy one. I would do much
  T' atone° them, for the love I bear to Cassio.
OTHELLO: Fire and brimstone!
DESDEMONA: My lord?
OTHELLO: Are you wise?
DESDEMONA: What, is he angry?
LODOVICO: May be the letter
  moved him;
  For, as I think, they do command him home,
  Deputing Cassio in his government.   235
DESDEMONA: By my troth, I am glad on't.
OTHELLO: Indeed?
DESDEMONA: My lord?
OTHELLO: I am glad to see you mad.°
DESDEMONA: Why, sweet Othello—
OTHELLO: Devil!

[*Strikes her.*]

DESDEMONA: I have not deserved this.   240
LODOVICO: My lord, this would not be believed in
  Venice,
  Though I should swear I saw't. 'Tis very much.
  Make her amends; she weeps.
OTHELLO: O devil, devil!
  If that the earth could teem° with woman's tears,
  Each drop she falls would prove a crocodile.°   245
  Out of my sight!
DESDEMONA: I will not stay to offend you.
                                          [*Going.*]
LODOVICO: Truly, an obedient lady.
  I do beseech your lordship call her back.
OTHELLO: Mistress!
DESDEMONA: My lord?
OTHELLO: What would you with her, sir?   250
LODOVICO: Who? I, my lord?

---

175. prizes: Values.   190. invention: Imagination.   193. condition: Disposition.   198. patent: License.   205. unprovide:
Disarm.   211. be his undertaker: Undertake to deal with him.

232. atone: Reconcile.   238. mad: I.e., waggish.   244. teem:
Breed.   245. crocodile: (Crocodiles were supposed to shed
hypocritical tears to lure men to destruction).

Paul Robeson in the 1930 London production of *Othello*.

Paul Robeson as Othello and Uta Hagen as
Desdemona in the 1943 Theatre Guild production,
directed by Margaret Webster.

OTHELLO: Ay! You did wish that I would make her
     turn.
   Sir, she can turn, and turn, and yet go on
   And turn again; and she can weep, sir, weep;
255 And she's obedient; as you say, obedient,
   Very obedient.—Proceed you in your tears.—
   Concerning this, sir—O well-painted passion!°—
   I am commanded home.—Get you away;
   I'll send for you anon.—Sir, I obey the mandate
260 And will return to Venice.—Hence, avaunt!

                         [*Exit Desdemona.*]

   Cassio shall have my place. And, sir, to-night
   I do entreat that we may sup together.
   You are welcome, sir, to Cyprus—Goats and
     monkeys!

                                        Exit.

LODOVICO: Is this the noble Moor whom our full
     Senate
265 Call all in all sufficient? Is this the nature
   Whom passion could not shake? whose solid virtue
   The shot of accident nor dart of chance
   Could neither graze nor pierce?
IAGO: He is much changed.
LODOVICO: Are his wits safe? Is he not light of brain?
270 IAGO: He's that he is; I may not breathe my censure.
   What he might be—if what he might he is not—
   I would to heaven he were!
LODOVICO: What, strike his wife?
IAGO: Faith, that was not so well; yet would I knew
   That stroke would prove the worst!
LODOVICO: Is it his use?°
275 Or did the letters work upon his blood
   And new-create this fault?
IAGO: Alas, alas!
   It is not honesty in me to speak
   What I have seen and known. You shall observe
     him,
   And his own courses will denote him so
280 That I may save my speech. Do but go after
   And mark how he continues.
LODOVICO: I am sorry that I am deceived in him.

                                      Exeunt.

Scene II

Within the castle.

Enter Othello and Emilia.

OTHELLO: You have seen nothing then?
EMILIA: Nor ever heard, nor ever did suspect.
OTHELLO: Yes, you have seen Cassio and she together.
EMILIA: But then I saw no harm, and then I heard
5   Each syllable that breath made up between them.
OTHELLO: What, did they never whisper?

257. **passion:** Grief.   274. **use:** Custom.

EMILIA: Never, my lord.
OTHELLO: Nor send you out o' th' way?
EMILIA: Never.
OTHELLO: To fetch her fan, her gloves, her mask, nor
     nothing?
EMILIA: Never, my lord.   10
OTHELLO: That's strange.
EMILIA: I durst, my lord, to wager she is honest,
   Lay down my soul at stake. If you think other,
   Remove your thought; it doth abuse your bosom.°
   If any wretch have put this in your head,   15
   Let heaven requite it with the serpent's curse!°
   For if she be not honest, chaste, and true,
   There's no man happy; the purest of their wives
   Is foul as slander.
OTHELLO: Bid her come hither. Go.

                              Exit Emilia.

   She says enough; yet she's a simple bawd   20
   That cannot say as much. This is a subtle whore,
   A closet lock and key of villainous secrets;
   And yet she'll kneel and pray; I have seen her do't.

Enter Desdemona and Emilia.

DESDEMONA: My lord, what is your will?
OTHELLO: Pray, chuck,
   come hither.
DESDEMONA: What is your pleasure?
OTHELLO: Let me see your eyes.   25
   Look in my face.
DESDEMONA: What horrible fancy's this?
OTHELLO [*to Emilia*]: Some of your function, mistress.
   Leave procreants° alone and shut the door;
   Cough or cry hem if anybody come.
   Your mystery, your mystery!° Nay, dispatch!   30

                              Exit Emilia.

DESDEMONA: Upon my knees, what doth your speech
     import?
   I understand a fury in your words,
   [But not the words.]
OTHELLO: Why, what art thou?
DESDEMONA: Your wife, my lord;
     your true
   And loyal wife.
OTHELLO: Come, swear it, damn thyself;   35
   Lest, being like one of heaven,° the devils
     themselves
   Should fear to seize thee. Therefore be double-
     damned—
   Swear thou art honest.°
DESDEMONA: Heaven doth truly know it.
OTHELLO: Heaven truly knows that thou art false as
     hell.

IV, II. 14. **abuse . . . bosom:** Deceive your heart.   16. **serpent's
curse:** (Cf. Genesis 3:14).   28. **procreants:** Mating couples.
30. **mystery:** Trade, occupation.   36. **being . . . heaven:** Looking like an angel.   38. **honest:** Chaste.

DESDEMONA: To whom, my lord? With whom? How
40   am I false?
OTHELLO: Ah, Desdemona! away! away! away!
DESDEMONA: Alas the heavy day! Why do you weep?
    Am I the motive of these tears, my lord?
    If haply you my father do suspect
45   An instrument° of this your calling back,
    Lay not your blame on me. If you have lost him,
    Why, I have lost him too.
OTHELLO: Had it pleased heaven
    To try me with affliction, had they rained
    All kinds of sores and shames on my bare head,
50   Steeped me in poverty to the very lips,
    Given to captivity me and my utmost hopes,
    I should have found in some place of my soul
    A drop of patience. But, alas, to make me
    A fixèd figure for the time of scorn°
55   To point his slow unmoving finger at!
    Yet could I bear that too; well, very well.
    But there where I have garnered up my heart,
    Where either I must live or bear no life,
    The fountain from the which my current runs
60   Or else dries up—to be discarded thence,
    Or keep it as a cistern for foul toads
    To knot and gender in—turn thy complexion
    there,°
    Patience, thou young and rose-lipped cherubin!
    Ay, there look grim as hell!
65 DESDEMONA: I hope my noble lord esteems me honest.
OTHELLO: O, ay; as summer flies are in the shambles,°
    That quicken° even with blowing. O thou weed,
    Who art so lovely fair, and smell'st so sweet,
    That the sense aches at thee, would thou hadst ne'er
    been born!
DESDEMONA: Alas, what ignorant sin have I
70   committed?
OTHELLO: Was this fair paper, this most goodly book,
    Made to write "whore" upon? What committed?
    Committed? O thou public commoner!°
    I should make very forges of my cheeks
75   That would to cinders burn up modesty,
    Did I but speak thy deeds. What committed?
    Heaven stops the nose at it, and the moon winks;°
    The bawdy wind, that kisses all it meets,
    Is hushed within the hollow mine of earth
80   And will not hear it. What committed?
    Impudent strumpet!
DESDEMONA: By heaven, you do me wrong!
OTHELLO: Are not you a strumpet?
DESDEMONA: No, as I am a Christian!
    If to preserve this vessel for my lord
    From any other foul unlawful touch
85   Be not to be a strumpet, I am none.

---

45. An instrument: To be the cause.   **54. time of scorn:** Scornful world.   **62. turn thy complexion there:** Change thy color at that point.   **66. shambles:** Slaughterhouse.   **67. quicken:** Come to life.   **73. commoner:** Harlot.   **77. winks:** Closes her eyes.

OTHELLO: What, not a whore?
DESDEMONA: No, as I shall be saved!
OTHELLO: Is't possible?
DESDEMONA: O, heaven forgive us!
OTHELLO: I cry you mercy° then.
    I took you for that cunning whore of Venice
    That married with Othello.—[*Calling.*] You,
    mistress,   90
    That have the office opposite to Saint Peter
    And keep the gate of hell!

Enter Emilia.

                    You, you, ay, you!
    We have done our course; there's money for your
    pains:
    I pray you turn the key, and keep our counsel.   *Exit.*
EMILIA: Alas, what does this gentleman conceive?   95
    How do you, madam? How do you, my good lady?
DESDEMONA: Faith, half asleep.°
EMILIA: Good madam, what's the matter with my lord?
DESDEMONA: With who?
EMILIA: Why, with my lord, madam.   100
DESDEMONA: Who is thy lord?
EMILIA: He that is yours, sweet lady.
DESDEMONA: I have none. Do not talk to me, Emilia.
    I cannot weep; nor answer have I none
    But what should go by water. Prithee to-night
    Lay on my bed my wedding sheets, remember;   105
    And call thy husband hither.
EMILIA: Here's a change indeed!
                              Exit.
DESDEMONA: 'Tis meet I should be used so, very meet.
    How have I been behaved, that he might stick
    The small'st opinion° on my least misuse?°

Enter Iago and Emilia.

IAGO: What is your pleasure, madam? How is't with
    you?   110
DESDEMONA: I cannot tell. Those that do teach young
    babes
    Do it with gentle means and easy tasks:
    He might have chid me so; for, in good faith,
    I am a child to chiding.
IAGO: What is the matter, lady?
EMILIA: Alas, Iago, my lord hath so bewhored her,   115
    Thrown such despite and heavy terms upon her
    As true hearts cannot bear.
DESDEMONA: Am I that name, Iago?
IAGO: What name, fair lady?
DESDEMONA: Such as she said my lord did say I was.
EMILIA: He called her whore. A beggar in his drink   120
    Could not have laid such terms upon his callet.°
IAGO: Why did he so?
DESDEMONA: I do not know; I am sure I am none such.

---

88. cry you mercy: Beg your pardon.   **97. half asleep:** I.e., stunned.   **109. small'st opinion:** Least suspicion.   **least misuse:** Slightest misconduct.   **121. callet:** Whore.

IAGO: Do not weep, do not weep. Alas the day!

125 EMILIA: Hath she forsook so many noble matches,
  Her father and her country, and her friends,
  To be called whore? Would it not make one weep?

DESDEMONA: It is my wretched fortune.

IAGO: Beshrew him for't!
  How comes this trick° upon him?

DESDEMONA: Nay, heaven doth know.

130 EMILIA: I will be hanged if some eternal villain,
  Some busy and insinuating rogue,
  Some cogging, cozening° slave, to get some office,
  Have not devised this slander. I'll be hanged else.

IAGO: Fie, there is no such man! It is impossible.

135 DESDEMONA: If any such there be, heaven pardon him!

EMILIA: A halter pardon him! and hell gnaw his bones!
  Why should he call her whore? Who keeps her
    company?
  What place? what time? what form? what likelihood?
  The Moor 's abused by some most villainous knave,
140 Some base notorious knave, some scurvy fellow.
  O heaven, that such companions° thou 'dst unfold,°
  And put in every honest hand a whip
  To lash the rascals naked through the world
  Even from the east to th' west!

IAGO: Speak within door.°

145 EMILIA: O, fie upon them! Some such squire he was
  That turned your wit the seamy side without
  And made you to suspect me with the Moor.

IAGO: You are a fool. Go to.

DESDEMONA: Alas, Iago,
  What shall I do to win my lord again?
150 Good friend, go to him; for, by this light of heaven,
  I know not how I lost him. Here I kneel:
  If e'er my will did trespass 'gainst his love
  Either in discourse° of thought or actual deed,
  Or that mine eyes, mine ears, or any sense
155 Delighted them in any other form,
  Or that I do not yet, and ever did,
  And ever will (though he do shake me off
  To beggarly divorcement) love him dearly,
  Comfort forswear° me! Unkindness may do much;
160 And his unkindness may defeat° my life,
  But never taint my love. I cannot say "whore."
  It does abhor me now I speak the word;
  To do the act that might the addition earn
  Not the world's mass of vanity could make me.

165 IAGO: I pray you be content. 'Tis but his humor.
  The business of the state does him offense,
  [And he does chide with you.]

DESDEMONA: If 'twere no other—

IAGO: 'Tis but so, I warrant.

[Trumpets within.]

Hark how these instruments summon you to supper.
The messengers of Venice stay the meat: 170
Go in, and weep not. All things shall be well.

Exeunt Desdemona and Emilia.

Enter Roderigo.

  How now, Roderigo?

RODERIGO: I do not find that thou deal'st justly with me.

IAGO: What in the contrary?

RODERIGO: Every day thou daff'st me with some   175
  device,° Iago, and rather, as it seems to me now,
  keep'st from me all conveniency° than suppliest me
  with the least advantage of hope. I will indeed no
  longer endure it; nor am I yet persuaded to put up in
  peace what already I have foolishly suffered.   180

IAGO: Will you hear me, Roderigo?

RODERIGO: Faith, I have heard too much; for your
  words and performances are no kin together.

IAGO: You charge me most unjustly.

RODERIGO: With naught but truth. I have wasted myself   185
  out of my means. The jewels you have had from me
  to deliver to Desdemona would half have corrupted a
  votarist.° You have told me she hath received them,
  and returned me expectations and comforts of sudden respect° and acquaintance; but I find none.   190

IAGO: Well, go to; very well.

RODERIGO: Very well! go to! I cannot go to, man; nor
  'tis not very well. By this hand, I say 'tis very scurvy,
  and begin to find myself fopped° in it.

IAGO: Very well.   195

RODERIGO: I tell you 'tis not very well. I will make myself known to Desdemona. If she will return me my
  jewels, I will give over my suit and repent my unlawful solicitation; if not, assure yourself I will seek satisfaction of you.   200

IAGO: You have said now.

RODERIGO: Ay, and said nothing but what I protest in-
  tendment of doing.

IAGO: Why, now I see there's mettle in thee; and even
  from this instant do build on thee a better opinion   205
  than ever before. Give me thy hand, Roderigo. Thou
  has taken against me a most just exception; but yet I
  protest I have dealt most directly° in thy affair.

RODERIGO: It hath not appeared.

IAGO: I grant indeed it hath not appeared, and your   210
  suspicion is not without wit and judgment. But,
  Roderigo, if thou hast that in thee indeed which I
  have greater reason to believe now than ever, I mean
  purpose, courage, and valor, this night show it. If
  thou the next night following enjoy not Desdemona,   215
  take me from this world with treachery and devise
  engines for° my life.

---

129. **trick:** Freakish behavior. 132. **cogging, cozening:** Cheating, defrauding. 141. **companions:** Rogues. **unfold:** Expose. 144. **within door:** With restraint. 153. **discourse:** Course. 159. **Comfort forswear:** Happiness forsake. 160. **defeat:** Destroy.

175–76. **thou . . . device:** You put me off with some trick. 177. **conveniency:** Favorable opportunities. 188. **votarist:** Nun. 190. **sudden respect:** Immediate notice. 194. **fopped:** Duped. 208. **directly:** Straightforwardly. 217. **engines for:** Plots against.

RODERIGO: Well, what is it? Is it within reason and compass?

220 IAGO: Sir, there is especial commission come from Venice to depute Cassio in Othello's place.

RODERIGO: Is that true? Why, then Othello and Desdemona return again to Venice.

IAGO: O, no; he goes into Mauritania and takes away
225 with him the fair Desdemona, unless his abode be lingered here° by some accident; wherein none can be so determinate° as the removing of Cassio.

RODERIGO: How do you mean removing of him?

IAGO: Why, by making him uncapable of Othello's
230 place—knocking out his brains.

RODERIGO: And that you would have me to do?

IAGO: Ay, if you dare do yourself a profit and a right. He sups to-night with a harlotry, and thither will I go to him. He knows not yet of his honorable fortune. If
235 you will watch his going thence, which I will fashion to fall out between twelve and one, you may take him at your pleasure. I will be near to second your attempt, and he shall fall between us. Come, stand not amazed at it, but go along with me. I will show
240 you such a necessity in his death that you shall think yourself bound to put it on him. It is now high supper time, and the night grows to waste. About it!

RODERIGO: I will hear further reason for this.

IAGO: And you shall be satisfied.   *Exeunt.*

Scene III

Within the castle.

Enter Othello, Lodovico, Desdemona, Emilia, and Attendants.

LODOVICO: I do beseech you, sir, trouble yourself no further.

OTHELLO: O, pardon me; 'twill do me good to walk.

LODOVICO: Madam, good night. I humbly thank your ladyship.

DESDEMONA: Your honor is most welcome.

OTHELLO: Will you walk, sir?
5 O, Desdemona—

DESDEMONA: My lord?

OTHELLO: Get you to bed on th' instant; I will be returned forthwith. Dismiss your attendant there. Look 't be done.

10 DESDEMONA: I will, my lord.

          Exit [Othello, with Lodovico and Attendants].

EMILIA: How goes it now? He looks gentler than he did.

DESDEMONA: He says he will return incontinent.°

He hath commanded me to go to bed,
And bade me to dismiss you.

EMILIA: Dismiss me?

DESDEMONA: It was his bidding; therefore, good Emilia,   15
Give me my nightly wearing, and adieu.
We must not now displease him.

EMILIA: I would you had never seen him!

DESDEMONA: So would not I. My love doth so approve him
That even his stubbornness,° his checks,° his frowns—   20
Prithee unpin me—have grace and favor in them.

EMILIA: I have laid those sheets you bade me on the bed.

DESDEMONA: All's one. Good faith, how foolish are our minds!
If I do die before thee, prithee shroud me
In one of those same sheets.

EMILIA: Come, come! You talk.   25

DESDEMONA: My mother had a maid called Barbary.
She was in love; and he she loved proved mad°
And did forsake her. She had a song of "Willow";
An old thing 'twas; but it expressed her fortune,
And she died singing it. That song to-night   30
Will not go from my mind; I have much to do
But to go hang my head all at one side
And sing it like poor Barbary. Prithee dispatch.

EMILIA: Shall I go fetch your nightgown?°

DESDEMONA: No, unpin me here.   35
This Lodovico is a proper man.

EMILIA: A very handsome man.

DESDEMONA: He speaks well.

EMILIA: I know a lady in Venice would have walked barefoot to Palestine for a touch of his nether lip.   40

DESDEMONA (*sings*):
"The poor soul sat sighing by a sycamore tree
Sing all a green willow;
Her hand on her bosom, her head on her knee,
Sing willow, willow, willow.
The fresh streams ran by her and murmured her moans;   45
Sing willow, willow, willow;
Her salt tears fell from her, and soft'ned the stones"—
Lay by these.
"Sing willow, willow, willow"—
Prithee hie thee;° he'll come anon.   50
"Sing all a green willow must be my garland.
Let nobody blame him; his scorn I approve"—
Nay, that's not next. Hark! who is 't that knocks?

EMILIA: It's the wind.

DESDEMONA (*sings*):
"I call my love false love; but what said he then?   55
Sing willow, willow, willow:

225–26. **abode . . . here:** Stay here be extended. **227. determinate:** Effective. **IV, III. 12. incontinent:** At once.

20. **stubbornness:** Roughness. **checks:** Rebukes. **27. mad:** Wild, faithless. **34. nightgown:** Dressing gown. **50. hie thee:** Hurry.

If I court moe women, you'll couch with moe
    men."
So get thee gone; good night. Mine eyes do itch.
Doth that bode weeping?
EMILIA: 'Tis neither here nor there.
DESDEMONA: I have heard it said so. O, these men,
60   these men!
    Dost thou in conscience think—tell me, Emilia—
    That there be women do abuse their husbands
    In such gross kind?
EMILIA: There be some such, no question.
DESDEMONA: Wouldst thou do such a deed for all the
    world?
EMILIA: Why, would not you?
65 DESDEMONA: No, by this heavenly light!
EMILIA: Nor I neither by this heavenly light.
    I might do't as well i' th' dark.
DESDEMONA: Wouldst thou do such a deed for all the
    world?
70 EMILIA: The world's a huge thing; it is a great price for a
    small vice.
DESDEMONA: In troth, I think thou wouldst not.
EMILIA: In troth, I think I should; and undo't when I had
    done it. Marry, I would not do such a thing for a
75   joint-ring,° nor for measures of lawn, nor for gowns,
    petticoats, nor caps, nor any petty exhibition;° but,
    for all the whole world—'Ud's pity! who would not
    make her husband a cuckold to make him a mon-
    arch? I should venture purgatory for't.
80 DESDEMONA: Beshrew me if I would do such a wrong
    For the whole world.
EMILIA: Why, the wrong is but a wrong i' th' world; and
    having the world for your labor, 'tis a wrong in your
    own world, and you might quickly make it right.
85 DESDEMONA: I do not think there is any such woman.
EMILIA: Yes, a dozen; and as many to th' vantage° as
    Would store° the world they played for.
    But I do think it is their husbands' faults
    If wives do fall. Say that they slack their duties
90   And pour our treasures into foreign laps;
    Or else break out in peevish° jealousies,
    Throwing restraint upon us; or say they strike us,
    Or scant our former having° in despite—
    Why, we have galls;° and though we have some
    grace,
95   Yet have we some revenge. Let husbands know
    Their wives have sense like them. They see, and
    smell,
    And have their palates both for sweet and sour,
    As husbands have. What is it that they do
    When they change us for others? Is it sport?
100   I think it is. And doth affection breed it?
    I think it doth. Is't frailty that thus errs?

It is so too. And have not we affections,
Desires for sport, and frailty, as men have?
Then let them use us well; else let them know,
The ills we do, their ills instruct us so.   105
DESDEMONA: Good night, good night. God me such
    usage° send,
    Not to pick bad from bad, but by bad mend!
                    Exeunt.

ACT V • *Scene I*

A street in Cyprus.

Enter Iago and Roderigo.

IAGO: Here, stand behind this bulk;° straight will he
    come.
    Wear thy good rapier bare, and put it home.
    Quick, quick! Fear nothing; I'll be at thy elbow.
    It makes us, or it mars us—think on that,
    And fix most firm thy resolution.   5
RODERIGO: Be near at hand; I may miscarry in't.
IAGO: Here, at thy hand. Be bold, and take thy stand.

[Stands aside.]

RODERIGO: I have no great devotion to the deed,
    And yet he hath given me satisfying reasons.
    'Tis but a man gone. Forth my sword! He dies! 10
IAGO: I have rubbed this young quat° almost to the
    sense,°
    And he grows angry. Now whether he kill Cassio,
    Or Cassio him, or each do kill the other,
    Every way makes my gain. Live Roderigo,
    He calls me to a restitution large   15
    Of gold and jewels that I bobbed° from him
    As gifts to Desdemona.
    It must not be. If Cassio do remain,
    He hath a daily beauty in his life
    That makes me ugly; and besides, the Moor   20
    May unfold me to him; there stand I in much peril.
    No, he must die. Be't so! I hear him coming.

Enter Cassio.

RODERIGO: I know his gait. 'Tis he. Villain, thou diest!

[Makes a pass at Cassio.]

CASSIO: That thrust had been mine enemy indeed
    But that my coat° is better than thou know'st. 25
    I will make proof of thine.

[Draws, and wounds Roderigo.]

RODERIGO: O, I am slain!

        [Iago darts from concealment behind Cassio,
             wounds him in the leg, and exits.]

---

75. **joint-ring:** Ring made in separable halves. 76. **exhibition:** Gift. 86. **to th' vantage:** Besides. 87. **store:** Populate.
91. **peevish:** Senseless. 93. **having:** Allowance. 94. **galls:**
Spirits to resent.

106. **usage:** Habits. V, I. 1. **bulk:** Projecting shop-front.
11. **quat:** Pimple. **sense:** Quick. 16. **bobbed:** Swindled.
25. **coat:** Undershirt of mail.

CASSIO: I am maimed for ever. Help, ho! Murder!
    murder!

[*Falls.*]
Enter Othello.

OTHELLO: The voice of Cassio. Iago keeps his word.
RODERIGO: O, villain that I am!
OTHELLO: It is even so.
30 CASSIO: O, help, ho! light! a surgeon!
OTHELLO: 'Tis he. O brave Iago, honest and just,
    That hast such noble sense of thy friend's wrong!
    Thou teachest me. Minion,° your dear lies dead,
    And your unblest fate hies.° Strumpet, I come.
    Forth of my heart those charms, thine eyes, are
35   blotted.
    Thy bed, lust-stained, shall with lust's blood be
        spotted.   *Exit Othello.*

Enter Lodovico and Gratiano.

CASSIO: What, ho? No watch? No passage?° Murder!
    murder!
GRATIANO: 'Tis some mischance. The cry is very
    direful.
CASSIO: O, help!
40 LODOVICO: Hark!
RODERIGO: O wretched villain!
LODOVICO: Two or three groan. It is a heavy° night.
    These may be counterfeits. Let's think't unsafe
    To come in to the cry without more help.
45 RODERIGO: Nobody come? Then shall I bleed to
        death.
LODOVICO: Hark!

Enter Iago, with a light.

GRATIANO: Here's one comes in his shirt, with light
    and weapons.
IAGO: Who's there? Whose noise is this that cries on°
    murder?
LODOVICO: We do not know.
IAGO: Did not you hear a cry?
CASSIO: Here, here! For heaven's sake, help me!
IAGO: What's
50   the matter?
GRATIANO: This is Othello's ancient, as I take it.
LODOVICO: The same indeed, a very valiant fellow.
IAGO: What are you here that cry so grievously?
CASSIO: Iago? O, I am spoiled, undone by villains!
55   Give me some help.
IAGO: O me, lieutenant! What villains have done this?
CASSIO: I think that one of them is hereabout
    And cannot make° away.
IAGO: O treacherous villains!

[*To Lodovico and Gratiano.*]

    What are you there? Come in, and give some help.

RODERIGO: O, help me here!   60
CASSIO: That's one of them.
IAGO: O murd'rous slave! O villain!

[*Stabs Roderigo.*]

RODERIGO: O damned Iago! O inhuman dog!
IAGO: Kill men i' th' dark?—Where be these bloody
    thieves?—
    How silent is this town!—Ho! murder! murder!—
    What may you be? Are you of good or evil?   65
LODOVICO: As you shall prove us, praise us.
IAGO: Signior Lodovico?
LODOVICO: He, sir.
IAGO: I cry you mercy. Here's Cassio hurt by villains.
GRATIANO: Cassio?   70
IAGO: How is't, brother?
CASSIO: My leg is cut in two.
IAGO: Marry,° heaven forbid!
    Light, gentlemen. I'll bind it with my shirt.

Enter Bianca.

BIANCA: What is the matter, ho? Who is't that cried?
IAGO: Who is't that cried?   75
BIANCA: O my dear Cassio! my sweet Cassio!
    O Cassio, Cassio, Cassio!
IAGO: O notable strumpet!—Cassio, may you suspect
    Who they should be that have thus mangled you?
CASSIO: No.   80
GRATIANO: I am sorry to find you thus. I have been to
    seek you.
IAGO: Lend me a garter. So. O for a chair°
    To bear him easily hence!
BIANCA: Alas, he faints! O Cassio, Cassio, Cassio!
IAGO: Gentlemen all, I do suspect this trash   85
    To be a party in this injury.—
    Patience a while, good Cassio.—Come, come!
    Lend me a light. Know we this face or no?
    Alas, my friend and my dear countryman
    Roderigo? No—Yes, sure.—O heaven, Roderigo!   90
GRATIANO: What, of Venice?
IAGO: Even he, sir. Did you know him?
GRATIANO: Know him? Ay.
IAGO: Signior Gratiano? I cry your gentle pardon.
    These bloody accidents must excuse my manners
    That so neglected you.
GRATIANO: I am glad to see you.   95
IAGO: How do you, Cassio?—O, a chair, a chair!
GRATIANO: Roderigo?
IAGO: He, he, 'tis he!

[*A chair brought in.*]

    O, that's well said;° the chair.
    Some good man bear him carefully from hence.   100
    I'll fetch the general's surgeon. [*To Bianca.*] For you,
        mistress,

---

33. **Minion:** Mistress. 34. **hies:** Hurries on. 37. **passage:**
Passersby. 42. **heavy:** Cloudy, dark. 48. **cries on:** Raises the
cry of. 58. **make:** Get.

72. **Marry:** (From "By Mary"). 82. **chair:** Litter. 99. **well
said:** Well done.

Save you your labor.—He that lies slain here,
      Cassio,
   Was my dear friend. What malice was between you?
CASSIO: None in the world; nor do I know the man.
IAGO [*to Bianca*]: What, look you pale?—O, bear
105   him out o' th' air.

                  [*Cassio and Roderigo are borne off.*]

   Stay you, good gentlemen.—Look you pale,
      mistress?—
   Do you perceive the gastness° of her eye?—
   Nay, if you stare, we shall hear more anon.
   Behold her well; I pray you look upon her.
110   Do you see, gentlemen? Nay, guiltiness will speak.
   Though tongues were out of use.

Enter Emilia.

EMILIA: 'Las, what's the matter? What's the matter,
      husband?
IAGO: Cassio hath here been set on in the dark
   By Roderigo, and fellows that are scaped.
115   He's almost slain, and Roderigo dead.
EMILIA: Alas, good gentlemen! alas, good Cassio!
IAGO: This is the fruits of whoring. Prithee, Emilia,
   Go know of Cassio where he supped to-night.

[*To Bianca.*]

   What, do you shake at that?
BIANCA: He supped at my house; but I therefore shake
120   not.
IAGO: O, did he so? I charge you go with me.
EMILIA: Fie, fie upon thee, strumpet!
BIANCA: I am no strumpet, but of life as honest°
   As you that thus abuse me.
EMILIA: As I? Foh! fie upon thee!
125 IAGO: Kind gentlemen, let's go see poor Cassio dressed.

[*To Bianca.*]

   Come, mistress, you must tell 's another tale.
   Emilia, run you to the citadel
   And tell my lord and lady what hath happed.

                              [*Exit Emilia.*]

   Will you go on afore?   *Exeunt* [*all but Iago*].
                  This is the night
130   That either makes me or fordoes° me quite.   [*Exit.*]

Scene II

A bedchamber in the castle.

Desdemona [asleep] in her bed. Enter Othello with a light.

OTHELLO: It is the cause, it is the cause,° my soul.
   Let me not name it to you, you chaste stars!

It is the cause. Yet I'll not shed her blood,
Nor scar that whiter skin of hers than snow,
And smooth as monumental alabaster.   5
Yet she must die, else she'll betray more men.
Put out the light, and then put out the light.
If I quench thee, thou flaming minister,°
I can again thy former light restore,
Should I repent me; but once put out thy light,   10
Thou cunning'st pattern of excelling nature,
I know not where is that Promethean heat°
That can thy light relume.° When I have plucked the
   rose,
I cannot give it vital growth again;
It needs must wither. I'll smell thee on the tree.   15

(*He kisses her.*)

O balmy breath, that dost almost persuade
Justice to break her sword! One more, one more!
Be thus when thou art dead, and I will kill thee,
And love thee after. One more, and that's the last!
So sweet was ne'er so fatal. I must weep,   20
But they are cruel tears. This sorrow's heavenly;
It strikes where it doth love. She wakes.
DESDEMONA: Who's there? Othello?
OTHELLO: Ay, Desdemona.
DESDEMONA: Will you come to bed, my lord?
OTHELLO: Have you prayed to-night, Desdemon?
DESDEMONA: Ay,
      my lord.   25
OTHELLO: If you bethink yourself of any crime°
   Unreconciled as yet to heaven and grace,
   Solicit for it straight.
DESDEMONA: Alack, my lord, what may you mean by
      that?
OTHELLO: Well, do it, and be brief; I will walk by.   30
   I would not kill thy unprepared spirit.
   No, heaven forfend!° I would not kill thy soul.
DESDEMONA: Talk you of killing?
OTHELLO: Ay, I do.
DESDEMONA: Then heaven
      Have mercy on me!
OTHELLO: Amen, with all my heart!
DESDEMONA: If you say so, I hope you will not kill me. 35
OTHELLO: Hum!
DESDEMONA: And yet I fear you; for you're fatal then
   When your eyes roll so. Why I should fear I know
      not,
   Since guiltiness I know not; but yet I feel I fear.
OTHELLO: Think on thy sins.
DESDEMONA: They are loves I bear to you.   40
OTHELLO: Ay, and for that thou diest.
DESDEMONA: That death 's unnatural that kills for
      loving.
   Alas, why gnaw you so your nether lip?
   Some bloody passion shakes your very frame.

---

107. **gastness:** Terror.   123. **honest:** Chaste.   130. **fordoes:**
Destroys.   V, II. 1. **cause:** Cause of justice.

8. **minister:** Servant.   12. **Promethean heat:** Divine fire.   13. **re-**
lume: Relight.   26. **crime:** Sin.   32. **forfend:** Forbid.

45   These are portents,° but yet I hope, I hope,
     They do not point on me.
OTHELLO: Peace and be still!
DESDEMONA: I will so. What's the matter?
OTHELLO: That handkerchief which I so loved and
     gave thee
     Thou gav'st to Cassio.
DESDEMONA: No, by my life and soul!
     Send for the man and ask him.
50 OTHELLO: Sweet soul, take heed,
     Take heed of perjury; thou art on thy deathbed.
DESDEMONA: Ay, but not yet to die.
OTHELLO: Yes, presently.°
     Therefore confess thee freely of thy sin;
     For to deny each article with oath
55   Cannot remove nor choke the strong conception°
     That I do groan withal. Thou art to die.
DESDEMONA: Then Lord have mercy on me!
OTHELLO: I say amen.
DESDEMONA: And have you mercy too! I never did
     Offend° you in my life; never loved Cassio
60   But with such general warranty of heaven
     As I might love. I never gave him token.
OTHELLO: By heaven, I saw my handkerchief in's hand!
     O perjured woman! thou dost stone my heart,°
     And mak'st me call what I intend to do
65   A murder, which I thought a sacrifice.
     I saw the handkerchief.
DESDEMONA: He found it then.
     I never gave it him. Send for him hither.
     Let him confess a truth.
OTHELLO: He hath confessed.
DESDEMONA: What, my lord?
OTHELLO: That he hath used thee.
DESDEMONA: How? Unlawfully?
70 OTHELLO: Ay.
DESDEMONA: He will not say so.
OTHELLO: No, his mouth is stopped.
     Honest Iago hath ta'en order° for't.
DESDEMONA: O, my fear interprets. What, is he dead?
OTHELLO: Had all his hairs been lives, my great
     revenge
75   Had stomach for them all.
DESDEMONA: Alas, he is betrayed, and I undone!
OTHELLO: Out, strumpet! Weep'st thou for him to my
     face?
DESDEMONA: O, banish me, my lord, but kill me not!
OTHELLO: Down, strumpet!
80 DESDEMONA: Kill me to-morrow; let me live to-night!
OTHELLO: Nay, if you strive—
DESDEMONA: But half an hour!
OTHELLO: Being done, there is no pause.
DESDEMONA: But while I say one prayer!
OTHELLO: It is too late.

---

45. **portents:** Signs of impending violence.   52. **presently:** At
once.   55. **conception:** Belief.   59. **Offend:** Wrong.   63. **stone
my heart:** Turn my heart to stone.   72. **ta'en order:** Taken
measures.

(*Smothers her.*)

[DESDEMONA: O Lord, Lord, Lord!]

Emilia at the door.

EMILIA (*calls within*): My lord, my lord! What, ho!
     my lord, my lord!   85
OTHELLO: What noise is this? Not dead? not yet
     quite dead?
     I that am cruel am yet merciful;
     I would not have thee linger in thy pain.
     So, so.
EMILIA (*within*): What, ho! my lord, my lord!
OTHELLO: Who's there?   90
EMILIA (*within*): O, good my lord, I would speak a
     word with you!
OTHELLO: Yes, 'tis Emilia.—By and by.°—She's
     dead.—
     'Tis like she comes to speak of Cassio's death.
     The noise was here. Ha! no more moving?
     Still as the grave.—Shall she come in? Were't
     good!—   95
     I think she stirs again. No.—What's best to do?
     If she come in, she'll sure speak to my wife.
     My wife! my wife! what wife! I have no wife.
     O, insupportable! O heavy hour!
     Methinks it should be now a huge eclipse   100
     Of sun and moon, and that th' affrighted globe
     Should yawn° at alteration.
EMILIA (*within*):   I do beseech you
     That I may speak with you, O good my lord!
OTHELLO: I had forgot thee. O, come in, Emilia.
     Soft, by and by.—Let me the curtains draw.—   105

[*Closes the bed-curtains.*]

     Where art thou?

[*Opens the door.*]
Enter Emilia.
                        What's the matter with thee now?
EMILIA: O my good lord, yonder's foul murder done!
OTHELLO: What? Now?
EMILIA: But now, my lord.
OTHELLO: It is the very error° of the moon.   110
     She comes more nearer earth than she was wont
     And makes men mad.
EMILIA: Cassio, my lord, hath killed a young
     Venetian Called Roderigo.
OTHELLO: Roderigo killed?
     And Cassio killed?
EMILIA: No, Cassio is not killed.   115
OTHELLO: Not Cassio killed? Then murder's out of
     tune,
     And sweet revenge grows harsh.
DESDEMONA: O, falsely, falsely murdered?

---

92. **By and by:** Just a moment (addressed to Emilia).
102. **yawn:** Open, as in an earthquake.   110. **error:** Straying
off course.

EMILIA: O, Lord!
    what cry is that?
OTHELLO: That? What?
120 EMILIA: Out and alas! that was my lady's voice.
    Help! help, ho! help! O lady, speak again!
    Sweet Desdemona! O sweet mistress, speak!
DESDEMONA: A guiltless death I die.
EMILIA: O, who hath done this deed?
125 DESDEMONA: Nobody—I myself. Farewell.
    Commend° me to my kind lord. O, farewell!

(*She dies.*)

OTHELLO: Why, how should she be murd'red?
EMILIA: Alas,
    who knows?
OTHELLO: You heard her say herself, it was not I.
EMILIA: She said so. I must needs report the truth.
130 OTHELLO: She's like a liar gone to burning hell!
    'Twas I that killed her.
EMILIA: O, the more angel she,
    And you the blacker devil!
OTHELLO: She turned to folly, and she was a whore.
EMILIA: Thou dost belie her, and thou art a devil.
OTHELLO: She was false as water.°
EMILIA: Thou art rash as fire
135   to say
    That she was false. O, she was heavenly true!
OTHELLO: Cassio did top her. Ask thy husband else.
    O, I were damned beneath all depth in hell
    But that I did proceed upon just grounds
140   To this extremity. Thy husband knew it all.
EMILIA: My husband?
OTHELLO: Thy husband.
EMILIA: That she was false to wedlock?
OTHELLO: Ay, with Cassio. Nay, had she been true,
145   If heaven would make me such another world
    Of one entire and perfect chrysolite,°
    I'ld not have sold her for it.
EMILIA: My husband?
OTHELLO: Ay 'twas he that told me first.
    An honest man he is, and hates the slime
    That sticks on filthy deeds.
150 EMILIA: My husband?
OTHELLO: What needs this iterance,° woman? I say thy
    husband.
EMILIA: O mistress, villainy hath made mocks with
    love!
    My husband say that she was false?
OTHELLO: He, woman.
    I say, thy husband. Dost understand the word?
155   My friend, thy husband; honest, honest Iago.
EMILIA: If he say so, may his pernicious soul
    Rot half a grain a day! he lies to th' heart.
    She was too fond of her most filthy bargain.
OTHELLO: Ha!

EMILIA: Do thy worst.   160
    This deed of thine is no more worthy heaven
    Than thou wast worthy her.
OTHELLO: Peace, you were best.
EMILIA: Thou hast not half the power to do me harm
    As I have to be hurt.° O gull! O dolt!
    As ignorant as dirt! thou hast done a deed—   165
    I care not for thy sword; I'll make thee known,
    Though I lost twenty lives. Help! help! Ho! help!
    The Moor hath killed my mistress! Murder!
    murder!

Enter Montano, Gratiano, Iago, and others.

MONTANO: What is the matter? How now, general?
EMILIA: O, are you come, Iago? You have done well,   170
    That men must lay their murders on your neck.
GRATIANO: What is the matter?
EMILIA: Disprove this villain, if thou be'st a man.
    He says thou told'st him that his wife was false.
    I know thou didst not; thou'rt not such a villain.   175
    Speak, for my heart is full.
IAGO: I told him what I thought, and told no more
    Than what he found himself was apt and true.
EMILIA: But did you ever tell him she was false?
IAGO: I did.   180
EMILIA: You told a lie, an odious damnèd lie!
    Upon my soul, a lie! a wicked lie!
    She false with Cassio? Did you say with Cassio?
IAGO: With Cassio, mistress. Go to, charm° your
    tongue.
EMILIA: I will not charm my tongue; I am bound to
    speak: 185
    My mistress here lies murdered in her bed—
ALL: O heavens forfend!
EMILIA: And your reports have set the murder on.
OTHELLO: Nay, stare not, masters. It is true indeed.
GRATIANO: 'Tis a strange truth.   190
MONTANO: O monstrous act!
EMILIA: Villainy, villainy, villainy!
    I think upon't—I think I smell't!—O villainy!
    I thought so then.—I'll kill myself for grief.—
    O villainy, villainy!
IAGO: What, are you mad? I charge you get you home.   195
EMILIA: Good gentlemen, let me have leave to speak.
    'Tis proper I obey him, but not now.
    Perchance, Iago, I will ne'er go home.
OTHELLO: O! O! O!   (*Falls on the bed.*)
EMILIA: Nay, lay thee down and roar!
    For thou hast killed the sweetest innocent   200
    That e'er did lift up eye.
OTHELLO: O, she was foul!

[*Rises.*]

    I scarce did know you, uncle. There lies your niece,
    Whose breath, indeed, these hands have newly
    stopped.

---

126. Commend: Remember.   **135. water:** (Which is yielding).
146. chrysolite: (Precious topaz).   **151. iterance:** Repetition.

164. to be hurt: To endure hurt.   **184. charm:** Cast a spell on.

I know this act shows° horrible and grim.

GRATIANO: Poor Desdemon! I am glad thy father's
205   dead.
Thy match was mortal to him, and pure grief
Shore his old thread in twain. Did he live now,
This sight would make him do a desperate turn;°
Yea, curse his better angel from his side,
210   And fall to reprobation.°

OTHELLO: 'Tis pitiful; but yet Iago knows
That she with Cassio hath the act of shame
A thousand times committed. Cassio confessed it;
And she did gratify° his amorous works
215   With that recognizance° and pledge of love
Which I first gave her. I saw it in his hand.
It was a handkerchief, an antique token
My father gave my mother.

EMILIA: O God! O heavenly God!

IAGO: Zounds, hold your peace!

220 EMILIA: 'Twill out, 'twill out! I peace?
No, I will speak as liberal as the north,°
Let heaven and men and devils, let them all,
All, all, cry shame against me, yet I'll speak.

IAGO: Be wise, and get you home.

EMILIA: I will not.

[Iago draws and threatens Emilia.]

GRATIANO: Fie!
225   Your sword upon a woman?

EMILIA: O thou dull Moor, that handkerchief thou
    speak'st of
I found by fortune, and did give my husband;
For often with a solemn earnestness—
More than indeed belonged to such a trifle—
He begged of me to steal't.

230 IAGO: Villainous whore!

EMILIA: She give it Cassio? No, alas, I found it,
And I did give't my husband.

IAGO: Filth, thou liest!

EMILIA: By heaven, I do not, I do not, gentlemen.
O murd'rous coxcomb! what should such a fool
Do with so good a wife?

235 OTHELLO: Are there no stones° in heaven
But what serves for the thunder? Precious villain!

The Moor runs at Iago [but is disarmed by Montano].
Iago kills his wife.

GRATIANO: The woman falls. Sure he hath killed his
    wife.

EMILIA: Ay, ay. O, lay me by my mistress' side.
                  Exit Iago.

GRATIANO: He's gone, but his wife's killed.

MONTANO: 'Tis a notorious° villain. Take you this
240   weapon,

Which I have here recovered from the Moor.
Come, guard the door without. Let him not pass,
But kill him rather. I'll after that same villain,
For 'tis a damnèd slave.

    Exit [Montano, with all but Othello and Emilia].

OTHELLO: I am not valiant neither;
But every puny whipster° gets my sword.   245
But why should honor outlive honesty?
Let it go all.

EMILIA: What did thy song bode, lady?
Hark, canst thou hear me? I will play the swan,
And die in music. [*Sings.*] "Willow, willow,
    willow."
Moor, she was chaste. She loved thee, cruel Moor: 250
So come my soul to bliss as I speak true.
So speaking as I think, alas, I die.

(She dies.)

OTHELLO: I have another weapon in this chamber;
It is a sword of Spain, the ice brook's° temper.
O, here it is.—Uncle, I must come forth.   255

GRATIANO (*within*): If thou attempt it, it will cost
    thee dear.
Thou hast no weapon, and perforce must suffer.

OTHELLO: Look in upon me then and speak with me,
Or, naked° as I am, I will assault thee.

[Enter Gratiano.]

GRATIANO: What is the matter?

OTHELLO: Behold, I have a weapon;   260
A better never did itself sustain
Upon a soldier's thigh. I have seen the day
That with this little arm and this good sword
I have made my way through more impediments
Than twenty times your stop.° But O vain boast!   265
Who can control his fate? 'Tis not so now.
Be not afraid, though you do see me weaponed.
Here is my journey's end, here is my butt,°
And very seamark° of my utmost sail:
Do you go back dismayed? 'Tis a lost° fear.   270
Man but a rush° against Othello's breast,
And he retires. Where should Othello go?
Now, how dost thou look now? O ill-starred
    wench!
Pale as thy smock! When we shall meet at compt,°
This look of thine will hurl my soul from heaven,   275
And fiends will snatch at it. Cold, cold, my girl?
Even like thy chastity.
O cursèd, cursèd slave! Whip me, ye devils,
From the possession of this heavenly sight!
Blow me about in winds! roast me in sulphur!   280

---

204. **shows:** Appears.   208. **turn:** Act.   210. **reprobation:** Rejection by God, damnation.   214. **gratify:** Reward.   215. **recognizance:** Token.   221. **liberal as the north:** Unchecked as the north wind blows.   235. **stones:** Bolts like those used for thunderbolts.   240. **notorious:** Notable.

245. **puny whipster:** Whippersnapper.   254. **ice brook:** I.e., a Spanish blade, tempered in cold running water.   259. **naked:** Disarmed.   265. **stop:** Power to stop.   268. **butt:** Limit. 269. **seamark:** Beacon, destination.   270. **lost:** Wasted. 271. **Man but a rush:** Wield only a reed.   274. **compt:** Final accounting, Last Judgment.

Wash me in steep-down gulfs of liquid fire!
Oh Desdemon! dead Desdemon! dead! Oh! Oh!

*Enter Lodovico, Montano, Iago [as prisoner], and Offi-
cers; Cassio in a chair.*

LODOVICO: Where is this rash and most unfortunate
    man?
OTHELLO: That's he that was Othello. Here I am.
285 LODOVICO: Where is that viper? Bring the villain forth.
OTHELLO: I look down towards his feet° — but that's
    a fable.
    If that thou be'st a devil, I cannot kill thee.

[*Wounds Iago.*]

LODOVICO: Wrench his sword from him.

[*Othello is disarmed.*]

IAGO: I bleed, sir, but not killed.
OTHELLO: I am not sorry neither. I'ld have thee live;
290   For in my sense, 'tis happiness to die.
LODOVICO: O thou Othello that wert once so good,
    Fall'n in the practice° of a damnèd slave,
    What shall be said to thee?
OTHELLO: Why, anything;
    An honorable murderer, if you will;
295   For naught did I in hate, but all in honor.
LODOVICO: This wretch hath part confessed his
    villainy.
    Did you and he consent in° Cassio's death?
OTHELLO: Ay.
CASSIO: Dear general, I never gave you cause.
300 OTHELLO: I do believe it, and I ask your pardon.
    Will you, I pray, demand that demi-devil
    Why he hath thus ensnared my soul and body?
IAGO: Demand me nothing. What you know, you
    know.
    From this time forth I never will speak word.
LODOVICO: What, not to pray?
305 GRATIANO: Torments will ope your lips.
OTHELLO: Well, thou dost best.
LODOVICO: Sir, you shall understand what hath
    befall'n,
    Which, as I think, you know not. Here is a letter
    Found in the pocket of the slain Roderigo;
310   And here another. The one of them imports
    The death of Cassio to be undertook
    By Roderigo.
OTHELLO: O villain!
CASSIO: Most heathenish and most gross!
LODOVICO: Now here's another discontented paper
315   Found in the pocket too; and this, it seems,
    Roderigo mean t' have sent this damnèd villain;
    But that, belike, Iago in the nick°
    Came in and satisfied him.

OTHELLO: O thou pernicious caitiff! —
    How came you, Cassio, by that handkerchief
    That was my wife's?
CASSIO: I found it in my chamber;   320
    And he himself confessed but even now
    That there he dropped it for a special purpose
    Which wrought to his desire.
OTHELLO: O fool! fool! fool!
CASSIO: There is besides in Roderigo's letter,
    How he upbraids Iago that he made him   325
    Brave me upon the watch; whereon it came
    That I was cast;° and even but now he spake,
    After long seeming dead — Iago hurt him,
    Iago set him on.
LODOVICO: You must forsake this room and go with
    us.   330
    Your power and your command is taken off,
    And Cassio rules in Cyprus. For this slave,
    If there be any cunning cruelty
    That can torment him much and hold him long,
    It shall be his. You shall close prisoner rest   335
    Till that the nature of your fault be known
    To the Venetian state. Come, bring away.
OTHELLO: Soft you! a word or two before you go.
    I have done the state some service, and they
    know't.
    No more of that. I pray you, in your letters,   340
    When you shall these unlucky° deeds relate,
    Speak of me as I am. Nothing extenuate,
    Nor set down aught in malice. Then must you
    speak
    Of one that loved not wisely, but too well;
    Of one not easily jealous, but, being wrought,   345
    Perplexed° in the extreme; of one whose hand,
    Like the base Judean,° threw a pearl away
    Richer than all his tribe; of one whose subdued°
    eyes,
    Albeit unusèd to the melting mood,
    Drop tears as fast as the Arabian trees   350
    Their med'cinable gum. Set you down this.
    And say besides that in Aleppo once,
    Where a malignant and a turbaned Turk
    Beat a Venetian and traduced the state,
    I took by th' throat the circumcisèd dog   355
    And smote him — thus.

(*He stabs himself.*)

LODOVICO: O bloody period!°
GRATIANO: All that's spoke is marred.
OTHELLO: I kissed thee ere I killed thee. No way but
    this,
    Killing myself, to die upon a kiss.

(*He [falls upon the bed and] dies.*)

---

286. **I . . . feet:** I.e., to see if they are cloven, like the Devil's.
292. **practice:** Plot.   297. **consent in:** Agree upon.   317. **nick:**
Nick of time.

327. **cast:** Dismissed.   341. **unlucky:** Fatal.   346. **Perplexed:**
Distracted.   347. **Judean:** Judas Iscariot (?) (quarto reads "In-
dian").   348. **subdued:** I.e., conquered by grief.   357. **period:**
Ending.

CASSIO: This did I fear, but thought he had no
360   weapon;
       For he was great of heart.
LODOVICO [*to Iago*]:   O Spartan dog,
       More fell° than anguish, hunger, or the sea!
       Look on the tragic loading of this bed.
       This is thy work. The object poisons sight;
365   Let it be hid.° Gratiano, keep the house,

And seize upon° the fortunes of the Moor,
For they succeed on you. To you, lord governor,
Remains the censure° of this hellish villain,
The time, the place, the torture. O, enforce it!
Myself will straight aboard, and to the state   370
This heavy act with heavy heart relate.

                                    Exeunt.

362. fell: Cruel.   **365. Let it be hid:** I.e., draw the bed curtains.

366. seize upon: Take legal possession of.   **368. censure:** Judicial sentence.

COMMENTARIES

Virginia Mason Vaughan offers insights into the way in which one of the greatest nineteenth-century English actors prepared for the role and what he felt he had to trim from the text in order to satisfy midcentury audiences. Margaret Webster, who directed the great performance of Paul Robeson in *Othello* in 1943, discusses the question of race in the play from the perspective of the mid-twentieth century. Her focus is on Desdemona as much as on Othello.

Virginia Mason Vaughan (b. 1947)
MACREADY'S OTHELLO   1994

In her discussion of Othello's performance history, Virginia Mason Vaughan describes one of the greatest Shakespearean actors of the mid-nineteenth century. William Charles Macready (1793–1873) was born in England and performed in London and throughout the United States. His care in producing Othello, *including his willingness to edit out sensitive lines, gives us an interesting insight into the history of the play's production.*

Alan Downer, Macready's biographer, describes the tragedian's acting methods: "In the study and rehearsal of a part, Macready searched for character traits which an audience would recognize as natural, and by the skillful use of pause, transition, and colloquialism strove to convey the poet's meaning."[1] One technique was the "Macready pause," a slight hesitation within the speech in imitation of a natural speaking voice. Macready used these pauses to make Othello seem more realistic. On 1 November 1836, he recorded: "I think

[1]Alan Downer, *The Eminent Tragedian: William Charles Macready* (Cambridge: Harvard University Press, 1966), p. 80. See also Bertram Joseph, *The Tragic Actor* (London: Routledge and Kegan Paul, 1959), pp. 284–320, for a discussion of Macready's acting style and the traits of his competitors, including Vandenhoff, Phelps, and Kean.

I acted Othello well with considerable spirit, and more *pause* than I generally allow myself, which is an undoubted improvement."[2] Again, on 7 November: "Acted Othello, not exactly well, but again derived great benefit from *taking time* between my sentences."[3] Macready also used specific stage business to achieve what he thought would be a more natural effect. Downer observes, for example, that "To further contribute to the reality of the senate scene in *Othello* he played with his back to the audience."[4]

The productions Macready mounted at Covent Garden and Drury Lane demonstrate his meticulousness over scenic design and costume. George Ellis prepared watercolor drawings of costumes and scenery from the Covent Garden *Othello* for Charles Kean; seven scenic drawings, now in the Folger Shakespeare Library,[5] show careful attention to detail. The first is a wash of the Rialto that was also used for *The Merchant of Venice,* complete with bridge, canal, gondola, and Renaissance buildings in the background. The second scene is the citadel of Famagusta on the isle of Cyprus. It consists of three layers: the front panel shows the castle wall and cannons pointing out to sea; the middle panel portrays a castle turret, while the back panel opens to a prospect across the harbor. The third scene is a gateway leading from outside the castle to the inside. The drunken revels of *Othello,* act ii, scene iii, would be staged before these gates. The fourth watercolor is an ornate chamber in the castle, suitable for the temptation scene, the fifth an antechamber in the castle, ornamented with carved scrolled walls. The sixth set is a piazza outside an Italian Renaissance building, flanked by columns. Last, of course, is the bedchamber. The bed, hidden in the center back alcove, is ornately decked with labial curtains. At first the bed's upstage location seems to marginalize Desdemona, but three sets of brightly colored curtains draped above lure the eye inward toward the recess. The entire set, in contrast to the grim action of the murder, is brightly colored in shades of blue, pink, and yellow.

Macready's elaborate scenery was symptomatic of his efforts to produce Shakespeare in historically accurate settings. Shattuck demonstrates the tragedian's meticulous attention to historical detail when he produced *King John.*[6] This concern was not confined to the history plays, however. For *Othello* accuracy meant realistic scenes from Renaissance Venice (the Rialto, bridge, canal, gondolas, and Doge's Palace) and Cyprus (the citadel at Famagusta). Though they were painted after the fact, these watercolors demonstrate the extravagant beauty of Macready's 1837 Covent Garden *Othello,* a beauty that set a high standard for subsequent spectacular, historically based productions.

Macready's quest for scenic harmony included detailed attention to costumes. For London productions no expense was spared. Watercolor sketches of the Covent Garden costumes[7] are just as detailed and colorful as the scenic designs. They too may have been used, where appropriate, in *The Merchant of*

[2]William Charles Macready, *The Diaries of William Charles Macready,* ed. William Toynbee (London: Chapman and Hall, Ltd., 1912), v. 1, p. 354.

[3]Ibid., p. 357.

[4]Downer, *Eminent Tragedian,* p. 75.

[5]The promptbooks described below are listed in Charles H. Shattuck's *The Shakespeare Promptbooks: A Descriptive Catalogue* (Urbana: University of Illinois Press, 1965). This particular promptbook, Folger 14, is listed in Shattuck as no. 26 (p. 359).

[6]See Charles H. Shattuck, *William Charles Macready's King John* (Urbana: University of Illinois Press, 1962).

[7]Folger Promptbook 15, Shattuck 27. (See note 5 above.)

Venice. Brabantio wears a red robe trimmed with ermine over a black doublet. Gratiano, in contrast, appears in a black robe with red doublet. Othello's red tunic is fringed with gold to match his gold cape. Iago is dressed in a buff doublet with a green vest and gold trim. He wears red hose and black shoes. Later, he changes to buff leggings and a blue jacket. Cassio is foppish. He sports a plumed hat, green vest, and a gold doublet slashed to show red beneath. Lodovico is more decorous in silver and blue, with hat, cape, doublet, and hose. Montano wears a long white gown trimmed in red with a gold sash. The Venetian guard appears in sixteenth-century armor, while servants are appareled in rough brown jackets and doublets. White lace signifies Desdemona's purity, whereas black (with a red underskirt) suggests Emilia's earthiness. Tissue of gold or silver bespeaks an exalted station.

Red, black, gold, white, and blue—the colors create that harmonious effect Macready so cherished. Othello's red aligned him with the Venetian Senators, figures of law and authority. Emilia's red petticoat picks up the color scheme, but *her* scarlet indicates easy virtue. Each scene is chromatically planned, even the bed curtains' labial folds—the shapes and colors, like the acting, should suggest the emotions represented onstage.

The grandeur of Macready's Covent Garden *Othello* is best conveyed by the Senate Council scene (I, iii). Macready's promptbook notes:

> The Senators are discov'd seated on an elevated platform, up the sides, and aX the back of the stage. Ten in Red Gowns- / including the Duke-Gratiano-and Brabantio / aX at back- Thirty- / including Lodovico / - in Black Gowns, with large open ermin'd sleeves, -at sides R & L. - The Duke's seat is slightly elevated above the others.- The Secretary is seated, - writing, and faces the duke.[8]

This scene was the culmination of Macready's search in *Othello* productions for historical accuracy; this was the Doge and his Council as he envisioned it from historical research and his own visits to Venice. Macready even covered the walls of the Doge's Hall with Titians and Tintorettos.[9] He was pleased with the result: his diary of 16 October 1837 exudes that "The Council of Forty was a scene of beautiful effect, one of the most real things I ever saw."[10]

Productions in the provinces and the United States could never be this elaborate, but traveling stars could carry their costumes with them; the Moor, at least, could be seen in appropriate splendor. Even through the swamps of Georgia, from Savannah to Mobile, Macready carted mammoth trunks of resplendent costumes so that he could represent his characters as he envisioned them.

Costumes aside, Macready's careful preparation was often wasted when he left London to play with provincial casts or journeyed to the backwoods of America. Although he was a difficult, egocentric man who often upstaged his fellow actors, as Kean had before him, one can sympathize with the meticulous actor faced with inadequate theatres and poorly prepared casts. In Liverpool, 31 January 1850, Macready found that "The Roderigo, Mr. Brown was

---

[8]Folger Promptbook 13, Shattuck 25.

[9]Julie Hankey, Ed., *Othello* by William Shakespeare (Bristol: Bristol Classical Press, 1987), p. 153.

[10]William Charles Macready, *Macready's Reminiscences: and Selections from His Diaries and Letters*, ed. Sir Frederick Pollock (New York: Harper & Brothers, 1875), p. 416.

drunk!"[11] Later that year in Birmingham, Macready acted with an Othello who "actually *belaboured* [him] in the third act; it was so bad that at last [he] was obliged to resist the gentleman's 'corporal chastisement' and decline his shaking and pummelling!"[12] Perhaps such treatment was Macready's just punishment for rough handling of Desdemonas like Helena Faucit Martin. The wonder is that the perfectionist Macready could act at all with provincial and American casts too reluctant to rehearse and rather short on theatrical talent.

That Macready traveled from city to city, cast to cast, and performed Shakespeare's *Othello* night after night testifies to the uniformity of mid-nineteenth-century productions. As manager at Covent Garden and Drury Lane, Macready supervised his ideal *Othello*, a carefully designed performance in which scenery, costumes, blocking, and acting created a harmonious experience. In the provinces or outside New York and Philadelphia, the council scene might have two Senators instead of forty, but the blocking was substantially the same. So was the text.

A collation of the 1839 Macready acting edition with its predecessors—Mrs. Inchbald's (c. 1808), Kemble's (1814), and Oxberry's (based on Edmund Kean's performances, 1819)—shows that Macready's Covent Garden *Othello* was somewhat more chaste and sensitive to the delicate feelings of his audiences than his predecessors'. Like Oxberry, but unlike Kemble and Inchbald, Macready's Iago makes no reference to "making the beast with two backs." Macready's Senate scene is by design much grander, requiring forty Senators rather than his predecessors' seven. Othello's cannibals and anthropophagi are quietly eliminated in keeping with the hero's dignity. On the Cyprus quay Macready drops Iago's reference to wives as "Players in your housewifery and housewives in your beds" (II, I, 111). Iago's observation that Othello "hath not yet made wanton the night with her . . ." (II, II, 16) is also removed. Instead of "Happiness to their sheets!" Iago cries, "Happiness to them!" In the temptation scene, lines 463 to 467 are cut, whereas Inchbald and Kemble had retained them. Macready and Oxberry also root out the kisses from Cassio's dream. The major cuts from the eighteenth century—clown, Bianca, fit, willow song scene—persist. Macready's fastidiousness climaxes in act IV, scene ii, where he removes "Oh thou weed . . . That the sense aches at thee" (67–69) and "Was this fair paper . . . made to write whore upon" (71–72). He also substitutes the tame "one" for "strumpet" and "whore." In the next scene, Desdemona is not allowed to ask for her nightly apparel. Macready restores the original "Let me the curtains draw" (V, II, 105), probably in reference to stage business. Hankey notes contemporary accounts of Macready's "thrilling effect" of thrusting his dark face through the curtains at Emilia's knock.[13] He closes the play—as Kean had done in performance—with Othello's last words.

Macready's purified text drops, in other words, all references to sheets, beds, going to bed, adultery, and sex. The bed behind half-closed curtains perhaps symbolizes the hidden sexuality underlying the play. While nothing remains in the revised language to offend a Victorian, the subject—adultery—was indeed salacious. Yet *Othello* was popular among all audiences, and no one apparently condemned the plot as immoral.

[11]Toynbee, *Diaries*, vol. II, p. 446.
[12]Ibid., p. 463.
[13]Hankey, *Othello*, p. 317.

Margaret Webster (1905–1972)

SHAKESPEARE WITHOUT TEARS

1942

Margaret Webster directed the notable Broadway performance of Othello *with Paul Robeson in 1943–1944. In this excerpt from her memoirs, she comments on the question of race and its importance to the play. She focuses on Desdemona and her motives in marrying a black man whom her father could not accept. Webster connects this important detail to Othello's "acceptance of the possibility of Desdemona's infidelity."*

The question of Othello's race is of paramount importance to the play. There has been much controversy as to Shakespeare's intention. It is improbable that he troubled himself greatly with ethnological exactness. The Moor, to an Elizabethan, was a blackamoor, an African, an Ethiopian. Shakespeare's other Moor, Aaron, in *Titus Andronicus,* is specifically black; he has thick lips and a fleece of woolly hair. The Prince of Morocco in *The Merchant of Venice* bears "the shadowed livery of the burnished sun," and even Portia recoils from his "complexion" which he himself is at great pains to excuse.

Othello is repeatedly described, both by himself and others, as black; not pale beige, but black; and for a century and a half after the play's first presentation he was so represented on the stage. But after this the close consideration of nice minds began to discern something not quite ladylike about Desdemona's marrying a black man with thick lips. They cannot have been more horrified than Brabantio, her father, who thought that only witchcraft could have caused "nature so preposterously to err," or more convinced of the disastrous outcome of such a match than Iago, who looked upon it as nothing but a "frail vow between an erring Barbarian and a supersubtle Venetian," and declared, with his invincible cynicism, that "when she is sated with his body, she will find the error of her choice: She must have change; she must!"

It is very apparent, and vital to the play, that Othello himself was very conscious of these same considerations and quiveringly aware of what the judgment of the world would be upon his marriage. It is one of the most potent factors in his acceptance of the possibility of Desdemona's infidelity. And she herself loses much in the quality of her steadfastness and courage if it be supposed that she simply married against her father's wishes a man who chanced to be a little darker than his fellows, instead of daring a marriage which would cause universal condemnation among the ladies of polite society. To scamp this consideration in the play is to deprive Othello of his greatest weakness, Desdemona of her highest strength, Iago of his skill and judgment, Emilia of a powerful factor in her behavior both to her master and her mistress, and Venice itself of an arrogance in toleration which was one of the principal hallmarks of its civilization—a civilization which frames, first and last, the soaring emotions of the play.

After these three tragedies, Shakespeare will never again take us into so passion-tossed a world, never set his actors to release themselves so fully from the normal restraints of polite behavior, never pound his audience into submission by the relentless power of words. He will give us a jealous man in Leontes,

Ron Canada as Iago and Patrick Stewart as Othello, in the Shakespeare Theater's 1997–1998 production of *Othello* in Washington, D.C., directed by Jude Kelly. In this version Stewart played Othello with an otherwise all-black cast.

an ambitious one in Octavius, an embittered outcast in Timon, but it will not be the sacrificial jealousy of Othello, the haunted ambition of Macbeth, or the madness of Lear. Nothing that happens in the later plays will carry us beyond the sphere where reason is still a comfortable guide. Nor will man ever again cry with such anguish to the stars to shield him from the unbearable responsibility of the world he has fashioned. The theatre will revert to its normal self, its walls solid and comfortably bounding the two hours' traffic of make-believe. There will be plenty of technical problems to be faced. *Antony and Cleopatra* especially will call for a width and range of vision; many of the plays to come will need adroit and lavish handling. But never again will the hearts of players and audience be so swept with the mystery of life and the bitter release of death.

Ben Jonson

Ben Jonson was known primarily as a writer of comedies such as *Every Man in His Humor* (1598) and *Every Man out of His Humor* (1599) in the reign of Elizabeth I, but his most interesting plays were performed during the reign (called the Jacobean period) of her successor, King James I. *Volpone* (1606) and *The Alchemist* (1610) stand today as Jonson's most often produced plays. Both are broad comedies: *Volpone* plays on the foxiness of a dying man who is eager to see which of his heirs is worthy, and *The Alchemist* is a satire on the wiliness of con men who pretend to know how to transmute base metal into gold. All of these plays were highly regarded in Jacobean times. In addition to his comedies, Jonson's tragedies *Sejanus* (1603) and *Catiline* (1611) earned him the description of "best in tragedy" from a contemporary who maintained a diary devoted to his experiences in the theater.

Jonson led an exciting life. Born after his father died, he was placed in the Westminster School at the expense of its master, William Camden, author of the famous survey *Britannia*. There Jonson learned Latin and Greek, but he himself said that instead of attending a university, he practiced his trade. Because Jonson's stepfather was a bricklayer, it has been assumed that Jonson learned that trade. He eventually grew tired of bricklaying and managed to get a job as an actor. In 1598, while a member of Philip Henslowe's theater, he killed a fellow actor in a brawl. He claimed self-defense and was granted "benefit of clergy," which was accorded those who could read and translate a Latin passage, but as punishment he carried a brand on his thumb from Tyburn, the place of execution and punishment, for the rest of his life.

For Jonson the stage was a way of making a living. He aspired to be a pure poet and was accorded great honor in his lifetime by other poets. But he could not, even with the patronage of important noblemen, eke out a sufficient living writing only poetry. Jonson was imprisoned in Elizabeth's reign for writing an offensive play, *The Isle of Dogs* (1597), and in the early years of King James's reign, which began on March 24, 1603, play writing continued to be dangerous. Toward the end of 1605, Jonson teamed with George Chapman and William Marston to write *Eastward Ho!*, a comedy that ridiculed the Scots (James I was a Scot). Jonson and Chapman were imprisoned, but Jonson eventually contacted enough important people to secure his release, probably in October, claiming that the few offensive lines had been written by Marston, who had fled London to avoid prison. Then in November the great Gunpowder Plot—remembered today with bonfires on November 5, Guy Fawkes Day—cast a dangerous shadow over him. Led by the Catholic conspirator Guy Fawkes, the Gunpowder Plot was a plan to kill the king, his advisors, and all members of the hierarchy of the Church and Parliament. Guy Fawkes's use of the pseudonym John Johnson, together with Jonson's conversion to Catholicism, may have resulted in the playwright's becoming a suspect. Luckily, he was well known in James's court and was able to demonstrate his loyalty and innocence.

For most of his life Jonson made his living by writing for the public stage, but he was by no means always successful. Although many of his plays are today regarded as among the most important of the late Renaissance, tastes changed during his lifetime, and by the end of his life he found himself no longer in vogue.

Jonson won considerable acclaim as a writer in the court of James I and Queen Anne. He composed entertainments and masques designed to be associated with important state occasions. The masque was a dramatic form that enjoyed great popularity for close to a century and a half. It was restricted to the entertainment and participation of royalty and courtiers. As its name implies, characters were sometimes masked to represent abstract ideas such as Blackness or Beauty or mythic characters such as Albion, an allegory for England itself.

Inigo Jones (1573–1652), brought to court by Queen Anne, collaborated with Jonson to make the Jacobean masque a dazzling spectacle. Jones was a painter and architect who had traveled abroad and returned to England with members of Anne's court when Anne ascended the British throne. He was responsible for designing costumes, scenery, special effects, and lighting. He introduced Italian theater machinery and techniques into his entertainments. The Jacobean masque was elaborate, sensational, and so enormously expensive that it is said to have contributed to the impoverishment of the crown inherited by James's successor, Charles I.

THE MASQUE OF BLACKNESS

Apparently dissatisfied with Samuel Daniel, the poet and writer who had produced the first masque for her court, Queen Anne turned to Ben Jonson and asked him to create a masque in which she and some of her court ladies could paint themselves black and pretend to be Moors. The source for her inspiration is unclear, but she may have encountered African emissaries in London or otherwise been aware of the presence of numerous Africans in London. During the later years of her reign, Queen Elizabeth felt there were too many black Africans in London and ordered them sent abroad. James does not seem to have followed her example.

The Masque of Blackness was the first of Ben Jonson's many masques. It was performed January 6, 1605, in the same theater and around the same time as *Othello*. Inigo Jones's machinery impressed the audience, which included foreign emissaries, such as the Venetian and Spanish ambassadors. Sir Dudley Carleton, present at the performance, was not pleased that the queen and her attendants had painted themselves black. He feared that kissing the hands of the masquers might blacken his face. He may have been familiar with earlier royal entertainments in which black characters were represented with long black gloves and black cloth masks.

Jonson's opening description of the setting is extensive because in masques the costumes and imaginative figures took on great importance. But his text is also ingenious. Given the assignment to produce a masque for blackamoors, he invented the conceit that "the Ethiops were as fair / As other dames, now black with black despair." Hence, the narrative moves these figures toward recovering their original brightness by seeking a nation whose name ends in "*-tania*" and residing there for thirteen days. Their journey takes them to Mauretania, Lusitania, and Aquitania, but none of those nations can avail them. Finally, Britannia fulfills their desire, and the masque ends with the prospect of their remaining another twelve nights.

The daughters of Niger are described as beautiful women, all the more beautiful because of their black skin and hair, but in Jonson's masque they encounter a Eurocentric point of view expressed by "some few / Poor brainsick men" who convince them that they should be "fair." The word "fair" in Elizabethan English means primarily beautiful, but it also means light in color. The point of the masque is to emphasize the beauty of the daughters (who are played by the queen and her attendants) and to restore them to their original fairness.

One important feature of the masque is the representation of figures in an allegorical fashion. In other words, Oceanus is not a psychologically real character but a figure who represents the ocean. Niger is the river, Aethiopia the nation. All the characters in the masque follow this pattern. When the queen and her attendants dance (line 302), they assume allegorical identities. The queen is Euphoris, or Happiness, and her symbol is a "golden tree laden with fruit." The dance that the queen and her attendants perform is the highlight of the masque, and the courtiers who participated felt it to be a joyful and exciting occasion.

The Masque of Blackness, like all Jacobean masques, was a multimedia event, like a modern "happening." The lines of dialogue are carefully crafted and the narrative suitably dramatic. But it is the music, the song, the dance, and the machinery of the setting—the rocking and moving seashell and the sudden appearances of characters—that make the masque successful and impressive. As far as we know, masques such as this were not performed more than once or twice, partly because of expense and partly because of the demand for novelty in a relatively small court.

The speaking characters were played by professional actors, but all the other roles were drawn from the court. That way the poetry could be heard and the drama maintained without stressing the courtiers, who would have had, with very few exceptions, no aspirations toward the stage.

The Masque of Blackness in Performance

Since the masque is preeminently a performance piece, we must credit the spectacle over the poetry and dialogue. Even Jonson, early in his collaboration, pays homage to Inigo Jones's innovations in the masque. Sir Dudley Carleton, who was present at the performance in the old banqueting house, had much to say about it. His comments help us imagine the scene:

> On Twelfth-Day . . . at night, we had the Queen's masque in the Banqueting House, or rather her pageant. There was a great engine at the lower end of the room, which had

Inigo Jones, Costume for a Nymph, Daughter of Niger. Jonson described the masquers: "The attire of [the] *Masquers* was alike, in all, without difference: the colors, *azure,* and *silver;* (their hair thick, and curled upright in tresses, like *Pyramids*), but returned on the top with a scroll and antique dressing of feathers, and jewels interlaced with ropes of pearl. And, for the front, ear, neck, and wrists, the ornament was of the most choice and orient pearl; best setting off from the black."

motion, and in it were the images of sea horses, with other terrible fishes, which were ridden by Moors; the indecorum was, that there was all fish and no water. At the further end was a great shell in the form of a scallop, wherein were four seats; on the lowest sat the Queen with my lady Bedford; on the rest were placed the ladies . . . their apparel was rich, but too courtesan-like for such great ones. Instead of vizards, their faces, and arms up to elbows, were painted black, which was disguise sufficient, for they were hard to be known; *but it became them nothing so well as their own red and white, and you cannot imagine a more ugly sight than a troop of lean-cheeked Moors.* The Spanish and Venetian Ambassadors were both present, and sat by the King in state; at which Monsieur Beaumont [the French ambassador] quarrels so extremely that he saith the whole court is Spanish . . . the night's work was concluded with a banquet in the great chamber, which was so seriously assaulted that down went tables and trestles before one bit was touched.

Masques are occasionally performed today but in nothing like their original form. The costs for the *Masque of Blackness* exceeded £3,000, a fortune of hundreds of thousands of dollars in today's money.

Ben Jonson (1572–1637)

THE MASQUE OF BLACKNESS

1605

List of Characters

OCEANUS
NIGER
AETHIOPIA
TRITONS, SEA-MAIDS, NYMPHS, THE DAUGHTERS OF
   NIGER, *and* OCEANIAE

The honor and splendor of these spectacles was such in the performance as, could those hours have lasted, this of mine now had been a most unprofitable work. But, when it is the fate even of the greatest and most
5 absolute° births to need and borrow a life of posterity, little had been done to the study of magnificence° in these° if presently with the rage of the people, who, as a part of greatness, are privileged by custom to deface their carcases,° the spirits had also perished. In duty,
10 therefore, to that majesty who gave them their authority and grace, and, no less than the most royal of predecessors, deserves eminent celebration for these solemnities, I add this later hand to redeem them° as well from ignorance as envy, two common evils, the one of censure, the
15 other of oblivion.

Pliny, Solinus, Ptolemy, and of late Leo the African, remember° unto us a river in Ethiopia famous by the name of Niger, of which the people were called *Nigritae*, now Negroes, and are the blackest nation of the world.
20 This river taketh spring out of a certain lake,° eastward, and after a long race falleth into the western ocean. Hence, because it was her majesty's will to have them° blackamores at first, the invention° was derived by me, and presented thus.

25 *First, for the scene, was drawn a Landtschap° consisting of small woods, and here and there a void place filled with huntings;° which falling,° an artificial sea was seen to shoot forth, as if it flowed to the land, raised with waves which seemed to move, and in some places*
30 *the billow to break, as imitating that orderly disorder which is common in nature. In front of this sea were placed six tritons in moving and sprightly actions, their*

upper parts human, save that their hairs were blue, as partaking of the sea color, their desinent° parts fish, mounted above their heads, and all varied in disposi-
35 *tion.° From their backs were borne out certain light pieces of taffeta as if carried by the wind, and their music made out of wreathed shells. Behind these a pair of sea-maids, for song, were as conspicuously seated; between which two great sea-horses, as big as the life, put*
40 *forth themselves, the one mounting aloft and writhing his head from the other, which seemed to sink forwards (so intended for variation, and that the figure behind might come off better); upon their backs Oceanus and Niger were advanced.*

45 *Oceanus presented in a human form, the color of his flesh blue, and shadowed° with a robe of sea-green; his head grey and horned, as he is described by the ancients; his beard of the like mixed color. He was garlanded with algae, or sea-grass, and in his hand a trident.*
50 *Niger in form and color of an Ethiop, his hair and rare° beard curled, shadowed with a blue and bright mantle; his front,° neck and wrists adorned with pearl; and crowned with an artificial wreath of cane and paper-rush.°*
55 *These induced° the masquers, which were twelve nymphs, Negroes, and the daughters of Niger, attended by so many of the Oceaniae,° which were their light-bearers.*

The masquers were placed in a great concave shell
60 *like mother of pearl, curiously° made to move on those waters and rise with the billow; the top thereof was stuck with a chevron of lights which, indented to the proportion of the shell, struck a glorious beam upon them as they were seated one above another; so that*
65 *they were all seen, but in an extravagant° order.*

On sides of the shell did swim six huge sea-monsters, varied in their shape and dispositions,° bearing on their backs the twelve torch-bearers, who were planted there in several greces,° so as the backs of some were seen,
70 *some in purfle,° or side, others in face; and all having their lights burning out of whelks or murex shells.*

The attire of the masquers was alike in all, without difference: the colors, azure and silver; their hair thick and curled upright in tresses, like pyramids, but re-
75

---

5. absolute: Perfect; here, noble. 6. magnificence: According to Aristotle, the virtue of monarchs. 7. these: I.e., masques. 7–9. people . . . carcases: At the end of the masque, the audience was traditionally permitted to tear down the scenery and plunder the decorations. 13. them: The "spirits" of line 9. 17. remember: Mention. 20. lake: Lake Chad. 22. them: The masquers. invention: Device of the masque. 25. Landtschap: Landscape. 27. huntings: Animals hunting their prey. which falling: The landscape-curtain was released from above, and fell to the floor in front of the stage to reveal the scene.

34. desinent: Terminal. 35–36. disposition: Arrangement. 47. shadowed: Covered. 52. rare: Thin. 53. front: Forehead. 55. paper-rush: Papyrus. 56. induced: Brought in. 58. Oceaniae: Sea nymphs, daughters of Oceanus. 61. curiously: Artfully. 66. extravagant: (1) Unusual; (2) moving about in an extraordinary way. 68. dispositions: Positions. 70. greces: Steps. 71. purfle: Profile.

*turned on the top with a scroll and antique dressing
of feathers and jewels interlaced with ropes of pearl.
And for the front,° ear, neck and wrists, the ornament
was of the most choice and orient pearl, best setting off*
80 *from the black.*

*For the light-bearers, sea-green, waved about the
skirts with gold and silver; their hair loose and flowing,
garlanded with sea-grass, and that stuck with branches
of coral.*

85 *These thus presented,° the scene behind seemed a
vast sea, and united with this that flowed forth, from
the termination or horizon of which (being the level of
the state,° which was placed in the upper end of the
hall) was drawn, by the lines of perspective, the whole*
90 *work shooting downwards from the eye; which decorum made it more conspicuous, and caught the eye afar
off with a wandering beauty. To which was added an
obscure and cloudy night-piece that made the whole set
off. So much for the bodily part, which was of Master*
95 *Inigo Jones° his design and act.*

*By this,° one of the tritons, with the two sea-maids,
began to sing to the others' loud music, their voices
being a tenor and two trebles.°*

SONG:
    Sound, sound aloud
100   The welcome of the orient flood
    Into the west;
    Fair Niger, son to great Oceanus,
    Now honored thus,
    With all his beauteous race,
105 Who, though but black in face,
    Yet are they bright,
    And full of life and light,
    To prove that beauty best
    Which not the color but the feature°
110   Assures unto the creature.
OCEANUS: Be silent now the ceremony's done,
    And Niger, say, how comes it, lovely son,
    That thou, the Ethiop's river, so far east,
    Art seen to fall into th'extremest west
115 Of me, the king of floods, Oceanus,
    And in mine empire's heart salute me thus?
    My ceaseless current now amazèd stands
    To see thy labor through so many lands
    Mix thy fresh billow with my brackish stream,
120 And in thy sweetness stretch thy diadem
    To these far distant and unequalled skies,
    This squarèd circle of celestial bodies.°
NIGER: Divine Oceanus, 'tis not strange at all
    That, since the immortal souls of creatures mortal

Mix with their bodies, yet reserve forever   125
A power of separation, I should sever
My fresh streams from thy brackish, like things
    fixed,
Though with thy powerful saltness thus far mixed.
Virtue, though chained to earth, will still live free,
And hell itself must yield to industry.°   130
OCEANUS: But what's the end of thy herculean labors
    Extended to these calm and blessèd shores?
NIGER: To do a kind and careful father's part,
    In satisfying every pensive heart
    Of these my daughters, my most lovèd birth: 135
    Who, though they were the first formed dames of
        earth,
    And in whose sparkling and refulgent eyes
    The glorious sun did still delight to rise;
    Though he—the best judge and most formal cause°
    Of all dames' beauties—in their firm hues draws 140
    Signs of his fervent'st love, and thereby shows
    That in their black° the perfect'st beauty grows,
    Since the fixed color of their curlèd hair,
    Which is the highest grace of dames most fair,
    No cares, no age can change, or there display   145
    The fearful tincture of abhorrèd grey,
    Since Death herself (herself being pale and blue)
    Can never alter their most faithful hue;
    All which are arguments to prove how far
    Their beauties conquer in great beauty's war,   150
    And more, how near divinity they be
    That stand from passion or decay so free.
    Yet since the fabulous voices of some few
    Poor brainsick men, styled poets here with you,
    Have with such envy of their graces sung   155
    The painted beauties other empires sprung,
    Letting their loose and wingèd fictions fly
    To infect all climates, yea, our purity;
    As of one Phaëton,° that fired the world,
    And that before his heedless flames were hurled   160
    About the globe, the Ethiops were as fair
    As other dames, now black with black despair;
    And in respect of their complexions changed,
    Are eachwhere since for luckless creatures ranged.
    Which when my daughters heard, as women are   165
    Most jealous of their beauties, fear and care
    Possessed them° whole; yea, and believing them,
    They wept such ceaseless tears into my stream
    That it hath thus far overflowed his shore
    To seek them patience, who have since e'ermore   170
    As the sun riseth charged his burning throne

78. front: Forehead.   **85. presented:** Having been presented.
87–88. level . . . state: Height of the royal throne.   **95. Inigo
Jones** (1573–1652): Architect and stage designer, Jonson's
collaborator throughout his career as court masque writer.
96. this: This time.   **98. trebles:** Sopranos.   **109. feature:**
Form.   **122. squarèd . . . bodies:** I.e., heavenly bodies perfectly transformed into an earthly realm.

130. hell . . . industry: From Horace, Odes I, iii, 36: "herculean effort overcame hell"; alluded to in the next line.
139. formal cause: Creator of the form or essence; Aristotelian
terminology.   **142. black:** Synonymous with ugly in Elizabethan English.   **159. Phaëton:** Son of Phoebus Apollo, the
sun god. He was allowed to drive the chariot of the sun, but
could not control the horses, and Zeus destroyed him lest he set
the world afire.   **167. them:** The poets. (Jonson)

With volleys of revilings, 'cause he shone
On their scorched cheeks with such intemperate
    fires,
And other dames made queens of all desires.
175 To frustrate which strange error oft I sought,
Though most in vain, against a settled thought
As women's are, till they confirmed at length
By miracle what I with so much strength
Of argument resisted; else they feigned.
180 For in the lake where their first spring they gained,
As they sat cooling their soft limbs one night,
Appeared a face all circumfused with light—
And sure they saw't, for Ethiops never dream—
Wherein they might decipher through the stream
185 These words:

That they a land must forthwith seek
Whose termination, of the Greek,
Sounds -tania; where bright Sol,° that heat
Their bloods, doth never rise or set,
190 But in his journey passeth by,
And leaves that climate of the sky
To comfort of a greater light,
Who forms all beauty with his sight.

In search of this have we three princedoms passed
195 That speak out -tania in their accents last;
Black Mauretania° first, and secondly
Swarth° Lusitania;° next we did descry
Rich Aquitania,° and yet cannot find
The place unto these longing nymphs designed.°
200 Instruct and aid me, great Oceanus:
What land is this that now appears to us?
OCEANUS: This land that lifts into the temperate air
His snowy cliff is Albion° the fair,
So called of Neptune's son, who ruleth here;
205 For whose dear guard, myself four thousand year,
Since old Deucalion's° days, have walked the round
About his empire, proud to see him crowned
Above my waves.

At this the moon was discovered in the upper part of
210 *the house, triumphant in a silver throne made in figure*
of a pyramis.° Her garments white and silver, the dress-
ing of her head antique, and crowned with a luminary,
or sphere of light, which striking on the clouds, and
heightened with silver, reflected as natural clouds do by
215 *the splendor of the moon. The heaven about her was*
vaulted with blue silk and set with stars of silver which
had in them their several lights burning. The sudden
sight of which made Niger to interrupt Oceanus with
this present° passion.

NIGER: O see, our silver star! 220
Whose pure, auspicious light greets us thus far!
Great Aethiopia,° goddess of our shore,
Since with particular worship we adore
Thy general brightness, let particular grace
Shine on my zealous daughters: show the place 225
Which long their longings urged their eyes to see.
Beautify them, which long have deified thee.
AETHIOPIA: Niger, be glad; resume thy native cheer.
Thy daughters' labors have their period° here,
And so thy errors.° I was that bright face 230
Reflected by the lake, in which thy race
Read mystic lines; which skill Pythagoras
First taught to men by a reverberate° glass.°
This blessèd isle doth with that -tania end,
Which there they saw inscribed, and shall extend 235
Wished satisfaction to their best desires.
Britannia, which the triple world° admires,
This isle hath now recovered for her name,°
Where reign those beauties that with so much fame
The sacred muses' sons have honorèd, 240
And from bright Hesperus° to Eos° spread.
With that great name Britannia, this blessed isle
Hath won her ancient dignity and style,°
A world divided from the world, and tried
The abstract of it in his general pride.° 245
For were the world with all his wealth a ring,
Britannia, whose new name° makes all tongues sing,
Might be a diamond worthy to enchase° it,
Ruled by a sun that to this height doth grace it,
Whose beams shine day and night, and are of force 250
To blanch an Ethiop, and revive a corse.°
His light sciential° is, and, past mere nature,
Can salve the rude defects of every creature.
    Call forth thy honored daughters, then,
    And let them, 'fore the Britain men, 255
Indent° the land with those pure traces°
They flow with in their native graces.
Invite them boldly to the shore;
Their beauties shall be scorched no more;
This sun is temperate, and refines 260
All things on which his radiance shines.

222. **Aethiopia:** The moon goddess. 229. **period:** End.
230. **errors:** With a quibble on "wanderings." 233. **reverberate:** Reflecting. 232–33. **Pythagoras . . . glass:** Pythagoras was supposedly able to reflect messages onto the moon by writing in blood on a mirror. 237. **triple world:** Heaven, earth, and the underworld. 238. **recovered . . . name:** See line 247 and gloss. 241. **Hesperus:** Evening, the west. **Eos:** Dawn, the east. 243. **style:** Characterization. 244–45. **tried . . . pride:** Experienced the ideal of it through England's own pride in herself. "His" refers to England, despite "her" two lines earlier. 247. **new name:** The name Great Britain was coined when James VI of Scotland became king also of England and Wales in 1604. It was not officially adopted, however, until 1707. 248. **enchase:** Set in. 251. **corse:** Corpse. 252. **sciential:** Endowed with the powers of science. 256. **Indent:** Leave footprints on. **traces:** Footsteps.

188. **Sol:** The sun. 196. **Mauretania:** The land of the Moors, including modern Morocco and part of Algeria. 197. **Swarth:** Swarthy. **Lusitania:** Portugal and western Spain. 198. **Aquitania:** Southwestern France. 199. **designed:** Indicated. 203. **Albion:** Traditional poetic name for England. 206. **Deucalion:** A Greek Noah, survivor of the universal flood. 211. **pyramis:** Pyramid. 219. *present:* Immediate.

Here the tritons sounded, and they danced on shore, every couple as they advanced severally presenting their fans, in one of which were inscribed their mixed names, in the other a mute hieroglyphic expressing their mixed qualities. (Which manner of symbol I rather chose than imprese,° as well for strangeness as relishing of antiquity, and more applying to that original doctrine of sculpture which the Egyptians are said first to have brought from the Ethiopians.)

	The names	The symbols
The queen	*Euphoris*°	A golden tree° laden with fruit.
1.		
Countess of Bedford	*Aglaia*°	
Lady Herbert	*Diaphane*°	The figure icosa-hedron° of crystal.
2.		
Countess of Derby	*Eucampse*°	
Lady Rich	*Ocyte*°	A pair of naked feet in a river.°
3.		
Countess of Suffolk	*Kathare*°	
Lady Bevill	*Notis*°	The salamander° simple.
4.		
Lady Effingham	*Psychrote*°	
Lady Elizabeth Howard	*Glycyte*°	A cloud full of rain,° dropping.
5.		
Lady Susan de Vere	*Malacia*°	
Lady Wroth	*Baryte*°	An urn, sphered with wine.°
6.		
Lady Walsingham	*Periphere*°	

The names of the Oceaniae were: *Doris, Petraea, Ocyrhoe, Cydippe, Glauce, Tyche, Beroe, Acaste, Clytia, Ianthe, Lycoris, Plexaure.*

---

267. **imprese:** Emblems.   272. *Euphoris:* Abundance.   **golden tree:** Symbol of fertility.   274. *Aglaia:* Splendor.   275. *Diaphane:* Transparent.   276. **icosahedron:** A twenty-sided figure symbolizing water.   277. *Eucampse:* Flexibility.   278. **Ocyte:** Swiftness.   279. **naked . . . river:** Symbolizing purity.   280. *Kathare:* Spotless.   281. *Notis:* Moisture.   **salamander:** Which is not harmed by fire and can extinguish it.   283. **Psychrote:** Coldness.   284. *Glycyte:* Sweetness.   284–85. **cloud . . . rain:** Symbolizing education.   286. *Malacia:* Delicacy.   287. *Baryte:* Weight.   287–88. **urn . . . wine:** Obscure, but the whole symbolizes the globe of earth.   289. *Periphere:* Revolving, circular.

Their own single dance ended, as they were about to make choice of their men, one from the sea was heard to call 'em with this charm, sung by a tenor voice.   295

SONG:
Come away, come away,
We grow jealous of your stay;
If you do not stop your ear,
We shall have more cause to fear
Sirens of the land, than they   300
To doubt the sirens of the sea.

Here they danced with their men several measures° and corantos.° All which ended, they were again accited° to sea with a song of two trebles,° whose cadences were iterated by a double echo from several parts of the land.   305

SONG:
                    Daughters of the subtle flood,
                        Do not let earth longer entertain you;
1ST ECHO: Let earth longer entertain you.
2ND ECHO: Longer entertain you.
                        'Tis to them enough of good   310
                    That you give this little hope to gain you.
1ST ECHO: Give this little hope to gain you.
2ND ECHO: Little hope to gain you.
                    If they love,
                        You shall quickly see;   315
                    For when to flight you move,
                    They'll follow you, the more you flee.
1ST ECHO: Follow you, the more you flee.
2ND ECHO: The more you flee.
                    If not, impute it each to other's matter;   320
                    They are but earth—
1ST ECHO: But earth,
2ND ECHO: Earth—
                                And what you vowed was water.
1ST ECHO: And what you vowed was water.   325
2ND ECHO: You vowed was water.
AETHIOPIA: Enough, bright nymphs, the night grows old,
And we are grieved we cannot hold
You longer light; but comfort take.
Your father only to the lake   330
Shall make return; yourselves, with feasts,
Must here remain the Ocean's guests.
Nor shall this veil the sun hath cast
Above your blood more summers last;
For which, you shall observe these rites: 335
Thirteen times thrice, on thirteen nights
(So often as I fill my sphere
With glorious light throughout the year),
You shall, when all things else do sleep
Save your chaste thoughts, with reverence steep   340

---

302. *measures:* Slow dances.   303. *corantos:* Dances with a running or gliding step.   **accited:** Summoned.   304. *trebles:* Sopranos.

Your bodies in that purer brine
And wholesome dew called rosmarine;°
Then with that soft and gentler° foam,
Of which the ocean yet yields some,
345   Whereof bright Venus, beauty's queen,
Is said to have begotten been,
You shall your gentler limbs o'er-lave,
And for your pains perfection have;
So that, this night, the year gone round,°
350   You do again salute this ground,
And in the beams of yond' bright sun
Your faces dry, and all is done.

*At which, in a dance they returned to the sea, where
they took their shell, and with this full song went out.*

---

342. rosmarine: Sea dew.   **343. gentler:** Very gentle.   **349. year
. . . round:** The sequel, however, was not produced until 1608.

Song:
Now Dian° with her burning face   355
   Declines apace,
   By which our waters know
   To ebb, that late did flow.
Back seas, back nymphs, but with a forward grace
   Keep, still, your reverence to the place;   360
And shout with joy of favor you have won
   In sight of Albion, Neptune's son.

*So ended the first masque, which, beside the singular
grace of music and dances, had that success in the nobility of performance as nothing needs to the illustration   365
but the memory by whom it was personated.*

---

355. Dian: The moon.

COMMENTARY

Eldred Jones (b. 1925)
AFRICA IN ENGLISH MASQUE AND PAGEANTRY   *1965*

In his book, Othello's Countrymen *(1965), Eldred Jones offers an extensive review
of the appearance of Africans in English entertainments. While the heyday of the
masque form is brief, it offered numerous opportunities to portray Africans even
before Ben Jonson's* Masque of Blackness. *What Jones demonstrates is that the traditions and attitudes depicted in the masques were deeply ingrained in English culture. Jonson relied on tradition as he developed his material.*

The English masque had only a short vogue. From its emergence as a distinct art
form with a name of its own, to its disappearance as a significant form, the period
stretches over less than a century and a half. Reckoning from the days when by the
combined efforts of Ben Jonson and Inigo Jones the masque rose to its final form,
the period shrinks to a little over three decades. But from its earliest beginnings to
its disappearance, figures from Africa frequently contributed to the splendor and
strangeness of both the spectacle and the poetry of the masque. Like the form itself,
these African figures were at first vague and ill-defined, bearing little relevance to
any overall theme, and frequently having no connection with Africa except in
name. But later, as the masque took a settled form, they became more defined and
more deliberately related both to their supposed place of origin and to the themes
of the masques in which they appeared. For instance, figures which in the earliest

masques would have been described as "Moors" or "Blackamoors" appear in Jonson's *Masque of Blacknesse* as the "Daughters of Niger" against a background of both ancient and modern authorities: "Pliny, Solinus, Ptolemy, and of late Leo the African."

Whatever may have been the character or the strength of the stimulus which the English masque undoubtedly received from Renaissance Italy, certain of its features are to be found in activities which had been part of English life since medieval times. The dance was the nucleus around which the other features of the masque came to be established, and dancing, especially the dance called "Morisce" or "Morisco," had been an essential part of English medieval village festivals from earliest times. One of the customs associated with Morris dancing was the blackening of the faces of the participants. This tradition of blackening was also a feature of other popular activities in medieval England. The folk processions, the sword dance, and the folk drama all show an employment of the grotesque of which blackening was only one feature.

One of the most interesting characters in the medieval mummers play was the king of Egypt, who had a black face and who was accepted by tradition as the father of St. George. The devils in the mystery plays were also usually portrayed as black, and indeed some local traditions required all the participants in the mummers play to have black faces. The term "Moriscoe" (with its associations with "Moor" and "Morocco") and the king of Egypt also suggest a possible link between the English medieval dramatic tradition and Africa.

The practice of blackening was transferred to the more sophisticated court "disguisings" of the sixteenth century. In the earliest surviving description of a courtly festivity which involved blackening, the terms "Egipcians," "Moreskoes," and "blacke Moors" appear. In this masquelike performance in 1510, Henry VIII and the Earl of Essex had come in "appareled after Turkey fashion," while "the torchebearers were appareyled in Crymosyn satyne and grene, lyke Moreskoes, their faces blacke. . . ." Later in the same proceedings, six ladies also appeared "their heads rouled in plesauntes and typpers lyke the Egipcians, embroudered with gold. Their faces, neckes, armes and handes, covered with fyne plesaunce blacke . . . so that the same ladies seemed to be nigrost [sic] or blacke Mores." In this festivity, as in earlier entertainments of this kind, the black characters were merely decorative. The strangeness of their appearance had an exotic impact, and that was all that was required at that time. But it was this tradition which, continuing, made Queen Anne request Ben Jonson to make the characters in his masque of 1605 "Black-mores at first."

The Elizabethan outdoor pageant also frequently employed "Moors," and here again this use seems to have been linked with the use of grotesque characters in the medieval pageant. A king of Moors appeared in a pageant undertaken by the London drapers in 1522, and a surviving list of expenses in connection with it gives some indication of his function. The relevant entry records

> payment of 5s. to John Wakelyn, for playing the king of Moors, (the company finding him his apparell, his stage, and wyld fire).

Robert Withington, who notes this entry, draws the interesting conclusion that the "wyld fire" seems to connect the king of Moors here with the "wild man" or "green man" whose function in medieval pageantry was to clear a way through the crowd for the procession by using "wyld-fire" or fireworks. The king of Moors seems then to have crept into the later "procession" or "entertainment" as a grotesque character, to compel the crowds back by his strange appearance and his use of fireworks. (Individual items of the king's costume suggest that his appearance was spectacular: "the said king's girdle, his garland or turban of white feathers and black satin, sylver paper for his shoes, &c.") In later outdoor pageants this crude function was refined so that the "Moor" or "king of Moors" appeared as a principal speaking character, often acting as the Presenter. In George Peele's pageant of 1585, for instance, the Presenter is described as "him that rid on a luzern before the Pageant, apparelled like a Moor." In Middleton's *Triumph of Truth* (1613) and Anthony Munday's *Chrysanaleia* (1616) similarly important functions were reserved for a Moor.

The popularity of Moors in masques can be judged by the number of references in surviving records either to masques specifically called masques of Moors, or to masques involving such characters, during the reigns of Edward VI, Elizabeth, and James I. The charges for a "Masque of Young Moors" given during Shrovetide 1547, in which King Edward took part, make very interesting reading, for they give illuminating information about the costuming of these characters. The blackening was effected through the use of black gloves, nether stockings, and face masks. These items are mentioned in the long list of charges: "To Rychard Lees of London mercer for viij yards d. of black vellett for gloves above thelbow for mores . . ."; "To hughe Eston the kynges hosyer for the makyng of xiiij peyres of nether stockes of lether black for mores"; a payment to "Nycholas modena straynger . . . for the trymyng Coloring and lyning of xvj vezars or maskes for moores." Some attempt was made to disguise the hair by giving the Moors "Cappes made with Cowrse budge." The elaborate costumes included "belles to hange at the skyrtes of the mores garments" and "dartes with brode heddes and ffethers of sylver. . . ." During the same reign, the accounts show that there was a masque involving Moors on 6 January 1551 and a masque of female Moors at Christmas 1551.

The accounts relating to the reign of Philip and Mary do not refer to any Moors in masques. In view of the apparent popularity of Moors in masques during Edward's reign, and the fact that a year after Elizabeth's accession they seem to have resumed their popularity and continued to hold it up to and during the reign of James I, this seems to indicate a significant temporary change of taste. One is led to speculate on whether portrayals of Moors were suspended out of deference to Philip, who, having had closer dealings with Moors, may have felt touchier on the subject than English monarchs.

Whatever the reasons were for the disappearance of Moors from masques during the reign of Philip and Mary, they reappeared in all their grandeur soon after Queen Elizabeth's accession. An inventory (dated 27 April 1560) of the wardrobe of the Office of the Revels refers to a masque of six Barbarians, and a masque of six Moors. The masque of Barbarians was performed on 1 January 1560, according to a note in the inventory, while the masque of Moors whose date is less certain is placed by E. K. Chambers on 29 January 1559.

There are no more references to masques involving African characters until 1579. (The records of the intervening years are either lost or are very incomplete.) But even this one masque referred to was not performed, although a Willyam Lyzard was paid "for patorns for the mores maske that should have served on Shrovetuesday." There are no other references to masques with Africans in Queen Elizabeth's reign.

Before we encounter our next Africans in masques, early in the reign of James I, a remarkable transformation had taken place. The masque had borrowed from the pageants and processions the use of poetry, and this new form had been employed by the gentlemen of the Inns of Court in their *Gesta Grayorum* (1595). Thus when the masque emerges under James I it emerges as a new form, a form worthy to engage the minds of serious poets. For a short while the English masque flourished as a serious art.

Queen Anne, who was to take a leading part in Ben Jonson's first court masque, expressed a wish "to have them [the masquers] Black-mores at first." This was not in itself a strange request. Now, however, more was involved than mere dressing-up. There had to be a poetic theme which would justify the introduction of black characters. It was therefore logical that Jonson should choose an African theme. His masquers thus emerged as "twelve Nymphs, Negro's, and the daughters of Niger . . ." since Negroes were "the blackest nation of the world." Niger himself was "in forme and colour of an Aethiope; his haire, and rare beard curled. . . ."

Around these characters Jonson weaves an ingenious story, using, whenever he so required, the fictions of the ancients to augment the fruits of his own imagination. The result is an engaging fable. The daughters of Niger had suddenly discovered, while reading Ovid, that they were not, after all, the most beautiful creatures in the world, and that their present color was the result of Phaeton's action:

> And, that, before his heedlesse flames were hurld
> About the Globe, the Aethiopes were as faire,
> As other Dames . . .

The now disillusioned and distracted girls cursed the sun for disfiguring them ("A custome of the Aethiopes, notable in Herod[otus] and Diod[orus] Sic[ulus]. See Plinie Nat. Hist. Lib. 5, cap. 8," adds a helpful Jonson) until they saw in a vision ("for Aethiopes never dreame") that they would recover their beauty if they traveled to a land with the termination "Tania." After passing through "'blacke Mauritania, Swarth Lusitania and Rich Aquitania," they arrive in Britannia, the end of their quest. Here the beams of a "Sunne" (James),

> are of force
> To blanch an Aethiope, and revive a Cor's [sic].

All they had to do was to bathe thirteen nights in the ocean, and they would gain whiteness and beauty.

Jonson, once he had hit on the idea of black characters, wove both the poetry and, insofar as he controlled Inigo Jones, costume and scenery around them. The costumes and setting were carefully based on pale colors — silver and azure — with "jewells interlaced with ropes of pearle . . . best setting off from the black." The poetry is shot through with contrasts — light and darkness, black and white, death and life, the sun and the moon, and, by total implication, Africa and Europe. Niger's daughters for instance are thus described:

> Who, though but blacke in face,
> Yet, are they bright,
> And full of life and light.

In what must have been a *tour de force* in Elizabethan ears, Niger maintains that the black complexion is the most beautiful:

> That, in their black, the perfectst beauty growes;
> Since the fix't colour of their curled haire,
> (Which is the highest grace of dames most faire)
> No cares, no age can change; or there display
> The fearefull tincture of abhorred *Gray*;
> Since *Death* her selfe (her selfe being pale and blue)
> Can never alter their most faithfull hiew.

Nothing as intricately harmonized as *The Masque of Blacknesse* had been attempted in the masque form before. It is a perfect blend of matter and manner; in it the extravagance which was germane to the masque is controlled by a disciplined imagination. This opinion was obviously not shared by Sir Dudley Carleton, whose comments on this presentation are preserved for us. Sir Dudley's criticisms of the scenery, that "there was all Fish and no Water," and of the apparel — "to light and Curtizan-light [*sic*] for such great ones" — show a literal rather than a literary mind. He, however, notes an interesting detail, namely that the masquers used paint (and not the usual velvet masks) to disguise their complexions:

> Instead of Vizzards, their Faces and Arms up to the Elbows, were painted black, which was Disguise sufficient, for they were hard to be known; but it became them nothing so well as their red and white, and you cannot imagine a more ugly Sight, then a Troop of lean-cheek'd Moors.

The thirteen days promised in *The Masque of Blacknesse* ran into three years before the daughters of Niger, by then washed white, were to return to the stage in *The Masque of Beauty*, which was presented in 1608.

Pedro Calderón de la Barca

Calderón is one of Spain's greatest poets and dramatists of the Golden Age—the early and mid-seventeenth century. This was a time when Lope de Vega (1562–1635) dominated the stage and fashioned the form of the popular drama as a three-act structure, with the opening act establishing the issues and characters, the second act developing the conflict, and the third act resolving the problems raised by the drama. Lope established the form of the *comedia* (tragicomic social drama) in his *The New Art of Play Writing* (1609). Calderón followed Lope's structure.

The Golden Age also produced Spain's greatest painters—El Greco (1541–1614), Murillo (1617–1682), and Velásquez (1599–1660). The activity and significance of art in this period may be underscored by noting that during most of this period, King Philip IV brought artists to court and provided them with studios. Velásquez painted many portraits of King Philip, who visited his studio daily. Likewise, the theater was nurtured by the court throughout this period. Lope was the first court playwright; when he died in 1635, Calderón took his place.

Calderón came from a well-to-do family ruled by a difficult and tyrannical father. He went first to the University of Alcalá and then to the university at Salamanca, where he studied law and probably theology. He changed his original plan to become a priest and began writing plays in 1623. Apparently the king or perhaps the powerful prime minister, Olivares, became aware of his work and brought him into the court circle, giving him the opportunity to produce a variety of plays. Despite the fact that Spain's power and wealth were eroding rapidly, Philip's court maintained a strenuous program of lavish entertainment. Some historians have seen this behavior as an escapist refusal to believe that most of the immense wealth in gold and silver brought back twice yearly from the Americas was already mortgaged on wars, insurrections, and entertainment. Not long after Calderón died, the nation was virtually bankrupt.

The opportunities afforded him at court made it possible for Calderón to produce elaborate entertainments, especially after Olivares built a new court suitable for more brilliant productions in 1634. The old court, the Alcázar, was dark, small, and depressing. The new court was large, elegant, and expressive. It demanded a steady stream of entertainments.

The popular stage was often an open-air theater similar to the Elizabethan theater of Shakespeare's time. Scenery was minimal, costumes rarely more than suggestions, and lighting natural. Plays were put on in the afternoon at 3 o'clock in the summer and at 2 o'clock in the winter. But at court, lighting was provided by candles and oil lamps, scenic backgrounds were possible, and costuming was imaginative.

In Calderón's remarkable output as a playwright he may have produced as many as a hundred one-act religious plays for the feast of Corpus Christi. These *auto sacramentales* are allegorical plays, usually about saints' lives and similar to medieval miracle plays. Some of these plays were widely admired, such as *The Constant Prince* (1629), about the martyrdom of Portuguese prince Ferdinand; *The Wonder-Working Magician* (1637), about a Faust character; and *The Two Lovers of Heaven* (1640). Nearly eighty of these plays survive.

Calderón wrote many secular dramas as well as *zarzuelas*, a form that combined music, dance, and drama and that developed into his operas, in which the dialogue is set to music. Among his most important secular plays are *The Surgeon of His Honor* (1635), *Life Is a Dream* (1635), *The Mayor of Zalamea* (1640), and *Daughter of the Air* (1653). Each of these plays is powerful, but *Life Is a Dream* has become the longest-lived and the most often produced of his plays. He wrote it in his favorite baroque style—*Gongorism*, named for an earlier baroque poet, Luis de Góngora y Argote (1561–1627), whose style is marked by references to mythology, stylistic excesses, and complexity of language and thought. In translation many of these stylistic effects are lost, although *Life Is a Dream* is marked by complexity of thought even in English.

In 1651 Calderón took religious orders and retired from the popular stage, but he continued to write for the court. He eventually became an honorary chaplain to Philip and spent much of his time at court in Madrid even while officially assigned to Toledo.

LIFE IS A DREAM

The central action of *Life Is a Dream* is the conversion, or "rebirth," of Prince Sigismund. The action of the subplot is the recovery of Rossaura's honor after her seduction by the foreign duke Aistulf. These two strands of action intertwine when Rossaura helps Sigismund begin to understand the true nature of the world, and he helps her regain her honor once he is recognized by the people of Poland as the true heir of his father.

Life Is a Dream, often called Spain's *Hamlet*, is one of Calderón's philosophical plays. It centers on self-discovery and the untrustworthiness of illusion. Like Hamlet, Sigismund spends part of the second act of the play trying to decide the truth of his experiences: Were they real, or were they a dream? Is life real or a dream? The concept of life as a dream comes from Eastern thought and was commonly discussed in the seventeenth century. Skepticism—the reluctance to believe in the knowledge gathered by the senses—was widespread in this age. Both Shakespeare and Calderón were influenced by the revival of classical skepticism, and both examined experience in an effort to discover truth.

When the play opens, Sigismund is imprisoned and baffled at his lack of freedom. He does not know that his horoscope predicted at his birth that he would grow up to be a tyrant who would conquer his father, King Vasily. As a result Vasily placed him in a prison with Clothold as his guard and tutor. But the aging Vasily, concerned with the succession of his throne, has second thoughts and suspects that the horoscope might be wrong. He releases Sigismund to observe his behavior: if he seems tyrannical, he will be reimprisoned and told that his moments of freedom were a dream; if he is prudent, he will inherit the crown.

Rossaura arrives searching for Aistulf, the man who wronged her. She is disguised as a man and is present when Vasily experiments with freeing Sigismund. Sigismund behaves tyrannically, doing what he wants when he wants with no thought for anyone else. He is in a sense a "natural" man because he had not been socialized in a normal family or in normal surroundings. But before he is returned to prison, he falls in love with Rossaura, and his love for her begins the process of his conversion.

Once returned to prison, Sigismund believes his experience of freedom was a dream until he reflects on Rossaura. His memory of her begins to convince him that he truly experienced freedom after all. Ultimately, the people resist the imposition of a foreign king, Aistulf, Duke of Muscovy, and storm the prison to free Sigismund. He is a changed man who realizes that he must temper his desires and consider other people's feelings. At the head of an army, he defeats his father, Vasily. When his father bows before him, he in turn bows before his father, thus demonstrating his allegiance and his conversion from a wrathful tyrant. Rossaura is a central part of Sigismund's metamorphosis. She may be an allegorical representation of beauty, feminine (and therefore civilizing) beauty, or humanity. Sigismund pledges to help her recover her honor. Prince Aistulf is revealed as a seducer, and Sigismund is a wiser and more compassionate person.

Life Is a Dream in Performance

Like *Hamlet*, Calderón's *Life Is a Dream* has been produced often since its first appearance in 1635. Ironically, modern productions in Spain are infrequent because the Spanish are reluctant to tamper with the original verse, which is difficult and unusual. On the other hand, Federico García Lorca produced it in Spain in 1932, respecting the conventions of classic Spanish theater. The Teatro Español produced a full version in 1982. Productions in other parts of the world have, since the first English version in London in 1899, been frequent and interesting. Among the several modern New York versions was the 1981 production directed by María Irene Fornés. Anne Bogart did a highly praised "pictorially 'Spanish'" production in Cambridge, Massachusetts, in 1989 using Edwin Honig's translation. José Rivera's somewhat vaudevillean adaptation appeared in Hartford in 1998 and in New York in 2000, titled *Sueño*.

Another recent production was that by the Royal Lyceum Theatre Company of Scotland at the Brooklyn Academy of Music in 1999. This was a high-energy, powerful drama that concentrated on the pain and bewilderment of Sigismund, who appeared much of the time bearing a large chain, symbolic of his imprisonment. The stage was simple: a twenty-five-foot circle of broken stones over which hung a huge picture-frame mirror tilted to show only part of the action and to mirror the reality of the stage action in an unreal way throughout. The director, Calixto Bieito, from Barcelona, compressed the action into one two-hour act, relying for clarity on some long speeches of exposition and explanation. He also included two Spanish musicians singing Flamenco songs and beating Flamenco rhythms in the background—a haunting accompaniment.

In February 2007, the South Coast Repertory Theatre of Costa Mesa, California, produced *Life Is a Dream* in another new translation and adaptation by the Pulitzer Prize–winning playwright Nilo Cruz. Cruz, author of *Anna in the Tropics*, has said that this is his favorite play in part because of its lyrical language and the questions it poses about the nature of humanity. The following new translation by Michael Kidd is in prose rather than poetry. It achieves great accuracy by avoiding the linguistic difficulties imposed by restrictive poetic forms in English.

Pedro Calderón de la Barca (1600–1681)
LIFE IS A DREAM   1635
TRANSLATED BY MICHAEL KIDD

Characters

ROSSAURA, *Lady*
BUGLE, *Rossaura's servant*
VASILY, *King of Poland*
SIGISMUND, *Vasily's son*
CLOTHOLD, *elderly adviser to Vasily and Sigismund's jailer*
AISTULF, *Duke of Muscovy and cousin to Sigismund*
STELLA, *Princess of Poland and cousin to Sigismund*
GUARDS
SERVANTS AND COURT ATTENDANTS
MUSICIANS
SOLDIERS

Setting: *Renaissance Poland.*

ACT 1 • Scene 1

Deserted mountainside at twilight, near the entrance to Sigismund's tower.

(Enter Rossaura at the top of the mountain, disguised as a man dressed for the road. As she makes her way down the mountain, she addresses the horse from which she has just been thrown.)

ROSSAURA: Monstrous hippogriff,° peer of the wind, you're as ill conceived as a bolt of lightning without

flame, a bird without color, a fish without scales, or a beast without instinct! Where do you speed off to bucking, lurching, and bolting before the obscure labyrinth of those barren crags? Stay, then, on this mountainside and let the beasts have their Phaëthon;° while I, a woman with no direction but that offered by the laws of destiny, shall descend in blindness and desperation the twisted face of this lofty cliff, whose scowling brow withers in the sun. Poorly, Poland, do you greet the foreigner, for you write his entrance to your sands in blood, and hardly is he come when he comes into hardship. My luck says it all, for where can an unlucky wretch turn for mercy?

(Enter Bugle.)

BUGLE: Make that two unlucky wretches, and don't pretend I'm asleep back at camp when you start lamenting. For if it was two of us who left our fatherland to seek adventures, and two of us who, amid misfortune and madness, arrived at this spot, and two of us who were thrown down the mountain, can't I rightly complain if you make me party to the sorrow and leave me out of the tally?

ROSSAURA: I didn't want to involve you in my laments, Bugle, and take away your right to consolation through the expression of your own distress, for there is such delight to be gained from lamenting, a

---

hippogriff: Mythological beast that is part horse, part eagle, and part lion.

Phaëthon: Son of Helios, who lets him drive the chariot of the sun for one day.

philosopher once said, that one should go in search of misfortunes just to be able to lament them.

BUGLE: That philosopher was a filthy drunk who deserves a thousand slaps in the face! I'd like to see how he enjoys lamenting then. But really, my lady, what are we to do now—on foot, alone, and lost at such an hour on a deserted mountainside with the sun fast headed for the horizon?

ROSSAURA: Who ever heard of such a strange turn of events? Yet unless my vision suffers from the deceptions of fantasy, I think I see some kind of building in the flickering twilight.

BUGLE: Either my desire is deceiving me, or I see the same thing.

ROSSAURA: Lying crudely among the barren crags, it's a palace so insignificant that even the sunlight barely reaches it. Its crude architecture is such that it could pass for a boulder that rolled off the mountaintop and settled at the foot of all these rocks and crags that strive toward the sun's warmth.

BUGLE: Let's draw closer and not lose more time in speculation, my lady, when it's better to be welcomed by the people who live inside.

(*They approach the tower.*)

ROSSAURA: The door—or better yet, the gloomy mouth—is open, and from its depths night, conceived inside, issues forth.

(*They hear the sound of chains from inside.*)

BUGLE: What's that sound, heavens!

ROSSAURA: I'm paralyzed, a mass of fire and ice.

BUGLE: I hear the sound of a chain; I'll be damned if it's not the ghost of a galley slave! My fear says it all.

(*Sigismund's voice is heard from inside the tower.*)

SIGISMUND: Oh, what a miserable, unlucky wretch am I!

ROSSAURA: What's that sad voice I hear! I'm confronted with new sufferings and torments!

BUGLE: And I with new fears.

ROSSAURA: Bugle!

BUGLE: My lady!

ROSSAURA: We must flee the rigors of this haunted tower!

BUGLE: I don't have the courage to flee even if I wanted to.

ROSSAURA: Is there not a faint light in that decrepit glow, that pale star which, in faltering swoons, quivering heat, and fleeting glimmers makes the dark room even more shadowy with its feeble light? Yes, for in its flicker I can make out, even from afar, a dark prison that serves as grave to a living corpse; and, to my even greater astonishment, clothed in the skins of a beast lies a man bound in chains and accompanied only by the light. Since we can't flee, let's listen to his misfortunes from here and see what he says.

(*As Rossaura and Bugle listen, a curtain is drawn to reveal Sigismund, dressed in animal skins and seated on the floor of the tower with a dim lantern. He bears on one leg a chain that allows him some mobility.*)

SIGISMUND: Oh, what a miserable, unlucky wretch am I! Please explain to me, heavens, given the way you treat me, what crime I committed against you with my birth; although if I was born, my crime is clear, and the severity of your sentence has sufficient cause, for birth itself is man's greatest crime. But I would just like to know, to ease my distress—leaving aside, heavens, the crime of birth—what else I did to merit further punishment. Weren't others born as well? And if so, what privileges were they granted that I've never enjoyed? Birds are born, and, with the regalia that decorates them in finest beauty, hardly do they attain the stature of a feathered flower or a winged bouquet when they cut swiftly through the ethereal chambers, overcoming the bond of the tranquil nest they leave behind. So how is it that I, with more soul, have less liberty? Beasts are born, and, with their coats of dappled beauty, hardly do they reflect the constellations above (thanks to divine artistry) when they become daring and cruel, and human necessity, harnessing their cruelty, makes them monsters in their labyrinth. So how is it that I, with gentler instinct, have less liberty? Fish are born, unbreathing miscarriages of algae and slime, and hardly do these scaly ships see themselves upon the waves when they begin to twist in all directions, testing the vastness of the ocean's icy depths. So how is it that I, with greater will, have less liberty? Streams are born, snakes winding through the flowers, and hardly do these silvery serpents begin to twist and turn among the blossoms when they celebrate with music the devotion of the majestic heavens that grant them passage through the open field. So how is it that I, with more life, have less liberty? (*He rises.*) My suffering rages in me like a volcano, a Mt. Etna, and I'd gladly rip the pieces of my heart from my breast! What law, what powers of justice or reason are capable of denying men the sweet privilege, the fundamental license that God grants to crystalline waters, to fish, to beasts, and to birds?

ROSSAURA: His words have filled me with fear and pity.

SIGISMUND: Who's been listening to me? Is that you, Clothold?

BUGLE: (*Aside.*) Say yes.

ROSSAURA: It's only a poor wretch—oh, miserable me!—who in these frigid caverns has overheard your melancholy words.

(*Sigismund grabs her, his chain permitting him to step slightly past the threshold of the tower [whose door has remained open].*)

SIGISMUND: Then you shall die by my hand so you won't know that I know that you know my frailties. Simply because you've overheard me, I'm going to rip you to shreds with my mighty arms!

BUGLE: I'm deaf and haven't heard a word you've said.

ROSSAURA: If you're human by birth, my kneeling at your feet will be sufficient cause for you to spare me.

ABOVE: John Ortiz as Sigismund hangs over Rossaura (Michi Barall) and Clarion (Jan Leslie Hardin), who contemplate the significance of his imprisonment. From José Rivera's Hartford Stage Company 1998 production of *Sueño*. This scene is visually reminiscent of Leonardo da Vinci's drawing of the "measure of man" as well as emblems of the crucifixion. RIGHT TOP: Sigismund (John Ortiz) in prison holding his symbolic chains while Rossaura looks on in José Rivera's production of *Sueño* at the Hartford Stage. RIGHT BOTTOM: George Anton as Sigismund in Calixto Bieito's Royal Lyceum Theatre production of *Life Is a Dream* at the Brooklyn Academy of Music, October 1999. The chains he carries symbolize his imprisonment and his torment.

SIGISMUND: Your voice has filled me with sympathy; your appearance, with wonder; and your deference, with confusion. Who are you? For although I know so little here of the world, for this tower is both my cradle and my grave; and although since birth, if mine can be called birth, I know only this crude wasteland where I live miserably, a living skeleton and a breathing cadaver; and although I've never seen or spoken to anyone but the one man who frequents this place and understands my misfortunes and from whom I know of heaven and earth; and although here—to give you more reason to be astonished and to call me a human monster—I am, amid bewilderment and illusion, a man among beasts and a beast among men; and although, amid such grim misfortunes, I have studied the art of government through the example of beasts and the counsel of birds and have measured the orbits of the gentle heavenly bodies; you alone—you—have stayed the agony of my anger, the bewilderment of my eyes, the amazement of my ears. Each glimpse of you increases my amazement, and the more I look at you the more I desire to look. My eyes must suffer from the dropsy,° since although drinking means death, they wish only to drink more, and thus, seeing that sight kills me, I'm dying to see. But let me see you and die, for now that I've succumbed I can't imagine, if seeing you brings me death, what not seeing you would bring. It would be beyond death; it would be savage ire, rage, and intense grief—thus do I qualify its severity—for to give life to an unfortunate wretch is tantamount to giving death to a happy soul.

ROSSAURA: I'm so astonished by looking at you and so amazed by listening to you that I can't think of what to say to you or what to ask you. I shall say only that heaven must have led me here today to console me, if he who is unfortunate can attain consolation from seeing another even more so. They tell the story of a wise man who one day reached a point of such poverty and misery that his only nourishment came from eating the grasses he picked. Can there be anyone else, he said to himself, poorer and sadder than I? And when he turned his head he found the answer, for there was another wise man gathering up the blades that he'd discarded. Up to this point I've lived resentful of the way fortune has treated me, and just when I asked myself, Can there be anyone else with more miserable luck? you responded mercifully, for, upon applying the moral of my story, I see that my sufferings would be your joys if you were to gather them up. And if by chance my sufferings might give you some relief, listen to them carefully, and feel free to take any that are left over. My name is...

CLOTHOLD: (*Offstage.*) Tower guards! Through sleep or cowardice you've given passage to two people who've broken through the prison perimeter.

dropsy: Disorder in which retention of liquid causes swelling.

ROSSAURA: (*Aside.*) What new confusion is this!

SIGISMUND: That's Clothold, my jailer; my misfortunes are never ending.

CLOTHOLD: (*Offstage.*) Come quickly and, with vigilance, before they can defend themselves, seize them or kill them! (*In unison with the Guards.*) Treason!

BUGLE: Tower guards! You let us in here, and since we have a choice, I think seizing us would be easier.

(*Enter Clothold, armed and accompanied by soldiers, all with their faces covered.*)

CLOTHOLD: Make sure you all keep your faces covered, for it's important that no one recognize us while we're here.

BUGLE: What's this, a damn costume party?

CLOTHOLD: O you, whose ignorance of this forbidden site has led you past its enclosed perimeter against the decree of the king, who has prohibited anyone from seeing the aberration that lies among these boulders; surrender your arms and your lives, or this pistol, a metallic viper, will spit forth a piercing venom of two bullets, deafening the air with its shots.

SIGISMUND: Before, O tyrannical master, you can offend or injure them, my life will become the spoils of these miserable fetters. For despite their restraint, by God, I'll tear myself to shreds with my own hands and teeth, here among these very crags, before I allow any misfortune to befall these strangers and end up bemoaning their mistreatment.

CLOTHOLD: If you know that your misfortunes, Sigismund, are so great that even before your birth you were sentenced to death by the dictates of heaven; if you know that these chains are meant to serve as a brake and rein to your arrogant fury, what are you boasting about? Guards, hide him away in his narrow cell and shut the door.

(*They lock him, struggling, back in the tower, and he speaks from within.*)

SIGISMUND: Oh, heavens, how rightly you act in stripping me of my liberty, because otherwise I would fight you like a giant who, to tear the sun off its crystal hinges, would pile mountains of marble atop foundations of stone!

CLOTHOLD: Perhaps, precisely so you won't do so, you suffer so many hardships today.

ROSSAURA: Given that his presumption has so offended you, I would be a fool if I didn't beg you humbly for my life, which lies in your power. Let yourself be moved by my sincerity, for it would be unduly severe of you to find favor with neither presumption nor humility.

BUGLE: And if humility and presumption don't move you, even though as characters they've moved and stirred a thousand allegorical plays, then I shall, neither humbly nor presumptuously but somewhere in between, ask you for your help and shelter.

CLOTHOLD: (*To the soldiers.*) Attention!

SOLDIERS: Sir!

CLOTHOLD: Strip them both of their arms and blindfold them, so they won't see how or from where they're leaving.

ROSSAURA: (*Touching her sword, still in its sheath.*) My sword can be surrendered to you alone because, after all, you're in charge here, and it is incapable of surrendering to those of lesser rank.

BUGLE: Mine is such that it can be given to the lowest of the low: here (*To one of the soldiers.*), you take it.

ROSSAURA: And if I am to die, I wish to leave you, as proof of my sincerity, an instrument whose value is determined by he who once wore it: I ask you to keep it safe because, although I don't know what secret it holds, I do know that this golden sword conceals great mysteries, for I have come to Poland to avenge a dishonor with nothing else to vouch for me. (*She unsheathes the sword and hands it to Clothold, who cannot contain his astonishment.*)

CLOTHOLD: (*Aside.*) Good heavens! How can this be! Now my sufferings and confusions, my anxieties and sorrows, are compounded.

(*To Rossaura.*) Who gave it to you?

ROSSAURA: A woman.

CLOTHOLD: What is her name?

ROSSAURA: I'm obliged not to reveal that.

CLOTHOLD: Well, how do you now infer or know that it holds some secret?

ROSSAURA: The woman who gave it to me said, "Leave for Poland and, through ingenuity, deliberation, or artifice, let the noble and powerful see you with this sword, for I know that one of them will favor and shelter you." She wouldn't mention his name for fear he might be dead.

CLOTHOLD: (*Aside.*) Heaven help me! What have I just heard! Is this an illusion or reality? This sword is the one I left with the lovely Viola, signaling that anyone who returned wearing it would find me as loving as a son and as devoted as a father. So what am I to do now—oh, miserable me!—amid such confusion, when he who wears the sword seeking favor can find only death, for he comes before me doomed by the king's edict? What terrible confusion! What sad fate! What inconstant luck! This is my son; his appearance confirms what I feel in my heart, which, longing to see him, calls to my breast, beats its wings within, and—unable to break the lock—acts as he who, confined indoors, leans out the window upon hearing a noise in the street. And thus, hearing the noise without knowing the cause, my heart rushes to look out through my eyes—the windows of my soul—through which it escapes in tears. What am I to do? Heaven help me! What am I to do? To take him to the king is to take him—oh, what sorrow!—to his death, but I can't hide him from the king without violating the laws of fealty. On the one hand I am swayed by self-interest, on the other by loyalty to the king. But how can I really have any doubt? Doesn't loyalty to the king come before one's own life and honor? So loyalty it shall be, and away with honor.

Besides, I recall now that he said he's come to Poland to avenge a dishonor, and everyone knows that a dishonored man is contemptible, so he can't be my son. He's *not* my son and does *not* share my noble blood. But then again, if the affront was inescapable—for honor is so fragile that it can be shattered with a single deed or blemished with a whisper—what more could a nobleman do in his defense, what more than to go looking for his remedy at all cost? He *is* my son, he *does* share my blood, for his valor is great! And thus, in such a dilemma, my best option is to go to the king, inform him that he's my son, and acknowledge that he must die. Perhaps the very conviction of my loyalty will move His Majesty to sympathy; and if I manage to earn my son's life, then I'll help him avenge his dishonor; but if the king remains steady in his severity and sentences him to death, then he will die without knowing I'm his father.
(*To Rossaura and Bugle.*) Come with me, foreigners. But don't fear, no, that you lack company in your misfortunes; for amid such terrible doubt I know not which is worse, to live or to die.

Scene 2

King's palace.

(*Enter, on one side, Aistulf in the company of soldiers, and on the other, Stella with her ladies-in-waiting. Music sounds.*)

AISTULF: The drums and bugles, together with the birds and fountains, do well in mixing their diverse greetings in the presence of your celestial gaze, a comet in the night sky; for, alike in their music and in the great wonder they inspire, before your heavenly image the birds act as feathered bugles and the bugles as metal birds. And thus you are greeted, my lady, as queen by the drumbeats, as Aurora° by the birds, as Pallas° by the bugles, and as Flora° by the fountains; because, in mocking the day that has already been banished by the night, you are Aurora in happiness, Flora in peace, Pallas in war, and queen in my soul.

STELLA: If words are to be backed up by actions, you do not fare well in pronouncing courtly compliments that are easily contradicted by such a display of military might (*Pointing to the soldiers.*), which I shall defiantly resist; for the flattery I'm hearing from you, as I see it, does not agree with the severe show of force I'm observing. And take note that it's a base action, worthy only of the deception and treachery of beasts, to flatter with the mouth and kill with the mind.

AISTULF: You're very poorly informed, Stella, if you doubt the earnestness of my compliments, so I

Aurora: The goddess of dawn. **Pallas:** The goddess Athena, who appears with lance and shield. **Flora:** The goddess of flowers.

beseech you: listen and I shall prove that I understand your concerns. When Eustorge the Third, king of Poland, died, he left Vasily as his heir, along with two daughters, from whom you and I were born. I won't tire you with details that have no place here. Clorilyn, your mother and my aunt, who now rests under a canopy of stars in a sweeter realm, was the eldest, and you're her daughter; next came my mother and your aunt, the graceful Grethissunda, may God keep her a thousand years. She married the Duke of Muscovy and gave birth to me. Now here's the issue, my lady: our Uncle Vasily, who's already succumbing to the inevitable contempt of time and who's always been more inclined to academic pursuits than to women, is widowed and childless, and you and I both aspire to his throne. You contend that you're the descendent of the eldest child; I, that I was born a man and that, even though my mother was younger than yours, I should receive preference. We have both informed our uncle of our intentions; he responded that he wished to resolve our dispute, and we settled on this place and this day. With this intention I left my estate in Muscovy; with the same intention I have arrived here and, instead of waging war against you, find that you are doing so against me. Oh, if only Love, a wise god, would sway the masses, so unerring in their predictions, to predict for both of us today a resolution of this matter that would make you queen—queen of my will, that is. Thus you would find yourself—to your greater glory—crowned by our uncle, rewarded by your own valor, and recognized as sovereign by my love.

STELLA: To such courtly elegance my heart responds no less in kind, for I, simply to make this imperial monarchy yours, would be happy to claim it as mine; although my love is not altogether satisfied by your intentions, for in all you say I fear you are contradicted by that locket hanging about your breast.

AISTULF: I'll resolve your doubts about that...but not now, for all those clamorous instruments indicate that the king and his court are approaching.

(*Flourish. Enter King Vasily—an old man—and his attendants.*)

STELLA: Wise Thales,°
AISTULF: Learned Euclid,°
STELLA: who governs today
AISTULF: who lives today
STELLA: by the constellations
AISTULF: by the stars
STELLA: and describes
AISTULF: and glosses and measures
STELLA: their courses;
AISTULF: their tracks;

Thales: Greek astronomer (c. 624–546 BCE) considered the first Western philosopher. **Euclid:** Greek mathematician and geometer (fl. 300 BCE).

STELLA: allow me, with obedient arms,
AISTULF: allow me, with tender embraces,
STELLA: to be the ivy upon your trunk
AISTULF: to surrender myself at your feet.
VASILY: Dear niece and nephew, I greet you with open arms. And, insofar as you both come here, true to my loving ways, with your own show of affection, you may trust that I shall leave no one with cause for complaint and that you will both remain each other's equal. And now, confessing weariness from the heavy burden of my years, I solicit only your silence, for the subject matter itself will solicit your amazement. You know well—and please listen carefully, my beloved niece and nephew, illustrious court of Poland, vassals, relatives, and friends—you know well that my science has earned me the nickname of Learned in world opinion; for, in defiance of time and forgetfulness, painters worthy of Timanthes° and sculptors worthy of Lysippus° proclaim me the great Vasily across the globe. You know also that the sciences I most study and admire lie in subtle mathematics, in whose name I rob time and exempt fame of the jurisdiction and task of making new revelations with the passing of each day. For when in my charts I see manifest the news of coming centuries, I earn the thanks owed to time for revealing what I have told. Those snowy spheres, those glass canopies illuminated by the sun's rays and encircled by the moon's beams, those diamond orbs, those crystalline globes adorned by the stars and crisscrossed by the Zodiac have received the greatest attention of my years; they are the books in which, on diamond-studded paper bound in sapphire, with diverse characters etched in gold lines, heaven records our deeds, whether adverse or auspicious. These books I read with such swiftness that I follow in spirit their rapid movements across the sky's corridors and pathways. If only heaven had taken my life as the first casualty of its ire before my ingenuity began to gloss the margins and index the pages in which I foresaw my tragedy! For even merit has a sharp edge for the unlucky, and he who is pricked by curiosity ends up destroying himself! I can say this to you with words, but my deeds will speak more clearly, so once again I ask for your silence as you listen in amazement. By Clorilyn, my wife, I had an unlucky son, upon whose birth the heavens ran out of appalling signs even before he had passed into the beautiful light of day from the darkness of the womb—a living tomb insofar as birth and death are akin. Time and again his mother, seized by the images and hallucinations of dreams, watched as a monster in human form broke forth defiantly from her entrails and, drenched in her blood, brought her death through its own birth, an inconceivable human viper. The day of the birth arrived, and, in fulfillment of the omens—for rarely

Timanthes: Greek painter (c. 400 BCE). *Lysippus:* Greek sculptor (c. 300 BCE).

or never does perverse prophecy misspeak—the child was born under a horoscope in which the sun, reddened by its blood, was entering into a wrathful duel with the moon; and, with the earth in between, the two divine torches fought with the full force of their luminous rays—a most unconventional battle. It was the greatest, most horrendous eclipse the sun has suffered since it shed tears of blood over Christ's death; and, caught in the midst of the raging fires, the earth presumed itself in the throes of extinction. The heavens darkened, buildings trembled, the clouds rained stones, and the rivers ran with blood. Under this miserable, under this fatal planet or sign, Sigismund was born and gave an indication of his nature, for, in bringing death to his mother, he said of his own savagery, "I am man, for I'm already beginning to repay kindness with cruelty." Resorting to my studies, I saw in them and in everything else that Sigismund would be the most reckless of men, the cruelest of princes, and the most perverse of monarchs; that through him the kingdom would become polarized and divided, a school of treason and an academy of vice; that, driven by his fury and wavering between bewilderment and malice, he would trample me underfoot; and that I would find myself vanquished and prostrate before him, the gray hair of my beard serving as (*Aside:* What anxiety it causes me just to say the words!) a rug beneath his feet. Who doesn't take danger seriously, especially one that arises from the studies on which his own self-worth depends? Thus, lending credence to the fates, whose soothsaying had foretold such disaster in their fatal prophecies, I determined to lock up the beast that had just been born, hoping that a wise man might rein in the influence of the stars. It was announced that the prince was stillborn, and I, ever cautious, had a tower built among the crags and bluffs of those mountains where the light of day scarcely makes its way, so heavily do the site's crude obelisks guard its entrance. The stern penalties and laws that, by public proclamation, prohibit anyone from entering the mountain's forbidden zone were made necessary by what I have told you. There lives Sigismund, in misery, destitution, and confinement; and only Clothold has spoken to him, dealt with him, and seen him. The only witness to his miseries, Clothold has also taught him the natural sciences and instructed him in the Catholic faith. Three conclusions may be drawn from all this. First, that I hold you in such esteem, Poland, that I wish to spare you the oppression and liability of a tyrannical king, because any ruler who would put his fatherland and empire in such danger could not be considered benevolent. Second is the consideration that to deprive my heir of the right he was given by human and divine sanction is not an act of Christian charity, for no law says that I, in trying to keep another from becoming tyrannical and reckless, may become so myself; yet if my son is a tyrant, to prevent him from committing crimes I must commit them myself. Third and last, I realize how erroneous it was to place easy credence in predictions of the future, since, even if the prince's inclination places obstacles in his path, they might not overcome him; because even the most contemptuous fate, the most wayward inclination, or the most perverse planet can only influence the will, not force it. And so, after hesitating and reflecting over my options, I've come up with a solution that is sure to bewilder your senses. Tomorrow I shall place Sigismund—for this is his name—without his knowing that he's my son and your king, under my canopy and upon my throne, where, acting in my place, he will govern and lead you and where you will all docilely swear obedience to him. In this way I shall accomplish three things, with which I can now respond to the three conclusions I pointed out earlier. First, if he turns out to be prudent, rational, and benevolent in complete contradiction of fate, which predicted so many things of him, you will all enjoy the reign of your rightful prince, who until now has been a courtier to mountains and a neighbor to beasts. Second, if he turns out to be presumptuous, brazen, reckless, and cruel and plays with free rein the field of his vices, I shall have fulfilled my obligation in good faith; and then, in ousting him, I shall act as any triumphant king, returning him to his cell not out of cruelty but rather as a punishment. Third, if he turns out to be the kind of prince I've just described, out of my love for you, my subjects, I shall give you a king and queen more worthy of my crown and scepter: for my niece and nephew, uniting their two claims to the throne and reconciled to each other through the sanctity of marriage, will have the title they have earned. This I command of you as king; this I ask of you as father; this I beg of you as a wise man; this I say to you as an old man. And finally, if the Roman philosopher Seneca, a native of Spanish soil, declared that kings are their countries' humble servants, this I beseech of you as your servant.

AISTULF: If it's up to me to respond, since it seems I'm the one with the greatest vested interest in this matter, I'll speak for everyone in saying let Sigismund come forward, for his being your son is reason enough.

ALL: Give us our prince, for we want him as our king!

VASILY: Dear subjects, I appreciate and value your goodwill. Accompany my niece and nephew, Atlas°-like pillars of my old age, to their quarters, and tomorrow you will behold him.

ALL: Long live the great King Vasily!

(*Exit all. Before Vasily can leave, Clothold enters with Rossaura and Bugle and detains him.*)

CLOTHOLD: May I speak with you?

VASILY: Oh, Clothold! You are most welcome.

CLOTHOLD: Although I should feel welcome bowing before your presence, this time, my lord, a morose

Atlas: Greek Titan who supported the earth on his back.

and contemptuous fate has suspended routine procedure and customary practice.

VASILY: What's the matter?

CLOTHOLD: A grave misfortune, my lord, has befallen me, when it could have been cause for the greatest joy.

VASILY: Explain.

CLOTHOLD: (*Pointing to Rossaura.*) This handsome young man, through either boldness or ignorance, entered the tower, my lord, where he saw the prince. And...

VASILY: Don't fret, Clothold. If it had happened before today, I confess I would have been disturbed. But I've just revealed the tower's secret, so it doesn't matter if he knows about it as long as I allow it. But come see me later, because I have many things to report to you and much to ask of you; for you are to be, let me advise you, the instrument of the greatest event the world has ever seen. And to these prisoners, so you won't think I'm punishing your oversight, I grant pardon. (*Exit.*)

CLOTHOLD: May you live a thousand centuries, great lord!

(*Aside.*) Heaven has improved my luck. I won't tell anyone now that he's my son, for I can get by without doing so.

(*To Rossaura and Bugle.*) Errant strangers, you are free to go.

ROSSAURA: I shall adorn your feet a thousand times with my kisses.

BUGLE: I'll just adore them from afar, for what's a letter or two between friends?

ROSSAURA: You have given me, sire, my life; and since I live in your debt, I shall be your eternal slave.

CLOTHOLD: What I've given you isn't life, for a well-born man has no life as long as he's dishonored; and given that you've come here to avenge a dishonor, as you yourself told me, I can't give you life because you bring none with you; for a life lived in contempt is no life.

(*Aside.*) In this way I'll spur him on.

ROSSAURA: I confess that I remain without life despite receiving it from you; but through vengeance I shall leave my honor so unblemished that my life, in surmounting all obstacles, may be recognized as your gift.

CLOTHOLD: Take back this burnished blade you brought with you, for I know that, when dyed in the blood of your enemy, it will be sufficient to avenge your dishonor; because any blade of mine—I mean "mine" in this instant, this brief period that I've held it in my power—is capable of avenging you.

ROSSAURA: In your name I arm myself with it a second time, and upon it I swear myself to revenge, even though my enemy be more powerful.

CLOTHOLD: How much more powerful is he?

ROSSAURA: So much so that I prefer not to tell you, not because I wouldn't entrust even greater matters to your prudence but because I fear losing the favor I have found in your devotion.

CLOTHOLD: On the contrary, it would be to your further advantage to tell me, for you would thus keep me from helping your enemy.
(*Aside.*) Oh, if only I knew who it was!

ROSSAURA: So you won't think I underestimate your trust, know that my enemy is none other than Aistulf, Duke of Muscovy.

CLOTHOLD: (*Aside.*) Good grief, that's much worse than I'd imagined!
(*To Rossaura.*) Let's clarify matters. If you were born a Muscovite, your natural lord cannot have dishonored you; return to your fatherland, then, and leave behind the burning tenacity that impels you.

ROSSAURA: I'm certain that, even though he's my prince, he has dishonored me.

CLOTHOLD: Impossible, even if he had dared to slap you in the face.
(*Aside.*) Heaven help me!

ROSSAURA: My dishonor was worse.

CLOTHOLD: State it then, for you can't say anything worse than I can imagine.

ROSSAURA: I would do so, but such is the respect with which I look upon you, the affection with which I worship you, the esteem in which I hold you that I dare not tell you that my external trappings are but a riddle, for their owner is not who you might think. So, if I am not what I appear to be and if Aistulf has come here to marry Stella, you be the judge of whether he can dishonor me or not. I have said enough.

(*Exit Rossaura and Bugle.*)

CLOTHOLD: Listen! Wait! Stop! What confusing labyrinth is this where reason has lost its thread? My honor is besmirched, the enemy is powerful, I'm a vassal, and the offended party is a woman—show me the way out, heavens! Although I'm not sure there is a way out of such a confusing abyss when all heaven is an omen and all earth is an aberration.

ACT 2 • *Scene 1*

King's palace.

(*Enter Vasily and Clothold.*)

CLOTHOLD: Everything you ordered has been carried out.

VASILY: Tell me, Clothold, how it went.

CLOTHOLD: In this way, my lord. With the soothing concoction you had brewed from a mixture of medicinal herbs, whose tyrannical properties and secret powers so dissipate, rob, and disorient human reasoning that they turn one into a living corpse, and whose potency robs one in his sleep of his senses and faculties—there's no reason to doubt that this is possible, for so many times, my lord, experiment has shown us, and it's true, that medicine is full of natural secrets, and there's no animal, plant, or rock that doesn't have a determined property; and if human malice has experimented with a thousand poisons in search of their lethal qualities, is it any surprise that, with just a little less potency, a poison that kills could be made to induce sleep? Not at all, for it's been demonstrated through hypotheses and proofs—with the concoction, I was saying, of opium, poppy leaves, and henbane,° I descended to Sigismund's narrow cell. I talked with him a bit about the lessons he's been taught by the silent nature of the mountains and sky, under whose divine instruction he learned rhetoric from the birds and the beasts. To elevate his spirit to the level of the task you have in store for him, I pointed to a majestic eagle and proposed for discussion the swiftness that allowed it, in scorning the sphere of the wind, to become a feathery flare or a runaway comet in the lofty regions of fire. I praised the headstrong flight, saying, "You are, after all, sovereign among birds, so it is natural that you should consider yourself superior to all the rest." He needed no further prompting, for whenever the topic of sovereign power is discussed, he reasons with ambition and pride because his blood, of course, incites, moves, and animates him to great things, and he said: "To think that in the restless realm of the birds there is one that can command the obedience of all! In this matter my misfortunes console me, since, if I'm subservient to another, it's only by force because I would never submit of my own free will to another man." Seeing him enraged by this idea—a constant theme of his grief—I invited him to drink from the potion, and hardly had the elixir passed from the glass to his chest when he surrendered himself to the arms of sleep and a cold sweat coursed through his veins and broke out upon his body, such that, if I hadn't known it was a simulated death, I would have doubted whether he was alive. At this moment the people to whom you have entrusted the success of this endeavor have arrived and, having placed him in a coach, are taking him to your quarters, which have been prepared with the majesty and grandeur worthy of his person. They will lay him upon your bed where, when the stupor wears off, they will attend to him as if he were you, my lord, for thus you have ordered. And if having obeyed you has earned me any favor, I ask only—and forgive me my impropriety—that you tell me what your intention is in bringing Sigismund to the palace in this way.

VASILY: Clothold, your doubt is well founded, and I would like to satisfy it for you alone. The influence of my son Sigismund's star, as you know, threatens a thousand misfortunes and tragedies. I wish to study whether heaven—which is incapable of lying, especially when it's already given us, in the prince's cruel character, so many examples of its accuracy—at

---

henbane: Leaves of a plant that, with opium, can produce hysteria.

least softens or tempers its judgment and, won over through valor and prudence, retracts its prediction; for man ultimately has mastery over the stars. I wish to study this matter by bringing the prince to a place where he'll discover he's my son and have his talent put to the test. If he shows virtue and overcomes his inclinations, he will become king; but if his cruel and tyrannical nature wins out, I shall return him to his chain. Now you'll ask why for the purposes of the experiment it was necessary to bring him asleep in this way. And I wish to satisfy all your doubts. If he were to discover today that he's my son and find himself tomorrow reduced a second time to his prison and misery, given his character he would no doubt lose all hope because, with the knowledge of who he is, what possible consolation could he harbor? And thus I have tried to hedge my bets by leaving myself the option of telling him that everything he saw was a dream. In this way two things may be studied. First, his character, for he acts in his waking hours on whatever his imagination and thoughts suggest. Second, a way to console him even if he finds himself obeyed now and later reawakens in his chains, for he will conclude that he dreamed everything—and he will be correct because in this world, Clothold, everyone who lives dreams.

CLOTHOLD: I wouldn't be lacking in reasons to prove that this is not a good idea. But it's too late now, for, from the look of things, the prince has awoken and is drawing near.

VASILY: I'm going to step out. You're his mentor; go to him and, with the truth, free him from whatever confusions are besieging his thoughts.

CLOTHOLD: So you give me permission to tell him everything?

VASILY: Yes, for it may be that when he finds out, the danger will be more easily overcome because it has been understood.

(*Exit Vasily; enter Bugle.*)

BUGLE: (*Aside.*) At the expense of a good beating from a blond, halberd°-brandishing sentry whose beard matched the color of his livery, I've pushed my way in to see what's going on; for the best way to get a good seat without bribing the usher is to take charge yourself, since in all public spectacles a shallow pocket can be overcome with a deep wit and an insolent attitude.

CLOTHOLD: (*Aside.*) That's Bugle, servant to she who— Good heavens!—she who, trafficking in misfortune, has escorted my dishonor to Poland.
(*To Bugle.*) Bugle, what's the news?

BUGLE: The news, my lord, is that the great generosity you show in your willingness to help Rossaura avenge her dishonor has encouraged her to resume dressing in women's clothes.

---

halberd: Lancelike weapon with an axe-head and sharp spike.

CLOTHOLD: A good decision, so that she not be judged indecent.

BUGLE: The news is that, changing her name and calling herself—wisely—your niece, she has enhanced her stature to such a degree that the extraordinary Princess Stella has welcomed her into the palace as her lady-in-waiting.

CLOTHOLD: It is fitting that my name accredit her honor once and for all.

BUGLE: The news is that she is hoping for the time and opportunity in which you can act on behalf of her honor.

CLOTHOLD: That's a safe bet, for time eventually settles all scores.

BUGLE: The news is that she is being pampered and attended to like a queen, thanks to calling herself your niece. And the news is that, living at her side, I'm dying of hunger; and nary a soul thinks of me, forgetting that I'm Bugle and that, when a bugle like me sounds off, it can inform the king, Aistulf, and Stella of everything that's happening, for bugles and servants are two things that don't go very well with secrecy. And if silence ever abandons me, I may become the subject of that familiar tune, *A bugle that heralds the sun / Sounds second to none.*

CLOTHOLD: Your complaint is well founded, and I shall attend to it; in the meantime, you may serve me.

BUGLE: Here comes Sigismund.

(*Enter Musicians, singing, and servants, who are busy dressing Sigismund in royal garments. The prince enters, astonished by his surroundings.*)

SIGISMUND: Heaven help me, what am I seeing! Heaven help me, what am I watching! The sight provokes more doubt than shock! I, in a sumptuous palace? I, dressed in fine fabrics and brocades? I, surrounded by such distinguished and gallant servants? I, waking from sleep in such an exquisite bed? I, amid so many people intent on dressing me? To say I'm dreaming is an error; I know quite well that I'm awake. Am I not Sigismund? Heavens, reveal the truth for me! Tell me, what could have happened to my mind as I slept that I should find myself here? But whatever it was, why waste time wondering about it? Better to enjoy being served and let come what may.

SERVANT 2: He's so melancholy!

SERVANT 1: Who wouldn't be after what he's been through?

BUGLE: Me.

SERVANT 2: Go speak to him now.

SERVANT 1: (*To Sigismund.*) Shall I have them sing again?

SIGISMUND: No, I don't want any more singing.

SERVANT 2: You seem so bewildered, I thought you might enjoy some entertainment.

SIGISMUND: My sorrows can't be comforted by their voices; military marches are the only music I enjoy listening to.

CLOTHOLD: Your Highness, my lord, allow me to kiss your hand; for my loyalty will be the first to offer you obedience.

SIGISMUND: (*Aside.*) This is Clothold, so how is it that he who mistreats me in prison now treats me with such respect? What's happening to me?

CLOTHOLD: In the immense confusion of your new surroundings, your thought and reason must be plagued by thousands of doubts. But I want to free you from all of them if possible . . . (*Solemnly.*) . . . because you need to know, my lord, that you are the crown prince of Poland. If you have lived secluded and hidden from sight, it was due to the inclemency of fate, which sanctions a thousand tragedies for this realm once the kingly laurel leaf adorns your august brow. Yet trusting that, with prudence, you can overcome the stars—because a virtuous man can do so—they've brought you to the palace from the tower in which you lived while your spirit was in the power of sleep. Your father, the king my lord, will come to see you shortly, and from him, Sigismund, you'll learn the rest.

SIGISMUND: You vile, contemptible traitor! What more need I learn, now that I know my true identity, in order to exercise my pride and power from this day forward? How could you commit such treason against your fatherland by hiding me away, for you have denied me my birthright against all reason and law!

CLOTHOLD: Oh, miserable me!

SIGISMUND: You have been a traitor to the law, a sycophant to the king, and a savage to me; and thus the king, the law, and I, amid such barbaric misfortune, condemn you to die by my hands.

SERVANT 2: My lord!

SIGISMUND: Let no one try to stop me, for it would be a useless endeavor, and, by God, if you get in my way, I'll throw you out that window.

SERVANT 1: Flee, Clothold!

CLOTHOLD: (*Aside.*) Poor Sigismund, what presumption you demonstrate, unaware that you're only dreaming!
(*He flees.*)

SERVANT 2: Beware that . . .

SIGISMUND: Stay out of my way.

SERVANT 2: . . . he was obeying his king.

SIGISMUND: When the law isn't just, the king needn't be obeyed; and what's more, I was his prince.

SERVANT 2: It wasn't for him to decide whether it was just or not.

SIGISMUND: You're asking for it, talking back to me that way.

BUGLE: The prince is right, and you've acted very wrongly.

SERVANT 1: Who gave you permission to speak?

BUGLE: I took it upon myself.

SIGISMUND: And who are you, pray tell?

BUGLE: A busybody, a job in which I reign supreme because I'm the nosiest person on the face of the earth.

SIGISMUND: You're the only one in this princely world I find entertaining.

BUGLE: My lord, I'm a great entertainer of all worldly princes.

(*Enter Aistulf, hat in hand.*)

AISTULF: Infinitely fortunate is this day, O prince, in which you proclaim yourself Poland's sun and fill its horizons with the resplendence and cheer of your divine aura, for you appear like the sun from underneath the mountains! Rise, then, and may the resplendent laurel leaf, so slow in crowning your brow, be as slow in withering. (*He dons his hat.*)

SIGISMUND: God keep you.

AISTULF: I shall forgive your meager greeting only because you don't know who I am. I am Aistulf, Duke of Muscovy, and your cousin; we must treat each other as equals.

SIGISMUND: I said "God keep you." What more do you wish? But since you don't find my greeting suitable to your high birth, next time I'll say "God damn you!"

SERVANT 2: (*To Aistulf.*) Consider, Your Highness, that he was raised in the mountains and treats everyone accordingly.
(*To Sigismund.*) Aistulf, my lord, prefers to be addressed as . . .

SIGISMUND: It irritated me the way he spoke so sternly, and the first thing he did was don his hat.

SERVANT 2: He's titled.

SIGISMUND: I'm more entitled!

SERVANT 2: All the same, it's fitting that more respect be observed between the two of you than between others.

SIGISMUND: What's it to you, anyway?

(*Enter Stella.*)

STELLA: Your Highness, my lord, I welcome you warmly to the royal family, which gratefully receives you and desires your presence and which, despite past deceptions, wishes you an august and exalted reign and a life measured in centuries rather than years.

SIGISMUND: Tell me now, who is this imperial beauty? Who is this human goddess at whose divine feet heaven surrenders its aura? Who is this beautiful woman?

BUGLE: She is, my lord, your cousin Stella.

SIGISMUND: Stella . . . Stellar? More like Solar! (*To Stella.*) Although it were well to wish me well on the wealth that I inherit, I deserve more well-wishing just for having seen you today; and thus, I appreciate your well-wishing for finding myself before such unmerited wealth. Stella—whose waking is enough to cheer the brightest shining star—what is left for the sun to do if you rise with the day? Allow me to kiss your hand, from whose snowy chalice the gentle breeze drinks in radiance. (*He moves to kiss her hand.*)

STELLA: (*Recoiling.*) Be a little more gentlemanly in the presence of the court.

AISTULF: (*Aside.*) If he takes her hand, I'm finished!

SERVANT 2: (*Aside.*) I can sense Aistulf's dismay; I must put a stop to this.

(*To Sigismund.*) Beware, my lord, that it's not right to be so forward, especially when Aistulf…

SIGISMUND: Didn't I tell you to stay out of my way?

SERVANT 2: I'm only saying what's right.

SIGISMUND: Everything you say annoys me. Nothing is right when it contradicts my delight.

SERVANT 2: But my lord, I remember hearing you say that it's well to obey and serve what's right.

SIGISMUND: You also heard me say that I'd throw anyone who got in my way off that balcony.

SERVANT 2: Men of my standing can't be treated that way.

SIGISMUND: Oh no? So help me God, I'll prove it!

(*He grabs* servant 2 *and rushes offstage, followed by the others. A scream is heard, and all but the servant return.*)

AISTULF: I can't believe what I've just seen!

STELLA: Help, everyone! (*Exit.*)

SIGISMUND: Did you see how he dropped from the balcony to the sea below? By God, I did it!

AISTULF: You should keep your rash impulses in greater check, for the difference between men and beasts is the same as that between a mountainside and a palace.

SIGISMUND: If you persist in scolding me with that smug attitude of yours, next time you might not have a head to wear your hat on.

(*Exit Aistulf; enter Vasily.*)

VASILY: What's going on here?

SIGISMUND: Nothing. I threw a man who irritated me off the balcony.

BUGLE: (*To Sigismund.*) Be aware that you're speaking to the king.

VASILY: The first day of your arrival has already cost a life?

SIGISMUND: He told me it couldn't be done, and I won the bet.

VASILY: It's very distressing that, when I come to see you as prince, expecting to find you mindful, triumphing over the fates and the stars, I find you acting with such severity and learn that your first deed in power is a grim murder. How can I now offer you love with open arms if I know your presumptuous embrace is trained in delivering death? Who ever looked without fear upon a naked dagger fresh from the kill? Who ever looked without emotion upon the bloody scene in which a man was murdered? Even the strongest among us responds to his instinct. And thus, recognizing your arms as the instrument of this murder and observing the bloody scene, I withdraw from your arms; and, although I had planned to encircle your neck with loving embraces, I must turn away without doing so, for I fear the grip of your arms. (*He turns his back on Sigismund.*)

SIGISMUND: I can survive without your embraces as I have until now, for when a father is capable of using such severity against me that he ungratefully casts me off, raises me like a beast, treats me like a monster, and solicits my death, it matters little that he withhold his embraces, for he has already denied me my humanity.

VASILY: (*Angrily turning back to face Sigismund.*) By God and heaven above, I wish I had never brought you into existence so as not to hear your voice and see your impudence now!

SIGISMUND: If you'd never brought me into existence, I'd have no complaint with you; but since you did, I do because you then took it from me; and although to give is the noblest and most exceptional of actions, to give only to take away later is the most despicable.

VASILY: What thanks I get for turning you from a poor and humble prisoner into the prince of Poland!

SIGISMUND: Well, what's there to thank you for in that? You've done nothing but usurp my free will. Old and decrepit, you're already at death's door, so what can you give me? Anything more than what's mine? You're my father and my king; hence all this grandeur is mine by the rights of natural law. Thus, even though you may have brought me here, I owe you nothing and could even denounce you for the time you've kept me without liberty, life, and honor; so it is you who should be thankful to me for not making you pay for what you've taken from me.

VASILY: You are barbaric and reckless; heaven has kept its word. And thus I appeal to heaven against your presumption and gall. And although you may now know who you are and understand the deception in which you have lived, and although you find yourself in a place where you consider yourself superior to everyone else, take my advice seriously: act with humility and gentleness because you might be dreaming even though you think yourself awake. (*Exit.*)

SIGISMUND: Might be dreaming even though I think myself awake? Impossible, for I feel and perceive the continuity between my past and present. And although you (*Gesturing toward the absent Vasily.*) may regret your decision to free me, there's no going back now; I know who I am, and you cannot—like it or not— take away my birthright to this throne. You may be used to the idea of seeing me in chains, but that was only when I didn't know who I was. But I know who I am now, and I know that I'm a composite of man and beast.

(*Enter Rossaura, dressed as a lady-in-waiting.*)

ROSSAURA: (*Aside.*) Now that I'm in the service of Stella, I'm in constant fear of running into Aistulf, for Clothold doesn't want him to know who I am or to see me because he says it's important for my honor. And I trust Clothold's intentions because I owe him a debt of gratitude for the shelter he has given my honor and life here in the palace.

BUGLE: What has pleased you most of everything you've seen and beheld today?

SIGISMUND: Nothing has completely bewildered me, for I've always known that anything is possible. Yet if I had to name something truly amazing in the world, it would be (*Gazing at Rossaura.*) the beauty of woman. I used to read in the books I had that what cost God the greatest deliberation was man, inasmuch as he is a world unto himself. Be that as it may, woman causes me more unease, for she is a heaven unto herself and is as superior to man in beauty as heaven is to earth, especially the one I'm looking at now.

ROSSAURA: (*Aside.*) The prince is here; I must withdraw.

SIGISMUND: Hey, woman, stop! Don't couple sunset and sunrise with your speedy retreat; for in coupling sunrise and sunset, warmth and cold shadow you will no doubt syncopate° the day.
(*Aside.*) But what's this I'm seeing!

ROSSAURA: (*Aside.*) What I'm seeing inspires both doubt and belief!

SIGISMUND: (*Aside.*) I've seen this beauty before!

ROSSAURA: (*Aside.*) I've seen this splendor, this grandeur reduced to the confines of a narrow prison!

SIGISMUND: (*Aside.*) Now I know I'm alive!
(*To Rossaura.*) Woman—for this term is the most loving sentiment a man can express—who are you? Without recognizing you I recognize my love for you, and such is the faith you inspire in me that I'm convinced I've seen you before. Who are you, beautiful woman?

ROSSAURA: (*Aside.*) I must keep my identity a secret.
(*To Sigismund.*) Just a lowly lady-in-waiting to Princess Stella.

SIGISMUND: You misspeak; you are the sun on whose flame that stellar beauty lives, for it takes its resplendence from your rays. I have seen how, in the fragrant realm of the flowers, the divine rose rules over all others, empress through her greater beauty. I have seen how, in the dark depths of the learned academy of precious gems, the diamond is crowned emperor because of his greater brilliance. I have seen how, in the beautiful corridors of the restless realm of the stars, the morning star, first in rank, rules as king. I have seen how, in the perfect spheres of heaven, the sun calls the planets to congress, presiding over them as the most dazzling source of daylight. So how is it that when, among flowers, gems, stars, and planets the most beautiful govern, you serve one of lesser beauty while you—ever more beautiful and lovely—are the sun, the morning star, the diamond, and the rose?

(*Enter Clothold, unseen.*)

CLOTHOLD: (*Aside.*) I must restrain Sigismund, for it was I, after all, who raised him. But what's going on here?

ROSSAURA: I cherish your kindness, but silence will be my most eloquent response; for when reason falters, my lord, the most articulate is the one who knows how to keep quiet. (*She turns to exit.*)

SIGISMUND: Stop; wait! How can you presume to leave my senses in the dark like that?

syncopate: To shorten (shorten the day).

ROSSAURA: I request Your Highness's permission to go.

SIGISMUND: To go so suddenly is not a request; it's called taking matters into your own hands.

ROSSAURA: Well, if you don't grant me permission, I shall have no other choice.

SIGISMUND: You'll force me from politeness to rudeness because resistance acts as a cruel venom upon my patience.

ROSSAURA: Well, even if that venom—full of fury, severity, and wrath—were to overcome your patience, it wouldn't dare attack my honor, nor could it.

SIGISMUND: You'll make me lose the fear your beauty inspires in me just to see if I can, for I'm strongly inclined to overcome the impossible. Today I threw a man off that balcony who said it couldn't be done, so have no doubt that I'll throw your honor out the window just to see if I can.

CLOTHOLD: (*Aside.*) His rashness knows no bounds. What am I to do, heavens, in the face of this mad desire that puts my honor at risk a second time?

ROSSAURA: Not in vain were the warnings that this unlucky realm would suffer, at the hands of your tyranny, terrible scandals of transgression, treason, ire, and death. Yet what can be expected of a man who—human in name only—is reckless, inhuman, cruel, presumptuous, barbaric, and tyrannical; a man who, after all, was born among beasts?

SIGISMUND: Precisely so you wouldn't insult me that way, I was polite with you, thinking I could win you over with such measures; but if my efforts mean nothing to you, then, by God, I might as well live up to your insults! (*To Bugle.*) You there, leave us alone, close the door, and make sure no one comes in!

(*Exit Bugle.*)

ROSSAURA: (*Aside.*) I'm finished!
(*To Sigismund.*) I'm warning you!

SIGISMUND: I'm a tyrant, remember? So your attempts to restrain me are in vain.

CLOTHOLD: (*Aside.*) Oh, what an awful predicament! I must stop him even if he kills me.
(*To Sigismund.*) My lord, listen to reason!

SIGISMUND: This is the second time you provoke my ire, you decrepit old madman. Do you take my anger and severity so lightly? How did you get in here?

CLOTHOLD: Summoned by the cries of her voice, I'm here to tell you to act more peacefully if you desire to rule; and you needn't resort to cruelty just because you have authority over others, because this may all be a dream.

SIGISMUND: You provoke my rage by lecturing me about reality. I'll kill you and see if it's a dream or reality?

(*As he goes to unsheathe his sword, Clothold detains him and kneels before him.*)

CLOTHOLD: I'm hoping this gesture will save my life.

SIGISMUND: Take your brazen hand off my blade!

CLOTHOLD: Until someone arrives who can restrain your severity and quick temper, I will not let you go.

ROSSAURA: Good heavens!

SIGISMUND: Let go I say, you decrepit madman, you barbaric traitor, or else . . .
(*They fight*) . . . I'll kill you with my bare hands!

ROSSAURA: Come quickly, everyone, he's going to kill Clothold! (*Exit.*)

(*As Aistulf enters, Clothold falls at his feet, and Aistulf steps between the two antagonists.*)

AISTULF: What's the meaning of this, kind prince? You would tarnish your gallant blade with the blood of an old man? Return your distinguished sword to its sheath.

SIGISMUND: As soon as I've drenched it in his contemptible blood.

AISTULF: His life seeks refuge at my feet, so my arrival must be for a reason.

SIGISMUND: Reason for you to die, since with your death I'll also make you pay for the anger you provoked in me earlier.

AISTULF: I fight in self-defense and thus commit no offense against the crown.

(*They unsheathe their swords. Enter Vasily and Stella.*)

CLOTHOLD: (*To Aistulf.*) Don't hurt him, my lord!

VASILY: What's this, swords drawn in the palace?

STELLA: (*Aside.*) It's Aistulf! Oh, miserable me, this is torture!

VASILY: What's going on here?

AISTULF: Nothing, my lord, now that you're here.

(*They sheathe their swords.*)

SIGISMUND: A great deal, my lord, even though you've arrived. I tried to kill that old man.

VASILY: You show no respect for his gray hair?

CLOTHOLD: Don't fret, my lord; my gray hair is unimportant.

SIGISMUND: It is in vain to hope that I will show respect for gray hair; why, I might even see yours (*Gesturing at Vasily.*) at my feet one day because I still haven't had my revenge for the unjust manner in which you raised me! (*Exit.*)

VASILY: Well, before that happens, you'll return to sleep in a place where, upon awakening, you'll believe that all that has happened to you, like everything of this world, was a dream.

(*Exit Vasily and Clothold, Stella and Aistulf remain onstage.*)

AISTULF: How seldom fate errs in predicting misfortune, for it is as accurate in foretelling evil as it is inaccurate in foretelling good! What an excellent astrologer it would be if it limited itself to the harshest predictions, for there's no doubt that they would always come true! This theory, Stella, is confirmed in the case of both Sigismund and myself, for in each of us there was a different prediction. In Sigismund's case it foresaw severity, presumption, misfortune, and death, and it was right in each instance because everything

has come true in the end. But in my case—where, my lady, once my eyes met your celestial gaze, of which the sun is but a shadow and the sky a mere hint, it predicted good fortune, triumph, acclaim, and wealth—it was both wrong and right; for when fate hints at favors, it's only right to expect contempt.

STELLA: I'm sure your compliments are heartfelt; yet I suspect they're intended for another lady, Aistulf, perhaps the one whose portrait you wore in the locket around your neck when you first came to see me. That being the case, your amorous sentiments are best directed toward her; go to her to claim your reward, for insincere compliments and misrepresentations are no more valid in courtship than they are at court.

(*Enter Rossaura, hidden.*)

ROSSAURA: (*Aside.*) Thank God my cruel misfortunes are finally coming to an end, for whoever suffers through this is prepared for anything!

AISTULF: I'll banish the locket's portrait from my breast to make way for your beautiful image. Where Stella's light is present, shadows have no place . . .
(*Aside.*) . . . nor does stellar light in the presence of the sun.
(*To Stella.*) I'll go get the locket.
(*Aside.*) Forgive me, lovely Rossaura, for the offense, but this is as faithful as men and women can be when they're apart. (*Exit.*)

ROSSAURA: (*Aside.*) I was so worried he'd see me that I didn't catch anything they said.

STELLA: Astraea?

ROSSAURA: My lady?

STELLA: I'm glad it's you because you're the only one I can trust with a secret.

ROSSAURA: You're too kind, my lady, to one who serves you.

STELLA: In the short time I've known you, Astraea, you've earned the keys to my volition; for this reason and because of who you are, I'm going to trust you with a secret I'm not even comfortable with myself.

ROSSAURA: You command my absolute loyalty.

STELLA: Well, to make a long story short, my first cousin Aistulf—it should be enough to say he's my *first* because some things are spoken through thought alone—is to marry me, if in fact fortune is willing to remedy so much adversity with a single act of joy. I was distressed the first day I saw him that he was wearing the portrait of another lady in a locket around his neck. I spoke to him about it politely; he's gentlemanly and well-intentioned, so he went to get the locket and is going to bring it here. But I feel too awkward accepting it from him directly. Stay here, and when he comes, tell him to hand it over to you. I'll say no more; you're discreet and beautiful and must know quite well what it means to be in love.

(*Exit.*)

ROSSAURA: If only I didn't! Heaven help me! What woman is careful and prudent enough to escape such a dilemma? Can there be anyone else in the world whom the merciless heavens assail with more misfortune and besiege with more sorrow? What shall I do amid such confusion, where it seems impossible to find a solution that comforts me or a comfort that consoles me? Since the first misfortune, nothing has happened or arisen that hasn't turned into another misfortune, and they seem to succeed one another like heirs. In imitation of the phoenix, they breed one another, living on what kills them; and their urn is always alive with their ashes. Misfortunes are cowardly, a philosopher once said, because they never seem to walk alone; but I say they're courageous, since they always push forward and never look back. Whoever is escorted by misfortunes need stop at nothing, for he need never fear that they will abandon him. I can say this because so many have occurred in my life that I've never found myself without them, nor do they tire until they find me wounded by fortune and in the arms of death. Oh, miserable me! What shall I do now under such circumstances? If I reveal my identity, Clothold, to whom I owe my life for his protection and esteem, might be offended, for he has asked me to keep quiet while awaiting his remedy to my dishonor. But if I don't reveal my identity, how can I keep up the charade when Aistulf arrives? For even if I manage to disguise my voice, my speech, and my eyes, my soul will expose them all as liars. What shall I do? But why deliberate over what to do when it's evident that, no matter how I prepare, deliberate, and think, when the moment arrives my grief will make me act as it sees fit? For no one can claim absolute rule over his sufferings. And since my soul dares not determine a course of action, let my grief culminate today and let my suffering reach its extreme, as long as I'm freed of doubting and guessing once and for all. But until then, give me strength, heavens, give me strength!

(*Enter Aistulf with the locket.*)

AISTULF: Here, my lady, is the locket... but... my god!

ROSSAURA: Why that look of bewilderment, my lord? Why are you so amazed?

AISTULF: To hear your voice, Rossaura, and to see you here before me.

ROSSAURA: I, Rossaura? You are mistaken, my lord, if you take me for another lady; for I am Astraea, and my humble station is not worthy of the joy caused by your confused affection.

AISTULF: Enough with the deception, Rossaura, for the soul never lies; and although mine may behold you as Astraea, it loves you as Rossaura.

ROSSAURA: I don't understand, my lord, so I don't know how to respond. All I can say is that Stella (who's at least as stellar as Venus) has ordered me to wait here for you and to ask you to hand over that locket—which seems like a very reasonable request—and to take it to her myself. Stella wishes it thus, for even the slightest of actions, if they end up compromising me, are stellar in design.

AISTULF: Try as you might, Rossaura, you're a most unconvincing liar! Tell your eyes to harmonize their music to your voice; otherwise it's inevitable that such a cacophonous instrument stutter and falter in attempting to adjust and calibrate the falsehoods of speech to the truth of feelings.

ROSSAURA: I repeat that I'm here only for the locket.

AISTULF: Well, since you insist on carrying on with this deception, I shall reply in kind. You may tell the princess, Astraea, that I hold her in such esteem that, when she asks me for a portrait, I consider it in poor taste to send it to her; rather, that she may treasure and revere it, I'm sending her the original. And you may take it to her directly, for you already bear it with you if you can bear yourself.

ROSSAURA: When a determined, willful, and courageous man agrees to undertake a mission, if he returns without reaching the goal—even if he acquires something more valuable in the process—he faces ridicule and humiliation. I'm here for a portrait, and even if I take back an original of greater worth, I'll be ridiculed. Give me the locket, my lord, for I will not return without it.

AISTULF: (*Taunting*) Well, I don't know how you expect to take it if I don't give it to you.

ROSSAURA: Like this. (*She grabs for the locket.*) Give it to me, you ingrate!

AISTULF: Forget it.

ROSSAURA: By God, it's not for another woman's hands! (*She continues struggling for the locket.*)

AISTULF: My, you're ferocious today!

ROSSAURA: And you're a two-timing scoundrel!

AISTULF: That's enough, my Rossaura.

ROSSAURA: I'm not your Rossaura, you swine!

(*They continue struggling. Enter Stella.*)

STELLA: Astraea, Aistulf! What's the meaning of this?

AISTULF: (*Aside.*) Oh no, it's Stella!

ROSSAURA: (*Aside.*) May love grant me the ingenuity to get my locket back.
(*To Stella.*) If you wish to know what's going on, my lady, I shall tell you.

AISTULF: (*Aside to Rossaura.*) What do you think you're doing?

ROSSAURA: You ordered me to wait here for Aistulf and to ask him for a locket on your behalf. I was left alone, and as related topics associate freely in the mind, your talk of lockets reminded me that I was carrying one of my own in my sleeve. I decided to look at it, for people always entertain themselves with nonsense when they're alone. I accidentally dropped it on the floor, and Aistulf, who'd just arrived to give you the other lady's locket, picked it up; and not only was he unwilling to hand over the one you'd asked him for, but he also decided to take mine. And since he wouldn't give it back even when I begged and beseeched him, I grew angry and impatient and tried to take it by force. That's mine in his hand now; you can easily tell from the resemblance it bears to me.

STELLA: Let go of the locket, Aistulf! (*She takes it from him.*)

AISTULF: My lady!

STELLA: (*Looking at the locket, then at Rossaura.*) A faithful copy of the original.

ROSSAURA: Then you agree it's mine?

STELLA: How could there be any doubt?

ROSSAURA: (*Triumphant.*) Now tell him to give you the other one.

STELLA: (*Dismayed.*) Take your locket and go.

ROSSAURA: (*Aside.*) At least I got my locket back. The rest is their problem. (*Exit.*)

STELLA: Now give me the locket I asked you for; for though I don't plan to look at you or speak to you ever again, I don't want it to remain in your power, no, if only because I so foolishly asked you for it.

AISTULF: (*Aside.*) How can I get out of this awful predicament?
(*To Stella.*) Although I should like, lovely Stella, to serve and obey you, I can't give you the locket you request because...

STELLA: You're a swine and a boorish suitor! I don't want it from you now because I wouldn't want to be reminded, in taking it, that I ever asked you for it! (*Exit.*)

AISTULF: Hey...listen...look...wait! Goddamn you, Rossaura! From where, how, or why did you show up in Poland today? You're going to end up destroying yourself and me with you? (*Exit.*)

Scene 2

The tower as described in Act 1.

(*Sigismund, bound in chains and dressed in animal skins as at the beginning of the play, is asleep on the floor. Enter Clothold, Bugle, and two servants.*)

CLOTHOLD: (*To the servants.*) Leave him here, for his presumption will end today where it began.

SERVANT 1: I've secured the chain as before.

BUGLE: Better never to wake up, Sigismund; you'll only find yourself destroyed, your luck reversed, your counterfeit pleasure reduced to a shadow of life and a glow of death.

CLOTHOLD: People who talk as much as you do should have a nice place in which to debate. (*To the servants.*) Seize him and lock him away in that cell.

BUGLE: Why me?

CLOTHOLD: Because a Bugle that knows so many secrets must be kept locked away where it can't sound off.

BUGLE: Have I, by chance, tried to kill my father? No. Am I the one who threw little Icarus off the balcony? Is my death or rebirth the issue here? Does my dreaming or sleeping matter? What's your purpose in locking me up?

CLOTHOLD: You're Bugle.

BUGLE: Well, I'll call myself Horn from now on, and I'll keep quiet as befits those with horns.

(*They lock him in the tower. Enter Vasily, his face hidden by a hood.*)

VASILY: Clothold?

CLOTHOLD: My lord! Why does Your Majesty come in disguise?

VASILY: A foolish curiosity to see what happens with Sigismund—oh, miserable me!—has lowered me to this level.

CLOTHOLD: Behold him there, reduced to the misery of his former self.

VASILY: Oh, unfortunate prince, born under such a sad sign! (*To Clothold.*) Go wake him now, for the lotus he drank should be wearing off.

CLOTHOLD: He is restless, my lord, and talking in his sleep.

VASILY: What could he be dreaming now? Let's listen.

SIGISMUND: (*In his sleep.*) A proper prince is he who punishes tyrants. Clothold shall die by my hands! My father shall kiss my feet!

CLOTHOLD: He threatens me with death.

VASILY: And me with severity and disrespect.

CLOTHOLD: He wishes to take my life.

VASILY: He schemes to have me bow before his feet.

SIGISMUND: (*In his sleep.*) On the broad public square that is the great stage of the world, my unequalled valor shall make its appearance! To satisfy my vengeance, all shall watch Prince Sigismund triumph over his father! (*He wakes up.*) But—oh, miserable me!—where am I?

VASILY: (*Aside to Clothold.*) He mustn't see me. You know what to do. I shall listen from over there. (*He steps back and remains out of Sigismund's view.*)

SIGISMUND: (*Touching himself.*) Is this really me? Is this me, reduced to prison and chains? Is this not the tower that is my grave? Yes. God help me, what a deluge of dreams!

CLOTHOLD: (*Aside.*) It's up to me to carry off the charade. (*To Sigismund.*) Are you finally waking up?

SIGISMUND: Yes, I'm finally waking up.

CLOTHOLD: Have you been sleeping all day? You haven't woken since I left to follow the flight of that majestic eagle while you stayed put?

SIGISMUND: No, nor am I awake now, for as I see it, Clothold, I'm still sleeping. I can't be very wrong because, if what seemed so palpable and true to me was only a dream, what I'm seeing now mustn't be trusted. And it's no surprise, given I can see in my sleep, that exhaustion should lead me to dream while awake.

CLOTHOLD: Tell me what you dreamed.

SIGISMUND: Even if it was a dream, I won't say what I dreamed, Clothold, but rather what I saw. I awoke to find myself—what flattering cruelty!—upon a bed that could have been, with a bit of detail and color, a mat of flowers woven by Spring. There a thousand noblemen, bowing at my feet, called me their prince and adorned me in fine clothes and precious gems. You appeared and turned the numbness of my senses into happiness by announcing the joyous news; for although I live in misery here, there I was Prince of Poland.

CLOTHOLD: You must have given me a handsome reward!

SIGISMUND: Not exactly. With a daring and mighty spirit, I twice tried to kill you for your treason.

CLOTHOLD: Such severity toward me?

SIGISMUND: I was lord over all, and I wanted revenge on everyone. My only love was for a woman, a love I still believe to be real because, while everything else has vanished, it alone has remained with me.

(*Exit Vasily.*)

CLOTHOLD: (*Aside.*) The king has left, filled with sympathy at the prince's remarks.

(*To Sigismund.*) Because we had spoken about that eagle beforehand, when you went to sleep you dreamed of empire. But in your dreams it would be fitting, Sigismund, to show more respect to he who raised you with such care; for even in dreams it pays to do what's right. (*Exit.*)

SIGISMUND: This is true; so we must repress this savage character, this fury, this ambition, just in case we dream again. And that will happen sooner or later, for we live in such an exceptional world that living is no more than dreaming; and experience teaches me that he who lives dreams what he is until waking. The king dreams that he's king, and he lives under this deception commanding, planning, and governing; and his acclaim, which he receives on loan, is scribbled in the wind and turned to ashes by death. What grave misfortune! To think that anyone should wish to govern knowing that he will awaken in the sleep of death! The rich man dreams of more riches, which only bring him more worries; the poor man dreams that he suffers in misery and poverty; the man who improves his lot dreams; the man who toils and petitions dreams; the man who insults and offends dreams. And in this world, in short, everyone dreams what he is although no one realizes it. I dream that I'm here, weighed down by these chains, and I've dreamt that I found myself in more flattering circumstances. What is life? A frenzy. What is life? A vain hope, a shadow, a fiction. The greatest good is fleeting, for all life is a dream and even dreams are but dreams.

ACT 3 • Scene 1

The tower.

(*Enter Bugle amid darkness. He addresses the audience.*)

BUGLE: In a haunted tower, because of what I know, I'm being held captive. What will they do to me because of my ignorance if they ax me because of my knowledge? To think that a fellow should be sentenced to a life of starving to death! Everyone will say I'm feeling sorry for myself. Well, they're right, because this silence, in my opinion, doesn't befit one named Bugle, and I can't shut up. My only company here, if I can bring myself to say so, are spiders and mice—what lovely goldfinches! My dreams last night filled my poor head with shawms,° trumpets, and tomfoolery; and with processions, crucifixes, and penitents marching up and down and fainting at the sight of one another's blood. Whereas I, to tell the truth, am fainting from hunger, for I find myself in a prison where the board is bare and the menu mean. If silence is considered saintly, then Saint Secret must be my day in the New Calendar,° for I fast in his honor and never feast! But the punishment I suffer is well deserved, for, unlike most servants, I kept my mouth shut, which is the greatest sacrilege.

(*A sound of drums and people is heard, and a voice speaks from offstage.*)

SOLDIER 1: This is his tower. Break down the door! Everyone in!

BUGLE: By God! They must be looking for me, for they know I'm here! What can they want with me?

(*Enter as many soldiers as possible.*)

SOLDIER 1: Inside, inside!

SOLDIER 2: (*Pointing to Bugle.*) There he is.

BUGLE: No he's not.

SOLDIERS: (*In unison.*) My lord!

BUGLE: (*Aside.*) Are these guys drunk or what?

SOLDIER 2: You are our prince; we will not accept and do not want anyone but our rightful lord, nor a foreign prince. Grant us all your feet, that we may bow before them.

SOLDIERS: (*In unison.*) Long live our great prince!

BUGLE: (*Aside.*) By God, it's for real! Can it be a custom of this kingdom to take a new prisoner each day, make him prince, and then return him to the tower? Apparently so, for I've seen it happen each day I've been here. I'll have to play my role.

SOLDIERS: (*In unison.*) Grant us the soles of your feet. (*They kneel to kiss his feet.*)

BUGLE: I can't because I need them for myself, and I wouldn't do you much good as a de-solate prince.

SOLDIER 2: We've all told your father that we'll accept only you as our prince, not the Muscovite.

BUGLE: You insulted my father that way? You've got a lot of nerve!

SOLDIER 1: It was the loyalty of our hearts speaking.

BUGLE: If it was out of loyalty, then I forgive you.

SOLDIER 2: Come forth and restore your rule. Long live Sigismund!

ALL SOLDIERS: (*In unison.*) Long live Sigismund!

BUGLE: (*Aside.*) They call me Sigismund? Why, it must be the name they reserve for all their bogus princes.

---

shawms: Musical instruments similar to an oboe.   **New Calendar:** Our Gregorian calendar, introduced in 1582.

(*Enter Sigismund.*)

SIGISMUND: Who calls my name?

BUGLE: (*Aside.*) Alas, is my time as prince already up?

SOLDIER 2: Which of you is Sigismund?

SIGISMUND: I am.

SOLDIER 2: (*To Bugle.*) You impudent fool! How dare you call yourself Sigismund?

BUGLE: Me, call myself Sigismund? That's not true. You're the ones who Sigismunded me, so you're the impudent fools.

SOLDIER 1: Great Prince Sigismund—the sight of whom validates the faith that led us to proclaim you our lord—your father, the great King Vasily, fearful lest the heavens bear out a fate that says he will end up at your feet, vanquished by his own son, is attempting to deny you your rightful authority and give it to Aistulf, Duke of Muscovy. For this purpose he convened his court, but the masses learned of the events and, realizing that they have a Polish-born prince, refuse to be ruled by a foreigner. And thus, nobly overlooking the inclemency of fate, they search for you where you are held prisoner so that, with the aid of their weapons, you may break out of this tower and recover your imperial crown and scepter, stripping them from a tyrant. Come forth, then, for a numerous army of outlaws and peasants hails you in the wilderness. Freedom is within your grasp; listen to its chant.

VOICES: (*Offstage, in unison.*) Long live Sigismund! Long live the prince.

SIGISMUND: (*Aside.*) What in heaven is going on! Am I again to dream of grandeur only to see it undone by time? Am I to glimpse again the shadows and outlines of majesty and splendor only to see them swept away by the wind? Must I learn the truth all over again—that human power is born humbly of risk and lives in constant jeopardy? It shall not happen; it shall not. Look at me, once again prisoner of my fortune. And since I know that this life is all a dream, be gone, shadows, you who today feign bodies and voices before my deadened senses when I know you have no body or voice. For I don't want counterfeit majesty and splendor, no! Fanciful illusions that unravel at the slightest touch of a breeze—just like the budding almond tree whose flowers, without warning and ignoring counsel, bloom early and expire at the first cold wind, withering and tarnishing the beauty, light, and color of their rosy bonnets— I see you, I recognize you, and I know you play the same game with everyone who sleeps. I won't be fooled this time, for I've learned the truth and know that life is a dream.

SOLDIER 2: (*Sensing Sigismund's doubt.*) If you think we're deceiving you, turn your gaze toward those imperious mountains, and you'll see all the people who wait there to obey your command.

SIGISMUND: I've seen this before as clearly and distinctly as I'm seeing it now, yet it was a dream.

SOLDIER 1: Great things are always announced in premonitions, which must be what you had if you dreamt this moment.

SIGISMUND: You're right; it was a premonition. (*Aside.*) And just in case it was correct, given that life is so short, let's dream, my soul, let's dream again. But this time we must be vigilant and aware that we shall awaken from this delight at the best moment; and if we keep that in mind, the truth will be easier to bear, for to be prepared for harm is to avoid it. And with the knowledge that, even if the premonition was correct, all power is borrowed and must be returned to its heavenly owner, let us stop at nothing. (*To the soldiers.*) Vassals, I appreciate your loyalty; you can count on me, bold and adroit, to liberate you from slavery to a foreigner. Sound the call to arms, and shortly you will see my immense valor in action. I shall take arms against my father and prove the heavens true; soon he will be at my mercy. (*Aside.*) Yet, given that I could wake up before then, wouldn't it be better not to make promises I can't keep?

ALL: (*Offstage, in unison.*) Long live Sigismund! Long live the prince!

(*Enter Clothold, on his way to visit Sigismund in the tower.*)

CLOTHOLD: What's all the commotion, heavens?

SIGISMUND: Clothold!

CLOTHOLD: My lord! (*Aside.*) My life will be the test of his cruelty.

BUGLE: (*Aside.*) I'll bet he hurls him off the mountain. (*Exit.*)

CLOTHOLD: I come before your regal feet, certain of my death. (*He kneels before Sigismund.*)

SIGISMUND: On your feet, father, on your feet; you will be the compass and guide to whom I entrust my achievements, for I know that I owe my upbringing to your ceaseless loyalty. Let me embrace you.

CLOTHOLD: (*He remains on his knees.*) What are you saying?

SIGISMUND: That I'm dreaming, and that I want to do what's right, for it pays to do what's right even in dreams.

CLOTHOLD: Well, my lord, if doing what's right is now your watchword, then you won't be offended if I do the same. You would wage war against your father, but I cannot counsel you or come to your aid against my king. I am at your mercy; kill me.

SIGISMUND: Swine! Traitor! Ingrate! (*Aside.*) But heavens! I should exercise more restraint, for I still don't know if I'm awake. (*To Clothold.*) Clothold, I envy and appreciate your valor. Go serve the king, and we'll see each other on the battlefield. (*To his soldiers.*) You there, sound the call to arms.

CLOTHOLD: (*Rising.*) You have my eternal gratitude. (*Exit.*)

SIGISMUND: Off we go, fortune, to restore my reign. Don't wake me if I'm sleeping, and don't put me to sleep if it's real. Yet, whether it's reality or a dream, doing what's right is what matters. If it's reality, then for the sake of reality; if it's a dream, then for the purpose of winning friends for when we awaken. (*Exit all amid the call to arms.*)

Scene 2

King's palace.

(*Enter Vasily and Aistulf.*)

VASILY: Who, Aistulf, is wise enough to curb the fury of a runaway horse? Who can detain the current of an imperious river in its downhill rush to the sea? Who is courageous enough to stay a boulder that has broken free of the mountaintop? Well, that's all easy in comparison to halting a willful and reckless mob. The proof is in the clashing cries of Poland's rival parties, which fill the mountains with thunderous echoes of "Long live Aistulf!" or "Long live Sigismund!" (*The voices indicated are heard offstage.*) The coronation site, fallen prey to wayward aspirations and hidden loyalties, has become a gloomy theater where importunate fortune stages her tragedies.

AISTULF: We must stay the celebration, my lord, and postpone the acclaim and flattering delights your favored hand promised me; for if Poland, which I hope to rule, today refuses obedience to me, it is to make me earn it first. Give me a horse and watch as I turn my arrogant thunder into a bolt of lightning. (*Exit.*)

VASILY: The inevitable has little remedy, and the foreseeable carries considerable risk; if it's meant to be, there's no defense against it, for trying to avoid it only precipitates its arrival. What harsh logic! What extreme circumstances! What tremendous horror! He who thinks he's running from danger ends up running into it. My attempts to forestall fate have ruined me. I, and I alone, have destroyed my fatherland.

(*Enter Stella.*)

STELLA: If you do not act quickly, Your Majesty, to put a stop to the chaos that has broken out and, spreading from one side to the next, polarizes streets and squares, you will soon find your kingdom swimming in waves of scarlet, drenched in the crimson of its own blood. Sorrow is already widespread as misfortune and tragedy take hold. Such is the ruin of your empire, such the might of harsh and bloody strife that it amazes the eyes and shocks the ears. The sun reels in confusion and the wind stifles its breezes; every rock is a tombstone and every flower marks a grave; every building is a mausoleum and every soldier a living skeleton.

(*Enter Clothold.*)

CLOTHOLD: Thank God I've made it here alive!

VASILY: Clothold! What can you tell us of Sigismund?

CLOTHOLD: A monstrous mob, impulsive and blind, broke into the tower and liberated the prince from its depths. Finding his power seconded a second time, he became courageous, proclaiming fiercely that he would prove the heavens right.

VASILY: Give me a horse, and I, ever courageous, shall defeat my ungrateful son face to face. In the defense of my crown, may steel triumph where learning has failed. (*Exit.*)

STELLA: And I, flanking the sun (*Gesturing toward Vasily as he exits.*), shall act as Bellona.° I hope to write my name next to yours, for I shall fly on loyal wings in competition with Pallas. (*Exit amid the call to arms.*)

(*Enter Rossaura, who detains Clothold.*)

ROSSAURA: I realize we're in the midst of war, but even if your heart is bursting with valor in its desire to aid the king, hear me out. You know that I arrived in Poland poor, humble, and unfortunate and that, aided by your stature, I found refuge in your devotion. You ordered me—oh, heavens!—to live in disguise in the palace and to attempt, concealing my jealousy, to keep away from Aistulf. But he saw me in the end, and he has so little respect for my honor that he speaks to Stella in front of me every night in the garden. I've stolen the key, with which you can enter the garden and put an end to my troubles. Willful, bold, and adamant, you can affirm my honor there since you're already resolved to avenge me with his death.

CLOTHOLD: It's true that from the moment I met you, Rossaura, I was moved by your sobs to do for you whatever my life allowed. The first thing I did was to get you to change that outfit you were wearing so that, if Aistulf saw you, he'd see you in your own clothes and not take for indecency the mad temerity that besmirches honor. I've since been trying to determine how to recover your lost honor even if it meant—so much does your honor preoccupy me!—killing Aistulf. What futile madness! Although, given that he's not my king, I'm neither frightened nor awed by him. I was planning to kill him when Sigismund tried to kill me, and just then he showed up and, overlooking all danger to himself, demonstrated a degree of altruism in my defense that went past courage to temerity. So tell me, how am I now to kill the person who saved my life when my soul is full of gratitude? And thus, with appreciation on one side and affection on the other, having given you life and received it from him, I don't know which party to attend to or to help; for to you I'm bound on account of giving, and to him I'm bound on account of receiving. And thus, in the matter at hand, there's no way to satisfy my heart because my active and passive tempers are at odds.

Bellona: Roman goddess of war.

ROSSAURA: I needn't remind you that, in men of exception, receiving is as base an act as giving is noble. Accepting this principle, you have no reason to be grateful to him given that, if he gave you life and you gave it to me, it's obvious that he forced your noble nature to commit a base act while I facilitated its generosity. Therefore you should consider yourself offended by him and indebted to me, for you have given to me what you received from him. And thus you should attend to my honor, which is at great risk, for it gives me precedence in the conflict between giving and receiving.

CLOTHOLD: Although nobility lives in those who give, gratitude for noble actions corresponds to those who receive. And as I have not held back in giving, my honorable name has become identified with generosity. Let me now become known as grateful, for I can do so while still being charitable, for giving and receiving are equally honorable.

ROSSAURA: You gave me life and, in doing so, said yourself that a life lived in dishonor is no life. Therefore I haven't actually received anything from you, for in reality your hand has dispensed death, not life. And if you must be charitable before grateful—as you just said—I expect you to give me my life, which you haven't done yet; and, since giving is more dignified, be charitable first, and later there will be time to be grateful.

CLOTHOLD: I'm convinced by your reasoning and shall indeed be charitable first. I shall, Rossaura, give you my inheritance, with which you may retire to a convent. This is a good solution to our problem since, in fleeing from a crime, you will take refuge in a sanctuary. For when a divided kingdom is burdened with misfortunes, I don't wish to multiply them, for I was born noble. With this remedy I can be loyal to my country, charitable to you, and grateful to Aistulf. It behooves you to accept this remedy, which we'll keep between the two of us, for I wouldn't do anything more even if—by God!—I were your father.

ROSSAURA: If you were my father, I would accept this insult; but since you're not, I refuse.

CLOTHOLD: Then what do you plan to do?

ROSSAURA: Kill the duke.

CLOTHOLD: Can a lady who never knew her father have such valor?

ROSSAURA: Yes.

CLOTHOLD: What drives you?

ROSSAURA: My reputation.

CLOTHOLD: Beware that Aistulf is about to become...

ROSSAURA: My honor trumps all else.

CLOTHOLD: ...your king and husband to Stella.

ROSSAURA: By God, it shall not happen!

CLOTHOLD: This is madness.

ROSSAURA: I know.

CLOTHOLD: You must overcome it.

ROSSAURA: I cannot.

CLOTHOLD: You'll lose...

ROSSAURA: I know.

CLOTHOLD: ...your life and your honor.

ROSSAURA: I know.

CLOTHOLD: Then what's your goal?

ROSSAURA: My death.

CLOTHOLD: That's sacrilege.

ROSSAURA: It's honorable.

CLOTHOLD: It's absurd.

ROSSAURA: Its valiant.

CLOTHOLD: It's reckless.

ROSSAURA: It's the product of rage and ire.

CLOTHOLD: So there's no compromising with your blind frenzy?

ROSSAURA: No.

CLOTHOLD: Who will help you?

ROSSAURA: I'll help myself.

CLOTHOLD: There's no other solution?

ROSSAURA: There's no other solution.

CLOTHOLD: Think about it; there must be another way.

ROSSAURA: Only another form of self-destruction. (*Exit.*)

CLOTHOLD: Well, if you're bent on destroying yourself, wait for me, my daughter, and we'll go down together. (*Exit.*)

Scene 3

A wilderness area, somewhere between the palace and the tower.

(*Amid the call to arms, soldiers, Bugle, and Sigismund march out, the latter dressed in animal skins.*)

SIGISMUND: If Rome at her most triumphant could see me today, how thrilled she would be at the rare opportunity of having her mighty armies led by a beast whose headstrong vigor strikes at the firmament itself! But let's come back to earth, my spirit. We mustn't exalt this tenuous acclaim if I'll be disappointed upon waking at having achieved so much only to lose it; for the lesser the acclaim, the less it will be missed if it's lost.

(*A bugle sounds offstage.*)

BUGLE: We are approached by a swift horse—forgive me, but its description requires considerable detail—upon which a careful map is drawn in which the body is formed of earth, the soul is made up of fire trapped in the chest, the frothy mouth partakes of the sea, and air is exhaled in its hot breath; the motley figure inspires chaos, for its body, soul, frothy mouth, and breath form a monster of earth, fire, sea, and wind. Upon its coarse coat of dapple gray sits a remarkable woman who, in seeking your presence, digs in the spurs and bids it fly rather than gallop.

SIGISMUND: Her aura is blinding.

BUGLE: By God, it's Rossaura! (*Exit.*)

SIGISMUND: Heaven has restored her to my presence.

(*Enter Rossaura with a splendid cloak, a sword, and a dagger.*)

ROSSAURA: Kind Sigismund, shining sun of Poland, whose heroic majesty is emerging into the day of its deeds from the night of its nothingness; may your ascent in the world be like that of the greatest of heavenly bodies, which, in the arms of dawn, recovers its shining throne among flowers and roses and, stepping out newly crowned, spreads light and casts rays over oceans and mountains, bathing high peaks and adorning frothy waves. Grant refuge to this unlucky woman who today throws herself at your feet, who, being both unfortunate and a woman, has two reasons to expect charity from a man who prides himself on his courage—either of which is enough, either of which is more than enough. Three times now you have beheld me, three times without knowing who I am, for on each occasion you've seen me in different attire and surroundings. The first time was in your cruel prison, where you took me for a man and your life made my misfortunes seem flattering. The second time—when you saw your majestic splendor reduced to a dream, a ghost, a shadow—you beheld me as a woman. The third time is today, where, like a monstrous hybrid, I mix the fine clothes of a woman with the weapons of a man. And so that pity may move you to act on my behalf, listen to the tragic events of my life. I was born at court in Muscovy to a noble mother who, to judge from her misfortunes, must have been quite beautiful. She caught the eye of a treacherous scoundrel, whom I don't name because I don't know him, although my own valor tells me something of his; and, as the product of his inclinations, I regret now not being born pagan so that I could madly convince myself that he was one of those gods who—transformed into a shower of gold, a swan, or a bull—are lamented by Danae, Leda, and Europa.° Although I thought these two-timing tales would simply embellish my speech, I realize now that they sum up perfectly what I wish to tell you; that my mother, swept away in the game of love, was more beautiful than any other woman and as unlucky as all of them. She was so completely duped by that foolish old ruse of a secret wedding vow that she relives it even today; and her betrayer was so like Aeneas° fleeing from responsibility that he even left her a sword. Its blade will remain covered for now, but I shall unsheathe it before my story is over. From this poorly tied knot that neither binds nor imprisons, from this secret wedding vow or wicked lie—for it's all the same—I was born, so similar to my mother that I could have passed for her double, if not in loveliness then in luck and circumstances. And thus I needn't say that her stormy fortune ran me through many shipwrecks of my own. The most I can tell you is the name of the lord who robs my honor and sacks my reputation: Aistulf. Oh, miserable me! At the mere mention of his name my heart fills with anger and bile, chafing at any allusion to the enemy. Aistulf was the ungrateful lord who, forgetting our shared pleasure—for when love is extinguished, all memories are forgotten—came to Poland, lured by his ambition, to marry Stella, his north star and my setting sun. Who would have guessed that, having been brought together through stellar design, we would now be separated by Stella's design? The humiliating offense left me sad, demented, and dead, yet still myself; that is to say, I felt the confusion of hell and the chaos of Babylonia° in my soul. And refusing to talk about it, because some sufferings and anguish are much better left to feelings than to words, I spoke my sufferings in silence until one day, when I was alone with my mother Viola—oh, heavens!—she broke them free of their prison, and they all poured out together, tripping over one another in their haste. I didn't try to keep them in, for when a person confesses his faults to someone he knows has similar faults, he feels free and uninhibited in doing so, for there are times when a bad example does some good. In any case, my mother listened devotedly to my laments and tried to console me with her own. How easily a guilty judge forgives! And learning a lesson from her own experience—whereby, having entrusted the remedy of her dishonor to idle liberty and lenient time, she now had no way to remedy my own misfortunes—she considered it best that I go after the duke and obligate him, with overpowering arguments, to pay the debt of my honor; and to make it easier, fortune had her dress me in the clothes of a man. She took down an old sword—this one you see me wearing. Now's the time to unsheathe it as I promised, for my mother, trusting in its unique appearance, said to me: "Make your way to Poland, Rossaura, and do your best to have the nobles there see you wearing this sword, for in one of them your fortunes may find a merciful welcome and your anguish, consolation." Thus I arrived in Poland. I'll quickly summarize what needn't be repeated in detail because it's already known: that a bucking beast led me to your cave, where you were astonished to see me; that Clothold took pity on me, asked the king for my life, and the king granted his request; that Clothold, informed of my identity, persuaded me to wear my normal clothes and enter the service of Stella, where I ingeniously thwarted Aistulf's courtship and marriage to her; that there, in the palace, you were again baffled at the sight of me, this time dressed as a woman, my past and present appearances confused in your mind; and finally, that Clothold, convinced of the importance that Aistulf marry the lovely Stella and rule jointly with her, advised me to forget my dishonor and end my crusade. But now, O valiant Sigismund,

Danae, Leda, and Europa: Three women seduced by Zeus in the forms of a shower of gold, a swan, and a white bull, respectively.   **Aeneas:** Hero of Virgil's *Aeneid*; he abandoned queen Dido.

Babylonia: Ancient Persian empire; site of the Tower of Babel.

that your turn at revenge has arrived, for heaven has allowed you to break free of that crude prison cell where sorrow made your soul savage and suffering made it unyielding; now that you are taking up arms against your fatherland and against your father, I am here to offer my help, combining the rich garments of Diana° and the arms of Pallas—cloth here and steel there—for I am at home in both. Let's move quickly then, brave chief! For we both have an interest in preventing or annulling this arranged marriage: I, to stop the man who promised to marry me from marrying another; you, to preempt the threat to our victory that the strength and power of their two states, once united, would represent. As a woman, I come to move you to the cause of my honor; as a man, I come to encourage you to recover your crown. As a woman, I come to beg your sympathy by throwing myself at your feet; as a man, I come to serve you by aiding your soldiers. As a woman, I come to request your support in my dishonor and anguish; as a man, I come to support you with my sword and my character. And finally, consider that if you try to seduce me today as a woman, as a man I will slay you in legitimate defense of my honor; for in restoring my good name I must act as a lovesick woman to plead for help and as a man to win respect.

SIGISMUND: (*Aside.*) Heavens, if I'm really dreaming, then stay my memory, for it's impossible for a dream to have so many twists and turns! God help me! Who could manage to escape them all or avoid thinking about any of them? Who ever heard of such baffling torments? If that grandeur in which I awoke was a dream, how is it that this woman can now describe it to me in such vivid detail? So it had to be real, not a dream. But if it was real, it's no less confusing, for why does my experience call it a dream? Are pleasures so akin to dreams that the real ones are taken for lies and the fake ones for authentic? Is there so little difference between the true and the false that it's debatable whether what is seen and enjoyed is real or made up? Is the copy so close to the original that it can pass inspection undetected? If so, and all grandeur and power, all majesty and splendor will eventually fade into shadow, then we must take advantage of this moment while we can, for it affords us enjoyment to be found only in dreams. Rossaura is in my power; my soul longs for her loveliness. Let's enjoy, then, the occasion and permit love to violate the ideals of valor and trust with which she kneels before me. This is a dream, and, that being the case, let's dream of joys now, for they're sure to become sorrows later. (*Pause.*) But my own argument can be used against me. If it's a dream, a show, who would risk losing divine glory for the sake of human vainglory? What past good is not a dream? Who has never thought, when he looks back on his heroic achievements, "It must have all been a dream"? If this is my lesson, if I

Diana: Roman goddess of hunting.

know that delight is a lovely flame and will be reduced to ashes by the first breeze that blows, then we must focus on the eternal, where fame is everlasting, joy never sleeps, and grandeur never rests. Rossaura is without honor, and a prince's responsibility is to dispense honor rather than to rob it. By God, I shall restore her honor before my own crown! But first, we must turn our back on this temptation. (*He struggles to divert his gaze from Rossaura.*)
(*To a soldier.*) Sound the call to arms, for today I must do battle before the dark shadows bury the sun's golden rays in waves of greenish black!

ROSSAURA: My lord, are you going to leave just like that? My worries and anguish don't merit a single word from you in reply? How can you not even look at me or listen to me? You won't even show me your face?

SIGISMUND: (*Without looking at her.*) Rossaura, honor demands that I be cruel to you now in order to be merciful later. My voice is silent so my honor may respond; I don't speak to you because I want my actions to speak for me; I don't look at you because it's essential, when your cruel suffering makes you so vulnerable, that he who is to look after your honor not look upon your beauty.

(*Exit Sigismund and soldiers.*)

ROSSAURA: What enigmatic talk is this, heavens? After so much sorrow, must I still put up with ambivalent responses?

(*Enter Bugle.*)

BUGLE: My lady, do you have a moment?
ROSSAURA: Oh, Bugle! Where have you been?
BUGLE: Locked away in a tower wondering what the cards had in store for me and when I might be put to death, for they could have knocked me off at any moment.
ROSSAURA: Why?
BUGLE: Because I know the secret of your identity. You see . . .

(*Offstage, the drums of war are heard.*)

BUGLE: . . . Clothold . . . but what's all that racket?
ROSSAURA: What could it be?
BUGLE: An armed squadron is spilling out of the besieged palace in hopes of resisting and defeating the regiment commanded by the fierce Sigismund.
ROSSAURA: Well, how can I stand here like a coward when such cruelty is unleashed without order or rules? I must fight by his side and astound the world. (*Exit.*)
SOLDIERS: (*Offstage, one group*) Long live our invincible king! (*Offstage, another group.*) Long live our freedom!
BUGLE: I say long live freedom *and* the king. Let them live with my blessing, for I have no problem with either as long as they look out for me. And now, amid such confusion, I must withdraw and be as

pitiless as Nero° as he watched Rome burn. Although I'd like to take pity on something, so it might as well be on me; if I hide, I can watch the whole spectacle from here among the crags. It's a safe place where death won't find me, so to hell with death! (*He makes an obscene gesture, directed at death, and hides.*)

(*The sound of clashing arms becomes stronger. Enter Vasily, Clothold, and Aistulf, in retreat.*)

VASILY: Has there ever been an unluckier king? Has there ever been a more persecuted father?

CLOTHOLD: Your army, now defeated, retreats in disorder.

AISTULF: The traitors have won.

VASILY: In battles such as this, the winners always consider themselves loyal and treat the losers as traitors. We must flee, Clothold, from the cruel and inhuman severity of a tyrannical son.

(*A shot is heard offstage, and Bugle falls down, wounded, from his hiding place.*)

BUGLE: Heaven help me!

AISTULF: Who is this unlucky soldier who has fallen at our feet, drenched in blood?

BUGLE: Just an unfortunate man who, in trying to run from death, ran right into her, for there's no hiding place she can't find. Which goes to show that he who most tries to flee from her reach is the one who will first fall within her reach. So return, return to the bloody fighting immediately, for you're safer amid arms and open fire than on the most shielded mountaintop, and there's no road that will protect you against the power of destiny and the inclemency of fate. And thus, although you hope to free yourselves from death by fleeing, consider that, if it's God's will that you die, then you shall die. (*He dies.*)

VASILY: "Consider that, if it's God's will that you die, then you shall die." How easily—oh, heavens!—we are brought from error and ignorance to greater understanding by this corpse that speaks through the mouth of an open wound, its hemorrhage a bloody tongue that teaches us that all attempts to cheat fate are in vain; for I, in attempting to save my fatherland from sedition and death, have in the end turned it over to the very people from whom I was attempting to save it!

CLOTHOLD: Although fate, my lord, sees all and is capable of finding its prey in even the darkest crags, it isn't of Christian temperament to conclude that there's no way around its wrath. There is, and a prudent man can triumph over fate; and now, if you wish to avoid further suffering and tragedy, you should find a place where you can protect yourself.

AISTULF: Clothold, my lord, speaks with the wisdom of old age and I with the courage of youth. Over there in the thicket stands a horse, swift miscarriage of the wind; use it to flee, and I shall guard your back.

Nero: (15–68 CE) was one of Rome's most sadistic and violent emperors.

VASILY: If it's God's will that I die or if death already awaits me here, today I shall seek her out and confront her face to face.

(*The call to arms is sounded, and Sigismund enters accompanied by his soldiers.*)

SOLDIER 1: Among the crags and thickets of the mountain hides the king.

SIGISMUND: Seek him out! I want every tree and shrub of these jagged peaks scrutinized, trunk by trunk and branch by branch!

CLOTHOLD: (*To Vasily.*) Flee, my lord!

VASILY: To what end?

AISTULF: What are you going to do?

VASILY: Step aside, Aistulf!

CLOTHOLD: What are you going to do?

VASILY: The only thing I haven't yet tried, Clothold. (*To Sigismund.*) If I'm the one you're looking for, you have me at your mercy, my prince. (*He kneels before Sigismund and remains on his knees throughout the prince's reply*) Use the snow of my hair as a white rug beneath your feet; trample my neck and tread upon my crown; humiliate me and drag my good name through the mud; take your vengeance on my honor and treat me as your captive. After so many warnings, fate shall honor its promise and heaven shall keep its word.

SIGISMUND: Illustrious Court of Poland, witness to so many amazing events, listen carefully, for your prince wishes to address you. What is determined by heaven from the blue slate inscribed by the finger of God— and encoded and printed on those immense blue spheres adorned with gold stars—never deceives or lies; the lies and deceptions come from the one who, wishing to use the information to his own ends, undertakes to decipher it. My father, who is present among us, in order to avoid the wrath of my character, turned me into a brute, a human beast; thus, whereas my graceful nobility, genteel lineage, and fine character should have made me congenial and humble, my living conditions and upbringing were sufficient to cultivate a ferocious disposition. What a way to cheat fate! If anyone were told, "One day you will be killed by an inhuman beast," would it be a good solution to wake one up while it was sleeping? If they said, "That sword you're wearing will one day be the death of you," to then take it out and point it at your chest would prove a futile remedy. If they said, "Your grave will lie beneath vast expanses of water and bear tombstones of silvery waves," you would be foolish to set sail when the imperious sea was whipping up rough, jagged mountains of snow and glass. My father has ended up just like the one who, threatened by beast, woke it up; like the one who, fearful of the sword, unsheathed it; and like the one who stirred up the waves of a tempest. And even if—and listen well—my wrath were a dormant beast, my fury a dull sword, and my severity a gentle tropical breeze, fortune is not to be overcome through injustice and vengeance but rather is provoked even further by such measures. Whoever wishes to overcome his fortune must do so through prudence and temperance. Foreseeing a danger doesn't mean you can protect yourself or guard against it before it occurs; yes, you can always take a few humble measures to protect yourself, but not until the moment is upon you, for there's no way of forestalling its arrival. Of this there's no better proof than the strange spectacle we've witnessed today: this bizarre, amazing event, this horrific aberration. Just look and you'll see—despite all efforts to the contrary—a father vanquished, a monarch crushed before my feet. This was the work of heaven, and no matter how he tried to prevent it, he was unable. But I—inferior to him in years, valor, and learning—shall succeed where he failed. Rise, my lord, and give me your hand; now that heaven has revealed the error in your attempts to overcome it, my neck humbly awaits your vengeance. I am at your mercy.

VASILY: My son, such noble action rekindles your presence in my heart. You are prince! The laurel and the palm are yours; let your deeds be your crown.

ALL: (*In unison.*) Long live Sigismund! Long live Sigismund!

(*Enter Rossaura.*)

SIGISMUND: (*Observing Rossaura.*) My valor promises me great victories, and today the greatest of all will be victory over myself. Aistulf, promise your hand to Rossaura immediately, for you know you're a debtor to her honor, and I intend to make you pay.

AISTULF: Although it's true I owe her something, bear in mind that she doesn't know who her father is; and it would be a low and infamous deed for someone like me to marry a woman who...

CLOTHOLD: Do not go on; hold your tongue and listen. Rossaura is just as noble as you, Aistulf, and I will argue her case with my sword if I have to. She is my daughter, and that's all you need to know.

AISTULF: What are you saying?

CLOTHOLD: Until I saw her promised in noble marriage and her honor avenged, I didn't want to reveal the secret. It's a very long story, but the point is that she's my daughter.

AISTULF: Well, that being the case, I shall honor my word. (*He takes Rossaura's hand.*)

SIGISMUND: And now, so that Stella won't feel left out given that she's lost a prince of such valor and reputation, by my own hand I shall wed her to a man who is, in merits and good fortune, if not greater than Aistulf, at least his equal. Give me your hand, my lady. (*He takes Stella's hand.*)

STELLA: I'm honored to be worthy of such joy.

SIGISMUND: To Clothold, who was unswerving in his loyalty to my father, I offer my warm embrace together with any favors he might ask of me.

SOLDIER 1: If that's how you reward someone who never came to your aid, what do I get for inciting the uprising against the king and for freeing you from the tower in which you were imprisoned?

SIGISMUND: The tower. And so that you'll spend the rest of your life there, you'll be under constant watch of the guards, for traitors serve no purpose once their treason has been exposed.

VASILY: Your ingenuity amazes us all.

AISTULF: What a change of character!

ROSSAURA: What discretion, what prudence!

SIGISMUND: What's so amazing, what's so shocking, given that my teacher was a dream? And I still fear, deep down inside, that one day I shall awaken to find myself locked away in my cramped prison. And if that doesn't happen, it's enough to dream it's so, for that's how I came to realize that all human joy is, in the end, as ephemeral as a dream. So I'd like to take advantage of this happy moment while I can...(*To the audience.*) and ask you to overlook our flaws, for forgiveness should come naturally to noble souls.

COMMENTARIES

Ed Morales
REVIEW OF JOSÉ RIVERA'S
PRODUCTION OF *SUEÑO*   *1998*

In this extensive discussion of José Rivera's adaptation of Life Is a Dream, *Morales examines the reasoning behind Rivera's reworking of Calderón's language and Rivera's emphasis on the philosophical issues that lie beneath the surface of the play. Morales also gives us some insight into the challenges faced by a modern producer of a seventeenth-century drama, especially in light of the ways in which both the theater and its audiences have changed.*

Sueño, José Rivera's adaptation of Calderón de la Barca's classic *La Vida es Sueño (Life Is a Dream)*, starts out impressively enough. When John Ortiz's hirsute, muscular, and scantily clad body appears onstage suspended in midair by long red ropes, Hartford Stage Company audiences can't help but hold their collective breath and expect a wild theatrical ride. Ortiz plays Segismundo, the son of a Spanish monarch held in a dungeon because of his original sin—killing his mother in childbirth—but about to be freed from his misery to have a go at his birthright as a ruler. The sharp contrast between his captivity and deliverance causes Segismundo to blur the line between reality and dreams and allows Calderón to explore the big philosophical questions (What is existence? *Is* life a dream, and if so, who is dreaming *us*? God?) that have made *La Vida es Sueño* so enduring. However, it's hard not to wonder what kind of resonance these issues can have for a twentieth-century audience, when a good chunk of reality is virtual or simulated.

At first glance, *Sueño*'s theatrical strategy seems to be a variation on what might be called the New York Shakespeare Festival style of reinventing the classics. The characters engage in a contemporary sassiness; they draw out some of the contemporaneous subtext from seventeenth-century situations; and traditionally cross-dressed roles are augmented by nontraditionally cross-dressed ones. But on closer inspection, Rivera's *Sueño* proves to be a true adaptation, not a recontextualization; there are no TV sets or gang paraphernalia in this production. The costumes are faithful to their origins in Spain. Indeed, it's not the surface aspects of the production that offer a contemporary spin on Calderón's metaphysical musings: it is the *language* that has been changed, shifting from the baroque Spanish verse of the 1600s to the contemporary rhythms of America at the end of the twentieth century.

From Segismundo's opening soliloquies, where he proclaims himself "a storm of chemical responses pretending to have a soul," Rivera has reclaimed Calderón's florid use of metaphor and made it his own, spiced with science, sarcasm, and sweetness. "I wanted to find the language Calderón would have used if he was a forty-two-year-old playwright living in California," the theater and television writer says on the phone from his home in Los Angeles. That blending of the contemporary and the antiquated can have some surprising results. For instance, when Segismundo says he is "God's wild virus," you can feel all the implications of imagined or real modern-day plagues while simultaneously acknowledging their roots in an empire engaged in conquering a New World.

Rivera was not only faced with the task of reinventing Calderón's language, but also the challenge of making the play, which is long on plot and short on characterization, "actable." By doing case studies of people who had experienced long-term isolation, Rivera was able to create a realistic psychological profile for Segismundo and enliven his character with appropriate behavior, particularly in the early scenes between him and Rosaura (Michi Barall), a young noblewoman bent on revenge. Long monologues were replaced with short, snappy, almost sit-com-esque interactions, a possible by-product of the time Rivera has done in Hollywood. (The writer professes to have given up television work, particularly since the demise of *Eerie, Indiana*, a series he created that some claim was too smart to remain on the air.)

In this way, the wordplay between Lord Astolfo (Damian Young) and Princess Estrella (Alene Dawson)—two scheming nobles who have their eyes on the throne—is one of the highlights of the production. "Flowers are dishrags compared to you," carps Astolfo in his parodic wooing of a noblewoman in line to succeed the reigning monarch. "Helen? A slutbox.... Aphrodite? Maggot poop." Young and Jan Leslie Harding, in her drag interpretation of Rosaura's clownish manservant Clarin (the character is traditionally played by a male), provide comic relief from the dark antics Segismundo engages in when he's given a chance to prove he might be worthy of nobility.

By showcasing these underlying comedic moments, *Sueño* moves away from the tragically cerebral aura that traditionally surrounds Calderón's work. Nevertheless, the play's dramatic impact is reinvigorated by Rivera's commitment to updating its contextual underpinnings. In the post-Freud era, there are echoes of the Oedipus complex in Segismundo's attacks on his father Basilio's kingship. Perhaps more important, their relationship strongly resembles the one between Prospero and Caliban in *The Tempest*. Segismundo is portrayed as a vulgar, uneducated beast, an id looking to inflict severe psychological, as well as physical, pain. Basilio, on the other hand, seems to be uncertain about his moral imperative: he is vaguely aware of his own complicity in the brutal conquest of the New World. Even as he obsesses over a lunar eclipse (the evil omen that marks the birth of his son), another spherical object, the Aztec calendar, lurks center stage for much of the play.

For Rivera, this zigzagging between the old and the new in some ways mirrors the ambivalence of the Hispanic phenomenon and may explain Latino interest in the Hartford Stage production. (The fact that the theater coordinated a major community relations drive didn't hurt either.) According to Rivera, while Hispanics may not feel directly connected to Spain, they still relate to intrinsic elements of the culture. "There's this code of honor that we all seem to be struggling with," muses Rivera. "Being Latino in the U.S. is like being caught in the middle between tradition and nontradition. But we have come to feel comfortable with contradiction."

While Rivera's rewrite may make Calderón's work more accessible and contemporary, *Sueño* has even more profound implications. Instead of saying, "If the Fates decree that now's your time to die / There's nothing you can do," Clarin declares, "If God wants your ass, he's going to get your ass." While the change works as humor, these lines are also helping Rivera establish the idea that the presence of mortal life is no longer just an extension of the proof of the existence of God. "In the original, Segismundo gets attached to the idea that if everything is a dream, the dreamer must be God," says Rivera. "What my version is trying to say is that the idea of God is unreliable."

In transferring Calderón's psyche into his own, Rivera is making a statement about American reality and the way it represents the difference between Old World and New World thinking. The romantic pairings that climax the original—Astolfo-Rosaura and Segismundo-Estrella—are reversed. Rosaura turns her back on nobility and urges Segismundo to join her in a quest for free will and the over-turning of the rigid class structures of Europe. It's a moment that brings out an idea buried in Calderón's text, that a New World is about to begin. In José Rivera's own sly and spiritual way, *Sueño* carries the enormous implication that we're on the verge of that kind of history happening all over again.

Matt Wolf
THE *HAMLET* OF SPAIN, IN A FEVERED STAGING   *1999*

Matt Wolf reviews the 1999 London production of Life Is a Dream, *connecting the play to Calderón's near-contemporary, William Shakespeare. In certain ways Wolf sees Segismundo as a version of Hamlet. Like Hamlet, Segismundo quests for the truth and is never sure he has found it. And like Hamlet, Segismundo has been denied a portion of his birthright.*

Imagine a play that suggests Shakespeare—particularly *Hamlet* or *The Tempest*—filtered through a Pirandellian prism, with an enormous gilt-edged mirror suspended forbiddingly above the action and a gravel-strewn set providing its own aural soundscape.

That is one way of describing the production of *Life Is a Dream* that the Royal Lyceum Theater Company of Scotland will present on Tuesday at the Brooklyn Academy of Music. The Spanish director Calixto Bieito's fevered staging of the defining seventeenth-century play by Pedro Calderón de la Barca will have six performances at the Harvey Theater as part of the 1999 Next Wave Festival.

In Spain, Calderón's play enjoys something of the status of *Hamlet*, with which it shares an interest in man at his most self-avowedly anguished. Indeed, professing in John Clifford's contemporary translation that "humankind's greatest crime is to be born," Calderón's antiheroic prince, Segismundo (played by George Anton), recalls the racked metaphysician that is Shakespeare's Danish prince.

Segismundo has been sequestered from birth in a tower because of fears by his father, the king, Basilio (Jeffery Kissoon), that his son will rise up against him. The prince is then briefly released upon adulthood, only to be imprisoned once more, a caged animal capable, we discover later, of very real mercy.

And though he finds a vengeful ally of sorts in Rosaura (Olwen Fouere), the spurned lover whose separate fate provides the main subplot, Segismundo ends the play a free and potentially noble man—if, that is, freedom and nobility mean anything in the elision between wakefulness and sleep that is the true terrain of *Life Is a Dream.*

"What I love about it is it's a very questioning play," said Mr. Clifford, the translator, from his home in Edinburgh. "It's asking fundamental questions, starting with 'What are we doing here?'" (His translation, he said, draws less from the accepted 1635 text than from an earlier published version dating to 1630.)

Mr. Bieito's production was first seen at the 1998 Edinburgh International Festival, where several critics found it a high point of the theater program ("The two hours pass like, well, a dream," wrote Charles Spencer in the *Daily Telegraph*). After a hiatus, the production toured last month to London as part of the Barbican International Theater Event (BITE '99) season.

His aim, Mr. Bieito said after the London opening, was to invigorate anew a play barely known in Britain or the United States, notwithstanding its affinities to the Elizabethans as well as to countless modernist writers, including Pirandello and Ionesco.

"For me, it was easier to work in Britain," said Mr. Bieito, thirty-five, of a rare directing assignment away from Barcelona, where he has lived since he was fifteen. Among his credits back home: a Catalan-language version in 1997 of the Broadway musical *Company*, whose songs include the very appropriately titled "Barcelona."

"In Spain," said the director, who doubles as his own designer (with Carles Pujol), "you have all the pressure all the time of tradition, of people thinking what *Life Is a Dream* must be." But in Scotland, he said, "I was freed to do the play and to renew it. Classical theater must not be classical, it must be fresh."

The result is a multicultural staging defiantly un-British in its impetuousness and vigor, especially coming from a writer who, Mr. Clifford said, "has an unfortunate reputation as a rigid Catholic theologian."

And Graham Sheffield, the Barbican's artistic director, said, "Calixto seems to have made the play modern without sacrificing its traditional roots; its physicality is frightening."

The play's animalistic passions more often than not fall to Mr. Anton, thirty-four, a Scot who spends much of the evening raising his voice and shedding his clothes as he charts Segismundo's journey from a Caliban figure to a Prospero of sorts.

The actor compared Mr. Bieito to a boxing coach. "When you were in the ring, as it were, he was hot," Mr. Anton said of his director. "He'd be at your side going, 'Quieter, quieter,' and then, 'Punch, punch, punch.'"

That may be because, said Mr. Kissoon, the performer, the director "wants to wake us up."

Late Seventeenth- and Eighteenth-Century Drama

The Restoration: Rebirth of Drama

Theater in England continued to thrive after Shakespeare's death, with a host of successful playwrights, including John Webster (1580?–1638?), Francis Beaumont (c. 1584–1616) and his collaborator John Fletcher (1579–1625), Philip Massinger (1583–1640), Thomas Middleton (1580–1627), John Ford (1586–c. 1655), and James Shirley (1596–1666). All these playwrights were busy working independently or in collaboration. Fletcher, chosen successor to Shakespeare at the Globe, furnished the theater with as many as four plays a year. But in 1642 long-standing religious and political conflicts between King Charles I and Parliament finally erupted into civil war, with the Parliament, under the influence of Puritanism, eventually winning.

The Puritans were religious extremists with narrow, specific values. They were essentially an emerging merchant class of well-to-do citizens who viewed the aristocracy as wastrels. Theater for them was associated with both the aristocracy and the low life. Theatergoing was synonymous with wasting time, the theaters were often a focus for immoral activity, and the neighborhoods around the theaters were as unsavory as any in England. Under the Puritan government, all theaters in England were closed for almost twenty years. When the new king, Charles II, was crowned in 1660, those that had not been converted to other uses had become completely outmoded.

As a young prince, Charles, with his mother and brother, had been sent to the Continent in the early stages of the civil war. When his father, Charles I, was beheaded, the future king and his family were in France, where they were in a position to see the remarkable achievements of French comedy and French classical tragedy. Charles II developed a taste for theater that accompanied him back to England. And when he returned in triumph to usher in the exciting and swashbuckling period known as the Restoration, he permitted favorites to build new theaters.

Theater on the Continent: Neoclassicism

Interaction among the leading European countries—England, Spain, and France—was sporadic at best in the seventeenth century because of intermittent wars among the nations, yet the development of theater in all three countries took similar turns throughout the early 1600s.

By the 1630s, the French were aware of Spanish achievements in the theater; Pierre Corneille (1606–1684), who emerged as France's leading playwright of the time, adapted a Spanish story by de Castro that became one of his most important plays, *Le Cid*.

By the time Charles II took up residence in France in the 1640s, the French had developed a suave, polished, and intellectually demanding approach to drama. Corneille and the neoclassicists were part of a large movement in European culture and the arts that tried to codify and emulate the achievement of the ancients. Qualities such as harmony, symmetry, balance in everything structural, and clear moral themes were most in evidence. Because NEOCLASSICISM valued thought over feeling, the thematic material in neoclassical drama was very important. That material was sometimes political, reflecting the values of Augustan Rome—27 BCE to 17 CE—when Caesar Augustus lived and when it was appropriate to think in terms of subordinating the self to the interests of the state. Neoclassical dramatists focused on honor, moral integrity, self-sacrifice, and heroic political subjects.

One school of critics held playwrights strictly to the Aristotelian concepts of the unities of time, place, character, and action. These "rules critics" demanded a perfect observance of the unities—that is, they wanted a play to have one plot, a single action that takes place in one day, and a single setting. In most cases the plays that satisfied them are now often thought of as static, cold, limited, and dull. Their perfection is seen today as rigid and emotionally icy.

Corneille's work did not please such critics, and they turned to a much younger competitor, Jean Racine (1639–1699), who brought the tradition of French tragedy to its fullest. Most of his plays are on classical subjects, beginning in 1667 with *Andromache*, continuing with *Britannicus* (1669), *Iphigenia* (1674), and *Mithridate* (1673), and ending in 1677 with his most famous and possibly best play, *Phaedra*.

Phaedra is a deeply passionate, moral play centering on the love of Phaedra for her stepson, Hippolytus. Venus is responsible for her incestuous love—which is the playwright's way of saying that Phaedra is impelled by the gods or by destiny, almost against her will.

The French stage, unlike the English, never substituted boys for female roles, and so plays such as *Phaedra* were opportunities for brilliant actresses. Phaedra, in particular, dominates the stage—she is a commanding and infinitely complex figure. It is no wonder that this play was a favorite of Sarah Bernhardt (1844–1923), one of France's greatest actresses.

French Comedy: Molière

At the same time that Racine commanded the tragic stage, Jean Baptiste Poquelin (1622–1673), known as Molière, began his dominance of the comic stage. He was aware of Racine's achievements and applauded them strongly. His career started with a small theater company that spent most of its time touring the countryside beyond Paris. When the company settled in Paris, its plays were influenced by some of the stock characters and situations of the commedia dell'arte, but they also began to reflect Molière's own genius for composition.

Seeing the company in 1658, King Louis XIV found it so much to his liking that he installed it in a theater and demanded to see more of its work. From that time on, Molière wrote, produced, and acted in one comedy after another, most of which have become part of the permanent repertoire of the French stage. Plays such as *The Misanthrope* (1666), *The Miser* (1669), *The Bourgeois Gentleman* (1670), *The Imaginary Invalid* (1673), and his satire on the theme of religious hypocrisy, *Tartuffe* (1669), are also staged all over the world.

Theater in England: The Restoration

The English Restoration began in 1660 with the return of King Charles II to England after nearly two decades in France. During the preceding twenty years, which began with the English Revolution in the 1640s, plays had been banned and theaters demolished under the reign of Oliver Cromwell.

The new age craved glitter, excitement, sensuality, and dramatic dazzle. Audiences wanted upbeat comedies that poked fun at stuffed shirts and old-fashioned institutions. Charles was influenced by the French theaters, which were often constructed on a pattern of the French tennis court—a long, narrow, rectangular space that served well for French performances.

The Great Fire of 1666, which destroyed most of London, occasioned extensive reconstruction that, in the 1670s, included the building of new theaters. They too were long and narrow, but, unlike most Elizabethan theaters, they were enclosed and depended on artificial lighting. Restoration theaters operated year-round, and the prices of seats depended on their location. The first-level boxes against the walls were the most expensive seats; the middle-priced seats—actually backless benches—filled the pit before the proscenium-arched stage (Figure 13); and the lowest-priced seats were in the upper ranges of the galleries.

The structure of the new theater permitted realistic scene design, with a receding space that accommodated painted backdrops. Actors could enter and leave by side doors directly on stage or could retreat to the flies through the scenic stage. The proscenium was not framed as in later theaters but, rather, permitted actors to move close to those sitting in the pit. The space allotted to the actors in the Drury Lane Theatre was considerable, facilitating rousing fight scenes and crowd scenes. The apron also produced an intimacy between actor and audience that encouraged a more natural presentation. The drama-starved audiences also favored a new style of comedy—one that was socially observant—and a new style of tragedy—one that may be called heroic, as in the plays of John Dryden (1631–1700), whose *All for Love* was a "rewrite" of Shakespeare's *Antony and Cleopatra*. New plays for the Restoration often consisted of rewritings of great Elizabethan plays (including a version of *King Lear* with a happy ending) or the reworking of plots of French, Italian, and Spanish plays. The age required high fashion, superficial brilliance, and sensual entertainment in the style of a sometimes lewd court and more open society.

Not everyone applauded these developments, however. The clergyman and critic Jeremy Collier, in *A Short View of the Immorality and Profaneness of the English Stage* (1698), attacked the contemporary theater for its immorality, its satiric portrayal of ministers of the church, and its casual references to the Bible. He condemned not only the theater of his age but also the plays of Shakespeare and the great Elizabethan dramatists, whose work was quite different in tone from the contemporary drama. The effect he had on theater was extensive, in part because James II took up an earlier cry to reform the theater. Major playwrights were fined for their productions, which certainly

FIGURE 13.   Theatre Royal, Drury Lane, 1676, designed by Sir Christopher Wren.

had a dampening effect on some later productions by important actors and companies.

Restoration Comedy in England

Among England's notable playwrights from 1660 through the eighteenth century were Aphra Behn (1640–1689), the first professional woman playwright on the English stage and author of *The Rover*, one of the most frequently performed plays of the period; William Wycherley (1640–1716), whose *The Plain Dealer*, indebted to Molière, and *The Country Wife* are regarded as his best work; William Congreve (1670–1729), whose *The Way of the World* is justly famous; and Richard Brinsley Sheridan (1751–1816), whose *School for Scandal* is still bright, lively, and engaging for modern audiences. Other important playwrights whose work is still performed are George Farquhar (1678–1707), especially known for *The Beaux Stratagem* (1707), John Gay (1685–1732), whose *Beggar's Opera* has been revived constantly since its first performance in 1728, and Oliver Goldsmith (1730–1774), author of *She Stoops to Conquer* (1773).

John Dryden (1631–1700), perhaps the most highly regarded English playwright from 1664 to 1677, collaborated in adaptations of Shakespeare's plays, but he became popular for his heroic dramas in rhymed verse: *The Indian Queen* (1664), its sequel *The Indian Emperor* (1665), *Tyrannick Love* (1669), and the two-part, ten-act *The Conquest of Granada* (1670). Montezuma is at the center of the first two plays; *Tyrannick Love* concerns the martyrdom of St. Catherine by the Roman emperor, Maximin. *The Conquest of Granada* traces internal conflicts among the Moors fighting for survival in Spain. Almanzor, the main character, is considered one of Dryden's most accomplished creations. *Aureng-Zebe* (1675), his last effort in heroic rhymed drama, focuses on Aureng-Zebe, emperor of India and among the most rational and moral of his characters. Its plot and love complications are extremely dense and its mood somewhat melancholy. Today the heroic plays of the 1660s resemble high-style melodramas, but they were enormously popular in their time.

Dryden was also successful writing comedies such as *The Wild Gallant* (1663) and *The Rival Ladies* (1664). His tragicomedies were popular in his time and represent some of his most imaginative dramatic efforts. *Marriage à-la-Mode* (1672) is still highly regarded, especially for Dryden's songs. Among his experiments in opera is a version of Milton's *Paradise Lost* that he called *The State of Innocence and the Fall of Man* (1677), in which he rhymed some of Milton's blank verse. This work was never performed, although it remains a curiosity of the age. Dryden is also noted for his critical writing on drama, such as his famous *Of Dramatick Poesie* (1668) and *Of Heroick Plays* (1672), which laid down the theory behind his dramas and opened the questions of dramatic practice for examination.

Marriages of convenience are often the target of Restoration playwrights. The aristocratic attitude toward marriage usually centered on the union of "suitable" mates whose families were of the same social level and who were financially attractive to one another. Consequently, impoverished gentlemen of good name would sometimes seek out wealthy women, and vice versa. The grounds for marriage were based sometimes on love but more often on financial or social convenience. As a result, conflicts in choosing marriage partners often involved elaborate dealings between parents and children, as in Oliver Goldsmith's comic play *She Stoops to Conquer*. Once married, however, husbands and wives played complex games of adultery and betrayal, negotiating terms of financial settlements while engaging in witty repartee and riposte, as in William Congreve's immortal *The Way of the World*. It is not until the end of the eighteenth century that the sentimental comedy appears, introducing recognizable emotional responses that appear to moderns as normal. Aristocratic attitudes toward marriage are evident in drama as late as the end of the nineteenth century, as in Oscar Wilde's *The Importance of Being Earnest*.

The English playwrights produced a wide range of comedy, drawing on their understanding of the audience's desire for bright, gay, and witty entertainment. The comedies of the period came to be known in the twentieth century as COMEDIES OF MANNERS because they reveal the foibles of the society that watched them. Society enjoyed laughing at itself. Although some of the English drama of the eighteenth century developed a moralistic tone and was often heavily classical, the earlier RESTORATION COMEDIES were less interested in reforming the society than in capitalizing on its faults.

Eighteenth-Century Drama

Eighteenth-century Europe absorbed much of the spirit of France and the French neoclassicists. England, like other European countries, began to see the effects of neoclassicism in the arts and literature. Emulation of classical art and classical values was common throughout Europe, and critics established standards of excellence in the arts to guarantee quality.

The most famous name in eighteenth-century English drama is David Garrick (1717–1779), the legendary actor and manager of the Drury Lane Theatre. The theaters, including his own, often reworked French drama and earlier English and Italian drama, but they began to develop a new SENTIMENTAL COMEDY to balance the neoclassical heroic tragedies of the period. It was a comedy in which the emotions of the audience were played on, manipulated, and exploited to arouse sympathy for the characters in the play.

Sentimental comedy flourished after 1720, but Colley Cibber (1671–1757) is sometimes credited with originating this form with his *Love's Last Shift* (1696). The play centers on Loveless, who wanders from his marriage only to find that his wife has disguised herself as a prostitute to win him back. As in all sentimental comedies, what the audience most wants is what it gets: a certain amount of tears, a contrasting amount of laughter, and a happy ending. Cibber was especially well known as an actor for his portrayal of fops, his way of poking satiric fun at his own society and its pretensions.

Sir Richard Steele (1672–1729) wrote one of the best-known sentimental comedies, *The Conscious Lovers* (1722). Steele's coauthor of *The Spectator*, Joseph Addison (1672–1719), also distinguished himself with his contribution to the heroic tragedy of the age, the long neoclassical *Cato* (1713). It was considered to be the finest example of the moral heroic style. Today it is not a playable drama because the action is too slow, the speeches too long, and the theme too obscure, although it is a perfect model of what the age preferred in heroic tragedy. George Lillo (1693–1739) in *The London Merchant* (1731) produced a bourgeois tragedy in which the main character was from the middle class. It was one of the most frequently produced plays of its time.

The audiences at the time enjoyed bright, amusing comedies that often criticized wayward youth, overprotective parents, dishonest financial dealings, and social expectations. Their taste in tragedies veered toward a moralizing heroism that extolled the values of the community and self-sacrifice on the part of the hero.

The Seventeenth- and Eighteenth-Century Actor

The tradition of acting in England had been largely interrupted for almost twenty years before the Restoration, but some important actors, such as Thomas Betterton (1635–1710), were able to continue many of the traditions of Shakespeare's staging. Betterton was especially noted for his performances as Hamlet, a part that was popular throughout the eighteenth century. Actors in this period in England were praised for their fine figure, their strong and mellow voice, and their use of facial expressions in revealing emotion at the proper dramatic moment. Contemporary commentary on acting stressed naturalness of expression as a prerequisite for excellence in an actor. However, the

FIGURE 14. Nell Gwynne, the best-known actress of her age, in a portrait by Sir Peter Lely (c. 1675).

age's concept of what was natural was much different from ours; the acting of the age would seem grossly exaggerated to us.

In France, women had been on stage for some time, and during the Restoration, actresses appeared on the English stage and proved enormously popular. Actresses were often the most important draw in English theaters in the seventeenth century. Nell Gwynne (1650–1687), one of the most famous actresses of the age (Figure 14), was also mistress to Charles II. She was discovered by her actor husband while selling flowers near a theater at age 15. Her lightheartedness and sometimes risqué manner were part of her stage appeal. The great diarist Samuel Pepys saw her in a comedy and vowed that "so great a performance of a comical part was never, I believe, in the world before." She was so remarkable that John Dryden, poet laureate, wrote comic parts specifically for her.

Actors in this period employed numerous stage tricks that were sometimes called claptraps, designed to elicit applause because they were conventional theatrical exaggerations (Hamlet's startled reaction when he first sees his father's ghost is a good example). Various actors "milked" the scene for applause by various ingenious means of showing horror and alarm. Even the "preg-nant" pause was used by Betterton and others to draw the audience in. Con-ventions such as broad gestures with the upstage hand and sudden kneeling on the downstage knee were widely employed for dramatic effect, along with impetuous turns to the audience, especially from the apron. Some of the older actors were also skilled at the rant—raising their voice, grotesquely twisting their body, and grimacing while driving home their point. These were tricks that actors such as David Garrick (1717–1779) often railed against in an effort to promote a more subdued style of acting. Although contemporary commen-tators note that he sometimes used mild forms of the very tricks he disliked, Garrick's purpose was to exhibit a natural style on stage, and he was widely complimented for having done so.

Garrick's greatest role was Richard III, and he was praised for his ability to reveal a variety of emotions in his face, especially in the tent scene on Bosworth field (Figure 15). He practiced moving from joy to horror to surprise to alarm to grief to guilt—and even more emotions, one after another—all in a con-vincing manner. Garrick and other eighteenth-century actors had the advan-tage of modern theaters such as the Drury Lane, which he managed, and the closeness of the apron reaching into the pit. The intimate, enclosed space made it possible for actors to be heard easily and to be seen well enough for their facial expressions to do the work that in ages past necessitated broad gestur-ing. The evolution of the theater's design made it possible for Garrick to achieve the effects for which he was so widely praised. Garrick occasionally went so far as to burlesque the overly theatrical style of some of his compe-titors, although sometimes only a portion of the audience got the joke.

FIGURE 15.   David Garrick as Shakespeare's Richard III, in a 1745 portrait by William Hogarth.

A good many fine actors maintained important reputations on the stage of the period: James Quin (1693–1766), said to be the finest Falstaff of his age; Charles Macklin (1699–1797), a playwright also known for his sensitive portrayal of Shylock and his virtual invention of the stage Irishman; Sarah Siddons (1755–1831) and her brother John Philip Kemble (1757–1823), praised for their smooth and careful acting style. Siddons and Kemble sometimes acted together to great acclaim, and their style evolved over time into a melodramatic exaggeration that was to become dominant in the early nineteenth century.

Drama in Japan

During the period of the Tokugawa shogunate (1603–1868), Japan attempted to seal itself off from the Western world. Although the Portuguese had a trading facility in Nagasaki, their influence was limited in range and scope. The great playwrights and actors of the Tokugawa period in Edo (Tokyo), Kyoto, and Osaka were generally unaware of traditions of Western drama, and in some cases they had never read or seen a foreign play.

Although Japan was essentially a military dictatorship at the time, the period was peaceful and prosperous, with a rising merchant middle class that demanded entertainment that represented their own values and interests. The shogun, or leader, was a warrior, and the warrior class—the samurai—had much to say about the forms of entertainment available. They were interested in theater partly because with peacetime came leisure time and the opportunity for indulgence. The pleasure district or "floating world" of Kyoto permitted prostitution and various theatrical and circus-like entertainments for men. It was in this atmosphere that traditions of kabuki theater and puppet theater flourished.

Kabuki began from a dance performed in 1603 by a woman entertainer named Okuni, whose popularity was such that she developed numerous imitators, especially prostitutes who danced kabuki in order to attract customers. The dance was enlarged with sketches from contemporary life accompanied by a popular three-stringed instrument called a *shamisen*. The role of the *shamisen* musician in kabuki plays was to establish the rhythms of speech and help stimulate the emotions of the audience. Kabuki quickly drew important actors who used elaborate makeup and brilliant costumes to perform multiact plays over an entire day.

After women were banned from the stage in 1629, men performed all the parts in kabuki plays. Audiences found kabuki exciting because it was designed to stimulate the masses. This popular entertainment form narrated stories of contemporary life and sometimes permitted people to grumble about inequities they perceived in their own society. Kabuki also produced a generation of highly gifted actors, many from the samurai class, who became a draw in their own right.

Partly because the actors became difficult and demanding, some of the important playwrights of the time, including Chikamatsu Monzaemon (1653–1725), turned to the *jōruri*, or puppet plays. Unlike actors, puppets made no demands on authors and never stole the show. They were also versatile enough to create remarkably subtle expressions of emotion, thought, and action. Some plays were produced in both kabuki and *jōruri* forms, but because incredible special effects were possible with puppets—effects that could not be achieved with actors—*jōruri* theater flourished in the early eighteenth century.

Chikamatsu, the greatest of Japanese playwrights, was born into a samurai family that had little influence in society. He drifted into kabuki theater and now enjoys the reputation of being Japan's first professional playwright. His early plays were for particularly important kabuki actors. He specialized in history plays, which were popular because they educated people not only about their own history, but also about faraway places. His domestic plays, especially his tragedies, which are primarily puppet plays, are more frequently produced today, partly because their subjects—middle-class suffering and emotional longing—seem more modern to us. *The Love Suicides at Sonezaki*, one of a series of love suicide plays, was so influential as to help cause the entire genre to be banned.

During this period, kabuki acting and stagecraft developed quickly, with highly stylized masks, extraordinary costumes, and complex sets. Eventually, complex stage machinery—trap doors and revolving stages—made the drama all the more interesting. The puppet stage depended on a chanter who recited the lines of all the characters and sometimes the narrator. Eventually, puppets operated by a single person gave way to more complex, three-person puppets requiring unusual coordination and skill and producing subtle expressions and effects. Today both forms of theater still exist in Japan and are performed throughout the world.

Late Seventeenth- and Eighteenth-Century Drama Timeline

DATE	THEATER	POLITICAL	SOCIAL/CULTURAL
1600–1700	**1603:** Okuni creates the first kabuki dance. **1606–1684:** French playwright Pierre Corneille, author of *Le Cid* (1636) **1622–1673:** Molière (born Jean Baptiste Poquelin), French dramatist and actor, author of *The Misanthrope* (1666), *Tartuffe* (1669), and *The Learned Ladies* (1672) **c. 1634–1691:** Sir George Etherege, author of *Love in a Tub* and *The Man of Mode* (1676) **1635–1710:** Thomas Betterton, perhaps the Restoration's most important actor **1639–1699:** Jean Racine, French playwright, author of *Phaedra* (1677) **1640–1689:** Aphra Behn, first professional woman playwright in the English theater, author of *The Rover* (1677–1680) **1650–1687:** Nell Gwynne, English actress and mistress of Charles II **1656:** First use of Italianate scenery in England in a production of *The Siege of Rhodes*, designed by John Webb **1658:** Molière's troupe, the Illustre Théâtre, is invited to perform at the court of King Louis XIV. The company is subsequently given permission to remain in Paris, as the Troupe de Monsieur, and allowed to use the Petit Bourbon for public performances. **1660:** Theatrical activity resumes in London (after being halted in 1642) when King Charles II issues patents to Thomas Killigrew and William Davenant. Women are permitted on the English stage for the first time.	**1603:** Beginning of the Tokugawa shogunate in Edo, Japan. A long period of peace. **1605:** Gun Powder Plot in London; execution of Guy Fawkes **1642:** Beginning of the English Civil War **1643:** Louis XIV becomes king of France at age four. **1649:** King Charles I of England is beheaded by Parliament. **1655:** Oliver Cromwell prohibits Anglican church services and divides England into eleven districts governed by major-generals. **1658:** Cromwell dissolves Parliament. **1660:** Restoration of the English monarchy and end of the Commonwealth. Charles II, son of the executed Charles I, is crowned.	**1606–1669:** Rembrandt van Rijn, Dutch painter **1608–1674:** John Milton, English author **1610:** Galileo's first observations through a telescope **1620:** Voyage of the *Mayflower* **1628:** William Harvey describes the circulation of blood. **1631–1700:** John Dryden, English author and playwright **1633:** John Donne's *Poems*, the complete collection of his poetry, is published. **1637:** René Descartes's *Discourse on Method*, exploration of mathematics and laws **1638:** Anne Hutchinson is expelled from the Massachusetts Bay Colony and founds Rhode Island. **1645:** Gian Lorenzo Bernini begins his "Ecstasy of St. Theresa." **1650:** Anne Bradstreet publishes *The Tenth Muse*, the first collection of poetry from the New World. **1660:** Samuel Pepys begins his diary. **1660:** Dutch Boers settle on the Cape of Good Hope. **1661–1731:** Daniel Defoe, English author

DATE	THEATER	POLITICAL	SOCIAL/CULTURAL
1600–1700 (continued)	**1664:** Japanese playwright Fukui Yagozaemon writes *The Outcast's Revenge,* the first full-length kabuki play. **1670–1729:** William Congreve, author of *Love for Love* (1695) and *The Way of the World* (1700) **1680:** The Comédie-Française, the first national theater, opens in Paris. **1695–1715:** Proliferation of female playwrights in England. Thirty-seven new plays by women are produced on the London stage during this period by playwrights such as Mary Pix (1666–1706), Susanna Centlivre (c. 1670–1723), Mary Delarivière Manley (c. 1672–1724), and Catharine Trotter (1679–1749). **1698:** Jeremy Collier's *A Short View of the Immorality and Profaneness of the English Stage,* the most effective of several attacks on the theater published at the turn of the century	**1664:** The British annex New Amsterdam and rename it New York. **1682:** Louis XIV moves the French court to Versailles. **1682–1725:** Peter the Great reigns as czar of Russia and calls for political and cultural reforms. **1685:** Louis XIV revokes the Edict of Nantes, and persecution of the Huguenots (French Protestants) ensues. **1688:** William of Orange invades England with the encouragement of prominent Protestants, who fear James II's Catholicism. James flees to France and then England. William III and Mary II (daughter of James II) are crowned in 1689. **1690:** An Irish uprising in favor of James II is suppressed by William III at the Battle of the Boyne. **1697:** The last remains of Mayan civilization are destroyed by the Spanish.	**1664–1666:** Isaac Newton (1642–1727), English mathematician and physicist, discovers the law of universal gravitation and begins to develop calculus. **1665:** Plague devastates London. **1666:** Great Fire of London **1685–1750:** J. S. Bach, German composer **1687:** Isaac Newton publishes *Mathematical Principles.* **1688–1704:** Alexander Pope, English poet **1692:** Salem witchcraft trials **1694–1778:** François Marie Arouet de Voltaire, French author often described as the embodiment of the Enlightenment
1700–1800	**1703:** Chikamatsu creates the genre of love suicide plays with *The Love Suicides at Sonezaki.* **1707–1793:** Carlo Goldoni, Italian playwright, author of *The Servant of Two Masters* (1743) **1717–1779:** David Garrick, greatest English actor of the eighteenth century and owner and manager of the Drury Lane Theatre in London **1720–1806:** Carlo Gozzi, Italian playwright, author of *King Stag* (1762) and *Turandot* (1762)	**1703:** Peter the Great lays the foundation for St. Petersburg. **1707:** The Act of Union unites Scotland and England, which become Great Britain. **1714:** The House of Hanover begins its rule of Great Britain with the accession of George I. **1715:** Louis XIV, France's Sun King, dies.	**1703–1758:** Jonathan Edwards, American theologian **1709–1784:** Samuel Johnson, English literary critic, scholar, poet, and lexicographer **1720:** First serialization of novels in newspapers **1724:** Emmanuel Kant, German metaphysics philosopher

Late Seventeenth- and Eighteenth-Century Drama Timeline (continued)

DATE	THEATER	POLITICAL	SOCIAL/CULTURAL
1700–1800 (continued)	**1728:** John Gay (1685–1732) writes *The Beggar's Opera*, arguably the most popular English play of the eighteenth century.		**1726:** Jonathan Swift writes *Gulliver's Travels*.
	1730–1774: Oliver Goldsmith, author of *The Vicar of Wakefield, The Deserted Village*, and *She Stoops to Conquer*		**1732:** Covent Garden opera house opens in London.
	1729–1781: Gotthold Ephraim Lessing, Germany's first important playwright, author of *Minna von Barnhelm* (1767) and *Emilia Galotti* (1772)		**1732:** Franz Josef Haydn, prolific Austrian composer
	1737: The Licensing Act in England prohibits the performance of any play not previously licensed by the Lord Chamberlain. A number of such laws regulating theatrical activity are enacted throughout the eighteenth century.	**1740:** Frederick the Great introduces freedom of press and worship in Prussia.	**1742:** Cotton factories are established in Birmingham and Northampton, England.
			1746–1828: Francisco de Goya, Spanish painter and political cartoonist
	1749–1832: Johann Wolfgang von Goethe, German writer. His early works include the play *Götz von Berlichingen* (1773) and the novel *The Sorrows of Young Werther* (1774).	**1756–1763:** Frederick begins the Seven Years War pitting Prussia and Great Britain against Russia, Austria, and France.	**1751:** Dennis Diderot, French writer and philosopher, publishes the first volume of his *Encyclopédie*.
			1756–1791: Wolfgang Amadeus Mozart, Austrian classical composer
	1751–1816: Richard Brinsley Sheridan, playwright and statesman, author of *The School for Scandal* (1777)	**1762:** Catherine the Great (b. 1729) becomes empress of Russia after overthrowing her husband, Peter III; she reigns until her death in 1796.	**1757–1827:** William Blake, Romantic poet and artist, author of *Songs of Innocence* and *Songs of Experience*
	1762: English actor-manager David Garrick prohibits audience members from sitting on the stage.	**1763:** The Treaty of Paris ends the Seven Years War. Prussia emerges as an important European power. France loses many colonial possessions.	**1759–1797:** Mary Wollstonecraft, English writer and early feminist, author of *Vindication of the Rights of Woman* (1792)
			1762: The Sorbonne library opens in Paris.
		1765: British Parliament passes the Stamp Act. Nine colonies draw up a declaration of rights and liberties.	
	c. 1769: Spectators are banned from sitting on the stage in Paris.	**1766:** Catherine the Great grants freedom of worship in Russia.	**1791:** James Boswell publishes his *Life of Johnson*.
		1776: U.S. Declaration of Independence	

Molière

Molière (1622–1673, born Jean Baptiste Poquelin) came from a family attached to the glittering court of King Louis XIV, the Sun King. His father had purchased an appointment to the king, and as a result the family was familiar with the exciting court life of Paris, although not on intimate terms with the courtiers who surrounded the king. Molière's father was a furnisher and upholsterer to the king; the family, while well-to-do and enjoying some power, was still apart from royalty and the privileged aristocracy.

Molière's education was exceptional. He went to Jesuit schools and spent more than five years at Collège de Clermont, which he left in 1641 having studied both the humanities and philosophy. His knowledge of philosophy was unusually deep, and his background in the classics was exceptionally strong. He also took a law degree in 1641, at Orléans, but never practiced. His father's dream was that his son should inherit his appointment as furnisher to the king, thereby guaranteeing himself a comfortable future.

That, however, was not to be. Instead of following the law, Molière decided at the last minute to abandon his secure future, change his name so as not to scandalize his family, and take up a career in the theater. He began by joining a company of actors run by the Béjart family. They established a theater based in Paris called the Illustre Théâtre. It was run by Madeleine Béjart, with whom Molière had a professional and personal relationship until she died in 1672. Eventually, Molière began writing plays, but only after he had worked extensively as an actor.

The famed commedia dell'arte actor Tiberio Fiorillo, known as Scaramouche, was a close friend of Molière and perhaps was responsible for Molière's choice of a career in theater. Scaramouche may have been part of the Illustre Théâtre, or he may have acted in it on occasion. Unfortunately, the Illustre Théâtre lasted only a year. It was one of several Parisian theatrical groups, and none of them prospered.

The company went bankrupt in 1644, and Molière, forced to leave Paris for about thirteen years, played in the provinces and remote towns. Before leaving Paris he had to be bailed out of debtors' prison. What was left of the Béjart group merged with another company on tour, and Molière became director of that company. During this time he suffered most of the indignities typical of the traveling life, including impoverishment.

In October 1658 Louis XIV saw Molière's troupe acting in one of his comedies at the Louvre. The royal court was so impressed with what it saw that the king gave him the use of a theater. Molière's work remained immensely popular and controversial. He acted in his own plays, produced his own plays, and wrote a succession of major works that are still favorites.

Because other companies envied his success and favor with the king, a number of "scandals" arose around some of his plays. The first play to invite controversy was *The School for Wives* (1662), in which Arnolphe reacts in horror

509

to the infidelities he sees in the wives all around him. He decides that his wife-to-be must be raised far from the world, where she will be ignorant of the wayward lives of the Parisians. A man who intends to seduce her tells Arnolphe (not knowing who he is) how he will get her out of Arnolphe's grasp. The play is highly comic, but groups of theatergoers protested that it was immoral and scandalous. In response Molière wrote *Criticism of the School for Wives* (1663), in which the debate over the play is enacted.

One of Molière's most popular plays is *The Misanthrope* (1666), which, though not his most comic play, is one of his most often produced and most thought-provoking. Molière himself acted the part of Alceste, and his wife acted opposite him as Célimène; most of the players realized that the play was making fun of their own marriage. It was not so serious a portrayal as to dampen the spirits of the audience, because Molière introduced enough humor to keep it light. Yet the play has enough substance to keep audiences concerned with the oppositions in sentiment between them. Alceste hates society and refuses to be polite and tell people nice things when he feels they deserve rebuke. Célimène loves society and especially loves the way she can dominate it and be its center, enjoying the attention of many suitors.

The Misanthrope examines the character of each person on stage and, by extension, the character of those in his audience — a privileged, refined stratum of society. One reason why the play did not satisfy its earliest audiences may be that the lovers adhere to their opposite views of the world and, as a result, do not marry in the end. A conventional comedy would have found a means to join them, but this is not a conventional comedy.

Among Molière's other successes are *The Miser* (1668), *The Bourgeois Gentleman* (1670), and his final play, *The Imaginary Invalid* (1673). Molière had a bad cough for most of the last decade of his life, which onstage he often made to seem the cough of the character he was playing. But Molière was genuinely ill; he died on stage, playing the title role of *The Imaginary Invalid*.

TARTUFFE

Molière first produced *Tartuffe, or The Hypocrite* in three acts at Versailles at a royal fête shortly after he finished it in 1664, but the production was private, and although he recognized the value of the play, the king immediately banned it from public production. However, he liked it enough to have it read at court as a private entertainment. While the king was away from court, Molière rewrote the play as *Panulphe, or the Hypocrite*, but that also was deemed too irreverent to be produced publicly.

Because Molière's satirical comedies were already thought to be problematic for French society, the clergy, who wielded considerable power with the king, kept careful watch on Molière's productions. The Society of the Holy Sacrament thought that it was being satirized in *Tartuffe* and protested the play as immoral and an attack on the Church. The Bishop of Autun also believed, perhaps correctly, that he was being satirized in the character of Tartuffe. As a result of the Church's anger, Molière was denounced as a "demon," and a writ of excommunication was ordered against all who performed in or went to see the play.

In 1669, after the dissolution of the Society of the Holy Sacrament, and after the king had managed to assuage the clergy, a permit was issued for the production of the present version of the play in five acts. Its immediate success established it as a permanent repertory piece, and it has been performed regularly ever since. Its satire on religious hypocrisy is timeless and meaningful in virtually all societies.

Tartuffe is a beggar who somehow cons Orgon, a wealthy man with a large estate, into taking him into his home. He also tricks him by convincing Orgon that he is a man of God who cares nothing for the material goods of the world and whose only duty is to God. Orgon's mother, Madame Pernelle, is thoroughly convinced that Tartuffe is virtuous and that he must be listened to and respected. Orgon's son Damis sees Tartuffe for a fraud but is silenced and disowned by his father, who will not listen to reason. He has made up his mind and cannot be swayed by argument.

Molière immediately introduces the comic convention of the father forcing his daughter to marry against her will when Orgon announces that Mariane must give up her love for Valère and marry Tartuffe. She is an obedient daughter and seems to comply, though reluctantly. In one of the most amusing scenes in drama (act II, scene 3), Mariane's maid Dorine cleverly persuades her to disobey her father and marry Valère. The interchange between Mariane and Valère in the following scene reveals the high spirits of both lovers, who demonstrate their stubbornness and whose irritation with each other is smoothed out by the clever maid, a staple of drama since the Greeks.

Tartuffe, who does not appear until act III, proposes adultery to Orgon's wife Elmire, who plays along with him to undo Orgon's plans to marry off Mariane. It is a wonderfully comic scene (act III, scene 3) marked by memorable lines, such as Tartuffe's "I offer you, my dear Elmire, / Love without scandal, pleasure without fear." Later he adds, "It's scandal, madame, which makes it an offense / And it's no sin to sin in confidence" (act IV, scene 5). Elmire finally plots to expose Tartuffe to her husband by having Orgon hide while Tartuffe tries to seduce her. But the plan almost backfires because Orgon madly signed over his estate to Tartuffe and upbraided his family for abusing a pious man.

The level of satire in the play is broad enough to bring laughter to virtually all audiences, and the portrait of a supposedly pious, religious, and zealous person who is fundamentally a hypocrite and fraud is so brilliantly established that Tartuffe has become the stereotype of the hypocrite. In our age, the many such frauds exposed in the press make it clear that little has changed since Molière's time.

Richard Wilbur's translation, in rhymed couplets, respects the original French, which is also in rhymed couplets. The French verse is twelve-syllable rhymed couplets, called Alexandrines. Rhyming is much easier to do in French than in English, but Wilbur produces some marvelous rhymes, such as Tartuffe's seductive lines "Madam, forget such fears, and be my pupil, / And I shall teach you how to conquer scruple" (act IV, scene 5, 99–100). The artificiality of rhyme mirrors the artificiality of some of the characters and of their society — probably even more effectively in modern English than it did in seventeenth-century France, when it was unusual for plays to be written in prose.

Molière observes the unities in *Tartuffe* by having the action take place in one day, in one setting, with no subplots. The result is that intensity builds relentlessly until the unusual resolution of the action, which comes at the very last minute. As in most comedies, the lovers are permitted to marry, the villain is revealed and chastised, and the family is restored to its rightful position. But in the process, society is exposed as gullible, naive, and easily manipulated. In this sense, the play is a moral play, rather than the dangerous immoral work that the clergy condemned.

Tartuffe in Performance

Molière played the part of Orgon at the first public performance in February 1669, at the Palais Royale in Paris. The Théâtre-Français, which still produces the play regularly, featured Nicholas Auge as Tartuffe in 1776. His first entrance in Act 3 was notable for his bringing out a gigantic handkerchief to hide Dorine's bosom, while delivering the line "Hide that breast" with a lustful leer and obvious lecherous looks — a convention later followed and developed by that company throughout the nineteenth century. One of the strangest productions was that of the Athénée theater in Paris in 1950, with Louis Jouvet as a truly pious Tartuffe struggling with himself over the temptation of Elmire! Jouvet's Tartuffe was not a slovenly, fat, lecherous figure with a dangling crucifix, as conventional Tartuffes were. Early audiences were annoyed at what they felt was a misreading of the text, and reviews indicate that there were very few laughs. However, the production ran for 139 performances. A similar interpretation in Paris in 1964 with Michel Auclair, a dashing leading man of the era, emphasized a possible unconscious homosexual connection between Tartuffe and Orgon as an explanation for Orgon's strange behavior. The stage was decorated with huge black-and-white religious paintings that emphasized a naked Christ, thus introducing the images of flesh even before the play began. In 1965 the Repertory Theatre of Lincoln Center produced the Richard Wilbur translation with Michael O'Sullivan as Tartuffe; the production ran for five months, alternating with an Arthur Miller play. Tyrone Guthrie's 1967 production at the Old Vic starred John Gielgud as Orgon but was criticized for its weak, rural clown Tartuffe. However, it was praised for avoiding modern psychological interpretations and sticking with the text in such a way that the *deus ex machina* of the king's messenger at the end was more intelligible as a force that restores proper order to a disordered world. Freyda Thomas adapted the play at Circle in the Square in New York in 1996 as *Tartuffe: Born Again*. This production portrayed Tartuffe as a modern televangelist, a comparison that begged to be made in the 1990s. In 2002 London's National Theatre produced a rollicking *Tartuffe* with Martin Clunes, a TV sitcom star of considerable girth, playing the role broadly for laughs in a translation that sometimes verged on the scatological. The Yale Repertory Theater productions took the same approach, first in 1984 and most recently in 2007. Austin Pendleton has performed his Tartuffe at Yale, and his comic interpretation will be long remembered.

Molière (1662–1673)

TARTUFFE   *1669*
TRANSLATED BY RICHARD WILBUR

Characters

MME PERNELLE, *Orgon's mother*
ORGON, *Elmire's husband*
ELMIRE, *Orgon's wife*
DAMIS, *Orgon's son, Elmire's stepson*
MARIANE, *Orgon's daughter, Elmire's stepdaughter, in love with Valère*
VALÈRE, *in love with Mariane*
CLÉANTE, *Orgon's brother-in-law*
TARTUFFE, *a hypocrite*
DORINE, *Mariane's lady's-maid*
M. LOYAL, *a bailiff*
A POLICE OFFICER
FLIPOTE, *Mme Pernelle's maid*

The scene throughout. Orgon's house in Paris.

ACT I • *Scene 1* [*Madame Pernelle and Flipote, her maid, Elmire, Mariane, Dorine, Damis, Cléante.*]

MADAME PERNELLE: Come, come, Flipote; it's time I left this place.
ELMIRE: I can't keep up, you walk at such a pace.
MADAME PERNELLE: Don't trouble, child; no need to show me out.
    It's not your manners I'm concerned about.
5 ELMIRE: We merely pay you the respect we owe.
    But, Mother, why this hurry? Must you go?
MADAME PERNELLE: I must. This house appalls me. No one in it
    Will pay attention for a single minute.
    Children, I take my leave much vexed in spirit.
10 I offer good advice, but you won't hear it.
    You all break in and chatter on and on.
    It's like a madhouse with the keeper gone.
DORINE: If . . .
MADAME PERNELLE: Girl, you talk too much, and I'm afraid
    You're far too saucy for a lady's-maid.
15 You push in everywhere and have your say.
DAMIS: But . . .
MADAME PERNELLE: You, boy, grow more foolish every day.
    To think my grandson should be such a dunce!
    I've said a hundred times, if I've said it once,
    That if you keep the course on which you've
20   started,
    You'll leave your worthy father broken-hearted.

MARIANE: I think . . .
MADAME PERNELLE: And you, his sister, seem so pure,
    So shy, so innocent, and so demure.
    But you know what they say about still waters.
    I pity parents with secretive daughters.
ELMIRE: Now, Mother . . .
MADAME PERNELLE: And as for you, child, let me add   25
    That your behavior is extremely bad,
    And a poor example for these children, too.
    Their dear, dead mother did far better than you.
    You're much too free with money, and I'm distressed
    To see you so elaborately dressed.   30
    When it's one's husband that one aims to please,
    One has no need of costly fripperies.
CLÉANTE: Oh, Madam, really . . .
MADAME PERNELLE: You are her brother, Sir,
    And I respect and love you; yet if I were
    My son, this lady's good and pious spouse,   35
    I wouldn't make you welcome in my house.
    You're full of worldly counsels which, I fear,
    Aren't suitable for decent folk to hear.
    I've spoken bluntly, Sir; but it behooves us
    Not to mince words when righteous fervor moves us.   40
DAMIS: Your man Tartuffe is full of holy speeches . . .
MADAME PERNELLE: And practices precisely what he preaches.
    He's a fine man, and should be listened to.
    I will not hear him mocked by fools like you.
DAMIS: Good God! Do you expect me to submit   45
    To the tyranny of that carping hypocrite?
    Must we forgo all joys and satisfactions
    Because that bigot censures all out actions?
DORINE: To hear him talk—and he talks all the time—
    There's nothing one can do that's not a crime.   50
    He rails at everything, your dear Tartuffe
MADAME PERNELLE: Whatever he reproves deserves reproof.
    He's out to save your souls, and all of you
    Must love him, as my son would have you do.
DAMIS: Ah no, Grandmother, I could never take   55
    To such a rascal, even for my father's sake.
    That's how I feel, and I shall not dissemble.
    His every action makes me seethe and tremble
    With helpless anger, and I have no doubt
    That he and I will shortly have it out.   60
DORINE: Surely it is a shame and a disgrace
    To see this man usurp the master's place—

To see this beggar who, when first he came,
Had not a shoe or shoestring to his name
65   So far forget himself that he behaves
As if the house were his, and we his slaves.
MADAME PERNELLE: Well, mark my words, your
    souls would fare far better
If you obeyed his precepts to the letter.
DORINE: You see him as a saint. I'm far less awed;
70   In fact, I see right through him. He's a fraud.
MADAME PERNELLE: Nonsense!
DORINE: His man Laurent's the same, or
    worse;
I'd not trust either with a penny purse.
MADAME PERNELLE: I can't say what his servant's
    morals may be;
His own great goodness I can guarantee.
75   You all regard him with distaste and fear
Because he tells you what you're loath to hear,
Condemns your sins, points out your moral flaws,
And humbly strives to further Heaven's cause.
DORINE: If sin is all that bothers him, why is it
80   He's so upset when folk drop in to visit?
Is Heaven so outraged by a social call
That he must prophesy against us all?
I'll tell you what I think: if you ask me,
He's jealous of my mistress' company.
MADAME PERNELLE: Rubbish! (To Elmire.) He's not
85   alone, child, in complaining
Of all your promiscuous entertaining.
Why, the whole neighborhood's upset, I know,
By all these carriages that come and go,
With crowds of guests parading in and out
90   And noisy servants loitering about.
In all of this, I'm sure there's nothing vicious;
But why give people cause to be suspicious?
CLÉANTE: They need no cause; they'll talk in any case.
Madam, this world would be a joyless place
95   If, fearing what malicious tongues might say,
We locked our doors and turned our friends away.
And even if one did so dreary a thing,
D'you think those tongues would cease their
    chattering?
One can't fight slander; it's a losing battle;
100 Let us instead ignore their tittle-tattle.
Let's strive to live by conscience' clear decrees,
And let the gossips gossip as they please.
DORINE: If there is talk against us, I know the source:
It's Daphne and her little husband, of course.
105 Those who have greatest cause for guilt and shame
Are quickest to besmirch a neighbor's name.
When there's a chance for libel, they never miss it;
When something can be made to seem illicit
They're off at once to spread the joyous news,
110 Adding to fact what fantasies they choose.
By talking up their neighbor's indiscretions
They seek to camouflage their own transgressions,
Hoping that others' innocent affairs
Will lend a hue of innocence to theirs,
115 Or that their own black guilt will come to seem

Part of a general shady color-scheme.
MADAME PERNELLE: All that is quite irrelevant. I
    doubt
That anyone's more virtuous and devout
Than dear Orante; and I'm informed that she
Condemns your mode of life most vehemently.   120
DORINE: Oh, yes, she's strict, devout, and has no
    taint
Of worldliness; in short, she seems a saint.
But it was time which taught her that disguise;
She's thus because she can't be otherwise.
So long as her attractions could enthrall,   125
She flounced and flirted and enjoyed it all,
But now that they're no longer what they were
She quits a world which fast is quitting her,
And wears a veil of virtue to conceal
Her bankrupt beauty and her lost appeal.   130
That's what becomes of old coquettes today;
Distressed when all their lovers fall away,
They see no recourse but to play the prude,
And so confer a style on solitude.
Thereafter, they're severe with everyone,   135
Condemning all our actions, pardoning none,
And claiming to be pure, austere, and zealous
When, if the truth were known, they're merely
    jealous,
And cannot bear to see another know
The pleasures time has forced them to forgo.   140
MADAME PERNELLE (initially to Elmire): That sort of
    talk is what you like to hear;
Therefore you'd have us all keep still, my dear,
While Madam rattles on the livelong day.
Nevertheless, I mean to have my say.
I tell you that you're blest to have Tartuffe   145
Dwelling, as my son's guest, beneath this roof;
That Heaven has sent him to forestall its wrath
By leading you, once more, to the true path;
That all he reprehends is reprehensible,
And that you'd better heed him, and be sensible.   150
These visits, balls, and parties in which you revel
Are nothing but inventions of the Devil.
One never hears a word that's edifying:
Nothing but chaff and foolishness and lying,
As well as vicious gossip in which one's neighbor 155
Is cut to bits with epee, foil, and saber.
People of sense are driven half-insane
At such affairs, where noise and folly reign
And reputations perish thick and fast.
As a wise preacher said on Sunday last,   160
Parties are Towers of Babylon, because
The guests all babble on with never a pause;
And then he told a story which, I think . . .
    (To Cléante.)
I heard that laugh, Sir, and I saw that wink!
Go find your silly friends and laugh some more!   165
Enough; I'm going; don't show me to the door.
I leave this household much dismayed and vexed;
I cannot say when I shall see you next.
    (Slapping Flipote.)

2

Wake up, don't stand there gaping into space!
170 I'll slap some sense into that stupid face.
Move, move, you slut.

Scene 2 [Cléante, Dorine.]

CLÉANTE: I think I'll stay behind;
I want no further pieces of her mind.
How that old lady . . .
DORINE: Oh, what wouldn't she say
If she could hear you speak of her that way!
5 She'd thank you for the *lady*, but I'm sure
She'd find the *old* a little premature.
CLÉANTE: My, what a scene she made, and what a din!
And how this man Tartuffe has taken her in!
DORINE: Yes, but her son is even worse deceived;
10 His folly must be seen to be believed.
In the late troubles, he played an able part
And served his king with wise and loyal heart,
But he's quite lost his senses since he fell
Beneath Tartuffe's infatuating spell.
15 He calls him brother, and loves him as his life,
Preferring him to mother, child, or wife.
In him and him alone will he confide;
He's made him his confessor and his guide;
He pets and pampers him with love more tender
20 Than any pretty mistress could engender,
Gives him the place of honor when they dine,
Delights to see him gorging like a swine,
Stuffs him with dainties till his guts distend,
And when he belches, cries "God bless you, friend!"
25 In short, he's mad; he worships him; he dotes;
His deeds he marvels at, his words he quotes,
Thinking each act a miracle, each word
Oracular as those that Moses heard.
Tartuffe, much pleased to find so easy a victim,
30 Has in a hundred ways beguiled and tricked him,
Milked him of money, and with his permission
Established here a sort of Inquisition.
Even Laurent, his lackey, dares to give
Us arrogant advice on how to live;
35 He sermonizes us in thundering tones
And confiscates our ribbons and colognes.
Last week he tore a kerchief into pieces
Because he found it pressed in a *Life of Jesus:*
He said it was a sin to juxtapose
40 Unholy vanities and holy prose.

Scene 3 [Elmire, Mariane, Damis, Cléante, Dorine.]

ELMIRE (*to Cléante*): You did well not to follow; she stood in the door
And said *verbatim* all she'd said before.
I saw my husband coming. I think I'd best
Go upstairs now, and take a little rest.
CLÉANTE: I'll wait and greet him here; then I must go.
5 I've really only time to say hello.
DAMIS: Sound him about my sister's wedding, please.
I think Tartuffe's against it, and that he's
Been urging Father to withdraw his blessing,
As you well know, I'd find that most distressing. 10
Unless my sister and Valère can marry,
My hopes to wed *his* sister will miscarry,
And I'm determined . . .
DORINE: He's coming.

Scene 4 [Orgon, Cléante, Dorine.]

ORGON: Ah, Brother, good-day.
CLÉANTE: Well, welcome back. I'm sorry I can't stay,
How was the country? Blooming, I trust, and green?
ORGON: Excuse me, Brother; just one moment.
(*To Dorine.*)
                                   Dorine . . .
(*To Cléante.*)   5
To put my mind at rest, I always learn
The household news the moment I return.
                              (*To Dorine.*)
Has all been well, these two days I've been gone?
How are the family? What's been going on?
DORINE: Your wife, two days ago, had a bad fever, 10
And a fierce headache which refused to leave her.
ORGON: Ah. And Tartuffe?
DORINE: Tartuffe? Why, he's round and red,
Bursting with health, and excellently fed.
ORGON: Poor fellow!
DORINE: That night, the mistress was unable
To take a single bite at the dinner-table. 15
Her headache-pains, she said, were simply hellish.
ORGON: Ah. And Tartuffe?
DORINE: He ate his meal with relish,
And zealously devoured in her presence
A leg of mutton and a brace of pheasants.
ORGON: Poor fellow!
DORINE: Well, the pains continued strong,
And so she tossed and tossed the whole night long, 20
Now icy-cold, now burning like a flame.
We sat beside her bed till morning came.
ORGON: Ah. And Tartuffe?
DORINE: Why, having eaten, he rose
And sought his room, already in a doze,
Got into his warm bed, and snored away 25
In perfect peace until the break of day.
ORGON: Poor fellow!
DORINE: After much ado, we talked her
Into dispatching someone for the doctor.
He bled her, and the fever quickly fell.

ORGON: Ah. And Tartuffe?
30 DORINE: He bore it very well.
　　　To keep his cheerfulness at any cost,
　　　And make up for the blood *Madame* had lost,
　　　He drank, at lunch, four beakers full of port.
ORGON: Poor fellow!
DORINE: Both are doing well, in short.
35 　I'll go and tell *Madame* that you've expressed
　　　Keen sympathy and anxious interest.

Scene 5   [*Orgon, Cléante.*]

CLÉANTE: That girl was laughing in your face, and
　　　though
　　　I've no wish to offend you, even so
　　　I'm bound to say that she had some excuse.
　　　How can you possibly be such a goose?
5 　　Are you so dazed by this man's hocus-pocus
　　　That all the world, save him, is out of focus?
　　　You've given him clothing, shelter, food, and care;
　　　Why must you also . . .
ORGON: Brother, stop right there.
　　　You do not know the man of whom you speak.
CLÉANTE: I grant you that. But my judgment's not so
10 　　weak
　　　That I can't tell, by his effect on others . . .
ORGON: Ah, when you meet him, you two will be
　　　like brothers!
　　　There's been no loftier soul since time began.
　　　He is a man who . . . a man who . . . an excellent man.
15 　To keep his precepts is to be reborn,
　　　And view this dunghill of a world with scorn.
　　　Yes, thanks to him I'm a changed man indeed.
　　　Under his tutelage my soul's been freed
　　　From earthly loves, and every human tie:
20 　My mother, children, brother, and wife could die,
　　　And I'd not feel a single moment's pain.
CLÉANTE: That's a fine sentiment, Brother; most
　　　humane.
ORGON: Oh, had you seen Tartuffe as I first knew
　　　him,
　　　Your heart, like mine, would have surrendered to
　　　him.
25 　He used to come into our church each day
　　　And humbly kneel nearby, and start to pray.
　　　He'd draw the eyes of everybody there
　　　By the deep fervor of his heartfelt prayer;
　　　He'd sigh and weep, and sometimes with a sound
30 　Of rapture he would bend and kiss the ground;
　　　And when I rose to go, he'd run before
　　　To offer me holy-water at the door.
　　　His serving-man, no less devout than he,
　　　Informed me of his master's poverty;
35 　I gave him gifts, but in his humbleness
　　　He'd beg me every time to give him less.
　　　"Oh, that's too much," he'd cry, "too much by
　　　twice!
　　　I don't deserve it. The half, Sir, would suffice."

And when I wouldn't take it back, he'd share
Half of it with the poor, right then and there.   40
At length, Heaven prompted me to take him in
To dwell with us, and free our souls from sin.
He guides our lives, and to protect my honor
Stays by my wife, and keeps an eye upon her;
He tells me whom she sees, and all she does,   45
And seems more jealous than I ever was!
And how austere he is! Why, he can detect
A mortal sin where you would least suspect;
In smallest trifles, he's extremely strict.
Last week, his conscience was severely pricked   50
Because, while praying, he had caught a flea
And killed it, so he felt, too wrathfully.
CLÉANTE: Good God, man! Have you lost your
　　　common sense—
　　　Or is this all some joke at my expense?
　　　How can you stand there and in all sobriety . . .   55
ORGON: Brother, your language savors of impiety.
　　　Too much free-thinking's made your faith unsteady,
　　　And as I've warned you many times already,
　　　'Twill get you into trouble before you're through.
CLÉANTE: So I've been told before by dupes like you: 60
　　　Being blind, you'd have all others blind as well;
　　　The clear-eyed man you call an infidel,
　　　And he who sees through humbug and pretense
　　　Is charged, by you, with want of reverence.
　　　Spare me your warnings, Brother; I have no fear   65
　　　Of speaking out, for you and Heaven to hear,
　　　Against affected zeal and pious knavery.
　　　There's true and false in piety, as in bravery,
　　　And just as those whose courage shines the most
　　　In battle, are the least inclined to boast,   70
　　　So those whose hearts are truly pure and lowly
　　　Don't make a flashy show of being holy.
　　　There's a vast difference, so it seems to me,
　　　Between true piety and hypocrisy:
　　　How do you fail to see it, may I ask?   75
　　　Is not a face quite different from a mask?
　　　Cannot sincerity and cunning art,
　　　Reality and semblance, be told apart?
　　　Are scarecrows just like men, and do you hold
　　　That a false coin is just as good as gold?   80
　　　Ah, Brother, man's a strangely fashioned creature
　　　Who seldom is content to follow Nature,
　　　But recklessly pursues his inclination
　　　Beyond the narrow bounds of moderation,
　　　And often, by transgressing Reason's laws,   85
　　　Perverts a lofty aim or noble cause.
　　　A passing observation, but it applies.
ORGON: I see, dear Brother, that you're profoundly
　　　wise;
　　　You harbor all the insight of the age.
　　　You are our one clear mind, our only sage,   90
　　　The era's oracle, its Cato° too,
　　　And all mankind are fools compared to you.

91. Cato: Roman statesman (234–149 BCE) noted for his virtue
and wisdom.

CLÉANTE: Brother, I don't pretend to be a sage,
Nor have I all the wisdom of the age.
95   There's just one insight I would dare to claim;
I know that true and false are not the same;
And just as there is nothing I more revere
Than a soul whose faith is steadfast and sincere,
Nothing that I more cherish and admire
100 Than honest zeal and true religious fire,
So there is nothing that I find more base
Than specious piety's dishonest face —
Than these bold mountebanks, these histrios
Whose impious mummeries and hollow shows
105 Exploit our love of Heaven, and make a jest
Of all that men think holiest and best;
These calculating souls who offer prayers
Not to their Maker, but as public wares,
And seek to buy respect and reputation
110 With lifted eyes and sighs of exaltation;
These charlatans, I say, whose pilgrim souls
Proceed, by way of Heaven, toward earthly goals,
Who weep and pray and swindle and extort,
Who preach the monkish life, but haunt the court,
115 Who make their zeal the partner of their vice—
Such men are vengeful, sly, and cold as ice,
And when there is an enemy to defame
They cloak their spite in fair religion's name,
Their private spleen and malice being made
120 To seem a high and virtuous crusade,
Until, to mankind's reverent applause,
They crucify their foe in Heaven's cause.
Such knaves are all too common; yet, for the wise,
True piety isn't hard to recognize,
125 And, happily, these present times provide us
With bright examples to instruct and guide us.
Consider Ariston and Périandre;
Look at Oronte, Alcidamas, Clitandre;
Their virtue is acknowledged; who could doubt it?
130 But you won't hear them beat the drum about it.
They're never ostentatious, never vain,
And their religion's moderate and humane;
It's not their way to criticize and chide:
They think censoriousness a mark of pride,
135 And therefore, letting others preach and rave,
They show, by deeds, how Christians should behave.
They think no evil of their fellow man,
But judge of him as kindly as they can.
They don't intrigue and wangle and conspire;
140 To lead a good life is their one desire;
The sinner wakes no rancorous hate in them;
It is the sin alone which they condemn;
Nor do they try to show a fiercer zeal
For Heaven's cause than Heaven itself could feel.
145 These men I honor, these men I advocate
As models for us all to emulate.
Your man is not their sort at all, I fear:
And, while your praise of him is quite sincere,

I think that you've been dreadfully deluded.
ORGON: Now then, dear Brother, is your speech concluded?   150
CLÉANTE: Why, yes.
ORGON: Your servant, Sir.

[*He turns to go.*]

CLÉANTE: No, Brother; wait.
There's one more matter. You agreed of late
That young Valère might have your daughter's hand.
ORGON: I did.
CLÉANTE: And set the date, I understand.
ORGON: Quite so.
CLÉANTE: You've now postponed it; is that true?   155
ORGON: No doubt.
CLÉANTE: The match no longer pleases you?
ORGON: Who knows?
CLÉANTE: D'you mean to go back on your word?
ORGON: I won't say that.
CLÉANTE: Has anything occurred
Which might entitle you to break your pledge?
ORGON: Perhaps.
CLÉANTE: Why must you hem, and haw, and hedge?   160
The boy asked me to sound you in this affair . . .
ORGON: It's been a pleasure.
CLÉANTE: But what shall I tell Valère?
ORGON: Whatever you like.
CLÉANTE: But what have you decided?
What are your plans?
ORGON: I plan, Sir, to be guided
By Heaven's will.
CLÉANTE: Come, Brother, don't talk rot.   165
You've given Valère your word; will you keep it, or not?
ORGON: Good day.
CLÉANTE: This looks like poor Valère's undoing;
I'll go and warn him that there's trouble brewing.

ACT II • Scene 1   [*Orgon, Mariane.*]

ORGON: Mariane.
MARIANE: Yes, Father?
ORGON: A word with you; come here.
MARIANE: What are you looking for?
ORGON (*peering into a small closet*):
                                      Eavesdroppers, dear.
I'm making sure we shan't be overheard.
Someone in there could catch our every word.
Ah, good, we're safe. Now, Mariane, my child,   5

You're a sweet girl who's tractable and mild,
Whom I hold dear, and think most highly of.
MARIANE: I'm deeply grateful, Father, for your love.
ORGON: That's well said, Daughter; and you can repay me
10 If, in all things, you'll cheerfully obey me.
MARIANE: To please you, Sir, is what delights me best.
ORGON: Good, good. Now, what d'you think of
   Tartuffe, our guest?
MARIANE: I, Sir?
ORGON: Yes. Weigh your answer; think it
   through.
MARIANE: Oh, dear. I'll say whatever you wish me to.
ORGON: That's wisely said, my Daughter. Say of him,
15   then,
That he's the very worthiest of men,
And that you're fond of him, and would rejoice
In being his wife, if that should be my choice.
Well?
MARIANE: What?
ORGON: What's that?
MARIANE: I . . .
ORGON: Well?
MARIANE: Forgive me,
   pray.
ORGON: Did you not hear me?
MARIANE: Of *whom*, Sir, must I
20   say
That I am fond of him, and would rejoice
In being his wife, if that should be your choice?
ORGON: Why, of Tartuffe.
MARIANE: But, Father, that's false, you
   know.
Why would you have me say what isn't so?
25 ORGON: Because I am resolved it shall be true.
That it's my wish should be enough for you.
MARIANE: You can't mean, Father . . .
ORGON: Yes, Tartuffe
   shall be
Allied by marriage to this family,
And he's to be your husband, is that clear?
30 It's a father's privilege . . .

Scene 2 [Dorine, Orgon, Mariane.]

ORGON (*to Dorine*):   What are you doing in
   here?
Is curiosity so fierce a passion
With you, that you must eavesdrop in this
   fashion?
DORINE: There's lately been a rumor going about—
Based on some hunch or chance remark, no
5   doubt—
That you mean Mariane to wed Tartuffe.
I've laughed it off, of course, as just a spoof.
ORGON: You find it so incredible?
DORINE: Yes, I do.
I won't accept that story, even from you.

ORGON: Well, you'll believe it when the thing is
   done.   10
DORINE: Yes, yes, of course. Go on and have your
   fun.
ORGON: I've never been more serious in my life.
DORINE: Ha!
ORGON: Daughter, I mean it; you're to be his wife.
DORINE: No, don't believe your father; it's all a hoax.
ORGON: See here, young woman . . .
DORINE: Come, Sir, no
   more jokes;   15
You can't fool us.
ORGON: How dare you talk that way?
DORINE: All right, then: we believe you, sad to say.
But how a man like you, who looks so wise
And wears a moustache of such splendid size,
Can be so foolish as to . . .
ORGON: Silence, please!   20
My girl, you take too many liberties.
I'm master here, as you must not forget.
DORINE: Do let's discuss this calmly; don't be upset.
You can't be serious, Sir, about this plan.
What should that bigot want with Mariane?   25
Praying and fasting ought to keep him busy.
And then, in terms of wealth and rank, what
   is he?
Why should a man of property like you
Pick out a beggar son-in-law?
ORGON: That will do.
Speak of his poverty with reverence.   30
His is a pure and saintly indigence
Which far transcends all worldly pride and pelf.
He lost his fortune, as he says himself,
Because he cared for Heaven alone, and so
Was careless of his interests here below.   35
I mean to get him out of his present straits
And help him to recover his estates—
Which, in his part of the world, have no small
   fame.
Poor though he is, he's a gentleman just the same.
DORINE: Yes, so he tells us; and, Sir, it seems to me   40
Such pride goes very ill with piety.
A man whose spirit spurns this dungy earth
Ought not to brag of lands and noble birth;
Such worldly arrogance will hardly square
With meek devotion and the life of prayer.   45
. . . But this approach, I see, has drawn a blank;
Let's speak, then, of his person, not his rank.
Doesn't it seem to you a trifle grim
To give a girl like her to a man like him?
When two are so ill-suited, can't you see   50
What the sad consequence is bound to be?
A young girl's virtue is imperilled, Sir,
When such a marriage is imposed on her;
For if one's bridegroom isn't to one's taste,
It's hardly an inducement to be chaste,   55
And many a man with horns upon his brow
Has made his wife the thing that she is now.
It's hard to be a faithful wife, in short,

To certain husbands of a certain sort,
60   And he who gives his daughter to a man she hates
Must answer for her sins at Heaven's gates.
Think, Sir, before you play so risky a role.
ORGON: This servant-girl presumes to save my soul!
DORINE: You would do well to ponder what I've said.
65   ORGON: Daughter, we'll disregard this dunderhead.
Just trust your father's judgment. Oh, I'm aware
That I once promised you to young Valère;
But now I hear he gambles, which greatly
          shocks me;
What's more, I've doubts about his orthodoxy.
70   His visits to church, I note, are very few.
DORINE: Would you have him go at the same hours
          as you,
And kneel nearby, to be sure of being seen?
ORGON: I can dispense with such remarks, Dorine.
(*To Mariane.*)
Tartuffe, however, is sure of Heaven's blessing,
75   And that's the only treasure worth possessing.
This match will bring you joys beyond all
          measure;
Your cup will overflow with every pleasure;
You two will interchange your faithful loves
Like two sweet cherubs, or two turtle-doves.
80   No harsh word shall be heard, no frown be seen,
And he shall make you happy as a queen.
DORINE: And she'll make him a cuckold, just wait
          and see.
ORGON: What language!
DORINE: Oh, he's a man of destiny;
He's *made* for horns, and what the stars demand
85   Your daughter's virtue surely can't withstand.
ORGON: Don't interrupt me further. Why can't you
          learn
That certain things are none of your concern?
DORINE: It's for your own sake that I interfere.

[*She repeatedly interrupts Orgon just as he is turning to
speak to his daughter.*]

ORGON: Most kind of you. Now, hold your tongue,
          d'you hear?
DORINE: If I didn't love you . . .
ORGON: Spare me your
90   affection.
DORINE: I'll love you, Sir, in spite of your objection.
ORGON: Blast!
DORINE: I can't bear, Sir, for your honor's sake,
To let you make this ludicrous mistake.
ORGON: You mean to go on talking?
DORINE: If I didn't protest
95   This sinful marriage, my conscience couldn't rest.
ORGON: If you don't hold your tongue, you little
          shrew . . .
DORINE: What, lost your temper? A pious man like
          you?
ORGON: Yes! Yes! You talk and talk. I'm maddened
          by it.
Once and for all, I tell you to be quiet.

DORINE: Well, I'll be quiet. But I'll be thinking hard.
ORGON: Think all you like, but you had better guard   100
That saucy tongue of yours, or I'll . . .
(*Turning back to Mariane.*)
                                                Now, child,
I've weighed this matter fully.
DORINE (*aside*):   It drives me wild
That I can't speak.

[*Orgon turns his head, and she is silent.*]

ORGON: Tartuffe is no young dandy,
But, still, his person . . .
DORINE (*aside*):   Is as sweet as candy.   105
ORGON: Is such that, even if you shouldn't care
For his other merits . . .

[*He turns and stands facing Dorine, arms crossed.*]

DORINE (*aside*):   They'll make a lovely pair.
If I were she, no man would marry me
Against my inclination, and go scot-free.
He'd learn, before the wedding-day was over,   110
How readily a wife can find a lover.
ORGON (*to Dorine*): It seems you treat my orders as
          a joke.
DORINE: Why, what's the matter? 'Twas not to you I
          spoke.
ORGON: What *were* you doing?
DORINE: Talking to myself,
          that's all.
ORGON: Ah! (*Aside.*) One more bit of impudence and
          gall,   115
And I shall give her a good slap in the face.

(*He puts himself in position to slap her; Dorine, whenever he glances at her, stands immobile and silent.*)

Daughter, you shall accept, and with good grace,
The husband I've selected . . . Your wedding-day . . .
(*To Dorine.*)
Why don't you talk to yourself?
DORINE: I've nothing to say.
ORGON: Come, just one word.
DORINE: No thank you, Sir, I
          pass.   120
ORGON: Come, speak; I'm waiting.
DORINE: I'd not be such an ass.
ORGON (*turning to Mariane*): In short, dear
          Daughter, I mean to be obeyed,
And you must bow to the sound choice I've made.
DORINE (*moving away*): I'd not wed such a monster,
          even in jest.

[*Orgon attempts to slap her, but misses.*]

ORGON: Daughter, that maid of yours is a thorough
          pest;   125
She makes me sinfully annoyed and nettled.
I can't speak further; my nerves are too
          unsettled.
She's so upset me by her insolent talk,
I'll calm myself by going for a walk.

Scene 3   [*Dorine, Mariane.*]

DORINE (*returning*): Well, have you lost your tongue,
    girl? Must I play
  Your part, and say the lines you ought to say?
  Faced with a fate so hideous and absurd,
  Can you not utter one dissenting word?
MARIANE: What good would it do? A father's power
5   is great.
DORINE: Resist him now, or it will be too late.
MARIANE: But . . .
DORINE: Tell him one cannot love at a
    father's whim,
  That you shall marry for yourself, not him;
  That once it's you who are to be the bride,
10 It's you, not he, who must be satisfied;
  And that if his Tartuffe is so sublime,
  He's free to marry him at any time.
MARIANE: I've bowed so long to Father's strict
    control,
  I couldn't oppose him now, to save my soul.
DORINE: Come, come, Mariane. Do listen to reason,
15   won't you?
  Valère has asked your hand. Do you love him, or
    don't you?
MARIANE: Oh, how unjust of you! What can you
    mean
  By asking such a question, dear Dorine?
  You know the depth of my affection for him;
20 I've told you a hundred times how I adore him.
DORINE: I don't believe in everything I hear;
  Who knows if your professions were sincere?
MARIANE: They were, Dorine, and you do me wrong
    to doubt it;
  Heaven knows that I've been all too frank
    about it.
DORINE: You love him, then?
MARIANE: Oh, more than I can
25   express.
DORINE: And he, I take it, cares for you no less?
MARIANE: I think so.
DORINE: And you both, with equal fire,
  Burn to be married?
MARIANE: That is our one desire.
DORINE: What of Tartuffe, then? What of your
    father's plan?
MARIANE: I'll kill myself, if I'm forced to wed that
30   man.
DORINE: I hadn't thought of that recourse. How
    splendid!
  Just die, and all your troubles will be ended!
  A fine solution. Oh, it maddens me
  To hear you talk in that self-pitying key.
35 MARIANE: Dorine, how harsh you are! It's most unfair.
  You have no sympathy for my despair.
DORINE: I've none at all for people who talk drivel
  And, faced with difficulties, whine and snivel.
MARIANE: No doubt I'm timid, but it would be
    wrong . . .

DORINE: True love requires a heart that's firm and
    strong.   40
MARIANE: I'm strong in my affection for Valère,
  But coping with my father is his affair.
DORINE: But if your father's brain has grown so
    cracked
  Over his dear Tartuffe that he can retract
  His blessing, though your wedding-day was
    named,   45
  It's surely not Valère who's to be blamed.
MARIANE: If I defied my father, as you suggest,
  Would it not seem unmaidenly, at best?
  Shall I defend my love at the expense
  Of brazenness and disobedience?   50
  Shall I parade my heart's desires, and flaunt . . .
DORINE: No, I ask nothing of you. Clearly you want
  To be Madame Tartuffe, and I feel bound
  Not to oppose a wish so very sound.
  What right have I to criticize the match?   55
  Indeed, my dear, the man's a brilliant catch.
  Monsieur Tartuffe! Now, there's a man of weight!
  Yes, yes, Monsieur Tartuffe, I'm bound to state,
  Is quite a person; that's not to be denied;
  'Twill be no little thing to be his bride.   60
  The world already rings with his renown;
  He's a great noble— in his native town;
  His ears are red, he has a pink complexion,
  And all in all, he'll suit you to perfection.
MARIANE: Dear God!
DORINE: Oh, how triumphant you will
    feel   65
  At having caught a husband so ideal!
MARIANE: Oh, do stop teasing, and use your
    cleverness
  To get me out of this appalling mess.
  Advise me, and I'll do whatever you say.
DORINE: Ah no, a dutiful daughter must obey   70
  Her father, even if he weds her to an ape.
  You've a bright future; why struggle to escape?
  Tartuffe will take you back where his family lives,
  To a small town aswarm with relatives—
  Uncles and cousins whom you'll be charmed to
    meet.   75
  You'll be received at once by the elite,
  Calling upon the bailiff's wife, no less—
  Even, perhaps, upon the mayoress,
  Who'll sit you down in the *best* kitchen chair.
  Then, once a year, you'll dance at the village fair 80
  To the drone of bagpipes—two of them, in fact—
  And see a puppet-show, or an animal act.
  Your husband . . .
MARIANE: Oh, you turn my blood to ice!
  Stop torturing me, and give me your advice.
DORINE (*threatening to go*): Your servant, Madam. 85
MARIANE: Dorine, I beg of you . . .
DORINE: No, you deserve it; this marriage must go
    through.
MARIANE: Dorine!
DORINE: No.

MARIANE: Not Tartuffe! You know I think him . . .
DORINE: Tartuffe's your cup of tea, and you shall
    drink him.
MARIANE: I've always told you everything, and
    relied . . .
90 DORINE: No. You deserve to be tartutified.
MARIANE: Well, since you mock me and refuse to care,
    I'll henceforth seek my solace in despair:
    Despair shall be my counsellor and friend,
    And help me bring my sorrows to an end.
                      [She starts to leave.]
DORINE: There now, come back; my anger has
95   subsided.
    You do deserve some pity, I've decided.
MARIANE: Dorine, if Father makes me undergo
    This dreadful martyrdom, I'll die, I know.
DORINE: Don't fret; it won't be difficult to discover
    Some plan of action . . . But here's Valère, your
100   lover.

Scene 4 [*Valère, Mariane, Dorine.*]

VALÈRE: Madam. I've just received some wondrous
    news
    Regarding which I'd like to hear your views.
MARIANE: What news?
VALÈRE: You're marrying Tartuffe.
MARIANE: I find
    That Father does have such a match in mind.
VALÈRE: Your father, Madam . . .
MARIANE: . . . has just this
5   minute said
    That it's Tartuffe he wishes me to wed.
VALÈRE: Can he be serious?
MARIANE: Oh, indeed he can;
    He's clearly set his heart upon the plan.
VALÈRE: And what position do you propose to take,
    Madam?
MARIANE: Why—I don't know.
10 VALÈRE: For heaven's sake—
    You don't know?
MARIANE: No.
VALÈRE: Well, well!
MARIANE: Advise me, do.
VALÈRE: Marry the man. That's my advice to you.
MARIANE: That's your advice?
VALÈRE: Yes.
MARIANE: Truly?
VALÈRE: Oh, absolutely.
    You couldn't choose more wisely, more astutely.
MARIANE: Thanks for this counsel; I'll follow it, of
15   course.
VALÈRE: Do, do; I'm sure 'twill cost you no remorse.
MARIANE: To give it didn't cause your heart to break.
VALÈRE: I gave it, Madam, only for your sake.
MARIANE: And it's for your sake that I take it, Sir.
DORINE (*withdrawing to the rear of the stage*): Let's
20   see which fool will prove the stubborner.

VALÈRE: So! I am nothing to you, and it was flat
    Deception when you . . .
MARIANE: Please, enough of that.
    You've told me plainly that I should agree
    To wed the man my father's chosen for me,
    And since you've deigned to counsel me so wisely, 25
    I promise, Sir, to do as you advise me.
VALÈRE: Ah, no, 'twas not by me that you were
    swayed.
    No, your decision was already made;
    Though now, to save appearances, you protest
    That you're betraying me at my behest. 30
MARIANE: Just as you say.
VALÈRE: Quite so. And I now see
    That you were never truly in love with me.
MARIANE: Alas, you're free to think so if you choose.
VALÈRE: I choose to think so, and here's a bit of news:
    You've spurned my hand, but I know where to
    turn 35
    For kinder treatment, as you shall quickly learn.
MARIANE: I'm sure you do. Your noble qualities
    Inspire affection . . .
VALÈRE: Forget my qualities, please.
    They don't inspire you overmuch, I find.
    But there's another lady I have in mind 40
    Whose sweet and generous nature will not scorn
    To compensate me for the loss I've borne.
MARIANE: I'm no great loss, and I'm sure that you'll
    transfer
    Your heart quite painlessly from me to her.
VALÈRE: I'll do my best to take it in my stride. 45
    The pain I feel at being cast aside
    Time and forgetfulness may put an end to.
    Or if I can't forget, I shall pretend to.
    No self-respecting person is expected
    To go on loving once he's been rejected. 50
MARIANE: Now, that's a fine, high-minded sentiment.
VALÈRE: One to which any sane man would assent.
    Would you prefer it if I pined away
    In hopeless passion till my dying day?
    Am I to yield you to a rival's arms 55
    And not console myself with other charms?
MARIANE: Go then: console yourself; don't hesitate.
    I wish you to; indeed, I cannot wait.
VALÈRE: You wish me to?
MARIANE: Yes.
VALÈRE: That's the final straw.
    Madam, farewell. Your wish shall be my law. 60

[*He starts to leave, and then returns: this repeatedly.*]

MARIANE: Splendid.
VALÈRE (*coming back again*):
               This breach, remember, is of your
    making;
    It's you who've driven me to the step I'm taking.
MARIANE: Of course.
VALÈRE: (*coming back again*):
             Remember, too, that I am merely
    Following your example.

MARIANE: I see that clearly.
65 VALÈRE: Enough. I'll go and do your bidding, then.
MARIANE: Good.
VALÈRE (*coming back again*):
                    You shall never see my face again.
MARIANE: Excellent.
VALÈRE (*walking to the door, then turning about*):
                    Yes?
MARIANE: What?
VALÈRE: What's that? What did
    you say?
MARIANE: Nothing. You're dreaming.
VALÈRE: Ah. Well, I'm on
    my way.
    Farewell, *Madame*.
        [*He moves slowly away.*]
MARIANE: Farewell.
DORINE (*to Mariane*):   If you ask me,
70 Both of you are as mad as mad can be.
    Do stop this nonsense, now. I've only let you
    Squabble so long to see where it would get you.
    Whoa there, Monsieure Valère!

[*She goes and seizes Valère by the arm; he makes a great
show of resistance.*]

VALÈRE: What's this, Dorine?
DORINE: Come here.
VALÈRE: No, no, my heart's too full of
    spleen.
75 Don't hold me back; her wish must be obeyed.
DORINE: Stop!
VALÈRE: It's too late now; my decision's made.
DORINE: Oh, pooh!
MARIANE (*aside*): He hates the sight of me, that's
    plain.
    I'll go, and so deliver him from pain.
DORINE (*leaving Valère, running after Mariane*): And
    now *you* run away! Come back.
MARIANE: No, no.
80 Nothing you say will keep me here. Let go!
VALÈRE (*aside*): She cannot bear my presence, I
    perceive.
    To spare her further torment, I shall leave.
DORINE (*leaving Mariane, running after Valère*):
    Again! You'll not escape, Sir; don't you try it.
    Come here, you two. Stop fussing, and be quiet.

[*She takes Valère by the hand, then Mariane, and draws
them together.*]

VALÈRE (*to Dorine*): What do you want of me?
85 MARIANE (*to Dorine*):   What
    is the point of this?
DORINE: We're going to have a little armistice.
                        (*To Valère.*)
    Now, weren't you silly to get so overheated?
VALÈRE: Didn't you see how badly I was treated?
DORINE (*to Mariane*): Aren't you a simpleton, to have
    lost your head?

MARIANE: Didn't you hear the hateful things he said? 90
DORINE (*to Valère*): You're both great fools. Her sole
    desire, Valère,
    Is to be yours in marriage. To that I'll swear.
                        (*To Mariane.*)
    He loves you only, and he wants no wife
    But you, Mariane. On that I'll stake my life.
MARIANE (*to Valère*): Then why you advised me so, 95
    I cannot see.
VALÈRE (*to Mariane*): On such a question, why ask
    advice of *me*?
DORINE: Oh, you're impossible. Give me your hands,
    you two.
                        (*To Valère.*)
    Yours first.
VALÈRE (*giving Dorine his hand*):
                    But why?
DORINE (*to Mariane*): And now a hand from you.
MARIANE (*also giving Dorine her hand*): What are
    you doing?
DORINE: There: a perfect fit.
    You suit each other better than you'll admit. 100

[*Valère and Mariane hold hands for some time without
looking at each other.*]

VALÈRE (*turning toward Mariane*): Ah, come, don't
    be so haughty. Give a man
    A look of kindness, won't you Mariane?
            [*Mariane turns toward Valère and smiles.*]
DORINE: I tell you, lovers are completely mad!
VALÈRE (*to Mariane*): Now come, confess that you
    were very bad
    To hurt my feeling as you did just now. 105
    I have a just complaint, you must allow.
MARIANE: *You* must allow that you were most
    unpleasant . . .
DORINE: Let's table that discussion for the present;
    Your father has a plan which must be stopped.
MARIANE: Advise us, then; what means must we
    adopt? 110
DORINE: We'll use all manner of means, and all at
    once.
                        (*To Mariane.*)
    Your father's addled; he's acting like a dunce.
    Therefore you'd better humor the old fossil.
    Pretend to yield to him, be sweet and docile,
    And then postpone, as often as necessary, 115
    The day on which you have agreed to marry.
    You'll thus gain time, and time will turn the trick.
    Sometimes, for instance, you'll be taken sick,
    And that will seem good reason for delay;
    Or some bad omen will make you change the day— 120
    You'll dream of muddy water, or you'll pass
    A dead man's hearse, or break a looking-glass.
    If all else fails, no man can marry you
    Unless you take his ring and say "I do."
    But now, let's separate. If they should find 125
    Us talking here, our plot might be divined.
                        (*To Valère.*)

Go to your friends, and tell them what's occurred,
And have them urge her father to keep his word.
Meanwhile, we'll stir her brother into action,
130   And get Elmire, as well, to join our faction.
Good-bye.
VALÈRE (*to Mariane*):
                    Though each of us will do his best,
It's your true heart on which my hopes shall rest.
MARIANE (*to Valère*): Regardless of what Father may
        decide,
None but Valère shall claim me as his bride.
VALÈRE: Oh, how those words content me! Come
135   what will . . .
DORINE: Oh, lovers, lovers! Their tongues are never
        still.
Be off, now.
VALÈRE (*turning to go, then turning back*):
                    One last word . . .
DORINE: No time to chat:
You leave by this door; and *you* leave by that.

[*Dorine pushes them, by the shoulders, toward opposing doors.*]

ACT III • *Scene 1*   [*Damis, Dorine.*]

DAMIS: May lightning strike me even as I speak,
May all men call me cowardly and weak,
If any fear or scruple holds me back
From settling things, at once, with that great
        quack!
5   DORINE: Now, don't give way to violent emotion.
Your father's merely talked about this notion,
And words and deeds are far from being one.
Much that is talked about is left undone.
DAMIS: No, I must stop that scoundrel's
        machinations;
I'll go and tell him off; I'm out of patience.
10   DORINE: Do calm down and be practical. I had
        rather
My mistress dealt with him—and with your father.
She has some influence with Tartuffe, I've noted.
He hangs upon her words, seems most devoted,
15   And may, indeed, be smitten by her charm.
Pray Heaven it's true! 'Twould do our cause no
        harm.
She sent for him, just now, to sound him out
On this affair you're so incensed about;
She'll find out where he stands, and tell him, too,
20   What dreadful strife and trouble will ensue
If he lends countenance to your father's plan.
I couldn't get in to see him, but his man
Says that he's almost finished with his prayers.
Go, now. I'll catch him when he comes
        downstairs.
25   DAMIS: I want to hear this conference, and I will.
DORINE: No, they must be alone.
DAMIS: Oh, I'll keep still.

DORINE: Not you. I know your temper. You'd start a
        brawl,
And shout and stamp your foot and spoil it all.
Go on.
DAMIS: I won't; I have a perfect right . . .
DORINE: Lord, you're a nuisance! He's coming; get
        out of sight.   30

[*Damis conceals himself in a closet at the rear of the stage.*]

Scene 2   [*Tartuffe, Dorine.*]

TARTUFFE (*observing Dorine, and calling to his
        manservant offstage*): Hang up my hair-shirt,
        put my scourge in place,
And pray, Laurent, for Heaven's perpetual grace.
I'm going to the prison now, to share
My last few coins with the poor wretches there.
DORINE (*aside*): Dear God, what affectation! What a
        fake!   5
TARTUFFE: You wished to see me?
DORINE: Yes . . .
TARTUFFE (*taking a handkerchief from his pocket*):
                              For mercy's sake,
Please take this handkerchief, before you speak.
DORINE: What?
TARTUFFE: Cover that bosom, girl. The flesh is
        weak,
And unclean thoughts are difficult to control.
Such sights as that can undermine the soul.   10
DORINE: Your soul, it seems, has very poor defenses,
And flesh makes quite an impact on your senses.
It's strange that you're so easily excited;
My own desires are not so soon ignited,
And if I saw you naked as a beast,   15
Not all your hide would tempt me in the least.
TARTUFFE: Girl, speak more modestly; unless you do,
I shall be forced to take my leave of you.
DORINE: Oh, no, it's I who must be on my way;
I've just one little message to convey.   20
Madame is coming down, and begs you, Sir,
To wait and have a word or two with her.
TARTUFFE: Gladly.
DORINE (*aside*):   *That* had a softening effect!
I think my guess about him was correct.
TARTUFFE: Will she be long?
DORINE: No: that's her step I hear.   25
Ah, here she is, and I shall disappear.

Scene 3   [*Elmire, Tartuffe.*]

TARTUFFE: May Heaven, whose infinite goodness we
        adore,
Preserve your body and soul forevermore,
And bless your days, and answer thus the plea
Of one who is its humblest votary.
ELMIRE: I thank you for that pious wish. But please,   5
Do take a chair and let's be more at ease.

Debra Gillett as Dorine and Martin Clunes as Tartuffe
in the "handkerchief" scene from London's National
Theatre production in 2002.

[*They sit down.*]

TARTUFFE: I trust that you are once more well and
    strong?
ELMIRE: Oh, yes: the fever didn't last for long.
TARTUFFE: My prayers are too unworthy. I am sure,
    To have gained from Heaven this most gracious
10   cure;
    But lately, Madam, my every supplication
    Has had for object your recuperation.
ELMIRE: You shouldn't have troubled so. I don't
    deserve it.
TARTUFFE: Your health is priceless, Madam, and to
    preserve it
15   I'd gladly give my own, in all sincerity.
ELMIRE: Sir, you outdo us all in Christian charity.
    You've been most kind. I count myself your
    debtor.
TARTUFFE: 'Twas nothing, Madam. I long to serve
    you better.
ELMIRE: There's a private matter I'm anxious to
    discuss.
20   I'm glad there's no one here to hinder us.
TARTUFFE: I too am glad; it floods my heart with bliss
    To find myself alone with you like this.
    For just this chance I've prayed with all my
    power—
    But prayed in vain, until this happy hour.

ELMIRE: This won't take long, Sir, and I hope
    you'll be   25
    Entirely frank and unconstrained with me.
TARTUFFE: Indeed, there's nothing I had rather do
    Than bare my inmost heart and soul to you.
    First, let me say that what remarks I've made
    About the constant visits you are paid   30
    Were prompted not by any mean emotion,
    But rather by a pure and deep devotion,
    A fervent zeal . . .
ELMIRE: No need for explanation.
    Your sole concern, I'm sure, was my salvation.
TARTUFFE (*taking Elmire's hand and pressing her
    fingertips*): Quite so; and such great fervor
    do I feel . . .   35
ELMIRE: Ooh! Please! You're pinching!
TARTUFFE: 'Twas from
    excess of zeal.
    I never meant to cause you pain, I swear.
    I'd rather . . .

[*He places his hand on Elmire's knee.*]

ELMIRE: What can your hand be doing there?
TARTUFFE: Feeling your gown; what soft, fine-woven
    stuff!
ELMIRE: Please, I'm extremely ticklish. That's enough.   40

[*She draws her chair away; Tartuffe pulls his after her.*]

TARTUFFE (*fondling the lace collar of her gown*): My,
    my, what lovely lacework on your dress!
    The workmanship's miraculous, no less.
    I've not seen anything to equal it.
ELMIRE: Yes, quite. But let's talk business for a bit.
    They say my husband means to break his word   45
    And give his daughter to you, Sir. Had you heard?
TARTUFFE: He did once mention it. But I confess
    I dream of quite a different happiness.
    It's elsewhere, Madam, that my eyes discern
    The promise of that bliss for which I yearn.   50
ELMIRE: I see: you care for nothing here below.
TARTUFFE: Ah, well—my heart's not made of stone,
    you know.
ELMIRE: All your desires mount heavenward, I'm
    sure,
    In scorn of all that's earthly and impure.
TARTUFFE: A love of heavenly beauty does not
    preclude   55
    A proper love for earthly pulchritude;
    Our senses are quite rightly captivated
    By perfect works our Maker has created.
    Some glory clings to all that Heaven has made;
    In you, all Heaven's marvels are displayed.   60
    On that fair face, such beauties have been
    lavished.
    The eyes are dazzled and the heart is ravished;
    How could I look on you, O flawless creature,
    And not adore the Author of all Nature,
    Feeling a love both passionate and pure   65
    For you, his triumph of self-portraiture?

At first, I trembled lest that love should be
A subtle snare that Hell had laid for me;
I vowed to flee the sight of you, eschewing
70   A rapture that might prove my soul's undoing;
But soon, fair being, I became aware
That my deep passion could be made to square
With rectitude, and with my bounden duty.
I thereupon surrendered to your beauty.
75   It is, I know, presumptuous on my part
To bring you this poor offering of my heart,
And it is not my merit, Heaven knows,
But your compassion on which my hopes repose.
You are my peace, my solace, my salvation;
80   On you depends my bliss—or desolation;
I bide your judgment and, as you think best,
I shall be either miserable or blest.
   ELMIRE: Your declaration is most gallant, Sir,
But don't you think it's out of character?
85   You'd have done better to restrain your passion
And think before you spoke in such a fashion.
It ill becomes a pious man like you . . .
   TARTUFFE: I may be pious, but I'm human too:
With your celestial charms before his eyes,
90   A man has not the power to be wise.
I know such words sound strangely, coming
      from me,
But I'm no angel, nor was meant to be,
And if you blame my passion, you must needs
Reproach as well the charms on which it feeds.
95   Your loveliness I had no sooner seen
Than you became my soul's unrivalled queen;
Before your seraph glance, divinely sweet,
My heart's defenses crumbled in defeat,
And nothing fasting, prayer, or tears might do
100 Could stay my spirit from adoring you.
My eyes, my sighs have told you in the past
What now my lips make bold to say at last,
And if, in your great goodness, you will deign
To look upon your slave, and ease his pain,—
105 If, in compassion for my soul's distress,
You'll stoop to comfort my unworthiness,
I'll raise to you, in thanks for that sweet manna,
An endless hymn, an infinite hosanna.
With me, of course, there need be no anxiety,
110 No fear of scandal or of notoriety.
These young court gallants, whom all the ladies
      fancy,
Are vain in speech, in action rash and chancy;
When they succeed in love, the world soon
      knows it;
No favor's granted them but they disclose it
115 And by the looseness of their tongues profane
The very altar where their hearts have lain.
Men of my sort, however, love discreetly,
And one may trust our reticence completely.
My keen concern for my good name insures
120 The absolute security of yours;
In short, I offer you, my dear Elmire,
Love without scandal, pleasure without fear.
   ELMIRE: I've heard your well-turned speeches to
      the end,
And what you urge I clearly apprehend.
Aren't you afraid that I may take a notion   125
To tell my husband of your warm devotion,
And that, supposing he were duly told,
His feelings toward you might grow rather cold?
   TARTUFFE: I know, dear lady, that your exceeding
      charity
Will lead your heart to pardon my temerity;   130
That you'll excuse my violent affection
As human weakness, human imperfection;
And that—O fairest!—you will bear in mind
That I'm but flesh and blood, and am not blind.
   ELMIRE: Some women might do otherwise, perhaps,   135
But I shall be discreet about your lapse;
I'll tell my husband nothing of what's occurred
If, in return, you'll give your solemn word
To advocate as forcefully as you can
The marriage of Valère and Mariane,   140
Renouncing all desires to dispossess
Another of his rightful happiness,
And . . .

Scene 4   [*Damis, Elmire, Tartuffe.*]

DAMIS (*emerging from the closet where he has been
      hiding*): No! We'll not hush up this vile affair;
I heard it all inside that closet there,
Where Heaven, in order to confound the pride
Of this great rascal, prompted me to hide.
Ah, now I have my long-awaited chance   5
To punish his deceit and arrogance,
And give my father clear and shocking proof
Of the black character of his dear Tartuffe.
   ELMIRE: Ah no, Damis; I'll be content if he
Will study to deserve my leniency.   10
I've promised silence—don't make me break my
      word;
To make a scandal would be too absurd.
Good wives laugh off such trifles, and forget them;
Why should they tell their husbands, and upset
      them?
   DAMIS: You have your reasons for taking such a
      course,   15
And I have reasons, too, of equal force.
To spare him now would be insanely wrong.
I've swallowed my just wrath for far too long
And watched this insolent bigot bringing strife
And bitterness into our family life.   20
Too long he's meddled in my father's affairs,
Thwarting my marriage-hopes, and poor Valère's.
It's high time that my father was undeceived,
And now I've proof that can't be disbelieved—
Proof that was furnished me by Heaven above.   25
It's too good not to take advantage of.
This is my chance, and I deserve to lose it
If, for one moment, I hesitate to use it.

ELMIRE: Damis . . .
DAMIS: No, I must do what I think right.
30   Madam, my heart is bursting with delight,
      And, say whatever you will, I'll not consent
      To lose the sweet revenge on which I'm bent.
      I'll settle matters without more ado;
      And here, most opportunely, is my cue.

Scene 5   [*Orgon, Damis, Tartuffe, Elmire.*]

DAMIS: Father, I'm glad you've joined us. Let us
         advise you
      Of some fresh news which doubtless will surprise
         you.
      You've just now been repaid with interest
      For all your loving-kindness to our guest.
5   He's proved his warm and grateful feelings
         toward you;
      It's with a pair of horns he would reward you.
      Yes, I surprised him with your wife, and heard
      His whole adulterous offer, every word.
      She, with her all too gentle disposition,
10   Would not have told you of his proposition;
      But I shall not make terms with brazen lechery,
      And feel that not to tell you would be treachery.
ELMIRE: And I hold that one's husband's peace of
         mind
      Should not be spoilt by tattle of this kind.
15   One's honor doesn't require it: to be proficient
      In keeping men at bay is quite sufficient.
      These are my sentiments, and I wish, Damis,
      That you had heeded me and held your peace.

Scene 6   [*Orgon, Damis, Tartuffe.*]

ORGON: Can it be true, this dreadful thing I hear?
TARTUFFE: Yes, Brother, I'm a wicked man, I fear:
      A wretched sinner, all depraved and twisted,
      The greatest villain that has ever existed.
      My life's one heap of crimes, which grows each
5   minute;
      There's naught but foulness and corruption in it;
      And I perceive that Heaven, outraged by me,
      Has chosen this occasion to mortify me.
      Charge me with any deed you wish to name;
10   I'll not defend myself, but take the blame.
      Believe what you are told, and drive Tartuffe
      Like some base criminal from beneath your
         roof;
      Yes, drive me hence, and with a parting curse:
      I shan't protest, for I deserve far worse.
ORGON (*to Damis*): Ah, you deceitful boy, how dare
15   you try
      To stain his purity with so foul a lie?
DAMIS: What! Are you taken in by such a bluff?
      Did you not hear . . . ?
ORGON: Enough, you rogue, enough!

TARTUFFE: Ah, Brother, let him speak: you're being
         unjust.
      Believe his story; the boy deserves your trust.   20
      Why, after all, should you have faith in me?
      How can you know what I might do, or be?
      Is it on my good actions that you base
      Your favor? Do you trust my pious face?
      Ah, no, don't be deceived by hollow shows;   25
      I'm far, alas, from being what men suppose;
      Though the world takes me for a man of worth,
      I'm truly the most worthless man on earth.
         (*To Damis.*)
      Yes, my dear son, speak out now: call me the chief
      Of sinners, a wretch, a murderer, a thief;   30
      Load me with all the names men most abhor;
      I'll not complain; I've earned them all, and more;
      I'll kneel here while you pour them on my head
      As a just punishment for the life I've led.
ORGON (*to Taruffe*): This is too much, dear Brother.   35
         (*To Damis.*)
                        Have you no heart?
DAMIS: Are you so hoodwinked by this rascal's art . . . ?
ORGON: Be still, you monster.
         (*To Tartuffe.*)
                        Brother, I pray you, rise.
         (*To Damis.*)
      Villain!
DAMIS: But . . .
ORGON: Silence!
DAMIS: Can't you realize . . . ?
ORGON: Just one word more, and I'll tear you limb
         from limb.
TARTUFFE: In God's name, Brother, don't be harsh
         with him.   40
      I'd rather far be tortured at the stake
      Than see him bear one scratch for my poor
         sake.
ORGON (*to Damis*): Ingrate!
TARTUFFE: If I must beg you, on bended knee,
      To pardon him . . .
ORGON (*falling to his knees, addressing Tartuffe*):
                        Such goodness cannot be!
         (*To Damis.*)
      Now, *there's* true charity!
DAMIS: What, you . . . ?
ORGON: Villain, be still!   45
      I know your motives; I know you wish him ill:
      Yes, all of you—wife, children, servants, all—
      Conspire against him and desire his fall,
      Employing every shameful trick you can
      To alienate me from this saintly man.   50
      Ah, but the more you seek to drive him away,
      The more I'll do to keep him. Without delay,
      I'll spite this household and confound its pride
      By giving him my daughter as his bride.
DAMIS: You're going to force her to accept his hand?   55
ORGON: Yes, and this very night, d'you understand?
      I shall defy you all, and make it clear
      That I'm the one who gives the orders here.

Come, wretch, kneel down and clasp his blessed
    feet,
60   And ask his pardon for your black deceit.
DAMIS: I ask that swindler's pardon? Why, I'd
    rather . . .
ORGON: So! You insult him, and defy your father!
    A stick! A stick! (*To Tartuffe.*) No, no—release
    me, do.
    (*To Damis.*)
    Out of my house this minute! Be off with you,
65   And never dare set foot in it again.
DAMIS: Well, I shall go, but . . .
ORGON: Well, go quickly, then.
    I disinherit you; an empty purse
    Is all you'll get from me—except my curse!

Scene 7   [*Orgon, Tartuffe.*]

ORGON: How he blasphemed your goodness! What
    a son!
TARTUFFE: Forgive him, Lord, as I've already done.
    (*To Orgon.*)
    You can't know how it hurts when someone
    tries
    To blacken me in my dear Brother's eyes.
ORGON: Ahh!
5 TARTUFFE: The mere thought of such ingratitude
    Plunges my soul into so dark a mood . . .
    Such horror grips my heart . . . I gasp for breath,
    And cannot speak, and feel myself near death.
ORGON:

[*He runs, in tears, to the door through which he has just
driven his son.*]

    You blackguard! Why did I spare you? Why did
    I not
10   Break you in little pieces on the spot?
    Compose yourself, and don't be hurt, dear friend.
TARTUFFE: These scenes, these dreadful quarrels, have
    got to end.
    I've much upset your household, and I perceive
    That the best thing will be for me to leave.
ORGON: What are you saying!
TARTUFFE: They're all against me
15   here;
    They'd have you think me false and insincere.
ORGON: Ah, what of that? Have I ceased believing
    in you?
TARTUFFE: Their adverse talk will certainly continue,
    And charges which you now repudiate
20   You may find credible at a later date.
ORGON: No, Brother, never.
TARTUFFE: Brother, a wife can sway
    Her husband's mind in many a subtle way.
ORGON: No, no.
TARTUFFE: To leave at once is the solution;
    Thus only can I end their persecution.
25 ORGON: No, no, I'll not allow it; you shall remain.

TARTUFFE: Ah, well; 'twill mean much martyrdom
    and pain,
    But if you wish it . . .
ORGON: Ah!
TARTUFFE: Enough; so be it.
    But one thing must be settled, as I see it.
    For your dear honor, and for our friendship's
    sake,
    There's one precaution I feel bound to take.   30
    I shall avoid your wife, and keep away . . .
ORGON: No, you shall not, whatever they may say.
    It pleases me to vex them, and for spite
    I'd have them see you with her day and night.
    What's more, I'm going to drive them to despair   35
    By making you my only son and heir;
    This very day, I'll give to you alone
    Clear deed and title to everything I own.
    A dear, good friend and son-in-law-to-be
    Is more than wife, or child, or kin to me.   40
    Will you accept my offer, dearest son?
TARTUFFE: In all things, let the will of Heaven be
    done.
ORGON: Poor fellow! Come, we'll go draw up the
    deed.
    Then let them burst with disappointed greed!

ACT IV • *Scene 1*   [*Cléante, Tartuffe.*]

CLÉANTE: Yes, all the town's discussing it, and truly,
    Their comments do not flatter you unduly.
    I'm glad we've met, Sir, and I'll give my view
    Of this sad matter in a word or two.
    As for who's guilty, that I shan't discuss;   5
    Let's say it was Damis who caused the fuss;
    Assuming, then, that you have been ill-used
    By young Damis, and groundlessly accused,
    Ought not a Christian to forgive, and ought
    He not to stifle every vengeful thought?   10
    Should you stand by and watch a father make
    His only son an exile for your sake?
    Again I tell you frankly, be advised:
    The whole town, high and low, is scandalized;
    This quarrel must be mended, and my advice is   15
    Not to push matters to a further crisis.
    No, sacrifice your wrath to God above,
    And help Damis regain his father's love.
TARTUFFE: Alas, for my part I should take great joy
    In doing so. I've nothing against the boy.   20
    I pardon all, I harbor no resentment;
    To serve him would afford me much contentment.
    But Heaven's interest will not have it so:
    If he comes back, then I shall have to go.
    After his conduct—so extreme, so vicious—   25
    Our further intercourse would look suspicious.
    God knows what people would think! Why, they'd
    describe
    My goodness to him as a sort of bribe;

They'd say that out of guilt I made pretense
30 Of loving-kindness and benevolence—
    That, fearing my accuser's tongue, I strove
    To buy his silence with a show of love.
    CLÉANTE: Your reasoning is badly warped and
        stretched,
    And these excuses, Sir, are most far-fetched.
35 Why put yourself in charge of Heaven's cause?
    Does Heaven need our help to enforce its laws?
    Leave vengeance to the Lord, Sir; while we live,
    Our duty's not to punish, but forgive;
    And what the Lord commands, we should obey
40 Without regard to what the world may say.
    What! Shall the fear of being misunderstood
    Prevent our doing what is right and good?
    No, no; let's simply do what Heaven ordains,
    And let no other thoughts perplex our brains.
45 TARTUFFE: Again, Sir, let me say that I've forgiven
    Damis, and thus obeyed the laws of Heaven;
    But I am not commanded by the Bible
    To live with one who smears my name with libel.
    CLÉANTE: Were you commanded, Sir, to indulge the
        whim
50 Of poor Orgon, and to encourage him
    In suddenly transferring to your name
    A large estate to which you have no claim?
    TARTUFFE: 'Twould never occur to those who know
        me best
    To think I acted from self-interest.
55 The treasures of this world I quite despise;
    Their specious glitter does not charm my eyes;
    And if I have resigned myself to taking
    The gift which my dear Brother insists on
        making,
    I do so only, as he well understands,
60 Lest so much wealth fall into wicked hands,
    Lest those to whom it might descend in time
    Turn it to purposes of sin and crime,
    And not, as I shall do, make use of it
    For Heaven's glory and mankind's benefit.
65 CLÉANTE: Forget these trumped-up fears. Your
        argument
    Is one the rightful heir might well resent;
    It is a moral burden to inherit
    Such wealth, but give Damis a chance to bear it.
    And would it not be worse to be accused
70 Of swindling, than to see that wealth misused?
    I'm shocked that you allowed Orgon to broach
    This matter, and that you feel no self-reproach;
    Does true religion teach that lawful heirs
    May freely be deprived of what is theirs?
75 And if the Lord has told you in your heart
    That you and young Damis must dwell apart,
    Would it not be the decent thing to beat
    A generous and honorable retreat,
    Rather than let the son of the house be sent,
80 For your convenience, into banishment?
    Sir, if you wish to prove the honesty
    Of your intentions . . .

TARTUFFE: Sir, it is half-past three.
    I've certain pious duties to attend to,
    And hope my prompt departure won't offend you.
CLÉANTE (alone): Damn.   85

Scene 2 [Elmire, Mariane, Cléante, Dorine.]

DORINE: Stay, Sir, and help Mariane,
        for Heaven's sake!
    She's suffering so, I fear her heart will break.
    Her father's plan to marry her off tonight
    Has put the poor child in a desperate plight.
    I hear him coming. Let's stand together, now,   5
    And see if we can't change his mind, somehow,
    About this match we all deplore and fear.

Scene 3 [Orgon, Elmire, Mariane, Cléante,
Dorine.]

ORGON: Halt! Glad to find you all assembled here.
    (To Mariane.)
    This contract, child, contains your happiness,
    And what it says I think your heart can guess.
MARIANE (falling to her knees): Sir, by that Heaven
        which sees me here distressed,
    And by whatever else can move your breast,   5
    Do not employ a father's power, I pray you,
    To crush my heart and force it to obey you,
    Nor by your harsh commands oppress me so
    That I'll begrudge the duty which I owe—
    And do not so embitter and enslave me   10
    That I shall hate the very life you gave me.
    If my sweet hopes must perish, if you refuse
    To give me to the one I've dared to choose,
    Spare me at least—I beg you, I implore—
    The pain of wedding one whom I abhor;   15
    And do not, by a heartless use of force,
    Drive me to contemplate some desperate course.
ORGON (feeling himself touched by her): Be firm, my
        soul. No human weakness, now.
MARIANE: I don't resent your love for him. Allow
    Your heart free rein, Sir; give him your property, 20
    And if that's not enough, take mine from me;
    He's welcome to my money; take it, do,
    But don't, I pray, include my person too.
    Spare me, I beg you; and let me end the tale
    Of my sad days behind a convent veil.   25
ORGON: A convent! Hah! When crossed in their
        amours,
    All lovesick girls have the same thought as yours.
    Get up! The more you loathe the man, and dread
        him,
    The more ennobling it will be to wed him.
    Marry Tartuffe, and mortify your flesh!   30
    Enough; don't start that whimpering afresh.
DORINE: But why . . . ?

ORGON: Be still, there. Speak when
   you're spoken to.
   Not one more bit of impudence out of you.
CLÉANTE: If I may offer a word of counsel here . . .
35 ORGON: Brother, in counseling you have no peer;
   All your advice is forceful; sound, and clever;
   I don't propose to follow it, however.
ELMIRE (*to Orgon*): I am amazed, and don't know
   what to say;
   Your blindness simply takes my breath away.
40 You are indeed bewitched, to take no warning
   From our account of what occurred this morning.
ORGON: Madam, I know a few plain facts, and one
   Is that you're partial to my rascal son;
   Hence, when he sought to make Tartuffe the
   victim
45 Of a base lie, you dared not contradict him.
   Ah, but you underplayed your part, my pet;
   You should have looked more angry, more upset.
ELMIRE: When men make overtures, must we reply
   With righteous anger and a battle-cry?
50 Must we turn back their amorous advances
   With sharp reproaches and with fiery glances?
   Myself, I find such offers merely amusing,
   And make no scenes and fusses in refusing;
   My taste is for good-natured rectitude,
55 And I dislike the savage sort of prude
   Who guards her virtue with her teeth and claws,
   And tears men's eyes out for the slightest cause:
   The Lord preserve me from such honor as that,
   Which bites and scratches like an alley-cat!
60 I've found that a polite and cool rebuff
   Discourages a lover quite enough.
ORGON: I know the facts, and I shall not be shaken.
ELMIRE: I marvel at your power to be mistaken.
   Would it, I wonder, carry weight with you
65 If I could *show* you that our tale was true?
ORGON: Show me?
ELMIRE: Yes.
ORGON: Rot.
ELMIRE: Come, what if I found a way
   To make you see the facts as plain as day?
ORGON: Nonsense.
ELMIRE: Do answer me; don't be absurd.
   I'm not now asking you to trust our word.
70 Suppose that from some hiding-place in here
   You learned the whole sad truth by eye and ear—
   What would you say of your good friend, after
   that?
ORGON: Why, I'd say . . . nothing, by Jehoshaphat!
   It can't be true.
ELMIRE: You've been too long deceived,
75 And I'm quite tired of being disbelieved.
   Come now: let's put my statements to the test,
   And you shall see the truth made manifest.
ORGON: I'll take that challenge. Now do your
   uttermost.
   We'll see how you make good your empty boast.
ELMIRE (*to Dorine*): Send him to me.

DORINE: He's crafty; it
   may be hard   80
   To catch the cunning scoundrel off his guard.
ELMIRE: No, amorous men are gullible. Their conceit
   So blinds them that they're never hard to cheat.
   Have him come down (*To Cléante and Mariane.*)
   Please leave us, for a bit.

Scene 4   [*Elmire, Orgon.*]

ELMIRE: Pull up this table, and get under it.
ORGON: What?
ELMIRE: It's essential that you be well-hidden.
ORGON: Why there?
ELMIRE: Oh, Heavens! Just do as you are
   bidden.
   I have my plans; we'll soon see how they fare.
   Under the table, now; and once you're there,   5
   Take care that you are neither seen nor heard.
ORGON: Well, I'll indulge you, since I gave my word
   To see you through this infantile charade.
ELMIRE: Once it is over, you'll be glad we played.

(*To her husband, who is now under the table.*)

   I'm going to act quite strangely, now, and you   10
   Must not be shocked at anything I do.
   Whatever I may say, you must excuse
   As part of that deceit I'm forced to use.
   I shall employ sweet speeches in the task
   Of making that imposter drop his mask;   15
   I'll give encouragement to his bold desires,
   And furnish fuel to his amorous fires.
   Since it's for your sake, and for his destruction,
   That I shall seem to yield to his seduction,
   I'll gladly stop whenever you decide   20
   That all your doubts are fully satisfied.
   I'll count on you, as soon as you have seen
   What sort of man he is, to intervene,
   And not expose me to his odious lust
   One moment longer than you feel you must.   25
   Remember: you're to save me from my plight
   Whenever . . . He's coming! Hush! Keep out of
   sight!

Scene 5   [*Tartuffe, Elmire, Orgon.*]

TARTUFFE: You wish to have a word with me, I'm
   told.
ELMIRE: Yes. I've a little secret to unfold.
   Before I speak, however, it would be wise
   To close that door, and look about for spies.

[*Tartuffe goes to the door, closes it, and returns.*]

   The very last thing that must happen now   5
   Is a repetition of this morning's row.
   I've never been so badly caught off guard.
   Oh, how I feared for you! You saw how hard

I tried to make that troublesome Damis
10   Control his dreadful temper, and hold his peace.
In my confusion, I didn't have the sense
Simply to contradict his evidence;
But as it happened, that was for the best,
And all has worked out in our interest.
15   This storm has only bettered your position;
My husband doesn't have the least suspicion,
And now, in mockery of those who do,
He bids me be continually with you.
And that is why, quite fearless of reproof,
20   I now can be alone with my Tartuffe,
And why my heart—perhaps too quick to yield—
Feels free to let its passion be revealed.
TARTUFFE: Madam, your words confuse me. Not long ago,
You spoke in quite a different style, you know.
25   ELMIRE: Ah, Sir, if that refusal made you smart,
It's little that you know of woman's heart.
Or what that heart is trying to convey
When it resists in such a feeble way!
Always, at first, our modesty prevents
30   The frank avowal of tender sentiments;
However high the passion which inflames us,
Still, to confess its power somehow shames us.
Thus we reluct, at first, yet in a tone
Which tells you that our heart is overthrown,
35   That what our lips deny, our pulse confesses,
And that, in time, all noes will turn to yesses.
I fear my words are all too frank and free,
And a poor proof of woman's modesty;
But since I'm started, tell me, if you will—
40   Would I have tried to make Damis be still,
Would I have listened, calm and unoffended,
Until your lengthy offer of love was ended,
And been so very mild in my reaction,
Had your sweet words not given me satisfaction?
45   And when I tried to force you to undo
The marriage-plans my husband has in view.
What did my urgent pleading signify
If not that I admired you, and that I
Deplored the thought that someone else might own
50   Part of a heart I wished for mine alone?
TARTUFFE: Madam, no happiness is so complete
As when, from lips we love, come words so sweet;
Their nectar floods my every sense, and drains
In honeyed rivulets through all my veins.
55   To please you is my joy, my only goal;
Your love is the restorer of my soul;
And yet I must beg leave, now, to confess
Some lingering doubts as to my happiness.
Might this not be a trick? Might not the catch
60   Be that you wish me to break off the match
With Mariane, and so have feigned to love me?
I shan't quite trust your fond opinion of me
Until the feelings you've expressed so sweetly
Are demonstrated somewhat more concretely,
65   And you have shown, by certain kind concessions,
That I may put my faith in your professions.

ELMIRE (She coughs, to warn her husband): Why be in such a hurry? Must my heart
Exhaust its bounty at the very start?
To make that sweet admission cost me dear,
But you'll not be content, it would appear,   70
Unless my store of favors is disbursed
To the last farthing, and at the very first.
TARTUFFE: The less we merit, the less we dare to hope,
And with our doubts, mere words can never cope.
We trust no promised bliss till we receive it;   75
Not till a joy is ours can we believe it.
I, who so little merit your esteem,
Can't credit this fulfillment of my dream,
And shan't believe it, Madam, until I savor
Some palpable assurance of your favor.   80
ELMIRE: My, how tyrannical your love can be,
And how it flusters and perplexes me!
How furiously you take one's heart in hand,
And make your every wish a fierce command!
Come, must you hound and harry me to death?   85
Will you not give me time to catch my breath?
Can it be right to press me with such force,
Give me no quarter, show me no remorse,
And take advantage, by your stern insistence,
Of the fond feelings which weaken my resistance?   90
TARTUFFE: Well, if you look with favor upon my love,
Why, then, begrudge me some clear proof thereof?
ELMIRE: But how can I consent without offense
To Heaven, toward which you feel such reverence?
TARTUFFE: If Heaven is all that holds you back, don't worry.   95
I can remove that hindrance in a hurry.
Nothing of that sort need obstruct our path.
ELMIRE: Must one not be afraid of Heaven's wrath?
TARTUFFE: Madam, forget such fears, and be my pupil,
And I shall teach you how to conquer scruple.   100
Some joys, it's true, are wrong in Heaven's eyes;
Yet Heaven is not averse to compromise;
There is a science, lately formulated,
Whereby one's conscience may be liberated,
And any wrongful act you care to mention   105
May be redeemed by purity of intention.
I'll teach you, Madam, the secrets of that science;
Meanwhile, just place on me your full reliance.
Assuage my keen desires, and feel no dread:
The sin, if any, shall be on my head.   110

[Elmire coughs, this time more loudly.]

You've a bad cough.
ELMIRE: Yes, yes. It's bad indeed.
TARTUFFE (producing a little paper bag): A bit of licorice may be what you need.
ELMIRE: No, I've a stubborn cold, it seems. I'm sure it
Will take much more than licorice to cure it.
TARTUFFE: How aggravating.

115 ELMIRE: Oh, more than I can say.
     TARTUFFE: If you're still troubled, think of things
           this way:
        No one shall know our joys, save us alone,
        And there's no evil till the act is known;
        It's scandal, Madam, which makes it an offense,
120   And it's no sin to sin in confidence.
     ELMIRE (*having coughed once more*): Well, clearly
           I must do as you require,
        And yield to your importunate desire.
        It is apparent, now, that nothing less
        Will satisfy you, and so I acquiesce.
125   To go so far is much against my will;
        I'm vexed that it should come to this; but still,
        Since you are so determined on it, since you
        Will not allow mere language to convince you,
        And since you ask for concrete evidence, I
130   See nothing for it, now, but to comply.
        If this is sinful, if I'm wrong to do it,
        So much the worse for him who drove me to it.
        The fault can surely not be charged to me.
     TARTUFFE: Madam, the fault is mine, if fault there be,
        And . . .
135 ELMIRE: Open the door a little, and peek out;
        I wouldn't want my husband poking about.
     TARTUFFE: Why worry about the man? Each day he
           grows
        More gullible; one can lead him by the nose.
        To find us here would fill him with delight,
140   And if he saw the worst, he'd doubt his sight.
     ELMIRE: Nevertheless, do step out for a minute
        Into the hall, and see that no one's in it.

Scene 6   [*Orgon, Elmire.*]

ORGON (*coming out from under the table*): That
        man's a perfect monster, I must admit!
     I'm simply stunned. I can't get over it.
ELMIRE: What, coming out so soon? How premature!
     Get back in hiding, and wait until you're sure.
5   Stay till the end, and be convinced completely;
     We mustn't stop till things are proved concretely.
ORGON: Hell never harbored anything so vicious!
ELMIRE: Tut, don't be hasty. Try to be judicious.
     Wait, and be certain that there's no mistake.
10   No jumping to conclusions, for Heaven's sake!

[*She places Orgon behind her, as Tartuffe re-enters.*]

Scene 7   [*Tartuffe, Elmire, Orgon.*]

TARTUFFE (*not seeing Orgon*): Madam, all things
        have worked out to perfection;
     I've given the neighboring rooms a full inspection;
     No one's about; and now I may at last . . .
ORGON (*intercepting him*): Hold on, my passionate
        fellow, not so fast!
5   I should advise a little more restraint.

Well, so you thought you'd fool me, my dear
     saint!
How soon you wearied of the saintly life—
Wedding my daughter, and coveting my wife!
I've long suspected you, and had a feeling
That soon I'd catch you at your double-dealing.   10
Just now, you've given me evidence galore;
It's quite enough; I have no wish for more.
ELMIRE (*to Tartuffe*): I'm sorry to have treated you
     so slyly,
But circumstances forced me to be wily.
TARTUFFE: Brother, you can't think . . .
ORGON: No more talk
     from you;   15
Just leave this household, without more ado.
TARTUFFE: What I intended . . .
ORGON: That seems fairly clear.
     Spare me your falsehoods and get out of here.
TARTUFFE: No, I'm the master, and you're the one
        to go!
This house belongs to me, I'll have you know,   20
And I shall show you that you can't hurt *me*
By this contemptible conspiracy,
That those who cross me know not what they do,
And that I've means to expose and punish you,
Avenge offended Heaven, and make you grieve   25
That ever you dared order me to leave.

Scene 8   [*Elmire, Orgon.*]

ELMIRE: What was the point of all that angry chatter?
ORGON: Dear God, I'm worried. This is no laughing
        matter.
ELMIRE: How so?
ORGON: I fear I understood his drift.
     I'm much disturbed about that deed of gift.
ELMIRE: You gave him . . . ?
ORGON: Yes, it's all been drawn
        and signed.   5
     But one thing more is weighing on my mind.
ELMIRE: What's that?
ORGON: I'll tell you; but first let's see if
        there's
     A certain strong-box in his room upstairs.

ACT V • Scene 1   [*Orgon, Cléante.*]

CLÉANTE: Where are you going so fast?
ORGON: God knows!
CLÉANTE: Then wait;
     Let's have a conference, and deliberate
     On how this situation's to be met.
ORGON: That strong-box has me utterly upset;
     This is the worst of many, many shocks.   5
CLÉANTE: Is there some fearful mystery in that box?
ORGON: My poor friend Argas brought that box to me
     With his own hands, in utmost secrecy;

'Twas on the very morning of his flight.
10   It's full of papers which, if they came to light,
      Would ruin him—or such is my impression.
CLÉANTE: Then why did you let it out of your
      possession?
ORGON: Those papers vexed my conscience, and it
      seemed best
      To ask the counsel of my pious guest.
15   The cunning scoundrel got me to agree
      To leave the strong-box in his custody,
      So that, in case of an investigation,
      I could employ a slight equivocation
      And swear I didn't have it, and thereby,
20   At no expense to conscience, tell a lie.
CLÉANTE: It looks to me as if you're out on a limb.
      Trusting him with that box, and offering him
      That deed of gift, were actions of a kind
      Which scarcely indicate a prudent mind.
25   With two such weapons, he has the upper hand,
      And since you're vulnerable, as matters stand,
      You erred once more in bringing him to bay.
      You should have acted in some subtler way.
ORGON: Just think of it: behind that fervent face,
30   A heart so wicked, and a soul so base!
      I took him in, a hungry beggar, and then . . .
      Enough, by God! I'm through with pious men:
      Henceforth I'll hate the whole false brotherhood,
      And persecute them worse than Satan could.
35 CLÉANTE: Ah, there you go—extravagant as ever!
      Why can you not be rational? You never
      Manage to take the middle course, it seems,
      But jump, instead, between absurd extremes.
      You've recognized your recent grave mistake
40   In falling victim to a pious fake;
      Now, to correct that error, must you embrace
      An even greater error in its place,
      And judge our worthy neighbors as a whole
      By what you've learned of one corrupted soul?
45   Come, just because one rascal made you swallow
      A show of zeal which turned out to be hollow,
      Shall you conclude that all men are deceivers,
      And that, today, there are no true believers?
      Let atheists make that foolish inference;
50   Learn to distinguish virtue from pretense,
      Be cautious in bestowing admiration,
      And cultivate a sober moderation.
      Don't humor fraud, but also don't asperse
      True piety; the latter fault is worse,
55   And it is best to err, if err one must,
      As you have done, upon the side of trust.

Scene 2   [Damis, Orgon, Cléante.]

DAMIS: Father, I hear that scoundrel's uttered threats
      Against you; that he pridefully forgets
      How, in his need, he was befriended by you,
      And means to use your gifts to crucify you.
5 ORGON: It's true, my boy. I'm too distressed for tears.

DAMIS: Leave it to me, Sir; let me trim his ears.
      Faced with such insolence, we must not waver.
      I shall rejoice in doing you the favor
      Of cutting short his life, and your distress.
CLÉANTE: What a display of young hotheadedness!   10
      Do learn to moderate your fits of rage.
      In this just kingdom, this enlightened age,
      One does not settle things by violence.

Scene 3   [Madame Pernelle, Mariane, Elmire,
Dorine, Damis, Orgon, Cléante.]

MADAME PERNELLE: I hear strange tales of very
      strange events.
ORGON: Yes, strange events which these two eyes
      beheld.
      The man's ingratitude is unparalleled.
      I save a wretched pauper from starvation,
      House him, and treat him like a blood relation,   5
      Shower him every day with my largesse,
      Give him my daughter, and all that I possess;
      And meanwhile the unconscionable knave

Angelika Thomas as Pernelle and Peter Jordan as Orgon in
Der Tartuffe at the 2006 Salzburg Festival.

Tries to induce my wife to misbehave;
10 And not content with such extreme rascality,
Now threatens me with my own liberality,
And aims, by taking base advantage of
The gifts I gave him out of Christian love,
15 To drive me from my house, a ruined man,
And make me end a pauper, as he began.

DORINE: Poor fellow!

MADAME PERNELLE: No, my son, I'll never bring
Myself to think him guilty of such a thing.

ORGON: How's that?

MADAME PERNELLE: The righteous always were
maligned.

ORGON: Speak clearly, Mother. Say what's on your
mind.

MADAME PERNELLE: I mean that I can smell a rat, my
20   dear.
You know how everybody hates him, here.

ORGON: That has no bearing on the case at all.

MADAME PERNELLE: I told you a hundred times,
when you were small,
That virtue in this world is hated ever;
25   Malicious men may die, but malice never.

ORGON: No doubt that's true, but how does it apply?

MADAME PERNELLE: They've turned you against him
by a clever lie.

ORGON: I've told you, I was there and saw it done.

MADAME PERNELLE: Ah, slanderers will stop at
nothing, Son.

ORGON: Mother, I'll lose my temper . . . For the last
30   time,
I tell you I was witness to the crime.

MADAME PERNELLE: The tongues of spite are busy
night and noon,
And to their venom no man is immune.

ORGON: You're talking nonsense. Can't you realize
35   I saw it; saw it; saw it with my eyes?
Saw, do you understand me? Must I shout it
Into your ears before you'll cease to doubt it?

MADAME PERNELLE: Appearances can deceive, my
son. Dear me,
We cannot always judge by what we see.

ORGON: Drat! Drat!

MADAME PERNELLE:
40   One often interprets things awry;
Good can seem evil to a suspicious eye.

ORGON: Was I to see his pawing at Elmire
As an act of charity?

MADAME PERNELLE: Till his guilt is clear,
A man deserves the benefit of the doubt.
You should have waited, to see how things turned
45   out.

ORGON: Great God in Heaven, what more proof did
I need?
Was I to sit there, watching, until he'd . . .
You drive me to the brink of impropriety.

MADAME PERNELLE: No, no, a man of such
surpassing piety
50   Could not do such a thing. You cannot shake me.

I don't believe it, and you shall not make me.

ORGON: You vex me so that, if you weren't my
mother,
I'd say to you . . . some dreadful thing or other.

DORINE: It's your turn now, Sir, not to be listened to;
You'd not trust us, and now she won't trust you.   55

CLÉANTE: My friends, we're wasting time which
should be spent
In facing up to our predicament.
I fear that scoundrel's threats weren't made in
sport.

DAMIS: Do you think he'd have the nerve to go to
court?

ELMIRE: I'm sure he won't: they'd find it all too crude   60
A case of swindling and ingratitude.

CLÉANTE: Don't be too sure. He won't be at a loss
To give his claims a high and righteous gloss;
And clever rogues with far less valid cause
Have trapped their victims in a web of laws.   65
I say again that to antagonize
A man so strongly armed was most unwise.

ORGON: I know it; but the man's appalling cheek
Outraged me so, I couldn't control my pique.

CLÉANTE: I wish to Heaven that we could devise   70
Some truce between you, or some compromise.

ELMIRE: If I had known what cards he held, I'd not
Have roused his anger by my little plot.

ORGON (to Dorine, as M. Loyal enters): What is that
fellow looking for? Who is he?
Go talk to him—and tell him that I'm busy.   75

Scene 4 [Monsieur Loyal, Madame Pernelle, Orgon,
Damis, Mariane, Dorine, Elmire, Cléante.]

MONSIEUR LOYAL: Good day, dear sister. Kindly let
me see
Your master.

DORINE: He's involved with company,
And cannot be disturbed just now, I fear.

MONSIEUR LOYAL: I hate to intrude; but what has
brought me here
Will not disturb your master, in any event.
Indeed, my news will make him most content.   5

DORINE: Your name?

MONSIEUR LOYAL: Just say that I bring greetings
from
Monsieur Tartuffe, on whose behalf I've come.

DORINE (to Orgon): Sir, he's a very gracious man,
and bears
A message from Tartuffe, which he declares,   10
Will make you most content.

CLÉANTE: Upon my word,
I think this man had best be seen, and heard.

ORGON: Perhaps he has some settlement to suggest.
How shall I treat him? What manner would be best?

CLÉANTE: Control your anger, and if he should mention   15
Some fair adjustment, give him your full attention.

MONSIEUR LOYAL: Good health to you, good Sir.
    May Heaven confound
    Your enemies, and may your joys abound.
ORGON (*aside, to Cléante*): A gentle salutation: it
    confirms
20   My guess that he is here to offer terms.
MONSIEUR LOYAL: I've always held your family most
    dear;
    I served your father, Sir, for many a year.
ORGON: Sir, I must ask your pardon; to my shame,
    I cannot now recall your face or name.
MONSIEUR LOYAL: Loyal's my name; I come from
25   Normandy,
    And I'm a bailiff, in all modesty.
    For forty years, praise God, it's been my boast
    To serve with honor in that vital post,
    And I am here, Sir, if you will permit
30   'The liberty, to serve you with this writ . . .
ORGON: To—*what?*
MONSIEUR LOYAL: Now, please, Sir, let us have no
    friction:
    It's nothing but an order of eviction.
    You are to move your goods and family out
    And make way for new occupants, without
35   Deferment or delay, and give the keys . . .
ORGON: I? Leave this house?
MONSIEUR LOYAL: Why yes, Sir, if you please.
    This house, Sir, from the cellar to the roof,
    Belongs now to the good Monsieur Tartuffe,
    And he is lord and master of your estate
40   By virtue of a deed of present date,
    Drawn in due form, with clearest legal phrasing . . .
DAMIS: Your insolence is utterly amazing!
MONSIEUR LOYAL: Young man, my business here is
    not with you,
    But with your wise and temperate father, who,
45   Like every worthy citizen, stands in awe
    Of justice, and would never obstruct the law.
ORGON: But . . .
MONSIEUR LOYAL:
          Not for a million, Sir, would you rebel
    Against authority; I know that well.
    You'll not make trouble, Sir, or interfere
50   With the execution of my duties here.
DAMIS: Someone may execute a smart tattoo
    On that black jacket of yours, before you're through.
MONSIEUR LOYAL: Sir, bid your son be silent. I'd much
    regret
    Having to mention such a nasty threat
55   Of violence, in writing my report.
DORINE (*aside*): This man Loyal's a most disloyal sort!
MONSIEUR LOYAL: I love all men of upright character,
    And when I agreed to serve these papers, Sir,
    It was your feelings that I had in mind.
60   I couldn't hear to see the case assigned
    To someone else, who might esteem you less
    And so subject you to unpleasantness.
ORGON: What's more unpleasant than telling a man
    to leave

His house and home?
MONSIEUR LOYAL: You'd like a short reprieve?
    If you desire it, Sir, I shall not press you,   65
    But wait until tomorrow to dispossess you.
    Splendid. I'll come and spend the night here, then,
    Most quietly, with half a score of men.
    For form's sake, you might bring me, just before
    You go to bed, the keys to the front door.   70
    My men, I promise, will be on their best
    Behavior, and will not disturb your rest.
    But bright and early, Sir, you must be quick
    And move out all your furniture, every stick:
    The men I've chosen are both young and strong,   75
    And with their help it shouldn't take you long.
    In short, I'll make things pleasant and convenient,
    And since I'm being so extremely lenient,
    Please show me, Sir, a like consideration,
    And give me your entire cooperation.
ORGON (*aside*): I may be all but bankrupt, but I vow   80
    I'd give a hundred louis, here and now,
    Just for the pleasure of landing one good clout
    Right on the end of that complacent snout.
CLÉANTE: Careful; don't make things worse.
DAMIS: My bootsole itches   85
    To give that beggar a good kick in the breeches.
DORINE: Monsieur Loyal, I'd love to hear the whack
    Of a stout stick across your fine broad back.
MONSIEUR LOYAL: Take care: a woman too may go
    to jail if
    She uses threatening language to a bailiff.   90
CLÉANTE: Enough, enough, Sir. This must not go on.
    Give me that paper, please, and then begone.
MONSIEUR LOYAL: Well, *au revoir*. God give you all
    good cheer!
ORGON: May God confound you, and him who sent
    you here!

Scene 5   [*Orgon, Cléante, Mariane, Elmire, Madame
Pernelle, Dorine, Damis.*]

ORGON: Now, Mother, was I right or not? This
    writ
    Should change your notion of Tartuffe a bit.
    Do you perceive his villainy at last?
MADAME PERNELLE: I'm thunderstruck. I'm utterly
    aghast.
DORINE: Oh, come, be fair. You mustn't take offense   5
    At this new proof of his benevolence.
    He's acting out of selfless love, I know.
    Material things enslave the soul, and so
    He kindly has arranged your liberation
    From all that might endanger your salvation.   10
ORGON: Will you not ever hold your tongue, you
    dunce?
CLÉANTE: Come, you must take some action, and at
    once.
ELMIRE: Go tell the world of the low trick he's tried.

15   The deed of gift is surely nullified
      By such behavior, and public rage will not
      Permit the wretch to carry out his plot.

Scene 6 [*Valère, Orgon, Cléante, Elmire, Mariane,*
Madame Pernelle, Damis, Dorine.]

VALÈRE: Sir, though I hate to bring you more bad
            news,
         Such is the danger that I cannot choose.
         A friend who is extremely close to me
         And knows my interest in your family
5   Has, for my sake, presumed to violate
         The secrecy that's due to things of state,
         And sends me word that you are in a plight
         From which your one salvation lies in flight.
         That scoundrel who's imposed upon you so
10   Denounced you to the King an hour ago
         And, as supporting evidence, displayed
         The strong-box of a certain renegade
         Whose secret papers, so he testified,
         You had disloyally agreed to hide.
15   I don't know just what charges may be pressed,
         But there's a warrant out for your arrest;
         Tartuffe has been instructed, furthermore,
         To guide the arresting officer to your door.
CLÉANTE: He's clearly done this to facilitate
20   His seizure of your house and your estate.
ORGON: That man, I must say, is a vicious beast!
VALÈRE: Quick, Sir; you mustn't tarry in the least.
         My carriage is outside, to take you hence;
         This thousand louis should cover all expense.
25   Let's lose no time, or you shall be undone;
         The sole defense, in this case, is to run.
         I shall go with you all the way, and place you
         In a safe refuge to which they'll never trace you.
ORGON: Alas, dear boy, I wish that I could show
            you
30   My gratitude for everything I owe you.
         But now is not the time; I pray the Lord
         That I may live to give you your reward.
         Farewell, my dears; be careful . . .
CLÉANTE: Brother, hurry.
         We shall take care of things; you needn't worry.

Scene 7 [*The Officer, Tartuffe, Valère, Orgon,*
Elmire, Mariane, Madame Pernelle, Dorine, Cléante,
Damis.]

TARTUFFE: Gently, Sir, gently; stay right where you are.
            No need for haste; your lodging isn't far.
            You're off to prison, by order of the Prince.
ORGON: This is the crowning blow, you wretch; and
            since
5   It means my total ruin and defeat,
         Your villainy is now at last complete.

TARTUFFE: You needn't try to provoke me; it's no use.
            Those who serve Heaven must expect abuse.
CLÉANTE: You are indeed most patient, sweet, and
            blameless.
DORINE: How he exploits the name of Heaven! It's
            shameless.   10
TARTUFFE: Your taunts and mockeries are all for
            naught;
            To do my duty is my only thought.
MARIANE: Your love of duty is most meritorious,
            And what you've done is little short of glorious.
TARTUFFE: All deeds are glorious, Madam, which
            obey   15
            The sovereign prince who sent me here today.
ORGON: I rescued you when you were destitute;
            Have you forgotten that, you thankless brute?
TARTUFFE: No, no, I well remember everything;
            But my first duty is to serve my King.   20
            That obligation is so paramount
            That other claims, beside it, do not count;
            And for it I would sacrifice my wife,
            My family, my friend, or my own life.
ELMIRE: Hypocrite!
DORINE: All that we most revere, he uses   25
            To cloak his plots and camouflage his ruses.
CLÉANTE: If it is true that you are animated
            By pure and loyal zeal, as you have stated,
            Why was this zeal not roused until you'd sought
            To make Orgon a cuckold, and been caught?   30
            Why weren't you moved to give your evidence
            Until your outraged host had driven you hence?
            I shan't say that the gift of all his treasure
            Ought to have damped your zeal in any measure;
            But if he is a traitor, as you declare,   35
            How could you condescend to be his heir?
TARTUFFE (*to the officer*): Sir, spare me all this
            clamor; it's growing shrill.
            Please carry out your orders, if you will.
OFFICER: Yes, I've delayed too long, Sir. Thank you
            kindly.
            You're just the proper person to remind me.   40
            Come, you are off to join the other boarders
            In the King's prison, according to his orders.
TARTUFFE: Who? I, Sir?
OFFICER: Yes.
TARTUFFE: To prison? This can't be true!
OFFICER: I owe an explanation, but not to you.
                                           (*To Orgon.*)
            Sir, all is well; rest easy, and be grateful.   45
            We serve a Prince to whom all sham is hateful,
            A Prince who sees into our inmost hearts,
            And can't be fooled by any trickster's arts.
            His royal soul, though generous and human,
            Views all things with discernment and acumen;   50
            His sovereign reason is not lightly swayed,
            And all his judgments are discreetly weighed.
            He honors righteous men of every kind,
            And yet his zeal for virtue is not blind,
            Nor does his love of piety numb his wits   55

John Lee Beatty's set design (with ensemble cast) for the Roundabout Theatre Company's 2002–2003 production.

And make him tolerant of hypocrites.
'Twas hardly likely that this man could cozen
A King who's foiled such liars by the dozen.
With one keen glance, the King perceived the
   whole
60   Perverseness and corruption of his soul,
And thus high Heaven's justice was displayed:
Betraying you, the rogue stood self-betrayed.
The King soon recognized Tartuffe as one
Notorious by another name, who'd done
65   So many vicious crimes that one could fill
Ten volumes with them, and be writing still.
But to be brief: our sovereign was appalled
By this man's treachery toward you, which he
   called
The last, worst villainy of a vile career,
70   And bade me follow the impostor here
To see how gross his impudence could be,
And force him to restore your property.
Your private papers, by the King's command,
I hereby seize and give into your hand.
75   The King, by royal order, invalidates

The deed which gave this rascal your estates,
And pardons, furthermore, your grave offense
In harboring an exile's documents.
By these decrees, our Prince rewards you for
Your loyal deeds in the late civil war,   80
And shows how heartfelt is his satisfaction
In recompensing any worthy action,
How much he prizes merit, and how he makes
More of men's virtues than of their mistakes.
DORINE: Heaven be praised!
MADAME PERNELLE: I breathe again, at last.   85
ELMIRE: We're safe.
MARIANE: I can't believe the danger's past.
ORGON (*to Tartuffe*): Well, traitor, now you see . . .
CLÉANTE: Ah, Brother, please,
   Let's not descend to such indignities.
   Leave the poor wretch to his unhappy fate,
   And don't say anything to aggravate   90
   His present woes; but rather hope that he
   Will soon embrace an honest piety,
   And mend his ways, and by a true repentance
   Move our just King to moderate his sentence.

Meanwhile, go kneel before your sovereign's
95   throne
And thank him for the mercies he has shown.
ORGON: Well said: let's go at once and, gladly
    kneeling,

Express the gratitude which all are feeling.
Then, when that first great duty has been done,
We'll turn with pleasure to a second one,   100
And give Valère, whose love has proven so true,
The wedded happiness which is his due.

COMMENTARY

Mel Gussow (1933–2005)
REVIEW OF *TARTUFFE*   *1991*

Mel Gussow, in his New York Times *review of the Yale Repertory Theatre's 1991 production of* Tartuffe, *comments on the effects of the stage set, which was dominated by huge mahogany doors, and on the visual elements that help qualify the diminutive stature of Tartuffe as played by the irrepressible Austin Pendleton.*

In Walton Jones's production of *Tartuffe* at the Yale Repertory Theater, a row of large mahogany-like doors is positioned against a *trompe l'oeil* background. The doors are used for quick entrances, exits, and punchlines. They slide across the stage on tracks, swing open and slam on cue, and are filled with concealed crannies for depositing plot-advancing objects.

In using the jack-in-the-box set, the design of Kevin Rupnik, the director offers a well-carpentered, occasionally tricked-up approach to Molière, but with merit in its breathlessness. It is enlivened by several performances, especially by that of Austin Pendleton in the title role.

Mr. Pendleton takes to Tartuffe as a hypocrite to a hairshirt. Although his characterization is larger than life, he is undeniably short, and he uses his lowness to comic effect, even to playing one scene on his knees behind a portable pulpit that is the height of a go-cart. From his first entrance in an itch-provoking gown that almost reaches to his bare feet, he plays Tartuffe like a saint set for martyrdom. When he throws away his propriety and makes an advance on Orgon's wife (Frances Conroy), he does so with a sudden gale of energy. "I may be pious," he proclaims, "but I'm human too," and he raises his hand as if signaling the cavalry into action.

When he is caught in a flagrantly compromising position with the lady of the house, he looks at the almost cuckolded Orgon with the expression of an innocent child. "Brother, you can't think . . . ," says Tartuffe, and the actor takes a long, laughable pause before realizing that his game is up.

The key to Mr. Pendleton's success is that he is portraying a fanatic. This could be regarded as a Pendleton specialty—on stage and also on television, as witness his Mr. Entertainment, a helplessly stagestruck song-and-dance man, the amateur Sinatra of *St. Elsewhere.*

With Tartuffe loose in the household, the interfering maid Dorine (a pert performance by Fran Brill) mobilizes her allies, who include most of the other characters in the play, for an all-out siege on the villain. Subplot humor is provided by her attempt to wake up her employer, Orgon (Jerome Dempsey), a nearsighted fool who holds fast to his astigmatism. Mr. Dempsey is a master of the slow burn, as demonstrated in the scene in which he, aroused from his gullibility, tries to convince his still skeptical mother of Tartuffe's deceit. Patiently he describes the dastard, and she blithely dismisses the charge as slander. His carefully timed delivery of the line "Mother, I'll lose my temper" is done with apoplectic finesse.

Barring a certain amount of busyness—too much swirling through those doors—and a tentativeness at the conclusion, this is a mirthful *Tartuffe* that begins the Yale Repertory season. A final word is due Richard Wilbur's verse translation. In common with his other versions of Molière comedies, it is an eloquent example of the adapter's art.

Aphra Behn

Although not technically the first English woman playwright or the first woman to earn a living by her pen, Aphra Behn (c. 1640–1689) was the first notably successful woman playwright. She wrote twenty plays, several novels, among them *Oroonoko* (c. 1688), and *Poems on Several Occasions* (1684). She also published translations and edited volumes of poetry.

Behn grew up in an England governed by the Puritan Commonwealth. Throughout the 1650s Oliver Cromwell was Protector, and the theaters were closed. The Puritans were, in her eyes, dull, hypocritical, and repressive. Her allegiance was with the Stuarts, whose King Charles I was beheaded by order of Parliament in 1649. His sons, Charles and James, were forced into exile on the Continent, along with many Stuart courtiers, such as the gallants who appear in *The Rover*. When Charles II was restored to the throne in 1660, the period known as the Restoration began. Behn was twenty years old.

Very little is known of her, and much of that is guesswork based on her writing. For example, *Oroonoko* is a novel set in Surinam, which was a British colony when she visited there with members of her family in 1663–1664. Before returning to London, she may have acted as a political informant under the name of Astrea. She married Mr. Behn, possibly a Dutch merchant in England, who died two years later. She seems to have been persuaded by the writer and theater manager Thomas Killigrew to become an English spy in Antwerp. She was residing there when the great fire of 1666 destroyed most of London. Her services were so little valued that she was not paid and ended up for a brief time in debtors' prison when she returned to England.

Once out of prison, she took advantage of her friendship with Thomas Betterton, who belonged to a theater company at Lincoln's Inn Fields. He played the lead in her first play, *The Forced Marriage* (1670), which ran successfully for six nights. The record for the first run of a play was thirteen nights. In 1670 Behn reached a mostly courtly audience, those politically aligned with Charles II or somehow involved in court politics.

Behn succeeded again with *The Amorous Prince* in 1671. Those first two plays were wholly original, but she quickly resorted to the Shakespearean device of adapting the work of others. Like Shakespeare, she made considerable changes and constantly improved the material she borrowed. After the success of *The Rover* (1677), she was accused of plagiarism and answered the charge in the Postscript to the play. She did borrow some characters and details from Thomas Killigrew's *Thomaso; or, The Wanderer,* a closet drama, or play intended to be read, not staged (1654; published 1664); but, as she says in her Postscript, no one would have taken notice if her play were not so successful — and written by a woman. Playwrights commonly adapted earlier material because they had to produce many plays in a short time to earn a meager living.

The theme of her first play, loveless and unhappy marriages arranged by families, recurs throughout Behn's work. All we know about her own marriage

539

is that it was brief; she did not remarry despite having long-term relationships. But she concerned herself with the fate of women in her society. A young woman could not hope to marry if she were not a virgin. Once she was married, a woman's property became her husband's, and her legal identity was melded with his. Consequently, she was at her husband's mercy since she had no recourse in law against any of his excesses.

However, the alternative to marriage was considered worse. If a woman was seduced, and people found out, she could expect to lose her status and forsake marriage. As a result, she would be forced to earn her own living, a harsh prospect since women were not given the same education as men and could not take part in any of the professions. One fate of many such women was to become prostitutes. In the meantime men pursued their goal of seduction, as they do in *The Rover* and other Behn plays, with no thought given to the welfare of the women they seduced. Furthermore, they frequently threatened women with rape if the women were uncompliant. The theme of rape echoes through Behn's plays. By necessity Behn had to appeal to a predominantly male audience, but even so she expresses some of her deeper concerns for the welfare of her sex. She exposes the unfairness and pain of arranged marriages and portrays women as complex and intelligent. Her work seems to reflect the influence of Shakespeare's female characters, such as Helena and Hermia in *A Midsummer Night's Dream* and Beatrice in *Much Ado about Nothing*.

Behn's plays include *Abdelazer* (1676), *The Town Fop* (1676), *The Lucky Chance* (1686), and *The Emperor of the Moon* (1687). Her last play, *The Widow Ranter* (1689), produced posthumously, was a failure. But it is an interesting portrait of the settlement of the Virginias, based on her experience in the New World. The prefaces to Behn's plays treat important issues, such as the unequal education of women. She points out, however, that in playwriting the lack of education in Greek and Latin is no handicap. She reminds her readers that Shakespeare and Jonson did very well with limited education and that "gownmen" (scholars) talked incessantly and to little account. What was needed for the stage was experience and a good ear, and Aphra Behn had both.

THE ROVER; OR, THE BANISHED CAVALIERS

The English rakes who swagger through this play are displaced Royalist cavaliers who lived perilously in exile during the Puritan interregnum of the 1650s as they awaited the restoration of Charles II to the throne. Their concerns in Naples are warlike and lusty. Their frequent dueling delighted the audiences of 1677 and caused *The Rover* to be one of Behn's best-received plays. Beneath the brawling, however, is a more serious struggle between the sexes.

It is pre-Lenten carnival time in Naples, when all the people dress in masquerade. The players in *The Rover* disguise themselves—Hellena as a gypsy or a page, Belvile as Antonio, the others in costumes that make them unrecognizable—from the first act to the last. Such masquerading permits the young men and women to meet and talk without supervision. Among the characters, the most stable are Florinda and Belvile, who love each other from the beginning and who end up married despite the objections of Florinda's brother Pedro and their father, who has promised Florinda to Don Vincentio, a wealthy old man.

Behn's favorite theme of arranged or forced marriage thus surfaces quickly in this play, and much of the action involves its circumvention. A related theme also develops quickly: forcible rape. The Cavaliers, or rakes, treat women of lower social class as if they were whores. In this play Florinda faces rape not once but twice. First Willmore, the Rover, treats her as "an errant harlot" and forces her to scream "rape" (III, v). When Frederick and Belvile intervene, Willmore explains that he was drunk and not to blame. Florinda's second close call comes with Blunt. When she runs into his apartment to escape discovery on the street, Blunt decides to avenge his disgrace at the hands of Lucetta by raping Florinda—thus punishing the entire sex for his mishandling. This time Frederick, without knowing who Florinda is, decides both to help Blunt and to rape her as well. When she gives them a ring that reveals her to be an aristocrat, a woman of quality, Frederick says, "'twould anger us vilely to be trussed up for a rape upon a maid of quality, when we only believe we ruffle a harlot" (IV, v, 150–52).

These scenes are painful from our modern perspective and must have been even more so to women in Behn's audience. Part of her purpose, though, is to point out that men treated women differently according to class. Aristocrats such as these cavaliers were sometimes willfully brutal toward women in a lower class. Behn builds sympathy for Florinda and, by extension, for all women who are treated viciously by men. It is conceivable that some men in the audiences of Behn's day might not have been conscious of her purpose, since they may have approved of behavior such as Blunt's and Frederick's.

Like Florinda, the other female characters in *The Rover* face obstacles with wit and resourcefulness, but not all the women are successful. Behn's portrait of the courtesan Angellica is laced with irony. Against her will and better judgment, Angellica finds herself falling in love with Willmore. When she takes Willmore as a lover without demanding from him the usual thousand crowns, her handmaid Moretta watches in horror, realizing that her mistress is giving away something she would normally sell at a dear price. Angellica is smitten by Willmore—just as Hellena is smitten by the same rover—but once Willmore enjoys Angellica's pleasures, he dismisses her from his mind. Angellica the courtesan knows that this is the way men relate to women. But Angellica the woman, who gave Willmore her "virgin heart," is as deceived as any woman could be.

Hellena, promised to the church as a nun by her father, begins the play revealing her plans to avoid the convent at all costs. Her brother Pedro does not say so, but he seems to expect that when she is in the convent he will have access to the 300,000 crowns her uncle has bequeathed her. Pedro attempts to force Hellena to "marry" the church in the same way that he attempts to force Florinda to marry a man she does not love. Neither sister will have any of it.

The play centers more on the success of Florinda and Hellena than it does on Belvile or Willmore. Hellena, by virtue of her wit—which is equal to Willmore's—and her understanding of social realities, forces Willmore to submit to her will. He is all for making love, but she demands that Hymen, the god of marriage, be invoked before their lovemaking. When he tells her that she should be content with love and not demand marriage, she replies, "What shall I get? A cradle full of noise and mischief, with a pack of repentance at my back?" (V, 514–16) She is more than his match. The play ends with Florinda, Hellena, and Valeria all winning the husbands of their choice on their own terms.

The Rover; or, The Banished Cavaliers in Performance

King Charles II attended the March 24, 1677, production of *The Rover*, and successive royal performances were commanded before different monarchs in 1724 and 1729. Some seventy performances of the play took place between 1700 and 1725, and even more were recorded between 1726 and 1760. However, after 1790 the play was not produced for many decades.

Today's productions indicate a modern understanding of the play's feminist themes and its subtle wit-play between the sexes. The Folger Theater Group in Washington, D.C., produced the work in 1982, playing it broadly for its humor. Critics praised the play for its vitality but complained that the production overdid the "business"—stage gestures, movement, and action—and the actors did not clearly deliver their lines. Christopher Reeve played Willmore in the Williamstown Theater production in 1987, with Kate Burton as Florinda. The director, John Rubinstein, moved the setting from Naples to the West Indies. One of the most interesting, although not wholly satisfying, productions was in 1986 by the Royal Shakespeare Company. Jeremy Irons played Willmore and Imogen Stubbs played Hellena. The director, John Barton, adapted the text using the earlier source play *Thomaso; or, The Wanderer* by Thomas Killigrew. Critics of the Royal Shakespeare production were struck by the modernity of Behn's play. The King's County Shakespeare Company of Brooklyn, New York, produced the play to some acclaim in 2003. D.J.R. Bruckner, in the *New York Times*, said the play was "as fresh as tomorrow." The cast used period costume and period weaponry, which is not always done with this play. The version of the play produced by the Chance Theatre Company of Anaheim, California, in 2005 employed modern casual dress, casting the women as adolescent girls having a fantasy and using stuffed animals and Barbie and Ken dolls as weapons. The modern productions focus on the feminist issues in the text.

Aphra Behn (c. 1640–1689)

THE ROVER; OR, THE BANISHED CAVALIERS

1677

PROLOGUE

Wits, like physicians, never can agree,
When of a different society.
And Rabel's drops° were never more cried down
By all the learned doctors of the town,
5   Than a new play whose author is unknown.
Nor can those doctors with more malice sue
(And powerful purses) the dissenting few,
Than those, with an insulting pride, do rail
At all who are not of their own cabal.°
10   If a young poet hit your humor right,
You judge him then out of revenge and spite.
So amongst men there are ridiculous elves,
Who monkeys hate for being too like themselves.
So that the reason of the grand debate
15   Why wit so oft is damned when good plays take,
Is that you censure as you love, or hate.
    Thus like a learned conclave poets sit,
Catholic° judges both of sense and wit,
And damn or save as they themselves think fit.
20   Yet those who to others' faults are so severe,
Are not so perfect but themselves may err.
Some write correct, indeed, but then the whole
(Bating° their own dull stuff i'th' play) is stole:
As bees do suck from flowers their honeydew,
25   So they rob others striving to please you.
    Some write their characters genteel and fine,
But then they do so toil for every line,
That what to you does easy seem, and plain,
Is the hard issue of their laboring brain.
30   And some th' effects of all their pains, we see,
Is but to mimic good extempore.°
Others, by long converse about the town,
Have wit enough to write a lewd lampoon,
But their chief skill lies in a bawdy song.
35   In short, the only wit that's now in fashion,
Is but the gleanings of good conversation.
As for the author of this coming play,
I asked him what he thought fit I should say
In thanks for your good company today:
40   He called me fool, and said it was well known
You came not here for our sakes, but your own.

New plays are stuffed with wits, and with deboches,°
That crowd and sweat like cits° in May-Day°
    coaches.°

        WRITTEN BY A PERSON OF QUALITY

The Actors' Names

[Men]
DON ANTONIO, *the Viceroy's son*
DON PEDRO, *a noble Spaniard, his friend*
BELVILE, *an English colonel in love with Florinda*
WILLMORE, *the Rover*
FREDERICK, *an English gentleman, and friend to Belvile and Blunt*
BLUNT, *an English country gentleman*
STEPHANO, *servant to Don Pedro*
PHILIPPO, *Lucetta's gallant*
SANCHO, *pimp to Lucetta*
BISKEY and SEBASTIAN, *two bravos° to Angellica*
OFFICER and SOLDIERS
[DIEGO,] *Page to Don Antonio*

[Women]
FLORINDA, *sister to Don Pedro*
HELLENA, *a gay young woman designed for a nun, and sister to Florinda*
VALERIA, *a kinswoman to Florinda*
ANGELLICA BIANCA, *a famous courtesan*
MORETTA, *her woman*
CALLIS, *governess to Florinda and Hellena*
LUCETTA, *a jilting wench*
SERVANTS, *other* MASQUERADERS, MEN *and* WOMEN

The Scene: *Naples, in Carnival time.*

ACT I • Scene I

(*A Chamber. Enter Florinda and Hellena.*)

FLORINDA: What an impertinent thing is a young girl bred in a nunnery! How full of questions! Prithee no more, Hellena; I have told thee more than thou understand'st already.

---

3. **Rabel's drops:** A patent medicine.   9. **cabal:** A small, secret political group.   18. **Catholic:** Having broad tastes or interests.   23. **Bating:** Leaving out.   31. **extempore:** A performance given without a script or rehearsal.

42. **deboches:** Orgies, debauches.   43. **cits:** Residents of cities. **May-Day:** May 1, celebrated as a spring festival.   **coaches:** Carriages on parade during a May Day celebration.   44. [**The Actors' Names**] **bravos:** Villains, adventurers.

HELLENA: The more's my grief. I would fain know as much as you, which makes me so inquisitive; nor is't enough I know you're a lover, unless you tell me too who 'tis you sigh for.

FLORINDA: When you're a lover I'll think you fit for a secret of that nature.

HELLENA: 'Tis true, I never was a lover yet, but I begin to have a shrewd guess what 'tis to be so, and fancy it very pretty to sigh, and sing, and blush, and wish, and dream and wish, and long and wish to see the man, and when I do, look pale and tremble, just as you did when my brother brought home the fine English colonel to see you. What do you call him? Don Belvile?

FLORINDA: Fie, Hellena.

HELLENA: That blush betrays you. I am sure 'tis so. Or is it Don Antonio the Viceroy's son? Or perhaps the rich old Don Vincentio, whom my father designs you for a husband? Why do you blush again?

FLORINDA: With indignation; and how near soever my father thinks I am to marrying that hated object, I shall let him see I understand better what's due to my beauty, birth, and fortune, and more to my soul, than to obey those unjust commands.

HELLENA: Now hang me, if I don't love thee for that dear disobedience. I love mischief strangely, as most of our sex do who are come to love nothing else. But tell me, dear Florinda, don't you love that fine *Anglese*?° For I vow, next to loving him myself, 'twill please me most that you do so, for he is so gay and so handsome.

FLORINDA: Hellena, a maid designed for a nun ought not to be so curious in a discourse of love.

HELLENA: And dost thou think that ever I'll be a nun? Or at least till I'm so old I'm fit for nothing else? Faith no, sister; and that which makes me long to know whether you love Belvile, is because I hope he has some mad companion or other that will spoil my devotion. Nay, I'm resolved to provide myself this Carnival, if there be e'er a handsome proper fellow of my humor above ground,° though I ask first.

FLORINDA: Prithee be not so wild.

HELLENA: Now you have provided yourself of a man you take no care of poor me. Prithee tell me, what dost thou see about me that is unfit for love? Have I not a world of youth? A humor gay? A beauty passable? A vigor desirable? Well shaped? Clean limbed? Sweet breathed? And sense enough to know how all these ought to be employed to the best advantage? Yes, I do and will; therefore lay aside your hopes of my fortune by my being a devote,° and tell me how you came acquainted with this Belvile. For I perceive you knew him before he came to Naples.

FLORINDA: Yes, I knew him at the siege of Pamplona; he was then a colonel of French horse,° who when the town was ransacked, nobly treated my brother and myself, preserving us from all insolences. And I must own, besides great obligations, I have I know not what that pleads kindly for him about my heart, and will suffer no other to enter. But see, my brother.

(*Enter Don Pedro, Stephano with a masking habit,° and Callis.*)

PEDRO: Good morrow, sister. Pray when saw you your lover Don Vincentio?

FLORINDA: I know not, sir. Callis, when was he here? For I consider it so little I know not when it was.

PEDRO: I have a command from my father here to tell you you ought not to despise him, a man of so vast a fortune, and such a passion for you. — Stephano, my things.

(*Puts on his masking habit.*)

FLORINDA: A passion for me? 'Tis more than e'er I saw, or he had a desire should be known. I hate Vincentio, sir, and I would not have a man so dear to me as my brother follow the ill customs of our country and make a slave of his sister. And, sir, my father's will I'm sure you may divert.

PEDRO: I know not how dear I am to you, but I wish only to be ranked in your esteem equal with the English colonel Belvile. Why do you frown and blush? Is there any guilt belongs to the name of that cavalier?

FLORINDA: I'll not deny I value Belvile. When I was exposed to such dangers as the licensed lust of common soldiers threatened when rage and conquest flew through the city, then Belvile, this criminal for my sake, threw himself into all dangers to save my honor. And will you not allow him my esteem?

PEDRO: Yes, pay him what you will in honor, but you must consider Don Vincentio's fortune, and the jointure° he'll make you.

FLORINDA: Let him consider my youth, beauty, and fortune, which ought not to be thrown away on his age and jointure.

PEDRO: 'Tis true, he's not so young and fine a gentleman as that Belvile. But what jewels will that cavalier present you with? Those of his eyes and heart?

HELLENA: And are not those better than any Don Vincentio has brought from the Indies?

PEDRO: Why, how now! Has your nunnery breeding taught you to understand the value of hearts and eyes?

HELLENA: Better than to believe Vincentio's deserve value from any woman. He may perhaps increase her bags, but not her family.°

---

33. *Anglese*: The English colonel Belvile.   45. **above ground**: In the real world (i.e., outside the convent).   55. **devote**: Nun.   59. **of French horse**: In the French cavalry.   64. [s.d.] *masking habit*: Costume for the Carnival masquerades.   90–91. **jointure**: An estate given by a husband to a wife in lieu of her dowry.   103–04. **increase her bags...family**: Give her material goods but not enhance her family's standing.

105 PEDRO: This is fine! Go! Up to your devotion! You are
not designed for the conversation of lovers.

HELLENA (*aside*): Nor saints yet a while, I hope.—Is't
not enough you make a nun of me, but you must cast
my sister away too, exposing her to a worse confine-
110 ment than a religious life?

PEDRO: The girl's mad! It is a confinement to be carried
into the country to an ancient villa belonging to the
family of the Vincentios these five hundred years, and
have no other prospect than that pleasing one of see-
115 ing all her own that meets her eyes: a fine air, large
fields, and gardens where she may walk and gather
flowers?

HELLENA: When, by moonlight? For I am sure she dares
not encounter with the heat of the sun; that were a
120 task only for Don Vincentio and his Indian breeding,
who loves it in the dog days.° And if these be her
daily divertissements,° what are those of the night?
To lie in a wide moth-eaten bed-chamber with furniture in fashion in the reign of King Sancho the First;°
125 the bed, that which his forefathers lived and died in.

PEDRO: Very well.

HELLENA: This apartment, new furbushed° and fitted
out for the young wife, he out of freedom makes his
dressing room; and being a frugal and a jealous cox-
130 comb,° instead of a valet to uncase° his feeble carcass, he desires you to do that office. Signs of favor,
I'll assure you, and such as you must not hope for
unless your woman be out of the way.

PEDRO: Have you done yet?

135 HELLENA: That honor being past, the giant stretches
itself, yawns and sighs a belch or two loud as a musket, throws himself into bed, and expects you in his
foul sheets; and ere you can get yourself undressed,
calls you with a snore or two. And are not these fine
140 blessings to a young lady?

PEDRO: Have you done yet?

HELLENA: And this man you must kiss, nay you must
kiss none but him too, and nuzzle through his beard
to find his lips. And this you must submit to for
145 threescore years, and all for a jointure.

PEDRO: For all your character of Don Vincentio, she is
as like to marry him as she was before.

HELLENA: Marry Don Vincentio! Hang me, such a wedlock would be worse than adultery with another man.
150 I had rather see her in the *Hostel de Dieu,*° to waste
her youth there in vows, and be a handmaid to lazars°
and cripples, than to lose it in such a marriage.

PEDRO: You have considered, sister, that Belvile has no
fortune to bring you to; banished his country, de-
155 spised at home, and pitied abroad.

HELLENA: What then? The Viceroy's son is better than

that old Sir Fifty. Don Vincentio! Don Indian! He
thinks he's trading to Gambo° still, and would barter
himself—that bell and bauble—for your youth and
fortune.   160

PEDRO: Callis, take her hence and lock her up all this
Carnival, and at Lent she shall begin her everlasting
penance in a monastery.

HELLENA: I care not; I had rather be a nun than be
obliged to marry as you would have me if I were de-   165
signed for't.

PEDRO: Do not fear the blessing of that choice. You shall
be a nun.

HELLENA (*aside*): Shall I so? You may chance to be mistaken in my way of devotion. A nun! Yes, I am like to   170
make a fine nun! I have an excellent humor for a
grate!° No, I'll have a saint of my own to pray to
shortly, if I like any that dares venture on me.

PEDRO: Callis, make it your business to watch this wild-
cat.—As for you, Florinda, I've only tried you all   175
this while and urged my father's will; but mine is that
you would love Antonio: He is brave and young, and
all that can complete the happiness of a gallant maid.
This absence of my father will give us opportunity to
free you from Vincentio by marrying here, which you   180
must do tomorrow.

FLORINDA: Tomorrow!

PEDRO: Tomorrow, or 'twill be too late. 'Tis not my
friendship to Antonio which makes me urge this, but
love to thee and hatred to Vincentio; therefore resolve 185
upon tomorrow.

FLORINDA: Sir, I shall strive to do as shall become your
sister.

PEDRO: I'll both believe and trust you. Adieu.

(*Exeunt*° *Pedro and Stephano.*)

HELLENA: As becomes his sister! That is to be as resolved 190
your way as he is his.

(*Hellena goes to Callis.*)

FLORINDA: I ne'er till now perceived my ruin near.
I've no defense against Antonio's love,
For he has all the advantages of nature,
The moving arguments of youth and fortune.   195

HELLENA: But hark you, Callis, you will not be so cruel
to lock me up indeed, will you?

CALLIS: I must obey the commands I have. Besides, do
you consider what a life you are going to lead?

HELLENA: Yes, Callis, that of a nun; and till then I'll be in- 200
debted a world of prayers to you if you'll let me now
see what I never did, the divertissements of a Carnival.

CALLIS: What, go in masquerade? 'Twill be a fine farewell to the world, I take it. Pray what would you do
there?   205

HELLENA: That which all the world does, as I am told:

Be as mad as the rest and take all innocent freedoms. Sister, you'll go too, will you not? Come, prithee be not sad. We'll outwit twenty brothers if you'll be 210 ruled by me. Come, put off this dull humor with your clothes, and assume one as gay and as fantastic as the dress my cousin Valeria and I have provided, and let's ramble.

FLORINDA: Callis, will you give us leave to go?

215 CALLIS (aside): I have a youthful itch of going myself.— Madam, if I thought your brother might not know it, and I might wait on you; for by my troth I'll not trust young girls alone.

FLORINDA: Thou seest my brother's gone already, and 220 thou shalt attend and watch us.

(Enter Stephano.)

STEPHANO: Madam, the habits are come, and your cousin Valeria is dressed and stays for you.

FLORINDA (aside): 'Tis well. I'll write a note, and if I chance to see Belvile and want an opportunity to 225 speak to him, that shall let him know what I've resolved in favor of him.

HELLENA: Come, let's in and dress us.   (Exeunt.)

Scene II

(A long street. Enter Belvile, melancholy; Blunt and Frederick.)

FREDERICK: Why, what the devil ails the colonel, in a time when all the world is gay to look like mere Lent thus? Hadst thou been long enough in Naples to have been in love, I should have sworn some such 5 judgment had befallen thee.

BELVILE: No, I have made no new amours since I came to Naples.

FREDERICK: You have left none behind you in Paris?

BELVILE: Neither.

10 FREDERICK: I cannot divine the cause then, unless the old cause, the want of money.

BLUNT: And another old cause, the want of a wench. Would not that revive you?

BELVILE: You are mistaken, Ned.

15 BLUNT: Nay, 'adsheartlikins,° then thou'rt past cure.

FREDERICK: I have found it out: Thou hast renewed thy acquaintance with the lady that cost thee so many sighs at the siege of Pamplona—pox on't, what d'ye call her—her brother's a noble Spaniard, nephew to 20 the dead general. Florinda. Ay, Florinda. And will nothing serve thy turn but that damned virtuous woman, whom on my conscience thou lov'st in spite too, because thou seest little or no possibility of gaining her.

25 BELVILE: Thou art mistaken; I have int'rest enough in that lovely virgin's heart to make me proud and vain,

were it not abated by the severity of a brother, who, perceiving my happiness—

FREDERICK: Has civilly forbid thee the house?

BELVILE: 'Tis so, to make way for a powerful rival, the 30 Viceroy's son, who has the advantage of me in being a man of fortune, a Spaniard, and her brother's friend; which gives him liberty to make his court, whilst I have recourse only to letters and distant looks from her window, which are as soft and kind as 35 those which heaven sends down on penitents.

BLUNT: Heyday! 'Adsheartlikins, simile! By this light the man is quite spoiled. Fred, what the devil are we made of that we cannot be thus concerned for a wench? 'Adsheartlikins, our Cupids are like the cooks of the 40 camp: They can roast or boil a woman, but they have none of the fine tricks to set 'em off; no hogoes° to make the sauce pleasant and the stomach sharp.

FREDERICK: I dare swear I have had a hundred as young, kind, and handsome as this Florinda; and dogs eat 45 me if they were not as troublesome to me i'th' morning as they were welcome o'er night.

BLUNT: And yet I warrant he would not touch another woman if he might have her for nothing.

BELVILE: That's thy joy, a cheap whore. 50

BLUNT: Why, 'adsheartlikins, I love a frank soul. When did you ever hear of an honest woman that took a man's money? I warrant 'em good ones. But gentlemen, you may be free; you have been kept so poor with parliaments and protectors that the little stock 55 you have is not worth preserving. But I thank my stars I had more grace than to forfeit my estate by cavaliering.

BELVILE: Methinks only following the court should be sufficient to entitle 'em to that. 60

BLUNT: 'Adsheartlikins, they know I follow it to do it no good, unless they pick a hole in my coat for lending you money now and then, which is a greater crime to my conscience, gentlemen, than to the commonwealth. 65

(Enter Willmore.)

WILLMORE: Ha! Dear Belvile! Noble colonel!

BELVILE: Willmore! Welcome ashore, my dear rover! What happy wind blew us this good fortune?

WILLMORE: Let me salute my dear Fred, and then command me.—How is't, honest lad? 70

FREDERICK: Fair, sir, the old compliment, infinitely the better to see my dear mad Willmore again. Prithee, why camest thou ashore? And where's the Prince?°

WILLMORE: He's well, and reigns still lord of the wat'ry element. I must aboard again within a day or two, 75 and my business ashore was only to enjoy myself a little this Carnival.

BELVILE: Pray know our new friend, sir; he's but bashful, a raw traveler, but honest, stout, and one of us.

---

15. 'adsheartlikins: Expostulation equivalent to "As God loves us."

42. hogoes: Relishes.   73. Prince: Charles II, in exile on the Continent during the reign of Cromwell.

(*Embraces Blunt.*)

80 WILLMORE: That you esteem him gives him an int'rest here.

BLUNT: Your servant, sir.

WILLMORE: But well, faith, I'm glad to meet you again in a warm climate, where the kind sun has its godlike
85 power still over the wine and women. Love and mirth are my business in Naples, and if I mistake not the place, here's an excellent market for chapmen° of my humor.

BELVILE: See, here be those kind merchants of love you
90 look for.

(*Enter several men in masking habits, some playing on music, others dancing after; women dressed like courtesans, with papers pinned on their breasts, and baskets of flowers in their hands.*)

BLUNT: 'Adsheartlikins, what have we here?

FREDERICK: Now the game begins.

WILLMORE: Fine pretty creatures! May a stranger have leave to look and love? What's here? "Roses for every
95 month"?   (*Reads the papers.*)

BLUNT: Roses for every month? What means that?

BELVILE: They are, or would have you think they're courtesans, who here in Naples are to be hired by the month.

100 WILLMORE: Kind and obliging to inform us, pray where do these roses grow? I would fain plant some of 'em in a bed of mine.

WOMAN: Beware such roses, sir.

WILLMORE: A pox of fear: I'll be baked with thee
105 between a pair of sheets, and that's thy proper still; so I might but strew such roses over me and under me. Fair one, would you would give me leave to gather at your bush this idle month; I would go near to make somebody smell of it all the year after.

110 BELVILE: And thou hast need of such a remedy, for thou stink'st of tar and ropes' ends like a dock or pesthouse.

(*The Woman puts herself into the hands of a man and exeunt.*)

WILLMORE: Nay, nay, you shall not leave me so.

BELVILE: By all means use no violence here.

WILLMORE: Death! Just as I was going to be damnably
115 in love, to have her led off! I could pluck that rose out of his hand, and even kiss the bed the bush grew in.

FREDERICK: No friend to love like a long voyage at sea.

BLUNT: Except a nunnery, Fred.

WILLMORE: Death! But will they not be kind? Quickly
120 be kind? Thou know'st I'm no tame sigher, but a rampant lion of the forest.

(*Advances from the farther end of the scenes two men dressed all over with horns° of several sorts, making grimaces at one another, with papers pinned on their backs.*)

87. **chapmen:** Merchants, in this case merchants of love.
121. [S.D.] **horns:** Emblem of the cuckold, a man whose wife is unfaithful.

BELVILE: Oh the fantastical rogues, how they're dressed! 'Tis a satire against the whole sex.

WILLMORE: Is this a fruit that grows in this warm coun-
125 try?

BELVILE: Yes, 'tis pretty to see these Italians start, swell, and stab at the word cuckold, and yet stumble at horns on every threshold.

WILLMORE: See what's on their back. (*Reads.*) "Flowers
130 of every night." Ah, rogue! And more sweet than roses of every month! This is a gardener of Adam's own breeding.

(*They dance.*)

BELVILE: What think you of these grave people? Is a wake in Essex half so mad or extravagant?

135 WILLMORE: I like their sober grave way; 'tis a kind of legal authorized fornication, where the men are not chid° for't, nor the women despised, as amongst our dull English. Even the monsieurs° want that part of good manners.

140 BELVILE: But here in Italy, a monsieur is the humblest best-bred gentleman: Duels are so baffled by bravos that an age shows not one but between a Frenchman and a hangman, who is as much too hard for him on the Piazza as they are for a Dutchman on the New
145 Bridge. But see, another crew.

(*Enter Florinda, Hellena, and Valeria, dressed like gypsies; Callis and Stephano, Lucetta, Philippo, and Sancho in masquerade.*)

HELLENA: Sister, there's your Englishman, and with him a handsome proper fellow. I'll to him, and instead of telling him his fortune, try my own.

WILLMORE: Gypsies, on my life. Sure these will prattle if a man cross their hands.° (*Goes to Hellena.*)—Dear,
150 pretty, and, I hope, young devil, will you tell an amorous stranger what luck he's like to have?

HELLENA: Have a care how you venture with me, sir, lest I pick your pocket, which will more vex your English humor than an Italian fortune will please you.

155 WILLMORE: How the devil cam'st thou to know my country and humor?

HELLENA: The first I guess by a certain forward impudence, which does not displease me at this time; and the loss of your money will vex you because I hope
160 you have but very little to lose.

WILLMORE: Egad, child, thou'rt i'th' right; it is so little I dare not offer it thee for a kindness. But cannot you divine what other things of more value I have about me that I would more willingly part with?

165 HELLENA: Indeed no, that's the business of a witch, and I am but a gypsy yet. Yet without looking in your hand, I have a parlous° guess 'tis some foolish heart you mean, an inconstant English heart, as little worth stealing as your purse.

170

137. **chid:** Chided, reproached.   138. **monsieurs:** Frenchmen.
150. **cross their hands:** Cross their hands with silver: pay them to tell his fortune.   168. **parlous:** Dangerously cunning, clever (from *perilous*).

WILLMORE: Nay, then thou dost deal with the devil, that's certain. Thou hast guessed as right as if thou hadst been one of that number it has languished for. I find you'll be better acquainted with it, nor can you take it in a better time; for I am come from sea, child, and Venus not being propitious to me in her own element,° I have a world of love in store. Would you would be good-natured and take some on't° off my hands.

HELLENA: Why, I could be inclined that way, but for a foolish vow I am going to make to die a maid.

WILLMORE: Then thou art damned without redemption, and as I am a good Christian, I ought in charity to divert so wicked a design. Therefore prithee, dear creature, let me know quickly when and where I shall begin to set a helping hand to so good a work.

HELLENA: If you should prevail with my tender heart, as I begin to fear you will, for you have horrible loving eyes, there will be difficulty in't that you'll hardly undergo for my sake.

WILLMORE: Faith, child, I have been bred in dangers, and wear a sword that has been employed in a worse cause than for a handsome kind woman. Name the danger; let it be anything but a long siege, and I'll undertake it.

HELLENA: Can you storm?

WILLMORE: Oh, most furiously.

HELLENA: What think you of a nunnery wall? For he that wins me must gain that first.

WILLMORE: A nun! Oh, now I love thee for't! There's no sinner like a young saint. Nay, now there's no deny-ing me; the old law had no curse to a woman like dying a maid: Witness Jeptha's daughter.°

HELLENA: A very good text this, if well handled; and I perceive, Father Captain, you would impose no severe penance on her who were inclined to console herself before she took orders.°

WILLMORE: If she be young and handsome.

HELLENA: Ay, there's it. But if she be not—

WILLMORE: By this hand, child, I have an implicit faith, and dare venture on thee with all faults. Besides, 'tis more meritorious to leave the world when thou hast tasted and proved the pleasure on't. Then 'twill be a virtue in thee, which now will be pure ignorance.

HELLENA: I perceive, good Father Captain, you design only to make me fit for heaven. But if, on the con-trary, you should quite divert me from it, and bring me back to the world again, I should have a new man to seek, I find. And what a grief that will be; for when I begin, I fancy I shall love like anything; I never tried yet.

WILLMORE: Egad, and that's kind! Prithee, dear crea-ture, give me credit for a heart, for faith, I'm a very honest fellow. Oh, I long to come first to the banquet of love! And such a swinging appetite I bring. Oh, I'm impatient. Thy lodging, sweetheart, thy lodging, or I'm a dead man!

HELLENA: Why must we be either guilty of fornication or murder if we converse with you men? And is there no difference between leave to love me, and leave to lie with me?

WILLMORE: Faith, child, they were made to go together.

LUCETTA (pointing to Blunt): Are you sure this is the man?

SANCHO: When did I mistake your game?

LUCETTA: This is a stranger, I know by his gazing; if he be brisk he'll venture to follow me, and then, if I understand my trade, he's mine. He's English, too, and they say that's a sort of good-natured loving people, and have generally so kind an opinion of themselves that a woman with any wit may flatter 'em into any sort of fool she pleases.

(She often passes by Blunt and gazes on him; he struts and cocks, and walks and gazes on her.)

BLUNT: 'Tis so, she is taken; I have beauties which my false glass° at home did not discover.

FLORINDA (aside): This woman watches me so, I shall get no opportunity to discover myself to him, and so miss the intent of my coming. — [To Belvile.] But as I was saying, sir, by this line you should be a lover. (Looking in his hand.)

BELVILE: I thought how right you guessed: All men are in love, or pretend to be so. Come, let me go; I'm weary of this fooling. (Walks away.)

FLORINDA: I will not, sir, till you have confessed whether the passion that you have vowed Florinda be true or false.

(She holds him; he strives to get from her.)

BELVILE: Florinda! (Turns quick toward her.)

FLORINDA: Softly.

BELVILE: Thou hast nam'd one will fix me here forever.

FLORINDA: She'll be disappointed then, who expects you this night at the garden gate. And if you fail not, as — (Looks on Callis, who observes 'em.) Let me see the other hand — you will go near to do, she vows to die or make you happy.

BELVILE: What canst thou mean?

FLORINDA: That which I say. Farewell.

(Offers to go.)

BELVILE: O charming sibyl,° stay; complete that joy which as it is will turn into distraction! Where must I be? At the garden gate? I know it. At night, you say? I'll sooner forfeit heaven than disobey.

(Enter Don Pedro and other maskers, and pass over the stage.)

---

176. **Venus...element:** Venus, the goddess of love, was suppos-edly born from the foam of the sea. 178. **on't:** Of it. 201. **Jeptha's daughter:** To fulfill a vow, Jeptha sacrificed his only child, a virgin daughter, whom he allowed to go off to the mountains for two months to "bewail" her virginity before he killed her. "And it became a custom in Israel that the daughters of Israel went year by year to lament the daughter of Jeptha... four days in the year" (Judges 11:39–40). 205. **took orders:** Entered the convent.

242. **false glass:** Lying mirror. 263. **sibyl:** A female prophet; fortune-teller.

CALLIS: Madam, your brother's here.
FLORINDA: Take this to instruct you farther.

(Gives him a letter, and goes off.)

270 FREDERICK: Have a care, sir, what you promise; this may
be a trap laid by her brother to ruin you.
BELVILE: Do not disturb my happiness with doubts.

(Opens the letter.)

WILLMORE: My dear pretty creature, a thousand blessings on thee! Still in this habit, you say? And after
dinner at this place?
275 HELLENA: Yes, if you will swear to keep your heart and
not bestow it between this and that.
WILLMORE: By all the little gods of love, I swear; I'll
leave it with you, and if you run away with it, those
deities of justice will revenge me.

(Exeunt all the women [except Lucetta].)

280 FREDERICK: Do you know the hand?
BELVILE: 'Tis Florinda's.
All blessings fall upon the virtuous maid.
FREDERICK: Nay, no idolatry; a sober sacrifice I'll allow
you.
285 BELVILE: Oh friends, the welcom'st news! The softest
letter! Nay, you shall all see it. And could you now be
serious, I might be made the happiest man the sun
shines on!
WILLMORE: The reason of this mighty joy?
290 BELVILE: See how kindly she invites me to deliver her
from the threatened violence of her brother. Will you
not assist me?
WILLMORE: I know not what thou mean'st, but I'll make
one at any mischief where a woman's concerned. But
295 she'll be grateful to us for the favor, will she not?
BELVILE: How mean you?
WILLMORE: How should I mean? Thou know'st there's
but one way for a woman to oblige me.
BELVILE: Do not profane; the maid is nicely virtuous.
300 WILLMORE: Who, pox, then she's fit for nothing but a
husband. Let her e'en go, colonel.
FREDERICK: Peace, she's the colonel's mistress, sir.
WILLMORE: Let her be the devil; if she be thy mistress,
I'll serve her. Name the way.
305 BELVILE: Read here this postscript. *(Gives him a letter.)*
WILLMORE *(reads)*: "At ten at night, at the garden gate,
of which, if I cannot get the key, I will contrive a
way over the wall. Come attended with a friend or
two."—Kind heart, if we three cannot weave a string
310 to let her down a garden wall, 'twere pity but the
hangman wove one for us all.
FREDERICK: Let her alone for that; your woman's wit,
your fair kind woman, will outtrick a broker or a
Jew, and contrive like a Jesuit° in chains. But see,
315 Ned Blunt is stolen out after the lure of a damsel.

(Exeunt Blunt and Lucetta.)

BELVILE: So, he'll scarce find his way home again unless
we get him cried by the bellman in the market place.
And 'twould sound prettily: "A lost English boy of
thirty."
320 FREDERICK: I hope 'tis some common crafty sinner, one
that will fit him. It may be she'll sell him for Peru:°
The rogue's sturdy, and would work well in a mine.
At least I hope she'll dress him for our mirth, cheat
him of all, then have him well-favoredly banged, and
325 turned out at midnight.
WILLMORE: Prithee what humor is he of, that you wish
him so well?
BELVILE: Why, of an English elder brother's humor: educated in a nursery, with a maid to tend him till fifteen,
330 and lies with his grandmother till he's of age; one that
knows no pleasure beyond riding to the next fair, or
going up to London with his right worshipful father
in parliament time, wearing gay clothes, or making
honorable love to his lady mother's laundry maid;
335 gets drunk at a hunting match, and ten to one then
gives some proofs of his prowess. A pox upon him,
he's our banker, and has all our cash about him; and
if he fail, we are all broke.
FREDERICK: Oh, let him alone for that matter; he's of a
340 damned stingy quality that will secure our stock. I
know not in what danger it were indeed if the jilt
should pretend she's in love with him, for 'tis a kind
believing coxcomb; otherwise, if he part with more
than a piece of eight,° geld° him—for which offer he
345 may chance to be beaten if she be a whore of the first
rank.
BELVILE: Nay, the rogue will not be easily beaten; he's
stout enough. Perhaps if they talk beyond his capacity he may chance to exercise his courage upon some
350 of them, else I'm sure they'll find it as difficult to beat
as to please him.
WILLMORE: 'Tis a lucky devil to light upon so kind a
wench!
FREDERICK: Thou hadst a great deal of talk with thy
355 little gypsy; couldst thou do no good upon her? For
mine was hardhearted.
WILLMORE: Hang her, she was some damned honest
person of quality, I'm sure, she was so very free and
witty. If her face be but answerable to her wit and
360 humor, I would be bound to constancy this month to
gain her. In the meantime, have you made no kind
acquaintance since you came to town? You do not
use to be honest° so long, gentlemen.
FREDERICK: Faith, love has kept us honest: We have
365 been all fir'd with a beauty newly come to town, the
famous Paduana° Angellica Bianca.
WILLMORE: What, the mistress of the dead Spanish
general?

---

314. Jew…Jesuit: Anti-Semitic and anti-Catholic attitudes of the time portrayed Jews and Jesuits as cunning and not worthy of trust.

321. sell him for Peru: Sell him as a slave.   **344. piece of eight:** Spanish money.   **geld:** Castrate.   **363. honest:** Sexually inactive.   **366. Paduana:** Angellica was born in Padua, Italy.

BELVILE: Yes, she's now the only ador'd beauty of all
370 the youth in Naples, who put on all their charms to
appear lovely in her sight: Their coaches, liveries, and
themselves all gay as on a monarch's birthday to
attract the eyes of this fair charmer, while she has
the pleasure to behold all languish for her that see
375 her.
FREDERICK: 'Tis pretty to see with how much love the
men regard her, and how much envy the women.
WILLMORE: What gallant has she?
BELVILE: None; she's exposed to sale, and four days in
380 the week she's yours, for so much a month.
WILLMORE: The very thought of it quenches all manner
of fire in me. Yet prithee, let's see her.
BELVILE: Let's first to dinner, and after that we'll pass the
day as you please. But at night ye must all be at my
385 devotion.
WILLMORE: I will not fail you.   [Exeunt.]

ACT II • Scene 1

(The long street. Enter Belvile and Frederick in masking
habits, and Willmore in his own clothes, with a vizard°
in his hand.)

WILLMORE: But why thus disguised and muzzled?
BELVILE: Because whatever extravagances we commit in
these faces, our own may not be obliged to answer
'em.
5 WILLMORE: I should have changed my eternal buff,°
too; but no matter, my little gypsy would not have
found me out then. For if she should change hers, it is
impossible I should know her unless I should hear her
prattle. A pox on't, I cannot get her out of my head.
10 Pray heaven, if ever I do see her again, she prove
damnably ugly, that I may fortify myself against her
tongue.
BELVILE: Have a care of love, for o' my conscience she
was not of a quality to give thee any hopes.
15 WILLMORE: Pox on 'em, why do they draw a man in
then? She has played with my heart so, that 'twill
never lie still till I have met with some kind wench
that will play the game out with me. Oh, for my arms
full of soft, white, kind woman—such as I fancy
20 Angellica.
BELVILE: This is her house, if you were but in stock to
get admittance. They have not dined yet; I perceive
the picture is not out.°

(Enter Blunt.)

WILLMORE: I long to see the shadow of the fair sub-
25 stance; a man may gaze on that for nothing.

BLUNT: Colonel, thy hand. And thine, Fred. I have been
an ass, a deluded fool, a very coxcomb from my birth
till this hour, and heartily repent my little faith.
BELVILE: What the devil's the matter with thee, Ned?
BLUNT: Oh, such a mistress, Fred! Such a girl!   30
WILLMORE: Ha! Where?
FREDERICK: Ay, where?
BLUNT: So fond, so amorous, so toying, and so fine! And
all for sheer love, ye rogue! Oh, how she looked and
kissed! And soothed my heart from my bosom! I can- 35
not think I was awake, and yet methinks I see and
feel her charms still. Fred, try if she have not left the
taste of her balmy kisses upon my lips. (Kisses him.)
BELVILE: Ha! Ha! Ha!
WILLMORE: Death, man, where is she?   40
BLUNT: What a dog was I to stay in dull England so
long! How have I laughed at the colonel when he
sighed for love! But now the little archer° has revenged him! And by this one dart I can guess at all his
joys, which then I took for fancies, mere dreams and 45
fables. Well, I'm resolved to sell all in Essex and plant
here forever.
BELVILE: What a blessing 'tis, thou hast a mistress thou
dar'st boast of; for I know thy humor is rather to
have a proclaimed clap than a secret amour.   50
WILLMORE: Dost know her name?
BLUNT: Her name? No, 'adsheartlikins. What care I for
names? She's fair, young, brisk and kind, even to rav-
ishment! And what a pox care I for knowing her by
any other title?   55
WILLMORE: Didst give her anything?
BLUNT: Give her? Ha! Ha! Ha! Why, she's a person of
quality. That's a good one! Give her? 'Adsheartlikins,
dost think such creatures are to be bought? Or are we
provided for such a purchase? Give her, quoth ye?   60
Why, she presented me with this bracelet for the toy
of a diamond I used to wear. No, gentlemen, Ned
Blunt is not everybody. She expects me again tonight.
WILLMORE: Egad, that's well; we'll all go.
BLUNT: Not a soul! No, gentlemen, you are wits; I am a 65
dull country rogue, I.
FREDERICK: Well, sir, for all your person of quality, I
shall be very glad to understand your purse be secure; 'tis our whole estate at present, which we are
loath to hazard in one bottom.° Come sir, unlade.   70
BLUNT: Take the necessary trifle useless now to me, that
am beloved by such a gentlewoman. 'Adsheartlikins,
money! Here, take mine too.
FREDERICK: No, keep that to be cozened,° that we may
laugh.   75
WILLMORE: Cozened? Death! Would I could meet with
one that would cozen me of all the love I could spare
tonight.
FREDERICK: Pox, 'tis some common whore, upon my life.

II, I. [S.D.] *vizard*: Face mask.   5. buff: Military coat made of buff (leather).   23. picture is not out: Hanging her picture outside the house is a sign that she is open for business. (See lines 111–12 later in the scene.)

43. little archer: Cupid.   70. hazard in one bottom: Keep in one place, as in the hold (bottom) of a ship.   74. cozened: Cheated.

80   BLUNT: A whore? Yes, with such clothes, such jewels, such a house, such furniture, and so attended! A whore!

BELVILE: Why yes, sir, they are whores, though they'll neither entertain you with drinking, swearing, or
85   bawdry; are whores in all those gay clothes and right° jewels; are whores with those great houses richly furnished with velvet beds, store of plate,° handsome attendance, and fine coaches; are whores, and errant° ones.

90   WILLMORE: Pox on't, where do these fine whores live?

BELVILE: Where no rogues in office, ycleped° constables, dare give 'em laws, nor the wine-inspired bullies of the town break their windows; yet they are whores though this Essex calf° believe 'em persons of quality.

95   BLUNT: 'Adsheartlikins, y'are all fools. There are things about this Essex calf that shall take with the ladies, beyond all your wit and parts. This shape and size, gentlemen, are not to be despised; my waist, too, tolerably long, with other inviting signs that shall be
100   nameless.

WILLMORE: Egad, I believe he may have met with some person of quality that may be kind to him.

BELVILE: Dost thou perceive any such tempting things about him that should make a fine woman, and of
105   quality, pick him out from all mankind to throw away her youth and beauty upon; nay, and her dear heart, too? No, no, Angellica has raised the price too high.

WILLMORE: May she languish for mankind till she die,
110   and be damned for that one sin alone.

(*Enter two Bravos and hang up a great picture of Angellica's against the balcony, and two little ones at each side of the door.*)

BELVILE: See there the fair sign to the inn where a man may lodge that's fool enough to give her price.

(*Willmore gazes on the picture.*)

BLUNT: 'Adsheartlikins, gentlemen, what's this?
BELVILE: A famous courtesan, that's to be sold.
115   BLUNT: How? To be sold? Nay, then I have nothing to say to her. Sold? What impudence is practiced in this country; with what order and decency whoring's established here by virtue of the Inquisition!° Come, let's be gone; I'm sure we're no chapmen for this
120   commodity.

FREDERICK: Thou art none, I'm sure, unless thou couldst have her in thy bed at a price of a coach in the street.

WILLMORE: How wondrous fair she is! A thousand crowns a month? By heaven, as many kingdoms were

too little! A plague of this poverty, of which I ne'er   125
complain but when it hinders my approach to beauty which virtue ne'er could purchase.

(*Turns from the picture.*)

BLUNT: What's this? (*Reads.*) "A thousand crowns a month"! 'Adsheartlikins, here's a sum! Sure 'tis a mistake. —[*To one of the Bravos.*] Hark you, friend,   130
does she take or give so much by the month?

FREDERICK: A thousand crowns! Why, 'tis a portion for the Infanta!°

BLUNT: Hark ye, friends, won't she trust?°

BRAVO: This is a trade, sir, that cannot live by credit.   135

(*Enter Don Pedro in masquerade, followed by Stephano.*)

BELVILE: See, here's more company; let's walk off a while.

(*Exeunt English,° Pedro reads.*)

PEDRO: Fetch me a thousand crowns; I never wished to buy this beauty at an easier rate. (*Passes off.*)

(*Enter Angellica and Moretta in the balcony, and draw a silk curtain.*)

ANGELLICA: Prithee, what said those fellows to thee?

BRAVO: Madam, the first were admirers of beauty only,   140
but no purchasers; they were merry with your price and picture, laughed at the sum, and so passed off.

ANGELLICA: No matter, I'm not displeased with their rallying; their wonder feeds my vanity, and he that wishes but to buy gives me more pride than he that   145
gives my price can make my pleasure.

BRAVO: Madam, the last I knew through all his disguises to be Don Pedro, nephew to the general, and who was with him in Pamplona.

ANGELLICA: Don Pedro? My old gallant's nephew?   150
When his uncle died he left him a vast sum of money; it is he who was so in love with me at Padua, and who used to make the general so jealous.

MORETTA: Is this he that used to prance before our window, and take such care to show himself an amorous   155
ass? If I am not mistaken, he is the likeliest man to give your price.

ANGELLICA: The man is brave and generous, but of a humor so uneasy and inconstant that the victory over his heart is as soon lost as won; a slave that can add   160
little to the triumph of the conqueror. But inconstancy's the sin of all mankind, therefore I'm resolved that nothing but gold shall charm my heart.

MORETTA: I'm glad on't; 'tis only interest that women of our profession ought to consider, though I wonder   165
what has kept you from that general disease of our sex so long; I mean, that of being in love.

ANGELLICA: A kind but sullen star under which I had the happiness to be born. Yet I have had no time for love; the bravest and noblest of mankind have purchased   170

---

86. **right:** Real.   87. **plate:** Silverware.   89. **errant:** Unmitigated.   91. **ycleped:** Past participle of *clepe*: called.   94. **Essex calf:** Derogatory term meaning "fool," referring to Essex, England, Blunt's home.   118. **Inquisition:** The Spanish Inquisition (1478–1834) forced prostitutes out of Spain and into neighboring countries.

132–33. **portion for the Infanta:** Dowry for the Spanish princess.   134. **trust:** Extend credit for payment.   136. [S.D.] *English:* All the English characters.

The King's County Shakespeare Company's 2003 production of *The Rover* with Tessa Martin and Jon Fordham.

my favors at so dear a rate, as if no coin but gold were current with our trade. But here's Don Pedro again; fetch me my lute, for 'tis for him or Don Antonio the Viceroy's son that I have spread my nets.

(*Enter at one door Don Pedro, Stephano; Don Antonio and Diego [his page] at the other door, with people following him in masquerade, antically attired, some with music. They both go up to the picture.*)

175   ANTONIO: A thousand crowns! Had not the painter flattered her, I should not think it dear.
PEDRO: Flattered her? By heaven, he cannot. I have seen the original, nor is there one charm here more than adorns her face and eyes; all this soft and sweet, with
180   a certain languishing air that no artist can represent.
ANTONIO: What I heard of her beauty before had fired my soul, but this confirmation of it has blown it to a flame.
PEDRO: Ha!
185   PAGE: Sir, I have known you throw away a thousand crowns on a worse face, and though y'are near your marriage, you may venture a little love here; Florinda will not miss it.
PEDRO (*aside*): Ha! Florinda! Sure 'tis Antonio.
190   ANTONIO: Florinda! Name not those distant joys; there's not one thought of her will check my passion here.
PEDRO [*aside*]: Florinda scorned! (*A noise of a lute above.*) And all my hopes defeated of the possession

of Angellica! (*Antonio gazes up.*) Her injuries, by heaven, he shall not boast of!
195
(*Song to a lute above.*)

SONG
[I]
When Damon first began to love
He languished in a soft desire,
And knew not how the gods to move,
To lessen or increase his fire.
For Caelia in her charming eyes   200
Wore all love's sweets, and all his cruelties.

II
But as beneath a shade he lay,
Weaving of flowers for Caelia's hair,
She chanced to lead her flock that way,
And saw the am'rous shepherd there.   205
She gazed around upon the place,
And saw the grove, resembling night,
To all the joys of love invite,
Whilst guilty smiles and blushes dressed her face.
At this the bashful youth all transport grew,   210
And with kind force he taught the virgin how
To yield what all his sighs could never do.

(*Angellica throws open the curtains and bows to Antonio, who pulls off his vizard and bows and blows up kisses. Pedro, unseen, looks in's face. [The curtains close.]*)

ANTONIO: By heaven, she's charming fair!

PEDRO (*aside*): 'Tis he, the false Antonio!

ANTONIO (*to the Bravo*): Friend, where must I pay my
215   off'ring of love?
     My thousand crowns I mean.

PEDRO: That off'ring I have designed to make,
     And yours will come too late.

ANTONIO: Prithee begone; I shall grow angry else,
220   And then thou art not safe.

PEDRO: My anger may be fatal, sir, as yours,
     And he that enters here may prove this truth.

ANTONIO: I know not who thou art, but I am sure
     thou'rt worth my killing, for aiming at Angellica.

                      (*They draw and fight.*)

(*Enter Willmore and Blunt, who draw and part 'em.*)

225 BLUNT: 'Adsheartlikins, here's fine doings.

WILLMORE: Tilting for the wench, I'm sure. Nay, gad, if
     that would win her I have as good a sword as the best
     of ye. Put up, put up, and take another time and
     place, for this is designed for lovers only.

                      (*They all put up.*)

PEDRO: We are prevented; dare you meet me tomorrow
230   on the Molo?°
     For I've a title to a better quarrel,
     That of Florinda, in whose credulous heart
     Thou'st made an int'rest, and destroyed my hopes.

ANTONIO: Dare!
235 I'll meet thee there as early as the day.

PEDRO: We will come thus disguised, that whosoever
     chance to get the better, he may escape unknown.

ANTONIO: It shall be so.

                (*Exeunt Pedro and Stephano.*)

—Who should this rival be? Unless the English
240 colonel, of whom I've often heard Don Pedro speak.
     It must be he, and time he were removed who lays a
     claim to all my happiness.

(*Willmore, having gazed all this while on the picture[s],
pulls down a little one.*)

WILLMORE: This posture's loose and negligent;
     The sight on't would beget a warm desire
245   In souls whom impotence and age had chilled.
     This must along with me.

BRAVO: What means this rudeness, sir? Restore the
     picture.

ANTONIO: Ha! Rudeness committed to the fair Angel-
250   lica!—Restore the picture, sir.

WILLMORE: Indeed I will not, sir.

ANTONIO: By heaven, but you shall.

WILLMORE: Nay, do not show your sword; if you do, by
     this dear beauty, I will show mine too.

255 ANTONIO: What right can you pretend to't?

WILLMORE: That of possession, which I will maintain.

230. Molo: Wharf.

You, perhaps, have a thousand crowns to give for the
original.

ANTONIO: No matter, sir, you shall restore the picture.

([*The curtains open.*] *Angellica and Moretta above.*)

ANGELLICA: Oh, Moretta, what's the matter?   260

ANTONIO: Or leave your life behind.

WILLMORE: Death! You lie; I will do neither.

(*They fight. The Spaniards join with Antonio, Blunt laying on like mad.*)

ANGELLICA: Hold, I command you, if for me you fight.

(*They leave off and bow.*)

WILLMORE [*aside*]: How heavenly fair she is! Ah, plague
     of her price!   265

ANGELLICA: You sir, in buff, you that appear a soldier,
     that first began this insolence—

WILLMORE: 'Tis true, I did so, if you call it insolence for
     a man to preserve himself. I saw your charming pic-
     ture and was wounded; quite through my soul each   270
     pointed beauty ran; and wanting a thousand crowns
     to procure my remedy, I laid this little picture to my
     bosom, which, if you cannot allow me, I'll resign.

ANGELLICA: No, you may keep the trifle.

ANTONIO: You shall first ask me leave, and this.   275

(*Fight again as before.*)

(*Enter Belvile and Frederick, who join with the English.*)

ANGELLICA: Hold! Will you ruin me?—Biskey! Sebas-
     tian! Part 'em!

(*The Spaniards are beaten off.*)

MORETTA: Oh, madam, we're undone. A pox upon that
     rude fellow; he's set on to ruin us. We shall never see
     good days again till all these fighting poor rogues are   280
     sent to the galleys.

(*Enter Belvile, Blunt, Frederick, and Willmore with's
shirt bloody.*)

BLUNT: 'Adsheartlikins, beat me at this sport and I'll
     ne'er wear sword more.

BELVILE (*to Willmore*): The devil's in thee for a mad fel-
     low; thou art always one at an unlucky adventure.   285
     Come, let's be gone whilst we're safe, and remember
     these are Spaniards, a sort of people that know how
     to revenge an affront.

FREDERICK: You bleed! I hope you are not wounded.

WILLMORE: Not much. A plague on your dons; if they   290
     fight no better they'll ne'er recover Flanders.° What
     the devil was't to them that I took down the picture?

BLUNT: Took it! 'Adsheartlikins, we'll have the great one
     too; 'tis ours by conquest. Prithee help me up and I'll
     pull it down.   295

291. ne'er recover Flanders: In 1659 the Spanish gave Flanders,
which had been part of the Spanish Netherlands, to France as
settlement to end a war.

ANGELLICA [*to Willmore*]: Stay, sir, and ere you affront me
farther let me know how you durst commit this outrage. To you I speak, sir, for you appear a gentleman.

300 WILLMORE: To me, madam?—Gentlemen, your servant.

(*Belvile stays him.°*)

BELVILE: Is the devil in thee? Dost know the danger of
ent'ring the house of an incensed courtesan?

WILLMORE: I thank you for your care, but there are
other matters in hand, there are, though we have no
305 great temptation. Death! Let me go!

FREDERICK: Yes, to your lodging if you will, but not in
here. Damn these gay harlots; by this hand I'll have
as sound and handsome a whore for a patacoon.°
Death, man, she'll murder thee!

310 WILLMORE: Oh, fear me not. Shall I not venture where a
beauty calls? A lovely charming beauty! For fear of
danger? When, by heaven, there's none so great as to
long for her whilst I want money to purchase her.

FREDERICK: Therefore 'tis loss of time unless you had
315 the thousand crowns to pay.

WILLMORE: It may be she may give a favor; at least I
shall have the pleasure of saluting her when I enter
and when I depart.

BELVILE: Pox, she'll as soon lie with thee as kiss thee,
320 and sooner stab than do either. You shall not go.

ANGELLICA: Fear not, sir, all I have to wound with is my
eyes.

BLUNT: Let him go. 'Adsheartlikins, I believe the gentlewoman means well.

325 BELVILE: Well, take thy fortune; we'll expect you in the
next street. Farewell, fool, farewell.

WILLMORE: Bye, colonel.   (*Goes in.*)

FREDERICK: The rogue's stark mad for a wench.

(*Exeunt.*)

Scene II

(*A fine chamber. Enter Willmore, Angellica, and Moretta.*)

ANGELLICA: Insolent sir, how durst you pull down my
picture?

WILLMORE: Rather, how durst you set it up to tempt
poor am'rous mortals with so much excellence,
5 which I find you have but too well consulted by the
unmerciful price you set upon't. Is all this heaven of
beauty shown to move despair in those that cannot
buy? And can you think th'effects of that despair
should be less extravagant than I have shown?

10 ANGELLICA: I sent for you to ask my pardon, sir, not to
aggravate your crime. I thought I should have seen
you at my feet imploring it.

WILLMORE: You are deceived. I came to rail at you, and
rail such truths too, as shall let you see the vanity of
15 that pride which taught you how to set such price on
sin.

For such it is whilst that which is love's due
Is meanly bartered for.

ANGELLICA: Ha! Ha! Ha! Alas, good captain, what pity
'tis your edifying doctrine will do no good upon me.   20
Moretta, fetch the gentleman a glass,° and let him
survey himself to see what charms he has.—(*Aside,
in a soft tone.*) And guess my business.

MORETTA: He knows himself of old: I believe those
breeches and he have been acquainted ever since he   25
was beaten at Worcester.°

ANGELLICA: Nay, do not abuse the poor creature.

MORETTA: Good weather-beaten corporal, will you
march off? We have no need of your doctrine, though
you have of our charity. But at present we have no   30
scraps; we can afford no kindness for God's sake. In
fine, sirrah, the price is too high i'th' mouth° for you,
therefore troop, I say.

WILLMORE: Here, good forewoman of the shop, serve
me and I'll be gone.   35

MORETTA: Keep it to pay your laundress; your linen
stinks of the gun room. For here's no selling by retail.

WILLMORE: Thou hast sold plenty of thy stale ware at a
cheap rate.

MORETTA: Ay, the more silly kind heart I, but this is an   40
age wherein beauty is at higher rates. In fine, you
know the price of this.

WILLMORE: I grant you 'tis here set down, a thousand
crowns a month. Pray, how much may come to my
share for a pistole?° Bawd, take your black lead° and   45
sum it up, that I may have a pistole's worth of this
vain gay thing, and I'll trouble you no more.

MORETTA: Pox on him, he'll fret me to death! Abominable fellow, I tell thee we only sell by the whole
piece.   50

WILLMORE: 'Tis very hard, the whole cargo or nothing.
Faith, madam, my stock will not reach it; I cannot be
your chapman. Yet I have countrymen in town, merchants of love like me; I'll see if they'll put in for a
share. We cannot lose much by it, and what we have   55
no use for, we'll sell upon the Friday's mart at "Who
gives more?"—I am studying, madam, how to purchase you, though at present I am unprovided of
money.

ANGELLICA (*aside*): Sure this from any other man would   60
anger me; nor shall he know the conquest he has
made.—Poor angry man, how I despise this railing.

WILLMORE: Yes, I am poor. But I'm a gentleman,
And one that scorns this baseness which you practice.
Poor as I am I would not sell myself,   65
No, not to gain your charming high-prized person.
Though I admire you strangely for your beauty,
Yet I contemn your mind.
And yet I would at any rate enjoy you;

21. glass: Mirror.   26. Worcester: Charles II was routed by
Cromwell at Worcester in 1651 and was forced into exile on
the Continent.   32. high i'th' mouth: High.   44–45. how
much…pistole: How much will my pistole (a Spanish coin)
buy?   45. black lead: Pencil.

300. [S.D.] *stays him:* Keeps him from leaving.   308. patacoon: Portuguese or Spanish coin of small denomination.

70   At your own rate; but cannot. See here
      The only sum I can command on earth:
      I know not where to eat when this is gone.
      Yet such a slave I am to love and beauty
      This last reserve I'll sacrifice to enjoy you.
75   Nay, do not frown, I know you're to be bought,
      And would be bought by me. By me,
      For a meaning trifling sum, if I could pay it down.
      Which happy knowledge I will still repeat,
      And lay it to my heart: It has a virtue in't,
      And soon will cure those wounds your eyes have
80   made.
      And yet, there's something so divinely powerful
          there—
      Nay, I will gaze, to let you see my strength.

(*Holds her, looks on her, and pauses and sighs.*)

      By heav'n, bright creature, I would not for the world
      Thy fame were half so fair as is thy face.

(*Turns her away from him.*)

ANGELLICA (*aside*): His words go through me to the
85   very soul.—
      If you have nothing else to say to me—
WILLMORE: Yes, you shall hear how infamous you are—
      For which I do not hate thee—
      But that secures my heart, and all the flames it feels
90   Are but so many lusts:
      I know it by their sudden bold intrusion.
      The fire's impatient and betrays; 'tis false.
      For had it been the purer flame of love,
      I should have pined and languished at your feet,
95   Ere found the impudence to have discovered it.
      I now dare stand your scorn and your denial.
MORETTA: Sure she's bewitched, that she can stand thus
      tamely and hear his saucy railing.—Sirrah, will you
      be gone?
100 ANGELLICA (*to Moretta*): How dare you take this lib-
      erty! Withdraw!—Pray tell me, sir, are not you guilty
      of the same mercenary crime? When a lady is pro-
      posed to you for a wife, you never ask how fair, dis-
      creet, or virtuous she is, but what's her fortune;
105   which, if but small, you cry "She will not do my busi-
      ness," and basely leave her, though she languish for
      you. Say, is not this as poor?
WILLMORE: It is a barbarous custom, which I will scorn
      to defend in our sex, and do despise in yours.
ANGELLICA: Thou'rt a brave fellow! Put up thy gold,
110   and know,
      That were thy fortune as large as is thy soul,
      Thou shouldst not buy my love
      Couldst thou forget those mean effects of vanity
      Which set me out to sale,
115 And as a lover prize my yielding joys.
      Canst thou believe they'll be entirely thine,
      Without considering they were mercenary?
WILLMORE: I cannot tell, I must bethink me first.
      (*Aside.*) Ha! Death, I'm going to believe her.
ANGELLICA: Prithee confirm that faith, or if thou canst
120   not,

Jeremy Irons, as Willmore, and Sinéad Cusack, as Angellica,
in the Royal Shakespeare Company's 1986 production
directed by John Barton.

      Flatter me a little: 'Twill please me from thy mouth.
WILLMORE (*aside*): Curse on thy charming tongue!
          Dost thou return
      My feigned contempt with so much subtlety?—
      Thou'st found the easiest way into my heart,
      Though I yet know that all thou say'st is false.   125

(*Turning from her in rage.*)

ANGELLICA: By all that's good, 'tis real;
      I never loved before, though oft a mistress.
      Shall my first vows be slighted?
WILLMORE (*aside*): What can she mean?
ANGELLICA (*in an angry tone*): I find you cannot credit
      me.   130
WILLMORE: I know you take me for an errant ass,
      An ass that may be soothed into belief,
      And then be used at pleasure;
      But, madam, I have been so often cheated
      By perjured, soft, deluding hypocrites,   135
      That I've no faith left for the cozening sex,
      Especially for women of your trade.
ANGELLICA: The low esteem you have of me perhaps
      May bring my heart again:
      For I have pride that yet surmounts my love.   140

(*She turns with pride; he holds her.*)

WILLMORE: Throw off this pride, this enemy to bliss,
      And show the power of love: 'Tis with those arms
      I can be only vanquished, made a slave.

ANGELLICA: Is all my mighty expectation vanished?
145 No, I will not hear thee talk; thou hast a charm
     In every word that draws my heart away,
     And all the thousand trophies I designed
     Thou hast undone. Why art thou soft?
     Thy looks are bravely rough, and meant for war.
150 Couldst thou not storm on still?
     I then perhaps had been as free as thou.
WILLMORE (aside): Death, how she throws her fire
         about my soul!—
     Take heed, fair creature, how you raise my hopes,
     Which once assumed pretends to all dominion:
155 There's not a joy thou hast in store
     I shall not then command.
     For which I'll pay you back my soul, my life!
     Come, let's begin th'account this happy minute!
ANGELLICA: And will you pay me then the price I ask?
WILLMORE: Oh, why dost thou draw me from an
160   awful worship,
     By showing thou art no divinity.
     Conceal the fiend, and show me all the angel!
     Keep me but ignorant, and I'll be devout
     And pay my vows forever at this shrine.

(Kneels and kisses her hand.)

165 ANGELLICA: The pay I mean is but thy love for mine.
     Can you give that?
WILLMORE: Entirely. Come, let's withdraw where I'll
     renew my vows, and breathe 'em with such ardor
     thou shalt not doubt my zeal.
170 ANGELLICA: Thou hast a power too strong to be resisted.

         (Exeunt Willmore and Angellica.)

MORETTA: Now my curse go with you! Is all our project
     fallen to this? To love the only enemy to our trade?
     Nay, to love such a shameroon;° a very beggar; nay, a
     pirate beggar, whose business is to rifle and be gone;
175 a no-purchase, no-pay tatterdemalion,° and English
     picaroon;° a rogue that fights for daily drink, and
     takes a pride in being loyally lousy? Oh, I could curse
     now, if I durst. This is the fate of most whores.
         Trophies, which from believing fops we win,
180   *Are spoils to those who cozen us again.*   [Exit.]

ACT III • Scene I

(A street. Enter Florinda, Valeria, Hellena, in antic° different dresses from what they were in before; Callis
attending.)

FLORINDA: I wonder what should make my brother in so
     ill a humor? I hope he has not found out our ramble
     this morning.

HELLENA: No, if he had, we should have heard on't at
     both ears, and have been mewed up° this afternoon,   5
     which I would not for the world should have hap-
     pened. Hey ho, I'm as sad as a lover's lute.
VALERIA: Well, methinks we have learnt this trade of
     gypsies as readily as if we had been bred upon the
     road to Loretto;° and yet I did so fumble when I told   10
     the stranger his fortune that I was afraid I should
     have told my own and yours by mistake. But me-
     thinks Hellena has been very serious ever since.
FLORINDA: I would give my garters she were in love, to be
     revenged upon her for abusing me. How is't, Hellena?   15
HELLENA: Ah, would I had never seen my mad mon-
     sieur. And yet, for all your laughing, I am not in love.
     And yet this small acquaintance, o' my conscience,
     will never out of my head.
VALERIA: Ha! Ha! Ha! I laugh to think how thou art fit-   20
     ted with a lover, a fellow that I warrant loves every
     new face he sees.
HELLENA: Hum, he has not kept his word with me here,
     and may be taken up. That thought is not very pleas-
     ant to me. What the deuce should this be now that I   25
     feel?
VALERIA: What is't like?
HELLENA: Nay, the Lord knows, but if I should be
     hanged I cannot choose but be angry and afraid
     when I think that mad fellow should be in love with   30
     anybody but me. What to think of myself I know not:
     Would I could meet with some true damned gypsy,
     that I might know my fortune.
VALERIA: Know it! Why there's nothing so easy: Thou
     wilt love this wand'ring inconstant till thou find'st   35
     thyself hanged about his neck, and then be as mad to
     get free again.
FLORINDA: Yes, Valeria, we shall see her bestride his
     baggage horse and follow him to the campaign.
HELLENA: So, so, now you are provided for there's no   40
     care taken of poor me. But since you have set my
     heart a-wishing, I am resolved to know for what, I
     will not die of the pip,° so I will not.
FLORINDA: Art thou mad to talk so? Who will like thee
     well enough to have thee, that hears what a mad   45
     wench thou art?
HELLENA: Like me? I don't intend every he that likes me
     shall have me, but he that I like. I should have stayed
     in the nunnery still if I had liked my lady abbess as
     well as she liked me. No, I came thence not, as my   50
     wise brother imagines, to take an eternal farewell of
     the world, but to love and to be beloved; and I will be
     beloved, or I'll get one of your men, so I will.
VALERIA: Am I put into° the number of lovers?

---

173. **shameroon:** Shameful person. **175. tatterdemalion:**
Ragamuffin. **176. picaroon:** Wandering rogue. **III, I. [S.D.]**
antic: Absurd, ludicrous, strange.

5. **mewed up:** Shut in, imprisoned. **10. Loretto:** Loreto is an
Italian town on the Adriatic coast, a destination for pilgrims
visiting the cottage of the Virgin Mary. **43. pip:** A disease of
poultry and birds, applied vaguely, usually humorously, to various ailments in humans. **54. Am I put into:** Do you include
me among?

55 HELLENA: You? Why, coz, I know thou'rt too good-
natured to leave us in any design; thou wouldst venture a cast° though thou comest off a loser, especially
with such a gamester. I observed your man, and your
willing ear incline that way; and if you are not a
60 lover, 'tis an art soon learnt—that I find.   (*Sighs.*)
FLORINDA: I wonder how you learnt to love so easily. I
had a thousand charms to meet my eyes and ears ere I
could yield, and 'twas the knowledge of Belvile's
merit, not the surprising person, took my soul. Thou
65 art too rash, to give a heart at first sight.
HELLENA: Hang your considering lover! I never thought
beyond the fancy that 'twas a very pretty, idle, silly
kind of pleasure to pass one's time with: to write little
soft nonsensical billets,° and with great difficulty and
70 danger receive answers in which I shall have my
beauty praised, my wit admired, though little or
none, and have the vanity and power to know I am
desirable. Then I have the more inclination that way
because I am to be a nun, and so shall not be sus-
75 pected to have any such earthly thoughts about me;
but when I walk thus—and sigh thus—they'll think
my mind's upon my monastery, and cry, "How
happy 'tis she's so resolved." But not a word of man.
FLORINDA: What a mad creature's this!
80 HELLENA: I'll warrant, if my brother hears either of you
sigh, he cries gravely, "I fear you have the indiscretion to be in love, but take heed of the honor of our
house, and your own unspotted fame"; and so he
conjures on till he has laid the soft winged god in
85 your hearts, or broke the bird's nest.° But see, here
comes your lover, but where's my inconstant? Let's
step aside, and we may learn something.
(*Go aside.*)

(*Enter Belvile, Frederick, and Blunt.*)

BELVILE: What means this! The picture's taken in.
BLUNT: It may be the wench is good-natured, and will be
90 kind gratis.° Your friend's a proper handsome fellow.
BELVILE: I rather think she has cut his throat and is fled;
I am mad he should throw himself into dangers. Pox
on't, I shall want him, too, at night. Let's knock and
ask for him.
95 HELLENA: My heart goes a-pit, a-pat, for fear 'tis my
man they talk of.
(*Knock; Moretta above.*)
MORETTA: What would you have?
BELVILE: Tell the stranger that entered here about two
hours ago that his friends stay here for him.
100 MORETTA: A curse upon him for Moretta: Would he
were at the devil! But he's coming to you.

(*Enter Willmore.*)

HELLENA: Ay, ay 'tis he. Oh, how this vexes me!

BELVILE: And how and how, dear lad, has fortune
smiled? Are we to break her windows, or raise up
altars to her, hah?   105
WILLMORE: Does not my fortune sit triumphant on my
brow? Dost not see the little wanton god there all gay
and smiling? Have I not an air about my face and
eyes that distinguish me from the crowd of common
lovers? By heaven, Cupid's quiver has not half so   110
many darts as her eyes! Oh, such a *bona roba*!° To
sleep in her arms is lying *in fresco*,° all perfumed air
about me.
HELLENA (*aside*): Here's fine encouragement for me to
fool on!   115
WILLMORE: Hark'ee, where didst thou purchase that
rich Canary° we drank today? Tell me, that I may
adore the spigot and sacrifice to the butt.° The juice
was divine; into which I must dip my rosary, and
then bless all things that I would have bold or fortu-   120
nate.
BELVILE: Well, sir, let's go take a bottle and hear the
story of your success.
FREDERICK: Would not French wine do better?
WILLMORE: Damn the hungry balderdash!° Cheerful   125
sack° has a generous virtue in't inspiring a successful
confidence, gives eloquence to the tongue and vigor
to the soul, and has in a few hours completed all my
hopes and wishes! There's nothing left to raise a new
desire in me. Come, let's be gay and wanton. And,   130
gentlemen, study; study what you want, for here are
friends that will supply gentlemen. [*Jingles gold.*]
Hark what a charming sound they make! 'Tis he and
she gold whilst here, and shall beget new pleasures
every moment.   135
BLUNT: But hark'ee, sir, you are not married, are you?
WILLMORE: All the honey of matrimony but none of the
sting, friend.
BLUNT: 'Adsheartlikins, thou'rt a fortunate rogue!
WILLMORE: I am so, sir: let these inform you! Ha, how   140
sweetly they chime! Pox of poverty: It makes a man a
slave, makes wit and honor sneak. My soul grew lean
and rusty for want of credit.
BLUNT: 'Adsheartlikins, this I like well; it looks like my
lucky bargain! Oh, how I long for the approach of   145
my squire, that is to conduct me to her house again.
Why, here's two provided for!
FREDERICK: By this light, y'are happy men.
BLUNT: Fortune is pleased to smile on us, gentlemen, to
smile on us.   150

(*Enter Sancho and pulls down Blunt by the sleeve; they
go aside.*)

SANCHO: Sir, my lady expects you. She has removed all
that might oppose your will and pleasure, and is impatient till you come.

56–57. **venture a cast:** Throw the dice.   69. **billets:** Brief letters, notes.   84–85. **laid...bird's nest:** Ruined your chances.
90. **gratis:** Free of charge.   111. *bona roba:* A courtesan.   112. *in fresco:* In the fresh air out
of doors.   117. **Canary:** A light sweet wine from the Canary
Islands.   118. **butt:** Large wine cask.   125. **hungry balderdash:**
Cheap mixture of liquor.   126. **sack:** Dry white Spanish wine.

BLUNT: Sir, I'll attend you.—Oh the happiest rogue! I'll
155 take no leave, lest they either dog me or stay me.
                                        (*Exit with Sancho.*)
BELVILE: But then the little gypsy is forgot?
WILLMORE: A mischief on thee for putting her into my
     thoughts! I had quite forgot her else, and this night's
     debauch had drunk her quite down.
160 HELLENA: Had it so, good captain!

(*Claps him on the back.*)

WILLMORE (*aside*): Ha! I hope she did not hear me!
HELLENA: What, afraid of such a champion?
WILLMORE: Oh, you're a fine lady of your word, are you
     not? To make a man languish a whole day—
165 HELLENA: In tedious search of me.
WILLMORE: Egad, child, thou'rt in the right. Hadst thou
     seen what a melancholy dog I have been ever since I
     was a lover, how I have walked the streets like a
     Capuchin,° with my hands in my sleeves—faith,
170 sweetheart, thou wouldst pity me.
HELLENA [*aside*]: Now if I should be hanged I can't be
     angry with him, he dissembles so heartily.—Alas,
     good captain, what pains you have taken; now were I
     ungrateful not to reward so true a servant.
175 WILLMORE: Poor soul, that's kindly said; I see thou
     barest a conscience. Come then, for a beginning
     show me thy dear face.
HELLENA: I'm afraid, my small acquaintance, you have
     been staying that swinging stomach you boasted of
180 this morning. I then remember my little collation°
     would have gone down with you without the sauce
     of a handsome face. Is your stomach so queasy now?
WILLMORE: Faith, long fasting, child, spoils a man's
     appetite. Yet if you durst treat, I could so lay about
185 me still—
HELLENA: And would you fall to before a priest says
     grace?
WILLMORE: O fie, fie, what an old out-of-fashioned
     thing hast thou named? Thou couldst not dash me
190 more out of countenance shouldst thou show me an
     ugly face.

(*Whilst he is seemingly courting Hellena, enter Angellica, Moretta, Biskey, and Sebastian, all in masquerade.
Angellica sees Willmore and stares.*)

ANGELLICA: Heavens, 'tis he! And passionately fond to
     see another woman!
MORETTA: What could you less expect from such a
195 swaggerer?
ANGELLICA: Expect? As much as I paid him: a heart
        entire,
     Which I had pride enough to think when'er I gave,
     It would have raised the man above the vulgar,
     Made him all soul, and that all soft and constant.
200 HELLENA: You see, captain, how willing I am to be
     friends with you, till time and ill luck make us lovers;
     and ask you the question first rather than put your

169. **Capuchin:** Franciscan monk.   180. **collation:** Snack.

modesty to the blush by asking me. For alas, I know
you captains are such strict men, and such severe
observers of your vows to chastity, that 'twill be hard   205
to prevail with your tender conscience to marry a
young willing maid.
WILLMORE: Do not abuse me, for fear I should take thee
     at thy word and marry thee indeed, which I'm sure
     will be revenge sufficient.   210
HELLENA: O' my conscience, that will be our destiny,
     because we are both of one humor: I am as incon-
     stant as you, for I have considered, captain, that a
     handsome woman has a great deal to do whilst her
     face is good. For then is our harvest-time to gather   215
     friends, and should I in these days of my youth catch
     a fit of foolish constancy, I were undone: 'tis loitering
     by daylight in our great journey. Therefore, I declare
     I'll allow but one year for love, one year for indiffer-
     ence, and one year for hate; and then go hang your-   220
     self, for I profess myself the gay, the kind, and the
     inconstant. The devil's in't if this won't please you!
WILLMORE: Oh, most damnably. I have a heart with a
     hole quite through it too; no prison mine, to keep a
     mistress in.   225
ANGELLICA (*aside*): Perjured man! How I believe thee
     now!
HELLENA: Well, I see our business as well as humors are
     alike: yours to cozen as many maids as will trust you,
     and I as many men as have faith. See if I have not as   230
     desperate a lying look as you can have for the heart
     of you. (*Pulls off her vizard; he starts.*) How do you
     like it, captain?
WILLMORE: Like it! By heaven, I never saw so much
     beauty! Oh, the charms of those sprightly black eyes!   235
     That strangely fair face, full of smiles and dimples!
     Those soft round melting cherry lips and small even
     white teeth! Not to be expressed, but silently adored!
     [*She replaces her mask.*] Oh, one look more, and strike
     me dumb, or I shall repeat nothing else till I'm mad.   240

(*He seems to court her to pull off her vizard; she refuses.*)

ANGELLICA: I can endure no more. Nor is it fit to inter-
     rupt him, for if I do, my jealousy has so destroyed my
     reason I shall undo him. Therefore I'll retire, and you,
     Sebastian (*to one of her Bravos*), follow that woman
     and learn who 'tis; while you (*to the other Bravo*) tell   245
     the fugitive I would speak to him instantly.   (*Exit.*)

(*This while Florinda is talking to Belvile, who stands
sullenly; Frederick courting Valeria.*)

VALERIA [*to Belvile*]: Prithee, dear stranger, be not so
     sullen, for though you have lost your love you see my
     friend frankly offers you hers to play with in the
     meantime.   250
BELVILE: Faith, madam, I am sorry I can't play at her
     game.
FREDERICK [*to Valeria*]: Pray leave your intercession and
     mind your own affair. They'll better agree apart: He's
     a modest sigher in company, but alone no woman   255
     'scapes him.

FLORINDA [*aside*]: Sure he does but rally. Yet, if it should be true? I'll tempt him farther.—Believe me, noble stranger, I'm no common mistress. And for a little
260 proof on't, wear this jewel.° Nay, take it, sir, 'tis right, and bills of exchange may sometimes miscarry.

BELVILE: Madam, why am I chose out of all mankind to be the object of your bounty?

VALERIA: There's another civil question asked.

265 FREDERICK [*aside*]: Pox of's modesty; it spoils his own markets and hinders mine.

FLORINDA: Sir, from my window I have often seen you, and women of my quality have so few opportunities for love that we ought to lose none.

270 FREDERICK [*to Valeria*]: Ay, this is something! Here's a woman! When shall I be blest with so much kindness from your fair mouth?—(*Aside to Belvile.*) Take the jewel, fool!

BELVILE: You tempt me strangely, madam, every way—

275 FLORINDA (*aside*): So, if I find him false, my whole repose is gone.

BELVILE: And but for a vow I've made to a very fair lady, this goodness had subdued me.

FREDERICK [*aside to Belvile*]: Pox on't, be kind, in pity
280 to me be kind. For I am to thrive here but as you treat her friend.

HELLENA: Tell me what you did in yonder house, and I'll unmask.

WILLMORE: Yonder house? Oh, I went to a—to—why,
285 there's a friend of mine lives there.

HELLENA: What, a she or a he friend?

WILLMORE: A man, upon honor, a man. A she friend? No, no, madam, you have done my business, I thank you.

290 HELLENA: And was't your man friend that had more darts in's eyes than Cupid carries in's whole budget of arrows?

WILLMORE: So—

HELLENA: "Ah, such a *bona roba*! To be in her arms is
295 lying *in fresco*, all perfumed air about me." Was this your man friend too?

WILLMORE: So—

HELLENA: That gave you the he and the she gold, that begets young pleasures?

300 WILLMORE: Well, well, madam, then you can see there are ladies in the world that will not be cruel. There are, madam, there are.

HELLENA: And there be men, too, as fine, wild, inconstant fellows as yourself. There be, captain, there be,
305 if you go to that now. Therefore, I'm resolved—

WILLMORE: Oh!

HELLENA: To see your face no more—

WILLMORE: Oh!

HELLENA: Till tomorrow.

310 WILLMORE: Egad, you frighted me.

HELLENA: Nor then neither, unless you'll swear never to see that lady more.

260. jewel: A locket with her picture in it.

WILLMORE: See her! Why, never to think of womankind again.

HELLENA: Kneel and swear.   315

(*Kneels, she gives him her hand.*)

WILLMORE: I do, never to think, to see, to love, nor lie, with any but thyself.

HELLENA: Kiss the book.

WILLMORE: Oh, most religiously.   (*Kisses her hand.*)

HELLENA: Now what a wicked creature am I, to damn a   320
proper fellow.

CALLIS (*to Florinda*): Madam, I'll stay no longer: 'tis e'en dark.

FLORINDA [*to Belvile*]: However, sir, I'll leave this with you, that when I'm gone you may repent the oppor-   325
tunity you have lost by your modesty.

(*Gives him the jewel, which is her picture, and exit.
He gazes after her.*)

WILLMORE [*to Hellena*]: 'Twill be an age till tomorrow, and till then I will most impatiently expect you. Adieu, my dear pretty angel.

(*Exeunt all the women.*)

BELVILE: Ha! Florinda's picture! 'Twas she herself. What   330
a dull dog was I! I would have given the world for one minute's discourse with her.

FREDERICK: This comes of your modesty. Ah, pox o' your vow; 'twas ten to one but we had lost the jewel by't.

BELVILE: Willmore, the blessed'st opportunity lost!   335
Florinda, friends, Florinda!

WILLMORE: Ah, rogue! Such black eyes! Such a face! Such a mouth! Such teeth! And so much wit!

BELVILE: All, all, and a thousand charms besides.

WILLMORE: Why, dost thou know her?   340

BELVILE: Know her! Ay, ay, and a pox take me with all my heart for being so modest.

WILLMORE: But hark'ee, friend of mine, are you my rival? And have I been only beating the bush all this while?

BELVILE: I understand thee not. I'm mad! See here—   345

(*Shows the picture.*)

WILLMORE: Ha! Whose picture's this? 'Tis a fine wench!

FREDERICK: The colonel's mistress, sir.

WILLMORE: Oh, oh, here. (*Gives the picture back.*) I thought't had been another prize. Come, come, a bottle will set thee right again.   350

BELVILE: I am content to try, and by that time 'twill be late enough for our design.

WILLMORE: Agreed.
       Love does all day the soul's great empire keep,
       But wine at night lulls the soft god asleep.   355

(*Exeunt.*)

Scene II

(*Lucetta's house. Enter Blunt and Lucetta with a light.*)

LUCETTA: Now we are safe and free: no fears of the coming home of my old jealous husband, which made me a little thoughtful when you came in first. But now love is all the business of my soul.

5 BLUNT: I am transported! — (*Aside.*) Pox on't, that I had but some fine things to say to her, such as lovers use. I was a fool not to learn of Fred a little by heart before I came. Something I must say. 'Adsheartlikins, sweet soul, I am not used to compliment, but I'm an honest gentleman, and thy humble servant.

10 LUCETTA: I have nothing to pay for so great a favor, but such a love as cannot but be great, since at first sight of that sweet face and shape it made me your absolute captive.

15 BLUNT (*aside*): Kind heart, how prettily she talks! Egad, I'll show her husband a Spanish trick: Send him out of the world and marry her; she's damnably in love with me, and will ne'er mind settlements,° and so there's that saved.

20 LUCETTA: Well, sir, I'll go and undress me, and be with you instantly.

BLUNT: Make haste then, for 'adsheartlikins, dear soul, thou canst not guess at the pain of a longing lover when his joys are drawn within the compass of a few minutes.

25 LUCETTA: You speak my sense, and I'll make haste to prove it.   (*Exit.*)

BLUNT: 'Tis a rare girl, and this one night's enjoyment with her will be worth all the days I ever passed in Essex. Would she would go with me into England, though to say truth, there's plenty of whores already. Put a pox on 'em, they are such mercenary prodigal whores that they want such a one as this, that's free and generous, to give 'em good examples. Why, what a house she has, how rich and fine!

35

(*Enter Sancho.*)

SANCHO: Sir, my lady has sent me to conduct you to her chamber.

BLUNT: Sir, I shall be proud to follow. — (*Aside.*) Here's one of her servants too; 'adsheartlikins, by this garb and gravity he might be a justice of peace in Essex, and is but a pimp here.

40

(*Exeunt.*)

Scene III

(*The scene changes to a chamber with an alcove bed in't, a table, etc.; Lucetta in bed. Enter Sancho and Blunt, who takes the candle of Sancho at the door.*)

SANCHO: Sir, my commission reaches no farther.

BLUNT: Sir, I'll excuse your compliment.

[*Exit Sancho.*]

—What, in bed, my sweet mistress?

LUCETTA: You see, I still outdo you in kindness.

5 BLUNT: And thou shalt see what haste I'll make to quit scores. Oh, the luckiest rogue!

18. will ne'er mind settlements: Won't require the gifts of property usually settled on a wife after marriage.

(*He undresses himself.*)

LUCETTA: Should you be false or cruel now—

BLUNT: False! 'Adsheartlikins, what dost thou take me for, a Jew? An insensible heathen? A pox of thy old jealous husband: An° he were dead, egad, sweet soul, it should be none of my fault if I did not marry thee.

10

LUCETTA: It never should be mine.

BLUNT: Good soul! I'm the fortunatest dog!

LUCETTA: Are you not undressed yet?

BLUNT: As much as my impatience will permit.

15

(*Goes toward the bed in his shirt, drawers, etc.*)

LUCETTA: Hold, sir, put out the light; it may betray us else.

BLUNT: Anything; I need no other light but that of thine eyes. — (*Aside.*) 'Adsheartlikins, there I think I had it.

(*Puts out the candle; the bed descends; he gropes about to find it.*)

Why, why, where am I got? What, not yet? Where are you, sweetest? — Ah, the rogue's silent now. A pretty love-trick this; how she'll laugh at me anon! — You need not, my dear rogue, you need not! I'm all on fire already; come, come, now call me, in pity. — Sure I'm enchanted! I have been round the chamber, and can find neither woman nor bed. I locked the door; I'm sure she cannot go that way, or if she could, the bed could not. — Enough, enough, my pretty wanton; do not carry the jest too far! (*Lights on a trap, and is let down.*) — Ha! Betrayed! Dogs! Rogues! Pimps! Help! Help!

20

25

30

(*Enter Lucetta, Philippo, and Sancho with a light.*)

PHILIPPO: Ha! Ha! Ha! He's dispatched finely.

LUCETTA: Now, sir, had I been coy, we had missed of this booty.

PHILIPPO: Nay, when I saw 'twas a substantial fool, I was mollified. But when you dote upon a serenading coxcomb, upon a face, fine clothes, and a lute, it makes me rage.

35

LUCETTA: You know I was never guilty of that folly, my dear Philippo, but with yourself. But come, let's see what we have got by this.

40

PHILIPPO: A rich coat; sword and hat; these breeches, too, are well lined! See here, a gold watch! A purse— Ha! Gold! At least two hundred pistoles! A bunch of diamond rings, and one with the family arms! A gold box, with a medal of his king, and his lady mother's picture! These were sacred relics, believe me. See, the waistband of his breeches have a mine of gold—old queen Bess's!° We have a quarrel to her ever since eighty-eight,° and may therefore justify the theft: The Inquisition might have committed it.

45

50

LUCETTA: See, a bracelet of bowed gold! These his sisters tied about his arm at parting. But well, for all this, I

10. An: If.   **48–49. old queen Bess's:** Queen Elizabeth I (reigned 1558–1603).   **50. eighty-eight:** The year the Spanish Armada was defeated by the English (1588).

55 fear his being a stranger may make a noise and hinder our trade with them hereafter.

PHILIPPO: That's our security: He is not only a stranger to us, but to the country too. The common shore° into which he is descended, thou know'st, conducts him into another street, which this light will hinder
60 him from ever finding again. He knows neither your name, nor that of the street where your house is; nay, nor the way to his own lodgings.

LUCETTA: And art thou not an unmerciful rogue, not to afford him one night for all this? I should not have
65 been such a Jew.

PHILIPPO: Blame me not, Lucetta, to keep as much of thee as I can to myself. Come, that thought makes me wanton; let's to bed. — Sancho, lock up these.

This is the fleece which fools do bear,
70 *Designed for witty men to shear.*   (*Exeunt.*)

Scene IV

(*The scene changes, and discovers Blunt creeping out of a common shore; his face, etc., all dirty.*)

BLUNT (*climbing up*): Oh, Lord, I am got out at last, and, which is a miracle, without a clue. And now to damning and cursing! But if that would ease me, where shall I begin? With my fortune, myself, or the
5 quean° that cozened me? What a dog was I to believe in woman! Oh, coxcomb! Ignorant conceited coxcomb! To fancy she could be enamored with my person! At first sight enamored! Oh, I'm a cursed puppy! 'Tis plain, fool was writ upon my forehead! She per-
10 ceived it; saw the Essex calf there. For what allurements could there be in this countenance, which I can endure because I'm acquainted with it. Oh dull, silly dog, to be thus soothed into a cozening! Had I been drunk, I might fondly have credited the young quean;
15 but as I was in my right wits to be thus cheated, confirms it: I am a dull believing English country fop. But my comrades! Death and the devil, there's the worst of all! Then a ballad will be sung tomorrow on the Prado,° to a lousy tune of the enchanted squire and
20 the annihilated damsel. But Fred — that rogue — and the colonel will abuse me beyond all Christian patience. Had she left me my clothes, I have a bill of exchange at home would have saved my credit. But now all hope is taken from me. Well, I'll home, if I
25 can find the way, with this consolation: that I am not the first kind believing coxcomb; but there are, gallants, many such good natures amongst ye.

And though you've better arts to hide your follies,
'Adsheartlikins, y'are all as errant cullies.°
(*Exit.*)

57. **common shore:** Sewer. 5. **quean:** Harlot, tramp.
18–19. **ballad…Prado:** A song satirizing him will be sung on the Prado, a fashionable promenade in Madrid, for common amusement. 29. *cullies:* A cully is one easily fooled; a simpleton.

Scene V

(*Scene: the garden in the night. Enter Florinda in an undress,° with a key and a little box.*)

FLORINDA: Well, thus far I'm in my way to happiness. I have got myself free from Callis; my brother too, I find by yonder light, is got into his cabinet,° and thinks not of me; I have by good fortune got the key of the garden back door. I'll open it to prevent
5 Belvile's knocking: A little noise will now alarm my brother. Now am I as fearful as a young thief. (*Unlocks the door.*) Hark! What noise is that? Oh, 'twas the wind that played amongst the boughs. Belvile stays long, methinks; it's time. Stay, for fear of
10 a surprise, I'll hide these jewels in yonder jasmine.

(*She goes to lay down the box.*)

(*Enter Willmore, drunk.*)

WILLMORE: What the devil is become of these fellows Belvile and Frederick? They promised to stay at the next corner for me, but who the devil knows the corner of a full moon? Now, whereabouts am I? Ha,
15 what have we here? A garden! A very convenient place to sleep in. Ha! What has God sent us here? A female! By this light, a woman! I'm a dog if it be not a very wench!

FLORINDA: He's come! Ha! Who's there?
20

WILLMORE: Sweet soul, let me salute thy shoestring.

FLORINDA [*aside*]: 'Tis not my Belvile. Good heavens, I know him not! — Who are you, and from whence come you?

WILLMORE: Prithee, prithee, child, not so many hard
25 questions! Let it suffice I am here, child. Come, come kiss me.

FLORINDA: Good gods! What luck is mine?

WILLMORE: Only good luck, child, parlous° good luck. Come hither. — 'Tis a delicate shining wench. By this
30 hand, she's perfumed, and smells like any nosegay. — Prithee, dear soul, let's not play the fool and lose time — precious time. For as Gad shall save me, I'm as honest a fellow as breathes, though I'm a little disguised° at present. Come, I say. Why, thou mayst be
35 free with me: I'll be very secret. I'll not boast who 'twas obliged me, not I; for hang me if I know thy name.

FLORINDA: Heavens! What a filthy beast is this!

WILLMORE: I am so, and thou ought'st the sooner to lie
40 with me for that reason. For look you, child, there will be no sin in't, because 'twas neither designed nor premeditated: 'Tis pure accident on both sides. That's a certain thing now. Indeed, should I make love to you, and you vow fidelity, and swear and lie till you
45 believed and yielded — that were to make it willful fornication, the crying sin of the nation. Thou art,

III, V. [S.D.] *undress:* Undergarment. 3. **cabinet:** Private room. 29. **parlous:** Excessively, with pun on *perilous*. 34–35. **disguised:** I.e., by liquor.

therefore, as thou art a good Christian, obliged in conscience to deny me nothing. Now, come be kind
50   without any more idle prating.

FLORINDA: Oh, I am ruined! Wicked man, unhand me!

WILLMORE: Wicked? Egad, child, a judge, were he young and vigorous, and saw those eyes of thine, would know 'twas they gave the first blow, the first
55   provocation. Come, prithee let's lose no time, I say. This is a fine convenient place.

FLORINDA: Sir, let me go, I conjure° you, or I'll call out.

WILLMORE: Ay, ay, you were best to call witness to see how finely you treat me. Do!

60   FLORINDA: I'll cry murder, rape, or anything, if you do not instantly let me go!

WILLMORE: A rape? Come, come, you lie, you baggage, you lie. What! I'll warrant you would fain have the world believe now that you are not so forward as
65   I. No, not you. Why at this time of night was your cobweb door set open, dear spider, but to catch flies? Ha! Come, or I shall be damnably angry. Why, what a coil° is here!

FLORINDA: Sir, can you think—

70   WILLMORE: That you would do't for nothing? Oh, oh, I find what you would be at. Look here, here's a pistole for you. Here's a work indeed! Here, take it, I say!

FLORINDA: For heaven's sake, sir, as you're a gentleman—

75   WILLMORE: So now, now, she would be wheedling me for more! What, you will not take it then? You are resolved you will not? Come, come, take it or I'll put it up again, for look ye, I never give more. Why, how now, mistress, are you so high i'th' mouth a pistole
80   won't down with you? Ha! Why, what a work's here! In good time! Come, no struggling to be gone. But an y'are good at a dumb wrestle, I'm for ye. Look ye, I'm for ye.   (*She struggles with him.*)

(*Enter Belvile and Frederick.*)

BELVILE: The door is open. A pox of this mad fellow!
85   I'm angry that we've lost him; I durst have sworn he had followed us.

FREDERICK: But you were so hasty, colonel, to be gone.

FLORINDA: Help! Help! Murder! Help! Oh, I am ruined!

BELVILE: Ha! Sure that's Florinda's voice! (*Comes up to
90   them.*) A man!—Villain, let go that lady!

(*A noise; Willmore turns and draws; Frederick interposes.*)

FLORINDA: Belvile! Heavens! My brother too is coming, and 'twill be impossible to escape. Belvile, I conjure you to walk under my chamber window, from whence I'll give you some instructions what to do.
95   This rude man has undone us.   (*Exit.*)

WILLMORE: Belvile!

(*Enter Pedro, Stephano, and other servants, with lights.*)

PEDRO: I'm betrayed! Run, Stephano, and see if Florinda be safe.
                                        (*Exit Stephano.*)

(*They fight, and Pedro's party beats 'em out.*)

—So, whoe'er they be, all is not well. I'll to Florinda's chamber.   (*Going out, meets Stephano.*)   100

STEPHANO: You need not, sir: The poor lady's fast asleep, and thinks no harm. I would not awake her, sir, for fear of frighting her with your danger.

PEDRO: I'm glad she's there.—Rascals, how came the garden door open?   105

STEPHANO: That question comes too late, sir. Some of my fellow servants masquerading, I'll warrant.

PEDRO: Masquerading! A lewd custom to debauch our youth! There's something more in this than I imagine.
                                        (*Exeunt.*)

Scene VI

(*Scene changes to the street. Enter Belvile in rage, Frederick holding him, Willmore melancholy.*)

WILLMORE: Why, how the devil should I know Florinda?

BELVILE: Ah, plague of your ignorance! If it had not been Florinda, must you be a beast? A brute? A senseless swine?

WILLMORE: Well, sir, you see I am endued° with patience: I can bear. Though egad, y'are very free with   5
me, methinks. I was in good hopes the quarrel would have been on my side, for so uncivilly interrupting me.

BELVILE: Peace, brute, whilst thou'rt safe. Oh, I'm distracted!   10

WILLMORE: Nay, nay, I'm an unlucky dog, that's certain.

BELVILE: Ah, curse upon the star that ruled my birth, or whatsoever other influence that makes me still so wretched.   15

WILLMORE: Thou break'st my heart with these complaints. There is no star in fault, no influence but sack, the cursed sack I drunk.

FREDERICK: Why, how the devil came you so drunk?

WILLMORE: Why, how the devil came you so sober?   20

BELVILE: A curse upon his thin skull, he was always beforehand that way.

FREDERICK: Prithee, dear colonel, forgive him; he's sorry for his fault.

BELVILE: He's always so after he has done a mischief. A   25
plague on all such brutes!

WILLMORE: By this light, I took her for an errant harlot.

BELVILE: Damn your debauched opinion! Tell me, sot, hadst thou so much sense and light about thee to distinguish her woman, and couldst not see something   30
about her face and person to strike an awful reverence into thy soul?

---

57. conjure: Entreat, implore.   **68. coil:** Noisy disturbance.   **5. endued:** Endowed.

WILLMORE: Faith no, I considered her as mere a woman
as I could wish.

35 BELVILE: 'Sdeath, I have no patience. Draw, or I'll kill
you!

WILLMORE: Let that alone till tomorrow, and if I set not
all right again, use your pleasure.

BELVILE: Tomorrow! Damn it,

40 The spiteful light will lead me to no happiness.
Tomorrow is Antonio's, and perhaps
Guides him to my undoing. Oh, that I could meet
This rival, this powerful fortunate!

WILLMORE: What then?

45 BELVILE: Let thy own reason, or my rage, instruct thee.

WILLMORE: I shall be finely informed then, no doubt.
Hear me, colonel, hear me; show me the man and I'll
do his business.

BELVILE: I know him no more than thou, or if I did I
50 should not need thy aid.

WILLMORE: This you say is Angellica's house; I promised the kind baggage to lie with her tonight.

(*Offers to go in.*)

(*Enter Antonio and his Page. Antonio knocks on the hilt
of's sword.*)

ANTONIO: You paid the thousand crowns I directed?

PAGE: To the lady's old woman, sir, I did.

55 WILLMORE: Who the devil have we here?

BELVILE: I'll now plant myself under Florinda's window,
and if I find no comfort there, I'll die.

(*Exeunt Belvile and Frederick.*)

(*Enter Moretta.*)

MORETTA: Page?

PAGE: Here's my lord.

60 WILLMORE: How is this? A picaroon going to board my
frigate? — Here's one chase gun for you!

(*Drawing his sword, justles Antonio, who turns and
draws. They fight; Antonio falls.*)

MORETTA: Oh, bless us! We're all undone!

(*Runs in and shuts the door.*)

PAGE: Help! Murder!

(*Belvile returns at the noise of fighting.*)

BELVILE: Ha! The mad rogue's engaged in some unlucky
65 adventure again.

(*Enter two or three Masqueraders.*)

MASQUERADER: Ha! A man killed!

WILLMORE: How, a man killed? Then I'll go home to
sleep.

(*Puts up and reels out. Exeunt Masqueraders another
way.*)

BELVILE: Who should it be? Pray heaven the rogue is
70 safe, for all my quarrel to him.

(*As Belvile is groping about, enter an Officer and six
Soldiers.*)

SOLDIER: Who's there?

OFFICER: So, here's one dispatched. Secure the murderer.

BELVILE: Do not mistake my charity for murder! I came
to his assistance!   (*Soldiers sieze on Belvile.*)   75

OFFICER: That shall be tried, sir. St. Jago! Swords drawn
in the Carnival time!   (*Goes to Antonio.*)

ANTONIO: Thy hand, prithee.

OFFICER: Ha! Don Antonio! Look well to the villain
there. — How is it, sir?   80

ANTONIO: I'm hurt.

BELVILE: Has my humanity made me a criminal?

OFFICER: Away with him!

BELVILE: What a curst chance is this!

(*Exeunt soldiers with Belvile.*)

ANTONIO [*aside*]: This is the man that has set upon me   85
twice. — (*To the officer.*) Carry him to my apartment
till you have further orders from me.

(*Exit Antonio, led.*)

ACT IV • *Scene* I

(*A fine room. Discovers Belvile as by dark alone.*)

BELVILE: When shall I be weary of railing on fortune,
who is resolved never to turn with smiles upon me?
Two such defeats in one night none but the devil and
that mad rogue could have contrived to have plagued
me with. I am here a prisoner. But where, heaven   5
knows. And if there be murder done, I can soon
decide the fate of a stranger in a nation without
mercy. Yet this is nothing to the torture my soul bows
with when I think of losing my fair, my dear
Florinda. Hark, my door opens. A light! A man, and   10
seems of quality. Armed, too! Now shall I die like a
dog, without defense.

(*Enter Antonio in a nightgown, with a light; his arm in a
scarf, and a sword under his arm. He sets the candle on
the table.*)

ANTONIO: Sir, I come to know what injuries I have done
you, that could provoke you to so mean an action as
to attack me basely without allowing time for my   15
defense?

BELVILE: Sir, for a man in my circumstances to plead
innocence would look like fear. But view me well,
and you will find no marks of coward on me, nor
anything that betrays that brutality you accuse me   20
with.

ANTONIO: In vain, sir, you impose upon my sense. You
are not only he who drew on me last night, but yesterday before the same house, that of Angellica. Yet
there is something in your face and mien° that makes   25
me wish I were mistaken.

25. mien: Demeanor, appearance.

BELVILE: I own I fought today in the defense of a friend of mine with whom you, if you're the same, and your party were first engaged. Perhaps you think this
30   crime enough to kill me; but if you do, I cannot fear you'll do it basely.

ANTONIO: No sir, I'll make you fit for a defense with this.   (*Gives him the sword.*)

BELVILE: This gallantry surprises me, nor know I how to
35   use this present, sir, against a man so brave.

ANTONIO: You shall not need. For know, I come to snatch you from a danger that is decreed against you: perhaps your life, or long imprisonment. And 'twas with so much courage you offended, I cannot see you
40   punished.

BELVILE: How shall I pay this generosity?

ANTONIO: It had been safer to have killed another than have attempted me. To show your danger, sir, I'll let you know my quality: And 'tis the Viceroy's son
45   whom you have wounded.

BELVILE: The Viceroy's son! — (*Aside.*) Death and confusion! Was this plague reserved to complete all the rest? Obliged by° him, the man of all the world I would destroy!

50 ANTONIO: You seem disordered, sir.

BELVILE: Yes, trust me, I am, and 'tis with pain that man receives such bounties who wants the power to pay 'em back again.

ANTONIO: To gallant spirits 'tis indeed uneasy, but you
55   may quickly overpay me, sir.

BELVILE (*aside*): Then I am well. Kind heaven, but set us even, that I may fight with him and keep my honor safe. — Oh, I'm impatient, sir, to be discounting the mighty debt I owe you. Command me quickly.

60 ANTONIO: I have a quarrel with a rival, sir, about the maid we love.

BELVILE (*aside*): Death, 'tis Florinda he means! That thought destroys my reason, and I shall kill him.

ANTONIO: My rival, sir, is one has all the virtues man
65   can boast of —

BELVILE (*aside*): Death, who should this be?

ANTONIO: He challenged me to meet him on the Molo as soon as day appeared, but last night's quarrel has made my arm unfit to guide a sword.

70 BELVILE: I apprehend you, sir. You'd have me kill the man that lays a claim to the maid you speak of. I'll do't. I'll fly to do't!

ANTONIO: Sir, do you know her?

BELVILE: No, sir, but 'tis enough she is admired by you.

75 ANTONIO: Sir, I shall rob you of the glory on't, for you must fight under my name and dress.

BELVILE: That opinion must be strangely obliging that makes you think I can personate the brave Antonio, whom I can but strive to imitate.

80 ANTONIO: You say too much to my advantage. Come, sir, the day appears that calls you forth. Within, sir, is the habit.°   (*Exit Antonio.*)

48. Obliged by: Favored by.   **82. habit:** Antonio's clothing.

BELVILE: Fantastic fortune, thou deceitful light,
That cheats the wearied traveler by night,
Though on a precipice each step you tread,   85
I am resolved to follow where you lead.   (*Exit.*)

Scene II

(*The Molo. Enter Florinda and Callis in masks, with Stephano.*)

FLORINDA (*aside*): I'm dying with my fears: Belvile's not coming as I expected under my window makes me believe that all those fears are true. — Canst thou not tell with whom my brother fights?

STEPHANO: No, madam, they were both in masquerade.   5
I was by when they challenged one another, and they had decided the quarrel then, but were prevented by some cavaliers; which made 'em put it off till now. But I am sure 'tis about you they fight.

FLORINDA (*aside*): Nay, then, 'tis with Belvile, for what   10
other lover have I that dares fight for me except Antonio, and he is too much in favor with my brother. If it be he, for whom shall I direct my prayers to heaven?

STEPHANO: Madam, I must leave you, for if my master see me, I shall be hanged for being your conductor. I   15
escaped narrowly for the excuse I made for you last night i'th' garden.

FLORINDA: I'll reward thee for't. Prithee, no more.
(*Exit Stephano.*)

(*Enter Don Pedro in his masking habit.*)

PEDRO: Antonio's late today; the place will fill, and we may be prevented.   (*Walks about.*)   20

FLORINDA (*aside*): Antonio? Sure I heard amiss.

PEDRO: But who will not excuse a happy lover
When soft fair arms confine the yielding neck,
And the kind whisper languishingly breathes
"Must you be gone so soon?"   25
Sure I had dwelt forever on her bosom —
But stay, he's here.

(*Enter Belvile dressed in Antonio's clothes.*)

FLORINDA [*aside*]: 'Tis not Belvile; half my fears are vanished.

PEDRO: Antonio!   30

BELVILE (*aside*): This must be he. — You're early, sir; I do not use to be outdone this way.

PEDRO: The wretched, sir, are watchful, and 'tis enough you've the advantage of me in Angellica.

BELVILE (*aside*): Angellica! Or° I've mistook my man, or   35
else Antonio! Can he forget his interest in Florinda and fight for common prize?

PEDRO: Come, sir, you know our terms.

BELVILE (*aside*): By heaven, not I. — No talking; I am ready, sir.   40

(*Offers to fight; Florinda runs in.*)

35. Or: Either.

FLORINDA (*to Belvile*): Oh, hold! Whoever you be, I do
    conjure you hold! If you strike here, I die!
PEDRO: Florinda!
BELVILE: Florinda imploring for my rival!
45 PEDRO: Away; this kindness is unseasonable.

(*Puts her by; they fight; she runs in just as Belvile disarms Pedro.*)

FLORINDA: Who are you, sir, that dares deny my prayers?
BELVILE: Thy prayers destroy him; if thou wouldst preserve him, do that thou'rt unacquainted with, and curse him.
                                (*She holds him.*)
50 FLORINDA: By all you hold most dear, by her you love,
    I do conjure you, touch him not.
BELVILE: By her I love?
    See, I obey, and at your feet resign
    The useless trophy of my victory.

(*Lays his sword at her feet.*)

55 PEDRO: Antonio, you've done enough to prove you love
    Florinda.
BELVILE: Love Florinda! Does heaven love adoration,
    prayer, or penitence? Love her? Here, sir, your sword
    again.

(*Snatches up the sword and gives it to him.*)

60   Upon this truth I'll fight my life away.
PEDRO: No, you've redeemed my sister, and my friendship.

(*He gives him Florinda, and pulls off his vizard to show his face, and puts it on again.*)

BELVILE: Don Pedro!
PEDRO: Can you resign your claims to other women,
65   and give your heart entirely to Florinda?
BELVILE: Entire, as dying saints' confessions are!
    I can delay my happiness no longer:
    This minute let me make Florinda mine.
PEDRO: This minute let it be. No time so proper: This
70   night my father will arrive from Rome, and possibly
    may hinder what we purpose.
FLORINDA: O, heavens! This minute?

(*Enter Masqueraders and pass over.*)

BELVILE: Oh, do not ruin me!
PEDRO: The place begins to fill, and that we may not be
75   observed, do you walk off to St. Peter's church,
    where I will meet you and conclude your happiness.
BELVILE: I'll meet you there.—(*Aside.*) If there be no
    more saints' churches in Naples.
FLORINDA: Oh, stay, sir, and recall your hasty doom!
80   Alas, I have not yet prepared my heart
    To entertain so strange a guest.
PEDRO: Away; this silly modesty is assumed too late.
BELVILE: Heaven, madam, what do you do?
FLORINDA: Do? Despise the man that lays a tyrant's
    claim
85   To what he ought to conquer by submission.

BELVILE: You do not know me. Move a little this way.
                         (*Draws her aside.*)
FLORINDA: Yes, you may force me even to the altar,
    But not the holy man that offers there
    Shall force me to be thine.

(*Pedro talks to Callis this while.*)

BELVILE: Oh, do not lose so blest an opportunity!   90

(*Pulls off his vizard.*)

    See, 'tis your Belvile, not Antonio,
    Whom your mistaken scorn and anger ruins.
FLORINDA: Belvile!
    Where was my soul it could not meet thy voice,
    And take this knowledge in.   95

(*As they are talking, enter Willmore, finely dressed, and Frederick.*)

WILLMORE: No intelligence? No news of Belvile yet?
    Well, I am the most unlucky rascal in nature. Ha! Am
    I deceived, or is it he? Look, Fred! 'Tis he, my dear
    Belvile!

(*Runs and embraces him; Belvile's vizard falls out on's hand.*)

BELVILE: Hell and confusion seize thee!   100
PEDRO: Ha! Belvile! I beg your pardon, sir.

(*Takes Florinda from him.*)

BELVILE: Nay, touch her not. She's mine by conquest, sir;
    I won her by my sword.
WILLMORE: Didst thou so? And egad, child, we'll keep
    her by the sword.   105

(*Draws on Pedro; Belvile goes between.*)

BELVILE: Stand off!
    Thou'rt so profanely lewd, so curst by heaven,
    All quarrels thou espousest must be fatal.
WILLMORE: Nay, an you be so hot, my valor's coy,
    And shall be courted when you want it next.   110
                          (*Puts up his sword.*)
BELVILE (*to Pedro*): You know I ought to claim a
    victor's right,
    But you're the brother to divine Florinda,
    To whom I'm such a slave. To purchase her
    I durst not hurt the man she holds so dear.
PEDRO: 'Twas by Antonio's, not by Belvile's
    sword   115
    This question should have been decided, sir.
    I must confess much to your bravery's due,
    Both now and when I met you last in arms;
    But I am nicely punctual in my word,
    As men of honor ought, and beg your pardon: 120
    For this mistake another time shall clear.

(*Aside to Florinda as they are going out.*)

    —This was some plot between you and Belvile,
    But I'll prevent you.
                       [*Exeunt Pedro and Florinda.*]

(*Belvile looks after her and begins to walk up and down in rage.*)

WILLMORE: Do not be modest now and lose the woman.
125   But if we shall fetch her back so—
BELVILE: Do not speak to me!
WILLMORE: Not speak to you? Egad, I'll speak to you, and will be answered, too.
BELVILE: Will you, sir?
130 WILLMORE: I know I've done some mischief, but I'm so dull a puppy that I'm the son of a whore if I know how or where. Prithee inform my understanding.
BELVILE: Leave me, I say, and leave me instantly!
WILLMORE: I will not leave you in this humor, nor till I
135   know my crime.
BELVILE: Death, I'll tell you, sir—

(*Draws and runs at Willmore; he runs out, Belvile after him; Frederick interposes.*)

(*Enter Angellica, Moretta, and Sebastian.*)

ANGELLICA: Ha! Sebastian, is that not Willmore?
    Haste! haste and bring him back.

[*Exit Sebastian.*]

FREDERICK [*aside*]: The colonel's mad: I never saw him
140   thus before. I'll after 'em lest he do some mischief, for I am sure Willmore will not draw on him. (*Exit.*)
ANGELLICA: I am all rage! My first desires defeated!
    For one for aught he knows that has no
    Other merit than her quality,
145   Her being Don Pedro's sister. He loves her!
    I know 'tis so. Dull, dull, insensible,
    He will not see me now, though oft invited,
    And broke his word last night. False perjured man!
    He that but yesterday fought for my favors,
150   And would have made his life a sacrifice
    To've gained one night with me,
    Must now be hired and courted to my arms.
MORETTA: I told you what would come on't, but Moretta's an old doting fool. Why did you give him
155   five hundred crowns, but to set himself out for other lovers? You should have kept him poor if you had meant to have had any good from him.
ANGELLICA: Oh, name not such mean trifles! Had I given
    Him all my youth has earned from sin,
160   I had not lost a thought nor sigh upon't.
    But I have given him my eternal rest,
    My whole repose, my future joys, my heart!
    My virgin heart, Moretta! Oh, 'tis gone!
MORETTA: Curse on him, here he comes. How fine she
165   has made him, too.

(*Enter Willmore and Sebastian; Angellica turns and walks away.*)

WILLMORE: How now, turned shadow?
    Fly when I pursue, and follow when I fly? (*Sings.*)
    Stay, gentle shadow of my dove,
      And tell me ere I go,

Whether the substance may not prove   170
    A fleeting thing like you.

(*As she turns she looks on him.*)

There's a soft kind look remaining yet.
ANGELLICA: Well, sir, you may be gay: All happiness, all joys pursue you still. Fortune's your slave, and gives you every hour choice of new hearts and beauties, till   175
you are cloyed° with the repeated bliss which others vainly languish for. But know, false man, that I shall be revenged.

(*Turns away in rage.*)

WILLMORE: So, gad, there are of those faint-hearted lovers, whom such a sharp lesson next their hearts   180
would make as impotent as fourscore.° Pox o' this whining; my business is to laugh and love. A pox on't, I hate your sullen lover: A man shall lose as much time to put you in humor now as would serve to gain a new woman.   185
ANGELLICA: I scorn to cool that fire I cannot raise,
    Or do the drudgery of your virtuous mistress.
WILLMORE: A virtuous mistress? Death, what a thing thou hast found out for me! Why, what the devil should I do with a virtuous woman, a sort of ill-   190
natured creatures that take a pride to torment a lover. Virtue is but an infirmity in woman, a disease that renders even the handsome ungrateful; whilst the ill-favored, for want of solicitations and address, only fancy themselves so. I have lain with a woman of   195
quality who has all the while been railing at whores.
ANGELLICA: I will not answer for your mistress's virtue,
    Though she be young enough to know no guilt;
    And I could wish you would persuade my heart
    'Twas the two hundred thousand crowns you
      courted.   200
WILLMORE: Two hundred thousand crowns! What story's this? What trick? What woman, ha?
ANGELLICA: How strange you make it. Have you forgot the creature you entertained on the Piazzo last night?   205
WILLMORE (*aside*): Ha! My gypsy worth two hundred thousand crowns! Oh, how I long to be with her! Pox, I knew she was of quality.
ANGELLICA: False man! I see my ruin in thy face.
    How many vows you breathed upon my bosom   210
    Never to be unjust. Have you forgot so soon?
WILLMORE: Faith, no; I was just coming to repeat 'em. But here's a humor indeed would make a man a saint. —(*Aside.*) Would she would be angry enough to leave me, and command me not to wait on her.   215

(*Enter Hellena dressed in man's clothes.*)

HELLENA: This must be Angellica: I know it by her mumping° matron here. Ay, ay, 'tis she. My mad captain's with her, too, for all his swearing. How this

---

176. cloyed: Full to bursting.   **181. as fourscore:** As an eighty-year-old.   **217. mumping:** Moping.

220 unconstant humor makes me love him!—Pray, good
grave gentlewoman, is not this Angellica?

MORETTA: My too young sir, it is.—[*Aside.*] I hope 'tis
one from Don Antonio.   (*Goes to Angellica.*)

HELLENA (*aside*): Well, something I'll do to vex him for
this.

225 ANGELLICA: I will not speak with him. Am I in humor to
receive a lover?

WILLMORE: Not speak with him? Why, I'll be gone, and
wait your idler minutes. Can I show less obedience to
the thing I love so fondly?

                              (*Offers to go.*)

230 ANGELLICA: A fine excuse this! Stay—

WILLMORE: And hinder your advantage? Should I repay
your bounties so ungratefully?

ANGELLICA [*to Hellena*]: Come hither, boy.—
[*To Willmore.*] That I may let you see

235 How much above the advantages you name
I prize one minute's joy with you.

WILLMORE (*impatient to be gone*): Oh, you destroy me
with this endearment.—[*Aside.*] Death, how shall
I get away?—Madam, 'twill not be fit I should be

240 seen with you. Besides, it will not be convenient. And
I've a friend—that's dangerously sick.

ANGELLICA: I see you're impatient. Yet you shall stay.

WILLMORE (*aside*): And miss my assignation with my
gypsy.

(*Walks about impatiently; Moretta brings Hellena, who
addresses herself to Angellica.*)

245 HELLENA: Madam,
You'll hardly pardon my intrusion
When you shall know my business,
And I'm too young to tell my tale with art;
But there must be a wondrous store of goodness

250 Where so much beauty dwells.

ANGELLICA: A pretty advocate, whoever sent thee.
Prithee proceed.

(*To Willmore, who is stealing off.*)

          —Nay, sir, you shall not go.

WILLMORE (*aside*): Then I shall lose my dear gypsy forever. Pox on't, she stays me out of spite.

255 HELLENA: I am related to a lady, madam,
Young, rich, and nobly born, but has the fate
To be in love with a young English gentleman.
Strangely she loves him, at first sight she loved him,
But did adore him when she heard him speak;

260 For he, she said, had charms in every word
That failed not to surprise, to wound and conquer.

WILLMORE (*aside*): Ha! Egad, I hope this concerns me.

ANGELLICA (*aside*): 'Tis my false man he means. Would
he were gone:
This praise will raise his pride, and ruin me.
                    (*To Willmore.*)—Well,

265 Since you are so impatient to be gone,
I will release you, sir.

WILLMORE (*aside*): Nay, then I'm sure 'twas me he
spoke of: This cannot be the effects of kindness in

her.—No, Madam, I've considered better on't, and
will not give you cause of jealousy.   270

ANGELLICA: But sir, I've business that—

WILLMORE: This shall not do; I know 'tis but to try me.

ANGELLICA: Well, to your story, boy.—(*Aside.*) Though
'twill undo me.

HELLENA: With this addition to his other beauties,   275
He won her unresisting tender heart.
He vowed, and sighed, and swore he loved her
dearly;
And she believed the cunning flatterer,
And thought herself the happiest maid alive.
Today was the appointed time by both   280
To consummate their bliss:
The virgin, altar, and the priest were dressed;
And whilst she languished for th'expected
bridegroom,
She heard he paid his broken vows to you.

WILLMORE (*aside*): So, this is some dear rogue that's in   285
love with me, and this way lets me know it. Or, if
it be not me, he means someone whose place I may
supply.

ANGELLICA: Now I perceive
The cause of thy impatience to be gone,   290
And all the business of this glorious dress.

WILLMORE: Damn the young prater; I know not what
he means.

HELLENA: Madam,
In your fair eyes I read too much concern   295
To tell my further business.

ANGELLICA: Prithee, sweet youth, talk on: Thou mayst
perhaps
Raise here a storm that may undo my passion,
And then I'll grant thee anything.

HELLENA: Madam, 'tis to entreat you (oh
unreasonable)   300
You would not see this stranger.
For if you do, she vows you are undone;
Though nature never made a man so excellent,
And sure he 'ad been a god, but for inconstancy.

WILLMORE (*aside*): Ah, rogue, how finely he's instructed!   305
'Tis plain, some woman that has seen me *en passant.*°

ANGELLICA: Oh, I shall burst with jealousy! Do you
know the man you speak of?

HELLENA: Yes, madam, he used to be in buff and scarlet.

ANGELLICA (*to Willmore*): Thou false as hell, what canst   310
thou say to this?

WILLMORE: By heaven—

ANGELLICA: Hold, do not damn thyself—

HELLENA: Nor hope to be believed.

(*He walks about; they follow.*)

ANGELLICA: Oh perjured man!   315
Is't thus you pay my generous passion back?

HELLENA: Why would you, sir, abuse my lady's faith?

ANGELLICA: And use me so unhumanely.

HELLENA: A maid so young, so innocent—

---

306. *en passant:* In passing.

320 WILLMORE: Ah, young devil!
ANGELLICA: Dost thou not know thy life is in my power?
HELLENA: Or think my lady cannot be revenged?
WILLMORE (*aside*): So, so, the storm comes finely on.
ANGELLICA: Now thou art silent: Guilt has struck thee
325   dumb.
    Oh, hadst thou still been so, I'd lived in safety.

(*She turns away and weeps.*)

WILLMORE (*aside to Hellena*): Sweetheart, the lady's name and house—quickly! I'm impatient to be with her.

(*Looks toward Angellica to watch her turning, and as she comes towards them he meets her.*)

330 HELLENA (*aside*): So, now is he for another woman.
WILLMORE: The impudent'st young thing in nature:
    I cannot persuade him out of his error, madam.
ANGELLICA: I know he's in the right; yet thou'st a tongue
    That would persuade him to deny his faith.

(*In rage walks away.*)

335 WILLMORE (*said softly to Hellena*): Her name, her name, dear boy!
HELLENA: Have you forgot it, sir?
WILLMORE (*aside*): Oh, I perceive he's not to know I am a stranger to his lady.—Yes, yes, I do know, but I
340   have forgot the—(*Angellica turns.*)—By heaven, such early confidence I never saw.
ANGELLICA: Did I not charge you with this mistress, sir?
    Which you denied, though I beheld your perjury.
    This little generosity of thine has rendered back my heart.   (*Walks away.*)
345 WILLMORE (*to Hellena*): So, you have made sweet work here, my little mischief. Look your lady be kind and good-natured now, or I shall have but a cursed bargain on't. (*Angellica turns toward them.*)—The rogue's bred up to mischief; art thou so great a fool
350   to credit him?
ANGELLICA: Yes, I do, and you in vain impose upon me. Come hither, boy. Is not this he you spake of?
HELLENA: I think it is. I cannot swear, but I vow he has just such another lying lover's look.

(*Hellena looks in his face; he gazes on her.*)

355 WILLMORE (*aside*): Ha! Do I not know that face? By heaven, my little gypsy! What a dull dog was I: Had I but looked that way I'd known her. Are all my hopes of a new woman banished?—Egad, if I do not fit thee for this, hang me.—[*To Angellica.*] Madam, I
360   have found out the plot.
HELLENA [*aside*]: Oh lord, what does he say? Am I discovered now?
WILLMORE: Do you see this young spark here?
HELLENA [*aside*]: He'll tell her who I am.
365 WILLMORE: Who do you think this is?

HELLENA [*aside*]: Ay, ay, he does know me.—Nay, dear captain, I am undone if you discover me.
WILLMORE: Nay, nay, no cogging;° she shall know what a precious mistress I have.
HELLENA: Will you be such a devil?   370
WILLMORE: Nay, nay, I'll teach you to spoil sport you will not make.—This small ambassador comes not from a person of quality, as you imagine and he says, but from a very errant gypsy: the talking'st, prating'st, canting'st little animal thou ever saw'st.   375
ANGELLICA: What news you tell me, that's the thing I mean.
HELLENA (*aside*): Would I were well off the place! If ever I go a-captain-hunting again—
WILLMORE: Mean that thing? That gypsy thing? Thou   380
    mayst as well be jealous of thy monkey or parrot as of her. A German motion° were worth a dozen of her, and a dream were a better enjoyment—a creature of a constitution fitter for heaven than man.
HELLENA (*aside*): Though I'm sure he lies, yet this vexes   385
    me.
ANGELLICA: You are mistaken: she's a Spanish woman made up of no such dull materials.
WILLMORE: Materials? Egad, an she be made of any that will either dispense or admit of love, I'll be   390
    bound to continence.
HELLENA (*aside to him*): Unreasonable man, do you think so?
WILLMORE: You may return, my little brazen head, and tell your lady, that till she be handsome enough to be   395
    beloved, or I dull enough to be religious, there will be small hopes of me.
ANGELLICA: Did you not promise, then, to marry her?
WILLMORE: Not I, by heaven.
ANGELLICA: You cannot undeceive my fears and torments, till you have vowed you will not marry her.   400
HELLENA (*aside*): If he swears that, he'll be revenged on me indeed for all my rogueries.
ANGELLICA: I know what arguments you'll bring against me: fortune and honor.   405
WILLMORE: Honor! I tell you, I hate it in your sex; and those that fancy themselves possessed of that foppery are the most impertinently troublesome of all womankind, and will transgress nine commandments to keep one. And to satisfy your jealousy, I   410
    swear—
HELLENA (*aside to him*): Oh, no swearing, dear captain.
WILLMORE: If it were possible I should ever be inclined to marry, it should be some kind young sinner: one that has generosity enough to give a favor handsomely to one that can ask it discreetly, one that has   415
    wit enough to manage an intrigue of love. Oh, how civil such a wench is to a man that does her the honor to marry her.
ANGELLICA: By heaven, there's no faith in anything he   420
    says.

(*Enter Sebastian.*)

368. **cogging:** Fawning, coaxing.   382. **motion:** Puppet show.

SEBASTIAN: Madam, Don Antonio—
ANGELLICA: Come hither.
HELLENA [*aside*]: Ha! Antonio! He may be coming
425   hither, and he'll certainly discover me. I'll therefore
       retire without a ceremony.   (*Exit Hellena.*)
ANGELLICA: I'll see him. Get my coach ready.
SEBASTIAN: It waits you, madam.
WILLMORE [*aside*]: This is lucky.—What, madam, now
430   I may be gone and leave you to the enjoyment of my
       rival?
ANGELLICA: Dull man, that canst not see how ill, how
       poor,
       That false dissimulation looks. Be gone,
       And never let me see thy cozening face again,
435   Lest I relapse and kill thee.
WILLMORE: Yes, you can spare me now. Farewell, till
       you're in better humor.—[*Aside.*] I'm glad of this
       release. Now for my gypsy:
       For though to worse we change, yet still we find
440   New joys, new charms, in a new miss that's kind.
                                        (*Exit Willmore.*)
ANGELLICA: He's gone, and in this ague° of my soul
       The shivering fit returns.
       Oh, with what willing haste he took his leave,
       As if the longed-for minute were arrived
445   Of some blest assignation.
       In vain I have consulted all my charms,
       In vain this beauty prized, in vain believed
       My eyes could kindle any lasting fires;
       I had forgot my name, my infamy,
450   And the reproach that honor lays on those
       That dare pretend a sober passion here.
       Nice reputation, though it leave behind
       More virtues than inhabit where that dwells,
       Yet that once gone, those virtues shine no more.
455   Then since I am not fit to be beloved,
       I am resolved to think on a revenge
       On him that soothed° me thus to my undoing.
                                        (*Exeunt.*)

Scene III

(*A street. Enter Florinda and Valeria in habits different
from what they have been seen in.*)

FLORINDA: We're happily escaped, and yet I tremble
       still.
VALERIA: A lover, and fear? Why, I am but half an one,
       and yet I have courage for any attempt. Would Hel-
5   lena were here: I would fain have had her as deep in
       this mischief as we; she'll fare but ill else, I doubt.
FLORINDA: She pretended a visit to the Augustine nuns;
       but I believe some other design carried her out; pray
       heaven we light on her. Prithee, what didst do with
10   Callis?

VALERIA: When I saw no reason would do good on her, I
       followed her into the wardrobe, and as she was look-
       ing for something in a great chest, I toppled her in by
       the heels, snatched the key of the apartment where
       you were confined, locked her in, and left her bawl-   15
       ing for help.
FLORINDA: 'Tis well you resolve to follow my fortunes,
       for thou darest never appear at home again after such
       an action.
VALERIA: That's according as the young stranger and I   20
       shall agree. But to our business. I delivered your note
       to Belvile when I got out under pretense of going to
       mass. I found him at his lodging, and believe me it
       came seasonably, for never was man in so desperate a
       condition. I told him of your resolution of making   25
       your escape today if your brother would be absent
       long enough to permit you; if not, to die rather than
       be Antonio's.
FLORINDA: Thou should'st have told him I was confined
       to my chamber upon my brother's suspicion that the   30
       business on the Molo was a plot laid between him
       and I.
VALERIA: I said all this, and told him your brother was
       now gone to his devotion; and he resolves to visit
       every church till he find him, and not only undeceive   35
       him in that, but caress him so as shall delay his return
       home.
FLORINDA: Oh heavens! He's here, and Belvile with him,
       too.
(*They put on their vizards.*)

(*Enter Don Pedro, Belvile, Willmore; Belvile and Don
Pedro seeming in serious discourse.*)

VALERIA: Walk boldly by them, and I'll come at a dis-   40
       tance, lest he suspect us.

(*She walks by them and looks back on them.*)

WILLMORE: Ha! A woman, and of excellent mien!
PEDRO: She throws a kind look back on you.
WILLMORE: Death, 'tis a likely wench and that kind
       look shall not be cast away. I'll follow her.   45
BELVILE: Prithee do not.
WILLMORE: Do not? By heavens, to the antipodies,°
       with such an invitation.

       (*She goes out, and Willmore follows her.*)

BELVILE: 'Tis a mad fellow for a wench.

(*Enter Frederick.*)

FREDERICK: Oh, colonel, such news!   50
BELVILE: Prithee what?
FREDERICK: News that will make you laugh in spite of
       fortune.
BELVILE: What, Blunt has had some damned trick put
       upon him? Cheated, banged, or clapped?°   55

441. **ague:** Fever, accompanied by shivering.   457. **soothed:**
Advised.

47. **antipodies:** Antipodes; parts of the earth diametrically opposite.   55. **clapped:** Given gonorrhea.

FREDERICK: Cheated, sir, rarely cheated of all but his shirt and drawers; the unconscionable whore too turned him out before consummation, so that, traversing the streets at midnight, the watch found him in this *fresco* and conducted him home. By heaven, 'tis such a sight, and yet I durst as well been hanged as laughed at him or pity him: He beats all that do but ask him a question, and is in such an humor.

PEDRO: Who is't has met with this ill usage, sir?

BELVILE: A friend of ours whom you must see for mirth's sake.—(*Aside.*) I'll employ him to give Florinda time for an escape.

PEDRO: What is he?

BELVILE: A young countryman of ours, one that has been educated at so plentiful a rate he yet ne'er knew the want of money; and 'twill be a great jest to see how simply he'll look without it. For my part, I'll lend him none: And the rogue know not how to put on a borrowing face and ask first, I'll let him see how good 'tis to play our parts whilst I play his. Prithee, Fred, do you go home and keep him in that posture till we come. (*Exeunt.*)

(*Enter Florinda from the farther end of the scene, looking behind her.*)

FLORINDA: I am followed still. Ha! My brother too advancing this way! Good heavens defend me from being seen by him! (*She goes off.*)

(*Enter Willmore, and after him Valeria, at a little distance.*)

WILLMORE: Ah, there she sails! She looks back as she were willing to be boarded; I'll warrant her prize.°

(*He goes out, Valeria following.*)

(*Enter Hellena, just as he goes out, with a page.*)

HELLENA: Ha, is not that my captain that has a woman in chase? 'Tis not Angellica.—Boy, follow those people at a distance, and bring me an account where they go in. (*Exit Page.*) —I'll find his haunts, and plague him everywhere. Ha! My brother!

(*Belvile, Willmore, Pedro cross the stage; Hellena runs off.*)

Scene IV

(*Scene changes to another street. Enter Florinda.*)

FLORINDA: What shall I do? My brother now pursues me. Will no kind power protect me from his tyranny? Ha! Here's a door open; I'll venture in, since nothing can be worse than to fall into his hands. My life and honor are at stake, and my necessity has no choice. (*She goes in.*)

(*Enter Valeria, Hellena's Page peeping after Florinda.*)

PAGE: Here she went in; I shall remember this house. (*Exit Boy.*)

VALERIA: This is Belvile's lodging, she's gone in as readily as if she knew it. Ha! Here's that mad fellow again; I dare not venture in. I'll watch my opportunity. (*Goes aside.*)

(*Enter Willmore, gazing about him.*)

WILLMORE: I have lost her hereabouts. Pox on't, she must not 'scape me so. (*Goes out.*)

Scene V

(*Scene changes to Blunt's chamber, discovers him sitting on a couch in his shirt and drawers, reading.*)

BLUNT: So, now my mind's a little at peace, since I have resolved revenge. A pox on this tailor, though, for not bringing home the clothes I bespoke. And a pox of all poor cavaliers: A man can never keep a spare suit for 'em, and I shall have these rogues come in and find me naked, and then I'm undone. But I'm resolved to arm myself: The rascals shall not insult over me too much. (*Puts on an old rusty sword and buff belt.*) Now, how like a morris dancer° I am equipped! A fine ladylike whore to cheat me thus without affording me a kindness for my money! A pox light on her, I shall never be reconciled to the sex more; she has made me as faithless as a physician, as uncharitable as a churchman, and as ill-natured as a poet. Oh, how I'll use all womankind hereafter! What would I give to have one of 'em within my reach now! Any mortal thing in petticoats, kind fortune, send me, and I'll forgive thy last night's malice.—Here's a cursed book, too—a warning to all young travelers—that can instruct me how to prevent such mischiefs now 'tis too late. Well, 'tis a rare convenient thing to read a little now and then, as well as hawk and hunt.

(*Sits down again and reads.*)

(*Enter to him Florinda.*)

FLORINDA: This house is haunted, sure: 'Tis well furnished, and no living thing inhabits it. Ha! A man! Heavens, how he's attired! Sure 'tis some rope dancer, or fencing master. I tremble now for fear, and yet I must venture now to speak to him.—Sir, if I may not interrupt your meditations—

(*He starts up and gazes.*)

BLUNT: Ha, what's here? Are my wishes granted? And is not that a she creature? 'Adsheartlikins, 'tis.—What wretched thing art thou, ha?

FLORINDA: Charitable sir, you've told yourself already

---

82. **warrant her prize:** Consider her worthy of pursuing.

IV, v, 9. **morris dancer:** The morris dance is a lively dance performed by men wearing costumes and bells.

what I am: a very wretched maid, forced by a strange unlucky accident to seek a safety here, and must be ruined if you do not grant it.

BLUNT: Ruined! Is there any ruin so inevitable as that which now threatens thee? Dost thou know, miserable woman, into what den of mischiefs thou art fallen; what abyss of confusion, ha? Dost not see something in my looks that frights thy guilty soul, and makes thee wish to change that shape of woman for any humble animal, or devil? For those were safer for thee, and less mischievous.

FLORINDA: Alas, what mean you, sir? I must confess, your looks have something in 'em makes me fear, but I beseech you, as you seem a gentleman, pity a harmless virgin that takes your house for sanctuary.

BLUNT: Talk on, talk on; and weep, too, till my faith so return. Do, flatter me out of my senses again. A harmless virgin with a pox; as much one as t'other, 'adsheartlikins. Why, what the devil, can I not be safe in my house for you, not in my chamber? Nay, not even being naked too cannot secure me? This is an impudence greater than has invaded me yet. Come, no resistance.   (*Pulls her rudely.*)

FLORINDA: Dare you be so cruel?

BLUNT: Cruel? 'Adsheartlikins, as a galley slave, or a Spanish whore. Cruel? Yes, I will kiss and beat thee all over, kiss and see thee all over; thou shalt lie with me too, not that I care for the enjoyment, but to let thee see I have ta'en deliberated malice to thee, and will be revenged on one whore for the sins of another. I will smile and deceive thee; flatter thee, and beat thee; embrace thee and rob thee, as she did me; fawn on thee, and strip thee stark naked; then hang thee out at my window by the heels, with a paper of scurvy verses fastened to thy breast in praise of damnable women. Come, come, along.

FLORINDA: Alas, sir, must I be sacrificed for the crimes of the most infamous of my sex? I never understood the sins you name.

BLUNT: Do, persuade the fool you love him, or that, one of you can be just or honest; tell me I was not an easy coxcomb, or any strange impossible tale: It will be believed sooner than thy false showers or protestations. A generation of damned hypocrites! To flatter my very clothes from my back! Dissembling witches! Are these the returns you make an honest gentleman that trusts, believes, and loves you? But if I be not even with you—Come along, or I shall—   (*Pulls her again.*)

(*Enter Frederick.*)

FREDERICK: Ha, what's here to do?

BLUNT: 'Adsheartlikins, Fred, I am glad thou art come, to be a witness of my dire revenge.

FREDERICK: What's this, a person of quality too, who is upon the ramble° to supply the defects of some grave impotent husband?

BLUNT: No, this has another pretense: Some very unfortunate accident brought her hither, to save a life pursued by I know not who or why, and forced to take sanctuary here at fool's haven. 'Adsheartlikins, to me of all mankind for protection? Is the ass to be cajoled again, think ye? No, young one, no prayers or tears shall mitigate my rage; therefore prepare for both my pleasures of enjoyment and revenge. For I am resolved to make up my loss here on thy body: I'll take it out in kindness and in beating.

FREDERICK: Now, mistress of mine, what do you think of this?

FLORINDA: I think he will not, dares not be so barbarous.

FREDERICK: Have a care, Blunt, she fetched a deep sigh; she is enamored with thy shirt and drawers. She'll strip thee even of that; there are of her calling such unconscionable baggages and such dexterous thieves, they'll flea° a man and he shall ne'er miss his skin till he feels the cold. There was a countryman of ours robbed of a row of teeth whilst he was a-sleeping, which the jilt made him buy again when he waked. You see, lady, how little reason we have to trust you.

BLUNT: 'Adsheartlikins, why this is most abominable!

FLORINDA: Some such devils there may be, but by all that's holy, I am none such. I entered here to save a life in danger.

BLUNT: For no goodness, I'll warrant her.

FREDERICK: Faith, damsel, you had e'en confessed the plain truth, for we are fellows not to be caught twice in the same trap. Look on that wreck: a tight vessel when he set out of haven, well trimmed and laden. And see how a female picaroon of this island of rogues has shattered him, and canst thou hope for any mercy?

BLUNT: No, no, gentlewoman, come along; 'adsheartlikins, we must be better acquainted.—We'll both lie with her, and then let me alone to bang her.

FREDERICK: I'm ready to serve you in matters of revenge that has a double pleasure in't.

BLUNT: Well said.—You hear, little one, how you are condemned by public vote to the bed within; there's no resisting your destiny, sweetheart.
(*Pulls her.*)

FLORINDA: Stay, sir. I have seen you with Belvile, an English cavalier. For his sake, use me kindly. You know him, sir.

BLUNT: Belvile? Why yes, sweeting, we do know Belvile, and wish he were with us now. He's a cormorant at whore and bacon:° He'd have a limb or two of thee, my virgin pullet. But 'tis no matter; we'll leave him the bones to pick.

FLORINDA: Sir, if you have any esteem for that Belvile, I conjure you to treat me with more gentleness; he'll thank you for the justice.

FREDERICK: Hark'ee, Blunt, I doubt we are mistaken in this matter.

---

85. upon the ramble: Rambling, wandering.

104. flea: Strip off the skin (flay).   **133–34. cormorant…
bacon:** Glutton for sex.

FLORINDA: Sir, if you find me not worth Belvile's care, use me as you please. And that you may think I merit better treatment than you threaten, pray take this present. 145

(*Gives him a ring; he looks on it.*)

BLUNT: Hum, a diamond! Why, 'tis a wonderful virtue now that lies in this ring, a mollifying virtue. 'Adsheartlikins, there's more persuasive rhetoric in't than all her sex can utter.

FREDERICK: I begin to suspect something, and 'twould anger us vilely to be trussed up for a rape upon a maid of quality, when we only believe we ruffle a harlot. 150

BLUNT: Thou art a credulous fellow, but 'adsheartlikins, I have no faith yet. Why, my saint prattled as parlously as this does; she gave me a bracelet, too, a devil on her! But I sent my man to sell it today for necessaries, and it proved as counterfeit as her vows of love. 155

FREDERICK: However, let it reprieve her till we see Belvile. 160

BLUNT: That's hard, yet I will grant it.

(*Enter a Servant.*)

SERVANT: Oh, sir, the colonel is just come in with his new friend and a Spaniard of quality, and talks of having you to dinner with 'em.

BLUNT: 'Adsheartlikins, I'm undone! I would not see 'em for the world. Hark'ee, Fred, lock up the wench in your chamber. 165

FREDERICK: Fear nothing, madam: Whate'er he threatens, you are safe whilst in my hands.

(*Exeunt Frederick and Florinda.*)

BLUNT: And sirrah, upon your life, say I am not at home, or that I'm asleep, or—or—anything. Away; I'll prevent their coming this way. 170

(*Locks the door, and exeunt.*)

ACT V

(*Blunt's chamber. After a great knocking as at his chamber door, enter Blunt softly crossing the stage, in his shirt and drawers as before.*)

[VOICES] (*call within*): Ned! Ned Blunt! Ned Blunt!

BLUNT: The rogues are up in arms. 'Adsheartlikins, this villainous Frederick has betrayed me: They have heard of my blessed fortune.

[VOICES] (*and knocking within*): Ned Blunt! Ned! Ned! 5

BELVILE [*within*]: Why, he's dead, sir, without dispute dead; he has not been seen today. Let's break open the door. Here, boy—

BLUNT: Ha, break open the door? 'Adsheartlikins, that mad fellow will be as good as his word. 10

BELVILE [*within*]: Boy, bring something to force the door.

(*A great noise within, at the door again.*)

BLUNT: So, now must I speak in my own defense, I'll try what rhetoric will do.—Hold, hold! What do you mean, gentlemen, what do you mean?

BELVILE (*within*): Oh, rogue, art alive? Prithee open the door and convince us. 15

BLUNT: Yes, I am alive, gentlemen, but at present a little busy.

BELVILE (*within*): How, Blunt grown a man of business? Come, come, open and let's see this miracle. 20

BLUNT: No, no, no, no, gentlemen, 'tis no great business. But—I am—at—my devotion. 'Adsheartlikins, will you not allow a man time to pray?

BELVILE (*within*): Turned religious? A greater wonder than the first! Therefore open quickly, or we shall unhinge, we shall. 25

BLUNT [*aside*]: This won't do.—Why hark'ee, colonel, to tell you the truth, I am about a necessary affair of life: I have a wench with me. You apprehend me?—The devil's in't if they be so uncivil as to disturb me now. 30

WILLMORE [*within*]: How, a wench? Nay then, we must enter and partake. No resistance. Unless it be your lady of quality, and then we'll keep our distance.

BLUNT: So, the business is out. 35

WILLMORE [*within*]: Come, come, lend's more hands to the door. Now heave, all together. (*Breaks open the door.*) So, well done, my boys.

(*Enter Belvile [and his Page], Willmore, Frederick, and Pedro. Blunt looks simply, they all laugh at him; he lays his hand on his sword, and comes up to Willmore.*)

BLUNT: Hark'ee, sir, laugh out your laugh quickly, d'ye hear, and be gone. I shall spoil your sport else, 'adsheartlikins, sir. I shall. The jest has been carried on too long.—(*Aside.*) A plague upon my tailor! 40

WILLMORE: 'Sdeath, how the whore has dressed him! Faith, sir, I'm sorry.

BLUNT: Are you so, sir? Keep't to yourself then, sir, I advise you, d'ye hear, for I can as little endure your pity as his mirth. 45

(*Lays his hand on's sword.*)

BELVILE: Indeed, Willmore, thou wert a little too rough with Ned Blunt's mistress. Call a person of quality whore, and one so young, so handsome, and so eloquent? Ha, ha, he. 50

BLUNT: Hark'ee, sir, you know me, and know I can be angry. Have a care, for 'adsheartlikins, I can fight, too, I can, sir. Do you mark me? No more.

BELVILE: Why so peevish, good Ned? Some disappointments, I'll warrant. What, did the jealous count, her husband, return just in the nick? 55

BLUNT: Or the devil, sir. (*They laugh.*) D'ye laugh? Look ye settle me a good sober countenance, and that quickly, too, or you shall know Ned Blunt is not— 60

BELVILE: Not everybody, we know that.

BLUNT: Not an ass to be laughed at, sir.

WILLMORE: Unconscionable sinner! To bring a lover so near his happiness—a vigorous passionate lover—

65 and then not only cheat him of his movables, but his very desires, too.

BELVILE: Ah, sir, a mistress is a trifle with Blunt; he'll have a dozen the next time he looks abroad. His eyes have charms not to be resisted; there needs no more

70 than to expose that taking person to the view of the fair, and he leads 'em all in triumph.

PEDRO: Sir, though I'm a stranger to you, I am ashamed at the rudeness of my nation; and could you learn who did it, would assist you to make an example of

75 'em.

BLUNT: Why ay, there's one speaks sense now, and hand-somely. And let me tell you, gentlemen, I should not have showed myself like a jack pudding° thus to have made you mirth, but that I have revenge within my

80 power. For know, I have got into my possession a female, who had better have fallen under any curse than the ruin I design her. 'Adsheartlikins, she as-saulted me here in my own lodgings, and had doubt-less committed a rape upon me, had not this sword

85 defended me.

FREDERICK: I know not that, but o' my conscience thou had ravished her, had she not redeemed herself with a ring. Let's see't, Blunt.

(*Blunt shows the ring.*)

BELVILE [*aside*]: Ha! The ring I gave Florinda when we

90 exchanged our vows! — Hark'ee, Blunt —

(*Goes to whisper to him.*)

WILLMORE: No whispering, good colonel, there's a woman in the case. No whispering.

BELVILE [*aside to Blunt*]: Hark'ee, fool, be advised, and conceal both the ring and the story for your reputa-

95 tion's sake. Do not let people know what despised cullies we English are; to be cheated and abused by one whore, and another rather bribe thee than be kind to thee, is an infamy to our nation.

WILLMORE: Come, come, where's the wench? We'll see

100 her; let her be what she will, we'll see her.

PEDRO: Ay, ay, let us see her. I can soon discover whether she be of quality, or for your diversion.

BLUNT: She's in Fred's custody.

WILLMORE: Come, come, the key —

(*To Frederick, who gives him the key; they are going.*)

105 BELVILE [*aside*]: Death, what shall I do? — Stay, gentle-men. — [*Aside.*] Yet if I hinder 'em, I shall discover all. — Hold, let's go one at once.° Give me the key.

WILLMORE: Nay, hold there, colonel, I'll go first.

FREDERICK: Nay, no dispute, Ned and I have the propri-

110 ety of her.

WILLMORE: Damn propriety! Then we'll draw cuts. (*Bel-vile goes to whisper* [*to*] *Willmore.*) Nay, no corrup-tion, good colonel. Come, the longest sword carries her.

---

78. **jack pudding:** Clown.   107. **one at once:** One after the other.

(*They all draw, forgetting Don Pedro, being a Spaniard, had the longest.*)

BLUNT: I yield up my interest to you, gentlemen, and   115 that will be revenge sufficient.

WILLMORE (*to Pedro*): The wench is yours. — [*Aside.*] Pox of his Toledo,° I had forgot that.

FREDERICK: Come, sir, I'll conduct you to the lady.

(*Exeunt Frederick and Pedro.*)

BELVILE (*aside*): To hinder him will certainly discover   120 her. — Dost know, dull beast, what mischief thou hast done?

(*Willmore walking up and down, out of humor.*)

WILLMORE: Ay, ay, to trust our fortune to lots! A devil on't, 'twas madness, that's the truth on't.

BELVILE: Oh, intolerable sot —   125

(*Enter Florinda running, masked, Pedro after her; Will-more gazing round her.*)

FLORINDA (*aside*): Good heaven defend me from dis-covery!

PEDRO: 'Tis but in vain to fly me; you're fallen to my lot.

BELVILE [*aside*]: Sure she's undiscovered yet, but now I fear there is no way to bring her off.   130

WILLMORE [*aside*]: Why, what a pox, is not this my woman, the same I followed but now?

(*Pedro talking to Florinda, who walks up and down.*)

PEDRO: As if I did not know ye, and your business here.

FLORINDA (*aside*): Good heaven, I fear he does indeed!

PEDRO: Come, pray be kind; I know you meant to be so   135 when you entered here, for these are proper gentle-men.

WILLMORE: But sir, perhaps the lady will not be im-posed upon: She'll choose her man.

PEDRO: I am better bred than not to leave her choice   140 free.

(*Enter Valeria, and is surprised at sight of Don Pedro.*)

VALERIA (*aside*): Don Pedro here! There's no avoiding him.

FLORINDA (*aside*): Valeria! Then I'm undone.

VALERIA (*to Pedro, running to him*): Oh, I have found   145 you, sir! The strangest accident — if I had breath — to tell it.

PEDRO: Speak! Is Florinda safe? Hellena well?

VALERIA: Ay, ay, sir. Florinda is safe. — [*Aside.*] From any fears of you.   150

PEDRO: Why, where's Florinda? Speak!

VALERIA: Ay, where indeed, sir; I wish I could inform you. But to hold you no longer in doubt —

FLORINDA (*aside*): Oh, what will she say?

VALERIA: She's fled away in the habit — of one of her   155 pages, sir. But Callis thinks you may retrieve her yet,

---

118. **Toledo:** His sword, which won the draw, was made in Toledo, Spain.

if you make haste away. She'll tell you, sir, the rest. — (*Aside.*) If you can find her out.

PEDRO: Dishonorable girl, she has undone my aim. —
160   [*To Belvile.*] Sir, you see my necessity of leaving you, and I hope you'll pardon it. My sister, I know, will make her flight to you, and if she do, I shall expect she should be rendered back.

BELVILE: I shall consult my love and honor, sir.

                            (*Exit Pedro.*)

165 FLORINDA (*to Valeria*): My dear preserver, let me embrace thee.

WILLMORE: What the devil's all this?

BLUNT: Mystery, by this light.

VALERIA: Come, come, make haste and get yourselves
170   married quickly, for your brother will return again.

BELVILE: I'm so surprised with fears and joys, so amazed to find you here in safety, I can scarce persuade my heart into a faith of what I see.

WILLMORE: Hark'ee, colonel, is this that mistress who
175   has cost you so many sighs, and me so many quarrels with you?

BELVILE: It is. — [*To Florinda.*] Pray give him the honor of your hand.

WILLMORE: Thus it must be received, then. (*Kneels and*
180   *kisses her hand.*) And with it give your pardon, too.

FLORINDA: The friend to Belvile may command me anything.

WILLMORE (*aside*): Death, would I might; 'tis a surprising beauty.

185 BELVILE: Boy, run and fetch a father instantly.

                            (*Exit Boy.*)

FREDERICK: So, now do I stand like a dog, and have not a syllable to plead my own cause with. By this hand, madam, I was never thoroughly confounded before, nor shall I ever more dare look up with confidence,
190   till you are pleased to pardon me.

FLORINDA: Sir, I'll be reconciled to you on one condition: that you'll follow the example of your friend in marrying a maid that does not hate you, and whose fortune, I believe, will not be unwelcome to you.

195 FREDERICK: Madam, had I no inclinations that way, I should obey your kind commands.

BELVILE: Who, Fred marry? He has so few inclinations for womankind that had he been possessed of paradise he might have continued there to this day, if no
200   crime but love could have disinherited him.

FREDERICK: Oh, I do not use to boast of my intrigues.

BELVILE: Boast! Why, thou cost nothing but boast. And I dare swear, wert thou as innocent from the sin of the grape as thou art from the apple, thou might'st yet
205   claim that right in Eden which our first parents lost by too much loving.

FREDERICK: I wish this lady would think me so modest a man.

VALERIA: She would be sorry then, and not like you half
210   so well. And I should be loath to break my word with you, which was, that if your friend and mine agreed, it should be a match between you and I.

                   (*She gives him her hand.*)

FREDERICK: Bear witness, colonel, 'tis a bargain.

                   (*Kisses her hand.*)

BLUNT (*to Florinda*): I have a pardon to beg, too; but
    'adsheartlikins, I am so out of countenance that I'm a 215
    dog if I can say anything to purpose.

FLORINDA: Sir, I heartily forgive you all.

BLUNT: That's nobly said, sweet lady. — Belvile, prithee present her her ring again, for I find I have not courage to approach her myself. 220

(*Gives him the ring; he gives it to Florinda.*)

(*Enter Boy.*)

BOY: Sir, I have brought the father that you sent for.

                          [*Exit Boy.*]

BELVILE: 'Tis well. And now, my dear Florinda, let's fly to complete that mighty joy we have so long wished and sighed for. — Come, Fred, you'll follow?

FREDERICK: Your example, sir, 'twas ever my ambition 225
    in war, and must be so in love.

WILLMORE: And must not I see this juggling° knot tied?

BELVILE: No, thou shalt do us better service and be our guard, lest Don Pedro's sudden return interrupt the ceremony. 230

WILLMORE: Content; I'll secure this pass.

    (*Exeunt Belvile, Florinda, Frederick, and Valeria.*)

(*Enter Boy.*)

BOY (*to Willmore*): Sir, there's a lady without would speak to you.

WILLMORE: Conduct her in; I dare not quit my post.

BOY [*to Blunt*]: And sir, your tailor waits you in your 235
    chamber.

BLUNT: Some comfort yet: I shall not dance naked at the wedding.

                   (*Exeunt Blunt and Boy.*)

(*Enter again the Boy, conducting in Angellica in a masking habit and a vizard. Willmore runs to her.*)

WILLMORE [*aside*]: This can be none but my pretty gypsy. — Oh, I see you can follow as well as fly. 240
    Come, confess thyself the most malicious devil in nature; you think you have done my business with Angellica —

ANGELLICA: Stand off, base villain!

(*She draws a pistol and holds it to his breast.*)

WILLMORE: Ha, 'tis not she! Who art thou, and what's 245
    thy business?

ANGELLICA: One thou hast injured, and who comes to kill thee for't.

WILLMORE: What the devil canst thou mean?

ANGELLICA: By all my hopes to kill thee — 250

(*Holds still the pistol to his breast; he going back, she following still.*)

WILLMORE: Prithee, on what acquaintance? For I know thee not.

---

227. juggling: Based on trickery or deception.

ANGELLICA: Behold this face so lost to thy
    remembrance,   (*Pulls off her vizard.*)
    And then call all thy sins about thy soul
255   And let 'em die with thee.
WILLMORE: Angellica!
ANGELLICA: Yes, traitor! Does not thy guilty blood run
    shivering through thy veins? Hast thou no horror at
    this sight, that tells thee thou hast not long to boast
260   thy shameful conquest?
WILLMORE: Faith, no, child. My blood keeps its old
    ebbs and flows still, and that usual heat too, that
    could oblige thee with a kindness, had I but opportu-
    nity.
265 ANGELLICA: Devil! Dost wanton with my pain? Have at
    thy heart!
WILLMORE: Hold, dear virago!° Hold thy hand a little; I
    am not now at leisure to be killed. Hold and hear
    me. — (*Aside.*) Death, I think she's in earnest.
270 ANGELLICA (*aside, turning from him*): Oh, if I take not
    heed, my coward heart will leave me to his mercy. —
    What have you, sir, to say? — But should I hear thee,
    thoud'st talk away all that is brave about me, and I
    have vowed thy death by all that's sacred.

(*Follows him with the pistol to his breast.*)

275 WILLMORE: Why then, there's an end of a proper hand-
    some fellow, that might 'a lived to have done good
    service yet. That's all I can say to't.
ANGELLICA (*pausingly*): Yet — I would give thee time
    for — penitence.
280 WILLMORE: Faith, child, I thank God I have ever took
    care to lead a good, sober, hopeful life, and am of a
    religion that teaches me to believe I shall depart in
    peace.
ANGELLICA: So will the devil! Tell me,
285   How many poor believing fools thou hast undone?
    How many hearts thou hast betrayed to ruin?
    Yet these are little mischiefs to the ills
    Thou'st taught mine to commit: Thou'st taught it
    love.
WILLMORE: Egad, 'twas shrewdly hurt the while.
290 ANGELLICA: Love, that has robbed it of its unconcern,
    Of all that pride that taught me how to value it.
    And in its room
    A mean submissive passion was conveyed,
    That made me humbly bow, which I ne'er did
295   To anything but heaven.
    Thou, perjured man, didst this; and with thy
      oaths,
    Which on thy knees thou didst devoutly make,
    Softened my yielding heart, and then I was a slave.
    Yet still had been content to've worn my chains,
300   Worn 'em with vanity and joy forever,
    Hadst thou not broke those vows that put them on.
    'Twas then I was undone.

(*All this while follows him with the pistol to his breast.*)

---

267. **virago:** A woman of great stature, strength, and courage.

WILLMORE: Broke my vows? Why, where hast thou
    lived? Amongst the gods? For I never heard of mortal
    man that has not broke a thousand vows.   305
ANGELLICA: Oh, impudence!
WILLMORE: Angellica, that beauty has been too long
    tempting, not to have made a thousand lovers lan-
    guish; who, in the amorous fever, no doubt have
    sworn like me. Did they all die in that faith, still   310
    adoring? I do not think they did.
ANGELLICA: No, faithless man; had I repaid their vows,
    as I did thine, I would have killed the ingrateful that
    had abandoned me.
WILLMORE: This old general has quite spoiled thee: 315
    Nothing makes a woman so vain as being flattered.
    Your old lover ever supplies the defects of age with
    intolerable dotage, vast charge, and that which you
    call constancy; and attributing all this to your own
    merits, you domineer, and throw your favors in's   320
    teeth, upbraiding him still with the defects of age,
    and cuckold him as often as he deceives your expec-
    tations. But the gay, young, brisk lover, that brings
    his equal fires, and can give you dart for dart, you'll
    find will be as nice as you sometimes.   325
ANGELLICA: All this thou'st made me know, for which I
    hate thee.
    Had I remained in innocent security,
    I should have thought all men were born my slaves,
    And worn my power like lightning in my eyes,
    To have destroyed at pleasure when offended.   330
    But when love held the mirror, the undeceiving
      glass
    Reflected all the weakness of my soul, and made me
      know
    My richest treasure being lost, my honor,
    All the remaining spoil could not be worth
    The conqueror's care or value.   335
    Oh, how I fell, like a long-worshiped idol,
    Discovering all the cheat.
    Would not the incense and rich sacrifice
    Which blind devotion offered at my altars
    Have fallen to thee?   340
    Why wouldst thou then destroy my fancied power?
WILLMORE: By heaven, thou'rt brave, and I admire
    thee strangely.
    I wish I were that dull, that constant thing
    Which thou wouldst have, and nature never meant
      me.
    I must, like cheerful birds, sing in all groves,   345
    And perch on every bough,
    Billing the next kind she that flies to meet me;
    Yet, after all, could build my nest with thee,
    Thither repairing when I'd loved my round,
    And still reserve a tributary flame.   350
    To gain your credit, I'll pay you back your charity,
    And be obliged for nothing but for love.

(*Offers her a purse of gold.*)

ANGELLICA: Oh, that thou wert in earnest!
    So mean a thought of me

355   Would turn my rage to scorn, and I should pity
            thee,
        And give thee leave to live;
        Which for the public safety of our sex,
        And my own private injuries, I dare not do.
        Prepare—   (*Follows still, as before.*)
360   I will no more be tempted with replies.
WILLMORE: Sure—
ANGELLICA: Another word will damn thee! I've heard
        thee talk too long.

(*She follows him with the pistol ready to shoot; he retires, still amazed. Enter Don Antonio, his arm in a
scarf, and lays hold on the pistol.*)

ANTONIO: Ha! Angellica!
365 ANGELLICA: Antonio! What devil brought thee hither?
ANTONIO: Love and curiosity, seeing your coach at door.
        Let me disarm you of this unbecoming instrument of
        death. (*Takes away the pistol.*) Amongst the number
        of your slaves was there not one worthy the honor to
370   have fought your quarrel?—[*To Willmore.*] Who are
        you, sir, that are so very wretched to merit death
        from her?
WILLMORE: One, sir, that could have made a better end
        of an amorous quarrel without you, than with you.
375 ANTONIO: Sure 'tis some rival. Ha! The very man took
        down her picture yesterday; the very same that set on
        me last night! Blessed opportunity—

(*Offers to shoot him.*)

ANGELLICA: Hold, you're mistaken, sir.
ANTONIO: By heaven, the very same!—Sir, what preten-
380   sions have you to this lady?
WILLMORE: Sir, I do not use to be examined, and am ill
        at all disputes but this—

(*Draws; Antonio offers to shoot.*)

ANGELLICA (*to Willmore*): Oh, hold! You see he's
            armed with certain death.
        —And you, Antonio, I command you hold,
385   By all the passion you've so lately vowed me.

(*Enter Don Pedro, sees Antonio, and stays.*)

PEDRO (*aside*): Ha! Antonio! And Angellica!
ANTONIO: When I refuse obedience to your will,
        May you destroy me with your mortal hate.
        By all that's holy, I adore you so,
390   That even my rival, who has charms enough
        To make him fall a victim to my jealousy,
        Shall live; nay, and have leave to love on still.
PEDRO (*aside*): What's this I hear?
ANGELLICA (*pointing to Willmore*): Ah thus, 'twas thus
            he talked, and I believed.
395   Antonio, yesterday
        I'd not have sold my interest in his heart
        For all the sword has won and lost in battle.
        —But now, to show my utmost of contempt,
        I give thee life; which, if thou wouldst preserve,
400   Live where my eyes may never see thee more.

        Live to undo someone whose soul may prove
        So bravely constant to revenge my love.

(*Goes out. Antonio follows, but Pedro pulls him back.*)

PEDRO: Antonio, stay.
ANTONIO: Don Pedro!
PEDRO: What coward fear was that prevented thee from   405
        meeting me this morning on the Molo?
ANTONIO: Meet thee?
PEDRO: Yes, me; I was the man that dared thee to't.
ANTONIO: Hast thou so often seen me fight in war, to
        find no better cause to excuse my absence? I sent my   410
        sword and one to do thee right, finding myself unca-
        pable to use a sword.
PEDRO: But 'twas Florinda's quarrel that we fought, and
        you, to show how little you esteemed her, sent me
        your rival, giving him your interest. But I have found   415
        the cause of this affront, and when I meet you fit for
        the dispute, I'll tell you my resentment.
ANTONIO: I shall be ready, sir, ere long, to do you rea-
        son.   (*Exit Antonio.*)
PEDRO: If I could find Florinda, now whilst my anger's   420
        high, I think I should be kind, and give her to Belvile
        in revenge.
WILLMORE: Faith, sir, I know not what you would do,
        but I believe the priest within has been so kind.
PEDRO: How? My sister married?   425
WILLMORE: I hope by this time he is, and bedded too, or
        he has not my longings about him.
PEDRO: Dares he do this? Does he not fear my power?
WILLMORE: Faith, not at all; if you will go in and thank
        him for the favor he has done your sister, so; if not, sir,   430
        my power's greater in this house than yours: I have a
        damned surly crew here that will keep you till the
        next tide, and then clap you on board for prize. My
        ship lies but a league off the Molo, and we shall show
        your donship a damned Tramontana° rover's trick.   435

(*Enter Belvile.*)

BELVILE: This rogue's in some new mischief. Ha! Pedro
        returned!
PEDRO: Colonel Belvile, I hear you have married my
        sister.
BELVILE: You have heard truth then, sir.   440
PEDRO: Have I so? Then, sir, I wish you joy.
BELVILE: How?
PEDRO: By this embrace I do, and I am glad on't.
BELVILE: Are you in earnest?
PEDRO: By our long friendship and my obligations to   445
        thee, I am; the sudden change I'll give you reasons for
        anon. Come, lead me to my sister, that she may know
        I now approve her choice.

(*Exit Belvile with Pedro.*)

(*Willmore goes to follow them. Enter Hellena, as before
in boy's clothes, and pulls him back.*)

435. **Tramontana:** Region of Italy north of the Alps.

WILLMORE: Ha! My gypsy! Now a thousand blessings
450   on thee for this kindness. Egad, child, I was e'en in
despair of ever seeing thee again; my friends are all
provided for within, each man his kind woman.

HELLENA: Ha! I thought they had served me some such
trick!

455   WILLMORE: And I was e'en resolved to go aboard, and
condemn myself to my lone cabin, and the thoughts
of thee.

HELLENA: And could you have left me behind? Would
you have been so ill natured?

460   WILLMORE: Why, 'twould have broke my heart, child.
But since we are met again, I defy foul weather to
part us.

HELLENA: And would you be a faithful friend now, if a
maid should trust you?

465   WILLMORE: For a friend I cannot promise: Thou art of a
form so excellent, a face and humor too good for
cold dull friendship. I am parlously afraid of being in
love, child; and you have not forgotten how severely
you have used me?

470   HELLENA: That's all one; such usage you must still look
for: to find out all your haunts, to rail at you to all
that love you, till I have made you love only me in
your own defense, because nobody else will love you.

WILLMORE: But hast thou no better quality to recom-
475   mend thyself by?

HELLENA: Faith, none, captain. Why, twill be the greater
charity to take me for thy mistress. I am a lone child,
a kind of orphan lover, and why I should die a maid,
and in a captain's hands too, I do not understand.

480   WILLMORE: Egad, I was never clawed away with broad-
sides from any female before. Thou hast one virtue I
adore—good nature. I hate a coy demure mistress,
she's as troublesome as a colt, I'll break none. No,
give me a mad mistress when mewed, and in flying,
485   one I dare trust upon the wing, that whilst she's kind
will come to the lure.°

HELLENA: Nay, as kind as you will, good captain, whilst
it lasts. But let's lose no time.

WILLMORE: My time's as precious to me as thine can be.
490   Therefore, dear creature, since we are so well agreed,
let's retire to my chamber; and if ever thou wert
treated with such savory love! Come, my bed's prepared for such a guest all clean and sweet as thy fair
self. I love to steal a dish and a bottle with a friend,
495   and hate long graces. Come, let's retire and fall to.

HELLENA: 'Tis but getting my consent, and the business
is soon done. Let but old gaffer Hymen° and his
priest say amen to's, and I dare lay my mother's
daughter by as proper a fellow as your father's son,
500   without fear or blushing.

WILLMORE: Hold, hold, no bug words,° child. Priest
and Hymen? Prithee add a hangman to 'em to make

up the consort. No, no, we'll have no vows but love,
child, nor witness but the lover: The kind deity
enjoins naught but love and enjoy. Hymen and priest   505
wait still upon portion and jointure; love and beauty
have their own ceremonies. Marriage is as certain a
bane to love as lending money is to friendship. I'll
neither ask nor give a vow, though I could be content
to turn gypsy and become a left-handed bridegroom   510
to have the pleasure of working that great miracle of
making a maid a mother, if you durst venture. 'Tis
upse gypsy° that, and if I miss I'll lose my labor.

HELLENA: And if you do not lose, what shall I get? A
cradle full of noise and mischief, with a pack of   515
repentance at my back? Can you teach me to weave
incle° to pass my time with? 'Tis upse gypsy that, too.

WILLMORE: I can teach thee to weave a true love's knot
better.

HELLENA: So can my dog.   520

WILLMORE: Well, I see we are both upon our guards,
and I see there's no way to conquer good nature but
by yielding. Here, give me thy hand: One kiss, and I
am thine.

HELLENA: One kiss! How like my page he speaks! I am   525
resolved you shall have none, for asking such a
sneaking sum. He that will be satisfied with one kiss
will never die of that longing. Good friend single-
kiss, is all your talking come to this? A kiss, a
caudle!° Farewell, captain single-kiss.   530

(*Going out; he stays her.*)

WILLMORE: Nay, if we part so, let me die like a bird
upon a bough, at the sheriff's charge. By heaven,
both the Indies shall not buy thee from me. I adore
thy humor and will marry thee, and we are so of one
humor it must be a bargain. Give me thy hand.   535
(*Kisses her hand.*) And now let the blind ones, love
and fortune, do their worst.

HELLENA: Why, god-a-mercy, captain!

WILLMORE: But hark'ee: the bargain is now made, but is
it not fit we should know each other's names, that   540
when we have reason to curse one another hereafter,
and people ask me who 'tis I give to the devil, I may
at least be able to tell what family you came of?

HELLENA: Good reason, captain, and where I have
cause, as I doubt not but I shall have plentiful, that I   545
may know at whom to throw my—blessings, I
beseech ye your name.

WILLMORE: I am called Robert the Constant.

HELLENA: A very fine name! Pray was it your faulkner°
or butler that christened you? Do they not use to   550
whistle when they call you?

WILLMORE: I hope you have a better, that a man may
name without crossing himself—you are so merry
with mine.

484–86. flying…lure: I.e., one who will be faithful as long as
that doesn't interfere with her wishes.   **497. Hymen:** God of
marriage.   **501. bug words:** Words that inspire fear.

513. upse gypsy: Gypsy fashion.   517. incle: Linen yarn or
tape.   530. caudle: A warm drink made of gruel and wine or
ale, sweetened and spiced, given to the sick.   549. faulkner:
Falconer, trainer of hawks.

555 HELLENA: I am called Hellena the Inconstant.

(*Enter Pedro, Belvile, Florinda, Frederick, Valeria.*)

PEDRO: Ha! Hellena!

FLORINDA: Hellena!

HELLENA: The very same. Ha! My brother! Now, captain, show your love and courage; stand to your arms
560 and defend me bravely, or I am lost forever.

PEDRO: What's this I hear? False girl, how came you
hither, and what's your business? Speak!

(*Goes roughly to her.*)

WILLMORE: Hold off, sir; you have leave to parley°
only.

(*Puts himself between.*)

HELLENA: I had e'en as good tell it, as you guess it. Faith,
565 brother, my business is the same with all living creatures of my age: to love and be beloved—and here's
the man.

PEDRO: Perfidious maid, hast thou deceived me too;
deceived thyself and heaven?

570 HELLENA: 'Tis time enough to make my peace with that;
Be you but kind, let me alone with heaven.

PEDRO: Belvile, I did not expect this false play from you.
Was't not enough you'd gain Florinda, which I pardoned, but your lewd friends too must be enriched
575 with the spoils of a noble family?

BELVILE: Faith, sir, I am as much surprised at this as you
can be. Yet, sir, my friends are gentlemen, and ought
to be esteemed for their misfortunes, since they have
the glory to suffer with the best of men and kings.
580 'Tis true, he's a rover of fortune, yet a prince aboard
his little wooden world.

PEDRO: What's this to the maintenance of a woman of
her birth and quality?

WILLMORE: Faith, sir, I can boast of nothing but a
585 sword which does me right where'er I come, and has
defended a worse cause than a woman's, and since I
loved her before I either knew her birth or name, I
must pursue my resolution and marry her.

PEDRO: And is all your holy intent of becoming a nun
590 debauched into a desire of man?

HELLENA: Why, I have considered the matter, brother,
and find the three hundred thousand crowns my
uncle left me, and you cannot keep from me, will be
better laid out in love than in religion, and turn to as
595 good an account. Let most voices carry it: for heaven
or the captain?

ALL CRY: A captain! A captain!

HELLENA: Look ye, sir, 'tis a clear case.

PEDRO: Oh, I am mad!—(*Aside.*) If I refuse, my life's in
600 danger.—Come, there's one motive induces me. Take
her; I shall now be free from fears of her honor.
Guard it you now, if you can; I have been a slave to't
long enough.   (*Gives her to him.*)

563. **parley:** Speak or discuss.

WILLMORE: Faith, sir, I am of a nation that are of opinion a woman's honor is not worth guarding when she   605
has a mind to part with it.

HELLENA: Well said, captain.

PEDRO (*to Valeria*): This was your plot, mistress, but I
hope you have married one that will revenge my
quarrel to you.   610

VALERIA: There's no altering destiny, sir.

PEDRO: Sooner than a woman's will; therefore I forgive
you all, and wish you may get my father's pardon as
easily, which I fear.

(*Enter Blunt dressed in a Spanish habit, looking very
ridiculous; his Man adjusting his band.*)

MAN: 'Tis very well, sir.   615

BLUNT: Well, sir! 'Adsheartlikins, I tell you 'tis damnable
ill, sir. A Spanish habit! Good Lord! Could the devil
and my tailor devise no other punishment for me but
the mode of a nation I abominate?

BELVILE: What's the matter, Ned?   620

BLUNT: Pray view me round, and judge.

(*Turns round.*)

BELVILE: I must confess thou art a kind of an odd figure.

BLUNT: In a Spanish habit with a vengeance! I had rather
be in the Inquisition for Judaism° than in this doublet
and breeches; a pillory were an easy collar to this,   625
three handfuls high; and these shoes, too, are worse
than the stocks, with the sole an inch shorter than my
foot. In fine, gentlemen, methinks I look like a bag of
bays° stuffed full of fool's flesh.

BELVILE: Methinks 'tis well, and makes thee look e'en   630
cavalier. Come, sir, settle your face and salute our
friends. Lady—

BLUNT (*to Hellena*): Ha! Sayst thou so, my little rover?
Lady, if you be one, give me leave to kiss your hand,
and tell you, 'adsheartlikins, for all I look so, I am   635
your humble servant. A pox of my Spanish habit!
(*Music is heard to play.*)

WILLMORE: Hark! What's this?

(*Enter Boy.*)

BOY: Sir, as the custom is, the gay people in masquerade,
who make every man's house their own, are coming
up.   640

(*Enter several men and women in masking habits, with
music; they put themselves in order and dance.*)

BLUNT: 'Adsheartlikins, would 'twere lawful to pull off
their false faces, that I might see if my doxy° were not
amongst 'em.

BELVILE (*to the maskers*): Ladies and gentlemen, since
you are come so *a propos*,° you must take a small   645
collation with us.

624. **Inquisition for Judaism:** The Spanish Inquisition, which
persecuted heretics, Jews, and Muslims.   628–29. **bag of bays:**
Spices wrapped in cloth and used for flavoring in cooking.
642. **doxy:** Mistress, prostitute.   645. *a propos:* In a timely
fashion; appropriately.

WILLMORE (*to Hellena*): Whilst we'll to the good man
    within, who stays to give us a cast of his office.°
    Have you no trembling at the near approach?
650 HELLENA: No more than you have in an engagement or
    a tempest.
WILLMORE: Egad, thou'rt a brave girl, and I admire thy
    love and courage.
      Lead on; no other dangers they can dread,
655   *Who venture in the storms o'th' marriage bed.*
                    (*Exeunt.*)

EPILOGUE

    The banished cavaliers! A roving blade!
    A popish carnival! A masquerade!
    The devil's in't if this will please the nation
    In these our blessed times of reformation,
5   When conventickling° is so much in fashion.
    And yet—
    That mutinous tribe less factions do beget,
    Than your continual differing in wit.
    Your judgment's, as your passion's, a disease:
10   Nor muse nor miss your appetite can please;
    You're grown as nice as queasy consciences,
    Whose each convulsion, when the spirit moves,
    Damns everything that maggot° disapproves.
      With canting° rule you would the stage refine,
15   And to dull method all our sense confine.
    With th'insolence of commonwealths you rule,
    Where each gay fop and politic grave fool
    On monarch wit impose, without control.
    As for the last, who seldom sees a play,
20   Unless it be the old Blackfriars° way;
    Shaking his empty noddle o'er bamboo,°
    He cries, "Good faith, these plays will never do!
    Ah, sir, in my young days, what lofty wit,
    What high-strained scenes of fighting there were writ.
25   These are slight airy toys. But tell me, pray,
    What has the House of Commons done today?"
    Then shows his politics, to let you see
    Of state affairs he'll judge as notably
    As he can do of wit and poetry.
30   The younger sparks, who hither do resort,
    Cry,
    "Pox o' your genteel things! Give us more sport'!

    Damn me, I'm sure 'twill never please the court."
      Such fops are never pleased, unless the play
    Be stuffed with fools as brisk and dull as they.   35
    Such might the half-crown spare, and in a glass
    At home behold a more accomplished ass.
    Where they may set their cravats, wigs, and faces,
    And practice all their buffoonry grimaces:
    See how this huff becomes, this damny,° stare,   40
    Which they at home may act because they dare,
    But must with prudent caution do elsewhere.
    Oh that our Nokes, or Tony Lee,° could show
    A fop but half so much to th' life as you.

POSTSCRIPT

This play had been sooner in print, but for a report
about the town (made by some either very malicious
or very ignorant) that 'twas *Thomaso*° altered; which
made the booksellers fear some trouble from the proprietor of that admirable play, which indeed has wit   5
enough to stock a poet, and is not to be pieced or
mended by any but the excellent author himself. That
I have stolen some hints from it, may be a proof that
I valued it more than to pretend to alter it, had I the
dexterity of some poets, who are not more expert in   10
stealing than in the art of concealing, and who even
that way outdo the Spartan boys.° I might have
appropriated all to myself; but I, vainly proud of my
judgment, hang out the sign of Angellica (the only
stolen object) to give notice where a great part of the   15
wit dwelt; though if the *Play of the Novella*° were as
well worth remembering as *Thomaso*, they might
(bating° the name) have as well said I took it from
thence. I will only say the plot and business (not to
boast on't) is my own; as for the words and charac-   20
ters, I leave the reader to judge and compare 'em with
Thomaso, to whom I recommend the great entertainment of reading it. Though had this succeeded ill, I
should have had no need of imploring that justice
from the critics, who are naturally so kind to any that   25
pretend to usurp their dominion, especially of our
sex: They would doubtless have given me the whole
honor on't. Therefore I will only say in English what
the famous Vergil does in Latin: I make verses, and
others have the fame.   30

---

648. **stays . . . office:** The priest waits to perform his office, i.e., to marry them. **5. conventickling:** A pun. A conventicle was a secret meeting of religious dissenters (those who were not members of the Church of England). **13. maggot:** Conscience. **14. canting:** Hypocritical. **20. Blackfriars:** The Blackfriars Theatre (1576–1655), considered old-fashioned in Behn's time. **21. o'er bamboo:** Over a cane, implying old age.

40. damny: Damn me. **43. Nokes . . . Lee:** The best low comedians of the day. James Nokes performed in Thomas Betterton's company. **3. *Thomaso*:** Thomas Killigrew's *Thomaso; or, The Wanderer* (1654; published 1664). **12. Spartan boys:** Those who hid in the Trojan horse. **16. *Play of the Novella*:** *The Novella* (1632) by Richard Brome, from which Behn borrowed several ideas. **18. bating:** Excepting.

COMMENTARY

Elaine Hobby (b. 1956)
COURTSHIP AND MARRIAGE IN *THE ROVER*   1989

*Elaine Hobby closely examines The Rover to help us understand the conventions
of romantic love in Aphra Behn's work. Her essay is especially enlightening on the
questions of marriage and rape and on the differences in the viewpoints of men and
women characters in the play. Hobby notes the complexities implied in the characterization of Angellica, the courtesan.*

Commonly, Behn's plays feature at least two pairs of young lovers, whose attitudes
to love and marriage serve as contrasting strategies in courtship. A common pattern
is that of the "constant couple," who remain true to one another, and finally marry,
despite parental opposition and, usually, confusions over one another's true identity
and conduct. These lovers are not, however, idyllically well matched or perfectly
happy. In *The Rover,* Florinda and Belvile are just such a constant couple. From the
beginning they are in love with one another, and resolved to accept no other partner.
Except for her stubbornness on this one issue, Florinda is all quiet obedience, failing
to argue her case against an arranged marriage. Her passivity is no ideal. Twice in
the course of the play she narrowly escapes being raped by the friends of her
beloved, and on each occasion is only saved because her obvious high social class
causes her attackers to hesitate, fearing retribution from her relatives. The second of
these incidents is a nightmare scene where, seeking refuge in Blunt's house, she is
regarded by him as the perfect target for his revenge against all women (and Lucetta
in particular) for making fun of him. When Frederick, the play's great upholder of
patriarchal morality, arrives, the two men agree to rape her.

> BLUNT: We'll both lie with her, and then let me alone to bang her.
> FREDERICK: I'm ready to serve you in matters of revenge that has a double pleasure in't.
>
> (IV, v, 123–26)

In a world where men can choose to rape a woman, any woman, for spite, there is
no safety for the romantic heroine. In Behn's plays, as in her novels, rape or the
threat of it is shown to be an almost routine masculine strategy to bully and manipulate women. In *The Amorous Prince,* Frederick threatens to rape Laura at knife-
point to humble her for scorning him, and in the same play Silvio threatens to rape
his "sister" Cleonte. Sir Timothy Tawdrey in *The Town-Fopp,* when threatening to
rape Phillis, tells her that old patriarchal lie: that all women want to be forcibly
taken. Phillis's fate is the most terrible of all. Having no economic choices (like
Philadelphia in Behn's novel *The Unfortunate Happy Lady*), she has no option but
to marry her would-be rapist.

Setting out with a theme of courtship and marriage, Behn writes about rape and
prostitution, constructing scenarios that show how closely connected these fates

are for women. Where Florinda's reliance on "true love" for her salvation twice brings her to the brink of being raped, the courtesan Angellica Bianca in the same play is betrayed by her final inability to escape from the tempting lies of romance. Early in the play, she makes a cool assessment of women's position, explaining that she had opted to sell her body for the solid return of financial reward, rather than trusting to illusory male fidelity: "Nothing but gold shall charm my heart" (II, i, 163). She knows, too, that marriage for money is a no less mercenary affair than prostitution. Disaster arrives, however, because she has seriously misjudged the power structure of her society. She arrives in town hoping to captivate either the viceroy's son Don Antonio, or Don Pedro, the nephew of her deceased "protector." Had she been married to her old lover, Don Pedro would have been her kin, and had some social duty to support her. As it is, she is left to live on her wits and her transitory physical charms. When Willmore, the "rover" of the title, finally rejects her in favor of the wealthy virgin Hellena, she is forced to recognize that her chosen independence was illusory. In a world where men make the rules, her only salable item is her virginity. Having sold that in the wrong market, she is damned.

When Angellica falls hopelessly for the feckless Willmore, she wants to believe that love and romance can be dissociated from social and economic structures, that "true love" in her world can be above financial considerations. She calls on him to see things her way and, blinded by this desire, does not recognize that he is using her for his pleasure.

> ANGELLICA: Thou'rt a brave fellow! Put up thy gold, and know,
>   That were thy fortune large as is thy soul,
>   Thou shouldst not buy my love
>   Couldst thou forget these mean effects of vanity
>   Which set me out to sale,
>   And as a lover prize my yielding joys.
>   Canst thou believe they'll be entirely thine,
>   Without considering they were mercenary?   (II, ii, 110–17)

In the course of the play, Willmore's repeated answer to this is a resounding "No." Having worshiped her beauty, tasted the pleasures of her body, and spent her money to attract a wealthier woman, he leaves her for a better catch.

Angellica is a troubling and uncomfortable figure in the play, disrupting the wit and airiness of scenes between Hellena and Willmore and undercutting the conventional "happy ending" of true lovers united. Realizing she has been betrayed by Willmore despite giving him "My virgin heart…Oh! 'tis gone!" (IV, ii, 163) she plots her revenge "for the public safety of our sex" (V, 357). Trapping him at gunpoint she decides, however, to let him live: he is not worth the trouble of an execution: "But now, to show my utmost of contempt, / I give thee life" (V, 398–99). Through Willmore, she has learned that male protestations of devotion, and all their courtly love rhetoric, are for them just a game. There is no true power, no safety, for women.[…]

In many of Behn's plays, men's obsessions with their courtship conventions prevent them from understanding the women they address. Romance is a male invention, and women are jeopardized and often betrayed if they believe such declarations of undying passion. The task for the witty heroine who is at the center of many of Behn's plays, as Hellena is in *The Rover,* is to discover as much as possible about her man's true intentions, beneath his courtly facade. Willmore refers to both Angellica and to Hellena as his "angel" in high-flown rhetoric, but where Angellica is briefly fooled by this worship, Hellena is quite clear-sighted about the limit of his commitment. As far as possible, she takes control of her situation, disguising herself and playing parts, testing out and then capturing the man she has chosen. Disguised, she watches him court and promise fidelity to Angellica, and in a bitter but witty scene mocks him, throwing back at him the overblown promises she has heard him make (III, 1). She has no interest in traditional courtship rituals, thinking them "a very pretty, idle, silly kind of pleasure to pass one's time with" (III, 1, 67–68), but she is not deceived by Willmore's forthright arguments in favor of unfettered sensuality. She knows already what Angellica shows the audience: Marriage is a necessity for women, otherwise, as she challenges Willmore, "What shall I get? A cradle full of noise and mischief, with a pack of repentance at my back?" (V, 514–16).

She gets her man, but it is a tawdry victory and the audience knows it, with Angellica there to remind them. Willmore has shown himself to be insensitive, capricious, and dangerous to women, and there is no reason to imagine that he will be faithful to Hellena for longer than the month that he originally resolves to sacrifice to gain her. In *The Second Part of the Rover,* where Willmore again chooses between two women (and this time chooses the prostitute), it is revealed in passing that Hellena had died at sea within three months of the marriage.

The world of courtship and marriage depicted by Behn in these plays is a bleak one. Bright, witty women like Hellena use daring and imagination in a desperate attempt to evade the arranged marriages or confinements to nunneries destined them by their families. They race against time, trying their best to negotiate when all power lies in others' hands. None of the dashing young blades they choose and test out are admirable characters, but they seem preferable to a fool like Haunce van Ezel (in *The Dutch Lover*) or an odious tyrant like Octavio (in *The Feign'd Curtizans*). Woven in with the wit and humor, music and spectacle, are hard, sober women's truths about the debauchery of the Restoration court and its acolytes. Armed with wit and driven by necessity, like her heroines, Aphra Behn succeeded in dramatizing in marketable form the dilemmas that faced her and her sisters.

Chikamatsu Monzaemon

Generally regarded as the most significant Japanese playwright, Chikamatsu Monzaemon (1653–1725) was born in the province of Echizen into a minor samurai family. His family name was Sugimori, but he changed it when he began writing plays. In his lifetime — during the celebrated Tokugawa shogunate (1603–1868) — hundreds of thousands of samurai did not serve the shogun or a *daimyo,* or master. Chikamatsu was among those called *rōnin,* samurai who lived without a master and who were therefore without a clear direction. Trained as warriors, the samurai, supported by the farmer class in Japan during the extended peace of the period, had little to do. Some of them left the samurai class and, like Chikamatsu, changed their names and went into theater or into some form of business.

The class structure of Japan at this time consisted essentially of peasant farmers, the samurai, the nobility, and merchants. (Some commentators add a class of artisans.) During the late seventeenth and eighteenth centuries, the merchants grew into a wealthy class and often held power over the nobility through debts and other obligations. Chikamatsu was especially interesting because he experienced life as part of the samurai class, but he also appears to have been connected with a Buddhist monastery as a youth. He may have taken his pseudonym from the Chikamatsu temple at which he stayed for some time. At age nineteen, he became a page in a noble family and experienced palace life. Some sources suggest that he was employed by nobleman Ogimachi Kimmochi (1653–1733), who wrote puppet plays; others suggest he worked for Lord Ichijo Eikan, a connoisseur of puppet plays. Regardless, it was probably this experience that impelled Chikamatsu to give up his position and become Japan's first professional playwright. In essence, Chikamatsu had personal experience in three of the four primary classes in Japanese culture.

Unfortunately, we do not know a great deal about Chikamatsu. We do not know which was his first play, nor do we know how many plays he wrote. Estimates run from 130 to 140 plays, the majority of which are *jōruri,* or puppet plays, and the rest kabuki plays using live actors.

Kabuki, whose linguistic root implies subversive behavior, began with a dance in the "floating world," or gay quarter of Kyoto. This was an area licensed for the entertainment of samurai and nobles and permitting prostitution and many forms of entertainment for men, including theater. If we think of Nō drama as refined and religious at heart, we can think of kabuki as profane and appealing to the masses. Its beginning was in 1603 in the dances of a woman named Okuni. Scholar James Brandon, an expert on classical Japanese theater, says of kabuki, "it was the rock entertainment of the seventeenth century. Okuni performed the first Japanese plays of contemporary urban life: numerous painted screens and scrolls show her outrageously garbed as a handsome young warrior, exotic Christian rosary draped on her bosom, conducting an assignation with a prostitute."[1] Eventually, prostitutes took up the practice of kabuki in narrative plays that were sometimes based on current events and that used live actors aiming at an essentially realistic theater. In 1629, the authorities eventually cracked down and banned women actors, giving rise to the highly specialized *onnagata,* male actors who represented women on stage.

Chikamatsu was most renowned for his puppet plays, but early in his career he also wrote for the kabuki theater. At that time puppet plays were known as *jōruri,* but the more common term today is *bunraku.* Both forms of theater, kabuki and bunraku, are performed in Japan and elsewhere today. Chikamatsu's earliest plays were probably written for the puppet theater in 1683. The puppet theater relied on chanters—virtuoso speakers with highly trained voices—to deliver the lines of the characters. One of the greatest chanters of this period, Takemoto Gidayū (1651–1714), is known to have produced a number of Chikamatsu's earliest plays, among them *Kagekiyo Victorious* (1686).

Chikamatsu's early kabuki plays seem to have been inspired by especially popular actors, among them the brilliant Sakata Tōjūrō (1647–1709). One problem with kabuki actors in the late seventeenth century was that many grew arrogant and difficult. They developed a cult of personality as strong as our contemporary film star system, resulting in a drama that focused not on the play itself but on the presence of the actor.

The puppet theater had the advantage of eliminating this complication. In addition, during the early part of the eighteenth century, the drama that was possible with puppets was similar to what is possible today with computer-generated imagery (CGI) in animated and live-action films. Impossible situations could be enacted with puppets: caesarian operations, quick transformations, dismemberments, and more. At the time when Chikamatsu wrote *jōruri* plays, each puppet was operated by a single person, usually dressed in black (as they are today) so as to permit the puppets to seem to be acting on their own. Each puppet head was painted in a way that signaled to the audience whether it was a good or a villainous figure. Chikamatsu went beyond these limitations, however, and created characters of some moral ambiguity and considerable complexity.

His works are usually divided into history plays and domestic plays, often domestic tragedies. The most successful of his history plays is *The Battles of Coxinga* (1715), set in China. Because Japan was essentially sealed off from foreigners and no Japanese were allowed to travel at this time, the foreign setting added to its appeal. Chikamatsu also invented the successful genre called *shinjū-mono,* or love-suicide play. *The Love Suicides at Sonezaki* (1703) was the first of a series of love-suicide plays written by Chikamatsu as well as other playwrights of the time. It was based on an actual event that constituted a minor scandal only weeks before he produced his play. He refined the genre in several more plays, *The Love Suicides at the Women's Temple* (1708) and the unusually modern and complex *The Love Suicides at Amijima* (c. 1720).

The genre was so popular that it became a societal threat. In response to these plays, a great many people committed their own love-suicides, and consequently the authorities banned all such plays in 1722. (Curiously, a similar cult of suicide developed in Europe after the publication of Goethe's *The Sorrows of Young Werther* [1774].)

---

[1]James Brandon, *The Cambridge Guide to Asian Theatre* (Cambridge: Cambridge University Press, 1993), p. 147.

After 1705 Chikamatsu moved to Osaka, where he was the resident playwright for Gidayū's puppet theater until his death in 1725. His work matured, and his subtle and complex use of language, especially rhyme patterns and puns, established him as one of Japan's greatest writers. He is noted for a technique known as the "pivot-word" — a word that has a double meaning, functioning one way in the beginning of a line and in another way in the rest of the line. His skill as a poet makes reading his plays almost as rewarding as seeing them enacted.

THE LOVE SUICIDES AT SONEZAKI

Sonezaki shinjū is the first of the *shinjū-mono,* or love-suicide plays. Chikamatsu wrote some dozen such plays himself, and other playwrights contributed their own. Taken from a current event, the story is direct and moving. Tokubei falls in love with Ohatsu, a young prostitute whose freedom he cannot afford to buy. In desperation, Tokubei sees only one way out of their dilemma, suicide.

In this play, Chikamatsu explores a number of interesting issues. It was not uncommon for a visitor to the floating world to fall in love with a courtesan. Japanese society maintained a clear double standard: men were permitted to enjoy the favors of prostitutes in the licensed areas, whereas their wives were threatened with execution if they committed adultery. In some plays a brother and father approved the killing of an unfaithful woman by her husband. Wives who maintained silence in face of such activity were praised. Those who complained or grew jealous were often divorced, and once divorced they were ruined. Prostitutes were unmarried entertainers whose job was to attract the attention of men and to please them. They were owned by the establishments they served and could be purchased for a high price.

One of the first things one notices about *The Love Suicides at Sonezaki* is that the characters are essentially part of what we would think of today as the middle class. The play is a representational drama, a domestic tragedy, that attempts to present characters speaking as they would if they were encountered in actual society. Tokubei works for a company that sells soy sauce. The villain Kuheiji is a powerful oil merchant. One of Ohatsu's customers is a "country bumpkin." What Chikamatsu reveals is the potential of ordinary people for experiencing powerful emotions. It would take another 150 years for such serious middle-class drama to appear on European stages.

The play is also interesting because it respects the Aristotelian unities even though Chikamatsu could have known nothing of Aristotle, or of any foreign play. The action takes place in a twenty-four-hour period, the characters develop clearly and consistently, and there is no subplot. As a result, the play seems modern to the Western reader.

Unfortunately, because it was connected with a specific current event, this play and other *shinjū* plays fell out of favor only a few years after the ban. Moreover, after Chikamatsu's death the puppet theater developed much more technically advanced production values. The development of three-person puppets permitted more surprising effects and more subtle and amazing movements that required considerable coordination among the puppeteers. Chikamatsu's plays were sometimes rewritten to take advantage of these and other developments, such as a revolving stage (about a century before a similar development in Europe). Therefore, most of the current texts of the plays have the marks of a modern rewriting. In the text given here, however, Chikamatsu's 1703 version, except for a brief introductory passage, appears as it was originally played.

Because the chanter controls the dialogue in the puppet play, he also acts as a narrator commenting on and advancing the action. The narrator chants some of the most beautiful poetry in the third scene. A passage known as the *michiyuki,* or "lovers' journey," offers Chikamatsu the opportunity to raise the level of diction and explore the emotions implied in the action of lovers journeying toward their death. It begins,

> Farewell to this world, and to the night farewell.
> We who walk the road to death, to what should we be likened?
> To the frost by the road that leads to the graveyard,
> Vanishing with each step we take ahead:
> How sad is this dream of a dream!

The conjunction of religion, Amida Buddhism, in this and other plays that have at their root an erotic content, is not unusual. Most of the better kabuki plays treated religion as important. Ohatsu and Tokubei end *The Love Suicides at Sonezaki* with a sense of religious assurance that may seem odd to Western audiences. At the heart of this play and other love-suicide dramas is the conflict of two important values of Japanese society: *giri,* the obligations one has to family and society, and *ninjō,* the personal human feelings to which one responds. Like yin and yang, these elements must be balanced. If one worries only about obligation to others and ignores emotion, one can miss important life experiences. If one is dominated only by personal emotion and desire, society itself will suffer. In this play Tokubei is torn between his obligation to his master and his feelings for Ohatsu. In addition, he is humiliated by the clever Kuheiji and loses his honor. Ohatsu realizes the situation Tokubei is in and proposes a way out for them both. The narrator, obviously moved by the lovers' situation, sees them as moving toward paradise.

One of the details that makes this play seem so modern, especially in relation to European plays of the eighteenth century, is its emphasis on money. Tokubei seems naïve in lending his money even to a good friend, considering what is at stake. But it is the forfeit of the money by Kuheiji's cleverness that drives Tokubei to the play's ultimate resolution. One way or another, Tokubei seems doomed because of the considerable sum of money he has received from his master.

The Love Suicides at Sonezaki in Performance

A key element of all *jōruri* puppet plays is the musician, who plays a three-string instrument called the *shamisen.* Performers on this instrument were successful entertainers before they collaborated with chanters and puppets, and even today the musician has a prominent role in both kabuki and bunraku (puppet) productions. The chanter stands or sits to the side of the stage, and the handlers of the puppets are usually in a lowered section of the stage so that they remain inconspicuous. In modern performances, the handlers are often dressed in absolute black, including face masks, and from a slight distance they are almost unnoticeable. The puppets are elaborate and capable of expressing considerable emotion, especially in conjunction with the shamisen musician.

The stage itself has grown wider since Chikamatsu's age, but it still relies on painted scenery and realistic representation of the various locations of the drama. Like a number of important puppet plays, *The Love Suicides at Sonezaki* has also been performed as a kabuki play with living actors, usually wearing masks and elaborate costumes. Contemporary productions of puppet plays, those of both Chikamatsu and other playwrights, take advantage of the scale of large Western theaters, a development that was adopted largely after World War II. These plays are remarkably effective in those spaces.

Chikamatsu Monzaemon (1653–1725)

THE LOVE SUICIDES AT SONEZAKI   *1703*

TRANSLATED BY DONALD KEENE

Cast of Characters

TOKUBEI, *aged 25, employee of a dealer in soy sauce*
KUHEIJI, *an oil merchant*
HOST *of Temma House*
CHŌZŌ, *an apprentice*
CUSTOMER *of Ohatsu*
TOWNSMEN
OHATSU, *aged 19, a courtesan*
HOSTESS
COURTESANS
SERVANTS

Scene One: The grounds of the Ikudama Shrine in Osaka. Time: May 21, 1703.

NARRATOR:
  This graceful young man has served many springs
  With the firm of Hirano in Uchihon Street;
  He hides the passion that burns in his breast
  Lest word escape and the scandal spread.
  He drinks peach wine, a cup at a time,
  And combs with care his elegant locks.
  "Toku" he is called, and famed for his taste,
  But now, his talents buried underground,
  He works as a clerk, his sleeves stained with oil,

A slave to his sweet remembrances of love.
Today he makes the rounds of his clients
With a lad who carries a cask of soy:
They have reached the shrine of Ikudama.
A woman's voice calls from a bench inside a refreshment stand.
OHATSU: Tokubei — that's you, isn't it?
NARRATOR: She claps her hands, and Tokubei nods in recognition.
TOKUBEI: Chōzō, I'll be following later. Make the rounds of the temples in Tera Street and the uptown mansions, and then return to the shop. Tell them that I'll be back soon. Don't forget to call on the dyer's in Azuchi Street and collect the money he owes us. And stay away from Dōtombori.
NARRATOR: He watches as long as the boy remains in sight, then lifts the bamboo blinds.
TOKUBEI: Ohatsu — what's the matter?
NARRATOR: He starts to remove his bamboo hat.
OHATSU: Please keep your hat on just now. I have a customer from the country today who's making a pilgrimage to all thirty-three temples of Kwannon. He's been boasting that he intends to spend the whole day drinking. At the moment he's gone off to hear the impersonators' show, but if he returns and finds us

together, there might be trouble. All the chair-bearers know you. It's best you keep your face covered.

But to come back to us. Lately you haven't written me a word. I've been terribly worried but, not knowing what the situation might be in your shop, I couldn't very well write you. I must have called a hundred times at the Tamba House, but they hadn't any news of you either. Somebody—yes, it was Taichi, the blind musician—asked his friends, and they said you'd gone back to the country. I couldn't believe it was true. You've really been too cruel. Didn't you even want to ask about me? Perhaps you hoped things would end that way, but I've been sick with worry. If you think I'm lying, feel this swelling!

NARRATOR: She takes his hand and presses it to her breast, weeping reproachful and entreating tears, exactly as if they were husband and wife. Man though he is, he also weeps.

TOKUBEI: You're right, entirely right, but what good would it have done to tell you and make you suffer? I've been going through such misery that I couldn't be more distracted if Bon, New Year, the Ten Nights, and every other feast in the calendar came all at once. My mind's been in a turmoil, and my finances in chaos. To tell the truth, I went up to Kyoto to raise some money, among other things. It's a miracle I'm still alive. If they make my story into a three-act play, I'm sure the audiences will weep.

NARRATOR: Words fail and he can only sigh.

OHATSU: And is this the comic relief of your tragedy? Why couldn't you have trusted me with your worries when you tell me even trivial little things? You must've had some reason for hiding. Why don't you take me into your confidence?

NARRATOR: She leans over his knee. Bitter tears soak her handkerchief.

TOKUBEI: Please don't cry or be angry with me. I wasn't hiding anything, but it wouldn't have helped to involve you. At any rate, my troubles have largely been settled, and I can tell you the whole story now.

My master has always treated me with particular kindness because I'm his nephew. For my part, I've served him with absolute honesty. There's never been a penny's discrepancy in the accounts. It's true that recently I used his name when I bought on credit a bolt of Kaga silk to make into a summer kimono, but that's the one and only time, and if I have to raise the money on the spot, I can always sell back the kimono without taking a loss. My master has been so impressed by my honesty that he proposed I marry his wife's niece with a dowry of two *kamme*,° and promised to set me up in business. That happened last year, but how could I shift my affections when I have you? I didn't give his suggestion a second thought, but in the meantime my mother—she's really my stepmother—conferred with my master, keeping it a secret from me. She went back to the

country with the two *kamme* in her clutches. Fool that I am, I never dreamt what had happened.

The trouble began last month when they tried to force me to marry. I got angry and said, "Master, you surprise me. You know how unwilling I am to get married, and yet you've inveigled my old mother into giving her consent. You've gone too far, master. I can't understand the mistress's attitude either. If I took as my wife this young lady whom I've always treated with the utmost deference and accepted her dowry in the bargain, I'd spend my whole life dancing attendance on my wife. How could I ever assert myself? I've refused once, and even if my father were to return from his grave, the answer would still be no."

The master was furious that I should have answered so bluntly. His voice shook with rage. "I know your real reasons. You're involved with Ohatsu, or whatever her name is, from the Temma House in Dōjima. That's why you seem so averse to my wife's niece. Very well—after what's been said, I'm no longer willing to give you the girl, and since there's to be no wedding, return the money. Settle without fail by the twenty-second of the month and clear your business accounts. I'll chase you from Osaka and never let you set foot here again!"

I too have my pride as a man. "Right you are!" I answered, and rushed off to my village. But my so-called mother wouldn't let the money from her grip, not if this world turned into the next. I went to Kyoto, hoping to borrow the money from the wholesale soy sauce dealers in the Fifth Ward. I've always been on good terms with them. But, as ill luck would have it, they had no money to spare. I retraced my steps to the country, and this time, with the intercession of the whole village, I managed to extract the money from my mother. I intended to return the dowry immediately and settle things for once and for all. But if I can't remain in Osaka, how shall I be able to meet you?

My bones may be crushed to powder, my flesh be torn away, and I may sink, an empty shell, in the slime of Shijimi River. Let that happen if it must, but if I am parted from you, what shall I do?

NARRATOR: He weeps, suffocated by his grief. Ohatsu, holding back the welling tears of sympathy, strengthens and comforts him.

OHATSU: How you've suffered! And when I think that it's been because of me, I feel happy, sad, and most grateful all at once. But please, show more courage. Pull yourself together. Your uncle may have forbidden you to set foot in Osaka again, but you haven't committed robbery or arson. I'll think of some way to keep you here. And if a time should come when we can no longer meet, did our promises of love hold only for this world? Others before us have chosen reunion through death. To die is simple enough—none will hinder and none be hindered on the journey to the Mountain of Death and the River of Three Ways.

kamme: A considerable sum of money.

NARRATOR: Ohatsu falters among these words of encouragement, choked by tears. She resumes.

OHATSU: The twenty-second is tomorrow. Return the money early, since you must return it anyway. Try to get in your master's good graces again.

TOKUBEI: I want to, and I'm impatient to return the money, but on the thirteenth of the month Kuheiji the oil merchant—I think you know him—begged me desperately for the money. He said he needed it only for one day, and promised to return it by the morning of the eighteenth. I decided to lend him the money since I didn't need it until the twenty-second, and it was for a friend close as a brother. He didn't get in touch with me on the eighteenth or nineteenth. Yesterday he was out and I couldn't see him. I intended to call on him this morning, but I've spent it making the rounds of my customers in order to wind up my business by tomorrow. I'll go to him this evening and settle everything. He's a man of honor and he knows my predicament. I'm sure nothing will go wrong. Don't worry. Oh—look there, Ohatsu!

NARRATOR:
"Hatsuse is far away,
Far too is Naniwa-dera:
So many temples are renowned
For the sound of their bells,
Voices of the Eternal Law.
If, on an evening in spring,
You visit a mountain temple
You will see…"
At the head of a band of revelers

TOKUBEI: Kuheiji! That's a poor performance! You've no business running off on excursions when you haven't cleared up your debt with me. Today we'll settle our account.

NARRATOR: He grasps Kuheiji's arm and restrains him. Kuheiji's expression is dubious.

KUHEIJI: What are you talking about, Tokubei? These people with me are all residents of the ward. We've had a meeting in Ueshio Street to raise funds for a pilgrimage to Ise. We've drunk a little saké, but we're on our way home now. What do you mean by grabbing my arm? Don't be rowdy!

NARRATOR: He removes his wicker hat and glares at Tokubei.

TOKUBEI: I'm not being rowdy. All I ask is that you return the two *kamme* of silver I lent you on the thirteenth, which you were supposed to repay on the eighteenth.

NARRATOR: Before he can finish speaking, Kuheiji bursts out laughing.

KUHEIJI: Are you out of your mind, Tokubei? I can't remember having borrowed a penny from you in all the years I've known you. Don't make any accusations which you'll regret.

NARRATOR: He shakes himself free. His companions also remove their hats. Tokubei pales with astonishment.

TOKUBEI: Don't say that, Kuheiji! You came to me in tears, saying that you couldn't survive your monthly bills, and I thought that this was the kind of emergency for which we'd been friends all these years. I lent you the money as an act of generosity, though I needed it desperately myself. I told you that I didn't even require a receipt, but you insisted on putting your seal to one, for form's sake. You made me write out a promissory note and you sealed it. Don't try to deny it, Kuheiji!

NARRATOR: Tokubei rebukes him heatedly.

KUHEIJI: What's that? I'd like to see the seal.

TOKUBEI: Do you think I'm afraid to show you?

NARRATOR: He produces the paper from his wallet.

TOKUBEI: If these gentlemen are from the ward, I am sure that they will recognize your seal. Will you still dispute it?

NARRATOR: When he unfolds the paper and displays it, Kuheiji claps his hands in recollection.

KUHEIJI: Yes, it's my seal all right. Oh, Tokubei, I never thought you'd do such a thing, not even if you were starving and forced to eat dirt. On the tenth of the month I lost a wallet containing the seal. I advertised for it everywhere, but without success, so as of the sixteenth of this month, as I've informed these gentlemen, I've changed my seal. Could I have affixed the seal I lost on the tenth to a document on the thirteenth? No—what happened was that you found my wallet, wrote the promissory note, and affixed my seal. Now you're trying to extort money from me—that makes you a worse criminal than a forger. You'd do better, Tokubei, to commit out-and-out robbery. You deserve to have your head cut off, but for old times' sake, I'll forgive you. Let's see if you can make any money out of this!

NARRATOR: He throws the note in Tokubei's face and glares at him fiercely in an extraordinary display of feigned innocence. Tokubei, furious, cries aloud.

TOKUBEI: You've been damned clever. You've put one over on me. I'm dishonored. What am I to do? Must I let you take my money brazenly from me? You've planned everything so cleverly that even if I go to court, I'm sure to lose. I'll take back my money with my fists! See here! I'm Tokubei of the Hirano-ya, a man of honor. Do you follow me? I'm not a man to trick a friend out of his money the way you have. Come on!

NARRATOR: He falls on Kuheiji.

KUHEIJI: You impudent little apprentice! I'll knock the insolence out of you!

NARRATOR: He seizes the front of Tokubei's kimono and they grapple, trading blows and shoves. Ohatsu rushes barefoot to them.

OHATSU (to townsmen): Please everybody, stop the fight! He's a friend of mine. Where are the chairbearers? Why don't they do something? Tokubei's being beaten!

NARRATOR: She writhes in anguish, but is helpless. Her customer, country bumpkin that he is, bundles her forcibly into a palanquin.

CUSTOMER: It won't do for you to get hurt.

OHATSU: Please wait just a moment! Oh, I'm so unhappy!

NARRATOR: The palanquin is rushed off, leaving only the echoes of her weeping voice.

Tokubei is alone; Kuheiji has five companions. Men rush out from the nearby booths and drive them all with sticks to the lotus pond. Who tramples Tokubei? Who beats him? There is no way to tell. His hair is disheveled, his sash undone. He stumbles and falls to this side and that.

TOKUBEI: Kuheiji, you swine! Do you think I'll let you escape alive?

NARRATOR: He staggers about searching for Kuheiji, but he has fled and vanished. Tokubei falls heavily in his tracks and, weeping bitterly, he cries aloud.

TOKUBEI (*to bystanders*): I feel humiliated and ashamed that you've seen me this way. There was not a false word in my accusation. I've always treated Kuheiji like a brother, and when he begged me for the money, saying he'd never forget it as long as he lived, I lent it to him, sure that he'd do the same for me, though the money was precious as life, and I knew that without it tomorrow, the twenty-first, I'd have to kill myself. He made me write the note in my own hand, then put his seal to it. But it was a seal which he had already reported as lost, and now he's turned the accusations against me! It's mortifying, infuriating—to be kicked and beaten this way, dishonored and forced to my knees. It would've been better if I had died while smashing and biting him!

NARRATOR: He strikes the ground and gnashes his teeth, clenches his fists and moans, a sight to stir compassion.

TOKUBEI: There's no point in my talking this way. Before three days have passed I, Tokubei, will make amends by showing all Osaka the purity at the bottom of my heart.

NARRATOR: The meaning of these words is later known.

TOKUBEI: I'm sorry to have bothered you all. Please forgive me.

NARRATOR: He speaks his apologies, picks up his battered hat and puts it on. His face, downcast in the sinking rays of the sun, is clouded by tears that engulf him. Dejectedly he leaves, a sight too pitiful to behold.

Scene Two: Inside the Temma House. Time: Evening of the same day.

NARRATOR:
The breezes of love are all-pervasive
By Shijimi River, where love-drowned guests
Like empty shells, bereft of their senses,
Wander the dark ways of love
Lit each night by burning lanterns,
Fireflies that glow in the four seasons,
Stars that shine on rainy nights.

By Plum Bridge, blossoms show even in summer.
Rustics on a visit, city connoisseurs,
All journey the varied roads of love,
Where adepts wander and novices play:
What a lively place this New Quarter is!

But alas for Ohatsu of the Temma House—even after she returns the day's events still weigh on her. She cannot swallow her saké, she feels on edge. As she sits weeping, some courtesans from the neighboring houses and other friends come for a little chat.

FIRST COURTESAN: Have you heard, Ohatsu? They say that Toku was given a thrashing for something bad he did. Is it true?

SECOND COURTESAN: No, my customer told me that Toku was trampled to death.

NARRATOR: They say he was fettered for fraud or trussed for counterfeiting a seal. Not one decent thing have they to report: every expression of sympathy makes their visit the more painful.

OHATSU: No, please, not another word. The more I hear, the worse my breast pains me. I'm sure I'll be the first to die. I wish I were dead already.

NARRATOR: She can only weep. But amidst her tears she happens to look outside and catches a glimpse of Tokubei, a pathetic figure wearing a wicker hat, even at night. Her heart leaps, and she wants to run to him, but in the sitting room are the master and his wife, and by the entrance stands the cook, while in the kitchen a maid is hovering: with so many sharp eyes watching, she cannot do as she pleases.

OHATSU: I feel terribly depressed. I think I'll step outside for a moment.

NARRATOR: She slips out softly.

OHATSU: What happened? I've heard rumors of every sort about you. They've driven me out of my mind with worry.

NARRATOR: She thrusts her face under the brim of his wicker hat and weeps in secret, soundless, painful tears. He too is lost in tears.

TOKUBEI: I've been made the victim of a clever plot, as no doubt you've heard, and the more I struggle, the worse off I am. Everything has turned against me now. I can't survive this night. I've made up my mind to it.

NARRATOR: As he whispers, voices are heard from within.

VOICES: Come inside, Ohatsu. There's enough gossip about you as it is.

OHATSU: There—did you hear? We can't go on talking. Do as I show you.

NARRATOR: She hides him under the train of her mantle. He crawls behind her to the garden door, where he slips beneath the porch at the step. Ohatsu sits by the entrance and, pulling the tobacco tray to her, lights her pipe. She assumes an air of unconcern.

At this moment Kuheiji and a couple of his loud-mouthed friends burst in, accompanied by a blind musician.

KUHEIJI: Hello, girls. You're looking lonesome. Would you like me for a customer? Hello there, host. I haven't seen you in ages.

NARRATOR: He strides arrogantly into the room.

HOST: Bring a tobacco tray and some saké cups.

NARRATOR: He makes the customary fuss over the guests.

KUHEIJI: No, don't bother about saké. We were drinking before we came. I have something to tell you. Tokubei, the number one customer of your Ohatsu, found a seal I'd lost and tried to cheat me out of two *kamme* in silver with a forged note. The facts were too much for him, and he finally met with some unpleasantness from which he was lucky to escape alive. His reputation has been ruined. Be on your guard if he comes here again. Everybody will tell you that I speak the truth, so even if Tokubei tells you the exact opposite, don't believe him for a moment. You'd do best not to let him in at all. Sooner or later he's bound to end up on the gallows.

NARRATOR: He pours out his words convincingly. Tokubei, underneath the porch, gnashes his teeth and trembles with rage. Ohatsu, afraid that he may reveal himself, calms him with her foot, calms him gently. The host is loath to answer yes or no, for Tokubei's a customer of long standing.

HOST: Well, then, how about some soup?

NARRATOR: Covering his confusion, he leaves the room. Ohatsu, weeping bitterly, exclaims.

OHATSU: You needn't try your clever words on me. Tokubei and I have been intimate for years. We've told each other our inmost secrets. He hasn't a particle of deceit in him, the poor boy. His generosity has been his undoing. He's been tricked, but he hasn't the evidence to prove it. After what has happened Tokubei has no choice but to kill himself. I wish I knew whether or not he was resolved to die.

NARRATOR: She pretends to be talking to herself, but with her foot she questions him. He nods, and taking her ankle, passes it across his throat, to let her know that he is bent on suicide.

OHATSU: I knew it. I knew it. No matter how long one lives, it comes to the same thing. Only death can wipe out the disgrace.

NARRATOR: Kuheiji is startled by her words.

KUHEIJI: What is Ohatsu talking about? Why should Tokubei kill himself? Well, if he kills himself, I'll take good care of you after he is gone! I think you've fallen for me too!

OHATSU: That's most generous of you, I'm sure. But would you object if, by way of thanks for your kindness, I killed you? Could I go on living even a moment if separated from Toku? Kuheiji, you dirty thief! Anyone hearing your silly lies can only suspect you. I'm sure that Toku intends to die with me, as I with him.

NARRATOR: She taps with her foot, and Tokubei, weeping, takes it in his hands and reverently touches it to his forehead. He embraces her knees and sheds tears

of love. She too can hardly conceal her emotions. Though no word is spoken, answering each other heart to heart, they silently weep. That no one knows makes it sadder still.

Kuheiji feels uncomfortable.

KUHEIJI: The wind's against us today. Let's get out of here. The whores in this place are certainly peculiar— they seem to have an aversion for customers like ourselves with plenty of money to spend. Let's stop at the Asa House and have a drink there. We'll rattle around a couple of gold pieces, then go home to bed. Oh—my wallet is so heavy I can hardly walk.

NARRATOR: Spewing forth all manner of abuse, they noisily depart. The host and his wife call to the servants.

HOST: It's time to put out the lights for the night. Lay out beds for the guests who are staying on. Ohatsu, you sleep upstairs. Get to bed early.

OHATSU (*to herself*): Master, mistress, I shall probably never see you again. Farewell. Farewell to all the servants too.

NARRATOR: Thus inwardly taking leave, she goes to her bedchamber. Later they will learn that this was a parting for life; how pitiful the foolish hearts of men who do not realize the truth in time!

HOST: See that the fire is out under the kettle. Don't let the mice get at the relishes.

NARRATOR: They shut the place and bar the gate. Hardly have their heads touched their pillows than all are snoring merrily. So short is the night that before they've had a chance to dream, two o'clock in the morning has come. Ohatsu is dressed for death, a black cloak dark as the ways of love thrown over her kimono of spotless white. She tiptoes to the staircase and looks down. Tokubei shows his face from under the porch. He beckons, nods, points, communicating his intent without a word. Below the stairs a servant girl is sleeping. A hanging lantern brightly shines. Ohatsu in desperation attaches her fan to a palm-leaf broom, and from the second step of the staircase attempts in vain to extinguish the flame. At last, by stretching every inch, she puts it out, only to tumble suddenly down the stairs. The lamp is out, and in the darkness the servant girl turns in her sleep. Trembling, the lovers grope for each other—a fearful moment. The host awakens in his room to the back.

HOST: What was that noise just now? Servants! The night lamp has gone out. Get up and light it!

NARRATOR: The servant girl, aroused, sleepily rubs her eyes and gets up from bed stark naked.

SERVANT: I can't find the flint box.

NARRATOR: She wanders about the room searching, and Ohatsu, faint with terror, dodges this way and that to avoid her. At last she catches Tokubei's hand, and softly they creep to the entranceway. They unfasten the latch, but the hinges creak, and frightened by the noise, they hesitate. Just then the maid begins to strike the flints; they time their actions to the rasping sound, and with each rasp open the door farther until, huddled together and their sleeves twisted round them, they pass through the door one after the other, feeling as though they tread on a tiger's tail. They exchange glances and cry out for joy, happy that they are to die—a painful, heart-rending sight. The life left them now is as brief as sparks that fly from blocks of flint.

Scene Three: The journey from Dōjima to the Sonezaki Shrine.

NARRATOR:
  Farewell to this world, and to the night farewell.
  We who walk the road to death, to what should
    we be likened?
  To the frost by the road that leads to the graveyard,
  Vanishing with each step we take ahead:
  How sad is this dream of a dream!
TOKUBEI:
  Ah, did you count the bell? Of the seven strokes
  That mark the dawn, six have sounded.
  The remaining one will be the last echo
  We shall hear in this life.
OHATSU:
  It will echo the bliss of nirvana.
NARRATOR:
  Farewell, and not to the bell alone—
  They look a last time on the grass, the trees, the sky.
  The clouds, the river go by unmindful of them;
  The Dipper's bright reflection shines in the water.
TOKUBEI:
  Let's pretend that Umeda Bridge
  Is the bridge the magpies built
  Across the Milky Way, and make a vow
  To be husband and wife stars for eternity.
OHATSU:
  I promise. I'll be your wife forever.
NARRATOR:
  They cling together—the river waters
  Will surely swell with the tears they shed.
  Across the river, in a teahouse upstairs,
  Some revelers, still not gone to bed,
  Are loudly talking under blazing lamps—
  No doubt gossiping about the good or bad
  Of this year's crop of lovers' suicides;
  Their hearts sink to hear these voices.
TOKUBEI:
  How strange! but yesterday, even today,
  We spoke as if such things did not concern us.
  Tomorrow we shall figure in their gossip.
  If the world will sing about us, let it sing.
NARRATOR:
  This is the song that now they hear.
    "I'm sure you'll never have me for your wife,
    I know my love means nothing to you..."
  Yes, for all our love, for all our grieving,
  Our lives, our lots, have not been as we wished.
  Never, until this very day, have we known

A single night of heart's relaxation—
Instead, the tortures of an ill-starred love.
  "What is this bond between us?
  I cannot forget you.
  But you would shake me off and go—
  I'll never let you!
  Kill me with your hands, then go.
  I'll never release you!"
  So she said in tears.
OHATSU:
  Of all the many songs, that one, tonight!
TOKUBEI:
  Who is it singing? We who listen
BOTH:
  Suffer the ordeal of those before us.
NARRATOR:
  They cling to each other, weeping bitterly.
  Any other night would not matter
  If tonight were only a little longer,
  But the heartless summer night, as is its wont,
  Breaks as cockcrows hasten their last hour.
TOKUBEI:
  It will be worse if we wait for dawn.
  Let us die in the wood of Tenjin.
NARRATOR:
  He leads her by the hand.
  At Umeda Embankment, the night ravens.
TOKUBEI:
  Tomorrow our bodies may be their meal.
OHATSU:
  It's strange, this is your unlucky year
  Of twenty-five, and mine of nineteen.
  It's surely proof how deep are our ties
  That we who love each other are cursed alike.
  All the prayers I have made for this world
  To the gods and to the Buddha, I here and now
  Direct to the future: in the world to come
  May we be reborn on the same lotus!
NARRATOR:
  One hundred eight the beads her fingers tell
  On her rosary;° tears increase the sum.
  No end to her grief, but the road has an end:
  Their minds are numbed, the sky is dark, the wind
    still,
  They have reached the thick wood of Sonezaki.
    Shall it be here, shall it be there? When they brush
    the grass, the falling dew vanishes even quicker
    than their lives, in this uncertain world a
    lightning flash—or was it something else?
OHATSU: I'm afraid. What was that now?
TOKUBEI: That was a human spirit. I thought we alone
  would die tonight, but someone else has preceded us.
  Whoever it may be, we'll have a companion on the
  journey to the Mountain of Death. *Namu Amida
  Butsu. Namu Amida Butsu.*°

rosary: A Buddhist rosary. *Namu Amida Butsu:* Calling the name of the Amida Buddha, an incarnation of Siddhartha Gautama, with sincerity should grant the individual eternal life in The Pure Land—hence Pure Land Buddhism.

NARRATOR: She weeps helplessly.

OHATSU: To think that others are dying tonight too! How heartbreaking!

NARRATOR: Man though he is, his tears fall freely.

TOKUBEI: Those two spirits flying together—do you suppose they belong to anyone else? They must be yours and mine!

OHATSU: Those two spirits? Then, are we dead already?

TOKUBEI: Normally, if we saw a spirit, we'd knot our clothes and murmur prayers to keep our souls with us, but now we hurry towards our end, hoping instead our two souls will find the same dwelling. Do not mistake the way, do not lose me!

NARRATOR: They embrace, flesh to flesh, then fall to the ground and weep—how pitiful they are! Their strings of tears unite like entwining branches, or the pine and palm that grow from a single trunk, a symbol of eternal love. Here the dew of their unhappy lives will at last settle.

TOKUBEI: Let this be the spot.

NARRATOR: He unfastens the sash of his cloak. Ohatsu removes her tear-stained outer robe, and throws it on the palm tree; the frond might now serve as a broom to sweep away the sad world's dust. Ohatsu takes a razor from her sleeve.

OHATSU: I had this razor prepared in case we were overtaken on the way and separated. I was determined not to forfeit our name as lovers. How happy I am that we are to die together as we hoped!

TOKUBEI: How wonderful of you to have thought of that! I am so confident in our love that I have no fears even about death. And yet it would be unfortunate if because of the pain we are to suffer people said that we looked ugly in death. Let us secure our bodies to this twin-trunked tree and die immaculately! We will become an unparalleled example of a lovers' suicide.

OHATSU: Yes, let us do that.

NARRATOR: Alas! She little thought she thus would use her light blue undersash! She draws it taut, and with her razor slashes it through.

OHATSU: The sash is cut, but you and I will never be torn apart.

NARRATOR: She sits, and he binds her twice, thrice to the tree, firmly so that she will not stir.

TOKUBEI: Is it tight?

OHATSU: Very tight.

NARRATOR: She looks at her husband, and he at her—they burst into tears.

BOTH: This is the end of our unhappy lives!

TOKUBEI: No I mustn't give way to grief.

NARRATOR: He lifts his head and joins his hands in prayer.

TOKUBEI: My parents died when I was a boy, and I grew up thanks to the efforts of my uncle, who was my master. It disgraces me to die without repaying his kindness. Instead I shall cause him trouble which will last even after my death. Please forgive my sins.

Soon I shall see my parents in the other world. Father, Mother, welcome me there!

NARRATOR: He weeps. Ohatsu also joins her hands.

OHATSU: I envy you. You say you will meet your parents in the world of the dead. My father and mother are in this world and in good health. I wonder when I shall see them again. I heard from them this spring, but I haven't seen them since the beginning of last autumn. Tomorrow, when word reaches the village of our suicides, how unhappy they will be! Now I must bid farewell for this life to my parents, my brothers and sisters. If at least my thoughts can reach you, please appear before me, if only in dreams. Dear Mother, beloved Father!

NARRATOR: She sobs and wails aloud. Her husband also cries out and sheds incessant tears in all too understandable emotion.

OHATSU: We could talk forever, but it serves no purpose. Kill me, kill me quickly!

NARRATOR: She hastens the moment of death.

TOKUBEI: I'm ready.

NARRATOR: He swiftly draws his dagger.

TOKUBEI: The moment has come. *Namu Amida. Namu Amida.*

NARRATOR: But when he tries to bring the blade against the skin of the woman he's loved, and held and slept with so many months and years, his eyes cloud over, his hand shakes. He tries to steady his weakening resolve, but still he trembles, and when he thrusts, the point misses. Twice or thrice the flashing blade deflects this way and that until a cry tells it has struck her throat.

TOKUBEI: *Namu Amida. Namu Amida. Namu Amida Butsu.*

NARRATOR: He twists the blade deeper and deeper, but the strength has left his arm. When he sees her weaken, he stretches forth his hands. The last agonies of death are indescribable.

TOKUBEI: Must I lag behind you? Let's draw our last breaths together.

NARRATOR: He thrusts and twists the razor in his throat, until it seems the handle or the blade must snap. His eyes grow dim, and his last painful breath is drawn away at its appointed hour. No one is there to tell the tale, but the wind that blows through Sonezaki Wood transmits it, and high and low alike gather to pray for these lovers who beyond a doubt will in the future attain Buddhahood. They have become models of true love.

COMMENTARY

Donald H. Shively (1921–2005)
THE DEVELOPMENT OF THEATER BUILDINGS   *1978*

Professor emeritus at the University of California–Berkeley, Donald Shively discusses the development of the kabuki theater from 1600, beginning with the theater of Nō drama, through its use of revolving stages in 1830. The experience of the audience was radically altered by the changes in theater design, especially the hanamichi, a runway that took the actor into the audience while still maintaining his distance from both the main action and the onlookers.

The earliest kabuki performances, as noted, were staged in rudimentary enclosures which could be hastily constructed if subscription *nō* stages were not already available in the amusement quarters at the edge of the cities. From about 1617 Kyoto began issuing licenses to operate theaters. As was true of houses of prostitution, the theaters were increasingly restricted to certain quarters of the city. In Kyoto they were clustered in the area of Shijō, just east of the river, and although as many as seven licenses were issued by 1669, it is not clear how many were in operation at one time.[1] This concentration parallels the establishment of the large prostitution quarters at Shimabara, several miles to the southwest, in 1641. The Shijō theater area and riverbank was a large amusement center in which kabuki was one of many dozens of diversions. There were smaller playhouses, puppet theaters, and a number of wayside entertainers who recited tales from military epics, the *Taiheiki* and *Heike monogatari*. There were fortune-tellers, dentists, *sumō* wrestlers, jugglers, and tightrope walkers. There were sideshows exhibiting such freaks as the female giant and the armless woman archer. There were exotic animals—tigers, bears, porcupines, eagles and peacocks, performing monkeys, and dancing dogs. Teahouses, restaurants, and refreshment stands lined the streets. Paintings of the period show these establishments crowded together, thronged with people of every description.[2]

Edo performances of women's kabuki and youths' kabuki took place as early as 1617 in the Yoshiwara and the nearby amusement area of Nakabashi. The first

---

[1]Dōmoto Kansei (Yatarō) *Kamigata engeki shi* (Tokyo: Shun'yōdō, 1934), p. 41; Takano Tatsuyuki, *Nihon engeki shi* (Tokyo: Tōkyō-dō, 1948), II: 265–269. Dōmoto believes that seven theaters were licensed as early as 1624, but Takano's opinion that this did not happen until 1669–1670 seems more probable.

[2]There are many illustrations of the scene at the Shijō riverbank, including performances of *onna kabuki, wakashu kabuki,* and a variety of sideshows in screen paintings of the second quarter of the seventeenth century, as in Kondō Ichitarō, *Japanese Genre Painting: The Lively Art of Renaissance Japan,* trans. R. A. Miller (Tokyo: Charles E. Tuttle Co., 1961), plates 4, 66–71, pp. 22 and 24; also Kikuchi Sadao et al., eds., *Kinsei fūzoku zukan* (Tokyo: Mainichi Shimbunsha, 1974), II:109; and Kyoto Kokuritsu Hakubutsukan, comp., *Rakuchū rakugai zu* (Tokyo: Kadokawa Shoten, 1966), unnumbered plates at back.

theater to be licensed was the Saruwaka-za in Nakabashi in 1624, later renamed Nakamura-za, which continued to operate at a succession of locations until 1893. It serves as a particularly remarkable example of the exercise of an hereditary license to operate a theater. This and later kabuki theaters were ordered to move from time to time and finally, after the Meireki fire of 1657 forced the Yoshiwara far outside the city, were restricted to Sakai-chō and Kobiki-chō and shortly limited to four in number. The Tokugawa government continued to follow a policy of treating the prostitution and theater quarters as parallel concerns. When the theater quarters burned in 1841, nearly two centuries later, they were ordered to move to Saruwaka-chō in Asakusa, close by the Yoshiwara. In Osaka too, where the issuing of regular licenses to theaters followed the Edo precedent, they were restricted from the 1660s to Dōtombori and Horie.

With the issuing of licenses permitting the construction of permanent theaters, the buildings became gradually more substantial. The mat fence was replaced by solid board walls, and a row of boxes (*sajiki*) was built along the two sides of the parquet (*doma*) for spectators who required more comfort and privacy. Later boxes were added at the rear of the parquet. City officials, seeking to keep kabuki a simple form of entertainment, forbade the construction of roofs over the parquet. But resourceful theater owners devised a method of stretching mats across the parquet to serve as makeshift shelters which provided shade from the sun and protection against light showers. Over a period of two centuries the theater buildings became gradually more elaborate and comfortable as the authorities made concessions, alternating between a resigned attitude and a stricter policy of sumptuary regulation.

Set back slightly from the street so as not to obstruct traffic, the theater façade was dominated by a tower on which ornamental spears were mounted to indicate possession of an official license. This spear (or drum) tower was draped with a cloth bunting featuring the large design of the theater's crest. The Nakamura-za first used the wheeling crane (*maizuru*) design. The Ichimura-za chose a rounded crane within an octagon.[3] Most theaters placed large billboards on the tower, the center board announcing in bold characters the name of the proprietor, those on either side the names of leading actors. Lower billboards, typically four in number if the offering was a four-act play, gave the title of each act. From the 1720s a tableau from each act was painted above the title.

Before these signs stood low platforms where barkers waved their fans to attract the attention of passersby and entice them into the theater. In addition to the cruder techniques of whistling and calling to onlookers, they would attempt to draw a crowd by staging impersonations of the leading actors, imitating their voices as they recited tantalizing lines from the play, and parodying their characteristic poses and gestures. Contemporary paintings record the remarkably exuberant commitment of these *kido geisha* (entrance performers) to their task.[4]

[3]The use of the crane became taboo in 1690 because the word for crane (*tsuru*) was used by the shōgun Tsunayoshi in his daughter's name, Tsuruhime. Thereafter the Nakamura-za used a gingko leaf design, and the Ichimura-za changed its crest to an orange-tree design. Suda Atsuo, *Nihon gekijō shi no kenkyū* (Tokyo: Sagami Shobō, 1957), p. 330.

[4]The six-fold screen (Tokyo National Museum) of the Nakamura-za with its new gingko-leaf crest and stage, attributed to Hishikawa Moronobu (d. 1694), appears in Kondō, plate 76 (identified inexplicably as the Morita-za); Gunji (1969), plate 416; and Suwa Haruo, *Kabuki kaika* (Tokyo: Kadokawa Shoten, 1970), plate 58.

The early theaters had only one entrance, located in the center of the building under the drum tower. It was a small opening with a high threshold which the customer had to step over while ducking under a low overhead. Aptly called the mouse-entrance (*nezumi kido*), it was a holdover from the enclosures used for subscription *nō* and was presumably designed to make it difficult for anyone to slip in quickly without paying. As the theaters grew larger in the eighteenth century, an entrance was provided on each side of the drum tower for admission to the parquet. The stoop entrance was abandoned and a short curtain (*noren*) hung across the top of the doorway, as is customary in Japanese shops. Tickets were purchased outside and other fees paid within for the rental of a reed mat (*hanjō*) and a length of smoldering cord to light one's pipe. On each side of the front of the building an entrance was added for guests going to boxes in order to avoid jostling by the plebs. Inside, stairs led to the upper level of boxes.

The price of tickets ranged widely between the cheapest and the best seats. In 1714, boxes in Edo theaters commanded 1200 *mon,* single spaces 200 *mon.* Parquet tickets averaged 64 *mon.* When space was available, single-act tickets were sold for 12 *mon.* Rental of a mat was 6 *mon* additional.[5] These prices increased rather steadily through much of the Tokugawa period, probably following the general inflationary trend, but exacerbated at certain times by the escalating salaries of the star actors. Attending a major theater was not cheap. The cost of a box seat in 1828 was 1 *ryō* 2 *bu,* the equivalent of 3 bales (*hyō*) of rice or a servant's salary for three or four months. When a performance was popular, the price of tickets rose abruptly.[6]

While the Nakamura-za in Edo provides a detailed illustration of the physical design of a theater, it should be noted that no two were identical. Theaters were, moreover, periodically rebuilt, for fires frequently ravaged Edo. In the 1690s the outer dimensions of the Nakamura-za were 71.5 feet by 97.5 feet, or 6,971 square feet.[7] At its largest in 1809, it measured 80 feet by 138.5 feet, or 11,080 square feet.[8] The structure remained a fraction of the size of the present Kabuki-za in Tokyo, which has 39,000 square feet of space on the ground floor, seating 1,078 people, approximately the same number as the Tokugawa structure. But the modern building has five floors with 120,000 square feet of floor space and accommodates an additional 1,522 people on the mezzanine and balconies.[9] The Nakamura-za of 1720 had a row of boxes along the two sides and across the back. Although only one tier was allowed at that time, by 1724 a second tier of boxes had been added. It was repeatedly forbidden to hang bamboo blinds across the front of the boxes and to install screens or other partitions which would provide privacy for the occupants. However, a number of paintings from this period show

[5]Takano, II:242–243.

[6]Gunji (1956), pp. 62–63; Gunji (1969), pp. 51–52. Only the large theaters of the three cities are discussed in this chapter, but there were also small, low-priced theaters known as *miyachi shibai* located on temple grounds, which were permitted to give performances for one hundred days during the year. Gunji (1956), pp. 38–42.

[7]Suda, p. 328.

[8]Zushi Yoshihiko, *Nihon no gekijō kaiko* (Tokyo: Sagami Shobō, 1947), p. 61. The largest Kyoto theaters seem to have been somewhat larger, at least in 1689 when one measured 106 by 196 feet, over 20,000 square feet. Suda, p. 330.

[9]Yoshida Teruji, ed., *Kabuki-za* (Tokyo: Kabuki-za Shuppanbu, 1951), p. 324.

such items in use, partially concealing from the gaze of the populace ladies-in-waiting of the shogun's or daimyo's households, members of the Buddhist clergy, and rich merchants.[10]

The parquet (*doma*) of the Nakamura-za, 52 feet wide and 82.4 feet deep in 1720, had a capacity of 800 persons. Later, the front half with its better seats was divided into partitions (*masu*) not quite five feet square which narrowly accommodated seven or eight people.[11] Rear parquet space was unreserved. The last back seats, called the *ōmukō* (greatly beyond) were so far from the stage that they were also known as the "deaf gallery." Thus, including boxes and the cheapest parquet seats, the theater held about 1,200.[12] Operating policy was to crowd in as many as possible. According to a book of 1703, "The people came in pushing and jostling, and eight persons sat knee over knee on a mat. It is very pleasant to see them pressed together like human *sushi*."[13]

By the early eighteenth century, wooden roofs occasionally sheltered part of the pit, although not officially sanctioned until 1724. Thereafter tile roofs were recommended to decrease the danger of fire from flying embers. Even after the theaters added roofs, artificial lighting remained proscribed because of the danger to the wooden structure from the open flame of oil lamps and candles. Performances, expected to end about 5 P.M., depended on natural light from windows with translucent paper-covered *shōji* installed on both sides of the theater behind or above the upper row of boxes.[14]

Dressing rooms, located directly behind the stage, were built in two stories by the 1670s. Before the end of the century the Morita-za in Edo added a third level.[15] This section of the building was built high to take as little ground space as necessary from the stage and parquet. A passageway leading to the dressing room section was constructed behind the boxes. Though intended for use by actors to gain access to the end of the runway (*hanamichi*), it was soon traveled by actors summoned to boxes or patrons visiting dressing rooms.[16] The usual arrangement called for baths and quarters for musicians, writers, and *wakashu* on the first floor, *onnagata* on the second, and players of men's roles on the third. A large rehearsal area also occupied the third level. Leading players had individual dressing rooms, although partitions had not received official sanction.[17]

The early kabuki stage basically recreated the square *nō* stage with pillars in the four corners supporting a thatched roof. The main platform had two narrow appendages, one to the right used by the chorus in the *nō*, the other at the rear for the musicians. Off the left of the stage a "bridge" (*hashigakari*) for entrances and

---

[10]Zushi, p. 60; Suda, pp. 331–333; Takano, II:341. Three-tiered boxes are mentioned in 1701, but this perhaps means two tiers raised above the floor, allowing space underneath. Suda, p. 331.

[11]From 1772, wooden partitions replaced ropes to divide the *masu,* and later the size of the *masu* was reduced until finally there was space for only four people. Suda, 339.

[12]Takano, II:343; Iizuka Tomoichirō, *Kabuki gairon* (Tokyo: Hakubunkan, 1928), p. 469; Gunji (1969), p. 50.

[13]"*(Kyō-Ōsaka) Yakusha hyōban iro jamisen,*" in *Kabuki hyōbanki shūsei* (Tokyo: Iwanami Shoten, 1973), III:327a; Takano, II:343.

[14]Suda, p. 333.

[15]Suda, p. 327.

[16]Suda, pp. 327, 329.

[17]Suda, pp. 335, 345.

exits extended back at an oblique angle with a railing on each side and a long roof. These features of the *nō* stage were gradually modified in the kabuki theater, although it is surprising how long they persisted. The stage itself was only 19 feet square at the outset. Rather than alter its design, more space was gained by greatly widening the bridge and eliminating its handrails. It then emerged as a secondary performing area, a rectangle set back slightly from the main stage. A platform was appended to the front of the stage (*tsuke-butai*) which jutted into the audience. Though these changes were not completed until the first decades of the eighteenth century, some stages had already become quite large. That of the Nakamura-za measured 32.5 feet by 37.7 feet in 1724. Not until 1796, however, was the roof over the main stage eliminated.[18]

One of the most distinctive inventions of the kabuki theater is the *hanamichi,* a five-foot-wide runway which extends from the left side of the stage to the rear of the audience. It is used for more dramatic entrances and exits and as an occasional pivot of activity. Its origins are unclear. The more obvious assumption, that it began as a second *hashigakari* directed through the audience, appears to be incorrect. Perhaps as early as the 1650s a small platform was attached to the stage slightly left of center where members of the audience placed gifts (*hana*) of money or goods for their favorite actors. These were called *hana* because the gift was attached to a flower (*hana*) branch. Such a platform appears in a drawing of the Nakamura-za in 1687.[19] By 1724, at least, the *hanamichi* was a runway 52 feet long, set at an oblique angle, probably ending toward the rear end of the row of boxes on the left side of the hall. Although the word *hanamichi* may originally have meant "a path for gifts," by the 1720s and perhaps several decades earlier, it was used primarily as an extension of the stage. Woodblock prints of the next decade show actors standing or seated upon it. Occasionally a small platform called the *nanori-dai* was added about the midway point where an actor could stand almost dead center of the parquet to announce the name and pedigree (*nanori*) of the character he was portraying. After 1780 another, narrower runway was sometimes erected on the right side of the hall. Perhaps as a result, the main *hanamichi* was set at right angles to the stage, parallel to its narrower companion.[20]

Most of the physical features of the theater discussed on the preceding pages are illustrated in a woodblock print by Okumura Masanobu (1686–1764) of the Ichimura-za in Edo in 1744. The *nō* stage with its roof and front pillars, the appended *hashigakari* stage right and *tsuke-butai* stage front, and the *hanamichi* are clearly evident. There is a raised walk (*ayumi*) across the hall for easier access by customers and vendors to the front part of the pit. A tea and a food vendor pass through the audience. The stage curtain is drawn to stage right. Boxes of the first tier were known as quail boxes (*uzura sajiki*) because their wooden bars made them resemble crates for keeping quail. The second tier of boxes retained eaves

---

[18]Suda, p. 337. The present Kabuki-za stage is 77 feet by 95 feet.

[19]Suda, p. 329. There is some evidence that it was used as part of the stage by 1668. Iizuka, p. 421; Takano, II:361–363.

[20]Suda, pp. 337–341.

Perspective view of Kyogen play stage by artist Okumura Masanobu.

Artist Utagawa Toyokuni III's woodblock print of an eighteenth-century stage, with the galleries at the edges of the stage and the two balconies, the arhat dais and the yoshino.

from the days, a few decades earlier, when there was no roof over the pit. Sliding doors of translucent paper let in daylight above the boxes.[21]

In such a theater the play moved easily into the audience. The tiers of boxes at the front of the hall were alongside the stage. Later in the eighteenth century a low balcony intruded behind the left corner of the stage (stage right). Known as the *rakandai* (arhat dais), its tightly lined-up spectators hovered over the stage like the five hundred arhats of a Buddhist painting. A seventeen-syllable satirical poem (*senryū*) observes: "The five hundred went home, having seen the actors' backs." A second balcony inevitably grew above this. It was called *tsūten* (passing through to heaven), or Yoshino (a mountain district noted for cherry blossoms), as its perspective barely penetrated the artificial cherry blossoms suspended from the ceiling of the hall. A woodblock print of the last decades of the Tokugawa period shows the plebs, crammed in these galleries at the edge of the stage, watching gleefully, mouths agape, as the actors perform, almost within reach.[22] When the play was a great success, the management, not impervious to the potential boon, seated customers on the stage itself. This practice is recorded by the satirical poems: "A big hit—the action is performed in a six-foot square," and "Spectators and actors are lined up together—a big hit."[23] With an audience thus gathered on three sides of the performers and cheap balcony seating available over one corner of the stage, no concept of a platform-framing proscenium arch emerged.

[21]The pillar at stage left bears the name of the play, *Nanakusa wakayagi Soga*, followed by the name of the theater, Ichimura-za. The other pillar gives the name of the scene, "Yaoya Oshichi kyōdai biraki." On the beam joining the pillars we see that the Ichimura-za has reclaimed its crane crest. On stage beside her shop counter stands the vegetable dealer (*yaoya*) Oshichi, played by Segawa Kikujirō in this performance of the first month of 1744. Kichizō, played by Onoe Kikugorō, approaches on the *hanamichi*. A stage attendant waves his fan to quiet the audience. This print is an example of the Western-style perspective picture (*ukie*, "floating picture") which came into vogue about 1736. Yoshida Teruji, *Kabuki-e no kenkyū* (Tokyo: Ryokuen Shobō, 1936, 1963), pp. 98–101. The print is in the collection of the Atami Bijutsu-kan.

[22]Detail of a print of a theater interior by Utagawa Toyokuni III (1786–1864), in the collection of the Waseda Daigaku Engeki Hakubutsukan (The Tsubouchi Memorial Theatre Museum, Waseda University). The entire print is reproduced in Gunji (1969), plate 448.

[23]Gunji (1956), pp. 59–60.

William Congreve

Although born in England, William Congreve (1670–1729) was educated in Ireland, first at Kilkenny School and then at Trinity College, Dublin. Jonathan Swift, whose poetry praised Congreve, was also at Kilkenny and Trinity during part of this time. They were lifelong friends and central figures in literary London. Later, Congreve read law at the Middle Temple in London and was able to make good use of his legal training in several of his plays.

Congreve's literary career began with a novel, *Incognita* (1691), which he wrote in his teens. John Dryden praised the novel and, later, his plays. After Congreve's first play was produced, the poet Thomas Southerne named Congreve the likely inheritor of Dryden's crown as poet laureate.

His first play, *The Old Bachelor* (1693), was an immediate success, establishing him as an important playwright. Later in 1693 he produced his second play, *The Double Dealer*, which had a mixed reception. Dryden, in a letter, said, "The women thinke he has exposed their Bitchery too much and the Gentlemen are offended with him; for the discovery of their follyes: & the way of their Intrigues, under the notion of Friendship to their Ladyes Husbands." Maskwell, the double dealer, is a classic manipulator who advances his own interests while damaging those of other characters. Congreve defended the play as a moral fable, and it was not until Queen Mary requested a command performance that the play was restored in the eyes of the public. *Love for Love* (1695) was for many years Congreve's most popular and best-liked play. It is the story of the worthy Valentine, who is about to lose an inheritance to a younger brother. In the end Valentine's intelligence wins out, and by pretending madness he secures his beloved, the wealthy heiress Angelica, as well as his own estate. Thomas Betterton, the acclaimed Restoration actor, played Valentine in the first performances; his theater company at Lincoln's Inn Fields produced all of Congreve's work. John Gielgud played Valentine in London, opening on April 8, 1943, to considerable acclaim and continuing for 471 performances through World War II. Laurence Olivier and Lynn Redgrave played in the 1965 revival, also a success. Congreve's one tragedy, *The Mourning Bride* (1697), was very successful, although it has not been revived in the twentieth century.

Congreve's career as a playwright lasted only seven years. He left the stage after the production of *The Way of the World* (1700), ostensibly because of its cool reception. Although not technically a failure, the play was not received with the enthusiasm Congreve thought it deserved. He was stung by the criticism of Jeremy Collier in *A Short View of the Immorality and Profaneness of the English Stage* (1698). Congreve was also annoyed by the rise of the new sentimental middle-class drama. He spent the rest of his life writing occasional poetry, such as *A Pindarique Ode on the Victorious Progress of Her Majesties Arms* (1706), and libretti for several operas: *The Judgment of Paris* (1701), *A Hymn to Harmony* (1703), and *The Tears of Amarylis* (1703). He spent much of his later years as a retiring gentleman in the company of the duchess of Marlborough, with whom he probably had a child, Lady Mary Godolphin, who inherited his estate.

Congreve was buried in the Poet's Corner of Westminster Abbey, near the grave of Aphra Behn, who is buried at the entrance to the cloisters. Critics in his time and in succeeding generations have regarded his plays as among the purest examples of the English comic style of the late seventeenth century. *The Way of the World* has been especially singled out for praise because even though it is witty, brisk, and amusing, it is pungent and serious at the core, with characters whose intelligence and essential worth help animate a drama that vies with the achievement of Molière.

THE WAY OF THE WORLD

The Way of the World (1700), Congreve's fifth and last play, has been his most enduring and—taking the long view—his most successful. It is an intellectual romp, with plot twists, disguises, and numerous complications. The names of the characters—Fainall, Mirabell, Wilfull, Witwoud, Waitwell, and Petulant— indicate Congreve's use of stock or TYPE CHARACTERS, characters immediately recognizable for their stereotypical behavior and traits. However, he always moves beneath the surfaces of types and reveals a satisfying complexity. Type characters have been used to advantage in all ages of comic drama, but especially so in the English Restoration.

Congreve's genius shows up in his witty use of REPARTEE, or quick replies. He is a master of the one-liner and the RIPOSTE, a sharp return in speech. Wit was a rapier in the late seventeenth century, to be used for the amusement of those intelligent enough to follow the exchanges. Early on, Witwoud says, "A wit should no more be sincere than a woman constant; one argues a decay of parts, as t'other of beauty." Mirabell tells Mrs. Fainall, "You should have just so much disgust for your husband as may be sufficient to make you relish your lover." Such witty comment on early eighteenth-century marriage, once we get to know Fainall and his essential viciousness, takes on a serious cast.

The plot of *The Way of the World* centers on marriage, adultery, and family fortunes. Man-about-town Mirabell wishes to marry Mrs. Millamant, who has inherited six thousand pounds and will receive another six thousand pounds if she marries in accord with the wishes of her aunt, Lady Wishfort (an older woman "full of the vigor of fifty-five"). Lady Wishfort, however, feels betrayed by Mirabell, who pretended to love her to get close to Millamant. Lady Wishfort wants Millamant to marry Sir Wilfull Witwoud, and Mirabell's efforts to make Lady Wishfort relent in this wish are carried forth on a wave of deception, disguise, and comic mixups. Mirabell and Millamant resemble traditional Shakespearean lovers such as Petruchio and Katharine in *The Taming of the Shrew* and Benedick and Beatrice in *Much Ado about Nothing*. They also resemble Aphra

Behn's Willmore and Hellena and Molière's Alceste and Célimène. Millamant is every bit a match for Mirabell, and as a result, their comic scenes are intense and engaging even as they reveal the limits of Congreve's society.

The "contract" scene in act IV, in which Millamant and Mirabell discuss their intentions to marry, is both funny and very serious. Their use of legal language in what is ostensibly a romantic situation is pointedly ironic. Millamant is no starry-eyed bride. She knows that once she is married, all her possessions will belong to her husband; she will be like his chattel, to do with as he pleases. Having had the advantage of studying the marriages around her, she covenants in this scene for her independence.

The villain in the play is Fainall. While having an affair with Mrs. Marwood, he discovers that she is seriously attracted to Mirabell. No longer interested in Mrs. Marwood, he cannot turn away from her because she can expose him to his wife as an adulterer. Fainall's wife is Lady Wishfort's daughter, once married to a Mr. Languish, who has died. Before becoming involved with Fainall, Mrs. Fainall was Mirabell's mistress, but when she feared she was pregnant, Mirabell arranged the hasty marriage to Fainall, knowing that Fainall needed the widow's money and that Mrs. Fainall needed the respectability of marriage. It turned out that Mrs. Fainall was not pregnant and now regrets her marriage. In act II when she asks Mirabell why she married, he responds, "Why do we daily commit disagreeable and dangerous actions? To save that idol, reputation." Of her husband Fainall, he says, "When you are weary of him, you know your remedy." (The epigraph at the beginning of the play warns us that adultery is the subject of the drama.) These circumstances demonstrate that Fainall, for all his villainy, is also being used by the Wishfort family.

Mirabell, like Fainall, is a manipulator but is not a villain at heart. He respects Millamant and manages ultimately to find a way to undo Fainall's schemes to control Millamant's fortune. The play does not end with everyone happy, but with Mirabell and Millamant possessing the advantage and looking forward to marriage and children. Eventually, all deceptions are revealed, the proper lovers are joined, and the complications are smoothed out. Because of its careful examination of the relationship between the sexes and of the impediments a sophisticated society can throw between them, *The Way of the World* is virtually a timeless comedy.

The Way of the World in Performance

After the play's initial poor reception, Alexander Pope praised *The Way of the World* as having "so much bullion in it as would serve to lace fifty modern comedies." It was revived relatively soon after 1701 in London, and according to theater historian Emmet Avery, it played 285 times in the eighteenth century. It was one of the first plays at the new Covent Garden Theatre on December 7, 1732, and is said to be among the most-produced English comedies ever since. It is manifestly a vehicle for female stars. The great actress Dame Peggy Ashcroft, along with Dame Edith Evans, starred in the London production of 1942. The play has been done steadily in the United States since the 1920s. The Tyrone Guthrie Theater in Minneapolis produced it in 1965 to rave notices; Jessica Tandy as Lady Wishfort essentially stole the show. Britain's Actor's Company brought it to the Brooklyn Academy of Music in 1974, with the characters wearing cutaway formal clothes, top hats, and tails instead of eighteenth-century garb. The production used telephones and other modern conveniences to demonstrate that the play is not a museum piece. Robin Phillips's 1976 Stratford, Ontario, production was described as "nothing short of brilliant." Maggie Smith played Millamant several times in the 1980s, joining Jessica Tandy in her role as Lady Wishfort. Smith's performance in the January 1985 London production underscored the fact that the role is ideal for a great comic actress. She made the play her own. A good number of recent productions, since Ray Vitra's for the Pearl Theater in New York's East Village in 2000, have been well reviewed, despite concerns regarding the text's intelligibility for unprepared audiences.

William Congreve (1670–1729)
THE WAY OF THE WORLD   1700

Audire est operae pretium, procedere recte
Qui moechis non vultis.   —HORACE, *Satires*°

—*Metuat doti deprensa.*°

PROLOGUE

(*Spoken by Mr. Fainall.*)

Of those few fools who with ill stars are curst,
Sure scribbling fools, call'd poets, fare the worst;
For they're a sort of fools which Fortune makes,
And after she has made 'em fools, forsakes.
5   With Nature's oafs 'tis quite a different case,
For Fortune favors all her idiot-race;
In her° own nest the cuckoo-eggs we find,
O'er which she broods to hatch the
        changeling-kind.°
No portion for her own she has to spare,
10   So much she dotes on her adopted care.
    Poets are bubbles,° by the town drawn in,
Suffer'd at first some trifling stakes to win;
But what unequal hazards do they run!
Each time they write, they venture all they've won;

The squire that's buttered° still, is sure to be
    undone.   15
This author, heretofore, has found your favor,
But pleads no merit from his past behavior.
To build on that might prove a vain presumption,
Should grants to poets made admit resumption;
And in Parnassus° he must lose his seat,   20
If that be found a forfeited estate.
    He owns, with toil he wrought the following
        scenes,
But, if they're naught, ne'er spare him for his pains;
Damn him the more; have no commiseration
For dullness on mature deliberation.   25
He swears he'll not resent one hiss'd-off scene,
Nor, like those peevish wits, his play maintain,
Who, to assert their sense, your taste arraign.
Some plot we think he has, and some new thought;
Some humor too, no farce; but that's a fault.   30
Satire, he thinks, you ought not to expect;
For so reform'd a town who dares correct?
To please, this time, has been his sole pretense;
He'll not instruct, lest it should give offense.
Should he by chance a knave or fool expose,   35
That hurts none here, sure here are none of those.
In short, our play shall (with your leave to show it)
Give you one instance of a passive poet,
Who to your judgments yields all resignation;
So save or damn, after your own discretion.   40

[Epigraphs] *Audire . . . vultis:* Horace, *Satires* I.2.37–38. "Ye that do not wish well to the proceedings of adulterers, it is worth your while to hear how they are hampered on all sides" (trans. Christopher Smart). *Metuat doti deprensa:* Ibid., line 131. The context of the lines in which the epigraph appears is "Nor am I apprehensive, while I am in her company, . . . lest the maid . . . should be in apprehension for her limbs, *the detected wife for her portion* [dowry], I for myself" (trans. Smart).   7. **her:** Fortune's.   8. **O'er which . . . changeling-kind:** The cuckoo lays its eggs in the nests of other birds to whom they are left to be hatched. The implication is that Fortune is favorable to fools.   11. **bubbles:** Dupes.

15. **buttered:** Abundantly flattered.   20. **Parnassus:** The Greek mountain sacred to Apollo and the Muses.

Dramatis Personae

Men

FAINALL, *in love with Mrs. Marwood*
MIRABELL, *in love with Mrs. Millamant*
WITWOUD,⎫
PETULANT,⎭ *followers of Mrs. Millamant*
SIR WILFULL, WITWOUD, *half brother to Witwoud, and
    nephew to Lady Wishfort*
WAITWELL, *servant to Mirabell*

Women

LADY WISHFORT, *enemy to Mirabell, for having falsely
    pretended love to her*
MRS. MILLAMANT, *a fine lady, niece to Lady Wishfort,
    and loves Mirabell*
MRS. MARWOOD, *friend to Mr. Fainall, and likes
    Mirabell*
MRS. FAINALL, *daughter to Lady Wishfort, and wife to
    Fainall, formerly friend to Mirabell*
FOIBLE, *woman to Lady Wishfort*
MINCING, *woman to Mrs. Millamant*
BETTY, *waiting-maid at a chocolate-house*
PEG, *maid to Lady Wishfort*
DANCERS, FOOTMEN, *and* ATTENDANTS

Scene: *London. The time equal to that of the presentation.*

ACT I

(*A Chocolate-House. Mirabell and Fainall, rising from
cards; Betty waiting.*)

MIRABELL: You are a fortunate man, Mr. Fainall.
FAINALL: Have we done?
MIRABELL: What you please. I'll play on to entertain
    you.
5 FAINALL: No, I'll give you your revenge another time,
    when you are not so indifferent; you are thinking of
    something else now, and play too negligently. The
    coldness of a losing gamester lessens the pleasure of
    the winner. I'd no more play with a man that slighted
10   his ill fortune than I'd make love to a woman who
    undervalued the loss of her reputation.
MIRABELL: You have a taste extremely delicate and are
    for refining on your pleasures.
FAINALL: Prithee, why so reserved? Something has put
15   you out of humor.
MIRABELL: Not at all. I happen to be grave today, and
    you are gay; that's all.
FAINALL: Confess, Millamant and you quarreled last
    night, after I left you; my fair cousin has some
20   humors° that would tempt the patience of a Stoic.°

---

20. humors: Moods. **Stoic:** One who subscribes to the Stoic
school of philosophy, which teaches freedom from passion and
indifference to pleasure and pain.

What, some coxcomb° came in, and was well
    received by her, while you were by.
MIRABELL: Witwoud and Petulant, and what was worse,
    her aunt, your wife's mother, my evil genius; or to
    sum up all in her own name, my old Lady Wishfort   25
    came in.
FAINALL: Oh, there it is then! She has a lasting passion
    for you, and with reason. What, then my wife was
    there?
MIRABELL: Yes, and Mrs. Marwood, and three or four   30
    more, whom I never saw before. Seeing me, they all
    put on their grave faces, whispered one another; then
    complained aloud of the vapors,° and after fell into a
    profound silence.
FAINALL: They had a mind to be rid of you.   35
MIRABELL: For which reason I resolved not to stir. At
    last the good old lady broke through her painful taci-
    turnity with an invective against long visits. I would
    not have understood her, but Millamant joining in
    the argument, I rose, and, with a constrained smile,   40
    told her, I thought nothing was so easy as to know
    when a visit began to be troublesome. She reddened,
    and I withdrew, without expecting° her reply.
FAINALL: You were to blame to resent what she spoke
    only in compliance with her aunt.   45
MIRABELL: She is more mistress of herself than to be
    under the necessity of such a resignation.
FAINALL: What? though half her fortune depends upon
    her marrying with my lady's approbation?
MIRABELL: I was then in such a humor that I should   50
    have been better pleased if she had been less discreet.
FAINALL: Now I remember, I wonder not they were
    weary of you. Last night was one of their cabal
    nights; they have 'em three times a week, and meet by
    turns at one another's apartments, where they come   55
    together like the coroner's inquest, to sit upon the
    murdered reputations of the week. You and I are
    excluded; and it was once proposed that all the male
    sex should be excepted. But somebody moved that,
    to avoid scandal, there might be one man of the com-   60
    munity; upon which motion Witwoud and Petulant
    were enrolled members.°
MIRABELL: And who may have been the foundress of
    this sect? My Lady Wishfort, I warrant, who pub-
    lishes her detestation of mankind, and full of the   65
    vigor of fifty-five, declares for a friend° and ratafia,°
    and let posterity shift for itself, she'll breed no more.
FAINALL: The discovery of your sham addresses to her,
    to conceal your love to her niece, has provoked this
    separation; had you dissembled better, things might   70
    have continued in the state of nature.
MIRABELL: I did as much as man could, with any

---

21. coxcomb: Conceited person, fop. **33. vapors:** Boredom.
43. expecting: Awaiting. **61–62. Witwoud . . . members:** The
implication is that Witwoud and Petulant are but half-men.
66. friend: Lover. When applied to a lady, the word carries the
meaning of "mistress." **ratafia:** Fruit-flavored liqueur.

reasonable conscience; I proceeded to the very last act of flattery with her, and was guilty of a song in her commendation. Nay, I got a friend to put her into a lampoon, and compliment her with the imputation of an affair with a young fellow, which I carried so far that I told her the malicious town took notice that she was grown fat of a sudden; and when she lay in of a dropsy,° persuaded her she was reported to be in labor. The devil's in't, if an old woman is to be flattered further, unless a man should endeavor downright personally to debauch° her; and that my virtue forbade me. But for the discovery of this amour I am indebted to your friend, or your wife's friend, Mrs. Marwood.

FAINALL: What should provoke her to be your enemy, unless she has made you advances which you have slighted? Women do not easily forgive omissions of that nature.

MIRABELL: She was always civil to me till of late. I confess I am not one of those coxcombs who are apt to interpret a woman's good manners to her prejudice, and think that she who does not refuse 'em everything can refuse 'em nothing.

FAINALL: You are a gallant man, Mirabell; and though you may have cruelty enough not to satisfy a lady's longing, you have too much generosity not to be tender of her honor. Yet you speak with an indifference which seems to be affected, and confesses you are conscious of a negligence.

MIRABELL: You pursue the argument with a distrust that seems to be unaffected, and confesses you are conscious of a concern for which the lady is more indebted to you than is your wife.

FAINALL: Fie, fie, friend! If you grow censorious, I must leave you. I'll look upon the gamesters in the next room.

MIRABELL: Who are they?

FAINALL: Petulant and Witwoud. (*To Betty.*) Bring me some chocolate.   (*Exit.*)

MIRABELL: Betty, what says your clock?

BETTY: Turned of the last canonical hour,° sir.

                                              (*Exit.*)

MIRABELL: How pertinently the jade° answers me! (*Looking on his watch.*) Ha? almost one o'clock! O, y'are come!

(*Enter a Footman.*)

Well, is the grand affair over? You have been something tedious.

FOOTMAN: Sir, there's such coupling at Pancras° that they stand behind one another, as 'twere in a country dance. Ours was the last couple to lead up, and no hopes appearing of dispatch, besides the parson growing hoarse, we were afraid his lungs would have failed before it came to our turn, so we drove round to Duke's place,° and there they were riveted in a trice.°

MIRABELL: So, so, you are sure they are married.

FOOTMAN: Married and bedded, sir; I am witness.

MIRABELL: Have you the certificate?

FOOTMAN: Here it is, sir.

MIRABELL: Has the tailor brought Waitwell's clothes home, and the new liveries?

FOOTMAN: Yes, sir.

MIRABELL: That's well. Do you go home again, d'ye hear, and adjourn the consummation till further order; bid Waitwell shake his ears, and Dame Partlet° rustle up her feathers, and meet me at one o'clock by Rosamond's Pond,° that I may see her before she returns to her lady; and as you tender your ears, be secret.

                                    (*Exit Footman.*)

(*Reenter Fainall and Betty.*)

FAINALL: Joy of your success, Mirabell; you look pleased.

MIRABELL: Aye, I have been engaged in a matter of some sort of mirth, which is not yet ripe for discovery. I am glad this is not a cabal night. I wonder, Fainall, that you who are married, and of consequence should be discreet, will suffer your wife to be of such a parry.

FAINALL: Faith, I am not jealous. Besides, most who are engaged are women and relations; and for the men, they are of a kind too contemptible to give scandal.

MIRABELL: I am of another opinion. The greater the coxcomb, always the more the scandal; for a woman who is not a fool can have but one reason for associating with a man who is one.

FAINALL: Are you jealous as often as you see Witwoud entertained by Millamant?

MIRABELL: Of her understanding I am, if not of her person.

FAINALL: You do her wrong; for, to give her her due, she has wit.

MIRABELL: She has beauty enough to make any man think so, and complaisance enough not to contradict him who shall tell her so.

FAINALL: For a passionate lover, methinks you are a man somewhat too discerning in the failings of your mistress.

MIRABELL: And for a discerning man, somewhat too passionate a lover; for I like her with all her faults, nay, like her for her faults. Her follies are so natural,

---

80. **dropsy:** An excessive accumulation of fluid in the body. 83. **debauch:** Seduce.   113. **canonical hour:** It was only during the canonical hours (eight in the morning to twelve noon) that marriages could be legally performed.   114. **jade:** Derogatory term for a woman.   119. **Pancras:** St. Pancras Church, where marriages were performed without license and outside the canonical hours.

125. **Duke's place:** St. James's Church, Aldgate. **riveted in a trice:** Married quickly. 135. **Dame Partlet:** Refers to Foible, who has just been married to Waitwell. "Partlet" derives from Pertelote, the hen in Chaucer's "Nun's Priest's Tale." 137. **Rosamond's Pond:** A lake in St. James's Park.

or so artful, that they become her, and those affectations which in another woman would be odious,
serve but to make her more agreeable. I'll tell thee,
Fainall, she once used me with that insolence, that in
revenge I took her to pieces, sifted° her, and separated her failings, I studied 'em, and got 'em by rote.°
The catalogue was so large that I was not without
hopes one day or other to hate her heartily: To which
end I so used° myself to think of 'em that at length,
contrary to my design and expectation, they gave me
every hour less and less disturbance, till in a few days
it became habitual to me to remember 'em without
being displeased. They are now grown as familiar to
me as my own frailties; and in all probability, in a
little time longer I shall like 'em as well.

FAINALL: Marry her, marry her! Be half as well acquainted
with her charms as you are with her defects, and my
life on't, you are your own man again.

MIRABELL: Say you so?

FAINALL: Aye, aye, I have experience; I have a wife, and
so forth.

(*Enter a Messenger.*)

MESSENGER: Is one Squire Witwoud here?

BETTY: Yes; what's your business?

MESSENGER: I have a letter for him, from his brother Sir
Wilfull, which I am charged to deliver into his own
hands.

BETTY: He's in the next room, friend; that way.

(*Exit Messenger.*)

MIRABELL: What, is the chief of that noble family in
town, Sir Wilfull Witwoud?

FAINALL: He is expected today. Do you know him?

MIRABELL: I have seen him. He promises to be an
extraordinary° person; I think you have the honor to
be related to him.

FAINALL: Yes, he is half brother to this Witwoud by a
former wife, who was sister to my Lady Wishfort, my
wife's mother. If you marry Millamant, you must call
cousins too.

MIRABELL: I had rather be his relation than his acquaintance.

FAINALL: He comes to town in order to equip himself
for travel.

MIRABELL: For travel! Why the man that I mean is
above forty.°

FAINALL: No matter for that; 'tis for the honor of
England that all Europe should know we have blockheads of all ages.

MIRABELL: I wonder there is not an act of parliament to
save the credit of the nation, and prohibit the expor-
tation of fools.

FAINALL: By no means; 'tis better as 'tis. 'Tis better to

trade with a little loss than to be quite eaten up with
being overstocked.

MIRABELL: Pray, are the follies of this knight-errant and
those of the squire his brother anything related?

FAINALL: Not at all; Witwoud grows by the knight, like
a medlar grafted on a crab.° One will melt in your
mouth, and t'other set your teeth on edge; one is all
pulp, and the other all core.

MIRABELL: So one will be rotten before he be ripe, and
the other will be rotten without ever being ripe at all.

FAINALL: Sir Wilfull is an odd mixture of bashfulness
and obstinacy. But when he's drunk, he's as loving as
the monster in *The Tempest*,° and much after the
same manner. To give t'other his due, he has something of good nature and does not always want wit.

MIRABELL: Not always; but as often as his memory fails
him, and his commonplace° of comparisons. He is a
fool with a good memory and sonic few scraps of
other folks' wit. He is one whose conversation can
never be approved, yet it is now and then to be
endured. He has indeed one good quality, he is not
exceptious;° for he so passionately affects the reputation of understanding raillery° that he will construe
an affront into a jest and call downright rudeness
and ill language, satire and fire.

FAINALL: If you have a mind to finish his picture, you
have an opportunity to do it at full length. Behold the
original!

(*Enter Witwoud.*)

WITWOUD: Afford me your compassion, my dears! Pity
me, Fainall! Mirabell, pity me!

MIRABELL: I do from my soul.

FAINALL: Why, what's the matter?

WITWOUD: No letters for me, Betty?

BETTY: Did not a messenger bring you one but now, sir?

WITWOUD: Aye, but no other?

BETTY: No, sir.

WITWOUD: That's hard, that's very hard. A messenger, a
mule, a beast of burden! He has brought me a letter
from the fool my brother, as heavy as a panegyric°
in a funeral sermon, or a copy of commendatory
verses from one poet to another. And what's worse,
'tis as sure a forerunner of the author as an epistle
dedicatory.

MIRABELL: A fool, and your brother, Witwoud!

WITWOUD: Aye, aye, my half brother. My half brother
he is, no nearer upon honor.

MIRABELL: Then 'tis possible he may be but half a fool.

---

173. sifted: Examined closely.   **174. by rote:** In a mechanical
way.   **177. used:** Accustomed.   **200. extraordinary:** Somewhat
eccentric.   **211. above forty:** It was customary for a gentleman
of quality to make a "grand tour" of continental capitals in his
early twenties.

224. medlar grafted on a crab: The medlar is like a crab apple
and is edible only when it begins to decay. The crab apple
is always sour.   **231. the monster in *The Tempest*:** Caliban
(or Sycorax) in the adaptation of Shakespeare's play by John
Dryden and Sir William Davenant (1667).   **235. commonplace:** Commonplace book; scrapbook.   **240. exceptious:**
Inclined to take exceptions.   **241. raillery:** Good-humored
ridicule; banter.   **257. panegyric:** Eulogy; especially involving
elaborate praise.

WITWOUD: Good, good, Mirabell, *le drôle*!° Good, good; hang him, don't let's talk of him. Fainall, how does your lady? Gad, I say anything in the world to get this fellow out of my head. I beg pardon that I should ask a man of pleasure and the town a question at once so foreign and domestic.° But I talk like an old maid at a marriage, I don't know what I say; but she's the best woman in the world.°

FAINALL: 'Tis well you don't know what you say, or else your commendation would go near to make me either vain or jealous.

WITWOUD: No man in town lives well with a wife but Fainall. Your judgment, Mirabell?

MIRABELL: You had better step and ask his wife, if you would he credibly informed.

WITWOUD: Mirabell.

MIRABELL: Aye.

WITWOUD: My dear, I ask ten thousand pardons; gad, I have forgot what I was going to say to you!

MIRABELL: I thank you heartily, heartily.

WITWOUD: No, but prithee excuse me; my memory is such a memory.

MIRABELL: Have a care of such apologies, Witwoud; for I never knew a fool but he affected to complain, either of the spleen° or his memory.

FAINALL: What have you done with Petulant?

WITWOUD: He's reckoning his money—my money it was. I have no luck today.

FAINALL: You may allow him to win of you at play, for you are sure to be too hard for him at repartee;° since you monopolize the wit that is between you, the fortune must be his, of course.

MIRABELL: I don't find that Petulant confesses the superiority of wit to be your talent, Witwoud.

WITWOUD: Come, come, you are malicious now, and would breed debates. Petulant's my friend, and a very honest fellow, and a very pretty fellow, and has a smattering—faith and troth,° a pretty deal of an odd sort of a small wit; nay, I'll do him justice. I'm his friend, I won't wrong him. And if he had any judgment in the world, he would not be altogether contemptible. Come, come, don't detract from the merits of my friend.

FAINALL: You don't take your friend to be over-nicely bred?

WITWOUD: No, no, hang him, the rogue has no manners at all, that I must own. No more breeding than a bum-baily,° that I grant you. 'Tis pity, faith; the fellow has fire and life.

MIRABELL: What, courage?

WITWOUD: Hum, faith I don't know as to that; I can't say as to that. Yes, faith, in a controversy he'll contradict anybody.

MIRABELL: Though 'twere a man whom he feared, or a woman whom he loved?

WITWOUD: Well, well, he does not always think before he speaks; we have all our failings. You are too hard upon him, you are, faith. Let me excuse him. I can defend most of his faults, except one or two. One he has, that's the truth on't; if he were my brother, I could not acquit him. That indeed I could wish were otherwise.

MIRABELL: Aye, marry, what's that, Witwoud?

WITWOUD: Oh, pardon me! Expose the infirmities of my friend? No, my dear, excuse me there.

FAINALL: What, I warrant he's unsincere, or 'tis some such trifle.

WITWOUD: No, no, what if he be? 'Tis no matter for that; his wit will excuse that. A wit should no more be sincere than a woman constant; one argues a decay of parts,° as t'other of beauty.

MIRABELL: Maybe you think him too positive?

WITWOUD: No, no, his being positive is an incentive to argument, and keeps up conversation.

FAINALL: Too illiterate?

WITWOUD: That! that's his happiness; his want of learning gives him the more opportunities to show his natural parts.

MIRABELL: He wants words?

WITWOUD: Aye, but I like him for that now; for his want of words gives me the pleasure very often to explain his meaning.

FAINALL: He's impudent?

WITWOUD: No, that's not it.

MIRABELL: Vain?

WITWOUD: No.

MIRABELL: What! he speaks unseasonable truths sometimes, because he has not wit enough to invent an evasion?

WITWOUD: Truths! ha! ha! ha! No, no; since you will have it, I mean he never speaks truth at all, that's all. He will lie like a chambermaid, or a woman of quality's porter. Now that is a fault.

(*Enter a Coachman.*)

COACHMAN: Is Master Petulant here, mistress?

BETTY: Yes.

COACHMAN: Three gentlewomen in a coach would speak with him.

FAINALL: O brave Petulant! Three!

BETTY: I'll tell him.

COACHMAN: You must bring two dishes of chocolate and a glass of cinnamon-water.°

(*Exeunt*° *Betty and Coachman.*)

---

266. *le drôle:* The wag.   271. **foreign and domestic:** Since he knows (by gossip) that the Fainall marriage is not working out very well, Witwoud plays on the words "foreign and domestic."   273. **best woman in the world:** I.e., Mrs. Fainall. Witwoud realizes that he has blundered into a rather delicate situation.   290. **spleen:** Ill humor; peevishness.   295. **repartee:** Adroitness and cleverness in making replies in conversation.   303. **troth:** Loyalty, faithfulness.   313. **bum-baily:** An under-bailiff, a minor court officer.

335. **parts:** Personal endowments.   365. **cinnamon-water:** A cordial of spirits, cinnamon, and hot water, prescribed to aid digestion.   [S.D.] *Exeunt:* Latin for "they go out."

WITWOUD: That should be for two fasting strumpets,° and a bawd troubled with wind.° Now you may know what the three are.

MIRABELL: You are very free with your friend's acquaintance.

WITWOUD: Aye, aye, friendship without freedom is as dull as love without enjoyment, or wine without toasting. But to tell you a secret, these are trulls° whom he allows coach-hire, and something more, by the week, to call on him once a day at public places.

MIRABELL: How!

WITWOUD: You shall see how he won't go to 'em, because there's no more company here to take notice of him. Why, this is nothing to what he used to do; before he found out this way, I have known him call for himself.

FAINALL: Call for himself? What dost thou mean?

WITWOUD: Mean! Why, he would slip you out° of this chocolate-house, just when you had been talking to him; as soon as your back was turned, whip, he was gone! Then trip to his lodging, clap on a hood and scarf, and a mask, slap into a hackney-coach, and drive hither to the door again in a trice, where he would send in for himself; that I mean, call for himself, wait for himself. Nay, and what's more, not finding himself, sometimes leave a letter for himself.

MIRABELL: I confess this is something extraordinary. I believe he waits for himself now, he is so long a-coming. Oh! I ask his pardon.

(*Enter Petulant and Betty.*)

BETTY: Sir, the coach stays.

PETULANT: Well, well, I come. 'Sbud,° a man had as good be a professed midwife as a professed whoremaster, at this rate! To be knocked up and raised at all hours, and in all places! Pox on 'em, I won't come! D'ye hear, tell 'em I won't come. Let 'em snivel and cry their hearts out.

FAINALL: You are very cruel, Petulant.

PETULANT: All's one, let it pass. I have a humor to be cruel.

MIRABELL: I hope they are not persons of condition° that you use at this rate.

PETULANT: Condition! Condition's a dried fig, if I am not in humor! By this hand, if they were your—a—a—your what-d'ye-call-'ems themselves, they must wait or rub off,° if I want appetite.°

MIRABELL: What-d'ye-call-'ems! What are they, Witwoud?

WITWOUD: Empresses, my dear; by your what-d'ye-call-'ems he means sultana queens.

PETULANT: Aye, Roxolanas.°

MIRABELL: Cry you mercy!   415

FAINALL: Witwoud says they are—

PETULANT: What does he say th'are?

WITWOUD: I? Fine ladies, I say.

PETULANT: Pass on, Witwoud. Harkee, by this light his relations: two co-heiresses his cousins, and an old   420
aunt, who loves caterwauling° better than a conventicle.°

WITWOUD: Ha! ha! ha! I had a mind to see how the rogue would come off. Ha! ha! ha! Gad, I can't be angry with him, if he had said they were my mother   425
and my sisters.

MIRABELL: No!

WITWOUD: No; the rogue's wit and readiness of invention charm me. Dear Petulant!

BETTY: They are gone, sir, in great anger.   430

PETULANT: Enough, let 'em trundle. Anger helps complexion, saves paint.°

FAINALL: This continence is all dissembled; this is in order to have something to brag of the next time he makes court to Millamant, and swear he has aban-   435
doned the whole sex for her sake.

MIRABELL: Have you not left off your impudent pretensions there yet? I shall cut your throat some time or other, Petulant, about that business.

PETULANT: Aye, aye, let that pass. There are other   440
throats to be cut.

MIRABELL: Meaning mine, sir?

PETULANT: Not I. I mean nobody; I know nothing. But there are uncles and nephews in the world, and they may be rivals. What then? All's one for that.   445

MIRABELL: How! harkee Petulant, come hither. Explain, or I shall call your interpreter.°

PETULANT: Explain! I know nothing. Why, you have an uncle, have you not, lately come to town, and lodges by my Lady Wishfort's?   450

MIRABELL: True.

PETULANT: Why, that's enough. You and he are not friends; and if he should marry and have a child, you may be disinherited, ha?

MIRABELL: Where hast thou stumbled upon all this   455
truth?

PETULANT: All's one for that; why, then say I know something.

MIRABELL: Come, thou art an honest fellow, Petulant, and shalt make love to my mistress, thou sha't,°   460
faith. What hast thou heard of my uncle?

PETULANT: I? Nothing I. If throats are to be cut, let swords clash! Snug's the word;° I shrug and am silent.

MIRABELL: Oh, raillery, raillery! Come, I know thou art   465
in the women's secrets. What, you're a cabalist; I

---

366. **strumpets:** Prostitutes.   367. **wind:** Air in the stomach or bowels.   373. **trulls:** Women of easy virtue.   382. **slip you out:** Slip out.   395. **'Sbud:** "God's blood," a mild oath.   404. **condition:** Social distinction.   409. **rub off:** Go away. **want appetite:** Lack desire for them.   414. **Roxolanas:** Roxolana is the name of the Turkish sultana in Davenant's *The Siege of Rhodes* (1656), one of the first "heroic plays."

421. **caterwauling:** Noisy quarreling.   421–22. **conventicle:** A meetinghouse of nonconformist religious sects, especially Presbyterians.   432. **paint:** Makeup.   447. **interpreter:** Possibly a second, as in a duel.   460. **sha't:** Slangy contraction for "shalt."   463. **Snug's the word:** In modern slang, "Mum's the word."

know you stayed at Millamant's last night, after I went. Was there any mention made of my uncle or me? Tell me. If thou hadst but good nature equal to thy wit, Petulant, Tony Witwoud, who is now thy competitor in fame, would show as dim by thee as a dead whiting's° eye by a pearl of orient;° he would no more be seen by thee than Mercury is by the sun.° Come, I'm sure thou wo't° tell me.

PETULANT: If I do, will you grant me common sense then for the future?

MIRABELL: Faith, I'll do what I can for thee, and I'll pray that Heaven may grant it thee in the meantime.

PETULANT: Well, harkee.

(*Mirabell and Petulant talk apart.*)

FAINALL: Petulant and you both will find Mirabell as warm a rival as a lover.

WITWOUD: Pshaw! pshaw! That she laughs at Petulant is plain. And for my part, but that it is almost a fashion to admire her, I should—Harkee, to tell you a secret, but let it go no further; between friends, I shall never break my heart for her.

FAINALL: How?

WITWOUD: She's handsome; but she's a sort of an uncertain woman.

FAINALL: I thought you had died for her.

WITWOUD: Umh—no—

FAINALL: She has wit.

WITWOUD: 'Tis what she will hardly allow anybody else. Now, demme,° I should hate that, if she were as handsome as Cleopatra. Mirabell is not so sure of her as he thinks for.

FAINALL: Why do you think so?

WITWOUD: We stayed pretty late there last night, and heard something of an uncle to Mirabell, who is lately come to town, and is between him and the best part of his estate. Mirabell and he are at some distance, as my Lady Wishfort has been told; and you know she hates Mirabell worse than a Quaker hates a parrot,° or than a fishmonger hates a hard frost.° Whether this uncle has seen Mrs. Millamant or not, I cannot say; but there were items of such a treaty being in embryo, and if it should come to life, poor Mirabell would be in some sort unfortunately fobbed,° i'faith.

FAINALL: 'Tis impossible Millamant should hearken to it.

WITWOUD: Faith, my dear, I can't tell; she's a woman, and a kind of a humorist.°

MIRABELL: And this° is the sum of what you could collect last night?

PETULANT: The quintessence. Maybe Witwoud knows more; he stayed longer. Besides, they never mind him; they say anything before him.

MIRABELL: I thought you had been the greatest favorite.

PETULANT: Aye, *tête à tête*,° but not in public, because I make remarks.

MIRABELL: You do?

PETULANT: Aye, aye, pox, I'm malicious, man! Now he's soft, you know; they are not in awe of him. The fellow's well bred; he's what you call a what-d'ye-call-'em, a fine gentleman; but he's silly withal.

MIRABELL: I thank you. I know as much as my curiosity requires. Fainall, are you for the Mall?°

FAINALL: Aye, I'll take a turn before dinner.

WITWOUD: Aye, we'll walk in the Park; the ladies talked of being there.

MIRABELL: I thought you were obliged to watch for your brother Sir Wilfull's arrival.

WITWOUD: No, no, he comes to his aunt's, my Lady Wishfort. Pox on him! I shall he troubled with him too; what shall I do with the fool?

PETULANT: Beg him for his estate, that I may beg you afterwards; and so have but one trouble with you both.

WITWOUD: O rare Petulant! Thou art as quick as fire in a frosty morning; thou shalt to the Mall with us, and we'll be very severe.

PETULANT: Enough, I'm in a humor to be severe.

MIRABELL: Are you? Pray then walk by yourselves: Let us not be accessory to your putting the ladies out of countenance with your senseless ribaldry,° which you roar out aloud as often as they pass by you; and when you have made a handsome woman blush, then you think you have been severe.

PETULANT: What, what? Then let 'em either show their innocence by not understanding what they hear, or else show their discretion by not hearing what they would not be thought to understand.

MIRABELL: But hast not thou then sense enough to know that thou oughtest to be most ashamed thyself, when thou hast put another out of countenance?

PETULANT: Not I, by this hand! I always take blushing either for a sign of guilt or ill breeding.

MIRABELL: I confess you ought to think so. You are in the right, that you may plead the error of your judgment in defense of your practice.

Where modesty's ill manners, 'tis but fit
That impudence and malice pass for wit.

(*Exeunt.*)

---

472. **whiting:** A kind of codfish.   **pearl of orient:** Said to be particularly brilliant.   473. **than Mercury is by the sun:** The planet nearest the sun and of very low magnitude. 474. **wo't:** Wilt.   494. **demme:** Contraction of "damn me." 503–04. **Quaker . . . parrot:** Parrots are proverbially known to swear.   504. **fishmonger . . . frost:** Fishmongers peddled fish and consequently hated very cold weather. 509. **fobbed:** Cheated.   513. **humorist:** A moody or capricious person, hence unreliable.

514. **And this:** During the dialogue of Fainall and Witwoud, Mirabell and Petulant have been talking "apart." They now reenter the general dialogue.   520. *tête à tête:* Head to head. 528. **Mall:** A fashionable walk in St. James's Park.   546. **ribaldry:** Coarse behavior or language.

Scene from an updated version of *The Way of the World*, directed by Sharon Ott in 1992 at the Huntington Theatre in Boston.

ACT II

(St. James's Park. Enter Mrs. Fainall and Mrs. Marwood.)

MRS. FAINALL: Aye, aye, dear Marwood, if we will be happy, we must find the means in ourselves, and among ourselves. Men are ever in extremes, either doting or averse. While they are lovers, if they have
5 fire and sense, their jealousies are insupportable. And when they cease to love (we ought to think at least) they loathe; they look upon us with horror and distaste; they meet us like the ghosts of what we were, and as from such, fly from us.
10 MRS. MARWOOD: True, 'tis an unhappy circumstance of life that love should ever die before us; and that the man so often should outlive the lover. But say what you will, 'tis better to be left than never to have been loved. To pass our youth in dull indifference, to
15 refuse the sweets of life because they once must leave us, is as preposterous as to wish to have been born old, because we one day must be old. For my part, my youth may wear and waste, but it shall never rust in my possession.

MRS. FAINALL: Then it seems you dissemble an aversion   20
to mankind, only in compliance to my mother's humor?

MRS. MARWOOD: Certainly. To be free,° I have no taste of those insipid dry discourses with which our sex of force must entertain themselves, apart from men. We   25
may affect endearments to each other, profess eternal friendships, and seem to dote like lovers; but 'tis not in our natures long to persevere. Love will resume his empire in our breasts; and every heart, or soon or late, receive and readmit him as its lawful tyrant.   30

MRS. FAINALL: Bless me, how have I been deceived! Why, you profess a libertine!°

23. free: Frank.   32. profess a libertine: Speak as one who leads a loose, unconventional life.

MRS. MARWOOD: You see my friendship by my freedom. Come, be as sincere, acknowledge that your sentiments agree with mine.

MRS. FAINALL: Never!

MRS. MARWOOD: You hate mankind?

MRS. FAINALL: Heartily, inveterately.

MRS. MARWOOD: Your husband?

MRS. FAINALL: Most transcendently; aye, though I say it, meritoriously.

MRS. MARWOOD: Give me your hand upon it.

MRS. FAINALL: There.

MRS. MARWOOD: I join with you; what I have said has been to try you.

MRS. FAINALL: Is it possible? Dost thou hate those vipers, men?

MRS. MARWOOD: I have done hating 'em; and am now come to despise 'em; the next thing I have to do, is eternally to forget 'em.

MRS. FAINALL: There spoke the spirit of an Amazon, a Penthesilea!°

MRS. MARWOOD: And yet I am thinking sometimes to carry my aversion further.

MRS. FAINALL: How?

MRS. MARWOOD: Faith, by marrying; if I could but find one that loved me very well and would be thoroughly sensible of ill usage, I think I should do myself the violence of undergoing the ceremony.

MRS. FAINALL: You would not make him a cuckold?

MRS. MARWOOD: No, but I'd make him believe I did, and that's as bad.

MRS. FAINALL: Why had not you as good do it?

MRS. MARWOOD: Oh, if he should ever discover it, he would then know the worst, and be out of his pain; but I would have him ever to continue upon the rack of fear and jealousy.

MRS. FAINALL: Ingenious mischief! Would thou wert married to Mirabell.

MRS. MARWOOD: Would I were!

MRS. FAINALL: You change color.

MRS. MARWOOD: Because I hate him.

MRS. FAINALL: So do I; but I can hear him named. But what reason have you to hate him in particular?

MRS. MARWOOD: I never loved him; he is, and always was, insufferably proud.

MRS. FAINALL: By the reason you give for your aversion, one would think it dissembled; for you have laid a fault to his charge of which his enemies must acquit him.

MRS. MARWOOD: Oh, then it seems you are one of his favorable enemies. Methinks you look a little pale, and now you flush again.

MRS. FAINALL: Do I? I think I am a little sick o' the sudden.

MRS. MARWOOD: What ails you?

MRS. FAINALL: My husband. Don't you see him? He turned short upon me unawares, and has almost overcome me.

(*Enter Fainall and Mirabell.*)

MRS. MARWOOD: Ha! ha! ha! He comes opportunely for you.

MRS. FAINALL: For you, for he has brought Mirabell with him.

FAINALL: My dear!

MRS. FAINALL: My soul!

FAINALL: You don't look well today, child.

MRS. FAINALL: D'ye think so?

MIRABELL: He is the only man that does, madam.

MRS. FAINALL: The only man that would tell me so at least; and the only man from whom I could hear it without mortification.

FAINALL: O my dear, I am satisfied of your tenderness; I know you cannot resent anything from me, especially what is in effect of my concern.

MRS. FAINALL: Mr. Mirabell, my mother interrupted you in a pleasant relation last night; I would fain hear it out.

MIRABELL: The persons concerned in that affair have yet a tolerable reputation. I am afraid Mr. Fainall will be censorious.

MRS. FAINALL: He has a humor more prevailing than his curiosity and will willingly dispense with the hearing of one scandalous story, to avoid giving an occasion to make another by being seen to walk with his wife. This way, Mr. Mirabell, and I dare promise you will oblige us both.

(*Exeunt Mrs. Fainall and Mirabell.*)

FAINALL: Excellent creature! Well, sure if I should live to be rid of my wife, I should be a miserable man.

MRS. MARWOOD: Aye!

FAINALL: For having only that one hope, the accomplishment of it, of consequence, must put an end to all my hopes; and what a wretch is he who must survive his hopes! Nothing remains when that day comes, but to sit down and weep like Alexander,° when he wanted other worlds to conquer.

MRS. MARWOOD: Will you not follow 'em?

FAINALL: Faith, I think not.

MRS. MARWOOD: Pray let us; I have a reason.

FAINALL: You are not jealous?

MRS. MARWOOD: Of whom?

FAINALL: Of Mirabell.

MRS. MARWOOD: If I am, is it inconsistent with my love to you that I am tender of your honor?

FAINALL: You would intimate, then, as if there were a fellow-feeling between my wife and him.

MRS. MARWOOD: I think she does not hate him to that degree she would be thought.

---

52. **Penthesilea:** Queen of the Amazons, the mythical race of women warriors. After befriending Priam following the death of Hector, she was killed by Achilles, who fell in love with her as she lay dying.

124. **Alexander:** Alexander the Great (356–323 BCE), the powerful ruler and conqueror.

FAINALL: But he, I fear, is too insensible.

MRS. MARWOOD: It may be you are deceived.

140 FAINALL: It may be so. I do now begin to apprehend it.

MRS. MARWOOD: What?

FAINALL: That I have been deceived, madam, and you are false.

MRS. MARWOOD: That I am false! What mean you?

145 FAINALL: To let you know I see through all your little arts. Come, you both love him; and both have equally dissembled your aversion. Your mutual jealousies of one another have made you clash till you have both struck fire. I have seen the warm confes-150 sion reddening on your cheeks and sparkling from your eyes.

MRS. MARWOOD: You do me wrong.

FAINALL: I do not. 'Twas for my ease to oversee° and willfully neglect the gross advances made him by my 155 wife; that by permitting her to be engaged, I might continue unsuspected in my pleasures, and take you oftener to my arms in full security. But could you think, because the nodding husband would not awake, that e'er the watchful lover slept?

160 MRS. MARWOOD: And wherewithal can you reproach me?

FAINALL: With infidelity, with loving another, with love of Mirabell.

MRS. MARWOOD: 'Tis false! I challenge you to show an 165 instance that can confirm your groundless accusation. I hate him.

FAINALL: And wherefore do you hate him? He is insensible, and your resentment follows his neglect. An instance? The injuries you have done him are a proof, 170 your interposing in his love. What cause had you to make discoveries of his pretended passion? to undeceive the credulous aunt, and be the officious obstacle of his match with Millamant?

MRS. MARWOOD: My obligations to my lady urged me; 175 I had professed a friendship to her, and could not see her easy nature so abused by that dissembler.

FAINALL: What, was it conscience then? Professed a friendship! Oh, the pious friendships of the female sex!

180 MRS. MARWOOD: More tender, more sincere, and more enduring, than all the vain and empty vows of men, whether professing love to us, or mutual faith to one another.

FAINALL: Ha! ha! ha! You are my wife's friend too.

185 MRS. MARWOOD: Shame and ingratitude! Do you reproach me? You, you upbraid me? Have I been false to her, through strict fidelity to you, and sacrificed my friendship to keep my love inviolate? And have you the baseness to charge me with the guilt, unmindful of 190 the merit? To you it should be meritorious, that I have been vicious, and do you reflect that guilt upon me, which should lie buried in your bosom?

FAINALL: You misinterpret my reproof. I meant but to remind you of the slight account you once could

make of strictest ties, when set in competition with 195 your love to me.

MRS. MARWOOD: 'Tis false; you urged it with deliberate malice! 'Twas spoke in scorn, and I never will forgive it.

FAINALL: Your guilt, not your resentment, begets your 200 rage. If yet you loved, you could forgive a jealousy; but you are stung to find that you are discovered.

MRS. MARWOOD: It shall be all discovered. You too shall be discovered, be sure you shall. I can but be exposed. If I do it myself, I shall prevent° your baseness. 205

FAINALL: Why, what will you do?

MRS. MARWOOD: Disclose it to your wife; own what has passed between us.

FAINALL: Frenzy!

MRS. MARWOOD: By all my wrongs I'll do't! I'll publish 210 to the world the injuries you have done me, both in my fame and fortune! With both I trusted you, you bankrupt in honor, as indigent of wealth.

FAINALL: Your fame I have preserved. Your fortune has been bestowed as the prodigality of your love would 215 have it, in pleasures which we both have shared. Yet, had not you been false, I had ere this repaid it. 'Tis true, had you permitted Mirabell with Millamant to have stolen their marriage, my lady had been incensed beyond all means of reconcilement, Milla-220 mant had forfeited the moiety° of her fortune, which then would have descended to my wife. And wherefore did I marry, but to make lawful prize of a rich widow's wealth, and squander it on love and you?

MRS. MARWOOD: Deceit and frivolous pretense! 225

FAINALL: Death, am I not married? What's pretense? Am I not imprisoned, fettered? Have I not a wife? nay a wife that was a widow, a young widow, a handsome widow; and would be again a widow, but that I have a heart of proof,° and something of a constitution to 230 bustle through the ways of wedlock and this world! Will you yet be reconciled to truth and me?

MRS. MARWOOD: Impossible. Truth and you are inconsistent. I hate you, and shall for ever.

FAINALL: For loving you? 235

MRS. MARWOOD: I loathe the name of love after such usage; and next to the guilt with which you would asperse me, I scorn you most. Farewell!

FAINALL: Nay, we must not part thus.

MRS. MARWOOD: Let me go. 240

FAINALL: Come, I'm sorry.

MRS. MARWOOD: I care not, let me go, break my hands, do! I'd leave 'em to get loose.

FAINALL: I would not hurt you for the world. Have I no other hold to keep you here? 245

MRS. MARWOOD: Well, I have deserved it all.

FAINALL: You know I love you.

MRS. MARWOOD: Poor dissembling! Oh, that—well, It is not yet—

153. oversee: Overlook.

205. prevent: Anticipate. 221. moiety: Half. 230. heart of proof: A heart that is proof against such wishes.

250   FAINALL: What? what is it not? what is it not yet? It is
       not yet too late—
       MRS. MARWOOD: No, it is not yet too late; I have that
       comfort.
       FAINALL: It is, to love another.
255   MRS. MARWOOD: But not to loathe, detest, abhor
       mankind, myself, and the whole treacherous world.
       FAINALL: Nay, this is extravagance. Come, I ask your
       pardon. No tears. I was to blame; I could not love
       you and be easy in my doubts. Pray, forbear. I believe
260   you. I'm convinced I've done you wrong; and any
       way, every way will make amends. I'll hate my wife
       yet more, damn her! I'll part with her, rob her of all
       she's worth, and we'll retire somewhere, anywhere,
       to another world. I'll marry thee; be pacified.
265   'Sdeath,° they come; hide your face, your tears. You
       have a mask;° wear it a moment. This way, this way.
       Be persuaded.

                                                      (*Exeunt.*)

(*Reenter Mirabell and Mrs. Fainall.*)

       MRS. FAINALL: They are here yet.
       MIRABELL: They are turning into the other walk.
270   MRS. FAINALL: While I only hated my husband, I could
       bear to see him; but since I have despised him, he's
       too offensive.
       MIRABELL: Oh, you should hate with prudence.
       MRS. FAINALL: Yes, for I have loved with indiscretion.
275   MIRABELL: You should have just so much disgust for
       your husband as may be sufficient to make you relish
       your lover.
       MRS. FAINALL: You have been the cause that I have
       loved without bounds, and would you set limits to
280   that aversion of which you have been the occasion?
       Why did you make me marry this man?
       MIRABELL: Why do we daily commit disagreeable and
       dangerous actions? To save that idol, reputation. If
       the familiarities of our loves had produced that con-
285   sequence of which you were apprehensive, where
       could you have fixed a father's name with credit, but
       on a husband?° I knew Fainall to be a man lavish of
       his morals, an interested and professing° friend, a
       false and a designing lover; yet one whose wit and
290   outward fair behavior have gained a reputation with
       the town enough to make that woman stand excused
       who has suffered herself to be won by his addresses.
       A better man ought not to have been sacrificed to the
       occasion; a worse had not answered to the purpose.
295   When you are weary of him, you know your remedy.

265. **'Sdeath:** "God's death," an oath.   266. **mask:** Ladies'
masks were fashionable and reputable except when worn at the
theater, where they were construed as the mark of a loose
woman.   283–87. **If the familiarities . . . husband:** Mirabell
refers to his affair with Mrs. Fainall, after the death of her first
husband, Mr. Languish, and prior to her marriage to Fainall.
She feared that she was pregnant by Mirabell, and as a result
Mirabell urged her marriage to Fainall.   288. **professing:** Self-
interested and dissembling.

       MRS. FAINALL: I ought to stand in some degree of credit
       with you, Mirabell.
       MIRABELL: In justice to you, I have made you privy to
       my whole design, and put it in your power to ruin or
       advance my fortune.   300
       MRS. FAINALL: Whom have you instructed to represent
       your pretended uncle?
       MIRABELL: Waitwell, my servant.
       MRS. FAINALL: He is an humble servant° to Foible, my
       mother's woman, and may win her to your interest.   305
       MIRABELL: Care is taken for that. She is won and worn
       by this time. They were married this morning.
       MRS. FAINALL: Who?
       MIRABELL: Waitwell and Foible. I would not tempt my
       servant to betray me by trusting him too far. If your   310
       mother, in hopes to ruin me, should consent to marry
       my pretended uncle, he might, like Mosca in *The
       Fox*,° stand upon terms;° so I made him sure before-
       hand.
       MRS. FAINALL: So if my poor mother is caught in a con-   315
       tract, you will discover the imposture betimes, and
       release her by producing a certificate of her gallant's
       former marriage?
       MIRABELL: Yes, upon condition that she consent to my
       marriage with her niece, and surrender the moiety of   320
       her fortune in her possession.°
       MRS. FAINALL: She talked last night of endeavoring at a
       match between Millamant and your uncle.
       MIRABELL: That was by Foible's direction, and my instruc-
       tion, that she might seem to carry it more privately.°   325
       MRS. FAINALL: Well, I have an opinion of your success
       for I believe my lady will do anything to get a hus-
       band; and when she has this, which you have pro-
       vided for her, I suppose she will submit to anything to
       get rid of him.   330
       MIRABELL: Yes, I think the good lady would marry any-
       thing that resembled a man, though 'twere no more
       than what a butler could pinch out of a napkin.°
       MRS. FAINALL: Female frailty! We must all come to it, if
       we live to be old and feel the craving of a false   335
       appetite when the true is decayed.
       MIRABELL: An old woman's appetite is depraved like
       that of a girl. 'Tis the green sickness° of a second

304. **servant:** Suitor.   312–13. **Mosca . . . Fox:** Mosca, the
crafty servant in Ben Jonson's play *Volpone; or, The Fox*
(1606).   313. **stand upon terms:** Insist on the proper terms of
a binding contract, as Mosca does in the denouement of the
Jonson play.   319–21. **condition that she . . . possession:** Lady
Wishfort has control of half of Mrs. Millamant's (her niece's)
fortune, which Millamant will acquire on her marriage, provided Lady Wishfort approves of the match; should Millamant
marry without her aunt's approval, she forfeits the half of her
fortune in trust.   325. **she might . . . privately:** I.e., to allay
any suspicions Lady Wishfort might have about the validity of
Mirabell's "uncle."   333. **pinch out of a napkin:** It was fashionable to pinch table napkins into curious and fancy shapes.
338. **green sickness:** An anemia prevalent in adolescent girls,
marked by a sallow yellow-green complexion.

childhood; and, like the faint offer of a latter spring,
340   serves but to usher in the fall, and withers in an
affected bloom.

MRS. FAINALL: Here's your mistress.

(*Enter Mrs. Millamant, Witwoud, and Mincing.*)

MIRABELL: Here she comes, i'faith, full sail, with her fan
spread and streamers out, and a shoal of fools for
345   tenders.° Ha, no, I cry her mercy!

MRS. FAINALL: I see but one poor empty sculler,° and he
tows her woman after him.

MIRABELL (*to Mrs. Millamant*): You seem to be unattended, madam. You used to have the *beau monde*°
350   throng after you, and a flock of gay, fine perukes°
hovering round you.

WITWOUD: Like moths about a candle. I had like to have
lost my comparison for want of breath.

MRS. MILLAMANT: Oh, I have denied myself airs today. I
355   have walked as fast through the crowd—

WITWOUD: As a favorite just disgraced, and with as few
followers.

MRS. MILLAMANT: Dear Mr. Witwoud, truce with your
similitudes;° for I'm as sick of 'em—

360   WITWOUD: As a physician of a good air. I cannot help it,
madam, though 'tis against myself.

MRS. MILLAMANT: Yet again! Mincing, stand between
me and his wit.

WITWOUD: Do, Mrs. Mincing, like a screen before a
365   great fire. I confess I do blaze today; I am too bright.

MRS. FAINALL: But, dear Millamant, why were you so
long?

MRS. MILLAMANT: Long! Lord, have I not made violent
haste? I have asked every living thing I met for you; I
370   have inquired after you, as after a new fashion.

WITWOUD: Madam, truce with your similitudes. No,
you met her husband, and did not ask him for her.

MIRABELL: By your leave, Witwoud, that were like
inquiring after an old fashion, to ask a husband for
375   his wife.

WITWOUD: Hum, a hit! a hit! a palpable hit!° I confess it.

MRS. FAINALL: You were dressed before I came abroad.

MRS. MILLAMANT: Aye, that's true. Oh, but then I
had—Mincing, what had I? Why was I so long?

380   MINCING: O mem,° your laship° stayed to peruse a
pecket° of letters.

MRS. MILLAMANT: Oh, aye, letters; I had letters. I am
persecuted with letters. I hate letters. Nobody knows
how to write letters, and yet one has 'em, one does
385   not know why. They serve one to pin up one's hair.

WITWOUD: Is that the way? Pray, madam, do you pin up
your hair with all your letters? I find I must keep
copies.

MRS. MILLAMANT: Only with those in verse, Mr.
Witwoud. I never pin up my hair with prose, I think I   390
tried once, Mincing.

MINCING: O mem, I shall never forget it.

MRS. MILLAMANT: Aye, poor Mincing tiffed° and tiffed
all the morning.

MINCING: Till I had the cremp in my fingers, I'll vow,   395
mem. And all to no purpose. But when your laship
pins it up with poetry, it sits so pleasant the next day
as anything, and is so pure and so crips.°

WITWOUD: Indeed, so crips?

MINCING: You're such a critic, Mr. Witwoud.   400

MRS. MILLAMANT: Mirabell, did you take exceptions
last night? Oh, aye, and went away. Now I think
on't, I'm angry. No, now I think on't, I'm pleased; for
I believe I gave you some pain.

MIRABELL: Does that please you?   405

MRS. MILLAMANT: Infinitely; I love to give pain.

MIRABELL: You would affect a cruelty which is not in
your nature; your true vanity is in the power of pleasing.

MRS. MILLAMANT: Oh, I ask your pardon for that. One's   410
cruelty is one's power; and when one parts with one's
cruelty, one parts with one's power; and when one has
parted with that, I fancy one's old and ugly.

MIRABELL: Aye, aye, suffer your cruelty to ruin the
object of your power, to destroy your lover, and then   415
how vain, how lost a thing you'll be! Nay, 'tis true:
You are no longer handsome when you've lost your
lover; your beauty dies upon the instant. For beauty
is the lover's gift; 'tis he bestows your charms, your
glass is all a cheat. The ugly and the old, whom the   420
looking-glass mortifies, yet after commendation° can
be flattered by it, and discover beauties in it; for that
reflects our praises, rather than your face.

MRS. MILLAMANT: Oh, the vanity of these men! Fainall,
d'ye hear him? If they did not commend us, we were   425
not handsome! Now, you must know they could not
commend one, if one was not handsome. Beauty the
lover's gift! Lord, what is a lover, that it can give?
Why, one makes lovers as fast as one pleases, and
they live as long as one pleases, and they die as soon   430
as one pleases; and then, if one pleases, one makes
more.

WITWOUD: Very pretty. Why, you make no more of
making of lovers, madam, than of making so many
card matches.°   435

MRS. MILLAMANT: One no more owes one's beauty to a
lover than one's wit to an echo. They can but reflect
what we look and say; vain empty things if we are
silent or unseen, and want a being.

---

345. tenders: Small boats that attend larger ships.   **346. sculler:**
A man operating a rowboat; i.e., Witwoud.   **349.** *beau*
monde: People of fashion.   **350. perukes:** Suitors, referring to
the wigs worn by gentlemen of the period.   **359. similitudes:**
Witwoud is a tireless (and tiresome) maker of comparisons,
or similes. See "his commonplace [book] of comparisons" in
act I.   **376. a palpable hit:** See Osric in *Hamlet*, V, II; "A hit, a
very palpable hit."   **380. mem:** Madam.   **laship:** Ladyship.
381. pecket: Packet.

393. tiffed: Arranged.   **398. crips:** Crisp.   **421. commenda-**
tion: Praise.   **435. card matches:** Matches made from pieces of
heavy paper tipped with sulfur.

440 MIRABELL: Yet to those two vain empty things you owe
two° the greatest pleasures of your life.
MRS. MILLAMANT: How so?
MIRABELL: To your lover you owe the pleasure of hearing yourselves praised; and to an echo the pleasure of
445 hearing yourselves talk.
WITWOUD: But I know a lady that loves talking so incessantly, she won't give an echo fair play; she has that
everlasting rotation of tongue, that an echo must
wait till she dies, before it can catch her last words.
450 MRS. MILLAMANT: Oh, fiction! Fainall, let us leave these
men.
MIRABELL (*aside to Mrs. Fainall*): Draw off Witwoud.
MRS. FAINALL: Immediately. I have a word or two for
Mr. Witwoud.

(*Exeunt Witwoud and Mrs. Fainall.*)

455 MIRABELL: I would beg a little private audience too. You
had the tyranny to deny me last night, though you
knew I came to impart a secret to you that concerned
my love.
MRS. MILLAMANT: You saw I was engaged.
460 MIRABELL: Unkind! You had the leisure to entertain a
herd of fools; things who visit you from their excessive idleness, bestowing on your easiness that time
which is the encumbrance of their lives. How can you
find delight in such society? It is impossible they
465 should admire you; they are not capable. Or if they
were, it should be to you as a mortification, for sure
to please a fool is some degree of folly.
MRS. MILLAMANT: I please myself. Besides, sometimes
to converse with fools is for my health.
470 MIRABELL: Your health! Is there a worse disease than
the conversation of fools?
MRS. MILLAMANT: Yes, the vapors; fools are physic° for
it, next to assafetida.°
MIRABELL: You are not in a course of fools?°
475 MRS. MILLAMANT: Mirabell, if you persist in this offensive freedom, you'll displease me. I think I must
resolve, after all, not to have you; we shan't agree.
MIRABELL: Not in our physic, it may be.
MRS. MILLAMANT: And yet our distemper,° in all likeli-
480 hood, will be the same; for we shall be sick of one
another. I shan't endure to be reprimanded nor
instructed; 'tis so dull to act always by advice, and so
tedious to be told of one's faults—I can't bear it.
Well, I won't have you, Mirabell, I'm resolved—I
485 think—you may go. Ha! ha! ha! What would you
give that you could help loving me?
MIRABELL: I would give something that you did not
know I could not help it.
MRS. MILLAMANT: Come, don't look grave then. Well,
490 what do you say to me?

MIRABELL: I say that a man may as soon make a friend
by his wit, or a fortune by his honesty, as win a
woman with plain dealing° and sincerity.
MRS. MILLAMANT: Sententious Mirabell! Prithee, don't
look with that violent and inflexible wise face, like   495
Solomon at the dividing of the child° in an old tapestry hanging.
MIRABELL: You are merry, madam, but I would persuade you for a moment to be serious.
MRS. MILLAMANT: What, with that face? No, if you   500
keep your countenance, 'tis impossible I should hold
mine. Well, after all, there is something very moving
in a lovesick face. Ha! ha! ha! Well, I won't laugh;
don't be peevish. Heigho! now I'll be melancholy, as
melancholy as a watchlight.° Well, Mirabell, if ever   505
you will win me, woo me now. Nay, if you are so
tedious, fare you well; I see they are walking away.
MIRABELL: Can you not find in the variety of your disposition one moment—
MRS. MILLAMANT: To hear you tell me Foible's married,   510
and your plot like to speed? No.
MIRABELL: But how you came to know it—
MRS. MILLAMANT: Without the help of the devil, you
can't imagine; unless she should tell me herself,
Which of the two it may have been, I will leave you   515
to consider; and when you have done thinking of
that, think of me.

(*Exeunt Mrs. Millamant with Mincing.*)

MIRABELL: I have something more—Gone! Think of
you! To think of a whirlwind, though 'twere in a
whirlwind, were a case of more steady contempla-   520
tion; a very tranquility of mind and mansion. A fellow that lives in a windmill has not a more whimsical
dwelling than the heart of a man that is lodged in a
woman. There is no point of the compass to which
they cannot turn, and by which they are not turned;   525
and by one as well as another; for motion, not
method, is their occupation. To know this, and yet
continue to be in love, is to be made wise from the
dictates of reason, and yet persevere to play the fool
by the force of instinct. Oh, here come my pair of   530
turtles!° What, billing so sweetly? Is not Valentine's
Day over with you yet?

(*Enter Waitwell and Foible.*)

Sirrah, Waitwell, why, sure you think you were married
for your own recreation, and not for my conveniency.

---

441. **two:** Two of.   472. **physic:** Medicine.   473. **assafetida:** A
gum resin prescribed by doctors as an antidote to "the vapors."
474. **course of fools:** Series of treatments.   479. **distemper:**
Illness.

493. **plain dealing:** Honesty, frankness.   496. **Solomon . . .
child:** The Old Testament Solomon, king of Israel, was known
for his wisdom. When confronted with two women both claiming to be the mother of a newborn baby, Solomon said he
would divide the baby in two and give one half to each woman.
When one of the women told the king not to slay the baby but
to let it live and give it whole to the other woman, Solomon
declared the first woman the baby's true mother (I Kings
3:16–28).   505. **watchlight:** A small night candle.   530–31.
pair of turtles: Turtle doves; lovers.

535 WAITWELL: Your pardon, sir. With submission, we have
       indeed been solacing° in lawful delights; but still with
       an eye to business, sir. I have instructed her as well as
       I could. If she can take your directions as readily as my
       instructions, sir, your affairs are in a prosperous way.
540 MIRABELL: Give you joy, Mrs. Foible.
    FOIBLE: O las, sir, I'm so ashamed! I'm afraid my lady
       has been in a thousand inquietudes for me. But I
       protest, sir, I made as much haste as I could.
    WAITWELL: That she did indeed, sir. It was my fault that
545   she did not make more.
    MIRABELL: That I believe.
    FOIBLE: But I told my lady as you instructed me, sir that
       I had a prospect of seeing Sir Rowland, your uncle;
       and that I would put her ladyship's picture in my
550   pocket to show him, which I'll be sure to say has
       made him so enamored of her beauty, that he burns
       with impatience to lie at her ladyship's feet and wor-
       ship the original.
    MIRABELL: Excellent Foible! Matrimony has made you
555   eloquent in love.
    WAITWELL: I think she has profited, sir. I think so.
    FOIBLE: You have seen Madam Millamant, sir?
    MIRABELL: Yes.
    FOIBLE: I told her, sir, because I did not know that you
560   might find an opportunity; she had so much com-
       pany last night.
    MIRABELL: Your diligence will merit more. In the mean-
       time—   (*Gives money.*)
    FOIBLE: O dear sir, your humble servant!
565 WAITWELL: Spouse.
    MIRABELL: Stand off, sir, not a penny! Go on and pros-
       per, Foible; the lease shall be made good and the farm
       stocked, if we succeed.°
    FOIBLE: I don't question your generosity, sir; and you
570   need not doubt of success. If you have no more com-
       mands, sir, I'll be gone, I'm sure my lady is at her toi-
       let and can't dress till I come. Oh, dear, I'm sure that
       (*looking out*) was Mrs. Marwood that went by in a
       mask; if she has seen me with you, I'm sure she'll tell
575   my lady. I'll make haste home and prevent her. Your
       servant, sir. B'w'y,° Waitwell.   (*Exit.*)
    WAITWELL: Sir Rowland, if you please. The jade's so
       pert upon her preferment° she forgets herself.
    MIRABELL: Come, sir, will you endeavor to forget your-
580   self, and transform into Sir Rowland?
    WAITWELL: Why, sir, it will be impossible I should
       remember myself. Married, knighted, and attended°
       all in one day! 'Tis enough to make any forget him-
       self. The difficulty will be how to recover my acquain-
585   tance and familiarity with my former self, and fall
       from my transformation to a reformation into Wait-
       well. Nay, I shan't be quite the same Waitwell nei-

ther; for, now I remember me, I'm married and can't
be my own man again.
   Aye, there's my grief; that's the sad change of life,   590
   To lose my title, and yet keep my wife.
                                           (*Exeunt.*)

ACT III

(*A room in Lady Wishfort's house. Lady Wishfort at her
toilet, Peg waiting.*)

LADY WISHFORT: Merciful! no news of Foible yet?
PEG: No, madam.
LADY WISHFORT: I have no more patience. If I have not
   fretted myself till I am pale again, there's no veracity
   in me! Fetch me the red; the red, do you hear, sweet-   5
   heart? An arrant ash-color, as I'm a person! Look
   you how this wench stirs! Why dost thou not fetch
   me a little red? Didst thou not hear me, mopus?°
PEG: The red ratafia° does your ladyship mean, or the
   cherry-brandy?   10
LADY WISHFORT: Ratafia, fool! No, fool! Not the
   ratafia, fool. Grant me patience! I mean the Spanish
   paper,° idiot; complexion, darling. Paint, paint, paint;
   dost thou understand that, changeling,° dangling thy
   hands like bobbins° before thee? Why dost thou not   15
   stir, puppet? thou wooden thing upon wires!
PEG: Lord, madam, your ladyship is so impatient! I cannot come at the paint, madam; Mrs. Foible has
   locked it up and carried the key with her.
LADY WISHFORT: A pox take you both! Fetch me the   20
   cherry-brandy then. (*Exit Peg.*) I'm as pale and as
   faint, I look like Mrs. Qualmsick, the curate's wife,
   that's always breeding. Wench, come, come, wench,
   what art thou doing? sipping? tasting? Save thee,
   dost thou not know the bottle?   25

(*Reenter Peg with a bottle and china cup.*)

PEG: Madam, I was looking for a cup.
LADY WISHFORT: A cup, save thee! and what a cup
   hast thou brought! Does thou take me for a fairy, to
   drink out of an acorn? Why didst thou not bring thy
   thimble? Hast thou ne'er a brass thimble clinking in   30
   thy pocket with a bit of nutmeg? I warrant thee.
   Come, fill, fill! So; again. (*One knocks.*) See who that
   is. Set down the bottle first. Here, here under the
   table. What, wouldst thou go with the bottle in thy
   hand, like a tapster?° As I'm a person, this wench has   35
   lived in an inn upon the road, before she came to me,
   like Maritornes the Asturian in *Don Quixote*!° No
   Foible yet?

---

536. **solacing:** Taking pleasure. 567–68. **the lease . . . suc-**
ceed: I.e., "If our little plot succeeds, I'll be even more generous." 576. **B'w'y:** A slurred form of "God be with you."
578. **preferment:** Her advancement in the world; her new status
as a wife. 582. **attended:** Waited upon.

8. **mopus:** Idiot; dull-witted girl. 9. **ratafia:** Fruit-flavored
brandy. 12–13. **Spanish paper:** Cosmetic rouge. 14. **change-**
ling: Simpleton. 15. **bobbins:** Spools of yarn. 35. **tapster:** A
person who taps beer in a tavern. 37. **Maritornes . . . *Don***
***Quixote*:** In Cervantes's *Don Quixote* (part 1, chapter 16),
Maritornes is an Austrian chambermaid with whom the Don
fancies himself in love.

PEG: No, madam; Mrs. Marwood.

40 LADY WISHFORT: Oh, Marwood; let her come in. Come in, good Marwood.

(*Enter Mrs. Marwood.*)

MRS. MARWOOD: I'm surprised to find your ladyship in *déshabillé*° at this time of day.

LADY WISHFORT: Foible's a lost thing; has been abroad
45 since morning, and never heard of since.

MRS. MARWOOD: I saw her but now, as I came masked through the park, in conference with Mirabell.

LADY WISHFORT: With Mirabell! You call my blood into my face, with mentioning that traitor. She durst not
50 have the confidence! I sent her to negotiate an affair in which, if I'm detected, I'm undone. If that wheedling villain has wrought upon Foible to detect me, I'm ruined. O my dear friend, I'm a wretch of wretches if I'm detected.

55 MRS. MARWOOD: O madam, you cannot suspect Mrs. Foible's integrity.

LADY WISHFORT: Oh, he carries poison in his tongue that would corrupt integrity itself! If she has given him an opportunity, she has as good as put her
60 integrity into his hands. Ah, dear Marwood, what's integrity to an opportunity? Hark! I hear her! Go, you thing, and send her in. (*Exit Peg.*) Dear friend, retire into my closet,° that I may examine her with more freedom. You'll pardon me, dear friend; I can
65 make bold with you. There are books over the chimney, Quarles° and Prynne,° and the *Short View of the Stage,*° with Bunyan's works,° to entertain you.
(*Exit Mrs. Marwood.*)

(*Enter Foible.*)

O Foible, where hast thou been? What hast thou been doing?

70 FOIBLE: Madam, I have seen the party.

LADY WISHFORT: But what hast thou done?

FOIBLE: Nay, 'tis your ladyship has done, and are to do; I have only promised. But a man so enamored, so transported! Well, if worshiping of pictures be a sin,
75 poor Sir Rowland, I say.

LADY WISHFORT: The miniature has been counted like. But hast thou not betrayed me, Foible? Hast thou not detected me to that faithless Mirabell? What hadst

thou to do with him in the Park? Answer me, has he
got nothing out of thee?   80

FOIBLE (*aside*): So the devil has been beforehand with me. What shall I say? (*Aloud.*) Alas, madam, could I help it, if I met that confident thing? Was I in fault? If you had heard how he used me, and all upon your ladyship's account, I'm sure you would not suspect   85
my fidelity. Nay, if that had been the worst, I could have borne; but he had a fling at your ladyship too. And then I could not hold; but i'faith I gave him his own.

LADY WISHFORT: Me? what did the filthy fellow say?   90

FOIBLE: O madam! 'tis a shame to say what he said, with his taunts and his fleers, tossing up his nose. "Humh!" says he. "What, you are a-hatching some plot," says he, "you are so early abroad, or catering," says he. "Ferreting for some disbanded° officer,   95
I warrant. Half-pay is but thin subsistence," says he. "Well, what pension does your lady propose? Let me see," says he. "What, she must come down pretty deep now, she's superannuated,"° says he, "and—"

LADY WISHFORT: Ods° my life, I'll have him, I'll have   100
him murdered! I'll have him poisoned! Where does he eat? I'll marry a drawer° to have him poisoned in his wine! I'll send for Robin° from Locket's° immediately.

FOIBLE: Poison him? Poisoning's too good fur him.   105
Starve him, madam, starve him; marry Sir Rowland, and get him disinherited. Oh, you would bless yourself to hear what he said!

LADY WISHFORT: A villain! "superannuated"!

FOIBLE: "Humh," says he. "I hear you are laying   110
designs against me too," says he, "and Mrs. Millamant is to marry my uncle" (he does not suspect a word of your ladyship); "but," says he, "I'll fit you for that." "I warrant you," says he. "I'll hamper you for that," says he. "You and your old frippery° too,"   115
says he. "I'll handle you—"

LADY WISHFORT: Audacious villain! "handle" me; would he durst! "Frippery! old frippery!" Was there ever such a foul-mouthed fellow? I'll be married tomorrow; I'll be contracted tonight.   120

FOIBLE: The sooner the better, madam.

LADY WISHFORT: Will Sir Rowland be here, sayest thou? When, Foible?

FOIBLE: Incontinently,° madam. No new sheriff's wife expects the return of her husband after knighthood   125
with that impatience in which Sir Rowland burns for the dear hour of kissing your ladyship's hands after dinner.

43. *déshabillé:* Casual attire.   63. closet: Private sitting room.
66. Quarles: Francis Quarles, devotional poet, author of
Emblems, Divine and Moral (1635).   Prynne: William Prynne,
Puritan author of *Histrio-Mastix* (1633), an attack on the
immorality of the stage.   66–67. *Short View of the Stage:* By
Jeremy Collier, an attack on "the Immorality and Profaneness
of the English Stage" (1698), directly aimed at the earlier plays
of Congreve. Dryden answered the censures of Collier in his
Preface to the *Fables* (1700).   67. Bunyan's works: John Bunyan,
the great Puritan writer and preacher. A one-volume edition of
the *Works of That Eminent Servant of Christ, Mr. John Bunyan*
had appeared in 1692.

95. disbanded: Discharged.   99. superannuated: Old and
infirm.   100. Ods: "God's."   102. drawer: One who draws
wine or ale; a waiter.   103. Robin: Common name for a
waiter. Locket's: A fashionable restaurant in Charing Cross.
115. old frippery: Old clothes, as applied to Lady Wishfort,
"old clotheshorse."   124. Incontinently: Immediately, and
with the added suggestion of passionate impatience.

LADY WISHFORT: "Frippery! superannuated! frippery!"
I'll frippery the villain; I'll reduce him to frippery and
rags! A tatterdemalion!° I hope to see him hung with
tatters, like a Long Lane penthouse° or a gibbet thief.
A slander-mouthed railer! I warrant the spendthrift
prodigal's in debt as much as the million lottery,° or
the whole court upon a birthday.° I'll spoil his credit
with his tailor. Yes, he shall have my niece with her
fortune, he shall!

FOIBLE: He! I hope to see him lodge in Ludgate° first,
and angle into Blackfriars° for brass farthings with
an old mitten.°

LADY WISHFORT: Aye, dear Foible; thank thee for that,
dear Foible. He has put me out of all patience. I shall
never recompose my features to receive Sir Rowland
with any economy of face.° This wretch has fretted
me that I am absolutely decayed. Look, Foible.

FOIBLE: Your ladyship has frowned a little too rashly,
indeed, madam. There are some cracks discernible in
the white varnish.

LADY WISHFORT: Let me see the glass. "Cracks," sayest
thou? Why I am arrantly fleaed;° I look like an old
peeled wall. Thou must repair me, Foible, before Sir
Rowland comes, or I shall never keep up to my
picture.°

FOIBLE: I warrant you, madam, a little art once made
your picture like you; and now a little of the same art
must make you like your picture. Your picture must
sit for you, madam.

LADY WISHFORT: But art thou sure Sir Rowland will not
fail to come? Or will 'a not fail when he does come?
Will he be importunate, Foible, and push? For if he
should not be importunate, I shall never break decorums. I shall die with confusion, if I am forced to
advance. Oh no, I can never advance! I shall swoon if
he should expect advances. No, I hope Sir Rowland
is better bred than to put a lady to the necessity of
breaking her forms. I won't be too coy neither. I
won't give him despair; but a little disdain is not
amiss, a little scorn is alluring.

FOIBLE: A little scorn becomes your ladyship.

LADY WISHFORT: Yes, but tenderness becomes me best,
a sort of dyingness. You see that picture has a sort of
a—ha, Foible? a swimmingness in the eyes, Yes, I'll
look so. My niece affects it; but she wants features. Is
Sir Rowland handsome? Let my toilet be removed.
I'll dress above. I'll receive Sir Rowland here. Is he
handsome? Don't answer me. I won't know; I'll be
surprised, I'll be taken by surprise.

FOIBLE: By storm, madam. Sir Rowland's a brisk man.

LADY WISHFORT: Is he! Oh, then he'll importune, if he's
a brisk man. I shall save decorums if Sir Rowland
importunes. I have a mortal terror at the apprehension of offending against decorums. Oh, I'm glad he's
a brisk man. Let my things be removed, good Foible.
(Exit.)

(Enter Mrs. Fainall.)

MRS. FAINALL: O Foible, I have been in a fright, lest I
should come too late! That devil Marwood saw you
in the Park with Mirabell, and I'm afraid will discover it to my lady.

FOIBLE: Discover what, madam?

MRS. FAINALL: Nay, nay, put not on that strange face. I
am privy to the whole design, and know that Waitwell, to whom thou wert this morning married, is to
personate Mirabell's uncle, and as such, winning my
lady, to involve her in those difficulties from which
Mirabell only must release her, by his making his
conditions to have my cousin and her fortune left to
her own disposal.

FOIBLE: O dear madam, I beg your pardon. It was not
my confidence in your ladyship that was deficient;
but I thought the former good correspondence
between your ladyship and Mr. Mirabell might have
hindered his communicating this secret.

MRS. FAINALL: Dear Foible, forget that.

FOIBLE: O dear madam, Mr. Mirabell is such a sweet,
winning gentleman, but your ladyship is the pattern
of generosity. Sweet lady, to be so good! Mr. Mirabell
cannot choose but be grateful. I find your ladyship
has his heart still. Now, madam, I can safely tell your
ladyship our success. Mrs. Marwood had told my
lady, but I warrant I managed myself. I turned it all
for the better. I told my lady that Mr. Mirabell railed
at her. I laid horrid things to his charge, I'll vow; and
my lady is so incensed that she'll be contracted to Sir
Rowland tonight, she says. I warrant I worked her
up, that he may have her for asking for, as they say of
a Welsh maidenhead.

MRS. FAINALL: O rare Foible!

FOIBLE: I beg your ladyship to acquaint Mr. Mirabell of
his success. I would be seen as little as possible to
speak to him; besides, I believe Madam Marwood
watches me. She has a month's mind;° but I know
Mr. Mirabell can't abide her. (Calls.) John! Remove
my lady's toilet. Madam, your servant. My lady is so
impatient, I fear she'll come for me if I stay.

---

131. **tatterdemalion:** Ragamuffin. 132. **Long Lane pent-
house:** A shed with a sloping roof in Long Lane, a district
famous for its shops of old and secondhand clothes. 134. **million lottery:** A wild scheme to raise a million pounds by the
sale of lottery tickets. 135. **the whole . . . birthday:** Since
custom demanded gifts on such an occasion, a royal birthday
was an expensive event. 138. **Ludgate:** The debtors' prison.
139. **angle into Blackfriars:** Ludgate Prison abutted on the
precinct of Blackfriars, the area of London between Ludgate
Hill and the river. 140. **old mitten:** It was the practice of
Ludgate prisoners to beg money from passersby, probably
by lowering an old mitten on a string from a high window.
144. **economy of face:** The sense is that Lady Wishfort has been
so distressed by Foible's account of Mirabell's words that her
makeup has been ruined, and the cosmetics necessary to make
her face presentable to Sir Rowland will be very expensive.
150. **fleaed:** Flayed; skinned. 152–53. **keep . . . picture:** I.e.,
"look as lovely as I do in my picture."

220. **month's mind:** A longing, desire.

MRS. FAINALL: I'll go with you up the back stairs, lest I
should meet her.   (*Exeunt.*)

225

(*Reenter Mrs. Marwood alone.*)

MRS. MARWOOD: Indeed, Mrs. Engine,° is it thus with
you? Are you become a go-between of this importance? Yes, I shall watch you. Why, this wench is the
passe-partout, a very master-key to everybody's

230
strong-box. My friend Fainall,° have you carried it so
swimmingly? I thought there was something in it; but
it seems it's over with you.° Your loathing is not from
a want of appetite then, but from a surfeit. Else you
could never be so cool to fall from a principal to be

235
an assistant; to procure for him! "A pattern of generosity," that I confess. Well, Mr. Fainall, you have
met with your match. O man, man! woman, woman!
the devil's an ass; if I were a painter, I would draw
him like an idiot, a driveller with a bib and bells.

240
Man should have his head and horns,° and woman
the rest of him. Poor simple fiend! "Madam Marwood has a month's mind, but he can't abide her."
'Twere better for him you had not been his confessor
in that affair, without° you could have kept his coun-

245
sel closer. I shall not prove another "pattern of generosity." He has not obliged me to that with those
excesses of himself; and now I'll have none of him.
Here comes the good lady, panting ripe; with a heart
full of hope, and a head full of care, like any chemist

250
upon the day of projection.°

(*Reenter Lady Wishfort.*)

LADY WISHFORT: O dear Marwood, what shall I say for
this rude forgetfulness? But my dear friend is all
goodness.
MRS. MARWOOD: No apologies, dear madam. I have

255
been very well entertained.
LADY WISHFORT: As I'm a person, I am in a very chaos
to think I should so forget myself, but I have such an
olio of affairs,° really I know not what to do. (*Calls.*)
Foible! I expect my nephew, Sir Wilfull, every mo-

260
ment too. (*Calls.*) Why, Foible! He means to travel
for improvement.
MRS. MARWOOD: Methinks Sir Wilfull should rather
think of marrying than travelling at his years. I hear
he is turned of forty.

LADY WISHFORT: Oh, he's in less danger of being spoiled

265
by his travels. I am against my nephew's marrying
too young. It will be time enough when he comes
back and has acquired discretion to choose for
himself.
MRS. MARWOOD: Methinks Mrs. Millamant and he

270
would make a very fit match. He may travel afterwards. 'Tis a thing very usual with young gentlemen.
LADY WISHFORT: I promise you I have thought on't; and
since 'tis your judgment, I'll think on't again. I assure
you I will; I value your judgment extremely. On my

275
word, I'll propose it.

(*Reenter Foible.*)

Come, come, Foible, I had forgot my nephew will be
here before dinner. I must make haste.
FOIBLE: Mr. Witwoud and Mr. Petulant are come to dine
with your ladyship.
LADY WISHFORT: Oh, dear, I can't appear till I am

280
dressed. Dear Marwood, shall I be free with you
again, and beg you to entertain 'em? I'll make all
imaginable haste. Dear friend, excuse me.

(*Exeunt Lady Wishfort and Foible.*)

(*Enter Mrs. Millamant and Mincing.*)

MRS. MILLAMANT: Sure never anything was so unbred
as that odious man! Marwood, your servant.

285
MRS. MARWOOD: You have a color; what's the matter?
MRS. MILLAMANT: That horrid fellow, Petulant, has
provoked me into a flame. I have broke my fan.
Mincing, lend me yours; is not all the powder out of
my hair?

290
MRS. MARWOOD: No. What has he done?
MRS. MILLAMANT: Nay, he has done nothing; he has
only talked. Nay, he has said nothing neither; but he
has contradicted everything that has been said. For
my part, I thought Witwoud and he would have

295
quarreled.
MINCING: I vow, mem, I thought once they would have
fit.°
MRS. MILLAMANT: Well, 'tis a lamentable thing, I swear,
that one has not the liberty of choosing one's acquain-

300
tance as one does one's clothes.
MRS. MARWOOD: If we had that liberty, we should be as
weary of one set of acquaintance, though never so
good, as we are of one suit, though never so fine. A
fool and a doily stuff° would now and then find days

305
of grace, and be worn for variety.
MRS. MILLAMANT: I could consent to wear 'em, if they
would wear alike; but fools never wear out, they are
such *drap-de-Berry*° things! without one could give
'em to one's chambermaid after a day or two.

310
MRS. MARWOOD: 'Twere better so indeed. Or what
think you of the playhouse? A fine, gay, glossy fool

226. **Mrs. Engine:** I.e., Foible, the agent of the plot, which Mrs.
Marwood has discovered by eavesdropping on the discourse
between Foible and Mrs. Fainall.   230. **Fainall:** Mrs. Fainall.
232. **it seems . . . you:** Among other things, Mrs. Marwood has
learned of Mrs. Fainall's affair with Mirabell before her marriage to Fainall.   240. **horns:** The traditional sign of the cuckold, a man whose wife is unfaithful.   244. **without:** Unless.
249–50. **like any chemist . . . projection:** The comparison refers
to the attempts of the alchemists to transmute base metals into
gold. The "day of projection" is the last day of the experiment,
when success or failure will be known.   257–58. **such an olio
of affairs:** I.e., "such a number of things on my mind."

298. **fit:** Fought.   305. **doily stuff:** A coarse woolen material.
309. *drap-de-Berry:* Woolen cloth, probably coarse, from the
French province of Berry.

should be given there, like a new masking habit, after the masquerade is over, and we have done with the
315 disguise. For a fool's visit is always a disguise, and never admitted by a woman of wit, but to blind° her affair with a lover of sense. If you would but appear barefaced now, and own Mirabell, you might as easily put off Petulant and Witwoud as your hood and
320 scarf. And indeed 'tis time, for the town has found it; the secret is grown too big for the pretense. 'Tis like Mrs. Primly's great belly, she may lace it down before, but it burnishes° on her hips. Indeed, Millamant, you can no more conceal it than my Lady
325 Strammel can her face, that goodly face, which, in defiance of her Rhenish-wine tea,° will not be comprehended in a mask.°

MRS. MILLAMANT: I'll take my death, Marwood, you are more censorious than a decayed beauty, or a discarded toast. Mincing, tell the men they may come
330 up. My aunt is not dressing here; their folly is less provoking than your malice. (*Exit Mincing.*) "The town has found it!" What has it found? That Mirabell loves me is no more a secret than it is a secret
335 that you discovered it to my aunt, or than the reason why you discovered it is a secret.

MRS. MARWOOD: You are nettled.°

MRS. MILLAMANT: You're mistaken. Ridiculous!

MRS. MARWOOD: Indeed, my dear, you'll tear another
340 fan, if you don't mitigate those violent airs.

MRS. MILLAMANT: O silly! ha! ha! ha! I could laugh immoderately. Poor Mirabell! His constancy to me has quite destroyed his complaisance for all the world beside. I swear, I never enjoined it him to be so coy. If
345 I had the vanity to think he would obey me, I would command him to show more gallantry. 'Tis hardly well-bred to be so particular° on one hand, and so insensible on the other. But I despair to prevail, and so let him follow his own way, ha! ha! ha! Pardon
350 me, dear creature, I must laugh, ha! ha! ha! though I grant you 'tis a little barbarous, ha! ha! ha!

MRS. MARWOOD: What pity 'tis, so much fine raillery, and delivered with so significant gesture, should be so unhappily directed to miscarry!
355 MRS. MILLAMANT: Ha? Dear creature, I ask your pardon. I swear I did not mind you.°

MRS. MARWOOD: Mr. Mirabell and you both may think it a thing impossible, when I shall tell him by telling you—
360 MRS. MILLAMANT: Oh, dear, what? For it is the same thing if I hear it, ha! ha! ha!

MRS. MARWOOD: That I detest him, hate him, madam.

316. blind: Camouflage.   **323. burnishes:** Is all the more evident.   **326. Rhenish-wine tea:** Rhenish white wine was supposed to reduce corpulence.   **326–27. will not . . . mask:** The sense is that the lady's face was so fat that no mask would fit it.   **337. nettled:** Annoyed.   **347. particular:** Attentive to one lady (i.e., Millamant).   **356. I did not mind you:** "I did not have you in mind."

MRS. MILLAMANT: O madam, why so do I. And yet the creature loves me, ha! ha! ha! How can one forbear laughing to think of it! I am a sibyl° if I am not
365 amazed to think what he can see in me. I'll take my death, I think you are handsomer and, within a year or two as young; if you could but stay for me, I should overtake you, but that cannot be. Well, that thought makes me melancholic. Now, I'll be sad.
370 MRS. MARWOOD: Your merry note may be changed sooner than you think.

MRS. MILLAMANT: D'ye say so? Then I'm resolved I'll have a song to keep up my spirits.

(*Reenter Mincing.*)

MINCING: The gentlemen stay but to comb,° madam,
375 and will wait on you.

MRS. MILLAMANT: Desire Mrs.—, that is in the next room, to sing the song I would have learnt yesterday. You shall hear it, madam, not that there's any great matter in it, but 'tis agreeable to my humor.
380

(*Song.*)

[*Set by Mr. John Eccles.*]

I
Love's but the frailty of the mind,
   When 'tis not with ambition join'd;
A sickly flame, which, if not fed, expires,
And feeding, wastes in self-consuming fires.

II
'Tis not to wound a wanton boy   385
   Or am'rous youth, that gives the joy;
But 'tis the glory to have pierc'd a swain,
For whom inferior beauties sigh'd in vain.

III
Then I alone the conquest prize,
   When I insult a rival's eyes;   390
If there's delight in love, 'tis when I see
That heart, which others bleed for, bleed for me.

(*Enter Petulant and Witwoud.*)

MRS. MILLAMANT: Is your animosity composed, gentlemen?

WITWOUD: Raillery, raillery, madam; we have no animosity. We hit off a little wit now and then, but no   395
animosity. The falling-out of wits is like the falling-out of lovers; we agree in the main, like treble and bass. Ha, Petulant?

PETULANT: Aye, in the main, but when I have a humor to   400
contradict.

WITWOUD: Aye, when he has a humor to contradict, then I contradict too. What, I know my cue. Then we contradict one another like two battledores; for contradictions beget one another like Jews.   405

365. sibyl: A female prophet or seer.   **375. comb:** I.e., comb their wigs.

PETULANT: If he says black's black, if I have a humor to say 'tis blue, let that pass; all's one for that. If I have a humor to prove it, it must be granted.

WITWOUD: Not positively must, but it may, it may.

410 PETULANT: Yes, it positively must, upon proof positive.

WITWOUD: Aye, upon proof positive it must; but upon proof presumptive it only may. That's a logical distinction now, madam.

MRS. MARWOOD: I perceive your debates are of impor-
415 tance and very learnedly handled.

PETULANT: Importance is one thing, and learning's another; but a debate's a debate, that I assert.

WITWOUD: Petulant's an enemy to learning; he relies altogether on his parts.

420 PETULANT: No, I'm no enemy to learning; it hurts not me.

MRS. MARWOOD: That's a sign indeed it's no enemy to you.

PETULANT: No, no, it's no enemy to anybody but them that have it.

425 MRS. MILLAMANT: Well, an illiterate man's my aversion; I wonder at the impudence of any illiterate man to offer to make love.

WITWOUD: That I confess I wonder at too.

MRS. MILLAMANT: Ah! to marry an ignorant that can
430 hardly read or write!

PETULANT: Why should a man be any further from being married, though he can't read, than he is from being hanged? The ordinary's° paid for setting the psalm, and the parish priest for reading the ceremony. And
435 for the rest which is to follow in both cases, a man may do it without book; so all's one for that.

MRS. MILLAMANT: D'ye hear the creature? Lord, here's company; I'll be gone.

(*Exeunt Mrs. Millamant and Mincing.*)

(*Enter Sir Wilfull Witwoud in a riding dress, and a Foot-man to Lady Wishfort.*)

WITWOUD: In the name of Bartlemew and his fair,° what
440 have we here?

MRS. MARWOOD: 'Tis your brother, I fancy. Don't you know him?

WITWOUD: Not I. Yes, I think it is he. I've almost forgot him; I have not seen him since the Revolution.°

445 FOOTMAN (*to Sir Wilfull*): Sir, my lady's dressing. Here's company; if you please to walk in, in the meantime.

SIR WILFULL: Dressing! What, it's but morning here, I warrant, with you in London; we should count it towards afternoon in our parts, down in Shropshire.
450 Why then, belike my aunt han't dined yet, ha, friend?

FOOTMAN: Your aunt, sir?

---

433. ordinary's: The ordinary was the chaplain of a prison, who prepared criminals for death.   **439. Bartlemew and his fair:** Bartholomew Fair was held in August of each year at Smithfield, Since it was specially renowned for its sale of country cloths, Witwoud may here be referring to the inappropriateness of his brother's riding habit in a London drawing room.   **444. Revolution:** The bloodless Revolution of 1688, which marked the defeat of James II and the accession to the throne of William and Mary.

SIR WILFULL: My aunt, sir! Yes, my aunt, sir, and your lady, sir; your lady is my aunt, sir. Why, what, dost thou not know me, friend? Why, then send somebody hither that does. How long hast thou lived with 455
thy lady, fellow, ha?

FOOTMAN: A week, sir; longer than anybody else in the house, except my lady's woman.

SIR WILFULL: Why then, belike thou dost not know thy lady, if thou seest her, ha, friend? 460

FOOTMAN: Why truly, sir, I cannot safely swear to her face in a morning, before she is dressed. 'Tis like I may give a shrewd guess at her by this time.

SIR WILFULL: Well, prithee try what thou canst do; if thou canst not guess, inquire her out, dost hear, fel- 465
low? And tell her, her nephew, Sir Wilfull Witwoud, is in the house.

FOOTMAN: I shall, sir.

SIR WILFULL: Hold ye, hear me, friend; a word with you in your ear. Prithee who are these gallants? 470

FOOTMAN: Really, sir, I can't tell; here come so many here, 'tis hard to know 'em all.   (*Exit.*)

SIR WILFULL: Oons,° this fellow knows less than a star-ling;° I don't think 'a knows his own name.

MRS. MARWOOD: Mr. Witwoud, your brother is not 475
behind-hand in forgetfulness; I fancy he has forgot you too.

WITWOUD: I hope so. The devil take him that remem-bers first, I say.

SIR WILFULL: Save you, gentlemen and lady! 480

MRS. MARWOOD: For shame, Mr. Witwoud; why won't you speak to him? And you, sir.

WITWOUD: Petulant, speak.

PETULANT: And you, sir.

SIR WILFULL: No offense, I hope. 485
                             (*Salutes Mrs. Marwood.*)

MRS. MARWOOD: No sure, sir.

WITWOUD: This is a vile dog; I see that already. No offense! Ha! ha! ha! to him; to him, Petulant, smoke° him.

PETULANT: It seems as if you had come a journey, sir; 490
hem, hem.   (*Surveying him round.*)

SIR WILFULL: Very likely, sir, that it may seem so.

PETULANT: No offense, I hope, sir.

WITWOUD: Smoke the boots, the boots; Petulant, the boots, ha! ha! ha! 495

SIR WILFULL: Maybe not, sir; thereafter as 'tis meant,° sir.

PETULANT: Sir, I presume upon the information of your boots.

SIR WILFULL: Why, 'tis like you may, sir. If you are not 500
satisfied with the information of my boots, sir, if you will step to the stable, you may inquire further of my horse, sir.

PETULANT: Your horse, sir! Your horse is an ass, sir!

---

473. Oons: "God's wounds," an oath.   **473–74. starling:** Pro-verbially a stupid bird.   **488. smoke:** "To affront a stranger at his coming in" (Summers, *Dictionary of the Canting Crew*).
496. as 'tis meant: "According to the way it is meant."

505 SIR WILFULL: Do you speak by way of offense, sir?

MRS. MARWOOD: The gentleman's merry, that's all, sir. (*Aside.*) 'Slife,° we shall have a quarrel betwixt an horse and an ass, before they find one another out. (*Aloud.*) You must not take anything amiss from

510 your friends, sir. You are among your friends here, though it may be you don't know it. If I am not mistaken, you are Sir Wilfull Witwoud.

SIR WILFULL: Right, lady; I am Sir Wilfull Witwoud, so I write myself; no offense to anybody, I hope; and

515 nephew to the Lady Wishfort of this mansion.

MRS. MARWOOD: Don't you know this gentleman, sir?

SIR WILFULL: Hum! What, sure 'tis not—yea by'r Lady, but 'tis. 'Sheart° I know not whether 'tis or no. Yea, but 'tis, by the Wrekin.° Brother Antony! What, Tony,

520 i'faith! What, dost thou not know me? By'r Lady, nor I thee, thou art so becravated° and so beperiwigged.° 'Sheart, why dost not speak? Art thou o'erjoyed?

WITWOUD: Odso, brother, is it you? Your servant, brother.

525 SIR WILFULL: Your servant! Why, yours, sir. Your servant again, 'sheart, and your friend and servant to that, and a—(*puff*) and a flapdragon for your service,° sir! and a hare's foot, and a hare's scut° for your service, sir, an you be so cold and so courtly!

530 WITWOUD: No offense, I hope, brother.

SIR WILFULL: 'Sheart, sir, but there is, and much offense! A pox, is this your Inns o' Court° breeding, not to know your friends and your relations, your elders and your betters?

535 WITWOUD: Why, brother Wilfull of Salop,° you may be as short as a Shrewsbury° cake, if you please. But I tell you 'tis not modish to know relations in town. You think you're in the country, where great lubberly° brothers slabber° and kiss one another when

540 they meet, like a call of serjeants.° 'Tis not the fashion here, 'tis not indeed, dear brother.

SIR WILFULL: The fashion's a fool; and you're a fop, dear brother. 'Sheart, I've suspected this. By'r Lady, I conjectured you were a fop, since you began to

545 change the style of your letters, and write in a scrap of paper, gilt round the edges, no broader than a *subpoena.*° I might expect this when you left off, "Honored brother," and "hoping you are in good health," and so forth, to begin with a "Rat me,° knight, I'm so

sick of a last night's debauch," ods heart, and then 550 tell a familiar tale of a cock and a bull,° and a whore and a bottle, and so conclude. You could write news before you were out of your time,° when you lived with honest Pumple Nose, the attorney of Furnival's Inn,° you could entreat to be remembered then to 555 your friends round the Wrekin. We could have gazettes, then, and *Dawks's Letter,*° and the *Weekly Bill,*° till of late days.

PETULANT: 'Slife, Witwoud, were you ever an attorney's clerk? of the family of the Furnivals? Ha! ha! ha! 560

WITWOUD: Aye, aye, but that was but for a while, not long, not long. Pshaw! I was not in my own power then; an orphan, and this fellow was my guardian. Aye, aye, I was glad to consent to that man to come to London. He had the disposal of me then. If I had 565 not agreed to that, I might have been bound prentice to a felt maker in Shrewsbury; this fellow would have bound me to a maker of felts.

SIR WILFULL: 'Sheart, and better than to be bound to a maker of fops, where, I suppose, you have served 570 your time; and now you may set up for yourself.

MRS. MARWOOD: You intend to travel, sir, as I'm informed.

SIR WILFULL: Belike I may, madam. I may chance to sail upon the salt seas, if my mind hold. 575

PETULANT: And the wind serve.

SIR WILFULL: Serve or not serve, I shan't ask license of you, sir; nor the weathercock your companion. I direct my discourse to the lady, sir. 'Tis like my aunt may have told you, madam. Yes, I have settled my 580 concerns, I may say now, and am minded to see foreign parts. If an how that the peace° holds, whereby, that is, taxes abate.

MRS. MARWOOD: I thought you had designed for France at all adventures.° 585

SIR WILFULL: I can't tell that; 'tis like I may, and 'tis like I may not. I am somewhat dainty in making a resolution, because when I make it, I keep it. I don't stand shill I, shall I,° then; if I say't, I'll do't. But I have thoughts to tarry a small matter in town, to learn 590 somewhat of your lingo first, before I cross the seas. I'd gladly have a spice of your French, as they say, whereby to hold discourse in foreign countries.

MRS. MARWOOD: Here's an academy in town for that use. 595

SIR WILFULL: There is? 'Tis like there may.

507. **'Slife:** "God's life."   518. **'Sheart:** "God's heart." 519. **Wrekin:** A hill in his native Shropshire.   521. **becravated:** Wearing a cravat, or tie. **beperiwigged:** Wearing a wig. 527–28. **flapdragon . . . service:** Derived from the game of catching raisins out of burning brandy; meaning "a fig for your service." 528. **scut:** Tail. 532. **Inns o' Court:** The center of the legal world of London, used for the city itself. Sir Wilfull, the country squire, simply asks if Witwoud's rudeness is a mark of city manners. 535. **Salop:** Another name for Shropshire. 536. **Shrewsbury:** The capital of Shropshire. 538–39. **lubberly:** Loutish. 539. **slabber:** Slobber. 540. **serjeants:** When sergeants-at-law are admitted to the bar. 546–47. **subpoena:** A legal summons. 549. **"Rat me":** Contraction of the oath "May God rot me."

551. **tale . . . bull:** A wildly exaggerated tale.   553. **out of your time:** I.e., before he had finished his legal apprenticeship. 554–55. **Furnival's Inn:** One of the Inns of Court (Chancery) attached to Lincoln's Inn. 557. ***Dawks's Letter:*** A newsletter with a wide circulation in the provinces.   557–58. ***Weekly Bill:*** It reported all deaths in and around London.   582. **peace:** The Treaty of Ryswick (1697), which temporarily terminated the war between France on the one hand and England and her Continental allies on the other.   585. **at all adventures:** In any case.   589. **shill I, shall I:** Shilly-shally. Sir Wilfull is saying that he is not an indecisive man.

MRS. MARWOOD: No doubt you will return very much improved.

WITWOUD: Yes, refined, like a Dutch skipper from a
600 whale-fishing.

(*Reenter Lady Wishfort with Fainall.*)

LADY WISHFORT: Nephew, you are welcome.

SIR WILFULL: Aunt, your servant.

FAINALL: Sir Wilfull, your most faithful servant.

SIR WILFULL: Cousin Fainall, give me your hand.

605 LADY WISHFORT: Cousin Witwoud, your servant; Mr. Petulant, your servant. Nephew, you are welcome again. Will you drink anything after your journey, nephew, before you eat? Dinner's almost ready.

SIR WILFULL: I'm very well, I thank you, aunt; however,
610 I thank you for your courteous offer. 'Sheart I was afraid you would have been in the fashion too, and have remembered to have forgot your relations. Here's your cousin Tony; belike I mayn't call him brother for fear of offense.

615 LADY WISHFORT: O, he's a rallier,° nephew. My cousin's a wit; and your great wits always rally their best friends to choose.° When you have been abroad, nephew, you'll understand raillery better.

(*Fainall and Mrs. Marwood talk apart.*)

SIR WILFULL: Why then, let him hold his tongue in the
620 meantime, and rail when that day comes.

(*Reenter Mincing.*)

MINCING: Mem, I come to acquaint your laship that dinner is impatient.

SIR WILFULL: Impatient? Why then, belike it won't stay till I pull off my boots. Sweetheart, can you help me
625 to a pair of slippers? My man's with the horses, I warrant.

LADY WISHFORT: Fie, fie, nephew, you would not pull off your boots here. Go down into the hall; dinner shall stay for you. My nephew's a little unbred; you'll
630 pardon him, madam. Gentlemen, will you walk? Marwood?

MRS. MARWOOD: I'll follow you, madam, before Sir Wilfull is ready.

(*Exeunt all but Mrs. Marwood and Fainall.*)

FAINALL: Why then, Foible's a bawd, an arrant, rank,
635 match-making bawd. And I, it seems, am a husband, a rank husband; and my wife a very arrant, rank wife, all in the way of the world. 'Sdeath, to be a cuckold by anticipation, a cuckold in embryo!° Sure I was born with budding antlers, like a young satyr, or

a citizen's child.° 'Sdeath! to be outwitted, to he out-
640 jilted, outmatrimonied! If I had kept my speed like a stag, 'twere somewhat; but to crawl after, with my horns, like a snail, and he out-stripped by my wife, 'tis scurvy wedlock.

MRS. MARWOOD: Then shake it off. You have often
645 wished for an opportunity to part; and now you have it. But first prevent their plot; the half of Millamant's fortune is too considerable to be parted with, to a foe, to Mirabell.

FAINALL: Damn him! that had been mine, had you not
650 made that fond° discovery. That had been forfeited, had they been married. My wife had added luster to my horns by that increase of fortune, I could have worn 'em tipped with gold, though my forehead had been furnished like a deputy lieutenant's hall.°
655

MRS. MARWOOD: They may prove a cap of mainte-nance° to you still, if you can away with° your wife. And she's no worse than when you had her. I dare swear she had given up her game before she was married.
660

FAINALL: Hum! that may be.

MRS. MARWOOD: You married her to keep you; and if you can contrive to have her keep you better than you expected, why should you not keep her longer than you intended?
665

FAINALL: The means, the means.

MRS. MARWOOD: Discover to my lady your wife's con-duct; threaten to part with her. My lady loves her, and will come to any composition° to save her repu-tation. Take the opportunity of breaking it, just upon
670 the discovery of this imposture. My lady will be enraged beyond bounds, and sacrifice niece and for-tune and all, at that conjuncture. And let me alone to keep her warm; if she should flag in her part, I will not fail to prompt her.
675

FAINALL: Faith, this has an appearance.°

MRS. MARWOOD: I'm sorry I hinted to my lady to endeavor a match between Millamant and Sir Wil-full; that may be an obstacle.

FAINALL: Oh, for that matter leave me to manage him;
680 I'll disable him for that. He will drink like a Dane;° after dinner, I'll set his hand in.°

---

615. **rallier:** A railer; one who delights in raillery, gentle mock-ery.   617. **to choose:** As they like.   637–38. **to be . . . embryo:** In their "talk apart," Mrs. Marwood has told Mr. Fainall what she has learned of his wife's affair with Mirabell before her marriage to Fainall.

640. **citizen's child:** I.e., a cuckold's child. Many a child of an honest citizen was fathered by a gentleman of the town. 651. **fond:** Foolish.   654–55. **forehead . . . hall:** I.e., though he had been cuckolded as many times as there are antlers of stags and deer decorating the country mansion of a deputy lieutenant. 656–57. **cap of maintenance:** A term in heraldry. The coat of arms of a royal bastard sometimes included a cap with two points behind, like the horns of a cuckold. Mrs. Marwood puns on the word *maintenance* since she is insinuating that, armed with this new information concerning his wife, Fainall may be in a better position to blackmail Lady Wishfort to the amount of Millamant's fortune that she controls. 657. **away with:** Continue to tolerate.   669. **come to any composition:** Agree to anything.   676. **an appearance:** Possibilities.   681. **drink like a Dane:** The Danes were known as heavy drinkers.   682. **I'll set . . . in:** I.e., "I'll involve him in the plot."

MRS. MARWOOD: Well, how do you stand affected towards your lady?

685 FAINALL: Why, faith, I'm thinking of it. Let me see. I am married already, so that's over. My wife has played the jade with me; well, that's over too. I never loved her, or if I had, why, that would have been over too by this time. Jealous of her I cannot be, for I am cer-

690 tain; so there's an end of jealousy. Weary of her I am, and shall be. No, there's no end of that; no, no, that were too much to hope. Thus far concerning my repose; now for my reputation. As to my own, I married not for it, so that's out of the question. And as to

695 my part in my wife's, why, she had parted with hers before; so bringing none to me, she can take none from me. 'Tis against all rule of play that I should lose to one who has not wherewithal to stake.

MRS. MARWOOD: Besides, you forget marriage is

700 honorable.

FAINALL: Hum! Faith, and that's well thought on. Marriage is honorable, as you say; and if so, wherefore should cuckoldom be a discredit, being derived from so honorable a root?

705 MRS. MARWOOD: Nay, I know not; if the root be honorable, why not the branches?°

FAINALL: So, so; why, this point's clear. Well, how do we proceed?

MRS. MARWOOD: I will contrive a letter which shall be

710 delivered to my lady at the time when that rascal who is to act Sir Rowland is with her. It shall come as from an unknown hand, for the less I appear to know of the truth, the better I can play the incendiary. Besides, I would not have Foible provoked if I

715 could help it, because you know she knows some passages.° Nay, I expect all will come out; but let the mine be sprung first, and then I care not if I am discovered.

FAINALL: If the worst come to the worst, I'll turn my

720 wife to grass,° I have already a deed of settlement of the best part of her estate, which I wheedled out of her; and that you shall partake at least.

MRS. MARWOOD: I hope you are convinced that I hate Mirabell now; you'll be no more jealous?

725 FAINALL: Jealous! No, by this kiss. Let husbands be jealous; but let the lover still believe. Or if he doubt, let it be only to endear his pleasure, and prepare the joy that follows, when he proves his mistress true. But let husbands' doubts convert to endless jealousy; or if

730 they have belief, let it corrupt to superstition and blind credulity. I am single, and will herd no more with 'em. True, I wear the badge, but I'll disown the order. And since I take my leave of 'em, I care not if I leave 'em a common motto to their common crest.

All husbands must or pain or shame endure   735
The wise too jealous are, fools too secure.

(*Exeunt.*)

ACT IV

([*Scene continues.*] *Enter Lady Wishfort and Foible.*)

LADY WISHFORT: Is Sir Rowland coming, sayest thou, Foible? and are things in order?

FOIBLE: Yes, madam, I have put wax-lights in the sconces, and placed the footmen in a row in the hall, in their best liveries, with the coachman and postil-   5
lion to fill up the equipage.

LADY WISHFORT: Have you pulvilled° the coachman and postillion, that they may not stink of the stable when Sir Rowland comes by?

FOIBLE: Yes, madam.   10

LADY WISHFORT: And are the dancers and the music ready, that he may be entertained in all points with correspondence to his passion?

FOIBLE: All is ready, madam.

LADY WISHFORT: And—well, and how do I look,   15
Foible?

FOIBLE: Most killing well, madam.

LADY WISHFORT: Well, and how shall I receive him? In what figure shall I give his heart the first impression? There is a great deal in the first impression. Shall I   20
sit? No, I won't sit, I'll walk; aye, I'll walk from the door upon his entrance; and then turn full upon him. No, that will be too sudden. I'll lie, aye, I'll lie down. I'll receive him in my little dressing-room; there's a couch. Yes, yes, I'll give the first impression on a   25
couch. I won't lie neither, but loll and lean upon one elbow; with one foot a little dangling off, jogging in a thoughtful way. Yes, and then as soon as he appears, start, aye, start and be surprised, and rise to meet him in a pretty disorder. Yes, oh, nothing is more alluring   30
than a levee° from a couch, in some confusion; it shows the foot to advantage, and furnishes with blushes and recomposing airs beyond comparison. Hark! there's a coach.

FOIBLE: 'Tis he, madam.   35

LADY WISHFORT: Oh dear, has my nephew made his addresses to Millamant? I ordered him.

FOIBLE: Sir Wilfull is set in to drinking, madam, in the parlor.

LADY WISHFORT: Ods my life, I'll send him to her. Call   40
her down, Foible; bring her hither. I'll send him as I go. When they are together, then come to me, Foible, that I may not be too long alone with Sir Rowland.

(*Exit.*)

---

706. **branches:** I.e., the cuckold's horns.   **715–16. she knows some passages:** I.e., Foible knows of Mrs. Marwood's affair with Mr. Fainall and may divulge it. Indeed, she does, in the denouement of act V.   **719–20. turn . . . grass:** Turn her out, as he would an animal to graze.

7. **pulvilled:** Scented with a sweet-smelling powder.   **31. levee:** Rising.

(*Enter Mrs. Millamant and Mrs. Fainall.*)

FOIBLE: Madam, I stayed here to tell your ladyship that
45   Mr. Mirabell has waited this half hour for an opportunity to talk with you, though my lady's orders were
to leave you and Sir Wilfull together. Shall I tell Mr.
Mirabell that you are at leisure?

MRS. MILLAMANT: No, what would the dear man have?
50   I am thoughtful, and would amuse myself; bid him
come another time.
          "There never yet was woman made,
          Nor shall, but to he curs'd."°
                              (*Repeating and walking about.*)
          That's hard!

55   MRS. FAINALL: You are very fond of Sir John Suckling
today, Millamant, and the poets.

MRS. MILLAMANT: He? Aye, and filthy verses; so I am.

FOIBLE: Sir Wilfull is coming, madam. Shall I send Mr.
Mirabell away?

60   MRS. MILLAMANT: Aye, if you please, Foible, send him
away, or send him hither; just as you will, dear
Foible. I think I'll see him; shall I? Aye, let the wretch
come.
                              (*Exit Foible.*)
          "Thyrsis, a youth of the inspired train."°
                              (*Repeating.*)
65   Dear Fainall, entertain Sir Wilfull. Thou hast philosophy to undergo° a fool; thou art married and hast
patience. I would confer with my own thoughts.

MRS. FAINALL: I am obliged to you, that you would
make me your proxy in this affair; but I have busi-
70   ness of my own.

(*Enter Sir Wilfull.*)

O Sir Wilfull, you are come at the critical instant.
There's your mistress up to the ears in love and contemplation; pursue your point, now or never.

SIR WILFULL: Yes; my aunt will have it so. I would
75   gladly have been encouraged with a bottle or two,
because I'm somewhat wary at first, before I am
acquainted. (*This while Millamant walks about
repeating to herself.*) But I hope, after a time, I shall
break my mind; that is, upon further acquaintance.
80   So for the present, cousin, I'll take my leave. If so he
you'll be so kind to make my excuse, I'll return to my
company.

MRS. FAINALL: Oh, fie, Sir Wilfull! What, you must not
be daunted.

85   SIR WILFULL: Daunted! No, that's not it. It is not so
much for that; for if so be that I set on't, I'll do't. But
only for the present; 'tis sufficient till further
acquaintance, that's all. Your servant.

MRS. FAINALL: Nay, I'll swear you shall never lose so
favorable an opportunity, if I can help it. I'll leave   90
you together and lock the door.   (*Exit.*)

SIR WILFULL: Nay, nay, cousin. I have forgot my gloves.
What d'ye do? 'Sheart, 'a has locked the door indeed,
I think. Nay, Cousin Fainall, open the door! Pshaw,
what a vixen trick is this? Nay, now 'a has seen me   95
too. Cousin, I made bold to pass through as it were. I
think this door's enchanted!

MRS. MILLAMANT (*repeating*):
          "I prithee spare me, gentle boy,
          Press me no more for that slight toy—"°   100

SIR WILFULL: Anan?° Cousin, your servant.

MRS. MILLAMANT (*repeating*):
          "That foolish trifle of a heart—"
          Sir Wilfull!

SIR WILFULL: Yes. Your servant. No offense, I hope,
cousin.

MRS. MILLAMANT (*repeating*):
          "I swear it will not do its part,   105
          Though thou dost shine, employ'st thy pow'r
          and art."
          Natural, easy Suckling!

SIR WILFULL: Anan? Suckling? No such suckling neither, cousin, nor stripling! I thank Heaven, I'm no
minor.   110

MRS. MILLAMANT: Ah, rustic! ruder than Gothic.°

SIR WILFULL: Well, well, I shall understand your lingo
one of these days, cousin; in the meanwhile I must
answer in plain English.

MRS. MILLAMANT: Have you any business with me, Sir   115
Wilfull?

SIR WILFULL: Not at present, cousin. Yes, I made bold
to see, to come and know if that how you were disposed to fetch a walk this evening; if so be that I
might not be troublesome, I would have fought° a   120
walk with you.

MRS. MILLAMANT: A walk! What then?

SIR WILFULL: Nay, nothing. Only for the walk's sake,
that's all.

MRS. MILLAMANT: I nauseate walking; 'tis a country   125
diversion. I loathe the country and everything that
relates to it.

SIR WILFULL: Indeed! hah! Look ye, look ye, you do?
Nay, 'tis like you may. Here are choice of pastimes
here in town, as plays and the like; that must be con-   130
fessed indeed.

MRS. MILLAMANT: *Ah, l'étourdi!*° I hate the town too.

SIR WILFULL: Dear heart, that's much. Hah! that you
should hate 'em both! Hah! 'tis like you may; there
are some can't relish the town, and others can't away   135

52–53. "There never . . . curs'd": The opening lines of a poem
by Sir John Suckling (1609–1642). **64. "Thyrsis . . . train":**
The first line of *The Story of Phoebus and Daphne, Applied,* a
poem by Edmund Waller (1606–1687), a poet much admired
by Dryden and renowned for the "sweetness" of his verse.
66. undergo: Put up with.

99–100. "I prithee . . . toy": The first two lines of a "Song" by
Suckling. The three lines quoted by Millamant in her next two
speeches complete the first stanza of the poem. **101. Anan:** "I
beg your pardon." **111. Gothic:** The Restoration and early
eighteenth century considered the civilization of the Goths and
"Gothic" art rude and barbarous. **120. fought:** A provincial
form of "fetched." **132. l'étourdi:** The silly fellow.

with the country. 'Tis like you may be one of those, cousin.

MRS. MILLAMANT: Ha! ha! ha! Yes, 'tis like I may. You have nothing further to say to me?

140 SIR WILFULL: Not at present, cousin. 'Tis like when I have an opportunity to be more private, I may break my mind in some measure. I conjecture you partly guess—however, that's as time shall try; but spare to
145 speak and spare to speed,° as they say.

MRS. MILLAMANT: If it is of no great importance, Sir Wilfull, you will oblige me to leave me; I have just now a little business—

SIR WILFULL: Enough, enough, cousin, yes, yes, all a case;° when you're disposed, when you're disposed.
150 Now's as well as another time; and another time as well as now. All's one for that. Yes, yes, if your concerns call you, there's no haste; it will keep cold, as they say. Cousin, your servant. I think this door's locked.

155 MRS. MILLAMANT: You may go this way, sir.

SIR WILFULL: Your servant; then with your leave I'll return to my company.

MRS. MILLAMANT: Aye, aye; ha! ha! ha!
"Like Phoebus sung the no less am'rous boy."°

(*Enter Mirabell.*)

160 MIRABELL: "Like Daphne, she, as lovely and as coy."°
Do you lock yourself up from me, to make my search more curious?° Or is this pretty artifice contrived, to signify that here the chase must end and my pursuit be crowned, for you can fly no further?

165 MRS. MILLAMANT: Vanity! No. I'll fly and be followed to the last moment. Though I am upon the very verge of matrimony, I expect you should solicit me as much as if I were wavering at the grate of a monastery, with one foot over the threshold. I'll be solicited to the
170 very last, nay, and afterwards.

MIRABELL: What, after the last?

MRS. MILLAMANT: Oh, I should think I was poor and had nothing to bestow, if I were reduced to an inglorious ease and freed from the agreeable fatigues of
175 solicitation.

MIRABELL: But do not you know that when favors are conferred upon instant and tedious solicitation, that they diminish in their value, and that both the giver loses the grace, and the receiver lessens his pleasure?

180 MRS. MILLAMANT: It may be in things of common application; but never sure in love. Oh, I hate a lover that can dare to think he draws a moment's air independent on the bounty of his mistress. There is not so impudent a thing in nature as the saucy look of an

assured man, confident of success. The pedantic arro- 185
gance of a very husband has not so pragmatical° an
air. Ah! I'll never marry, unless I am first made sure of
my will and pleasure.

MIRABELL: Would you have 'em both before marriage?
Or will you be contented with the first now, and stay 190
for the other till after grace?

MRS. MILLAMANT: Ah! don't be impertinent. My dear
liberty, shall I leave thee? My faithful solitude, my
darling contemplation, must I bid you then adieu?
Ay-h adieu, my morning thoughts, agreeable wak- 195
ings, indolent slumbers, all ye *douceurs,*° ye *sommeils du matin,*° adieu. I can't do't, 'tis more than
impossible. Positively, Mirabell, I'll lie abed in a
morning as long as I please.

MIRABELL: Then I'll get up in a morning as early as I 200
please.

MRS. MILLAMANT: Ah! idle creature, get up when you
will. And d'ye hear, I won't be called names after I'm
married; positively I won't be called names.

MIRABELL: Names! 205

MRS. MILLAMANT: Aye, as wife, spouse, my dear, joy,
jewel, love, sweetheart, and the rest of that nauseous
cant, in which men and their wives are so fulsomely
familiar; I shall never bear that. Good Mirabell,
don't let us be familiar or fond, nor kiss before folks, 210
like my Lady Fadler and Sir Francis; nor go to Hyde
Park together the first Sunday in a new chariot, to
provoke eyes and whispers, and then never be seen
there together again, as if we were proud of one
another the first week, and ashamed of one another 215
ever after. Let us never visit together, nor go to a play
together. But let us be very strange and well-bred; let
us be as strange as if we had been married a great
while, and as well-bred as if we were not married at
all. 220

MIRABELL: Have you any more conditions to offer?
Hitherto your demands are pretty reasonable.

MRS. MILLAMANT: Trifles! As liberty to pay and receive
visits to and from whom I please; to write and receive
letters, without interrogatories° or wry faces on your 225
part; to wear what I please, and choose conversation
with regard only to my own taste; to have no obligation upon me to converse with wits that I don't like,
because they are your acquaintance, or to be intimate
with fools, because they may be your relations. Come 230
to dinner when I please; dine in my dressing-room
when I'm out of humor, without giving a reason. To
have my closet inviolate; to be sole empress of my
tea-table, which you must never presume to approach without first asking leave. And lastly, wherever 235
I am, you shall always knock at the door before you
come in. These articles subscribed, if I continue to

143–44. spare to speak . . . speed: Proverb meaning "If you hold
your tongue, you won't get along in the world."   148–49. all
a case: Idiomatic for "It's all the same."   159. "Like Phoebus . . . boy": The third line of Waller's *Story of Phoebus and
Daphne, Applied.*   160. "Like Daphne . . . coy": The fourth
line of Waller's poem. Mirabell completes the couplet begun by
Millamant.   162. curious: Difficult.

186. pragmatical: Officious.   196. *douceurs:* Sweet pleasures.
196–97. *sommeils du matin:* Morning sleep.   225. interrogatories: Prying questions.

endure you a little longer, I may by degrees dwindle
into a wife.

240 MIRABELL: Your bill of fare is something advanced in
this latter account. Well, have I liberty to offer conditions, that when you are dwindled into a wife, I may
not be beyond measure enlarged into a husband?

MRS. MILLAMANT: You have free leave. Propose your
245 utmost; speak and spare not.

MIRABELL: I thank you. *Imprimis*° then, I covenant°
that your acquaintance be general; that you admit no
sworn confidante, or intimate of your own sex; no
she-friend to screen her affairs under your counte-
250 nance, and tempt you to make trial of a mutual
secrecy. No decoy-duck to wheedle° you a fop,
scrambling° to the play in a mask; then bring you
home in a pretended fright, when you think you shall
be found out, and rail at me for missing the play, and
255 disappointing the frolic which you had to pick me up
and prove my constancy.

MRS. MILLAMANT: Detestable *imprimis*! I go to the play
in a mask!

MIRABELL: *Item*,° I article that you continue to like your
260 own face, as long as I shall; and while it passes current with me, that you endeavor not to new-coin it.
To which end, together with all vizards for the day, I
prohibit all masks for the night, made of oiled skins
and I know not what: hog's bones, hare's gall, pig
265 water, and the marrow of a roasted cat.° In short, I
forbid all commerce with the gentle-woman in What-
d'ye-call-it Court. *Item*, I shut my doors against all
bawds with baskets, and pennyworths of muslin,
china, fans, atlases,° etc. *Item*, when you shall be
270 breeding—

MRS. MILLAMANT: Ah! name it not.

MIRABELL: Which may be presumed, with a blessing on
our endeavors—

MRS. MILLAMANT: Odious endeavors!

275 MIRABELL: I denounce against all strait-lacing, squeezing for a shape, till you mold my boy's head like a
sugar-loaf, and instead of a man child, make me
father to a crooked billet.° Lastly, to the dominion of
the tea-table I submit, but with *proviso* that you
280 exceed not in your province, but restrain yourself to
native and simple tea-table drinks, as tea, chocolate,
and coffee, as likewise to genuine and authorized
tea-table talk, such as mending of fashions, spoiling
reputations, railing at absent friends, and so forth;
285 but that on no account you encroach upon the men's
prerogative, and presume to drink healths, or toast
fellows; for prevention of which, I banish all foreign
forces, all auxiliaries to the tea-table, as orange
brandy, all aniseed, cinnamon, citron, and Barbados
290 waters, together with ratafia and the most noble

246. *Imprimis:* First. covenant: Decree. 251. wheedle:
Procure. 252. scrambling: Going without suitable dignity.
259. *Item:* In addition. 264–65. hog's bones . . . cat: All
were ingredients in cosmetics. 269. atlases: A kind of satin.
278. billet: Stick.

spirit of clary.° But for cowslip wine, poppy water,
and all dormitives,° those I allow. These *provisos*
admitted, in other things I may prove a tractable and
complying husband.

MRS. MILLAMANT: O horrid *provisos*! filthy strongwa- 295
ters! I toast fellows, odious men! I hate your odious
provisos.

MIRABELL: Then we're agreed. Shall I kiss your hand
upon the contract? And here comes one to be a witness to the sealing of the deed. 300

(*Reenter Mrs. Fainall.*)

MRS. MILLAMANT: Fainall, what shall I do? Shall I have
him? I think I must have him.

MRS. FAINALL: Aye, aye, take him, take him; what
should you do?

MRS. MILLAMANT: Well then—I'll take my death I'm in 305
a horrid fright. Fainall, I shall never say it. Well—I
think—I'll endure you.

MRS. FAINALL: Fie! fie! have him, have him, and tell him
so in plain terms; for I am sure you have a mind to him. 310

MRS. MILLAMANT: Are you? I think I have; and the horrid man looks as if he thought so too. Well, you
ridiculous thing you, I'll have you; I won't be kissed,
nor I won't be thanked. Here, kiss my hand though.
So, hold your tongue now; don't say a word. 315

MRS. FAINALL: Mirabell, there's a necessity for your
obedience; you have neither time to talk nor stay. My
mother is coming; and in my conscience, if she should
see you, would fall into fits and maybe not recover,
time enough to return to Sir Rowland, who, as Foible 320
tells me, is in a fair way to succeed. Therefore spare
your ecstacies for another occasion, and slip down
the back stairs, where Foible waits to consult you.

MRS. MILLAMANT: Aye, go, go. In the meantime I suppose you have said something to please me. 325

MIRABELL: I am all obedience.   (*Exit.*)

MRS. FAINALL: Yonder Sir Wilfull's drunk, and so noisy
that my mother has been forced to leave Sir Rowland
to appease him; but he answers her only with singing
and drinking. What they may have done by this time 330
I know not; but Petulant and he were upon quarreling as I came by.

MRS. MILLAMANT: Well, if Mirabell should not make a
good husband, I am a lost thing; for I find I love him
violently. 335

MRS. FAINALL: So it seems; for you mind not what's said
to you. If you doubt him, you had best take up with
Sir Wilfull.

MRS. MILLAMANT: How can you name that superannuated lubber? Foh! 340

(*Enter Witwoud, from drinking.*)

MRS. FAINALL: So, is the fray made up, that you have left
'em?

288–91. orange brandy . . . clary: All these "auxiliaries" were
cordials made of brandy and variously flavored. 292. dormitives: Sedatives.

WITWOUD: Left 'em? I could stay no longer. I have laughed like ten christenings; I am tipsy with laugh-
345   ing. If I had stayed any longer I should have burst; I must have been let out and pieced in the sides like an unsized camlet.° Yes, yes, the fray is composed; my lady came in like a *noli prosequi*° and stopped the proceedings.
350 MRS. MILLAMANT: What was the dispute?
WITWOUD: That's the jest; there was no dispute. They could neither of 'em speak for rage, and so fell asput-tering at one another like two roasting apples.

(*Enter Petulant, drunk.*)

Now, Petulant? All's over, all's well? Gad, my head
355   begins to whim° it about. Why dost thou not speak? Thou art both as drunk and as mute as a fish.
PETULANT: Look you, Mrs. Millamant, if you can love me, dear nymph, say it, and that's the conclusion. Pass on, or pass off; that's all.
360 WITWOUD: Thou hast uttered volumes, folios, in less than *decimo sexto*,° my dear Lacedemonian.° Sirrah, Petulant, thou art an epitomizer of words.°
PETULANT: Witwoud, you are an annihilator of sense.
WITWOUD: Thou art a retailer of phrases and dost deal
365   in remnants of remnants, like a maker of pincush-ions; thou art in truth (metaphorically speaking) a speaker of shorthand.
PETULANT: Thou art (without a figure) just one half of an ass, and Baldwin° yonder, thy half brother, is the rest.
370   A Gemini° of asses split would make just four of you.
WITWOUD: Thou dost bite, my dear mustard seed; kiss me for that.
PETULANT: Stand off! I'll kiss no more males. I have kissed your twin yonder in a humor of reconciliation,
375   till he (*hiccup*) rises upon my stomach like a radish.
MRS. MILLAMANT: Eh! filthy creature! What was the quarrel?
PETULANT: There was no quarrel; there might have been a quarrel.
380 WITWOUD: If there had been words enow between 'em to have expressed provocation, they had gone together by the ears like a pair of castanets.
PETULANT: You were the quarrel.
MRS. MILLAMANT: Me!
385 PETULANT: If I have a humor to quarrel, I can make less matters conclude premises. If you are not handsome, what then, if I have a humor to prove it? If I shall

have my reward, say so; if not, fight for your face the next time yourself. I'll go sleep.
WITWOUD: Do, wrap thyself up like a wood louse, and   390
dream revenge; and hear me, if thou canst learn to write by tomorrow morning, pen me a challenge. I'll carry it for thee.
PETULANT: Carry your mistress's monkey a spider! Go flea dogs, and read romances! I'll go to bed to my   395
maid.   (*Exit.*)
MRS. FAINALL: He's horridly drunk. How came you all in this pickle?
WITWOUD: A plot! a plot! to get rid of the knight. Your husband's advice; but he sneaked off.   400

(*Reenter Sir Wilfull drunk, and Lady Wishfort.*)

LADY WISHFORT: Out upon't, out upon't! At years of discretion, and comport yourself at this rantipole° rate!
SIR WILFULL: No offense, aunt.
LADY WISHFORT: Offense? As I'm a person, I'm ashamed of you. Fogh! how you stink of wine! D'ye   405
think my niece will ever endure such a borachio!° you're an absolute borachio.
SIR WILFULL: Borachio!
LADY WISHFORT: At a time when you should commence an amour, and put your best foot foremost—   410
SIR WILFULL: 'Sheart, an you grutch° me your liquor, make a hill. Give me more drink, and take my purse.

(*Sings.*) "Prithee fill me the glass
         Till it laugh in my face,   415
With ale that is potent and mellow;
         He that whines for a lass
         Is an ignorant ass,
For a bumper has not its fellow."

But if you would have me marry my cousin, say the word, and I'll do't. Wilfull will do't; that's the word.   420
Wilfull will do't; that's my crest. My motto I have forgot.
LADY WISHFORT: My nephew's a little overtaken,° cousin, but 'tis with drinking your health. O' my word you are obliged to him.   425
SIR WILFULL: *In vino veritas*,° aunt. If I drunk your health today, cousin, I am a borachio. But if you have a mind to be married, say the word, and send for the piper; Wilfull will do't. If not, dust it away, and let's have t'other round. Tony! Ods-heart, where's Tony?   430
Tony's an honest fellow; but he spits after a bumper, and that's a fault.

347. unsized camlet: I.e., like a piece of unstiffened satin.
348. *noli prosequi:* A legal term meaning that the plaintiff does not wish to continue the prosecution. 355. whim: Spin.
361. *decimo sexto:* A very tiny book. Lacedemonian: Spar-tan. (The Spartans were known to be very laconic people, that is, terse in their speech.) 362. thou art . . . words: I.e., "You say much in few words." 369. Baldwin: The name of the ass in the medieval tale *Reynard the Fox*. 370. Gemini: Matched pair of twins. The constellation Gemini derives its name from the twin stars Castor and Pollux.

402. rantipole: Wild. 406. borachio: Spanish for "wine bag," a drunkard. Shakespeare has a character named Borachio in *Much Ado about Nothing*. 411. grutch: Grudge. 423. over-taken: Overcome by drink. 426. *In vino veritas:* "In wine (there is) truth."

(*Sings.*) "We'll drink, and we'll never ha' done, boys,
    Put the glass then around with the sun, boys;
435 Let Apollo's example invite us;
    For he's drunk every night,
    And that makes him so bright,
  That he's able next morning to light us."

The sun's a good pimple,° an honest soaker, he has a
440 cellar at your Antipodes.° If I travel, aunt, I touch at
your Antipodes; your Antipodes are a good, rascally
sort of topsy-turvy fellows. If I had a bumper, I'd
stand upon my head and drink a health to 'em. A
match or no match, cousin, with the hard name.
445 Aunt, Wilfull will do't. If she has her maidenhead, let
her look to't, if she has not, let her keep her own
counsel in the meantime, and cry out at the nine
months' end.

MRS. MILLAMANT: Your pardon, madam, I can stay no
450 longer. Sir Wilfull grows very powerful. Egh! how he
smells! I shall be overcome if I stay. Come, cousin.

(*Exeunt Mrs. Millamant and Mrs. Fainall.*)

LADY WISHFORT: Smells! he would poison a tallow-
chandler° and his family! Beastly creature, I know
not what to do with him. Travel, quotha! aye, travel,
455 travel, get thee gone, get thee but far enough, to the
Saracens, or the Tartars, or the Turks, for thou art
not fit to live in a Christian commonwealth, thou
beastly pagan!

SIR WILFULL: Turks, no; no Turks, aunt; your Turks are
460 infidels, and believe not in the grape. Your Maho-
metan, your Mussulman, is a dry stinkard.° No
offense, aunt. My map says that your Turk is not so
honest a man as your Christian. I cannot find by the
map that your mufti° is orthodox; whereby it is a
465 plain case that orthodox is a hard word, aunt, and
(*hiccup*) Greek for claret.

(*Sings.*) "To drink is a Christian diversion,
Unknown to the Turk or the Persian
    Let Mahometan fools
470   Live by heathenish rules,
And be damn'd over teacups and coffee!
    But let British lads sing,
    Crown a health to the king,
And a fig for your sultan and sophy!"°

475 Ah, Tony!

(*Enter Foible, and whispers [to] Lady Wishfort.*)

LADY WISHFORT (*aside to Foible*): Sir Rowland impatient? Good lack! what shall I do with this beastly
tumbril?° (*Aloud.*) Go lie down and sleep, you sot!
or, as I'm a person, I'll have you bastinadoed° with
broomsticks. Call up the wenches with broomsticks. 480

(*Exit Foible.*)

SIR WILFULL: Ahey! Wenches, where are the wenches?
LADY WISHFORT: Dear Cousin Witwoud, get him away,
and you will bind me to you inviolably. I have an
affair of moment that invades me with some precipi-
tation. You will oblige me to all futurity. 485
WITWOUD: Come, knight. Pox on him, I don't know
what to say to him. Will you go to a cock match?
SIR WILFULL: With a wench, Tony? Is she a shakebag,°
Sirrah? Let me bite your cheek° for that.
WITWOUD: Horrible! he has a breath like a bagpipe! 490
Aye, aye, come, will you march, my Salopian?°
SIR WILFULL: Lead on, little Tony, I'll follow thee, my
Anthony, my Tantony. Sirrah, thou shalt be my
Tantony, and I'll be thy pig.°
  "And a fig for your sultan and sophy." 495

(*Exit singing with Witwoud.*)

LADY WISHFORT: This will never do. It will never make
a match; at least before he has been abroad.

(*Enter Waitwell, disguised as Sir Rowland.*)

Dear Sir Rowland, I am confounded with confusion
at the retrospection of my own rudeness! I have more
pardons to ask than the Pope distributes in the Year 500
of Jubilee.° But I hope, where there is likely to be so
near an alliance, we may unbend the severity of decorum, and dispense with a little ceremony.
WAITWELL: My impatience, madam, is the effect of my
transport; and till I have the possession of your 505
adorable person, I am tantalized on the rack, and do
but hang, madam, on the tenter° of expectation.
LADY WISHFORT: You have excess of gallantry, Sir Rowland, and press things to a conclusion with a most
prevailing vehemence. But a day or two for decency 510
of marriage—
WAITWELL: For decency of funeral, madam! The delay
will break my heart; or, if that should fail, I shall be
poisoned. My nephew will get an inkling of my
designs, and poison me—and I would willingly 515
starve him before I die; I would gladly go out of the
world with that satisfaction. That would be some

---

439. **pimple:** Drinking companion. 440. **Antipodes:** The opposite end of the world, or its inhabitants. 452–53. **tallow-chandler:** Candle maker. 461. **dry stinkard:** A miserable nondrinker. Mohammedans drink neither wine nor spirits. 464. **mufti:** An expert in Mohammedan religious law. 474. **sophy:** A former title of the Persian shah.

478. **tumbril:** Dump-cart. 479. **bastinadoed:** Beaten. 488. **shakebag:** A term in cock fighting for a very game or sporting cock. 489. **bite your cheek:** I.e., "give you a big kiss." 491. **Salopian:** Shropshireman. 494. **pig:** In art and legend, the pig is associated with St. Anthony the Great. 500–01. **Year of Jubilee:** The year (approximately every twenty-fifth) in which the pope grants general remission from the consequences of sin. 507. **tenter:** A tenterhook.

comfort to me, if I could but live so long as to be revenged on that unnatural viper.

520 LADY WISHFORT: Is he so unnatural, say you? Truly I would contribute much both to the saving of your life, and the accomplishment of your revenge. Not that I respect myself, though he has been a perfidious wretch to me.

525 WAITWELL: Perfidious to you!

LADY WISHFORT: O Sir Rowland, the hours that he has died away at my feet, the tears that he has shed, the oaths that he has sworn, the palpitations that he has felt, the trances and the tremblings, the ardors and 530 the ecstasies, the kneelings and the risings, the heart-heavings and the hand-gripings, the pangs and the pathetic regards of his protesting eyes! Oh, no memory can register!

WAITWELL: What, my rival! Is the rebel my rival? 'A 535 dies.

LADY WISHFORT: No, don't kill him at once, Sir Rowland; starve him gradually, inch by inch.

WAITWELL: I'll do't. In three weeks he shall be barefoot; in a month out at knees with begging an alms. He 540 shall starve upward and upward, till he has nothing living but his head, and then go out in a stink like a candle's end upon a save-all.°

LADY WISHFORT: Well, Sir Rowland, you have the way. You are no novice in the labyrinth of love; you have 545 the clue. But as I am a person, Sir Rowland, you must not attribute my yielding to any sinister appetite, or indigestion of widowhood: nor impute my complacency to any lethargy of continence. I hope you do not think me prone to any iteration° of nuptials.

550 WAITWELL: Far be it from me—

LADY WISHFORT: If you do, I protest I must recede, or think that I have made a prostitution of decorums; but in the vehemence of compassion, and to save the life of a person of so much importance—

555 WAITWELL: I esteem it so.

LADY WISHFORT: Or else you wrong my condescension.

WAITWELL: I do not, I do not!

LADY WISHFORT: Indeed you do.

WAITWELL: I do not, fair shrine of virtue!

560 LADY WISHFORT: If you think the least scruple of carnality° was an ingredient—

WAITWELL: Dear madam, no. You are all camphire° and frankincense, all chastity and odor.

LADY WISHFORT: Or that—

(Reenter Foible.)

565 FOIBLE: Madam, the dancers are ready; and there's one with a letter, who must deliver it into your own hands.

LADY WISHFORT: Sir Rowland, will you give me leave? Think favorably, judge candidly, and conclude you have found a person who would suffer racks in honor's cause, dear Sir Rowland, and will wait on 570 you incessantly.° *(Exit.)*

WAITWELL: Fie, fie! What a slavery have I undergone! Spouse, hast thou any cordial? I want spirits.

FOIBLE: What a washy° rogue art thou, to pant thus for a quarter of an hour's lying and swearing to a fine 575 lady!

WAITWELL: Oh, she is the antidote to desire! Spouse, thou wilt fare the worse for't. I shall have no appetite to "iteration of nuptials" this eight-and-forty hours. By this hand I'd rather be a chair-man° in the dog 580 days° than act Sir Rowland till this time tomorrow!

(Reenter Lady Wishfort, with a letter.)

LADY WISHFORT: Call in the dancers. Sir Rowland, we'll sit, if you please, and see the entertainment. *(Dance.)* Now, with your permission, Sir Rowland, I will peruse my letter. I would open it in your presence, 585 because I would not make you uneasy. If it should make you uneasy, I would burn it—speak if it does—but you may see, the superscription is like a woman's hand.

FOIBLE *(aside to Waitwell):* By Heaven! Mrs. Mar- 590 wood's; I know it. My heart aches. Get it from her.

WAITWELL: A woman's hand? No, madam, that's no woman's hand; I see that already. That's somebody whose throat must be cut.

LADY WISHFORT: Nay, Sir Rowland, since you give me a 595 proof of your passion by your jealousy, I promise you I'll make a return, by a frank communication. You shall see it; we'll open it together. Look you here. *(Reads.)* "Madam, though unknown to you." Look you there; 'tis from nobody that I know. "I have that 600 honor for your character, that I think myself obliged to let you know you are abused. He who pretends to be Sir Rowland is a cheat and a rascal." Oh, heavens! what's this?

FOIBLE *(aside):* Unfortunate! all's ruined! 605

WAITWELL: How, how, let me see, let me see! *(Reading.)* "A rascal, and disguised and suborned° for that imposture." O villainy! O villainy! "by the contrivance of—"

LADY WISHFORT: I shall faint, I shall die, oh! 610

FOIBLE *(aside to Waitwell):* Say 'tis your nephew's hand. Quickly, his plot, swear, swear it!

WAITWELL: Here's a villain! Madam, don't you perceive it? don't you see it?

LADY WISHFORT: Too well, too well! I have seen too 615 much.

---

542. **save-all:** A device in a candlestick to ensure that the candle will be completely burned.   549. **iteration:** Repetition. The sense seems to be that Lady Wishfort hopes Sir Rowland will not suspect her of a willingness to marry just any man. 560–61. **carnality:** Sensuality, lust.   562. **camphire:** Camphor was believed to reduce sexual desire.

571. **incessantly:** Immediately.   574. **washy:** Weak.   580. **chairman:** A sedan-chair carrier.   580–81. **dog days:** The sultriest days of the summer, a period of about six weeks beginning in early July.   607. **suborned:** Bribed.

Robert Hack, Carol Schultz, and Mikel Sarah Lambert in the Pearl Theatre Company's 2000 performance of *The Way of the World*, directed by Ray Vitra.

WAITWELL: I told you at first I knew the hand. A woman's hand? The rascal writes a sort of a large hand, your Roman hand. I saw there was a throat to be cut presently. If he were my son, as he is my nephew, I'd pistol him!

620

FOIBLE: Oh, treachery! But are you sure, Sir Rowland, it is his writing?

WAITWELL: Sure? Am I here? Do I live? Do I love this pearl of India? I have twenty letters in my pocket from him in the same character.°

625

LADY WISHFORT: How!

FOIBLE: Oh, what luck it is, Sir Rowland, that you were present at this juncture! This was the business that brought Mr. Mirabell disguised to Madam Millamant this afternoon. I thought something was contriving, when he stole by me and would have hid his face.

630

626. **character:** Handwriting.   640. **discompose:** Distress, upset.   668. **arrant knight:** I.e., a true knight-errant.   **arrant:** Downright.

LADY WISHFORT: How, how! I heard the villain was in the house indeed; and now I remember, my niece went away abruptly, when Sir Wilfull was to have made his addresses.

635

FOIBLE: Then, then, madam, Mr. Mirabell waited for her in her chamber, bur I would not tell your ladyship to discompose° you when you were to receive Sir Rowland.

640

WAITWELL: Enough, his date is short.

FOIBLE: No, good Sir Rowland, don't incur the law.

WAITWELL: Law? I care not for law. I can but die, and 'tis in a good cause. My lady shall be satisfied of my truth and innocence, though it cost me my life.

645

LADY WISHFORT: No, dear Sir Rowland, don't fight; if you should be killed, I must never show my face; or hanged! Oh, consider my reputation, Sir Rowland! No, you shan't fight. I'll go in and examine my niece; I'll make her confess. I conjure you, Sir Rowland, by all your love, not to fight.

650

WAITWELL: I am charmed, madam; I obey. But some proof you must let me give you; I'll go for a black box, which contains the writings of my whole estate, and deliver that into your hands.

655

LADY WISHFORT: Aye, dear Sir Rowland, that will be some comfort; bring the black box.

WAITWELL: And may I presume to bring a contract to be signed this night? May I hope so far?

660

LADY WISHFORT: Bring what you will; but come alive, pray come alive. Oh, this is a happy discovery!

WAITWELL: Dead or alive I'll come, and married we will be in spite of treachery; aye, and get an heir that shall defeat the last remaining glimpse of hope in my abandoned nephew. Come, my buxom widow.

665

Ere long you shall substantial proof receive,
That I'm an arrant knight—°

FOIBLE (*aside*):   Or arrant° knave.

(*Exeunt.*)

ACT V

([*Scene continues.*] *Enter Lady Wishfort and Foible.*)

LADY WISHFORT: Out of my house, out of my house, thou viper! thou serpent, that I have fostered! thou bosom traitress, that I raised from nothing! Begone! begone! begone! go! go! That I took from washing of old gauze and weaving of dead hair, with a bleak blue nose, over a chafing-dish of starved embers, and dining behind a traverse rag,° in a shop no bigger than a birdcage! Go, go! starve again, do, do!

5

FOIBLE: Dear madam, I'll beg your pardon on my knees.

LADY WISHFORT: Away! out! out! Go set up for yourself again! Do, drive a trade, do, with your three-penny-worth of small ware flaunting upon a pack-thread under a brandy-seller's bulk,° or against a dead wall

10

7. **traverse rag:** A curtain or hanging that serves as a screen.
13. **bulk:** A booth where brandy is sold.

15 by a ballad-monger! Go, hang out an old frisoneer-gorget,° with a yard of yellow colberteen° again. Do; an old gnawed mask, two rows of pins, and a child's fiddle; a glass necklace with the beads broken, and a quilted nightcap with one ear. Go, go, drive a trade!
20 These were your commodities, you treacherous trull! this was the merchandise you dealt in, when I took you into my house, placed you next myself, and made you governante of my whole family! You have forgot this, have you, now you have feathered your nest?

FOIBLE: No, no, dear madam. Do but hear me; have but
25 a moment's patience. I'll confess all. Mr. Mirabell seduced me; I am not the first that he has wheedled with his dissembling tongue. Your ladyship's own wisdom has been deluded by him, then how should I, a poor ignorant, defend myself? O madam, if you
30 knew but what he promised me, and how he assured me your ladyship should come to no damage! Or else the wealth of the Indies should not have bribed me to conspire against so good, so sweet, so kind a lady as you have been to me.

35 LADY WISHFORT: No damage? What, to betray me, to marry me to a cast-servingman?° To make me a receptacle, a hospital for a decayed pimp? "No damage"? O thou frontless° impudence, more than a big-bellied actress!

40 FOIBLE: Pray do but hear me, madam; he could not marry your ladyship, madam. No indeed; his marriage was to have been void in law, for he was married to me first, to secure your ladyship. He could not have bedded your ladyship; for if he had consum-
45 mated with your ladyship, he must have run the risk of the law and been put upon his clergy.° Yes indeed, I inquired of the law in that case before I would meddle or make.°

LADY WISHFORT: What, then I have been your property,
50 have I? I have been convenient to you, it seems! While you were catering for Mirabell, I have been broker° for you? What, have you made a passive bawd of me? This exceeds all precedent; I am brought to fine uses, to become a botcher° of second-
55 hand marriages between Abigails° and Andrews!° I'll couple you! Yes, I'll baste you together, you and your Philander!° I'll Duke's-Place you, as I'm a person! Your turtle is in custody already; you shall coo in the

same cage, if there be constable or warrant in the parish.   (*Exit.*)   60

FOIBLE: Oh, that ever I was born! Oh, that I was ever married! A bride! aye, I shall he a Bridewell-bride.° Oh!

(*Enter Mrs. Fainall.*)

MRS. FAINALL: Poor Foible, what's the matter?

FOIBLE: O madam, my lady's gone for a constable. I   65
shall be had to a justice, and put to Bridewell to beat hemp. Poor Waitwell's gone to prison already.

MRS. FAINALL: Have a good heart, Foible; Mirabell's gone to give security for him. This is all Marwood's and my husband's doing.   70

FOIBLE: Yes, yes, I know it, madam; she was in my lady's closet, and overheard all that you said to me before dinner. She sent the letter to my lady; and that missing effect, Mr. Fainall laid this plot to arrest Waitwell, when he pretended to go for the papers; and in   75
the meantime Mrs. Marwood declared all to my lady.

MRS. FAINALL: Was there no mention made of me in the letter? My mother does not suspect my being in the confederacy? I fancy Marwood has not told her, though she has told my husband.   80

FOIBLE: Yes, madam; but my lady did not see that part. We stifled the letter before she read so far. Has that mischievous devil told Mr. Fainall of your ladyship then?

MRS. FAINALL: Aye, all's out, my affair with Mirabell,   85
everything discovered. This is the last day of our living together; that's my comfort.

FOIBLE: Indeed, madam, and so 'tis a comfort if you knew all. He has been even with your ladyship; which I could have told you long enough since, but I   90
love to keep peace and quietness by my good will. I had rather bring friends together than set 'em at distance. But Mrs. Marwood and he are nearer related than ever their parents thought for.

MRS. FAINALL: Sayest thou so, Foible? Canst thou prove   95
this?

FOIBLE: I can take my oath of it, madam; so can Mrs. Mincing. We have had many a fair word from Madam Marwood, to conceal something that passed in our chamber one evening when you were at Hyde   100
Park and we were thought to have gone awalking; but we went up unawares, though we were sworn to secrecy too. Madam Marwood took a book and swore us upon it, but it was but a book of poems. So long as it was not a Bible oath, we may break it with   105
a safe conscience.

MRS. FAINALL: This discovery is the most opportune thing I could wish. Now, Mincing?

(*Enter Mincing.*)

14–15. frisoneer-gorget: A kind of wimple, or head covering, made of coarse woolen cloth.   **15. colberteen:** A French lace of inferior quality.   **36. cast-servingman:** A discharged servant.   **38. frontless:** Shameless.   **46. put upon his clergy:** Forced to plead benefit of clergy. Clergy (and, later, people who could read or write) could claim exemption from punishment imposed by a secular court.   **48. meddle or make:** A colloquialism for "get mixed up in this business."   **52. broker:** Marriage broker.   **54. botcher:** A maker or mender.   **55. Abigails:** A maidservant in Beaumont and Fletcher's play *The Scornful Lady*.   **Andrews:** A manservant in Fletcher and Massinger's *The Elder Brother*.   **57. Philander:** The lover in Beaumont and Fletcher's *The Laws of Candy*.

62. Bridewell-bride: Bridewell was a house of correction.

MINCING: My lady° would speak with Mrs. Foible,
110   mem. Mr. Mirabell is with her; he has set your spouse
at liberty, Mrs. Foible, and would have you hide
yourself in my lady's closet till my old lady's anger is
abated. Oh, my old lady is in a perilous passion at
something Mr. Fainall has said, he swears, and my
115   old lady cries. There's a fearful hurricane, I vow. He
says, mem, how that he'll have my lady's fortune
made over to him, or he'll be divorced.
MRS. FAINALL: Does your lady or Mirabell know that?
MINCING: Yes, mem, they have sent me to see if Sir Wil-
120   full be sober and to bring him to them. My lady is
resolved to have him, I think, rather than lose such a
vast sum as six thousand pound. Oh, come, Mrs.
Foible, I hear my old lady.
MRS. FAINALL: Foible, you must tell Mincing that she
125   must prepare to vouch° when I call her.
FOIBLE: Yes, yes, madam.
MINCING: O yes, mem, I'll vouch anything for your
ladyship's service, be what it will.

(*Exeunt Mincing and Foible.*)

(*Reenter Lady Wishfort, with, Mrs. Marwood.*)

LADY WISHFORT: O my dear friend, how can I enumer-
130   ate the benefits that I have received from your goodness? To you I owe the timely discovery of the false
vows of Mirabell, to you I owe the detection of the
impostor, Sir Rowland. And now you are become an
intercessor with my son-in-law, to save the honor of
135   my house, and compound for the frailties of my
daughter. Well, friend, you are enough to reconcile
me to the bad world, or else I would retire to deserts
and solitudes, and feed harmless sheep by groves and
purling streams. Dear Marwood, let us leave the
140   world, and retire by ourselves and be shepherdesses.
MRS. MARWOOD: Let us first dispatch the affair in hand,
madam. We shall have leisure to think of retirement
afterwards. Here is one who is concerned in the treaty.
LADY WISHFORT: O daughter, daughter, is it possible
145   thou shouldst be my child, bone of my bone, and
flesh of my flesh, and, as I may say, another me, and
yet transgress the most minute particle of severe
virtue? Is it possible° you should lean aside to iniquity,
who have been cast in the direct mold of virtue? I
150   have not only been a mold but a pattern for you, and
a model for you, after you were brought into the
world.
MRS. FAINALL: I don't understand your ladyship.
LADY WISHFORT: Not understand? Why, have you not
155   been naught?° Have you not been sophisticated?° Not
understand? Here I am ruined to compound° for your
caprices and your cuckoldoms. I must pawn my plate
and my jewels, and ruin my niece, and all little enough.

MRS. FAINALL: I am wronged and abused, and so are   160
you. 'Tis a false accusation, as false as hell, as false as
your friend there, aye, or your friend's friend, my
false husband.
MRS. MARWOOD: My friend, Mrs. Fainall? Your husband my friend? What do you mean?   165
MRS. FAINALL: I know what I mean, madam, and so do
you; and so shall the world at a time convenient.
MRS. MARWOOD: I am sorry to see you so passionate,
madam. More temper° would look more like innocence. But I have done. I am sorry my zeal to serve   170
your ladyship and family should admit of miscon-
struction, or make me liable to affronts. You will
pardon me, madam, if I meddle no more with an
affair in which I am not personally concerned.
LADY WISHFORT: O dear friend, I am so ashamed that   175
you should meet with such returns! (*To Mrs. Fainall.*)
You ought to ask pardon on your knees, ungrateful
creature; she deserves more from you than all your
life can accomplish. (*To Mrs. Marwood.*) Oh, don't
leave me destitute in this perplexity! No, stick to me, 180
my good genius.
MRS. FAINALL: I tell you, madam, you're abused. Stick
to you? Aye, like a leech, to suck your best blood;
she'll drop off when she's full. Madam, you shan't
pawn a bodkin,° nor part with a brass counter,° in   185
composition for me. I defy 'em all. Let 'em prove
their aspersions; I know my own innocence, and dare
stand a trial.   (*Exit.*)
LADY WISHFORT: Why, if she should be innocent, if she
should be wronged after all, ha? I don't know what   190
to think; and, I promise you, her education has been
unexceptionable.° I may say it; for I chiefly made it
my own care to initiate her very infancy in the rudiments of virtue, and to impress upon her tender years
a young odium° and aversion to the very sight of   195
men. Aye, friend, she would ha' shrieked if she had
but seen a man, till she was in her teens. As I'm a person 'tis true. She was never suffered to play with a
male child, though but in coats; nay, her very babies°
were of the feminine gender. Oh, she never looked a   200
man in the face but her own father, or the chaplain,
and him we made a shift° to put upon her for a
woman, by the help of his long garments and his
sleek face, till she was going in her fifteen.°
MRS. MARWOOD: 'Twas much she should be deceived so 205
long.
LADY WISHFORT: I warrant you, or she would never
have borne to have been catechized by him; and have
heard his long lectures against singing and dancing,
and such debaucheries, and going to filthy plays and 210

---

109. **My lady:** I.e., Millamant.   125. **vouch:** Testify.
155. **naught:** Naughty, wicked.   **sophisticated:** Corrupted,
debauched.   156. **compound:** Compensate. Lady Wishfort
refers to Mr. Fainall's blackmailing tactics.

169. **temper:** Temperateness.   185. **bodkin:** Needle or hairpin.
brass counter: A farthing (a quarter of a penny).   192. **unexceptionable:** Exemplary.   195. **odium:** Dislike.   199. **babies:**
Dolls.   202. **made a shift:** Devised a plan.   204. **in her fifteen:**
Into her fifteenth year.

profane music meetings, where the lewd trebles squeak nothing but bawdy, and the basses roar blasphemy. Oh, she would have swooned at the sight or name of an obscene playbook! And can I think, after
215 all this, that my daughter can be naught? What, a whore? and thought it excommunication to set her foot within the door of a playhouse! O dear friend, I can't believe it, no, no! As she says, let him prove it, let him prove it.
220 MRS. MARWOOD: Prove it, madam? What, and have your name prostituted in a public court? yours and your daughter's reputation worried at the bar by a pack of bawling lawyers? To be ushered in with an *Oyez°* of scandal, and have your case opened by an
225 old fumbling lecher in a quoif° like a man-midwife; to bring your daughter's infamy to light; to be a theme for legal punsters and quibblers by the statute, and become a jest against a rule of court, where there is no precedent for a jest in any record, not even in
230 Doomsday Book;° to discompose the gravity of the bench, and provoke naughty interrogatories in more naughty law Latin, while the good judge, tickled with the proceeding, simpers under a gray beard, and fidges° off and on his cushion as if he had swallowed
235 cantharides,° or sat upon cow-itch!°
LADY WISHFORT: Oh, 'tis very hard!
MRS. MARWOOD: And then to have my young revelers of the Temple° take notes, like prentices at a conventicle;° and after, talk it over again in Commons,° or
240 before drawers in an eating-house.
LADY WISHFORT: Worse and worse!
MRS. MARWOOD: Nay, this is nothing; if it would end here, 'twere well. But it must, after this, be consigned by the shorthand writers to the public press; and
245 from thence be transferred to the hands, nay into the throats and lungs of hawkers,° with voices more licentious than the loud flounder-man's.° And this you must hear till you are stunned; nay, you must hear nothing else for some days.
250 LADY WISHFORT: Oh, 'tis insupportable! No, no, dear friend; make it up, make it up; aye, aye, I'll compound. I'll give up all, myself and my all, my niece and her all, anything, everything for composition.

MRS. MARWOOD: Nay, madam, I advise nothing; I only
255 lay before you, as a friend, the inconveniencies which perhaps you have overseen. Here comes Mr. Fainall; if he will be satisfied to huddle up all in silence, I shall be glad. You must think I would rather congratulate than condole with you.

(*Enter Fainall.*)

LADY WISHFORT: Aye, aye, I do not doubt it, dear Mar-
260 wood; no, no, I do not doubt it.
FAINALL: Well, madam, I have suffered myself to be overcome by the importunity of this lady, your friend, and am content you shall enjoy your own proper estate during life, on condition you oblige
265 yourself never to marry, under such penalty as I think convenient.
LADY WISHFORT: Never to marry?
FAINALL: No more Sir Rowlands; the next imposture may not be so timely detected.
270 MRS. MARWOOD: That condition, I dare answer, my lady will consent to, without difficulty; she has already but too much experienced the perfidiousness of men. Besides, madam, when we retire to our pastoral solitude, we shall bid adieu to all other thoughts.
275 LADY WISHFORT: Aye, that's true; but in case of necessity, as of health, or some such emergency—
FAINALL: Oh, if you are prescribed marriage, you shall be considered; I will only reserve to myself the power to choose for you. If your physic be wholesome, it
280 matters not who is your apothecary. Next, my wife shall settle on me the remainder of her fortune, not made over already; and for her maintenance depend entirely on my discretion.
LADY WISHFORT: This is most inhumanly savage,
285 exceeding the barbarity of a Muscovite° husband.
FAINALL: I learned it from his Czarish majesty's retinue,° in a winter evening's conference over brandy and pepper, amongst other secrets of matrimony and policy, as they are at present practiced in the northern
290 hemisphere. But this must be agreed unto, and that positively. Lastly, I will be endowed, in right of my wife, with that six thousand pound, which is the moiety of Mrs. Millamant's fortune in your possession; and which she has forfeited (as will appear by
295 the last will and testament of your deceased husband, Sir Jonathan Wishfort) by her disobedience in contracting herself against your consent or knowledge, and by refusing the offered match with Sir Wilfull Witwoud, which you, like a careful aunt, had pro-
300 vided for her.
LADY WISHFORT: My nephew was *non compos,°* and could not make his addresses.
FAINALL: I come to make demands. I'll hear no objections.
LADY WISHFORT: You will grant me time to consider?
305

224. *Oyez:* The court crier's call for silence. 225. quoif: Coif, the lawyer's white cap. 230. Doomsday Book: A record of a survey of the lands of England made by order of William the Conqueror. 234. fidges: Fidgets. 235. cantharides: A powder made from dried beetles and used medicinally as a skin irritant. cow-itch: Cowage, a plant that causes intense itching. 238. Temple: The courts of law. 238–39. prentices at a conventicle: It was customary for a Puritan master to require his apprentice to take notes on the Sunday sermon in the meetinghouse (conventicle). 239. Commons: The dining hall. 246. hawkers: Peddlers. 247. flounder-man: An actual flounder seller, well known to the Londoners of the day and noted for his "loud, but not unmusical" voice.

286. Muscovite: Russian. 287. Czarish majesty's retinue: Referring to Peter the Great's visit to England in 1697. 302. **non compos:** I.e., *non compos mentis,* not in his right mind.

FAINALL: Yes, while the instrument° is drawing, to which you must set your hand till more sufficient deeds can he perfected; which I will take care shall be done with all possible speed. In the meanwhile I will

310   go for the said instrument, and till my return you may balance this matter in your own discretion.

(Exit.)

LADY WISHFORT: This insolence is beyond all precedent, all parallel; must I be subject to this merciless villain?

MRS. MARWOOD: 'Tis severe indeed, madam, that you

315   should smart for your daughter's wantonness.

LADY WISHFORT: 'Twas against my consent that she married this barbarian, but she would have him, though her year° was not out. Ah! her first husband, my son Languish, would not have carried it thus.

320   Well, that was my choice, this is hers; she is matched now with a witness.° I shall he mad! Dear friend, is there no comfort for me? Must I live to be confiscated at this rebel-rate?° Here come two more of my Egyptian plagues° too.

(Enter Mrs. Millamant and Sir Wilfull Witwoud.)

325   SIR WILFULL: Aunt, your servant.

LADY WISHFORT: Out, caterpillar, call not me aunt! I know thee not!

SIR WILFULL: I confess I have been a little in disguise,° as they say. 'Sheart! and I'm sorry for't. What would

330   you have? I hope I committed no offense, aunt, and if I did, I am willing to make satisfaction; and what can a man say fairer? If I have broke anything, I'll pay for't, an it cost a pound. And so let that content for what's past, and make no more words. For what's to

335   come, to pleasure you I'm willing to marry my cousin. So pray let's all be friends; she and I are agreed upon the matter before a witness.

LADY WISHFORT: How's this, dear niece? Have I any comfort? Can this be true?

340   MRS. MILLAMANT: I am content to be a sacrifice to your repose, madam; and to convince you that I had no hand in the plot, as you were misinformed, I have laid my commands on Mirabell to come in person, and be a witness that I give my hand to this flower of

345   knighthood; and for the contract that passed between Mirabell and me, I have obliged him to make a resignation of it in your ladyship's presence. He is without, and waits your leave for admittance.

LADY WISHFORT: Well, I'll swear I am something revived

350   at this testimony of your obedience; but I cannot admit that traitor. I fear I cannot fortify myself to support his appearance. He is as terrible to me as a

Gorgon;° if I see him, I fear I shall turn to stone, petrify incessantly.

355   MRS. MILLAMANT: If you disoblige him, he may resent your refusal, and insist upon the contract still. Then 'tis the last time he will be offensive to you.

LADY WISHFORT: Are you sure it will be the last time? If I were sure of that! Shall I never see him again?

360   MRS. MILLAMANT: Sir Wilfull, you and he are to travel together, are you not?

SIR WILFULL: 'Sheart, the gentleman's a civil gentleman, aunt; let him come in. Why, we are sworn brothers and fellow travelers. We are to be Pylades and

365   Orestes,° he and I. He is to be my interpreter in foreign parts. He has been overseas once already; and with *proviso* that I marry my cousin, will cross 'em once again, only to bear me company. 'Sheart, I'll call him in. An I set on't once, he shall come in; and see

370   who'll hinder him.

(Goes to the door and hems.)

MRS. MARWOOD: This is precious fooling, if it would pass; but I'll know the bottom of it.

LADY WISHFORT: O dear Marwood, you are not going?

MRS. MARWOOD: Not far, madam; I'll return immediately.   *(Exit.)*   375

(Reenter Sir Wilfull with Mirabell.)

SIR WILFULL: Look up, man, I'll stand by you; 'spud and she do frown, she can't kill you, besides, harkee, she dare not frown desperately, because her face is none of her own. 'Sheart, an she should, her forehead would wrinkle like the coat of a cream cheese; but   380 mum for that, fellow traveler.

MIRABELL: If a deep sense of the many injuries I have offered to so good a lady, with a sincere remorse and a hearty contrition, can but obtain the least glance of compassion, I am too happy. Ah, madam, there was   385 a time! But let it be forgotten. I confess I have deservedly forfeited the high place I once held, of sighing at your feet. Nay, kill me not, by turning from me in disdain. I come not to plead for favor; nay, not for pardon. I am a suppliant only for pity. I am going   390 where I shall never behold you more.

SIR WILFULL: How, fellow traveler! You shall go by yourself then.

MIRABELL: Let me be pitied first, and afterwards forgotten. I ask no more.   395

SIR WILFULL: By'r lady, a very reasonable request, and will cost you nothing, aunt. Come, come, forgive and forget, aunt; why, you must, an you are a Christian.

MIRABELL: Consider, madam, in reality you could not receive much prejudice; it was an innocent device,   400

---

306. **instrument:** formal agreement.   318. **her year:** Period of mourning for her first husband.   321. **with a witness:** Colloquialism meaning "with a vengeance."   322–23. **Must I live . . . rebel-rate:** The sense is "Must I live to see my property and fortune confiscated in this piratical fashion?"   324. **Egyptian plagues:** Referring to the plagues of Egypt recorded in Exodus 7ff.   328. **disguise:** Drunk.

353. **Gorgon:** Any one of the three sisters in Greek legend (Medusa was one) whose hair was wreathed with snakes and whose glance turned the beholder to stone.   364. **Pylades and Orestes:** In Greek legend Pylades was the loyal and trusted friend of Orestes, son of Agamemnon and brother of Elektra.

though I confess it had a face of guiltiness. It was at most an artifice which love contrived, and errors which love produces have ever been accounted venial. At least think it is punishment enough that I have lost what in my heart I hold most dear, that to your cruel indignation I have offered up this beauty, and with her my peace and quiet; nay, all my hopes of future comfort.

SIR WILFULL: An he does not move me, would I may never be o' the quorum!° An it were not as good a deed as to drink, to give her to him again, I would I might never take shipping! Aunt, if you don't forgive quickly, I shall melt, I can tell you that. My contract went no farther than a little mouth-glue, and that's hardly dry; one doleful sigh more from my fellow traveler, and 'tis dissolved.

LADY WISHFORT: Well, nephew, upon your account—ah, he has a false insinuating tongue! Well, sir, I will stifle my just resentment at my nephew's request. I will endeavor what I can to forget, but on *proviso* that you resign the contract with my niece immediately.

MIRABELL: It is in writing, and with papers of concern; but I have sent my servant for it, and will deliver it to you, with all acknowledgments for your transcendent goodness.

LADY WISHFORT (*aside*): Oh, he has witchcraft in his eyes and tongue! When I did not see him, I could have bribed a villain to his assassination; but his appearance rakes the embers which have so long lain smothered in my breast.

(*Reenter Fainall and Mrs. Marwood.*)

FAINALL: Your date of deliberation, madam, is expired. Here is the instrument; are you prepared to sign?

LADY WISHFORT: If I were prepared, I am not empowered. My niece exerts a lawful claim, having matched herself by my direction to Sir Wilfull.

FAINALL: That sham is too gross to pass on me, though 'tis imposed on you, madam.

MRS. MILLAMANT: Sir, I have given my consent.

MIRABELL: And, sir, I have resigned my pretensions.

SIR WILFULL: And, sir, I assert my right; and will maintain it in defiance of you, sir, and of your instrument. 'Sheart, an you talk of an instrument, sir, I have an old fox° by my thigh shall hack your instrument of ram vellum° to shreds, sir! It shall not be sufficient for a *mittimus*° or a tailor's measure.° Therefore withdraw your instrument, sir, or, by'r lady, I shall draw mine.

LADY WISHFORT: Hold, nephew, hold!

MRS. MILLAMANT: Good Sir Wilfull, respite° your valor.

FAINALL: Indeed? Are you provided of your guard, with your single beefeater° there? But I'm prepared for

you, and insist upon my first proposal. You shall submit your own estate to my management and absolutely make over my wife's to my sole use, as pursuant to the purpose and tenor of this other covenant. (*To Mrs. Millamant.*) I suppose, madam, your consent is not requisite in this case; nor, Mr. Mirabell, your resignation; nor, Sir Wilfull, your right. You may draw your fox if you please, sir, and make a Bear Garden° flourish somewhere else; for here it will not avail.—This, my Lady Wishfort, must be subscribed, or your darling daughter's turned adrift, like a leaky hulk, to sink or swim, as she and the current of this lewd town can agree.

LADY WISHFORT: Is there no means, no remedy to stop my ruin? Ungrateful wretch! dost thou not owe thy being, thy subsistence, to my daughter's fortune?

FAINALL: I'll answer you when I have the rest of it in my possession.

MIRABELL (*to Lady Wishfort*): But that you would not accept of a remedy from my hands—I own I have not deserved you should owe any obligation to me; or else perhaps I could advise—

LADY WISHFORT: Oh, what? what? to save me and my child from ruin, from want, I'll forgive all that's past; nay, I'll consent to anything to come, to be delivered from this tyranny.

MIRABELL: Aye, madam, but that is too late; my reward is intercepted. You have disposed of her who only could have made me a compensation for all my services. But be it as it may, I am resolved I'll serve you; you shall not be wronged in this savage manner.

LADY WISHFORT: How! Dear Mr. Mirabell, can you be so generous at last? But it is not possible. Harkee, I'll break my nephew's match; you shall have my niece yet, and all her fortune, if you can but save me from this imminent danger.

MIRABELL: Will you? I take you at your word. I ask no more. I must have leave for two criminals to appear.

LADY WISHFORT: Aye, aye; anybody, anybody!

MIRABELL: Foible is one, and a penitent.

(*Reenter Mrs. Fainall, Foible, and Mincing.*)

MRS. MARWOOD (*to Fainall*): O my shame! (*Mirabell and Lady Wishfort go to Mrs. Fainall and Foible.*) These corrupt things are brought hither to expose me.

FAINALL: If it must all come out, why let 'em know it; 'tis but the way of the world. That shall not urge me to relinquish or abate one tittle of my terms; no, I will insist the more.

FOIBLE: Yes indeed, madam; I'll take my Bible oath of it.

MINCING: And so will I, mem.

LADY WISHFORT: O Marwood. Marwood, art thou false? my friend deceive me? Hast thou been a wicked accomplice with that profligate man?

MRS. MARWOOD: Have you so much ingratitude and injustice, to give credit against your friend to the aspersions of two such mercenary trulls?

MINCING: "Mercenary," mem? I scorn your words. 'Tis true we found you and Mr. Fainall in the blue garret; by the same token, you swore us to secrecy upon Messalina's poems.° "Mercenary?" No, if we would have been mercenary, we should have held our tongues; you would have bribed us sufficiently.

FAINALL: Go, you are an insignificant thing! Well, what are you the better for this? Is this Mr. Mirabell's expedient? I'll be put off no longer. You thing, that was a wife, shall smart for this! I will not leave thee wherewithal to hide thy shame; your body shall be naked as your reputation.

MRS. FAINALL: I despise you, and defy your malice! You have aspersed me wrongfully. I have proved your falsehood. Go, you and your treacherous—I will not name it, but starve together, perish!

FAINALL: Not while you are worth a groat,° indeed, my dear. Madam, I'll be fooled no longer.

LADY WISHFORT: Ah, Mr. Mirabell, this is small comfort, the detection of this affair.

MIRABELL: Oh, in good time. Your leave for the other offender and penitent to appear, madam.

(*Enter Waitwell, with a box of writings.*)

LADY WISHFORT: O Sir Rowland? Well, rascal?

WAITWELL: What your ladyship pleases. I have brought the black box at last, madam.

MIRABELL: Give it me. Madam, you remember your promise.

LADY WISHFORT: Aye, dear sir.

MIRABELL: Where are the gentlemen?

WAITWELL: At hand, sir, rubbing their eyes; just risen from sleep.

FAINALL: 'Sdeath, what's this to me? I'll not wait your private concerns.

(*Enter Petulant and Witwoud.*)

PETULANT: How now? What's the matter? Whose hand's out?°

WITWOUD: Heyday! what, are you all got together, like players at the end of the last act?

MIRABELL: You may remember, gentlemen, I once requested your hands as witnesses to a certain parchment.

WITWOUD: Aye, I do; my hand I remember. Petulant set his mark.

MIRABELL: You wrong him, his name is fairly written, as shall appear. You do not remember, gentlemen, anything of what that parchment contained?

(*Undoing the box.*)

WITWOUD: No.

PETULANT: Not I. I writ. I read nothing.

MIRABELL: Very well; now you shall know. Madam, your promise.

LADY WISHFORT: Aye, aye, sir, upon my honor.

MIRABELL: Mr. Fainall, it is now time that you should know that your lady, while she was at her own disposal, and before you had by your insinuations wheedled her out of a pretended settlement of the greatest part of her fortune—

FAINALL: Sir! pretended!

MIRABELL: Yes, sir. I say that this lady, while a widow, having it seems received some cautions respecting your inconstancy and tyranny of temper, which from her own partial opinion and fondness of you she could never have suspected—she did, I say, by the wholesome advice of friends and of sages learned in the laws of this land, deliver this same as her act and deed to me in trust, and to the uses within mentioned. You may read if you please (*holding out the parchment*), though perhaps what is written on the back may serve your occasions.

FAINALL: Very likely, sir. What's here? Damnation! (*Reads.*) "A deed of conveyance of the whole estate real of Arabella Languish, widow, in trust to Edward Mirabell." Confusion!

MIRABELL: Even so, sir; 'tis the way of the world, sir, of the widows of the world. I suppose this deed may bear an elder° date than what you have obtained from your lady?

FAINALL: Perfidious fiend! Then thus I'll be revenged.

(*Offers to run at Mrs. Fainall.*)

SIR WILFULL: Hold, sir! Now you may make your Bear Garden flourish somewhere else, sir.

FAINALL: Mirabell, you shall hear of this, sir; be sure you shall. (*To Sir Wilfull.*) Let me pass, oaf!

(*Exit.*)

MRS. FAINALL (*to Mrs. Marwood*): Madam, you seem to stifle your resentment; you had better give it vent.

MRS. MARWOOD: Yes, it shall have vent, and to your confusion; or I'll perish in the attempt.   (*Exit.*)

LADY WISHFORT: O daughter, daughter, 'tis plain thou hast inherited thy mother's prudence.

MRS. FAINALL: Thank Mr. Mirabell, a cautious friend, to whose advice all is owing.

LADY WISHFORT: Well, Mr. Mirabell, you have kept your promise, and I must perform mine. First, I pardon, for your sake, Sir Rowland there, and Foible. The next thing is to break the matter to my nephew, and how to do that—

MIRABELL: For that, madam, give yourself no trouble; let me have your consent. Sir Wilfull is my friend; he has had compassion upon lovers, and generously engaged a volunteer° in this action, for our service, and now designs to prosecute his travels.

---

509. **Messalina's poems:** Mincing means a volume of "miscellaneous" poems. Her mistake presents an amusing irony, since Messalina, the wife of the Roman Emperor Claudius, was notorious for her avarice, treachery, and dissoluteness.   522. **groat:** An old silver coin worth about fourpence.   539–40. **Whose hand's out:** "What is the trouble?"

579. **elder:** Earlier.   602. **a volunteer:** As a volunteer.

SIR WILFULL: 'Sheart, aunt, I have no mind to marry.
605   My cousin's a fine lady, and the gentleman loves her,
      and she loves him, and they deserve one another; my
      resolution is to see foreign parts. I have set on't, and
      when I'm set on't, I must do't. And if these two gentle-
      men would travel too, I think they may be spared.
610 PETULANT: For my part, I say little; I think things are
      best off or on.°
      WITWOUD: Egad, I understand nothing of the matter;
      I'm in a maze yet, like a dog in a dancing school.
      LADY WISHFORT: Well, sir, take her, and with her all the
615   joy I can give you.
      MRS. MILLAMANT: Why does not the man take me?
      Would you have me give myself to you over again?
      MIRABELL: Aye, and over and over again; (*kisses her
      hand*) for I would have you as often as possibly I can.
620   Well, Heaven grant I love you not too well; that's all
      my fear.
      SIR WILFULL: 'Sheart, you'll have time enough to toy°
      after you're married; or if you will toy now, let us
      have a dance in the meantime, that we who are not
625   lovers may have some other employment besides
      looking on.
      MIRABELL: With all my heart, dear Sir Wilfull. What
      shall we do for music?
      FOIBLE: Oh, sir, some that were provided for Sir Row-
630   land's entertainment are yet within call.
                                              (*A dance.*)
      LADY WISHFORT: As I am a person, I can hold out no
      longer. I have wasted my spirits so today already that
      I am ready to sink under the fatigue; and I cannot but
      have some fears upon me yet that my son Fainall will
635   pursue same desperate course.
      MIRABELL: Madam, disquiet not yourself on that
      account; to my knowledge his circumstances are
      such, he must of force° comply. For my part, I will
      contribute all that in me lies to a reunion; in the
640   meantime, madam (*to Mrs. Fainall*), let me before
      these witnesses restore to you this deed of trust; it
      may be a means, well-managed, to make you live eas-
      ily together.
            From hence let those be warn'd, who mean to
                  wed,
645   Lest mutual falsehood stain the bridal bed;
            For each deceiver to his cost may find
            That marriage frauds too oft are paid in kind.
                                          (*Exeunt omnes.*)°

EPILOGUE

(*Spoken by Mrs. Millamant.*)

      After our Epilogue this crowd dismisses,
      I'm thinking how this play'll be pull'd to pieces.
      But pray consider, ere you doom its fall,
      How hard a thing 'twould be to please you all.
      There are some critics so with spleen diseas'd,   5
      They scarcely come inclining to be pleas'd;
      And sure he must have more than mortal skill,
      Who pleases any one against his will.
      Then, all bad poets we are sure are foes,
      And how their number's swell'd the town well
            knows;   10
      In shoals I've mark'd 'em judging in the pit;
      Though they're on no pretense for judgment fit,
      But that they have been damn'd for want of wit.
      Since when they, by their own offenses taught,
      Set up for spies on plays, and finding fault.   15
      Others there are whose malice we'd prevent;
      Such who watch plays with scurrilous intent
      To mark out who by characters are meant.
      And though no perfect likeness they can trace,
      Yet each pretends to know the copy'd face.   20
      These with false glosses° feed their own ill nature,
      And turn to libel what was meant a satire.°
      May such malicious fops this fortune find,
      To think themselves alone the fools design'd;
      If any are so arrogantly vain,   25
      To think they singly can support a scene,
      And furnish fool enough to entertain.
      For well the learn'd and the judicious know
      That satire scorns to stoop so meanly low
      As any one abstracted° fop to show.   30
      For, as when painters form a matchless face
      They from each fair one catch some diff'rent grace;
      And shining features in one portrait blend,
      To which no single beauty must pretend;
      So poets oft do in one piece expose   35
      Whole *belles assemblées*° of coquettes and beaux.

---

611. off or on: One way or the other.   **622. toy:** Play.   **638. of
force:** Of necessity.   **647. [S.D.]** *omnes:* Latin for "all."

21. glosses: Marginal notes.   **21–22. nature . . . satire:**
According to seventeenth-century pronunciation, "nature"
and "satire" were good rhymes.   **30. abstracted:** Particular.
36. *belles assemblées:* Fine gatherings.

COMMENTARIES

Howard Taubman (1907–1996)
REVIEW OF *THE WAY OF THE WORLD*   1930

Howard Taubman reviewed one of the notable modern productions of The Way of the World, *starring Zoe Caldwell, a British actress who went on to win numerous awards. The question of accents, which Taubman discusses, is important for any audience, since the lines are often rapid-fire and the wit razor-sharp. Caldwell's authenticity and style charmed Taubman, who was pleased enough with the production to forgive its minor flaws.*

There are many good reasons to justify going out of one's way for the Minnesota Theater Company's *The Way of the World*, and hardly the least of them is Congreve himself. But an excellent one is to enjoy the impeccable high-comedy playing of Zoe Caldwell as Millamant.

Jessica Tandy brings a raffish gusto to Lady Wishfort, Nancy Wickwire is a cool, suave intriguer as Marwood, Robert Pastene is all showy manners and hard bargainer as Fainall, Robert Milli conveys the shrewd charm of Mirabell. But it is Miss Caldwell who is unfaltering in every velvet thrust.

Not an inflection or a gesture is out of place in this handsomely composed portrait of a wise and witty young woman of the London world of 1700. In Tanya Moiseiwitch's modish clothes, with their headdresses and trains, Miss Caldwell moves with the poised self-knowledge of one who has stepped out of a Restoration drawing room.

Her face with its pale make-up, obviously the careful concern of a young woman of breeding who will not look vulgarly outdoorsy, rarely betrays an emotion. The eyes are detached but brighten occasionally with mischief. The voice is silken, but what humor there is in the phrasing—not catchpenny humor but the sense of fun that sparkles in a civilized mind.

When Miss Caldwell talks of being persecuted by letters, there is amusement in the weariness of her tone. When she reads the poems of Sir John Suckling to confuse addle-brained Sir Wilfull, it is as if only she and we were privy to the dry jesting.

When she sets forth the conditions on which she will agree to marry Mirabell, she does so with a mingling of seriousness and laughter that suits perfectly Congreve's milieu and style. And Mr. Milli's response in kind gives the necessary fillip to a scene that has not lost its edge in 265 years.

Douglas Campbell has directed *The Way of the World* with a relish of its manners and mannerisms. Miss Moiseiwitch's designs with their suggestion of colorful elegancies turn the open stage of the Tyrone Guthrie Theater into a garden or boudoir with equal felicity.

The over-all tone of the production, with its occasional background of Purcell music and with its ingratiating concluding dance, is admirable. But the Minnesota

Douglas Campbell's set design and ensemble cast, including Zoe Caldwell and Jessica Tandy, in the Minnesota Theater Company's 1965 performance of *The Way of the World* at the Tyrone Guthrie Theater.

Theater Company would be deluding itself if it thought that it had met all the challenges implicit in a Congreve revival.

The balance of the performance is not always right. One or two players handle the Restoration extravagances self-consciously, making their points too obviously. Several others lack the flexibility of movement and diction needed for this kind of work.

And what is to be done about the mélange of accents with which Congreve's glittering English is spoken?

Consider Miss Tandy, Miss Wickwire and Miss Caldwell, all of whom know their business and speak well. Miss Wickwire's speech has the flatness of the American timbre. Miss Tandy's seems now to be an accommodation between her native English and the American approach. Miss Caldwell's enunciation and rhythm have the ring of authenticity. As for some of the company's younger members, they are struggling in deep, unfamiliar waters.

But if we are going to wait for perfection, we will never attempt revivals of the classics. It is better to do a Congreve with forces not equal in all parts than not to do him at all, provided, of course, you have such delightful exemplars as Miss Caldwell to show the irresistible way.

Arnold Aronson (b. 1948)
COMEDY, MANNERS, AND BRICKBATS   *1991*

Arnold Aronson centers his comments on The Way of the World *on the 1991 production at the Public Theater in New York. He reviews Jeremy Collier's attack on
the theaters of the time and then comments on the current production. His discussion is less a review than an effort to position the comedy in relation to historical
events and early eighteenth-century attitudes toward sex and marriage.*

Currently at the Public Theater and opening Tuesday is an elitist play that has been
attacked roundly by conservative moralists, led by a demagogic clergyman. But it
will not be shut down by incensed watchdog groups, since the play is nearly 300
years old: William Congreve's classic *The Way of the World*, in a revival directed
by David Greenspan.

First presented in 1700, the work is generally considered the artistic culmination
of the Restoration comedy of manners. The exquisite language, rapier-sharp repartee, and labyrinthine plot make the play somewhat daunting for modern audiences
and actors. Yet the antipathy faced by Congreve and his colleagues in the late seventeenth century was not unlike that [encountered by] many theater artists today.

Jeremy Collier, a parson who campaigned against the stage with a vengeance,
attacked Restoration playwrights in his famous 1698 diatribe, *A Short View of the
Immorality and Profaneness of the English Stage*. He criticized them for "smutti-
ness of expression" and "swearing" and condemned a theater that "degrades
human nature, sinks reason into appetite, and breaks down the distinction between
man and beast." He was joined by the monarchs William and Mary and by members of Parliament who sought to restrict public behavior in the theater.

How could the situation have reached this state less than 100 years after Shakespeare? Whereas Elizabethan London had supported some half-dozen theaters
catering to thousands of spectators, Restoration London never filled more than
two theaters attended by an audience numbering in the hundreds, most of whom
were associated with the court.

The transition began in 1642 when the Puritan rebellion led by Oliver Cromwell
overthrew the monarchy. All the theaters were closed, and most of the courtiers
escaped to Paris, where they remained until 1660, when Charles II took the throne.
The returning nobility brought back a taste for French theater, especially its novel
practice—for the English—of employing actresses. Under Charles II and James II
the theater nearly became the private domain of the court. Thus the fops, pompous
gallants, wits, and hypocrites who populate the plays (and bear the names of their
characteristics—such as, in this play, Witwoud and Lady Wishfort, pronounced
"Wish-for-it") are typically seen as both vicious caricatures and realistic portraits
of the audience.

The plots usually revolve around sexual intrigue, and infidelity seems taken for
granted—it is *The Way of the World*. Easily lost in this play is the fact that the
seemingly admirable Mirabell (André Braugher) had an affair with Lady Wishfort's
(Ruth Maleczech) daughter (Mary Shultz), and when he thought she might be pregnant, foisted her on his friend Fainall (René Rivera), who marries her, though he is
having an affair with Mrs. Marwood (Caris Corfman).

The accusations of immorality focused, not surprisingly, on sexual content and disregarded the fact that such plays were satirical. The playwrights tried to defend themselves, through pamphlets and jibes in their texts. But the attackers achieved their end. The theaters began to censor themselves, the small audiences declined further, and Congreve ceased writing. A decade later, plays were emphasizing moral virtues, and comedies, like those by George Farquhar, stressed sentiment and natural goodness, while the settings changed to the countryside, where city slickers received their comeuppance.

What critics at the time failed to realize was that Restoration comedies are not about sex. A kiss is rare and seems almost vulgar when it occurs. The plays are about human passions sublimated into a brilliant display of language. It is excess and lack of control that [are] evil in Congreve's world. Rationality, order, and command over passions and language are rewarded. This may not be the same as morality, but it *is* civility.

Nineteenth-Century Drama through the Turn of the Twentieth Century

The Nineteenth-Century Theater

Technically, theaters changed more during the period between 1800 and 1900 than in any comparable earlier period. The introduction of gas jets early in the century had a major effect. Now, light could be dimmed or raised as needed; the house could be gradually and entirely darkened. With gaslight onstage, selective lighting contributed to the emotional effect of plays and allowed actors to move deeper into the stage instead of playing important scenes on the apron. With the advent of elaborate scenery, as in the Drottningholm Theater in Sweden, lighting devices were often placed behind the proscenium pillars and scenery so that actors were more visible when they stood within the proscenium. The changes did not take place overnight, but as new theaters were built in the early nineteenth century (and as older theaters were refurbished), the apron shrank and the front doors leading to it disappeared. That change reinforced the nineteenth-century practice of treating the proscenium opening as the imaginary "fourth wall" of a room. The elaborate framing of Chicago's Auditorium (1889, Figure 16) allowed for complex lighting systems as well as for framing of the proscenium, which acts as a "window" into the dramatic action.

Numerous other technical innovations were introduced into the new theaters, such as London's Drury Lane Theatre, which was rebuilt in 1812. Highly sophisticated machinery lifted actors from below the stage, and flies or fly galleries above the stage permitted scene changes and other dramatic alterations and effects. At Theatre Royal, Drury Lane (Figure 17), the remodeling changed the shape of the apron and made space for the orchestra. The actors moving forward onto the apron were not able to reach the audience, which necessitated a change in the style of acting. Histrionic gestures were still visible, but intimate expressions of disdain or hatred were not as likely to elicit a response in the audience. Music, especially in the first half of the century, was usually part of the theater experience. In the United States various kinds of entertainment might share a bill with a play, and the entire experience might last five hours or more. At times it was thought impossible to succeed with a play if there were not dances or music between the acts.

FIGURE 16.   Elaborately decorated proscenium arch. Auditorium, Chicago, 1889. (Courtesy of the Chicago Historical Society, HB-31105C, photograph by Hedrich Blessing.)

Drury Lane drew a considerable audience among the middle classes, and the entertainment was lively and often sentimental. However, the great plays of Shakespeare were still being produced—though usually in modified forms and often with happy endings, even in the tragedies. France and England naturally influenced each other throughout the century, especially in stage design. The English stage designs in turn influenced North American designs.

The Nineteenth-Century Actor

Throughout the first half of the century in the United States, English actors essentially set the standard for acting. Edmund Kean and William Charles Macready were influenced by David Garrick, whose approach aimed at a "natural" style, although by our standards it was still an enlarged and over-done mode of acting. For them, however, it was a realistic and emotionally true

FIGURE 17.   Theatre Royal, Drury Lane, 1812

method of acting that toned down the ranting of earlier ages, as well as the use of broad rhetorical gestures designed to dazzle the audience. English audiences were experienced enough to no longer need the exaggerated style that had appealed to some earlier theatergoers.

American actors, such as Edwin Forrest, Ira Aldrige, and Charlotte Cushman, continued a tradition of broad rhetorical acting, with some of the familiar gestures and exaggerations that in earlier times thrilled English audiences. The English actors felt that the American audiences were less sophisticated and thus much more susceptible to the high drama of an actor such as Forrest.

One of the strangest events in the history of theater occurred on May 10, 1849, when the styles of two actors, the American Edwin Forrest (1806–1872) (Figure 18) and the Englishman William Charles Macready (1793–1873) (Figure 19)—both playing the role of Macbeth—were the subject of a serious riot! Forrest's American style featured exaggerated gestures and dramatic vocal

FIGURE 18.   Edwin Forrest as Macbeth.

FIGURE 19.   William Charles Macready as Macbeth.

expostulations—as in Figure 18, which shows his upstage hand gesturing profoundly and his cape rustling in a powerful wind. Macready, by contrast, was typically described as intellectual, cool, and refined in his gestures (Figure 19 shows him as Macbeth in the costume of an older-generation Scots lord). Writing in his diary six years before the riot when Macready and Forrest were friends, Macready said of American acting, "From what I can learn the audiences of the United States have been accustomed to exaggeration in all its forms, and have applauded what has been most extravagant; it is not, therefore, surprising that they should bestow such little applause on me, not having their accustomed cues." Of Forrest, whom he had seen as Lear, he said,

> I had a very high opinion of his powers of mind when I saw him exactly seventeen years ago; I said then, if he would cultivate those powers and really study, where, as in England, his taste could be formed, he would make one of the very first actors of this or any day. But I thought he would not do so, as his countrymen were, by their extravagant applause, possessing him with the idea and with the fact, as far as remuneration was concerned, that it was unnecessary. I reluctantly, as far as my feelings towards him are interested, record my opinion that my prophetic soul foresaw the consequence. He has great physical power. But I could discern no imagination, no original thought, no poetry at all in his acting.

Macready is credited with having insisted on several important changes in the production of Shakespeare's plays. He restored them to their original texts—not without criticism—and he insisted on doing considerable research to guarantee authenticity of costuming and other historical details. In addition, he changed the way actors approached a play. Previously they memorized their lines in isolation and came to the theater as they pleased, with no special thought to the overall nature of the drama at hand. Macready insisted that the actors respect the spirit of the play and unify their styles so they would be acting in concert. This approach was, ultimately, the beginning of the modern style of acting that dominated the later half of the century.

The Astor Place Riot in 1849 took place because Macready's restrained style was thought to be effete and foppish in comparison with Forrest's. The unruly mobs of New York, egged on by several instigators who preferred Forrest over Macready, threw paving stones, rocks, and vegetables in the audience of the Opera House and became so threatening that no one could hear the performance. The police were called in to restore order. When they failed, the National Guard was called up to control the throngs of 20,000. Like the police, the Guard faltered for a time, but it eventually gathered itself and fired point blank into the mob after a warning salvo over their heads. The death toll was approximately 20, but upwards of 100 were wounded. This was not the first theater riot, but it was the most famous and the most disastrous. Although Macready never returned, he left his mark on American theater, which began to evolve a more relaxed and realistic style of acting. The generations of actors in melodrama that followed were not always as restrained as Macready, but they were usually not as enthusiastic as Forrest.

Romantic Drama

Early-nineteenth-century English Romantic poets produced a variety of plays espousing a new philosophy of the individual, a philosophy of democracy, and a cry for personal liberation, but unfortunately their plays failed to capture the popular stage. William Wordsworth's *The Borderers* (1796–1797), concerning political struggles on the border between England and Scotland, was a failure. A relatively recent production (1989) at Yale University revealed its static, declamatory nature. Even a play with an inherently dramatic subject such as *The Fall of Robespierre* (1794) by Robert Southey and Samuel Taylor Coleridge—concerning the violent excesses of the French Revolution of 1789—could not stir popular audiences. John Keats wrote *Otho the Great* (1819) about a tenth-century dispute between brothers and a father and son. He hoped that the great actor and producer Edmund Kean would want to produce the play, but Kean declined. Percy Bysshe Shelley wrote *The Cenci* (1819) when he was in Italy, hoping it would be produced on the English stage, but it was banned by the censors. The style of Shelley's play has been compared with John Webster's *The Dutchess of Malfi* (1613); its themes include violent death and insanity. George Gordon, Lord Byron, wrote several plays that had admirers but were not successful. *Manfred* (1817) is a CLOSET DRAMA—a play meant to be read, not produced. It presents a powerful portrait of a brooding intellect that could, in some ways, be compared with Hamlet. Allardyce Nicoll, the British drama historian and critic, has said of this and other Romantic plays that "audiences and readers familiar with *Lear* and *Macbeth* and *Othello* could not be expected to feel a thrill of wonder and delight in the contemplation of works so closely akin to these in general aim and yet so far removed from them in freshness of imaginative power."

French and German Romantic dramatists were more successful than their English counterparts. Johann Wolfgang von Goethe (1749–1832), one of Germany's most important playwrights, produced a number of successful plays in the late eighteenth century. Then came his masterpiece, *Faust* (1808, 1832), in two parts, with a scope and grandeur of concept that challenged the theaters of his day. The play opens in heaven, with Mephistopheles presenting his plan for tempting Faust; Faust signs over his soul to Mephistopheles in return for one moment of perfect joy. Faust was willing to risk all in his efforts to live life to its fullest, and despite his sins he was admired as a hero. Faust's self-analytic individualism, marked by a love of excess and a capacity for deep feeling and frightening intensity, has fascinated the German mind ever since Goethe rediscovered him. His development of Faust as a psychologically complex character contrasts with Christopher Marlowe's version in *Doctor Faustus*.

Another important force in German theater was Johann Cristoph Friedrich von Schiller (1759–1805), whose early play *The Robbers* (1781) was written when he was twenty-two. This still-popular (and still-produced) play reminds English audiences of the legend of Robin Hood since its hero, Karl von Moor, is a robber admirable for his generosity and seriousness. His adversary is his evil brother, who dominates the castle, the emblem of local repressive political power. Schiller was a highly successful playwright throughout the late eighteenth century. In the early nineteenth century he produced several popular historical plays, such as *Maria Stuart* (1800) on Scotland's Queen Mary, the ill-fated cousin of Queen Elizabeth I. *The Maid of Orleans* (1801) told the story of Joan of Arc, the French heroine who led her army to victory only to be burned at the stake to satisfy political and religious exigencies. Both plays evoke deep sympathy for their heroines and both have been noted for their sentimentality. His last play, *William Tell* (1804), like *The Robbers*, tells the story of a heroic individual's fight against the oppressive forces of an evil baron. Schiller made the story of William Tell universal, and his theatrical successes were soon known throughout Europe and the Americas.

In France, the Romantic tragedy held sway for some time in the 1830s. Victor Hugo (1802–1885) had a great success in *Hernani* (1830), although critics and writers who insisted on classical rules were so disturbed by its innovation that they made disturbances in the theater. They attended only to jeer the pardon of Hernani, an outlaw, by Don Carlos, king of Spain. At the end Hernani and Donna Sol, his loved one, drink a poison so as to die together because they could not live together. Alexandre Dumas (1802–1879), soon to be famous as a novelist, produced a number of successful, influential plays, among them *Henry III and His Court* (1829) and *The Tower of Nesle* (1832).

Melodrama

MELODRAMA developed in Germany and France in the mid- and late eighteenth century. The *melo* in *melodrama* means "song"; incidental music was a hallmark of melodrama. In England certain regulations separated Covent Garden, Drury Lane, and the Haymarket—the three "major" theaters with exclusive licenses to produce spoken drama—from the "minor" theaters, which had to produce musical plays such as burlettas, which resembled our comic operettas. Eventually, the minor theaters began to produce plays with spoken dialogue and accompanying music, heralding a new, popular style. Melodrama proved to be one of the most durable innovations of the late eighteenth century.

In Germany August Friedrich Ferdinand von Kotzebue (1761–1819) and in France Guilbert de Pixérécourt (1773–1844), who coined the term *melodrama*, began developing the melodramatic play. Many of these dramas used background music that altered according to the mood of the scene, a tradition that continues today in films and on television. Nineteenth-century melodramas featured familiar crises: the virtuous maiden fallen into the hands of an unscrupulous landlord; the father who, lamenting over a portrait of his dead wife, discovers that he is speaking to his—until then—lost daughter. Nineteenth-century melodramas had well-defined heroes, heroines, and villains. The plots were filled with surprises and unlikely twists designed to amaze and delight the audience. Most of the plays were explicitly sentimental, depending on a strong emotional appeal with clear-cut and relatively decisive endings.

Though not popular later on, the plays of Kotzebue and Pixérécourt pleased their contemporary audiences and helped establish melodrama as a dominant style for the first six decades of the nineteenth century. Kotzebue published thirty-six plays (twenty-two were produced) and enjoyed immense popularity in England and the United States. Translated into several languages, his works influenced later popular playwrights, who admired his ability to invent and resolve complex plot situations. An example of the ending of *La-Peyrouse* (1798) may provide a taste of the mode. The hero, cast ashore on a desert island, falls in love with the "savage" Malvina. When he rejoins his wife, Adelaide, he is presented with the problem of what to do with Malvina. Here is the women's solution:

> MALVINA (*turning affectionately, yet with trembling, to Adelaide*): I have prayed for thee, and for myself—let us be sisters!
> ADELAIDE: Sisters! (*She remains some moments lost in thought.*) Sisters! Sweet girl, you have awakened a consoling idea in my bosom! Yes, we will be sisters, and this man shall be our brother! Share him we cannot, nor can either possess him singly. (*With enthusiasm.*) We, the sisters, will inhabit one hut, he shall dwell in another. We will educate our children, he shall assist us both—by day we will make but one family, at night we will separate—how say you? will you consent? . . . (*Extending her arms to La-Peyrouse.*) A sisterly embrace!

In France Pixérécourt produced a similar and highly successful drama that pleased his audiences. Not everyone was pleased, however. Goethe resigned his office from the Weimar Court Theatre when Pixérécourt's *The Dog of Montargis* was produced in 1816 because he did not want to be associated with any play that had a dog as its hero.

Not all these plays have been forgotten. Alexandre Dumas's *La Dame aux camélias* (Camille) was a theatrical hit in 1852 and has remained popular ever since, inspiring the Verdi opera *La Traviata* (1853) and revivals and adaptations up to the present, including the British playwright Pam Gems's feminist version (1987), starring Kathleen Turner. Based on a woman Dumas knew in Paris, it is the story of a wealthy young man who falls in love with a courtesan, Marguerite Gauthier. Like Angellica in *The Rover*, she has manipulated men throughout her life, but now she is truly in love with Armand. The young man's father opposes the match, but even he is moved by the majesty of their love. Eventually, the father faces Marguerite and convinces her that if she really loves his son, she will let him go since their union can bring nothing but harm to Armand. She then feigns contempt for Armand and dismisses him, broken-hearted. Later, after they have been separated and she has fallen deathly ill, Armand learns the truth and rushes to her. On her deathbed Armand professes his love as she dies in his arms.

In the United States, George Aiken produced another long-lasting and influential drama, *Uncle Tom's Cabin* (1852), based on Harriet Beecher Stowe's novel. Stowe, a prominent northern abolitionist, poured all her anger at slavery into her novel. Aiken's stage version played for three hundred nights in its first production and across the nation more than a quarter of a million times. Some of its characters—Uncle Tom, Little Eva, Sambo, Topsy, and Simon Legree— live on in the popular imagination, but despite the contemporary interest in Stowe and in this play, the paternalistic subtitle, "Life among the Lowly," marks its era.

The Well-Made Play

Early in the nineteenth century, a Frenchman with an unusual theatrical gift for pleasing popular audiences began a career that spanned fifty successful years. Eugène Scribe (1791–1861) may have produced as many as four or five hundred plays. He employed collaborators and mined novels and stories for his plots, producing tragedies, comedies, opera libretti, and vaudeville one-act pieces. He quickly determined that the plot held the attention of the audience and that rambling character studies were of lesser interest. Consequently, he developed a formula for dramatic action and made sure that all his works fit into it. The result was the creation of a "factory" for making plays. Among the elements of Scribe's formula were the following:

1. A careful exposition telling the audience what the situation is, usually including one or more secrets to be revealed later.

2. Surprises, such as letters to be opened at a critical moment and identities to be revealed later.

3. Suspense that builds steadily throughout the play, usually sustained by cliff-hanging situations and characters who miss each other by way of carefully timed entrances and exits. At critical moments, characters lose important papers or misplace identifying jewelry, for instance.

4. A CLIMAX late in the play when the secrets are revealed and the hero confronts his antagonists and succeeds.

5. A DENOUEMENT, the resolution of the drama when all the loose ends are drawn together and explanations are made that render all the action plausible.

It should be evident from this description that the WELL-MADE PLAY still thrives, not only on the stage but also in films and on television. Scribe's emphasis on plot was sensational for his time, and his success was unrivaled; however, none of his plays has survived in contemporary performance. Only one, *Adrienne Lecouvreur* (1849), the story of a famous actress poisoned by a rival, is mentioned by critics as interesting because of its depth of characterization. Scribe was superficial and brilliant—a winning combination in theater at the time. He had numerous imitators and prepared the way for later developments in theater.

The Rise of Realism

Technical changes in theaters during the latter part of the nineteenth century continued at a rapid pace. When limelight was added to gas, the result was bright, intense lighting onstage; in the last decades of the century, electric light heralded a new era in lighting design. Good lighting generally demanded detailed and authentic scenery; the dreamy light produced by gas often hid imperfections that were now impossible to disguise. The new Madison Square Theater (1879) in New York City was built with elevators that allowed its stage, complete with detailed and realistic scenery as well as actors, to be raised into position. European theaters had developed similar capacities.

In the 1840s accurate period costumes began to be the norm for historical plays. In the Elizabethan theater, contemporary clothing had been worn onstage, but by the mid-1800s costume designers were researching historical periods and producing costumes that aimed at historical accuracy.

In addition to offering lifelike scenery, lighting, and costumes, the theaters of the latter part of the century also featured plays whose circumstances and language were recognizable, contemporary, and believable. Even the sentimental melodramas seemed more realistic than productions of *King Lear* or *Macbeth*, plays that were still popular. The work of Scribe, including his historical plays, used a relatively prosaic everyday language. The situations may not seem absolutely lifelike to our eyes, but in their day they prepared the way for realism.

Changes in philosophy also contributed to the development of a realistic drama. Émile Zola (1840–1902) preached a doctrine of NATURALISM, demanding that drama avoid the artificiality of convoluted plot and urging a drama of natural, lifelike action. He intended his work to help change social conditions in France. His naturalistic novel *Nana* (1880) focused on a courtesan whose life came to a terrifying end. The play *Thérèse Raquin* (1873), based on Zola's novel of the same name, told the story of a woman and her lover who murder her husband and then commit suicide out of a sense of mutual guilt. There are no twists, surprises, or even much suspense in the play. Zola's subjects seem to have been uniformly grim, and naturalism became associated with the darker side of life.

REALISM, which avoided mechanical "clockwork" plots with their artificially contrived conclusions, began in the later years of the eighteenth century (some scholars claim to see evidence of it even earlier, in the work of Thomas Middleton) and progressed steadily to the end of the nineteenth century. In the realistic plays of Henrik Ibsen (1828–1906) and August Strindberg (1849–1912), the details of the setting, the costuming, and the circumstances of the action were so fully realized as to convince audiences that they were listening in on life itself. (See Figure 20 for an example of a realistic stage setting.)

In Britain, Oscar Wilde (1854–1900), poet, novelist, and playwright, offered an alternative to both melodrama and realistic drama near the end of the century. Wilde had spent much of his literary life promoting the philosophy of art for art's sake. He asserted that the pleasure of poetry was in its sounds, images,

FIGURE 20.   Realistic setting in a 1941 production of Anton Chekhov's *The Cherry Orchard*. (Courtesy of the Harvard Theatre Collection, Houghton Library.)

and thoughts. Poetry and drama did not serve religious, political, social, or even personal goals. For Wilde, art served itself. He was such a brilliant conversationalist that the Irish poet-playwright W. B. Yeats declared him the only person he ever heard who spoke complete, rounded sentences that sounded as if he had written and polished them the night before. His witticisms were often barbed and vicious but always incisive and perceptive. He became famous for his bright, witty comedies. *The Importance of Being Earnest* (1895), sometimes wrongly accused of being about nothing, is the most often performed. It is an unsentimental, witty, and sometimes brittle comedy that dissects English upper-class attitudes that most of his audience would have taken for granted.

Wilde competed with numerous comic playwrights in England and abroad, such as the enormously successful Arthur Wing Pinero (1855–1934) and W. S. Gilbert (1836–1911) in England and Georges Feydeau (1862–1921) in France. None, though, could manage the unusual combination of wit and seriousness that marks Wilde's achievement. Another important competitor was another Irish playwright (Wilde was Irish), Bernard Shaw (1856–1950), whose plays were also comic and serious, such as *Arms and the Man* (1894), *You Never Can Tell* (1898), and *Pygmalion* (1913). But Shaw is probably best known for his plays of ideas — plays in which an underlying idea or principle drives the action — such as *Mrs. Warren's Profession* (1898), *Man and Superman* (1903), and *Major Barbara* (1905).

After a disappointing beginning as a playwright, Anton Chekhov (1860–1904) worked with the Moscow Arts Theatre under the directorship of Konstantin Stanislavski (1865–1938), one of the most influential figures in modern Western drama. Stanislavski emphasized "inner realism," having the actor become the character even in situations off stage by developing improvisational experiences to let the actor explore the character in situations other than those within the play. The Stanislavski Method helped the actor become the part, rather than just play the part. Chekhov and Stanislavski worked together to produce Chekhov's plays at a time when Chekhov felt himself a failure as a dramatist.

The first production of Chekhov's *The Seagull* (1896), his sixth major staged play, was a failure. Stanislavski convinced Chekhov to give it to his company to produce, resulting in an important triumph. Chekhov then reworked an earlier play into *Uncle Vanya* (1899) for Stanislavski, and it, too, was a hit. *Three Sisters* (1901) was not successful in its first performances, but it later became known as one of Chekhov's finest works. His last play, *The Cherry Orchard* (1904), was put on by Stanislavski's company and has become one of the most important works of twentieth-century drama. Chekhov died of a heart attack soon after the play's first production. Today Chekhov's legacy continues, and all his major plays are staged throughout the world. Thus one of the most important nineteenth-century writers led the way to new developments in twentieth-century drama that are still evident today on the stage, as well as in films and on television.

Nineteenth-Century Drama Timeline

DATE	THEATER	POLITICAL	SOCIAL/CULTURAL
1700–1800	**1759–1805:** Friedrich von Schiller, German playwright, author of *The Robbers* (1781) and *Maria Stuart* (1800)		
	1761–1819: August Friedrich Ferdinand von Kotzebue, German playwright and one of the early developers of melodrama	**1775:** The American War of Independence begins at Concord, Massachusetts.	**1770–1827:** Ludwig van Beethoven, German composer
		1776: The Declaration of Independence is signed.	**1775–1817:** Jane Austen, English novelist
	1767–1787: *Sturm und Drang* period in German drama featuring the work of Goethe, Schiller, and others who rebelled against eighteenth-century rationalism	**1783:** Peace of Versailles: Britain recognizes the independence of the United States.	
	1773: The Swedish National Theater is established in Stockholm.	**1789:** French revolutionaries storm the Bastille as the French revolution sweeps over French society.	**1792–1822:** Percy Bysshe Shelley, English Romantic poet
	1773–1844: Guilbert de Pixérécourt, French playwright generally credited with originating the melodrama	**1793:** Louis XVI and his queen, Marie Antoinette, are guillotined. The reign of terror, a purge instituted by the revolutionary government of France, claims 35,000 lives in one year.	**1793:** Eli Whitney (1765–1825) invents the cotton gin. **1795:** British forces occupy the Cape of Good Hope. **1795–1821:** John Keats, English Romantic poet
	1791–1861: Eugène Scribe, French playwright, developer of the "well-made" play, author of *Adrienne Lecouvreur* (1849)	**1799:** Napoleon Bonaparte overthrows the Directory of France, the moderate government that replaced the government of terror.	**1798:** *Lyrical Ballads* is published by Wordsworth and Coleridge. **1799–1837:** Alexander Pushkin, Russian poet
	1793–1873: William Charles Macready, English actor		
1800–1900	**1806–1872:** Edwin Forrest, America's first great native-born actor	**1803:** The Louisiana Purchase doubles the area of the United States.	**1802–1885:** Victor Hugo, French novelist
		1804: Napoleon I (1769–1821) declares himself emperor of France.	**1803–1882:** Ralph Waldo Emerson, American Transcendental philosopher, clergyman, and author
	1808 and 1832: German writer Johann Wolfgang von Goethe (1749–1832) produces his masterpiece, *Faust* (in two parts).	**1805:** Admiral Horatio Nelson's victory over Napoleon at Trafalgar establishes the supremacy of British naval forces.	**1805:** Gas lighting is introduced in Great Britain.
	1809–1852: Nikolai Gogol, Russian playwright, author of *The Inspector General* (1836)	**1811–1820:** The Regency period: George, Prince of Wales, acts as regent for George III, who was declared insane.	**1809–1852:** Louis Braille, French inventor of reading system for the blind
	1812: Theatre Royal, Drury Lane, is rebuilt.		
	1813–1837: Georg Büchner, German playwright, author of *Danton's Death* (1835) and *Woyzeck* (1836)	**1812:** The United States declares war on Britain. **1814:** Treaty of Ghent ends the War of 1812; Britain is defeated.	**1812–1870:** Charles Dickens, English novelist

Nineteenth-Century Drama Timeline (continued)

DATE	THEATER	POLITICAL	SOCIAL/CULTURAL
1800–1900 (continued)	**1816:** Chestnut Street Theater in Philadelphia is the first theater to illuminate its stage with gas lighting.	**1815:** Napoleon is decisively defeated at the Battle of Waterloo.	**1816–1855:** Charlotte Brontë, English novelist
	1820–1890: Dion Boucicault, Irish American actor and writer of popular melodramas, among them *The Octoroon* (1859) and *The Colleen Bawn* (1860)	**1818:** Shaka ascends the Zulu throne in Southern Africa and initiates a period of military reform; he is assassinated in 1828.	**1817–1862:** Henry David Thoreau, American Transcendental writer and naturalist
		1820: Accession of George IV	**1820–1906:** Susan B. Anthony, American leader of the women's suffrage movement
	1828–1906: Henrik Ibsen, Norwegian playwright. Among his best-known works are *A Doll House* (1879) and *Hedda Gabler* (1890).	**1820:** The Missouri Compromise admits Maine as a free state and Missouri as a slave state.	**1821–1881:** Fyodor Dostoevsky, Russian novelist
		1821: Mexico declares its independence.	**1828–1910:** Leo Tolstoy, Russian novelist and philosopher
	1830: *Hernani*, by the French novelist and playwright Victor Hugo (1802–1885), traditionally marks the beginning of French romanticism.	**1823:** The Monroe Doctrine closes the American continent to European colonization.	**1830–1886:** Emily Dickinson, American poet
			1831: William Lloyd Garrison (1805–1879), American abolitionist, founds the *Liberator*.
	1837: William Charles Macready (1793–1873), an English actor, is the first to use the limelight (or Drummond light), a prototype of the spotlight.	**1837:** Queen Victoria begins her sixty-four-year reign in Great Britain.	**1833–1897:** Johannes Brahms, German composer
		1839: Beginning of the First Opium War between Britain and China. The war ends in 1842 with the Treaty of Nanjing, which turns over Hong Kong to Britain and opens several Chinese ports to Western trade.	**1839:** Louis Daguerre (1789–1851) invents the daguerreotype, an early type of photograph.
	1840–1902: Émile Zola, French writer and promoter of naturalism in literature. Among his works is the novel (also a play) *Thérèse Raquin* (1873).		**1840–1893:** Peter Ilyich Tchaikovsky, Russian composer
			1843–1916: Henry James, American realist novelist
			1844: The telegraph is used for the first time.
			1845: Frederick Douglass (c. 1817–1895), African American abolitionist, publishes *Narrative of the Life of Frederick Douglass*.
			1845–1849: The great potato famine in Ireland kills nearly a million Irish; 1,600,000 immigrate to the United States.
	1849: The Astor Place Riot in New York is a result of the rivalry between the actors William Charles Macready and Edwin Forrest; twenty-two people are killed.	**1846–1848:** Mexican War over the United States' annexation of Texas. The Treaty of Guadalupe Hidalgo (1848) cedes Texas to the United States.	**1848:** The First U.S. Women's Rights Convention is held in Seneca Falls, New York.
			1848: California gold rush
	1849–1923: Sarah Bernhardt, French performer, perhaps the greatest actress of the nineteenth century		**1848:** Karl Marx, German political philosopher, writes *The Communist Manifesto*, with Friedrich Engels.
			1850: Tennyson succeeds Wordsworth as poet laureate of Great Britain.
	1849–1912: August Strindberg, Swedish playwright. Among his works are *Miss Julie* (1888) and *A Dream Play* (1902).	**1852:** Napoleon III declares himself emperor of France and rules until 1871.	**1851:** Herman Melville (1819–1891) publishes *Moby Dick*.
			1852: Harriet Beecher Stowe (1811–1896) publishes *Uncle Tom's Cabin*.

Nineteenth-Century Drama Timeline (continued)

DATE	THEATER	POLITICAL	SOCIAL/CULTURAL
1800–1900 (continued)	**1854–1900:** Oscar Wilde, Irish writer. His plays include *A Woman of No Importance* (1893) and *The Importance of Being Earnest* (1895). **1856–1950:** Bernard Shaw, Irish playwright. Among his works are *Mrs. Warren's Profession* (1898), *Major Barbara* (1905), and *Pygmalion* (1913). **1860–1904:** Anton Chekhov, Russian writer, author of *The Seagull* (1896) and *The Cherry Orchard* (1903) **1870–1900:** Golden Age of Peking (Beijing) Opera **1871–1896:** Gilbert and Sullivan write their comic operas, among them *H.M.S. Pinafore* (1878) and *The Pirates of Penzance* (1879). **1876:** Opening of Richard Wagner's Festival Theater in Bayreuth, Germany. Among his works is the four-part *Der Ring des Nibelungen* (1853–1874). **1881:** The Savoy Theatre is the first theater in London to be completely illuminated by electric light. **1887:** Théâtre Libre is founded in Paris by André Antoine to pursue naturalism in subject matter and staging. **1890–1930:** Vaudeville becomes one of the most popular forms of entertainment in the United States. **1896:** The first revolving stage is installed by Karl Lautenschlager at the Residenz Theater in Munich. **1898:** The Moscow Art Theatre is founded under the direction of Konstantin Stanislavsky and Vladimir Nemirovich-Danchenko.	**1857:** Czar Alexander II begins emancipation of serfs in Russia. **1860:** Abraham Lincoln is elected president. South Carolina secedes from the Union. **1861:** Italy is unified under Victor Emmanuel II. **1861–1865:** The Civil War is fought in the United States. **1862:** Otto von Bismarck is appointed prime minister of Prussia. **1865:** Abraham Lincoln is assassinated by the actor John Wilkes Booth at Ford's Theatre in Washington, D.C. **1869:** The Suez Canal opens. **1870–1871:** Franco-Prussian War **1871:** The German Empire is founded under Kaiser Wilhelm I. **1876:** At the Battle of the Little Bighorn, the Sioux defeat General George Custer's troops. **1885:** The Congo becomes a personal possession of King Leopold II of Belgium. **1890:** The Battle of Wounded Knee ends the American Indians' wars of resistance; two hundred Indians are killed by the U.S. Army. **1898:** The Spanish-American War. Cuban patriots demand independence and receive the military support of the United States. The 1898 Treaty of Paris gives Puerto Rico, Guam, the Philippines, and Cuba to the United States. **1899–1902:** The Boer War (South African War) ends British supremacy in South Africa.	**1854–1856:** Scottish explorer David Livingstone crosses Africa. **1859:** Charles Darwin (1809–1882) publishes *On the Origin of Species by Natural Selection*. **1860s:** Louis Pasteur (1822–1895), French chemist, develops pasteurization. **1865–1939:** William Butler Yeats, Irish poet and playwright **1869:** The first transcontinental railroad in the United States is completed. **1869–1959:** Frank Lloyd Wright, preeminent American architect **1876:** Alexander Graham Bell (1847–1922) invents the telephone. **1877:** Thomas Edison (1847–1931) invents the phonograph. **1879:** Thomas Edison invents the lightbulb. **1898–1976:** Paul Robeson, African American singer, actor, and civil rights activist

Henrik Ibsen

Using the new style of realism, Henrik Ibsen (1828–1906) slowly and painfully became the most influential modern dramatist. Subjects that had been ignored on the stage became the center of his work. But his rise to fame was anything but direct. His family was extremely poor, and as a youth he worked in a drugstore in Grimstad, a seaport town in Norway. At seventeen he had an illegitimate child with a servant girl. At twenty-one he wrote his first play, in verse. In 1850, at the age of twenty-two, he left Grimstad for Oslo (then called Christiana) to become a student, but within a year he joined the new National Theater and stayed for six years, writing and directing.

In the 1850s he wrote numerous plays that did not bring him recognition: *St. John's Eve* (1853), *Lady Inger of Østraat* (1855), *Olaf Liljekrans* (1857),

Henrik Ibsen at age sixty-eight, seventeen years after the first production of *A Doll House*. He was the most influential playwright in Europe when this photograph was taken in 1896.

and *The Vikings at Helgeland* (1857). In the early 1860s, with a wife and daughter to support, he went through a period of serious self-doubt and despair, and his first play in five years, *Love's Comedy* (1862), was turned down for performance. Eventually he got a job with the Christiana Theater and had a rare success with *The Pretenders* (1864), a historical play about thirteenth-century warriors vying for the vacant throne of Norway.

His breakthrough came with the publication in 1866 of the verse play *Brand,* which was written to be read, not performed. (It was first produced in 1885.) It is the portrait of a clergyman who takes the strictures of religion so seriously that he rejects the New Testament doctrine of love and accepts the Old Testament doctrine of the will of God. He destroys himself in the process and ends the play on a mountaintop in the Ice Church, facing an avalanche about to kill him. Out of the clouds comes the answer to his questions of whether love or will achieves salvation: "He is the God of Love." *Brand* made Ibsen famous. He followed it with another successful closet drama, *Peer Gynt* (1867), about a character, quite unlike Brand, who avoids the rigors of morality and ends up uncertain whether he has been saved or condemned.

Despite these successes, Ibsen still struggled for recognition. It was not until 1877 that he had his first success in a play that experimented with the new realistic style of drama: *The Pillars of Society,* which probed behind the hypocrisies of Karsten Bernick, a merchant who prospers by all manner of double-dealing and betrayal of his relatives. Eventually, he admits his crimes but, instead of being punished, is welcomed back into society and is more successful than ever. This play gave Ibsen a reputation in Germany, where it was frequently performed, and prepared him for his great successes. *A Doll House* (1879), which he wrote in Italy, came two years later. It was more fully realistic in style than *The Pillars of Society* and, though immensely successful in Scandinavia, did not become widely known elsewhere for another ten years.

His next play, *Ghosts* (1881), was denounced violently because it dared to treat a subject that had been taboo on the stage: syphilis. *Ghosts* introduced a respectable family, the Alvings, who harbor the secret that their late father contracted the disease and passed it on to Oswald, his son. In addition, the theme of incest is suggested in the presence of Alving's illegitimate daughter, Regina, who falls in love with Oswald. This kind of material was so foreign to the late-nineteenth-century stage that Ibsen was vilified and isolated by the literary community in Norway. He chose exile for a time in Rome, Amalfi, and Munich.

Ibsen's last years were filled with activity. He wrote some of his best-known plays in rapid succession: *An Enemy of the People* (1882), *The Wild Duck* (1884), *Hedda Gabler* (1890), *The Master Builder* (1892), and *John Gabriel Borkman* (1896). In 1891 he returned to live in Norway, where he died fifteen years later.

The most influential European dramatist in the late nineteenth century, Ibsen inspired emerging writers in the United States, Ireland, and many other nations. But his full influence was not felt until the early decades of the twentieth century, when other writers were able to spread the revolutionary doctrine that was implied in realism as practiced by Ibsen and Strindberg. Being direct, honest, and unsparing in treating character and theme became the normal mode of serious drama after Ibsen.

A DOLL HOUSE

Once Henrik Ibsen found his voice as a realist playwright, he began to develop plays centering on social problems and the problems of the individual struggling against the demands of society. In *A Doll House* (1879) he focused on the repression of women. It was a subject that deeply offended conservatives and was very much on the minds of progressive and liberal Scandinavians. It was therefore a rather daring theme. The play opens with the dutiful, eager wife Nora Helmer twittering like a lark and pattering like a squirrel, pleasing her husband, Torvald. Helmer is consumed with propriety. As far as he is concerned, Nora is only a woman, an empty-headed ornament in a house designed to keep his life functioning smoothly.

Nora is portrayed as a macaroon-eating, sweet-toothed creature looking for ways to please her husband. When she reveals that she borrowed the money that took them to Italy for a year to save her husband's life, she shows us that she is made of much stronger stuff than anyone has given her credit for. Yet the manner in which she borrowed the money is technically criminal because she had to forge her father's signature, and she now finds herself at the mercy of the lender, Nils Krogstad.

From a modern perspective, Nora's action seems daring and imaginative rather than merely illegal and surreptitious. Torvald Helmer's moralistic position is to us essentially stifling. He condemns Nora's father for a similar failure

For this 1906 production of Ibsen's *The Wild Duck,* the director, André Antoine, had the set constructed of Norwegian pine to achieve a high degree of realism.

Edvard Munch's 1906 stage design for Max Reinhardt's production of Ibsen's *Ghosts* at the Kammerspiele in Berlin. Although *Ghosts* (1881) was written in Ibsen's realistic style, Munch's expressionistic lines and shadows seem to reflect the tendency in Ibsen's late plays to move beyond realism to a more dreamlike structure.

to secure proper signatures, just as he condemns Nils Krogstad for doing the same. He condemns people for their crimes without considering their circumstances or motives. He is moralistic rather than moral.

The atmosphere of the Helmer household is oppressive. Everything is set up to amuse Torvald, and he lacks any awareness that other people might be his equal. Early in the play Ibsen establishes Nora's longings: she explains that to pay back her loan she has had to take in copying work, and, rather than resenting her labor, she observes that it made her feel wonderful, the way a man must feel. Ibsen said that his intention in the play was not primarily to promote the emancipation of women; it was to establish, as Ibsen's biographer Michael Meyer says, "that the primary duty of anyone was to find out who he or she really was and to become that person."

However, the play from the first was seen as addressing the problems of women, especially married women who were treated as their husbands' property. When the play was first performed, the slam of the door at Nora's leaving was much louder than it is today. It was shocking to late-nineteenth-century society, which took Torvald Helmer's attitudes for granted. The first audiences probably were split in their opinions about Nora's actions. As Meyer reminds us, "No play had ever before contributed so momentously to the social debate, or been so widely and furiously discussed among people who were not normally interested in theatrical or even artistic matters." Although the critics in Copenhagen (where the play was first produced) and London were very negative, the audiences were filled with curiosity and flocked to the theaters to see the play.

What the audiences saw was that once Nora is awakened, the kind of life Torvald imagines for her is death to Nora. Torvald cannot see how his self-absorbed concern and fear for his own social standing reveal his limitations and selfishness. Nora sees immediately the limits of his concern, and her only choice is to leave him so that she can grow morally and spiritually.

What she does and where she goes have been a matter of speculation since the play was first performed. Ibsen refused to encourage any specific conjecture. It is enough that she has the courage to leave. But the ending of the play bothered audiences as well as critics, and it was performed in Germany in 1880 with a happy ending that Ibsen himself wrote to forestall anyone else's doing so. The first German actress to play the part insisted that she would personally never leave her children and therefore would not do the play as written. In the revised version, instead of leaving, Nora is led to the door of her children's room and falls weeping as the curtain goes down. The so-called happy-ending version was played for a while in England and elsewhere. No one was satisfied with this ending, and eventually the play reverted to its original form.

Through the proscenium arch of the theater in Ibsen's day audiences were permitted to eavesdrop on themselves, since Ibsen clearly was analyzing their own mores. In a way the audience was looking at a dollhouse, but instead of containing miniature furniture and miniature people, it contained replicas of those watching. That very sense of intimacy, made possible by the late-nineteenth-century theater, heightened the intensity of the play.

A Doll House in Performance

A Doll House was first produced in the Royal Theatre, Copenhagen, in December 1879. Despite its immediate popular success in Scandinavia and Germany, two years passed before the play appeared elsewhere and ten years before it appeared in England and America in a complete and accurate text. Further, the early German version (February 1880), with Hedwig Niemann-Raabe as Nora, had to be revised with a happy ending because the actress refused to play the original ending. Fortunately, the "happy ending," in which Nora does not leave home, was not successful and Niemann-Raabe eventually played the part as written. An adaptation (also with the happy ending) titled *The Child Wife* was produced in Milwaukee in 1882. The first professional London production of the play in 1889 found favor with the public, but it was attacked in the press for being "unnatural, immoral and, in its concluding scene, essentially undramatic." Among other things, Ibsen was being condemned for not providing a vibrant plot.

Among the play's memorable performances was Ethel Barrymore's version in New York in 1905. Barrymore was praised for a brilliant interpretation of "the child wife." Ruth Gordon played the part to acclaim in 1937, as did Claire Bloom in 1971 on the stage and in 1973 in film. Jane Fonda played the role in Joseph Losey's film version of 1973. The Norwegian actress Liv Ullmann performed the role in Lincoln Center in 1975 and was praised as "the most enchanting," the "most honest" Nora that the critic Walter Kerr had seen. Other critics were less kind, but it was a successful run. One of the most riveting of modern productions starred Janet McTeer in Anthony Page's revival of *A Doll House*. This production began in London in 1997 and transferred to New York for a Broadway run the same year. Ben Brantley of the *New York Times* said of it, "Nothing can prepare you for the initial shock of Ms. McTeer's performance, which transforms the passive Nora Helmer, Ibsen's childlike plaything of a wife, into an electric, even aggressive presence" revealing "previously hidden nuances in Ibsen's landmark work." This production was faithful to the production values of Ibsen's original, using an essentially Victorian-era setting with period costumes. McTeer's energy transformed the play and gave Nora a new dimension that made the audience feel that she would do better than merely survive when she left her home. Lee Breuer's 2005 production of *Mabou Mines Dollhouse* set the stage as a dollhouse and used actresses who were six feet tall and actors who were five feet tall and shorter. The effect on the audience was to emphasize the power relationships between men and women. Controversy followed the Mabou Mines Theater Company tour, but it also awakened audiences to some of the underlying forces of the play. The play is performed regularly in college and regional theaters in the United States and elsewhere.

Henrik Ibsen (1828–1906)

A DOLL HOUSE   1879
TRANSLATED BY ROLF FJELDE

The Characters

TORVALD HELMER, *a lawyer*
NORA, *his wife*
DR. RANK
MRS. LINDE
NILS KROGSTAD, *a bank clerk*
THE HELMERS' THREE SMALL CHILDREN
ANNE-MARIE, *their nurse*
HELENE, *a maid*
A DELIVERY BOY

The action takes place in Helmer's residence.

ACT I

(*A comfortable room, tastefully but not expensively furnished. A door to the right in the back wall leads to the entryway; another to the left leads to Helmer's study. Between these doors, a piano. Midway in the left-hand wall a door, and further back a window. Near the window a round table with an armchair and a small sofa. In the right-hand wall, toward the rear, a door, and nearer the foreground a porcelain stove with two armchairs and a rocking chair beside it. Between the stove and the side door, a small table. Engravings on the walls. An*

As Fjelde explains in his foreword to the translation, he does not use the possessive "A Doll's House" because "the house is not Nora's, as the possessive implies." Fjelde believes that Ibsen includes Torvald with Nora in the original title, "for the two of them at the play's opening are still posing like the little marzipan bride and groom atop the wedding cake."

étagère° with china figures and other small art objects; a small bookcase with richly bound books; the floor carpeted; a fire burning in the stove. It is a winter day.)
(*A bell rings in the entryway; shortly after we hear the door being unlocked. Nora comes into the room, humming happily to herself; she is wearing street clothes and carries an armload of packages, which she puts down on the table to the right. She has left the hall door open, and through it a Delivery Boy is seen holding a Christmas tree and a basket, which he gives to the Maid who let them in.*)

NORA: Hide the tree well, Helene. The children mustn't get a glimpse of it till this evening, after it's trimmed. (*To the Delivery Boy, taking out her purse.*) How much?
DELIVERY BOY: Fifty, ma'am.
NORA: There's a crown. No, keep the change. (*The Boy thanks her and leaves. Nora shuts the door. She laughs softly to herself while taking off her street things. Drawing a bag of macaroons from her pocket, she eats a couple, then steals over and listens at her husband's study door.*) Yes, he's home. (*Hums again as she moves to the table right.*)
HELMER (*from the study*): Is that my little lark twittering out there?
NORA (*busy opening some packages*): Yes, it is.
HELMER: Is that my squirrel rummaging around?
NORA: Yes!
HELMER: When did my squirrel get in?
NORA: Just now. (*Putting the macaroon bag in her pocket and wiping her mouth.*) Do come in, Torvald, and see what I've bought.

[S.D.] étagère: Cabinet with shelves.

HELMER: Can't be disturbed. (*After a moment he opens the door and peers in, pen in hand.*) Bought, you say? All that there? Has the little spendthrift been out throwing money around again?

NORA: Oh, but Torvald, this year we really should let ourselves go a bit. It's the first Christmas we haven't had to economize.

HELMER: But you know we can't go squandering.

NORA: Oh yes, Torvald, we can squander a little now. Can't we? Just a tiny, wee bit. Now that you've got a big salary and are going to make piles and piles of money.

HELMER: Yes—starting New Year's. But then it's a full three months till the raise comes through.

NORA: Pooh! We can borrow that long.

HELMER: Nora! (*Goes over and playfully takes her by the ear.*) Are your scatterbrains off again? What if today I borrowed a thousand crowns, and you squandered them over Christmas week, and then on New Year's Eve a roof tile fell on my head, and I lay there—

NORA (*putting her hand on his mouth*): Oh! Don't say such things!

HELMER: Yes, but what if it happened—then what?

NORA: If anything so awful happened, then it just wouldn't matter if I had debts or not.

HELMER: Well, but the people I'd borrowed from?

NORA: Them? Who cares about them! They're strangers.

HELMER: Nora, Nora, how like a woman! No, but seriously, Nora, you know what I think about that. No debts! Never borrow! Something of freedom's lost—and something of beauty, too—from a home that's founded on borrowing and debt. We've made a brave stand up to now, the two of us; and we'll go right on like that the little while we have to.

NORA (*going toward the stove*): Yes, whatever you say, Torvald.

HELMER (*following her*): Now, now, the little lark's wings mustn't droop. Come on, don't be a sulky squirrel. (*Taking out his wallet.*) Nora, guess what I have here.

NORA (*turning quickly*): Money!

HELMER: There, see. (*Hands her some notes.*) Good grief, I know how costs go up in a house at Christmastime.

NORA: Ten—twenty—thirty—forty. Oh, thank you, Torvald; I can manage no end on this.

HELMER: You really will have to.

NORA: Oh yes, I promise I will! But come here so I can show you everything I bought. And so cheap! Look, new clothes for Ivar here—and a sword. Here a horse and a trumpet for Bob. And a doll and a doll's bed here for Emmy; they're nothing much, but she'll tear them to bits in no time anyway. And here I have dress material and handkerchiefs for the maids. Old Anne-Marie really deserves something more.

HELMER: And what's in that package there?

NORA (*with a cry*): Torvald, no! You can't see that till tonight!

HELMER: I see. But tell me now, you little prodigal, what have you thought of for yourself?

NORA: For myself? Oh, I don't want anything at all.

HELMER: Of course you do. Tell me just what—within reason—you'd most like to have.

NORA: I honestly don't know. Oh, listen, Torvald—

HELMER: Well?

NORA (*fumbling at his coat buttons, without looking at him*): If you want to give me something, then maybe you could—you could—

HELMER: Come on, out with it.

NORA (*hurriedly*): You could give me money, Torvald. No more than you think you can spare; then one of these days I'll buy something with it.

HELMER: But Nora—

NORA: Oh, please, Torvald darling, do that! I beg you, please. Then I could hang the bills in pretty gilt paper on the Christmas tree. Wouldn't that be fun?

HELMER: What are those little birds called that always fly through their fortunes?

NORA: Oh yes, spendthrifts; I know all that. But let's do as I say, Torvald; then I'll have time to decide what I really need most. That's very sensible, isn't it?

HELMER (*smiling*): Yes, very—that is, if you actually hung onto the money I give you, and you actually used it to buy yourself something. But it goes for the house and for all sorts of foolish things, and then I only have to lay out some more.

NORA: Oh, but Torvald—

HELMER: Don't deny it, my dear little Nora. (*Putting his arm around her waist.*) Spendthrifts are sweet, but they use up a frightful amount of money. It's incredible what it costs a man to feed such birds.

NORA: Oh, how can you say that! Really, I save everything I can.

HELMER (*laughing*): Yes, that's the truth. Everything you can. But that's nothing at all.

NORA (*humming, with a smile of quiet satisfaction*): Hm, if you only knew what expenses we larks and squirrels have, Torvald.

HELMER: You're an odd little one. Exactly the way your father was. You're never at a loss for scaring up money; but the moment you have it, it runs right out through your fingers; you never know what you've done with it. Well, one takes you as you are. It's deep in your blood. Yes, these things are hereditary, Nora.

NORA: Ah, I could wish I'd inherited many of Papa's qualities.

HELMER: And I couldn't wish you anything but just what you are, my sweet little lark. But wait; it seems to me you have a very—what should I call it?—a very suspicious look today—

NORA: I do?

HELMER: You certainly do. Look me straight in the eye.

NORA (*looking at him*): Well?

HELMER (*shaking an admonitory finger*): Surely my sweet tooth hasn't been running riot in town today, has she?

NORA: No. Why do you imagine that?

HELMER: My sweet tooth really didn't make a little detour through the confectioner's?

NORA: No, I assure you, Torvald—

HELMER: Hasn't nibbled some pastry?

NORA: No, not at all.

HELMER: Not even munched a macaroon or two?

NORA: No, Torvald, I assure you, really—

HELMER: There, there now. Of course I'm only joking.

NORA (*going to the table, right*): You know I could never think of going against you.

HELMER: No, I understand that; and you *have* given me your word. (*Going over to her.*) Well, you keep your little Christmas secrets to yourself, Nora darling. I expect they'll come to light this evening, when the tree is lit.

NORA: Did you remember to ask Dr. Rank?

HELMER: No. But there's no need for that, it's assumed he'll be dining with us. All the same, I'll ask him when he stops by here this morning. I've ordered some fine wine. Nora, you can't imagine how I'm looking forward to this evening.

NORA: So am I. And what fun for the children, Torvald!

HELMER: Ah, it's so gratifying to know that one's gotten a safe, secure job, and with a comfortable salary. It's a great satisfaction, isn't it?

NORA: Oh, it's wonderful!

HELMER: Remember last Christmas? Three whole weeks before, you shut yourself in every evening till long after midnight, making flowers for the Christmas tree, and all the other decorations to surprise us. Ugh, that was the dullest time I've ever lived through.

NORA: It wasn't at all dull for me.

HELMER (*smiling*): But the outcome *was* pretty sorry, Nora.

NORA: Oh, don't tease me with that again. How could I help it that the cat came in and tore everything to shreds.

HELMER: No, poor thing, you certainly couldn't. You wanted so much to please us all, and that's what counts. But it's just as well that the hard times are past.

NORA: Yes, it's really wonderful.

HELMER: Now I don't have to sit here alone, boring myself, and you don't have to tire your precious eyes and your fair little delicate hands—

NORA (*clapping her hands*): No, is it really true, Torvald, I don't have to? Oh, how wonderfully lovely to hear! (*Taking his arm.*) Now I'll tell you just how I've thought we should plan things. Right after Christmas—(*The doorbell rings.*) Oh, the bell. (*Straightening the room up a bit.*) Somebody would have to come. What a bore!

HELMER: I'm not at home to visitors, don't forget.

MAID (*from the hall doorway*): Ma'am, a lady to see you—

NORA: All right, let her come in.

MAID (*to Helmer*): And the doctor's just come too.

HELMER: Did he go right to my study?

MAID: Yes, he did.

(*Helmer goes into his room. The Maid shows in Mrs. Linde, dressed in traveling clothes, and shuts the door after her.*)

MRS. LINDE (*in a dispirited and somewhat hesitant voice*): Hello, Nora.

NORA (*uncertain*): Hello—

MRS. LINDE: You don't recognize me.

NORA: No, I don't know—but wait, I think— (*Exclaiming.*) What! Kristine! Is it really you?

MRS. LINDE: Yes, it's me.

NORA: Kristine! To think I didn't recognize you. But then, how could I? (*More quietly.*) How you've changed, Kristine!

MRS. LINDE: Yes, no doubt I have. In nine—ten long years.

NORA: Is it so long since we met! Yes, it's all of that. Oh, these last eight years have been a happy time, believe me. And so now you've come in to town, too. Made the long trip in the winter. That took courage.

MRS. LINDE: I just got here by ship this morning.

NORA: To enjoy yourself over Christmas, of course. Oh, how lovely! Yes, enjoy ourselves, we'll do that. But take your coat off. You're not still cold? (*Helping her.*) There now, let's get cozy here by the stove. No, the easy chair there! I'll take the rocker here. (*Seizing her hands.*) Yes, now you have your old look again; it was only in that first moment. You're a bit more pale, Kristine—and maybe a bit thinner.

MRS. LINDE: And much, much older, Nora.

NORA: Yes, perhaps a bit older; a tiny, tiny bit; not much at all. (*Stopping short; suddenly serious.*) Oh, but thoughtless me, to sit here, chattering away. Sweet, good Kristine, can you forgive me?

MRS. LINDE: What do you mean, Nora?

NORA (*softly*): Poor Kristine, you've become a widow.

MRS. LINDE: Yes, three years ago.

NORA: Oh, I knew it, of course; I read it in the papers. Oh, Kristine, you must believe me; I often thought of writing you then, but I kept postponing it, and something always interfered.

MRS. LINDE: Nora dear, I understand completely.

NORA: No, it was awful of me, Kristine. You poor thing, how much you must have gone through. And he left you nothing?

MRS. LINDE: No.

NORA: And no children?

MRS. LINDE: No.

NORA: Nothing at all, then?

MRS. LINDE: Not even a sense of loss to feed on.

NORA (*looking incredulously at her*): But Kristine, how could that be?

MRS. LINDE (*smiling wearily and smoothing her hair*): Oh, sometimes it happens, Nora.

NORA: So completely alone. How terribly hard that must be for you. I have three lovely children. You can't see them now; they're out with the maid. But now you must tell me everything—

MRS. LINDE: No, no, no, tell me about yourself.

NORA: No, you begin. Today I don't want to be selfish. I want to think only of you today. But there is something I must tell you. Did you hear of the wonderful luck we had recently?

MRS. LINDE: No, what's that?

NORA: My husband's been made manager in the bank, just think!

MRS. LINDE: Your husband? How marvelous!

NORA: Isn't it? Being a lawyer is such an uncertain living, you know, especially if one won't touch any cases that aren't clean and decent. And of course Torvald would never do that, and I'm with him completely there. Oh, we're simply delighted, believe me! He'll join the bank right after New Year's and start getting a huge salary and lots of commissions. From now on we can live quite differently—just as we want. Oh, Kristine, I feel so light and happy! Won't it be lovely to have stacks of money and not a care in the world?

MRS. LINDE: Well, anyway, it would be lovely to have enough for necessities.

NORA: No, not just for necessities, but stacks and stacks of money!

MRS. LINDE (smiling): Nora, Nora, aren't you sensible yet? Back in school you were such a free spender.

NORA (with a quiet laugh): Yes, that's what Torvald still says. (Shaking her finger.) But "Nora, Nora" isn't as silly as you all think. Really, we've been in no position for me to go squandering. We've had to work, both of us.

MRS. LINDE: You too?

NORA: Yes, at odd jobs—needlework, crocheting, embroidery, and such—(casually) and other things too. You remember that Torvald left the department when we were married? There was no chance of promotion in his office, and of course he needed to earn more money. But that first year he drove himself terribly. He took on all kinds of extra work that kept him going morning and night. It wore him down, and then he fell deathly ill. The doctors said it was essential for him to travel south.

MRS. LINDE: Yes, didn't you spend a whole year in Italy?

NORA: That's right. It wasn't easy to get away, you know. Ivar had just been born. But of course we had to go. Oh, that was a beautiful trip, and it saved Torvald's life. But it cost a frightful sum, Kristine.

MRS. LINDE: I can well imagine.

NORA: Four thousand, eight hundred crowns it cost. That's really a lot of money.

MRS. LINDE: But it's lucky you had it when you needed it.

NORA: Well, as it was, we got it from Papa.

MRS. LINDE: I see. It was just about the time your father died.

NORA: Yes, just about then. And, you know, I couldn't make that trip out to nurse him. I had to stay here, expecting Ivar any moment, and with my poor sick Torvald to care for. Dearest Papa, I never saw him again, Kristine. Oh, that was the worst time I've known in all my marriage.

MRS. LINDE: I know how you loved him. And then you went off to Italy?

NORA: Yes. We had the means now, and the doctors urged us. So we left a month after.

MRS. LINDE: And your husband came back completely cured?

NORA: Sound as a drum!

MRS. LINDE: But—the doctor?

NORA: Who?

MRS. LINDE: I thought the maid said he was a doctor, the man who came in with me.

NORA: Yes, that was Dr. Rank—but he's not making a sick call. He's our closest friend, and he stops by at least once a day. No, Torvald hasn't had a sick moment since, and the children are fit and strong, and I am, too. (Jumping up and clapping her hands.) Oh, dear God, Kristine, what a lovely thing to live and be happy! But how disgusting of me—I'm talking of nothing but my own affairs. (Sits on a stool close by Kristine, arms resting across her knees.) Oh, don't be angry with me! Tell me, is it really true that you weren't in love with your husband? Why did you marry him, then?

MRS. LINDE: My mother was still alive, but bedridden and helpless—and I had my two younger brothers to look after. In all conscience, I didn't think I could turn him down.

NORA: No, you were right there. But was he rich at the time?

MRS. LINDE: He was very well off, I'd say. But the business was shaky, Nora. When he died, it all fell apart, and nothing was left.

NORA: And then—?

MRS. LINDE: Yes, so I had to scrape up a living with a little shop and a little teaching and whatever else I could find. The last three years have been like one endless workday without a rest for me. Now, it's over, Nora. My poor mother doesn't need me, for she's passed on. Nor the boys, either; they're working now and can take care of themselves.

NORA: How free you must feel—

MRS. LINDE: No—only unspeakably empty. Nothing to live for now. (Standing up anxiously.) That's why I couldn't take it any longer out in that desolate hole. Maybe here it'll be easier to find something to do and keep my mind occupied. If I could only be lucky enough to get a steady job, some office work—

NORA: Oh, but Kristine, that's so dreadfully tiring, and you already look so tired. It would be much better for you if you could go off to a bathing resort.

MRS. LINDE (going toward the window): I have no father to give me travel money, Nora.

NORA (rising): Oh, don't be angry with me.

MRS. LINDE (going to her): Nora dear, don't you be angry with me. The worst of my kind of situation is all the bitterness that's stored away. No one to work for, and yet you're always having to snap up your opportunities. You have to live; and so you grow self-ish. When you told me the happy change in your lot, do you know I was delighted less for your sakes than for mine?

NORA: How so? Oh, I see. You think maybe Torvald could do something for you.

MRS. LINDE: Yes, that's what I thought.

NORA: And he will, Kristine! Just leave it to me; I'll bring it up so delicately—find something attractive to humor him with. Oh, I'm so eager to help you.

MRS. LINDE: How very kind of you, Nora, to be so concerned over me—doubly kind, considering you really know so little of life's burdens yourself.

NORA: I—? I know so little—?

MRS. LINDE (*smiling*): Well, my heavens—a little needlework and such—Nora, you're just a child.

NORA (*tossing her head and pacing the floor*): You don't have to act so superior.

MRS. LINDE: Oh?

NORA: You're just like the others. You all think I'm incapable of anything serious—

MRS. LINDE: Come now—

NORA: That I've never had to face the raw world.

MRS. LINDE: Nora dear, you've just been telling me all your troubles.

NORA: Hm! Trivial! (*Quietly.*) I haven't told you the big thing.

MRS. LINDE: Big thing? What do you mean?

NORA: You look down on me so, Kristine, but you shouldn't. You're proud that you worked so long and hard for your mother.

MRS. LINDE: I don't look down on a soul. But it is true: I'm proud—and happy, too—to think it was given to me to make my mother's last days almost free of care.

NORA: And you're also proud thinking of what you've done for your brothers.

MRS. LINDE: I feel I've a right to be.

NORA: I agree. But listen to this, Kristine—I've also got something to be proud and happy for.

MRS. LINDE: I don't doubt it. But whatever do you mean?

NORA: Not so loud. What if Torvald heard! He mustn't, not for anything in the world. Nobody must know, Kristine. No one but you.

MRS. LINDE: But what is it, then?

NORA: Come here. (*Drawing her down beside her on the sofa.*) It's true—I've also got something to be proud and happy for. I'm the one who saved Torvald's life.

MRS. LINDE: Saved—? Saved how?

NORA: I told you about the trip to Italy. Torvald never would have lived if he hadn't gone south—

MRS. LINDE: Of course; your father gave you the means—

NORA (*smiling*): That's what Torvald and all the rest think, but—

MRS. LINDE: But—?

NORA: Papa didn't give us a pin. I was the one who raised the money.

MRS. LINDE: You? That whole amount?

NORA: Four thousand, eight hundred crowns. What do you say to that?

MRS. LINDE: But Nora, how was it possible? Did you win the lottery?

NORA (*disdainfully*): The lottery? Pooh! No art to that.

MRS. LINDE: But where did you get it from then?

NORA (*humming, with a mysterious smile*): Hmm, tra-la-la-la.

MRS. LINDE: Because you couldn't have borrowed it.

NORA: No? Why not?

MRS. LINDE: A wife can't borrow without her husband's consent.

NORA (*tossing her head*): Oh, but a wife with a little business sense, a wife who knows how to manage—

MRS. LINDE: Nora, I simply don't understand—

NORA: You don't have to. Whoever said I *borrowed* the money? I could have gotten it other ways. (*Throwing herself back on the sofa.*) I could have gotten it from some admirer or other. After all, a girl with my ravishing appeal—

MRS. LINDE: You lunatic.

NORA: I'll bet you're eaten up with curiosity, Kristine.

MRS. LINDE: Now listen here, Nora—you haven't done something indiscreet?

NORA (*sitting up again*): Is it indiscreet to save your husband's life?

MRS. LINDE: I think it's indiscreet that without his knowledge you—

NORA: But that's the point: He mustn't know! My Lord, can't you understand? He mustn't ever know the close call he had. It was to *me* the doctors came to say his life was in danger—that nothing could save him but a stay in the south. Didn't I try strategy then! I began talking about how lovely it would be for me to travel abroad like other young wives; I begged and I cried; I told him please to remember my condition, to be kind and indulge me; and then I dropped a hint that he could easily take out a loan. But at that, Kristine, he nearly exploded. He said I was frivolous, and it was his duty as man of the house not to indulge me in whims and fancies—as I think he called them. Aha, I thought, now you'll just have to be saved—and that's when I saw my chance.

MRS. LINDE: And your father never told Torvald the money wasn't from him?

NORA: No, never. Papa died right about then. I'd considered bringing him into my secret and begging him never to tell. But he was too sick at the time—and then, sadly, it didn't matter.

MRS. LINDE: And you've never confided in your husband since?

NORA: For heaven's sake, no! Are you serious? He's so strict on that subject. Besides—Torvald, with all his masculine pride—how painfully humiliating for him if he ever found out he was in debt to me. That would just ruin our relationship. Our beautiful, happy home would never be the same.

MRS. LINDE: Won't you ever tell him?

NORA (*thoughtfully, half smiling*): Yes—maybe sometime years from now, when I'm no longer so attractive. Don't laugh! I only mean when Torvald loves me less than now, when he stops enjoying my dancing and dressing up and reciting for him. Then it might be wise to have something in reserve—(*Breaking off.*) How ridiculous! That'll never happen—Well, Kristine, what do you think of my big secret? I'm capable of something too, hm? You can imagine, of course, how this thing hangs over me. It really hasn't been easy meeting the payments on time. In the business world there's what they call quarterly interest and what they call amortization, and these are always so terribly hard to manage. I've had to skimp a little here and there, wherever I could, you know. I could hardly spare anything from my house allowance, because Torvald has to live well. I couldn't let the children go poorly dressed; whatever I got for them, I felt I had to use up completely—the darlings!

MRS. LINDE: Poor Nora, so it had to come out of your own budget, then?

NORA: Yes, of course. But I was the one most responsible, too. Every time Torvald gave me money for new clothes and such, I never used more than half; always bought the simplest, cheapest outfits. It was a godsend that everything looks so well on me that Torvald never noticed. But it did weigh me down at times, Kristine. It *is* such a joy to wear fine things. You understand.

MRS. LINDE: Oh, of course.

NORA: And then I found other ways of making money. Last winter I was lucky enough to get a lot of copying to do. I locked myself in and sat writing every evening till late in the night. Ah, I was tired so often, dead tired. But still it was wonderful fun, sitting and working like that, earning money. It was almost like being a man.

MRS. LINDE: But how much have you paid off this way so far?

NORA: That's hard to say, exactly. These accounts, you know, aren't easy to figure. I only know that I've paid out all I could scrape together. Time and again I haven't known where to turn. (*Smiling.*) Then I'd sit here dreaming of a rich old gentleman who had fallen in love with me—

MRS. LINDE: What! Who is he?

NORA: Oh, really! And that he'd died, and when his will was opened, there in big letters it said, "All my fortune shall be paid over in cash, immediately, to that enchanting Mrs. Nora Helmer."

MRS. LINDE: But Nora dear—who *was* this gentleman?

NORA: Good grief, can't you understand? The old man never existed; that was only something I'd dream up time and again whenever I was at my wits' end for money. But it makes no difference now; the old fossil can go where he pleases for all I care; I don't need him or his will—because now I'm free. (*Jumping up.*) Oh, how lovely to think of that, Kristine! Carefree! To know you're carefree, utterly carefree; to be

able to romp and play with the children, and to keep up a beautiful, charming home—everything just the way Torvald likes it! And think, spring is coming, with big blue skies. Maybe we can travel a little then. Maybe I'll see the ocean again. Oh yes, it *is* so marvelous to live and be happy!

(*The front doorbell rings.*)

MRS. LINDE (*rising*): There's the bell. It's probably best that I go.

NORA: No, stay. No one's expected. It must be for Torvald.

MAID (*from the hall doorway*): Excuse me, ma'am—there's a gentleman here to see Mr. Helmer, but I didn't know—since the doctor's with him—

NORA: Who is the gentleman?

KROGSTAD (*from the doorway*): It's me, Mrs. Helmer.

(*Mrs. Linde starts and turns away toward the window.*)

NORA (*stepping toward him, tense, her voice a whisper*): You? What is it? Why do you want to speak to my husband?

KROGSTAD: Bank business—after a fashion. I have a small job in the investment bank, and I hear now your husband is going to be our chief—

NORA: In other words, it's—

KROGSTAD: Just dry business, Mrs. Helmer. Nothing but that.

NORA: Yes, then please be good enough to step into the study. (*She nods indifferently as she sees him out by the hall door, then returns and begins stirring up the stove.*)

MRS. LINDE: Nora—who was that man?

NORA: That was a Mr. Krogstad—a lawyer.

MRS. LINDE: Then it really was him.

NORA: Do you know that person?

MRS. LINDE: I did once—many years ago. For a time he was a law clerk in our town.

NORA: Yes, he's been that.

MRS. LINDE: How he's changed.

NORA: I understand he had a very unhappy marriage.

MRS. LINDE: He's a widower now.

NORA: With a number of children. There now, it's burning. (*She closes the stove door and moves the rocker a bit to one side.*)

MRS. LINDE: They say he has a hand in all kinds of business.

NORA: Oh? That may be true; I wouldn't know. But let's not think about business. It's so dull.

(*Dr. Rank enters from Helmer's study.*)

RANK (*still in the doorway*): No, no, really—I don't want to intrude, I'd just as soon talk a little while with your wife. (*Shuts the door, then notices Mrs. Linde.*) Oh, beg pardon. I'm intruding here too.

NORA: No, not at all. (*Introducing him.*) Dr. Rank, Mrs. Linde.

RANK: Well now, that's a name much heard in this house. I believe I passed the lady on the stairs as I came.

MRS. LINDE: Yes, I take the stairs very slowly. They're rather hard on me.

RANK: Uh-hm, some touch of internal weakness?

MRS. LINDE: More overexertion, I'd say.

RANK: Nothing else? Then you're probably here in town to rest up in a round of parties?

MRS. LINDE: I'm here to look for work.

RANK: Is that the best cure for overexertion?

MRS. LINDE: One has to live, Doctor.

RANK: Yes, there's a common prejudice to that effect.

NORA: Oh, come on, Dr. Rank—you really do want to live yourself.

RANK: Yes, I really do. Wretched as I am, I'll gladly prolong my torment indefinitely. All my patients feel like that. And it's quite the same, too, with the morally sick. Right at this moment there's one of those moral invalids in there with Helmer—

MRS. LINDE (*softly*): Ah!

NORA: Who do you mean?

RANK: Oh, it's a lawyer, Krogstad, a type you wouldn't know. His character is rotten to the root—but even he began chattering all-importantly about how he had to live.

NORA: Oh? What did he want to talk to Torvald about?

RANK: I really don't know. I only heard something about the bank.

NORA: I didn't know that Krog—that this man Krogstad had anything to do with the bank.

RANK: Yes, he's gotten some kind of berth down there. (*To Mrs. Linde.*) I don't know if you also have, in your neck of the woods, a type of person who scuttles about breathlessly, sniffing out hints of moral corruption, and then maneuvers his victim into some sort of key position where he can keep an eye on him. It's the healthy these days that are out in the cold.

MRS. LINDE: All the same, it's the sick who most need to be taken in.

RANK (*with a shrug*): Yes, there we have it. That's the concept that's turning society into a sanatorium.

(*Nora, lost in her thoughts, breaks out into quiet laughter and claps her hands.*)

RANK: Why do you laugh at that? Do you have any real idea of what society is?

NORA: What do I care about dreary old society? I was laughing at something quite different—something terribly funny. Tell me, Doctor—is everyone who works in the bank dependent now on Torvald?

RANK: Is that what you find so terribly funny?

NORA (*smiling and humming*): Never mind, never mind! (*Pacing the floor.*) Yes, that's really immensely amusing: that we—that Torvald has so much power now over all those people. (*Taking the bag out of her pocket.*) Dr. Rank, a little macaroon on that?

RANK: See here, macaroons! I thought they were contraband here.

NORA: Yes, but these are some that Kristine gave me.

MRS. LINDE: What? I—?

NORA: Now, now, don't be afraid. You couldn't possibly know that Torvald had forbidden them. You see, he's worried they'll ruin my teeth. But hmp! Just this once! Isn't that so, Dr. Rank? Help yourself! (*Puts a macaroon in his mouth.*) And you too, Kristine. And I'll also have one, only a little one—or two, at the most. (*Walking about again.*) Now I'm really tremendously happy. Now's there's just one last thing in the world that I have an enormous desire to do.

RANK: Well! And what's that?

NORA: It's something I have such a consuming desire to say so Torvald could hear.

RANK: And why can't you say it?

NORA: I don't dare. It's quite shocking.

MRS. LINDE: Shocking?

RANK: Well, then it isn't advisable. But in front of us you certainly can. What do you have such a desire to say so Torvald could hear?

NORA: I have such a huge desire to say—to hell and be damned!

RANK: Are you crazy?

MRS. LINDE: My goodness, Nora!

RANK: Go on, say it. Here he is.

NORA (*hiding the macaroon bag*): Shh, shh, shh!

(*Helmer comes in from his study, hat in hand, overcoat over his arm.*)

NORA (*going toward him*): Well, Torvald dear, are you through with him?

HELMER: Yes, he just left.

NORA: Let me introduce you—this is Kristine, who's arrived here in town.

HELMER: Kristine—? I'm sorry, but I don't know—

NORA: Mrs. Linde, Torvald dear. Mrs. Kristine Linde.

HELMER: Of course. A childhood friend of my wife's, no doubt?

MRS. LINDE: Yes, we knew each other in those days.

NORA: And just think, she made the long trip down here in order to talk with you.

HELMER: What's this?

MRS. LINDE: Well, not exactly—

NORA: You see, Kristine is remarkably clever in office work, and so she's terribly eager to come under a capable man's supervision and add more to what she already knows—

HELMER: Very wise, Mrs. Linde.

NORA: And then when she heard that you'd become a bank manager—the story was wired out to the papers—then she came in as fast as she could and—Really, Torvald, for my sake you can do a little something for Kristine, can't you?

HELMER: Yes, it's not at all impossible. Mrs. Linde, I suppose you're a widow?

MRS. LINDE: Yes.

HELMER: Any experience in office work?

MRS. LINDE: Yes, a good deal.

HELMER: Well, it's quite likely that I can make an opening for you—

NORA (*clapping her hands*): You see, you see!

HELMER: You've come at a lucky moment, Mrs. Linde.

MRS. LINDE: Oh, how can I thank you?

HELMER: Not necessary. (*Putting his overcoat on.*) But today you'll have to excuse me—

RANK: Wait, I'll go with you. (*He fetches his coat from the hall and warms it at the stove.*)

NORA: Don't stay out long, dear.

HELMER: An hour; no more.

NORA: Are you going too, Kristine?

MRS. LINDE (*putting on her winter garments*): Yes, I have to see about a room now.

HELMER: Then perhaps we can all walk together.

NORA (*helping her*): What a shame we're so cramped here, but it's quite impossible for us to—

MRS. LINDE: Oh, don't even think of it! Good-bye, Nora dear, and thanks for everything.

NORA: Good-bye for now. Of course you'll be back this evening. And you too, Dr. Rank. What? If you're well enough? Oh, you've got to be! Wrap up tight now.

(*In a ripple of small talk the company moves out into the hall; children's voices are heard outside on the steps.*)

NORA: There they are! There they are! (*She runs to open the door. The children come in with their nurse, Anne-Marie.*) Come in, come in! (*Bends down and kisses them.*) Oh, you darlings—! Look at them, Kristine. Aren't they lovely!

RANK: No loitering in the draft here.

HELMER: Come, Mrs. Linde—this place is unbearable now for anyone but mothers.

(*Dr. Rank, Helmer, and Mrs. Linde go down the stairs. Anne-Marie goes into the living room with the children. Nora follows, after closing the hall door.*)

NORA: How fresh and strong you look. Oh, such red cheeks you have! Like apples and roses. (*The children interrupt her throughout the following.*) And it was so much fun? That's wonderful. Really? You pulled both Emmy and Bob on the sled? Imagine, all together! Yes, you're a clever boy, Ivar. Oh, let me hold her a bit, Anne-Marie. My sweet little doll baby! (*Takes the smallest from the nurse and dances with her.*) Yes, yes, Mama will dance with Bob as well. What? Did you throw snowballs? Oh, if I'd only been there! No, don't bother, Anne-Marie—I'll undress them myself. Oh yes, let me. It's such fun. Go in and rest; you look half frozen. There's hot coffee waiting for you on the stove. (*The nurse goes into the room to the left. Nora takes the children's winter things off, throwing them about, while the children talk to her all at once.*) Is that so? A big dog chased you? But it didn't bite? No, dogs never bite little, lovely doll babies. Don't peek in the packages, Ivar! What is it? Yes, wouldn't you like to know. No, no, it's an ugly something. Well? Shall we play? What shall we play? Hide-and-seek? Yes, let's play hide-and-seek. Bob must hide first. I must? Yes, let me hide first. (*Laughing and shouting, she and the children play in and out of the living room and the*

adjoining room to the right. At last Nora hides under the table. The children come storming in, search, but cannot find her, then hear her muffled laughter, dash over to the table, lift the cloth up and find her. Wild shouting. She creeps forward as if to scare them. More shouts. Meanwhile, a knock at the hall door; no one has noticed it. Now the door half opens, and Krogstad appears. He waits a moment; the game goes on.*)

KROGSTAD: Beg pardon, Mrs. Helmer—

NORA (*with a strangled cry, turning and scrambling to her knees*): Oh! What do you want?

KROGSTAD: Excuse me. The outer door was ajar; it must be someone forgot to shut it—

NORA (*rising*): My husband isn't home, Mr. Krogstad.

KROGSTAD: I know that.

NORA: Yes—then what do you want here?

KROGSTAD: A word with you.

NORA: With—? (*To the children, quietly.*) Go in to Anne-Marie. What? No, the strange man won't hurt Mama. When he's gone, we'll play some more. (*She leads the children into the room to the left and shuts the door after them. Then, tense and nervous:*) You want to speak to me?

KROGSTAD: Yes, I want to.

NORA: Today? But it's not yet the first of the month—

KROGSTAD: No, it's Christmas Eve. It's going to be up to you how merry a Christmas you have.

NORA: What is it you want? Today I absolutely can't—

KROGSTAD: We won't talk about that till later. This is something else. You do have a moment to spare, I suppose?

NORA: Oh yes, of course—I do, except—

KROGSTAD: Good. I was sitting over at Olsen's Restaurant when I saw your husband go down the street—

NORA: Yes?

KROGSTAD: With a lady.

NORA: Yes. So?

KROGSTAD: If you'll pardon my asking: Wasn't that lady a Mrs. Linde?

NORA: Yes.

KROGSTAD: Just now come into town?

NORA: Yes, today.

KROGSTAD: She's a good friend of yours?

NORA: Yes, she is. But I don't see—

KROGSTAD: I also knew her once.

NORA: I'm aware of that.

KROGSTAD: Oh? You know all about it. I thought so. Well, then let me ask you short and sweet: Is Mrs. Linde getting a job in the bank?

NORA: What makes you think you can cross-examine me, Mr. Krogstad—you, one of my husband's employees? But since you ask, you might as well know—yes, Mrs. Linde's going to be taken on at the bank. And I'm the one who spoke for her, Mr. Krogstad. Now you know.

KROGSTAD: So I guessed right.

NORA (*pacing up and down*): Oh, one does have a tiny bit of influence, I should hope. Just because I am a woman, don't think it means that—When one has a subordinate position, Mr. Krogstad, one really ought to be careful about pushing somebody who—hm—

KROGSTAD: Who has influence?

NORA: That's right.

KROGSTAD (*in a different tone*): Mrs. Helmer, would you be good enough to use your influence on my behalf?

NORA: What? What do you mean?

KROGSTAD: Would you please make sure that I keep my subordinate position in the bank?

NORA: What does that mean? Who's thinking of taking away your position?

KROGSTAD: Oh, don't play the innocent with me. I'm quite aware that your friend would hardly relish the chance of running into me again; and I'm also aware now whom I can thank for being turned out.

NORA: But I promise you—

KROGSTAD: Yes, yes, yes, to the point: There's still time, and I'm advising you to use your influence to prevent it.

NORA: But Mr. Krogstad, I have absolutely no influence.

KROGSTAD: You haven't? I thought you were just saying—

NORA: You shouldn't take me so literally. I! How can you believe that I have any such influence over my husband?

KROGSTAD: Oh, I've known your husband from our student days. I don't think the great bank manager's more steadfast than any other married man.

NORA: You speak insolently about my husband, and I'll show you the door.

KROGSTAD: The lady has spirit.

NORA: I'm not afraid of you any longer. After New Year's, I'll soon be done with the whole business.

KROGSTAD (*restraining himself*): Now listen to me, Mrs. Helmer. If necessary, I'll fight for my little job in the bank as if it were life itself.

NORA: Yes, so it seems.

KROGSTAD: It's not just a matter of income; that's the least of it. It's something else—All right, out with it! Look, this is the thing. You know, just like all the others, of course, that once, a good many years ago, I did something rather rash.

NORA: I've heard rumors to that effect.

KROGSTAD: The case never got into court; but all the same, every door was closed in my face from then on. So I took up those various activities you know about. I had to grab hold somewhere; and I dare say I haven't been among the worst. But now I want to drop all that. My boys are growing up. For their sakes, I'll have to win back as much respect as possible here in town. That job in the bank was like the first rung in my ladder. And now your husband wants to kick me right back down in the mud again.

NORA: But for heaven's sake, Mr. Krogstad, it's simply not in my power to help you.

KROGSTAD: That's because you haven't the will to—but I have the means to make you.

NORA: You certainly won't tell my husband that I owe you money?

KROGSTAD: Hm—what if I told him that?

NORA: That would be shameful of you. (*Nearly in tears.*) This secret—my joy and my pride—that he should learn it in such a crude and disgusting way—learn it from you. You'd expose me to the most horrible unpleasantness—

KROGSTAD: Only unpleasantness?

NORA (*vehemently*): But go on and try. It'll turn out the worse for you, because then my husband will really see what a crook you are, and then you'll never be able to hold your job.

KROGSTAD: I asked if it was just domestic unpleasantness you were afraid of?

NORA: If my husband finds out, then of course he'll pay what I owe at once, and then we'd be through with you for good.

KROGSTAD (*a step closer*): Listen, Mrs. Helmer—you've either got a very bad memory, or else no head at all for business. I'd better put you a little more in touch with the facts.

NORA: What do you mean?

KROGSTAD: When your husband was sick, you came to me for a loan of four thousand, eight hundred crowns.

NORA: Where else could I go?

KROGSTAD: I promised to get you that sum—

NORA: And you got it.

KROGSTAD: I promised to get you that sum, on certain conditions. You were so involved in your husband's illness, and so eager to finance your trip, that I guess you didn't think out all the details. It might just be a good idea to remind you. I promised you the money on the strength of a note I drew up.

NORA: Yes, and that I signed.

KROGSTAD: Right. But at the bottom I added some lines for your father to guarantee the loan. He was supposed to sign down there.

NORA: Supposed to? He did sign.

KROGSTAD: I left the date blank. In other words, your father would have dated his signature himself. Do you remember that?

NORA: Yes, I think—

KROGSTAD: Then I gave you the note for you to mail to your father. Isn't that so?

NORA: Yes.

KROGSTAD: And naturally you sent it at once—because only some five, six days later you brought me the note, properly signed. And with that, the money was yours.

NORA: Well, then; I've made my payments regularly, haven't I?

KROGSTAD: More or less. But—getting back to the point—those were hard times for you then, Mrs. Helmer.

NORA: Yes, they were.

KROGSTAD: Your father was very ill, I believe.

NORA: He was near the end.

KROGSTAD: He died soon after?

NORA: Yes.

KROGSTAD: Tell me, Mrs. Helmer, do you happen to recall the date of your father's death? The day of the month, I mean.

NORA: Papa died the twenty-ninth of September.

KROGSTAD: That's quite correct; I've already looked into that. And now we come to a curious thing—(*taking out a paper*) which I simply cannot comprehend.

NORA: Curious thing? I don't know—

KROGSTAD: This is the curious thing: that your father co-signed the note for your loan three days after his death.

NORA: How—? I don't understand.

KROGSTAD: Your father died the twenty-ninth of September. But look. Here your father dated his signature October second. Isn't that curious, Mrs. Helmer? (*Nora is silent.*) Can you explain it to me? (*Nora remains silent.*) It's also remarkable that the words "October second" and the year aren't written in your father's hand, but rather in one that I think I know. Well, it's easy to understand. Your father forgot perhaps to date his signature, and then someone or other added it, a bit sloppily, before anyone knew of his death. There's nothing wrong in that. It all comes down to the signature. And there's no question about *that*, Mrs. Helmer. It really *was* your father who signed his own name here, wasn't it?

NORA (*after a short silence, throwing her head back and looking squarely at him*): No, it wasn't. *I* signed Papa's name.

KROGSTAD: Wait, now—are you fully aware that this is a dangerous confession?

NORA: Why? You'll soon get your money.

KROGSTAD: Let me ask you a question—why didn't you send the paper to your father?

NORA: That was impossible. Papa was so sick. If I'd asked him for his signature, I also would have had to tell him what the money was for. But I couldn't tell him, sick as he was, that my husband's life was in danger. That was just impossible.

KROGSTAD: Then it would have been better if you'd given up the trip abroad.

NORA: I couldn't possibly. The trip was to save my husband's life. I couldn't give that up.

KROGSTAD: But didn't you ever consider that this was a fraud against me?

NORA: I couldn't let myself be bothered by that. You weren't any concern of mine. I couldn't stand you, with all those cold complications you made, even though you knew how badly off my husband was.

KROGSTAD: Mrs. Helmer, obviously you haven't the vaguest idea of what you've involved yourself in. But I can tell you this: It was nothing more and nothing worse that I once did—and it wrecked my whole reputation.

NORA: You? Do you expect me to believe that you ever acted bravely to save your wife's life?

KROGSTAD: Laws don't inquire into motives.

NORA: Then they must be very poor laws.

KROGSTAD: Poor or not—if I introduce this paper in court, you'll be judged according to law.

NORA: This I refuse to believe. A daughter hasn't a right to protect her dying father from anxiety and care? A

Nora (Claire Bloom) is troubled as Helmer (Donald Madden) kisses her in Patrick Garland's 1971 production.

wife hasn't a right to save her husband's life? I don't know much about laws, but I'm sure that somewhere in the books these things are allowed. And you don't know anything about it—you who practice the law? You must be an awful lawyer, Mr. Krogstad.

KROGSTAD: Could be. But business—the kind of business we two are mixed up in—don't you think I know about that? All right. Do what you want now. But I'm telling you *this*: If I get shoved down a second time, you're going to keep me company. (*He bows and goes out through the hall.*)

NORA (*pensive for a moment, then tossing her head*): Oh, really! Trying to frighten me! I'm not so silly as all that. (*Begins gathering up the children's clothes, but soon stops.*) But—? No, but that's impossible! I did it out of love.

THE CHILDREN (*in the doorway, left*): Mama, that strange man's gone out the door.

NORA: Yes, yes, I know it. But don't tell anyone about the strange man. Do you hear? Not even Papa!

THE CHILDREN: No, Mama. But now will you play again?

NORA: No, not now.

Krogstad (Robert Gerringer) explains the seriousness of her actions to Nora.

THE CHILDREN: Oh, but Mama, you promised.
NORA: Yes, but I can't now. Go inside; I have too much to do. Go in, go in, my sweet darlings. (*She herds them gently back in the room and shuts the door after them. Settling on the sofa, she takes up a piece of embroidery and makes some stitches, but soon stops abruptly.*) No! (*Throws the work aside, rises, goes to the hall door and calls out.*) Helene! Let me have the tree in here. (*Goes to the table, left, opens the table drawer, and stops again.*) No, but that's utterly impossible!
MAID (*with the Christmas tree*): Where should I put it, ma'am?
NORA: There. The middle of the floor.
MAID: Should I bring anything else?
NORA: No, thanks. I have what I need.

(*The Maid, who has set the tree down, goes out.*)

NORA (*absorbed in trimming the tree*): Candles here— and flowers here. That terrible creature! Talk, talk, talk! There's nothing to it at all. The tree's going to

be lovely. I'll do anything to please you Torvald. I'll sing for you, dance for you—

(*Helmer comes in from the hall, with a sheaf of papers under his arm.*)

NORA: Oh! You're back so soon?
HELMER: Yes. Has anyone been here?
NORA: Here? No.
HELMER: That's odd. I saw Krogstad leaving the front door.
NORA: So? Oh yes, that's true. Krogstad was here a moment.
HELMER: Nora, I can see by your face that he's been here, begging you to put in a good word for him.
NORA: Yes.
HELMER: And it was supposed to seem like your own idea? You were to hide it from me that he'd been here. He asked you that, too, didn't he?
NORA: Yes, Torvald, but—
HELMER: Nora, Nora, and you could fall for that? Talk with that sort of person and promise him anything? And then in the bargain, tell me an untruth.
NORA: An untruth—?
HELMER: Didn't you say that no one had been here? (*Wagging his finger.*) My little songbird must never do that again. A songbird needs a clean beak to warble with. No false notes. (*Putting his arm about her waist.*) That's the way it should be, isn't it? Yes, I'm sure of it. (*Releasing her.*) And so, enough of that. (*Sitting by the stove.*) Ah, how snug and cozy it is here. (*Leafing among his papers.*)
NORA (*busy with the tree, after a short pause*): Torvald!
HELMER: Yes.
NORA: I'm so much looking forward to the Stenborgs' costume party, day after tomorrow.
HELMER: And I can't wait to see what you'll surprise me with.
NORA: Oh, that stupid business!
HELMER: What?
NORA: I can't find anything that's right. Everything seems so ridiculous, so inane.
HELMER: So my little Nora's come to *that* recognition?
NORA (*going behind his chair, her arms resting on its back*): Are you very busy, Torvald?
HELMER: Oh—
NORA: What papers are those?
HELMER: Bank matters.
NORA: Already?
HELMER: I've gotten full authority from the retiring management to make all necessary changes in personnel and procedure. I'll need Christmas week for that. I want to have everything in order by New Year's.
NORA: So that was the reason this poor Krogstad—
HELMER: Hm.
NORA (*still leaning on the chair and slowly stroking the nape of his neck*): If you weren't so very busy, I would have asked you an enormous favor, Torvald.

The *Mabou Mines Dollhouse*, a 2005 interpretation of Ibsen's play by Lee Breuer and the Mabou Mines troupe, paired female actors at least six feet tall with male actors five feet tall or shorter.

HELMER: Let's hear. What is it?

NORA: You know, there isn't anyone who has your good taste—and I want so much to look well at the costume party. Torvald, couldn't you take over and decide what I should be and plan my costume?

HELMER: Ah, is my stubborn little creature calling for a lifeguard?

NORA: Yes, Torvald, I can't get anywhere without your help.

HELMER: All right—I'll think it over. We'll hit on something.

NORA: Oh, how sweet of you. (*Goes to the tree again. Pause.*) Aren't the red flowers pretty—? But tell me, was it really such a crime that this Krogstad committed?

HELMER: Forgery. Do you have any idea what that means?

NORA: Couldn't he have done it out of need?

HELMER: Yes, or thoughtlessness, like so many others. I'm not so heartless that I'd condemn a man categorically for just one mistake.

NORA: No, of course not, Torvald!

HELMER: Plenty of men have redeemed themselves by openly confessing their crimes and taking their punishment.

NORA: Punishment—?

HELMER: But now Krogstad didn't go that way. He got himself out by sharp practices, and that's the real cause of his moral breakdown.

NORA: Do you really think that would—?

HELMER: Just imagine how a man with that sort of guilt in him has to lie and cheat and deceive on all sides, has to wear a mask even with the nearest and dearest he has, even with his own wife and children. And with the children, Nora—that's where it's most horrible.

NORA: Why?

HELMER: Because that kind of atmosphere of lies infects the whole life of a home. Every breath the children take in is filled with the germs of something degenerate.

NORA (*coming closer behind him*): Are you sure of that?

HELMER: Oh, I've seen it often enough as a lawyer. Almost everyone who goes bad early in life has a mother who's a chronic liar.

NORA: Why just—the mother?

HELMER: It's usually the mother's influence that's dominant, but the father's works in the same way, of course. Every lawyer is quite familiar with it. And still this Krogstad's been going home year in, year out, poisoning his own children with lies and pretense; that's why I call him morally lost. (*Reaching his hands out toward her.*) So my sweet little Nora must promise me never to plead his cause. Your hand on it. Come, come, what's this? Give me your hand. There, now. All settled. I can tell you it'd be impossible for me to work alongside of him. I literally feel physically revolted when I'm anywhere near such a person.

NORA (*withdraws her hand and goes to the other side of the Christmas tree*): How hot it is here! And I've got so much to do.

HELMER (*getting up and gathering his papers*): Yes, and I have to think about getting some of these read through before dinner. I'll think about your costume, too. And something to hang on the tree in gilt paper, I may even see about that. (*Putting his hand on her head.*) Oh you, my darling little songbird. (*He goes into his study and closes the door after him.*)

NORA (*softly, after a silence*): Oh, really! It isn't so. It's impossible. It must be impossible.

ANNE-MARIE (*in the doorway left*): The children are begging so hard to come in to Mama.

NORA: No, no, no, don't let them in to me! You stay with them, Anne-Marie.

ANNE-MARIE: Of course, ma'am. (*Closes the door.*)

NORA (*pale with terror*): Hurt my children—! Poison my home? (*A moment's pause; then she tosses her head.*) That's not true. Never. Never in all the world.

ACT II

(*Same room. Beside the piano the Christmas tree now stands stripped of ornament, burned-down candle stubs on its ragged branches. Nora's street clothes lie on the sofa. Nora, alone in the room, moves restlessly about; at last she stops at the sofa and picks up her coat.*)

NORA (*dropping the coat again*): Someone's coming! (*Goes toward the door, listens.*) No—there's no one. Of course—nobody's coming today, Christmas Day— or tomorrow, either. But maybe—(*Opens the door and looks out.*) No, nothing in the mailbox. Quite empty. (*Coming forward.*) What nonsense! He won't do anything serious. Nothing terrible could happen. It's impossible. Why, I have three small children.

(*Anne-Marie, with a large carton, comes in from the room to the left.*)

ANNE-MARIE: Well, at last I found the box with the masquerade clothes.

NORA: Thanks. Put it on the table.

ANNE-MARIE (*does so*): But they're all pretty much of a mess.

NORA: Ahh! I'd love to rip them in a million pieces!

ANNE-MARIE: Oh, mercy, they can be fixed right up. Just a little patience.

NORA: Yes, I'll go get Mrs. Linde to help me.

ANNE-MARIE: Out again now? In this nasty weather? Miss Nora will catch cold—get sick.

NORA: Oh, worse things could happen—How are the children?

ANNE-MARIE: The poor mites are playing with their Christmas presents, but—

NORA: Do they ask for me much?

ANNE-MARIE: They're so used to having Mama around, you know.

NORA: Yes, but Anne-Marie, I *can't* be together with them as much as I was.

ANNE-MARIE: Well, small children get used to anything.

NORA: You think so? Do you think they'd forget their mother if she was gone for good?

ANNE-MARIE: Oh, mercy—gone for good!

NORA: Wait, tell me. Anne-Marie—I've wondered so often—how could you ever have the heart to give your child over to strangers?

ANNE-MARIE: But I had to, you know, to become little Nora's nurse.

NORA: Yes, but how could you *do* it?

ANNE-MARIE: When I could get such a good place? A girl who's poor and who's gotten in trouble is glad enough for that. Because that slippery fish, he didn't do a thing for me, you know.

NORA: But your daughter's surely forgotten you.

ANNE-MARIE: Oh, she certainly has not. She's written to me, both when she was confirmed and when she was married.

NORA (*clasping her about the neck*): You old Anne-Marie, you were a good mother for me when I was little.

ANNE-MARIE: Poor little Nora, with no other mother but me.

NORA: And if the babies didn't have one, then I know that you'd—What silly talk! (*Opening the carton.*) Go in to them. Now I'll have to—Tomorrow you can see how lovely I'll look.

ANNE-MARIE: Oh, there won't be anyone at the party as lovely as Miss Nora. (*She goes off into the room, left.*)

NORA (*begins unpacking the box, but soon throws it aside*): Oh, if I dared to go out. If only nobody would come. If only nothing would happen here while I'm out. What craziness—nobody's coming. Just don't think. This muff—needs a brushing. Beautiful gloves, beautiful gloves. Let it go. Let it go! One, two, three, four, five, six—(*With a cry.*) Oh, there they are! (*Poises to move toward the door, but remains irresolutely standing. Mrs. Linde enters from the hall, where she has removed her street clothes.*)

NORA: Oh, it's you, Kristine. There's no one else out there? How good that you've come.

MRS. LINDE: I hear you were up asking for me.

NORA: Yes, I just stopped by. There's something you really can help me with. Let's get settled on the sofa. Look, there's going to be a costume party tomorrow evening at the Stenborgs' right above us, and now Torvald wants me to go as a Neapolitan peasant girl and dance the tarantella that I learned in Capri.

MRS. LINDE: Really, are you giving a whole performance?

NORA: Torvald says yes, I should. See, here's the dress. Torvald had it made for me down there; but now it's all so tattered that I just don't know—

MRS. LINDE: Oh, we'll fix that up in no time. It's nothing more than the trimmings—they're a bit loose here and there. Needle and thread? Good, now we have what we need.

NORA: Oh, how sweet of you!

MRS. LINDE (*sewing*): So you'll be in disguise tomorrow, Nora. You know what? I'll stop by then for a moment and have a look at you all dressed up. But listen, I've absolutely forgotten to thank you for that pleasant evening yesterday.

NORA (*getting up and walking about*): I don't think it was as pleasant as usual yesterday. You should have come to town a bit sooner, Kristine—Yes, Torvald really knows how to give a home elegance and charm.

MRS. LINDE: And you do, too, if you ask me. You're not your father's daughter for nothing. But tell me, is Dr. Rank always so down in the mouth as yesterday?

NORA: No, that was quite an exception. But he goes around critically ill all the time—tuberculosis of the spine, poor man. You know, his father was a disgusting thing who kept mistresses and so on—and that's why the son's been sickly from birth.

MRS. LINDE (*lets her sewing fall to her lap*): But my dearest Nora, how do you know about such things?

NORA (*walking more jauntily*): Hmp! When you've had three children, then you've had a few visits from—from women who know something of medicine, and they tell you this and that.

MRS. LINDE (*resumes sewing; a short pause*): Does Dr. Rank come here every day?

NORA: Every blessed day. He's Torvald's best friend from childhood, and *my* good friend, too. Dr. Rank almost belongs to this house.

MRS. LINDE: But tell me—is he quite sincere? I mean, doesn't he rather enjoy flattering people?

NORA: Just the opposite. Why do you think that?

MRS. LINDE: When you introduced us yesterday, he was proclaiming that he'd often heard my name in this house; but later I noticed that your husband hadn't the slightest idea who I really was. So how could Dr. Rank—?

NORA: But it's all true, Kristine. You see, Torvald loves me beyond words, and, as he puts it, he'd like to keep me all to himself. For a long time he'd almost be jealous if I even mentioned any of my old friends back home. So of course I dropped that. But with Dr. Rank I talk a lot about such things because he likes hearing about them.

MRS. LINDE: Now listen, Nora; in many ways you're still like a child. I'm a good deal older than you, with a little more experience. I'll tell you something: You ought to put an end to all this with Dr. Rank.

NORA: What should I put an end to?

MRS. LINDE: Both parts of it, I think. Yesterday you said something about a rich admirer who'd provide you with money—

NORA: Yes, one who doesn't exist—worse luck. So?

MRS. LINDE: Is Dr. Rank well off?

NORA: Yes, he is.

MRS. LINDE: With no dependents?

NORA: No, no one. But—

MRS. LINDE: And he's over here every day?

NORA: Yes, I told you that.

MRS. LINDE: How can a man of such refinement be so grasping?

NORA: I don't follow you at all.

MRS. LINDE: Now don't try to hide it, Nora. You think I can't guess who loaned you the forty-eight hundred crowns?

NORA: Are you out of your mind? How could you think such a thing! A friend of ours, who comes here every single day. What an intolerable situation that would have been!

MRS. LINDE: Then it really wasn't him.

NORA: No, absolutely not. It never even crossed my mind for a moment—And he had nothing to lend in those days; his inheritance came later.

MRS. LINDE: Well, I think that was a stroke of luck for you, Nora dear.

NORA: No, it never would have occurred to me to ask Dr. Rank—Still, I'm quite sure that if I had asked him—

MRS. LINDE: Which you won't, of course.

NORA: No, of course not. I can't see that I'd ever need to. But I'm quite positive that if I talked to Dr. Rank—

MRS. LINDE: Behind your husband's back?

NORA: I've got to clear up this other thing; *that's* also behind his back. I've *got* to clear it all up.

MRS. LINDE: Yes, I was saying that yesterday, but—

NORA (*pacing up and down*): A man handles these problems so much better than a woman—

MRS. LINDE: One's husband does, yes.

NORA: Nonsense. (*Stopping.*) When you pay everything you owe, then you get your note back, right?

MRS. LINDE: Yes, naturally.

NORA: And can rip it into a million pieces and burn it up—that filthy scrap of paper!

MRS. LINDE (*looking hard at her, laying her sewing aside, and rising slowly*): Nora, you're hiding something from me.

NORA: You can see it in my face?

MRS. LINDE: Something's happened to you since yesterday morning. Nora, what is it?

NORA (*hurrying toward her*): Kristine! (*Listening.*) Shh! Torvald's home. Look, go in with the children a while. Torvald can't bear all this snipping and stitching. Let Anne-Marie help you.

MRS. LINDE (*gathering up some of the things*): All right, but I'm not leaving here until we've talked this out. (*She disappears into the room, left, as Torvald enters from the hall.*)

NORA: Oh, how I've been waiting for you, Torvald dear.

HELMER: Was that the dressmaker?

NORA: No, that was Kristine. She's helping me fix up my costume. You know, it's going to be quite attractive.

HELMER: Yes, wasn't that a bright idea I had?

NORA: Brilliant! But then wasn't I good as well to give in to you?

HELMER: Good—because you give in to your husband's judgment? All right, you little goose, I know you didn't mean it like that. But I won't disturb you. You'll want to have a fitting, I suppose.

NORA: And you'll be working?

HELMER: Yes. (*Indicating a bundle of papers.*) See. I've been down to the bank. (*Starts toward his study.*)

NORA: Torvald.

HELMER (*stops*): Yes.

NORA: If your little squirrel begged you, with all her heart and soul, for something—?

HELMER: What's that?

NORA: Then would you do it?

HELMER: First, naturally, I'd have to know what it was.

NORA: Your squirrel would scamper about and do tricks, if you'd only be sweet and give in.

HELMER: Out with it.

NORA: Your lark would be singing high and low in every room—

HELMER: Come on, she does that anyway.

NORA: I'd be a wood nymph and dance for you in the moonlight.

HELMER: Nora—don't tell me it's that same business from this morning?

NORA (*coming closer*): Yes, Torvald, I beg you, please!

HELMER: And you actually have the nerve to drag that up again?

NORA: Yes, yes, you've got to give in to me; you *have* to let Krogstad keep his job in the bank.

HELMER: My dear Nora, I've slated his job for Mrs. Linde.

NORA: That's awfully kind of you. But you could just fire another clerk instead of Krogstad.

HELMER: This is the most incredible stubbornness! Because you go and give an impulsive promise to speak up for him, I'm expected to—

NORA: That's not the reason, Torvald. It's for your own sake. That man does writing for the worst papers; you said it yourself. He could do you any amount of harm. I'm scared to death of him—

HELMER: Ah, I understand. It's the old memories haunting you.

NORA: What do you mean by that?

HELMER: Of course, you're thinking about your father.

NORA: Yes, all right. Just remember how those nasty gossips wrote in the papers about Papa and slandered him so cruelly. I think they'd have had him dismissed if the department hadn't sent you up to investigate, and if you hadn't been so kind and openminded toward him.

HELMER: My dear Nora, there's a notable difference between your father and me. Your father's official career was hardly above reproach. But mine is; and I hope it'll stay that way as long as I hold my position.

NORA: Oh, who can ever tell what vicious minds can invent? We could be so snug and happy now in our quiet, carefree home—you and I and the children, Torvald! That's why I'm pleading with you so—

HELMER: And just by pleading for him you make it impossible for me to keep him on. It's already known at the bank that I'm firing Krogstad. What if it's rumored around now that the new bank manager was vetoed by his wife—

NORA: Yes, what then—?

HELMER: Oh yes—as long as our little bundle of stubbornness gets her way—! I should go and make myself ridiculous in front of the whole office—give people the idea I can be swayed by all kinds of outside pressure. Oh, you can bet I'd feel the effects of that soon enough! Besides—there's something that rules Krogstad right out at the bank as long as I'm the manager.

NORA: What's that?

HELMER: His moral failings I could maybe overlook if I had to—

NORA: Yes, Torvald, why not?

HELMER: And I hear he's quite efficient on the job. But he was a crony of mine back in my teens—one of those rash friendships that crop up again and again to embarrass you later in life. Well, I might as well say it straight out: We're on a first-name basis. And that tactless fool makes no effort at all to hide it in front of others. Quite the contrary—he thinks that entitles him to take a familiar air around me, and so every other second he comes booming out with his, "Yes, Torvald!" and "Sure thing, Torvald!" I tell you, it's been excruciating for me. He's out to make my place in the bank unbearable.

NORA: Torvald, you can't be serious about all this.

HELMER: Oh no? Why not?

NORA: Because these are such petty considerations.

HELMER: What are you saying? Petty? You think I'm petty!

NORA: No, just the opposite, Torvald dear. That's exactly why—

HELMER: Never mind. You call my motives petty; then I might as well be just that. Petty! All right! We'll put a stop to this for good. (*Goes to the hall door and calls.*) Helene!

NORA: What do you want?

HELMER (*searching among his papers*): A decision. (*The Maid comes in.*) Look here; take this letter; go out with it at once. Get hold of a messenger and have him deliver it. Quick now. It's already addressed. Wait, here's some money.

MAID: Yes, sir. (*She leaves with the letter.*)

HELMER (*straightening his papers*): There, now, little Miss Willful.

NORA (*breathlessly*): Torvald, what was that letter?

HELMER: Krogstad's notice.

NORA: Call it back, Torvald! There's still time. Oh, Torvald, call it back! Do it for my sake—for your sake, for the children's sake! Do you hear, Torvald; do it! You don't know how this can harm us.

HELMER: Too late.

NORA: Yes, too late.

HELMER: Nora, dear, I can forgive you this panic, even though basically you're insulting me. Yes, you are! Or isn't it an insult to think that *I* should be afraid of a courtroom hack's revenge? But I forgive you anyway, because this shows so beautifully how much you love me. (*Takes her in his arms.*) This is the way it should be, my darling Nora. Whatever comes, you'll see: When it really counts, I have strength and courage enough as a man to take on the whole weight myself.

NORA (*terrified*): What do you mean by that?

HELMER: The whole weight, I said.

NORA (*resolutely*): No, never in all the world.

HELMER: Good. So we'll share it, Nora, as man and wife. That's as it should be. (*Fondling her.*) Are you happy now? There, there, there—not these frightened dove's eyes. It's nothing at all but empty fantasies— Now you should run through your tarantella and practice your tambourine. I'll go to the inner office, and shut both doors, so I won't hear a thing; you can make all the noise you like. (*Turning in the doorway.*) And when Rank comes, just tell him where he can find me. (*He nods to her and goes with his papers into the study, closing the door.*)

NORA (*standing as though rooted, dazed with fright, in a whisper*): He really could do it. He will do it. He'll do it in spite of everything. No, not that, never, never! Anything but that! Escape! A way out—(*The doorbell rings.*) Dr. Rank! Anything but that! Anything, whatever it is! (*Her hands pass over her face, smoothing it; she pulls herself together, goes over and opens the hall door. Dr. Rank stands outside, hanging his fur coat up. During the following scene, it begins getting dark.*)

NORA: Hello, Dr. Rank. I recognized your ring. But you mustn't go in to Torvald yet; I believe he's working.

RANK: And you?

NORA: For you, I always have an hour to spare—you know that. (*He has entered, and she shuts the door after him.*)

RANK: Many thanks. I'll make use of these hours while I can.

NORA: What do you mean by that? While you can?

RANK: Does that disturb you?

NORA: Well, it's such an odd phrase. Is anything going to happen?

RANK: What's going to happen is what I've been expecting so long—but I honestly didn't think it would come so soon.

NORA (*gripping his arm*): What is it you've found out? Dr. Rank, you have to tell me!

RANK (*sitting by the stove*): It's all over with me. There's nothing to be done about it.

NORA (*breathing easier*): Is it you—then—?

RANK: Who else? There's no point in lying to one's self. I'm the most miserable of all my patients, Mrs. Helmer. These past few days I've been auditing my internal accounts. Bankrupt! Within a month I'll probably be laid out and rotting in the churchyard.

NORA: Oh, what a horrible thing to say.

RANK: The thing itself is horrible. But the worst of it is all the other horror before it's over. There's only one final examination left; when I'm finished with that, I'll know about when my disintegration will begin. There's something I want to say. Helmer with his sensitivity has such a sharp distaste for anything ugly. I don't want him near my sickroom.

NORA: Oh, but Dr. Rank—

RANK: I won't have him in there. Under no condition. I'll lock my door to him—As soon as I'm completely sure of the worst, I'll send you my calling card marked with a black cross, and you'll know then the wreck has started to come apart.

NORA: No, today you're completely unreasonable. And I wanted you so much to be in a really good humor.

RANK: With death up my sleeve? And then to suffer this way for somebody else's sins. Is there any justice in that? And in every single family, in some way or another, this inevitable retribution of nature goes on—

NORA (*her hands pressed over her ears*): Oh, stuff! Cheer up! Please—be gay!

RANK: Yes, I'd just as soon laugh at it all. My poor, innocent spine, serving time for my father's gay army days.

NORA (*by the table, left*): He was so infatuated with asparagus tips and pâté de foie gras, wasn't that it?

RANK: Yes—and with truffles.

NORA: Truffles, yes. And then with oysters, I suppose?

RANK: Yes, tons of oysters, naturally.

NORA: And then the port and champagne to go with it. It's so sad that all these delectable things have to strike at our bones.

RANK: Especially when they strike at the unhappy bones that never shared in the fun.

NORA: Ah, that's the saddest of all.

RANK (*looks searchingly at her*): Hm.

NORA (*after a moment*): Why did you smile?

RANK: No, it was you who laughed.

NORA: No, it was you who smiled, Dr. Rank!

RANK (*getting up*): You're even a bigger tease than I'd thought.

NORA: I'm full of wild ideas today.

RANK: That's obvious.

NORA (*putting both hands on his shoulders*): Dear, dear Dr. Rank, you'll never die for Torvald and me.

RANK: Oh, that loss you'll easily get over. Those who go away are soon forgotten.

NORA (*looks fearfully at him*): You believe that?

RANK: One makes new connections, and then—

NORA: Who makes new connections?

RANK: Both you and Torvald will when I'm gone. I'd say you're well under way already. What was that Mrs. Linde doing here last evening?

NORA: Oh, come—you can't be jealous of poor Kristine?

RANK: Oh yes, I am. She'll be my successor here in the house. When I'm down under, that woman will probably—

NORA: Shh! Not so loud. She's right in there.

RANK: Today as well. So you see.

NORA: Only to sew on my dress. Good gracious, how unreasonable you are. (*Sitting on the sofa.*) Be nice now, Dr. Rank. Tomorrow you'll see how beautifully I'll dance; and you can imagine then that I'm dancing only for you—yes, and of course for Torvald, too—that's understood. (*Takes various items out of the carton.*) Dr. Rank, sit over here and I'll show you something.

RANK (*sitting*): What's that?

NORA: Look here. Look.

RANK: Silk stockings.

NORA: Flesh-colored. Aren't they lovely? Now it's so dark here, but tomorrow—No, no, no, just look at the feet. Oh well, you might as well look at the rest.

RANK: Hm—

NORA: Why do you look so critical? Don't you believe they'll fit?

RANK: I've never had any chance to form an opinion on that.

NORA (*glancing at him a moment*): Shame on you. (*Hits him lightly on the ear with the stockings.*) That's for you. (*Puts them away again.*)

RANK: And what other splendors am I going to see now?

NORA: Not the least bit more, because you've been naughty. (*She hunts a little and rummages among her things.*)

RANK (*after a short silence*): When I sit here together with you like this, completely easy and open, then I don't know—I simply can't imagine—whatever would have become of me if I'd never come into this house.

NORA (*smiling*): Yes, I really think you feel completely at ease with us.

RANK (*more quietly, staring straight ahead*): And then to have to go away from it all—

NORA: Nonsense, you're not going away.

RANK (*his voice unchanged*): —and not even be able to leave some poor show of gratitude behind, scarcely a fleeting regret—no more than a vacant place that anyone can fill.

NORA: And if I asked you now for—No—

RANK: For what?

NORA: For a great proof of your friendship—

RANK: Yes, yes?

NORA: No, I mean—for an exceptionally big favor—

RANK: Would you really, for once, make me so happy?

NORA: Oh, you haven't the vaguest idea what it is.

RANK: All right, then tell me.

NORA: No, but I can't, Dr. Rank—it's all out of reason. It's advice and help, too—and a favor—

RANK: So much the better. I can't fathom what you're hinting at. Just speak out. Don't you trust me?

NORA: Of course. More than anyone else. You're my best and truest friend, I'm sure. That's why I want to talk to you. All right, then, Dr. Rank There's something you can help me prevent. You know how deeply, how inexpressibly dearly Torvald loves me; he'd never hesitate a second to give up his life for me.

RANK (*leaning close to her*): Nora—do you think he's the only one—

NORA (*with a slight start*): Who—?

RANK: Who'd gladly give up his life for you.

NORA (*heavily*): I see.

RANK: I swore to myself you should know this before I'm gone. I'll never find a better chance. Yes, Nora, now you know. And also you know now that you can trust me beyond anyone else.

NORA (*rising, natural and calm*): Let me by.

RANK (*making room for her, but still sitting*): Nora—

NORA (*in the hall doorway*): Helene, bring the lamp in. (*Goes over to the stove.*) Ah, dear Dr. Rank, that was really mean of you.

RANK (*getting up*): That I've loved you just as deeply as somebody else? Was *that* mean?

NORA: No, but that you came out and told me. That was quite unnecessary—

RANK: What do you mean? Have you known—?

(*The Maid comes in with the lamp, sets it on the table, and goes out again.*)

RANK: Nora—Mrs. Helmer—I'm asking you: Have you known about it?

NORA: Oh, how can I tell what I know or don't know? Really, I don't know what to say—Why did you have to be so clumsy, Dr. Rank! Everything was so good.

RANK: Well, in any case, you now have the knowledge that my body and soul are at your command. So won't you speak out?

NORA (*looking at him*): After that?

RANK: Please, just let me know what it is.

NORA: You can't know anything now.

RANK: I have to. You mustn't punish me like this. Give me the chance to do whatever is humanly possible for you.

NORA: Now there's nothing you can do for me. Besides, actually, I don't need any help. You'll see—it's only my fantasies. That's what it is. Of course! (*Sits in the rocker, looks at him, and smiles.*) What a nice one you are, Dr. Rank. Aren't you a little bit ashamed, now that the lamp is here?

Cheryl Campbell as Nora in the 1981–1982 Royal Shakespeare Company production of *A Doll House*.

RANK: No, not exactly. But perhaps I'd better go—for good?

NORA: No, you certainly can't do that. You must come here just as you always have. You know Torvald can't do without you.

RANK: Yes, but you?

NORA: You know how much I enjoy it when you're here.

RANK: That's precisely what threw me off. You're a mystery to me. So many times I've felt you'd almost rather be with me than with Helmer.

NORA: Yes—you see, there are some people that one loves most and other people that one would almost prefer being with.

RANK: Yes, there's something to that.

NORA: When I was back home, of course I loved Papa most. But I always thought it was so much fun when I could sneak down to the maids' quarters, because they never tried to improve me, and it was always so amusing, the way they talked to each other.

RANK: Aha, so it's their place that I've filled.

NORA (*jumping up and going to him*): Oh, dear, sweet Dr. Rank, that's not what I meant at all. But you can understand that with Torvald it's just the same as with Papa—

Nora and Torvald (Stephen Moore).

(*The Maid enters from the hall.*)

MAID: Ma'am—please! (*She whispers to Nora and hands her a calling card.*)

NORA (*glancing at the card*): Ah! (*Slips it into her pocket.*)

RANK: Anything wrong?

NORA: No, no, not at all. It's only some—it's my new dress—

RANK: Really? But—there's your dress.

NORA: Oh, that. But this is another one—I ordered it—Torvald mustn't know—

RANK: Ah, now we have the big secret.

NORA: That's right. Just go in with him—he's back in the inner study. Keep him there as long as—

RANK: Don't worry. He won't get away. (*Goes into the study.*)

NORA (*to the Maid*): And he's standing waiting in the kitchen?

MAID: Yes, he came up by the back stairs.

NORA: But didn't you tell him somebody was here?

MAID: Yes, but that didn't do any good.

NORA: He won't leave?

MAID: No, he won't go till he's talked with you, ma'am.

NORA: Let him come in, then—but quietly. Helene, don't breathe a word about this. It's a surprise for my husband.

MAID: Yes, yes, I understand—(*Goes out.*)

NORA: This horror—it's going to happen. No, no, no, it can't happen, it mustn't. (*She goes and bolts Helmer's door. The Maid opens the hall door for Krogstad and shuts it behind him. He is dressed for travel in a fur coat, boots, and a fur cap.*)

NORA (*going toward him*): Talk softly. My husband's home.

KROGSTAD: Well, good for him.

NORA: What do you want?

KROGSTAD: Some information.

NORA: Hurry up, then. What is it?

KROGSTAD: You know, of course, that I got my notice.

NORA: I couldn't prevent it, Mr. Krogstad. I fought for you to the bitter end, but nothing worked.

KROGSTAD: Does your husband's love for you run so thin? He knows everything I can expose you to, and all the same he dares to—

NORA: How can you imagine he knows anything about this?

KROGSTAD: Ah, no—I can't imagine it either, now. It's not at all like my fine Torvald Helmer to have so much guts—

NORA: Mr. Krogstad, I demand respect for my husband!

KROGSTAD: Why, of course—all due respect. But since the lady's keeping it so carefully hidden, may I presume to ask if you're also a bit better informed than yester-day about what you've actually done?

NORA: More than you ever could teach me.

KROGSTAD: Yes, I *am* such an awful lawyer.

NORA: What is it you want from me?

KROGSTAD: Just a glimpse of how you are, Mrs. Helmer. I've been thinking about you all day long. A cashier, a night-court scribbler, a—well, a type like me also has a little of what they call a heart, you know.

NORA: Then show it. Think of my children.

KROGSTAD: Did you or your husband ever think of mine? But never mind. I simply wanted to tell you that you don't need to take this thing too seriously. For the present, I'm not proceeding with any action.

NORA: Oh no, really! Well—I knew that.

KROGSTAD: Everything can be settled in a friendly spirit. It doesn't have to get around town at all; it can stay just among us three.

NORA: My husband must never know anything of this.

KROGSTAD: How can you manage that? Perhaps you can pay me the balance?

NORA: No, not right now.

KROGSTAD: Or you know some way of raising the money in a day or two?

NORA: No way that I'm willing to use.

KROGSTAD: Well, it wouldn't have done you any good, anyway. If you stood in front of me with a fistful of bills, you still couldn't buy your signature back.

NORA: Then tell me what you're going to do with it.

KROGSTAD: I'll just hold onto it—keep it on file. There's no outsider who'll even get wind of it. So if you've been thinking of taking some desperate step—

NORA: I have.

KROGSTAD: Been thinking of running away from home—

NORA: I have!

KROGSTAD: Or even of something worse—

NORA: How could you guess that?

KROGSTAD: You can drop those thoughts.

NORA: How could you guess I was thinking of *that*?

KROGSTAD: Most of us think about *that* at first. I thought about it too, but I discovered I hadn't the courage—

NORA (*lifelessly*): I don't either.

KROGSTAD (*relieved*): That's true, you haven't the courage? You too?

NORA: I don't have it—I don't have it.

KROGSTAD: It would be terribly stupid, anyway. After that first storm at home blows out, why, then—I have here in my pocket a letter for your husband—

NORA: Telling everything?

KROGSTAD: As charitably as possible.

NORA (*quickly*): He mustn't ever get that letter. Tear it up. I'll find some way to get money.

KROGSTAD: Beg pardon, Mrs. Helmer, but I think I just told you—

NORA: Oh, I don't mean the money I owe you. Let me know how much you want from my husband, and I'll manage it.

KROGSTAD: I don't want any money from your husband.

NORA: What do you want, then?

KROGSTAD: I'll tell you what. I want to recoup, Mrs. Helmer; I want to get on in the world—and there's where your husband can help me. For a year and a half I've kept myself clean of anything disreputable—all that time struggling with the worst conditions; but I was satisfied, working my way up step by step. Now I've been written right off, and I'm just not in the mood to come crawling back. I tell you, I want to move on. I want to get back in the bank—in a better position. Your husband can set up a job for me—

NORA: He'll never do that!

KROGSTAD: He'll do it. I know him. He won't dare breathe a word of protest. And once I'm in there together with him, you just wait and see! Inside of a year, I'll be the manager's right-hand man. It'll be Nils Krogstad, not Torvald Helmer, who runs the bank.

NORA: You'll never see the day!

KROGSTAD: Maybe you think you can—

NORA: I have the courage now—for *that*.

KROGSTAD: Oh, you don't scare me. A smart, spoiled lady like you—

NORA: You'll see; you'll see!

KROGSTAD: Under the ice, maybe? Down in the freezing, coal-black water? There, till you float up in the spring, ugly unrecognizable, with your hair falling out—

NORA: You don't frighten me.

KROGSTAD: Nor do you frighten me. One doesn't do these things, Mrs. Helmer. Besides what good would it be? I'd still have him safe in my pocket.

NORA: Afterwards? When I'm no longer—?

KROGSTAD: Are you forgetting that *I'll* be in control then over your final reputation? (*Nora stands speechless, staring at him.*) Good; now I've warned you. Don't do anything stupid. When Helmer's read my letter, I'll be waiting for his reply. And bear in mind that it's your husband himself who's forced me back to my old ways. I'll never forgive him for that. Good-bye, Mrs. Helmer. (*He goes out through the hall.*)

NORA (*goes to the hall door, opens it a crack, and listens*): He's gone. Didn't leave the letter. Oh no, no, that's impossible too! (*Opening the door more and more.*) What's that? He's standing outside—not going down-stairs. He's thinking it over? Maybe he'll—? (*A letter falls in the mailbox; then Krogstad's footsteps are heard, dying away down a flight of stairs. Nora gives a muffled cry and runs over toward the sofa table. A short pause.*) In the mailbox. (*Slips warily over to the hall door.*) It's lying there. Torvald, Torvald—now we're lost!

MRS. LINDE (*entering with the costume from the room, left*): There now, I can't see anything else to mend. Perhaps you'd like to try—

NORA (*in a hoarse whisper*): Kristine, come here.

MRS. LINDE (*tossing the dress on the sofa*): What's wrong? You look upset.

NORA: Come here. See that letter? There! Look—through the glass in the mailbox.

MRS. LINDE: Yes, yes, I see it.

NORA: That letter's from Krogstad—

MRS. LINDE: Nora—it's Krogstad who loaned you the money!

NORA: Yes, and now Torvald will find out everything.

MRS. LINDE: Believe me, Nora, it's best for both of you.

NORA: There's more you don't know. I forged a name.

MRS. LINDE: But for heaven's sake—?

NORA: I only want to tell you that, Kristine, so that you can be my witness.

MRS. LINDE: Witness? Why should I—?

NORA: If I should go out of my mind—it could easily happen—

MRS. LINDE: Nora!

NORA: Or anything else occurred—so I couldn't be present here—

MRS. LINDE: Nora, Nora, you aren't yourself at all!

NORA: And someone should try to take on the whole weight, all of the guilt, you follow me—

MRS. LINDE: Yes, of course, but why do you think—?

NORA: Then you're the witness that it isn't true, Kristine. I'm very much myself; my mind right now is perfectly clear; and I'm telling you: Nobody else has known about this; I alone did everything. Remember that.

MRS. LINDE: I will. But I don't understand all this.

NORA: Oh, how could you ever understand it? It's the miracle now that's going to take place.

MRS. LINDE: The miracle?

NORA: Yes, the miracle. But it's so awful, Kristine. It mustn't take place, not for anything in the world.

MRS. LINDE: I'm going right over and talk with Krogstad.

NORA: Don't go near him; he'll do you some terrible harm!

MRS. LINDE: There was a time once when he'd gladly have done anything for me.

NORA: He?

MRS. LINDE: Where does he live?

NORA: Oh, how do I know? Yes. (Searches in her pocket.) Here's his card. But the letter, the letter—!

HELMER (from the study, knocking on the door): Nora!

NORA (with a cry of fear): Oh! What is it? What do you want?

HELMER: Now, now, don't be so frightened. We're not coming in. You locked the door—are you trying on the dress?

NORA: Yes, I'm trying it. I'll look just beautiful, Torvald.

MRS. LINDE (who has read the card): He's living right around the corner.

NORA: Yes, but what's the use? We're lost. The letter's in the box.

MRS. LINDE: And your husband has the key?

NORA: Yes, always.

MRS. LINDE: Krogstad can ask for his letter back unread; he can find some excuse—

NORA: But it's just this time that Torvald usually—

MRS. LINDE: Stall him. Keep him in there. I'll be back as quick as I can. (She hurries out through the hall entrance.)

NORA (goes to Helmer's door, opens it, and peers in): Torvald!

HELMER (from the inner study): Well—does one dare set foot in one's own living room at last? Come on, Rank, now we'll get a look—(In the doorway.) But what's this?

NORA: What, Torvald dear?

HELMER: Rank had me expecting some grand masquerade.

RANK (in the doorway): That was my impression, but I must have been wrong.

NORA: No one can admire me in my splendor—not till tomorrow.

HELMER: But Nora dear, you look so exhausted. Have you practiced too hard?

NORA: No, I haven't practiced at all yet.

HELMER: You know, it's necessary—

NORA: Oh, it's absolutely necessary, Torvald. But I can't get anywhere without your help. I've forgotten the whole thing completely.

HELMER: Ah, we'll soon take care of that.

NORA: Yes, take care of me, Torvald, please! Promise me that? Oh, I'm so nervous. That big party—You must give up everything this evening for me. No business—don't even touch your pen. Yes? Dear Torvald, promise?

HELMER: It's a promise. Tonight I'm totally at your service—you little helpless thing. Hm—but first there's one thing I want to—(Goes toward the hall door.)

NORA: What are you looking for?

HELMER: Just to see if there's any mail.

NORA: No, no, don't do that, Torvald!

HELMER: Now what?

NORA: Torvald, please. There isn't any.

HELMER: Let me look, though. (Starts out. Nora, at the piano, strikes the first notes of the tarantella. Helmer, at the door, stops.) Aha!

NORA: I can't dance tomorrow if I don't practice with you.

HELMER (going over to her): Nora dear, are you really so frightened?

NORA: Yes, so terribly frightened. Let me practice right now; there's still time before dinner. Oh, sit down and play for me, Torvald. Direct me. Teach me, the way you always have.

HELMER: Gladly, if it's what you want. (Sits at the piano.)

NORA (snatches the tambourine up from the box, then a long, varicolored shawl, which she throws around herself, whereupon she springs forward and cries out): Play for me now! Now I'll dance!

(Helmer plays and Nora dances. Rank stands behind Helmer at the piano and looks on.)

HELMER (as he plays): Slower. Slow down.

NORA: Can't change it.

HELMER: Not so violent, Nora!

NORA: Has to be just like this.

HELMER (*stopping*): No, no, that won't do at all.

NORA (*laughing and swinging her tambourine*): Isn't that what I told you?

RANK: Let me play for her.

HELMER (*getting up*): Yes, go on. I can teach her more easily then.

(*Rank sits at the piano and plays, Nora dances more and more wildly. Helmer has stationed himself by the stove and repeatedly gives her directions; she seems not to hear them; her hair loosens and falls over her shoulders; she does not notice, but goes on dancing. Mrs. Linde enters.*)

MRS. LINDE (*standing dumbfounded at the door*): Ah—!

NORA (*still dancing*): See what fun, Kristine!

HELMER: But Nora darling, you dance as if your life were at stake.

NORA: And it is.

HELMER: Rank, stop! This is pure madness. Stop it, I say!

(*Rank breaks off playing, and Nora halts abruptly.*)

HELMER (*going over to her*): I never would have believed it. You've forgotten everything I taught you.

NORA (*throwing away the tambourine*): You see for yourself.

HELMER: Well, there's certainly room for instruction here.

NORA: Yes, you see how important it is. You've got to teach me to the very last minute. Promise me that, Torvald?

HELMER: You can bet on it.

NORA: You mustn't, either today or tomorrow, think about anything else but me; you mustn't open any letters—or the mailbox—

HELMER: Ah, it's still the fear of that man—

NORA: Oh yes, yes, that too.

HELMER: Nora, it's written all over you—there's already a letter from him out there.

NORA: I don't know. I guess so. But you mustn't read such things now; there mustn't be anything ugly between us before it's all over.

RANK (*quietly to Helmer*): You shouldn't deny her.

HELMER (*putting his arm around her*): The child can have her way. But tomorrow night, after you've danced—

NORA: Then you'll be free.

MAID (*in the doorway, right*): Ma'am, dinner is served.

NORA: We'll be wanting champagne, Helene.

MAID: Very good, ma'am. (*Goes out.*)

HELMER: So—a regular banquet, hm?

NORA: Yes, a banquet—champagne till daybreak! (*Calling out.*) And some macaroons, Helene. Heaps of them—just this once.

HELMER (*taking her hands*): Now, now, now—no hysterics. Be my own little lark again.

NORA: Oh, I will soon enough. But go on in—and you, Dr. Rank. Kristine, help me put up my hair.

RANK (*whispering, as they go*): There's nothing wrong—really wrong, is there?

HELMER: Oh, of course not. It's nothing more than this childish anxiety I was telling you about. (*They go out, right.*)

NORA: Well?

MRS. LINDE: Left town.

NORA: I could see by your face.

MRS. LINDE: He'll be home tomorrow evening. I wrote him a note.

NORA: You shouldn't have. Don't try to stop anything now. After all, it's a wonderful joy, this waiting here for the miracle.

MRS. LINDE: What is it you're waiting for?

NORA: Oh, you can't understand that. Go in to them; I'll be along in a moment.

(*Mrs. Linde goes into the dining room. Nora stands a short while as if composing herself; then she looks at her watch.*)

NORA: Five. Seven hours to midnight. Twenty-four hours to the midnight after, and then the tarantella's done. Seven and twenty-four? Thirty-one hours to live.

HELMER (*in the doorway, right*): What's become of the little lark?

NORA (*going toward him with open arms*): Here's your lark!

ACT III

(*Same scene. The table, with chairs around it, has been moved to the center of the room. A lamp on the table is lit. The hall door stands open. Dance music drifts down from the floor above. Mrs. Linde sits at the table, absently paging through a book, trying to read, but apparently unable to focus her thoughts. Once or twice she pauses, tensely listening for a sound at the outer entrance.*)

MRS. LINDE (*glancing at her watch*): Not yet—and there's hardly any time left. If only he's not—(*Listening again.*) Ah, there it is. (*She goes out in the hall and cautiously opens the outer door. Quiet footsteps are heard on the stairs. She whispers.*) Come in. Nobody's here.

KROGSTAD (*in the doorway*): I found a note from you at home. What's back of all this?

MRS. LINDE: I just *had* to talk to you.

KROGSTAD: Oh? And it just *had* to be here in this house?

MRS. LINDE: At my place it was impossible; my room hasn't a private entrance. Come in, we're all alone. The maid's asleep, and the Helmers are at the dance upstairs.

KROGSTAD (*entering the room*): Well, well, the Helmers are dancing tonight? Really?

MRS. LINDE: Yes, why not?

KROGSTAD: How true—why not?

MRS. LINDE: All right, Krogstad, let's talk.

KROGSTAD: Do we two have anything more to talk about?

MRS. LINDE: We have a great deal to talk about.

KROGSTAD: I wouldn't have thought so.

MRS. LINDE: No, because you've never understood me, really.

KROGSTAD: Was there anything more to understand—except what's all too common in life? A calculating woman throws over a man the moment a better catch comes by.

MRS. LINDE: You think I'm so thoroughly calculating? You think I broke it off lightly?

KROGSTAD: Didn't you?

MRS. LINDE: Nils—is that what you really thought?

KROGSTAD: If you cared, then why did you write me the way you did?

MRS. LINDE: What else could I do? If I had to break off with you, then it was my job as well to root out everything you felt for me.

KROGSTAD (*wringing his hands*): So that was it. And this—all this, simply for money!

MRS. LINDE: Don't forget I had a helpless mother and two small brothers. We couldn't wait for you, Nils; you had such a long road ahead of you then.

KROGSTAD: That may be; but you still hadn't the right to abandon me for somebody else's sake.

MRS. LINDE: Yes—I don't know. So many, many times I've asked myself if I did have that right.

KROGSTAD (*more softly*): When I lost you, it was as if all the solid ground dissolved from under my feet. Look at me; I'm a half-drowned man now, hanging onto a wreck.

MRS. LINDE: Help may be near.

KROGSTAD: It was near—but then you came and blocked it off.

MRS. LINDE: Without my knowing it, Nils. Today for the first time I learned that it's you I'm replacing at the bank.

KROGSTAD: All right—I believe you. But now that you know, will you step aside?

MRS. LINDE: No, because that wouldn't benefit you in the slightest.

KROGSTAD: Not "benefit" me, hm! I'd step aside anyway.

MRS. LINDE: I've learned to be realistic. Life and hard, bitter necessity have taught me that.

KROGSTAD: And life's taught me never to trust fine phrases.

MRS. LINDE: Then life's taught you a very sound thing. But you do have to trust in actions, don't you?

KROGSTAD: What does that mean?

MRS. LINDE: You said you were hanging on like a half-drowned man to a wreck.

KROGSTAD: I've good reason to say that.

MRS. LINDE: I'm also like a half-drowned woman on a wreck. No one to suffer with; no one to care for.

KROGSTAD: You made your choice.

MRS. LINDE: There wasn't any choice then.

KROGSTAD: So—what of it?

MRS. LINDE: Nils, if only we two shipwrecked people could reach across to each other.

KROGSTAD: What are you saying?

MRS. LINDE: Two on one wreck are at least better off than each on his own.

KROGSTAD: Kristine!

MRS. LINDE: Why do you think I came into town?

KROGSTAD: Did you really have some thought of me?

MRS. LINDE: I have to work to go on living. All my born days, as long as I can remember, I've worked, and it's been my best and my only joy. But now I'm completely alone in the world; it frightens me to be so empty and lost. To work for yourself—there's no joy in that. Nils, give me something—someone to work for.

KROGSTAD: I don't believe all this. It's just some hysterical feminine urge to go out and make a noble sacrifice.

MRS. LINDE: Have you ever found me to be hysterical?

KROGSTAD: Can you honestly mean this? Tell me—do you know everything about my past?

MRS. LINDE: Yes.

KROGSTAD: And you know what they think I'm worth around here.

MRS. LINDE: From what you were saying before, it would seem that with me you could have been another person.

KROGSTAD: I'm positive of that.

MRS. LINDE: Couldn't it happen still?

KROGSTAD: Kristine—you're saying this in all seriousness? Yes, you are! I can see it in you. And do you really have the courage, then—?

MRS. LINDE: I need to have someone to care for, and your children need a mother. We both need each other. Nils, I have faith that you're good at heart—I'll risk everything together with you.

KROGSTAD (*gripping her hands*): Kristine, thank you, thank you—Now I know I can win back a place in their eyes. Yes—but I forgot—

MRS. LINDE (*listening*): Shh! The tarantella. Go now! Go on!

KROGSTAD: Why? What is it?

MRS. LINDE: Hear the dance up there? When that's over, they'll be coming down.

KROGSTAD: Oh, then I'll go. But—it's all pointless. Of course, you don't know the move I made against the Helmers.

MRS. LINDE: Yes, Nils, I know.

KROGSTAD: And all the same, you have the courage to—?

MRS. LINDE: I know how far despair can drive a man like you.

KROGSTAD: Oh, if I only could take it all back.

MRS. LINDE: You easily could—your letter's still lying in the mailbox.

KROGSTAD: Are you sure of that?

MRS. LINDE: Positive. But—

KROGSTAD (*looks at her searchingly*): Is that the meaning of it, then? You'll save your friend at any price. Tell me straight out. Is that it?

MRS. LINDE: Nils—anyone who's sold herself for somebody else once isn't going to do it again.

KROGSTAD: I'll demand my letter back.

MRS. LINDE: No, no.

KROGSTAD: Yes, of course. I'll stay here till Helmer comes down; I'll tell him to give me my letter again—that it only involves my dismissal—that he shouldn't read it—

MRS. LINDE: No, Nils, don't call the letter back.

KROGSTAD: But wasn't that exactly why you wrote me to come here?

MRS. LINDE: Yes, in that first panic. But it's been a whole day and night since then, and in that time I've seen such incredible things in this house. Helmer's got to learn everything; this dreadful secret has to be aired; those two have to come to a full understanding; all these lies and evasions can't go on.

KROGSTAD: Well, then, if you want to chance it. But at least there's one thing I can do, and do right away—

MRS. LINDE (listening): Go now, go, quick! The dance is over. We're not safe another second.

KROGSTAD: I'll wait for you downstairs.

MRS. LINDE: Yes, please do; take me home.

KROGSTAD: I can't believe it; I've never been so happy. (He leaves by way of the outer door; the door between the room and the hall stays open.)

MRS. LINDE (straightening up a bit and getting together her street clothes): How different now! How different! Someone to work for, to live for—a home to build. Well, it is worth the try! Oh, if they'd only come! (Listening.) Ah, there they are. Bundle up. (She picks up her hat and coat. Nora's and Helmer's voices can be heard outside; a key turns in the lock, and Helmer brings Nora into the hall almost by force. She is wearing the Italian costume with a large black shawl about her; he has on evening dress, with a black domino open over it.)

NORA (struggling in the doorway): No, no, no, not inside! I'm going up again. I don't want to leave so soon.

HELMER: But Nora dear—

NORA: Oh, I beg you, please, Torvald. From the bottom of my heart, please—only an hour more!

HELMER: Not a single minute, Nora darling. You know our agreement. Come on, in we go; you'll catch cold out here. (In spite of her resistance, he gently draws her into the room.)

MRS. LINDE: Good evening.

NORA: Kristine!

HELMER: Why, Mrs. Linde—are you here so late?

MRS. LINDE: Yes, I'm sorry, but I did want to see Nora in costume.

NORA: Have you been sitting here, waiting for me?

MRS. LINDE: Yes. I didn't come early enough; you were all upstairs; and then I thought I really couldn't leave without seeing you.

HELMER (removing Nora's shawl): Yes, take a good look. She's worth looking at, I can tell you that, Mrs. Linde. Isn't she lovely?

MRS. LINDE: Yes, I should say—

HELMER: A dream of loveliness, isn't she? That's what everyone thought at the party, too. But she's horribly stubborn—this sweet little thing. What's to be done with her? Can you imagine, I almost had to use force to pry her away.

NORA: Oh, Torvald, you're going to regret you didn't indulge me, even for just a half hour more.

HELMER: There, you see. She danced her tarantella and got a tumultuous hand—which was well earned, although the performance may have been a bit too naturalistic—I mean it rather overstepped the proprieties of art. But never mind—what's important is, she made a success, an overwhelming success. You think I could let her stay on after that and spoil the effect? Oh no; I took my lovely little Capri girl—my capricious little Capri girl, I should say—took her under my arm; one quick tour of the ballroom, a curtsy to every side, and then—as they say in novels—the beautiful vision disappeared. An exit should always be effective, Mrs. Linde, but that's what I can't get Nora to grasp. Phew, It's hot in here. (Flings the domino on a chair and opens the door to his room.) Why's it dark in here? Oh yes, of course. Excuse me. (He goes in and lights a couple of candles.)

NORA (in a sharp, breathless whisper): So?

MRS. LINDE (quietly): I talked with him.

NORA: And—?

MRS. LINDE: Nora—you must tell your husband everything.

NORA (dully): I knew it.

MRS. LINDE: You've got nothing to fear from Krogstad, but you have to speak out.

NORA: I won't tell.

MRS. LINDE: Then the letter will.

NORA: Thanks, Kristine. I know now what's to be done. Shh!

HELMER (reentering): Well, then, Mrs. Linde—have you admired her?

MRS. LINDE: Yes, and now I'll say good night.

HELMER: Oh, come, so soon? Is this yours, this knitting?

MRS. LINDE: Yes, thanks. I nearly forgot it.

HELMER: Do you knit, then?

MRS. LINDE: Oh yes.

HELMER: You know what? You should embroider instead.

MRS. LINDE: Really? Why?

HELMER: Yes, because it's a lot prettier. See here, one holds the embroidery so, in the left hand, and then one guides the needle with the right—so—in an easy, sweeping curve—right?

MRS. LINDE: Yes, I guess that's—

HELMER: But, on the other hand, knitting—it can never be anything but ugly. Look, see here, the arms tucked in, the knitting needles going up and down—there's something Chinese about it. Ah, that was really a glorious champagne they served.

MRS. LINDE: Yes, good night, Nora, and don't be stubborn anymore.

HELMER: Well put, Mrs. Linde!

MRS. LINDE: Good night, Mr. Helmer.

HELMER (*accompanying her to the door*): Good night, good night. I hope you get home all right. I'd be very happy to—but you don't have far to go. Good night, good night. (*She leaves. He shuts the door after her and returns.*) There, now, at last we got her out the door. She's a deadly bore, that creature.

NORA: Aren't you pretty tired, Torvald?

HELMER: No, not a bit.

NORA: You're not sleepy?

HELMER: Not at all. On the contrary, I'm feeling quite exhilarated. But you? Yes, you really look tired and sleepy.

NORA: Yes, I'm very tired. Soon now I'll sleep.

HELMER: See! You see! I was right all along that we shouldn't stay longer.

NORA: Whatever you do is always right.

HELMER (*kissing her brow*): Now my little lark talks sense. Say, did you notice what a time Rank was having tonight?

NORA: Oh, was he? I didn't get to speak with him.

HELMER: I scarcely did either, but it's a long time since I've seen him in such high spirits. (*Gazes at her a moment, then comes nearer her.*) Hm—it's marvelous, though, to be back home again—to be completely alone with you. Oh, you bewitchingly lovely young woman!

NORA: Torvald, don't look at me like that!

HELMER: Can't I look at my richest treasure? At all that beauty that's mine, mine alone—completely and utterly.

NORA (*moving around to the other side of the table*): You mustn't talk to me that way tonight.

HELMER (*following her*): The tarantella is still in your blood. I can see—and it makes you even more enticing. Listen. The guests are beginning to go. (*Dropping his voice.*) Nora—it'll soon be quiet through this whole house.

NORA: Yes, I hope so.

HELMER: You do, don't you, my love? Do you realize—when I'm out at a party like this with you—do you know why I talk to you so little, and keep such a distance away; just send you a stolen look now and then—you know why I do it? It's because I'm imagining then that you're my secret darling, my secret young bride-to-be, and that no one suspects there's anything between us.

NORA: Yes, yes; oh, yes, I know you're always thinking of me.

HELMER: And then when we leave and I place the shawl over those fine young rounded shoulders—over that wonderful curving neck—then I pretend that you're my young bride, that we're just coming from the wedding, that for the first time I'm bringing you into my house—that for the first time I'm alone with you—completely alone with you, your trembling young beauty! All this evening I've longed for nothing but you. When I saw you turn and sway in the tarantella—my blood was pounding till I couldn't stand it—that's why I brought you down here so early—

NORA: Go away, Torvald! Leave me alone. I don't want all this.

HELMER: What do you mean? Nora, you're teasing me. You will, won't you? Aren't I your husband—?

(*A knock at the outside door.*)

NORA (*startled*): What's that?

HELMER (*going toward the hall*): Who is it?

RANK (*outside*): It's me. May I come in a moment?

HELMER (*with quiet irritation*): Oh, what does he want now? (*Aloud.*) Hold on. (*Goes and opens the door.*) Oh, how nice that you didn't just pass us by!

RANK: I thought I heard your voice, and then I wanted so badly to have a look in. (*Lightly glancing about.*) Ah, me, these old familiar haunts. You have it snug and cozy in here, you two.

HELMER: You seemed to be having it pretty cozy upstairs, too.

RANK: Absolutely. Why shouldn't I? Why not take in everything in life? As much as you can, anyway, and as long as you can. The wine was superb—

HELMER: The champagne especially.

RANK: You noticed that too? It's amazing how much I could guzzle down.

NORA: Torvald also drank a lot of champagne this evening.

RANK: Oh?

NORA: Yes, and that always makes him so entertaining.

RANK: Well, why shouldn't one have a pleasant evening after a well-spent day?

HELMER: Well spent? I'm afraid I can't claim that.

RANK (*slapping him on the back*): But I can, you see!

NORA: Dr. Rank, you must have done some scientific research today.

RANK: Quite so.

HELMER: Come now—little Nora talking about scientific research!

NORA: And can I congratulate you on the results?

RANK: Indeed you may.

NORA: Then they were good?

RANK: The best possible for both doctor and patient—certainty.

NORA (*quickly and searchingly*): Certainty?

RANK: Complete certainty. So don't I owe myself a gay evening afterwards?

NORA: Yes, you're right, Dr. Rank.

HELMER: I'm with you—just so long as you don't have to suffer for it in the morning.

RANK: Well, one never gets something for nothing in life.

NORA: Dr. Rank—are you very fond of masquerade parties?

RANK: Yes, if there's a good array of odd disguises—

NORA: Tell me, what should we two go as at the next masquerade?

HELMER: You little featherhead—already thinking of the next!

RANK: We two? I'll tell you what: You must go as Charmed Life—

HELMER: Yes, but find a costume for that!

RANK: Your wife can appear just as she looks every day.

HELMER: That was nicely put. But don't you know what you're going to be?

RANK: Yes, Helmer, I've made up my mind.

HELMER: Well?

RANK: At the next masquerade I'm going to be invisible.

HELMER: That's a funny idea.

RANK: They say there's a hat—black, huge—have you never heard of the hat that makes you invisible? You put it on, and then no one on earth can see you.

HELMER (*suppressing a smile*): Ah, of course.

RANK: But I'm quite forgetting what I came for. Helmer, give me a cigar, one of the dark Havanas.

HELMER: With the greatest pleasure. (*Holds out his case.*)

RANK: Thanks. (*Takes one and cuts off the tip.*)

NORA (*striking a match*): Let me give you a light.

RANK: Thank you. (*She holds the match for him; he lights the cigar.*) And now good-bye.

HELMER: Good-bye, good-bye, old friend.

NORA: Sleep well, Doctor.

RANK: Thanks for that wish.

NORA: Wish me the same.

RANK: You? All right, if you like—Sleep well. And thanks for the light. (*He nods to them both and leaves.*)

HELMER (*his voice subdued*): He's been drinking heavily.

NORA (*absently*): Could be. (*Helmer takes his keys from his pocket and goes out in the hall.*) Torvald—what are you after?

HELMER: Got to empty the mailbox; it's nearly full. There won't be room for the morning papers.

NORA: Are you working tonight?

HELMER: You know I'm not. Why—what's this? Someone's been at the lock.

NORA: At the lock—?

HELMER: Yes, I'm positive. What do you suppose—? I can't imagine one of the maids—? Here's a broken hairpin. Nora, it's yours—

NORA (*quickly*): Then it must be the children—

HELMER: You'd better break them of that. Hm, hm—well, opened it after all. (*Takes the contents out and calls into the kitchen.*) Helene! Helene, would you put out the lamp in the hall. (*He returns to the room, shutting the hall door, then displays the handful of mail.*) Look how it's piled up. (*Sorting through them.*) Now what's this?

NORA (*at the window*): The letter! Oh, Torvald, no!

HELMER: Two calling cards—from Rank.

NORA: From Dr. Rank?

HELMER (*examining them*): "Dr. Rank, Consulting Physician." They were on top. He must have dropped them in as he left.

NORA: Is there anything on them?

HELMER: There's a black cross over the name. See? That's a gruesome notion. He could almost be announcing his own death.

NORA: That's just what he's doing.

HELMER: What! You've heard something? Something he's told you?

NORA: Yes. That when those cards came, he'd be taking his leave of us. He'll shut himself in now and die.

HELMER: Ah, my poor friend! Of course I knew he wouldn't be here much longer. But so soon—And then to hide himself away like a wounded animal.

NORA: If it has to happen, then it's best it happens in silence—don't you think so, Torvald?

HELMER (*pacing up and down*): He's grown right into our lives. I simply can't imagine him gone. He with his suffering and loneliness—like a dark cloud setting off our sunlit happiness. Well, maybe it's best this way. For him, at least. (*Standing still.*) And maybe for us too, Nora. Now we're thrown back on each other, completely. (*Embracing her.*) Oh you, my darling wife, how can I hold you close enough? You know what, Nora—time and again I've wished you were in some terrible danger, just so I could stake my life and soul and everything, for your sake.

NORA (*tearing herself away, her voice firm and decisive*): Now you must read your mail, Torvald.

HELMER: No, no, not tonight. I want to stay with you, dearest.

NORA: With a dying friend on your mind?

HELMER: You're right. We've both had a shock. There's ugliness between us—these thoughts of death and corruption. We'll have to get free of them first. Until then—we'll stay apart.

NORA (*clinging about his neck*): Torvald—good night! Good night!

HELMER (*kissing her on the cheek*): Good night, little songbird. Sleep well, Nora. I'll be reading my mail now. (*He takes the letters into his room and shuts the door after him.*)

NORA (*with bewildered glances, groping about, seizing Helmer's domino, throwing it around her, and speaking in short, hoarse, broken whispers*): Never see him again. Never, never. (*Putting her shawl over her head.*) Never see the children either—them, too. Never, never. Oh, the freezing black water! The depths—down—Oh, I wish it were over—He has it now; he's reading it—now. Oh no, no, not yet. Torvald, good-bye, you and the children—(*She starts for the hall; as she does, Helmer throws open his door and stands with an open letter in his hand.*)

HELMER: Nora!

NORA (*screams*): Oh—!

HELMER: What is this? You know what's in this letter?

NORA: Yes, I know. Let me go! Let me out!

HELMER (*holding her back*): Where are you going?

NORA (*struggling to break loose*): You can't save me, Torvald!

HELMER (*slumping back*): True! Then it's true what he writes? How horrible! No, no, it's impossible—it can't be true.

NORA: It *is* true. I've loved you more than all this world.

HELMER: Ah, none of your slippery tricks.

NORA (*taking one step toward him*): Torvald—!

HELMER: What *is* this you've blundered into!

NORA: Just let me loose. You're not going to suffer for my sake. You're not going to take on my guilt.

HELMER: No more playacting. (*Locks the hall door.*) You stay right here and give me a reckoning. You understand what you've done? Answer! You understand?

NORA (*looking squarely at him, her face hardening*): Yes. I'm beginning to understand everything now.

HELMER (*striding about*): Oh, what an awful awakening! In all these eight years—she who was my pride and joy—a hypocrite, a liar—worse, worse—a criminal! How infinitely disgusting it all is! The shame! (*Nora says nothing and goes on looking straight at him. He stops in front of her.*) I should have suspected something of the kind. I should have known. All your father's flimsy values—Be still! All your father's flimsy values have come out in you. No religion, no morals, no sense of duty—Oh, how I'm punished for letting him off! I did it for your sake, and you repay me like this.

NORA: Yes, like this.

HELMER: Now you've wrecked all my happiness—ruined my whole future. Oh, it's awful to think of. I'm in a cheap little grafter's hands; he can do anything he wants with me, ask for anything, play with me like a puppet—and I can't breathe a word. I'll be swept down miserably into the depths on account of a featherbrained woman.

NORA: When I'm gone from this world, you'll be free.

HELMER: Oh, quit posing. Your father had a mess of those speeches too. What good would that ever do me if you were gone from this world, as you say? Not the slightest. He can still make the whole thing known; and if he does, I could be falsely suspected as your accomplice. They might even think that I was behind it—that I put you up to it. And all that I can thank you for—you that I've coddled the whole of our marriage. Can you see now what you've done to me?

NORA (*icily calm*): Yes.

HELMER: It's so incredible, I just can't grasp it. But we'll have to patch up whatever we can. Take off the shawl. I said, take it off! I've got to appease him somehow or other. The thing has to be hushed up at any cost. And as for you and me, it's got to seem like everything between us is just as it was—to the outside world, that is. You'll go right on living in this house, of course. But you can't be allowed to bring up the children; I don't dare trust you with them—Oh, to have to say this to someone I've loved so much! Well, that's done with. From now on happiness doesn't matter; all that matters is saving the bits and pieces, the appearance—(*The doorbell rings. Helmer starts.*) What's that? And so late. Maybe the worst—? You think he'd—? Hide, Nora! Say you're sick. (*Nora remains standing motionless. Helmer goes and opens the door.*)

MAID (*half dressed, in the hall*): A letter for Mrs. Helmer.

HELMER: I'll take it. (*Snatches the letter and shuts the door.*) Yes, it's from him. You don't get it; I'm reading it myself.

NORA: Then read it.

HELMER (*by the lamp*): I hardly dare. We may be ruined, you and I. But—I've got to know. (*Rips open the letter, skims through a few lines, glances at an enclosure, then cries out joyfully.*) Nora! (*Nora looks inquiringly at him.*) Nora! Wait—better check it again—Yes, yes, it's true. I'm saved. Nora, I'm saved!

NORA: And I?

HELMER: You too, of course. We're both saved, both of us. Look. He's sent back your note. He says he's sorry and ashamed—that a happy development in his life—oh, who cares what he says! Nora, we're saved! No one can hurt you. Oh, Nora, Nora—but first, this ugliness all has to go. Let me see—(*Takes a look at the note.*) No, I don't want to see it; I want the whole thing to fade like a dream. (*Tears the note and both letters to pieces, throws them into the stove and watches them burn.*) There—now there's nothing left—He wrote that since Christmas Eve you—Oh, they must have been three terrible days for you, Nora.

NORA: I fought a hard fight.

HELMER: And suffered pain and saw no escape but—No, we're not going to dwell on anything unpleasant. We'll just be grateful and keep on repeating: It's over now, it's over! You hear me, Nora? You don't seem to realize—it's over. What's it mean—that frozen look? Oh, poor little Nora, I understand. You can't believe I've forgiven you. But I have, Nora; I swear I have. I know that what you did, you did out of love for me.

NORA: That's true.

HELMER: You loved me the way a wife ought to love her husband. It's simply the means that you couldn't judge. But you think I love you any the less for not knowing how to handle your affairs? No, no—just lean on me; I'll guide you and teach you. I wouldn't be a man if this feminine helplessness didn't make you twice as attractive to me. You mustn't mind those sharp words I said—that was all in the first confusion of thinking my world had collapsed. I've forgiven you, Nora; I swear I've forgiven you.

NORA: My thanks for your forgiveness. (*She goes out through the door, right.*)

HELMER: No, wait—(*Peers in.*) What are you doing in there?

NORA (*inside*): Getting out of my costume.

HELMER (*by the open door*): Yes, do that. Try to calm yourself and collect your thoughts again, my frightened little songbird. You can rest easy now; I've got wide wings to shelter you with. (*Walking about close by the door.*) How snug and nice our home is, Nora. You're safe here; I'll keep you like a hunted dove I've rescued out of a hawk's claws. I'll bring peace to your poor, shuddering heart. Gradually it'll happen, Nora;

you'll see. Tomorrow all this will look different to you; then everything will be as it was. I won't have to go on repeating I forgive you; you'll feel it for yourself. How can you imagine I'd ever conceivably want to disown you—or even blame you in any way? Ah, you don't know a man's heart, Nora. For a man there's something indescribably sweet and satisfying in knowing he's forgiven his wife—and forgiven her out of a full and open heart. It's as if she belongs to him in two ways now: In a sense he's given her fresh into the world again, and she's become his wife and his child as well. From now on that's what you'll be to me—you little, bewildered, helpless thing. Don't be afraid of anything, Nora; just open your heart to me, and I'll be conscience and will to you both—(*Nora enters in her regular clothes.*) What's this? Not in bed? You've changed your dress?

NORA: Yes, Torvald, I've changed my dress.

HELMER: But why now, so late?

NORA: Tonight I'm not sleeping.

HELMER: But Nora dear—

NORA (*looking at her watch*): It's still not so very late. Sit down, Torvald; we have a lot to talk over. (*She sits at one side of the table.*)

HELMER: Nora—what is this? That hard expression—

NORA: Sit down. This'll take some time. I have a lot to say.

HELMER (*sitting at the table directly opposite her*): You worry me, Nora. And I don't understand you.

NORA: No, that's exactly it. You don't understand me. And I've never understood you either—until tonight. No, don't interrupt. You can just listen to what I say. We're closing out accounts, Torvald.

HELMER: How do you mean that?

NORA (*after a short pause*): Doesn't anything strike you about our sitting here like this?

HELMER: What's that?

NORA: We've been married now eight years. Doesn't it occur to you that this is the first time we two, you and I, man and wife, have ever talked seriously together?

HELMER: What do you mean—seriously?

NORA: In eight whole years—longer even—right from our first acquaintance, we've never exchanged a serious word on any serious thing.

HELMER: You mean I should constantly go and involve you in problems you couldn't possibly help me with?

NORA: I'm not talking of problems. I'm saying that we've never sat down seriously together and tried to get to the bottom of anything.

HELMER: But dearest, what good would that ever do you?

NORA: That's the point right there: You've never understood me. I've been wronged greatly, Torvald—first by Papa, and then by you.

HELMER: What! By us—the two people who've loved you more than anyone else?

NORA (*shaking her head*): You never loved me. You've thought it fun to be in love with me, that's all.

HELMER: Nora, what a thing to say!

NORA: Yes, it's true now, Torvald. When I lived at home with Papa, he told me all his opinions, so I had the same ones too; or if they were different I hid them, since he wouldn't have cared for that. He used to call me his doll-child, and he played with me the way I played with my dolls. Then I came into your house—

HELMER: How can you speak of our marriage like that?

NORA (*unperturbed*): I mean, then I went from Papa's hands into yours. You arranged everything to your own taste, and so I got the same taste as you—or I pretended to; I can't remember. I guess a little of both, first one, then the other. Now when I look back, it seems as if I'd lived here like a beggar—just from hand to mouth. I've lived by doing tricks for you, Torvald. But that's the way you wanted it. It's a great sin what you and Papa did to me. You're to blame that nothing's become of me.

HELMER: Nora, how unfair and ungrateful you are! Haven't you been happy here?

NORA: No, never. I thought so—but I never have.

HELMER: Not—not happy!

NORA: No, only lighthearted. And you've always been so kind to me. But our home's been nothing but a playpen. I've been your doll-wife here, just as at home I was Papa's doll-child. And in turn the children have been my dolls. I thought it was fun when you played with me, just as they thought it fun when I played with them. That's been our marriage, Torvald.

HELMER: There's some truth in what you're saying—under all the raving exaggeration. But it'll all be different after this. Playtime's over; now for the schooling.

NORA: Whose schooling—mine or the children's?

HELMER: Both yours and the children's, dearest.

NORA: Oh, Torvald, you're not the man to teach me to be a good wife to you.

HELMER: And you can say that?

NORA: And I—how am I equipped to bring up children?

HELMER: Nora!

NORA: Didn't you say a moment ago that that was no job to trust me with?

HELMER: In a flare of temper! Why fasten on that?

NORA: Yes, but you were so very right. I'm not up to the job. There's another job I have to do first. I have to try to educate myself. You can't help me with that. I've got to do it alone. And that's why I'm leaving you now.

HELMER (*jumping up*): What's that?

NORA: I have to stand completely alone, if I'm ever going to discover myself and the world out there. So I can't go on living with you.

HELMER: Nora, Nora!

NORA: I want to leave right away. Kristine should put me up for the night—

HELMER: You're insane! You've no right! I forbid you!

NORA: From here on, there's no use forbidding me anything. I'll take with me whatever is mine. I don't want a thing from you, either now or later.

HELMER: What kind of madness is this!

NORA: Tomorrow I'm going home—I mean, home where I came from. It'll be easier up there to find something to do.

HELMER: Oh, you blind, incompetent child!

NORA: I must learn to be competent, Torvald.

HELMER: Abandon your home, your husband, your children! And you're not even thinking what people will say.

NORA: I can't be concerned about that. I only know how essential this is.

HELMER: Oh, it's outrageous. So you'll run out like this on your most sacred vows.

NORA: What do you think are my most sacred vows?

HELMER: And I have to tell you that! Aren't they your duties to your husband and children?

NORA: I have other duties equally sacred.

HELMER: That isn't true. What duties are they?

NORA: Duties to myself.

HELMER: Before all else, you're a wife and a mother.

NORA: I don't believe in that anymore. I believe that before all else, I'm a human being, no less than you—or anyway, I ought to try to become one. I know the majority thinks you're right, Torvald, and plenty of books agree with you, too. But I can't go on believing what the majority says, or what's written in books. I have to think over these things myself and try to understand them.

HELMER: Why can't you understand your place in your own home? On a point like that, isn't there one everlasting guide you can turn to? Where's your religion?

NORA: Oh, Torvald, I'm really not sure what religion is.

HELMER: What—?

NORA: I only know what the minister said when I was confirmed. He told me religion was this thing and that. When I get clear and away by myself, I'll go into that problem too. I'll see if what the minister said was right, or, in any case, if it's right for me.

HELMER: A young woman your age shouldn't talk like that. If religion can't move you, I can try to rouse your conscience. You do have some moral feeling? Or, tell me—has that gone too?

NORA: It's not easy to answer that, Torvald. I simply don't know. I'm all confused about these things. I just know I see them so differently from you. I find out for one thing, that the law's not at all what I'd thought—but I can't get it through my head that the law is fair. A woman hasn't a right to protect her dying father or save her husband's life! I can't believe that.

HELMER: You talk like a child. You don't know anything of the world you live in.

NORA: No, I don't. But now I'll begin to learn for myself. I'll try to discover who's right, the world or I.

HELMER: Nora, you're sick; you've got a fever. I almost think you're out of your head.

NORA: I've never felt more clearheaded and sure in my life.

HELMER: And—clearheaded and sure—you're leaving your husband and children?

NORA: Yes.

Janet McTeer as Nora Helmer in Anthony Page's production of *A Doll House* at the Belasco Theater on Broadway, 1997. McTeer's interpretation of the role electrified audiences, who, according to Ben Brantley, found "previously hidden nuances in Ibsen's landmark work."

HELMER: Then there's only one possible reason.

NORA: What?

HELMER: You no longer love me.

NORA: No. That's exactly it.

HELMER: Nora! You can't be serious!

NORA: Oh, this is so hard, Torvald—you've been so kind to me always. But I can't help it. I don't love you anymore.

HELMER (*struggling for composure*): Are you also clearheaded and sure about that?

NORA: Yes, completely. That's why I can't go on staying here.

HELMER: Can you tell me what I did to lose your love?

NORA: Yes, I can tell you. It was this evening when the miraculous thing didn't come—then I knew you weren't the man I'd imagined.

HELMER: Be more explicit; I don't follow you.

NORA: I've waited now so patiently eight long years—for, my Lord, I know miracles don't come every day. Then this crisis broke over me, and such a certainty filled me: *Now* the miraculous event would occur. While Krogstad's letter was lying out there, I never for an instant dreamed that you could give in to his terms. I was so utterly sure you'd say to him: Go on, tell your tale to the whole wide world. And when he'd done that—

HELMER: Yes, what then? When I'd delivered my own wife into shame and disgrace—!

NORA: When he'd done that, I was so utterly sure that you'd step forward, take the blame on yourself and say: I am the guilty one.

HELMER: Nora—!

NORA: You're thinking I'd never accept such a sacrifice from you? No, of course not. But what good would my protests be against you? That was the miracle I was waiting for, in terror and hope. And to stave that off, I would have taken my life.

HELMER: I'd gladly work for you day and night, Nora—and take on pain and deprivation. But there's no one who gives up honor for love.

NORA: Millions of women have done just that.

HELMER: Oh, you think and talk like a silly child.

NORA: Perhaps. But you neither think nor talk like the man I could join myself to. When your big fright was over—and it wasn't from any threat against me, only for what might damage you—when all the danger was past, for you it was just as if nothing had happened. I was exactly the same, your little lark, your doll, that you'd have to handle with double care now that I'd turned out so brittle and frail. (*Gets up.*) Torvald—in that instant it dawned on me that for eight years I've been living here with a stranger, and that I'd even conceived three children—oh, I can't stand the thought of it! I could tear myself to bits.

HELMER (*heavily*): I see. There's a gulf that's opened between us—that's clear. Oh, but Nora, can't we bridge it somehow?

NORA: The way I am now, I'm no wife for you.

HELMER: I have the strength to make myself over.

NORA: Maybe—if your doll gets taken away.

HELMER: But to part! To part from you! No, Nora, no—I can't imagine it.

NORA (*going out, right*): All the more reason why it has to be. (*She reenters with her coat and a small overnight bag, which she puts on a chair by the table.*)

HELMER: Nora, Nora, not now! Wait till tomorrow.

NORA: I can't spend the night in a strange man's room.

HELMER: But couldn't we live here like brother and sister—

NORA: You know very well how long that would last. (*Throws her shawl about her.*) Good-bye, Torvald. I won't look in on the children. I know they're in better hands than mine. The way I am now, I'm no use to them.

HELMER: But someday, Nora—someday—?

NORA: How can I tell? I haven't the least idea what'll become of me.

HELMER: But you're my wife, now and wherever you go.

NORA: Listen, Torvald—I've heard that when a wife deserts her husband's house just as I'm doing, then the law frees him from all responsibility. In any case, I'm freeing you from being responsible. Don't feel yourself bound, any more than I will. There has to be absolute freedom for us both. Here, take your ring back. Give me mine.

HELMER: That too?

NORA: That too.

HELMER: There it is.

NORA: Good. Well, now it's all over. I'm putting the keys here. The maids know all about keeping up the house—better than I do. Tomorrow, after I've left town, Kristine will stop by to pack up everything that's mine from home. I'd like those things shipped up to me.

HELMER: Over! All over! Nora, won't you ever think about me?

NORA: I'm sure I'll think of you often, and about the children and the house here.

HELMER: May I write you?

NORA: No—never. You're not to do that.

HELMER: Oh, but let me send you—

NORA: Nothing. Nothing.

HELMER: Or help you if you need it.

NORA: No. I accept nothing from strangers.

HELMER: Nora—can I never be more than a stranger to you?

NORA (*picking up the overnight bag*): Ah, Torvald—it would take the greatest miracle of all—

HELMER: Tell me the greatest miracle!

NORA: You and I both would have to transform ourselves to the point that—Oh, Torvald, I've stopped believing in miracles.

HELMER: But I'll believe. Tell me! Transform ourselves to the point that—?

NORA: That our living together could be a true marriage. (*She goes out down the hall.*)

HELMER (*sinks down on a chair by the door, face buried in his hands*): Nora! Nora! (*Looking about and rising.*) Empty. She's gone. (*A sudden hope leaps in him.*) The greatest miracle—?

(*From below, the sound of a door slamming shut.*)

COMMENTARIES

Ibsen wrote about his own work, both in his letters to producers and actors and in his notes describing the development of his plays. Such notes reveal his concern, his insights as he wrote the plays, and his motives. Sometimes what he says about the plays does not completely square with modern interpretations. On the other hand, he explains in his notes that the circumstances of women in modern society were much on his mind when he was working on *A Doll House*.

Ibsen's "Notes for the Modern Tragedy" is remarkable for suggesting a separate sensibility (spiritual law) for men and for women. His observations about the society in which women live—and in which Nora is confounded—sound as if they could have been written a century later than they were. Muriel C. Bradbrook's discussion of *A Doll House* focuses on the moral bankruptcy of Nora's situation, which is to say the situation of all wives of the period.

Henrik Ibsen (1828–1906)
NOTES FOR THE MODERN TRAGEDY   1878

TRANSLATED BY A. G. CHATER

Ibsen's first notes for A Doll House *were jotted down on October 19, 1878. They show that his thinking on the relations between men and women was considerably sophisticated and that the material for the play had been gestating. His comments indicate that the essentially male society he knew was one of his central concerns in the play.*

There are two kinds of spiritual law, two kinds of conscience, one in man and another, altogether different, in woman. They do not understand each other; but in practical life the woman is judged by man's law, as though she were not a woman but a man.

The wife in the play ends by having no idea of what is right or wrong; natural feeling on the one hand and belief in authority on the other have altogether bewildered her.

A woman cannot be herself in the society of the present day, which is an exclusively masculine society, with laws framed by men and with a judicial system that judges feminine conduct from a masculine point of view.

She has committed forgery, and she is proud of it; for she did it out of love for her husband, to save his life. But this husband with his commonplace principles of honor is on the side of the law and looks at the question from the masculine point of view.

Spiritual conflicts. Oppressed and bewildered by the belief in authority, she loses faith in her moral right and ability to bring up her children. Bitterness. A mother in modern society, like certain insects who go away and die when she has done her duty in the propagation of the race. Love of life, of home, of husband and children and family. Now and then a womanly shaking off of her thoughts. Sudden return of anxiety and terror. She must bear it all alone. The catastrophe approaches, inexorably, inevitably. Despair, conflict, and destruction.

(Krogstad has acted dishonorably and thereby become well-to-do; now his prosperity does not help him, he cannot recover his honor.)

Muriel C. Bradbrook (1909–1993)
A DOLL'S HOUSE: IBSEN THE MORALIST   *1948*

In her important study of Ibsen, Ibsen: The Norwegian, *Muriel C. Bradbrook discusses all the important plays, but she reserves a special place for* A Doll House. *In her analysis she suggests that Nora slowly discovers the fundamental bankruptcy of her marriage. Bradbrook calls it "eight years' prostitution." She also shows the true extent of Torvald's possessiveness and immaturity. As Bradbrook says, the true moment of recognition — in the Greek tragic sense — occurs when Nora sees both herself and Torvald in their true nature. Bradbrook also helps us see the full implication of Nora's leaving her home. She can never hope again for the comforts she has enjoyed as Torvald's wife.*

Poor Nora, living by playing her tricks like a little pet animal, sensing how to manage Torvald by those pettinesses in his character she does not know she knows of, is too vulnerably sympathetic to find her life-work in reading John Stuart Mill. At the end she still does not understand the strange world in which she has done wrong by forging a signature. She does understand that she has lived by what Virginia Woolf called "the slow waterlogged sinking of her will into his." And this picture is built up for her and for us by the power of structural implication, a form of writing particularly suited to drama, where the latent possibilities of a long stretch of past time can be thrown into relief by a crisis. In *A Doll's House,* the past is not only lighted up by the present, as a transparency might be lit up with a lamp; the past is changed by the present so that it becomes a different thing. Nora's marriage becomes eight years' prostitution, as she gradually learns the true nature of her relations with Torvald and the true nature of Torvald's feelings for her.

In act I, no less than six different episodes bring out the war that is secretly waged between his masculine dictatorship and her feminine wiles:

Her wheedling him for money with a simple transference: "Let us do as *you* suggest. . . ."

Her promise to Christine: "Just leave it to me: I will broach the matter very cleverly." She is evidently habituated to and aware of her own technique.

Her description of how she tried to coax Torvald into taking the holiday and how she was saving up the story of the bond "for when I am no longer as good-looking as I am now." She knows the precarious nature of her hold.

Her method of asking work for Christine by putting Christine also into a (completely bogus) position of worshiping subservience to Torvald.

Her boast to Krogstad about her influence. Whilst this may be a justifiable triumph over her tormentor, it is an unconscious betrayal of Torvald (witness his fury in act II at the idea of being thought uxorious).

After this faceted exposition, the treatment grows much broader. Nora admits Torvald's jealousy: Yet she flirts with Rank, aware but not acknowledging the grounds of her control. The pressure of implication remains constant throughout: It is comparable with the effect of a dialect, coloring all that is said. To take a few lines at random from the dialogue of Nora and Rank in act II:

> NORA (*putting her hand on his shoulder*): Dear, dear Dr. Rank! Death mustn't take you away from Torvald and me. [Nora is getting demonstrative as she senses Rank's responsiveness, and her hopes of obtaining a loan from him rise. Hence her warmth of feeling, purely seductive.]
> RANK: It is a loss you will easily recover from. Those who are gone away are soon forgotten. [Poor Rank is reminded by that "Torvald and me" how little he really counts to Nora.]
> NORA (*anxiously*): Do you believe that? [Rank has awakened her thoughts of what may happen if *she* has to go away.]

Her methods grow more desperate—the open appeal to Torvald to keep Krogstad and the frantic expedient of the tarantella. In the last act her fate is upon her; yet in spite of all her terror and Torvald's tipsy amorousness, she still believes in his chivalry and devotion. This extraordinary self-deception is perhaps the subtlest and most telling implication of all. Practice had left her theory unshaken: So when the crash comes, she cries, "I have been living with a strange man," yet it was but the kind of man her actions had always implied him to be. Her vanity had completely prevented her from recognizing what she was doing, even though she had become such an expert at doing it.

Torvald is more gradually revealed. In the first act he appears indulgent, perhaps a trifle inclined to nag about the macaroons and to preach, but virtually a more efficient David Copperfield curbing a rather better-trained Dora. In the second act, his resentment and his pleasure alike uncover the deeper bases of his dominance. His anger at the prospect of being thought under his wife's influence and his fury at the imputation of narrow-mindedness show that it is really based on his own cowardice, the need for something weaker to bully: This is confirmed when he gloats over Nora's panic as evidence of her love for him, and over her agitation in the tarantella ("you little helpless thing!"). His love of order and his fastidiousness, when joined to such qualities, betray a set personality; and the last act shows that he has neither control nor sympathy on the physical level. But he is no fool, and his integrity is not all cowardice. Doubtless, debt or forgery really was abhorrent to him.

The climax of the play comes when Nora sees Torvald and sees herself: It is an *anagnorisis*, a recognition. Her life is cored like an apple. For she has had no life apart from this. Behind the irrelevant program for self-education there stands a woman, pitifully inexperienced, numbed by emotional shock, but with a newfound will to face what has happened, to accept her bankruptcy, as, in a very different way, Peer Gynt had at last accepted his.

"Yes, I am beginning to understand. . . ." she says. "What you did," observes the now magnanimous Torvald, "you did out of love for me." "That is true," says Nora: And she calls him to a "settling of accounts," not in any spirit of hostility but in an attempt to organize vacancy. "I have made nothing of my life. . . . I must stand quite alone . . . it is necessary to me . . ." That is really the program. *Ainsi tout leur a craqué dans les mains.*°

The spare and laminated speech gains its effect by inference and riddle. But these are the characteristic virtues of Norse. Irony is its natural weapon. Ibsen was working with the grain of the language. It was no accident that it fell to a Norwegian to take that most finely tooled art, the drama, and bring it to a point and precision so nice that literally not a phrase is without its direct contribution to the structure. The unrelenting cohesion of *A Doll's House* is perhaps, like that of the *Oedipus the King,* too hard on the playgoer; he is allowed no relief. Nora cannot coo to her baby without saying: "My sweet little *baby doll!*" or play with her children without choosing, significantly, *Hide and Seek.* Ibsen will not allow the smallest action to escape from the psychopathology of everyday life. However, a play cannot be acted so that every moment is tense with significance, and, in practice, an actor, for the sake of light and shade, will probably slur some of Ibsen's points, deliberately or unconsciously. The tension between the characters is such that the slightest movement of one sets all the others quivering. But this is partly because they are seen with such detachment, like a clear-cut intaglio. The play is, above all, articulated.

That is not to say that it is the mere dissection of a problem. Perhaps Rank and Mrs. Linde would have been more subtly wrought into the action at a later date; but the tight control kept over Nora and Torvald does not mean that they can be exhausted by analysis or staled by custom. They are so far in advance of the characters of *Pillars of Society* that they are capable of the surprising yet inevitable development that marks the character conceived "in the round," the character that is, in Ibsen's phrase, fully "seen."

Consider, for example, Torvald's soliloquy whilst Nora is taking off her masquerade dress. It recalls at one moment Dickens's most unctuous hypocrites — "Here I will protect you like a hunted dove that I have saved from the claws of the hawk!" — at another Meredith's Willoughby Patterne° — "Only be frank and open with me and I will be both will and conscience to you" — yet from broadest caricature to sharpest analysis, it remains the self-glorified strut of the one character, the bank clerk in his pride, cousin to Peer Gynt, that typical Norwegian, and to Hjalmer Ekdal, the toiling breadwinner of the studio.

Whilst the Ibsenites might have conceded that Torvald is Art, they would probably have contended that Nora is Truth. Nora, however, is much more than a Revolting Wife. She is not a sour misanthropist or a fighting suffragette, but a lovely young woman who knows that she still holds her husband firmly infatuated after eight years of marriage. . . .

In leaving her husband Nora is seeking a fuller life as a human being. She is emancipating herself. Yet the seeking itself is also a renunciation, a kind of death — "I must stand alone." No less than Falk, or the hero of *On the Vidda,* she gives up something that has been her whole life. She is as broken as Torvald in the end: But she is a strong character and he is a weak one. In the "happy ending" which Ibsen

---

Ainsi . . . mains: Thus everything has shattered in their hands.
Willoughby Patterne: The protagonist in George Meredith's novel *The Egoist* (1879), an arrogant aristocrat who lacks awareness of the needs and desires of the women in his life.

reluctantly allowed to be used, it was the sight of the children that persuaded her to stay, and unless it is remembered that leaving Torvald means leaving the children, the full measure of Nora's decision cannot be taken. An actress gets her chance to make this point in the reply to Torvald's plea that Nora should stay for the children's sake.

It should be remembered, too, that the seriousness of the step she takes is lost on the present generation. She was putting herself outside society, inviting insult, destitution, and loneliness. She went out into a very dark night.

August Strindberg

The Swedish playwright August Strindberg (1849–1912) wrote fifty-eight plays, more than a dozen novels, and more than a hundred short stories, all collected now in fifty-five volumes. Much of the time he was producing this astonishing body of work, he was the victim of persistent paranoia, suffered the destruction of three marriages, and lived through a major nervous breakdown.

He was a man of enormous complexity whose work has traditionally been broken into two parts. The first consists of the work he wrote up to 1894, which includes *The Father* (1877), *Miss Julie* (1888), *The Creditors* (1889), and other naturalistic plays; the second consists of work he wrote after 1897, including *To Damascus* (1898–1901), *There Are Crimes and Crimes* (1899), *Easter* and *The Dance of Death* (both 1901), *A Dream Play* (1902), and *Ghost Sonata* (1907). These are largely expressionist plays. EXPRESSIONISM disregarded the strict demands of naturalism to present a "slice of life" without artistic shaping of plot and resolution. Instead, expressionist drama used materials that resembled dreams—or nightmares—and focused on symbolic actions and a subjective interpretation of the world. Strindberg's later drama is often symbolic, taut, and psychological. His novel *Inferno* (1897) not only marks the transition between his early and late work; it gives this period of his life its name. Strindberg's *Inferno* period was a time of madness and paranoic behavior that virtually redirected his life for more than three years. During this time he was convinced that the secrets of life were wrapped in the occult, and his energies went into alchemical experiments and studies of cabalistic lore.

The first period of his dramatic career began with *Master Olof* (1872), a historical drama that he chose to write in prose, which he felt was a more natural medium than verse, the convention for such plays at the time. The play was turned down, and he rewrote it in verse in 1876. It was rejected for a second time by the Royal Dramatic Theater but was finally produced the following year. At that time, Strindberg recorded, "In 1877 Antoine opened his Théâtre Libre in Paris, and *Thérèse Raquin*, although nothing but an adapted novel, became the dominant model. It was the powerful theme and the concentrated form that showed innovation, although the unity of time was not yet observed, and curtain falls were retained. It was then I wrote my dramas: *Lady Julie, The Father*, and *Creditors*." *Thérèse Raquin*, Émile Zola's naturalistic play, inspired Strindberg to move further toward his own interpretation of naturalism, which is perhaps most evident in *Miss Julie*. Strindberg was more subjective in his approach to naturalism, less scientific and deterministic, than Zola. Whereas Zola's approach might be described as "photographic" realism, Strindberg's was more selective and impressionistic but no less honest and true. He saw his characters operating out of "a whole series of deeply buried motives." They were not necessarily the product of their biology or their social circumstances, as the naturalists of Zola's stripe sometimes implied. Yet Strindberg saw clearly that class distinctions helped determine the behavior of many people. He seemed to accept the view that people were not created by their class but rather belonged to their class because of the kind of people they were. Strindberg probed deeply into the psychology of his characters, whose emotional lives, rather than outward social qualities, determined their actions.

Strindberg is often described as a woman-hater, a misogynist. For periods of his life he seems to have been misogynistic, but he was nonetheless extremely contradictory in both behavior and belief. There is no simple way to talk about Strindberg's attitude toward women. On the one hand, he is conventional in his thinking that women belong in the home. On the other hand, he married a highly successful actress, Siri von Essen. As he said in a letter in 1895, "Woman is to me the earth and all its glory, the bond that binds, and of all the evil the worst evil I have seen is the female sex." A decade later in *A Blue Book*, he wrote, "When I approach a woman as a lover, I look up to her, I see something of the mother in her, and this I respect. I assume a subordinate position, become childish and puerile and actually am subordinate, like most men. . . . I put her on a pedestal." As in many things, including his attitude toward dramatic techniques and style, Strindberg is a mass of contradictions and complexities of the sort sometimes associated with genius.

MISS JULIE

Miss Julie, the daughter of a count, and Jean, the count's valet, come from strikingly different social backgrounds. In ordinary circumstances, they might not have been on friendly terms, much less have become lovers, as they do. But the count is away, and Miss Julie and Jean are drawn into a sexual liaison marked by a struggle for dominance and control. Miss Julie's fiancé has been disposed of before the play begins because he refused to debase himself slavishly to her will. She is a free spirit, but her breeding is suspect because her mother, like her, took a lover and defied the count. Miss Julie's mother rebelled against her husband and punished him by burning their house down after the insurance expired. As further punishment and abasement, she humiliated the count by arranging to have her lover lend him the money to rebuild the house. Thus, Miss Julie's heritage is one of independence, rebellion, and unorthodoxy.

Under her mother's tutelage, Miss Julie was raised to manipulate men, but she cannot accept them totally. She also seems to feel a mixture of contempt for herself as a woman along with her contempt for men. In his preface to the play, Strindberg says that Julie is a modern "man-hating half-woman" who sells herself for honors of various kinds. (See the commentary on p. 715.)

The play has a mysterious quality. It takes place on Midsummer Eve, when lovers reveal themselves to one another and when almost anything can happen. In primitive fertility rites it was a time associated with sexual awakening. The cook, Kristine, mentions that it is the feast of St. John and alludes to his beheading for spurning Salome's advances. Jean (French for John) in one tense moment of the play beheads Julie's pet bird as a sign of the violence pent up in him. This incident foreshadows Miss Julie's death.

The fairy-tale quality that creeps into the play—as in *A Midsummer Night's Dream*, set on the same day—may seem out of place in a realistic drama, but it is profoundly compelling. It is also typical of Strindberg, who often uses symbolism to suggest a dream quality and deepen the significance of the action. (Dreams are a part of reality that modern playwrights have taken great pains to explore.)

The count himself, Julie's father, never appears in the play, but his presence is always ominous and intense, again much as in a fairy tale. Jean tells Miss Julie that he would willingly kill himself if the count were to order it. Kristine, like a witch, demands retribution because she was spurned by Jean, who was once her lover. Near the end of the play she prevents Julie and Jean from running away from the count by impounding the horses in the stable, thus taking revenge on both of them.

Although Julie may be seen as the princess, Jean has very little claim to being Prince Charming of the play, especially since he has little strength of character. He feels superior to his station as a valet, and Strindberg in his preface refers to him as a nobleman. However, like Kristine, he is coarse beneath his outwardly polished appearance. His highest ambition is to be the proprietor of a first-class hotel, a prospect he wants to share with Julie.

One of the most striking passages in the play is the story Jean tells Julie almost reluctantly. He tries to explain to her what it feels like to be "down below," where she has never been. When he was a boy, he thought of the apple trees in her father's garden as part of the "Garden of Eden, guarded by angry angels." He entered this enchanted place with his mother to weed onions and wandered into the outhouse—a building like a Turkish pavilion whose function he could not guess. While he was exploring it, he heard someone coming and had to exit beneath the outhouse and hide himself under a pile of weeds and "wet dirt that stank." From his hiding place he saw Julie in a pink dress and white stockings. He rushed to the millpond and jumped in to wash the filth off himself. Ironically, only a few moments after he tells her this story, he calls her a whore, and she, in response, says, "Oh, God in heaven, end my wretched life! Take me away from the filth I'm sinking into! Save me! Save me!"

Miss Julie falls under the power of her lover and cannot redirect her life; she sinks deeper and deeper into "filth." She has few choices at the end of the play, and the conclusion to *Miss Julie* is swift. The contrast between the willfulness of Julie and the caution of Jean makes their situation especially desperate. When Julie leaves at the end of the play to seal her fate, we sense the terrible weight of their society's values. Those values are symbolized by the return of the count and the expectations he had of Julie's behavior while he was gone.

Miss Julie in Performance

The first planned professional production of *Miss Julie* was canceled at the last minute by censors in Copenhagen on March 1, 1889. Although the play was performed privately on March 14, 1889, in Copenhagen University's Students' Union, it was not performed professionally in Stockholm until 1906. Some important early productions of the play were in Paris in Antoine's distinguished Théâtre Libre in 1893 and in Berlin in Max Reinhardt's Kleine Theater in 1904. Reinhardt produced seventeen of Strindberg's plays and was one of his great champions. In 1907 Strindberg produced the play in his own Intimate Theatre in Stockholm, where it ran intermittently for 134 showings. He even arranged a special performance for Bernard Shaw. The first London production was in 1912, but since the 1930s it has been revived many times, with many distinguished actors in all three major roles.

Among the notable modern productions is the Old Vic's 1966 version directed by Michael Elliott, with Maggie Smith and Albert Finney starring. The Baxter Theatre of Johannesburg, South Africa, produced the play in 1985 with the black actor John Kani as Jean and the white Afrikaner actress Sandra Prinsloo as Julie. Some white audiences considered that casting outrageous. The sensational Ingmar Bergman production at the Brooklyn Academy of Music in 1991 stretched the play to two hours and made it more of a domestic tragedy—as John Simon said, "more like us, more believable, and, therefore, more terrifying."

The translation of *Miss Julie* by dramatist Frank McGuinness was produced at the Theatre Royal in London in 2000, with Christopher Eccleston and Aisling O'Sullivan in a carefully built period kitchen with period costumes. The sexual dynamic of the play was central to a production designed to attract a younger audience. In New York in 2005, the Rattlestick Playwrights Theatre produced a well-reviewed version adapted by Craig Lucas that emphasized the physicality of the protagonists and went so far as to show their lovemaking silhouetted behind a scrim during a scene change.

Filmed at least five times, *Miss Julie* has been televised as well. It is one of the most frequently produced modern plays.

August Strindberg (1849–1912)

MISS JULIE   *1888*
TRANSLATED BY HARRY G. CARLSON

Characters

MISS JULIE, *25 years old*
JEAN, *her father's valet, 30 years old*
KRISTINE, *her father's cook, 35 years old*

(*The action takes place in the Count's kitchen on midsummer eve.*)

Setting: (*A large kitchen, the ceiling and side walls of which are hidden by draperies. The rear wall runs diagonally from down left to up right. On the wall down left are two shelves with copper, iron, and pewter utensils; the shelves are lined with scalloped paper. Visible to the right is most of a set of large, arched glass doors, through which can be seen a fountain with a statue of Cupid, lilac bushes in bloom, and the tops of some Lombardy poplars. At down left is the corner of a large tiled stove; a portion of its hood is showing. At right, one end of the servants' white pine dining table juts out; several chairs stand around it. The stove is decorated with birch branches; juniper twigs are strewn on the floor. On the end of the table stands a large Japanese spice jar, filled with lilac blossoms. An ice box, a sink, and a washstand. Above the door is an old-fashioned bell on a spring; to the left of the door, the mouthpiece of a speaking tube is visible.*)

(*Kristine is frying something on the stove. She is wearing a light-colored cotton dress and an apron. Jean enters. He is wearing livery and carries a pair of high riding boots with spurs, which he puts down on the floor where they can be seen by the audience.*)

JEAN: Miss Julie's crazy again tonight; absolutely crazy!
KRISTINE: So you finally came back?
JEAN: I took the Count to the station and when I returned past the barn I stopped in for a dance. Who do I see but Miss Julie leading off the dance with the gamekeeper! But as soon as she saw me she rushed over to ask me for the next waltz. And she's been waltzing ever since—I've never seen anything like it. She's crazy!
KRISTINE: She always has been, but never as bad as the last two weeks since her engagement was broken off.
JEAN: Yes, I wonder what the real story was there. He was a gentleman, even if he wasn't rich. Ah! These

people have such romantic ideas. (*Sits at the end of the table.*) Still, it's strange, isn't it? I mean that she'd rather stay home with the servants on midsummer eve instead of going with her father to visit relatives?

KRISTINE: She's probably embarrassed after that row with her fiancé.

JEAN: Probably! He gave a good account of himself, though. Do you know how it happened, Kristine? I saw it, you know, though I didn't let on I had.

KRISTINE: No! You saw it?

JEAN: Yes, I did.———That evening they were out near the stable, and she was "training" him—as she called it. Do you know what she did? She made him jump over her riding crop, the way you'd teach a dog to jump. He jumped twice and she hit him each time. But the third time he grabbed the crop out of her hand, hit her with it across the cheek, and broke it in pieces. Then he left.

KRISTINE: So, that's what happened! I can't believe it!

JEAN: Yes, that's the way it went!———What have you got for me that's tasty, Kristine?

KRISTINE (*serving him from the pan*): Oh, it's only a piece of kidney I cut from the veal roast.

JEAN (*smelling the food*): Beautiful! That's my favorite *délice*.° (*Feeling the plate.*) But you could have warmed the plate!

KRISTINE: You're fussier than the Count himself, once you start! (*She pulls his hair affectionately.*)

JEAN (*angry*): Stop it, leave my hair alone! You know I'm touchy about that.

KRISTINE: Now, now, it's only love, you know that. (*Jean eats. Kristine opens a bottle of beer.*)

JEAN: Beer? On midsummer eve? No thank you! I can do better than that. (*Opens a drawer in the table and takes out a bottle of red wine with yellow sealing wax.*) See that? Yellow seal! Give me a glass! A wine glass! I'm drinking this *pur*.°

KRISTINE (*returns to the stove and puts on a small saucepan*): God help the woman who gets you for a husband! What a fussbudget.

JEAN: Nonsense! You'd be damned lucky to get a man like me. It certainly hasn't done you any harm to have people call me your sweetheart. (*Tastes the wine.*) Good! Very good! Just needs a little warming. (*Warms the glass between his hands.*) We bought this in Dijon. Four francs a liter, not counting the cost of the bottle, or the customs duty.———What are you cooking now? It stinks like hell!

KRISTINE: Oh, some slop Miss Julie wants to give Diana.

JEAN: Watch your language, Kristine. But why should you have to cook for that damn mutt on midsummer eve? Is she sick?

KRISTINE: Yes, she's sick! She sneaked out with the gatekeeper's dog—and now there's hell to pay. Miss Julie won't have it!

JEAN: Miss Julie has too much pride about some things and not enough about others, just like her mother

was. The Countess was most at home in the kitchen and the cowsheds, but a *one*-horse carriage wasn't elegant enough for her. The cuffs of her blouse were dirty, but she had to have her coat of arms on her cufflinks.———And Miss Julie won't take proper care of herself either. If you ask me, she just isn't refined. Just now, when she was dancing in the barn, she pulled the gamekeeper away from Anna and made him dance with her. *We* wouldn't behave like that, but that's what happens when aristocrats pretend they're common people—they get *common*!——— But she is quite a woman! Magnificent! What shoulders, and what—et cetera!

KRISTINE: Oh, don't overdo it! I've heard what Clara says, and she dresses her.

JEAN: Ha, Clara! You're all jealous of each other! I've been out riding with her. . . . And the way she dances!

KRISTINE: Listen, Jean! You're going to dance with me, when I'm finished here, aren't you?

JEAN: Of course I will.

KRISTINE: Promise?

JEAN: Promise? When I say I'll do something, I do it! By the way, the kidney was very good. (*Corks the bottle.*)

JULIE (*in the doorway to someone outside*): I'll be right back! You go ahead for now! (*Jean sneaks the bottle back into the table drawer and gets up respectfully. Miss Julie enters and crosses to Kristine by the stove.*) Well? Is it ready? (*Kristine indicates that Jean is present.*)

JEAN (*gallantly*): Are you ladies up to something secret?

JULIE (*flicking her handkerchief in his face*): None of your business!

JEAN: Hmm! I like the smell of violets!

JULIE (*coquettishly*): Shame on you! So you know about perfumes, too? You certainly know how to dance. Ah, ah! No peeking! Go away.

JEAN (*boldly but respectfully*): Are you brewing up a magic potion for midsummer eve? Something to prophesy by under a lucky star, so you'll catch a glimpse of your future husband!

JULIE (*caustically*): You'd need sharp eyes to see him! (*To Kristine.*) Pour out half a bottle and cork it well.——— Come and dance a schottische° with me, Jean . . .

JEAN (*hesitating*): I don't want to be impolite to anyone, and I've already promised this dance to Kristine . . .

JULIE: Oh, she can have another one—can't you, Kristine? Won't you lend me Jean?

KRISTINE: It's not up to me, ma'am. (*To Jean.*) If the mistress is so generous, it wouldn't do for you to say no. Go on, Jean, and thank her for the honor.

JEAN: To be honest, and no offense intended, I wonder whether it's wise for you to dance twice running with the same partner, especially since these people are quick to jump to conclusions . . .

JULIE (*flaring up*): What's that? What sort of conclusions? What do you mean?

---

délice: Delight.   *pur*: Pure; the first drink from the bottle.

schottische: A Scottish round dance resembling a polka.

JEAN (*submissively*): If you don't understand, ma'am, I must speak more plainly. It doesn't look good to play favorites with your servants. . . .

JULIE: Play favorites! What an idea! I'm astonished! As mistress of the house, I honor your dance with my presence. And when I dance, I want to dance with someone who can lead, so I won't look ridiculous.

JEAN: As you order, ma'am! I'm at your service!

JULIE (*gently*): Don't take it as an order! On a night like this we're all just ordinary people having fun, so we'll forget about rank. Now, take my arm!——— Don't worry, Kristine! I won't steal your sweetheart! (*Jean offers his arm and leads Miss Julie out.*)

Mime

(*The following should be played as if the actress playing Kristine were really alone. When she has to, she turns her back to the audience. She does not look toward them, nor does she hurry as if she were afraid they would grow impatient. Schottische music played on a fiddle sounds in the distance. Kristine hums along with the music. She clears the table, washes the dishes, dries them, and puts them away. She takes off her apron. From a table drawer she removes a small mirror and leans it against the bowl of lilacs on the table. She lights a candle, heats a hairpin over the flame, and uses it to set a curl on her forehead. She crosses to the door and listens, then returns to the table. She finds the handkerchief Miss Julie left behind, picks it up, and smells it. Then, preoccupied, she spreads it out, stretches it, smoothes out the wrinkles, and folds it into quarters, and so forth.*)

JEAN (*enters alone*): God, she really *is* crazy! What a way to dance! Everybody's laughing at her behind her back. What do you make of it, Kristine?

KRISTINE: Ah! It's that time of the month for her, and she always gets peculiar like that. Are you going to dance with me now?

JEAN: You're not mad at me, are you, for leaving . . . ?

KRISTINE: Of course not!——— Why should I be, for a little thing like that? Besides, I know my place . . .

JEAN (*puts his arm around her waist*): You're a sensible girl, Kristine, and you'd make a good wife . . .

JULIE (*entering; uncomfortably surprised; with forced good humor*): What a charming escort—running away from his partner.

JEAN: On the contrary, Miss Julie. Don't you see how I rushed back to the partner I abandoned!

JULIE (*changing her tone*): You know, you're a superb dancer!——— But why are you wearing livery on a holiday? Take it off at once!

JEAN: Then I must ask you to go outside for a moment. You see, my black coat is hanging over here . . . (*Gestures and crosses right.*)

JULIE: Are you embarrassed about changing your coat in front of me? Well, go in your room then. Either that or stay and I'll turn my back.

JEAN: With your permission, ma'am! (*He crosses right. His arm is visible as he changes his jacket.*)

JULIE (*to Kristine*): Tell me, Kristine—you two are so close—. Is Jean your fiancé?

KRISTINE: Fiancé? Yes, if you wish. We can call him that.

JULIE: What do you mean?

KRISTINE: You had a fiancé yourself, didn't you? So . . .

JULIE: Well, we were properly engaged . . .

KRISTINE: But nothing came of it, did it? (*Jean returns dressed in a frock coat and bowler hat.*)

JULIE: *Très gentil, monsieur Jean! Très gentil!*

JEAN: *Vous voulez plaisanter, madame!*

JULIE: *Et vous voulez parler français!°* Where did you learn that?

JEAN: In Switzerland, when I was wine steward in one of the biggest hotels in Lucerne!

JULIE: You look like a real gentleman in that coat! *Charmant!°* (*Sits at the table.*)

JEAN: Oh, you're flattering me!

JULIE (*offended*): Flattering you?

JEAN: My natural modesty forbids me to believe that you would really compliment someone like me, and so I took the liberty of assuming that you were exaggerating, which polite people call flattering.

JULIE: Where did you learn to talk like that? You must have been to the theater often.

JEAN: Of course. And I've done a lot of traveling.

JULIE: But you come from here, don't you?

JEAN: My father was a farmhand on the district attorney's estate nearby. I used to see you when you were little, but you never noticed me.

JULIE: No! Really?

JEAN: Sure. I remember one time especially . . . but I can't talk about that.

JULIE: Oh, come now! Why not? Just this once!

JEAN: No, I really couldn't, not now. Some other time, perhaps.

JULIE: Why some other time? What's so dangerous about now?

JEAN: It's not dangerous, but there are obstacles.——— Her, for example. (*Indicating Kristine, who has fallen asleep in a chair by the stove.*)

JULIE: What a pleasant wife she'll make! She probably snores, too.

JEAN: No, she doesn't, but she talks in her sleep.

JULIE (*cynically*): How do *you* know?

JEAN (*audaciously*): I've heard her! (*Pause, during which they stare at each other.*)

JULIE: Why don't you sit down?

JEAN: I couldn't do that in your presence.

JULIE: But if I order you to?

JEAN: Then I'd obey.

JULIE: Sit down, then.———No, wait. Can you get me something to drink first?

JEAN: I don't know what we have in the ice box. I think there's only beer.

Très gentil . . . français!: Very pleasing, Mr. Jean! Very pleasing. You would trifle with me, madam! And you want to speak French!   *Charmant!*: Charming!

JULIE: Why do you say "only"? My tastes are so simple I prefer beer to wine. (*Jean takes a bottle of beer from the ice box and opens it. He looks for a glass and a plate in the cupboard and serves her.*)

JEAN: Here you are, ma'am.

JULIE: Thank you. Won't you have something yourself?

JEAN: I'm not partial to beer, but if it's an order . . .

JULIE: An order?———Surely a gentleman can keep his lady company.

JEAN: You're right, of course. (*Opens a bottle and gets a glass.*)

JULIE: Now, drink to my health! (*He hesitates.*) What? A man of the world—and shy?

JEAN (*in mock romantic fashion, he kneels and raises his glass*): Skål to my mistress!

JULIE: Bravo!———Now kiss my shoe, to finish it properly. (*Jean hesitates, then boldly seizes her foot and kisses it lightly.*) Perfect! You should have been an actor.

JEAN (*rising*): That's enough now, Miss Julie! Someone might come in and see us.

JULIE: What of it?

JEAN: People talk, that's what! If you knew how their tongues were wagging just now at the dance, you'd . . .

JULIE: What were they saying? Tell me!———Sit down!

JEAN (*sits*): I don't want to hurt you, but they were saying things———suggestive things, that, that . . . well, you can figure it out for yourself! You're not a child. If a woman is seen drinking alone with a man—let alone a servant—at night—then . . .

JULIE: Then what? Besides, we're not alone. Kristine is here.

JEAN: Asleep!

JULIE: Then I'll wake her up. (*Rising.*) Kristine! Are you asleep? (*Kristine mumbles in her sleep.*)

JULIE: Kristine!———She certainly can sleep!

KRISTINE (*in her sleep*): The Count's boots are brushed—put the coffee on—right away, right away—uh, huh—oh!

JULIE (*grabbing Kristine's nose*): Will you wake up!

JEAN (*severely*): Leave her alone—let her sleep!

JULIE (*sharply*): What?

JEAN: Someone who's been standing over a stove all day has a right to be tired by now. Sleep should be respected . . .

JULIE (*changing her tone*): What a considerate thought—it does you credit—thank you! (*Offering her hand.*) Come outside and pick some lilacs for me! (*During the following, Kristine awakens and shambles sleepily off right to bed.*)

JEAN: Go with you?

JULIE: With me!

JEAN: We couldn't do that! Absolutely not!

JULIE: I don't understand. Surely you don't imagine . . .

JEAN: No, I don't, but the others might.

JULIE: What? That I've fallen in love with a servant?

JEAN: I'm not a conceited man, but such things happen—and for these people, nothing is sacred.

JULIE: I do believe you're an aristocrat!

JEAN: Yes, I am.

JULIE: And I'm stepping down . . .

JEAN: Don't step down, Miss Julie, take my advice. No one'll believe you stepped down voluntarily. People will always say you fell.

JULIE: I have a higher opinion of people than you. Come and see!———Come! (*She stares at him broodingly.*)

JEAN: You're very strange, do you know that?

JULIE: Perhaps! But so are you!———For that matter, everything is strange. Life, people, everything. Like floating scum, drifting on and on across the water, until it sinks down and down! That reminds me of a dream I have now and then. I've climbed up on top of a pillar. I sit there and see no way of getting down. I get dizzy when I look down, and I must get down, but I don't have the courage to jump. I can't hold on firmly, and I long to be able to fall, but I don't fall. And yet I'll have no peace until I get down, no rest unless I get down, down on the ground! And if I did get down to the ground, I'd want to be under the earth . . . Have you ever felt anything like that?

JEAN: No. I dream that I'm lying under a high tree in a dark forest. I want to get up, up on top, and look out over the bright landscape, where the sun is shining, and plunder the bird's nest up there, where the golden eggs lie. And I climb and climb, but the trunk's so thick and smooth, and it's so far to the first branch. But I know if I just reached that first branch, I'd go right to the top, like up a ladder. I haven't reached it yet, but I will, even if it's only in a dream!

JULIE: Here I am chattering with you about dreams. Come, let's go out! Just into the park! (*She offers him her arm, and they start to leave.*)

JEAN: We'll have to sleep on nine midsummer flowers, Miss Julie, to make our dreams come true! (*They turn at the door. Jean puts his hand to his eye.*)

JULIE: Did you get something in your eye?

JEAN: It's nothing—just a speck—it'll be gone in a minute.

JULIE: My sleeve must have brushed against you. Sit down and let me help you. (*She takes him by the arm and seats him. She tilts his head back and with the tip of a handkerchief tries to remove the speck.*) Sit still, absolutely still! (*She slaps his hand.*) Didn't you hear me?———Why, you're trembling; the big, strong man is trembling! (*Feels his biceps.*) What muscles you have!

JEAN (*warning*): Miss Julie!

JULIE: Yes, *monsieur* Jean.

JEAN: *Attention! Je ne suis qu'un homme!*°

JULIE Will you sit still!———There! Now it's gone! Kiss my hand and thank me.

JEAN (*rising*): Miss Julie, listen to me!———Kristine has gone to bed!———Will you listen to me!

Attention! Je ne suis qu'un homme!: Watch out! I am only a man!

JULIE: Kiss my hand first!

JEAN: Listen to me!

JULIE: Kiss my hand first!

JEAN: All right, but you've only yourself to blame!

JULIE: For what?

JEAN: For what? Are you still a child at twenty-five? Don't you know that it's dangerous to play with fire?

JULIE: Not for me. I'm insured.

JEAN (*boldly*): No, you're not! But even if you were, there's combustible material close by.

JULIE: Meaning you?

JEAN: Yes! Not because it's me, but because I'm young——

JULIE: And handsome—what incredible conceit! A Don Juan perhaps! Or a Joseph!° Yes, that's it, I do believe you're a Joseph!

JEAN: Do you?

JULIE: I'm almost afraid so. (*Jean boldly tries to put his arm around her waist and kiss her. She slaps his face.*) How dare you?

JEAN: Are you serious or joking?

JULIE: Serious.

JEAN: Then so was what just happened. You play games too seriously, and that's dangerous. Well, I'm tired of games. You'll excuse me if I get back to work. I haven't done the Count's boots yet and it's long past midnight.

JULIE: Put the boots down!

JEAN: No! It's the work I have to do. I never agreed to be your playmate, and never will. It's beneath me.

JULIE: You're proud.

JEAN: In certain ways, but not in others.

JULIE: Have you ever been in love?

JEAN: We don't use that word, but I've been fond of many girls, and once I was sick because I couldn't have the one I wanted. That's right, sick, like those princes in the Arabian Nights—who couldn't eat or drink because of love.

JULIE: Who was she? (*Jean is silent.*) Who was she?

JEAN: You can't force me to tell you that.

JULIE: But if I ask you as an equal, as a—friend! Who was she?

JEAN: You!

JULIE (*sits*): How amusing . . .

JEAN: Yes, if you like! It was ridiculous!——You see, that was the story I didn't want to tell you earlier. Maybe I will now. Do you know how the world looks from down below?——Of course you don't. Neither do hawks and falcons, whose backs we can't see because they're usually soaring up there above us. I grew up in a shack with seven brothers and sisters and a pig, in the middle of a wasteland, where there wasn't a single tree. But from our window I could see the tops of apple trees above the wall of your father's garden. That was the Garden of Eden, guarded by

Don Juan . . . Joseph: Don Juan in Spanish legend is a seducer of women; in Genesis, Joseph resists the advances of Potiphar's wife.

angry angels with flaming swords. All the same, the other boys and I managed to find our way to the Tree of Life.——Now you think I'm contemptible, I suppose.

JULIE: Oh, all boys steal apples.

JEAN: You say that, but you think I'm contemptible anyway. Oh well! One day I went into the Garden of Eden with my mother, to weed the onion beds. Near the vegetable garden was a small Turkish pavilion in the shadow of jasmine bushes and over-grown with honeysuckle. I had no idea what it was used for, but I'd never seen such a beautiful building. People went in and came out again, and one day the door was left open. I sneaked close and saw walls covered with pictures of kings and emperors, and red curtains with fringes at the windows—now you know the place I mean. I——(*Breaks off a sprig of lilac and holds it in front of Miss Julie's nose.*)——I'd never been inside the manor house, never seen anything except the church—but this was more beautiful. From then on, no matter where my thoughts wandered, they returned—there. And gradually I got a longing to experience, just once, the full pleasure of—*enfin,*° I sneaked in, saw, and marveled! But then I heard someone coming! There was only one exit for ladies and gentlemen, but for me there was another, and I had no choice but to take it! (*Miss Julie, who has taken the lilac sprig, lets it fall on the table.*) Afterwards, I started running. I crashed through a raspberry bush, flew over a strawberry patch, and came up onto the rose terrace. There I caught sight of a pink dress and a pair of white stockings—it was you. I crawled under a pile of weeds, and I mean under—under thistles that pricked me and wet dirt that stank. And I looked at you as you walked among the roses, and I thought: If it's true that a thief can enter heaven and be with the angels, then why can't a farm-hand's son here on God's earth enter the manor house garden and play with the Count's daughter?

JULIE (*romantically*): Do you think all poor children would have thought the way you did?

JEAN (*at first hesitant, then with conviction*): If *all* poor—yes—of course. Of course!

JULIE: It must be terrible to be poor!

JEAN (*with exaggerated suffering*): Oh, Miss Julie! Oh!——A dog can lie on the Countess's sofa, a horse can have his nose patted by a young lady's hand, but a servant——(*Changing his tone.*)——oh, I know—now and then you find one with enough stuff in him to get ahead in the world, but how often?——Anyhow, do you know what I did then?——I jumped in the millstream with my clothes on, was pulled out, and got a beating. But the following Sunday, when my father and all the others went to my grandmother's, I arranged to stay home. I scrubbed myself with soap and water, put on my best clothes, and went to church so that I could see you!

enfin: Finally.

I saw you and returned home, determined to die. But I wanted to die beautifully and pleasantly, without pain. And then I remembered that it was dangerous to sleep under an elder bush. We had a big one, and it was in full flower. I plundered its treasures and bedded down under them in the oat bin. Have you ever noticed how smooth oats are?—and soft to the touch, like human skin . . . ! Well, I shut the lid and closed my eyes. I fell asleep and woke up feeling very sick. But I didn't die, as you can see. What was I after?———I don't know. There was no hope of winning you, of course.——— You were a symbol of the hopelessness of ever rising out of the class in which I was born.

JULIE: You're a charming storyteller. Did you ever go to school?

JEAN: A bit, but I've read lots of novels and been to the theater often. And then I've listened to people like you talk—that's where I learned most.

JULIE: Do you listen to what we say?

JEAN: Naturally! And I've heard plenty, too, driving the carriage or rowing the boat. Once I heard you and a friend . . .

JULIE: Oh?———What did you hear?

JEAN: I'd better not say. But I was surprised a little. I couldn't imagine where you learned such words. Maybe at bottom there isn't such a great difference between people as we think.

JULIE: Shame on you! We don't act like you when we're engaged.

JEAN (staring at her): Is that true?——— You don't have to play innocent with me, Miss . . .

JULIE: The man I gave my love to was a swine.

JEAN: That's what you all say—afterwards.

JULIE: All?

JEAN: I think so. I know I've heard that phrase before, on similar occasions.

JULIE: What occasions?

JEAN: Like the one I'm talking about. The last time . . .

JULIE (rising): Quiet! I don't want to hear any more!

JEAN: That's interesting—that's what she said, too. Well, if you'll excuse me, I'm going to bed.

JULIE (gently): To bed? On midsummer eve?

JEAN: Yes! Dancing with the rabble out there doesn't amuse me much.

JULIE: Get the key to the boat and row me out on the lake. I want to see the sun come up.

JEAN: Is that wise?

JULIE: Are you worried about your reputation?

JEAN: Why not? Why should I risk looking ridiculous and getting fired without a reference, just when I'm trying to establish myself. Besides, I think I owe something to Kristine.

JULIE: So, now it's Kristine . . .

JEAN: Yes, but you, too.———Take my advice, go up and go to bed!

JULIE: Am I to obey you?

JEAN: Just this once—for your own good! Please! It's very late. Drowsiness makes people giddy and liable to lose their heads! Go to bed! Besides—unless I'm mistaken—I hear the others coming to look for me. And if they find us together, you'll be lost!

(The Chorus approaches, singing.)

The swineherd found his true love
a pretty girl so fair,
The swineherd found his true love
but let the girl beware.

For then he saw the princess
the princess on the golden hill,
but then saw the princess,
so much fairer still.

So the swineherd and the princess
they danced the whole night through,
and he forgot his first love,
to her he was untrue.

And when the long night ended,
and in the light of day, of day,
the dancing too was ended,
and the princess could not stay.

Then the swineherd lost his true love,
and the princess grieves him still,
and never more she'll wander
from atop the golden hill.

JULIE: I know all these people and I love them, just as they love me. Let them come in and you'll see.

JEAN: No, Miss Julie, they don't love you. They take your food, but they spit on it! Believe me! Listen to them, listen to what they're singing!———No. don't listen to them!

JULIE (listening): What are they singing?

JEAN: It's a dirty song! About you and me!

JULIE: Disgusting! Oh! How deceitful!———

JEAN: The rabble is always cowardly! And in a battle like this, you don't fight; you can only run away!

JULIE: Run away? But where? We can't go out—or into Kristine's room.

JEAN: True. But there's my room. Necessity knows no rules. Besides, you can trust me. I'm your friend and I respect you.

JULIE: But suppose—suppose they look for you in there?

JEAN: I'll bolt the door, and if anyone tries to break in, I'll shoot!———Come! (On his knees.) Come!

JULIE (urgently): Promise me. . . ?

JEAN: I swear! (Miss Julie runs off right. Jean hastens after her.)

Ballet

(Led by a fiddler, the servants and farm people enter, dressed festively, with flowers in their hats. On the table they place a small barrel of beer and a keg of schnapps, *both garlanded. Glasses are brought out, and the drinking starts. A dance circle is formed and "The Swineherd and the Princess" is sung. When the dance is finished, everyone leaves, singing.)*

(Miss Julie enters alone. She notices the mess in the kitchen, wrings her hands, then takes out her powder puff and powders her nose.)

JEAN *(enters, agitated)*: There, you see? And you heard them. We can't possibly stay here now, you know that.

JULIE: Yes, I know. But what can we do?

JEAN: Leave, travel, far away from here.

JULIE: Travel? Yes, but where?

JEAN: To Switzerland, to the Italian lakes. Have you ever been there?

JULIE: No. Is it beautiful?

JEAN: Oh, an eternal summer—oranges growing everywhere, laurel trees, always green . . .

JULIE: But what'll we do there?

JEAN: I'll open a hotel—with first-class service for first-class people.

JULIE: Hotel?

JEAN: That's the life, you know. Always new faces, new languages. No time to worry or be nervous. No hunting for something to do—there's always work to be done: bells ringing night and day, train whistles blowing, carriages coming and going, and all the while gold rolling into the till! That's the life!

JULIE: Yes, it sounds wonderful. But what'll I do?

JEAN: You'll be mistress of the house: the jewel in our crown! With your looks . . . and your manner—oh—success is guaranteed! It'll be wonderful! You'll sit in your office like a queen and push an electric button to set your slaves in motion. The guests will file past your throne and timidly lay their treasures before you.——— You have no idea how people tremble when they get their bill.———I'll salt the bills° and you'll sweeten them with your prettiest smile.———Let's get away from here———*(Takes a timetable out of his pocket.)*———Right away, on the next train! We'll be in Malmö six-thirty tomorrow morning, Hamburg at eight-forty; from Frankfort to Basel will take a day, then on to Como by way of the St. Gotthard Tunnel, in, let's see, three days. Three days!

JULIE: That's all very well! But Jean—you must give me courage!———Tell me you love me! Put your arms around me!

JEAN *(hesitating)*: I want to—but I don't dare. Not in this house, not again. I love you—never doubt that—you don't doubt it, do you, Miss Julie?

JULIE *(shy; very feminine)*: "Miss!"———Call me Julie! There are no barriers between us anymore. Call me Julie!

JEAN *(tormented)*: I can't! There'll always be barriers between us as long as we stay in this house.——— There's the past and there's the Count. I've never met anyone I had such respect for.———When I see his

salt the bills: Inflate or pad the bills.

gloves lying on a chair, I feel small.———When I hear that bell up there ring, I jump like a skittish horse.———And when I look at his boots standing there so stiff and proud, I feel like bowing! *(Kicking the boots.)* Superstitions and prejudices we learned as children—but they can easily be forgotten. If I can just get to another country, a republic, people will bow and scrape when they see my livery—*they'll* bow and scrape, you hear, not me! I wasn't born to cringe. I've got stuff in me, I've got character, and if I can only grab onto that first branch, you watch me climb! I'm a servant today, but next year I'll own my own hotel. In ten years I'll have enough to retire. Then I'll go to Rumania and be decorated. I could—mind you I said *could*—end up a count!

JULIE: Wonderful, wonderful!

JEAN: Ah, in Rumania you just buy your title, and so you'll be a countess after all. My countess!

JULIE: But I don't care about that—that's what I'm putting behind me! Show me you love me, otherwise—otherwise, what am I?

JEAN: I'll show you a thousand times—afterwards! Not here! And whatever you do, no emotional outbursts, or we'll both be lost! We must think this through coolly, like sensible people. *(He takes out a cigar, snips the end, and lights it.)* You sit there, and I'll sit here. We'll talk as if nothing happened.

JULIE *(desperately)*: Oh, my God! Have you no feelings?

JEAN: Me? No one has more feelings than I do, but I know how to control them.

JULIE: A little while ago you could kiss my shoe—and now!

JEAN *(harshly)*: Yes, but that was before. Now we have other things to think about.

JULIE: Don't speak harshly to me!

JEAN: I'm not—just sensibly! We've already done one foolish thing, let's not have any more. The Count could return any minute, and by then we've got to decide what to do with our lives. What do you think of my plans for the future? Do you approve?

JULIE: They sound reasonable enough. I have only one question: For such a big undertaking you need capital—do you have it?

JEAN *(chewing on the cigar)*: Me? Certainly! I have my professional expertise, my wide experience, and my knowledge of languages. That's capital enough, I should think!

JULIE: But all that won't even buy a train ticket.

JEAN: That's true. That's why I'm looking for a partner to advance me the money.

JULIE: Where will you find one quickly enough?

JEAN: That's up to you, if you want to come with me.

JULIE: But I can't; I have no money of my own. *(Pause.)*

JEAN: Then it's all off . . .

JULIE: And . . .

JEAN: Things stay as they are.

JULIE: Do you think I'm going to stay in this house as your lover? With all the servants pointing their fingers at me? Do you imagine I can face my father after

Marin Hinkle as Julie and Reg Rogers as Jean in the Rattlestick Playwrights Theatre 2005 production of *Miss Julie*, directed by Craig Lucas.

this? No! Take me away from here, away from shame and dishonor——Oh, what have I done! My God, my God! (*She cries.*)

JEAN: Now, don't start that old song!——What have you done? The same as many others before you.

JULIE (*screaming convulsively*): And now you think I'm contemptible!——I'm falling, I'm falling!

JEAN: Fall down to my level and I'll lift you up again.

JULIE: What terrible power drew me to you? The attraction of the weak to the strong? The falling to the rising? Or was it love? Was this love? Do you know what love is?

JEAN: Me? What do you take me for? You don't think this was my first time, do you?

JULIE: The things you say, the thoughts you think!

JEAN: That's the way I was taught, and that's the way I am! Now don't get excited and don't play the grand lady, because we're in the same boat now!—— Come on, Julie, I'll pour you a glass of something special! (*He opens a drawer in the table, takes out a wine bottle, and fills two glasses already used.*)

JULIE: Where did you get that wine?

JEAN: From the cellar.

JULIE: My father's burgundy!

JEAN: That'll do for his son-in-law, won't it?

JULIE: And I drink beer! Beer!

JEAN: That only shows I have better taste.

JULIE: Thief!

JEAN: Planning to tell?

JULIE: Oh, oh! Accomplice of a common thief! Was I drunk? Have I been walking in a dream the whole evening? Midsummer eve! A time of innocent fun!

JEAN: Innocent, eh?

JULIE (*pacing back and forth*): Is there anyone on earth more miserable than I am at this moment?

JEAN: Why should you be? After such a conquest? Think of Kristine in there. Don't you think she has feelings, too?

JULIE: I thought so awhile ago, but not any more. No, a servant is a servant . . .

JEAN: And a whore is a whore!

JULIE (*on her knees, her hands clasped*): Oh, God in heaven, end my wretched life! Take me away from the filth I'm sinking into! Save me! Save me!

JEAN: I can't deny I feel sorry for you. When I lay in that onion bed and saw you in the rose garden, well . . . I'll be frank . . . I had the same dirty thoughts all boys have.

Helen Mirren as Miss Julie in a 1971 production of Strindberg's play.

JULIE: And you wanted to die for me!

JEAN: In the oat bin? That was just talk.

JULIE: A lie, in other words!

JEAN (*beginning to feel sleepy*): More or less! I got the idea from a newspaper story about a chimney sweep who curled up in a firewood bin full of lilacs because he got a summons for not supporting his illegitimate child . . .

JULIE: So, that's what you're like . . .

JEAN: I had to think of something. And that's the kind of story women always go for.

JULIE: Swine!

JEAN: *Merde!*

JULIE: And now you've seen the hawk's back . . .

JEAN: Not exactly its *back* . . .

JULIE: And I was to be the first branch . . .

JEAN: But the branch was rotten . . .

JULIE: I was to be the sign on the hotel . . .

JEAN: And I the hotel . . .

JULIE: Sit at your desk, entice your customers, pad their bills . . .

JEAN: That I'd do myself . . .

JULIE: How can anyone be so thoroughly filthy?

JEAN: Better clean up then!

JULIE: You lackey, you menial, stand up, when I speak to you!

JEAN: Menial's strumpet, lackey's whore, shut up and get out of here! Who are you to lecture me on coarseness? None of my kind is ever as coarse as you were tonight. Do you think one of your maids would throw herself at a man the way you did? Have you ever seen any girl of my class offer herself like that? I've only seen it among animals and streetwalkers.

JULIE (*crushed*): You're right. Hit me, trample on me. I don't deserve any better. I'm worthless. But help me! If you see any way out of this, help me, Jean, please!

JEAN (*more gently*): I'd be lying if I didn't admit to a sense of triumph in all this, but do you think that a person like me would have dared even to look at someone like you if you hadn't invited it? I'm still amazed . . .

JULIE: And proud . . .

JEAN: Why not? Though I must say it was too easy to be really exciting.

JULIE: Go on, hit me, hit me harder!

JEAN (*rising*): No! Forgive me for what I've said! I don't hit a man when he's down, let alone a woman. I can't deny though, that I'm pleased to find out that what looked so dazzling to us from below was only tinsel, that the hawk's back was only gray, after all, that the lovely complexion was only powder, that those polished fingernails had black edges, and that a dirty handkerchief is still dirty, even if it smells of perfume . . . ! On the other hand, it hurts me to find out that what I was striving for wasn't finer, more substantial. It hurts me to see you sunk so low that you're inferior to your own cook. It hurts like watching flowers beaten down by autumn rains and turned into mud.

JULIE: You talk as if you were already above me.

JEAN: I am. You see, I could make you a countess, but you could never make me a count.

JULIE: But I'm the child of a count—something you could never be!

JEAN: That's true. But I could be the father of counts—if . . .

JULIE: But you're a thief. I'm not.

JEAN: There are worse things than being a thief! Besides, when I'm working in a house, I consider myself sort of a member of the family, like one of the children. And you don't call it stealing when a child snatches a berry off a full bush. (*His passion is aroused again.*) Miss Julie, you're a glorious woman, much too good for someone like me! You were drinking and you lost your head. Now you want to cover up your mistake by telling yourself that you love me! You don't. Maybe there was a physical attraction—but then your love is no better than mine. ———— I could never be satisfied to be no more than an animal to you, and I could never arouse real love in you.

JULIE: Are you sure of that?

JEAN: You're suggesting it's possible——— Oh, I could fall in love with you, no doubt about it. You're beautiful, you're refined——— (*approaching and taking her hand*)——— cultured, lovable when you want to be, and once you start a fire in a man, it never goes out. (*Putting his arm around her waist.*) You're like hot, spicy wine, and one kiss from you . . . (*He tries to lead her out, but she slowly frees herself.*)

JULIE: Let me go!? ——— You'll never win me like that.

JEAN: *How* then?———Not like that? Not with caresses and pretty speeches. Not with plans about the future or rescue from disgrace! *How* then?

JULIE: How? How? I don't know!———I have no idea!——— I detest you as I detest rats, but I can't escape from you.

JEAN: Escape with me!

JULIE (*pulling herself together*): Escape? Yes, we must escape!——— But I'm so tired. Give me a glass of wine? (*Jean pours the wine. She looks at her watch.*) But we must talk first. We still have a little time. (*She drains the glass, then holds it out for more.*)

JEAN: Don't drink so fast. It'll go to your head.

JULIE: What does it matter?

JEAN: What does it matter? It's vulgar to get drunk! What did you want to tell me?

JULIE: We must escape! But first we must talk, I mean I must talk. You've done all the talking up to now. You told about your life, now I want to tell about mine, so we'll know all about each other before we go off together.

JEAN: Just a minute! Forgive me! If you don't want to regret it afterwards, you'd better think twice before revealing any secrets about yourself.

JULIE: Aren't you my friend?

JEAN: Yes, sometimes! But don't rely on me.

JULIE: You're only saying that. ——— Besides, everyone already knows my secrets. ——— You see, my mother was a commoner—very humble background. She was brought up believing in social equality, women's rights, and all that. The idea of marriage repelled her. So, when my father proposed, she replied that she would never become his wife, but he could be her lover. He insisted that he didn't want the woman he loved to be less respected than he. But his passion ruled him, and when she explained that the world's respect meant nothing to her, he accepted her conditions.

But now his friends avoided him and his life was restricted to taking care of the estate, which couldn't satisfy him. I came into the world—against my mother's wishes, as far as I can understand. She wanted to bring me up as a child of nature, and, what's more, to learn everything a boy had to learn, so that I might be an example of how a woman can be as good as a man. I had to wear boy's clothes and learn to take care of horses, but I was never allowed in the cowshed. I had to groom and harness the horses and go hunting—and even had to watch them slaughter animals—that was disgusting! On the estate men were put on women's jobs and women on men's jobs—with the result that the property became run down and we became the laughingstock of the district. Finally, my father must have awakened from his trance because he rebelled and changed everything his way. My parents were then married quietly. Mother became ill—I don't know what illness it was—but she often had convulsions, hid in the attic and in the garden, and sometimes stayed out all night. Then came the great fire, which you've heard about. The house, the stables, and the cowshed all burned down, under very curious circumstances, suggesting arson, because the accident happened the day after the insurance had expired. The quarterly premium my father sent in was delayed because of a messenger's carelessness and didn't arrive in time. (*She fills her glass and drinks.*)

JEAN: Don't drink any more!

JULIE: Oh, what does it matter. ——— We were left penniless and had to sleep in the carriages. My father had no idea where to find money to rebuild the house because he had so slighted his old friends that they had forgotten him. Then my mother suggested that he borrow from a childhood friend of hers, a brick manufacturer who lived nearby. Father got the loan without having to pay interest, which surprised him. And that's how the estate was rebuilt. ——— (*Drinks again.*) Do you know who started the fire?

JEAN: The Countess, your mother.

JULIE: Do you know who the brick manufacturer was?

JEAN: Your mother's lover?

JULIE: Do you know whose money it was?

JEAN: Wait a moment—no, I don't.

JULIE: It was my mother's.

JEAN: You mean the Count's, unless they didn't sign an agreement when they were married.

JULIE: They didn't. ———My mother had a small inheritance which she didn't want under my father's control, so she entrusted it to her—friend.

JEAN: Who stole it!

JULIE: Exactly! He kept it. ———All this my father found out, but he couldn't bring it to court, couldn't repay his wife's lover, couldn't prove it was his wife's money! It was my mother's revenge for being forced into marriage against her will. It nearly drove him to suicide—there was a rumor that he tried with a pistol, but failed. So, he managed to live through it and my mother had to suffer for what she'd done. You can imagine that those were a terrible five years for me. I loved my father, but I sided with my mother because I didn't know the circumstances. I learned from her to hate men—you've heard how she hated the whole male sex—and I swore to her I'd never be a slave to any man.

JEAN: But you got engaged to that lawyer.

JULIE: In order to make him my slave.

JEAN: And he wasn't willing?

JULIE: He was willing, all right, but I wouldn't let him. I got tired of him.

JEAN: I saw it—out near the stable.

JULIE: What did you see?

JEAN: I saw—how he broke off the engagement.

JULIE: That's a lie! I was the one who broke it off. Has he said that he did? That swine . . .

JEAN: He was no swine, I'm sure. So, you hate men, Miss Julie?

JULIE: Yes!———Most of the time! But sometimes—when the weakness comes, when passion burns! Oh, God, will the fire never die out?

JEAN: Do you hate me, too?

JULIE: Immeasurably! I'd like to have you put to death, like an animal . . .

JEAN: I see—the penalty for bestiality—the woman gets two years at hard labor and the animal is put to death. Right?

JULIE: Exactly!

JEAN: But there's no prosecutor here—and no animal. So, what'll we do?

JULIE: Go away!

JEAN: To torment each other to death?

JULIE: No! To be happy for—two days, a week, as long as we can be happy, and then—die . . .

JEAN: Die? That's stupid! It's better to open a hotel!

JULIE (without listening): ———on the shore of Lake Como, where the sun always shines, where the laurels are green at Christmas and the oranges glow.

JEAN: Lake Como is a rainy hole, and I never saw any oranges outside the stores. But tourists are attracted there because there are plenty of villas to be rented out to lovers, and that's a profitable business.——— Do you know why? Because they sign a lease for six months—and then leave after three weeks!

JULIE (naively): Why after three weeks?

JEAN: They quarrel, of course! But they still have to pay the rent in full! And so you rent the villas out again. And that's the way it goes, time after time. There's never a shortage of love—even if it doesn't last long!

JULIE: You don't want to die with me?

JEAN: I don't want to die at all! For one thing, I like living, and for another, I think suicide is a crime against the Providence which gave us life.

JULIE: You believe in God? You?

JEAN: Of course I do. And I go to church every other Sunday.———To be honest, I'm tired of all this, and I'm going to bed.

JULIE: Are you? And do you think I can let it go at that? A man owes something to the woman he's shamed.

JEAN (taking out his purse and throwing a silver coin on the table): Here! I don't like owing anything to anybody.

JULIE (pretending not to notice the insult): Do you know what the law states . . .

JEAN: Unfortunately the law doesn't state any punishment for the woman who seduces a man!

JULIE (as before): Do you see any way out but to leave, get married, and then separate?

JEAN: Suppose I refuse such a *mésalliance?*°

JULIE: *Mésalliance* . . .

JEAN: Yes, for me! You see, I come from better stock than you. There's no arsonist in my family.

JULIE: How do you know?

JEAN: You can't prove otherwise. We don't keep charts on our ancestors—there's just the police records! But I've read about your family. Do you know who the founder was? He was a miller who let the king sleep with his wife one night during the Danish War. I don't have any noble ancestors like that. I don't have any noble ancestors at all, but I could become one myself.

JULIE: This is what I get for opening my heart to someone unworthy, for giving my family's honor . . .

JEAN: Dishonor!———Well, I told you so: When people drink, they talk, and talk is dangerous!

JULIE: Oh, how I regret it!———How I regret it!——— If you at least loved me.

JEAN: For the last time———what do you want? Shall I cry; shall I jump over your riding crop? Shall I kiss you and lure you off to Lake Como for three weeks, and then God knows what...? What shall I do? What do you want? This is getting painfully embarrassing! But that's what happens when you stick your nose in women's business. Miss Julie! I see that you're unhappy. I know you're suffering, but I can't understand you. We don't have such romantic ideas; there's not this kind of hate between us. Love is a game we play when we get time off from work, but we don't have all day and night, like you. I think you're sick, really sick. Your mother was crazy, and her ideas have poisoned your life.

JULIE: Be kind to me. At least now you're talking like a human being.

JEAN: Be human yourself, then. You spit on me, and you won't let me wipe myself off———

JULIE: Help me! Help me! Just tell me what to do, where to go!

JEAN: In God's name, if I only knew myself!

JULIE: I've been crazy, out of my mind, but isn't there any way out?

JEAN: Stay here and keep calm! No one knows anything!

JULIE: Impossible! The others know and Kristine knows.

JEAN: No they don't, and they'd never believe a thing like that!

JULIE (hesitantly): But—it could happen again!

JEAN: That's true!

JULIE: And then?

JEAN (frightened): Then?———Why didn't I think about that? Yes, there is only one thing to do—get away from here! Right away! I can't come with you,

---

mésalliance: Misalliance or mismatch, especially regarding relative social status.

then we'd be finished, so you'll have to go alone—away—anywhere!

JULIE: Alone?———Where?———I can't do that!

JEAN: You must! And before the Count gets back! If you stay, you know what'll happen. Once you make a mistake like this, you want to continue because the damage has already been done.... Then you get bolder and bolder—until finally you're caught! So leave! Later you can write to the Count and confess everything—except that it was me! He'll never guess who it was, and he's not going to be eager to find out, anyway.

JULIE: I'll go if you come with me.

JEAN: Are you out of your head? Miss Julie runs away with her servant! In two days it would be in the newspapers, and that's something your father would never live through.

JULIE: I can't go and I can't stay! Help me! I'm so tired, so terribly tired.———Order me! Set me in motion—I can't think or act on my own . . .

JEAN: What miserable creatures you people are! You strut around with your noses in the air as if you were the lords of creation! All right, I'll order you. Go upstairs and get dressed! Get some money for the trip, and then come back down!

JULIE (*in a half-whisper*): Come up with me!

JEAN: To your room?———Now you're crazy again! (*Hesitates for a moment.*) No! Go, at once! (*Takes her hand to lead her out.*)

JULIE (*as she leaves*): Speak kindly to me, Jean!

JEAN: An order always sounds unkind—now you know how it feels. (*Jean, alone, sighs with relief. He sits at the table, takes out a notebook and pencil, and begins adding up figures, counting aloud as he works. He continues in dumb show until Kristine enters, dressed for church. She is carrying a white tie and shirt front.*)

KRISTINE: Lord Jesus, what a mess! What have you been up to?

JEAN: Oh, Miss Julie dragged everybody in here. You mean you didn't hear anything? You must have been sleeping soundly.

KRISTINE: Like a log.

JEAN: And dressed for church already?

KRISTINE: Of course! You remember you promised to come with me to communion today!

JEAN: Oh, yes, that's right.———And you brought my things. Come on, then! (*He sits down. Kristine starts to put on his shirt front and tie. Pause. Jean begins sleepily.*) What's the gospel text for today?

KRISTINE: On St. John's Day?—the beheading of John the Baptist, I should think!

JEAN: Ah, that'll be a long one, for sure.———Hey, you're choking me!———Oh, I'm sleepy, so sleepy!

KRISTINE: Yes, what have you been doing, up all night? Your face is absolutely green.

JEAN: I've been sitting here gabbing with Miss Julie.

KRISTINE: She has no idea what's proper, that one! (*Pause.*)

JEAN: You know, Kristine . . .

KRISTINE: What?

JEAN: It's really strange when you think about it.———Her!

KRISTINE: What's so strange?

JEAN: Everything! (*Pause.*)

KRISTINE (*looking at the half-empty glasses standing on the table*): Have you been drinking together, too?

JEAN: Yes.

KRISTINE: Shame on you!———Look me in the eye!

JEAN: Well?

KRISTINE: Is it possible? Is it possible?

JEAN (*thinking it over for a moment*): Yes, it is.

KRISTINE: Ugh! I never would have believed it! No, shame on you, shame!

JEAN: You're not jealous of her, are you?

KRISTINE: No, not of her! If it had been Clara or Sofie I'd have scratched your eyes out!———I don't know why, but that's the way I feel.———Oh, it's disgusting!

JEAN: Are you angry at her, then?

KRISTINE: No, at you! That was an awful thing to do, awful! Poor girl!———No, I don't care who knows it—I won't stay in a house where we can't respect the people we work for.

JEAN: Why should we respect them?

KRISTINE: You're so clever, you tell me! Do you want to wait on people who can't behave decently? Do you? You disgrace yourself that way, if you ask me.

JEAN: But it's a comfort to know they aren't any better than us.

KRISTINE: Not for me. If they're no better, what do we have to strive for to better ourselves.———And think of the Count! Think of him! As if he hasn't had enough misery in his life! Lord Jesus! No, I won't stay in this house any longer!———And it had to be with someone like you! If it had been that lawyer, if it had been a real gentleman . . .

JEAN: What do you mean?

KRISTINE: Oh, you're all right for what you are, but there are men and gentlemen, after all!———No, this business with Miss Julie I can never forget. She was so proud, so arrogant with men, you wouldn't have believed she could just go and give herself—and to someone like you! And she was going to have poor Diana shot for running after the gatekeepers' mutt!———Yes, I'm giving my notice, I mean it—I won't stay here any longer. On the twenty-fourth of October, I leave!

JEAN: And then?

KRISTINE: Well, since the subject has come up, it's about time you looked around for something since we're going to get married, in any case.

JEAN: Where am I going to look? I couldn't find a job like this if I was married.

KRISTINE: No, that's true. But you can find work as a porter or as a caretaker in some government office. The state doesn't pay much, I know, but it's secure, and there's a pension for the wife and children . . .

JEAN (*grimacing*): That's all very well, but it's a bit early for me to think about dying for a wife and children. My ambitions are a little higher than that.

KRISTINE: Your ambitions, yes! Well, you have obligations, too! Think about them!

JEAN: Don't start nagging me about obligations. I know what I have to do! (*Listening for something outside.*) Besides, this is something we have plenty of time to think over. Go and get ready for church.

KRISTINE: Who's that walking around up there?

JEAN: I don't know, unless it's Clara.

KRISTINE (*going*): You don't suppose it's the Count, who came home without us hearing him?

JEAN (*frightened*): The Count? No, I don't think so. He'd have rung.

KRISTINE (*going*): Well, God help us! I've never seen anything like this before. (*The sun has risen and shines through the treetops in the park. The light shifts gradually until it slants in through the windows. Jean goes to the door and signals. Miss Julie enters, dressed in travel clothes and carrying a small bird cage, covered with a cloth, which she places on a chair.*)

JULIE: I'm ready now.

JEAN: Shh! Kristine is awake.

JULIE (*very nervous during the following*): Does she suspect something?

JEAN: She doesn't know anything. But my God, you look awful!

JULIE: Why? How do I look?

JEAN: You're pale as a ghost and—excuse me, but your face is dirty.

JULIE: Let me wash up then.———(*She goes to the basin and washes her hands and face.*) Give me a towel!———Oh———the sun's coming up.

JEAN: Then the goblins will disappear.

JULIE: Yes, there must have been goblins out last night!———Jean, listen, come with me! I have some money now.

JEAN (*hesitantly*): Enough?

JULIE: Enough to start with. Come with me! I just can't travel alone on a day like this—midsummer day on a stuffy train—jammed in among crowds of people staring at me. Eternal delays at every station, while I'd wish I had wings. No, I can't, I can't! And then there'll be memories, memories of midsummer days when I was little. The church—decorated with birch leaves and lilacs; dinner at the big table with relatives and friends, the afternoons in the park, dancing, music, flowers, and games. Oh, no matter how far we travel, the memories will follow in the baggage car, with remorse and guilt!

JEAN: I'll go with you—but right away, before it's too late. Right this minute!

JULIE: Get dressed, then! (*Picking up the bird cage.*)

JEAN: But no baggage! It would give us away!

JULIE: No, nothing! Only what we can have in the compartment with us.

JEAN (*has taken his hat*): What've you got there? What is it?

JULIE: It's only my greenfinch. I couldn't leave her behind.

JEAN: What? Bring a bird cage with us? You're out of your head! Put it down!

JULIE: It's the only thing I'm taking from my home—the only living being that loves me, since Diana was unfaithful. Don't be cruel! Let me take her!

JEAN: Put the cage down, I said!———And don't talk so loudly—Kristine will hear us!

JULIE: No, I won't leave her in the hands of strangers! I'd rather you killed her.

JEAN: Bring the thing here, then, I'll cut its head off!

JULIE: Oh! But don't hurt her! Don't . . . no, I can't.

JEAN: Bring it here! I can!

JULIE (*taking the bird out of the cage and kissing it*): Oh, my little Serena, must you die and leave your mistress?

JEAN: Please don't make a scene! Your whole future is at stake! Hurry up! (*He snatches the bird from her, carries it over to the chopping block, and picks up a meat cleaver. Miss Julie turns away.*) You should have learned how to slaughter chickens instead of how to fire pistols. (*He chops off the bird's head.*) Then you wouldn't feel faint at the sight of blood.

JULIE (*screaming*): Kill me, too! Kill me! You, who can slaughter an innocent animal without blinking an eye! Oh, how I hate, how I detest you! There's blood between us now! I curse the moment I set eyes on you! I curse the moment I was conceived in my mother's womb!

JEAN: What good does cursing do? Let's go!

JULIE (*approaching the chopping block, as if drawn against her will*): No, I don't want to go yet. I can't . . . until I see . . . Shh! I hear a carriage———(*She listens, but her eyes never leave the cleaver and the chopping block.*) Do you think I can't stand the sight of blood? You think I'm so weak . . . Oh—I'd like to see your blood and your brains on a chopping block!———I'd like to see your whole sex swimming in a sea of blood, like my little bird . . . I think I could drink from your skull! I'd like to bathe my feet in your open chest and eat your heart roasted whole!———You think I'm weak. You think I love you because my womb craved your seed. You think I want to carry your spawn under my heart and nourish it with my blood—bear your child and take your name! By the way, what is your family name? I've never heard it.———Do you have one? I was to be Mrs. Bootblack—or Madame Pigsty.———You dog, who wears my collar, you lackey, who bears my coat of arms on your buttons—do I have to share you with my cook, compete with my own servant? Oh! Oh! Oh!———You think I'm a coward who wants to run away! No, now I'm staying—and let the storm break! My father will come home . . . to find his desk broken open . . . and his money gone! Then he'll ring—that bell . . . twice for his valet—and then he'll send for the police . . . and then I'll tell everything! Everything! Oh, what a relief it'll be to have it all end—if only it will end!———And then he'll have a stroke and die . . . That'll be the end of all of us—and there'll be peace . . . quiet . . . eternal rest!———And then our coat of arms will be broken against his coffin—the family title extinct—but the valet's line will go on in an orphanage . . . win laurels in the gutter, and end in jail!

JEAN: There's the blue blood talking! Very good, Miss Julie! Just don't let that miller out of the closet! (*Kristine enters, dressed for church, with a psalm-book in her hand.*)

JULIE (*rushing to Kristine and falling into her arms, as if seeking protection*): Help me, Kristine! Help me against this man!

KRISTINE (*unmoved and cold*): What a fine way to behave on a Sunday morning! (*Sees the chopping block.*) And look at this mess!———What does all this mean? Why all this screaming and carrying on?

JULIE: Kristine! You're a woman and my friend! Beware of this swine!

JEAN (*uncomfortable*): While you ladies discuss this, I'll go in and shave. (*Slips off right.*)

JULIE: You must listen to me so you'll understand!

KRISTINE: No, I could never understand such disgusting behavior! Where are you off to in your traveling clothes?———And he had his hat on.———Well? ———Well?

JULIE: Listen to me, Kristine! Listen, and I'll tell you everything———

KRISTINE: I don't want to hear it . . .

JULIE: But you must listen to me . . .

KRISTINE: What about? If it's about this silliness with Jean, I'm not interested, because it's none of my business. But if you're thinking of tricking him into running out, we'll soon put a stop to that!

JULIE (*extremely nervous*): Try to be calm now, Kristine, and listen to me! I can't stay here, and neither can Jean—so we must go away . . .

KRISTINE: Hm, hm!

JULIE (*brightening*): You see, I just had an idea——— What if all three of us go—abroad—to Switzerland and start a hotel together?———I have money, you see—and Jean and I could run it—and I thought you, you could take care of the kitchen . . . Wouldn't that be wonderful?———Say yes! And come with us, and then everything will be settled!———Oh, do say yes! (*Embracing Kristine and patting her warmly.*)

KRISTINE (*coolly, thoughtfully*): Hm, hm!

JULIE (*presto tempo*):° You've never traveled, Kristine. ———You must get out and see the world. You can't imagine how much fun it is to travel by train— always new faces—new countries.———And when we get to Hamburg, we'll stop off at the zoo—you'll like that.———and then we'll go to the theater and

the opera—and when we get to Munich, dear, there we have museums, with Rubens and Raphael, the great painters, as you know.———You've heard of Munich, where King Ludwig lived—the king who went mad.———And then we'll see his castles— they're still there and they're like castles in fairy tales. ———And from there it isn't far to Switzerland— and the Alps.———Imagine—the Alps have snow on them even in the middle of summer!———And oranges grow there and laurel trees that are green all year round———(*Jean can be seen in the wings right, sharpening his razor on a strop which he holds with his teeth and his left hand. He listens to the conversation with satisfaction, nodding now and then in approval. Miss Julie continues tempo prestissimo.*)° And then we'll start a hotel—and I'll be at the desk, while Jean greets the guests . . . does the shopping . . . writes letters.———You have no idea what a life it'll be—the train whistles blowing and the carriages arriving and the bells ringing in the rooms and down in the restaurant.———And I'll make out the bills—and I know how to salt them! . . . You'll never believe how timid travelers are when they have to pay their bills!———And you—you'll be in charge of the kitchen.———Naturally, you won't have to stand over the stove yourself.———And since you're going to be seen by people, you'll have to wear beautiful clothes.———And you, with your looks—no, I'm not flattering you—one fine day you'll grab yourself a husband!———You'll see!— ——A rich Englishman—they're so easy to——— (*Slowing down.*)———catch—and then we'll get rich—and build ourselves a villa on Lake Como.— ——It's true it rains there a little now and then, but ———(*Dully.*)———the sun has to shine sometimes—although it looks dark—and then . . . of course we could always come back home again——— —(*Pause.*)———here—or somewhere else———

KRISTINE: Listen, Miss Julie, do you believe all this?

JULIE (*crushed*): Do I believe it?

KRISTINE: Yes!

JULIE (*wearily*): I don't know. I don't believe in anything anymore. (*She sinks down on the bench and cradles her head in her arms on the table.*) Nothing! Nothing at all!

KRISTINE (*turning right to where Jean is standing*): So, you thought you'd run out!

JEAN (*embarrassed; puts the razor on the table*): Run out? That's no way to put it. You hear Miss Julie's plan, and even if she is tired after being up all night, it's still a practical plan.

KRISTINE: Now you listen to me! Did you think I'd work as a cook for that . . .

JEAN (*sharply*): You watch what you say in front of your mistress! Do you understand?

---

presto tempo: At a rapid pace.

tempo prestissimo: At a very rapid pace.

KRISTINE: Mistress!

JEAN: Yes!

KRISTINE: Listen to him! Listen to him!

JEAN: Yes, you listen! It'd do you good to listen more and talk less! Miss Julie is your mistress. If you despise her, you have to despise yourself for the same reason!

KRISTINE: I've always had enough self-respect———

JEAN: ———to be able to despise other people!

KRISTINE: ———to stop me from doing anything that's beneath me. You can't say that the Count's cook has been up to something with the groom or the swineherd! Can you?

JEAN: No, you were lucky enough to get hold of a gentleman!

KRISTINE: Yes, a gentleman who sells the Count's oats from the stable.

JEAN: You should talk—taking a commission from the grocer and bribes from the butcher.

KRISTINE: What?

JEAN: And you say you can't respect your employers any longer. You, you, you!

KRISTINE: Are you coming to church with me, now? You could use a good sermon after your fine deed!

JEAN: No, I'm not going to church today. You'll have to go alone and confess what you've been up to.

KRISTINE: Yes, I'll do that, and I'll bring back enough forgiveness for you, too. The Savior suffered and died on the Cross for all our sins, and if we go to Him with faith and a penitent heart, He takes all our sins on Himself.

JEAN: Even grocery sins?

JULIE: And do you believe that, Kristine?

KRISTINE: It's my living faith, as sure as I stand here. It's the faith I learned as a child, Miss Julie, and kept ever since. "Where sin abounded, grace did much more abound!"

JULIE: Oh, if I only had your faith. If only . . .

KRISTINE: Well, you see, we can't have it without God's special grace, and that isn't given to everyone———

JULIE: Who is it given to then?

KRISTINE: That's the great secret of the workings of grace, Miss Julie, and God is no respecter of persons, for the last shall be the first . . .

JULIE: Then He does respect the last.

KRISTINE (continuing): . . . and it is easier for a camel to go through the eye of a needle, than for a rich man to enter the Kingdom of God. That's how it is, Miss Julie! Anyhow, I'm going now—alone, and on the way I'm going to tell the groom not to let any horses out, in case anyone wants to leave before the Count gets back!———Goodbye! (Leaves.)

JEAN: What a witch!———And all this because of a greenfinch!———

JULIE (dully): Never mind the greenfinch!———Can you see any way out of this? Any end to it?

JEAN (thinking): No!

JULIE: What would you do in my place?

JEAN: In your place? Let's see—as a person of position, as a woman who had—fallen. I don't know—wait, now I know.

JULIE (taking the razor and making a gesture): You mean like this?

JEAN: Yes! But—understand—I wouldn't do it! That's the difference between us!

JULIE: Because you're a man and I'm a woman? What sort of difference is that?

JEAN: The usual difference—between a man and a woman.

JULIE (with the razor in her hand): I want to, but I can't!———My father couldn't either, the time he should have done it.

JEAN: No, he shouldn't have! He had to revenge himself first.

JULIE: And now my mother is revenged again, through me.

JEAN: Didn't you ever love your father, Miss Julie?

JULIE: Oh yes, deeply, but I've hated him, too. I must have done so without realizing it! It was he who brought me up to despise my own sex, making me half woman, half man. Whose fault is what's happened? My father's, my mother's, my own? My own? I don't have anything that's my own. I don't have a single thought that I didn't get from my father, not an emotion that I didn't get from my mother, and this last idea—that all people are equal—I got that from my fiancé.———That's why I called him a swine! How can it be my fault? Shall I let Jesus take on the blame, the way Kristine does?———No, I'm too proud to do that and too sensible—thanks to my father's teachings.———And as for someone rich not going to heaven, that's a lie. But Kristine won't get in—how will she explain the money she has in the savings bank? Whose fault is it?———What does it matter whose fault it is? I'm still the one who has to bear the blame, face the consequences . . .

JEAN: Yes, but . . . (The bell rings sharply twice. Miss Julie jumps up. Jean changes his coat.) The Count is back! Do you suppose Kristine—(He goes to the speaking tube, taps the lid, and listens.)

JULIE: He's been to his desk!

JEAN: It's Jean, sir! (Listening; the audience cannot hear the Count's voice.) Yes, sir! (Listening.) Yes, sir! Right away! (Listening.) At once, sir! (Listening.) I see, in half an hour!

JULIE (desperately frightened): What did he say? Dear Lord, what did he say?

JEAN: He wants his boots and his coffee in half an hour.

JULIE: So, in half an hour! Oh, I'm so tired. I'm not able to do anything. I can't repent, can't run away, can't stay, can't live—can't die! Help me now! Order me, and I'll obey like a dog! Do me this last service, save my honor, save his name! You know what I should do, but don't have the will to . . . You will it, you order me to do it!

JEAN: I don't know why———but now I can't either———I don't understand.———It's as if this coat made it impossible for me to order you to do anything.———And now, since the Count spoke to me—I—I can't really explain it—but—ah, it's the damn lackey in me!———I think if the Count came down here now—and ordered me to cut my throat, I'd do it on the spot.

JULIE: Then pretend you're he, and I'm you!——— You gave such a good performance before when you knelt at my feet.——— You were a real nobleman.——— Or—have you ever seen a hypnotist in the theater? (*Jean nods.*) He says to his subject: "Take the broom," and he takes it. He says: "Sweep," and he sweeps———

JEAN: But the subject has to be asleep.

JULIE (*ecstatically*): I'm already asleep.———The whole room is like smoke around me . . . and you look like an iron stove . . . shaped like a man in black, with a tall hat—and your eyes glow like coals when the fire is dying—and your face is a white patch, like ashes———(*The sunlight has reached the floor and now shines on Jean.*)———it's so warm and good——— (*She rubs her hands as if warming them before a fire.*) ———and bright—and so peaceful!

JEAN (*taking the razor and putting it in her hand*): Here's the broom! Go now while it's bright—out to the barn—and . . . (*Whispers in her ear.*)

JULIE (*awake*): Thank you. I'm going now to rest! But just tell me—that those who are first can also receive the gift of grace. Say it, even if you don't believe it.

JEAN: The first? No, I can't———But wait—Miss Julie —now I know! You're no longer among the first— you're now among—the last!

JULIE: That's true.———I'm among the very last. I'm the last one of all! Oh!———But now I can't go! ———Tell me once more to go!

JEAN: No, now I can't either! I can't!

JULIE: And the first shall be the last!

JEAN: Don't think, don't think! You're taking all my strength from me, making me a coward.———What was that? I thought the bell moved!———No! Shall we stuff paper in it?———To be so afraid of a bell! ———But it isn't just a bell.———There's someone behind it—a hand sets it in motion—and something else sets the hand in motion.———Maybe if you cover your ears—cover your ears! But then it rings even louder! rings until someone answers.——— And then it's too late! And then the police come— and—then———(*The bell rings twice loudly. Jean flinches, then straightens up.*) It's horrible! But there's no other way!———Go! (*Miss Julie walks firmly out through the door.*)

COMMENTARY

August Strindberg (1849–1912)
FROM THE PREFACE TO *MISS JULIE*   1888
TRANSLATED BY HARRY G. CARLSON

Strindberg's preface sets out his intentions in writing Miss Julie, *a play concerned with the problem of "social climbing or falling, of higher or lower, better or worse, man or woman." He discusses the struggle for dominance between Miss Julie and Jean, and he characterizes Miss Julie as a woman forced to "wreak vengeance" on herself.*

Miss Julie is a modern character. Not that the man-hating half-woman has not existed in all ages but because now that she has been discovered, she has come out in the open to make herself heard. The half-woman is a type who pushes her way ahead, selling herself nowadays for power, decorations, honors, and diplomas, as formerly she used to do for money. The type implies a retrogressive step in evolution, an inferior species who cannot endure. Unfortunately, they are able to pass on their wretchedness; degenerate men seem unconsciously to choose their mates from among them. And so they breed, producing an indeterminate sex for whom life is a torture. Fortunately, the offspring go under either because they are out of harmony with reality or because their repressed instincts break out uncontrollably or because their hopes of achieving equality with men are crushed. The type is tragic, revealing the drama of a desperate struggle against Nature, tragic as the romantic heritage now being dissipated by naturalism, which has a contrary aim: happiness, and happiness belongs only to the strong and skillful species.

But Miss Julie is also: a relic of the old warrior nobility now giving way to a new nobility of nerve and intellect, a victim of her own flawed constitution, a victim of the discord caused in a family by a mother's "crime," a victim of the delusions and conditions of her age — and together these are the equivalent of the concept of Destiny, or Universal Law, of antiquity. Guilt has been abolished by the naturalist, along with God, but the consequences of an action — punishment, imprisonment or the fear of it — that he cannot erase, for the simple reason that they remain, whether he pronounces acquittal or not. Those who have been injured are not as kind and understanding as an unscathed outsider can afford to be. Even if her father felt constrained not to seek revenge, his daughter would wreak vengeance upon herself, as she does here, out of an innate or acquired sense of honor, which the upper classes inherit — from where? From barbarism, from the ancient Aryan home of the race, from medieval chivalry. It is a beautiful thing, but nowadays a hindrance to the survival of the race. It is the nobleman's harikari, which compels him to slit open his own stomach when someone insults him and which survives in a modified form in the duel, that privilege of the nobility. That is why Jean, the servant, lives, while Miss Julie cannot live without honor. The slave's advantage over the nobleman is that he lacks this fatal preoccupation with honor. But in all of us Aryans there is something of the nobleman, or a Don Quixote. And so we sympathize with the suicide, whose act means a loss of honor. We are noblemen enough to be pained when we see the mighty fallen and as superfluous as a corpse, yes, even if the fallen should rise again and make amends through an honorable act. The servant Jean is a race-founder, someone in whom the process of differentiation can be detected. Born the son of a tenant farmer, he has educated himself in the things a gentleman should know. He has been quick to learn, has finely developed senses (smell, taste, sight) and a feeling for what is beautiful. He is already moving up in the world and is not embarrassed about using other people's help. He is alienated from his fellow servants, despising them as parts of a past he has already put behind him. He fears and flees them because they know his secrets, pry into his intentions, envy his rise, and look forward eagerly to his fall. Hence his dual, indecisive nature, vacillating between sympathy for people in high social positions and hatred for those who currently occupy those positions. He is an aristocrat, as he himself says, has learned the secrets of good society, is polished on the surface but coarse beneath, wears a frock coat tastefully but without any guarantee that his body is clean.

He has respect for Miss Julie, but is afraid of Kristine because she knows his dangerous secrets. He is sufficiently callous not to let the night's events disturb his plans for the future. With both a slave's brutality and a master's lack of squeamishness, he can see blood without fainting and shake off misfortune easily. Consequently, he comes through the struggle unscathed and will probably end up an innkeeper. And even if *he* does not become a Rumanian count, his son will become a university student and possibly a county police commissioner. . . .

Apart from the fact that Jean is rising in the world, he is superior to Miss Julie because he is a man. Sexually, he is an aristocrat because of his masculine strength, his more keenly developed senses, and his capacity for taking the initiative. His sense of inferiority is mostly due to the social circumstances in which he happens to be living, and he can probably shed it along with his valet's jacket.

His slave mentality expresses itself in the fearful respect he has for the Count (the boots) and his religious superstition; but he respects the Count mainly as the occupant of the kind of high position to which he himself aspires; and the respect remains even after he has conquered the daughter of the house and seen how empty the lovely shell was.

I do not believe that love in any "higher" sense can exist between two people of such different natures, and so I have Miss Julie's love as something she fabricates in order to protect and excuse herself; and I have Jean suppose himself capable of loving her under other social circumstances. I think it is the same with love as with the hyacinth, which must take root in darkness *before* it can produce a sturdy flower. Here a flower shoots up, blooms, and goes to seed all at once, and that is why it dies so quickly.

A STYLISTIC CASEBOOK

American Melodrama

The rise in popularity of melodrama in nineteenth-century America—in contrast to the dominance of heroic drama, tragedy, and social satire of the previous century in England and Europe—has been attributed to the less sophisticated audiences in American cities. After the Revolutionary War and the War of 1812, the nation had freed itself from England's social domination and established its own mores, demanding an entertainment that was more intelligible, less subtle, and more immediate. The American audiences for melodramas included a more socially mixed population than the English eighteenth-century's upper middle class. American audiences also enjoyed certain plays by Shakespeare and a few other important playwrights, but the overwhelming demand was for sentimental comedies and crime dramas that involved suspense, surprise, and excitement.

Melodrama is sometimes considered a less significant form of drama than the standard repertory of tragedies and comedies because it relies on stereotypes, simplified moral situations, conventional pieties that are never examined critically, and the inevitable happy ending that resolves all of the essentially artificial complications. The resolutions are often achieved by unexpected and unlikely means, such as a revealing birthmark that qualifies the lowly hero as the lost child of a noble family, who is then able to marry the Lady whom he has just saved from death. Many of the situations are unrealistic, and the complexities that might be the sole subject of a more serious drama are usually omitted altogether. Modern musicals have generally followed this formula with considerable success.

Although their plots were unrealistic, sentimental plays relied on spectacle that was realistic in appearance and effect. For example, complex water effects were common in the mid- and late century, and machines that permitted horses to race on stage provided thrills and excitement. Trap doors, revolving stages, and scenery lowered from the flies all helped to intensify the spectacle of the melodrama. These innovations were enhanced by the replacement of gas lights with electric lights in the late 1880s. Bright or controllable light made it possible—and necessary—to achieve a high level of realism in the scenery and settings. The *mise en scene*, or design elements, such as furnishings, costumes, interior details, or outdoor scenes, all had to be realistic because they were so much more visible! This period was remarkable for major improvements in scene painting and scene construction, which was the primary draw for much of the audience. Actors, more visible in bright lights, and capable of powerful dramatic effects in contrasting low lights, seized their advantage, especially in suspenseful scenes implying great danger and in tragic scenes that verged on the operatic. All of these new developments in lighting, set, and costume design paralleled and complemented the rise of melodrama in the United States.

Writing plays was not a lucrative profession in nineteenth-century America, but acting in them often was, which is why many playwrights acted in the plays that made them famous. Born in France, Anna Cora Mowatt began her stage career in the United States after her husband died. Despite the fact that she had no training, she was an immediate success as an actor. Her play *Fashion* (1845) satirizes the ambitious attempts of American socialites to emulate the latest European styles.

The most successful American play of the nineteenth century was *Uncle Tom's Cabin* (1852), a melodrama by George L. Aiken. The play was derived from Harriet Beecher Stowe's novel, which had been published only six months before. Stowe came from a very religious family that condemned the stage outright, so there was never any question of her adapting the novel as a play. Aiken never received permission to write the play, and he earned very little money for his efforts, even though at least 500,000 people attended the play over its lifetime on the stage. The play depends on stereotypes, simplified situations, considerable sentimentality, and unlikely events. It also relied on spectacular effects that shocked and surprised the eager audiences. The play was faithful to Stowe's disapproval of slavery and emerged as successful antislavery propaganda that, according to Abraham Lincoln, contributed to the start of the Civil War.

The Civil War (1860–1865) interrupted the development of theater in many parts of the nation, but it also became a major theme of later plays and melodramas. Bronson Howard's Civil War drama *Shenandoah* (1888) was enormously successful, even though it avoids discussion of the reasons for the war or the nature of the war itself. William Gillette's *Secret Service* (1895) and his earlier Civil War drama *Held by the Enemy* (1886) were successful in large part because he played the primary roles. He was already a matinee idol when he began a lifelong engagement playing the title role in *Sherlock Holmes* (1899), which ran well into the twentieth century and made him a wealthy man.

A prime ingredient of many melodramas of the period was the sensational crime that had to be solved before the play ended. Dion Boucicault, an Irish transplant in America, was the master of the sentimental melodrama and among the most productive playwrights of the age. His pre-Civil War drama *The Octoroon, or Life in Louisiana* (1859) also treated the question of slavery and was set on a southern plantation. Boucicault's play was very popular, in part because it treated the theme in such a way that southerners thought it approved the southern way of life, whereas northerners thought it fueled the abolitionist cause of ending slavery. With the primary focus on solving a murder by ingenious technical means, the question of slavery was played down.

Today, when we read or see the sentimental melodramas of the nineteenth century, we may react to exaggerated dialogue and conventional platitudes much the way Hamlet reacted to the old style of acting when he instructs the players in *Hamlet*. The language may be easy to imitate because it seems so completely artificial, but it is important to understand that the audiences of this period felt such dialogue was artistic. To them, the more high-flown, artificial, and stagy, the better. Instead of parodying it, these audiences imitated it. Thus we must recognize that the drama that dominated the American theater scene in this century reflects the tastes of the audiences that demanded and rewarded it.

Anna Cora Mowatt
FROM *FASHION*   1845

Anna Cora Mowatt (1819–1870) was eight years old when she left France for the United States with her American parents. Her father was an exporter and raised her in a comfortable upper-middle-class family. She was interested in the theater and acting from a very young age, appearing in a play when she was only five. When she was fifteen, Mowatt eloped with a wealthy lawyer, James Mowatt, and lived on Long Island, where she was part of a social circle similar to the one portrayed in her play. She began writing fiction in the 1830s, but in 1840 her husband lost a great deal of money and became ill. Her writing, including the six-act play *Gulzara, or the Persian Star* (1840), took on greater importance and was a means of supporting the entire family, including her three young adopted children. Her task was made more difficult by her suffering from tuberculosis, which made brief periods of convalescence necessary.

During one of her periods of convalescence, Mowatt wrote the five-act comedy *Fashion*. The play was first performed in 1845 and enjoyed remarkable popular and critical success at the Park Theater in New York and at the Walnut Street Theater in Philadelphia a few days later, establishing her as a major force in dramatic literature. Although she did not act in the first performances, Mowatt played the part of Gertrude later in the year. She continued to act, appearing in Bulwer-Lytton's *The Lady of Lyons* at the Park Theater in June 1845, and was an immediate success. Her husband died in 1851, and her own health became so problematic that she had to retire in 1854. She remarried a southerner and eventually split with him over the question of slavery. She moved to Paris, to Florence, and then to England, where she lived until her death in 1870.

Fashion

In *Fashion*, Mowatt satirizes the American pretensions to European styles and the American worship of European aristocracy. This play is in many ways a farce, although its underlying message is clear. The excerpt here includes the complete act V, wherein all the intrigues and deceptions are clarified and the problems of the play are resolved. In earlier acts, we are introduced to the important characters:

Adam Trueman, a wealthy, 72-year-old farmer from the frontier, rugged and, as his name suggests, a man who is a true American and plainspoken

Count Jolimaitre, a fraud acting as a Count

Mrs. Tiffany, a spendthrift duped by the Count

Mr. Tiffany, a businessman who forges documents in order to maintain his wife's lavish lifestyle

Snobson, his clerk who knows about the forgeries and who blackmails Tiffany by demanding that he be permitted to marry Tiffany's daughter

Seraphina, Tiffany's daughter, who falls for the Count

Gertrude, a governess who was raised in Geneva

Captain Howard, an officer in the U.S. Army who loves Gertrude

The fact is that all these characters are essentially stereotypes: the rustic American backwoodsman, the elegant con man, the vain and easily fooled wife, the bland and helpless husband, the villainous servant-clerk, the empty-headed girl, the misunderstood and undervalued heroine, and the dashing but empty military man.

According to Mowatt, Trueman is the one character who was drawn from life, having been modeled on a farmer whom she knew. He has all the lines that seem to establish the moral tone of the play and the desirable moral position of those in society. He delivers speeches such as, "Fashion! And pray what is *fashion*, madam? An agreement between certain persons to live without using their souls! To substitute etiquette for virtue — decorum for purity — manners for morals! To affect a shame for the works of their Creator! And expend all their rapture upon the works of their tailors and dressmakers" (act IV). He plays the critical role in resolving the action in act V.

In act IV, Gertrude concocts a scheme for exposing the fraudulent Count, but her plan backfires and act V begins with people believing she has compromised herself with the Count. She had attempted to set up a tryst between Millinette, the French ladies' maid, and the Count, but she was discovered before she could bring the two of them together. As act V begins, she is under suspicion and tries, by being honest, to clear her name. A large part of the play's appeal in 1845 was its moral: confirming the value of American straightforwardness, and warning against sacrificing a family's financial security for the sake of fashion.

ACT V • *Scene 1*

Mrs. Tiffany's Drawing Room—same Scene as Act First. Gertrude seated at a table, with her head leaning on her hand; in the other hand she holds a pen. A sheet of paper and an ink-stand before her.

GERTRUDE: How shall I write to them? What shall I say? Prevaricate I cannot—(*Rises and comes forward.*) and yet if I write the truth—simple souls! how can they comprehend the motives for my conduct? Nay—the truly pure see no imaginary evil in others! It is only vice, that reflecting its own image, suspects, even the innocent. I have no time to lose—I must prepare them for my return. (*Resumes her seat and writes.*) What a true pleasure there is in daring to be frank! (*After writing a few lines more, pauses.*) Not so frank either,—there is one name that I cannot mention. Ah! that he should suspect—should despise me. (*Writes.*)

(*Enter Trueman.*)

TRUEMAN: There she is! If this girl's soul had only been as fair as her face,—yet she dared to speak the truth,—I'll not forget that! A woman who refuses to tell a lie has one spark of heaven in her still. (*Approaches her.*) Gertrude, (*Gertrude starts and looks up.*) what are you writing there? Plotting more mischief, eh, girl?

GERTRUDE: I was writing a few lines to some friends in Geneva.

TRUEMAN: The Wilsons, eh?

GERTRUDE (*surprised, rising*): Are you acquainted with them, Sir?

TRUEMAN: I shouldn't wonder if I was. I suppose you have taken good care not to mention the dark room—that foreign puppy in the closet—the pleasant surprise—and all that sort of thing, eh?

GERTRUDE: I have no reason for concealment, Sir! for I have done nothing of which I am ashamed!

TRUEMAN: Then I can't say much for your modesty.

GERTRUDE: I should not wish you to say more than I deserve.

TRUEMAN: There's a bold minx! (*Aside.*)

GERTRUDE: Since my affairs seem to have excited your interest—I will not say *curiosity*, perhaps you even feel a desire to inspect my correspondence? There, (*Handing the letter.*) I pride myself upon my good nature,—you may like to take advantage of it?

TRUEMAN: With what an air she carries it off? (*Aside.*) Take advantage of it? So I will. (*Reads.*) What's this? "French chambermaid—Count—impostor—infatuation—Seraphina—Millinette—disguised myself—expose him." Thunder and lightning! I see it all! Come and kiss me, girl! (*Gertrude evinces surprise.*) No, no—I forgot—it won't do to come to that yet! She's a rare girl! I'm out of my senses with joy! I don't know what to do with myself! Tol, de rol, de rol, de ra. (*Capers and sings.*)

GERTRUDE: What a remarkable old man! (*Aside.*) Then you do me justice, Mr. Trueman?

TRUEMAN: I say I don't! Justice? You're above all dependence upon justice! Hurrah! I've found one true woman at last? *True*? (*Pauses thoughtfully.*) Humph! I didn't think of that flaw! Plotting and manoeuvering—not much truth in that? An honest girl should be above stratagems!

GERTRUDE: But my *motive,* Sir, was good.

TRUEMAN: That's not enough—your *actions* must be *good* as well as your *motives*! Why could you not tell the silly girl that man was an imposter?

GERTRUDE: I did inform her of my suspicions—she ridiculed them; the plan I chose was an imprudent one, but I could not devise—

TRUEMAN: I hate devising! Give me a woman with the *firmness* to be *frank*! But no matter—I had no right to look for an angel out of Paradise; and I am as happy—as happy as a Lord! that is, ten times happier than any Lord ever was! Tol, de rol, de rol! Oh! you—you—I'll thrash every fellow that says a word against you!

GERTRUDE: You will have plenty of employment then, Sir, for I do not know of one just now who would speak in my favor!

TRUEMAN: Not *one*, eh? Why, where's your dear Mr. Twinkle? I know all about it—can't say that I admire your choice of a husband! But there's no accounting for a girl's taste.

GERTRUDE: Mr. Twinkle! Indeed you are quite mistaken!

TRUEMAN: No—really? Then you're not taken with him, eh?

GERTRUDE: Not even with his rhymes.

TRUEMAN: Hang that old mother meddle-much! What a fool she has made of me. And so you're quite free, and I may choose a husband for you myself? Heart-whole, eh?

GERTRUDE: I—I—I trust there is nothing *unsound* about my heart.

TRUEMAN: There it is again. Don't prevaricate, girl! I tell you an *evasion* is a *lie in contemplation*, and I hate lying! Out with the truth! Is your heart *free* or not?

GERTRUDE: Nay, Sir, since you *demand* an answer, permit *me* to demand by what right you ask the question?

(*Enter Howard.*)

Colonel Howard here!

TRUEMAN: I'm out again! What's the Colonel to her? (*Retires up.*)

HOWARD (*crosses to her*): I have come, Gertrude, to bid you farewell. To-morrow I resign my commission and leave this city, perhaps for ever. You, Gertrude, it is you who have exiled me! After last evening—

TRUEMAN (*coming forward to Howard*): What the plague have you got to say about last evening?

HOWARD: Mr. Trueman!

TRUEMAN: What have you got to say about last evening? and what have you to say to that little girl at all? It's Tiffany's precious daughter you're in love with.

HOWARD: Miss Tiffany? Never! I never had the slightest pretension—

TRUEMAN: That lying old woman! But I'm glad of it! Oh! Ah! Um! (*Looking significantly at Gertrude and then at Howard.*) I see how it is. So you don't choose to marry Seraphina, eh? Well now, whom do you choose to marry? (*Glancing at Gertrude.*)

HOWARD: I shall not marry at all!

TRUEMAN: You won't? (*Looking at them both again.*) Why you don't mean to say that you don't like—(*Points with his thumb to Gertrude.*)

GERTRUDE: Mr. Trueman, I may have been wrong to boast of my good nature, but do not presume too far upon it.

HOWARD: You like frankness, Mr. Trueman, therefore I will speak plainly. I have long cherished a dream from which I was last night rudely awakened.

TRUEMAN: And that's what you call speaking plainly? Well, I differ with you! But I can guess what you mean. Last night you suspected Gertrude there of—(*angrily*) of what no man shall ever suspect her again while I'm above ground! You did her injustice,—it was a mistake! There, now that matter's settled. Go, and ask her to forgive you,—she's woman enough to do it! Go, go!

HOWARD: Mr. Trueman, you have forgotten to whom you dictate.

TRUEMAN: Then you won't do it? you won't ask her pardon?

HOWARD: Most undoubtedly I will not—not at any man's bidding. I must first know—

TRUEMAN: You won't do it? Then if I don't give you a lesson in politeness—

HOWARD: It will be because you find me your *tutor* in the same science. I am not a man to brook an insult, Mr. Trueman! but we'll not quarrel in presence of the lady.

TRUEMAN: Won't we? I don't know that—

GERTRUDE: Pray, Mr. Trueman—Colonel Howard, pray desist, Mr. Trueman, for my sake! (*Taking hold of his arm to hold him back.*) Colonel Howard, if you will read this letter it will explain everything. (*Hands letter to Howard, who reads.*)

TRUEMAN: He don't deserve an explanation! Didn't I tell him that it was a mistake? Refuse to beg your pardon! I'll teach him, I'll teach him!

HOWARD (*after reading*): Gertrude, how have I wronged you!

TRUEMAN: Oh, you'll beg her pardon now? (*Between them.*)

HOWARD: Hers, Sir, and yours! Gertrude, I fear—

TRUEMAN: You needn't,—she'll forgive you. You don't know these women as well as I do,—they're always ready to pardon; it's their nature, and they can't help it. Come along, I left Antony and his wife in the dining room; we'll go and find them. I've a story of my own to tell! As for you, Colonel, you may follow. Come along. Come along!

(*Leads out Gertrude, followed by Howard.*)
(*Enter Mr. and Mrs. Tiffany, Mr. Tiffany with a bundle of bills in his hand.*)

MRS. TIFFANY: I beg you won't mention the subject again, Mr. Tiffany. Nothing is more plebeian than a discussion upon economy—nothing more *ungenteel* than looking over and fretting over one's bills!

TIFFANY: Then I suppose, my dear, it is quite as ungenteel to *pay* one's bills?

MRS. TIFFANY: Certainly! I hear the *ee-light* never condescend to do anything of the kind. The honor of their invaluable patronage is sufficient for the persons they employ!

TIFFANY: *Patronage* then is a newly invented food upon which the working classes fatten? What convenient appetites poor people must have! Now listen to what I am going to say. As soon as my daughter marries Mr. Snobson—

(*Enter Prudence, a three-cornered note in her hand.*)

PRUDENCE: Oh, dear! oh, dear! what shall we do! Such a misfortune! Such a disaster! Oh, dear! oh, dear!

MRS. TIFFANY: Prudence, you are the most tiresome creature! What *is* the matter?

PRUDENCE (*passing up and down the stage*): Such a disgrace to the whole family! But I always expected it. Oh, dear! oh, dear!

MRS. TIFFANY (*following her up and down the stage*): What are you talking about, Prudence? Will you tell me what has happened?

PRUDENCE (*still pacing, Mrs. Tiffany following*): Oh! I can't, I can't! You'll feel so dreadfully! How could she do such a thing! But I expected nothing else! I never did, I never did!

MRS. TIFFANY (*still following*): Good gracious! what do you mean, Prudence? Tell me, will you tell me? I shall get into such a passion! What *is* the matter?

PRUDENCE (*still pacing*): Oh, Betsy, Betsy! That your daughter should have come to that? Dear me, dear me!

TIFFANY: Seraphina? Did you say Seraphina? What has happened to her? what has she done?

(*Following Prudence up and down the stage on the opposite side from Mrs. Tiffany.*)

MRS. TIFFANY (*still following*): What *has* she done? what *has* she done?

PRUDENCE: Oh! something dreadful—dreadful—shocking!

TIFFANY (*still following*): Speak quickly and plainly—you torture me by this delay, Prudence, be calm, and speak! What is it?

PRUDENCE (*stopping*): Zeke just told me—he carried her travelling trunk himself—she gave him a whole dollar! Oh, my!

TIFFANY: Her trunk? where? where?

PRUDENCE: Round the corner!

MRS. TIFFANY: What did she want with her trunk? You are the most vexatious creature, Prudence! There is no bearing your ridiculous conduct!

PRUDENCE: Oh, you will have worse to bear—worse! Seraphina's gone!

TIFFANY: Gone! where?

PRUDENCE: Off!—eloped—eloped with the Count! Dear me, dear me! I always told you she would!

TIFFANY: Then I am ruined!

(*Stands with his face buried in his hands.*)

MRS. TIFFANY: Oh, what a ridiculous girl! And she might have had such a splendid wedding! What could have possessed her?

TIFFANY: The devil himself possessed her, for she has ruined me past all redemption! Gone, Prudence, did you say gone? Are you *sure* they are gone?

PRUDENCE: Didn't I tell you so! Just look at this note—one might know by the very fold of it—

TIFFANY (*snatching the note*): Let me see it! (*Opens the note and reads.*) "My dear Ma,—When you receive this I shall be a *countess!* Isn't it a sweet title? The Count and I were forced to be married privately, for reasons which I will explain in my next. You must pacify Pa, and put him in a good humour before I come back, though now I'm to be a countess I suppose I shouldn't care!" Undutiful huzzy! "We are going to make a little excursion and will be back in a week.

"Your dutiful daughter—Seraphina." A man's curse is sure to spring up at his own hearth,—here is mine! The solo curb upon that villain gone, I am wholly in his power! Oh! the first downward step from honor—he who takes it cannot pause in his mad descent and is sure to be hurried on to ruin!

MRS. TIFFANY: Why, Mr. Tiffany, how you do take on! And I dare say to elope was the most fashionable way after all!

(*Enter Trueman, leading Gertrude, and followed by Howard.*)

TRUEMAN: Where are all the folks? Here, Antony, you are the man I want. We've been hunting for you all over the house. Why—what's the matter? There's a face for a thriving city merchant! Ah! Antony, you never wore such a hang-dog look as that when you trotted about the country with your pack upon your back! Your shoulders are no broader now—but they've a heavier load to carry—that's plain!

MRS. TIFFANY: Mr. Trueman, such allusions are highly improper! What would my daughter, *the Countess,* say!

GERTRUDE: The Countess? Oh! Madam!

MRS. TIFFANY: Yes, the Countess!" My daughter Seraphina, the Countess *dee* Jolimaitre! What have you to say to that? No wonder you are surprised after your *recherché, abimé* conduct! I have told you already, Miss Gertrude, that you were not a proper person to enjoy the inestimable advantages of my patronage. You are dismissed—do you understand? Discharged!

TRUEMAN: Have you done? Very well, it's my turn now. Antony, perhaps what I have to say don't concern you as much as some others—but I want you to listen to me. You remember, Antony, (*his tone becomes serious*), a blue-eyed, smiling girl—

TIFFANY: Your daughter, Sir? I remember her well.

TRUEMAN: None ever saw her to forget her! Give me your hand, man. There—that will do! Now let me go on. I never coveted wealth—yet twenty years ago I found myself the richest farmer in Catteraugus. This cursed money made my girl an object of speculation. Every idle fellow that wanted to feather his nest was sure to come courting Ruth. There was one—my heart misgave me the instant I laid eyes upon him—for he was a city chap, and not over fond of the truth. But Ruth—ah! she was too pure herself to look for guile! His fine words and his fair looks—the old story—she was taken with him—I said, "no"—but the girl liked her own way better than her old father's—girls always do! and one morning—the rascal robbed me—not of my money, he would have been welcome to that—but of the only treasure I cherished—my daughter!

TIFFANY: But you forgave her!

TRUEMAN: I did! I knew she would never forgive herself—that was punishment enough! The scoundrel thought he was marrying my gold with my daughter—he was mistaken! I took care that they should never want; but that was all. She loved him—what will not woman love? The villain broke her heart—mine was tougher, or it wouldn't have stood what it did. A year after they were married, he forsook her! She came back to her old home—her old father! It couldn't last long—she pined—and pined—and—then—she died! Don't think me an old fool—though I am one—for grieving won't bring her back. (*Bursts into tears.*)

TIFFANY: It was a heavy loss!

TRUEMAN: So heavy, that I should not have cared how soon I followed her, but for the child she left! As I pressed that child in my arms, I swore that my unlucky wealth should never curse it, as it had cursed its mother! It was all I had to love—but I sent it away—and the neighbors thought it was dead. The girl was brought up tenderly but humbly by my wife's relatives in Geneva. I had her taught true independence—she had hands—capacities—and should use them! Money should never buy her a husband! for I resolved not to claim her until she had made her choice, and found the man who was willing to take her for herself alone. She turned out a rare girl! and it's time her old grandfather claimed her. Here he is to do it! And there stands Ruth's child! Old Adam's heiress! Gertrude, Gertrude!—my child! (*Gertrude rushes into his arms.*)

PRUDENCE (*after a pause*): Do tell; I want to know! But I knew it! I always said Gertrude would turn out somebody, after all!

MRS. TIFFANY: Dear me! Gertrude an heiress! My dear Gertrude, I always thought you a very charming girl—quite YOU-NICK—an heiress! I must give her a ball! I'll introduce her into society myself—of course an heiress must make a sensation! (*Aside.*)

HOWARD: I am too bewildered even to wish her joy. Ah! there will be plenty to do that now—but the gulf between us is wider than ever. (*Aside.*)

TRUEMAN: Step forward, young man, and let us know what you are muttering about. I said I would never claim her until she had found the man who loved her for herself. I *have* claimed her—yet I never break my word—I think I *have* found that man! and here he is. (*Strikes Howard on the shoulder.*) Gertrude's yours! There—never say a word, man—don't bore me with your thanks—you can cancel all obligations by making that child happy! There—take her!—Well, girl, and what do you say?

GERTRUDE: That I rejoice too much at having found a parent for my first act to be one of disobedience! (*Gives her hand to Howard.*)

TRUEMAN: How very dutiful! and how disinterested!

(*Tiffany retires up—and paces the stage, exhibiting great agitation.*)

PRUDENCE (*to Trueman*): All the *single folks* are getting married!

TRUEMAN: No they are not. You and I are single folks, and we're not likely to get married.

MRS. TIFFANY: My dear Mr. Trueman—my sweet Gertrude, when my daughter, the Countess, returns, she will be delighted to hear of this *deenooment*! I assure you that the Countess will be quite charmed!

GERTRUDE: The Countess? Pray, Madam, where *is* Seraphina?

MRS. TIFFANY: The Countess *dee* Jolimaitre, my dear, is at this moment on her way to—to Washington! Where after visiting all the fashionable curiosities of the day—including the President—she will return to grace her native city!

GERTRUDE: I hope you are only jesting, Madam? Seraphina is not married?

MRS. TIFFANY: Excuse me, my dear, my daughter had this morning the honor of being united to the Count *dee* Jolimaitre!

GERTRUDE: Madam! He is an imposter!

MRS. TIFFANY: Good gracious! Gertrude, how can you talk in that disrespectful way of a man of rank? An heiress, my dear, should have better manners! The Count—

(*Enter Millinette, crying.*)

MILLINETTE: Oh! Madame! I will tell everything—oh! dat monstre! He break my heart!

MRS. TIFFANY: Millinette, what is the matter?

MILLINETTE: Oh! he promise to marry me—I love him much—and now Zeke say he run away vid Mademoiselle Seraphina!

MRS. TIFFANY: What insolence! The girl is mad! Count Jolimaitre marry my *femmy de chamber*!

MILLINETTE: Oh! Madame, he is not one Count, not at all! Dat is only de title he go by in dis country. De foreigners always take de large title ven dey do come here. His name *à Paris* vas Gustave Treadmill. But he not one Frenchman at all, but he do live one long time *à Paris*. First he live vid Monsieur Vermicelle—dere he vas de head cook! Den he live vid Monsieur Tire-nez, de barber! After dat he live wid Monsieur le Comte Frippon-fin—and dere he vas le Comte's valet! Dere, now I tell everyting I feel one great deal better!

MRS. TIFFANY: Oh! good gracious! I shall faint! Not a Count! What will everybody say? It's no such thing! I say he *is* a Count! One can see the foreign *jenny says quoi* in his face! Don't you think I can tell a Count when I see one? I say he *is* a Count!

(*Enter Snobson, his hat on—his hands thrust in his pocket—evidently a little intoxicated.*)

SNOBSON: I won't stand it! I say I won't

TIFFANY (*rushing up to him*): Mr. Snobson, for heaven's sake—(*Aside.*)

SNOBSON: Keep off! I'm a hard customer to get the better of! You'll see if I don't come out strong!

TRUEMAN (*quietly knocking off Snobson's hat with his stick*): Where are your manners, man?

SNOBSON: My business ain't with you, Catteraugus; you've waked up the wrong passenger!—Now the way I'll put it into Tiff will be a caution. I'll make him wince! That extra mint julep has put the true pluck in me. Now for it! (*Aside*) Mr. Tiffany, Sir—you need n't think to come over me, Sir—you'll have to get up a little earlier in the morning before you do *that*, Sir! I'd like to know, Sir, how you came to assist your daughter in running away with that foreign loafer? It was a downright swindle, Sir. After the conversation I and you had on that subject she wasn't your property, Sir.

TRUEMAN: What, Antony, is that the way your city clerk bullies his boss?

SNOBSON: You're drunk, Catteraugus—don't expose your-self—you're drunk! Taken a little too much toddy, my old boy! Be quiet! I'll look after you, and they won't find it out. If you want to be busy, you may take care of my *hat*—I feel so deuced weak in the chest, I don't think I *could* pick it up myself.—Now to put the screws to Tiff. (*Aside.*) Mr. Tiffany, Sir—you have broken your word, as no virtuous individual—no honorable member—of—the—com—mu—ni—ty—

TIFFANY: Have some pity, Mr. Snobson, I beseech you! I had nothing to do with my daughter's elopement! I will agree to anything you desire—your salary shall be doubled—trebled—(*Aside to him.*)

SNOBSON (*aloud*): No you don't. No bribery and corruption.

TIFFANY: I implore you to be silent. You shall become partner of the concern, if you please—only do not speak. You are not yourself at this moment. (*Aside to him.*)

SNOBSON: Ain't I, though? I feel *twice* myself. I feel like two Snobsons rolled into one, and I'm chock full of the spunk of a dozen! Now Mr. Tiffany, Sir—

TIFFANY: I shall go distracted! Mr. Snobson, if you have one spark of manly feeling— (*Aside to him.*)

TRUEMAN: Antony, why do you stand disputing with that drunken jackass? Where's your nigger? Let him kick the critter out, and be of use for once in his life.

SNOBSON: Better be quiet, Catteraugus. This ain't your hash, so keep your spoon out of the dish. Don't expose yourself, old boy.

TRUEMAN: Turn him out, Antony!

SNOBSON: He daren't do it! Ain't I up to him? Ain't he in my power? Can't I knock him into a cocked hat with a word? And now he's got my steam up—I *will* do it!

TIFFANY (*beseechingly*): Mr. Snobson—my friend—

SNOBSON: It's no go—steam's up—and I don't stand at anything!

TRUEMAN: You won't *stand* here long unless you mend your manners—you're not the first man I've *upset* because he didn't know his place.

SNOBSON: I know where Tiff's place is, and that's in the *States' Prison*! It's bespoke already. He would have it! He wouldn't take pattern of me, and behave like a gentleman! He's a *forger*, Sir! (*Tiffany throws himself into a chair in an attitude of despair; the others stand transfixed with astonishment.*) He's been forging Dick Anderson's endorsements of his notes these ten months. He's got a couple in the bank that will send him to the wall anyhow—if he can't make a raise. I took them there myself! Now you know what he's worth. I said I'd expose him, and I have done it!

MRS. TIFFANY: Get out of the house! You ugly, little, drunken brute, get out! It's not true. Mr. Trueman, put him out; you have got a stick—put him out!

(*Enter Seraphina, in her bonnet and shawl—a parasol in her hand.*)

SERAPHINA: I hope Zeke hasn't delivered my note.

(*Stops in surprise at seeing the persons assembled.*)

MRS. TIFFANY: Oh, here is the Countess! (*Advances to embrace her.*)

TIFFANY (*starting from his seat, and seizing Seraphina violently by the arm*): Are—you—married?

SERAPHINA: Goodness. Pa, how you frighten me! No, I'm not married, *quite*.

TIFFANY: Thank heaven.

MRS. TIFFANY (*drawing Seraphina aside*): What's the matter? Why did you come back?

SERAPHINA: The clergyman wasn't at home—I came back for my jewels—the Count said nobility couldn't get on without them.

TIFFANY: I may be saved yet! Seraphina, my child, you will not see me disgraced—ruined! I have been a kind father to you—at least I have tried to be one—although your mother's extravagance made a *madman* of me! The Count is an imposter—you seemed to like him—(*pointing to Snobson*). Heaven forgive me! (*Aside.*) Marry *him* and save *me*. You, Mr. Trueman, you will be my friend in this hour of extreme need—you will advance the sum which I require—I pledge myself to return it. My wife—my child—who will support them were I—the thought makes me frantic! You will aid me? You had a child yourself.

TRUEMAN: But I did not *sell* her—it was her own doings. Shame on you, Antony! Put a price on your own flesh and blood! Shame on such foul traffic!

TIFFANY: Save me—I conjure you—for my father's sake.

TRUEMAN: For your *father's* SON's sake I will *not* aid you in becoming a greater villain than you are!

GERTRUDE: Mr. Trueman—Father, I should say—save him—do not embitter our happiness by permitting this calamity to fall upon another—

TRUEMAN: Enough—I did not need your voice, child. I am going to settle this matter my own way.

(*Goes up to Snobson—who has seated himself and fallen asleep—tilts him out of the chair.*)

SNOBSON (*waking up*): Eh? Where's the fire? Oh! it's you, Catteraugus.

TRUEMAN: If I comprehend aright, you have been for some time aware of your principal's forgeries?

(*As he says this, he beckons to Howard, who advances as witness.*)

SNOBSON: You've hit the nail, Catteraugus! Old chap saw that I was up to him six months ago; left off throwing dust into my eyes—

TRUEMAN: Oh, he did!

SNOBSON: Made no bones of forging Anderson's name at my elbow.

TRUEMAN: Forged at your elbow? You saw him do it?

SNOBSON: I did.

TRUEMAN: Repeatedly.

SNOBSON: Re—pea—ted—ly.

TRUEMAN: Then you, Rattlesnake, if he goes to the States' Prison, you'll take up your quarters there too. You are an accomplice, an *accessory*!

(*Trueman walks away and seats himself, Howard rejoins Gertrude. Snobson stands for some time bewildered.*)

SNOBSON: The deuce, so I am! I never thought of that! I must make myself scarce. I'll be off! Tif, I say, Tif! (*Going up to him and speaking confidentially*) that drunken old rip has got us in his power. Let's give him the slip and be off. They want men of genius at the West,—we're sure to get on! You—you can set up for a writing master, and teach copying *signatures*; and I—I'll give lectures on *temperance*! You won't come, eh? Then I'm off without you. Good bye, Catteraugus! Which is the way to California? (*Steals off.*)

TRUEMAN: There's one debt your city owes me. And now let us see what other nuisances we can abate. Antony, I'm not given to preaching, therefore I shall not say much about what you have done. Your face speaks for itself,—the crime has brought its punishment along with it.

TIFFANY: Indeed it has, Sir! In *one* year I have lived a *century* of misery.

TRUEMAN: I believe you, and upon one condition I will assist you—

TIFFANY: My friend—my first, ever kind friend,—only name it!

TRUEMAN: You must sell your house and all these gew gaws, and bundle your wife and daughter off to the country. There let them learn economy, true independence, and home virtues, instead of foreign follies. As for yourself, continue your business—but let moderation, in future, be your counsellor, and let *honesty* be your confidential clerk.

TIFFANY: Mr. Trueman, you have made existence once more precious to me! My wife and daughter shall quit the city to-morrow, and—

PRUDENCE: It's all coming right! It's all coming right! We'll go to the county of Catteraugus. (*Walking up to Trueman.*)

TRUEMAN: No, you won't—I make that a stipulation. Antony; keep clear of Catteraugus. None of your fashionable examples there!

(*Jolimaitre appears in the Conservatory and peeps into the room unperceived.*)

COUNT: What can detain Seraphina? We ought to be off!

MILLINETTE (*turns round, perceives him, runs and forces him into the room.*): Here he is! Ah, Gustave, mon cher Gustave! I have you now and we never part no more. Don't frown, Gustave, don't frown.

TRUEMAN: Come forward, Mr. Count! and for the edification of fashionable society confess that you're an imposter.

COUNT: An imposter? Why, you abominable old—

TRUEMAN: Oh, your feminine friend has told us all about it, the cook—the valet—barber and all that sort of thing. Come, confess, and something may be done for you.

COUNT: Well, then, I do confess I am no count; but really, ladies and gentlemen, I may recommend myself as the most capital cook.

MRS. TIFFANY: Oh, Seraphina!

SERAPHINA: Oh, Ma! (*They embrace and retire up.*)

TRUEMAN: Promise me to call upon the whole circle of your fashionable acquaintances with your own advertisements and in your cook's attire, and I will set you up in business to-morrow. Better turn stomachs than turn heads!

MILLINETTE: But you will marry me?

COUNT: Give us your hand, Millinette! Sir, command me for the most delicate *paté*—the daintiest *croquette à la royale*—the most transcendent *omelette soufflée* that ever issued from a French pastry-cook's oven. I hope you will pardon my conduct, but I heard that in America, where you pay homage to titles while you profess to scorn them—where *Fashion* makes the basest coin current—where you have no kings, no princes, no *nobility*—

TRUEMAN: Stop there! I object to your use of that word. When justice is found only among lawyers—health among physicians—and patriotism among politicians, *then* may you say that there is no *nobility* where there are no titles! But we *have* kings, princes, and nobles in abundance—of *Nature's stamp*, if not of *Fashion's*,—we have honest men, warm hearted and brave, and we have women—gentle, fair, and true, to whom no *title* could add *nobility*.

EPILOGUE

PRUDENCE: I told you so! And now you hear and see.
    I told you *Fashion* would the fashion be!
TRUEMAN: Then both its point and moral I distrust.
COUNT: Sir, is that liberal?
HOWARD: Or is it just?
TRUEMAN: The guilty have escaped!
TIFFANY: Is, therefore, sin. Made charming? Ah! there's punishment within!
    Guilt ever carries his own scourge along.
GERTRUDE: Virtue her own reward!
TRUEMAN: You're right, I'm wrong.
MRS. TIFFANY: How we have been deceived!
PRUDENCE: I told you so.
SERAPHINA: To lose at once a title and a beau!
COUNT: A count no more, I'm no more of *account*.
TRUEMAN: But to a nobler title you may mount,
    And be in time—who knows?—an honest man!
COUNT: Eh, Millinette?
MILLINETTE: Oh, *oui*—I know you can!
GERTRUDE (*to audience*): But ere we close the scene, a word with you,—
    We charge you answer,—Is this picture true?
    Some little mercy to our efforts show,
    Then let the world your honest verdict know.
    Here let it see portrayed its ruling passion,
    And learn to prize at its just value—*Fashion*.

George L. Aiken
FROM *UNCLE TOM'S CABIN, OR LIFE AMONG THE LOWLY*

1852

Harriet Beecher Stowe's novel *Uncle Tom's Cabin* was published only six months before George Aiken's play was first produced in 1852. At least one friend of Stowe's asked for her permission to stage the novel and was refused because Stowe, the daughter of a famous minister and the wife of a theologian, was convinced that the stage was unholy and led Christians to bad behavior. But she did not have the means to protect her novel from Aiken's adaptation, which in its first production lasted three hundred performances and was an instant success. Historians estimate that the play was seen by at least half a million people from 1852 to the early years of the twentieth century.

Very little is known about George Aiken (1830–1876). He had written some dime novels before he wrote this play, and so far as we know, he wrote no other plays. However, we do know that, like most playwrights of the period, he received very little for his script: $40 and a gold watch. His money was made from acting in the drama itself. He played two roles in different productions: George Shelby, the white master who wants to buy back Uncle Tom in Act VI (included here), and George Harris, the black slave who ultimately fights for and gains his freedom in Canada in the acts that precede this one.

There were several different dramatic versions of Stowe's novel in the nineteenth century, but Aiken's became the standard and was used as the basis of subsequent films in the early twentieth century because it was the only version that was published in book form. Stowe, who had never before been to a theater, eventually was spirited into a Washington theater by a friend who arranged for Stowe to be seated in the manager's box through a private entrance and covered her so she would not be recognized. The friend later reported that Stowe was moved to joy and tears, along with the rest of the audience.

Uncle Tom's Cabin

The play was originally written as two plays, which is one reason why this version has six acts. The final scene, a wordless tableau, was added in 1853 to prevent people from leaving the theater abruptly, and on a down note, after Tom's death. The play also has two primary plots. The first, which opens the play, is that of the slave George Harris. Harris complains about his master to his wife Eliza, whose Christian beliefs console her with the thought that she must obey her master and suffer slavery. George is not content with resignation and speaks almost blasphemously about what he feels is a careless God. He is perceptive and articulate as well:

> My master! And who made him my master? That's what I think of! What right has he to me? I'm as much of a man as he is! What right has he to make a dray-horse of me?—to take me from things I can do better than he can, and put me to work that any horse can do? He tries to do it; he says he'll bring me down and humble me, and he puts me to just the hardest, meanest and dirtiest work, on purpose.

George is a highly sympathetic character, and, aided by a frontierman called Phineas Fletcher, who kills the slave hunter Loker, George and Eliza and their child cross over the half-frozen Ohio River to the North and eventually into Canada to begin a new life.

As in the novel, the portraits of blacks are uniformly sympathetic, and the portraits of whites are uniformly unsympathetic. The white characters are either violent and cruel, like Simon Legree, or well-meaning and weak, like George Shelby. Stowe's primary purpose was propagandistic—to protest and portray slavery as inhuman and cruel—and Aiken's play follows her lead entirely. The use of stereotypes advances the purposes of the novel and play.

A scene from a 1901 stage production of *Uncle Tom's Cabin*, showing Eliza and George's flight through ice and snow to eventual freedom in Canada.

The second plot is that of Uncle Tom, the "good slave." He accepts his lot in life as he thinks a Christian should. Even here in act VI he offers to sacrifice himself for his oppressor if need be, because it is the Christian thing to do. Such behavior pleased the primarily white audiences of the nineteenth century, especially in the decade before the Civil War, when the question of slavery was hotly debated in the North. However, black commentators were not eager to accept the portrayal of any such obedient slave as being either desirable or realistic.

Because of financial setbacks that befall his master, Mr. Shelby, Uncle Tom is "sold down the river" into a frightening environment. But while on the river boat he meets Eva, a little white girl whose sense of Christian charity matches Tom's, and the two of them form a special bond. When Eva falls off the boat, Tom saves her life, and Eva's father, St. Clare, buys Tom from the slave trader. He and Eva become friends who understand each other, but Eva dies of an illness. She is seen in a vision that helps people change their lives, and St. Clare promises to free Tom. However, he is killed in a fight, and ultimately Tom is bought by the evil Simon Legree, who embodies the stereotype of the cruel and inhuman slave driver. His brutality to the humane and sympathetic Uncle Tom makes Tom into a martyr in act VI.

ACT VI • Scene 1

Dark landscape. An old, roofless shed.

(*Tom is discovered in shed, lying on some old cotton bagging. Cassy kneels by his side, holding a cup to his lips.*)

CASSY: Drink all ye want. I knew how it would be. It isn't the first time I've been out in the night, carrying water to such as you.

TOM (*returning cup*); Thank you, missis.

CASSY: Don't call me missis. I'm a miserable slave like yourself—a lower one than you can ever be! It's no use, my poor fellow, this you've been trying to do. You were a brave fellow. You had the right on your side; but it's all in vain for you to struggle. You are in the Devil's hands: he is the strongest, and you must give up.

TOM: Oh! how can I give up?

CASSY: You see *you* don't know anything about it; I do. Here you are, on a lone plantation, ten miles from any other, in the swamps; not a white person here who could testify, if you were burned alive. There's no law here that can do you, or any of us, the least good; and this man! there's no earthly thing that he is not bad enough to do. I could make one's hair rise, arid their teeth chatter, if I should only tell what I've seen and been knowing to here; and it's no use resisting! Did I *want* to live with him? Wasn't I a woman delicately bred? and he!—Father in Heaven! what was he and is he? And yet I've lived with him these five years, and cursed every moment of my life, night and day.

TOM: Oh, heaven! have you quite forgot us poor critters?

CASSY: And what are these miserable low dogs you work with, that you should suffer on their account? Every one of them would turn against you the first time they get a chance. They are all of them as low and cruel to each other as they can be; there's no use in your suffering to keep from hurting them!

TOM: What made 'em cruel? If I give out, I shall get used to it and grow, little by little, just like 'em. No, no, missis, I've lost everything, wife, and children, and home, and a kind master, and he would have set me free if he'd only lived a day longer—I've lost everything in *this* world, and now I can't lose heaven, too; no, I can't get to be wicked besides all.

CASSY: But it can't be that He will lay sin to our account; he won't charge it to us when we are forced to it; he'll charge it to them that drove us to it. Can I do anything more for you? Shall I give you some more water?

TOM: Oh missis! I wish you'd go to Him who can give you living waters!

CASSY: Go to Him! Where is He? Who is He?

TOM: Our Heavenly Father!

CASSY: I used to see the picture of Him, over the altar, when I was a girl; but *he isn't here!* there's nothing here but sin, and long, long despair! There, there, don't talk any more, my poor fellow. Try to sleep, if you can. I must hasten back, lest my absence be noted. Think of me when I am gone, Uncle Tom, and pray, pray for me. (*Exit Cassy. Tom sinks back to sleep.*)

Scene 2

Street in New Orleans.

(*Enter George Shelby.*)

GEORGE: At length my mission of mercy is nearly finished; I have reached my journey's end. I have now but to find the house of Mr. St. Clare, re-purchase old Uncle Tom, and convey him back to his wife and children, in old Kentucky. Some one approaches; he may, perhaps, be able to give me the information I require. I will accost him.

(*Enter Marks.*)

Pray, sir, can you tell me where Mr. St. Clare dwells?

MARKS: Where I don't think you'll be in a hurry to seek him.

GEORGE: And where is that?

MARKS: In the grave!

GEORGE: Stay, sir! you may be able to give me some information concerning Mr. St. Clare.

MARKS: I beg pardon, sir, I am a lawyer; I can't afford to *give* anything.

GEORGE: But you would have no objections to selling it?

MARKS: Not the slightest.

GEORGE: What do you value it at?

MARKS: Well, say five dollars, that's reasonable.

GEORGE: There they are. (*Gives money.*) Now answer me to the best of your ability. Has the death of St. Clare caused his slaves to be sold?

MARKS: It has.

GEORGE: How were they sold?

MARKS: At auction—they went dirt cheap.

GEORGE: How were they bought—all in one lot?

MARKS: No, they went to different bidders.

GEORGE: Was you present at the sale?

MARKS: I was.

GEORGE: Do you remember seeing a negro among them called Tom.

MARKS: What, Uncle Tom?

GEORGE: The same—who bought him?

MARKS: A Mr. Legree.

GEORGE: Where is his plantation?

MARKS: Up in Louisiana, on the Red River; but a man never could find it unless he had been there before.

GEORGE: Who could I get to direct me there?

MARKS: Well, stranger, I don't know of any one just at present, 'cept myself, could find it for you; it's such an out-of-the-way sort of hole; and if you are a mind to come down handsomely, why, I'll do it.

GEORGE: The reward shall be ample.

MARKS: Enough said, stranger; let's take the steamboat at once. (*Exeunt.*)

Scene 3

A rough chamber.

(*Enter Legree. Sits.*)

LEGREE: Plague on that Sambo, to kick up this yer row between me and the new hands.

(*Cassy steals on, and stands behind him.*)

The fellow won't be fit to work for a week now, right in the press of the season.

CASSY: Yes, just like you.

LEGREE: Hah! you she-devil! you've come back, have you? (*Rises.*)

CASSY: Yes, I have; come to have my own way, too.

LEGREE: You lie, you jade! I'll be up to my word. Either behave yourself, or stay down in the quarters and fare and work with the rest.

CASSY: I'd rather, ten thousand times, live in the dirtiest hole in the quarters, than be under your hoof!

LEGREE: But you are under my hoof, for all that, that's one comfort; so sit down here and listen to reason. (*Grasps her wrist.*)

CASSY: Simon Legree, take care! (*Legree lets go his hold.*) You're afraid of me, Simon, and you've reason to be; for I've got the Devil in me!

LEGREE: I believe to my soul you have. After all, Cassy, why can't you be friends with me, as you used to?

CASSY (*bitterly*): Used to!

LEGREE: I wish, Cassy, you'd behave yourself decently.

CASSY: *You* talk about behaving decently! and what have you been doing? You haven't even sense enough to keep from spoiling one of your best hands, right in the most pressing season, just for your devilish temper.

LEGREE: I was a fool, it's a fact, to let any such brangle come up; but when Tom set up his will he had to be broke in.

CASSY: You'll never break *him* in.

LEGREE: Won't I? I'd like to know if I won't! He'll be the first nigger that ever come it round me! I'll break every bone in his body but he shall give up.

(*Enter Sambo, with a paper in his hand; he stands bowing.*)

LEGREE: What's that, you dog?

SAMBO: It's a witch thing, mas'r.

LEGREE: A what?

SAMBO: Something that niggers gits from witches. Keep 'em from feeling when they's flogged. He had it tied round his neck with a black string.

(*Legree takes the paper and opens it. A silver dollar drops on the stage, and a long curl of light hair twines around his finger.*)

LEGREE: Damnation. (*Stamping and writhing, as if the hair burned him.*) Where did this come from? Take if off! burn it up! burn it up! (*Throws the curl away.*) What did you bring it to me for?

SAMBO (*trembling*): I beg pardon, mas'r; I thought you would like to see 'um.

LEGREE: Don't you bring me any more of your devilish things. (*Shakes his fist at Sambo who runs off. Legree kicks the dollar after him.*) Blast it! where did he get that? If it didn't look just like — whoo! I thought I'd forgot that. Curse me if I think there's any such thing as forgetting anything, any how.

CASSY: What is the matter with you, Legree? What is there in a simple curl of fair hair to appal a man like you — you who are familiar with every form of cruelty.

LEGREE: Cassy, to-night the past has been recalled to me — the past that I have so long and vainly striven to forget.

CASSY: Hast aught on this earth power to move a soul like thine?

LEGREE: Yes, for hard and reprobate as I now seem, there has been a time when I have been rocked on the bosom of a mother, cradled with prayers and pious hymns, my now seared brow bedewed with the waters of holy baptism.

CASSIE (*aside*): What sweet memories of childhood can thus soften down that heart of iron?

LEGREE: In early childhood a fair-haired woman has led me, at the sound of Sabbath bells, to worship and to pray. Born of a hard-tempered sire, on whom that gentle woman had wasted a world of unvalued love, I followed in the steps of my father. Boisterous, unruly and tyrannical, I despised all her counsel, and would have none of her reproof, and, at an early age, broke from her to seek my fortunes on the sea. I never came home but once after that; and then my mother, with the yearning of a heart that must love something, and had nothing else to love, clung to me, and sought with passionate prayers and entreaties to win me from a life of sin.

CASSY: That was your day of grace, Legree; then good angels called you, and mercy held you by the hand.

LEGREE: My heart inly relented; there was a conflict, but sin got the victory, and I set all the force of my rough nature against the conviction of my conscience. I drank and swore, was wilder and more brutal than ever. And one night, when my mother, in the last agony of her despair, knelt at my feet, I spurned her from me, threw her senseless on the floor, and with brutal curses fled to my ship.

CASSY: Then the fiend took thee for his own.

LEGREE: The next I heard of my mother was one night while I was carousing among drunken companions. A letter was put in my hands. I opened and a lock of long, curling hair fell from it, and twined about my fingers, even as that lock twined but now. The letter told me that my mother was dead, and that dying she blest and forgave me! (*Buries his face in his hands.*)

CASSY: Why did you not even then renounce your evil ways?

LEGREE: There is a dread, unhallowed necromancy of evil, that turns things sweetest and holiest to phantoms of horror and affright. That pale, loving mother, — her dying prayers, her forgiving love,—wrought in my demoniac heart of sin only as a damning sentence, bringing with it a fearful looking for of judgment and fiery indignation.

CASSY: And yet you would not strive to avert the doom that threatened you.

LEGREE: I burned the lock of hair and I burned the letter; and when I saw them hissing and crackling in the flame, inly shuddered as I thought of everlasting fires! I tried to drink and revel, and swear away the memory; but often in the deep night, whose solemn stillness arraigns the soul in forced communion with itself, I have seen that pale mother rising by my bed-side, and felt the soft twining of that hair around my fingers, 'till the cold sweat would roll down my face, and I would spring from my bed in horror—horror! (*Falls in chair. After a pause.*) What the devil ails me? Large drops of sweat stand on my forehead, and my heart beats heavy and thick with fear. I thought I saw something white rising and glimmering in the gloom before me, and it seemed to bear my mother's face! I know one thing; I'll let that fellow Tom alone, after this. What did I want with his cussed paper? I believe I am bewitched sure enough! I've been shivering and sweating ever since! Where did he get that hair? It couldn't have been that! I *burn'd* that up, I know I did! It would be a joke if hair could rise from the dead! I'll have Sambo and Quimbo up here to sing and dance one of their dances, and keep off these horrid notions. Here, Sambo! Quimbo! (*Exit.*)

CASSY: Yes, Legree, that golden tress was charmed; each hair had in it a spell of terror and remorse for thee, and was used by a mightier power to bind thy cruel hands from inflicting uttermost evil on the helpless! (*Exit.*)

Scene 4

Street.

(*Enter Marks, meeting Cute, who enters, dressed in an old faded uniform.*)

MARKS: By the land, stranger, but it strikes me that I've seen you somewhere before.

CUTE: By chowder! do you know now, that's just what I was going to say?

MARKS: Isn't your name Cute?

CUTE: You're right, I calculate. Yours is Marks, I reckon.

MARKS: Just so.

CUTE: Well, I swow, I'm glad to see you. (*They shake hands.*) How's your wholesome?

MARKS: Hearty as ever. Well, who would have thought of ever seeing you again. Why, I thought you was in Vermont?

CUTE: Well, so I was. You see I went there after that rich relation of mine—but the speculation didn't turn out well.

MARKS: How so?

CUTE: Why, you see, she took a shine to an old fellow—Deacon Abraham Perry—and married him.

MARKS: Oh, that rather put your nose out of joint in that quarter.

CUTE: Busted me right up, I tell you. The deacon did the handsome thing though; he said if I would leave the neighbourhood and go out South again, he'd stand the damage. I calculate I didn't give him much time to change his mind, and so, you see, here I am again.

MARKS: What are you doing in that soldier rig?

CUTE: Oh, this is my sign.

MARKS: Your sign?

CUTE: Yes; you see, I'm engaged just at present in an all-fired good speculation; I'm a Fillibusterow.

MARKS: A what?

CUTE: A Fillibusterow! Don't you know what that is? It's Spanish for Cuban Volunteer; and means a chap that goes the whole porker for glory and all that ere sort of thing.

MARKS: Oh! you've joined the order of the Lone Star!

CUTE: You've hit it. You see I bought this uniform at a second-hand clothing store; I puts it on and goes to a benevolent individual and I says to him,—appealing to his feelings,— I'm one of the fellows that went to Cuba and got massacred by the bloody Spaniards. I'm in a destitute condition—give me a trifle to pay my passage back, so I can whop the tyrannical cusses and avenge my brave fellow soger what got slewed there.

MARKS: How pathetic!

CUTE: I tell you it works up the feelings of benevolent individuals dreadfully. It draws tears from their eyes and money from their pockets. By chowder! one old chap gave me a hundred dollars to help on the cause.

MARKS: I admire a genius like yours.

CUTE: But I say, what are you up to?

MARKS: I am the travelling companion of a young gentleman by the name of Shelby, who is going to the plantation of a Mr. Legree, on the Red River, to buy an old darky who used to belong to his father.

CUTE: Legree—Legree? Well, now, I calculate I've heard that ere name afore.

MARKS: Do you remember that man who drew a bowie knife on you in New Orleans?

CUTE: By chowder! I remember the circumstance just as well as if it was yesterday; but I can't say that I recollect much about the man, for you see I was in something of a hurry about that time and didn't stop to take a good look at him.

MARKS: Well, that man was this same Mr. Legree.

CUTE: Do you know, now, I should like to pay that critter off?

MARKS: Then I'll give you an opportunity.

CUTE: Chowder! how will you do that?

MARKS: Do you remember the gentleman that interfered between you and Legree?

CUTE: Yes—well?

MARKS: He received the blow that was intended for you, and died from the effects of it. So, you see, Legree is a murderer, and we are the only witnesses of the deed. His life is in our hands.

CUTE: Let's have him right up and make him dance on nothing to the tune of Yankee Doodle!

MARKS: Stop a bit. Don't you see a chance for a profitable speculation?

CUTE: A speculation! Fire away, don't be bashful; I'm the man for a speculation.

MARKS: I have made a deposition to the Governor of the State of all the particulars of that affair at Orleans.

CUTE: What did you do that for?

MARKS: To get a warrant for his arrest.

CUTE: Oh! and have you got it?

MARKS: Yes; here it is. (*Takes out paper.*)

CUTE: Well, now, I don't see how you are going to make anything by that bit of paper?

MARKS: But I do. I shall say to Legree, I have got a warrant against you for murder; my friend, Mr. Cute, and myself are the only witnesses who can appear against you. Give us a thousand dollars, and we will tear up the warrant and be silent.

CUTE: Then Mr. Legree forks over a thousand dollars, and your friend Cute pockets five hundred of it. Is that the calculation?

MARKS: If you will join me in the undertaking.

CUTE: I'll do it, by chowder!

MARKS: Your hand to bind the bargain.

CUTE: I'll stick by you thro' thick and thin.

MARKS: Enough said.

CUTE: Then shake. (*They shake hands.*)

MARKS: But I say, Cute, he may be contrary and show fight.

CUTE: Never mind, we've got the law on our side, and we're bound to stir him up. If he don't come down handsomely, we'll present him with a neck-tie made of hemp!

MARKS: I declare you're getting spunky.

CUTE: Well, I reckon I am. Let's go and have something to drink. Tell you what, Marks, if we don't get *him*, we'll have his hide, by chowder! (*Exeunt, arm in arm.*)

Scene 5

Rough chamber.

(*Enter Legree, followed by Sambo.*)

LEGREE: Go and send Cassy to me.

SAMBO: Yes, mas'r. (*Exit.*)

LEGREE: Curse the woman! she's got a temper worse than the devil! I shall do her an injury one of these days if she isn't careful.

(*Re-enter Sambo, frightened.*)

What's the matter with you, you black scoundrel?

SAMBO: S'help me, mas'r, she isn't dere.

LEGREE: I suppose she's about the house somewhere?

SAMBO: No, she isn't, mas'r; I's been all over de house and I can't find nothing of her nor Emmeline.

LEGREE: Bolted, by the Lord! Call out the dogs! saddle my horse! Stop! are you sure they really have gone?

SAMBO: Yes, mas'r; I's been in every room 'cept the haunted garret, and dey wouldn't go dere.

LEGREE: I have it! Now, Sambo, you jest go and walk that Tom up here, right away! (*Exit Sambo.*) The old cuss is at the bottom of this yer whole matter; and I'll have it out of his infernal black hide, or I'll know the reason why! I *hate* him—I *hate* him! And isn't he *mine?* Can't I do what I like with him? Who's to hinder, I wonder?

(*Tom is dragged on by Sambo and Quimbo.*)

LEGREE (*grimly confronting Tom*): Well, Tom, do you know I've made up my mind to *kill* you?

TOM: It's very likely, Mas'r.

LEGREE: *I—have—done—just—that—thing,* Tom, unless you tell me what do you know about these yer gals? (*Tom is silent.*) D'ye hear? Speak!

TOM: I hain't got anything to tell, mas'r.

LEGREE: Do you dare to tell me, you old black rascal, you don't know? Speak! Do you know anything?

TOM: I know, mas'r; but I can't tell anything. I *can die!*

LEGREE: Hark ye, Tom! ye think, 'cause I have let you off before, I don't mean what I say; but, this time, I have made *up my mind,* and counted the cost. You've always stood it out agin me; now, I'll *conquer ye or kill ye!* one or t'other. I'll count every drop of blood there is in you, and take 'em one by one, 'till ye give up!

TOM: Mas'r, if you was sick, or in trouble, or dying, and I could save, I'd *give* you my heart's blood; and, if taking every drop of blood in this poor old body would save your precious soul, I'd give 'em freely. Do the worst you can, my troubles will be over soon; but if you don't repent, yours won't never end.

(*Legree strikes Tom down with the butt of his whip.*)

LEGREE: How do you like that?

SAMBO: He's most gone, mas'r!

TOM (*rises feebly on his hands*): There ain't no more you can do! I forgive you with all my soul. (*Sinks back, and is carried off by Sambo and Quimbo.*)

LEGREE: I believe he's done for finally. Well, his mouth is shut up at last—that's one comfort.

(*Enter George Shelby, Marks and Cute.*)

Strangers! Well, what do you want?

GEORGE: I understand that you bought in New Orleans a negro named Tom?

LEGREE: Yes, I did buy such a fellow, and a devil of a bargain I had of it, too! I believe he's trying to die, but I don't know as he'll make it out.

GEORGE: Where is he? Let me see him!

SAMBO: Dere he is! (*Points to Tom.*)

LEGREE: How dare you speak? (*Drives Sambo and Quimbo off. George exits.*)

CUTE: Now's the time to nab him.

MARKS: How are you, Mr. Legree?

LEGREE: What the devil brought you here?

MARKS: This little bit of paper. I arrest you for the murder of Mr. St. Clare. What do you say to that?

LEGREE: This is my answer! (*Makes a blow at Marks, who dodges, and Cute receives the blow. He cries out and runs off. Marks fires at Legree, and follows Cute.*) I am hit!—the game's up! (*Falls dead. Quimbo and Sambo return and carry him off laughing.*)

(*George Shelby enters, supporting Tom. Music. They advance and Tom falls, centre.*)

GEORGE: Oh! dear Uncle Tom! do wake—do speak once more! look up! Here's Master George—your own little Master George. Don't you know me?

TOM (*opening his eyes and speaking in a feeble tone*): Mas'r George! Bless de Lord! it's all I wanted! They hav'n't forgot me! It warms my soul; it does my old heart good! Now I shall die content!

GEORGE: You sha'n't die! you mustn't die, nor think of it. I have come to buy you, and take you home.

TOM: Oh, Mas'r George, you're too late. The Lord has bought me, and is going to take me home.

GEORGE: Oh! don't die. It will kill me—it will break my heart to think what you have suffered, poor, poor fellow!

TOM: Don't call me poor fellow. I *have* been poor fellow; but that's all past and gone now. I'm right in the door, going into glory! Oh, Mas'r George! *Heaven has come!* I've got the victory! the Lord has given it to me! Glory be to His name! (*Dies.*)

(*Solemn music. George covers Uncle Tom with his cloak, and kneels over him. Clouds work on and conceal them, and then work off.*)

Scene 7

(*Gorgeous clouds, tinted with sunlight. Eva, robed in white, is discovered on the back of a milk-white dove, with expanded wings, as if just soaring upward. Her hands are extended in benediction over St. Clare and Uncle Tom, who are kneeling and gazing up to her. Impressive music. Slow curtain.*)

Bronson Howard

FROM *SHENANDOAH* 1888

Bronson Howard (1842–1908) has the distinction of being the first professional American playwright and the first to make a handsome living writing plays. He was followed by many more playwrights, but he demonstrated that there was money to be made not just by acting on stage but also by providing the texts for actors. He originally studied to attend Yale University, but an eye problem kept him home in Detroit, where he worked on the *Free Press.* He began producing plays very early in his career, in 1864, with *Fantine,* a dramatization of a segment of *Les Miserables;* its success was limited but encouraging. He left Detroit for the *Tribune* and the *Post* in New York, where, after the Civil War, he wrote *Saratoga* (1870), a farce produced by another important American playwright and producer, Augustin Daly. His play ran for 101 nights, guaranteeing him a living in the theater.

Among his eighteen plays, *The Banker's Daughter* (1878) and *The Henrietta* (1887) are significant because they both emphasize issues in American business, which Howard felt was one of the most important themes in American drama. None of these plays offered a significant analysis of American culture. Howard excelled in mild satire of the kind that helps audiences laugh at themselves without feeling the need to change their behavior. Howard's gift was that he understood what his late-nineteenth-century audiences really wanted and gave it to them. He was the essence of the popular playwright.

Howard's success was based in part on reflecting to his audience an image of itself. For them, the language of even the most elevated and high-brow speeches was stirring and moved them emotionally in ways that it simply does not today. We need to remember, when we read his work, that the nineteenth-century audience felt he offered a reliable portrait of human behavior. That is why Howard was so powerful a figure in American melodrama.

Howard's stagecraft was marked in some measure by the increasing availability of theaters around the country that emphasized the proscenium arch at the expense of the apron in front of it. The overacting of those who depended on asides to the audience (as in both *Fashion* and *Uncle Tom's Cabin* and, indeed, most melodramas before the Civil War) was rendered nearly impossible by Howard's practice of keeping the action within the proscenium. This also established a sense of realism and of detachment from the audience. The asides in *Shenandoah* are few and brief, although soliloquy sometimes does the same work that asides had done in earlier plays. One of Howard's means of building emotional intensity, as in *Shenandoah*, was to write each act as a single scene. This was in stark contrast with such melodramas as *Uncle Tom's Cabin* and Dion Boucicault's *The Octoroon*, in which all the acts are punctuated with numerous scenes and scene changes.

Howard's fortunes improved profoundly when he teamed with Charles Frohman, the American impresario and theater producer, whose skills helped Howard make *Shenandoah* one of America's most successful nineteenth-century dramas. Howard is said to have earned at least $100,000 from this play alone. He went on to establish, in 1891, what is now known as The Dramatists Guild as a means of helping dramatists earn royalties from their work. What he understood better than most playwrights before him was the business of the theater. Howard's posthumously published *Autobiography of a Play* (1914) recounts his experiences as a dramatist.

Shenandoah

The memory of the Civil War was still painful for many people in 1888, but dramas were beginning to use the war as their subject. Most, like Howard's *Shenandoah,* skirted many important issues, such as slavery and the motives for the secession of the states. Although *Shenandoah* begins in act I with the main characters anticipating the opening salvo of southern forces preparing to shell Fort Sumter, in Charlestown, South Carolina, their concerns are more immediately focused on the romances of Kerchival West, a northerner in love with a southern girl, Gertrude Ellingham, and Robert Ellingham, a southerner married to Kerchival's sister Madeline West. Once the cannonade is heard at the end of act I, Kerchival and Robert, best of friends, face the possibility that they will meet on the field of battle. Both join their respective armies as colonels, and Kerchival and Gertrude are separated until act III, when Kerchival is wounded and Gertrude helps nurse him.

Act III, included here, focuses more on the war itself than the rest of the play. Soldiers appear on stage; prisoners of war and their wounded appear; the sounds of cannons and of muskets punctuate the act as Kerchival tries to shake off his

An 1898 poster advertisement for Bronson Howard's *Shenandoah*.

wound, rejoin his command, and attack the enemy. He is held back by General Haverill, who mistakenly thinks his wife has been unfaithful to him with Kerchival. Ultimately, Kerchival is arrested, Haverill moves out, and the Union soldiers are temporarily routed by Confederate General Early. The threat of infidelity during their three-year separation hangs over Kerchival and Gertrude as well, but by the end of act III it is clear that Gertrude has remained true to her love for Kerchival. The act ends with a reversal. The Union troops, harried by Kerchival, are turned back to the battle by the arrival of Union General Sheridan, who rides on stage on Gertrude's horse, Jack. Even Gertrude, the southerner, cheers him on. The drama of act III is responsible for much of the success of the play. It offers all the spectacle that an audience in search of thrilling inspiration could have wanted.

Act IV, the last act of the drama, ties everything together. Mrs. Haverill is no longer under suspicion, and both pairs of lovers (Kerchival and Gertrude, and Ellingham and Madeline) are reunited. The older married couple, the Haverills, are also together. Howard's purposes in using these romantic models may have been to symbolize the separation and reunion of the states themselves, in a nation now whole again when the play ends.

ACT III

(The scene is the same as in Act II. It is now bright daylight, with sunshine flecking the foreground and bathing the distant valley and mountains. As the curtain rises Jenny Buckthorn is sitting on the low stone post, in the center of the stage, looking toward the left. She imitates a Trumpet Signal on her closed fists.)

JENNY: What a magnificent line! Guides posts! Every man and every horse is eager for the next command. There comes the flag! *(As the scene progresses, trumpet signals are heard without and she follows their various meanings in her speech.)* To the standard! The regiment is going to the front. Oh! I do wish I could go with it. I always do, the moment I hear the trumpets. Boots and Saddles! Mount! I wish I was in command of the regiment. It was born in me. Fours right! There they go! Look at those horses' ears! Forward. *(A military band is heard without, playing "The Battle Cry of Freedom." Jenny takes the attitude of holding a bridle and trotting.)* Bappity—plap— plap—plap, etc. *(She imitates the motions of a soldier on horseback, stepping down to the rock at side of post; thence to the ground and about the stage, with the various curvellings of a spirited horse. A chorus of soldiers is heard without, with the band. The music becomes more and more distant. Jenny gradually stops as the music is dying away, and stands, listening. As it dies entirely away, she suddenly starts to an enthusiastic attitude.)* Ah! If I were only a man! The enemy! On Third Battalion, left, front, into line, march! Draw sabres! Charge! *(Imitates a trumpet signal. As she finishes, she rises to her full height, with both arms raised, and trembling with enthusiasm.)* Ah! *(She suddenly drops her arms and changes to an attitude and expression of disappointment—pouting.)* And the first time Old Margery took me to Father, in her arms, she had to tell him I was a girl. Father was as much disgusted as I was. But he'd never admit it; he says I'm as good a soldier as any of 'em—just as I am.

(Enter Barket, on the veranda, his arm in a sling.)

BARKET: Miss Jenny!
JENNY: Barket! The regiment has marched away to the front, and we girls are left here, with just you and a corporal's guard to look after us.
BARKET: I've been watching the byes mesilf. *(Coming down.)* If a little military sugar-plum like you, Miss Jenny, objects to not goin' wid 'em, what do you think of an ould piece of hard tack like me? I can't join the regiment till I've taken you and Miss Madeline back to Winchester, by your father's orders. But it is n't the first time I've escorted you, Miss Jenny. Many a time, when you was a baby, on the Plains, I commanded a special guard to accompany ye's from one fort to anither, and we gave the command in a whisper, so as not to wake ye's up.
JENNY: I told you to tell Father that I'd let him know when Madeline and I were ready to go.
BARKET: I tould him that I'd as soon move a train of army mules.
JENNY: I suppose we must start for home again to-day?
BARKET: Yes, Miss Jenny, in charge of an ould Sargeant wid his arm in a sling and a couple of convalescent throopers. This department of the United States Army will move to the rear in half an hour.
JENNY: Madeline and I only came yesterday morning.
BARKET: Whin your father got ye's a pass to the front, we all thought the fightin' in the Shenandoey Valley was over. It looks now as if it was just beginning. This is no place for women, now. Miss Gertrude Ellingham ought to go wid us, but she won't.
JENNY: Barket! Captain Heartsease left the regiment yesterday, and he has n't rejoined it; he is n't with them, now, at the head of his company. Where is he?
BARKET: I can't say where he is, Miss Jenny. *(Aside.)* Lyin' unburied in the woods, where he was shot, I'm afraid.
JENNY: When Captain Heartsease does rejoin the regiment, Barket, please say to him for me, that—that I—I may have some orders for him, when we next meet. *(Exit, on veranda.)*
BARKET: Whin they nixt mate. They tell us there is no such thing as marriage in Hiven. If

Miss Jenny and Captain Heartsease mate there, they'll invint somethin' that's mighty like it. While I was lyin' wounded in General Buckthorn's house at Washington, last summer, and ould Margery was taking care of me, Margery tould me, confidentially, that they was in love wid aitch ither; and I think she was about right. I've often seen Captain Heartsease take a sly look at a little lace handkerchief, just before we wint into battle. (*Looking off the stage.*) Here's General Buckthorn himself. He and I must make it as aisy as we can for Miss Jenny's poor heart.

(*Enter General Buckthorn.*)

BUCKTHORN: Sergeant Barket! You have n't started with those girls yet?

BARKET: They're to go in half an hour, sir.

BUCKTHORN: Be sure they do go. Is General Haverill here?

BARKET: Yes, sur; in the house with some of his staff, and the Surgeon.

BUCKTHORN: Ah! The Surgeon. How is Colonel West, this morning, after the wound he received last night?

BARKET: He says, himself, that he's as well as iver he was; but the Colonel and Surgeon don't agray on that subject. The dochter says he must n't lave his room for a month. The knife wint dape; and there's something wrong inside of him. But the Colonel bein' on the outside himself, can't see it. He's as cross as a bear, baycause they would n't let him go to the front this morning, at the head of his regiment. I happened to raymark that the Chaplain was prayin' for his raycovery. The Colonel said he'd courtmartial him if he did n't stop that—quick; there's more important things for the Chaplain to pray for in his official capacity. Just at that moment the trumpets sounded, "Boots and Saddles." I had to dodge one of his boots, and the Surgeon had a narrow escape from the ither one. It was lucky for us both his saddle was n't in the room.

BUCKTHORN: That looks encouraging. I think Kerchival will get on.

BARKET: Might I say a word to you, sur, about Miss Jenny?

BUCKTHORN: Certainly, Barket. You and old Margery and myself have been a sort of tri-angular mother, so to speak, to the little girl since her own poor mother left her to our care, when she was only a baby, in the old fort on the Plains. (*He unconsciously rests his arm over Barket's shoulder, familiarly, and then suddenly draws up.*) Ahem! (*Gruffly.*) What is it? Proceed.

BARKET: Her mother's bosom would have been the softest place for her poor little head to rest upon, now, sur.

BUCKTHORN (*touching his eyes*): Well!

BARKET: Ould Margery tould me in Washington that Miss Jenny and Captain Heartsease were in love wid aitch ither.

BUCKTHORN (*starting*): In love!

BARKET: I approved of the match.

BUCKTHORN: What the devil!

(*Barket salutes quickly and starts up stage and out. Buckthorn moves up after him, and stops at the post. Barket stops in the road.*)

BARKET: So did ould Margery.

BUCKTHORN (*angrily*): March! (*Barket salutes suddenly and marches off.*) Heartsease! That young jackanapes! A mere fop; he'll never make a soldier. My girl in love with —bah! I don't believe it; she's too good a soldier, herself.

(*Enter Haverill, on the veranda.*)

Ah, Haverill!

HAVERILL: General Buckthorn! Have you heard anything of General Sheridan since I sent that dispatch to him last evening?

BUCKTHORN: He received it at midnight and sent back word that he considers it a ruse of the enemy. General Wright agrees with him. The reconnoissance yesterday showed no hostile force, on our right, and Crook reports that Early is retreating up the valley. But General Sheridan may, perhaps, give up his journey to Washington, and he has ordered some changes in our line, to be executed this afternoon at four o'clock. I rode over to give you your instructions in person. You may order General McCuen to go into camp on the right of Meadow Brook, with the second division.

(*Haverill is writing in his note-book.*)
(*Enter Jenny, on the veranda.*)

JENNY: Oh, Father! I'm so glad you've come. I've got something to say to you.

(*Running down and jumping into his arms, kissing him. He turns with her, and sets her down, squarely on her feet and straight before him.*)

BUCKTHORN: And I've got something to say to you—about Captain Heartsease.
JENNY: Oh! That's just what I wanted to talk about.
BUCKTHORN: Fall in! Front face! (*She jumps into military position, turning toward him.*) What's this I hear from Sergeant Barket? He says you've been falling in love.
JENNY: I have (*Saluting.*)
BUCKTHORN: Young woman! Listen to my orders. Fall out! (*Turns sharply and marches to Haverill.*) Order the Third Brigade of Cavalry, under Colonel Lowell, to occupy the left of the pike.
JENNY: Father! (*Running to him and seizing the tail of his coat.*) Father, dear!
BUCKTHORN: Close in Colonel Powell on the extreme left—(*slapping his coat-tails out of Jenny's hands, without looking around*)—and hold Custer on the second line, at Old Forge Road. That is all at present. (*Turning to Jenny.*) Goodbye, my darling! (*Kisses her.*) Remember your orders! You little pet! (*Chuckling, as he taps her chin; draws up suddenly and turns to Haverill.*) General! I bid you good-day.
HAVERILL: Good-day, General Buckthorn.

(*They salute with great dignity. Buckthorn starts up stage; Jenny springs after him, seizing his coat-tails.*)

JENNY: But I want to talk with you, Father; I can't fall out. I—I—have n't finished yet.

(*Clinging to his coat, as Buckthorn marches out rapidly, in the road, holding back with all her might.*)

HAVERILL: It may have been a ruse of the enemy, but I hope that General Sheridan has turned back from Washington. (*Looking at his note-book.*) We are to make changes in our line at four o'clock this afternoon. (*Returning the book to his pocket, he stands in thought.*) The Surgeon tells me that Kerchival West will get on well enough if he remains quiet; otherwise not. He shall not die by the hand of a common assassin; he has no right to die like that. My wife gave my own picture of herself to him— not to my son—and she looked so like an angel when she took it from my hand! They were both false to me, and they have been true to each other. I will save his life for myself.

(*Enter Gertrude, on the veranda.*)

GERTRUDE: General Haverill! (*Anxiously, coming down.*) Colonel West persists in disobeying the injunctions of the Surgeon. He is preparing to join his regiment at the front. Give him your orders to remain here. Compel him to be prudent!
HAVERILL (*quickly*): The honor of death at the front is not in reserve for him.
GERTRUDE: Eh? What did you say, General?
HAVERILL: Gertrude! I wish to speak to you, as your father's old friend; and I was once your guardian. Your father was my senior officer in the Mexican War. Without his care I should have been left dead in a foreign land. He, himself, afterwards fell fighting for the old flag.
GERTRUDE: The old flag. (*Aside.*) My father died for it, and he—(*looking toward the left*)—is suffering for it—the old flag!
HAVERILL: I can now return the kindness your father did to me, by protecting his daughter from something that may be worse than death.
GERTRUDE: What do you mean?
HAVERILL: Last night I saw you kneeling at the side of Kerchival West; you spoke to him with all the tender passion of a Southern woman. You said you loved him. But you

spoke into ears that could not hear you. Has he ever heard those words from your lips? Have you ever confessed your love to him before?

GERTRUDE: Never. Why do you ask?

HAVERILL: Do not repeat those words. Keep your heart to yourself, my girl.

GERTRUDE: General! Why do you say this to me? And at such a moment—when his life—

HAVERILL: His life! (*Turning sharply.*) It belongs to me!

GERTRUDE: Oh!

KERCHIVAL: Sergeant! (*Without. He steps into the road, looking back. Haverill comes down.*) See that my horse is ready at once. General! (*Saluting.*) Are there any orders for my regiment beyond those given to Major Wilson, in my absence, this morning? I am about to ride on after the troops and reassume my command.

HAVERILL (*quietly*): It is my wish, Colonel, that you remain here under the care of the Surgeon.

KERCHIVAL: My wound is a mere trifle. This may be a critical moment in the campaign, and I cannot rest here. I must be with my own men.

HAVERILL (*quietly*): I beg to repeat the wish I have already expressed.

(*Kerchival walks to him, and speaks apart, almost under his breath, but very earnest in tone.*)

KERCHIVAL: I have had no opportunity, yet, to explain certain matters, as you requested me to do yesterday; but whatever there may be between us, you are now interfering with my duty and my privilege as a soldier; and it is my right to be at the head of my regiment.

HAVERILL (*quietly*): It is my positive order that you do not reassume your command.

KERCHIVAL: General Haverill, I protest against this—

HAVERILL (*quietly*): You are under arrest, sir.

KERCHIVAL: Arrest!

GERTRUDE: Ah!

(*Kerchival unclasps his belt and offers his sword to Haverill.*)

HAVERILL (*quietly*): Keep your sword; I have no desire to humiliate you; but hold yourself subject to further orders from me.

KERCHIVAL: My regiment at the front!—and I under arrest! (*Exit.*)

HAVERILL: Gertrude! If your heart refuses to be silent—if you feel that you must confess your love to that man—first tell him what I have said to you, and refer him to me for an explanation. (*Exit.*)

GERTRUDE: What can he mean? He would save me from something worse than death, he said. "His life—It belongs to me!" What can he mean? Kerchival told me that he loved me—it seems many years since that morning in Charleston—and when we met again, yesterday, he said that he had never ceased to love me. I will not believe that he has told me a falsehood. I have given him my love, my whole soul and my faith. (*Drawing up to her full height.*) My perfect faith!

(*Jenny runs in, to the road, and up the slope. She looks down the hill, then toward the left and enters.*)

JENNY: A flag of truce, Gertrude. And a party of Confederate soldiers, with an escort, coming up the hill. They are carrying someone; he is wounded.

(*Enter, up the slope, a Lieutenant of Infantry with an escort of Union Soldiers, their arms at right shoulder, and a party of Confederate Soldiers bearing a rustic stretcher. Lieutenant Frank Bedloe lies on the stretcher. Major Hardwick, a Confederate Surgeon, walks at his side. Madeline appears at the veranda, watching them. Gertrude stands with her back to the audience. The Lieutenant gives orders in a low tone, and the front escort moves toward the right, in the road. The Confederate bearers and the Surgeon pass through the gate. The rear escort moves on in the road, under the Lieutenant's orders. The bearers halt in the front of the stage; on a sign from the Surgeon, they leave the stretcher on the ground, stepping back.*)

MAJOR HARDWICK: Is General Haverill here?

GERTRUDE: Yes; what can we do, sir?

MADELINE: The General is just about mounting with his staff, to ride away. Shall I go for him, sir?

MAJOR HARDWICK: Say to him, please, that Colonel Robert Ellingham, of the Tenth Virginia, sends his respects and sympathy. He instructed me to bring this young officer to this point, in exchange for himself, as agreed upon between them last evening.

(*Exit Madeline.*)

JENNY: Is he unconscious or sleeping, sir?

MAJOR HARDWICK: Hovering between life and death. I thought he would bear the removal better. He is waking. Here, my lad! (*Placing his canteen to the lips of Frank, who moves, reviving.*) We have reached the end of our journey.

FRANK: My father!

MAJOR HARDWICK: He is thinking of his home.

(*Frank rises on one arm, assisted by the Surgeon.*)

FRANK: I have obeyed General Haverill's orders, and I have a report to make.

GERTRUDE: We have already sent for him. (*Stepping to him.*) He will be here in a moment.

FRANK (*looking into her face, brightly*): Is not this—Miss—Gertrude Ellingham?

GERTRUDE: You know me? You have seen me before?

FRANK: Long ago! Long ago! You know the wife of General Haverill?

GERTRUDE: I have no dearer friend in the world.

FRANK: She will give a message for me to the dearest friend *I* have in the world. My little wife! I must not waste even the moment we are waiting. Doctor! My note-book! (*Trying to get it from his coat. The Surgeon takes it out. A torn and blood stained lace handkerchief also falls out. Gertrude kneels at his side.*) Ah! I—I—have a message from another—(*holding up the handkerchief*)—from Captain Heartsease. (*Jenny makes a quick start toward him.*) He lay at my side in the hospital, when they brought me away; he had only strength enough to put this in my hand, and he spoke a woman's name; but I—I—forget what it is. The red spots upon it are the only message he sent.

(*Gertrude takes the handkerchief and looks back at Jenny, extending her hand. Jenny moves to her, takes the handkerchief and turns back, looking down on it. She drops her face into her hands and goes out sobbing, on the veranda.*)

(*Enter Madeline on the veranda.*)

MADELINE: General Haverill is coming. I was just in time. He was already on his horse.

FRANK: Ah! He is coming. (*Then suddenly.*) Write! Write! (*Gertrude writes in the note-book as he dictates.*) "To—my wife—Edith:—Tell our little son, when he is old enough to know—how his father died; not how he lived. And tell her who filled my own mother's place so lovingly—she is your mother, too—that my father's portrait of her, which she gave to me in Charleston, helped me to be a better man!" And— Oh! I must not forget this—"It was taken away from me while I was a prisoner in Richmond, and it is in the possession of Captain Edward Thornton, of the Confederate Secret Service. But her face is still beside your own in my heart. My best— warmest, last—love—to you, darling." I will sign it.

(*Gertrude holds the book, and he signs it, then sinks back very quietly, supported by the Surgeon. Gertrude rises and walks away.*)

MADELINE: General Haverill is here.

(*The Surgeon lays the fold of the blanket over Frank's face and rises.*)

GERTRUDE: Doctor!

MAJOR HARDWICK: He is dead.

(*Madeline, on the veranda, turns and looks away. The Lieutenant orders the guard, "Present Arms."*)

(*Enter Haverill, on the veranda. He salutes the guard as he passes. The Lieutenant orders, "Carry Arms." Haverill comes down.*)

HAVERILL: I am too late?

MAJOR HARDWICK: I'm sorry, General. His one eager thought as we came was to reach here in time to see you.

(*Haverill moves to the bier, looks down at it, then folds back the blanket from the face. He starts slightly as he first sees it.*)

HAVERILL: Brave boy! I hoped once to have a son like you. I shall be in your father's place to-day, at your grave. (*He replaces the blanket and steps back.*) We will carry him to his comrades in the front. He shall have a soldier's burial, in sight of the mountain-top beneath which he sacrificed his young life; that shall be his monument.

MAJOR HARDWICK: Pardon me, General. We Virginians are your enemies, but you cannot honor this young soldier more than we do. Will you allow my men the privilege of carrying him to his grave?

(*Haverill inclines his head. The Surgeon motions to the Confederate Soldiers, who step to the bier and raise it gently.*)

HAVERILL: Lieutenant!

(*The Lieutenant orders the guard "Left Face." The Confederate bearers move through the gate, preceded by Lieutenant Hardwick. Haverill draws his sword, reverses it, and moves up behind the bier with bowed head. The Lieutenant orders "Forward March," and the cortège disappears. While the girls are still watching it, the heavy sound of distant artillery is heard, with booming reverberations among the hills and in the valley.*)

MADELINE: What is that sound, Gertrude?

GERTRUDE: Listen!

(*Another and more prolonged distant sound, with long reverberations.*)

MADELINE: Again! Gertrude!

(*Gertrude raises her hand to command silence; listens. Distant cannon again.*)

GERTRUDE: It is the opening of a battle.

MADELINE: Ah! (*Running down stage. The sounds are heard again, prolonged.*)

GERTRUDE: How often have I heard that sound! (*Coming down.*) This is war, Madeline! You are face to face with it now.

MADELINE: And Robert is there! He may be in the thickest of the danger—at this very moment.

GERTRUDE: Yes. Let our prayers go up for him; mine do, with all a sister's heart.

(*Kerchival enters on veranda, without coat or vest, his sash about his waist, looking back as he comes in.*)

Kerchival!

KERCHIVAL: Go on! Go on! Keep the battle to yourselves. I'm out of it. (*The distant cannon and reverberations are rising in volume.*)

MADELINE: I pray for Robert Ellingham—and for the *cause* in which he risks his life! (*Kerchival looks at her, suddenly; also Gertrude.*) Heaven forgive me if I am wrong, but I am praying for the enemies of my country. His people are my people, his enemies are my enemies. Heaven defend him and his, in this awful hour.

KERCHIVAL: Madeline! My sister!

MADELINE: Oh, Kerchival! (*Turning and dropping her face on his breast.*) I cannot help it—I cannot help it!

KERCHIVAL: My poor girl! Every woman's heart, the world over, belongs not to any country or any flag, but to her husband—and her lover. Pray for the man you love, sister—it would be treason not to. (*Passes her before him to the left of the stage. Looks across to Gertrude.*) Am I right? (*Gertrude drops her head. Madeline moves up veranda and out.*) Is what I have said to Madeline true?

GERTRUDE: Yes! (*Looks up.*) Kerchival!

KERCHIVAL: Gertrude! (*Hurries across to her, clasps her in his arms. He suddenly staggers and brings his hand to his breast.*)

GERTRUDE: Your wound!

(*Supporting him as he reels and sinks into seat.*)

KERCHIVAL: Wound! I have no wound! You do love me! (*Seizing her hand.*)

GERTRUDE: Let me call the Surgeon, Kerchival.

KERCHIVAL: You can be of more service to me than he can. (*Detaining her. Very heavy sounds of the battle; she starts, listening.*) Never mind that! It's only a battle. You love me!

GERTRUDE: Be quiet, Kerchival, dear. I do love you. I told you so, when you lay bleeding here, last night. But you could not hear me. (*At his side, resting her arm about him, stroking his head.*) I said that same thing to—to—another, more than three years ago. It is in that letter that General Buckthorn gave you. (*Kerchival starts.*) No—no —you must be very quiet, or I will not say another word. If you obey me, I will repeat that part of the letter, every word; I know it by heart, for I read it a dozen times. The letter is from Mrs. Haverill.

KERCHIVAL (*quietly*): Go on.

GERTRUDE: "I have kept your secret, my darling, but I was sorely tempted to betray the confidence you reposed in me at Charleston. If Kerchival West—(*she retires backward from him as she proceeds*)—had heard you say, as I did, when your face was hidden in my bosom, that night, that you loved him with your whole heart—"

KERCHIVAL: Ah!

(*Starting to his feet. He sinks back. She springs to support him.*)

GERTRUDE: I will go for help.

KERCHIVAL: Do not leave me at such a moment as this. You have brought me a new life. (*Bringing her to her knees before him and looking down at her.*) Heaven is just opening before me. (*His hands drop suddenly and his head falls back.*)

GERTRUDE: Ah! Kerchival? You are dying!

(*Musketry. A sudden sharp burst of musketry, mingled with the roar of artillery nearby. Kerchival starts, seizing Gertrude's arm and holding her away, still on her knees. He looks eagerly toward the left.*)

KERCHIVAL: The enemy is close upon us!

(*Barket runs in, up the slope.*)

BARKET: Colonel Wist! The devils have sprung out of the ground. They're pouring over our lift flank like Noah's own flood. The Union Army has started back for Winchester, on its way to the North Pole; our own regiment, Colonel, is coming over the hill in full retrate.

KERCHIVAL: My own regiment! (*Starting up.*) Get my horse, Barket. (*Turns.*) Gertrude, my life! (*Embraces Gertrude.*)

BARKET: Your horse is it? I'm wid ye! There's a row at Finnegan's ball, and we're in it. (*Springs to the road, and runs out.*)

KERCHIVAL (*turns away; stops*): I am under arrest.

(*The retreat begins. Fugitives begin to straggle across the stage from the left.*)

GERTRUDE: You must not go, Kerchival; it will kill you.

KERCHIVAL: Arrest be damned! (*Starts up toward the center, raising his arms above his head with clenched fist, and rising to full height.*) Stand out of my way, you cowards!

(*They cower away from him as he rushes out among them. The stream of fugitives passing across the stage swells in volume. Gertrude runs through them and up to the elevation, turning.*)

GERTRUDE: Men! Are you soldiers? Turn back! There is a leader for you! Turn back! Fight for your flag—and mine!—the flag my father died for! Turn back! (*She looks out toward the left and then turns toward the front.*) He has been marked for death already, and I—I can only pray. (*Dropping to her knees.*)

(The stream of fugitives continues, now over the elevation also. Rough and torn uniforms, bandaged arms and legs; some limping and supported by others, some dragging their muskets after them, others without muskets, others using them as crutches. There is a variety of uniforms, both cavalry and infantry; flags are dragged on the ground, the rattle of near musketry and roar of cannon continue; two or three wounded fugitives drop down beside the hedge. Benson staggers in and drops upon a rock near the post. Artillerists, rough, torn and wounded, drag and force a field-piece across. Corporal Dunn, wounded, staggers to the top of elevation. There is a lull in the sounds of the battle. Distant cheers are heard without.)

DUNN: Listen, fellows! Stop! Listen! Sheridan! General Sheridan is coming! *(Cheers from those on stage. Gertrude rises quickly. The wounded soldiers rise, looking over the hedge. All on stage stop, looking eagerly toward the left. The cheers without come nearer, with shouts of "Sheridan! Sheridan!")* The horse is down; he is worn out.

GERTRUDE: No! He is up again! He is on my Jack! Now, for your life, Jack, and for me! You've never failed me yet. *(The cheers without now swell to full volume and are taken up by those on the stage. The horse sweeps by with General Sheridan.)* Jack! Jack!! Jack!!!

(Waving her arms as he passes. She throws up her arms and falls backward, caught by Dunn. The stream of men is reversed and surges across the stage to the left, in the road and on the elevation, with shouts, and throwing up of hats. The field-piece is forced up the slope with a few bold, rough movements; the artillerists are loading it, and the stream of returning fugitives is still surging by in the road as the curtain falls.)

Dion Boucicault (1820–1890)
NOTES ON ACTING

Boucicault was an Irish playwright and a gifted actor who had been the darling of the English stage with plays such as London Assurance *(1841),* The Vampire *(1852),* The Octoroon, or Life in Louisiana *(1859),* The Colleen Bawn *(1860),* The Shaughraun *(1874), and many others. His* Rip Van Winkle *(1866) made Joseph Jefferson, an American actor, a star. Jefferson played the part for most of the rest of his life. All of Boucicault's popular plays were melodramas, and his skill in writing for the popular stage was such that he has sometimes been regarded as the century's leading melodramatist. He lived for some time in America and died in New York. His comments on acting give us insight into the expectations for performance in the nineteenth century.*

I must now go to a subject of a rather delicate nature, and that is really the first part of my subject — the voice. You know there are certain voices on the stage — you are perfectly aware of this — that the actor does not use off the stage; that are exclusively confined to tragedy. It is not the actor's ordinary voice. The idea is that the tragedian never has to use his own voice. Why? What is the reason? Before this century the great French tragedians before Talma and the great English tragedians before Kean used their treble voice — the teapot style. They did it as if they played on the flute. Then came the period when the tragedian played his part on the double bass.... There was no reason for it. Now we perform that part in the present age in what is called the medium voice. The reason is this. It is the transcendental drama tragedy. When I call it transcendental I mean unreal, poetic, to distinguish it from the realistic or the drama of ordinary life. The transcendental drama assumes that the dialogues are uttered by beings larger than life, who express ideas that no human being could pour out. The actor has accustomed himself to feel that he is in a different region; and, therefore, he feels if he uses his ordinary voice it might jar on the transcendental effect. I have fought out this very question with the great tragedians in France; and it seemed as if the tragedians were afraid of destroying the delicate illusion of the audience, who are sent about four hundred years back, as if they were living with people whom they had never seen and had no knowledge of. The consequence is those characters are too big for any ordinary human being, and the actor tries to make his manner and his voice correspond.

• • •

To the young beginner I would say, when you go upon the stage do not be full of yourself, but be full of your part. That is mistaking vanity for genius, and is the fault of many more than perhaps you are aware of. If actors' and actresses' minds be employed upon themselves, and not on the character they wish and aspire to perform, they never really get out of themselves. Many think they are studying their character when they are only studying themselves. They get their costume, they put it on, see how it fits, they cut and contrive it, but all that is not studying their character, but their costume. Actors and actresses frequently come to me and say, "Have you any part that will fit me?" They never dream of saying, "Have you any part that I can fit? that I can expand myself or contract myself into; that I can put myself inside of; that I, as a Protean, can shape myself into, even alter my voice and everything that nature has given to me, and be what you have contrived? I do not want you to contrive like a tailor to fit me." That is what is constantly happening....

It was not so forty years ago. They had their faults many of them, but they did not constitute costume and make-up as the study of character, which it is not. I will tell you what did happen forty years ago. I was producing a comedy in which Mr. Farren, the father of the gentleman who so ably bears the same name (old Farren), played a leading part. He did not ask what he was going to wear, but he came to me, and said, "Who did you draw this party from; had you any type?" I said, "Yes, I had," and mentioned the names of two old fogies, who, at that time, were well known in London society. One he knew, the other he did not. He went and studied Sir Harcourt Courtley, and he studied by the speediest method, for the study was absolutely and literally out of the mouth of the man himself. That will give you an idea how they studied character....

That is the way to study character, to get at the bottom of human nature, and I am happy to say that, amongst some young actors who have come out within the last ten or fifteen years, I have seen a natural instinct for the study of character and for the drawing of character most admirably, and much more faithfully than they drew it twenty or thirty years ago. There is a study of character that we may call good and true that has been accomplished within the last fifteen or sixteen years.

Now, I will say something by way of anecdote to show how utterly unnecessary it is for you to bother your minds so much about your dress. I was producing *The Shaughraun* in New York. I generally had enough to employ my time. I get the actors and actresses to study their characters, and generally leave myself to the last. But the last morning before the play was produced I saw my dresser hobbling about, but afraid to come to the stage. At last he said, "Have you thought of your costume?" I said I had not done any such thing. It was about three o'clock in the afternoon, and I had to play about seven o'clock in the evening. I went upstairs, and said, "Have you got a red coat?" "Yes; we have got a uniform red hunting coat." "Oh, that is of no use!" "We have got one that was used in *She Stoops to Conquer*." That was brought, but it had broad lapels, and looked to belong to about one hundred and fifty years ago. "Oh!" said the man, "there is an old coat that was worn by Mr. Beckett as Goldfinch." When he came to that it reached all down to my feet, and was too long in the sleeves. So I cut them off with a big pair of shears, and by the shears and the scissors I got some sort of a fit. Then I got an old hunting cap, a pair of breeches, and sent for some old boots that cost about 2s 6d, and did not fit me, and that is how I came on the stage. The editor of one of the newspapers said, "Where on earth did you get that extraordinary costume from?"

Believe me, I mention these circumstances simply to show that the study of character should be from the inside; not from the outside! Great painters, I am told, used to draw a human figure in the nude form, and, when they were proposing to finish their pictures, to paint the costumes; then the costumes came right. That is exactly how an actor ought to study his art. He ought to paint his character in the nude form and put the costume on the last thing.

Now, let me give this particular advice to all persons going on the stage. Many of you are already on the stage, but others may be going on. Having arrived at that conclusion as to what your line is going to be, always try to select those kinds of characters and the line that is most suited and more nearly conforms to your own natural gifts. Nature knows best. If you happen to have a short, sharp face, a hard voice, an angular figure, you are suited for the intellectual characters of the drama, such as Hamlet and so forth. If you are of a soft, passionate nature—if you have a soft voice and that sort of sensuous disposition which seems to lubricate your entire form, your limbs, so that your movements are gentle and softer than others, then this character is fitted for a Romeo or an Othello. You will find, if you look back at the records of actors, there are few great actors that have shone in the two different lines, the intellectual and the sensual drama. Kemble could do Hamlet, but he could not do Othello. Kean could do Othello, but he could not do Hamlet. The one was passionate and sensual, the other was an intellectual, a noble, grand actor.

Now, after you have made this preliminary study you will recollect that in every great character, there are three characters really. We are all free men, in one sense, speaking, of course, of our inner life; but we have three characters. First there is the man by himself—as he is to himself—as he is to God. That is one man, the inner man, as he is when alone; the unclothed man. Then there is the native man, the domestic man, as he is to his family. Still there is a certain amount of disguise. He is not as he is to other men. Then there is the man as he stands before the world at large; as he is outside in society. Those are the three characters. They are all in the one man, and the dramatist does not know his business unless he puts them into one character. Look at Hamlet in his soliloquies, he is passionate, he is violent, he is intemperate in himself, he knows his faults and lashes his own weakness. But he has no sooner done that when Horatio comes on the stage with a few friends. Horatio is the mild, soft, gentle companion; with his arm round his neck, Hamlet forgets the other man; he gets a little on, but he is the same man to Horatio as he is to his mother, when he gets her in the closet. But when he encounters the world at large, he is the Prince! the condescending man! You have seen Hamlet played, and if you watched closely, you have seen those three phases of his character have been given on this stage! So it is in nearly all characters — comic or otherwise. You will find that the three characters always combine in the man....

Now, ladies and gentlemen, I have kept you a long time. All I say now is that I have to give you most heartily and conscientiously, as an old man, an old dramatist, and an old actor, this advice. Whatever is done by an actor let it be done with circumspection, without anxiety or hurry, remembering that vehemence is not passion, that the public will feel and appreciate when the actor is not full of himself, but when he is full of character, with that deliberation without slowness, that calmness of resolution without coldness, that self-possession without over-weening confidence, which should combine in the actor so as to give grace to comic and importance to tragic presence. The audience are impressed with the unaffected character of one who moves forward with a fixed purpose, full of momentous designs. He expresses a passion with which they will sympathize, and radiates a command which they will obey....

Gary A. Richardson
MELODRAMA AS NATIONAL HISTORY

In his critical history of American drama, Gary Richardson (b. 1949) gives us a clear sense of the importance of melodrama in the developing nation. The demands for entertainment in the period were considerable, especially with the tensions that grew between the North and the South through the difficult period of the 1850s and the postwar years of the 1860s and 1870s. Drama played a role in clarifying national goals, just as it did in healing national wounds. In some ways, melodrama was ideally suited for exploring historical issues.

While Daly was seeking to bring new light to the tensions of city life and class conflict and Boucicault was endeavoring to humanize Irish immigrants, another group of playwrights was busily reinterpreting recent national history in an attempt to reunite the nation emotionally by examining its most recent and most deeply felt social and political wound, the Civil War. In a series of plays in the 1880s and 1890s, American melodramatists presented plays which examined the causes of the war, the nature of its conflicts and the grounds upon which a reconciliation had been or might be accomplished. Using the strengths of melodrama—a simplified moral universe, easily comprehensible characters, and exciting action—these playwrights sought to integrate the recent past for their audiences by presenting a dramatized history which testified to the enduring values—individual dignity, political freedom, and the indivisibility of the union—ostensibly reaffirmed by the war. The results not only indicate the flexibility of melodrama as a form but also belie in substantial ways the stereotype of melodrama as a naive drama whose orientation wholly neglects political or social commentary.

In their use of history, these dramatists were in one sense continuing a tradition even older than melodrama, for from the Greeks onward, dramatists have found historical material particularly appealing.[1] Ranging from what Lindenberger calls documentary drama—which purports to enact chronicled "facts"—to the "unhistorical history play"—which is concerned with historical issues but is not based upon "real" events—history plays provide a convenient method of casting the present into relief

---

[1]Herbert Lindenberger, *Historical Drama: The Relation of Literature and Reality* (Chicago: University of Chicago Press, 1975), 6.

by juxtaposing it with the audience's past.[2] The history play allows for a simultaneous examination of past and present institutions, beliefs, and values, and depicts in a condensed framework the manner in which and the degree to which continuity has been maintained. The effect is most often a psychic uniting of the audience with its past, providing viewers the opportunity to identify with those elements that are still appealing and to repudiate those which seem antiquated. Because the audience is never in doubt as to the "plot's" resolution, the audience's "interest tends to shift from the *what* to the *how*."[3] While this shift may, as in the case of such tragic histories as *Antony and Cleopatra* or *Maria Stuart*, generate complex characterizations, historical drama by no means demands them. As Brecht's *Mutter Courage* indicates, historical drama's delineation of the historical process itself may occasionally even demand a simplification of character. Thus, the melodrama's ostensibly unambiguous characterizations present no inhibition to the uniting of history and melodrama. The melding of melodrama and historical drama provides, in fact, an ideal means of uniting the public world with private affairs, personalizing the tides of history while exalting private concerns by playing them out upon a stage dignified by its concern with historical process.

Besides their use of recent history, all the Civil War plays of the 1880s and 1890s are united by their appropriation of one of the pervasive myths about the South—its uniqueness as a region. While this myth is of long duration, in the years immediately preceding the Civil War it found one of its most ardent and popular spokesmen in William Gilmore Simms. In a series of romantic novels which displaced antebellum southern cultural assumptions to the romanticized, temporally distanced and privileged past of the American Revolution and its aftermath, Simms established in copious detail the idealized pastoral and political foundations of the Old South. As Kolodny has pointed out, this bucolic vision combined the mythic Earth Mother with the pervasive American longing for a new edenic garden.[4] For southerners, the result was a conception of the land as a surrogate mother whose nurturing power was inextricably tied to the maintenance of long-established and seemingly divinely sanctioned patterns of life. So the southern resistance to change stemmed at least in part from a subconscious desire to resist a second expulsion from the Garden. An outgrowth of this subconsciously feminized landscape was the conflation of the land with southern womanhood in a way unavailable to other sections of the country. So powerful and pervasive was this identification that Simms's admonition to his son is typical: "remember that you are to defend your mother country and your natural mother from a hoard of mercenaries and plunderers."[5] The melodramatic heroine's central role as the embodiment of cultural values made the southern woman a particularly appealing focus for these dramatists. It is therefore not surprising that the plays often present the reuniting of the country as a stormy romance in which a northern hero overcomes the initial resistance of a southern heroine. The private institution of marriage becomes a metaphor for the public reuniting of the political nation after what amounts to a lovers' spat. Before the reunion, however, came the dissolution and an examination of the causes of the discord.

[2]Lindenberger, 14–29.
[3]Lindenberger, 24.
[4]Annette Kolodny, *The Lady of the Land: Metaphor as Experience and History in American Life and Letters* (Chapel Hill: University of North Carolina Press, 1975), 115–32.
[5]Kolodny, 115.

The thorniest issue facing postwar playwrights was the emotional wellspring of the war, slavery.... [I]n the years immediately preceding the Civil War, slavery and its victims had generated a large number of plays in which both joy and pathos served an overtly political purpose. In most cases, only two alternatives were available to slaves in these dramas. In the first, exemplified by George Harris in Aiken's *Uncle Tom's Cabin*, the slave, usually a mulatto, repudiated slavery and triumphantly escaped to freedom. However, most plays traced the lives of characters who chose the other alternative, as illustrated by Zoe in Boucicault's *The Octoroon* and Uncle Tom in *Uncle Tom's Cabin*. In these propaganda pieces, the long-suffering protagonists endured slavery until death freed them from persecution. But the plots and characters which had sustained strong abolitionist sentiment in the 1850s were not abandoned after the war. Bartley Campbell's *The White Slave* (1882) indicates the manner in which many of the prewar melodramatic devices were utilized in order to retroactively deterge slavery of its moral stigma and thereby provide an emotional warrant for post–Civil War racial prejudice, both northern and southern.

Writing after abolition and the Civil War had made slavery a moot issue—but in an America in which much of the overt racial bigotry had re-emerged in, for instance, the de facto disenfranchisement of former slaves in the South and the increasing indifference of northern politicians to the cause of blacks—Campbell effectively eviscerates the traditional political commentary of the slavery plays. By manipulating the slavery play's conventions, consciously or unconsciously, Campbell relieved late-nineteenth-century white America from meaningfully confronting its abiding racial prejudice. The conventions that had once divided northern and southern whites by arguing against the institution of slavery served, paradoxically, in 1882 to reunite regionally factionalized whites behind a resurgent myth of white moral and cultural supremacy, thus aiding in the reestablishment of the mentality that had made slavery possible.

Michael R. Booth
A DEFENSE OF NINETEENTH-CENTURY DRAMA

In this excerpt from a longer article published in 1974, the distinguished critic of nineteenth-century British drama Michael R. Booth defends the popular theater of that day against those who feel that its very popularity disqualifies it from serious consideration. To claims that plays of the nineteenth century were generally subliterary and primarily theatrical spectacle, Booth responds that these are the very characteristics that establish their general worth. His focus is on English melodramas such as Baron Edward Bulwer-Lytton's The Lady of Lyons *and Edward Fitzball's* Jonathan Bradford *or his* Murder at the Roadside Inn, *the first melodrama based on a real crime. That these plays were good entertainment is something that Booth applauds, and he concludes with the wish that contemporary theater might consider returning to that goal as a way of preserving drama as a living art form.*

One of the major claims that I make for nineteenth-century drama is ironically, perhaps, for the very aspect of it critics have found most distasteful: that in the nineteenth century the drama was for the last time in English history an entertainment for all classes of society, a truly popular drama in both senses of the word. From the meanest penny gaff in Whitechapel to the Rubens Room in Windsor Castle, and from the lowest street urchin to the monarch of the land, the English enjoyed theater in confusingly multifarious forms. Its very popularity and lack of intellectuality made it in its own time the object of intellectual, middle-class attack. Today the middle class has won a Pyrrhic victory, and despite occasional valiant attempts to broaden the class appeal of theater, it is now, and has been for some time, essentially a middle-class minority entertainment catering to an estimated maximum potential audience of 2 percent of the population of Britain and North America. Some regard this development as a gain; I see it not only as a loss but also as a blow to the viability of theater as a form of entertainment that may ultimately—unless its broad base of popular appeal is regained—prove fatal. The nineteenth century, then, is an age we should value for the universality of its theater, and today, when popular cultures are the focus of much academic study, there is no reason why the popular aspects of nineteenth-century drama should not command respectful attention.

Presumably the art of the Romantic movement—poetry, novel, music, and painting—would elicit postures of veneration from the same critics who condemn the "claptrap" of melodrama. Presumably some of these critics have done scholarly work in the Romantic field; Professor Otten, for instance, certainly has, since his book is a result of it. But they do not appear to realize, or else do not value, the fact that the Gothic melodrama of brigands, tyrants, castles, gloomy dungeons, fleeing heroines, mysterious apparitions, and tenebrous forests lit by flashes of lightning— a melodrama that flourished from about 1795 to 1825—represents the Romantic movement in the popular theater; that the passionate libertarian sentiments, the turbulent expression of emotion, the heroic individuality, the power of guilt and remorse, the new richness of scene-painting (especially of romantic landscapes), the sweep of rhetoric, the wild flights of joy and the dark depths of despondency so characteristic of Gothic and Eastern melodrama are the stuff of Romantic poetry, painting, and music. If the scholar wishes to examine the manifestations of the Romantic movement apart from and below the great heights of the great artists, he would do well to read the despised melodramas (which he might find hugely enjoyable reading) and investigate the means of their staging. The experience would not only be revealing, but should also possess comparative value.

Two principal charges against nineteenth-century drama are that it was divorced from literature and therefore inconsequential and trivial; furthermore, since it was written purely for the "theater" (that naughty pejorative again), it was therefore separated from the real world around it and bore little or no relation to the serious concerns of life and thought. The first charge is true in the sense that except for Bulwer-Lytton, the important poets and novelists of the century were not generally fortunate in the theater, their efforts varying from occasional successes, often caused by ingenious staging or skilful adaptation by other hands, such as Coleridge's *Remorse* (1813) and Tennyson's *Becket* (1893), to utter disasters or rejection by managers. In fact, one of the troubles with early nineteenth-century tragedy is that it was *too* conscious of literature and anxious to emulate dead Elizabethan modes of playwriting, looking to a past age of drama for themes and styles rather than to its own period, plenteously endowed with dramatic substance. The relationship between the stage and the novel was very close, and although the novelists did not on the whole establish reputations as dramatists, their novels—from Ann Radcliffe through Scott and Dickens to Mrs. Henry Wood, Ouida, and Anthony Hope—were continuously adapted for stage performance. Not only that: all the major tendencies of nineteenth-century drama can be found in the novel—a strong emphasis on narrative and moral line, a great deal of sensation, shining virtue, and dark-hued vice; romantic passion, and a romantic landscape (in the earlier period); eccentric native humor; domestic idealism, domestic bliss, and domestic agony; sentiment and pathos, a fondness for the happy ending; and a more than cursory examination of themes relating to wealth (inherited and newly acquired), commerce, class conflict, industrial strife, the urban environment, social problems and social protest. Nobody has accused the nineteenth-century novel of being divorced from contemporary life and thought, and if nineteenth-century drama deals with this material—as indeed it does—then the second charge cannot be sustained. When it is recalled that nineteenth-century playwrights were effectively prevented by the absolute power of the Examiner of Plays from dealing seriously with sex, religion, and politics, it is remarkable how much they reflected and commented on the life of their times; the fact that they were writing principally for audiences seeking entertainment at a popular and non-intellectual level makes this achievement not insignificant, and certainly not worthy of dismissive contempt.

Oscar Wilde

Oscar Fingal O'Flahertie Wills Wilde (1854–1900) was born to a famous eye surgeon who maintained a home in Dublin's most exclusive neighborhood. Wilde's mother, known by her literary name, Speranza, was noted for collecting Irish folk stories in the western hills in the late 1870s. Her work was important to later literature, but it was especially important for its timing, since most of the storytellers in Ireland were gone by the turn of the century.

Wilde was a brilliant classics scholar at Trinity College, Dublin, where his tutor was the legendary Mahaffy, who later traveled with him in France. After Trinity, he went to Magdalen College, Oxford, where he took a distinguished degree. Among his influences in Oxford was Slade Professor of Art John Ruskin, with whom Wilde had long walks and talks. Ruskin had published important books on northern Gothic art and on Italian art, especially the art of Venice. Art was one of Wilde's primary passions, especially decoration and the decorative arts. He agreed with Walter Pater, a contemporary art critic, that art must best serve the needs of art. He felt, for example, that poetry did not serve religious, political, social, or biographical goals. Its ends were aesthetic and its pleasures were in its sounds, images, and thoughts.

Partly because of his brilliance and partly because he was one of the age's greatest conversationalists, he was soon in the company of the famous and amusing people of his generation. Some of his conversational gift is apparent in his plays.

By his own admission, his life was marked by an overindulgence in sensuality: "What paradox was to me in the sphere of thought, perversity became to me in the sphere of passion." He married Constance Lloyd in 1884 and soon had two sons. But by 1891 he had already had several homosexual liaisons, one of which was to bring him to ruin. His relationship with the much younger Lord Alfred Douglas ended with Douglas's father, the marquis of Queensberry, publicly denouncing Wilde as a sodomite. Wilde sued for libel but lost. As a result, in 1895 he was tried for sodomy, convicted, and sentenced to two years' hard labor. Wilde's actions have been seen as self-destructive, but they are also consistent with his efforts to force society to examine its own hypocrisy. Unfortunately, his efforts in court and prison ruined him, and he died in exile in Paris three years after his release.

His best-known novel, *The Picture of Dorian Gray* (1891; expanded 1894), is the story of a young man whose sensual life eats away at him and eventually destroys him. The novel's failure when it was first published led Wilde to try the stage, where he was a signal success. Remarkably, all his plays were written in the period between 1891 and his imprisonment in 1895. Most of his plays—*Salomé* (1891), *Lady Windermere's Fan* (1892), *A Woman of No Importance* (1893), *An Ideal Husband* (1895), and *The Importance of Being Earnest* (1895)—rank as witty, insightful, and sharp commentaries on the upper-class British society he knew best. They owe a great deal to eighteenth-century comedies, such as William Congreve's *The Way of the World*. But they also owe a great deal to

British and European farces and comedies of his own time, many of which he seems to have studied closely. Unlike those plays—many have never been published and no longer exist—Wilde's are still funny and still seem pertinent even though the class he criticized has long vanished.

The Importance of Being Earnest was a remarkable success when it opened at the St. James Theatre on Valentine's Day 1895, but it closed in two months after fewer than one hundred performances when the scandal of Wilde's conviction became public. Wilde's reputation as playwright was made and broken in a matter of a few years, and it was not restored until after his death.

THE IMPORTANCE OF BEING EARNEST

The play was originally written in four acts, but because the producer requested it be cut, Wilde reworked it into three acts, agreeing that the excisions made the play stronger. Its subtitle, *A Trivial Comedy for Serious People*, has prompted commentators to think of the play as farcical fluff, a play about little or nothing that is nonetheless profoundly amusing. The *New York Times* commented after its first U.S. opening, "The thing is as slight in structure and as devoid of purpose as a paper balloon, but it is extraordinarily funny." Recent critics have challenged this view on the grounds that the play's subject matter centers on the questions of identity and reality. One current view is that its surfaces are slight but that beneath the surface is a commentary on a society that judges things only by appearance.

The primary characters are Algernon Moncrieff and Jack Worthing, young gentlemen of marriageable age. Among the women are Algernon's cousin Gwendolen Fairfax, who adores the name Ernest and is in love with Jack; Lady Bracknell, her mother; and Cecily Cardew, Jack's ward. Bunbury, referred to by Algernon, seems to be a character, but is instead an invention. He is a convenience for Algernon, a country friend whose illnesses Algernon uses to avoid social events he dislikes, such as Lady Bracknell's dinners. Jack, who lives in the country, has created a similar figure to help him escape to town—an imaginary brother Ernest. In town, Jack pretends to be Ernest, and all his town acquaintances, including Algernon and Gwendolen, know Jack by that name.

The similarities with Restoration comedies are striking. The question of marriage is central in the play, and attitudes toward marriage in Wilde's social class are among the targets of his satire. When Lady Bracknell probes into Jack Worthing's background, she discovers the distressing news about his family "line"; Jack is a foundling who had been left in a handbag in Victoria Station. His family "line" is the Brighton Line! Gwendolen could also have stepped from a Restoration comedy. She is determined to have Jack Worthing, and when he seems sluggish about proposing she prompts him, offering a critique of his proposal by telling him he seems inexperienced at it.

The play owes perhaps even more to the farces of the 1880s and 1890s and a great deal to the well-made plays of Eugène Scribe and his successors. Critics often compare Wilde to Alexandre Dumas, the author of *La Dame aux camélias (Camille)*, because both writers fashioned their plays with a considerable degree of artificiality, planting information in the first act that would prove the solution to problems in the last act. They also play with questions of identity, disguise, and revelation at the last minute in much the way Wilde does here when he reveals the identity of Ernest.

In melodramas and well-made plays, the revelation at the end was not that the potential husband had the right name so much as that he had the right background: he was an aristocrat and not the commoner he seemed to be. Wilde has fun with this convention and many others. In an instant, he ridicules the trick of revealing the hero to be "marriageable" because of his birth by emphasizing the triviality of a name. Yet names are of great importance (as Shakespeare tells us in *Romeo and Juliet*), and the earnestness implied in Ernest is one ingredient that helps Jack Worthing succeed.

Critic Kerry Powell has demonstrated that almost every device in *The Importance of Being Earnest* was drawn from a contemporary farce or comedy. The device of the child lost in a piece of luggage was used in *The Lost Child* (1863), and *The Foundling* (1894) actually takes place in Brighton. The name Banbury and the concept of "Bunburying" come from *The Godpapa* (1891). Even the device of baptism was used in *Crimes and Christening* (1891). Wilde was adept at taking the theater conventions his audience was most familiar with and using them to his own ends—to entertain his audience, but at the same time to help him put an extra edge on his satire.

The Importance of Being Earnest in Performance

After the first production closed down in 1895, the play was revived in London in 1898 and 1902, but an even more successful production in 1909 saw 324 performances. The benchmark for a truly successful play in those days seems to have been one hundred performances, and Wilde would have felt vindicated by the 1909 production, had he lived to see it. *The Importance of Being Earnest* has been produced so often in Great Britain and the United States that only a few productions can be taken into account here. The first New York production was in 1902. John Gielgud and Edith Evans played in the 1939 London production and then again in 1942. In 1947 Gielgud played in New York with Clifton Webb and Estelle Winwood. The reviews were especially strong, calling the play "as insolently monocled in manner and as killingly high-toned in language as mischievous tomfoolery can make it."

The play inspired at least five musicals between 1927 and 1984. The 1979 production at Stratford, Ontario, was called "a perfect play in a perfect production." An unsuccessful production by the Berlin Play Actors in 1987 used all men and relied on insights drawn from transvestite performers, but it was badly received. University productions of the play are fairly common, although, like the Yale Repertory production in 1986, they are not always able to pull off the comic demands of the play's exacting language. The original four-act version of the play, discovered in 1977 in the New York Public Library, was produced in Ohio in the John Carroll University's Marinello Theater in 1985. It was more a curiosity than a triumph. The 1993 production at the Aldwych in London received great praise for its dazzling sets that "matched Wilde's word pictures with bold stage pictures." Maggie Smith played Lady Bracknell. Sir Peter Hall toured his Theatre Royal Bath company successfully in 2006 with a strikingly energetic Lynn Redgrave as Lady Bracknell. The production at the Brooklyn Academy of Music was well received, although the Harvey Theatre's stage was faulted for not wholly accommodating the proscenium frame necessary for the drama.

The play is a witty tour de force of language. Its surfaces gleam, and the best productions play it straight. A contemporary spate of films has made Wilde's work available to a wide audience.

Oscar Wilde (1854–1900)

THE IMPORTANCE OF BEING EARNEST   1895
A TRIVIAL COMEDY FOR SERIOUS PEOPLE

The Persons of the Play

JOHN WORTHING, J.P., *of the Manor House, Woolton, Hertfordshire*
ALGERNON MONCRIEFF, *his friend*
REV. CANON CHASUBLE, D.D., *rector of Woolton*
MERRIMAN, *butler to Mr. Worthing*
LANE, *Mr. Moncrieff's manservant*
LADY BRACKNELL
HON. GWENDOLEN FAIRFAX, *her daughter*
CECILY CARDEW, *John Worthing's ward*
MISS PRISM, *her governess*

The Scenes of the Play

Act I: *Algernon Moncrieff's Flat in Half Moon Street, W.*
Act II: *The Garden at the Manor House, Woolton*
Act III: *Morning Room at the Manor House, Woolton*

ACT I

(*Scene: Morning room in Algernon's flat in Half Moon Street. The room is luxuriously and artistically furnished. The sound of a piano is heard in the adjoining room. Lane is arranging afternoon tea on the table, and after the music has ceased, Algernon enters.*)

ALGERNON: Did you hear what I was playing, Lane?
LANE: I didn't think it polite to listen, sir.
ALGERNON: I'm sorry for that, for your sake. I don't play accurately—anyone can play accurately—but I play with wonderful expression. As far as the piano is concerned, sentiment is my forte. I keep science for Life.

LANE: Yes, sir.
ALGERNON: And, speaking of the science of Life, have you got the cucumber sandwiches cut for Lady Bracknell?
LANE: Yes, sir.   (*Hands them on a salver.*)
ALGERNON (*inspects them, takes two, and sits down on the sofa*): Oh!—by the way, Lane, I see from your book that on Thursday night, when Lord Shoreham and Mr. Worthing were dining with me, eight bottles of champagne are entered as having been consumed.
LANE: Yes, sir; eight bottles and a pint.
ALGERNON: Why is it that at a bachelor's establishment the servants invariably drink the champagne? I ask merely for information.
LANE: I attribute it to the superior quality of the wine, sir. I have often observed that in married households the champagne is rarely of a first-rate brand.
ALGERNON: Good heavens! Is marriage so demoralizing as that?
LANE: I believe it *is* a very pleasant state, sir. I have had very little experience of it myself up to the present. I have only been married once. That was in consequence of a misunderstanding between myself and a young person.
ALGERNON (*languidly*): I don't know that I am much interested in your family life, Lane.
LANE: No, sir; it is not a very interesting subject. I never think of it myself.
ALGERNON: Very natural, I am sure. That will do, Lane, thank you.
LANE: Thank you, sir.   (*Lane goes out.*)
ALGERNON: Lane's views on marriage seem somewhat lax. Really, if the lower orders don't set us a good example, what on earth is the use of them? They

seem, as a class, to have absolutely no sense of moral responsibility.

(*Enter Lane.*)

LANE: Mr. Ernest Worthing.

(*Enter Jack. Lane goes out.*)

ALGERNON: How are you, my dear Ernest? What brings you up to town?

JACK: Oh, pleasure, pleasure! What else should bring one anywhere? Eating as usual, I see, Algy!

ALGERNON (*Stiffly*): I believe it is customary in good society to take some slight refreshment at five o'clock. Where have you been since last Thursday?

JACK (*sitting down on the sofa*): In the country.

ALGERNON: What on earth do you do there?

JACK (*pulling off his gloves*): When one is in town one amuses oneself. When one is in the country one amuses other people. It is excessively boring.

ALGERNON: And who are the people you amuse?

JACK (*airily*): Oh, neighbors, neighbors.

ALGERNON: Got nice neighbors in your part of Shropshire?

JACK: Perfectly horrid! Never speak to one of them.

ALGERNON: How immensely you must amuse them! (*Goes over and takes sandwich.*) By the way, Shropshire is your county, is it not?

JACK: Eh? Shropshire? Yes, of course. Hallo! Why all these cups? Why cucumber sandwiches? Why such reckless extravagance in one so young? Who is coming to tea?

ALGERNON: Oh! merely Aunt Augusta and Gwendolen.

JACK: How perfectly delightful!

ALGERNON: Yes, that is all very well; but I am afraid Aunt Augusta won't quite approve of your being here.

JACK: May I ask why?

ALGERNON: My dear fellow, the way you flirt with Gwendolen is perfectly disgraceful. It is almost as bad as the way Gwendolen flirts with you.

JACK: I am in love with Gwendolen. I have come up to town expressly to propose to her.

ALGERNON: I thought you had come up for pleasure? — I call that business.

JACK: How utterly unromantic you are!

ALGERNON: I really don't see anything romantic in proposing. It is very romantic to be in love. But there is nothing romantic about a definite proposal. Why, one may be accepted. One usually is, I believe. Then the excitement is all over. The very essence of romance is uncertainty. If ever I get married, I'll certainly try to forget the fact.

JACK: I have no doubt about that, dear Algy. The Divorce Court was specially invented for people whose memories are so curiously constituted.

ALGERNON: Oh! there is no use speculating on that subject. Divorces are made in heaven — (*Jack puts out his hand to take a sandwich. Algernon at once interferes.*) Please don't touch the cucumber sandwiches. They are ordered specially for Aunt Augusta. (*Takes one and eats it.*)

JACK: Well, you have been eating them all the time.

ALGERNON: That is quite a different matter. She is my aunt. (*Takes plate from below.*) Have some bread and butter. The bread and butter is for Gwendolen. Gwendolen is devoted to bread and butter.

JACK (*advancing to table and helping himself*): And very good bread and butter it is too.

ALGERNON: Well, my dear fellow, you need not eat as if you were going to eat it all. You behave as if you were married to her already. You are not married to her already, and I don't think you ever will be.

JACK: Why on earth do you say that?

ALGERNON: Well, in the first place, girls never marry the men they flirt with. Girls don't think it right.

JACK: Oh, that is nonsense!

ALGERNON: It isn't. It is a great truth. It accounts for the extraordinary number of bachelors that one sees all over the place. In the second place, I don't give my consent.

JACK: Your consent!

ALGERNON: My dear fellow, Gwendolen is my first cousin. And before I allow you to marry her, you will have to clear up the whole question of Cecily.

(*Rings bell.*)

JACK: Cecily! What on earth do you mean? What do you mean, Algy, by Cecily? I don't know anyone of the name of Cecily.

(*Enter Lane.*)

ALGERNON: Bring me that cigarette case Mr. Worthing left in the smoking room the last time he dined here.

LANE: Yes, sir.   (*Lane goes out.*)

JACK: Do you mean to say you have had my cigarette case all this time? I wish to goodness you had let me know. I have been writing frantic letters to Scotland Yard about it. I was very nearly offering a large reward.

ALGERNON: Well, I wish you would offer one. I happen to he more than usually hard up.

JACK: There is no good offering a large reward now that the thing is found.

(*Enter Lane with the cigarette case on a salver. Algernon takes it at once. Lane goes out.*)

ALGERNON: I think that is rather mean of you, Ernest, I must say. (*Opens case and examines it.*) However, it makes no matter, for, now that I look at the inscription inside, I find that the thing isn't yours after all.

JACK: Of course it's mine. (*Moving to him.*) You have seen me with it a hundred times, and you have no right whatsoever to read what is written inside. It is a very ungentlemanly thing to read a private cigarette case.

ALGERNON: Oh! it is absurd to have a hard-and-fast rule about what one should read and what one shouldn't. More than half of modern culture depends on what one shouldn't read.

JACK: I am quite aware of the fact, and I don't propose to discuss modern culture. It isn't the sort of thing one should talk of in private. I simply want my cigarette case back.

ALGERNON: Yes; but this isn't your cigarette case. This cigarette case is a present from someone of the name of Cecily, and you said you didn't know anyone of that name.

JACK: Well, if you want to know, Cecily happens to be my aunt.

ALGERNON: Your aunt!

JACK: Yes. Charming old lady she is, too. Lives at Tunbridge Wells. Just give it back to me, Algy.

ALGERNON (*retreating to back of sofa*): But why does she call herself little Cecily if she is your aunt and lives at Tunbridge Wells? (*Reading.*) "From little Cecily with her fondest love."

JACK (*moving to sofa and kneeling upon it*): My dear fellow, what on earth is there in that? Some aunts are tall, some aunts are not tall. That is a matter that surely an aunt may be allowed to decide for herself. You seem to think that every aunt should be exactly like your aunt! That is absurd! For heaven's sake give me back my cigarette case.

(*Follows Algernon round the room.*)

ALGERNON: Yes. But why does your aunt call you her uncle? "From little Cecily, with her fondest love to her dear Uncle Jack." There is no objection, I admit, to an aunt being a small aunt, but why an aunt, no matter what her size may be, should call her own nephew her uncle, I can't quite make out. Besides, your name isn't Jack at all; it is Ernest.

JACK: It isn't Ernest; it's Jack.

ALGERNON: You have always told me it was Ernest. I have introduced you to everyone as Ernest. You answer to the name of Ernest. You look as if your name was Ernest. You are the most earnest looking person I ever saw in my life. It is perfectly absurd your saying that your name isn't Ernest. It's on your cards. Here is one of them (*taking it from case*) "Mr. Ernest Worthing, B.4, The Albany." I'll keep this as a proof that your name is Ernest if ever you attempt to deny it to me, or to Gwendolen, or to anyone else.

(*Puts the card in his pocket.*)

JACK: Well, my name is Ernest in town and Jack in the country, and the cigarette case was given to me in the country.

ALGERNON: Yes, but that does not account for the fact that your small Aunt Cecily, who lives at Tunbridge Wells, calls you her dear uncle. Come, old boy, you had much better have the thing out at once.

JACK: My dear Algy, you talk exactly as if you were a dentist. It is very vulgar to talk like a dentist when one isn't a dentist. It produces a false impression.

ALGERNON: Well, that is exactly what dentists always do. Now, go on! Tell me the whole thing. I may mention that I have always suspected you of being a confirmed and secret Bunburyist; and I am quite sure of it now.

JACK: Bunburyist? What on earth do you mean by a Bunburyist?

ALGERNON: I'll reveal to you the meaning of that incomparable expression as soon as you are kind enough to inform me why you are Ernest in town and Jack in the country.

JACK: Well, produce my cigarette case first.

ALGERNON: Here it is. (*Hands cigarette case.*) Now produce your explanation, and pray make it improbable.

(*Sits on sofa.*)

JACK: My dear fellow, there is nothing improbable about my explanation at all. In fact it's perfectly ordinary. Old Mr. Thomas Cardew, who adopted me when I was a little boy, made me in his will guardian to his granddaughter, Miss Cecily Cardew. Cecily, who addresses me as her uncle from motives of respect that you could not possibly appreciate, lives at my place in the country under the charge of her admirable governess, Miss Prism.

ALGERNON: Where is that place in the country, by the way?

JACK: That is nothing to you, dear boy. You are not going to be invited — I may tell you candidly that the place is not in Shropshire.

ALGERNON: I suspected that, my dear fellow! I have Bunburyed all over Shropshire on two separate occasions. Now, go on. Why are you Ernest in town and Jack in the country?

JACK: My dear Algy, I don't know whether you will be able to understand my real motives. You are hardly serious enough. When one is placed in the position of guardian, one has to adopt a very high moral tone on all subjects. It's one's duty to do so. And as a high moral tone can hardly be said to conduce very much to either one's health or one's happiness, in order to get up to town I have always pretended to have a younger brother of the name of Ernest, who lives in the Albany, and gets into the most dreadful scrapes. That, my dear Algy, is the whole truth pure and simple.

ALGERNON: The truth is rarely pure and never simple. Modern life would be very tedious if it were either and modern literature a complete impossibility!

JACK: That wouldn't be at all a bad thing.

ALGERNON: Literary criticism is not your forte, my dear fellow. Don't try it. You should leave that to people who haven't been at a university. They do it so well in the daily papers. What you really are is a Bunburyist. I was quite right in saying you were a Bunburyist. You are one of the most advanced Bunburyists I know.

JACK: What on earth do you mean?

ALGERNON: You have invented a very useful younger brother called Ernest, in order that you may be able to come up to town as often as you like. I have invented an invaluable permanent invalid called Bunbury, in order that I may be able to go down into the country whenever I choose. Bunbury is perfectly invaluable. If it wasn't for Bunbury's extraordinary bad health, for instance, I wouldn't be able to dine with you at Willis's tonight, for I have been really engaged to Aunt Augusta for more than a week.

JACK: I haven't asked you to dine with me anywhere tonight.

ALGERNON: I know. You are absurdly careless about sending out invitations. It is very foolish of you. Nothing annoys people so much as not receiving invitations.

JACK: You had much better dine with your Aunt Augusta.

ALGERNON: I haven't the smallest intention of doing anything of the kind. To begin with, I dined there on Monday, and once a week is quite enough to dine with one's own relations. In the second place, whenever I do dine there I am always treated as a member of the family, and sent down with° either no woman at all, or two. In the third place, I know perfectly well whom she will place me next to, tonight. She will place me next Mary Farquhar, who always flirts with her own husband across the dinner table. That is not very pleasant. Indeed, it is not even decent — and that sort of thing is enormously on the increase. The amount of women in London who flirt with their own husbands is perfectly scandalous. It looks so bad. It is simply washing one's clean linen in public. Besides, now that I know you to be a confirmed Bunburyist I naturally want to talk to you about Bunburying. I want to tell you the rules.

JACK: I'm not a Bunburyist at all. If Gwendolen accepts me, I am going to kill my brother, indeed I think I'll kill him in any case. Cecily is a little too much interested in him. It is rather a bore. So I am going to get rid of Ernest. And I strongly advise you to do the same with Mr. — with your invalid friend who has the absurd name.

ALGERNON: Nothing will induce me to part with Bunbury, and if you ever get married, which seems to me extremely problematic, you will be very glad to know Bunbury. A man who marries without knowing Bunbury has a very tedious time of it.

JACK: That is nonsense. If I marry a charming girl like Gwendolen, and she is the only girl I ever saw in my life that I would marry, I certainly won't want to know Bunbury.

ALGERNON: Then your wife will. You don't seem to realize, that in married life three is company and two is none.

JACK (sententiously): That, my dear young friend, is the theory that the corrupt French drama has been propounding for the last fifty years.

ALGERNON: Yes; and that the happy English home has proved in half the time.

JACK: For heaven's sake, don't try to be cynical. It's perfectly easy to be cynical.

ALGERNON: My dear fellow, it isn't easy to be anything nowadays. There's such a lot of beastly competition about. (The sound of an electric bell is heard.) Ah! that must be Aunt Augusta. Only relatives, or creditors, ever ring in that Wagnerian° manner. Now, if I

---

sent down with: Assigned a woman to escort into the dining room for dinner. **Wagnerian:** Referring to the operas of Richard Wagner (1813–1883), whose music was popularly thought to be loud.

---

get her out of the way for ten minutes, so that you can have an opportunity for proposing to Gwendolen, may I dine with you tonight at Willis's?

JACK: I suppose so, if you want to.

ALGERNON: Yes, but you must be serious about it. I hate people who are not serious about meals. It is so shallow of them.

(Enter Lane.)

LANE: Lady Bracknell and Miss Fairfax.

(Algernon goes forward to meet them. Enter Lady Bracknell and Gwendolen.)

LADY BRACKNELL: Good afternoon, dear Algernon, I hope you are behaving very well.

ALGERNON: I'm feeling very well, Aunt Augusta.

LADY BRACKNELL: That's not quite the same thing. In fact the two things rarely go together.

(Sees Jack and bows to him with icy coldness.)

ALGERNON (to Gwendolen): Dear me, you are smart!

GWENDOLEN: I am always smart! Aren't I, Mr. Worthing?

JACK: You're quite perfect, Miss Fairfax.

GWENDOLEN: Oh! I hope I am not that. It would leave no room for developments, and I intend to develop in many directions.

(Gwendolen and Jack sit down together in the corner.)

LADY BRACKNELL: I'm sorry if we are a little late Algernon, but I was obliged to call on dear Lady Harbury. I hadn't been there since her poor husband's death. I never saw a woman so altered; she looks quite twenty years younger. And now I'll have a cup of tea, and one of those nice cucumber sandwiches you promised me.

ALGERNON: Certainly, Aunt Augusta.

(Goes over to tea table.)

LADY BRACKNELL: Won't you come and sit here, Gwendolen?

GWENDOLEN: Thanks, Mama, I'm quite comfortable where I am.

ALGERNON (picking up empty plate in horror): Good heavens! Lane! Why are there no cucumber sandwiches? I ordered them specially.

LANE (gravely): There were no cucumbers in the market this morning, sir. I went down twice.

ALGERNON: No cucumbers?

LANE: No, sir. Not even for ready money.

ALGERNON: That will do, Lane, thank you.

LANE: Thank you, sir. (Goes out.)

ALGERNON: I am greatly distressed, Aunt Augusta, about there being no cucumbers, not even for ready money.

LADY BRACKNELL: It really makes no matter, Algernon. I had some crumpets with Lady Harbury, who seems to me to be living entirely for pleasure now.

ALGERNON: I hear her hair has turned quite gold from grief.

LADY BRACKNELL: It certainly has changed its color. From what cause I, of course, cannot say. (*Algernon crosses and hands tea.*) Thank you. I've quite a treat for you tonight, Algernon. I am going to send you down with Mary Farquhar. She is such a nice woman, and so attentive to her husband. It's delightful to watch them.

ALGERNON: I am afraid, Aunt Augusta, I shall have to give up the pleasure of dining with you tonight after all.

LADY BRACKNELL (*frowning*): I hope not, Algernon. It would put my table completely out. Your uncle would have to dine upstairs. Fortunately he is accustomed to that.

ALGERNON: It is a great bore, and, I need hardly say, a terrible disappointment to me, but the fact is I have just had a telegram to say that my poor friend Bunbury is very ill again. (*Exchanges glances with Jack.*) They seem to think I should be with him.

LADY BRACKNELL: It is very strange. This Mr. Bunbury seems to suffer from curiously bad health.

ALGERNON: Yes; poor Bunbury is a dreadful invalid.

LADY BRACKNELL: Well, I must say, Algernon, that I think it is high time that Mr. Bunbury made up his mind whether he was going to live or to die. This shilly-shallying with the question is absurd. Nor do I in any way approve of the modern sympathy with invalids. I consider it morbid. Illness of any kind is hardly a thing to be encouraged in others. Health is the primary duty of life. I am always telling that to your poor uncle, but he never seems to take much notice—as far as any improvement in his ailments goes. I should be much obliged if you would ask Mr. Bunbury, from me, to be kind enough not to have a relapse on Saturday, for I rely on you to arrange my music for me. It is my last reception, and one wants something that will encourage conversation, particularly at the end of the season when everyone has practically said whatever they had to say, which, in most cases, was probably not much.

ALGERNON: I'll speak to Bunbury, Aunt Augusta, if he is still conscious, and I think I can promise you he'll be all right by Saturday. Of course the music is a great difficulty. You see, if one plays good music, people don't listen, and if one plays bad music people don't talk. But I'll run over the program I've drawn out, if you will kindly come into the next room for a moment.

LADY BRACKNELL: Thank you, Algernon. It is very thoughtful of you. (*Rising, and following Algernon.*) I'm sure the program will be delightful, after a few expurgations. French songs I cannot possibly allow. People always seem to think that they are improper, and either look shocked, which is vulgar, or laugh, which is worse. But German sounds a thoroughly respectable language, and indeed, I believe is so. Gwendolen, you will accompany me.

GWENDOLEN: Certainly, Mama.

(*Lady Bracknell and Algernon go into the music room. Gwendolen remains behind.*)

JACK: Charming day it has been, Miss Fairfax.

GWENDOLEN: Pray don't talk to me about the weather Mr. Worthing. Whenever people talk to me about the weather, I always feel quite certain that they mean something else. And that makes me so nervous.

JACK: I do mean something else.

GWENDOLEN: I thought so. In fact, I am never wrong.

JACK: And I would like to be allowed to take advantage of Lady Bracknell's temporary absence—

GWENDOLEN: I would certainly advise you to do so. Mama has a way of coming back suddenly into a room that I have often had to speak to her about.

JACK (*nervously*): Miss Fairfax, ever since I met you I have admired you more than any girl—I have ever met since—I met you.

GWENDOLEN: Yes, I am quite aware of the fact. And I often wish that in public, at any rate, you had been more demonstrative. For me you have always had an irresistible fascination. Even before I met you I was far from indifferent to you. (*Jack looks at her in amazement.*) We live, as I hope you know Mr. Worthing, in an age of ideals. The fact is constantly mentioned in the more expensive monthly magazines, and has reached the provincial pulpits I am told: And my ideal has always been to love someone of the name of Ernest. There is something in that name that inspires absolute confidence. The moment Algernon first mentioned to me that he had a friend called Ernest, I knew I was destined to love you.

JACK: You really love me, Gwendolen?

GWENDOLEN: Passionately!

JACK: Darling! You don't know how happy you've made me.

GWENDOLEN: My own Ernest!

JACK: But you don't mean to say that you couldn't love me if my name wasn't Ernest?

GWENDOLEN: But your name is Ernest.

JACK: Yes, I know it is. But supposing it was something else? Do you mean to say you couldn't love me then?

GWENDOLEN (*glibly*): Ah! that is clearly a metaphysical speculation, and like most metaphysical speculations has very little reference at all to the actual facts of real life, as we know them.

JACK: Personally, darling, to speak quite candidly, I don't much care about the name of Ernest—I don't think the name suits me at all.

GWENDOLEN: It suits you perfectly. It is a divine name. It has a music of its own. It produces vibrations.

JACK: Well, really, Gwendolen, I must say that I think there are lots of other much nicer names. I think Jack, for instance, a charming name.

GWENDOLEN: Jack?—No, there is very little music in the name Jack, if any at all, indeed. It does not thrill. It produces absolutely no vibrations—I have known several Jacks, and they all, without exception, were more than usually plain. Besides, Jack is a notorious domesticity for John! And I pity any woman who is married to a man called John. She would probably never be allowed to know the entrancing pleasure of a single moment's solitude. The only really safe name is Ernest.

JACK: Gwendolen, I must get christened at once—I mean we must get married at once. There is no time to be lost.

GWENDOLEN: Married, Mr. Worthing?

JACK (*astounded*): Well—surely. You know that I love you, and you led me to believe, Miss Fairfax that you were not absolutely indifferent to me.

GWENDOLEN: I adore you. But you haven't proposed to me yet. Nothing has been said at all about marriage. The subject has not even been touched on.

JACK: Well—may I propose to you now?

GWENDOLEN: I think it would be an admirable opportunity. And to spare you any possible disappointment, Mr. Worthing, I think it only fair to tell you quite frankly beforehand that I am fully determined to accept you.

JACK: Gwendolen!

GWENDOLEN: Yes, Mr. Worthing, what have you got to say to me?

JACK: You know what I have got to say to you.

GWENDOLEN: Yes, but you don't say it.

JACK: Gwendolen, will you marry me?

(*Goes on his knees.*)

GWENDOLEN: Of course I will, darling. How long you have been about it! I am afraid you have had very little experience in how to propose.

JACK: My own one, I have never loved anyone in the world but you.

GWENDOLEN: Yes, but men often propose for practice. I know my brother Gerald does. All my girlfriends tell me so. What wonderfully blue eyes you have, Ernest! They are quite, quite blue. I hope you will always look at me just like that, especially when there are other people present.

(*Enter Lady Bracknell.*)

LADY BRACKNELL: Mr. Worthing! Rise, sir, from this semirecumbent posture. It is most indecorous.

GWENDOLEN: Mama! (*He tries to rise; she restrains him.*) I must beg you to retire. This is no place for you. Besides, Mr. Worthing has not quite finished yet.

LADY BRACKNELL: Finished what, may I ask?

GWENDOLEN: I am engaged to Mr. Worthing, Mama.

(*They rise together.*)

LADY BRACKNELL: Pardon me, you are not engaged to anyone. When you do become engaged to someone, I, or your father, should his health permit him, will inform you of the fact. An engagement should come on a young girl as a surprise, pleasant or unpleasant, as the case may be. It is hardly a matter that she could be allowed to arrange for herself—And now I have a few questions to put to you, Mr. Worthing. While I am making these inquiries, you, Gwendolen, will wait for me below in the carriage.

GWENDOLEN (*reproachfully*): Mama!

LADY BRACKNELL: In the carriage, Gwendolen! (*Gwendolen goes to the door. She and Jack blow kisses to each other behind Lady Bracknell's back. Lady Bracknell looks vaguely about as if she could not understand what the noise was. Finally turns round.*) Gwendolen, the carriage!

GWENDOLEN: Yes, Mama.

(*Goes out, looking back at Jack.*)

LADY BRACKNELL (*sitting down*): You can take a seat, Mr. Worthing.

(*Looks in her pocket for notebook and pencil.*)

JACK: Thank you, Lady Bracknell, I prefer standing.

LADY BRACKNELL (*pencil and notebook in hand*): I feel bound to tell you that you are not down on my list of eligible young men, although I have the same list as the dear Duchess of Bolton has. We work together, in fact. However, I am quite ready to enter your name, should your answers be what a really affectionate mother requires. Do you smoke?

JACK: Well, yes, I must admit I smoke.

LADY BRACKNELL: I am glad to hear it. A man should always have an occupation of some kind. There are far too many idle men in London as it is. How old are you?

JACK: Twenty-nine.

LADY BRACKNELL: A very good age to be married at. I have always been of opinion that a man who desires to get married should know either everything or nothing. Which do you know?

JACK (*after some hesitation*): I know nothing, Lady Bracknell.

LADY BRACKNELL: I am pleased to hear it. I do not approve of anything that tampers with natural ignorance. Ignorance is like a delicate exotic fruit; touch it and the bloom is gone. The whole theory of modern education is radically unsound. Fortunately in England, at any rate, education produces no effect whatsoever. If it did, it would prove a serious danger to the upper classes, and probably lead to acts of violence in Grosvenor Square. What is your income?

JACK: Between seven and eight thousand a year.

LADY BRACKNELL (*makes a note in her book*): In land, or in investments?

JACK: In investments, chiefly.

LADY BRACKNELL: That is satisfactory. What between the duties expected of one during one's lifetime, and the duties exacted from one after one's death, land has ceased to be either a profit or a pleasure. It gives one position, and prevents one from keeping it up. That's all that can be said about land.

JACK: I have a country house with some land, of course, attached to it, about fifteen hundred acres, I believe; but I don't depend on that for my real income. In fact, as far as I can make out, the poachers are the only people who make anything out of it.

LADY BRACKNELL: A country house! How many bedrooms? Well, that point can be cleared up afterwards. You have a town house, I hope? A girl with a simple, unspoiled nature, like Gwendolen, could hardly be expected to reside in the country.

JACK: Well, I own a house in Belgrave Square, but it is let by the year to Lady Bloxham. Of course, I can get it back whenever I like, at six months' notice.

LADY BRACKNELL: Lady Bloxham? I don't know her.

JACK: Oh, she goes about very little. She is a lady considerably advanced in years.

LADY BRACKNELL: Ah, nowadays that is no guarantee of respectability of character. What number in Belgrave Square?

JACK: 149.

LADY BRACKNELL (*shaking her head*): The unfashionable side. I thought there was something. However, that could easily be altered.

JACK: Do you mean the fashion, or the side?

LADY BRACKNELL (*sternly*): Both, if necessary, I presume. What are your politics?

JACK: Well, I am afraid I really have none. I am a Liberal Unionist.

LADY BRACKNELL: Oh, they count as Tories. They dine with us. Or come in the evening, at any rate. Now to minor matters. Are your parents living?

JACK: I have lost both my parents.

LADY BRACKNELL: Both? To lose one parent may be regarded as a misfortune—to lose *both* seems like carelessness. Who was your father? He was evidently a man of some wealth. Was he born in what the Radical papers call the purple of commerce, or did he rise from the ranks of the aristocracy?

JACK: I am afraid I really don't know. The fact is, Lady Bracknell, I said I had lost my parents. It would be nearer the truth to say that my parents seem to have lost me—I don't actually know who I am by birth. I was—well, I was found.

LADY BRACKNELL: Found!

JACK: The late Mr. Thomas Cardew, an old gentleman of a very charitable and kindly disposition, found me, and gave me the name of Worthing, because he happened to have a first-class ticket for Worthing in his pocket at the time. Worthing is a place in Sussex. It is a seaside resort.

LADY BRACKNELL: Where did the charitable gentleman who had a first-class ticket for this seaside resort find you?

JACK (*gravely*): In a handbag.

LADY BRACKNELL: A handbag?

JACK (*very seriously*): Yes, Lady Bracknell. I was in a handbag—a somewhat large, black leather handbag, with handles to it—an ordinary handbag in fact.

LADY BRACKNELL: In what locality did this Mr. James, or Thomas, Cardew come across this ordinary handbag?

JACK: In the cloakroom at Victoria Station. It was given to him in mistake for his own.

LADY BRACKNELL: The cloakroom at Victoria Station?

JACK: Yes. The Brighton line.

LADY BRACKNELL: The line is immaterial. Mr. Worthing, I confess I feel somewhat bewildered by what you have just told me. To be born, or at any rate bred, in a handbag, whether it had handles or not, seems to me to display a contempt for the ordinary decencies of family life that reminds one of the worst excesses of the French Revolution. And I presume you know what that unfortunate movement led to? As for the particular locality in which the handbag was found, a cloakroom at a railway station might serve to conceal a social indiscretion—has probably, indeed, been used for that purpose before now—but it could hardly be regarded as an assured basis for a recognized position in good society.

JACK: May I ask you then what you would advise me to do? I need hardly say I would do anything in the world to ensure Gwendolen's happiness.

LADY BRACKNELL: I would strongly advise you, Mr. Worthing, to try and acquire some relations as soon as possible, and to make a definite effort to produce at any rate one parent of either sex, before the season is quite over.

JACK: Well, I don't see how I could possibly manage to do that. I can produce the handbag at any moment. It is in my dressing room at home. I really think that should satisfy you, Lady Bracknell.

LADY BRACKNELL: Me, sir! What has it to do with me? You can hardly imagine that I and Lord Bracknell would dream of allowing our only daughter—a girl brought up with the utmost care—to marry into a cloakroom, and form an alliance with a parcel? Good morning, Mr. Worthing!

(*Lady Bracknell sweeps out in majestic indignation.*)

JACK: Good morning! (*Algernon, from the other room, strikes up the Wedding March. Jack looks perfectly furious, and goes to the door.*) For goodness' sake don't play that ghastly tune, Algy! How idiotic you are!

(*The music stops, and Algernon enters cheerily.*)

ALGERNON: Didn't it go off all right, old boy? You don't mean to say Gwendolen refused you? I know it is a way she has. She is always refusing people. I think it is most ill-natured of her.

JACK: Oh, Gwendolen is as right as a trivet. As far as she is concerned, we are engaged. Her mother is perfectly unbearable. Never met such a Gorgon°—I don't really know what a Gorgon is like, but I am quite sure that Lady Bracknell is one. In any case, she is a monster, without being a myth, which is rather unfair. I beg your pardon, Algy, I suppose I shouldn't talk about your own aunt in that way before you.

ALGERNON: My dear boy, I love hearing my relations abused. It is the only thing that makes me put up with them at all. Relations are simply a tedious pack of people, who haven't got the remotest knowledge

---

Gorgon: In Greek myth, one of three very ugly sisters who had, among other characteristics, serpents for hair.

of how to live, nor the smallest instinct about when to die.

JACK: Oh, that is nonsense!

ALGERNON: It isn't!

JACK: Well, I won't argue about the matter. You always want to argue about things.

ALGERNON: That is exactly what things were originally made for.

JACK: Upon my word, if I thought that, I'd shoot myself—(*A pause.*) You don't think there is any chance of Gwendolen becoming like her mother in about a hundred and fifty years, do you Algy?

ALGERNON: All women become like their mothers. That is their tragedy. No man does. That's his.

JACK: Is that clever?

ALGERNON: It is perfectly phrased! and quite as true as any observation in civilized life should be.

JACK: I am sick to death of cleverness. Everybody is clever nowadays. You can't go anywhere without meeting clever people. The thing has become an absolute public nuisance. I wish to goodness we had a few fools left.

ALGERNON: We have.

JACK: I should extremely like to meet them. What do they talk about?

ALGERNON: The fools? Oh! about the clever people, of course.

JACK: What fools!

ALGERNON: By the way, did you tell Gwendolen the truth about your being Ernest in town, and Jack in the country?

JACK (*in a very patronizing manner*): My dear fellow, the truth isn't quite the sort of thing one tells to a nice sweet refined girl. What extraordinary ideas you have about the way to behave to a woman!

ALGERNON: The only way to behave to a woman is to make love to her if she is pretty, and to someone else if she is plain.

JACK: Oh, that is nonsense.

ALGERNON: What about your brother? What about the profligate Ernest?

JACK: Oh, before the end of the week I shall have got rid of him. I'll say he died in Paris of apoplexy. Lots of people die of apoplexy, quite suddenly, don't they?

ALGERNON: Yes, but it's hereditary, my dear fellow. It's a sort of thing that runs in families. You had much better say a severe chill.

JACK: You are sure a severe chill isn't hereditary, or anything of that kind?

ALGERNON: Of course it isn't!

JACK: Very well, then. My poor brother Ernest is carried off suddenly in Paris, by a severe chill. That gets rid of him.

ALGERNON: But I thought you said that—Miss Cardew was a little too much interested in your poor brother Ernest? Won't she feel his loss a good deal?

JACK: Oh, that is all right. Cecily is not a silly romantic girl, I am glad to say. She has got a capital appetite,

goes long walks, and pays no attention at all to her lessons.

ALGERNON: I would rather like to see Cecily.

JACK: I will take very good care you never do. She is excessively pretty, and she is only just eighteen.

ALGERNON: Have you told Gwendolen yet that you have an excessively pretty ward who is only just eighteen?

JACK: Oh! one doesn't blurt these things out to people. Cecily and Gwendolen are perfectly certain to be extremely great friends. I'll bet you anything you like that half an hour after they have met, they will be calling each other sister.

ALGERNON: Women only do that when they have called each other a lot of other things first. Now, my dear boy, if we want to get a good table at Willis's, we really must go and dress. Do you know it is nearly seven?

JACK (*irritably*): Oh! it always is nearly seven.

ALGERNON: Well, I'm hungry.

JACK: I never knew you when you weren't—

ALGERNON: What shall we do after dinner? Go to a theater?

JACK: Oh, no! I loathe listening.

ALGERNON: Well, let us go to the Club?

JACK: Oh, no! I hate talking.

ALGERNON: Well, we might trot round to the Empire° at ten?

JACK: Oh, no! I can't bear looking at things. It is so silly.

ALGERNON: Well, what shall we do?

JACK: Nothing!

ALGERNON: It is awfully hard work doing nothing. However, I don't mind hard work where there is no definite object of any kind.

(*Enter Lane.*)

LANE: Miss Fairfax.

(*Enter Gwendolen. Lane goes out.*)

ALGERNON: Gwendolen, upon my word!

GWENDOLEN: Algy, kindly turn your back. I have something very particular to say to Mr. Worthing.

ALGERNON: Really, Gwendolen, I don't think I can allow this at all.

GWENDOLEN: Algy, you always adopt a strictly immoral attitude towards life. You are not quite old enough to do that.

(*Algernon retires to the fireplace.*)

JACK: My own darling!

GWENDOLEN: Ernest, we may never be married. From the expression on Mama's face I fear we never shall. Few parents nowadays pay any regard to what their children say to them. The old-fashioned respect for the young is fast dying out. Whatever influence I ever had over Mama, I lost at the age of three. But although she may prevent us from becoming man and wife, and I may marry someone else, and marry often,

---

Empire: Empire Theatre, a London music hall that was also a rendezvous for prostitutes.

Scene from the Huntington Theatre Company's 1994 production of *The Importance of Being Earnest.*

nothing that she can possibly do can alter my eternal devotion to you.

JACK: Dear Gwendolen!

GWENDOLEN: The story of your romantic origin, as related to me by Mama, with unpleasing comments, has naturally stirred the deeper fibers of my nature. Your Christian name has an irresistible fascination. The simplicity of your character makes you exquisitely incomprehensible to me. Your town address at the Albany I have. What is your address in the country?

JACK: The Manor House, Woolton, Hertfordshire.

(*Algernon, who has been carefully listening, smiles to himself, and writes the address on his shirt cuff. Then picks up the Railway Guide.*)

GWENDOLEN: There is a good postal service, I suppose? It may be necessary to do something desperate. That of course will require serious consideration. I will communicate with you daily.

JACK: My own one!

GWENDOLEN: How long do you remain in town?

JACK: Till Monday.

GWENDOLEN: Good! Algy, you may turn round now.

ALGERNON: Thanks, I've turned round already.

GWENDOLEN: You may also ring the bell.

JACK: You will let me see you to your carriage, my own darling?

GWENDOLEN: Certainly.

JACK (*to Lane, who now enters*): I will see Miss Fairfax out.

LANE: Yes, sir.   (*Jack and Gwendolen go off.*)

(*Lane presents several letters on a salver to Algernon. It is to be surmised that they are bills, as Algernon, after looking at the envelopes, tears them up.*)

ALGERNON: A glass of sherry, Lane.

LANE: Yes, sir.

ALGERNON: Tomorrow, Lane, I'm going Bunburying.

LANE: Yes, sir.

ALGERNON: I shall probably not be back till Monday. You can put up my dress clothes, my smoking jacket, and all the Bunbury suits—

LANE: Yes, sir.   (*Handing sherry.*)

ALGERNON: I hope tomorrow will be a fine day, Lane.

LANE: It never is, sir.

ALGERNON: Lane, you're a perfect pessimist.

LANE: I do my best to give satisfaction, sir.

(*Enter Jack. Lane goes off.*)

JACK: There's a sensible, intellectual girl! the only girl I ever cared for in my life. (*Algernon is laughing immoderately.*) What on earth are you so amused at?

ALGERNON: Oh, I'm a little anxious about poor Bunbury, that is all.

JACK: If you don't take care, your friend Bunbury will get you into a serious scrape some day.

ALGERNON: I love scrapes. They are the only things that are never serious.

JACK: Oh, that's nonsense, Algy. You never talk anything but nonsense.

ALGERNON: Nobody ever does.

(*Jack looks indignantly at him, and leaves the room. Algernon lights a cigarette, reads his shirt cuff, and smiles.*)

ACT II

(*Scene: Garden at the Manor House. A flight of gray stone steps leads up to the house. The garden, an old-fashioned one, full of roses. Time of year, July. Basket chairs, and a table covered with books, are set under a large yew tree. Miss Prism discovered seated at the table. Cecily is at the back watering flowers.*)

MISS PRISM (*calling*): Cecily, Cecily! Surely such a utilitarian occupation as the watering of flowers is rather Moulton's duty than yours? Especially at a moment when intellectual pleasures await you. Your German grammar is on the table. Pray open it at page fifteen. We will repeat yesterday's lesson.

CECILY (*coming over very slowly*): But I don't like German. It isn't at all a becoming language. I know perfectly well that I look quite plain after my German lesson.

MISS PRISM: Child, you know how anxious your guardian is that you should improve yourself in every way. He laid particular stress on your German, as he was leaving for town yesterday. Indeed, he always lays stress on your German when he is leaving for town.

CECILY: Dear Uncle Jack is so very serious! Sometimes he is so serious that I think he cannot be quite well.

MISS PRISM (*drawing herself up*): Your guardian enjoys the best of health, and his gravity of demeanor is especially to be commended in one so comparatively young as he is. I know no one who has a higher sense of duty and responsibility.

CECILY: I suppose that is why he often looks a little bored when we three are together.

MISS PRISM: Cecily! I am surprised at you. Mr. Worthing has many troubles in his life. Idle merriment and triviality would be out of place in his conversation. You must remember his constant anxiety about that unfortunate young man his brother.

CECILY: I wish Uncle Jack would allow that unfortunate young man, his brother, to come down here sometimes.

We might have a good influence over him, Miss Prism. I am sure you certainly would. You know German, and geology, and things of that kind influence a man very much.

(*Cecily begins to write in her diary.*)

MISS PRISM (*shaking her head*): I do not think that even I could produce any effect on a character that according to his own brother's admission is irretrievably weak and vacillating. Indeed I am not sure that I would desire to reclaim him. I am not in favor of this modern mania for turning bad people into good people at a moment's notice. As a man sows so let him reap. You must put away your diary, Cecily. I really don't see why you should keep a diary at all.

CECILY: I keep a diary in order to enter the wonderful secrets of my life. If I didn't write them down I should probably forget all about them.

MISS PRISM: Memory, my dear Cecily, is the diary that we all carry about with us.

CECILY: Yes, but it usually chronicles the things that have never happened, and couldn't possibly have happened. I believe that Memory is responsible for nearly all the three-volume novels that Mudie sends us.

MISS PRISM: Do not speak slightingly of the three-volume novel, Cecily. I wrote one myself in earlier days.

CECILY: Did you really, Miss Prism? How wonderfully clever you are! I hope it did not end happily? I don't like novels that end happily. They depress me so much.

MISS PRISM: The good ended happily, and the bad unhappily. That is what Fiction means.

CECILY: I suppose so. But it seems very unfair. And was your novel ever published?

MISS PRISM: Alas! no. The manuscript unfortunately was abandoned. I use the word in the sense of lost or mislaid. To your work, child, these speculations are profitless.

CECILY (*smiling*): But I see dear Dr. Chasuble coming up through the garden.

MISS PRISM (*rising and advancing*): Dr. Chasuble! This is indeed a pleasure.

(*Enter Canon Chasuble.*)

CHASUBLE: And how are we this morning? Miss Prism, you are, I trust, well?

CECILY: Miss Prism has just been complaining of a slight headache. I think it would do her so much good to have a short stroll with you in the park, Dr. Chasuble.

MISS PRISM: Cecily, I have not mentioned anything about a headache.

CECILY: No, dear Miss Prism, I know that, but I felt instinctively that you had a headache. Indeed I was thinking about that, and not about my German lesson, when the Rector came in.

CHASUBLE: I hope, Cecily, you are not inattentive.

CECILY: Oh, I am afraid I am.

CHASUBLE: That is strange. Were I fortunate enough to be Miss Prism's pupil, I would hang upon her lips.

(*Miss Prism glares.*) I spoke metaphorically.—My metaphor was drawn from bees. Ahem! Mr. Worthing, I suppose, has not returned from town yet?

MISS PRISM: We do not expect him till Monday afternoon.

CHASUBLE: Ah yes, he usually likes to spend his Sunday in London. He is not one of those whose sole aim is enjoyment, as, by all accounts, that unfortunate young man his brother seems to be. But I must not disturb Egeria° and her pupil any longer.

MISS PRISM: Egeria? My name is Laetitia, Doctor.

CHASUBLE (*bowing*): A classical allusion merely, drawn from the Pagan authors. I shall see you both no doubt at Evensong?

MISS PRISM: I think, dear Doctor, I will have a stroll with you. I find I have a headache after all, and a walk might do it good.

CHASUBLE: With pleasure, Miss Prism, with pleasure. We might go as far as the schools and back.

MISS PRISM: That would be delightful. Cecily, you will read your Political Economy in my absence. The chapter on the Fall of the Rupee° you may omit. It is somewhat too sensational. Even these metallic problems have their melodramatic side.

　　　　　　(*Goes down the garden with Dr. Chasuble.*)

CECILY (*picks up books and throws them back on table*): Horrid Political Economy! Horrid Geography! Horrid, horrid German!

(*Enter Merriman with a card on a salver.*)

MERRIMAN: Mr. Ernest Worthing has just driven over from the station. He has brought his luggage with him.

CECILY (*takes the card and reads it*): "Mr. Ernest Worthing, B.4, The Albany, W." Uncle Jack's brother! Did you tell him Mr. Worthing was in town?

MERRIMAN: Yes, Miss. He seemed very much disappointed. I mentioned that you and Miss Prism were in the garden. He said he was anxious to speak to you privately for a moment.

CECILY: Ask Mr. Ernest Worthing to come here. I suppose you had better talk to the housekeeper about a room for him.

MERRIMAN: Yes, Miss.　　　　　(*Merriman goes off.*)

CECILY: I have never met any really wicked person before. I feel rather frightened. I am so afraid he will look just like everyone else.

(*Enter Algernon, very gay and debonair.*)

He does!

ALGERNON (*raising his hat*): You are my little cousin Cecily, I'm sure.

CECILY: You are under some strange mistake. I am not little. In fact, I believe I am more than usually tall for my age (*Algernon is rather taken aback.*) But I am

your cousin Cecily. You, I see from your card, are Uncle Jack's brother, my cousin Ernest, my wicked cousin Ernest.

ALGERNON: Oh! I am not really wicked at all, Cousin Cecily. You mustn't think that I am wicked.

CECILY: If you are not, then you have certainly been deceiving us all in a very inexcusable manner. I hope you have not been leading a double life, pretending to be wicked and being really good all the time. That would be hypocrisy.

ALGERNON (*looks at her in amazement*): Oh! Of course I have been rather reckless.

CECILY: I am glad to hear it.

ALGERNON: In fact, now you mention the subject, I have been very bad in my own small way.

CECILY: I don't think you should be so proud of that, though I am sure it must have been very pleasant.

ALGERNON: It is much pleasanter being here with you.

CECILY: I can't understand how you are here at all. Uncle Jack won't be back till Monday afternoon.

ALGERNON: That is a great disappointment. I am obliged to go up by the first train on Monday morning. I have a business appointment that I am anxious—to miss.

CECILY: Couldn't you miss it anywhere but in London?

ALGERNON: No: the appointment is in London.

CECILY: Well, I know, of course, how important it is not to keep a business engagement, if one wants to retain any sense of the beauty of life, but still I think you had better wait till Uncle Jack arrives. I know he wants to speak to you about your emigrating.

ALGERNON: About my what?

CECILY: Your emigrating. He has gone up to buy your outfit.

ALGERNON: I certainly wouldn't let Jack buy my outfit. He has no taste in neckties at all.

CECILY: I don't think you will require neckties. Uncle Jack is sending you to Australia.

ALGERNON: Australia! I'd sooner die.

CECILY: Well, he said at dinner on Wednesday night, that you would have to choose between this world, the next world, and Australia.

ALGERNON: Oh, well! The accounts I have received of Australia and the next world are not particularly encouraging. This world is good enough for me, Cousin Cecily.

CECILY: Yes, but are you good enough for it?

ALGERNON: I'm afraid I'm not that. That is why I want you to reform me. You might make that your mission, if you don't mind, Cousin Cecily.

CECILY: I'm afraid I've no time, this afternoon.

ALGERNON: Well, would you mind my reforming myself this afternoon?

CECILY: It is rather quixotic° of you. But I think you should try.

ALGERNON: I will. I feel better already.

CECILY: You are looking a little worse.

Egeria: Roman goddess of water.　　**Fall of the Rupee:** Reference to the Indian rupee, whose steady deflation between 1873 and 1893 caused the Indian government finally to close the mints.

quixotic: Foolishly impractical, from the idealistic hero of Cervantes' *Don Quixote*.

ALGERNON: That is because I am hungry.

CECILY: How thoughtless of me. I should have remembered that when one is going to lead an entirely new life, one requires regular and wholesome meals. Won't you come in?

ALGERNON: Thank you. Might I have a buttonhole° first? I never have any appetite unless I have a buttonhole first.

CECILY: A Maréchal Niel?°

ALGERNON: No, I'd sooner have a pink rose.

CECILY: Why?   (*Cuts a flower.*)

ALGERNON: Because you are like a pink rose, Cousin Cecily.

CECILY: I don't think it can be right for you to talk to me like that. Miss Prism never says such things to me.

ALGERNON: Then Miss Prism is a shortsighted old lady. (*Cecily puts the rose in his buttonhole.*) You are the prettiest girl I ever saw.

CECILY: Miss Prism says that all good looks are a snare.

ALGERNON: They are a snare that every sensible man would like to be caught in.

CECILY: Oh! I don't think I would care to catch a sensible man. I shouldn't know what to talk to him about.

(*They pass into the house. Miss Prism and Dr. Chasuble return.*)

MISS PRISM: You are too much alone, dear Dr. Chasuble. You should get married. A misanthrope I can understand—a womanthrope, never!

CHASUBLE (*with a scholar's shudder*): Believe me, I do not deserve so neologistic a phrase. The precept as well as the practice of the Primitive Church was distinctly against matrimony.

MISS PRISM (*sententiously*): That is obviously the reason why the Primitive Church has not lasted up to the present day. And you do not seem to realize, dear Doctor, that by persistently remaining single, a man converts himself into a permanent public temptation. Men should be more careful; this very celibacy leads weaker vessels astray.

CHASUBLE: But is a man not equally attractive when married?

MISS PRISM: No married man is ever attractive except to his wife.

CHASUBLE: And often, I've been told, not even to her.

MISS PRISM: That depends on the intellectual sympathies of the woman. Maturity can always be depended on. Ripeness can be trusted. Young women are green. (*Dr. Chasuble starts.*) I spoke horticulturally. My metaphor was drawn from fruits. But where is Cecily?

CHASUBLE: Perhaps she followed us to the schools.

(*Enter Jack slowly from the back of the garden. He is dressed in the deepest mourning, with crepe hatband and black gloves.*)

MISS PRISM: Mr. Worthing!

CHASUBLE: Mr. Worthing?

---

buttonhole: Boutonniere.   **Maréchal Niel:** A yellow rose.

MISS PRISM: This is indeed a surprise. We did not look for you till Monday afternoon.

JACK (*shakes Miss Prism's hand in a tragic manner*): I have returned sooner than I expected. Dr. Chasuble, I hope you are well?

CHASUBLE: Dear Mr. Worthing, I trust this garb of woe does not betoken some terrible calamity?

JACK: My brother.

MISS PRISM: More shameful debts and extravagance?

CHASUBLE: Still leading his life of pleasure?

JACK (*shaking his head*): Dead!

CHASUBLE: Your brother Ernest dead?

JACK: Quite dead.

MISS PRISM: What a lesson for him! I trust he will profit by it.

CHASUBLE: Mr. Worthing, I offer you my sincere condolence. You have at least the consolation of knowing that you were always the most generous and forgiving of brothers.

JACK: Poor Ernest! He had many faults, but it is a sad, sad blow.

CHASUBLE: Very sad indeed. Were you with him at the end?

JACK: No. He died abroad, in Paris, in fact. I had a telegram last night from the manager of the Grand Hotel.

CHASUBLE: Was the cause of death mentioned?

JACK: A severe chill, it seems.

MISS PRISM: As a man sows, so shall he reap.

CHASUBLE (*raising his hand*): Charity, dear Miss Prism, charity! None of us are perfect. I myself am peculiarly susceptible to drafts. Will the interment take place here?

JACK: No. He seemed to have expressed a desire to be buried in Paris.

CHASUBLE: In Paris! (*Shakes his head.*) I fear that hardly points to any very serious state of mind at the last. You would no doubt wish me to make some slight allusion to this tragic domestic affliction next Sunday. (*Jack presses his hand convulsively.*) My sermon on the meaning of the manna in the wilderness can be adapted to almost any occasion, joyful, or, as in the present case, distressing. (*All sigh.*) I have preached it at harvest celebrations, christenings, confirmations, on days of humiliation and festal days. The last time I delivered it was in the Cathedral, as a charity sermon on behalf of the Society for the Prevention of Discontent among the Upper Orders. The Bishop, who was present, was much struck by some of the analogies I drew.

JACK: Ah! that reminds me, you mentioned christenings I think, Dr. Chasuble? I suppose you know how to christen all right? (*Dr. Chasuble looks astounded.*) I mean, of course, you are continually christening, aren't you?

MISS PRISM: It is, I regret to say, one of the Rector's most constant duties in this parish. I have often spoken to the poorer classes on the subject. But they don't seem to know what thrift is.

CHASUBLE: But is there any particular infant in whom you are interested, Mr. Worthing? Your brother was, I believe, unmarried, was he not?

JACK: Oh yes.

MISS PRISM (*bitterly*): People who live entirely for pleasure usually are.

JACK: But it is not for any child, dear Doctor. I am very fond of children. No! the fact is, I would like to be christened myself, this afternoon, if you have nothing better to do.

CHASUBLE: But surely, Mr. Worthing, you have been christened already?

JACK: I don't remember anything about it.

CHASUBLE: But have you any grave doubts on the subject?

JACK: I certainly intend to have. Of course I don't know if the thing would bother you in any way, or if you think I am a little too old now.

CHASUBLE: Not at all. The sprinkling, and, indeed, the immersion of adults is a perfectly canonical practice.

JACK: Immersion!

CHASUBLE: You need have no apprehensions. Sprinkling is all that is necessary, or indeed I think advisable. Our weather is so changeable. At what hour would you wish the ceremony performed?

JACK: Oh, I might trot round about five if that would suit you.

CHASUBLE: Perfectly, perfectly! In fact I have two similar ceremonies to perform at that time. A case of twins that occurred recently in one of the outlying cottages on your own estate. Poor Jenkins the carter, a most hardworking man.

JACK: Oh! I don't see much fun in being christened along with other babies. It would be childish. Would half-past five do?

CHASUBLE: Admirably! Admirably! (*Takes out watch.*) And now, dear Mr. Worthing, I will not intrude any longer into a house of sorrow. I would merely beg you not to be too much bowed down by grief. What seem to us bitter trials are often blessings in disguise.

MISS PRISM: This seems to me a blessing of an extremely obvious kind.

(*Enter Cecily from the house.*)

CECILY: Uncle Jack! Oh, I am pleased to see you back. But what horrid clothes you have got on! Do go and change them.

MISS PRISM: Cecily!

CHASUBLE: My child! my child!

(*Cecily goes towards Jack; he kisses her brow in a melancholy manner.*)

CECILY: What is the matter, Uncle Jack? Do look happy! You look as if you had toothache, and I have got such a surprise for you. Who do you think is in the dining room? Your brother!

JACK: Who?

CECILY: Your brother Ernest. He arrived about half an hour ago.

JACK: What nonsense! I haven't got a brother.

CECILY: Oh, don't say that. However badly he may have behaved to you in the past he is still your brother. You couldn't be so heartless as to disown him. I'll tell him to come out. And you will shake hands with him, won't you, Uncle Jack?

(*Runs back into the house.*)

CHASUBLE: These are very joyful tidings.

MISS PRISM: After we had all been resigned to his loss, his sudden return seems to me peculiarly distressing.

JACK: My brother is in the dining room? I don't know what it all means. I think it is perfectly absurd.

(*Enter Algernon and Cecily hand in hand. They come slowly up to Jack.*)

JACK: Good heavens!   (*Motions Algernon away.*)

ALGERNON: Brother John, I have come down from town to tell you that I am very sorry for all the trouble I have given you, and that I intend to lead a better life in the future.

(*Jack glares at him and does not take his hand.*)

CECILY: Uncle Jack, you are not going to refuse your own brother's hand?

JACK: Nothing will induce me to take his hand. I think his coming down here disgraceful. He knows perfectly well why.

CECILY: Uncle Jack, do be nice. There is some good in everyone. Ernest has just been telling me about his poor invalid friend Mr. Bunbury whom he goes to visit so often. And surely there must be much good in one who is kind to an invalid, and leaves the pleasures of London to sit by a bed of pain.

JACK: Oh! he has been talking about Bunbury has he?

CECILY: Yes, he has told me all about poor Mr. Bunbury, and his terrible state of health.

JACK: Bunbury! Well, I won't have him talk to you about Bunbury or about anything else. It is enough to drive one perfectly frantic.

ALGERNON: Of course I admit that the faults were all on my side. But I must say that I think that Brother John's coldness to me is peculiarly painful. I expected a more enthusiastic welcome, especially considering it is the first time I have come here.

CECILY: Uncle Jack, if you don't shake hands with Ernest I will never forgive you.

JACK: Never forgive me?

CECILY: Never, never, never!

JACK: Well, this is the last time I shall ever do it.

(*Shakes hands with Algernon and glares.*)

CHASUBLE: It's pleasant, is it not, to see so perfect a reconciliation? I think we might leave the two brothers together.

MISS PRISM: Cecily, you will come with us.

CECILY: Certainly, Miss Prism. My little task of reconciliation is over.

CHASUBLE: You have done a beautiful action today, dear child.

MISS PRISM: We must not be premature in our judgments.
CECILY: I feel very happy.   (*They all go off.*)
JACK: You young scoundrel, Algy, you must get out of this place as soon as possible. I don't allow any Bunburying here.

(*Enter Merriman.*)

MERRIMAN: I have put Mr. Ernest's things in the room next to yours, sir. I suppose that is all right?
JACK: What?
MERRIMAN: Mr. Ernest's luggage, sir. I have unpacked it and put it in the room next to your own.
JACK: His luggage?
MERRIMAN: Yes, sir. Three portmanteaus, a dressing case, two hatboxes, and a large luncheon basket.
ALGERNON: I am afraid I can't stay more than a week this time.
JACK: Merriman, order the dog cart at once. Mr. Ernest has been suddenly called back to town.
MERRIMAN: Yes, sir.   (*Goes back into the house.*)
ALGERNON: What a fearful liar you are, Jack. I have not been called back to town at all.
JACK: Yes, you have.
ALGERNON: I haven't heard anyone call me.
JACK: Your duty as a gentleman calls you back.
ALGERNON: My duty as a gentleman has never interfered with my pleasures in the smallest degree.
JACK: I can quite understand that.
ALGERNON: Well, Cecily is a darling.
JACK: You are not to talk of Miss Cardew like that. I don't like it.
ALGERNON: Well, I don't like your clothes. You look perfectly ridiculous in them. Why on earth don't you go up and change? It is perfectly childish to be in deep mourning for a man who is actually staying for a whole week in your house as a guest. I call it grotesque.
JACK: You are certainly not staying with me for a whole week as a guest or anything else. You have got to leave—by the four-five train.
ALGERNON: I certainly won't leave you so long as you are in mourning. It would be most unfriendly. If I were in mourning you would stay with me, I suppose. I should think it very unkind if you didn't.
JACK: Well, will you go if I change my clothes?
ALGERNON: Yes, if you are not too long. I never saw anybody take so long to dress, and with such little result.
JACK: Well, at any rate, that is better than being always overdressed as you are.
ALGERNON: If I am occasionally a little overdressed, I make up for it by being always immensely overeducated.
JACK: Your vanity is ridiculous, your conduct an outrage, and your presence in my garden utterly absurd. However, you have got to catch the four-five, and I hope you will have a pleasant journey back to town. This Bunburying, as you call it, has not been a great success for you.

(*Goes into the house.*)

ALGERNON: I think it has been a great success. I'm in love with Cecily, and that is everything.

(*Enter Cecily at the back of the garden. She picks up the can and begins to water the flowers.*)

But I must see her before I go, and make arrangements for another Bunbury. Ah, there she is.
CECILY: Oh, I merely came back to water the roses. I thought you were with Uncle Jack.
ALGERNON: He's gone to order the dog cart for me.
CECILY: Oh, is he going to take you for a nice drive?
ALGERNON: He's going to send me away.
CECILY: Then have we got to part?
ALGERNON: I am afraid so. It's a very painful parting.
CECILY: It is always painful to part from people whom one has known for a very brief space of time. The absence of old friends one can endure with equanimity. But even a momentary separation from anyone to whom one has just been introduced is almost unbearable.
ALGERNON: Thank you.

(*Enter Merriman.*)

MERRIMAN: The dog cart is at the door, sir.

(*Algernon looks appealingly at Cecily.*)

CECILY: It can wait, Merriman—for—five minutes.
MERRIMAN: Yes, miss.   (*Exit Merriman.*)
ALGERNON: I hope, Cecily, I shall not offend you if I state quite frankly and openly that you seem to me to be in every way the visible personification of absolute perfection.
CECILY: I think your frankness does you great credit, Ernest. If you will allow me I will copy your remarks into my diary.
          (*Goes over to table and begins writing in diary.*)
ALGERNON: Do you really keep a diary? I'd give anything to look at it. May I?
CECILY: Oh no. (*Puts her hand over it.*) You see, it is simply a very young girl's record of her own thoughts and impressions, and consequently meant for publication. When it appears in volume form I hope you will order a copy. But pray, Ernest, don't stop. I delight in taking down from dictation. I have reached "absolute perfection." You can go on. I am quite ready for more.
ALGERNON (*somewhat taken aback*): Ahem! Ahem!
CECILY: Oh, don't cough, Ernest. When one is dictating one should speak fluently and not cough. Besides, I don't know how to spell a cough.

(*Writes as Algernon speaks.*)

ALGERNON (*speaking very rapidly*): Cecily, ever since I first looked upon your wonderful and incomparable beauty, I have dared to love you wildly, passionately, devotedly, hopelessly.
CECILY: I don't think that you should tell me that you love me wildly, passionately, devotedly, hopelessly. Hopelessly doesn't seem to make much sense, does it?
ALGERNON: Cecily!

(*Enter Merriman.*)

MERRIMAN: The dog cart is waiting, sir.

ALGERNON: Tell it to come round next week, at the same hour.

MERRIMAN (*looks at Cecily, who makes no sign*): Yes, sir.   (*Merriman retires.*)

CECILY: Uncle Jack would be very much annoyed if he knew you were staying on till next week, at the same hour.

ALGERNON: Oh, I don't care about Jack. I don't care for anybody in the whole world but you. I love you, Cecily. You will marry me, won't you?

CECILY: You silly boy! Of course. Why, we have been engaged for the last three months.

ALGERNON: For the last three months?

CECILY: Yes, it will be exactly three months on Thursday.

ALGERNON: But how did we become engaged?

CECILY: Well, ever since dear Uncle Jack first confessed to us that he had a younger brother who was very wicked and bad, you of course have formed the chief topic of conversation between myself and Miss Prism. And of course a man who is much talked about is always very attractive. One feels there must be something in him after all. I daresay it was foolish of me, but I fell in love with you, Ernest.

ALGERNON: Darling! And when was the engagement actually settled?

CECILY: On the 14th of February last. Worn out by your entire ignorance of my existence, I determined to end the matter one way or the other, and after a long struggle with myself I accepted you under this dear old tree here. The next day I bought this little ring in your name, and this is the little bangle with the true lovers' knot I promised you always to wear.

ALGERNON: Did I give you this? It's very pretty, isn't it?

CECILY: Yes, you've wonderfully good taste, Ernest. It's the excuse I've always given for your leading such a bad life. And this is the box in which I keep all your dear letters.

(*Kneels at table, opens box, and produces letters tied up with blue ribbon.*)

ALGERNON: My letters! But my own sweet Cecily, I have never written you any letters.

CECILY: You need hardly remind me of that, Ernest. I remember only too well that I was forced to write your letters for you. I wrote always three times a week, and sometimes oftener.

ALGERNON: Oh, do let me read them, Cecily!

CECILY: Oh, I couldn't possibly. They would make you far too conceited. (*Replaces box.*) The three you wrote me after I had broken off the engagement are so beautiful, and so badly spelled, that even now I can hardly read them without crying a little.

ALGERNON: But was our engagement ever broken off?

CECILY: Of course it was. On the 22nd of last March. You can see the entry if you like. (*Shows diary.*)

"Today I broke off my engagement with Ernest. I feel it is better to do so. The weather still continues charming."

ALGERNON: But why on earth did you break it off? What had I done? I had done nothing at all. Cecily, I am very much hurt indeed to hear you broke it off. Particularly when the weather was so charming.

CECILY: It would hardly have been a really serious engagement if it hadn't been broken off at least once. But I forgave you before the week was out.

ALGERNON (*crossing to her, and kneeling*): What a perfect angel you are, Cecily.

CECILY: You dear romantic boy. (*He kisses her; she puts her fingers through his hair.*) I hope your hair curls naturally, does it?

ALGERNON: Yes, darling, with a little help from others.

CECILY: I am so glad.

ALGERNON: You'll never break off our engagement again, Cecily?

CECILY: I don't think I could break it off now that I have actually met you. Besides, of course, there is the question of your name.

ALGERNON (*nervously*): Yes, of course.

CECILY: You must not laugh at me, darling, but it had always been a girlish dream of mine to love someone whose name was Ernest. (*Algernon rises, Cecily also.*) There is something in that name that seems to inspire absolute confidence. I pity any poor married woman whose husband is not called Ernest.

ALGERNON: But, my dear child, do you mean to say you could not love me if I had some other name?

CECILY: But what name?

ALGERNON: Oh, any name you like — Algernon — for instance —

CECILY: But I don't like the name of Algernon.

ALGERNON: Well, my own dear, sweet, loving little darling, I really can't see why you should object to the name of Algernon. It is not at all a bad name. In fact, it is rather an aristocratic name. Half of the chaps who get into the Bankruptcy Court are called Algernon. But seriously, Cecily — (*moving to her*) — if my name was Algy, couldn't you love me?

CECILY (*rising*): I might respect you, Ernest, I might admire your character, but I fear that I should not be able to give you my undivided attention.

ALGERNON: Ahem! Cecily! (*Picking up hat.*) Your Rector here is, I suppose, thoroughly experienced in the practice of all the rites and ceremonials of the Church?

CECILY: Oh yes. Dr. Chasuble is a most learned man. He has never written a single book, so you can imagine how much he knows.

ALGERNON: I must see him at once on a most important christening — I mean on most important business.

CECILY: Oh!

ALGERNON: I shan't be away more than half an hour.

CECILY: Considering that we have been engaged since February the 14th, and that I only met you today for the first time, I think it is rather hard that you should leave me for so long a period as half an hour. Couldn't you make it twenty minutes?

ALGERNON: I'll be back in no time.

(*Kisses her and rushes down the garden.*)

CECILY: What an impetuous boy he is! I like his hair so much. I must enter his proposal in my diary.

(*Enter Merriman.*)

MERRIMAN: A Miss Fairfax has just called to see Mr. Worthing. On very important business Miss Fairfax states.

CECILY: Isn't Mr. Worthing in his library?

MERRIMAN: Mr. Worthing went over in the direction of the Rectory some time ago.

CECILY: Pray ask the lady to come out here; Mr. Worthing is sure to be back soon. And you can bring tea.

MERRIMAN: Yes, miss.   (*Goes out.*)

CECILY: Miss Fairfax! I suppose one of the many good elderly women who are associated with Uncle Jack in some of his philanthropic work in London. I don't quite like women who are interested in philanthropic work. I think it is so forward of them.

(*Enter Merriman.*)

MERRIMAN: Miss Fairfax.

(*Enter Gwendolen. Exit Merriman.*)

CECILY (*advancing to meet her*): Pray let me introduce myself to you. My name is Cecily Cardew.

GWENDOLEN: Cecily Cardew? (*Moving to her and shaking hands.*) What a very sweet name! Something tells me that we are going to be great friends. I like you already more than I can say. My first impressions of people are never wrong.

CECILY: How nice of you to like me so much after we have known each other such a comparatively short time. Pray sit down.

GWENDOLEN (*still standing up*): I may call you Cecily, may I not?

CECILY: With pleasure!

GWENDOLEN: And you will always call me Gwendolen, won't you?

CECILY: If you wish.

GWENDOLEN: Then that is all quite settled, is it not?

CECILY: I hope so.

(*A pause. They both sit down together.*)

GWENDOLEN: Perhaps this might be a favorable opportunity for my mentioning who I am. My father is Lord Bracknell. You have never heard of Papa, I suppose?

CECILY: I don't think so.

GWENDOLEN: Outside the family circle, Papa, I am glad to say, is entirely unknown. I think that is quite as it should be. The home seems to me to be the proper sphere for the man. And certainly once a man begins to neglect his domestic duties he becomes painfully effeminate, does he not? And I don't like that. It makes men so very attractive. Cecily, Mama, whose views on education are remarkably strict, has brought me up to be extremely shortsighted; it is part of her system, so do you mind my looking at you through my glasses?

CECILY: Oh! not at all, Gwendolen. I am very fond of being looked at.

GWENDOLEN (*after examining Cecily carefully through a lorgnette*): You are here on a short visit I suppose?

CECILY: Oh no! I live here.

GWENDOLEN (*severely*): Really? Your mother, no doubt, or some female relative of advanced years, resides here also?

CECILY: Oh no! I have no mother, nor, in fact, any relations.

GWENDOLEN: Indeed?

CECILY: My dear guardian, with the assistance of Miss Prism, has the arduous task of looking after me.

GWENDOLEN: Your guardian?

CECILY: Yes, I am Mr. Worthing's ward.

GWENDOLEN: Oh! It is strange he never mentioned to me that he had a ward. How secretive of him! He grows more interesting hourly. I am not sure, however, that the news inspires me with feelings of unmixed delight. (*Rising and going to her.*) I am very fond of you, Cecily; I have liked you ever since I met you! But I am bound to state that now that I know that you are Mr. Worthing's ward, I cannot help expressing a wish you were — well just a little older than you seem to be — and not quite so very alluring in appearance. In fact, if I may speak candidly —

CECILY: Pray do! I think that whenever one has anything unpleasant to say, one should always be quite candid.

GWENDOLEN: Well, to speak with perfect candor, Cecily, I wish that you were fully forty-two, and more than usually plain for your age. Ernest has a strong upright nature. He is the very soul of truth and honor. Disloyalty would be as impossible to him as deception. But even men of the noblest possible moral character are extremely susceptible to the influence of the physical charms of others. Modern, no less than Ancient History, supplies us with many most painful examples of what I refer to. If it were not so, indeed, History would be quite unreadable.

CECILY: I beg your pardon, Gwendolen, did you say Ernest?

GWENDOLEN: Yes.

CECILY: Oh, but it is not Mr. Ernest Worthing who is my guardian. It is his brother — his elder brother.

GWENDOLEN (*sitting down again*): Ernest never mentioned to me that he had a brother.

CECILY: I am sorry to say they have not been on good terms for a long time.

GWENDOLEN: Ah! that accounts for it. And now that I think of it I have never heard any man mention his brother. The subject seems distasteful to most men. Cecily, you have lifted a load from my mind. I was growing almost anxious. It would have been terrible if any cloud had come across a friendship like ours, would it not? Of course you are quite, quite sure that it is not Mr. Ernest Worthing who is your guardian?

CECILY: Quite sure. (*A pause.*) In fact, I am going to be his.

GWENDOLEN (*inquiringly*): I beg your pardon?

CECILY (*rather shy and confidingly*): Dearest Gwendolen, there is no reason why I should make a secret of it to you. Our little county newspaper is sure to chronicle the fact next week. Mr. Ernest Worthing and I are engaged to be married.

GWENDOLEN (*quite politely, rising*): My darling Cecily, I think there must be some slight error. Mr. Ernest Worthing is engaged to me. The announcement will appear in the *Morning Post* on Saturday at the latest.

CECILY (*very politely, rising*): I am afraid you must be under some misconception. Ernest proposed to me exactly ten minutes ago.   (*Shows diary.*)

GWENDOLEN (*examines diary through her lorgnette carefully*): It is certainly very curious, for he asked me to be his wife yesterday afternoon at 5:30. If you would care to verify the incident, pray do so. (*Produces diary of her own.*) I never travel without my diary. One should always have something sensational to read in the train. I am so sorry, dear Cecily, if it is any disappointment to you, but I am afraid *I* have the prior claim.

CECILY: It would distress me more than I can tell you, dear Gwendolen, if it caused you any mental or physical anguish, but I feel bound to point out that since Ernest proposed to you he clearly has changed his mind.

GWENDOLEN (*meditatively*): If the poor fellow has been entrapped into any foolish promise I shall consider it my duty to rescue him at once, and with a firm hand.

CECILY (*thoughtfully and sadly*): Whatever unfortunate entanglement my dear boy may have got into, I will never reproach him with it after we are married.

GWENDOLEN: Do you allude to me, Miss Cardew, as an entanglement? You are presumptuous. On an occasion of this kind it becomes more than a moral duty to speak one's mind. It becomes a pleasure.

CECILY: Do you suggest, Miss Fairfax, that I entrapped Ernest into an engagement? How dare you? This is no time for wearing the shallow mask of manners. When I see a spade I call it a spade.

GWENDOLEN (*satirically*): I am glad to say that I have never seen a spade. It is obvious that our social spheres have been widely different.

(*Enter Merriman, followed by the Footman. He carries a salver, tablecloth, and plate stand. Cecily is about to retort. The presence of the servants exercises a restraining influence, under which both girls chafe.*)

MERRIMAN: Shall I lay tea here as usual, miss?

CECILY (*sternly, in a calm voice*): Yes, as usual.

(*Merriman begins to clear table and lay cloth. A long pause. Cecily and Gwendolen glare at each other.*)

GWENDOLEN: Are there many interesting walks in the vicinity, Miss Cardew?

CECILY: Oh! Yes! a great many. From the top of one of the hills quite close one can see five counties.

GWENDOLEN: Five counties! I don't think I should like that. I hate crowds.

CECILY (*sweetly*): I suppose that is why you live in town?

(*Gwendolen bites her lip, and beats her foot nervously with her parasol.*)

GWENDOLEN (*looking round*): Quite a well-kept garden this is, Miss Cardew.

CECILY: So glad you like it, Miss Fairfax.

GWENDOLEN: I had no idea there were any flowers in the country.

CECILY: Oh, flowers are as common here, Miss Fairfax, as people are in London.

GWENDOLEN: Personally I cannot understand how anybody manages to exist in the country, if anybody who is anybody does. The country always bores me to death.

CECILY: Ah! This is what the newspapers call agricultural depression, is it not? I believe the aristocracy are suffering very much from it just at present. It is almost an epidemic amongst them, I have been told. May I offer you some tea, Miss Fairfax?

GWENDOLEN (*with elaborate politeness*): Thank you. (*Aside.*) Detestable girl! But I require tea!

CECILY (*sweetly*): Sugar?

GWENDOLEN (*superciliously*): No, thank you. Sugar is not fashionable anymore.

(*Cecily looks angrily at her, takes up the tongs, and puts four lumps of sugar into the cup.*)

CECILY (*severely*): Cake or bread and butter?

GWENDOLEN (*in a bored manner*): Bread and butter, please. Cake is rarely seen at the best houses nowadays.

CECILY (*cuts a very large slice of cake, and puts it on the tray*): Hand that to Miss Fairfax.

(*Merriman does so, and goes out with Footman. Gwendolen drinks the tea and makes a grimace. Puts down cup at once, reaches out her hand to the bread and butter, looks at it, and finds it is cake. Rises in indignation.*)

GWENDOLEN: You have filled my tea with lumps of sugar, and though I asked most distinctly for bread and butter, you have given me cake. I am known for the gentleness of my disposition, and the extraordinary sweetness of my nature, but I warn you, Miss Cardew, you may go too far.

CECILY (*rising*): To save my poor, innocent, trusting boy from the machinations of any other girl there are no lengths to which I would not go.

GWENDOLEN: From the moment I saw you I distrusted you. I felt that you were false and deceitful. I am never deceived in such matters. My first impressions of people are invariably right.

CECILY: It seems to me, Miss Fairfax, that I am trespassing on your valuable time. No doubt you have many other calls of a similar character to make in the neighborhood.

(*Enter Jack.*)

GWENDOLEN (*catching sight of him*): Ernest! My own Ernest!

JACK: Gwendolen! Darling!   (*Offers to kiss her.*)

GWENDOLEN (*drawing back*): A moment! May I ask if you are engaged to be married to this young lady? (*Points to Cecily.*)

JACK (*laughing*): To dear little Cecily! Of course not! What could have put such an idea into your pretty little head?

GWENDOLEN: Thank you. You may!
                                   (*Offers her cheek.*)

CECILY (*very sweetly*): I knew there must be some misunderstanding, Miss Fairfax. The gentleman whose arm is at present round your waist is my dear guardian, Mr. John Worthing.

GWENDOLEN: I beg your pardon?

CECILY: This is Uncle Jack.

GWENDOLEN (*receding*): Jack! Oh!

(*Enter Algernon.*)

CECILY: Here is Ernest.

ALGERNON (*goes straight over to Cecily without noticing anyone else*): My own love!
                                   (*Offers to kiss her.*)

CECILY (*drawing back*): A moment, Ernest! May I ask you—are you engaged to be married to this young lady?

ALGERNON (*looking round*): To what young lady? Good heavens! Gwendolen!

CECILY: Yes! to good heavens, Gwendolen, I mean to Gwendolen.

ALGERNON (*laughing*): Of course not! What could have put such an idea into your pretty little head?

CECILY: Thank you. (*Presenting her cheek to be kissed.*) You may.   (*Algernon kisses her.*)

GWENDOLEN: I felt there was some slight error, Miss Cardew. The gentleman who is now embracing you is my cousin, Mr. Algernon Moncrieff.

CECILY (*breaking away from Algernon*): Algernon Moncrieff! Oh!

(*The two girls move towards each other and put their arms round each other's waists as if for protection.*)

CECILY: Are you called Algernon?

ALGERNON: I cannot deny it.

CECILY: Oh!

GWENDOLEN: Is your name really John?

JACK (*standing rather proudly*): I could deny it if I liked. I could deny anything if I liked. But my name certainly is John. It has been John for years.

CECILY (*to Gwendolen*): A gross deception has been practiced on both of us.

GWENDOLEN: My poor wounded Cecily!

CECILY: My sweet wronged Gwendolen!

GWENDOLEN (*slowly and seriously*): You will call me sister, will you not?

(*They embrace. Jack and Algernon groan and walk up and down.*)

CECILY (*rather brightly*): There is just one question I would like to be allowed to ask my guardian.

GWENDOLEN: An admirable idea! Mr. Worthing, there is just one question I would like to be permitted to put to you. Where is your brother Ernest? We are both engaged to be married to your brother Ernest, so it is a matter of some importance to us to know where your brother Ernest is at present.

JACK (*slowly and hesitatingly*): Gwendolen—Cecily—it is very painful for me to be forced to speak the truth. It is the first time in my life that I have ever been reduced to such a painful position, and I am really quite inexperienced in doing anything of the kind. However I will tell you quite frankly that I have no brother Ernest. I have no brother at all. I never had a brother in my life, and I certainly have not the smallest intention of ever having one in the future.

CECILY (*surprised*): No brother at all?

JACK (*cheerily*): None!

GWENDOLEN (*severely*): Had you never a brother of any kind?

JACK (*pleasantly*): Never. Not even of any kind.

GWENDOLEN: I am afraid it is quite clear, Cecily, that neither of us is engaged to be married to anyone.

CECILY: It is not a very pleasant position for a young girl suddenly to find herself in. Is it?

GWENDOLEN: Let us go into the house. They will hardly venture to come after us there.

CECILY: No, men are so cowardly, aren't they?

(*They retire into the house with scornful looks.*)

JACK: This ghastly state of things is what you call Bunburying, I suppose?

ALGERNON: Yes, and a perfectly wonderful Bunbury it is. The most wonderful Bunbury I have ever had in my life.

JACK: Well, you've no right whatsoever to Bunbury here.

ALGERNON: That is absurd. One has a right to Bunbury anywhere one chooses. Every serious Bunburyist knows that.

JACK: Serious Bunburyist! Good heavens!

ALGERNON: Well, one must be serious about something, if one wants to have any amusement in life. I happen to be serious about Bunburying. What on earth you are serious about I haven't got the remotest idea. About everything, I should fancy. You have such an absolutely trivial nature.

JACK: Well, the only small satisfaction I have in the whole of this wretched business is that your friend Bunbury is quite exploded. You won't be able to run down to the country quite so often as you used to do, dear Algy. And a very good thing too.

ALGERNON: Your brother is a little off color, isn't he, dear Jack? You won't be able to disappear to London quite so frequently as your wicked custom was. And not a bad thing either.

JACK: As for your conduct towards Miss Cardew, I must say that your taking in a sweet, simple, innocent girl like that is quite inexcusable. To say nothing of the fact that she is my ward.

ALGERNON: I can see no possible defense at all for your deceiving a brilliant, clever, thoroughly experienced young lady like Miss Fairfax. To say nothing of the fact that she is my cousin.

JACK: I wanted to be engaged to Gwendolen, that is all. I love her.

ALGERNON: Well, I simply wanted to be engaged to Cecily. I adore her.

JACK: There is certainly no chance of your marrying Miss Cardew.

ALGERNON: I don't think there is much likelihood, Jack, of you and Miss Fairfax being united.

JACK: Well, that is no business of yours.

ALGERNON: If it was my business, I wouldn't talk about it. (*Begins to eat muffins.*) It is very vulgar to talk about one's business. Only people like stockbrokers do that, and then merely at dinner parties.

JACK: How you can sit there, calmly eating muffins when we are in this horrible trouble. I can't make out. You seem to me to be perfectly heartless.

ALGERNON: Well, I can't eat muffins in an agitated manner. The butter would probably get on my cuffs. One should always eat muffins quite calmly. It is the only way to eat them.

JACK: I say it's perfectly heartless your eating muffins at all, under the circumstances.

ALGERNON: When I am in trouble, eating is the only thing that consoles me. Indeed, when I am in really great trouble, as anyone who knows me intimately will tell you, I refuse everything except food and drink. At the present moment I am eating muffins because I am unhappy. Besides, I am particularly fond of muffins.   (*Rising.*)

JACK (*rising*): Well, that is no reason why you should eat them all in that greedy way.

(*Takes muffins from Algernon.*)

ALGERNON (*offering tea cake*): I wish you would have tea cake instead. I don't like tea cake.

JACK: Good heavens! I suppose a man may eat his own muffins in his own garden.

ALGERNON: But you have just said it was perfectly heartless to eat muffins.

JACK: I said it was perfectly heartless of you, under the circumstances. That is a very different thing.

ALGERNON: That may be, but the muffins are the same. (*He seizes the muffin dish from Jack.*)

JACK: Algy, I wish to goodness you would go.

ALGERNON: You can't possibly ask me to go without having some dinner. It's absurd. I never go without my dinner. No one ever does, except vegetarians and people like that. Besides I have just made arrangements, with Dr. Chasuble to be christened at a quarter to six under the name of Ernest.

JACK: My dear fellow, the sooner you give up that nonsense the better. I made arrangements this morning with Dr. Chasuble to be christened myself at 5:30, and I naturally will take the name of Ernest. Gwendolen would wish it. We can't both be christened Ernest. It's absurd. Besides, I have a perfect right to be christened if I like. There is no evidence at all that I ever have been christened by anybody. I should think it extremely probable I never was, and so does Dr. Chasuble. It is entirely different in your case. You have been christened already.

ALGERNON: Yes, but I have not been christened for years.

JACK: Yes, but you have been christened. That is the important thing.

ALGERNON: Quite so. So I know my constitution can stand it. If you are not quite sure about your ever having been christened, I must say I think it rather dangerous your venturing on it now. It might make you very unwell. You can hardly have forgotten that someone very closely connected with you was very nearly carried off this week in Paris by a severe chill.

JACK: Yes, but you said yourself that a severe chill was not hereditary.

ALGERNON: It usen't to be, I know—but I daresay it is now. Science is always making wonderful improvements in things.

JACK (*picking up the muffin dish*): Oh, that is nonsense; you are always talking nonsense.

ALGERNON: Jack, you are at the muffins again! I wish you wouldn't. There are only two left. (*Takes them.*) I told you I was particularly fond of muffins.

JACK: But I hate tea cake.

ALGERNON: Why on earth then do you allow tea cake to be served up for your guests? What ideas you have of hospitality!

JACK: Algernon! I have already told you to go. I don't want you here. Why don't you go!

ALGERNON: I haven't quite finished my tea yet! and there is still one muffin left.

(*Jack groans, and sinks into a chair. Algernon still continues eating.*)

ACT III

(*Scene: Morning room at the Manor House. Gwendolen and Cecily are at the window, looking out into the garden.*)

GWENDOLEN: The fact that they did not follow us at once into the house, as anyone else would have done, seems to me to show that they have some sense of shame left.

CECILY: They have been eating muffins. That looks like repentance.

GWENDOLEN (*after a pause*): They don't seem to notice us at all. Couldn't you cough?

CECILY: But I haven't got a cough.

GWENDOLEN: They're looking at us. What effrontery!

CECILY: They're approaching. That's very forward of them.

GWENDOLEN: Let us preserve a dignified silence.

CECILY: Certainly. It's the only thing to do now.

(*Enter Jack followed by Algernon. They whistle some dreadful popular air from a British opera.*)

GWENDOLEN: This dignified silence seems to produce an unpleasant effect.

CECILY: A most distasteful one.

GWENDOLEN: But we will not be the first to speak.

CECILY: Certainly not.

GWENDOLEN: Mr. Worthing, I have something very particular to ask you. Much depends on your reply.

CECILY: Gwendolen, your common sense is invaluable. Mr. Moncrieff, kindly answer me the following question. Why did you pretend to be my guardian's brother?

ALGERNON: In order that I might have an opportunity of meeting you.

CECILY (*to Gwendolen*): That certainly seems a satisfactory explanation, does it not?

GWENDOLEN: Yes, dear, if you can believe him.

CECILY: I don't. But that does not affect the wonderful beauty of his answer.

GWENDOLEN: True. In matters of grave importance, style, not sincerity is the vital thing. Mr. Worthing, what explanation can you offer to me for pretending to have a brother? Was it in order that you might have an opportunity of coming up to town to see me as often as possible?

JACK: Can you doubt it, Miss Fairfax?

GWENDOLEN: I have the gravest doubts upon the subject. But I intend to crush them. This is not the moment for German skepticism. (*Moving to Cecily.*) Their explanations appear to be quite satisfactory, especially Mr. Worthing's. That seems to me to have the stamp of truth upon it.

CECILY: I am more than content with what Mr. Moncrieff said. His voice alone inspires one with absolute credulity.

GWENDOLEN: Then you think we should forgive them?

CECILY: Yes. I mean no.

GWENDOLEN: True! I had forgotten. There are principles at stake that one cannot surrender. Which of us should tell them? The task is not a pleasant one.

CECILY: Could we not both speak at the same time?

GWENDOLEN: An excellent idea! I nearly always speak at the same time as other people. Will you take the time from me?

CECILY: Certainly.

(*Gwendolen beats time with uplifted finger.*)

GWENDOLEN and CECILY (*speaking together*): Your Christian names are still an insuperable barrier. That is all!

JACK and ALGERNON (*speaking together*): Our Christian names! Is that all? But we are going to be christened this afternoon.

GWENDOLEN (*to Jack*): For my sake you are prepared to do this terrible thing?

JACK: I am!

CECILY (*to Algernon*): To please me you are ready to face this fearful ordeal?

ALGERNON: I am!

GWENDOLEN: How absurd to talk of the equality of the sexes! Where questions of self-sacrifice are concerned, men are infinitely beyond us.

JACK: We are! (*Clasps hands with Algernon.*)

CECILY: They have moments of physical courage of which we women know absolutely nothing.

GWENDOLEN (*to Jack*): Darling!

ALGERNON (*to Cecily*): Darling!

(*They fall into each other's arms.*)

(*Enter Merriman. When he enters he coughs loudly, seeing the situation.*)

MERRIMAN: Ahem! Ahem! Lady Bracknell!

JACK: Good heavens!

(*Enter Lady Bracknell. The couples separate, in alarm. Exit Merriman.*)

LADY BRACKNELL: Gwendolen! What does this mean?

GWENDOLEN: Merely that I am engaged to be married to Mr. Worthing, Mama.

LADY BRACKNELL: Come here. Sit down. Sit down immediately. Hesitation of any kind is a sign of mental decay in the young, of physical weakness in the old. (*Turns to Jack.*) Apprised, sir, of my daughter's sudden flight by her trusty maid, whose confidence I purchased by means of a small coin, I followed her at once by a luggage train. Her unhappy father is, I am glad to say, under the impression that she is attending a more than usually lengthy lecture by the University Extension Scheme on the influence of a permanent income on thought. I do not propose to undeceive him. Indeed I have never undeceived him on any question. I would consider it wrong. But of course, you will clearly understand that all communication between yourself and my daughter must cease immediately from this moment. On this point, as indeed on all points, I am firm.

JACK: I am engaged to be married to Gwendolen, Lady Bracknell!

LADY BRACKNELL: You are nothing of the kind, sir. And now, as regards Algernon! — Algernon!

ALGERNON: Yes, Aunt Augusta.

LADY BRACKNELL: May I ask if it is in this house that your invalid friend Mr. Bunbury resides?

ALGERNON (*stammering*): Oh! No! Bunbury doesn't live here. Bunbury is somewhere else at present. In fact, Bunbury is dead.

LADY BRACKNELL: Dead! When did Mr. Bunbury die? His death must have been extremely sudden.

ALGERNON (*airily*): Oh! I killed Bunbury this afternoon. I mean poor Bunbury died this afternoon.

LADY BRACKNELL: What did he die of?

ALGERNON: Bunbury? Oh, he was quite exploded.

LADY BRACKNELL: Exploded! Was he the victim of a revolutionary outrage? I was not aware that Mr. Bunbury was interested in social legislation. If so, he is well punished for his morbidity.

ALGERNON: My dear Aunt Augusta, I mean he was found out! The doctors found out that Bunbury could not live, that is what I mean — so Bunbury died.

Eric Stoltz and Schuyler Grant propose a toast in the Irish Repertory Theatre's 1996 production of *The Importance of Being Earnest.*

LADY BRACKNELL: He seems to have had great confidence in the opinion of his physicians. I am glad, however, that he made up his mind at the last to some definite course of action, and acted under proper medical advice. And now that we have finally got rid of this Mr. Bunbury, may I ask, Mr. Worthing, who is that young person whose hand my nephew Algernon is now holding in what seems to me a peculiarly unnecessary manner?

JACK: That lady is Miss Cecily Cardew, my ward.

(*Lady Bracknell bows coldly to Cecily.*)

ALGERNON: I am engaged to be married to Cecily, Aunt Augusta.

LADY BRACKNELL: I beg your pardon?

CECILY: Mr. Moncrieff and I are engaged to be married, Lady Bracknell.

LADY BRACKNELL (*with a shiver, crossing to the sofa and sitting down*): I do not know whether there is anything peculiarly exciting in the air of this particular part of Hertfordshire, but the number of engagements that go on seems to me considerably above the proper average that statistics have laid down for our guidance. I think some preliminary inquiry on my part would not be out of place. Mr. Worthing, is Miss Cardew at all connected with any of the larger railway stations in London? I merely desire information. Until yesterday I had no idea that there were any families or persons whose origin was a Terminus.

(*Jack looks perfectly furious, but restrains himself.*)

JACK (*in a clear, cold voice*): Miss Cardew is the granddaughter of the late Mr. Thomas Cardew of 149, Belgrave Square, S.W.; Gervase Park, Dorking, Surrey; and the Sporran, Fifeshire, N.B.

LADY BRACKNELL: That sounds not unsatisfactory. Three addresses always inspire confidence, even in tradesmen. But what proof have I of their authenticity?

JACK: I have carefully preserved the Court Guides of the period. They are open to your inspection, Lady Bracknell.

LADY BRACKNELL (*grimly*): I have known strange errors in that publication.

JACK: Miss Cardew's family solicitors are Messrs. Markby, Markby, and Markby.

LADY BRACKNELL: Markby, Markby, and Markby? A firm of the very highest position in their profession. Indeed I am told that one of the Mr. Markbys is occasionally to be seen at dinner parties. So far I am satisfied.

JACK (*very irritably*): How extremely kind of you, Lady Bracknell! I have also in my possession, you will be pleased to hear, certificates of Miss Cardew's birth, baptism, whooping cough, registration, vaccination, confirmation, and the measles; both the German and the English variety.

LADY BRACKNELL: Ah! A life crowded with incident I see; though perhaps somewhat too exciting for a young girl. I am not myself in favor of premature experiences. (*Rises, looks at her watch.*) Gwendolen! the time approaches for our departure. We have not a moment to lose. As a matter of form, Mr. Worthing, I had better ask you if Miss Cardew has any little fortune?

JACK: Oh! about a hundred and thirty thousand pounds in the Funds. That is all. Good-bye, Lady Bracknell. So pleased to have seen you.

LADY BRACKNELL (*sitting down again*): A moment, Mr. Worthing. A hundred and thirty thousand pounds! And in the Funds! Miss Cardew seems to me a most attractive young lady, now that I look at her. Few girls of the present day have any really solid qualities, any of the qualities that last, and improve with time. We live, I regret to say, in an age of surfaces. (*To Cecily.*) Come over here, dear. (*Cecily goes across.*) Pretty child! your dress is sadly simple, and your hair seems almost as Nature might have left it. But we can soon alter all that. A thoroughly experienced French maid produces a really marvelous result in a very brief space of time: I remember recommending one to young Lady Lancing, and after three months her own husband did not know her.

JACK (*aside*): And after six months nobody knew her.

LADY BRACKNELL (*glares at Jack for a few moments. Then bends, with a practiced smile, to Cecily*): Kindly turn round, sweet child. (*Cecily turns completely round.*) No, the side view is what I want. (*Cecily presents her profile.*) Yes, quite as I expected. There are distinct social possibilities in your profile. The two weak points in our age are its want of principle and its want of profile. The chin a little higher, dear. Style largely depends on the way the chin is worn. They are worn very high, just at present. Algernon!

ALGERNON: Yes, Aunt Augusta!

LADY BRACKNELL: There are distinct social possibilities in Miss Cardew's profile.

ALGERNON: Cecily is the sweetest, dearest, prettiest girl in the whole world. And I don't care twopence about social possibilities.

LADY BRACKNELL: Never speak disrespectfully of Society, Algernon. Only people who can't get into it do that. (*To Cecily.*) Dear child, of course you know that Algernon has nothing but his debts to depend upon. But I do not approve of mercenary marriages. When I married Lord Bracknell I had no fortune of any kind. But I never dreamed for a moment of allowing that to stand in my way. Well, I suppose I must give my consent.

ALGERNON: Thank you, Aunt Augusta.

LADY BRACKNELL: Cecily, you may kiss me!

CECILY (*kisses her*): Thank you, Lady Bracknell.

LADY BRACKNELL: You may also address me as Aunt Augusta for the future.

CECILY: Thank you, Aunt Augusta.

LADY BRACKNELL: The marriage, I think, had better take place quite soon.

ALGERNON: Thank you, Aunt Augusta.

CECILY: Thank you, Aunt Augusta.

LADY BRACKNELL: To speak frankly, I am not in favor of long engagements. They give people the opportunity of finding our each other's character before marriage, which I think is never advisable.

JACK: I beg your pardon for interrupting you, Lady Bracknell, but this engagement is quite out of the question. I am Miss Cardew's guardian, and she cannot marry without my consent until she comes of age. That consent I absolutely decline to give.

LADY BRACKNELL: Upon what grounds may I ask? Algernon is an extremely, I may almost say an ostentatiously, eligible young man. He has nothing, but he looks everything. What more can one desire?

JACK: It pains me very much to have to speak frankly to you, Lady Bracknell, about your nephew, but the fact is that I do not approve at all of his moral character. I suspect him of being untruthful.

(*Algernon and Cecily look at him in indignant amazement.*)

LADY BRACKNELL: Untruthful! My nephew Algernon? Impossible! He is an Oxonian.°

JACK: I fear there can be no possible doubt about the matter. This afternoon, during my temporary absence in London on an important question of romance, he obtained admission to my house by means of the false pretense of being my brother. Under an assumed name he drank, I've just been informed by my butler, an entire pint bottle of my Perrier-Jouêt, Brut, '89; a wine I was specially reserving for myself. Continuing his disgraceful deception, he succeeded in the course of the afternoon in alienating the affections of my only ward. He subsequently stayed to tea, and devoured every single muffin. And what makes his conduct all the more heartless is, that he was perfectly well aware from the first that I have no brother, that I never had a brother, and that I don't intend to have a brother, not even of any kind. I distinctly told him so myself yesterday afternoon.

LADY BRACKNELL: Ahem! Mr. Worthing, after careful consideration I have decided entirely to overlook my nephew's conduct to you.

JACK: That is very generous of you, Lady Bracknell. My own decision, however, is unalterable. I decline to give my consent.

LADY BRACKNELL (*to Cecily*): Come here, sweet child. (*Cecily goes over.*) How old are you, dear?

Oxonian: Educated at Oxford University.

Lady Bracknell (Lynn Redgrave), with Algernon (Robert Petkoff) and Cecily (Charlotte Parry), in Sir Peter Hall's Theatre Royal Bath production, 2006.

CECILY: Well, I am really only eighteen, but I always admit to twenty when I go to evening parties.

LADY BRACKNELL: You are perfectly right in making some slight alteration. Indeed, no woman should ever be quite accurate about her age. It looks so calculating— (*In a meditative manner.*) Eighteen but admitting to twenty at evening parties. Well, it will not be very long before you are of age and free from the restraints of tutelage. So I don't think your guardian's consent is, after all, a matter of any importance.

JACK: Pray excuse me, Lady Bracknell, for interrupting you again, but it is only fair to tell you that according to the terms of her grandfather's will Miss Cardew does not come legally of age till she is thirty-five.

LADY BRACKNELL: That does not seem to me to be a grave objection. Thirty-five is a very attractive age. London society is full of women of the very highest birth who have, of their own free choice, remained thirty-five for years. Lady Dumbleton is an instance in point. To my own knowledge she has been thirty-five ever since she arrived at the age of forty, which was many years ago now. I see no reason why our dear Cecily should not be even still more attractive at the age you mention than she is at present. There will be a large accumulation of property.

CECILY: Algy, could you wait for me till I was thirty-five?

ALGERNON: Of course I could, Cecily. You know I could.

CECILY: Yes, I felt it instinctively, but I couldn't wait all that time. I hate waiting even five minutes for anybody. It always makes me rather cross. I am not punctual myself, I know, but I do like punctuality in others, and waiting, even to be married, is quite out of the question.

ALGERNON: Then what is to be done, Cecily?

CECILY: I don't know, Mr. Moncrieff.

LADY BRACKNELL: My dear Mr. Worthing, as Miss Cardew states positively that she cannot wait till she is thirty-five—a remark which I am bound to say seems to me to show a somewhat impatient nature— I would beg of you to reconsider your decision.

JACK: But my dear Lady Bracknell, the matter is entirely in your own hands. The moment you consent to my marriage with Gwendolen, I will most gladly allow your nephew to form an alliance with my ward.

LADY BRACKNELL (*rising and drawing herself up*): You must be quite aware that what you propose is out of the question.

JACK: Then a passionate celibacy is all that any of us can look forward to.

LADY BRACKNELL: That is not the destiny I propose for Gwendolen. Algernon, of course, can choose for himself. (*Pulls out her watch.*) Come, dear; (*Gwendolen rises*) we have already missed five, if not six, trains. To miss any more might expose us to comment on the platform.

(*Enter Dr. Chasuble.*)

CHASUBLE: Everything is quite ready for the christenings.

LADY BRACKNELL: The christenings, sir! Is not that somewhat premature?

CHASUBLE (*looking rather puzzled, and pointing to Jack and Algernon*): Both these gentlemen have expressed a desire for immediate baptism.

LADY BRACKNELL: At their age? The idea is grotesque and irreligious! Algernon, I forbid you to be baptized. I will not hear of such excesses. Lord Bracknell would be highly displeased if he learned that that was the way in which you wasted your time and money.

CHASUBLE: Am I to understand then that there are to be no christenings at all this afternoon?

JACK: I don't think that, as things are now, it would be of much practical value to either of us, Dr. Chasuble.

CHASUBLE: I am grieved to hear such sentiments from you, Mr. Worthing. They savor of the heretical views of the Anabaptists,° views that I have completely refuted in four of my unpublished sermons. However, as your present mood seems to be one peculiarly secular, I will return to the church at once. Indeed, I have just been informed by the pew opener that for the last hour and a half Miss Prism has been waiting for me in the vestry.

LADY BRACKNELL (*starting*): Miss Prism! Did I hear you mention a Miss Prism?

CHASUBLE: Yes, Lady Bracknell. I am on my way to join her.

LADY BRACKNELL: Pray allow me to detain you for a moment. This matter may prove to be one of vital importance to Lord Bracknell and myself. Is this Miss Prism a female of repellent aspect, remotely connected with education?

CHASUBLE (*somewhat indignantly*): She is the most cultivated of ladies, and the very picture of respectability.

LADY BRACKNELL: It is obviously the same person. May I ask what position she holds in your household?

CHASUBLE (*severely*): I am a celibate, madam.

JACK (*interposing*): Miss Prism, Lady Bracknell, has been for the last three years Miss Cardew's esteemed governess and valued companion.

LADY BRACKNELL: In spite of what I hear of her, I must see her at once. Let her be sent for.

CHASUBLE (*looking off*): She approaches; she is nigh.

(*Enter Miss Prism hurriedly.*)

MISS PRISM: I was told you expected me in the vestry, dear Canon. I have been waiting for you there for an hour and three-quarters.

(*Catches sight of Lady Bracknell who has fixed her with a stony glare. Miss Prism grows pale and quails. She looks anxiously round as if desirous to escape.*)

LADY BRACKNELL (*in a severe, judicial voice*): Prism! (*Miss Prism bows her head in shame.*) Come here, Prism! (*Miss Prism approaches in a humble manner.*) Prism! Where is that baby? (*General consternation. The Canon starts back in horror. Algernon and Jack pretend to be anxious to shield Cecily and Gwendolen from hearing the details of a terrible public scandal.*) Twenty-eight years ago, Prism, you

Anabaptists: A religious sect beginning in the sixteenth century and advocating adult baptism and church membership by adults only.

left Lord Bracknell's house, Number 104, Upper Grosvenor Street, in charge of a perambulator that contained a baby, of the male sex. You never returned. A few weeks later, through the elaborate investigations of the Metropolitan police, the perambulator was discovered at midnight, standing by itself in a remote corner of Bayswater. It contained the manuscript of a three-volume novel of more than usually revolting sentimentality. (*Miss Prism starts in involuntary indignation.*) But the baby was not there! (*Everyone looks at Miss Prism.*) Prism! Where is that baby?   (*A pause.*)

MISS PRISM: Lady Bracknell, I admit with shame that I do not know. I only wish I did. The plain facts of the case are these. On the morning of the day you mention, a day that is forever branded on my memory, I prepared as usual to take the baby out in its perambulator. I had also with me a somewhat old, but capacious handbag in which I had intended to place the manuscript of a work of fiction that I had written during my few unoccupied hours. In a moment of mental abstraction, for which I never can forgive myself, I deposited the manuscript in the bassinette, and placed the baby in the handbag.

JACK (*who has been listening attentively*): But where did you deposit the handbag?

MISS PRISM: Do not ask me, Mr. Worthing.

JACK: Miss Prism, this is a matter of no small importance to me. I insist on knowing where you deposited the handbag that contained that infant.

MISS PRISM: I left it in the cloakroom of one of the larger railway stations in London.

JACK: What railway station?

MISS PRISM (*quite crushed*): Victoria. The Brighton line.
                                        (*Sinks into a chair.*)

JACK: I must retire to my room for a moment. Gwendolen, wait here for me.

GWENDOLEN: If you are not too long, I will wait here for you all my life.

                    (*Exit Jack in great excitement.*)

CHASUBLE: What do you think this means, Lady Bracknell?

LADY BRACKNELL: I dare not even suspect, Dr. Chasuble. I need hardly tell you that in families of high position strange coincidences are not supposed to occur. They are hardly considered the thing.

(*Noises heard overhead as if someone was throwing trunks about. Everyone looks up.*)

CECILY: Uncle Jack seems strangely agitated.

CHASUBLE: Your guardian has a very emotional nature.

LADY BRACKNELL: This noise is extremely unpleasant. It sounds as if he was having an argument. I dislike arguments of any kind. They are always vulgar, and often convincing.

CHASUBLE (*looking up*): It has stopped now.
                                (*The noise is redoubled.*)

LADY BRACKNELL: I wish he would arrive at some conclusion.

GWENDOLEN: This suspense is terrible. I hope it will last.

(*Enter Jack with a handbag of black leather in his hand.*)

JACK (*rushing over to Miss Prism*): Is this the handbag, Miss Prism? Examine it carefully before you speak. The happiness of more than one life depends on your answer.

MISS PRISM (*calmly*): It seems to be mine. Yes, here is the injury it received through the upsetting of a Gower Street omnibus in younger and happier days. Here is the stain on the lining caused by the explosion of a temperance beverage, an incident that occurred at Leamington. And here, on the lock, are my initials. I had forgotten that in an extravagant mood I had had them placed there. The bag is undoubtedly mine. I am delighted to have it so unexpectedly restored to me. It has been a great inconvenience being without it all these years.

JACK (*in a pathetic voice*): Miss Prism, more is restored to you than this handbag. I was the baby you placed in it.

MISS PRISM (*amazed*): You?

JACK (*embracing her*): Yes—mother!

MISS PRISM (*recoiling in indignant astonishment*): Mr. Worthing! I am unmarried!

JACK: Unmarried! I do not deny that is a serious blow. But after all, who has the right to cast a stone against one who has suffered? Cannot repentance wipe out an act of folly? Why should there be one law for men, and another for women? Mother, I forgive you. (*Tries to embrace her again.*)

MISS PRISM (*still more indignant*): Mr. Worthing, there is some error. (*Pointing to Lady Bracknell.*) There is the lady who can tell you who you really are.

JACK (*after a pause*): Lady Bracknell, I hate to seem inquisitive, but would you kindly inform me who I am?

LADY BRACKNELL: I am afraid that the news I have to give you will not altogether please you. You are the son of my poor sister, Mrs. Moncrieff, and consequently Algernon's elder brother.

JACK: Algy's elder brother! Then I have a brother after all. I knew I had a brother! I always said I had a brother! Cecily,—how could you have ever doubted that I had a brother. (*Seizes hold of Algernon.*) Dr. Chasuble, my unfortunate brother. Miss Prism, my unfortunate brother. Gwendolen, my unfortunate brother. Algy, you young scoundrel, you will have to treat me with more respect in the future. You have never behaved to me like a brother in all your life.

ALGERNON: Well, not till today, old boy, I admit. I did my best, however, though I was out of practice.
(*Shakes hands.*)

GWENDOLEN (*to Jack*): My own! But what own are you? What is your Christian name, now that you have become someone else?

JACK: Good heavens!—I had quite forgotten that point. Your decision on the subject of my name is irrevocable, I suppose?

GWENDOLEN: I never change, except in my affections.

CECILY: What a noble nature you have, Gwendolen!

JACK: Then the question had better be cleared up at once. Aunt Augusta, a moment. At the time when Miss Prism left me in the handbag, had I been christened already?

LADY BRACKNELL: Every luxury that money could buy, including christening, had been lavished upon you by your fond and doting parents.

JACK: Then I was christened! That is settled. Now, what name was I given? Let me know the worst.

LADY BRACKNELL: Being the eldest son you were naturally christened after your father.

JACK (*irritably*): Yes, but what was my father's Christian name?

LADY BRACKNELL (*meditatively*): I cannot at the present moment recall what the General's Christian name was. But I have no doubt he had one. He was eccentric, I admit. But only in later years. And that was the result of the Indian climate, and marriage, and indigestion, and other things of that kind.

JACK: Algy! Can't you recollect what our father's Christian name was?

ALGERNON: My dear boy, we were never even on speaking terms. He died before I was a year old.

JACK: His name would appear in the Army Lists of the period, I suppose, Aunt Augusta?

LADY BRACKNELL: The General was essentially a man of peace, except in his domestic life. But I have no doubt his name would appear in any military directory.

JACK: The Army Lists of the last forty years are here. These delightful records should have been my constant study. (*Rushes to bookcase and tears the books out.*) M. Generals—Mallam, Maxbohm, Magley, what ghastly names they have—Markby, Migsby, Mobbs, Moncrieff! Lieutenant 1840, Captain, Lieutenant-Colonel, Colonel, General 1869, Christian names, Ernest John. (*Puts book very quietly down and speaks quite calmly.*) I always told you, Gwendolen, my name was Ernest, didn't I? Well, it is Ernest after all. I mean it naturally is Ernest.

LADY BRACKNELL: Yes, I remember now that the General was called Ernest. I knew I had some particular reason for disliking the name.

GWENDOLEN: Ernest! My own Ernest! I felt from the first that you could have no other name!

JACK: Gwendolen, it is a terrible thing for a man to find out suddenly that all his life he has been speaking nothing but the truth. Can you forgive me?

GWENDOLEN: I can. For I feel that you are sure to change.

JACK: My own one!

CHASUBLE (*to Miss Prism*): Laetitia! (*Embraces her.*)

MISS PRISM (*enthusiastically*): Frederick! At last!

ALGERNON: Cecily! (*Embraces her.*) At last!

JACK: Gwendolen! (*Embraces her.*) At last!

LADY BRACKNELL: My nephew, you seem to be displaying signs of triviality.

JACK: On the contrary, Aunt Augusta, I've now realized for the first time in my life the vital Importance of Being Earnest.

COMMENTARY

Joseph Donohue

INTERVIEW WITH SIR PETER HALL, DIRECTOR OF
THE IMPORTANCE OF BEING EARNEST   2006

The distinguished director is interviewed by professor Joseph Donohue concerning his reasons for directing Wilde's play for contemporary audiences. Hall explains why he believes the play is always timely and what he feels are its central issues. He also explores the gender issues buried in the play.

Q: Is there anything about the present time, the world situation, or our understanding of Oscar Wilde himself that makes mounting a production of *The Importance of Being Earnest* particularly appropriate now?

A: This is the second time I've done the play, and I believe it's an absolutely unique and original object. I don't think that you can write it off as a farce or a farcical comedy; I think it's as original as *Waiting for Godot*, and heaven knows what Wilde would've done if he had been spared, if we hadn't murdered him, because it is absolutely original. In that sense, it's a masterpiece, and in that sense, it's always timely. It's not easy to do, but I think the important thing about Wilde — I've done *Ideal Husband* several times, and *Earnest* twice — the important thing is to understand what his wit is about. It's not about standing on the stage and having like a tennis match of facetiousness of who can win. If you look at Wilde's plays carefully, the wit always covers over something which is very painful, or very extraordinary, something that can't be actually understood or said, for whatever reason. Wilde said, "Give a man a mask and he will tell you the truth," and Wilde's mask, for his characters, is always wit. It's like the English stiff upper lip of the nineteenth century. So you've got to look at *The Importance of Being Earnest* as a deeply serious play about the double life, about sexual desire, about the marriage market, and if you play it very seriously, it's excruciatingly funny. If you don't play it seriously, I think the comedy wears off.

But, why do it now? Well, I think it's always time to do it, in a sense. I don't think there's a deeply contemporary need to do it or anything. Masterpieces need revaluing for each generation.

Q: The original production of *The Importance of Being Earnest*, at George Alexander's St. James Theatre, in London in 1895, featured a three-act play text, cut down — probably mostly by Alexander himself — from the four-act play originally written by Wilde. Earlier, the author had written to Alexander offering him the play and telling him that the two men's parts of Jack and Algy were of equal prominence. In cutting the play to three acts Alexander seems to have made sure that his own part, Jack Worthing, outshone the part of Algy. That choice was memorialized in the first edition of the play. What text do you plan to use for the production? The standard choice is the first edition text, based on Alexander's three-act play, but have you considered using at least some material from the original four-act text? If you chose to do that, would you try to restore more of a balance between the two roles of Jack and Algy, or do you like the greater centrality of Jack as the three-act text presents it? Do you have some other comments about the balancing of pairs of contrasting characters in the play—for example, Gwendolen and Cecily, Miss Prism and Canon Chasuble?

A: We're using the three-act text. When we did the play before, I looked into the fourth act very carefully and actually rehearsed some of it and did some of it, but not in performance. Whoever edited it to the three-act version, whether it was George Alexander or Wilde himself or a collaboration, I personally think they did well. There's something prolix and a little self-indulgent about the fourth act. Of course it's got some good things in it, but I don't think they finally help.

I don't understand the comment about an imbalance between the two roles. Algy is a superb part; he gets all the laughs. Ernest is the center of the play in the sense that Ernest is the man who has not yet come to terms with who he is, not come to terms with his own sexuality, among other things, and therefore needs to lead a double life. I think that's a wonderfully rich and extraordinary part. I don't think that Algy is a supporting role at all.

I think classically, from Plautus onward and certainly [in] Shakespeare, comedy is about couples. Couples who find out they're now mature enough to get married, or relate to each other in terms of love. I think the balancing of the characters is classic comedy.

Q: Is the play essentially a comedy, or essentially a farce? Or is it a mixed breed?

A: I never understand why people need to put some kind of label on things. It's like saying, "Are Shakespeare's late plays romances or comedies, or comedy/romances, or what are they?" They're plays, and they're very original, and as I said, I think *The Importance of Being Earnest* is one of the most original plays in the English language. I certainly don't think it can be dismissed as a farce any more than I think that it can be just looked at as a serious play. It's the most extraordinary combination of critical comedy which illuminates what the people are about, and what their quest is, and what their pains are, and what their anguishes are. It's very serious, but it's excruciatingly funny. I don't know of any label for that; it's why I think Oscar Wilde is so original.

Q: Is the author in the play?

A: Well, the author's in the play. The author's in the play all the while. He's partly Algy always wanting to go off on some secret mission, for some nefarious, probably sexual, purpose. He's also Ernest trying to be a pillar of the community but actually leading a double life. Of course, *Ideal Husband* is another case in point. The first great play in the English language about bisexuality, if you actually look at it. And I don't think any writer leaves himself outside when he sits down to write his play. I think that looking at *The Importance of Being Earnest* as autobiography is altogether too crude. Certainly Wilde is there all the time.

Q: Lady Bracknell is a notorious blocking character—standing in the way, for over two acts, of Jack and Gwendolen's happiness. And yet hers is one of the most delicious roles in all of British comedy—or farce! How do these two aspects of the character factor into your direction of Lynn Redgrave in the role? Will there be some pressure for her to differentiate her approach to the role from such famous portrayers as Edith Evans or Judi Dench?

A: I was fortunate enough to do my other *Importance of Being Earnest* with Judi Dench, so perhaps I'm uniquely qualified to answer the question. I simply don't understand it, actually. I think what's wonderful about Lady Bracknell is that she's such a materialist, such a total exponent of the marriage market. She's out to sell her daughter to the highest bidder. She reveals that [she] had absolutely no money herself, but her marriage enabled her to become rich. She is, in many respects, a monster. But like other monsters, like Fagin, we like the enormity of their desires; we get a charge out of seeing someone behave quite so absolutely. . . . I don't think at all that Lady Bracknell wrecks the play, blocks the play, distorts the play. I think if she's played as a comic turn she wrecks the play; I've seen that happen. But if you understand what a rapacious lady she is, she really makes the serious heart of the play very evident. It's a curious thing, comedy—it has to be highly serious, and that's certainly true of Lady Bracknell.

Anton Chekhov

Anton Chekhov (1860–1904) spent most of his childhood in relative poverty. His family managed to set up its household in Moscow after years spent in remote Taganrog, six hundred miles to the south. He studied medicine in Moscow and eventually received his degree. Although he practiced medicine most of his life, he said that if medicine was his wife, literature was his mistress. His earliest literary efforts were for the purpose of relieving his family's poverty, but it was not long before he earned more from writing than from medicine. By 1896 he had written more than three hundred short stories, most of them published in newspapers. Many of them are classics.

His first theatrical works, apart from his short farces, were not successful. *Ivanov* (1887–1889), rushed to production, was a failure, but its revised 1889 version, reflecting much of his personal life, was successful. *The Wood Demon* (1889), also a failure, helped Chekhov eventually produce his great plays: *The Seagull* (1896); *Uncle Vanya* (1897); *Three Sisters* (1901); and his last, *The Cherry Orchard* (1903). These plays essentially reshaped modern drama, creating a style that critic Richard Peace describes as a "subtle blend of naturalism and symbolism."

The Seagull attracted the attention of the Moscow Art Theatre. The play was not a success in its first production in 1896, but two years later it became one of the theater's triumphs. Konstantin Stanislavsky, the great Russian director and actor, played Trigorin, the lead character, but Chekhov felt that he was overacting. They often had disagreements about the playwright's work, but the Moscow Art Theatre supported Chekhov fully.

The surfaces of Chekhov's plays are so lifelike that at times one feels his dramatic purposes are submerged, and to an extent that is true. Chekhov is the master of the SUBTEXT, a technique in which the surface of the dialogue seems innocuous or meandering, but deeper meanings are implied. Madame Ranevskaya's musings about her childhood in act I of *The Cherry Orchard* contrast with the purposeful dialogue of Lopakhin. Her long speeches in act III talking about the "millstone" she loves in Paris are also meanderings, but they reveal an idealistic character doomed to suffer at the hands of a new generation of realists who have no time for her ramblings and sentimentalism.

Because Chekhov's subtexts are always present, to read his work requires close attention. One must constantly probe, analyze, ask what is implied by what is being said. Chekhov resists "explaining" his plays by having key characters give key thematic speeches. Instead, the meaning builds slowly. Our grasp of what a situation or circumstance finally means will change as we read and as we gather more understanding of the subtleties veiled by surfaces.

Chekhov's style is remarkable for its clarity; its surface is direct, simple, and effective. Even his short stories have a clear dramatic center, and the characters he chose to observe are exceptionally modern in that they are neither heroes nor villains. The dramatic concept of a larger-than-life Oedipus or of *Hamlet*'s

787

devilish Claudius is nowhere to be seen in his work. Chekhov's characters are limited, recognizable, and in many ways completely ordinary.

Chekhov's genius was in showing such characters' ambitions, pain, and successes. He was quite aware of important social changes taking place in Russia; the old aristocratic classes, who once owned serfs, were being reduced to a genteel impoverishment, while the children of former slaves were beginning to succeed in business and real estate ventures. Since Chekhov's grandfather had been a serf who bought his freedom in 1841, it is likely that Chekhov was especially supportive of such social change; we see evidence of that in his best plays.

THE CHERRY ORCHARD

The Cherry Orchard (1903) premiered on Chekhov's birthday, January 17, in 1904. The Moscow Art Theatre performance was directed by Konstantin Stanislavsky, an actor-director who pioneered a new method of realistic acting. (Stanislavsky is still read and admired the world over. His techniques were modified in the United States and form the basis of METHOD ACTING.) For the subtle effects that Chekhov wanted, however, he found Stanislavsky too stagey, flamboyant, and melodramatic. They argued hotly over what should happen in his plays, and often Stanislavsky prevailed.

One argument was over whether *The Cherry Orchard* was a tragedy. Chekhov steadfastly called it a comedy, but Stanislavsky saw the ruin of Madame Ranevskaya and the destruction of the cherry orchard as tragic. Chekhov perhaps saw it the same way, but he also considered its potential as the beginning of a new, more realistic life for Madame Ranevskaya and her brother Gayev. Their impracticality was an important cause of their having lost their wealth and estate.

How audiences interpret Lopakhin depends on how they view the ambition of the new class of businessmen whose zeal, work, and cleverness earn them the estates that previously they could have hoped only to work on. Social change is fueled by money, which replaces an inherited aristocracy with ambitious moneymakers who earn the power to force changes on the old, less flexible aristocrats. In Russia, massive social change was eventually effected by revolution and the institution of communism. But *The Cherry Orchard* shows that change would have come to Russia in any event.

Perhaps Chekhov's peasant blood helped him see the play as more of a comedy than a tragedy, even though he portrays the characters with greater complexity than we might expect in comedy. Lopakhin is not a simple, unsympathetic character; Trofimov is not a simple dreamer. We need to look closely at what they do and why they do it. For example, when thinking about preserving the beauties of the cherry orchard, Trofimov reminds people that all of Russia is an orchard, that the world is filled with beautiful places. Such a view makes it difficult for him to feel nostalgia for aristocratic privilege.

Trofimov sounds a striking note about the practice of slavery in Russia. He tells Madame Ranevskaya and Gayev that they are living on credit, that they must repay debts to the Russian people. The cherry orchard is beautiful because each tree represents the soul of a serf. The beautiful class of people to which the impractical Madame Ranevskaya belongs owes its beauty and grace to the institution of slavery, and soon the note will be presented for payment. The sound of the breaking string in act I, repeated at the end of the play, is Chekhov's way of symbolizing the losses and changes represented in the play.

Madame Ranevskaya, however, cannot change. Her habits of mind are fully formed before the play begins; nothing that Lopakhin can say will help change her. Even though she knows she is dangerously in debt, she gives a gold coin to a beggar. *Noblesse oblige*—the duty of the upper class to help the poor—is still part of her ethos, even if it also involves her own ruin.

A sense of tragedy is apparent in Madame Ranevskaya's feelings and her helplessness. She seems incapable of transforming herself, no matter how much she may wish to change. We see her as a victim of fate, a fate that is formed by her expectations and training. But the play also contains comic and nonsensical moments, as, for example, in the by-play of Varya, Yasha, and Yepikhodov over a game of billiards in act III. In his letters Chekhov mentions that the play is happy and frivolous, "in places even a farce."

The Cherry Orchard in Performance

Since its first production in 1904, *The Cherry Orchard* has played to responsive audiences in Europe and abroad. It was produced in London in 1911, Berlin in 1919, and New York in 1923 (in Russian). Eva Le Gallienne produced it in New York in her English version in 1928. In 1968 she directed the play with Uta Hagen as Madame Ranevskaya. Tyrone Guthrie directed it at the Old Vic in 1933 and again in 1941. John Gielgud, Peggy Ashcroft, Judi Dench, and Dorothy Tutin performed in a powerful and well-reviewed version in London in 1961. When Joseph Papp produced an all-black *Cherry Orchard* in 1973, James Earl Jones was praised as a powerful Lopakhin.

Andrei Serban's 1977 production for Joseph Papp at Lincoln Center in New York was praised for its extraordinary stage effects. According to the reviewer at *Time* magazine,

> Serban's best images effectively magnify the play's conflict between the old order and the bright new world that is its doom: a frieze of peasants laboring beneath modern telegraph wires, a group of aristocrats watching the setting sun silhouette a factory on the horizon.

The American playwright Jean Claude van Italie has revised the text for contemporary audiences. His version, produced at the John Drew Theater of Guild Hall in East Hampton in July 1985, was directed by Elinor Renfield. Amanda Plummer played Anya, and Joanna Merlin played Madame Ranevskaya. Peter Brook's 1987 New York production, with Brian Dennehy as a notable Lopakhin, had little scenery beyond a great number of Oriental rugs. It was played without intermissions at breakneck speed. *New York Times* critic Frank Rich said of it, "On this director's magic carpets, *The Cherry Orchard* flies." Other modern treatments of Chekhov's plays include Michael Picardie's adaptation of *The Cherry Orchard* to South Africa and Brian Friel's adaptation to Ireland. Mustapha Matura's *Trinidad Sisters* (1988) moves *Three Sisters* to Trinidad, demonstrating the universal appeal of Chekhov's plays. In 1997 Galina Volchek staged a Russian-language version in the Martin Beck Theater on

Broadway. Critic Peter Marks said the play was "communicated vividly." Theater critic David Finkle described the 2006 production by the Shakespeare Theatre of New Jersey as "the essence of Anton Chekhov." The set of this production, unlike most, included several trees in bloom so that the audience could actually see the orchard that was to be cut away for new housing.

Anton Chekhov (1860–1904)

THE CHERRY ORCHARD

TRANSLATED BY ANN DUNNIGAN

1903

Characters

RANEVSKAYA, LYUBOV ANDREYEVNA, *a landowner*
ANYA, *her daughter, seventeen years old*
VARYA, *her adopted daughter, twenty-four years old*
GAYEV, LEONID ANDREYEVICH, *Madame Ranevskaya's brother*
LOPAKHIN, YERMOLAI ALEKSEYEVICH, *a merchant*
TROFIMOV, PYOTR SERGEYEVICH, *a student*
SEMYONOV-PISHCHIK, BORIS BORISOVICH, *a landowner*
CHARLOTTA IVANOVNA, *a governess*
YEPIKHODOV, SEMYON PANTELEYEVICH, *a clerk*
DUNYASHA, *a maid*
FIRS, *an old valet, eighty-seven years old*
YASHA, *a young footman*
A STRANGER
THE STATIONMASTER
A POST OFFICE CLERK
GUESTS, SERVANTS

The action takes place on Madame Ranevskaya's estate.

ACT I

(*A room that is still called the nursery. One of the doors leads into Anya's room. Dawn; the sun will soon rise. It is May, the cherry trees are in bloom, but it is cold in the orchard; there is a morning frost. The windows in the room are closed. Enter Dunyasha with a candle, and Lopakhin with a book in his hand.*)

LOPAKHIN: The train is in, thank God. What time is it?

DUNYASHA: Nearly two. (*Blows out the candle.*) It's already light.

LOPAKHIN: How late is the train, anyway? A couple of hours at least. (*Yawns and stretches.*) I'm a fine one! What a fool I've made of myself! Came here on purpose to meet them at the station, and then overslept.... Fell asleep in the chair. It's annoying.... You might have waked me.

DUNYASHA: I thought you had gone. (*Listens.*) They're coming now, I think!

LOPAKHIN (*listens*): No...they've got to get the luggage and one thing and another. (*Pause.*) Lyubov Andreyevna has lived abroad for five years, I don't know what she's like now.... She's a fine person. Sweet-tempered, simple. I remember when I was a boy of fifteen, my late father—he had a shop in the village then—gave me a punch in the face and made my nose bleed.... We had come into the yard here for some reason or other, and he'd had a drop too much. Lyubov Andreyevna—I remember as if it were yesterday—still young, and so slender, led me to the washstand in this very room, the nursery. "Don't cry, little peasant," she said, "it will heal in time for your wedding...." (*Pause.*) Little peasant... my father was a peasant, it's true, and here I am in a white waistcoat and tan shoes. Like a pig in a pastry shop.... I may be rich, I've made a lot of money, but if you think about it, analyze it, I'm a peasant through and through. (*Turning pages of the book.*) Here I've been reading this book, and I didn't understand a thing. Fell asleep over it. (*Pause.*)

DUNYASHA: The dogs didn't sleep all night: They can tell that their masters are coming.

LOPAKHIN: What's the matter with you, Dunyasha, you're so...

DUNYASHA: My hands are trembling. I'm going to faint.

LOPAKHIN: You're much too delicate, Dunyasha. You dress like a lady, and do your hair like one, too. It's not right. You should know your place.

(*Enter Yepikhodov with a bouquet, he wears a jacket and highly polished boots that squeak loudly. He drops the flowers as he comes in.*)

YEPIKHODOV (*picking up the flowers*): Here, the gardener sent these. He says you're to put them in the dining room. (*Hands the bouquet to Dunyasha.*)

LOPAKHIN: And bring me some kvas.°

DUNYASHA: Yes, sir. (*Goes out.*)

YEPIKHODOV: There's a frost this morning—three degrees—and the cherry trees are in bloom. I cannot approve of our climate. (*Sighs.*) I cannot. Our climate is not exactly conducive. And now, Yermolai Alekseyevich, permit me to append: The day before yesterday I bought myself a pair of boots, which, I venture to assure you, squeak so that it's quite infeasible. What should I grease them with?

LOPAKHIN: Leave me alone. You make me tired.

YEPIKHODOV: Every day some misfortune happens to me. But I don't complain, I'm used to it, I even smile.

(*Dunyasha enters, serves Lopakhin the kvas.*)

YEPIKHODOV: I'm going. (*Stumbles over a chair and upsets it.*) There! (*As if in triumph.*) Now you see, excuse the expression...the sort of circumstance, incidentally.... It's really quite remarkable! (*Goes out.*)

DUNYASHA: You know, Yermolai Alekseyich, I have to confess that Yepikhodov has proposed to me.

LOPAKHIN: Ah!

DUNYASHA: And I simply don't know.... He's a quiet man, but sometimes, when he starts talking, you can't understand a thing he says. It's nice, and full of feeling, only it doesn't make sense. I sort of like him. He's madly in love with me. But he's an unlucky fellow: Every day something happens to him. They tease him about it around here; they call him Two-and-twenty Troubles.

LOPAKHIN (*listening*): I think I hear them coming...

DUNYASHA: They're coming! What's the matter with me? I'm cold all over.

LOPAKHIN: They're really coming. Let's go and meet them. Will she recognize me? It's five years since we've seen each other.

DUNYASHA (*agitated*): I'll faint this very minute...oh, I'm going to faint!

(*Two carriages are heard driving up to the house. Lopakhin and Dunyasha go out quickly. The stage is empty. There is a hubbub in the adjoining rooms. Firs hurriedly crosses the stage leaning on a stick. He has been to meet Lyubov Andreyevna and wears old fashioned livery and a high hat. He mutters something to himself, not a word of which can be understood. The noise offstage grows louder and louder. A voice: "Let's go through here...." Enter Lyubov Andreyevna, Anya, Charlotta Ivanovna with a little dog on a chain, all in traveling dress; Varya wearing a coat and kerchief; Gayev, Semyonov-Pishchik, Lopakhin, Dunyasha with a bundle and parasol; servants with luggage—all walk through the room.*)

ANYA: Let's go this way. Do you remember, Mama, what room this is?

kvas: A Russian beer.

LYUBOV ANDREYEVNA (*joyfully, through tears*): The nursery!

VARYA: How cold it is! My hands are numb. (*To Lyubov Andreyevna.*) Your rooms, both the white one and the violet one, are just as you left them, Mama.

LYUBOV ANDREYEVNA: The nursery...my dear, lovely nursery....I used to sleep here when I was little.... (*Weeps.*) And now, like a child, I...(*Kisses her brother, Varya, then her brother again.*) Varya hasn't changed; she still looks like a nun. And I recognized Dunyasha....(*Kisses Dunyasha.*)

GAYEV: The train was two hours late. How's that? What kind of management is that?

CHARLOTTA (*to Pishchik*): My dog even eats nuts.

PISHCHIK (*amazed*): Think of that now!

(*They all go out except Anya and Dunyasha.*)

DUNYASHA: We've been waiting and waiting for you.... (*Takes off Anya's coat and hat.*)

ANYA: I didn't sleep for four nights on the road...now I feel cold.

DUNYASHA: It was Lent when you went away, there was snow and frost then, but now? My darling! (*Laughs and kisses her.*) I've waited so long for you, my joy, my precious...I must tell you at once, I can't wait another minute....

ANYA (*listlessly*): What now?

DUNYASHA: The clerk, Yepikhodov, proposed to me just after Easter.

ANYA: You always talk about the same thing.... (*Straightening her hair.*) I've lost all my hairpins.... (*She is so exhausted she can hardly stand.*)

DUNYASHA: I really don't know what to think. He loves me—he loves me so!

ANYA (*looking through the door into her room, tenderly*): My room, my windows...it's just as though I'd never been away. I am home! Tomorrow morning I'll get up and run into the orchard.... Oh, if I could only sleep! I didn't sleep during the entire journey, I was so tormented by anxiety.

DUNYASHA: Pyotr Sergeich arrived the day before yesterday.

ANYA (*joyfully*): Petya!

DUNYASHA: He's asleep in the bathhouse, he's staying there. "I'm afraid of being in the way," he said. (*Looks at her pocket watch.*) I ought to wake him up, but Varvara Mikhailovna told me not to. "Don't you wake him," she said.

(*Enter Varya with a bunch of keys at her waist.*)

VARYA: Dunyasha, coffee, quickly...Mama's asking for coffee.

DUNYASHA: This very minute. (*Goes out.*)

VARYA: Thank God, you've come! You're home again. (*Caressing her.*) My little darling has come back! My pretty one is here!

ANYA: I've been through so much.

VARYA: I can imagine!

ANYA: I left in Holy Week, it was cold then. Charlotta

never stopped talking and doing her conjuring tricks the entire journey. Why did you saddle me with Charlotta?

VARYA: You couldn't have traveled alone, darling. At seventeen!

ANYA: When we arrived in Paris, it was cold, snowing. My French is awful.... Mama was living on the fifth floor, and when I got there, she had all sorts of Frenchmen and ladies with her, and an old priest with a little book, and it was full of smoke, dismal. Suddenly I felt sorry for Mama, so sorry. I took her head in my arms and held her close and couldn't let her go. Afterward she kept hugging me and crying....

VARYA (through her tears): Don't talk about it, don't talk about it....

ANYA: She had already sold her villa near Mentone, and she had nothing left, nothing. And I hadn't so much as a kopeck left, we barely managed to get there. But Mama doesn't understand! When we had dinner in a station restaurant, she always ordered the most expensive dishes and tipped each of the waiters a ruble. Charlotta is the same. And Yasha also ordered a dinner, it was simply awful. You know, Yasha is Mama's footman; we brought him with us.

VARYA: I saw the rogue.

ANYA: Well, how are things? Have you paid the interest?

VARYA: How could we?

ANYA: Oh, my God, my God!

VARYA: In August the estate will be put up for sale.

ANYA: My God!

(Lopakhin peeps in at the door and moos like a cow.)

LOPAKHIN: Moo-o-o! (Disappears.)

VARYA (through her tears): What I couldn't do to him! (Shakes her fist.)

ANYA (embracing Varya, softly): Varya, has he proposed to you? (Varya shakes her head.) But he loves you.... Why don't you come to an understanding, what are you waiting for?

VARYA: I don't think anything will ever come of it. He's too busy, he has no time for me...he doesn't even notice me. I've washed my hands of him, it makes me miserable to see him.... Everyone talks of our wedding, they all congratulate me, and actually there's nothing to it—it's all like a dream.... (In a different tone.) You have a brooch like a bee.

ANYA (sadly): Mama bought it. (Goes into her own room; speaks gaily, like a child.) In Paris I went up in a balloon!

VARYA: My darling is home! My pretty one has come back!

(Dunyasha has come in with the coffeepot and prepares coffee.)

VARYA (stands at the door of Anya's room): You know, darling, all day long I'm busy looking after the house, but I keep dreaming. If we could marry you to a rich man I'd be at peace. I could go into a hermitage, then to Kiev, to Moscow, and from one holy place to another....I'd go on and on. What a blessing!

ANYA: The birds are singing in the orchard. What time is it?

VARYA: It must be after two. Time you were asleep, darling. (Goes into Anya's room.) What a blessing!

(Yasha enters with a lap robe and a traveling bag.)

YASHA (crosses the stage mincingly): May one go through here?

DUNYASHA: A person would hardly recognize you, Yasha. Your stay abroad has done wonders for you.

YASHA: Hm....And who are you?

DUNYASHA: When you left here I was only that high— (indicating with her hand). I'm Dunyasha, Fyodor Kozoyedov's daughter. You don't remember?

YASHA: Hm....A little cucumber! (Looks around, then embraces her; she cries out and drops a saucer. He quickly goes out.)

VARYA (in a tone of annoyance, from the doorway): What's going on here?

DUNYASHA (tearfully): I broke a saucer.

VARYA: That's good luck.

ANYA: We ought to prepare Mama: Petya is here....

VARYA: I gave orders not to wake him.

ANYA (pensively): Six years ago Father died, and a month later brother Grisha drowned in the river...a pretty little seven-year-old boy. Mama couldn't bear it and went away...went without looking back.... (Shudders.) How I understand her, if she only knew! (Pause.) And Petya Trofimov was Grisha's tutor, he may remind her....

(Enter Firs wearing a jacket and a white waistcoat.)

FIRS (goes to the coffeepot, anxiously): The mistress will have her coffee here. (Puts on white gloves.) Is the coffee ready? (To Dunyasha, sternly.) You! Where's the cream?

DUNYASHA: Oh, my goodness! (Quickly goes out.)

FIRS (fussing over the coffeepot): Ah, what an addlepate! (Mutters to himself.) They've come back from Paris....The master used to go to Paris...by carriage.... (Laughs.)

VARYA: What is it, Firs?

FIRS: If you please? (Joyfully.) My mistress has come home! At last! Now I can die.... (Weeps with joy.)

(Enter Lyubov Andreyevna, Gayev, and Semyonov-Pishchik, the last wearing a sleeveless peasant coat of fine cloth and full trousers. Gayev, as he comes in, goes through the motions of playing billiards.)

LYUBOV ANDREYEVNA: How does it go? Let's see if I can remember...cue ball into the corner! Double the rail to center table.

GAYEV: Cut shot into the corner! There was a time, sister, when you and I used to sleep here in this very room, and now I'm fifty-one, strange as it may seem....

LOPAKHIN: Yes, time passes.

GAYEV: How's that?

LOPAKHIN: Time, I say, passes.

GAYEV: It smells of patchouli here.

ANYA: I'm going to bed. Good night, Mama. (*Kisses her mother.*)

LYUBOV ANDREYEVNA: My precious child. (*Kisses her hands.*) Are you glad to be home? I still feel dazed.

ANYA: Good night, Uncle.

GAYEV (*kisses her face and hands*): God bless you. How like your mother you are! (*To his sister.*) At her age you were exactly like her, Lyuba.

(*Anya shakes hands with Lopakhin and Pishchik and goes out, closing the door after her.*)

LYUBOV ANDREYEVNA: She's exhausted.

PISHCHIK: Must have been a long journey.

VARYA: Well, gentlemen? It's after two, high time you were going.

LYUBOV ANDREYEVNA (*laughs*): You haven't changed, Varya. (*Draws Varya to her and kisses her.*) I'll just drink my coffee and then we'll all go. (*Firs places a cushion under her feet.*) Thank you, my dear. I've got used to coffee. I drink it day and night. Thanks, dear old man. (*Kisses him.*)

VARYA: I'd better see if all the luggage has been brought in.

LYUBOV ANDREYEVNA: Is this really me sitting here? (*Laughs.*) I feel like jumping about and waving my arms. (*Buries her face in her hands.*) What if it's only a dream! God knows I love my country, love it dearly. I couldn't look out the train window, I was crying so! (*Through tears.*) But I must drink my coffee. Thank you, Firs, thank you, my dear old friend. I'm so glad you're still alive.

FIRS: The day before yesterday.

GAYEV: He's hard of hearing.

LOPAKHIN: I must go now, I'm leaving for Kharkov about five o'clock. It's so annoying! I wanted to have a good look at you, and have a talk. You're as splendid as ever.

PISHCHIK (*breathing heavily*): Even more beautiful.... Dressed like a Parisienne.... There goes my wagon, all four wheels!

LOPAKHIN: Your brother here, Leonid Andreich, says I'm a boor, a moneygrubber, but I don't mind. Let him talk. All I want is that you should trust me as you used to, and that your wonderful, touching eyes should look at me as they did then. Merciful God! My father was one of your father's serfs, and your grandfather's, but you yourself did so much for me once, that I've forgotten all that and love you as if you were my own kin — more than my kin.

LYUBOV ANDREYEVNA: I can't sit still, I simply cannot. (*Jumps up and walks about the room in great excitement.*) I cannot bear this joy.... Laugh at me, I'm silly.... My dear little bookcase...(*kisses bookcase*) my little table...

GAYEV: Nurse died while you were away.

LYUBOV ANDREYEVNA (*sits down and drinks coffee*): Yes, God rest her soul. They wrote me.

GAYEV: And Anastasy is dead. Petrushka Kosoi left me and is now with the police inspector in town. (*Takes a box of hard candies from his pocket and begins to suck one.*)

PISHCHIK: My daughter, Dashenka...sends her regards...

LOPAKHIN: I wish I could tell you something very pleasant and cheering. (*Glances at his watch.*) I must go directly, there's no time to talk, but...well, I'll say it in a couple of words. As you know, the cherry orchard is to be sold to pay your debts. The auction is set for August twenty-second, but you need not worry, my dear, you can sleep in peace, there is a way out. This is my plan. Now, please listen! Your estate is only twenty versts° from town, the railway runs close by, and if the cherry orchard and the land along the river were cut up into lots and leased for summer cottages, you'd have, at the very least, an income of twenty-five thousand a year.

GAYEV: Excuse me, what nonsense!

LYUBOV ANDREYEVNA: I don't quite understand you, Yermolai Alekseich.

LOPAKHIN: You will get, at the very least, twenty-five rubles a year for a two-and-a-half-acre lot, and if you advertise now, I guarantee you won't have a single plot of ground left by autumn, everything will be snapped up. In short, I congratulate you, you are saved. The site is splendid, the river is deep. Only, of course, the ground must be cleared...you must tear down all the old outbuildings, for instance, and this house, which is worthless, cut down the old cherry orchard —

LYUBOV ANDREYEVNA: Cut it down? Forgive me, my dear, but you don't know what you are talking about. If there is one thing in the whole province that is interesting, not to say remarkable, it's our cherry orchard.

LOPAKHIN: The only remarkable thing about this orchard is that it is very big. There's a crop of cherries every other year, and then you can't get rid of them, nobody buys them.

GAYEV: This orchard is even mentioned in the *Encyclopedia.*

LOPAKHIN (*glancing at his watch*): If we don't think of something and come to a decision, on the twenty-second of August the cherry orchard, and the entire estate, will be sold at auction. Make up your minds! There is no other way out, I swear to you. None whatsoever.

FIRS: In the old days, forty or fifty years ago, the cherries were dried, soaked, marinated, and made into jam, and they used to —

GAYEV: Be quiet, Firs.

FIRS: And they used to send cartloads of dried cherries to Moscow and Kharkov. And that brought in money! The dried cherries were soft and juicy in those days, sweet, fragrant....They had a method then...

LYUBOV ANDREYEVNA: And what has become of that method now?

---

versts: A verst is approximately equal to a kilometer, a little more than half a mile.

FIRS: Forgotten. Nobody remembers....

PISHCHIK: How was it in Paris? What's it like there? Did you eat frogs?

LYUBOV ANDREYEVNA: I ate crocodiles.

PISHCHIK: Think of that now!

LOPAKHIN: There used to be only the gentry and the peasants living in the country, but now these summer people have appeared. All the towns, even the smallest ones, are surrounded by summer cottages. And it is safe to say that in another twenty years these people will multiply enormously. Now the summer resident only drinks tea on his porch, but it may well be that he'll take to cultivating his acre and then your cherry orchard will be a happy, rich, luxuriant —

GAYEV (*indignantly*): What nonsense!

(*Enter Varya and Yasha.*)

VARYA: There are two telegrams for you, Mama. (*Picks out a key and with a jingling sound opens an old-fashioned bookcase.*) Here they are.

LYUBOV ANDREYEVNA: From Paris. (*Tears up the telegrams without reading them.*) That's all over....

GAYEV: Do you know, Lyuba, how old this bookcase is? A week ago I pulled out the bottom drawer, and what do I see? Some figures burnt into it. The bookcase was made exactly a hundred years ago. What do you think of that? Eh? We could have celebrated its jubilee. It's an inanimate object, but nevertheless, for all that, it's a bookcase.

PISHCHIK: A hundred years...think of that now!

GAYEV: Yes...that is something.... (*Feeling the bookcase.*) Dear, honored bookcase. I salute thy existence, which for over one hundred years has served the glorious ideals of goodness and justice; thy silent appeal to fruitful endeavor, unflagging in the course of a hundred years, tearfully sustaining through generations of our family, courage and faith in a better future, and fostering in us ideals of goodness and social consciousness....

(*A pause.*)

LOPAKHIN: Yes...

LYUBOV ANDREYEVNA: You are the same as ever, Lyonya.

GAYEV (*somewhat embarrassed*): Carom into the corner, cut shot to center table.

LOPAKHIN (*looks at his watch*): Well, time for me to go.

YASHA (*hands medicine to Lyubov Andreyevna*): Perhaps you will take your pills now.

PISHCHIK: Don't take medicaments, dearest lady, they do neither harm nor good. Let me have them, honored lady. (*Takes the pillbox, shakes the pills into his hand, blows on them, puts them into his mouth and washes them down with kvas.*) There!

LYUBOV ANDREYEVNA (*alarmed*): Why, you must be mad!

PISHCHIK: I've taken all the pills.

LOPAKHIN: What a glutton!

(*Everyone laughs.*)

FIRS: The gentleman stayed with us during Holy Week...ate half a bucket of pickles.... (*Mumbles.*)

LYUBOV ANDREYEVNA: What is he saying?

VARYA: He's been muttering like that for three years now. We've grown used to it.

YASHA: He's in his dotage.

(*Charlotta Ivanovna, very thin, tightly laced, in a white dress with a lorgnette at her belt, crosses the stage.*)

LOPAKHIN: Forgive me, Charlotta Ivanovna, I haven't had a chance to say how do you do to you. (*Tries to kiss her hand.*)

CHARLOTTA (*pulls her hand away*): If I permit you to kiss my hand you'll be wanting to kiss my elbow next, then my shoulder.

LOPAKHIN: I have no luck today. (*Everyone laughs.*) Charlotta Ivanovna, show us a trick!

LYUBOV ANDREYEVNA: Charlotta, show us a trick!

CHARLOTTA: No. I want to sleep. (*Goes out.*)

LOPAKHIN: In three weeks we'll meet again. (*Kisses Lyubov Andreyevna's hand.*) Good-bye till then. Time to go. (*To Gayev.*) Good-bye. (*Kisses Pishchik.*) Good-bye. (*Shakes hands with Varya, then with Firs and Yasha.*) I don't feel like going. (*To Lyubov Andreyevna.*) If you make up your mind about the summer cottages and come to a decision, let me know; I'll get you a loan of fifty thousand or so. Think it over seriously.

VARYA (*angrily*): Oh, why don't you go!

LOPAKHIN: I'm going, I'm going. (*Goes out.*)

GAYEV: Boor. Oh, pardon. Varya's going to marry him, he's Varya's young man.

VARYA: Uncle dear, you talk too much.

LYUBOV ANDREYEVNA: Well, Varya, I shall be very glad. He's a good man.

PISHCHIK: A man, I must truly say...most worthy.... And my Dashenka...says, too, that...says all sorts of things. (*Snores but wakes up at once.*) In any case, honored lady, oblige me...a loan of two hundred and forty rubles...tomorrow the interest on my mortgage is due....

VARYA (*in alarm*): We have nothing, nothing at all!

LYUBOV ANDREYEVNA: I really haven't any money.

PISHCHIK: It'll turn up. (*Laughs.*) I never lose hope. Just when I thought everything was lost, that I was done for, lo and behold—the railway line ran through my land...and they paid me for it. And before you know it, something else will turn up, if not today—tomorrow....Dashenka will win two hundred thousand... she's got a lottery ticket.

LYUBOV ANDREYEVNA: The coffee is finished, we can go to bed.

FIRS (*brushing Gayev's clothes, admonishingly*): You've put on the wrong trousers again. What am I to do with you?

VARYA (*softly*): Anya's asleep. (*Quietly opens the window.*) The sun has risen, it's no longer cold. Look, Mama dear, what wonderful trees! Oh, Lord, the air! The starlings are singing!

GAYEV (*opens another window*): The orchard is all white. You haven't forgotten, Lyuba? That long avenue there that runs straight—straight as a stretched-out strap;

it gleams on moonlight nights. Remember? You've not forgotten?

LYUBOV ANDREYEVNA (*looking out the window at the orchard*): Oh, my childhood, my innocence! I used to sleep in this nursery, I looked out from here into the orchard, happiness awoke with me each morning, it was just as it is now, nothing has changed. (*Laughing with joy.*) All, all white! Oh, my orchard! After the dark, rainy autumn and the cold winter, you are young again, full of happiness, the heavenly angels have not forsaken you.... If I could cast off this heavy stone weighing on my breast and shoulders, if I could forget my past!

GAYEV: Yes, and the orchard will be sold for our debts, strange as it may seem....

LYUBOV ANDREYEVNA: Look, our dead mother walks in the orchard...in a white dress! (*Laughs with joy.*) It is she!

GAYEV: Where?

VARYA: God be with you, Mama dear.

LYUBOV ANDREYEVNA: There's no one there, I just imagined it. To the right, as you turn to the summerhouse, a slender white sapling is bent over...it looks like a woman.

(*Enter Trofimov wearing a shabby student's uniform and spectacles.*)

LYUBOV ANDREYEVNA: What a wonderful orchard! The white masses of blossoms, the blue sky —

TROFIMOV: Lyubov Andreyevna! (*She looks around at him.*) I only want to pay my respects, then I'll go at once. (*Kisses her hand ardently.*) I was told to wait until morning, but I hadn't the patience.

(*Lyubov Andreyevna looks at him, puzzled.*)

VARYA (*through tears*): This is Petya Trofimov.

TROFIMOV: Petya Trofimov, I was Grisha's tutor.... Can I have changed so much?

(*Lyubov Andreyevna embraces him, quietly weeping.*)

GAYEV (*embarrassed*): There, there, Lyuba.

VARYA (*crying*): Didn't I tell you, Petya, to wait till tomorrow?

LYUBOV ANDREYEVNA: My Grisha...my little boy... Grisha...my son....

VARYA: What can we do, Mama dear? It's God's will.

TROFIMOV (*gently, through tears*): Don't, don't....

LYUBOV ANDREYEVNA (*quietly weeping*): My little boy dead, drowned.... Why? Why, my friend? (*In a lower voice.*) Anya is sleeping in there, and I'm talking loudly...making all this noise....But Petya, why do you look so bad? Why have you grown so old?

TROFIMOV: A peasant woman in the train called me a mangy gentleman.

LYUBOV ANDREYEVNA: You were just a boy then, a charming little student, and now your hair is thin — and spectacles! Is it possible you are still a student? (*Goes toward the door.*)

TROFIMOV: I shall probably be an eternal student.

LYUBOV ANDREYEVNA (*kisses her brother, then Varya*): Now, go to bed.... You've grown older too, Leonid.

PISHCHIK (*follows her*): Well, seems to be time to sleep....Oh, my gout! I'm staying the night. Lyubov Andreyevna, my soul, tomorrow morning...two hundred and forty rubles....

GAYEV: He keeps at it.

PISHCHIK: Two hundred and forty rubles...to pay the interest on my mortgage.

LYUBOV ANDREYEVNA: I have no money, my friend.

PISHCHIK: My dear, I'll pay it back....It's a trifling sum.

LYUBOV ANDREYEVNA: Well, all right, Leonid will give it to you....Give it to him, Leonid.

GAYEV: Me give it to him!...Hold out your pocket!

LYUBOV ANDREYEVNA: It can't be helped, give it to him.... He needs it.... He'll pay it back.

(*Lyubov Andreyevna, Trofimov, Pishchik, and Firs go out. Gayev, Varya, and Yasha remain.*)

GAYEV: My sister hasn't yet lost her habit of squandering money. (*To Yasha.*) Go away, my good fellow, you smell of the henhouse.

YASHA (*with a smirk*): And you, Leonid Andreyevich, are just the same as ever.

GAYEV: How's that? (*To Varya.*) What did he say?

VARYA: Your mother has come from the village; she's been sitting in the servants' room since yesterday, waiting to see you....

YASHA: Let her wait, for God's sake!

VARYA: Aren't you ashamed?

YASHA: A lot I need her! She could have come tomorrow. (*Goes out.*)

VARYA: Mama's the same as ever, she hasn't changed a bit. She'd give away everything, if she could.

GAYEV: Yes....(*A pause.*) If a great many remedies are suggested for a disease, it means that the disease is incurable. I keep thinking, racking my brains, I have many remedies, a great many, and that means in effect, that I have none. It would be good to receive a legacy from someone, good to marry our Anya to a very rich man, good to go to Yaroslav and try our luck with our aunt, the Countess. She is very, very rich, you know.

VARYA (*crying*): If only God would help us!

GAYEV: Stop bawling. Auntie's very rich, but she doesn't like us. In the first place, sister married a lawyer, not a nobleman...(*Anya appears in the doorway.*) She married beneath her, and it cannot be said that she has conducted herself very virtuously. She is good, kind, charming, and I love her dearly, but no matter how much you allow for extenuating circumstances, you must admit she leads a sinful life. You feel it in her slightest movement.

VARYA (*in a whisper*): Anya is standing in the doorway.

GAYEV: What? (*Pause.*) Funny, something got into my right eye...I can't see very well. And Thursday, when I was in the district court...

(*Anya enters.*)

VARYA: Why aren't you asleep, Anya?

ANYA: I can't get to sleep. I just can't.

GAYEV: My little one! (*Kisses Anya's face and hands.*) My child.... (*Through tears.*) You are not my niece, you are my angel, you are everything to me. Believe me, believe...

ANYA: I believe you, Uncle. Everyone loves you and respects you, but, Uncle dear, you must keep quiet, just keep quiet. What were you saying just now about my mother, about your own sister? What made you say that?

GAYEV: Yes, yes.... (*Covers his face with her hand.*) Really, it's awful! My God! God help me! And today I made a speech to the bookcase...so stupid! And it was only when I had finished that I realized it was stupid.

VARYA: It's true, Uncle dear, you ought to keep quiet. Just don't talk, that's all.

ANYA: If you could keep from talking, it would make things easier for you, too.

GAYEV: I'll be quiet. (*Kisses Anya's and Varya's hands.*) I'll be quiet. Only this is about business. On Thursday I was in the district court, well, a group of us gathered together and began talking about one thing and another, this and that, and it seems it might be possible to arrange a loan on a promissory note to pay the interest at the bank.

VARYA: If only God would help us!

GAYEV: On Tuesday I'll go and talk it over again. (*To Varya.*) Stop bawling. (*To Anya.*) Your mama will talk to Lopakhin; he, of course, will not refuse her.... And as soon as you've rested, you will go to Yaroslav to the Countess, your great-aunt. In that way we shall be working from three directions—and our business is in the hat. We'll pay the interest, I'm certain of it.... (*Puts a candy in his mouth.*) On my honor, I'll swear by anything you like, the estate shall not be sold. (*Excitedly.*) By my happiness, I swear it! Here's my hand on it, call me a worthless, dishonorable man if I let it come to auction! I swear by my whole being!

ANYA (*a calm mood returns to her, she is happy*): How good you are, Uncle, how clever! (*Embraces him.*) Now I am at peace! I'm at peace! I'm happy!

(*Enter Firs.*)

FIRS (*reproachfully*): Leonid Andreich, have you no fear of God? When are you going to bed?

GAYEV: Presently, presently. Go away, Firs. I'll...all right, I'll undress myself. Well, children, bye-bye.... Details tomorrow, and now go to sleep. (*Kisses Anya and Varya.*) I am a man of the eighties.... They don't think much of that period today, nevertheless, I can say that in the course of my life I have suffered not a little for my convictions. It is not for nothing that the peasant loves me. You have to know the peasant! You have to know from what—

ANYA: There you go again, Uncle!

VARYA: Uncle dear, do be quiet.

FIRS (*angrily*): Leonid Andreich!

GAYEV: I'm coming, I'm coming....Go to bed. A clean double rail shot to center table....(*Goes out; Firs hobbles after him.*)

ANYA: I'm at peace now. I would rather not go to Yaroslav, I don't like my great-aunt, but still, I'm at peace, thanks to Uncle. (*She sits down.*)

VARYA: We must get some sleep. I'm going now. Oh, something unpleasant happened while you were away. In the old servants' quarters, as you know, there are only the old people: Yefimushka, Polya, Yevstignei, and, of course, Karp. They began letting in all sorts of rogues to spend the night—I didn't say anything. But then I heard they'd been spreading a rumor that I'd given an order for them to be fed nothing but dried peas. Out of stinginess, you see.... It was all Yevstignei's doing.... Very well, I think, if that's how it is, you just wait. I send for Yevstignei... (*yawning*) he comes.... "How is it, Yevstignei," I say, "that you could be such a fool...." (*Looks at Anya.*) She's fallen asleep. (*Takes her by the arm.*) Come to your little bed.... Come along. (*Leading her.*) My little darling fell asleep. Come.... (*They go.*)

(*In the distance, beyond the orchard, a shepherd is playing on a reed pipe. Trofimov crosses the stage and, seeing Varya and Anya, stops.*)

VARYA: Sh! She's asleep...asleep.... Come along, darling.

ANYA (*softly, half-asleep*): I'm so tired.... Those bells... Uncle...dear...Mama and Uncle...

VARYA: Come, darling, come along. (*They go into Anya's room.*)

TROFIMOV (*deeply moved*): My sunshine! My spring!

ACT II

(*A meadow. An old, lopsided, long-abandoned little chapel; near it a well, large stones that apparently were once tombstones, and an old bench. A road to the Gayev manor house can be seen. On one side, where the cherry orchard begins, tall poplars loom. In the distance a row of telegraph poles, and far, far away, on the horizon, the faint outline of a large town, which is visible only in very fine, clear weather. The sun will soon set. Charlotta, Yasha, and Dunyasha are sitting on the bench; Yepikhodov stands near playing something sad on the guitar. They are all lost in thought. Charlotta wears an old forage cap; she has taken a gun from her shoulder and is adjusting the buckle on the sling.*)

CHARLOTTA (*reflectively*): I haven't got a real passport, I don't know how old I am, but it always seems to me that I'm quite young. When I was a little girl, my father and mother used to travel from one fair to another giving performances—very good ones. And I did the *salto mortale*° and all sorts of tricks. Then

salto mortale: Somersault.

when Papa and Mama died, a German lady took me to live with her and began teaching me. Good. I grew up and became a governess. But where I come from and who I am—I do not know.... Who my parents were—perhaps they weren't even married—I don't know. (*Takes a cucumber out of her pocket and eats it.*) I don't know anything. (*Pause.*) One wants so much to talk, but there isn't anyone to talk to...I have no one.

YEPIKHODOV (*plays the guitar and sings*): "What care I for the clamorous world, what's friend or foe to me?"...How pleasant it is to play a mandolin!

DUNYASHA: That's a guitar, not a mandolin. (*Looks at herself in a hand mirror and powders her face.*)

YEPIKHODOV: To a madman, in love, it is a mandolin.... (*Sings.*) "Would that the heart were warmed by the flame of requited love..."

(*Yasha joins in.*)

CHARLOTTA: How horribly these people sing!...Pfui! Like jackals!

DUNYASHA (*to Yasha*): Really, how fortunate to have been abroad!

YASHA: Yes, to be sure. I cannot but agree with you there. (*Yawns, then lights a cigar.*)

YEPIKHODOV: It stands to reason. Abroad everything has long since been fully constituted.

YASHA: Obviously.

YEPIKHODOV: I am a cultivated man, I read all sorts of remarkable books, but I am in no way able to make out my own inclinations, what it is I really want, whether, strictly speaking, to live or to shoot myself; nevertheless, I always carry a revolver on me. Here it is. (*Shows revolver.*)

CHARLOTTA: Finished. Now I'm going. (*Slings the gun over her shoulder.*) You're a very clever man, Yepikhodov, and quite terrifying; women must be mad about you. Brrr! (*Starts to go.*) These clever people are all so stupid, there's no one for me to talk to.... Alone, always alone, I have no one...and who I am, and why I am, nobody knows....(*Goes out unhurriedly.*)

YEPIKHODOV: Strictly speaking, all else aside, I must state regarding myself, that fate treats me unmercifully, as a storm does a small ship. If, let us assume, I am mistaken, then why, to mention a single instance, do I wake up this morning, and there on my chest see a spider of terrifying magnitude?...Like that. (*Indicates with both hands.*) And likewise, I take up some kvas to quench my thirst, and there see something in the highest degree unseemly, like a cockroach. (*Pause.*) Have you read Buckle?° (*Pause.*) If I may trouble you, Avdotya Fyodorovna, I should like to have a word or two with you.

Buckle: Thomas Henry Buckle (1821–1862) was a radical historian who formulated a scientific basis for history emphasizing the interrelationship of climate, food production, population, and wealth.

DUNYASHA: Go ahead.

YEPIKHODOV: I prefer to speak with you alone.... (*Sighs.*)

DUNYASHA (*embarrassed*): Very well...only first bring me my little cape...you'll find it by the cupboard.... It's rather damp here....

YEPIKHODOV: Certainly, ma'am...I'll fetch it, ma'am.... Now I know what to do with my revolver....(*Takes the guitar and goes off playing it.*)

YASHA: Two-and-twenty Troubles! Between ourselves, a stupid fellow. (*Yawns.*)

DUNYASHA: God forbid that he should shoot himself. (*Pause.*) I've grown so anxious, I'm always worried. I was only a little girl when I was taken into the master's house, and now I'm quite unused to the simple life, and my hands are white as can be, just like a lady's. I've become so delicate, so tender and ladylike, I'm afraid of everything....Frightfully so. And, Yasha, if you deceive me, I just don't know what will become of my nerves.

YASHA (*kisses her*): You little cucumber! Of course, a girl should never forget herself. What I dislike above everything is when a girl doesn't conduct herself properly.

DUNYASHA: I'm passionately in love with you, you're educated, you can discuss anything. (*Pause.*)

YASHA (*yawns*): Yes....As I see it, it's like this: If a girl loves somebody, that means she's immoral. (*Pause.*) Very pleasant smoking a cigar in the open air....(*Listens.*) Someone's coming this way....It's the masters. (*Dunyasha impulsively embraces him.*) You go home, as if you'd been to the river to bathe; take that path, otherwise they'll see you and suspect me of having a rendezvous with you. I can't endure that sort of thing.

DUNYASHA (*with a little cough*): My head is beginning to ache from your cigar....(*Goes out.*)

(*Yasha remains, sitting near the chapel. Lyubov Andreyevna, Gayev, and Lopakhin enter.*)

LOPAKHIN: You must make up your mind once and for all—time won't stand still. The question, after all, is quite simple. Do you agree to lease the land for summer cottages or not? Answer in one word: Yes or no? Only one word!

LYUBOV ANDREYEVNA: Who is it that smokes those disgusting cigars out here? (*Sits down.*)

GAYEV: Now that the railway line is so near, it's made things convenient. (*Sits down.*) We went to town and had lunch...cue ball to the center! I feel like going to the house first and playing a game.

LYUBOV ANDREYEVNA: Later.

LOPAKHIN: Just one word! (*Imploringly.*) Do give me an answer!

GAYEV (*yawning*): How's that?

LYUBOV ANDREYEVNA (*looks into her purse*): Yesterday I had a lot of money, and today there's hardly any left. My poor Varya tries to economize by feeding everyone milk soup, and in the kitchen the old people get nothing but dried peas, while I squander money

Laila Robins, Edmond Genest, and Alison Weller in the Shakespeare Theatre of New Jersey's 2006 production of *The Cherry Orchard*, which included a set with trees in bloom.

foolishly.... (*Drops the purse, scattering gold coins.*) There they go.... (*Vexed.*)

YASHA: Allow me, I'll pick them up in an instant. (*Picks up the money.*)

LYUBOV ANDREYEVNA: Please do, Yasha. And why did I go to town for lunch?...That miserable restaurant of yours with its music, and tablecloths smelling of soap.... Why drink so much, Lyonya? Why eat so much? Why talk so much? Today in the restaurant again you talked too much, and it was all so pointless. About the seventies, about the decadents. And to whom? Talking to waiters about the decadents!

LOPAKHIN: Yes.

GAYEV (*waving his hand*): I'm incorrigible, that's evident.... (*Irritably to Yasha.*) Why do you keep twirling about in front of me?

YASHA (*laughs*): I can't help laughing when I hear your voice.

GAYEV (*to his sister*): Either he or I —

LYUBOV ANDREYEVNA: Go away, Yasha, run along.

YASHA (*hands Lyubov Andreyevna her purse*): I'm going, right away. (*Hardly able to contain his laughter.*) This very instant.... (*Goes out.*)

LOPAKHIN: That rich man, Deriganov, is prepared to buy the estate. They say he's coming to the auction himself.

LYUBOV ANDREYEVNA: Where did you hear that?

LOPAKHIN: That's what they're saying in town.

LYUBOV ANDREYEVNA: Our aunt in Yaroslav promised to send us something, but when and how much, no one knows.

LOPAKHIN: How much do you think she'll send? A hundred thousand? Two hundred?

LYUBOV ANDREYEVNA: Oh...ten or fifteen thousand, and we'll be thankful for that.

LOPAKHIN: Forgive me, but I have never seen such frivolous, such queer, unbusinesslike people as you, my friends. You are told in plain language that your estate is to be sold, and it's as though you don't understand it.

LYUBOV ANDREYEVNA: But what are we to do? Tell us what to do.

LOPAKHIN: I tell you every day. Every day I say the same thing. Both the cherry orchard and the land must be leased for summer cottages, and it must be done now, as quickly as possible—the auction is close at hand. Try to understand! Once you definitely decide on the cottages, you can raise as much money as you like, and then you are saved.

LYUBOV ANDREYEVNA: Cottages, summer people—forgive me, but it's so vulgar.

GAYEV: I agree with you, absolutely.

LOPAKHIN: I'll either burst into tears, start shouting, or fall into a faint! I can't stand it! You've worn me out! (*To Gayev.*) You're an old woman!

GAYEV: How's that?

LOPAKHIN: An old woman! (*Starts to go.*)

LYUBOV ANDREYEVNA (*alarmed*): No, don't go, stay, my dear. I beg you. Perhaps we'll think of something!

LOPAKHIN: What is there to think of?

LYUBOV ANDREYEVNA: Don't go away, please. With you here it's more cheerful somehow.... (*Pause.*) I keep

ABOVE: The spare set in Ron Daniels's 1993 production of *The Cherry Orchard* at the American Repertory Theatre highlights the characters' emotional isolation. RIGHT: Claire Bloom as Madame Ranevskaya.

expecting something to happen, like the house caving in on us.

GAYEV (*in deep thought*): Double rail shot into the corner.... Cross table to the center....

LYUBOV ANDREYEVNA: We have sinned so much....

LOPAKHIN: What sins could you have —

GAYEV (*puts a candy into his mouth*): They say I've eaten up my entire fortune in candies.... (*Laughs.*)

LYUBOV ANDREYEVNA: Oh, my sins.... I've always squandered money recklessly, like a madwoman, and I married a man who did nothing but amass debts. My husband died from champagne — he drank terribly —

then, to my sorrow, I fell in love with another man, lived with him, and just at that time — that was my first punishment, a blow on the head — my little boy was drowned...here in the river. And I went abroad, went away for good, never to return, never to see this river.... I closed my eyes and ran, beside myself, and *he* after me...callously, without pity. I bought a villa near Mentone, because he fell ill there, and for three years I had no rest, day or night. The sick man wore me out, my soul dried up. Then last year, when the villa was sold to pay my debts, I went to Paris, and there he stripped me of everything, and left me for another woman; I tried to poison myself.... So stupid, so shameful.... And suddenly I felt a longing for Russia, for my own country, for my little girl.... (*Wipes away her tears.*) Lord, Lord, be merciful, forgive my sins! Don't punish me anymore! (*Takes a telegram out of her pocket.*) This came today from Paris.... He asks my forgiveness, begs me to return.... (*Tears up telegram.*) Do I hear music? (*Listens.*)

GAYEV: That's our famous Jewish band. You remember, four violins, a flute, and double bass.

LYUBOV ANDREYEVNA: It's still in existence? We ought to send for them sometime and give a party.

LOPAKHIN (*listens*): I don't hear anything.... (*Sings softly.*) "The Germans, for pay, will turn Russians into Frenchmen, they say." (*Laughs.*) What a play I saw yesterday at the theater—very funny!

LYUBOV ANDREYEVNA: There was probably nothing funny about it. Instead of going to see plays you ought to look at yourselves a little more often. How drab your lives are, how full of futile talk!

LOPAKHIN: That's true. I must say, this life of ours is stupid.... (*Pause.*) My father was a peasant, an idiot; he understood nothing, taught me nothing; all he did was beat me when he was drunk, and always with a stick. As a matter of fact, I'm as big a blockhead and idiot as he was. I never learned anything, my handwriting's disgusting, I write like a pig—I'm ashamed to have people see it.

LYUBOV ANDREYEVNA: You ought to get married, my friend.

LOPAKHIN: Yes... that's true.

LYUBOV ANDREYEVNA: To our Varya. She's a nice girl.

LOPAKHIN: Yes.

LYUBOV ANDREYEVNA: She's a girl who comes from simple people, works all day long, but the main thing is she loves you. Besides, you've liked her for a long time now.

LOPAKHIN: Well? I've nothing against it.... She's a good girl. (*Pause.*)

GAYEV: I've been offered a place in the bank. Six thousand a year.... Have you heard?

LYUBOV ANDREYEVNA: How could you! You stay where you are....

(*Firs enters carrying an overcoat.*)

FIRS (*to Gayev*): If you please, sir, put this on, it's damp.

GAYEV (*puts on the overcoat*): You're a pest, old man.

FIRS: Never mind.... You went off this morning without telling me. (*Looks him over.*)

LYUBOV ANDREYEVNA: How you have aged, Firs!

FIRS: What do you wish, madam?

LOPAKHIN: She says you've grown very old!

FIRS: I've lived a long time. They were arranging a marriage for me before your papa was born.... (*Laughs.*) I was already head footman when the emancipation came. At that time I wouldn't consent to my freedom, I stayed with the masters.... (*Pause.*) I remember, everyone was happy, but what they were happy about, they themselves didn't know.

LOPAKHIN: It was better in the old days. At least they flogged them.

FIRS (*not hearing*): Of course. The peasants kept to the masters, the masters kept to the peasants; but now they have all gone their own ways, you can't tell about anything.

GAYEV: Be quiet, Firs. Tomorrow I must go to town. I've been promised an introduction to a certain general who might let us have a loan.

LOPAKHIN: Nothing will come of it. And you can rest assured, you won't even pay the interest.

LYUBOV ANDREYEVNA: He's raving. There is no such general.

(*Enter Trofimov, Anya, and Varya.*)

GAYEV: Here come our young people.

ANYA: There's Mama.

LYUBOV ANDREYEVNA (*tenderly*): Come, come along, my darlings. (*Embraces Anya and Varya.*) If you only knew how I love you both! Sit here beside me—there, like that.

(*They all sit down.*)

LOPAKHIN: Our eternal student is always with the young ladies.

TROFIMOV: That's none of your business.

LOPAKHIN: He'll soon be fifty, but he's still a student.

TROFIMOV: Drop your stupid jokes.

LOPAKHIN: What are you so angry about, you queer fellow?

TROFIMOV: Just leave me alone.

LOPAKHIN (*laughs*): Let me ask you something: What do you make of me?

TROFIMOV: My idea of you, Yermolai Alekseich, is this: You're a rich man, you will soon be a millionaire. Just as the beast of prey, which devours everything that crosses its path, is necessary in the metabolic process, so are you necessary.

(*Everyone laughs.*)

VARYA: Petya, you'd better tell us something about the planets.

LYUBOV ANDREYEVNA: No, let's go on with yesterday's conversation.

TROFIMOV: What was it about?

GAYEV: About the proud man.

TROFIMOV: We talked a long time yesterday, but we didn't get anywhere. In the proud man, in your sense of the word, there's something mystical. And you may be right from your point of view, but if you look at it simply, without being abstruse, why even talk about pride? Is there any sense in it if, physiologically, man is poorly constructed, if, in the vast majority of cases, he is coarse, ignorant, and profoundly unhappy? We should stop admiring ourselves. We should just work, and that's all.

GAYEV: You die, anyway.

TROFIMOV: Who knows? And what does it mean—to die? It may be that man has a hundred senses, and at his death only the five that are known to us perish, and the other ninety-five go on living.

LYUBOV ANDREYEVNA: How clever you are, Petya!

LOPAKHIN (*ironically*): Terribly clever!

TROFIMOV: Mankind goes forward, perfecting its powers. Everything that is now unattainable will some day be comprehensible and within our grasp, only we must work, and help with all our might those who are seeking the truth. So far, among us here in Russia, only a very few work. The great majority of the intelligentsia that I know seek nothing, do nothing, and as yet are incapable of work. They call themselves the intelligentsia, yet they belittle their servants, treat the peasants like animals, are wretched students, never read anything serious, and do absolutely nothing; they only talk about science and know very little about art. They all look serious, have grim expressions, speak of weighty matters, and philosophize; and meanwhile anyone can see that the workers eat abominably, sleep without pillows, thirty or forty to a room, and everywhere there are bedbugs, stench, dampness, and immorality.... It's obvious that all our fine talk is merely to delude ourselves and others. Show me the day nurseries they are always talking about—and where are the reading rooms? They only write about them in novels, but in reality they don't exist. There is nothing but filth, vulgarity, asiaticism.°... I'm afraid of those very serious countenances, I don't like them, I'm afraid of serious conversations. We'd do better to remain silent.

LOPAKHIN: You know, I get up before five in the morning, and I work from morning to night; now, I'm always handling money, my own and other people's, and I see what people around me are like. You have only to start doing something to find out how few honest, decent people there are. Sometimes, when I can't sleep, I think: "Lord, Thou gavest us vast forests, boundless fields, broad horizons, and living in their midst we ourselves ought truly to be giants...."

LYUBOV ANDREYEVNA: Now you want giants! They're good only in fairy tales, otherwise they're frightening.

(*Yepikhodov crosses at the rear of the stage, playing the guitar.*)

LYUBOV ANDREYEVNA (*pensively*): There goes Yepikhodov...

ANYA (*pensively*): There goes Yepikhodov...

GAYEV: The sun has set, ladies and gentlemen.

TROFIMOV: Yes.

GAYEV (*in a low voice, as though reciting*): Oh, Nature, wondrous Nature, you shine with eternal radiance, beautiful and indifferent; you, whom we call mother, unite within yourself both life and death, giving life and taking it away....

asiaticism: Trofimov, expressing a common prejudice of the time, refers to Asian apathy.

VARYA (*beseechingly*): Uncle dear!

ANYA: Uncle, you're doing it again!

TROFIMOV: You'd better cue ball into the center.

GAYEV: I'll be silent, silent.

(*All sit lost in thought. The silence is broken only by the subdued muttering of Firs. Suddenly a distant sound is heard, as if from the sky, like the sound of a snapped string mournfully dying away.*)

LYUBOV ANDREYEVNA: What was that?

LOPAKHIN: I don't know. Somewhere far off in a mine shaft a bucket's broken loose. But somewhere very far away.

GAYEV: It might be a bird of some sort...like a heron.

TROFIMOV: Or an owl...

LYUBOV ANDREYEVNA (*shudders*): It's unpleasant somehow.... (*Pause.*)

FIRS: The same thing happened before the troubles: An owl hooted and the samovar hissed continually.

GAYEV: Before what troubles?

FIRS: Before the emancipation.

LYUBOV ANDREYEVNA: Come along, my friends, let us go, evening is falling. (*To Anya.*) There are tears in your eyes—what is it, my little one?

(*Embraces her.*)

ANYA: It's all right, Mama. It's nothing.

TROFIMOV: Someone is coming.

(*A Stranger appears wearing a shabby white forage cap and an overcoat. He is slightly drunk.*)

STRANGER: Permit me to inquire, can I go straight through here to the station?

GAYEV: You can. Follow the road.

STRANGER: I am deeply grateful to you. (*Coughs.*) Splendid weather.... (*Reciting.*) "My brother, my suffering brother...come to the Volga, whose groans"...(*To Varya.*) Mademoiselle, will you oblige a hungry Russian with thirty kopecks?

(*Varya, frightened, cries out.*)

LOPAKHIN (*angrily*): There's a limit to everything.

LYUBOV ANDREYEVNA (*panic-stricken*): Here you are—take this....(*Fumbles in her purse.*) I have no silver.... Never mind, here's a gold piece for you....

STRANGER: I am deeply grateful to you. (*Goes off.*)

(*Laughter.*)

VARYA (*frightened*): I'm leaving...I'm leaving.... Oh, Mama, dear, there's nothing in the house for the servants to eat, and you give him a gold piece!

LYUBOV ANDREYEVNA: What's to be done with such a silly creature? When we get home I'll give you all I've got. Yermolai Alekseyevich, you'll lend me some more!

LOPAKHIN: At your service.

LYUBOV ANDREYEVNA: Come, my friends, it's time to go. Oh, Varya, we have definitely made a match for you. Congratulations!

VARYA (*through tears*): Mama, that's not something to joke about.

LOPAKHIN: "Aurelia, get thee to a nunnery..."°

GAYEV: Look, my hands are trembling: It's a long time since I've played a game of billiards.

LOPAKHIN: "Aurelia, O Nymph, in thy orisons, be all my sins remember'd!"

LYUBOV ANDREYEVNA: Let us go, my friends, it will soon be suppertime.

VARYA: He frightened me. My heart is simply pounding.

LOPAKHIN: Let me remind you, ladies and gentlemen: On the twenty-second of August the cherry orchard is to be sold. Think about that!—Think!

(*All go out except Trofimov and Anya.*)

ANYA (*laughs*): My thanks to the stranger for frightening Varya, now we are alone.

TROFIMOV: Varya is so afraid we might suddenly fall in love with each other that she hasn't left us alone for days. With her narrow mind she can't understand that we are above love. To avoid the petty and the illusory, which prevent our being free and happy— that is the aim and meaning of life. Forward! We are moving irresistibly toward the bright star that burns in the distance! Forward! Do not fall behind, friends!

ANYA (*clasping her hands*): How well you talk! (*Pause.*) It's marvelous here today!

TROFIMOV: Yes, the weather is wonderful.

ANYA: What have you done to me, Petya, that I no longer love the cherry orchard as I used to? I loved it so tenderly, it seemed to me there was no better place on earth than our orchard.

TROFIMOV: All Russia is our orchard. It is a great and beautiful land, and there are many wonderful places in it. (*Pause.*) Just think, Anya: Your grandfather, your great-grandfather, and all your ancestors were serf-owners, possessors of living souls. Don't you see that from every cherry tree, from every leaf and trunk, human beings are peering out at you? Don't you hear their voices? To possess living souls—that has corrupted all of you, those who lived before and you who are living now, so that your mother, you, your uncle, no longer perceive that you are living in debt, at someone else's expense, at the expense of those whom you wouldn't allow to cross your threshold.... We are at least two hundred years behind the times, we have as yet absolutely nothing, we have no definite attitude toward the past, we only philosophize, complain of boredom, or drink vodka. Yet it's quite clear that to begin to live we must first atone for the past, be done with it, and we can atone for it only by suffering, only by extraordinary, unceasing labor. Understand this, Anya.

ANYA: The house we live in hasn't really been ours for a long time, and I shall leave it, I give you my word.

TROFIMOV: If you have the keys of the household, throw them into the well and go. Be as free as the wind.

ANYA (*in ecstasy*): How well you put that!

TROFIMOV: Believe me, Anya, believe me! I am not yet thirty, I am young, still a student, but I have already been through so much! As soon as winter comes, I am hungry, sick, worried, poor as a beggar, and— where has not fate driven me! Where have I not been? And yet always, every minute of the day and night, my soul was filled with inexplicable premonitions. I have a premonition of happiness, Anya, I can see it...

ANYA: The moon is rising.

(*Yepikhodov is heard playing the same melancholy song on the guitar. The moon rises. Somewhere near the poplars Varya is looking for Anya and calling: "Anya, where are you?"*)

TROFIMOV: Yes, the moon is rising. (*Pause.*) There it is— happiness...it's coming, nearer and nearer, I can hear its footsteps. And if we do not see it, if we do not recognize it, what does it matter? Others will see it.

VARYA'S VOICE: Anya! Where are you?

TROFIMOV: That Varya again! (*Angrily.*) It's revolting!

ANYA: Well? Let's go down to the river. It's lovely there.

TROFIMOV: Come on. (*They go.*)

VARYA'S VOICE: Anya! Anya!

ACT III

(*The drawing room, separated by an arch from the ballroom. The chandelier is lighted. The Jewish band that was mentioned in act II is heard playing in the hall. It is evening. In the ballroom they are dancing a grand rond. The voice of Semyonov-Pishchik: "Promenade à une paire!"° They all enter the drawing room: Pishchik and Charlotta Ivanovna are the first couple, Trofimov and Lyubov Andreyevna the second, Anya and the Post-Office Clerk the third, Varya and the Stationmaster the fourth, etc. Varya, quietly weeping, dries her tears as she dances. Dunyasha is in the last couple. As they cross the drawing room Pishchik calls: "Grand rond, balancez!" and "Les cavaliers à genoux et remerciez vos dames!"° Firs, wearing a dress coat, brings in a tray with seltzer water. Pishchik and Trofimov come into the drawing room.*)

PISHCHIK: I'm a full-blooded man, I've already had two strokes, and dancing's hard work for me, but as they say, "If you run with the pack, you can bark or not, but at least wag your tail." At that, I'm as strong as a horse. My late father—quite a joker he was, God rest his soul—used to say, talking about our origins, that the ancient line of Semyonov-Pishchik was descended from the very horse that Caligula had

---

"**Aurelia...nunnery**": From Hamlet's famous line rejecting Ophelia (Lopakhin's next line is also from Shakespeare's *Hamlet*).

"***Promenade à une paire!***": French for "Walk in pairs!"
"***Grand rond...dames!***": Instructions in the dance: "Large circle!" and "Gentlemen, kneel down and thank your ladies!"

seated in the Senate.° ... (*Sits down.*) But the trouble is—no money! A hungry dog believes in nothing but meat.... (*Snores but wakes up at once.*) It's the same with me—I can think of nothing but money....

TROFIMOV: You know, there really is something equine about your figure.

PISHCHIK: Well, a horse is a fine animal.... You can sell a horse.

(*There is the sound of a billiard game in the next room. Varya appears in the archway.*)

TROFIMOV (*teasing her*): Madame Lopakhina! Madame Lopakhina!

VARYA (*angrily*): Mangy gentleman!

TROFIMOV: Yes, I am a mangy gentleman, and proud of it!

VARYA (*reflecting bitterly*): Here we've hired musicians, and what are we going to pay them with? (*Goes out.*)

TROFIMOV (*to Pishchik*): If the energy you have expended in the course of your life trying to find money to pay interest had gone into something else, ultimately, you might very well have turned the world upside down.

PISHCHIK: Nietzsche...the philosopher...the greatest, most renowned...a man of tremendous intellect... says in his works that it is possible to forge banknotes.

TROFIMOV: And have you read Nietzsche?

PISHCHIK: Well...Dashenka told me. I'm in such a state now that I'm just about ready for forging.... The day after tomorrow I have to pay three hundred and ten rubles...I've got a hundred and thirty.... (*Feels in his pocket, grows alarmed.*) The money is gone! I've lost the money! (*Tearfully.*) Where is my money? (*Joyfully.*) Here it is, inside the lining.... I'm all in a sweat....

(*Lyubov Andreyevna and Charlotta Ivanovna come in.*)

LYUBOV ANDREYEVNA (*humming a* Lezginka):° Why does Leonid take so long? What is he doing in town? (*To Dunyasha.*) Dunyasha, offer the musicians some tea.

TROFIMOV: In all probability, the auction didn't take place.

LYUBOV ANDREYEVNA: It was the wrong time to have the musicians, the wrong time to give a dance.... Well, never mind.... (*Sits down and hums softly.*)

CHARLOTTA (*gives Pishchik a deck of cards*): Here's a deck of cards for you. Think of a card.

PISHCHIK: I've thought of one.

CHARLOTTA: Now shuffle the pack. Very good. And now, my dear Mr. Pishchik, hand it to me. *Eins, zwei, drei!*° Now look for it—it's in your side pocket.

PISHCHIK (*takes the card out of his side pocket*): The eight of spades—absolutely right! (*Amazed.*) Think of that, now!

CHARLOTTA (*holding the deck of cards in the palm of her hand, to Trofimov*): Quickly, tell me, which card is on top?

TROFIMOV: What? Well, the queen of spades.

CHARLOTTA: Right! (*To Pishchik.*) Now which card is on top?

PISHCHIK: The ace of hearts.

CHARLOTTA: Right! (*Claps her hands and the deck of cards disappears.*) What lovely weather we're having today! (*A mysterious feminine voice, which seems to come from under the floor, answers her: "Oh, yes, splendid weather, madam."*) You are so nice, you're my ideal.... (*The voice: "And I'm very fond of you, too, madam."*)

STATIONMASTER (*applauding*): Bravo, Madame Ventriloquist!

PISHCHIK (*amazed*): Think of that, now! Most enchanting Charlotta Ivanovna...I am simply in love with you....

CHARLOTTA: In love? (*Shrugs her shoulders.*) Is it possible that you can love? *Guter Mensch, aber schlechter Musikant.*°

TROFIMOV (*claps Pishchik on the shoulder*): You old horse, you!

CHARLOTTA: Attention, please! One more trick. (*Takes a lap robe from a chair.*) Here's a very fine lap robe; I should like to sell it. (*Shakes it out.*) Doesn't anyone want to buy it?

PISHCHIK (*amazed*): Think of that, now!

CHARLOTTA: *Eins, zwei, drei!* (*Quickly raises the lap robe, behind it stands Anya, who curtsies, runs to her mother, embraces her, and runs back into the ballroom amid the general enthusiasm.*)

LYUBOV ANDREYEVNA (*applauding*): Bravo, bravo!

CHARLOTTA: Once again! *Eins, zwei, drei.* (*Raises the lap robe; behind it stands Varya, who bows.*)

PISHCHIK (*amazed*): Think of that, now!

CHARLOTTA: The end! (*Throws the robe at Pishchik, makes a curtsy, and runs out of the room.*)

PISHCHIK (*hurries after her*): The minx!... What a woman! What a woman! (*Goes out.*)

LYUBOV ANDREYEVNA: And Leonid still not here. What he is doing in town so long, I do not understand! It must be all over by now. Either the estate is sold, or the auction didn't take place—but why keep us in suspense so long!

VARYA (*trying to comfort her*): Uncle has bought it, I am certain of that.

TROFIMOV (*mockingly*): Yes.

VARYA: Great-aunt sent him power of attorney to buy it in her name and transfer the debt. She's doing it for Anya's sake. And I am sure, with God's help, Uncle will buy it.

LYUBOV ANDREYEVNA: Our great-aunt in Yaroslav sent fifteen thousand to buy the estate in her name—she doesn't trust us—but that's not even enough to pay the interest. (*Covers her face with her hands.*) Today my fate will be decided, my fate...

TROFIMOV (*teasing Varya*): Madame Lopakhina!

Caligula...Senate: Caligula (CE 12–41), a cavalry soldier, was Roman emperor (CE 37–41).
Lezginka: A lively Russian tune for a dance. *Eins, zwei, drei!*: "One, two, three" (German).

Guter Mensch, aber schlechter Musikant: "Good man, but poor musician" (German).

VARYA (*angrily*): Eternal student! Twice already you've been expelled from the university.

LYUBOV ANDREYEVNA: Why are you so cross, Varya? If he teases you about Lopakhin, what of it? Go ahead and marry Lopakhin if you want to. He's a nice man, he's interesting. And if you don't want to, don't. Nobody's forcing you, my pet.

VARYA: To be frank, Mama dear, I regard this matter seriously. He is a good man, I like him.

LYUBOV ANDREYEVNA: Then marry him. I don't know what you're waiting for!

VARYA: Mama, I can't propose to him myself. For the last two years everyone's been talking to me about him; everyone talks, but he is either silent or he jokes. I understand. He's getting rich, he's absorbed in business, he has no time for me. If I had some money, no matter how little, if it were only a hundred rubles, I'd drop everything and go far away. I'd go into a nunnery.

TROFIMOV: A blessing!

VARYA (*to Trofimov*): A student ought to be intelligent! (*In a gentle tone, tearfully.*) How homely you have grown, Petya, how old! (*To Lyubov Andreyevna, no longer crying.*) It's just that I cannot live without work, Mama. I must be doing something every minute.

(*Yasha enters.*)

YASHA (*barely able to suppress his laughter*): Yepikhodov has broken a billiard cue! (*Goes out.*)

VARYA: But why is Yepikhodov here? Who gave him permission to play billiards? I don't understand these people....(*Goes out.*)

LYUBOV ANDREYEVNA: Don't tease her, Petya. You can see she's unhappy enough without that.

TROFIMOV: She's much too zealous, always meddling in other people's affairs. All summer long she's given Anya and me no peace—afraid a romance might develop. What business is it of hers? Besides, I've given no occasion for it, I am far removed from such banality. We are above love!

LYUBOV ANDREYEVNA: And I suppose I am beneath love. (*In great agitation.*) Why isn't Leonid here? If only I knew whether the estate had been sold or not! The disaster seems to me so incredible that I don't even know what to think, I'm lost....I could scream this very instant...I could do something foolish. Save me, Petya. Talk to me, say something....

TROFIMOV: Whether or not the estate is sold today— does it really matter? That's all done with long ago; there's no turning back, the path is overgrown. Be calm, my dear. One must not deceive oneself; at least once in one's life one ought to look the truth straight in the eye.

LYUBOV ANDREYEVNA: What truth? You can see where there is truth and where there isn't, but I seem to have lost my sight, I see nothing. You boldly settle all the important problems, but tell me, my dear boy, isn't it because you are young and have not yet had to suffer for a single one of your problems? You boldly look ahead, but isn't it because you neither see nor expect anything dreadful, since life is still hidden from your young eyes? You're bolder, more honest, deeper than we are, but think about it, be just a little bit magnanimous, and spare me. You see, I was born here, my mother and father lived here, and my grandfather. I love this house, without the cherry orchard my life has no meaning for me, and if it must be sold, then sell me with the orchard....(*Embraces Trofimov and kisses him on the forehead.*) And my son was drowned here....(*Weeps.*) Have pity on me, you good, kind man.

TROFIMOV: You know I feel for you with all my heart.

LYUBOV ANDREYEVNA: But that should have been said differently, quite differently....(*Takes out her handkerchief and a telegram falls to the floor.*) My heart is heavy today, you can't imagine. It's so noisy here, my soul quivers at every sound, I tremble all over, and yet I can't go to my room. When I am alone the silence frightens me. Don't condemn me, Petya...I love you as if you were my own. I would gladly let you marry Anya, I swear it, only you must study, my dear, you must get your degree. You do nothing, fate simply tosses you from place to place—it's so strange....Isn't that true? Isn't it? And you must do something about your beard, to make it grow somehow....(*Laughs.*) You're so funny!

TROFIMOV (*picks up the telegram*): I have no desire to be an Adonis.°

LYUBOV ANDREYEVNA: That's a telegram from Paris. I get them every day. One yesterday, one today. That wild man has fallen ill again, he's in trouble again.... He begs my forgiveness, implores me to come, and really, I ought to go to Paris to be near him. Your face is stern, Petya, but what can one do, my dear? What am I to do? He is ill, he's alone and unhappy, and who will look after him there, who will keep him from making mistakes, who will give him his medicine on time? And why hide it or keep silent, I love him, that's clear. I love him, love him....It's a millstone round my neck, I'm sinking to the bottom with it, but I love that stone, I cannot live without it. (*Presses Trofimov's hand.*) Don't think badly of me, Petya, and don't say anything to me, don't say anything....

TROFIMOV (*through tears*): For God's sake, forgive my frankness: You know that he robbed you!

LYUBOV ANDREYEVNA: No, no, no, you mustn't say such things! (*Covers her ears.*)

TROFIMOV: But he's a scoundrel! You're the only one who doesn't know it! He's a petty scoundrel, a nonentity —

LYUBOV ANDREYEVNA (*angry, but controlling herself*): You are twenty-six or twenty-seven years old, but you're still a schoolboy!

TROFIMOV: That may be!

LYUBOV ANDREYEVNA: You should be a man, at your age you ought to understand those who love. And you ought to be in love yourself. (*Angrily.*) Yes, yes!

Adonis: From Greek myth, a beautiful young man.

It's not purity with you, it's simply prudery, you're a ridiculous crank, a freak —

TROFIMOV (*horrified*): What is she saying!

LYUBOV ANDREYEVNA: I am above love! You're not above love, you're just an addlepate, as Firs would say. Not to have a mistress at your age!

TROFIMOV (*in horror*): This is awful! What is she saying!…(*Goes quickly toward the ballroom.*) This is awful…I can't…I won't stay here.…(*Goes out, but immediately returns.*) All is over between us! (*Goes out to the hall.*)

LYUBOV ANDREYEVNA (*calls after him*): Petya, wait! You absurd creature, I was joking! Petya!

(*In the hall there is the sound of someone running quickly downstairs and suddenly falling with a crash. Anya and Varya scream, but a moment later laughter is heard.*)

LYUBOV ANDREYEVNA: What was that?

(*Anya runs in.*)

ANYA (*laughing*): Petya fell down the stairs! (*Runs out.*)

LYUBOV ANDREYEVNA: What a funny boy that Petya is!

(*The Stationmaster stands in the middle of the ballroom and recites A. Tolstoy's° "The Sinner." Everyone listens to him, but he has no sooner spoken a few lines than the sound of a waltz is heard from the hall and the recitation is broken off. They all dance. Trofimov, Anya, Varya, and Lyubov Andreyevna come in from the hall.*)

LYUBOV ANDREYEVNA: Come, Petya…come, you pure soul…please, forgive me.… Let's dance.… (*They dance.*)

(*Anya and Varya dance. Firs comes in, puts his stick by the side door. Yasha also comes into the drawing room and watches the dancers.*)

YASHA: What is it, grandpa?

FIRS: I don't feel well. In the old days, we used to have generals, barons, admirals, dancing at our balls, but now we send for the post office clerk and the stationmaster, and even they are none too eager to come. Somehow I've grown weak. The late master, their grandfather, dosed everyone with sealing wax, no matter what ailed them. I've been taking sealing wax every day for twenty years or more, maybe that's what's kept me alive.

YASHA: You bore me, grandpa. (*Yawns.*) High time you croaked.

FIRS: Ah, you…addlepate! (*Mumbles.*)

(*Trofimov and Lyubov Andreyevna dance from the ballroom into the drawing room.*)

LYUBOV ANDREYEVNA: *Merci.* I'll sit down a while. (*Sits.*) I'm tired.

(*Anya comes in.*)

A. Tolstoy: Aleksey Konstantinovich Tolstoy (1817–1875), Russian novelist, dramatist, and poet.

ANYA (*excitedly*): There was a man in the kitchen just now saying that the cherry orchard was sold today.

LYUBOV ANDREYEVNA: Sold to whom?

ANYA: He didn't say. He's gone. (*Dances with Trofimov; they go into the ballroom.*)

YASHA: That was just some old man babbling. A stranger.

FIRS: Leonid Andreich is not back yet, still hasn't come. And he's wearing the light, between-seasons overcoat; like enough he'll catch cold. Ah, when they're young they're green.

LYUBOV ANDREYEVNA: This is killing me. Yasha, go and find out who it was sold to.

YASHA: But that old man left long ago. (*Laughs.*)

LYUBOV ANDREYEVNA (*slightly annoyed*): Well, what are you laughing at? What are you so happy about?

YASHA: That Yepikhodov is very funny! Hopeless! Two-and-twenty Troubles.

LYUBOV ANDREYEVNA: Firs, if the estate is sold, where will you go?

FIRS: Wherever you tell me to go, I'll go.

LYUBOV ANDREYEVNA: Why do you look like that? Aren't you well? You ought to go to bed.

FIRS: Yes.…(*With a smirk.*) Go to bed, and without me who will serve, who will see to things? I'm the only one in the whole house.

YASHA (*to Lyubov Andreyevna*): Lyubov Andreyevna! Permit me to make a request, be so kind! If you go back to Paris again, do me the favor of taking me with you. It is positively impossible for me to stay here. (*Looking around, then in a low voice.*) There's no need to say it, you can see for yourself, it's an uncivilized country, the people have no morals, and the boredom! The food they give us in the kitchen is unmentionable, and besides, there's this Firs who keeps walking about mumbling all sorts of inappropriate things. Take me with you, be so kind!

(*Enter Pishchik.*)

PISHCHIK: May I have the pleasure of a waltz with you, fairest lady? (*Lyubov Andreyevna goes with him.*) I really must borrow a hundred and eighty rubles from you, my charmer…I really must.…(*Dancing.*) Just a hundred and eighty rubles.…(*They pass into the ballroom.*)

YASHA (*softly sings*): "Wilt thou know my soul's unrest…"

(*In the ballroom a figure in a gray top hat and checked trousers is jumping about, waving its arms; there are shouts of "Bravo, Charlotta Ivanovna!"*)

DUNYASHA (*stopping to powder her face*): The young mistress told me to dance—there are lots of gentlemen and not enough ladies—but dancing makes me dizzy, and my heart begins to thump. Firs Nikolayevich, the post office clerk just said something to me that took my breath away.

(*The music grows more subdued.*)

FIRS: What did he say to you?

DUNYASHA: "You," he said, "are like a flower."

YASHA (*yawns*): What ignorance.... (*Goes out.*)

DUNYASHA: Like a flower....I'm such a delicate girl, I just adore tender words.

FIRS: You'll get your head turned.

(*Enter Yepikhodov.*)

YEPIKHODOV: Avdotya Fyodorovna, you are not desirous of seeing me....I might almost be some sort of insect. (*Sighs.*) Ah, life!

DUNYASHA: What is it you want?

YEPIKHODOV: Indubitably, you may be right. (*Sighs.*) But, of course, if one looks at it from a point of view, then, if I may so express myself, and you will forgive my frankness, you have completely reduced me to a state of mind. I know my fate, every day some misfortune befalls me, but I have long since grown accustomed to that; I look upon my fate with a smile. But you gave me your word, and although I —

DUNYASHA: Please, we'll talk about it later, but leave me in peace now. Just now I'm dreaming.... (*Plays with her fan.*)

YEPIKHODOV: Every day a misfortune, and yet, if I may so express myself, I merely smile, I even laugh.

(*Varya enters from the ballroom.*)

VARYA: Are you still here, Semyon? What a disrespectful man you are, really! (*To Dunyasha.*) Run along, Dunyasha. (*To Yepikhodov.*) First you play billiards and break a cue, then you wander about the drawing room as though you were a guest.

YEPIKHODOV: You cannot, if I may so express myself, penalize me.

VARYA: I am not penalizing you, I'm telling you. You do nothing but wander from one place to another, and you don't do your work. We keep a clerk, but for what, I don't know.

YEPIKHODOV (*offended*): Whether I work, or wander about, or eat, or play billiards, these are matters to be discussed only by persons of discernment, and my elders.

VARYA: You dare say that to me! (*Flaring up.*) You dare? You mean to say I have no discernment? Get out of here! This instant!

YEPIKHODOV (*intimidated*): I beg you to express yourself in a more delicate manner.

VARYA (*beside herself*): Get out, this very instant! Get out! (*He goes to the door, she follows him.*) Two-and-twenty Troubles! Don't let me set eyes on you again!

YEPIKHODOV (*goes out, his voice is heard behind the door*): I shall lodge a complaint against you!

VARYA: Oh, you're coming back? (*Seizes the stick left near the door by Firs.*) Come, come on....Come, I'll show you....Ah, so you're coming, are you? Then take that—(*Swings the stick just as Lopakhin enters.*)

LOPAKHIN: Thank you kindly.

VARYA (*angrily and mockingly*): I beg your pardon.

LOPAKHIN: Not at all. I humbly thank you for your charming reception.

VARYA: Don't mention it. (*Walks away, then looks back and gently asks.*) I didn't hurt you, did I?

LOPAKHIN: No, it's nothing. A huge bump coming up, that's all.

(*Voices in the ballroom: "Lopakhin has come! Yermolai Alekseich!" Pishchik enters.*)

PISHCHIK: As I live and breathe! (*Kisses Lopakhin.*) There is a whiff of cognac about you, dear soul. And we've been making merry here, too.

(*Enter Lyubov Andreyevna.*)

LYUBOV ANDREYEVNA: Is that you, Yermolai Alekseich? What kept you so long? Where's Leonid?

LOPAKHIN: Leonid Andreich arrived with me, he's coming...

LYUBOV ANDREYEVNA (*agitated*): Well, what happened? Did the sale take place? Tell me!

LOPAKHIN (*embarrassed, fearing to reveal his joy*): The auction was over by four o'clock.... We missed the train, had to wait till half past nine. (*Sighing heavily.*) Ugh! My head is swimming....

(*Enter Gayev; he carries his purchases in one hand and wipes away his tears with the other.*)

LYUBOV ANDREYEVNA: Lyonya, what happened? Well, Lyonya? (*Impatiently, through tears.*) Be quick, for God's sake!

GAYEV (*not answering her, simply waves his hand. To Firs, weeping*): Here, take these....There's anchovies, Kerch herrings....I haven't eaten anything all day.... What I have been through! (*The click of billiard balls is heard through the open door to the billiard room, and Yasha's voice: "Seven and eighteen!" Gayev's expression changes, he is no longer weeping.*) I'm terribly tired. Firs, help me change. (*Goes through the ballroom to his own room, followed by Firs.*)

PISHCHIK: What happened at the auction? Come on, tell us!

LYUBOV ANDREYEVNA: Is the cherry orchard sold?

LOPAKHIN: It's sold.

LYUBOV ANDREYEVNA: Who bought it?

LOPAKHIN: I bought it. (*Pause.*)

(*Lyubov Andreyevna is overcome; she would fall to the floor if it were not for the chair and table near which she stands. Varya takes the keys from her belt and throws them on the floor in the middle of the drawing room and goes out.*)

LOPAKHIN: I bought it! Kindly wait a moment, ladies and gentlemen, my head is swimming. I can't talk.... (*Laughs.*) We arrived at the auction, Deriganov was already there. Leonid Andreich had only fifteen thousand, and straight off Deriganov bid thirty thousand over and above the mortgage. I saw how the land lay, so I got into the fight and bid forty. He bid forty-five. I bid fifty-five. In other words, he kept raising it by five thousand, and I by ten. Well, it finally came to an end. I bid ninety thousand above the mortgage, and it was knocked down to me. The cherry orchard is now mine! Mine! (*Laughs uproariously.*) Lord! God in heaven! The cherry orchard is mine! Tell me I'm drunk, out of my mind, that I imagine it.... (*Stamps his feet.*) Don't laugh at me! If my father and my grandfather could only rise from their graves and see all that has happened, how their Yermolai, their beaten, half-literate Yermolai, who used to run about barefoot in winter, how that same Yermolai has bought an estate, the most beautiful estate in the whole world! I bought the estate where my father and grandfather were slaves, where they weren't even allowed in the kitchen. I'm asleep, this is just some dream of mine, it only seems to be.... It's the fruit of your imagination, hidden in the darkness of uncertainty.... (*Picks up the keys, smiling tenderly.*) She threw down the keys, wants to show that she's not mistress here anymore.... (*Jingles the keys.*) Well, no matter. (*The orchestra is heard tuning up.*) Hey, musicians, play, I want to hear you! Come on, everybody, and see how Yermolai Lopakhin will lay the ax to the cherry orchard, how the trees will fall to the ground! We're going to build summer cottages and our grandsons and great-grandsons will see a new life here.... Music! Strike up!

(*The orchestra plays. Lyubov Andreyevna sinks into a chair and weeps bitterly.*)

LOPAKHIN (*reproachfully*): Why didn't you listen to me, why? My poor friend, there's no turning back now. (*With tears.*) Oh, if only all this could be over quickly, if somehow our discordant, unhappy life could be changed!

PISHCHIK (*takes him by the arm; speaks in an undertone*): She's crying. Let's go into the ballroom, let her be alone.... Come on.... (*Leads him into the ballroom.*)

LOPAKHIN: What's happened? Musicians, play so I can hear you! Let everything be as I want it! (*Ironically.*) Here comes the new master, owner of the cherry orchard! (*Accidentally bumps into a little table, almost upsetting the candelabrum.*) I can pay for everything! (*Goes out with Pishchik.*)

(*There is no one left in either the drawing room or the ballroom except Lyubov Andreyevna, who sits huddled up and weeping bitterly. The music plays softly. Anya and Trofimov enter hurriedly. Anya goes to her mother and kneels before her. Trofimov remains in the doorway of the ballroom.*)

ANYA: Mama!... Mama, you're crying! Dear, kind, good Mama, my beautiful one, I love you... I bless you. The cherry orchard is sold, it's gone, that's true, true, but don't cry, Mama, life is still before you, you still have your good, pure soul.... Come with me, come, darling, we'll go away from here!... We'll plant a new orchard, more luxuriant than this one.

You will see it and understand; and joy, quiet, deep joy, will sink into your soul, like the evening sun, and you will smile, Mama! Come, darling, let us go....

ACT IV

(*The scene is the same as act I. There are neither curtains on the windows nor pictures on the walls, and only a little furniture piled up in one corner, as if for sale. There is a sense of emptiness. Near the outer door, at the rear of the stage, suitcases, traveling bags, etc., are piled up. Through the open door on the left the voices of Varya and Anya can be heard. Lopakhin stands waiting. Yasha is holding a tray with little glasses of champagne. In the hall, Yepikhodov is tying up a box. Offstage, at the rear, there is a hum of voices. It is the peasants who have come to say good-bye. Gayev's voice: "Thanks, brothers, thank you."*)

YASHA: The peasants have come to say good-bye. In my opinion, Yermolai Alekseich, peasants are good-natured, but they don't know much.

(*The hum subsides. Lyubov Andreyevna enters from the hall with Gayev. She is not crying, but she is pale, her face twitches, and she cannot speak.*)

GAYEV: You gave them your purse, Lyuba. That won't do! That won't do!

LYUBOV ANDREYEVNA: I couldn't help it! I couldn't help it! (*They both go out.*)

LOPAKHIN (*in the doorway, calls after them*): Please, do me the honor of having a little glass at parting. I didn't think of bringing champagne from town, and at the station I found only one bottle. Please! What's the matter, friends, don't you want any? (*Walks away from the door.*) If I'd known that, I wouldn't have bought it. Well, then I won't drink any either. (*Yasha carefully sets the tray down on a chair.*) At least you have a glass, Yasha.

YASHA: To those who are departing! Good luck! (*Drinks.*) This champagne is not the real stuff, I can assure you.

LOPAKHIN: Eight rubles a bottle. (*Pause.*) It's devilish cold in here.

YASHA: They didn't light the stoves today; it doesn't matter, since we're leaving. (*Laughs.*)

LOPAKHIN: Why are you laughing?

YASHA: Because I'm pleased.

LOPAKHIN: It's October, yet it's sunny and still outside, like summer. Good for building. (*Looks at his watch, then calls through the door.*) Bear in mind, ladies and gentlemen, only forty-six minutes till train time! That means leaving for the station in twenty minutes. Better hurry up!

(*Trofimov enters from outside wearing an overcoat.*)

TROFIMOV: Seems to me it's time to start. The carriages are at the door. What the devil has become of my rubbers? They're lost. (*Calls through the door.*) Anya, my rubbers are not here. I can't find them.

LOPAKHIN: I've got to go to Kharkov. I'm taking the same train you are. I'm going to spend the winter in Kharkov. I've been hanging around here with you, and I'm sick and tired of loafing. I can't live without work, I don't know what to do with my hands; they dangle in some strange way, as if they didn't belong to me.

TROFIMOV: We'll soon be gone, then you can take up your useful labors again.

LOPAKHIN: Here, have a little drink.

TROFIMOV: No, I don't want any.

LOPAKHIN: So you're off for Moscow?

TROFIMOV: Yes, I'll see them into town, and tomorrow I'll go to Moscow.

LOPAKHIN: Yes.... Well, I expect the professors haven't been giving any lectures: They're waiting for you to come!

TROFIMOV: That's none of your business.

LOPAKHIN: How many years is it you've been studying at the university?

TROFIMOV: Can't you think of something new? That's stale and flat. (*Looks for his rubbers.*) You know we'll probably never see each other again, so allow me to give you one piece of advice at parting: Don't wave your arms about! Get out of that habit—of arm-waving. And another thing, building cottages and counting on the summer residents in time becoming independent farmers—that's just another form of arm-waving. Well, when all's said and done, I'm fond of you anyway. You have fine, delicate fingers, like an artist; you have a fine delicate soul.

LOPAKHIN (*embraces him*): Good-bye, my dear fellow. Thank you for everything. Let me give you some money for the journey, if you need it.

TROFIMOV: What for? I don't need it.

LOPAKHIN: But you haven't any!

TROFIMOV: I have. Thank you. I got some money for a translation. Here it is in my pocket. (*Anxiously.*) But where are my rubbers?

VARYA (*from the next room*): Here, take the nasty things! (*Flings a pair of rubbers onto the stage.*)

TROFIMOV: What are you so cross about, Varya? Hm.... But these are not my rubbers.

LOPAKHIN: In the spring I sowed three thousand acres of poppies, and now I've made forty thousand rubles clear. And when my poppies were in bloom, what a picture it was! So, I'm telling you, I've made forty thousand, which means I'm offering you a loan because I can afford to. Why turn up your nose? I'm a peasant—I speak bluntly.

TROFIMOV: Your father was a peasant, mine was a pharmacist—which proves absolutely nothing. (*Lopakhin takes out his wallet.*) No, don't—even if you gave me two hundred thousand I wouldn't take it. I'm a free man. And everything that is valued so highly and held so dear by all of you, rich and poor alike, has not the slightest power over me—it's like a feather floating in the air. I can get along without you, I can pass you by, I'm strong and proud.

Mankind is advancing toward the highest truth, the highest happiness attainable on earth, and I am in the front ranks!

LOPAKHIN: Will you get there?

TROFIMOV: I'll get there. (*Pause.*) I'll either get there or I'll show others the way to get there.

(*The sound of axes chopping down trees is heard in the distance.*)

LOPAKHIN: Well, good-bye, my dear fellow. It's time to go. We turn up our noses at one another, but life goes on just the same. When I work for a long time without stopping, my mind is easier, and it seems to me that I, too, know why I exist. But how many there are in Russia, brother, who exist nobody knows why. Well, it doesn't matter, that's not what makes the wheels go round. They say Leonid Andreich has taken a position in the bank, six thousand a year.... Only, of course, he won't stick it out, he's too lazy....

ANYA (*in the doorway*): Mama asks you not to start cutting down the cherry orchard until she's gone.

TROFIMOV: Yes, really, not to have had the tact...(*Goes out through the hall.*)

LOPAKHIN: Right away, right away.... Ach, what people....(*Follows Trofimov out.*)

ANYA: Has Firs been taken to the hospital?

YASHA: I told them this morning. They must have taken him.

ANYA (*to Yepikhodov, who is crossing the room*): Semyon Panteleich, please find out if Firs has been taken to the hospital.

YASHA (*offended*): I told Yegor this morning. Why ask a dozen times?

YEPIKHODOV: It is my conclusive opinion that the venerable Firs is beyond repair; it's time he was gathered to his fathers. And I can only envy him. (*Puts a suitcase down on a hatbox and crushes it.*) There you are! Of course! I knew it! (*Goes out.*)

YASHA (*mockingly*): Two-and-twenty Troubles!

VARYA (*through the door*): Has Firs been taken to the hospital?

ANYA: Yes, he has.

VARYA: Then why didn't they take the letter to the doctor?

ANYA: We must send it on after them....(*Goes out.*)

VARYA (*from the adjoining room*): Where is Yasha? Tell him his mother has come to say good-bye to him.

YASHA (*waves his hand*): They really try my patience.

(*Dunyasha has been fussing with the luggage; now that Yasha is alone she goes up to him.*)

DUNYASHA: You might give me one little look, Yasha. You're going away...leaving me.... (*Cries and throws herself on his neck.*)

YASHA: What's there to cry about? (*Drinks champagne.*) In six days I'll be in Paris again. Tomorrow we'll take the express, off we go, and that's the last you'll see of us. I can hardly believe it. *Vive la France!* This place is not for me, I can't live here....It can't be helped.

I've had enough of this ignorance—I'm fed up with it. (*Drinks champagne.*) What are you crying for? Behave yourself properly, then you won't cry.

DUNYASHA (*looks into a small mirror and powders her face*): Send me a letter from Paris. You know, I loved you, Yasha, how I loved you! I'm such a tender creature, Yasha!

YASHA: Here they come. (*Busies himself with the luggage, humming softly.*)

(*Enter Lyubov Andreyevna, Gayev, Charlotta Ivanovna.*)

GAYEV: We ought to be leaving. There's not much time now. (*Looks at Yasha.*) Who smells of herring?

LYUBOV ANDREYEVNA: In about ten minutes we should be getting into the carriages. (*Glances around the room.*) Good-bye, dear house, old grandfather. Winter will pass, spring will come, and you will no longer be here, they will tear you down. How much these walls have seen! (*Kisses her daughter warmly.*) My treasure, you are radiant, your eyes are sparkling like two diamonds. Are you glad? Very?

ANYA: Very! A new life is beginning, Mama!

GAYEV (*cheerfully*): Yes, indeed, everything is all right now. Before the cherry orchard was sold we were all worried and miserable, but afterward, when the question was finally settled once and for all, everybody calmed down and felt quite cheerful....I'm in a bank now, a financier...cue ball into the center... and you, Lyuba, say what you like, you look better, no doubt about it.

LYUBOV ANDREYEVNA: Yes. My nerves are better, that's true. (*Her hat and coat are handed to her.*) I sleep well. Carry out my things, Yasha, it's time. (*To Anya.*) My little girl, we shall see each other soon.... I shall go to Paris and live there on the money your great-aunt sent to buy the estate—long live Auntie!— but that money won't last long.

ANYA: You'll come back soon, Mama, soon...won't you? I'll study hard and pass my high school examinations, and then I can work and help you. We'll read all sorts of books together, Mama.... Won't we? (*Kisses her mother's hand.*) We'll read in the autumn evenings, we'll read lots of books, and a new and wonderful world will open up before us....(*Dreaming.*) Mama, come back....

LYUBOV ANDREYEVNA: I'll come, my precious. (*Embraces her.*)

(*Enter Lopakhin, Charlotta Ivanovna is softly humming a song.*)

GAYEV: Happy Charlotta: She's singing!

CHARLOTTA (*picks up a bundle and holds it like a baby in swaddling clothes*): Bye, baby, bye....(*A baby's crying is heard, "Wah! Wah!"*) Be quiet, my darling, my dear little boy. (*"Wah! Wah!"*) I'm so sorry for you! (*Throws the bundle down.*) You will find me a position, won't you? I can't go on like this.

LOPAKHIN: We'll find something, Charlotta Ivanovna, don't worry.

GAYEV: Everyone is leaving us, Varya's going away...all of a sudden nobody needs us.

CHARLOTTA: I have nowhere to go in town. I must go away. (*Hums.*) It doesn't matter...

(*Enter Pishchik.*)

LOPAKHIN: Nature's wonder!

PISHCHIK (*panting*): Ugh! Let me catch my breath.... I'm exhausted.... My esteemed friends.... Give me some water....

GAYEV: After money, I suppose? Excuse me, I'm fleeing from temptation....(*Goes out.*)

PISHCHIK: It's a long time since I've been to see you... fairest lady.... (*To Lopakhin*) So you're here.... Glad to see you, you intellectual giant.... Here... take it...four hundred rubles...I still owe you eight hundred and forty...

LOPAKHIN (*shrugs his shoulders in bewilderment*): I must be dreaming.... Where did you get it?

PISHCHIK: Wait...I'm hot.... A most extraordinary event. Some Englishmen came to my place and discovered some kind of white clay on my land. (*To Lyubov Andreyevna*) And four hundred for you... fairest, most wonderful lady.... (*Hands her the money.*) The rest later. (*Takes a drink of water.*) Just now a young man in the train was saying that a certain...great philosopher recommends jumping off roofs.... "Jump!" he says, and therein lies the whole problem. (*In amazement.*) Think of that, now!... Water!

LOPAKHIN: Who were those Englishmen?

PISHCHIK: I leased them the tract of land with the clay on it for twenty-four years....And now, excuse me, I have no time...I must be trotting along...I'm going to Znoikov's...to Kardamanov's...I owe everybody. (*Drinks.*) Keep well...I'll drop in on Thursday...

LYUBOV ANDREYEVNA: We're just moving into town, and tomorrow I go abroad...

PISHCHIK: What? (*Alarmed.*) Why into town? That's why I see the furniture...suitcases.... Well, never mind.... (*Through tears.*) Never mind.... Men of the greatest intellect, those Englishmen.... Never mind.... Be happy...God will help you.... Never mind.... Everything in this world comes to an end.... (*Kisses Lyubov Andreyevna's hand.*) And should the news reach you that my end has come, just remember this old horse, and say: "There once lived a certain Semyonov-Pishchik, God rest his soul."... Splendid weather.... Yes.... (*Goes out greatly disconcerted, but immediately returns and speaks from the doorway.*) Dashenka sends her regards. (*Goes out.*)

LYUBOV ANDREYEVNA: Now we can go. I am leaving with two things on my mind. First—that Firs is sick. (*Looks at her watch.*) We still have about five minutes....

ANYA: Mama, Firs has already been taken to the hospital. Yasha sent him there this morning.

LYUBOV ANDREYEVNA: My second concern is Varya. She's used to getting up early and working, and now, with no work to do, she's like a fish out of water. She's grown pale and thin, and cries all the time, poor girl.... (*Pauses.*) You know very well, Yermolai Alekseich, that I dreamed of marrying her to you, and everything pointed to your getting married. (*Whispers to Anya, who nods to Charlotta, and they both go out.*) She loves you, you are fond of her, and I don't know—I don't know why it is you seem to avoid each other. I can't understand it!

LOPAKHIN: To tell you the truth, I don't understand it myself. The whole thing is strange, somehow.... If there's still time, I'm ready right now.... Let's finish it up—and *basta*,° but without you I feel I'll never be able to propose to her.

LYUBOV ANDREYEVNA: Splendid! After all, it only takes a minute. I'll call her in at once....

LOPAKHIN: And we even have the champagne. (*Looks at the glasses.*) Empty! Somebody's already drunk it. (*Yasha coughs.*) That's what you call lapping it up.

LYUBOV ANDREYEVNA (*animatedly*): Splendid! We'll leave you.... Yasha, *allez!*° I'll call her.... (*At the door.*) Varya, leave everything and come here. Come! (*Goes out with Yasha.*)

LOPAKHIN (*looking at his watch*): Yes.... (*Pause.*)

(*Behind the door there is smothered laughter and whispering; finally Varya enters.*)

VARYA (*looking over the luggage for a long time*): Strange, I can't seem to find it...

LOPAKHIN: What are you looking for?

VARYA: I packed it myself, and I can't remember... (*Pause.*)

LOPAKHIN: Where are you going now, Varya Mikhailovna?

VARYA: I? To the Ragulins'.... I've agreed to go there to look after the house...as a sort of housekeeper.

LOPAKHIN: At Yashnevo? That would be about seventy versts from here. (*Pause.*) Well, life in this house has come to an end....

VARYA (*examining the luggage*): Where can it be?... Perhaps I put it in the trunk.... Yes, life in this house has come to an end...there'll be no more...

LOPAKHIN: And I'm off for Kharkov...by the next train. I have a lot to do. I'm leaving Yepikhodov here...I've taken him on.

VARYA: Really!

LOPAKHIN: Last year at this time it was already snowing, if you remember, but now it's still and sunny. It's cold though.... About three degrees of frost.

VARYA: I haven't looked. (*Pause.*) And besides, our thermometer's broken. (*Pause.*)

(*A voice from the yard calls: "Yermolai Alekseich!"*)

LOPAKHIN (*as if he had been waiting for a long time for the call*): Coming! (*Goes out quickly.*)

basta: Italian for "enough."   *allez!*: French for "go!"

(*Varya sits on the floor, lays her head on a bundle of clothes, and quietly sobs. The door opens and Lyubov Andreyevna enters cautiously.*)

LYUBOV ANDREYEVNA: Well? (*Pause.*) We must be going.

VARYA (*no longer crying, dries her eyes*): Yes, it's time, Mama dear. I can get to the Ragulins' today, if only we don't miss the train.

LYUBOV ANDREYEVNA (*in the doorway*): Anya, put your things on!

(*Enter Anya, then Gayev and Charlotta Ivanovna. Gayev wears a warm overcoat with a hood. The servants and coachmen come in. Yepikhodov bustles about the luggage.*)

LYUBOV ANDREYEVNA: Now we can be on our way.

ANYA (*joyfully*): On our way!

GAYEV: My friends, my dear, cherished friends! Leaving this house forever, can I pass over in silence, can I refrain from giving utterance, as we say farewell, to those feelings that now fill my whole being —

ANYA (*imploringly*): Uncle!

VARYA: Uncle dear, don't!

GAYEV (*forlornly*): Double the rail off the white to center table...yellow into the side pocket.... I'll be quiet....

(*Enter Trofimov, then Lopakhin.*)

TROFIMOV: Well, ladies and gentlemen, it's time to go!

LOPAKHIN: Yepikhodov, my coat!

LYUBOV ANDREYEVNA: I'll sit here just one more minute. It's as though I had never before seen what the walls of this house were like, what the ceilings were like, and now I look at them hungrily, with such tender love...

GAYEV: I remember when I was six years old, sitting on this windowsill on Whitsunday, watching my father going to church...

LYUBOV ANDREYEVNA: Have they taken all the things?

LOPAKHIN: Everything, I think. (*Puts on his overcoat.*) Yepikhodov, see that everything is in order.

YEPIKHODOV (*in a hoarse voice*): Rest assured, Yermolai Alekseich!

LOPAKHIN: What's the matter with your voice?

YEPIKHODOV: Just drank some water...must have swallowed something.

YASHA (*contemptuously*): What ignorance!

LYUBOV ANDREYEVNA: When we go—there won't be a soul left here....

LOPAKHIN: Till spring.

VARYA (*pulls an umbrella out of a bundle as though she were going to hit someone; Lopakhin pretends to be frightened*): Why are you—I never thought of such a thing!

TROFIMOV: Ladies and gentlemen, let's get into the carriages—it's time now! The train will soon be in!

VARYA: Petya, there they are—your rubbers, by the suitcase. (*Tearfully.*) And what dirty old things they are!

TROFIMOV (*putting on his rubbers*): Let's go, ladies and gentlemen!

GAYEV (*extremely upset, afraid of bursting into tears*): The train...the station....Cross table to the center, double the rail...on the white into the corner.

LYUBOV ANDREYEVNA: Let us go!

GAYEV: Are we all here? No one in there? (*Locks the side door on the left.*) There are some things stored in there, we must lock up. Let's go!

ANYA: Good-bye, house! Good-bye, old life!

TROFIMOV: Hail to the new life! (*Goes out with Anya.*)

(*Varya looks around the room and slowly goes out. Yasha and Charlotta with her dog go out.*)

LOPAKHIN: And so, till spring. Come along, my friends.... Till we meet! (*Goes out.*)

(*Lyubov Andreyevna and Gayev are left alone. As though they had been waiting for this, they fall onto each other's necks and break into quiet, restrained sobs, afraid of being heard.*)

GAYEV (*in despair*): My sister, my sister....

LYUBOV ANDREYEVNA: Oh, my dear, sweet, lovely orchard!...My life, my youth, my happiness, good-bye!...Good-bye!

ANYA'S VOICE (*gaily calling*): Mama!

TROFIMOV'S VOICE (*gay and excited*): Aa-oo!

LYUBOV ANDREYEVNA: One last look at these walls, these windows.... Mother loved to walk about in this room....

GAYEV: My sister, my sister!

ANYA'S VOICE: Mama!

TROFIMOV'S VOICE: Aa-oo!

LYUBOV ANDREYEVNA: We're coming! (*They go out.*)

(*The stage is empty. There is the sound of doors being locked, then of the carriages driving away. It grows quiet. In the stillness there is the dull thud of an ax on a tree, a forlorn, melancholy sound. Footsteps are heard. From the door on the right Firs appears. He is dressed as always in a jacket and white waistcoat, and wears slippers. He is ill.*)

FIRS (*goes to the door and tries the handle*): Locked. They have gone.... (*Sits down on the sofa.*) They've forgotten me.... Never mind.... I'll sit here awhile.... I expect Leonid Andreich hasn't put on his fur coat and has gone off in his overcoat. (*Sighs anxiously.*) And I didn't see to it....When they're young, they're green! (*Mumbles something which cannot be understood.*) I'll lie down awhile.... There's no strength left in you, nothing's left, nothing.... Ach, you...addlepate! (*Lies motionless.*)

(*A distant sound is heard that seems to come from the sky, the sound of a snapped string mournfully dying away. A stillness falls, and nothing is heard but the thud of the ax on a tree far away in the orchard.*)

COMMENTARIES

Anton Chekhov (1860–1904)
FROM *LETTERS OF ANTON CHEKOV*
1888–1903

TRANSLATED BY MICHAEL HENRY HEIM WITH SIMON KARLINSKY

Chekhov, like Ibsen, was an inveterate letter writer. In letters to family members and colleagues, he wrote quite frankly about his hopes, expectations, and difficulties regarding his work. Chekhov's letters concerning his purpose as an artist and his play The Cherry Orchard *give us some insight into his anxieties and hopes that he had for his work. His awareness of the difficulties he faced in his writing helps us understand how his plays developed into complex and demanding works.*

October 4, 1888

The people I fear are those who look for tendentiousness between the lines and are determined to see me as either liberal or conservative. I am neither liberal, nor conservative, nor gradualist, nor monk, nor indifferentist. I should like to be a free artist and nothing else. That is why I cultivate no particular predilection for policemen, butchers, scientists, writers, or the younger generation. I look upon tags and labels as prejudices. My holy of holies is the human body, health, intelligence, talent, inspiration, love and the most absolute freedom imaginable, freedom from violence and lies.

November 25, 1892

Keep in mind that the writers we call eternal or simply good, the writers who intoxicate us, have one highly important trait in common: They are moving towards something definite and beckon you to follow, and you feel with your entire being, not only with your mind, that they have a certain goal, like the ghost of Hamlet's father, which had a motive for coming and stirring Hamlet's imagination. Depending on their caliber, some have immediate goals—the abolition of serfdom, the liberation of one's country, politics, beauty, or simply vodka...—while the goals of others are more remote—God, life after death, the happiness of mankind, etc. The best of them are realistic and describe life as it is, but because each line is saturated with the consciousness of its goal, you feel life as it should be in addition to life as it is, and you are captivated by it. But what about us? Us! We describe life as it is and stop dead right there. We wouldn't lift a hoof if you lit into us with a whip. We have neither immediate nor remote goals, and there is an emptiness in our souls. We have no politics, we don't believe in revolution, there is no God, we're not afraid of ghosts, and I personally am not even afraid of death or blindness. If you want nothing, hope for nothing, and fear nothing, you cannot be an artist.

To K. S. Stanislavsky°
Yalta. Oct. 30, 1903

When I was writing Lopakhin, I thought of it as a part for you. If for any reason you don't care for it, take the part of Gayev. Lopakhin is a merchant, of course, but he is a very decent person in every sense. He must behave with perfect decorum, like an educated man, with no petty ways or tricks of any sort, and it seemed to me this part, the central one of the play, would come out brilliantly in your hands.... In choosing an actor for the part you must remember that Varya, a serious and religious girl, is in love with Lopakhin; she wouldn't be in love with a mere money-grubber....

To Vl. I. Nemirovich-Danchenko°
Yalta. Nov. 2, 1903

...Pishchik is a Russian, an old man, worn out by the gout, age, and satiety; stout, dressed in a sleeveless undercoat (à la Simov [an actor in the Moscow Art Theatre]), boots without heels. Lopakhin—a white waistcoat, yellow shoes; when walking, swings his arms, a broad stride, thinks deeply while walking, walks as if on a straight line. Hair not short, and therefore often throws back his head; while in thought he passes his hand through his beard, combing it from the back forward, i.e., from the neck toward the mouth. Trofimov, I think, is clear. Varya—black dress, wide belt.

Three years I spent writing "The Cherry Orchard," and for three years I have been telling you that it is necessary to invite an actress for the role of Lyubov Andreyevna. And now you see you are trying to solve a puzzle that won't work out.

To K. S. Alekseyev (Stanislavsky)
Yalta. Nov. 5, 1903

The house in the play is two-storied, a large one. But in the third act does it not speak of a stairway leading down? Nevertheless, this third act worries me....N. has it that the third act takes place in "some kind of hotel"; ...evidently I made an error in the play. The action does not pass in "some kind of hotel," but in a *drawing-room*. If I mention a hotel in the play, which I cannot now doubt, after Vl. Iv.'s [Nemirovich-Danchenko] letter, please telegraph me. We must correct it; we cannot issue it thus, with grave errors distorting its meaning.

The house must be large, solid; wooden (like Aksakov's, which, I think, S. T. Morozov has seen) or stone, it is all the same. It is very old and imposing; country residents do not take such houses; such houses are usually wrecked and the material employed for the construction of a country house. The furniture is ancient, stylish, solid; ruin and debt have not affected the surroundings.

When they buy such a house, they reason thus: it is cheaper and easier to build a new and smaller one than to repair this old one.

Your shepherd played well. That was most essential.

K. S. Stanislavsky: Konstantin Stanislavsky (1863–1938), director with the Moscow Art Theatre, which produced most of Chekhov's plays.
Vl. I. Nemirovich-Danchenko: Vladimir Ivanovich Nemirovich-Danchenko (1858–1943), novelist and codirector of the Moscow Art Theatre.

Peter Brook (b. 1925)
ON CHEKHOV   *1987*

Peter Brook has established himself as one of the most distinguished directors of recent years. He was educated at Oxford University and has been a director of the Royal Shakespeare Company in England. In 1987 he directed The Cherry Orchard *at the Brooklyn Academy of Music. Some of his thoughts as he prepared to direct the play are presented here, showing his awareness of Chekhov's "film sense" in a play that was written just as film was emerging as a popular form. He is also aware of Chekhov's personal vision of death and sees it expressed in the circumstances of the play.*

Chekhov always looked for what's natural; he wanted performances and productions to be as limpid as life itself. Chekhov's writing is extremely concentrated, employing a minimum of words; in a way, it is similar to Pinter or Beckett. As with them, it is construction that counts, rhythm, the purely theatrical poetry that comes not from beautiful words but from the right word at the right moment. In the theater, someone can say "yes" in such a way that the "yes" is no longer ordinary — it can become a beautiful word, because it is the perfect expression of what cannot be expressed in any other way. With Chekhov, periods, commas, points of suspension are all of a fundamental importance, as fundamental as the "pauses" precisely indicated by Beckett. If one fails to observe them, one loses the rhythm and tensions of the play. In Chekhov's work, the punctuation represents a series of coded messages which record characters' relationships and emotions, the moments at which ideas come together or follow their own course. The punctuation enables us to grasp what the words conceal.

Chekhov is like a perfect filmmaker. Instead of cutting from one image to another — perhaps from one place to another — he switches from one emotion to another just before it gets too heavy. At the precise moment when the spectator risks becoming too involved in a character, an unexpected situation cuts across: Nothing is stable. Chekhov portrays individuals and a society in a state of perpetual change, he is the dramatist of life's movement, simultaneously smiling and serious, amusing and bitter — completely free from the "music," the Slav "nostalgia" that Paris nightclubs still preserve. He often stated that his plays were comedies — this was the central issue of his conflict with Stanislavsky.

But it's wrong to conclude that *The Cherry Orchard* should be performed as a vaudeville. Chekhov is an infinitely detailed observer of the human comedy. As a doctor, he knew the meaning of certain kinds of behavior, how to discern what was essential, to expose what he diagnosed. Although he shows tenderness and an attentive sympathy, he never sentimentalizes. One doesn't imagine a doctor shedding tears over the illnesses of his patients. He learns how to balance compassion with distance.

In Chekhov's work, death is omnipresent — he knew it well — but there is nothing negative or unsavory in its presence. The awareness of death is balanced with a desire to live. His characters possess a sense of the present moment, and the need to taste it fully. As in great tragedies, one finds a harmony between life and death.

Chekhov died young, having traveled, written, and loved enormously, having taken part in the events of his day, in great schemes of social reform. He died shortly after asking for some champagne, and his coffin was transported in a wagon bearing the inscription "Fresh Oysters." His awareness of death, and of the precious moments that could be lived, endows his work with a sense of the relative: in other words, a viewpoint from which the tragic is always a bit absurd.

In Chekhov's work, each character has its own existence: not one of them resembles another, particularly in *The Cherry Orchard*, which presents a micro-cosm of the political tendencies of the time. There are those who believe in social transformations, others attached to a disappearing past. None of them can achieve satisfaction or plenitude, and seen from outside, their existences might well appear empty, senseless. But they all burn with intense desires. They are not disillusioned, quite the contrary: In their own ways, they are all searching for a better quality of life, emotionally and socially. Their drama is that society—the outside world—blocks their energy. The complexity of their behavior is not indicated in the words, it emerges from the mosaic construction of an infinite number of details. What is essential is to see that these are not plays about lethargic people. They are hypervi-tal people in a lethargic world, forced to dramatize the minutest happening out of a passionate desire to live. They have not given up.

Bernard Shaw

The Irish playwright Bernard Shaw[1] (1856–1950) was astonishing not only for the range of his writing but also for the length and vigor of his life. He was a public figure for most of his days, with an especially keen ability to catch public attention and to make his presence felt. His early work was devoted to criticism in newspapers and then to a series of fairly successful novels. He began writing plays in his late thirties; once he began, he realized that he had discovered his vocation, and he went on to write more than fifty. Some of them, such as *Arms and the Man* (1894), *Candida* (1897), *Mrs. Warren's Profession* (1898), *Man and Superman* (1901–1903), *Major Barbara* (1905), *Pygmalion* (1913), *Heartbreak House* (1919), and *St. Joan* (1923), are among the most often performed plays by any English-language writer of his time.

Shaw's gift of analysis and philosophical reflection created in his works a new kind of drama that has sometimes been named for him—Shavian. The term implies a deep interest in ideas rather than in character and a propensity for elaborate discourse between characters who represent different points of view. Shaw assumed that drama should amuse and entertain, but of much greater importance was his didactic motive. Drama should teach a lesson about something of great moral importance.

This is not to say that Shaw was unable to be entertaining. Some of his comedies, still played today, are bright and witty. *You Never Can Tell* (1898), a comedy about male-female relationships whose main character is a dentist, and *Pygmalion*, a comedy in which a man teaches a cockney girl how to speak with an upper-class accent with unexpected results, are both funny plays. *Pygmalion* was redone as a musical, *My Fair Lady*, and has been Shaw's most financially successful play.

Still, Shaw was basically a philosophical writer. His plays can usually be seen as having a specific theme on which the characters constantly discourse. Whether it was the relationship of England and Ireland, the state of the medical profession, genetics and propagation, or poverty, Shaw always focused on an issue, and he even commented that Shakespeare's shortcoming was that his plays have no message.

Shaw frequently wrote elaborate and lengthy prefaces to his published plays. In his prefaces, Shaw takes time to explain—and fully explore—the messages of his plays. He discusses the questions of genetic planning and the improvement of the race in his preface to *Man and Superman*; in the preface to *Candida* he discusses the relationship of pity to love.

Shaw's lifelong socialism affected his work and his thinking, and he himself was a socialist politician for a short period. Consequently, it is not uncommon to see political concerns expressed and debated in his plays.

[1]Shaw was born George Bernard Shaw and is sometimes referred to as GBS. He disliked the name George and preferred to be addressed as Bernard Shaw.

Shaw's political ideas were shaped by his concern for economics as a discipline. In 1884 he joined the Fabian Society, which had been established a year earlier as a group to study and promote socialism, and remained active until 1911. Fabianism, unlike Marxism or communism, held that society need not be destroyed by revolution but could become an instrument of socialist reform. For this reason Fabianism was known as evolutionary socialism. *Fabian Essays* (1889), which Shaw edited, was used by study groups that sprouted up throughout Great Britain to spread Fabian socialist ideas through politics, religion, and society. The result of this movement was the organization of a new political party, the Labour Party (1893), which still exists. The socialist government of Britain in the 1960s and 1970s was a direct outgrowth of Fabian theories.

While Shaw studied economics, he grew to believe that all social values were built on an economic base. He developed this idea in his Fabian essays and maintained it throughout his plays. He also maintained a presence as a critic of theater and accepted Ibsen as a major playwright at a time when most London critics found Ibsen's work unacceptable. Shaw's *Quintessence of Ibsenism* (1891; revised after Ibsen's death in 1913) is still a useful commentary on that playwright's work.

MRS. WARREN'S PROFESSION

Shaw once described this play as being in "my most odious vein." It was written in 1894 and inspired by Janet Achurch, the actress who played Nora in Ibsen's *A Doll House*. Achurch told Shaw the story of a play she was writing based on Guy de Maupassant's short story "Yvette." Shaw adopted the idea and hoped that when he finished his play, Achurch would play Vivie, the heroine. Shaw owed a great deal to other playwrights who had touched on similar themes—although none as directly as Shaw—but his story of a mother-daughter relationship in which the mother was a prostitute was original in that it proposed a "new woman" for the heroine, Vivie, and refused to permit Mrs. Warren to express shame for her professional decisions. This was a highly daring play for its time.

Indeed, the play had only two private performances in London in 1902 before it premiered in the United States in 1905. The play was banned or protested in several cities, especially after its first performances. By the time it was given its first public performances in London in 1926, Shaw had lost interest in the play and simply felt it was too late in production. The Comédie-Française considered it too amoral to produce as late as 1955, which demonstrates that Shaw hit a nerve that was still sensitive well beyond his own day.

The form of the play is essentially conventional for its time, although Shaw consciously employed techniques of Henrik Ibsen, whom he admired enough to have written the seminal study *The Quintessence of Ibsenism* (1891). He had learned from Ibsen how to address social issues directly and how to produce a female character whose ambiguities intrigue an audience. Ibsen's emphasis on the "new woman"—the independent woman who could make her own decisions and her own way—is evident in *Mrs. Warren's Profession*.

The men in the play are generally dependent on the women. Mrs. Warren has a good business sense and has used the capital provided her by Sir George Crofts so well that Crofts need no longer worry about his own welfare. In one sense he is a kept man, living on the earnings of a woman. The Reverend Samuel Gardner has converted from a roué and former client of Mrs. Warren to an overly pious churchman worried about his reputation. His son, Frank, may or may not be a brother to Vivie, and although the play ends with Vivie declaring that she doesn't care whether he is her brother or not, the theme of incest seems underdeveloped. Yet Shaw felt it was an essential ingredient of the play. Frank plans not to work, is shiftless and indolent, and would be content to be supported by Vivie and her mother's money just as Crofts is content to bask in the security provided by Mrs. Warren.

The underlying theme of economic opportunities for women drives this play. The Victorians felt that prostitution, widespread in England, was one of the most serious social diseases of the time. But Shaw is keen enough in his analysis of English social life to realize that prostitutes were often forced into the profession because the alternatives were even worse. Mrs. Warren explains to Vivie in act II that she watched her two half-sisters follow the path of respectability: "One of them worked in a whitelead factory twelve hours a day for nine shillings a week until she died of lead poisoning. She only expected to get her hands a little paralyzed; but she died. The other was always held up to us as a model because she married a Government laborer in the Deptford victualling yard, and kept his room and the three children neat and tidy on eighteen shillings a week—until he took to drink."

The unrespectable sisters, Liz and Mrs. Warren, followed "the life" and ended up in control of their own situation. Liz, retired in a cathedral town, is emblematic of the height of respectability. Vivie is in a position to reject her mother's life, as well as Croft's offer of marriage and wealth and Frank's offer of marriage and love. But she is in this position because her mother provided her with a man's education at Cambridge. She describes herself as a "wrangler"—a term meaning an honors student in mathematics but also implying achievement in debate. This position was formerly available only to men (as Praed implies when he says nothing like that happened "in my day").

Vivie ends the play in the secure knowledge that she will succeed in the law profession and that the limited options available to her mother will never be her only options. Vivie, then, is heroic, and the play is comic in form.

Mrs. Warren's Profession in Performance

Mrs. Warren's Profession was produced privately in London on January 5, 1902, at the New Lyric Theater. On October 27, 1902, it was produced at the Hyperion Theater in New Haven, Connecticut, its first American production. H. Granville Barker, a distinguished actor and writer, played the part of Frank, and Fanny Brough was Mrs. Warren. It was performed again in New York in

1905 with the well-known actor Richard Mansfield, but the police commissioner closed the play for "offending public decency." A special court hearing in 1906 proclaimed the play "not pleasant" but did not declare it indecent.

After performances in Berlin (1907) and Glasgow (1913), the play's first public performance in England took place in Birmingham in 1925, when the British censors finally cleared the play of charges of indecency. It ran in London at the Strand Theatre in 1926 for eighty-six performances.

John Loder and Estelle Winwood played Crofts and Mrs. Warren off-Broadway in 1950 for twenty-eight performances. Ruth Gordon and Lynn Redgrave played Mrs. Warren and Vivie in a 1976 New York Shakespeare Festival production in Lincoln Center that lasted for sixty-nine performances. Edward Herrmann played Frank, and Milo O'Shea played Reverend Gardner. Current productions of the play abound. The Irish Classical Theater Co. in Buffalo, New York, staged a well-received performance in April 2003. That same year, the celebrated British director Peter Hall chose Brenda Blethyn for the lead and his daughter Rebecca Hall for Vivie in the London West End production at the Strand Theatre. The reviews praised Blethyn and the rest of the cast, but they especially honored Shaw for attacking hypocrisy. Former fashion model Twiggy Lawson played Mrs. Warren in a Wiltshire, England, production in July 2003. These contemporary productions demonstrate the validity of Shaw's views.

Bernard Shaw (1856–1950)

MRS. WARREN'S PROFESSION   *1898*

Characters

VIVIE WARREN
PRAED
MRS WARREN
SIR GEORGE CROFTS
FRANK GARDNER
REVEREND SAMUEL GARDNER

ACT I

Summer afternoon in a cottage garden on the eastern slope of a hill a little south of Haslemere in Surrey. Looking up the hill, the cottage is seen in the left hand corner of the garden, with its thatched roof and porch, and a large latticed window to the left of the porch. Farther back a little wing is built out, making an angle with the right side wall. From the end of this wing a paling curves across and forward, completely shutting in the garden, except for a gate on the right. The common rises uphill beyond the paling to the sky line. Some folded canvas garden chairs are leaning against the side bench in the porch. A lady's bicycle is propped against the wall, under the window. A little to the right of the porch a hammock is slung from two posts. A big canvas umbrella, stuck in the ground, keeps the sun off the hammock, in which a young lady lies reading and making notes, her head towards the cottage and her feet towards the gate. In front of the hammock, and within reach of her hand, is a common kitchen chair, with a pile of serious-looking books and a supply of writing paper upon it.

A gentleman walking on the common comes into sight from behind the cottage. He is hardly past middle age, with something of the artist about him, unconventionally but carefully dressed, and clean-shaven except for a moustache, with an eager, susceptible face and very amiable and considerate manners. He has silky black hair, with waves of grey and white in it. His eyebrows are white, his moustache black. He seems not certain of his way. He looks over the paling; takes stock of the place; and sees the young lady.

THE GENTLEMAN (*taking off his hat*): I beg your pardon. Can you direct me to Hindhead View—Mrs Alison's?

THE YOUNG LADY (*glancing up from her book*): This is Mrs Alison's. (*She resumes her work.*)

THE GENTLEMAN: Indeed! Perhaps—may I ask are you Miss Vivie Warren?

THE YOUNG LADY (*sharply, as she turns on her elbow to get a good look at him*): Yes.

THE GENTLEMAN (*daunted and conciliatory*): I'm afraid I appear intrusive. My name is Praed. (*Vivie at once throws her books upon the chair, and gets out of the hammock.*) Oh, pray dont let me disturb you.

VIVIE (*striding to the gate and opening it for him*): Come in, Mr Praed. (*He comes in.*) Glad to see you. (*She proffers her hand and takes his with a resolute and hearty grip. She is an attractive specimen of the sensible, able, highly educated young middle-class Englishwoman. Age 22. Prompt, strong, confident, self-possessed. Plain, business-like dress, but not dowdy. She wears a chatelaine at her belt, with a fountain pen and a paper knife among its pendants.*)

PRAED: Very kind of you indeed, Miss Warren. (*She shuts the gate with a vigorous slam: he passes in to the middle of the garden, exercising his fingers, which are slightly numbed by her greeting.*) Has your mother arrived?

VIVIE (*quickly, evidently scenting aggression*): Is she coming?

PRAED (*surprised*): Didnt you expect us?

VIVIE: No.

PRAED: Now, goodness me, I hope Ive not mistaken the day. That would be just like me, you know. Your mother arranged that she was to come down from London and that I was to come over from Horsham to be introduced to you.

VIVIE (*not at all pleased*): Did she? Hm! My mother has rather a trick of taking me by surprise—to see how I behave myself when she's away, I suppose. I fancy I shall take my mother very much by surprise one of these days, if she makes arrangements that concern me without consulting me beforehand. She hasnt come.

PRAED (*embarrassed*): I'm really very sorry.

VIVIE (*throwing off her displeasure*): It's not your fault, Mr Praed, is it? And I'm very glad youve come, believe me. You are the only one of my mother's friends I have asked her to bring to see me.

PRAED (*relieved and delighted*): Oh, now this is really very good of you, Miss Warren!

VIVIE: Will you come indoors; or would you rather sit out here whilst we talk?

PRAED: It will be nicer out here, dont you think?

VIVIE: Then I'll go and get you a chair. (*She goes to the porch for a garden chair.*)

PRAED (*following her*): Oh, pray, pray! Allow me. (*He lays hands on the chair.*)

VIVIE (*letting him take it*): Take care of your fingers: theyre rather dodgy things, those chairs. (*She goes across to the chair with the books on it; pitches them into the hammock; and brings the chair forward with one swing.*)

PRAED (*who has just unfolded his chair*): Oh, now do let me take that hard chair! I like hard chairs.

VIVIE: So do I. (*She sits down.*) Sit down, Mr Praed. (*This invitation she gives with genial peremptoriness, his anxiety to please her clearly striking her as a sign of weakness of character on his part.*)

PRAED: By the way, though, hadnt we better go to the station to meet your mother?

VIVIE (*coolly*): Why? She knows the way. (*Praed hesitates, and then sits down in the garden chair, rather disconcerted.*) Do you know, you are just like what I expected. I hope you are disposed to be friends with me.

PRAED (*again beaming*): Thank you, my dear Miss Warren: thank you. Dear me! I'm so glad your mother hasnt spoilt you!

VIVIE: How?

PRAED: Well, in making you too conventional. You know, my dear Miss Warren, I am a born anarchist. I hate authority. It spoils the relations between parent and child—even between mother and daughter. Now I was always afraid that your mother would strain her authority to make you very conventional. It's such a relief to find that she hasnt.

VIVIE: Oh! have I been behaving unconventionally?

PRAED: Oh no: oh dear no. At least not conventionally unconventionally, you understand. (*She nods. He goes on, with a cordial outburst.*) But it was so charming of you to say that you were disposed to be friends with me! You modern young ladies are splendid—perfectly splendid!

VIVIE (*dubiously*): Eh? (*Watching him with dawning disappointment as to the quality of his brains and character.*)

PRAED: When I was your age, young men and women were afraid of each other: there was no good fellowship—nothing real—only gallantry copied out of novels, and as vulgar and affected as it could be. Maidenly reserve!—gentlemanly chivalry!—always saying no when you meant yes!—simple purgatory for shy and sincere souls!

VIVIE: Yes, I imagine there must have been a frightful waste of time—especially women's time.

PRAED: Oh, waste of life, waste of everything. But things are improving. Do you know, I have been in a positive state of excitement about meeting you ever since your magnificent achievements at Cambridge—a thing unheard of in my day. It was perfectly splendid, your tieing with the third wrangler.° Just the right place, you know. The first wrangler is always a dreamy, morbid fellow, in whom the thing is pushed to the length of a disease.

VIVIE: It doesnt pay. I wouldnt do it again for the same money.

---

wrangler: An honors student in mathematics. The term also implies achievement in debate.

PRAED (*aghast*): The same money!

VIVIE: I did it for £50. Perhaps you dont know how it was. Mrs Latham, my tutor at Newnham, told my mother that I could distinguish myself in the mathematical tripos° if I went in for it in earnest. The papers were full just then of Phillipa Summers beating the senior wrangler—you remember about it; and nothing would please my mother but that I should do the same thing. I said flatly that it was not worth my while to face the grind since I was not going in for teaching; but I offered to try for fourth wrangler or thereabouts for £50. She closed with me at that, after a little grumbling; and I was better than my bargain. But I wouldnt do it again for that. £200 would have been nearer the mark.

PRAED (*much damped*): Lord bless me! Thats a very practical way of looking at it.

VIVIE: Did you expect to find me an unpractical person?

PRAED: No, no. But surely it's practical to consider not only the work these honors cost, but also the culture they bring.

VIVIE: Culture! My dear Mr Praed: do you know what the mathematical tripos means? It means grind, grind, grind for six to eight hours a day at mathematics, and nothing but mathematics. I'm supposed to know something about science; but I know nothing except the mathematics it involves. I can make calculations for engineers, electricians, insurance companies, and so on; but I know next to nothing about engineering or electricity or insurance. I dont even know arithmetic well. Outside mathematics, lawn-tennis, eating, sleeping, cycling, and walking, I'm a more ignorant barbarian than any woman could possibly be who hadnt gone in for the tripos.

PRAED (*revolted*): What a monstrous, wicked, rascally system! I knew it! I felt at once that it meant destroying all that makes womanhood beautiful.

VIVIE: I dont object to it on that score in the least. I shall turn it to very good account, I assure you.

PRAED: Pooh! In what way?

VIVIE: I shall set up in chambers in the City and work at actuarial calculations and conveyancing. Under cover of that I shall do some law, with one eye on the Stock Exchange all the time. Ive come down here by myself to read law—not for a holiday, as my mother imagines. I hate holidays.

PRAED: You make my blood run cold. Are you to have no romance, no beauty in your life?

VIVIE: I dont care for either, I assure you.

PRAED: You cant mean that.

VIVIE: Oh yes I do. I like working and getting paid for it. When I'm tired of working, I like a comfortable chair, a cigar, a little whisky, and a novel with a good detective story in it.

PRAED (*in a frenzy of repudiation*): I dont believe it. I am an artist; and I cant believe it: I refuse to believe it.

tripos: An examination for the B.A. degree with honors at Cambridge University.

(*Enthusiastically.*) Ah, my dear Miss Warren, you havnt discovered yet, I see, what a wonderful world art can open up to you.

VIVIE: Yes I have. Last May I spent six weeks in London with Honoria Fraser. Mamma thought we were doing a round of sightseeing together; but I was really at Honoria's chambers in Chancery Lane every day, working away at actuarial calculations for her, and helping her as well as a greenhorn could. In the evenings we smoked and talked, and never dreamt of going out except for exercise. And I never enjoyed myself more in my life. I cleared all my expenses, and got initiated into the business without a fee into the bargain.

PRAED: But bless my heart and soul, Miss Warren, do you call that trying art?

VIVIE: Wait a bit. That wasnt the beginning. I went up to town on an invitation from some artistic people in Fitzjohn's Avenue: one of the girls was a Newnham chum. They took me to the National Gallery, to the Opera, and to a concert where the band played all the evening—Beethoven and Wagner and so on. I wouldnt go through that experience again for anything you could offer me. I held out for civility's sake until the third day; and then I said, plump out, that I couldnt stand any more of it, and went off to Chancery Lane. Now you know the sort of perfectly splendid modern young lady I am. How do you think I shall get on with my mother?

PRAED (*startled*): Well, I hope—er—

VIVIE: It's not so much what you hope as what you believe, that I want to know.

PRAED: Well, frankly, I am afraid your mother will be a little disappointed. Not from any shortcoming on your part—I dont mean that. But you are so different from her ideal.

VIVIE: What is her ideal like?

PRAED: Well, you must have observed, Miss Warren, that people who are dissatisfied with their own bringing up generally think that the world would be all right if everybody were to be brought up quite differently. Now your mother's life has been—er—I suppose you know—

VIVIE: I know nothing. (*Praed is appalled. His consternation grows as she continues.*) Thats exactly my difficulty. You forget, Mr. Praed, that I hardly know my mother. Since I was a child I have lived in England, at school or college, or with people paid to take charge of me. I have been boarded out all my life; and my mother has lived in Brussels or Vienna and never let me go to her. I only see her when she visits England for a few days. I dont complain: it's been very pleasant; for people have been very good to me; and there has always been plenty of money to make things smooth. But dont imagine I know anything about my mother. I know far less than you do.

PRAED (*very ill at ease*): In that case—(*He stops, quite at a loss. Then, with a forced attempt at gaiety*) But what nonsense we are talking! Of course you and your mother will get on capitally. (*He rises, and looks abroad at the view.*) What a charming little place you have here!

VIVIE (*unmoved*): If you think you are doing anything but confirming my worst suspicions by changing the subject like that, you must take me for a much greater fool than I hope I am.

PRAED: Your worst suspicions! Oh, pray dont say that. Now dont.

VIVIE: Why wont my mother's life bear being talked about?

PRAED: Pray think, Miss Vivie. It is natural that I should have a certain delicacy in talking to my old friend's daughter about her behind her back. You will have plenty of opportunity of talking to her about it when she comes. (*Anxiously*) I wonder what is keeping her.

VIVIE: No: she wont talk about it either. (*Rising*) However, I wont press you. Only, mind this, Mr Praed. I strongly suspect there will be a battle royal when my mother hears of my Chancery Lane project.

PRAED (*ruefully*): I'm afraid there will.

VIVIE: I shall win the battle, because I want nothing but my fare to London to start there to-morrow earning my own living by devilling° for Honoria. Besides, I have no mysteries to keep up; and it seems she has. I shall use that advantage over her if necessary.

PRAED (*greatly shocked*): Oh no! No, pray. Youd not do such a thing.

VIVIE: Then tell me why not.

PRAED: I really cannot. I appeal to your good feeling. (*She smiles at his sentimentality.*) Besides, you may be too bold. Your mother is not to be trifled with when she's angry.

VIVIE: You cant frighten me, Mr Praed. In that month at Chancery Lane I had opportunities of taking the measure of one or two women very like my mother, who came to consult Honoria. You may back me to win. But if I hit harder in my ignorance than I need, remember that it is you who refuse to enlighten me. Now, let us drop the subject. (*She takes her chair and replaces it near the hammock with the same vigorous swing as before.*)

PRAED (*taking a desperate resolution*): One word, Miss Warren. I had better tell you. It's very difficult; but—

(*Mrs Warren and Sir George Crofts arrive at the gate. Mrs Warren is a woman between 40 and 50, good-looking, showily dressed in a brilliant hat and a gay blouse fitting tightly over her bust and flanked by fashionable sleeves. Rather spoiled and domineering, but, on the whole, a genial and fairly presentable old blackguard of a woman.*

Crofts is a tall, powerfully-built man of about 50, fashionably dressed in the style of a young man. Nasal voice, reedier than might be expected from his strong frame.

---

devilling: To aid a professional (such as a lawyer or literary person) without fee or monetary recognition. This would constitute an apprenticeship.

Clean-shaven, bulldog jaws, large flat ears, and thick neck, gentlemanly combination of the most brutal types of city man, sporting man, and man about town.)

VIVIE: Here they are. (*Coming to them as they enter the garden.*) How do, mater. Mr Praed's been here this half hour, waiting for you.

MRS WARREN: Well, if youve been waiting, Praddy, it's your own fault: I thought youd have had the gumption to know I was coming by the 3:10 train. Vivie: put your hat on, dear: youll get sunburnt. Oh, I forgot to introduce you. Sir George Crofts: my little Vivie.

(*Crofts advances to Vivie with his most courtly manner. She nods, but makes no motion to shake hands.*)

CROFTS: May I shake hands with a young lady whom I have known by reputation very long as the daughter of one of my oldest friends?

VIVIE (*who has been looking him up and down sharply*): If you like. (*She takes his tenderly proffered hand and gives it a squeeze that makes him open his eyes; then turns away, and says to her mother.*) Will you come in, or shall I get a couple more chairs? (*She goes into the porch for the chairs.*)

MRS WARREN: Well, George, what do you think of her?

CROFTS (*ruefully*): She has a powerful fist. Did you shake hands with her, Praed?

PRAED: Yes: it will pass off presently.

CROFTS: I hope so. (*Vivie reappears with two more chairs. He hurries to her assistance.*) Allow me.

MRS WARREN (*patronizingly*): Let Sir George help you with the chairs, dear.

VIVIE (*almost pitching the two into his arms*): Here you are. (*She dusts her hands and turns to Mrs Warren.*) Youd like some tea, wouldnt you?

MRS WARREN (*sitting in Praed's chair and fanning herself*): I'm dying for a drop to drink.

VIVIE: I'll see about it. (*She goes into the cottage. Sir George has by this time managed to unfold a chair and plant it beside Mrs Warren, on her left. He throws the other on the grass and sits down, looking dejected and rather foolish, with the handle of his stick in his mouth. Praed, still very uneasy, fidgets about the garden on their right.*)

MRS WARREN (*to Praed, looking at Crofts*): Just look at him, Praddy: he looks cheerful, dont he? He's been worrying my life out these three years to have that little girl of mine shewn to him; and now that Ive done it, he's quite out of countenance. (*Briskly.*) Come! sit up, George; and take your stick out of your mouth. (*Crofts sulkily obeys.*)

PRAED: I think, you know—if you dont mind my saying so—that we had better get out of the habit of thinking of her as a little girl. You see she has really distinguished herself; and I'm not sure, from what I have seen of her, that she is not older than any of us.

MRS WARREN (*greatly amused*): Only listen to him, George! Older than any of us! Well, she has been stuffing you nicely with her importance.

PRAED: But young people are particularly sensitive about being treated in that way.

MRS WARREN: Yes; and young people have to get all that nonsense taken out of them, and a good deal more besides. Dont you interfere, Praddy. I know how to treat my own child as well as you do. (*Praed, with a grave shake of his head, walks up the garden with his hands behind his back. Mrs Warren pretends to laugh, but looks after him with perceptible concern. Then she whispers to Crofts*) Whats the matter with him? What does he take it like that for?

CROFTS (*morosely*): Youre afraid of Praed.

MRS WARREN: What! Me! Afraid of dear old Praddy! Why, a fly wouldnt be afraid of him.

CROFTS: Youre afraid of him.

MRS WARREN (*angry*): I'll trouble you to mind your own business, and not try any of your sulks on me. I'm not afraid of you, anyhow. If you cant make yourself agreeable, youd better go home. (*She gets up, and, turning her back on him, finds herself face to face with Praed.*) Come, Praddy, I know it was only your tender-heartedness. Youre afraid I'll bully her.

PRAED: My dear Kitty: you think I'm offended. Dont imagine that: pray dont. But you know I often notice things that escape you; and though you never take my advice, you sometimes admit afterwards that you ought to have taken it.

MRS WARREN: Well, what do you notice now?

PRAED: Only that Vivie is a grown woman. Pray, Kitty, treat her with every respect.

MRS WARREN (*with genuine amazement*): Respect! Treat my own daughter with respect! What next, pray!

VIVIE (*appearing at the cottage door and calling to Mrs Warren*): Mother: will you come up to my room and take your bonnet off before tea?

MRS WARREN: Yes, dearie. (*She laughs indulgently at Praed and pats him on the cheek as she passes him on her way to the porch. She follows Vivie into the cottage.*)

CROFTS (*furtively*): I say, Praed.

PRAED: Yes.

CROFTS: I want to ask you a rather particular question.

PRAED: Certainly. (*He takes Mrs Warren's chair and sits close to Crofts.*)

CROFTS: Thats right: they might hear us from the window. Look here: did Kitty ever tell you who that girl's father is?

PRAED: Never.

CROFTS: Have you any suspicion of who it might be?

PRAED: None.

CROFTS (*not believing him*): I know, of course, that you perhaps might feel bound not to tell if she had said anything to you. But it's very awkward to be uncertain about it now that we shall be meeting the girl every day. We dont exactly know how we ought to feel towards her.

PRAED: What difference can that make? We take her on her own merits. What does it matter who her father was?

CROFTS (*suspiciously*): Then you know who he was?

PRAED (*with a touch of temper*): I said no just now. Did you not hear me?

CROFTS: Look here, Praed. I ask you as a particular favor. If you do know (*movement of protest from Praed*)—I only say, if you know, you might at least set my mind at rest about her. The fact is, I feel attracted towards her. Oh, dont be alarmed: it's quite an innocent feeling. Thats what puzzles me about it. Why, for all I know, *I* might be her father.

PRAED: You! Impossible! Oh no, nonsense!

CROFTS (*catching him up cunningly*): You know for certain that I'm not?

PRAED: I know nothing about it, I tell you, any more than you. But really, Crofts—oh no, it's out of the question. Theres not the least resemblance.

CROFTS: As to that, theres no resemblance between her and her mother that I can see. I suppose she's not your daughter, is she?

PRAED (*He meets the question with an indignant stare; then recovers himself with an effort and answers gently and gravely*): Now listen to me, my dear Crofts. I have nothing to do with that side of Mrs Warren's life, and never had. She has never spoken to me about it; and of course I have never spoken to her about it. Your delicacy will tell you that a handsome woman needs some friends who are not—well, not on that footing with her. The effect of her own beauty would become a torment to her if she could not escape from it occasionally. You are probably on much more confidential terms with Kitty than I am. Surely you can ask her the question yourself.

CROFTS (*rising impatiently*): I have asked her, often enough. But she's so determined to keep the child all to herself that she would deny that it ever had a father if she could. No: theres nothing to be got out of her—nothing that one can believe, anyhow. I'm thoroughly uncomfortable about it, Praed.

PRAED (*rising also*): Well, as you are, at all events, old enough to be her father, I dont mind agreeing that we both regard Miss Vivie in a parental way, as a young girl whom we are bound to protect and help. All the more, as the real father, whoever he was, was probably a black-guard. What do you say?

CROFTS (*aggressively*): I'm no older than you, if you come to that.

PRAED: Yes you are, my dear fellow: you were born old. I was born a boy: Ive never been able to feel the assurance of a grown-up man in my life.

MRS WARREN (*calling from within the cottage*): Praddee! George! Tea-ea-ea-ea!

CROFTS (*hastily*): She's calling us. (*He hurries in. Praed shakes his head bodingly, and is following slowly when he is hailed by a young gentleman who has just appeared on the common, and is making for the gate. He is a pleasant, pretty, smartly dressed, and entirely good-for-nothing young fellow, not long turned 20, with a charming voice and agreeably disrespectful manners. He carries a very light sporting magazine rifle.*)

THE YOUNG GENTLEMAN: Hallo! Praed!

PRAED: Why, Frank Gardner! (*Frank comes in and shakes hands cordially.*) What on earth are you doing here?

FRANK: Staying with my father.

PRAED: The Roman father?

FRANK: He's rector here. I'm living with my people this autumn for the sake of economy. Things came to a crisis in July: the Roman father had to pay my debts. He's stony broke in consequence; and so am I. What are you up to in these parts? Do you know the people here?

PRAED: Yes: I'm spending the day with a Miss Warren.

FRANK (*enthusiastically*): What! Do you know Vivie? Isnt she a jolly girl! I'm teaching her to shoot—you see (*shewing the rifle*)! I'm so glad she knows you: youre just the sort of fellow she ought to know. (*He smiles, and raises the charming voice almost to a singing tone as he exclaims.*) It's ever so jolly to find you here, Praed. Aint it now?

PRAED: I'm an old friend of her mother's. Mrs Warren brought me over to make her daughter's acquaintance.

FRANK: The mother! Is she here?

PRAED: Yes—inside, at tea.

MRS WARREN (*calling from within*): Prad-dee-ee-ee-eee! The tea-cake'll be cold.

PRAED (*calling*): Yes, Mrs Warren. In a moment. Ive just met a friend here.

MRS WARREN: A what?

PRAED (*louder*): A friend.

MRS WARREN: Bring him up.

PRAED: All right. (*To Frank.*) Will you accept the invitation?

FRANK (*incredulous, but immensely amused*): Is that Vivie's mother?

PRAED: Yes.

FRANK: By Jove! What a lark! Do you think she'll like me?

PRAED: Ive no doubt youll make yourself popular, as usual. Come in and try (*moving towards the house*).

FRANK: Stop a bit. (*Seriously.*) I want to take you into my confidence.

PRAED: Pray dont. It's only some fresh folly, like the barmaid at Redhill.

FRANK: It's ever so much more serious than that. You say youve only just met Vivie for the first time?

PRAED: Yes.

FRANK (*rhapsodically*): Then you can have no idea what a girl she is. Such character! Such sense! And her cleverness! Oh, my eye, Praed, but I can tell you she is clever! And the most loving little heart that—

CROFTS (*putting his head out of the window*): I say, Praed: what are you about? Do come along. (*He disappears.*)

FRANK: Hallo! Sort of chap that would take a prize at a dog show, aint he? Who's he?

PRAED: Sir George Crofts, an old friend of Mrs Warren's. I think we had better come in.

(*On their way to the porch they are interrupted by a call from the gate. Turning, they see an elderly clergyman looking over it.*)

THE CLERGYMAN (*calling*): Frank!

FRANK: Hello! (*To Praed.*) The Roman father. (*To the clergyman.*) Yes, gov'nor: all right: presently. (*To Praed.*) Look here, Praed: youd better go in to tea. I'll join you directly.

PRAED: Very good. (*He raises his hat to the clergyman, who acknowledges the salute distantly. Praed goes into the cottage. The clergyman remains stiffly outside the gate, with his hands on the top of it. The Rev. Samuel Gardner, a beneficed clergyman of the Established Church, is over 50. He is a pretentious, booming, noisy person, hopelessly asserting himself as a father and a clergyman without being able to command respect in either capacity.*)

REV. SAMUEL: Well, sir. Who are your friends here, if I may ask?

FRANK: Oh, it's all right, gov'nor! Come in.

REV. SAMUEL: No, sir; not until I know whose garden I am entering.

FRANK: It's all right. It's Miss Warren's.

REV. SAMUEL: I have not seen her at church since she came.

FRANK: Of course not: she's a third wrangler—ever so intellectual!—took a higher degree than you did; so why should she go to hear you preach?

REV. SAMUEL: Dont be disrespectful, sir.

FRANK: Oh, it dont matter: nobody hears us. Come in. (*He opens the gate, unceremoniously pulling his father with it into the garden.*) I want to introduce you to her. She and I get on rattling well together: she's charming. Do you remember the advice you gave me last July, gov'nor?

REV. SAMUEL (*severely*): Yes. I advised you to conquer your idleness and flippancy, and to work your way into an honorable profession and live on it and not upon me.

FRANK: No: thats what you thought of afterwards. What you actually said was that since I had neither brains nor money, I'd better turn my good looks to account my marrying somebody with both. Well, look here. Miss Warren has brains: you cant deny that.

REV. SAMUEL: Brains are not everything.

FRANK: No, of course not: theres the money—

REV. SAMUEL (*interrupting him austerely*): I was not thinking of money, sir. I was speaking of higher things—social position, for instance.

FRANK: I dont care a rap about that.

REV. SAMUEL: But I do, sir.

FRANK: Well, nobody wants you to marry her. Anyhow, she has what amounts to a high Cambridge degree; and she seems to have as much money as she wants.

REV. SAMUEL (*sinking into a feeble vein of humor*): I greatly doubt whether she has as much money as you will want.

FRANK: Oh, come: I havnt been so very extravagant. I live ever so quietly; I dont drink; I dont bet much; and I never go regularly on the razzle-dazzle as you did when you were my age.

REV. SAMUEL (*booming hollowly*): Silence, sir.

FRANK: Well, you told me yourself, when I was making ever such an ass of myself about the barmaid at Red-hill, that you once offered a woman £50 for the letters you wrote to her when—

REV. SAMUEL (*terrified*): Sh-sh-sh, Frank, for Heaven's sake! (*He looks round apprehensively. Seeing no one within earshot he plucks up courage to boom again, but more subduedly.*) You are taking an ungentlemanly advantage of what I confided to you for your own good, to save you from an error you would have repented all your life long. Take warning by your father's follies, sir; and dont make them an excuse for your own.

FRANK: Did you ever hear the story of the Duke of Wellington and his letters?

REV. SAMUEL: No, sir; and I dont want to hear it.

FRANK: The old Iron Duke didnt throw away £50—not he. He just wrote: "My dear Jenny: Publish and be damned! Yours affectionately, Wellington." Thats what you should have done.

REV. SAMUEL (*piteously*): Frank, my boy: when I wrote those letters I put myself into that woman's power. When I told you about her I put myself, to some extent, I am sorry to say, in your power. She refused my money with these words, which I shall never forget: "Knowledge is power," she said; "and I never sell power." Thats more than twenty years ago; and she has never made use of her power or caused me a moment's uneasiness. You are behaving worse to me than she did, Frank.

FRANK: Oh yes I dare say! Did you ever preach at her the way you preach at me every day?

REV. SAMUEL (*wounded almost to tears*): I leave you, sir. You are incorrigible. (*He turns towards the gate.*)

FRANK (*utterly unmoved*): Tell them I shant be home to tea, will you, gov'nor, like a good fellow? (*He goes towards the cottage door and is met by Vivie coming out, followed by Praed, Crofts, and Mrs Warren.*)

VIVIE (*to Frank*): Is that your father, Frank? I do so want to meet him.

FRANK: Certainly. (*Calling after his father*) Gov'nor. (*The Rev Samuel turns at the gate, fumbling nervously at his hat. Praed comes down the garden on the opposite side, beaming in anticipation of civilities. Crofts prowls about near the hammock, poking it with his stick to make it swing. Mrs Warren halts on the threshold, staring hard at the clergyman.*) Let me introduce—my father: Miss Warren.

VIVIE (*going to the clergyman and shaking his hand*): Very glad to see you here, Mr Gardner. Let me introduce everybody. Mr Gardner—Mr Frank Gardner—Mr Praed—Sir George Crofts, and—(*As the men are raising their hats to one another, Vivie is interrupted by an exclamation from her mother, who swoops down on the Reverend Samuel.*)

MRS WARREN: Why, it's Sam Gardner, gone into the church! Dont you know us, Sam? This is George Crofts, as large as life and twice as natural. Dont you remember me?

REV. SAMUEL (*very red*): I really—er—

MRS WARREN: Of course you do. Why, I have a whole album of your letters still: I came across them only the other day.

REV. SAMUEL (*miserably confused*): Miss Vavasour, I believe.

MRS WARREN (*correcting him quickly in a loud whisper*): Tch! Nonsense—Mrs. Warren: dont you see my daughter there?

ACT II

(*Inside the cottage after nightfall. Looking eastward from within instead of westward from without, the latticed window, with its curtains drawn, is now seen in the middle of the front wall of the cottage, with the porch door to the left of it. In the left-hand side wall is the door leading to the wing. Farther back against the same wall is a dresser with a candle and matches on it, and Frank's rifle standing beside them, with the barrel resting in the plate-rack. In the centre a table stands with a lighted lamp on it. Vivie's books and writing materials are on a table to the right of the window, against the wall. The fireplace is on the right, with a settle: there is no fire. Two of the chairs are set right and left of the table.*

The cottage door opens, showing a fine starlit night without; and Mrs Warren, her shoulders wrapped in a shawl borrowed from Vivie, enters, followed by Frank. She has had enough of walking, and gives a gasp of relief as she unpins her hat; takes it off; sticks the pin through the crown; and puts it on the table.)

MRS WARREN: O Lord! I dont know which is the worst of the country, the walking or the sitting at home with nothing to do. I could do a whisky and soda now very well, if only they had such a thing in this place.

FRANK (*helping her to take off her shawl, and giving her shoulders the most delicate possible little caress with his fingers as he does so*): Perhaps Vivie's got some.

MRS WARREN (*glancing back at him for an instant from the corner of her eye as she detects the pressure*): Nonsense! What would a young girl like her be doing with such things! Never mind: it dont matter. (*She throws herself wearily into a chair at the table.*) I wonder how she passes her time here! I'd a good deal rather be in Vienna.

FRANK: Let me take you there. (*He folds the shawl neatly; hangs it on the back of the other chair; and sits down opposite Mrs Warren.*)

MRS WARREN: Get out! I'm beginning to think youre a chip of the old block.

FRANK: Like the gov'nor, eh?

MRS WARREN: Never you mind. What do you know about such things? Youre only a boy.

FRANK: Do come to Vienna with me? It'd be ever such larks.

MRS WARREN: No, thank you. Vienna is no place for you—at least not until youre a little older. (*She nods at him to emphasize this piece of advice. He makes a mock-piteous face, belied by his laughing eyes. She looks at him; then rises and goes to him.*) Now, look here, little boy (*taking his face in her hands and turning it up to her*): I know you through and through by your likeness to your father, better than you know yourself. Dont you go taking any silly ideas into your head about me. Do you hear?

FRANK (*gallantly wooing her with his voice*): Cant help it, my dear Mrs Warren: it runs in the family. (*She pretends to box his ears; then looks at the pretty, laughing, upturned face for a moment, tempted. At last she kisses him, and immediately turns away, out of patience with herself.*)

MRS WARREN: There! I shouldnt have done that. I am wicked. Never you mind, my dear: it's only a motherly kiss. Go and make love to Vivie.

FRANK: So I have.

MRS WARREN (*turning on him with a sharp note of alarm in her voice*): What!

FRANK: Vivie and I are ever such chums.

MRS WARREN: What do you mean? Now see here: I wont have any young scamp tampering with my little girl. Do you hear? I wont have it.

FRANK (*quite unabashed*): My dear Mrs Warren: dont you be alarmed. My intentions are honorable—ever so honorable; and your little girl is jolly well able to take care of herself. She dont need looking after half so much as her mother. She aint so handsome, you know.

MRS WARREN (*taken aback by his assurance*): Well, you have got a nice, healthy two inches thick of cheek all over you. I dont know where you got it—not from your father, anyhow. (*Voices and footsteps in the porch.*) Sh! I hear the others coming in. (*She sits down hastily.*) Remember: youve got your warning. (*The Rev. Samuel comes in, followed by Crofts.*) Well, what became of you two? And wheres Praddy and Vivie?

CROFTS (*putting his hat on the settle and his stick in the chimney corner*): They went up the hill. We went to the village. I wanted a drink. (*He sits down on the settle, putting his legs up along the seat.*)

MRS WARREN: Well, she oughtnt to go off like that without telling me. (*To Frank*) Get your father a chair, Frank: where are your manners? (*Frank springs up and gracefully offers his father his chair; then takes another from the wall and sits down at the table, in the middle, with his father on his right and Mrs Warren on his left.*) George: where are you going

to stay to-night? You cant stay here. And whats Praddy going to do?

CROFTS: Gardner'll put me up.

MRS WARREN: Oh, no doubt youve taken care of yourself! But what about Praddy?

CROFTS: Dont know. I suppose he can sleep at the inn.

MRS WARREN: Havnt you room for him, Sam?

REV. SAMUEL: Well, er—you see, as rector here, I am not free to do as I like exactly. Er—what is Mr Praed's social position?

MRS WARREN: Oh, he's all right: he's an architect. What an old stick-in-the-mud you are, Sam!

FRANK: Yes, it's all right, gov'nor. He built that place down in Monmouthshire for the Duke of Beaufort—Tintern Abbey they call it. You must have heard of it. (*He winks with lightning smartness at Mrs Warren, and regards his father blandly.*)

REV. SAMUEL: Oh, in that case, of course we shall only be too happy. I suppose he knows the Duke of Beaufort personally.

FRANK: Oh, ever so intimately! We can stick him in Georgina's old room.

MRS WARREN: Well, thats settled. Now if those two would only come in and let us have supper. Theyve no right to stay out after dark like this.

CROFTS (*aggressively*): What harm are they doing you?

MRS WARREN: Well, harm or not, I dont like it.

FRANK: Better not wait for them, Mrs Warren. Praed will stay out as long as possible. He has never known before what it is to stray over the heath on a summer night with my Vivie.

CROFTS (*sitting up in some consternation*): I say, you know. Come!

REV. SAMUEL (*startled out of his professional manner into real force and sincerity*): Frank, once for all, its out of the question. Mrs Warren will tell you that its not to be thought of.

CROFTS: Of course not.

FRANK (*with enchanting placidity*): Is that so, Mrs Warren?

MRS WARREN (*reflectively*): Well, Sam, I dont know. If the girl wants to get married, no good can come of keeping her unmarried.

REV. SAMUEL (*astounded*): But married to him!—your daughter to my son! Only think: it's impossible.

CROFTS: Of course it's impossible. Dont be a fool, Kitty.

MRS WARREN (*nettled*): Why not? Isnt my daughter good enough for your son?

REV. SAMUEL: But surely, my dear Mrs Warren, you know the reason—

MRS WARREN (*defiantly*): I know no reasons. If you know any, you can tell them to the lad, or to the girl, or to your congregation, if you like.

REV. SAMUEL (*helplessly*): You know very well that I couldnt tell anyone the reasons. But my boy will believe me when I tell him there are reasons.

FRANK: Quite right, Dad: he will. But has your boy's conduct ever been influenced by your reasons?

CROFTS: You cant marry her; and thats all about it. (*He gets up and stands on the hearth, with his back to the fireplace, frowning determinedly.*)

MRS WARREN (*turning on him sharply*): What have you got to do with it, pray?

FRANK (*with his prettiest lyrical cadence*): Precisely what I was going to ask, myself, in my own graceful fashion.

CROFTS (*to Mrs Warren*): I suppose you dont want to marry the girl to a man younger than herself and without either a profession or twopence to keep her on. Ask Sam, if you dont believe me. (*To the Rev. Samuel.*) How much more money are you going to give him?

REV. SAMUEL: Not another penny. He has had his patrimony; and he spent the last of it in July. (*Mrs Warren's face falls.*)

CROFTS (*watching her*): There! I told you. (*He resumes his place on the settle and puts up his legs on the seat again, as if the matter were finally disposed of.*)

FRANK (*plaintively*): This is ever so mercenary. Do you suppose Miss Warren's going to marry for money? If we love one another—

MRS WARREN: Thank you. Your love's a pretty cheap commodity, my lad. If you have no means of keeping a wife, that settles it: you cant have Vivie.

FRANK (*much amused*): What do you say, gov'nor, eh?

REV. SAMUEL: I agree with Mrs Warren.

FRANK: And good old Crofts has already expressed his opinion.

CROFTS (*turning angrily on his elbow*): Look here: I want none of your cheek.

FRANK (*pointedly*): I'm ever so sorry to surprise you, Crofts; but you allowed yourself the liberty of speaking to me like a father a moment ago. One father is enough, thank you.

CROFTS (*contemptuously*): Yah! (*He turns away again.*)

FRANK (*rising*): Mrs Warren: I cannot give my Vivie up, even for your sake.

MRS WARREN (*muttering*): Young scamp!

FRANK (*continuing*): And as you no doubt intend to hold out other prospects to her, I shall lose no time in placing my case before her. (*They stare at him; and he begins to declaim gracefully*)

He either fears his fate too much,
Or his deserts are small,
That dares not put it to the touch
To gain or lose it all.

(*The cottage door opens whilst he is reciting; and Vivie and Praed come in. He breaks off. Praed puts his hat on the dresser. There is an immediate improvement in the company's behaviour. Crofts takes down his legs from the settle and pulls himself together as Praed joins him at the fireplace. Mrs Warren loses her ease of manner and takes refuge in querulousness.*)

MRS WARREN: Wherever have you been, Vivie?

VIVIE (*taking off her hat and throwing it carelessly on the table*): On the hill.

MRS WARREN: Well, you shouldnt go off like that without letting me know. How could I tell what had become of you—and night coming on too!

VIVIE (*going to the door of the inner room and opening it, ignoring her mother*): Now, about supper? We shall be rather crowded in here, I'm afraid.

MRS WARREN: Did you hear what I said, Vivie?

VIVIE (*quietly*): Yes, mother. (*Reverting to the supper difficulty.*) How many are we? (*Counting.*) One, two, three, four, five, six. Well, two will have to wait until the rest are done: Mrs Allison has only plates and knives for four.

PRAED: Oh, it doesnt matter about me. I—

VIVIE: You have had a long walk and are hungry, Mr Praed: you shall have your supper at once. I can wait myself. I want one person to wait with me. Frank: are you hungry?

FRANK: Not the least in the world—completely off my peck, in fact.

MRS WARREN (*to Crofts*): Neither are you, George. You can wait.

CROFTS: Oh, hang it, Ive eaten nothing since tea-time. Cant Sam do it?

FRANK: Would you starve my poor father?

REV. SAMUEL (*testily*): Allow me to speak for myself, sir. I am perfectly willing to wait.

VIVIE (*decisively*): Theres no need. Only two are wanted. (*She opens the door of the inner room.*) Will you take my mother in, Mr Gardner. (*The Rev. Samuel takes Mrs Warren; and they pass into the next room. Praed and Crofts follow. All except Praed clearly disapprove of the arrangement, but do not know how to resist it. Vivie stands at the door looking in at them.*) Can you squeeze past to that corner, Mr Praed: it's rather a tight fit. Take care of your coat against the white-wash—thats right. Now, are you all comfortable?

PRAED (*within*): Quite, thank you.

MRS WARREN (*within*): Leave the door open, dearie. (*Frank looks at Vivie; then steals to the cottage door and softly sets it wide open.*) Oh Lor, what a draught! Youd better shut it, dear. (*Vivie shuts it promptly. Frank noiselessly shuts the cottage door.*)

FRANK (*exulting*): Aha! Got rid of em. Well, Vivvums: what do you think of my governor?

VIVIE (*preoccupied and serious*): Ive hardly spoken to him. He doesnt strike me as being a particularly able person.

FRANK: Well, you know, the old man is not altogether such a fool as he looks. You see, he's rector here; and in trying to live up to it he makes a much bigger ass of himself than he really is. No, the gov'nor aint so bad, poor old chap; and I dont dislike him as much as you might expect. He means well. How do you think youll get on with him?

VIVIE (*rather grimly*): I dont think my future life will be much concerned with him, or with any of that old circle of my mother's, except perhaps Praed. What do you think of my mother?

FRANK: Really and truly?

VIVIE: Yes, really and truly.

FRANK: Well, she's ever so jolly. But she's rather a caution, isnt she? And Crofts! Oh, my eye, Crofts!

VIVIE: What a lot, Frank!

FRANK: What a crew!

VIVIE (*with intense contempt for them*): If I thought that *I* was like that—that I was going to be a waster, shifting along from one meal to another with no purpose, and no character, and no grit in me, I'd open an artery and bleed to death without one moment's hesitation.

FRANK: Oh no, you wouldnt. Why should they take any grind when they can afford not to? I wish I had their luck. No: what I object to is their form. It isnt the thing: it's slovenly, ever so slovenly.

VIVIE: Do you think your form will be any better when youre as old as Crofts, if you dont work?

FRANK: Of course I do—ever so much better. Vivvums mustnt lecture: her little boy's incorrigible. (*He attempts to take her face caressingly in his hands.*)

VIVIE (*striking his hands down sharply*): Off with you: Vivvums is not in a humor for petting her little boy this evening.

FRANK: How unkind!

VIVIE (*stamping at him*): Be serious. I'm serious.

FRANK: Good. Let us talk learnedly. Miss Warren: do you know that all the most advanced thinkers are agreed that half the diseases of modern civilization are due to starvation of the affections in the young. Now, *I*—

VIVIE (*cutting him short*): You are getting tiresome. (*She opens the inner door*) Have you room for Frank there? He's complaining of starvation.

MRS WARREN (*within*): Of course there is (*clatter of knives and glasses as she moves the things on the table.*) Here: theres room now beside me. Come along, Mr Frank.

FRANK (*aside to Vivie, as he goes*): Her little boy will be ever so even with his Vivvums for this. (*He goes into the other room.*)

MRS WARREN (*within*): Here, Vivie: come on you too, child. You must be famished. (*She enters, followed by Crofts, who holds the door open for Vivie with marked deference. She goes out without looking at him; and he shuts the door after her.*) Why, George, you cant be done: youve eaten nothing.

CROFTS: Oh, all I wanted was a drink. (*He thrusts his hands in his pockets, and begins prowling about the room, restless and sulky.*)

MRS WARREN: Well, I like enough to eat. But a little of that cold beef and cheese and lettuce goes a long way. (*With a sigh of only half repletion she sits down lazily at the table.*)

CROFTS: What do you go encouraging that young pup for?

MRS WARREN (*on the alert at once*): Now see here, George: what are you up to about that girl? Ive been watching your way of looking at her. Remember: I know you and what your looks mean.

CROFTS: Theres no harm in looking at her, is there?

MRS WARREN: I'd put you out and pack you back to London pretty soon if I saw any of your nonsense. My girl's little finger is more to me than your whole body and soul. (*Crofts receives this with a sneering grin. Mrs Warren, flushing a little at her failure to impose on him in the character of a theatrically devoted mother, adds in a lower key*) Make your mind easy: the young pup has no more chance than you have.

CROFTS: Maynt a man take an interest in a girl?

MRS WARREN: Not a man like you.

CROFTS: How old is she?

MRS WARREN: Never you mind how old she is.

CROFTS: Why do you make such a secret of it?

MRS WARREN: Because I choose.

CROFTS: Well, I'm not fifty yet; and my property is as good as ever it was—

MRS WARREN (*interrupting him*): Yes; because youre as stingy as youre vicious.

CROFTS (*continuing*): And a baronet isnt to be picked up every day. No other man in my position would put up with you for a mother-in-law. Why shouldnt she marry me?

MRS WARREN: You!

CROFTS: We three could live together quite comfortably. I'd die before her and leave her a bouncing widow with plenty of money. Why not? It's been growing in my mind all the time Ive been walking with that fool inside there.

MRS WARREN (*revolted*): Yes: it's the sort of thing that would grow in your mind. (*He halts in his prowling; and the two look at one another, she steadfastly, with a sort of awe behind her contemptuous disgust: he stealthily, with a carnal gleam in his eye and a loose grin, tempting her.*)

CROFTS (*suddenly becoming anxious and urgent as he sees no sign of sympathy in her*): Look here, Kitty: youre a sensible woman: you neednt put on any moral airs. I'll ask no more questions; and you need answer none. I'll settle the whole property on her; and if you want a cheque for yourself on the wedding day, you can name any figure you like—in reason.

MRS WARREN: So it's come to that with you, George, like all the other worn out old creatures!

CROFTS (*savagely*): Damn you! (*She rises and turns fiercely on him; but the door of the inner room is opened just then; and the voices of the others are heard returning. Crofts, unable to recover his presence of mind, hurries out of the cottage. The clergyman comes back.*)

REV. SAMUEL (*looking round*): Where is Sir George?

MRS WARREN: Gone out to have a pipe. (*She goes to the fireplace, turning her back on him to compose herself. The clergyman goes to the table for his hat. Meanwhile Vivie comes in, followed by Frank, who collapses into the nearest chair with an air of extreme exhaustion. Mrs Warren looks round at Vivie and says, with her affectation of maternal patronage even*) *more forced than usual.*) Well, dearie: have you had a good supper?

VIVIE: You know what Mrs Alison's suppers are. (*She turns to Frank and pets him.*) Poor Frank! was all the beef gone? did it get nothing but bread and cheese and ginger beer? (*Seriously, as if she had done quite enough trifling for one evening.*) Her butter is really awful. I must get some down from the stores.

FRANK: Do, in Heaven's name!

(*Vivie goes to the writing-table and makes a memorandum to order the butter. Praed comes in from the inner room, putting up his handkerchief, which he has been using as a napkin.*)

REV. SAMUEL: Frank, my boy: it is time for us to be thinking of home. Your mother does not know yet that we have visitors.

PRAED: I'm afraid we're giving trouble.

FRANK: Not the least in the world, Praed: my mother will be delighted to see you. She's a genuinely intellectual, artistic woman; and she sees nobody here from one year's end to another except the gov'nor; so you can imagine how jolly dull it pans out for her. (*To the Rev. Samuel.*) Youre not intellectual or artistic, are you, pater? So take Praed home at once; and I'll stay here and entertain Mrs Warren. Youll pick up Crofts in the garden. He'll be excellent company for the bull-pup.

PRAED (*taking his hat from the dresser, and coming close to Frank*): Come with us, Frank. Mrs Warren has not seen Miss Vivie for a long time; and we have prevented them from having a moment together yet.

FRANK (*quite softened, and looking at Praed with romantic admiration*): Of course: I forgot. Ever so thanks for reminding me. Perfect gentleman, Praddy. Always were—my ideal through life. (*He rises to go, but pauses a moment between the two older men, and puts his hand on Praed's shoulder.*) Ah, if you had only been my father instead of this unworthy old man! (*He puts his other hand on his father's shoulder.*)

REV. SAMUEL (*blustering*): Silence, sir, silence: you are profane.

MRS WARREN (*laughing heartily*): You should keep him in better order, Sam. Good-night. Here: take George his hat and stick with my compliments.

REV. SAMUEL (*taking them*): Good-night. (*They shake hands. As he passes Vivie he shakes hands with her also and bids her good-night. Then, in booming command, to Frank*) Come along, sir, at once. (*He goes out. Meanwhile Frank has taken his cap from the dresser and his rifle from the rack. Praed shakes hands with Mrs Warren and Vivie and goes out, Mrs Warren accompanying him idly to the door and looking out after him as he goes across the garden. Frank silently begs a kiss from Vivie; but she, dismissing him with a stern glance, takes a couple of books and some paper from the writing-table, and sits down with them at the middle table, so as to have the benefit of the lamp.*)

FRANK (*at the door, taking Mrs Warren's hand*): Goodnight, dear Mrs Warren. (*He squeezes her hand. She snatches it away, her lips tightening, and looks more than half disposed to box his ears. He laughs mischievously and runs off, clapping-to° the door behind him.*)

MRS WARREN (*coming back to her place at the table, opposite Vivie, resigning herself to an evening of boredom now that the men are gone*): Did you ever in your life hear anyone rattle on so? Isnt he a tease? (*She sits down.*) Now that I think of it, dearie, dont you go encouraging him. I'm sure he's a regular good-for-nothing.

VIVIE: Yes: I'm afraid poor Frank is a thorough good-for-nothing. I shall have to get rid of him; but I shall feel sorry for him, though he's not worth it, poor lad. That man Crofts does not seem to me to be good for much either, is he?

MRS WARREN (*galled by Vivie's cool tone*): What do you know of men, child, to talk that way about them? Youll have to make up your mind to see a good deal of Sir George Crofts, as he's a friend of mine.

VIVIE (*quite unmoved*): Why? Do you expect that we shall be much together—you and I, I mean?

MRS WARREN (*staring at her*): Of course—until youre married. Youre not going back to college again.

VIVIE: Do you think my way of life would suit you? I doubt it.

MRS WARREN: Your way of life! What do you mean?

VIVIE (*cutting a page of her book with the paper knife on her chatelaine*): Has it really never occurred to you, mother, that I have a way of life like other people?

MRS WARREN: What nonsense is this youre trying to talk? Do you want to shew your independence, now that youre a great little person at school? Dont be a fool, child.

VIVIE (*indulgently*): Thats all you have to say on the subject, is it, mother?

MRS WARREN (*puzzled, then angry*): Dont you keep on asking me questions like that. (*Violently*) Hold your tongue. (*Vivie works on, losing no time, and saying nothing.*) You and your way of life, indeed! What next? (*She looks at Vivie again. No reply.*) Your way of life will be what I please, so it will. (*Another pause.*) Ive been noticing these airs in you ever since you got that tripos or whatever you call it. If you think I'm going to put up with them youre mistaken; and the sooner you find it out, the better. (*Muttering.*) All I have to say on the subject, indeed! (*Again raising her voice angrily.*) Do you know who youre speaking to, Miss?

VIVIE (*looking across at her without raising her head from her book*): No. Who are you? What are you?

MRS WARREN (*rising breathless*): You young imp!

clapping-to: Slamming.

VIVIE: Everybody knows my reputation, my social standing, and the profession I intend to pursue. I know nothing about you. What is that way of life which you invite me to share with you and Sir George Crofts, pray?

MRS WARREN: Take care. I shall do something I'll be sorry for after, and you too.

VIVIE (*putting aside her books with cool decision*): Well, let us drop the subject until you are better able to face it. (*Looking critically at her mother*) You want some good walks and a little lawn tennis to set you up. You are shockingly out of condition: you were not able to manage twenty yards uphill to-day without stopping to pant; and your wrists are mere rolls of fat. Look at mine. (*She holds out her wrists.*)

MRS WARREN (*after looking at her helplessly, begins to whimper*): Vivie —

VIVIE (*springing up sharply*): Now pray dont begin to cry. Anything but that. I really cannot stand whimpering. I will go out of the room if you do.

MRS WARREN (*piteously*): Oh, my darling, how can you be so hard on me? Have I no rights over you as your mother?

VIVIE: Are you my mother?

MRS WARREN (*appalled*): Am I your mother! Oh, Vivie!

VIVIE: Then where are our relatives — my father — our family friends? You claim the rights of a mother: the right to call me fool and child; to speak to me as no woman in authority over me at college dare speak to me; to dictate my way of life; and to force on me the acquaintance of a brute whom anyone can see to be the most vicious sort of London man about town. Before I give myself the trouble to resist such claims, I may as well find out whether they have any real existence.

MRS WARREN (*distracted, throwing herself on her knees*): Oh no, no. Stop, stop. I am your mother: I swear it. Oh, you cant mean to turn on me — my own child: it's not natural. You believe me, dont you? Say you believe me.

VIVIE: Who was my father?

MRS WARREN: You dont know what youre asking. I cant tell you.

VIVIE (*determinedly*): Oh yes you can, if you like. I have a right to know; and you know very well that I have that right. You can refuse to tell me, if you please; but if you do, you will see the last of me to-morrow morning.

MRS WARREN: Oh, it's too horrible to hear you talk like that. You wouldnt — you couldnt leave me.

VIVIE (*ruthlessly*): Yes, without a moment's hesitation, if you trifle with me about this. (*Shivering with disgust.*) How can I feel sure that I may not have the contaminated blood of that brutal waster in my veins?

MRS WARREN: No, no. On my oath it's not he, nor any of the rest that you have ever met. I'm certain of that, at least. (*Vivie's eyes fasten sternly on her mother as the significance of this flashes on her.*)

VIVIE (*slowly*): You are certain of that, at least. Ah! You mean that that is all you are certain of. (*Thoughtfully.*) I see. (*Mrs Warren buries her face in her hands.*) Dont do that, mother: you know you dont feel it a bit. (*Mrs Warren takes down her hands and looks up deplorably at Vivie, who takes out her watch and says*) Well, that is enough for to-night. At what hour would you like breakfast? Is half-past eight too early for you?

MRS WARREN (*wildly*): My God, what sort of woman are you?

VIVIE (*coolly*): The sort the world is mostly made of, I should hope. Otherwise I dont understand how it gets its business done. Come (*taking her mother by the wrist, and pulling her up pretty resolutely*): pull yourself together. Thats right.

MRS WARREN (*querulously*): Youre very rough with me, Vivie.

VIVIE: Nonsense. What about bed? It's past ten.

MRS WARREN (*passionately*): Whats the use of my going to bed? Do you think I could sleep?

VIVIE: Why not? I shall.

MRS WARREN: You! youve no heart. (*She suddenly breaks out vehemently in her natural tongue — the dialect of a woman of the people — with all her affectations of maternal authority and conventional manners gone, and an overwhelming inspiration of true conviction and scorn in her.*) Oh, I wont bear it: I wont put up with the injustice of it. What right have you to set yourself up above me like this? You boast of what you are to me — to me, who gave you the chance of being what you are. What chance had I? Shame on you for a bad daughter and a stuck-up prude!

VIVIE (*cool and determined, but no longer confident; for her replies, which have sounded convincingly sensible and strong to her so far, now begin to ring rather woodenly and even priggishly against the new tone of her mother*): Dont think for a moment I set myself above you in any way. You attacked me with the conventional authority of a mother: I defended myself with the conventional superiority of a respectable woman. Frankly, I am not going to stand any of your nonsense; and when you drop it I shall not expect you to stand any of mine. I shall always respect your right to your own opinions and your own way of life.

MRS WARREN: My own opinions and my own way of life! Listen to her talking! Do you think I was brought up like you — able to pick and choose my own way of life? Do you think I did what I did because I liked it, or thought it right, or wouldnt rather have gone to college and been a lady if I'd had the chance?

VIVIE: Everybody has some choice, mother. The poorest girl alive may not be able to choose between being Queen of England or Principal of Newnham; but she can choose between ragpicking and flowerselling, according to her taste. People are always blaming their circumstances for what they are. I dont believe in circumstances. The people who get on in this world are the people who get up and look for the circumstances they want, and, if they cant find them, make them.

MRS WARREN: Oh, it's easy to talk, very easy, isnt it? Here!—would you like to know what my circumstances were?

VIVIE: Yes: you had better tell me. Wont you sit down?

MRS WARREN: Oh, I'll sit down: dont you be afraid. (*She plants her chair farther forward with brazen energy, and sits down. Vivie is impressed in spite of herself.*) D'you know what your gran'mother was?

VIVIE: No.

MRS WARREN: No, you dont. I do. She called herself a widow and had a fried-fish shop down by the Mint, and kept herself and four daughters out of it. Two of us were sisters: that was me and Liz; and we were both good-looking and well made. I suppose our father was a well-fed man: mother pretended he was a gentleman; but I dont know. The other two were only half sisters—undersized, ugly, starved looking, hard working, honest poor creatures: Liz and I would have half-murdered them if mother hadnt half-murdered us to keep our hands off them. They were the respectable ones. Well, what did they get by their respectability? I'll tell you. One of them worked in a white-lead factory twelve hours a day for nine shillings a week until she died of lead poisoning. She only expected to get her hands a little paralyzed; but she died. The other was always held up to us as a model because she married a Government laborer in the Deptford victualling yard, and kept his room and the three children neat and tidy on eighteen shillings a week—until he took to drink. That was worth being respectable for, wasnt it?

VIVIE (*now thoughtfully attentive*): Did you and your sister think so?

MRS WARREN: Liz didnt, I can tell you: she had more spirit. We both went to a church school—that was part of the ladylike airs we gave ourselves to be superior to the children that knew nothing and went nowhere—and we stayed there until Liz went out one night and never came back. I know the schoolmistress thought I'd soon follow her example; for the clergyman was always warning me that Lizzie'd end by jumping off Waterloo Bridge. Poor fool: that was all he knew about it! But I was more afraid of the white-lead factory than I was of the river; and so would you have been in my place. That clergyman got me a situation as scullery maid in a temperance restaurant where they sent out for anything you liked. Then I was waitress; and then I went to the bar at Waterloo station—fourteen hours a day serving drinks and washing glasses for four shillings a week and my board. That was considered a great promotion for me. Well, one cold, wretched night, when I was so tired I could hardly keep myself awake, who should come up for a half of Scotch but

Lizzie, in a long fur cloak, elegant and comfortable, with a lot of sovereigns in her purse.

VIVIE (*grimly*): My aunt Lizzie!

MRS WARREN: Yes; and a very good aunt to have, too. She's living down at Winchester now, close to the cathedral, one of the most respectable ladies there—chaperones girls at the county ball, if you please. No river for Liz, thank you! You remind me of Liz a little: she was a first-rate business woman—saved money from the beginning—never let herself look too like what she was—never lost her head or threw away a chance. When she saw I'd grown up good-looking she said to me across the bar "What are you doing there, you little fool? wearing out your health and your appearance for other people's profit!" Liz was saving money then to take a house for herself in Brussels; and she thought we two could save faster than one. So she lent me some money and gave me a start; and I saved steadily and first paid her back, and then went into business with her as her partner. Why shouldnt I have done it? The house in Brussels was real high class—a much better place for a woman to be in than the factory where Anne Jane got poisoned. None of our girls were ever treated as I was treated in the scullery of that temperance place, or at the Waterloo bar, or at home. Would you have had me stay in them and become a worn out old drudge before I was forty?

VIVIE (*intensely interested by this time*): No; but why did you choose that business? Saving money and good management will succeed in any business.

MRS WARREN: Yes, saving money. But where can a woman get the money to save in any other business? Could you save out of four shillings a week and keep yourself dressed as well? Not you. Of course, if youre a plain woman and cant earn anything more; or if you have a turn for music, or the stage, or newspaper-writing: thats different. But neither Liz nor I had any turn for such things: all we had was our appearance and our turn for pleasing men. Do you think we were such fools as to let other people trade in our good looks by employing us as shopgirls, or barmaids, or waitresses, when we could trade in them ourselves and get all the profits instead of starvation wages? Not likely.

VIVIE: You were certainly quite justified—from the business point of view.

MRS WARREN: Yes; or any other point of view. What is any respectable girl brought up to do but to catch some rich man's fancy and get the benefit of his money by marrying him?—as if a marriage ceremony could make any difference in the right or wrong of the thing! Oh, the hypocrisy of the world makes me sick! Liz and I had to work and save and calculate just like other people; elseways we should be as poor as any good-for-nothing, drunken waster of a woman that thinks her luck will last for ever. (*With great energy.*) I despise such people: theyve no character; and if theres a thing I hate in a woman, it's want of character.

VIVIE: Come now, mother: frankly! Isnt it part of what you call character in a woman that she should greatly dislike such a way of making money?

MRS WARREN: Why, of course. Everybody dislikes having to work and make money; but they have to do it all the same. I'm sure Ive often pitied a poor girl, tired out and in low spirits, having to try to please some man that she doesnt care two straws for—some half-drunken fool that thinks he's making himself agreeable when he's teasing and worrying and disgusting a woman so that hardly any money could pay her for putting up with it. But she has to bear with disagreeables and take the rough with the smooth, just like a nurse in a hospital or anyone else.

BELOW: Vivie, played by Kate Goehring, listens to her mother, Mariette Hartley, reveal her secret in Bernard Shaw's *Mrs. Warren's Profession* at the Huntington Theatre, Boston, 1999.

RIGHT: Vivie and her mother console each other in *Mrs. Warren's Profession*, Huntington Theatre, Boston, 1999.

It's not work that any woman would do for pleasure, goodness knows; though to hear the pious people talk you would suppose it was a bed of roses.

VIVIE: Still you consider it worth while. It pays.

MRS WARREN: Of course it's worth while to a poor girl, if she can resist temptation and is good-looking and well conducted and sensible. It's far better than any other employment open to her. I always thought that oughtnt to be. It cant be right, Vivie, that there shouldnt be better opportunities for women. I stick to that: it's wrong. But it's so, right or wrong; and a girl must make the best of it. But of course its not worth while for a lady. If you took to it youd be a fool; but I should have been a fool if I'd taken to anything else.

VIVIE (*more and more deeply moved*): Mother: suppose we were both as poor as you were in those wretched old days, are you quite sure that you wouldnt advise me to try the Waterloo bar, or marry a laborer, or even go into the factory?

MRS WARREN (*indignantly*): Of course not. What sort of mother do you take me for! How could you keep your self-respect in such starvation and slavery? And whats a woman worth? whats life worth? without self-respect! Why am I independent and able to give my daughter a first-rate education, when other women that had just as good opportunities are in the gutter? Because I always knew how to respect myself and control myself. Why is Liz looked up to in a cathedral town? The same reason. Where would we be now if we'd minded the clergyman's foolishness? Scrubbing floors for one and sixpence a day and nothing to look forward to but the workhouse infirmary. Dont you be led astray by people who dont know the world, my girl. The only way for a woman to provide for herself decently is for her to be good to some man that can afford to be good to her. If she's in his own station of life, let her make him marry her; but if she's far beneath him she cant expect it—why should she? It wouldnt be for her own happiness. Ask any lady in London society that has daughters; and she'll tell you the same, except that I tell you straight and she'll tell you crooked. Thats all the difference.

VIVIE (*fascinated, gazing at her*): My dear mother: you are a wonderful woman—you are stronger than all England. And are you really and truly not one wee bit doubtful—or—or—ashamed?

MRS WARREN: Well, of course, dearie, it's only good manners to be ashamed of it: it's expected from a woman. Women have to pretend to feel a great deal that they dont feel. Liz used to be angry with me for plumping out the truth about it. She used to say that when every woman could learn enough from what was going on in the world before her eyes, there was no need to talk about it to her. But then Liz was such a perfect lady! She had the true instinct of it; while I was always a bit of a vulgarian. I used to be so pleased when you sent me your photographs to see

that you were growing up like Liz: youve just her ladylike, determined way. But I cant stand saying one thing when everyone knows I mean another. Whats the use in such hypocrisy? If people arrange the world that way for women, theres no good pretending that it's arranged the other way. I never was a bit ashamed really. I consider that I had a right to be proud that we managed everything so respectably, and never had a word against us, and that the girls were so well taken care of. Some of them did very well: one of them married an ambassador. But of course now I darent talk about such things: whatever would they think of us! (*She yawns.*) Oh dear! I do believe I'm getting sleepy after all. (*She stretches herself lazily, thoroughly relieved by her explosion, and placidly ready for her night's rest.*)

VIVIE: I believe it is I who will not be able to sleep now. (*She goes to the dresser and lights the candle. Then she extinguishes the lamp, darkening the room a good deal.*) Better let in some fresh air before locking up. (*She opens the cottage door, and finds that it is broad moonlight.*) What a beautiful night! Look! (*She draws aside the curtains of the window. The landscape is seen bathed in the radiance of the harvest moon rising over Blackdown.*)

MRS WARREN (*with a perfunctory glance at the scene*): Yes, dear; but take care you dont catch your death of cold from the night air.

VIVIE (*contemptuously*): Nonsense.

MRS WARREN (*querulously*): Oh yes: everything I say is nonsense, according to you.

VIVIE (*turning to her quickly*): No: really that is not so, mother. You have got completely the better of me tonight, though I intended it to be the other way. Let us be good friends now.

MRS WARREN (*shaking her head a little ruefully*): So it has been the other way. But I suppose I must give in to it. I always got the worst of it from Liz; and now I suppose it'll be the same with you.

VIVIE: Well, never mind. Come: good-night, dear old mother. (*She takes her mother in her arms.*)

MRS WARREN (*fondly*): I brought you up well, didnt I, dearie?

VIVIE: You did.

MRS WARREN: And youll be good to your poor old mother for it, wont you?

VIVIE: I will, dear. (*Kissing her*) Good-night.

MRS WARREN (*with unction*): Blessings on my own dearie darling—a mother's blessing! (*She embraces her daughter protectingly, instinctively looking upward as if to call down a blessing.*)

ACT III

(*In the Rectory garden next morning, with the sun shining and the birds in full song. The garden wall has a five-barred wooden gate, wide enough to admit a carriage, in the middle. Beside the gate hangs a bell on a coiled spring, communicating with a pull outside. The carriage drive comes down the middle of the garden and then swerves to its left, where it ends in a little gravelled circus opposite the Rectory porch. Beyond the gate is seen the dusty high road, parallel with the wall, bounded on the farther side by a strip of turf and an unfenced pine wood. On the lawn, between the house and the drive, is a clipped yew tree, with a garden bench in its shade. On the opposite side the garden is shut in by a box hedge; and there is a sundial on the turf, with an iron chair near it. A little path leads off through the box hedge, behind the sundial.*

Frank, seated on the chair near the sundial, on which he has placed the morning papers, is reading the Standard. *His father comes from the house, red-eyed and shivery, and meets Frank's eye with misgiving.)*

FRANK (*looking at his watch*): Half past eleven. Nice hour for a rector to come down to breakfast!

REV. SAMUEL: Dont mock, Frank: dont mock. I am a little — er — (*Shivering*) —

FRANK: Off colour?

REV. SAMUEL (*repudiating the expression*): No, sir: unwell this morning. Wheres your mother?

FRANK: Dont be alarmed: she's not here. Gone to town by the 11.13 with Bessie. She left several messages for you. Do you feel equal to receiving them now, or shall I wait till youve breakfasted?

REV. SAMUEL: I have breakfasted, sir. I am surprised at your mother going to town when we have people staying with us. Theyll think it very strange.

FRANK: Possibly she has considered that. At all events, if Crofts is going to stay here, and you are going to sit up every night with him until four, recalling the incidents of your fiery youth, it is clearly my mother's duty, as a prudent housekeeper, to go up to the stores and order a barrel of whisky and a few hundred siphons.

REV. SAMUEL: I did not observe that Sir George drank excessively.

FRANK: You were not in a condition to, gov'nor.

REV. SAMUEL: Do you mean to say that *I* —

FRANK (*calmly*): I never saw a beneficed clergyman less sober. The anecdotes you told about your past career were so awful that I really dont think Praed would have passed the night under your roof if it hadnt been for the way my mother and he took to one another.

REV. SAMUEL: Nonsense, sir. I am Sir George Crofts' host. I must talk to him about something; and he has only one subject. Where is Mr Praed now?

FRANK: He is driving my mother and Bessie to the station.

REV. SAMUEL: Is Crofts up yet?

FRANK: Oh, long ago. He hasnt turned a hair: he's in much better practice than you — has kept it up ever since, probably. He's taken himself off somewhere to smoke. (*Frank resumes his paper. The Rev. Samuel*

turns disconsolately towards the gate; then comes back irresolutely.)

REV. SAMUEL: Er — Frank.

FRANK: Yes.

REV. SAMUEL: Do you think the Warrens will expect to be asked here after yesterday afternoon?

FRANK: Theyve been asked already. Crofts informed us at breakfast that you told him to bring Mrs Warren and Vivie over here to-day, and to invite them to make this house their home. It was after that communication that my mother found she must go to town by the 11.13 train.

REV. SAMUEL (*with despairing vehemence*): I never gave any such invitation. I never thought of such a thing.

FRANK (*compassionately*): How do you know, gov'nor, what you said and thought last night? Hallo! heres Praed back again.

PRAED (*coming in through the gate*): Good morning.

REV. SAMUEL: Good morning. I must apologize for not having met you at breakfast. I have a touch of — of —

FRANK: Clergyman's sore throat, Praed. Fortunately not chronic.

PRAED (*changing the subject*): Well, I must say your house is in a charming spot here. Really most charming.

REV. SAMUEL: Yes: it is indeed. Frank will take you for a walk, Mr Praed, if you like. I'll ask you to excuse me: I must take the opportunity to write my sermon while Mrs Gardner is away and you are all amusing yourselves. You wont mind, will you?

PRAED: Certainly not. Dont stand on the slightest ceremony with me.

REV. SAMUEL: Thank you. I'll — er — er — (*He stammers his way to the porch and vanishes into the house.)*

PRAED (*sitting down on the turf near Frank, and hugging his ankles*): Curious thing it must be writing a sermon every week.

FRANK: Ever so curious, if he did it. He buys em. He's gone for some soda water.

PRAED: My dear boy: I wish you would be more respectful to your father. You know you can be so nice when you like.

FRANK: My dear Praddy: you forget that I have to live with the governor. When two people live together — it dont matter whether theyre father and son, husband and wife, brother and sister — they cant keep up the polite humbug which comes so easy for ten minutes on an afternoon call. Now the governor, who unites to many admirable domestic qualities the irresoluteness of a sheep and the pompousness and aggressiveness of a jackass —

PRAED: No, pray, pray, my dear Frank, remember! He is your father.

FRANK: I give him due credit for that. But just imagine his telling Crofts to bring the Warrens over here! He must have been ever so drunk. You know, my dear Praddy, my mother wouldnt stand Mrs Warren for a moment. Vivie mustnt come here until she's gone back to town.

PRAED: But your mother doesnt know anything about Mrs Warren, does she?

FRANK: I dont know. Her journey to town looks as if she did. Not that my mother would mind in the ordinary way: she has stuck like a brick to lots of women who had got into trouble. But they were all nice women. Thats what makes the real difference. Mrs Warren, no doubt, has her merits; but she's ever so rowdy; and my mother simply wouldnt put up with her. So—hallo! (*This exclamation is provoked by the reappearance of the clergyman, who comes out of the house in haste and dismay.*)

REV. SAMUEL: Frank: Mrs Warren and her daughter are coming across the heath with Crofts: I saw them from the study windows. What am I to say about your mother?

FRANK (*jumping up energetically*): Stick on your hat and go out and say how delighted you are to see them; and that Frank's in the garden; and that mother and Bessie have been called to the bedside of a sick relative, and were ever so sorry they couldnt stop; and that you hope Mrs Warren slept well; and—and—say any blessed thing except the truth, and leave the rest to Providence.

REV. SAMUEL: But how are we to get rid of them afterwards?

FRANK: Theres no time to think of that now. Here! (*He bounds into the porch and returns immediately with a clerical felt hat, which he claps on his father's head.*) Now: off with you. Praed and I'll wait here, to give the thing an unpremeditated air. (*The clergyman, dazed but obedient, hurries off through the gate. Praed gets up from the turf, and dusts himself.*)

FRANK: We must get that old lady back to town somehow, Praed. Come! honestly, dear Praddy, do you like seeing them together—Vivie and the old lady?

PRAED: Oh, why not?

FRANK (*his teeth on edge*): Dont it make your flesh creep ever so little?—that wicked old devil, up to every villainy under the sun, I'll swear, and Vivie—ugh!

PRAED: Hush, pray. Theyre coming. (*The clergyman and Crofts are seen coming along the road, followed by Mrs Warren and Vivie walking affectionately together.*)

FRANK: Look: she actually has her arm round the old woman's waist. It's her right arm: she began it. She's gone sentimental, by God! Ugh! ugh! Now do you feel the creeps? (*The clergyman opens the gate; and Mrs Warren and Vivie pass him and stand in the middle of the garden looking at the house. Frank, in an ecstasy of dissimulation, turns gaily to Mrs Warren, exclaiming*) Ever so delighted to see you, Mrs Warren. This quiet old rectory garden becomes you perfectly.

MRS WARREN: Well, I never! Did you hear that, George? He says I look well in a quiet old rectory garden.

REV. SAMUEL (*still holding the gate for Crofts, who loafs through it, heavily bored*): You look well everywhere, Mrs Warren.

FRANK: Bravo, gov'nor! Now look here: lets have an awful jolly time of it before lunch. First lets see the church. Everyone has to do that. It's a regular old thirteenth century church, you know: the gov'nor's ever so fond of it, because he got up a restoration fund and had it completely rebuilt six years ago. Praed will be able to show its points.

REV. SAMUEL (*mooning hospitably at them*): I shall be pleased, I'm sure, if Sir George and Mrs Warren really care about it.

MRS WARREN: Oh, come along and get it over. Itll do George good: I'll lay he doesnt trouble church much.

CROFTS (*turning back towards the gate*): Ive no objection.

REV. SAMUEL: Not that way. We go through the fields, if you dont mind. Round here. (*He leads the way by the little path through the box hedge.*)

CROFTS: Oh, all right. (*He goes with the parson. Praed follows with Mrs Warren. Vivie does not stir, but watches them until they have gone, with all the lines of purpose in her face marking it strongly.*)

FRANK: Aint you coming?

VIVIE: No. I want to give you a warning, Frank. You were making fun of my mother just now when you said that about the rectory garden. That is barred in future. Please treat my mother with as much respect as you treat your own.

FRANK: My dear Viv: she wouldnt appreciate it. She's not like my mother: the same treatment wouldnt do for both cases. But what on earth has happened to you? Last night we were perfectly agreed as to your mother and her set. This morning I find you attitudinizing sentimentally with your arm round your parent's waist.

VIVIE (*flushing*): Attitudinizing!

FRANK: That was how it struck me. First time I ever saw you do a second-rate thing.

VIVIE (*controlling herself*): Yes, Frank: there has been a change; but I dont think it a change for the worse. Yesterday I was a little prig.

FRANK: And to-day?

VIVIE (*wincing; then looking at him steadily*): To-day I know my mother better than you do.

FRANK: Heaven forbid!

VIVIE: What do you mean?

FRANK: Viv: theres a freemasonry among thoroughly immoral people that you know nothing of. Youve too much character. Thats the bond between your mother and me: thats why I know her better than youll ever know her.

VIVIE: You are wrong: you know nothing about her. If you knew the circumstances against which my mother had to struggle—

FRANK (*adroitly finishing the sentence for her*): I should know why she is what she is, shouldnt I? What difference would that make? Circumstances or no circumstances, Viv, you wont be able to stand your mother.

VIVIE (*very angry*): Why not?

FRANK: Because she's an old wretch, Viv. If you ever put your arm round her waist in my presence again, I'll shoot myself there and then as a protest against an exhibition which revolts me.

VIVIE: Must I choose between dropping your acquaintance and dropping my mother's?

FRANK (*gracefully*): That would put the old lady at ever such a disadvantage. No, Viv: your infatuated little boy will have to stick to you in any case. But he's all the more anxious that you shouldnt make mistakes. It's no use, Viv: your mother's impossible. She may be a good sort; but she's a bad lot, a very bad lot.

VIVIE (*hotly*): Frank—! (*He stands his ground. She turns away and sits down on the bench under the yew tree, struggling to recover her self-command. Then she says*) Is she to be deserted by all the world because she's what you call a bad lot? Has she no right to live?

FRANK: No fear of that, Viv: she wont ever be deserted. (*He sits on the bench beside her.*)

VIVIE: But I am to desert her, I suppose.

FRANK (*babyishly, lulling her and making love to her with his voice*): Mustnt go live with her. Little family group of mother and daughter wouldnt be a success. Spoil our little group.

VIVIE (*falling under the spell*): What little group?

FRANK: The babes in the wood: Vivie and little Frank. (*He slips his arm round her waist and nestles against her like a weary child.*) Lets go and get covered up with leaves.

VIVIE (*rythmically, rocking him like a nurse*): Fast asleep, hand in hand, under the trees.

FRANK: The wise little girl with her silly little boy.

VIVIE: The dear little boy with his dowdy little girl.

FRANK: Ever so peaceful, and relieved from the imbecility of the little boy's father and the questionableness of the little girl's—

VIVIE (*smothering the word against her breast*): Sh-sh-sh-sh! little girl wants to forget all about her mother. (*They are silent for some moments, rocking one another. Then Vivie wakes up with a shock, exclaiming*) What a pair of fools we are! Come: sit up. Gracious! your hair. (*She smooths it.*) I wonder do all grown up people play in that childish way when nobody is looking. I never did it when I was a child.

FRANK: Neither did I. You are my first playmate. (*He catches her hand to kiss it, but checks himself to look round first. Very unexpectedly, he sees Crofts emerging from the box hedge.*) Oh damn!

VIVIE: Why damn, dear?

FRANK (*whispering*): Sh! Here's this brute Crofts. (*He sits farther away from her with an unconcerned air.*)

VIVIE: Dont be rude to him, Frank. I particularly wish to be polite to him. It will please my mother. (*Frank makes a wry face.*)

CROFTS: Could I have a few words with you, Miss Vivie?

VIVIE: Certainly.

CROFTS (*to Frank*): Youll excuse me, Gardner. Theyre waiting for you in the church, if you dont mind.

FRANK (*rising*): Anything to oblige you, Crofts—except church. If you want anything, Vivie, ring the gate bell, and a domestic will appear. (*He goes into the house with unruffled suavity.*)

CROFTS (*watching him with a crafty air as he disappears, and speaking to Vivie with an assumption of being on privileged terms with her*): Pleasant young fellow that, Miss Vivie. Pity he has no money, isnt it?

VIVIE: Do you think so?

CROFTS: Well, whats he to do? No profession, no property. Whats he good for?

VIVIE: I realize his disadvantages, Sir George.

CROFTS (*a little taken aback at being so precisely interpreted*): Oh, it's not that. But while we're in this world we're in it; and money's money. (*Vivie does not answer.*) Nice day, isnt it?

VIVIE (*with scarcely veiled contempt for this effort at conversation*): Very.

CROFTS (*with brutal good humor, as if he liked her pluck*): Well, thats not what I came to say. (*Affecting frankness*) Now listen, Miss Vivie. I'm quite aware that I'm not a young lady's man.

VIVIE: Indeed, Sir George?

CROFTS: No; and to tell you the honest truth I dont want to be either. But when I say a thing I mean it; when I feel sentiment I feel it in earnest; and what I value I pay hard money for. Thats the sort of man I am.

VIVIE: It does you great credit, I'm sure.

CROFTS: Oh, I dont mean to praise myself. I have my faults, Heaven knows: no man is more sensible of that than I am. I know I'm not perfect: thats one of the advantages of being a middle-aged man; for I'm not a young man, and I know it. But my code is a simple one, and, I think, a good one. Honor between man and man; fidelity between man and woman; and no cant about this religion or that religion, but an honest belief that things are making for good on the whole.

VIVIE (*with biting irony*): "A power, not ourselves, that makes for righteousness," eh?

CROFTS (*taking her seriously*): Oh, certainly, not ourselves, of course. You understand what I mean. (*He sits down beside her, as one who has found a kindred spirit.*) Well, now as to practical matters. You may have an idea that Ive flung my money about; but I havnt: I'm richer to-day than when I first came into the property. Ive used my knowledge of the world to invest my money in ways that other men have overlooked; and whatever else I may be, I'm a safe man from the money point of view.

VIVIE: It's very kind of you to tell me all this.

CROFTS: Oh well, come, Miss Vivie: you neednt pretend you dont see what I'm driving at. I want to settle down with a Lady Crofts. I suppose you think me very blunt, eh?

VIVIE: Not at all: I am much obliged to you for being so definite and business-like. I quite appreciate the offer: the money, the position, Lady Crofts, and so on. But I think I will say no, if you dont mind. I'd rather not. (*She rises, and strolls across to the sundial to get out of his immediate neighborhood.*)

CROFTS (*not at all discouraged, and taking advantage of the additional room left him on the seat to spread himself comfortably, as if a few preliminary refusals were part of the inevitable routine of courtship*): I'm in no hurry. It was only just to let you know in case young Gardner should try to trap you. Leave the question open.

VIVIE (*sharply*): My no is final. I wont go back from it. (*She looks authoritatively at him. He grins; leans forward with his elbows on his knees to prod with his stick at some unfortunate insect in the grass; and looks cunningly at her. She turns away impatiently.*)

CROFTS: I'm a good deal older than you—twenty-five years—quarter of a century. I shant live for ever; and I'll take care that you shall be well off when I'm gone.

VIVIE: I am proof against even that inducement, Sir George. Dont you think youd better take your answer? There is not the slightest chance of my altering it.

CROFTS (*rising, after a final slash at a daisy, and beginning to walk to and fro*): Well, no matter. I could tell you some things that would change your mind fast enough; but I wont, because I'd rather win you by honest affection. I was a good friend to your mother: ask her whether I wasnt. She'd never have made the money that paid for your education if it hadnt been for my advice and help, not to mention the money I advanced her. There are not many men would have stood by her as I have. I put not less than £40,000 into it, from first to last.

VIVIE (*staring at him*): Do you mean to say you were my mother's business partner?

CROFTS: Yes. Now just think of all the trouble and the explanations it would save if we were to keep the whole thing in the family, so to speak. Ask your mother whether she'd like to have to explain all her affairs to a perfect stranger.

VIVIE: I see no difficulty, since I understand that the business is wound up, and the money invested.

CROFTS (*stopping short, amazed*): Wound up! Wind up a business thats paying 35 per cent in the worst years! Not likely. Who told you that?

VIVIE (*her color quite gone*): Do you mean that it is still—? (*She stops abruptly, and puts her hand on the sundial to support herself. Then she gets quickly to the iron chair and sits down.*) What business are you talking about?

CROFTS: Well, the fact is it's not what would be considered exactly a high-class business in my set—the county set, you know—our set it will be if you think better of my offer. Not that theres any mystery about it: dont think that. Of course you know by your mother's being in it that it's perfectly straight and honest. Ive known her for many years; and I can say of her that she'd cut off her hands sooner than touch anything that was not what it ought to be. I'll tell you all about it if you like. I dont know whether youve found in travelling how hard it is to find a really comfortable private hotel.

VIVIE (*sickened, averting her fate*): Yes: go on.

CROFTS: Well, thats all it is. Your mother has a genius for managing such things. We've got two in Brussels, one in Berlin, one in Vienna, and two in Buda-Pesth. Of course there are others besides ourselves in it; but we hold most of the capital; and your mother's indispensable as managing director. Youve noticed, I daresay, that she travels a good deal. But you see you cant mention such things in society. Once let out the word hotel and everybody says you keep a public-house. You wouldnt like people to say that of your mother, would you? Thats why we're so reserved about it. By the bye, youll keep it to yourself, wont you? Since it's been a secret so long, it had better remain so.

VIVIE: And this is the business you invite me to join you in?

CROFTS: Oh no. My wife shant be troubled with business. Youll not be in it more than youve always been.

VIVIE: *I* always been! What do you mean?

CROFTS: Only that youve always lived on it. It paid for your education and the dress you have on your back. Dont turn up your nose at business, Miss Vivie; where would your Newnhams and Girtons be without it?

VIVIE (*rising, almost beside herself*): Take care. I know what this business is.

CROFTS (*starting, with a suppressed oath*): Who told you?

VIVIE: Your partner—my mother.

CROFTS (*black with rage*): The old—(*Vivie looks quickly at him. He swallows the epithet and stands swearing and raging foully to himself. But he knows that his cue is to be sympathetic. He takes refuge in generous indignation.*) She ought to have had more consideration for you. *I'd* never have told you.

VIVIE: I think you would probably have told me when we were married: it would have been a convenient weapon to break me in with.

CROFTS (*quite sincerely*): I never intended that. On my word as a gentleman I didnt.

(*Vivie wonders at him. Her sense of the irony of his protest cools and braces her. She replies with contemptuous self-possession.*)

VIVIE: It does not matter. I suppose you understand that when we leave here to-day our acquaintance ceases.

CROFTS: Why? Is it for helping your mother?

VIVIE: My mother was a very poor woman who had no reasonable choice but to do as she did. You were a rich gentleman; and you did the same for the sake of 35 per cent. You are a pretty common sort of scoundrel, I think. That is my opinion of you.

CROFTS (*after a stare—not at all displeased, and much more at his ease on these frank terms than on their former ceremonious ones*): Ha, ha, ha, ha! Go it, little missie, go it: it doesnt hurt me and it amuses you. Why the devil shouldnt I invest my money that way? I take the interest on my capital like other people: I hope you dont think I dirty my own hands with the work. Come: you wouldnt refuse the acquaintance of my mother's cousin the Duke of Belgravia because some of the rents he gets are earned in queer ways. You wouldnt cut the Archbishop of Canterbury, I suppose, because the Ecclesiastical Commissioners have a few publicans and sinners among their tenants. Do you remember your Crofts scholarship at Newnham? Well, that was founded by my brother the M.P. He gets his 22 per cent out of a factory with 600 girls in it, and not one of them getting wages enough to live on. How d'ye suppose most of them manage? Ask your mother. And do you expect me to turn my back on 35 per cent when all the rest are pocketing what they can, like sensible men? No such fool! If youre going to pick and choose your acquaintances on moral principles, youd better clear out of this country, unless you want to cut yourself out of all decent society.

VIVIE (*conscience stricken*): You might go on to point out that I myself never asked where the money I spent came from. I believe I am just as bad as you.

CROFTS (*greatly reassured*): Of course you are; and a very good thing too! What harm does it do after all? (*Rallying her jocularly*) So you dont think me such a scoundrel now you come to think it over. Eh?

VIVIE: I have shared profits with you; and I admitted you just now to the familiarity of knowing what I think of you.

CROFTS (*with serious friendliness*): To be sure you did. You wont find me a bad sort; I dont go in for being superfine intellectually; but Ive plenty of honest human feeling; and the old Crofts breed comes out in a sort of instinctive hatred of anything low, in which I'm sure youll sympathize with me. Believe me, Miss Vivie, the world isnt such a bad place as the croakers make out. So long as you dont fly openly in the face of society, society doesnt ask any inconvenient questions; and it makes precious short work of the cads who do. There are no secrets better kept than the secrets that everybody guesses. In the society I can introduce you to, no lady or gentleman would so far forget themselves as to discuss my business affairs or your mother's. No man can offer you a safer position.

VIVIE (*studying him curiously*): I suppose you really think youre getting on famously with me.

CROFTS: Well, I hope I may flatter myself that you think better of me than you did at first.

VIVIE (*quietly*): I hardly find you worth thinking about at all now. (*She rises and turns towards the gate, pausing on her way to contemplate him and say almost gently, but with intense conviction*) When I think of the society that tolerates you, and the laws that protect you—when I think of how helpless nine out of ten young girls would be in the hands of you and my mother—the unmentionable woman and her capitalist bully—

CROFTS (*livid*): Damn you!

VIVIE: You need not. I am among the damned already.

(*She raises the latch of the gate to open it and go out. He follows her and puts his hand heavily on the top bar to prevent its opening.*)

CROFTS (*panting with fury*): Do you think I'll put up with this from you, you young devil, you?

VIVIE (*unmoved*): Be quiet. Some one will answer the bell. (*Without flinching a step she strikes the bell with the back of her hand. It clangs harshly; and he starts back involuntarily. Almost immediately Frank appears at the porch with his rifle.*)

FRANK (*with cheerful politeness*): Will you have the rifle, Viv; or shall I operate?

VIVIE: Frank: have you been listening?

FRANK: Only for the bell, I assure you; so that you shouldnt have to wait. I think I showed great insight into your character, Crofts.

CROFTS: For two pins I'd take that gun from you and break it across your head.

FRANK (*stalking him cautiously*): Pray dont. I'm ever so careless in handling firearms. Sure to be a fatal accident, with a reprimand from the coroner's jury for my negligence.

VIVIE: Put the rifle away, Frank: it's quite unnecessary.

FRANK: Quite right, Viv. Much more sportsmanlike to catch him in a trap. (*Crofts, understanding the insult, makes a threatening movement.*) Crofts: there are fifteen cartridges in the magazine here; and I am a dead shot at the present distance and at an object of your size.

CROFTS: Oh, you neednt be afraid. I'm not going to touch you.

FRANK: Ever so magnanimous of you under the circumstances! Thank you.

CROFTS: I'll just tell you this before I go. It may interest you, since youre so fond of one another. Allow me, Mister Frank, to introduce you to your half-sister, the eldest daughter of the Reverend Samuel Gardner. Miss Vivie: Your half-brother. Good morning. (*He goes out through the gate and along the road.*)

FRANK (*after a pause of stupefaction, raising the rifle*): Youll testify before the coroner that it's an accident, Viv. (*He takes aim at the retreating figure of Crofts. Vivie seizes the muzzle and pulls it round against her breast.*)

VIVIE: Fire now. You may.

FRANK (*dropping his end of the rifle hastily*): Stop! take care. (*She lets it go. It falls on the turf.*) Oh, youve given your little boy such a turn. Suppose it had gone off—ugh! (*He sinks on the garden seat, overcome.*)

VIVIE: Suppose it had: do you think it would not have been a relief to have some sharp physical pain tearing through me?

FRANK (*coaxingly*): Take it ever so easy, dear Viv. Remember: even if the rifle scared that fellow into telling the truth for the first time in his life, that only makes us the babes in the wood in earnest. (*He holds out his arms to her.*) Come and be covered up with leaves again.

VIVIE (*with a cry of disgust*): Ah, not that, not that. You make all my flesh creep.

FRANK: Why, whats the matter?

VIVIE: Good-bye. (*She makes for the gate.*)

FRANK (*jumping up*): Hallo! Stop! Viv! Viv! (*She turns in the gateway*) Where are you going to? Where shall we find you?

VIVIE: At Honoria Fraser's chambers, 67 Chancery Lane, for the rest of my life. (*She goes off quickly in the opposite direction to that taken by Crofts.*)

FRANK: But I say—wait—dash it! (*He runs after her.*)

ACT IV

(*Honoria Fraser's chambers in Chancery Lane. An office at the top of New Stone Buildings, with a plate-glass window, distempered walls, electric light, and a patent stove. Saturday afternoon. The chimneys of Lincoln's Inn and the western sky beyond are seen through the window. There is a double writing-table in the middle of the room, with a cigar box, ash pans, and a portable electric reading lamp almost snowed up in heaps of papers and books. This table has knee holes and chairs right and left and is very untidy. The clerk's desk, closed and tidy, with its high stool, is against the wall, near a door communicating with the inner rooms. In the opposite wall is the door leading to the public corridor. Its upper panel is of opaque glass, lettered in black on the outside, "Fraser and Warren." A baize screen hides the corner between this door and the window.*

Frank, in a fashionable light-colored coaching suit, with his stick, gloves, and white hat in his hands, is pacing up and down the office. Somebody tries the door with a key.)

FRANK (*calling*): Come in. It's not locked.

(*Vivie comes in, in her hat and jacket. She stops and stares at him.*)

VIVIE (*sternly*): What are you doing here?

FRANK: Waiting to see you. Ive been here for hours. Is this the way you attend to your business? (*He puts his hat and stick on the table, and perches himself with a vault on the clerk's stool, looking at her with every appearance of being in a specially restless, teasing, flippant mood.*)

VIVIE: Ive been away exactly twenty minutes for a cup of tea. (*She takes off her hat and jacket and hangs them up behind the screen.*) How did you get in?

FRANK: The staff had not left when I arrived. He's gone to play cricket on Primrose Hill. Why dont you employ a woman, and give your sex a chance?

VIVIE: What have you come for?

FRANK (*springing off the stool and coming close to her*): Viv: lets go and enjoy the Saturday half-holiday somewhere, like the staff. What do you say to Richmond, and then a music hall, and a jolly supper?

VIVIE: Cant afford it. I shall put in another six hours work before I go to bed.

FRANK: Cant afford it, cant we? Aha! Look here. (*He takes out a handful of sovereigns and makes them chink.*) Gold, Viv, gold!

VIVIE: Where did you get it?

FRANK: Gambling, Viv, gambling. Poker.

VIVIE: Pah! It's meaner than stealing it. No: I'm not coming. (*She sits down to work at the table, with her back to the glass door, and begins turning over the papers.*)

FRANK (*remonstrating piteously*): But, my dear Viv, I want to talk to you ever so seriously.

VIVIE: Very well: sit down in Honoria's chair and talk here. I like ten minutes chat after tea. (*He murmurs.*) No use groaning: I'm inexorable. (*He takes the opposite seat disconsolately.*) Pass that cigar box, will you?

FRANK (*pushing the cigar box across*): Nasty womanly habit. Nice men dont do it any longer.

VIVIE: Yes: they object to the smell in the office; and weve had to take to cigarets. See! (*She opens the box and takes out a cigaret, which she lights. She offers him one; but he shakes his head with a wry face. She settles herself comfortably in her chair, smoking.*) Go ahead.

FRANK: Well, I want to know what youve done—what arrangements youve made.

VIVIE: Everything was settled twenty minutes after I arrived here. Honoria has found the business too much for her this year; and she was on the point of sending for me and proposing a partnership when I walked in and told her I hadnt a farthing in the world. So I installed myself and packed her off for a fortnight's holiday. What happened at Haslemere when I left?

FRANK: Nothing at all. I said youd gone to town on particular business.

VIVIE: Well?

FRANK: Well, either they were too flabbergasted to say anything, or else Crofts had prepared your mother. Anyhow, she didnt say anything; and Crofts didnt say anything; and Praddy only stared. After tea they got up and went; and Ive not seen them since.

VIVIE (*nodding placidly with one eye on a wreath of smoke*): Thats all right.

FRANK (*looking round disparagingly*): Do you intend to stick in this confounded place?

VIVIE (*blowing the wreath decisively away, and sitting straight up*): Yes. These two days have given me back all my strength and self-possession. I will never take a holiday again as long as I live.

FRANK (*with a very wry face*): Mps! You look quite happy—and as hard as nails.

VIVIE (*grimly*): Well for me that I am!

FRANK (*rising*): Look here, Viv: we must have an explanation. We parted the other day under a complete misunderstanding.

VIVIE (*putting away the cigaret*): Well: clear it up.

FRANK: You remember what Crofts said?

VIVIE: Yes.

FRANK: That revelation was supposed to bring about a complete change in the nature of our feeling for one another. It placed us on the footing of brother and sister.

VIVIE: Yes.

FRANK: Have you ever had a brother?

VIVIE: No.

FRANK: Then you dont know what being brother and sister feels like? Now I have lots of sisters: Jessie and Georgina and the rest. The fraternal feeling is quite familiar to me; and I assure you my feeling for you is not the least in the world like it. The girls will go their way; I will go mine; and we shant care if we never see one another again. Thats brother and sister. But as to you, I cant be easy if I have to pass a week without seeing you. Thats not brother and sister. It's exactly what I felt an hour before Crofts made his revelation. In short, dear Viv, it's love's young dream.

VIVIE (bitingly): The same feeling, Frank, that brought your father to my mother's feet. Is that it?

FRANK (revolted): I very strongly object, Viv, to have my feelings compared to any which the Reverend Samuel is capable of harboring; and I object still more to a comparison of you to your mother. Besides, I dont believe the story. I have taxed my father with it, and obtained from him what I consider tantamount to a denial.

VIVIE: What did he say?

FRANK: He said he was sure there must be some mistake.

VIVIE: Do you believe him?

FRANK: I am prepared to take his word as against Crofts'.

VIVIE: Does it make any difference? I mean in your imagination or conscience; for of course it makes no real difference.

FRANK (shaking his head): None whatever to me.

VIVIE: Nor to me.

FRANK (staring): But this is ever so surprising! I thought our whole relations were altered in your imagination and conscience, as you put it, the moment those words were out of that brute's muzzle.

VIVIE: No: it was not that. I didnt believe him. I only wish I could.

FRANK: Eh?

VIVIE: I think brother and sister would be a very suitable relation for us.

FRANK: You really mean that?

VIVIE: Yes. It's the only relation I care for, even if we could afford any other. I mean that.

FRANK (raising his eyebrows like one on whom a new light has dawned, and speaking with quite an effusion of chivalrous sentiment): My dear Viv: why didnt you say so before? I am ever so sorry for persecuting you. I understand, of course.

VIVIE (puzzled): Understand what?

FRANK: Oh, I'm not a fool in the ordinary sense—only in the Scriptural sense of doing all the things the wise man declared to be folly, after trying them himself on the most extensive scale. I see I am no longer Vivvum's little boy. Dont be alarmed: I shall never call you Vivvums again—at least unless you get tired of your new little boy, whoever he may be.

VIVIE: My new little boy!

FRANK (with conviction): Must be a new little boy. Always happens that way. No other way, in fact.

VIVIE: None that you know of, fortunately for you.

(Someone knocks at the door.)

FRANK: My curse upon yon caller, whoe'er he be!

VIVIE: It's Praed. He's going to Italy and wants to say good-bye. I asked him to call this afternoon. Go and let him in.

FRANK: We can continue our conversation after his departure for Italy. I'll stay him out. (He goes to the door and opens it.) How are you, Praddy. Delighted to see you. Come in. (Praed, dressed for travelling, comes in, in high spirits, excited by the beginning of his journey.)

PRAED: How do you do, Miss Warren. (She presses his hand cordially, though a certain sentimentality in his high spirits jars on her.) I start in an hour from Holborn Viaduct. I wish I could persuade you to try Italy.

VIVIE: What for?

PRAED: Why, to saturate yourself with beauty and romance, of course. (Vivie, with a shudder, turns her chair to the table, as if the work waiting for her there were a consolation and support to her. Praed sits opposite to her. Frank places a chair just behind Vivie, and drops lazily and carelessly into it, talking at her over his shoulder.)

FRANK: No use, Praddy. Viv is a little Philistine. She is indifferent to my romance, and insensible to my beauty.

VIVIE: Mr Praed: once for all, there is no beauty and no romance in life for me. Life is what it is; and I am prepared to take it as it is.

PRAED (enthusiastically): You will not say that if you come to Verona and on to Venice. You will cry with delight at living in such a beautiful world.

FRANK: This is most eloquent, Praddy. Keep it up.

PRAED: Oh, I assure you I have cried—I shall cry again, I hope—at fifty! At your age, Miss Warren, you would not need to go so far as Verona. Your spirits would absolutely fly up at the mere sight of Ostend. You would be charmed with the gaiety, the vivacity, the happy air of Brussels. (Vivie recoils) Whats the matter?

FRANK: Hallo, Viv!

VIVIE (to Praed, with deep reproach): Can you find no better example of your beauty and romance than Brussels to talk to me about?

PRAED (puzzled): Of course it's very different from Verona. I dont suggest for a moment that—

VIVIE (bitterly): Probably the beauty and romance come to much the same in both places.

PRAED (*completely sobered and much concerned*): My dear Miss Warren: I—(*looking enquiringly at Frank*) Is anything the matter?

FRANK: She thinks your enthusiasm frivolous, Praddy. She's had ever such a serious call.

VIVIE (*sharply*): Hold your tongue, Frank. Dont be silly.

FRANK (*calmly*): Do you call this good manners, Praed?

PRAED (*anxious and considerate*): Shall I take him away, Miss Warren? I feel sure we have disturbed you at your work. (*He is about to rise.*)

VIVIE: Sit down: I'm not ready to go back to work yet. You both think I have an attack of nerves. Not a bit of it. But there are two subjects I want dropped, if you dont mind. One of them (*to Frank*) is love's young dream in any shape or form: the other (*to Praed*) is the romance and beauty of life, especially as exemplified by the gaiety of Brussels. You are welcome to any illusions you may have left on these subjects: I have none. If we three are to remain friends, I must be treated as a woman of business, permanently single (*to Frank*) and permanently unromantic (*to Praed*).

FRANK: I also shall remain permanently single until you change your mind. Praddy: change the subject. Be eloquent about something else.

PRAED (*diffidently*): I'm afraid theres nothing else in the world that I can talk about. The Gospel of Art is the only one I can preach. I know Miss Warren is a great devotee of the Gospel of Getting On; but we cant discuss that without hurting your feelings, Frank, since you are determined not to get on.

FRANK: Oh, dont mind my feelings. Give me some improving advice by all means: it does me ever so much good. Have another try to make a successful man of me, Viv. Come: lets have it all: energy, thrift, foresight, self-respect, character. Dont you hate people who have no character, Viv?

VIVIE (*wincing*): Oh, stop, stop: let us have no more of that horrible cant. Mr Praed: if there are really only those two gospels in the world, we had better all kill ourselves; for the same taint is in both, through and through.

FRANK (*looking critically at her*): There is a touch of poetry about you to-day, Viv, which has hitherto been lacking.

PRAED (*remonstrating*): My dear Frank: arnt you a little unsympathetic?

VIVIE (*merciless to herself*): No: it's good for me. It keeps me from being sentimental.

FRANK (*bantering her*): Checks your strong natural propensity that way, dont it?

VIVIE (*almost hysterically*): Oh yes: go on: dont spare me. I was sentimental for one moment in my life—beautifully sentimental—by moonlight; and now—

FRANK (*quickly*): I say, Viv: take care. Dont give yourself away.

VIVIE: Oh, do you think Mr Praed does not know all about my mother? (*Turning on Praed*) You had better have told me that morning, Mr Praed. You are very old fashioned in your delicacies, after all.

PRAED: Surely it is you who are a little old fashioned in your prejudices, Miss Warren. I feel bound to tell you, speaking as an artist, and believing that the most intimate human relationships are far beyond and above the scope of the law, that though I know that your mother is an unmarried woman, I do not respect her the less on that account. I respect her more.

FRANK (*airily*): Hear, hear!

VIVIE (*staring at him*): Is that all you know?

PRAED: Certainly that is all.

VIVIE: Then you neither of you know anything. Your guesses are innocence itself compared to the truth.

PRAED (*startled and indignant, preserving his politeness with an effort*): I hope not. (*More emphatically*) I hope not, Miss Warren. (*Frank's face shows that he does not share Praed's incredulity. Vivie utters an exclamation of impatience. Praed's chivalry droops before their conviction. He adds, slowly*) If there is anything worse—that is, anything else—are you sure you are right to tell us, Miss Warren?

VIVIE: I am sure that if I had the courage I should spend the rest of my life in telling it to everybody—in stamping and branding it into them until they felt their share in its shame and horror as I feel mine. There is nothing I despise more than the wicked convention that protects these things by forbidding a woman to mention them. And yet I cant tell you. The two infamous words that describe what my mother is are ringing in my ears and struggling on my tongue; but I cant utter them: my instinct is too strong for me. (*She buries her face in her hands. The two men, astonished, stare at one another and then at her. She raises her head again desperately and takes a sheet of paper and a pen.*) Here: let me draft you a prospectus.

FRANK: Oh, she's mad. Do you hear, Viv, mad. Come: pull yourself together.

VIVIE: You shall see. (*She writes.*) "Paid up capital: not less than £40,000 standing in the name of Sir George Crofts, Baronet, the chief shareholder." What comes next?—I forget. Oh yes: "Premises at Brussels, Berlin, Vienna and Buda-Pesth. Managing director: Mrs Warren"; and now dont let us forget her qualifications: the two words. There! (*She pushes the paper to them.*) Oh, no: dont read it: dont! (*She snatches it back and tears it to pieces; then seizes her head in her hands and hides her face on the table. Frank, who has watched the writing carefully over her shoulder, and opened his eyes very widely at it, takes a card from his pocket; scribbles a couple of words; and silently hands it to Praed, who looks at it with amazement. Frank then remorsefully stoops over Vivie.*)

FRANK (*whispering tenderly*): Viv, dear: thats all right. I read what you wrote: so did Praddy. We understand. And we remain, as this leaves us at present, yours ever so devotedly. (*Vivie slowly raises her head.*)

PRAED: We do indeed, Miss Warren. I declare you are the most splendidly courageous woman I ever met.

(*This sentimental compliment braces Vivie. She throws it away from her with an impatient shake, and forces herself to stand up, though not without some support from the table.*)

FRANK: Dont stir, Viv, if you dont want to. Take it easy.

VIVIE: Thank you. You can always depend on me for two things, not to cry and not to faint. (*She moves a few steps towards the door of the inner rooms, and stops close to Praed to say*) I shall need much more courage than that when I tell my mother that we have come to the parting of the ways. Now I must go into the next room for a moment to make myself neat again, if you dont mind.

PRAED: Shall we go away?

VIVIE: No: I'll be back presently. Only for a moment.

(*She goes into the other room, Praed opening the door for her.*)

PRAED: What an amazing revelation! I'm extremely disappointed in Crofts: I am indeed.

FRANK: I'm not in the least. I feel he's perfectly accounted for at last. But what a facer for me, Praddy! I cant marry her now.

PRAED (*sternly*): Frank! (*The two look at one another, Frank unruffled, Praed deeply indignant.*) Let me tell you, Gardner, that if you desert her now you will behave very despicably.

FRANK: Good old Praddy! Ever chivalrous! But you mistake: it's not the moral aspect of the case: it's the money aspect. I really cant bring myself to touch the old woman's money now.

PRAED: And was that what you were going to marry on?

FRANK: What else? *I* havnt any money, nor the smallest turn for making it. If I married Viv now she would have to support me; and I should cost her more than I am worth.

PRAED: But surely a clever, bright fellow like you can make something by your own brains.

FRANK: Oh yes, a little. (*He takes out his money again.*) I made all that yesterday—in an hour and a half. But I made it in a highly speculative business. No, dear Praddy: even if Jessie and Georgina marry millionaires and the governor dies after cutting them off with a shilling, I shall have only four hundred a year. And he wont die until he's three score and ten: he hasnt originality enough. I shall be on short allowance for the next twenty years. No short allowance for Viv, if I can help it. I withdraw gracefully and leave the field to the gilded youth of England. So thats settled. I shant worry her about it: I'll just send her a little note after we're gone. She'll understand.

PRAED (*grasping his hand*): Good fellow, Frank! I heartily beg your pardon. But must you never see her again?

FRANK: Never see her again! Hang it all, be reasonable. I shall come along as often as possible, and be her brother. I can not understand the absurd consequences you romantic people expect from the most ordinary transactions. (*A knock at the door.*) I wonder who this is. Would you mind opening the door? If it's a client it will look more respectable than if I appeared.

PRAED: Certainly. (*He goes to the door and opens it. Frank sits down in Vivie's chair to scribble a note.*) My dear Kitty: come in, come in.

(*Mrs Warren comes in, looking apprehensively round for Vivie. She has done her best to make herself matronly and dignified. The brilliant hat is replaced by a sober bonnet, and the gay blouse covered by a costly black silk mantle. She is pitiably anxious and ill at ease—evidently panic-stricken.*)

MRS WARREN (*to Frank*): What! Youre here, are you?

FRANK (*turning in his chair from his writing, but not rising*): Here, and charmed to see you. You come like a breath of spring.

MRS WARREN: Oh, get out with your nonsense. (*In a low voice*) Wheres Vivie?

(*Frank points expressively to the door of the inner room, but says nothing.*)

MRS WARREN (*sitting down suddenly and almost beginning to cry*): Praddy: wont she see me, dont you think?

PRAED: My dear Kitty: dont distress yourself. Why should she not?

MRS WARREN: Oh, you never can see why not: youre too amiable. Mr Frank: did she say anything to you?

FRANK (*folding his note*): She must see you, if (*very expressively*) you wait until she comes in.

MRS WARREN (*frightened*): Why shouldnt I wait?

(*Frank looks quizzically at her; puts his note carefully on the ink-bottle, so that Vivie cannot fail to find it when next she dips her pen; then rises and devotes his attention entirely to her.*)

FRANK: My dear Mrs Warren: suppose you were a sparrow—ever so tiny and pretty a sparrow hopping in the roadway—and you saw a steam roller coming in your direction, would you wait for it?

MRS WARREN: Oh, dont bother me with your sparrows. What did she run away from Haslemere like that for?

FRANK: I'm afraid she'll tell you if you wait until she comes back.

MRS WARREN: Do you want me to go away?

FRANK: No. I always want you to stay. But I advise you to go away.

MRS WARREN: What! And never see her again!

FRANK: Precisely.

MRS WARREN (*crying again*): Praddy: dont let him be cruel to me. (*She hastily checks her tears and wipes her eyes.*) She'll be so angry if she sees Ive been crying.

FRANK (*with a touch of real compassion in his airy tenderness*): You know that Praddy is the soul of kindness, Mrs Warren. Praddy: what do you say? Go or stay?

PRAED (*to Mrs Warren*): I really should be very sorry to cause you unnecessary pain; but I think perhaps you had better not wait. The fact is—(*Vivie is heard at the inner door.*)

FRANK: Sh! Too late. She's coming.

MRS WARREN: Dont tell her I was crying. (*Vivie comes in. She stops gravely on seeing Mrs Warren, who greets her with hysterical cheerfulness.*) Well, dearie. So here you are at last.

VIVIE: I am glad you have come: I want to speak to you. You said you were going, Frank, I think.

FRANK: Yes. Will you come with me, Mrs Warren? What do you say to a trip to Richmond, and the theatre in the evening? There is safety in Richmond. No steam roller there.

VIVIE: Nonsense, Frank. My mother will stay here.

MRS WARREN (*scared*): I dont know: perhaps I'd better go. We're disturbing you at your work.

VIVIE (*with quiet decision*): Mr Praed: please take Frank away. Sit down, mother. (*Mrs Warren obeys helplessly.*)

PRAED: Come, Frank. Good-bye, Miss Vivie.

VIVIE (*shaking hands*): Good-bye. A pleasant trip.

PRAED: Thank you: thank you. I hope so.

FRANK (*to Mrs Warren*): Good-bye: youd ever so much better have taken my advice. (*He shakes hands with her. Then airily to Vivie*) Bye-bye, Viv.

VIVIE: Good-bye. (*He goes out gaily without shaking hands with her. Praed follows. Vivie, composed and extremely grave, sits down in Honoria's chair, and waits for her mother to speak. Mrs Warren, dreading a pause, loses no time in beginning.*)

MRS WARREN: Well, Vivie, what did you go away like that for without saying a word to me? How could you do such a thing! And what have you done to poor George? I wanted him to come with me; but he shuffled out of it. I could see that he was quite afraid of you. Only fancy: he wanted me not to come. As if (*trembling*) I should be afraid of you, dearie. (*Vivie's gravity deepens.*) But of course I told him it was all settled and comfortable between us, and that we were on the best of terms. (*She breaks down.*) Vivie: whats the meaning of this? (*She produces a paper from an envelope; comes to the table; and hands it across.*) I got it from the bank this morning.

VIVIE: It is my month's allowance. They sent it to me as usual the other day. I simply sent it back to be placed to your credit, and asked them to send you the lodgment receipt. In future I shall support myself.

MRS WARREN (*not daring to understand*): Wasnt it enough? Why didnt you tell me? (*With a cunning gleam in her eye*) I'll double it: I was intending to double it. Only let me know how much you want.

VIVIE: You know very well that that has nothing to do with it. From this time I go my own way in my own business and among my own friends. And you will go yours. (*She rises*) Good-bye.

MRS WARREN (*appalled*): Good-bye?

VIVIE: Yes: good-bye. Come: dont let us make a useless scene: you understand perfectly well. Sir George Crofts has told me the whole business.

MRS WARREN (*angrily*): Silly old—(*She swallows an epithet, and turns white at the narrowness of her escape from uttering it.*) He ought to have his tongue cut out. But I explained it all to you; and you said you didnt mind.

VIVIE (*steadfastly*): Excuse me: I do mind. You explained how it came about. That does not alter it.

(*Mrs Warren, silenced for a moment, looks forlornly at Vivie, who waits like a statue, secretly hoping that the combat is over. But the cunning expression comes back into Mrs Warren's face; and she bends across the table, sly and urgent, half whispering*)

MRS WARREN: Vivie: do you know how rich I am?

VIVIE: I have no doubt you are very rich.

MRS WARREN: But you dont know all that that means: youre too young. It means a new dress every day; it means theatres and balls every night; it means having the pick of all the gentlemen in Europe at your feet; it means a lovely house and plenty of servants; it means the choicest of eating and drinking; it means everything you like, everything you want, everything you can think of. And what are you here? A mere drudge, toiling and moiling early and late for your bare living and two cheap dresses a year. Think over it. (*Soothingly*) Youre shocked, I know. I can enter into your feelings; and I think they do you credit; but trust me, nobody will blame you: you may take my word for that. I know what young girls are; and I know youll think better of it when youve turned it over in your mind.

VIVIE: So thats how it's done, is it? You must have said all that to many a woman, mother, to have it so pat.

MRS WARREN (*passionately*): What harm am I asking you to do? (*Vivie turns away contemptuously. Mrs Warren follows her desperately*) Vivie: listen to me: you dont understand: youve been taught wrong on purpose: you dont know what the world is really like.

VIVIE (*arrested*): Taught wrong on purpose! What do you mean?

MRS WARREN: I mean that youre throwing away all your chances for nothing. You think that people are what they pretend to be—that the way you were taught at school and college to think right and proper is the way things really are. But it's not: it's all only a pretence, to keep the cowardly, slavish common run of people quiet. Do you want to find that out, like other women, at forty, when youve thrown yourself away and lost your chances; or wont you take it in good time now from your own mother, that loves you and swears to you that it's truth—gospel truth? (*Urgently*) Vivie: the big people, the clever people, the managing people, all know it. They do as I do, and think what I think. I know plenty of them. I know them to speak to, to introduce you to, to make friends of for you. I dont mean anything wrong: thats what you dont understand: your head is full of ignorant ideas about me. What do the people that taught you know about life or about people like me? When did they ever meet me, or speak to me, or let anyone tell them about me?—the fools! Would they ever have done anything for you if I hadnt paid them? Havnt I told you that I want you to be respectable? Havnt I brought you up to be respectable? And how can you keep it up without my money and my influence and Lizzie's friends? Cant you see that youre cutting your own throat as well as breaking my heart in turning your back on me?

VIVIE: I recognise the Crofts philosophy of life, mother. I heard it all from him that day at the Gardners'.

MRS WARREN: You think I want to force that played-out old sot on you! I dont, Vivie: on my oath I dont.

VIVIE: It would not matter if you did: you would not succeed. (*Mrs Warren winces, deeply hurt by the implied indifference towards her affectionate intention. Vivie, neither understanding this nor concerning herself about it, goes on calmly*) Mother: you dont at all know the sort of person I am. I dont object to Crofts more than to any other coarsely built man of his class. To tell you the truth, I rather admire him for being strong-minded enough to enjoy himself in his own way and make plenty of money instead of living the usual shooting, hunting, dining-out, tailoring, loafing life of his set merely because all the rest do it. And I'm perfectly aware that if I'd been in the same circumstances as my aunt Liz, I'd have done exactly what she did. I dont think I'm more prejudiced or straitlaced than you: I think I'm less. I'm certain I'm less sentimental. I know very well that fashionable morality is all a pretence, and that if I took your money and devoted the rest of my life to spending it fashionably, I might be as worthless and vicious as the silliest woman could possibly want to be without having a word said to me about it. But I dont want to be worthless. I shouldnt enjoy trotting about the park to advertize my dressmaker and carriage builder, or being bored at the opera to show off a shop windowful of diamonds.

MRS WARREN (*bewildered*): But—

VIVIE: Wait a moment: Ive not done. Tell me why you continue your business now that you are independent of it. Your sister, you told me, has left all that behind her. Why dont you do the same?

MRS WARREN: Oh, it's all very easy for Liz: she likes good society, and has the air of being a lady. Imagine me in a cathedral town! Why, the very rooks in the trees would find me out even if I could stand the dulness of it. I must have work and excitement, or I should go melancholy mad. And what else is there for me to do? The life suits me: I'm fit for it and not for anything else. If I didnt do it somebody else would; so I dont do any real harm by it. And then it brings in money; and I like making money. No: it's no use: I cant give it up—not for anybody. But what need you know about it? I'll never mention it. I'll keep Crofts away. I'll not trouble you much: you see I have to be constantly running about from one place to another. Youll be quit of me altogether when I die.

VIVIE: No. I am my mother's daughter. I am like you: I must have work, and must make more money than I spend. But my work is not your work, and my way not your way. We must part. It will not make much difference to us: instead of meeting one another for perhaps a few months in twenty years, we shall never meet: thats all.

MRS WARREN (*her voice stifled in tears*): Vivie: I meant to have been more with you: I did indeed.

VIVIE: It's no use, mother: I am not to be changed by a few cheap tears and entreaties any more than you are, I dare say.

MRS WARREN (*wildly*): Oh, you call a mother's tears cheap.

VIVIE: They cost you nothing; and you ask me to give you the peace and quietness of my whole life in exchange for them. What use would my company be to you if you could get it? What have we two in common that could make either of us happy together?

MRS WARREN (*lapsing recklessly into her dialect*): We're mother and daughter. I want my daughter. Ive a right to you. Who is to care for me when I'm old? Plenty of girls have taken to me like daughters and cried at leaving me; but I let them all go because I had you to look forward to. I kept myself lonely for you. Youve no right to turn on me now and refuse to do your duty as a daughter.

VIVIE (*jarred and antagonized by the echo of the slums in her mother's voice*): My duty as a daughter! I thought we should come to that presently. Now once for all, mother, you want a daughter and Frank wants a wife. I dont want a mother; and I dont want a husband. I have spared neither Frank nor myself in sending him about his business. Do you think I will spare you?

MRS WARREN (*violently*): Oh, I know the sort you are—no mercy for yourself or anyone else. *I* know. My experience has done that for me anyhow: I can tell the pious, canting, hard, selfish woman when I meet her. Well, keep yourself to yourself: *I* dont want you. But listen to this. Do you know what I would do with you if you were a baby again—aye, as sure as there's a Heaven above us?

VIVIE: Strangle me, perhaps.

MRS WARREN: No: I'd bring you up to be a real daughter to me, and not what you are now, with your pride and your prejudices and the college education you stole from me—yes, stole: deny it if you can: what was it but stealing? I'd bring you up in my own house, so I would.

VIVIE (*quietly*): In one of your own houses.

MRS WARREN (*screaming*): Listen to her! listen to how she spits on her mother's grey hairs! Oh, may you live to have your own daughter tear and trample on you as you have trampled on me. And you will: you will. No woman ever had luck with a mother's curse on her.

VIVIE: I wish you wouldnt rant, mother. It only hardens me. Come: I suppose I am the only young woman you ever had in your power that you did good to. Dont spoil it all now.

MRS WARREN: Yes, Heaven forgive me, it's true; and you are the only one that ever turned on me. Oh, the injustice of it, the injustice, the injustice! I always wanted to be a good woman. I tried honest work; and I was slave-driven until I cursed the day I ever heard of honest work. I was a good mother; and because I made my daughter a good woman she turns me out as if I was a leper. Oh, if I only had my life to live over again! I'd talk to that lying clergyman in the school. From this time forth, so help me Heaven in my last hour, I'll do wrong and nothing but wrong. And I'll prosper on it.

VIVIE: Yes: it's better to choose your line and go through with it. If I had been you, mother, I might have done as you did; but I should not have lived one life and believed in another. You are a conventional woman at heart. That is why I am bidding you good-bye now. I am right, am I not?

MRS WARREN (*taken aback*): Right to throw away all my money!

VIVIE: No: right to get rid of you? I should be a fool not to? Isnt that so?

MRS WARREN (*sulkily*): Oh well, yes, if you come to that, I suppose you are. But Lord help the world if everybody took to doing the right thing! And now I'd better go than stay where I'm not wanted. (*She turns to the door.*)

VIVIE (*kindly*): Wont you shake hands?

MRS WARREN (*after looking at her fiercely for a moment with a savage impulse to strike her*): No, thank you. Good-bye.

VIVIE (*matter-of-factly*): Good-bye. (*Mrs Warren goes out, slamming the door behind her. The strain on Vivie's face relaxes; her grave expression breaks up into one of joyous content; her breath goes out in a half sob, half laugh of intense relief. She goes buoyantly to her place at the writing-table; pushes the electric lamp out of the way; pulls over a great sheaf of papers; and is in the act of dipping her pen in the ink when she finds Frank's note. She opens it unconcernedly and reads it quickly, giving a little laugh at some quaint turn of expression in it.*) And good-bye, Frank. (*She tears the note up and tosses the pieces into the wastepaper basket without a second thought. Then she goes at her work with a plunge, and soon becomes absorbed in her figures.*)

COMMENTARIES

Bernard Shaw (1856–1950)

PLAYS UNPLEASANT: *MRS. WARREN'S PROFESSION*   1898

Shaw included Mrs. Warren's Profession *in a group of three plays he titled "unpleasant." In this excerpt from one of his prefaces (1898), he explains that the subjects of these plays are not to be taken lightly by an audience out for an evening of fun but are serious and meant to be considered carefully.*

In *Mrs Warren's Profession* I have gone straight at the fact that, as Mrs Warren puts it, "the only way for a woman to provide for herself decently is for her to be good to some man that can afford to be good to her." There are some questions on which I am, like most Socialists, an extreme Individualist. I believe that any society which desires to found itself on a high standard of integrity of character in its units should organize itself in such a fashion as to make it possible too for all men and all women to maintain themselves in reasonable comfort by their industry without selling their affections and their convictions. At present we not only condemn women as a sex to attach themselves to "breadwinners," licitly or illicitly, on pain of heavy privation and disadvantage; but we have great prostitute classes of men: for instance, dramatists and journalists, to whom I myself belong, not to mention the legions of lawyers, doctors, clergymen, and platform politicians who are daily using their highest faculties to belie their real sentiments: a sin compared to which that of a woman who sells the use of her person for a few hours is too venial to be worth mentioning; for rich men without conviction are more dangerous in modern society than poor women without chastity. Hardly a pleasant subject this!

I must, however, warn my readers that my attacks are directed against themselves, not against my stage figures. They cannot too thoroughly understand that the guilt of defective social organization does not lie alone on the people who actually work the commercial makeshifts which the defects make inevitable, and who often, like Sartorius and Mrs Warren, display valuable executive capacities and even high moral virtues in their administration, but with the whole body of citizens whose public opinion, public action, and public contribution as ratepayers alone can replace Sartorius's slums with decent dwellings, Charteris's intrigues with reasonable marriage contracts, and Mrs Warren's profession with honorable industries guarded by a humane industrial code and a "moral minimum" wage.

Bernard Shaw (1856–1950)
FROM THE PREFACE TO *MRS. WARREN'S PROFESSION*   1902

Most of Shaw's prefaces to his plays address the issues of the plays themselves. This preface concentrates on the efforts of authorities to censor the play and prevent its production. Shaw gives us his views on censorship and on the public attitudes that viewed the play as threatening to public morality. However, he also goes on to comment on the issues of prostitution in the late nineteenth century and its relationship to the society that sustained it. As he puts it, even his supportive critics would not see themselves as responsible for the existence of the Mrs. Warrens among them.

The Author's Apology

Mrs Warren's Profession has been performed at last, after a delay of only eight years; and I have once more shared with Ibsen the triumphant amusement of startling all but the strongest-headed of the London theater critics clean out of the practice of their profession. No author who has ever known the exultation of sending the Press into an hysterical tumult of protest, of moral panic, of involuntary and frantic confession of sin, of a horror of conscience in which the power of distinguishing between the work of art on the stage and the real life of the spectator is confused and overwhelmed, will ever care for the stereotyped compliments which every successful farce or melodrama elicits from the newspapers. Give me that critic who rushed from my play to declare furiously that Sir George Crofts ought to be kicked. What a triumph for the actor, thus to reduce a jaded London journalist to the condition of the simple sailor in the Wapping gallery, who shouts execrations at Iago and warnings to Othello not to believe him! But dearer still than such simplicity is that sense of the sudden earthquake shock to the foundations of morality which sends a pallid crowd of critics into the street shrieking that the pillars of society are cracking and the ruin of the State at hand. Even the Ibsen champions of ten years ago remonstrate with me just as the veterans of those brave days remonstrated with them. Mr Grein, the hardy iconoclast who first launched my plays on the stage alongside *Ghosts* and *The Wild Ducks,* exclaims that I have shattered his ideals. Actually his ideals! What would Dr. Relling say? And Mr William Archer himself disowns me because I "cannot touch pitch without wallowing in it." Truly my play must be more needed than I knew; and yet I thought I knew how little the others know.

Do not suppose, however, that the consternation of the Press reflects any consternation among the general public. Anybody can upset the theater critics, in a turn of the wrist, by substituting for the romantic commonplaces of the stage the moral commonplaces of the pulpit, the platform, or the library. Play *Mrs Warren's Profession* to an audience of clerical members of the Christian Social Union and of women well experienced in Rescue, Temperance, and Girls' Club work, and no moral panic will arise: every man and woman present will know that as long as poverty makes virtue hideous and the spare pocket-money of rich bachelordom makes vice dazzling, their daily hand-to-hand fight against prostitution with prayer and persuasion, shelters and scanty alms, will be a losing one. There was a time when they were able to urge that though "the white-lead factory where Anne Jane was poisoned" may be a far more terrible place than Mrs Warren's house, yet hell is still more dreadful. Nowadays they no longer believe in hell; and the girls among whom they are working know that they did not believe in it, and would laugh at them if they did. So well have the rescuers learnt that Mrs Warren's defense of herself and indictment of society is the thing that most needs saying, that those who know me personally reproach me, not for writing this play, but for wasting my energies on "pleasant plays" for the amusement of frivolous people, when I can build up such excellent stage sermons on their own work. *Mrs Warren's Profession* is the one play of mine which I could submit to a censorship without doubt of the result; only, it must not be the censorship of the minor theater critic, nor of an innocent court official like the King's Reader of Plays, much less of people who consciously profit by Mrs Warren's profession, or who personally make use of it, or who hold the widely whispered view that it is an indispensable safety-valve for the protection of domestic virtue, or, above all, who are smitten with a sentimental affection for our fallen sister, and would "take her up tenderly, lift her with care, fashioned so slenderly, young, and *so* fair." Nor am I prepared to accept the verdict of the medical gentlemen who would compulsorily examine and register Mrs Warren, whilst leaving Mrs Warren's patrons, especially her military patrons, free to destroy her health and anybody else's without fear of reprisals. But I should be quite content to have my play judged by, say, a joint committee of the Central Vigilance Society and the Salvation Army. And the sterner moralists the members of the committee were, the better.[. . .]

I now come to those critics who, intellectually baffled by the problem in *Mrs Warren's Profession,* have made a virtue of running away from it. I will illustrate their method by a quotation from Dickens, taken from the fifth chapter of *Our Mutual Friend.*

> "Hem!" began Wegg. "This, Mr Boffin and Lady, is the first chapter of the first wollume of the *Decline and Fall of——*" here he looked hard at the book, and stopped.
>
> "What's the matter, Wegg?"

"Why, it comes into my mind, do you know, sir," said Wegg with an air of insinuating frankness (having first again looked hard at the book), "that you made a little mistake this morning, which I had meant to set you right in; only something put it out of my head. I think you said Rooshan Empire, sir?"

"It is Rooshan; ain't it, Wegg?"

"No, sir. Roman. Roman."

"What's the difference, Wegg?"

"The difference, sir?" Mr Wegg was faltering and in danger of breaking down, when a bright thought flashed upon him. "The difference, sir? There you place me in a difficulty, Mr Boffin. Suffice it to observe, that the difference is best postponed to some other occasion when Mrs Boffin does not honour us with her company. In Mrs Boffin's presence, sir, we had better drop it."

Mr Wegg thus came out of his disadvantage with quite a chivalrous air, and not only that, but by dint of repeating with a manly delicacy, "In Mrs Boffin's presence, sir, we had better drop it!" turned the disadvantage on Boffin, who felt that he had committed himself in a very painful manner.

I am willing to let Mr Wegg drop it on these terms, provided I am allowed to mention here that *Mrs Warren's Profession* is a play for women; that it was written for women; that it has been performed and produced mainly through the determination of women that it should be performed and produced; that the enthusiasm of women made its first performance excitingly successful; and that not one of these women had any inducement to support it except their belief in the timeliness and the power of the lesson the play teaches. Those who were "surprised to see ladies present" were men; and when they proceeded to explain that the journals they represented could not possibly demoralize the public by describing such a play, their editors cruelly devoted the space saved by their delicacy to an elaborate and respectful account of the progress of a young lord's attempt to break the bank at Monte Carlo. A few days sooner Mrs Warren would have been crowded out of their papers by an exceptionally abominable police case. [. . .]

My old Independent Theater manager, Mr Grein, besides that reproach to me for shattering his ideals, complains that Mrs Warren is not wicked enough, and names several romancers who would have clothed her black soul with all the terrors of tragedy. I have no doubt they would; but if you please, my dear Mr. Grein, that is just what I did not want to do. Nothing would please our sanctimonious British public more than to throw the whole guilt of Mrs Warren's profession on Mrs Warren herself. Now the whole aim of my play is to throw that guilt on the British public itself. You may remember that when he produced my first play, *Widowers' Houses*, exactly the same misunderstanding arose. When the virtuous young gentleman rose up in wrath against the slum landlord, the slum landlord very effectually shewed him that slums are the product, not of individual Harpagons, but of the indifference of virtuous young gentlemen to the condition of the city they live in, provided they live at the west end of it on money earned by somebody else's labor. The notion that prostitution is created by the wickedness of Mrs Warren is as silly as the notion—prevalent, nevertheless, to some extent in Temperance circles—that drunkenness is created by the wickedness of the publican. Mrs Warren is not a whit a worse woman than the reputable daughter who cannot endure her. Her indifference to the ultimate social consequences of her means of making money, and her discovery of that means by the ordinary method of taking the line of least resistance to getting it, are too common in English society to call for any special remark. Her vitality, her thrift, her energy, her outspokenness, her wise care of her daughter, and the managing capacity which has enabled her and her sister to climb from the fried fish shop down by the Mint to the establishments of which she boasts, are all high English social virtues. Her defense of herself is so overwhelming that it provokes the *St James's Gazette* to declare that "the tendency of the play is wholly evil" because "it contains one of the boldest and most specious defenses of an immoral life for poor women that has ever been penned." Happily the *St James's Gazette* here speaks in its haste. Mrs Warren's defense of herself is not only bold and specious, but valid and unanswerable. But it is no defense at all of the vice which she organizes. It is no defense of an immoral life to say that the alternative offered by society collectively to poor women is a miserable life, starved, overworked, fetid, ailing, ugly. Though it is quite natural and *right* for Mrs Warren to choose what is, according to her lights, the least immoral alternative, it is none the less infamous of society to offer such alternatives. For the alternatives offered are not morality and immorality, but two sorts of immorality. The man who cannot see that starvation, overwork, dirt, and disease are as immoral as prostitution—that they are the vices and crimes of a nation, and not merely its misfortunes—is (to put it as politely as possible) a hopelessly Private Person.

The notion that Mrs Warren must be a fiend is only an example of the violence and passion which the slightest reference to sex rouses in undisciplined minds, and which makes it seem natural to our lawgivers to punish silly and negligible indecencies with a ferocity unknown in dealing with, for example, ruinous financial swindling. Had my play been entitled *Mr Warren's Profession*, and Mr Warren been a bookmaker, nobody would have expected me to make him a villain as well. Yet gambling is a vice, and bookmaking an institution, for which there is absolutely nothing to be said. The moral and economic evil done by trying to get other people's money without working for it (and this is the essence of gambling) is not only enormous but uncompensated. There are no two sides to the question of gambling, no circumstances which force us to tolerate it lest its suppression lead to worse things, no consensus of opinion among responsible classes, such as magistrates and military commanders, that it is a necessity, no Athenian records of gambling made splendid by the talents of its professors, no contention that instead of violating morals it only violates a legal institution which is in many respects oppressive and unnatural, no possible plea that the instinct on which it is founded is a vital one. Prostitution can confuse the issue with all these excuses: gambling has none of them. Consequently, if Mrs Warren must needs be a demon, a bookmaker must be a cacodemon. Well, does anybody who knows the sporting world really believe that bookmakers are worse than their neighbors? On the contrary, they have to be a good deal better; for in that world nearly everybody whose social rank does not exclude such an occupation would be a bookmaker if he could; but the strength of character required for handling large sums of money and for strict settlements and unflinching payment of losses is so rare that successful bookmakers are rare too. It may seem that at least public spirit cannot be one of a bookmaker's virtues; but I can testify from personal experience that excellent public work is done with money subscribed by bookmakers. It is true that there are abysses in bookmaking: for example, welshing. Mr Grein hints that there are abysses in Mrs Warren's profession also. So there are in every profession: the error lies in supposing that every member of them sounds these depths. I sit on a public body which prosecutes Mrs Warren zealously; and I can assure Mr Grein that she is often leniently dealt with because she has conducted her business "respectably" and held herself above its vilest branches. The degrees in infamy are as numerous and as scrupulously observed as the degrees in the peerage: the moralist's notion that there are depths at which the moral atmosphere ceases is as delusive as the rich man's notion that there are no social jealousies or snobberies among the very poor. No: had I drawn Mrs Warren as a fiend in human form, the very people who now rebuke me for flattering her would probably be the first to deride me for deducing character logically from occupation instead of observing it accurately in society.

One critic is so enslaved by this sort of logic that he calls my portraiture of the Reverend Samuel Gardner an attack on religion. According to this view Subaltern Iago is an attack on the army, Sir John Falstaff an attack on knighthood, and King Claudius an attack on royalty. Here again the clamor for naturalness and human feeling, raised by so many critics when they are confronted by the real thing on the stage, is really a clamor for the most mechanical and superficial sort of logic. The dramatic reason for making the clergyman what Mrs Warren calls "an old stick-in-the-mud," whose son, in spite of much capacity and charm, is a cynically worthless member of society, is to set up a mordant contrast between him and the woman of infamous profession, with her well brought-up, straightforward, hardworking daughter. The critics who have missed the contrast have doubtless observed often enough that many clergymen are in the Church through no genuine calling, but simply because, in circles which can command preferment, it is the refuge of "the fool of the family"; and that clergymen's sons are often conspicuous reactionists against the restraints imposed on them in childhood by their father's profession. These critics must know, too, from history if not from experience, that women as unscrupulous as Mrs Warren have distinguished themselves as administrators and rulers, both commercially and politically. But both observation and knowledge are left behind when journalists go to the theater. Once in their stalls, they assume that it is "natural" for clergymen to be saintly, for soldiers to be heroic, for lawyers to be hard-hearted, for sailors to be simple and generous, for doctors to perform miracles with little bottles, and for Mrs Warren to be a beast and a demon. All this is not only not natural, but not dramatic. A man's profession only enters into the drama of his life when it comes into conflict with his nature. The result of this conflict is tragic in Mrs Warren's case, and comic in the clergyman's case (at least we are savage enough to laugh at it); but in both cases it is illogical, and in both cases natural. I repeat, the critics who accuse me of sacrificing nature to logic are so sophisticated by their profession that to them logic is nature, and nature absurdity.

A CULTURAL CASEBOOK

The "Woman Question" in the Late Nineteenth Century

The "woman question" was central to great controversy that swept throughout Europe and the United States during the nineteenth century and brought the circumstances of women to the attention of society. Prior to the industrial revolution, women worked side by side with men in the fields or in home-based industries. With the creation of a moneyed class made possible by the fruits of factory labor, however, women similar to Ibsen's Nora Helmer sought economic independence. Although wealthy and newly middle-class women were considered "angels of the house"—responsible for managing the household, supervising the children, and supporting their husbands' efforts—eventually these women began to see the limitations of their role. As the philosopher John Stuart Mill put it, women were expected to be willing slaves, but some of them, like Nora in Ibsen's *A Doll House*, rebelled.

Ibsen's Nora Helmer and Strindberg's Miss Julie offer views into the opportunities for women in the age. Marriage is the key to Nora's sense of self and satisfaction until she realizes how little her efforts to save her husband are appreciated. For Miss Julie, romance is not synonymous with marriage, but she realizes, too, that her virtue, once spent, can no longer give her power over men such as Jean. These plays demonstrate the limits of women's power in the second half of the nineteenth century.

The limited legal status of married women was increasingly unsatisfactory to wives during the latter part of the nineteenth century, and laws were passed to help them retain control over some of their own property as distinct from their husbands' property. Because divorce was difficult or impossible, separation usually ended in the ostracism of the woman. Many women in this era worked for reform, and several of the dramas of Ibsen and other Scandinavian writers argued for better treatment of women in society.

The economic limitations imposed on women were severe. Women of the upper-middle classes were expected not to work at all, whereas women of the lower classes living in cities had few choices. Women who did factory work risked injury and disease. As Mrs. Warren eloquently explains in Shaw's *Mrs. Warren's Profession*, even late in the nineteenth century, factory women aged quickly, had no job security, were dispensable, and often ended badly. One alternative was the choice made by Mrs. Warren, who avoided the early death of her sister Jane, victim of lead poisoning in a factory, by becoming a prostitute and then a madam.

In the Victorian era prostitution remained an almost universal fact of life. It was licensed in some places, tolerated in others, and subject to graft in yet others. In England, the Contagious Diseases Acts, instituted between 1860 and 1870, supposedly protected sailors and other military personnel from venereal disease. The laws required all prostitutes in military regions to be examined by appointed officials. Prostitutes adjudged "sick" were confined in hospitals with little or no hope of being released. Politically active women who had been at the forefront of the equal rights movement and the quest for the vote were outraged at this unequal treatment of the participants in the act of prostitution. Eventually, their protests forced the government to repeal the Contagious Diseases Acts.

Some of the following documents point out the economic and social issues involved in prostitution in the period. Descriptions from brothel directories reveal the widely accepted "business" of running a brothel. Madams, "landladies" of the brothels, were managers who had risen from the ranks, and their number was not large, as Barbara Meil Hobson explains in "Successful Madams." The small number of madams who actually achieved financial independence is a point to remember when considering the achievement of Mrs. Warren in Shaw's play.

As this collection of documents attests, the debate over the "woman question" was conducted in the houses of Parliament, in the daily newspapers of many nations, and in the essays, dramas, and writings of authors such as August Strindberg. The plays of Ibsen, Strindberg, Shaw, and other writers of the period must be seen against the backdrop of the struggle for women's rights.

John Stuart Mill (1806–1873)
ON THE SUBJECTION OF WOMEN   1869

John Stuart Mill was an important philosopher in the mid-nineteenth century. He held to a philosophy of utilitarianism, which stressed the usefulness of actions and principles. His views on the subjection of women note that the superior strength of men had been turned into principles of law and behavior as if women were meant to be subjugated. According to Mill, women have been forced into wrongful submission.

From the very earliest twilight of human society, every woman (owing to the value attached to her by men, combined with her inferiority in muscular strength) was found in a state of bondage to some man. Laws and systems of polity always begin by recognizing the relations they find already existing between individuals. They convert what was a mere physical fact into a legal right, give it the sanction of society, and principally aim at the substitution of public and organized means of asserting and protecting these rights, instead of the irregular and lawless conflict of physical strength. Those who had already been compelled to obedience became in this manner legally bound to it.

All causes, social and natural, combine to make it unlikely that women should be collectively rebellious to the power of men. They are so far in a position different from all other subject classes, that their masters require something more from them than actual service. Men do not want solely the obedience of women, they want their sentiments. All men, except the most brutish, desire to have, in the woman most nearly connected with them, not a forced slave but a willing one, not a slave merely, but a favorite. They have therefore put everything in practice to enslave their minds. The masters of all other slaves rely, for maintaining obedience, on fear; either fear of themselves, or religious fears. The masters of women wanted more than simple obedience, and they turned the whole force of education to effect their purpose. All women are brought up from the very earliest years in the belief that their ideal of character is the very opposite to that of men; not self-will, and government by self-control, but submission, and yielding to the control of others. All the moralities tell them that it is the duty of women, and all the current sentimentalities that it is their nature, to live for others; to make complete abnegation of themselves, and to have no life but in their affections. And by their affections are meant the only ones they are allowed to have—those to the men with whom they are connected, or to the children who constitute an additional and indefeasible tie between them and a man. When we put together three things—first, the natural attraction between opposite sexes; secondly, the wife's entire dependence on the husband, every privilege or pleasure she has being either his gift, or depending entirely on his will; and lastly, that the principal object of human pursuit, consideration, and all objects of social ambition, can in general be sought or obtained by her only through him, it would be a miracle if the object of being attractive to men had not become the polar star of feminine education and formation of character. And, this great means of influence over the minds of women having been acquired, an instinct of selfishness made men avail themselves of it to the utmost as a means of holding women in subjection, by representing to them meekness, submissiveness, and resignation of all individual will into the hands of a man, as an essential part of sexual attractiveness. What is now called the nature of women is an eminently artificial thing—the result of forced repression in some directions, unnatural stimulation in others.

August Strindberg (1849–1912)

THE WOMAN QUESTION: WOMEN'S RIGHTS   1884

TRANSLATED FROM THE SWEDISH BY MARY SANDBACH

Though he eventually developed a reputation as a misogynist, the playwright August Strindberg published a forward-looking book on marriage early in his career. He was married to the actress Siri von Essen and living in Switzerland when he wrote The Last Word on the Woman Question *(1883). But it was hardly his last word on the subject. The very next year he wrote the novel* Getting Married. *The following excerpt is from the preface to part 1 of that work. Feminism had been a growing movement in Scandinavia and elsewhere, and while Strindberg's views may seem compatible with feminist ideals, he wrote the following declaration of women's rights in a state of irritation. He was apparently sick and tired of the woman question by 1884.*

Meanwhile, under present conditions, it is both impossible and harmful to detach the Woman Question from its context. Woman's desire for emancipation is identical with man's restless longing for freedom. Let us therefore liberate man from his prejudices, and we shall see that the emancipation of women will follow. But we must work together for our objective as friends, not as enemies. The woman of the future, be it a nearer or a more distant future, shall have an indisputable right to demand certain things and, in order to dispel the suspicion that I entertain reactionary ideas, I will now set these out under the following heading:

Woman's Rights

Which the laws of nature would grant her, but of which, thanks to our perverse social system (and not as a result of male tyranny), she has been deprived.

1. The right to the same education as men. I cannot too often repeat that by this I do not mean to imagine that she will be raised to man's level by learning all the unnecessary things with which he now has to stuff himself. Posterity, which will put an end to the difference between elementary and secondary schools, which will put an end to matriculation, and all other examinations, will one day feel obliged to establish a single civic examination which everyone will take, and which will replace confirmation. This examination will be the same for men and women, and will only require those examined to have a thorough knowledge of the arts of reading, writing, and arithmetic, a knowledge of the laws of their country, a knowledge of their civic rights and duties, and also of one living language. He who wants after that to learn what Cicero thought of Lucius Sulla, and what Moses intended to do with the children of Israel may do so, that is if he has time for such luxuries, for posterity will demand that every citizen shall support himself by bodily toil as nature intended.

2. Boys and girls shall attend the same schools, so that both sexes learn to know each other early in life. Things will not then be as they are today, when boys imagine that girls are angels, and girls that boys are knights. In this way we shall avoid all the silent sins of fantasy and precocity, for they are a result of the way in which the sexes are isolated.

3. The girl shall have the same freedom to "run wild" and choose what company she pleases.

4. There shall be complete equality between the sexes, which will do away with that revolting form of hypocrisy called gallantry, or politeness to ladies. A girl will not expect a boy to get up and give her his seat, for that is the hallmark of the subservient slave; and a brother will not get into the habit of expecting his sister to make his bed, or sew on his shirt buttons, for these are things he must do for himself.

5. Woman shall have the vote. In the future, when her confirmation consists of an examination in the laws that govern the community in which she lives, and when this community is obliged to present an annual report to its members, as companies do today, a woman will be just as well able to decide for whom or for what she will vote as a man.

6. Woman shall be eligible for all occupations, which should not be any more difficult to arrange under self-government than it is today when, inconsequently enough, she can become the monarch. Self-government will not be the same as government by professionals, but will be more like local government, that is a commission which can be performed in leisure moments. Is anyone wiser and better suited to govern than an old mother, who has learned through motherhood and running a household both how to rule and how to administrate? (Our forefathers had such a veneration for the wisdom of older women that they believed them to possess supernatural knowledge.)

7. This measure will mean that the moral code will become less rigid, and the law less strict, for a mother has learned to be more tolerant than anyone, and no one knows better than she how patient and how unexacting you must be with the erring children of man.

8. Woman shall be exempt from military service. Anyone who regards this as unjust should take into consideration the fact that nature exacts compensation from her in the form of heavy maternal duties. For that matter military service will not in future be regarded as particularly glorious. It will simply be a duty.

9. By a just distribution of the combined riches of nature the community of the future will ensure that all who are born receive sustenance and instruction. Marriage as a guarantee for these advantages will therefore become unnecessary. Man and wife will conclude a contract, verbal or written, for a union of any length they may decide, which they will have the right to dissolve when they please, without reference to law or gospel. It is true that this will not prevent a situation in which two males want to possess the same female, but the struggle will be less cruel, and the female will be the one to choose,—which is not the case at present—for no one in future will be obliged to marry for money or position, as neither of these things will exist. Selection will therefore be natural, and consequently the race will improve.

So much for the woman of the future and marriage. But there are things we can do to make reasonable improvements in the married state under present conditions. These are:

1. That boys and girls shall be allowed to mix more freely.

2. That the education of boys shall be simplified, so that it will not be unjust if the education of girls is simplified too.

3. The girl (like the boy) shall no longer be forced to learn so much about the past, but she shall be obliged to acquaint herself with the way in which society is governed today.

4. She may be given the vote at the earliest possible moment.

5. False gallantry will cease of itself, and men and women will associate together as men do now. But things shall not be as at present, when men have all male banquets, which end with a toast to the ladies, while the latter sit at home eating porridge and milk.

6. Civil marriage shall be introduced, and this will make divorce easier. Not that it is likely to become more frequent, but easier divorce will make the bonds feel less irksome, and will disabuse the man of the idea that he owns the woman. Children will still hold married couples together, unless the circumstances are very difficult.

Civil marriage would do away with the horrible legal ruling that necessitates warnings by the clergy, or obligatory "desertion."

7. The paragraphs in our laws about a husband's rights as a guardian shall be rescinded.

8. A woman shall come of age at eighteen without any reservations.

9. Deeds of settlement and the judicial division of property shall be obligatory on all married couples.

10. A woman (when her education is the same as that given to men) shall have the right to fill any post and practice any profession she pleases. (But if two million women were let loose on the labor market at the moment the result would be ruthless competition. Here—under present conditions—we must perhaps condescend to an inconsistency, unless by any chance, a surplus of labor accelerated the adoption of the new social system.)

11. When he marries a man shall be obliged to take out a life insurance policy, so that in the event of his death, his wife and children will not be left destitute. This is more especially his duty if he takes a woman away from a gainful occupation.

12. A woman shall keep her own name. She shall not have the right to take her husband's title in its feminine form, for a title under present conditions is a possession, often expensively acquired, and worth money. This proviso is necessary if there is to be equality, and it will prevent many women from being tempted to buy a title with their wealth. Boys shall take their father's name, and girls their mother's.

13. Separate bedrooms shall be the rule from the beginning. For a practice so offensive to "decency" as a common bedchamber brings its own punishment, and gives rise to confusion, distaste, satiety, and even worse things in a relationship. This rule will make a woman's position freer, and will give her the right to possess her own body.

14. If a woman is solely her husband's wife, and the mother of his children and has no independent occupation, she shall receive an allowance for clothes and recreation. She shall not have a salary, or receive clothes as presents, for which she has to say thank you. Moreover, she shall have the *right* to pay for her amusements herself, even when she is out with her husband, and thus be spared from always being *treated*.

15. If a married woman is gainfully occupied and does not run her own home, she shall be obliged to contribute from her earnings as much to the household as her husband does. If she also works in her home she shall be allowed to keep what she earns, for her work at home will thus come to be regarded as an extra contribution, and not as now, as the services rendered by a slave.

Johan Thorsten Sellin (1897–1994)
MARRIAGE AND DIVORCE IN SWEDEN   *1922*

Johan Thorsten Sellin discusses the rights of Swedish women in marriage before the sweeping changes invoked by the law of 1920. Prior to that time the wife was essentially at the mercy of her husband's decisions. She was bound to obey her husband's wishes on virtually all important issues, and her children were her husband's to educate or train as he liked. A wife's limitations were established under law.

Before the law of 1920 went into effect, the status of the wife, as far as the law was concerned, was, in spite of improvements, rather unfavorable in many respects, giving unmistakable evidence of the double standard, which the present law has succeeded in abolishing. She, first of all, followed her husband's estate in life; if he for some reason or other became poor, she was obliged to accept this fact with resignation, even though he might have been the cause of the poverty. Her husband's nationality was hers, and the choice of domicile was in his hands. Her only right to refuse to live where he determined to live depended on whether or not his decision would cause her life to be placed in jeopardy, expose her to injustice, or force her to move abroad. In the last mentioned case, she could refuse to comply with his wishes only if his business at the time of the marriage was not likely to take him abroad or if he was not appointed to some official position which necessitated foreign residence.

A wife was in duty bound to expend her energies and efforts for her family and her home, in accordance with her husband's wishes. This meant that she could not accept outside work without his permission, unless the needs of the family made it imperative. Although the law gave him no power to compel her to follow his wishes, he could refuse to support her or could ask the clergy to "warn" her, the first step toward separation from bed and board. With her husband's permission[1] she could conduct a business or engage in other profitable employment, but if he were legally disqualified to engage in business (due to official position as custom officer, public prosecutor, or tax collector) she shared his disability, even though she may have had his permission. If she failed to heed her husband's refusal, she could be fined like any other individual who conducted a business without license. When she worked lawfully, i.e., with her husband's permission, her earnings belonged to her, although it is not certain that what she purchased with these earnings became hers to do with as she chose.

A married mother had nothing to say in the bringing up of her own children, i.e., the law gave her no such right. Her husband was their guardian until they reached majority, [he] chose their life's work, and [he] gave away his daughters in marriage. If he abused his guardianship, the court could appoint someone else guardian, but in no instance could the mother be so appointed while the family remained undisrupted. She was thereby classified with "feeble-minded persons, heavy debtors, spendthrifts, enemies of the child, persons not yet twenty-five years of age, or so old and crippled that he cannot discharge his duties as guardian, etc." Only in case the husband went insane, deserted his wife, or for other reasons was unable to exercise his guardianship could she be substituted, and if he died, she took his place as guardian of her children—until she remarried. In case husband and wife belonged to different religious faiths, the former decided in which faith the children should be brought up.

As a rule, all the property of the spouses was joint, since in the majority of marriages no private property or income existed. Of this joint property the husband was the sole manager. His administrative powers extended even to his wife's private property, with the exception of her private real property. He decided upon the amount to be spent for the household expenses, for the education of the children, and even for his wife's personal needs. The latter had no right to demand anything from her husband, except necessities, even though she may have been the source of the entire family fortune. Most important of all, perhaps, was the fact that no matter how he managed the joint property, he owed his wife no accounting.

[1]The industrial and commercial acts of 1846 prohibited a woman to engage in business without her husband's permission and security.

Richard Panofsky (b. 1943)

A NINETEENTH-CENTURY HUSBAND'S LETTER
TO HIS WIFE   *1844*

Richard Panofsky, a professor at the University of Massachusetts at Dartmouth, has provided a translated letter from a man named Marcus (1807–1865) to his wife Ulrike (1816–1888). The couple and their six children lived in nineteenth-century Hamburg, Germany. The letter establishes the conditions under which Marcus would take his wife back into his house after she had left him and the children. It also establishes exactly what he expects of his wife. According to Panofsky, Ulrike returned.

June 23, 1844

Dear Wife,

You have sinned greatly—and maybe I too; but this much is certain: Adam sinned after Eve had already sinned. So it is with us; you, alone, carry the guilt of all the misfortune which, however, I helped to enlarge later by my behavior. Listen now, since I still believe certain things to be necessary in order that we may have a peaceful life. If we want not only to be content for a day but forever, you will have to follow my wishes. So examine yourself and determine if you are strong enough to conquer your false ambitions and your stubbornness to submit to all the conditions, the fulfillment of which I cannot ignore. Every sensible person will tell you that all I ask of you is what is easily understood. If you insist on remaining stubborn, then do not return to my house, for you will never be happy with me; your husband, children, and the entire city threaten indifference or even contempt.

But if you decide to act *sensibly* and *correctly*, that is *justly* and *kindly*, then be certain that many in the world will envy you.

I am including here the paper which I read to you in front of the rabbi; ask anyone in your residence if the wishes expressed by me are not quite reasonable, and are of a kind to which every wife can agree for the welfare of domestic happiness. In any case, act in a way you think best.

When you decide to return, write to tell me on which day and hour you depart from Berlin and give me your itinerary whether by way of Kuestrin and Pinne or by way of Wollstein. I will then meet you at Wollstein or Pinne. I expect you will bring Solomon with you.

Don't travel unprepared. If you need money, ask your father.

May God enlighten your heart and mind.

I remain your so far unhappy,

[MARCUS]

Greetings to my parents, brothers, and sisters; also your brother. Show them what you wish, this letter, the enclosure, whatever you want. The children are fortunately healthy.

If you want to return with joy and peace, write me by return mail. In that case, I would rather send you a carriage. Maybe Madam Fraenkel will come along. . . .

[*Enclosure*]

My wife promises—for which every wife is obligated to her husband—to follow my wishes in everything and to strictly obey my orders. It is already self-evident that

our marital relations have often been disturbed by the fact that my wife does not follow my wishes but believes herself to be entitled to act on her own, even if this is
totally against my orders. In order not to have to remind my wife every second what
my wishes are regarding homemaking and public conduct—wishes which I have
often expressed—I want to make here a few rules which shall serve as a code of
conduct. A home is best run if the work for each hour is planned ahead of time, if
possible.

Servants get up no later than 5:00 A.M. in summer and 6:00 A.M. in winter, the
children an hour later. The cook prepares breakfast. The nursemaid puts out
clothes for every child, prepares water and sponge, cleans the combs, etc. The cook
should stay in the kitchen unless there is time to clean the rooms. At least once a
week the rooms should be cleaned whenever possible, but not all on the same day.

Every Wednesday, the people in the house should do a laundry. Every last
Wednesday in the month, there shall be a large laundry with an outside washerwoman. At least every Monday, the seamstress shall come into the house to fix
what is necessary.

Every Thursday or Friday, bread is baked for the week; I think it is best to buy
grain and have it ground, but to knead it at home.

Every Friday special bread (Barches) should be bought for the evening meal.

The kitchen list will be prepared and discussed every Thursday evening, jointly,
by me and my wife; but my wish is to be decisive.

After this, provisions are to be bought every Friday at the market. For this purpose, my wife, herself, will go to the market on Fridays, accompanied by a servant;
she can substitute a special woman who does errands (Faktorfrau) if she wishes,
but not a servant.

All expenditures have to be written down daily and punctually.

The children receive a bath every Thursday evening. The children's clothes must
be kept in a specially appointed chest, with a separate compartment for each child
with the child's name upon it. The boys' suits and girls' dresses are to be kept separately. To keep used laundry, there must be a hamper easily accessible. Equally
important is the food storage box in which provisions are kept in order, locked and
safe from vermin.

The kitchen should be kept in order. Once a week all woodwork and copper
must be scoured. The lights and lamps have to be cleaned daily. Toward servants,
one has to be strict and just. Therefore, one should not call them names which
aren't suitable for a decent wife. One should give them enough nourishing food.
Disobedience and obstinacy are to be referred to me.

My wife will never make visits in my absence. However, she should visit the synagogue every Saturday—at least once a month; also she should go for a walk with
the children at least once a week.

Helen Watterson Moody (1859–1928)
What It Means to Be a Wife   *1899*

The Ladies' Home Journal, *by no means a radical magazine in 1899, attempted to
show wives how best to serve their husbands and themselves. Helen Watterson*

Moody, a frequent contributor to the Journal, *emphasizes methods by which a wife can "Keep Love Secure."*

When a woman marries she assumes two new sets of relations—those of sentiment, through which she becomes the loving, faithful companion of one man and the mother of his children, and the economic relation, through which she becomes one of the great conserving and distributing agents of the world. Since I shall speak of these last two conditions later, I will now only consider that one sentimental relation whose beauty and holiness, if rightly assumed, give foundation to all the rest—that of wifehood.

Marriage is, or should be, primarily a relation of sentiment, yet the happiness of married life is decided by quite other things than sentiment—sturdy and steady moral qualities, good sense, and fair executive ability. I think the recognition of the fact that, though love is the supreme thing in married life, love alone is not enough, always comes to a newly married couple with a sense of surprise.

The Only Way to Keep Love Secure

In the first months of married life, love is so sufficient, and loving so simple, that there seems no other need in life. But by-and-by, when care begins to shadow them, when duties present themselves, and, strangely enough, conflict with each other, when convictions clash and tastes differ, then both husband and wife begin to realize that back of love must stand what I have called "steady and sturdy moral qualities"—justice, patience, honesty, and sincerity, and magnanimity. Indeed, on these depends the very continuance of love in marriage, for it is not possible to go on loving unless that is found which is worthy of love. I say this advisedly. I know the world is full of men and women who think, either because they like to think so, or sadly, because they must, that one can love where one does not respect. It seems to me that this does not ennoble one's ideal of love. One may pity, may have an infinite yearning tenderness over what one cannot respect, but love is of royal birth and recognizes only what is as royal as itself. The way, then, to keep love secure in married life is not so much to be anxiously watching and guarding lest it should escape, or crying that love has spread its wings because the first holiday romance is replaced by graver feeling, but by living along simply and honestly and frankly together, on a high plane, looking most and always toward "whatsoever things are true, whatsoever things are honest, whatsoever things are just, whatsoever things are pure, whatsoever things are lovely, whatsoever things are of good report." Then Love will be not a captive, but a most willing guest.

Marriage Is a Serious and Steady Occupation

That is why I say that the real happiness of married life depends largely upon the personal character that is put into it. Next in importance I place sound, good sense; and I mean by this that underlying sense of proportion by which one is able to discriminate the insignificant, the passing, the unimportant, from the grave, the permanent, the important—that capacity for steady, balancing thought which keeps one from impulsive words and rash deeds. A woman who is blessed with good sense does not consider at the start that marriage is a role to be skillfully and successfully enacted, or a grand frolic of which she is to be the admired and indulged center, or a mere incident in a life crowded with other activities. She knows that marriage is a serious and steady vocation, and that the true wife is one who enters

RIGHT: Scene in a brothel, from the *National Police Gazette,* July 26, 1879. (© Collection of The New-York Historical Society)
BELOW: A scene from Hogarth's *Harlot's Progress:* A madam welcomes a newly arrived woman who will soon become part of the establishment. One of her customers looks on eagerly.

marriage not thinking how much she can get out of it, but how much she can put into it. It is this larger conception of marriage which makes women dwell by their own firesides in sweet content with what is commonly called the "narrow limits of home," knowing well that no true home is narrow since it must give cover to "the whole primal mysteries of life—food, raiment, and work to earn them withal: love and marriage, birth and death, right-doing and wrong-doing—all these commonplaces of humanity which are most divine because they are most commonplace."

The way to make home a wide place to dwell in, is to bring a wide personality to dwell in it. Any home is just as wide as the maker, and can be no wider. When a woman understands this she is able to keep her head steady and her heart undisturbed over newspaper sketches about other women, in which each one of them is made to do the most remarkable and entirely unnecessary combination of things. [. . .]

Married Women Can Find Time If They Will

When I hear a married woman lament the lack of wide opportunities in her life I find myself wondering, in a kind of daze, what she means. If I inquire particularly, I usually discover that by lack of opportunities she means either the time for study and self-cultivation which she deeply desires, or else an opportunity for public activity and recognition. Well, both of these are good in their proper places, and there are few wives who will not be able to find some hours in the week to give to either one or the other. I suspect that in the case of those women who say they actually do not get time for study or music, or for an occasional club meeting, the trouble lies in the fact that they do not want to enough. For be sure of this, that in the long run a man or a woman usually finds time in life to do the thing that he or she wants to do most. A woman may desire the opportunity for self-culture and growth, but if she in her heart really prefers an hour of neighborhood gossip, or a piece of drawn linen for her luncheon table, or a vulgar profusion in the menu she offers her guests, she will have these and not the study. If, on the other hand, the intellectual quickening that comes from communion with big and earnest minds be the one thing in life that she feels she must have, be sure that in some degree she will have it—not enough of it, possibly, to satisfy her, but enough to make her life richer, because she will make her living less complex in order that she may have it.

Flora Tristan (1803–1844)

LONDON JOURNAL: PROSTITUTES IN LONDON . . .
ALL THE STREETS ARE FULL OF THEM   *1842*

TRANSLATED FROM THE FRENCH BY JEAN HAWKES

Flora Tristan, a French feminist, visited London often. Her journal was published in France in 1840 and translated into English in 1842. Among her many observations, her comments on the prostitutes of London establish the fact of their presence in remarkable numbers. Waterloo Bridge remained a notorious site for plying the trade of prostitution both in the late nineteenth century and afterward. Tristan's detailed account implies a deep sympathy for the women involved.

There are so many prostitutes in London that one sees them everywhere at any time of day; all the streets are full of them, but at certain times they flock in from outlying districts in which most of them live, and mingle with the crowds in theaters and public places. It is rare for them to take men home; their landlords would object, and besides their lodgings are unfit. They take their "captures" to the houses reserved for their trade. . . .

Between seven and eight o'clock one evening, accompanied by two friends armed with canes, I went to take a look at the new suburb which lies on either side of the long broad thoroughfare called Waterloo Road at the end of Waterloo Bridge. This neighborhood is almost entirely inhabited by prostitutes and people who live off prostitution; it is courting danger to go there alone at night. It was a hot summer evening; in every window and doorway women were laughing and joking with their protectors. Half dressed, some of them *naked to the waist,* they were a revolting sight, and the criminal, cynical expressions of their companions filled me with apprehension. These men are for the most part very good looking— young, vigorous, and well made—but their coarse and common air marks them as animals whose sole instinct is to satisfy their appetites. . . .

We went on our way and explored all the streets in the vicinity of Waterloo Road, then we sat upon the bridge to watch the women of the neighborhood flock past, as they do every night between the hours of eight and nine, on their way to the West End, where they ply their trade all through the night and return home between eight and nine in the morning. They infest the promenades and any other place where people gather, such as the approaches to the Stock Exchange, the various public buildings and the theaters, which they invade as soon as entry is reduced to half price. . . . After the play they move on to the "finishes"; these are squalid taverns or vast resplendent gin-palaces where people go to spend what remains of the night. . . .

I had heard descriptions of the debauchery to be seen at finishes, but could never bring myself to believe them. Now I was in London for the fourth time with the firm resolve to discover everything for myself. I determined to overcome my repugnance and go in person to one of these finishes. . . . The same friends who had accompanied me to the Waterloo Road again offered to be my guides. . . .

From the outside these "gin-palaces" with their carefully fastened shutters seem to be quietly slumbering; but no sooner has the doorkeeper admitted you by the little door reserved for the initiates than you are dazzled by the light of a thousand gas lamps. Upstairs there is a spacious salon divided down the middle; in one half there is a row of tables separated one from the other by wooden screens, as in all English restaurants. . . . In the other half there is a dais where the prostitutes parade in all their finery; seeking to arouse the men with their glances and remarks. . . .

Towards midnight the regular clients begin to arrive; several finishes are frequented by men in high society, and this is where the cream of the aristocracy gather. At first the young noblemen recline on the sofas, smoking and exchanging pleasantries with the women; then, when they have drunk enough for the fumes of champagne and Madeira to go to their heads, the illustrious scions of the English nobility, the very honorable members of Parliament remove their coats, untie their cravats, take off their waistcoats and braces, and proceed to set up their private boudoir in a public place. Why not make themselves at home, since they are paying out so much money for the right to display their contempt. . . . The orgy rises to a crescendo; between four and five o'clock in the morning it reaches its height.

At this point it takes a good deal of courage to remain in one's seat, a mute spectator of all that takes place. What a worthy use these English lords make of their immense fortunes! How fine and generous they are when they have lost the use of their reason and offer fifty, even a hundred guineas to a prostitute if she will lend herself to all the obscenities that drunkenness engenders. . . .

For in a finish there is no lack of entertainment. One of the favorite sports is to *ply a woman with drink* until she falls dead drunk upon the floor, then to make her swallow a draught compounded of *vinegar, mustard, and pepper;* this invariably throws the poor creature into horrible convulsions, and her spasms and contortions provoke the *honorable company* to gales of laughter and infinite amusement. Another diversion much appreciated at these fashionable gatherings is to empty the contents of the nearest glass upon the women as they lie insensible on the ground. I have seen satin dresses of no recognizable color, only a confused mass of stains; wine, brandy, beer, tea, coffee, cream, etc. . . . daubed all over them in a thousand fantastic shapes. . . . The air is heavy with the noxious odors of food, drink, tobacco, and others more fetid still which seize you by the throat, grip your temples in a vice, and make your senses reel: it is indescribably horrible! . . . However, this life, which continues relentlessly night after night, is the prostitute's sole hope of a fortune, for she has no hold on the Englishman when he is sober. *The sober Englishman is chaste to the point of prudery.*

It is usually between seven and eight o'clock in the morning when people leave the finish. The servants go out to look for cabs, and anyone still on his feet gathers up his clothes and returns home; as for the rest, the pot-boys dress them in the first garments that come to hand, bundle them into a cab, and tell the cabman where to deliver them. Often nobody knows their address; then they are deposited in the cellar and left to sleep in the straw. This place is known as the drunkards hole, and there they stay until they have recovered their wits sufficiently to say where they wish to be taken.

A LETTER TO THE *TIMES* (LONDON) FROM A PROSTITUTE

1858

After a concerted effort on the part of prominent London citizens to reduce prostitution in London, a prostitute who referred to herself as "one of that abandoned sisterhood" came forth with the following letter filled with suggestions about how to improve the circumstances of the prostitute and her customers. She hopes to avoid the "persecution" of individuals while London attempts to deal with a vice it considers a nuisance.

Sir:

Certain Persons have, as you know, commenced a crusade against London Prostitutes, and, if one of that abandoned sisterhood may presume to address you, grant me your attention.

The precept and example set me by parents, now, thank God, in their graves; the education likewise "thrown away" upon me, and my subsequent experience as a governess in a highly respectable family, were not necessary to the conviction that the class among which I may be numbered consists of outcasts whose undisguised pursuit is an offense to the laws of God and man.

I know that we are cut off from the moral, social, and religious worlds. . . . We need not be told of our ruin and degradation, because we never "fall" without being alive to the fact. A woman seduced may forgive her wrongs . . . it is impossible for her to forget what she is; society will not permit her to do so. . . . Do not suppose, then, that I would attempt to defend what transpires nightly in the Haymarket, in Coventry Street, or wherever women of my caste congregate. I do not ask you to countenance anything of the kind. No, Sir, give "Vice its own image" and do your duty.

But, while you yourself refrain from going a step too far, pray give a warning to others. It is one thing to put down a nuisance. It is another to persecute individuals. I will anticipate much that may fairly be said, and admit that if I live avowedly in defiance of those regulations which the community has established as essential to its well being. . . . I must expect to be checked in such openly vicious courses, for I believe the liberty of the subject should end where injustice to others begins. But pray tell those good gentlemen who are bent on "putting us down," that theirs is not only a delicate, but a difficult undertaking, and they should be careful lest they have more to answer for than they dream of in their philosophy.

The vice of London, Sir, is seen to float upon its surface; let it pass as the weed on its way to the ocean. If it accumulates so as to become offensive, disperse it. If it is otherwise annoying and cannot conveniently be avoided, deal with it accordingly.

Appoint commissioners who are fitted for the office, intelligent, respectable, and responsible gentlemen, and make it worth their while to devote themselves entirely to the reduction of the scandal complained of. Empower these officials to have us taken up and punished for riot or impropriety of any kind. But let not the "pelting petty officer," the ignorant constable of a few shillings a week, and it may be an unfeeling and unthinking brute, interfere with us as he will. Recollect it was man who made us what we are. It is man who pays for the finery, the rouge, and the gin . . . it is man who, when we apply ourselves to industry and honesty, employs us upon starvation wages; and if man had his way, and women's nature were not superior to his, there would be no virtue extant. Say, then, is it for man to persecute even the most profligate among us?

Pray, Sir, think of this, and tell those gentlemen whose speeches I read to act upon it. They may be husbands and fathers . . . and I allow for their parental solicitude. But if they be Christians they will imitate one who said, "Go, and sin no more," and not "move on," "anywhere, anywhere, out of the world."

Your humble servant,

ONE MORE UNFORTUNATE

Barbara Meil Hobson
SUCCESSFUL MADAMS   1987

In this brief excerpt Hobson describes prostitutes who became "successful entrepreneurs" and achieved positions similar to that of Mrs. Warren in Bernard Shaw's play. However, very few prostitutes ever became financially independent. Mrs. Warren is remarkable for her success, not for her profession.

The Gentleman's Directory,
Temples of Love, address
listings, 1870. Published
directories such as this one
informed men where to find
the best brothels. Even
newspapers carried discreet
advertisements when
prostitutes changed houses so
they would not lose their
regular clientele. (© Collection
of The New York Historical
Society)

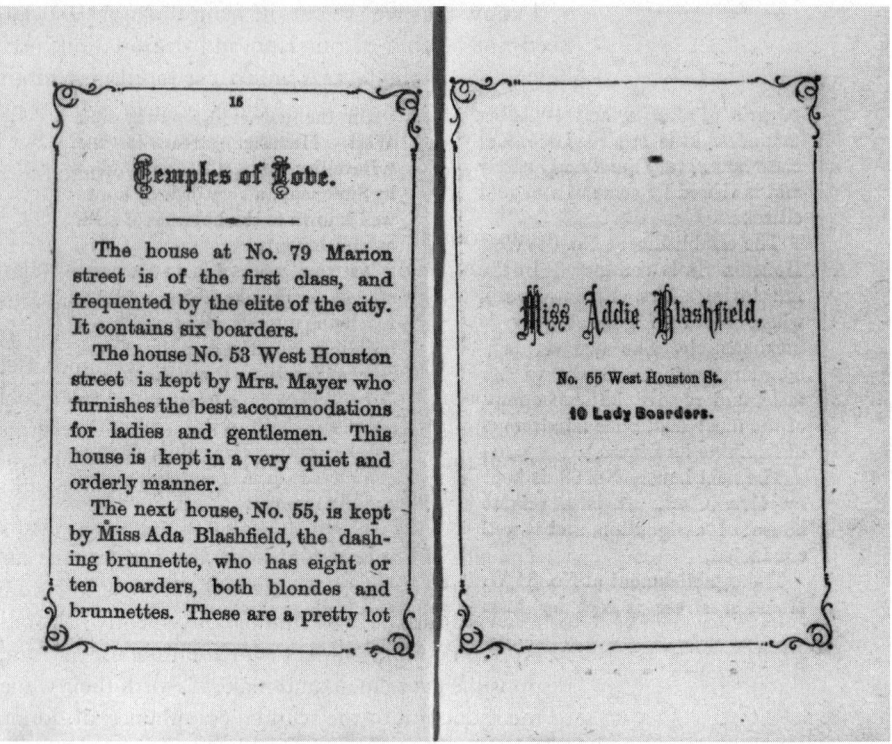

On the other hand, the image of the prostitute as someone who accumulates savings from her trade, wisely invests her capital, and obtains a small fortune was not very realistic either. We know of some famous successful madams at the turn of the century, including the Everleigh sisters, who operated gilded palaces of vice in Chicago, and Nell Kimball, the famous "queen" of Storeyville. They were the successful entrepreneurs of the demimonde, and they even published their memoirs.

What little we know of typical prostitutes' futures suggests that few women achieved upward economic mobility through prostitution. The nineteenth-century police registers tell us that women in regulated prostitution were most likely to reenter traditional working class occupations. [. . .] The fees Swedish prostitutes had to pay for medical examinations, the percentages madams took for room and board, and the expenses for dress and cosmetics did not leave very much money for savings. Prostitutes in the high-class brothels in nineteenth-century American cities were paid high prices for their sexual services. But madams usually took 50 percent of a prostitute's receipts, and expenses were high. In addition, prostitutes in many of these cities had to take a cut from their earnings for police protection. Research on nineteenth-century St. Paul documents that career paths within prostitution were limited. Only four out of sixty-one brothel prostitutes listed in official records became madams, a revealing statistic in a city where prostitution was aboveboard — unofficially licensed.

Drama in the Early and Mid-Twentieth Century

The realist tradition in drama had certain EXPRESSIONIST qualities evident in the symbolic actions in Strindberg's *Miss Julie* and certain romantic fantasies in later plays of Ibsen. But the surfaces of the plays appear realistic, consisting of a sequence of events that we might imagine happening in real life. The subject matter is also in the tradition of naturalism because it is drawn from life and not beautified or toned down for the middle-class audience.

But in the early to mid-twentieth century realistic drama took a new turn, incorporating distortions of reality that border on the unreal or *surreal*. From the time of Anton Chekhov in 1903 to Samuel Beckett in the 1950s, drama exploited the possibilities of realism, antirealism, and the poetic expansion of expressionism.

The Heritage of Realism

In the late nineteenth century realism was often perceived as too severe for an audience that had loved melodrama. Realistic plays forced comfortable audiences to observe psychological and physical problems that their status as members of the middle class usually allowed them to avoid. Audiences often protested loudly at this painful experience.

Early in the twentieth century, Susan Glaspell (1876–1948) began writing plays for the pleasure of having them read in her own living room in Provincetown, Massachusetts. *Trifles* (1916) told the story of a murdered husband in a deadpan fashion without alluding directly to the abusive nature of the husband and the ultimate resistance of the wife. The play may be said to be realistic on the surface, but its deep structure is symbolic, and its indirectness implies an experimental attitude toward the writing of plays.

The technique of realism could, however, be adapted for many different purposes, and eventually realism was reshaped to satisfy middle-class sensibilities by commercial playwrights, who produced popular, pleasant plays. By the 1920s in Europe and the 1930s in America, theatergoing audiences expected plays to be realistic. Even the light comedies dominating the commercial stage were in a more or less realistic mode. Anything that disturbed the illusion of realism was thought to be a flaw.

Reactions to the comfortable use of realistic techniques were numerous, especially after World War I. One extreme reaction was that of DADAISM. Through the Dadaists' chief propagandist, Tristan Tzara (1896–1963), the group promoted an art that was essentially enigmatic and incoherent to the average person. That was its point. The Dadaists blamed World War I on sensible, middle-class people who were logical and well intentioned but never questioned convention. The brief plays that were performed in many Dadaist clubs in Europe often featured actors speaking simultaneously so that nothing they said could be understood. The purpose was to confound the normal expectations of theatergoers.

Other developments were also making it possible for playwrights to experiment and move away from a strict reliance on "comfortable" realism. By World War I, motion pictures began to make melodramatic entertainment available to most people in the world. Even when films were silent, they relied on techniques that had been common on the nineteenth-century stage. Their growing domination of popular dramatic entertainment provided an outlet for the expectations of middle-class audiences and freed more imaginative playwrights to experiment and develop in different directions.

Realism and Myth

The incorporation of myth in drama offered new opportunities to expand the limits of realism. Sigmund Freud's theories of psychoanalysis at the turn of the century stimulated a new interest in myth and dreams as a psychological link between people. Freud studied Greek myths for clues to the psychic state of his patients, and he published a number of commentaries on Greek plays and on *Hamlet*. (See excerpts on pp. 101–104 and pp. 396–397.) The psychologist Carl Jung, a follower of Freud who eventually split with him, helped give a powerful impetus to the interest in dreams and the symbolism of myth by suggesting that all members of a culture share an inborn knowledge of the basic myths of the culture. Jung postulated a collective unconscious, a repository of mythic material in the mind that all humans inherit as part of their birthright. This theory gave credence to the power of myth in everyday life; along with Freud's theories, it is one of the most important ideas empowering drama and other art forms in the twentieth century. Playwrights who used elements of myth in their plays produced a poetic form of realism that deals with a level of truth common to all humans.

Myth and Culture

Some non-European drama depends on interpretation of local myth in relation to the culture or cultures that produce it. Wole Soyinka's background as a Nigerian familiar with Yoruba culture and myth, along with his formal education in England, prepared him for a career that expanded the horizons of drama for both Nigerian and European audiences.

Soyinka's experimentation has spanned two traditions — modern European theater and modern ritual theater of the Yoruba people of Nigeria. Traditional Yoruba drama develops from religious celebrations and annual festivals and includes music and dance. Soyinka's plays, including *The Strong Breed* (1962), concern themselves with African traditions and issues, but often, they also explore mythic forces that link European and African cultures. His plays have been produced throughout the world and have demonstrated the universality of the community and the anxiety it sometimes breeds in the individual. Soyinka has also written critical studies on Yoruba tragedy and has interpreted, translated, and produced Greek tragedy.

Poetic Realism

The Abbey Theatre in Dublin, which functioned with distinction from the turn of the century, produced major works by John Millington Synge, W. B. Yeats, Sean O'Casey, and Lady Gregory. Lady Gregory's peasant plays concentrated on the charming, the amusing, and occasionally the grotesque. She tried to represent the dialect she heard in the west of Ireland, a dialect that was distinctive, poetic, and colorful. She also took advantage of local Irish myths and used some of them for her most powerful plays, such as *Dervorgilla* and *Grania*, both portraits of passionate women from Irish legend and myth.

John Millington Synge, like Lady Gregory, was interested in the twin forces of myth and peasant dialects. His plays are difficult to fit into a realist mold, although their surfaces are sometimes naturalistic. Some audiences reacted violently to his portrayals of peasant life because they were unflattering. Synge's plays were sometimes directly connected with ancient Irish myth, as in *Deirdre of the Sorrows* (1910), which concerns a willful Irish princess who runs off with a young warrior and his brothers on the eve of her wedding to an old king. The story ends sadly for Deirdre, and she is regarded as a fated heroine and assumes almost the stature of a Greek tragic figure. Synge's most popular one-act play, *Riders to the Sea* (1904), reveals his gift for emulating the Irish way of speaking English in Ireland's western county of Mayo. His creation of peasant dialogue remains one of his most important contributions to modern drama.

In the United States, Eugene O'Neill, influenced by Strindberg, experimented with realism, first by presenting stark, powerful plays that disturbed his audiences. *The Hairy Ape* (1922) portrayed a primitive coal stoker on a passenger liner who awakened base emotions in the more refined passengers. In *The Emperor Jones* (1921) O'Neill produced the first important American expressionist play. The shifting scenery, created by lighting, was dreamlike and at times frightening. The experience of the play reflected the frightening psychic experiences of the main character, Brutus Jones.

O'Neill also experimented with more poetic forms of realism. In *Desire under the Elms* (1924), he explores the myth of Phaedra—centering on her incestuous love for her husband's son—but sets it in rural New England on a rock-hard farm. In the tradition of realism, the play treats unpleasant themes: sons' distrust of their father and their dishonoring him, lust between a son and his stepmother, and the murder of a baby to "prove" love. But it is not simply realistic. Without its underpinning of myth, the play would be sordid, but the myth helps us see that fate operates even today, not in terms of messages from the gods but rather in terms of messages from our hearts and bodies. Lust is a force in nature that drives and destroys.

Meanwhile, in Fascist Spain, Federico García Lorca, also a poetic realist, was uncovering dark emotional centers of the psyche in his *House of Bernarda Alba* (1936), which explores erotic forces repressed and then set loose. Lorca was opposed to Fascism and was murdered by a Fascist agent. His plays reveal a bleakness of spirit that helps us imagine the darkness—moral and psychological—that enveloped Europe in the 1940s.

Social Realism

Ten years after *Desire under the Elms* enjoyed popularity, a taste for plays based on SOCIAL REALISM developed. This was realism with a political conscience. Because the world was in the throes of a depression that reduced many people to destitution and homelessness, drama began to aim at awakening governments to the consequences of unbridled capitalism and the depressions that freewheeling economies produced.

Plays such as Jack Kirkland's *Tobacco Road* (1933), adapted from Erskine Caldwell's novel, presented a grim portrait of rural poverty in America. Sidney Kingsley's *Dead End* (1935) portrayed the lives of virtually homeless boys on the Lower East Side of Manhattan. In the same year Maxwell Anderson produced a verse tragedy, *Winterset*, with gangsters and gangsterism at its core. Also in 1935 Clifford Odets produced *Waiting for Lefty*, an openly leftist labor drama. These plays' realist credentials lay primarily in their effort to show audiences portraits of life that might shock their middle-class sensibilities.

Realism and Expressionism

O'Neill's later plays shed the underpinnings of myth and developed a powerful realistic style as seen in *The Iceman Cometh* (1939), set in a dingy bar filled with patrons living on the edge, listening to Theodor Hickman (Hickey) and Harry Hope give their philosophy of life. At this time he also wrote a haunting one-act play, *Hughie* (1941), set in a shabby hotel lobby late at night. In it, Erie Smith, a small-time gambler, shares his views of life with the hotel night manager, Charlie Hughes. The play is simple but intense and moving. One of O'Neill's greatest plays, *Long Day's Journey into Night*, written in 1941 but not published or produced until 1956, took him in a new direction. For the first time, he began an analysis of his own tortured family background, which included alcoholism and drug addiction. The play was so searing and painful that he sequestered it with Random House, instructing publisher Bennett Cerf not to publish it until twenty-five years after his death. O'Neill's wife, however, broke the will and had the play produced. It has since become the vehicle for some of the best performances of the latter part of the twentieth century.

After Eugene O'Neill's experiments, later American dramatists looked for new ways to expand the resources of realism while retaining its power. The use of EXPRESSIONISM — often poetic in language and effect — was one solution that appealed to both Tennessee Williams and Arthur Miller. Expressionism developed in the first and second decades of the twentieth century. The movement began in Germany and was influenced by some of Strindberg's work. Because expressionism takes many forms, there is no simple way to define the term except to see it as an alternative to realistic drama. Instead of having realistic sets, the stage may sometimes be barren or flooded with light or draped. Characters sometimes become symbolic; dialogue is often sharp, abrupt, enigmatic. The German theater saw its earliest developments in Frank Wedekind, whose first play, *Spring Awakening*, which explored sexual repression, abandoned a naturalistic style. Wedekind's work influenced later German playwrights such as George Kaiser, Ernst Toller, Erwin Piscator, and Bertolt Brecht, whose *Threepenny Opera* (1928) incorporated some of the hallmarks of expressionism, such as a music-hall atmosphere and broadly drawn characters.

Later American playwrights modified the characteristics of expressionism; they melded expressionist elements, such as fantastic sets and highly poetic diction, with a relatively realistic style. Tennessee Williams's *The Glass Menagerie*

FIGURE 21.   Expressionistic setting in Arthur Miller's *Death of a Salesman*.

(1944) and Arthur Miller's *Death of a Salesman* (1949) both use expressionist techniques. Williams's poetic stage directions make clear that he is drawing on nonrealistic dramatic devices. He describes the scene as "memory and . . . therefore nonrealistic." He calls for an interior "rather dim and poetic," and he uses a character who also steps outside the staged action to serve as a narrator — one who "takes whatever license with dramatic convention as is convenient to his purposes." As the narrator tells his story, the walls of the building seem to melt away, revealing the inside of a house and the lives and fantasies of his mother and sister, both caught in their own distorted visions of life.

Arthur Miller's original image for *Death of a Salesman* was the inside of Willy Loman's mind; Jo Mielziner's expressionist set represented his idea as a cross-section of Loman's house. As the action in one room concluded, lights went up to begin action in another (Figure 21). This evocative staging influenced the production of numerous plays by later writers. In the original set, a scrim, or gauze screen, was painted with branches and leaves. When this scrim was lit from the front for memory scenes, the set was transformed to evoke an earlier time when the sons were boys.

Miller used expressionist techniques to create the hallucinatory sequences when Willy talks with Ben, the man who walked into the jungle poor and walked out a millionaire, and when Biff recalls seeing Willy with the woman in Boston.

Although expressionism made some inroads in American theater, the techniques of realism persisted and developed. Lorraine Hansberry's *A Raisin in the Sun* (1959) uses basically realistic staging and dialogue to portray the difficulties of the members of one family in reaching for opportunity to overcome poverty. For Williams and Miller, expressionism offered a way to bring other worlds to bear on the staged action—the worlds of dream and fantasy. Hansberry does not use the expressionist techniques of Miller. Her only exotic touch is the visit of the African young man, Asagai, who offers a moment of cultural counterpoint. Hansberry's realism is essentially conservative.

Antirealism

SURREALISM (literally, "beyond realism") in the early twentieth century was based originally on an interpretation of experience not through the lucid mind of the waking person but through the mind of the dreamer, the unconscious mind that Freud described. Surrealism augmented or, for some playwrights, supplanted realism and became a means of distorting reality for emotional purposes.

When Pirandello's six characters come onstage looking for their author in *Six Characters in Search of an Author* (1921), no one believes that they are characters rather than actors. Pirandello's play is an examination of the realities we take for granted in drama. He turns the world of expectation in drama upside down. He reminds us that what we assume to be real is always questionable: we cannot be sure of anything; we must presume that things are true, and in some cases we must take them on faith.

Pirandello's philosophy dominated his stories, plays, and novels. His questioning of the certainty of human knowledge was designed to undermine his audience's faith in an absolute reality. Modern physicists have concurred with philosophers, ancient and modern, who question everyday reality. Pirandello was influenced by the modern theories of relativity that physicists were developing, and he found in them validation of his own attack on certainty.

Epic Theater

Bertolt Brecht (1898–1956) began writing plays just after World War I. He was a political dramatist who rejected the theater of his day, which valued the realistic "well-made play," in which all the parts fit perfectly together and function almost as a machine. His feeling was that such plays were too mechanical, like a "clockwork mouse."

Exploring the style of his predecessor Irwin Piscator, Brecht developed EPIC THEATER. The term implies a sequence of actions or episodes of the kind found in Homer's *Iliad*. In epic theater the sense of dramatic illusion is constantly voided by reminders from the stage that one is watching a play. Stark, harsh lighting, blank stages, placards announcing changes of scenes, bands playing music onstage, and long, discomfiting pauses make it impossible for an audience to become totally immersed in a realistic illusion. Brecht, offering a genuine alternative to realistic drama, wanted the audience to analyze the play's thematic content rather than to sit back and be entertained. He believed that realistic drama convinced audiences that the play's vision of reality described not just things as they are but things as they must be. Such drama, Brecht asserted, helped maintain the social problems that it portrayed by reinforcing, rather than challenging, their realities.

Brecht's *Mother Courage* (written in 1939 and produced in 1941) is an antiwar drama staged early in World War II. The use of song, an unreal setting, and an unusual historical perspective (the Thirty Years' War in the seventeenth century) help to achieve the "defamiliarization" that Brecht thought drama ought to produce in its audiences. The techniques of epic theater in *Galileo* (1938–1939) and *The Good Woman of Setzuan* (1943)—a study of the immoralities that prosper under capitalism—were imitated by playwrights in the 1950s. Hardly a major play in that period is free of Brecht's influence.

Eugène Ionesco (1909–1994) is said to have been the first of the postwar absurdist dramatists, with his production of *The Bald Soprano* and *The Lesson* (both in 1951). Ionesco called them "anti-plays" because they avoided the normal causal relationship of actions and realistic expectations of conventional drama.

Absurdist Drama

The critic Martin Esslin coined the term THEATER OF THE ABSURD when describing the work of Samuel Beckett (1906–1989), the Irish playwright whose dramas often dispense with almost everything that makes the well-made play well made. Some of his plays have no actors onstage—amplified breathing is the only hint of human presence in one case. Some have little or no plot; others have no words. His theater is minimalist, offering a stage reality that seems cut to the bone, without the usual realistic devices of plot, character development, and intricate setting.

The theater of the absurd assumes that the world is meaningless, that meaning is a human concept, and that individuals must create significance and not rely on institutions or traditions to provide it. The absurdist movement grew out of EXISTENTIALISM, a postwar French philosophy demanding that the individual face the emptiness of the universe and create meaning in a life that has no essential meaning within itself. *Waiting for Godot* (1952) captured the modern imagination and established a landmark in absurdist drama.

In *Waiting for Godot* two tramps, Vladimir and Estragon, meet near a tree where they expect Godot to arrive to talk with them. The play has two acts that both end with a small boy explaining that Godot cannot come today but will come tomorrow. Godot is not coming, and the tramps who wait for Godot will wait forever. While they wait they entertain themselves with vaudeville routines and eventually are met by a rich man, Pozzo, and his slave, Lucky. Lucky, on the command "Think, pig," speaks in a stream of garbled phrases that evoke Western philosophy and religion but that remain incoherent. Pozzo and Lucky have no interest in joining Vladimir and Estragon in waiting for Godot. They leave the two alone, waiting—afraid to leave for fear of missing Godot, but uncertain that Godot will ever arrive.

Beckett seems to be saying that in an absurd world, such gestures are necessary to create the sense of significance that people need to live. His characters' awareness of an audience and his refusal to create a drama in which an audience can "lose" itself in a comfortable surface of realistic illusion are all, in their own way, indebted to Brecht.

Beckett's *Krapp's Last Tape* (1958) places some extraordinary limitations on performance. Krapp is the only person onstage throughout the play, and his dialogues are with tapes of himself made many years before. The situation is absurd, but as Beckett reveals to us, the absurd has its own complexities, and situations such as Krapp's can sustain complex interpretations. Beckett expects his audience to analyze the drama, not merely to be entertained.

The illusion of reality is shed almost entirely in *Endgame* (1957). Hamm cannot move. His parents, both legless, are in trashcans onstage. Clov performs all the play's movement on a barren, cellarlike stage.

Beckett's *Happy Days* (1961) is generally thought to be his most optimistic play. Winnie, who talks almost nonstop throughout, seems mired in trivia and the details of everyday life. Yet, she can pause for philosophical observations on the nature of her existence and position herself thoughtfully in regard to the world. In the first act she is buried in a mound of earth up to her waist, and in the second act she is buried up to her neck, but her positive attitude intensifies. She is doing the best she can. Willy, her husband, hardly says a word and does not begin to act until the last minute of the play, at which time his action is ambiguous. *Happy Days*, while similar to Beckett's other absurdist plays, still intrigues audiences in the twenty-first century. It speaks to the hopeful among us, but it also offers a view of life that is far from sugar coated. It is absurd in the sense that it does not offer an easy answer to the questions raised by the limitations of Winnie's and Willy's existence.

The great plays of this period reflect the values of the cultures from which they spring. They make comments on life in the modern world and question the values that the culture takes for granted. The drama of this part of the twentieth century is a drama of examination.

The Early- and Mid-Twentieth-Century Stage

The physical stage continued its evolution into the twentieth century, although it depended on the proscenium arch and the concept of the "fourth wall" most of the time, especially in the development of the musical theater, which was, to an extent, a substitute for the nineteenth-century melodrama. With early silent films and then mid-century musicals, the popular stage was still home to melodramatic entertainment.

One of the primary aims of early-twentieth-century theater designs was to create spaces in which the audience and the actors became more intimate than in the pure proscenium theater, which treated the audience almost as voyeurs. The smaller theaters, such as the Vieux Colombier (Figure 22), opened the proscenium and extended the stage forward, making it possible for actors to be much closer to the audience and to produce a more involving experience.

In France and England, so-called little theaters developed quickly even before the first world war, taking advantage of this newfound intimacy. In the United States, the growth of "little" theaters led to the founding, in 1915, of the Provincetown Players with Eugene O'Neill and Susan Glaspell. This company held its early performances at the end of a wharf in an old abandoned fish house in Provincetown, Massachusetts (see Figure 23).

Eventually the Provincetown Players moved to New York City, where the Provincetown Playhouse still exists, now connected with New York University. Most major cities (Boston, New York, Chicago, and Detroit) and even some smaller cities produced plays in "little" theaters, some of which still exist. The Theatre Guild also formed in 1919 in the United States for the purpose of producing plays that were not likely to have a broad commercial appeal. It became one of the most distinguished theater companies of its time.

FIGURE 22.   The Vieux
Colombier, Paris, 1920.

Antonin Artaud (1896–1948), while working directly on stage in Paris for only a few years in the 1920s, made a lasting impression on drama theory and theatrical space. His concept of the "theater of cruelty" helped shape the modern theater as we know it. The cruelty he proposed was psychological in that he wanted the audience to relinquish its comfortable and privileged position in the theater and to feel the discomfort produced by facing unpleasant ideas and events. This was a complete departure from earlier melodrama, which soothed the audience with happy endings and avoided raising profound and unanswerable questions. Artaud proposed avoiding standard theaters altogether and moving the drama into a barn or warehouse or similar open space. Even today, many small theater companies follow his lead and perform in such spaces as garages and storefronts.

Technical developments in larger theaters naturally continued throughout the early part of the century, with improved lighting, revolving stages, and complex arrangements of flies that lowered and then raised elaborate scenery for set changes. Some experiments in staging brought the audience to all sides of the stage so that they were virtually "involved" in such necessary moments as entrances and exits. Theater in the round developed in the 1930s, and it helped create some of the most intense experiences in the mid-century, particularly those that depended on surrealist effects. Artaud was a proponent of theater in the round because the audience could never feel separated from the action, as it would in a proscenium theater. Many of the stage settings in the larger theaters in Europe and the United States generated exciting visual designs for expressionist and surrealist plays that are still talked about as visionary productions.

FIGURE 23.   The original theater of the Provincetown Players was a converted fishing shack on Lewis Wharf, in Provincetown, Massachusetts.

Expressionist drama, as in *Miss Julie* and other late-nineteenth-century exper-imental works, often attempted to examine transformations of the inner life of the character through the use of symbolism. Expressionist plays favored a certain form of abstraction, represented in their stage settings, that attempted to be emo-tionally representational rather than realistic in the usual sense. The stage set-tings for O'Neill's plays, as well as those for Elmer Rice's *The Adding Machine* (1923), have been interpreted in many interesting ways, but they are often described as symbolic. In a Queens College production of Rice's *The Adding Machine*, the primary character is Mr. Zero, who eventually kills Boss. The sets are visually allusive to the machine, as in Figure 24, where the interior of the machine suggests a virtual cave as Mr. Zero approaches Heaven. The play itself is a commentary on the influence of the machine on modern life, and it may be even more relevant in the twenty-first century than it was in the twentieth.

The Early- and Mid-Twentieth-Century Actor

From the Moscow Art Theater in the late 1890s to the Group Theatre in the United States in 1931, the most persistent influence on acting and acting theory was Constantin Stanislavsky (1863–1938) (Figure 25). Stanislavsky, his adopted

FIGURE 24.   Elmer Rice's *The Adding Machine*, Queens College Drama, Theater, and Dance Production, 1999.

name for the stage, was born into a prosperous Russian family but decided to make his own way acting and directing. His productions of Gorky and Chekhov were legendary, and it was while working on these plays that he developed acting techniques that actors are still using today. He wished above all to encourage a natural style of acting that would be instantly recognized as offering insight into the truth of life. Years of successful melodramas had produced an exaggerated mode of acting, both "theatrical" in the pejorative sense and rhetorical in its demand for attention. It was against this "star" system, which relied entirely on stars of the magnitude of Edwin Forrest, William Macready, Edmund Kean, Junius Brutus Booth, William Gillette, Sarah Bernhardt, and others, that Stanislavsky rebelled.

Instead, Stanislavsky insisted that the actor prepare for a role using a method rooted in modern psychology—searching for the subconscious energy that would inform the actor and permit him to understand a character's most profound feelings. Applying Stanislavsky's method, the actor should first analyze the scenes carefully to establish the underlying motive of the character and then attempt to recreate within himself the motivation and the emotional content of the action by reflecting on his own life and drawing from a personal store of emotional experience. Only then was the actor ready to go on stage and perform the scene.

Stanislavsky also developed exercises for actors, some of which he discusses in *An Actor Prepares* (1936). One of the exercises on his principle of concentration of attention requires that the actor concentrate on something on stage. It must

FIGURE 25.   Constantin Stanislavsky as Gayev in Chekhov's *The Cherry Orchard*, 1923.

arrest the actor's attention and utterly absorb the actor in order to generate the closeness to truth that Stanislavsky demanded from his company. As he said, "Here we are dealing with powers of observation that are subconscious in their origin. Our ordinary type of attention is not sufficiently far-reaching to carry out the process of penetrating another person's soul." Some of the most famous actors of the twentieth century, including Marlon Brando, Al Pacino, Jane Fonda, and Jack Nicholson, employed the basic principles of "The Method," which they learned as students of Lee Strasberg's Actor's Studio in New York City in the 1940s and 1950s.

Some form of naturalism was dominant on the stage in the first half of the century, but expressionist plays such as O'Neill's *The Emperor Jones* (1920), *The Hairy Ape* (1922), and *The Great God Brown* (1926) depended on a style of acting that verged on distortion and exaggeration. The characters were meant to be larger than life, so the style of acting followed suit, but it could not be described as overly theatrical in the style that Stanislavsky and others condemned. Many of the best actors of the period also worked in films. Examples include Emile Jannings (1887–1950), Sir Cedric Hardwicke (1893–1964), Sibyl Thorndike (1882–1976), John Barrymore (1882–1942), and Laurette Taylor (1884–1946). Each was renowned, but much of their best work was done in film and not on the stage. Most of these distinguished actors relied on

FIGURE 26.   Bertolt Brecht (1898–1956) in Berlin, Germany, 1931.

conventional acting training rather than following Stanislavsky, although most of them were aware of his ideas and were, if only indirectly, affected by them.

On a theoretical level, the work of Bertolt Brecht (1898–1956) (Figure 26) reinforced Artaud's ideas about acting and the structure of drama in Europe and elsewhere between the two world wars. Brecht's concept of epic theater and the "alienation effect" took root and influenced theaters and actors everywhere. For example, Brecht insisted on controlling the amount of empathy an actor on stage might evoke. He also wished to avoid "magic" on stage, by which he meant the creation of an illusion of reality. In this sense, he was anti-Aristotelian. He said,

> On the Epic stage, no attempt is made to create the atmosphere of a particular place (a room at evening, a street in autumn), or to generate a mood by a broken speech-rhythm. The actor does not warm the audience up by unloosing a flood of temperament, nor cast a spell over them by tightening his muscles. In short, no effort is made to put the audience into a trance and give them the illusion of witnessing natural, unrehearsed events.

Brecht's staging was often symbolic in nature, and his actors were often out-fitted in oversized clothing and spoke in an unnatural fashion. His staging employed dance and/or music as needed. A Communist protesting the brutalities of the Nazis, Brecht expressed a political message between the wars, as in his extraordinary play *Galileo*, which was written in 1938 and 1939 and was first produced in Hollywood in 1947, with Charles Laughton in the title role. Galileo had been punished by the Catholic Church for his discovery that the earth revolves around the sun, not the other way around. Brecht's *Galileo* became a symbol for people resisting tyranny of all kinds. Brecht, like many other playwrights in the first half of the twentieth century, was searching for ways to express serious thought through the medium of drama. They knew they could not rely on the ordinary realistic styles of the late nineteenth century, so they had to invent new ways to write and new ways to act.

Early- and Mid-Twentieth-Century Drama Timeline

DATE	THEATER	POLITICAL	SOCIAL/CULTURAL
1850–1900	**1854–1931:** David Belasco, American producer. Belasco uses pictorial realism in staging and creates "stars" on the New York stage.	**1857:** Sepoy mutiny in India against British officers	**1853:** U.S. Navy arrives in Tokyo Bay to negotiate a trade treaty.
	1862–1928: Adolphe Appia, influential Swiss designer	**1860–65:** Civil War in the United States	**1861:** Russia emancipates its serfs.
	1863–1938: Constantin Stanislavsky, Russian actor and director	**1867:** Dominion of Canada formed	**1863:** U.S. Emancipation Proclamation frees slaves.
	1871–1909: John Millington Synge, Irish playwright, author of *Riders to the Sea* (1904) and *The Playboy of the Western World* (1907)	**1868–1912:** Meiji period in Japan **1871:** Feudalism in Japan ends.	**1869:** The Suez Canal opens.
	1872–1966: Edward Gordon Craig, influential English theatrical designer		
	1873–1943: Max Reinhardt, Austrian director, producer, and theorist		**1876:** General George Custer's troops are destroyed at Little Big Horn by Sioux-Cheyennes.
	1880–1964: Sean O'Casey, Irish playwright, author of *Juno and the Paycock* (1924) and *The Plough and the Stars* (1926)		**1880–1914:** All of Africa (except Ethiopia) is rapidly colonized by European and Turkish authorities.
	1887–1954: Robert Edmond Jones, revolutionary American scenic designer		
	1888–1953: Eugene O'Neill, American playwright. Among his works are *Desire under the Elms* (1924), *Mourning Becomes Electra* (1931), and *Long Day's Journey into Night* (1941).	**1889:** First Japanese Constitution is enacted.	
	1896–1948: Antonin Artaud, French playwright, poet, actor, and director	**1895:** China is defeated in war by Japan. Korea becomes independent.	
	1898–1956: Bertolt Brecht, German playwright, author of *The Threepenny Opera* (1928), *Mother Courage* (1941), and *The Good Woman of Setzuan* (1943)	**1898:** Boer War in South Africa **1898:** Spanish-American War. Cuba is freed from Spain.	
	1898: The Irish Literary Society is founded by W. B. Yeats (1865–1939) and Lady Augusta Gregory (1863–1932). The group leads the way in creating an indigenous Irish theater.		

Early- and Mid-Twentieth-Century Drama Timeline (continued)

DATE	THEATER	POLITICAL	SOCIAL/CULTURAL
1900–1950	**1904:** The Abbey Theatre, evolved from the Irish Literary Society founded by Yeats and Lady Gregory, opens in Dublin.	**1900:** The Boxer Rebellion attempts to curtail Western commercial interests in China.	**1900–1971:** Louis Armstrong, African American jazz trumpet player
	1905–1984: Lillian Hellman, American playwright, author of *The Children's Hour* (1934) and *The Little Foxes* (1939). Other important American female playwrights of the period include Rachel Crothers (1876–1958), Zona Gale (1874–1938), and Susan Glaspell (1876–1948).	**1901:** Queen Victoria of Great Britain dies and is succeeded by her son Edward VII.	**1900:** Sigmund Freud (1856–1939) writes *The Interpretation of Dreams*.
		1904–1905: Russo-Japanese War. Russia is defeated, and Japan emerges as a world power.	**1901:** Ragtime music becomes popular in the United States.
		1905: The Sinn Fein party is founded in Dublin.	**1903:** Wilbur and Orville Wright's first flight
	1906–1989: Samuel Beckett, Irish playwright who wrote some of his plays in French. Among his works are *Waiting for Godot* (1952) and *Endgame* (1957).		**1905:** The first movie theater in the United States opens in New York City.
			1905–1914: More than 10 million immigrants arrive in the United States.
			1906: An earthquake and subsequent fire ravage San Francisco.
			1907: Picasso's (1881–1973) *Les Demoiselles d'Avignon* is significant to cubism movement in art.
	1911–1983: Tennessee Williams, American playwright, author of *The Glass Menagerie* (1944), *A Streetcar Named Desire* (1947), and *Cat on a Hot Tin Roof* (1955)		**1908:** Henry Ford (1863–1947) designs the Model T.
		1912: Sun Yat Sen is elected president of the Republic of China and founds the Kuomintang.	**1910:** W. E. B. DuBois (1868–1963), African American civil rights leader and author, establishes the NAACP.
		1914: World War I begins with the assassination of Austrian Archduke Franz Ferdinand in Sarajevo.	**1912:** The ocean liner *Titanic* sinks, killing 1,513 passengers.
	1915: Arthur Miller, American playwright, born. Among his works are *Death of a Salesman* (1949) and *The Crucible* (1953).		**1913:** Niels Bohr (1885–1962) formulates his theory of atomic structure.
		1916: The Easter Rising in Ireland is suppressed by the British.	**1914:** The Panama Canal is completed.
	1915: George Cram Cook, Eugene O'Neill, and Susan Glaspell found the Provincetown Players in Provincetown, Massachusetts.	**1917:** The Russian Revolution overthrows the czar and establishes Bolshevik control under V. I. Lenin.	**1915:** D. W. Griffith's film *The Birth of a Nation* is released.
			c. 1916: Albert Einstein (1879–1955) formulates his theory of relativity.
	1917: J. L. Williams's *Why Marry?* receives the first Pulitzer Prize for drama.		**1916:** Jazz music evolves in New Orleans, Chicago, and New York City.
		1919: The Treaty of Versailles formally ends World War I.	**1918:** Influenza epidemic kills 22 million people worldwide by 1922.
	1918: Formation of the Theatre Guild in New York City		**1919:** The Bauhaus, an influential school of art and architecture, is established by Walter Gropius in Germany.
	1919: Actors Equity Association is officially recognized as a union in the United States.	**1920:** The Nineteenth Amendment recognizes the right of American women to vote.	**1920:** Prohibition begins in the United States.
	1920: Théâtre National Populaire is founded in Paris.	**1921:** Southern Ireland becomes the independent Republic of Ireland.	**1933:** Prohibition is repealed.

DATE	THEATER	POLITICAL	SOCIAL/CULTURAL
1900–1950 (continued)	**1921:** Italian playwright Luigi Pirandello (1867–1936) writes *Six Characters in Search of an Author*. **1923–1924:** Moscow Art Theater visits the United States for the first time. **1927:** Neil Simon born. His plays include *The Odd Couple* (1965), *Chapter Two* (1979), and *Biloxi Blues* (1984). **1928:** Bertolt Brecht and Kurt Weill produce *The Threepenny Opera* in Berlin. **1930–1965:** Lorraine Hansberry, African American playwright, author of *A Raisin in the Sun* (1959) **1930:** María Irene Fornés, Cuban playwright, born. Among her works are *Fefu and Her Friends* (1977) and *The Conduct of Life* (1985). **1931:** The Group Theatre is founded by Harold Clurman, Cheryl Crawford, and Lee Strasberg and operates for ten years. **1934:** Wole Soyinka, Nigerian playwright, born. His works include *The Strong Breed* (1962) and *A Play of Giants* (1984). **1934:** Socialist realism is declared the official artistic policy in Soviet theater.	**1921:** Ku Klux Klan activities become violent throughout southern United States. **1921:** Sacco and Vanzetti, Italian anarchists, are sentenced to death in the United States. **1922:** Fascist dictator Benito Mussolini gains power in Italy. **1924–1972:** J. Edgar Hoover, director of the Federal Bureau of Investigation **1925:** Adolf Hitler reorganizes the Nazi Party and publishes volume 1 of *Mein Kampf*. **1928:** The Kellogg-Briand Pact, outlawing war, is signed in Paris by 65 states. **c. 1928:** Joseph Stalin comes to power in the Soviet Union. **1929:** The U.S. stock market crash begins the Great Depression. **1933:** New Deal economic reforms attempt to stimulate recovery from the Depression. **1933:** Adolf Hitler comes to power in Germany. German labor unions and political parties other than the Nazi Party are suppressed. Nazis erect their first concentration camp; persecution of Jews begins in Germany. **1935:** Roosevelt signs the U.S. Social Security Act. **1935:** The Nuremberg laws in Nazi Germany deprive German Jews of their citizenship and civil rights. **1935–1936:** Italy's conquest of Ethiopia **1936:** Chiang Kai-shek declares war on Japan.	**1922:** T. S. Eliot (1888–1965) publishes *The Waste Land*. **1922:** James Joyce (1882–1941) publishes *Ulysses*. **1923:** George Gershwin (1898–1937) performs *Rhapsody in Blue*. **1925:** F. Scott Fitzgerald (1896–1940) publishes *The Great Gatsby*. **1925:** Margaret Sanger (1883–1966) organizes the first international birth control conference. **1920s:** Harlem Renaissance: African American literature, music, and art flourish in New York City. Langston Hughes (1902–1967), Zora Neale Hurston (1901–1960), Jean Toomer (1894–1967), and many others publish. **1925:** John T. Scopes, schoolteacher, is tried for violating a Tennessee law that prohibits the teaching of the theory of evolution. **1926:** Ernest Hemingway (1899–1961) publishes *The Sun Also Rises*. **1926:** Duke Ellington's (1899–1974) first records appear. **1927:** *The Jazz Singer* is the first "talkie" movie. **1927:** Charles Lindbergh (1902–1974) makes the first solo nonstop transatlantic flight. **1927:** Virginia Woolf (1882–1941), English novelist, publishes *To the Lighthouse*. **1929:** William Faulkner (1897–1962) publishes *The Sound and the Fury*. **1931:** Robert Frost (1874–1963) wins the Pulitzer Prize for *Collected Poems*. **1931:** The Empire State Building in New York City is completed. **1932:** Aldous Huxley (1894–1963) publishes *Brave New World*.

Early- and Mid-Twentieth-Century Drama Timeline (continued)

DATE	THEATER	POLITICAL	SOCIAL/CULTURAL
1900–1950 (continued)	**1935:** The American plays *Dead End* by Sidney Kingsley, *Winterset* by Maxwell Anderson, and *Waiting for Lefty* by Clifford Odets are produced.	**1936–1939:** Civil War in Spain results in Generalissimo Franco's consolidation of power.	**1937:** Amelia Earhart (1897–1937), the first woman to fly across the Atlantic, vanishes over the Pacific Ocean.
	1935–1939: The Federal Theatre Project operates in the United States under the auspices of the Works Progress Administration.	**1939:** Germany invades Poland.	**1938:** Joe Louis (1914–1981), African American heavyweight boxer, defeats German Max Schmeling.
	1936: Federico García Lorca, Spanish playwright, writes *The House of Bernarda Alba*.	**1939:** Great Britain and France declare war on Germany and its allies.	
	1937: Peter Stein, influential German director, born. Among his important productions are *Peer Gynt* (1971) and the *Oresteia* (1980).	**1940:** Germany invades France.	
		1941: Japan attacks Pearl Harbor, and the United States enters World War II.	
	1938: Antonín Artaud, French playwright and theorist, writes *The Theater and Its Double*.	**1942:** Germany begins killing Jews and others in gas chambers.	
		1942: The U.S. Army interns Japanese Americans in prison camps.	**1943:** Penicillin is first used in the treatment of chronic diseases.
		1944: Allies liberate France.	**1940s:** The era of great musical theater begins in the United States, featuring the songs of Cole Porter (1891–1964), Richard Rodgers (1902–1979), and Oscar Hammerstein (1895–1960), among many others.
	1946: The Living Theatre is founded by Judith Malina and Julian Beck.	**1945:** Hitler commits suicide in Berlin, and Germany signs an unconditional surrender.	
		1945: The United States drops atomic bombs on Hiroshima and Nagasaki, Japan.	
		1946: Juan Perón is elected president of Argentina.	
	1947: The Actors Studio is founded in New York City by Robert Lewis, Elia Kazan, and Cheryl Crawford. Lee Strasberg assumes control by 1948.	**1947:** India proclaims independence and is divided into Pakistan and India.	**1947:** Jackie Robinson (1919–1972) becomes the first African American to sign a contract with a major league baseball club.
	1947: Beginning of the regional theater movement in the United States. Margo Jones opens an arena theater in Dallas, Nina Vance founds the Alley Theatre in Houston, and the Arena Stage opens in 1949 in Washington, D.C.	**1948:** The Republic of Israel is proclaimed by Jewish leaders in Palestine.	
		1948: Indian leader Mahatma Gandhi is assassinated.	
		1949: Mao Zedong announces the establishment of the People's Republic of China.	
	1949: The Berliner Ensemble is founded in East Berlin.	**1949:** The North Atlantic Treaty Organization unites Canada, Western Europe, and the United States as allies.	
		1949: The apartheid system is established in South Africa.	

John Millington Synge

John Millington Synge (1871–1909) was one of the brilliant discoveries of the Irish Literary Renaissance, which was largely the product of Lady Gregory and William Butler Yeats, the codirectors of the Abbey Theatre in Dublin. The Abbey ranks as one of the most influential and successful national theaters in European history. From 1904 to the present, it has been devoted to producing plays by Irish writers, some of whom have gone on to be ranked among the greatest of their age. Besides Synge, Bernard Shaw, Lady Gregory, Yeats, Sean O'Casey, and Brian Friel are among the many who contributed to the reputation of the Abbey.

Synge was gifted in languages, with a degree in German from Trinity College, Dublin. Also a violinist, he went to Paris to study music and live the bohemian life of the artist. It was there, in 1896, that Yeats and Lady Gregory met Synge and persuaded him to return to Ireland and write plays for what was to become the Abbey. They convinced him to spend time in the Aran Islands, the wildest part of Ireland. Yeats felt the Arans were an important source of the literary energy of the nation because the Islanders' colorful language sounded like English filtered through Irish Gaelic.

Synge wrote a number of important plays within less than ten years. Most of them remain in the repertory of modern drama: *In the Shadow of the Glen* (1903), *Riders to the Sea* (1904), *The Well of the Saints* (1905), *The Tinker's Wedding* (1907), *The Playboy of the Western World* (1907), and *Deirdre of the Sorrows* (1910). With the exception of *The Tinker's Wedding*, which is so anticlerical that it has never been given a production at the Abbey, they are all still regularly produced there.

Synge was not always a popular playwright in Ireland. He felt that he faithfully represented peasant ways, but his Dublin audiences often protested that he insulted the Irish. Synge's kind of realism, though not especially harsh or critical, was an unvarnished view of the west of Ireland. The Abbey audiences wanted an idealized portrait of their countrymen and countrywomen, not straightforward and sometimes embarrassing portraits such as the one Synge offered them in *The Playboy of the Western World*. That play caused riots in the Abbey Theatre when first performed because of its nationalistic elements, its gritty, honest portrayal of country people, and its use of "indecent" language. Regarding this last, it is said that his use of the image of "chosen females standing in their shifts"—shifts referring to women's slips or chemises—incensed audiences.

Synge was shocked at the uproar; he had never expected his play to stimulate such a response. The question of realism was probably not on Synge's mind at all. *Playboy* is a less realistic play than *Riders to the Sea,* and both are rooted not in any effort to force the audience to look at life as it is really lived but, rather, in the mythic and symbolic forces that underlie everyone's experiences of heroism, life, and death. The deep roots of both plays are in Irish myth and the Christian religion. Synge was amazed that audiences ignored those important aspects and focused on other, less significant issues.

Synge's early death robbed world drama of a figure who certainly would have been among the greatest writers of the century. As it is, his work is remarkable; but in his last play, *Deirdre of the Sorrows*, which he never finished, we can see the promise of a body of work that would have taken its place with the best plays of our time.

RIDERS TO THE SEA

Riders to the Sea (1904) was the first success that Synge produced for the Abbey Theatre. In some ways it is still one of the most impressive plays to come out of the Irish Literary Renaissance. It is a one-act play, which the Abbey found congenial for its early programs, but its brevity in no way diminishes its power.

The play is set in the west of Ireland, the part least touched by English influence. Aran Islanders speak both Gaelic and English, but their English is marked with a very expressive and idiosyncratic flavor, which Synge tries to replicate in this play. The syntax of Synge's peasants benefits from his musician's ear as well as from his having lived in an inn in Wicklow, where he eavesdropped on the local Irish kitchen girls speaking naturally and unaffectedly.

Riders to the Sea owes much of its power to the local speech and the local way of life portrayed faithfully in the play. In his preface to *The Playboy of the Western World*, Synge credits Irish writers with the advantage of listening "for a few years more" to a language that is "rich as a nut." Maurya's long speeches at the end of *Riders to the Sea* are filled with the rhythms of the sea and the agony of someone who has suffered as much as the world can demand. Even the speeches of the lesser characters have an extraordinarily expressive flavor.

The drama depicts the sufferings of a superstitious peasant woman, yet it contains the same kinds of intensity of dramatic action found in Greek tragedies. It maintains a unity of time, place, character, and action, as well as an intense sense of fate and impending doom. Synge may well have begun developing a new genre of folk tragedy, just as Arthur Miller later began developing a genre of middle-class tragedy in *Death of a Salesman*. *Riders to the Sea* is permeated by a sense of fate; and Maurya, whose name is remarkably close in sound to *moira*, the Greek word for "fate," senses the inevitability of the premature death of her last son on the sea. The feeling of inevitability is heightened by the discussion between the daughters about the son Michael, who has been feared lost at sea, by their identification of his sock that was recovered from the sea, and by the willful insistence of the last son, Bartley, on riding the mares across the sea to the mainland, knowingly risking his life. (In fact, men

SYNGE • RIDERS TO THE SEA

did swim their animals from the islands to the mainland, and they often went out to meet the large boats that came near. Even today those waters are difficult, and Aran Islanders still use the same black curraghs their ancestors used to ferry themselves, their goods, and their livestock between the mainland and their homes.) Maurya's horrifying vision of Michael and Bartley on the mares confirms her premonitions and fears. It also injects an element of supernatural intensity.

Perhaps because of its tragic Greek pattern, *Riders to the Sea* has a mythic force. The sense of destiny that Maurya feels is built into her life. Her resignation and deep faith help her grow in our imagination and give her a heroic dimension. Synge's approach to realism is much different from Ibsen's or Chekhov's. It is more elemental, based on the spiritual life of the folk as expressed in the eloquence of their language.

Riders to the Sea in Performance

All of Synge's plays were written for the early Abbey Theatre, founded in 1904 by Lady Gregory and W. B. Yeats to perform Irish plays. At that time all performances were in Molesworth Hall, leased facilities. Synge's *In the Shadow of the Glen* was one of the first plays to be performed by the company, then known as the Irish National Theatre. The play opened in October 1903, coinciding with an Irish holiday, Samhain (pronounced *sow-in*). Although controversial, it was a success. *Riders to the Sea* was Synge's second play, produced in Molesworth Hall in February 1904. At this time the Abbey had already attracted some excellent actors. Bartley was played by W. G. Fay, who was instrumental in shaping the Abbey. Sarah Allgood, destined to become a standard player in American films in the 1930s and 1940s, played Cathleen. The production was well received by press and public.

Riders to the Sea has usually been paired with other Irish plays in production. The Abbey Theatre Company still produces the play regularly and often takes it on tour. One of the most memorable tours was in 1957, when the Abbey brought the play to the tiny Theatre East in New York. Despite the theater's small size, the effect of the play, which had not been seen in an Abbey performance in the United States since 1911, was electrifying. The finest Irish actress of the age, Siobhan McKenna, played Maurya.

Ralph Vaughan Williams used Synge's play as the basis for his opera *Riders to the Sea* (1925–1932). One of its most recent productions was at the University of California at Santa Barbara Opera Theatre in February, 2008. The opera explores the deep emotional valences of Synge's original.

Riders to the Sea enjoys frequent production by both high school and college students. Its brevity and power make it a strong vehicle for amateur productions.

John Millington Synge (1871–1909)

RIDERS TO THE SEA

Persons in the Play

MAURYA (*an old woman*)
BARTLEY (*her son*)
CATHLEEN (*her daughter*)
NORA (*a younger daughter*)
MEN *and* WOMEN

Scene: *An Island off the West of Ireland.*

(*Cottage kitchen, with nets, oilskins, spinning wheel, some new boards standing by the wall, etc. Cathleen, a girl of about twenty, finishes kneading cake, and puts it down in the pot-oven by the fire; then wipes her hands, and begins to spin at the wheel. Nora, a young girl, puts her head in at the door.*)

NORA (*in a low voice*): Where is she?

CATHLEEN: She's lying down, God help her, and may be sleeping, if she's able.

(*Nora comes in softly and takes a bundle from under her shawl.*)

CATHLEEN (*spinning the wheel rapidly*): What is it you have?

NORA: The young priest is after bringing them. It's a shirt and a plain stocking were got off a drowned man in Donegal.

(*Cathleen stops her wheel with a sudden movement, and leans out to listen.*)

NORA: We're to find out if it's Michael's they are, some time herself will be down looking by the sea.

CATHLEEN: How would they be Michael's, Nora? How would he go the length of that way to the far north?

NORA: The young priest says he's known the like of it. "If it's Michael's they are," says he, "you can tell herself he's got a clean burial by the grace of God, and if they're not his, let no one say a word about them, for she'll be getting her death," says he, "with crying and lamenting."

(*The door which Nora half closed is blown open by a gust of wind.*)

CATHLEEN (*looking out anxiously*): Did you ask him would he stop Bartley going this day with the horses to the Galway fair?

NORA: "I won't stop him," says he, "but let you not be afraid. Herself does be saying prayers half through the night, and the Almighty God won't leave her destitute," says he, "with no son living."

CATHLEEN: Is the sea bad by the white rocks, Nora?

NORA: Middling bad, God help us. There's a great roaring in the west, and it's worse it'll be getting when the tide's turned to the wind. (*She goes over to the table with the bundle.*) Shall I open it now?

CATHLEEN: Maybe she'd wake up on us, and come in before we'd done. (*Coming to the table.*) It's a long time we'll be, and the two of us crying.

NORA (*goes to the inner door and listens*): She's moving about on the bed. She'll be coming in a minute.

CATHLEEN: Give me the ladder, and I'll put them up in the turf-loft, the way she won't know of them at all, and maybe when the tide turns she'll be going down to see would he be floating from the east.

(*They put the ladder against the gable of the chimney; Cathleen goes up a few steps and hides the bundle in the turf-loft. Maurya comes from the inner room.*)

MAURYA (*looking up at Cathleen and speaking querulously*): Isn't it turf enough you have for this day and evening?

CATHLEEN: There's a cake baking at the fire for a short space (*throwing down the turf*) and Bartley will want it when the tide turns if he goes to Connemara.

(*Nora picks up the turf and puts it round the pot-oven.*)

MAURYA (*sitting down on a stool at the fire*): He won't go this day with the wind rising from the south and west. He won't go this day, for the young priest will stop him surely.

NORA: He'll not stop him, mother, and I heard Eamon Simon and Stephen Pheety and Colum Shawn saying he would go.

MAURYA: Where is he itself?

NORA: He went down to see would there be another boat sailing in the week, and I'm thinking it won't be long till he's here now, for the tide's turning at the green head, and the hooker's tacking from the east.

CATHLEEN: I hear some one passing the big stones.

NORA (*looking out*): He's coming now, and he in a hurry.

BARTLEY (*comes in and looks round the room. Speaking sadly and quietly*): Where is the bit of new rope, Cathleen, was bought in Connemara?

CATHLEEN (*coming down*): Give it to him, Nora; it's on a nail by the white boards. I hung it up this morning, for the pig with the black feet was eating it.

NORA (*giving him a rope*): Is that it, Bartley?

MAURYA: You'd do right to leave that rope, Bartley, hanging by the boards. (*Bartley takes the rope.*) It will be wanting in this place, I'm telling you, if Michael is washed up tomorrow morning, or the

The fateful first scene of *Riders to the Sea* in the 1998 Royal Shakespeare Company/The Other Place production directed by John Crowley. Mairead McKinley (foreground) and Aislinn Mangan (background) play the daughters, Cathleen and Nora. Stella McCusker plays their mother, Maurya.

next morning, or any morning in the week, for it's a deep grave we'll make him by the grace of God.

BARTLEY (*beginning to work with the rope*): I've no halter the way I can ride down on the mare, and I must go now quickly. This is the one boat going for two weeks or beyond it, and the fair will be a good fair for horses I heard them saying below.

MAURYA: It's a hard thing they'll be saying below if the body is washed up and there's no man in it to make the coffin, and I after giving a big price for the finest white boards you'd find in Connemara.

(*She looks round at the boards.*)

BARTLEY: How would it be washed up, and we after looking each day for nine days, and a strong wind blowing a while back from the west and south?

MAURYA: If it wasn't found itself, that wind is raising the sea, and there was a star up against the moon, and it rising in the night. If it was a hundred horses, or a thousand horses you had itself, what is the price of a thousand horses against a son where there is one son only?

BARTLEY (*working at the halter, to Cathleen*): Let you go down each day, and see the sheep aren't jumping in on the rye, and if the jobber comes you can sell the pig with the black feet if there is a good price going.

MAURYA: How would the like of her get a good price for a pig?

BARTLEY (*to Cathleen*): If the west wind holds with the last bit of the moon let you and Nora get up weed enough for another cock for the kelp. It's hard set we'll be from this day with no one in it but one man to work.

MAURYA: It's hard set we'll be surely the day you're drownd'd with the rest. What way will I live and the girls with me, and I an old woman looking for the grave?

(*Bartley lays down the halter, takes off his old coat, and puts on a newer one of the same flannel.*)

BARTLEY (*to Nora*): Is she coming to the pier?

NORA (*looking out*): She's passing the green head and letting fall her sails.

BARTLEY (*getting his purse and tobacco*): I'll have half an hour to go down, and you'll see me coming again in two days, or in three days, or maybe in four days if the wind is bad.

MAURYA (*turning round to the fire, and putting her shawl over her head*): Isn't it a hard and cruel man won't hear a word from an old woman, and she holding him from the sea?

CATHLEEN: It's the life of a young man to be going on the sea, and who would listen to an old woman with one thing and she saying it over?

BARTLEY (*taking the halter*): I must go now quickly. I'll ride down on the red mare, and the gray pony'll run behind me.... The blessing of God on you.

(*He goes out.*)

MAURYA (*crying out as he is in the door*): He's gone now, God spare us, and we'll not see him again. He's gone now, and when the black night is falling I'll have no son left me in the world.

CATHLEEN: Why wouldn't you give him your blessing and he looking round in the door? Isn't it sorrow enough is on every one in this house without your sending him out with an unlucky word behind him, and a hard word in his ear?

(*Maurya takes up the tongs and begins raking the fire aimlessly without looking round.*)

NORA (*turning toward her*): You're taking away the turf from the cake.

CATHLEEN (*crying out*): The Son of God forgive us, Nora, we're after forgetting his bit of bread.

(*She comes over to the fire.*)

NORA: And it's destroyed he'll be going till dark night, and he after eating nothing since the sun went up.

CATHLEEN (*turning the cake out of the oven*): It's destroyed he'll be, surely. There's no sense left on any person in a house where an old woman will be talking forever.

(*Maurya sways herself on her stool.*)

CATHLEEN (*cutting off some of the bread and rolling it in a cloth; to Maurya*): Let you go down now to the spring well and give him this and he passing. You'll see him then and the dark word will be broken, and you can say "God speed you," the way he'll be easy in his mind.

MAURYA (*taking the bread*): Will I be in it as soon as himself?

CATHLEEN: If you go now quickly.

MAURYA (*standing up unsteadily*): It's hard set I am to walk.

CATHLEEN (*looking at her anxiously*): Give her the stick, Nora, or maybe she'll slip on the big stones.

NORA: What stick?

CATHLEEN: The stick Michael brought from Connemara.

MAURYA (*taking a stick Nora gives her*): In the big world the old people do be leaving things after them for their sons and children, but in this place it is the young men do be leaving things behind for them that do be old.

(*She goes out slowly. Nora goes over to the ladder.*)

CATHLEEN: Wait, Nora, maybe she'd turn back quickly. She's that sorry, God help her, you wouldn't know the thing she'd do.

NORA: Is she gone round by the bush?

CATHLEEN (*looking out*): She's gone now. Throw it down quickly, for the Lord knows when she'll be out of it again.

NORA (*getting the bundle from the loft*): The young priest said he'd be passing tomorrow, and we might go down and speak to him below if it's Michael's they are surely.

CATHLEEN (*taking the bundle*): Did he say what way they were found?

NORA (*coming down*): "There were two men," says he, "and they rowing round with poteen before the cocks crowed, and the oar of one of them caught the body, and they passing the black cliffs of the north."

CATHLEEN (*trying to open the bundle*): Give me a knife, Nora, the string's perished with the salt water, and there's a black knot on it you wouldn't loosen in a week.

NORA (*giving her a knife*): I've heard tell it was a long way to Donegal.

CATHLEEN (*cutting the string*): It is surely. There was a man in here a while ago—the man sold us that knife—and he said if you set off walking from the rocks beyond, it would be seven days you'd be in Donegal.

NORA: And what time would a man take, and he floating?

(*Cathleen opens the bundle and takes out a bit of a stocking. They look at them eagerly.*)

CATHLEEN (*in a low voice*): The Lord spare us, Nora! isn't it a queer hard thing to say if it's his they are surely?

NORA: I'll get his shirt off the hook the way we can put the one flannel on the other. (*She looks through some clothes hanging in the corner.*) It's not with them, Cathleen, and where will it be?

CATHLEEN: I'm thinking Bartley put it on him in the morning, for his own shirt was heavy with the salt in it (*pointing to the corner*). There's a bit of a sleeve was of the same stuff. Give me that and it will do.

(*Nora brings it to her and they compare the flannel.*)

CATHLEEN: It's the same stuff, Nora; but if it is itself aren't there great rolls of it in the shops of Galway, and isn't it many another man may have a shirt of it as well as Michael himself?

NORA (*who has taken up the stocking and counted the stitches, crying out*): It's Michael, Cathleen, it's Michael; God spare his soul, and what will herself say when she hears this story, and Bartley on the sea?

CATHLEEN (*taking the stocking*): It's a plain stocking.

NORA: It's the second one of the third pair I knitted, and I put up three score stitches, and I dropped four of them.

CATHLEEN (*counts the stitches*): It's that number is in it. (*Crying out.*) Ah, Nora, isn't it a bitter thing to think of him floating that way to the far north, and no one to keen him but the black hags that do be flying on the sea?

NORA (*swinging herself round, and throwing out her arms on the clothes*): And isn't it a pitiful thing when there is nothing left of a man who was a great rower and fisher, but a bit of an old shirt and a plain stocking?

CATHLEEN (*after an instant*): Tell me is herself coming, Nora? I hear a little sound on the path.

NORA (*looking out*): She is, Cathleen. She's coming up to the door.

CATHLEEN: Put these things away before she'll come in. Maybe it's easier she'll be after giving her blessing to Bartley, and we won't let on we've heard anything the time he's on the sea.

NORA (*helping Cathleen to close the bundle*): We'll put them here in the corner.

(*They put them into a hole in the chimney corner. Cathleen goes back to the spinning wheel.*)

NORA: Will she see it was crying I was?

CATHLEEN: Keep your back to the door the way the light'll not be on you.

(*Nora sits down at the chimney corner, with her back to the door. Maurya comes in very slowly, without looking at the girls, and goes over to her stool at the other side of the fire. The cloth with the bread is still in her hand. The girls look at each other, and Nora points to the bundle of bread.)*

CATHLEEN (*after spinning for a moment*): You didn't give him his bit of bread?

(*Maurya begins to keen softly, without turning round.*)

CATHLEEN: Did you see him riding down?

(*Maurya goes on keening.*)

CATHLEEN (*a little impatiently*): God forgive you; isn't it a better thing to raise your voice and tell what you seen, than to be making lamentation for a thing that's done? Did you see Bartley, I'm saying to you.
MAURYA (*with a weak voice*): My heart's broken from this day.
CATHLEEN (*as before*): Did you see Bartley?
MAURYA: I seen the fearfulest thing.
CATHLEEN (*leaves her wheel and looks out*): God forgive you; he's riding the mare now over the green head, and the gray pony behind him.
MAURYA (*starts, so that her shawl falls back from her head and shows her white tossed hair. With a frightened voice*): The gray pony behind him.
CATHLEEN (*coming to the fire*): What is it ails you, at all?
MAURYA (*speaking very slowly*): I've seen the fearfulest thing any person has seen, since the day Bride Dara seen the dead man with the child in his arms.
CATHLEEN AND NORA: Uah.

(*They crouch down in front of the old woman at the fire.*)

NORA: Tell us what it is you seen.
MAURYA: I went down to the spring well, and I stood there saying a prayer to myself. Then Bartley came along, and he riding on the red mare with the gray pony behind him. (*She puts up her hands, as if to hide something from her eyes.*) The Son of God spare us, Nora!
CATHLEEN: What is it you seen?
MAURYA: I seen Michael himself.
CATHLEEN (*speaking softly*): You did not, mother. It wasn't Michael you seen, for his body is after being found in the far north, and he's got a clean burial by the grace of God.
MAURYA (*a little defiantly*): I'm after seeing him this day, and he riding and galloping. Bartley came first on the red mare; and I tried to say "God speed you," but something choked the words in my throat. He went by quickly; and "the blessing of God on you," says he, and I could say nothing. I looked up then, and I crying, at the gray pony, and there was Michael upon it—with fine clothes on him, and new shoes on his feet.
CATHLEEN (*begins to keen*): It's destroyed we are from this day. It's destroyed, surely.
NORA: Didn't the young priest say the Almighty God wouldn't leave her destitute with no son living?

MAURYA (*in a low voice, but clearly*): It's little the like of him knows of the sea.... Bartley will be lost now, and let you call in Eamon and make me a good coffin out of the white boards, for I won't live after them. I've had a husband, and a husband's father, and six sons in this house—six fine men, though it was a hard birth I had with every one of them and they coming to the world—and some of them were found and some of them were not found, but they're gone now the lot of them.... There were Stephen, and Shawn, were lost in the great wind, and found after in the Bay of Gregory of the Golden Mouth, and carried up the two of them on the one plank, and in by that door.

(*She pauses for a moment, the girls start as if they heard something through the door that is half open behind them.*)

NORA (*in a whisper*): Did you hear that, Cathleen? Did you hear a noise in the northeast?
CATHLEEN (*in a whisper*): There's some one after crying out by the seashore.
MAURYA (*continues without hearing anything*): There was Sheamus and his father, and his own father again, were lost in a dark night, and not a stick or sign was seen of them when the sun went up. There was Patch after was drowned out of a curagh° that turned over. I was sitting here with Bartley, and he a baby, lying on my two knees, and I seen two women, and three women, and four women coming in, and they crossing themselves, and not saying a word. I looked out then, and there were men coming after them, and they holding a thing in the half of a red sail, and water dripping out of it—it was a dry day, Nora—and leaving a track to the door.

(*She pauses again with her hand stretched out toward the door. It opens softly and old women begin to come in, crossing themselves on the threshold, and kneeling down in front of the stage with red petticoats over their heads.*)

MAURYA (*half in a dream, to Cathleen*): Is it Patch or Michael, or what is it at all?
CATHLEEN: Michael is after being found in the far north, and when he is found there how could he be here in this place?
MAURYA: There does be a power of young men floating round in the sea, and what way would they know if it was Michael they had, or another man like him, for when a man is nine days in the sea, and the wind blowing, it's hard set his own mother would be to say what man was it.
CATHLEEN: It's Michael, God spare him, for they're after sending us a bit of his clothes from the far north.

(*She reaches out and hands Maurya the clothes that belonged to Michael. Maurya stands up slowly and takes them in her hands. Nora looks out.*)

curagh: A small boat with a hide- or tarpaulin-covered frame.

Maurya (Stella McCusker) mourns the death of her last son, Bartley (Stephen Kennedy).

NORA: They're carrying a thing among them and there's water dripping out of it and leaving a track by the big stones.

CATHLEEN (*in a whisper to the women who have come in*): Is it Bartley it is?

ONE OF THE WOMEN: It is surely, God rest his soul.

(*Two younger women come in and pull out the table. Then men carry in the body of Bartley, laid on a plank, with a bit of a sail over it, and lay it on the table.*)

CATHLEEN (*to the women, as they are doing so*): What way was he drowned?

ONE OF THE WOMEN: The gray pony knocked him into the sea, and he was washed out where there is a great surf on the white rocks.

(*Maurya has gone over and knelt down at the head of the table. The women are keening softly and swaying themselves with a slow movement. Cathleen and Nora kneel at the other end of the table. The men kneel near the door.*)

MAURYA (*raising her head and speaking as if she did not see the people around her*): They're all gone now, and there isn't anything more the sea can do to me.... I'll have no call now to be up crying and praying when the wind breaks from the south, and you can hear the surf is in the east, and the surf is in the west, making a great stir with the two noises, and they hitting one on the other. I'll have no call now to be going down and getting Holy Water in the dark nights after Samhain,° and I won't care what way the

Samhain: Feast of All Saints, November 1.

sea is when the other women will be keening. (*To Nora.*) Give me the Holy Water, Nora, there's a small sup still on the dresser.

(*Nora gives it to her.*)

MAURYA (*drops Michael's clothes across Bartley's feet, and sprinkles the Holy Water over him*): It isn't that I haven't prayed for you, Bartley, to the Almighty God. It isn't that I haven't said prayers in the dark night till you wouldn't know what I'll be saying; but it's a great rest I'll have now, and it's time surely. It's a great rest I'll have now, and great sleeping in the long nights after Samhain, if it's only a bit of wet flour we do have to eat, and maybe a fish that would be stinking.

(*She kneels down again, crossing herself, and saying prayers under her breath.*)

CATHLEEN (*to an old man*): Maybe yourself and Eamon would make a coffin when the sun rises. We have fine white boards herself bought, God help her, thinking Michael would be found, and I have a new cake you can eat while you'll be working.

THE OLD MAN (*looking at the boards*): Are there nails with them?

CATHLEEN: There are not, Colum; we didn't think of the nails.

ANOTHER MAN: It's a great wonder she wouldn't think of the nails, and all the coffins she's seen made already.

CATHLEEN: It's getting old she is, and broken.

(*Maurya stands up again very slowly and spreads out the pieces of Michael's clothes beside the body, sprinkling them with the last of the Holy Water.*)

NORA (*in a whisper to Cathleen*): She's quiet now and easy; but the day Michael was drowned you could hear her crying out from this to the spring well. It's fonder she was of Michael, and would any one have thought that?

CATHLEEN (*slowly and clearly*): An old woman will be soon tired with anything she will do, and isn't it nine days herself is after crying and keening, and making great sorrow in the house?

MAURYA (*puts the empty cup mouth downward on the table, and lays her hands together on Bartley's feet*): They're all together this time, and the end is come. May the Almighty God have mercy on Bartley's soul, and on Michael's soul, and on the souls of Sheamus and Patch, and Stephen and Shawn (*bending her head*); and may He have mercy on my soul, Nora, and on the soul of every one is left living in the world.

(*She pauses, and the keen rises a little more loudly from the women, then sinks away.*)

MAURYA (*continuing*): Michael has a clean burial in the far north, by the grace of the Almighty God. Bartley will have a fine coffin out of the white boards, and a deep grave surely. What more can we want than that? No man at all can be living forever, and we must be satisfied.

(*She kneels down again and the curtain falls slowly.*)

COMMENTARY

John Millington Synge (1871–1909)
FROM *THE ARAN ISLANDS*   *1907*

For several weeks a year from 1898 to 1902, Synge traveled to the Aran Islands, off the west coast of Ireland near Galway. He spent part of his time learning Gaelic and part of it keeping a journal. He wrote mostly about his experiences in this remote part of Ireland, so distant from Dublin civilization that Synge sometimes felt he was in a time warp. This excerpt, published in 1907 but written before Riders to the Sea, portrays the people he met on the Aran Islands. Synge said he learned how people speak on the islands in part from overhearing servant girls, such as those he describes here, talking among themselves in the kitchen beneath his room. His musical training enabled him to catch the intonations of English as it was spoken by native Gaelic speakers.

I am settled at last on Inishmaan in a small cottage with a continual drone of Gaelic coming from the kitchen that opens into my room.

Early this morning the man of the house came over for me with a four-oared curagh° — that is, a curagh with four rowers and four oars on either side, as each man uses two — and we set off a little before noon.

It gave me a moment of exquisite satisfaction to find myself moving away from civilization in this rude canvas canoe of a model that has served primitive races since men first went on the sea.

We had to stop for a moment at a hulk that is anchored in the bay, to make some arrangements for the fish-curing of the middle island, and my crew called out as

---

curagh: Small boat in the general shape of a canoe.

soon as we were within earshot that they had a man with them who had been in France a month from this day.

When we started again, a small sail was run up in the bow, and we set off across the sound with a leaping oscillation that had no resemblance to the heavy movement of a boat.

The sail is only used as an aid, so the men continued to row after it had gone up, and as they occupied the four cross-seats I lay on the canvas at the stern and the frame of slender laths, which bent and quivered as the waves passed under them.

When we set off it was a brilliant morning of April, and the green, glittering waves seemed to toss the canoe among themselves, yet as we drew nearer this island a sudden thunderstorm broke out behind the rocks we were approaching, and lent a momentary tumult to this still vein of the Atlantic.

We landed at a small pier, from which a rude track leads up to the village between small fields and bare sheets of rock like those in Aranmor. The youngest son of my boatman, a boy of about seventeen, who is to be my teacher and guide, was waiting for me at the pier and guided me to his house, while the men settled the curagh and followed slowly with my baggage.

My room is at one end of the cottage, with a boarded floor and ceiling, and two windows opposite each other. Then there is the kitchen with earth floor and open rafters, and two doors opposite each other opening into the open air, but no windows. Beyond it there are two small rooms of half the width of the kitchen with one window apiece.

The kitchen itself, where I will spend most of my time, is full of beauty and distinction. The red dresses of the women who cluster round the fire on their stools give a glow of almost Eastern richness, and the walls have been toned by the turf-smoke to a soft brown that blends with the grey earth-colour of the floor. Many sorts of fishing-tackle, and the nets and oilskins of the men, are hung upon the walls or among the open rafters; and right overhead, under the thatch, there is a whole cowskin from which they make pampooties.°

Every article on these islands has an almost personal character, which gives this simple life, where all art is unknown, something of the artistic beauty of medieval life. The curaghs and spinning-wheels, the tiny wooden barrels that are still much used in the place of earthenware, the homemade cradles, churns, and baskets, are all full of individuality, and being made from materials that are common here, yet to some extent peculiar to the island, they seem to exist as a natural link between the people and the world that is about them.

The simplicity and unity of the dress increases in another way the local air of beauty. The women wear red petticoats and jackets of the island wool stained with madder, to which they usually add a plaid shawl twisted round their chests and tied at the back. When it rains they throw another petticoat over their heads with the waistband round their faces, or, if they are young, they use a heavy shawl like those worn in Galway. Occasionally other wraps are worn, and during the thunderstorm I arrived in I saw several girls with men's waistcoats buttoned round their bodies. Their skirts do not come much below the knee, and show their powerful legs in the heavy indigo stockings with which they are all provided.

The men wear three colours: the natural wool, indigo, and a grey flannel that is woven of alternate threads of indigo and the natural wool. In Aranmor many of the

pampooties: Soft slippers of sealskin or rawhide.

younger men have adopted the usual fisherman's jersey, but I have only seen one on this island.

As flannel is cheap—the women spin the yarn from the wool of their own sheep, and it is then woven by a weaver in Kilronan for fourpence a yard—the men seem to wear an indefinite number of waistcoats and woollen drawers one over the other. They are usually surprised at the lightness of my own dress, and one old man I spoke to for a minute on the pier, when I came ashore, asked me if I was not cold with "my little clothes."

As I sat in the kitchen to dry the spray from my coat, several men who had seen me walking up came in to talk to me, usually murmuring on the threshold, "The blessing of God on this place," or some similar words.

The courtesy of the old woman of the house is singularly attractive, and though I could not understand much of what she said—she has no English—I could see with how much grace she motioned each visitor to a chair, or stool, according to his age, and said a few words to him till he drifted into our English conversation.

For the moment my own arrival is the chief subject of interest, and the men who come in are eager to talk to me.

Some of them express themselves more correctly than the ordinary peasant, others use the Gaelic idioms continually and substitute "he" or "she" for "it," as the neuter pronoun is not found in modern Irish.

A few of the men have a curiously full vocabulary, others know only the commonest words in English, and are driven to ingenious devices to express their meaning. Of all the subjects we can talk of war seems their favourite, and the conflict between America and Spain° is causing a great deal of excitement. Nearly all the families have relations who have had to cross the Atlantic, and all eat of the flour and bacon that is brought from the United States, so they have a vague fear that "if anything happened to America," their own island would cease to be habitable.

Foreign languages are another favourite topic, and as these men are bilingual they have a fair notion of what it means to speak and think in many different idioms. Most of the strangers they see on the islands are philological students, and the people have been led to conclude that linguistic studies, particularly Gaelic studies, are the chief occupation of the outside world.

"I have seen Frenchmen, and Danes, and Germans," said one man, "and there does be a power of Irish books along with them, and they reading them better than ourselves. Believe me there are few rich men now in the world who are not studying the Gaelic."

They sometimes ask me the French for simple phrases, and when they have listened to the intonation for a moment, most of them are able to reproduce it with admirable precision.

No one who has not lived for weeks among these grey clouds and seas can realize the joy with which the eye rests on the red dresses of the women, especially when a number of them are to be found together, as happened early this morning.

I heard that the young cattle were to be shipped for a fair on the mainland, which is to take place in a few days, and I went down on the pier, a little after dawn, to watch them.

conflict between America and Spain: Spanish-American War, 1898.

The bay was shrouded in the greys of coming rain, yet the thinness of the cloud threw a silvery light on the sea, and an unusual depth of blue to the mountains of Connemara.

As I was going across the sandhills one dun-sailed hooker° glided slowly out to begin her voyage, and another beat up to the pier. Troops of red cattle, driven mostly by the women, were coming up from several directions, forming, with the green of the long tract of grass that separates the sea from the rocks, a new unity of colour.

The pier itself was crowded with bullocks and a great number of the people. I noticed one extraordinary girl in the throng who seemed to exert an authority on all who came near her. Her curiously-formed nostrils and narrow chin gave her a witch-like expression, yet the beauty of her hair and skin made her singularly attractive.

When the empty hooker was made fast its deck was still many feet below the level of the pier, so the animals were slung down by a rope from the mast-head, with much struggling and confusion. Some of them made wild efforts to escape, nearly carrying their owners with them into the sea, but they were handled with wonderful dexterity, and there was no mishap.

When the open hold was filled with young cattle, packed as tightly as they could stand, the owners with their wives or sisters, who go with them to prevent extravagance in Galway, jumped down on the deck, and the voyage was begun. Immediately afterwards a rickety old hooker beat up with turf° from Connemara, and while she was unlading all the men sat along the edge of the pier and made remarks upon the rottenness of her timber till the owners grew wild with rage.

The tide was now too low for more boats to come to the pier, so a move was made to a strip of sand towards the southeast, where the rest of the cattle were shipped through the surf. Here the hooker was anchored about eighty yards from the shore, and a curagh was rowed round to tow out the animals. Each bullock was caught in its turn and girded with a sling of rope by which it could be hoisted on board. Another rope was fastened to the horns and passed out to a man in the stern of the curagh. Then the animal was forced down through the surf and out of its depth before it had much time to struggle. Once fairly swimming, it was towed out to the hooker and dragged on board in a half-drowned condition.

The freedom of the sand seemed to give a stronger spirit of revolt, and some of the animals were only caught after a dangerous struggle. The first attempt was not always successful, and I saw one three-year-old lift two men with his horns, and drag another fifty yards along the sand by his tail before he was subdued.

While this work was going on a crowd of girls and women collected on the edge of the cliff and kept shouting down a confused babble of satire and praise.

When I came back to the cottage I found that among the women who had gone to the mainland was a daughter of the old woman's, and that her baby of about nine months had been left in the care of its grandmother.

As I came in she was busy getting ready my dinner, and old Pat Dirane, who usually comes at this hour, was rocking the cradle. It is made of clumsy wicker-work, with two pieces of rough wood fastened underneath to serve as rockers, and all the time I am in my room I can hear it bumping on the floor with extraordinary

---

hooker: A commercial fishing boat.
turf: Peat used for fuel.

violence. When the baby is awake it sprawls on the floor, and the old woman sings it a variety of inarticulate lullabies that have much musical charm.

Another daughter, who lives at home, has gone to the fair also, so the old woman has both the baby and myself to take care of as well as a crowd of chickens that live in a hole beside the fire. Often when I want tea, or when the old woman goes for water, I have to take my own turn at rocking the cradle.

Susan Glaspell

"The biggest stories are written about the things which draw human beings closer together."

— SUSAN GLASPELL

Although Susan Glaspell (1876–1948) was already established as a novelist, she became an important figure in early-twentieth-century drama. She was born in Davenport, Iowa, graduated from Drake University in Des Moines, and went to work as a reporter on the *Des Moines Daily News* in 1899. While there she began writing short fiction and novels, and with the beginnings of publishing success, she returned to Davenport to write. Her first novel, *The Glory of the Conquered: The Story of a Great Love* (1909), earned enough for her to spend a year in Paris. *The Visioning* (1911) was set on an army base and presented a less sentimentalized world than her first book. Back in the United States in 1911, she published her book of short stories, *Lifted Masks* (1912). One of her best novels, *Fidelity*, published in 1915, tells the story of a woman who leaves her loving husband and family to run off with a married man.

In 1908 Glaspell first met her future husband, George Cram (Jig) Cook, a traveled intellectual and Harvard graduate who was teaching at Iowa University. After that initial meeting, Cook married another woman, but five years later he was divorced for the second time. Glaspell and Cook were reintroduced in 1913 by mutual friends and eventually felt they were fated for each other. Because the scandal of Cook's divorces made it virtually impossible for them to live in Iowa, the couple moved to New York and Provincetown, Massachusetts.

In Provincetown, Cook wanted to involve himself in a new kind of drama, and the two of them wrote *Suppressed Desires* (1915), which they first produced in their living room. The playhouse eventually relocated to a neglected fish house on a wharf and was a local success. *Suppressed Desires* was a satire that poked fun at the trend of using Freudian theories to explain everyday life. In a letter to the *New York Times* (February 13, 1920) Glaspell wrote that the play "is having fun with the people who went off their heads about psychoanalysis—went 'bugs'—when this subject reached the first circle in New York to know of it." *Trifles*, written entirely by Glaspell, followed in 1916. Its story line developed from a murder in Des Moines that Glaspell was familiar with from her days as a journalist.

The Provincetown Players, which Glaspell and Cook founded, quickly became an influential platform for a number of important American writers, such as Edna St. Vincent Millay and Eugene O'Neill, whose first play, *Bound East for Cardiff*, was produced at the Wharf Theatre in 1916. Eventually the Provincetown Players relocated to New York, where they attracted more important playwrights and produced additional plays by Glaspell and O'Neill.

Glaspell's one-act plays, including *Close the Book* (1917), *A Woman's Honor* (1918), and *Tickless Time* (1919), were collected in 1920. Her first full-length play, *Bernice* (1919), centered on interpreting the character of a dead woman. Its success led to another full-length play, *The Verge* (1921), about a woman who tries to make a new reality around herself and begins with creating new kinds of plants. Some critics saw the protagonist as an admirable new woman;

others saw her as neurotic. *The Inheritors* (1921), also a full-length drama, focuses on the third-generation inheritors of a Midwestern college who clash because one family has liberal views and one has conservative views. Her last play, winner of the Pulitzer Prize, was *Alison's House* (1930), based on the life of Emily Dickinson. The latter part of Glaspell's life was spent writing fiction, especially four novels set in the Midwest that traced the struggles of women to maintain their ideals and values. *The Morning Is Near Us* sold over 100,000 copies in 1940 and was only one of her best-selling novels.

Jig Cook, a writer himself and a partner in many of Glaspell's ventures, spent the last two years of his life living in Delphi, Greece, in the manner of the peasants living on Mount Parnassus near the temple of Apollo. He died in 1924, and when Glaspell returned to the United States, she wrote a memoir of their life together called *The Road to the Temple*. In 1925 she broke with the Provincetown Players, who had moved in directions she did not approve of under the directorship of Eugene O'Neill. O'Neill tried to mollify Glaspell, but she never accepted his use of the theater company she and her husband had cofounded. When she died in 1948, she and O'Neill were essentially unreconciled.

TRIFLES

Trifles (1916) was apparently written as a companion piece for Eugene O'Neill's first produced play, the one-act *Bound East for Cardiff*. The two were performed together to make a complete evening presentation. In one sense *Trifles* is a murder mystery, but in another it is a critique of the gender-rigid attitudes of the officials whose responsibility it is to investigate the death of John Wright. Its main character, Minnie Foster Wright, is never presented but only described as a sweet woman who loved to sing when she was young but who married a man who slowly stifled her joy in living.

The setting of the play is a kitchen where the women, Mrs. Peters and Mrs. Hale, remain throughout the action. They examine the condition of the room and, by extension, the condition of Minnie Foster Wright. The men, examining the crime scene, the upstairs bedroom, spend much of the time offstage. They believe they are examining the important evidence, yet when they return with their findings, they are unable to understand what led to the death of John Wright, who to them seems quite a normal farmer.

The women, however, by examining the messy condition of the kitchen, the state of Minnie's preserves, and the quilt she was working on, begin to understand the motive behind Wright's murder. When they get to the dead body of the songbird Minnie had valued, they understand things in a way that the men cannot. The men observe that women are concerned with trifles, things of no importance. But the truth is that the women understand the fate of Minnie Foster Wright and John Wright in a way that would be almost impossible for the men, given their sense of what is significant and what is a trifle.

In many ways the play is a study of gender differences and the way men's expectations and their sense of reality can distort the truth and deform a woman's life. In 1917 Glaspell wrote a short story, using all the same material, called "A Jury of Her Peers," implying that the only peers of Minnie Foster Wright would be women like Mrs. Hale and Mrs. Peters. In 1917, however, women could not vote and in most states could not serve on juries.

Trifles in Performance

The original production, which may have included Eugene O'Neill among its cast members, was well received, but after Glaspell's death, most of her work fell out of fashion. *The Verge*, however, is still highly regarded in England and is often performed there. *Trifles* was neglected until the early 1960s, when feminist interest helped revive Glaspell's plays. Teacher and writer Sylvan Barnet included the play in his drama anthology, helping to bring it to the attention of contemporary viewers. Now produced most often by school and college groups, the play enjoys considerable popularity.

Susan Glaspell (1876–1948)

TRIFLES

1916

Characters

GEORGE HENDERSON, *county attorney*
HENRY PETERS, *sheriff*
LEWIS HALE, *a neighboring farmer*
MRS. PETERS
MRS. HALE

Scene: *The kitchen in the now abandoned farmhouse of John Wright, a gloomy kitchen, and left without having been put in order—the walls covered with a faded wall paper. Down right is a door leading to the parlor. On the right wall above this door is a built-in kitchen cupboard with shelves in the upper portion and drawers below. In the rear wall at right, up two steps is a door opening onto stairs leading to the second floor. In the rear wall at left is a door to the shed and from there to the outside. Between these two doors is an old-fashioned black iron stove. Running along the left wall from the shed door is an old iron sink and sink shelf, in which is set a hand pump. Downstage of the sink is an uncurtained window. Near the window is an old wooden rocker. Center stage is an unpainted wooden kitchen table with straight chairs on either side. There is a small chair down right. Unwashed pans under the sink, a loaf of bread outside the breadbox, a dish towel on the table—other signs of incompleted work. At the rear the shed door opens and the Sheriff comes in followed by the County Attorney and Hale. The Sheriff and Hale are men in middle life, the County Attorney is a young man; all are much bundled up and go at once to the stove. They are followed by the two women—the Sheriff's wife, Mrs. Peters, first: she is a slight wiry woman, a thin nervous face. Mrs. Hale is larger and would ordinarily be called more comfortable looking, but she is disturbed now and looks fearfully about as she enters. The women have come in slowly, and stand close together near the door.*

COUNTY ATTORNEY (*at stove rubbing his hands*): This feels good. Come up to the fire, ladies.

MRS. PETERS (*after taking a step forward*): I'm not—cold.

SHERIFF (*unbuttoning his overcoat and stepping away from the stove to right of table as if to mark the beginning of official business*): Now, Mr. Hale, before we move things about, you explain to Mr. Henderson just what you saw when you came here yesterday morning.

COUNTY ATTORNEY (*crossing down to left of the table*): By the way, has anything been moved? Are things just as you left them yesterday?

SHERIFF (*looking about*): It's just about the same. When it dropped below zero last night I thought I'd better send Frank out this morning to make a fire for us— (*sits right of center table*) no use getting pneumonia with a big case on, but I told him not to touch anything except the stove—and you know Frank.

COUNTY ATTORNEY: Somebody should have been left here yesterday.

SHERIFF: Oh—yesterday. When I had to send Frank to Morris Center for that man who went crazy—I want you to know I had my hands full yesterday. I knew you could get back from Omaha by today and as long as I went over everything here myself———

COUNTY ATTORNEY: Well, Mr. Hale, tell just what happened when you came here yesterday morning.

HALE (*crossing down to above table*): Harry and I had started to town with a load of potatoes. We came along the road from my place and as I got here I said, "I'm going to see if I can't get John Wright to go in with me on a party telephone." I spoke to Wright about it once before and he put me off, saying folks talked too much anyway, and all he asked was peace and quiet—I guess you know about how much he talked himself; but I thought maybe if I went to the house and talked about it before his wife, though I said to Harry that I didn't know as what his wife wanted made much difference to John———

COUNTY ATTORNEY: Let's talk about that later, Mr. Hale. I do want to talk about that, but tell now just what happened when you got to the house.

HALE: I didn't hear or see anything; I knocked at the door, and still it was all quiet inside. I knew they must be up, it was past eight o'clock. So I knocked again, and I thought I heard someone say, "Come in." I wasn't sure, I'm not sure yet, but I opened the door—this door (*indicating the door by which the two women are still standing*) and there in that rocker—(*pointing to it*) sat Mrs. Wright. (*They all look at the rocker down left.*)

COUNTY ATTORNEY: What—was she doing?

HALE: She was rockin' back and forth. She had her apron in her hand and was kind of—pleating it.

COUNTY ATTORNEY: And how did she—look?

HALE: Well, she looked queer.

COUNTY ATTORNEY: How do you mean—queer?

HALE: Well, as if she didn't know what she was going to do next. And kind of done up.

COUNTY ATTORNEY (*takes out notebook and pencil and sits left of center table*): How did she seem to feel about your coming?

HALE: Why, I don't think she minded—one way or other. She didn't pay much attention. I said, "How do, Mrs. Wright, it's cold, ain't it?" And she said, "Is it?"—and went on kind of pleating at her apron. Well, I was surprised: she didn't ask me to come up to the stove, or to set down, but just sat there, not even looking at me, so I said, "I want to see John." And then she—laughed. I guess you would call it a laugh. I thought of Harry and the team outside, so I said a little sharp: "Can't I see John?" "No," she says, kind o' dull like. "Ain't he home?" says I. "Yes," says she,

"he's home." "Then why can't I see him?" I asked her, out of patience. "'Cause he's dead," says she. "*Dead?*" says I. She just nodded her head, not getting a bit excited, but rockin' back and forth. "Why—where is he?" says I, not knowing what to say. She just pointed upstairs—like that. (*Himself pointing to the room above.*) I started for the stairs, with the idea of going up there. I walked from there to here—then I says, "Why, what did he die of?" "He died of a rope round his neck," says she, and just went on pleatin' at her apron. Well, I went out and called Harry. I thought I might—need help. We went upstairs and there he was lyin'———

COUNTY ATTORNEY: I think I'd rather have you go into that upstairs, where you can point it all out. Just go on now with the rest of the story.

HALE: Well, my first thought was to get that rope off. It looked . . . (*stops: his face twitches*) . . . but Harry, he went up to him, and he said, "No, he's dead all right, and we'd better not touch anything." So we went right back downstairs. She was still sitting that same way. "Has anybody been notified?" I asked. "No," says she, unconcerned. "Who did this, Mrs. Wright?" said Harry. He said it businesslike—and she stopped pleatin' of her apron. "I don't know," she says. "You don't *know*?" says Harry. "No," says she. "Weren't you sleepin' in the bed with him?" says Harry. "Yes," says she, "but I was on the inside." "Somebody slipped a rope round his head and strangled him and you didn't wake up?" says Harry. "I didn't wake up," she said after him. We must 'a' looked as if we didn't see how that could be, for after a minute she said, "I sleep sound." Harry was going to ask her more questions but I said maybe we ought to let her tell her story first to the coroner, or the sheriff, so Harry went fast as he could to Rivers' place, where there's a telephone.

COUNTY ATTORNEY: And what did Mrs. Wright do when she knew that you had gone for the coroner?

HALE: She moved from the rocker to that chair over there (*pointing to a small chair in the down right corner*) and just sat there with her hands held together and looking down. I got a feeling that I ought to make some conversation, so I said I had come in to see if John wanted to put in a telephone, and at that she started to laugh, and then she stopped and looked at me—scared. (*The County Attorney, who has had his notebook out, makes a note.*) I dunno, maybe it wasn't scared. I wouldn't like to say it was. Soon Harry got back, and then Dr. Lloyd came and you, Mr. Peters, and so I guess that's all I know that you don't.

COUNTY ATTORNEY (*rising and looking around*): I guess we'll go upstairs first—and then out to the barn and around there. (*To the Sheriff.*) You're convinced that there was nothing important here—nothing that would point to any motive?

SHERIFF: Nothing here but kitchen things. (*The County Attorney, after again looking around the kitchen,*

An early performance by the Provincetown Players of *Trifles* shows the small space and simple staging of the Wharf Theatre.

opens the door of a cupboard closet in right wall. He brings a small chair from right — gets on it and looks on a shelf. Pulls his hand away, sticky.)

COUNTY ATTORNEY: Here's a nice mess. (*The women draw nearer up to center.*)

MRS. PETERS (*to the other woman*): Oh, her fruit; it did freeze. (*To the Lawyer.*) She worried about that when it turned so cold. She said the fire'd go out and her jars would break.

SHERIFF (*rises*): Well, can you beat the woman! Held for murder and worryin' about her preserves.

COUNTY ATTORNEY (*getting down from chair*): I guess before we're through she may have something more serious than preserves to worry about. (*Crosses down right center.*)

HALE: Well, women are used to worrying over trifles. (*The two women move a little closer together.*)

COUNTY ATTORNEY (*with the gallantry of a young politician*): And yet, for all their worries, what would we do without the ladies? (*The women do not unbend. He goes below the center table to the sink, takes a dipperful of water from the pail, and pouring it into a basin, washes his hands. While he is doing this the Sheriff and Hale cross to cupboard, which they inspect. The County Attorney starts to wipe his hands on the roller towel, turns it for a cleaner place.*) Dirty towels! (*Kicks his foot against the pans under the sink.*) Not much of a housekeeper, would you say, ladies?

MRS. HALE (*stiffly*): There's a great deal of work to be done on a farm.

COUNTY ATTORNEY: To be sure. And yet (*with a little bow to her*) I know there are some Dickson County farmhouses which do not have such roller towels. (*He gives it a pull to expose its full-length again.*)

MRS. HALE: Those towels get dirty awful quick. Men's hands aren't always clean as they might be.

COUNTY ATTORNEY: Ah, loyal to your sex, I see. But you and Mrs. Wright were neighbors. I suppose you were friends, too.

MRS. HALE (*shaking her head*): I've not seen much of her of late years. I've not been in this house — it's more than a year.

COUNTY ATTORNEY (*crossing to women up center*): And why was that? You didn't like her?

MRS. HALE: I liked her all well enough. Farmer's wives have their hands full, Mr. Henderson. And then——

COUNTY ATTORNEY: Yes——?

MRS. HALE (*looking about*): It never seemed a very cheerful place.

COUNTY ATTORNEY: No — it's not cheerful. I shouldn't say she had the homemaking instinct.

MRS. HALE: Well, I don't know as Wright had, either.

COUNTY ATTORNEY: You mean that they didn't get on very well?

MRS. HALE: No, I don't mean anything. But I don't think a place'd be any cheerfuller for John Wright's being in it.

COUNTY ATTORNEY: I'd like to talk more of that a little later. I want to get the lay of things upstairs now. (*He goes past the women to up right where the steps lead to a stair door.*)

SHERIFF: I suppose anything Mrs. Peters does'll be all right. She was to take in some clothes for her, you know, and a few little things. We left in such a hurry yesterday.

COUNTY ATTORNEY: Yes, but I would like to see what you take, Mrs. Peters, and keep an eye out for anything that might be of use to us.

MRS. PETERS: Yes, Mr. Henderson. (*The men leave by up right door to stairs. The women listen to the men's steps on the stairs, then look about the kitchen.*)

MRS. HALE (*crossing left to sink*): I'd hate to have men coming into my kitchen, snooping around and criticizing. (*She arranges the pans under sink which the lawyer had shoved out of place.*)

MRS. PETERS: Of course it's no more than their duty. (*Crosses to cupboard up right.*)

MRS. HALE: Duty's all right, but I guess that deputy sheriff that came out to make the fire might have got a little of this on. (*Gives the roller towel a pull.*) Wish I'd thought of that sooner. Seems mean to talk about her for not having things slicked up when she had to come away in such a hurry. (*Crosses right to Mrs. Peters at cupboard.*)

MRS. PETERS (*who has been looking through cupboard, lifts one end of towel that covers a pan*): She had bread set. (*Stands still.*)

MRS. HALE (*eyes fixed on a loaf of bread beside the breadbox, which is on a low shelf of the cupboard*): She was going to put this in there. (*Picks up loaf, abruptly drops it. In a manner of returning to familiar things.*) It's a shame about her fruit. I wonder if it's all gone. (*Gets up on chair and looks.*) I think there's some here that's all right, Mrs. Peters. Yes — here; (*holding it toward the window*) this is cherries, too. (*Looking again.*) I declare I believe that's the only one. (*Gets down, jar in hand. Goes to the sink and wipes it off on the outside.*) She'll feel awful bad after all her hard work in the hot weather. I remember the afternoon I put up my cherries last summer. (*She puts the jar on the big kitchen table, center of the room. With a sigh, is about to sit down in the rocking chair. Before she is seated realizes what chair it is; with a slow look at it, steps back. The chair which she has touched rocks back and forth. Mrs. Peters moves to center table and they both watch the chair rock for a moment or two.*)

MRS. PETERS (*shaking off the mood which the empty rocking chair has evoked. Now in a businesslike manner she speaks*): Well I must get those things from the front room closet. (*She goes to the door at the right but, after looking into the other room, steps back.*) You coming with me, Mrs. Hale? You could help me carry them. (*They go in the other room; reappear, Mrs. Peters carrying a dress, petticoat, and skirt, Mrs. Hale following with a pair of shoes.*) My, it's cold in there. (*She puts the clothes on the big table and hurries to the stove.*)

MRS. HALE (*right of center table examining the skirt*): Wright was close. I think maybe that's why she kept so much to herself. She didn't even belong to the Ladies' Aid. I suppose she felt she couldn't do her part, and then you don't enjoy things when you feel shabby. I heard she used to wear pretty clothes and

be lively, when she was Minnie Foster, one of the town girls singing in the choir. But that — oh, that was thirty years ago. This all you want to take in?

MRS. PETERS: She said she wanted an apron. Funny thing to want, for there isn't much to get you dirty in jail, goodness knows. But I suppose just to make her feel more natural. (*Crosses to cupboard.*) She said they was in the top drawer in this cupboard. Yes, here. And then her little shawl that always hung behind the door. (*Opens stair door and looks.*) Yes, here it is. (*Quickly shuts door leading upstairs.*)

MRS. HALE (*abruptly moving toward her*): Mrs. Peters?

MRS. PETERS: Yes, Mrs. Hale? (*At up right door.*)

MRS. HALE: Do you think she did it?

MRS. PETERS (*in a frightened voice*): Oh, I don't know.

MRS. HALE: Well, I don't think she did. Asking for an apron and her little shawl. Worrying about her fruit.

MRS. PETERS (*starts to speak, glances up, where footsteps are heard in the room above. In a low voice*): Mr. Peters says it looks bad for her. Mr. Henderson is awful sarcastic in a speech and he'll make fun of her sayin' she didn't wake up.

MRS. HALE: Well, I guess John Wright didn't wake when they was slipping that rope under his neck.

MRS. PETERS (*crossing slowly to table and placing shawl and apron on table with other clothing*): No, it's strange. It must have been done awful crafty and still. They say it was such a — funny way to kill a man, rigging it all up like that.

MRS. HALE (*crossing to left of Mrs. Peters at table*): That's just what Mr. Hale said. There was a gun in the house. He says that's what he can't understand.

MRS. PETERS: Mr. Henderson said coming out that what was needed for the case was a motive: something to show anger, or — sudden feeling.

MRS. HALE (*who is standing by the table*): Well, I don't see any signs of anger around here. (*She puts her hand on the dish towel, which lies on the table, stands looking down at table, one-half of which is clean, the other half messy.*) It's wiped to here. (*Makes a move as if to finish work, then turns and looks at loaf of bread outside the breadbox. Drops towel. In that voice of coming back to familiar things.*) Wonder how they are finding things upstairs. (*Crossing below table to down right.*) I hope she had it a little more red-up° up there. You know, it seems kind of *sneaking*. Locking her up in town and then coming out here and trying to get her own house to turn against her!

MRS. PETERS: But, Mrs. Hale, the law is the law.

MRS. HALE: I s'pose 'tis. (*Unbuttoning her coat.*) Better loosen up your things, Mrs. Peters. You won't feel them when you go out. (*Mrs. Peters takes off her fur tippet, goes to hang it on chair back left of table, stands looking at the work basket on floor near down left window.*)

---

red-up: (slang) Ready for company.

MRS. PETERS: She was piecing a quilt. (*She brings the large sewing basket to the center table and they look at the bright pieces, Mrs. Hale above the table and Mrs. Peters left of it.*)

MRS. HALE: It's a log cabin pattern. Pretty, isn't it? I wonder if she was goin' to quilt it or just knot it? (*Footsteps have been heard coming down the stairs. The Sheriff enters followed by Hale and the County Attorney.*)

SHERIFF: They wonder if she was going to quilt it or just knot it! (*The men laugh, the women look abashed.*)

COUNTY ATTORNEY (*rubbing his hands over the stove*): Frank's fire didn't do much up there, did it? Well, let's go out to the barn and get that cleared up. (*The men go outside by up left door.*)

MRS. HALE (*resentfully*): I don't know as there's anything so strange, our takin' up our time with little things while we're waiting for them to get the evidence. (*She sits in chair right of table smoothing out a block with decision.*) I don't see as it's anything to laugh about.

MRS. PETERS (*apologetically*): Of course they've got awful important things on their minds. (*Pulls up a chair and joins Mrs. Hale at the left of the table.*)

MRS. HALE (*examining another block*): Mrs. Peters, look at this one. Here, this is the one she was working on, and look at the sewing! All the rest of it has been so nice and even. And look at this! It's all over the place! Why, it looks as if she didn't know what she was about! (*After she has said this they look at each other, then start to glance back at the door. After an instant Mrs. Hale has pulled at a knot and ripped the sewing.*)

MRS. PETERS: Oh, what are you doing, Mrs. Hale?

MRS. HALE (*mildly*): Just pulling out a stitch or two that's not sewed very good. (*Threading a needle.*) Bad sewing always made me fidgety.

MRS. PETERS (*with a glance at the door, nervously*): I don't think we ought to touch things.

MRS. HALE: I'll just finish up this end. (*Suddenly stopping and leaning forward.*) Mrs. Peters?

MRS. PETERS: Yes, Mrs. Hale?

MRS. HALE: What do you suppose she was so nervous about?

MRS. PETERS: Oh—I don't know. I don't know as she was nervous. I sometimes sew awful queer when I'm just tired. (*Mrs. Hale starts to say something, looks at Mrs. Peters, then goes on sewing.*) Well, I must get these things wrapped up. They may be through sooner than we think. (*Putting apron and other things together.*) I wonder where I can find a piece of paper, and string. (*Rises.*)

MRS. HALE: In that cupboard, maybe.

MRS. PETERS (*crosses right looking in cupboard*): Why, here's a bird-cage. (*Holds it up.*) Did she have a bird, Mrs. Hale?

MRS. HALE: Why, I don't know whether she did or not—I've not been here for so long. There was a man around last year selling canaries cheap, but I

Mrs. Hale (Sarah Einerson) and Mrs. Peters (Mary-Margaret Pyeatt) discovering the truth about the dead songbird in the 2000 Echo Theater production of Susan Glaspell's *Trifles*, performed in Dallas, Texas, and directed by Ellen Locy. The production was an entry in Dallas's second annual Festival of Independent Theatres (FIT).

don't know as she took one; maybe she did. She used to sing real pretty herself.

MRS. PETERS (*glancing around*): Seems funny to think of a bird here. But she must have had one, or why would she have a cage? I wonder what happened to it?

MRS. HALE: I s'pose maybe the cat got it.

MRS. PETERS: No, she didn't have a cat. She's got that feeling some people have about cats—being afraid of them. My cat got in her room and she was real upset and asked me to take it out.

MRS. HALE: My sister Bessie was like that. Queer, ain't it?

MRS. PETERS (*examining the cage*): Why, look at this door. It's broke. One hinge is pulled apart. (*Takes a step down to Mrs. Hale's right.*)

MRS. HALE (*looking too*): Looks as if someone must have been rough with it.

MRS. PETERS: Why, yes. (*She brings the cage forward and puts it on the table.*)

MRS. HALE (*glancing toward up left door*): I wish if they're going to find any evidence they'd be about it. I don't like this place.

MRS. PETERS: But I'm awful glad you came with me, Mrs. Hale. It would be lonesome for me sitting here alone.

MRS. HALE: It would, wouldn't it? (*Dropping her sewing.*) But I tell you what I do wish, Mrs. Peters. I wish I had come over sometimes when *she* was here. I—(*looking around the room*)—wish I had.

MRS. PETERS: But of course you were awful busy, Mrs. Hale—your house and your children.

MRS. HALE (*rises and crosses left*): I could've come. I stayed away because it weren't cheerful—and that's why I ought to have come. I—(*looking out left window*)—I've never liked this place. Maybe it's because it's down in a hollow and you don't see the road. I dunno what it is, but it's a lonesome place and always was. I wish I had come over to see Minnie Foster sometimes. I can see now—(*Shakes her head.*)

MRS. PETERS (*left of table and above it*): Well, you mustn't reproach yourself, Mrs. Hale. Somehow we just don't see how it is with other folks until—something turns up.

MRS. HALE: Not having children makes less work—but it makes a quiet house, and Wright out to work all day, and no company when he did come in. (*Turning from window.*) Did you know John Wright, Mrs. Peters?

MRS. PETERS: Not to know him; I've seen him in town. They say he was a good man.

MRS. HALE: Yes—good; he didn't drink, and kept his word as well as most, I guess, and paid his debts. But he was a hard man, Mrs. Peters. Just to pass the time of day with him—(*Shivers.*) Like a raw wind that gets to the bone. (*Pauses, her eye falling on the cage.*) I should think she would 'a' wanted a bird. But what do you suppose went with it?

MRS. PETERS: I don't know, unless it got sick and died. (*She reaches over and swings the broken door, swings it again, both women watch it.*)

MRS. HALE: You weren't raised round here, were you? (*Mrs. Peters shakes her head.*) You didn't know—her?

MRS. PETERS: Not till they brought her yesterday.

MRS. HALE: She—come to think of it, she was kind of like a bird herself—real sweet and pretty, but kind of timid and—fluttery. How—she—did—change. (*Silence: then as if struck by a happy thought and relieved to get back to everyday things. Crosses right*

above Mrs. Peters to cupboard, replaces small chair used to stand on to its original place down right.*) Tell you what, Mrs. Peters, why don't you take the quilt in with you? It might take up her mind.

MRS. PETERS: Why, I think that's a real nice idea, Mrs. Hale. There couldn't possibly be any objection to it could there? Now, just what would I take? I wonder if her patches are in here—and her things. (*They look in the sewing basket.*)

MRS. HALE (*crosses to right of table*): Here's some red. I expect this has got sewing things in it. (*Brings out a fancy box.*) What a pretty box. Looks like something somebody would give you. Maybe her scissors are in here. (*Opens box. Suddenly puts her hand to her nose.*) Why——(*Mrs. Peters bends nearer, then turns her face away.*) There's something wrapped up in this piece of silk.

MRS. PETERS: Why, this isn't her scissors.

MRS. HALE (*lifting the silk*): Oh, Mrs. Peters—it's———(*Mrs. Peters bends closer.*)

MRS. PETERS: It's the bird.

MRS. HALE: But, Mrs. Peters—look at it! Its neck! Look at its neck! It's all—other side *to*.

MRS. PETERS: Somebody—wrung—its—neck. (*Their eyes meet. A look of growing comprehension, of horror. Steps are heard outside. Mrs. Hale slips box under quilt pieces, and sinks into her chair. Enter Sheriff and County Attorney. Mrs. Peters steps down left and stands looking out of window.*)

COUNTY ATTORNEY (*as one turning from serious things to little pleasantries*): Well, ladies, have you decided whether she was going to quilt it or knot it? (*Crosses to center above table.*)

MRS. PETERS: We think she was going to—knot it. (*Sheriff crosses to right of stove, lifts stove lid, and glances at fire, then stands warming hands at stove.*)

COUNTY ATTORNEY: Well, that's interesting, I'm sure. (*Seeing the bird-cage.*) Has the bird flown?

MRS. HALE (*putting more quilt pieces over the box*): We think the—cat got it.

COUNTY ATTORNEY (*preoccupied*): Is there a cat? (*Mrs. Hale glances in a quick covert way at Mrs. Peters.*)

MRS. PETERS (*turning from window takes a step in*): Well, not *now*. They're superstitious, you know. They leave.

COUNTY ATTORNEY (*to Sheriff Peters, continuing an interrupted conversation*): No sign at all of anyone having come from the outside. Their own rope. Now let's go up again and go over it piece by piece. (*They start upstairs.*) It would have to have been someone who knew just the———(*Mrs. Peters sits down left of table. The two women sit there not looking at one another, but as if peering into something and at the same time holding back. When they talk now it is in the manner of feeling their way over strange ground, as if afraid of what they are saying, but as if they cannot help saying it.*)

MRS. HALE (*hesistatively and in hushed voice*): She liked the bird. She was going to bury it in that pretty box.

MRS. PETERS (*in a whisper*): When I was a girl—my kitten—there was a boy took a hatchet, and before my eyes—and before I could get there———(*Covers her face an instant.*) If they hadn't held me back I would have—(*catches herself, looks upstairs where steps are heard, falters weakly*)—hurt him.

MRS. HALE (*with a slow look around her*): I wonder how it would seem never to have had any children around. (*Pause.*) No, Wright wouldn't like the bird—a thing that sang. She used to sing. He killed that, too.

MRS. PETERS (*moving uneasily*): We don't know who killed the bird.

MRS. HALE: I knew John Wright.

MRS. PETERS: It was an awful thing was done in this house that night, Mrs. Hale. Killing a man while he slept, slipping a rope around his neck that choked the life out of him.

MRS. HALE: His neck. Choked the life out of him. (*Her hand goes out and rests on the bird-cage.*)

MRS. PETERS (*with rising voice*): We don't know who killed him. We don't *know*.

MRS. HALE (*her own feelings not interrupted*): If there'd been years and years of nothing, then a bird to sing to you, it would be awful—still, after the bird was still.

MRS. PETERS (*something within her speaking*): I know what stillness is. When we homesteaded in Dakota, and my first baby died—after he was two years old, and me with no other then———

MRS. HALE (*moving*): How soon do you suppose they'll be through looking for the evidence?

MRS. PETERS: I know what stillness is. (*Pulling herself back.*) The law has got to punish crimes, Mrs. Hale.

MRS. HALE (*not as if answering that*): I wish you'd seen Minnie Foster when she wore a white dress with blue ribbons and stood up there in the choir and sang. (*A look around the room.*) Oh, I *wish* I'd come over here once in a while! That was a crime! That was a crime! Who's going to punish that?

MRS. PETERS (*looking upstairs*): We mustn't—take on.

MRS. HALE: I might have known she needed help! I know how things can be—for women. I tell you, it's queer, Mrs. Peters. We live close together and we live far apart. We all go through the same things—it's all just a different kind of the same thing. (*Brushes her eyes, noticing the jar of fruit, reaches out for it.*) If I was you I wouldn't tell her her fruit was gone. Tell her it *ain't*. Tell her it's all right. Take this in to prove it to her. She—she may never know whether it was broke or not.

MRS. PETERS (*takes the jar, looks about for something to wrap it in; takes petticoat from the clothes brought from the other room, very nervously begins winding this around the jar. In a false voice*): My, it's a good thing the men couldn't hear us. Wouldn't they just laugh! Getting all stirred up over a little thing like a—dead canary. As if that could have anything to do with—with—wouldn't they *laugh!* (*The men are heard coming downstairs.*)

MRS. HALE (*under her breath*): Maybe they would—maybe they wouldn't.

COUNTY ATTORNEY: No, Peters, it's all perfectly clear except a reason for doing it. But you know juries when it comes to women. If there was some definite thing. (*Crosses slowly to above table. Sheriff crosses down right. Mrs. Hale and Mrs. Peters remain seated at either side of table.*) Something to show—something to make a story about—a thing that would connect up with this strange way of doing it———(*The women's eyes meet for an instant. Enter Hale from outer door.*)

HALE (*remaining by door*): Well, I've got the team around. Pretty cold out there.

COUNTY ATTORNEY: I'm going to stay awhile by myself. (*To the Sheriff.*) You can send Frank out for me, can't you? I want to go over everything. I'm not satisfied that we can't do better.

SHERIFF: Do you want to see what Mrs. Peters is going to take in? (*The Lawyer picks up the apron, laughs.*)

COUNTY ATTORNEY: Oh, I guess they're not very dangerous things the ladies have picked out. (*Moves a few things about, disturbing the quilt pieces which cover the box. Steps back.*) No, Mrs. Peters doesn't need supervising. For that matter a sheriff's wife is married to the law. Ever think of it that way, Mrs. Peters?

MRS. PETERS: Not—just that way.

SHERIFF (*chuckling*): Married to the law. (*Moves to down right door to the other room.*) I just want you to come in here a minute, George. We ought to take a look at these windows.

COUNTY ATTORNEY (*scoffingly*): Oh, windows!

SHERIFF: We'll be right out, Mr. Hale. (*Hale goes outside. The Sheriff follows the County Attorney into the room. Then Mrs. Hale rises, hands tight together, looking intensely at Mrs. Peters, whose eyes make a slow turn, finally meeting Mrs. Hale's. A moment Mrs. Hale holds her, then her own eyes point the way to where the box is concealed. Suddenly Mrs. Peters throws back quilt pieces and tries to put the box in the bag she is carrying. It is too big. She opens box, starts to take bird out, cannot touch it, goes to pieces, stands there helpless. Sound of a knob turning in the other room. Mrs. Hale snatches the box and puts it in the pocket of her big coat. Enter County Attorney and Sheriff, who remains down right.*)

COUNTY ATTORNEY (*crosses to up left door facetiously*): Well, Henry, at least we found out that she was not going to quilt it. She was going to—what is it you call it, ladies?

MRS. HALE (*standing center below table facing front, her hand against her pocket*): We call it—knot it, Mr. Henderson.

COMMENTARY

Christine Dymkowski (*b. 1950*)
ON THE EDGE: THE PLAYS OF SUSAN GLASPELL   1988

Christine Dymkowski sees Trifles *as a play that occupies the edge—the marginalized space reserved for women. The male figures in the play assume that their interests are central to the murder investigation, whereas Glaspell demonstrates that the most significant issues in the investigation are on the edge of men's attention, where they can never see them.*

The paradoxically central nature of the edge informs Glaspell's theatrical methods and themes. Her first play, *Trifles* (1916), illustrates its use in several ways, the irony of the title already having been noted. The plot revolves around the visit to a farmhouse by County Attorney Henderson and Sheriff Peters to investigate the murder of John Wright; they are accompanied by the farmer who discovered the murder and, almost incidentally, by the farmer's and sheriff's wives. The men's assumption is that Minnie Wright, already in custody for the crime, has killed her husband, and they are there to search the house for clues to a motive. The audience undoubtedly sees them as protagonists at the start of the play.

The stage directions immediately call attention to the women's marginality: the men, "much bundled up" against the freezing cold, "go at once to the stove" in the Wrights' kitchen, while the women who follow them in do so "slowly, and stand close together near the door." The separateness of the female and male worlds is thus immediately established visually and then reinforced by the dialogue:

> MRS. PETERS (*to the other woman*): Oh, her fruit; it did freeze. (*To the Lawyer.*) She worried about that when it turned so cold. . . .
> SHERIFF: Well, can you beat the women [*sic*]! Held for murder and worryin' about her preserves.
> COUNTY ATTORNEY: I guess before we're through she may have something more serious than preserves to worry about.
> HALE: Well, women are used to worrying over trifles.
> (*The two women move a little closer together.*)

Not surprisingly, the women are relegated to the kitchen, while the men's attention turns to the rest of the house, particularly the bedroom where the crime was committed: "You're convinced that there was nothing important here—nothing that would point to any motive," Henderson asks Peters, and is assured that there is "Nothing here but kitchen things." However, while the men view the kitchen as marginal to their purpose, the drama stays centered there where the women are: contrary to expectation, it becomes the central focus of the play.

Ironically, it is the kitchen that holds the clues to the desperation and loneliness of Minnie's life and yields the women the answers for which the men search in vain;

moreover, the understanding that they do reach goes beyond the mere solving of the crime to a redefinition of what the crime was. Mrs. Hale blames herself for a failure of imagination: "Oh, I *wish* I'd come over here once in a while! That was a crime! That was a crime! Who's going to punish that? . . . I might have known she needed help! I know how things can be—for women. I tell you, it's queer, Mrs. Peters. We live close together and we live far apart. We all go through the same things—it's all just a different kind of the same thing." The empathy both women feel for Minnie leads them to suppress the evidence they have found, patiently enduring the men's condescension instead of competing with them on their own ground. Conventional moral values are overturned, just as the expected form of the murder mystery is ignored: the play differentiates between justice and law and shows that the traditional "solution" is no such thing.

Just as Glaspell sets the play in the seemingly marginal kitchen, she makes the absent Minnie Wright its focus, a tactic she was to use again in *Bernice* and *Alison's House;* although noted by critics, this use of an absent central character has not received much comment. It is yet another way in which Glaspell makes central the apparently marginal—indeed, in stage terms, the nonexistent.

Luigi Pirandello

Luigi Pirandello (1867–1936) was an Italian short-story writer and novelist, a secondary school teacher, and finally a playwright. His life was complicated by business failures that wiped out his personal income and threw his wife into a psychological depression that Pirandello quite bluntly described as madness. Out of his acquaintance with madness—he remained with his wife for fourteen years after she lost touch with reality—Pirandello claimed to have developed much of his attitude toward the shifting surfaces of appearances.

Pirandello's short stories and novels show the consistent pattern of his plays: a deep examination of what we know to be real and a questioning of our confidence in our beliefs. His novel *Shoot* (1915) questions the surfaces of cinema reality, which contemporary Italy had embraced with great enthusiasm. His relentless examination of the paradoxes of experience has given him a reputation for pessimism. He himself said, "I think of life as a very sad piece of buffoonery," and he insisted that people bear within them a deep need to deceive themselves "by creating a reality . . . which . . . is discovered to be vain and illusory."

For most of his early career Pirandello was not a popular playwright in Italy, and therefore much of his dramatic work was first performed abroad. In 1923 he was known as an important novelist and came to the attention of Benito Mussolini (1883–1945), the Fascist dictator of Italy. Pirandello joined the Italian Fascist party as a means of establishing the National Art Theatre in Rome, which enjoyed considerable state support. When asked why he was a Fascist, he said, "I am a Fascist because I am an Italian." After Pirandello won the Nobel Prize for literature in 1934, one account has him breaking with Fascism entirely over the Italian invasion of Ethiopia, and another account has him giving over his Nobel medal to be melted down for the Ethiopian campaign. Like some of his dramas, his behavior seems to reflect profound uncertainties that persist to this day.

Pirandello's influence in modern theater resulted from his experimentation with the concept of realism that dominated drama from the time of Strindberg and Ibsen. The concept of the imaginary "fourth wall" of the stage through which the audience observed the action of characters in their living rooms had become the norm in theater. Pirandello, however, questioned all thought of norms by subjecting the very idea of reality to philosophical scrutiny. His questioning helped playwrights around the world expand their approaches to theater in the early part of the twentieth century. Pirandello was one of the first, and one of the best, experimentalists.

SIX CHARACTERS IN SEARCH OF AN AUTHOR

Pirandello's play is part of a trilogy: *Six Characters in Search of an Author* (1921), *Each in His Own Way* (1924), and *Tonight We Improvise* (1930). These plays all examine the impossibility of knowing reality. There is no objective truth to know, Pirandello tells us, and what we think of as reality is totally subjective, something that each of us maintains independently of other people and that none of us can communicate. We are, in other words, apart—sealed into our own limited world.

These ideas were hardly novel. Playwrights had dealt with them before, even during the Elizabethan age, at a time when—because of the Protestant Reformation—the absolute systems of reality promoted by the Roman Catholic Church had crumbled. Pirandello's plays were also produced during a period—the 1920s—when his culture was uncertain, frightened, and still reeling in shock from the destruction of World War I. In this depressed time, Pirandello's audience saw in his work a reflection of their own dispirited, fearful selves.

In a sense, *Six Characters in Search of an Author* is about the relationship between art and life, and especially about the relationship between drama and life. The premise of the play is absurd. In the middle of a rehearsal of a Pirandello play, several characters appear and request that an author be present to cobble them into a play. The stage manager assumes that they are presenting themselves as actors to be in a play, but they explain that they are not actors. They are real characters. This implies a paradox: that characters are independent of the actors who play them (we are used to the characters being only on paper). When they demand actors to represent them, we know that one limit of impossibility has been reached.

The characters who appear are, in a sense, types: a father, a mother, a stepdaughter, a son, two silent figures—the boy and the child—and, finally, a milliner, Madame Pace. They share the stage with the actors of the company, who are rehearsing the Pirandello play *Mixing It Up*. The six characters have been abandoned by their creator, the author who has absconded, leaving them in search of a substitute. The stepdaughter, late in the play, surmises that their author abandoned them "in a fit of depression, of disgust for the ordinary theater as the public knows it and likes it."

Pirandello uses his characters and their situation to comment on the life of the theater in the 1920s, and he also uses them to begin a series of speculations on the relationship of a public to the actors they see in plays, the characters the actors play, and the authors who create them. To an extent, the relationship between an author and his or her characters always implies a metaphor for the relationship between a creator and all creation. It is tempting to think of Samuel Beckett years later in his *Waiting for Godot* imagining an "author" having abandoned his creations because they failed to satisfy him. The six characters—or creations—who invade the stage in Pirandello's play have a firm sense of themselves and their actions. They bring with them a story—as all characters in plays do—and they invite the manager to participate in their stories, just as characters invite audiences to become one with their narratives.

One of the more amusing scenes depicts the characters' reactions to seeing actors play their parts. Since they are "real" characters, they have the utmost authority in knowing how their parts should be played, and they end up laughing at the inept efforts of the actors in act II. When the manager disputes with them, wondering why they protest so vigorously, they explain that they want to make sure the truth is told. The truth: the concept seems so simple on the surface, but in the situation that Pirandello has conceived, it is loaded with complexities that the stage manager cannot fathom.

By the time the question of truth has been raised, the manager has begun to get a sense of the poignancy of the story that these characters have to tell. He has also begun to see that he must let them continue to tell their story—except that they are not telling it, they are living it. When the climax of their story is reached in the last moments of the play, the line between what is acted and what is lived onstage has become almost completely blurred. When the play ends, it is difficult to know what has truly occurred and what has truly been acted out.

Six Characters in Search of an Author has endured because it still rings true in its examination of the relationship between art and life, illusion and reality. The very word *illusion* is rejected by the characters—as characters, they are part of the illusion of reality. They reject the thought that they are literature, asserting, "This is Life, this is passion!"

Six Characters in Search of an Author in Performance

The first production of *Six Characters in Search of an Author* in Rome in May 1921 resulted in a riot that threatened the author and his daughter. The calmer London production in March 1922 in the Kingsway Theatre garnered positive reviews, and the audiences, although at times puzzled, were responsive to what the *Christian Science Monitor* called "one of the freshest and most original productions seen for a long time." The first production in New York was directed by Brock Pemberton at the Princess Theater in October 1922 with the distinguished American actress Florence Eldridge as the stepdaughter. One newspaper critic said, "Pirandello turns a powerful microscope on the dramatist's mental workshop—the modus operandi of play production—and after having destroyed our illusion, like a prestidigitator who shows us how a trick is done, expects us to believe in him."

Pirandello directed the play in Italian in London in 1925, and despite the audience's general inability to understand the language, the New Oxford Theatre was filled for every night of its run. He brought the company to the United States after the British censor determined that the play was "unsuitable for English audiences" and closed the play in London. It was not officially licensed for performance in England again until 1928.

Revivals of the play have been numerous. Three productions in New York in the 1930s preceded revivals in 1948 and 1955. London saw productions in February 1932 and November 1950. By the 1930s audience confusion had simmered down, and in 1932 one London critic declared, "Repetition cannot dull the brilliance of the play's attack on theatrical shams." Sir Ralph Richardson performed in London's West End in 1963. In 1955, Tyrone Guthrie's Phoenix Theater used a translation and adaptation by Guthrie and Michael Wager. The production was not successful, although critics liked the translation. Robert Brustein received extraordinary praise for his American Repertory Theatre (ART) production in 1985. Instead of having the six characters interrupt a Pirandello play, they interrupt the rehearsal of a Molière play, *Sganarelle*, which has roots in Italian commedia dell'arte, and which had been a highly successful ART production. This self-reference—in Pirandellian fashion—helped to blur the line between the realities on and off the stage. Boston critic Kevin Kelly said of the performance, "Brustein immediately links the paradox in Pirandello's theme about reality in illusion / illusion in reality to . . . the pragmatic fantasy of theater itself." The play was revived by Brustein and ART once more in 1996 to great acclaim.

Luigi Pirandello *(1867–1936)*

SIX CHARACTERS IN SEARCH OF AN AUTHOR   *1921*
A COMEDY IN THE MAKING

TRANSLATED BY EDWARD STORER

Characters of the Comedy in the Making

THE FATHER
THE MOTHER
THE STEPDAUGHTER
THE SON
THE BOY } *do not speak*
THE CHILD
MADAME PACE

Actors of the Company

THE MANAGER
LEADING LADY
LEADING MAN
SECOND LADY LEAD
L'INGÉNUE
JUVENILE LEAD
OTHER ACTORS AND ACTRESSES
PROPERTY MAN
PROMPTER
MACHINIST
MANAGER'S SECRETARY
DOOR-KEEPER
SCENE SHIFTERS

Scene: *Daytime. The stage of a theater.*

(N.B.: *The Comedy is without acts or scenes. The performance is interrupted once, without the curtain being lowered, when the Manager and the chief characters withdraw to arrange a scenario. A second interruption of the action takes place when, by mistake, the stage hands let the curtain down.*)

ACT I

(*The spectators will find the curtain raised and the stage as it usually is during the daytime. It will be half dark, and empty, so that from the beginning the public may have the impression of an impromptu performance.*)

(*Prompter's box and a small table and chair for the Manager*)

(*Two other small tables and several chairs scattered about as during rehearsals.*)

(*The Actors and Actresses of the company enter from the back of the stage: first one, then another, then two together; nine or ten in all. They are about to rehearse a Pirandello play: Mixing It Up. Some of the company move off toward their dressing rooms. The Prompter, who has the "book" under his arm, is waiting for the Manager in order to begin the rehearsal.*)

(The Actors and Actresses, some standing, some sitting, chat and smoke. One perhaps reads a paper; another cons his part.)

(Finally, the Manager enters and goes to the table prepared for him. His Secretary brings him his mail, through which he glances. The Prompter takes his seat, turns on a light, and opens the "book.")

THE MANAGER *(throwing a letter down on the table)*: I can't see. *(To Property Man.)* Let's have a little light, please!

PROPERTY MAN: Yes, sir, yes, at once. *(A light comes down on to the stage.)*

THE MANAGER *(clapping his hands)*: Come along! Come along! Second act of "Mixing It Up." *(Sits down.)*

(The Actors and Actresses go from the front of the stage to the wings, all except the three who are to begin the rehearsal.)

THE PROMPTER *(reading the "book")*: "Leo Gala's house. A curious room serving as dining-room and study."

THE MANAGER *(to Property Man)*: Fix up the old red room.

PROPERTY MAN *(noting it down)*: Red set. All right!

THE PROMPTER *(continuing to read from the "book")*: "Table already laid and writing desk with books and papers. Bookshelves. Exit rear to Leo's bedroom. Exit left to kitchen. Principal exit to right."

THE MANAGER *(energetically)*: Well, you understand: The principal exit over there; here, the kitchen. *(Turning to actor who is to play the part of Socrates.)* You make your entrances and exits here. *(To Property Man.)* The baize doors at the rear, and curtains.

PROPERTY MAN *(noting it down)*: Right!

PROMPTER *(reading as before)*: "When the curtain rises, Leo Gala, dressed in cook's cap and apron, is busy beating an egg in a cup. Philip, also dressed as a cook, is beating another egg. Guidi Venanzi is seated and listening."

LEADING MAN *(to Manager)*: Excuse me, but must I absolutely wear a cook's cap?

THE MANAGER *(annoyed)*: I imagine so. It says so there anyway. *(Pointing to the "book.")*

LEADING MAN: But it's ridiculous!

THE MANAGER *(jumping up in a rage)*: Ridiculous? Ridiculous? Is it my fault if France won't send us any more good comedies, and we are reduced to putting on Pirandello's works, where nobody understands anything, and where the author plays the fool with us all? *(The Actors grin. The Manager goes to Leading Man and shouts.)* Yes sir, you put on the cook's cap and beat eggs. Do you suppose that with all this egg-beating business you are on an ordinary stage? Get that out of your head. You represent the shell of the eggs you are beating! *(Laughter and comments among the Actors.)* Silence! and listen to my explanations, please! *(To Leading Man.)* "The empty form of reason without the fullness of instinct, which is blind."— You stand for reason, your wife is instinct.

It's a mixing up of the parts, according to which you who act your own part become the puppet of yourself. Do you understand?

LEADING MAN: I'm hanged if I do.

THE MANAGER: Neither do I. But let's get on with it. It's sure to be a glorious failure anyway. *(Confidentially.)* But I say, please face three-quarters. Otherwise, what with the abstruseness of the dialogue, and the public that won't be able to hear you, the whole thing will go to hell. Come on! come on!

PROMPTER: Pardon sir, may I get into my box? There's a bit of a draft.

THE MANAGER: Yes, yes, of course!

(At this point, the Door-Keeper has entered from the stage door and advances toward the Manager's table, taking off his braided cap. During this maneuver, the Six Characters enter, and stop by the door at back of stage, so that when the Door-Keeper is about to announce their coming to the Manager, they are already on the stage. A tenuous light surrounds them, almost as if irradiated by them—the faint breath of their fantastic reality.)

(This light will disappear when they come forward toward the actors. They preserve, however, something of the dream lightness in which they seem almost suspended; but this does not detract from the essential reality of their forms and expressions.)

(He who is known as the Father is a man of about 50: hair, reddish in color, thin at the temples; he is not bald, however, thick mustaches, falling over his still fresh mouth, which often opens in an empty and uncertain smile. He is fattish, pale; with an especially wide forehead. He has blue, oval-shaped eyes, very clear and piercing. Wears light trousers and a dark jacket. He is alternatively mellifluous and violent in his manner.)

(The Mother seems crushed and terrified as if by an intolerable weight of shame and abasement. She is dressed in modest black and wears a thick widow's veil of crepe. When she lifts this, she reveals a waxlike face. She always keeps her eyes downcast.)

(The Stepdaughter is dashing, almost impudent, beautiful. She wears mourning too, but with great elegance. She shows contempt for the timid half-frightened manner of the wretched Boy (14 years old, and also dressed in black); on the other hand, she displays a lively tenderness for her little sister, the Child (about four), who is dressed in white, with a black silk sash at the waist.)

(The Son (22) is tall, severe in his attitude of contempt for the Father, supercilious and indifferent to the Mother. He looks as if he had come on the stage against his will.)

DOOR-KEEPER *(cap in hand)*: Excuse me, sir . . .

THE MANAGER *(rudely)*: Eh? What is it?

DOOR-KEEPER *(timidly)*: These people are asking for you, sir.

THE MANAGER *(furious)*: I am rehearsing, and you know perfectly well no one's allowed to come in during rehearsals! *(Turning to the Characters.)* Who are you, please? What do you want?

THE FATHER *(coming forward a little, followed by the*

others who seem embarrassed): As a matter of fact . . . we have come here in search of an author . . .

THE MANAGER (*half angry, half amazed*): An author? What author?

THE FATHER: Any author, sir.

THE MANAGER: But there's no author here. We are not rehearsing a new piece.

THE STEPDAUGHTER (*vivaciously*): So much the better, so much the better! We can be your new piece.

AN ACTOR (*coming forward from the others*): Oh, do you hear that?

THE FATHER (*to Stepdaughter*): Yes, but if the author isn't here . . . (*To Manager.*) unless you would be willing . . .

THE MANAGER: You are trying to be funny.

THE FATHER: No, for Heaven's sake, what are you saying? We bring you a drama, sir.

THE STEPDAUGHTER: We may be your fortune.

THE MANAGER: Will you oblige me by going away? We haven't time to waste with mad people.

THE FATHER (*mellifluously*): Oh sir, you know well that life is full of infinite absurdities, which, strangely enough, do not even need to appear plausible, since they are true.

THE MANAGER: What the devil is he talking about?

THE FATHER: I say that to reverse the ordinary process may well be considered a madness: that is, to create credible situations, in order that they may appear true. But permit me to observe that if this be madness, it is the sole *raison d'être*° of your profession, gentlemen. (*The Actors look hurt and perplexed.*)

THE MANAGER (*getting up and looking at him*): So our profession seems to you one worthy of madmen then?

THE FATHER: Well, to make seem true that which isn't true . . . without any need . . . for a joke as it were . . . Isn't that your mission, gentlemen: to give life to fantastic characters on the stage?

THE MANAGER (*interpreting the rising anger of the Company*): But I would beg you to believe, my dear sir, that the profession of the comedian is a noble one. If today, as things go, the playwrights give us stupid comedies to play and puppets to represent instead of men, remember we are proud to have given life to immortal works here on these very boards! (*The Actors, satisfied, applaud their Manager.*)

THE FATHER (*interrupting furiously*): Exactly, perfectly, to living beings more alive than those who breathe and wear clothes: beings less real perhaps, but truer! I agree with you entirely. (*The Actors look at one another in amazement.*)

THE MANAGER: But what do you mean? Before, you said . . .

THE FATHER: No, excuse me, I meant it for you, sir, who were crying out that you had no time to lose with madmen, while no one better than yourself knows that nature uses the instrument of human fantasy in order to pursue her high creative purpose.

raison d'être: French for "reason to exist."

THE MANAGER: Very well,—but where does all this take us?

THE FATHER: Nowhere! It is merely to show you that one is born to life in many forms, in many shapes, as tree, or as stone, as water, as butterfly, or as woman. So one may also be born a character in a play.

THE MANAGER (*with feigned comic dismay*): So you and these other friends of yours have been born characters?

THE FATHER: Exactly, and alive as you see! (*Manager and Actors burst out laughing.*)

THE FATHER (*hurt*): I am sorry you laugh, because we carry in us a drama, as you can guess from this woman here veiled in black.

THE MANAGER (*losing patience at last and almost indignant*): Oh, chuck it! Get away please! Clear out of here! (*To Property Man.*) For Heaven's sake, turn them out!

THE FATHER (*resisting*): No, no, look here, we . . .

THE MANAGER (*roaring*): We come here to work, you know.

LEADING ACTOR: One cannot let oneself be made such a fool of.

THE FATHER (*determined, coming forward*): I marvel at your incredulity, gentlemen. Are you not accustomed to see the characters created by an author spring to life in yourselves and face each other? Just because there is no "book" (*pointing to the Prompter's box*) which contains us, you refuse to believe . . .

THE STEPDAUGHTER (*advances toward Manager, smiling and coquettish*): Believe me, we are really six most interesting characters, sir; sidetracked however.

THE FATHER: Yes, that is the word! (*To Manager all at once.*) In the sense, that is, that the author who created us alive no longer wished, or was no longer able, materially to put us into a work of art. And this was a real crime, sir, because he who has had the luck to be born a character can laugh even at death. He cannot die. The man, the writer, the instrument of the creation will die, but his creation does not die. And to live for ever, it does not need to have extraordinary gifts or to be able to work wonders. Who was Sancho Panza? Who was Don Abbondio?° Yet they live eternally because— live germs as they were—they had the fortune to find a fecundating matrix, a fantasy which could raise and nourish them: make them live for ever!

THE MANAGER: That is quite all right. But what do you want here, all of you?

THE FATHER: We want to live.

THE MANAGER (*ironically*): For Eternity?

THE FATHER: No, sir, only for a moment . . . in you.

AN ACTOR: Just listen to him!

LEADING LADY: They want to live, in us . . . !

JUVENILE LEAD (*pointing to the Stepdaughter*): I've no objection, as far as that one is concerned!

Sancho Panza . . . Don Abbondio: Memorable characters in novels: the squire in Cervantes's *Don Quixote* and the priest in Manzoni's *I Promessi Sposi* (*The Betrothed*), respectively.

THE FATHER: Look here! look here! The comedy has to be made. (*To the Manager.*) But if you and your actors are willing, we can soon concert it among ourselves.

THE MANAGER (*annoyed*): But what do you want to concert? We don't go in for concerts here. Here we play dramas and comedies!

THE FATHER: Exactly! That is just why we have come to you.

THE MANAGER: And where is the "book"?

THE FATHER: It is in us! (*The Actors laugh.*) The drama is in us, and we are the drama. We are impatient to play it. Our inner passion drives us on to this.

THE STEPDAUGHTER (*disdainful, alluring, treacherous, full of impudence*): My passion, sir! Ah, if you only knew! My passion for him! (*Points to the Father and makes a pretense of embracing him. Then she breaks out into a loud laugh.*)

THE FATHER (*angrily*): Behave yourself! And please don't laugh in that fashion.

THE STEPDAUGHTER: With your permission, gentlemen, I, who am a two months orphan, will show you how I can dance and sing. (*Sings and then dances Prenez garde à Tchou-Tchin-Tchou.*)

Les chinois sont un peuple malin,
De Shangaî à Pékin,
Ils ont mis des écriteaux partout:
Prenez garde à Tchou-Tchin-Tchou.°

ACTORS AND ACTRESSES: Bravo! Well done! Tip-top!

THE MANAGER: Silence! This isn't a café concert, you know! (*Turning to the Father in consternation.*) Is she mad?

THE FATHER: Mad? No, she's worse than mad.

THE STEPDAUGHTER (*to Manager*): Worse? Worse? Listen! Stage this drama for us at once! Then you will see that at a certain moment I . . . when this little darling here. . . . (*Takes the Child by the hand and leads her to the Manager.*) Isn't she a dear? (*Takes her up and kisses her.*) Darling! Darling! (*Puts her down again and adds feelingly.*) Well, when God suddenly takes this dear little child away from that poor mother there; and this imbecile here (*seizing hold of the Boy roughly and pushing him forward*) does the stupidest things, like the fool he is, you will see me run away. Yes, gentlemen, I shall be off. But the moment hasn't arrived yet. After what has taken place between him and me (*indicates the Father with a horrible wink*) I can't remain any longer in this society, to have to witness the anguish of this mother here for that fool. . . . (*Indicates the Son.*) Look at him! Look at him! See how indifferent, how frigid he is, because he is the legitimate son. He despises me, despises him (*pointing to the Boy*), despises this baby

Prenez . . . Tchou: This French popular song is an adaptation of "Chu-Chin-Chow," an old Broadway show tune. "The Chinese are a sly people; / From Shanghai to Peking, / They've stuck up warning signs: / Beware of Tchou-Tchin-Tchou." (The words are funnier in French because *chou* means "cabbage.")

here; because . . . we are bastards. (*Goes to the Mother and embraces her.*) And he doesn't want to recognize her as his mother—she who is the common mother of us all. He looks down upon her as if she were only the mother of us three bastards. Wretch! (*She says all this very rapidly, excitedly. At the word "bastards" she raises her voice, and almost spits out the final "Wretch!"*)

THE MOTHER (*to the Manager, in anguish*): In the name of these two little children, I beg you. . . . (*She grows faint and is about to fall.*) Oh God!

THE FATHER (*coming forward to support her as do some of the Actors*): Quick, a chair, a chair for this poor widow!

THE ACTORS: Is it true? Has she really fainted?

THE MANAGER: Quick, a chair! Here!

(*One of the Actors brings a chair, the others proffer assistance. The Mother tries to prevent the Father from lifting the veil which covers her face.*)

THE FATHER: Look at her! Look at her!

THE MOTHER: No, no; stop it please!

THE FATHER (*raising her veil*): Let them see you!

THE MOTHER (*rising and covering her face with her hands, in desperation*): I beg you, sir, to prevent this man from carrying out his plan which is loathsome to me.

THE MANAGER (*dumbfounded*): I don't understand at all. What is the situation? (*To the Father.*) Is this lady your wife?

THE FATHER: Yes, gentlemen: my wife!

THE MANAGER: But how can she be a widow if you are alive? (*The Actors find relief for their astonishment in a loud laugh.*)

THE FATHER: Don't laugh! Don't laugh like that, for Heaven's sake. Her drama lies just here in this: she has had a lover, a man who ought to be here.

THE MOTHER (*with a cry*): No! No!

THE STEPDAUGHTER: Fortunately for her, he is dead. Two months ago as I said. We are in mourning, as you see.

THE FATHER: He isn't here, you see, not because he is dead. He isn't here—look at her a moment and you will understand—because her drama isn't a drama of the love of two men for whom she was incapable of feeling anything except possibly a little gratitude—gratitude not for me but for the other. She isn't a woman, she is a mother, and her drama—powerful, sir, I assure you—lies, as a matter of fact, all in these four children she has had by two men.

THE MOTHER: I had them? Have you got the courage to say that I wanted them? (*To the Company.*) It was his doing. It was he who gave me that other man, who forced me to go away with him.

THE STEPDAUGHTER: It isn't true.

THE MOTHER (*startled*): Not true, isn't it?

THE STEPDAUGHTER: No, it isn't true, it just isn't true.

THE MOTHER: And what can you know about it?

THE STEPDAUGHTER: It isn't true. Don't believe it. (*To Manager.*) Do you know why she says so? For that fellow there. (*Indicates the Son.*) She tortures herself, destroys herself on account of the neglect of that son there, and she wants him to believe that if she abandoned him when he was only two years old, it was because he (*indicates the Father*) made her do so.

THE MOTHER (*vigorously*): He forced me to it, and I call God to witness it. (*To the Manager.*) Ask him (*indicates Husband*) if it isn't true. Let him speak. You (*to Daughter*) are not in a position to know anything about it.

THE STEPDAUGHTER: I know you lived in peace and happiness with my father while he lived. Can you deny it?

THE MOTHER: No, I don't deny it. . . .

THE STEPDAUGHTER: He was always full of affection and kindness for you. (*To the Boy, angrily.*) It's true, isn't it? Tell them! Why don't you speak, you little fool?

THE MOTHER: Leave the poor boy alone. Why do you want to make me appear ungrateful, daughter? I don't want to offend your father. I have answered him that I didn't abandon my house and my son through any fault of mine, nor from any wilful passion.

THE FATHER: It is true. It was my doing.

LEADING MAN (*to the Company*): What a spectacle!

LEADING LADY: We are the audience this time.

JUVENILE LEAD: For once, in a way.

THE MANAGER (*beginning to get really interested*): Let's hear them out. Listen!

THE SON: Oh yes, you're going to hear a fine bit now. He will talk to you of the Demon of Experiment.

THE FATHER: You are a cynical imbecile. I've told you so already a hundred times. (*To the Manager.*) He tries to make fun of me on account of this expression which I have found to excuse myself with.

THE SON (*with disgust*): Yes, phrases! phrases!

THE FATHER: Phrases! Isn't everyone consoled when faced with a trouble or fact he doesn't understand, by a word, some simple word, which tells us nothing and yet calms us?

THE STEPDAUGHTER: Even in the case of remorse. In fact, especially then.

THE FATHER: Remorse? No, that isn't true. I've done more than use words to quiet the remorse in me.

THE STEPDAUGHTER: Yes, there was a bit of money too. Yes, yes, a bit of money. There were the hundred lire he was about to offer me in payment, gentlemen. . . . (*Sensation of horror among the Actors.*)

THE SON (*to the Stepdaughter*): This is vile.

THE STEPDAUGHTER: Vile? There they were in a pale blue envelope on a little mahogany table in the back of Madame Pace's shop. You know Madame Pace—one of those ladies who attract poor girls of good family into their ateliers, under the pretext of their selling *robes et manteaux*.°

THE SON: And he thinks he has bought the right to tyrannize over us all with those hundred lire he was going to pay; but which, fortunately—note this, gentlemen—he had no chance of paying.

robes et manteaux: French for "dresses and capes."

THE STEPDAUGHTER: It was a near thing, though, you know! (*Laughs ironically.*)

THE MOTHER (*protesting*): Shame, my daughter, shame!

THE STEPDAUGHTER: Shame indeed! This is my revenge! I am dying to live that scene . . . The room . . . I see it . . . Here is the window with the mantles exposed, there the divan, the looking-glass, a screen, there in front of the window the little mahogany table with the blue envelope containing one hundred lire. I see it. I see it. I could take hold of it. . . . But you, gentlemen, you ought to turn your backs now: I am almost nude, you know. But I don't blush: I leave that to him. (*Indicating Father.*)

THE MANAGER: I don't understand this at all.

THE FATHER: Naturally enough. I would ask you, sir, to exercise your authority a little here, and let me speak before you believe all she is trying to blame me with. Let me explain.

THE STEPDAUGHTER: Ah yes, explain it in your own way.

THE FATHER: But don't you see that the whole trouble lies here? In words, words. Each one of us has within him a whole world of things, each man of us his own special world. And how can we ever come to an understanding if I put in the words I utter the sense and value of things as I see them; while you who listen to me must inevitably translate them according to the conception of things each one of you has within himself. We think we understand each other, but we never really do. Look here! This woman (*indicating the Mother*) takes all my pity for her as a specially ferocious form of cruelty.

THE MOTHER: But you drove me away.

THE FATHER: Do you hear her? I drove her away! She believes I really sent her away.

THE MOTHER: You know how to talk, and I don't but, believe me, sir (*to Manager*), after he had married me . . . who knows why? . . . I was a poor insignificant woman. . . .

THE FATHER: But, good Heavens! it was just for your humility that I married you. I loved this simplicity in you. (*He stops when he sees she makes signs to contradict him, opens his arms wide in sign of desperation, seeing how hopeless it is to make himself understood.*) You see she denies it. Her mental deafness, believe me, is phenomenal, the limit: (*touches his forehead*) deaf, deaf, mentally deaf! She has plenty of feeling. Oh yes, a good heart for the children; but the brain—deaf, to the point of desperation—!

THE STEPDAUGHTER: Yes, but ask him how his intelligence has helped us.

THE FATHER: If we could see all the evil that may spring from good, what should we do? (*At this point the Leading Lady, who is biting her lips with rage at seeing the Leading Man flirting with the Stepdaughter, comes forward and speaks to the Manager.*)

LEADING LADY: Excuse me, but are we going to rehearse today?

THE MANAGER: Of course, of course; but let's hear them out.

JUVENILE LEAD: This is something quite new.

L'INGÉNUE: Most interesting!

LEADING LADY: Yes, for the people who like that kind of thing. (*Casts a glance at Leading Man.*)

THE MANAGER (*to Father*): You must please explain yourself quite clearly. (*Sits down.*)

THE FATHER: Very well then: listen! I had in my service a poor man, a clerk, a secretary of mine, full of devotion, who became friends with her. (*Indicating the Mother.*) They understood one another, were kindred souls in fact, without, however, the least suspicion of any evil existing. They were incapable even of thinking of it.

THE STEPDAUGHTER: So he thought of it—for them!

THE FATHER: That's not true. I meant to do good to them—and to myself, I confess, at the same time. Things had come to the point that I could not say a word to either of them without their making a mute appeal, one to the other, with their eyes. I could see them silently asking each other how I was to be kept in countenance, how I was to be kept quiet. And this, believe me, was just about enough of itself to keep me in a constant rage, to exasperate me beyond measure.

THE MANAGER: And why didn't you send him away then—this secretary of yours?

THE FATHER: Precisely what I did, sir. And then I had to watch this poor woman drifting forlornly about the house like an animal without a master, like an animal one has taken in out of pity.

THE MOTHER: Ah yes . . . !

THE FATHER (*suddenly turning to the Mother*): It's true about the son anyway, isn't it?

THE MOTHER: He took my son away from me first of all.

THE FATHER: But not from cruelty. I did it so that he should grow up healthy and strong by living in the country.

THE STEPDAUGHTER (*pointing to him ironically*): As one can see.

THE FATHER (*quickly*): Is it my fault if he has grown up like this? I sent him to a wet nurse in the country, a peasant, as *she* did not seem to me strong enough, though she is of humble origin. That was, anyway, the reason I married her. Unpleasant all this may be, but how can it be helped? My mistake possibly, but there we are! All my life I have had these confounded aspirations towards a certain moral sanity. (*At this point the Stepdaughter bursts into a noisy laugh.*) Oh, stop it! Stop it! I can't stand it.

THE MANAGER: Yes, please stop it, for Heaven's sake.

THE STEPDAUGHTER: But imagine moral sanity from him, if you please—the client of certain ateliers like that of Madame Pace!

THE FATHER: Fool! That is the proof that I am a man! This seeming contradiction, gentlemen, is the strongest proof that I stand here a live man before you. Why, it is just for this very incongruity in my nature that I have had to suffer what I have. I could not live by the side of that woman (*indicating the Mother*) any longer; but not so much for the boredom she inspired me with as for the pity I felt for her.

THE MOTHER: And so he turned me out—.

THE FATHER: —well provided for! Yes, I sent her to that man, gentlemen . . . to let her go free of me.

THE MOTHER: And to free himself.

THE FATHER: Yes, I admit it. It was also a liberation for me. But great evil has come of it. I meant well when I did it, and I did it more for her sake than mine. I swear it. (*Crosses his arms on his chest; then turns suddenly to the Mother.*) Did I ever lose sight of you until that other man carried you off to another town, like the angry fool he was? And on account of my pure interest in you . . . my pure interest, I repeat, that had no base motive in it . . . I watched with the tenderest concern the new family that grew up around her. She can bear witness to this. (*Points to the Stepdaughter.*)

THE STEPDAUGHTER: Oh yes, that's true enough. When I was a kiddie so so high, you know, with plaits over my shoulders and knickers longer than my skirts, I used to see him waiting outside the school for me to come out. He came to see how I was growing up.

THE FATHER: This is infamous, shameful!

THE STEPDAUGHTER: No. Why?

THE FATHER: Infamous! infamous! (*Then excitedly to Manager, explaining.*) After she (*indicating the Mother*) went away, my house seemed suddenly empty. She was my incubus, but she filled my house. I was like a dazed fly alone in the empty rooms. This boy here (*indicating the Son*) was educated away from home, and when he came back, he seemed to me to be no more mine. With no mother to stand between him and me, he grew up entirely for himself, on his own, apart, with no tie of intellect or affection binding him to me. And then—strange but true—I was driven, by curiosity at first and then by some tender sentiment, towards her family, which had come into being through my will. The thought of her began gradually to fill up the emptiness I felt all around me. I wanted to know if she were happy in living out the simple daily duties of life. I wanted to think of her as fortunate and happy because far away from the complicated torments of my spirit. And so, to have proof of this, I used to watch that child coming out of school.

THE STEPDAUGHTER: Yes, yes. True. He used to follow me in the street and smiled at me, waved his hand, like this. I would look at him with interest, wondering who he might be. I told my mother, who guessed at once. (*The Mother agrees with a nod.*) Then she didn't want to send me to school for some days; and when I finally went back, there he was again—looking so ridiculous—with a paper parcel in his hands. He came close to me, caressed me, and drew out a fine straw hat from the parcel, with a bouquet of flowers—all for me!

THE MANAGER: A bit discursive this, you know!

THE SON (*contemptuously*): Literature! Literature!

Scene from the 1985
American Repertory Theatre
production of *Six Characters
in Search of an Author*,
directed by Robert Brustein.

THE FATHER: Literature indeed! This is life, this is passion!

THE MANAGER: It may be, but it won't act.

THE FATHER: I agree. This is only the part leading up. I don't suggest this should be staged. She (*pointing to the Stepdaughter*), as you see, is no longer the flapper with plaits down her back—

THE STEPDAUGHTER:—and knickers showing below the skirt!

THE FATHER: The drama is coming now, sir; something new, complex, most interesting.

THE STEPDAUGHTER: As soon as my father died . . .

THE FATHER:—there was absolute misery for them. They came back here, unknown to me. Through her stupidity! (*Pointing to the Mother.*) It is true she can barely write her own name; but she could anyhow have got her daughter to write to me that they were in need . . .

THE MOTHER: And how was I to divine all this sentiment in him?

THE FATHER: That is exactly your mistake, never to have guessed any of my sentiments.

THE MOTHER: After so many years apart, and all that had happened . . .

THE FATHER: Was it my fault if that fellow carried you away? It happened quite suddenly, for after he had obtained some job or other, I could find no trace of them; and so, not unnaturally, my interest in them dwindled. But the drama culminated unforeseen and violent on their return, when I was impelled by my miserable flesh that still lives. . . . Ah! what misery, what wretchedness is that of the man who is alone and disdains debasing *liaisons!* Not old enough to do without women, and not young enough to go and look for one without shame. Misery? It's worse than misery; it's a horror; for no woman can any longer give him love; and when a man feels this. . . . One ought to do without, you say? Yes, yes, I know. Each of us when he appears before his fellows is clothed in a certain dignity. But every man knows what unconfessable things pass within the secrecy of his own heart. One gives way to the temptation, only to rise from it again, afterwards, with a great eagerness to reestablish one's dignity, as if it were a tombstone to place on the grave of one's shame, and a monument to hide and sign the memory of our weaknesses. Everybody's in the same case. Some folks haven't the courage to say certain things, that's all!

THE STEPDAUGHTER: All appear to have the courage to do them though.

THE FATHER: Yes, but in secret. Therefore, you want more courage to say these things. Let a man but speak these things out, and folks at once label him a cynic. But it isn't true. He is like all the others, better indeed, because he isn't afraid to reveal with the light of the intelligence the red shame of human bestiality on which most men close their eyes so as not to see it.

Woman—for example, look at her case! She turns tantalizing inviting glances on you. You seize her. No sooner does she feel herself in your grasp than she closes her eyes. It is the sign of her mission, the sign by which she says to man: "Blind yourself, for I am blind."

THE STEPDAUGHTER: Sometimes she can close them no

more: when she no longer feels the need of hiding her shame to herself, but dry-eyed and dispassionately, sees only that of the man who has blinded himself without love. Oh, all these intellectual complications make me sick, disgust me—all this philosophy that uncovers the beast in man, and then seeks to save him, excuse him . . . I can't stand it, sir. When a man seeks to "simplify" life bestially, throwing aside every relic of humanity, every chaste aspiration, every pure feeling, all sense of ideality, duty, modesty, shame . . . then nothing is more revolting and nauseous than a certain kind of remorse—crocodiles' tears, that's what it is.

THE MANAGER: Let's come to the point. This is only discussion.

THE FATHER: Very good, sir! But a fact is like a sack which won't stand up when it's empty. In order that it may stand up, one has to put into it the reason and sentiment which have caused it to exist. I couldn't possibly know that after the death of that man, they had decided to return here, that they were in misery, and that she (*pointing to the Mother*) had gone to work as a modiste,° and at a shop of the type of that of Madame Pace.

THE STEPDAUGHTER: A real high-class modiste, you must know, gentlemen. In appearance, she works for the leaders of the best society; but she arranges matters so that these elegant ladies serve her purpose . . . without prejudice to other ladies who are . . . well . . . only so so.

THE MOTHER: You will believe me, gentlemen, that it never entered my mind that the old hag offered me work because she had her eye on my daughter.

THE STEPDAUGHTER: Poor mamma! Do you know, sir, what that woman did when I brought her back the work my mother had finished? She would point out to me that I had torn one of my frocks, and she would give it back to my mother to mend. It was I who paid for it, always I; while this poor creature here believed she was sacrificing herself for me and these two children here, sitting up at night sewing Madame Pace's robes.

THE MANAGER: And one day you met there . . .

THE STEPDAUGHTER: Him, him. Yes sir, an old client. There's a scene for you to play! Superb!

THE FATHER: She, the Mother arrived just then . . .

THE STEPDAUGHTER (*treacherously*): Almost in time!

THE FATHER (*crying out*): No, in time! in time! Fortunately I recognized her . . . in time. And I took them back home with me to my house. You can imagine now her position and mine; she, as you see her; and I who cannot look her in the face.

THE STEPDAUGHTER: Absurd! How can I possibly be expected—after that—to be a modest young miss, a fit person to go with his confounded aspirations for "a solid moral sanity"?

THE FATHER: For the drama lies all in this—in the con-

modiste: A person who makes fashionable clothing for women.

science that I have, that each one of us has. We believe this conscience to be a single thing, but it is many-sided. There is one for this person, and another for that. Diverse consciences. So we have this illusion of being one person for all, of having a personality that is unique in all our acts. But it isn't true. We perceive this when, tragically perhaps, in something we do, we are as it were, suspended, caught up in the air on a kind of hook. Then we perceive that all of us was not in that act, and that it would be an atrocious injustice to judge us by that action alone, as if all our existence were summed up in that one deed. Now do you understand the perfidy of this girl? She surprised me in a place, where she ought not to have known me, just as I could not exist for her; and she now seeks to attach to me a reality such as I could never suppose I should have to assume for her in a shameful and fleeting moment of my life. I feel this above all else. And the drama, you will see, acquires a tremendous value from this point. Then there is the position of the others . . . his. . . . (*Indicating the Son.*)

THE SON (*shrugging his shoulders scornfully*): Leave me alone! I don't come into this.

THE FATHER: What? You don't come into this?

THE SON: I've got nothing to do with it, and don't want to have; because you know well enough I wasn't made to be mixed up in all this with the rest of you.

THE STEPDAUGHTER: We are only vulgar folk! He is the fine gentleman. You may have noticed, Mr. Manager, that I fix him now and again with a look of scorn while he lowers his eyes—for he knows the evil he has done me.

THE SON (*scarcely looking at her*): I?

THE STEPDAUGHTER: You! you! I owe my life on the streets to you. Did you or did you not deny us, with your behavior, I won't say the intimacy of home, but even that mere hospitality which makes guests feel at their ease? We were intruders who had come to disturb the kingdom of your legitimacy. I should like to have you witness, Mr. Manager, certain scenes between him and me. He says I have tyrannized over everyone. But it was just his behavior which made me insist on the reason for which I had come into the house,—this reason he calls "vile"— into his house, with my mother who is his mother too. And I came as mistress of the house.

THE SON: It's easy for them to put me always in the wrong. But imagine, gentlemen, the position of a son, whose fate it is to see arrive one day at his home a young woman of impudent bearing, a young woman who inquires for his father, with whom who knows what business she has. This young man has then to witness her return bolder than ever, accompanied by that child there. He is obliged to watch her treat his father in an equivocal and confidential manner. She asks for money of him in a way that lets one suppose he must give it to her, *must*, do you understand, because he has every obligation to do so.

THE FATHER: But I have, as a matter of fact, this obligation. I owe it to your mother.

THE SON: How should I know? When had I ever seen or heard of her? One day there arrive with her (*indicating Stepdaughter*) that lad and this baby here. I am told: "This is *your* mother too, you know." I divine from her manner (*indicating Stepdaughter again*) why it is they have come home. I had rather not say what I feel and think about it. I shouldn't even care to confess to myself. No action can therefore be hoped for from me in this affair. Believe me, Mr. Manager, I am an "unrealized" character, dramatically speaking; and I find myself not at all at ease in their company. Leave me out of it, I beg you.

THE FATHER: What? It is just because you are so that . . .

THE SON: How do you know what I am like? When did you ever bother your head about me?

THE FATHER: I admit it. I admit it. But isn't that a situation in itself? This aloofness of yours which is so cruel to me and to your mother, who returns home and sees you almost for the first time grown up, who doesn't recognize you but knows you are her son. . . . (*Pointing out the Mother to the Manager.*) See, she's crying!

THE STEPDAUGHTER (*angrily, stamping her foot*): Like a fool!

THE FATHER (*indicating Stepdaughter*): She can't stand him, you know. (*Then referring again to the Son.*) He says he doesn't come into the affair, whereas he is really the hinge of the whole action. Look at that lad who is always clinging to his mother, frightened and humiliated. It is on account of this fellow here. Possibly his situation is the most painful of all. He feels himself a stranger more than the others. The poor little chap feels mortified, humiliated at being brought into a home out of charity as it were. (*In confidence.*) He is the image of his father. Hardly talks at all. Humble and quiet.

THE MANAGER: Oh, we'll cut him out. You've no notion what a nuisance boys are on the stage. . . .

THE FATHER: He disappears soon, you know. And the baby too. She is the first to vanish from the scene. The drama consists finally in this: when that mother reenters my house, her family born outside of it, and shall we say superimposed on the original, ends with the death of the little girl, the tragedy of the boy and the flight of the elder daughter. It cannot go on, because it is foreign to its surroundings. So after much torment, we three remain: I, the mother, that son. Then, owing to the disappearance of that extraneous family, we too find ourselves strange to one another. We find we are living in an atmosphere of mortal desolation which is the revenge, as he (*indicating Son*) scornfully said of the Demon of Experiment, that unfortunately hides in me. Thus, sir, you see when faith is lacking, it becomes impossible to create certain states of happiness, for we lack the necessary humility. Vaingloriously, we try to substitute ourselves for this faith, creating thus for the rest of the world a reality which we believe after their fashion, while, actually, it doesn't exist. For each one of us has his own reality to be respected before God, even when it is harmful to one's very self.

THE MANAGER: There is something in what you say. I assure you all this interests me very much. I begin to think there's the stuff for a drama in all this, and not a bad drama either.

THE STEPDAUGHTER (*coming forward*): When you've got a character like me . . .

THE FATHER (*shutting her up, all excited to learn the decision of the Manager*): You be quiet!

THE MANAGER (*reflecting, heedless of interruption*): It's new . . . hem . . . yes. . . .

THE FATHER: Absolutely new!

THE MANAGER: You've got a nerve though, I must say, to come here and fling it at me like this . . .

THE FATHER: You will understand, sir, born as we are for the stage . . .

THE MANAGER: Are you amateur actors then?

THE FATHER: No, I say born for the stage, because . . .

THE MANAGER: Oh, nonsense. You're an old hand, you know.

THE FATHER: No sir, no. We act that role for which we have been cast, that role which we are given in life. And in my own case, passion itself, as usually happens, becomes a trifle theatrical when it is exalted.

THE MANAGER: Well, well, that will do. But you see, without an author. . . . I could give you the address of an author if you like . . .

THE FATHER: No, no. Look here! You must be the author.

THE MANAGER: I? What are you talking about?

THE FATHER: Yes, you, you! Why not?

THE MANAGER: Because I have never been an author: that's why.

THE FATHER: Then why not turn author now? Everybody does it. You don't want any special qualities. Your task is made much easier by the fact that we are all here alive before you. . . .

THE MANAGER: It won't do.

THE FATHER: What? When you see us live our drama. . . .

THE MANAGER: Yes, that's all right. But you want someone to write it.

THE FATHER: No, no. Someone to take it down, possibly, while we play it, scene by scene! It will be enough to sketch it out at first, and then try it over.

THE MANAGER: Well . . . I am almost tempted. It's a bit of an idea. One might have a shot at it.

THE FATHER: Of course. You'll see what scenes will come out of it. I can give you one, at once . . .

THE MANAGER: By Jove, it tempts me. I'd like to have a go at it. Let's try it out. Come with me to my office. (*Turning to the Actors.*) You are at liberty for a bit, but don't step out of the theater for long. In a quarter of an hour, twenty minutes, all back here again! (*To the Father.*) We'll see what can be done. Who knows if we don't get something really extraordinary out of it?

THE FATHER: There's no doubt about it. They (*indicating the Characters*) had better come with us too, hadn't they?

THE MANAGER: Yes, yes. Come on! come on! (*Moves away and then turning to the Actors.*) Be punctual, please! (*Manager and the Six Characters cross the stage and go off. The other Actors remain, looking at one another in astonishment.*)

LEADING MAN: Is he serious? What the devil does he want to do?

JUVENILE LEAD: This is rank madness.

THIRD ACTOR: Does he expect to knock up a drama in five minutes?

JUVENILE LEAD: Like the improvisers!

LEADING LADY: If he thinks I'm going to take part in a joke like this. . . .

JUVENILE LEAD: I'm out of it anyway.

FOURTH ACTOR: I should like to know who they are. (*Alludes to Characters.*)

THIRD ACTOR: What do you suppose? Madmen or rascals!

JUVENILE LEAD: And he takes them seriously!

L'INGÉNUE: Vanity! He fancies himself as an author now.

LEADING MAN: It's absolutely unheard of. If the stage has come to this . . . well I'm . . .

FIFTH ACTOR: It's rather a joke.

THIRD ACTOR: Well, we'll see what's going to happen next.

(*Thus talking, the Actors leave the stage, some going out by the little door at the back, others retiring to their dressing rooms.*)

(*The curtain remains up.*)

(*The action of the play is suspended for twenty minutes.*)

ACT II

(*The stage call-bells ring to warn the company that the play is about to begin again.*)

(*The Stepdaughter comes out of the Manager's office along with the Child and the Boy. As she comes out of the office, she cries:—*)

Nonsense! nonsense! Do it yourselves! I'm not going to mix myself up in this mess. (*Turning to the Child and coming quickly with her on to the stage.*) Come on, Rosetta, let's run!

(*The Boy follows them slowly, remaining a little behind and seeming perplexed.*)

THE STEPDAUGHTER (*stops, bends over the Child and takes the latter's face between her hands*): My little darling! You're frightened, aren't you? You don't know where we are, do you? (*Pretending to reply to a question of the Child.*) What is the stage? It's a place, baby, you know, where people play at being serious, a place where they act comedies. We've got to act a comedy now, dead serious, you know; and

you're in it also, little one. (*Embraces her, pressing the little head to her breast, and rocking the Child for a moment.*) Oh darling, darling, what a horrid comedy you've got to play! What a wretched part they've found for you! A garden . . . a fountain . . . look . . . just suppose, kiddie, it's here. Where, you say? Why, right here in the middle. It's all pretense you know. That's the trouble, my pet: it's all make-believe here. It's better to imagine it though, because if they fix it up for you, it'll only be painted cardboard, painted cardboard for the rockery, the water, the plants. . . . Ah, but I think a baby like this one would sooner have a make-believe fountain than a real one, so she could play with it. What a joke it'll be for the others! But for you, alas! not quite such a joke: you who are real, baby dear, and really play by a real fountain that is big and green and beautiful, with ever so many bamboos around it that are reflected in the water, and a whole lot of little ducks swimming about. . . . No, Rosetta, no, your mother doesn't bother about you on account of that wretch of a son there. I'm in the devil of a temper, and as for that lad. . . . (*Seizes Boy by the arm to force him to take one of his hands out of his pockets.*) What have you got there? What are you hiding? (*Pulls his hand out of his pocket, looks into it, and catches the glint of a revolver.*) Ah! where did you get this? (*The Boy, very pale in the face, looks at her, but does not answer.*) Idiot! If I'd been in your place, instead of killing myself, I'd have shot one of those two, or both of them: father and son.

(*The Father enters from the office, all excited from his work. The Manager follows him.*)

THE FATHER: Come on, come on dear! Come here for a minute! We've arranged everything. It's all fixed up.

THE MANAGER (*also excited*): If you please, young lady, there are one or two points to settle still. Will you come along?

THE STEPDAUGHTER (*following him toward the office*): Ouff! what's the good, if you've arranged everything.

(*The Father, Manager, and Stepdaughter go back into the office again [off] for a moment. At the same time, the Son, followed by the Mother, comes out.*)

THE SON (*looking at the three entering office*): Oh this is fine, fine! And to think I can't even get away!

(*The Mother attempts to look at him, but lowers her eyes immediately when he turns away from her. She then sits down. The Boy and the Child approach her. She casts a glance again at the Son, and speaks with humble tones, trying to draw him into conversation.*)

THE MOTHER: And isn't my punishment the worst of all? (*Then seeing from the Son's manner that he will not bother himself about her.*) My God! Why are you so cruel? Isn't it enough for one person to support all this torment? Must you then insist on others seeing it also?

THE SON (*half to himself, meaning the Mother to hear, however*): And they want to put it on the stage! If there was at least a reason for it! He thinks he has got at the meaning of it all. Just as if each one of us in every circumstance of life couldn't find his own explanation of it! (*Pauses.*) He complains he was discovered in a place where he ought not to have been seen, in a moment of his life which ought to have remained hidden and kept out of the reach of that convention which he has to maintain for other people. And what about my case? Haven't I had to reveal what no son ought ever to reveal: how father and mother live and are man and wife for themselves quite apart from that idea of father and mother which we give them? When this idea is revealed, our life is then linked at one point only to that man and that woman; and as such it should shame them, shouldn't it?

(*The Mother hides her face in her hands. From the dressing rooms and the little door at the back of the stage the Actors and Stage Manager return, followed by the Property Man and the Prompter. At the same moment, the Manager comes out of his office, accompanied by the Father and the Stepdaughter.*)

THE MANAGER: Come on, come on, ladies and gentlemen! Heh! you there, machinist!

MACHINIST: Yes sir?

THE MANAGER: Fix up the parlor with the floral decorations. Two wings and a drop with a door will do. Hurry up!

(*The Machinist runs off at once to prepare the scene and arranges it while the Manager talks with the Stage Manager, the Property Man, and the Prompter on matters of detail.*)

THE MANAGER (*to Property Man*): Just have a look, and see if there isn't a sofa or a divan in the wardrobe . . .

PROPERTY MAN: There's the green one.

THE STEPDAUGHTER: No no! Green won't do. It was yellow, ornamented with flowers—very large! and most comfortable!

PROPERTY MAN: There isn't one like that.

THE MANAGER: It doesn't matter. Use the one we've got.

THE STEPDAUGHTER: Doesn't matter? It's most important!

THE MANAGER: We're only trying it now. Please don't interfere. (*To Property Man.*) See if we've got a shop window—long and narrowish.

THE STEPDAUGHTER: And the little table! The little mahogany table for the pale blue envelope!

PROPERTY MAN (*to Manager*): There's that little gilt one.

THE MANAGER: That'll do fine.

THE FATHER: A mirror.

THE STEPDAUGHTER: And the screen! We must have a screen. Otherwise how can I manage?

PROPERTY MAN: That's all right, Miss. We've got any amount of them.

THE MANAGER (*to the Stepdaughter*): We want some clothes pegs too, don't we?

THE STEPDAUGHTER: Yes, several, several!

THE MANAGER: See how many we've got and bring them all.

PROPERTY MAN: All right!

(*The Property Man hurries off to obey his orders. While he is putting the things in their places, the Manager talks to the Prompter and then with the Characters and the Actors.*)

THE MANAGER (*to Prompter*): Take your seat. Look here: this is the outline of the scenes, act by act. (*Hands him some sheets of paper.*) And now I'm going to ask you to do something out of the ordinary.

PROMPTER: Take it down in shorthand?

THE MANAGER (*pleasantly surprised*): Exactly! Can you do shorthand?

PROMPTER: Yes, a little.

THE MANAGER: Good! (*Turning to a Stage Hand.*) Go and get some paper from my office, plenty, as much as you can find.

(*The Stage Hand goes off and soon returns with a handful of paper which he gives to the Prompter.*)

THE MANAGER (*to Prompter*): You follow the scenes as we play them, and try and get the points down, at any rate the most important ones. (*Then addressing the Actors.*) Clear the stage, ladies and gentlemen! Come over here (*pointing to the left*) and listen attentively.

LEADING LADY: But, excuse me, we . . .

THE MANAGER (*guessing her thought*): Don't worry! You won't have to improvise.

LEADING MAN: What have we to do then?

THE MANAGER: Nothing. For the moment you just watch and listen. Everybody will get his part written out afterwards. At present we're going to try the thing as best we can. They're going to act now.

THE FATHER (*as if fallen from the clouds into the confusion of the stage*): We? What do you mean, if you please, by a rehearsal?

THE MANAGER: A rehearsal for them. (*Points to the Actors.*)

THE FATHER: But since we are the characters . . .

THE MANAGER: All right: "characters" then, if you insist on calling yourselves such. But here, my dear sir, the characters don't act. Here the actors do the acting. The characters are there, in the "book" (*pointing toward Prompter's box*)—when there is a "book"!

THE FATHER: I won't contradict you; but excuse me, the actors aren't the characters. They want to be, they pretend to be, don't they? Now if these gentlemen here are fortunate enough to have us alive before them . . .

THE MANAGER: Oh, this is grand! You want to come before the public yourselves then?

THE FATHER: As we are. . . .

THE MANAGER: I can assure you it would be a magnificent spectacle!

LEADING MAN: What's the use of us here anyway then?

THE MANAGER: You're not going to pretend that you can

act? It makes me laugh! (*The Actors laugh.*) There, you see, they are laughing at the notion. But, by the way, I must cast the parts. That won't be difficult. They cast themselves. (*To the Second Lady Lead.*) You play the Mother. (*To the Father.*) We must find her a name.

THE FATHER: Amalia, sir.

THE MANAGER: But that is the real name of your wife. We don't want to call her by her real name.

THE FATHER: Why ever not, if it is her name? . . . Still, perhaps, if that lady must . . . (*Makes a slight motion of the hand to indicate the Second Lady Lead.*) I see this woman here (*means the Mother*) as Amalia. But do as you like. (*Gets more and more confused.*) I don't know what to say to you. Already, I begin to hear my own words ring false, as if they had another sound . . .

THE MANAGER: Don't you worry about it. It'll be our job to find the right tones. And as for her name, if you want her Amalia, Amalia it shall be; and if you don't like it, we'll find another! For the moment though, we'll call the characters in this way: (*To Juvenile Lead.*) You are the Son. (*To the Leading Lady.*) You naturally are the Stepdaughter. . . .

THE STEPDAUGHTER (*excitedly*): What? what? I, that woman there? (*Bursts out laughing.*)

THE MANAGER (*angry*): What is there to laugh at?

LEADING LADY (*indignant*): Nobody has ever dared to laugh at me. I insist on being treated with respect; otherwise I go away.

THE STEPDAUGHTER: No, no, excuse me . . . I am not laughing at you. . . .

THE MANAGER (*to Stepdaughter*): You ought to feel honored to be played by . . .

LEADING LADY (*at once, contemptuously*): "That woman there" . . .

THE STEPDAUGHTER: But I wasn't speaking of you, you know. I was speaking of myself—whom I can't see at all in you! That is all. I don't know . . . but . . . you . . . aren't in the least like me. . . .

THE FATHER: True. Here's the point. Look here, sir, our temperaments, our souls. . . .

THE MANAGER: Temperament, soul, be hanged! Do you suppose the spirit of the piece is in you? Nothing of the kind!

THE FATHER: What, haven't we our own temperaments, our own souls?

THE MANAGER: Not at all. Your soul or whatever you like to call it takes shape here. The actors give body and form to it, voice and gesture. And my actors—I may tell you—have given expression to much more lofty material than this little drama of yours, which may or may not hold up on the stage. But if it does, the merit of it, believe me, will be due to my actors.

THE FATHER: I don't dare contradict you, sir, but, believe me, it is a terrible suffering for us who are as we are, with these bodies of ours, these features to see. . . .

THE MANAGER (*cutting him short and out of patience*):

Good heavens! The make-up will remedy all that, man, the make-up. . . .

THE FATHER: Maybe. But the voice, the gestures . . .

THE MANAGER: Now, look here! On the stage, you as yourself, cannot exist. The actor here acts you, and that's an end to it!

THE FATHER: I understand. And now I think I see why our author who conceived us as we are, all alive, didn't want to put us on the stage after all. I haven't the least desire to offend your actors. Far from it! But when I think that I am to be acted by . . . I don't know by whom. . . .

LEADING MAN (*on his dignity*): By me, if you've no objection!

THE FATHER (*humbly, mellifluously*): Honored, I assure you, sir. (*Bows.*) Still, I must say that try as this gentleman may, with all his good will and wonderful art, to absorb me into himself. . . .

LEADING MAN: Oh chuck it! "Wonderful art!" Withdraw that, please!

THE FATHER: The performance he will give, even doing his best with make-up to look like me. . . .

LEADING MAN: It will certainly be a bit difficult! (*The Actors laugh.*)

THE FATHER: Exactly! It will be difficult to act me as I really am. The effect will be rather—apart from the make-up—according as to how he supposes I am, as he senses me—if he does sense me—and not as I inside of myself feel myself to be. It seems to me then that account should be taken of this by everyone whose duty it may become to criticize us. . . .

THE MANAGER: Heavens! The man's starting to think about the critics now! Let them say what they like. It's up to us to put on the play if we can. (*Looking around.*) Come on! come on! Is the stage set? (*To the Actors and Characters.*) Stand back—stand back! Let me see, and don't let's lose any more time! (*To the Stepdaughter.*) Is it all right as it is now?

THE STEPDAUGHTER: Well, to tell the truth, I don't recognize the scene.

THE MANAGER: My dear lady, you can't possibly suppose that we can construct that shop of Madame Pace piece by piece here? (*To the Father.*) You said a white room with flowered wallpaper, didn't you?

THE FATHER: Yes.

THE MANAGER: Well then. We've got the furniture right more or less. Bring that little table a bit further forward. (*The Stage Hands obey the order. To Property Man.*) You go and find an envelope, if possible, a pale blue one; and give it to that gentleman. (*Indicates Father.*)

PROPERTY MAN: An ordinary envelope?

MANAGER AND FATHER: Yes, yes, an ordinary envelope.

PROPERTY MAN: At once, sir. (*Exit.*)

THE MANAGER: Ready, everyone! First scene—the Young Lady. (*The Leading Lady comes forward.*) No, no, you must wait. I meant her. (*Indicating the Stepdaughter.*) You just watch—

THE STEPDAUGHTER (*adding at once*): How I shall play it, how I shall live it! . . .

LEADING LADY (*offended*): I shall live it also, you may be sure, as soon as I begin!

THE MANAGER (*with his hands to his head*): Ladies and gentlemen, if you please! No more useless discussions! Scene I: the Young Lady with Madame Pace: Oh! (*Looks around as if lost.*) And this Madame Pace, where is she?

THE FATHER: She isn't with us, sir.

THE MANAGER: Then what the devil's to be done?

THE FATHER: But she is alive too.

THE MANAGER: Yes, but where is she?

THE FATHER: One minute. Let me speak! (*Turning to the Actresses.*) If these ladies would be so good as to give me their hats for a moment. . . .

THE ACTRESSES (*half surprised, half laughing, in chorus*): What? Why? Our hats? What does he say?

THE MANAGER: What are you going to do with the ladies' hats? (*The Actors laugh.*)

THE FATHER: Oh nothing. I just want to put them on these pegs for a moment. And one of the ladies will be so kind as to take off her mantle. . . .

THE ACTORS: Oh, what d'you think of that? Only the mantle? He must be mad.

SOME ACTRESSES: But why? Mantles as well?

THE FATHER: To hang them up here for a moment. Please be so kind, will you?

THE ACTRESSES (*taking off their hats, one or two also their cloaks, and going to hang them on the racks*): After all, why not? There you are! This is really funny. We've got to put them on show.

THE FATHER: Exactly; just like that, on show.

THE MANAGER: May we know why?

THE FATHER: I'll tell you. Who knows if, by arranging the stage for her, she does not come here herself, attracted by the very articles of her trade? (*Inviting the Actors to look toward the exit at back of stage.*) Look! Look!

(*The door at the back of stage opens and Madame Pace enters and takes a few steps forward. She is a fat, oldish woman with puffy oxygenated hair. She is rouged and powdered, dressed with a comical elegance in black silk. Round her waist is a long silver chain from which hangs a pair of scissors. The Stepdaughter runs over to her at once amid the stupor of the Actors.*)

THE STEPDAUGHTER (*turning toward her*): There she is! There she is!

THE FATHER (*radiant*): It's she! I said so, didn't I! There she is!

THE MANAGER (*conquering his surprise, and then becoming indignant*): What sort of a trick is this?

LEADING MAN (*almost at the same time*): What's going to happen next?

JUVENILE LEAD: Where does she come from?

L'INGÉNUE: They've been holding her in reserve, I guess.

LEADING LADY: A vulgar trick!

THE FATHER (*dominating the protests*): Excuse me, all of you! Why are you so anxious to destroy in the name of a vulgar, commonplace sense of truth, this reality which comes to birth attracted and formed by the magic of the stage itself, which has indeed more right to live here than you, since it is much truer than you—if you don't mind my saying so? Which is the actress among you who is to play Madame Pace? Well, here is Madame Pace herself. And you will allow, I fancy, that the actress who acts her will be less true than this woman here, who is herself in person. You see my daughter recognized her and went over to her at once. Now you're going to witness the scene!

(*But the scene between the Stepdaughter and Madame Pace has already begun despite the protest of the Actors and the reply of the Father. It has begun quietly, naturally, in a manner impossible for the stage. So when the Actors, called to attention by the Father, turn round and see Madame Pace, who has placed one hand under the Stepdaughter's chin to raise her head, they observe her at first with great attention, but hearing her speak in an unintelligible manner their interest begins to wane.*)

THE MANAGER: Well? well?

LEADING MAN: What does she say?

LEADING LADY: One can't hear a word.

JUVENILE LEAD: Louder! Louder please!

THE STEPDAUGHTER (*leaving Madame Pace, who smiles a Sphinx-like smile, and advancing toward the Actors*): Louder? Louder? What are you talking about? These aren't matters which can be shouted at the top of one's voice. If I have spoken them out loud, it was to shame him and have my revenge. (*Indicates Father.*) But for Madame it's quite a different matter.

THE MANAGER: Indeed? indeed? But here, you know people have got to make themselves heard, my dear. Even we who are on the stage can't hear you. What will it be when the public's in the theater? And anyway, you can very well speak up now among yourselves, since we shan't be present to listen to you as we are now. You've got to pretend to be alone in a room at the back of a shop where no one can hear you.

(*The Stepdaughter coquettishly and with a touch of malice makes a sign of disagreement two or three times with her finger.*)

THE MANAGER: What do you mean by no?

THE STEPDAUGHTER (*sotto voce,° mysteriously*): There's someone who will hear us if she (*indicating Madame Pace*) speaks out loud.

THE MANAGER (*in consternation*): What? Have you got someone else to spring on us now? (*The Actors burst out laughing.*)

THE FATHER: No, no sir. She is alluding to me. I've got to be here—there behind that door, in waiting; and

sotto voce: In a soft voice or stage whisper.

Madame Pace knows it. In fact, if you will allow me, I'll go there at once, so I can be quite ready. (*Moves away.*)

THE MANAGER (*stopping him*): No! wait! wait! We must observe the conventions of the theater. Before you are ready . . .

THE STEPDAUGHTER (*interrupting him*): No, get on with it at once! I'm just dying, I tell you, to act this scene. If he's ready, I'm more than ready.

THE MANAGER (*shouting*): But, my dear young lady, first of all, we must have the scene between you and this lady. . . . (*Indicates Madame Pace.*) Do you understand?

THE STEPDAUGHTER: Good Heavens! She's been telling me what you know already: that mama's work is badly done again, that the material's ruined; and that if I want her to continue to help us in our misery I must be patient. . . .

MADAME PACE (*coming forward with an air of great importance*): Yes indeed, sir, I no wanta take advantage of her, I no wanta be hard. . . .

(*Note: Madame Pace is supposed to talk in a jargon half Italian, half English.*)

THE MANAGER (*alarmed*): What? What? She talks like that? (*The Actors burst out laughing again.*)

THE STEPDAUGHTER (*also laughing*): Yes yes, that's the way she talks, half English, half Italian! Most comical it is!

MADAME PACE: Itta seem not verra polite gentlemen laugha atta me eeff I trya best speaka English.

THE MANAGER: *Diamine!*° Of course! Of course! Let her talk like that! Just what we want. Talk just like that, Madame, if you please! The effect will be certain. Exactly what was wanted to put a little comic relief into the crudity of the situation. Of course she talks like that! Magnificent!

THE STEPDAUGHTER: Magnificent? Certainly! When certain suggestions are made to one in language of that kind, the effect is certain, since it seems almost a joke. One feels inclined to laugh when one hears her talk about an "old signore" "who wanta talka nicely with you." Nice old signore, eh, Madame?

MADAME PACE: Not so old my dear, not so old! And even if you no like him, he won't make any scandal!

THE MOTHER (*jumping up amid the amazement and consternation of the Actors, who had not been noticing her. They move to restrain her*): You old devil! You murderess!

THE STEPDAUGHTER (*running over to calm her Mother*): Calm yourself, Mother, calm yourself! Please don't. . . .

THE FATHER (*going to her also at the same time*): Calm yourself! Don't get excited! Sit down now!

THE MOTHER: Well then, take that woman away out of my sight!

Diamine!: Italian for "Well, I'll be damned!"

THE STEPDAUGHTER (*to Manager*): It is impossible for my mother to remain here.

THE FATHER (*to Manager*): They can't be here together. And for this reason, you see: that woman there was not with us when we came. . . . If they are on together, the whole thing is given away inevitably, as you see.

THE MANAGER: It doesn't matter. This is only a first rough sketch—just to get an idea of the various points of the scene, even confusedly. . . . (*Turning to the Mother and leading her to her chair.*) Come along, my dear lady, sit down now, and let's get on with the scene. . . .

(*Meanwhile, the Stepdaughter, coming forward again, turns to Madame Pace.*)

THE STEPDAUGHTER: Come on, Madame, come on!

MADAME PACE (*offended*): No, no, *grazie*. I do not do anything witha your mother present.

THE STEPDAUGHTER: Nonsense! Introduce this "old signore" who wants to talk nicely to me. (*Addressing the Company imperiously.*) We've got to do this scene one way or another, haven't we? Come on! (*To Madame Pace.*) You can go!

MADAME PACE: Ah yes! I go'way! I go'way! Certainly! (*Exits furious.*)

THE STEPDAUGHTER (*to the Father*): Now you make your entry. No, you needn't go over there. Come here. Let's suppose you've already come in. Like that, yes! I'm here with bowed head, modest like. Come on! Out with your voice! Say "Good morning, Miss" in that peculiar tone, that special tone. . . .

THE MANAGER: Excuse me, but are you the Manager, or am I? (*To the Father, who looks undecided and perplexed.*) Get on with it, man! Go down there to the back of the stage. You needn't go off. Then come right forward here.

(*The Father does as he is told, looking troubled and perplexed at first. But as soon as he begins to move, the reality of the action affects him, and he begins to smile and to be more natural. The Actors watch intently.*)

THE MANAGER (*sotto voce, quickly to the Prompter in his box*): Ready! ready! Get ready to write now.

THE FATHER (*coming forward and speaking in a different tone*): Good afternoon, Miss!

THE STEPDAUGHTER (*head bowed down slightly, with restrained disgust*): Good afternoon!

THE FATHER (*looks under her hat which partly covers her face. Perceiving she is very young, he makes an exclamation, partly of surprise, partly of fear lest he compromise himself in a risky adventure*): Ah . . . but . . . ah . . . I say . . . this is not the first time that you have come here, is it?

THE STEPDAUGHTER (*modestly*): No sir.

THE FATHER: You've been here before, eh? (*Then seeing her nod agreement.*) More than once? (*Waits for her to answer, looks under her hat, smiles, and then says:*) Well then, there's no need to be so shy, is there? May I take off your hat?

THE STEPDAUGHTER (*anticipating him and with veiled disgust*): No sir . . . I'll do it myself. (*Takes it off quickly.*)

(*The Mother, who watches the progress of the scene with the Son and the other two children who cling to her, is on thorns; and follows with varying expressions of sorrow, indignation, anxiety, and horror the words and actions of the other two. From time to time she hides her face in her hands and sobs.*)

THE MOTHER: Oh, my God, my God!

THE FATHER (*playing his part with a touch of gallantry*): Give it to me! I'll put it down. (*Takes hat from her hands.*) But a dear little head like yours ought to have a smarter hat. Come and help me choose one from the stock, won't you?

L'INGÉNUE (*interrupting*): I say . . . those are our hats you know.

THE MANAGER (*furious*): Silence! silence! Don't try and be funny, if you please. . . . We're playing the scene now, I'd have you notice. (*To the Stepdaughter.*) Begin again, please!

THE STEPDAUGHTER (*continuing*): No thank you, sir.

THE FATHER: Oh, come now. Don't talk like that. You must take it. I shall be upset if you don't. There are some lovely little hats here; and then — Madame will be pleased. She expects it, anyway, you know.

THE STEPDAUGHTER: No, no! I couldn't wear it!

THE FATHER: Oh, you're thinking about what they'd say at home if they saw you come in with a new hat? My dear girl, there's always a way round these little matters, you know.

THE STEPDAUGHTER (*all keyed up*): No, it's not that. I couldn't wear it because I am . . . as you see . . . you might have noticed . . .

(*Showing her black dress.*)

THE FATHER: . . . in mourning! Of course: I beg your pardon: I'm frightfully sorry. . . .

THE STEPDAUGHTER (*forcing herself to conquer her indignation and nausea*): Stop! Stop! It's I who must thank you. There's no need for you to feel mortified or specially sorry. Don't think any more of what I've said. (*Tries to smile.*) I must forget that I am dressed so. . . .

THE MANAGER (*interrupting and turning to the Prompter*): Stop a minute! Stop! Don't write that down. Cut out that last bit. (*Then to the Father and Stepdaughter.*) Fine! it's going fine! (*To the Father only.*) And now you can go on as we arranged. (*To the Actors.*) Pretty good that scene, where he offers her the hat, eh?

THE STEPDAUGHTER: The best's coming now. Why can't we go on?

THE MANAGER: Have a little patience! (*To the Actors.*) Of course, it must be treated rather lightly.

LEADING MAN: Still, with a bit of go in it!

LEADING LADY: Of course! It's easy enough! (*To Leading Man.*) Shall you and I try it now?

LEADING MAN: Why, yes! I'll prepare my entrance. (*Exit in order to make his entrance.*)

THE MANAGER (*to Leading Lady*): See here! The scene between you and Madame Pace is finished. I'll have it written out properly after. You remain here . . . oh, where are you going?

LEADING LADY: One minute. I want to put my hat on again. (*Goes over to hatrack and puts her hat on her head.*)

THE MANAGER: Good! You stay here with your head bowed down a bit.

THE STEPDAUGHTER: But she isn't dressed in black.

LEADING LADY: But I shall be, and much more effectively than you.

THE MANAGER (*to Stepdaughter*): Be quiet please, and watch! You'll be able to learn something. (*Clapping his hands.*) Come on! come on! Entrance, please!

(*The door at rear of stage opens, and the Leading Man enters with the lively manner of an old gallant. The rendering of the scene by the Actors from the very first words is seen to be quite a different thing, though it has not in any way the air of a parody. Naturally, the Stepdaughter and the Father, not being able to recognize themselves in the Leading Lady and the Leading Man, who deliver their words in different tones and with a different psychology, express, sometimes with smiles, sometimes with gestures, the impression they receive.*)

LEADING MAN: Good afternoon, Miss . . .

THE FATHER (*at once unable to contain himself*): No! no!

(*The Stepdaughter, noticing the way the Leading Man enters, bursts out laughing.*)

THE MANAGER (*furious*): Silence! And you, please, just stop that laughing. If we go on like this, we shall never finish.

THE STEPDAUGHTER: Forgive me, sir but it's natural enough. This lady (*indicating Leading Lady*) stands there still; but if she is supposed to be me, I can assure you that if I heard anyone say "Good afternoon" in that manner and in that tone, I should burst out laughing as I did.

THE FATHER: Yes, yes, the manner, the tone . . .

THE MANAGER: Nonsense! Rubbish! Stand aside and let me see the action.

LEADING MAN: If I've got to represent an old fellow who's coming into a house of an equivocal character . . .

THE MANAGER: Don't listen to them, for Heaven's sake! Do it again! It goes fine. (*Waiting for the Actors to begin again.*) Well?

LEADING MAN: Good afternoon, Miss.

LEADING LADY: Good afternoon.

LEADING MAN (*imitating the gesture of the Father when he looked under the hat, and then expressing quite clearly first satisfaction and then fear*): Ah, but . . . I say . . . this is not the first time that you have come here, is it?

THE MANAGER: Good, but not quite so heavily. Like this. (*Acts himself.*) "This isn't the first time that you have come here" . . . (*To Leading Lady.*) And you say: "No, sir."

LEADING LADY: No, sir.

LEADING MAN: You've been here before, more than once.

THE MANAGER: No, no, stop! Let her nod "yes" first. "You've been here before, eh?" (*The Leading Lady lifts up her head slightly and closes her eyes as though in disgust. Then she inclines her head twice.*)

THE STEPDAUGHTER (*unable to contain herself*): Oh my God! (*Puts a hand to her mouth to prevent herself from laughing.*)

THE MANAGER (*turning round*): What's the matter?

THE STEPDAUGHTER: Nothing, nothing!

THE MANAGER (*to Leading Man*): Go on!

LEADING MAN: You've been here before, eh? Well then, there's no need to be so shy, is there? May I take off your hat?

(*The Leading Man says this last speech in such a tone and with such gestures that the Stepdaughter, though she has her hand to her mouth, cannot keep from laughing.*)

LEADING LADY (*indignant*): I'm not going to stop here to be made a fool of by that woman there.

LEADING MAN: Neither am I! I'm through with it!

THE MANAGER (*shouting to Stepdaughter*): Silence! for once and all, I tell you!

THE STEPDAUGHTER: Forgive me! forgive me!

THE MANAGER: You haven't any manners: that's what it is! You go too far.

THE FATHER (*endeavoring to intervene*): Yes, it's true, but excuse her . . .

THE MANAGER: Excuse what? It's absolutely disgusting.

THE FATHER: Yes, sir, but believe me, it has such a strange effect when . . .

THE MANAGER: Strange? Why strange? Where is it strange?

THE FATHER: No, sir; I admire your actors — this gentleman here, this lady; but they are certainly not us!

THE MANAGER: I should hope not. Evidently they cannot be you, if they are actors.

THE FATHER: Just so: actors! Both of them act our parts exceedingly well. But, believe me, it produces quite a different effect on us. They want to be us, but they aren't, all the same.

THE MANAGER: What is it then anyway?

THE FATHER: Something that is . . . that is theirs — and no longer ours . . .

THE MANAGER: But naturally, inevitably, I've told you so already.

THE FATHER: Yes, I understand . . . I understand . . .

THE MANAGER: Well then, let's have no more of it! (*Turning to the Actors.*) We'll have the rehearsals by ourselves, afterwards, in the ordinary way. I never could stand rehearsing with the author present. He's never satisfied! (*Turning to Father and Stepdaughter.*) Come on! Let's get on with it again; and try and see if you can't keep from laughing.

THE STEPDAUGHTER: Oh, I shan't laugh any more. There's a nice little bit coming from me now: you'll see.

THE MANAGER: Well then: when she says "Don't think any more of what I've said, I must forget, etc.," you (*addressing the Father*) come in sharp with "I understand"; and then you ask her . . .

THE STEPDAUGHTER (*interrupting*): What?

THE MANAGER: Why she is in mourning.

THE STEPDAUGHTER: Not at all! See here: when I told him that it was useless for me to be thinking about my wearing mourning, do you know how he answered me? "Ah well," he said, "then let's take off this little frock."

THE MANAGER: Great! Just what we want, to make a riot in the theater!

THE STEPDAUGHTER: But it's the truth!

THE MANAGER: What does that matter? Acting is our business here. Truth up to a certain point, but no further.

THE STEPDAUGHTER: What do you want to do then?

THE MANAGER: You'll see, you'll see! Leave it to me.

THE STEPDAUGHTER: No sir! What you want to do is to piece together a little romantic sentimental scene out of my disgust, out of all the reasons, each more cruel and viler than the other, why I am what I am. He is to ask me why I'm in mourning; and I'm to answer with tears in my eyes, that it is just two months since papa died. No sir, no! He's got to say to me, as he did say, "Well, let's take off this little dress at once." And I, with my two months' mourning in my heart, went there behind that screen, and with these fingers tingling with shame . . .

THE MANAGER (*running his hands through his hair*): For Heaven's sake! What are you saying?

THE STEPDAUGHTER (*crying out excitedly*): The truth! The truth!

THE MANAGER: It may be. I don't deny it, and I can understand all your horror; but you must surely see that you can't have this kind of thing on the stage. It won't go.

THE STEPDAUGHTER: Not possible, eh? Very well! I'm much obliged to you — but I'm off.

THE MANAGER: Now be reasonable! Don't lose your temper!

THE STEPDAUGHTER: I won't stop here! I won't! I can see you fixed it all up with him in your office. All this talk about what is possible for the stage . . . I understand! He wants to get at his complicated "cerebral drama," to have his famous remorses and torments acted; but I want to act my part, *my part!*

THE MANAGER: (*annoyed, shaking his shoulders*): Ah! Just *your* part! But, if you will pardon me, there are other parts than yours: His (*indicating the Father*) and hers (*indicating the Mother*)! On the stage you can't have a character becoming too prominent and overshadowing all the others. The thing is to pack them all into a neat little framework and then act what is actable. I am aware of the fact that everyone has his own interior life which he wants very much to put forward. But the difficulty lies in this fact: to set out just so much as is necessary for the stage, taking the other characters into consideration, and at the same time hint at the unrevealed interior life of each. I am willing to admit, my dear young lady, that from your point of view it would be a fine idea if each character could tell the public all his troubles in a nice monologue or a regular one hour lecture. (*Good humoredly.*) You must restrain yourself, my dear, and in your own interest, too; because this fury of yours, this exaggerated disgust you show, may make a bad impression, you know. After you have confessed to me that there were others before him at Madame Pace's and more than once . . .

THE STEPDAUGHTER (*bowing her head, impressed*): It's true. But remember those others mean him for me all the same.

THE MANAGER (*not understanding*): What? The others? What do you mean?

THE STEPDAUGHTER: For one who has gone wrong, sir, he who was responsible for the first fault is responsible for all that follow. He is responsible for my faults, was, even before I was born. Look at him, and see if it isn't true!

THE MANAGER: Well, well! And does the weight of so much responsibility seem nothing to you? Give him a chance to act it, to get it over!

THE STEPDAUGHTER: How? How can he act all his "noble remorses," all his "moral torments," if you want to spare him the horror of being discovered one day—after he had asked her what he did ask her—in the arms of her, that already fallen woman, that child, sir, that child he used to watch come out of school? (*She is moved.*)

(*The Mother at this point is overcome with emotion and breaks out into a fit of crying. All are touched. A long pause.*)

THE STEPDAUGHTER (*as soon as the Mother becomes a little quieter, adds resolutely and gravely*): At present, we are unknown to the public. Tomorrow, you will act us as you wish, treating us in your own manner. But do you really want to see drama, do you want to see it flash out as it really did?

THE MANAGER: Of course! That's just what I do want, so I can use as much of it as is possible.

THE STEPDAUGHTER: Well then, ask that Mother there to leave us.

THE MOTHER (*changing her low plaint into a sharp cry*): No! No! Don't permit it, sir, don't permit it!

THE MANAGER: But it's only to try . . .

THE MOTHER: I can't bear it. I can't.

THE MANAGER: But since it has happened already . . . I don't understand!

THE MOTHER: It's taking place now. It happens all the time. My torment isn't a pretended one. I live and feel every minute of my torture. Those two children there—have you heard them speak? They can't speak anymore. They cling to me to keep my torment

actual and vivid for me. But for themselves, they do not exist, they aren't anymore. And she (*indicating the Stepdaughter*) has run away, she has left me, and is lost. If I now see her here before me, it is only to renew for me the tortures I have suffered for her too.

THE FATHER: The eternal moment! She (*indicating the Stepdaughter*) is here to catch me, fix me, and hold me eternally in the stocks for that one fleeting and shameful moment of my life. She can't give it up! And you, sir, cannot either fairly spare me . . .

THE MANAGER: I never said I didn't want to act it. It will form, as a matter of fact, the nucleus of the whole first act right up to her surprise. (*Indicates the Mother.*)

THE FATHER: Just so! This is my punishment: the passion in all of us that must culminate in her final cry.

THE STEPDAUGHTER: I can hear it still in my ears. It's driven me mad, that cry!—You can put me on as you like; it doesn't matter. Fully dressed, if you like—provided I have at least the arm bare; because, standing like this (*she goes close to the Father and leans her head on his breast*) with my head so, and my arms round his neck, I saw a vein pulsing in my arm here; and then, as if that live vein had awakened disgust in me, I closed my eyes like this, and let my head sink on his breast. (*Turning to the Mother.*) Cry out, mother! Cry out! (*Buries head in Father's breast, and with her shoulders raised as if to prevent her hearing the cry, adds in tones of intense emotion.*) Cry out as you did then!

THE MOTHER (*coming forward to separate them*): No! My daughter, my daughter! (*And after having pulled her away from him.*) You brute! you brute! She is my daughter! Don't you see she's my daughter?

THE MANAGER (*walking backward toward footlights*): Fine! fine! Damned good! And then, of course—curtain!

THE FATHER (*going toward him excitedly*): Yes, of course, because that's the way it really happened.

THE MANAGER (*convinced and pleased*): Oh, yes, no doubt about it. Curtain here, curtain!

(*At the reiterated cry of the Manager, the Machinist lets the curtain down, leaving the Manager and the Father in front of it before the footlights.*)

THE MANAGER: The darned idiot! I said "curtain" to show the act should end there, and he goes and lets it down in earnest. (*To the Father, while he pulls the curtain back to go on to the stage again.*) Yes, yes, it's all right. Effect certain! That's the right ending. I'll guarantee the first act at any rate.

ACT III

(*When the curtain goes up again, it is seen that the stage hands have shifted the bit of scenery used in the last part and have rigged up instead at the back of the stage a drop, with some trees, and one or two wings. A portion of a fountain basin is visible. The Mother is sitting on the right with the two children by her side. The Son is on the same side, but away from the others. He seems bored, angry, and full of shame. The Father and the Stepdaughter are also seated toward the right front. On the other side (left) are the Actors, much in the positions they occupied before the curtain was lowered. Only the Manager is standing up in the middle of the stage, with his hand closed over his mouth, in the act of meditating.)*

THE MANAGER (*shaking his shoulders after a brief pause*): Ah yes: the second act! Leave it to me, leave it all to me as we arranged, and you'll see! It'll go fine!

THE STEPDAUGHTER: Our entry into his house (*indicates Father*) in spite of him . . . (*Indicates the Son.*)

THE MANAGER (*out of patience*): Leave it to me, I tell you!

THE STEPDAUGHTER: Do let it be clear, at any rate, that it is in spite of my wishes.

THE MOTHER (*from her corner, shaking her head*): For all the good that's come of it . . .

THE STEPDAUGHTER (*turning toward her quickly*): It doesn't matter. The more harm done us, the more remorse for him.

THE MANAGER (*impatiently*): I understand! Good Heavens! I understand! I'm taking it into account.

THE MOTHER (*supplicatingly*): I beg you, sir, to let it appear quite plain that for conscience' sake I did try in every way . . .

THE STEPDAUGHTER (*interrupting indignantly and continuing for the Mother*): . . . to pacify me, to dissuade me from spiting him. (*To Manager.*) Do as she wants: satisfy her, because it is true! I enjoy it immensely. Anyhow, as you can see, the meeker she is, the more she tries to get at his heart, the more distant and aloof does he become.

THE MANAGER: Are we going to begin this second act or not?

THE STEPDAUGHTER: I'm not going to talk any more now. But I must tell you this: you can't have the whole action take place in the garden, as you suggest. It isn't possible!

THE MANAGER: Why not?

THE STEPDAUGHTER: Because he (*indicates the Son again*) is always shut up alone in his room. And then there's all the part of that poor dazed-looking boy there which takes place indoors.

THE MANAGER: Maybe! On the other hand, you will understand—we can't change scenes three or four times in one act.

LEADING MAN: They used to once.

THE MANAGER: Yes, when the public was up to the level of that child there.

LEADING LADY: It makes the illusion easier.

THE FATHER (*irritated*): The illusion! For Heaven's sake, don't say illusion. Please don't use that word, which is particularly painful for . . .

THE MANAGER (*astounded*): And why, if you please?

THE FATHER: It's painful, cruel, really cruel; and you ought to understand that.

THE MANAGER: But why? What ought we to say then? The illusion, I tell you, sir, which we've got to create for the audience. . . .

LEADING MAN: With our acting.

THE MANAGER: The illusion of a reality.

THE FATHER: I understand; but you, perhaps, do not understand us. Forgive me! You see . . . here for you and your actors, the thing is only—and rightly so . . . a kind of game. . . .

LEADING LADY (*interrupting indignantly*): A game! We're not children here, if you please! We are serious actors.

THE FATHER: I don't deny it. What I mean is the game, or play, of your art, which has to give, as the gentleman says, a perfect illusion of reality.

THE MANAGER: Precisely—!

THE FATHER: Now, if you consider the fact that we (*indicates himself and the other five Characters*), as we are, have no other reality outside of this illusion. . . .

THE MANAGER (*astonished, looking at his Actors, who are also amazed*): And what does that mean?

THE FATHER (*after watching them for a moment with a wan smile*): As I say, sir, that which is a game of art for you is our sole reality. (*Brief pause. He goes a step or two nearer the Manager and adds.*) But not only for us, you know, by the way. Just you think it over well. (*Looks him in the eyes.*) Can you tell me who you are?

THE MANAGER (*perplexed, half-smiling*): What? Who am I? I am myself.

THE FATHER: And if I were to tell you that that isn't true, because you and I . . . ?

THE MANAGER: I should say you were mad—! (*The Actors laugh.*)

THE FATHER: You're quite right to laugh: because we are all making believe here. (*To Manager.*) And you can therefore object that it's only for a joke that that gentleman there (*indicates the Leading Man*), who naturally is himself, has to be me, who am on the contrary myself—this thing you see here. You see I've caught you in a trap! (*The Actors laugh.*)

THE MANAGER (*annoyed*): But we've had all this over once before. Do you want to begin again?

THE FATHER: No, no! That wasn't my meaning! In fact, I should like to request you to abandon this game of art (*looking at the Leading Lady as if anticipating her*) which you are accustomed to play here with your actors, and to ask you seriously once again: who are you?

THE MANAGER (*astonished and irritated, turning to his Actors*): If this fellow here hasn't got a nerve! A man who calls himself a character comes and asks me who I am!

THE FATHER (*with dignity, but not offended*): A character, sir, may always ask a man who he is. Because a character has really a life of his own, marked with his especial characteristics; for which reason he is always "somebody." But a man—I'm not speaking of you now—may very well be "nobody."

THE MANAGER: Yes, but you are asking these questions of me, the boss, the manager! Do you understand?

THE FATHER: But only in order to know if you, as you really are now, see yourself as you once were with all the illusions that were yours then, with all the things both inside and outside of you as they seemed to you—as they were then indeed for you. Well, sir, if you think of all those illusions that mean nothing to you now, of all those things which don't even *seem* to you to exist anymore, while once they *were* for you, don't you feel that—I won't say these boards—but the very earth under your feet is sinking away from you when you reflect that in the same way this *you* as you feel it today—all this present reality of yours—is fated to seem a mere illusion to you tomorrow?

THE MANAGER (*without having understood much, but astonished by the specious argument*): Well, well! And where does all this take us anyway?

THE FATHER: Oh, nowhere! It's only to show you that if we (*indicating the Characters*) have no other reality beyond the illusion, you too must not count over-much on your reality as you feel it today, since, like that of yesterday, it may prove an illusion for you tomorrow.

THE MANAGER (*determining to make fun of him*): Ah, excellent! Then you'll be saying next that you, with this comedy of yours that you brought here to act, are truer and more real than I am.

THE FATHER (*with the greatest seriousness*): But of course, without doubt!

THE MANAGER: Ah, really?

THE FATHER: Why, I thought you'd understand that from the beginning.

THE MANAGER: More real than I?

THE FATHER: If your reality can change from one day to another. . . .

THE MANAGER: But everyone knows it can change. It is always changing, the same as anyone else's.

THE FATHER (*with a cry*): No, sir, not ours! Look here! That is the very difference! Our reality doesn't change: it can't change! It can't be other than what it is, because it is already fixed for ever. It's terrible. Ours is an immutable reality which should make you shudder when you approach us if you are really conscious of the fact that your reality is a mere transitory and fleeting illusion, taking this form today and that tomorrow, according to the conditions, according to your will, your sentiments, which in turn are controlled by an intellect that shows them to you today in one manner and tomorrow . . . who knows how? . . . Illusions of reality represented in this fatuous comedy of life that never ends, nor can ever end! Because if tomorrow it were to end . . . then why, all would be finished.

THE MANAGER: Oh for God's sake, will you *at least* finish with this philosophizing and let us try and shape this comedy which you yourself have brought me here? You argue and philosophize a bit too much, my dear sir. You know you seem to me almost,

almost . . . (*Stops and looks him over from head to foot.*) Ah, by the way, I think you introduced yourself to me as a—what shall . . . we say—a "character," created by an author who did not afterward care to make a drama of his own creations.

THE FATHER: It is the simple truth, sir.

THE MANAGER: Nonsense! Cut that out, please! None of us believes it, because it isn't a thing, as you must recognize yourself, which one can believe seriously. If you want to know, it seems to me you are trying to imitate the manner of a certain author whom I heartily detest—I warn you—although I have unfortunately bound myself to put on one of his works. As a matter of fact, I was just starting to rehearse it, when you arrived. (*Turning to the Actors.*) And this is what we've gained—out of the frying-pan into the fire!

THE FATHER: I don't know to what author you may be alluding, but believe me I feel what I think; and I seem to be philosophizing only for those who do not think what they feel, because they blind themselves with their own sentiment. I know that for many people this self-blinding seems much more "human"; but the contrary is really true. For man never reasons so much and becomes so introspective as when he suffers, since he is anxious to get at the cause of his sufferings, to learn who has produced them, and whether it is just or unjust that he should have to bear them. On the other hand, when he is happy, he takes his happiness as it comes and doesn't analyze it, just as if happiness were his right. The animals suffer without reasoning about their sufferings. But take the case of a man who suffers and begins to reason about it. Oh no! it can't be allowed! Let him suffer like an animal, and then—ah yes, he is "human"!

THE MANAGER: Look here! Look here! You're off again, philosophizing worse than ever.

THE FATHER: Because I suffer, sir! I'm not philosophizing: I'm crying aloud the reason of my sufferings.

THE MANAGER (*makes brusque movement as he is taken with a new idea*): I should like to know if anyone has ever heard of a character who gets right out of his part and perorates and speechifies as you do. Have you ever heard of a case? I haven't.

THE FATHER: You have never met such a case, sir, because authors, as a rule, hide the labor of their creations. When the characters are really alive before their author, the latter does nothing but follow them in their action, in other words, in the situations which they suggest to him; and he has to will them the way they will themselves—for there's trouble if he doesn't. When a character is born, he acquires at once such an independence, even of his own author, that he can be imagined by everybody even in many other situations where the author never dreamed of placing him; and so he acquires for himself a meaning which the author never thought of giving him.

THE MANAGER: Yes, yes, I know this.

THE FATHER: What is there then to marvel at in us? Imagine such a misfortune for characters as I have described to you: to be born of an author's fantasy, and be denied life by him; and then answer me if these characters left alive, and yet without life, weren't right in doing what they did do and are doing now, after they have attempted everything in their power to persuade him to give them their stage life. We've all tried him in turn, I, she (*indicating the Step-daughter*) and she (*indicating the Mother*).

THE STEPDAUGHTER: It's true. I too have sought to tempt him, many, many times, when he has been sitting at his writing table, feeling a bit melancholy, at the twi-light hour. He would sit in his armchair too lazy to switch on the light, and all the shadows that crept into his room were full of our presence coming to tempt him. (*As if she saw herself still there by the writing table, and was annoyed by the presence of the Actors.*) Oh, if you would only go away, go away and leave us alone—mother here with that son of hers—I with that child—that boy there always alone—and then I with him (*just hints at the Father*)—and then I alone, alone . . . in those shadows! (*Makes a sudden movement as if in the vision she has of herself illu-minating those shadows she wanted to seize hold of herself.*) Ah! my life! my life! Oh, what scenes we pro-posed to him—and I tempted him more than any of the others!

THE FATHER: Maybe. But perhaps it was your fault that he refused to give us life: because you were too insis-tent, too troublesome.

THE STEPDAUGHTER: Nonsense! Didn't he make me so himself? (*Goes close to the Manager to tell him as if in confidence.*) In my opinion he abandoned us in a fit of depression, of disgust for the ordinary theater as the public knows it and likes it.

THE SON: Exactly what it was, sir; exactly that!

THE FATHER: Not at all! Don't believe it for a minute. Listen to me! You'll be doing quite right to modify, as you suggest, the excesses both of this girl here, who wants to do too much, and of this young man, who won't do anything at all.

THE SON: No, nothing!

THE MANAGER: You too get over the mark occasionally, my dear sir, if I may say so.

THE FATHER: I? When? Where?

THE MANAGER: Always! Continuously! Then there's this insistence of yours in trying to make us believe you are a character. And then too, you must really argue and philosophize less, you know, much less.

THE FATHER: Well, if you want to take away from me the possibility of representing the torment of my spirit which never gives me peace, you will be sup-pressing me: that's all. Every true man, sir, who is a little above the level of the beasts and plants does not live for the sake of living, without knowing how to live; but he lives so as to give a meaning and a value of his own to life. For me this is *everything*. I cannot give up this, just to represent a mere fact as she (*indi-cating the Stepdaughter*) wants. It's all very well for

her, since her "vendetta" lies in the "fact." I'm not going to do it. It destroys my *raison d'être*.

THE MANAGER: Your *raison d'être*! Oh, we're going ahead fine! First she starts off, and then you jump in. At this rate, we'll never finish.

THE FATHER: Now, don't be offended! Have it your own way—provided, however, that within the limits of the parts you assign us each one's sacrifice isn't too great.

THE MANAGER: You've got to understand that you can't go on arguing at your own pleasure. Drama is action, sir, action and not confounded philosophy.

THE FATHER: All right. I'll do just as much arguing and philosophizing as everybody does when he is consid-ering his own torments.

THE MANAGER: If the drama permits! But for Heaven's sake, man, let's get along and come to the scene.

THE STEPDAUGHTER: It seems to me we've got too much action with our coming into his house. (*Indicating Father.*) You said, before, you couldn't change the scene every five minutes.

THE MANAGER: Of course not. What we've got to do is to combine and group up all the facts in one simulta-neous, close-knit action. We can't have it as you want, with your little brother wandering like a ghost from room to room, hiding behind doors and meditating a project which—what did you say it did to him?

THE STEPDAUGHTER: Consumes him, sir, wastes him away!

THE MANAGER: Well, it may be. And then at the same time, you want the little girl there to be playing in the garden . . . one in the house, and the other in the gar-den; isn't that it?

THE STEPDAUGHTER: Yes, in the sun, in the sun! That is my only pleasure: to see her happy and careless in the garden after the misery and squalor of the horrible room where we all four slept together. And I had to sleep with her—I, do you understand?—with my vile contaminated body next to hers; with her hold-ing me fast in her loving little arms. In the garden, whenever she spied me, she would run to take me by the hand. She didn't care for the big flowers, only the little ones; and she loved to show me them and pet me.

THE MANAGER: Well then, we'll have it in the garden. Everything shall happen in the garden; and we'll group the other scenes there. (*Calls a Stage Hand.*) Here, a backcloth with trees and something to do as a fountain basin. (*Turning round to look at the back of the stage.*) Ah, you've fixed it up. Good! (*To Step-daughter.*) This is just to give an idea, of course. The Boy, instead of hiding behind the doors, will wander about here in the garden, hiding behind the trees. But it's going to be rather difficult to find a child to do that scene with you where she shows you the flowers. (*Turning to the Boy.*) Come forward a little, will you please? Let's try it now! Come along! come along! (*Then seeing him come shyly forward, full of fear and looking lost.*) It's a nice business, this lad here. What's the matter with him? We'll have to give him a word or two to say. (*Goes close to him, puts a hand on his shoulders, and leads him behind one of the trees.*) Come on! come on! Let me see you a little! Hide here . . . yes, like that. Try and show your head just a little as if you were looking for someone. . . . (*Goes back to observe the effect, when the Boy at once goes through the action.*) Excellent! fine! (*Turning to Stepdaughter.*) Suppose the little girl there were to surprise him as he looks round, and run over to him, so we could give him a word or two to say?

THE STEPDAUGHTER: It's useless to hope he will speak, as long as that fellow there is here. . . . (*Indicates the Son.*) You must send him away first.

THE SON (*jumping up*): Delighted! Delighted! I don't ask for anything better. (*Begins to move away.*)

THE MANAGER (*at once stopping him*): No! No! Where are you going? Wait a bit!

(*The Mother gets up alarmed and terrified at the thought that he is really about to go away. Instinctively she lifts her arms to prevent him, without, however, leaving her seat.*)

THE SON (*to Manager, who stops him*): I've got nothing to do with this affair. Let me go, please! Let me go!

THE MANAGER: What do you mean by saying you've got nothing to do with this?

THE STEPDAUGHTER (*calmly, with irony*): Don't bother to stop him: he won't go away.

THE FATHER: He has to act the terrible scene in the garden with his mother.

THE SON (*suddenly resolute and with dignity*): I shall act nothing at all. I've said so from the very beginning. (*To the Manager.*) Let me go!

THE STEPDAUGHTER (*going over to the Manager*): Allow me? (*Puts down the Manager's arm which is restraining the Son.*) Well, go away then, if you want to! (*The Son looks at her with contempt and hatred. She laughs and says.*) You see, he can't, he can't go away! He is obliged to stay here, indissolubly bound to the chain. If I, who fly off when that happens which has to happen because I can't bear him — if I am still here and support that face and expression of his, you can well imagine that he is unable to move. He has to remain here, has to stop with that nice father of his, and that mother whose only son he is. (*Turning to the Mother.*) Come on, mother, come along! (*Turning to Manager to indicate her.*) You see, she was getting up to keep him back. (*To the Mother, beckoning her with her hand.*) Come on, come on! (*Then to Manager.*) You can imagine how little she wants to show these actors of yours what she really feels; but so eager is she to get near him that . . . There, you see? She is willing to act her part. (*And in fact, the Mother approaches him; and as soon as the Stepdaughter has finished speaking, opens her arms to signify that she consents.*)

THE SON (*suddenly*): No! no! If I can't go away, then I'll stop here; but I repeat: I act nothing!

THE FATHER (*to Manager excitedly*): You can force him, sir.

THE SON: Nobody can force me.

THE FATHER: I can.

THE STEPDAUGHTER: Wait a minute, wait . . . First of all, the baby has to go to the fountain. . . . (*Runs to take the Child and leads her to the fountain.*)

THE MANAGER: Yes, yes of course; that's it. Both at the same time.

(*The Second Lady Lead and the Juvenile Lead at this point separate themselves from the group of Actors. One watches the Mother attentively; the other moves about studying the movements and manner of the Son whom he will have to act.*)

THE SON (*to Manager*): What do you mean by both at the same time? It isn't right. There was no scene between me and her. (*Indicates the Mother.*) Ask her how it was!

THE MOTHER: Yes, it's true. I had come into his room. . . .

THE SON: Into my room, do you understand? Nothing to do with the garden.

THE MANAGER: It doesn't matter. Haven't I told you we've got to group the action?

THE SON (*observing the Juvenile Lead studying him*): What do you want?

JUVENILE LEAD: Nothing! I was just looking at you.

THE SON (*turning toward the Second Lady Lead*): Ah! she's at it too: to re-act her part! (*Indicating the Mother.*)

THE MANAGER: Exactly! And it seems to me that you ought to be grateful to them for their interest.

THE SON: Yes, but haven't you yet perceived that it isn't possible to live in front of a mirror which not only freezes us with the image of ourselves, but throws our likeness back at us with a horrible grimace?

THE FATHER: That is true, absolutely true. You must see that.

THE MANAGER (*to Second Lady Lead and Juvenile Lead*): He's right! Move away from them!

THE SON: Do as you like. I'm out of this!

THE MANAGER: Be quiet, you, will you? And let me hear your mother! (*To Mother.*) You were saying you had entered. . . .

THE MOTHER: Yes, into his room, because I couldn't stand it any longer. I went to empty my heart to him of all the anguish that tortures me. . . . But as soon as he saw me come in. . . .

THE SON: Nothing happened! There was no scene. I went away, that's all! I don't care for scenes!

THE MOTHER: It's true, true. That's how it was.

THE MANAGER: Well now, we've got to do this bit between you and him. It's indispensable.

THE MOTHER: I'm ready . . . when you are ready. If you could only find a chance for me to tell him what I feel here in my heart.

THE FATHER (*going to Son in a great rage*): You'll do this for your mother, for your mother, do you understand?

THE SON (*quite determined*): I do nothing!

THE FATHER (*taking hold of him and shaking him*): For God's sake, do as I tell you! Don't you hear your mother asking you for a favor? Haven't you even got the guts to be a son?

THE SON (*taking hold of the Father*): No! No! And for God's sake stop it, or else.... (*General agitation. The Mother, frightened, tries to separate them.*)

THE MOTHER (*pleading*): Please! please!

THE FATHER (*not leaving hold of the Son*): You've got to obey, do you hear?

THE SON (*almost crying from rage*): What does it mean, this madness you've got? (*They separate.*) Have you no decency, that you insist on showing everyone our shame? I won't do it! I won't! And I stand for the will of our author in this. He didn't want to put us on the stage, after all!

THE MANAGER: Man alive! You came here ...

THE SON (*indicating Father*): He did! I didn't!

THE MANAGER: Aren't you here now?

THE SON: It was his wish, and he dragged us along with him. He's told you not only the things that did happen, but also things that have never happened at all.

THE MANAGER: Well, tell me then what did happen. You went out of your room without saying a word?

THE SON: Without a word, so as to avoid a scene!

THE MANAGER: And then what did you do?

THE SON: Nothing ... walking in the garden.... (*Hesitates for a moment with expression of gloom.*)

THE MANAGER (*coming closer to him, interested by his extraordinary reserve*): Well, well ... walking in the garden....

THE SON (*exasperated*): Why on earth do you insist? It's horrible!

(*The Mother trembles, sobs, and looks toward the fountain.*)

THE MANAGER (*slowly observing the glance and turning toward the Son with increasing apprehension*): The baby?

THE SON: There in the fountain....

THE FATHER (*pointing with tender pity to the Mother*): She was following him at the moment....

THE MANAGER (*to the Son anxiously*): And then you....

THE SON: I ran over to her; I was jumping in to drag her out when I saw something that froze my blood ... the boy standing stock still, with eyes like a madman's, watching his little drowned sister, in the fountain! (*The Stepdaughter bends over the fountain to hide the Child. She sobs.*) Then.... (*A revolver shot rings out behind the trees where the Boy is hidden.*)

THE MOTHER (*with a cry of terror runs over in that direction together with several of the Actors amid general confusion*): My son! My son! (*Then amid the cries and exclamations one hears her voice.*) Help! Help!

THE MANAGER (*pushing the Actors aside while they lift up the Boy and carry him off*): Is he really wounded?

SOME ACTORS: He's dead! dead!

OTHER ACTORS: No, no, it's only make-believe, it's only pretense!

THE FATHER (*with a terrible cry*): Pretense? Reality, sir, reality!

THE MANAGER: Pretense? Reality? To hell with it all! Never in my life has such a thing happened to me. I've lost a whole day over these people, a whole day!

Federico García Lorca

Federico García Lorca (1898–1936) lived through some of the most troubling times of modern Spain. He was born in the countryside near Granada, and maintained a lifelong love of the Spanish village and country people. His father was a wealthy farmer, and his mother was a teacher who encouraged his early love of literature, art, and music. Lorca's talents were extraordinary. A fine pianist, he counted among his friends some of Spain's greatest musicians, including Manuel de Falla. Lorca painted throughout his life and maintained a close friendship with Salvador Dalí. His career in the university was not especially distinguished, but as a student he became famous for readings of his own poetry. He produced an early play, *The Butterfly's Evil Spell*, in 1920, the year before he published his first book of poems. His political leanings throughout his life were liberal and reformist, but his early years were spent living under a Spanish dictatorship. General elections ended Spain's monarchy and established the Second Spanish Republic in 1931, but Fascist leaders, notably Francisco Franco, began agitating for control. Standing for a free republic and prominent as a leftist, Lorca was killed suddenly and without explanation by Franco's forces in 1936, just two days before the start of the Spanish Civil War.

Lorca's dramatic work had developed steadily. His second play, *The Girl Who Waters the Sweet Basil Flower and the Inquisitive Prince* (1923), was a puppet show. Lorca, who especially enjoyed this form of drama, had bought his own puppet theater when he was fifteen. He designed the sets, and Manuel de Falla provided the music. Unfortunately, the manuscript for this play has been lost. Text for another puppet play of the same period, *The Billy-Club Puppets*, does exist, as do copies of some later dramatic sketches: *Buster Keaton's Promenade* (1926), which takes off on Buster Keaton's film character, and *The Public* (1933), one of several experimental surrealist plays. His first real success was *Mariana Pineda* (1927), produced in Granada. After suffering a personal crisis, perhaps connected to his growing awareness of his homosexuality, Lorca spent a year in New York, from which experience he wrote *The Poet in New York*, published—much later—in 1940.

Lorca returned to Spain and produced a number of plays in the early 1930s, such as *The Shoemaker's Prodigious Wife* (1930), *The Love of Don Perlimplín with Belisa in the Garden* (1933), and *Doña Rosita, the Spinster* (1935), the last of his plays to be produced during his lifetime. His three most important plays are generally referred to as folk tragedies: *Blood Wedding* (1933) and *Yerma* (1934) were produced in Madrid, and *The House of Bernarda Alba* was produced in Buenos Aires in 1945. These three plays were influenced by a great

Spanish actress and producer, Margarita Xirgu, for whom the title role of Yerma was created.

Lorca's reputation flourished after the end of World War II, but because Spain's Fascist government continued until Franco's death in 1975, Lorca's work could not be produced in his native country until the 1980s. His gift was in combining poetry, music, original set designs, and a sense of the language of the country people who inspired his work. He had a feel for the pagan forces that informed the country people and aimed to show their creative power in everyday life. He celebrated instinctive, primitive religious feeling, the joy of living, the sexual energy of the universe, and the fullness of life.

THE HOUSE OF BERNARDA ALBA

Lorca diverged from his earlier poetic style when he created this play, subtitled "a drama about women in the villages of Spain." He is on record as having said, "Not a drop of poetry! Reality! Realism!" Supposed to be as realistic and detailed as a "photographic document," the play pointed to some of the harsher realities of life for women in rural Spain. Indeed, only women appear in the play. Pepe el Romano, a young handsome man, betrothed to Angustias, Bernarda's eldest daughter (apparently for her money), is mentioned often but never appears. In the beginning of the third act, a stallion making loud sounds in his stall represents the symbolic force of sex in nature. Bernarda Alba demands that the stallion be freed before it brings the walls down, but at the same time she determines to keep her daughters hidden away in her house and under her thumb. The focus of the play is on Bernarda Alba's determination to preserve her dignity in her village. She wants to make sure that no one talks about her family disparagingly; she must keep up appearances even at the risk of smothering the sexual energies of her five daughters.

When the play opens, Bernarda's second husband has just died, and she declares that the household shall mourn for eight years. Her daughters would be shut in and not see a man for any of that time. However, since Angustias has her own money from her father, Bernarda's first husband, she is courted by Pepe el Romano. At the same time Pepe secretly expresses his true affection to Angustias's sister Adela, who is much closer to him in age and who would be a more suitable wife. Bernarda, however, is adamant about the period of mourning and eventually chases Pepe away with a shotgun after discovering that he has given in to his desires.

This is a play about the tyranny of Bernarda over her daughters. It portrays her desire to be respected in the community at all costs, even the cost of living a lie. It is also a play about "Women without men." Some critics have seen in the prisonlike atmosphere (note the constant reference to bars) a suggestion of the religious convent and the sexual repression it implies. The Cistercians, known as Bernardas, were an order of nuns familiar to Lorca. But Lorca is exploring a number of powerful forces in life: the power of the family and tradition, the power of religion and its strictures of moral behavior, the power of economic necessity and the way it distorts lives, and the power of a political force that maintains itself through absolute authority. Most of these forces were evident in the Spain Lorca knew throughout his life. From 1932 much of his time was spent traveling with, and writing for, a government-sponsored touring company, La Barraca, that put on classic Spanish plays in remote towns around the nation. He had plenty of opportunity to observe everyday life in rural Spain. This play reveals some of its nature.

The House of Bernarda Alba in Performance

The first production of the play, in 1945, was in Buenos Aires, which Lorca visited shortly before he died, impressing those he met with his genius. South America has long found his work important; Lorca's play was produced in various South American countries long before it appeared in Spain. Eric Bentley staged a minimalist production of the play at the Abbey Theatre in Dublin in 1950, with Peggy Hayes as Bernarda and Angela Newmann as Adela. He describes this production in his *In Search of Theater* (1953), saying, "Ireland and Spain are two of the remaining vestiges of Catholic-peasant civilization. Lorca's play springs from this civilization, gives it amazingly full expression, and is a bitter rejection of it."

The play was given a limited production in Paris in the Studio des Champs-Élysées in 1946, employing a fine set with stark white walls and black wrought-iron bars across the windows. A New York production at the ANTA Playhouse lasted for seventeen performances in January 1951. Bentley had earlier speculated that the play would be very difficult to communicate to 1950s London or New York audiences, and he seems to have been correct. It was produced in New York again by Teatro Hispano, directed by Max Ferra, in early 1972. Bernarda was played by the Cuban actress Ofelia González. Numerous productions in Europe followed; one of the most powerful was in 1986 at the Lyric Theatre in Hammersmith, London, directed by Nuria Espert. The sets and the lighting served to intensify the sense of overwhelming heat from the Andalusian sun. Paul Preston, in his review in the *Times Literary Supplement*, said, "Glenda Jackson's Bernarda is as stiff-backed as the most humorless prison governor or mother superior, dominating her brood with snarling sarcasm and fulminating looks." Joan Plowright played a powerful Poncia, but Patricia Hayes, as Bernarda's mother, was singled out for a stunning performance: "wearing muslin rags over white flesh like a feverish and ecstatic moth" (Michael Ratcliffe in the *Observer*). The play moved into the West End (London's Broadway) to the Globe Theatre in 1987 with the same cast. Among recent productions was the 1993 production in Northern Ireland at the adventurous women's company, the Charabanc Theatre Company. Lynne Parker adapted and directed the play to exceptional reviews, and the production toured twenty towns throughout Ireland and Northern Ireland before settling in at the Project Arts Centre in Dublin. The reviews of the production celebrated its excellence and explored the women's issues in the drama. The Orange Tree Theatre in Richmond, which is billed as "London's only theatre in the round," staged a very well reviewed production in March–April 2003. Auriol Smith directed a translation that she and Rebecca Morahan had done. Lynn Farley played Bernarda Alba. The 2005 production of *The House of Bernarda Alba* at the National Theatre in London was described by Philip Fisher in the *British Theatre Guide:* "This new version by Sir David Hare is all shimmering sensuality in the massive hothouse of a room created by designer Vicki Mortimer and lighting designer Paule Constable." In June 2007, the National Asian American Theater Company produced a very well-received adaptation that was praised for capturing the intensity of Lorca's original. Clearly, this play resonates in modern times.

Federico García Lorca (1898–1936)

THE HOUSE OF BERNARDA ALBA   *1936*
A DRAMA ABOUT WOMEN IN THE VILLAGES OF SPAIN
TRANSLATED BY JAMES GRAHAM-LUJÁN AND RICHARD L. O'CONNELL

Characters

BERNARDA (*age 60*)
MARÍA JOSEFA, *Bernarda's Mother* (*age 80*)
ANGUSTIAS, *Bernarda's Daughter* (*age 39*)
MAGDALENA, *Bernarda's Daughter* (*age 30*)
AMELIA, *Bernarda's Daughter* (*age 27*)
MARTIRIO, *Bernarda's Daughter* (*age 24*)
ADELA, *Bernarda's Daughter* (*age 20*)
A MAID (*age 50*)
LA PONCIA, *A Maid* (*age 60*)
PRUDENCIA (*age 50*)
WOMEN IN MOURNING

The writer states that these Three Acts are intended as a photographic document.

ACT 1

(*A very white room in Bernarda Alba's house. The walls are white. There are arched doorways with jute curtains tied back with tassels and ruffles. Wicker chairs. On the walls, pictures of unlikely landscapes full of nymphs or legendary kings.*

It is summer. A great brooding silence fills the stage. It is empty when the curtain rises. Bells can be heard tolling outside.)

FIRST SERVANT (*entering*): The tolling of those bells hits me right between the eyes.

PONCIA (*she enters, eating bread and sausage*): More than two hours of mumbo jumbo. Priests are here from all the towns. The church looks beautiful. At the first responsory for the dead, Magdalena fainted.

FIRST SERVANT: She's the one who's left most alone.

PONCIA: She's the only one who loved her father. Ay! Thank God we're alone for a little. I came over to eat.

FIRST SERVANT: If Bernarda sees you . . . !

PONCIA: She's not eating today so she'd just as soon we'd all die of hunger! Domineering old tyrant! But she'll be fooled! I opened the sausage crock.

FIRST SERVANT (*with an anxious sadness*): Couldn't you give me some for my little girl, Poncia?

PONCIA: Go ahead! And take a fistful of peas too. She won't know the difference today.

VOICE (*within*): Bernarda!

PONCIA: There's the grandmother! Isn't she locked up tight?

FIRST SERVANT: Two turns of the key.

PONCIA: You'd better put the cross-bar up too. She's got the fingers of a lock-picker!

VOICE (*within*): Bernarda!

PONCIA (*shouting*): She's coming! (*to the servant*) Clean everything up good. If Bernarda doesn't find things shining, she'll pull out the few hairs I have left.

SERVANT: What a woman!

PONCIA: Tyrant over everyone around her. She's perfectly capable of sitting on your heart and watching you die for a whole year without turning off that cold little smile she wears on her wicked face. Scrub, scrub those dishes!

SERVANT: I've got blood on my hands from so much polishing of everything.

PONCIA: She's the cleanest, she's the decentest, she's the highest everything! A good rest her poor husband's earned!

(*The bells stop.*)

SERVANT: Did all the relatives come?

PONCIA: Just hers. His people hate her. They came to see him dead and make the sign of the cross over him; that's all.

SERVANT: Are there enough chairs?

PONCIA: More than enough. Let them sit on the floor. When Bernarda's father died people stopped coming under this roof. She doesn't want them to see her in her "domain." Curse her!

SERVANT: She's been good to you.

PONCIA: Thirty years washing her sheets. Thirty years eating her leftovers. Nights of watching when she had a cough. Whole days peeking through a crack in the shutters to spy on the neighbors and carry her the tale. Life without secrets one from the other. But in spite of that—curse her! May the "pain of the piercing nail" strike her in the eyes.

SERVANT: Poncia!

PONCIA: But I'm a good watchdog! I bark when I'm told and bite beggars' heels when she sics me on 'em. My sons work in her fields—both of them already married, but one of these days I'll have enough.

SERVANT: And then . . . ?

PONCIA: Then I'll lock myself up in a room with her and spit in her face—a whole year. "Bernarda, here's for this, that and the other!" Till I leave her—just like a lizard the boys have squashed. For that's what she is—she and her whole family! Not that I envy her her life. Five girls are left her, five ugly daughters—not counting Angustias the eldest, by her first husband, who has money—the rest of them, plenty of eyelets to embroider, plenty of linen petticoats, but bread and grapes when it comes to inheritance.

SERVANT: Well, *I'd* like to have what they've got!

PONCIA: All we have is our hands and a hole in God's earth.

SERVANT: And that's the only earth they'll ever leave to us—to us who have nothing!

PONCIA (*at the cupboard*): This glass has some specks.

SERVANT: Neither soap nor rag will take them off.

(*The bells toll.*)

PONCIA: The last prayer! I'm going over and listen. I certainly like the way our priest sings. In the Pater Noster his voice went up, and up—like a pitcher filling with water little by little. Of course, at the end his voice cracked, but it's glorious to hear it. No, there never was anybody like the old Sacristan—Tronchapinos. At my mother's Mass, may she rest in peace, he sang. The walls shook—and when he said "Amen," it was as if a wolf had come into the church.

(*Imitating him.*)

A-a-a-a-men!

(*She starts coughing.*)

SERVANT: Watch out—you'll strain your windpipe!

PONCIA: I'd rather strain something else!

(*Goes out laughing.*)
(*The servant scrubs. The bells toll.*)

SERVANT (*imitating the bells*): Dong, dong, dong. Dong, dong, dong. May God forgive him!

BEGGAR WOMAN (*at the door, with a little girl*): Bléssed be God!

SERVANT: Dong, dong, dong. I hope he waits many years for us! Dong, dong, dong.

BEGGAR (*loudly, a little annoyed*): Bléssed be God!

SERVANT (*annoyed*): Forever and ever!

BEGGAR: I came for the scraps.

(*The bells stop tolling.*)

SERVANT: You can go right out the way you came in. Today's scraps are for me.

BEGGAR: But you have somebody to take care of you—and my little girl and I are all alone!

SERVANT: Dogs are alone too, and they live.

BEGGAR: They always give them to me.

SERVANT: Get out of here! Who let you in anyway? You've already tracked up the place.

(*The beggar woman and little girl leave. The servant goes on scrubbing.*)

Floors finished with oil, cupboards, pedestals, iron beds—but us servants, we can suffer in silence—and live in mud huts with a plate and a spoon. I hope someday not a one will be left to tell it.

(*The bells sound again.*)

Yes, yes—ring away. Let them pelt you in a coffin with gold inlay and brocade to carry it on—you're no less dead than I'll be, so take what's coming to you, Antonio María Benavides—stiff in your broadcloth suit and your high boots—take what's coming to you! You'll never again lift my skirts behind the corral door!

(*From the rear door, two by two, women in mourning with large shawls and black skirts and fans, begin to enter. They come in slowly until the stage is full.*)

SERVANT (*breaking into a wail*): Oh, Antonio María Benavides, now you'll never see these walls, nor break bread in this house again! I'm the one who loved you most of all your servants.

(*Pulling her hair.*)

Must I love on after you've gone? Must I go on living?

(*The two hundred women finish coming in, and Bernarda and her five daughters enter. Bernarda leans on a cane.*)

BERNARDA (*to the servant*): Silence!

SERVANT (*weeping*): Bernarda!

BERNARDA: Less shrieking and more work. You should have had all this cleaner for the wake. Get out. This isn't your place.

(*The servant goes off crying.*)

The poor are like animals—they seem to be made of different stuff.

FIRST WOMAN: The poor feel their sorrows too.

BERNARDA: But they forget them in front of a plateful of peas.

FIRST GIRL (*timidly*): Eating is necessary for living.

BERNARDA: At your age one doesn't talk in front of older people.

WOMAN: Be quiet, child.

BERNARDA: I've never taken lessons from anyone. Sit down.

(*They sit down. Pause. Loudly.*)

Magdalena, don't cry. If you want to cry, get under your bed. Do you hear me?

SECOND WOMAN (*to Bernarda*): Have you started to work the fields?

BERNARDA: Yesterday.

THIRD WOMAN: The sun comes down like lead.

FIRST WOMAN: I haven't known heat like this for years.

(*Pause. They all fan themselves.*)

BERNARDA: Is the lemonade ready?

PONCIA: Yes, Bernarda.

(*She brings in a large tray full of little white jars which she distributes.*)

BERNARDA: Give the men some.

PONCIA: They're already drinking in the patio.

BERNARDA: Let them get out the way they came in. I don't want them walking through here.

A GIRL (*to Angustias*): Pepe el Romano was with the men during the service.

ANGUSTIAS: There he was.

BERNARDA: His mother was there. She saw his mother. Neither she nor I saw Pepe . . .

GIRL: I thought . . .

BERNARDA: The one who *was* there was Darajalí, the widower. Very close to your Aunt. We all of us saw him.

SECOND WOMAN (*aside, in a low voice*): Wicked, worse than wicked woman!

THIRD WOMAN: A tongue like a knife!

BERNARDA: Women in church shouldn't look at any man but the priest—and him only because he wears skirts. To turn your head is to be looking for the warmth of corduroy.

FIRST WOMAN: Sanctimonious old snake!

PONCIA (*between her teeth*): Itching for a man's warmth.

BERNARDA (*beating with her cane on the floor*): Blesséd be God!

ALL (*crossing themselves*): Forever blesséd and praised.

BERNARDA: Rest in peace with holy company at your head.

ALL: Rest in peace!

BERNARDA: With the Angel Saint Michael, and his sword of justice.

ALL: Rest in peace!

BERNARDA: With the key that opens, and the hand that locks.

ALL: Rest in peace!

BERNARDA: With the most blesséd, and the little lights of the field.

ALL: Rest in peace!

BERNARDA: With our holy charity, and all souls on land and sea.

ALL: Rest in peace!

BERNARDA: Grant rest to your servant, Antonio María Benavides, and give him the crown of your blesséd glory.

ALL: Amen.

BERNARDA (*she rises and chants*): *Requiem aeternam donat eis domine.*

ALL (*standing and chanting in the Gregorian fashion*): *Et lux perpetua luce ab eis.*°

(*They cross themselves.*)

FIRST WOMAN: May you have health to pray for his soul. (*They start filing out.*)

THIRD WOMAN: You won't lack loaves of hot bread.

SECOND WOMAN: Nor a roof for your daughters.

(*They are all filing in front of Bernarda and going out. Angustias leaves by the door to the patio.*)

FOURTH WOMAN: May you go on enjoying your wedding wheat.

PONCIA (*she enters, carrying a money bag*): From the men—this bag of money for Masses.

BERNARDA: Thank them—and let them have a glass of brandy.

GIRL (*to Magdalena*): Magdalena . . .

Requiem aeternam . . . ab eis: Eternal rest grant to him, O Lord And let perpetual light shine on him.

BERNARDA (*to Magdalena, who is starting to cry*): Sh-h-h-h!

(*She beats with her cane on the floor.*)
(*All the women have gone out.*)

BERNARDA (*to the women who have just left*): Go back to your houses and criticize everything you've seen! I hope it'll be many years before you pass under the archway of my door again.

PONCIA: You've nothing to complain about. The whole town came.

BERNARDA: Yes, to fill my house with the sweat from their wraps and the poison of their tongues.

AMELIA: Mother, don't talk like that.

BERNARDA: What other way is there to talk about this cursèd village with no river — this village full of wells where you drink water always fearful it's been poisoned?

PONCIA: Look what they've done to the floor!

BERNARDA: As though a herd of goats had passed through.

(*Poncia cleans the floor.*)

Adela, give me a fan.

ADELA: Take this one.

(*She gives her a round fan with green and red flowers.*)

BERNARDA (*throwing the fan on the floor*): Is that the fan to give to a widow? Give me a black one and learn to respect your father's memory.

MARTIRIO: Take mine.

BERNARDA: And you?

MARTIRIO: I'm not hot.

BERNARDA: Well, look for another, because you'll need it. For the eight years of mourning, not a breath of air will get in this house from the street. We'll act as if we'd sealed up doors and windows with bricks. That's what happened in my father's house — and in my grandfather's house. Meantime, you can all start embroidering your hope-chest linens. I have twenty bolts of linen in the chest from which to cut sheets and coverlets. Magdalena can embroider them.

MAGDALENA: It's all the same to me.

ADELA (*sourly*): If you don't want to embroider them — they can go without. That way yours will look better.

MAGDALENA: Neither mine nor yours. I know I'm not going to marry. I'd rather carry sacks to the mill. Anything except sit here day after day in this dark room.

BERNARDA: That's what a woman is for.

MAGDALENA: Cursed be all women.

BERNARDA: In this house you'll do what I order. You can't run with the story to your father any more. Needle and thread for women. Whiplash and mules for men. That's the way it has to be for people who have certain obligations.

(*Adela goes out.*)

VOICE: Bernarda! Let me out!

BERNARDA (*calling*): Let her out now!

(*The first servant enters.*)

FIRST SERVANT: I had a hard time holding her. In spite of her eighty years, your mother's strong as an oak.

BERNARDA: It runs in the family. My grandfather was the same way.

SERVANT: Several times during the wake I had to cover her mouth with an empty sack because she wanted to shout out to you to give her dishwater to drink at least, and some dogmeat, which is what she says you feed her.

MARTIRIO: She's mean!

BERNARDA (*to servant*): Let her get some fresh air in the patio.

SERVANT: She took her rings and the amethyst earrings out of the box, put them on, and told me she wants to get married.

(*The daughters laugh.*)

BERNARDA: Go with her and be careful she doesn't get near the well.

SERVANT: You don't need to be afraid she'll jump in.

BERNARDA: It's not that — but the neighbors can see her there from their windows.

(*The servant leaves.*)

MARTIRIO: We'll go change our clothes.

BERNARDA: Yes, but don't take the kerchiefs from your heads.

(*Adela enters.*)

And Angustias?

ADELA (*meaningfully*): I saw her looking out through the cracks of the back door. The men had just gone.

BERNARDA: And you, what were *you* doing at the door?

ADELA: I went there to see if the hens had laid.

BERNARDA: But the men had already gone!

ADELA (*meaningfully*): A group of them were still standing outside.

BERNARDA (*furiously*): Angustias! Angustias!

ANGUSTIAS (*entering*): Did you want something?

BERNARDA: For what — and at whom — were you looking?

ANGUSTIAS: Nobody.

BERNARDA: Is it decent for a woman of your class to be running after a man the day of her father's funeral? Answer me! Whom were you looking at?

(*Pause.*)

ANGUSTIAS: I . . .

BERNARDA: Yes, you!

ANGUSTIAS: Nobody.

BERNARDA: Soft! Honeytongue!

(*She strikes her.*)

PONCIA (*running to her*): Bernarda, calm down!

(*She holds her. Angustias weeps.*)

BERNARDA: Get out of here, all of you!

(*They all go out.*)

PONCIA: She did it not realizing what she was doing— although it's bad, of course. It really disgusted me to see her sneak along to the patio. Then she stood at the window listening to the men's talk, which, as usual, was not the sort one should listen to.

BERNARDA: That's what they come to funerals for. (*With curiosity.*) What were they talking about?

PONCIA: They were talking about Paca la Roseta. Last night they tied her husband up in a stall, stuck her on a horse behind the saddle, and carried her away to the depths of the olive grove.

BERNARDA: And what did she do?

PONCIA: She? She was just as happy—they say her breasts were exposed and Maximiliano held on to her as if he were playing a guitar. Terrible!

BERNARDA: And what happened?

PONCIA: What had to happen. They came back almost at daybreak. Paca la Roseta with her hair loose and a wreath of flowers on her head.

BERNARDA: She's the only bad woman we have in the village.

PONCIA: Because she's not from here. She's from far away. And those who went with her are the sons of outsiders too. The men from here aren't up to a thing like that.

BERNARDA: No, but they like to see it, and talk about it, and suck their fingers over it.

PONCIA: They were saying a lot more things.

BERNARDA (*looking from side to side with a certain fear*): What things?

PONCIA: I'm ashamed to talk about them.

BERNARDA: And my daughter heard them?

PONCIA: Of course!

BERNARDA: That one takes after her Aunts: white and mealy-mouthed and casting sheep's eyes at any little barber's compliment. Oh, what one has to go through and put up with so people will be decent and not too wild!

PONCIA: It's just that your daughters are of an age when they ought to have husbands. Mighty little trouble they give you. Angustias must be much more than thirty now.

BERNARDA: Exactly thirty-nine.

PONCIA: Imagine. And she's never had a beau . . .

BERNARDA (*furiously*): None of them has ever had a beau and they've never needed one! They get along very well.

PONCIA: I didn't mean to offend you.

BERNARDA: For a hundred miles around there's no one good enough to come near them. The men in this town are not of their class. Do you want me to turn them over to the first shepherd?

PONCIA: You should have moved to another town.

BERNARDA: That's it. To sell them!

PONCIA: No, Bernarda, to change. . . . Of course, any place else, they'd be the poor ones.

BERNARDA: Hold your tormenting tongue!

PONCIA: One can't even talk to you. Do we, or do we not share secrets?

BERNARDA: We do not. You're a servant and I pay you. Nothing more.

PONCIA: But . . .

FIRST SERVANT (*entering*): Don Arturo's here. He's come to see about dividing the inheritance.

BERNARDA: Let's go. (*to the servant*) You start white-washing the patio. (*to La Poncia*) And you start putting all the dead man's clothes away in the chest.

PONCIA: We could give away some of the things.

BERNARDA: Nothing—not a button even! Not even the cloth we covered his face with.

(*She goes out slowly, leaning on her cane. At the door she turns to look at the two servants. They go out. She leaves.*)

(*Amelia and Martirio enter.*)

AMELIA: Did you take the medicine?

MARTIRIO: For all the good it'll do me.

AMELIA: But you took it?

MARTIRIO: I do things without any faith, but like clock-work.

AMELIA: Since the new doctor came you look livelier.

MARTIRIO: I feel the same.

AMELIA: Did you notice? Adelaida wasn't at the funeral.

MARTIRIO: I know. Her sweetheart doesn't let her go out even to the front doorstep. Before, she was gay. Now, not even powder on her face.

AMELIA: These days a girl doesn't know whether to have a beau or not.

MARTIRIO: It's all the same.

AMELIA: The whole trouble is all these wagging tongues that won't let us live. Adelaida has probably had a bad time.

MARTIRIO: She's afraid of our mother. Mother is the only one who knows the story of Adelaida's father and where he got his lands. Everytime she comes here, Mother twists the knife in the wound. Her father killed his first wife's husband in Cuba so he could marry her himself. Then he left her there and went off with another woman who already had one daughter, and then he took up with this other girl, Adelaida's mother, and married her after his second wife died insane.

AMELIA: But why isn't a man like that put in jail?

MARTIRIO: Because men help each other cover up things like that and no one's able to tell on them.

AMELIA: But Adelaida's not to blame for any of that.

MARTIRIO: No. But history repeats itself. I can see that everything is a terrible repetition. And she'll have the same fate as her mother and grandmother—both of them wife to the man who fathered her.

AMELIA: What an awful thing!

MARTIRIO: It's better never to look at a man. I've been afraid of them since I was a little girl. I'd see them in the yard, yoking the oxen and lifting grain sacks, shouting and stamping, and I was always afraid to grow up for fear one of them would suddenly take me in his arms. God has made me weak and ugly and has definitely put such things away from me.

AMELIA: Don't say that! Enrique Humanas was after you and he liked you.

MARTIRIO: That was just people's ideas! One time I stood in my nightgown at the window until daybreak because he let me know through his shepherd's little girl that he was going to come, and he didn't. It was all just talk. Then he married someone else who had more money than I.

AMELIA: And ugly as the devil.

MARTIRIO: What do men care about ugliness? All they care about is lands, yokes of oxen, and a submissive bitch who'll feed them.

AMELIA: Ay!

(*Magdalena enters.*)

MAGDALENA: What are you doing?

MARTIRIO: Just here.

AMELIA: And you?

MAGDALENA: I've been going through all the rooms. Just to walk a little, and look at Grandmother's needlepoint pictures — the little woolen dog, and the black man wrestling with the lion — which we liked so much when we were children. Those were happier times. A wedding lasted ten days and evil tongues weren't in style. Today people are more refined. Brides wear white veils, just as in the cities, and we drink bottled wine, but we rot inside because of what people might say.

MARTIRIO: Lord knows what went on then!

AMELIA (*to Magdalena*): One of your shoelaces has come untied.

MAGDALENA: What of it?

AMELIA: You'll step on it and fall.

MAGDALENA: One less!

MARTIRIO: And Adela?

MAGDALENA: Ah! She put on the green dress she made to wear for her birthday, went out to the yard, and began shouting: "Chickens! Chickens, look at me!" I had to laugh.

AMELIA: If Mother had only seen her!

MAGDALENA: Poor little thing! She's the youngest one of us and still has her illusions. I'd give something to see her happy.

(*Pause. Angustias crosses the stage, carrying some towels.*)

ANGUSTIAS: What time is it?

MAGDALENA: It must be twelve.

ANGUSTIAS: So late?

AMELIA: It's about to strike.

(*Angustias goes out.*)

MAGDALENA (*meaningfully*): Do you know what?

(*Pointing after Angustias.*)

AMELIA: No.

MAGDALENA: Come on!

MARTIRIO: I don't know what you're talking about!

MAGDALENA: Both of you know it better than I do, always with your heads together, like two little sheep, but not letting anybody else in on it. I mean about Pepe el Romano!

MARTIRIO: Ah!

MAGDALENA (*mocking her*): Ah! The whole town's talking about it. Pepe el Romano is coming to marry Angustias. Last night he was walking around the house and I think he's going to send a declaration soon.

MARTIRIO: I'm glad. He's a good man.

AMELIA: Me too. Angustias is well off.

MAGDALENA: Neither one of you is glad.

MARTIRIO: Magdalena! What do you mean?

MAGDALENA: If he were coming because of Angustias' looks, for Angustias as a woman, I'd be glad too, but he's coming for her money. Even though Angustias is our sister, we're her family here and we know she's old and sickly, and always has been the least attractive one of us! Because if she looked like a dressed-up stick at twenty, what can she look like now, now that she's forty?

MARTIRIO: Don't talk like that. Luck comes to the one who least expects it.

AMELIA: But Magdalena's right after all! Angustias has all her father's money; she's the only rich one in the house and that's why, now that Father's dead and the money will be divided, they're coming for her.

MAGDALENA: Pepe el Romano is twenty-five years old and the best looking man around here. The natural thing would be for him to be after you, Amelia, or our Adela, who's twenty — not looking for the least likely one in this house, a woman who, like her father, talks through her nose.

MARTIRIO: Maybe he likes that!

MAGDALENA: I've never been able to bear your hypocrisy.

MARTIRIO: Heavens!

(*Adela enters.*)

MAGDALENA: Did the chickens see you?

ADELA: What did you want me to do?

AMELIA: If Mother sees you, she'll drag you by your hair!

ADELA: I had a lot of illusions about this dress. I'd planned to put it on the day we were going to eat watermelons at the well. There wouldn't have been another like it.

MARTIRIO: It's a lovely dress.

ADELA: And one that looks very good on me. It's the best thing Magdalena's ever cut.

MAGDALENA: And the chickens, what did they say to you?

ADELA: They presented me with a few fleas that riddled my legs.

(*They laugh.*)

MARTIRIO: What you can do is dye it black.

MAGDALENA: The best thing you can do is give it to Angustias for her wedding with Pepe el Romano.

ADELA (*with hidden emotion*): But Pepe el Romano . . .

AMELIA: Haven't you heard about it?

ADELA: No.

MAGDALENA: Well, now you know!

ADELA: But it can't be!

MAGDALENA: Money can do anything.

ADELA: Is that why she went out after the funeral and stood looking through the door?

(*Pause.*)

And that man would . . .

MAGDALENA: Would do anything.

(*Pause.*)

MARTIRIO: What are you thinking, Adela?

ADELA: I'm thinking that this mourning has caught me at the worst moment of my life for me to bear it.

MAGDALENA: You'll get used to it.

ADELA (*bursting out, crying with rage*): I will not get used to it! I can't be locked up. I don't want my skin to look like yours. I don't want my skin's whiteness lost in these rooms. Tomorrow I'm going to put on my green dress and go walking in the streets. I want to go out!

(*The first servant enters.*)

MAGDALENA (*in a tone of authority*): Adela!

SERVANT: The poor thing! How she misses her father. . . .

(*She goes out.*)

MARTIRIO: Hush!

AMELIA: What happens to one will happen to all of us.

(*Adela grows calm.*)

MAGDALENA: The servant almost heard you.

SERVANT (*entering*): Pepe el Romano is coming along at the end of the street.

(*Amelia, Martirio and Magdalena run hurriedly.*)

MAGDALENA: Let's go see him!

(*They leave rapidly.*)

SERVANT (*to Adela*): Aren't you going?

ADELA: It's nothing to me.

SERVANT: Since he has to turn the corner, you'll see him better from the window of your room.

(*The servant goes out. Adela is left on the stage, standing doubtfully; after a moment, she also leaves rapidly, going toward her room. Bernarda and La Poncia come in.*)

BERNARDA: Damned portions and shares.

PONCIA: What a lot of money is left to Angustias!

BERNARDA: Yes.

PONCIA: And for the others, considerably less.

BERNARDA: You've told me that three times now, when you know I don't want it mentioned! Considerably less; a lot less! Don't remind me any more.

(*Angustias comes in, her face heavily made up.*)

Angustias!

ANGUSTIAS: Mother.

BERNARDA: Have you dared to powder your face? Have you dared to wash your face on the day of your father's death?

ANGUSTIAS: He wasn't my father. Mine died a long time ago. Have you forgotten that already?

BERNARDA: You owe more to this man, father of your sisters, than to your own. Thanks to him, your fortune is intact.

ANGUSTIAS: We'll have to see about that first!

BERNARDA: Even out of decency! Out of respect!

ANGUSTIAS: Let me go out, mother!

BERNARDA: Let you go out? After I've taken that powder off your face, I will. Spineless! Painted hussy! Just like your aunts!

(*She removes the powder violently with her handkerchief.*)

Now get out!

PONCIA: Bernarda, don't he so hateful!

BERNARDA: Even though my mother is crazy, I still have my five senses and I know what I'm doing.

(*They all enter.*)

MAGDALENA: What's going on here?

BERNARDA: Nothing's "going on here"!

MAGDALENA (*to Angustias*): If you're fighting over the inheritance, you're the richest one and can hang on to it all.

ANGUSTIAS: Keep your tongue in your pocketbook!

BERNARDA (*beating on the floor*): Don't fool yourselves into thinking you'll sway me. Until I go out of this house feet first I'll give the orders for myself and for you!

(*Voices are heard and María Josefa, Bernarda's mother, enters. She is very old and has decked out her head and breast with flowers.*)

MARÍA JOSEFA: Bernarda, where is my mantilla? Nothing, nothing of what I own will be for any of you. Not my rings nor my black moiré dress. Because not a one of you is going to marry — not a one. Bernarda, give me my necklace of pearls.

BERNARDA (*to the servant*): Why did you let her get in here?

SERVANT (*trembling*): She got away from me!

MARÍA JOSEFA: I ran away because I want to marry — I want to get married to a beautiful manly man from the shore of the sea. Because here the men run from women.

BERNARDA: Hush, hush, Mother!

MARÍA JOSEFA: No, no — I won't hush. I don't want to see these single women, longing for marriage, turning their hearts to dust; and I want to go to my home town. Bernarda, I want a man to get married to and be happy with!

BERNARDA: Lock her up!
MARÍA JOSEFA: Let me go out, Bernarda!

(*The servant seizes María Josefa.*)

BERNARDA: Help her, all of you!

(*They all grab the old woman.*)

MARÍA JOSEFA: I want to get away from here! Bernarda! To get married by the shore of the sea—by the shore of the sea!

(*Quick curtain.*)

ACT 2

(*A white room in Bernarda's house. The doors on the left lead to the bedrooms. Bernarda's daughters are seated on low chairs, sewing. Magdalena is embroidering. La Poncia is with them.*)

ANGUSTIAS: I've cut the third sheet.
MARTIRIO: That one goes to Amelia.
MAGDALENA: Angustias, shall I put Pepe's initials here too?
ANGUSTIAS (*dryly*): No.
MAGDALENA (*calling, from off stage to Adela*): Adela, aren't you coming?
AMELIA: She's probably stretched out on the bed.
PONCIA: Something's wrong with that one. I find her restless, trembling, frightened—as if a lizard were between her breasts.
MARTIRIO: There's nothing, more or less, wrong with her than there is with all of us.
MAGDALENA: All of us except Angustias.

ANGUSTIAS: I feel fine, and anybody who doesn't like it can pop.
MAGDALENA: We all have to admit the nicest things about you are your figure and your tact.
ANGUSTIAS: Fortunately, I'll soon be out of this hell.
MAGDALENA: Maybe you won't get out!
MARTIRIO: Stop this talk!
ANGUSTIAS: Besides, a good dowry is better than dark eyes in one's face!
MAGDALENA: All you say just goes in one ear and out the other.
AMELIA (*to La Poncia*): Open the patio door and see if we can get a bit of a breeze.

(*La Poncia opens the door.*)

MARTIRIO: Last night I couldn't sleep because of the heat.
AMELIA: Neither could I.
MAGDALENA: I got up for a bit of air. There was a black storm cloud and a few drops even fell.
PONCIA: It was one in the morning and the earth seemed to give off fire. I got up too. Angustias was still at the window with Pepe.
MAGDALENA (*with irony*): That late? What time did he leave?
ANGUSTIAS: Why do you ask, if you saw him?
AMELIA: He must have left about one-thirty.
ANGUSTIAS: Yes. How did you know?
AMELIA: I heard him cough and heard his mare's hoofbeats.
PONCIA: But I heard him leave around four.
ANGUSTIAS: It must have been someone else!
PONCIA: No, I'm sure of it!
AMELIA: That's what it seemed to me, too.
MAGDALENA: That's very strange!

Cherry Morris as Maria Josefa, Penelope Wilton as Bernarda Alba, and Justine Mitchell as Magdalena in David Hare's 2005 production of *The House of Bernarda Alba* at the National Theatre, London.

The National Asian American
Theater Company's 2007
production of *The House
of Bernarda Alba*.

(*Pause.*)

PONCIA: Listen, Angustias, what did he say to you the
   first time he came by your window?
ANGUSTIAS: Nothing. What should he say? Just talked.
MARTIRIO: It's certainly strange that two people who
   never knew each other should suddenly meet at a
   window and be engaged.
ANGUSTIAS: Well, I didn't mind.
AMELIA: I'd have felt very strange about it.
ANGUSTIAS: No, because when a man comes to a window
   he knows, from all the busybodies who come and go
   and fetch and carry, that he's going to be told "yes."

MARTIRIO: All right, but he'd have to ask you.
ANGUSTIAS: Of course!
AMELIA (*inquisitively*): And how did he ask you?
ANGUSTIAS: Why, no way:— "You know I'm after you. I
   need a good, well brought up woman, and that's you
   —if it's agreeable."
AMELIA: These things embarrass me!
ANGUSTIAS: They embarrass me too, but one has to go
   through it!
PONCIA: And did he say anything more?
ANGUSTIAS: Yes, he did all the talking.
MARTIRIO: And you?

The women stand as witnesses in a scene from *The House of Bernarda Alba*, directed by Julia Robinson at the Alba Tomi Theatre in New York in 1987.

ANGUSTIAS: I couldn't have said a word. My heart was almost coming out of my mouth. It was the first time I'd ever been alone at night with a man.

MAGDALENA: And such a handsome man.

ANGUSTIAS: He's not bad looking!

PONCIA: Those things happen among people who have an idea how to do things, who talk and say and move their hand. The first time my husband, Evaristo the Short-tailed, came to my window . . . Ha! Ha! Ha!

AMELIA: What happened?

PONCIA: It was very dark. I saw him coming along and as he went by he said, "Good evening." "Good evening," I said. Then we were both silent for more than half an hour. The sweat poured down my body. Then Evaristo got nearer and nearer as if he wanted to squeeze in through the bars and said in a very low voice — "Come here and let me feel you!"

(*They all laugh. Amelia gets up, runs, and looks through the door.*)

AMELIA: Ay, I thought mother was coming!

MAGDALENA: What she'd have done to us!

(*They go on laughing.*)

AMELIA: Sh-h-h! She'll hear us.

PONCIA: Then he acted very decently. Instead of getting some other idea, he went to raising birds, until he died. You aren't married but it's good for you to know, anyway, that two weeks after the wedding a man gives up the bed for the table, then the table for the tavern, and the woman who doesn't like it can just rot, weeping in a corner.

AMELIA: You liked it.

PONCIA: I learned how to handle him!

MARTIRIO: Is it true that you sometimes hit him?

PONCIA: Yes, and once I almost poked out one of his eyes!

MAGDALENA: All women ought to be like that!

PONCIA: I'm one of your mother's school. One time I don't know what he said to me, and then I killed all his birds — with the pestle!

(*They laugh.*)

MAGDALENA: Adela, child! Don't miss this.

AMELIA: Adela!

(*Pause.*)

MAGDALENA: I'll go see!

(*She goes out.*)

PONCIA: That child is sick!

MARTIRIO: Of course. She hardly sleeps!

PONCIA: What *does* she do, then?

MARTIRIO: How do I know what she does?

PONCIA: You probably know better than we do, since you sleep with just a wall between you.

ANGUSTIAS: Envy gnaws on people.

AMELIA: Don't exaggerate.

ANGUSTIAS: I can tell it in her eyes. She's getting the look of a crazy woman.

MARTIRIO: Don't talk about crazy women. This is one place you're not allowed to say that word.

(*Magdalena and Adela enter.*)

MAGDALENA: Didn't you say she was asleep?

ADELA: My body aches.

MARTIRIO (*with a hidden meaning*): Didn't you sleep well last night?

ADELA: Yes.

MARTIRIO: Then?

ADELA (*loudly*): Leave me alone. Awake or asleep, it's no affair of yours. I'll do whatever I want to with my body.

MARTIRIO: I was just concerned about you!

ADELA: Concerned?—curious! Weren't you sewing? Well, continue! I wish I were invisible so I could pass through a room without being asked where I was going!

SERVANT (*entering*): Bernarda is calling you. The man with the laces is here.

(*All but Adela and La Poncia go out, and as Martirio leaves, she looks fixedly at Adela.*)

ADELA: Don't look at me like that! If you want, I'll give you my eyes, for they're younger, and my back to improve that hump you have, but look the other way when I go by.

PONCIA: Adela, she's your sister, and the one who most loves you besides!

ADELA: She follows me everywhere. Sometimes she looks in my room to see if I'm sleeping. She won't let me breathe, and always, "Too bad about that face!" "Too bad about that body! It's going to waste!" But I won't let that happen. My body will be for whomever I choose.

PONCIA (*insinuatingly, in a low voice*): For Pepe el Romano, no?

ADELA (*frightened*): What do you mean?

PONCIA: What I said, Adela!

ADELA: Shut up!

PONCIA (*loudly*): Don't you think I've noticed?

ADELA: Lower your voice!

PONCIA: Then forget what you're thinking about!

ADELA: What do you know?

PONCIA: We old ones can see through walls. Where do you go when you get up at night?

ADELA: I wish you were blind!

PONCIA: But my head and hands are full of eyes, where something like this is concerned. I couldn't possibly guess your intentions. Why did you sit almost naked at your window, and with the light on and the window open, when Pepe passed by the second night he came to talk with your sister?

ADELA: That's not true!

PONCIA: Don't be a child! Leave your sister alone. And if you like Pepe el Romano, keep it to yourself.

(*Adela weeps.*)

Besides, who says you can't marry him? Your sister Angustias is sickly. She'll die with her first child. Narrow waisted, old—and out of my experience I can tell you she'll die. Then Pepe will do what all widowers do in these parts: he'll marry the youngest and most beautiful, and that's you. Live on that hope, forget him, anything; but don't go against God's law.

ADELA: Hush!

PONCIA: I won't hush!

ADELA: Mind your own business. Snooper, traitor!

PONCIA: I'm going to stick to you like a shadow!

ADELA: Instead of cleaning the house and then going to bed and praying for the dead, you root around like an old sow about goings on between men and women—so you can drool over them.

PONCIA: I keep watch; so people won't spit when they pass our door.

ADELA: What a tremendous affection you've suddenly conceived for my sister.

PONCIA: I don't have any affection for any of you. I want to live in a decent house. I don't want to be dirtied in my old age!

ADELA: Save your advice. It's already too late. For I'd leap not over you, just a servant, but over my mother to put out this fire I feel in my legs and my mouth. What can you possibly say about me? That I lock myself in my room and will not open the door? That I don't sleep? I'm smarter than you! See if you can catch the hare with your hands.

PONCIA: Don't defy me, Adela, don't defy me! Because I can shout, light lamps, and make bells ring.

ADELA: Bring four thousand yellow flares and set them about the walls of the yard. No one can stop what has to happen.

PONCIA: You like him that much?

ADELA: That much! Looking in his eyes I seem to drink his blood in slowly.

PONCIA: I won't listen to you.

ADELA: Well, you'll have to. I've been afraid of you. But now I'm stronger than you!

(*Angustias enters.*)

ANGUSTIAS: Always arguing!

PONCIA: Certainly. She insists that in all this heat I have to go bring her I don't know what from the store.

ANGUSTIAS: Did you buy me the bottle of perfume?

PONCIA: The most expensive one. And the face powder. I put them on the table in your room.

(*Angustias goes out.*)

ADELA: And be quiet!

PONCIA: We'll see!

(*Martirio and Amelia enter.*)

MARTIRIO (*to Adela*): Did you see the laces?

AMELIA: Angustias', for her wedding sheets, are beautiful.

ADELA (*to Martirio, who is carrying some lace*): And these?

MARTIRIO: They're for me. For a nightgown.

ADELA (*with sarcasm*): One needs a sense of humor around here!

MARTIRIO (*meaningfully*): But only for me to look at. I don't have to exhibit myself before anybody.

PONCIA: No one ever sees us in our nightgowns.

MARTIRIO (*meaningfully, looking at Adela*): Sometimes they don't! But I love nice underwear. If I were rich, I'd have it made of Holland Cloth. It's one of the few tastes I've left.

PONCIA: These laces are beautiful for babies caps and christening gowns. I could never afford them for my own. Now let's see if Angustias will use them for hers. Once she starts having children, they'll keep her running night and day.

MAGDALENA: I don't intend to sew a stitch on them.

AMELIA: And much less bring up some stranger's children. Look how our neighbors across the road are— making sacrifices for four brats.

PONCIA: They're better off than you. There at least they laugh and you can hear them fight.

MARTIRIO: Well, you go work for them, then.

PONCIA: No, fate has sent me to this nunnery!

(*Tiny bells are heard distantly as though through several thicknesses of wall.*)

MAGDALENA: It's the men going back to work.

PONCIA: It was three o'clock a minute ago.

MARTIRIO: With this sun!

ADELA (*sitting down*): Ay! If only we could go out in the fields too!

MAGDALENA (*sitting down*): Each class does what it has to!

MARTIRIO (*sitting down*): That's it!

AMELIA (*sitting down*): Ay!

PONCIA: There's no happiness like that in the fields right at this time of year. Yesterday morning the reapers arrived. Forty or fifty handsome young men.

MAGDALENA: Where are they from this year?

PONCIA: From far, far away. They came from the mountains! Happy! Like weathered trees! Shouting and throwing stones! Last night a woman who dresses in sequins and dances, with an accordion, arrived, and fifteen of them made a deal with her to take her to the olive grove. I saw them from far away. The one who talked with her was a boy with green eyes—tight knit as a sheaf of wheat.

AMELIA: Really?

ADELA: Are you sure?

PONCIA: Years ago another one of those women came here, and I myself gave my eldest son some money so he could go. Men need things like that.

ADELA: Everything's forgiven *them*.

AMELIA: To be born a woman's the worst possible punishment.

MAGDALENA: Even our eyes aren't our own.

(*A distant song is heard, coming nearer.*)

PONCIA: There they are. They have a beautiful song.

AMELIA: They're going out to reap now.

CHORUS:
> The reapers have set out
> Looking for ripe wheat;
> They'll carry off the hearts
> Of any girls they meet.

(*Tambourines and carrañacas are heard. Pause. They all listen in the silence cut by the sun.*)

AMELIA: And they don't mind the sun!

MARTIRIO: They reap through flames.

ADELA: How I'd like to be a reaper so I could come and go as I pleased. Then we could forget what's eating us all.

MARTIRIO: What do you have to forget?

ADELA: Each one of us has something.

MARTIRIO (*intensely*): Each one!

PONCIA: Quiet! Quiet!

CHORUS (*very distantly*):
> Throw wide your doors and windows,
> You girls who live in the town
> The reaper asks you for roses
> With which to deck his crown.

PONCIA: What a song!

MARTIRIO (*with nostalgia*):
> Throw wide your doors and windows,
> You girls who live in the town.

ADELA (*passionately*):
> The reaper asks you for roses
> With which to deck his crown.

(*The song grows more distant.*)

PONCIA: Now they're turning the corner.

ADELA: Let's watch them from the window of my room.

PONCIA: Be careful not to open the shutters too much because they're likely to give them a push to see who's looking.

(*The three leave. Martirio is left sitting on the low chair with her head between her hands.*)

AMELIA (*drawing near her*): What's wrong with you?

MARTIRIO: The heat makes me feel ill.

AMELIA: And it's no more than that?

MARTIRIO: I was wishing it were November, the rainy days, the frost—anything except this unending summertime.

AMELIA: It'll pass and come again.

MARTIRIO: Naturally.

(*Pause.*)

What time did you go to sleep last night?

AMELIA: I don't know. I sleep like a log. Why?

MARTIRIO: Nothing. Only I thought I heard someone in the yard.

AMELIA: Yes?

MARTIRIO: Very late.

AMELIA: And weren't you afraid?

MARTIRIO: No. I've heard it other nights.

AMELIA: We'd better watch out! Couldn't it have been the shepherds?

MARTIRIO: The shepherds come at six.

AMELIA: Maybe a young, unbroken mule?

MARTIRIO (*to herself, with double meaning*): That's it! That's it. An unbroken little mule.

AMELIA: We'll have to set a watch.

MARTIRIO: No. No. Don't say anything. It may be I've just imagined it.

AMELIA: Maybe.

(*Pause. Amelia starts to go.*)

MARTIRIO: Amelia!

AMELIA (*at the door*): What?

(*Pause.*)

MARTIRIO: Nothing.

(*Pause.*)

AMELIA: Why did you call me?

(*Pause.*)

MARTIRIO: It just came out. I didn't mean to.

(*Pause.*)

AMELIA: Lie down for a little.

ANGUSTIAS (*she bursts in furiously, in a manner that makes a great contrast with previous silence*): Where's that picture of Pepe I had under my pillow? Which one of you has it?

MARTIRIO: No one.

AMELIA: You'd think he was a silver St. Bartholomew.°

ANGUSTIAS: Where's the picture?

(*Poncia, Magdalena and Adela enter.*)

ADELA: What picture?

ANGUSTIAS: One of you has hidden it from me.

MAGDALENA: Do you have the effrontery to say that?

ANGUSTIAS: I had it in my room, and now it isn't there.

MARTIRIO: But couldn't it have jumped out into the yard at midnight? Pepe likes to walk around in the moonlight.

ANGUSTIAS: Don't joke with me! When he comes I'll tell him.

PONCIA: Don't do that! Because it'll turn up.

(*Looking at Adela.*)

ANGUSTIAS: I'd like to know which one of you has it.

ADELA (*looking at Martirio*): Somebody has it! But not me!

MARTIRIO (*with meaning*): Of course not you!

silver St. Bartholomew: A medallion used for good fortune.

BERNARDA (*entering with her cane*): What scandal is this in my house in the heat's heavy silence? The neighbors must have their ears glued to the walls.

ANGUSTIAS: They've stolen my sweetheart's picture!

BERNARDA (*fiercely*): Who? Who?

ANGUSTIAS: They have!

BERNARDA: Which one of you?

(*Silence.*)

Answer me!

(*Silence.*) (*To La Poncia.*)

Search their rooms! Look in their beds. This comes of not tying you up with shorter leashes. But I'll teach you now! (*to Angustias*) Are you sure?

ANGUSTIAS: Yes.

BERNARDA: Did you look everywhere?

ANGUSTIAS: Yes, Mother.

(*They all stand in an embarrassed silence.*)

BERNARDA: At the end of my life—to make me drink the bitterest poison a mother knows. (*to Poncia*) Did you find it?

PONCIA: Here it is.

BERNARDA: Where did you find it?

PONCIA: It was . . .

BERNARDA: Say it! Don't be afraid.

PONCIA (*wonderingly*): Between the sheets in Martirio's bed.

BERNARDA (*to Martirio*): Is that true?

MARTIRIO: It's true.

BERNARDA (*advancing on her, beating her with her cane*): You'll come to a bad end yet, you hypocrite! Trouble maker!

MARTIRIO (*fiercely*): Don't hit me, Mother!

BERNARDA: All I want to!

MARTIRIO: If I let you! You hear me? Get back!

PONCIA: Don't be disrespectful to your mother!

ANGUSTIAS (*holding Bernarda*): Let her go, please!

BERNARDA: Not even tears in your eyes.

MARTIRIO: I'm not going to cry just to please you.

BERNARDA: Why did you take the picture?

MARTIRIO: Can't I play a joke on my sister? What else would I want it for?

ADELA (*leaping forward, full of jealousy*): It wasn't a joke! You never liked to play jokes. It was something else bursting in her breast—trying to come out. Admit it openly now.

MARTIRIO: Hush, and don't make me speak; for if I should speak the walls would close together one against the other with shame.

ADELA: An evil tongue never stops inventing lies.

BERNARDA: Adela!

MAGDALENA: You're crazy.

AMELIA: And you stone us all with your evil suspicions.

MARTIRIO: But some others do things more wicked!

ADELA: Until all at once they stand forth stark naked and the river carries them along.

BERNARDA: Spiteful!

ANGUSTIAS: It's not my fault Pepe el Romano chose me!

ADELA: For your money.

ANGUSTIAS: Mother!

BERNARDA: Silence!

MARTIRIO: For your fields and your orchards.

MAGDALENA: That's only fair.

BERNARDA: Silence, I say! I saw the storm coming but I didn't think it'd burst so soon. Oh, what an avalanche of hate you've thrown on my heart! But I'm not old yet—I have five chains for you, and this house my father built, so not even the weeds will know of my desolation. Out of here!

(*They go out. Bernarda sits down desolately. La Poncia is standing close to the wall. Bernarda recovers herself, and beats on the floor.*)

I'll have to let them feel the weight of my hand! Bernarda, remember your duty!

PONCIA: May I speak?

BERNARDA: Speak. I'm sorry you heard. A stranger is always out of place in a family.

PONCIA: What I've seen, I've seen.

BERNARDA: Angustias must get married right away.

PONCIA: Certainly. We'll have to get her away from here.

BERNARDA: Not her, him!

PONCIA: Of course. He's the one to get away from here. You've thought it all out.

BERNARDA: I'm not thinking. These are things that shouldn't and can't be thought out. I give orders.

PONCIA: And you think he'll be satisfied to go away?

BERNARDA (*rising*): What are you imagining now?

PONCIA: He will, of course, marry Angustias.

BERNARDA: Speak up! I know you well enough to see that your knife's out for me.

PONCIA: I never knew a warning could be called murder.

BERNARDA: Have you some "warning" for me?

PONCIA: I'm not making any accusations, Bernarda. I'm only telling you to open your eyes and you'll see.

BERNARDA: See what?

PONCIA: You've always been smart, Bernarda. You've seen other people's sins a hundred miles away. Many times I've thought you could read minds. But, your children are your children, and now you're blind.

BERNARDA: Are you talking about Martirio?

PONCIA: Well, yes—about Martirio . . .

(*With curiosity.*)

I wonder why she hid the picture?

BERNARDA (*shielding her daughter*): After all, she says it was a joke. What else could it be?

PONCIA (*scornfully*): Do you believe that?

BERNARDA (*sternly*): I don't merely believe it. It's so!

PONCIA: Enough of this. We're talking about your family. But if we were talking about your neighbor across the way, what would it be?

BERNARDA: Now you're beginning to pull the point of the knife out.

PONCIA (*always cruelly*): No, Bernarda. Something very grave is happening here. I don't want to put the blame on your shoulders, but you've never given your daughters any freedom. Martirio is lovesick. I don't care what you say. Why didn't you let her marry Enrique Humanas? Why, on the very day he was coming to her window did you send him a message not to come?

BERNARDA (*loudly*): I'd do it a thousand times over! My blood won't mingle with the Humanas' while I live! His father was a shepherd.

PONCIA: And you see now what's happening to you with these airs!

BERNARDA: I have them because I can afford to. And you don't have them because you know where you came from!

PONCIA (*with hate*): Don't remind me! I'm old now. I've always been grateful for your protection.

BERNARDA (*emboldened*): You don't seem so!

PONCIA (*with hate, behind softness*): Martirio will forget this.

BERNARDA: And if she doesn't—the worse for her. I don't believe this is that "very grave thing" that's happening here. Nothing's happening here. It's just that you wish it would! And if it should happen one day, you can be sure it won't go beyond these walls.

PONCIA: I'm not so sure of that! There are people in town who can also read hidden thoughts, from afar.

BERNARDA: How you'd like to see me and my daughters on our way to a whorehouse!

PONCIA: No one knows her own destiny!

BERNARDA: I know my destiny! And my daughters! The whorehouse was for a certain woman, already dead. . . .

PONCIA (*fiercely*): Bernarda, respect the memory of my mother!

BERNARDA: Then don't plague me with your evil thoughts!

(*Pause.*)

PONCIA: I'd better stay out of everything.

BERNARDA: That's what you ought to do. Work and keep your mouth shut. The duty of all who work for a living.

PONCIA: But we can't do that. Don't you think it'd be better for Pepe to marry Martirio or . . . yes! . . . Adela?

BERNARDA: No, I *don't* think so.

PONCIA (*with meaning*): Adela! She's Romano's real sweetheart!

BERNARDA: Things are never the way we want them!

PONCIA: But it's hard work to turn them from their destined course. For Pepe to be with Angustias seems wrong to me—and to other people—and even to the wind. Who knows if they'll get what they want?

BERNARDA: There you go again! Sneaking up on me—giving me bad dreams. But I won't listen to you, because if all you say should come to pass—I'd scratch your face.

PONCIA: Frighten someone else with that.

BERNARDA: Fortunately, my daughters respect me and have never gone against my will!

PONCIA: That's right! But, as soon as they break loose they'll fly to the rooftops!

BERNARDA: And I'll bring them down with stones!

PONCIA: Oh, yes! You were always the bravest one!

BERNARDA: I've always enjoyed a good fight!

PONCIA: But aren't people strange. You should see Angustias' enthusiasm for her lover, at her age! And he seems very smitten too. Yesterday my oldest son told me that when he passed by with the oxen at four-thirty in the morning they were still talking.

BERNARDA: At four-thirty?

ANGUSTIAS (*entering*): That's a lie!

PONCIA: That's what he told me.

BERNARDA (*to Angustias*): Speak up!

ANGUSTIAS: For more than a week Pepe has been leaving at one. May God strike me dead if I'm lying.

MARTIRIO (*entering*): I heard him leave at four too.

BERNARDA: But did you see him with your eyes?

MARTIRIO: I didn't want to look out. Don't you talk now through the side window?

ANGUSTIAS: We talk through my bedroom window.

(*Adela appears at the door.*)

MARTIRIO: Then . . .

BERNARDA: What's going on here?

PONCIA: If you're not careful, you'll find out! At least Pepe was at *one* of your windows—and at four in the morning too!

BERNARDA: Are you sure of that?

PONCIA: You can't be sure of anything in this life!

ADELA: Mother, don't listen to someone who wants us to lose everything we have.

BERNARDA: I know how to take care of myself! If the townspeople want to come bearing false witness against me, they'll run into a stone wall! Don't any of you talk about this! Sometimes other people try to stir up a wave of filth to drown us.

MARTIRIO: I don't like to lie.

PONCIA: So there must be something.

BERNARDA: There won't be anything. I was born to have my eyes always open. Now I'll watch without closing them 'til I die.

ANGUSTIAS: I have the right to know.

BERNARDA: You don't have any right except to obey. No one's going to fetch and carry for me. (*to La Poncia*) And don't meddle in our affairs. No one will take a step without my knowing it.

SERVANT (*entering*): There's a big crowd at the top of the street, and all the neighbors are at their doors!

BERNARDA (*to Poncia*): Run see what's happening!

(*The girls are about to run out.*)

Where are you going? I always knew you for window-watching women and breakers of your mourning. All of you, to the patio!

(*They go out. Bernarda leaves. Distant shouts are heard.*)
(*Martirio and Adela enter and listen, not daring to step farther than the front door.*)

MARTIRIO: You can be thankful I didn't happen to open my mouth.

ADELA: I would have spoken too.

MARTIRIO: And what were you going to say? Wanting isn't doing!

ADELA: I do what I can and what happens to suit me. You've wanted to, but haven't been able.

MARTIRIO: You won't go on very long.

ADELA: I'll have everything!

MARTIRIO: I'll tear you out of his arms!

ADELA (*pleadingly*): Martirio, let me be!

MARTIRIO: None of us will have him!

ADELA: He wants me for his house!

MARTIRIO: I saw how he embraced you!

ADELA: I didn't want him to. It's as if I were dragged by a rope.

MARTIRIO: I'll see you dead first!

(*Magdalena and Angustias look in. The tumult is increasing. A servant enters with Bernarda. Poncia also enters from another door.*)

PONCIA: Bernarda!

BERNARDA: What's happening?

PONCIA: Librada's daughter, the unmarried one, had a child and no one knows whose it is!

ADELA: A child?

PONCIA: And to hide her shame she killed it and hid it under the rocks, but the dogs, with more heart than most Christians, dug it out and, as though directed by the hand of God, left it at her door. Now they want to kill her. They're dragging her through the streets—and down the paths and across the olive groves the men are coming, shouting so the fields shake.

BERNARDA: Yes, let them all come with olive whips and hoe handles—let them all come and kill her!

ADELA: No, not to kill her!

MARTIRIO: Yes—and let us go out too!

BERNARDA: And let whoever loses her decency pay for it!

(*Outside a woman's shriek and a great clamor is heard.*)

ADELA: Let her escape! Don't you go out!

MARTIRIO (*looking at Adela*): Let her pay what she owes!

BERNARDA (*at the archway*): Finish her before the guards come! Hot coals in the place where she sinned!

ADELA (*holding her belly*): No! No!

BERNARDA: Kill her! Kill her!

(*Curtain.*)

ACT 3

(*Four white walls, lightly washed in blue, of the interior patio of Bernarda Alba's house. The doorways, illumined by the lights inside the rooms, give a tenuous glow to the stage. At the center there is a table with a shaded oil lamp about which Bernarda and her daughters are eating. La Poncia serves them. Prudencia sits apart. When the curtain rises, there is a great silence interrupted only by the noise of plates and silverware.*)

PRUDENCIA: I'm going. I've made you a long visit.

(*She rises.*)

BERNARDA: But wait, Prudencia. We never see one another.
PRUDENCIA: Have they sounded the last call to rosary?
PONCIA: Not yet.

(*Prudencia sits down again.*)

BERNARDA: And your husband, how's he getting on?
PRUDENCIA: The same.
BERNARDA: We never see him either.
PRUDENCIA: You know how he is. Since he quarrelled with his brothers over the inheritance, he hasn't used the front door. He takes a ladder and climbs over the back wall.
BERNARDA: He's a real man! And your daughter?
PRUDENCIA: He's never forgiven her.
BERNARDA: He's right.
PRUDENCIA: I don't know what he told you. I suffer because of it.
BERNARDA: A daughter who's disobedient stops being a daughter and becomes an enemy.
PRUDENCIA: I let water run. The only consolation I've left is to take refuge in the church, but, since I'm losing my sight, I'll have to stop coming so the children won't make fun of me.

(*A heavy blow is heard against the walls.*)

What's that?
BERNARDA: The stallion. He's locked in the stall and he kicks against the wall of the house.

(*Shouting.*)

Tether him and take him out in the yard!

(*In a lower voice.*)

He must be too hot.
PRUDENCIA: Are you going to put the new mares to him?
BERNARDA: At daybreak.
PRUDENCIA: You've known how to increase your stock.
BERNARDA: By dint of money and struggling.
PONCIA (*interrupting*): And she has the best herd in these parts. It's a shame that prices are low.
BERNARDA: Do you want a little cheese and honey?
PRUDENCIA: I have no appetite.

(*The blow is heard again.*)

PONCIA: My God!
PRUDENCIA: It quivered in my chest.
BERNARDA (*rising, furiously*): Do I have to say things twice? Let him out to roll on the straw.

(*Pause. Then, as though speaking to the stableman.*)

Well then, lock the mares in the corral, but let him run free or he may kick down the walls.

(*She returns to the table and sits again.*)

Ay, what a life!
PRUDENCIA: You have to fight like a man.
BERNARDA: That's it.

(*Adela gets up from the table.*)

Where are you going?
ADELA: For a drink of water.
BERNARDA (*raising her voice*): Bring a pitcher of cool water. (*to Adela*) You can sit down. (*Adela sits down.*)
PRUDENCIA: And Angustias, when will she get married?
BERNARDA: They're coming to ask for her within three days.
PRUDENCIA: You must be happy.
ANGUSTIAS: Naturally!
AMELIA (*to Magdalena*): You've spilled the salt!
MAGDALENA: You can't possibly have worse luck than you're having.
AMELIA: It always brings bad luck.
BERNARDA: That's enough!
PRUDENCIA (*to Angustias*): Has he given you the ring yet?
ANGUSTIAS: Look at it.

(*She holds it out.*)

PRUDENCIA: It's beautiful. Three pearls. In my day, pearls signified tears.
ANGUSTIAS: But things have changed now.
ADELA: I don't think so. Things go on meaning the same. Engagement rings should be diamonds.
PONCIA: The most appropriate.
BERNARDA: With pearls or without them, things are as one proposes.
MARTIRIO: Or as God disposes.
PRUDENCIA: I've been told your furniture is beautiful.
BERNARDA: It cost sixteen thousand *reales*.°
PONCIA (*interrupting*): The best is the wardrobe with the mirror.
PRUDENCIA: I never saw a piece like that.
BERNARDA: We had chests.
PRUDENCIA: The important thing is that everything be for the best.
ADELA: And that you never know.
BERNARDA: There's no reason why it shouldn't be.

(*Bells are heard very distantly.*)

PRUDENCIA: The last call. (*to Angustias*) I'll be coming back to have you show me your clothes.
ANGUSTIAS: Whenever you like.
PRUDENCIA: Good evening—God bless you!
BERNARDA: Good-bye, Prudencia.

---

reales: Spanish silver coin. Sixteen thousand would have been a great sum.

ALL FIVE DAUGHTERS (*at the same time*): God go with you!

(*Pause. Prudencia goes out.*)

BERNARDA: Well, we've eaten.

(*They rise.*)

ADELA: I'm going to walk as far as the gate to stretch my legs and get a bit of fresh air.

(*Magdalena sits down in a low chair and leans against the wall.*)

AMELIA: I'll go with you.
MARTIRIO: I too.
ADELA (*with contained hate*): I'm not going to get lost!
AMELIA: One needs company at night.

(*They go out. Bernarda sits down. Angustias is clearing the table.*)

BERNARDA: I've told you once already! I want you to talk to your sister Martirio. What happened about the picture was a joke and you must forget it.
ANGUSTIAS: You know she doesn't like me.
BERNARDA: Each one knows what she thinks inside. I don't pry into anyone's heart, but I want to put up a good front and have family harmony. You understand?
ANGUSTIAS: Yes.
BERNARDA: Then that's settled.
MAGDALENA (*she is almost asleep*): Besides, you'll be gone in no time.

(*She falls asleep.*)

ANGUSTIAS: Not soon enough for me.
BERNARDA: What time did you stop talking last night?
ANGUSTIAS: Twelve-thirty.
BERNARDA: What does Pepe talk about?
ANGUSTIAS: I find him absent-minded. He always talks to me as though he were thinking of something else. If I ask him what's the matter, he answers—"We men have our worries."
BERNARDA: You shouldn't ask him. And when you're married, even less. Speak if he speaks, and look at him when he looks at you. That way you'll get along.
ANGUSTIAS: But, Mother, I think he's hiding things from me.
BERNARDA: Don't try to find out. Don't ask him, and above all, never let him see you cry.
ANGUSTIAS: I should be happy, but I'm not.
BERNARDA: It's all the same.
ANGUSTIAS: Many nights I watch Pepe very closely through the window bars and he seems to fade away—as though he were hidden in a cloud of dust like those raised by the flocks.
BERNARDA: That's just because you're not strong.
ANGUSTIAS: I hope so!
BERNARDA: Is he coming tonight?
ANGUSTIAS: No, he went into town with his mother.
BERNARDA: Good, we'll get to bed early. Magdalena!
ANGUSTIAS: She's asleep.

(*Adela, Martirio and Amelia enter.*)

AMELIA: What a dark night!
ADELA: You can't see two steps in front of you.
MARTIRIO: A good night for robbers, for anyone who needs to hide.
ADELA: The stallion was in the middle of the corral. White. Twice as large. Filling all the darkness.
AMELIA: It's true. It was frightening. Like a ghost.
ADELA: The sky has stars as big as fists.
MARTIRIO: This one stared at them till she almost cracked her neck.
ADELA: Don't you like them up there?
MARTIRIO: What goes on over the roof doesn't mean a thing to me. I have my hands full with what happens under it.
ADELA: Well, that's the way it goes with you!
BERNARDA: And it goes the same for you as for her.
ANGUSTIAS: Good night.
ADELA: Are you going to bed now?
ANGUSTIAS: Yes, Pepe isn't coming tonight.

(*She goes out.*)

ADELA: Mother, why, when a stars falls or lightning flashes, does one say:
    Holy Barbara, blessed on high
    May your name be in the sky
    With holy water written high?
BERNARDA: The old people know many things we've forgotten.
AMELIA: I close my eyes so I won't see them.
ADELA: Not I. I like to see what's quiet and been quiet for years on end, running with fire.
MARTIRIO: But all that has nothing to do with us.
BERNARDA: And it's better not to think about it.
ADELA: What a beautiful night! I'd like to stay up till very late and enjoy the breeze from the fields.
BERNARDA: But we have to go to bed. Magdalena!
AMELIA: She's just dropped off.
BERNARDA: Magdalena!
MAGDALENA (*annoyed*): Leave me alone!
BERNARDA: To bed!
MAGDALENA (*rising, in a bad humor*): You don't give anyone a moment's peace!

(*She goes off grumbling.*)

AMELIA: Good night!

(*She goes out.*)

BERNARDA: You two get along, too.
MARTIRIO: How is it Angustias' sweetheart isn't coming tonight?
BERNARDA: He went on a trip.
MARTIRIO (*looking at Adela*): Ah!
ADELA: I'll see you in the morning!

(*She goes out. Martirio drinks some water and goes out slowly, looking at the door to the yard. La Poncia enters.*)

PONCIA: Are you still here?

BERNARDA: Enjoying this quiet and not seeing anywhere the "very grave thing" that's happening here — according to you.

PONCIA: Bernarda, let's not go any further with this.

BERNARDA: In this house there's no question of a yes or a no. My watchfulness can take care of anything.

PONCIA: Nothing's happening outside. That's true, all right. Your daughters act and are as though stuck in a cupboard. But neither you nor anyone else can keep watch inside a person's heart.

BERNARDA: My daughters breathe calmly enough.

PONCIA: That's your business, since you're their mother. I have enough to do just with serving you.

BERNARDA: Yes, you've turned quiet now.

PONCIA: I keep my place — that's all.

BERNARDA: The trouble is you've nothing to talk about. If there were grass in this house, you'd make it your business to put the neighbors' sheep to pasture here.

PONCIA: I hide more than you think.

BERNARDA: Do your sons still see Pepe at four in the morning? Are they still repeating this house's evil litany?

PONCIA: They say nothing.

BERNARDA: Because they can't. Because there's nothing for them to sink their teeth in. And all because my eyes keep constant watch!

PONCIA: Bernarda, I don't want to talk about this because I'm afraid of what you'll do. But don't you feel so safe.

BERNARDA: Very safe!

PONCIA: Who knows, lightning might strike suddenly. Who knows but what all of a sudden, in a rush of blood, your heart might stop.

BERNARDA: Nothing will happen here. I'm on guard now against all your suspicions.

PONCIA: All the better for you.

BERNARDA: Certainly, all the better!

SERVANT (entering): I've just finished with the dishes. Is there anything else, Bernarda?

BERNARDA (rising): Nothing. I'm going to get some rest.

PONCIA: What time do you want me to call you?

BERNARDA: No time. Tonight I intend to sleep well.

(She goes out.)

PONCIA: When you're powerless against the sea, it's easier to turn your back on it and not look at it.

SERVANT: She's so proud! She herself pulls the blindfold over her eyes.

PONCIA: I can do nothing. I tried to head things off, but now they frighten me too much. You feel this silence? — in each room there's a thunderstorm and the day it breaks, it'll sweep all of us along with it. But I've said what I had to say.

SERVANT: Bernarda thinks nothing can stand against her, yet she doesn't know the strength a man has among women alone.

PONCIA: It's not all the fault of Pepe el Romano. It's true last year he was running after Adela; and she was crazy about him — but she ought to keep her place and not lead him on. A man's a man.

SERVANT: And some there are who believe he didn't have to talk many times with Adela.

PONCIA: That's true.

(In a low voice.)

And some other things.

SERVANT: I don't know what's going to happen here.

PONCIA: How I'd like to sail across the sea and leave this house, this battleground, behind!

SERVANT: Bernarda's hurrying the wedding and it's possible nothing will happen.

PONCIA: Things have gone much too far already. Adela is set no matter what comes, and the rest of them watch without rest.

SERVANT: Martirio too . . . ?

PONCIA: That one's the worst. She's a pool of poison. She sees El Romano is not for her, and she'd sink the world if it were in her hand to do so.

SERVANT: How bad they all are!

PONCIA: They're women without men, that's all. And in such matters even blood is forgotten. Sh-h-h-h!

(She listens.)

SERVANT: What's the matter?

PONCIA (she rises): The dogs are barking.

SERVANT: Someone must have passed by the back door.

(Adela enters wearing a white petticoat and corselet.)

PONCIA: Aren't you in bed yet?

ADELA: I want a drink of water.

(She drinks from a glass on the table.)

PONCIA: I imagined you were asleep.

ADELA: I got thirsty and woke up. Aren't you two going to get some rest?

SERVANT: Soon now.

(Adela goes out.)

PONCIA: Let's go.

SERVANT: We've certainly earned some sleep. Bernarda doesn't let me rest the whole day.

PONCIA: Take the light.

SERVANT: The dogs are going mad.

PONCIA: They're not going to let us sleep.

(They go out. The stage is left almost dark. María Josefa enters with a lamb in her arms.)

MARÍA JOSEFA (singing):
    Little lamb, child of mine,
    Let's go to the shore of the sea,
    The tiny ant will be at his doorway,
    I'll nurse you and give you your bread.
    Bernarda, old leopard-face,
    And Magdalena, hyena-face,
    Little lamb . . .
    Rock, rock-a-bye,
    Let's go to the palms at Bethlehem's gate.

(She laughs.)

Neither you nor I would want to sleep
The door will open by itself
And on the beach we'll go and hide
In a little coral cabin.
Bernarda, old leopard-face,
And Magdalena, hyena-face,
Little lamb . . .
Rock, rock-a-bye,
Let's go to the palms at Bethlehem's gate.

(*She goes off singing.*)
(*Adela enters. She looks about cautiously and disappears out the door leading to the corral. Martirio enters by another door and stands in anguished watchfulness near the center of the stage. She also is in petticoats. She covers herself with a small black scarf. María Josefa crosses before her.*)

MARTIRIO: Grandmother, where are you going?
MARÍA JOSEFA: You are going to open the door for me? Who are you?
MARTIRIO: How did you get out here?
MARÍA JOSEFA: I escaped. You, who are you?
MARTIRIO: Go back to bed.
MARÍA JOSEFA: You're Martirio. Now I see you. Martirio, face of a martyr. And when are you going to have a baby? I've had this one.
MARTIRIO: Where did you get that lamb?
MARÍA JOSEFA: I know it's a lamb. But can't a lamb be a baby? It's better to have a lamb than not to have anything. Old Bernarda, leopard-face, and Magdalena, hyena-face!
MARTIRIO: Don't shout.
MARÍA JOSEFA: It's true. Everything's very dark. Just because I have white hair you think I can't have babies, but I can—babies and babies and babies. This baby will have white hair, and I'd have *this* baby, and another, and this *one* other; and with all of us with snow white hair we'll be like the waves—one, then another, and another. Then we'll all sit down and all of us will have white heads, and we'll be seafoam. Why isn't there any seafoam here? Nothing but mourning shrouds here.
MARTIRIO: Hush, hush.
MARÍA JOSEFA: When my neighbor had a baby, I'd carry her some chocolate and later she'd bring me some, and so on—always and always and always. You'll have white hair, but your neighbors won't come. Now I have to go away, but I'm afraid the dogs will bite me. Won't you come with me as far as the fields? I don't like fields. I like houses, but open houses, and the neighbor women asleep in their beds with their little tiny tots, and the men outside sitting in their chairs. Pepe el Romano is a giant. All of you love him. But he's going to devour you because you're grains of wheat. No, not grains of wheat. Frogs with no tongues!
MARTIRIO (*angrily*): Come, off to bed with you.

(*She pushes her.*)

MARÍA JOSEFA: Yes, but then you'll open the door for me, won't you?
MARTIRIO: Of course.
MARÍA JOSEFA (*weeping*):
   Little lamb, child of mine,
   Let's go to the shore of the sea,
   The tiny ant will be at his doorway,
   I'll nurse you and give you your bread.

(*Martirio locks the door through which María Josefa came out and goes to the yard door. There she hesitates, but goes two steps farther.*)

MARTIRIO (*in a low voice*): Adela! (*Pause. She advances to the door. Then, calling.*) Adela!

(*Adela enters. Her hair is disarranged.*)

ADELA: And what are you looking for me for?
MARTIRIO: Keep away from him.
ADELA: Who are you to tell me that?
MARTIRIO: That's no place for a decent woman.
ADELA: How you wish *you'd* been there!
MARTIRIO (*shouting*): This is the moment for me to speak. This can't go on.
ADELA: This is just the beginning. I've had strength enough to push myself forward—the spirit and looks you lack. I've seen death under this roof, and gone out to look for what was mine, what belonged to me.
MARTIRIO: That soulless man came for another woman. You pushed yourself in front of him.
ADELA: He came for the money, but his eyes were always on me.
MARTIRIO: I won't allow you to snatch him away. He'll marry Angustias.
ADELA: You know better than I he doesn't love her.
MARTIRIO: I know.
ADELA: You know because you've seen—he loves me, me!
MARTIRIO (*desperately*): Yes.
ADELA (*close before her*): He loves me, *me!* He loves me, *me!*
MARTIRIO: Stick me with a knife if you like, but don't tell me that again.
ADELA: That's why you're trying to fix it so I won't go away with him. It makes no difference to you if he puts his arms around a woman he doesn't love. Nor does it to me. He could be a hundred years with Angustias, but for him to have his arms around me seems terrible to you—because you too love him! You love him!
MARTIRIO (*dramatically*): Yes! Let me say it without hiding my head. Yes! my breast's bitter, bursting like a pomegranate. I love him!
ADELA (*impulsively, hugging her*): Martirio, Martirio, I'm not to blame!
MARTIRIO: Don't put your arms around me! Don't try to smooth it over. My blood's no longer yours, and even though I try to think of you as a sister, I see you as just another woman.

(*She pushes her away.*)

ADELA: There's no way out here. Whoever has to drown—let her drown. Pepe is mine. He'll carry me to the rushes along the river bank. . . .

MARTIRIO: He won't!

ADELA: I can't stand this horrible house after the taste of his mouth. I'll be what he wants me to be. Everybody in the village against me, burning me with their fiery fingers; pursued by those who claim they're decent, and I'll wear, before them all, the crown of thorns that belongs to the mistress of a married man.

MARTIRIO: Hush!

ADELA: Yes, yes. (*In a low voice.*) Let's go to bed. Let's let him marry Angustias. I don't care any more, but I'll go off alone to a little house where he'll come to see me whenever he wants, whenever he feels like it.

MARTIRIO: That'll never happen! Not while I have a drop of blood left in my body.

ADELA: Not just weak you, but a wild horse I could force to his knees with just the strength of my little finger.

MARTIRIO: Don't raise that voice of yours to me. It irritates me. I have a heart full of a force so evil that, without my wanting to be, I'm drowned by it.

ADELA: You show us the way to love our sisters. God must have meant to leave me alone in the midst of darkness because I can see you as I've never seen you before.

(*A whistle is heard and Adela runs toward the door, but Martirio gets in front of her.*)

MARTIRIO: Where are you going?

ADELA: Get away from that door!

MARTIRIO: Get by me if you can!

ADELA: Get away!

(*They struggle.*)

MARTIRIO (*shouts*): Mother! Mother!

ADELA: Let me go!

(*Bernarda enters. She wears petticoats and a black shawl.*)

BERNARDA: Quiet! Quiet! How poor I am without even a man to help me!

MARTIRIO (*pointing to Adela*): She was with him. Look at those skirts covered with straw!

BERNARDA (*going furiously toward Adela*): That's the bed of a bad woman!

ADELA (*facing her*): There'll be an end to prison voices here! (*Adela snatches away her mother's cane and breaks it in two.*) This is what I do with the tyrant's cane. Not another step. No one but Pepe commands me!

(*Magdalena enters.*)

MAGDALENA: Adela!

(*La Poncia and Angustias enter.*)

ADELA: I'm his. (*to Angustias*) Know that—and go out in the yard and tell him. He'll be master in this house.

ANGUSTIAS: My God!

BERNARDA: The gun! Where's the gun?

(*She rushes out. La Poncia runs ahead of her. Amelia enters and looks on frightened, leaning her head against the wall. Behind her comes Martirio.*)

ADELA: No one can hold me back!

(*She tries to go out.*)

ANGUSTIAS (*holding her*): You're not getting out of here with your body's triumph! Thief! Disgrace of this house!

MAGDALENA: Let her go where we'll never see her again!

(*A shot is heard.*)

BERNARDA (*entering*): Just try looking for him now!

MARTIRIO (*entering*): That does away with Pepe el Romano.

ADELA: Pepe! My God! Pepe!

(*She runs out.*)

PONCIA: Did you kill him?

MARTIRIO: No. He raced away on his mare!

BERNARDA: It was my fault. A woman can't aim.

MAGDALENA: Then, why did you say . . . ?

MARTIRIO: For her! I'd like to pour a river of blood over her head!

PONCIA: Curse you!

MAGDALENA: Devil!

BERNARDA: Although it's better this way!

(*A thud is heard.*)

Adela! Adela!

PONCIA (*at her door*): Open this door!

BERNARDA: Open! Don't think the walls will hide your shame!

SERVANT (*entering*): All the neighbors are up!

BERNARDA (*in a low voice, but like a roar*): Open! Or I'll knock the door down!

(*Pause. Everything is silent.*)

Adela!

(*She walks away from the door.*)

A hammer!

(*La Poncia throws herself against the door. It opens and she goes in. As she enters, she screams and backs out.*)

What is it?

PONCIA (*she puts her hands to her throat*): May we never die like that!

(*The sisters fall back. The servant crosses herself. Bernarda screams and goes forward.*)

Don't go in!

BERNARDA: No, not I! Pepe, you're running now, alive in the darkness, under the trees, but another day you'll fall. Cut her down! My daughter died a virgin. Take her to another room and dress her as though she were a virgin. No one will say anything about this! She died a virgin. Tell them, so that at dawn, the bells will ring twice.

MARTIRIO: A thousand times happy she, who had him.

BERNARDA: And I want no weeping. Death must be looked at face to face. Silence!

(*To one daughter.*)

Be still, I said!

(*To another daughter.*)

Tears when you're alone! We'll drown ourselves in a sea of mourning. She, the youngest daughter of Bernarda Alba, died a virgin. Did you hear me? Silence, silence, I said. Silence!

Eugene O'Neill

Eugene O'Neill (1888–1953) is a major figure in American drama. His enormous output began in the tradition of realism established by Strindberg and Ibsen, and his early plays, such as *Anna Christie* (1921), introduced Americans to the techniques of the great European realists. Realism for Americans was a move away from the sentimental comedies and the melodramas that dominated the American stage from before the Civil War to World War I. Some of O'Neill's plays, such as *Strange Interlude* (1928) and *Dynamo* (1929), were expressionist in style, demonstrating his considerable range. O'Neill rejected the kind of theater in which his father had thrived. James O'Neill had long been a stage star, traveling across the country in his production of *The Count of Monte Cristo*, which had made him rich but had also made him a prisoner of a single role.

Eugene O'Neill won the Pulitzer Prize for drama three times in the 1920s and once posthumously in 1957 for *Long Day's Journey into Night*, which was written in 1941. He won the Nobel Prize for literature in 1936. Although not popular successes in his own day, his plays—including those published posthumously—are now mainstays of the American theater. Some of America's finest actors have taken a strong interest in his work, both producing his plays and acting in them on the stage and on television. From the 1950s to the 1990s, the late Colleen Dewhurst and Jason Robards, Jr., in particular, gave some magnificent performances and interpretations of O'Neill's work.

The young O'Neill was a romantic in the popular sense of the word. After a year at Princeton University, he began to travel on the sea. His jaunts took him to South America, and he once wound up virtually broke and without resources in Buenos Aires. When he returned to America, he studied for a year at Harvard with George Pierce Baker, the most famous drama teacher of his day. Eventually, he took up residence in Provincetown, Massachusetts, where a group of people dedicated to theater—including the playwright Susan Glaspell—began to put on plays in their living rooms. When their audiences spilled over, the group created the Provincetown Playhouse, the theater in which some of O'Neill's earliest pieces were first performed.

The subjects of many of O'Neill's plays were not especially appealing to general theater audiences. Those who hoped for light comedy and a good laugh or light melodrama and a good cry found the intensity of his dark vision of the world to be overwhelming. They came for mere entertainment, and he was providing them with frightening visions of the soul's interior. The glum and painful surroundings of *Anna Christie* (1921) and the brutality of the lower-class coal stoker in *The Hairy Ape* (1922) were foreign to the comfortable middle-class audiences who supported commercial theater in America. They found O'Neill's characters to be haunted by family agonies, affections never given, ambitions never realized, pains never assuaged. Despite his remarkable abilities and the power of his drama, audiences often did not know what to make of him. To a large extent, his acceptance came on waves of shock, as had the acceptance of the Scandinavian realists.

O'Neill's early work is marked by a variety of experiments with theatrical effects and moods. He tried to use the primary influences of Greek drama in such plays as *Desire under the Elms* (1924), which has been described by critics as Greek tragedy, and *Mourning Becomes Electra* (1931), based on the *Oresteia*, which took three days to perform. But many of his early plays now seem dated and strange. His most impressive plays are his later work, such as *Ah, Wilderness!* (1933), *The Iceman Cometh* (1939), *Long Day's Journey into Night* (1939–1941), *A Moon for the Misbegotten* (1943), and *A Touch of the Poet* (1935–1942), which was performed posthumously in 1957.

O'Neill's personal life had been darkened by the alcoholism of his father and brother and the drug addiction of his mother. O'Neill himself had to fight alcoholism and depression brought on by the instability of his life and family. The darkness of his dramas may or may not be related to his personal life experiences, but they reflect his understanding of the human condition. His experiments with Greek concepts of fate are tempered and strengthened by his interpretation of Freud's theories about the unconscious, the ruling force of the sexual drive, and the effects of trauma on childhood. *Desire under the Elms* brings together all these elements with the influence of the land—the environment of Puritan New England—and illustrates perfectly his awareness of the limits of human free will and the power of the forces that work on us all.

DESIRE UNDER THE ELMS

Desire under the Elms (1924) is Eugene O'Neill's first effort at writing in the style of Greek tragedy. He did not follow the Greek tradition and choose a great figure of noble birth about whom the fates would unravel their mystery. Rather, he was deliberately democratic, choosing a New England farmer and his family as the protagonists of his drama. Just as fate animates a Greek tragedy, the emotional forces of jealousy, resentment, lust, and incestuous love animate *Desire under the Elms*.

O'Neill set his play on a typically rocky New England soil, which in many ways bears a striking resemblance to the rocky soil of Athens and the Greek coastline. The unyielding toughness of life on that land contrasts with the easy life to be made from gold mining in California. Ephraim Cabot, the seventy-five-year-old father, has been made hard and physically powerful by his work. He has just taken a third wife, the young and scheming Abbie. His youngest son, Eben, has decided to stay on the farm, whereas his two other sons plan to go to California and put New England behind them.

The sense of having been dispossessed of his farm by his new stepmother drives Eben to hate Abbie, who has married the elder Cabot merely to inherit his farm. At first the sparring between Abbie and Eben is based on calculating self-interest, but eventually their feelings overpower them. Lust turns to love, and the son they produce is passed off as old Cabot's, although the townspeople have no illusion about whose child it is.

The farm itself is a powerful presence in the play. Whenever old Cabot thinks he should give up and follow the promise of easy money in California, he feels God's presence urging him to stay. God operates for Ephraim as the oracle in *Oedipus Rex* does, giving him a message that is painful but must be obeyed. The rocks on the farm are unforgiving, and so is the fate that Abbie and Eben face. Theirs is an impossible love; everything they do to prove their love condemns them even more. The forces of fate center on the farm. When the play opens, Eben says of it, "God! Purty!" When the play ends, the sheriff praises the farm and says he surely would like to own it, striking a clear note of irony: the agony of the play is rooted in lust—lust for the farm that parallels the lust between Abbie and Eben.

The play is haunted by the ghost of Eben's mother, whom Ephraim married primarily for her farm. Her ghost is exorcised only after the cycle of retribution has begun. Old Cabot has committed a crime against her, and now he must become the victim.

The language of the dialogue is that of New England in the mid-nineteenth century. Living in New England, O'Neill understood the ways and the language of its people. He seems to have imagined the "downeast" flavor of Maine in the language, and he has been careful to build the proper pronunciation into the dialogue. This folksy way of speaking helps emphasize the peasantlike qualities in these New England farmers. O'Neill's careful use of language is reminiscent of Synge's masterful representation of the Irish-English speech in *Playboy of the Western World*.

The language of O'Neill's characters has a rocky toughness at times. Characters are laconic—they often answer in a single word: "Ay-eh." Faithful to his vision of the simple speech of country folk, O'Neill avoids giving them elaborate poetic soliloquies. Instead, he shows how, despite their limited language, rural people feel profound emotions and act on them.

O'Neill carefully links Abbie with Queen Phaedra, who in Euripides' play *Hippolytus* and in Racine's seventeenth-century play *Phaedra* finds herself uncontrollably desiring her husband's son as a lover. Racine and Racine's audience could easily imagine such intense emotions overwhelming a noblewoman because they thought that nobility felt more intensely and lived more intensely than ordinary people. But O'Neill is trying to make his audience see that even unlettered farm people can feel as deeply as tragic heroes of any age do. The Cabots are victims of passion. They share their fate with the great families of the Greek tragedies.

Desire under the Elms in Performance

Desire under the Elms was first performed in Greenwich Village in 1924 under the auspices of the Provincetown Players. A year later it appeared on Broadway for thirty-six weeks, a long run for a tragedy. Its first reviewers were courteous but puzzled. They compared the play with earlier O'Neill works, remarking on its "tragic gloom and irony" and praising its language. At the Los Angeles production in 1926, the cast was arrested for "giving an obscene play." The sexual themes offended theatergoers in California, and even those who defended the play admitted that the text would be offensive to some members of the audience.

Because the English censor banned the play until 1938, its first European production was in Prague's National Theatre in 1925. Its Czech title translated as "The Farm under the Elms." The director used a highly stylized set influenced by the Moscow Art Theater and later described as "a sort of two-storied wooded edifice. . . rather like a log cabin multiplied by four."

Other earlier European productions followed in Moscow in 1932, in Stockholm in 1933, and finally in London in 1940. The 1952 New York revival was not successful. The 1963 revival at the Circle in the Square in New York starred George C. Scott and his wife, Colleen Dewhurst. Jose Quintero, a notable interpreter of O'Neill, directed. Critics complained about "awkward" echoes of Greek tragedy while admitting that the play had an uncanny power despite its flaws. It ran for 380 performances.

The play has often been revived: in Boston in 1967; at the Berkshire Theater Festival in 1974; at the Roundabout Theater in New York, directed by Terry Schrieber, in 1984; and by numerous local theater groups. In 1978 Edward Thomas staged it at Connecticut College in New London as an opera. A creditable production, it emphasized the play's American folk qualities. Dan Wackerman directed an off-Broadway production in 1997 and added an African American character named Silent Woman. She did not speak but added the issue of race to this issue-laden play. Even more recently, in 2005, the American Repertory Theatre staged the play under the direction on János Szász with an innovative, expressionistic set designed by Riccardo Hernandez.

Eugene O'Neill (1888–1953)

DESIRE UNDER THE ELMS

1924

Characters

EPHRAIM CABOT
SIMEON ⎤
PETER ⎬ *his sons*
EBEN ⎦
ABBIE PUTNAM
YOUNG GIRL, TWO FARMERS, *the* FIDDLER, *a* SHERIFF, *and other folk from the neighboring farms.*

Scene: *The action of the entire play takes place in, and immediately outside of, the Cabot farmhouse in New England, in the year 1850. The south end of the house faces front to a stone wall with a wooden gate at center opening on a country road. The house is in good condition but in need of paint. Its walls are a sickly grayish, the green of the shutters faded. Two enormous elms are on each side of the house. They bend their trailing branches down over the roof. They appear to protect and at the same time subdue. There is a sinister maternity in their aspect, a crushing, jealous absorption. They have developed from their intimate contact with the life of man in the house an appalling humaneness. They brood oppressively over the house. They are like exhausted women resting their sagging breasts and hands and hair on its roof, and when it rains their tears trickle down monotonously and rot on the shingles.*

There is a path running from the gate around the right corner of the house to the front door. A narrow porch is on this side. The end wall facing us has two windows in its upper story, two larger ones on the floor below. The two upper are those of the father's bedroom and that of the brothers. On the left, ground floor, is the kitchen—on the right, the parlor, the shades of which are always drawn down.

PART I • *Scene I*

(*Exterior of the farmhouse. It is sunset of a day at the beginning of summer in the year 1850. There is no wind and everything is still. The sky above the roof is suffused with deep colors, the green of the elms glows, but the house is in shadow, seeming pale and washed out by contrast.*)

(*A door opens and Eben Cabot comes to the end of the porch and stands looking down the road to the right. He has a large bell in his hand and this he swings mechanically, awakening a deafening clangor. Then he puts his hands on his hips and stares up at the sky. He sighs with a puzzled awe and blurts out with halting appreciation.*)

EBEN: God! Purty! (*His eyes fall and he stares about him frowningly. He is twenty-five, tall and sinewy. His face is well formed, good-looking, but its expression is resentful and defensive. His defiant, dark eyes remind one of a wild animal's in captivity. Each day is a cage in which he finds himself trapped but inwardly unsubdued. There is a fierce repressed vitality about him. He has black hair, mustache, a thin curly trace of beard. He is dressed in rough farm clothes.*)

(*He spits on the ground with intense disgust, turns, and goes back into the house.*)

(*Simeon and Peter come in from their work in the fields. They are tall men, much older than their half-brother [Simeon is thirty-nine and Peter thirty-seven], built on a squarer, simpler model, fleshier in body, more bovine and homelier in face, shrewder and more practical. Their shoulders stoop a bit from years of farm work. They clump heavily along in their clumsy thick-soled boots caked with earth. Their clothes, their faces, hands, bare arms, and throats are earth-stained. They smell of earth. They stand together for a moment in front of the house and, as if with the one impulse, stare dumbly up at the sky, leaning on their hoes. Their faces have a compressed, unresigned expression. As they look upward, this softens.*)

SIMEON (*grudgingly*): Purty.
PETER: Ay-eh.
SIMEON (*suddenly*): Eighteen year ago.
PETER: What?
SIMEON: Jenn. My woman. She died.
PETER: I'd fergot.
SIMEON: I rec'lect—now an' agin. Makes it lonesome. She'd hair long's a hoss' tail—an' yeller like gold!

PETER: Waal—she's gone. (*This with indifferent finality—then after a pause.*) They's gold in the West, Sim.
SIMEON (*still under the influence of sunset—vaguely*): In the sky?
PETER: Waal—in a manner o' speakin'—that's the promise. (*Growing excited.*) Gold in the sky—in the West—Golden Gate—Californi-a!—Goldest West!—fields o' gold!
SIMEON (*excited in his turn*): Fortunes layin' just atop o' the ground waitin' t' be picked! Solomon's mines, they says! (*For a moment they continue looking up at the sky—then their eyes drop.*)
PETER (*with sardonic bitterness*): Here—it's stones atop o' the ground—stones atop o' stones—makin' stone walls—year atop o' year—him 'n' yew 'n' me 'n' then Eben—makin' stone walls fur him to fence us in!
SIMEON: We've wuked. Give our strength. Give our years. Plowed 'em under in the ground—(*He stamps rebelliously.*)—rottin'—makin' soil for his crops! (*A pause.*) Waal—the farm pays good for hereabouts.
PETER: If we plowed in Californi-a, they'd be lumps o' gold in the furrow!
SIMEON: Californi-a's t'other side o' earth, a'most. We got t' calc'late—
PETER (*after a pause*): 'Twould be hard fur me, too, to give up what we've 'arned here by our sweat. (*A pause. Eben sticks his head out of the dining room window, listening.*)
SIMEON: Ay-eh. (*A pause.*) Mebbe—he'll die soon.
PETER (*doubtfully*): Mebbe.
SIMEON: Mebbe—fur all we knows—he's dead now.
PETER: Ye'd need proof.
SIMEON: He's been gone two months—with no word.
PETER: Left us in the fields an evenin' like this. Hitched up an' druv off into the West. That's plum onnateral. He hadn't never been off this farm 'ceptin' t' the village in thirty year or more, not since he married Eben's maw. (*A pause. Shrewdly.*) I calc'late we might git him declared crazy by the court.
SIMEON: He skinned 'em too slick. He got the best o' all on 'em. They'd never b'lieve him crazy. (*A pause.*) We got t' wait—till he's underground.
EBEN (*with a sardonic chuckle*): Honor thy father! (*They turn startled, and stare at him. He grins, then scowls.*) I pray he's died. (*They stare at him. He continues matter-of-factly.*) Supper's ready.
SIMEON AND PETER (*together*): Ay-eh.
EBEN (*gazing up at the sky*): Sun's downin' purty.
SIMEON AND PETER (*together*): Ay-eh. They's gold in the West.
EBEN: Ay-eh. (*Pointing.*) Yonder atop o' the hill pasture, ye mean?
SIMEON AND PETER (*together*): In Californi-a!
EBEN: Hunh? (*Stares at them indifferently for a second, then drawls.*) Waal—supper's gittin' cold. (*He turns back into kitchen.*)
SIMEON (*startled—smacks his lips*): I air hungry!
PETER (*sniffing*): I smells bacon!

SIMEON (*with hungry appreciation*): Bacon's good!

PETER (*in same tone*): Bacon's bacon! (*They turn, shouldering each other, their bodies bumping and rubbing together as they hurry clumsily to their food, like two friendly oxen toward their evening meal. They disappear around the right corner of house and can be heard entering the door.*)

Scene II

(*The color fades from the sky. Twilight begins. The interior of the kitchen is now visible. A pine table is at center, a cook-stove in the right rear corner, four rough wooden chairs, a tallow candle on the table. In the middle of the rear wall is fastened a big advertising poster with a ship in full sail and the word "California" in big letters. Kitchen utensils hang from nails. Everything is neat and in order but the atmosphere is of a men's camp kitchen rather than that of a home.*)

(*Places for three are laid. Eben takes boiled potatoes and bacon from the stove and puts them on the table, also a loaf of bread and a crock of water. Simeon and Peter shoulder in, slump down in their chairs without a word. Eben joins them. The three eat in silence for a moment, the two elder as naturally unrestrained as beasts of the field, Eben picking at his food without appetite, glancing at them with a tolerant dislike.*)

SIMEON (*suddenly turns to Eben*): Looky here! Ye'd oughtn't t' said that, Eben.

PETER: 'Twa'n't righteous.

EBEN: What?

SIMEON: Ye prayed he'd died.

EBEN: Waal—don't yew pray it? (*A pause.*)

PETER: He's our Paw.

EBEN (*violently*): Not mine!

SIMEON (*dryly*): Ye'd not let no one else say that about yer Maw! Ha! (*He gives one abrupt sardonic guffaw. Peter grins.*)

EBEN (*very pale*): I meant—I hain't his'n—I hain't like him—he hain't me!

PETER (*dryly*): Wait till ye've growed his age!

EBEN (*intensely*): I'm Maw—every drop o' blood! (*A pause. They stare at him with indifferent curiosity.*)

PETER (*reminiscently*): She was good t' Sim 'n' me. A good Stepmaw's scurse.

SIMEON: She was good t' everyone.

EBEN (*greatly moved, gets to his feet and makes an awkward bow to each of them—stammering*): I be thankful t' ye. I'm her—her heir. (*He sits down in confusion.*)

PETER (*after a pause—judicially*): She was good even t' him.

EBEN (*fiercely*): An' fur thanks he killed her!

SIMEON (*after a pause*): No one never kills nobody. It's allus somethin'. That's the murderer.

EBEN: Didn't he slave Maw t' death?

PETER: He's slaved himself t' death. He's slaved Sim 'n' me 'n' yew t' death—on'y none o' us hain't died—yit.

SIMEON: It's somethin'—drivin' him—t' drive us!

EBEN (*vengefully*): Waal—I hold him t' jedgment! (*Then scornfully.*) Somethin'! What's somethin'?

SIMEON: Dunno.

EBEN (*sardonically*): What's drivin' yew to Californi-a, mebbe? (*They look at him in surprise.*) Oh, I've heerd ye! (*Then, after a pause.*) But ye'll never go t' the gold fields!

PETER (*assertively*): Mebbe!

EBEN: Whar'll ye git the money?

PETER: We kin walk. It's an a'mighty ways—Californi-a—but if yew was t' put all the steps we've walked on this farm end t' end we'd be in the moon!

EBEN: The Injuns'll skulp ye on the plains.

SIMEON (*with grim humor*): We'll mebbe make 'em pay a hair fur a hair!

EBEN (*decisively*): But t'aint that. Ye won't never go because ye'll wait here fur yer share o' the farm, thinkin' allus he'll die soon.

SIMEON (*after a pause*): We've a right.

PETER: Two-thirds belongs t'us.

EBEN (*jumping to his feet*): Ye've no right! She wa'n't yewr Maw! It was her farm! Didn't he steal it from her? She's dead. It's my farm.

SIMEON (*sardonically*): Tell that t' Paw—when he comes! I'll bet ye a dollar he'll laugh—fur once in his life. Ha! (*He laughs himself in one single mirthless bark.*)

PETER (*amused in turn, echoes his brother*): Ha!

SIMEON (*after a pause*): What've ye got held agin us, Eben? Year arter year it's skulked in yer eye—somethin'.

PETER: Ay-eh.

EBEN: Ay-eh. They's somethin'. (*Suddenly exploding.*) Why didn't ye never stand between him 'n' my Maw when he was slavin' her to her grave—t' pay her back fur the kindness she done t' yew? (*There is a long pause. They stare at him in surprise.*)

SIMEON: Waal—the stock'd got t' be watered.

PETER: 'R they was woodin' t' do.

SIMEON: 'R plowin'.

PETER: 'R hayin'.

SIMEON: 'R spreadin' manure.

PETER: 'R weedin'.

SIMEON: 'R prunin'.

PETER: 'R milkin'.

EBEN (*breaking in harshly*): An' makin' walls—stone atop o' stone—makin' walls till yer heart's a stone ye heft up out o' the way o' growth onto a stone wall t' wall in yer heart!

SIMEON (*matter-of-factly*): We never had no time t' meddle.

PETER (*to Eben*): Yew was fifteen afore yer Maw died—an' big fur yer age. Why didn't ye never do nothin'?

EBEN (*harshly*): They was chores t' do, wasn't they? (*A pause—then slowly.*) It was on'y arter she died I come to think o' it. Me cookin'—doin' her work—that made me know her, suffer her sufferin'—she'd come back t' help—come back t' bile potatoes—come back t' fry bacon—come back t' bake biscuits—come back all cramped up t' shake the fire, an' carry ashes, her eyes weepin' an' bloody with smoke an' cinders same's they used t' be. She still comes back—stands by the stove thar in the evenin'—she can't find it nateral sleepin' an' restin' in peace. She can't git used t' bein' free—even in her grave.

SIMEON: She never complained none.

EBEN: She'd got too tired. She'd got too used t' bein' too tired. That was what he done. (*With vengeful passion.*) An' sooner'r later, I'll meddle. I'll say the thin's I didn't say then t' him! I'll yell 'em at the top o' my lungs. I'll see t' it my Maw gits some rest an' sleep in her grave! (*He sits down again, relapsing into a brooding silence. They look at him with a queer indifferent curiosity.*)

PETER (*after a pause*): Whar in tarnation d'ye s'pose he went, Sim?

SIMEON: Dunno. He druv off in the buggy, all spick an' span, with the mare all breshed an' shiny, druv off clackin' his tongue an' wavin' his whip. I remember it right well. I was finishin' plowin', it was spring an' May an' sunset, an' gold in the West, an' he druv off into it. I yells "Whar ye goin', Paw?" an' he hauls up by the stone wall a jiffy. His old snake's eyes was glitterin' in the sun like he'd been drinkin' a jugful an' he says with a mule's grin: "Don't ye run away till I come back!"

PETER: Wonder if he knowed we was wantin' fur Californi-a?

SIMEON: Mebbe. I didn't say nothin' and he says, lookin' kinder queer an' sick: "I been hearin' the hens cluckin' an' the roosters crowin' all the durn day. I been listenin't the cows lowin' an' everythin' else kickin' up till I can't stand it no more. It's spring an' I'm feelin' damned," he says. "Damned like an old bare hickory tree fit on'y fur burnin'," he says. An' then I calc'late I must've looked a mite hopeful, fur he adds real spry and vicious: "But don't git no fool idee I'm dead. I've sworn t' live a hundred an' I'll do it, if on'y t' spite yer sinful greed! An' now I'm ridin' out t' learn God's message t' me in the spring, like the prophets done. An' yew git back t' yer plowin'," he says. An' he druv off singin' a hymn. I thought he was drunk—'r I'd stopped him goin'.

EBEN (*scornfully*): No, ye wouldn't! Ye're scared o' him. He's stronger—inside—than both o' ye put together!

PETER (*sardonically*): An' yew—be yew Samson?°

EBEN: I'm gittin' stronger. I kin feel it growin' in me—growin' an' growin'—till it'll bust out—! (*He gets up and puts on his coat and a hat. They watch him, gradually breaking into grins. Eben avoids their eyes sheepishly.*) I'm goin' out fur a spell—up the road.

Samson: A biblical hero known for his great physical strength.

PETER: T' the village.

SIMEON: T' see Minnie?

EBEN (*defiantly*): Ay-eh!

PETER (*jeeringly*): The Scarlet Woman!

SIMEON: Lust—that's what's growin' in ye!

EBEN: Waal—she's purty!

PETER: She's been purty fur twenty year.

SIMEON: A new coat o' paint'll make a heifer out of forty.

EBEN: She hain't forty!

PETER: If she hain't, she's teeterin' on the edge.

EBEN (*desperately*): What d'yew know—

PETER: All they is . . . Sim knew her—an' then me arter—

SIMEON: An' Paw kin tell yew somethin' too! He was fust!

EBEN: D'ye mean t' say he . . . ?

SIMEON (*with a grin*): Ay-eh! We air his heirs in everythin'!

EBEN (*intensely*): That's more to it! That grows on it! It'll bust soon! (*Then violently.*) I'll go smash my fist in her face! (*He pulls open the door in rear violently.*)

SIMEON (*with a wink at Peter—drawlingly*): Mebbe—but the night's wa'm—purty—by the time ye git thar mebbe ye'll kiss her instead!

PETER: Sart'n he will! (*They both roar with coarse laughter. Eben rushes out and slams the door—then the outside front door—comes around the corner of the house and stands still by the gate, staring up at the sky.*)

SIMEON (*looking after him*): Like his Paw.

PETER: Dead spit an' image!

SIMEON: Dog'll eat dog!

PETER: Ay-eh. (*Pause. With yearning.*) Mebbe a year from now we'll be in Californi-a.

SIMEON: Ay-eh. (*A pause. Both yawn.*) Let's git t'bed. (*He blows out the candle. They go out door in rear. Eben stretches his arms up to the sky—rebelliously.*)

EBEN: Waal—thar's a star, an' somewhar's they's him, an' here's me, an' thar's Min up the road—in the same night. What if I does kiss her? She's like t'night, she's soft 'n' wa'm, her eyes kin wink like a star, her mouth's wa'm, her arms're wa'm, she smells like a wa'm plowed field, she's purty . . . Ay-eh! By God A'mighty she's purty, an' I don't give a damn how many sins she's sinned afore mine or who she's sinned 'em with, my sin's as purty as any one on 'em! (*He strides off down the road to the left.*)

Scene III

(*It is the pitch darkness just before dawn. Eben comes in from the left and goes around to the porch, feeling his way, chuckling bitterly and cursing half-aloud to himself.*)

EBEN: The cussed old miser! (*He can be heard going in the front door. There is a pause as he goes upstairs, then a loud knock on the bedroom door of the brothers.*) Wake up!

SIMEON (*startledly*): Who's thar?

EBEN (*Pushing open the door and coming in, a lighted candle in his hand. The bedroom of the brothers is revealed. Its ceiling is the sloping roof. They can stand upright only close to the center dividing wall of the upstairs. Simeon and Peter are in a double bed, front. Eben's cot is to the rear. Eben has a mixture of silly grin and vicious scowl on his face.*): I be!

PETER (*angrily*): What in hell's-fire. . . ?

EBEN: I got news fur ye! Ha! (*He gives one abrupt sardonic guffaw.*)

SIMEON (*angrily*): Couldn't ye hold it 'til we'd got our sleep?

EBEN: It's nigh sunup. (*Then explosively.*) He's gone an' married agen!

SIMEON AND PETER (*explosively*): Paw?

EBEN: Got himself hitched to a female 'bout thirty-five—an' purty, they says . . .

SIMEON (*aghast*): It's a durn lie!

PETER: Who says?

SIMEON: They been stringin' ye!

EBEN: Think I'm a dunce, do ye? The hull village says. The preacher from New Dover, he brung the news— told it t'our preacher—New Dover, that's whar the old loon got himself hitched—that's whar the woman lived—

PETER (*no longer doubting—stunned*): Waal . . . !

SIMEON (*the same*): Waal . . . !

EBEN (*sitting down on a bed—with vicious hatred*): Ain't he a devil out o' hell? It's jest t' spite us—the damned old mule!

PETER (*after a pause*): Everythin'll go t'her now.

SIMEON: Ay-eh. (*A pause—dully.*) Waal—if it's done—

PETER: It's done us. (*Pause—then persuasively.*) They's gold in the fields o' Californi-a, Sim. No good a-stayin' here now.

SIMEON: Jest what I was a-thinkin'. (*Then with decision.*) S'well fust's last! Let's light out and git this mornin'.

PETER: Suits me.

EBEN: Ye must like walkin'.

SIMEON (*sardonically*): If ye'd grow wings on us we'd fly thar!

EBEN: Ye'd like ridin' better—on a boat, wouldn't ye? (*Fumbles in his pocket and takes out a crumpled sheet of foolscap.*) Waal, if ye sign this ye kin ride on a boat. I've had it writ out an' ready in case ye'd ever go. It says fur three hundred dollars t' each ye agree yewr shares o' the farm is sold t' me. (*They look suspiciously at the paper. A pause.*)

SIMEON (*wonderingly*): But if he's hitched agen—

PETER: An' whar'd yew git that sum o' money, anyways?

EBEN (*cunningly*): I know whar it's hid. I been waitin'— Maw told me. She knew whar it lay fur years, but she was waitin' . . . It's her'n—the money he hoarded from her farm an' hid from Maw. It's my money by rights now.

PETER: Whar's it hid?

EBEN (*cunningly*): Whar yew won't never find it without me. Maw spied on him—'r she'd never knowed. (*A pause. They look at him suspiciously, and he at them.*) Waal, is it fa'r trade?

SIMEON: Dunno.

PETER: Dunno.

SIMEON (*looking at window*): Sky's grayin'.

PETER: Ye better start the fire, Eben.

SIMEON: An' fix some vittles.

EBEN: Ay-eh. (*Then with a forced jocular heartiness.*) I'll git ye a good one. If ye're startin' t' hoof it t' Californi-a ye'll need somethin' that'll stick t' yer ribs. (*He turns to the door, adding meaningly.*) But ye kin ride on a boat if ye'll swap. (*He stops at the door and pauses. They stare at him.*)

SIMEON (*suspiciously*): Whar was ye all night?

EBEN (*defiantly*): Up t' Min's. (*Then slowly.*) Walkin' thar, fust I felt 's if I'd kiss her; then I got a-thinkin' o' what ye'd said o' him an' her an' I says, I'll bust her nose fur that! Then I got t' the village an' heerd the news an' I got madder'n hell an' run all the way t' Min's not knowin' what I'd do—(*He pauses—then sheepishly but more defiantly.*) Waal—when I seen her, I didn't hit her—nor I didn't kiss her nuther—I begun t' beller like a calf an' cuss at the same time, I was so durn mad—an' she got scared—an' I jest grabbed holt an' tuk her! (*Proudly.*) Yes, sirree! I tuk her. She may've been his'n—an' your'n, too—but she's mine now!

SIMEON (*dryly*): In love, air yew?

EBEN (*with lofty scorn*): Love! I don't take no stock in sech slop!

PETER (*winking at Simeon*): Mebbe Eben's aimin' t' marry, too.

SIMEON: Min'd make a true faithful he'pmeet! (*They snicker.*)

EBEN: What do I care fur her—'ceptin' she's round an' wa'm? The p'int is she was his'n—an' now she b'longs t' me! (*He goes to the door—then turns— rebelliously.*) An' Min hain't sech a bad un. They's worse'n Min in the world, I'll bet ye! Wait'll we see this cow the Old Man's hitched t'! She'll beat Min, I got a notion! (*He starts to go out.*)

SIMEON (*suddenly*): Mebbe ye'll try t' make her your'n, too?

PETER: Ha! (*He gives a sardonic laugh of relish at this idea.*)

EBEN (*spitting with disgust*): Her—here—sleepin' with him—stealin' my Maw's farm! I'd as soon pet a skunk 'r kiss a snake! (*He goes out. The two stare after him suspiciously. A pause. They listen to his steps receding.*)

PETER: He's startin' the fire.

SIMEON: I'd like t' ride t' Californi-a—but—

PETER: Min might o' put some scheme in his head.

SIMEON: Mebbe it's all a lie 'bout Paw marryin'. We'd best wait an' see the bride.

PETER: An' don't sign nothin' till we does!

SIMEON: Nor till we've tested it's good money! (*Then with a grin.*) But if Paw's hitched we'd be sellin' Eben somethin' we'd never git nohow!

PETER: We'll wait an' see. (*Then with sudden vindictive anger.*) An' till he comes, let's yew 'n' me not wuk a lick, let Eben tend to thin's if he's a mind t', let's us jest sleep an' eat an' drink likker, an' let the hull damned farm go t' blazes!

SIMEON (*excitedly*): By God, we've 'arned a rest! We'll play rich fur a change. I hain't a-going to stir outa bed till breakfast's ready.

PETER: An' on the table!

SIMEON (*after a pause—thoughtfully*): What d'ye cal'c'late she'll be like—our new Maw? Like Eben thinks?

PETER: More'n' likely.

SIMEON (*vindictively*): Waal—I hope she's a she-devil that'll make him wish he was dead an' livin' in the pit o' hell fur comfort!

PETER (*fervently*): Amen!

SIMEON (*imitating his father's voice*): "I'm ridin' out t' learn God's message t' me in the spring like the prophets done," he says. I'll bet right then an' thar he knew plumb well he was goin' whorin', the stinkin' old hypocrite!

Scene IV

(*Same as scene II—shows the interior of the kitchen with a lighted candle on table. It is gray dawn outside. Simeon and Peter are just finishing their breakfast. Eben sits before his plate of untouched food, brooding frowningly.*)

PETER (*glancing at him rather irritably*): Lookin' glum don't help none.

SIMEON (*sarcastically*): Sorrowin' over his lust o' the flesh!

PETER (*with a grin*): Was she yer fust?

EBEN (*angrily*): None o'yer business. (*A pause.*) I was thinkin' o' him. I got a notion he's gittin' near—I kin feel him comin' on like yew kin feel malaria chill afore it takes ye.

PETER: It's too early yet.

SIMEON: Dunno. He'd like t' catch us nappin'—jest t' have somethin' t' hoss us 'round over.

PETER (*Mechanically gets to his feet. Simeon does the same.*): Waal—let's git t'wuk. (*They both plod mechanically toward the door before they realize. Then they stop short.*)

SIMEON (*grinning*): Ye're a cussed fool, Pete—and I be wuss! Let him see we hain't wukin'! We don't give a durn!

PETER (*as they go back to the table*): Not a damned durn! It'll serve t' show him we're done with him. (*They sit down again. Eben stares from one to the other with surprise.*)

SIMEON (*grins at him*): We're aimin' t' start bein' lilies o' the field.

PETER: Nary a toil 'r spin 'r lick o' wuk do we put in!

SIMEON: Ye're sole owner—till he comes—that's what ye wanted. Waal, ye got t' be sole hand, too.

PETER: The cows air bellerin'. Ye better hustle at the milkin'.

EBEN (*with excited joy*): Ye mean ye'll sign the paper?

SIMEON (*dryly*): Mebbe.

PETER: Mebbe.

SIMEON: We're considerin'. (*Peremptorily.*) Ye better git t' wuk.

EBEN (*with queer excitement*): It's Maw's farm agen! It's my farm! Them's my cows! I'll milk my durn fingers off fur cows o' mine! (*He goes out door in rear, they stare after him indifferently.*)

SIMEON: Like his Paw.

PETER: Dead spit 'n' image!

SIMEON: Waal—let dog eat dog! (*Eben comes out of front door and around the corner of the house. The sky is beginning to grow flushed with sunrise. Eben stops by the gate and stares around him with glowing, possessive eyes. He takes in the whole farm with his embracing glance of desire.*)

EBEN: It's purty! It's damned purty! It's mine! (*He suddenly throws his head back boldly and glares with hard, defiant eyes at the sky.*) Mine, d'ye hear? Mine! (*He turns and walks quickly off left, rear, toward the barn. The two brothers light their pipes.*)

SIMEON (*putting his muddy boots up on the table, tilting back his chair, and puffing defiantly*): Waal—this air solid comfort—fur once.

PETER: Ay-eh. (*He follows suit. A pause. Unconsciously they both sigh.*)

SIMEON (*suddenly*): He never was much o' a hand at milkin', Eben wa'n't.

PETER (*with a snort*): His hands air like hoofs! (*A pause.*)

SIMEON: Reach down the jug thar! Let's take a swaller. I'm feelin' kind o' low.

PETER: Good idee! (*He does so—gets two glasses—they pour out drinks of whisky.*) Here's t' the gold in Californi-a!

SIMEON: An' luck t' find it! (*They drink—puff resolutely—sigh—take their feet down from the table.*)

PETER: Likker don't pear t' sot right.

SIMEON: We hain't used t' it this early. (*A pause. They become very restless.*)

PETER: Gittin' close in this kitchen.

SIMEON (*with immense relief*): Let's git a breath o' air. (*They arise briskly and go out rear—appear around house and stop by the gate. They stare up at the sky with a numbed appreciation.*)

PETER: Purty!

SIMEON: Ay-eh. Gold's t' the East now.

PETER: Sun's startin' with us fur the Golden West.

SIMEON (*staring around the farm, his compressed face tightened, unable to conceal his emotion*): Waal—it's our last mornin'—mebbe.

PETER (*the same*): Ay-eh.

SIMEON (*stamps his foot on the earth and addresses it desperately*): Waal—ye've thirty year o' me buried in ye—spread out over ye—blood an' bone an' sweat—rotted away—fertilizin' ye—richin' yer soul—prime manure, by God, that's what I been t' ye!

PETER: Ay-eh! An' me.

SIMEON: An' yew, Peter. (*He sighs—then spits.*) Waal—no use'n cryin' over spilt milk.

PETER: They's gold in the West—an' freedom, mebbe. We been slaves t' stone walls here.

SIMEON (*defiantly*): We hain't nobody's slaves from this out—nor nothin's slaves nuther. (*A pause—restlessly.*) Speaking o' milk, wonder how Eben's managin'?

PETER: I s'pose he's managin'.

SIMEON: Mebbe we'd ought t' help—this once.

PETER: Mebbe. The cows knows us.

SIMEON: An' likes us. They don't know him much.

PETER: An' the hosses, an' pigs, an' chickens. They don't know him much.

SIMEON: They knows us like brothers—an' likes us! (*Proudly.*) Hain't we raised 'em t' be fust-rate, number one prize stock?

PETER: We hain't—not no more.

SIMEON (*dully*): I was fergittin'. (*Then resignedly.*) Waal, let's go help Eben a spell an' git waked up.

PETER: Suits me. (*They are starting off down left, rear, for the barn when Eben appears from there hurrying toward them, his face excited.*)

EBEN (*breathlessly*): Waal—har they be! The old mule an' the bride! I seen 'em from the barn down below at the turnin'.

PETER: How could ye tell that far?

EBEN: Hain't I as far-sight as he's near-sight? Don't I know the mare 'n' buggy, an' two people settin' in it? Who else . . . ? An' I tell ye I kin feel 'em a'comin', too! (*He squirms as if he had the itch.*)

PETER (*beginning to be angry*): Waal—let him do his own unhitchin'!

SIMEON (*angry in his turn*): Let's hustle in an' git our bundles an' be a-goin' as he's a-comin'. I don't want never t' step inside the door agen arter he's back. (*They both start back around the corner of the house. Eben follows them.*)

EBEN (*anxiously*): Will ye sign it afore ye go?

PETER: Let's see the color o' the old skinflint's money an' we'll sign. (*They disappear left. The two brothers clump upstairs to get their bundles. Eben appears in the kitchen, runs to window, peers out, comes back and pulls up a strip of flooring in under stove, takes out a canvas bag and puts it on table, then sets the floorboard back in place. The two brothers appear a moment after. They carry old carpetbags.*)

EBEN (*puts his hand on bag guardingly*): Have ye signed?

SIMEON (*shows paper in his hand*): Ay-eh. (*Greedily.*) Be that the money?

EBEN (*opens bag and pours out pile of twenty-dollar gold pieces*): Twenty-dollar pieces—thirty of 'em. Count 'em. (*Peter does so, arranging them in stacks of five, biting one or two to test them.*)

PETER: Six hundred. (*He puts them in bag and puts it inside his shirt carefully.*)

SIMEON (*handing paper to Eben*): Har ye be.

EBEN (*after a glance, folds it carefully and hides it under his shirt—gratefully*): Thank yew.

PETER: Thank yew fur the ride.

SIMEON: We'll send ye a lump o' gold fur Christmas. (*A pause. Eben stares at them and they at him.*)

PETER (*awkwardly*): Waal—we're a-goin'.

SIMEON: Comin' out t' the yard?

EBEN: No. I'm waitin' in here a spell. (*Another silence. The brothers edge awkwardly to door in rear—then turn and stand.*)

SIMEON: Waal—good-by.

PETER: Good-by.

EBEN: Good-by. (*They go out. He sits down at the table, faces the stove and pulls out the paper. He looks from it to the stove. His face, lighted up by the shaft of sunlight from the window, has an expression of trance. His lips move. The two brothers come out to the gate.*)

PETER (*looking off toward barn*): Thar he be—unhitchin'.

SIMEON (*with a chuckle*): I'll bet ye he's riled!

PETER: An thar she be.

SIMEON: Let's wait 'n' see what our new Maw looks like.

PETER (*with a grin*): An' give him our partin' cuss!

SIMEON (*grinning*): I feel like raisin' fun. I feel light in my head an' feet.

PETER: Me, too. I feel like laffin' till I'd split up the middle.

SIMEON: Reckon it's the likker?

PETER: No. My feet feel itchin' t' walk an' walk—an' jump high over thin's—an'. . . .

SIMEON: Dance? (*A pause.*)

PETER (*puzzled*): It's plumb onnateral.

SIMEON (*a light coming over his face*): I calc'late it's 'cause school's out. It's holiday. Fur once we're free!

PETER (*dazedly*): Free?

SIMEON: The halter's broke—the harness is busted—the fence bars is down—the stone walls air crumblin' an' tumblin'! We'll be kickin' up an' tearin' away down the road!

PETER (*drawing a deep breath—oratorically*): Anybody that wants this stinkin' old rock-pile of a farm kin hev it. T'ain't our'n, no sirree!

SIMEON (*takes the gate off its hinges and puts it under his arm*): We harby 'bolishes shet gates, an' open gates, an' all gates, by thunder!

PETER: We'll take it with us fur luck an' let 'er sail free down some river.

SIMEON (*as a sound of voices comes from left, rear*): Har they comes! (*The two brothers congeal into two stiff, grim-visaged statues. Ephraim Cabot and Abbie Putnam come in. Cabot is seventy-five, tall and gaunt, with great, wiry, concentrated power, but stoop-shouldered from toil. His face is as hard as if it were hewn out of a boulder, yet there is a weakness in it, a petty pride in its own narrow strength. His eyes are small, close together, and extremely near-sighted, blinking continually in the effort to focus on objects, their stare having a straining, ingrowing quality. He is dressed in his dismal black Sunday suit. Abbie is thirty-five, buxom, full of vitality. Her round face is pretty but marred by its rather gross sensuality. There is strength and obstinacy in her jaw, a hard determination in her eyes, and about her whole personality the same unsettled, untamed, desperate quality which is so apparent in Eben.)*

CABOT (*as they enter—a queer strangled emotion in his dry cracking voice*): Har we be t' hum, Abbie.

ABBIE (*with lust for the word*): Hum! (*Her eyes gloating on the house without seeming to see the two stiff figures at the gate.*) It's purty—purty! I can't b'lieve it's r'ally mine.

CABOT (*sharply*): Yewr'n? Mine! (*He stares at her penetratingly. She stares back. He adds relentlessly.*) Our'n—mebbe! It was lonesome too long. I was growin' old in the spring. A hum's got t' hev a woman.

ABBIE (*her voice taking possession*): A woman's got t' hev a hum!

CABOT (*nodding uncertainly*): Ay-eh. (*Then irritably.*) Whar be they? Ain't thar nobody about—'r wukin'—'r nothin'?

ABBIE (*Sees the brothers. She returns their stare of cold appraising contempt with interest—slowly.*): Thar's two men loafin' at the gate an' starin' at me like a couple o' strayed hogs.

CABOT (*straining his eyes*): I kin see 'em—but I can't make out. . . .

SIMEON: It's Simeon.

PETER: It's Peter.

CABOT (*exploding*): Why hain't ye wukin'?

SIMEON (*dryly*): We're waitin' t' welcome ye hum—yew an' the bride!

CABOT (*confusedly*): Huh? Waal—this be yer new Maw, boys. (*She stares at them and they at her.*)

SIMEON (*turns away and spits contemptuously*): I see her!

PETER (*spits also*): An I see her!

ABBIE (*with the conqueror's conscious superiority*): I'll go in an' look at *my* house. (*She goes slowly around to porch.*)

SIMEON (*with a snort*): *Her* house!

PETER (*calls after her*): Ye'll find Eben inside. Ye better not tell him it's *yewr* house.

ABBIE (*mouthing the name*): Eben. (*Then quietly.*) I'll tell Eben.

CABOT (*with a contemptuous sneer*): Ye needn't heed Eben. Eben's a dumb fool—like his Maw—soft an' simple!

SIMEON (*with his sardonic burst of laughter*): Ha! Eben's a chip o' yew—spit 'n' image—hard 'n' bitter's a hickory tree! Dog'll eat dog. He'll eat ye yet, old man!

CABOT (*commandingly*): Ye git t' wuk.

SIMEON (*as Abbie disappears in house—winks at Peter and says tauntingly*): So that thar's our new Maw, be it? Whar in hell did ye dig her up? (*He and Peter laugh.*)

PETER: Ha! Ye'd better turn her in the pen with the other sows. (*They laugh uproariously, slapping their thighs.*)

CABOT (*so amazed at their effrontery that he stutters in confusion*): Simeon! Peter! What's come over ye? Air ye drunk?

SIMEON: We're free, old man—free o' yew an' the hull damned farm! (*They grow more and more hilarious and excited.*)

PETER: An' we're startin' out fur the gold fields o' Californi-a!

SIMEON: Ye kin take this place an' burn it!

PETER: An' bury it—fur all we cares!

SIMEON: We're free, old man! (*He cuts a caper.*)

PETER: Free! (*He gives a kick in the air.*)

SIMEON (*in a frenzy*): Whoop!

PETER: Whoop! (*They do an absurd Indian war dance about the old man who is petrified between rage and the fear that they are insane.*)

SIMEON: We're free as Injuns! Lucky we don't skulp ye!

PETER: An' burn yer barn an' kill the stock!

SIMEON: An' rape yer new woman! Whoop! (*He and Peter stop their dance, holding their sides, rocking with wild laughter.*)

CABOT (*edging away*): Lust fur gold—fur the sinful, easy gold o' Californi-a! It's made ye mad!

SIMEON (*tauntingly*): Wouldn't ye like us to send ye back some sinful gold, ye old sinner?

PETER: They's gold besides what's in Californi-a! (*He retreats back beyond the vision of the old man and takes the bag of money and flaunts it in the air above his head, laughing.*)

SIMEON: And sinfuller, too!

PETER: We'll be voyagin' on the sea! Whoop! (*He leaps up and down.*)

SIMEON: Livin' free! Whoop! (*He leaps in turn.*)

CABOT (*suddenly roaring with rage*): My cuss on ye!

SIMEON: Take our'n in trade fur it! Whoop!

CABOT: I'll hev ye both chained up in the asylum!

PETER: Ye old skinflint! Good-by!

SIMEON: Ye old blood sucker! Good-by!

CABOT: Go afore I . . . !

PETER: Whoop! (*He picks a stone from the road. Simeon does the same.*)

SIMEON: Maw'll be in the parlor.

PETER: Ay-eh! One! Two!

CABOT (*frightened*): What air ye . . . ?

PETER: Three! (*They both throw, the stones hitting the parlor window with a crash of glass, tearing the shade.*)

SIMEON: Whoop!

PETER: Whoop!

CABOT (*in a fury now, rushing toward them*): If I kin lay hands on ye—I'll break yer bones fur ye! (*But they beat a capering retreat before him, Simeon with the gate still under his arm. Cabot comes back, panting with impotent rage. Their voices as they go off take up the song of the gold-seekers to the old tune of "Oh, Susannah!")*

"I jumped aboard the Liza ship,
And traveled on the sea,
And every time I thought of home
I wished it wasn't me!
Oh! Californi-a,
That's the land fur me!
I'm off to Californi-a!
With my wash bowl on my knee."

(In the meantime, the window of the upper bedroom on right is raised and Abbie sticks her head out. She looks down at Cabot—with a sigh of relief.)

ABBIE: Waal—that's the last o' them two, hain't it? *(He doesn't answer. Then in possessive tones).* This here's a nice bedroom, Ephraim. It's a r'al nice bed. Is it my room, Ephraim?

CABOT *(grimly—without looking up):* Our'n! *(She cannot control a grimace of aversion and pulls back her head slowly and shuts the window. A sudden horrible thought seems to enter Cabot's head.)* They been up to somethin'! Mebbe—mebbe they've pizened the stock—'r somethin'! *(He almost runs off down toward the barn. A moment later the kitchen door is slowly pushed open and Abbie enters. For a moment she stands looking at Eben. He does not notice her at first. Her eyes take him in penetratingly with a calculating appraisal of his strength as against hers. But under this her desire is dimly awakened by his youth and good looks. Suddenly he becomes conscious of her presence and looks up. Their eyes meet. He leaps to his feet, glowering at her speechlessly.)*

ABBIE *(in her most seductive tones which she uses all through this scene):* Be you—Eben? I'm Abbie— *(She laughs.)* I mean, I'm yer new Maw.

EBEN *(viciously):* No, damn ye!

ABBIE *(as if she hadn't heard—with a queer smile):* Yer Paw's spoke a lot o' yew. . . .

EBEN: Ha!

ABBIE: Ye mustn't mind him. He's an old man. *(A long pause. They stare at each other.)* I don't want t' pretend playin' Maw t' ye, Eben. *(Admiringly.)* Ye're too big an' too strong fur that. I want t' be frens with ye. Mebbe with me fur a fren ye'd find ye'd like livin' here better. I kin make it easy fur ye with him, mebbe. *(With a scornful sense of power.)* I calc'late I kin git him t' do most anythin' fur me.

EBEN *(with bitter scorn):* Ha! *(They stare again, Eben obscurely moved, physically attracted to her—in forced stilted tones.)* Yew kin go t' the devil!

ABBIE *(calmly):* If cussin' me does ye good, cuss all ye've a mind t'. I'm all prepared t' have ye agin me—at fust. I don't blame ye nuther. I'd feel the same at any stranger comin' t' take my Maw's place. *(He shudders. She is watching him carefully.)* Yew must've cared a lot fur yewr Maw, didn't ye? My Maw died

afore I'd growed. I don't remember her none. *(A pause.)* But yew won't hate me long, Eben. I'm not the wust in the world—an' yew an' me've got a lot in common. I kin tell that by lookin' at ye. Waal—I've had a hard life, too—oceans o' trouble an' nuthin' but wuk fur reward. I was a orphan early an' had t' wuk fur others in other folks' hums. Then I married an' he turned out a drunken spreer an' so he had to wuk fur others an' me too agen in other folks' hums, an' the baby died, an' my husband got sick an' died too, an' I was glad sayin' now I'm free fur once, on'y I diskivered right away all I was free fur was t'wuk agen in other folks' hums, doin' other folks' wuk till I'd most give up hope o' ever doin' my own wuk in my own hum, an' then your Paw come . . . *(Cabot appears returning from the barn. He comes to the gate and looks down the road the brothers have gone. A faint strain of their retreating voices is heard: "Oh, Californi-a! That's the place for me." He stands glowering, his fist clenched, his face grim with rage.)*

EBEN *(fighting against his growing attraction and sympathy—harshly):* An' bought yew—like a harlot! *(She is stung and flushes angrily. She has been sincerely moved by the recital of her troubles. He adds furiously.)* An' the price he's payin' ye—this farm—was my Maw's, damn ye!—an' mine now!

ABBIE *(with a cool laugh of confidence):* Yewr'n? We'll see 'bout that! *(Then strongly.)* Waal—what if I did need a hum? What else'd I marry an old man like him fur?

EBEN *(maliciously):* I'll tell him ye said that!

ABBIE *(smiling):* I'll say ye're lyin' a-purpose—an' he'll drive ye off the place!

EBEN: Ye devil!

ABBIE *(defying him):* This be my farm—this be my hum—this be my kitchen—!

EBEN *(furiously, as if he were going to attack her):* Shut up, damn ye!

ABBIE *(walks up to him—a queer coarse expression of desire in her face and body—slowly):* An' upstairs— that be my bedroom—an' my bed! *(He stares into her eyes, terribly confused and torn. She adds softly.)* I hain't bad nor mean—'ceptin' fur an enemy—but I got t' fight fur what's due me out o' life, if I ever 'spect t' git it. *(Then putting her hand on his arm— seductively.)* Let's yew 'n' me be frens, Eben.

EBEN *(stupidly—as if hypnotized):* Ay-eh. *(Then furiously flinging off her arm.)* No, ye durned old witch! I hate ye! *(He rushes out the door.)*

ABBIE *(looks after him smiling satisfiedly—then half to herself, mouthing the word):* Eben's nice. *(She looks at the table, proudly.)* I'll wash up *my* dishes now. *(Eben appears outside, slamming the door behind him. He comes around corner, stops on seeing his father, and stands staring at him with hate.)*

CABOT *(raising his arms to heaven in the fury he can no longer control):* Lord God o' Hosts, smite the undutiful sons with Thy wust cuss!

EBEN *(breaking in violently):* Yew 'n' yewr God! Allus cussin' folks—allus naggin' 'em!

CABOT (*oblivious to him—summoningly*): God o' the old! God o' the lonesome!

EBEN (*mockingly*): Naggin' His sheep t' sin! T' hell with yewr God! (*Cabot turns. He and Eben glower at each other.*)

CABOT (*harshly*): So it's yew. I might've knowed it. (*Shaking his finger threateningly at him.*) Blasphemin' fool! (*Then quickly.*) Why hain't ye t' wuk?

EBEN: Why hain't yew? They've went. I can't wuk it all alone.

CABOT (*contemptuously*): Nor noways! I'm wuth ten o' ye yit, old's I be! Ye'll never be more'n half a man! (*Then, matter-of-factly.*) Waal—let's git t' the barn. (*They go. A last faint note of the "Californi-a" song is heard from the distance. Abbie is washing her dishes.*)

PART II • *Scene I*

(*The exterior of the farmhouse, as in part I—a hot Sunday afternoon two months later. Abbie, dressed in her best, is discovered sitting in a rocker at the end of the porch. She rocks listlessly, enervated by the heat, staring in front of her with bored, half-closed eyes.*)

(*Eben sticks his head out of his bedroom window. He looks around furtively and tries to see—or hear—if anyone is on the porch, but although he has been careful to make no noise, Abbie has sensed his movement. She stops rocking, her face grows animated and eager, she waits attentively. Eben seems to feel her presence, he scowls back his thoughts of her and spits with exaggerated disdain—then withdraws back into the room. Abbie waits, holding her breath as she listens with passionate eagerness for every sound within the house.*)

(*Eben comes out. Their eyes meet; his falter. He is confused, he turns away and slams the door resentfully. At this gesture, Abbie laughs tantalizingly, amused but at the same time piqued and irritated. He scowls, strides off the porch to the path and starts to walk past her to the road with a grand swagger of ignoring her existence. He is dressed in his store suit, spruced up, his face shines from soap and water. Abbie leans forward on her chair, her eyes hard and angry now, and, as he passes her, gives a sneering, taunting chuckle.*)

EBEN (*stung—turns on her furiously*): What air yew cacklin' 'bout?

ABBIE (*triumphant*): Yew!

EBEN: What about me?

ABBIE: Ye look all slicked up like a prize bull.

EBEN (*with a sneer*): Waal—ye hain't so durned purty yerself, be ye? (*They stare into each other's eyes, his held by hers in spite of himself, hers glowingly possessive. Their physical attraction becomes a palpable force quivering in the hot air.*)

ABBIE (*softly*): Ye don't mean that, Eben. Ye may think ye mean it, mebbe, but ye don't. Ye can't. It's agin nature, Eben. Ye been fightin' yer nature ever since the day I

come—tryin' t' tell yerself I hain't purty t' ye. (*She laughs a low humid laugh without taking her eyes from his. A pause—her body squirms desirously—she murmurs languorously.*) Hain't the sun strong an' hot? Ye kin feel it burnin' into the earth—Nature—makin' thin's grow—bigger 'n' bigger—burnin' inside ye—makin' ye want t' grow—into somethin' else—till ye're jined with it—an' it's your'n—but it owns ye, too—ant makes ye grow bigger—like a tree—like them elums—(*She laughs again softly, holding his eyes. He takes a step toward her, compelled against his will.*) Nature'll beat ye, Eben. Ye might's well own up t' it fust 's last.

EBEN (*trying to break from her spell—confusedly*): If Paw'd hear ye goin' on.... (*Resentfully.*) But ye've made such a damned idjit out o' the old devil...! (*Abbie laughs.*)

ABBIE: Waal—hain't it easier fur yew with him changed softer?

EBEN (*defiantly*): No. I'm fightin' him—fightin' yew—fightin' fur Maw's rights t' her hum! (*This breaks her spell for him. He glowers at her.*) An' I'm onto ye. Ye hain't foolin' me a mite. Ye're aimin' t' swaller up everythin' an' make it your'n. Waal, you'll find I'm a heap sight bigger hunk nor yew kin chew! (*He turns from her with a sneer.*)

ABBIE (*trying to regain her ascendancy—seductively*): Eben!

EBEN: Leave me be! (*He starts to walk away.*)

ABBIE (*more commandingly*): Eben!

EBEN (*stops—resentfully*): What d'ye want?

ABBIE (*trying to conceal a growing excitement*): Whar air ye goin'?

EBEN (*with malicious nonchalance*): Oh—up the road a spell.

ABBIE: T' the village?

EBEN (*airily*): Mebbe.

ABBIE (*excitedly*): T' see that Min, I s'pose?

EBEN: Mebbe.

ABBIE (*weakly*): What d'ye want t' waste time on her fur?

EBEN (*revenging himself now—grinning at her*): Ye can't beat Nature, didn't ye say? (*He laughs and again starts to walk away.*)

ABBIE (*bursting out*): An ugly old hake!

EBEN (*with a tantalizing sneer*): She's purtier'n yew be!

ABBIE: That every wuthless drunk in the country has....

EBEN (*tauntingly*): Mebbe—but she's better'n yew. She owns up fa'r 'n' squar' t' her doin's.

ABBIE (*furiously*): Don't ye dare compare....

EBEN: She don't go sneakin' an' stealin'—what's mine.

ABBIE (*savagely seizing on his weak point*): Your'n? Yew mean—my farm?

EBEN: I mean the farm yew sold yerself fur like any other old whore—my farm!

ABBIE (*stung—fiercely*): Ye'll never live t' see the day when even a stinkin' weed on it'll belong t' ye! (*Then in a scream.*) Git out o' my sight! Go on t' yer slut—disgracin' yer Paw 'n' me! I'll git yer Paw t' horsewhip ye off the place if I want t'! Ye're only livin' here 'cause I tolerate ye! Git along! I hate the sight o' ye! (*She stops, panting and glaring at him.*)

EBEN (*returning her glance in kind*): An' I hate the sight o' yew! (*He turns and strides off up the road. She follows his retreating figure with concentrated hate. Old Cabot appears coming up from the barn. The hard, grim expression of his face has changed. He seems in some queer way softened, mellowed. His eyes have taken on a strange, incongruous dreamy quality. Yet there is no hint of physical weakness about him—rather he looks more robust and younger. Abbie sees him and turns away quickly with unconcealed aversion. He comes slowly up to her.*)

CABOT (*mildly*): War yew an' Eben quarrelin' agen?

ABBIE (*shortly*): No.

CABOT: Ye was talkie' a'mighty loud. (*He sits down on the edge of porch.*)

ABBIE (*snappishly*): If ye heerd us they hain't no need askin' questions.

CABOT: I didn't hear what ye said.

ABBIE (*relieved*): Waal—it wa'n't nothin' t' speak on.

CABOT (*after a pause*): Eben's queer.

ABBIE (*bitterly*): He's the dead spit 'n' image o' yew!

CABOT (*queerly interested*): D'ye think so, Abbie? (*After a pause, ruminatingly.*) Me 'n' Eben's allus fit 'n' fit. I never could b'ar him noways. He's so thunderin' soft—like his Maw.

ABBIE (*scornfully*): Ay-eh! 'Bout as soft as yew be!

CABOT (*as if he hadn't heard*): Mebbe I been too hard on him.

ABBIE (*jeeringly*): Waal—ye're gittin' soft now—soft as slop! That's what Eben was sayin'.

CABOT (*his face instantly grim and ominous*): Eben was sayin'? Waal, he'd best not do nothin' t' try me 'r he'll soon diskiver. . . . (*A pause. She keeps her face turned away. His gradually softens. He stares up at the sky.*) Purty, hain't it?

ABBIE (*crossly*): I don't see nothin' purty.

CABOT: The sky. Feels like a wa'm field up thar.

ABBIE (*sarcastically*): Air yew aimin' t' buy up over the farm too? (*She snickers contemptuously.*)

CABOT (*strangely*): I'd like t' own my place up thar. (*A pause.*) I'm gittin' old, Abbie. I'm gittin' ripe on the bough. (*A pause. She stares at him mystified. He goes on.*) It's allus lonesome cold in the house—even when it's bilin' hot outside. Hain't yew noticed?

ABBIE: No.

CABOT: It's wa'm down t' the barn—nice smellin' an' warm—with the cows. (*A pause.*) Cows is queer.

ABBIE: Like yew?

CABOT: Like Eben. (*A pause.*) I'm gittin' t' feel resigned t' Eben—jest as I got t' feel 'bout his Maw. I'm gittin' t' learn to b'ar his softness—jest like her'n. I calc'late I c'd a'most take t' him—if he wa'n't sech a dumb fool! (*A pause.*) I s'pose it's old age a-creepin' in my bones.

ABBIE (*indifferently*): Waal—ye hain't dead yet.

CABOT (*roused*): No, I hain't, yew bet—not by a hell of a sight—I'm sound 'n' tough as hickory! (*Then moodily.*) But arter three score and ten the Lord warns ye t' prepare. (*A pause.*) That's why Eben's come in my head. Now that his cussed sinful brothers is gone their path t' hell, they's no one left but Eben.

ABBIE (*resentfully*): They's me, hain't they? (*Agitatedly.*) What's all this sudden likin' ye've tuk to Eben? Why don't ye say nothin' 'bout me? Hain't I yer lawful wife?

CABOT (*simply*): Ay-eh. Ye be. (*A pause—he stares at her desirously—his eyes grow avid—then with a sudden movement he seizes her hands and squeezes them, declaiming in a queer camp meeting preacher's tempo.*) Yew air my Rose o' Sharon! Behold, yew air fair; yer eyes air doves; yer lips air like scarlet; yer two breasts air like two fawns; yer navel be like a round goblet; yer belly be like a heap o' wheat. . . . (*He covers her hand with kisses. She does not seem to notice. She stares before her with hard angry eyes.*)

ABBIE (*jerking her hands away—harshly*): So ye're plannin' t' leave the farm t' Eben, air ye?

CABOT (*dazedly*): Leave . . . ? (*Then with resentful obstinacy.*) I hain't a-givin' it t' no one!

ABBIE (*remorselessly*): Ye can't take it with ye.

CABOT (*thinks a moment—then reluctantly*): No, I calc'late not. (*After a pause—with a strange passion.*) But if I could, I would, by the Eternal! 'R if I could, in my dyin' hour, I'd set it afire an' watch it burn—this house an' every ear o' corn an' every tree down t' the last blade o' hay! I'd sit an' know it was all a-dying with me an' no one else'd ever own what was mine, what I'd made out o' nothin' with my own sweat 'n' blood! (*A pause—then he adds with a queer affection.*) 'Ceptin' the cows. Them I'd turn free.

ABBIE (*harshly*): An' me?

CABOT (*with a queer smile*): Ye'd be turned free, too.

ABBIE (*furiously*): So that's the thanks I git fur marryin' ye—t' have ye change kind to Eben who hates ye, an' talk o' turnin' me out in the road.

CABOT (*hastily*): Abbie! Ye know I wa'n't. . . .

ABBIE (*vengefully*): Just let me tell ye a thing or two 'bout Eben! Whar's he gone? T' see that harlot, Min! I tried fur t' stop him. Disgracin' yew an' me—on the Sabbath, too!

CABOT (*rather guiltily*): He's a sinner—nateral-born. It's lust eatin' his heart.

ABBIE (*enraged beyond endurance—wildly vindictive*): An' his lust fur me! Kin ye find excuses fur that?

CABOT (*stares at her—after a dead pause*): Lust—fur yew?

ABBIE (*defiantly*): He was tryin' t' make love t' me—when ye heerd us quarrelin'.

CABOT (*stares at her—then a terrible expression of rage comes over his face—he springs to his feet shaking all over*): By the A'mighty God—I'll end him!

ABBIE (*frightened now for Eben*): No! Don't ye!

CABOT (*violently*): I'll git the shotgun an' blow his soft brains t' the top o' them elums!

ABBIE (*throwing her arms around him*): No, Ephraim!

CABOT (*pushing her away violently*): I will, by God!

ABBIE (*in a quieting tone*): Listen, Ephraim. 'Twa'n't nothin' bad—on'y a boy's foolin'—'twa'n't meant serious—jest jokin' an' teasin'. . . .

CABOT: Then why did ye say—lust?

ABBIE: It must hev sounded wusser'n I meant. An' I was mad at thinkin'—ye'd leave him the farm.

CABOT (*quieter but still grim and cruel*): Waal then, I'll horsewhip him off the place if that much'll content ye.

ABBIE (*reaching out and taking his hand*): No. Don't think o' me! Ye mustn't drive him off. 'Tain't sensible. Who'll ye get to help ye on the farm? They's no one hereabouts.

CABOT (*considers this—then nodding his appreciation*): Ye got a head on ye. (*Then irritably.*) Waal, let him stay. (*He sits down on the edge of the porch. She sits beside him. He murmurs contemptuously.*) I oughtn't t' git riled so—at that 'ere fool calf. (*A pause.*) But har's the p'int. What son o' mine'll keep on here t' the farm—when the Lord does call me? Simeon an' Peter air gone t' hell—an' Eben's follerin' 'em.

ABBIE: They's me.

CABOT: Ye're on'y a woman.

ABBIE: I'm yewr wife.

CABOT: That hain't me. A son is me—my blood—mine. Mine ought t' git mine. An' then it's still mine—even though I be six foot under. D'ye see?

ABBIE (*giving him a look of hatred*): Ay-eh. I see. (*She becomes very thoughtful, her face growing shrewd, her eyes studying Cabot craftily.*)

CABOT: I'm gittin' old—ripe on the bough. (*Then with a sudden forced reassurance.*) Not but what I hain't a hard nut t' crack even yet—an' fur many a year t' come! By the Eternal, I kin break most o' the young fellers' backs at any kind o' work any day o' the year!

ABBIE (*suddenly*): Mebbe the Lord'll give *us* a son.

CABOT (*turns and stares at her eagerly*): Ye mean—a son—t' me 'n' yew?

ABBIE (*with a cajoling smile*): Ye're a strong man yet, hain't ye? 'Tain't noways impossible, be it? We know that. Why d'ye stare so? Hain't ye never thought o' that afore? I been thinkin' o' it all along. Ay-eh—an' I been prayin' it'd happen, too.

CABOT (*his face growing full of joyous pride and a sort of religious ecstasy*): Ye been prayin', Abbie?—fur a son?—t' us?

ABBIE: Ay-eh. (*With a grim resolution.*) I want a son now.

CABOT (*excitedly clutching both of her hands in his*): It'd be the blessin' o' God, Abbie—the blessin' o' God A'mighty on me—in my old age—in my lonesomeness! They hain't nothin' I wouldn't do fur ye then, Abbie. Ye'd hev on'y t' ask it—anythin' ye'd a mind t'!

ABBIE (*interrupting*): Would ye will the farm t' me then—t' me an' it . . . ?

CABOT (*vehemently*): I'd do anythin' ye axed, I tell ye! I swar it! May I be everlastin' damned t' hell if I wouldn't! (*He sinks to his knees pulling her down*

with him. He trembles all over with the fervor of his hopes.*) Pray t' the Lord agen, Abbie. It's the Sabbath! I'll jine ye! Two prayers air better nor one. "An' God hearkened unto Rachel"! An' God hearkened unto Abbie! Pray, Abbie! Pray fur him to hearken! (*He bows his head, mumbling. She pretends to do likewise but gives him a side glance of scorn and triumph.*)

Scene II

(*About eight in the evening. The interior of the two bedrooms on the top floor is shown. Eben is sitting on the side of his bed in the room on the left. On account of the heat he has taken off everything but his undershirt and pants. His feet are bare. He faces front, brooding moodily, his chin propped on his hands, a desperate expression on his face.*)

(*In the other room Cabot and Abbie are sitting side by side on the edge of their bed, an old four-poster with feather mattress. He is in his nightshirt, she in her nightdress. He is still in the queer, excited mood into which the notion of a son has thrown him. Both rooms are lighted dimly and flickeringly by tallow candles.*)

CABOT: The farm needs a son.

ABBIE: I need a son.

CABOT: Ay-eh. Sometimes ye air the farm an' sometimes the farm be yew. That's why I clove t'ye in my lonesomeness. (*A pause. He pounds his knee with his fist.*) Me an' the farm has got t' beget a son!

ABBIE: Ye'd best go t' sleep. Ye're gittin' thin's all mixed.

CABOT (*with an impatient gesture*): No, I hain't. My mind's clear's a well. Ye don't know me, that's it. (*He stares hopelessly at the floor.*)

ABBIE (*indifferently*): Mebbe. (*In the next room Eben gets up and paces up and down distractedly. Abbie hears him. Her eyes fasten on the intervening wall with concentrated attention. Eben stops and stares. Their hot glances seem to meet through the wall. Unconsciously he stretches out his arms for her and she half rises. Then aware, he mutters a curse at himself and flings himself face downward on the bed, his clenched fists above his head, his face buried in the pillow. Abbie relaxes with a faint sigh but her eyes remain fixed on the wall; she listens with all her attention for some movement from Eben.*)

CABOT (*suddenly raises his head and looks at her—scornfully*): Will ye ever know me—'r will any man 'r woman? (*Shaking his head.*) No. I calc'late wa'n't t' be. (*He turns away. Abbie looks at the wall. Then, evidently unable to keep silent about his thoughts, without looking at his wife, he puts out his hand and clutches her knee. She starts violently, looks at him, sees he is not watching her, concentrates again on the wall, and pays no attention to what he says.*) Listen, Abbie. When I come here fifty odd year ago—I was jest twenty an' the strongest an' hardest ye ever seen—ten times as strong an' fifty times as hard as Eben. Waal—this place was nothin' but fields o' stones. Folks laughed when I tuk it. They couldn't know what I knowed. When ye kin make corn sprout out o' stones, God's livin' in yew! They wa'n't strong enuf fur that! They reckoned God was easy. They laughed. They don't laugh no more. Some died hereabouts. Some went West an' died. They're all underground—fur follerin' arter an easy God. God hain't easy. (*He shakes his head slowly.*) An' I growed hard. Folks kept allus sayin' he's a hard man like 'twas sinful t' be hard, so's at last I said back at 'em: Waal then, by thunder, ye'll git me hard an' see how ye like it! (*Then suddenly.*) But I give in t' weakness once. 'Twas arter I'd been here two year. I got weak—despairful—they was so many stones. They was a party leavin', givin' up, goin' West. I jined 'em. We tracked on 'n' on. We come t' broad medders, plains, whar the soil was black an' rich as gold. Nary a stone. Easy. Ye'd on'y to plow an' sow an' then set an' smoke yer pipe an' watch thin's grow. I could o' been a rich man—but somethin' in me fit me an' fit me—the voice o' God sayin': "This hain't wuth nothin' t' Me. Git ye back t' hum!" I got afeerd o' that voice an' I lit out back t' hum here, leavin' my claim an' crops t' whoever'd a mind t' take 'em. Ay-eh. I actoolly give up what was rightful mine! God's hard, not easy! God's in the stones! Build my church on a rock—out o' stones an' I'll be in them! That's what He meant t' Peter! (*He sighs heavily—a pause.*) Stones. I picked 'em up an' piled 'em into walls. Ye kin read the years of my life in them walls, every day a hefted stone, climbin' over the hills up and down, fencin' in the fields that was mine, whar I'd made thin's grow out o' nothin'—like the will o' God, like the servant o' His hand. It wa'n't easy. It was hard an' He made me hard fur it. (*He pauses.*) All the time I kept gittin' lonesomer. I tuk a wife. She bore Simeon an' Peter. She was a good woman. She wuked hard. We was married twenty year. She never knowed me. She helped but she never knowed what she was helpin'. I was allus lonesome. She died. After that it wa'n't so lonesome fur a spell. (*A pause.*) I lost count o' the years. I had no time t' fool away countin' 'em. Sim an' Peter helped. The farm growed. It was all mine! When I thought o' that I didn't feel lonesome. (*A pause.*) But ye can't hitch yer mind t' one thin' day an' night. I tuk another wife—Eben's Maw. Her folks was contestin' me at law over my deeds t' the farm—my farm! That's why Eben keeps a-talkin' his fool talk o' this bein' his Maw's farm. She bore Eben. She was purty—but soft. She tried t' be hard. She couldn't. She never knowed me nor nothin'. It was lonesomer 'n hell with her. After a matter o' sixteen odd years, she died. (*A pause.*) I lived with the boys. They hated me 'cause I was hard. I hated them 'cause they was soft. They coveted the farm without knowin' what it meant. It made me bitter 'n wormwood. It aged me—them coveting what I'd made fur

mine. Then this spring the call come—the voice o' God cryin' in my wilderness, in my lonesomeness—t' go out an' seek an' find! (*Turning to her with strange passion.*) I sought ye an' I found ye! Yew air my Rose o' Sharon! Yer eyes air like.... (*She has turned a blank face, resentful eyes to his. He stares at her for a moment—then harshly.*) Air ye any the wiser fur all I've told ye?

ABBIE (*confusedly*): Mebbe.

CABOT (*pushing her away from him—angrily*): Ye don't know nothin'—nor never will. If ye don't hev a son t' redeem ye.... (*This in a tone of cold threat.*)

ABBIE (*resentfully*): I've prayed, hain't I?

CABOT (*bitterly*): Pray agen—fur understandin'!

ABBIE (*a veiled threat in her tone*): Ye'll have a son out o' me, I promise ye.

CABOT: How kin ye promise?

ABBIE: I got second-sight mebbe. I kin foretell. (*She gives a queer smile.*)

CABOT: I believe ye have. Ye give me the chills sometimes. (*He shivers.*) It's cold in this house. It's oneasy. They's thin's pokin' about in the dark—in the corners. (*He pulls on his trousers, tucking in his nightshirt, and pulls on his boots.*)

ABBIE (*surprised*): Whar air ye goin'?

CABOT (*queerly*): Down whar it's restful—whar it's warm—down t' the barn. (*Bitterly.*) I kin talk t' the cows. They know. They know the farm an' me. They'll give me peace. (*He turns to go out the door.*)

ABBIE (*a bit frightenedly*): Air ye ailin' tonight, Ephraim?

CABOT: Growin'. Growin' ripe on the bough. (*He turns and goes, his boots clumping down the stairs. Eben sits up with a start, listening. Abbie is conscious of his movement and stares at the wall. Cabot comes out of the house around the corner and stands by the gate, blinking at the sky. He stretches up his hands in a tortured gesture.*) God A'mighty, call from the dark! (*He listens as if expecting an answer. Then his arms drop, he shakes his head and plods off toward the barn. Eben and Abbie stare at each other through the wall. Eben sighs heavily and Abbie echoes it. Both become terribly nervous, uneasy. Finally Abbie gets up and listens, her ear to the wall. He acts as if he saw every move she was making, he becomes resolutely still. She seems driven into a decision—goes out the door in rear determinedly. His eyes follow her. Then as the door of his room is opened softly, he turns away, waits in an attitude of strained fixity. Abbie stands for a second staring at him, her eyes burning with desire. Then with a little cry she runs over and throws her arms about his neck, she pulls his head back and covers his mouth with kisses. At first, he submits dumbly; then he puts his arms about her neck and returns her kisses, but finally, suddenly aware of his hatred, he hurls her away from him, springing to his feet. They stand speechless and breathless, panting like two animals.*)

ABBIE (*at last—painfully*): Ye shouldn't, Eben—ye shouldn't—I'd make ye happy!

Abbie in the 1988 Pushkin Theatre (Moscow) production of *Desire under the Elms*, directed by Mark Lamos of the Hartford Stage Company.

EBEN (*harshly*): I don't want t' be happy—from yew!

ABBIE (*helplessly*): Ye do, Eben! Ye do! Why d'ye lie?

EBEN (*viciously*): I don't take t'ye, I tell ye! I hate the sight o' ye!

ABBIE (*with an uncertain troubled laugh*): Waal, I kissed ye anyways—an' ye kissed back—yer lips was burnin'—ye can't lie 'bout that! (*Intensely.*) If ye don't care, why did ye kiss me back—why was yer lips burnin'?

EBEN (*wiping his mouth*): It was like pizen on 'em. (*Then tauntingly.*) When I kissed ye back, mebbe I thought 'twas someone else.

ABBIE (*wildly*): Min?

EBEN: Mebbe.

ABBIE (*torturedly*): Did ye go t' see her? Did ye r'ally go? I thought ye mightn't. Is that why ye throwed me off jest now?

EBEN (*sneeringly*): What if it be?

ABBIE (*raging*): Then ye're a dog, Eben Cabot!

EBEN (*threateningly*): Ye can't talk that way t' me!

ABBIE (*with a shrill laugh*): Can't I? Did ye think I was in love with ye—a weak thin' like yew? Not much! I on'y wanted ye fur a purpose o' my own—an' I'll hev ye fur it yet 'cause I'm stronger'n yew be!

EBEN (*resentfully*): I knowed well it was on'y part o' yer plan t' swaller everythin'!

ABBIE (*tauntingly*): Mebbe!

EBEN (*furious*): Git out o' my room!

ABBIE: This air my room an' ye're on'y hired help!

EBEN (*threateningly*): Git out afore I murder ye!

ABBIE (*quite confident now*): I hain't a mite afeerd. Ye want me, don't ye? Yes, ye do! An' yer Paw's son'll never kill what he wants! Look at yer eyes! They's lust fur me in 'em, burnin' 'em up! Look at yer lips now! They're tremblin' an' longin' t' kiss me, an' yer teeth t' bite! (*He is watching her now with a horrible fascination. She laughs a crazy triumphant laugh.*) I'm a-goin' t' make all o' this hum my hum! They's one room hain't mine yet, but it's a-goin' t' be tonight. I'm a-goin' down now an' light up! (*She makes him a mocking bow.*) Won't ye come courtin' me in the best parlor, Mister Cabot?

EBEN (*staring at her—horribly confused—dully*): Don't ye dare! It hain't been opened since Maw died an' was laid out thar! Don't ye . . . ! (*But her eyes are fixed on his so burningly that his will seems to wither before hers. He stands swaying toward her helplessly.*)

ABBIE (*holding his eyes and putting all her will into her words as she backs out the door*): I'll expect ye afore long, Eben.

EBEN (*Stares after her for a while, walking toward the door. A light appears in the parlor window. He murmurs.*): In the parlor? (*This seems to arouse connotations, for he comes back and puts on his white shirt, collar, half ties the tie mechanically, puts on coat, takes his hat, stands barefooted looking about him in bewilderment, mutters wonderingly.)* Maw! Whar air yew? (*Then goes slowly toward the door in rear.*)

Scene III

(*A few minutes later. The interior of the parlor is shown. A grim, repressed room like a tomb in which the family has been interred alive. Abbie sits on the edge of the horsehair sofa. She has lighted all the candles and the room is revealed in all its preserved ugliness. A change has come over the woman. She looks awed and frightened now, ready to run away.*)

(*The door is opened and Eben appears. His face wears an expression of obsessed confusion. He stands staring at her, his arms hanging disjointedly from his shoulders, his feet bare, his hat in his hand.*)

ABBIE (*after a pause—with a nervous, formal politeness*): Won't ye set?

EBEN (*dully*): Ay-eh. (*Mechanically he places his hat carefully on the floor near the door and sits stiffly beside her on the edge of the sofa. A pause. They both remain rigid, looking straight ahead with eyes full of fear.*)

ABBIE: When I fust come in—in the dark—they seemed somethin' here.

EBEN (*simply*): Maw.

ABBIE: I kin still feel—somethin'. . . .

EBEN: It's Maw.

ABBIE: At fust I was feered o' it. I wanted t' yell an' run. Now—since yew come—seems like it's growin' soft an' kind t' me. (*Addressing the air—queerly.*) Thank yew.

EBEN: Maw allus loved me.

ABBIE: Mebbe it knows I love yew, too. Mebbe that makes it kind t' me.

EBEN (*dully*): I dunno. I should think she'd hate ye.

ABBIE (*with certainty*): No. I kin feel it don't—not no more.

EBEN: Hate ye fur stealin' her place—here in her hum—settin' in her parlor whar she was laid—(*He suddenly stops, staring stupidly before him.*)

ABBIE: What is it, Eben?

EBEN (*in a whisper*): Seems like Maw didn't want me t' remind ye.

ABBIE (*excitedly*): I knowed, Eben! It's kind t' me! It don't b'ar me no grudges fur what I never knowed an' couldn't help!

EBEN: Maw b'ars him a grudge.

ABBIE: Waal, so does all o' us.

EBEN: Ay-eh. (*With passion.*) I does, by God!

ABBIE (*taking one of his hands in hers and patting it*): Thar! Don't git riled thinkin' o' him. Think o' yer Maw who's kind t' us. Tell me about yer Maw, Eben.

Raymond J. Barry and Amelia Campbell in the American Repertory Theatre's 2004–2005 production of *Desire under the Elms*, directed by János Szász.

EBEN: They hain't nothin' much. She was kind. She was good.

ABBIE (*Putting one arm over his shoulder. He does not seem to notice—passionately.*): I'll be kind an' good t' ye!

EBEN: Sometimes she used t' sing fur me.

ABBIE: I'll sing fur ye!

EBEN: This was her hum. This was her farm.

ABBIE: This is my hum! This is my farm!

EBEN: He married her t' steal 'em. She was soft an' easy. He couldn't 'preciate her.

ABBIE: He can't 'preciate me!

EBEN: He murdered her with his hardness.

ABBIE: He's murderin' me!

EBEN: She died. (*A pause.*) Sometimes she used to sing fur me. (*He bursts into a fit of sobbing.*)

ABBIE (*both her arms around him—with wild passion*): I'll sing fur ye! I'll die fur ye! (*In spite of her overwhelming desire for him, there is a sincere maternal love in her manner and voice—a horribly frank mixture of lust and mother love.*) Don't cry, Eben! I'll take yer Maw's place! I'll be everythin' she was t' ye! Let me kiss ye, Eben! (*She pulls his head around. He makes a bewildered pretense of resistance. She is tender.*) Don't be afeered! I'll kiss ye pure, Eben—same 's if I was a Maw t' ye—an' ye kin kiss me back 's if yew was my son—my boy—sayin' good-night t' me! Kiss me, Eben. (*They kiss in restrained fashion. Then suddenly wild passion overcomes her. She kisses him lustfully again and again and he flings his arms about her and returns her kisses. Suddenly, as in the bedroom, he frees himself from her violently and springs to his feet. He is trembling all over, in a strange state of terror. Abbie strains her arms toward him with fierce pleading.*) Don't ye leave me, Eben! Can't ye see it hain't enuf—lovin' ye like a Maw—can't ye see it's got t' be that an' more—much more—a hundred times more—fur me t' be happy—fur yew t' be happy?

EBEN (*to the presence he feels in the room*): Maw! Maw! What d'ye want? What air ye tellin' me?

ABBIE: She's tellin' ye t' love me. She knows I love ye an' I'll be good t' ye. Can't ye feel it? Don't ye know? She's tellin' ye t' love me, Eben!

EBEN: Ay-eh. I feel—mebbe she—but—I can't figger out—why—when ye've stole her place—here in her hum—in the parlor whar she was—

ABBIE (*fiercely*): She knows I love ye!

EBEN (*his face suddenly lighting up with a fierce, triumphant grin*): I see it! I sees why. It's her vengeance on him—so's she kin rest quiet in her grave!

ABBIE (*wildly*): Vengeance o' God on the hull o' us! What d'we give a durn! I love ye, Eben! God knows I love ye! (*She stretches out her arms for him.*)

EBEN (*throws himself on his knees beside the sofa and grabs her in his arms—releasing all his pent-up passion*): An' I love ye, Abbie!—now I kin say it! I been dyin' fur want o' ye—every hour since ye come! I love ye! (*Their lips meet in a fierce, bruising kiss.*)

Scene IV

(*Exterior of the farmhouse. It is just dawn. The front door at right is opened and Eben comes out and walks around to the gate. He is dressed in his working clothes. He seems changed. His face wears a bold and confident expression, he is grinning to himself with evident satisfaction. As he gets near the gate, the window of the parlor is heard opening and the shutters are flung back and Abbie sticks her head out. Her hair tumbles over her shoulders in disarray, her face is flushed, she looks at Eben with tender, languorous eyes and calls softly.*)

ABBIE: Eben. (*As he turns—playfully.*) Jest one more kiss afore ye go. I'm goin' to miss ye fearful all day.

EBEN: An' me yew, ye kin bet! (*He goes to her. They kiss several times. He draws away, laughingly.*) Thar. That's enuf, hain't it? Ye won't hev none left fur next time.

ABBIE: I got a million o' 'em left fur yew! (*Then a bit anxiously.*) D'ye r'ally love me, Eben?

EBEN (*emphatically*): I like ye better'n any gal I ever knowed! That's gospel!

ABBIE: Likin' hain't lovin'.

EBEN: Waal then—I love ye. Now air yew satisfied?

ABBIE: Ay-eh, I be. (*She smiles at him adoringly.*)

EBEN: I better git t' the barn. The old critter's liable t' suspicion an' come sneakin' up.

ABBIE (*with a confident laugh*): Let him! I kin allus pull the wool over his eyes. I'm goin' t' leave the shutters open and let in the sun 'n' air. This room's been dead long enuf. Now it's goin' t' be my room!

EBEN (*frowning*): Ay-eh.

ABBIE (*hastily*): I meant—our room.

EBEN: Ay-eh.

ABBIE: We made it our'n last night, didn't we? We give it life—our lovin' did. (*A pause.*)

EBEN (*with a strange look*): Maw's gone back t' her grave. She kin sleep now.

ABBIE: May she rest in peace! (*Then tenderly rebuking.*) Ye oughtn't t' talk o' sad thin's—this mornin'.

EBEN: It jest come up in my mind o' itself.

ABBIE: Don't let it. (*He doesn't answer. She yawns.*) Waal, I'm a-goin' t' steal a wink o' sleep. I'll tell the Old Man I hain't feelin' pert. Let him git his own vittles.

EBEN: I see him comin' from the barn. Ye better look smart an' git upstairs.

ABBIE: Ay-eh. Good-by. Don't ferget me. (*She throws him a kiss. He grins—then squares his shoulders and awaits his father confidently. Cabot walks slowly up from the left, staring up at the sky with a vague face.*)

EBEN (*jovially*): Mornin', Paw. Star-gazin' in daylight?

CABOT: Purty, hain't it?

EBEN (*looking around him possessively*): It's a durned purty farm.

CABOT: I mean the sky.

EBEN (*grinning*): How d'ye know? Them eyes o' your'n can't see that fur. (*This tickles his humor and he slaps his thigh and laughs.*) Ho-ho! That's a good un!

CABOT (*grimly sarcastic*): Ye're feelin' right chipper, hain't ye? Whar'd ye steal the likker?

EBEN (*good-naturedly*): 'Tain't likker. Jest life. (*Suddenly holding out his hand—soberly.*) Yew 'n' me is quits. Let's shake hands.

CABOT (*suspiciously*): What's come over ye?

EBEN: Then don't. Mebbe it's jest as well. (*A moment's pause.*) What's come over me? (*Queerly.*) Didn't ye feel her passin'—goin' back t' her grave?

CABOT (*dully*): Who?

EBEN: Maw. She kin rest now an' sleep content. She's quit with ye.

CABOT (*confusedly*): I rested. I slept good—down with the cows. They know how t' sleep. They're teachin' me.

EBEN (*suddenly jovial again*): Good fur the cows! Waal—ye better git t' work.

CABOT (*grimly amused*): Air yew bossin' me, ye calf?

EBEN (*beginning to laugh*): Ay-eh! I'm bossin' yew! Ha-ha-ha! See how ye like it! Ha-ha-ha! I'm the prize rooster o' this roost. Ha-ha-ha! (*He goes off toward the barn laughing.*)

CABOT (*looks after him with scornful pity*): Soft-headed. Like his Maw. Dead spit 'n' image. No hope in him! (*He spits with contemptuous disgust.*) A born fool! (*Then matter-of-factly.*) Waal—I'm gittin' peckish. (*He goes toward door.*)

PART III • *Scene I*

(*A night in late spring the following year. The kitchen and the two bedrooms upstairs are shown. The two bedrooms are dimly lighted by a tallow candle in each. Eben is sitting on the side of the bed in his room, his chin propped on his fists, his face a study of the struggle he is making to understand his conflicting emotions. The noisy laughter and music from below where a kitchen dance is in progress annoy and distract him. He scowls at the floor.*)

(*In the next room a cradle stands beside the double bed.*)

(*In the kitchen all is festivity. The stove has been taken down to give more room to the dancers. The chairs, with wooden benches added, have been pushed back against the walls. On these are seated, squeezed in tight against one another, farmers and their wives and their young folks of both sexes from the neighboring farms. They are all chattering and laughing loudly. They evidently have some secret joke in common. There is no end of winking, of nudging, of meaning nods of the head toward Cabot who, in a state of extreme hilarious excitement increased by the amount he has drunk, is standing near the rear door where there is a small keg of whisky and serving drinks to all the men. In the left corner, front, dividing the attention with her husband, Abbie is sitting in a rocking chair, a shawl wrapped about her shoulders. She is very pale, her face is thin and drawn, her eyes are fixed anxiously on the open door in rear as if waiting for someone.*)

(*The musician is tuning up his fiddle, seated in the far right corner. He is a lanky young fellow with a long, weak face. His pale eyes blink incessantly and he grins about him slyly with a greedy malice.*)

ABBIE (*suddenly turning to a young girl on her right*): Whar's Eben?

YOUNG GIRL (*eyeing her scornfully*): I dunno, Mrs. Cabot. I hain't seen Eben in ages. (*Meaningly.*) Seems like he's spent most o' his time t' hum since yew come.

ABBIE (*vaguely*): I tuk his Maw's place.

YOUNG GIRL: Ay-eh. So I've heerd. (*She turns away to retail this bit of gossip to her mother sitting next to her. Abbie turns to her left to a big stoutish middle-aged man whose flushed face and starting eyes show the amount of "likker" he has consumed.*)

ABBIE: Ye hain't seen Eben, hev ye?

MAN: No, I hain't. (*Then he adds with a wink.*) If yew hain't, who would?

ABBIE: He's the best dancer in the county. He'd ought t' come an' dance.

MAN (*with a wink*): Mebbe he's doin' the dutiful an' walkin' the kid t' sleep. It's a boy, hain't it?

ABBIE (*nodding vaguely*): Ay-eh—born two weeks back—purty's a picter.

MAN: They all is—t' their Maws. (*Then in a whisper, with a nudge and a leer.*) Listen, Abbie—if ye ever git tired o' Eben, remember me! Don't fergit now! (*He looks at her uncomprehending face for a second—then grunts disgustedly.*) Waal—guess I'll likker agin. (*He goes over and joins Cabot who is arguing noisily with an old farmer over cows. They all drink.*)

ABBIE (*this time appealing to nobody in particular*): Wonder what Eben's a-doin'? (*Her remark is repeated down the line with many a guffaw and titter until it reaches the fiddler. He fastens his blinking eyes on Abbie.*)

FIDDLER (*raising his voice*): Bet I kin tell ye, Abbie, what Eben's doin'! He's down t' the church offerin' up prayers o' thanksgivin'. (*They all titter expectantly.*)

A MAN: What fur? (*Another titter.*)

FIDDLER: 'Cause unto him a—(*He hesitates just long enough.*) brother is born! (*A roar of laughter. They all look from Abbie to Cabot. She is oblivious, staring at the door. Cabot, although he hasn't heard the words, is irritated by the laughter and steps forward, glaring about him. There is an immediate silence.*)

CABOT: What're ye all bleatin' about—like a flock o' goats? Why don't ye dance, damn ye? I axed ye here t' dance—t' eat, drink an' be merry—an' thar ye set cacklin' like a lot o' wet hens with the pip! Ye've swilled my likker an' guzzled my vittles like hogs, hain't ye? Then dance fur me, can't ye? That's fa'r an' squar', hain't it? (*A grumble of resentment goes around but they are all evidently in too much awe of him to express it openly.*)

FIDDLER (*slyly*): We're waitin' fur Eben. (*A suppressed laugh.*)

CABOT (*with a fierce exultation*): T'hell with Eben! Eben's done fur now! I got a new son! (*His mood switching with drunken suddenness.*) But ye needn't t' laugh at Eben, none o' ye! He's my blood, if he be a dumb fool. He's better nor any o' yew! He kin do a day's work a'most up t' what I kin—an' that'd put any o' yew pore critters t' shame!

FIDDLER: An' he kin do a good night's work, too! (*A roar of laughter.*)

CABOT: Laugh, ye damn fools! Ye're right jist the same, Fiddler. He kin work day an' night too, like I kin, if need be!

OLD FARMER (*from behind the keg where he is weaving drunkenly back and forth—with great simplicity*): They hain't many t' touch ye, Ephraim—a son at seventy-six. That's a hard man fur ye! I be on'y sixty-eight an' I couldn't do it. (*A roar of laughter in which Cabot joins uproariously.*)

CABOT (*slapping him on the back*): I'm sorry fur ye, Hi. I'd never suspicion sech weakness from a boy like yew!

OLD FARMER: An' I never reckoned yew had it in ye nuther, Ephraim. (*There is another laugh.*)

CABOT (*suddenly grim*): I got a lot in me—a hell of a lot—folks don't know on. (*Turning to the fiddler.*) Fiddle 'er up, durn ye! Give 'em somethin' t' dance t'! What air ye, an ornament? Hain't this a celebration? Then grease yer elbow an' go it!

FIDDLER (*seizes a drink which the Old Farmer holds out to him and downs it*): Here goes! (*He starts to fiddle "Lady of the Lake." Four young fellows and four girls form in two lines and dance a square dance. The Fiddler shouts directions for the different movements, keeping his words in the rhythm of the music and interspersing them with jocular personal remarks to the dancers themselves. The people seated along the walls stamp their feet and clap their hands in unison. Cabot is especially active in this respect. Only Abbie remains apathetic, staring at the door as if she were alone in a silent room.*)

FIDDLER: Swing your partner t' the right! That's it, Jim! Give her a b'ar hug. Her Maw hain't lookin'. (*Laughter.*) Change partners! That suits ye, don't it, Essie, now ye got Reub afore ye? Look at her redden up, will ye? Waal, life is short an' so's love, as the feller says. (*Laughter.*)

CABOT (*excitedly, stamping his foot*): Go it, boys! Go it, gals!

FIDDLER (*with a wink at the others*): Ye're the spryest seventy-six ever I sees, Ephraim! Now if ye'd on'y good eyesight . . . ! (*Suppressed laughter. He gives Cabot no chance to retort but roars.*) Promenade! Ye're walkin' like a bride down the aisle, Sarah! Waal, while they's life they's allus hope, I've heerd tell. Swing your partner to the left! Gosh A'mighty, look at Johnny Cook high-steppin'! They hain't goin' t' be much strength left fur howin' in the corn lot t'morrow. (*Laughter.*)

CABOT: Go it! Go it! (*Then suddenly, unable to restrain himself any longer, he prances into the midst of the dancers, scattering them, waving his arms about wildly.*) Ye're all hoofs! Git out o' my road! Give me room! I'll show ye dancin'. Ye're all too soft! (*He pushes them roughly away. They crowd back toward the walls, muttering, looking at him resentfully.*)

FIDDLER (*jeeringly*): Go it, Ephraim! Go it! (*He starts "Pop, Goes the Weasel," increasing the tempo with every verse until at the end he is fiddling crazily as fast as he can go.*)

CABOT (*Starts to dance, which he does very well and with tremendous vigor. Then he begins to improvise, cuts incredibly grotesque capers, leaping up and cracking his heels together, prancing around in a circle with body bent in an Indian war dance, then suddenly straightening up and kicking as high as he can with both legs. He is like a monkey on a string. And all the while he intersperses his antics with shouts and derisive comments.*): Whoop! Here's dancin' fur ye! Whoop! See that! Seventy-six, if I'm a day! Hard as iron yet! Beatin' the young 'uns like I allus done! Look at me! I'd invite ye t' dance on my hundredth birthday on'y ye'll all be dead by then. Ye're a sickly generation! Yer hearts air pink, not red! Yer veins is full o' mud an' water! I be the on'y man in the county! Whoop! See that! I'm a Injun! I've killed Injuns in the West afore ye was born—an' skulped 'em too! They's a arrer wound on my backside I c'd show ye! The hull tribe chased me. I outrun 'em all—with the arrer stuck in me! An' I tuk vengeance on 'em. Ten eyes fur an eye, that was my motter! Whoop! Look at me! I kin kick the ceilin' off the room! Whoop!

FIDDLER (*stops playing—exhaustedly*): God A'mighty, I got enuf. Ye got the devil's strength in ye.

CABOT (*delightedly*): Did I beat yew, too? Waal, ye played smart. Hev a swig. (*He pours whisky for himself and Fiddler. They drink. The others watch Cabot silently with cold, hostile eyes. There is a dead pause. The Fiddler rests. Cabot leans against the keg, panting, glaring around him confusedly. In the room above, Eben gets to his feet and tiptoes out the door in rear, appearing a moment later in the other bedroom. He moves silently, even frightenedly, toward the cradle and stands there looking down at the baby. His face is as vague as his reactions are confused, but there is a trace of tenderness, of interested discovery. At the same moment that he reaches the cradle, Abbie seems to sense something. She gets up weakly and goes to Cabot.*)

ABBIE: I'm goin' up t' the baby.

CABOT (*with real solicitation*): Air ye able fur the stairs? D'ye want me t' help ye, Abbie?

ABBIE: No. I'm able. I'll be down agen soon.

CABOT: Don't ye git wore out! He needs ye, remember—our son does! (*He grins affectionately, patting her on the back. She shrinks from his touch.*)

ABBIE (*dully*): Don't—tech me. I'm goin'—up. (*She goes. Cabot looks after her. A whisper goes around the room. Cabot turns. It ceases. He wipes his forehead streaming with sweat. He is breathing pantingly.*)

CABOT: I'm a-goin' out t' git fresh air. I'm feelin' a mite dizzy. Fiddle up thar! Dance, all o' ye! Here's likker fur them as wants it. Enjoy yerselves. I'll be back. (*He goes, closing the door behind him.*)

FIDDLER (*sarcastically*): Don't hurry none on our account! (*A suppressed laugh. He imitates Abbie.*) Whar's Eben? (*More laughter.*)

A WOMAN (*loudly*): What's happened in this house is plain as the nose on yer face! (*Abbie appears in the doorway upstairs and stands looking in surprise and adoration at Eben who does not see her.*)

A MAN: Ssshh! He's li'ble t' be listenin' at the door. That'd be like him. (*Their voices die to an intensive whispering. Their faces are concentrated on this gossip. A noise as of dead leaves in the wind comes from the room. Cabot has come out from the porch and stands by the gate, leaning on it, staring at the sky blinkingly. Abbie comes across the room silently. Eben does not notice her until quite near.*)

EBEN (*starting*): Abbie!

ABBIE: Ssshh! (*She throws her arms around him. They kiss—then bend over the cradle together.*) Ain't he purty?—dead spit 'n' image o' yew!

EBEN (*pleased*): Air he? I can't tell none.

ABBIE: E-zactly like!

EBEN (*frowningly*): I don't like this. I don't like lettin' on what's mine's his'n. I been doin' that all my life. I'm gittin' t' the end o' b'arin' it!

ABBIE (*putting her finger on his lips*): We're doin' the best we kin. We got t' wait. Somethin's bound t' happen. (*She puts her arms around him.*) I got t' go back.

EBEN: I'm goin' out. I can't b'ar it with the fiddle playin' an' the laughin'.

ABBIE: Don't git feelin' low. I love ye, Eben. Kiss me. (*He kisses her. They remain in each other's arms.*)

CABOT (*at the gate, confusedly*): Even the music can't drive it out—somethin'. Ye kin feel it droppin' off the elums, climbin' up the roof, sneakin' down the chimney, pokin' in the corners! They's no peace in houses, they's no rest livin' with folks. Somethin's always livin' with ye. (*With a deep sigh.*) I'll go t' the barn an' rest a spell. (*He goes wearily toward the barn.*)

FIDDLER (*tuning up*): Let's celebrate the old skunk gittin' fooled! We kin have some fun now he's went. (*He starts to fiddle "Turkey in the Straw." There is real merriment now. The young folks get up to dance.*)

Scene II

(*A half hour later—exterior—Eben is standing by the gate looking up at the sky, an expression of dumb pain bewildered by itself on his face. Cabot appears, returning from the barn, walking wearily, his eyes on the ground. He sees Eben and his whole mood immediately changes. He becomes excited, a cruel, triumphant grin comes to his lips, he strides up and slaps Eben on the back. From within comes the whining of the fiddle and the noise of stamping feet and laughing voices.*)

CABOT: So har ye be!

EBEN (*startled, stares at him with hatred for a moment—then dully*): Ay-eh.

CABOT (*surveying him jeeringly*): Why hain't ye been in t' dance? They was all axin' fur ye.

EBEN: Let 'em ax!

CABOT: They's a hull passel o' purty gals.

EBEN: T' hell with 'em!

CABOT: Ye'd ought t' be marryin' one o' 'em soon.

EBEN: I hain't marryin' no one.

CABOT: Ye might 'arn a share o' a farm that way.

EBEN (*with a sneer*): Like yew did, ye mean? I hain't that kind.

CABOT (*stung*): Ye lie! 'Twas yer Maw's folks aimed t' steal my farm from me.

EBEN: Other folks don't say so. (*After a pause—defiantly.*) An' I got a farm, anyways!

CABOT (*derisively*): Whar?

EBEN (*stamps a foot on the ground*): Har!

CABOT (*throws his head back and laughs coarsely*): Ho-ho! Ye hev, hev ye? Waal, that's a good un!

EBEN (*controlling himself—grimly*): Ye'll see!

CABOT (*stares at him suspiciously, trying to make him out—a pause—then with scornful confidence*): Ay-eh. I'll see. So'll ye. It's ye that's blind—blind as a mole underground. (*Eben suddenly laughs, one short sardonic bark: "Ha." A pause. Cabot peers at him with renewed suspicion.*) What air ye hawin' 'bout? (*Eben turns away without answering. Cabot grows angry.*) God A'mighty, yew air a dumb dunce! They's nothin' in that thick skull o' your'n but noise—like a empty keg it be! (*Eben doesn't seem to hear. Cabot's rage grows.*) Yewr farm! God A'mighty! If ye wa'n't a born donkey ye'd know ye'll never own stick nor stone on it, specially now arter him bein' born. It's his'n, I tell ye—his'n arter I die—but I'll live a hundred jest t' fool ye all—an' he'll be growed then—yewr age a'most! (*Eben laughs again his sardonic "Ha." This drives Cabot into a fury.*) Ha? Ye think ye kin git 'round that someways, do ye? Waal, it'll be her'n, too—Abbie's—ye won't git 'round her—she knows yer tricks—she'll be too much fur ye—she wants the farm her'n—she was afeerd o' ye—she told me ye was sneakin' 'round tryin' t' make love t' her t' git her on yer side . . . ye . . . ye mad fool, ye! (*He raises his clenched fists threateningly.*)

EBEN (*is confronting him, choking with rage*): Ye lie, ye old skunk! Abbie never said no sech thing!

CABOT (*suddenly triumphant when he sees how shaken Eben is*): She did. An' I says, I'll blow his brains t' the top o' them elums—an' she says no that hain't sense, who'll ye git t' help ye on the farm in his place—an' then she says yew'n me ought t' have a son—I know we kin, she says—an' I says, if we do, ye kin have anythin' I've got ye've a mind t'. An' she says, I wants Eben cut off so's this farm'll be mine when ye die! (*With terrible gloating.*) An' that's what's happened, hain't it? An' the farm's her'n! An' the dust o' the road—that's you'rn! Ha! Now who's hawin'?

EBEN (*has been listening, petrified with grief and rage—suddenly laughs wildly and brokenly*): Ha-ha-ha! So that's her sneakin' game—all along!—like I suspicioned at fust—t' swaller it all—an' me, too . . . ! (*Madly.*) I'll murder her! (*He springs toward the porch but Cabot is quicker and gets in between.*)

CABOT: No, ye don't!

EBEN: Git out o' my road! (*He tries to throw Cabot aside. They grapple in what becomes immediately a murderous struggle. The old man's concentrated strength is too much for Eben. Cabot gets one hand on his throat and presses him back across the stone wall. At the same moment, Abbie comes out on the porch. With a stifled cry she runs toward them.*)

ABBIE: Eben! Ephraim! (*She tugs at the hand on Eben's throat.*) Let go, Ephraim! Ye're chokin' him!

CABOT (*Removes his hand and flings Eben sideways full length on the grass, gasping and choking. With a cry, Abbie kneels beside him, trying to take his head on her lap, but he pushes her away. Cabot stands looking down with fierce triumph.*): Ye needn't t've fret, Abbie, I wa'n't aimin' t' kill him. He hain't wuth hangin' fur—not by a hell of a sight! (*More and more triumphantly.*) Seventy-six an' him not thirty yit—an' look whar he be fur thinkin' his Paw was easy! No, by God, I hain't easy! An' him upstairs, I'll raise him t' be like me! (*He turns to leave them.*) I'm goin' in an' dance!—sing an' celebrate! (*He walks to the porch—then turns with a great grin.*) I don't calc'late it's left in him, but if he gits pesky, Abbie, ye jest sing out. I'll come a-runnin' an' by the Etarnal, I'll put him across my knee an' birch him! Ha-ha-ha! (*He goes into the house laughing. A moment later his loud "whoop" is heard.*)

ABBIE (*tenderly*): Eben. Air ye hurt? (*She tries to kiss him but he pushes her violently away and struggles to a sitting position.*)

EBEN (*gaspingly*): T'hell—with ye!

ABBIE (*not believing her ears*): It's me, Eben—Abbie—don't ye know me?

EBEN (*glowering at her with hatred*): Ay-eh—I know ye—now! (*He suddenly breaks down, sobbing weakly.*)

ABBIE (*fearfully*): Eben—what's happened t' ye—why did ye look at me 's if ye hated me?

EBEN (*violently, between sobs and gasps*): I do hate ye! Ye're a whore—a damn trickin' whore!

ABBIE (*shrinking back horrified*): Eben! Ye don't know what ye're sayin'!

EBEN (*scrambling to his feet and following her—accusingly*): Ye're nothin' but a stinkin' passel o' lies! Ye've been lyin' t' me every word ye spoke, day an' night, since we fust—done it. Ye've kept sayin' ye loved me. . . .

ABBIE (*frantically*): I do love ye! (*She takes his hand but he flings hers away.*)

EBEN (*unheeding*): Ye've made a fool o' me—a sick, dumb fool—a-purpose! Ye've been on'y playin' yer sneakin', stealin' game all along—gittin' me t' lie with ye so's ye'd hev a son he'd think was his'n, an' makin' him promise he'd give ye the farm and let me eat dust, if ye did git him a son! (*Staring at her with anguished, bewildered eyes.*) They must be a devil livin' in ye! T'ain't human t' be as bad as that be!

ABBIE (*stunned—dully*): He told yew . . . ?

EBEN: Hain't it true? It hain't no good in yew lyin'.

ABBIE (*pleadingly*): Eben, listen—ye must listen—it was long ago—afore we done nothin'—yew was scornin' me—goin' t' see Min—when I was lovin' ye—an' I said it t' him t' git vengeance on ye!

EBEN (*Unheedingly. With tortured passion.*): I wish ye was dead! I wish I was dead along with ye afore this come! (*Ragingly.*) But I'll git my vengeance too! I'll pray Maw t' come back t' help me—t' put her cuss on yew an' him!

ABBIE (*brokenly*): Don't ye, Eben! Don't ye! (*She throws herself on her knees before him, weeping.*) I didn't mean t' do bad t'ye! Fergive me, won't ye?

EBEN (*not seeming to hear her—fiercely*): I'll git squar' with the old skunk—an' yew! I'll tell him the truth 'bout the son he's so proud o'! Then I'll leave ye here t' pizen each other—with Maw comin' out o' her grave at nights—an' I'll go t' the gold fields o' Californi-a whar Sim an' Peter be!

ABBIE (*terrified*): Ye won't—leave me? Ye can't!

EBEN (*with fierce determination*): I'm a-goin', I tell ye! I'll git rich thar an' come back an' fight him fur the farm he stole—an' I'll kick ye both out in the road—t' beg an' sleep in the woods—an' yer son along with ye—t' starve an' die! (*He is hysterical at the end.*)

ABBIE (*with a shudder—humbly*): He's yewr son, too, Eben.

EBEN (*torturedly*): I wish he never was born! I wish he'd die this minit! I wish I'd never sot eyes on him! It's him—yew havin' him—a-purpose t' steal—that's changed everythin'!

ABBIE (*gently*): Did ye believe I loved ye—afore he come?

EBEN: Aye-eh—like a dumb ox!

ABBIE: An' ye don't believe no more?

EBEN: B'lieve a lyin' thief! Ha!

ABBIE (*shudders—then humbly*): An' did ye r'ally love me afore?

EBEN (*brokenly*): Ay-eh—an' ye was trickin' me!

ABBIE: An' ye don't love me now!

EBEN (*violently*): I hate ye, I tell ye!

ABBIE: An' ye're truly goin' West—goin' t' leave me—all account o' him being born?

EBEN: I'm a-goin' in the mornin'—or may God strike me t' hell!

ABBIE (*after a pause—with a dreadful cold intensity—slowly*): If that's what his comin's done t' me—killin' yewr love—takin' yew away—my on'y joy—the on'y joy I ever knowed—like heaven t' me—purtier'n heaven—then I hate him, too, even if I be his Maw!

EBEN (*bitterly*): Lies! Ye love him! He'll steal the farm fur ye! (*Brokenly.*) But t'ain't the farm so much—not no more—it's yew foolin' me—gittin' me t' love ye—lyin' yew loved me—jest t' git a son t' steal!

ABBIE (*distractedly*): He won't steal! I'd kill him fust! I do love ye! I'll prove t' ye . . . !

EBEN (*harshly*): T'ain't no use lyin' no more. I'm deaf t' ye! (*He turns away.*) I hain't seein' ye agen. Good-by!

ABBIE (*pale with anguish*): Hain't ye even goin' t' kiss me—not once—arter all we loved?

EBEN (*in a hard voice*): I hain't wantin' t' kiss ye never agen! I'm wantin' t' forgit I ever sot eyes on ye!

ABBIE: Eben!—ye mustn't—wait a spell—I want t' tell ye. . . .

EBEN: I'm a-goin' in t' git drunk. I'm a-goin' t' dance.

ABBIE (*clinging to his arm—with passionate earnestness*): If I could make it—'s if he'd never come up between us—if I could prove t' ye I wa'n't schemin' t' steal from ye—so's everythin' could be jest the same with us, lovin' each other jest the same, kissin' an' happy the same's we've been happy afore he come—if I could do it—ye'd love me agen, wouldn't ye? Ye'd kiss me agen? Ye wouldn't never leave me, would ye?

EBEN (*moved*): I calc'late not. (*Then shaking her hand off his arm—with a bitter smile.*) But ye hain't God, be ye?

ABBIE (*exultantly*): Remember ye've promised! (*Then with strange intensity.*) Mebbe I kin take back one thin' God does!

EBEN (*peering at her*): Ye're gittin' cracked, hain't ye? (*Then going toward door.*) I'm a-goin' t' dance.

ABBIE (*calls after him intensely*): I'll prove t' ye! I'll prove I love ye better'n. . . . (*He goes in the door, not seeming to hear. She remains standing where she is, looking after him—then she finishes desperately.*) Better'n everythin' else in the world!

Scene III

(*Just before dawn in the morning—shows the kitchen and Cabot's bedroom. In the kitchen, by the light of a tallow candle on the table, Eben is sitting, his chin propped on his hands, his drawn face blank and expressionless. His carpetbag is on the floor beside him. In the bedroom, dimly lighted by a small whale-oil lamp, Cabot lies asleep. Abbie is bending over the cradle, listening, her face full of terror yet with an undercurrent of desperate triumph. Suddenly, she breaks down and sobs, appears about to throw herself on her knees beside the cradle, but the old man turns restlessly, groaning in his sleep, and she controls herself, and, shrinking away from the cradle with a gesture of horror, backs swiftly toward the door in rear and goes out. A moment later she comes into the kitchen and, running to Eben, flings her arms about his neck and kisses him wildly. He hardens himself, he remains unmoved and cold, he keeps his eyes straight ahead.*)

ABBIE (*hysterically*): I done it, Eben! I told ye I'd do it! I've proved I love ye—better'n everythin'—so's ye can't never doubt me no more!

EBEN (*dully*): Whatever ye done, it hain't no good now.

ABBIE (*wildly*): Don't ye say that! Kiss me, Eben, won't ye? I need ye t' kiss me arter what I done! I need ye t' say ye love me!

EBEN (*kisses her without emotion—dully*): That's fur good-by. I'm a-goin' soon.

ABBIE: No! No! Ye won't go—not now!

EBEN (*going on with his own thoughts*): I been a-thinkin'—an' I hain't goin' t' tell Paw nothin'. I'll

leave Maw t' take vengeance on ye. If I told him, the old skunk'd jest be stinkin' mean enuf to take it out on that baby. (*His voice showing emotion in spite of him.*) An' I don't want nothin' bad t' happen t' him. He hain't t' blame fur yew. (*He adds with a certain queer pride.*) An' he looks like me! An' by God, he's mine! An' some day I'll be a-comin' back an' . . . !

ABBIE (*too absorbed in her own thoughts to listen to him—pleadingly*): They's no cause fur ye t' go now—they's no sense—it's all the same's it was—they's nothin' come b'tween us now—arter what I done!

EBEN (*Something in her voice arouses him. He stares at her a bit frightenedly.*): Ye look mad, Abbie. What did ye do?

ABBIE: I—I killed him, Eben.

EBEN (*amazed*): Ye killed him?

ABBIE (*dully*): Ay-eh.

EBEN (*recovering from his astonishment—savagely*): An' serves him right! But we got t' do somethin' quick t' make it look s'if the old skunk'd killed himself when he was drunk. We kin prove by 'em all how drunk he got.

ABBIE (*wildly*): No! No! Not him! (*Laughing distractedly.*) But that's what I ought t' done, hain't it? I oughter killed him instead! Why didn't ye tell me?

EBEN (*appalled*): Instead? What d'ye mean?

ABBIE: Not him.

EBEN (*his face grown ghastly*): Not—not that baby!

ABBIE (*dully*): Ay-eh!

EBEN (*falls to his knees as if he'd been struck—his voice trembling with horror*): Oh, God A'mighty! A'mighty God! Maw, whar was ye, why didn't ye stop her?

ABBIE (*simply*): She went back t' her grave that night we fust done it, remember? I hain't felt her about since. (*A pause. Eben hides his head in his hands, trembling all over as if he had the ague. She goes on dully.*) I left the piller over his little face. Then he killed himself. He stopped breathin'. (*She begins to weep softly.*)

EBEN (*rage beginning to mingle with grief*): He looked like me. He was mine, damn ye!

ABBIE (*slowly and brokenly*): I didn't want t' do it. I hated myself fur doin' it. I loved him. He was so purty—dead spit 'n' image o' yew. But I loved yew more—an' yew was goin' away—far off whar I'd never see ye agen, never kiss ye, never feel ye pressed agin me agen—an' ye said ye hated me fur havin' him—ye said ye hated him an' wished he was dead—ye said if it hain't been fur him comin' it'd be the same's afore between us.

EBEN (*unable to endure this, springs to his feet in a fury, threatening her, his twitching fingers seeming to reach out for her throat*): Ye lie! I never said—I never dreamed ye'd—I'd cut off my head afore I'd hurt his finger!

ABBIE (*piteously, sinking on her knees*): Eben, don't ye look at me like that—hatin' me—not after what I done fur ye—fur us—so's we could be happy agen—

EBEN (*furiously now*): Shut up, or I'll kill ye! I see yer game now—the same old sneakin' trick—ye're aimin' t' blame me fur the murder ye done!

ABBIE (*moaning—putting her hands over her ears*): Don't ye, Eben! Don't ye! (*She grasps his legs.*)

EBEN (*his mood suddenly changing to horror, shrinks away from her*): Don't ye tech me! Ye're pizen! How could ye—t' murder a pore little critter—Ye must've swapped yer soul t' hell! (*Suddenly raging.*) Ha! I kin see why ye done it! Not the lies ye jest told—but 'cause ye wanted t' steal agen—steal the last thin' ye'd left me—my part o' him—no, the hull o' him— ye saw he looked like me—ye knowed he was all mine—an' ye couldn't b'ar it—I know ye! Ye killed him fur bein' mine! (*All this has driven him almost insane. He makes a rush past her for the door—then turns—shaking both fists at her, violently.*) But I'll take vengeance now! I'll git the Sheriff! I'll tell him everythin'! Then I'll sing "I'm off to Californi-a!" an' go—gold—Golden Gate—gold sun—fields o' gold in the West! (*This last he half shouts, half croons incoherently, suddenly breaking off passionately.*) I'm a-goin' fur the Sheriff t' come an' git ye! I want ye tuk away, locked up from me! I can't stand t' luk at ye! Murderer an' thief 'r not, ye still tempt me! I'll give ye up t' the Sheriff! (*He turns and runs out, around the corner of house, panting and sobbing, and breaks into a swerving sprint down the road.*)

ABBIE (*struggling to her feet, runs to the door, calling after him*): I love ye, Eben! I love ye! (*She stops at the door weakly, swaying, about to fall.*) I don't care what ye do—if ye'll on'y love me agen—(*She falls limply to the floor in a faint.*)

Scene IV

(*About an hour later. Same as scene III. Shows the kitchen and Cabot's bedroom. It is after dawn. The sky is brilliant with the sunrise. In the kitchen, Abbie sits at the table, her body limp and exhausted, her head bowed down over her arms, her face hidden. Upstairs, Cabot is still asleep but awakens with a start. He looks toward the window and gives a snort of surprise and irritation— throws back the covers and begins hurriedly pulling on his clothes. Without looking behind him, he begins talking to Abbie whom he supposes beside him.*)

CABOT: Thunder 'n' lightin', Abbie! I hain't slept this late in fifty year! Looks 's if the sun was full riz a'most. Must've been the dancin' an' likker. Must be gittin' old. I hope Eben's t' wuk. Ye might've tuk the trouble t' rouse me, Abbie. (*He turns—sees no one there—surprised.*) Waal—whar air she? Gittin' vittles, I calc'late. (*He tiptoes to the cradle and peers down—proudly.*) Mornin', sonny. Purty's a picter! Sleepin' sound. He don't beller all night like most o' 'em. (*He goes quietly out the door in rear—a few moments later enters kitchen—sees Abbie—with*

satisfaction.) So thar ye be. Ye got any vittles cooked?

ABBIE (*without moving*): No.

CABOT (*coming to her, almost sympathetically*): Ye feelin' sick?

ABBIE: No.

CABOT (*Pats her on shoulder. She shudders.*): Ye'd best lie down a spell. (*Half jocularly.*) Yer son'll be needin' ye soon. He'd ought t' wake up with a gnashin' appetite, the sound way he's sleepin'.

ABBIE (*shudders—then in a dead voice*): He hain't never goin' t' wake up.

CABOT (*jokingly*): Takes after me this mornin'. I hain't slept so late in . . .

ABBIE: He's dead.

CABOT (*stares at her—bewilderedly*): What. . . .

ABBIE: I killed him.

CABOT (*stepping back from her—aghast*): Air ye drunk— 'r crazy—'r . . . ?

ABBIE (*suddenly lifts her head and turns on him— wildly*): I killed him, I tell ye! I smothered him. Go up an' see if ye don't b'lieve me!

(*Cabot stares at her a second, then bolts out the rear door, can be heard bounding up the stairs, and rushes into the bedroom and over to the cradle. Abbie has sunk back lifelessly into her former position. Cabot puts his hand down on the body in the crib. An expression of fear and horror comes over his face.*)

CABOT (*shrinking away—tremblingly*): God A'mighty! God A'mighty. (*He stumbles out the door—in a short while returns to the kitchen—comes to Abbie, the stunned expression still on his face—hoarsely.*) Why did ye do it? Why? (*As she doesn't answer, he grabs her violently by the shoulder and shakes her.*) I ax ye why ye done it! Ye'd better tell me 'r . . . !

ABBIE (*gives him a furious push which sends him staggering back and springs to her feet—with wild rage and hatred*): Don't ye dare tech me! What right hev ye t' question me 'bout him? He wa'n't yewr son! Think I'd have a son by yew? I'd die fust! I hate the sight o' ye an' allus did! It's yew I should've murdered, if I'd had good sense! I hate ye! I love Eben. I did from the fust. An' he was Eben's son—mine an' Eben's—not your'n!

CABOT (*stands looking at her dazedly—a pause—finding his words with an effort—dully*): That was it— what I felt—pokin' 'round the corners—while ye lied—holdin' yerself from me—sayin' ye'd already conceived—(*He lapses into crushed silence—then with a strange emotion.*) He's dead, sart'n. I felt his heart. Pore little critter! (*He blinks back one tear, wiping his sleeve across his nose.*)

ABBIE (*hysterically*): Don't ye! Don't ye! (*She sobs unrestrainedly.*)

CABOT (*with a concentrated effort that stiffens his body into a rigid line and hardens his face into a stony mask—through his teeth to himself*): I got t' be— like a stone—a rock o' jedgment! (*A pause. He gets complete control over himself—harshly*.) If he was Eben's, I be glad he air gone! An' mebbe I suspicioned it all along. I felt they was somethin' onnateral—somewhars—the house got so lonesome—an' cold drivin' me down t' the barn—t' the beasts o' the field. . . . Ay-eh. I must've suspicioned—somethin'. Ye didn't fool me—not altogether, leastways—I'm too old a bird—growin' ripe on the bough. . . . (*He becomes aware he is wandering, straightens again, looks at Abbie with a cruel grin*.) So ye'd liked t' hev murdered me 'steed o' him, would ye? Waal, I'll live to a hundred! I'll live t' see ye hung! I'll deliver ye up t' the jedgment o' God an' the law! I'll git the Sheriff now. (*Starts for the door*.)

ABBIE (*dully*): Ye needn't. Eben's gone fur him.

CABOT (*amazed*): Eben—gone fur the Sheriff?

ABBIE: Ay-eh.

CABOT: T' inform agen ye?

ABBIE: Ay-eh.

CABOT (*considers this—a pause—then in a hard voice*): Waal, I'm thankful fur him savin' me the trouble. I'll git t' wuk. (*He goes to the door—then turns—in a voice full of strange emotion*.) He'd ought t' been my son, Abbie. Ye'd ought t' loved me. I'm a man. If ye'd loved me, I'd never told no Sheriff on ye no matter what ye did, if they was t' brile me alive!

ABBIE (*defensively*): They's more to it nor yew know, makes him tell.

CABOT (*dryly*): Fur yewr sake, I hope they be. (*He goes out—comes around to the gate—stares up at the sky. His control relaxes. For a moment he is old and weary. He murmurs despairingly*.) God A'mighty, I be lonesomer'n ever! (*He hears running footsteps from the left, immediately is himself again. Eben runs in, panting exhaustedly, wild-eyed and mad looking. He lurches through the gate. Cabot grabs him by the shoulder. Eben stares at him dumbly*.) Did ye tell the Sheriff?

EBEN (*nodding stupidly*): Ay-eh.

CABOT (*gives him a push away that sends him sprawling—laughing with withering contempt*): Good fur ye! A prime chip o' yer Maw ye be! (*He goes toward the barn, laughing harshly. Eben scrambles to his feet. Suddenly Cabot turns—grimly threatening*.) Git off this farm when the Sheriff takes her—or, by God, he'll have t' come back an' git me fur murder, too! (*He stalks off. Eben does not appear to have heard him. He runs to the door and comes into the kitchen. Abbie looks up with a cry of anguished joy. Eben stumbles over and throws himself on his knees beside her sobbing brokenly*.)

EBEN: Fergive me!

ABBIE (*happily*): Eben! (*She kisses him and pulls his head over against her breast*.)

EBEN: I love ye! Fergive me!

ABBIE (*ecstatically*): I'd fergive ye all the sins in hell fur sayin' that! (*She kisses his head, pressing it to her with a fierce passion of possession*.)

EBEN (*brokenly*): But I told the Sheriff. He's comin' fur ye!

ABBIE: I kin b'ar what happens t' me—now!

EBEN: I woke him up. I told him. He says, wait 'til I git dressed. I was waiting. I got to thinkin' o' yew. I got to thinkin' how I'd loved ye. It hurt like somethin' was bustin' in my chest an' head. I got t' cryin'. I knowed sudden I loved ye yet, an' allus would love ye!

ABBIE (*caressing his hair—tenderly*): My boy, hain't ye?

EBEN: I begun t' run back. I cut across the fields an' through the woods. I thought ye might have time t' run away—with me—an'. . .

ABBIE (*shaking her head*): I got t' take my punishment—t' pay fur my sin.

EBEN: Then I want t' share it with ye.

ABBIE: Ye didn't do nothin'.

EBEN: I put it in yer head. I wisht he was dead! I as much as urged ye t' do it!

ABBIE: No. It was me alone!

EBEN: I'm as guilty as yew be! He was the child o' our sin.

ABBIE (*lifting her head as if defying God*): I don't repent that sin! I hain't askin' God t' fergive that!

EBEN: Nor me—but it led up t' the other—an' the murder ye did, ye did 'count o' me—an' it's my murder, too, I'll tell the Sheriff—an' if ye deny it, I'll say we planned it t'gether—an' they'll all b'lieve me, fur they suspicion everythin' we've done, an' it'll seem likely an' true to 'em. An' it is true—way down. I did help ye—somehow.

ABBIE (*laying her head on his—sobbing*): No! I don't want yew t' suffer!

EBEN: I got t' pay fur my part o' the sin! An' I'd suffer wuss leavin' ye, goin' West, thinkin' o' ye day an' night, bein' out when yew was in—(*lowering his voice*) 'r bein' alive when yew was dead. (*A pause*.) I want t' share with ye, Abbie—prison 'r death 'r hell 'r anythin'! (*He looks into her eyes and forces a trembling smile*.) If I'm sharin' with ye, I won't feel lonesome, leastways.

ABBIE (*weakly*): Eben! I won't let ye! I can't let ye!

EBEN (*kissing her—tenderly*): Ye can't he'p yerself. I got ye beat fur once!

ABBIE (*forcing a smile—adoringly*): I hain't beat—s'long's I got ye!

EBEN (*hears the sound of feet outside*): Ssshh! Listen! They've come t' take us!

ABBIE: No, it's him. Don't give him no chance to fight ye, Eben. Don't say nothin'—no matter what he says. An' I won't neither. (*It is Cabot. He comes up from the barn in a great state of excitement and strides into the house and then into the kitchen. Eben is kneeling beside Abbie, his arm around her, hers around him. They stare straight ahead*.)

CABOT (*Stares at them, his face hard. A long pause—vindictively*.): Ye make a slick pair o' murderin' turtle doves! Ye'd ought t' be both hung on the same limb an' left thar t' swing in the breeze an' rot—a warnin' t' old fools like me t' b'ar their lonesomeness alone—an' fur young fools like ye t' hobble their lust.

(*A pause. The excitement returns to his face, his eyes snap, he looks a bit crazy.*) I couldn't work today. I couldn't take no interest. T' hell with the farm! I'm leavin' it! I've turned the cows an' other stock loose! I've druv 'em into the woods whar they kin be free! By freein' 'em, I'm freein' myself! I'm quittin' here today! I'll set fire t' house an' barn an' watch 'em burn, an' I'll leave yer Maw t' haunt the ashes, an' I'll will the fields back t' God, so that nothin' human kin never touch 'em! I'll be a-goin' to Californi-a—t' jine Simeon an' Peter—true sons o' mine if they be dumb fools—an' the Cabots'll find Solomon's Mines t'gether! (*He suddenly cuts a mad caper.*) Whoop! What was the song they sung? "Oh, Californi-a! That's the land fur me." (*He sings this—then gets on his knees by the floorboard under which the money was hid.*) An' I'll sail thar on one o' the finest clippers I kin find! I've got the money! Pity ye didn't know whar this was hidden so's ye could steal. . . . (*He has pulled up the board. He stares—feels—stares again. A pause of dead silence. He slowly turns, slumping into a sitting position on the floor, his eyes like those of a dead fish, his face the sickly green of an attack of nausea. He swallows painfully several times—forces a weak smile at last.*) So—ye did steal it!

EBEN (*emotionlessly*): I swapped it t' Sim an' Peter fur their share o' the farm—t' pay their passage t' Californi-a.

CABOT (*with one sardonic*): Ha! (*He begins to recover. Gets slowly to his feet—strangely.*) I calc'late God give it to 'em—not yew! God's hard, not easy! Mebbe they's easy gold in the West but it hain't God's gold. It hain't fur me. I kin hear His voice warnin' me agen t' be hard an' stay on my farm. I kin see His hand usin' Eben t' steal t' keep me from weakness. I kin feel I be in the palm o' His hand, His fingers guidin' me. (*A pause—then he mutters sadly.*) It's a-goin' t' be lonesomer now than ever it war afore—an' I'm gittin'

old, Lord—ripe on the bough. . . . (*Then stiffening.*) Waal—what d'ye want? God's lonesome, hain't He? God's hard an' lonesome! (*A pause. The Sheriff with two men comes up the road from the left. They move cautiously to the door. The Sheriff knocks on it with the butt of his pistol.*)

SHERIFF: Open in the name o' the law! (*They start.*)

CABOT: They've come fur ye. (*He goes to the rear door.*) Come in, Jim! (*The three men enter. Cabot meets them in doorway.*) Jest a minit, Jim. I got 'em safe here. (*The Sheriff nods. He and his companions remain in the doorway.*)

EBEN (*suddenly calls*): I lied this mornin', Jim. I helped her to do it. Ye kin take me, too.

ABBIE (*brokenly*): No!

CABOT: Take 'em both. (*He comes forward—stares at Eben with a trace of grudging admiration.*) Purty good—fur yew! Waal, I got t' round up the stock. Good-by.

EBEN: Good-by.

ABBIE: Good-by. (*Cabot turns and strides past the men—comes out and around the corner of the house, his shoulders squared, his face stony, and stalks grimly toward the barn. In the meantime the Sheriff and men have come into the room.*)

SHERIFF (*embarrassedly*): Waal—we'd best start.

ABBIE: Wait. (*Turns to Eben.*) I love ye, Eben.

EBEN: I love ye, Abbie. (*They kiss. The three men grin and shuffle embarrassedly. Eben takes Abbie's hand. They go out the door in rear, the men following, and come from the house, walking hand in hand to the gate. Eben stops there and points to the sunrise sky.*) Sun's a-rizin'. Purty, hain't it?

ABBIE: Ay-eh. (*They both stand for a moment looking up raptly in attitudes strangely aloof and devout.*)

SHERIFF (*looking around at the farm enviously—to his companions*): It's a jim-dandy farm, no denyin'. Wished I owned it!

COMMENTARY

Louise Kennedy
"HE KNOWS THAT IT'S OK NOT TO KNOW": DIRECTOR JÁNOS SZÁSZ APPROACHES *DESIRE* WITH AN OPEN MIND
(2005)

In this Boston Globe *review, Louise Kennedy discusses an international director's approach to Eugene O'Neill's* Desire under the Elms. *János Szász (b. 1958), who first read this play in Hungarian, talks about the impact it had on him. He also discusses the play's Greek roots and its universality. In the process, we learn about the decisions about staging and set design that helped him create a powerful production in 2005 at the American Repertory Theatre in Cambridge, Massachusetts.*

Raymond J. Barry has just finished rehearsing a confrontation with Amelia Campbell, who plays the young wife, Abbie, to his hard old farmer, Ephraim Cabot, in János Szász's forthcoming production of Eugene O'Neill's *Desire under the Elms* at the American Repertory Theatre. Barry takes a breath, recovering from the scene's wild seesaw from fury to anguish to lust, and turns to Szász. "I have another idea, but I know it's wrong," the actor tells the director. "But I just want to do it, and get it out of my system." Szász assents, and they play the scene again. This time, instead of sticking close to Abbie as they fight, Barry's Cabot moves away downstage, bringing his inner torment closer to the audience. What had felt like an odd interjection into an argument now plays as a natural turning inward that then powers his movement back to her. "I love it," Szász says when the scene ends. "It's much better." "Isn't that interesting?" Barry says. "Because I thought it was wrong, and it's not wrong. It's much better."

That process of experimentation and discovery, Barry says later, has made working on *Desire* a rich, if intense, experience. The intensity comes in part, of course, from the play itself, a profoundly dark exploration of a love triangle enmeshing Abbie, Cabot, and Cabot's youngest son, Eben. Written in 1924, it marked a new level of maturity in O'Neill's work, as he at last found the balance of realism and expressionism, psychology and myth he had been seeking. Reactions were mixed, with some critics hailing it as a masterpiece and others condemning it as obscene; the play, though frequently revived and made into a 1958 film with Burl Ives and Sophia Loren, remained controversial for many years because of its incestuous themes and violent climax.

For this production, Barry is especially grateful to have, in Szász, a world-class director (his films include *Woyzeck*, and he's directed several ART productions, including *Uncle Vanya*) who's not afraid to admit he's not sure how to approach a given scene. "He knows that it's OK not to know," says Barry, whose long career in theater and film includes fifteen years with Open Theater founder Joseph Chaikin and *Born on the Fourth of July* with Oliver Stone. "Directors are under

Riccardo Hernandez's set model for the American Repertory Theatre's 2004–2005 production of *Desire under the Elms*.

enormous pressure, so you can understand how some guys would come in thinking, 'I'd better be really smart.' But it's better if you can operate from a kind of wonderment, rather than certainty."

Perhaps because he's Hungarian and not American, Szász is fearless in his approach to O'Neill, Barry says. "He feels no qualms about cutting; he feels no qualms about overlaying two scenes." For his part, Szász says he didn't realize until he began working on *Desire* that "it's a kind of American icon: spooky and big and not easy to go closer to. But I don't think so. I just feel, reading the lines, it's absolutely a drama about love, passion." Of course, he first read the play in a Hungarian translation, which took the dense and orthographically challenging dialect of the original, set in 1850 New England but with diction that often reads more like Appalachian, and transposed it into the patois of Hungarian peasants. And that introduction to the play made its ageless, universal themes all the more starkly apparent. "It is a kind of Greek tragedy," Szász says. "We wanted to try to make it timeless."

For that reason, one major change he and the cast quickly agreed upon, with the encouragement of ART artistic director Robert Woodruff, was to jettison the accent that O'Neill had laboriously spelled out—an accent so impenetrable, Szász says, that when he first read the English version, "I couldn't understand a word." (That's a problem that Barry shared; he saw a New York production, with "very fine artists," years ago, "and I couldn't understand what they were saying.") "We are not using the accent," Szász says. "It takes us away from understanding. For the audience to focus on the accent, the emotion would be lost."

Szász has also made substantial cuts; in last weekend's run-throughs, he reduced the running time from two-hours-plus to about an hour and forty minutes. "Some things are a little too melodramatic for János's taste," Barry says. "You get the point, you get the sadness; you don't have to push it." What remains, says Mickey Solis, who plays Eben, is the spare, sharp structure of O'Neill's tragic story, in which old Ephraim Cabot's marriage to young Abbie Putnam, followed by Abbie's irresistible entanglement with Eben, sets sorrows spinning downward into fresh disaster. And, far from making the actors' jobs easier, Solis says, the cuts made it harder. "We cut a bunch of it, and it didn't save me! Nothing saved me," Solis says with a laugh. "All he did was just get deeper to the bone. He cut the fat, and so I've just got to get to it, and get to it *now*."

Solis, who graduates this year from the ART/MXAT Institute for Advanced Theatre Training and worked with Szász on *Spring's Awakening* last season, says another thing the director cut was his own original conception of the show. "When he first came in, his concept was very iconically American," Solis says, with such references as *Midnight Cowboy* and the *Easy Rider* soundtrack coloring the early discussions. "But early on that kind of became what it needed to be to tell the story, rather than his idea. The remnants of this very American story still exist, but he kept exploring." That's characteristic of great directors, as Solis puts it: "to have a strong, strong vision, but above all to know you have to tell the story in the strongest way possible." For Szász, the strongest way possible turns out to be with "a naked stage," with the haunting façade of the play's New England farmhouse looming over a barren, rock-strewn wasteland. And when the audience members enter the theater, he says, "they immediately step into the dirt. Earth, dirt, dust, stone. And a kind of Greek tragedy."

Bertolt Brecht

Among the most inventive and influential of modern playwrights, Bertolt Brecht (1898–1956) has left a legacy of important plays and theories about how those plays should be produced. Throughout most of his career he felt that drama should inform and awaken sensibilities, not just entertain or anesthetize an audience. Most of his plays concern philosophical and political issues, and some of them so threatened the Nazi regime that his works were burned publicly in Germany during the Third Reich.

At nineteen, Brecht worked as an orderly in a hospital during the last months of World War I. Seeing so much carnage and misery in the medical wards made him a lifelong pacifist. After the war he began writing plays while a student in Munich. His first successes in the Munich theater took the form of commentary on returned war veterans and on the questions of duty and heroism—which he treated negatively. His rejection of spiritual concepts was influenced by his readings of Hegel and the doctrines of Marx's dialectical materialism. Marx's theories predicted class struggles and based most social values in economic realities. Brecht eventually moved to Berlin, the theatrical center of Germany, and by 1926 was on his way to becoming a Communist.

Finding the political pressures in early Nazi Germany too frightening and dangerous for his writing, Brecht went into exile in 1933. He lived for a time in Scandinavia and later in the United States. After World War II Brecht and his wife returned to Berlin where, in 1949, he founded the Berliner Ensemble, which produced most of his later work. Brecht chose East Berlin as his home, in part because he felt his work could best be understood in a Communist setting. One irony is that his work has been even more widely appreciated and accepted in the West than in the former Communist eastern bloc.

Brecht wrote his most popular play in 1928, a musical in collaboration with the German composer Kurt Weill: *The Threepenny Opera*. The model for this play, the English writer John Gay's 1728 ballad opera *The Beggar's Opera*, provided Brecht with a perfect platform on which to comment satirically on the political and economic circumstances in Germany two hundred years after Gay wrote. The success of the Brecht–Weill collaboration—the work is still performed regularly—is due in part to Brecht's capacity to create appealing underworld characters such as Polly Peachum and Macheath, known as Mack the Knife. Brecht's wife, Helene Weigel, played Mrs. Peachum, the madam of the brothel in which the action takes place. Kurt Weill's second wife, Lotte Lenya, was an overnight sensation in the part of Jenny. She had a highly acclaimed reprise in New York almost twenty-five years later.

Brecht's most successful plays are *Galileo* (1938–1939), *Mother Courage* (1939), *The Good Woman of Setzuan* (1943), *The Private Lives of the Master*

Race (1945), and *The Caucasian Chalk Circle* (1948). But these represent only a tiny fraction of a mass of work, including plays, poetry, criticism, and fiction. His output is extraordinary in volume and quality. It includes plays borrowed not only from Gay but also from Sophocles, Molière, Gorky, Shakespeare, and John Webster, among others.

Brecht developed a number of theories regarding drama. He used the term *epic theater* to distinguish his own theater from traditional Aristotelian drama. Brecht expected his audience to observe critically, to draw conclusions, and to participate in an intellectual argument with the work at hand. The confrontational relationship he intended was designed to engage the audience in analyzing what they saw rather than in identifying with the main characters or in enjoying a wash of sentimentality or emotion.

One of the ways Brecht achieved his ends was by making the theatricality of the production's props, lights, sets, and equipment visible, thereby reminding the members of the audience that they were seeing a play. He used the term ALIENATION to define the effect he wanted his theater to have on an audience. He hoped that by alienating his audience from the drama, he would keep them emotionally detached and intellectually alert. Brecht's theater was political. He saw a connection between an audience that could analyze theater critically and an audience that could analyze reality critically—and see that social, political, and economic conditions were not "natural" or fixed immutably but could (and should) be changed.

Brecht's theories produced interesting results and helped stimulate audiences that expected to be entertained by realistic or sentimental plays. His style spread rapidly throughout the world of theater, and it is still being used and developed by contemporary playwrights such as Heiner Müller and performers such as Pina Bausch.

MOTHER COURAGE

Since *Mother Courage* was first produced in 1941 in Zurich, it has become a classic of modern theater, performed successfully in the United States and most other Western countries. Brecht conceived of the drama as a powerful antiwar play. He set it in Germany during the Thirty Years' War, in which the German Protestants, supported by countries such as France, Denmark, and England, fought against the Hapsburg empire, which was allied with the Holy Roman Empire and the German Catholic princes. The war was actually a combination of many wars fought during the period of thirty years. It was bloody and seemingly interminable, devastating Germany's towns and citizenry as well as its agriculture and commerce. The armies fought to control territory, economic markets, and the religious differences between German Lutherans and Roman Catholics.

Brecht was not interested in the immediate causes underlying the Thirty Years' War. He was making a case against war entirely, regardless of its cause. To do this, he deliberately avoided making his play realistic. The stage setting is essentially barren, and the play is structured in scenes that are very intense but that avoid any sense of continuity of action. Audiences cannot become involved in unfolding action; they must always remain conscious of themselves as audience. Moreover, the lighting is high-intensity, almost cruel at times, spotlighting the action in a way that is completely unnatural. In the early productions, Brecht included slide projections of the headings that accompany each of the twelve scenes so that the audience was always reminded of the presence of the playwright and the fact that they were seeing a play. These headings provided yet another break in the continuity of the action.

Although the printed text does not convey it, the play as Brecht produced it employed long silences, some of which were unsettling to the audience. When Swiss Cheese, Mother Courage's "honest son," has a moment of rest in scene 3, he is in an intense ring of stage light as he comments on sitting in the sun in his shirtsleeves. As Swiss Cheese relaxes for the last time, the intense light becomes an ironic device: it seems to expose him as a thief, and he is dragged off to his death. While he is Mother Courage's "honest son," circumstances make it seem that he has been corrupted by the war, like everyone else.

Mother Courage herself lives off the war by selling goods to the soldiers. She and her children haul their wagon across the battlefields with no concern for who is winning, who is losing, or even where they are. Her only ambition is to stock her wagon, sell her goods, and make sure she does not get stuck with any useless inventory. When the chaplain tells her that peace has broken out, she laments their condition because without war the family has no livelihood.

As Mother Courage continues to pull her wagon across field after field, she learns how to survive. But she also loses her children, one by one, to the war. Eilif, seduced into joining the army by a recruitment officer, is led into battle thinking that war is a heroic adventure. Swiss Cheese thinks he found a good deal in a paymaster's uniform. Both are wrong: there is no security in war, and they eventually perish.

Kattrin, the daughter, is likewise a victim of the violence of war. Having been violated by a Swedish soldier, she becomes mute. Near the end of the play she is treated violently again, and the terrible scar on her face leaves her unmarriageable. At the end Kattrin dies while sounding an alarm to warn the sleeping town of an imminent attack.

Finally, Mother Courage is left alone. She picks up her wagon and finds that she can maneuver it herself. The play ends as she circles the stage, with everything around her consumed by war.

Brecht's stated intentions were somewhat thwarted by the reactions of the play's first audiences. They were struck by the power of Brecht's characterization of Mother Courage and treated her with immense sympathy. They saw her as an indomitable woman whose strength in the face of adversity was so great that she could not be overwhelmed. But Brecht intended the audience to analyze Mother Courage further and to see in her a reflection of society's wrong values. She conducts business on the field of battle, paying no attention to the moral question of war itself. She makes her living from the war but cannot see that it is the war that causes her anguish.

In response to the audiences' sympathetic reactions, Brecht revised the play, adding new lines to help audiences see the venality of Mother Courage's motives. But subsequent audiences have continued to treat her as a survivor—almost a biblical figure. Brecht's German critics saw her as one whose endurance of all the terrors of war testifies to the resilience of humankind. No matter how one decides to interpret her, Mother Courage remains one of the most unusual and haunting characters in modern drama.

Mother Courage in Performance

Brecht wrote *Mother Courage* in three months, beginning in September 1939, while he and Helene Weigel were in Sweden in exile from Nazi Germany. Its first production was on April 19, 1941, in Zurich, Switzerland, while Brecht waited in Sweden for entry papers to the United States. Brecht and Weigel returned to Europe after the war. In 1948 they went to East Berlin to work with a new theater group explicitly to produce *Mother Courage* with Helene Weigel in the title role in January 1949. In October 1950 Brecht directed Thérèsa Giehse as Courage in Munich. Other productions were staged in provincial German towns and in other European cities, such as Rotterdam and Paris, both in 1951.

Brecht's productions are sometimes regarded as "canonical," although contemporary directors often modify his original plans. He usually began the performance with a half-curtain and a four-person orchestra playing an overture. Next, an unseen record player played a song associated with Courage; as Courage came on stage, she sang the second verse of her song herself. The stage had only a CYCLORAMA, a large curved curtain used as a backdrop, and a circle marked on the floor. This defined the space that was Mother Courage's world, and various sets were placed on the circle to accommodate successive scenes. The circle itself was a revolving turntable on which the wagon moved, going essentially nowhere. Brecht used placards to signal changes in time and place as well as to indicate events in the life of Mother Courage and her children. The lighting was generally bright, and the effect was lively and colorful.

Brecht was not widely produced in the West during the cold war, but Leon Epp directed *Mother Courage* at the Volkstheater in Vienna in 1963. In the same year Jerome Robbins produced the play at the Martin Beck Theatre on Broadway, with sets by Ming Cho Lee. Anne Bancroft played Mother Courage, and Zohra Lampert was Kattrin. The reviews praised Bancroft for achieving a "lonely magnificence" at the end of the play and maintained that Brecht generated a considerable emotional intensity despite his theoretical distaste for such effects.

The next year Joseph Slowik produced the play in the Goodman Theater in Chicago with a partial student cast and the distinguished Eugenie Leontovich as Mother Courage. In England *Mother Courage* was produced twice in the 1950s in London. In 1961 and 1965 it was produced by the Old Vic. Numerous local theaters put on the play in the late 1960s and 1970s. In 1980 Ntozake Shange adapted it for its second New York production and reset it in the period after the American Civil War; Gloria Foster and Morgan Freeman had the major roles. Frank Rich praised the acting and the energy of the play but feared that Brecht's original vision was altered almost beyond recognition: Mother Courage becomes "an innocent victim of an entire system," which is exactly what Brecht argued against.

The Royal Shakespeare Company produced the play in London in 1984 with Judi Dench as Courage and Zoë Wanamaker as Kattrin. Both received fine reviews, as did the production itself. Diana Rigg was Mother Courage in the production at the Olivier Theatre in London (November 1995–January 1996), which featured a new colloquial translation by the playwright David Hare and reset the play in the period of World War I. Like all these productions, it maintained the circular set that Brecht had originally used and experimented with Brecht's theories of alienation and distancing. The success of these productions indicates the play's appeal for our time.

Gwendolyn Mulamba played Mother Courage in the Classical Theater of Harlem's production in New York City in February 2004. Christopher McElroen directed. In the summer of 2006, Kevin Kline and Meryl Streep starred in George Wolfe's production of *Mother Courage* at Shakespeare in the Park Public Theater, based on a new translation of the play by Tony Kushner. Clearly, Brecht's play speaks to all of us in the twenty-first century.

Bertolt Brecht (1898–1956)

MOTHER COURAGE AND HER CHILDREN   *1939*
A CHRONICLE OF THE THIRTY YEARS' WAR

TRANSLATED BY JOHN WILLETT

Characters

MOTHER COURAGE
KATTRIN, *her dumb daughter*
EILIF, *the elder son*
SWISS CHEESE, *the younger son*
THE RECRUITER
THE SERGEANT
THE COOK
THE GENERAL
THE CHAPLAIN
THE ARMOURER
YVETTE POTTIER
THE MAN WITH THE PATCH
ANOTHER SERGEANT
THE ANCIENT COLONEL
A CLERK
A YOUNG SOLDIER
AN OLDER SOLDIER

A PEASANT
THE PEASANT'S WIFE
THE YOUNG MAN
THE OLD WOMAN
ANOTHER PEASANT
HIS WIFE
THE YOUNG PEASANT
THE ENSIGN
SOLDIERS
A VOICE

SCENE 1

(*Spring 1624. The Swedish Commander-in-Chief Count Oxenstierna is raising troops in Dalecarlia for the Polish campaign. The canteen woman Anna Fierling, known under the name of Mother Courage, loses one son.*)

(*Country road near a town.*)
(*A sergeant and a recruiter stand shivering.*)

RECRUITER: How can you muster a unit in a place like this? I've been thinking about suicide, sergeant. Here am I, got to find our commander four companies before the twelfth of the month, and people round here are so nasty I can't sleep nights. S'pose I get hold of some bloke and shut my eye to his pigeon chest and varicose veins, I get him proper drunk, he signs on the line, I'm just settling up, he goes for a piss, I follow him to the door because I smell a rat; bob's your uncle, he's off like a flea with the itch. No notion of word of honour, loyalty, faith, sense of duty. This place has shattered my confidence in the human race, sergeant.

SERGEANT: It's too long since they had a war here; stands to reason. Where's their sense of morality to come from? Peace—that's just a mess; takes a war to restore order. Peacetime, the human race runs wild. People and cattle get buggered about, who cares? Everyone eats just as he feels inclined, a hunk of cheese on top of his nice white bread, and a slice of fat on top of the cheese. How many young blokes and good horses in that town there, nobody knows; they never thought of counting. I been in places ain't seen a war for nigh seventy years: folks hadn't got names to them, couldn't tell one another apart. Takes a war to get proper nominal rolls and inventories—shoes in bundles and corn in bags, and man and beast properly numbered and carted off, cause it stands to reason: no order, no war.

RECRUITER: Too true.

SERGEANT: Same with all good things, it's a job to get a war going. But once it's blossomed out there's no holding it; folk start fighting shy of peace like punters what can't stop for fear of having to tot up what they lost. Before that it's war they're fighting shy of. It's something new to them.

RECRUITER: Hey, here's a cart coming. Two tarts with two young fellows. Stop her, sergeant. If this one's a flop I'm not standing around in your spring winds any longer, I can tell you.

(*Sound of a jew's-harp. Drawn by two young fellows, a covered cart rolls in. On it sit Mother Courage and her dumb daughter Kattrin.*)

MOTHER COURAGE: Morning, sergeant.

SERGEANT (*blocking the way*): Morning, all. And who are you?

MOTHER COURAGE: Business folk. (*Sings.*)

You captains, tell the drums to slacken
And give your infanteers a break:
It's Mother Courage with her waggon
Full of the finest boots they make.
With crawling lice and looted cattle
With lumbering guns and straggling kit—
How can you flog them into battle
Unless you get them boots that fit?

The new year's come. The watchmen shout.
The thaw sets in. The dead remain.
Whatever life has not died out
It staggers to its feet again.

Captains, how can you make them face it—
Marching to death without a brew?
Courage has rum with which to lace it
And boil their souls and bodies through.
Their musket primed, their stomach hollow—
Captains, your men don't look so well.
So feed them up and let them follow
While you command them into hell.
The new year's come. The watchmen shout.
The thaw sets in. The dead remain.
Wherever life has not died out
It staggers to its feet again.

SERGEANT: Halt! Who are you with, you trash?

THE ELDER SON: Second Finnish Regiment.

SERGEANT: Where's your papers?

MOTHER COURAGE: Papers?

THE YOUNGER SON: What, mean to say you don't know Mother Courage?

SERGEANT: Never heard of her. What's she called Courage for?

MOTHER COURAGE: Courage is the name they gave me because I was scared of going broke, sergeant, so I drove me cart right through the bombardment of Riga with fifty loaves of bread aboard. They were going mouldy, it was high time, hadn't any choice really.

SERGEANT: Don't be funny with me. Your papers.

MOTHER COURAGE (*pulling a bundle of papers from a tin box and climbing down off the cart*): That's all my papers, sergeant. You'll find a whole big missal from Altötting in Bavaria for wrapping gherkins in, and a road map of Moravia, the Lord knows when I'll ever get there, might as well chuck it away, and here's a stamped certificate that my horse hasn't got foot-and-mouth, only he's dead worse luck, cost fifteen florins he did—not me luckily. That enough paper for you?

SERGEANT: You pulling my leg? I'll knock that sauce out of you. S'pose you know you got to have a licence.

MOTHER COURAGE: Talk proper to me, do you mind, and don't you dare say I'm pulling your leg in front of my unsullied children, 'tain't decent, I got no time for you. My honest face, that's me licence with the Second Regiment, and if it's too difficult for you to read there's nowt I can do about it. Nobody's putting a stamp on that.

RECRUITER: Sergeant, methinks I smell insubordination in this individual. What's needed in our camp is obedience.

MOTHER COURAGE: Sausage, if you ask me.

SERGEANT: Name.

MOTHER COURAGE: Anna Fierling.

SERGEANT: You all called Fierling then?

MOTHER COURAGE: What'd you mean? It's me's called Fierling, not them.

SERGEANT: Aren't all this lot your children?

MOTHER COURAGE: You bet they are, but why should they all have to be called the same, eh? (*Pointing to her elder son.*) For instance, that one's called Eilif Nojocki—Why? his father always claimed he was called Kojocki or Mojocki or something. The boy remembers him clearly, except that the one he remembers was someone else, a Frenchie with a little beard. Aside from that he's got his father's wits; that man knew how to snitch a peasant's pants off his bum without him noticing. This way each of us has his own name, see.

SERGEANT: What, each one different?

MOTHER COURAGE: Don't tell me you ain't never come across that.

SERGEANT: So I s'pose he's a Chinaman? (*Pointing to the younger son.*)

MOTHER COURAGE: Wrong. Swiss.

SERGEANT: After the Frenchman?

MOTHER COURAGE: What Frenchman? I never heard tell of no Frenchman. You keep muddling things up, we'll be hanging around here till dark. A Swiss, but called Fejos, and the name has nowt to do with his father. He was called something quite different and was a fortifications engineer, only drunk all the time.

(*Swiss Cheese beams and nods; dumb Kattrin too is amused.*)

SERGEANT: How in hell can he be called Fejos?

MOTHER COURAGE: I don't like to be rude, sergeant, but you ain't got much imagination, have you? Course he's called Fejos, because when he arrived I was with a Hungarian, very decent fellow, had terrible kidney trouble though he never touched a drop. The boy takes after him.

SERGEANT: But he wasn't his father . . .

MOTHER COURAGE: Took after him just the same. I call him Swiss Cheese. (*Pointing to her daughter.*) And that's Kattrin Haupt, she's half German.

SERGEANT: Nice family, I must say.

MOTHER COURAGE: Aye, me cart and me have seen the world.

SERGEANT: I'm writing all this down. (*He writes.*) And you're from Bamberg in Bavaria; how d'you come to be here?

MOTHER COURAGE: Can't wait till war chooses to visit Bamberg, can I?

RECRUITER (*to Eilif*): You two should be called Jacob Ox and Esau Ox, pulling the cart like that. I s'pose you never get out of harness?

EILIF: Ma, can I clobber him one? I wouldn't half like to.

MOTHER COURAGE: And I says you can't; just you stop where you are. And now two fine officers like you, I bet you could use a good pistol, or a belt buckle, yours is on its last legs, sergeant.

SERGEANT: I could use something else. Those boys are healthy as young birch trees, I observe: chests like

barrels, solid leg muscles. So why are they dodging their military service, may I ask?

MOTHER COURAGE (*quickly*): Nowt doing, sergeant. Yours is no trade for my kids.

RECRUITER: But why not? There's good money in it, glory too. Flogging boots is women's work. (*To Eilif.*) Come here, let's see if you've muscles in you or if you're a chicken.

MOTHER COURAGE: He's a chicken. Give him a fierce look, he'll fall over.

RECRUITER: Killing a young bull that happens to be in his way. (*Wants to lead him off.*)

MOTHER COURAGE: Let him alone, will you? He's nowt for you folk.

RECRUITER: He was crudely offensive and talked about clobbering me. The two of us are going to step into that field and settle it man to man.

EILIF: Don't you worry, mum, I'll fix him.

MOTHER COURAGE: Stop there! You varmint! I know you, nowt but fights. There's a knife down his boot. A slasher, that's what he is.

RECRUITER: I'll draw it out of him like a milk-tooth. Come along, sonny.

MOTHER COURAGE: Sergeant, I'll tell the colonel. He'll have you both in irons. The lieutenant's going out with my daughter.

SERGEANT: No rough stuff, chum. (*To Mother Courage.*) What you got against military service? Wasn't his own father a soldier? Died a soldier's death, too? Said it yourself.

MOTHER COURAGE: He's nowt but a child. You want to take him off to slaughterhouse, I know you lot. They'll give you five florins for him.

RECRUITER: First he's going to get a smart cap and boots, eh?

EILIF: Not from you.

MOTHER COURAGE: Let's both go fishing, said angler to worm. (*To Swiss Cheese.*) Run off, call out they're trying to kidnap your brother. (*She pulls a knife.*) Go on, you kidnap him, just try. I'll slit you open, trash. I'll teach you to make war with him. We're doing an honest trade in ham and linen, and we're peaceable folk.

SERGEANT: Peaceable I don't think; look at your knife. You should be ashamed of yourself; put that knife away, you old harridan. A minute back you were admitting you live off the war, how else should you live, what from? But how's anyone to have war without soldiers?

MOTHER COURAGE: No need for it to be my kids.

SERGEANT: Oh, you'd like war to eat the pips but spit out the apple? It's to fatten up your kids, but you won't invest in it. Got to look after itself, eh? And you called Courage, fancy that. Scared of the war that keeps you going? Your sons aren't scared of it, I can see that.

EILIF: Take more than a war to scare me.

SERGEANT: And why? Look at me: has army life done all that badly by me? Joined up at seventeen.

MOTHER COURAGE: Still got to reach seventy.

SERGEANT: I don't mind waiting.

MOTHER COURAGE: Under the sod, eh?

SERGEANT: You trying to insult me, saying I'll die?

MOTHER COURAGE: S'pose it's true? S'pose I can see the mark's on you? S'pose you look like a corpse on leave to me? Eh?

SWISS CHEESE: She's got second sight, Mother has.

RECRUITER: Go ahead, tell the sergeant's fortune, might amuse him.

MOTHER COURAGE: Gimme helmet. (*He gives it to her.*)

SERGEANT: It don't mean a bloody sausage. Anything for a laugh though.

MOTHER COURAGE (*taking out a sheet of parchment and tearing it up*): Eilif, Swiss Cheese and Kattrin, may all of us be torn apart like this if we lets ourselves get too mixed up in the war. (*To the sergeant.*) Just for you I'm doing it for free. Black's for death. I'm putting a big black cross on this slip of paper.

SWISS CHEESE: Leaving the other one blank, see?

MOTHER COURAGE: Then I fold them across and shake them. All of us is jumbled together like this from our mother's womb, and now draw a slip and you'll know. (*The sergeant hesitates.*)

RECRUITER (*to Eilif*): I don't take just anybody, they all know I'm choosey, but you got the kind of fire I like to see.

SERGEANT (*fishing in the helmet*): Too silly. Load of eyewash.

SWISS CHEESE: Drawn a black cross, he has. Write him off.

RECRUITER: They're having you on; not everybody's name's on a bullet.

SERGEANT (*hoarsely*): You've put me in the shit.

MOTHER COURAGE: Did that yourself the day you became a soldier. Come along, let's move on now. 'Tain't every day we have a war, I got to get stirring.

SERGEANT: God damn it, you can't kid me. We're taking that bastard of yours for a soldier.

EILIF: Swiss Cheese'd like to be a soldier too.

MOTHER COURAGE: First I've heard of that. You'll have to draw too, all three of you. (*She goes to the rear to mark crosses on further slips.*)

RECRUITER (*to Eilif*): One of the things they say against us is that it's all holy-holy in the Swedish camp; but that's a malicious rumour to do us down. There's no hymn-singing but Sundays, just a single verse, and then only for those got voices.

MOTHER COURAGE (*coming back with the slips, which she drops into the sergeant's helmet*): Trying to get away from their ma, the devils, off to war like calves to salt-lick. But I'm making you draw lots, and that'll show you the world is no vale of joys with "Come along, son, we need a few more generals." Sergeant, I'm so scared they won't get through the war. Such dreadful characters, all three of them. (*She hands the helmet to Eilif.*) Hey, come on, fish out your slip. (*He fishes one out, unfolds it. She snatches it from him.*) There you are, it's a cross. Oh, wretched mother that I am, o pain-racked giver of birth! Shall he die? Aye, in the springtime of life he is doomed. If he becomes a soldier he shall bite the dust, it's plain to see. He is too foolhardy, like his dad was. And if he ain't sensible he'll go the way of all flesh, his slip proves it. (*Shouts at him.*) You going to be sensible?

EILIF: Why not?

MOTHER COURAGE: Sensible thing is stay with your mother, never mind if they poke fun at you and call you chicken, just you laugh.

RECRUITER: If you're pissing in your pants I'll make do with your brother.

MOTHER COURAGE: I told you laugh. Go on, laugh. Now you draw, Swiss Cheese. I'm not so scared on account you're honest. (*He fishes in the helmet.*) Oh, why look at your slip in that strange way? It's got to be a blank. There can't be any cross on it. Surely I'm not going to lose you. (*She takes the slip.*) A cross? What, you too? Is that because you're so simple, perhaps? O Swiss Cheese, you too will be sunk if you don't stay utterly honest all the while, like I taught you from childhood when you brought the change back from the baker's. Else you can't save yourself. Look, sergeant, that's a black cross, ain't it?

SERGEANT: A cross, that's right. Can't think how I come to get one. I always stay in the rear. (*To the recruiter.*) There's no catch. Her own family get it too.

SWISS CHEESE: I get it too. But I listen to what I'm told.

MOTHER COURAGE (*to Kattrin*): And now you're the only one I know's all right, you're a cross yourself; got a kind heart you have. (*Holds the helmet up to her on the cart, but takes the slip out herself.*) No, that's too much. That can't be right; must have made a mistake shuffling. Don't be too kind-hearted, Kattrin, you'll have to give it up, there's a cross above your path too. Lie doggo, girl, it can't be that hard once you're born dumb. Right, all of you know now. Look out for yourselves, you'll need to. And now up we get and on we go. (*She climbs on to the cart.*)

RECRUITER (*to the sergeant*): Do something.

SERGEANT: I don't feel very well.

RECRUITER: Must of caught a chill taking your helmet off in that wind. Involve her in a deal. (*Aloud.*) Might as well have a look at that belt-buckle, sergeant. After all, our friends here have to live by their business. Hey, you people, the sergeant wants to buy that belt-buckle.

MOTHER COURAGE: Half a florin. Two florins is what a belt like that's worth. (*Climbs down again.*)

SERGEANT: 'Tain't new. Let me get out of this damned wind and have a proper look at it. (*Goes behind the cart with the buckle.*)

MOTHER COURAGE: Ain't what I call windy.

SERGEANT: I s'pose it might be worth half a florin, it's silver.

MOTHER COURAGE (*joining him behind the cart*): It's six solid ounces.

RECRUITER (*to Eilif*): And then we men'll have one together. Got your bounty money here, come along. (*Eilif stands undecided.*)

MOTHER COURAGE: Half a florin it is.

SERGEANT: It beats me. I'm always at the rear. Sergeant's the safest job there is. You can send the others up front, cover themselves with glory. Me dinner hour's properly spoiled. Shan't be able to hold nowt down, I know.

MOTHER COURAGE: Mustn't let it prey on you so's you can't eat. Just stay at the rear. Here, take a swig of brandy, man. (*Gives him a drink.*)

RECRUITER (*has taken Eilif by the arm and is leading him away up stage*): Ten florins bounty money, then you're a gallant fellow fighting for the king and women'll be after you like flies. And you can clobber me for free for insulting you.

(*Exeunt both.°*)

(*Dumb Kattrin leans down from the cart and makes hoarse noises.*)

MOTHER COURAGE: All right, Kattrin, all right. Sergeant's just paying. (*Bites the half-florin.*) I got no faith in any kind of money. Burnt child, that's me, sergeant. This coin's good, though. And now let's get moving. Where's Eilif?

SWISS CHEESE: Went off with the recruiter.

MOTHER COURAGE (*stands quite still, then*): You simpleton. (*To Kattrin.*) 'Tain't your fault, you can't speak, I know.

SERGEANT: Could do with a swig yourself, ma. That's life. Plenty worse things than being a soldier. Want to live off war, but keep yourself and family out of it, eh?

MOTHER COURAGE: You'll have to help your brother pull now, Kattrin.

(*Brother and sister hitch themselves to the cart and start pulling. Mother Courage walks alongside. The cart rolls on.*)

SERGEANT (*looking after them*):
Like the war to nourish you?
Have to feed it something too.

SCENE 2

(*In the years 1625 and 1626 Mother Courage crosses Poland in the train of the Swedish armies. Before the fortress of Wallhof she meets her son again. Successful sale of a capon and heyday of her dashing son.*)
(*The general's tent.*)
(*Beside it, his kitchen. Thunder of cannon. The cook is arguing with Mother Courage, who wants to sell him a capon.*)

THE COOK: Sixty hellers for a miserable bird like that?

MOTHER COURAGE: Miserable bird? This fat brute? Mean to say some greedy old general — and watch

Exeunt both: They both leave.

your step if you got nowt for his dinner — can't afford sixty hellers for him?

THE COOK: I can get a dozen like that for ten hellers just down the road.

MOTHER COURAGE: What, a capon like this you can get just down the road? In time of siege, which means hunger that tears your guts. A rat you might get: "might" I say because they're all being gobbled up, five men spending best part of day chasing one hungry rat. Fifty hellers for a giant capon in time of siege!

THE COOK: But it ain't us having the siege, it's t'other side. We're conducting the siege, can't you get that in your head?

MOTHER COURAGE: But we got nowt to eat too, even worse than them in the town. Took it with them, didn't they? They're having a high old time, everyone says. And look at us! I been to the peasants, there's nowt there.

THE COOK: There's plenty. They're sitting on it.

MOTHER COURAGE (*triumphantly*): They ain't. They're bust, that's what they are. Just about starving. I saw some, were grubbing up roots from sheer hunger, licking their fingers after they boiled some old leather strap. That's way it is. And me got a capon here and supposed to take forty hellers for it.

THE COOK: Thirty, not forty. I said thirty.

MOTHER COURAGE: Here, this ain't just any old capon. It was such a gifted beast, I been told, it could only eat to music, had a military march of its own. It could count, it was that intelligent. And you say forty hellers is too much? General will make mincemeat of you if there's nowt on his table.

THE COOK: See what I'm doing? (*He takes a piece of beef and puts his knife to it.*) Here I got a bit of beef, I'm going to roast it. Make up your mind quick.

MOTHER COURAGE: Go on, roast it. It's last year's.

THE COOK: Last night's. That animal was still alive and kicking, I saw him myself.

MOTHER COURAGE: Alive and stinking, you mean.

THE COOK: I'll cook him five hours if need be. I'll just see if he's still tough. (*He cuts into it.*)

MOTHER COURAGE: Put plenty of pepper on it so his lordship the general don't smell the pong.

(*The general, a chaplain and Eilif enter the tent.*)

THE GENERAL (*slapping Eilif on the shoulder*): Now then, Eilif my son, into your general's tent with you and sit thou at my right hand. For you accomplished a deed of heroism, like a pious cavalier; and doing what you did for God, and in a war of religion at that, is something I commend in you most highly, you shall have a gold bracelet as soon as we've taken this town. Here we are, come to save their souls for them, and what do those insolent dung-encrusted yokels go and do? Drive their beef away from us. They stuff it into those priests of theirs all right, back and front, but you taught 'em manners, ha! So here's a pot of red wine for you, the two of us'll knock it back at one gulp. (*They do so.*) Piss all for the chaplain, the old bigot. And now, what would you like for dinner, my darling?

EILIF: A bit of meat, why not?

THE GENERAL: Cook! Meat!

THE COOK: And then he goes and brings guests when there's nowt there.

(*Mother Courage silences him so she can listen.*)

EILIF: Hungry job cutting down peasants.

MOTHER COURAGE: Jesus Christ, it's my Eilif.

THE COOK: Your what?

MOTHER COURAGE: My eldest boy. It's two years since I lost sight of him, they pinched him from me on the road, must think well of him if the general's asking him to dinner, and what kind of a dinner can you offer? Nowt. You heard what the visitor wishes to

Shakespeare in the Park Public Theater's outdoor 2006 performance of *Mother Courage and Her Children*, starring Meryl Streep and Kevin Kline.

pay for a sign that there's still true faith to be found in my army. As for that shepherd of souls he can just look on, because all he does is preach, without the least idea how it's to be carried out. And now, my son Eilif, tell us more about the neat way you smashed those yokels and captured the twenty oxen. Let's hope they get here soon.

EILIF: A day or two at most.

MOTHER COURAGE: Thoughtful of our Eilif not to bring the oxen in till tomorrow, else you lot wouldn't have looked twice at my capon.

EILIF: Well, it was like this, see. I'd heard peasants had been driving the oxen they'd hidden, out of the forest into one particular wood, on the sly and mostly by night. That's where people from the town were s'posed to come and pick them up. So I holds off and lets them drive their oxen together, reckoning they'd be better than me at finding 'em. I had my blokes slavering after the meat, cut their emergency rations even further for a couple of days till their mouths was watering at the least sound of any word beginning with "me-," like "measles" say.

THE GENERAL: Very clever of you.

EILIF: Possibly. The rest was a piece of cake. Except that the peasants had cudgels and outnumbered us three to one and made a murderous attack on us. Four of 'em shoved me into a thicket, knocked my sword from my hand and bawled out "Surrender!" What's the answer, I wondered; they're going to make mincemeat of me.

THE GENERAL: What did you do?

EILIF: I laughed.

THE GENERAL: You did what?

EILIF: Laughed. So we got talking. I put it on a business footing from the start, told them "Twenty florins a head's too much. I'll give you fifteen." As if I was meaning to pay. That threw them, and they began scratching their heads. In a flash I'd picked up my sword and was hacking 'em to pieces. Necessity's the mother of invention, eh, sir?

THE GENERAL: What is your view, pastor of souls?

THE CHAPLAIN: That phrase is not strictly speaking in the Bible, but when Our Lord turned the five loaves into five hundred there was no war on and he could tell people to love their neighbours as they'd had enough to eat. Today it's another story.

THE GENERAL (*laughs*): Quite another story. You can have a swig after all for that, you old Pharisee.° (*To Eilif.*) Hacked 'em to pieces, did you, so my gallant lads can get a proper bite to eat? What do the Scriptures say? "Whatsoever thou doest for the least of my brethren, thou doest for me." And what did you do for them? Got them a good square meal of beef, because they're not accustomed to mouldy bread, the old way was to fix a cold meal of rolls and wine in your helmet before you went out to fight for God.

Pharisee: A member of a Jewish sect current in biblical days; the term is now commonly used to refer to a hypocritical, self-righteous person.

Lotte Lenya as Mother Courage, pulling her wagon in Brecht's 1979 Berliner Ensemble production of his play.

eat: meat. Take my tip, you settle for the capon, it'll be a florin.

THE GENERAL (*has sat down with Eilif, and bellows*): Food, Lamb, you foul cook, or I'll have your hide.

THE COOK: Give it over, dammit, this is blackmail.

MOTHER COURAGE: Didn't someone say it was a miserable bird?

THE COOK: Miserable; give it over, and a criminal price, fifty hellers.

MOTHER COURAGE: A florin, I said. For my eldest boy, the general's guest, no expense is too great for me.

THE COOK (*gives her the money*): You might at least pluck it while I see to the fire.

MOTHER COURAGE (*sits down to pluck the fowl*): He won't half be surprised to see me. He's my dashing clever son. Then I got a stupid one too, he's honest though. The girl's nowt. One good thing, she don't talk.

THE GENERAL: Drink up, my son, this is my best Falernian; only got a barrel or two left, but that's nothing to

EILIF: Aye, in a flash I'd picked up my sword and was hacking them to pieces.

THE GENERAL: You've the makings of a young Caesar. You ought to see the King.

EILIF: I have from a distance. He kind of glows. I'd like to model myself on him.

THE GENERAL: You've got something in common already. I appreciate soldiers like you, Eilif, men of courage. Somebody like that I treat as I would my own sort. (*He leads him over to the map.*) Have a look at the situation, Eilif; it's a long haul still.

MOTHER COURAGE (*who has been listening and now angrily plucks the fowl*): That must be a rotten general.

THE COOK: He's ravenous all right, but why rotten?

MOTHER COURAGE: Because he's got to have men of courage, that's why. If he knew how to plan a proper campaign what would he be needing men of courage for? Ordinary ones would do. It's always the same; whenever there's a load of special virtues around it means something stinks.

THE COOK: I thought it meant things is all right.

MOTHER COURAGE: No, that they stink. Look, s'pose some general or king is bone stupid and leads his men up shit creek, then those men've got to be fearless, there's another virtue for you. S'pose he's stingy and hires too few soldiers, then they got to be a crowd of Hercules's. And s'pose he's slapdash and don't give a bugger, then they got to be clever as monkeys else their number's up. Same way they got to show exceptional loyalty each time he gives them impossible jobs. Nowt but virtues no proper country and no decent king or general would ever need. In decent countries folk don't have to have virtues, the whole lot can be perfectly ordinary, average intelligence, and for all I know cowards.

THE GENERAL: I'll wager your father was a soldier.

EILIF: A great soldier, I been told. My mother warned me about it. There's a song I know.

THE GENERAL: Sing it to us. (*Roars.*) When's that dinner coming?

EILIF: It's called The Song of the Girl and the Soldier. (*He sings it, dancing a war dance with his sabre.*)

The guns blaze away, and the bay'nit'll slay
And the water can't hardly be colder.
What's the answer to ice? Keep off's my advice!
That's what the girl told the soldier.
Next thing the soldier, wiv' a round up the spout
Hears the band playing and gives a great shout:
Why, it's marching what makes you a soldier!
So it's down to the south and then northwards once more:
See him catching that bay'nit in his naked paw!
That's what his comrades done told her.

Oh, do not despise the advice of the wise
Learn wisdom from those that are older
And don't try for things that are out of your reach—

That's what the girl told the soldier.
Next thing the soldier, his bay'nit in place
Wades into the river and laughs in her face
Though the water comes up to his shoulder.
When the shingle roof glints in the light o' the moon
We'll be wiv' you again, not a moment too soon!
That's what his comrades done told her.

MOTHER COURAGE (*takes up the song in the kitchen, beating on a pot with her spoon*):

You'll go out like a light! And the sun'll take flight
For your courage just makes us feel colder.
Oh, that vanishing light! May God see that it's right!—
That's what the girl told the soldier.

EILIF: What's that?

MOTHER COURAGE (*continues singing*):

Next thing the soldier, his bay'nit in place
Was caught by the current and went down without trace
And the water couldn't hardly be colder.
Then the shingle roof froze in the light o' the moon
As both soldier and ice drifted down to their doom—
And d'you know what his comrades done told her?

He went out like a light. And the sunshine took flight
For his courage just made 'em feel colder.
Oh, do not despise the advice of the wise!
That's what the girl told the soldier.

THE GENERAL: The things they get up to in my kitchen these days.

EILIF (*Has gone into the kitchen. He flings his arms round his mother.*): Fancy seeing you again, ma! Where's the others?

MOTHER COURAGE (*in his arms*): Snug as a bug in a rug. They made Swiss Cheese paymaster of the Second Finnish; any road he'll stay out of fighting that way, I couldn't keep him out altogether.

EILIF: How's the old feet?

MOTHER COURAGE: Bit tricky getting me shoes on of a morning.

THE GENERAL (*has joined them*): So you're his mother, I hope you've got plenty more sons for me like this one.

EILIF: Ain't it my lucky day? You sitting out there in the kitchen, ma, hearing your son commended . . .

MOTHER COURAGE: You bet I heard. (*Slaps his face.*)

EILIF (*holding his cheek*): What's that for? Taking the oxen?

MOTHER COURAGE: No. Not surrendering when those four went for you and wanted to make mincemeat of you. Didn't I say you should look after yourself? You Finnish devil!

(*The general and the chaplain stand in the doorway laughing.*)

SCENE 3

(*Three years later Mother Courage is taken prisoner along with elements of a Finnish regiment. She manages to save her daughter, likewise her covered cart, but her honest son is killed.*)
(*Military camp.*)
(*Afternoon. A flagpole with the regimental pay. From her cart, festooned now with all kinds of goods, Mother Courage has stretched a washing line to a large cannon, across which she and Kattrin are folding the washing. She is bargaining at the same time with an armourer over a sack of shot. Swiss Cheese, now wearing a paymaster's uniform, is looking on. A comely person, Yvette Pottier, is sewing a gaily coloured hat, a glass of brandy before her. She is in her stockinged feet, having laid aside her red high-heeled boots.*)

THE ARMOURER: I'll let you have that shot for a couple of florins. It's cheap at the price, I got to have the money because the colonel's been boozing with his officers since two days back, and the drink's run out.
MOTHER COURAGE: That's troops' munitions. They catch me with that, I'm for court-martial. You crooks flog the shot, and troops got nowt to fire at enemy.
THE ARMOURER: Have a heart, can't you; you scratch my back and I'll scratch yours.
MOTHER COURAGE: I'm not taking army property. Not at that price.
THE ARMOURER: You can sell it on the q.t. tonight to the Fourth Regiment's armourer for five florins, eight even, if you let him have a receipt for twelve. He's right out of ammunition.
MOTHER COURAGE: Why not you do it?
THE ARMOURER: I don't trust him, he's a pal of mine.
MOTHER COURAGE (*takes the sack*): Gimme. (*To Kattrin.*) Take it away and pay him a florin and a half. (*The armourer protests.*) I said a florin and a half. (*Kattrin drags the sack upstage, the armourer following her. Mother Courage addresses Swiss Cheese.*) Here's your woollies, now look after them, it's October and autumn may set in any time. I ain't saying it's got to, cause I've learned nowt's got to come when you think it will, not even seasons of the year. But your regimental accounts got to add up right, come what may. Do they add up right?
SWISS CHEESE: Yes, mother.
MOTHER COURAGE: Don't you forget they made you paymaster cause you was honest, not dashing like your brother, and above all so stupid I bet you ain't even thought of clearing off with it, no not you. That's a big consolation to me. And don't lose those woollies.

SWISS CHEESE: No, mother, I'll put them under my mattress. (*Begins to go.*)
THE ARMOURER: I'll go along with you, paymaster.
MOTHER COURAGE: And don't you start learning him none of your tricks.

(*The armourer leaves with Swiss Cheese without any farewell gesture.*)

YVETTE (*waving to him*): No reason not to say goodbye, armourer.
MOTHER COURAGE (*to Yvette*): I don't like to see them together. He's wrong company for our Swiss Cheese. Oh well, war's off to a good start. Easily take four, five years before all countries are in. A bit of foresight, don't do nothing silly, and business'll flourish. Don't you know you ain't s'posed to drink before midday with your complaint?
YVETTE: Complaint, who says so, it's a libel.
MOTHER COURAGE: They all say so.
YVETTE: Because they're all telling lies, Mother Courage, and me at my wits' end cause they're all avoiding me like something the cat brought in thanks to those lies, what the hell am I remodelling my hat for? (*She throws it away.*) That's why I drink before midday. Never used to, gives you crows' feet, but now what the hell? All the Second Finnish know me. Ought to have stayed at home when my first fellow did me wrong. No good our sort being proud. Eat shit, that's what you got to do, or down you go.
MOTHER COURAGE: Now don't you start up again about that Pieter of yours and how it all happened, in front of my innocent daughter too.
YVETTE: She's the one should hear it, put her off love.
MOTHER COURAGE: Nobody can put 'em off that.
YVETTE: Then I'll go on, get it off my chest. It all starts with yours truly growing up in lovely Flanders, else I'd never of seen him and wouldn't be stuck here now in Poland, cause he was an army cook, fair-haired, a Dutchman but thin for once. Kattrin, watch out for the thin ones, only in those days I didn't know that, or that he'd got a girl already, or that they all called him Puffing Piet cause he never took his pipe out of his mouth when he was on the job, it meant that little to him. (*She sings the Song of Fraternisation.*)

When I was only sixteen
The foe came into our land.
He laid aside his sabre
And with a smile he took my hand.
After the May parade
The May light starts to fade.
The regiment dressed by the right
The drums were beaten, that's the drill.
The foe took us behind the hill
And fraternised all night.

There were so many foes then
But mine worked in the mess.
I loathed him in the daytime.

At night I loved him none the less.
After the May parade
The May light starts to fade.
The regiment dressed by the right
The drums were beaten, that's the drill.
The foe took us behind the hill
And fraternised all night.

The love which came upon me
Was wished on me by fate.
My friends could never grasp why
I found it hard to share their hate.
The fields were wet with dew
When sorrow first I knew.
The regiment dressed by the right
The drums were beaten, that's the drill.
And then the foe, my lover still
Went marching out of sight.

I followed him, fool that I was, but I never found him, and that was five years back. (*She walks unsteadily behind the cart.*)

MOTHER COURAGE: You left your hat here.

YVETTE: Anyone wants it can have it.

MOTHER COURAGE: Let that be a lesson, Kattrin. Don't you start anything with them soldiers. Love makes the world go round, I'm warning you. Even with fellows not in the army it's no bed of roses. He says he'd like to kiss the ground your feet walk on — reminds me, did you wash them yesterday? — and after that you're his skivvy. Be thankful you're dumb, then you can't contradict yourself and won't be wanting to bite your tongue off for speaking the truth; it's a godsend, being dumb is. And here comes the general's cook, now what's he after?

(*Enter the cook and the chaplain.*)

THE CHAPLAIN: I have a message for you from your son Eilif, and the cook has come along because you made such a profound impression on him.

THE COOK: I just came along to get a bit of air.

MOTHER COURAGE: That you can always do here if you behave yourself, and if you don't I can deal with you. What does he want? I got no spare cash.

THE CHAPLAIN: Actually I had a message for his brother the paymaster.

MOTHER COURAGE: He ain't here now nor anywhere else neither. He ain't his brother's paymaster. He's not to lead him into temptation nor be clever at his expense. (*Giving him money from the purse slung round her.*) Give him this, it's a sin, he's banking on mother's love and ought to be ashamed of himself.

THE COOK: Not for long, he'll have to be moving off with the regiment, might be to his death. Give him a bit extra, you'll be sorry later. You women are tough, then later on you're sorry. A little glass of brandy wouldn't have been a problem, but it wasn't offered and, who knows, a bloke may lie beneath the green sod and none of you people will ever be able to dig him up again.

THE CHAPLAIN: Don't give way to your feelings, cook. To fall in battle is a blessing, not an inconvenience, and why? It is a war of faith. None of your common wars but a special one, fought for the faith and therefore pleasing to God.

THE COOK: Very true. It's a war all right in one sense, what with requisitioning, murder and looting and the odd bit of rape thrown in, but different from all the other wars because it's a war of faith; stands to reason. But it's thirsty work at that, you must admit.

THE CHAPLAIN (*to Mother Courage, indicating the cook*): I tried to stop him, but he says he's taken a shine to you, you figure in his dreams.

THE COOK (*lighting a stumpy pipe*): Just want a glass of brandy from a fair hand, what harm in that? Only I'm groggy already cause the chaplain here's been telling such jokes all the way along you bet I'm still blushing.

MOTHER COURAGE: Him a clergyman too. I'd best give the pair of you a drink or you'll start making me immoral suggestions cause you've nowt else to do.

THE CHAPLAIN: Behold a temptation, said the court preacher, and fell. (*Turning back to look at Kattrin as he leaves.*) And who is this entrancing young person?

MOTHER COURAGE: That ain't an entrancing but a decent young person. (*The chaplain and the cook go behind the cart with Mother Courage. Kattrin looks after them, then walks away from her washing towards the hat. She picks it up and sits down, pulling the red boots towards her. Mother Courage can be heard in the background talking politics with the chaplain and the cook.*)

MOTHER COURAGE: Those Poles here in Poland had no business sticking their noses in. Right, our king moved in on them, horse and foot, but did they keep the peace? no, went and stuck their noses into their own affairs, they did, and fell on king just as he was quietly clearing off. They committed a breach of peace, that's what, so blood's on their own head.

THE CHAPLAIN: All our king minded about was freedom. The emperor had made slaves of them all, Poles and Germans alike, and the king had to liberate them.

THE COOK: Just what I say, your brandy's first rate, I weren't mistaken in your face, but talk of the king, it cost the king dear trying to give freedom to Germany, what with giving Sweden the salt tax, what cost the poor folk a bit, so I've heard, on top of which he had to have the Germans locked up and drawn and quartered cause they wanted to carry on slaving for the emperor. Course the king took a serious view when anybody didn't want to be free. He set out by just trying to protect Poland against bad people, particularly the emperor, then it started to become a habit till he ended up protecting the whole of Germany. They didn't half kick. So the poor old king's had nowt but trouble for all his kindness and expenses, and that's something he had to make up for by taxes of course, which caused bad blood, not that he'd let a little matter like that depress him. One thing he had on his side, God's word, that was a help. Because otherwise folk would of been saying he done it all for himself and to make a bit on the side. So he's always had a good conscience, which was the main point.

MOTHER COURAGE: Anyone can see you're no Swede or you wouldn't be talking that way about the Hero King.

THE CHAPLAIN: After all he provides the bread you eat.

THE COOK: I don't eat it, I bake it.

MOTHER COURAGE: They'll never beat him, and why, his men got faith in him. (*Seriously.*) To go by what the big shots say, they're waging war for almighty God and in the name of everything that's good and lovely. But look closer, they ain't so silly, they're waging it for what they can get. Else little folk like me wouldn't be in it at all.

THE COOK: That's the way it is.

THE CHAPLAIN: As a Dutchman you'd do better to glance at the flag above your head before venting your opinions here in Poland.

MOTHER COURAGE: All good Lutherans here. Prosit!°

(*Kattrin has put on Yvette's hat and begun strutting around in imitation of her way of walking.*)

(*Suddenly there is a noise of cannon fire and shooting. Drums. Mother Courage, the cook and the chaplain rush out from behind the cart, the two last-named still carrying their glasses. The armourer and another soldier run up to the cannon and try to push it away.*)

MOTHER COURAGE: What's happening? Wait till I've taken my washing down, you louts! (*She tries to rescue her washing.*)

THE ARMOURER: The Catholics! Broken through. Don't know if we'll get out of here. (*To the soldier.*) Get that gun shifted! (*Runs on.*)

THE COOK: God, I must find the general. Courage, I'll drop by in a day or two for another talk.

MOTHER COURAGE: Wait, you forgot your pipe.

THE COOK (*in the distance*): Keep it for me. I'll be needing it.

MOTHER COURAGE: Would happen just as we're making a bit of money.

THE CHAPLAIN: Ah well, I'll be going too. Indeed, if the enemy is so close as that it might be dangerous. Blessèd are the peacemakers is the motto in wartime. If only I had a cloak to cover me.

MOTHER COURAGE: I ain't lending no cloaks, not on your life. I been had too often.

THE CHAPLAIN: But my faith makes it particularly dangerous for me.

MOTHER COURAGE (*gets him a cloak*): Goes against my conscience, this does. Now you run along.

THE CHAPLAIN: Thank you, dear lady, that's very generous of you, but I think it might be wiser for me to remain seated here; it could arouse suspicion and bring the enemy down on me if I were seen to run.

MOTHER COURAGE (*to the soldier*): Leave it, you fool, who's going to pay you for that? I'll look after it for you, you're risking your neck.

THE SOLDIER (*running away*): You can tell 'em I tried.

MOTHER COURAGE: Cross my heart. (*Sees her daughter with the hat.*) What you doing with that strumpet's hat? Take that lid off, you gone crazy? And the enemy arriving any minute! (*Pulls the hat off Kattrin's head.*) Want 'em to pick you up and make a prostitute of you? And she's gone and put those boots on, whore of Babylon! Off with those boots! (*Tries to tug them off her.*) Jesus Christ, chaplain, gimme a hand, get those boots off her, I'll be right back. (*Runs to the cart.*)

YVETTE (*arrives, powdering her face*): Fancy that, the Catholics are coming. Where's my hat? Who's been kicking it around? I can't go about looking like this if the Catholics are coming. What'll they think of me? No mirror either. (*To the chaplain.*) How do I look? Too much powder?

THE CHAPLAIN: Exactly right.

YVETTE: And where are them red boots? (*Fails to find them as Kattrin hides her feet under her skirt.*) I left them here all right. Now I'll have to get to me tent barefoot. It's an outrage.

(*Exit.*)

(*Swiss Cheese runs in carrying in a small box.*)

MOTHER COURAGE (*Arrives with her hands full of ashes. To Kattrin.*): Here some ashes. (*To Swiss Cheese.*) What's that you're carrying?

SWISS CHEESE: Regimental cash box.

MOTHER COURAGE: Chuck it away. No more paymastering for you.

SWISS CHEESE: I'm responsible. (*He goes to the rear.*)

MOTHER COURAGE (*to the chaplain*): Take your clerical togs off, padre, or they'll spot you under that cloak. (*She rubs Kattrin's face with ash.*) Keep still, will you? There you are, a bit of muck and you'll be safe. What a disaster. Sentries were drunk. Hide your light under a bushel, it says. Take a soldier, specially a Catholic one, add a clean face, and there's your instant whore. For weeks they get nowt to eat, then soon as they manage to get it by looting they're falling on anything in skirts. That ought to do. Let's have a look. Not bad. Looks like you been grubbing in muckheap. Stop trembling. Nothing'll happen to you like that. (*To Swiss Cheese.*) Where d'you leave cash box?

SWISS CHEESE: Thought I'd put it in cart.

MOTHER COURAGE (*horrified*): What, my cart? Sheer criminal idiocy. Only take me eyes off you one instant. Hang us all three, they will.

SWISS CHEESE: I'll put it somewhere else then, or clear out with it.

MOTHER COURAGE: You sit on it, it's too late now.

THE CHAPLAIN (*who is changing his clothes downstage*): For heaven's sake, the flag!

MOTHER COURAGE (*hauls down the regimental flag*): Bozhe moi! I'd given up noticing it were there. Twenty-five years I've had it.

Prosit!: Cheers!

(*The thunder of cannon intensifies.*)
(*A morning three days later. The cannon has gone. Mother Courage, Kattrin, the chaplain and Swiss Cheese are sitting gloomily over a meal.*)

SWISS CHEESE: That's three days I been sitting around with nowt to do, and sergeant's always been kind to me but any moment now he'll start asking where's Swiss Cheese with the pay box?

MOTHER COURAGE: You thank your stars they ain't after you.

THE CHAPLAIN: What can I say? I can't even hold a service here, it might make trouble for me. Whosoever hath a full heart, his tongue runneth over, it says, but heaven help me if mine starts running over.

MOTHER COURAGE: That's how it goes. Here they sit, one with his faith and the other with his cash box. Dunno which is more dangerous.

THE CHAPLAIN: We are all of us in God's hands.

MOTHER COURAGE: Oh, I don't think it's as bad as that yet, though I must say I can't sleep nights. If it weren't for you, Swiss Cheese, things'd be easier. I think I got meself cleared. I told 'em I didn't hold with Antichrist, the Swedish one with horns on, and I'd observed left horn was a bit unserviceable. Half way through their interrogation I asked where I could get church candles not too dear. I knows the lingo cause Swiss Cheese's dad were Catholic, often used to make jokes about it, he did. They didn't believe me all that much, but they ain't got no regimental canteen lady. So they're winking an eye. Could turn out for the best, you know. We're prisoners, but same like fleas on dog.

THE CHAPLAIN: That's good milk. But we'll need to cut down our Swedish appetites a bit. After all, we've been defeated.

MOTHER COURAGE: Who's been defeated? Look, victory and defeat ain't bound to be same for the big shots up top as for them below, not by no means. Can be times the bottom lot find a defeat really pays them. Honour's lost, nowt else. I remember once up in Livonia our general took such a beating from enemy I got a horse off our baggage train in the confusion, pulled me cart seven months, he did, before we won and they checked up. As a rule you can say victory and defeat both come expensive to us ordinary folk. Best thing for us is when politics get bogged down solid. (*To Swiss Cheese.*) Eat up.

SWISS CHEESE: Got no appetite for it. What's sergeant to do when pay day comes round?

MOTHER COURAGE: They don't have pay days on a retreat.

SWISS CHEESE: It's their right, though. They needn't retreat if they don't get paid. Needn't stir a foot.

MOTHER COURAGE: Swiss Cheese, you're that conscientious it makes me quite nervous. I brought you up to be honest, you not being clever, but you got to know where to stop. Chaplain and me, we're off now to buy Catholic flag and some meat. Dunno anyone so good at sniffing meat, like sleepwalking it is, straight to target. I'd say he can pick out a good piece by the way his mouth starts watering. Well, thank goodness they're letting me go on trading. You don't ask tradespeople their faith but their prices. And Lutheran trousers keep cold out too.

THE CHAPLAIN: What did the mendicant say when he heard the Lutherans were going to turn everything in town and country topsy-turvy? "They'll always need beggars." (*Mother Courage disappears into the cart.*) So she's still worried about the cash box. So far they've taken us all for granted as part of the cart, but how long for?

SWISS CHEESE: I can get rid of it.

THE CHAPLAIN: That's almost more dangerous. Suppose you're seen. They have spies. Yesterday a fellow popped up out of the ditch in front of me just as I was relieving myself first thing. I was so scared I only just suppressed an ejaculatory prayer. That would have given me away all right. I think what they'd like best is to go sniffing people's excrement to see if they're Protestants. The spy was a little runt with a patch over one eye.

MOTHER COURAGE (*clambering out of the cart with a basket*): What have I found, you shameless creature? (*She holds up the red boots in triumph.*) Yvette's red high-heeled boots! Coolly went and pinched them, she did. Cause you put it in her head she was an enchanting young person. (*She lays them in the basket.*) I'm giving them back. Stealing Yvette's boots! She's wrecking herself for money. That's understandable. But you'd do it for nothing, for pleasure. What did I tell you: you're to wait till it's peace. No soldiers for you. You're not to start exhibiting yourself till it's peacetime.

THE CHAPLAIN: I don't find she exhibits herself.

MOTHER COURAGE: Too much for my liking. Let her be like a stone in Dalecarlia, where there's nowt else, so folk say "Can't see that cripple," that's how I'd lief have her. Then nowt'll happen to her. (*To Swiss Cheese.*) You leave that box where it is, d'you hear? And keep an eye on your sister, she needs it. The pair of you'll have me in grave yet. Sooner be minding a bagful of fleas.

(*She leaves with the chaplain. Kattrin clears away the dishes.*)

SWISS CHEESE: Won't be able to sit out in the sun in shirt-sleeves much longer. (*Kattrin points at a tree.*) Aye, leaves turning yellow. (*Kattrin asks by gestures if he wants a drink.*) Don't want no drink. I'm thinking. (*Pause.*) Said she can't sleep. Best if I got rid of that box, found a good place for it. All right, let's have a glass. (*Kattrin goes behind the cart.*) I'll stuff it down the rat-hole by the river for the time being. Probably pick it up tonight before first light and take it to Regiment. How far can they have retreated in three days? Bet sergeant's surprised. I'm agreeably disappointed in you, Swiss Cheese, he'll say. I make you responsible for the cash, and you go and bring it back.

(*As Kattrin emerges from behind the cart with a full glass in her hand, two men confront her. One is a sergeant, the other doffs his hat to her. He has a patch over one eye.*)

THE MAN WITH THE PATCH: God be with you, mistress. Have you seen anyone round here from Second Finnish Regimental Headquarters?

(*Kattrin, badly frightened, runs downstage, spilling the brandy. The two men look at one another, then withdraw on seeing Swiss Cheese sitting there.*)

SWISS CHEESE (*interrupted in his thoughts*): You spilt half of it. What are those faces for? Jabbed yourself in eye? I don't get it. And I'll have to be off, I've thought it over, it's the only way. (*He gets up. She does everything possible to make him realise the danger. He only shrugs her off.*) Wish I knew what you're trying to say. Sure you mean well, poor creature, just can't get words out. What's it matter your spilling my brandy, I'll drink plenty more glasses yet, what's one more or less? (*He gets the box from the cart and takes it under his tunic.*) Be back in a moment. Don't hold me up now, or I'll be angry. I know you mean well. Too bad you can't speak.

(*As she tries to hold him back he kisses her and tears himself away. Exit. She is desperate, running hither and thither uttering little noises. The chaplain and Mother Courage return. Kattrin rushes to her mother.*)

MOTHER COURAGE: What's all this? Pull yourself together, love. They done something to you? Where's Swiss Cheese? Tell it me step by step, Kattrin. Mother understands you. What, so that bastard did take the box? I'll wrap it round his ears, the little hypocrite. Take your time and don't gabble, use your hands, I don't like it when you howl like a dog, what'll his reverence say? Makes him uncomfortable. What, a one-eyed man came along?

THE CHAPLAIN: That one-eyed man is a spy. Have they arrested Swiss Cheese? (*Kattrin shakes her head, shrugs her shoulders.*) We're done for.

MOTHER COURAGE (*fishes in her basket and brings out a Catholic flag, which the chaplain fixes to the mast*): Better hoist new flag.

THE CHAPLAIN (*bitterly*): All good Catholics here.

(*Voices are heard from the rear. The two men bring in Swiss Cheese.*)

SWISS CHEESE: Let me go, I got nowt. Don't twist my shoulder, I'm innocent.

SERGEANT: Here's where he came from. You know each other.

MOTHER COURAGE: Us? How?

SWISS CHEESE: I don't know her. Got no idea who she is, had nowt to do with them. I bought me dinner here, ten hellers it cost. You might have seen me sitting here, it was too salty.

SERGEANT: Who are you people, eh?

MOTHER COURAGE: We're law-abiding folk. That's right, he bought a dinner. Said it was too salty.

SERGEANT: Trying to pretend you don't know each other, that it?

MOTHER COURAGE: Why should I know him? Can't know everyone. I don't go asking 'em what they're called and are they a heretic; if he pays he ain't a heretic. You a heretic?

SWISS CHEESE: Go on.

THE CHAPLAIN: He sat there very properly, never opening his mouth except when eating. Then he had to.

SERGEANT: And who are you?

MOTHER COURAGE: He's just my potboy. Now I expect you gentlemen are thirsty, I'll get you a glass of brandy, you must be hot and tired with running.

SERGEANT: No brandy on duty. (*To Swiss Cheese.*) You were carrying something. Must have hidden it by the river. Was a bulge in your tunic when you left here.

MOTHER COURAGE: You sure it was him?

SWISS CHEESE: You must be thinking of someone else. I saw someone bounding off with a bulge in his tunic. I'm the wrong man.

MOTHER COURAGE: I'd say it was a misunderstanding too, such things happen. I'm a good judge of people, I'm Courage, you heard of me, everyone knows me, and I tell you that's an honest face he has.

SERGEANT: We're on the track of the Second Finnish Regiment's cash box. We got the description of the fellow responsible for it. Been trailing him two days. It's you.

SWISS CHEESE: It's not me.

SERGEANT: And you better cough it up, or you're a goner, you know. Where is it?

MOTHER COURAGE (*urgently*): Of course he'd give it over rather than be a goner. Right out he'd say: I got it, here it is, you're too strong. He ain't all that stupid. Speak up, stupid idiot, here's the sergeant giving you a chance.

SWISS CHEESE: S'pose I ain't got it.

SERGEANT: Then come along. We'll get it out of you. (*They lead him off.*)

MOTHER COURAGE (*calls after them*): He'd tell you. He's not that stupid. And don't you twist his shoulder! (*Runs after them.*)

(*Evening of the same day. The chaplain and dumb Kattrin are cleaning glasses and polishing knives.*)

THE CHAPLAIN: Cases like that, where somebody gets caught, are not unknown in religious history. It reminds me of the Passion of Our Lord and Saviour. There's an old song about that. (*He sings the Song of the Hours.°*)

In the first hour Jesus mild
Who had prayed since even

Song of the Hours: Translated by Ralph Manheim.

Was betrayed and led before
Pontius the heathen.

Pilate found him innocent
Free from fault and error
Therefore, having washed his hands
Sent him to King Herod.

In the third hour he was scourged
Stripped and clad in scarlet
And a plaited crown of thorns
Set upon his forehead.

On the Son of Man they spat
Mocked him and made merry.
Then the cross of death was brought
Given him to carry.

At the sixth hour with two thieves
To the cross they nailed him
And the people and the thieves
Mocked him and reviled him.

This is Jesus King of Jews
Cried they in derision
Till the sun withdrew its light
From that awful vision.

At the ninth hour Jesus wailed
Why hast thou me forsaken?
Soldiers brought him vinegar
Which he left untaken.

Then he yielded up the ghost
And the earth was shaken.
Rended was the temple's veil
And the saints were wakened.

Soldiers broke the two thieves' legs
As the night descended.
Thrust a spear in Jesus' side
When his life had ended.

Still they mocked, as from his wound
Flowed the blood and water
And blasphemed the Son of Man
With their cruel laughter.

MOTHER COURAGE (*entering excitedly*): It's touch and go. They say sergeant's open to reason though. Only we mustn't let on it's Swiss Cheese else they'll say we helped him. It's a matter of money, that's all. But where's money to come from? Hasn't Yvette been round? I ran into her, she's got her hooks on some colonel, maybe he'd buy her a canteen business.

THE CHAPLAIN: Do you really wish to sell?

MOTHER COURAGE: Where's money for sergeant to come from?

THE CHAPLAIN: What'll you live on, then?

MOTHER COURAGE: That's just it.

(*Yvette Pottier arrives with an extremely ancient colonel.*)

YVETTE (*embracing Mother Courage*): My dear Courage, fancy seeing you so soon. (*Whispers.*) He's not unwilling. (*Aloud.*) This is my good friend who advises me in business matters. I happened to hear you wanted to sell your cart on account of circumstances. I'll think it over.

MOTHER COURAGE: Pledge it, not sell, just not too much hurry, tain't every day you find a cart like this in wartime.

YVETTE (*disappointed*): Oh, pledge. I thought it was for sale. I'm not so sure I'm interested. (*To the colonel.*) How do you feel about it?

THE COLONEL: Just as you feel, pet.

MOTHER COURAGE: I'm only pledging it.

YVETTE: I thought you'd got to have the money.

MOTHER COURAGE (*firmly*): I got to have it, but sooner run myself ragged looking for a bidder than sell outright. And why? The cart's our livelihood. It's a chance for you, Yvette; who knows when you'll get another like it and have a special friend to advise you, am I right?

YVETTE: Yes, my friend thinks I should clinch it, but I'm not sure. If it's only a pledge . . . so you agree we ought to buy outright?

THE COLONEL: I agree, pet.

MOTHER COURAGE: Best look and see if you can find anything for sale then; maybe you will if you don't rush it, take your friend along with you, say a week or fortnight, might find something suits you.

YVETTE: Then let's go looking. I adore going around looking for things, I adore going around with you, Poldi, it's such fun, isn't it? No matter if it takes a fortnight. How soon would you pay the money back if you got it?

MOTHER COURAGE: I'd pay back in two weeks, maybe one.

YVETTE: I can't make up my mind, Poldi chéri, you advise me. (*Takes the colonel aside.*) She's got to sell, I know, no problem there. And there's that ensign, you know, the fair-haired one, he'd be glad to lend me the money. He's crazy about me, says there's someone I remind him of. What do you advise?

THE COLONEL: You steer clear of him. He's no good. He's only making use of you. I said I'd buy you something, didn't I, pussykins?

YVETTE: I oughtn't to let you. Of course if you think the ensign might try to take advantage . . . Poldi, I'll accept it from you.

THE COLONEL: That's how I feel too.

YVETTE: Is that your advice?

THE COLONEL: That is my advice.

YVETTE (*to Courage once more*): My friend's advice would be to accept. Make me out a receipt saying the cart's mine once two weeks are up, with all its contents, we'll check it now, I'll bring the two hundred florins later. (*To the colonel.*) You go back to the camp, I'll follow, I got to check it all and see there's nothing missing from my cart. (*She kisses him. He leaves. She climbs up on the cart.*) Not all that many boots, are there?

MOTHER COURAGE: Yvette, it's no time for checking your cart, s'posing it is yours. You promised you'd talk to sergeant about Swiss Cheese, there ain't a minute to lose, they say in an hour he'll be court-martialled.

YVETTE: Just let me count the shirts.

MOTHER COURAGE (*pulling her down by the skirt*): You bloody vampire. Swiss Cheese's life's at stake. And not a word about who's making the offer, for God's sake, pretend it's your friend, else we're all done for cause we looked after him.

YVETTE: I fixed to meet that one-eyed fellow in the copse, he should be there by now.

THE CHAPLAIN: It doesn't have to be the whole two hundred either, I'd go up to a hundred and fifty, that may be enough.

MOTHER COURAGE: Since when has it been your money? You kindly keep out of this. You'll get your hotpot all right, don't worry. Hurry up and don't haggle, it's life or death. (*Pushes Yvette off.*)

THE CHAPLAIN: Far be it from me to interfere, but what are we going to live on? You're saddled with a daughter who can't earn her keep.

MOTHER COURAGE: I'm counting on regimental cash box, Mr. Clever. They'll allow it as his expenses.

THE CHAPLAIN: But will she get the message right?

MOTHER COURAGE: It's her interest I should spend her two hundred so she gets the cart. She's set on that, God knows how long that colonel of hers'll last. Kattrin, polish the knives, there's the pumice. And you, stop hanging round like Jesus on Mount of Olives,° get moving, wash them glasses, we'll have fifty or more of cavalry in tonight and I don't want to hear a lot of "I'm not accustomed to having to run about, oh my poor feet, we never ran in church." Thank the Lord they're corruptible. After all, they ain't wolves, just humans out for money. Corruption in humans is same as compassion in God. Corruption's our only hope. Long as we have it there'll be lenient sentences and even an innocent man'll have a chance of being let off.

YVETTE (*comes in panting*): They'll do it for two hundred. But it's got to be quick. Soon be out of their hands. Best thing is I go right away to my colonel with the one-eyed man. He's admitted he had the box, they put the thumbscrews on him. But he chucked it in the river soon as he saw they were on his track. The box is a write-off. I'll go and get the money from my colonel, shall I?

MOTHER COURAGE: Box is a write-off? How'm I to pay back two hundred then?

Jesus on Mount of Olives: The Bible shows Jesus on the Mount of Olives when he preaches the Sermon on the Mount and when he prays in anguish before his betrayal by Peter.

YVETTE: Oh, you thought you'd get it from the box, did you? And I was to be Joe Soap I suppose? Better not count on that. You'll have to pay up if you want Swiss Cheese back, or would you sooner I dropped the whole thing so's you can keep your cart?

MOTHER COURAGE: That's something I didn't allow for. Don't worry, you'll get your cart, I've said goodbye to it, had it seventeen years, I have. I just need a moment to think, it's bit sudden, what'm I to do, two hundred's too much for me, pity you didn't beat 'em down. Must keep a bit back, else any Tom, Dick and Harry'll be able to shove me in ditch. Go and tell them I'll pay hundred and twenty florins, else it's all off, either way I'm losing me cart.

YVETTE: They won't do it. That one-eyed man's impatient already, keeps looking over his shoulder, he's so worked up. Hadn't I best pay them the whole two hundred?

MOTHER COURAGE (*in despair*): I can't pay that. Thirty years I been working. She's twenty-five already, and no husband. I got her to think of too. Don't push me, I know what I'm doing. Say a hundred and twenty, or it's off.

YVETTE: It's up to you. (*Rushes off.*)

(*Without looking at either the chaplain or her daughter, Mother Courage sits down to help Kattrin polish knives.*)

MOTHER COURAGE: Don't smash them glasses, they ain't ours now. Watch what you're doing, you'll cut yourself. Swiss Cheese'll be back, I'll pay two hundred if it comes to the pinch. You'll get your brother, love. For eighty florins we could fill a pack with goods and start again. Plenty of folk has to make do.

THE CHAPLAIN: The Lord will provide, it says.

MOTHER COURAGE: See they're properly dry. (*She cleans knives in silence. Kattrin suddenly runs behind the cart, sobbing.*)

YVETTE (*comes running in*): They won't do it. I told you so. The one-eyed man wanted to leave right away, said there was no point. He says he's just waiting for the drum-roll; that means sentence has been pronounced. I offered a hundred and fifty. He didn't even blink. I had to convince him to stay there so's I could have another word with you.

MOTHER COURAGE: Tell him I'll pay the two hundred. Hurry! (*Yvette runs off. They sit in silence. The chaplain has stopped polishing the glasses.*) I reckon I bargained too long.

(*In the distance drumming is heard. The chaplain gets up and goes to the rear. Mother Courage remains seated. It grows dark. The drumming stops. It grows light once more. Mother Courage is sitting exactly as before.*)

YVETTE (*arrives, very pale*): Well, you got what you asked for, with your haggling and trying to keep your cart. Eleven bullets they gave him, that's all. You don't deserve I should bother any more about you. But I did hear they don't believe the box really is in the river. They've an idea it's here and anyhow that you're connected with him. They're going to bring him here, see if you gives yourself away when you sees him. Thought I'd better warn you so's you don't recognise him, else you'll all be for it. They're right on my heels, best tell you quick. Shall I keep Kattrin away? (*Mother Courage shakes her head.*) Does she know? She mayn't have heard the drumming or know what it meant.

MOTHER COURAGE: She knows. Get her.

(*Yvette fetches Kattrin, who goes to her mother and stands beside her. Mother Courage takes her hand. Two lansequenets come carrying a stretcher with something lying on it covered by a sheet. The sergeant marches beside them. They set down the stretcher.*)

SERGEANT: Here's somebody we dunno the name of. It's got to be listed, though, so everything's shipshape. He had a meal here. Have a look, see if you know him. (*He removes the sheet.*) Know him? (*Mother Courage shakes her head.*) What, never see him before he had that meal here? (*Mother Courage shakes her head.*) Pick him up. Chuck him in the pit. He's got nobody knows him. (*They carry him away.*)

SCENE 4

(*Mother Courage sings the Song of the Grand Capitulation.*)
(*Outside an officer's tent.*)
(*Mother Courage is waiting. A clerk looks out of the tent.*)

THE CLERK: I know you. You had a paymaster from the Lutherans with you, what was in hiding. I'd not complain if I were you.

MOTHER COURAGE: But I got a complaint to make. I'm innocent, would look as how I'd a bad conscience if I let this pass. Slashed everything in me cart to pieces with their sabres, they did, then wanted I should pay five taler fine for nowt, I tell you, nowt.

CLERK: Take my tip, better shut up. We're short of canteens, so we let you go on trading, specially if you got a bad conscience and pay a fine now and then.

MOTHER COURAGE: I got a complaint.

CLERK: Have it your own way. Then you must wait till the captain's free. (*Withdraws inside the tent.*)

YOUNG SOLDIER (*enters aggressively*): Bouque la Madonne! Where's that bleeding pig of a captain what's took my reward money to swig with his tarts? I'll do him.

OLDER SOLDIER (*running after him*): Shut up. They'll put you in irons.

YOUNG SOLDIER: Out of there, you thief! I'll slice you into pork chops, I will. Pocketing my prize money after I'd swum the river, only one in the whole squadron, and now I can't even buy meself a beer.

I'm not standing for that. Come on out there so I can cut you up!

OLDER SOLDIER: Blessed Mother of God, he's asking for trouble.

MOTHER COURAGE: Is it some reward he weren't paid?

YOUNG SOLDIER: Lemme go, I'll slash you too while I'm at it.

OLDER SOLDIER: He rescued the colonel's horse and got no reward for it. He's young yet, still wet behind the ears.

MOTHER COURAGE: Let him go, he ain't a dog you got to chain up. Wanting your reward is good sound sense. Why be a hero otherwise?

YOUNG SOLDIER: So's he can sit in there and booze. You're shit-scared, the lot of you. I done something special and I want my reward.

MOTHER COURAGE: Don't you shout at me, young fellow. Got me own worries, I have; any road you should spare your voice, be needing it when captain comes, else there he'll be and you too hoarse to make a sound, which'll make it hard for him to clap you in irons till you turn blue. People what shouts like that can't keep it up ever; half an hour, and they have to be rocked to sleep, they're so tired.

YOUNG SOLDIER: I ain't tired and to hell with sleep. I'm hungry. They make our bread from acorns and hemp-seed, and they even skimp on that. He's whoring away my reward and I'm hungry. I'll do him.

MOTHER COURAGE: Oh I see, you're hungry. Last year that general of yours ordered you all off roads and across fields so corn should be trampled flat; I could've got ten florins for a pair of boots s'pose I'd had boots and s'pose anyone'd been able to pay ten florins. Thought he'd be well away from that area this year, he did, but here he is, still there, and hunger is great. I see what you're angry about.

YOUNG SOLDIER: I won't have it, don't talk to me, it ain't fair and I'm not standing for that.

MOTHER COURAGE: And you're right; but how long? How long you not standing for unfairness? One hour, two hours? Didn't ask yourself that, did you, but it's the whole point, and why, once you're in irons it's too bad if you suddenly finds you can put up with unfairness after all.

YOUNG SOLDIER: What am I listening to you for, I'd like to know? Bouque la Madonne, where's that captain?

MOTHER COURAGE: You been listening to me because you knows it's like what I say, your anger has gone up in smoke already, it was just a short one and you needed a long one, but where you going to get it from?

YOUNG SOLDIER: Are you trying to tell me asking for my reward is wrong?

MOTHER COURAGE: Not a bit. I'm just telling you your anger ain't long enough, it's good for nowt, pity. If you'd a long one I'd be trying to prod you on. Cut him up, the swine, would be my advice to you in that case; but how about if you don't cut him up cause you feels your tail going between your legs? Then I'd look silly and captain'd take it out on me.

OLDER SOLDIER: You're perfectly right, he's just a bit crazy.

YOUNG SOLDIER: Very well, let's see if I don't cut him up. (*Draws his sword.*) When he arrives I'm going to cut him up.

CLERK (*looks out*): The captain'll be here in one minute. Sit down.

(*The young soldier sits down.*)

MOTHER COURAGE: He's sitting now. See, what did I say? You're sitting now. Ah, how well they know us, no one need tell 'em how to go about it. Sit down! and, bingo, we're sitting. And sitting and sedition don't mix. Don't try to stand up, you won't stand the way you was standing before. I shouldn't worry about what I think; I'm no better, not one moment. Bought up all our fighting spirit, they have. Eh? S'pose I kick back, might be bad for business. Let me tell you a thing or two about the Grand Capitulation. (*She sings the Song of the Grand Capitulation.*)

Back when I was young, I was brought to realise
What a very special person I must be
(Not just any old cottager's daughter, what with
    my looks and my talents and my urge towards
    Higher Things)
And insisted that my soup should have no hairs
    in it.
No one makes a sucker out of me!
(All or nothing, only the best is good enough, each
    man for himself, nobody's telling *me* what to do.)
Then I heard a tit
Chirp: Wait a bit!
    And you'll be marching with the band
    In step, responding to command
    And striking up your little dance:
    Now we advance.
    And now: parade, form square!
    Then men swear God's there—
    Not the faintest chance!

In no time at all anyone who looked could see
That I'd learned to take my medicine with good
    grace.
(Two kids on my hands and look at the price of
    bread, and things they expect of you!)
When they finally came to feel that they were
    through with me
They'd got me grovelling on my face.
(Takes all sorts to make a world, you scratch my
    back and I'll scratch yours, no good banging
    your head against a brick wall.)
Then I heard that tit
Chirp: Wait a bit!
    And you'll be marching with the band
    In step, responding to command
    And striking up your little dance:
    Now they advance.

    And now: parade, form square!
    Then men swear God's there—
    Not the faintest chance!

I've known people tried to storm the summits:
There's no star too bright or seems too far away.
(Dogged does it, where there's a will there's a way,
    by hook or by crook.)
As each peak disclosed fresh peaks to come, it's
Strange how much a plain straw hat could weigh.
(You have to cut your coat according to your cloth.)
Then I hear the tit
Chirp: Wait a bit!
    And they'll be marching with the band
    In step, responding to command
    And striking up their little dance:
    Now they advance.
    And now: parade, form square!
    Then men swear God's there—
    Not the faintest chance!

MOTHER COURAGE (*to the young soldier*): That's why I reckon you should stay there with your sword drawn if you're truly set on it and your anger's big enough, because you got grounds, I agree, but if your anger's a short one best leave right away.

YOUNG SOLDIER: Oh stuff it. (*He staggers off with the older soldier following.*)

CLERK (*sticks his head out*): Captain's here now. You can make your complaint.

MOTHER COURAGE: I changed me mind. I ain't complaining.

(*Exit.*)

SCENE 5

(*Two years have gone by. The war is spreading to new areas. Ceaselessly on the move, Courage's little cart crosses Poland, Moravia, Bavaria, Italy then Bavaria again. 1631. Tilly's victory at Magdeburg costs Mother Courage four officers' shirts.*)

(*Mother Courage's cart has stopped in a badly shot-up village. Thin military music in the distance. Two soldiers at the bar being served by Kattrin and Mother Courage. One of them has a lady's fur coat over his shoulders.*)

MOTHER COURAGE: Can't pay, that it? No money, no schnapps. They give us victory parades, but catch them giving men their pay.

SOLDIER: I want my schnapps. I missed the looting. That double-crossing general only allowed an hour's looting in the town. He ain't an inhuman monster, he said. Town must of paid him.

THE CHAPLAIN (*stumbles in*): There are people still lying in that yard. The peasant's family. Somebody give me a hand. I need linen.

(*The second soldier goes off with him. Kattrin becomes very excited and tries to make her mother produce linen.*)

MOTHER COURAGE: I got none. All my bandages was sold to regiment. I ain't tearing up my officer's shirts for that lot.

CHAPLAIN (*calling back*): I need linen, I tell you.

MOTHER COURAGE (*blocking Kattrin's way into the cart by sitting on the step*): I'm giving nowt. They'll never pay, and why, nowt to pay with.

CHAPLAIN (*bending over a woman he has carried in*): Why d'you stay around during the gunfire?

PEASANT WOMAN (*feebly*): Farm.

MOTHER COURAGE: Catch them abandoning anything. But now I'm s'posed to foot the bill. I won't do it.

FIRST SOLDIER: Those are Protestants. What they have to be Protestants for?

MOTHER COURAGE: They ain't bothering about faith. They lost their farm.

SECOND SOLDIER: They're no Protestants. They're Catholics like us.

FIRST SOLDIER: No way of sorting 'em out in a bombardment.

A PEASANT (*brought in by the chaplain*): My arm's gone.

THE CHAPLAIN: Where's that linen?

MOTHER COURAGE: I can't give nowt. What with expenses, taxes, loan interest and bribes. (*Making guttural noises, Kattrin raises a plank and threatens her mother with it.*) You gone plain crazy? Put that plank away or I'll paste you one, you cow. I'm giving nowt, don't want to, got to think of meself. (*The chaplain lifts her off the steps and sets her on the ground, then starts pulling out shirts and tearing them into strips.*) My officers' shirts! Half a florin apiece! I'm ruined. (*From the house comes the cry of a child in pain.*)

THE PEASANT: The baby's in there still. (*Kattrin dashes in.*)

THE CHAPLAIN (*to the woman*): Don't move. They'll get it out.

MOTHER COURAGE: Stop her, roof may fall in.

THE CHAPLAIN: I'm not going back in there.

MOTHER COURAGE (*torn both ways*): Don't waste my precious linen.

(*Kattrin brings a baby out of the ruins.*)

MOTHER COURAGE: How nice, found another baby to cart around? Give it to its ma this instant, unless you'd have me fighting for hours to get it off you, like last time, d'you hear? (*To the second soldier.*) Don't stand there gawping, you go back and tell them cut out that music, we can see it's a victory with our own eyes. All your victories mean to me is losses.

THE CHAPLAIN (*tying a bandage*): Blood's coming through.

(*Kattrin is rocking the baby and making lullaby noises.*)

MOTHER COURAGE: Look at her, happy as a queen in all this misery; give it back at once, its mother's coming round. (*She catches the first soldier, who has been attacking the drinks and is trying to make off with one of the bottles.*) Psia krew! Thought you'd score another victory, you animal? Now pay.

FIRST SOLDIER: I got nowt.

MOTHER COURAGE (*pulling the fur coat off his back*): Then leave that coat, it's stolen any road.

THE CHAPLAIN: There's still someone under there.

SCENE 6

(*Outside the Bavarian town of Ingolstadt Courage participates in the funeral of the late Imperial commander Tilly. Discussions are held about war heroes and the war's duration. The chaplain complains that his talents are lying fallow, and dumb Kattrin gets the red boots. The year is 1632.*)

(*Inside a canteen tent.*)

(*It has a bar towards the rear. Rain. Sound of drums and Funeral music. The chaplain and the regimental clerk are playing a board game. Mother Courage and her daughter are stocktaking.*)

THE CHAPLAIN: Now the funeral procession will be moving off.

MOTHER COURAGE: Too bad about commander in chief—twenty-two pairs those socks—he fell by accident, they say. Mist over fields, that was the trouble. General had just been haranguing a regiment saying they must fight to last man and last round, he was riding back when mist made him lose direction so he was up front and a bullet got him in midst of battle—only four hurricane lamps left. (*A whistle from the rear. She goes to the bar.*) You scrimshankers, dodging your commander in chief's funeral, scandal I call it. (*Pours drinks.*)

THE CLERK: They should never of paid troops out before the funeral. Instead of going now they're all getting pissed.

THE CHAPLAIN (*to the clerk*): Aren't you supposed to go to the funeral?

THE CLERK: Dodged it cause of the rain.

MOTHER COURAGE: It's different with you, your uniform might get wet. I heard they wanted to toll bells for funeral as usual, except it turned out all churches had been blown to smithereens by his orders, so poor old commander in chief won't be hearing no bells as they let the coffin down. They're going to let off three salvoes instead to cheer things up—seventeen belts.

SHOUTS (*from the bar*): Hey, Missis, a brandy!

MOTHER COURAGE: Let's see your money. No, I ain't having you in my tent with your disgusting boots. You can drink outside, rain or no rain. (*To the clerk.*) I'm only letting in sergeants and up. Commander in chief had been having his worries, they say. S'posed to have been trouble with Second Regiment cause he stopped their pay, said it was a war of faith and they should do it for free. (*Funeral march. All look to the rear.*)

THE CHAPLAIN: Now they'll be filing past the noble corpse.

MOTHER COURAGE: Can't help feeling sorry for those generals and emperors, there they are maybe thinking they're doing something extra special what folk'll talk about in years to come, and earning a public monument, like conquering the world for instance, that's a fine ambition for a general, how's he to know any better? I mean, he plagues hisself to death, then it all breaks down on account of ordinary folk what just wants their beer and bit of a chat, nowt higher. Finest plans get bolloxed up by the pettiness of them as should be carrying them out, because emperors can't do nowt themselves, they just counts on soldiers and people to back 'em up whatever happens, am I right?

THE CHAPLAIN (laughs): Courage, you're right, aside from the soldiers. They do their best. Give me that lot outside there, for instance, drinking their brandy in the rain, and I'd guarantee to make you one war after another for a hundred years if need be, and I'm no trained general.

MOTHER COURAGE: You don't think war might end, then?

THE CHAPLAIN: What, because the commander in chief's gone? Don't be childish. They're two a penny, no shortage of heroes.

MOTHER COURAGE: Ee, I'm not asking for fun of it, but because I'm thinking whether to stock up, prices are low now, but if war's going to end it's money down the drain.

THE CHAPLAIN: I realise it's a serious question. There've always been people going round saying "the war can't go on for ever." I tell you there's nothing to stop it going on for ever. Of course there can be a bit of a breathing space. The war may need to get its second wind, it may even have an accident so to speak. There's no guarantee against that; nothing's perfect on this earth of ours. A perfect war, the sort you might say couldn't be improved on, that's something we shall probably never see. It can suddenly come to a standstill for some quite unforeseen reason, you can't allow for everything. A slight case of negligence, and it's bogged down up to the axles. And then it's a matter of hauling the war out of the mud again. But emperor and kings and popes will come to its rescue. So on the whole it has nothing serious to worry about, and will live to a ripe old age.

A SOLDIER (sings at the bar):

A schnapps, landlord, you're late!
A soldier cannot wait
To do his emperor's orders.

Make it a double, this is a holiday.

MOTHER COURAGE: S'pose I went by what you say . . .

THE CHAPLAIN: Think it out for yourself. What's to compete with the war?

THE SOLDIER (at the rear):

Your breast, my girl, you're late!
A soldier cannot wait
To ride across the borders.

THE CLERK (unexpectedly): And what about peace? I'm from Bohemia and I'd like to go home some day.

THE CHAPLAIN: Would you indeed? Ah, peace. Where is the hole once the cheese has been eaten?

THE SOLDIER (at the rear):

Lead trumps, my friend, you're late!
A soldier cannot wait.
His emperor needs him badly.

Your blessing, priest, you're late!
A soldier cannot wait.
Must lay his life down gladly.

THE CLERK: In the long run life's impossible if there's no peace.

THE CHAPLAIN: I'd say there's peace in war too; it has its peaceful moments. Because war satisfies all requirements, peaceable ones included, they're catered for, and it would simply fizzle out if they weren't. In war you can do a crap like in the depths of peacetime, then between one battle and the next you can have a beer, then even when you're moving up you can lay your head on your arms and have a bit of shuteye in the ditch, it's entirely possible. During a charge you can't play cards maybe, but nor can you in the depths of peacetime when you're ploughing, and after a victory there are various openings. You may get a leg blown off, then you start by making a lot of fuss as though it were serious, but afterwards you calm down or get given a schnapps, and you end up hopping around and the war's no worse off than before. And what's to stop you being fruitful and multiplying in the middle of all the butchery, behind a barn or something, in the long run you can't be held back from it, and then the war will have your progeny and can use them to carry on with. No, the war will always find an outlet, mark my words. Why should it ever stop?

(Kattrin has ceased working and is staring at the chaplain.)

MOTHER COURAGE: I'll buy fresh stock then. If you say so. (Kattrin suddenly flings a basket full of bottles to the ground and runs off.) Kattrin! (Laughs.) Damn me if she weren't waiting for peace. I promised her she'd get a husband soon as peace came. (Hurries after her.)

THE CLERK (standing up): I won. You been talking too much. Pay up.

MOTHER COURAGE (returning with Kattrin): Don't be silly, war'll go on a bit longer, and we'll make a bit more money, and peacetime'll be all the nicer for it. Now you go into town, that's ten minutes' walk at most, fetch things from Golden Lion, the expensive ones, we can fetch rest in cart later, it's all arranged, regimental clerk here will go with you. Nearly everybody's attending commander in chief's funeral, nowt can happen to you. Careful now, don't let them steal nowt, think of your dowry.

(Kattrin puts a cloth over her head and leaves with the clerk.)

THE CHAPLAIN: Is that all right to let her go with the clerk?

MOTHER COURAGE: She's not that pretty they'd want to ruin her.

THE CHAPLAIN: I admire the way you run your business and always win through. I see why they called you Courage.

MOTHER COURAGE: Poor folk got to have courage. Why, they're lost. Simply getting up in morning takes some doing in their situation. Or ploughing a field, and in a war at that. Mere fact they bring kids into world shows they got courage, cause there's no hope for them. They have to hang one another and slaughter one another, so just looking each other in face must call for courage. Being able to put up with emperor and pope shows supernatural courage, cause those two cost 'em their lives. *(She sits down, takes a little pipe from her purse and smokes.)* You might chop us a bit of kindling.

THE CHAPLAIN *(reluctantly removing his coat and preparing to chop up sticks)*: I happen to be a pastor of souls, not a woodcutter.

MOTHER COURAGE: I got no soul, you see. Need firewood, though.

THE CHAPLAIN: Where's that stumpy pipe from?

MOTHER COURAGE: Just a pipe.

THE CHAPLAIN: What d'you mean, "just," it's a quite particular pipe, that.

MOTHER COURAGE: Aha?

THE CHAPLAIN: That stumpy pipe belongs to the Oxenstierna Regiment's cook.

MOTHER COURAGE: If you know that already why ask, Mr. Clever?

THE CHAPLAIN: Because I didn't know if you were aware what you're smoking. You might just have been rummaging around in your things, come across some old pipe or other, and used it out of sheer absence of mind.

MOTHER COURAGE: And why not?

THE CHAPLAIN: Because you didn't. You're smoking that deliberately.

MOTHER COURAGE: And why shouldn't I?

THE CHAPLAIN: Courage, I'm warning you. It's my duty. Probably you'll never clap eyes on the gentleman again, and that's no loss but your good fortune. He didn't make at all a reliable impression on me. Quite the opposite.

MOTHER COURAGE: Really? Nice fellow that.

THE CHAPLAIN: So he's what you would call a nice fellow? I wouldn't. Far be it from me to bear him the least ill-will, but nice is not what I would call him.

More like one of those Don Juans, a slippery one. Have a look at that pipe if you don't believe me. You must admit it tells you a good deal about his character.

MOTHER COURAGE: Nowt that I can see. Worn out, I'd call it.

THE CHAPLAIN: Practically bitten through, you mean. A man of wrath. That is the pipe of an unscrupulous man of wrath; you must see that if you have any discrimination left.

MOTHER COURAGE: Don't chop my chopping block in two.

THE CHAPLAIN: I told you I'm not a woodcutter by trade. I studied to be a pastor of souls. My talent and abilities are being abused in this place, by manual labour. My God-given endowments are denied expression. It's a sin. You have never heard me preach. One sermon of mine can put a regiment in such a frame of mind it'll treat the enemy like a flock of sheep. Life to them is a smelly old foot cloth which they fling away in a vision of final victory. God has given me the gift of speech. I can preach so you'll lose all sense of sight and hearing.

MOTHER COURAGE: I don't wish to lose my sense of sight and hearing. Where'd that leave me?

THE CHAPLAIN: Courage, I have often thought that your dry way of talking conceals more than just a warm heart. You too are human and need warmth.

MOTHER COURAGE: Best way for us to get this tent warm is have plenty of firewood.

THE CHAPLAIN: Don't change the subject. Seriously, Courage, I sometimes ask myself what it would be like if our relationship were to become somewhat closer. I mean, given that the whirlwind of war has so strangely whirled us together.

MOTHER COURAGE: I'd say it was close enough. I cook meals for you and you run around and chop firewood for instance.

THE CHAPLAIN *(coming closer)*: You know what I mean by closer; it's not a relationship founded on meals and wood-chopping and other such base necessities. Let your head speak, harden thyself not.

MOTHER COURAGE: Don't you come at me with that axe. That'd be too close a relationship.

THE CHAPLAIN: You shouldn't make a joke of it. I'm a serious person and I've thought about what I'm saying.

MOTHER COURAGE: Be sensible, padre. I like you. I don't want to row you. All I'm after is get myself and children through all this with my cart. I don't see it as mine, and I ain't in the mood for private affairs. Right now I'm taking a gamble, buying stores just when commander in chief's fallen and all the talk's of peace. Where d'you reckon you'd turn if I'm ruined? Don't know, do you? You chop us some kindling wood, then we can keep warm at night, that's quite something these times. What's this? *(She gets up. Enter Kattrin, out of breath, with a wound above her eye. She is carrying a variety of stuff: parcels, leather goods, a drum and so on.)*

MOTHER COURAGE: What happened, someone assault you? On way back? She was assaulted on her way back. Bet it was that trooper was getting drunk here. I shouldn't have let you go, love. Drop that stuff. Not too bad, just a flesh wound you got. I'll bandage it and in a week it'll be all right. Worse than wild beasts, they are. (*She ties up the wound.*)

THE CHAPLAIN: It's not them I blame. They never went raping back home. The fault lies with those that start wars, it brings humanity's lowest instincts to the surface.

MOTHER COURAGE: Calm down. Didn't clerk come back with you? That's because you're respectable, they don't bother. Wound ain't a deep one, won't leave no mark. There you are, all bandaged up. You'll get something, love, keep calm. Something I put aside for you, wait till you see. (*She delves into a sack and brings out Yvette's red high-heeled boots.*) Made you open your eyes, eh? Something you always wanted. They're yours. Put 'em on quick, before I change me mind. Won't leave no mark, and what if it does? Ones I'm really sorry for's the ones they fancy. Drag them around till they're worn out, they do. Those they don't care for they leaves alive. I seen girls before now had pretty faces, then in no time looking fit to frighten a hyaena. Can't even go behind a bush without risking trouble, horrible life they lead. Same like with trees, straight well-shaped ones get chopped down to make beams for houses and crooked ones live happily ever after. So it's a stroke of luck for you really. Them boots'll be all right, I greased them before putting them away.

(*Kattrin leaves the boots where they are and crawls into the cart.*)

THE CHAPLAIN: Let's hope she's not disfigured.

MOTHER COURAGE: She'll have a scar. No use her waiting for peacetime now.

THE CHAPLAIN: She didn't let them steal the things.

MOTHER COURAGE: Maybe I shouldn't have dinned that into her so. Wish I knew what went on in that head of hers. Just once she stayed out all night, once in all those years. Afterwards she went around like before, except she worked harder. Couldn't get her to tell what had happened. Worried me quite a while, that did. (*She collects the articles brought by Kattrin, and sorts them angrily.*) That's war for you. Nice way to get a living!

(*Sound of cannon fire.*)

THE CHAPLAIN: Now they'll be burying the commander in chief. This is a historic moment.

MOTHER COURAGE: What I call a historic moment is them bashing my daughter over the eye. She's half wrecked already, won't get no husband now, and her so crazy about kids; anyway, she's only dumb from war, soldier stuffed something in her mouth when she was little. As for Swiss Cheese I'll never see

him again, and where Eilif is God alone knows. War be damned.

SCENE 7

(*Mother Courage at the peak of her business career.*)
(*High road.*)
(*The chaplain, Mother Courage, and Kattrin are pulling the cart, which is hung with new wares. Mother Courage is wearing a necklace of silver coins.*)

MOTHER COURAGE: I won't have you folk spoiling my war for me. I'm told it kills off the weak, but they're write-off in peacetime too. And war gives its people a better deal. (*She sings.*)

> And if you feel your forces fading
> You won't be there to share the fruits.
> But what is war but private trading
> That deals in blood instead of boots?

And what's the use of settling down? Them as does are first to go. (*Sings.*)

> Some people think to live by looting
> The goods some others haven't got.
> You think it's just a line they're shooting
> Until you hear they have been shot.

> And some I saw dig six feet under
> In haste to lie down and pass out.
> Now they're at rest perhaps they wonder
> Just what was all their haste about.

(*They pull it further.*)

SCENE 8

(*The same year sees the death of the Swedish king Gustavus Adolphus at the battle of Lützen. Peace threatens to ruin Mother Courage's business. Courage's dashing son performs one heroic deed too many and comes to a sticky end.*)
(*Camp.*)
(*A summer morning. In front of the cart stand an old woman and her son. The son carries a large sack of bedding.*)

MOTHER COURAGE'S VOICE (*from inside the cart*): Does it need to be this ungodly hour?

THE YOUNG MAN: We walked twenty miles in the night and got to be back today.

MOTHER COURAGE'S VOICE: What am I to do with bedding? Folk've got no houses.

THE YOUNG MAN: Best have a look first.

THE OLD WOMAN: This place is no good either. Come on.

THE YOUNG MAN: What, and have them sell the roof over our head for taxes? She might pay three florins if you throw in the bracelet. (*Bells start ringing.*) Listen, mother.

VOICES (*from the rear*): Peace! Swedish king's been killed.

MOTHER COURAGE (*Sticks her head out of the cart. She has not yet done her hair.*): What's that bell-ringing about in mid-week?

THE CHAPLAIN (*crawling out from under the cart*): What are they shouting? Peace?

MOTHER COURAGE: Don't tell me peace has broken out just after I laid in new stock.

THE CHAPLAIN (*calling to the rear*): That true? Peace?

VOICES: Three weeks ago, they say, only no one told us.

THE CHAPLAIN (*to Courage*): What else would they be ringing the bells for?

VOICES: A whole lot of Lutherans have driven into town, they brought the news.

THE YOUNG MAN: Mother, it's peace. What's the matter?

(*The old woman has collapsed.*)

MOTHER COURAGE (*speaking into the cart*): Holy cow! Kattrin, peace! Put your black dress on, we're going to church. Least we can do for Swiss Cheese. Is it true, though?

THE YOUNG MAN: The people here say so. They've made peace. Can you get up? (*The old woman stands up dumbfounded.*) I'll get the saddlery going again. I promise. It'll all work out. Father will get his bedding back. Can you walk? (*To the chaplain.*) She came over queer. It's the news. She never thought there'd be peace again. Father always said so. We're going straight home. (*They go off.*)

MOTHER COURAGE'S VOICE: Give her a schnapps.

THE CHAPLAIN: They've already gone.

MOTHER COURAGE'S VOICE: What's up in camp?

THE CHAPLAIN: They're assembling. I'll go on over. Shouldn't I put on my clerical garb?

MOTHER COURAGE'S VOICE: Best check up before parading yourself as heretic. I'm glad about peace, never mind if I'm ruined. Any road I'll have got two of me children through the war. Be seeing Eilif again now.

THE CHAPLAIN: And who's that walking down the lines? Bless me, the army commander's cook.

THE COOK (*somewhat bedraggled and carrying a bundle*): What do I behold? The padre!

THE CHAPLAIN: Courage, we've got company.

(*Mother Courage clambers out.*)

THE COOK: I promised I'd drop over for a little talk soon as I had the time. I've not forgotten your brandy, Mrs. Fierling.

MOTHER COURAGE: Good grief, the general's cook! After all these years! Where's my eldest boy Eilif?

THE COOK: Hasn't he got here? He left before me, he was on his way to see you too.

THE CHAPLAIN: I shall don my clerical garb, just a moment.

(*Goes off behind the cart.*)

MOTHER COURAGE: Then he may be here any minute. (*Calls into the cart.*) Kattrin, Eilif's on his way. Get cook a glass of brandy, Kattrin! (*Kattrin does not appear.*) Drag your hair down over it, that's all right. Mr. Lamb's no stranger. (*Fetches the brandy herself.*) She don't like to come out, peace means nowt to her. Took too long coming, it did. They gave her a crack over one eye, you barely notice it now but she thinks folks are staring at her.

THE COOK: Ah yes. War. (*He and Mother Courage sit down.*)

MOTHER COURAGE: Cooky, you caught me at bad moment. I'm ruined.

THE COOK: What? That's hard.

MOTHER COURAGE: Peace'll wring my neck. I went and took chaplain's advice, laid in fresh stocks only t'other day. And now they're going to demobilise and I'll be left sitting on me wares.

THE COOK: What'd you want to go and listen to padre for? If I hadn't been in such a hurry that time, the Catholics arriving so quickly and all, I'd warned you against that man. All piss and wind, he is. So he's the authority around here, eh?

MOTHER COURAGE: He's been doing washing-up for me and helping pull.

THE COOK: Him pull! I bet he told you some of those jokes of his too, I know him, got a very unhealthy view of women, he has, all my good influence on him went for nowt. He ain't steady.

MOTHER COURAGE: You steady then?

THE COOK: Whatever else I ain't, I'm steady. Mud in your eye!

MOTHER COURAGE: Steady, that's nowt. I only had one steady fellow, thank God. Hardest I ever had to work in me life; he flogged the kids' blankets soon as autumn came, and he called me mouth-organ an unchristian instrument. Ask me, you ain't saying much for yourself admitting you're steady.

THE COOK: Still tough as nails, I see; but that's what I like about you.

MOTHER COURAGE: Now don't tell me you been dreaming of me nails.

THE COOK: Well, well, here we are, along with armistice bells and your brandy like what nobody else ever serves, it's famous, that is.

MOTHER COURAGE: I don't give two pins for your armistice bells just now. Can't see 'em handing out all the back pay what's owing, so where does that leave me with my famous brandy? Had your pay yet?

THE COOK (*hesitantly*): Not exactly. That's why we all shoved off. If that's how it is, I thought, I'll go and visit friends. So here I am sitting with you.

MOTHER COURAGE: Other words you got nowt.

THE COOK: High time they stopped that bloody clanging. Wouldn't mind getting into some sort of trade. I'm fed up being cook to that lot. I'm s'posed to rustle them up meals out of tree roots and old bootsoles, then they fling the hot soup in my face. Cook these days is a dog's life. Sooner do war service, only of course it's peacetime now. (*He sees the chaplain reappearing in his old garments.*) More about that later.

THE CHAPLAIN: It's still all right, only had a few moths in it.

THE COOK: Can't see why you bother. You won't get your old job back, who are you to inspire now to earn his pay honourably and lay down his life? What's more I got a bone to pick with you, cause you advised this lady to buy a lot of unnecessary goods saying war would go on for ever.

THE CHAPLAIN (*heatedly*): I'd like to know what concern that is of yours.

THE COOK: Because it's unscrupulous, that sort of thing is. How dare you meddle in other folks' business arrangements with your unwanted advice?

THE CHAPLAIN: Who's meddling? (*To Courage.*) I never knew this gentleman was such an intimate you had to account to him for everything.

MOTHER COURAGE: Keep your hair on, cook's only giving his personal opinion and you can't deny your war was a flop.

THE CHAPLAIN: You should not blaspheme against peace, Courage. You are a hyaena of the battlefield.

MOTHER COURAGE: I'm what?

THE COOK: If you're going to insult this lady you'll have to settle with me.

THE CHAPLAIN: It's not you I'm talking to. Your intentions are only too transparent. (*To Courage.*) But when I see you picking up peace betwixt your finger and your thumb like some dirty old snot-rag, then my humanity feels outraged; for then I see that you don't want peace but war, because you profit from it; in which case you shouldn't forget the ancient saying that whosoever sups with the devil needs a long spoon.

MOTHER COURAGE: I got no use for war, and war ain't got much use for me. But I'm not being called no hyaena, you and me's through.

THE CHAPLAIN: Then why grumble about peace when everybody's breathing sighs of relief? Because of some old junk in your cart?

MOTHER COURAGE: My goods ain't old junk but what I lives by, and you too up to now.

THE CHAPLAIN: Off war, in other words. Aha.

THE COOK (*to the chaplain*): You're old enough to know it's always a mistake offering advice. (*To Courage.*) Way things are, your best bet's to get rid of certain goods quick as you can before prices hit rockbottom. Dress yourself and get moving, not a moment to lose.

MOTHER COURAGE: That ain't bad advice. I'll do that, I guess.

THE CHAPLAIN: Because cooky says it.

MOTHER COURAGE: Why couldn't you say it? He's right, I'd best go off to market. (*Goes inside the cart.*)

THE COOK: That's one to me, padre. You got no presence of mind. What you should of said was: what, me

offer advice, all I done was discuss politics. Better not take me on. Cockfighting don't suit that get-up.

THE CHAPLAIN: If you don't stop your gob I'll murder you, get-up or no get-up.

THE COOK (*pulling off his boots and unwrapping his footcloths*): Pity the war made such a godless shit of you, else you'd easily get another parsonage now it's peacetime. Cooks won't be needed, there's nowt to cook, but faith goes on just the same, nowt changed in that direction.

THE CHAPLAIN: Mr. Lamb, I'm asking you not to elbow me out. Since I came down in the world I've become a better person. I couldn't preach to anyone now.

(*Enter Yvette Pottier in black, dressed up to the nines, carrying a cane. She is much older and fatter, and heavily powdered. She is followed by a manservant.*)

YVETTE: Hullo there, everybody. Is this Mother Courage's establishment?

THE CHAPLAIN: It is. And with whom have we the honour . . . ?

YVETTE: With the Countess Starhemberg, my good man. Where's Courage?

THE CHAPLAIN (*calls into the cart*): The Countess Starhemberg wishes to speak to you.

MOTHER COURAGE'S VOICE: Just coming.

YVETTE: It's Yvette.

MOTHER COURAGE'S VOICE: Oh, Yvette!

YVETTE: Come to see how you are. (*Sees the cook turn round aghast.*) Pieter!

THE COOK: Yvette!

YVETTE: Well I never! How d'you come to be here?

THE COOK: Got a lift.

THE CHAPLAIN: You know each other then? Intimately?

YVETTE: I should think so. (*She looks the cook over.*) Fat.

THE COOK: Not all that skinny yourself.

YVETTE: All the same I'm glad to see you, you shit. Gives me a chance to say what I think of you.

THE CHAPLAIN: You say it, in full; but don't start till Courage is out here.

MOTHER COURAGE (*coming out with all kinds of goods*): Yvette! (*They embrace.*) But what are you in mourning for?

YVETTE: Suits me, don't it? My husband the colonel died a few years back.

MOTHER COURAGE: That old fellow what nearly bought the cart?

YVETTE: His elder brother.

MOTHER COURAGE: Then you're sitting pretty. Nice to find somebody what's made it in this war.

YVETTE: Up and down and up again, that's the way it went.

MOTHER COURAGE: I'm not hearing a word against colonels, they make a mint of money.

THE CHAPLAIN: I would put my boots back on if I were you. (*To Yvette.*) You promised you would say what you think of the gentleman.

THE COOK: Don't kick up a stink here, Yvette.

MOTHER COURAGE: Yvette, this is a friend of mine.

YVETTE: That's old Puffing Piet.

THE COOK: Let's drop the nicknames. I'm called Lamb.

MOTHER COURAGE (laughs): Puffing Piet! Him as made all the women crazy! Here, I been looking after your pipe for you.

THE CHAPLAIN: Smoking it, too.

YVETTE: What luck I can warn you against him. Worst of the lot, he was, rampaging along the whole Flanders coastline. Got more girls in trouble than he has fingers.

THE COOK: That's all a long while ago. Tain't true anyhow.

YVETTE: Stand up when a lady brings you into the conversation! How I loved this man! All the time he had a little dark girl with bandy legs, got her in trouble too of course.

THE COOK: Got you into high society more like, far as I can see.

YVETTE: Shut your trap, you pathetic remnant! Better watch out for him, though; fellows like that are still dangerous even when on their last legs.

MOTHER COURAGE (to Yvette): Come along, got to get rid of my stuff afore prices start dropping. You might be able to put a word in for me at regiment, with your connections. (Calls into the cart.) Kattrin, church is off, I'm going to market instead. When Eilif turns up, one of you give him a drink. (Exit with Yvette.)

YVETTE (as she leaves): Fancy a creature like that ever making me leave the straight and narrow path. Thank my lucky stars I managed to reach the top all the same. But I've cooked your goose, Puffing Piet, and that's something that'll be credited to me one day in the world to come.

THE CHAPLAIN: I would like to take as a text for our little talk "The mills of God grind slowly." Weren't you complaining about my jokes?

THE COOK: Dead out of luck, I am. It's like this, you see: I thought I might get a hot meal. Here am I starving, and now they'll be talking about me and she'll get quite a wrong picture. I think I'll clear out before she's back.

THE CHAPLAIN: I think so too.

THE COOK: Padre, I'm fed up already with this bloody peace. Human race has to go through fire and sword cause it's sinful from the cradle up. I wish I could be roasting a fat capon once again for the general, wherever he's got to, in mustard sauce with a carrot or two.

THE CHAPLAIN: Red cabbage. Red cabbage for a capon.

THE COOK: You're right, but carrots was what he had to have.

THE CHAPLAIN: No sense of what's fitting.

THE COOK: Not that it stopped you guzzling your share.

THE CHAPLAIN: With misgivings.

THE COOK: Anyway you must admit those were the days.

THE CHAPLAIN: I might admit it if pressed.

THE COOK: Now you've called her a hyaena your days here are finished. What you staring at?

THE CHAPLAIN: Eilif! (Eilif arrives, followed by soldiers with pikes. His hands are fettered. His face is chalky-white.) What's wrong?

EILIF: Where's mother?

THE CHAPLAIN: Gone into town.

EILIF: I heard she was around. They've allowed me to come and see her.

THE COOK (to the soldiers): What you doing with him?

A SOLDIER: Something not nice.

THE CHAPLAIN: What's he been up to?

THE SOLDIER: Broke into a peasant's place. The wife's dead.

THE CHAPLAIN: How could you do a thing like that?

EILIF: It's what I did last time, ain't it?

THE COOK: Aye, but it's peace now.

EILIF: Shut up. All right if I sit down till she comes?

THE SOLDIER: We've no time.

THE CHAPLAIN: In wartime they recommended him for that, sat him at the general's right hand. Dashing, it was, in those days. Any chance of a word with the provost-marshal?

THE SOLDIER: Wouldn't do no good. Taking some peasant's cattle, what's dashing about that?

THE COOK: Dumb, I call it.

EILIF: If I'd been dumb you'd of starved, clever bugger.

THE COOK: But as you were clever you're going to be shot.

THE CHAPLAIN: We'd better fetch Kattrin out anyhow.

EILIF: Sooner have a glass of schnapps, could do with that.

THE SOLDIER: No time, come along.

THE CHAPLAIN: And what shall we tell your mother?

EILIF: Tell her it wasn't any different, tell her it was the same thing. Or tell her nowt. (The soldiers propel him away.)

THE CHAPLAIN: I'll accompany you on your grievous journey.

EILIF: Don't need any bloody parsons.

THE CHAPLAIN: Wait and see. (Follows him.)

THE COOK (calls after them): I'll have to tell her, she'll want to see him.

THE CHAPLAIN: I wouldn't tell her anything. At most that he was here and will come again, maybe tomorrow. By then I'll be back and can break it to her. (Hurries off.)

(The cook looks after him, shaking his head, then walks restlessly around. Finally he comes up to the cart.)

THE COOK: Hoy! Don't you want to come out? I can understand you hiding away from peace. Like to do the same myself. Remember me, I'm general's cook? I was wondering if you'd a bit of something to eat while I wait for your mum. I don't half feel like a bit of pork, or bread even, just to fill the time. (Peers inside.) Head under blanket. (Sound of gunfire off.)

MOTHER COURAGE (runs in, out of breath and with all her goods still): Cooky, peacetime's over. War's been on again three days now. Heard news before selling me stuff, thank God. They're having a shooting match with Lutherans in town. We must get cart away at once. Kattrin, pack up! What you in the dumps for? What's wrong?

THE COOK: Nowt.

MOTHER COURAGE: Something is. I see it way you look.

THE COOK: Cause war's starting up again, I s'pose. Looks as if it'll be tomorrow night before I get next hot food inside me.

MOTHER COURAGE: You're lying, cooky.

THE COOK: Eilif was here. Had to leave almost at once, though.

MOTHER COURAGE: Was he now? Then we'll be seeing him on the march. I'm joining our side this time. How's he look?

THE COOK: Same as usual.

MOTHER COURAGE: Oh, he'll never change. Take more than war to steal him from me. Clever, he is. You going to help me get packed? (*Begins to pack up.*) What's his news? Still in general's good books? Say anything about his deeds of valour?

THE COOK (*glumly*): Repeated one of them, I'm told.

MOTHER COURAGE: Tell it me later, we got to move off. (*Kattrin appears.*) Kattrin, peacetime's finished now. We're moving on. (*To the cook.*) How about you?

THE COOK: Have to join up again.

MOTHER COURAGE: Why don't you . . . Where's padre?

THE COOK: Went into town with Eilif.

MOTHER COURAGE: Then you come along with us a way. Need somebody to help me.

THE COOK: That business with Yvette, you know . . .

MOTHER COURAGE: Done you no harm in my eyes. Opposite. Where there's smoke there's fire, they say. You coming along?

THE COOK: I won't say no.

MOTHER COURAGE: The Twelfth moved off already. Take the shaft. Here's a bit of bread. We must get round behind to Lutherans. Might even be seeing Eilif tonight. He's my favourite one. Short peace, wasn't it? Now we're off again. (*She sings as the cook and Kattrin harness themselves up.*)

From Ulm to Metz, from Metz to Munich
Courage will see the war gets fed.
The war will show a well-filled tunic
Given its daily shot of lead.
But lead alone can hardly nourish
It must have soldiers to subsist.
It's you it needs to make it flourish.
The war's still hungry. So enlist!

SCENE 9

(*It is the seventeenth year of the great war of faith. Germany has lost more than half her inhabitants. Those who survive the bloodbath are killed off by terrible epidemics. Once fertile areas are ravaged by famine, wolves roam the burnt-out towns. In autumn 1634 we find Courage in the Fichtelgebirge, off the main axis of the Swedish armies. The winter this year is early and harsh.*

Business is bad, so that there is nothing to do but beg. The cook gets a letter from Utrecht and is sent packing.) (*Outside a semi-dilapidated parsonage.*) (*Grey morning in early winter. Gusts of wind. Mother Courage and the cook in shabby sheepskins, drawing the cart.*)

THE COOK: It's all dark, nobody up yet.

MOTHER COURAGE: Except it's parson's house. Have to crawl out of bed to ring bells. Then he'll have hot soup.

THE COOK: What from, when the whole village is burnt? We seen it.

MOTHER COURAGE: It's lived in, though, dog was barking.

THE COOK: S'pose parson's got, he'll give nowt.

MOTHER COURAGE: Maybe if we sing. . . .

THE COOK: I've had enough. (*Abruptly.*) Got a letter from Utrecht saying mother died of cholera and inn's mine. Here's letter if you don't believe me. No business of yours the way aunty goes on about my mode of existence, but have a look.

MOTHER COURAGE: (*Reads the letter.*) Lamb, I'm tired too of always being on the go. I feel like butcher's dog, dragging meat round customers and getting nowt off it. I got nowt left to sell, and folk got nowt left to buy nowt with. Saxony a fellow in rags tried landing me a stack of old books for two eggs, Württemberg they wanted to swap their plough for a titchy bag of salt. What's to plough for? Nowt growing no more, just brambles. In Pomerania villages are s'posed to have started in eating the younger kids, and nuns have been caught sticking folk up.

THE COOK: World's dying out.

MOTHER COURAGE: Sometimes I sees meself driving through hell with me cart selling brimstone, or across heaven with packed lunches for hungry souls. Give me my kids what's left, let's find some place they ain't shooting, and I'd like a few more years undisturbed.

THE COOK: You and me could get that inn going, Courage, think it over. Made up me mind in the night, I did: back to Utrecht with or without you, and starting today.

MOTHER COURAGE: Have to talk to Kattrin. That's a bit quick for me; I'm against making decisions all freezing cold and nowt inside you. Kattrin! (*Kattrin climbs out of the cart.*) Kattrin, got something to tell you. Cook and I want to go to Utrecht. He's been left an inn there. That'd be a settled place for you, let you meet a few people. Lots of 'em respect somebody mature, looks ain't everything. I'd like it too. I get on with cook. Say one thing for him, got a head for business. We'd have our meals for sure, not bad, eh? And your own bed too; like that, wouldn't you? Road's no life really. God knows how you might finish up. Lousy already, you are. Have to make up our minds, see, we could move with the Swedes, up north, they're somewhere up that way. (*She points to the left.*) Reckon that's fixed, Kattrin.

THE COOK: Anna, I got something private to say to you.

MOTHER COURAGE: Get back in cart, Kattrin.

(*Kattrin climbs back.*)

THE COOK: I had to interrupt, cause you don't understand, far as I can see. I didn't think there was need to say it, sticks out a mile. But if it don't, then let me tell you straight, no question of taking her along, not on your life. You get me, eh.

(*Kattrin sticks her head out of the cart behind them and listens.*)

MOTHER COURAGE: You mean I'm to leave Kattrin back here?

THE COOK: Use your imagination. Inn's got no room. It ain't one of the sort got three bar parlours. Put our backs in it we two'll get a living, but not three, no chance of that. She can keep cart.

MOTHER COURAGE: Thought she might find husband in Utrecht.

THE COOK: Go on, make me laugh. Find a husband, how? Dumb and that scar on top of it. And at her age?

MOTHER COURAGE: Don't talk so loud.

THE COOK: Loud or soft, no getting over facts. And that's another reason why I can't have her in the inn. Customers don't want to be looking at that all the time. Can't blame them.

MOTHER COURAGE: Shut your big mouth. I said not so loud.

THE COOK: Light's on in parson's house. We can try singing.

MOTHER COURAGE: Cooky, how's she to pull the cart on her own? War scares her. She'll never stand it. The dreams she must have . . . I hear her nights groaning. Mostly after a battle. What's she seeing in those dreams, I'd like to know. She's got a soft heart. Lately I found she'd got another hedgehog tucked away what we'd run over.

THE COOK: Inn's too small. (*Calls out.*) Ladies and gentlemen, domestic staff and other residents! We are now going to give you a song concerning Solomon, Julius Caesar and other famous personages what had bad luck. So's you can see we're respectable folk, which makes it difficult to carry on, particularly in winter. (*They sing.*)

> You saw sagacious Solomon
> You know what came of him.
> To him complexities seemed plain.
> He cursed the hour that gave birth to him
> And saw that everything was vain.
> How great and wise was Solomon!
> The world however didn't wait
> But soon observed what followed on.
> It's wisdom that had brought him to this state—
> How fortunate the man with none!

Yes, the virtues are dangerous stuff in this world, as this fine song proves, better not to have them and have a pleasant life and breakfast instead, hot soup for instance. Look at me: I haven't any but I'd like some. I'm a serving soldier but what good did my courage do me in all them battles, nowt,

here I am starving and better have been shit-scared and stayed at home. For why?

> You saw courageous Caesar next
> You know what he became.
> They deified him in his life
> Then had him murdered just the same.
> And as they raised the fatal knife
> How loud he cried: You too, my son!
> The world however didn't wait
> But soon observed what followed on.
> It's courage that had brought him to that state.
> How fortunate the man with none!

(*Sotto voce.*) Don't even look out. (*Aloud.*) Ladies and gentlemen, domestic staff and other inmates! All right, you may say, gallantry never cooked a man's dinner, what about trying honesty? You can eat all you want then, or anyhow not stay sober. How about it?

> You heard of honest Socrates
> The man who never lied:
> They weren't so grateful as you'd think
> Instead the rulers fixed to have him tried
> And handed him the poisoned drink.
> How honest was the people's noble son!
> The world however didn't wait
> But soon observed what followed on.
> It's honesty that brought him to that state.
> How fortunate the man with none!

Ah yes, they say, be unselfish and share what you've got, but how about if you got nowt? It's all very well to say the do-gooders have a hard time, but you still got to have something. Aye, unselfishness is a rare virtue, cause it just don't pay.

> Saint Martin couldn't bear to see
> His fellows in distress.
> He met a poor man in the snow
> And shared his cloak with him, we know.
> Both of them therefore froze to death.
> His place in Heaven was surely won!
> The world however didn't wait
> But soon observed what followed on.
> Unselfishness had brought him to that state.
> How fortunate the man with none!

That's how it is with us. We're respectable folk, stick together, don't steal, don't murder, don't burn places down. And all the time you might say we're sinking lower and lower, and it's true what the song says, and soup is few and far between, and if we weren't like this but thieves and murderers I dare say we'd be eating our fill. For virtues aren't their own reward, only wickednesses are, that's how the world goes and it didn't ought to.

> Here you can see respectable folk
> Keeping to God's own laws.
> So far he hasn't taken heed.

You who sit safe and warm indoors
Help to relieve our bitter need!
How virtuously we had begun!
The world however didn't wait
But soon observed what followed on.
It's fear of God that brought us to that state.
How fortunate the man with none!

VOICE (*from above*): Hey, you there! Come on up! There's hot soup if you want.

MOTHER COURAGE: Lamb, me stomach won't stand nowt. 'Tain't that it ain't sensible, what you say, but is that your last word? We got on all right.

THE COOK: Last word. Think it over.

MOTHER COURAGE: I've nowt to think. I'm not leaving her here.

THE COOK: That's proper senseless, nothing I can do about it though. I'm not a brute, just the inn's a small one. So now we better get on up, or there'll be nowt here either and wasted time singing in the cold.

MOTHER COURAGE: I'll get Kattrin.

THE COOK: Better bring a bit back for her. Scare them if they sees three of us coming. (*Exeunt both.*)

(*Kattrin climbs out of the cart with a bundle. She looks around to see if the other two have gone. Then she takes an old pair of trousers of the cook's and a skirt of her mother's, and lays them side by side on one of the wheels, so that they are easily seen. She has finished and is picking up her bundle to go, when Mother Courage comes back from the house.*)

MOTHER COURAGE (*with a plate of soup*): Kattrin! Will you stop there? Kattrin! Where you off to with that bundle? Has devil himself taken you over? (*She examines the bundle.*) She's packed her things. You been listening? I told him nowt doing, Utrecht, his rotten inn, what'd we be up to there? You and me, inn's no place for us. Still plenty to be got out of war. (*She sees the trousers and the skirt.*) You're plain stupid. S'pose I'd seen that, and you gone away? (*She holds Kattrin back as she tries to break away.*) Don't you start thinking it's on your account I given him the push. It was cart, that's it. Catch me leaving my cart I'm used to, it ain't you, it's for cart. We'll go off in t'other direction, and we'll throw cook's stuff out so he finds it, silly man. (*She climbs in and throws out a few other articles in the direction of the trousers.*) There, he's out of our business now, and I ain't having nobody else in, ever. You and me'll carry on now. This winter will pass, same as all the others. Get hitched up, it looks like snow.

(*They both harness themselves to the cart, then wheel it round and drag it off. When the cook arrives he looks blankly at his kit.*)

SCENE 10

(*During the whole of 1635 Mother Courage and her daughter Kattrin travel over the highroads of central Germany, in the wake of the increasingly bedraggled armies.*)
(*High road.*)
(*Mother Courage and Kattrin are pulling the cart. They pass a peasant's house inside which there is a voice singing.*)

THE VOICE:

The roses in our arbour
Delight us with their show:
They have such lovely flowers
Repaying all our labour
After the summer showers.
Happy are those with gardens now:
They have such lovely flowers.
When winter winds are freezing
As through the woods they blow
Our home is warm and pleasing.
We fixed the thatch above it
With straw and moss we wove it.
Happy are those with shelter now
When winter winds are freezing.

(*Mother Courage and Kattrin pause to listen, then continue pulling.*)

SCENE 11

(*January 1636. The emperor's troops are threatening the Protestant town of Halle. The stone begins to speak. Mother Courage loses her daughter and trudges on alone. The war is a long way from being over.*)
(*The cart is standing, much the worse for wear, alongside a peasant's house with a huge thatched roof, backing on a wall of rock. It is night.*)
(*An ensign and three soldiers in heavy armour step out of the wood.*)

THE ENSIGN: I want no noise now. Anyone shouts, shove your pike into him.

FIRST SOLDIER: Have to knock them up, though, if we're to find a guide.

THE ENSIGN: Knocking sounds natural. Could be a cow bumping the stable wall.

(*The soldiers knock on the door of the house. The peasant's wife opens it. They stop her mouth. Two soldiers go in.*)

MAN'S VOICE (*within*): What is it?

(*The soldiers bring out the peasant and his son.*)

THE ENSIGN (*pointing at the cart, where Kattrin's head has appeared*): There's another one. (*A Soldier drags her out.*) Anyone else live here beside you lot?

THE PEASANTS: This is our son. And she's dumb. Her mother's gone into town to buy stuff. For their business, cause so many people's getting out and selling things cheap. They're just passing through. Canteen folk.

THE ENSIGN: I'm warning you, keep quiet, or if there's the least noise you get a pike across your nut. Now I want someone to come with us and show us the path to the town. (*Points to the young peasant.*) Here, you.

THE YOUNG PEASANT: I don't know no path.

SECOND SOLDIER (*grinning*): He don't know no path.

THE ENSIGN (*to the second soldier*): Stick your pike in his ribs.

THE YOUNG PEASANT (*forced to his knees, with the pike threatening him*): I won't do it, not to save my life.

FIRST SOLDIER: I know what'll change his mind. (*Goes towards the stable.*) Two cows and an ox. Listen, you: if you're not reasonable I'll chop up your cattle.

THE YOUNG PEASANT: No, not that!

THE PEASANT'S WIFE (*weeps*): Please spare our cattle, captain, it'd be starving us to death.

THE ENSIGN: They're dead if he goes on being obstinate.

FIRST SOLDIER: I'm taking the ox first.

THE YOUNG PEASANT (*to his father*): Have I got to? (*The wife nods.*) Right.

THE PEASANT'S WIFE: And thank you kindly, captain, for sparing us, for ever and ever, Amen.

(*The peasant stops his wife from further expressions of gratitude.*)

FIRST SOLDIER: I knew the ox was what they minded about most, was I right?

(*Guided by the young peasant, the ensign and his men continue on their way.*)

THE PEASANT: What are they up to, I'd like to know. Nowt good.

THE PEASANT'S WIFE: Perhaps they're just scouting. What you doing?

THE PEASANT (*putting a ladder against the roof and climbing up it*): Seeing if they're on their own. (*From the top.*) Something moving in the wood. Can see something down by the quarry. And there are men in armour in the clearing. And a gun. That's at least a regiment. God's mercy on the town and everyone in it!

THE PEASANT'S WIFE: Any lights in the town?

THE PEASANT: No. They'll all be asleep. (*Climbs down.*) If those people get in they'll butcher the lot.

THE PEASANT'S WIFE: Sentries're bound to spot them first.

THE PEASANT: Sentry in the tower up the hill must have been killed, or he'd have blown his bugle.

THE PEASANT'S WIFE: If only there were more of us.

THE PEASANT: Just you and me and that cripple.

THE PEASANT'S WIFE: Nowt we can do, you'd say. . . .

THE PEASANT: Nowt.

THE PEASANT'S WIFE: Can't possibly run down there in the blackness.

THE PEASANT: Whole hillside's crawling with 'em. We could give a signal.

THE PEASANT'S WIFE: What, and have them butcher us too?

THE PEASANT: You're right, nowt we can do.

THE PEASANT'S WIFE (*to Kattrin*): Pray, poor creature, pray! Nowt we can do to stop bloodshed. You can't talk, maybe, but at least you can pray. He'll hear you if no one else can. I'll help you. (*All kneel, Kattrin behind the two peasants.*) Our Father, which art in Heaven, hear Thou our prayer, let not the town be destroyed with all what's in it sound asleep and suspecting nowt. Arouse Thou them that they may get up and go to the walls and see how the enemy approacheth with picks and guns in the blackness across fields below the slope. (*Turning to Kattrin.*) Guard Thou our mother and ensure that the watchman sleepeth not but wakes up, or it will be too late. Succour our brother-in-law also, he is inside there with his four children, spare Thou them, they are innocent and know nowt. (*To Kattrin, who gives a groan.*) One of them's not two yet, the eldest's seven. (*Kattrin stands up distractedly.*) Our Father, hear us, for only Thou canst help; we look to be doomed, for why, we are weak and have no pike and nowt and can risk nowt and are in Thy hand along with our cattle and all the farm, and same with the town, it too is in Thy hand and the enemy is before the walls in great strength.

(*Unobserved, Kattrin has slipped away to the cart and taken from it something which she hides beneath her apron; then she climbs up the ladder on to the stable roof.*)

THE PEASANT'S WIFE: Forget not the children, what are in danger, the littlest ones especially, the old folk what can't move, and every living creature.

THE PEASANT: And forgive us our trespasses as we forgive them that trespass against us. Amen.

(*Sitting on the roof, Kattrin begins to beat the drum which she has pulled out from under her apron.*)

THE PEASANT'S WIFE: Jesus Christ, what's she doing?

THE PEASANT: She's out of her mind.

THE PEASANT'S WIFE: Quick, get her down.

(*The peasant hurries to the ladder, but Kattrin pulls it up on to the roof.*)

THE PEASANT'S WIFE: She'll do us in.

THE PEASANT: Stop drumming at once, you cripple!

THE PEASANT'S WIFE: Bringing the Catholics down on us!

THE PEASANT (*looking for stones to throw*): I'll stone you.

THE PEASANT'S WIFE: Where's your feelings? Where's your heart? We're done for if they come down on us. Slit our throats, they will.

(*Kattrin stares into the distance towards the town and carries on drumming.*)

THE PEASANT'S WIFE (*to her husband*): I told you we shouldn't have allowed those vagabonds on to farm. What do they care if our last cows are taken?

THE ENSIGN (*runs in with his soldiers and the young peasant*): I'll cut you to ribbons, all of you!

THE PEASANT'S WIFE: Please, sir, it's not our fault, we couldn't help it. It was her sneaked up there. A foreigner.

THE ENSIGN: Where's the ladder?

THE PEASANT: There.

THE ENSIGN (*calls up*): I order you, throw that drum down.

(*Kattrin goes on drumming.*)

THE ENSIGN: You're all in this together. It'll be the end of you.

THE PEASANT: They been cutting pine trees in that wood. How about if we got one of the trunks and poked her off. . . .

FIRST SOLDIER (*to the ensign*): Permission to make a suggestion, sir! (*He whispers something in the ensign's ear.*) Listen, we got a suggestion could help you. Get down off there and come into town with us right away. Show us which your mother is and we'll see she ain't harmed.

(*Kattrin goes on drumming.*)

THE ENSIGN (*pushes him roughly aside*): She doesn't trust you; with a mug like yours it's not surprising. (*Calls up.*) Suppose I gave you my word? I can give my word of honour as an officer.

(*Kattrin drums harder.*)

THE ENSIGN: Is nothing sacred to her?

THE YOUNG PEASANT: There's more than her mother involved, sir.

FIRST SOLDIER: This can't go on much longer. They're bound to hear in the town.

THE ENSIGN: We'll have somehow to make a noise that's louder than her drumming. What can we make a noise with?

FIRST SOLDIER: Thought we weren't s'posed to make no noise.

THE ENSIGN: A harmless one, you fool. A peaceful one.

THE PEASANT: I could chop wood with my axe.

THE ENSIGN: Good: you chop. (*The peasant fetches his axe and attacks a tree-trunk.*) Chop harder! Harder! You're chopping for your life.

(*Kattrin has been listening, drumming less loudly the while. She now looks wildly round, and goes on drumming.*)

THE ENSIGN: Not loud enough. (*To the first soldier.*) You chop too.

THE PEASANT: Only got the one axe. (*Stops chopping.*)

THE ENSIGN: We'll have to set the farm on fire. Smoke her out, that's it.

THE PEASANT: It wouldn't help, captain. If the townspeople see a fire here they'll know what's up.

(*Kattrin has again been listening as she drums. At this point she laughs.*)

THE ENSIGN: Look at her laughing at us. I'm not having that. I'll shoot her down, and damn the consequences. Fetch the harquebus.

(*Three soldiers hurry off. Kattrin goes on drumming.*)

THE PEASANT'S WIFE: I got it, captain. That's their cart. If we smash it up she'll stop. Cart's all they got.

THE ENSIGN (*to the young peasant*): Smash it up. (*Calls up.*) We're going to smash up your cart if you don't stop drumming. (*The young peasant gives the cart a few feeble blows.*)

THE PEASANT'S WIFE: Stop it, you animal!

(*Desperately looking towards the cart, Kattrin emits pitiful noises. But she goes on drumming.*)

THE ENSIGN: Where are those clodhoppers with the harquebus?

FIRST SOLDIER: Can't have heard nowt in town yet, else we'd be hearing their guns.

THE ENSIGN (*calls up*): They can't hear you at all. And now we're going to shoot you down. For the last time: throw down that drum!

THE YOUNG PEASANT (*suddenly flings away his plank*): Go on drumming! Or they'll all be killed! Go on, go on. . . .

(*The soldier knocks him down and beats him with his pike. Kattrin starts to cry, but she goes on drumming.*)

THE PEASANT'S WIFE: Don't strike his back! For God's sake, you're beating him to death!

(*The soldiers hurry in with the harquebus.*)

SECOND SOLDIER: Colonel's frothing at the mouth, sir. We're all for court-martial.

THE ENSIGN: Set it up! Set it up! (*Calls up while the gun is being erected.*) For the very last time: stop drumming! (*Kattrin, in tears, drums as loud as she can.*) Fire! (*The soldiers fire. Kattrin is hit, gives a few more drumbeats and then slowly crumples.*)

THE ENSIGN: That's the end of that.

(*But Kattrin's last drumbeats are taken up by the town's cannon. In the distance can be heard a confused noise of tocsins and gunfire.*)

FIRST SOLDIER: She's made it.

SCENE 12

(*Before first light. Sound of the fifes and drums of troops marching off into the distance.*)

(*In front of the cart Mother Courage is squatting by her daughter. The peasant family are standing near her.*)

THE PEASANTS (*with hostility*): You must go, missis. There's only one more regiment behind that one. You can't go on your own.

MOTHER COURAGE: I think she's going to sleep. (*She sings.*)

Lullaby baby
What's that in the hay?
Neighbours' kids grizzle
But my kids are gay.

Neighbours' are in tatters
And you're dressed in lawn
Cut down from the raiment an
Angel has worn.
Neighbours' kids go hungry
And you shall eat cake
Suppose it's too crumbly
You've only to speak.
Lullaby baby
What's that in the hay?
The one lies in Poland
The other — who can say?

Better if you'd not told her nowt about your brother-in-law's kids.

THE PEASANT: If you'd not gone into town to get your cut it might never of happened.

MOTHER COURAGE: Now she's asleep.

THE PEASANT'S WIFE: She ain't asleep. Can't you see she's passed over?

THE PEASANT: And it's high time you got away yourself. There are wolves around and, what's worse, marauders.

MOTHER COURAGE: Aye.

(*She goes and gets a tarpaulin to cover the dead girl with.*)

THE PEASANT'S WIFE: Ain't you got nobody else? What you could go to?

MOTHER COURAGE: Aye, one left. Eilif.

THE PEASANT (*as Mother Courage covers the dead girl*): Best look for him, then. We'll mind her, see she gets proper burial. Don't you worry about that.

MOTHER COURAGE: Here's money for expenses.

(*She counts out coins into the peasant's hands. The peasant and his son shake hands with her and carry Kattrin away.*)

THE PEASANT'S WIFE (*as she leaves*): I'd hurry.

MOTHER COURAGE (*harnessing herself to the cart*): Hope I can pull cart all right by meself. Be all right, nowt much inside it. Got to get back in business again.

(*Another regiment with its fifes and drums marches past in the background.*)

MOTHER COURAGE (*tugging the cart*): Take me along! (*Singing is heard from offstage.*)

With all its luck and all its danger
The war is dragging on a bit
Another hundred years or longer
The common man won't benefit.
Filthy his food, no soap to shave him
The regiment steals half his pay.
But still a miracle may save him:
Tomorrow is another day!
　　The new year's come. The watchmen shout.
　　The thaw sets in. The dead remain.
　　Wherever life has not died out
　　It staggers to its feet again.

COMMENTARIES

Bertolt Brecht (1898–1956)

THE ALIENATION EFFECT   *1964*

TRANSLATED BY JOHN WILLETT

In this short description, Brecht explains some of his theories of staging and acting. His alienation effect (A-effect) reminds the audience that the characters on stage are dramatic constructs, not real people suffering real emotions. As he explains, the A-effect is the opposite of traditional acting, which is designed to produce an empathy between actor and audience. The A-effect rejects that empathy.

What follows represents an attempt to describe a technique of acting which was applied in certain theaters with a view to taking the incidents portrayed and alienating them from the spectator. The aim of this technique, known as the alienation effect, was to make the spectator adopt an attitude of inquiry and criticism in his approach to the incident. The means were artistic.

The first condition for the A-effect's application to this end is that stage and auditorium must be purged of everything "magical" and that no "hypnotic tensions" should be set up. This ruled out any attempt to make the stage convey the flavor of a particular place (a room at evening, a road in the autumn), or to create atmosphere by relaxing the tempo of the conversation. The audience was not "worked up" by a display of temperament or "swept away" by acting with tautened muscles; in short, no attempt was made to put it in a trance and give it the illusion of watching an ordinary unrehearsed event. As will be seen presently, the audience's tendency to plunge into such illusions has to be checked by specific artistic means.

The first condition for the achievement of the A-effect is that the actor must invest what he has to show with a definite gest of showing. It is of course necessary to drop the assumption that there is a fourth wall cutting the audience off from the stage and the consequent illusion that the stage action is taking place in reality and without an audience. That being so, it is possible for the actor in principle to address the audience directly.

It is well known that contact between audience and stage is normally made on the basis of empathy. Conventional actors devote their efforts so exclusively to bringing about this psychological operation that they may be said to see it as the principal aim of their art. Our introductory remarks will already have made it clear that the technique which produces an A-effect is the exact opposite of that which aims at empathy. The actor applying it is bound not to try to bring about the empathy operation.

Yet in his efforts to reproduce particular characters and show their behavior he need not renounce the means of empathy entirely. He uses these means just as any normal person with no particular acting talent would use them if he wanted to portray someone else, i.e., show how he behaves. This showing of other people's behavior happens time and again in ordinary life (witnesses of an accident demonstrating to newcomers how the victim behaved, a facetious person imitating a friend's walk, etc.), without those involved making the least effort to subject their spectators to an illusion. At the same time they do feel their way into their characters' skins with a view to acquiring their characteristics.

As has already been said, the actor too will make use of this psychological operation. But whereas the usual practice in acting is to execute it during the actual performance, in the hope of stimulating the spectator into a similar operation, he will achieve it only at an earlier stage, at some time during rehearsals.

To safeguard against an unduly "impulsive," frictionless and uncritical creation of characters and incidents, more reading rehearsals can be held than usual. The actor should refrain from living himself into the part prematurely in any way, and should go on functioning as long as possible as a reader (which does not mean a reader-aloud). An important step is memorizing one's first impressions.

When reading his part the actor's attitude should be one of a man who is astounded and contradicts. Not only the occurrence of the incidents, as he reads about them, but the conduct of the man he is playing, as he experiences it, must be weighed up by him and their peculiarities understood; none can be taken as given, as something that "was bound to turn out that way," that was "only to be expected from a character like that." Before memorizing the words he must memorize what he felt astounded at and where he felt impelled to contradict. For these are dynamic forces that he must preserve in creating his performance.

When he appears on the stage, besides what he actually is doing he will at all essential points discover, specify, imply what he is not doing; that is to say he will act in such a way that the alternative emerges as clearly as possible, that his acting allows the other possibilities to be inferred and only represents one out of the possible variants. He will say for instance "You'll pay for that," and not say "I forgive you." He detests his children; it is not the case that he loves them. He moves down stage left and not up stage right. Whatever he doesn't do must be contained and conserved in what he does. In this way every sentence and every gesture signifies a decision; the character remains under observation and is tested. The technical term for this procedure is "fixing the 'not . . . but.'"

The actor does not allow himself to become completely transformed on the stage into the character he is portraying. He is not Lear, Harpagon, Schweik; he shows them. He reproduces their remarks as authentically as he can; he puts forward their way of behaving to the best of his abilities and knowledge of men; but he never tries to persuade himself (and thereby others) that this amounts to a complete transformation. Actors will know what it means if I say that a typical kind of acting without this complete transformation takes place when a producer or colleague shows one how to play a particular passage. It is not his own part, so he is not completely transformed; he underlines the technical aspect and retains the attitude of someone just making suggestions.

Once the idea of total transformation is abandoned the actor speaks his part not as if he were improvising it himself but like a quotation. At the same time he obviously has to render all the quotation's overtones, the remark's full human and concrete shape; similarly the gesture he makes must have the full substance of a human gesture even though it now represents a copy.

Given this absence of total transformation in the acting there are three aids which may help to alienate the actions and remarks of the characters being portrayed:

1. Transposition into the third person.
2. Transposition into the past.
3. Speaking the stage directions out loud.

Using the third person and the past tense allows the actor to adopt the right attitude of detachment. In addition he will look for stage directions and remarks that comment on his lines, and speak them aloud at rehearsal ("He stood up and exclaimed angrily, not having eaten: . . . ," or "He had never been told so before, and didn't know if it was true or not," or "He smiled, and said with forced nonchalance: . . ."). Speaking the stage directions out loud in the third person results in a clash between two tones of voice, alienating the second of them, the text proper. This style of acting is further alienated by taking place on the stage after having already been outlined and announced in words. Transposing it into the past gives the speaker a standpoint from which he can look back at his sentence. The sentence too is thereby alienated without the speaker adopting an unreal point of view; unlike the spectator, he has read the play right through and is better placed to judge the sentence in accordance with the ending, with its consequences, than the former, who knows less and is more of a stranger to the sentence.

This composite process leads to an alienation of the text in the rehearsals which generally persists in the performance too. The directness of the relationship with the audience allows and indeed forces the actual speech delivery to be varied in accordance with the greater or smaller significance attaching to the sentences. Take the case of witnesses addressing a court. The underlinings, the characters' insistence on their remarks, must be developed as a piece of effective virtuosity. If the actor turns to the audience it must be a whole-hearted turn rather than the asides and soliloquizing technique of the old-fashioned theater. To get the full A-effect from the poetic medium the actor should start at rehearsal by paraphrasing the verse's content in vulgar prose, possibly accompanying this by the gestures designed for the verse. A daring and beautiful handling of verbal media will alienate the text. (Prose can be alienated by translation into the actor's native dialect.)

Gesture will be dealt with below, but it can at once be said that everything to do with the emotions has to be externalized; that is to say, it must be developed into a gesture. The actor has to find a sensibly perceptible outward expression for his character's emotions, preferably some action that gives away what is going on inside him. The emotion in question must be brought out, must lose all its restrictions so that it can be treated on a big scale. Special elegance, power and grace of gesture bring about the A-effect.

A masterly use of gesture can be seen in Chinese acting. The Chinese actor achieves the A-effect by being seen to observe his own movements.

Whatever the actor offers in the way of gesture, verse structure, etc., must be finished and bear the hallmarks of something rehearsed and rounded-off. The impression to be given is one of ease, which is at the same time one of difficulties overcome. The actor must make it possible for the audience to take his own art, his mastery of technique, lightly too. He puts an incident before the spectator with perfection and as he thinks it really happened or might have happened. He does not conceal the fact that he has rehearsed it, any more than an acrobat conceals his training, and he emphasizes that it is his own (actor's) account, view, version of the incident.

Because he doesn't identify himself with him he can pick a definite attitude to adopt towards the character whom he portrays, can show what he thinks of him and invite the spectator, who is likewise not asked to identify himself, to criticize the character portrayed.

The attitude which he adopts is a socially critical one. In his exposition of the incidents and in his characterization of the person he tries to bring out those features which come within society's sphere. In this way his performance becomes a discussion (about social conditions) with the audience he is addressing. He prompts the spectator to justify or abolish these conditions according to what class he belongs to.

The object of the A-effect is to alienate the social gest underlying every incident. By social gest is meant the mimetic and gestural expression of the social relationships prevailing between people of a given period.

It helps to formulate the incident for society, and to put it across in such a way that society is given the key, if titles are thought up for the scenes. These titles must have a historical quality.

This brings us to a crucial technical device: historicization.

The actor must play the incidents as historical ones. Historical incidents are unique, transitory incidents associated with particular periods. The conduct of the persons involved in them is not fixed and "universally human"; it includes elements that have been or may be overtaken by the course of history, and is subject to criticism from the immediately following period's point of view. The conduct of those born before us is alienated[1] from us by an incessant evolution.

It is up to the actor to treat present-day events and modes of behavior with the same detachment as the historian adopts with regard to those of the past. He must alienate these characters and incidents from us.

Characters and incidents from ordinary life, from our immediate surroundings, being familiar, strike us as more or less natural. Alienating them helps to make them seem remarkable to us. Science has carefully developed a technique of getting irritated with the everyday, "self-evident," universally accepted occurrence, and there is no reason why this infinitely useful attitude should not be taken over by art. It is an attitude which arose in science as a result of the growth in human productive powers. In art the same motive applies.

As for the emotions, the experimental use of the A-effect in the epic theater's German productions indicated that this way of acting too can stimulate them, though possibly a different class of emotion is involved from those of the orthodox theater. A critical attitude on the audience's part is a thoroughly artistic one. Nor does the actual practice of the A-effect seem anything like so unnatural as its description. Of course it is a way of acting that his nothing to do with stylization as commonly practiced. The main advantage of the epic theater with its A-effect, intended purely to show the world in such a way that it becomes manageable, is precisely its quality of being natural and earthly, its humor and its renunciation of all the mystical elements that have stuck to the orthodox theater from the old days.

[1]*Entfremdet.*

Bertolt Brecht (1898–1956)
NOTES FOR *MOTHER COURAGE*, SCENE 12   1949

TRANSLATED BY ERIC BENTLEY AND HUGO SCHMIDT

For some of his work, Brecht produced booklets that supply a great deal of background information that does not appear in the text of the plays. Brecht's manner of producing his plays was important to him. Although he did not expect every successive production to adhere strictly to the standards he established in commentaries such as this, he hoped his intentions would be substantially respected.

Twelfth Scene
Courage Moves On

The peasants have to convince Courage that Kattrin is dead. Kattrin's lullaby. Mother Courage pays for Kattrin's funeral and receives the expressions of sympathy of the peasants. Mother Courage harnesses herself to her empty covered wagon. Still hoping to get back into business, she follows the tattered army.

Basic Arrangement

The wagon stands on the empty stage. Mother Courage holds dead Kattrin's head in her lap. The peasants stand at the foot of the dead girl, huddled together and hostile. Courage talks as if her daughter were only sleeping, and deliberately overhears the reproach of the peasants that she was to blame for Kattrin's death.

Kattrin's lullaby. The mother's face is bent low over the face of the daughter. The song does not conciliate those who listen.

Mother Courage pays for Kattrin's funeral and receives expressions of sympathy from the peasants. After she has realized that her last child is dead, Courage gets up laboriously and hobbles around the corpse (right), along the footlights, behind the wagon. She returns with a tent cloth, and answers over her shoulder the peasant's question whether she had no one to turn to: "Oh yes, one. Eilif." And places the cloth over the body, with her back toward the footlights. At the head of the corpse, she pulls the cloth all the way over the face, then again takes her place behind the corpse. The peasant and his son shake hands with her and bow ceremoniously before carrying the body out (to the right). The peasant woman, too, shakes hands with Courage, walks to the right and stops once more, undecided. The two women exchange a few words, then the peasant woman exits.

Mother Courage harnesses herself to her empty covered wagon. Still hoping to get back into business, she follows the tattered army. Slowly, the old woman walks to the wagon, rolls up the rope which Dumb Kattrin had been pulling to this point, takes a stick, looks at it, slips it through the sling of the second rope, tucks the stick under her arm, and starts pulling. The turntable begins to move, and Courage circles the stage once. The curtain closes when she is upstage right for the second time.

The Peasants

The attitude of the peasants toward Courage is hostile. She got them into difficulties, and they will be saddled with her if she does not catch up with the regiments. Besides, she is to blame for the accident herself, in their opinion. And moreover the canteen woman is not part of the resident population, and now, in time of war, she belongs to the fleecers, cutthroats, and marauders in the wake of the armies. When they condole with her by shaking her hand, they merely follow custom.

The Bow

During this entire scene, Weigel, as Courage, showed an almost animal indifference. All the more beautiful was the deep bow that she made when the body was carried away.

The Lullaby

The lullaby must be sung without sentimentality and without the desire to arouse sentimentality. Otherwise, its significance does not get across. The thought that is the basis of this song is a murderous one: the child of this mother was supposed to be better off than other children of other mothers. Through a slight stress on the "you," Weigel revealed the treacherous hope of Courage to get her child, and perhaps only hers, through the war alive. The child to whom the most common things were denied was promised the uncommon.

Paying for the Funeral

Even when paying for the funeral, Weigel gave another hint at the character of Courage. She fished a few coins from her leather purse, put one back, and gave the rest to the peasant. The overpowering impression she gave of having been destroyed was not in the least diminished by this.

The Last Verse

While Courage slowly harnessed herself to her wagon, the last verse of her song was sung from the box in which the band had been placed. It expresses one more time her undestroyed hope to get something out of war anyway. It becomes more impressive in that it does not aim at the illusion that the song is actually sung by army units moving past in the distance.

Giehse in the Role
of Courage

When covering up the body, Giehse put her head under the cloth, looking at her daughter one more time, before finally dropping it over her face.

Before she began pulling away her covered wagon—another beautiful variant—she looked into the distance, to figure out where to go, and before she started pulling, she blew her nose with her index finger.

Take Your Time

At the end of the play it is necessary that one see the wagon roll away. Naturally, the audience gets the idea when the wagon starts. If the movement is extended, a moment of irritation arises ("that's long enough, now"). If it is prolonged even further, deeper understanding sets in.

Pulling the Wagon in the
Last Scene

For the 12th scene, farm house and stable with roof (of the 11th scene) were cleared away, and only the wagon and Dumb Kattrin's body were left. The act of dragging the wagon off—the large letters "Saxony" were pulled up (out of sight) when the music begins—took place on a completely empty stage: whereby one remembered the setting of the first scene. Courage and her wagon moved in a complete circle on the revolving stage. She passed the footlights once more. As usual, the stage was bathed in light.

Discoveries of the Realists

Wherein lies the effectiveness of Weigel's gesture when she mechanically puts one coin back into her purse, after having fished her money out, as she hands the peasant the funeral money for dead Kattrin? She shows that this tradeswoman, in all her grief, does not completely forget to count, since money is so hard to come by. And she shows this as a discovery about human nature that is shaped by certain conditions. This little feature has the power and the suddenness of a discovery. The art of the realists consists of digging out the truth from under the rubble of the evident, of connecting the particular with the general, of pinning down the unique within the larger process.

A Change of Text

After "I'll manage, there isn't much in it now," Courage added, in the Munich and then also in the Berlin production: "I must start up again in business."

Mother Courage Learns
Nothing

In the last scene, Weigel's Courage appeared like an eighty-year-old woman. And she comprehends nothing. She reacts only to the statements that are connected with war, such as that one must not remain behind. She overhears the crude reproach of the peasants that Kattrin's death was her fault.

Courage's inability to learn from the unproductiveness of war was a prophecy in the year 1938 when the play was written. At the Berlin production in 1948 the desire was voiced that Courage should at least come to a realization in the play. To make it possible for the spectator to get something out of this realistic play, i.e., to make the spectator learn a lesson, theaters have to arrive at an acting style that does not seek an identification of the spectator with the protagonist.

Judging on the basis of reports of spectators and newspaper reviews, the Zurich world premiere—although artistically on a high level—presented only the image of war as a natural catastrophe and an inevitable fate, and thereby it underscored to the middle-class spectator in the orchestra his own indestructibility, his ability to survive. But even to the likewise middle-class Courage, the decision "Join in or don't join in" was always left open in the play. The production, it seems, must also have presented Courage's business dealings, profiteering, willingness to take risks, as quite natural, "eternally human" behavior, so that she had no other choice. Today, it is true, the man of the middle class can no longer stay out of war, as Courage could have. To him, a production of the play can probably teach nothing but a real hatred of war, and a certain insight into the fact that the big deals of which war consists are not made by the little people. In that sense, the play is more of a lesson than reality is, because here in the play the situation of war is more of an experimental situation, made for the sake of insights. I.e., the spectator attains the attitude of a student—as long as the acting style is correct. The part of the audience that belongs to the proletariat, i.e., the class that actually can struggle against and overcome war, should be given insight into the connection between business and war (again provided the acting style is correct): the proletariat as a class can do away with war by doing away with capitalism. Of course, as far as the proletarian part of the audience is concerned, one must also take into consideration the fact that this class is busy drawing its own conclusions—inside as well as outside the theater.

The Epic Element

The Epic element was certainly visible in the production at the Deutsches Theater—in the arrangement, in the presentation of the characters, in the minute execution of details, and in the pacing of the entire play. Also, contradictory elements were not eliminated but stressed, and the parts, visible as such, made a convincing whole. However, the goal of Epic Theater was not reached. Much became clear, but clarification was in the end absent. Only in a few recasting-rehearsals did it clearly emerge, for then the actors were only "pretending," i.e., they only showed to the newly added colleague the positions and intonations, and then the whole thing received that preciously loose, unlabored, non-urgent element that incites the spectator to have his own independent thoughts and feelings.

That the production did not have an Epic foundation was never remarked, however: which was probably the reason the actors did not dare provide one.

Concerning the Notes Themselves

We hope that the present notes, offering various explanations and inventions essential to the production of a play, will not have an air of spurious seriousness. It is admittedly hard to establish the lightness and casualness that are of the essence of theater. The arts, even when they are instructive, are forms of amusement.

Tennessee Williams

Tennessee Williams (1911–1983) was one of a handful of post–World War II American playwrights to achieve an international reputation. He was born Thomas Lanier Williams in Columbus, Mississippi, the first son of a traveling shoe salesman who eventually moved the family to a dark and dreary tenement in St. Louis. A precocious child, Williams was given a typewriter by his mother when he was eleven years old. The instrument helped him create fantasy worlds that seemed more real, more important to him than the dark and sometimes threatening world in which he lived. His parents, expecting a third child, their son Dakin, moved out of the tenement and bought a house whose gloominess depressed virtually everyone in it. His mother and father found themselves arguing, and his older sister, Rose, took refuge from the real world by closeting herself with a collection of glass animals.

Both Rose and Tennessee responded badly to their environment, and both had breakdowns. Tennessee was so ill that he suffered a partial paralysis of his legs, a disorder that made him a victim of bullies at school and a disappointment to his father at home. He could never participate in sports and was always somewhat frail; however, he was very advanced intellectually and published his first story when he was sixteen.

His education was sporadic. He attended the University of Missouri but, failing ROTC because of his physical limitations, soon dropped out to work in a shoe company. He then went to Washington University in St. Louis but dropped out again. Finally, he earned a bachelor's degree in playwriting at the State University of Iowa when he was twenty-four. During this time he was writing plays, some of which were produced at Washington University. Two years after he graduated, the Theatre Guild produced his first commercial play, *Battle of Angels* (1940), in Boston. It was such a distinct failure that he feared his fledgling career was stunted, but he kept writing and managed to live for a few years on foundation grants. It was not until the production of *The Glass Menagerie* (1944 in Chicago, 1945 in New York) that he achieved the kind of notice he knew he deserved. His first real success, the play was given the New York Drama Critics' Circle Award, the sign of his having achieved a measure of professional recognition and financial independence.

After trying several jobs, including an unsuccessful attempt at screenwriting, he had no more worries about work after *The Glass Menagerie* ran on Broadway for 561 performances. In 1947 his second success, *A Streetcar Named Desire*, starring the then-unknown Marlon Brando, was an even bigger box-office smash. It ran for 855 performances and won the Pulitzer Prize. By the time Tennessee Williams was thirty-six, he was regarded as one of the most important playwrights in America.

Williams followed these successes with a number of plays that were not all as well received as his first works. *Summer and Smoke* (1948), *The Rose Tattoo* (1951), and *Camino Real* (1953) were met with measured enthusiasm from the public, although the critics thought highly of Williams's work. These plays were followed by the saga of a southern family, *Cat on a Hot Tin Roof*, which won all the major drama prizes in 1955, including the Pulitzer.

Williams's energy was unfailing in the next several years. He authored a screenplay, *Baby Doll*, with the legendary director Elia Kazan, in 1956. In 1958 he wrote a one-act play, *Suddenly Last Summer*, and in 1959 *Sweet Bird of Youth*. Some of his later plays are *The Night of the Iguana* (1961), *The Milk Train Doesn't Stop Here Anymore* (1963), and *Small Craft Warnings* (1972). He also wrote a novel and several volumes of short stories, establishing himself as an important writer in many genres. His sudden death in 1983 was a blow to the theater world.

THE GLASS MENAGERIE

Tennessee Williams has often been accused of exorcising his family demons in his plays and of sometimes cloaking events in a personal symbolism that is impossible for an audience to penetrate totally. *The Glass Menagerie* (1944) certainly derives from his personal experience growing up in St. Louis in a tenement, the setting for the play. The characters are drawn from his own family, particularly the character Laura, who is based on his sister. But the symbolism in the play is not so obscure as to give an audience special difficulty.

In a way Williams thought of the play as a tribute to his sister, Rose. Rose's depressions were so severe that eventually she received a lobotomy, which rendered her more passive and more hopeless than before. The operation did not achieve anything positive, and Williams felt somewhat responsible because he had not urged the family to refuse the treatment.

In the play Amanda Wingfield is obsessed with finding gentlemen callers and a suitable career for her daughter, Laura, who walks with a slight limp and is exceedingly shy. Amanda lives in a world of imagination, endlessly retelling stories about a glorious past filled with suitors she could have had before she married. Amanda bullies Laura, whose only defense is to bury herself in her own fantasy world of spun-glass animals. Tom, the son and narrator of the play, is also a victim of Amanda's bullying, but he is more independent and better able to withstand her assaults.

Both children are great disappointments to Amanda. Tom is aloof, indolent, something like his father, who is present only in his picture on the wall. Laura calls herself a cripple and has no self-esteem or hope for a future such as the one her mother conceives for her. Laura's shyness is almost uncontrollable. It has ruined any hope of a business career, to Amanda's intense distress. When Tom brings home Jim, and his sister recognizes him as a boy she admired from afar in high school, Laura is nearly too shy to come to the dinner table. And when it becomes clear that Jim is not the gentleman caller of Amanda's dreams, Amanda and Laura are left to face reality or to continue living in their fantasy worlds.

Amanda confronts Tom at the end of the play and asserts that he "live[s] in a dream" and "manufacture[s] illusions." She could be speaking about any character in the play, including Jim, who lives according to popular illusions about self-fulfillment. But the Wingfields in particular pay dearly for their illusions, perhaps Laura more than anyone because of her mother's inability to relinquish intense but unrealistic hopes for her daughter.

Williams's written presentation of the play provides more insights than usual for a reading audience. His stage directions are elaborate, poetic, and exceptionally evocative. Through Tom, as narrator, he says that the play is not realistic but rather is a memory play, an enactment of moments in Tom's memory.

Williams specifies a setting that is almost dreamlike, using Brechtian devices such as the visual images and screen legends flashed at appropriate moments. He uses music to establish a mood or stimulate an association. Because modern productions rarely follow Williams's directions, the dreamlike quality is sometimes lost. In fact, ironically, modern productions of this play are often realistic rather than symbolic, although they usually maintain the mood that Williams hoped to achieve.

The Glass Menagerie in Performance

The first production of *The Glass Menagerie* opened in Chicago on December 26, 1944, during World War II. Audiences were not drawn to it at first, but the critics' positive reviews began to attract people to the theater. In March 1945, when it was playing to full houses, the play transferred to New York and began a run of 561 performances. It won the Drama Critics' Circle Award as the best American play of the 1944–1945 season. Two road companies then toured the play around the country. The first London performance, in the large and distinguished Theatre Royal in Haymarket in July 1948, was directed by John Gielgud and starred Helen Hayes as Amanda Wingfield. A film version followed in 1950.

Revivals of the play have been both numerous and successful. Laurette Taylor, who played Amanda in the original New York production, set a standard with her interpretation of Williams's poetic language. Maureen Stapleton, whose more vigorous approach contrasted sharply with Taylor's, took the role in the 1965 production at the Brooks Atkinson Theater in New York. The critic Howard Taubman said, "Maureen Stapleton does not cause one to forget Miss Taylor. . . . Through the magic of her own sensitivity, she gives Amanda a strong, binding thread of sadness and tenderness." Katharine Hepburn's first television performance was as Amanda in 1973. "She gives a brilliant, multifaceted performance that is surely the acting tour de force of the year," said critic Percy Shain. Jessica Tandy performed the role in 1983 at the Eugene O'Neill Theater in New York, with Amanda Plummer as Laura. *New York Times* critic Frank Rich declared, "This Amanda is tough, and even her most comic badgerings leave a bitter aftertaste." The British director of that production, John Dexter, used some of the flash cards that Williams specified in the original published version but that had been omitted from previous productions. They flashed important speeches on the scrim during the performance.

Joanne Woodward played Amanda in the 1986 revival at the Long Wharf Theater in New Haven in a version that had been performed at the Williamstown Theatre Festival in 1982. Treat Williams was the son, James Naughton was the gentleman caller, and the Long Wharf production was impressively dreamlike and powerful. Woodward's husband, Paul Newman, directed the 1987 film version of the play. Jessica Lange and Christian Slater took the play to Broadway in 2005 in what Ben Brantley called a "narcotized" production. Lange has made a serious effort to interpret several of Williams's plays.

Tennessee Williams (1911–1983)
THE GLASS MENAGERIE   *1944*

nobody, not even the rain, has such small hands— E. E. CUMMINGS

Production Notes by Tennessee Williams

Being a "memory play," *The Glass Menagerie* can be presented with unusual freedom of convention. Because of its considerably delicate or tenuous material, atmospheric touches and subtleties of direction play a particularly important part. Expressionism and all other unconventional techniques in drama have only one valid aim, and this is a closer approach to truth. When a play employs unconventional techniques, it is not, or certainly shouldn't be, trying to escape its responsibility of dealing with reality, or interpreting experience, but is actually or should be attempting to find a closer approach, or more penetrating and vivid expression of things as they are. The straight realistic play with its genuine frigidaire and authentic ice cubes, its characters that speak exactly as its audience speaks, corresponds to the academic landscape and has the same virtue of a photographic likeness. Everyone should know nowadays the unimportance of the photographic in art: that truth, life, or reality is an organic thing which the poetic imagination can represent or suggest, in essence, only through transformation, through changing into other forms than those which were merely present in appearance.

These remarks are not meant as a preface only to this particular play. They have to do with a conception of a new, plastic theatre which must take the place of the exhausted theatre of realistic conventions if the theatre is to resume vitality as a part of our culture.

The Screen Device. There is *only one important difference between the original and acting version of the play* and that is the *omission* in the latter of the device which I tentatively included in my *original* script. This device was the use of a screen on which were projected magic-lantern slides bearing images or titles. I do not regret the omission of this device from the present Broadway production. The extraordinary power of Miss Taylor's performance made it suitable to have the utmost simplicity in the physical production. But I think it may be interesting to some readers to see how this device was conceived. So I am putting it into the published manuscript. These images and legends, projected from behind, were cast on a section of wall between the front-room and dining-room areas, which should be indistinguishable from the rest when not in use.

The purpose of this will probably be apparent. It is to give accent to certain values in each scene. Each scene contains a particular point (or several) which is structurally the most important. In an episodic play, such as this, the basic structure or narrative line may be obscured from the audience; the effect may seem fragmentary rather than architectural. This may not be the fault of the play so much as a lack of attention in the audience. The legend or image upon the screen will strengthen the effect of what is merely allusion in the writing and allow the primary point to be made more simply and lightly than if the entire responsibility were on the spoken lines. Aside from this structural value, I think the screen will have a definite emotional appeal, less definable but just as important. An imaginative producer or director may invent many other uses for this device than those indicated in the present script. In fact the possibilities of the device seem much larger to me than the instance of this play can possibly utilize.

The Music. Another extra-literary accent in this play is provided by the use of music. A single recurring tune, "The Glass Menagerie," is used to give emotional emphasis to suitable passages. This tune is like circus music, not when you are on the grounds or in the immediate vicinity of the parade, but when you are at some distance and very likely thinking of something else. It seems under those circumstances to continue almost interminably and it weaves in and out of your preoccupied consciousness; then it is the lightest, most delicate music in the world and perhaps the saddest. It expresses the surface vivacity of life with the underlying strain of immutable and inexpressible sorrow. When you look at a piece of delicately spun glass you think of two things: how beautiful it is and how easily it can be broken. Both of those ideas should be woven into the recurring tune, which dips in and out of the play as if it were carried on a wind that changes. It serves as a thread of connection and allusion between the narrator with his separate point in time and space and the subject of his story. Between each episode it returns as reference to the emotion, nostalgia, which is the first condition of the play. It is primarily Laura's music and therefore comes out most clearly when the play focuses upon her and the lovely fragility of glass which is her image.

The Lighting. The lighting in the play is not realistic. In keeping with the atmosphere of memory, the stage is dim. Shafts of light are focused on selected areas or actors, sometimes in contradistinction to what is the apparent center. For instance, in the quarrel scene between Tom and Amanda, in which Laura has no active part, the clearest pool of light is on her figure. This is also true of the supper scene, when her silent figure on the sofa should remain the visual center. The light upon Laura should be distinct from the others, having a peculiar pristine clarity such as light used in early religious portraits of female saints or madonnas. A certain correspondence to light in religious paintings, such as El Greco's, where the figures are radiant in atmosphere that is relatively dusky, could be effectively used throughout the play. (It will also permit a more effective use of the screen.) A free, imaginative use of light can be of enormous value in giving a mobile, plastic quality to plays of a more or less static nature.

Characters

AMANDA WINGFIELD, *the mother. A little woman of great but confused vitality clinging frantically to another time and place. Her characterization must be carefully created, not copied from type. She is not paranoiac, but her life is paranoia. There is much to admire in Amanda, and as much to love and pity as there is to laugh at. Certainly she has endurance and a kind of heroism, and though her foolishness makes her unwittingly cruel at times, there is tenderness in her slight person.*

LAURA WINGFIELD, *her daughter. Amanda, having failed to establish contact with reality, continues to live vitally in her illusions, but Laura's situation is even graver. A childhood illness has left her crippled, one leg slightly shorter than the other, and held in a brace. This defect need not be more than suggested on the stage. Stemming from this, Laura's separation increases till she is like a piece of her own glass collection, too exquisitely fragile to move from the shelf.*

TOM WINGFIELD, *her son. And the narrator of the play. A poet with a job in a warehouse. His nature is not remorseless, but to escape from a trap he has to act without pity.*

JIM O'CONNOR, *the gentleman caller. A nice, ordinary, young man.*

Scene: *An alley in St. Louis.*
Part I: *Preparation for a Gentleman Caller.*
Part II: *The Gentleman Calls.*
Time: *Now and the Past.*

SCENE 1

(*The Wingfield apartment is in the rear of the building, one of those vast hive-like conglomerations of cellular living-units that flower as warty growths in overcrowded urban centers of lower middle-class population and are symptomatic of the impulse of this largest and fundamentally enslaved section of American society to avoid fluidity and differentiation and to exist and function as one interfused mass of automatism.*)

(*The apartment faces an alley and is entered by a fire escape, a structure whose name is a touch of accidental poetic truth, for all of these huge buildings are always burning with the slow and implacable fires of human desperation. The fire escape is included in the set — that is, the landing of it and steps descending from it.*)

(*The scene is memory and is therefore nonrealistic. Memory takes a lot of poetic license. It omits some details; others are exaggerated, according to the emotional value of the articles it touches, for memory is seated predominantly in the heart. The interior is therefore rather dim and poetic.*)

(*At the rise of the curtain, the audience is faced with the dark, grim rear wall of the Wingfield tenement. This building, which runs parallel to the footlights, is flanked on both sides by dark, narrow alleys which run into murky canyons of tangled clotheslines, garbage cans, and the sinister latticework of neighboring fire escapes. It is up and down these side alleys that exterior entrances and exits are made, during the play. At the end of Tom's opening commentary, the dark tenement wall slowly reveals (by means of a transparency) the interior of the ground floor Wingfield apartment.*)

(*Downstage is the living room, which also serves as a sleeping room for Laura, the sofa unfolding to make her bed. Upstage, center, and divided by a wide arch or second proscenium with transparent faded portieres (or second curtain), is the dining room. In an old-fashioned what-not in the living room are seen scores of transparent glass animals. A blown-up photograph of the father hangs on the wall of the living room, facing the audience, to the left of the archway. It is the face of a very handsome young man in a doughboy's First World War cap. He is gallantly smiling, ineluctably smiling, as if to say, "I will be smiling forever."*)

(*The audience hears and sees the opening scene in the dining room through both the transparent fourth wall of the building and the transparent gauze portieres of the dining-room arch. It is during this revealing scene that the fourth wall slowly ascends, out of sight. This transparent exterior wall is not brought down again until the very end of the play, during Tom's final speech.*)

(*The narrator is an undisguised convention of the play. He takes whatever license with dramatic convention is convenient to his purposes.*)

(*Tom enters dressed as a merchant sailor from alley, stage left, and strolls across the front of the stage to the fire escape. There he stops and lights a cigarette. He addresses the audience.*)

TOM: Yes, I have tricks in my pocket, I have things up my sleeve. But I am the opposite of a stage magician. He gives you illusion that has the appearance of truth. I give you truth in the pleasant disguise of illusion. To begin with, I turn back time. I reverse it to that quaint period, the thirties, when the huge middle class of America was matriculating in a school for the blind. Their eyes had failed them, or they had failed their eyes, and so they were having their fingers pressed forcibly down on the fiery Braille alphabet of a dissolving economy. In Spain there was revolution. Here there was only shouting and confusion. In Spain there was Guernica. Here there were disturbances of labor, sometimes pretty violent, in otherwise peaceful cities such as Chicago, Cleveland, Saint Louis. . . . This is the social background of the play.

(*Music.*)

The play is memory. Being a memory play, it is dimly lighted, it is sentimental, it is not realistic. In memory everything seems to happen to music. That explains the fiddle in the wings. I am the narrator of the play, and also a character in it. The other characters are my mother, Amanda, my sister, Laura, and a gentleman caller who appears in the final scenes. He is the most realistic character in the play, being an emissary from a world of reality that we were somehow set apart from. But since I have a poet's weakness for symbols, I am using this character also as a symbol; he is the long delayed but always expected something that we live for. There is a fifth character in the play who doesn't appear except in this larger-than-life photograph over the mantel. This is our father who left us a long time ago. He was a telephone man who fell in love with long distances; he gave up his job with the telephone company and skipped the light fantastic out of town . . . The last we heard of him was a picture postcard from Mazatlan, on the Pacific coast of Mexico, containing a message of two words — "Hello — Good-bye!" and no address. I think the rest of the play will explain itself. . . .

(*Amanda's voice becomes audible through the portieres.*)

(*Legend on Screen: "Où Sont les Neiges."*)°

(*He divides the portieres and enters the upstage area.*)

(*Amanda and Laura are seated at a drop-leaf table. Eating is indicated by gestures without food or utensils. Amanda faces the audience. Tom and Laura are seated in profile.*)

(*The interior has lit up softly and through the scrim we see Amanda and Laura seated at the table in the upstage area.*)

AMANDA (*calling*): Tom?

TOM: Yes, Mother.

AMANDA: We can't say grace until you come to the table!

TOM: Coming, Mother. (*He bows slightly and withdraws, reappearing a few moments later in his place at the table.*)

AMANDA (*to her son*): Honey, don't *push* with your *fingers*. If you have to push with something, the thing to push with is a crust of bread. And chew — chew! Animals have sections in their stomachs which enable them to digest food without mastication, but human beings are supposed to chew their food before they swallow it down. Eat food leisurely, son, and really enjoy it. A well-cooked meal has lots of delicate flavors that have to be held in the mouth for appreciation. So chew your food and give your salivary glands a chance to function!

(*Tom deliberately lays his imaginary fork down and pushes his chair back from the table.*)

TOM: I haven't enjoyed one bite of this dinner because of your constant directions on how to eat it. It's you that makes me rush through meals with your hawk-like

Où Sont les Neiges: Where are the snows [of yesteryear].

attention to every bite I take. Sickening—spoils my appetite—all this discussion of animals' secretion—salivary glands—mastication!

AMANDA (*lightly*): Temperament like a Metropolitan° star! (*He rises and crosses downstage.*) You're not excused from the table.

TOM: I'm getting a cigarette.

AMANDA: You smoke too much.

(*Laura rises.*)

LAURA: I'll bring in the blancmange.

(*He remains standing with his cigarette by the portieres during the following.*)

AMANDA (*rising*): No, sister, no, sister—you be the lady this time and I'll be the darky.

LAURA: I'm already up.

AMANDA: Resume your seat, little sister—I want you to stay fresh and pretty—for gentlemen callers!

LAURA: I'm not expecting any gentlemen callers.

AMANDA (*crossing out to kitchenette. Airily*): Sometimes they come when they are least expected! Why, I remember one Sunday afternoon in Blue Mountain— (*Enters kitchenette.*)

TOM: I know what's coming!

LAURA: Yes. But let her tell it.

TOM: Again?

LAURA: She loves to tell it.

(*Amanda returns with bowl of dessert.*)

AMANDA: One Sunday afternoon in Blue Mountain— your mother received—*seventeen!*—gentlemen callers! Why, sometimes there weren't chairs enough to accommodate them all. We had to send the nigger over to bring in folding chairs from the parish house.

TOM (*remaining at portieres*): How did you entertain those gentlemen callers?

AMANDA: I understood the art of conversation!

TOM: I bet you could talk.

AMANDA: Girls in those days *knew* how to talk, I can tell you.

TOM: Yes?

(*Image: Amanda as a girl on a porch greeting callers.*)

AMANDA: They knew how to entertain their gentlemen callers. It wasn't enough for a girl to be possessed of a pretty face and a graceful figure—although I wasn't slighted in either respect. She also needed to have a nimble wit and a tongue to meet all occasions.

TOM: What did you talk about?

AMANDA: Things of importance going on in the world! Never anything coarse or common or vulgar. (*She addresses Tom as though he were seated in the vacant chair at the table though he remains by portieres. He plays this scene as though he held the book.*) My callers were gentlemen—all! Among my callers were some of the most prominent young

Metropolitan: The Metropolitan Opera in New York City.

planters of the Mississippi Delta—planters and sons of planters!

(*Tom motions for music and a spot of light on Amanda.*) (*Her eyes lift, her face glows, her voice becomes rich and elegiac.*)
(*Screen legend: "Où Sont les Neiges."*)

There was young Champ Laughlin who later became vice-president of the Delta Planters Bank. Hadley Stevenson who was drowned in Moon Lake and left his widow one hundred and fifty thousand in Government bonds. There were the Cutrere brothers, Wesley and Bates. Bates was one of my bright particular beaux! He got in a quarrel with that wild Wainright boy. They shot it out on the floor of Moon Lake Casino. Bates was shot through the stomach. Died in the ambulance on his way to Memphis. His widow was also well-provided for, came into eight or ten thousand acres, that's all. She married him on the rebound—never loved her—carried my picture on him the night he died! And there was that boy that every girl in the Delta had set her cap for! That beautiful, brilliant young Fitzhugh boy from Greene County!

TOM: What did he leave his widow?

AMANDA: He never married! Gracious, you talk as though all of my old admirers had turned up their toes to the daisies!

TOM: Isn't this the first you mentioned that still survives?

AMANDA: That Fitzhugh boy went North and made a fortune—came to be known as the Wolf of Wall Street! He had the Midas touch, whatever he touched turned to gold! And I could have been Mrs. Duncan J. Fitzhugh, mind you! But—I picked your *father*!

LAURA (*rising*): Mother, let me clear the table.

AMANDA: No, dear, you go in front and study your typewriter chart. Or practice your shorthand a little. Stay fresh and pretty!—It's almost time for our gentlemen callers to start arriving. (*She flounces girlishly toward the kitchenette.*) How many do you suppose we're going to entertain this afternoon?

(*Tom throws down the paper and jumps up with a groan.*)

LAURA (*alone in the dining room*): I don't believe we're going to receive any, Mother.

AMANDA (*reappearing, airily*): What? No one—not one? You must be joking! (*Laura nervously echoes her laugh. She slips in a fugitive manner through the half-open portieres and draws them gently behind her. A shaft of very clear light is thrown on her face against the faded tapestry of the curtains. Music: "The Glass Menagerie" under faintly. Lightly.*) Not one gentleman caller? It can't be true! There must be a flood, there must have been a tornado!

LAURA: It isn't a flood, it's not a tornado, Mother. I'm just not popular like you were in Blue Mountain. . . . (*Tom utters another groan. Laura glances at him with a faint, apologetic smile. Her voice catching a little.)* Mother's afraid I'm going to be an old maid.

(The scene dims out with "Glass Menagerie" music.)

SCENE 2

("Laura, Haven't You Ever Liked Some Boy?")

(On the dark stage the screen is lighted with the image of blue roses.)

(Gradually Laura's figure becomes apparent and the screen goes out.)

(The music subsides.)

(Laura is seated in the delicate ivory chair at the small clawfoot table.)

(She wears a dress of soft violet material for a kimono—her hair tied back from her forehead with a ribbon.)

(She is washing and polishing her collection of glass.)

(Amanda appears on the fire escape steps. At the sound of her ascent, Laura catches her breath, thrusts the bowl of ornaments away and seats herself stiffly before the diagram of the typewriter keyboard as though it held her spellbound. Something has happened to Amanda. It is written in her face as she climbs to the landing: a look that is grim and hopeless and a little absurd.)

(She has on one of those cheap or imitation velvety-looking cloth coats with imitation fur collar. Her hat is five or six years old, one of those dreadful cloche hats that were worn in the late twenties, and she is clasping an enormous black patent-leather pocketbook with nickel clasp and initials. This is her full-dress outfit, the one she usually wears to the D.A.R.°)

(Before entering she looks through the door.)

(She purses her lips, opens her eyes wide, rolls them upward and shakes her head.)

(Then she slowly lets herself in the door. Seeing her mother's expression Laura touches her lips with a nervous gesture.)

LAURA: Hello, Mother, I was—*(She makes a nervous gesture toward the chart on the wall. Amanda leans against the shut door and stares at Laura with a martyred look.)*

AMANDA: Deception? Deception? *(She slowly removes her hat and gloves, continuing the swift suffering stare. She lets the hat and gloves fall on the floor—a bit of acting.)*

LAURA *(shakily)*: How was the D.A.R. meeting? *(Amanda slowly opens her purse and removes a dainty white handkerchief which she shakes out delicately and delicately touches to her lips and nostrils.)* Didn't you go to the D.A.R. meeting, Mother?

D.A.R.: Daughters of the American Revolution, a patriotic organization for women whose ancestors were involved in the American Revolutionary War.

AMANDA *(faintly, almost inaudibly)*:—No.—No. *(Then more forcibly).* I did not have the strength—to go to the D.A.R. In fact, I did not have the courage! I wanted to find a hole in the ground and hide myself in it forever! *(She crosses slowly to the wall and removes the diagram of the typewriter keyboard. She holds it in front of her for a second, staring at it sweetly and sorrowfully—then bites her lips and tears it in two pieces.)*

LAURA *(faintly)*: Why did you do that, Mother? *(Amanda repeats the same procedure with the chart of the Gregg Alphabet.)* Why are you—

AMANDA: Why? Why? How old are you, Laura?

LAURA: Mother, you know my age.

AMANDA: I thought that you were an adult; it seems that I was mistaken. *(She crosses slowly to the sofa and sinks down and stares at Laura.)*

LAURA: Please don't stare at me, Mother.

(Amanda closes her eyes and lowers her head. Count ten.)

AMANDA: What are we going to do, what is going to become of us, what is the future?

(Count ten.)

LAURA: Has something happened, Mother? *(Amanda draws a long breath and takes out the handkerchief again. Dabbing process.)* Mother, has—something happened?

AMANDA: I'll be all right in a minute. I'm just bewildered—*(Count five.)*—by life. . . .

LAURA: Mother, I wish that you would tell me what's happened.

AMANDA: As you know, I was supposed to be inducted into my office at the D.A.R. this afternoon. *(Image: a swarm of typewriters.)* But I stopped off at Rubicam's Business College to speak to your teachers about your having a cold and ask them what progress they thought you were making down there.

LAURA: Oh. . . .

AMANDA: I went to the typing instructor and introduced myself as your mother. She didn't know who you were. Wingfield, she said. We don't have any such student enrolled at the school! I assured her she did, that you had been going to classes since early in January. "I wonder," she said, "if you could be talking about that terribly shy little girl who dropped out of school after only a few days' attendance?" "No," I said, "Laura, my daughter, has been going to school every day for the past six weeks!" "Excuse me," she said. She took the attendance book out and there was your name, unmistakably printed, and all the dates you were absent until they decided that you had dropped out of school. I still said, "No, there must have been some mistake! There must have been some mix-up in the records!" And she said, "No—I remember her perfectly now. Her hands shook so that she couldn't hit the right keys! The first time we gave a speed test, she broke down completely—was sick at the stomach and almost had to be carried into the wash-room! After that morning she never showed up any more. We phoned the house but never got any answer"—while I was working at Famous and Barr, I suppose, demonstrating those—Oh! I felt so weak I could barely keep on my feet. I had to sit down while they got me a glass of water! Fifty dollars' tuition, all of our plans—my hopes and ambitions for you—just gone up the spout, just gone up the spout like that. (*Laura draws a long breath and gets awkwardly to her feet. She crosses to the victrola and winds it up.*) What are you doing?

LAURA: Oh! (*She releases the handle and returns to her seat.*)

AMANDA: Laura, where have you been going when you've gone out pretending that you were going to business college?

LAURA: I've just been going out walking.

AMANDA: That's not true.

LAURA: It is. I just went walking.

AMANDA: Walking? Walking? In winter? Deliberately courting pneumonia in that light coat? Where did you walk to, Laura?

LAURA: All sorts of places—mostly in the park.

AMANDA: Even after you'd started catching that cold?

LAURA: It was the lesser of two evils, Mother. (*Image: winter scene in park.*) I couldn't go back up. I—threw up—on the floor!

AMANDA: From half past seven till after five every day you mean to tell me you walked around in the park, because you wanted to make me think that you were still going to Rubicam's Business College?

LAURA: It wasn't as bad as it sounds. I went inside places to get warmed up.

AMANDA: Inside where?

LAURA: I went in the art museum and the bird houses at the Zoo. I visited the penguins every day! Sometimes I did without lunch and went to the movies. Lately I've been spending most of my afternoons in the Jewel-box, that big glass house where they raise the tropical flowers.

AMANDA: You did all this to deceive me, just for the deception? (*Laura looks down.*) Why?

LAURA: Mother, when you're disappointed, you get that awful suffering look on your face, like the picture of Jesus' mother in the museum!

AMANDA: Hush!

LAURA: I couldn't face it.

(*Pause. A whisper of strings.*)
(*Legend: "The Crust of Humility."*)

AMANDA (*hopelessly fingering the huge pocketbook*): So what are we going to do the rest of our lives? Stay home and watch the parades go by? Amuse ourselves with the glass menagerie, darling? Eternally play those worn-out phonograph records your father left as a painful reminder of him? We won't have a business career—we've given that up because it gave us nervous indigestion! (*Laughs wearily.*) What is there left but dependency all our lives? I know so well what

becomes of unmarried women who aren't prepared to occupy a position. I've seen such pitiful cases in the South—barely tolerated spinsters living upon the grudging patronage of sister's husband or brother's wife!—stuck away in some little mousetrap of a room—encouraged by one in-law to visit another—little birdlike women without any nest—eating the crust of humility all their life! Is that the future that we've mapped out for ourselves? I swear it's the only alternative I can think of! It isn't a very pleasant alternative, is it? Of course—some girls do *marry*. (*Laura twists her hands nervously.*) Haven't you ever liked some boy?

LAURA: Yes. I liked one once. (*Rises.*) I came across his picture a while ago.

AMANDA (*with some interest*): He gave you his picture?

LAURA: No, it's in the yearbook.

AMANDA (*disappointed*): Oh—a high-school boy.

(*Screen image: Jim as high school hero bearing a silver cup.*)

LAURA: Yes. His name was Jim. (*Laura lifts the heavy annual from the clawfoot table.*) Here he is in *The Pirates of Penzance.*

AMANDA (*absently*): The what?

LAURA: The operetta the senior class put on. He had a wonderful voice and we sat across the aisle from each other Mondays, Wednesdays, and Fridays in the Aud. Here he is with the silver cup for debating! See his grin?

AMANDA (*absently*): He must have had a jolly disposition.

LAURA: He used to call me—Blue Roses.

(*Image: blue roses.*)

AMANDA: Why did he call you such a name as that?

LAURA: When I had that attack of pleurosis—he asked me what was the matter when I came back. I said pleurosis—he thought that I said Blue Roses! So that's what he always called me after that. Whenever he saw me, he'd holler, "Hello, Blue Roses!" I didn't care for the girl that he went out with. Emily Meisenbach. Emily was the best-dressed girl at Soldan. She never struck me, though, as being sincere . . . It says in the Personal Section—they're engaged. That's—six years ago! They must be married by now.

AMANDA: Girls that aren't cut out for business careers usually wind up married to some nice man. (*Gets up with a spark of revival.*) Sister, that's what you'll do!

(*Laura utters a startled, doubtful laugh. She reaches quickly for a piece of glass.*)

LAURA: But, Mother—

AMANDA: Yes? (*Crossing to photograph.*)

LAURA (*in a tone of frightened apology*): I'm—crippled!

(*Image: screen.*)

AMANDA: Nonsense! Laura, I've told you never, never to use that word. Why, you're not crippled, you just have a little defect—hardly noticeable, even! When people have some slight disadvantage like that, they cultivate other things to make up for it—develop charm—and vivacity—and—*charm!* That's all you have to do! (*She turns again to the photograph.*) One thing your father had *plenty of*—was *charm!*

(*Tom motions to the fiddle in the wings.*)
(*The scene fades out with music.*)

SCENE 3

(*Legend on screen: "After the Fiasco—"*)
(*Tom speaks from the fire escape landing.*)

TOM: After the fiasco at Rubicam's Business College, the idea of getting a gentleman caller for Laura began to play a more important part in Mother's calculations. It became an obsession. Like some archetype of the universal unconscious, the image of the gentleman caller haunted our small apartment. . . . (*Image: young man at door with flowers.*) An evening at home rarely passed without some allusion to this image, this specter, this hope. . . . Even when he wasn't mentioned, his presence hung in Mother's preoccupied look and in my sister's frightened, apologetic manner—hung like a sentence passed upon the Wingfields! Mother was a woman of action as well as words. She began to take logical steps in the planned direction. Late that winter and in the early spring— realizing that extra money would be needed to properly feather the nest and plume the bird—she conducted a vigorous campaign on the telephone, roping in subscribers to one of those magazines for matrons called *The Home-maker's Companion,* the type of journal that features the serialized sublimations of ladies of letters who think in terms of delicate cuplike breasts, slim, tapering waists, rich, creamy thighs, eyes like wood smoke in autumn, fingers that soothe and caress like strains of music, bodies as powerful as Etruscan sculpture.

(*Screen image: glamor magazine cover.*)
(*Amanda enters with phone on long extension cord. She is spotted in the dim stage.*)

AMANDA: Ida Scott? This is Amanda Wingfield! We *missed* you at the D.A.R. last Monday! I said to myself: She's probably suffering with that sinus condition! How is that sinus condition? Horrors! Heaven have mercy!—You're a Christian martyr, yes, that's what you are, a Christian martyr! Well I just now happened to notice that your subscription to the *Companion'*s about to expire! Yes, it expires with the next issue, honey!—just when that wonderful new serial by Bessie Mae Hopper is getting off to such an exciting start. Oh, honey, it's something that you can't miss! You remember how *Gone with the Wind* took everybody by storm? You simply couldn't go out if you hadn't read it. All everybody *talked* was Scarlett O'Hara. Well, this is a book that critics already compare to *Gone with the Wind.* It's the

Gone with the Wind of the post–World War generation!—What?—Burning?—Oh, honey, don't let them burn, go take a look in the oven and I'll hold the wire! Heavens—I think she's hung up!

(*Dim out.*)
(*Legend on screen: "You Think I'm in Love with Continental Shoemakers?"*)
(*Before the stage is lighted, the violent voices of Tom and Amanda are heard.*)
(*They are quarreling behind the portieres. In front of them stands Laura with clenched hands and panicky expression.*)
(*A clear pool of light on her figure throughout this scene.*)

TOM: What in Christ's name am I—
AMANDA (*shrilly*): Don't you use that—
TOM: Supposed to do!
AMANDA: Expression! Not in my—
TOM: Ohhh!
AMANDA: Presence! Have you gone out of your senses?
TOM: I have, that's true, *driven* out!
AMANDA: What is the matter with you, you—big— big—IDIOT!
TOM: Look—I've got *no thing*, no single thing—
AMANDA: Lower your voice!
TOM: In my life here that I can call my own! Everything is—
AMANDA: Stop that shouting!
TOM: Yesterday you confiscated my books! You had the nerve to—
AMANDA: I took that horrible novel back to the library—yes! That hideous book by that insane Mr. Lawrence. (*Tom laughs wildly.*) I cannot control the output of diseased minds or people who cater to them—(*Tom laughs still more wildly.*) BUT I WON'T ALLOW SUCH FILTH BROUGHT INTO MY HOUSE! No, no, no, no, no!
TOM: House, house! Who pays rent on it, who makes a slave of himself to—
AMANDA (*fairly screeching*): Don't you DARE to—
TOM: No, no, *I* mustn't say things! *I've* got to just—
AMANDA: Let me tell you—
TOM: I don't want to hear any more! (*He tears the portieres open. The upstage area is lit with a turgid smoky red glow.*)

(*Amanda's hair is in metal curlers and she wears a very old bathrobe, much too large for her slight figure, a relic of the faithless Mr. Wingfield.*)
(*An upright typewriter and a wild disarray of manuscripts are on the dropleaf table. The quarrel was probably precipitated by Amanda's interruption of his creative labor. A chair lying overthrown on the floor.*)
(*Their gesticulating shadows are cast on the ceiling by the fiery glow.*)

AMANDA: You *will* hear more, you—
TOM: No, I won't hear more, I'm going out!
AMANDA: You come right back in—

TOM: Out, out out! Because I'm—

AMANDA: Come back here, Tom Wingfield! I'm not through talking to you!

TOM: Oh, go—

LAURA (*desperately*): Tom!

AMANDA: You're going to listen, and no more insolence from you! I'm at the end of my patience! (*He comes back toward her.*)

TOM: What do you think I'm at? Aren't I supposed to have any patience to reach the end of, Mother? I know, I know. It seems unimportant to you, what I'm *doing*—what I *want* to do—having a little *difference* between them! You don't think that—

AMANDA: I think you've been doing things that you're ashamed of. That's why you act like this. I don't believe that you go every night to the movies. Nobody goes to the movies night after night. Nobody in their right minds goes to the movies as often as you pretend to. People don't go to the movies at nearly midnight, and movies don't let out at two A.M. Come in stumbling. Muttering to yourself like a maniac! You get three hours' sleep and then go to work. Oh, I can picture the way you're doing down there. Moping, doping, because you're in no condition.

TOM (*wildly*): No, I'm in no condition!

AMANDA: What right have you got to jeopardize your job? Jeopardize the security of us all? How do you think we'd manage if you were—

TOM: Listen! You think I'm crazy *about* the *warehouse*? (*He bends fiercely toward her slight figure.*) You think I'm in love with the Continental Shoemakers? You think I want to spend fifty-five *years* down there in that—*celotex interior!* with—*fluorescent—tubes!* Look! I'd rather somebody picked up a crowbar and battered out my brains—than go back mornings! I *go!* Every time you come in yelling that God damn "*Rise and Shine!*" "*Rise and Shine!*" I say to myself, "*How lucky dead* people are!" But I get up. I *go!* For sixty-five dollars a month I give up all that I dream of doing and being *ever!* And you say self—*self's* all I ever think of. Why, listen, if self is what I thought of, Mother, I'd be where he is— GONE! (*Pointing to father's picture.*) As far as the system of transportation reaches! (*He starts past her. She grabs his arm.*) Don't grab at me, Mother!

AMANDA: Where are you going?

TOM: I'm going to the *movies!*

AMANDA: I don't believe that lie!

TOM (*Crouching toward her, overtowering her tiny figure. She backs away, gasping.*): I'm going to opium dens! Yes, opium dens, dens of vice and criminals' hangouts, Mother. I've joined the Hogan gang, I'm a hired assassin, I carry a tommy-gun in a violin case! I run a string of cathouses in the Valley! They call me Killer, Killer Wingfield, I'm leading a double life, a simple, honest warehouse worker by day, by night, a dynamic *czar* of the *underworld, Mother.* I go to gambling casinos, I spin away fortunes on the roulette table! I wear a patch over one eye and a false mustache, sometimes I put on green whiskers. On those occasions they call me—*El Diablo!* Oh, I could tell you things to make you sleepless! My enemies plan to dynamite this place. They're going to blow us all sky-high some night! I'll be glad, very happy, and so will you! You'll go up, up on a broomstick, over Blue Mountain with seventeen gentlemen callers! You ugly—babbling old—*witch*.... (*He goes through a series of violent, clumsy movements, seizing his overcoat, lunging to the door, pulling it fiercely open. The women watch him, aghast. His arm catches in the sleeve of the coat as he struggles to pull it on. For a moment he is pinioned by the bulky garment. With an outraged groan he tears the coat off again, splitting the shoulders of it, and hurls it across the room. It strikes against the shelf of Laura's glass collection, there is a tinkle of shattering glass. Laura cries out as if wounded.*)

(*Music legend: "The Glass Menagerie."*)

LAURA (*shrilly*): My glass!—menagerie.... (*She covers her face and turns away.*)

(*But Amanda is still stunned and stupefied by the "ugly witch" so that she barely notices this occurrence. Now she recovers her speech.*)

AMANDA (*in an awful voice*): I won't speak to you— until you apologize! (*She crosses through portieres and draws them together behind her. Tom is left with Laura. Laura clings weakly to the mantel with her face averted. Tom stares at her stupidly for a moment. Then he crosses to shelf. Drops awkwardly to his knees to collect the fallen glass, glancing at Laura as if he would speak but couldn't.*)

(*"The Glass Menagerie" steals in as the scene dims out.*)

SCENE 4

(*The interior is dark. Faint light in the alley.*)

(*A deep-voiced bell in a church is tolling the hour of five as the scene commences.*)

(*Tom appears at the top of the alley. After each solemn boom of the bell in the tower, he shakes a little noisemaker or rattle as if to express the tiny spasm of man in contrast to the sustained power and dignity of the Almighty. This and the unsteadiness of his advance make it evident that he has been drinking.*)

(*As he climbs the few steps to the fire escape landing light steals up inside. Laura appears in nightdress, observing Tom's empty bed in the front room.*)

(*Tom fishes in his pockets for the door key, removing a motley assortment of articles in the search, including a perfect shower of movie ticket stubs and an empty bottle. At last he finds the key, but just as he is about to insert it, it slips from his fingers. He strikes a match and crouches below the door.*)

TOM (*bitterly*): One crack—and it falls through!

(*Laura opens the door.*)

LAURA: Tom! Tom, what are you doing?

TOM: Looking for a door key.

LAURA: Where have you been all this time?

TOM: I have been to the movies.

LAURA: All this time at the movies?

TOM: There was a very long program. There was a Garbo picture and a Mickey Mouse and a travelogue and a newsreel and a preview of coming attractions. And there was an organ solo and a collection for the milk fund—simultaneously—which ended up in a terrible fight between a fat lady and an usher!

LAURA (*innocently*): Did you have to stay through everything?

TOM: Of course! And, oh, I forgot! There was a big stage show! The headliner on this stage show was Malvolio the Magician. He performed wonderful tricks, many of them, such as pouring water back and forth between pitchers. First it turned to wine and then it turned to beer and then it turned to whiskey. I know it was whiskey it finally turned into because he needed somebody to come up out of the audience to help him, and I came up—both shows! It was Kentucky Straight Bourbon. A very generous fellow, he gave souvenirs. (*He pulls from his back pocket a shimmering rainbow-colored scarf.*) He gave me this. This is his magic scarf. You can have it, Laura. You wave it over a canary cage and you get a bowl of goldfish. You wave it over the goldfish bowl and they fly away canaries. . . . But the wonderfullest trick of all was the coffin trick. We nailed him into a coffin and he got out of the coffin without removing one nail. (*He has come inside.*) There is a trick that would come in handy for me—get me out of this 2 by 4 situation! (*Flops onto bed and starts removing shoes.*)

LAURA: Tom—Shhh!

TOM: What you shushing me for?

LAURA: You'll wake up Mother.

TOM: Goody, goody! Pay 'er back for all those "Rise an' Shines." (*Lies down, groaning.*) You know it don't take much intelligence to get yourself into a nailed-up coffin, Laura. But who in hell ever got himself out of one without removing one nail?

(*As if in answer, the father's grinning photograph lights up.*)

(*Scene dims out.*)

(*Immediately following: The church bell is heard striking six. At the sixth stroke the alarm clock goes off in Amanda's room, and after a few moments we hear her calling: "Rise and Shine! Rise and Shine! Laura, go tell your brother to rise and shine!"*)

TOM (*sitting up slowly*): I'll rise—but I won't shine.

(*The light increases.*)

AMANDA: Laura, tell your brother his coffee is ready.

(*Laura slips into front room.*)

LAURA: Tom! it's nearly seven. Don't make Mother nervous. (*He stares at her stupidly. Beseechingly.*) Tom, speak to Mother this morning. Make up with her, apologize, speak to her!

TOM: She won't to me. It's her that started not speaking.

LAURA: If you just say you're sorry she'll start speaking.

TOM: Her not speaking—is that such a tragedy?

LAURA: Please—please!

AMANDA (*calling from kitchenette*): Laura, are you going to do what I asked you to do, or do I have to get dressed and go out myself?

LAURA: Going, going—soon as I get on my coat! (*She pulls on a shapeless felt hat with nervous, jerky movement, pleadingly glancing at Tom. Rushes awkwardly for coat. The coat is one of Amanda's, inaccurately made over, the sleeves too short for Laura.*) Butter and what else?

AMANDA (*entering upstage*): Just butter. Tell them to charge it.

LAURA: Mother, they make such faces when I do that.

AMANDA: Sticks and stones may break my bones, but the expression on Mr. Garfinkel's face won't harm us! Tell your brother his coffee is getting cold.

LAURA (*at door*): Do what I asked you, will you, will you, Tom?

(*He looks sullenly away.*)

AMANDA: Laura, go now or just don't go at all!

LAURA (*rushing out*): Going—going! (*A second later she cries out. Tom springs up and crosses to the door. Amanda rushes anxiously in. Tom opens the door.*)

TOM: Laura?

LAURA: I'm all right. I slipped, but I'm all right.

AMANDA (*peering anxiously after her*): If anyone breaks a leg on those fire escape steps, the landlord ought to be sued for every cent he possesses! (*She shuts door. Remembers she isn't speaking and returns to other room.*)

(*As Tom enters listlessly for his coffee, she turns her back to him and stands rigidly facing the window on the gloomy gray vault of the areaway. Its light on her face with its aged but childish features is cruelly sharp, satirical as a Daumier print.*)

(*Music under: "Ave Maria."*)

(*Tom glances sheepishly but sullenly at her averted figure and slumps at the table. The coffee is scalding hot; he sips it and gasps and spits it back in the cup. At his gasp, Amanda catches her breath and half turns. Then catches herself and turns back to window.*)

(*Tom blows on his coffee, glancing sidewise at his mother. She clears her throat. Tom clears his. He starts to rise. Sinks back down again, scratches his head, clears his throat again. Amanda coughs. Tom raises his cup in both hands to blow on it, his eyes staring over the rim of it at his mother for several moments. Then he slowly sets the cup down and awkwardly and hesitantly rises from the chair.*)

TOM (*hoarsely*): Mother. I—I apologize. Mother.

(*Amanda draws a quick, shuddering breath. Her face*)

works grotesquely. She breaks into childlike tears.)
I'm sorry for what I said, for everything that I said, I
didn't mean it.

AMANDA (*sobbingly*): My devotion has made me a
witch and so I make myself hateful to my children!

TOM: *No, you don't.*

AMANDA: I worry so much, don't sleep, it makes me
nervous!

TOM (*gently*): I understand that.

AMANDA: I've had to put up a solitary battle all these
years. But you're my right-hand bower! Don't fall
down, don't fail!

TOM (*gently*): I try, Mother.

AMANDA (*with great enthusiasm*): Try and you will SUC-
CEED! (*The notion makes her breathless.*) Why,
you—you're just *full* of natural endowments! Both
of my children—they're *unusual* children! Don't you
think I know it? I'm so—*proud!* Happy and—feel
I've—so much to be thankful for but—Promise me
one thing, son!

TOM: What, Mother?

AMANDA: Promise, son, you'll—never be a drunkard!

TOM (*turns to her grinning*): I will never be a drunkard,
Mother.

AMANDA: That's what frightened me so, that you'd be
drinking! Eat a bowl of Purina!

TOM: Just coffee, Mother.

AMANDA: Shredded wheat biscuit?

TOM: No, no, Mother, just coffee.

AMANDA: You can't put in a day's work on an empty
stomach. You've got ten minutes—don't gulp!
Drinking too-hot liquids makes cancer of the stomach. . . . Put cream in.

TOM: No, thank you.

AMANDA: To cool it.

TOM: No! No, thank you, I want it black.

AMANDA: I know, but it's not good for you. We have
to do all that we can to build ourselves up. In these
trying times we live in, all that we have to cling to
is—each other. . . . That's why it's so important to—
Tom, I—I sent out your sister so I could discuss
something with you. If you hadn't spoken I would
have spoken to you. (*Sits down.*)

TOM (*gently*): What is it, Mother, that you want to
discuss?

AMANDA: *Laura!*

(*Tom puts his cup down slowly.*)
  (*Legend on screen: "Laura."*)
  (*Music: "The Glass Menagerie."*)

TOM:—Oh.—Laura . . .

AMANDA (*touching his sleeve*): You know how Laura is.
So quiet but—still water runs deep! She notices things
and I think she—broods about them. (*Tom looks up.*)
A few days ago I came in and she was crying.

TOM: What about?

AMANDA: You.

TOM: Me?

AMANDA: She has an idea that you're not happy here.

TOM: What gave her that idea?

AMANDA: What gives her any idea? However, you do act
strangely. I—I'm not criticizing, understand *that!* I
know your ambitions do not lie in the warehouse, that
like everybody in the whole wide world—you've had
to—make sacrifices, but—Tom—Tom—life's not
easy, it calls for—Spartan endurance! There's so many
things in my heart that I cannot describe to you! I've
never told you but I—*loved your father.* . . .

TOM (*gently*): I know that, Mother.

AMANDA: And you—when I see you taking after his
ways! Staying out late—and—well, you *had* been
drinking the night you were in that—terrifying condition! Laura says that you hate the apartment and
that you go out nights to get away from it! Is that
true, Tom?

TOM: No. You say there's so much in your heart that
you can't describe to me. That's true of me, too.
There's so much in my heart that I can't describe to
you! So let's respect each other's—

AMANDA: But, why—*why,* Tom—are you always so
restless? Where do you go to, nights?

TOM: I—go to the movies.

AMANDA: Why do you go to the movies so much, Tom?

TOM: I go to the movies because—I like adventure.
Adventure is something I don't have much of at
work, so I go to the movies.

LEFT: Laurette Taylor as Amanda in the original 1944 production of *The Glass Menagerie*. RIGHT: Julie Haydon as Laura. ABOVE: Jo Mielziner's drawing of the set for the original production of *The Glass Menagerie*.

AMANDA: But, Tom, you go to the movies *entirely* too *much!*

TOM: I like a lot of adventure.

(*Amanda looks baffled, then hurt. As the familiar inquisition resumes he becomes hard and impatient again. Amanda slips back into her querulous attitude toward him.*)

(*Image on screen: sailing vessel with Jolly Roger.°*)

AMANDA: Most young men find adventure in their careers.

TOM: Then most young men are not employed in a warehouse.

AMANDA: The world is full of young men employed in warehouses and offices and factories.

TOM: Do all of them find adventure in their careers?

AMANDA: They do or they do without it! Not everybody has a craze for adventure.

TOM: Man is by instinct a lover, a hunter, a fighter, and none of those instincts are given much play at the warehouse!

AMANDA: Man is by instinct! Don't quote instinct to me! Instinct is something that people have got away from! It belongs to animals! Christian adults don't want it!

TOM: What do Christian adults want, then, Mother?

AMANDA: Superior things! Things of the mind and the spirit! Only animals have to satisfy instincts! Surely your aims are somewhat higher than theirs! Than monkeys—pigs—

TOM: I reckon they're not.

AMANDA: You're joking. However, that isn't what I wanted to discuss.

TOM (*rising*): I haven't much time.

AMANDA (*pushing his shoulders*): Sit down.

TOM: You want me to punch in red at the warehouse, Mother?

AMANDA: You have five minutes. I want to talk about Laura.

(*Legend: "Plans and Provisions."*)

TOM: All right! What about Laura?

AMANDA: We have to be making plans and provisions for her. She's older than you, two years, and nothing has happened. She just drifts along doing nothing. It frightens me terribly how she just drifts along.

TOM: I guess she's the type that people call home girls.

AMANDA: There's no such type, and if there is, it's a pity! That is unless the home is hers, with a husband!

TOM: What?

AMANDA: Oh, I can see the handwriting on the wall as plain as I see the nose in front of my face! It's terrifying! More and more you remind me of your father! He was out all hours without explanation—Then *left! Good-bye!* And me with a bag to hold. I saw that letter you got from the Merchant Marine. I know what you're dreaming of. I'm not standing

here blindfolded. Very well, then. Then *do* it! But not till there's somebody to take your place.

TOM: What do you mean?

AMANDA: I mean that as soon as Laura has got somebody to take care of her, married, a home of her own, independent—why, then you'll be free to go wherever you please, on land, on sea, whichever way the wind blows you! But until that time you've got to look out for your sister. I don't say me because I'm old and don't matter! I say for your sister because she's young and dependent. I put her in business college—a dismal failure! Frightened her so it made her sick to her stomach. I took her over to the Young People's League at the church. Another fiasco. She spoke to nobody, nobody spoke to her. Now all she does is fool with those pieces of glass and play those worn-out records. What kind of a life is that for a girl to lead!

TOM: What can I do about it?

AMANDA: Overcome selfishness! Self, self, self is all that you ever think of! (*Tom springs up and crosses to get his coat. It is ugly and bulky. He pulls on a cap with earmuffs.*) Where is your muffler? Put your wool muffler on! (*He snatches it angrily from the closet and tosses it around his neck and pulls both ends tight.*) Tom! I haven't said what I had in mind to ask you.

TOM: I'm too late to—

AMANDA (*catching his arms—very importunately. Then shyly*): Down at the warehouse, aren't there some—nice young men?

TOM: No!

AMANDA: There *must* be—*some*...

TOM: Mother—

(*Gesture.*)

AMANDA: Find out one that's clean-living—doesn't drink and—ask him out for sister!

TOM: What?

AMANDA: For *sister!* To *meet!* Get *acquainted!*

TOM (*stamping to door*): Oh, my go-osh!

AMANDA: Will you? (*He opens door. Imploringly.*) Will you? (*He starts down.*) Will you? Will you, dear?

TOM (*calling back*): YES!

(*Amanda closes the door hesitantly and with a troubled but faintly hopeful expression.*)
(*Screen image: glamor magazine cover.*)
(*Spot° Amanda at phone.*)

AMANDA: Ella Cartwright? This is Amanda Wingfield! How are you, honey? How is that kidney condition? (*Count five.*) Horrors! (*Count five.*) You're a Christian martyr, yes, honey, that's what you are, a Christian martyr! Well, I just happened to notice in my little red book that your subscription to the Companion has just run out! I knew that you wouldn't want to miss out on the wonderful serial starting in this new issue.

Jolly Roger: The black flag with white skull and crossbones used by pirates.

Spot: Spotlight.

It's by Bessie Mae Hopper, the first thing she's written since *Honeymoon for Three.* Wasn't that a strange and interesting story? Well, this one is even lovelier, I believe. It has a sophisticated society background. It's all about the horsey set on Long Island!

(*Fade out.*)

SCENE 5

(*Legend on screen "Annunciation." Fade with music.*)
    (*It is early dusk of a spring evening. Supper has just been finished in the Wingfield apartment. Amanda and Laura in light colored dresses are removing dishes from the table, in the upstage area, which is shadowy, their movements formalized almost as a dance or ritual, their moving forms as pale and silent as moths.*)
    (*Tom, in white shirt and trousers, rises from the table and crosses toward the fire escape.*)

AMANDA (*as he passes her*): Son, will you do me a favor?
TOM: What?
AMANDA: Comb your hair! You look so pretty when your hair is combed! (*Tom slouches on sofa with evening paper. Enormous caption "Franco Triumphs."*) There is only one respect in which I would like you to emulate your father.
TOM: What respect is that?
AMANDA: The care he always took of his appearance. He never allowed himself to look untidy. (*He throws down the paper and crosses to fire escape.*) Where are you going?
TOM: I'm going out to smoke.
AMANDA: You smoke too much. A pack a day at fifteen cents a pack. How much would that amount to in a month? Thirty times fifteen is how much, Tom? Figure it out and you will be astounded at what you could save. Enough to give you a night school course in accounting at Washington U! Just think what a wonderful thing that would be for you, son!

(*Tom is unmoved by the thought.*)

TOM: I'd rather smoke. (*He steps out on landing, letting the screen door slam.*)
AMANDA (*sharply*): I know! That's the tragedy of it. . . .
    (*Alone, she turns to look at her husband's picture.*)

(*Dance music: "All the World is Waiting for the Sunrise!"*)

TOM (*to the audience*): Across the alley from us was the Paradise Dance Hall. On evenings in spring the windows and doors were open and the music came outdoors. Sometimes the lights were turned out except for a large glass sphere that hung from the ceiling. It would turn slowly about and filter the dusk with delicate rainbow colors. Then the orchestra played a waltz or a tango, something that had a slow and sensuous rhythm. Couples would come outside, to the relative privacy of the alley. You could see them kissing behind ash-pits and telephone poles. This was the compensation for lives that passed like mine, without any change or adventure. Adventure and change were imminent in this year. They were waiting around the corner for all these kids. Suspended in the mist over Berchtesgaden, caught in the folds of Chamberlain's umbrella—In Spain there was Guernica!° But here there was only hot swing music and liquor, dance halls, bars, and movies, and sex that hung in the gloom like a chandelier and flooded the world with brief, deceptive rainbows. . . . All the world was waiting for bombardments!

(*Amanda turns from the picture and comes outside.*)

AMANDA (*sighing*): A fire escape landing's a poor excuse for a porch. (*She spreads a newspaper on a step and sits down, gracefully and demurely as if she were settling into a swing on a Mississippi veranda.*) What are you looking at?
TOM: The moon.
AMANDA: Is there a moon this evening?
TOM: It's rising over Garfinkel's Delicatessen.
AMANDA: So it is! A little silver slipper of a moon. Have you made a wish on it yet?
TOM: Um-hum.
AMANDA: What did you wish for?
TOM: That's a secret.
AMANDA: A secret, huh? Well, I won't tell mine either. I will be just as mysterious as you.
TOM: I bet I can guess what yours is.
AMANDA: Is my head so transparent?
TOM: You're not a sphinx.
AMANDA: No, I don't have secrets. I'll tell you what I wished for on the moon. Success and happiness for my precious children! I wish for that whenever there's a moon, and when there isn't a moon, I wish for it, too.
TOM: I thought perhaps you wished for a gentleman caller.
AMANDA: Why do you say that?
TOM: Don't you remember asking me to fetch one?
AMANDA: I remember suggesting that it would be nice for your sister if you brought home some nice young man from the warehouse. I think I've made that suggestion more than once.
TOM: Yes, you have made it repeatedly.
AMANDA: Well?
TOM: We are going to have one.
AMANDA: *What?*
TOM: A gentleman caller!

(*The annunciation is celebrated with music.*)
    (*Amanda rises.*)
    (*Image on screen: caller with bouquet.*)

Berchtesgaden . . . Chamberlain . . . Guernica: All references to the approaches of World War II in Europe. Berchtesgaden was Hitler's summer home; Neville Chamberlain was the prime minister of England who signed the Munich Pact, which was regarded as a capitulation to Hitler; and the Spanish town Guernica was destroyed by German bombs during the Spanish Civil War in the late 1930s.

AMANDA: You mean you have asked some nice young man to come over?

TOM: Yep. I've asked him to dinner.

AMANDA: You really did?

TOM: I did!

AMANDA: You did, and did he—*accept?*

TOM: He did!

AMANDA: Well, well—well, well! That's—lovely!

TOM: I thought that you would be pleased.

AMANDA: It's definite, then?

TOM: Very definite.

AMANDA: Soon?

TOM: Very soon.

AMANDA: For heaven's sake, stop putting on and tell me some things, will you?

TOM: What things do you want me to tell you?

AMANDA: *Naturally* I would like to know when he's *coming!*

TOM: He's coming tomorrow.

AMANDA: *Tomorrow?*

TOM: Yep. Tomorrow.

AMANDA: But, Tom!

TOM: Yes, Mother?

AMANDA: Tomorrow gives me no time!

TOM: Time for what?

AMANDA: Preparations! Why didn't you phone me at once, as soon as you asked him, the minute that he accepted? Then, don't you see, I could have been getting ready!

TOM: You don't have to make any fuss.

AMANDA: Oh, Tom, Tom, Tom, of course I have to make a fuss! I want things nice, not sloppy! Not thrown together. I'll certainly have to do some fast thinking, won't I?

TOM: I don't see why you have to think at all.

AMANDA: You just don't know. We can't have a gentleman caller in a pigsty! All my wedding silver has to be polished, the monogrammed table linen ought to be laundered! The windows have to be washed and fresh curtains put up. And how about clothes? We have to *wear* something, don't we?

TOM: Mother, this boy is no one to make a fuss over!

AMANDA: Do you realize he's the first young man we've introduced to your sister? It's terrible, dreadful, disgraceful that poor little sister has never received a single gentleman caller! Tom, come inside! (*She opens the screen door.*)

TOM: What for?

AMANDA: I want to ask you some things.

TOM: If you're going to make such a fuss, I'll call it off, I'll tell him not to come.

AMANDA: You certainly won't do anything of the kind. Nothing offends people worse than broken engagements. It simply means I'll have to work like a Turk! We won't be brilliant, but we'll pass inspection. Come on inside. (*Tom follows, groaning.*) Sit down.

TOM: Any particular place you would like me to sit?

AMANDA: Thank heavens I've got that new sofa! I'm also making payments on a floor lamp I'll have sent out! And put the chintz covers on, they'll brighten things up! Of course I'd hoped to have these walls repapered. . . . What is the young man's name?

TOM: His name is O'Connor.

AMANDA: That, of course, means fish°—tomorrow is Friday!° I'll have that salmon loaf—with Durkee's dressing! What does he do? He works at the warehouse?

TOM: Of course! How else would I—

AMANDA: Tom, he—doesn't drink?

TOM: Why do you ask me that?

AMANDA: Your father *did!*

TOM: Don't get started on that!

AMANDA: He *does* drink, then?

TOM: Not that I know of!

AMANDA: Make sure, be certain! The last thing I want for my daughter's a boy who drinks!

TOM: Aren't you being a little premature? Mr. O'Connor has not yet appeared on the scene!

AMANDA: But will tomorrow. To meet your sister, and what do I know about his character? Nothing! Old maids are better off than wives of drunkards!

TOM: Oh, my God!

AMANDA: Be still!

TOM (*leaning forward to whisper*): Lots of fellows meet girls whom they don't marry!

AMANDA: Oh, talk sensibly, Tom—and don't be sarcastic! (*She has gotten a hairbrush.*)

TOM: What are you doing?

AMANDA: I'm brushing that cowlick down! What is this young man's position at the warehouse?

TOM (*submitting grimly to the brush and the interrogation*): This young man's position is that of a shipping clerk, Mother.

AMANDA: Sounds to me like a fairly responsible job, the sort of a job *you* would be in if you just had more *get-up*. What is his salary? Have you got any idea.

TOM: I would judge it to be approximately eighty-five dollars a month.

AMANDA: Well—not princely, but—

TOM: Twenty more than I make.

AMANDA: Yes, how well I know! But for a family man, eighty-five dollars a month is not much more than you can just get by on. . . .

TOM: Yes, but Mr. O'Connor is not a family man.

AMANDA: He might be, mightn't he? Some time in the future?

TOM: I see. Plans and provisions.

AMANDA: You are the only young man that I know of who ignores the fact that the future becomes the present, the present the past, and the past turns into everlasting regret if you don't plan for it!

TOM: I will think that over and see what I can make of it.

AMANDA: Don't be supercilious with your mother! Tell me some more about this—what do you call him?

TOM: James D. O'Connor. The D. is for Delaney.

---

fish . . . Friday: Until the 1960s Catholics were prohibited from eating meat on Fridays.

AMANDA: Irish on *both* sides! *Gracious!* And doesn't drink?

TOM: Shall I call him up and ask him right this minute?

AMANDA: The only way to find out about those things is to make discreet inquiries at the proper moment. When I was a girl in Blue Mountain and it was suspected that a young man drank, the girl whose attentions he had been receiving, if any girl *was,* would sometimes speak to the minister of his church, or rather her father would if her father was living, and sort of feel him out on the young man's character. That is the way such things are discreetly handled to keep a young woman from making a tragic mistake!

TOM: Then how did you happen to make a tragic mistake?

AMANDA: That innocent look of your father's had everyone fooled! He *smiled*—the world was *enchanted!* No girl can do worse than put herself at the mercy of a handsome appearance! I hope that Mr. O'Connor is not too good-looking.

TOM: No, he's not too good-looking. He's covered with freckles and hasn't too much of a nose.

AMANDA: He's not right-down homely, though?

TOM: Not right-down homely. Just medium homely, I'd say.

AMANDA: Character's what to look for in a man.

TOM: That's what I've always said, Mother.

AMANDA: You've never said anything of the kind and I suspect you would never give it a thought.

TOM: Don't be suspicious of me.

AMANDA: At least I hope he's the type that's up and coming.

TOM: I think he really goes in for self-improvement.

AMANDA: What reason have you to think so?

TOM: He goes to night school.

AMANDA (*beaming*): Splendid! What does he do, I mean study?

TOM: Radio engineering and public speaking!

AMANDA: Then he has visions of being advanced in the world! Any young man who studies public speaking is aiming to have an executive job some day! And radio engineering? A thing for the future! Both of these facts are very illuminating. Those are the sort of things that a mother should know concerning any young man who comes to call on her daughter. Seriously or—not.

TOM: One little warning. He doesn't know about Laura. I didn't let on that we had dark ulterior motives. I just said, why don't you come have dinner with us? He said okay and that was the whole conversation.

AMANDA: I bet it was! You're eloquent as an oyster. However, he'll know about Laura when he gets here. When he sees how lovely and sweet and pretty she is, he'll thank his lucky stars he was asked to dinner.

TOM: Mother, you mustn't expect too much of Laura.

AMANDA: What do you mean?

TOM: Laura seems all those things to you and me because she's ours and we love her. We don't even notice she's crippled anymore.

AMANDA: Don't say crippled! You know that I never allow that word to be used!

TOM: But face facts, Mother. She is and—that's not all—

AMANDA: What do you mean not all?

TOM: Laura is very different from other girls.

AMANDA: I think the difference is all to her advantage.

TOM: Not quite all—in the eyes of others—strangers—she's terribly shy and lives in a world of her own and those things make her seem a little peculiar to people outside the house.

AMANDA: Don't say peculiar.

TOM: Face the facts. She is.

(*The dance-hall music changes to a tango that has a minor and somewhat ominous tone.*)

AMANDA: In what way is she peculiar—may I ask?

TOM (*gently*): She lives in a world of her own—a world of—little glass ornaments, Mother.... (*Gets up. Amanda remains holding brush, looking at him, troubled.*) She plays old phonograph records and—that's about all—(*He glances at himself in the mirror and crosses to door.*)

AMANDA (*sharply*): Where are you going?

TOM: I'm going to the movies. (*Out screen door.*)

AMANDA: Not to the movies, every night to the movies! (*Follows quickly to screen door.*) I don't believe you always go to the movies! (*He is gone. Amanda looks worriedly after him for a moment. Then vitality and optimism return and she turns from the door. Crossing to portieres.*) Laura! Laura! (*Laura answers from kitchenette.*)

LAURA: Yes, Mother.

AMANDA: Let those dishes go and come in front! (*Laura appears with dish towel. Gaily.*) Laura, come here and make a wish on the moon!

LAURA (*entering*): Moon—moon?

AMANDA: A little silver slipper of a moon. Look over your left shoulder, Laura, and make a wish! (*Laura looks faintly puzzled as if called out of sleep. Amanda seizes her shoulders and turns her at an angle by the door.*) Now! Now, darling, *wish!*

LAURA: What shall I wish for, Mother?

AMANDA (*her voice trembling and her eyes suddenly filling with tears*): Happiness! Good Fortune!

(*The violin rises and the stage dims out.*)

SCENE 6

(*Image: high school hero.*)

TOM: And so the following evening I brought Jim home to dinner. I had known Jim slightly in high school. In high school Jim was a hero. He had tremendous Irish good nature and vitality with the scrubbed and polished look of white chinaware. He seemed to move in a continual spotlight. He was a star in basketball, captain of the debating club, president of the senior class and the glee club and he sang the male lead in the annual light operas. He was always running or bounding, never just walking. He seemed always at the point of defeating the law of gravity. He was shooting with such velocity through his adolescence that you would logically expect him to arrive at nothing short of the White House by the time he was thirty. But Jim apparently ran into more interference after his graduation from Soldan. His speed had definitely slowed. Six years after he left high school he was holding a job that wasn't much better than mine.

(*Image: clerk.*)

He was the only one at the warehouse with whom I was on friendly terms. I was valuable to him as someone who could remember his former glory, who had seen him win basketball games and the silver cup in debating. He knew of my secret practice of retiring to a cabinet of the washroom to work on poems when business was slack in the warehouse. He called me Shakespeare. And while the other boys in the warehouse regarded me with suspicious hostility, Jim took a humorous attitude toward me. Gradually his attitude affected the others, their hostility wore off and they also began to smile at me as people smile at an oddly fashioned dog who trots across their path at some distance.

   I knew that Jim and Laura had known each other at Soldan, and I had heard Laura speak admiringly of his voice. I didn't know if Jim remembered her or not. In high school Laura had been as unobtrusive as Jim had been astonishing. If he did remember Laura, it was not as my sister, for when I asked him to dinner, he grinned and said, "You know, Shakespeare, I never thought of you as having folks!"
   He was about to discover that I did. . . .

(*Light up stage.*)
(*Legend on screen: "The Accent of a Coming Foot."*)
(*Friday evening. It is about five o'clock of a late spring evening which comes "scattering poems in the sky."*)
(*A delicate lemony light is in the Wingfield apartment.*)
(*Amanda has worked like a Turk in preparation for the gentleman caller. The results are astonishing. The new floor lamp with its rose-silk shade is in place, a colored paper lantern conceals the broken light fixture in the ceiling, new billowing white curtains are at the windows, chintz covers are on chairs and sofa, a pair of new sofa pillows make their initial appearance.*)
(*Open boxes and tissue paper are scattered on the floor.*)
(*Laura stands in the middle with lifted arms while Amanda crouches before her, adjusting the hem of the new dress, devout and ritualistic. The dress is colored and designed by memory. The arrangement of Laura's hair is changed; it is softer and more becoming. A fragile, unearthly prettiness has come out in Laura: she is like a piece of translucent glass touched by light, given a momentary radiance, not actual, not lasting.*)

AMANDA (*impatiently*): Why are you trembling?
LAURA: Mother, you've made me so nervous!
AMANDA: How have I made you nervous?
LAURA: By all this fuss! You make it seem so important!
AMANDA: I don't understand you, Laura. You couldn't be satisfied with just sitting home, and yet whenever I try to arrange something for you, you seem to resist it. (*She gets up.*) Now take a look at yourself. No, wait! Wait just a moment—I have an idea!
LAURA: What is it now?

(*Amanda produces two powder puffs which she wraps in handkerchiefs and stuffs in Laura's bosom.*)

LAURA: Mother, what are you doing?
AMANDA: They call them "Gay Deceivers"!
LAURA: I won't wear them!
AMANDA: You will!
LAURA: Why should I?
AMANDA: Because, to be painfully honest, your chest is flat.
LAURA: You make it seem like we were setting a trap.
AMANDA: All pretty girls are a trap, a pretty trap, and men expect them to be. (*Legend: "A Pretty Trap."*) Now look at yourself, young lady. This is the prettiest you will ever be! I've got to fix myself now! You're going to be surprised by your mother's appearance! (*She crosses through portieres, humming gaily.*)

(*Laura moves slowly to the long mirror and stares solemnly at herself.*)
   (*A wind blows the white curtains inward in a slow, graceful motion and with a faint, sorrowful sighing.*)

AMANDA (*offstage*): It isn't dark enough yet. (*She turns slowly before the mirror with a troubled look.*)

(*Legend on screen: "This Is My Sister: Celebrate Her with Strings!" Music.*)

AMANDA (*laughing, off*): I'm going to show you something. I'm going to make a spectacular appearance!
LAURA: What is it, Mother?
AMANDA: Possess your soul in patience—you will see! Something I've resurrected from that old trunk! Styles haven't changed so terribly much after all. . . . (*She parts the portieres.*) Now just look at your mother! (*She wears a girlish frock of yellowed voile with a blue silk sash. She carries a bunch of jonquils—the legend of her youth is nearly revived. Feverishly.*) This is the dress in which I led the cotillion. Won the cakewalk twice at Sunset Hill, wore one spring to the Governor's ball in Jackson! See how I sashayed around the ballroom, Laura? (*She raises her skirt and does a mincing step around the room.*) I wore it on Sundays for my gentlemen callers! I had it on the day I met your father—I had malaria fever all that spring. The change of climate from East Tennessee to the Delta—weakened resistance—I had a little temperature all the time—not enough to be serious—just enough to make me restless and giddy! Invitations poured in—parties all over the Delta!—"Stay in bed," said Mother, "you have

fever!"—but I just wouldn't.—I took quinine but kept on going, going!—Evenings, dances!—Afternoons, long, long rides! Picnics—lovely!—So lovely, that country in May.—All lacy with dogwood, literally flooded with jonquils!—That was the spring I had the craze for jonquils. Jonquils became an absolute obsession. Mother said, "Honey, there's no more room for jonquils." And still I kept on bringing in more jonquils. Whenever, wherever I saw them, I'd say, "Stop! Stop! I see jonquils!" I made the young men help me gather the jonquils! It was a joke, Amanda and her jonquils! Finally there were no more vases to hold them, every available space was filled with jonquils. No vases to hold them? All right, I'll hold them myself! And then I—(*She stops in front of the picture. Music.*) met your father! Malaria fever and jonquils and then—this—boy.... (*She switches on the rose-colored lamp.*) I hope they get here before it starts to rain. (*She crosses upstage and places the jonquils in bowl on table.*) I gave your brother a little extra change so he and Mr. O'Connor could take the service car home.

LAURA (*with altered look*): What did you say his name was?

AMANDA: O'Connor.

LAURA: What is his first name?

AMANDA: I don't remember. Oh, yes, I do. It was—Jim!

(*Laura sways slightly and catches hold of a chair.*)
(*Legend on screen: "Not Jim!"*)

LAURA (*faintly*): Not—Jim!

AMANDA: Yes, that was it, it was Jim! I've never known a Jim that wasn't nice!

(*Music: ominous.*)

LAURA: Are you sure his name is Jim O'Connor?

AMANDA: Yes. Why?

LAURA: Is he the one that Tom used to know in high school?

AMANDA: He didn't say so. I think he just got to know him at the warehouse.

LAURA: There was a Jim O'Connor we both knew in high school—(*Then, with effort.*) If that is the one that Tom is bringing to dinner—you'll have to excuse me, I won't come to the table.

AMANDA: What sort of nonsense is this?

LAURA: You asked me once if I'd ever liked a boy. Don't you remember I showed you this boy's picture?

AMANDA: You mean the boy you showed me in the yearbook?

LAURA: Yes, that boy.

AMANDA: Laura, Laura, were you in love with that boy?

LAURA: I don't know, Mother. All I know is I couldn't sit at the table if it was him!

AMANDA: It won't be him! It isn't the least bit likely. But whether it is or not, you will come to the table. You will not be excused.

LAURA: I'll have to be, Mother.

AMANDA: I don't intend to humor your silliness, Laura. I've had too much from you and your brother, both!

So just sit down and compose yourself till they come. Tom has forgotten his key so you'll have to let them in, when they arrive.

LAURA (*panicky*): Oh, Mother—*you* answer the door!

AMANDA (*lightly*): I'll be in the kitchen—busy!

LAURA: Oh, Mother, please answer the door, don't make me do it!

AMANDA (*crossing into kitchenette*): I've got to fix the dressing for the salmon. Fuss, fuss—silliness!—over a gentleman caller!

(*Door swings shut. Laura is left alone.*)
(*Legend: "Terror!"*)
(*She utters a low moan and turns off the lamp—sits stiffly on the edge of the sofa, knotting her fingers together.*)
(*Legend on screen: "The Opening of a Door!"*)
(*Tom and Jim appear on the fire escape steps and climb to landing. Hearing their approach, Laura rises with a panicky gesture. She retreats to the portieres.*)
(*The doorbell. Laura catches her breath and touches her throat. Low drums.*)

AMANDA (*calling*): Laura, sweetheart! The door!

(*Laura stares at it without moving.*)

JIM: I think we just beat the rain.

TOM: Uh-huh. (*He rings again, nervously. Jim whistles and fishes for a cigarette.*)

AMANDA (*very, very gaily*): Laura, that is your brother and Mr. O'Connor! Will you let them in, darling?

(*Laura crosses toward kitchenette door.*)

LAURA (*breathlessly*): Mother—you go to the door!

(*Amanda steps out of kitchenette and stares furiously at Laura. She points imperiously at the door.*)

LAURA: Please, please!

AMANDA (*in a fierce whisper*): What is the matter with you, you silly thing?

LAURA (*desperately*): Please, you answer it, *please!*

AMANDA: I told you I wasn't going to humor you, Laura. Why have you chosen this moment to lose your mind?

LAURA: Please, please, please, you go!

AMANDA: You'll have to go to the door because I can't!

LAURA (*despairingly*): I can't either!

AMANDA: *Why?*

LAURA: I'm *sick!*

AMANDA: I'm sick, too—of your nonsense! Why can't you and your brother be normal people? Fantastic whims and behavior! (*Tom gives a long ring.*) Preposterous goings on! Can you give me one reason—(*Calls out lyrically.*) COMING! JUST ONE SECOND!—why should you be afraid to open a door? Now you answer it, Laura!

LAURA: Oh, oh, oh... (*She returns through the portieres. Darts to the victrola and winds it frantically and turns it on.*)

AMANDA: Laura Wingfield, you march right to that door!

LAURA: Yes—yes, Mother!

(*A faraway, scratchy rendition of "Dardanella" softens the air and gives her strength to move through it. She slips to the door and draws it cautiously open.*)

(*Tom enters with the caller, Jim O'Connor.*)

Tom: Laura, this is Jim. Jim, this is my sister, Laura.

JIM (*stepping inside*): I didn't know that Shakespeare had a sister!

LAURA (*retreating stiff and trembling from the door*): How—how do you do?

JIM (*heartily extending his hand*): Okay!

(*Laura touches it hesitantly with hers.*)

JIM: Your hand's *cold*, Laura!

LAURA: Yes, well—I've been playing the victrola....

JIM: Must have been playing classical music on it! You ought to play a little hot swing music to warm you up!

LAURA: Excuse me—I haven't finished playing the victrola....

(*She turns awkwardly and hurries into the front room. She pauses a second by the victrola. Then catches her breath and darts through the portieres like a frightened deer.*)

JIM (*grinning*): What was the matter?

Tom: Oh—with Laura? Laura is—terribly shy.

JIM: Shy, huh? It's unusual to meet a shy girl nowadays. I don't believe you ever mentioned you had a sister.

Tom: Well, now you know. I have one. Here is the *Post Dispatch*. You want a piece of it?

JIM: Uh-huh.

Tom: What piece? The comics?

JIM: Sports! (*Glances at it.*) Ole Dizzy Dean is on his bad behavior.

Tom (*disinterest*): Yeah? (*Lights cigarette and crosses back to fire escape door.*)

JIM: Where are *you* going?

Tom: I'm going out on the terrace.

JIM (*goes after him*): You know, Shakespeare—I'm going to sell you a bill of goods!

Tom: What goods?

JIM: A course I'm taking.

Tom: Huh?

JIM: In public speaking! You and me, we're not the warehouse type.

Tom: Thanks—that's good news. But what has public speaking got to do with it?

JIM: It fits you for—executive positions!

Tom: Awww.

JIM: I tell you it's done a helluva lot for me.

(*Image: executive at desk.*)

Tom: In what respect?

JIM: In every! Ask yourself what is the difference between you an' me and men in the office down front? Brains?—No!—Ability?—No! Then what? Just one little thing—

TOM: What is that one little thing?

JIM: Primarily it amounts to—social poise! Being able to square up to people and hold your own on any social level!

AMANDA (*offstage*): Tom?

TOM: Yes, Mother?

AMANDA: Is that you and Mr. O'Connor?

TOM: Yes, Mother.

AMANDA: Well, you just make yourselves comfortable in there.

TOM: Yes, Mother.

AMANDA: Ask Mr. O'Connor if he would like to wash his hands.

JIM: Aw,—no—no—thank you—I took care of that at the warehouse. Tom—

TOM: Yes?

JIM: Mr. Mendoza was speaking to me about you.

TOM: Favorably?

JIM: What do you think?

TOM: Well—

JIM: You're going to be out of a job if you don't wake up.

TOM: I am waking up—

JIM: You show no signs.

TOM: The signs are interior.

(*Image on screen: the sailing vessel with Jolly Roger again.*)

TOM: I'm planning to change. (*He leans over the rail speaking with quiet exhilaration. The incandescent marquees and signs of the first-run movie houses light his face from across the alley. He looks like a voyager.*) I'm right at the point of committing myself to a future that doesn't include the warehouse and Mr. Mendoza or even a night school course in public speaking.

JIM: What are you gassing about?

TOM: I'm tired of the movies.

FAR LEFT: Amanda (Ruby Dee) and Laura (Tonia Rowe) in the 1989 Arena Stage production of *The Glass Menagerie*, directed by Tazewell Thompson. LEFT: Laura, Amanda, and Tom (Jonathan Earl Peck). RIGHT: Scene from *The Glass Menagerie*.

JIM: Movies!

TOM: Yes, movies! Look at them—(*A wave toward the marvels of Grand Avenue.*) All of those glamorous people—having adventures—hogging it all, gobbling the whole thing up! You know what happens? People go to the *movies* instead of *moving!* Hollywood characters are supposed to have all the adventures for everybody in America, while everybody in America sits in a dark room and watches them have them! Yes, until there's a war. That's when adventure becomes available to the masses! *Everyone's* dish, not only Gable's! Then the people in the dark room come out of the dark room to have some adventures themselves—Goody, goody!—It's our turn now, to go to the South Sea Island—to make a safari—to be exotic, far-off!—But I'm not patient. I don't want to wait till then. I'm tired of the *movies* and I am *about* to *move!*

JIM (*incredulously*): Move?

TOM: Yes.

JIM: When?

TOM: Soon!

JIM: Where? Where?

(*Theme three music seems to answer the question, while Tom thinks it over. He searches among his pockets.*)

TOM: I'm starting to boil inside. I know I seem dreamy, but inside—well, I'm boiling!—Whenever I pick up a shoe, I shudder a little thinking how short life is and what I am doing!—Whatever that means. I know it doesn't mean shoes—except as something to wear on a traveler's feet! (*Finds paper.*) Look—

JIM: What?

TOM: I'm a member.

JIM (*reading*): The Union of Merchant Seamen.

TOM: I paid my dues this month, instead of the light bill.

JIM: You will regret it when they turn the lights off.

TOM: I won't be here.

JIM: How about your mother?

TOM: I'm like my father. The bastard son of a bastard! See how he grins? And he's been absent going on sixteen years!

JIM: You're just talking, you drip. How does your mother feel about it?

TOM: Shhh!—Here comes Mother! Mother is not acquainted with my plans!

AMANDA (*enters portieres*): Where are you all?

TOM: On the terrace, Mother.

(*They start inside. She advances to them. Tom is distinctly shocked at her appearance. Even Jim blinks a little. He is making his first contact with girlish Southern vivacity and in spite of the night school course in public speaking is somewhat thrown off the beam by the unexpected outlay of social charm.*)

(*Certain responses are attempted by Jim but are swept aside by Amanda's gay laughter and chatter. Tom is embarrassed but after the first shock Jim reacts very warmly. Grins and chuckles, is altogether won over.*)

(*Image: Amanda as a girl.*)

AMANDA (*coyly smiling, shaking her girlish ringlets*): Well, well, well, so this is Mr. O'Connor. Introductions entirely unnecessary. I've heard so much about you from my boy. I finally said to him, Tom—good gracious!—why don't you bring this paragon to supper? I'd like to meet this nice young man at the warehouse!—Instead of just hearing him sing your praises so much! I don't know why my son is so standoffish—that's not Southern behavior! Let's sit down and—I think we could stand a little more air in here! Tom, leave the door open. I felt a nice fresh breeze a moment ago. Where has it gone to? Mmm, so warm already! And not quite summer, even. We're going to burn up when summer really gets started. However, we're having—we're having a very light supper. I think light things are better fo' this time of year. The same as light clothes are. Light clothes an' light food are what warm weather calls fo'. You know our blood gets so thick during th' winter—it takes a while fo' us to *adjust* ou'selves!—when the season changes . . . It's come so quick this year. I wasn't prepared. All of a sudden—heavens! Already summer!—I ran to the trunk an' pulled out this light dress—Terribly old! Historical almost! But feels so good—so good an' co-ol, y'know. . . .

TOM: Mother—

AMANDA: Yes, honey?

TOM: How about—supper?

AMANDA: Honey, you go ask Sister if supper is ready! You know that Sister is in full charge of supper! Tell her you hungry boys are waiting for it. (*To Jim.*) Have you met Laura?

JIM: She—

AMANDA: Let you in? Oh, good, you've met already! It's rare for a girl as sweet an' pretty as Laura to be domestic! But Laura is, thank heavens, not only pretty but also very domestic. I'm not at all. I never was a bit. I never could make a thing but angel food cake. Well, in the South we had so many servants. Gone, gone, gone. All vestiges of gracious living! Gone completely! I wasn't prepared for what the future brought me. All of my gentlemen callers were sons of planters and so of course I assumed that I would be married to one and raise my family on a large piece of land with plenty of servants. But man proposes—and woman accepts the proposal!—To vary that old, old saying a little bit—I married no planter! I married a man who worked for the telephone company!—That gallantly smiling gentleman over there! (*Points to the picture.*) A telephone man who—fell in love with long distance!—Now he travels and I don't even know where!—But what am I going on for about my—tribulations! Tell me yours—I hope you don't have any! Tom?

TOM (*returning*): Yes, Mother?

AMANDA: Is supper nearly ready?

TOM: It looks to me like supper is on the table.

AMANDA: Let me look—(*She rises prettily and looks through portieres.*) Oh, lovely!—But where is Sister?

TOM: Laura is not feeling well and she says that she thinks she'd better not come to the table.

AMANDA: What?—Nonsense!—Laura? Oh, Laura!

LAURA (*offstage, faintly*): Yes, Mother.

AMANDA: You really must come to the table. We won't be seated until you come to the table! Come in, Mr. O'Connor. You sit over there, and I'll—Laura? Laura Wingfield! You're keeping us waiting, honey! We can't say grace until you come to the table!

(*The back door is pushed weakly open and Laura comes in. She is obviously quite faint, her lips trembling, her eyes wide and staring. She moves unsteadily toward the table.*)
  (*Legend: "Terror!"*)
  (*Outside a summer storm is coming abruptly. The white curtains billow inward at the windows and there is a sorrowful murmur and deep blue dusk.*)
  (*Laura suddenly stumbles—she catches at a chair with a faint moan.*)

TOM: Laura!

AMANDA: Laura! (*There is a clap of thunder.*) (*Legend: "Ah!"*) (*Despairingly.*) Why, Laura, you *are* sick, darling! Tom, help your sister into the living room, dear! Sit in the living room, Laura—rest on the sofa. Well! (*To the gentleman caller.*) Standing over the hot stove made her ill!—I told her that it was just too warm this evening, but—(*Tom comes back in. Laura is on the sofa.*) Is Laura all right now?

TOM: Yes.

AMANDA: What *is* that? Rain? A nice cool rain has come up! (*She gives the gentleman caller a frightened look.*) I think we may—have grace—now . . . (*Tom looks at her stupidly.*) Tom, honey—you say grace!

TOM: Oh . . . "For these and all thy mercies—" (*They bow their heads, Amanda stealing a nervous glance at Jim. In the living room Laura, stretched on the sofa, clenches her hand to her lips, to hold back a shuddering sob.*) God's Holy Name be praised—

(*The scene dims out.*)

SCENE 7

(*A Souvenir*)
  (*Half an hour later. Dinner is just being finished in the upstage area which is concealed by the drawn portieres.*)
  (*As the curtain rises Laura is still huddled upon the sofa, her feet drawn under her, her head resting on a pale blue pillow, her eyes wide and mysteriously watchful. The new floor lamp with its shade of rose-colored silk gives a soft, becoming light to her face, bringing out the fragile, unearthly prettiness which usually escapes attention. There is a steady murmur of rain, but it is slackening and stops soon after the scene begins; the air outside becomes pale and luminous as the moon breaks out.*)

(*A moment after the curtain rises, the lights in both rooms flicker and go out.*)

JIM: Hey, there, Mr. Light Bulb!

(*Amanda laughs nervously.*)
  (*Legend: "Suspension of a Public Service."*)

AMANDA: Where was Moses when the lights went out? Ha-ha. Do you know the answer to that one, Mr. O'Connor?

JIM: No, Ma'am, what's the answer?

AMANDA: In the dark! (*Jim laughs appreciably.*) Everybody sit still. I'll light the candles. Isn't it lucky we have them on the table? Where's a match? Which of you gentlemen can provide a match?

JIM: Here.

AMANDA: Thank you, sir.

JIM: Not at all, Ma'am!

AMANDA: I guess the fuse has burnt out. Mr. O'Connor, can you tell a burnt-out fuse? I know I can't and Tom is a total loss when it comes to mechanics. (*Sound: getting up: voices recede a little to kitchenette.*) Oh, be careful you don't bump into something. We don't want our gentleman caller to break his neck. Now wouldn't that be a fine howdy-do?

JIM: Ha-ha! Where is the fuse box?

AMANDA: Right here next to the stove. Can you see anything?

JIM: Just a minute.

AMANDA: Isn't electricity a mysterious thing? Wasn't it Benjamin Franklin who tied a key to a kite? We live in such a mysterious universe, don't we? Some people say that science clears up all the mysteries for us. In my opinion it only creates more! Have you found it yet?

JIM: No, Ma'am. All these fuses look okay to me.

AMANDA: Tom!

TOM: Yes, Mother?

AMANDA: That light bill I gave you several days ago. The one I told you we got the notices about?

TOM: Oh.—Yeah.

(*Legend: "Ha!"*)

AMANDA: You didn't neglect to pay it by any chance?

TOM: Why, I—

AMANDA: Didn't! I might have known it!

JIM: Shakespeare probably wrote a poem on that light bill, Mrs. Wingfield.

AMANDA: I might have known better than to trust him with it! There's such a high price for negligence in this world!

JIM: Maybe the poem will win a ten-dollar prize.

AMANDA: We'll just have to spend the remainder of the evening in the nineteenth century, before Mr. Edison made the Mazda lamp!

JIM: Candlelight is my favorite kind of light.

AMANDA: That shows you're romantic! But that's no excuse for Tom. Well, we got through dinner. Very considerate of them to let us get through dinner before they plunged us into everlasting darkness, wasn't it, Mr. O'Connor?

JIM: Ha-ha!

AMANDA: Tom, as a penalty for your carelessness you can help me with the dishes.

JIM: Let me give you a hand.

AMANDA: Indeed you will not!

JIM: I ought to be good for something.

AMANDA: Good for something? (*Her tone is rhapsodic.*) *You?* Why, Mr. O'Connor, nobody, *nobody's* given me this much entertainment in years—as you have!

JIM: Aw, now, Mrs. Wingfield!

AMANDA: I'm not exaggerating, not one bit! But Sister is all by her lonesome. You go keep her company in the parlor! I'll give you this lovely old candelabrum that used to be on the altar at the church of the Heavenly Rest. It was melted a little out of shape when the church burnt down. Lightning struck it one spring. Gypsy Jones was holding a revival at the time and he intimated that the church was destroyed because the Episcopalians gave card parties.

JIM: Ha-ha.

AMANDA: And how about coaxing Sister to drink a little wine? I think it would be good for her! Can you carry both at once?

JIM: Sure. I'm Superman!

AMANDA: Now, Thomas, get into this apron!

(*The door of kitchenette swings closed on Amanda's gay laughter; the flickering light approaches the portieres.*)

(*Laura sits up nervously as he enters. Her speech at first is low and breathless from the almost intolerable strain of being alone with a stranger.*)

(*The legend: "I Don't Suppose You Remember Me at All!"*)

(*In her first speeches in this scene, before Jim's warmth overcomes her paralyzing shyness, Laura's voice is thin and breathless as though she has just run up a steep flight of stairs.*)

(*Jim's attitude is gently humorous. In playing this scene it should be stressed that while the incident is apparently unimportant, it is to Laura the climax of her secret life.*)

JIM: Hello, there, Laura.

LAURA (*faintly*): Hello. (*She clears her throat.*)

JIM: How are you feeling now? Better?

LAURA: Yes. Yes, thank you.

JIM: This is for you. A little dandelion wine. (*He extends it toward her with extravagant gallantry.*)

LAURA: Thank you.

JIM: Drink it—but don't get drunk! (*He laughs heartily. Laura takes the glass uncertainly; laughs shyly.*) Where shall I set the candles?

LAURA: Oh—oh, anywhere . . .

JIM: How about here on the floor? Any objections?

LAURA: No.

JIM: I'll spread a newspaper under to catch the drippings. I like to sit on the floor. Mind if I do?

LAURA: Oh, no.

JIM: Give me a pillow?

LAURA: What?

JIM: A pillow!

LAURA: Oh . . . (*Hands him one quickly.*)

JIM: How about you? Don't you like to sit on the floor?

LAURA: Oh—yes.

JIM: Why don't you, then?

LAURA: I—will.

JIM: Take a pillow! (*Laura does. Sits on the other side of the candelabrum. Jim crosses his legs and smiles engagingly at her.*) I can't hardly see you sitting way over there.

LAURA: I can—see you.

JIM: I know, but that's not fair, I'm in the limelight. (*Laura moves her pillow closer.*) Good! Now I can see you! Comfortable?

LAURA: Yes.

JIM: So am I. Comfortable as a cow. Will you have some gum?

LAURA: No, thank you.

JIM: I think that I will indulge, with your permission. (*Musingly unwraps it and holds it up.*) Think of the fortune made by the guy that invented the first piece of chewing gum. Amazing, huh? The Wrigley Building is one of the sights of Chicago.—I saw it summer before last when I went up to the Century of Progress. Did you take in the Century of Progress?

LAURA: No, I didn't.

JIM: Well, it was quite a wonderful exposition. What impressed me most was the Hall of Science. Gives you an idea of what the future will be in America, even more wonderful than the present time is! (*Pause. Smiling at her.*) Your brother tells me you're shy. Is that right, Laura?

LAURA: I—don't know.

JIM: I judge you to be an old-fashioned type of girl. Well, I think that's a pretty good type to be. Hope you don't think I'm being too personal—do you?

LAURA (*hastily, out of embarrassment*): I believe I *will* take a piece of gum, if you—don't mind. (*Clearing her throat.*) Mr. O'Connor, have you—kept up with your singing?

JIM: Singing? Me?

LAURA: Yes. I remember what a beautiful voice you had.

JIM: When did you hear me sing?

(*Voice offstage in the pause.*)

Voice: (*offstage*): O blow, ye winds, heigh-ho,
    A-roving I will go!
        I'm off to my love
            With a boxing glove—
    Ten thousand miles away!

JIM: You say you've heard me sing?

LAURA: Oh, yes! Yes, very often . . . I—don't suppose you remember me—at all?

JIM (*smiling doubtfully*): You know I have an idea I've seen you before. I had that idea soon as you opened the

door. It seemed almost like I was about to remember
your name. But the name that I started to call you—
wasn't a name! And so I stopped myself before I said it.

LAURA: Wasn't it—Blue Roses?

JIM (*Springs up. Grinning.*): Blue Roses! My gosh, yes—
Blue Roses! That's what I had on my tongue when
you opened the door! Isn't it funny what tricks your
memory plays? I didn't connect you with the high
school somehow or other. But that's where it was; it
was high school. I didn't even know you were Shakespeare's sister! Gosh, I'm sorry.

LAURA: I didn't expect you to. You—barely knew me!

JIM: But we did have a speaking acquaintance, huh?

LAURA: Yes, we—spoke to each other.

JIM: When did you recognize me?

LAURA: Oh, right away!

JIM: Soon as I came in the door?

LAURA: When I heard your name I thought it was probably you. I knew that Tom used to know you a little in
high school. So when you came in the door—Well,
then I was—sure.

JIM: Why didn't you *say* something, then?

LAURA (*breathlessly*): I didn't know what to say, I was—
too surprised!

JIM: For goodness' sakes! You know, this sure is funny!

LAURA: Yes! Yes, isn't it, though...

JIM: Didn't we have a class in something together?

LAURA: Yes, we did.

JIM: What class was that?

LAURA: It was—singing—Chorus!

JIM: Aw!

LAURA: I sat across the aisle from you in the Aud.

JIM: Aw.

LAURA: Mondays, Wednesdays, and Fridays.

JIM: Now I remember—you always came in late.

LAURA: Yes, it was so hard for me, getting upstairs. I had
that brace on my leg—it clumped so loud!

JIM: I never heard any clumping.

LAURA (*wincing at the recollection*): To me it sounded
like—thunder!

JIM: Well, well, well, I never even noticed.

LAURA: And everybody was seated before I came in. I
had to walk in front of all those people. My seat was
in the back row. I had to go clumping all the way up
the aisle with everyone watching!

JIM: You shouldn't have been self-conscious.

LAURA: I know, but I was. It was always such a relief
when the singing started.

JIM: Aw, yes, I've placed you now! I used to call you Blue
Roses. How was it that I got started calling you that?

LAURA: I was out of school a little while with pleurosis.
When I came back you asked me what was the mat-
ter. I said I had pleurosis—you thought I said Blue
Roses. That's what you always called me after that!

JIM: I hope you didn't mind.

LAURA: Oh, no—I liked it. You see, I wasn't acquainted
with many—people....

JIM: As I remember you sort of stuck by yourself.

LAURA: I—I—never had much luck at—making friends.

JIM: I don't see why you wouldn't.

LAURA: Well, I—started out badly.

JIM: You mean being—

LAURA: Yes, it sort of—stood between me—

JIM: You shouldn't have let it!

LAURA: I know, but it did, and—

JIM: You were shy with people!

LAURA: I tried not to be but never could—

JIM: Overcome it?

LAURA: No, I—I never could!

JIM: I guess being shy is something you have to work out
of kind of gradually.

LAURA (*sorrowfully*): Yes—I guess it—

JIM: Takes time!

LAURA: Yes—

JIM: People are not so dreadful when you know them.
That's what you have to remember! And everybody
has problems, not just you, but practically everybody
has got some problems. You think of yourself as having the only problems, as being the only one who is
disappointed. But just look around you and you will
see lots of people as disappointed as you are. For
instance, I hoped when I was going to high school
that I would be further along at this time, six years
later, than I am now—You remember that wonderful write-up I had in *The Torch*?

LAURA: Yes! (*She rises and crosses to table.*)

JIM: It said I was bound to succeed in anything I went
into! (*Laura returns with the annual.*) Holy Jeez! *The
Torch*! (*He accepts it reverently. They smile across it
with mutual wonder. Laura crouches beside him and
they begin to turn through it. Laura's shyness is dissolving in his warmth.*)

LAURA: Here you are in *Pirates of Penzance*!

JIM (*wistfully*): I sang the baritone lead in that operetta.

LAURA (*rapidly*): So—*beautifully*!

JIM (*protesting*): Aw—

LAURA: Yes, yes—beautifully—beautifully!

JIM: You heard me?

LAURA: All three times!

JIM: No!

LAURA: Yes!

JIM: All three performances?

LAURA (*looking down*): Yes.

JIM: Why?

LAURA: I—wanted to ask you to—autograph my program.

JIM: Why didn't you ask me to?

LAURA: You were always surrounded by your own
friends so much that I never had a chance to.

JIM: You should have just—

LAURA: Well, I—thought you might think I was—

JIM: Thought I might think you was—what?

LAURA: Oh—

JIM (*with reflective relish*): I was beleaguered by females
in those days.

LAURA: You were terribly popular!

JIM: Yeah—

LAURA: You had such a—friendly way—

JIM: I was spoiled in high school.

LAURA: Everybody—liked you!

JIM: Including you?

LAURA: I—yes, I—I did, too—(*She gently closes the book in her lap.*)

JIM: Well, well, well!—Give me that program, Laura. (*She hands it to him. He signs it with a flourish.*) There you are—better late than never!

LAURA: Oh, I—what a—surprise!

JIM: My signature isn't worth very much right now. But some day—maybe—it will increase in value! Being disappointed is one thing and being discouraged is something else. I am disappointed but I am not discouraged. I'm twenty-three years old. How old are you?

LAURA: I'll be twenty-four in June.

JIM: That's not old age!

LAURA: No, but—

JIM: You finished high school?

LAURA (*with difficulty*): I didn't go back.

JIM: You mean you dropped out?

LAURA: I made bad grades in my final examinations. (*She rises and replaces the book and the program. Her voice strained.*) How is—Emily Meisenbach getting along?

JIM: Oh, that kraut-head!

LAURA: Why do you call her that?

JIM: That's what she was.

LAURA: You're not still—going with her?

JIM: I never see her.

LAURA: It said in the Personal Section that you were—engaged!

JIM: I know, but I wasn't impressed by that—propaganda!

LAURA: It wasn't—the truth?

JIM: Only in Emily's optimistic opinion!

LAURA: Oh—

(*Legend: "What Have You Done since High School?"*)

(*Jim lights a cigarette and leans indolently back on his elbows smiling at Laura with a warmth and charm which lights her inwardly with altar candles. She remains by the table and turns in her hands a piece of glass to cover her tumult.*)

JIM (*after several reflective puffs on a cigarette*): What have you done since high school? (*She seems not to hear him.*) Huh? (*Laura looks up.*) I said what have you done since high school, Laura?

LAURA: Nothing much.

JIM: You must have been doing something these six long years.

LAURA: Yes.

JIM: Well, then, such as what?

LAURA: I took a business course at business college—

JIM: How did that work out?

LAURA: Well, not very—well—I had to drop out, it gave me—indigestion—

(*Jim laughs gently.*)

JIM: What are you doing now?

LAURA: I don't do anything—much. Oh, please don't think I sit around doing nothing! My glass collection takes up a good deal of my time. Glass is something you have to take good care of.

JIM: What did you say—about glass?

LAURA: Collection I said—I have one—(*She clears her throat and turns away again, acutely shy.*)

JIM (*abruptly*): You know what I judge to be the trouble with you? Inferiority complex! Know what that is? That's what they call it when someone low-rates himself! I understand it because I had it, too. Although my case was not so aggravated as yours seems to be. I had it until I took up public speaking, developed my voice, and learned that I had an aptitude for science. Before that time I never thought of myself as being outstanding in any way whatsoever! Now I've never made a regular study of it, but I have a friend who says I can analyze people better than doctors that make a profession of it. I don't claim that to be necessarily true, but I can sure guess a person's psychology, Laura! (*Takes out his gum.*) Excuse me, Laura. I always take it out when the flavor is gone. I'll use this scrap of paper to wrap it in. I know how it is to get it stuck on a shoe. Yep—that's what I judge to be your principal trouble. A lack of confidence in yourself as a person. You don't have the proper amount of faith in yourself. I'm basing that fact on a number of your remarks and also on certain observations I've made. For instance that clumping you thought was so awful in high school. You say that you even dreaded to walk into class. You see what you did? You dropped out of school, you gave up an education because of a clump, which as far as I know was practically non-existent! A little physical defect is what you have. Hardly noticeable even! Magnified thousands of times by imagination! You know what my strong advice to you is? Think of yourself as *superior* in some way!

LAURA: In what way would I think?

JIM: Why, man alive, Laura! Just look about you a little. What do you see? A world full of common people! All of 'em born and all of 'em going to die! Which of them has one-tenth of your good points! Or mine! Or anyone else's, as far as that goes—Gosh! Everybody excels in some one thing. Some in many! (*Unconsciously glances at himself in the mirror.*) All you've got to do is discover in what! Take me, for instance. (*He adjusts his tie at the mirror.*) My interest happens to lie in electro-dynamics. I'm taking a course in radio engineering at night school, Laura, on top of a fairly responsible job at the warehouse. I'm taking that course and studying public speaking.

LAURA: Ohhhh.

JIM: Because I believe in the future of television! (*Turning back to her.*) I wish to be ready to go up right along with it. Therefore I'm planning to get in on the ground floor. In fact, I've already made the right connections and all that remains is for the industry itself to get under way! Full steam—(*His eyes are starry.*) Knowledge—Zzzzzp! *Money*—Zzzzzzp!—*Power!* That's the cycle democracy is built on! (*His attitude is convincingly dynamic. Laura stares at him, even her shyness eclipsed in her absolute wonder. He suddenly grins.*) I guess you think I think a lot of myself!

LAURA: No—o-o-o, I—

JIM: Now how about you? Isn't there something you take more interest in than anything else?

LAURA: Well, I do—as I said—have my—glass collection—

(*A peal of girlish laughter from the kitchen.*)

JIM: I'm not right sure I know what you're talking about. What kind of glass is it?

LAURA: Little articles of it, they're ornaments mostly! Most of them are little animals made out of glass, the tiniest little animals in the world. Mother calls them a glass menagerie! Here's an example of one, if you'd like to see it! This one is one of the oldest. It's nearly thirteen. (*He stretches out his hand.*) (*Music: "The Glass Menagerie."*) Oh, be careful—if you breathe, it breaks!

JIM: I'd better not take it. I'm pretty clumsy with things.

LAURA: Go on, I trust you with him! (*Places it in his palm.*) There now—you're holding him gently! Hold him over the light, he loves the light! You see how the light shines through him?

JIM: It sure does shine!

LAURA: I shouldn't be partial, but he is my favorite one.

JIM: What kind of a thing is this one supposed to be?

LAURA: Haven't you noticed the single horn on his forehead?

JIM: A unicorn, huh?

LAURA: Mmm-hmmm!

JIM: Unicorns, aren't they extinct in the modern world?

LAURA: I know!

JIM: Poor little fellow, he must feel sort of lonesome.

LAURA (*smiling*): Well, if he does he doesn't complain about it. He stays on a shelf with some horses that don't have horns and all of them seem to get along nicely together.

JIM: How do you know?

LAURA (*lightly*): I haven't heard any arguments among them!

JIM (*grinning*): No arguments, huh? Well, that's a pretty good sign! Where shall I set him?

LAURA: Put him on the table. They all like a change of scenery once in a while!

JIM (*stretching*): Well, well, well, well—Look how big my shadow is when I stretch!

LAURA: Oh, oh, yes—it stretches across the ceiling!

JIM (*crossing to door*): I think it's stopped raining. (*Opens fire escape door.*) Where does the music come from?

LAURA: From the Paradise Dance Hall across the alley.

JIM: How about cutting the rug a little, Miss Wingfield?

LAURA: Oh, I—

JIM: Or is your program filled up? Let me have a look at it. (*Grasps imaginary card.*) Why, every dance is taken! I'll just have to scratch some out. (*Waltz music:*

"*La Golondrina.*") Ahhh, a waltz! (*He executes some sweeping turns by himself then holds his arms toward Laura.*)

LAURA (*breathlessly*): I—can't dance!

JIM: There you go, that inferiority stuff!

LAURA: I've never danced in my life!

JIM: Come on, try!

LAURA: Oh, but I'd step on you!

JIM: I'm not made out of glass.

LAURA: How—how—how do we start?

JIM: Just leave it to me. You hold your arms out a little.

LAURA: Like this?

JIM: A little bit higher. Right. Now don't tighten up, that's the main thing about it—relax.

LAURA (*laughing breathlessly*): It's hard not to.

JIM: Okay.

LAURA: I'm afraid you can't budge me.

JIM: What do you bet I can't? (*He swings her into motion.*)

LAURA: Goodness, yes, you can!

JIM: Let yourself go, now, Laura, just let yourself go.

LAURA: I'm—

JIM: Come on!

LAURA: Trying!

JIM: Not so stiff—Easy does it!

LAURA: I know but I'm—

JIM: Loosen th' backbone! There now, that's a lot better.

LAURA: Am I?

JIM: Lots, lots better! (*He moves her about the room in a clumsy waltz.*)

LAURA: Oh, my!

JIM: Ha-ha!

LAURA: Oh, my goodness!

JIM: Ha-ha-ha! (*They suddenly bump into the table. Jim stops.*) What did we hit on?

LAURA: Table.

JIM: Did something fall off it? I think—

LAURA: Yes.

JIM: I hope that it wasn't the little glass horse with the horn!

LAURA: Yes.

JIM: Aw, aw, aw. Is it broken?

LAURA: Now it is just like all the other horses.

JIM: It's lost its—

LAURA: Horn! It doesn't matter. Maybe it's a blessing in disguise.

JIM: You'll never forgive me. I bet that that was your favorite piece of glass.

LAURA: I don't have favorites much. It's no tragedy, Freckles. Glass breaks so easily. No matter how careful you are. The traffic jars the shelves and things fall off them.

JIM: Still I'm awfully sorry that I was the cause.

LAURA (*smiling*): I'll just imagine he had an operation. The horn was removed to make him feel less—freakish! (*They both laugh.*) Now he will feel more at home with the other horses, the ones that don't have horns . . .

JIM: Ha-ha, that's very funny! (*Suddenly serious.*) I'm glad to see that you have a sense of humor. You know—you're—well—very different! Surprisingly different from anyone else I know! (*His voice becomes soft and hesitant with a genuine feeling.*) Do you mind me telling you that? (*Laura is abashed beyond speech.*) I mean it in a nice way . . . (*Laura nods shyly, looking away.*) You make me feel sort of—I don't know how to put it! I'm usually pretty good at expressing things, but—This is something that I don't know how to say! (*Laura touches her throat and clears it—turns the broken unicorn in her hands.*) (*Even softer.*) Has anyone ever told you that you were pretty? (*Pause: Music.*) (*Laura looks up slowly, with wonder, and shakes her head.*) Well, you are! In a very different way from anyone else. And all the nicer because of the difference, too. (*His voice becomes low and husky. Laura turns away, nearly faint with the novelty of her emotions.*) I wish that you were my sister. I'd teach you to have some confidence in yourself. The different people are not like other people, but being different is nothing to be ashamed of. Because other people are not such wonderful people. They're one hundred times one thousand. You're one times one! They walk all over the earth. You just stay here. They're common as—weeds, but—you—well, you're—*Blue Roses!*

(*Image on screen: blue roses.*)
(*Music changes.*)

LAURA: But blue is wrong for—roses . . .
JIM: It's right for you—You're—pretty!
LAURA: In what respect am I pretty?
JIM: In all respects—believe me! Your eyes—your hair—are pretty! (*He catches hold of her hand.*) You think I'm making this up because I'm invited to dinner and have to be nice. Oh, I could do that! I could put on an act for you, Laura, and say lots of things without being very sincere. But this time I am. I'm talking to you sincerely. I happened to notice you had this inferiority complex that keeps you from feeling comfortable with people. Somebody needs to build your confidence up and make you proud instead of shy and turning away and—blushing—Somebody ought to—Ought to—*kiss* you, Laura! (*His hand slips slowly up her arm to her shoulder.*) (*Music swells tumultuously.*) (*He suddenly turns her about and kisses her on the lips. When he releases her Laura sinks on the sofa with a bright, dazed look. Jim backs away and fishes in his pocket for a cigarette.*) (*Legend on screen: "Souvenir."*) Stumble-john! (*He lights the cigarette, avoiding her look. There is a peal of girlish laughter from Amanda in the kitchen. Laura slowly raises and opens her hand. It still contains the little broken glass animal. She looks at it with a tender, bewildered expression.*) Stumble-john! I shouldn't have done that—That was way off the beam. You don't smoke, do you? (*She looks up, smiling, not hearing the question. He sits beside her a little gingerly. She looks at him speechlessly—waiting. He coughs decorously and moves a little farther aside as he considers the situation and senses her feelings, dimly, with per-*

turbation. Gently.) Would you—care for a—mint? (*She doesn't seem to hear him but her look grows brighter even.*) Peppermint—Life Saver? My pocket's a regular drugstore—wherever I go . . . (*He pops a mint in his mouth. Then gulps and decides to make a clean breast of it. He speaks slowly and gingerly.*) Laura, you know, if I had a sister like you, I'd do the same thing as Tom. I'd bring out fellows and—introduce her to them. The right type of boys of a type to—appreciate her. Only—well—he made a mistake about me. Maybe I've got no call to be saying this. That may not have been the idea in having me over. But what if it was? There's nothing wrong about that. The only trouble is that in my case—I'm not in a situation to—do the right thing. I can't take down your number and say I'll phone. I can't call up next week and—ask for a date. I thought I had better explain the situation in case you misunderstood it and—hurt your feelings. . . . (*Pause. Slowly, very slowly, Laura's look changes, her eyes returning slowly from his to the ornament in her palm.*)

(*Amanda utters another gay laugh in the kitchen.*)

LAURA (*faintly*): You—won't—call again?
JIM: No, Laura, I can't. (*He rises from the sofa.*) As I was just explaining, I've—got strings on me, Laura, I've—been going steady! I go out all the time with a girl named Betty. She's a home-girl like you, and Catholic, and Irish, and in a great many ways we—get along fine. I met her last summer on a moonlight boat trip up the river to Alton, on the *Majestic.* Well—right away from the start it was—love! (*Legend: Love!*) (*Laura sways slightly forward and grips the arm of the sofa. He fails to notice, now enrapt in his own comfortable being.*) Being in love has made a new man of me! (*Leaning stiffly forward, clutching the arm of the sofa, Laura struggles visibly with her storm. But Jim is oblivious, she is a long way off.*) The power of love is really pretty tremendous! Love is something that—changes the whole world, Laura! (*The storm abates a little and Laura leans back. He notices her again.*) It happened that Betty's aunt took sick, she got a wire and had to go to Centralia. So Tom—when he asked me to dinner—I naturally just accepted the invitation, not knowing that you—that he—that I—(*He stops awkwardly.*) Huh—I'm a stumble-john! (*He flops back on the sofa. The holy candles in the altar of Laura's face have been snuffed out! There is a look of almost infinite desolation. Jim glances at her uneasily.*) I wish that you would—say something. (*She bites her lip which was trembling and then bravely smiles. She opens her hand again on the broken glass ornament. Then she gently takes his hand and raises it level with her own. She carefully places the unicorn in the palm of his hand, then pushes his fingers closed upon it.*) What are you—doing that for? You want me to have him?—Laura? (*She nods.*) What for?
LAURA: A—souvenir . . .

(*She rises unsteadily and crouches beside the victrola to wind it up.*)

(*Legend on screen: "Things Have a Way of Turning out so Badly."*)

(*Or Image: "Gentleman Caller Waving Good-bye!—Gaily."*)

(*At this moment Amanda rushes brightly back in the front room. She bears a pitcher of fruit punch in an old-fashioned cut-glass pitcher and a plate of macaroons. The plate has a gold border and poppies painted on it.*)

AMANDA: Well, well, well! Isn't the air delightful after the shower? I've made you children a little liquid refreshment. (*Turns gaily to the gentleman caller.*) Jim, do you know that song about lemonade?
"Lemonade, lemonade
   Made in the shade and stirred with a spade—
Good enough for any old maid!"

JIM (*uneasily*): Ha-ha! No—I never heard it.

AMANDA: Why, Laura! You look so serious!

JIM: We were having a serious conversation.

AMANDA: Good! Now you're better acquainted!

JIM (*uncertainly*): Ha-ha! Yes.

AMANDA: You modern young people are much more serious-minded than my generation. I was so gay as a girl!

JIM: You haven't changed, Mrs. Wingfield.

AMANDA: Tonight I'm rejuvenated! The gaiety of the occasion, Mr. O'Connor! (*She tosses her head with a peal of laughter. Spills lemonade.*) Oooo! I'm baptizing myself!

JIM: Here—let me—

AMANDA (*setting the pitcher down*): There now. I discovered we had some maraschino cherries. I dumped them in, juice and all!

JIM: You shouldn't have gone to that trouble, Mrs. Wingfield.

AMANDA: Trouble, trouble? Why it was loads of fun! Didn't you hear me cutting up in the kitchen? I bet your ears were burning! I told Tom how out-done with him I was for keeping you to himself so long a time! He should have brought you over much, much sooner! Well, now that you've found your way, I want you to be a very frequent caller! Not just occasional but all the time. Oh, we're going to have a lot of gay times together! I see them coming! Mmm, just breathe that air! So fresh, and the moon's so pretty! I'll skip back out—I know where my place is when young folks are having a—serious conversation!

JIM: Oh, don't go out, Mrs. Wingfield. The fact of the matter is I've got to be going.

AMANDA: Going, now? You're joking! Why, it's only the shank of the evening, Mr. O'Connor!

JIM: Well, you know how it is.

AMANDA: You mean you're a young workingman and have to keep workingmen's hours. We'll let you off early tonight. But only on the condition that next time you stay later. What's the best night for you? Isn't Saturday night the best night for you workingmen?

JIM: I have a couple of time clocks to punch, Mrs. Wingfield. One at morning, another one at night!

AMANDA: My, but you *are* ambitious! You work at night, too?

JIM: No, Ma'am, not work but—Betty! (*He crosses deliberately to pick up his hat. The band at the Paradise Dance Hall goes into a tender waltz.*)

AMANDA: Betty? Betty? Who's—Betty! (*There is an ominous cracking sound in the sky.*)

JIM: Oh, just a girl. The girl I go steady with! (*He smiles charmingly. The sky falls.*)

(*Legend: "The Sky Falls."*)

AMANDA (*a long-drawn exhalation*): Ohhhh . . . Is it a serious romance, Mr. O'Connor?

JIM: We're going to be married the second Sunday in June.

AMANDA: Ohhhh—how nice! Tom didn't mention that you were engaged to be married.

JIM: The cat's not out of the bag at the warehouse yet. You know how they are. They call you Romeo and stuff like that. (*He stops at the oval mirror to put on his hat. He carefully shapes the brim and the crown to give a discreetly dashing effect.*) It's been a wonderful evening, Mrs. Wingfield. I guess this is what they mean by Southern hospitality.

AMANDA: It really wasn't anything at all.

JIM: I hope it don't seem like I'm rushing off. But I promised Betty I'd pick her up at the Wabash depot, an' by the time I get my jalopy down there her train'll be in. Some women are pretty upset if you keep 'em waiting.

AMANDA: Yes, I know—The tyranny of women! (*Extends her hand.*) Good-bye, Mr. O'Connor. I wish you luck—and happiness—and success! All three of them, and so does Laura!—Don't you, Laura?

LAURA: Yes!

JIM (*taking her hand*): Good-bye, Laura. I'm certainly going to treasure that souvenir. And don't you forget the good advice I gave you. (*Raises his voice to a cheery shout.*) So long, Shakespeare! Thanks again, ladies—Good night!

(*He grins and ducks jauntily out.*)

(*Still bravely grimacing, Amanda closes the door on the gentleman caller. Then she turns back to the room with a puzzled expression. She and Laura don't dare to face each other. Laura crouches beside the victrola to wind it.*)

AMANDA (*faintly*): Things have a way of turning out so badly. I don't believe that I would play the victrola. Well, well—well—Our gentleman caller was engaged to be married! Tom!

TOM (*from back*): Yes, Mother?

AMANDA: Come in here a minute. I want to tell you something awfully funny.

TOM (*enters with macaroon and a glass of the lemonade*): Has the gentleman caller gotten away already?

AMANDA: The gentleman caller has made an early departure. What a wonderful joke you played on us!

TOM: How do you mean?

AMANDA: You didn't mention that he was engaged to be married.

TOM: Jim? Engaged?

AMANDA: That's what he just informed us.

TOM: I'll be jiggered! I didn't know about that.

AMANDA: That seems very peculiar.

TOM: What's peculiar about it?

AMANDA: Didn't you call him your best friend down at the warehouse?

TOM: He is, but how did I know?

AMANDA: It seems extremely peculiar that you wouldn't know your best friend was going to be married!

TOM: The warehouse is where I work, not where I know things about people!

AMANDA: You don't know things anywhere! You live in a dream; you manufacture illusions! (*He crosses to door.*) Where are you going?

TOM: I'm going to the movies.

AMANDA: That's right, now that you've had us make such fools of ourselves. The effort, the preparations, all the expense! The new floor lamp, the rug, the clothes for Laura! All for what? To entertain some other girl's fiancé! Go to the movies, go! Don't think about us, a mother deserted, an unmarried sister who's crippled and has no job! Don't let anything interfere with your selfish pleasure! Just go, go, go — to the movies!

TOM: All right, I will! The more you shout about my selfishness to me the quicker I'll go, and I won't go to the movies!

AMANDA: Go, then! Then go to the moon — you selfish dreamer!

(*Tom smashes his glass on the floor. He plunges out on the fire escape, slamming the door. Laura screams — cut by door.*)

(*Dance hall music up. Tom goes to the rail and grips it desperately, lifting his face in the chill white moonlight penetrating the narrow abyss of the alley.*)

(*Legend on screen: "And so Good-bye . . . "*)

(*Tom's closing speech is timed with the interior pantomime. The interior scene is played as though viewed through soundproof glass. Amanda appears to be making a comforting speech to Laura who is huddled upon the sofa. Now that we cannot hear the mother's speech, her silliness is gone and she has dignity and tragic beauty. Laura's dark hair hides her face until at the end of the speech she lifts it to smile at her mother. Amanda's gestures are slow and graceful, almost dancelike, as she comforts the daughter. At the end of her speech she glances a moment at the father's picture — then withdraws through the portieres. At close of Tom's speech, Laura blows out the candles, ending the play.*)

TOM: I didn't go to the moon, I went much further — for time is the longest distance between two places — Not long after that I was fired for writing a poem on the lid of a shoebox. I left Saint Louis. I descended the steps of this fire escape for a last time and followed, from then on, in my father's footsteps, attempting to find in motion what was lost in space — I traveled around a great deal. The cities swept about me like dead leaves, leaves that were brightly colored but torn away from the branches. I would have stopped, but I was pursued by something. It always came upon me unawares, taking me altogether by surprise. Perhaps it was a familiar bit of music. Perhaps it was only a piece of transparent glass — Perhaps I am walking along a street at night, in some strange city, before I have found companions. I pass the lighted window of a shop where perfume is sold. The window is filled with pieces of colored glass, tiny transparent bottles in delicate colors, like bits of a shattered rainbow. Then all at once my sister touches my shoulder. I turn around and look into her eyes . . . Oh, Laura, Laura, I tried to leave you behind me, but I am more faithful than I intended to be! I reach for a cigarette, I cross the street, I run into the movies or a bar, I buy a drink, I speak to the nearest stranger — anything that can blow your candles out! (*Laura bends over the candles.*) — for nowadays the world is lit by lightning! Blow out your candles, Laura — and so good-bye. . . .

(*She blows the candles out.*)
(*The scene dissolves.*)

COMMENTARIES

Tennessee Williams is a fascinating figure in American drama. He was a forceful personality who charmed his friends and the public alike, although his life was often filled with uncertainties and unresolved problems. Some of his best work derived from his private agonies. His work was taken seriously almost from the first, and a body of criticism has developed around it, including biographies, personal reminiscences of collaborators, critical commentaries, and scholarship.

In the *New York Times* review of *The Glass Menagerie* (included here), Lewis Nichols describes Laurette Taylor's performance as Amanda as "completely perfect." Donald Spoto, who wrote *The Kindness of Strangers: The Life of Tennessee Williams* (1985), says that Taylor, a powerful actress whose career had seemed finished when the part was offered to her, almost refused the role at first. But her interpretation established a point of reference to which later actresses had to pay homage. Spoto helps us understand the power of collaboration between actor and playwright that sometimes helps both expand their understanding of the work.

Benjamin Nelson explains that "*The Glass Menagerie* exhibits several of Williams's weaknesses as well as his strengths as a playwright." He discusses Williams's characterizations, especially of Laura and Amanda. He also points to "poetic passages" in the play that he feels are weaknesses. Ultimately, Nelson poses an interesting dramatic question: Is the play a tragedy? The search for an answer to this question involves a full consideration of the play's strengths and weaknesses, its success or failure.

Lewis Nichols (1903–1982)
REVIEW OF *THE GLASS MENAGERIE*   *1945*

Lewis Nichols's review of the New York premiere of The Glass Menagerie *focused on the stellar performance of Laurette Taylor, who played the Mother, Amanda. Nichols also points out the quality of Williams's writing and his ear for "faintly sardonic dialogue." He saw the play as a superb vehicle for sublime acting.*

The theatre opened its Easter basket the night before and found it a particularly rich one. Preceded by warm and tender reports from Chicago, *The Glass Menagerie* opened at the Playhouse on Saturday, and immediately it was clear that for once the advance notes were not in error. Tennessee Williams's simple play forms the framework for some of the finest acting to be seen in many a day. "Memorable" is an overworked word, but that is the only one to describe Laurette Taylor's performance. March left the theatre like a lioness.

Miss Taylor's picture of a blowsy, impoverished woman who is living on memories of a flower-scented Southern past is completely perfect. It combines qualities of humor and human understanding. The Mother of the play is an amusing figure and a pathetic one. Aged, with two children, living in an apartment off an alley in St. Louis, she recalls her past glories, her seventeen suitors, the old and better life. She is a bit of a scold, a bit of a snob; her finery has worn threadbare, but she has kept it for occasions of state. Miss Taylor makes her a person known by any other name to everyone in her audience. That is art.

In the story the Mother is trying to do the best she can for her children. The son works in a warehouse, although he wants to go to far places. The daughter, a cripple, never has been able to finish school. She is shy, she spends her time collecting glass animals—the title comes from this—and playing old phonograph records. The Mother thinks it is time she is getting married, but there has never been a Gentleman Caller at the house. Finally the son brings home another man from the warehouse and out comes the finery and the heavy if bent candlestick. Even the Gentleman Caller fails. He is engaged to another girl.

Mr. Williams's play is not all of the same caliber. A strict perfectionist could easily find a good many flaws. There are some unconnected odds and ends which have little to do with the story: Snatches of talk about the war, bits of psychology, occasional moments of rather flowery writing. But Mr. Williams has a real ear for faintly sardonic dialogue, unexpected phrases and an affection for his characters. Miss Taylor takes these many good passages and makes them sing. She plays softly and part of the time seems to be mumbling—a mumble that can be heard at the top of the gallery. Her accents, like the author's phrases, are unexpected, her gestures are vague and fluttery. There is no doubt she was a Southern belle; there is no doubt she is a great actress.

Eddie Dowling, who is coproducer, and, with Margo Jones, codirector, has the double job of narrator and the player of The Son. The narration is like that of *Our Town* and *I Remember Mama* and it probably is not essential to *The Glass Menagerie*. In the play itself Mr. Dowling gives his quiet, easy performance. Julie Haydon, very ethereal and slight, is good as the daughter, as is Anthony Ross as the Gentleman Caller. The Caller had been the hero in high school, but he, too, had been unsuccessful. Jo Mielziner's setting fits the play, as does Paul Bowles's music. In fact, everything fits. *The Glass Menagerie*, like spring, is a pleasure to have in the neighborhood.

Donald Spoto (b. 1941)
LAURETTE TAYLOR IN *THE GLASS MENAGERIE*   1985

Before the part of Amanda Wingfield was offered to her, Laurette Taylor had thought her career as an actress was over. Donald Spoto, Tennessee Williams's biographer, gives us a vision of how persistence and devotion to someone of genuine talent produced a legend in American acting.

That month [December 1944], the details moved together swiftly. [Actor-producer-director Eddie] Dowling, who had directed actress Julie Haydon in *The Time of Your Life*,° convinced her that (although she was thirty-four) she would be credible as the lame, fragile Laura, a character at least a decade younger. She, in turn, took the play to her friend and mentor (later her husband), the formidable critic George Jean Nathan, whose approval she felt obligatory. At the same time, the forty-nine-year-old Dowling announced—without a smile—that he would play young (twentyish) Tom, the shoe-warehouse clerk and aspiring poet; for the role of the gentleman caller, Anthony Ross was hired. The remaining role to be cast was Amanda Wingfield—the "little woman of great but confused vitality," as Williams described her in the play, "clinging frantically to another time and place." The role demanded not mere competence, but the nuances of dramatic greatness. Nathan suggested Laurette Taylor. Dowling and [Audrey] Wood [Williams's agent] and Williams saw his wisdom; they also panicked.

Laurette Taylor, then sixty, had been up to the 1930s one of the great ladies of the American stage. Those who had seen her in *Peg O'My Heart* (in 1912) or *The Furies* (in 1928) or *Outward Bound* (in 1938) knew her gifts. But for almost ten years she had herself become a woman of great but confused vitality, and a confirmed alcoholic.

The Time of Your Life: A play (1939) by William Saroyan.

At that time, Taylor was living in sad withdrawal from the theater, at a hotel on East 60th Street, where she was daily attended by a drama student named Eloise Sheldon. In return for acting lessons, the young woman cared for the practical details of Taylor's life and offered devoted companionship. The play reached Taylor by the circuitous route of Wood to Dowling to Haydon to Nathan to Sheldon to Taylor. It also bore a new title — *The Glass Menagerie.*

"Of course her first reaction was to turn it down," Eloise Sheldon Armen recalled years later; "she thought her career was over. But we prevailed on her to see that no one could bring this character to life the way she could." At last, with the loving encouragement of Eloise — "a small flame," as Laurette Taylor's daughter apprecia- tively wrote of the young student, "guiding [Taylor] back to the paths of everyday life" — she accepted the part. She did not, however, stop drinking, nor did she seem to give much attention to memorizing lines before or during rehearsals.

In November, Dowling (with, Williams insisted, Margo Jones as codirector) began rehearsals in New York prior to a scheduled Chicago tryout at the end of December. Terrified that something like the history of *Battle of Angels* would be repeated — not because of the new play's content (which could not have been more different) but because he no longer believed the play was anything but "rather dull, too nice" — Williams fled New York for St. Louis. There he was interviewed on his life and work and hopes by the drama critic of the *Star-Times,* a man named William Inge. The resulting article was full of inaccuracies, half-truths, and Williams's typical alterations of personal history; the resulting friendship was much more intense and dramatic.

But Audrey and Dowling would not allow Williams to be an absentee author, and in December he was summoned to Chicago. The situation, he quickly realized, was as bleak as the fierce winter that had already descended.

First of all, Laurette Taylor — with only a week remaining before the December 26 premiere — attended the final rehearsals in what can only be called an alcoholic stupor, barely summarizing the dialogue and so broadly defining the woman's Southern accent and character that, as Williams wrote . . . , she made the play sound like the Aunt Jemima Pancake Hour. In addition, Jo Mielziner's stage designs were being followed with great difficulty, and the music Williams had commis- sioned from his old acquaintance Paul Bowles sounded harsh through the theater's crude sound system. Luggage had not arrived; a winter storm raged; the Civic The- atre was inconvenient to Chicago's main theater district; there was no budget for advertising or publicity; and everyone in the company (except Eddie Dowling and Julie Haydon) — cast, crew, author — submerged the fear of failure in strong drink. Margo Jones, Williams wrote . . . , was like a scoutmaster leading a wayward and desperate troop to their doom.

As late as Christmas Eve, the lines of the play had been neither "frozen" (fixed by the producer and playwright to be performed as written) nor completely memo- rized. Laurette Taylor managed only a martini mumble, Dowling was demanding rewrites, and the cast was stumbling into props and one another. "Mr. Dowling," Williams said quietly that night, "art is experience remembered in tranquillity. And I find no tranquillity in Chicago."

The night after Christmas, *The Glass Menagerie* was somehow performed for a small, diffident audience. By the afternoon of the twenty-seventh, the box office had taken in only four hundred dollars, and the producers prepared a closing notice. But then Audrey telephoned them to read two brief reviews: Critic Claudia Cassidy, writing in the *Chicago Daily Tribune,* said the play had "the stamina of success . . . [it] knows people and how they tick. . . . If it is your play, as it is mine, it reaches out . . . and you are caught in its spell." And Ashton Stevens, in the *Herald American,* said *The Glass Menagerie* "has the courage of true poetry couched in colloquial prose."

Before the end of that day, the mayor of Chicago, at the urging of the Civic Theatre's management, authorized a fifty-percent ticket subsidy for municipal employees. On the third night, Laurette Taylor was not simply discharging a half-formed role, she was creating a legend, she had begun to draw a more wonderful portrait than anyone could have imagined—not Eddie Dowling (who resented the critics' subsequent raves about her), not Tennessee Williams nor Audrey Wood, not anyone connected with the play.

"Actually," according to the playwright, "she directed many of the scenes, particularly the ones between mother and daughter, and she did a top-notch job. She was continually working on her part, putting in little things and taking them out— almost every night in Chicago there was something new, but she never disturbed the central characterization. Everything she did was absolutely in character."

The closing notice was removed—not, however, because box-office business dramatically improved, but because Claudia Cassidy and Ashton Stevens had been championing the play, returning almost nightly and telling and writing about it almost daily. "It gripped players and audiences alike," Cassidy wrote on January 7, 1945, "and created one of those rare evenings in the theater that make 'stagestruck' an honorable word." By the middle of the month, no tickets were available. In an unusual example of journalistic salvation, a play was for once not lost but kept alive because of critical support.

Benjamin Nelson
PROBLEMS IN *THE GLASS MENAGERIE*

1961

Benjamin Nelson's analysis of Williams's play recognizes the power of the circumstances portrayed in the play. Nelson is concerned, however, that the characters, especially Laura, are not as fully and carefully drawn as they need to be to make the play truly powerful. He also criticizes Williams for creating a universe that "does not allow tragedy."

The Glass Menagerie exhibits several of Williams's weaknesses as well as his strengths as a playwright. The great strength of the play is of course the delicate, sympathetic, yet objective creation of meaningful people in a meaningful situation. Williams has caught a decisive and desperate moment in the lives of four individuals and given it illumination and a sense of deep meaning—no small feat for any writer.

His characterizations are not equally realized. He has been unable to create Laura on more than a single dimension, while Amanda is overwhelming in her multifaceted delineation. On a more technical level the play manifests a doubt on the part of its author toward the power of the written word. As a backdrop for *The Glass Menagerie,* Williams originally wished to use a screen to register emotions and present images from the past, present, and future. For example, when Jim O'Connor confesses to the family that he is going steady with another girl, the legend on the screen is to read, "The Sky Falls." Fortunately, [actor-director] Eddie

Dowling deleted these touches of the poet from his production, but the play still abounds with a number of pretentious statements on the part of Tom as Narrator.

I assume that the final scene between Amanda and Laura is played in pantomime because Williams wished to portray Amanda's dignity through her gestures and her daughter's reaction rather than through the mother's speech, which during the course of the drama has been either shrill, simpering, or saucy. But in relegating this scene to background silence while Tom makes a self-conscious statement about drifting like a dead leaf "attempting to find in motion what was lost in space," he has substituted a painfully pretentious narration for what could have been an intense and luminous moment between the two women.

Again, on the credit side of the author, his play presents genuine situation, motivation, and, as Joseph Wood Krutch has noted, "a hard substantial core of shrewd observation and deft, economical characterization." But Mr. Krutch also noted that "this hard core is enveloped in a fuzzy haze of pretentious, sentimental, pseudopoetic verbiage."[1] In *The Glass Menagerie,* the strained lyricism runs parallel with dialogue that is fresh, alive, and highly characteristic, particularly in the speech of Amanda. This dialogue fortunately dominates the proceedings, but the excess of self-conscious "poetical" passages is quite apparent and is a fault of which Williams is to be guilty in much of his later work.

But the great weakness of *The Glass Menagerie* does not lie in its author's artistic or technical deficiencies. The weakness lies at the core of the play and evolves out of what is to become the playwright's hardening philosophical commitment. We can begin to comprehend this when we ask ourselves whether or not *The Glass Menagerie* is a tragedy. It presents a tragic situation and characters who, despite their moodiness and foolishness and self-deception, possess a sense of the tragic. With the possible exception of Laura, they are intensely genuine and the destruction of their dreams and aspirations bears the illusion of great importance. But the play is not a tragedy. The universe of *The Glass Menagerie* does not allow tragedy.

Everyone in the play is a failure and in the course of their drama they all perish a little. Amanda, the most heroic of the quartet, is pitiful but not tragic because from the outset she is doomed to failure despite her desperate struggle to right things. None of these people are given the opportunity to triumph against a fate which is as malignant as it is implacable. Their struggle is a rear-guard action against life, a continuous retreat. This retreat may be moving, pathetic, melodramatic, or boisterous, but it is always a withdrawal. After all, what is the world outside the glass menagerie?

> There was only hot swing music and liquor, dance halls, bars, and movies, and sex that hung in the gloom like a chandelier and flooded the world with brief, deceptive rainbows. . . . All the world was waiting for bombardments! (p. 1084)

The world outside the Wingfield apartment is a world of illusions, also, even more deceptive and destructive than those held by Amanda and Laura. It is the world of *Stairs to the Roof* and this time the escape is not to a new star but into the individual and personal illusions fostered by each of the characters as his private defense against destruction. Jim waits for the day when his "zzzzzp!" will at last disperse his fear and uncertainty; Laura creates her own sparkling, cold world which gives the illusion of warmth but is as eternal in its unreality as the glass from which it is composed; Amanda strikes out with all her power against her fate by clinging to the past as to a shield; and Tom, recognizing the plight of his family, can

---

[1]Joseph Wood Krutch, *The Nation* 14 April 1945:24.

do no more than drift away from them, rudderless, frightened, and never really as far from Amanda and Laura as he knows he should be.

Not one of these individuals can cope with his situation. They struggle and their hopes and the destruction of these hopes possess a sense of great importance because Williams has created genuine people in an intensely genuine situation, but they lack the completeness to truly cope with their dilemma. They are not responsible for what has happened to them and they are much too helpless to do more than delay the inevitable. And destruction is inevitable because it is implicit in the universe of Tennessee Williams.

> For the sins of the world are really only its partialities, and these are what sufferings must atone for. . . . The nature of man is full of such makeshift arrangements, devised by himself to cover his incompletion. He feels a part of himself to be like a missing wall or a room left unfurnished and he tries as well as he can to make up for it. The use of imagination, resorting to dreams or the loftier purpose of art, is a mask he devises to cover his incompletion. Or violence such as a war, between two men or among a number of nations, is also a blind and senseless compensation for that which is not yet formed in human nature. Then there is still another compensation. This one is found in the principle of atonement, the surrender of self to violent treatment by others with the idea of thereby cleansing one's self of his guilt.[2]

This statement emanates from the core of Williams's thought and is perhaps his most illuminating commentary about himself and his work. It represents a philosophy, or let us say an attitude toward man in his universe, which is to manifest itself in all his work. It is taken from his short story "Desire and the Black Masseur," which deals with the final compensation cited in the above quotation: purification through violence. In this tale, a man atones for what the author feels is a cosmic fragmentation and guilt by allowing—and actually furthering—his destruction by a cannibal. In *Battle of Angels* and *The Purification,* we find this same kind of violent cleansing.

The Glass Menagerie is a far cry from any of these works; it is the most nonviolent drama written by Williams. Nevertheless it adheres to the belief set forth in the short story. The underlying belief in *The Glass Menagerie* is that there is very little, if any, reason for living. Man is by nature incomplete because his universe is fragmented. There is nothing to be done about this condition because nothing *can* be done about it. Human guilt becomes a corollary of universal guilt and man's life is an atonement for the human condition. In each character in *The Glass Menagerie* there is a part "like a missing wall or a room left unfurnished and he tries as well as he can to make up for it." The mask devised by Laura and Amanda and Tom and Jim is "the use of imagination, resorting to dreams." The Wingfields are broken, fragmented people because "the sins of the world are really only its partialities." They are really not at all responsible for their condition, and thus are in no way able to cope with it. They are trapped in a determined universe. Without some kind of responsibility on the part of the protagonist there is opportunity neither for tragic elevation nor tragic fall. The Wingfields were doomed the moment they were born. At best their struggles will allow them to survive . . . for a time. They will never be allowed to triumph. Thus their struggles, their hopes, and even their eventual destruction can never move far beyond pathos. The beauty and magic of *The Glass Menagerie* is that this pathos is genuine, objective, and deeply moving.

[2]Williams, "Desire and the Black Masseur," *One Arm and Other Stories* (New York, New Directions, 1948), 85.

Arthur Miller

Arthur Miller (1915–2005) was the dean of American playwrights after the opening of *Death of a Salesman* in 1949. His steady output as a writer and a playwright began with his first publications after college in 1939, when he worked in the New York Federal Theatre Project, a branch of the Works Progress Administration (WPA), Franklin D. Roosevelt's huge Depression-era effort to put Americans back to work.

Miller, the son of a Jewish immigrant, was born and raised during his early years in the Harlem section of Manhattan and later in Brooklyn after his father's business failed. In high school Miller thought of himself more as an athlete than as a student, and he had trouble getting teachers' recommendations for college. After considerable struggle and waiting, he entered the University of Michigan, where his talent as a playwright emerged under the tutelage of Kenneth Rowe, his playwriting professor. His undergraduate plays won important university awards, and he became noticed by the Theatre Guild, a highly respected theater founded to present excellent plays (not necessarily commercial successes). His career was under way.

From 1939 to 1947 Miller wrote radio plays, screenplays, articles, stories, and a novel. His work covered a wide range of material, much of it growing out of his childhood memories of a tightly knit and somewhat eccentric family that provided him with a large gallery of characters. But he also dealt with political issues and problems of anti-Semitism, which was widespread in the 1930s and 1940s. Miller's political concerns have been a constant presence in his work since his earliest writings.

All My Sons (1947) was his first successful play. It ran on Broadway for three hundred performances, a remarkable record for a serious drama. The story centers on a man who knowingly produces defective parts for airplanes and then blames the subsequent crashes on his business partner, who is ruined and imprisoned. When the guilty man's son finds out the truth, he confronts his father and rebukes him. Ultimately, the man realizes not only that he has lost his son because of his deceit but that the dead pilots were also "all my sons." The play won the New York Drama Critics' Circle Award.

Miller's next play, *Death of a Salesman* (1949), was written in six weeks. Focusing on the American ideal of business success, its conclusions were a challenge to standard American business values. Willy Loman, first performed by Lee J. Cobb, was intended to be a warning for Americans in the postwar period of the cost of growing wealth and affluence.

His next play, *The Crucible* (1953), portrayed witch-hunts of seventeenth-century New England, but most people recognized the subtext: it was about contemporary anti-Communist witch-hunts. In the late 1940s and early 1950s the House Un-American Activities Committee (HUAC) held hearings to uncover suspected Communists in all areas of American life, particularly the arts. Many writers, artists, and performers came under close, often unfair, scrutiny by HUAC for their own political views and allegiances and were often asked to testify against their friends. Many were blacklisted (prevented from working in commercial theaters and movie companies), some were imprisoned for not testifying at others' trials, and some had their reputations and careers destroyed.

Arthur Miller was fearless in facing down HUAC, and he was convicted of contempt of court for not testifying against his friends. For a time he too was blacklisted, but his contempt citation was reversed, and he was not imprisoned. Given his personal political stance during this dangerous time, it is not a surprise to find that he usually chooses to write about matters of social concern.

In the 1990s Miller became the darling of the London stage, while at the same time being somewhat neglected in the United States. One full-scale play, *Broken Glass* (1994), played in regional theater before going to a brief run on Broadway and then a longer run in London's West End. The play concerns a woman who becomes paralyzed in response to *Kristallnacht* (night of crystal), a night of violent rampages against Jews and Jewish property that resulted in 91 Jewish dead, hundreds injured, and 7,500 businesses and 177 synagogues gutted. After November 9, 1938, it was clear that Jews were no longer safe in Hitler's Germany. The subject of the play is intense, significant, and still timely.

The Ride Down Mount Morgan had its premiere in London in 1991; it then took seven years to open in New York in 1998. Its protagonist, Lyman Felt, played by Patrick Stewart in New York, was conceived as a Reaganite go-getter of the late 1980s: economically rapacious, sexually voracious, and amoral. When Felt's Porsche crashes on a ride down Mount Morgan, his two wives discover one another at the hospital. The play proceeds from there, examining the ethical values that permit Felt to live as he does. George Wolfe produced the play at the Joseph Papp Public Theatre. The Broadway production opened at the Ambassador Theater in April 2000, again with Patrick Stewart. The play was nominated for a Tony Award.

DEATH OF A SALESMAN

Death of a Salesman (1949) was a hit from its first performances and has remained at the center of modern American drama ever since. It has been successful in China, where there were no salesmen in 1983, and in Europe, where many salesmen dominate certain industries. Everywhere this play has touched the hearts and minds of its audiences. Its success is a phenomenon of American drama.

The play was first performed in an experimental environment. Miller had originally conceived of a model of a man's head as the stage setting. He has said: "The first image that occurred to me which was to result in *Death of a*

Salesman was of an enormous face the height of the proscenium arch which would appear and then open up, and we would see the inside of a man's head. In fact, *The Inside of His Head* was the first title." This technique was not used, but when Miller worked with the director and producer of the first production, he helped develop a setting that became a model for the "American style" in drama. The multilevel set permitted the play to shift from Willy Loman and his wife, Linda, having a conversation in their kitchen to their sons' bedroom on the second level of the house. The set permitted portions of the stage to be reserved for Willy's visions of his brother, Ben, and for scenes outside the house such as Willy's interlude with the woman in Boston.

In a way, the setup of the stage respected Miller's original plan, but instead of portraying a cross-section of Willy's head, it presented a metaphor for a cross-section of his life. The audience was not looking in on just a living room, as in the nineteenth-century Ibsenist approach, but on an entire house and an entire life.

Using a cross section of a house as a metaphor was an especially important device in this play because of the play's allusions to Greek tragedy. The great Greek tragedies usually portray the destruction of a house—such as the house of Atreus—in which "house" stands for a whole family, not a building. When Shakespeare's Hamlet dies, for example, his entire line dies with him. The death in *Death of a Salesman* implies the destruction of a family holding certain beliefs that have been wrong from the start.

The life of the salesman has given Willy a sense of dignity and worth, and he imagines that the modern world has corrupted that sense by robbing salesmen of the value of their personality. He thinks that the modern world has failed him, but he is wrong. His original belief—that what counts is not *what* you know but *whom* you know and how well you are liked—lies at the heart of his failure. When the play opens, he already has failed at the traveling salesman's job because he can no longer drive to his assigned territory. He cannot sell what he needs to sell.

Willy has inculcated his beliefs in his sons, Happy and Biff, and both are as ineffectual as their father. Willy doted on Biff and encouraged him to become a high school football star at the expense of his studies. But when Biff cannot pass an important course, and his plans to make up the work are subverted by his disillusionment in his father, his dreams of a college football career vanish. He cannot change and recover from this defeat. Happy, like his father, builds castles in the air and assumes somehow that he will be successful, though he has nothing to back himself up with. He wants the glory—and he spends time in fanciful imaginings, as Willy does—but he cannot do the basic work that makes it possible to achieve glory. Ironically, it is the "anemic" Bernard—who studies hard, stresses personal honesty and diligence, and never brags—who is successful.

Linda supports Willy's illusions, allowing him to be a fraud by sharing—or pretending to believe—in his dream. Willy has permitted himself to feel that integrity, honesty, and fidelity are not as important as being well liked.

The play ends with Willy still unable to face the deceptions he has perpetuated. He commits suicide, believing that his sons will be able to follow in his footsteps and succeed where he did not; he thinks that his insurance money will save the house and the family. What he does not realize is that his sons are no more capable than he is. They have been corrupted by his thinking, his values, his beliefs. And they cannot solve the problems that overwhelmed him.

Death of a Salesman has been given a privileged position in American drama because it is a modern tragedy. Aristotle felt that only characters of noble birth could be tragic heroes, but Miller confounds this theory, as Eugene O'Neill did, by showing the human integrity in even the most humble characters. Miller's Willy Loman is not a peasant, nor is he noble. In fact, Miller took a frightening risk in producing a figure that we find hard to like. Willy wants to be well liked, but as an audience we find it difficult to like a person who whines, complains, and accepts petty immorality as a normal way of life. Despite his character, we are awed by his fate.

One Chinese commentator said, after the Chinese production, that China is filled with such dreamers as Willy. Certainly America has been filled with them. Willy stands as an aspect of our culture, commercial and otherwise, that is at the center of our reflection of ourselves. Perhaps we react so strongly to Willy because we are afraid that we might easily become a Willy Loman if we are not vigilant about our moral views, our psychological well-being, and the limits of our commitment to success. Willy Loman has mesmerized audiences in America in many different economic circumstances: prosperity, recession, rapid growth, and cautious development. No matter what those circumstances, we have looked at the play as if looking in a mirror. What we have seen has always involved us, although it has not always made us pleased with ourselves.

Death of a Salesman in Performance

Death of a Salesman opened on Broadway on February 10, 1949, and won virtually every prize available for drama, including the Pulitzer Prize and the New York Drama Critics' Circle Award for best play. It ran on Broadway for an incredible 742 performances. Elia Kazan, director, was instrumental in establishing the play's innovative staging. Lee J. Cobb was cast as Willy, Mildred Dunnock as Linda, Arthur Kennedy as Biff, and Cameron Mitchell as Happy. The London production in July 1949, with Paul Muni as Willy and Kevin McCarthy as Biff, lasted 204 performances. Robert Coleman said of the New York production: "An explosion of emotional dynamite was set off last evening in the Morosco [Theater]. . . . In fashioning *Death of a Salesman* for them, author Arthur Miller and director Elia Kazan have collaborated on as exciting and devastating a theatrical blast as the nerves of modern playgoers can stand." Of Cobb, Howard Barnes said, "Cobb contributes a mammoth and magnificent portrayal of the central character. In his hands the salesman's frustration and final suicide are a matter of tremendous import."

An all-black production was directed by Lee Sankowich in Baltimore in 1972. Miller, in the audience on that production's opening night, commented that the play had been well received in "many countries and cultures" and that the Baltimore production further underscored the universality of the play. George C. Scott was praised for the power of his performance as Willy in New York's Circle in the Square production in 1975. A Chinese production directed by Arthur Miller was enormously successful in 1983. In the most celebrated revival of the play Dustin Hoffman portrayed Willy, John Malkovich played Biff, and Michael Rudman directed at the Broadhurst Theatre in New York in 1984. The critic Benedict Nightingale said of that production, "Somewhere at the core of him

WILLY: When the hell did I lose my temper? I simply asked him if he was making any money. Is that a criticism?

LINDA: But, dear, how could he make any money?

WILLY (*worried and angered*): There's such an undercurrent in him. He became a moody man. Did he apologize when I left this morning?

LINDA: He was crestfallen, Willy. You know how he admires you. I think if he finds himself, then you'll both be happier and not fight any more.

WILLY: How can he find himself on a farm? Is that a life? A farmhand? In the beginning, when he was young, I thought, well, a young man, it's good for him to tramp around, take a lot of different jobs. But it's more than ten years now and he has yet to make thirty-five dollars a week!

LINDA: He's finding himself, Willy.

WILLY: Not finding yourself at the age of thirty-four is a disgrace!

LINDA: Shh!

WILLY: The trouble is he's lazy, goddammit!

LINDA: Willy, please!

WILLY: Biff is a lazy bum!

LINDA: They're sleeping. Get something to eat. Go on down.

WILLY: Why did he come home? I would like to know what brought him home.

LINDA: I don't know. I think he's still lost, Willy. I think he's very lost.

WILLY: Biff Loman is lost. In the greatest country in the world a young man with such — personal attractiveness, gets lost. And such a hard worker. There's one thing about Biff — he's not lazy.

LINDA: Never.

WILLY (*with pity and resolve*): I'll see him in the morning; I'll have a nice talk with him. I'll get him a job selling. He could be big in no time. My God! Remember how they used to follow him around in high school? When he smiled at one of them their faces lit up. When he walked down the street . . . (*He loses himself in reminiscences.*)

LINDA (*trying to bring him out of it*): Willy, dear, I got a new kind of American-type cheese today. It's whipped.

WILLY: Why do you get American when I like Swiss?

LINDA: I just thought you'd like a change —

WILLY: I don't want a change! I want Swiss cheese. Why am I always being contradicted?

LINDA (*with a covering laugh*): I thought it would be a surprise.

WILLY: Why don't you open a window in here, for God's sake?

LINDA (*with infinite patience*): They're all open, dear.

WILLY: The way they boxed us in here. Bricks and windows, windows and bricks.

LINDA: We should've bought the land next door.

WILLY: The street is lined with cars. There's not a breath of fresh air in the neighborhood. The grass don't grow anymore, you can't raise a carrot in the back yard. They should've had a law against apartment houses. Remember those two beautiful elm trees out there? When I and Biff hung the swing between them?

LINDA: Yeah, like being a million miles from the city.

WILLY: They should've arrested the builder for cutting those down. They massacred the neighborhood. (*Lost.*) More and more I think of those days, Linda. This time of year it was lilac and wisteria. And then the peonies would come out, and the daffodils. What fragrance in this room!

LINDA: Well, after all, people had to move somewhere.

WILLY: No, there's more people now.

LINDA: I don't think there's more people. I think —

WILLY: There's more people! That's what's ruining this country! Population is getting out of control. The competition is maddening! Smell the stink from that apartment house! And another one on the other side . . . How can they whip cheese?

(*On Willy's last line, Biff and Happy raise themselves up in their beds, listening.*)

LINDA: Go down, try it. And be quiet.

WILLY (*turning to Linda, guiltily*): You're not worried about me, are you, sweetheart?

BIFF: What's the matter?

HAPPY: Listen!

LINDA: You've got too much on the ball to worry about.

WILLY: You're my foundation and my support, Linda.

LINDA: Just try to relax, dear. You make mountains out of molehills.

WILLY: I won't fight with him any more. If he wants to go back to Texas, let him go.

LINDA: He'll find his way.

WILLY: Sure. Certain men just don't get started till later in life. Like Thomas Edison, I think. Or B. F. Goodrich. One of them was deaf. (*He starts for the bedroom doorway.*) I'll put my money on Biff.

LINDA: And Willy — if it's warm Sunday we'll drive in the country. And we'll open the windshield, and take lunch.

WILLY: No, the windshields don't open on the new cars.

LINDA: But you opened it today.

WILLY: Me? I didn't. (*He stops.*) Now isn't that peculiar! Isn't that a remarkable — (*He breaks off in amazement and fright as the flute is heard distantly.*)

LINDA: What, darling?

WILLY: That is the most remarkable thing.

LINDA: What, dear?

WILLY: I was thinking of the Chevvy. (*Slight pause.*) Nineteen twenty-eight . . . when I had that red Chevvy — (*Breaks off.*) That funny? I coulda sworn I was driving that Chevvy today.

LINDA: Well, that's nothing. Something must've reminded you.

WILLY: Remarkable. Ts. Remember those days? The way Biff used to simonize that car? The dealer refused to believe there was eighty thousand miles on it. (*He shakes his head.*) Heh! (*To Linda.*) Close your eyes, I'll be right up. (*He walks out of the bedroom.*)

HAPPY (*to Biff*): Jesus, maybe he smashed up the car again!

LINDA (*calling after Willy*): Be careful on the stairs, dear! The cheese is on the middle shelf! (*She turns, goes over to the bed, takes his jacket, and goes out of the bedroom.*)

(*Light has risen on the boys' room. Unseen, Willy is heard talking to himself, "Eighty thousand miles," and a little laugh. Biff gets out of bed, comes downstage a bit, and stands attentively. Biff is two years older than his brother Happy, well built, but in these days bears a worn air and seems less self-assured. He has succeeded less, and his dreams are stronger and less acceptable than Happy's. Happy is tall, powerfully made. Sexuality is like a visible color on him, or a scent that many women have discovered. He, like his brother, is lost, but in a different way, for he has never allowed himself to turn his face toward defeat and is thus more confused and hard-skinned, although seemingly more content.*)

HAPPY (*getting out of bed*): He's going to get his license taken away if he keeps that up. I'm getting nervous about him, y'know, Biff?

BIFF: His eyes are going.

HAPPY: No, I've driven with him. He sees all right. He just doesn't keep his mind on it. I drove into the city with him last week. He stops at a green light and then it turns red and he goes. (*He laughs.*)

BIFF: Maybe he's color-blind.

HAPPY: Pop? Why he's got the finest eye for color in the business. You know that.

BIFF (*sitting down on his bed*): I'm going to sleep.

HAPPY: You're not still sour on Dad, are you, Biff?

BIFF: He's all right, I guess.

WILLY (*underneath them, in the living room*): Yes, sir, eighty thousand miles—eighty-two thousand!

BIFF: You smoking?

HAPPY (*holding out a pack of cigarettes*): Want one?

BIFF (*taking a cigarette*): I can never sleep when I smell it.

WILLY: What a simonizing job, heh!

HAPPY (*with deep sentiment*): Funny, Biff, y'know? Us sleeping in here again? The old beds. (*He pats his bed affectionately.*) All the talk that went across those two beds, huh? Our whole lives.

BIFF: Yeah. Lotta dreams and plans.

HAPPY (*with a deep and masculine laugh*): About five hundred women would like to know what was said in this room.

(*They share a soft laugh.*)

BIFF: Remember that big Betsy something—what the hell was her name—over on Bushwick Avenue?

HAPPY (*combing his hair*): With the collie dog!

BIFF: That's the one. I got you in there, remember?

HAPPY: Yeah, that was my first time—I think. Boy, there was a pig. (*They laugh, almost crudely.*) You taught me everything I know about women. Don't forget that.

BIFF: I bet you forgot how bashful you used to be. Especially with girls.

HAPPY: Oh, I still am, Biff.

BIFF: Oh, go on.

HAPPY: I just control it, that's all. I think I got less bashful and you got more so. What happened, Biff? Where's the old humor, the old confidence? (*He shakes Biff's knee. Biff gets up and moves restlessly about the room.*) What's the matter?

BIFF: Why does Dad mock me all the time?

HAPPY: He's not mocking you, he—

BIFF: Everything I say there's a twist of mockery on his face. I can't get near him.

HAPPY: He just wants you to make good, that's all. I wanted to talk to you about Dad for a long time, Biff. Something's—happening to him. He—talks to himself.

BIFF: I noticed that this morning. But he always mumbled.

HAPPY: But not so noticeable. It got so embarrassing I sent him to Florida. And you know something? Most of the time he's talking to you.

BIFF: What's he say about me?

HAPPY: I can't make it out.

BIFF: What's he say about me?

HAPPY: I think the fact that you're not settled, that you're still kind of up in the air...

BIFF: There's one or two other things depressing him, Happy.

HAPPY: What do you mean?

BIFF: Never mind. Just don't lay it all to me.

HAPPY: But I think if you just got started—I mean—is there any future for you out there?

BIFF: I tell ya, Hap, I don't know what the future is. I don't know—what I'm supposed to want.

HAPPY: What do you mean?

BIFF: Well, I spent six or seven years after high school trying to work myself up. Shipping clerk, salesman, business of one kind or another. And it's a measly manner of existence. To get on that subway on the hot mornings in summer. To devote your whole life to keeping stock, or making phone calls, or selling or buying. To suffer fifty weeks of the year for the sake of a two-week vacation, when all you really desire is to be outdoors, with your shirt off. And always to have to get ahead of the next fella. And still—that's how you build a future.

HAPPY: Well, you really enjoy it on a farm? Are you content out there?

BIFF (*with rising agitation*): Hap, I've had twenty or thirty different kinds of jobs since I left home before the war, and it always turns out the same. I just realized it lately. In Nebraska when I herded cattle, and the Dakotas, and Arizona, and now in Texas. It's why I came home now, I guess, because I realized it. This farm I work on, it's spring there now, see? And they've got about fifteen new colts. There's nothing more inspiring or—beautiful than the sight of a mare and a new colt. And it's cool there now, see?

Texas is cool now, and it's spring. And whenever spring comes to where I am, I suddenly get the feeling, my God, I'm not gettin' anywhere! What the hell am I doing, playing around with horses, twenty-eight dollars a week! I'm thirty-four years old, I oughta be makin' my future. That's when I come running home. And now, I get here, and I don't know what to do with myself. (*After a pause.*) I've always made a point of not wasting my life, and every time I come back here I know that all I've done is to waste my life.

HAPPY: You're a poet, you know that, Biff? You're a— you're an idealist!

BIFF: No, I'm mixed up very bad. Maybe I oughta get married. Maybe I oughta get stuck into something. Maybe that's my trouble. I'm like a boy. I'm not married, I'm not in business, I just—I'm like a boy. Are you content, Hap? You're a success, aren't you? Are you content?

HAPPY: Hell, no!

BIFF: Why? You're making money, aren't you?

HAPPY (*moving about with energy, expressiveness*): All I can do now is wait for the merchandise manager to die. And suppose I get to be merchandise manager? He's a good friend of mine, and he just built a terrific estate on Long Island. And he lived there about two months and sold it, and now he's building another one. He can't enjoy it once it's finished. And I know that's just what I would do. I don't know what the hell I'm workin' for. Sometimes I sit in my apartment—all alone. And I think of the rent I'm paying. And it's crazy. But then, it's what I always wanted. My own apartment, a car, and plenty of women. And still, goddammit, I'm lonely.

BIFF (*with enthusiasm*): Listen, why don't you come out West with me?

HAPPY: You and I, heh?

BIFF: Sure, maybe we could buy a ranch. Raise cattle, use our muscles. Men built like we are should be working out in the open.

HAPPY (*avidly*): The Loman Brothers, heh?

BIFF (*with vast affection*): Sure, we'd be known all over the counties!

HAPPY (*enthralled*): That's what I dream about, Biff. Sometimes I want to just rip my clothes off in the middle of the store and outbox that goddam merchandise manager. I mean I can outbox, outrun and outlift anybody in that store, and I have to take orders from those common, petty sons-of-bitches till I can't stand it anymore.

BIFF: I'm tellin' you, kid, if you were with me I'd be happy out there.

HAPPY (*enthused*): See, Biff, everybody around me is so false that I'm constantly lowering my ideals...

BIFF: Baby, together we'd stand up for one another, we'd have someone to trust.

HAPPY: If I were around you—

BIFF: Hap, the trouble is we weren't brought up to grub for money. I don't know how to do it.

HAPPY: Neither can I!

BIFF: Then let's go!

HAPPY: The only thing is—what can you make out there?

BIFF: But look at your friend. Builds an estate and then hasn't the peace of mind to live in it.

HAPPY: Yeah, but when he walks into the store the waves part in front of him. That's fifty-two thousand dollars a year coming through the revolving door, and I got more in my pinky finger than he's got in his head.

BIFF: Yeah, but you just said—

HAPPY: I gotta show some of those pompous, self-important executives over there that Hap Loman can make the grade. I want to walk into the store the way he walks in. Then I'll go with you, Biff. We'll be together yet, I swear. But take those two we had tonight. Now weren't they gorgeous creatures?

BIFF: Yeah, yeah, most gorgeous I've had in years.

HAPPY: I get that any time I want, Biff. Whenever I feel disgusted. The only trouble is, it gets like bowling or something. I just keep knockin' them over and it doesn't mean anything. You still run around a lot?

BIFF: Naa. I'd like to find a girl—steady, somebody with substance.

HAPPY: That's what I long for.

BIFF: Go on! You'd never come home.

HAPPY: I would! Somebody with character, with resistance! Like Mom, y'know? You're gonna call me a bastard when I tell you this. That girl Charlotte I was with tonight is engaged to be married in five weeks. (*He tries on his new hat.*)

BIFF: No kiddin'!

HAPPY: Sure, the guy's in line for the vice-presidency of the store. I don't know what gets into me, maybe I just have an overdeveloped sense of competition or something, but I went and ruined her, and furthermore I can't get rid of her. And he's the third executive I've done that to. Isn't that a crummy characteristic? And to top it all, I go to their weddings! (*Indignantly, but laughing.*) Like I'm not supposed to take bribes. Manufacturers offer me a hundred-dollar bill now and then to throw an order their way. You know how honest I am, but it's like this girl, see. I hate myself for it. Because I don't want the girl, and, still, I take it and— I love it!

BIFF: Let's go to sleep.

HAPPY: I guess we didn't settle anything, heh?

BIFF: I just got one idea that I think I'm going to try.

HAPPY: What's that?

BIFF: Remember Bill Oliver?

HAPPY: Sure, Oliver is very big now. You want to work for him again?

BIFF: No, but when I quit he said something to me. He put his arm on my shoulder, and he said, "Biff, if you ever need anything, come to me."

HAPPY: I remember that. That sounds good.

BIFF: I think I'll go to see him. If I could get ten thousand or even seven or eight thousand dollars I could buy a beautiful ranch.

HAPPY: I bet he'd back you. 'Cause he thought highly of you, Biff. I mean, they all do. You're well liked, Biff. That's why I say to come back here, and we both have the apartment. And I'm tellin' you, Biff, any babe you want...

BIFF: No, with a ranch I could do the work I like and still be something. I just wonder though. I wonder if Oliver still thinks I stole that carton of basketballs.

HAPPY: Oh, he probably forgot that long ago. It's almost ten years. You're too sensitive. Anyway, he didn't really fire you.

BIFF: Well, I think he was going to. I think that's why I quit. I was never sure whether he knew or not. I know he thought the world of me, though. I was the only one he'd let lock up the place.

WILLY (below): You gonna wash the engine, Biff?

HAPPY: Shh!

(Biff looks at Happy, who is gazing down, listening. Willy is mumbling in the parlor.)

HAPPY: You hear that?

(They listen. Willy laughs warmly.)

BIFF (growing angry): Doesn't he know Mom can hear that?

WILLY: Don't get your sweater dirty, Biff!

(A look of pain crosses Biff's face.)

HAPPY: Isn't that terrible? Don't leave again, will you? You'll find a job here. You gotta stick around. I don't know what to do about him, it's getting embarrassing.

WILLY: What a simonizing job!

BIFF: Mom's hearing that!

WILLY: No kiddin', Biff, you got a date? Wonderful!

HAPPY: Go on to sleep. But talk to him in the morning, will you?

BIFF (reluctantly getting into bed): With her in the house. Brother!

HAPPY (getting into bed): I wish you'd have a good talk with him.

(The light on their room begins to fade.)

BIFF (to himself in bed): That selfish, stupid...

HAPPY: Sh . . . Sleep, Biff.

(Their light is out. Well before they have finished speaking, Willy's form is dimly seen below in the darkened kitchen. He opens the refrigerator, searches in there, and takes out a bottle of milk. The apartment houses are fading out, and the entire house and surroundings become covered with leaves. Music insinuates itself as the leaves appear.)

WILLY: Just wanna be careful with those girls, Biff, that's all. Don't make any promises. No promises of any kind. Because a girl, y'know, they always believe what you tell 'em, and you're very young, Biff, you're too young to be talking seriously to girls.

(Light rises on the kitchen. Willy, talking, shuts the refrigerator door and comes downstage to the kitchen table. He pours milk into a glass. He is totally immersed in himself, smiling faintly.)

WILLY: Too young entirely, Biff. You want to watch your schooling first. Then when you're all set, there'll be plenty of girls for a boy like you. (He smiles broadly at a kitchen chair.) That so? The girls pay for you? (He laughs.) Boy, you must really be makin' a hit.

(Willy is gradually addressing—physically—a point offstage, speaking through the wall of the kitchen, and his voice has been rising in volume to that of a normal conversation.)

WILLY: I been wondering why you polish the car so careful. Ha! Don't leave the hubcaps, boys. Get the chamois to the hubcaps. Happy, use newspaper on the windows, it's the easiest thing. Show him how to do it, Biff! You see, Happy? Pad it up, use it like a pad. That's it, that's it, good work. You're doin' all right, Hap. (He pauses, then nods in approbation for a few seconds, then looks upward.) Biff, first thing we gotta do when we get time is clip that big branch over the house. Afraid it's gonna fall in a storm and hit the roof. Tell you what. We get a rope and sling her around, and then we climb up there with a couple of saws and take her down. Soon as you finish the car, boys, I wanna see ye. I got a surprise for you, boys.

BIFF (offstage): Whatta ya got, Dad?

WILLY: No, you finish first. Never leave a job till you're finished—remember that. (Looking toward the "big trees.") Biff, up in Albany I saw a beautiful hammock. I think I'll buy it next trip, and we'll hang it right between those two elms. Wouldn't that be something? Just swingin' there under those branches. Boy, that would be...

(Young Biff and Young Happy appear from the direction Willy was addressing. Happy carries rags and a pail of water. Biff, wearing a sweater with a block "S," carries a football.)

BIFF (pointing in the direction of the car offstage): How's that, Pop, professional?

WILLY: Terrific. Terrific job, boys. Good work, Biff.

HAPPY: Where's the surprise, Pop?

WILLY: In the back seat of the car.

HAPPY: Boy! (He runs off.)

BIFF: What is it, Dad? Tell me, what'd you buy?

WILLY (laughing, cuffs him): Never mind, something I want you to have.

BIFF (turns and starts off): What is it, Hap?

HAPPY (offstage): It's a punching bag!

BIFF: Oh, Pop!

WILLY: It's got Gene Tunney's signature on it!

(Happy runs onstage with a punching bag.)

BIFF: Gee, how'd you know we wanted a punching bag?

Biff (Kevin Anderson), Willy (Brian Dennehy), and Happy (Ted Koch) in a bright moment in Robert Falls's 1999 Broadway revival of *Death of a Salesman*.

WILLY: Well, it's the finest thing for the timing.

HAPPY (*lies down on his back and pedals with his feet*): I'm losing weight, you notice, Pop?

WILLY (*to Happy*): Jumping rope is good too.

BIFF: Did you see the new football I got?

WILLY (*examining the ball*): Where'd you get a new ball?

BIFF: The coach told me to practice my passing.

WILLY: That so? And he gave you the ball, heh?

BIFF: Well, I borrowed it from the locker room. (*He laughs confidentially.*)

WILLY (*laughing with him at the theft*): I want you to return that.

HAPPY: I told you he wouldn't like it!

BIFF (*angrily*): Well, I'm bringing it back!

WILLY (*stopping the incipient argument, to Happy*): Sure, he's gotta practice with a regulation ball, doesn't he? (*To Biff.*) Coach'll probably congratulate you on your initiative!

BIFF: Oh, he keeps congratulating my initiative all the time, Pop.

WILLY: That's because he likes you. If somebody else took that ball there'd be an uproar. So what's the report, boys, what's the report?

BIFF: Where'd you go this time, Dad? Gee we were lonesome for you.

WILLY (*pleased, puts an arm around each boy and they come down to the apron*): Lonesome, heh?

BIFF: Missed you every minute.

WILLY: Don't say? Tell you a secret, boys. Don't breathe it to a soul. Someday I'll have my own business, and I'll never have to leave home anymore.

HAPPY: Like Uncle Charley, heh?

WILLY: Bigger than Uncle Charley! Because Charley is not—liked. He's liked, but he's not—well liked.

BIFF: Where'd you go this time, Dad?

WILLY: Well, I got on the road, and I went north to Providence. Met the Mayor.

BIFF: The Mayor of Providence!

WILLY: He was sitting in the hotel lobby.

BIFF: What'd he say?

WILLY: He said, "Morning!" And I said, "You got a fine city here, Mayor." And then he had coffee with me. And then I went to Waterbury. Waterbury is a fine city. Big clock city, the famous Waterbury clock. Sold a nice bill there. And then Boston—Boston is the cradle of the Revolution. A fine city. And a couple of other towns in Mass., and on to Portland and Bangor and straight home!

BIFF: Gee, I'd love to go with you sometime, Dad.

WILLY: Soon as summer comes.

HAPPY: Promise?

WILLY: You and Hap and I, and I'll show you all the towns. America is full of beautiful towns and fine, upstanding people. And they know me, boys, they know me up and down New England. The finest people. And when I bring you fellas up, there'll be open sesame for all of us, 'cause one thing, boys: I have friends. I can park my car in any street in New England, and the cops protect it like their own. This summer, heh?

BIFF AND HAPPY (*together*): Yeah! You bet!

WILLY: We'll take our bathing suits.

HAPPY: We'll carry your bags, Pop!

WILLY: Oh, won't that be something! Me comin' into the Boston stores with you boys carryin' my bags. What a sensation!

(*Biff is prancing around, practicing passing the ball.*)

WILLY: You nervous, Biff, about the game?

BIFF: Not if you're gonna be there.

WILLY: What do they say about you in school, now that they made you captain?

HAPPY: There's a crowd of girls behind him every time the classes change.

BIFF (*taking Willy's hand*): This Saturday, Pop, this Saturday—just for you, I'm going to break through for a touchdown.

HAPPY: You're supposed to pass.

BIFF: I'm takin' one play for Pop. You watch me, Pop, and when I take off my helmet, that means I'm breakin' out. Then you watch me crash through that line!

WILLY (*kisses Biff*): Oh, wait'll I tell this in Boston!

(*Bernard enters in knickers. He is younger than Biff, earnest and loyal, a worried boy.*)

BERNARD: Biff, where are you? You're supposed to study with me today.

WILLY: Hey, looka Bernard. What're you lookin' so anemic about, Bernard?

BERNARD: He's gotta study, Uncle Willy. He's got Regents next week.

HAPPY (*tauntingly, spinning Bernard around*): Let's box, Bernard!

BERNARD: Biff! (*He gets away from Happy.*) Listen, Biff, I heard Mr. Birnbaum say that if you don't start studyin' math he's gonna flunk you, and you won't graduate. I heard him!

WILLY: You better study with him, Biff. Go ahead now.

BERNARD: I heard him!

BIFF: Oh, Pop, you didn't see my sneakers! (*He holds up a foot for Willy to look at.*)

WILLY: Hey, that's a beautiful job of printing!

BERNARD (*wiping his glasses*): Just because he printed University of Virginia on his sneakers doesn't mean they've got to graduate him, Uncle Willy!

WILLY (*angrily*): What're you talking about? With scholarships to three universities they're gonna flunk him?

BERNARD: But I heard Mr. Birnbaum say—

WILLY: Don't be a pest, Bernard! (*To his boys.*) What an anemic!

BERNARD: Okay, I'm waiting for you in my house, Biff.

(*Bernard goes off. The Lomans laugh.*)

WILLY: Bernard is not well liked, is he?

BIFF: He's liked, but he's not well liked.

HAPPY: That's right, Pop.

WILLY: That's just what I mean. Bernard can get the best marks in school, y'understand, but when he gets out in the business world, y'understand, you are going to be five times ahead of him. That's why I thank Almighty God you're both built like Adonises. Because the man who makes an appearance in the business world, the man who creates personal interest, is the man who gets ahead. Be liked and you will never want. You take me, for instance. I never have to wait in line to see a buyer. "Willy Loman is here!" That's all they have to know, and I go right through.

BIFF: Did you knock them dead, Pop?

WILLY: Knocked 'em cold in Providence, slaughtered 'em in Boston.

HAPPY (*on his back, pedaling again*): I'm losing weight, you notice, Pop?

(*Linda enters as of old, a ribbon in her hair, carrying a basket of washing.*)

LINDA (*with youthful energy*): Hello, dear!

WILLY: Sweetheart!

LINDA: How'd the Chevvy run?

WILLY: Chevrolet, Linda, is the greatest car ever built. (*To the boys.*) Since when do you let your mother carry wash up the stairs?

BIFF: Grab hold there, boy!

HAPPY: Where to, Mom?

LINDA: Hang them up on the line. And you better go down to your friends, Biff. The cellar is full of boys. They don't know what to do with themselves.

BIFF: Ah, when Pop comes home they can wait!

WILLY (*laughs appreciatively*): You better go down and tell them what to do, Biff.

BIFF: I think I'll have them sweep out the furnace room.

WILLY: Good work, Biff.

BIFF (*goes through wall-line of kitchen to doorway at back and calls down*): Fellas! Everybody sweep out the furnace room! I'll be right down!

VOICES: All right! Okay, Biff.

BIFF: George and Sam and Frank, come out back! We're hangin' up the wash! Come on, Hap, on the double! (*He and Happy carry out the basket.*)

LINDA: The way they obey him!

WILLY: Well, that's training, the training. I'm tellin' you, I was sellin' thousands and thousands, but I had to come home.

LINDA: Oh, the whole block'll be at that game. Did you sell anything?

WILLY: I did five hundred gross in Providence and seven hundred gross in Boston.

LINDA: No! Wait a minute, I've got a pencil. (*She pulls pencil and paper out of her apron pocket.*) That makes your commission . . . Two hundred—my God! Two hundred and twelve dollars!

WILLY: Well, I didn't figure it yet, but . . .

LINDA: How much did you do?

WILLY: Well, I—I did—about a hundred and eighty gross in Providence. Well, no—it came to—roughly two hundred gross on the whole trip.

LINDA (*without hesitation*): Two hundred gross. That's . . . (*She figures.*)

WILLY: The trouble was that three of the stores were half-closed for inventory in Boston. Otherwise I woulda broke records.

LINDA: Well, it makes seventy dollars and some pennies. That's very good.

WILLY: What do we owe?

LINDA: Well, on the first there's sixteen dollars on the refrigerator—

WILLY: Why sixteen?

LINDA: Well, the fan belt broke, so it was a dollar eighty.

WILLY: But it's brand new.

LINDA: Well, the man said that's the way it is. Till they work themselves in, y'know.

(*They move through the wall-line into the kitchen.*)

WILLY: I hope we didn't get stuck on that machine.

LINDA: They got the biggest ads of any of them!

WILLY: I know, it's a fine machine. What else?

LINDA: Well, there's nine-sixty for the washing machine. And for the vacuum cleaner there's three and a half due on the fifteenth. Then the roof, you got twenty-one dollars remaining.

WILLY: It don't leak, does it?

LINDA: No, they did a wonderful job. Then you owe Frank for the carburetor.

WILLY: I'm not going to pay that man! That goddam Chevrolet, they ought to prohibit the manufacture of that car!

LINDA: Well, you owe him three and a half. And odds and ends, comes to around a hundred and twenty dollars by the fifteenth.

WILLY: A hundred and twenty dollars! My God, if business don't pick up I don't know what I'm gonna do!

LINDA: Well, next week you'll do better.

WILLY: Oh, I'll knock 'em dead next week. I'll go to Hartford. I'm very well liked in Hartford. You know, the trouble is, Linda, people don't seem to take to me.

(*They move onto the forestage.*)

LINDA: Oh, don't be foolish.

WILLY: I know it when I walk in. They seem to laugh at me.

LINDA: Why? Why would they laugh at you? Don't talk that way, Willy.

(*Willy moves to the edge of the stage. Linda goes into the kitchen and starts to darn stockings.*)

WILLY: I don't know the reason for it, but they just pass me by. I'm not noticed.

LINDA: But you're doing wonderful, dear. You're making seventy to a hundred dollars a week.

WILLY: But I gotta be at it ten, twelve hours a day. Other men—I don't know—they do it easier. I don't know why—I can't stop myself—I talk too much. A man oughta come in with a few words. One thing about Charley. He's a man of few words, and they respect him.

LINDA: You don't talk too much, you're just lively.

WILLY (*smiling*): Well, I figure, what the hell, life is short, a couple of jokes. (*To himself.*) I joke too much! (*The smile goes.*)

LINDA: Why? You're—

WILLY: I'm fat. I'm very—foolish to look at, Linda. I didn't tell you, but Christmas time I happened to be calling on F. H. Stewarts, and a salesman I know, as I was going in to see the buyer I heard him say something about—walrus. And I—I cracked him right across the face. I won't take that. I simply will not take that. But they do laugh at me. I know that.

LINDA: Darling . . .

WILLY: I gotta overcome it. I know I gotta overcome it. I'm not dressing to advantage, maybe.

LINDA: Willy, darling, you're the handsomest man in the world—

WILLY: Oh, no, Linda.

LINDA: To me you are. (*Slight pause.*) The handsomest.

(*From the darkness is heard the laughter of a woman. Willy doesn't turn to it, but it continues through Linda's lines.*)

LINDA: And the boys, Willy. Few men are idolized by their children the way you are.

(*Music is heard as behind a scrim, to the left of the house, The Woman, dimly seen, is dressing.*)

WILLY (*with great feeling*): You're the best there is, Linda, you're a pal, you know that? On the road—on the road I want to grab you sometimes and just kiss the life outa you.

(*The laughter is loud now, and he moves into a brightening area at the left, where The Woman has come from behind the scrim and is standing, putting on her hat, looking into a "mirror" and laughing.*)

WILLY: 'Cause I get so lonely—especially when business is bad and there's nobody to talk to. I get the feeling that I'll never sell anything again, that I won't make a living for you, or a business, a business for the boys.

(*He talks through The Woman's subsiding laughter; The Woman primps at the "mirror."*) There's so much I want to make for—

THE WOMAN: Me? You didn't make me, Willy. I picked you.

WILLY (*pleased*): You picked me?

THE WOMAN (*who is quite proper-looking, Willy's age*): I did. I've been sitting at that desk watching all the salesmen go by, day in, day out. But you've got such a sense of humor, and we do have such a good time together, don't we?

WILLY: Sure, sure. (*He takes her in his arms.*) Why do you have to go now?

THE WOMAN: It's two o'clock...

WILLY: No, come on in! (*He pulls her.*)

THE WOMAN: ... my sisters'll be scandalized. When'll you be back?

WILLY: Oh, two weeks about. Will you come up again?

THE WOMAN: Sure thing. You do make me laugh. It's good for me. (*She squeezes his arm, kisses him.*) And I think you're a wonderful man.

WILLY: You picked me, heh?

THE WOMAN: Sure. Because you're so sweet. And such a kidder.

WILLY: Well, I'll see you next time I'm in Boston.

THE WOMAN: I'll put you right through to the buyers.

WILLY (*slapping her bottom*): Right. Well, bottoms up!

THE WOMAN (*slaps him gently and laughs*): You just kill me, Willy. (*He suddenly grabs her and kisses her roughly.*) You kill me. And thanks for the stockings. I love a lot of stockings. Well, good night.

WILLY: Good night. And keep your pores open!

THE WOMAN: Oh, Willy!

(*The Woman bursts out laughing, and Linda's laughter blends in. The Woman disappears into the dark. Now the area at the kitchen table brightens. Linda is sitting where she was at the kitchen table, but now is mending a pair of her silk stockings.*)

LINDA: You are, Willy. The handsomest man. You've got no reason to feel that—

WILLY (*coming out of The Woman's dimming area and going over to Linda*): I'll make it all up to you, Linda, I'll—

LINDA: There's nothing to make up, dear. You're doing fine, better than—

WILLY (*noticing her mending*): What's that?

LINDA: Just mending my stockings. They're so expensive—

WILLY (*angrily, taking them from her*): I won't have you mending stockings in this house! Now throw them out!

(*Linda puts the stockings in her pocket.*)

BERNARD (*entering on the run*): Where is he? If he doesn't study!

WILLY (*moving to the forestage, with great agitation*): You'll give him the answers!

BERNARD: I do, but I can't on a Regents! That's a state exam! They're liable to arrest me!

WILLY: Where is he? I'll whip him, I'll whip him!

LINDA: And he'd better give back that football, Willy, it's not nice.

WILLY: Biff! Where is he? Why is he taking everything?

LINDA: He's too rough with the girls, Willy. All the mothers are afraid of him!

WILLY: I'll whip him!

BERNARD: He's driving the car without a license!

(*The Woman's laugh is heard.*)

WILLY: Shut up!

LINDA: All the mothers—

WILLY: Shut up!

BERNARD (*backing quietly away and out*): Mr. Birnbaum says he's stuck up.

WILLY: Get outa here!

BERNARD: If he doesn't buckle down he'll flunk math! (*He goes off.*)

LINDA: He's right, Willy, you've gotta—

WILLY (*exploding at her*): There's nothing the matter with him! You want him to be a worm like Bernard? He's got spirit, personality...

(*As he speaks, Linda, almost in tears, exits into the living room. Willy is alone in the kitchen, wilting and staring. The leaves are gone. It is night again, and the apartment houses look down from behind.*)

WILLY: Loaded with it. Loaded! What is he stealing? He's giving it back, isn't he? Why is he stealing? What did I tell him? I never in my life told him anything but decent things.

(*Happy in pajamas has come down the stairs; Willy suddenly becomes aware of Happy's presence.*)

HAPPY: Let's go now, come on.

WILLY (*sitting down at the kitchen table*): Huh! Why did she have to wax the floors herself? Everytime she waxes the floors she keels over. She knows that!

HAPPY: Shh! Take it easy. What brought you back tonight?

WILLY: I got an awful scare. Nearly hit a kid in Yonkers. God! Why didn't I go to Alaska with my brother Ben that time! Ben! That man was a genius, that man was success incarnate! What a mistake! He begged me to go.

HAPPY: Well, there's no use in—

WILLY: You guys! There was a man started with the clothes on his back and ended up with diamond mines!

HAPPY: Boy, someday I'd like to know how he did it.

WILLY: What's the mystery? The man knew what he wanted and went out and got it! Walked into a jungle, and comes out, the age of twenty-one, and he's rich! The world is an oyster, but you don't crack it open on a mattress!

HAPPY: Pop, I told you I'm gonna retire you for life.

WILLY: You'll retire me for life on seventy goddam dollars a week? And your women and your car and your apartment, and you'll retire me for life! Christ's sake,

I couldn't get past Yonkers today! Where are you guys, where are you? The woods are burning! I can't drive a car!

(*Charley has appeared in the doorway. He is a large man, slow of speech, laconic, immovable. In all he says, despite what he says, there is pity, and, now, trepidation. He has a robe over pajamas, slippers on his feet. He enters the kitchen.*)

CHARLEY: Everything all right?
HAPPY: Yeah, Charley, everything's...
WILLY: What's the matter?
CHARLEY: I heard some noise. I thought something happened. Can't we do something about the walls? You sneeze in here, and in my house hats blow off.
HAPPY: Let's go to bed, Dad. Come on.

(*Charley signals to Happy to go.*)

WILLY: You go ahead, I'm not tired at the moment.
HAPPY (*to Willy*): Take it easy, huh? (*He exits.*)
WILLY: What're you doin' up?
CHARLEY (*sitting down at the kitchen table opposite Willy*): Couldn't sleep good. I had a heartburn.
WILLY: Well, you don't know how to eat.
CHARLEY: I eat with my mouth.
WILLY: No, you're ignorant. You gotta know about vitamins and things like that.
CHARLEY: Come on, let's shoot. Tire you out a little.
WILLY (*hesitantly*): All right. You got cards?
CHARLEY (*taking a deck from his pocket*): Yeah, I got them. Someplace. What is it with those vitamins?
WILLY (*dealing*): They build up your bones. Chemistry.
CHARLEY: Yeah, but there's no bones in a heartburn.
WILLY: What are you talkin' about? Do you know the first thing about it?
CHARLEY: Don't get insulted.
WILLY: Don't talk about something you don't know anything about.

(*They are playing. Pause.*)

CHARLEY: What're you doin' home?
WILLY: A little trouble with the car.
CHARLEY: Oh. (*Pause.*) I'd like to take a trip to California.
WILLY: Don't say.
CHARLEY: You want a job?
WILLY: I got a job, I told you that. (*After a slight pause.*) What the hell are you offering me a job for?
CHARLEY: Don't get insulted.
WILLY: Don't insult me.
CHARLEY: I don't see no sense in it. You don't have to go on this way.
WILLY: I got a good job. (*Slight pause.*) What do you keep comin' in here for?
CHARLEY: You want me to go?
WILLY (*after a pause, withering*): I can't understand it. He's going back to Texas again. What the hell is that?
CHARLEY: Let him go.

WILLY: I got nothin' to give him, Charley, I'm clean, I'm clean.
CHARLEY: He won't starve. None a them starve. Forget about him.
WILLY: Then what have I got to remember?
CHARLEY: You take it too hard. To hell with it. When a deposit bottle is broken you don't get your nickel back.
WILLY: That's easy enough for you to say.
CHARLEY: That ain't easy for me to say.
WILLY: Did you see the ceiling I put up in the living room?
CHARLEY: Yeah, that's a piece of work. To put up a ceiling is a mystery to me. How do you do it?
WILLY: What's the difference?
CHARLEY: Well, talk about it.
WILLY: You gonna put up a ceiling?
CHARLEY: How could I put up a ceiling?
WILLY: Then what the hell are you bothering me for?
CHARLEY: You're insulted again.
WILLY: A man who can't handle tools is not a man. You're disgusting.
CHARLEY: Don't call me disgusting, Willy.

(*Uncle Ben, carrying a valise and an umbrella, enters the forestage from around the right corner of the house. He is a stolid man, in his sixties, with a mustache and an authoritative air. He is utterly certain of his destiny, and there is an aura of far places about him. He enters exactly as Willy speaks.*)

WILLY: I'm getting awfully tired, Ben.

(*Ben's music is heard. Ben looks around at everything.*)

CHARLEY: Good, keep playing; you'll sleep better. Did you call me Ben?

(*Ben looks at his watch.*)

WILLY: That's funny. For a second there you reminded me of my brother Ben.
BEN: I only have a few minutes. (*He strolls, inspecting the place. Willy and Charley continue playing.*)
CHARLEY: You never heard from him again, heh? Since that time?
WILLY: Didn't Linda tell you? Couple of weeks ago we got a letter from his wife in Africa. He died.
CHARLEY: That so.
BEN (*chuckling*): So this is Brooklyn, eh?
CHARLEY: Maybe you're in for some of his money.
WILLY: Naa, he had seven sons. There's just one opportunity I had with that man...
BEN: I must make a train, William. There are several properties I'm looking at in Alaska.
WILLY: Sure, sure! If I'd gone with him to Alaska that time, everything would've been totally different.
CHARLIE: Go on, you'd froze to death up there.
WILLY: What're you talking about?
BEN: Opportunity is tremendous in Alaska, William. Surprised you're not up there.

WILLY: Sure, tremendous.
CHARLEY: Heh?
WILLY: There was the only man I ever met who knew the answers.
CHARLEY: Who?
BEN: How are you all?
WILLY (*taking a pot, smiling*): Fine, fine.
CHARLEY: Pretty sharp tonight.
BEN: Is Mother living with you?
WILLY: No, she died a long time ago.
CHARLEY: Who?
BEN: That's too bad. Fine specimen of a lady, Mother.
WILLY (*to Charley*): Heh?
BEN: I'd hoped to see the old girl.
CHARLEY: Who died?
BEN: Heard anything from Father, have you?
WILLY (*unnerved*): What do you mean, who died?
CHARLEY (*taking a pot*): What're you talkin' about?
BEN (*looking at his watch*): William, it's half-past eight!
WILLY (*as though to dispel his confusion he angrily stops Charley's hand*): That's my build!
CHARLEY: I put the ace—
WILLY: If you don't know how to play the game I'm not gonna throw my money away on you!
CHARLEY (*rising*): It was my ace, for God's sake!
WILLY: I'm through, I'm through!
BEN: When did Mother die?
WILLY: Long ago. Since the beginning you never knew how to play cards.
CHARLEY (*picks up the cards and goes to the door*): All right! Next time I'll bring a deck with five aces.
WILLY: I don't play that kind of game!
CHARLEY (*turning to him*): You ought to be ashamed of yourself!
WILLY: Yeah?
CHARLEY: Yeah! (*He goes out.*)
WILLY (*slamming the door after him*): Ignoramus!
BEN (*as Willy comes toward him through the wall-line of the kitchen*): So you're William.
WILLY (*shaking Ben's hand*): Ben! I've been waiting for you so long! What's the answer? How did you do it?
BEN: Oh, there's a story in that.

(*Linda enters the forestage, as of old, carrying the wash basket.*)

LINDA: Is this Ben?
BEN (*gallantly*): How do you do, my dear.
LINDA: Where've you been all these years? Willy's always wondered why you—
WILLY (*pulling Ben away from her impatiently*): Where is Dad? Didn't you follow him? How did you get started?
BEN: Well, I don't know how much you remember.
WILLY: Well, I was just a baby, of course, only three or four years old—
BEN: Three years and eleven months.
WILLY: What a memory, Ben!
BEN: I have many enterprises, William, and I have never kept books.

WILLY: I remember I was sitting under the wagon in—was it Nebraska?
BEN: It was South Dakota, and I gave you a bunch of wild flowers.
WILLY: I remember you walking away down some open road.
BEN (*laughing*): I was going to find Father in Alaska.
WILLY: Where is he?
BEN: At that age I had a very faulty view of geography, William. I discovered after a few days that I was heading due south, so instead of Alaska, I ended up in Africa.
LINDA: Africa!
WILLY: The Gold Coast!
BEN: Principally diamond mines.
LINDA: Diamond mines!
BEN: Yes, my dear. But I've only a few minutes—
WILLY: No! Boys! Boys! (*Young Biff and Happy appear.*) Listen to this. This is your Uncle Ben, a great man! Tell my boys, Ben!
BEN: Why, boys, when I was seventeen I walked into the jungle, and when I was twenty-one I walked out. (*He laughs.*) And by God I was rich.
WILLY (*to the boys*): You see what I been talking about? The greatest things can happen!
BEN (*glancing at his watch*): I have an appointment in Ketchikan Tuesday week.
WILLY: No, Ben! Please tell about Dad. I want my boys to hear. I want them to know the kind of stock they spring from. All I remember is a man with a big beard, and I was in Mamma's lap, sitting around a fire, and some kind of high music.
BEN: His flute. He played the flute.
WILLY: Sure, the flute, that's right!

(*New music is heard, a high, rollicking tune.*)

BEN: Father was a very great and a very wild-hearted man. We would start in Boston, and he'd toss the whole family into the wagon, and then he'd drive the team right across the country; through Ohio, and Indiana, Michigan, Illinois, and all the Western states. And we'd stop in the towns and sell the flutes that he'd made on the way. Great inventor Father. With one gadget he made more in a week than a man like you could make in a lifetime.
WILLY: That's just the way I'm bringing them up, Ben—rugged, well liked, all-around.
BEN: Yeah? (*To Biff.*) Hit that, boy—hard as you can. (*He pounds his stomach.*)
BIFF: Oh, no, sir!
BEN (*taking boxing stance*): Come on, get to me! (*He laughs.*)
WILLY: Go to it, Biff! Go ahead, show him!
BIFF: Okay! (*He cocks his fists and starts in.*)
LINDA (*to Willy*): Why must he fight, dear?
BEN (*sparring with Biff*): Good boy! Good boy!
WILLY: How's that, Ben, heh?
HAPPY: Give him the left, Biff!
LINDA: Why are you fighting?

BEN: Good boy! (*Suddenly comes in, trips Biff, and stands over him, the point of his umbrella poised over Biff's eye.*)

LINDA: Look out, Biff!

BIFF: Gee!

BEN (*patting Biff's knee*): Never fight fair with a stranger, boy. You'll never get out of the jungle that way. (*Taking Linda's hand and bowing.*) It was an honor and a pleasure to meet you, Linda.

LINDA (*withdrawing her hand coldly, frightened*): Have a nice—trip.

BEN (*to Willy*): And good luck with your—what do you do?

WILLY: Selling.

BEN: Yes. Well . . . (*He raises his hand in farewell to all.*)

WILLY: No, Ben, I don't want you to think . . . (*He takes Ben's arm to show him.*) It's Brooklyn, I know, but we hunt too.

BEN: Really, now.

WILLY: Oh, sure, there's snakes and rabbits and—that's why I moved out here. Why, Biff can fell any one of these trees in no time! Boys! Go right over to where they're building the apartment house and get some sand. We're gonna rebuild the entire front stoop right now! Watch this, Ben!

BIFF: Yes, sir! On the double, Hap!

HAPPY (*as he and Biff run off*): I lost weight, Pop, you notice?

(*Charley enters in knickers, even before the boys are gone.*)

CHARLEY: Listen, if they steal any more from that building the watchman'll put the cops on them!

LINDA (*to Willy*): Don't let Biff . . .

(*Ben laughs lustily.*)

WILLY: You shoulda seen the lumber they brought home last week. At least a dozen six-by-tens worth all kinds a money.

CHARLEY: Listen, if that watchman—

WILLY: I gave them hell, understand. But I got a couple of fearless characters there.

CHARLEY: Willy, the jails are full of fearless characters.

BEN (*clapping Willy on the back, with a laugh at Charley*): And the stock exchange, friend!

WILLY (*joining in Ben's laughter*): Where are the rest of your pants?

CHARLEY: My wife bought them.

WILLY: Now all you need is a golf club and you can go upstairs and go to sleep. (*To Ben.*) Great athlete! Between him and his son Bernard they can't hammer a nail!

BERNARD (*rushing in*): The watchman's chasing Biff!

WILLY (*angrily*): Shut up! He's not stealing anything!

LINDA (*alarmed, hurrying off left*): Where is he? Biff, dear! (*She exits.*)

WILLY (*moving toward the left, away from Ben*): There's nothing wrong. What's the matter with you?

BEN: Nervy boy. Good!

WILLY (*laughing*): Oh, nerves of iron, that Biff!

CHARLEY: Don't know what it is. My New England man comes back and he's bleedin', they murdered him up there.

WILLY: It's contacts, Charley, I got important contacts!

CHARLEY (*sarcastically*): Glad to hear it, Willy. Come in later, we'll shoot a little casino. I'll take some of your Portland money. (*He laughs at Willy and exits.*)

WILLY (*turning to Ben*): Business is bad, it's murderous. But not for me, of course.

BEN: I'll stop by on my way back to Africa.

WILLY (*longingly*): Can't you stay a few days? You're just what I need, Ben, because I—I have a fine position here, but I—well, Dad left when I was such a baby and I never had a chance to talk to him and I still feel—kind of temporary about myself.

BEN: I'll be late for my train.

(*They are at opposite ends of the stage.*)

WILLY: Ben, my boys—can't we talk? They'd go into the jaws of hell for me, see, but I—

BEN: William, you're being first-rate with your boys. Outstanding, manly chaps!

WILLY (*hanging on to his words*): Oh, Ben, that's good to hear! Because sometimes I'm afraid that I'm not teaching them the right kind of—Ben, how should I teach them?

BEN (*giving great weight to each word, and with a certain vicious audacity*): William, when I walked into the jungle, I was seventeen. When I walked out I was twenty-one. And, by God, I was rich! (*He goes off into darkness around the right corner of the house.*)

WILLY: . . . was rich! That's just the spirit I want to imbue them with! To walk into a jungle! I was right! I was right! I was right!

(*Ben is gone, but Willy is still speaking to him as Linda, in nightgown and robe, enters the kitchen, glances around for Willy, then goes to the door of the house, looks out and sees him. Comes down to his left. He looks at her.*)

LINDA: Willy, dear? Willy?

WILLY: I was right!

LINDA: Did you have some cheese? (*He can't answer.*) It's very late, darling. Come to bed, heh?

WILLY (*looking straight up*): Gotta break your neck to see a star in this yard.

LINDA: You coming in?

WILLY: Whatever happened to that diamond watch fob? Remember? When Ben came from Africa that time? Didn't he give me a watch fob with a diamond in it?

LINDA: You pawned it, dear. Twelve, thirteen years ago. For Biff's radio correspondence course.

WILLY: Gee, that was a beautiful thing. I'll take a walk.

LINDA: But you're in your slippers.

WILLY (*starting to go around the house at the left*): I was right! I was! (*Half to Linda, as he goes, shaking his head.*) What a man! There was a man worth talking to. I was right!

LINDA (*calling after Willy*): But in your slippers, Willy!

(*Willy is almost gone when Biff, in his pajamas, comes down the stairs and enters the kitchen.*)

BIFF: What is he doing out there?

LINDA: Sh!

BIFF: God Almighty, Mom, how long has he been doing this?

LINDA: Don't, he'll hear you.

BIFF: What the hell is the matter with him?

LINDA: It'll pass by morning.

BIFF: Shouldn't we do anything?

LINDA: Oh, my dear, you should do a lot of things, but there's nothing to do, so go to sleep.

(*Happy comes down the stair and sits on the steps.*)

HAPPY: I never heard him so loud, Mom.

LINDA: Well, come around more often, you'll hear him. (*She sits down at the table and mends the lining of Willy's jacket.*)

BIFF: Why didn't you ever write me about this, Mom?

LINDA: How would I write to you? For over three months you had no address.

BIFF: I was on the move. But you know I thought of you all the time. You know that, don't you, pal?

LINDA: I know, dear, I know. But he likes to have a letter. Just to know that there's still a possibility for better things.

BIFF: He's not like this all the time, is he?

LINDA: It's when you come home he's always the worst.

BIFF: When I come home?

LINDA: When you write you're coming, he's all smiles and talks about the future, and—he's just wonderful. And then the closer you seem to come, the more shaky he gets, and then, by the time you get here, he's arguing, and he seems angry at you. I think it's just that maybe he can't bring himself to—to open up to you. Why are you so hateful to each other? Why is that?

BIFF (*evasively*): I'm not hateful, Mom.

LINDA: But you no sooner come in the door than you're fighting!

BIFF: I don't know why. I mean to change. I'm tryin', Mom, you understand?

LINDA: Are you home to stay now?

BIFF: I don't know. I want to look around, see what's goin'.

LINDA: Biff, you can't look around all your life, can you?

BIFF: I just can't take hold, Mom. I can't take hold of some kind of a life.

LINDA: Biff, a man is not a bird, to come and go with the springtime.

BIFF: Your hair . . . (*He touches her hair.*) Your hair got so gray.

LINDA: Oh, it's been gray since you were in high school. I just stopped dyeing it, that's all.

BIFF: Dye it again, will ye? I don't want my pal looking old. (*He smiles.*)

LINDA: You're such a boy! You think you can go away for a year and . . . You've got to get it into your head now that one day you'll knock on this door and there'll be strange people here—

BIFF: What are you talking about? You're not even sixty, Mom.

LINDA: But what about your father?

BIFF (*lamely*): Well, I meant him too.

HAPPY: He admires Pop.

LINDA: Biff, dear, if you don't have any feeling for him, then you can't have any feeling for me.

BIFF: Sure I can, Mom.

LINDA: No. You can't just come to see me, because I love him. (*With a threat, but only a threat, of tears.*) He's the dearest man in the world to me, and I won't have anyone making him feel unwanted and low and blue. You've got to make up your mind now, darling, there's no leeway any more. Either he's your father and you pay him that respect, or else you're not to come here. I know he's not easy to get along with—nobody knows that better than me—but . . .

WILLY (*from the left, with a laugh*): Hey, hey, Biffo!

BIFF (*starting to go out after Willy*): What the hell is the matter with him? (*Happy stops him.*)

LINDA: Don't—don't go near him!

BIFF: Stop making excuses for him! He always, always wiped the floor with you. Never had an ounce of respect for you.

HAPPY: He's always had respect for—

BIFF: What the hell do you know about it?

HAPPY (*surlily*): Just don't call him crazy!

BIFF: He's got no character—Charley wouldn't do this. Not in his own house—spewing out that vomit from his mind.

HAPPY: Charley never had to cope with what he's got to.

BIFF: People are worse off than Willy Loman. Believe me, I've seen them!

LINDA: Then make Charley your father, Biff. You can't do that, can you? I don't say he's a great man. Willy Loman never made a lot of money. His name was never in the paper. He's not the finest character that ever lived. But he's a human being, and a terrible thing is happening to him. So attention must be paid. He's not to be allowed to fall into his grave like an old dog. Attention, attention must be finally paid to such a person. You called him crazy—

BIFF: I didn't mean—

LINDA: No, a lot of people think he's lost his—balance. But you don't have to be very smart to know what his trouble is. The man is exhausted.

HAPPY: Sure!

LINDA: A small man can be just as exhausted as a great man. He works for a company thirty-six years this March, opens up unheard-of territories to their trademark, and now in his old age they take his salary away.

HAPPY (*indignantly*): I didn't know that, Mom.

LINDA: You never asked, my dear! Now that you get your spending money someplace else you don't trouble your mind with him.

HAPPY: But I gave you money last—

LINDA: Christmas time, fifty dollars! To fix the hot water it cost ninety-seven fifty! For five weeks he's been on straight commission, like a beginner, an unknown!

BIFF: Those ungrateful bastards!

LINDA: Are they any worse than his sons? When he brought them business, when he was young, they were glad to see him. But now his old friends, the old buyers that loved him so and always found some order to hand him in a pinch—they're all dead, retired. He used to be able to make six, seven calls a day in Boston. Now he takes his valises out of the car and puts them back and takes them out again and he's exhausted. Instead of walking he talks now. He drives seven hundred miles, and when he gets there no one knows him anymore, no one welcomes him. And what goes through a man's mind, driving seven hundred miles home without having earned a cent? Why shouldn't he talk to himself? Why? When he has to go to Charley and borrow fifty dollars a week and pretend to me that it's his pay? How long can that go on? How long? You see what I'm sitting here and waiting for? And you tell me he has no character? The man who never worked a day but for your benefit? When does he get the medal for that? Is this his reward—to turn around at the age of sixty-three and find his sons, who he loved better than his life, one a philandering bum—

HAPPY: Mom!

LINDA: That's all you are, my baby! (*To Biff.*) And you! What happened to the love you had for him? You were such pals! How you used to talk to him on the phone every night! How lonely he was till he could come home to you!

BIFF: All right, Mom. I'll live here in my room, and I'll get a job. I'll keep away from him, that's all.

LINDA: No, Biff. You can't stay here and fight all the time.

BIFF: He threw me out of this house, remember that.

LINDA: Why did he do that? I never knew why.

BIFF: Because I know he's a fake and he doesn't like anybody around who knows!

LINDA: Why a fake? In what way? What do you mean?

BIFF: Just don't lay it all at my feet. It's between me and him—that's all I have to say. I'll chip in from now on. He'll settle for half my pay check. He'll be all right. I'm going to bed. (*He starts for the stairs.*)

LINDA: He won't be all right.

BIFF (*turning on the stairs, furiously*): I hate this city and I'll stay here. Now what do you want?

LINDA: He's dying, Biff.

(*Happy turns quickly to her, shocked.*)

BIFF (*after a pause*): Why is he dying?

LINDA: He's been trying to kill himself.

BIFF (*with great horror*): How?

LINDA: I live from day to day.

BIFF: What're you talking about?

LINDA: Remember I wrote you that he smashed up the car again? In February?

BIFF: Well?

LINDA: The insurance inspector came. He said that they have evidence. That all these accidents in the last year—weren't—weren't—accidents.

HAPPY: How can they tell that? That's a lie.

LINDA: It seems there's a woman . . . (*She takes a breath as*)

BIFF (*sharply but contained*): ⎱ What woman?
LINDA (*simultaneously*): ⎰ . . . and this woman . . .

LINDA: What?

BIFF: Nothing. Go ahead.

LINDA: What did you say?

BIFF: Nothing. I just said what woman?

HAPPY: What about her?

LINDA: Well, it seems she was walking down the road and saw his car. She says that he wasn't driving fast at all, and that he didn't skid. She says he came to that little bridge, and then deliberately smashed into the railing, and it was only the shallowness of the water that saved him.

BIFF: Oh, no, he probably just fell asleep again.

LINDA: I don't think he fell asleep.

BIFF: Why not?

LINDA: Last month . . . (*With great difficulty.*) Oh, boys, it's so hard to say a thing like this! He's just a big stupid man to you, but I tell you there's more good in him than in many other people. (*She chokes, wipes her eyes.*) I was looking for a fuse. The lights blew out, and I went down the cellar. And behind the fuse box—it happened to fall out—was a length of rubber pipe—just short.

HAPPY: No kidding!

LINDA: There's a little attachment on the end of it. I knew right away. And sure enough, on the bottom of the water heater there's a new little nipple on the gas pipe.

HAPPY (*angrily*): That—jerk.

BIFF: Did you have it taken off?

LINDA: I'm—I'm ashamed to. How can I mention it to him? Every day I go down and take away that little rubber pipe. But, when he comes home, I put it back where it was. How can I insult him that way? I don't know what to do. I live from day to day, boys. I tell you, I know every thought in his mind. It sounds so old-fashioned and silly, but I tell you he put his whole life into you and you've turned your backs on him. (*She is bent over in the chair, weeping, her face in her hands.*) Biff, I swear to God! Biff, his life is in your hands!

HAPPY (*to Biff*): How do you like that damned fool!

BIFF (*kissing her*): All right, pal, all right. It's all settled now. I've been remiss. I know that, Mom. But now I'll stay, and I swear to you, I'll apply myself. (*Kneeling in front of her, in a fever of self-reproach.*) It's just—you see, Mom, I don't fit in business. Not that I won't try. I'll try, and I'll make good.

HAPPY: Sure you will. The trouble with you in business was you never tried to please people.

BIFF: I know, I—

HAPPY: Like when you worked for Harrison's. Bob Harrison said you were tops, and then you go and do some damn fool thing like whistling whole songs in the elevator like a comedian.

BIFF (*against Happy*): So what? I like to whistle sometimes.

HAPPY: You don't raise a guy to a responsible job who whistles in the elevator!

LINDA: Well, don't argue about it now.

HAPPY: Like when you'd go off and swim in the middle of the day instead of taking the line around.

BIFF (*his resentment rising*): Well, don't you run off? You take off sometimes, don't you? On a nice summer day?

HAPPY: Yeah, but I cover myself!

LINDA: Boys!

HAPPY: If I'm going to take a fade the boss can call any number where I'm supposed to be and they'll swear to him that I just left. I'll tell you something that I hate to say, Biff, but in the business world some of them think you're crazy.

BIFF (*angered*): Screw the business world!

HAPPY: All right, screw it! Great, but cover yourself!

LINDA: Hap, Hap!

BIFF: I don't care what they think! They've laughed at Dad for years, and you know why? Because we don't belong in this nuthouse of a city! We should be mixing cement on some open plain, or—or carpenters. A carpenter is allowed to whistle!

(*Willy walks in from the entrance of the house, at left.*)

WILLY: Even your grandfather was better than a carpenter. (*Pause. They watch him.*) You never grew up. Bernard does not whistle in the elevator, I assure you.

BIFF (*as though to laugh Willy out of it*): Yeah, but you do, Pop.

WILLY: I never in my life whistled in an elevator! And who in the business world thinks I'm crazy?

BIFF: I didn't mean it like that, Pop. Now don't make a whole thing out of it, will ye?

WILLY: Go back to the West! Be a carpenter, a cowboy, enjoy yourself!

LINDA: Willy, he was just saying—

WILLY: I heard what he said!

HAPPY (*trying to quiet Willy*): Hey, Pop, come on now . . .

WILLY (*continuing over Happy's line*): They laugh at me, heh? Go to Filene's, go to the Hub, go to Slattery's, Boston. Call out the name Willy Loman and see what happens! Big shot!

BIFF: All right, Pop.

WILLY: Big!

BIFF: All right!

WILLY: Why do you always insult me?

BIFF: I didn't say a word. (*To Linda.*) Did I say a word?

LINDA: He didn't say anything, Willy.

WILLY (*going to the doorway of the living room*): All right, good night, good night.

LINDA: Willy, dear, he just decided . . .

WILLY (*to Biff*): If you get tired hanging around tomorrow, paint the ceiling I put up in the living room.

BIFF: I'm leaving early tomorrow.

HAPPY: He's going to see Bill Oliver, Pop.

WILLY (*interestedly*): Oliver? For what?

BIFF (*with reserve, but trying, trying*): He always said he'd stake me. I'd like to go into business, so maybe I can take him up on it.

LINDA: Isn't that wonderful?

WILLY: Don't interrupt. What's wonderful about it? There's fifty men in the City of New York who'd stake him. (*To Biff.*) Sporting goods?

BIFF: I guess so. I know something about it and—

WILLY: He knows something about it! You know sporting goods better than Spalding, for God's sake! How much is he giving you?

BIFF: I don't know, I didn't even see him yet, but—

WILLY: Then what're you talkin' about?

BIFF (*getting angry*): Well, all I said was I'm gonna see him, that's all!

WILLY (*turning away*): Ah, you're counting your chickens again.

BIFF (*starting left for the stairs*): Oh, Jesus, I'm going to sleep!

WILLY (*calling after him*): Don't curse in this house!

BIFF (*turning*): Since when did you get so clean?

HAPPY (*trying to stop them*): Wait a . . .

WILLY: Don't use that language to me! I won't have it!

HAPPY (*grabbing Biff, shouts*): Wait a minute! I got an idea. I got a feasible idea. Come here, Biff, let's talk this over now, let's talk some sense here. When I was down in Florida last time, I thought of a great idea to sell sporting goods. It just came back to me. You and I, Biff—we have a line, the Loman Line. We train a couple of weeks, and put on a couple of exhibitions, see?

WILLY: That's an idea!

HAPPY: Wait! We form two basketball teams, see? Two water polo teams. We play each other. It's a million dollars' worth of publicity. Two brothers, see? The Loman Brothers. Displays in the Royal Palms—all the hotels. And banners over the ring and the basketball court: "Loman Brothers." Baby, we could sell sporting goods!

WILLY: That is a one-million-dollar idea!

LINDA: Marvelous!

BIFF: I'm in great shape as far as that's concerned.

HAPPY: And the beauty of it is, Biff, it wouldn't be like a business. We'd be out playin' ball again . . .

BIFF (*enthused*): Yeah, that's . . .

WILLY: Million-dollar . . .

HAPPY: And you wouldn't get fed up with it, Biff. It'd be the family again. There'd be the old honor, and comradeship, and if you wanted to go off for a swim or somethin'—well, you'd do it! Without some smart cooky gettin' up ahead of you!

WILLY: Lick the world! You guys together could absolutely lick the civilized world.

BIFF: I'll see Oliver tomorrow. Hap, if we could work that out...

LINDA: Maybe things are beginning to—

WILLY (*wildly enthused, to Linda*): Stop interrupting! (*To Biff.*) But don't wear sport jacket and slacks when you see Oliver.

BIFF: No, I'll—

WILLY: A business suit, and talk as little as possible, and don't crack any jokes.

BIFF: He did like me. Always liked me.

LINDA: He loved you!

WILLY (*to Linda*): Will you stop! (*To Biff.*) Walk in very serious. You are not applying for a boy's job. Money is to pass. Be quiet, fine, and serious. Everybody likes a kidder, but nobody lends him money.

HAPPY: I'll try to get some myself, Biff. I'm sure I can.

WILLY: I see great things for you kids, I think your troubles are over. But remember, start big and you'll end big. Ask for fifteen. How much you gonna ask for?

BIFF: Gee, I don't know—

WILLY: And don't say "Gee." "Gee" is a boy's word. A man walking in for fifteen thousand dollars does not say "Gee!"

BIFF: Ten, I think, would be top though.

WILLY: Don't be so modest. You always started too low. Walk in with a big laugh. Don't look worried. Start off with a couple of your good stories to lighten things up. It's not what you say, it's how you say it— because personality always wins the day.

LINDA: Oliver always thought the highest of him—

WILLY: Will you let me talk?

BIFF: Don't yell at her, Pop, will ye?

WILLY (*angrily*): I was talking, wasn't I?

BIFF: I don't like you yelling at her all the time, and I'm tellin' you, that's all.

WILLY: What're you, takin' over this house?

LINDA: Willy—

WILLY (*turning to her*): Don't take his side all the time, goddammit!

BIFF (*furiously*): Stop yelling at her!

WILLY (*suddenly pulling on his cheek, beaten down, guilt ridden*): Give my best to Bill Oliver—he may remember me. (*He exits through the living room doorway.*)

LINDA (*her voice subdued*): What'd you have to start that for? (*Biff turns away.*) You see how sweet he was as soon as you talked hopefully? (*She goes over to Biff.*) Come up and say good night to him. Don't let him go to bed that way.

HAPPY: Come on, Biff, let's buck him up.

LINDA: Please, dear. Just say good night. It takes so little to make him happy. Come. (*She goes through the living room doorway, calling upstairs from within the living room.*) Your pajamas are hanging in the bathroom, Willy!

HAPPY (*looking toward where Linda went out*): What a woman! They broke the mold when they made her. You know that, Biff?

BIFF: He's off salary. My God, working on commission!

HAPPY: Well, let's face it: he's no hot-shot selling man. Except that sometimes, you have to admit, he's a sweet personality.

BIFF (*deciding*): Lend me ten bucks, will ye? I want to buy some new ties.

HAPPY: I'll take you to a place I know. Beautiful stuff. Wear one of my striped shirts tomorrow.

BIFF: She got gray. Mom got awful old. Gee, I'm gonna go in to Oliver tomorrow and knock him for a—

HAPPY: Come on up. Tell that to Dad. Let's give him a whirl. Come on.

BIFF (*steamed up*): You know, with ten thousand bucks, boy!

HAPPY (*as they go into the living room*): That's the talk, Biff, that's the first time I've heard the old confidence out of you! (*From within the living room, fading off.*) You're gonna live with me, kid, and any babe you want just say the word . . . (*The last lines are hardly heard. They are mounting the stairs to their parents' bedroom.*)

LINDA (*entering her bedroom and addressing Willy, who is in the bathroom. She is straightening the bed for him.*): Can you do anything about the shower? It drips.

WILLY (*from the bathroom*): All of a sudden everything falls to pieces. Goddam plumbing, oughta be sued, those people. I hardly finished putting it in and the thing . . . (*His words rumble off.*)

LINDA: I'm just wondering if Oliver will remember him. You think he might?

WILLY (*coming out of the bathroom in his pajamas*): Remember him? What's the matter with you, you crazy? If he'd've stayed with Oliver he'd be on top by now! Wait'll Oliver gets a look at him. You don't know the average caliber any more. The average young man today—(*he is getting into bed*)—is got a caliber of zero. Greatest thing in the world for him was to bum around.

(*Biff and Happy enter the bedroom. Slight pause.*)

WILLY (*stops short, looking at Biff*): Glad to hear it, boy.

HAPPY: He wanted to say good night to you, sport.

WILLY (*to Biff*): Yeah. Knock him dead, boy. What'd you want to tell me?

BIFF: Just take it easy, Pop. Good night. (*He turns to go.*)

WILLY (*unable to resist*): And if anything falls off the desk while you're talking to him—like a package or something—don't you pick it up. They have office boys for that.

LINDA: I'll make a big breakfast—

WILLY: Will you let me finish? (*To Biff.*) Tell him you were in the business in the West. Not farm work.

BIFF: All right, Dad.

LINDA: I think everything—

WILLY (*going right through her speech*): And don't under-sell yourself. No less than fifteen thousand dollars.

BIFF (*unable to bear him*): Okay. Good night, Mom. (*He starts moving.*)

WILLY: Because you got a greatness in you, Biff, remember that. You got all kinds of greatness . . . (*He lies back, exhausted. Biff walks out.*)

LINDA (*calling after Biff*): Sleep well, darling!

HAPPY: I'm gonna get married, Mom. I wanted to tell you.

LINDA: Go to sleep, dear.

HAPPY (*going*): I just wanted to tell you.

WILLY: Keep up the good work. (*Happy exits.*) God . . . remember that Ebbets Field game? The championship of the city?

LINDA: Just rest. Should I sing to you?

WILLY: Yeah. Sing to me. (*Linda hums a soft lullaby.*) When that team came out—he was the tallest, remember?

LINDA: Oh, yes. And in gold.

(*Biff enters the darkened kitchen, takes a cigarette, and leaves the house. He comes downstage into a golden pool of light. He smokes, staring at the night.*)

WILLY: Like a young god. Hercules—something like that. And the sun, the sun all around him. Remember how he waved to me? Right up from the field, with the representatives of three colleges standing by? And the buyers I brought, and the cheers when he came out—Loman, Loman, Loman! God Almighty, he'll be great yet. A star like that, magnificent, can never really fade away!

(*The light on Willy is fading. The gas heater begins to glow through the kitchen wall, near the stairs, a blue flame beneath red coils.*)

LINDA (*timidly*): Willy dear, what has he got against you?

WILLY: I'm so tired. Don't talk anymore.

(*Biff slowly returns to the kitchen. He stops, stares toward the heater.*)

LINDA: Will you ask Howard to let you work in New York?

WILLY: First thing in the morning. Everything'll be all right.

(*Biff reaches behind the heater and draws out a length of rubber tubing. He is horrified and turns his head toward Willy's room, still dimly lit, from which the strains of Linda's desperate but monotonous humming rise.*)

WILLY (*staring through the window into the moonlight*): Gee, look at the moon moving between the buildings!

(*Biff wraps the tubing around his hand and quickly goes up the stairs.*)

ACT II

(*Music is heard, gay and bright. The curtain rises as the music fades away. Willy, in shirt sleeves, is sitting at the kitchen table, sipping coffee, his hat in his lap. Linda is filling his cup when she can.*)

WILLY: Wonderful coffee. Meal in itself.

LINDA: Can I make you some eggs?

WILLY: No. Take a breath.

LINDA: You look so rested, dear.

WILLY: I slept like a dead one. First time in months. Imagine, sleeping till ten on a Tuesday morning. Boys left nice and early, heh?

LINDA: They were out of here by eight o'clock.

WILLY: Good work!

LINDA: It was so thrilling to see them leaving together. I can't get over the shaving lotion in this house!

WILLY (*smiling*): Mmm—

LINDA: Biff was very changed this morning. His whole attitude seemed to be hopeful. He couldn't wait to get downtown to see Oliver.

WILLY: He's heading for a change. There's no question, there simply are certain men that take longer to get—solidified. How did he dress?

LINDA: His blue suit. He's so handsome in that suit. He could be a—anything in that suit!

(*Willy gets up from the table. Linda holds his jacket for him.*)

WILLY: There's no question, no question at all. Gee, on the way home tonight I'd like to buy some seeds.

LINDA (*laughing*): That'd be wonderful. But not enough sun gets back there. Nothing'll grow any more.

WILLY: You wait, kid, before it's all over we're gonna get a little place out in the country, and I'll raise some vegetables, a couple of chickens . . .

LINDA: You'll do it yet, dear.

(*Willy walks out of his jacket. Linda follows him.*)

WILLY: And they'll get married, and come for a weekend. I'd build a little guest house. 'Cause I got so many fine tools, all I'd need would be a little lumber and some peace of mind.

LINDA (*joyfully*): I sewed the lining . . .

WILLY: I could build two guest houses, so they'd both come. Did he decide how much he's going to ask Oliver for?

LINDA (*getting him into the jacket*): He didn't mention it, but I imagine ten or fifteen thousand. You going to talk to Howard today?

WILLY: Yeah. I'll put it to him straight and simple. He'll just have to take me off the road.

LINDA: And Willy, don't forget to ask for a little advance, because we've got the insurance premium. It's the grace period now.

WILLY: That's a hundred . . . ?

LINDA: A hundred and eight, sixty-eight. Because we're a little short again.

WILLY: Why are we short?

LINDA: Well, you had the motor job on the car . . .

WILLY: That goddam Studebaker!

LINDA: And you got one more payment on the refrigerator . . .

WILLY: But it just broke again!

LINDA: Well, it's old, dear.

WILLY: I told you we should've bought a well-advertised machine. Charley bought a General Electric and it's twenty years old and it's still good, that son-of-a-bitch.

LINDA: But, Willy—

WILLY: Whoever heard of a Hastings refrigerator? Once in my life I would like to own something outright before it's broken! I'm always in a race with the junkyard! I just finished paying for the car and it's on its last legs. The refrigerator consumes belts like a goddamn maniac. They time those things. They time them so when you finally paid for them, they're used up.

LINDA (buttoning up his jacket as he unbuttons it): All told, about two hundred dollars would carry us, dear. But that includes the last payment on the mortgage. After this payment, Willy, the house belongs to us.

WILLY: It's twenty-five years!

LINDA: Biff was nine years old when we bought it.

WILLY: Well, that's a great thing. To weather a twenty-five year mortgage is—

LINDA: It's an accomplishment.

WILLY: All the cement, the lumber, the reconstruction I put in this house! There ain't a crack to be found in it anymore.

LINDA: Well, it served its purpose.

WILLY: What purpose? Some stranger'll come along, move in, and that's that. If only Biff would take this house, and raise a family . . . (He starts to go.) Good-by, I'm late.

LINDA (suddenly remembering): Oh, I forgot! You're supposed to meet them for dinner.

WILLY: Me?

LINDA: At Frank's Chop House on Forty-eighth near Sixth Avenue.

WILLY: Is that so! How about you?

LINDA: No, just the three of you. They're gonna blow you to a big meal!

WILLY: Don't say! Who thought of that?

LINDA: Biff came to me this morning, Willy, and he said, "Tell Dad, we want to blow him to a big meal." Be there six o'clock. You and your two boys are going to have dinner.

WILLY: Gee whiz! That's really somethin'. I'm gonna knock Howard for a loop, kid. I'll get an advance, and I'll come home with a New York job. Goddammit, now I'm gonna do it!

LINDA: Oh, that's the spirit, Willy!

WILLY: I will never get behind a wheel the rest of my life!

LINDA: It's changing, Willy, I can feel it changing!

WILLY: Beyond a question. G'by, I'm late. (He starts to go again.)

LINDA (calling after him as she runs to the kitchen table for a handkerchief): You got your glasses?

WILLY (feels for them, then comes back in): Yeah, yeah, got my glasses.

LINDA (giving him the handkerchief): And a handkerchief.

WILLY: Yeah, handkerchief.

LINDA: And your saccharine?

WILLY: Yeah, my saccharine.

LINDA: Be careful on the subway stairs.

(She kisses him, and a silk stocking is seen hanging from her hand. Willy notices it.)

WILLY: Will you stop mending stockings? At least while I'm in the house. It gets me nervous. I can't tell you. Please.

(Linda hides the stocking in her hand as she follows Willy across the forestage in front of the house.)

LINDA: Remember, Frank's Chop House.

WILLY (passing the apron): Maybe beets would grow out there.

LINDA (laughing): But you tried so many times.

WILLY: Yeah. Well, don't work hard today. (He disappears around the right corner of the house.)

LINDA: Be careful!

(As Willy vanishes, Linda waves to him. Suddenly the phone rings. She runs across the stage and into the kitchen and lifts it.)

LINDA: Hello? Oh, Biff! I'm so glad you called, I just . . . Yes, sure, I just told him. Yes, he'll be there for dinner at six o'clock, I didn't forget. Listen, I was just dying to tell you. You know that little rubber pipe I told you about? That he connected to the gas heater? I finally decided to go down the cellar this morning and take it away and destroy it. But it's gone! Imagine? He took it away himself, it isn't there! (She listens.) When? Oh, then you took it. Oh—nothing, it's just that I'd hoped he'd taken it away himself. Oh, I'm not worried, darling, because this morning he left in such high spirits, it was like the old days! I'm not afraid any more. Did Mr. Oliver see you? . . . Well, you wait there then. And make a nice impression on him, darling. Just don't perspire too much before you see him. And have a nice time with Dad. He may have big news too! . . . That's right, a New York job. And be sweet to him tonight, dear. Be loving to him. Because he's only a little boat looking for a harbor. (She is trembling with sorrow and joy.) Oh, that's wonderful, Biff, you'll save his life. Thanks, darling. Just put your arm around him when he comes into the restaurant. Give him a smile. That's the boy . . . Good-by, dear. . . . You got your comb? . . . That's fine. Good-by, Biff dear.

(In the middle of her speech, Howard Wagner, thirty-six, wheels in a small typewriter table on which is a wire-recording machine and proceeds to plug it in. This is on the left forestage. Light slowly fades on Linda as it rises on Howard. Howard is intent on threading the machine and only glances over his shoulder as Willy appears.)

WILLY: Pst! Pst!

HOWARD: Hello, Willy, come in.

WILLY: Like to have a little talk with you, Howard.

HOWARD: Sorry to keep you waiting. I'll be with you in a minute.

WILLY: What's that, Howard?

HOWARD: Didn't you ever see one of these? Wire recorder.

WILLY: Oh. Can we talk a minute?

HOWARD: Records things. Just got delivery yesterday. Been driving me crazy, the most terrific machine I ever saw in my life. I was up all night with it.

WILLY: What do you do with it?

HOWARD: I bought it for dictation, but you can do anything with it. Listen to this. I had it home last night. Listen to what I picked up. The first one is my daughter. Get this. (*He flicks the switch and "Roll out the Barrel" is heard being whistled.*) Listen to that kid whistle.

WILLY: That is lifelike, isn't it?

HOWARD: Seven years old. Get that tone.

WILLY: Ts, ts. Like to ask a little favor if you...

(*The whistling breaks off, and the voice of Howard's daughter is heard.*)

HIS DAUGHTER: Now you, Daddy.

HOWARD: She's crazy for me! (*Again the same song is whistled.*) That's me! Ha! (*He winks.*)

WILLY: You're very good!

(*The whistling breaks off again. The machine runs silent for a moment.*)

HOWARD: Sh! Get this now, this is my son.

HIS SON: "The capital of Alabama is Montgomery; the capital of Arizona is Phoenix; the capital of Arkansas is Little Rock; the capital of California is Sacramento..." (*and on, and on.*)

HOWARD (*holding up five fingers*): Five years old, Willy!

WILLY: He'll make an announcer some day!

HIS SON (*continuing*): "The capital..."

HOWARD: Get that—alphabetical order! (*The machine breaks off suddenly.*) Wait a minute. The maid kicked the plug out.

WILLY: It certainly is a—

HOWARD: Sh, for God's sake!

HIS SON: "It's nine o'clock, Bulova watch time. So I have to go to sleep."

WILLY: That really is—

HOWARD: Wait a minute! The next is my wife.

(*They wait.*)

HOWARD'S VOICE: "Go on, say something." (*Pause.*) "Well, you gonna talk?"

HIS WIFE: "I can't think of anything."

HOWARD'S VOICE: "Well, talk—it's turning."

HIS WIFE (*shyly, beaten*): "Hello." (*Silence.*) "Oh, Howard, I can't talk into this..."

HOWARD (*snapping the machine off*): That was my wife.

WILLY: That is a wonderful machine. Can we—

HOWARD: I tell you, Willy, I'm gonna take my camera, and my bandsaw, and all my hobbies, and out they

go. This is the most fascinating relaxation I ever found.

WILLY: I think I'll get one myself.

HOWARD: Sure, they're only a hundred and a half. You can't do without it. Supposing you wanna hear Jack Benny, see? But you can't be at home at that hour. So you tell the maid to turn the radio on when Jack Benny comes on, and this automatically goes on with the radio...

WILLY: And when you come home you...

HOWARD: You can come home twelve o'clock, one o'clock, any time you like, and you get yourself a Coke and sit yourself down, throw the switch, and there's Jack Benny's program in the middle of the night!

WILLY: I'm definitely going to get one. Because lots of times I'm on the road, and I think to myself, what I must be missing on the radio!

HOWARD: Don't you have a radio in the car?

WILLY: Well, yeah, but who ever thinks of turning it on?

HOWARD: Say, aren't you supposed to be in Boston?

WILLY: That's what I want to talk to you about, Howard. You got a minute? (*He draws a chair in from the wing.*)

HOWARD: What happened? What're you doing here?

WILLY: Well...

HOWARD: You didn't crack up again, did you?

WILLY: Oh, no. No...

HOWARD: Geez, you had me worried there for a minute. What's the trouble?

WILLY: Well, tell you the truth, Howard. I've come to the decision that I'd rather not travel anymore.

HOWARD: Not travel! Well, what'll you do?

WILLY: Remember, Christmas time, when you had the party here? You said you'd try to think of some spot for me here in town.

HOWARD: With us?

WILLY: Well, sure.

HOWARD: Oh, yeah, yeah. I remember. Well, I couldn't think of anything for you, Willy.

WILLY: I tell ya, Howard. The kids are all grown up, y'know. I don't need much anymore. If I could take home—well, sixty-five dollars a week, I could swing it.

HOWARD: Yeah, but Willy, see I—

WILLY: I tell ya why, Howard. Speaking frankly and between the two of us, y'know—I'm just a little tired.

HOWARD: Oh, I could understand that, Willy. But you're a road man, Willy, and we do a road business. We've only got a half-dozen salesmen on the floor here.

WILLY: God knows, Howard, I never asked a favor of any man. But I was with the firm when your father used to carry you in here in his arms.

HOWARD: I know that, Willy, but—

WILLY: Your father came to me the day you were born and asked me what I thought of the name Howard, may he rest in peace.

HOWARD: I appreciate that, Willy, but there just is no spot here for you. If I had a spot I'd slam you right in, but I just don't have a single solitary spot.

(*He looks for his lighter. Willy has picked it up and gives it to him. Pause.*)

WILLY (*with increasing anger*): Howard, all I need to set my table is fifty dollars a week.

HOWARD: But where am I going to put you, kid?

WILLY: Look, it isn't a question of whether I can sell merchandise, is it?

HOWARD: No, but it's business, kid, and everybody's gotta pull his own weight.

WILLY (*desperately*): Just let me tell you a story, Howard—

HOWARD: 'Cause you gotta admit, business is business.

WILLY (*angrily*): Business is definitely business, but just listen for a minute. You don't understand this. When I was a boy—eighteen, nineteen—I was already on the road. And there was a question in my mind as to whether selling had a future for me. Because in those days I had a yearning to go to Alaska. See, there were three gold strikes in one month in Alaska, and I felt like going out. Just for the ride, you might say.

HOWARD (*barely interested*): Don't say.

WILLY: Oh, yeah, my father lived many years in Alaska. He was an adventurous man. We've got quite a little streak of self-reliance in our family. I thought I'd go out with my older brother and try to locate him, and maybe settle in the North with the old man. And I was almost decided to go, when I met a salesman in the Parker House. His name was Dave Singleman. And he was eighty-four years old, and he'd drummed merchandise in thirty-one states. And old Dave, he'd go up to his room, y'understand, put on his green velvet slippers—I'll never forget—and pick up his phone and call the buyers, and without ever leaving his room, at the age of eighty-four, he made his living. And when I saw that, I realized that selling was the greatest career a man could want. 'Cause what could be more satisfying than to be able to go, at the age of eighty-four, into twenty or thirty different cities, and pick up a phone, and be remembered and loved and helped by so many different people? Do you know? When he died—and by the way he died the death of a salesman, in his green velvet slippers in the smoker of the New York, New Haven and Hartford, going into Boston—when he died, hundreds of salesmen and buyers were at his funeral. Things were sad on a lotta trains for months after that. (*He stands up. Howard has not looked at him.*) In those days there was personality in it, Howard. There was respect and comradeship, and gratitude in it. Today, it's all cut and dried, and there's no chance for bringing friendship to bear—or personality. You see what I mean? They don't know me any more.

HOWARD (*moving away, to the right*): That's just the thing, Willy.

WILLY: If I had forty dollars a week—that's all I'd need. Forty dollars, Howard.

HOWARD: Kid, I can't take blood from a stone, I—

WILLY (*desperation is on him now*): Howard, the year Al Smith was nominated, your father came to me and—

HOWARD (*starting to go off*): I've got to see some people, kid.

WILLY (*stopping him*): I'm talking about your father! There were promises made across this desk! You mustn't tell me you've got people to see—I put thirty-four years into this firm, Howard, and now I can't pay my insurance! You can't eat the orange and throw the peel away—a man is not a piece of fruit! (*After a pause.*) Now pay attention. Your father—in 1928 I had a big year. I averaged a hundred and seventy dollars a week in commissions.

HOWARD (*impatiently*): Now, Willy, you never averaged—

WILLY (*banging his hand on the desk*): I averaged a hundred and seventy dollars a week in the year of 1928! And your father came to me—or rather I was in the office here—it was right over this desk—and he put his hand on my shoulder—

HOWARD (*getting up*): You'll have to excuse me, Willy, I gotta see some people. Pull yourself together. (*Going out.*) I'll be back in a little while.

(*On Howard's exit, the light on his chair grows very bright and strange.*)

WILLY: Pull myself together! What the hell did I say to him? My God, I was yelling at him! How could I? (*Willy breaks off, staring at the light, which occupies the chair, animating it. He approaches this chair, standing across the desk from it.*) Frank, Frank, don't you remember what you told me that time? How you put your hand on my shoulder, and Frank . . . (*He leans on the desk and as he speaks the dead man's name he accidentally switches on the recorder, and instantly*)

HOWARD'S SON: "... of New York is Albany. The capital of Ohio is Cincinnati, the capital of Rhode Island is ..." (*The recitation continues.*)

WILLY (*leaping away with fright, shouting*): Ha! Howard! Howard! Howard!

HOWARD (*rushing in*): What happened?

WILLY (*pointing at the machine, which continues nasally, childishly, with the capital cities*): Shut it off! Shut it off!

HOWARD (*pulling the plug out*): Look, Willy . . .

WILLY (*pressing his hands to his eyes*): I gotta get myself some coffee. I'll get some coffee . . .

(*Willy starts to walk out. Howard stops him.*)

HOWARD (*rolling up the cord*): Willy, look . . .

WILLY: I'll go to Boston.

HOWARD: Willy, you can't go to Boston for us.

WILLY: Why can't I go?

HOWARD: I don't want you to represent us. I've been meaning to tell you for a long time now.

WILLY: Howard, are you firing me?

HOWARD: I think you need a good long rest, Willy.

WILLY: Howard—

HOWARD: And when you feel better, come back, and we'll see if we can work something out.

WILLY: But I gotta earn money, Howard. I'm in no position to—

HOWARD: Where are your sons? Why don't your sons give you a hand?

WILLY: They're working on a very big deal.

HOWARD: This is no time for false pride, Willy. You go to your sons and you tell them that you're tired. You've got two great boys, haven't you?

WILLY: Oh, no question, no question, but in the meantime...

HOWARD: Then that's that, heh?

WILLY: All right, I'll go to Boston tomorrow.

HOWARD: No, no.

WILLY: I can't throw myself on my sons. I'm not a cripple!

HOWARD: Look, kid, I'm busy this morning.

WILLY (grasping Howard's arm): Howard, you've got to let me go to Boston!

HOWARD (hard, keeping himself under control): I've got a line of people to see this morning. Sit down, take five minutes, and pull yourself together, and then go home, will ya? I need the office, Willy. (He starts to go, turns, remembering the recorder, starts to push off the table holding the recorder.) Oh, yeah. Whenever you can this week, stop by and drop off the samples. You'll feel better, Willy, and then come back and we'll talk. Pull yourself together, kid, there's people outside.

(Howard exits, pushing the table off left. Willy stares into space, exhausted. Now the music is heard—Ben's music—first distantly, then closer, closer. As Willy speaks, Ben enters from the right. He carries valise and umbrella.)

WILLY: Oh, Ben, how did you do it? What is the answer? Did you wind up the Alaska deal already?

BEN: Doesn't take much time if you know what you're doing. Just a short business trip. Boarding ship in an hour. Wanted to say good-by.

WILLY: Ben, I've got to talk to you.

BEN (glancing at his watch): Haven't the time, William.

WILLY (crossing the apron to Ben): Ben, nothing's working out. I don't know what to do.

BEN: Now, look here, William. I've bought timberland in Alaska and I need a man to look after things for me.

WILLY: God, timberland! Me and my boys in those grand outdoors!

BEN: You've a new continent at your doorstep, William. Get out of these cities, they're full of talk and time payments and courts of law. Screw on your fists and you can fight for a fortune up there.

WILLY: Yes, yes! Linda, Linda!

(Linda enters as of old, with the wash.)

LINDA: Oh, you're back?

BEN: I haven't much time.

WILLY: No, wait! Linda, he's got a proposition for me in Alaska.

LINDA: But you've got—(To Ben.) He's got a beautiful job here.

WILLY: But in Alaska, kid, I could—

LINDA: You're doing well enough, Willy!

BEN (to Linda): Enough for what, my dear?

LINDA (frightened of Ben and angry at him): Don't say those things to him! Enough to be happy right here, right now. (To Willy, while Ben laughs.) Why must everybody conquer the world? You're well liked, and the boys love you, and someday—(To Ben)—why, old man Wagner told him just the other day that if he keeps it up he'll be a member of the firm, didn't he, Willy?

WILLY: Sure, sure. I am building something with this firm, Ben, and if a man is building something he must be on the right track, mustn't he?

BEN: What are you building? Lay your hand on it. Where is it?

WILLY (hesitantly): That's true, Linda, there's nothing.

LINDA: Why? (To Ben.) There's a man eighty-four years old—

WILLY: That's right, Ben, that's right. When I look at that man I say, what is there to worry about?

BEN: Bah!

WILLY: It's true, Ben. All he has to do is go into any city, pick up the phone, and he's making his living and you know why?

BEN (picking up his valise): I've got to go.

WILLY (holding Ben back): Look at this boy!

(Biff, in his high school sweater, enters carrying suitcase. Happy carries Biff's shoulder guards, gold helmet, and football pants.)

WILLY: Without a penny to his name, three great universities are begging for him, and from there the sky's the limit, because it's not what you do, Ben. It's who you know and the smile on your face! It's contacts, Ben, contacts! The whole wealth of Alaska passes over the lunch table at the Commodore Hotel, and that's the wonder, the wonder of this country, that a man can end with diamonds here on the basis of being liked! (He turns to Biff.) And that's why when you get out on that field today it's important. Because thousands of people will be rooting for you and loving you. (To Ben, who has again begun to leave.) And Ben! when he walks into a business office his name will sound out like a bell and all the doors will open to him! I've seen it, Ben, I've seen it a thousand times! You can't feel it with your hand like timber, but it's there!

BEN: Good-by, William.

WILLY: Ben, am I right? Don't you think I'm right? I value your advice.

BEN: There's a new continent at your doorstep, William. You could walk out rich. Rich! (He is gone.)

WILLY: We'll do it here, Ben! You hear me? We're gonna do it here!

(*Young Bernard rushes in. The gay music of the Boys is heard.*)

BERNARD: Oh, gee, I was afraid you left already!
WILLY: Why? What time is it?
BERNARD: It's half-past one!
WILLY: Well, come on, everybody! Ebbets Field next stop! Where's the pennants? (*He rushes through the wall-line of the kitchen and out into the living room.*)
LINDA (*to Biff*): Did you pack fresh underwear?
BIFF (*who has been limbering up*): I want to go!
BERNARD: Biff, I'm carrying your helmet, ain't I?
HAPPY: No, I'm carrying the helmet.
BERNARD: Oh, Biff, you promised me.
HAPPY: I'm carrying the helmet.
BERNARD: How am I going to get in the locker room?
LINDA: Let him carry the shoulder guards. (*She puts her coat and hat on in the kitchen.*)
BERNARD: Can I, Biff? 'Cause I told everybody I'm going to be in the locker room.
HAPPY: In Ebbets Field it's the clubhouse.
BERNARD: I meant the clubhouse. Biff!
HAPPY: Biff!
BIFF (*grandly, after a slight pause*): Let him carry the shoulder guards.
HAPPY (*as he gives Bernard the shoulder guards*): Stay close to us now.

(*Willy rushes in with the pennants.*)

WILLY (*handing them out*): Everybody wave when Biff comes out on the field. (*Happy and Bernard run off.*) You set now, boy?

(*The music has died away.*)

BIFF: Ready to go, Pop. Every muscle is ready.
WILLY (*at the edge of the apron*): You realize what this means?
BIFF: That's right, Pop.
WILLY (*feeling Biff's muscles*): You're comin' home this afternoon captain of the All-Scholastic Championship Team of the City of New York.
BIFF: I got it, Pop. And remember, pal, when I take off my helmet, that touchdown is for you.
WILLY: Let's go! (*He is starting out, with his arm around Biff, when Charley enters, as of old, in knickers.*) I got no room for you, Charley.
CHARLEY: Room? For what?
WILLY: In the car.
CHARLEY: You goin' for a ride? I wanted to shoot some casino.
WILLY (*furiously*): Casino! (*Incredulously.*) Don't you realize what today is?
LINDA: Oh, he knows, Willy. He's just kidding you.
WILLY: That's nothing to kid about!
CHARLEY: No, Linda, what's goin' on?
LINDA: He's playing in Ebbets Field.
CHARLEY: Baseball in this weather?
WILLY: Don't talk to him. Come on, come on! (*He is pushing them out.*)

CHARLEY: Wait a minute, didn't you hear the news?
WILLY: What?
CHARLEY: Don't you listen to the radio? Ebbets Field just blew up.
WILLY: You go to hell! (*Charley laughs. Pushing them out.*) Come on, come on! We're late.
CHARLEY (*as they go*): Knock a homer, Biff, knock a homer!
WILLY (*the last to leave, turning to Charley*): I don't think that was funny, Charley. This is the greatest day of his life.
CHARLEY: Willy, when are you going to grow up?
WILLY: Yeah, heh? When this game is over, Charley, you'll be laughing out of the other side of your face. They'll be calling him another Red Grange. Twenty-five thousand a year.
CHARLEY (*kidding*): Is that so?
WILLY: Yeah, that's so.
CHARLEY: Well, then, I'm sorry, Willy. But tell me something.
WILLY: What?
CHARLEY: Who is Red Grange?
WILLY: Put up your hands. Goddam you, put up your hands!

(*Charley, chuckling, shakes his head and walks away, around the left corner of the stage. Willy follows him. The music rises to a mocking frenzy.*)

WILLY: Who the hell do you think you are, better than everybody else? You don't know everything, you big, ignorant, stupid . . . Put up your hands!

(*Light rises, on the right side of the forestage, on a small table in the reception room of Charley's office. Traffic sounds are heard. Bernard, now mature, sits whistling to himself. A pair of tennis rackets and an overnight bag are on the floor beside him.*)

WILLY (*offstage*): What are you walking away for? Don't walk away! If you're going to say something say it to my face! I know you laugh at me behind my back. You'll laugh out of the other side of your goddam face after this game. Touchdown! Touchdown! Eighty thousand people! Touchdown! Right between the goal posts.

(*Bernard is a quiet, earnest, but self-assured young man. Willy's voice is coming from right upstage now. Bernard lowers his feet off the table and listens. Jenny, his father's secretary, enters.*)

JENNY (*distressed*): Say, Bernard, will you go out in the hall?
BERNARD: What is that noise? Who is it?
JENNY: Mr. Loman. He just got off the elevator.
BERNARD (*getting up*): Who's he arguing with?
JENNY: Nobody. There's nobody with him. I can't deal with him anymore, and your father gets all upset everytime he comes. I've got a lot of typing to do, and your father's waiting to sign it. Will you see him?

WILLY (*entering*): Touchdown! Touch—(*He sees Jenny.*) Jenny, Jenny, good to see you. How're ya? Workin'? Or still honest?

JENNY: Fine. How've you been feeling?

WILLY: Not much any more, Jenny. Ha, ha! (*He is surprised to see the rackets.*)

BERNARD: Hello, Uncle Willy?

WILLY (*almost shocked*): Bernard! Well, look who's here! (*He comes quickly, guiltily, to Bernard and warmly shakes his hand.*)

BERNARD: How are you? Good to see you.

WILLY: What are you doing here?

BERNARD: Oh, just stopped by to see Pop. Get off my feet till my train leaves. I'm going to Washington in a few minutes.

WILLY: Is he in?

BERNARD: Yes, he's in his office with the accountant. Sit down.

WILLY (*sitting down*): What're you going to do in Washington?

BERNARD: Oh, just a case I've got there, Willy.

WILLY: That so? (*Indicating the rackets.*) You going to play tennis there?

BERNARD: I'm staying with a friend who's got a court.

WILLY: Don't say. His own tennis court. Must be fine people, I bet.

BERNARD: They are, very nice. Dad tells me Biff's in town.

WILLY (*with a big smile*): Yeah, Biff's in. Working on a very big deal, Bernard.

BERNARD: What's Biff doing?

WILLY: Well, he's been doing very big things in the West. But he decided to establish himself here. Very big. We're having dinner. Did I hear your wife had a boy?

BERNARD: That's right. Our second.

WILLY: Two boys! What do you know!

BERNARD: What kind of a deal has Biff got?

WILLY: Well, Bill Oliver—very big sporting-goods man— he wants Biff very badly. Called him in from the West. Long distance, carte blanche, special deliveries. Your friends have their own private tennis court?

BERNARD: You still with the old firm, Willy?

WILLY (*after a pause*): I'm—I'm overjoyed to see how you made the grade, Bernard, overjoyed. It's an encouraging thing to see a young man really— really—Looks very good for Biff—very—(*He breaks off, then.*) Bernard—(*He is so full of emotion, he breaks off again.*)

BERNARD: What is it, Willy?

WILLY (*small and alone*): What—what's the secret?

BERNARD: What secret?

WILLY: How—how did you? Why didn't he ever catch on?

BERNARD: I wouldn't know that, Willy.

WILLY (*confidentially, desperately*): You were his friend, his boyhood friend. There's something I don't understand about it. His life ended after that Ebbets Field game. From the age of seventeen nothing good ever happened to him.

BERNARD: He never trained himself for anything.

WILLY: But he did, he did. After high school he took so many correspondence courses. Radio mechanics; television; God knows what, and never made the slightest mark.

BERNARD (*taking off his glasses*): Willy, do you want to talk candidly?

WILLY (*rising, faces Bernard*): I regard you as a very brilliant man, Bernard. I value your advice.

BERNARD: Oh, the hell with the advice, Willy. I couldn't advise you. There's just one thing I've always wanted to ask you. When he was supposed to graduate, and the math teacher flunked him—

WILLY: Oh, that son-of-a-bitch ruined his life.

BERNARD: Yeah, but, Willy, all he had to do was go to summer school and make up that subject.

WILLY: That's right, that's right.

BERNARD: Did you tell him not to go to summer school?

WILLY: Me? I begged him to go. I ordered him to go!

BERNARD: Then why wouldn't he go?

WILLY: Why? Why! Bernard, that question has been trailing me like a ghost for the last fifteen years. He flunked the subject, and laid down and died like a hammer hit him!

BERNARD: Take it easy, kid.

WILLY: Let me talk to you—I got nobody to talk to. Bernard, Bernard, was it my fault? Y'see? It keeps going around in my mind, maybe I did something to him. I got nothing to give him.

BERNARD: Don't take it so hard.

WILLY: Why did he lay down? What is the story there? You were his friend!

BERNARD: Willy, I remember, it was June, and our grades came out. And he'd flunked math.

WILLY: That son-of-a-bitch!

BERNARD: No, it wasn't right then. Biff just got very angry, I remember, and he was ready to enroll in summer school.

WILLY (*surprised*): He was?

BERNARD: He wasn't beaten by it at all. But then, Willy, he disappeared from the block for almost a month. And I got the idea that he'd gone up to New England to see you. Did he have a talk with you then?

(*Willy stares in silence.*)

BERNARD: Willy?

WILLY (*with a strong edge of resentment in his voice*): Yeah, he came to Boston. What about it?

BERNARD: Well, just that when he came back—I'll never forget this, it always mystifies me. Because I'd thought so well of Biff, even though he'd always taken advantage of me. I loved him, Willy, y'know? And he came back after that month and took his sneakers—remember those sneakers with "University of Virginia" printed on them? He was so proud of those, wore them every day. And he took them down in the cellar, and burned them up in the furnace. We had a fist fight. It lasted at least half an hour. Just the two of us, punching each other down the cellar, and crying right through it. I've often thought of how strange it was that I knew he'd given up his life. What happened in Boston, Willy?

(*Willy looks at him as at an intruder.*)

BERNARD: I just bring it up because you asked me.

WILLY (*angrily*): Nothing. What do you mean, "What happened?" What's that got to do with anything?

BERNARD: Well, don't get sore.

WILLY: What are you trying to do, blame it on me? If a boy lays down is that my fault?

BERNARD: Now, Willy, don't get—

WILLY: Well, don't—don't talk to me that way! What does that mean, "What happened?"

(*Charley enters. He is in his vest, and he carries a bottle of bourbon.*)

CHARLEY: Hey, you're going to miss that train. (*He waves the bottle.*)

BERNARD: Yeah, I'm going. (*He takes the bottle.*) Thanks, Pop. (*He picks up his rackets and bag.*) Good-by, Willy, and don't worry about it. You know, "If at first you don't succeed..."

WILLY: Yes, I believe in that.

BERNARD: But sometimes, Willy, it's better for a man just to walk away.

WILLY: Walk away?

BERNARD: That's right.

WILLY: But if you can't walk away?

BERNARD (*after a slight pause*): I guess that's when it's tough. (*Extending his hand.*) Good-by, Willy.

WILLY (*shaking Bernard's hand*): Good-by, boy.

CHARLEY (*an arm on Bernard's shoulder*): How do you like this kid? Gonna argue a case in front of the Supreme Court.

BERNARD (*protesting*): Pop!

WILLY (*genuinely shocked, pained, and happy*): No! The Supreme Court!

BERNARD: I gotta run. 'By, Dad!

CHARLEY: Knock 'em dead, Bernard!

(*Bernard goes off.*)

WILLY (*as Charley takes out his wallet*): The Supreme Court! And he didn't even mention it!

CHARLEY (*counting out money on the desk*): He don't have to—he's gonna do it.

WILLY: And you never told him what to do, did you? You never took any interest in him.

CHARLEY: My salvation is that I never took any interest in anything. There's some money—fifty dollars. I got an accountant inside.

WILLY: Charley, look ... (*With difficulty.*) I got my insurance to pay. If you can manage it—I need a hundred and ten dollars.

(*Charley doesn't reply for a moment; merely stops moving.*)

WILLY: I'd draw it from my bank but Linda would know, and I...

CHARLEY: Sit down, Willy.

WILLY (*moving toward the chair*): I'm keeping an account of everything, remember. I'll pay every penny back. (*He sits.*)

CHARLEY: Now listen to me, Willy.

WILLY: I want you to know I appreciate...

CHARLEY (*sitting down on the table*): Willy, what're you doin'? What the hell is goin' on in your head?

WILLY: Why? I'm simply...

CHARLEY: I offered you a job. You make fifty dollars a week. And I won't send you on the road.

WILLY: I've got a job.

CHARLEY: Without pay? What kind of a job is a job without pay? (*He rises.*) Now, look, kid, enough is enough. I'm no genius but I know when I'm being insulted.

WILLY: Insulted!

CHARLEY: Why don't you want to work for me?

WILLY: What's the matter with you? I've got a job.

CHARLEY: Then what're you walkin' in here every week for?

WILLY (*getting up*): Well, if you don't want me to walk in here—

CHARLEY: I'm offering you a job.

WILLY: I don't want your goddam job!

CHARLEY: When the hell are you going to grow up?

WILLY (*furiously*): You big ignoramus, if you say that to me again I'll rap you one! I don't care how big you are! (*He's ready to fight.*)

(*Pause.*)

CHARLEY (*kindly, going to him*): How much do you need, Willy?

WILLY: Charley, I'm strapped. I'm strapped. I don't know what to do. I was just fired.

CHARLEY: Howard fired you?

WILLY: That snotnose. Imagine that? I named him. I named him Howard.

CHARLEY: Willy, when're you gonna realize that them things don't mean anything? You named him Howard, but you can't sell that. The only thing you got in this world is what you can sell. And the funny thing is that you're a salesman, and you don't know that.

WILLY: I've always tried to think otherwise, I guess. I always felt that if a man was impressive, and well liked, that nothing—

CHARLEY: Why must everybody like you? Who liked J. P. Morgan?° Was he impressive? In a Turkish bath he'd look like a butcher. But with his pockets on he was very well liked. Now listen, Willy, I know you don't like me, and nobody can say I'm in love with you, but I'll give you a job because—just for the hell of it, put it that way. Now what do you say?

WILLY: I—I just can't work for you, Charley.

CHARLEY: What're you, jealous of me?

WILLY: I can't work for you, that's all, don't ask me why.

J. P. Morgan: (1837–1913), wealthy financier and art collector whose money was made chiefly in banking, railroads, and steel.

CHARLEY (*angered, takes out more bills*): You been jealous of me all your life, you dammed fool! Here, pay your insurance. (*He puts the money in Willy's hand.*)

WILLY: I'm keeping strict accounts.

CHARLEY: I've got some work to do. Take care of yourself. And pay your insurance.

WILLY (*moving to the right*): Funny, y'know? After all the highways, and the trains, and the appointments, and the years, you end up worth more dead than alive.

CHARLEY: Willy, nobody's worth nothin' dead. (*After a slight pause.*) Did you hear what I said?

(*Willy stands still, dreaming.*)

CHARLEY: Willy!

WILLY: Apologize to Bernard for me when you see him. I didn't mean to argue with him. He's a fine boy. They're all fine boys, and they'll end up big—all of them. Someday they'll all play tennis together. Wish me luck, Charley. He saw Bill Oliver today.

CHARLEY: Good luck.

WILLY (*on the verge of tears*): Charley, you're the only friend I got. Isn't that a remarkable thing? (*He goes out.*)

CHARLEY: Jesus!

(*Charley stares after him a moment and follows. All light blacks out. Suddenly raucous music is heard, and a red glow rises behind the screen at right. Stanley, a young waiter, appears, carrying a table, followed by Happy, who is carrying two chairs.*)

STANLEY (*putting the table down*): That's all right, Mr. Loman, I can handle it myself. (*He turns and takes the chairs from Happy and places them at the table.*)

HAPPY (*glancing around*): Oh, this is better.

STANLEY: Sure, in the front there you're in the middle of all kinds of noise. Whenever you got a party, Mr. Loman, you just tell me and I'll put you back here. Y'know, there's a lotta people they don't like it private, because when they go out they like to see a lotta action around them because they're sick and tired to stay in the house by theirself. But I know you, you ain't from Hackensack. You know what I mean?

HAPPY (*sitting down*): So how's it coming, Stanley?

STANLEY: Ah, it's a dog life. I only wish during the war they'd a took me in the Army. I coulda been dead by now.

HAPPY: My brother's back, Stanley.

STANLEY: Oh, he come back, heh? From the Far West.

HAPPY: Yeah, big cattle man, my brother, so treat him right. And my father's coming too.

STANLEY: Oh, your father too!

HAPPY: You got a couple of nice lobsters?

STANLEY: Hundred percent, big.

HAPPY: I want them with the claws.

STANLEY: Don't worry, I don't give you no mice. (*Happy laughs.*) How about some wine? It'll put a head on the meal.

HAPPY: No. You remember, Stanley, that recipe I brought you from overseas? With the champagne in it?

STANLEY: Oh, yeah, sure. I still got it tacked up yet in the kitchen. But that'll have to cost a buck apiece anyways.

HAPPY: That's all right.

STANLEY: What'd you, hit a number or somethin'?

HAPPY: No, it's a little celebration. My brother is—I think he pulled off a big deal today. I think we're going into business together.

STANLEY: Great! That's the best for you. Because a family business, you know what I mean?—that's the best.

HAPPY: That's what I think.

STANLEY: 'Cause what's the difference? Somebody steals? It's in the family. Know what I mean? (*Sotto voce.°*) Like this bartender here. The boss is goin' crazy what kinda leak he's got in the cash register. You put it in but it don't come out.

HAPPY (*raising his head*): Sh!

STANLEY: What?

HAPPY: You notice I wasn't lookin' right or left, was I?

STANLEY: No.

HAPPY: And my eyes are closed.

STANLEY: So what's the—?

HAPPY: Strudel's comin'.

STANLEY (*catching on, looks around*): Ah, no, there's no—

(*He breaks off as a furred, lavishly dressed girl enters and sits at the next table. Both follow her with their eyes.*)

STANLEY: Geez, how'd ya know?

HAPPY: I got radar or something. (*Staring directly at her profile.*) Ooooooooo . . . Stanley.

STANLEY: I think that's for you, Mr. Loman.

HAPPY: Look at that mouth. Oh, God. And the binoculars.

STANLEY: Geez, you got a life, Mr. Loman.

HAPPY: Wait on her.

STANLEY (*going to the girl's table*): Would you like a menu, ma'am?

GIRL: I'm expecting someone, but I'd like a—

HAPPY: Why don't you bring her—excuse me, miss, do you mind? I sell champagne, and I'd like you to try my brand. Bring her a champagne, Stanley.

GIRL: That's awfully nice of you.

HAPPY: Don't mention it. It's all company money. (*He laughs.*)

GIRL: That's a charming product to be selling, isn't it?

HAPPY: Oh, gets to be like everything else. Selling is selling, y'know.

GIRL: I suppose.

HAPPY: You don't happen to sell, do you?

GIRL: No, I don't sell.

HAPPY: Would you object to a compliment from a stranger? You ought to be on a magazine cover.

GIRL (*looking at him a little archly*): I have been.

(*Stanley comes in with a glass of champagne.*)

Sotto voce: In a soft voice or stage whisper.

HAPPY: What'd I say before, Stanley? You see? She's a cover girl.
STANLEY: Oh, I could see, I could see.
HAPPY (to the Girl): What magazine?
GIRL: Oh, a lot of them. (She takes the drink.) Thank you.
HAPPY: You know what they say in France, don't you? "Champagne is the drink of the complexion" — Hya, Biff!

(Biff has entered and sits with Happy.)

BIFF: Hello, kid. Sorry I'm late.
HAPPY: I just got here. Uh, Miss —?
GIRL: Forsythe.
HAPPY: Miss Forsythe, this is my brother.
BIFF: Is Dad here?
HAPPY: His name is Biff. You might've heard of him. Great football player.
GIRL: Really? What team?
HAPPY: Are you familiar with football?
GIRL: No, I'm afraid I'm not.
HAPPY: Biff is quarterback with the New York Giants.
GIRL: Well, that is nice, isn't it? (She drinks.)
HAPPY: Good health.
GIRL: I'm happy to meet you.
HAPPY: That's my name. Hap. It's really Harold, but at West Point they called me Happy.
GIRL (now really impressed): Oh, I see. How do you do? (She turns her profile.)
BIFF: Isn't Dad coming?
HAPPY: You want her?
BIFF: Oh, I could never make that.
HAPPY: I remember the time that idea would never come into your head. Where's the old confidence, Biff?
BIFF: I just saw Oliver —
HAPPY: Wait a minute. I've got to see that old confidence again. Do you want her? She's on call.
BIFF: Oh, no. (He turns to look at the Girl.)
HAPPY: I'm telling you. Watch this. (Turning to the Girl): Honey? (She turns to him.) Are you busy?
GIRL: Well, I am . . . but I could make a phone call.
HAPPY: Do that, will you, honey? And see if you can get a friend. We'll be here for a while. Biff is one of the greatest football players in the country.
GIRL (standing up): Well, I'm certainly happy to meet you.
HAPPY: Come back soon.
GIRL: I'll try.
HAPPY: Don't try, honey, try hard.

(The Girl exits. Stanley follows, shaking his head in bewildered admiration.)

HAPPY: Isn't that a shame now? A beautiful girl like that? That's why I can't get married. There's not a good woman in a thousand. New York is loaded with them, kid!
BIFF: Hap, look —
HAPPY: I told you she was on call!
BIFF (strangely unnerved): Cut it out, will ya? I want to say something to you.

HAPPY: Did you see Oliver?
BIFF: I saw him all right. Now look, I want to tell Dad a couple of things and I want you to help me.
HAPPY: What? Is he going to back you?
BIFF: Are you crazy? You're out of your goddam head, you know that?
HAPPY: Why? What happened?
BIFF (breathlessly): I did a terrible thing today, Hap. It's been the strangest day I ever went through. I'm all numb, I swear.
HAPPY: You mean he wouldn't see you?
BIFF: Well, I waited six hours for him, see? All day. Kept sending my name in. Even tried to date his secretary so she'd get me to him, but no soap.
HAPPY: Because you're not showin' the old confidence Biff. He remembered you, didn't he?
BIFF (stopping Happy with a gesture): Finally, about five o'clock, he comes out. Didn't remember who I was or anything. I felt like such an idiot, Hap.
HAPPY: Did you tell him my Florida idea?
BIFF: He walked away. I saw him for one minute. I got so mad I could've torn the walls down! How the hell did I ever get the idea I was a salesman there? I even believed myself that I'd been a salesman for him! And then he gave me one look and—I realized what a ridiculous lie my whole life has been! We've been talking in a dream for fifteen years. I was a shipping clerk.
HAPPY: What'd you do?
BIFF (with great tension and wonder): Well, he left, see. And the secretary went out. I was all alone in the waiting room. I don't know what came over me, Hap. The next thing I know I'm in his office—paneled walls, everything. I can't explain it. I—Hap, I took his fountain pen.
HAPPY: Geez, did he catch you?
BIFF: I ran out. I ran down all eleven flights. I ran and ran and ran.
HAPPY: That was an awful dumb—what'd you do that for?
BIFF (agonized): I don't know, I just—wanted to take something, I don't know. You gotta help me, Hap. I'm gonna tell Pop.
HAPPY: You crazy? What for?
BIFF: Hap, he's got to understand that I'm not the man somebody lends that kind of money to. He thinks I've been spiting him all these years and it's eating him up.
HAPPY: That's just it. You tell him something nice.
BIFF: I can't.
HAPPY: Say you got a lunch date with Oliver tomorrow.
BIFF: So what do I do tomorrow?
HAPPY: You leave the house tomorrow and come back at night and say Oliver is thinking it over. And he thinks it over for a couple of weeks, and gradually it fades away and nobody's the worse.
BIFF: But it'll go on forever!
HAPPY: Dad is never so happy as when he's looking forward to something!

(*Willy enters.*)

HAPPY: Hello, scout!
WILLY: Gee, I haven't been here in years!

(*Stanley has followed Willy in and sets a chair for him. Stanley starts off but Happy stops him.*)

HAPPY: Stanley!

(*Stanley stands by, waiting for an order.*)

BIFF (*going to Willy with guilt, as to an invalid*): Sit down, Pop. You want a drink?
WILLY: Sure, I don't mind.
BIFF: Let's get a load on.
WILLY: You look worried.
BIFF: N-no. (*To Stanley.*) Scotch all around. Make it doubles.
STANLEY: Doubles, right. (*He goes.*)
WILLY: You had a couple already, didn't you?
BIFF: Just a couple, yeah.
WILLY: Well, what happened, boy? (*Nodding affirmatively, with a smile.*) Everything go all right?
BIFF (*takes a breath, then reaches out and grasps Willy's hand*): Pal . . . (*He is smiling bravely, and Willy is smiling too.*) I had an experience today.
HAPPY: Terrific, Pop.
WILLY: That so? What happened?
BIFF (*high, slightly alcoholic, above the earth*): I'm going to tell you everything from first to last. It's been a strange day. (*Silence. He looks around, composes himself as best he can, but his breath keeps breaking the rhythm of his voice.*) I had to wait quite a while for him, and—
WILLY: Oliver?
BIFF: Yeah, Oliver. All day, as a matter of cold fact. And a lot of—instances—facts, Pop, facts about my life came back to me. Who was it, Pop? Who ever said I was a salesman with Oliver?
WILLY: Well, you were.
BIFF: No, Dad, I was a shipping clerk.
WILLY: But you were practically—
BIFF (*with determination*): Dad, I don't know who said it first, but I was never a salesman for Bill Oliver.
WILLY: What're you talking about?
BIFF: Let's hold on to the facts tonight, Pop. We're not going to get anywhere bullin' around. I was a shipping clerk.
WILLY (*angrily*): All right, now listen to me—
BIFF: Why don't you let me finish?
WILLY: I'm not interested in stories about the past or any crap of that kind because the woods are burning, boys, you understand? There's a big blaze going on all around. I was fired today.
BIFF (*shocked*): How could you be?
WILLY: I was fired, and I'm looking for a little good news to tell your mother, because the woman has waited and the woman has suffered. The gist of it is that I haven't got a story left in my head, Biff. So don't give

me a lecture about facts and aspects. I am not interested. Now what've you got to say to me?

(*Stanley enters with three drinks. They wait until he leaves.*)

WILLY: Did you see Oliver?
BIFF: Jesus, Dad!
WILLY: You mean you didn't go up there?
HAPPY: Sure he went up there.
BIFF: I did. I—saw him. How could they fire you?
WILLY (*on the edge of his chair*): What kind of a welcome did he give you?
BIFF: He won't even let you work on commission?
WILLY: I'm out! (*Driving.*) So tell me, he gave you a warm welcome?
HAPPY: Sure, Pop, sure!
BIFF (*driven*): Well, it was kind of—
WILLY: I was wondering if he'd remember you. (*To Happy.*) Imagine, man doesn't see him for ten, twelve years and gives him that kind of a welcome!
HAPPY: Damn right!
BIFF (*trying to return to the offensive*): Pop, look—
WILLY: You know why he remembered you, don't you? Because you impressed him in those days.
BIFF: Let's talk quietly and get this down to the facts, huh?
WILLY (*as though Biff had been interrupting*): Well, what happened? It's great news, Biff. Did he take you into his office or'd you talk in the waiting room?
BIFF: Well, he came in, see, and—
WILLY (*with a big smile*): What'd he say? Betcha he threw his arm around you.
BIFF: Well, he kinda—
WILLY: He's a fine man. (*To Happy.*) Very hard man to see, y'know.
HAPPY (*agreeing*): Oh, I know.
WILLY (*to Biff*): Is that where you had the drinks?
BIFF: Yeah, he gave me a couple of—no, no!
HAPPY (*cutting in*): He told him my Florida idea.
WILLY: Don't interrupt. (*To Biff.*) How'd he react to the Florida idea?
BIFF: Dad, will you give me a minute to explain?
WILLY: I've been waiting for you to explain since I sat down here! What happened? He took you into his office and what?
BIFF: Well—I talked. And—and he listened, see.
WILLY: Famous for the way he listens, y'know. What was his answer?
BIFF: His answer was—(*He breaks off, suddenly angry.*) Dad, you're not letting me tell you what I want to tell you!
WILLY (*accusing, angered*): You didn't see him, did you?
BIFF: I did see him!
WILLY: What'd you insult him or something? You insulted him, didn't you?
BIFF: Listen, will you let me out of it, will you just let me out of it!
HAPPY: What the hell!
WILLY: Tell me what happened!

BIFF (*to Happy*): I can't talk to him!

(*A single trumpet note jars the ear. The light of green leaves stains the house, which holds the air of night and a dream. Young Bernard enters and knocks on the door of the house.*)

YOUNG BERNARD (*frantically*): Mrs. Loman, Mrs. Loman!

HAPPY: Tell him what happened!

BIFF (*to Happy*): Shut up and leave me alone!

WILLY: No, no! You had to go and flunk math!

BIFF: What math? What're you talking about?

YOUNG BERNARD: Mrs. Loman, Mrs. Loman!

(*Linda appears in the house, as of old.*)

WILLY (*wildly*): Math, math, math!

BIFF: Take it easy, Pop!

YOUNG BERNARD: Mrs. Loman!

WILLY (*furiously*): If you hadn't flunked you'd've been set by now!

BIFF: Now, look, I'm gonna tell you what happened, and you're going to listen to me.

YOUNG BERNARD: Mrs. Loman!

BIFF: I waited six hours—

HAPPY: What the hell are you saying?

BIFF: I kept sending in my name but he wouldn't see me. So finally he . . . (*He continues unheard as light fades low on the restaurant.*)

YOUNG BERNARD: Biff flunked math!

LINDA: No!

YOUNG BERNARD: Birnbaum flunked him! They won't graduate him!

LINDA: But they have to. He's gotta go to the university. Where is he? Biff! Biff!

YOUNG BERNARD: No, he left. He went to Grand Central.

LINDA: Grand— You mean he went to Boston!

YOUNG BERNARD: Is Uncle Willy in Boston?

LINDA: Oh, maybe Willy can talk to the teacher. Oh, the poor, poor boy!

(*Light on house area snaps out.*)

BIFF (*at the table, now audible, holding up a gold fountain pen*): . . . so I'm washed up with Oliver, you understand? Are you listening to me?

WILLY (*at a loss*): Yeah, sure. If you hadn't flunked—

BIFF: Flunked what? What're you talking about?

WILLY: Don't blame everything on me! I didn't flunk math—you did! What pen?

HAPPY: That was awful dumb, Biff, a pen like that is worth—

WILLY (*seeing the pen for the first time*): You took Oliver's pen?

BIFF (*weakening*): Dad, I just explained it to you.

WILLY: You stole Bill Oliver's fountain pen!

BIFF: I didn't exactly steal it! That's just what I've been explaining to you!

HAPPY: He had it in his hand and just then Oliver walked in, so he got nervous and stuck it in his pocket!

WILLY: My God, Biff!

BIFF: I never intended to do it, Dad!

OPERATOR'S VOICE: Standish Arms, good evening!

WILLY (*shouting*): I'm not in my room!

BIFF (*frightened*): Dad, what's the matter? (*He and Happy stand up.*)

OPERATOR: Ringing Mr. Loman for you!

WILLY: I'm not there, stop it!

BIFF (*horrified, gets down on one knee before* Willy): Dad, I'll make good, I'll make good. (*Willy tries to get to his feet. Biff holds him down.*) Sit down now.

WILLY: No, you're no good, you're no good for anything.

BIFF: I am, Dad, I'll find something else, you understand? Now don't worry about anything. (*He holds up* Willy's *face.*) Talk to me, Dad.

OPERATOR: Mr. Loman does not answer. Shall I page him?

WILLY (*attempting to stand, as though to rush and silence the* Operator): No, no, no!

HAPPY: He'll strike something, Pop.

WILLY: No, no . . .

BIFF (*desperately, standing over* Willy): Pop, listen! Listen to me! I'm telling you something good. Oliver talked to his partner about the Florida idea. You listening? He—he talked to his partner, and he came to me . . . I'm going to be all right, you hear? Dad, listen to me, he said it was just a question of the amount!

WILLY: Then you . . . got it?

HAPPY: He's gonna be terrific, Pop!

WILLY (*trying to stand*): Then you got it, haven't you? You got it! You got it!

BIFF (*agonized, holds* Willy *down*): No, no. Look, Pop. I'm supposed to have lunch with them tomorrow. I'm just telling you this so you'll know that I can still make an impression, Pop. And I'll make good somewhere, but I can't go tomorrow, see?

WILLY: Why not? You simply—

BIFF: But the pen, Pop!

WILLY: You give it to him and tell him it was an oversight!

HAPPY: Sure, have lunch tomorrow!

BIFF: I can't say that—

WILLY: You were doing a crossword puzzle and accidentally used his pen!

BIFF: Listen, kid, I took those balls years ago, now I walk in with his fountain pen? That clinches it, don't you see? I can't face him like that! I'll try elsewhere.

PAGE'S VOICE: Paging Mr. Loman!

WILLY: Don't you want to be anything?

BIFF: Pop, how can I go back?

WILLY: You don't want to be anything, is that what's behind it?

BIFF (*now angry at* Willy *for not crediting his sympathy*): Don't take it that way! You think it was easy walking into that office after what I'd done to him? A team of horses couldn't have dragged me back to Bill Oliver!

WILLY: Then why'd you go?

BIFF: Why did I go? Why did I go! Look at you! Look at what's become of you!

(*Off left, The Woman laughs.*)

WILLY: Biff, you're going to go to that lunch tomorrow, or—

BIFF: I can't go. I've got no appointment!

HAPPY: Biff, for . . . !

WILLY: Are you spiting me?

BIFF: Don't take it that way! Goddammit!

WILLY (*strikes Biff and falters away from the table*): You rotten little louse! Are you spiting me?

THE WOMAN: Someone's at the door, Willy!

BIFF: I'm no good, can't you see what I am?

HAPPY (*separating them*): Hey, you're in a restaurant! Now cut it out, both of you! (*The girls enter.*) Hello, girls, sit down.

(*The Woman laughs, off left.*)

MISS FORSYTHE: I guess we might as well. This is Letta.

THE WOMAN: Willy, are you going to wake up?

BIFF (*ignoring Willy*): How're ya, miss, sit down. What do you drink?

MISS FORSYTHE: Letta might not be able to stay long.

LETTA: I gotta get up very early tomorrow. I got jury duty. I'm so excited! Were you fellows ever on a jury?

BIFF: No, but I been in front of them! (*The girls laugh.*) This is my father.

LETTA: Isn't he cute? Sit down with us, Pop.

HAPPY: Sit him down, Biff!

BIFF (*going to him*): Come on, slugger, drink us under the table. To hell with it! Come on, sit down, pal.

(*On Biff's last insistence, Willy is about to sit.*)

THE WOMAN (*now urgently*): Willy, are you going to answer the door!

(*The Woman's call pulls Willy back. He starts right, befuddled.*)

BIFF: Hey, where are you going?

WILLY: Open the door.

BIFF: The door?

WILLY: The washroom . . . the door . . . where's the door?

BIFF (*leading Willy to the left*): Just go straight down.

(*Willy moves left.*)

THE WOMAN: Willy, Willy, are you going to get up, get up, get up, get up?

(*Willy exits left.*)

LETTA: I think it's sweet you bring your daddy along.

MISS FORSYTHE: Oh, he isn't really your father!

BIFF (*at left, turning to her resentfully*): Miss Forsythe, you've just seen a prince walk by. A fine, troubled prince. A hard-working, unappreciated prince. A pal, you understand? A good companion. Always for his boys.

LETTA: That's so sweet.

HAPPY: Well, girls, what's the program? We're wasting time. Come on, Biff. Gather round. Where would you like to go?

BIFF: Why don't you do something for him?

HAPPY: Me!

BIFF: Don't you give a damn for him, Hap?

HAPPY: What're you talking about? I'm the one who—

BIFF: I sense it, you don't give a good goddam about him. (*He takes the rolled-up hose from his pocket and puts it on the table in front of Happy.*) Look what I found in the cellar, for Christ's sake. How can you bear to let it go on?

HAPPY: Me? Who goes away? Who runs off and—

BIFF: Yeah, but he doesn't mean anything to you. You could help him—I can't! Don't you understand what I'm talking about? He's going to kill himself, don't you know that?

HAPPY: Don't I know it! Me!

BIFF: Hap, help him! Jesus . . . help him . . . Help me, help me, I can't bear to look at his face! (*Ready to weep, he hurries out, up right.*)

HAPPY (*starting after him*): Where are you going?

MISS FORSYTHE: What's he so mad about?

HAPPY: Come on, girls, we'll catch up with him.

MISS FORSYTHE (*as Happy pushes her out*): Say, I don't like that temper of his!

HAPPY: He's just a little overstrung, he'll be all right!

WILLY (*off left, as The Woman laughs*): Don't answer! Don't answer!

LETTA: Don't you want to tell your father—

HAPPY: No, that's not my father. He's just a guy. Come on, we'll catch Biff, and, honey, we're going to paint this town! Stanley, where's the check! Hey, Stanley!

(*They exit. Stanley looks toward left.*)

STANLEY (*calling to Happy indignantly*): Mr. Loman! Mr. Loman!

(*Stanley picks up a chair and follows them off. Knocking is heard off left. The Woman enters, laughing. Willy follows her. She is in a black slip; he is buttoning his shirt. Raw, sensuous music accompanies their speech.*)

WILLY: Will you stop laughing? Will you stop?

THE WOMAN: Aren't you going to answer the door? He'll wake the whole hotel.

WILLY: I'm not expecting anybody.

THE WOMAN: Whyn't you have another drink, honey, and stop being so damn self-centered?

WILLY: I'm so lonely.

THE WOMAN: You know you ruined me, Willy? From now on, whenever you come to the office, I'll see that you go right through to the buyers. No waiting at my desk anymore, Willy. You ruined me.

WILLY: That's nice of you to say that.

THE WOMAN: Gee, you are self-centered! Why so sad? You are the saddest, self-centeredest soul I ever did see-saw. (*She laughs. He kisses her.*) Come on inside, drummer boy. It's silly to be dressing in the middle of the night. (*As knocking is heard.*) Aren't you going to answer the door?

WILLY: They're knocking on the wrong door.

THE WOMAN: But I felt the knocking. And he heard us talking in here. Maybe the hotel's on fire!

WILLY (*his terror rising*): It's a mistake.

THE WOMAN: Then tell him to go away!

WILLY: There's nobody there.

THE WOMAN: It's getting on my nerves, Willy. There's somebody standing out there and it's getting on my nerves!

WILLY (*pushing her away from him*): All right, stay in the bathroom here, and don't come out. I think there's a law in Massachusetts about it, so don't come out. It may be that new room clerk. He looked very mean. So don't come out. It's a mistake, there's no fire.

(*The knocking is heard again. He takes a few steps away from her, and she vanishes into the wing. The light follows him, and now he is facing Young Biff, who carries a suitcase. Biff steps toward him. The music is gone.*)

BIFF: Why didn't you answer?

WILLY: Biff! What are you doing in Boston?

BIFF: Why didn't you answer? I've been knocking for five minutes, I called you on the phone—

WILLY: I just heard you. I was in the bathroom and had the door shut. Did anything happen home?

BIFF: Dad—I let you down.

WILLY: What do you mean?

BIFF: Dad...

WILLY: Biffo, what's this about? (*Putting his arm around Biff.*) Come on, let's go downstairs and get you a malted.

BIFF: Dad, I flunked math.

WILLY: Not for the term?

BIFF: The term. I haven't got enough credits to graduate.

WILLY: You mean to say Bernard wouldn't give you the answers?

BIFF: He did, he tried, but I only got a sixty-one.

WILLY: And they wouldn't give you four points?

BIFF: Birnbaum refused absolutely. I begged him, Pop, but he won't give me those points. You gotta talk to him before they close the school. Because if he saw the kind of man you are, and you just talked to him in your way, I'm sure he'd come through for me. The class came right before practice, see, and I didn't go enough. Would you talk to him? He'd like you, Pop. You know the way you could talk.

WILLY: You're on. We'll drive right back.

BIFF: Oh, Dad, good work! I'm sure he'll change it for you!

WILLY: Go downstairs and tell the clerk I'm checkin' out. Go right down.

BIFF: Yes, sir! See, the reason he hates me, Pop—one day he was late for class so I got up at the blackboard and imitated him. I crossed my eyes and talked with a lithp.

WILLY (*laughing*): You did? The kids like it?

BIFF: They nearly died laughing!

WILLY: Yeah? What'd you do?

BIFF: The thquare root of thixthy twee is ... (*Willy bursts out laughing; Biff joins.*) And in the middle of it he walked in!

(*Willy laughs and The Woman joins in offstage.*)

WILLY (*without hesitation*): Hurry downstairs and—

BIFF: Somebody in there?

WILLY: No, that was next door.

(*The Woman laughs offstage.*)

BIFF: Somebody got in your bathroom!

WILLY: No, it's the next room, there's a party—

THE WOMAN (*enters, laughing. She lisps this.*): Can I come in? There's something in the bathtub, Willy, and it's moving!

(*Willy looks at Biff, who is staring open-mouthed and horrified at The Woman.*)

WILLY: Ah—you better go back to your room. They must be finished painting by now. They're painting her room so I let her take a shower here. Go back, go back ... (*He pushes her.*)

THE WOMAN (*resisting*): But I've got to get dressed, Willy, I can't—

WILLY: Get out of here! Go back, go back ... (*Suddenly striving for the ordinary.*) This is Miss Francis, Biff, she's a buyer. They're painting her room. Go back, Miss Francis, go back...

THE WOMAN: But my clothes, I can't go out naked in the hall!

WILLY (*pushing her offstage*): Get outa here! Go back, go back!

(*Biff slowly sits down on his suitcase as the argument continues offstage.*)

THE WOMAN: Where's my stockings? You promised me stockings, Willy!

WILLY: I have no stockings here!

THE WOMAN: You had two boxes of size nine sheers for me, and I want them!

WILLY: Here, for God's sake, will you get outa here!

THE WOMAN (*enters holding a box of stockings*): I just hope there's nobody in the hall. That's all I hope. (*To Biff.*) Are you football or baseball?

BIFF: Football.

THE WOMAN (*angry, humiliated*): That's me too. G'night. (*She snatches her clothes from Willy, and walks out.*)

WILLY (*after a pause*): Well, better get going. I want to get to the school first thing in the morning. Get my suits out of the closet. I'll get my valise. (*Biff doesn't move.*) What's the matter! (*Biff remains motionless, tears falling.*) She's a buyer. Buys for J. H. Simmons. She lives down the hall—they're painting. You don't imagine—(*He breaks off. After a pause.*) Now listen, pal, she's just a buyer. She sees merchandise in her room and they have to keep it looking just so ... (*Pause. Assuming command.*) All right, get my suits. (*Biff doesn't move.*) Now stop crying and do as I say.

I gave you an order. Biff, I gave you an order! Is that what you do when I give you an order? How dare you cry! (*Putting his arm around Biff.*) Now look, Biff, when you grow up you'll understand about these things. You mustn't—you mustn't overemphasize a thing like this. I'll see Birnbaum first thing in the morning.

BIFF: Never mind.

WILLY (*getting down beside Biff*): Never mind! He's going to give you those points. I'll see to it.

BIFF: He wouldn't listen to you.

WILLY: He certainly will listen to me. You need those points for the U. of Virginia.

BIFF: I'm not going there.

WILLY: Heh? If I can't get him to change that mark you'll make it up in summer school. You've got all summer to—

BIFF (*his weeping breaking from him*): Dad...

WILLY (*infected by it*): Oh, my boy...

BIFF: Dad...

WILLY: She's nothing to me, Biff. I was lonely, I was terribly lonely.

BIFF: You—you gave her Mama's stockings! (*His tears break through and he rises to go.*)

WILLY (*grabbing for Biff*): I gave you an order!

BIFF: Don't touch me, you—liar!

WILLY: Apologize for that!

BIFF: You fake! You phony little fake! You fake! (*Overcome, he turns quickly and weeping fully goes out with his suitcase. Willy is left on the floor on his knees.*)

WILLY: I gave you an order! Biff, come back here or I'll beat you! Come back here! I'll whip you!

(*Stanley comes quickly in from the right and stands in front of Willy.*)

WILLY (*shouts at Stanley*): I gave you an order...

STANLEY: Hey, let's pick it up, pick it up, Mr. Loman. (*He helps Willy to his feet.*) Your boys left with the chippies. They said they'll see you home.

(*A second waiter watches some distance away.*)

WILLY: But we were supposed to have dinner together.

(*Music is heard, Willy's theme.*)

STANLEY: Can you make it?

WILLY: I'll—sure, I can make it. (*Suddenly concerned about his clothes.*) Do I—I look all right?

STANLEY: Sure, you look all right. (*He flicks a speck off Willy's lapel.*)

WILLY: Here—here's a dollar.

STANLEY: Oh, your son paid me. It's all right.

WILLY (*putting it in Stanley's hand*): No, take it. You're a good boy.

STANLEY: Oh, no, you don't have to...

WILLY: Here—here's some more, I don't need it anymore. (*After a slight pause.*) Tell me—is there a seed store in the neighborhood?

STANLEY: Seeds? You mean like to plant?

(*As Willy turns, Stanley slips the money back into his jacket pocket.*)

WILLY: Yes. Carrots, peas...

STANLEY: Well, there's hardware stores on Sixth Avenue, but it may be too late now.

WILLY (*anxiously*): Oh, I'd better hurry. I've got to get some seeds. (*He starts off to the right.*) I've got to get some seeds, right away. Nothing's planted. I don't have a thing in the ground.

(*Willy hurries out as the light goes down. Stanley moves over to the right after him, watches him off. The other waiter has been staring at Willy.*)

STANLEY (*to the waiter*): Well, whatta you looking at?

(*The waiter picks up the chairs and moves off right. Stanley takes the table and follows him. The light fades on this area. There is a long pause, the sound of the flute coming over. The light gradually rises on the kitchen, which is empty. Happy appears at the door of the house, followed by Biff. Happy is carrying a large bunch of long-stemmed roses. He enters the kitchen, looks around for Linda. Not seeing her, he turns to Biff, who is just outside the house door, and makes a gesture with his hands, indicating "Not here, I guess." He looks into the living room and freezes. Inside, Linda, unseen, is seated, Willy's coat on her lap. She rises ominously and quietly and moves toward Happy, who backs up into the kitchen, afraid.*)

HAPPY: Hey, what're you doing up? (*Linda says nothing but moves toward him implacably.*) Where's Pop? (*He keeps backing to the right, and now Linda is in full view in the doorway to the living room.*) Is he sleeping?

LINDA: Where were you?

HAPPY (*trying to laugh it off*): We met two girls, Mom, very fine types. Here, we brought you some flowers. (*Offering them to her.*) Put them in your room, Ma.

(*She knocks them to the floor at Biff's feet. He has now come inside and closed the door behind him. She stares at Biff, silent.*)

HAPPY: Now what'd you do that for? Mom, I want you to have some flowers—

LINDA (*cutting Happy off, violently to Biff*): Don't you care whether he lives or dies?

HAPPY (*going to the stairs*): Come upstairs, Biff.

BIFF (*with a flare of disgust, to Happy*): Go away from me! (*To Linda.*) What do you mean, lives or dies? Nobody's dying around here, pal.

LINDA: Get out of my sight! Get out of here!

BIFF: I wanna see the boss.

LINDA: You're not going near him!

BIFF: Where is he? (*He moves into the living room and Linda follows.*)

LINDA (*shouting after Biff*): You invite him for dinner. He looks forward to it all day—(*Biff appears in his parents' bedroom, looks around, and exits*)—and then you desert him there. There's no stranger you'd do that to!

HAPPY: Why? He had a swell time with us. Listen, when I—(*Linda comes back into the kitchen*)—desert him I hope I don't outlive the day!

LINDA: Get out of here!

HAPPY: Now look, Mom . . .

LINDA: Did you have to go to women tonight? You and your lousy rotten whores!

(*Biff reenters the kitchen.*)

HAPPY: Mom, all we did was follow Biff around trying to cheer him up! (*To Biff.*) Boy, what a night you gave me!

LINDA: Get out of here, both of you, and don't come back! I don't want you tormenting him any more. Go on now, get your things together! (*To Biff.*) You can sleep in his apartment. (*She starts to pick up the flowers and stops herself.*) Pick up this stuff, I'm not your maid anymore. Pick it up, you bum, you!

(*Happy turns his back to her in refusal. Biff slowly moves over and gets down on his knees, picking up the flowers.*)

LINDA: You're a pair of animals! Not one, not another living soul would have had the cruelty to walk out on that man in a restaurant!

BIFF (*not looking at her*): Is that what he said?

LINDA: He didn't have to say anything. He was so humiliated he nearly limped when he came in.

HAPPY: But, Mom, he had a great time with us—

BIFF (*cutting him off violently*): Shut up!

(*Without another word, Happy goes upstairs.*)

LINDA: You! You didn't even go in to see if he was all right!

BIFF (*still on the floor in front of Linda, the flowers in his hand; with self-loathing*): No. Didn't. Didn't do a damned thing. How do you like that, heh? Left him babbling in a toilet.

LINDA: You louse. You . . .

BIFF: Now you hit it on the nose! (*He gets up, throws the flowers in the wastebasket.*) The scum of the earth, and you're looking at him!

LINDA: Get out of here!

BIFF: I gotta talk to the boss, Mom. Where is he?

LINDA: You're not going near him. Get out of this house!

BIFF (*with absolute assurance, determination*): No. We're gonna have an abrupt conversation, him and me.

LINDA: You're not talking to him.

(*Hammering is heard from outside the house, off right. Biff turns toward the noise.*)

LINDA (*suddenly pleading*): Will you please leave him alone?

BIFF: What's he doing out there?

LINDA: He's planting the garden!

BIFF (*quietly*): Now? Oh, my God!

(*Biff moves outside, Linda following. The light dies down on them and comes up on the center of the apron as Willy walks into it. He is carrying a flashlight, a hoe, and a handful of seed packets. He raps the top of the hoe sharply to fix it firmly, and then moves to the left, measuring off the distance with his foot. He holds the flashlight to look at the seed packets, reading off the instructions. He is in the blue of night.*)

WILLY: Carrots . . . quarter-inch apart. Rows . . . one-foot rows. (*He measures it off.*) One foot. (*He puts down a package and measures off.*) Beets. (*He puts down another package and measures again.*) Lettuce. (*He reads the package, puts it down.*) One foot—(*He breaks off as Ben appears at the right and moves slowly down to him.*) What a proposition, ts, ts. Terrific, terrific. 'Cause she's suffered, Ben, the woman has suffered. You understand me? A man can't go out the way he came in, Ben, a man has got to add up to something. You can't, you can't—(*Ben moves toward him as though to interrupt.*) You gotta consider, now. Don't answer so quick. Remember, it's a guaranteed twenty-thousand-dollar proposition. Now look, Ben, I want you to go through the ins and outs of this thing with me. I've got nobody to talk to, Ben, and the woman has suffered, you hear me?

BEN (*standing still, considering*): What's the proposition?

WILLY: It's twenty thousand dollars on the barrelhead. Guaranteed, gilt-edged, you understand?

BEN: You don't want to make a fool of yourself. They might not honor the policy.

WILLY: How can they dare refuse? Didn't I work like a coolie to meet every premium on the nose? And now they don't pay off? Impossible!

BEN: It's called a cowardly thing, William.

WILLY: Why? Does it take more guts to stand here the rest of my life ringing up a zero?

BEN (*yielding*): That's a point, William. (*He moves, thinking, turns.*) And twenty thousand—that is something one can feel with the hand, it is there.

WILLY (*now assured, with rising power*): Oh, Ben, that's the whole beauty of it! I see it like a diamond, shining in the dark, hard and rough, that I can pick up and touch in my hand. Not like—like an appointment! This would not be another damned-fool appointment, Ben, and it changes all the aspects. Because he thinks I'm nothing, see, and so he spites me. But the funeral—(*Straightening up.*) Ben, that funeral will be massive! They'll come from Maine, Massachusetts, Vermont, New Hampshire! All the old-timers with the strange license plates—that boy will be thunderstruck, Ben, because he never realized—I am known! Rhode Island, New York, New Jersey—I am known, Ben and he'll see it with his eyes once and for all. He'll see what I am, Ben! He's in for a shock, that boy!

BEN (*coming down to the edge of the garden*): He'll call you a coward.

WILLY (*suddenly fearful*): No, that would be terrible.

BEN: Yes. And a damned fool.

WILLY: No, no, he mustn't, I won't have that! (*He is broken and desperate.*)

BEN: He'll hate you, William.

(*The gay music of the Boys is heard.*)

WILLY: Oh, Ben, how do we get back to all the great times? Used to be so full of light, and comradeship, the sleigh-riding in winter, and the ruddiness on his cheeks. And always some kind of good news coming up, always something nice coming up ahead. And never even let me carry the valises in the house, and simonizing, simonizing that little red car! Why, why can't I give him something and not have him hate me?

BEN: Let me think about it. (*He glances at his watch.*) I still have a little time. Remarkable proposition, but you've got to be sure you're not making a fool of yourself.

(*Ben drifts off upstage and goes out of sight. Biff comes down from the left.*)

WILLY (*suddenly conscious of Biff, turns and looks up at him, then begins picking up the packages of seeds in confusion*): Where the hell is that seed? (*Indignantly.*) You can't see nothing out here! They boxed in the whole goddam neighborhood!

BIFF: There are people all around here. Don't you realize that?

WILLY: I'm busy. Don't bother me.

BIFF (*taking the hoe from Willy*): I'm saying good-by to you, Pop. (*Willy looks at him, silent, unable to move.*) I'm not coming back any more.

WILLY: You're not going to see Oliver tomorrow?

BIFF: I've got no appointment, Dad.

WILLY: He put his arm around you, and you've got no appointment?

BIFF: Pop, get this now, will you? Everytime I've left it's been a fight that sent me out of here. Today I realized something about myself and I tried to explain it to you and I—I think I'm just not smart enough to make any sense out of it for you. To hell with whose fault it is or anything like that. (*He takes Willy's arm.*) Let's just wrap it up, heh? Come on in, we'll tell Mom. (*He gently tries to pull Willy to left.*)

WILLY (*frozen, immobile, with guilt in his voice*): No, I don't want to see her.

BIFF: Come on! (*He pulls again, and Willy tries to pull away.*)

WILLY (*highly nervous*): No, no, I don't want to see her.

BIFF (*tries to look into Willy's face, as if to find the answer there*): Why don't you want to see her?

WILLY (*more harshly now*): Don't bother me, will you?

BIFF: What do you mean, you don't want to see her? You don't want them calling you yellow, do you? This isn't your fault; it's me, I'm a bum. Now come inside! (*Willy strains to get away.*) Did you hear what I said to you?

(*Willy pulls away and quickly goes by himself into the house. Biff follows.*)

LINDA (*to Willy*): Did you plant, dear?

BIFF (*at the door, to Linda*): All right, we had it out. I'm going and I'm not writing any more.

LINDA (*going to Willy in the kitchen*): I think that's the best way, dear. 'Cause there's no use drawing it out, you'll just never get along.

(*Willy doesn't respond.*)

BIFF: People ask where I am and what I'm doing, you don't know, and you don't care. That way it'll be off your mind and you can start brightening up again. All right? That clears it, doesn't it? (*Willy is silent, and Biff goes to him.*) You gonna wish me luck, scout? (*He extends his hand.*) What do you say?

LINDA: Shake his hand, Willy.

WILLY (*turning to her, seething with hurt*): There's no necessity to mention the pen at all, y'know.

BIFF (*gently*): I've got no appointment, Dad.

WILLY (*erupting fiercely*): He put his arm around . . . ?

BIFF: Dad, you're never going to see what I am, so what's the use of arguing? If I strike oil I'll send you a check. Meantime forget I'm alive.

WILLY (*to Linda*): Spite, see?

BIFF: Shake hands, Dad.

WILLY: Not my hand.

BIFF: I was hoping not to go this way.

WILLY: Well, this is the way you're going. Good-by.

(*Biff looks at him a moment, then turns sharply and goes to the stairs.*)

WILLY (*stops him with*): May you rot in hell if you leave this house!

BIFF (*turning*): Exactly what is it that you want from me?

WILLY: I want you to know, on the train, in the mountains, in the valleys, wherever you go, that you cut down your life for spite!

BIFF: No, no.

WILLY: Spite, spite, is the word of your undoing! And when you're down and out, remember what did it. When you're rotting somewhere beside the railroad tracks, remember, and don't you dare blame it on me!

BIFF: I'm not blaming it on you!

WILLY: I won't take the rap for this, you hear?

(*Happy comes down the stairs and stands on the bottom step, watching.*)

BIFF: That's just what I'm telling you!

WILLY (*sinking into a chair at a table, with full accusation*): You're trying to put a knife in me—don't think I don't know what you're doing!

BIFF: All right, phony! Then let's lay it on the line. (*He whips the rubber tube out of his pocket and puts it on the table.*)

HAPPY: You crazy . . .

Dustin Hoffman as Willy Loman in the 1985 television version of *Death of a Salesman*.

LINDA: Biff! (*She moves to grab the hose, but Biff holds it down with his hand.*)

BIFF: Leave it there! Don't move it!

WILLY (*not looking at it*): What is that?

BIFF: You know goddam well what that is.

WILLY (*caged, wanting to escape*): I never saw that.

BIFF: You saw it. The mice didn't bring it into the cellar! What is this supposed to do, make a hero out of you? This supposed to make me sorry for you?

WILLY: Never heard of it.

BIFF: There'll be no pity for you, you hear it? No pity!

WILLY (*to Linda*): You hear the spite!

BIFF: No, you're going to hear the truth—what you are and what I am!

LINDA: Stop it!

WILLY: Spite!

HAPPY (*coming down toward Biff*): You cut it now!

BIFF (*to Happy*): The man don't know who we are! The man is gonna know! (*To Willy.*) We never told the truth for ten minutes in this house!

HAPPY: We always told the truth!

BIFF (*turning on him*): You big blow, are you the assistant buyer? You're one of the two assistants to the assistant, aren't you?

HAPPY: Well, I'm practically...

BIFF: You're practically full of it! We all are! and I'm through with it. (*To Willy.*) Now hear this, Willy, this is me.

WILLY: I know you!

BIFF: You know why I had no address for three months? I stole a suit in Kansas City and I was in jail. (*To Linda, who is sobbing.*) Stop crying. I'm through with it.

(*Linda turns away from them, her hands covering her face.*)

WILLY: I suppose that's my fault!

BIFF: I stole myself out of every good job since high school!

WILLY: And whose fault is that?

BIFF: And I never got anywhere because you blew me so full of hot air I could never stand taking orders from anybody! That's whose fault it is!

WILLY: I hear that!

LINDA: Don't, Biff!

BIFF: It's goddam time you heard that! I had to be boss big shot in two weeks, and I'm through with it!

WILLY: Then hang yourself! For spite, hang yourself!

BIFF: No! Nobody's hanging himself, Willy! I ran down eleven flights with a pen in my hand today. And suddenly I stopped, you hear me? And in the middle of that office building, do you hear this? I stopped in the middle of that building and I saw—the sky. I saw the things that I love in this world. The work and the food and time to sit and smoke. And I looked at the pen and said to myself, what the hell am I grabbing this for? Why am I trying to become what I don't want to be? What am I doing in an office, making a contemptuous begging fool of myself, when all I want is out there, waiting for me the minute I say I know who I am! Why can't I say that, Willy? (*He tries to make Willy face him, but Willy pulls away and moves to the left.*)

WILLY (*with hatred, threateningly*): The door of your life is wide open!

BIFF: Pop! I'm a dime a dozen, and so are you!

WILLY (*turning on him now in an uncontrolled outburst*): I am not a dime a dozen! I am Willy Loman, and you are Biff Loman!

(*Biff starts for Willy, but is blocked by Happy. In his fury, Biff seems on the verge of attacking his father.*)

BIFF: I am not a leader of men, Willy, and neither are you. You were never anything but a hard-working drummer who landed in the ash can like all the rest of them! I'm one dollar an hour, Willy! I tried seven states and couldn't raise it. A buck an hour! Do you gather my meaning? I'm not bringing home any prizes any more, and you're going to stop waiting for me to bring them home!

WILLY (*directly to Biff*): You vengeful, spiteful mutt!

(*Biff breaks from Happy. Willy, in fright, starts up the stairs. Biff grabs him.*)

BIFF (*at the peak of his fury*): Pop, I'm nothing! I'm nothing, Pop. Can't you understand that? There's no spite in it any more. I'm just what I am, that's all.

(*Biff's fury has spent itself and he breaks down, sobbing, holding on to Willy, who dumbly fumbles for Biff's face.*)

WILLY (*astonished*): What're you doing? What're you doing? (*To Linda.*) Why is he crying?

BIFF (*crying, broken*): Will you let me go, for Christ's sake? Will you take that phony dream and burn it before something happens? (*Struggling to contain himself he pulls away and moves to the stairs.*) I'll go in the morning. Put him—put him to bed. (*Exhausted, Biff moves up the stairs to his room.*)

WILLY (*after a long pause, astonished, elevated*): Isn't that—isn't that remarkable? Biff—he likes me!

LINDA: He loves you, Willy!

HAPPY (*deeply moved*): Always did, Pop.

WILLY: Oh, Biff! (*Staring wildly.*) He cried! Cried to me. (*He is choking with his love, and now cries out his promise.*) That boy—that boy is going to be magnificent!

(*Ben appears in the light just outside the kitchen.*)

BEN: Yes, outstanding, with twenty thousand behind him.

LINDA (*sensing the racing of his mind, fearfully, carefully*): Now come to bed, Willy. It's all settled now.

WILLY (*finding it difficult not to rush out of the house*): Yes, we'll sleep. Come on. Go to sleep, Hap.

BEN: And it does take a great kind of a man to crack the jungle.

(*In accents of dread, Ben's idyllic music starts up.*)

HAPPY (*his arm around Linda*): I'm getting married, Pop, don't forget it. I'm changing everything. I'm gonna run that department before the year is up. You'll see, Mom. (*He kisses her.*)

BEN: The jungle is dark but full of diamonds, Willy.

(*Willy turns, moves, listening to Ben.*)

LINDA: Be good. You're both good boys, just act that way, that's all.

HAPPY: 'Night, Pop. (*He goes upstairs.*)

LINDA (*to Willy*): Come, dear.

BEN (*with greater force*): One must go in to fetch a diamond out.

WILLY (*to Linda, as he moves slowly along the edge of kitchen, toward the door*): I just want to get settled down, Linda. Let me sit alone for a little.

LINDA (*almost uttering her fear*): I want you upstairs.

WILLY (*taking her in his arms*): In a few minutes, Linda. I couldn't sleep right now. Go on, you look awful tired. (*He kisses her.*)

BEN: Not like an appointment at all. A diamond is rough and hard to the touch.

WILLY: Go on now. I'll be right up.

LINDA: I think this is the only way, Willy.

WILLY: Sure, it's the best thing.

BEN: Best thing!

WILLY: The only way. Everything is gonna be—go on, kid, get to bed. You look so tired.

LINDA: Come right up.

WILLY: Two minutes.

(*Linda goes into the living room, then reappears in her bedroom. Willy moves just outside the kitchen door.*)

Biff (Kevin Anderson) and
Willy (Brian Dennehy) try to
console one another in Robert
Falls's 1999 production of
Death of a Salesman.

WILLY: Loves me. (*Wonderingly.*) Always loved me. Isn't that a remarkable thing? Ben, he'll worship me for it!

BEN (*with promise*): It's dark there, but full of diamonds.

WILLY: Can you imagine that magnificence with twenty thousand dollars in his pocket?

LINDA (*calling from her room*): Willy! Come up!

WILLY (*calling into the kitchen*): Yes! yes. Coming! It's very smart, you realize that, don't you, sweetheart? Even Ben sees it. I gotta go, baby. 'By! 'By! (*Going over to Ben, almost dancing.*) Imagine? When the mail comes he'll be ahead of Bernard again!

BEN: A perfect proposition all around.

WILLY: Did you see how he cried to me? Oh, if I could kiss him, Ben!

BEN: Time, William, time!

WILLY: Oh, Ben, I always knew one way or another we were gonna make it, Biff and I!

BEN (*looking at his watch*): The boat. We'll be late. (*He moves slowly off into the darkness.*)

WILLY (*elegiacally, turning to the house*): Now when you kick off, boy, I want a seventy-yard boot, and get right down the field under the ball, and when you hit, hit low and hit hard, because it's important, boy. (*He swings around and faces the audience.*) There's all kinds of important people in the stands, and the first thing you know . . . (*Suddenly realizing he is alone.*) Ben! Ben, where do I . . . ? (*He makes a sudden movement of search.*) Ben, how do I . . . ?

LINDA (*calling*): Willy, you coming up?

WILLY (*uttering a gasp of fear, whirling about as if to quiet her*): Sh! (*He turns around as if to find his way; sounds, faces, voices, seem to be swarming in upon*

him and he flicks at them, crying, Sh! Sh! *Suddenly music, faint and high, stops him. It rises in intensity, almost to an unbearable scream. He goes up and down on his toes, and rushes off around the house.*) Shhh!

LINDA: Willy?

(*There is no answer. Linda waits. Biff gets up off his bed. He is still in his clothes. Happy sits up. Biff stands listening.*)

LINDA (*with real fear*): Willy, answer me! Willy!

(*There is the sound of a car starting and moving away at full speed.*)

LINDA: No!

BIFF (*rushing down the stairs*): Pop!

(*As the car speeds off, the music crashes down in a frenzy of sound, which becomes the soft pulsation of a single cello string. Biff slowly returns to his bedroom. He and Happy gravely don their jackets. Linda slowly walks out of her room. The music has developed into a dead march. The leaves of day are appearing over everything. Charley and Bernard, somberly dressed, appear and knock on the kitchen door. Biff and Happy slowly descend the stairs to the kitchen as Charley and Bernard enter. All stop a moment when Linda, in clothes of mourning, bearing a little bunch of roses, comes through the draped doorway into the kitchen. She goes to Charley and takes his arm. Now all move toward the audience, through the wall-line of the kitchen. At the limit of the apron, Linda lays down the flowers, kneels, and sits back on her heels. All stare down at the grave.*)

REQUIEM

CHARLEY: It's getting dark, Linda.

(*Linda doesn't react. She stares at the grave.*)

BIFF: How about it, Mom? Better get some rest, heh? They'll be closing the gate soon.

(*Linda makes no move. Pause.*)

HAPPY (*deeply angered*): He had no right to do that. There was no necessity for it. We would've helped him.

CHARLEY (*grunting*): Hmmm.

BIFF: Come along, Mom.

LINDA: Why didn't anybody come?

CHARLEY: It was a very nice funeral.

LINDA: But where are all the people he knew? Maybe they blame him.

CHARLEY: Naa. It's a rough world, Linda. They wouldn't blame him.

LINDA: I can't understand it. At this time especially. First time in thirty-five years we were just about free and clear. He only needed a little salary. He was even finished with the dentist.

CHARLEY: No man only needs a little salary.

LINDA: I can't understand it.

BIFF: There were a lot of nice days. When he'd come home from a trip; or on Sundays, making the stoop; finishing the cellar; putting on the new porch; when he built the extra bathroom; and put up the garage. You know something, Charley, there's more of him in that front stoop than in all the sales he ever made.

CHARLEY: Yeah. He was a happy man with a batch of cement.

LINDA: He was so wonderful with his hands.

BIFF: He had the wrong dreams. All, all, wrong.

HAPPY (*almost ready to fight Biff*): Don't say that!

BIFF: He never knew who he was.

CHARLEY (*stopping Happy's movement and reply. To Biff*): Nobody dast blame this man. You don't understand: Willy was a salesman. And for a salesman, there is no rock bottom to the life. He don't put a bolt to a nut, he don't tell you the law or give you medicine. He's a man way out there in the blue, riding on a smile and a shoeshine. And when they start not smiling back—that's an earthquake. And then you get yourself a couple of spots on your hat, and you're finished. Nobody dast blame this man. A salesman is got to dream, boy. It comes with the territory.

BIFF: Charley, the man didn't know who he was.

HAPPY (*infuriated*): Don't say that!

BIFF: Why don't you come with me, Happy?

HAPPY: I'm not licked that easily. I'm staying right in this city, and I'm gonna beat this racket! (*He looks at Biff, his chin set.*) The Loman Brothers!

BIFF: I know who I am, kid.

HAPPY: All right, boy. I'm gonna show you and everybody else that Willy Loman did not die in vain. He had a good dream. It's the only dream you can have—to come out number-one man. He fought it out here, and this is where I'm gonna win it for him.

BIFF (*with a hopeless glance at Happy, bends toward his mother*): Let's go, Mom.

LINDA: I'll be with you in a minute. Go on, Charley. (*He hesitates.*) I want to, just for a minute. I never had a chance to say good-by.

(*Charley moves away, followed by Happy. Biff remains a slight distance up and left of Linda. She sits there, summoning herself. The flute begins, not far away, playing behind her speech.*)

LINDA: Forgive me, dear. I can't cry. I don't know what it is, but I can't cry. I don't understand it. Why did you ever do that? Help me, Willy, I can't cry. It seems to me that you're just on another trip. I keep expecting you. Willy, dear, I can't cry. Why did you do it? I search and search and I search, and I can't understand it, Willy. I made the last payment on the house today. Today, dear. And there'll be nobody home. (*A sob rises in her throat.*) We're free and clear. (*Sobbing more fully, released.*) We're free. (*Biff comes slowly toward her.*) We're free . . . We're free . . .

(*Biff lifts her to her feet and moves out up right with her in his arms. Linda sobs quietly. Bernard and Charley come together and follow them, followed by Happy. Only the music of the flute is left on the darkening stage as over the house the hard towers of the apartment buildings rise into sharp focus, and the curtain falls.*)

COMMENTARIES

Arthur Miller (1915–2005)

IN MEMORIAM   *1932*

"In Memoriam," a short story about a salesman that Arthur Miller wrote in 1932 when he was seventeen, was published in 1995 after it was discovered in the Arthur Miller Archive at the University of Texas's Harry Ransom library. A note on the manuscript indicates that the real Schoenzeit threw himself in front of an elevated railway train the day after the incident the story records. While not providing the model for Death of a Salesman, *the story reminds us that Miller had experience with men like Willy Loman.*

Sitting here now, thinking of him, he seems to be a romantic figure, but really he wasn't. Yet I couldn't venture to call him "commonplace." I never knew him intimately, yet I feel as though I knew him more closely, more thoroughly, than I know myself. His was a salesman's profession, if one may describe such dignified slavery as a profession, and though he tried to interest himself in his work he never became entirely molded into the pot of that business. His emotions were displayed at the wrong times always, and he never quite knew when to laugh. Perhaps, if I may say so, he never was complete. He had lost something vital. There was an air of quiet solitude, of cryptic wondering about both him and his name.

Although he was ever simply and immaculately dressed, I always imagined he had been dressed by someone else.

When I first heard his name, I wondered if he hadn't forgotten some other and had merely been called this by men. His last name was Schoenzeit; the first I never learned, but it had to be Alfred. He always seemed to need that name. Especially when he sat at the small glass-topped table in my father's showroom, slowly perusing the columns of the *Times,* with tears of perspiration dotting the reddened ridge that his gray felt hat had made around his head. The shined, bulgy-toed shoes placed flatly and it seemed carefully on the carpet, his overcoat folded neatly on a chair, the bow of his tie stuck so perfectly into the crevice of a starched, rounded collar completed a setting where I am sure he never belonged.

Schoenzeit, as everyone called him, often was gay. I might add "happy," but of the last I shall never be sure. He laughed as superciliously as any of the others when someone was the object of a quip. But these occasions were rare and never lasted, as far as he was concerned. Always he returned to his fogged manner, and after the joke had faded from his mind the light which seemed to brighten his countenance, too, disappeared, and he was once more enigmatic and incomprehensible.

I had, on several occasions, been alone with him, and may truthfully say I deeply pitied such a dejected soul. At one time it was necessary for him to go to the Bronx to interview a large retail drygoods store, and I was instructed to carry his samples.

It was late spring, the sky was cloudless and blue, a yellow sun was slowly warming the cool morning air, and the usual city hurriers were plying their trade.

I had six coats in my arms, holding them against my chest, while he walked, leaning very slightly forward, by my side. His feet must have hurt him, for he pointed them outward, laying them flat on the ground at every step. When walking, he seemed to be striving against a stiff wind, his eyebrows peaked together, forming tiny creases at the bridge of his nose. His hat, placed straight on his head, shaded his eyes, which gazed seekingly ahead.

It was necessary to walk from Eighth to Third Avenue in order to reach the Elevated, and he offered many times to rest. I must have looked tired, because he turned to me once and laughed, saying in his cracked yet resonant baritone, "Hard work, eh, kid? Some business..." Of course, I didn't admit my weariness, and pitching my head to one side, raising my eyebrows and smiling, assured him that I was enjoying it as much as he was.

In due time, we approached the El, and about a block away he slowly and lightly touched my arm and, still looking ahead, he asked, "Arthur, do you get paid from the firm for carfare?" He said this in a low tone, as though he were trying to hide his point until it was absolutely necessary to take the plunge.

I thought for a moment and answered, "Well, whenever I have to go anywhere out of walking distance I am given money to ride, but I have no standing allowance for such purposes." He seemed to falter, and flushed a trifle before answering, and for a second I felt both rage and pity for this decrepit soul, who, it seemed, aged many years as he turned to me. I knew then that he felt as though his life were ended, that he was merely being pushed by outside forces. And though his body went on as before, the soul inside had crumpled and broken beyond repair.

He was asking me now for carfare. I knew he would rather have been pulled apart by a tiger, but he was asking me for carfare, a nickel to hold out to a corpulent, uninterested machine for his fare. My heart bled for him at that moment, and as we mounted the long stairway to the trains I realized that as low and shakingly embarrassed as I felt, his senses were that much more tormented and destroyed. And I marvelled at his poise under the circumstances. The coats were warm now against me, and I was thankful to God himself for this refuge for my gawky body which, with the expression of my eyes, must reveal to him my sensations.

I tried as best I could to make this situation seem as if it were common-place— I who had carried samples for so many salesmen. And when we reached the turnstile, I balanced my burden on one knee while I dipped my free hand into my pocket. Behind my throat, I cursed myself for not having the change. I turned from him in order to get the nickels required, and when I lifted my eyes to his figure I prayed, until my temples seemed to burst, for his salvation. At that moment, he looked so broken, so dejected and lost that I hastily lowered my gaze. He appeared to me then, as he stood there at the turnstile, like a small dog who has messed in the house, standing now, after his beating, waiting for his master to open the door to the back yard.

During the entire ride uptown, we two spoke but sparingly. The bright streets below changed constantly as we racketed past, and the windows of the houses facing the trains offered a haven for my confused and weary imagination.

He sold nothing that day and was profusely maltreated by the attending force at the buying office who, by virtue of their superior intelligence and ties to match, were vindicated even when they were consciously adding to the vicissitudes of a seller's life.

On the return trip, Alfred, as I subconsciously called him, became more voluble and questioned me as to my ambitions and my occupations in my leisure time. Upon hearing that I owned an old car, he immediately became interested and spoke a little less haltingly than was his wont. From constant rebuff, he was loath to venture an opinion, and often embarrassed us both by ending a bountiful conversation unexpectedly.

He accompanied me to my father's place and, placing his hand on the small of my back, patted me lightly, and said with a faint smile, "Thanks, Arthur — and I'll . . . see you tomorrow."

With that farewell, he was off into the crowd, and his restless body faded slowly into the dark overcoats of unknowns as it willingly shrank from my sight.

I never saw him again and had forgotten him entirely when I heard of his death.

"Schoenzeit is dead," and my only recollection of that second when I heard those words is a slow exhaling of my breath and a cool, soft, glowing smile within my soul.

Arthur Miller (1915–2005)

TRAGEDY AND THE COMMON MAN   *1949*

One of the curious debates that arose around Death of a Salesman *was the question of whether it was a genuine tragedy. One of the requirements for traditional tragedy is that the hero be of noble birth. Miller countered that notion with a clear statement of modern purpose regarding tragedy.*

In this age few tragedies are written. It has often been held that the lack is due to a paucity of heroes among us, or else that modern man has had the blood drawn out of his organs of belief by the skepticism of science, and the heroic attack on life cannot feed on an attitude of reserve and circumspection. For one reason or another, we are often held to be below tragedy — or tragedy above us. The inevitable conclusion is, of course, that the tragic mode is archaic, fit only for the very highly placed, the kings or the kingly, and where this admission is not made in so many words it is most often implied.

I believe that the common man is as apt a subject for tragedy in its highest sense as kings were. On the face of it this ought to be obvious in the light of modern psychiatry, which bases its analysis upon classic formulations, such as the Oedipus and Orestes complexes, for instance, which were enacted by royal beings, but which apply to everyone in similar emotional situations.

More simply, when the question of tragedy in art is not at issue, we never hesitate to attribute to the well-placed and the exalted the very same mental processes as the lowly. And finally, if the exaltation of tragic action were truly a property of the high-bred character alone, it is inconceivable that the mass of mankind should cherish tragedy above all other forms, let alone be capable of understanding it.

As a general rule, to which there may be exceptions unknown to me, I think the tragic feeling is evoked in us when we are in the presence of a character who is ready to lay down his life, if need be, to secure one thing — his sense of personal dignity. From Orestes to Hamlet, Medea to Macbeth, the underlying struggle is that of the individual attempting to gain his "rightful" position in his society.

Sometimes he is one who has been displaced from it, sometimes one who seeks to attain it for the first time, but the fateful wound from which the inevitable events spiral is the wound of indignity, and its dominant force is indignation. Tragedy, then, is the consequence of a man's total compulsion to evaluate himself justly.

In the sense of having been initiated by the hero himself, the tale always reveals what has been called his "tragic flaw," a failing that is not peculiar to grand or elevated characters. Nor is it necessarily a weakness. The flaw, or crack in the character, is really nothing—and need be nothing—but his inherent unwillingness to remain passive in the face of what he conceives to be a challenge to his dignity, his image of his rightful status. Only the passive, only those who accept their lot without active retaliation, are "flawless." Most of us are in that category.

But there are among us today, as there always have been, those who act against the scheme of things that degrades them, and in the process of action everything we have accepted out of fear or insensitivity or ignorance is shaken before us and examined, and from this total onslaught by an individual against the seemingly stable cosmos surrounding us—from this total examination of the "unchangeable" environment—comes the terror and the fear that is classically associated with tragedy.

More important, from this total questioning of what has previously been unquestioned, we learn. And such a process is not beyond the common man. In revolutions around the world, these past thirty years, he has demonstrated again and again this inner dynamic of all tragedy.

Insistence upon the rank of the tragic hero, or the so-called nobility of his character, is really but a clinging to the outward forms of tragedy. If rank or nobility of character was indispensable, then it would follow that the problems of those with rank were the particular problems of tragedy. But surely the right of one monarch to capture the domain from another no longer raises our passions, nor are our concepts of justice what they were to the mind of an Elizabethan king.

The quality in such plays that does shake us, however, derives from the underlying fear of being displaced, the disaster inherent in being torn away from our chosen image of what and who we are in this world. Among us today this fear is as strong, and perhaps stronger, than it ever was. In fact, it is the common man who knows this fear best.

Now, if it is true that tragedy is the consequence of a man's total compulsion to evaluate himself justly, his destruction in the attempt posits a wrong or an evil in his environment. And this is precisely the morality of tragedy and its lesson. The discovery of the moral law, which is what the enlightenment of tragedy consists of, is not the discovery of some abstract or metaphysical quantity.

The tragic right is a condition of life, a condition in which the human personality is able to flower and realize itself. The wrong is the condition which suppresses man, perverts the flowing out of his love and creative instinct. Tragedy enlightens—and it must, in that it points the heroic finger at the enemy of man's freedom. The thrust for freedom is the quality in tragedy which exalts. The revolutionary questioning of the stable environment is what terrifies. In no way is the common man debarred from such thoughts or such actions.

Seen in this light, our lack of tragedy may be partially accounted for by the turn which modern literature has taken toward the purely psychiatric view of life, or the purely sociological. If all our miseries, our indignities, are born and bred within our minds, then all action, let alone the heroic action, is obviously impossible.

And if society alone is responsible for the cramping of our lives, then the protagonist must needs be so pure and faultless as to force us to deny his validity as a character. From neither of these views can tragedy derive, simply because neither represents a balanced concept of life. Above all else, tragedy requires the finest appreciation by the writer of cause and effect.

No tragedy can therefore come about when its author fears to question absolutely everything, when he regards any institution, habit, or custom as being either everlasting, immutable, or inevitable. In the tragic view the need of man to wholly realize himself is the only fixed star, and whatever it is that hedges his nature and lowers it is ripe for attack and examination. Which is not to say that tragedy must preach revolution.

The Greeks could probe the very heavenly origin of their ways and return to confirm the rightness of laws. And Job could face God in anger, demanding his right, and end in submission. But for a moment everything is in suspension, nothing is accepted, and in this stretching and tearing apart of the cosmos, in the very action of so doing, the character gains "size," the tragic stature which is spuriously attached to the royal or the highborn in our minds. The commonest of men may take on that stature to the extent of his willingness to throw all he has into the contest, the battle to secure his rightful place in his world.

There is a misconception of tragedy with which I have been struck in review after review, and in many conversations with writers and readers alike. It is the idea that tragedy is of necessity allied to pessimism. Even the dictionary says nothing more about the word than that it means a story with a sad or unhappy ending. This impression is so firmly fixed that I almost hesitate to claim that in truth tragedy implies more optimism in its author than does comedy, and that its final result ought to be the reinforcement of the onlooker's brightest opinions of the human animal.

For, if it is true to say that in essence the tragic hero is intent upon claiming his whole due as a personality, and if this struggle must be total and without reservation, then it automatically demonstrates the indestructible will of man to achieve his humanity.

The possibility of victory must be there in tragedy. Where pathos rules, where pathos is finally derived, a character has fought a battle he could not possibly have won. The pathetic is achieved when the protagonist is, by virtue of his witlessness, his insensitivity, or the very air he gives off, incapable of grappling with a much superior force.

Pathos truly is the mode for the pessimist. But tragedy requires a nicer balance between what is possible and what is impossible. And it is curious, although edifying, that the plays we revere, century after century, are the tragedies. In them, and in them alone, lies the belief—optimistic, if you will—in the perfectibility of man.

It is time, I think, that we who are without kings, took up this bright thread of our history and followed it to the only place it can possibly lead in our time—the heart and spirit of the average man.

A PRODUCTION CASEBOOK

Death of a Salesman

The original staging of *Death of a Salesman* presented enormous challenges to everyone involved with the production. In many ways the play was radical in conception. Not only was the theory of tragedy challenged by the choice of a traveling salesman as the hero, but the approach to the drama itself—the sense that one needed to get inside Willy Loman's head—made the first production quite different from what theater-goers in 1949 would have expected. Arthur Miller's original title for the play, *The Inside of His Head*, was a rough guide to staging problems. The final production designs bestowed a novel transparency on the Lomans' house, so that the audience was not just looking through a fourth wall, as in conventional stagings, but looking through a small world.

The designer for the stage, Jo Mielziner (1901–1976), was committed to innovation in stage design both before and after he was given the chance to work with director Elia Kazan on this project. In his notes, he discusses the ways in which the illusional realistic theater seemed to be limited in spite of extraordinary technical resources—the use of projections, film (or video), and multilevel staging—all of which could achieve effects that could only be suggested previously. He approached the problems of the play enthusiastically, as his journal excerpts and Brenda Murphy's essay on the design process for this set both reveal. While working on *Death of a Salesman,* he was approached by Josh Logan to work on *South Pacific*, an upbeat and timeless American musical that must have provided an emotional relief of sorts while he dealt with the complexities of Miller's dark play.

It is perhaps unfair to refer to the play as dark, but when Miller sent the script to Elia Kazan, already a distinguished director, Kazan called him and said, "What a sad play." Miller thought that Kazan was rejecting the play. At that time Miller was famous as the author of *All My Sons,* but he was not at all confident that his new play would be acceptable for the stage. However, Kazan, whose voice sounded almost funereal, went on to talk about his own father; Miller later said Kazan was the first of many people who saw their own fathers in Willy Loman. The conversation with Kazan ended with a commitment to produce the play within the year. Kazan's "Directing *Death of a Salesman*" essay offers an overview of his experience as the play's director.

The problem of finding the right actor to play Willy Loman naturally challenged Kazan, who had Lee J. Cobb in mind right away, even though Miller felt that the actor who played the part should be small in stature. Cobb was so large a man that Miller referred to him as "the walrus," and for a very long time Miller had no confidence in Cobb's ability to play the part. Deep into rehearsals, Cobb internalized the role and shocked Miller into seeing him as perfect. From the beginning, Cobb was convinced that this play was a masterpiece and that it would alter theater history.

As June Schlueter and James K. Flanagan point out, Willy Loman might well be the most memorable character in modern theater. Consequently, it is no surprise that a great variety of significant actors have played the role of Willy. In more recent years, Dustin Hoffman was notable as Willy and, because of his small size, closer to what Miller had originally intended. Interestingly, Hoffman played Bernard in 1965 with Lee J. Cobb as Willy when they produced a long-playing-record version of the play. Hume Cronyn and Brian Dennehy were both important in the part also, although Cronyn was almost *too* small in stature. Arthur Miller describes Ying Ruocheng, who translated the play into Chinese for Miller's 1983 production in Beijing, as a "brilliant" Willy.

Casting for the play involved a great deal of thought and agreement between the author and director. Arthur Miller, in his "The American Theater" essay, gives us some interesting insights into the complexities and challenges that both actors and producers face. He includes an engrossing description of the way Mildred Dunnock, a distinguished and well-known actress, kept coming back for an audition even after being told she was not right for the role of Linda. What this demonstrates is that minds can be changed even when firm decisions have been made — and that people can misjudge the ability of actors to do the work that needs doing. As it turned out, Mildred Dunnock was perfect for the part and breathed life into it as few actresses have done since.

Some of the interesting questions concerning the universality of the play were answered in the Asian productions, which have been enthusiastically received. One such production was the Taiwanese production reviewed by professor and director Catherine Diamond. The Beijing production was especially exciting because it came at a time when China's attitude toward capitalism was beginning to shift. The all-black productions of the play, as well as versions in which some of the characters were played by black actors, presented their own issues. Brenda Murphy considers some of the questions that those renditions raised in her essay "Racial Consciousness in Casting *Death of a Salesman*." Any view that sees Willy Loman as restricted to a specific place and time seems to have been contradicted by the remarkable range of productions and producers, all of whom have faced considerable problems in staging and casting.

Perhaps the only generalization that can really be made is that the challenges the play presents seem to have been avenues into a boundless upwelling of creativity.

Jo Mielziner (1901–1976)

DESIGNING A PLAY: *DEATH OF A SALESMAN*   1948–49

A seasoned and already respected set designer, Jo Mielziner reveals the detailed and demanding work that went into making the innovative designs for the first production of Death of a Salesman. *The late nights; the collaboration with electricians and carpenters, not to mention those with the director and producer; and all the worries and difficulties of conception — all these are revealed in the journal Mielziner kept as a record of his work on the play.*

FIGURE 27.   Jo Mielziner's early sketch for the design of the original 1949 production of *Death of a Salesman*.

FIGURE 28.   Jo Mielziner's painting of the original set, showing the backdrop of apartment buildings.

December 15, 1948

During my midweek check-up of unfinished *Salesman* chores, I realized that a large number of basic decisions still had to be made about the small scenes outside Willy Loman's house. Since rehearsals were due to start a couple of days after Christmas, I appealed to Kazan for a good long session.

During the previous weeks I had been receiving from Arthur Miller, scene by scene, the final version of the rehearsal script. Although he had done the basic rewriting, he had made no attempt to say how the transitions from one scene to another would be made. This was a problem for the director and the designer to work out together as we studied the model, the ground plan, and the cut-out cardboard symbols representing the props.

FIGURE 29.   Mildred Dunnock (Linda), Lee J. Cobb (Willy), Arthur Kennedy (Biff), and Cameron Mitchell (Happy) on the original set of *Death of a Salesman* in 1949.

I pointed out to Kazan how difficult it would be in an office scene, for instance, to remove two desks, two chairs, and a hat rack (which the present script called for) and at the same time have an actor walk quickly across the stage and appear in "a hotel room in Boston where he meets a girl." I urged him to do even more cutting, not in the text but in the props called for in this latest version of the script. We finally got the office pared down to one desk and one chair. Then I suggested going so far as to use the same desk for both office scenes — first in Heiser's office and then, with a change of other props, in Charley's office. As usual, Kazan's imagination rose to the suggestion. He replied, "Sure, let's cut this down to the bone — we can play on practically anything." This is effective abstraction, giving the spectator the opportunity to "fill in."

I had felt from the outset that the cemetery scene at the end of the play would be done on the forestage, and I had actually drawn up a design for a trick trapdoor out of which would rise the small gravestone that we had thought necessary for this scene. I had shown Kazan the working drawing for the gravestone, explained how it would operate, and mentioned that because of union rules the man operating this mechanism would be doing this and nothing else, thereby adding a member to the crew for the sake of one effect. I had also mentioned that since the trap would be very close to the audience the sound of its opening might disturb the solemnity of the scene.

With some malice aforethought, I had also done a drawing showing the Salesman's widow sitting on the step leading to the forestage, with her two sons standing behind her, their heads bowed; on the floor at her feet was a small bouquet of flowers. The whole scene was bathed in a magic-lantern projection of autumn leaves. Here, again, leaves were symbolic. With this kind of lighting I thought I could completely obliterate the house in the background and evoke a sense of sadness and finality that might enable us to eliminate the gravestone itself.

My hints were not lost. "I get your point," Kazan said. "Let's do it without the gravestone. No matter how quietly you move it into place, everybody nearby is going to be so busy thinking, 'How is that done?' that they'll miss the mood of the scene."

I felt that this extreme simplicity would be the best theatre possible, and later, in dress rehearsal, it proved to be the right answer.

Kazan and I went over all the prop problems, especially the small hand props—who would bring them on, what actors would be handling them, were stagehands necessary on the set, how long could we black out the stage successfully for the changes?

A blackout is always difficult. As a rule, only a few seconds are permissible for a well-rehearsed stagehand to cross the stage in the darkness, pick up a prop, and exit without being seen by the audience. The eyes of those seated close to the stage soon become used to the sudden change of light, and figures onstage can be observed after six or eight seconds of the dark; gradually, everyone in the theatre can make them out. Stage blackouts are never complete anyway because there are masked and dimmed lights in the wings that must stay on for the control of the switchboard, the stage manager's desk with its telephones and master cue sheets, and the prop tables where the master property man gives hand props to actors waiting for entrance cues.

When we came to the scene in the Boston hotel room, Kazan said, "I don't need anything; just give me the feeling of a hotel room." I showed him a sketch of a panel of cheap wallpaper which I planned to project from the theatre balcony onto a background that was really a section of the trellis at one side of the Salesman's house. Projected images used in conjunction with scenery can be very valuable. In this case, the associations evoked by faded old wallpaper gave the audience a complete picture. Both the house and the exterior trellis faded away. The audience saw the Salesman in that cheap hotel room with that woman. I stress the phrase "in that room." Actors should never play against a scenic background but within the setting.

Kazan felt that the right actress cast in the role of the girl who visits Willy Loman in the hotel room, dressed in the right costume, plus the visual image of the wallpaper, would be enough to make this short scene come alive. There is no question that when a good actor is backed up by simple scenic treatment, his strong qualities are stressed. Of course, this can work in reverse, but Arthur Miller was lucky in the casting of *Salesman;* even the bit roles were played by vivid actors.

During these last weeks before rehearsals began, the producer's office was finishing the always difficult financing of the production, arranging details in preparation for the tryout and the New York run, organizing theatre parties, completing the casting. Arthur Miller was correcting and polishing the rehearsal version of the script. And Kazan was in constant communication with the author as well as the technical staff. I was busy enough myself. Although my wife and children were enjoying Christmas vacation in the country, I wasn't to join them until the day before Christmas.

January 19, 1949   This day was all mine. The stage was ready for me to set the lighting levels for the entire production. Backstage, property men were still unpacking and arranging hand props, and carpenters were finishing the masking of light leaks and cleaning up the paraphernalia; the acting company was still in New York for final run-throughs and costume fittings. The production stage manager had come down to

Philadelphia to make notes from my lighting cues and to take over running the crew backstage; one of his assistants stayed in New York to be with Kazan and the company. The company manager was already in Philadelphia and had reported happily that advance sales were promising.

I had asked Del Hughes, the production stage manager, to enlist a couple of local drama students as volunteer stand-ins for my lighting rehearsal. For this process, without the company on hand, I always try to have someone on the set each time I set a light. It is easy to become so absorbed in lighting an empty stage that you wind up illuminating the scenery for its own sake; if I have stand-ins, not only can I see exactly what they themselves look like in the acting light, but I have figures in the foreground to give perspective when I am lighting the background.

I began by taking out every light in the theatre except those over the fire exits. We had to find out how much light the electricians needed on their boards, how much the fly men needed in the fly loft, and how much the property man needed in the wings; with these necessities as a base, I would know how much light there was to start with. Then, with my assistant sitting in back of me, the complete blueprint in my hands which showed the number of each pipe and area, and a speaker in front of me, I called out to Richard Raven, the chief electrician, "Light first pipe playing area right, blue circuit."

As the process went on, I could judge two things: what my predetermined color would look like on the set, and how well my assistant and the crew had angled the units. One by one, I looked at every group of lamps, every individual spot, every color, and every circuit. Then I looked at each projection individually.

The next phase was to create the mood of the background. For the opening of the play I had decided to start with lights behind the drop, which would illuminate the windows of the neighboring buildings painted on the face of the drop. I always start by telling my electrician, "When I call for something, don't bring it on full power, but start with it low on the dimmer." Dimmer controls have markings from one to ten, one being full power, nine and ten being lowest intensity. In this case, I said on the intercom, "Bring the tenth pipe amber up slowly from the bottom." When it reached about halfway, I said, "Hold it." Then I went to the lights on the face of the drop; for this we had two pipes of border lights. I had planned one to cover the top half of the drop; the other was to pick up and carry the bottom half. Each of these pipes contained three colors; one color at a time, I brought the lights up to a certain level, blending the three elements. In this way I gradually established the mood for the opening scene.

I next worked with a series of light pipes that gave a blue backlighting to the Loman house; this brought out the plastic element in that part of the set which was built three-dimensionally. When I had established these, I called backstage on the intercom to the chief electrician, "Mark it up carefully." It takes patience to sit in the dark of the auditorium and wait for what seems an endless time; but the boys on the switchboard, in this case three of them, have to look at each one of the many dimmer handles and mark meticulously at just what point I had called out to hold. This has to be checked and double-checked and then written down on each one of their cue sheets.

Because of the refusal of theatre owners to provide modern electronic lighting systems, almost all of the professional theatres in America are still forced to use the same manual switchboards that were in use fifty and more years ago. While university theatres and community playhouses throughout the country are decades ahead, the professional theatre still hauls in antiquated, heavy (even if serviceable) manual boards. All this, of course, means extra money for the management of a play. In this respect a theatrical producer is not unlike a person who might rent an expensive Fifth Avenue apartment and find a kitchen with an outlet plug for a stove and a refrigerator, but no stove or refrigerator. In most of the New York theatres even the outlets are inadequate in power for modern lighting. Many a time, not only in New York but in try out on the road, I have had every fuse in the place blow out because the electric service was being taxed beyond the limit.

I welcomed the chief electrician's voice on the intercom, saying, "O.K., Mr. M., we're all marked up; what next?" I was ready now for the playing areas, and the stage manager brought on the two young people who were going to stand in for the actors. I placed them first in the bedroom. The opening scene occurs late at night when the Salesman arrives home; I wanted just enough glow to bring out the forms in bed. I then traced through the entrance of Willy Loman and had the electricians mark down the "pre-set," the lights that can be set behind the curtain before it rises. When this was done, I planned the "follow-up"; this is the next cue, which the stage manager gives when he sees that the house curtain is all the way up and the lights in the auditorium can be brought up; these lights, of course, cannot be pre-set, since their beams would hit the house curtain when it was down, creating ugly patterns on its surface.

I had to be careful to judge the effect of light on the faces of people who were not in make-up and costume. For instance, the young lady stand-in had appeared in a white blouse, and I had borrowed a throw from the bed to put around her shoulders. The mere presence of that much white would have given me the illusion that I was getting much more light than was actually there. When I finished with a scene and was waiting for it to be noted on the electricians' cue sheets, I had the property man bring out the props that went with the scene at hand; this gave me a chance to see them not only in terms of distance but also in relationship to their surroundings. The color of the "oilcloth" on the kitchen table, for example, proved to be satisfactory on the surfaces facing the audience but too light on the top surface, where the bounce from the overhead spotlights brought it into competition with the actors' faces. This was swiftly remedied by spraying down the table top.

Knowing that we had about a hundred and fifty light cues to set, we decided to work straight through the night until we had at least a basic scheme and a basic cue for every part of the production. There was no time for polishing or for going back to rehearse the timing of cues, things I usually have been able to do on this day. As it was, we worked until midnight, sent out for coffee and sandwiches for all, and didn't finish the final scene until 4:30 in the morning. This added up to twenty and a half hours of pretty intense work, and the week had just begun.

During the afternoon Alex North and the musicians had arrived from New York, and I used what little time I had, while waiting for the electrical crew to do their mark-ups, to work out some details about the music. I checked to see that the dressing room which was to be the "sound studio" was properly equipped with microphones and a communication system. We had to put blankets on the floor and on the walls before North was satisfied with the quality of the sound as it came into the auditorium over the speaker system. At the same time the assistant electrician rigged a signal-and-sound system for the musicians so that the stage manager's voice announcing cue warnings and cues would be clear and unmistakable.

The process of lighting a musical is basically the same as for a play like *Death of a Salesman*, but there is less refinement in the musical because the picture is broader and the contrasts greater; less subtlety is needed, more vitality desired. Another difference is that in a legitimate play, with the acting areas more limited and the sets fewer, there is much greater need for extreme control of lighting equipment. During this day of setting the lighting for *Salesman* I occasionally had the two follow-spot men turn on their new and beautifully engineered lights, and the effect was fascinating. In the opening scene, for instance, when the Salesman makes his tiptoe entrance carrying his bags, we dimmed the follow-spot far down and played the beam just on the face of the stand-in. The effect was magical; there was so little light that there was no shadow behind him, and yet there was enough warmth in it so that the face stood out in the gray-blue night light. I was sure that this new experiment would come through very serviceably indeed.

How different this subtle and complex lighting was from earlier times! When I designed *Of Thee I Sing* in 1931 for Sam Harris, he was disturbed that I was not willing to use the 1900 type of stage lighting that had characterized his previous productions. This consisted of border lights, footlights, and old-fashioned floodlights for what were known as "entrances." There was no control of any segment of the stage, only a system of dimming and raising lights for the total acting area, with all people, all objects, and all scenery treated alike.

After Harris had finally agreed to let me try out "modern lighting," I was busy one day with the electrician, who had laid out several dozen new spotlights on the stage in preparation for hanging them. Harris walked on, gave a quizzical glance at the equipment, started to leave, and then turned and said, "You know, kid, my name is Sam Harris, not Uncle Sam." But the lighting stayed in and Harris' productions started to look like their contemporaries.

January 24, 1949

At last: Opening Night. Nerves take over backstage on this night of nights, and it is the rare actor or stage manager who isn't in a cold sweat until the performance moves into high gear. But from the very beginning of my career I have been favored. As I sit out front, I become fatalistic: I've done what I've done; good, bad, or indifferent, there it stands. I can no longer do anything about it. If something goes wrong, I may cringe, but I rarely get up to go backstage.

One of the fascinating aspects of theatre is the feeling I get when I am watching a familiar performance as a member of an audience for the first time. I do not mean an audience of fellow professionals or the people with whom I have been working for weeks on the production, but an audience of ordinary theatre-goers who are seeing the show for the first time. I become intensely aware of their response, and my own reactions, both intellectual and emotional, change completely from what they were the night before when only my fellow workers were around me. I become part of a community of 800 people, and my responses reflect the communal atmosphere.

The first public performance of *Death of a Salesman* gave us all the feeling that the play had it. There were scenes that didn't go well; others seemed a little long, and would later be cut or changed. But from the very beginning, long before any applause, there was a sense that the play really held the audience. There is nothing esoteric about being able to make a fairly reliable verdict on whether a show is going to be a hit after seeing an out-of-town performance. If there are serious doubts, the chances are that the play will not succeed. Of course, some plays received coolly out of town can become moderate successes on Broadway, but out of the more than 250 productions I have designed I cannot remember one really first-rate show that did not reveal its strength on first exposure.

Brenda Murphy (b. 1950)

DEATH OF A SALESMAN: THE DESIGN PROCESS   1995

Brenda Murphy examines the process by which the design for the set began to take shape. The distinguished set designer Jo Mielziner was presented with a highly novel concept in the action of the play, and his solution has spawned many imitations. His solution was to concentrate on the salesman's house, presenting it in a dramatic cross-section.

While the casting proceeded, the biggest unanswered question about the script, the design concept, was being addressed. On September 24, Jo Mielziner received a call from Kermit Bloomgarden asking whether he could come straight over and talk to him about "something very interesting." After learning that Kazan hoped to begin rehearsal of the play in two weeks, Mielziner left the meeting with the *Salesman* script to read. During that afternoon and evening, Mielziner began to understand the difficulty of the job he was faced with: "It was not only that there were so many different scenic locations but that the action demanded instantaneous time changes from the present to the past and back again. Actors playing a contemporaneous scene suddenly went back fifteen years in exactly the same setting—the Salesman's house."

As he looked for a design solution to the many changes in scene and time demanded by the script, Mielziner hit on the concept that was to become the key to the production:

> The most important visual symbol in the play—the real background of the story—was the Salesman's house. Therefore, why should that house not be the main set, with all the other scenes—the corner of a graveyard, a hotel room in Boston, the corner of a business office, a lawyer's consultation room, and so on—played on a forestage? If I designed these little scenes in segments and fragments, with easily moved props and fluid lighting effects, I might be able, without ever lowering the curtain, to achieve the easy flow that the author dearly wanted.

The problem was that developing this design scheme would require more than the two weeks that remained before rehearsals were scheduled to begin. Miller would have to make substantial revisions in the script to change blackouts at the end of each scene to instantaneous scene changes, and Kazan would have to reconceive the whole production. What's more, if the play's opening was delayed, the pre-Broadway theatre bookings and the New York opening would have to be canceled and rescheduled. Mielziner asked for a meeting with Bloomgarden, Miller, and Kazan for that afternoon.

A long discussion followed Mielziner's presentation of his ideas on September 25. In the end, the aesthetic advantages of the single-set design scheme built around the material symbol of the house were determined to far outweigh the difficulties:

> To Arthur Miller, a design scheme allowing him as author to blend scenes at will without even the shortest break for physical changes was a significant decision. To Kazan, with his strong sense of movement, stimulated by his already proven genius as a film director, the scheme would permit use of some of the best cinematic techniques.

In the end, it was decided to postpone the start of rehearsals until the end of December and the New York opening until 10 February, allowing enough time for Miller's revisions and Kazan's rethinking of the direction as well as for the development of the design. Kazan was to consider Mielziner's "concept of a house standing like a specter behind all the scenes of the play, always present as it might be always present in Willy's mind, wherever his travels take him, even behind the office he visits, even behind the Boston hotel room and above his grave plot," the "single most critically important contribution and the key to the way [he] directed the play." Eloquently described by Miller on the opening pages of the published play, it has served the same purpose for millions of readers who have never seen a production of *Death of a Salesman*.

Mielziner set to work immediately to realize his ideas scenically. He made a number of rough sketches over the next few days, along with a ground plan of the stage, and worked on a breakdown of the script, which gave a page reference for each key scene and a notation of the needed lighting, scenery, props, and elevations. On September 28, he flew to Boston, where Kazan was rehearsing the pre-Broadway previews for *Love Life*, and went over his ideas at a breakfast meeting, leaving his director "after a brief hour with about ninety-percent approval." During the next week, Mielziner made about twenty black-and-white sketches representing the scenic design of the whole production and set his assistants to work on translating his sketches into an accurate floor plan and building a scale model of the set. When he met on October 4 with Bloomgarden, Kazan, and Miller, the designer had "a group of ground plans and sketches that . . . solved the major puzzles and were at least indications of the right style" for the production.

Mielziner's set was the culmination of a style of design he had been developing in his productions of Tennessee Williams's plays. In *The Glass Menagerie, A Streetcar Named Desire*, and *Summer and Smoke,* he had combined translucent scenery, expert lighting effects, and sets that went, as the eye traveled upward, from drab realistic interiors to light, delicate frameworks that were mere suggestions of buildings. The result was a style that was beginning to be recognized as his signature and that signaled to audiences a subjective realism in the play that juxtaposed ostensibly objective reality with a character's fantasy as easily as the scenery juxtaposed realism with symbolic abstraction.

Mielziner's *Salesman* set developed from his careful reading of the dialogue and the brief descriptive note that Miller had given him. Miller's note read: "[The house] had once been surrounded by open country, but it was now hemmed in with apartment houses. Trees that used to shade the house against the open sky and hot summer sun now were for the most part dead or dying." In the dialogue, Mielziner had underlined the lines "Boxed us in here"; "Bricks and windows, windows and bricks"; and "beautiful elm trees out there." From these visual suggestions, he conceived a tri-level set for the house, with Willy and Linda's bedroom on the lower floor, at stage right, one step up from the kitchen, which, at center stage, formed the largest playing space. On the far left of the kitchen were steps leading up to the boys' bedroom, above and behind the kitchen. All three rooms could be seen simultaneously. Although there was no wall between the parents' bedroom and the kitchen, the rear wall of each room was hung with translucent backdrops stenciled with "wallpaper" patterns. The lower floor also contained a bed, several chairs, a table, a telephone stand, and a refrigerator. Mielziner's original sketches also showed the hot water heater in the kitchen, but it was eventually hidden behind a curtain because it had become intrusive.

Rising above the lower floor there were only the skeletal rafters representing the gabled roof line and a platform holding the boys' beds and a chest. Behind the house was a translucent backdrop with two trees, the outline of the roof, and the boys' dormer window painted on the facing side. On the back were painted the outlines of bare, rectangular buildings with rectangular windows. When lit from the front with a soft golden light, the backdrop showed the Lomans' house as it used to be, a small but brave structure rising with hope and light to the sky. When lit from the back with a threatening reddish glow, it showed the house in the play's present, its fragile skeleton threatened by the huge, glowering apartment buildings.

On October 4, the main design problems that remained were lack of room for movement on the stage and transitions in time. The lack of room was solved only on December 8, when Kazan convinced Bloomgarden to take eleven seats out of the first row (at a cost of $323.40 per week in receipts) in order to extend the forestage. One of the biggest transition problems was getting Biff and Hap from the scene in their bedroom dressed in pajamas to the immediately following scene in which they appear to Willy in the kitchen as they were in the past, dressed in football uniforms. To manage this without closing the curtain or blacking the stage out, Mielziner had elevators built into the boys' beds so the actors could be moved unnoticed from one scene to the other. In order to give them time for a costume change, Miller expanded Willy's monologue about polishing the car by several minutes.

As the autumn progressed, Mielziner confronted the questions of lighting and props. Arthur Miller remembers that Mielziner and lighting expert Eddie Kook together "once worked an entire afternoon lighting a chair." The chair was the one that Willy addresses as if it were his old boss Frank Wagner in Howard's office, reminding him of the promises he had made. As Willy speaks to it, "the chair must become alive, quite as though his old boss were in it as he addresses him." Miller marveled that, "rather than being lit, the chair subtly seemed to begin emanating light" in the production. To achieve this effect, all of the surrounding lights on the stage had to be dimmed imperceptibly, rather than bringing up the spotlight on the chair, which would produce an effect too obvious to the audience.

This effect, and the attention that Mielziner and Kook gave to it, provide a good illustration of the designer's attitude toward the lighting of *Death of a Salesman*. Always a designer who made full artistic use of the scenic expression of lighting, Mielziner had decided that lighting was the key to *Salesman*'s time shifts. He decided to signify the passage of time on stage by creating two environments for the house through the lighting. When the set was first revealed, the audience saw the muslin backdrop lit from behind to show the oppressive apartment houses towering over the fragile house. When the scene shifted to the past, the lights behind the backdrop were dimmed out, and the buildings faded out as soft amber light and images of green leaves were projected onto the backdrop from a number of projection units that were carefully placed backstage, throughout the auditorium, and on the balcony. Mielziner felt that this visual symbol of the spring leaves, "liberating the house from the oppression of the surrounding structures and giving the stage a feeling of the free outdoors," was an "integral part of the Salesman's life story and had to be an easily recognized symbol of the springtime of that life." Combined with the music provided by Alex North, this lighting change would bring the audience effectively into the past along with Willy as each daydream began.

The painstaking work involved in the lighting of the original *Death of a Salesman* is almost inconceivable in these days of computerized stage lighting. Each of the 141 lighting units on the eight pipe battens above the stage had to be carefully hung and angled, and each light cue individually adjusted and marked up so that it could be re-created manually during each performance. It took three days for the hanging and angling, and another twenty-hour-day to set the approximately 150 light cues when the production was moved into the theater. In addition to the projection units, Mielziner had also persuaded Bloomgarden of the necessity of two special follow-spots, which could be manipulated to produce particular effects. Because their fine adjustments needed careful attention, each of these lights required a trained technician for its operation throughout the performance, a significant expense. Mielziner used the projection units to address spatial as well as temporal difficulties. He and Kazan had agreed early on that the most minimal of visual suggestions would suffice in creating the sets for the scenes to be played on the forestage—the Boston hotel room, the restaurant, and Howard's and Charley's offices. He created the hotel room by projecting a seedy wallpaper design from the theater balcony onto a section of the trellis at the side of the house. With the rest of the stage dimmed, this was enough to evoke the environment where Biff is disillusioned when he surprises Willy with The Woman.

This suggestiveness went along with the minimalism that Mielziner and Kazan had agreed on in the props. A few objects, such as the beds, the chairs, and the table, were required by the action on the stage. Most of the props, such as the refrigerator, the hot water heater, Willy's sample cases, the silk stockings, the rubber tubing, the hoe and seeds, and the gold fountain pen, served a necessary function but also took on a symbolic resonance. Kazan and Mielziner also agreed on several props which served primarily as material signifiers for the audience of some theme in the play, such as Biff's football trophy on a shelf over Willy's bed and a deflated football in the boys' room. The fact that props were kept to a minimum, with no attempt at realism, helped to foreground the few objects that did appear, encouraging the audience to perceive their symbolic significance.

Throughout the production process, the impulse was toward greater abstraction and symbolism, less realism. A good example is the Requiem scene, in which the original plan was to have a gravestone rise from a trick trapdoor in the forestage. Mielziner persuaded Kazan to use a simple bouquet of flowers to signify the grave instead, using a projection of autumn leaves to complete the symbolic statement of death in opposition to the life and hope suggested by the spring leaves in the daydream scenes. What made the production's style unique, however, was the juxtaposition of the abstract and poetic with the real and prosaic. The props that were introduced into the abstract suggestiveness of the set were authentic, battered objects that the Lomans might very well have owned. The kitchen table was covered with a cloth painted with an "oilcloth" design. The refrigerator was a careful reproduction of a typical model from the 1929 Sears Roebuck catalogue. It was vital to the production's aesthetic that these objects signify a specific time, place, class, and way of life in juxtaposition with the insistent visions in Willy's mind, and that they resonate with symbolic significance in the context of the play as a total experience.

Brenda Murphy (b. 1950)

RACIAL CONSCIOUSNESS IN CASTING
DEATH OF A SALESMAN

1995

A number of interesting issues came to the surface when the 1972 Baltimore production of Death of a Salesman *cast all black actors. Race-blind casting had been common with other classic American plays and often with Shakespeare and other European plays. This play provided unexpected surprises, however, as Murphy explains.*

The Center Stage production in 1972 brought to the fore the issue of race and ethnicity in casting the play. Although it was the first professional production cast with African-Americans, it was not the first to raise the color issue. As early as 1960, Miller had turned down a request from Terry Carter to do a "Negro version" of *Salesman* Off-Broadway. Although Carter assured Miller that care would be taken to avoid interracial casting that might "distort" the play—the entire Loman family, as well as The Woman, Miss Forsythe, and Letta were to be played by black actors—the request was refused, presumably because of Miller's ban on professional productions in New York.[1] According to Miller, however, he approved a production in New York during the sixties that would have featured African-American Frederick O'Neal as Willy, although the production never materialized.[2] O'Neal had played Willy in a 1962 production directed by Esther Merle Jackson at Clark College in Atlanta with an all-black cast.

The Center Stage production featured Richard Ward, who had been a hit in *Ceremonies of Dark Old Men* at the theatre in the previous year. Miller attended the opening night of the all-black production, and contributed a note to the program, saying:

> I have felt for many years that particularly with this play, which has been so well received in so many countries and cultures, the black actor would have an opportunity, if indeed that is needed anymore, to demonstrate to all his common humanity and his talent.[3]

The production was not particularly successful, chiefly because some inexperienced actors were cast in the minor roles. In several interviews, Ward made it clear that he had wanted to do the play with an integrated cast, particularly with Charley played by a white man, showing that "a white man and a black man can live next door to each other and care for each other . . . their children can grow up together and love each other."[4] Miller also was quoted as saying he would like to see the play done with an integrated cast, "just because it would allow a greater selection of players."[5]

---

[1]Unpublished letter from Terry Carter to Kay Brown, January 1960, HRHRC. [Harry Ransom Humanities Research Center]

[2]Unpublished letter from Arthur Miller to George [C. Scott], 28 April 1975, HRHRC.

[3]Quoted in Mel Gussow, "Stage: Black *Salesman*," *New York Times*, 9 April 1972: 69.

[4]Quoted in Carl Schoettler, "Actor in *Death of a Salesman* Went on Stage at Age 13," Baltimore *Evening Sun*, 3 April 1972: C6. See also Larry Siddons, "A Black Willy Loman Talks of *Salesman*'s Soul," *New York Post*, 4 April 1972: 60.

[5]Quoted in Siddons, "A Black Willy Loman."

The producers reported that they had thought about an integrated cast, but decided that it "might be an attempt to make a statement that's not in the play." They had wanted to make Charley white, "but some black leaders in Baltimore pointed out that the neighbor ends up success[ful], and that a 'be white, be a success' message might come across."[6]

Not surprisingly, the production was analyzed almost exclusively in terms of the race issue. Mel Gussow asserted in the *New York Times* that "Black time has caught up to *Salesman*," and contended that "what makes this more than just an intriguing experiment, but an exciting concept, is not only what it tells us about *Death of a Salesman*, but what it tells us about the black experience."[7] In Gussow's view, "Willy Loman's values are white values — the elevation of personality, congeniality, conformity, salesmanship in the sense of selling oneself," so that in the context of an all-black production, "Willy becomes a black man embracing the white world as an example to be emulated."[8] Hollie West of the *Washington Post* found the concept less revealing. Putting black actors "in roles written for whites," she contended, required the actors to "shed the badge of their color. Without the nuances of black dialogue and a consciousness reflecting the unique customs and traditions of black life, such actors may ask the question: Am I playing a white black man?"[9] West did not think the production succeeded in transferring the circumstances of the lower-middle-class white family in New York during the 1930s and 1940s to "the black circumstances of the same period."[10] Although she found Ward's performance as Willy entirely convincing, she found historical and social reality impinging on the dramatic illusion of the other characters: "Have black women been willing to play secondary roles when their husbands were failing, as in the case of Mrs. Loman?" she asked. "Would Biff have been considered an outcast among thousands of similar black men a generation ago?"[11]

Despite his support for Richard Ward's desire for interracial casting in the Baltimore production, Miller made it clear three years later that he found the question of race in casting an extremely complex one. A year after taking over the direction of the Philadelphia Drama Guild production from Scott, Miller approved an Off-Broadway revival of *Salesman* at the Circle in the Square Theatre that Scott was to direct, with himself in the title role. When he learned that Scott was planning to cast a black actor as Charley, Miller wrote him a four-page single-spaced letter, warning him to consider carefully what the implications of this casting would be. So-called color-blind casting, he believed, only worked when it was entirely color-blind, with Biff black and Happy white, for example. This, however, took the play out of the realm of realism, and made its relation to the social reality it depicted purely metaphorical, a conception which needed to be thoroughly thought through.[12]

In 1975, casting one "white" role with a black actor immediately foregrounded the issue of race. In the case of Charley, Miller did not think this would work. It would suggest that Willy, in daring to have a black man for his best friend during the thirties, would have it in him to rebel against accepted social values and prejudices, a

[6]*Ibid.*
[7]Gussow, "Black *Salesman.*"
[8]*Ibid.*
[9]Hollie I. West, "*Death of a Salesman*," *Washington Post*, 14 April 1972: D1.
[10]*Ibid.*, D7.
[11]*Ibid.*
[12]Unpublished letter from Arthur Miller to George [C. Scott], 28 April 1975, HRHRC.

quality antithetical to his character. It would also take away the sense that Charley is fundamentally the same as Willy, except for Willy's ruling passion, which destroys him. Miller felt that Charley should face the same conditions in life that Willy does, that he should be a representative of the American system when it functions as it should. He felt that adding the issue of race to this relationship would distort its dynamics as he had intended them to work.

Elia Kazan (1909–2003)
DIRECTING *DEATH OF A SALESMAN*   1988

Kazan speaks very personally about his involvement with Death of a Salesman, *beginning with his first reading of the script. He explains that the experience was like that of a brother speaking to him, someone who had shared his life experiences. And although he had directed the plays of Tennessee Williams and films such as* On the Waterfront, Death of a Salesman *was his favorite. The way in which he internalized the play may well parallel the responses of many readers and theatergoers, who might go home and wonder, as Kazan did, "Was I a good father? No? Why hadn't I done better?"*

Of all the plays I've directed, *Death of a Salesman* is my favorite. When I read it again recently, it hit me as hard as it had when I read it the first time, thirty-eight years ago — just as hard and in the same place, immediately, on page two! I am a man who has trained himself to let no pain show, but I felt tears coming as I turned that page. I suppose the play revives the memory, long at rest, of my father, a salesman of another product, of his hopes for his sons in this new country and the gently twisted Anatolian° smile on his face when he'd ask me, a muddle-headed kid of sixteen, "Who going support me my old age? Hey, you Elia, what you saying to that?" When I had nothing to say to that, but looked away, feeling threatened, he'd shrug and mutter — I'd hear it — "Hopeh-less case." That and more from those years of my life, as well as other memories, without words or faces, lying in wait with their burden of sadness, swarmed up when I read that damned disturbing play last week, just as they had when Art Miller, the day after he finished it in 1948, gave it to me.

After I'd read it that first time, I didn't wait for the next morning to see if I'd have a more "balanced" judgment, didn't delay as I generally did in those years to hear what Molly° might say about it, but called Art as I turned the back cover and told him his play had "killed" me. "I wrote it in eight weeks," he replied.

When I say this was my favorite play, I don't mean it was the best play. I am not a critic, and I do believe Williams wrote better. They were both Puritans, they were both concerned with morality — Tennessee more open about his "sins" and his problems, Miller more guarded. Still *Salesman* is the play that got to me most deeply. It's as if a brother was speaking of our common experience, a man who'd been through precisely the same life with his family that I had with mine. Art does

Anatolian: Of the main portion of Turkey, in western Asia. Kazan was born Elia Kazanjoglous to a Greek family in Istanbul, then the capital of the multiethnic Turkish Ottoman Empire.
Molly: His wife, Molly Day Thatcher (1907–1963).

an extraordinary thing there; he shows us a man who represents everything Art believes to be misguided about the system we live in, then goes on to make us feel affection and concern, pity and even love for this man. Then he goes deeper and we are aware of a tragic weight. Is it for the Salesman? Is it for ourselves? And along with arousing this sympathetic pain, his horrendous hero is able to make us laugh. He is ridiculous and he is tragic all at once. How is that accomplished? I don't know any other play in any other language that does all these things at the same time. But Arthur Miller did them all—that one time and never again.

I believe the reason he was able to do this was not that he was more understanding than anyone else about his fellow Americans and the system we live in, or knew better than the rest of us what was wrong with our civilization. It was because of his uncle. I remember—and I hope I remember correctly—that he derived Willy Loman from his uncle, "a very small man," the original stage direction reads, "who wears little shoes and little vests..." and "His emotions, in a word, are mercurial." Which is the way Art expected the part would be cast, not with Lee Cobb, certainly not great lumbering Leo Jacob Cobb. Art had this most ambivalent feeling about an actual person, thought him completely wrongheaded, believed he'd misguided his family and that everything he said that was meant to be serious was rubbish, but he still felt great affection for him and enjoyed his company and relished his passionate, nonsensical talk. The man made Art laugh, and Art likes to laugh. In short, he had the living model with that impossible combination of qualities in his own family, and he was smart enough, Art was, and talented enough to recognize that he had a character who could arouse affection and pity at the same time he evoked total condemnation and that both these reactions were significant separately, but together, in the same person, they were much more meaningful; together they could be tragic; together they were all of us.

Studying the play, as I was preparing to direct it, I began to see my father differently; I stopped being angry at him. I was ready at last to forget what I'd considered tyrannical and appreciate what he'd done for me. To gain an understanding of the play, one of the first things I did was sum up the similarities of my father to Willy Loman. George Kazan was a man full of violence that he dared release only at home, where it was safe to be angry. But the possibility that he might blow up at any time kept us all in terrible fear.

He also had about him, my father along with Willy, the euphoria of a salesman. When it came time to seduce a customer, he was expressive to a theatrical degree. "Feel it!" I remember him shouting at a buyer, as he lifted the end of a large Kashan carpet and thrust it into the man's hand. "Go on, take it in your hand. Give yourself the pleasure. No charge. Like butter, right? Eh? What you say? Like sweet butter! Tell me where you find piece goods like this piece goods, tell me that much." And so on. People in the trade said he was a great salesman. But when I watched these mercantile revels, they embarrassed me.

"Baba" dressed as a salesman and had his shoes shined every day. Even when he went to my aunt's apple farm in the Catskills for a weekend's vacation, he'd bring along other rug merchants, to talk about prices and the market and the sources "on the other side," then to play poker or pinochle most of the night. Sundays, when he would supervise the shish-ke-bab, bending over the hot wood coals and carefully turning the spits thrust through the cubes of well-marinated lamb leg, he wore a hard collar and a bow tie. Sometimes he even wore the jacket of his business suit and a flat-brimmed straw hat. In the Catskills on a Sunday, he was a merchant waiting for Monday.

It's the essence of the salesman's philosophy that your success or failure depends on your impressing others not only with the goods you have for sale but with yourself. You must gain their approval of your personality, make them believe that anything you say is true, even when you know it's grossly exaggerated or even totally false. That is how my father lived, by saying with the passion of unqualified conviction what was useful in winning a customer. Come to think of it, it was not different from what actors do on stage; they must make an audience believe the poetry and the nonsense, even when they don't believe it themselves. They are rewarded not with a sale but with applause.

Like Willy, my father considered his eldest son a special failure and oh, God, this hurt him! And me! But how could I blame him for what he expected of me and didn't get? Obviously what his wife had produced for him, this silent, secretive, mysteriously sullen son, was not going to rally to his side and sell rugs, not any to anyone, ever. Father preferred his next two boys: one was bound to study medicine—Father already called him "the doctor"—and the other actually did show, for a time, an interest in the business that had been my father's life. But he was afraid to tell himself the truth about his eldest son, the truth being that I didn't give a damn about the Oriental rug trade and, despite his persisting hopes, would never go into it; and if I did, would soon defect; and if I stayed, be no damn good. But just as Willy did, George Kazan kept pumping up hope, and the burden of that hope was on my back.

Willy had Linda, ever-faithful, fiercely devoted Linda; my father had my mother, Athena. She'd stand behind him every night as he gulped the dinner she'd spent the day preparing, would sit to eat her own meal only after he'd moved to the sofa; typically Anatolian that, taking a quick nap after his *yehmek*.° Old lions sleep after eating what the lioness provides.

There is an unarticulated tragedy when a woman discovers that the man she married is not what she hoped he was when she married him. Both Linda and Willy's best friend, Charley, saw through him but still loved him. Like Linda, my mother would not tolerate any criticism of my father from me; not while he was alive. If I indicated some disaffection, she'd turn on me and tell me he was a good man; "he never goes to other woman," she'd say, and someday I'd come to appreciate what he'd done for us all. He'd brought her to America, you see, not found her here, and she appreciated this. She protected him until the day he died; but when he was finally quiet in the grave, she surprised me one day by saying, "Your father was a stupid man." And soon afterward she said, "These years"—those following his death—"are best years of my life."

Art's play had such deep value for me because it forced me to understand my parents better. Even recently, when I read the play again, it made me wonder about the way I was treating my youngest son, ask myself if I was being as understanding of him as I should be. It disturbed me that I'd discovered my father's traits—even his facial expressions!—in myself. It disturbed me greatly when my youngest son told me that for years he'd lived in terror of my anger. I was repeating the pressure patterns of my father, and I was ashamed when I read Art's play and realized this. That damned play cut me where I was most vulnerable: Was I a good father? No? Why hadn't I done better?

I know it did this for many men; it was the only play I ever directed where men in the audience cried. I recall hearing sobs at the end of a performance, and they were mostly from men.

yehmek: Meal.

All the critics rushed to nail down the theme of the play, and Miller helped them with what's in the dialogue: "The man didn't know who he was," spoken over the grave, and a line even closer to the meaning, "He had the wrong dream," which is stated and restated. But it seemed to me that I, as the director, had to take another step and ask what that "wrong dream" was. I came to believe that the point was far more lethal than anything Art put into words. It's in the very fabric of the work, in the legend itself, which is where a theme should be. The Christian faith of this God-fearing civilization says we should love our brother as ourselves. Miller's story tells us that actually—as we have to live—we live by an opposite law, by which the purpose of life is to get the better of your brother, destroying him if necessary, yes, by in effect killing him. Even sex becomes a kind of aggression—to best your boss by taking his woman! That contrast between the ideal and the practice specific to our time is the sense in which the play is a "social drama," and this theme, so shameful and so final, permeates the work's fabric and is projected through the example of human behavior so there can be no avoiding it. Here is an antisystem play that is not "agitprop." We are out of the thirties at last—the audience does not have to suffer instruction or correction. The essence of our society, the capitalist system, is being destroyed not by rhetoric but by that unchallengeable vocabulary, action between people, which makes you believe that the terrible things that happen are true, are inevitable, and concern us all. Furthermore, the conflict we watch is between people who have every traditional reason to love each other. Miller makes us reach out for the lesson; it is not thrust down our throats. The question remains: Why do we live by that law when we know—and Art shows us this—that the result is so humanly destructive?

Art was trained first of all by Henrik Ibsen. The play has a strong structure. The viewer is immediately made aware, first by the title, then by Willy's revealing that he found himself driving off the road, that we are gathered together to watch the course of a suicide. That promise of terror and tragedy lies under every scene in the action that follows and makes the tension continuous. You wait in anxiety as you watch this ridiculous, tragic, misguided, frantically obsessed man—whether Cobb plays him, or the actor is a smaller man like Miller's uncle, doesn't matter. What you watch is yourself, struggling against the fate you've made for yourself.

This production became the other half (with *Streetcar*)° of a theatre legend. The fascinating game of what is fact and what is public relations buildup began to be played. In the accounts of the production and in the remeasuring of the people involved, what had actually happened was replaced by what a hungry press needed—good copy!—and what the imaginations of the people who saw the production were prepared to believe. Furthermore, within each of the people involved there was a swell of confidence. We became convinced of our ability to do anything we chose to do. Success seemed the natural course for us all, the inevitable reward of our efforts. The great success of the play certified our worth. Truth was soon out of sight; we all puffed up. Our producers, Bloomgarden and Fried, Lee Cobb, Arthur Miller, and Elia Kazan were never the same again.

The play became, to the surprise of many theatre people, including its producers, a great success, selling out immediately. Kermit Bloomgarden, an excellent "line" producer, who had the ability to see to it that everything necessary for

---

Streetcar: *A Streetcar Named Desire* by Tennessee Williams, which Kazan directed earlier in 1947. It was still running when *Death of a Salesman* opened.

mounting a show arrived on time and in good working order, was now offered to the public as something more, the leading producer of "class" plays that no one else dared produce on Broadway. His pressman immediately set about creating an enlarged reputation. But how Kermit was able to acquire *Death of a Salesman* and what he thought of it is more interesting than this "puff." Daring is not a feature of the true story; luck is.

At the end of the triumphant opening night performance, Eddie Kook, who'd provided the equipment for lighting the show, was sitting behind Cheryl Crawford, listening to the applause storm. Eddie noticed tears in Cheryl's eyes and commented on the play's power. "That's not why I'm crying," she said. "I had this play and let it get away." This was true. When Art and I weren't sure which producer to entrust it to, I suggested we give it to Cheryl. To my surprise, the force it would have with an audience did not strike her. She hesitated; the time allowed for hesitation in the theatre is brief. Cheryl seemed especially dubious about the play's commercial potential. She'd given it to friends to read; they hadn't been sure either. Since a lively enthusiasm is a necessity for a successful ride through the obstacle course of a Broadway production, and Cheryl didn't show any, I told her to forget the play.

Now luck was loose. Art and I decided to pass the script on to another good friend, Kermit, and his associate, Walter Fried. They'd accepted the play for production, but, as had been the case with Cheryl, they were not sure of its box office strength. Kermit told me he'd consulted theatre owners and box office treasurers, and everyone had cautioned him that the word "Death" in a title invited death to the ticket window; this had been proven time and again, so they maintained.

One morning when I was in Kermit's side office, working on casting, he burst in and declared that he was convinced the title of the play had to be changed. He said there was an "upbeat" phrase in the play that would make a fine title, commercial as well as meaningful. Fried and he were determined that *Free and Clear* should be our title. When my reaction was negative, then obdurate, then—when they persisted—scornful, they asked if I'd mind if they talked to Miller without me there. I don't know why I was so damned gracious, because my emotions were violently hostile, but I did say, "Go ahead," and they summoned the author quickly for consultation. Art had to pass the small office where I was waiting with the door open. When he came by, I pulled him in, and without telling him what their proposal was, I said, "They want to talk to you about something I'm dead against. Don't you dare say yes." Art went in, they talked without me; our title was not changed.

But Kermit was a man who made it a matter of pride that he never changed his mind. Perhaps he thought that I, along with others who knew his original concerns about Miller's title, might think him weak if he altered his stand. Kermit had a horror of appearing weak. On opening night, he was cornered by Irving Hoffman, who wrote theatre reviews for the *Hollywood Reporter,* and although Irving didn't ask him what he thought of the title, Kermit volunteered, "I still don't like the title, but it's Arthur Miller's play and he wants the title we have and that's all right with me." Perhaps Kermit was throwing up a defense for himself in case Hoffman didn't like the title either. His anxiety about what Hoffman might think was not altogether unfounded. The "head" of the review in the *Hollywood Reporter* read: "Tragically We Roll Along."

The imaginative qualities of Art's play, the nonrealistic aspects, worked successfully on stage and added a great deal to the force of the theme. They were indeed innovative, and Art deserved all the praise he's been given. How they came to be in the production, however, is a story that brings credit to the theatre as an institution, as well as confirming a string of influences. As Tennessee Williams admired and was stirred by *All My Sons* ("It has the kind of eloquence we need now," he'd written me), so did Art benefit from *A Streetcar Named Desire*. I remember the night he came to see *Streetcar*. After the performance he appeared to be full of wonder at the theatre's expressive possibilities. He told me he was amazed at how simply and successfully the nonrealistic elements in the play— *"Flores! Flores para los muertos!"°*—blended with the realistic ones. These two men, completely different humans who never mixed socially, influenced each other's work and owed each other a debt.

After *Death of a Salesman* had made theatre history, it was published, and the sentence that follows "The Curtain rises" on the first printed pages is: "Before us is the Salesman's home . . . an air of a dream clings to the place, a dream rising out of reality." However, the stage direction in the original manuscript that Art gave me to read directly he'd finished it does not mention a home as a scenic element. It reads: "A pinpoint travelling spot lights a small area on stage left. The Salesman is revealed. He takes out his keys and opens an invisible door." It was a play waiting for a directorial solution.

The concept of a house standing like a specter behind all the scenes of the play, always present as it might be always present in Willy's mind, wherever his travels take him, even behind the office he visits, even behind the Boston hotel room and above his grave plot, is not even suggested in the original script. Although the spectral home is a directorial vision, it was not my idea any more than it was Art's. It was urged on us by the scenic designer, Jo Mielziner. I went for it—it solved many problems for me—and when we took it to Miller, he approved of it. In this production, it was the single most critically important contribution and the key to the way I directed the play. Both Miller and I were praised for what Jo had conceived; he never got the credit he deserved. Art rewrote his stage direction for the book based on Jo's design. A published play is often the record of a collaboration: The director's stage directions are incorporated, as are some of the contributions of others working on the show— actors' "business," designer's solutions, and so on. The theatre is not an exclusively literary form. Although the playscript is the essentially important element, after that is finished, actors, designers, directors, technicians "write" the play together.

Lee J. Cobb became the great star of that season; people marveled at his power and his brilliance. This adulation may have done him more harm than good. When I recommended that we cast Cobb as Willy, I knew him well from our days in the Group° and a road tour we'd played of *Golden Boy*. Our friendship had started close, but like many actors' friendships, it thinned out. I knew him for a mass of contradictions: loving and hateful, anxious yet still supremely pleased with himself, smug but full of doubt, guilty and arrogant, fiercely competitive but very withdrawn, publicly private, suspicious but always reaching for trust, boastful with a modest air, begging for total acceptance no matter what he did to others. In other words, the part was him; I knew that Willy was in Cobb, there to be pulled out.

Flores! . . . muertos!: Flowers! Flowers for the dead!
Group: The Group Theatre was founded in New York in 1931.

When he received his fabulous notices, Lee awarded himself a status even higher than any the theatre world gave him. He was great as Willy Loman until he was told he was great and believed it—then he was less great. He was at his best during the last week of the tryout in Philadelphia, before his New York triumph. After we opened on Broadway, he began to share the audience's admiration for his performance and their pity for the character he played. Life on Broadway would not, because it could not, satisfy this man's hunger for unqualified recognition. He withdrew from our play before he should have, claiming that he was dangerously exhausted—which we might have appreciated except that we all saw he was dramatizing it beyond its measure. He said he was on the verge of a breakdown and demanded that I consult with his analyst. I did; we had a bad scene. I still don't know how serious Lee's trouble was; he was a very good actor and determined to prove that he had to leave the show.

Once he was "available" again, no more parts like Willy came his way. He began to masquerade as a martyr to an unappreciative theatre. Something pouting in his character waited for "justice," meaning that a role of great worth was his due and had to come soon. He'd certainly be the Lear of our time, he boasted. Friends agreed. But the theatre is no more just than life, and nothing came along that he found acceptable. Today, Cobb is remembered for Willy Loman and that is all; it became the story of his life.

Many actors are remembered because of a single great performance, but this comfort from history did not satisfy Cobb. When another season's crop of new plays came along with nothing for him, he decided to return west and to films. I brought him back east to my "location" in Hoboken, to play the corrupt labor boss in *Waterfront,* and he did well, even had an Academy Award nomination. But after that the roles offered him in films were beneath his talent. He felt aggrieved and insulted, and found that the people who dominated the film community were no less arrogant than I. To save his pride, he responded with arrogance. To release his tensions, he gambled more frequently and more seriously. I know only what I heard, the outside of the story. He disappeared from my view. Then suddenly he was dead, too young and—I agree—insufficiently rewarded. What a waste!

Thinkers who think about the theatre have said that success is a problem more difficult than failure—an astonishing thought to anyone who'd been hungry for recognition as long as I'd been. I didn't find success a problem; I was not uncomfortable sitting on a peak. I was credited with all kinds of magic and became the coy object of artistic temptation and commercial seduction. Every play of worth intended for Broadway was offered me first. I had to shrug them off. In films it was only a matter of what I wanted to do, name it. I could see no limit to what I might accomplish. I began to make notes on ambitious future projects, those I'd once only dreamed of. Now they were within reach; all I had to do was extend my hand. And work! That was easy; I had perfect health and boundless energy. I enjoyed the devotion and the intimate friendship of the two best playwrights of the day; one was writing a play, the other a film, both intended for me. I didn't have an enemy, not that I knew of; no, nothing but admiring followers. I was so successful there was no reason for anyone to be jealous of me: I was too far ahead of the pack. I was certain all this would endure—why would it not?—sure that my success would swell, my friendships deepen, my creative associations become richer. No longer suffering from self-doubt, I quit my analyst.

In time I had to confront some facts. I am a mediocre director except when a play or a film touches a part of my life's experience. Other times my cleverness and facility will not overcome my inadequacies. When I rely on mechanics, I do only what a good stage manager should be able to do. I am not catholic in my tastes. I dislike Beckett—his work. I am not an intellectual. I don't have great range. I am no good with music or with spectacles. The classics are beyond me. I enjoy humor and the great clowns, but I can't make up jokes or amusing bits of byplay and visual humor. What I need I steal. I have no ear for poetry. I have a pretty good eye but not a great eye. I do have courage, even some daring. I am able to talk to actors; I don't fear them and their questions. I've been able to arouse them to better work. I have strong, even violent, feelings, and they are assets. I am not shy about ripping the cover-guard off my own experiences; this encourages actors to overcome their inhibitions. I enjoy working with performers; they sense this and have been happy as well as successful with me. This is useful.

Molly used to say that I was too hard on myself. But I don't feel the above is inaccurate. I prefer this measure to the pumped-up state of fame I had after *Death of a Salesman* and *A Streetcar Named Desire*. It took me some years to face what I was as a director; in fact, it took a painful defeat at the Lincoln Center Repertory Theatre. At the time I'm writing about, I was mired in media mud; I'm afraid that for a time I believed what I read. When I see my photographs from that period, I don't like what I see. For three years I was on the very top, then life twisted, as it will; by surviving a great deal of pain and trouble, I became a different person. But that's looking too far ahead.

Arthur Miller (1915–2005)
FROM "THE AMERICAN THEATER"   1978

Reflecting on the process of casting both the main character, Willy, and Willy's wife, Linda, Miller considers some of the reasons for choosing one actor over another. He reminds us that the choices that producers and directors make are usually sound and sensible. Some actors have a great track record and recommend themselves in terms of their recent successes. Others have a quality that a director might remember and see as appropriate for the part. In addition, there are other actors who see themselves as the only viable choice for the part they want; their job, perhaps the most difficult, is to convince the decision makers that they are the right choice.

The basis upon which actors are hired or not hired is sometimes quite sound; for example, they may have been seen recently in a part which leads the director to believe they are right for the new role; but quite as often a horde of applicants is waiting beyond the door of the producer's private office and neither he nor the director nor the author has the slightest knowledge of any of them. It is at this point that things become painful, for the strange actor sits before them, so nervous and frightened that he either starts talking and can't stop, and sometimes says he can't stop, or is unable to say anything at all and says that. During the casting of one of my plays there entered a middle-aged woman who was so frightened she suddenly started to sing. The play being no musical, this was slightly beside the point, but the producer, the director, and myself, feeling so guilty ourselves, sat there and heard her through.

To further complicate matters there is each year the actor or actress who suddenly becomes what they call "hot." A hot performer is one not yet well-known, but who, for some mysterious reason, is generally conceded to be a coming star. It is possible, naturally, that a hot performer really has talent, but it is equally possible, and much more likely, that she or he is not a whit more attractive or more talented than a hundred others. Nevertheless, there comes a morning when every producer in these five blocks — some of them with parts the performer could never play — simply has to have him or her. Next season, of course, nobody hears about the new star and it starts all over again with somebody else.

All that is chancy in life, all that is fortuitous, is magnified to the bursting point at casting time; and that, I suspect, is one of the attractions of this whole affair, for it makes the ultimate winning of a part so much more zesty. It is also, to many actors, a most degrading process and more and more of them refuse to submit to these interviews until after the most delicate advances of friendship and hospitality are made to them. And their use of agents as intermediaries is often an attempt to soften the awkwardness of their applying for work.

The theatrical agents, in keeping with the unpredictable lunacy of the business, may be great corporations like the Music Corporation of America, which has an entire building on Madison Avenue, and will sell you anything from a tap dancer to a movie star, a symphony orchestra, saxophonists, crooners, scene designers, actors, and playwrights, to a movie script complete with cast; or they may be like Jane Broder, who works alone and can spread out her arms and touch both walls of her office. They may even be like Carl Cowl, who lives around the corner from me in Brooklyn. Carl is an ex-seaman who still ships out when he has no likely scripts on hand to sell, and when things get too nerve-racking he stays up all night playing Mozart on his flute. MCA has antique desks, English eighteenth-century prints, old broken clocks and inoperative antique barometers hanging on its paneled walls, but Carl Cowl had a hole in his floor that the cat got into, and when he finally got the landlord to repair it he was happy and sat down to play his flute again; but he heard meowing, and they had to rip the floor open again to let out the cat. Still, Carl is not incapable of landing a hit play and neither more nor less likely than MCA to get it produced, and that is another handicraft aspect of this much publicized small business, a quality of opportunity which keeps people coming into it. The fact is that theatrical agents do not sell anyone or anything in the way one sells merchandise. Their existence is mainly due to the need theater people have for a home, some semblance of order in their lives, some sense of being wanted during the long periods when they have nothing to do. To have an agent is to have a kind of reassurance that you exist. The actor is hired, however, mainly because he is wanted for the role.

By intuition, then, by rumor, on the recommendation of an agent — usually heartfelt; out of sheer exhaustion, and upsurge of sudden hope or what not, several candidates for each role are selected in the office of the producer, and are called for readings on the stage of a theater.

It is here that the still unsolved mystery begins, the mystery of what makes a stage performer. There are persons who, in an office, seem exciting candidates for a role, but as soon as they step onto a stage the observers out front — if they are experienced—know that the blessing was not given them. For myself, I know it when, regardless of how well the actor is reading, my eyes begin to wander up to the brick wall back of the stage. Conversely, there are many who make little impression in an office, but once on the stage it is impossible to take one's attention from them. It is a question neither of technique nor of ability, I think, but some quality of surprise inherent in the person.

For instance, when we were searching for a woman to play Linda, the mother in *Death of a Salesman,* a lady came in whom we all knew but could never imagine in the part. We needed a woman who looked as though she had lived in a house dress all her life, even somewhat coarse and certainly less than brilliant. Mildred Dunnock insisted she was that woman, but she was frail, delicate, not long ago a teacher in a girl's college, and a cultivated citizen who probably would not be out of place in a cabinet post. We told her this, in effect, and she understood, and left.

And the next day the line of women formed again in the wings, and suddenly there was Milly again. Now she had padded herself from neck to hem line to look a bit bigger, and for a moment none of us recognized her, and she read again. As soon as she spoke we started to laugh at her ruse; but we saw, too, that she *was* a little more worn now, and seemed less well-maintained, and while she was not quite ordinary, she reminded you of women who were. But we all agreed, when she was finished reading, that she was not right, and she left.

Next day she was there again in another getup, and the next and the next, and each day she agreed with us that she was wrong; and to make a long story short when it came time to make the final selection it had to be Milly, and she turned out to be magnificent. But in this case we had known her work; there was no doubt that she was an excellent actress. The number of talented applicants who are turned down because they are unknown is very large. Such is the crap-shooting chanciness of the business, its chaos, and part of its charm. In a world where one's fate so often seems machined and standardized, and unlikely to suddenly change, these five blocks are like a stockade inside which are people who insist that the unexpected, the sudden chance, must survive. And to experience it they keep coming on all the trains.

But to understand its apparently deathless lure for so many it is necessary, finally, to have participated in the first production of a new play. When a director takes his place at the beaten-up wooden table placed at the edge of the stage, and the cast for the first time sit before him in a semicircle, and he gives the nod to the actor who has the opening lines, the world seems to be filling with a kind of hope, a kind of regeneration that, at the time, anyway, makes all the sacrifices worth while.

The production of a new play, I have often thought, is like another chance in life, a chance to emerge cleansed of one's imperfections. Here, as when one was very young, it seems possible again to attain even greatness, or happiness, or some otherwise unattainable joy. And when production never loses that air of hope through all its three-and-a-half-week rehearsal period, one feels alive as at no other imaginable occasion. At such a time, it seems to all concerned that the very heart of life's mystery is what must be penetrated. They watch the director and each other and they listen with the avid attention of deaf mutes who have suddenly learned to speak and hear. Above their heads there begins to form a tantalizing sort of cloud, a question, a challenge to penetrate the mystery of why men move and speak and act.

It is a kind of glamour that can never be reported in a newspaper column, and yet it is the center of all the lure theater has. It is a kind of soul-testing that ordinary people rarely experience except in the greatest emergencies. The actor who has always regarded himself as a strong spirit discovers now that his vaunted power somehow sounds querulous, and he must look within himself to find his strength. The actress who has made her way on her charm discovers that she appears not charming so much as shallow now, and must evaluate herself all over again, and create anew what she always took for granted. And the great performers are merely those who have been able to face themselves without remorse.

In the production of a good play with a good cast and a knowing director a kind of banding together occurs; there is formed a fraternity whose members share a mutual sense of destiny. In these five blocks, where the rapping of the tap-dancer's feet and the bawling of the phonographs in the record-shop doorways mix with the roar of the Broadway traffic; where the lonely, the perverted, and the lost wander like the souls in Dante's hell and the life of the spirit seems impossible, there are still little circles of actors in the dead silence of empty theaters, with a director in their center, and a new creation of life taking place.

There are always certain moments in such rehearsals, moments of such wonder that the memory of them serves to further entrap all who witness them into this most insecure of all professions. Remembering such moments the resolution to leave and get a "real" job vanishes, and they are hooked again.

I think of Lee Cobb, the greatest dramatic actor I ever saw, when he was creating the role of Willy Loman in *Death of a Salesman*. When I hear people scoffing at actors as mere exhibitionists, when I hear them ask why there must be a theater if it cannot support itself as any business must, when I myself grow sick and weary of the endless waste and the many travesties of this most abused of all arts, I think then of Lee Cobb making that role and I know that the theater can yet be one of the chief glories of mankind.

He sat for days on the stage like a great lump, a sick seal, a mourning walrus. When it came his time to speak lines, he whispered meaninglessly. Kazan, the director, pretended certainty, but from where I sat he looked like an ant trying to prod an elephant off his haunches. Ten days went by. The other actors were by now much further advanced: Milly Dunnock, playing Linda, was already creating a role; Arthur Kennedy as Biff had long since begun to reach for his high notes; Cameron Mitchell had many scenes already perfected; but Cobb stared at them, heavy-eyed, morose, even persecuted, it seemed.

And then, one afternoon, there on the stage of the New Amsterdam way up on top of a movie theater on Forty-second Street (this roof theater had once been Ziegfeld's private playhouse in the gilded times, and now was barely heated and misty with dust), Lee rose from his chair and looked at Milly Dunnock and there was a silence. And then he said, "I was driving along, you understand, and then all of a sudden I'm going off the road...."

And the theater vanished. The stage vanished. The chill of an age-old recognition shuddered my spine; a voice was sounding in the dimly lit air up front, a created spirit, an incarnation, a Godlike creation was taking place; a new human being was being formed before all our eyes, born for the first time on this earth, made real by an act of will, by an artist's summoning up of all his memories and his intelligence; a birth was taking place above the meaningless traffic below; a man was here transcending the limits of his body and his own history. Through the complete concentration of his mind he had even altered the stance of his body, which now was strangely not the body of Lee Cobb (he was thirty-seven then) but of a sixty-year-old salesman; a mere glance of his eye created a window beside him, with the gentle touch of his hand on this empty stage a bed appeared, and when he glanced up at the emptiness above him a ceiling was there, and there was even a crack in it where his stare rested.

I knew then that something astounding was being made here. It would have been almost enough for me without even opening the play. The actors, like myself and Kazan and the producer, were happy, of course, that we might have a hit; but there was a good deal more. There was a new fact of life, there was an alteration of history for all of us that afternoon.

There is a certain immortality involved in theater, not created by monuments and books, but through the knowledge the actor keeps to his dying day that on a certain afternoon, in an empty and dusty theater, he cast a shadow of a being that was not himself but the distillation of all he had ever observed; all the unsingable heartsong the ordinary man may feel but never utter, he gave voice to. And by that he somehow joins the ages.

And that is the glamour that remains, but it will not be found in the gossip columns. And it is enough, once discovered, to make people stay with the theater, and others to come seeking it.

I think also that people keep coming into these five blocks because the theater is still so simple, so old-fashioned. And that is why, however often its obsequies are intoned, it somehow never really dies. Because underneath our shiny fronts of stone, our fascination with gadgets, and our new toys that can blow the earth into a million stars, we are still outside the doorway through which the great answers wait. Not all the cameras in Christendom nor all the tricky lights will move us one step closer to a better understanding of ourselves, but only, as it always was, the truly written word, the profoundly felt gesture, the naked and direct contemplation of man which is the enduring glamour of the stage.

June Schlueter (b. 1948) *and James K. Flanagan*
MEMORABLE WILLY   *1987*

The authors contend that there may be no more memorable character on the modern stage than Willy Loman. To an extent they base their statement on the effect that Willy has on the audience's imagination. The later audiences of the play seem to have been affected by Willy Loman even more than the original 1949 audience. The society had changed in twenty-five years, but in a direction that made Willy's values seem less connected with the Depression of the 1930s and more connected with the affluence of the 1970s.

When Walter Goodman reviewed the 1975 revival of *Death of a Salesman,* in which George C. Scott replaced Lee J. Cobb as the self-deluded drummer, he claimed that the play, though applauded in 1949 as the great American tragedy, might well mean more in 1975. Goodman argues that the sympathetic reception of so unmitigated a failure as Willy Loman could be expected from a people who had lived through the Great Depression and World War II, but identification with this loser of a salesman could not have lasted beyond the two-hour life of the play. For this audience was on its way to becoming the Affluent Society; in 1949, Willy Loman was "an anachronism, a relic of a Depression mentality." By 1975, however, America had again become a society ready to acknowledge that "attention must be paid," even to this unlikable, inept failure, whose condition rather than personality was moving. For the 1975 audience had lived through an unpopular, unnecessary war, which brought none of the enthusiasm or the nationalism of World War II; and it was disillusioned with two decades of an energetic prosperity that could not pause for failures nor accommodate a man who yearned to plant seeds or look at the moon.[1]

In 1984, Willy Loman appeared once again on the Broadway stage, this time a bit thinner and a bit smaller—more like the original "shrimp" Miller had created than the "walrus" into which Willy was metamorphosed when Lee J. Cobb was cast. Dustin Hoffman's portrayal of Willy was powerful and convincing, suggesting that the method actor had clearly found some coincidence between himself and the character that enabled him to create the role. But where America was in the mid-1980s did not seem to concern the critics. *Death of a Salesman* was no longer being viewed as time-bound commentary on capitalism and its victims, and audience response was not being judged in terms of economic or social circumstance. Miller's play had clearly earned its author's description of it as a play that raises "questions . . . whose answers define humanity,"[2] a description dramatically endorsed in 1983 when the play opened at the Beijing People's Art Theater in China.

That production, the first in China of an American play directed by an American, challenged the assumption that *Salesman* was culture-bound, meeting with enthusiastic responses in a country where peasants constitute 90 percent of the population and where there are no salesmen. Speaking of the opening in *"Salesman" in Beijing*, Miller noticed the odd laughs, the cruel laughs, beneath which he sensed "a comprehension of Willy's character, a recognition. Which I suppose means they share these embarrassing weaknesses?"[3] Harry Moses, producer of the Bill Moyers show on PBS, which ran a special program on the production of *Death of a Salesman* in Beijing, told Miller the day after opening night that the last shot on the program would be of a young Chinese who spoke English, saying that "China was full of Willys, dreamers of the dream."[4]

But the problem with Willy—aside from his self-delusion, his ineptness, his self-pity, his misplaced pride, and his fraudulent morality—is that he has dreamed the wrong dream. About to be fired from his job, Willy cries out to the young upstart Howard, "You can't eat the orange and throw the peel away—a man is not a piece of fruit!" Though only the peel of Willy's dream remains, he refuses to discard it, deluding himself into believing that the dream of being a salesman with green velvet slippers, who was not only liked but well liked by the hundreds who mourned his death, was right for him.

There may well be no character in modern drama more memorable than Willy Loman. The image of the tired salesman, valise in hand, shoulders sloping, suit

[1]Walter Goodman, "Miller's *Salesman*, Created in 1949, May Mean More to 1975." *New York Times*, June 15, 1975, pp. 1, 5.

[2]Arthur Miller, introduction to *Arthur Miller's Collected Plays* (New York: Viking Press, 1957), p. 32.

[3]Arthur Miller, *"Salesman" in Beijing* (New York: Viking Press, 1984), p. 238.

[4]Miller, *"Salesman" in Beijing*, p. 245.

jacket hanging loosely about his weary frame, which appeared on the jacket of the Viking edition of the play for years, has sustained its power in the imagination of the theatergoing public. It has become a symbol of the pursuer of the American—and the universal—dream who met with the harsh consequences of not being able to keep up. Willy Loman is indeed a low man; no tragic hero of high degree, he is circumstantially and psychologically down. Surrounded by high-rise apartment buildings that deflect the sun from the backyard, Willy's little house in Brooklyn stands as a symbol of time past, when the world still had room for vegetable gardens and for salesmen who carried on their trade on the strength of a smile. There is a collective guilt in Willy's failure in which every theatergoer participates; it is a guilt occasioned by the knowledge that society cannot accommodate its failures in a system that relentlessly demands success.

Catherine Diamond
DEATH OF A SALESMAN IN TAIPEI
1993

Diamond, who is a professor and director of the only English-language theater in Taiwan, felt that the Taiwanese production of Death of a Salesman *reflected Chinese values almost as much as it did American values. The political complexities of the production indicate the difficulties that the National Theater of Taipei overcame in order to produce the play. Diamond points to some of the interesting cultural differences that might be invisible to an American audience but that would be of considerable importance to the Chinese.*

DEATH OF A SALESMAN. By Arthur Miller. The Performance Workshop. The National Theater, Taipei, Taiwan, Republic of China. 18–26 April 1992.

In 1987, Yang Shipeng, director of the Hong Kong Repertory Theatre, was invited to direct a play at Taiwan's new National Theater. He requested permission from Arthur Miller to use a Taiwanese translation of *Death of a Salesman* because he could not use the Ying Ruocheng translation Miller used in Beijing. Miller initially gave his permission with the caveat that the translation be used only in Taiwan. The production was postponed and later, Yang heard from Miller's agent that only the Ying Ruocheng translation was acceptable. The reason for this change of mind has never been clearly determined, but the Taiwan press put the blame on Miller, insinuating his pro-communist sympathies. On the other hand, perhaps Miller, irritated that Taiwan's refusal of the mainland translation was based purely on political rather than artistic grounds, revoked his initial permission.

In 1991, Yang again wrote to Miller, asking whether he could use the Ying Ruocheng translation with some of his own emendations. Miller answered affirmatively. In both his alteration of the translation, in which he substituted Taipei idiom for the original Beijing idiom, and in his directing style, Yang strove for what he believed would appear most natural to the Taipei audience, neither emphasizing the play's Americanisms nor trying to adapt the story to a Taiwanese local.

The actors played the essence of relationships rather than their specifically American manifestations. However, there were some fundamental differences in social values that made it difficult for the audience to comprehend Willy's character

The 1992 Chinese production of *Death of a Salesman,* at the National Theater in Taipei, Taiwan, directed by Yang Shipeng.

and to sympathize with him. For example, virtually no Chinese father harbors aspirations for his son to become a professional sportsman, but desires instead for him to go to university—an American school preferably—and become a professor, doctor, manager, or lawyer. As an actor in Miller's *Salesman in Beijing* expressed it: "Every man wants his son to be a dragon." The audience clearly understood Willy's hopes for Biff and his ensuing disappointment, but since Taiwanese society so clearly admires the path taken by Willy's neighbor, the successful businessman Charley and his bookish son Bernard, people laughed at Willy's delusions, often failing to empathize with his particular dreams of success.

Despite some confusion caused by Willy's highly individualized character, other aspects of the play were almost written for modern day Taipei. The similarities between the United States in the wheeling-dealing 1920s and laissez faire capitalism in 1990s Taiwan are uncanny. Out-of-town extramarital affairs, children suffering from parental expectations, the high cost of housing, overcrowding, disappearance of green spaces, job obsolescence, increasing competition for jobs, and the struggle to maintain the esteem of others while facing failure are well-known phenomena in the postindustrial, newly-wealthy metropolis of Taipei. Yet the production did not challenge the audience to reflect upon these problems or the social values that cause them.

Director Yang had a clearcut goal of presenting an American play without any concessions to the Chinese actors or the Chinese audience, yet certain changes were inevitable. In the translation itself, the flavor of individual characters's speech gets attenuated, especially Happy's, which is slangy.

Another significant difference was in acting style. Modern Chinese stage acting tends to be broad, exaggerated and emphatic. This has roots in the traditional drama and is reinforced by television dramas which tend to be either contemporary soap operas or historical melodramas. Consequently the male actors in particular engaged in a great deal of demonstrative acting—pointing, waving their hands around, and touching each other to get attention. Seasoned stage actor Li Lichun played Willy's poignant scenes with admirable restraint, but Deng Chenghui, as the loyal wife Linda, evoked more sympathy. Her voice never broke until her last line at Willy's grave: "We're free . . . we're free," and, because she held back her tears until the very end, the audience wept with her, moved more by her devotion than Willy's fall and final sacrifice.

In his Beijing production, Miller initially felt apprehensive that his play might be reduced to a political message—an indictment of American capitalism. This aspect was wholly absent from the Taipei production, where it might have been more justified. Instead, both director and actors stressed the pathos of the Loman family. Yang Shipeng wanted to move the audience, but to what end, his production never made clear.

Eugène Ionesco

Eugène Ionesco (1909–1994) was born in Slatina, a small town in Romania not far from Bucharest, to a Romanian father and a French mother. In 1911 the family moved to Paris, where his father studied law, and from 1917 to 1919 he and his sister attended boarding school in the country village of La Chapelle-Anthenaise. In a complex turn of events, his father divorced his mother secretly in Romania and took Eugène and his sister to live with him and his new wife. The move left Eugène very unhappy because he was more attached to his mother than to his father, and his father was a domineering and sometimes violent man. Eugène eventually left home when he was seventeen, while his sister, unable to tolerate their stepmother, rejoined their mother.

Ionesco studied French at the University of Bucharest. There he began his writing career and was noticed by a number of Romanian writers. Ionesco's first volume of poetry, *Elegies for Minuscule Creatures,* was published in 1931, but he later disowned it as the musings of an immature writer. He married in 1936, three months before his mother died, and taught high school French in Romania until 1939, when he returned to France. Although he and his wife were forced to return to Romania when World War II began, Ionesco was permitted to teach in Bucharest until he made his way to Marseilles in 1942 and weathered the rest of the war virtually in hiding and in relative poverty.

After the war Ionesco and his family (a daughter was born in 1944) moved back to Paris. While working as a proofreader he also used textbooks to teach himself English. His amusement at the essential nonsense of the phrases and expressions he encountered in the books led him to write his first play, *The Bald Soprano* (1950). In the play, he employs the kinds of clichéd expressions that appear in such books. Ultimately, as the critics have said, the play is about the certainty of a failure of communication.

Failure of communication is present in many of Ionesco's plays, and some commentators have pointed to the problems of his childhood as the source of his anxiety. Early in his life his parents were separated and his father presumed dead. Then his father reappeared, only to divorce Ionesco's mother later and gain custody of their children in 1922 on the specious grounds that his wife deserted the family. Ionesco's journals of his early years record a tumultuous family life in which his mother appears as a virtual household slave. Some recurrent issues in his plays—including females as victims or as robotic extensions of the husband's will, and masculine figures as dark, tyrannical, and threatening—have led critics to credit his childhood experiences with having colored the main lines of his drama.

From the first performance of *The Bald Soprano,* soon linked with *The Lesson* (1951), Ionesco was considered a leader in a new wave of postwar drama. The first performance of *The Bald Soprano* entertained an audience of three, but all three were influential literary people in Paris, and the resultant word-of-mouth praise soon brought more people into the theater. In a short time Ionesco was associated with the absurdist writers, and his plays were thought to be the beginning of absurdist drama. He was linked repeatedly with Samuel Beckett.

Ionesco was more comfortable with the term *anti-play,* which is what he applied to *The Bald Soprano.* His theory was that realistic theater was dead, or certainly backward-looking. As an experimenter in avant-garde drama, Ionesco created fantasies that avoided realistic imitation and instead used symbol and language to convey a deeper level of meaning. He was not interested in the contemporary realistic drama or in the light entertainment of his day. He was also uninterested in the experiments of directors who tried to shock audiences. Instead, he intended the language in his plays to produce insight.

The ultimate success of *The Bald Soprano* and *The Lesson* has been remarkable. They established Ionesco as a powerful force in absurdist drama, along with Samuel Beckett. In his next play, *The Chairs* (1952), Old Woman and Old Man hire an Orator to deliver their message to the world. Instead of an audience, they draw only a collection of empty chairs. After they throw themselves out a window, calling, "Long live the Emperor!" the Orator steps forward to reveal that he can speak only gibberish. As an absurdist play, *The Chairs* remains a classic.

Among Ionesco's other important plays are *Rhinoceros* (1959), *Exit the King* (1962), *Killing Game* (1970), and *Macbett* (1972). His later plays seem to move away from the stark experimentation of the early drama, a disappointment to some of his fans. However, audiences have disagreed. *Rhinoceros,* about people who mutate into animals, is one of his best-received plays among general theatergoers. In the last twenty years of his life, Ionesco wrote several prose works and concentrated on painting and lithography.

THE BALD SOPRANO

Ionesco's first produced play, or "anti-play," was inspired by his efforts to learn English from a French primer. He realized that the phrases used to illustrate the use of the English language were filled with simple but important insights that, fractured though they were in the exercises he studied, contained their own logic. But when he wrote *The Bald Soprano,* Ionesco was not so much interested in the logic implied in specific phrases as in the way language communicated or failed to communicate ideas. His experimentation in this play involves language, both as it seems to make sense and as it totally breaks down into gibberish. As a dramatic experiment, the play is determinedly nonrepresentational and stubbornly non-Aristotelian. The audience is not asked to become emotionally involved in the lives of the Smiths and the Martins. Nor is the audience led to assume that the action on stage represents real life. Instead, the audience's experience is that of seeing a play about how language and logic work, while always knowing that they are seeing a play.

The Bald Soprano is the opposite of the well-made bourgeois play designed to delight the bourgeois audience. Yet the characters, the Smiths and the Martins, are absolute stereotypes of the English bourgeoisie. The set for the play usually relies on middle-class wallpaper designs, appropriate overstuffed chairs or sofas, and chintzy decorations. The irony of the contrast between the set, the characters, and the language is part of the play's strength. And even though Ionesco has said that the play has no psychology (meaning that the characters are not developed), the Smiths and the Martins, who seem to have no clear function in life other than to attend each other's dinners, are distinct from the maid Marie and the Fire Chief, who both have jobs and functions in society that distinguish them from the bourgeoisie. Thus when they meet, they recognize each other through their useful purposes in life.

Marie at one point calls herself Sherlock Holmes, the famous fictional detective who solved cases by a process of deduction, examining evidence and events until an inevitable conclusion emerged. The Martins, when they arrive at the Smiths', perform an act of deduction when they look at one another and try to figure out how they know each other. They begin by retracing their steps, one by one, as they traveled to the Smiths' home. At each instance of discovering they have both had the same experience, they marvel, until, finally, they identify themselves as sharing the same bed and having a child with one white eye and one red eye. They then realize who they are. However, Marie points out that they are wrong. The red and white eyes are actually reversed left from right from what the Martins say they are, and thus the extensive deductive process they just developed proves inconclusive. In other words, there is no guarantee that logic will reveal the truth, and the failure of logic is demonstrated over and over again throughout the play.

Ionesco experiments here with absurdism. Logic fails, language is slippery and undependable, and even the daily signs we rely on — the bells of the clocks and the bell of the door — are unreliable. The play breaks all the normal rules of drama and even of daily life. The very title, The Bald Soprano, seems absurd in view of the fact that there is no bald soprano in the play and the expression is used just once by the Fire Chief as a throwaway line.

The Bald Soprano in Performance

The first performance was given in 1951 in a small theater in Paris and directed by Nicolas Bataille. In February 1957, Bataille moved the production to the Theatre de la Huchette, where it has played with many of the same cast ever since, making it the longest-running play in the world! It has usually been performed with Ionesco's The Lesson, which may make a similar claim to longevity. Again and again, audiences seem to find these plays resonant with their own time. The Theatre de la Huchette has used the same set for all these years. In 1987 the Cubiculo Theater in New York produced the play, with John Turturro as Mr. Smith, to excellent reviews. Joseph Chaikin, a major figure in American drama, directed. Christopher Isherwood praised the Atlantic Theater Company's 2004 production in New York, in part by relating the language of the play to the upcoming elections, which he described as "always a joy for students of the uses and abuses of language." In a well-received production at the Shakespeare Theater of New Jersey in August 2007, the living room was placed in designer Mimi Lien's giant wooden packing case. In his review, Robert Daniels said, "One need only observe the picture frames on the wall that echo the chintzy flowery print of the wallpaper to be coaxed into the insanity that follows."

THE BALD SOPRANO

1950

TRANSLATED BY DONALD M. ALLEN

ANTI-PLAY

The Characters

MR. SMITH
MRS. SMITH
MR. MARTIN
MRS. MARTIN
MARY, *the maid*
THE FIRE CHIEF

Scene: *A middle-class English interior, with English armchairs. An English evening. Mr. Smith, an Englishman, seated in his English armchair and wearing English slippers, is smoking his English pipe and reading an English newspaper, near an English fire. He is wearing English spectacles and a small gray English mustache. Beside him, in another English armchair, Mrs. Smith, an Englishwoman, is darning some English socks. A long moment of English silence. The English clock strikes 17 English strokes.*

MRS. SMITH: There, it's nine o'clock. We've drunk the soup, and eaten the fish and chips, and the English salad. The children have drunk English water. We've eaten well this evening. That's because we live in the suburbs of London and because our name is Smith.

MR. SMITH [*continues to read, clicks his tongue.*]

MRS. SMITH: Potatoes are very good fried in fat; the salad oil was not rancid. The oil from the grocer at the corner is better quality than the oil from the grocer across the street. It is even better than the oil from the grocer at the bottom of the street. However, I prefer not to tell them that their oil is bad.

MR. SMITH [*continues to read, clicks his tongue.*]

MRS. SMITH: However, the oil from the grocer at the corner is still the best.

MR. SMITH [*continues to read, clicks his tongue.*]

MRS. SMITH: Mary did the potatoes very well, this evening. The last time she did not do them well. I do not like them when they are well done.

MR. SMITH [*continues to read, clicks his tongue.*]

MRS. SMITH: The fish was fresh. It made my mouth water. I had two helpings. No, three helpings. That made me go to the w.c. You also had three helpings. However, the third time you took less than the first two times, while as for me, I took a great deal more. I eat better than you this evening. Why is that? Usually, it is you who eats more. It is not appetite you lack.

MR. SMITH [*clicks his tongue.*]

MRS. SMITH: But still, the soup was perhaps a little too salt. It was saltier than you. Ha, ha, ha. It also had too many leeks and not enough onions. I regret I didn't advise Mary to add some aniseed stars. The next time I'll know better.

MR. SMITH [*continues to read, clicks his tongue.*]

MRS. SMITH: Our little boy wanted to drink some beer; he's going to love getting tiddly. He's like you. At table did you notice how he stared at the bottle? But I poured some water from the jug into his glass. He was thirsty and he drank it. Helen is like me: she's a good manager, thrifty, plays the piano. She never asks to drink English beer. She's like our little daughter who drinks only milk and eats only porridge. It's obvious that she's only two. She's named Peggy. The quince and bean pie was marvelous. It would have been nice, perhaps, to have had a small glass of Australian Burgundy with the sweet, but I did not bring the bottle to the table because I did not wish to set the children a bad example of gluttony. They must learn to be sober and temperate.

MR. SMITH [*continues to read, clicks his tongue.*]

MRS. SMITH: Mrs. Parker knows a Rumanian grocer by the name of Popesco Rosenfeld, who has just come from Constantinople.° He is a great specialist in yogurt. He has a diploma from the school of yogurt-making in Adrianople.° Tomorrow I shall buy a large pot of native Rumanian yogurt from him. One doesn't often find such things here in the suburbs of London.

MR. SMITH [*continues to read, clicks his tongue.*]

MRS. SMITH: Yogurt is excellent for the stomach, the kidneys, the appendicitis, and apotheosis. It was Doctor Mackenzie-King who told me that, he's the one who takes care of the children of our neighbors, the Johns. He's a good doctor. One can trust him. He never prescribes any medicine that he's not tried out on himself first. Before operating on Parker, he had his own liver operated on first, although he was not the least bit ill.

MR. SMITH: But how does it happen that the doctor pulled through while Parker died?

Constantinople: Major city in Turkey that was once the capital of the Roman empire.   **Adrianople:** City in Turkey named after the Emperor Hadrian. It was renamed Edirne in 1918.

MRS. SMITH: Because the operation was successful in the doctor's case and it was not in Parker's.

MR. SMITH: Then Mackenzie is not a good doctor. The operation should have succeeded with both of them or else both should have died.

MRS. SMITH: Why?

MR. SMITH: A conscientious doctor must die with his patient if they can't get well together. The captain of a ship goes down with his ship into the briny deep, he does not survive alone.

MRS. SMITH: One cannot compare a patient with a ship.

MR. SMITH: Why not? A ship has its diseases too; moreover, your doctor is as hale as a ship; that's why he should have perished at the same time as his patient, like the captain and his ship.

MRS. SMITH: Ah! I hadn't thought of that . . . Perhaps it is true . . . And then, what conclusion do you draw from this?

MR. SMITH: All doctors are quacks. And all patients too. Only the Royal Navy is honest in England.

MRS. SMITH: But not sailors.

MR. SMITH: Naturally [*A pause. Still reading his paper:*] Here's a thing I don't understand. In the newspaper they always give the age of deceased persons but never the age of the newly born. That doesn't make sense.

MRS. SMITH: I never thought of that!

[*Another moment of silence. The clock strikes seven times. Silence. The clock strikes three times. Silence. The clock doesn't strike.*]

MR. SMITH [*still reading his paper*]: Tsk, it says here that Bobby Watson died.

MRS. SMITH: My God, the poor man! When did he die?

MR. SMITH: Why do you pretend to be astonished? You know very well that he's been dead these past two years. Surely you remember that we attended his funeral a year and a half ago.

MRS. SMITH: Oh yes, of course I do remember. I remembered it right away, but I don't understand why you yourself were so surprised to see it in the paper.

MR. SMITH: It wasn't in the paper. It's been three years since his death was announced. I remembered it through an association of ideas.

MRS. SMITH: What a pity! He was so well preserved.

MR. SMITH: He was the handsomest corpse in Great Britain. He didn't look his age. Poor Bobby, he'd been dead for four years and he was still warm. A veritable living corpse. And how cheerful he was!

MRS. SMITH: Poor Bobby.

MR. SMITH: Which poor Bobby do you mean?

MRS. SMITH: It is his wife that I mean. She is called Bobby too, Bobby Watson. Since they both had the same name, you could never tell one from the other when you saw them together. It was only after his death that you could really tell which was which. And there are still people today who confuse her with the deceased and offer their condolences to him. Do you know her?

MR. SMITH: I only met her once, by chance, at Bobby's burial.

MRS. SMITH: I've never seen her. Is she pretty?

MR. SMITH: She has regular features and yet one cannot say that she is pretty. She is too big and stout. Her features are not regular but still one can say that she is very pretty. She is a little too small and too thin. She's a voice teacher.

[*The clock strikes five times. A long silence.*]

MRS. SMITH: And when do they plan to be married, those two?

MR. SMITH: Next spring, at the latest.

MRS. SMITH: We shall have to go to their wedding, I suppose.

MR. SMITH: We shall have to give them a wedding present. I wonder what?

MRS. SMITH: Why don't we give them one of the seven silver salvers° that were given us for our wedding and which have never been of any use to us? [*Silence.*]

MRS. SMITH: How sad for her to be left a widow so young.

MR. SMITH: Fortunately, they had no children.

MRS. SMITH: That was all they needed! Children! Poor woman, how could she have managed!

MR. SMITH: She's still young. She might very well remarry. She looks so well in mourning.

MRS. SMITH: But who would take care of the children? You know very well that they have a boy and a girl. What are their names?

MR. SMITH: Bobby and Bobby like their parents. Bobby Watson's uncle, old Bobby Watson, is a rich man and very fond of the boy. He might very well pay for Bobby's education.

MRS. SMITH: That would be proper. And Bobby Watson's aunt, old Bobby Watson, might very well, in her turn, pay for the education of Bobby Watson, Bobby Watson's daughter. That way Bobby, Bobby Watson's mother, could remarry. Has she anyone in mind?

MR. SMITH: Yes, a cousin of Bobby Watson's.

MRS. SMITH: Who? Bobby Watson?

MR. SMITH: Which Bobby Watson do you mean?

MRS. SMITH: Why, Bobby Watson, the son of old Bobby Watson, the late Bobby Watson's other uncle.

MR. SMITH: No, it's not that one, it's someone else. It's Bobby Watson, the son of old Bobby Watson, the late Bobby Watson's aunt.

MRS. SMITH: Are you referring to Bobby Watson the commercial traveler?

MR. SMITH: All the Bobby Watsons are commercial travelers.

MRS. SMITH: What a difficult trade! However, they do well at it.

MR. SMITH: Yes, when there's no competition.

MRS. SMITH: And when is there no competition?

MR. SMITH: On Tuesdays, Thursdays, and Tuesdays.

Salvers: Silver trays to carry calling cards or drinks.

MRS. SMITH: Ah! Three days a week? And what does Bobby Watson do on those days?

MR. SMITH: He rests, he sleeps.

MRS. SMITH: But why doesn't he work those three days if there's no competition?

MR. SMITH: I don't know everything. I can't answer all your idiotic questions!

MRS. SMITH: [offended]: Oh! Are you trying to humiliate me?

MR. SMITH [all smiles]: You know very well that I'm not.

MRS. SMITH: Men are all alike! You sit there all day long, a cigarette in your mouth, or you powder your nose and rouge your lips, fifty times a day, or else you drink like a fish.

MR. SMITH: But what would you say if you saw men acting like women do, smoking all day long, powdering, rouging their lips, drinking whisky?

MRS. SMITH: It's nothing to me! But if you're only saying that to annoy me . . . I don't care for that kind of joking, you know that very well!

[She hurls the socks across the stage and shows her teeth. She gets up.]

MR. SMITH [also getting up and going towards his wife, tenderly]: Oh, my little ducky daddles, what a little spitfire you are! You know that I only said it as a joke! [He takes her by the waist and kisses her.] What a ridiculous pair of old lovers we are! Come, let's put out the lights and go bye-byes.

MARY [entering]: I'm the maid. I have spent a very pleasant afternoon. I've been to the cinema with a man and I've seen a film with some women. After the cinema, we went to drink some brandy and milk and then read the newspaper.

MRS. SMITH: I hope that you've spent a pleasant afternoon, that you went to the cinema with a man and that you drank some brandy and milk.

MR. SMITH: And the newspaper.

MARY: Mr. and Mrs. Martin, your guests, are at the door. They were waiting for me. They didn't dare come in by themselves. They were supposed to have dinner with you this evening.

MRS. SMITH: Oh, yes. We were expecting them. And we were hungry. Since they didn't put in an appearance, we were going to start dinner without them. We've had nothing to eat all day. You should not have gone out!

MARY: But it was you who gave me permission.

MR. SMITH: We didn't do it on purpose.

MARY [bursts into laughter, then she bursts into tears. Then she smiles]: I bought me a chamber pot.

MRS. SMITH: My dear Mary, please open the door and ask Mr. and Mrs. Martin to step in. We will change quickly. [Mr. and Mrs. Smith exit right. Mary opens the door at the left by which Mr. and Mrs. Martin enter.]

MARY: Why have you come so late! You are not very polite. People should be punctual. Do you understand? But sit down there, anyway, and wait now that you're here.

[She exits. Mr. and Mrs. Martin sit facing each other, without speaking. They smile timidly at each other. The dialogue which follows must be spoken in voices that are drawling, monotonous, a little singsong, without nuances.]

MR. MARTIN: Excuse me, madam, but it seems to me, unless I'm mistaken, that I've met you somewhere before.

MRS. MARTIN: I, too, sir. It seems to me that I've met you somewhere before.

MR. MARTIN: Was it, by any chance, at Manchester that I caught a glimpse of you, madam?

MRS. MARTIN: That is very possible. I am originally from the city of Manchester. But I do not have a good memory, sir. I cannot say whether it was there that I caught a glimpse of you or not!

MR. MARTIN: Good God, that's curious! I, too, am originally from the city of Manchester, madam!

MRS. MARTIN: That is curious!

MR. MARTIN: Isn't that curious! Only, I, madam, I left the city of Manchester about five weeks ago.

MRS. MARTIN: That is curious! What a bizarre coincidence! I, too, sir, I left the city of Manchester about five weeks ago.

MR. MARTIN: Madam, I took the 8:30 morning train which arrives in London at 4:45.

MRS. MARTIN: That is curious! How very bizarre! And what a coincidence! I took the same train, sir, I too.

MR. MARTIN: Good Lord, how curious! Perhaps then, madam, it was on the train that I saw you?

MRS. MARTIN: It is indeed possible; that is, not unlikely. It is plausible and, after all, why not!—But I don't recall it, sir!

MR. MARTIN: I traveled second class, madam. There is no second class in England, but I always travel second class.

MRS. MARTIN: That is curious! How very bizarre! And what a coincidence! I, too, sir, I traveled second class.

MR. MARTIN: How curious that is! Perhaps we did meet in second class, my dear lady!

MRS. MARTIN: That is certainly possible, and it is not at all unlikely. But I do not remember very well, my dear sir!

MR. MARTIN: My seat was in coach No. 8, compartment 6, my dear lady.

MRS. MARTIN: How curious that is! My seat was also in coach No. 8, compartment 6, my dear sir!

MR. MARTIN: How curious that is and what a bizarre coincidence! Perhaps we met in compartment 6, my dear lady?

MRS. MARTIN: It is indeed possible, after all! But I do not recall it, my dear sir!

MR. MARTIN: To tell the truth, my dear lady, I do not remember it either, but it is possible that we caught a glimpse of each other there, and as I think of it, it seems to me even very likely.

MRS. MARTIN: Oh! truly, of course, truly, sir!

MR. MARTIN: How curious it is! I had seat No. 3, next to the window, my dear lady.

MRS. MARTIN: Oh, good Lord, how curious and bizarre! I had seat No. 6, next to the window, across from you, my dear sir.

MR. MARTIN: Good God, how curious that is and what a coincidence! We were then seated facing each other, my dear lady! It is there that we must have seen each other!

MRS. MARTIN: How curious it is! It is possible, but I do not recall it, sir!

MR. MARTIN: To tell the truth, my dear lady, I do not remember it either. However, it is very possible that we saw each other on that occasion.

MRS. MARTIN: It is true, but I am not at all sure of it, sir.

MR. MARTIN: Dear madam, were you not the lady who asked me to place her suitcase in the luggage rack and who thanked me and gave me permission to smoke?

MRS. MARTIN: But of course, that must have been I, sir. How curious it is, how curious it is, and what a coincidence!

MR. MARTIN: How curious it is, how bizarre, what a coincidence! And well, well, it was perhaps at that moment that we came to know each other, madam?

MRS. MARTIN: How curious it is and what a coincidence! It is indeed possible, my dear sir! However, I do not believe that I recall it.

MR. MARTIN: Nor do I, madam. [A moment of silence. The clock strikes twice, then once.] Since coming to London, I have resided in Bromfield Street, my dear lady.

MRS. MARTIN: How curious that is, how bizarre! I, too, since coming to London, I have resided in Bromfield Street, my dear sir.

MR. MARTIN: How curious that is, well then, well then, perhaps we have seen each other in Bromfield Street, my dear lady.

MRS. MARTIN: How curious that is, how bizarre! It is indeed possible, after all! But I do not recall it, my dear sir.

MR. MARTIN: I reside at No. 19, my dear lady.

MRS. MARTIN: How curious that is. I also reside at No. 19, my dear sir.

MR. MARTIN: Well then, well then, well then, well then, perhaps we have seen each other in that house, dear lady.

MRS. MARTIN: It is indeed possible but I do not recall it, dear sir.

MR. MARTIN: My flat is on the fifth floor, No. 8, my dear lady.

MRS. MARTIN: How curious it is, good Lord, how bizarre! And what a coincidence! I too reside on the fifth floor, in flat No. 8, dear sir!

MR. MARTIN [musing]: How curious it is, how curious it is, how curious it is, and what a coincidence! You know, in my bedroom there is a bed, and it is covered with a green eiderdown. This room, with the bed and the green eiderdown, is at the end of the corridor between the w.c. and the bookcase, dear lady!

MRS. MARTIN: What a coincidence, good Lord, what a coincidence! My bedroom, too, has a bed with a green eiderdown and is at the end of the corridor, between the w.c., dear sir, and the bookcase!

MR. MARTIN: How bizarre, curious, strange! Then, madam, we live in the same room and we sleep in the same bed, dear lady. It is perhaps there that we have met!

MRS. MARTIN: How curious it is and what a coincidence! It is indeed possible that we have met there, and perhaps even last night. But I do not recall it, dear sir!

MR. MARTIN: I have a little girl, my little daughter, she lives with me, dear lady. She is two years old, she's blonde, she has a white eye and a red eye, she is very pretty, her name is Alice, dear lady.

MRS. MARTIN: What a bizarre coincidence! I, too, have a little girl. She is two years old, has a white eye and a red eye, she is very pretty, and her name is Alice, too, dear sir!

MR. MARTIN [in the same drawling, monotonous voice]: How curious it is and what a coincidence! And bizarre! Perhaps they are the same, dear lady!

MRS. MARTIN: How curious it is! It is indeed possible, dear sir. [A rather long moment of silence. The clock strikes 29 times.]

MR. MARTIN [after having reflected at length, gets up slowly and, unhurriedly, moves toward Mrs. Martin, who, surprised by his solemn air, has also gotten up very quietly. Mr. Martin, in the same flat, monotonous voice, slightly singsong]: Then, dear lady, I believe that there can be no doubt about it, we have seen each other before and you are my own wife . . . Elizabeth, I have found you again!

[Mrs. Martin approaches Mr. Martin without haste. They embrace without expression. The clock strikes once, very loud. This striking of the clock must be so loud that it makes the audience jump. The Martins do not hear it.]

MRS. MARTIN: Donald, it's you, darling!

[They sit together in the same armchair, their arms around each other, and fall asleep. The clock strikes several more times. Mary, on tiptoe, a finger to her lips, enters quietly and addresses the audience.]

MARY: Elizabeth and Donald are now too happy to be able to hear me. I can therefore let you in on a secret. Elizabeth is not Elizabeth, Donald is not Donald. And here is the proof: the child that Donald spoke of is not Elizabeth's daughter, they are not the same person. Donald's daughter has one white eye and one red eye like Elizabeth's daughter. Whereas Donald's child has a white right eye and a red left eye, Elizabeth's child has a red right eye and a white left eye! Thus all of Donald's system of deduction collapses when it comes up against this last obstacle which destroys his whole theory. In spite of the extraordinary coincidences which seem to be definitive proofs, Donald and Elizabeth, not being the parents of the same child, are not Donald and Elizabeth. It is in vain that he thinks he is Donald, it is in vain that she thinks she is Elizabeth. He believes in vain that she is Elizabeth. She believes in vain that he is Donald— they are sadly deceived. But who is the true Donald? Who is the true Elizabeth? Who has any interest in prolonging this confusion? I don't know. Let's not try to know. Let's leave things as they are. [*She takes several steps toward the door, then returns and says to the audience*:] My real name is Sherlock Holmes. [*She exits.*]

[*The clock strikes as much as it likes. After several seconds, Mr. and Mrs. Martin separate and take the chairs they had at the beginning.*]

MR. MARTIN: Darling, let's forget all that has not passed between us, and, now that we have found each other again, let's try not to lose each other any more, and live as before.

MRS. MARTIN: Yes, darling.

[*Mr. and Mrs. Smith enter from the right, wearing the same clothes.*]

MRS. SMITH: Good evening, dear friends! Please forgive us for having made you wait so long. We thought that we should extend you the courtesy to which you are entitled and as soon as we learned that you had been kind enough to give us the pleasure of coming to see us without prior notice we hurried to dress for the occasion.

MR. SMITH [*furious*]: We've had nothing to eat all day. And we've been waiting four whole hours for you. Why have you come so late?

[*Mr. and Mrs. Smith sit facing their guests. The striking of the clock underlines the speeches, more or less strongly, according to the case. The Martins, particularly Mrs. Martin, seem embarrassed and timid. For this reason the conversation begins with difficulty and the words are uttered, at the beginning, awkwardly. A long embarrassed silence at first, then other silences and hesitations follow.*]

MR. SMITH: Hm. [*Silence.*]
MRS. SMITH: Hm, hm. [*Silence.*]
MRS. MARTIN: Hm, hm, hm. [*Silence.*]
MR. MARTIN: Hm, hm, hm, hm. [*Silence.*]
MRS. MARTIN: Oh, but definitely. [*Silence.*]
MR. MARTIN: We all have colds. [*Silence.*]
MR. SMITH: Nevertheless, it's not chilly. [*Silence.*]
MRS. SMITH: There's no draft. [*Silence.*]
MR. MARTIN: Oh no, fortunately. [*Silence.*]
MR. SMITH: Oh dear, oh dear, oh dear. [*Silence.*]
MR. MARTIN: Don't you feel well? [*Silence.*]
MRS. SMITH: No, he's wet his pants. [*Silence.*]
MRS. MARTIN: Oh, sir, at your age, you shouldn't. [*Silence.*]

Scene from the Cubiculo Theater's 1987 production of *The Bald Soprano*, starring John Turturro as Mr. Smith.

MR. SMITH: The heart is ageless. [*Silence.*]
MR. MARTIN: That's true. [*Silence.*]
MRS. SMITH: So they say. [*Silence.*]
MRS. MARTIN: They also say the opposite. [*Silence.*]
MR. SMITH: The truth lies somewhere between the two. [*Silence.*]
MR. MARTIN: That's true. [*Silence.*]
MRS. SMITH [*to the Martins*]: Since you travel so much, you must have many interesting things to tell us.
MR. MARTIN [*to his wife*]: My dear, tell us what you've seen today.
MRS. MARTIN: It's scarcely worth the trouble, for no one would believe me.
MR. SMITH: We're not going to question your sincerity!
MRS. SMITH: You will offend us if you think that.

RIGHT: John
Turturro as
Mr. Smith in the
Cubiculo Theater
production, 1987.

The Shakespeare Theater of New Jersey's August 2007 performance of *The Bald Soprano*, starring Kelly McAndrew and Mathew Floyd Miller, and featuring set designer Mimi Lien's wooden packing case (LEFT), which contained the living room (ABOVE). (Photo by Andrew Murad.)

MR. MARTIN [*to his wife*]: You will offend them, my dear, if you think that . . .

MRS. MARTIN [*graciously*]: Oh well, today I witnessed something extraordinary. Something really incredible.

MR. MARTIN: Tell us quickly, my dear.

MR. SMITH: Oh, this is going to be amusing.

MRS. SMITH: At last.

MRS. MARTIN: Well, today, when I went shopping to buy some vegetables, which are getting to be dearer and dearer . . .

MRS. SMITH: Where is it all going to end!

MR. SMITH: You shouldn't interrupt, my dear, it's very rude.

MRS. MARTIN: In the street, near a café, I saw a man, properly dressed, about fifty years old, or not even that, who . . .

MR. SMITH: Who, what?

MRS. SMITH: Who, what?

MR. SMITH [*to his wife*]: Don't interrupt, my dear, you're disgusting.

MRS. SMITH: My dear, it is you who interrupted first, you boor.

MR. SMITH [*to his wife*]: Hush. [*To Mrs. Martin:*] What was this man doing?

MRS. MARTIN: Well, I'm sure you'll say that I'm making it up—he was down on one knee and he was bent over.

MR. MARTIN, MR. SMITH, MRS. SMITH: Oh!

MRS. MARTIN: Yes, bent over.

MR. SMITH: Not possible.

MRS. MARTIN: Yes, bent over. I went near him to see what he was doing . . .

MR. SMITH: And?

MRS. MARTIN: He was tying his shoe lace which had come undone.

MR. MARTIN, MR. SMITH, MRS. SMITH: Fantastic!

MR. SMITH: If someone else had told me this, I'd not believe it.

MR. MARTIN: Why not? One sees things even more extraordinary every day, when one walks around. For instance, today in the Underground I myself saw a man, quietly sitting on a seat, reading his newspaper.

MRS. SMITH: What a character!

MR. SMITH: Perhaps it was the same man!

[*The doorbell rings.*]

MR. SMITH: Goodness, someone is ringing.

MRS. SMITH: There must be somebody there. I'll go and see. [*She goes to see, she opens the door and closes it, and comes back.*] Nobody. [*She sits down again.*]

MR. MARTIN: I'm going to give you another example . . .

[*Doorbell rings again.*]

MR. SMITH: Goodness, someone is ringing.

MRS. SMITH: There must be somebody there. I'll go and see. [*She goes to see, opens the door, and comes back.*] No one. [*She sits down again.*]

MR. MARTIN [*who has forgotten where he was*]: Uh . . .

MRS. MARTIN: You were saying that you were going to give us another example.

MR. MARTIN: Oh, yes . . .

[*Doorbell rings again.*]

MR. SMITH: Goodness, someone is ringing.

MRS. SMITH: I'm not going to open the door again.

MR. SMITH: Yes, but there must be someone there!

MRS. SMITH: The first time there was no one. The second time, no one. Why do you think that there is someone there now?

MR. SMITH: Because someone has rung!

MRS. MARTIN: That's no reason.

MR. MARTIN: What? When one hears the doorbell ring, that means someone is at the door ringing to have the door opened.

MRS. MARTIN: Not always. You've just seen otherwise!

MR. MARTIN: In most cases, yes.

MR. SMITH: As for me, when I go to visit someone, I ring in order to be admitted. I think that everyone does the same thing and that each time there is a ring there must be someone there.

MRS. SMITH: That is true in theory. But in reality things happen differently. You have just seen otherwise.

MRS. MARTIN: Your wife is right.

MR. MARTIN: Oh! You women! You always stand up for each other.

MRS. SMITH: Well, I'll go and see. You can't say that I am obstinate, but you will see that there's no one there! [*She goes to look, opens the door and closes it.*] You see, there's no one there. [*She returns to her seat.*]

MRS. SMITH: Oh, these men who always think they're right and who're always wrong!

[*The doorbell rings again.*]

MR. SMITH: Goodness, someone is ringing. There must be someone there.

MRS. SMITH [*in a fit of anger*]: Don't send me to open the door again. You've seen that it was useless. Experience teaches us that when one hears the doorbell ring it is because there is never anyone there.

MRS. MARTIN: Never.

MR. MARTIN: That's not entirely accurate.

MR. SMITH: In fact it's false. When one hears the doorbell ring it is because there is someone there.

MRS. SMITH: He won't admit he's wrong.

MRS. MARTIN: My husband is very obstinate, too.

MR. SMITH: There's someone there.

MR. MARTIN: That's not impossible.

MRS. SMITH [*to her husband*]: No.

MR. SMITH: Yes.

MRS. SMITH: I tell you *no*. In any case you are not going to disturb me again for nothing. If you wish to know, go and look yourself!

MR. SMITH: I'll go.

[*Mrs. Smith shrugs her shoulders. Mrs. Martin tosses her head.*]

MR. SMITH [*opening the door*]: Oh! how do you do. [*He glances at Mrs. Smith and the Martins, who are all surprised.*] It's the Fire Chief!

FIRE CHIEF [*he is of course in uniform and is wearing an enormous shining helmet*]: Good evening, ladies and gentlemen. [*The Smiths and the Martins are still slightly astonished. Mrs. Smith turns her head away, in a temper, and does not reply to his greeting.*] Good evening, Mrs. Smith. You appear to be angry.

MRS. SMITH: Oh!

MR. SMITH: You see it's because my wife is a little chagrined at having been proved wrong.

MR. MARTIN: There's been an argument between Mr. and Mrs. Smith, Mr. Fire Chief.

MRS. SMITH [*to Mr. Martin*]: This is no business of yours! [*To Mr. Smith:*] I beg you not to involve outsiders in our family arguments.

MR. SMITH: Oh, my dear, this is not so serious. The Fire Chief is an old friend of the family. His mother courted me, and I knew his father. He asked me to give him my daughter in marriage if ever I had one. And he died waiting.

MR. MARTIN: That's neither his fault, nor yours.

FIRE CHIEF: Well, what is it all about?

MRS. SMITH: My husband was claiming . . .

MR. SMITH: No, it was you who was claiming.

MR. MARTIN: Yes, it was she.

MRS. MARTIN: No, it was he.

FIRE CHIEF: Don't get excited. You tell me, Mrs. Smith.

MRS. SMITH: Well, this is how it was. It is difficult for me to speak openly to you, but a fireman is also a confessor.

FIRE CHIEF: Well then?

MRS. SMITH: We were arguing because my husband said that each time the doorbell rings there is always someone there.

MR. MARTIN: It is plausible.

MRS. SMITH: And I was saying that each time the doorbell rings there is never anyone there.

MR. MARTIN: It might seem strange.

MRS. SMITH: But it has been proved, not by theoretical demonstrations, but by facts.

MR. SMITH: That's false, since the Fire Chief is here. He rang the bell, I opened the door, and there he was.

MRS. MARTIN: When?

MR. MARTIN: But just now.

MRS. SMITH: Yes, but it was only when you heard the doorbell ring the fourth time that there was someone there. And the fourth time does not count.

MRS. MARTIN: Never. It is only the first three times that count.

MR. SMITH: Mr. Fire Chief, permit me in my turn to ask you several questions.

FIRE CHIEF: Go right ahead.

MR. SMITH: When I opened the door and saw you, it was really you who had rung the bell?

FIRE CHIEF: Yes, it was I.

MR. MARTIN: You were at the door? And you rang in order to be admitted?

FIRE CHIEF: I do not deny it.

MR. SMITH [*to his wife, triumphantly*]: You see? I was right. When you hear the doorbell ring, that means someone rang it. You certainly cannot say that the Fire Chief is not someone.

MRS. SMITH: Certainly not. I repeat to you that I was speaking of only the first three times, since the fourth time does not count.

MRS. MARTIN: And when the doorbell rang the first time, was it you?

FIRE CHIEF: No, it was not I.

MRS. MARTIN: You see? The doorbell rang and there was no one there.

MR. MARTIN: Perhaps it was someone else?

MR. SMITH: Were you standing at the door for a long time?

FIRE CHIEF: Three-quarters of an hour.

MR. SMITH: And you saw no one?

FIRE CHIEF: No one. I am sure of that.

MRS. MARTIN: And did you hear the bell when it rang the second time?

FIRE CHIEF: Yes, and that wasn't I either. And there was still no one there.

MRS. SMITH: Victory! I was right.

MR. SMITH [*to his wife*]: Not so fast. [*To the Fire Chief:*] And what were you doing at the door?

FIRE CHIEF: Nothing. I was just standing there. I was thinking of many things.

MR. MARTIN [*to the Fire Chief*]: But the third time—it was not you who rang?

FIRE CHIEF: Yes, it was I.

MR. SMITH: But when the door was opened nobody was in sight.

FIRE CHIEF: That was because I had hidden myself—as a joke.

MRS. SMITH: Don't make jokes, Mr. Fire Chief. This business is too sad.

MR. MARTIN: In short, we still do not know whether, when the doorbell rings, there is someone there or not!

MRS. SMITH: Never anyone.

MR. SMITH: Always someone.

FIRE CHIEF: I am going to reconcile you. You both are partly right. When the doorbell rings, sometimes there is someone, other times there is no one.

MR. MARTIN: This seems logical to me.

MRS. MARTIN: I think so too.

FIRE CHIEF: Life is very simple, really. [*To the Smiths:*] Go on and kiss each other.

MRS. SMITH: We just kissed each other a little while ago.

MR. MARTIN: They'll kiss each other tomorrow. They have plenty of time.

MRS. SMITH: Mr. Fire Chief, since you have helped us settle this, please make yourself comfortable, take off your helmet and sit down for a moment.

FIRE CHIEF: Excuse me, but I can't stay long. I should like to remove my helmet, but I haven't time to sit down. [*He sits down, without removing his helmet.*] I must admit that I have come to see you for another reason. I am on official business.

MRS. SMITH: And what can we do for you, Mr. Fire Chief?

FIRE CHIEF: I must beg you to excuse my indiscretion [*terribly embarrassed*] . . . uhm [*He points a finger at the Martins*] . . . you don't mind . . . in front of them . . .

MRS. MARTIN: Say whatever you like.

MR. MARTIN: We're old friends. They tell us everything.

MR. SMITH: Speak.

FIRE CHIEF: Eh, well—is there a fire here?

MRS. SMITH: Why do you ask us that?

FIRE CHIEF: It's because—pardon me—I have orders to extinguish all the fires in the city.

MRS. MARTIN: All?

FIRE CHIEF: Yes, all.

MRS. SMITH [*confused*]: I don't know . . . I don't think so. Do you want me to go and look?

MR. SMITH [*sniffing*]: There can't be one here. There's no smell of anything burning.

FIRE CHIEF [*aggrieved*]: None at all? You don't have a little fire in the chimney, something burning in the attic or in the cellar? A little fire just starting, at least?

MRS. SMITH: I am sorry to disappoint you but I do not believe there's anything here at the moment. I promise that I will notify you when we do have something.

FIRE CHIEF: Please don't forget, it would be a great help.

MRS. SMITH: That's a promise.

FIRE CHIEF [*to the Martins*]: And there's nothing burning at your house either?

MRS. MARTIN: No, unfortunately.

MR. MARTIN [*to the Fire Chief*]: Things aren't going so well just now.

FIRE CHIEF: Very poorly. There's been almost nothing, a few trifles—a chimney, a barn. Nothing important. It doesn't bring in much. And since there are no returns, the profits on output are very meager.

MR. SMITH: Times are bad. That's true all over. It's the same this year with business and agriculture as it is with fires, nothing is prospering.

MR. MARTIN: No wheat, no fires.

FIRE CHIEF: No floods either.

MRS. SMITH: But there is some sugar.

MR. SMITH: That's because it is imported.

MRS. MARTIN: It's harder in the case of fires. The tariffs are too high!

FIRE CHIEF: All the same, there's an occasional asphyxiation by gas, but that's unusual too. For instance, a young woman asphyxiated herself last week—she had left the gas on.

MRS. MARTIN: Had she forgotten it?

FIRE CHIEF: No, but she thought it was her comb.

MR. SMITH: These confusions are always dangerous!

MRS. SMITH: Did you go to see the match dealer?

FIRE CHIEF: There's nothing doing there. He is insured against fires.

MR. MARTIN: Why don't you go see the Vicar of Wakefield, and use my name?

FIRE CHIEF: I don't have the right to extinguish clergymen's fires. The Bishop would get angry. Besides they extinguish their fires themselves, or else they have them put out by vestal virgins.

MR. SMITH: Go see the Durands.

FIRE CHIEF: I can't do that either. He's not English. He's only been naturalized. And naturalized citizens have the right to have houses, but not the right to have them put out if they're burning.

MRS. SMITH: Nevertheless, when they set fire to it last year, it was put out just the same.

FIRE CHIEF: He did that all by himself. Clandestinely. But it's not I who would report him.

MR. SMITH: Neither would I.

MRS. SMITH: Mr. Fire Chief, since you are not too pressed, stay a little while longer. You would be doing us a favor.

FIRE CHIEF: Shall I tell you some stories?

MRS. SMITH: Oh, by all means, how charming of you. [She kisses him.]

MR. SMITH, MRS. MARTIN, MR. MARTIN: Yes, yes, some stories, hurrah!

[They applaud.]

MR. SMITH: And what is even more interesting is the fact that firemen's stories are all true, and they're based on experience.

FIRE CHIEF: I speak from my own experience. Truth, nothing but the truth. No fiction.

MR. MARTIN: That's right. Truth is never found in books, only in life.

MRS. SMITH: Begin!

MR. MARTIN: Begin!

MRS. MARTIN: Be quiet, he is beginning.

FIRE CHIEF [coughs slightly several times]: Excuse me, don't look at me that way. You embarrass me. You know that I am shy.

MRS. SMITH: Isn't he charming! [She kisses him.]

FIRE CHIEF: I'm going to try to begin anyhow. But promise me that you won't listen.

MRS. MARTIN: But if we don't listen to you we won't hear you.

FIRE CHIEF: I didn't think of that!

MRS. SMITH: I told you, he's just a boy.

MR. MARTIN, MR. SMITH: Oh, the sweet child! [They kiss him.]

MRS. MARTIN: Chin up!

FIRE CHIEF: Well, then! [He coughs again in a voice shaken by emotion:] "The Dog and the Cow," an experimental fable. Once upon a time another cow asked another dog: "Why have you not swallowed your trunk?" "Pardon me," replied the dog, "it is because I thought that I was an elephant."

MRS. MARTIN: What is the moral?

FIRE CHIEF: That's for you to find out.

MR. SMITH: He's right.

MRS. SMITH [furious]: Tell us another.

FIRE CHIEF: A young calf had eaten too much ground glass. As a result, it was obliged to give birth. It brought forth a cow into the world. However, since the calf was male, the cow could not call him Mamma. Nor could she call him Papa, because the calf was too little. The calf was then obliged to get married and the registry office carried out all the details completely à la mode.

MR. SMITH: À la mode de Caen.

MR. MARTIN: Like tripes.

FIRE CHIEF: You've heard that one?

MRS. SMITH: It was in all the papers.

MRS. MARTIN: It happened not far from our house.

FIRE CHIEF: I'll tell you another: "The Cock." Once upon a time, a cock wished to play the dog. But he had no luck because everyone recognized him right away.

MRS. SMITH: On the other hand, the dog that wished to play the cock was never recognized.

MR. SMITH: I'll tell you one: "The Snake and the Fox." Once upon a time, a snake came up to a fox and said: "It seems to me that I know you!" The fox replied to him: "Me too." "Then," said the snake, "give me some money." "A fox doesn't give money," replied the tricky animal, who, in order to escape, jumped down into a deep ravine full of strawberries and chicken honey. But the snake was there waiting for him with a Mephistophelean° laugh. The fox pulled out his knife, shouting: "I'm going to teach you how to live!" Then he took to flight, turning his back. But he had no luck. The snake was quicker. With a well-chosen blow of his fist, he struck the fox in the middle of his forehead, which broke into a thousand pieces, while he cried: "No! No! Four times no! I'm not your daughter."

MRS. MARTIN: It's interesting.

MRS. SMITH: It's not bad.

MR. MARTIN [shaking Mr. Smith's hand]: My congratulations.

FIRE CHIEF [jealous]: Not so good. And anyway, I've heard it before.

MR. SMITH: It's terrible.

MRS. SMITH: But it wasn't even true.

MRS. MARTIN: Yes, unfortunately.

MR. MARTIN [to Mrs. Smith]: It's your turn, dear lady.

MRS. SMITH: I only know one. I'm going to tell it to you. It's called "The Bouquet."

MR. SMITH: My wife has always been romantic.

MR. MARTIN: She's a true Englishwoman.

MRS. SMITH: Here it is: Once upon a time, a fiancé gave a bouquet of flowers to his fiancée, who said, "Thanks"; but before she had said, "Thanks," he, without saying a single word, took back the flowers he had given her in order to teach her a good lesson, and he said, "I take them back." He said, "Goodbye," and took them back and went off in all directions.

MR. MARTIN: Oh, charming! [He either kisses or does not kiss Mrs. Smith.]

Mephistophelean: Devilish, controlling; after Mephistopheles in Christopher Marlowe's *Doctor Faustus*.

MRS. MARTIN: You have a wife, Mr. Smith, of whom all the world is jealous.

MR. SMITH: It's true. My wife is intelligence personified. She's even more intelligent than I. In any case, she is much more feminine, everyone says so.

MRS. SMITH [*to the Fire Chief*]: Let's have another, Mr. Fire Chief.

FIRE CHIEF: Oh, no, it's too late.

MR. MARTIN: Tell us one, anyway.

FIRE CHIEF: I'm too tired.

MR. SMITH: Please do us a favor.

MR. MARTIN: I beg you.

FIRE CHIEF: No.

MRS. MARTIN: You have a heart of ice. We're sitting on hot coals.

MRS. SMITH [*falls on her knees sobbing, or else she does not do this*]: I implore you!

FIRE CHIEF: Righto.

MR. SMITH [*in Mrs. Martin's ear*]: He agrees! He's going to bore us again.

MRS. MARTIN: Shh.

MRS. SMITH: No luck. I was too polite.

FIRE CHIEF: "The Headcold." My brother-in law had, on the paternal side, a first cousin whose maternal uncle had a father-in-law whose paternal grandfather had married as his second wife a young native whose brother he had met on one of his travels, a girl of whom he was enamored and by whom he had a son who married an intrepid lady pharmacist who was none other than the niece of an unknown fourth-class petty officer of the Royal Navy and whose adopted father had an aunt who spoke Spanish fluently and who was, perhaps, one of the granddaughters of an engineer who died young, himself the grandson of the owner of a vineyard which produced mediocre wine, but who had a second cousin, a stay-at-home, a sergeant-major, whose son had married a very pretty young woman, a divorcée, whose first husband was the son of a loyal patriot who, in the hope of making his fortune, had managed to bring up one of his daughters so that she could marry a footman who had known Rothschild, and whose brother, after having changed his trade several times, married and had a daughter whose stunted great-grandfather wore spectacles which had been given him by a cousin of his, the brother-in-law of a man from Portugal, natural son of a miller, not too badly off, whose foster-brother had married the daughter of a former country doctor, who was himself a foster-brother of the son of a forrester, himself the natural son of another country doctor, married three times in a row, whose third wife . . .

MR. MARTIN: I knew that third wife, if I'm not mistaken. She ate chicken sitting on a hornet's nest.

FIRE CHIEF: It's not the same one.

MRS. SMITH: Shh!

FIRE CHIEF: As I was saying . . . whose third wife was the daughter of the best midwife in the region and who, early left a widow . . .

MR. SMITH: Like my wife.

FIRE CHIEF: . . . Had married a glazier who was full of life and who had had, by the daughter of a station master, a child who had burned his bridges . . .

MRS. SMITH: His britches?

MR. MARTIN: No his bridge game.

FIRE CHIEF: And had married an oyster woman, whose father had a brother, mayor of a small town, who had taken as his wife a blonde schoolteacher, whose cousin, a fly fisherman . . .

MR. MARTIN: A fly by night?

FIRE CHIEF: . . . Had married another blonde school-teacher, named Marie, too, whose brother was married to another Marie, also a blonde schoolteacher . . .

MR. SMITH: Since she's blonde, she must be Marie.

FIRE CHIEF: . . . And whose father had been reared in Canada by an old woman who was the niece of a priest whose grandmother, occasionally in the winter, like everyone else, caught a cold.

MRS. SMITH: A curious story. Almost unbelievable.

MR. MARTIN: If you catch a cold, you should get yourself a colt.

MR. SMITH: It's a useless precaution, but absolutely necessary.

MRS. MARTIN: Excuse me, Mr. Fire Chief, but I did not follow your story very well. At the end, when we got to the grandmother of the priest, I got mixed up.

MR. SMITH: One always gets mixed up in the hands of a priest.

MRS. SMITH: Oh yes, Mr. Fire Chief, begin again. Everyone wants to hear.

FIRE CHIEF: Ah, I don't know whether I'll be able to. I'm on official business. It depends on what time it is.

MRS. SMITH: We don't have the time, here.

FIRE CHIEF: But the clock?

MR. SMITH: It runs badly. It is contradictory, and always indicates the opposite of what the hour really is.

[*Enter Mary.*]

MARY: Madam . . . sir . . .

MRS. SMITH: What do you want?

MR. SMITH: What have you come in here for?

MARY: I hope, madam and sir will excuse me . . . and these ladies and gentlemen too . . . I would like . . . I would like . . . to tell you a story, myself.

MRS. MARTIN: What is she saying?

MR. MARTIN: I believe that our friends' maid is going crazy . . . she wants to tell us a story, too.

FIRE CHIEF: Who does she think she is? [*He looks at her.*] Oh!

MRS. SMITH: Why are you butting in?

MR. SMITH: This is really uncalled for, Mary . . .

FIRE CHIEF: Oh! But it is she! Incredible!

MR. SMITH: And you?

MARY: Incredible! Here!

MRS. SMITH: What does all this mean?

MR. SMITH: You know each other?

FIRE CHIEF: And how!

[*Mary throws herself on the neck of the Fire Chief.*]

MARY: I'm so glad to see you again . . . at last!

MR. AND MRS. SMITH: Oh!

MR. SMITH: This is too much, here, in our home, in the suburbs of London.

MRS. SMITH: It's not proper! . . .

FIRE CHIEF: It was she who extinguished my first fires.

MARY: I'm your little firehose.

MR. MARTIN: If that is the case . . . dear friends . . . these emotions are understandable, human, honorable . . .

MRS. MARTIN: All that is human is honorable.

MRS. SMITH: Even so, I don't like to see it . . . here among us . . .

MR. SMITH: She's not been properly brought up . . .

FIRE CHIEF: Oh, you have too many prejudices.

MRS. MARTIN: What I think is that a maid, after all — even though it's none of my business — is never anything but a maid . . .

MR. MARTIN: Even if she can sometimes be a rather good detective.

FIRE CHIEF: Let me go.

MARY: Don't be upset! . . . They're not so bad really.

MR. SMITH: Hm . . . hm . . . you two are very touching, but at the same time, a little . . . a little . . .

MR. MARTIN: Yes, that's exactly the word.

MR. SMITH: . . . A little too exhibitionistic . . .

MR. MARTIN: There is a native British modesty — forgive me for attempting, yet again, to define my thought — not understood by foreigners, even by specialists, thanks to which, if I may thus express myself . . . of course, I don't mean to refer to you . . .

MARY: I was going to tell you . . .

MR. SMITH: Don't tell us anything . . .

MARY: Oh yes!

MRS. SMITH: Go, my little Mary, go quietly to the kitchen and read your poems before the mirror . . .

MR. MARTIN: You know, even though I'm not a maid, I also read poems before the mirror.

MRS. MARTIN: This morning when you looked at yourself in the mirror you didn't see yourself.

MR. MARTIN: That's because I wasn't there yet . . .

MARY: All the same, I could, perhaps, recite a little poem for you.

MRS. SMITH: My little Mary, you are frightfully obstinate.

MARY: I'm going to recite a poem, then, is that agreed? It is a poem entitled "The Fire" in honor of the Fire Chief:

The Fire

The polypoids were burning in the wood
  A stone caught fire
  The castle caught fire
  The forest caught fire
  The men caught fire
  The women caught fire
  The birds caught fire
  The fish caught fire
  The water caught fire
  The sky caught fire

  The ashes caught fire
  The smoke caught fire
  The fire caught fire
  Everything caught fire
  Caught fire, caught fire.

[*She recites the poem while the Smiths are pushing her offstage.*]

MRS. MARTIN: That sent chills up my spine . . .

MR. MARTIN: And yet there's a certain warmth in those lines . . .

FIRE CHIEF: I thought it was marvelous.

MRS. SMITH: All the same . . .

MR. SMITH: You're exaggerating . . .

FIRE CHIEF: Just a minute . . . I admit . . . all this is very subjective . . . but this is my conception of the world. My world. My dream. My ideal . . . And now this reminds me that I must leave. Since you don't have the time here, I must tell you that in exactly three-quarters of an hour and sixteen minutes, I'm having a fire at the other end of the city. Consequently, I must hurry. Even though it will be quite unimportant.

MRS. SMITH: What will it be? A little chimney fire?

FIRE CHIEF: Oh, not even that. A straw fire and a little heartburn.

MR. SMITH: Well, we're sorry to see you go.

MRS. SMITH: You have been very entertaining.

MRS. MARTIN: Thanks to you, we have passed a truly Cartesian quarter of an hour.

FIRE CHIEF [*moving towards the door, then stopping*]: Speaking of that — the bald soprano? [*General silence, embarrassment.*]

MRS. SMITH: She always wears her hair in the same style.

FIRE CHIEF: Ah! Then goodbye, ladies and gentlemen.

MR. MARTIN: Good luck, and a good fire!

FIRE CHIEF: Let's hope so. For everybody.

[*Fire Chief exits. All accompany him to the door and then return to their seats.*]

MRS. MARTIN: I can buy a pocketknife for my brother, but you can't buy Ireland for your grandfather.

MR. SMITH: One walks on his feet, but one heats with electricity or coal.

MR. MARTIN: He who sells an ox today, will have an egg tomorrow.

MRS. SMITH: In real life, one must look out of the window.

MRS. MARTIN: One can sit down on a chair, when the chair doesn't have any.

MR. SMITH: One must always think of everything.

MR. MARTIN: The ceiling is above, the floor is below.

MRS. SMITH: When I say yes, it's only a manner of speaking.

MRS. MARTIN: To each his own.

MR. SMITH: Take a circle, caress it, and it will turn vicious.

MRS. SMITH: A schoolmaster teaches his pupils to read, but the cat suckles her young when they are small.

MRS. MARTIN: Nevertheless, it was the cow that gave us tails.

MR. SMITH: When I'm in the country, I love the solitude and the quiet.

MR. MARTIN: You are not old enough yet for that.

MRS. SMITH: Benjamin Franklin was right; you are more nervous than he.

MRS. MARTIN: What are the seven days of the week?

MR. SMITH: Monday, Tuesday, Wednesday, Thursday, Friday, Saturday, Sunday.

MR. MARTIN: Edward is a clerk; his sister Nancy is a typist, and his brother William a shop-assistant.

MRS. SMITH: An odd family!

MRS. MARTIN: I prefer a bird in the bush to a sparrow in a barrow.

MR. SMITH: Rather a steak in a chalet than gristle in a castle.

MR. MARTIN: An Englishman's home is truly his castle.

MRS. SMITH: I don't know enough Spanish to make myself understood.

MRS. MARTIN: I'll give you my mother-in-law's slippers if you'll give me your husband's coffin.

MR. SMITH: I'm looking for a monophysite priest to marry to our maid.

MR. MARTIN: Bread is a staff, whereas bread is also a staff, and an oak springs from an oak every morning at dawn.

MRS. SMITH: My uncle lives in the country, but that's none of the midwife's business.

MR. MARTIN: Paper is for writing, the cat's for the rat. Cheese is for scratching.

MRS. SMITH: The car goes very fast, but the cook beats batter better.

MR. SMITH: Don't be turkeys; rather kiss the conspirator.

MR. MARTIN: Charity begins at home.

MRS. SMITH: I'm waiting for the aqueduct to come and see me at my windmill.

MR. MARTIN: One can prove that social progress is definitely better with sugar.

MR. SMITH: To hell with polishing!

[*Following this last speech of Mr. Smith's, the others are silent for a moment, stupefied. We sense that there is a certain nervous irritation. The strokes of the clock are more nervous too. The speeches which follow must be said, at first, in a glacial, hostile tone. The hostility and the nervousness increase. At the end of this scene, the four characters must be standing very close to each other, screaming their speeches, raising their fists, ready to throw themselves upon each other.*]

MR. MARTIN: One doesn't polish spectacles with black wax.

MRS. SMITH: Yes, but with money one can buy anything.

MR. MARTIN: I'd rather kill a rabbit than sing in the garden.

MR. SMITH: Cockatoos, cockatoos, cockatoos, cockatoos, cockatoos, cockatoos, cockatoos, cockatoos, cockatoos.

MRS. SMITH: Such caca, such caca, such caca, such caca, such caca, such caca, such caca, such caca, such caca.

MR. MARTIN: Such cascades of cacas, such cascades of cacas, such cascades of cacas, such cascades of cacas, such cascades of cacas, such cascades of cacas, such cascades of cacas, such cascades of cacas.

MR. SMITH: Dogs have fleas, dogs have fleas.

MRS. MARTIN: Cactus, coccyx! crocus! cockaded! cockroach!

MRS. SMITH: Incasker, you incask us.

MR. MARTIN: I'd rather lay an egg in a box than go and steal an ox.

MRS. MARTIN [*opening her mouth very wide*]: Ah! oh! ah! oh! Let me gnash my teeth.

MR. SMITH: Crocodile!

MR. MARTIN: Let's go and slap Ulysses.

MR. SMITH: I'm going to live in my cabana among my cacao trees.

MRS. MARTIN: Cacao trees on cacao farms don't bear coconuts, they yield cocoa! Cacao trees on cacao farms don't bear coconuts, they yield cocoa! Cacao trees on cacao farms don't bear coconuts, they yield cocoa.

MRS. SMITH: Mice have lice, lice haven't mice.

MRS. MARTIN: Don't ruche my brooch!

MR. MARTIN: Don't smooch the brooch!

MR. SMITH: Groom the goose, don't goose the groom.

MRS. MARTIN: The goose grooms.

MRS. SMITH: Groom your tooth.

MR. MARTIN: Groom the bridegroom, groom the bridegroom.

MR. SMITH: Seducer seduced!

MRS. SMITH: Scaramouche!°

MRS. SMITH: Sainte-Nitouche!°

MR. MARTIN: Go take a douche.

MR. SMITH: I've been goosed.

MRS. MARTIN: Sainte-Nitouche stoops to my cartouche.

MRS. SMITH: "Who'd stoop to blame? . . . and I never choose to stoop."

MR. MARTIN: Robert!

MR. SMITH: Browning!°

MRS. MARTIN, MR. SMITH: Rudyard.

MRS. SMITH, MR. MARTIN: Kipling.°

MRS. MARTIN, MR. SMITH: Robert Kipling!

MRS. SMITH, MR. MARTIN: Rudyard Browning.

MRS. MARTIN: Silly gobblegobblers, silly gobblegobblers.

MR. MARTIN: Marietta, spot the pot!

MRS. SMITH: Krishnamurti,° Krishnamurti, Krishnamurti!

MR. SMITH: The pope elopes! The pope's got no horoscope. The horoscope's bespoke.

MRS. MARTIN: Bazaar, Balzac, bazooka!

MR. MARTIN: Bizarre, beaux-arts, brassieres!

Scaramouche: A novel by Rafael Sabatini about the French Revolution. **Sainte-Nitouche:** A poem by Edward Arlington Robinson about a burial. **Robert Browning:** British poet (1812–1899), once England's most popular poet. **Rudyard Kipling:** British novelist and poet (1865–1936), popular patriotic writer. **Krishnamurti:** Indian figure associated with a spiritual organization.

MR. SMITH: A, e, i, o, u, a, e, i, o, u, a, e, i, o, u, i!

MRS. MARTIN: B, c, d, f, g, l, m, n, p, r, s, t, v, w, x, z!

MR. MARTIN: From sage to stooge, from stage to serge!

MRS. SMITH [*imitating a train*]: Choo, choo, choo, choo, choo, choo, choo, choo, choo, choo, choo!

MR. SMITH: It's!

MRS. MARTIN: Not!

MR. MARTIN: That!

MRS. SMITH: Way!

MR. SMITH: It's!

MRS. MARTIN: O!

MR. MARTIN: Ver!

MRS. SMITH: Here!

[*All together, completely infuriated, screaming in each other's ears. The light is extinguished. In the darkness we hear, in an increasingly rapid rhythm:*]

ALL TOGETHER: It's not that way, it's over here, it's not that way, it's over here, it's not that way, it's over here, it's not that way, it's over here!

[*The words cease abruptly. Again, the lights come on. Mr. and Mrs. Martin are seated like the Smiths at the beginning of the play. The play begins again with the Martins, who say exactly the same lines as the Smiths in the first scene, while the curtain softly falls.*]

COMMENTARY

Eugène Ionesco (1909–1994)

THE TRAGEDY OF LANGUAGE

1960

HOW AN ENGLISH PRIMER BECAME MY FIRST PLAY

TRANSLATED BY JACK UNDANK

Eugène Ionesco comments on his inspiration for writing The Bald Soprano, *reminiscing about his efforts to learn English from a French-English primer. What he eventually learned was not the English language but insights about language itself. These are what he put to work in his play.*

In 1948, before writing my first play, *The Bald Soprano,* I had no idea of becoming a playwright. My only ambition, quite simply, was to learn English. The study of English does not necessarily lead to play writing. On the contrary, it was because I had no luck with English that I turned to the stage. Nor did I write these plays to avenge my failure, although some have said that my *Bald Soprano* was a satire of the English bourgeoisie. If I had wanted to learn Italian, Russian, or Turkish and not succeeded, they would have claimed, by the same token, that the play resulting from that futile effort was a satire of Italian, Russian, or Turkish society. Perhaps I ought to explain. Here is what happened: nine or ten years ago, in order to learn English conversation, I bought a French-English Primer. I set to work. Conscientiously, I copied whole sentences from my Primer with the purpose of memorizing them. Rereading them attentively, I learned not English, but some astonishing truths: that, for example, there are seven days in the week, something, moreover, I already knew; that the floor is down, the ceiling up, things I already knew as well perhaps, but which I had never seriously thought about or had forgotten and which seemed to me, suddenly, as stupefying as they were indisputably true.

I probably have enough of a philosophical bent to have realized that what I was copying into my notebook were not simple English sentences in French translation, but fundamental truths, profound observations. I didn't give up English quite yet. Fortunately so, because, after universal truths, the author of the Primer went on to disclose private ones; probably inspired by the Platonic method, he expressed them by means of dialogue. From the third lesson onward, two characters were presented whose real or fictive existence I am still not sure of: Mr. and Mrs. Smith, an English couple. To my great astonishment, Mrs. Smith informed her husband that they had several children, that they lived in the vicinity of London, that their name was Smith, that Mr. Smith was a clerk, that they had a servant, Mary, English like themselves, that for the past twenty years they have had friends by the name of Mr. and Mrs. Martin, that their house was a palace, for "the home of an Englishman is his true palace."

I really supposed that Mr. Smith was probably somewhat abreast of all this, but can one be sure; there are people that absent-minded. Moreover, it is wise to remind our fellow men of things they may forget or of which they are insufficiently conscious. Besides these permanent, private truths, there were other truths, truths of the moment, which became apparent: for example, the fact that the Smiths had just finished their dinner and that it was nine o'clock at night, according to the clock — English time.

I should like to point out the irrefutable, perfectly axiomatic character of Mrs. Smith's assertions as well as the entirely Cartesian manner of the author of my English Primer, for what was truly remarkable about it was its eminently methodical procedure in its quest for truth. In the fifth lesson, the Smiths' friends, the Martins, arrive; the four of them begin to chat, and, starting from basic axioms, they build more complex truths: "the country is quieter than the big city," some of them contend; "yes, but the city is more heavily populated and there are also more shops," the others reply — which is equally true and proves, moreover, that opposing truths can very well coexist.

It was then that my idea came to me. Perfecting my knowledge of English was now out of the question. To concentrate on enriching my English vocabulary, to learn words, to translate into another language what I could just as well say in French, without bearing in mind the "content" of those words, what they revealed, would have been to stumble into that sin of formalism which our thought-directors of today rightly condemn. My ambition had become greater: to communicate to my contemporaries the essential truths of which the French-English Primer had made me aware. And what is more, the dialogues of the Smiths, the Martins, the Smiths and the Martins, were really theater, theater and dialogue being one and the same thing. I had only to put it into a play. That is how I came to write *The Bald Soprano,* a pointedly didactic, theatrical work. And why is this work called *The Bald Soprano* and not *English Without Toil,* the title I first thought of giving it, or *The English Hour,* a title I thought of subsequently? That is too long a story: one of the reasons why *The Bald Soprano* has its present title is that no soprano, bald or otherwise, appears in it. That ought to be sufficient comment. A good part of the play is composed of sentence fragments drawn from my English Primer and set end to end. The Smiths and Martins of the Primer are the Smiths and Martins of my play; they are one and the same, mouth the same maxims, perform the same actions or the same "inactions." In all "didactic theater," you are not supposed to be original, to say what you yourself think: that would be a serious mishandling of objective *truth*; you have only to transmit, humbly, the instruction that has been transmitted to you, ideas that have been handed down. How could I take the slightest liberty with words expressing absolute truth in so edifying a fashion? My play, *authentically* didactic, was not meant to be original nor intended to show my talent to advantage.

. . . Nevertheless, the text of *The Bald Soprano* was a lesson (and an act of plagiarism) only at the start. A strange phenomenon took place, I don't know how: the text began imperceptibly to change before my eyes, and in spite of me. The very simple, luminously clear statements I had copied diligently into my schoolboy's notebook, left to themselves, fermented after a while, became denatured, expanded and overflowed. The repartee which I had, in careful and precise succession, copied from the Primer, became a jumble. Which is what happened to that certain, irrefutable truth: "the floor is down, the ceiling is up." Assertions—as categorical as they were solid: the seven days of the week are Monday, Tuesday, Wednesday, Thursday, Friday, Saturday, Sunday—collapsed, and Mr. Smith, my hero, now proposed that the week consisted of three days, namely: Tuesday, Thursday, and Tuesday. My characters, my good bourgeois, the Martins, husband and wife, were suddenly afflicted with amnesia: although they continued to speak to and see one another every day, they no longer recognized each other. Other alarming things happened: the Smiths now told of the death of a certain Bobby Watson whose identity was unrecognizable because, as they mentioned elsewhere, three quarters of the town's inhabitants, men, women, children, cats, and pseudo-philosophers were named Bobby Watson. A fifth character now unexpectedly burst upon the scene and added to the confusion of the couples' peaceable domesticity: the Fire Chief, who told stories which had something to do with a young bull supposedly giving birth to an enormous heifer, with a mouse giving birth to a mountain—then, the fireman went off to catch a fire which he had foreseen three days in advance (he had marked it on his calendar) and which was scheduled to break out at the other end of town. Whereupon the Smiths resumed their conversation. Alas! the wise and fundamental truths they exchanged, each carefully linked to the next, had gone wild, their language had become disjointed; the characters disintegrated: their words became meaningless absurdities; the entire cast ended up quarreling. It was impossible to grasp my heroes' motives in this quarrel. They didn't fling retorts at one another, not even sentence fragments or words; all they spoke were syllables, consonants and vowels! . . .

. . . It represented, for me, a kind of collapse of reality. Words had become empty, noisy shells without meaning; the characters as well, of course, had become psychologically empty. Everything appeared to me in an unfamiliar light, people moving in a timeless time, in a spaceless space. . .

While writing the play (for it had become a kind of play or anti-play, that is, a parody of a play, a comedy of comedy), I felt sick, dizzy, nauseous. I had to interrupt my work from time to time and, wondering all the while what demon was prodding me on, lie down on my couch for fear of seeing my work sink into nothingness, and me with it. All the same, once I had finished, I was very proud. I fancied myself having written something like *the tragedy of language*! . . . When it was staged, I was almost amazed to hear the audience laugh; they took it lightly (and still do), believing that it was a comedy, if not an outright farce. Some people (Jean Pouillon among them), those who sensed the uneasiness in it, were not fooled. Others noticed that I was poking fun at Bernstein's theater and his actors.

Nicolas Bataille's troupe was the first to notice this; they acted out the play (especially in its initial performances) as though it were a melodrama.

Serious and learned critics, analyzing the work later on, interpreted it as no more than a criticism of the Théâtre de Boulevard (popular theater). I have just said that I believe that interpretation valid; however, in my mind, it is not a satire of petty bourgeois mentality associated with any particular society. It is, above all, concerned with a kind of universal petty bourgeoisie, the petty bourgeoisie being the personification of accepted ideas and slogans, the ubiquitous conformist. His automatic use of language is, of course, what gives him away. The text of *The Bald Soprano* or of the English (or Russian or Portuguese) Primer, composed of ready-made expressions and the most tired clichés, made me aware of the automatic quality of language and human behavior, "empty talk," speaking because there is nothing personal to say, the absence of inner life, the mechanical aspect of daily existence, man bathing in his social environment, becoming an indistinguishable part of it. The Smiths, the Martins, can no longer talk because they can no longer think; they can no longer think *because they can no longer be moved, can no longer feel passions*; they can no longer be, they can "become" anybody, anything, for, having lost their identity, they assume the identity of others, become part of the world of the impersonal; they are interchangeable: you can put Martin in place of Smith and vice versa, no one will notice. The tragic character does not change, he is crushed; he is himself, he is *real*. Comic characters, fools, are people who do not exist.

Samuel Beckett

Samuel Beckett (1906–1989) was born in Dublin to an upper-middle-class Protestant family. After a privileged education at the Portora Royal School, he went to Trinity College, Dublin, where he studied French and Italian. He was an exceptionally good student and, in 1928 after graduation, taught English at the École Normale Supérieure in Paris.

Beckett early on straddled two literary cultures: Irish and Anglo-Irish. Most of the literary energy in Ireland in the 1920s and 1930s was split between the essentially conservative Anglo-Irish Protestants, such as W. B. Yeats and Lady Gregory, and the more avant-garde Catholics, such as James Joyce, with whom Beckett formed an enduring personal and literary friendship in Paris. Although much younger than Joyce, Beckett developed a close artistic sympathy with him. Beckett's first published work (1929) was one of the earliest critical essays on Joyce's most radical literary composition, the not-yet-published *Finnegans Wake*.

When he was first in France, Beckett's reading of French philosophers, especially Descartes, exerted a strong influence on his work. Beckett's earliest writings appeared in Eugene Jolas's avant-garde literary journal *transition*, which put him in the center of Parisian literary activity in the late 1920s. After 1930, his series of short stories published under the title *More Pricks Than Kicks* (1934) established him as an important writer. After settling in Paris in 1937, Beckett wrote the novel *Murphy* (1938), on a recognizably Irish theme of economic impoverishment, alienation, and inward meditation and spiritual complexity.

When World War II began in 1939, Beckett took up the cause of the French Resistance. After his activity caught the eye of the Gestapo, for two years he lay low in unoccupied France by working as a farmhand and also writing another novel, *Watt* (written in 1944 but published in 1953). After the war he took up residence again in Paris and began writing most of his work in French. His greatest novels were written in the five years after the war, and they are often referred to as his trilogy: *Molloy, Malone Dies,* and *The Unnamable*. These three novels are about men who have become disaffected with society and who have strange and compelling urgencies to be alone and to follow exacting and repetitive patterns of behavior. In a sense, they are archetypes of the kinds of protagonists that Beckett created in most of his work.

Beckett's first published play, *Waiting for Godot* (1952), was produced in Paris (1953), in London (1955), and in Miami (1956). From the first, its repetitive, whimsical, and sometimes nonsensical style established the play as a major postwar statement. In a barren setting, Vladimir and Estragon, two tramps who echo the comic vision of Charlie Chaplin, wait for Godot to come. They amuse themselves by doing vaudeville routines, but their loneliness and isolation are painfully apparent to the audience. Godot has promised to come, and as they wait, Vladimir and Estragon speculate on whether or not he will.

The comic moments in the play, along with the enigma of Vladimir and Estragon's fruitless waiting, combined to capture the imagination of audiences and the press. They saw the play as a modern statement about the condition of humankind, although there was never any agreement on just what the statement was. Godot sends a boy to say that he will indeed come, but when the play ends, he has not arrived. The implication seems to be that he will never arrive. Most audiences saw Godot as a metaphor for God. Despite the critics' constant inquiries, Beckett never confirmed the view that Godot was God and kept Godot's identity open-ended.

The play itself was open-ended, as Beckett had hoped, and therefore could be interpreted in many ways. One interpretation was to see the play as a commentary on the futility of religion; another was to suggest that the play underscored the loneliness of humankind in an empty universe; yet a third implied that it was up to individuals, represented by the hapless Vladimir and Estragon, to shape the significance of their own lives, and their waiting represented that effort.

Many of the themes in *Waiting for Godot* are apparent in Beckett's later plays. The radio play *All That Fall* (1957) was followed by the very successful *Krapp's Last Tape* (1958). Also in 1957, *Endgame,* a play on the theme of the end of the world, was produced, followed in 1961 by *Happy Days.* Beckett experimented with minimalist approaches to drama, exemplified in *Act without Words I* and *Act without Words II,* both mime plays. Other plays experiment with minimalism in setting, props, and—in the mime plays—even words.

Beckett's plays reveal the deep influence of French postwar philosophers, such as Albert Camus and Jean-Paul Sartre, both existentialists. Their philosophy declares that people are not essentially good, bad, kind, or anything else but are what they make of themselves. Beckett's adaptation of existentialism sometimes borders on pessimism, because his vision seems to negate many of the consolations of religious and secular philosophy. His style is antirealist, but the search for beliefs that are reasonable and plausible in a fundamentally absurd world, and the plight of individuals who must make their own meanings, are central to most of his work.

Beckett's view of the world is not cheerful. But his vision is consistent, honest, and sympathetic to the persistence of his characters, who endure even in the face of apparent defeat. The significance of Beckett's achievements was recognized in 1969 when he was awarded the Nobel Prize for literature.

KRAPP'S LAST TAPE

Krapp's Last Tape was first performed in 1958 at the Royal Court Theatre in London, a theater that developed an impressive reputation for producing avant-garde drama. By the time this play was produced, Samuel Beckett had achieved a worldwide reputation as an avant-garde playwright. His absurdist drama *Waiting for Godot* had been staged in 1953 and had caused a sensation as one of the first major works of the literature of the absurd that caught the attention of a large, popular audience.

The absurdist writers inherited the philosopher Nietzsche's view that god, as an idea that could explain the meaning of life, was dead. Therefore, the universe was meaningless, or absurd, and people must search out their own meanings and shape their own lives.

Krapp is in many ways a typical Beckett protagonist. He is totally alone, with no friends that he can count on and no connections with the lives of others except through memory. Yet he is in constant contact with his past self, through the medium of tape recordings he made on previous birthdays. The tapes attempt a kind of summary of events in the life of a lonely and withdrawn man. Krapp of the present time (which the stage directions tell us is actually a future time) looks back on the younger man who represents a version of himself that embarrasses him. He constantly says he is glad that the year on this particular tape—his thirty-ninth year—is over.

Krapp has deliberately chosen the way he lives now, and in listening to himself on tape he maintains a continual contact with his earlier personae and congratulates himself on no longer being the man he was. He fears that his best years may be gone but is convinced that he is better now.

Krapp borrows a page from the philosophy of Socrates, who said, "The unexamined life is not worth living." In his way, Krapp examines his life as intensely as anyone could. He listens to the young man he was, watches himself grow older, if not wiser, and cavorts onstage like a magpie. He keeps a ledger filled with his thoughts—as if they might add up to something meaningful. He examines himself in detail: his opinions, the strength of his voice, the thoughts he is able to form at any given moment. He thinks about his mother, who turns out to be the only woman with whom he had any genuine relationship.

He scrutinizes himself but seems to come to no definitive conclusions, other than satisfaction that he is not the man he was. To some extent his feelings reflect one critical point: His past, which absorbs all his energy, organizational skill, and technical know-how, was not devoted to a life that was lived. It was devoted to a life that was left unlived; Krapp has avoided the world. Krapp's is a life of denial.

Krapp's Last Tape in Performance

The use of the tape recorder was very effective in the play's first performances, when the technology of recording was still a novelty. In one production given by London's Young Vic company in the mid-1970s, the sound tapes were replaced by television tapes, with several monitors onstage. Television works as well as sound tapes and in some ways is even more striking to an audience. The lighting in early productions was harsh, brilliant, and totally revealing.

Audiences are impressed by Krapp's antiquity, his grizzledness, his sense that his youth is gone and good riddance. The audience may or may not give him much sympathy, but it will always see him as a strange, compelling figure, someone who is almost pitiable for the way he "lost" his life while all the time imagining he was preserving it.

The first production in 1958 was at the Royal Court Theatre with Patrick Magee, for whom the play was written. In its earliest form, the play was titled *Magee Monologue*. But since then a number of important actors have taken the role. The Young Vic production in the mid-1970s with Jack Magowran upgraded Krapp to videotape and produced a lively and stimulating production with multiple video monitors. The 1986 production in New York with Rick Cluchey was praised for the power of its writing, although Cluchey's performance was considered "routine." The costuming suggested a clown, and Beckett's required banana peel was nearby. John Hurt was a memorable Krapp in London's 2000 production at the New Ambassadors Theatre in the West End. That performance began with a single lamp in a black stage lighting a circle over Krapp sitting at a table, staring at a totally silenced audience. The first thing he does is open a drawer and cast a banana peel on the floor. The 2005 production at the Burton Taylor Theatre in Oxford featured an "outstanding" performance from Aaron Costa Ganis, who, as a very young man, had to stretch to create the illusion of a sixty-nine-year-old. The most striking production of the play, however, was again in the Royal Court in October 2006, when Harold Pinter played the part of Krapp. There were no bananas in this production, but Pinter used an electric wheelchair, which seemed natural to the character. The Upstairs Theatre in which the play was performed is very small, and Hildegarde Bechtler's set was spare and grim with gloomy lighting by Paule Constable. Pinter was sometimes only five or six feet away from parts of the audience. Pinter's own health was threatened seriously before the performance, which gave an edge to the issues of mortality that dominate the play. James Knowlson, in a review in London's *Times Online*, said that "this is probably the finest performance we shall ever be privileged to see."

Samuel Beckett (1906–1989)

KRAPP'S LAST TAPE

1958

(*A late evening in the future.*)

(*Krapp's den.*)

(*Front center a small table, the two drawers of which open toward audience.*)

(*Sitting at the table, facing front, i.e., across from the drawers, a wearish° old man: Krapp.*)

(*Rusty black narrow trousers too short for him. Rusty black sleeveless waistcoat, four capacious pockets. Heavy silver watch and chain. Grimy white shirt open at neck, no collar. Surprising pair of dirty white boots, size ten at least, very narrow and pointed.*)

(*White face. Purple nose. Disordered gray hair. Unshaven.*)

(*Very near-sighted [but unspectacled]. Hard of hearing.*)

(*Cracked voice. Distinctive intonation.*)

(*Laborious walk.*)

(*On the table a tape recorder with microphone and a number of cardboard boxes containing reels of recorded tapes.*)

(*Table and immediately adjacent area in strong white light. Rest of stage in darkness.*)

(*Krapp remains a moment motionless, heaves a great sigh, looks at his watch, fumbles in his pockets, takes out an envelope, puts it back, fumbles, takes out a small bunch of keys, raises it to his eyes, chooses a key, gets up and moves to front of table. He stoops, unlocks first drawer, peers into it, feels about inside it, takes out a reel of tape, peers at it, puts it back, locks drawer, unlocks second drawer, peers into it, feels about inside it, takes out a large banana, peers at it, locks drawer, puts keys back in his pocket. He turns, advances to edge of stage, halts, strokes banana, peels it, drops skin at his feet, puts end of banana in his mouth, and remains motionless, staring vacuously before him. Finally he bites off the end,*)

---

wearish: Sickly, withered.

turns aside, and begins pacing to and fro at edge of stage, in the light, i.e., not more than four or five paces either way, meditatively eating banana. He treads on skin, slips, nearly falls, recovers himself, stoops and peers at skin and finally pushes it, still stooping, with his foot over the edge of stage into pit. He resumes his pacing, finishes banana, returns to table, sits down, remains a moment motionless, heaves a great sigh, takes keys from his pockets, raises them to his eyes, chooses key, gets up and moves to front of table, unlocks second drawer, takes out a second large banana, peers at it, locks drawer, puts back keys in his pocket, turns, advances to edge of stage, halts, strokes banana, peels it, tosses skin into pit, puts end of banana in his mouth, and remains motionless, staring vacuously before him. Finally he has an idea, puts banana in his waistcoat pocket, the end emerging, and goes with all the speed he can muster backstage into darkness. Ten seconds. Loud pop of cork. Fifteen seconds. He comes back into light carrying an old ledger and sits down at table. He lays ledger on table, wipes his mouth, wipes his hands on the front of his waistcoat, brings them smartly together and rubs them.)

KRAPP (briskly): Ah! (He bends over ledger, turns the pages, finds the entry he wants, reads.) Box . . . threee . . . spool . . . five. (He raises his head and stares front. With relish.) Spool! (Pause.) Spooool! (Happy smile. Pause. He bends over table, starts peering and poking at the boxes.) Box . . . threee . . . threee . . . four . . . two . . . (with surprise) nine! good God! . . . seven . . . ah! the little rascal! (He takes up box, peers at it.) Box threee. (He lays it on table, opens it and peers at

The original 1958 production of *Krapp's Last Tape* with Patrick Magee, for whom the play was written. (Photo by Ida Kar; 2¼-inch square film negative, 1958.)

spools inside.) Spool . . . (he peers at ledger) . . . five . . . (he peers at spools) . . . five . . . five . . . ah! the little scoundrel! (He takes out a spool, peers at it.) Spool five. (He lays it on table, closes box three, puts it back with the others, takes up the spool.) Box thrree, spool five. (He bends over the machine, looks up. With relish.) Spooool! (Happy smile. He bends, loads spool on machine, rubs his hands.) Ah! (He peers at ledger, reads entry at foot of page.) Mother at rest at last . . . Hm . . . The black ball . . . (He raises his head, stares blankly front. Puzzled.) Black ball? . . . (He peers again at ledger, reads.) The dark nurse . . . (He raises his head, broods, peers again at ledger, reads.) Slight improvement in bowel condition . . . Hm . . . Memorable . . . what? (He peers closer.) Equinox, memorable equinox. (He raises his head, stares blankly front. Puzzled.) Memorable equinox? . . . (Pause. He shrugs his shoulders, peers again at ledger, reads.) Farewell to—(he turns the page)—love.

(He raises his head, broods, bends over machine, switches on and assumes listening posture, i.e., leaning forward, elbows on table, hand cupping ear toward machine, face front.)

TAPE (strong voice, rather pompous, clearly Krapp's at a much earlier time): Thirty-nine today, sound as a— (Settling himself more comfortably he knocks one of the boxes off the table, curses, switches off, sweeps boxes and ledger violently to the ground, winds tape back to beginning, switches on, resumes posture.) Thirty-nine today, sound as a bell, apart from my old weakness, and intellectually I have now every reason to suspect at the . . . (hesitates) . . . crest of the wave—or thereabouts. Celebrated the awful occasion, as in recent years, quietly at the Winehouse. Not a soul. Sat before the fire with closed eyes, separating the grain from the husks. Jotted down a few notes, on the back of an envelope. Good to be back in my den, in my old rags. Have just eaten I regret to say three bananas and only with difficulty refrained from a fourth. Fatal things for a man with my condition. (Vehemently.) Cut 'em out! (Pause.) The new light above my table is a great improvement. With all this darkness round me I feel less alone. (Pause.) In a way. (Pause.) I love to get up and move about in it, then back here to . . . (hesitates) . . . me. (Pause.) Krapp.

(Pause.)

The grain, now what I wonder do I mean by that, I mean . . . (hesitates) . . . I suppose I mean those things worth having when all the dust has—when all *my* dust has settled. I close my eyes and try and imagine them.

(Pause. Krapp closes his eyes briefly.)

Extraordinary silence this evening, I strain my ears and do not hear a sound. Old Miss McGlome always sings at this hour. But not tonight. Songs of her girlhood, she says. Hard to think of her as a girl. Wonderful woman though. Connaught, I fancy. (Pause.)

John Hurt as Krapp in the 2000 production at the New Ambassadors Theatre in London's West End.

Shall I sing when I am her age, if I ever am? No. (*Pause.*) Did I sing as a boy? No. (*Pause.*) Did I ever sing? No.

(*Pause.*)

Just been listening to an old year, passages at random. I did not check in the book, but it must be at least ten or twelve years ago. At that time I think I was still living on and off with Bianca in Kedar Street. Well out of that, Jesus yes! Hopeless business. (*Pause.*) Not much about her, apart from a tribute to her eyes. Very warm. I suddenly saw them again. (*Pause.*) Incomparable! (*Pause.*) Ah well . . . (*Pause.*) These old P.M.s are gruesome, but I often find them— (*Krapp switches off, broods, switches on*)—a help before embarking on a new . . . (*hesitates*) . . . retrospect. Hard to believe I was ever that young whelp. The voice! Jesus! And the aspirations! (*Brief laugh in which Krapp joins.*) And the resolutions! (*Brief laugh in which Krapp joins.*) To drink less, in particular. (*Brief laugh of Krapp alone.*) Statistics. Seventeen hundred hours, out of the preceding eight thousand odd, consumed on licensed premises alone. More than 20%, say 40% of his waking life. (*Pause.*) Plans for a less . . . (*hesitates*) . . . engrossing sexual life. Last illness of his father. Flagging pursuit of happiness. Unattainable laxation. Sneers at what he calls

his youth and thanks to God that it's over. (*Pause.*) False ring there. (*Pause.*) Shadows of the opus . . . magnum. Closing with a—(*brief laugh*)—yelp to Providence. (*Prolonged laugh in which Krapp joins.*) What remains of all that misery? A girl in a shabby green coat, on a railway-station platform? No?

(*Pause.*)

When I look—

(*Krapp switches off, broods, looks at his watch, gets up, goes backstage into darkness. Ten seconds. Pop of cork. Ten seconds. Second cork. Ten seconds. Third cork. Ten seconds. Brief burst of quavering song.*)

KRAPP (*sings*): Now the day is over,
    Night is drawing nigh-igh,
    Shadows—

(*Fit of coughing. He comes back into light, sits down, wipes his mouth, switches on, resumes his listening posture.*)

TAPE:—back on the year that is gone, with what I hope is perhaps a glint of the old eye to come, there is of

Harold Pinter as Krapp in the Royal Court Theatre's 2006 production.

course the house on the canal where mother lay a-dying, in the late autumn, after her long viduity (*Krapp gives a start*), and the—(*Krapp switches off, winds back tape a little, bends his ear closer to machine, switches on*)—a-dying, after her long viduity, and the—

(*Krapp switches off, raises his head, stares blankly before him. His lips move in the syllables of "viduity." No sound. He gets up, goes backstage into darkness, comes back with an enormous dictionary, lays it on table, sits down and looks up the word.*)

KRAPP (*reading from dictionary*): State—or condition of being—or remaining—a widow—or widower. (*Looks up. Puzzled.*) Being—or remaining? . . . (*Pause. He peers again at dictionary. Reading.*) "Deep weeds of viduity" . . . Also of an animal, especially a bird . . . the vidua or weaver-bird . . . Black plumage of male . . . (*He looks up. With relish.*) The vidua-bird!

(*Pause. He closes dictionary, switches on, resumes listening posture.*)

TAPE: —bench by the weir from where I could see her window. There I sat, in the biting wind, wishing she were gone. (*Pause.*) Hardly a soul, just a few regulars, nursemaids, infants, old men, dogs. I got to know them quite well—oh by appearance of course I mean! One dark young beauty I recollect particularly, all white and starch, incomparable bosom, with a big black hooded perambulator, most funereal thing. Whenever I looked in her direction she had her eyes on me. And yet when I was bold enough to speak to her—not having been introduced—she threatened to call a policeman. As if I had designs on her virtue! (*Laugh. Pause.*) The face she had! The eyes! Like . . . (*hesitates*) . . . chrysolite! (*Pause.*) Ah well . . . (*Pause.*) I was there when—(*Krapp switches off, broods, switches on again*)—the blind went down, one of those dirty brown roller affairs, throwing a ball for a little white dog, as chance would have it. I happened to look up and there it was. All over and done with, at last. I sat on for a few moments with the ball in my hand and the dog yelping and pawing at me. (*Pause.*) Moments. Her moments, my moments. (*Pause.*) The dog's moments. (*Pause.*) In the end I held it out to him and he took it in his mouth, gently, gently. A small, old, black, hard, solid rubber ball. (*Pause.*) I shall feel it, in my hand, until my dying day. (*Pause.*) I might have kept it. (*Pause.*) But I gave it to the dog.

(*Pause.*)

Ah well . . .

(*Pause.*)

Spiritually a year of profound gloom and indigence until that memorable night in March, at the end of the jetty, in the howling wind, never to be forgotten,

when suddenly I saw the whole thing. The vision, at last. This I fancy is what I have chiefly to record this evening, against the day when my work will be done and perhaps no place left in my memory, warm or cold, for the miracle that . . . (*hesitates*) . . . for the fire that set it alight. What I suddenly saw then was this, that the belief I had been going on all my life, namely—(*Krapp switches off impatiently, winds tape forward, switches on again*)—great granite rocks the foam flying up in the light of the lighthouse and the wind-gauge spinning like a propellor, clear to me at last that the dark I have always struggled to keep under is in reality my most—(*Krapp curses, switches off, winds tape forward, switches on again*)—unshatterable association until my dissolution of storm and night with the light of the understanding and the fire—(*Krapp curses louder, switches off, winds tape forward, switches on again*)—my face in her breasts and my hand on her. We lay there without moving. But under us all moved, and moved us, gently, up and down, and from side to side.

(*Pause.*)

Past midnight. Never knew such silence. The earth might be uninhabited.

(*Pause.*)

Here I end—

(*Krapp switches off, winds tape back, switches on again.*)

—upper lake, with the punt, barbed off the bank, then pushed out into the stream and drifted. She lay stretched out on the floorboards with her hands under her head and her eyes closed. Sun blazing down, bit of a breeze, water nice and lively. I noticed a scratch on her thigh and asked her how she came by it. Picking gooseberries, she said. I said again I thought it was hopeless and no good going on, and she agreed, without opening her eyes. (*Pause.*) I asked her to look at me and after a few moments—(*pause*)—after a few moments she did, but the eyes just slits, because of the glare. I bent over her to get them in the shadow and they opened. (*Pause. Low.*) Let me in. (*Pause.*) We drifted in among the flags and stuck. The way they went down, sighing, before the stem! (*Pause.*) I lay down across her with my face in her breasts and my hand on her. We lay there without moving. But under us all moved, and moved us, gently, up and down, and from side to side.

(*Pause.*)

Past midnight. Never knew—

(*Krapp switches off, broods. Finally he fumbles in his pockets, encounters the banana, takes it out, peers at it, puts it back, fumbles, brings out the envelope, fumbles, puts back envelope, looks at his watch, gets up and goes backstage into darkness. Ten seconds. Sound of bottle*) *against glass, then brief siphon. Ten seconds. Bottle against glass alone. Ten seconds. He comes back a little unsteadily into light, goes to front of table, takes out keys, raises them to his eyes, chooses key, unlocks first drawer, peers into it, feels about inside, takes out reel, peers at it, locks drawer, puts keys back in his pocket, goes and sits down, takes reel off machine, lays it on dictionary, loads virgin reel on machine, takes envelope from his pocket, consults back of it, lays it on table, switches on, clears his throat, and begins to record.)*

KRAPP: Just been listening to that stupid bastard I took myself for thirty years ago, hard to believe I was ever as bad as that. Thank God that's all done with anyway. *(Pause.)* The eyes she had! *(Broods, realizes he is recording silence, switches off, broods. Finally.)* Everything there, everything, all the—*(Realizes this is not being recorded, switches on.)* Everything there, everything on this old muckball, all the light and dark and famine and feasting of . . . *(hesitates)* . . . the ages! *(In a shout.)* Yes! *(Pause.)* Let that go! Jesus! Take his mind off his homework! Jesus! *(Pause. Weary.)* Ah well, maybe he was right. *(Pause.)* Maybe he was right. *(Broods. Realizes. Switches off. Consults envelope.)* Pah! *(Crumples it and throws it away. Broods. Switches on.)* Nothing to say, not a squeak. What's a year now? The sour cud and the iron stool. *(Pause.)* Reveled in the word spool. *(With relish.)* Spooool! Happiest moment of the past half million. *(Pause.)* Seventeen copies sold, of which eleven at trade price to free circulating libraries beyond the seas. Getting known. *(Pause.)* One pound six and something, eight I have little doubt. *(Pause.)* Crawled out once or twice, before the summer was cold. Sat shivering in the park, drowned in dreams and burning to be gone. Not a soul. *(Pause.)* Last fancies. *(Vehemently.)* Keep 'em under! *(Pause.)* Scalded the eyes out of me reading *Effie* again, a page a day, with tears again. Effie . . . *(Pause.)* Could have been happy with her, up there on the Baltic, and the pines, and the dunes. *(Pause.)* Could I? *(Pause.)* And she? *(Pause.)* Pah! *(Pause.)* Fanny came in a couple of times. Bony old ghost of a whore. Couldn't do much, but I suppose better than a kick in the crutch. The last time wasn't so bad. How do you manage it, she said, at your age? I told her I'd been saving up for her all my life. *(Pause.)* Went to Vespers once, like when I was in short trousers. *(Pause. Sings.)* Now the day is over,

Night is drawing nigh-igh,
Shadows—*(coughing, then almost inaudible)*—of the evening
Steal across the sky.
(Gasping.) Went to sleep and fell off the pew. *(Pause.)* Sometimes wondered in the night if a last effort mightn't—*(Pause.)* Ah finish your booze now and get to your bed. Go on with this drivel in the morning. Or leave it at that. *(Pause.)* Leave it at that. *(Pause.)* Lie propped up in the dark—and wander. Be again in the dingle on a Christmas Eve, gathering holly, the red-berried. *(Pause.)* Be again on Croghan on a Sunday morning, in the haze, with the bitch, stop and listen to the bells. *(Pause.)* And so on. *(Pause.)* Be again, be again. *(Pause.)* All that old misery. *(Pause.)* Once wasn't enough for you. *(Pause.)* Lie down across her.

(Long pause. He suddenly bends over machine, switches off, wrenches off tape, throws it away, puts on the other, winds it forward to the passage he wants, switches on, listens staring front.)

TAPE: —gooseberries, she said. I said again I thought it was hopeless and no good going on, and she agreed, without opening her eyes. *(Pause.)* I asked her to look at me and after a few moments—*(pause)*—after a few moments she did, but the eyes just slits, because of the glare. I bent over her to get them in the shadow and they opened. *(Pause. Low.)* Let me in. *(Pause.)* We drifted in among the flags and stuck. The way they went down, sighing, before the stem! *(Pause.)* I lay down across her with my face in her breasts and my hand on her. We lay there without moving. But under us all moved, and moved us, gently, up and down, and from side to side.

(Pause. Krapp's lips move. No sound.)

Past midnight. Never knew such silence. The earth might be uninhabited.

(Pause.)

Here I end this reel. Box—*(pause)*—three, spool—*(pause)*—five. *(Pause.)* Perhaps my best years are gone. When there was a chance of happiness. But I wouldn't want them back. Not with the fire in me now. No, I wouldn't want them back.

(Krapp motionless staring before him. The tape runs on in silence.)

COMMENTARIES

Samuel Beckett's plays are considered difficult, obscure, experimental, and, since Martin Esslin defined the term, absurd. Absurd literature might seem to require no commentary because absurdity ought to have no significant content, but quite the opposite is true. One of the anomalies of absurdist literature is that it may require more commentary than other kinds of literature.

Martin Esslin's essay defined the term by which we describe work by Beckett and a few other playwrights influenced by him. The essay tries to establish the character of absurd drama, its limits, and its importance. Audiences were certainly baffled by Beckett's work, starting with his very successful *Waiting for Godot* and including *Krapp's Last Tape* and *Happy Days*. All these plays are restricted by space and in action. Their very essence is restriction. Esslin shows the possible range of significance in Beckett's plays and explains that if we see them properly, we can understand how they interpret experience.

Ruby Cohn is interested in performance problems and discusses Beckett's own experiences in staging and directing *Krapp's Last Tape*. Her observations provide insight into Beckett's hopes for the play and into his understanding of the way the play works onstage. Absurdist drama is not without meaning; rather, it seems capable of absorbing a wide range of meanings and of reflecting the interpreter's attitudes and observations in remarkably subtle ways.

Martin Esslin (1918–2002)
THE THEATER OF THE ABSURD

Martin Esslin was a drama critic whose work has had wide currency. He was the first to write extensively about the theater of the absurd, a term that has come to describe the plays of Samuel Beckett and a number of other post–World War II playwrights such as Eugène Ionesco and Harold Pinter. The question of what use playwrights make of the absurd and why it is an appropriate term to reflect the achievement of Beckett is explored briefly in this excerpt.

The Theater of the Absurd shows the world as an incomprehensible place. The spectators see the happenings on the stage entirely from the outside, without ever understanding the full meaning of these strange patterns of events, as newly arrived visitors might watch life in a country of which they have not yet mastered the language. The confrontation of the audience with characters and happenings which they are not quite able to comprehend makes it impossible for them to share the aspirations and emotions depicted in the play. Brecht's famous "Verfremdungs-effekt" (alienation effect), the inhibition of any identification between spectator and actor, which Brecht could never successfully achieve in his own highly rational theater, really comes into its own in the Theater of the Absurd. It is impossible to identify oneself with characters one does not understand or whose motives remain a closed book, and so the distance between the public and the happenings on the stage can he maintained. Emotional identification with the characters is replaced by a puzzled, critical attention. For while the happenings on the stage are absurd, they yet remain recognizable as somehow related to real life with *its* absurdity, so that eventually the spectators are brought face to face with the irrational side of their existence. Thus, the absurd and fantastic goings-on of the Theater of the Absurd will, in the end, be found to reveal the irrationality of the human condition and the illusion of what we thought was its apparent logical structure.

If the dialogue in these plays consists of meaningless clichés and the mechanical, circular repetition of stereotyped phrases—how many meaningless clichés and stereotyped phrases do we use in our day-to-day conversation? If the characters change their personality halfway through the action, how consistent and truly integrated are the people we meet in our real life? And if people in these plays appear as mere marionettes, helpless puppets without any will of their own, passively at the mercy of blind fate and meaningless circumstance, do we, in fact, in our overorganized world, still possess any genuine initiative or power to decide our own destiny? The spectators of the Theater of the Absurd are thus confronted with a grotesquely heightened picture of their own world: a world without faith, meaning, and genuine freedom of will. In this sense, the Theater of the Absurd is the true theater of our time.

The theater of most previous epochs reflected an accepted moral order, a world whose aims and objectives were clearly present to the minds of all its public, whether it was the audience of the medieval mystery plays with their solidly accepted faith in the Christian world order or the audience of the drama of Ibsen, Shaw, or Hauptmann with their unquestioned belief in evolution and progress. To such audiences, right and wrong were never in doubt, nor did they question the then accepted goals of human endeavor. Our own time, at least in the Western world, wholly lacks such a generally accepted and completely integrated world picture. The decline of religious faith, the destruction of the belief in automatic social and biological progress, the discovery of vast areas of irrational and unconscious forces within the human psyche, the loss of a sense of control over rational human development in an age of totalitarianism and weapons of mass destruction, have all contributed to the erosion of the basis for a dramatic convention in which the action proceeds within a fixed and self-evident framework of generally accepted values. Faced with the vacuum left by the destruction of a universally accepted and unified set of beliefs, most serious playwrights have felt the need to fit their work into the frame of values and objectives expressed in one of the contemporary ideologies: Marxism, psychoanalysis, aestheticism, or nature worship. But these, in the eyes of a writer like Adamov, are nothing but superficial rationalizations which try to hide the depth of man's predicament, his loneliness and his anxiety. Or, as Ionesco puts it:

> As far as I am concerned, I believe sincerely in the poverty of the poor, I deplore it; it is real; it can become a subject for the theatre; I also believe in the anxieties and serious troubles the rich may suffer from; but it is neither in the misery of the former nor in the melancholia of the latter, that I, for one, find my dramatic subject matter. Theatre is for me the outward projection onto the stage of an inner world; it is in my dreams, in my anxieties, in my obscure desires, in my internal contradictions that I, for one, reserve for myself the right of finding my dramatic subject matter. As I am not alone in the world, as each of us, in the depth of his being, is at the same time part and parcel of all others, my dreams, my desires, my anxieties,

my obsessions do not belong to me alone. They form part of an ancestral heritage, a very ancient storehouse which is a portion of the common property of all mankind. It is this, which, transcending their outward diversity, reunites all human beings and constitutes our profound common patrimony, the universal language.[1]

In other words, the commonly acceptable framework of beliefs and values of former epochs which has now been shattered is to be replaced by the community of dreams and desires of a collective unconscious. And, to quote Ionesco again:

> . . . the new dramatist is one . . . who tries to link up with what is most ancient; new language and subject matter in a dramatic structure which aims at being clearer, more stripped of inessentials and more purely theatrical; the rejection of traditionalism to rediscover tradition; a synthesis of knowledge and invention, of the real and imaginary, of the particular and the universal, or as they say now, of the individual and the collective. . . . By expressing my deepest obsessions, I express my deepest humanity. I become one with all others, spontaneously, over and above all the barriers of caste and different psychologies. I express my solitude and become one with all other solitudes.[2]

What is the tradition with which the Theater of the Absurd—at first sight the most revolutionary and radically new movement—is trying to link itself? It is in fact a very ancient and a very rich tradition, nourished from many and varied sources: the verbal exuberance and extravagant inventions of Rabelais, the age-old clowning of the Roman mimes and the Italian *Commedia dell'Arte*, the knock-about humor of circus clowns like Grock; the wild, archetypal symbolism of English nonsense verse, the baroque horror of Jacobean dramatists like Webster or Tourneur, the harsh, incisive and often brutal tones of the German drama of Grabbe, Büchner, Kleist, and Wedekind with its delirious language and grotesque inventiveness; and the Nordic paranoia of the dreams and persecution fantasies of Strindberg.

Ruby Cohn (b. 1922)
BECKETT DIRECTING

Ruby Cohn has written books and articles about Beckett and has become one of the most important Beckett scholars. This discussion focuses on the way in which Beckett works with actors, directors, and other people in the theater. Cohn's description of the directions Beckett gave to the actors in Krapp's Last Tape *reveals his imaginative attitude toward the play. The thought that he once felt Krapp should wear clown white and behave farcically could certainly affect the way we interpret the play. Cohn is careful to give us information about the way Beckett responded to performances and actors, thus emphasizing the play as a performed work of art, not just something to read.*

After the intricate cross-relationships and complex repetitive texture of *Endgame*, directing *Krapp's Last Tape* might seem like child's play. It will be recalled that Beckett wrote the one-character piece in English for actor Pat Magee, who was first

[1]Eugène Ionesco, "L'Impromptu de l'Alma," *Théâtre II*, Paris, 1958.
[2]Ionesco, "The Avant-Garde Theatre," *World Theatre*, 8.3 (Autumn 1959).

directed by Donald McWhinnie. In 1958 in London Beckett worked closely with actor and director. The three of them played hard and then pub-crawled, but there was no pub crawling in 1969 in Berlin, where Krapp's role went to ponderous Martin Held.

James Knowlson has discussed the complex symbolism of *Krapp's Last Tape*, succinctly summarized in Beckett's Director's Notebook:

> Krapp decrees physical (ethical) incompatibility of light (Spiritual) and dark (Sensual) only when he intuits possibility of their reconciliation as rational-irrational. He turns from fact of anti-mind alien to mind to thought of anti-mind constituent of mind.[1]

Despite this esoteric and symbolic background, the surface of *Krapp's Last Tape* is realistic, but Beckett's Director's Notebook dwells on realistic and nonrealistic detail.

Unlike the *Endgame* notebook, that for *Krapp* does not divide the play into rehearsal scenes. Instead, Beckett lists twenty-seven matters needing directorial attention, from the metaphysical "1. *Choix-hasard*" (choice-guess) to the very physical "27. *Endgültig Werkstatt*" (final . . . Werkstatt [version]). Beckett calculates that Krapp has been recording for forty-five years, since there are nine boxes, each containing five spools of tape. The notebook designates the tape recorder as a masturbatory agent, and Beckett instructed Held to hold the box erotically. His separation of speech from motion, introduced into *Come and Go* and *Endgame*, becomes the fulcrum of performance: "Play therefore composed of two approximately equal parts, listening-immobility and nonlistening-motion." For the *écoute* (listening) Beckett began rehearsals with a provisional tape of thirty-nine-year-old Krapp, but this was replaced.

Beckett wished abrupt and vivid disjunction between still listening and agitated nonlistening. Toward this end, he amplified his stage directions and simplified his stage picture. He eliminated Krapp's clown makeup and endowed him with worn-out rather than farcical clothes. Krapp's table was clean at the start, and Beckett excised the comic business with keys and envelope, but he introduced fumbling rheumatic fingers. He suggested to Held a moving "rest" gesture; Krapp hugs himself shivering. Realistically, an old man seeks warmth; symbolically, Krapp loves himself.

Because of Beckett's stage simplification, we more easily grasp similarities between the young and the old Krapp. Action begins when Krapp peers short-sightedly at his large silver watch, and it proves to be time for his banana. After two bananas are eaten onstage, Krapp on tape mentions three. The man who has stepped from his spotlighted circle into darkness and back listens to a tape announcing that he loves to return from darkness to himself, Krapp. And yet, Krapp-Held looks in astonishment at the tape recorder when he hears the voice say: "Me. (*pause*) Krapp." For Krapp as for Rimbaud, "*Je est un autre*" ("I is another").

Separating speech from motion, Beckett moved Krapp toward pathos, although the effect in *Endgame* was lugubriously comic. In the opening mime Krapp makes clumsy comic gestures, but it is a rheumatic old man who makes them, and it is a lonely old man who personifies tapes as "little rascal" and "little scoundrel." Whenever Krapp-Held rises from the table, he leans heavily on both hands. Whenever Krapp walks away from the table, he crosses in front and to the right; he fears the darkness at his left. His love-hate relation with objects is comic, for pathos is a

---

[1] Quoted in Pierre Chabert, "Beckett as Director," *Gambit* (28): 62.

greater danger to *Krapp's Last Tape* than to *Endgame*. Beckett dissolved pathos by beating time for Krapp-Held's nonverbal and comic noises—wheezing, walking, turning pages, drinking, and even slamming objects on his table.

When taped speech fills the theater, Krapp listens motionless, comic gestures spent. His head is bent at an angle of 45 degrees, his left hand caresses the tape recorder, and the fingers of his right hand sometimes drum impatiently. Unrecorded in Beckett's notebook is the frequent ternary rhythm evident in performance. Krapp listens to three main events; there are three breaks in the equinox account and three in the "Farewell to Love." At the play's beginning Krapp walks three times out of his spotlight into darkness and back. He disappears through his backstage curtain three times—for his ledger, pile of tapes, and tape recorder, the increased weight of the objects revealed by increased fatigue. In the later action Beckett changed the three backstage exits to offstage drinking, search for a dictionary, offstage drinking and search for a microphone. Krapp consults his watch three times; he moves the tape ahead three times and back three times. After he records, he looks at the machine three times before he wrenches off his last tape.

Within this ternary pattern Krapp shows emotional variety—his lubricity on peeling a banana, his impatience with a younger self, his contained grief at his mother's death, his boast to a whore, his extrapolation of a novel, his fear of dark at his left, his inability to sustain love, which he perhaps regrets when he plays and replays the "Farewell to Love." Krapp-Held squinted when he tremulously spoke of eyes—in the words of the notebook, *"ein Traumgefressener Mensch"* ("A man consumed by dreams").

With improved vision of his own (after operations to remove cataracts), Beckett returned to *Krapp* in 1975—in his French translation, to accompany the French premiere of *Not I* at the Petit d'Orsay. Ten years after *L'Hypothèse* Beckett and Chabert again worked together on a one-character play. In Paris as in Berlin, the central image remained a Krapp who was "one body with the machine." As in *L'Hypothèse* Beckett divided the small stage into areas: the central table (place of reverie) and the backstage alcove (place of practicality).

Because of [the young actor Pierre] Chabert's relative youth, Beckett dressed him in a frayed dressing gown to hide his tall frame, a toque to hide his abundant hair, and black half gloves that evoke premonitions of death. Pale and thin, Krapp-Chabert shivered with an old man's cold, and his myopic eyes seemed intent on piercing the dark. He stretched to listen so as to compensate for his deafness, one hand curled round the recorder handle. Immobile, he sucked at his cheeks, leaving his mouth open. Tall, he bumped the overhead light when he rose from the table, and the light continued to move while he listened, still, to the "moves" of the "Farewell to Love."

Musically trained, Chabert readily responded to Beckett's sonata breakdown of the dialogue into b-A(b)-A-B-a, A being the taped voice, B the live voice, and small letters standing for short duration. Much of the brief (three-week) rehearsal period was devoted to the B-voice, sharp and staccato in b and (b), but rhythmically varied in B; the high-pitched quaver of the conventional stage old man was especially to be avoided. In both A and B, Beckett wished counterpoint between objectivity and self-disgust or between objectivity and fascination with a woman or a word.

In Paris Beckett revised key scenes of both nonlistening and listening. When Krapp goes backstage to drink, he leaves a curtain open, so that his guzzling shadow is seen in a long light rectangle, projected from a Chinese lantern on a screen. This space is sharply different from the dream-memory space of Krapp's table. Thus, Krapp versus his past is theatricalized audibly as Krapp versus his taped voice; visually as a shrunken actual Krapp versus his enlarged shadow. In the three playbacks of the love scene, Krapp listens first with bowed head, then with his face on the table, and finally, after a long look over his left shoulder into darkness, with stony erectness. Krapp-Chabert's last playback of "Farewell to Love" is clarified as his stoic farewell to life as well. After the stage lights go out, the tape-recorder light continues to glow—a small *memento mori.*

A little over two years later, in 1977, Beckett found himself directing an English *Krapp* in Berlin's Akademie der Künste, as a favor to his friend Rick Cluchey. Despite two previous productions, he made extensive director's notes, which have been published in the San Quentin Drama Workshop Program and in Bethanien Center Publications. His headings summarize the areas of his concern: "Tape Montage, Costume, Props [a long list], Lighting, Opening, *Hain* ["friend Death" in a poem by Matthias Claudius], Drinks, Song, Microphone, End." Visual details were carried over from the Paris production—a dressing gown, modified banana business, enlarged shadow of drinking, erect posture at the end as at the beginning.

This time Beckett divided the play into four rehearsal scenes: (1) Beginning to ledger note: "Farewell to—love"; (2) "Thirty-nine today . . ." to "A girl in a shabby green coat. . . . No?" (with "Connaught" replaced by "Kerry" and the hymn cut); (3) "When I look back—" to preparations for recording. (Watch business is cut. Looking up "viduity" in the dictionary, near-sighted Krapp first reads "vicar" and "vicious"); (4) From the newly introduced "Fanny" before "Just been listening . . ." to the end. ("One pound . . . doubt" disappears. "Finger and thumb" replaces "a kick in the crutch," and "dozed away" replaces "went to sleep.")

In contrast to Held's erotic recorder, Cluchey's is both friend and enemy, alternately caressed and cursed. Even more sharply than earlier, the Akademie *Krapp* points up opposites: stillness-movement, silence-noise, dark-light, black-white. As a corollary to such polarity, Beckett had Cluchey emphasize the "or"s in the "viduity" definition.

Beckett never spoke to the Workshop members of the symbolic genesis of the play, but they worried together in the inadequately equipped Akademie about nuances of light and sound. To the ternary rhythms of the earlier productions Beckett added long still "brood"s after the words "Incomparable," "crystolite," and "side by side." He sought tonal interest for the often-repeated phrase "Ah well," which had nearly become the play's title. Live Krapp's "Be again, be again" was to sound like the churchbells of his youth. Clinging to rhythm in the face of death, Krapp-Cluchey was sometimes rehearsed with Beckett beating time—for the little rushes of seven steps to and from the table, for the longer series of thirteen steps to and from the alcove, for the offstage drinking sounds (clink of bottle against glass, bottle down, drink, glass down, cough-sigh), and for the long *Hain* (sudden stiffening, slow head turn to left, hold, slow return to right, resume tape). Although the American group knew little German, they prattled glibly of the *Hain,* unaware that it derived from the Matthias Claudius poem. Seeking the precise shuffle sound he wanted from Krapp's run-walk, Beckett gave Cluchey his own worn slippers. In the last week (of nearly four) of rehearsals Beckett changed Krapp-Cluchey's listening position, right hand embracing the recorder, left hand behind it, head angled about 60 degrees to the table. Under a conical dunce-cap light, the metallic rotating tape was reflected on Cluchey's left cheek—a kind of shadow pulse. San Quentin technical men Hauptle and Thorpe conferred on how to eliminate it, but Beckett told them softly, "I love it."

Lorraine Hansberry

Lorraine Hansberry (1930–1965), like John Millington Synge, died tragically young. Her loss to the American stage is incalculable; her successes were only beginning, and at her death she seemed on the verge of a remarkable career.

Hansberry grew up in a middle-class black family in Chicago. Her father, who was successful in real estate, founded one of the first banks in Chicago to solicit black patronage. However, he spent much of his life vainly trying to find a way to make a decent life for himself and his family in America. He eventually gave up on the United States, and when he died in 1945, he was scouting for a place in Mexico where he could move his family to live comfortably.

Lorraine Hansberry went to college after her father died, and her first ambition was to become a visual artist. She attended the Art Institute of Chicago and numerous other schools before moving to New York. Once there, she became interested in some drama groups and soon married the playwright Howard Nemiroff. She began writing, sharing parts of her first play with friends in her own living room. They helped raise money to stage the play, and, with black director Lloyd Richards and little-known Sidney Poitier as Walter Lee Younger, *A Raisin in the Sun* (1959) thrust her into the drama spotlight.

In 1959, only twenty-nine years old, Hansberry was the most promising woman writing for the American stage. She was also the first black American to win the New York Drama Critics' Circle Award for the best play of the year. She died of cancer the day her second produced play, *The Sign in Sidney Brustein's Window,* closed. She had finished a third play, *Les Blancs,* which was brought to Broadway by Nemiroff in 1970. Neither of her other plays was as popular as *Raisin,* but the two later plays demonstrate a deepening concern for and understanding of some of the key issues of racial and sexual politics that interested her throughout her career.

The hero in *The Sign in Sidney Brustein's Window* is a Jewish intellectual in the 1950s in Greenwich Village. Feeling that all the radical struggle of the 1930s has been lost, he agitates for personal involvement, for emotional and intellectual action. This idealistic play anticipates the political agitation in the United States during the mid-1960s and early 1970s. *Les Blancs* takes as its central character a black African intellectual, Tshembe, and explores his relationship to both Europe and Africa. In his uneasiness with both cultures he discovers that he cannot live outside his own history. *Les Blancs* reveals some of Hansberry's deep interest in Pan-Africanism and the search for a personal heritage.

A posthumous work was put together by Howard Nemiroff from Hansberry's notes, letters, and early writings. Titled *To Be Young, Gifted, and Black* (1971), it has helped solidify her achievements. Although we will never know just how Hansberry's career would have developed had she lived, her gifts were so remarkable that we can only lament that she is not writing for the stage today.

A RAISIN IN THE SUN

When produced on Broadway in 1959, *A Raisin in the Sun* was somewhat prophetic. Lorraine Hansberry's themes of blacks pressing forward with legitimate demands and expressing interest in their African heritage were to become primary themes of black culture in the 1960s, in the 1970s, and, indeed, to this day. The title of her play is from a poem by Langston Hughes, one of the poets of the Harlem Renaissance. It warns of the social explosions that might occur if society permits blacks to remain unequal and unfree.

The work appeared at the beginning of renewed political activity on the part of African Americans; it reveals its historical position in the use of the word *Negro*, which black activists rejected in the 1960s as an enslaving euphemism. This play illustrates the American dream as it is felt not just by African Americans but by all Americans: if you work hard, save your money, are honorable, and hope, then you can one day buy your own home and have the kind of space and privacy that permit people to live with dignity. Yet this very theme has plagued the play from the beginning: its apparent emphasis on middle-class, bourgeois values. On the surface, it seems to celebrate a mild form of consumerism—the desire for the house in the suburbs with the TV set inside to anesthetize its occupants. Hansberry was shocked when such criticisms, from black critics as well as white, were leveled at the play. She had written it very carefully to explore just those issues in a context that demonstrated that black families' needs paralleled those of white families, while also having a different dimension that most white families could not understand.

Hansberry was quick to admit that Walter Lee Younger was affected by the same craziness influencing all Americans who lusted after possessions and the power they might confer. Walter wants to take his father's insurance money to buy a liquor store in partnership with a con man. Lena Younger argues against her son's plan as a profanation of her husband's memory as well as an abuse of the American dream: she believes that the product of a liquor store will further poison the community. What she wants is not a consumer product but the emblem of identity and security that she feels her family deserves.

Hansberry is painfully honest in this play. Walter Lee's weaknesses are recognizable. His male chauvinistic behavior undoes him. He is caught up in the old, failing pattern of male dominance over women. But none of the women in his life will tolerate his behavior. Hansberry also admits the social distinctions among African Americans. George Murchison is a young man from a wealthy black family, and when Beneatha tells Lena that she will not marry George, she says, "The only people in the world who are more snobbish than rich white people are rich colored people." Beneatha's desire to be a doctor is obviously not rooted in consumerism any more than in the middle-class need to be comfortable and rich.

The confusion caused in the family by a native African, Asagai, is realistically portrayed. In the early days of the Pan-African movement in the 1960s, blacks were often bemused by the way Africans presented themselves. Interest in Africa on the part of the American blacks was distorted by Tarzan movies and *National Geographic* articles, none of which presented black Africans as role models. Therefore, the adjustment to black African pride, though it was made swiftly, was not without difficulties. The Youngers are presented as no more sophisticated about black Africans than the rest of black society would be.

The dignity of the Younger family finally triumphs. When Walter Lee stands up for himself, he is asserting not macho domination but black manhood—a manhood that needs no domination over women. He is expressing not a desire for a big house—as he had done when he reflected on the possessions of his rich employer—but a desire to demonstrate to members of the Clybourne Park Improvement Association that the Youngers are their social equals and that they have a right to live wherever they choose.

A *Raisin in the Sun* in Performance

Lloyd Richards directed the first production at the Ethel Barrymore Theater in New York on March 11, 1959. The play won major prizes, and Sidney Poitier as a passionate Walter Lee Younger was a signal success. *New York Times* critic Brooks Atkinson said, "Since the performance is also honest and since Sidney Poitier is a candid actor, *A Raisin in the Sun* has vigor as well as veracity and is likely to destroy the complacency of any one who sees it." Critics were astonished that a first play could have the sophistication and depth they saw onstage.

The Theatre Guild staged the play in 1960 in Boston with a different cast, but the production received similar reviews. The film version, with most of the New York cast, was directed by Daniel Petrie in 1961. A revival in Chicago in 1983 at the Art Institute of Chicago—Hansberry's alma mater—was not altogether successful, but critics felt the text held up well. The Chicago revival, like the 1985 Merrimack Repertory Theater revival in Lowell, Massachusetts, demonstrated only that the play needs strong actors to have the desired impact. A twenty-fifth-anniversary production was directed by Lloyd Richards at the Yale Repertory Theatre in 1983. This production was taken to New York in 1986 and enjoyed a successful run. The setting was a realistic interior, emphasizing the play's realistic style. Critic Mel Gussow felt the revival demonstrated that the play is "an enduring work of contemporary theater." The production also revealed that Hansberry's language had not become dated, nor had the social issues of the play become any less critical and important twenty-five years later. In fact, a production starring hip-hop artist and fashion mogul Sean "P. Diddy" Combs and Audra McDonald during the 2004 season in New York City got good reviews. This production was shown on television in 2008 in a version that gained the play a brand-new audience. Like the proletarian plays of Sean O'Casey, who inspired Lorraine Hansberry, this play continues to move us because the problems it examines are serious and still remain.

Lorraine Hansberry *(1930–1965)*

A Raisin in the Sun

1959

HARLEM (A DREAM DEFERRED)

What happens to a dream deferred?

> *Does it dry up*
> *like a raisin in the sun?*
> *Or fester like a sore—*
> *And then run?*
> *Does it stink like rotten meat?*

Or crust and sugar over—
like a syrupy sweet?

Maybe it just sags
like a heavy load.

Or does it explode?   — LANGSTON HUGHES

Characters

RUTH YOUNGER
TRAVIS YOUNGER
WALTER LEE YOUNGER (*brother*)
BENEATHA YOUNGER
LENA YOUNGER (*Mama*)
JOSEPH ASAGAI
GEORGE MURCHISON
MRS. JOHNSON
KARL LINDNER
BOBO
MOVING MEN

The action of the play is set in Chicago's Southside, sometime between World War II and the present.

Act I

Scene I: *Friday morning.*
Scene II: *The following morning.*

Act II

Scene I: *Later, the same day.*
Scene II: *Friday night, a few weeks later.*
Scene III: *Moving day, one week later.*

Act III

An hour later.

ACT I • Scene I

(*The Younger living room would be a comfortable and well-ordered room if it were not for a number of indestructible contradictions to this state of being. Its furnishings are typical and undistinguished and their primary feature now is that they have clearly had to accommodate the living of too many people for too many years—and they are tired. Still, we can see that at some time, a time probably no longer remembered by the family [except perhaps for Mama], the furnishings of*

this room were actually selected with care and love and even hope—and brought to this apartment and arranged with taste and pride.)

(*That was a long time ago. Now the once loved pattern of the couch upholstery has to fight to show itself from under acres of crocheted doilies and couch covers which have themselves finally come to be more important than the upholstery. And here a table or a chair has been moved to disguise the worn places in the carpet; but the carpet has fought back by showing its weariness, with depressing uniformity, elsewhere on its surface.*)

(*Weariness has, in fact, won in this room. Everything has been polished, washed, sat on, used, scrubbed too often. All pretenses but living itself have long since vanished from the very atmosphere of this room.*)

(*Moreover, a section of this room, for it is not really a room unto itself, though the landlord's lease would make it seem so, slopes backward to provide a small kitchen area, where the family prepares the meals that are eaten in the living room proper, which must also serve as dining room. The single window that has been provided for these "two" rooms is located in this kitchen area. The sole natural light the family may enjoy in the course of a day is only that which fights its way through this little window.*)

(*At left, a door leads to a bedroom which is shared by Mama and her daughter, Beneatha. At right, opposite, is a second room [which in the beginning of the life of this apartment was probably a breakfast room] which serves as a bedroom for Walter and his wife, Ruth.*)

(*Time: Sometime between World War II and the present.*)

(*Place: Chicago's Southside.*)

(*At rise: It is morning dark in the living room. Travis is asleep on the make-down bed at center. An alarm clock sounds from within the bedroom at right, and presently Ruth enters from that room and closes the door behind her. She crosses sleepily toward the window. As she passes her sleeping son she reaches down and shakes him a little. At the window she raises the shade and a dusky Southside morning light comes in feebly. She fills a pot with water and puts it on to boil. She calls to the boy, between yawns, in a slightly muffled voice.)*

(Ruth is about thirty. We can see that she was a pretty girl, even exceptionally so, but now it is apparent that life has been little that she expected, and disappointment has already begun to hang in her face. In a few years, before thirty-five even, she will be known among her people as a "settled woman.")

(She crosses to her son and gives him a good, final, rousing shake.)

RUTH: Come on now, boy, it's seven thirty! *(Her son sits up at last, in a stupor of sleepiness.)* I say hurry up, Travis! You ain't the only person in the world got to use a bathroom! *(The child, a sturdy, handsome little boy of ten or eleven, drags himself out of the bed and almost blindly takes his towels and "today's clothes" from drawers and a closet and goes out to the bathroom, which is in an outside hall and which is shared by another family or families on the same floor. Ruth crosses to the bedroom door at right and opens it and calls in to her husband.)* Walter Lee! . . . It's after seven thirty! Lemme see you do some waking up in there now! *(She waits.)* You better get up from there, man! It's after seven thirty I tell you. *(She waits again.)* All right, you just go ahead and lay there and next thing you know Travis be finished and Mr. Johnson'll be in there and you'll be fussing and cussing round here like a madman! And be late too! *(She waits, at the end of patience.)* Walter Lee—it's time for you to GET UP!

(She waits another second and then starts to go into the bedroom, but is apparently satisfied that her husband has begun to get up. She stops, pulls the door to, and returns to the kitchen area. She wipes her face with a moist cloth and runs her fingers through her sleep-disheveled hair in a vain effort and ties an apron around her housecoat. The bedroom door at right opens and her husband stands in the doorway in his pajamas, which are rumpled and mismated. He is a lean, intense young man in his middle thirties, inclined to quick nervous movements and erratic speech habits—and always in his voice there is a quality of indictment.)

WALTER: Is he out yet?

RUTH: What you mean *out?* He ain't hardly got in there good yet.

WALTER *(wandering in, still more oriented to sleep than to a new day)*: Well, what was you doing all that yelling for if I can't even get in there yet? *(Stopping and thinking.)* Check coming today?

RUTH: They *said* Saturday and this is just Friday and I hopes to God you ain't going to get up here first thing this morning and start talking to me 'bout no money—'cause I 'bout don't want to hear it.

WALTER: Something the matter with you this morning?

RUTH: No—I'm just sleepy as the devil. What kind of eggs you want?

WALTER: Not scrambled. *(Ruth starts to scramble eggs.)* Paper come? *(Ruth points impatiently to the rolled up Tribune on the table, and he gets it and spreads it out and vaguely reads the front page.)* Set off another bomb yesterday.

RUTH *(maximum indifference)*: Did they?

WALTER *(looking up)*: What's the matter with you?

RUTH: Ain't nothing the matter with me. And don't keep asking me that this morning.

WALTER: Ain't nobody bothering you. *(Reading the news of the day absently again.)* Say Colonel McCormick is sick.

RUTH *(affecting tea-party interest)*: Is he now? Poor thing.

WALTER *(sighing and looking at his watch)*: Oh, me. *(He waits.)* Now what is that boy doing in that bathroom all this time? He just going to have to start getting up earlier. I can't be being late to work on account of him fooling around in there.

RUTH *(turning on him)*: Oh, no he ain't going to be getting up no earlier no such thing! It ain't his fault that he can't get to bed no earlier nights 'cause he got a bunch of crazy good-for-nothing clowns sitting up running their mouths in what is supposed to be his bedroom after ten o'clock at night . . .

WALTER: That's what you mad about, ain't it? The things I want to talk about with my friends just couldn't be important in your mind, could they?

(He rises and finds a cigarette in her handbag on the table and crosses to the little window and looks out, smoking and deeply enjoying this first one.)

RUTH *(almost matter of factly, a complaint too automatic to deserve emphasis)*: Why you always got to smoke before you eat in the morning?

WALTER *(at the window)*: Just look at 'em down there . . . Running and racing to work . . . *(He turns and faces his wife and watches her a moment at the stove, and then, suddenly.)* You look young this morning, baby.

RUTH *(indifferently)*: Yeah?

WALTER: Just for a second—stirring them eggs. Just for a second it was—you looked real young again. *(He reaches for her; she crosses away. Then, drily.)* It's gone now—you look like yourself again!

RUTH: Man, if you don't shut up and leave me alone.

WALTER *(looking out to the street again)*: First thing a man ought to learn in life is not to make love to no colored woman first thing in the morning. You all some eeeevil people at eight o'clock in the morning.

(Travis appears in the hall doorway, almost fully dressed and quite wide awake now, his towels and pajamas across his shoulders. He opens the door and signals for his father to make the bathroom in a hurry.)

TRAVIS *(watching the bathroom)*: Daddy, come on!

(Walter gets his bathroom utensils and flies out to the bathroom.)

RUTH: Sit down and have your breakfast, Travis.

TRAVIS: Mama, this is Friday. (*Gleefully*.) Check coming tomorrow, huh?

RUTH: You get your mind off money and eat your breakfast.

TRAVIS (*eating*): This is the morning we supposed to bring the fifty cents to school.

RUTH: Well, I ain't got no fifty cents this morning.

TRAVIS: Teacher say we have to.

RUTH: I don't care what teacher say. I ain't got it. Eat your breakfast, Travis.

TRAVIS: I *am* eating.

RUTH: Hush up now and just eat!

(*The boy gives her an exasperated look for her lack of understanding and eats grudgingly.*)

TRAVIS: You think Grandmama would have it?

RUTH: No! And I want you to stop asking your grandmother for money, you hear me?

TRAVIS (*outraged*): Gaaaleee! I don't ask her, she just gimme it sometimes!

RUTH: Travis Willard Younger—I got too much on me this morning to be—

TRAVIS: Maybe Daddy—

RUTH: *Travis!*

(*The boy hushes abruptly. They are both quiet and tense for several seconds.*)

TRAVIS (*presently*): Could I maybe go carry some groceries in front of the supermarket for a little while after school then?

RUTH: Just hush, I said. (*Travis jabs his spoon into his cereal bowl viciously and rests his head in anger upon his fists.*) If you through eating, you can get over there and make up your bed.

(*The boy obeys stiffly and crosses the room, almost mechanically, to the bed and more or less folds the bedding into a heap, then angrily gets his books and cap.*)

TRAVIS (*sulking and standing apart from her unnaturally*): I'm gone.

RUTH (*looking up from the stove to inspect him automatically*): Come here. (*He crosses to her and she studies his head.*) If you don't take this comb and fix this here head, you better! (*Travis puts down his books with a great sigh of oppression and crosses to the mirror. His mother mutters under her breath about his "slubbornness."*) 'Bout to march out of here with that head looking just like chickens slept in it! I just don't know where you get your slubborn ways . . . And get your jacket, too. Looks chilly out this morning.

TRAVIS (*with conspicuously brushed hair and jacket*): I'm gone.

RUTH: Get carfare and milk money—(*waving one finger*)—and not a single penny for no caps, you hear me?

TRAVIS (*with sullen politeness*): Yes'm.

(*He turns in outrage to leave. His mother watches after him as in his frustration he approaches the door almost*

comically. *When she speaks to him, her voice has become a very gentle tease.*)

RUTH (*mocking; as she thinks he would say it*): Oh, Mama makes me so mad sometimes, I don't know what to do! (*She waits and continues to his back as he stands stock-still in front of the door.*) I wouldn't kiss that woman good-bye for nothing in this world this morning! (*The boy finally turns around and rolls his eyes at her, knowing the mood has changed and he is vindicated; he does not, however, move toward her yet.*) Not for nothing in this world! (*She finally laughs aloud at him and holds out her arms to him and we see that it is a way between them, very old and practiced. He crosses to her and allows her to embrace him warmly but keeps his face fixed with masculine rigidity. She holds him back from her presently and looks at him and runs her fingers over the features of his face. With utter gentleness—*) Now—whose little old angry man are you?

TRAVIS (*the masculinity and gruffness start to fade at last*): Aw gaalee—Mama . . .

RUTH (*mimicking*): Aw—gaaaaalleeeee, Mama! (*She pushes him, with rough playfulness and finality, toward the door.*) Get on out of here or you going to be late.

TRAVIS (*in the face of love, new aggressiveness*): Mama, could I *please* go carry groceries?

RUTH: Honey, it's starting to get so cold evenings.

WALTER (*coming in from the bathroom and drawing a make-believe gun from a make-believe holster and shooting at his son*): What is it he wants to do?

RUTH: Go carry groceries after school at the supermarket.

WALTER: Well, let him go . . .

TRAVIS (*quickly, to the ally*): I *have* to—she won't gimme the fifty cents . . .

WALTER (*to his wife only*): Why not?

RUTH (*simply, and with flavor*): 'Cause we don't have it.

WALTER (*to Ruth only*): What you tell the boy things like that for? (*Reaching down into his pants with a rather important gesture.*) Here, son—

(*He hands the boy the coin, but his eyes are directed to his wife's. Travis takes the money happily.*)

TRAVIS: Thanks, Daddy.

(*He starts out. Ruth watches both of them with murder in her eyes. Walter stands and stares back at her with defiance and suddenly reaches into his pocket again on an afterthought.*)

WALTER (*without even looking at his son, still staring hard at his wife*): In fact, here's another fifty cents . . . Buy yourself some fruit today—or take a taxicab to school or something!

TRAVIS: Whoopee—

(*He leaps up and clasps his father around the middle with his legs, and they face each other in mutual appreciation; slowly Walter Lee peeks around the boy to*

*catch the violent rays from his wife's eyes and draws his
head back as if shot.*)

WALTER: You better get down now—and get to school,
man.

TRAVIS (*at the door*): O.K. Good-bye.

(*He exits.*)

WALTER (*after him, pointing with pride*): That's my boy.
(*She looks at him in disgust and turns back to her
work.*) You know what I was thinking 'bout in the
bathroom this morning?

RUTH: No.

WALTER: How come you always try to be so pleasant!

RUTH: What is there to be pleasant 'bout!

WALTER: You want to know what I was thinking 'bout
in the bathroom or not!

RUTH: I know what you thinking 'bout.

WALTER (*ignoring her*): 'Bout what me and Willy Harris
was talking about last night.

RUTH (*immediately—a refrain*): Willy Harris is a good-
for-nothing loudmouth.

WALTER: Anybody who talks to me has got to be a good-
for-nothing loudmouth, ain't he! And what you know
about who is just a good-for-nothing loudmouth?
Charlie Atkins was just a "good-for-nothing loudmouth" too, wasn't he! When he wanted me to go in
the dry-cleaning business with him. And now—he's
grossing a hundred thousand a year. A hundred thousand dollars a year! You still call *him* a loudmouth!

RUTH (*bitterly*): Oh, Walter Lee . . .

(*She folds her head on her arms over the table.*)

WALTER (*rising and coming to her and standing over her*):
You tired, ain't you? Tired of everything. Me, the boy,
the way we live—this beat-up hole—everything.
Ain't you? (*She doesn't look up, doesn't answer.*) So
tired—moaning and groaning all the time, but you
wouldn't do nothing to help, would you? You couldn't
be on my side that long for nothing, could you?

RUTH: Walter, please leave me alone.

WALTER: A man needs for a woman to back him up . . .

RUTH: Walter—

WALTER: Mama would listen to you. You know she listen to you more than she do me and Bennie. She
think more of you. All you have to do is just sit down
with her when you drinking your coffee one morning
and talking 'bout things like you do and—(*He sits
down beside her and demonstrates graphically what
he thinks her methods and tone should be.*)—you
just sip your coffee, see, and say easy like that you
been thinking 'bout that deal Walter Lee is so interested in, 'bout the store and all, and sip some more
coffee, like what you saying ain't really that important to you—And the next thing you know, she be
listening good and asking you questions and when I
come home—I can tell her the details. This ain't no
fly-by-night proposition, baby. I mean we figured it
out, me and Willy and Bobo.

RUTH (*with a frown*): Bobo?

WALTER: Yeah. You see, this little liquor store we got in
mind cost seventy-five thousand and we figured the
initial investment on the place be 'bout thirty thousand, see. That be ten thousand each. Course, there's
a couple of hundred you got to pay so's you don't
spend your life just waiting for them clowns to let
your license get approved—

RUTH: You mean graft?

WALTER (*frowning impatiently*): Don't call it that. See
there, that just goes to show you what women understand about the world. Baby, don't *nothing* happen
for you in this world 'less you pay *somebody* off!

RUTH: Walter, leave me alone! (*She raises her head and
stares at him vigorously—then says, more quietly.*)
Eat your eggs, they gonna be cold.

WALTER (*straightening up from her and looking off*):
That's it. There you are. Man say to his woman: I got
me a dream. His woman say: Eat your eggs. (*Sadly, but
gaining in power.*) Man say: I got to take hold of this
here world, baby! And a woman will say: Eat your
eggs and go to work. (*Passionately now.*) Man say: I
got to change my life, I'm choking to death, baby! And
his woman say—(*in utter anguish as he brings his fists
down on his thighs*)—Your eggs is getting cold!

RUTH (*softly*): Walter, that ain't none of our money.

WALTER (*not listening at all or even looking at her*): This
morning, I was lookin' in the mirror and thinking
about it . . . I'm thirty-five years old; I been married
eleven years and I got a boy who sleeps in the living
room—(*very, very quietly*)—and all I got to give
him is stories about how rich white people live . . .

RUTH: Eat your eggs, Walter.

WALTER (*slams the table and jumps up*):—DAMN MY
EGGS—DAMN ALL THE EGGS THAT EVER WAS!

RUTH: Then go to work.

WALTER (*looking up at her*): See—I'm trying to talk to
you 'bout myself—(*shaking his head with the repetition*)—and all you can say is eat them eggs and go to
work.

RUTH (*wearily*): Honey, you never say nothing new. I listen to you every day, every night and every morning,
and you never say nothing new. (*Shrugging.*) So you
would rather *be* Mr. Arnold than be his chauffeur.
So—I would *rather* be living in Buckingham Palace.

WALTER: That is just what is wrong with the colored
woman in this world . . . Don't understand about
building their men up and making 'em feel like they
somebody. Like they can do something.

RUTH (*drily, but to hurt*): There *are* colored men who do
things.

WALTER: No thanks to the colored woman.

RUTH: Well, being a colored woman, I guess I can't help
myself none.

(*She rises and gets the ironing board and sets it up and
attacks a huge pile of rough-dried clothes, sprinkling
them in preparation for the ironing and then rolling
them into tight fat balls.*)

WALTER (*mumbling*): We one group of men tied to a race of women with small minds!

(*His sister Beneatha enters. She is about twenty, as slim and intense as her brother. She is not as pretty as her sister-in-law, but her lean, almost intellectual face has a handsomeness of its own. She wears a bright red flannel nightie, and her thick hair stands wildly about her head. Her speech is a mixture of many things; it is different from the rest of the family's insofar as education has permeated her sense of English — and perhaps the Midwest rather than the South has finally — at last — won out in her inflection; but not altogether, because over all of it is a soft slurring and transformed use of vowels which is the decided influence of the Southside. She passes through the room without looking at either Ruth or Walter and goes to the outside door and looks, a little blindly, out to the bathroom. She sees that it has been lost to the Johnsons. She closes the door with a sleepy vengeance and crosses to the table and sits down a little defeated.*)

BENEATHA: I am going to start timing those people.

WALTER: You should get up earlier.

BENEATHA (*Her face in her hands. She is still fighting the urge to go back to bed.*): Really — would you suggest dawn? Where's the paper?

WALTER (*pushing the paper across the table to her as he studies her almost clinically, as though he has never seen her before*): You a horrible-looking chick at this hour.

BENEATHA (*drily*): Good morning, everybody.

WALTER (*senselessly*): How is school coming?

BENEATHA (*in the same spirit*): Lovely. Lovely. And you know, biology is the greatest. (*Looking up at him.*) I dissected something that looked just like you yesterday.

WALTER: I just wondered if you've made up your mind and everything.

BENEATHA (*gaining in sharpness and impatience*): And what did I answer yesterday morning — and the day before that?

RUTH (*from the ironing board, like someone disinterested and old*): Don't be so nasty, Bennie.

BENEATHA (*still to her brother*): And the day before that and the day before that!

WALTER (*defensively*): I'm interested in you. Something wrong with that? Ain't many girls who decide —

WALTER AND BENEATHA (*in unison*): — "to be a doctor."

(*Silence.*)

WALTER: Have we figured out yet just exactly how much medical school is going to cost?

RUTH: Walter Lee, why don't you leave that girl alone and get out of here to work?

BENEATHA (*exits to the bathroom and bangs on the door*): Come on out of there, please!

(*She comes back into the room.*)

WALTER (*looking at his sister intently*): You know the check is coming tomorrow.

BENEATHA (*turning on him with a sharpness all her own*): That money belongs to Mama, Walter, and it's for her to decide how she wants to use it. I don't care if she wants to buy a house or a rocketship or just nail it up somewhere and look at it. It's hers. Not ours — *hers*.

WALTER (*bitterly*): Now ain't that fine! You just got your mother's interest at heart, ain't you, girl? You such a nice girl — but if Mama got that money she can always take a few thousand and help you through school too — can't she?

BENEATHA: I have never asked anyone around here to do anything for me!

WALTER: No! And the line between asking and just accepting when the time comes is big and wide — ain't it!

BENEATHA (*with fury*): What do you want from me, Brother — that I quit school or just drop dead, which!

WALTER: I don't want nothing but for you to stop acting holy 'round here. Me and Ruth done made some sacrifices for you — why can't you do something for the family?

RUTH: Walter, don't be dragging me in it.

Sean "P. Diddy" Combs as Walter in the 2004 Broadway production of *A Raisin in the Sun* at the Royale Theater.

Claudia McNeil as Lena (Mama) and Sidney Poitier as Walter in the 1961 film version of *A Raisin in the Sun*.

WALTER: You are in it—Don't you get up and go work in somebody's kitchen for the last three years to help put clothes on her back?

RUTH: Oh, Walter—that's not fair . . .

WALTER: It ain't that nobody expects you to get on your knees and say thank you, Brother; thank you, Ruth; thank you, Mama—and thank you, Travis, for wearing the same pair of shoes for two semesters—

BENEATHA (*dropping to her knees*): Well—I *do*—all right?—thank everybody! And forgive me for ever wanting to be anything at all! (*Pursuing him on her knees across the floor.*) FORGIVE ME, FORGIVE ME, FORGIVE ME!

RUTH: Please stop it! Your mama'll hear you.

WALTER: Who the hell told you you had to be a doctor? If you so crazy 'bout messing 'round with sick people—then go be a nurse like other women—or just get married and be quiet . . .

BENEATHA: Well—you finally got it said . . . It took you three years but you finally got it said. Walter, give up; leave me alone—it's Mama's money.

WALTER: *He was my father, too!*

BENEATHA: So what? He was mine, too—and Travis' grandfather—but the insurance money belongs to Mama. Picking on me is not going to make her give it to you to invest in any liquor stores—(*under breath, dropping into a chair*)—and I for one say, God bless Mama for that!

WALTER (*to Ruth*): See—did you hear? Did you hear!

RUTH: Honey, please go to work.

WALTER: Nobody in this house is ever going to understand me.

BENEATHA: Because you're a nut.

WALTER: Who's a nut?

BENEATHA: You—you are a nut. Thee is mad, boy.

WALTER (*looking at his wife and his sister from the door, very sadly*): The world's most backward race of people, and that's a fact.

BENEATHA (*turning slowly in her chair*): And then there are all those prophets who would lead us out of the wilderness—(*Walter slams out of the house.*)—into the swamps!

RUTH: Bennie, why you always gotta be pickin' on your brother? Can't you be a little sweeter sometimes? (*Door opens. Walter walks in. He fumbles with his cap, starts to speak, clears throat, looks everywhere but at Ruth. Finally.*)

WALTER (*to Ruth*): I need some money for carfare.

RUTH (*looks at him, then warms; teasing, but tenderly*): Fifty cents? (*She goes to her bag and gets money.*) Here—take a taxi!

(*Walter exits. Mama enters. She is a woman in her early sixties, full-bodied and strong. She is one of those women of a certain grace and beauty who wear it so unobtrusively that it takes a while to notice. Her dark brown face is surrounded by the total whiteness of her hair, and, being a woman who has adjusted to many things in life and overcome many more, her face is full of strength. She has, we can see, wit and faith of a kind that keep her eyes lit and full of interest and expectancy. She is, in a word, a beautiful woman. Her bearing is perhaps most like the noble bearing of the women of the Hereros of Southwest Africa—rather as if she imagines that as she walks she still bears a basket or a vessel upon her head. Her speech, on the other hand, is as careless as her carriage is*

Ester Rolle as Lena Younger comforts her daughter-in-law Ruth in the Huntington Theatre Company's 1994 production of *A Raisin in the Sun*. Also in the scene are Marguerite Hannah as Ruth and B. W. Gonzalez as Beneatha.

precise—she is inclined to slur everything—but her voice is perhaps not so much quiet as simply soft.)

MAMA: Who that 'round here slamming doors at this hour?

(*She crosses through the room, goes to the window, opens it, and brings in a feeble little plant growing doggedly in a small pot on the window sill. She feels the dirt and puts it back out.*)

RUTH: That was Walter Lee. He and Bennie was at it again.

MAMA: My children and they tempers. Lord, if this little old plant don't get more sun than it's been getting it ain't never going to see spring again. (*She turns from the window.*) What's the matter with you this morning, Ruth? You looks right peaked. You aiming to iron all them things? Leave some for me. I'll get to 'em this afternoon. Bennie honey, it's too drafty for you to be sitting 'round half dressed. Where's your robe?

BENEATHA: In the cleaners.

MAMA: Well, go get mine and put it on.

BENEATHA: I'm not cold, Mama, honest.

MAMA: I know—but you so thin . . .

BENEATHA (*irritably*): Mama, I'm not cold.

MAMA (*seeing the make-down bed as Travis has left it*): Lord have mercy, look at that poor bed. Bless his heart—he tries, don't he?

(*She moves to the bed Travis has sloppily made up.*)

RUTH: No—he don't half try at all 'cause he knows you going to come along behind him and fix everything. That's just how come he don't know how to do nothing right now—you done spoiled that boy so.

MAMA (*folding bedding*): Well—he's a little boy. Ain't supposed to know 'bout housekeeping. My baby, that's what he is. What you fix for his breakfast this morning?

RUTH (*angrily*): I feed my son, Lena!

MAMA: I ain't meddling—(*Under breath; busybodyish.*) I just noticed all last week he had cold cereal, and when it starts getting this chilly in the fall a child ought to have some hot grits or something when he goes out in the cold—

RUTH (*furious*): I gave him hot oats—is that all right!

MAMA: I ain't meddling. (*Pause.*) Put a lot of nice butter on it? (*Ruth shoots her an angry look and does not reply.*) He likes lots of butter.

RUTH (*exasperated*): Lena—

MAMA (*To Beneatha. Mama is inclined to wander conversationally sometimes.*): What was you and your brother fussing 'bout this morning?

BENEATHA: It's not important, Mama.

(*She gets up and goes to look out at the bathroom, which is apparently free, and she picks up her towels and rushes out.*)

MAMA: What was they fighting about?

RUTH: Now you know as well as I do.

MAMA (*shaking her head*): Brother still worrying hisself sick about that money?

RUTH: You know he is.

MAMA: You had breakfast?

RUTH: Some coffee.

MAMA: Girl, you better start eating and looking after yourself better. You almost thin as Travis.

RUTH: Lena—

MAMA: Un-hunh?

RUTH: What are you going to do with it?

MAMA: Now don't you start, child. It's too early in the morning to be talking about money. It ain't Christian.

RUTH: It's just that he got his heart set on that store—

MAMA: You mean that liquor store that Willy Harris want him to invest in?

RUTH: Yes—

MAMA: We ain't no business people, Ruth. We just plain working folks.

RUTH: Ain't nobody business people till they go into business. Walter Lee say colored people ain't never going to start getting ahead till they start gambling on some different kinds of things in the world—investments and things.

MAMA: What done got into you, girl? Walter Lee done finally sold you on investing.

RUTH: No. Mama, something is happening between Walter and me. I don't know what it is—but he needs something—something I can't give him anymore. He needs this chance, Lena.

MAMA (*frowning deeply*): But liquor, honey—

RUTH: Well—like Walter say—I spec people going to always be drinking themselves some liquor.

MAMA: Well—whether they drinks it or not ain't none of my business. But whether I go into business selling it to 'em *is*, and I don't want that on my ledger this late in life. (*Stopping suddenly and studying her daughter-in-law.*) Ruth Younger, what's the matter with you today? You look like you could fall over right there.

RUTH: I'm tired.

MAMA: Then you better stay home from work today.

RUTH: I can't stay home. She'd be calling up the agency and screaming at them, "My girl didn't come in today—send me somebody! My girl didn't come in!" Oh, she just have a fit . . .

MAMA: Well, let her have it. I'll just call her up and say you got the flu—

RUTH (*laughing*): Why the flu?

MAMA: 'Cause it sounds respectable to 'em. Something white people get, too. They know 'bout the flu. Otherwise they think you been cut up or something when you tell 'em you sick.

RUTH: I got to go in. We need the money.

MAMA: Somebody would of thought my children done all but starved to death the way they talk about money here late. Child, we got a great big old check coming tomorrow.

RUTH (*sincerely, but also self-righteously*): Now that's your money. It ain't got nothing to do with me. We all feel like that—Walter and Bennie and me—even Travis.

MAMA (*thoughtfully, and suddenly very far away*): Ten thousand dollars—

RUTH: Sure is wonderful.

MAMA: Ten thousand dollars.

RUTH: You know what you should do, Miss Lena? You should take yourself a trip somewhere. To Europe or South America or someplace—

MAMA (*throwing up her hands at the thought*): Oh, child!

RUTH: I'm serious. Just pack up and leave! Go on away and enjoy yourself some. Forget about the family and have yourself a ball for once in your life—

MAMA (*drily*): You sound like I'm just about ready to die. Who'd go with me? What I look like wandering 'round Europe by myself?

RUTH: Shoot—these here rich white women do it all the time. They don't think nothing of packing up they suitcases and piling on one of them big steamships and—swoosh!—they gone, child.

MAMA: Something always told me I wasn't no rich white woman.

RUTH: Well—what are you going to do with it then?

MAMA: I ain't rightly decided. (*Thinking. She speaks now with emphasis.*) Some of it got to be put away for Beneatha and her schoolin'—and ain't nothing going to touch that part of it. Nothing. (*She waits several seconds, trying to make up her mind about something, and looks at Ruth a little tentatively before going on.*) Been thinking that we maybe could meet the notes on a little old two-story somewhere, with a yard where Travis could play in the summertime, if we use part of the insurance for a down payment and everybody kind of pitch in. I could maybe take on a little day work again, few days a week—

RUTH (*studying her mother-in-law furtively and concentrating on her ironing, anxious to encourage without seeming to*): Well, Lord knows, we've put enough rent into this here rat trap to pay for four houses by now . . .

MAMA (*looking up at the words "rat trap" and then looking around and leaning back and sighing—in a suddenly reflective mood—*): "Rat trap"—yes, that's all it is. (*Smiling.*) I remember just as well the day me and Big Walter moved in here. Hadn't been married but two weeks and wasn't planning on living here no more than a year. (*She shakes her head at the dissolved dream.*) We was going to set away, little by little, don't you know, and buy a little place out in Morgan Park. We had even picked out the house. (*Chuckling a little.*) Looks right dumpy today. But Lord, child, you should know, all the dreams I had 'bout buying that house and fixing it up and making me a little garden in the back—(*She waits and stops smiling.*) And didn't none of it happen.

(*Dropping her hands in a futile gesture.*)

RUTH (*keeps her head down, ironing*): Yes, life can be a barrel of disappointments, sometimes.

MAMA: Honey, Big Walter would come in here some nights back then and slump down on that couch there and just look at the rug, and look at me and look at the rug and then back at me—and I'd know he was down then . . . really down. (*After a second very long and thoughtful pause; she is seeing back to times that only she can see.*) And then, Lord, when I lost that baby—little Claude—I almost thought I was going to lose Big Walter too. Oh, that man grieved hisself! He was one man to love his children.

RUTH: Ain't nothin' can tear at you like losin' your baby.

MAMA: I guess that's how come that man finally worked hisself to death like he done. Like he was fighting his own war with this here world that took his baby from him.

RUTH: He sure was a fine man, all right. I always liked Mr. Younger.

MAMA: Crazy 'bout his children! God knows there was plenty wrong with Walter Younger—hard-headed, mean, kind of wild with women—plenty wrong with him. But he sure loved his children. Always wanted them to have something—be something. That's where Brother gets all these notions, I reckon. Big Walter used to say, he'd get right wet in the eyes sometimes, lean his head back with the water standing in his eyes and say, "Seem like God didn't see fit to give the black man nothing but dreams—but He did give us children to make them dreams seem worthwhile." (*She smiles.*) He could talk like that, don't you know.

RUTH: Yes, he sure could. He was a good man, Mr. Younger.

MAMA: Yes, a fine man—just couldn't never catch up with his dreams, that's all.

(*Beneatha comes in, brushing her hair and looking up to the ceiling, where the sound of a vacuum cleaner has started up.*)

BENEATHA: What could be so dirty on that woman's rugs that she has to vacuum them every single day?

RUTH: I wish certain young women 'round here who I could name would take inspiration about certain rugs in a certain apartment I could also mention.

BENEATHA (*shrugging*): How much cleaning can a house need, for Christ's sakes.

MAMA (*not liking the Lord's name used thus*): Bennie!

RUTH: Just listen to her—just listen!

BENEATHA: Oh, God!

MAMA: If you use the Lord's name just one more time—

BENEATHA (*a bit of a whine*): Oh, Mama—

RUTH: Fresh—just fresh as salt, this girl!

BENEATHA (*drily*): Well—if the salt loses its savor—

MAMA: Now that will do. I just ain't going to have you 'round here reciting the scriptures in vain—you hear me?

BENEATHA: How did I manage to get on everybody's wrong side by just walking into a room?

RUTH: If you weren't so fresh—

BENEATHA: Ruth, I'm twenty years old.

MAMA: What time you be home from school today?

BENEATHA: Kind of late. (*With enthusiasm.*) Madeline is going to start my guitar lessons today.

(*Mama and Ruth look up with the same expression.*)

MAMA: Your *what* kind of lessons?

BENEATHA: Guitar.

RUTH: Oh, Father!

MAMA: How come you done taken it in your mind to learn to play the guitar?

BENEATHA: I just want to, that's all.

MAMA (*smiling*): Lord, child, don't you know what to do with yourself? How long it going to be before you get tired of this now—like you got tired of that little play-acting group you joined last year? (*Looking at Ruth.*) And what was it the year before that?

RUTH: The horseback-riding club for which she bought that fifty-five-dollar riding habit that's been hanging in the closet ever since!

MAMA (*to Beneatha*): Why you got to flit so from one thing to another, baby?

BENEATHA (*sharply*): I just want to learn to play the guitar. Is there anything wrong with that?

MAMA: Ain't nobody trying to stop you. I just wonders sometimes why you has to flit so from one thing to another all the time. You ain't never done nothing with all that camera equipment you brought home—

BENEATHA: I don't flit! I—I experiment with different forms of expression—

RUTH: Like riding a horse?

BENEATHA: —People have to express themselves one way or another.

MAMA: What is it you want to express?

BENEATHA (*angrily*): Me! (*Mama and Ruth look at each other and burst into raucous laughter.*) Don't worry—I don't expect you to understand.

MAMA (*to change the subject*): Who you going out with tomorrow night?

BENEATHA (*with displeasure*): George Murchison again.

MAMA (*pleased*): Oh—you getting a little sweet on him?

RUTH: You ask me, this child ain't sweet on nobody but herself—(*Under breath.*) Express herself!

(*They laugh.*)

BENEATHA: Oh—I like George all right, Mama. I mean I like him enough to go out with him and stuff, but—

RUTH (*for devilment*): What does *and stuff* mean?

BENEATHA: Mind your own business.

MAMA: Stop picking at her now, Ruth. (*She chuckles—then a suspicious sudden look at her daughter as she turns in her chair for emphasis.*) What DOES it mean?

BENEATHA (*wearily*): Oh, I just mean I couldn't ever really be serious about George. He's—he's so shallow.

RUTH: Shallow—what do you mean he's shallow? He's *Rich!*

MAMA: Hush, Ruth.

BENEATHA: I know he's rich. He knows he's rich, too.

RUTH: Well—what other qualities a man got to have to satisfy you, little girl?

BENEATHA: You wouldn't even begin to understand. Anybody who married Walter could not possibly understand.

MAMA (*outraged*): What kind of way is that to talk about your brother?

BENEATHA: Brother is a flip—let's face it.

MAMA (*to Ruth, helplessly*): What's a flip?

RUTH (*glad to add kindling*): She's saying he's crazy.

BENEATHA: Not crazy. Brother isn't really crazy yet—he—he's an elaborate neurotic.

MAMA: Hush your mouth!

BENEATHA: As for George. Well. George looks good—he's got a beautiful car and he takes me to nice places and, as my sister-in-law says, he is probably the richest boy I will ever get to know and I even like him sometimes—but if the Youngers are sitting around waiting to see if their little Bennie is going to tie up the family with the Murchisons, they are wasting their time.

RUTH: You mean you wouldn't marry George Murchison if he asked you someday? That pretty, rich thing? Honey, I knew you was odd—

BENEATHA: No I would not marry him if all I felt for him was what I feel now. Besides, George's family wouldn't really like it.

MAMA: Why not?

BENEATHA: Oh, Mama—The Murchisons are honest-to-God-real-*live*-rich colored people, and the only people in the world who are more snobbish than rich white people are rich colored people. I thought everybody knew that. I've met Mrs. Murchison. She's a scene!

MAMA: You must not dislike people 'cause they well off, honey.

BENEATHA: Why not? It makes just as much sense as disliking people 'cause they are poor, and lots of people do that.

RUTH (*A wisdom-of-the-ages manner. To Mama.*): Well, she'll get over some of this—

BENEATHA: Get over it? What are you talking about, Ruth? Listen, I'm going to be a doctor. I'm not worried about who I'm going to marry yet—if I ever get married.

MAMA AND RUTH: *If!*

MAMA: Now, Bennie—

BENEATHA: Oh, I probably will . . . but first I'm going to be a doctor, and George, for one, still thinks that's pretty funny. I couldn't be bothered with that. I am going to be a doctor and everybody around here better understand that!

MAMA (*kindly*): 'Course you going to be a doctor, honey, God willing.

BENEATHA (*drily*): God hasn't got a thing to do with it.

MAMA: Beneatha—that just wasn't necessary.

BENEATHA: Well—neither is God. I get sick of hearing about God.

MAMA: Beneatha!

BENEATHA: I mean it! I'm just tired of hearing about God all the time. What has He got to do with anything? Does he pay tuition?

MAMA: You 'bout to get your fresh little jaw slapped!

RUTH: That's just what she needs, all right!

BENEATHA: Why? Why can't I say what I want to around here, like everybody else?

MAMA: It don't sound nice for a young girl to say things like that—you wasn't brought up that way. Me and your father went to trouble to get you and Brother to church every Sunday.

BENEATHA: Mama, you don't understand. It's all a matter of ideas, and God is just one idea I don't accept. It's not important. I am not going out and be immoral or commit crimes because I don't believe in God. I don't even think about it. It's just that I get tired of Him getting credit for all the things the human race achieves through its own stubborn effort. There simply is no blasted God—there is only man and it is *he* who makes miracles!

(*Mama absorbs this speech, studies her daughter and rises slowly and crosses to Beneatha and slaps her powerfully across the face. After, there is only silence and the daughter drops her eyes from her mother's face, and Mama is very tall before her.*)

MAMA: Now—you say after me, in my mother's house there is still God. (*There is a long pause and Beneatha stares at the floor wordlessly. Mama repeats the phrase with precision and cool emotion.*) In my mother's house there is still God.

BENEATHA: In my mother's house there is still God.

(*A long pause.*)

MAMA (*Walking away from Beneatha, too disturbed for triumphant posture. Stopping and turning back to her daughter.*): There are some ideas we ain't going to have in this house. Not long as I am at the head of this family.
BENEATHA: Yes, ma'am.

(*Mama walks out of the room.*)

RUTH (*almost gently, with profound understanding*): You think you a woman, Bennie—but you still a little girl. What you did was childish—so you got treated like a child.
BENEATHA: I see. (*Quietly.*) I also see that everybody thinks it's all right for Mama to be a tyrant. But all the tyranny in the world will never put a God in the heavens!

(*She picks up her books and goes out. Pause.*)

RUTH (*goes to Mama's door*): She said she was sorry.
MAMA (*coming out, going to her plant*): They frightens me, Ruth. My children.
RUTH: You got good children, Lena. They just a little off sometimes—but they're good.
MAMA: No—there's something come down between me and them that don't let us understand each other and I don't know what it is. One done almost lost his mind thinking 'bout money all the time and the other done commence to talk about things I can't seem to understand in no form or fashion. What is it that's changing, Ruth.
RUTH (*soothingly, older than her years*): Now . . . you taking it all too seriously. You just got strong-willed children and it takes a strong woman like you to keep 'em in hand.
MAMA (*looking at her plant and sprinkling a little water on it*): They spirited all right, my children. Got to admit they got spirit—Bennie and Walter. Like this little old plant that ain't never had enough sunshine or nothing—and look at it . . .

(*She has her back to Ruth, who has had to stop ironing and lean against something and put the back of her hand to her forehead.*)

RUTH (*trying to keep Mama from noticing*): You . . . sure . . . loves that little old thing, don't you? . . .
MAMA: Well, I always wanted me a garden like I used to see sometimes at the back of the houses down home. This plant is close as I ever got to having one. (*She looks out of the window as she replaces the plant.*) Lord, ain't nothing as dreary as the view from this window on a dreary day, is there? Why ain't you singing this morning, Ruth? Sing that "No Ways Tired." That song always lifts me up so—(*She turns at last to see that Ruth has slipped quietly to the floor, in a state of semiconsciousness.*) Ruth! Ruth honey—what's the matter with you . . . Ruth!

Scene II

(*It is the following morning; a Saturday morning, and house cleaning is in progress at the Youngers'. Furniture has been shoved hither and yon and Mama is giving the kitchen-area walls a washing down. Beneatha, in dungarees, with a handkerchief tied around her face, is spraying insecticide into the cracks in the walls. As they work, the radio is on and a Southside disk jockey program is inappropriately filling the house with a rather exotic saxophone blues. Travis, the sole idle one, is leaning on his arms, looking out of the window.*)

TRAVIS: Grandmama, that stuff Bennie is using smells awful. Can I go downstairs, please?
MAMA: Did you get all them chores done already? I ain't seen you doing much.
TRAVIS: Yes'm—finished early. Where did Mama go this morning?
MAMA (*looking at Beneatha*): She had to go on a little errand.

(*The phone rings. Beneatha runs to answer it and reaches it before Walter, who has entered from bedroom.*)

TRAVIS: Where?
MAMA: To tend to her business.
BENEATHA: Haylo . . . (*Disappointed.*) Yes, he is. (*She tosses the phone to Walter, who barely catches it.*) It's Willie Harris again.
WALTER (*as privately as possible under Mama's gaze*): Hello, Willie. Did you get the papers from the lawyer? . . . No, not yet. I told you the mailman doesn't get here till ten-thirty . . . No, I'll come there . . . Yeah! Right away. (*He hangs up and goes for his coat.*)
BENEATHA: Brother, where did Ruth go?
WALTER (*as he exits*): How should I know!
TRAVIS: Aw come on, Grandma. Can I go outside?
MAMA: Oh, I guess so. You stay right in front of the house, though, and keep a good lookout for the postman.
TRAVIS: Yes'm. (*He darts into bedroom for stickball and bat, reenters, and sees Beneatha on her knees spraying under sofa with behind upraised. He edges closer to the target, takes aim, and lets her have it. She screams.*) Leave them poor little cockroaches alone, they ain't bothering you none! (*He runs as she swings the spraygun at him viciously and playfully.*) Grandma! Grandma!
MAMA: Look out there, girl, before you be spilling some of that stuff on that child!
TRAVIS (*safely behind the bastion of Mama*): That's right—look out, now! (*He exits.*)
BENEATHA (*drily*): I can't imagine that it would hurt him—it has never hurt the roaches.

MAMA: Well, little boys' hides ain't as tough as South-side roaches. You better get over there behind the bureau. I seen one marching out of there like Napoleon yesterday.

BENEATHA: There's really only one way to get rid of them, Mama—

MAMA: How?

BENEATHA: Set fire to this building! Mama, where did Ruth go?

MAMA (*looking at her with meaning*): To the doctor, I think.

BENEATHA: The doctor? What's the matter? (*They exchange glances.*) You don't think—

MAMA (*with her sense of drama*): Now I ain't saying what I think. But I ain't never been wrong 'bout a woman neither.

(*The phone rings.*)

BENEATHA (*at the phone*): Hay-lo . . . (*Pause, and a moment of recognition.*) Well—when did you get back! . . . And how was it? . . . Of course I've missed you—in my way . . . This morning? No . . . house cleaning and all that and Mama hates it if I let people come over when the house is like this . . . You *have?* Well, that's different . . . What is it—Oh, what the hell, come on over . . . Right, see you then. *Arrivederci.*

(*She hangs up.*)

MAMA (*who has listened vigorously, as is her habit*): Who is that you inviting over here with this house looking like this? You ain't got the pride you was born with!

BENEATHA: Asagai doesn't care how houses look, Mama—he's an intellectual.

MAMA: *Who?*

BENEATHA: Asagai—Joseph Asagai. He's an African boy I met on campus. He's been studying in Canada all summer.

MAMA: What's his name?

BENEATHA: Asagai, Joseph. Ah-sah-guy . . . He's from Nigeria.

MAMA: Oh, that's the little country that was founded by slaves way back . . .

BENEATHA: No, Mama—that's Liberia.

MAMA: I don't think I never met no African before.

BENEATHA: Well, do me a favor and don't ask him a whole lot of ignorant questions about Africans. I mean, do they wear clothes and all that—

MAMA: Well, now, I guess if you think we so ignorant 'round here maybe you shouldn't bring your friends here—

BENEATHA: It's just that people ask such crazy things. All anyone seems to know about when it comes to Africa is Tarzan—

MAMA (*indignantly*): Why should I know anything about Africa?

BENEATHA: Why do you give money at church for the missionary work?

MAMA: Well, that's to help save people.

BENEATHA: You mean save them from *heathenism*—

MAMA (*innocently*): Yes.

BENEATHA: I'm afraid they need more salvation from the British and the French.

(*Ruth comes in forlornly and pulls off her coat with dejection. They both turn to look at her.*)

RUTH (*dispiritedly*): Well, I guess from all the happy faces—everybody knows.

BENEATHA: You pregnant?

MAMA: Lord have mercy, I sure hope it's a little old girl. Travis ought to have a sister.

(*Beneatha and Ruth give her a hopeless look for this grandmotherly enthusiasm.*)

BENEATHA: How far along are you?

RUTH: Two months.

BENEATHA: Did you mean to? I mean did you plan it or was it an accident?

MAMA: What do you know about planning or not planning?

BENEATHA: Oh, Mama.

RUTH (*wearily*): She's twenty years old, Lena.

BENEATHA: Did you plan it, Ruth?

RUTH: Mind your own business.

BENEATHA: It is my business—where is he going to live, on the *roof?* (*There is silence following the remark as the three women react to the sense of it.*) Gee—I didn't mean that, Ruth, honest. Gee, I don't feel like that at all. I—I think it is wonderful.

RUTH (*dully*): Wonderful.

BENEATHA: Yes—really.

MAMA (*looking at Ruth, worried*): Doctor say everything going to be all right?

RUTH (*far away*): Yes—she says everything is going to be fine . . .

MAMA (*immediately suspicious*): "She"—What doctor you went to?

(*Ruth folds over, near hysteria.*)

MAMA (*worriedly hovering over Ruth*): Ruth honey—what's the matter with you—you sick?

(*Ruth has her fists clenched on her thighs and is fighting hard to suppress a scream that seems to be rising in her.*)

BENEATHA: What's the matter with her, Mama?

MAMA (*working her fingers in Ruth's shoulders to relax her*): She be all right. Women gets right depressed sometimes when they get her way. (*Speaking softly, expertly, rapidly.*) Now you just relax. That's right . . . just lean back, don't think 'bout nothing at all . . . nothing at all—

RUTH: I'm all right . . .

(*The glassy-eyed look melts and then she collapses into a fit of heavy sobbing. The bell rings.*)

BENEATHA: Oh, my God—that must be Asagai.

MAMA (*to Ruth*): Come on now, honey. You need to lie down and rest awhile . . . then have some nice hot food.

(*They exit, Ruth's weight on her mother-in-law. Beneatha, herself profoundly disturbed, opens the door to admit a rather dramatic-looking young man with a large package.*)

ASAGAI: Hello, Alaiyo—

BENEATHA (*holding the door open and regarding him with pleasure*): Hello . . . (*Long pause.*) Well—come in. And please excuse everything. My mother was very upset about my letting anyone come here with the place like this.

ASAGAI (*coming into the room*): You look disturbed too . . . Is something wrong?

BENEATHA (*still at the door, absently*): Yes . . . we've all got acute ghetto-itus. (*She smiles and comes toward him, finding a cigarette and sitting.*) So—sit down! No! Wait! (*She whips the spraygun off sofa where she had left it and puts the cushions back. At last perches on arm of sofa. He sits.*) So, how was Canada?

ASAGAI (*a sophisticate*): Canadian.

BENEATHA (*looking at him*): Asagai, I'm very glad you are back.

ASAGAI (*looking back at her in turn*): Are you really?

BENEATHA: Yes—very.

ASAGAI: Why?—you were quite glad when I went away. What happened?

BENEATHA: You went away.

ASAGAI: Ahhhhhhhh.

BENEATHA: Before—you wanted to be so serious before there was time.

ASAGAI: How much time must there be before one knows what one feels?

BENEATHA (*Stalling this particular conversation. Her hands pressed together, in a deliberately childish gesture.*): What did you bring me?

ASAGAI (*handing her the package*): Open it and see.

BENEATHA (*eagerly opening the package and drawing out some records and the colorful robes of a Nigerian woman*): Oh, Asagai! . . . You got them for me! . . . How beautiful . . . and the records too! (*She lifts out the robes and runs to the mirror with them and holds the drapery up in front of herself.*)

ASAGAI (*coming to her at the mirror*): I shall have to teach you how to drape it properly. (*He flings the material about her for the moment and stands back to look at her.*) Ah—Oh-pay-gay-day, oh-gbah-mu-shay. (*A Yoruba exclamation for admiration.*) You wear it well . . . very well . . . mutilated hair and all.

BENEATHA (*turning suddenly*): My hair—what's wrong with my hair?

ASAGAI (*shrugging*): Were you born with it like that?

BENEATHA (*reaching up to touch it*): No . . . of course not.

(*She looks back to the mirror, disturbed.*)

ASAGAI (*smiling*): How then?

BENEATHA: You know perfectly well how . . . as crinkly as yours . . . that's how.

ASAGAI: And it is ugly to you that way?

BENEATHA (*quickly*): Oh, no—not ugly . . . (*More slowly, apologetically.*) But it's so hard to manage when it's, well—raw.

ASAGAI: And so to accommodate that—you mutilate it every week?

BENEATHA: It's not mutilation!

ASAGAI (*laughing aloud at her seriousness*): Oh . . . please! I am only teasing you because you are so very serious about these things. (*He stands back from her and folds his arms across his chest as he watches her pulling at her hair and frowning in the mirror.*) Do you remember the first time you met me at school? . . . (*He laughs.*) You came up to me and you said—and I thought you were the most serious little thing I had ever seen—you said: (*He imitates her.*) "Mr. Asagai—I want very much to talk with you. About Africa. You see, Mr. Asagai, I am looking for my *identity!*"

(*He laughs.*)

BENEATHA (*turning to him, not laughing*): Yes—

(*Her face is quizzical, profoundly disturbed.*)

ASAGAI (*still teasing and reaching out and taking her face in his hands and turning her profile to him*): Well . . . it is true that this is not so much a profile of a Hollywood queen as perhaps a queen of the Nile— (*A mock dismissal of the importance of the question.*) But what does it matter? Assimilationism is so popular in your country.

BENEATHA (*wheeling, passionately, sharply*): I am not an assimilationist!

ASAGAI (*the protest hangs in the room for a moment and Asagai studies her, his laughter fading*): Such a serious one. (*There is a pause.*) So—you like the robes? You must take excellent care of them—they are from my sister's personal wardrobe.

BENEATHA (*with incredulity*): You—you sent all the way home—for me?

ASAGAI (*with charm*): For you—I would do much more . . . Well, that is what I came for. I must go.

BENEATHA: Will you call me Monday?

ASAGAI: Yes . . . We have a great deal to talk about. I mean about identity and time and all that.

BENEATHA: Time?

ASAGAI: Yes. About how much time one needs to know what one feels.

BENEATHA: You see! You never understood that there is more than one kind of feeling which can exist between a man and a woman—or, at least, there should be.

ASAGAI (*shaking his head negatively but gently*): No. Between a man and a woman there need be only one kind of feeling. I have that for you . . . Now even . . . right this moment . . .

BENEATHA: I know—and by itself—it won't do. I can find that anywhere.

ASAGAI: For a woman it should be enough.

BENEATHA: I know—because that's what it says in all the novels that men write. But it isn't. Go ahead and laugh—but I'm not interested in being someone's little episode in America or—(*with feminine vengeance*)—one of them! (*Asagai has burst into laughter again.*) That's funny as hell, huh!

ASAGAI: It's just that every American girl I have known has said that to me. White—black—in this you are all the same. And the same speech, too!

BENEATHA (*angrily*): Yuk, yuk, yuk!

ASAGAI: It's how you can be sure that the world's most liberated women are not liberated at all. You all talk about it too much!

(*Mama enters and is immediately all social charm because of the presence of a guest.*)

BENEATHA: Oh—Mama—this is Mr. Asagai.

MAMA: How do you do?

ASAGAI (*total politeness to an elder*): How do you do, Mrs. Younger. Please forgive me for coming at such an outrageous hour on a Saturday.

MAMA: Well, you are quite welcome. I just hope you understand that our house don't always look like this. (*Chatterish.*) You must come again. I would love to hear all about—(*not sure of the name*)—your country. I think it's so sad the way our American Negroes don't know nothing about Africa 'cept Tarzan and all that. And all that money they pour into these churches when they ought to be helping you people over there drive out them French and Englishmen done taken away your land.

(*The mother flashes a slightly superior look at her daughter upon completion of the recitation.*)

ASAGAI (*taken aback by this sudden and acutely unrelated expression of sympathy*): Yes . . . yes . . .

MAMA (*smiling at him suddenly and relaxing and looking him over*): How many miles is it from here to where you come from?

ASAGAI: Many thousands.

MAMA (*looking at him as she would Walter*): I bet you don't half look after yourself, being away from your mama either. I spec you better come 'round here from time to time to get yourself some decent home-cooked meals . . .

ASAGAI (*moved*): Thank you. Thank you very much. (*They are all quiet, then—*) Well . . . I must go. I will call you Monday, Alaiyo.

MAMA: What's that he call you?

ASAGAI: Oh—"Alaiyo." I hope you don't mind. It is what you would call a nickname, I think. It is a Yoruba word. I am a Yoruba.

MAMA (*looking at Beneatha*): I—I thought he was from—(*Uncertain.*)

ASAGAI (*understanding*): Nigeria is my country. Yoruba is my tribal origin—

BENEATHA: You didn't tell us what Alaiyo means . . . for all I know, you might be calling me Little Idiot or something . . .

ASAGAI: Well . . . let me see . . . I do not know how just to explain it . . . The sense of a thing can be so different when it changes languages.

BENEATHA: You're evading.

ASAGAI: No—really it is difficult . . . (*Thinking.*) It means . . . it means One for Whom Bread—Food—Is Not Enough. (*He looks at her.*) Is that all right?

BENEATHA (*understanding, softly*): Thank you.

MAMA (*looking from one to the other and not understanding any of it*): Well . . . that's nice . . . You must come see us again—Mr. ——

ASAGAI: Ah-sah-guy . . .

MAMA: Yes . . . Do come again.

ASAGAI: Good-bye.

(*He exits.*)

MAMA (*after him*): Lord, that's a pretty thing just went out here! (*Insinuatingly, to her daughter.*) Yes, I guess I see why we done commence to get so interested in Africa 'round here. Missionaries my aunt Jenny!

(*She exits.*)

BENEATHA: Oh, Mama! . . .

(*She picks up the Nigerian dress and holds it up to her in front of the mirror again. She sets the headdress on haphazardly and then notices her hair again and clutches at it and then replaces the headdress and frowns at herself. Then she starts to wriggle in front of the mirror as she thinks a Nigerian woman might. Travis enters and stands regarding her.*)

TRAVIS: What's the matter, girl, you cracking up?

BENEATHA: Shut up.

(*She pulls the headdress off and looks at herself in the mirror and clutches at her hair again and squinches her eyes as if trying to imagine something. Then, suddenly, she gets her raincoat and kerchief and hurriedly prepares for going out.*)

MAMA (*coming back into the room*): She's resting now. Travis, baby, run next door and ask Miss Johnson to please let me have a little kitchen cleanser. This here can is empty as Jacob's kettle.

TRAVIS: I just came in.

MAMA: Do as you told. (*He exits and she looks at her daughter.*) Where you going?

BENEATHA (*halting at the door*): To become a queen of the Nile!

(*She exits in a breathless blaze of glory. Ruth appears in the bedroom doorway.*)

MAMA: Who told you to get up?

RUTH: Ain't nothing wrong with me to be lying in no bed for. Where did Bennie go?

MAMA (*drumming her fingers*): Far as I could make out—to Egypt. (*Ruth just looks at her.*) What time is it getting to?

RUTH: Ten twenty. And the mailman going to ring that bell this morning just like he done every morning for the last umpteen years.

(*Travis comes in with the cleanser can.*)

TRAVIS: She say to tell you that she don't have much.

MAMA (*angrily*): Lord, some people I could name sure is tight-fisted! (*Directing her grandson.*) Mark two cans of cleanser down on the list there. If she that hard up for kitchen cleanser, I sure don't want to forget to get her none!

RUTH: Lena—maybe the woman is just short on cleanser—

MAMA (*not listening*):—Much baking powder as she done borrowed from me all these years, she could of done gone into the baking business!

(*The bell sounds suddenly and sharply and all three are stunned—serious and silent—mid-speech. In spite of all the other conversations and distractions of the morning, this is what they have been waiting for, even Travis, who looks helplessly from his mother to his grandmother. Ruth is the first to come to life again.*)

RUTH (*to Travis*): Get down them steps, boy!

(*Travis snaps to life and flies out to get the mail.*)

MAMA (*her eyes wide, her hand to her breast*): You mean it done really come?

RUTH (*excited*): Oh, Miss Lena!

MAMA (*collecting herself*): Well . . . I don't know what we all so excited about 'round here for. We known it was coming for months.

RUTH: That's a whole lot different from having it come and being able to hold it in your hands . . . a piece of paper worth ten thousand dollars . . . (*Travis bursts back into the room. He holds the envelope high above his head, like a little dancer, his face is radiant and he is breathless. He moves to his grandmother with sudden slow ceremony and puts the envelope into her hands. She accepts it, and then merely holds it and looks at it.*) Come on! Open it . . . Lord have mercy, I wish Walter Lee was here!

TRAVIS: Open it, Grandmama!

MAMA (*staring at it*): Now you all be quiet. It's just a check.

RUTH: Open it . . .

MAMA (*still staring at it*): Now don't act silly . . . We ain't never been no people to act silly 'bout no money—

RUTH (*swiftly*): We ain't never had none before—OPEN IT!

(*Mama finally makes a good strong tear and pulls out the thin blue slice of paper and inspects it closely. The boy and his mother study it raptly over Mama's shoulders.*)

MAMA: *Travis!* (*She is counting off with doubt.*) Is that the right number of zeros.

TRAVIS: Yes'm . . . ten thousand dollars. Gaalee, Grandmama, you rich.

MAMA (*She holds the check away from her, still looking at it. Slowly her face sobers into a mask of unhappiness.*): Ten thousand dollars. (*She hands it to Ruth.*) Put it away somewhere, Ruth. (*She does not look at Ruth; her eyes seem to be seeing something somewhere very far off.*) Ten thousand dollars they give you. Ten thousand dollars.

TRAVIS (*to his mother, sincerely*): What's the matter with Grandmama—don't she want to be rich?

RUTH (*distractedly*): You go on out and play now, baby. (*Travis exits. Mama starts wiping dishes absently, humming intently to herself. Ruth turns to her, with kind exasperation.*) You've gone and got yourself upset.

MAMA (*not looking at her*): I spec if it wasn't for you all . . . I would just put that money away or give it to the church or something.

RUTH: Now what kind of talk is that. Mr. Younger would just be plain mad if he could hear you talking foolish like that.

MAMA (*stopping and staring off*): Yes . . . he sure would. (*Sighing.*) We got enough to do with that money, all right. (*She halts then, and turns and looks at her daughter-in-law hard; Ruth avoids her eyes and Mama wipes her hands with finality and starts to speak firmly to Ruth.*) Where did you go today, girl?

RUTH: To the doctor.

MAMA (*impatiently*): Now, Ruth . . . you know better than that. Old Doctor Jones is strange enough in his way but there ain't nothing 'bout him make somebody slip and call him "she"—like you done this morning.

RUTH: Well, that's what happened—my tongue slipped.

MAMA: You went to see that woman, didn't you?

RUTH (*defensively, giving herself away*): What woman you talking about?

MAMA (*angrily*): That woman who—

(*Walter enters in great excitement.*)

WALTER: Did it come?

MAMA (*quietly*): Can't you give people a Christian greeting before you start asking about money?

WALTER (*to Ruth*): Did it come? (*Ruth unfolds the check and lays it quietly before him, watching him intently with thoughts of her own. Walter sits down and grasps it close and counts off the zeros.*) Ten thousand dollars—(*He turns suddenly, frantically to his mother and draws some papers out of his breast pocket.*) Mama—look. Old Willy Harris put everything on paper—

MAMA: Son—I think you ought to talk to your wife . . . I'll go on out and leave you alone if you want—

WALTER: I can talk to her later—Mama, look—

MAMA: Son—

WALTER: WILL SOMEBODY PLEASE LISTEN TO ME TODAY!

MAMA (*quietly*): I don't 'low no yellin' in this house, Walter Lee, and you know it—(*Walter stares at them in frustration and starts to speak several times.*) And there ain't going to be no investing in no liquor stores.

WALTER: But, Mama, you ain't even looked at it.

MAMA: I don't aim to have to speak on that again.

(*A long pause.*)

WALTER: You ain't looked at it and you don't aim to have to speak on that again? You ain't even looked at it and *you* have decided—(*Crumpling his papers.*) Well, *you* tell that to my boy tonight when you put him to sleep on the living room couch . . . (*Turning to Mama and speaking directly to her.*) Yeah—and tell it to my wife, Mama, tomorrow when she has to go out of here to look after somebody else's kids. And tell it to *me*, Mama, every time we need a new pair of curtains and I have to watch *you* go out and work in somebody's kitchen. Yeah, you tell me then!

(*Walter starts out.*)

RUTH: Where you going?

WALTER: I'm going out!

RUTH: Where?

WALTER: Just out of this house somewhere—

RUTH (*getting her coat*): I'll come too.

WALTER: I don't want you to come!

RUTH: I got something to talk to you about, Walter.

WALTER: That's too bad.

MAMA (*still quietly*): Walter Lee—(*She waits and he finally turns and looks at her.*) Sit down.

WALTER: I'm a grown man, Mama.

MAMA: Ain't nobody said you wasn't grown. But you still in my house and my presence. And as long as you are—you'll talk to your wife civil. Now sit down.

RUTH (*suddenly*): Oh, let him go on out and drink himself to death! He makes me sick to my stomach! (*She flings her coat against him and exits to bedroom.*)

WALTER (*violently flinging the coat after her*): And you turn mine too, baby! (*The door slams behind her.*) That was my biggest mistake—

MAMA (*still quietly*): Walter, what is the matter with you?

WALTER: Matter with me? Ain't nothing the matter with *me*!

MAMA: Yes there is. Something eating you up like a crazy man. Something more than me not giving you this money. The past few years I been watching it happen to you. You get all nervous acting and kind of wild in the eyes—(*Walter jumps up impatiently at her words.*) I said sit there now, I'm talking to you!

WALTER: Mama—I don't need no nagging at me today.

MAMA: Seem like you getting to a place where you always tied up in some kind of knot about something. But if anybody ask you 'bout it you just yell at 'em and bust out the house and go out and drink somewheres. Walter Lee, people can't live with that. Ruth's a good, patient girl in her way—but you getting to be too much. Boy, don't make the mistake of driving that girl away from you.

WALTER: Why—what she do for me?

MAMA: She loves you.

WALTER: Mama—I'm going out. I want to go off somewhere and be by myself for a while.

MAMA: I'm sorry 'bout your liquor store, son. It just wasn't the thing for us to do. That's what I want to tell you about—

WALTER: I got to go out, Mama—

(*He rises.*)

MAMA: It's dangerous, son.

WALTER: What's dangerous?

MAMA: When a man goes outside his home to look for peace.

WALTER (*beseechingly*): Then why can't there never be no peace in this house then?

MAMA: You done found it in some other house?

WALTER: No—there ain't no woman! Why do women always think there's a woman somewhere when a man gets restless. (*Picks up the check.*) Do you know what this money means to me? Do you know what this money can do for us? (*Puts it back.*) Mama—Mama—I want so many things . . .

MAMA: Yes, son—

WALTER: I want so many things that they are driving me kind of crazy . . . Mama—look at me.

MAMA: I'm looking at you. You a good-looking boy. You got a job, a nice wife, a fine boy and—

WALTER: A job. (*Looks at her.*) Mama, a job? I open and close car doors all day long. I drive a man around in his limousine and I say, "Yes, sir, no, sir; very good, sir; shall I take the Drive, sir?" Mama, that ain't no kind of job . . . that ain't nothing at all. (*Very quietly.*) Mama, I don't know if I can make you understand.

MAMA: Understand what, baby?

WALTER (*quietly*): Sometimes it's like I can see the future stretched out in front of me—just plain as day. The future, Mama. Hanging over there at the edge of my days. Just waiting for me—a big, looming blank space—full of *nothing*. Just waiting for *me*. But it don't have to be. (*Pause. Kneeling beside her chair.*) Mama—sometimes when I'm downtown and I pass them cool, quiet-looking restaurants where them white boys are sitting back and talking 'bout things . . . sitting there turning deals worth millions of dollars . . . sometimes I see guys don't look much older than me—

MAMA: Son—how come you talk so much 'bout money?

WALTER (*with immense passion*): Because it is life, Mama!

MAMA (*quietly*): Oh—(*Very quietly.*) So now it's life. Money is life. Once upon a time freedom used to be life—now it's money. I guess the world really do change . . .

WALTER: No—it was always money, Mama. We just didn't know about it.

MAMA: No . . . something has changed. (*She looks at him.*) You something new, boy. In my time we was worried about not being lynched and getting to the North if we could and how to stay alive and still have a pinch of dignity too . . . Now here come you and Beneatha—talking 'bout things we ain't never even thought about hardly, me and your daddy. You ain't satisfied or proud of nothing we done. I mean that you had a home, that we kept you out of trouble till you was grown, that you don't have to ride to work on the back of nobody's streetcar—You my children—but how different we done become.

WALTER (*A long beat. He pats her hand and gets up.*): You just don't understand, Mama, you just don't understand.

MAMA: Son—do you know your wife is expecting another baby? (*Walter stands, stunned, and absorbs what his mother has said.*) That's what she wanted to talk to you about. (*Walter sinks down into a chair.*) This ain't for me to be telling—but you ought to know. (*She waits.*) I think Ruth is thinking 'bout getting rid of that child.

WALTER (*slowly understanding*):—No—no—Ruth wouldn't do that.

MAMA: When the world gets ugly enough—a woman will do anything for her family. *The part that's already living.*

WALTER: You don't know Ruth, Mama, if you think she would do that.

(*Ruth opens the bedroom door and stands there a little limp.*)

RUTH (*beaten*): Yes I would too, Walter. (*Pause.*) I gave her a five-dollar down payment.

(*There is total silence as the man stares at his wife and the mother stares at her son.*)

MAMA (*presently*): Well—(*Tightly.*) Well—son, I'm waiting to hear you say something ... (*She waits.*) I'm waiting to hear how you be your father's son. Be the man he was ... (*Pause. The silence shouts.*) Your wife says she going to destroy your child. And I'm waiting to hear you talk like him and say we a people who give children life, not who destroys them—(*She rises.*) I'm waiting to see you stand up and look like your daddy and say we done give up one baby to poverty and that we ain't going to give up nary another one ... I'm waiting.

WALTER: Ruth—(*He can say nothing.*)

MAMA: If you a son of mine, tell her! (*Walter picks up his keys and his coat and walks out. She continues, bitterly.*) You ... you are a disgrace to your father's memory. Somebody get me my hat!

ACT II • *Scene I*

(*Time: Later the same day.*)

(*At rise: Ruth is ironing again. She has the radio going. Presently Beneatha's bedroom door opens and Ruth's mouth falls and she puts down the iron in fascination.*)

RUTH: What have we got on tonight!

BENEATHA (*emerging grandly from the doorway so that we can see her thoroughly robed in the costume Asagai brought*): You are looking at what a well-dressed Nigerian woman wears—(*She parades for Ruth, her hair completely hidden by the headdress;*

she is coquettishly fanning herself with an ornate oriental fan, mistakenly more like Butterfly° than any Nigerian that ever was.*) Isn't it beautiful? (*She promenades to the radio and, with an arrogant flourish, turns off the good loud blues that is playing.*) Enough of this assimilationist junk! (*Ruth follows her with her eyes as she goes to the phonograph and puts on a record and turns and waits ceremoniously for the music to come up. Then, with a shout—*) OCOMOGOSIAY!

(*Ruth jumps. The music comes up, a lovely Nigerian melody. Beneatha listens, enraptured, her eyes far away— "back to the past." She begins to dance. Ruth is dumfounded.*)

RUTH: What kind of dance is that?

BENEATHA: A folk dance.

RUTH (*Pearl Bailey*): What kind of folks do that, honey?

BENEATHA: It's from Nigeria. It's a dance of welcome.

RUTH: Who you welcoming?

BENEATHA: The men back to the village.

RUTH: Where they been?

BENEATHA: How should I know—out hunting or something. Anyway, they are coming back now ...

RUTH: Well, that's good.

BENEATHA (*with the record*): Alundi, alundi
Alundi alunya
Jop pu a jeepua
Ang gu soooooooooo

Ai yai yue ...
Ayehaye—alundi ...

(*Walter comes in during this performance; he has obviously been drinking. He leans against the door heavily and watches his sister, at first with distaste. Then his eyes look off— "back to the past"—as he lifts both his fists to the roof, screaming.*)

WALTER: YEAH ... AND ETHIOPIA STRETCH FORTH HER HANDS AGAIN! ...

RUTH (*drily, looking at him*): Yes—and Africa sure is claiming her own tonight. (*She gives them both up and starts ironing again.*)

WALTER (*all in a drunken, dramatic shout*): Shut up! ... I'm digging them drums ... them drums move me! ... (*He makes his weaving way to his wife's face and leans in close to her.*) In my *heart of hearts*—(*he thumps his chest*)—I am much warrior!

RUTH (*without even looking up*): In your heart of hearts you are much drunkard.

WALTER (*coming away from her and starting to wander around the room, shouting*): Me and Jomo ... (*Intently, in his sister's face. She has stopped dancing to watch him in this unknown mood.*) That's my man, Kenyatta. (*Shouting and*

Butterfly: Madame Butterfly, the title character in the opera by Puccini, set in Japan.

thumping his chest.) FLAMING SPEAR! HOT DAMN!
(*He is suddenly in possession of an imaginary spear
and actively spearing enemies all over the room.*)
OCOMOGOSIAY . . .

BENEATHA (*to encourage Walter, thoroughly caught up
with this side of him*): OCOMOGOSIAY, FLAMING SPEAR!

WALTER: THE LION IS WAKING . . . OWIMOWEH! (*He
pulls his shirt open and leaps up on the table and gestures with his spear.*)

BENEATHA: OWIMOWEH!

WALTER (*On the table, very far gone, his eyes pure glass
sheets. He sees what we cannot, that he is a leader of
his people, a great chief, a descendant of Chaka, and
that the hour to march has come.*): Listen, my black
brothers—

BENEATHA: OCOMOGOSIAY!

WALTER:—Do you hear the waters rushing against the
shores of the coastlands—

BENEATHA: OCOMOGOSIAY!

WALTER:—Do you hear the screeching of the cocks in
yonder hills beyond where the chiefs meet in council
for the coming of the mighty war—

BENEATHA: OCOMOGOSIAY!

(*And now the lighting shifts subtly to suggest the world
of Walter's imagination, and the mood shifts from pure
comedy. It is the inner Walter speaking: the Southside
chauffeur has assumed an unexpected majesty.*)

WALTER:—Do you hear the beating of the wings of the
birds flying low over the mountains and the low
places of our land—

BENEATHA: OCOMOGOSIAY!

WALTER:—Do you hear the singing of the women singing
the war songs of our fathers to the babies in the great
houses? Singing the sweet war songs! (*The doorbell
rings.*) OH, DO YOU HEAR, MY *BLACK* BROTHERS!

BENEATHA (*completely gone*): We hear you, Flaming
Spear—

(*Ruth shuts off the phonograph and opens the door.
George Murchison enters.*)

WALTER: Telling us to prepare for the GREATNESS OF THE
TIME! (*Lights back to normal. He turns and sees
George.*) Black Brother!

(*He extends his hand for the fraternal clasp.*)

GEORGE: Black Brother, hell!

RUTH (*having had enough, and embarrassed for the
family*): Beneatha, you got company—what's the
matter with you? Walter Lee Younger, get down off
that table and stop acting like a fool . . .

(*Walter comes down off the table suddenly and makes
a quick exit to the bathroom.*)

RUTH: He's had a little to drink . . . I don't know what
her excuse is.

GEORGE (*to Beneatha*): Look honey, we're going *to* the
theater—we're not going to be *in* it . . . so go
change, huh?

(*Beneatha looks at him and slowly, ceremoniously, lifts
her hands and pulls off the headdress. Her hair is
close-cropped and unstraightened. George freezes mid-
sentence and Ruth's eyes all but fall out of her head.*)

GEORGE: What in the name of—

RUTH (*touching Beneatha's hair*): Girl, you done lost
your natural mind? Look at your head!

GEORGE: What have you done to your head—I mean
your hair!

BENEATHA: Nothing—except cut it off.

RUTH: Now that's the truth—it's what ain't been done
to it! You expect this boy to go out with you with
your head all nappy like that?

BENEATHA (*looking at George*): That's up to George. If
he's ashamed of his heritage—

GEORGE: Oh, don't be so proud of yourself, Bennie—
just because you look eccentric.

BENEATHA: How can something that's natural be
eccentric?

GEORGE: That's what being eccentric means—being
natural. Get dressed.

BENEATHA: I don't like that, George.

RUTH: Why must you and your brother make an argument out of everything people say?

BENEATHA: Because I hate assimilationist Negroes!

RUTH: Will somebody please tell me what assimila-
whoever means!

GEORGE: Oh, it's just a college girl's way of calling people
Uncle Toms—but that isn't what it means at all.

RUTH: Well, what does it mean?

BENEATHA (*cutting George off and staring at him as she
replies to Ruth*): It means someone who is willing to
give up his own culture and submerge himself completely in the dominant, and in this case *oppressive*
culture!

GEORGE: Oh, dear, dear, dear! Here we go! A lecture on
the African past! On our Great West African Heritage! In one second we will hear all about the great
Ashanti empires; the great Songhay civilizations; and
the great sculpture of Bénin—and then some poetry
in the Bantu—and the whole monologue will end
with the word *heritage!* (*Nastily.*) Let's face it, baby,
your heritage is nothing but a bunch of raggedy-
assed spirituals and some grass huts!

BENEATHA: GRASS HUTS! (*Ruth crosses to her and
forcibly pushes her toward the bedroom.*) See
there . . . you are standing there in your splendid
ignorance talking about people who were the first to
smelt iron on the face of the earth! (*Ruth is pushing
her through the door.*) The Ashanti were performing
surgical operations when the English—(*Ruth pulls
the door to, with Beneatha on the other side, and
smiles graciously at George. Beneatha opens the
door and shouts the end of the sentence defiantly at
George*)—were still tatooing themselves with blue
dragons! (*She goes back inside.*)

RUTH: Have a seat, George. (*They both sit. Ruth folds
her hands rather primly on her lap, determined to*

demonstrate the civilization of the family.) Warm, ain't it? I mean for September. (*Pause*.) Just like they always say about Chicago weather: If it's too hot or cold for you, just wait a minute and it'll change. (*She smiles happily at this cliché of clichés*.) Everybody say it's got to do with them bombs and things they keep setting off. (*Pause*.) Would you like a nice cold beer?

GEORGE: No, thank you. I don't care for beer. (*He looks at his watch*.) I hope she hurries up.

RUTH: What time is the show?

GEORGE: It's an eight-thirty curtain. That's just Chicago, though. In New York standard curtain time is eight forty.

(*He is rather proud of this knowledge*.)

RUTH (*properly appreciating it*): You get to New York a lot?

GEORGE (*offhand*): Few times a year.

RUTH: Oh—that's nice. I've never been to New York.

(*Walter enters. We feel he has relieved himself, but the edge of unreality is still with him*.)

WALTER: New York ain't got nothing Chicago ain't. Just a bunch of hustling people all squeezed up together—being "Eastern."

(*He turns his face into a screw of displeasure*.)

GEORGE: Oh—you've been?

WALTER: *Plenty* of times.

RUTH (*shocked at the lie*): Walter Lee Younger!

WALTER (*staring her down*): Plenty! (*Pause*.) What we got to drink in this house? Why don't you offer this man some refreshment. (*To George*.) They don't know how to entertain people in this house, man.

GEORGE: Thank you—I don't really care for anything.

WALTER (*feeling his head; sobriety coming*): Where's Mama?

RUTH: She ain't come back yet.

WALTER (*looking Murchison over from head to toe, scrutinizing his carefully casual tweed sports jacket over cashmere V-neck sweater over soft eyelet shirt and tie, and soft slacks, finished off with white buckskin shoes*): Why all you college boys wear them faggoty-looking white shoes?

RUTH: Walter Lee!

(*George Murchison ignores the remark*.)

WALTER (*to Ruth*): Well, they look crazy as hell—white shoes, cold as it is.

RUTH (*crushed*): You have to excuse him—

WALTER: No he don't! Excuse me for what? What you always excusing me for! I'll excuse myself when I needs to be excused! (*A pause*.) They look as funny as them black knee socks Beneatha wears out of here all the time.

RUTH: It's the college *style*, Walter.

WALTER: Style, hell. She looks like she got burnt legs or something!

RUTH: Oh, Walter—

WALTER (*an irritable mimic*): Oh, Walter! Oh, Walter! (*To Murchison*.) How's your old man making out? I understand you all going to buy that big hotel on the Drive? (*He finds a beer in the refrigerator, wanders over to Murchison, sipping and wiping his lips with the back of his hand, and straddling a chair backward to talk to the other man*.) Shrewd move. Your old man is all right, man. (*Tapping his head and half winking for emphasis*.) I mean he knows how to operate. I mean he thinks *big*, you know what I mean, I mean for a *home*, you know? But I think he's kind of running out of ideas now. I'd like to talk to him. Listen, man, I got some plans that could turn this city upside down. I mean think like he does. *Big*. Invest big, gamble big, hell, lose *big* if you have to, you know what I mean. It's hard to find a man on this whole Southside who understands my kind of thinking—you dig? (*He scrutinizes Murchison again, drinks his beer, squints his eyes, and leans in close, confidential, man to man*.) Me and you ought to sit down and talk sometimes, man. Man, I got me some ideas . . .

MURCHISON (*with boredom*): Yeah—sometimes we'll have to do that, Walter.

WALTER (*understanding the indifference, and offended*): Yeah—well, when you get the time, man. I know you a busy little boy.

RUTH: Walter, please—

WALTER (*bitterly, hurt*): I know ain't nothing in this world as busy as you colored college boys with your fraternity pins and white shoes . . .

RUTH (*covering her face with humiliation*): Oh, Walter Lee—

WALTER: I see you all all the time—with the books tucked under your arms—going to your (*British A—a mimic*) "clahsses." And for what! What the hell you learning over there? Filling up your heads—(*counting off on his fingers*)—with the sociology and the psychology—but they teaching you how to be a man? How to take over and run the world? They teaching you how to run a rubber plantation or a steel mill? Naw—just to talk proper and read books and wear them faggoty-looking white shoes . . .

GEORGE (*looking at him with distaste, a little above it all*): You're all wacked up with bitterness, man.

WALTER (*intently, almost quietly, between the teeth, glaring at the boy*): And you—ain't you bitter, man? Ain't you just about had it yet? Don't you see no stars gleaming that you can't reach out and grab? You happy?—You contented son-of-a-bitch—you happy? You got it made? Bitter? Man, I'm a volcano. Bitter? Here I am a giant—surrounded by ants! Ants who can't even understand what it is the giant is talking about.

RUTH (*passionately and suddenly*): Oh, Walter—ain't you with nobody!

WALTER (*violently*): No! 'Cause ain't nobody with me! Not even my own mother!

RUTH: Walter, that's a terrible thing to say!

(*Beneatha enters, dressed for the evening in a cocktail dress and earrings, hair natural.*)

GEORGE: Well—hey—(*Crosses to Beneatha; thoughtful, with emphasis, since this is a reversal.*) You look great!

WALTER (*seeing his sister's hair for the first time*): What's the matter with your head?

BENEATHA (*tired of the jokes now*): I cut it off, Brother.

WALTER (*coming close to inspect it and walking around her*): Well, I'll be damned. So that's what they mean by the African bush . . .

BENEATHA: Ha ha. Let's go, George.

GEORGE (*looking at her*): You know something? I like it. It's sharp. I mean it really is. (*Helps her into her wrap.*)

RUTH: Yes—I think so, too. (*She goes to the mirror and starts to clutch at her hair.*)

WALTER: Oh no! You leave yours alone, baby. You might turn out to have a pin-shaped head or something!

BENEATHA: See you all later.

RUTH: Have a nice time.

GEORGE: Thanks. Good night. (*Half out the door, he reopens it. To Walter.*) Good night, Prometheus!°

(*Beneatha and George exit.*)

WALTER (*to Ruth*): Who is Prometheus?

RUTH: I don't know. Don't worry about it.

WALTER (*in fury, pointing after George*): See there— they get to a point where they can't insult you man to man—they got to go talk about something ain't nobody never heard of!

RUTH: How do you know it was an insult? (*To humor him.*) Maybe Prometheus is a nice fellow.

WALTER: Prometheus! I bet there ain't even no such thing! I bet that simple-minded clown—

RUTH: Walter—

(*She stops what she is doing and looks at him.*)

WALTER (*yelling*): Don't start!

RUTH: Start what?

WALTER: Your nagging! Where was I? Who was I with? How much money did I spend?

RUTH (*plaintively*): Walter Lee—why don't we just try to talk about it . . .

WALTER (*not listening*): I been out talking with people who understand me. People who care about the things I got on my mind.

RUTH (*wearily*): I guess that means people like Willy Harris.

WALTER: Yes, people like Willy Harris.

RUTH (*with a sudden flash of impatience*): Why don't you all just hurry up and go into the banking business and stop talking about it!

WALTER: Why? You want to know why? 'Cause we all tied up in a race of people that don't know how to do nothing but moan, pray, and have babies!

Prometheus: Defiantly inventive Titan who stole fire from the gods and gave it to humans.

(*The line is too bitter even for him and he looks at her and sits down.*)

RUTH: Oh, Walter . . . (*Softly.*) Honey, why can't you stop fighting me?

WALTER (*without thinking*): Who's fighting you? Who even cares about you?

(*This line begins the retardation of his mood.*)

RUTH: Well—(*She waits a long time, and then with resignation starts to put away her things.*) I guess I might as well go on to bed . . . (*More or less to herself.*) I don't know where we lost it . . . but we have . . . (*Then, to him.*) I—I'm sorry about this new baby, Walter. I guess maybe I better go on and do what I started . . . I guess I just didn't realize how bad things was with us . . . I guess I just didn't really realize—(*She starts out to the bedroom and stops.*) You want some hot milk?

WALTER: Hot milk?

RUTH: Yes—hot milk.

WALTER: Why hot milk?

RUTH: 'Cause after all that liquor you come home with you ought to have something hot in your stomach.

WALTER: I don't want no milk.

RUTH: You want some coffee then?

WALTER: No, I don't want no coffee. I don't want nothing hot to drink. (*Almost plaintively.*) Why you always trying to give me something to eat?

RUTH (*standing and looking at him helplessly*): What else can I give you, Walter Lee Younger?

(*She stands and looks at him and presently turns to go out again. He lifts his head and watches her going away from him in a new mood which began to emerge when he asked her "Who cares about you?"*)

WALTER: It's been rough, ain't it, baby? (*She hears and stops but does not turn around and he continues to her back.*) I guess between two people there ain't never as much understood as folks generally thinks there is. I mean like between me and you—(*She turns to face him.*) How we gets to the place where we scared to talk softness to each other. (*He waits, thinking hard himself.*) Why you think it got to be like that? (*He is thoughtful, almost as a child would be.*) Ruth, what is it gets into people ought to be close?

RUTH: I don't know, honey. I think about it a lot.

WALTER: On account of you and me, you mean? The way things are with us. The way something done come down between us.

RUTH: There ain't so much between us, Walter . . . Not when you come to me and try to talk to me. Try to be with me . . . a little even.

WALTER (*total honesty*): Sometimes . . . sometimes . . . I don't even know how to try.

RUTH: Walter—

WALTER: Yes?

RUTH (*coming to him, gently and with misgiving, but coming to him*): Honey . . . life don't have to be like this. I mean sometimes people can do things so that things are better . . . You remember how we used to talk when Travis was born . . . about the way we were going to live . . . the kind of house . . . (*She is stroking his head.*) Well, it's all starting to slip away from us . . .

(*He turns her to him and they look at each other and kiss, tenderly and hungrily. The door opens and Mama enters — Walter breaks away and jumps up. A beat.*)

WALTER: Mama, where have you been?

MAMA: My — them steps is longer than they used to be. Whew! (*She sits down and ignores him.*) How you feeling this evening, Ruth?

(*Ruth shrugs, disturbed at having been interrupted and watching her husband knowingly.*)

WALTER: Mama, where have you been all day?

MAMA (*still ignoring him and leaning on the table and changing to more comfortable shoes*): Where's Travis?

RUTH: I let him go out earlier and he ain't come back yet. Boy, is he going to get it!

WALTER: Mama!

MAMA (*as if she has heard him for the first time*): Yes, son?

WALTER: Where did you go this afternoon?

MAMA: I went downtown to tend to some business that I had to tend to.

WALTER: What kind of business?

MAMA: You know better than to question me like a child, Brother.

WALTER (*rising and bending over the table*): Where were you, Mama? (*Bringing his fists down and shouting.*) Mama, you didn't go do something with that insurance money, something crazy?

(*The front door opens slowly, interrupting him, and Travis peeks his head in, less than hopefully.*)

TRAVIS (*to his mother*): Mama, I —

RUTH: "Mama I" nothing! You're going to get it, boy! Get on in that bedroom and get yourself ready!

TRAVIS: But I —

MAMA: Why don't you all never let the child explain hisself.

RUTH: Keep out of it now, Lena.

(*Mama clamps her lips together, and Ruth advances toward her son menacingly.*)

RUTH: A thousand times I have told you not to go off like that —

MAMA (*holding out her arms to her grandson*): Well — at least let me tell him something. I want him to be the first one to hear . . . Come here, Travis. (*The boy obeys, gladly.*) Travis — (*she takes him by the shoulder and looks into his face*) — you know that money we got in the mail this morning?

TRAVIS: Yes'm —

MAMA: Well — what you think your grandmama gone and done with that money?

TRAVIS: I don't know, Grandmama.

MAMA (*putting her finger on his nose for emphasis*): She went out and she bought you a house! (*The explosion comes from Walter at the end of the revelation and he jumps up and turns away from all of them in a fury. Mama continues, to Travis.*) You glad about the house? It's going to be yours when you get to be a man.

TRAVIS: Yeah — I always wanted to live in a house.

MAMA: All right, gimme some sugar then — (*Travis puts his arms around her neck as she watches her son over the boy's shoulder. Then, to Travis, after the embrace.*) Now when you say your prayers tonight, you thank God and your grandfather — 'cause it was him who give you the house — in his way.

RUTH (*taking the boy from Mama and pushing him toward the bedroom*): Now you get out of here and get ready for your beating.

TRAVIS: Aw, Mama —

RUTH: Get on in there — (*Closing the door behind him and turning radiantly to her mother-in-law.*) So you went and did it!

MAMA (*quietly, looking at her son with pain*): Yes, I did.

RUTH (*raising both arms classically*): PRAISE GOD! (*Looks at Walter a moment, who says nothing. She crosses rapidly to her husband.*) Please, honey — let me be glad . . . you be glad too. (*She has laid her hands on his shoulders, but he shakes himself free of her roughly, without turning to face her.*) Oh, Walter . . . a home . . . a home. (*She comes back to Mama.*) Well — where is it? How big is it? How much it going to cost?

MAMA: Well —

RUTH: When we moving?

MAMA (*smiling at her*): First of the month.

RUTH (*throwing back her head with jubilance*): *Praise God!*

MAMA (*tentatively, still looking at her son's back turned against her and Ruth*): It's — it's a nice house too . . . (*She cannot help speaking directly to him. An imploring quality in her voice, her manner, makes her almost like a girl now.*) Three bedrooms — nice big one for you and Ruth . . . Me and Beneatha still have to share our room, but Travis have one of his own and (*with difficulty*) I figure if the — new baby — is a boy, we could get one of them double-decker outfits . . . And there's a yard with a little patch of dirt where I could maybe get to grow me a few flowers . . . And a nice big basement . . .

RUTH: Walter honey, be glad —

MAMA (*still to his back, fingering things on the table*): 'Course I don't want to make it sound fancier than it is . . . It's just a plain little old house — but it's made good and solid — and it will be *ours*. Walter Lee — it makes a difference in a man when he can walk on floors that belong to *him* . . .

RUTH: Where is it?

MAMA (*frightened at this telling*): Well — well — it's out there in Clybourne Park —

(*Ruth's radiance fades abruptly, and Walter finally turns slowly to face his mother with incredulity and hostility.*)

RUTH: Where?

MAMA (*matter-of-factly*): Four o six Clybourne Street, Clybourne Park.

RUTH: Clybourne Park? Mama, there ain't no colored people living in Clybourne Park.

MAMA (*almost idiotically*): Well, I guess there's going to be some now.

WALTER (*bitterly*): So that's the peace and comfort you went out and bought for us today!

MAMA (*raising her eyes to meet his finally*): Son—I just tried to find the nicest place for the least amount of money for my family.

RUTH (*trying to recover from the shock*): Well—well—'course I ain't one never been 'fraid of no crackers,° mind you—but—well, wasn't there no other houses nowhere?

MAMA: Them houses they put up for colored in them areas way out all seem to cost twice as much as other houses. I did the best I could.

RUTH (*struck senseless with the news, in its various degrees of goodness and trouble, she sits a moment, her fists propping her chin in thought, and then she starts to rise, bringing her fists down with vigor, the radiance spreading from cheek to cheek again*): Well—well—All I can say is—if this is my time in life—MY TIME—to say good-bye—(*and she builds with momentum as she starts to circle the room with an exuberant, almost tearfully happy release*)—to these Goddamned cracking walls!—(*she pounds the walls*)—and these marching roaches!—(*she wipes at an imaginary army of marching roaches*)—and this cramped little closet which ain't now or never was no kitchen! . . . then I say it loud and good, HALLELUJAH! AND GOOD-BYE MISERY . . . I DON'T NEVER WANT TO SEE YOUR UGLY FACE AGAIN! (*She laughs joyously, having practically destroyed the apartment, and flings her arms up and lets them come down happily, slowly, reflectively, over her abdomen, aware for the first time perhaps that the life therein pulses with happiness and not despair.*) Lena?

MAMA (*moved, watching her happiness*): Yes, honey?

RUTH (*looking off*): Is there—is there a whole lot of sunlight?

MAMA (*understanding*): Yes, child, there's a whole lot of sunlight.

(*Long pause.*)

RUTH (*collecting herself and going to the door of the room Travis is in*): Well—I guess I better see 'bout Travis. (*To Mama.*) Lord, I sure don't feel like whipping nobody today!

(*She exits.*)

crackers: White people, often used to refer disparagingly to poor whites.

MAMA (*the mother and son are left alone now and the mother waits a long time, considering deeply, before she speaks*): Son—you—you understand what I done, don't you? (*Walter is silent and sullen.*) I— I just seen my family falling apart today . . . just falling to pieces in front of my eyes . . . We couldn't of gone on like we was today. We was going backwards 'stead of forwards—talking 'bout killing babies and wishing each other was dead . . . When it gets like that in life—you just got to do something different, push on out and do something bigger . . . (*She waits.*) I wish you say something, son . . . I wish you'd say how deep inside you you think I done the right thing—

WALTER (*crossing slowly to his bedroom door and finally turning there and speaking measuredly*): What you need me to say you done right for? *You* the head of this family. You run our lives like you want to. It was your money and you did what you wanted with it. So what you need for me to say it was all right for? (*Bitterly, to hurt her as deeply as he knows is possible.*) So you butchered up a dream of mine—you— who always talking 'bout your children's dreams . . .

MAMA: Walter Lee—

(*He just closes the door behind him. Mama sits alone, thinking heavily.*)

Scene II

(*Time: Friday night. A few weeks later.*)

(*At rise: Packing crates mark the intention of the family to move. Beneatha and George come in, presumably from an evening out again.*)

GEORGE: O.K. . . . O.K., whatever you say . . . (*They both sit on the couch. He tries to kiss her. She moves away.*) Look, we've had a nice evening; let's not spoil it, huh? . . .

(*He again turns her head and tries to nuzzle in and she turns away from him, not with distaste but with momentary lack of interest; in a mood to pursue what they were talking about.*)

BENEATHA: I'm *trying* to talk to you.

GEORGE: We always talk.

BENEATHA: Yes—and I love to talk.

GEORGE (*exasperated; rising*): I know it and I don't mind it sometimes . . . I want you to cut it out, see— The moody stuff, I mean. I don't like it. You're a nice-looking girl . . . all over. That's all you need, honey, forget the atmosphere. Guys aren't going to go for the atmosphere—they're going to go for what they see. Be glad for that. Drop the Garbo routine. It doesn't go with you. As for myself, I want a nice— (*groping*)—simple (*thoughtfully*)—sophisticated girl . . . not a poet—O.K.?

(*He starts to kiss her, she rebuffs him again, and he jumps up.*)

BENEATHA: Why are you angry, George?

GEORGE: Because this is stupid! I don't go out with you to discuss the nature of "quiet desperation" or to hear all about your thoughts—because the world will go on thinking what it thinks regardless—

BENEATHA: Then why read books? Why go to school?

GEORGE (*with artificial patience, counting on his fingers*): It's simple. You read books—to learn facts—to get grades—to pass the course—to get a degree. That's all—it has nothing to do with thoughts.

(*A long pause.*)

BENEATHA: I see. (*He starts to sit.*) Good night, George.

(*George looks at her a little oddly and starts to exit. He meets Mama coming in.*)

GEORGE: Oh—hello, Mrs. Younger.

MAMA: Hello, George, how you feeling?

GEORGE: Fine—fine, how are you?

MAMA: Oh, a little tired. You know them steps can get you after a day's work. You all have a nice time tonight?

GEORGE: Yes—a fine time. A fine time.

MAMA: Well, good night.

GEORGE: Good night. (*He exits. Mama closes the door behind her.*)

MAMA: Hello, honey. What you sitting like that for?

BENEATHA: I'm just sitting.

MAMA: Didn't you have a nice time?

BENEATHA: No.

MAMA: No? What's the matter?

BENEATHA: Mama, George is a fool—honest. (*She rises.*)

MAMA (*Hustling around unloading the packages she has entered with. She stops.*): Is he, baby?

BENEATHA: Yes.

(*Beneatha makes up Travis's bed as she talks.*)

MAMA: You sure?

BENEATHA: Yes.

MAMA: Well—I guess you better not waste your time with no fools.

(*Beneatha looks up at her mother, watching her put groceries in the refrigerator. Finally she gathers up her things and starts into the bedroom. At the door she stops and looks back at her mother.*)

BENEATHA: Mama—

MAMA: Yes, baby—

BENEATHA: Thank you.

MAMA: For what?

BENEATHA: For understanding me this time.

(*She exits quickly and the mother stands, smiling a little, looking at the place where Beneatha just stood. Ruth enters.*)

RUTH: Now don't you fool with any of this stuff, Lena—

MAMA: Oh, I just thought I'd sort a few things out. Is Brother here?

RUTH: Yes.

MAMA (*with concern*): Is he—

RUTH (*reading her eyes*): Yes.

(*Mama is silent and someone knocks on the door. Mama and Ruth exchange weary and knowing glances and Ruth opens it to admit the neighbor, Mrs. Johnson,° who is a rather squeaky wide-eyed lady of no particular age, with a newspaper under her arm.*)

MAMA (*changing her expression to acute delight and a ringing cheerful greeting*): Oh—hello there, Johnson.

JOHNSON (*this is a woman who decided long ago to be enthusiastic about EVERYTHING in life and she is inclined to wave her wrist vigorously at the height of her exclamatory comments*): Hello there, yourself! H'you this evening, Ruth?

RUTH (*not much of a deceptive type*): Fine, Mis' Johnson, h'you?

JOHNSON: Fine. (*Reaching out quickly, playfully, and patting Ruth's stomach.*) Ain't you starting to poke out none yet! (*She mugs with delight at the over-familiar remark and her eyes dart around looking at the crates and packing preparation; Mama's face is a cold sheet of endurance.*) Oh, ain't we getting ready round here, though! Yessir! Lookathere! I'm telling you the Youngers is really getting ready to "move on up a little higher!"—Bless God!

MAMA (*a little drily, doubting the total sincerity of the Blesser*): Bless God.

JOHNSON: He's good, ain't He?

MAMA: Oh yes, He's good.

JOHNSON: I mean sometimes He works in mysterious ways . . . but He works, don't He!

MAMA (*the same*): Yes, he does.

JOHNSON: I'm just soooooo happy for y'all. And this here child—(*about Ruth*) looks like she could just pop open with happiness, don't she. Where's all the rest of the family?

MAMA: Bennie's gone to bed—

JOHNSON: Ain't no . . . (*the implication is pregnancy*) sickness done hit you—I hope . . . ?

MAMA: No—she just tired. She was out this evening.

JOHNSON (*all is a coo, an emphatic coo*): Aw—ain't that lovely. She still going out with the little Murchison boy?

MAMA (*drily*): Ummmm huh.

JOHNSON: That's lovely. You sure got lovely children, Younger. Me and Isaiah talks all the time 'bout what fine children you was blessed with. We sure do.

MAMA: Ruth, give Mis' Johnson a piece of sweet potato pie and some milk.

JOHNSON: Oh honey, I can't stay hardly a minute—I just dropped in to see if there was anything I could

---

Mrs. Johnson: This character and the scene of her visit were cut from the original production and early editions of the play.

do. (*Accepting the food easily.*) I guess y'all seen the news what's all over the colored paper this week . . .

MAMA: No—didn't get mine yet this week.

JOHNSON (*lifting her head and blinking with the spirit of catastrophe*): You mean you ain't read 'bout them colored people that was bombed out their place out there?

(*Ruth straightens with concern and takes the paper and reads it. Johnson notices her and feeds commentary.*)

JOHNSON: Ain't it something how bad these here white folks is getting here in Chicago! Lord, getting so you think you right down in Mississippi! (*With a tremendous and rather insincere sense of melodrama.*) 'Course I thinks it's wonderful how our folks keeps on pushing out. You hear some of these Negroes round here talking 'bout how they don't go where they ain't wanted and all that—but not me, honey! (*This is a lie.*) Wilhemenia Othella Johnson goes anywhere, any time she feels like it! (*With head movement for emphasis.*) Yes I do! Why if we left it up to these here crackers the poor niggers wouldn't have nothing—(*She clasps her hand over her mouth.*) Oh, I always forgets you don't 'low that word in your house.

MAMA (*quietly, looking at her*): No—I don't 'low it.

JOHNSON (*vigorously again*): Me neither! I was just telling Isaiah yesterday when he come using it in front of me—I said, "Isaiah, it's just like Mis' Younger says all the time—"

MAMA: Don't you want some more pie?

JOHNSON: No—no thank you; this was lovely. I got to get on over home and have my midnight coffee. I hear some people say it don't let them sleep but I finds I can't close my eyes right lessen I done had that laaaast cup of coffee . . . (*She waits. A beat. Undaunted.*) My Good-night coffee, I calls it!

MAMA (*with much eye-rolling and communication between herself and Ruth*): Ruth, why don't you give Mis' Johnson some coffee.

(*Ruth gives Mama an unpleasant look for her kindness.*)

JOHNSON (*accepting the coffee*): Where's Brother tonight?

MAMA: He's lying down.

JOHNSON: Mmmmmmm, he sure gets his beauty rest, don't he? Good-looking man. Sure is a good-looking man! (*Reaching out to pat Ruth's stomach again.*) I guess that's how come we keep on having babies around here. (*She winks at Mama.*) One thing 'bout Brother, he always know how to have a *good* time. And soooooo ambitious! I bet it was his idea y'all moving out to Clybourne Park. Lord—I bet this time next month y'all's names will have been in the papers plenty—(*Holding up her hands to mark off each word of the headline she can see in front of her.*) "NEGROS INVADE CLYBOURNE PARK—BOMBED!"

MAMA (*she and Ruth look at the woman in amazement*): We ain't exactly moving out there to get bombed.

JOHNSON: Oh, honey—you know I'm praying to God every day that don't nothing like that happen! But you have to think of life like it is—and these here Chicago peckerwoods is some baaaad peckerwoods.

MAMA (*wearily*): We done thought about all that Mis' Johnson.

(*Beneatha comes out of the bedroom in her robe and passes through to the bathroom. Mrs. Johnson turns.*)

JOHNSON: Hello there, Bennie!

BENEATHA (*crisply*): Hello, Mrs. Johnson.

JOHNSON: How is school?

BENEATHA (*crisply*): Fine, thank you. (*She goes out.*)

JOHNSON (*insulted*): Getting so she don't have much to say to nobody.

MAMA: The child was on her way to the bathroom.

JOHNSON: I know—but sometimes she act like ain't got time to pass the time of day with nobody ain't been to college. Oh—I ain't criticizing her none. It's just—you know how some of our young people gets when they get a little education. (*Mama and Ruth say nothing, just look at her.*) Yes—well. Well, I guess I better get on home. (*Unmoving.*) 'Course I can understand how she must be proud and everything—being the only one in the family to make something of herself. I know just being a chauffeur ain't never satisfied Brother none. He shouldn't feel like that, though. Ain't nothing wrong with being a chauffeur.

MAMA: There's plenty wrong with it.

JOHNSON: What?

MAMA: Plenty. My husband always said being any kind of a servant wasn't a fit thing for a man to have to be. He always said a man's hands was made to make things, or to turn the earth with—not to drive nobody's car for 'em—or—(*she looks at her own hands*) carry they slop jars. And my boy is just like him—he wasn't meant to wait on nobody.

JOHNSON (*rising, somewhat offended*): Mmmmmmmmm. The Youngers is too much for me! (*She looks around.*) You sure one proud-acting bunch of colored folks. Well—I always thinks like Booker T. Washington said that time—"Education has spoiled many a good plow hand"—

MAMA: Is that what old Booker T. said?

JOHNSON: He sure did.

MAMA: Well, it sounds just like him. The fool.

JOHNSON (*indignantly*): Well—he was one of our great men.

MAMA: Who said so?

JOHNSON (*nonplussed*): You know, me and you ain't never agreed about some things, Lena Younger. I guess I better be going—

RUTH (*quickly*): Good night—

JOHNSON: Good night. Oh—(*Thrusting it at her.*) You can keep the paper! (*With a trill.*) 'Night.

MAMA: Good night, Mis' Johnson.

(*Mrs. Johnson exits.*)

RUTH: If ignorance was gold . . .

MAMA: Shush. Don't talk about folks behind their backs.

RUTH: You do.

MAMA: I'm old and corrupted. (*Beneatha enters.*) You was rude to Mis' Johnson, Beneatha, and I don't like it at all.

BENEATHA (*at her door*): Mama, if there are two things we, as a people, have got to overcome, one is the Klu Klux Klan—and the other is Mrs. Johnson. (*She exits.*)

MAMA: Smart aleck.

(*The phone rings.*)

RUTH: I'll get it.

MAMA: Lord, ain't this a popular place tonight.

RUTH (*at the phone*): Hello—Just a minute. (*Goes to door.*) Walter, it's Mrs. Arnold. (*Waits. Goes back to the phone. Tense.*) Hello. Yes, this is his wife speaking . . . He's lying down now. Yes . . . well, he'll be in tomorrow. He's been very sick. Yes—I know we should have called, but we were so sure he'd be able to come in today. Yes—yes, I'm very sorry. Yes . . . Thank you very much. (*She hangs up. Walter is standing in the doorway of the bedroom behind her.*) That was Mrs. Arnold.

WALTER (*indifferently*): Was it?

RUTH: She said if you don't come in tomorrow that they are getting a new man . . .

WALTER: Ain't that sad—ain't that crying sad.

RUTH: She said Mr. Arnold has had to take a cab for three days . . . Walter, you ain't been to work for three days! (*This is a revelation.*) Where you been, Walter Lee Younger? (*Walter looks at her and starts to laugh.*) You're going to lose your job.

WALTER: That's right . . . (*He turns on the radio.*)

RUTH: Oh, Walter, and with your mother working like a dog every day—

(*A steamy, deep blues pours into the room.*)

WALTER: That's sad too—Everything is sad.

MAMA: What you been doing for these three days, son?

WALTER: Mama—you don't know all the things a man what got leisure can find to do in this city . . . What's this—Friday night? Well—Wednesday I borrowed Willy Harris's car and I went for a drive . . . just me and myself and I drove and drove . . . Way out . . . way past South Chicago, and I parked the car and I sat and looked at the steel mills all day long. I just sat in the car and looked at them big black chimneys for hours. Then I drove back and I went to the Green Hat. (*Pause.*) And Thursday—Thursday I borrowed the car again and I got in it and I pointed it the other way and I drove the other way—for hours—way, way up to Wisconsin, and I looked at the farms. I just drove and looked at the farms. Then I drove back and I went to the Green Hat. (*Pause.*) And today—today I didn't get the car. Today I just walked. All over the Southside. And I looked at the Negroes and they looked at me and finally I just sat down on the curb at Thirty-ninth and South Parkway and I just sat there and watched the Negroes go by. And then I went to the Green Hat. You all sad? You all depressed? And you know where I am going right now—

(*Ruth goes out quietly.*)

MAMA: Oh, Big Walter, is this the harvest of our days?

WALTER: You know what I like about the Green Hat? I like this little cat they got there who blows a sax . . . He blows. He talks to me. He ain't but 'bout five feet tall and he's got a conked head and his eyes is always closed and he's all music—

MAMA (*rising and getting some papers out of her handbag*): Walter—

WALTER: And there's this other guy who plays the piano . . . and they got a sound. I mean they can work on some music . . . They got the best little combo in the world in the Green Hat . . . You can just sit there and drink and listen to them three men play and you realize that don't nothing matter worth a damn, but just being there—

MAMA: I've helped do it to you, haven't I, son? Walter I been wrong.

WALTER: Naw—you ain't never been wrong about nothing, Mama.

MAMA: Listen to me, now. I say I been wrong, son. That I been doing to you what the rest of the world been doing to you. (*She turns off the radio.*) Walter—(*She stops and he looks up slowly at her and she meets his eyes pleadingly.*) What you ain't never understood is that I ain't got nothing, don't own nothing, ain't never really wanted nothing that wasn't for you. There ain't nothing as precious to me . . . There ain't nothing worth holding on to, money, dreams, nothing else—if it means—if it means it's going to destroy my boy. (*She takes an envelope out of her handbag and puts it in front of him and he watches her without speaking or moving.*) I paid the man thirty-five hundred dollars down on the house. That leaves sixty-five hundred dollars. Monday morning I want you to take this money and take three thousand dollars and put it in a savings account for Beneatha's medical schooling. The rest you put in a checking account—with your name on it. And from now on any penny that come out of it or that go in it is for you to look after. For you to decide. (*She drops her hands a little helplessly.*) It ain't much, but it's all I got in the world and I'm putting it in your hands. I'm telling you to be the head of this family from now on like you supposed to be.

WALTER (*stares at the money*): You trust me like that, Mama?

MAMA: I ain't never stop trusting you. Like I ain't never stop loving you.

(*She goes out, and Walter sits looking at the money on the table. Finally, in a decisive gesture, he gets up and, in mingled joy and desperation, picks up the money. At the same moment, Travis enters for bed.*)

TRAVIS: What's the matter, Daddy? You drunk?

WALTER (*sweetly, more sweetly than we have ever known him*): No, Daddy ain't drunk. Daddy ain't going to never be drunk again . . .

TRAVIS: Well, good night, Daddy.

(*The father has come from behind the couch and leans over, embracing his son.*)

WALTER: Son, I feel like talking to you tonight.

TRAVIS: About what?

WALTER: Oh, about a lot of things. About you and what kind of man you going to be when you grow up. . . . Son—son, what do you want to be when you grow up?

TRAVIS: A bus driver.

WALTER (*laughing a little*): A what? Man, that ain't nothing to want to be!

TRAVIS: Why not?

WALTER: 'Cause, man—it ain't big enough—you know what I mean.

TRAVIS: I don't know then. I can't make up my mind. Sometimes Mama asks me that too. And sometimes when I tell her I just want to be like you—she says she don't want me to be like that and sometimes she says she does. . . .

WALTER (*gathering him up in his arms*): You know what, Travis? In seven years you going to be seventeen years old. And things is going to be very different with us in seven years Travis. . . . One day when you are seventeen I'll come home—home from my office downtown somewhere—

TRAVIS: You don't work in no office, Daddy.

WALTER: No—but after tonight. After what your daddy gonna do tonight, there's going to be offices—a whole lot of offices. . . .

TRAVIS: What you gonna do tonight, Daddy?

WALTER: You wouldn't understand yet, son, but your daddy's gonna make a transaction . . . a business transaction that's going to change our lives. . . . That's how come one day when you 'bout seventeen years old I'll come home and I'll be pretty tired, you know what I mean, after a day of conferences and secretaries getting things wrong the way they do . . . 'cause an executive's life is hell man—(*The more he talks the farther away he gets.*) And I'll pull the car up on the driveway . . . just a plain black Chrysler, I think, with white walls—no—black tires. More elegant. Rich people don't have to be flashy . . . though I'll have to get something a little sportier for Ruth—maybe a Cadillac convertible to do her shopping in. . . . And I'll come up the steps to the house and the gardener will be clipping away at the hedges and he'll say, "Good evening, Mr. Younger." And I'll say, "Hello, Jefferson, how are you this evening?" And I'll go inside and Ruth will come downstairs and meet me at the door and we'll kiss each other and she'll take my arm and we'll go up to your room to see you sitting on the floor with the catalogues of all the great schools in America

around you. . . . All the great schools in the world! And—and I'll say, all right son—it's your seventeenth birthday, what is it you've decided? . . . Just tell me where you want to go to school and you'll go. Just tell me, what it is you want to be—and you'll *be* it. . . . Whatever you want to be—Yessir! (*He holds his arms open for Travis.*) You just name it, son . . . (*Travis leaps into them*) and I hand you the world!

(*Walter's voice has risen in pitch and hysterical promise and on the last line he lifts Travis high.*)

Scene III

(*Time: Saturday, moving day, one week later.*)

(*Before the curtain rises, Ruth's voice, a strident, dramatic church alto, cuts through the silence.*)

(*It is, in the darkness, a triumphant surge, a penetrating statement of expectation: "Oh, Lord, I don't feel no ways tired! Children, oh, glory hallelujah!"*)

(*As the curtain rises we see that Ruth is alone in the living room, finishing up the family's packing. It is moving day. She is nailing crates and tying cartons. Beneatha enters, carrying a guitar case, and watches her exuberant sister-in-law.*)

RUTH: Hey!

BENEATHA (*putting away the case*): Hi.

RUTH (*pointing at a package*): Honey—look in that package there and see what I found on sale this morning at the South Center. (*Ruth gets up and moves to the package and draws out some curtains.*) Lookahere—hand-turned hems!

BENEATHA: How do you know the window size out there?

RUTH (*who hadn't thought of that*): Oh—Well, they bound to fit something in the whole house. Anyhow, they was too good a bargain to pass up. (*Ruth slaps her head, suddenly remembering something.*) Oh, Bennie—I meant to put a special note on that carton over there. That's your mama's good china and she wants 'em to be very careful with it.

BENEATHA: I'll do it.

(*Beneatha finds a piece of paper and starts to draw large letters on it.*)

RUTH: You know what I'm going to do soon as I get in that new house?

BENEATHA: What?

RUTH: Honey—I'm going to run me a tub of water up to here . . . (*With her fingers practically up to her nostrils.*) And I'm going to get in it—and I am going to sit . . . and sit . . . and sit in that hot water and the first person who knocks to tell *me* to hurry up and come out—

BENEATHA: Gets shot at sunrise.

RUTH (*laughing happily*): You said it, sister! (*Noticing how large Beneatha is absent-mindedly making the note.*) Honey, they ain't going to read that from no airplane.

BENEATHA (*laughing herself*): I guess I always think things have more emphasis if they are big, somehow.

RUTH (*looking up at her and smiling*): You and your brother seem to have that as a philosophy of life. Lord, that man—done changed so 'round here. You know—you know what we did last night? Me and Walter Lee?

BENEATHA: What?

RUTH (*smiling to herself*): We went to the movies. (*Looking at Beneatha to see if she understands.*) We went to the movies. You know the last time me and Walter went to the movies together?

BENEATHA: No.

RUTH: Me neither. That's how long it been. (*Smiling again.*) But we went last night. The picture wasn't much good, but that didn't seem to matter. We went—and we held hands.

BENEATHA: Oh, Lord!

RUTH: We held hands—and you know what?

BENEATHA: What?

RUTH: When we come out of the show it was late and dark and all the stores and things was closed up . . . and it was kind of chilly and there wasn't many people on the streets . . . and we was still holding hands, me and Walter.

BENEATHA: You're killing me.

(*Walter enters with a large package. His happiness is deep in him; he cannot keep still with his newfound exuberance. He is singing and wiggling and snapping his fingers. He puts his package in a corner and puts a phonograph record which he has brought in with him, on the record player. As the music, soulful and sensuous, comes up he dances over to Ruth and tries to get her to dance with him. She gives in at last to his raunchiness and in a fit of giggling allows herself to be drawn into his mood. They dip and she melts into his arms in a classic, body-melding "slow drag."*)

BENEATHA (*regarding them a long time as they dance, then drawing in her breath for a deeply exaggerated comment which she does not particularly mean*): Talk about—olddddddddddd—fashionedddddddd—Negroes!

WALTER (*stopping momentarily*): What kind of Negroes?

(*He says this in fun. He is not angry with her today, nor with anyone. He starts to dance with his wife again.*)

BENEATHA: Old-fashioned.

WALTER (*as he dances with Ruth*): You know, when these *New Negroes* have their convention—(*pointing at his sister*)—that is going to be the chairman of the Committee on Unending Agitation. (*He goes on dancing, then stops.*) Race, race, race! . . . Girl, I do believe you are the first person in the history of the entire human race to successfully brainwash yourself. (*Beneatha breaks up and he goes on dancing. He stops again,*

enjoying his tease.) Damn, even the N double A C P takes a holiday sometimes! (*Beneatha and Ruth laugh. He dances with Ruth some more and starts to laugh and stops and pantomimes someone over an operating table.*) I can just see that chick someday looking down at some poor cat on an operating table and before she starts to slice him, she says . . . (*pulling his sleeves back maliciously*) "By the way, what are your views on civil rights down there? . . ."

(*He laughs at her again and starts to dance happily. The bell sounds.*)

BENEATHA: Sticks and stones may break my bones but . . . words will never hurt me!

(*Beneatha goes to the door and opens it as Walter and Ruth go on with the clowning. Beneatha is somewhat surprised to see a quiet-looking middle-aged white man in a business suit holding his hat and a briefcase in his hand and consulting a small piece of paper.*)

MAN: Uh—how do you do, miss. I am looking for a Mrs.—(*he looks at the slip of paper*) Mrs. Lena Younger? (*He stops short, struck dumb at the sight of the oblivious Walter and Ruth.*)

BENEATHA (*smoothing her hair with slight embarrassment*): Oh—yes, that's my mother. Excuse me. (*She closes the door and turns to quiet the other two.*) Ruth! Brother! (*Enunciating precisely but soundlessly: "There's a white man at the door!" They stop dancing, Ruth cuts off the phonograph, Beneatha opens the door. The man casts a curious quick glance at all of them.*) Uh—come in please.

MAN (*coming in*): Thank you.

BENEATHA: My mother isn't here just now. Is it business?

MAN: Yes . . . well, of a sort.

WALTER (*freely, the Man of the House*): Have a seat. I'm Mrs. Younger's son. I look after most of her business matters.

(*Ruth and Beneatha exchange amused glances.*)

MAN (*regarding Walter, and sitting*): Well—My name is Karl Lindner . . .

WALTER (*stretching out his hand*): Walter Younger. This is my wife—(*Ruth nods politely*)—and my sister.

LINDNER: How do you do.

WALTER (*amiably, as he sits himself easily on a chair, leaning forward on his knees with interest and looking expectantly into the newcomer's face*): What can we do for you, Mr. Lindner!

LINDNER (*some minor shuffling of the hat and briefcase on his knees*): Well—I am a representative of the Clybourne Park Improvement Association—

WALTER (*pointing*): Why don't you sit your things on the floor?

LINDNER: Oh—yes. Thank you. (*He slides the briefcase and hat under the chair.*) And as I was saying—I am from the Clybourne Park Improvement Association and we have had it brought to our attention at the last meeting that you people—or at least your mother—has bought a piece of residential property at—(*he digs for the slip of paper again*)—four o six Clybourne Street . . .

WALTER: That's right. Care for something to drink? Ruth, get Mr. Lindner a beer.

LINDNER (*upset for some reason*): Oh—no, really. I mean thank you very much, but no thank you.

RUTH: (*innocently*): Some coffee?

LINDNER: Thank you, nothing at all.

(*Beneatha is watching the man carefully.*)

LINDNER: Well, I don't know how much you folks know about our organization. (*He is a gentle man; thoughtful and somewhat labored in his manner.*) It is one of these community organizations set up to look after—oh, you know, things like block upkeep and special projects and we also have what we call our New Neighbors Orientation Committee . . .

BENEATHA (*drily*): Yes—and what do they do?

LINDNER (*turning a little to her and then returning the main force to Walter*): Well—it's what you might call a sort of welcoming committee, I guess. I mean they, we—I'm the chairman of the committee—go around and see the new people who move into the neighborhood and sort of give them the lowdown on the way we do things out in Clybourne Park.

BENEATHA (*with appreciation of the two meanings, which escape Ruth and Walter*): Un-huh.

LINDNER: And we also have the category of what the association calls—(*he looks elsewhere*)—uh—special community problems . . .

BENEATHA: Yes—and what are some of those?

WALTER: Girl, let the man talk.

LINDNER (*with understated relief*): Thank you. I would sort of like to explain this thing in my own way. I mean I want to explain to you in a certain way.

WALTER: Go ahead.

LINDNER: Yes. Well. I'm going to try to get right to the point. I'm sure we'll all appreciate that in the long run.

BENEATHA: Yes.

WALTER: Be still now!

LINDNER: Well—

RUTH (*still innocently*): Would you like another chair—you don't look comfortable.

LINDNER (*more frustrated than annoyed*): No, thank you very much. Please. Well—to get right to the point I—(*a great breath, and he is off at last*) I am sure you people must be aware of some of the incidents which have happened in various parts of the city when colored people have moved into certain areas—(*Beneatha exhales heavily and starts tossing a piece of fruit up and down in the air.*) Well—because we have what I think is going to be a unique type of organization in American community life—not only do we deplore that kind of thing—but we are trying to do something about it. (*Beneatha stops tossing and turns with a new and quizzical interest to the man.*) We feel—(*gaining confidence in his mission because of the interest in the faces of the people he is talking to*)—we feel that most of the trouble in this world, when you come right down to it—(*he hits his knee for emphasis*)—most of the trouble exists because people just don't sit down and talk to each other.

RUTH (*nodding as she might in church, pleased with the remark*): You can say that again, mister.

LINDNER (*more encouraged by such affrmation*): That we don't try hard enough in this world to understand the other fellow's problem. The other guy's point of view.

RUTH: Now that's right.

(*Beneatha and Walter merely watch and listen with genuine interest.*)

LINDNER: Yes—that's the way we feel out in Clybourne Park. And that's why I was elected to come here this afternoon and talk to you people. Friendly like, you know, the way people should talk to each other and see if we couldn't find some way to work this thing out. As I say, the whole business is a matter of *caring* about the other fellow. Anybody can see that you are a nice family of folks, hard-working and honest I'm sure. (*Beneatha frowns slightly, quizzically, her head tilted regarding him.*) Today everybody knows what it means to be on the outside of *something.* And of course, there is always somebody who is out to take advantage of people who don't always understand.

WALTER: What do you mean?

LINDNER: Well—you see our community is made up of people who've worked hard as the dickens for years to build up that little community. They're not rich and fancy people; just hard-working, honest people who don't really have much but those little homes and a dream of the kind of community they want to raise their children in. Now, I don't say we are perfect and there is a lot wrong in some of the things they want. But you've got to admit that a man, right or wrong, has the right to want to have the neighborhood he lives in a certain kind of way. And at the moment the overwhelming majority of our people out there feel that people get along better, take more of a common interest in the life of the community, when they share a common background. I want you to believe me when I tell you that race prejudice simply doesn't enter into it. It is a matter of the people of Clybourne Park believing, rightly or wrongly, as I say, that for the happiness of all concerned that our Negro families are happier when they live in their *own* communities.

BENEATHA (*with a grand and bitter gesture*): This, friends, is the Welcoming Committee!

WALTER (*dumfounded, looking at Lindner*): Is this what you came marching all the way over here to tell us?

LINDNER: Well, now we've been having a fine conversation. I hope you'll hear me all the way through.

WALTER (*tightly*): Go ahead, man.

LINDNER: You see—in the face of all the things I have said, we are prepared to make your family a very generous offer . . .

BENEATHA: Thirty pieces and not a coin less!

WALTER: Yeah!

LINDNER (*putting on his glasses and drawing a form out of the briefcase*): Our association is prepared, through the collective effort of our people, to buy the house from you at a financial gain to your family.

RUTH: Lord have mercy, ain't this the living gall!

WALTER: All right, you through?

LINDNER: Well, I want to give you the exact terms of the financial arrangement—

WALTER: We don't want to hear no exact terms of no arrangements. I want to know if you got any more to tell us 'bout getting together?

LINDNER (*taking off his glasses*): Well—I don't suppose that you feel . . .

WALTER: Never mind how I feel—you got any more to say 'bout how people ought to sit down and talk to each other? . . . Get out of my house, man.

(*He turns his back and walks to the door.*)

LINDNER (*looking around at the hostile faces and reaching and assembling his hat and briefcase*): Well—I don't understand why you people are reacting this way. What do you think you are going to gain by moving into a neighborhood where you just aren't wanted and where some elements—well—people can get awful worked up when they feel that their whole way of life and everything they've ever worked for is threatened.

WALTER: Get out.

LINDNER (*at the door, holding a small card*): Well—I'm sorry it went like this.

WALTER: Get out.

LINDNER (*almost sadly regarding Walter*): You just can't force people to change their hearts, son.

(*He turns and puts his card on a table and exits. Walter pushes the door to with stinging hatred, and stands looking at it. Ruth just sits and Beneatha just stands. They say nothing. Mama and Travis enter.*)

MAMA: Well—this all the packing got done since I left out of here this morning. I testify before God that my children got all the energy of the *dead!* What time the moving men due?

BENEATHA: Four o'clock. You had a caller, Mama.

(*She is smiling, teasingly.*)

MAMA: Sure enough—who?

BENEATHA (*her arms folded saucily*): The Welcoming Committee.

(*Walter and Ruth giggle.*)

MAMA (*innocently*): Who?

BENEATHA: The Welcoming Committee. They said they're sure going to be glad to see you when you get there.

WALTER (*devilishly*): Yeah, they said they can't hardly wait to see your face.

(*Laughter.*)

MAMA (*sensing their facetiousness*): What's the matter with you all?

WALTER: Ain't nothing the matter with us. We just telling you 'bout the gentleman who came to see you this afternoon. From the Clybourne Park Improvement Association.

MAMA: What he want?

RUTH (*in the same mood as Beneatha and Walter*): To welcome you, honey.

WALTER: He said they can't hardly wait. He said the one thing they don't have, that they just *dying* to have out there is a fine family of fine colored people! (*To Ruth and Beneatha.*) Ain't that right!

RUTH (*mockingly*): Yeah! He left his card—

BENEATHA (*handing card to Mama*): In case.

(*Mama reads and throws it on the floor—understanding and looking off as she draws her chair up to the table on which she has put her plant and some sticks and some cord.*)

MAMA: Father, give us strength. (*Knowingly—and without fun.*) Did he threaten us?

BENEATHA: Oh—Mama—they don't do it like that anymore. He talked Brotherhood. He said everybody ought to learn how to sit down and hate each other with good Christian fellowship.

(*She and Walter shake hands to ridicule the remark.*)

MAMA (*sadly*): Lord, protect us . . .

RUTH: You should hear the money those folks raised to buy the house from us. All we paid and then some.

BENEATHA: What they think we going to do—eat 'em?

RUTH: No, honey, marry 'em.

MAMA (*shaking her head*): Lord, Lord, Lord . . .

RUTH: Well—that's the way the crackers crumble. (*A beat.*) Joke.

BENEATHA (*laughingly noticing what her mother is doing*): Mama, what are you doing?

MAMA: Fixing my plant so it won't get hurt none on the way . . .

BENEATHA: Mama, you going to take *that* to the new house?

MAMA: Un-huh—

BENEATHA: That raggedy-looking old thing?

MAMA (*stopping and looking at her*): It expresses ME!

RUTH (*with delight, to Beneatha*): So there, Miss Thing!

(*Walter comes to Mama suddenly and bends down behind her and squeezes her in his arms with all his strength. She is overwhelmed by the suddenness of it and, though delighted, her manner is like that of Ruth and Travis.*)

MAMA: Look out now, boy! You make me mess up my thing here!

WALTER (*his face lit, he slips down on his knees beside her, his arms still about her*): Mama . . . you know what it means to climb up in the chariot?

MAMA (*gruffly, very happy*): Get on away from me now . . .

RUTH (*near the gift-wrapped package, trying to catch Walter's eye*): Psst—

WALTER: What the old song say, Mama . . .

RUTH: Walter—Now?

(*She is pointing at the package.*)

WALTER (*speaking the lines, sweetly, playfully, in his mother's face*): I got wings . . . you got wings . . . All God's Children got wings . . .

MAMA: Boy—get out of my face and do some work . . .

WALTER: When I get to heaven gonna put on my wings, Gonna fly all over God's heaven . . .

BENEATHA (*teasingly, from across the room*): Everybody talking 'bout heaven ain't going there!

WALTER (*to Ruth, who is carrying the box across to them*): I don't know, you think we ought to give her that . . . Seems to me she ain't been very appreciative around here.

MAMA (*eyeing the box, which is obviously a gift*): What is that?

WALTER (*taking it from Ruth and putting it on the table in front of Mama*): Well—what you all think? Should we give it to her?

RUTH: Oh—she was pretty good today.

MAMA: I'll good you—

(*She turns her eyes to the box again.*)

BENEATHA: Open it, Mama.

(*She stands up, looks at it, turns, and looks at all of them, and then presses her hands together and does not open the package.*)

WALTER (*sweetly*): Open it, Mama. It's for you. (*Mama looks in his eyes. It is the first present in her life without its being Christmas. Slowly she opens her package and lifts out, one by one, a brand-new sparkling set of gardening tools. Walter continues, prodding.*) Ruth made up the note—read it . . .

MAMA (*picking up the card and adjusting her glasses*): "To our own Mrs. Miniver—Love from Brother, Ruth and Beneatha." Ain't that lovely . . .

TRAVIS (*tugging at his father's sleeve*): Daddy, can I give her mine now?

WALTER: All right, son. (*Travis flies to get his gift.*)

MAMA: Now I don't have to use my knives and forks no more . . .

WALTER: Travis didn't want to go in with the rest of us, Mama. He got his own. (*Somewhat amused.*) We don't know what it is . . .

TRAVIS (*racing back in the room with a large hatbox and putting it in front of his grandmother*): Here!

MAMA: Lord have mercy, baby. You done gone and bought your grandmother a hat?

TRAVIS (*very proud*): Open it!

(*She does and lifts out an elaborate, but very elaborate, wide gardening hat, and all the adults break up at the sight of it.*)

RUTH: Travis, honey, what is that?

TRAVIS (*who thinks it is beautiful and appropriate*): It's a gardening hat! Like the ladies always have on in the magazines when they work in their gardens.

BENEATHA (*giggling fiercely*): Travis—we were trying to make Mama Mrs. Miniver—not Scarlett O'Hara!

MAMA (*indignantly*): What's the matter with you all! This here is a beautiful hat! (*Absurdly.*) I always wanted me one just like it!

(*She pops it on her head to prove it to her grandson, and the hat is ludicrous and considerably oversized.*)

RUTH: Hot dog! Go, Mama!

WALTER (*doubled over with laughter*): I'm sorry, Mama—but you look like you ready to go out and chop you some cotton sure enough!

(*They all laugh except Mama, out of deference to Travis's feelings.*)

MAMA (*gathering the boy up to her*): Bless your heart—this is the prettiest hat I ever owned—(*Walter, Ruth, and Beneatha chime in—noisily, festively, and insincerely congratulating Travis on his gift.*) What are we all standing around here for? We ain't finished packin' yet. Bennie, you ain't packed one book.

(*The bell rings.*)

BENEATHA: That couldn't be the movers . . . it's not hardly two good yet—

(*Beneatha goes into her room. Mama starts for door.*)

WALTER (*turning, stiffening*): Wait—wait—I'll get it.

(*He stands and looks at the door.*)

MAMA: You expecting company, son?

WALTER (*just looking at the door*): Yeah—yeah . . .

(*Mama looks at Ruth, and they exchange innocent and unfrightened glances.*)

MAMA (*not understanding*): Well, let them in, son.

BENEATHA (*from her room*): We need some more string.

MAMA: Travis—you run to the hardware and get me some string cord.

(*Mama goes out and Walter turns and looks at Ruth. Travis goes to a dish for money.*)

RUTH: Why don't you answer the door, man?

WALTER (*suddenly bounding across the floor to embrace her*): 'Cause sometimes it hard to let the future begin! (*Stooping down in her face.*) I got wings! You got wings! All God's children got wings!

(*He crosses to the door and throws it open. Standing there is a very slight little man in a not too prosperous business suit and with haunted frightened eyes and a hat pulled down tightly, brim up, around his forehead. Travis passes between the men and exits. Walter leans deep in the man's face, still in his jubilance.*) When I get to heaven gonna put on my wings, Gonna fly all over

God's heaven . . . (*The little man just stares at him.*) Heaven—(*Suddenly he stops and looks past the little man into the empty hallway.*) Where's Willy, man?

BOBO: He ain't with me.

WALTER (*not disturbed*): Oh—come on in. You know my wife.

BOBO (*dumbly, taking off his hat*): Yes—h'you, Miss Ruth.

RUTH (*quietly, a mood apart from her husband already, seeing Bobo*): Hello, Bobo.

WALTER: You right on time today . . . Right on time. That's the way! (*He slaps Bobo on his back.*) Sit down . . . lemme hear.

(*Ruth stands stiffly and quietly in back of them, as though somehow she senses death, her eyes fixed on her husband.*)

BOBO (*his frightened eyes on the floor, his hat in his hands*): Could I please get a drink of water, before I tell you about it, Walter Lee?

(*Walter does not take his eyes off the man. Ruth goes blindly to the tap and gets a glass of water and brings it to Bobo.*)

WALTER: There ain't nothing wrong, is there?

BOBO: Lemme tell you—

WALTER: Man—didn't nothing go wrong?

BOBO: Lemme tell you—Walter Lee. (*Looking at Ruth and talking to her more than to Walter.*) You know how it was. I got to tell you how it was. I mean first I got to tell you how it was all the way . . . I mean about the money I put in, Walter Lee . . .

WALTER (*with taut agitation now*): What about the money you put in?

BOBO: Well—it wasn't much as we told you—me and Willy—(*He stops.*) I'm sorry, Walter. I got a bad feeling about it. I got a real bad feeling about it . . .

WALTER: Man, what you telling me about all this for? . . . Tell me what happened in Springfield . . .

BOBO: Springfield.

RUTH (*like a dead woman*): What was supposed to happen in Springfield?

BOBO (*to her*): This deal that me and Walter went into with Willy—Me and Willy was going to go down to Springfield and spread some money 'round so's we wouldn't have to wait so long for the liquor license . . . That's what we were going to do. Everybody said that was the way you had to do, you understand, Miss Ruth?

WALTER: Man—what happened down there?

BOBO (*a pitiful man, near tears*): I'm trying to tell you, Walter.

WALTER (*screaming at him suddenly*): THEN TELL ME, GODDAMMIT . . . WHAT'S THE MATTER WITH YOU?

BOBO: Man . . . I didn't go to no Springfield, yesterday.

WALTER (*halted, life hanging in the moment*): Why not?

BOBO (*the long way, the hard way to tell*): 'Cause I didn't have no reasons to . . .

WALTER: Man, what are you talking about!

BOBO: I'm talking about the fact that when I got to the train station yesterday morning—eight o'clock like we planned . . . Man—*Willy didn't never show up.*

WALTER: Why . . . where was he . . . where is he?

BOBO: That's what I'm trying to tell you . . . I don't know . . . I waited six hours . . . I called his house . . . and I waited . . . six hours . . . I waited in that train station six hours . . . (*Breaking into tears.*) That was all the extra money I had in the world . . . (*Looking up at Walter with the tears running down his face.*) Man, *Willy is gone.*

WALTER: Gone, what you mean Willy is gone? Gone where? You mean he went by himself. You mean he went off to Springfield by himself—to take care of getting the license—(*Turns and looks anxiously at Ruth.*) You mean maybe he didn't want too many people in on the business down there? (*Looks to Ruth again, as before.*) You know Willy got his own ways. (*Looks back to Bobo.*) Maybe you was late yesterday and he just went on down there without you. Maybe—maybe—he's been callin' you at home tryin' to tell you what happened or something. Maybe—maybe—he just got sick. He's somewhere—he's got to be somewhere. We just got to find him—me and you got to find him. (*Grabs Bobo senselessly by the collar and starts to shake him.*) We got to!

BOBO (*in sudden angry, frightened agony*): What's the matter with you, Walter! *When a cat take off with your money he don't leave you no road maps!*

WALTER (*turning madly, as though he is looking for Willy in the very room*): Willy! . . . Willy . . . don't do it . . . Please don't do it . . . Man, not with that money . . . Man, please, not with that money . . . Oh, God . . . Don't let it be true . . . (*He is wandering around, crying out for Willy and looking for him or perhaps for help from God.*) Man . . . I trusted you . . . Man, I put my life in your hands . . . (*He starts to crumple down on the floor as Ruth just covers her face in horror. Mama opens the door and comes into the room, with Beneatha behind her.*) Man . . . (*He starts to pound the floor with his fists, sobbing wildly.*) THAT MONEY IS MADE OUT MY FATHER'S FLESH——

BOBO (*standing over him helplessly*): I'm sorry, Walter . . . (*Only Walter's sobs reply. Bobo puts on his hat.*) I had my life staked on this deal, too . . .

(*He exits.*)

MAMA (*to Walter*): Son—(*She goes to him, bends down to him, talks to his bent head.*) Son . . . Is it gone? Son, I gave you sixty-five hundred dollars. Is it gone? All of it? Beneatha's money too?

WALTER (*lifting his head slowly*): Mama . . . I never . . . went to the bank at all . . .

MAMA (*not wanting to believe him*): You mean . . . your sister's school money . . . you used that too . . . Walter? . . .

WALTER: Yessss! All of it . . . It's all gone . . .

(*There is total silence. Ruth stands with her face covered with her hands; Beneatha leans forlornly against a wall, fingering a piece of red ribbon from the mother's gift. Mama stops and looks at her son without recognition and then, quite without thinking about it, starts to beat him senselessly in the face. Beneatha goes to them and stops it.*)

BENEATHA: Mama!

(*Mama stops and looks at both of her children and rises slowly and wanders vaguely, aimlessly away from them.*)

MAMA: I seen . . . him . . . night after night . . . come in . . . and look at that rug . . . and then look at me . . . the red showing in his eyes . . . the veins moving in his head . . . I seen him grow thin and old before he was forty . . . working and working and working like somebody's old horse . . . killing himself . . . and you—you give it all away in a day— (*She raises her arms to strike him again.*)

BENEATHA: Mama—

MAMA: Oh, God . . . (*She looks up to Him.*) Look down here—and show me the strength.

BENEATHA: Mama—

MAMA (*folding over*): Strength . . .

BENEATHA (*plaintively*): Mama . . .

MAMA: Strength!

ACT III

(*An hour later.*)

(*At curtain, there is a sullen light of gloom in the living room, gray light not unlike that which began the first scene of act I. At left we can see Walter within his room, alone with himself. He is stretched out on the bed, his shirt out and open, his arms under his head. He does not smoke, he does not cry out, he merely lies there, looking up at the ceiling, much as if he were alone in the world.*)

(*In the living room Beneatha sits at the table, still surrounded by the now almost ominous packing crates. She sits looking off. We feel that this is a mood struck perhaps an hour before, and it lingers now, full of the empty sound of profound disappointment. We see on a line from her brother's bedroom the sameness of their attitudes. Presently the bell rings and Beneatha rises without ambition or interest in answering. It is Asagai, smiling broadly, striding into the room with energy and happy expectation and conversation.*)

ASAGAI: I came over . . . I had some free time. I thought I might help with the packing. Ah, I like the look of packing crates! A household in preparation for a journey! It depresses some people . . . but for me . . . it is another feeling. Something full of the flow of life, do you understand? Movement, progress . . . It makes me think of Africa.

BENEATHA: Africa!

ASAGAI: What kind of a mood is this? Have I told you how deeply you move me?

BENEATHA: He gave away the money, Asagai . . .

ASAGAI: Who gave away what money?

BENEATHA: The insurance money. My brother gave it away.

ASAGAI: Gave it away?

BENEATHA: He made an investment! With a man even Travis wouldn't have trusted with his most worn-out marbles.

ASAGAI: And it's gone?

BENEATHA: Gone!

ASAGAI: I'm very sorry . . . And you, now?

BENEATHA: Me? . . . Me? . . . Me, I'm nothing . . . Me. When I was very small . . . we used to take our sleds out in the wintertime and the only hills we had were the ice-covered stone steps of some houses down the street. And we used to fill them in with snow and make them smooth and slide down them all day . . . and it was very dangerous, you know . . . far too steep . . . and sure enough one day a kid named Rufus came down too fast and hit the sidewalk and we saw his face just split open right there in front of us . . . And I remember standing there looking at his bloody open face thinking that was the end of Rufus. But the ambulance came and they took him to the hospital and they fixed the broken bones and they sewed it all up . . . and the next time I saw Rufus he just had a little line down the middle of his face . . . I never got over that . . .

ASAGAI: What?

BENEATHA: That that was what one person could do for another, fix him up—sew up the problem, make him all right again. That was the most marvelous thing in the world . . . I wanted to do that. I always thought it was the one concrete thing in the world that a human being could do. Fix up the sick, you know—and make them whole again. This was truly being God . . .

ASAGAI: You wanted to be God?

BENEATHA: No—I wanted to cure. It used to be so important to me. I wanted to cure. It used to matter. I used to care. I mean about people and how their bodies hurt . . .

ASAGAI: And you've stopped caring?

BENEATHA: Yes—I think so.

ASAGAI: Why?

BENEATHA (*bitterly*): Because it doesn't seem deep enough, close enough to what ails mankind! It was a child's way of seeing things—or an idealist's.

ASAGAI: Children see things very well sometimes—and idealists even better.

BENEATHA: I know that's what you think. Because you are still where I left off. You with all your talk and dreams about Africa! You still think you can patch up the world. Cure the Great Sore of Colonialism— (*loftily, mocking it*) with the Penicillin of Independence—!

ASAGAI: Yes!

BENEATHA: Independence *and then what?* What about all the crooks and thieves and just plain idiots who will come into power and steal and plunder the same as before—only now they will be black and do it in the name of the new Independence—WHAT ABOUT THEM?!

ASAGAI: That will be the problem for another time. First we must get there.

BENEATHA: And where does it end?

ASAGAI: End? Who even spoke of an end? To life? To living?

BENEATHA: An end to misery! To stupidity! Don't you see there isn't any real progress, Asagai, there is only one large circle that we march in, around and around, each of us with our own little picture in front of us—our own little mirage that we think is the future.

ASAGAI: That is the mistake.

BENEATHA: What?

ASAGAI: What you just said—about the circle. It isn't a circle—it is simply a long line—as in geometry, you know, one that reaches into infinity. And because we cannot see the end—we also cannot see how it changes. And it is very odd but those who see the changes—who dream, who will not give up—are called idealists . . . and those who see only the circle—we call *them* the "realists"!

BENEATHA: Asagai, while I was sleeping in that bed in there, people went out and took the future right out of my hands! And nobody asked me, nobody consulted me—they just went out and changed my life!

ASAGAI: Was it your money?

BENEATHA: What?

ASAGAI: Was it your money he gave away?

BENEATHA: It belonged to all of us.

ASAGAI: But did you earn it? Would you have had it at all if your father had not died?

BENEATHA: No.

ASAGAI: Then isn't there something wrong in a house—in a world—where all dreams, good or bad, must depend on the death of a man? I never thought to see *you* like this, Alaiyo. You! Your brother made a mistake and you are grateful to him so that now you can give up the ailing human race on account of it! You talk about what good is struggle, what good is anything! Where are we all going and why are we bothering!

BENEATHA: AND YOU CANNOT ANSWER IT!

ASAGAI (*shouting over her*): I LIVE THE ANSWER! (*Pause.*) In my village at home it is the exceptional man who can even read a newspaper . . . or who ever sees a book at all. I will go home and much of what I will have to say will seem strange to the people of my village. But I will teach and work and things will happen, slowly and swiftly. At times it will seem that nothing changes at all . . . and then again the sudden dramatic events which make history leap into the future. And then quiet again. Retrogression even. Guns, murder, revolution. And I even will have

moments when I wonder if the quiet was not better than all that death and hatred. But I will look about my village at the illiteracy and disease and ignorance and I will not wonder long. And perhaps . . . perhaps I will be a great man . . . I mean perhaps I will hold on to the substance of truth and find my way always with the right course . . . and perhaps for it I will be butchered in my bed some night by the servants of empire . . .

BENEATHA: *The martyr!*

ASAGAI (*he smiles*): . . . or perhaps I shall live to be a very old man, respected and esteemed in my new nation . . . And perhaps I shall hold office and this is what I'm trying to tell you, Alaiyo: Perhaps the things I believe now for my country will be wrong and outmoded, and I will not understand and do terrible things to have things my way or merely to keep my power. Don't you see that there will be young men and women—not British soldiers then, but my own black countrymen—to step out of the shadows some evening and slit my then useless throat? Don't you see they have always been there . . . that they always will be. And that such a thing as my own death will be an advance? They who might kill me even . . . actually replenish all that I was.

BENEATHA: Oh, Asagai, I know all that.

ASAGAI: Good! Then stop moaning and groaning and tell me what you plan to do.

BENEATHA: Do?

ASAGAI: I have a bit of a suggestion.

BENEATHA: What?

ASAGAI (*rather quietly for him*): That when it is all over—that you come home with me—

BENEATHA (*staring at him and crossing away with exasperation*): Oh—Asagai—at this moment you decide to be romantic!

ASAGAI (*quickly understanding the misunderstanding*): My dear, young creature of the New World—I do not mean across the city—I mean across the ocean: home—to Africa.

BENEATHA (*slowly understanding and turning to him with murmured amazement*): To Africa?

ASAGAI: Yes! . . . (*Smiling and lifting his arms playfully.*) Three hundred years later the African Prince rose up out of the seas and swept the maiden back across the middle passage over which her ancestors had come—

BENEATHA (*unable to play*): To—to Nigeria?

ASAGAI: Nigeria. Home. (*Coming to her with genuine romantic flippancy.*) I will show you our mountains and our stars; and give you cool drinks from gourds and teach you the old songs and the ways of our people—and, in time, we will pretend that—(*very softly*)—you have only been away for a day. Say that you'll come—(*He swings her around and takes her full in his arms in a kiss which proceeds to passion.*)

BENEATHA (*pulling away suddenly*): You're getting me all mixed up—

ASAGAI: Why?

BENEATHA: Too many things—too many things have happened today. I must sit down and think. I don't know what I feel about anything right this minute.

(*She promptly sits down and props her chin on her fist.*)

ASAGAI (*charmed*): All right, I shall leave you. No—don't get up. (*Touching her, gently, sweetly.*) Just sit awhile and think . . . Never be afraid to sit awhile and think. (*He goes to door and looks at her.*) How often I have looked at you and said, "Ah—so this is what the New World hath finally wrought . . ."

(*He exits. Beneatha sits on alone. Presently Walter enters from his room and starts to rummage through things, feverishly looking for something. She looks up and turns in her seat.*)

BENEATHA (*hissingly*): Yes—just look at what the New World hath wrought! . . . Just look! (*She gestures with bitter disgust.*) There he is! *Monsieur le petit bourgeois noir*°—himself! There he is—Symbol of a Rising Class! Entrepreneur! Titan° of the system! (*Walter ignores her completely and continues frantically and destructively looking for something and hurling things to floor and tearing things out of their place in his search. Beneatha ignores the eccentricity of his actions and goes on with the monologue of insult.*) Did you dream of yachts on Lake Michigan, Brother? Did you see yourself on that Great Day sitting down at the Conference Table, surrounded by all the mighty bald-headed men in America? All halted, waiting, breathless, waiting for your pronouncements on industry? Waiting for you—Chairman of the Board! (*Walter finds what he is looking for—a small piece of white paper—and pushes it in his pocket and puts on his coat and rushes out without ever having looked at her. She shouts after him.*) I look at you and I see the final triumph of stupidity in the world!

(*The door slams and she returns to just sitting again. Ruth comes quickly out of Mama's room.*)

RUTH: Who was that?
BENEATHA: Your husband.
RUTH: Where did he go?
BENEATHA: Who knows—maybe he has an appointment at U.S. Steel.
RUTH (*anxiously, with frightened eyes*): You didn't say nothing bad to him, did you?
BENEATHA: Bad? Say anything bad to him? No—I told him he was a sweet boy and full of dreams and everything is strictly peachy keen, as the ofay° kids say!

(*Mama enters from her bedroom. She is lost, vague, trying to catch hold, to make some sense of her former command of the world, but it still eludes her. A sense of*

_____
Monsieur . . . noir: Mr. Black Lower Middle Class.   **Titan:** Person of great power; originally, a god.   **ofay:** White person, usually used disparagingly.

waste overwhelms her gait; a measure of apology rides on her shoulders. She goes to her plant, which has remained on the table, looks at it, picks it up and takes it to the window sill and sits it outside, and she stands and looks at it a long moment. Then she closes the window, straightens her body with effort, and turns around to her children.*)

MAMA: Well—ain't it a mess in here, though? (*A false cheerfulness, a beginning of something.*) I guess we all better stop moping around and get some work done. All this unpacking and everything we got to do. (*Ruth raises her head slowly in response to the sense of the line; and Beneatha in similar manner turns very slowly to look at her mother.*) One of you all better call the moving people and tell 'em not to come.
RUTH: Tell 'em not to come?
MAMA: Of course, baby. Ain't no need in 'em coming all the way here and having to go back. They charges for that too. (*She sits down, fingers to her brow, thinking.*) Lord, ever since I was a little girl, I always remembers people saying, "Lena—Lena Eggleston, you aims too high all the time. You needs to slow down and see life a little more like it is. Just slow down some." That's what they always used to say down home—"Lord, that Lena Eggleston is a high-minded thing. She'll get her due one day!"
RUTH: No, Lena . . .
MAMA: Me and Big Walter just didn't never learn right.
RUTH: Lena, no! We gotta go. Bennie—tell her . . . (*She rises and crosses to Beneatha with her arms outstretched. Beneatha doesn't respond.*) Tell her we can still move . . . the notes ain't but a hundred and twenty-five a month. We got four grown people in this house—we can work . . .
MAMA (*to herself*): Just aimed too high all the time—
RUTH (*turning and going to Mama fast—the words pouring out with urgency and desperation*): Lena—I'll work . . . I'll work twenty hours a day in all the kitchens in Chicago . . . I'll strap my baby on my back if I have to and scrub all the floors in America and wash all the sheets in America if I have to—but we got to MOVE! We got to get OUT OF HERE!!

(*Mama reaches out absently and pats Ruth's hand.*)

MAMA: No—I sees things differently now. Been thinking 'bout some of the things we could do to fix this place up some. I seen a second-hand bureau over on Maxwell Street just the other day that could fit right there. (*She points to where the new furniture might go. Ruth wanders away from her.*) Would need some new handles on it and then a little varnish and it look like something brand-new. And—we can put up them new curtains in the kitchen . . . Why this place be looking fine. Cheer us all up so that we forget trouble ever come . . . (*To Ruth.*) And you could get some nice screens to put up in your room round the baby's bassinet . . . (*She looks at both of them, pleadingly.*)

Sometimes you just got to know when to give up some things . . . and hold on to what you got. . . .

(*Walter enters from the outside, looking spent and leaning against the door, his coat hanging from him.*)

MAMA: Where you been, son?

WALTER (*breathing hard*): Made a call.

MAMA: To who, son?

WALTER: To The Man. (*He heads for his room.*)

MAMA: What man, baby?

WALTER (*stops in the door*): The Man, Mama. Don't you know who The Man is?

RUTH: Walter Lee?

WALTER: *The Man.* Like the guys in the streets say — The Man. Captain Boss — Mistuh Charley . . . Old Cap'n Please Mr. Bossman . . .

BENEATHA (*suddenly*): Lindner!

WALTER: That's right! That's good. I told him to come right over.

BENEATHA (*fiercely, understanding*): For what? What do you want to see him for!

WALTER (*looking at his sister*): We going to do business with him.

MAMA: What you talking 'bout, son?

WALTER: Talking 'bout life, Mama. You all always telling me to see life like it is. Well — I laid in there on my back today . . . and I figured it out. Life just like it is. Who gets and who don't get. (*He sits down with his coat on and laughs.*) Mama, you know it's all divided up. Life is. Sure enough. Between the takers and the "tooken." (*He laughs.*) I've figured it out finally. (*He looks around at them.*) Yeah. Some of us always getting "tooken." (*He laughs.*) People like Willy Harris, they don't never get "tooken." And you know why the rest of us do? 'Cause we all mixed up. Mixed up bad. We get to looking 'round for the right and the wrong; and we worry about it and cry about it and stay up nights trying to figure out 'bout the wrong and the right of things all the time . . . And all the time, man, them takers is out there operating, just taking and taking. Willy Harris? Shoot — Willy Harris don't even count. He don't even count in the big scheme of things. But I'll say one thing for old Willy Harris . . . he's taught me something. He's taught me to keep my eye on what counts in this world. Yeah — (*Shouting out a little.*) Thanks, Willy!

RUTH: What did you call that man for, Walter Lee?

WALTER: Called him to tell him to come on over to the show. Gonna put on a show for the man. Just what he wants to see. You see, Mama, the man came here today and he told us that them people out there where you want us to move — well they so upset they willing to pay us *not* to move! (*He laughs again.*) And — and oh, Mama — you would of been proud of the way me and Ruth and Bennie acted. We told him to get out . . . Lord have mercy! We told the man to get out! Oh, we was some proud folks this afternoon, yeah. (*He lights a cigarette.*) We were still full of that old-time stuff . . .

RUTH (*coming toward him slowly*): You talking 'bout taking them people's money to keep us from moving in that house?

WALTER: I ain't just talking 'bout it, baby — I'm telling you that's what's going to happen!

BENEATHA: Oh, God! Where is the bottom! Where is the real honest-to-God bottom so he can't go any farther!

WALTER: See — that's the old stuff. You and that boy that was here today. You all want everybody to carry a flag and a spear and sing some marching songs, huh? You wanna spend your life looking into things and trying to find the right and the wrong part, huh? Yeah. You know what's going to happen to that boy someday — he'll find himself sitting in a dungeon, locked in forever — and the takers will have the key! Forget it, baby! There ain't no causes — there ain't nothing but taking in this world, and he who takes most is smartest — and it don't make a damn bit of difference *how.*

MAMA: You making something inside me cry, son. Some awful pain inside me.

WALTER: Don't cry, Mama. Understand. That white man is going to walk in that door able to write checks for more money than we ever had. It's important to him and I'm going to help him . . . I'm going to put on the show, Mama.

MAMA: Son — I come from five generations of people who was slaves and sharecroppers — but ain't nobody in my family never let nobody pay 'em no money that was a way of telling us we wasn't fit to walk the earth. We ain't never been that poor. (*Raising her eyes and looking at him.*) We ain't never been that — dead inside.

BENEATHA: Well — we are dead now. All the talk about dreams and sunlight that goes on in this house. It's all dead now.

WALTER: What's the matter with you all! I didn't make this world! It was give to me this way! Hell, yes, I want me some yachts someday! Yes, I want to hang some real pearls 'round my wife's neck. Ain't she supposed to wear no pearls? Somebody tell me — tell me, who decides which women is suppose to wear pearls in this world. I tell you I am a *man* — and I think my wife should wear some pearls in this world!

(*This last line hangs a good while and Walter begins to move about the room. The word "Man" has penetrated his consciousness; he mumbles it to himself repeatedly between strange agitated pauses as he moves about.*)

MAMA: Baby, how you going to feel on the inside?

WALTER: Fine! . . . Going to feel fine . . . a man . . .

MAMA: You won't have nothing left then, Walter Lee.

WALTER (*coming to her*): I'm going to feel fine, Mama. I'm going to look that son-of-a-bitch in the eyes and say — (*he falters*) — and say, "All right, Mr. Lindner — (*he falters even more*) — that's *your* neighborhood out there! You got the right to keep it like you want! You got the right to have it like you want! Just write the check and — the house is yours." And — and I am going to say—(*His voice almost breaks.*) "And you—you people just put the money in my hand and you won't have to live next to this bunch of stinking niggers! . . ." (*He straightens up and moves away from his mother, walking around the room.*) And maybe—maybe I'll just get down on my black knees . . . (*He does so; Ruth and Bennie and Mama watch him in frozen horror.*) "Captain, Mistuh, Bossman—(*Groveling and grinning and wringing his hands in profoundly anguished imitation of the slow-witted movie stereotype.*) A-hee-hee-hee! Oh, yassuh boss! Yassssssuh! Great white—(*voice breaking, he forces himself to go on*)—Father, just gi' ussen de money, fo' God's sake, and we's—we's ain't gwine come out deh and dirty up yo' white folks neighborhood . . ." (*He breaks down completely.*) And I'll feel fine! Fine! fine! (*He gets up and goes into the bedroom.*)

BENEATHA: That is not a man. That is nothing but a toothless rat.

MAMA: Yes—death done come in this here house. (*She is nodding, slowly, reflectively.*) Done come walking in my house on the lips of my children. You what supposed to be my beginning again. You—what supposed to be my harvest. (*To Beneatha.*) You—you mourning your brother?

BENEATHA: He's no brother of mine.

MAMA: What you say?

BENEATHA: I said that that individual in that room is no brother of mine.

MAMA: That's what I thought you said. You feeling like you better than he is today? (*Beneatha does not answer.*) Yes? What you tell him a minute ago? That he wasn't a man? Yes? You give him up for me? You done wrote his epitaph too—like the rest of the world? Well, who give you the privilege?

BENEATHA: Be on my side for once! You saw what he just did, Mama! You saw him—down on his knees. Wasn't it you who taught me to despise any man who would do that? Do what he's going to do?

MAMA: Yes—I taught you that. Me and your daddy. But I thought I taught you something else too . . . I thought I taught you to love him.

BENEATHA: Love him? There is nothing left to love.

MAMA: There is *always* something left to love. And if you ain't learned that, you ain't learned nothing. (*Looking at her.*) Have you cried for that boy today? I don't mean for yourself and for the family 'cause we lost the money. I mean for him: what he been through and what it done to him. Child, when do you think is the time to love somebody the most? When they done good and made things easy for everybody? Well then, you ain't through learning—because that ain't the time at all. It's when he's at his lowest and can't believe in hisself 'cause the world done whipped him so! When you starts measuring somebody, measure him right, child, measure him right. Make sure you done taken into account what hills and valleys he come through before he got to wherever he is.

(*Travis bursts into the room at the end of the speech, leaving the door open.*)

TRAVIS: Grandmama—the moving men are downstairs! The truck just pulled up.

MAMA (*turning and looking at him*): Are they, baby? They downstairs?

(*She sighs and sits. Lindner appears in the doorway. He peers in and knocks lightly, to gain attention, and comes in. All turn to look at him.*)

LINDNER (*hat and briefcase in hand*): Uh—hello . . .

(*Ruth crosses mechanically to the bedroom door and opens it and lets it swing open freely and slowly as the lights come up on Walter within, still in his coat, sitting at the far corner of the room. He looks up and out through the room to Lindner.*)

RUTH: He's here.

(*A long minute passes and Walter slowly gets up.*)

LINDNER (*coming to the table with efficiency, putting his briefcase on the table and starting to unfold papers and unscrew fountain pens*): Well, I certainly was glad to hear from you people. (*Walter has begun the trek out of the room, slowly and awkwardly, rather like a small boy, passing the back of his sleeve across his mouth from time to time.*) Life can really be so much simpler than people let it be most of the time. Well—with whom do I negotiate? You, Mrs. Younger, or your son here? (*Mama sits with her hands folded on her lap and her eyes closed as Walter advances. Travis goes closer to Lindner and looks at the papers curiously.*) Just some official papers, sonny.

RUTH: Travis, you go downstairs—

MAMA (*opening her eyes and looking into Walter's*): No. Travis, you stay right here. And you make him understand what you doing, Walter Lee. You teach him good. Like Willy Harris taught you. You show where our five generations done come to. (*Walter looks from her to the boy, who grins at him innocently.*) Go ahead, son—(*She folds her hands and closes her eyes.*) Go ahead.

WALTER (*at last crosses to Lindner, who is reviewing the contract*): Well, Mr. Lindner. (*Beneatha turns away.*) We called you—(*there is a profound, simple groping quality in his speech*)—because, well, me and my family (*he looks around and shifts from one foot to the other*) Well—we are very plain people . . .

LINDNER: Yes—

WALTER: I mean—I have worked as a chauffeur most of my life—and my wife here, she does domestic work in people's kitchens. So does my mother. I mean—we are plain people . . .

LINDNER: Yes, Mr. Younger—

WALTER (*really like a small boy, looking down at his shoes and then up at the man*): And—uh—well, my father, well, he was a laborer most of his life. . . .

LINDNER (*absolutely confused*): Uh, yes—yes, I under-stand. (*He turns back to the contract.*)

WALTER (*a beat; staring at him*): And my father—(*With sudden intensity.*) My father almost *beat a man to death* once because this man called him a bad name or something, you know what I mean?

LINDNER (*looking up, frozen*): No, no, I'm afraid I don't—

WALTER (*A beat. The tension hangs; then Walter steps back from it.*): Yeah. Well—what I mean is that we come from people who had a lot of *pride.* I mean—we are very proud people. And that's my sister over there and she's going to be a doctor—and we are very proud—

LINDNER: Well—I am sure that is very nice, but—

WALTER: What I am telling you is that we called you over here to tell you that we are very proud and that this—(*Signaling to Travis.*) Travis, come here. (*Travis crosses and Walter draws him before him facing the man.*) This is my son, and he makes the sixth generation of our family in this country. And we have all thought about your offer—

LINDNER: Well, good . . . good—

WALTER: And we have decided to move into our house because my father—my father—he earned it for us brick by brick. (*Mama has her eyes closed and is rocking back and forth as though she were in church, with her head nodding the Amen yes.*) We don't want to make no trouble for nobody or fight no causes, and we will try to be good neighbors. And that's *all* we got to say about that. (*He looks the man absolutely in the eyes.*) We don't want your money. (*He turns and walks away.*)

LINDNER (*looking around at all of them*): I take it then—that you have decided to occupy . . .

BENEATHA: That's what the man said.

LINDNER (*to Mama in her reverie*): Then I would like to appeal to you, Mrs. Younger. You are older and wiser and understand things better I am sure . . .

MAMA: I am afraid you don't understand. My son said we was going to move and there ain't nothing left for me to say. (*Briskly.*) You know how these young folks is nowadays, mister. Can't do a thing with 'em! (*As he opens his mouth, she rises.*) Goodbye.

LINDNER (*folding up his materials*): Well—if you are that final about it . . . there is nothing left for me to say. (*He finishes, almost ignored by the family, who are concentrating on Walter Lee. At the door Lindner halts and looks around.*) I sure hope you people know what you're getting into.

(*He shakes his head and exits.*)

RUTH (*looking around and coming to life*): Well, for God's sake—if the moving men are here—LET'S GET THE HELL OUT OF HERE!

MAMA (*into action*): Ain't it the truth! Look at all this here mess. Ruth, put Travis's good jacket on him . . . Walter Lee, fix your tie and tuck your shirt in, you look like somebody's hoodlum! Lord have mercy, where is my plant? (*She flies to get it amid the general bustling of the family, who are deliberately trying to ignore the nobility of the past moment.*) You all start on down . . . Travis child, don't go empty-handed . . . Ruth, where did I put that box with my skillets in it? I want to be in charge of it myself . . . I'm going to make us the biggest dinner we ever ate tonight . . . Beneatha, what's the matter with them stockings? Pull them things up, girl . . .

(*The family starts to file out as two moving men appear and begin to carry out the heavier pieces of furniture, bumping into the family as they move about.*)

BENEATHA: Mama, Asagai asked me to marry him today and go to Africa—

MAMA (*in the middle of her getting-ready activity*): He did? You ain't old enough to marry nobody—(*Seeing the moving men lifting one of her chairs precariously.*) Darling, that ain't no bale of cotton, please handle it so we can sit in it again! I had that chair twenty-five years . . .

(*The movers sigh with exasperation and go on with their work.*)

BENEATHA (*girlishly and unreasonably trying to pursue the conversation*): To go to Africa, Mama—be a doctor in Africa . . .

MAMA (*distracted*): Yes, baby—

WALTER: *Africa!* What he want you to go to Africa for?

BENEATHA: To practice there . . .

WALTER: Girl, if you don't get all them silly ideas out your head! You better marry yourself a man with some loot . . .

BENEATHA (*angrily, precisely as in the first scene of the play*): What have you got to do with who I marry!

WALTER: Plenty. Now I think George Murchison—

BENEATHA: *George Murchison!* I wouldn't marry him if he was Adam and I was Eve!

(*Walter and Beneatha go out yelling at each other vigorously and the anger is loud and real till their voices diminish. Ruth stands at the door and turns to Mama and smiles knowingly.*)

MAMA (*fixing her hat at last*): Yeah—they something all right, my children . . .

RUTH: Yeah—they're something. Let's go, Lena.

MAMA (*stalling, starting to look around at the house*): Yes—I'm coming. Ruth—

RUTH: Yes?

MAMA (*quietly, woman to woman*): He finally come into his manhood today, didn't he? Kind of like a rainbow after the rain . . .

RUTH (*biting her lip lest her own pride explode in front of Mama*): Yes, Lena.

(*Walter's voice calls for them raucously.*)

WALTER (*offstage*): Y'all come on! These people charges by the hour you know!

MAMA (*waving Ruth out vaguely*): All right, honey—
    go on down. I be down directly.

(*Ruth hesitates, then exits. Mama stands, at last alone in
the living room, her plant on the table before her as the
lights start to come down. She looks around at all the
walls and ceilings and suddenly, despite herself, while
the children call below, a great heaving thing rises in her
and she puts her fist to her mouth to stifle it, takes a final
desperate look, pulls her coat about her, pats her hat,
and goes out. The lights dim down. The door opens and
she comes back in, grabs her plant, and goes out for the
last time.*)

Wole Soyinka

Wole Soyinka (b. 1934) is one of Nigeria's several important writers who have
achieved international fame, winning the Nobel Prize for literature in 1986.
His work includes novels, poems, and plays, but he admits that "there is no
question at all that I think the Nobel Prize is for my drama."

Soyinka studied at University College, Ibadan, Nigeria, and began his literary career as an undergraduate, publishing poetry in the distinguished African
literary magazine *Black Orpheus*. His work, especially his drama, has been an
investigation of political, religious, and other forces in Nigerian culture. *The
Swamp Dwellers* (1958) is a powerful play condemning African superstition.
The Lion and the Jewel (1959) offers a comic view of Nigerian attitudes
toward European values left over from the colonial period. Among his other
plays are *The Trials of Brother Jero* (1960), about a corrupt evangelist, and
Kongi's Harvest (1964). *A Dance of the Forests* (1960) was written to celebrate
Nigerian independence, but it also alerted people to Nigeria's past violence and
warned against its return.

Nigeria went through a bitter civil war in 1967, and Soyinka's political sympathies led to a term in prison, where he was placed in solitary confinement.
He continued his writing, smuggling poems out of prison to give hope to his
political allies. He even criticized his own tribe, the Yoruba, for murdering
members of the Ibo during the war against Biafra.

Soyinka had studied at the University of Leeds after his schooling in Ibadan.
Most of his writing is in English, but he still writes some of his poetry in his
tribal language, Yoruba. He has recommended Swahili as the national language of Nigeria. Soyinka has spoken out against cultural parochialism,
including its manifestation in the negritude movement, which rejects Western
culture as a form of pollution. He expressed his philosophy to another great
African writer, Leopold Senghor: "A tiger is not forever shouting about his
tigritude"; a duiker antelope does not have to "prove his duikertude; you will
know him by his elegant leap."

Soyinka has been chair of the drama department at Ife University as well as
of his own University College, Ibadan. He has also lectured in Cambridge,
England, and in universities in North America. One of his works, *A Play of
Giants* (1984), is a scathing attack on abuse of power, indicting African tyrants
such as Idi Amin, Jean-Bedel Bokassa, and others.

For all of his criticism of Nigerian politics, Soyinka has rooted his work in
the religion and folklore of the Yoruba people. Ifa, the Yoruba religion,
depends on a complex cosmology that sees experience as layered in interactive
animal, mineral, and vegetable spheres. African critic Femi Osofisan has
described Yoruba cosmology as holding "coeval the three historical, actual,
and prospective planes of entity; . . . the animal and vegetable essences are cor-
respondent; . . . the acknowledged deities are both anthropomorphic and sym-
biotic, each fusing in his personality a series of antinomies." Osofisan also

notes "the comprehensive union of religious and secular intuition in the traditional Yoruba." Ifa plays a role in *The Strong Breed*, but the play is nonetheless understandable to those not familiar with the religion. Soyinka must be thought of as a traditional dramatist, writing in the tradition of his Yoruba people but reaching a worldwide audience.

THE STRONG BREED

The Strong Breed (1962), written at a time of political uncertainty in Nigeria, examines the interrelationship of ritual and community in African culture, describing one process by which a society renews itself. The "strong breed" are those men capable of the sacrifice needed annually to purify the community of its sins and to allow it to start over again. The community's sacrifice signals the beginning of a new year.

As the new year approaches, the elders of the community, Jaguna and Oroge, search for the appropriate "carrier" who can bear the burden of the community's guilt. The tradition in their community is to choose a stranger. Despite the elders' reluctance, Eman, one of the strong breed who has exiled himself from his own community, seems a logical choice until another outsider, the idiot Ifada, comes on the scene. Ifada seems heaven-sent to serve the community, but when he is chosen, he protests in terrified confusion. Eman explains to Jaguna and Oroge that no community should force a carrier to perform unwillingly. If he is unwilling, the guilt will not be carried away. Eman then offers himself as a willing sacrifice in Ifada's place.

The mythic pattern of sacrifice and renewal is basic to much Yoruba myth. Part of the tradition of Yoruba ritual drama is the reenactment of myths that resemble Eman's willing sacrifice. These are celebrated annually on the feast of Obatala, the god of creation. *The Strong Breed* has also been connected to ritual tragedies enacted in honor of Ogun, who suffers greatly for the good of the community.

The Strong Breed is informed by Soyinka's studies of Greek tragedy. Like Greek tragic figures, Soyinka's strong breed are genetically linked: they are fathers and sons who inherit their fathers' power. Soyinka's *The Bacchae of Euripides* (1973) deals with inspiration, intoxication, and mass hysteria. *Death and the King's Horseman* (1976), centering on death, also explores Greek themes of fate and inevitability. Soyinka demonstrates the universality of Greek themes in both European and African experience.

Certain patterns link Eman with Oedipus. Once Eman is identified by his father as one of the strong breed, he prepares himself for his mission by leaving his community. Like Oedipus, he unwittingly goes to another community where he ultimately must be sacrificed. Eman also resembles Christ: he is a teacher and healer; he refuses to exploit those around him; he lifts up the weak and has empathy for everyone, including the idiot Ifada. And, as in the case of Christ, those for whom he sacrifices himself do not hold him in high regard.

Despite its Greek and Christian overtones, the story is grounded in Yoruba tradition, with its initiation rites and concepts of heredity, community, and sacrifice. Soyinka's stagecraft includes traditional Yoruba music and dance as well as traditional Yoruba images, such as the effigy—the carrier doll—and the appearance of the human carrier in the form of Ifada. Soyinka demonstrates that everything in the past is part of the present by overlaying the ghosts of Omae, the woman Eman was to marry; his father (the Old Man); his tutor; and the priest. The past shapes the present just as his father's blood runs in his veins and shapes everything he does as a man.

The play leaves us wondering if Eman's sacrifice was wasteful or redeeming. Is the community led by Jaguna and Oroge worth dying for? Will Eman's death benefit Sunma, Ifada, and the Girl who betrayed him to his killers? Or does Eman die only because he is one of the strong breed, whose mission is to serve as the sacrifice for the community? Even the latter interpretation might imply a positive ending for the play, although it would be a different ending than suggesting that Eman has died *for* this village and thus has secured its renewal. Yoruba tradition implies that even if the community is unworthy, it shares in purification by the sacrifice of the willing. The subtlety of the issues in this play invites multiple interpretations.

The Strong Breed in Performance

In Ibadan in 1963, Soyinka created a twenty-five-minute version of *The Strong Breed* that omitted the flashbacks at the end of the play when Eman's past returns to him. This was done for Esso World Theatre and was included in the film *Culture in Transition*. The play was produced in its full-length version in 1964 at the Greenwich Mews Theatre in New York, and it has been performed by theater groups in several African nations. An African university theater group produced the play in its full-length version in Malawi in 1976 with Anthony Nazombe as Eman. In September 2002, Ahmed Yerima directed the Nigerian National Theater in an interpreted version at the Muson Center in Lagos. That was followed by another performance at the French Cultural Center in October, also in Lagos. Yerima stressed the cultural significance of the play and the appropriateness of this production at a time of political uncertainty and reconciliation. Another production in Durban, South Africa, at the University of Natal, took place in November 2003. African directors insist on interpreting passages through mime and dance, thus imparting an emotional valence to the play.

Wole Soyinka (b. 1934)
THE STRONG BREED

1962

Characters

EMAN, *a stranger*
SUNMA, *Jaguna's daughter*
IFADA, *an idiot*
A GIRL
JAGUNA
OROGE

ATTENDANT STALWARTS, *the villagers*
From Eman's past:
OLD MAN, *his father*
OMAE, *his betrothed*
TUTOR
PRIEST
ATTENDANTS, *the villagers*

The scenes are described briefly, but very often a dark-ened stage with lit areas will not only suffice but is nec-essary. Except for the one indicated place, there can be no break in the action. A distracting scene change would be ruinous.

(A mud house, with space in front of it. Eman, in light buba and trousers stands at the window, looking out. Inside, Sunma is clearing the table of what looks like a modest clinic, putting the things away in a cupboard. Another rough table in the room is piled with exercise books, two or three worn textbooks, etc. Sunma appears agitated. Outside, just below the window crouches Ifada. He looks up with a shy smile from time to time, waiting for Eman to notice him.)

SUNMA (*hesitant*): You will have to make up your mind soon, Eman. The lorry leaves very shortly.

(As Eman does not answer, Sunma continues her work, more nervously. Two villagers, obvious travelers, pass hurriedly in front of the house, the man has a small raf-fia sack, the woman a cloth-covered basket, the man enters first, turns and urges the woman who is just emerging to hurry.)

SUNMA (*seeing them, her tone is more intense*): Eman, are we going or aren't we? You will leave it till too late.

EMAN (*quietly*): There is still time—if you want to go.

SUNMA: If I want to go . . . and you?

(Eman makes no reply.)

SUNMA (*bitterly*): You don't really want to leave here. You never want to go away—even for a minute.

(Ifada continues his antics. Eman eventually pats him on the head and the boy grins happily. Leaps up suddenly and returns with a basket of oranges which he offers to Eman.)

EMAN: My gift for today's festival enh?

(Ifada nods, grinning.)

EMAN: They look ripe—that's a change.

SUNMA (*she has gone inside the room. Looks round the door*): Did you call me?

EMAN: No. (*She goes back.*) And what will you do tonight, Ifada? Will you take part in the dancing? Or perhaps you will mount your own masquerade?

(Ifada shakes his head, regretfully.)

EMAN: You won't? So you haven't any? But you would like to own one.

(Ifada nods eagerly.)

EMAN: Then why don't you make your own?

(Ifada stares, puzzled by this idea.)

EMAN: Sunma will let you have some cloth you know. And bits of wool . . .

SUNMA (*coming out*): Who are you talking to, Eman?

EMAN: Ifada. I am trying to persuade him to join the young maskers.

SUNMA (*losing control*): What does he want here? Why is he hanging round us?

EMAN (*amazed*): What . . . ? I said Ifada, Ifada.

SUNMA: Just tell him to go away. Let him go and play somewhere else!

EMAN: What is this? Hasn't he always played here?

SUNMA: I don't want him here. (*Rushes to the window.*) Get away, idiot. Don't bring your foolish face here anymore, do you hear? Go on, go away from here . . .

EMAN (*restraining her*): Control yourself, Sunma. What on earth has got into you?

(Ifada, hurt and bewildered, backs slowly away.)

SUNMA: He comes crawling round here like some hor-rible insect. I never want to lay my eyes on him again.

EMAN: I don't understand. It *is* Ifada you know. Ifada! The unfortunate one who runs errands for you and doesn't hurt a soul.

SUNMA: I cannot bear the sight of him.

EMAN: You can't do what? It can't be two days since he last fetched water for you.

SUNMA: What else can he do except that? He is useless. Just because we have been kind to him . . . Others would have put him in an asylum.

EMAN: You are not making sense. He is not a madman, he is just a little more unlucky than other children. (*Looks keenly at her.*) But what is the matter?

SUNMA: It's nothing. I only wish we had sent him off to one of those places for creatures like him.

EMAN: He is quite happy here. He doesn't bother any-one and he makes himself useful.

SUNMA: Useful! Is that one of any use to anybody? Boys of his age are already earning a living but all he can do is hang around and drool at the mouth.

EMAN: But he does work. You know he does a lot for you.

SUNMA: Does he? And what about the farm you started for him! Does he ever work on it? Or have you for-gotten that it was really for Ifada you cleared that bush. Now you have to go and work it yourself. You spend all your time on it and you have no room for anything else.

EMAN: That wasn't his fault. I should first have asked him if he was fond of farming.

SUNMA: Oh, so he can choose? As if he shouldn't be thankful for being allowed to live.

EMAN: Sunma!

SUNMA: He does not like farming but he knows how to feast his dumb mouth on the fruits.

EMAN: But I want him to. I encourage him.

SUNMA: Well keep him. I don't want to see him anymore.

EMAN (*after some moments*): But why? You cannot be telling all the truth. What has he done?

SUNMA: The sight of him fills me with revulsion.

EMAN (*goes to her and holds her*): What really is it? (*Sunma avoids his eyes.*) It is almost as if you are forcing yourself to hate him. Why?

SUNMA: That is not true. Why should I?

EMAN: Then what is the secret? You've even played with him before.

SUNMA: I have always merely tolerated him. But I cannot anymore. Suddenly my disgust won't take him anymore. Perhaps . . . perhaps it is the new year. Yes, yes, it must be the new year.

EMAN: I don't believe that.

SUNMA: It must be. I am a woman, and these things matter. I don't want a misshape near me. Surely for one day in the year, I may demand some wholesomeness.

EMAN: I do not understand you. (*Sunma is silent.*) It was cruel of you. And to Ifada who is so helpless and alone. We are the only friends he has.

SUNMA: No, just you. I have told you, with me it has always been only an act of kindness. And now I haven't any pity left for him.

EMAN: No. He is not a wholesome being.

(*He turns back to looking through the window.*)

SUNMA (*half-pleading*): Ifada can rouse your pity. And yet if anything, I need more kindness from you. Every time my weakness betrays me, you close your mind against me . . . Eman . . . Eman . . .

(*A Girl comes in view, dragging an effigy° by a rope attached to one of its legs. She stands for a while gazing at Eman. Ifada, who has crept back shyly to his accustomed position, becomes somewhat excited when he sees the effigy. The Girl is unsmiling. She possesses in fact a kind of inscrutability which does not make her hard but is unsettling.*)

GIRL: Is the teacher in?

EMAN (*smiling*): No.

GIRL: Where is he gone?

EMAN: I don't really know. Shall I ask?

GIRL: Yes, do.

EMAN (*turning slightly*): Sunma, a girl outside wants to know . . .

(*Sunma turns away, goes into the inside room.*)

EMAN: Oh. (*Returns to the Girl, but his slight gaiety is lost.*) There is no one at home who can tell me.

GIRL: Why are you not in?

EMAN: I don't really know. Maybe I went somewhere.

GIRL: All right. I will wait until you get back.

(*She pulls the effigy to her, sits down.*)

EMAN (*slowly regaining his amusement*): So you are all ready for the new year.

GIRL (*without turning round*): I am not going to the festival.

EMAN: Then why have you got that?

GIRL: Do you mean my carrier? I am unwell you know. My mother says it will take away my sickness with the old year.

EMAN: Won't you share the carrier with your playmates?

GIRL: Oh, no. Don't you know I play alone? The other children won't come near me. Their mothers would beat them.

effigy: A figure or likeness in human shape.

EMAN: But I have never seen you here. Why don't you come to the clinic?

GIRL: My mother said No.

(*Gets up, begins to move off.*)

EMAN: You are not going away?

GIRL: I must not stay talking to you. If my mother caught me . . .

EMAN: All right, tell me what you want before you go.

GIRL (*stops. For some moments she remains silent*): I must have some clothes for my carrier.

EMAN: Is that all? You wait a moment.

(*Sunma comes out as he takes down a buba from the wall. She goes to the window and glares almost with hatred at the Girl. The Girl retreats hastily, still impassive.*)

By the way, Sunma, do you know who that girl is?

SUNMA: I hope you don't really mean to give her that.

EMAN: Why not? I hardly ever use it.

SUNMA: Just the same, don't give it to her. She is not a child. She is as evil as the rest of them.

EMAN: What has got into you today?

SUNMA: All right, all right. Do what you wish.

(*She withdraws. Baffled, Eman returns to the window.*)

EMAN: Here . . . will this do? Come and look at it.

GIRL: Throw it.

EMAN: What is the matter? I am not going to eat you.

GIRL: No one lets me come near them.

EMAN: But I am not afraid of catching your disease.

GIRL: Throw it.

(*Eman shrugs and tosses the buba. She takes it without a word and slips it on the effigy, completely absorbed in the task. Eman watches for a while, then joins Sunma in the inner room.*)

GIRL (*after a long, cool survey of Ifada*): You have a head like a spider's egg, and your mouth dribbles like a roof. But there is no one else. Would you like to play?

(*Ifada nods eagerly, quite excited.*)

GIRL: You will have to get a stick.

(*Ifada rushes around, finds a big stick, and whirls it aloft, bearing down on the carrier.*)

GIRL: Wait. I don't want you to spoil it. If it gets torn I shall drive you away. Now, let me see how you are going to beat it.

(*Ifada hits it gently.*)

GIRL: You may hit harder than that. As long as there is something left to hang at the end. (*She appraises him up and down.*) You are not very tall . . . will you be able to hang it from a tree?

(*Ifada nods, grinning happily.*)

GIRL: You will hang it up and I will set fire to it. (*Then, with surprising venom.*) But just because you are helping me, don't think it is going to cure you. I am the one who will get well at midnight, do you under-stand? It is my carrier and it is for me alone. (*She pulls at the rope to make sure that it is well attached to the leg.*) Well don't stand there drooling. Let's go.

(*She begins to walk off, dragging the effigy in the dust. Ifada remains where he is for some moments, seemingly puzzled. Then his face breaks into a large grin and he leaps after the procession, belaboring the effigy with all his strength. The stage remains empty for some moments. Then the horn of a lorry is sounded and Sunma rushes out. The hooting continues for some time with a rhythmic pattern. Eman comes out.*)

EMAN: I am going to the village . . . I shan't be back before nightfall.

SUNMA (*blankly*): Yes.

EMAN (*hesitates*): Well what do you want me to do?

SUNMA: The lorry was hooting just now.

EMAN: I didn't hear it.

SUNMA: It will leave in a few minutes. And you did promise we could go away.

EMAN: I promised nothing. Will you go home by your-self or shall I come back for you?

SUNMA: You don't even want me here?

EMAN: But you have to go home haven't you?

SUNMA: I had hoped we would watch the new year together — in some other place.

EMAN: Why do you continue to distress yourself?

SUNMA: Because you will not listen to me. Why do you continue to stay where nobody wants you?

EMAN: That is not true.

SUNMA: It is. You are wasting your life on people who really want you out of their way.

EMAN: You don't know what you are saying.

SUNMA: You think they love you? Do you think they care at all for what you — or I — do for them?

EMAN: *Them?* These are your own people. Sometimes you talk as if you were a stranger too.

SUNMA: I wonder if I really sprang from here. I know they are evil and I am not. From the oldest to the smallest child, they are nourished in evil and unwholesomeness in which I have no part.

EMAN: You knew this when you returned?

SUNMA: You reproach me then for trying at all?

EMAN: I reproach you with nothing. But you must leave me out of your plans. I can have no part in them.

SUNMA (*nearly pleading*): Once I could have run away. I would have gone and never looked back.

EMAN: I cannot listen when you talk like that.

SUNMA: I swear to you, I do not mind what happens afterwards. But you must help me tear myself away from here. I can no longer do it by myself . . . It is only a little thing. And we have worked so hard this past year . . . surely we can go away for a week . . . even a few days would be enough.

EMAN: I have told you, Sunma . . .

SUNMA (*desperately*): Two days, Eman. Only two days.

EMAN (*distressed*): But I tell you I have no wish to go.

SUNMA (*suddenly angry*): Are you so afraid then?

EMAN: Me? Afraid of what?

SUNMA: You think you will not want to come back.

EMAN (*pitying*): You cannot dare me that way.

SUNMA: Then why won't you leave here, even for an hour? If you are so sure that your life is settled here, why are you afraid to do this thing for me? What is so wrong that you will not go into the next town for a day or two?

EMAN: I don't want to. I do not have to persuade you or myself about anything. I simply have no desire to go away.

SUNMA (*his quiet confidence appears to incense her*): You are afraid. You accuse me of losing my sense of mission, but you are afraid to put yours to the test.

EMAN: You are wrong, Sunma. I have no sense of mis-sion. But I have found peace here and I am content with that.

SUNMA: I haven't. For a while I thought that too, but I found there could be no peace in the midst of so much cruelty. Eman, tonight at least, the last night of the old year . . .

EMAN: No, Sunma. I find this too distressing; you should go home now.

SUNMA: It is the time for making changes in one's life, Eman. Let's breathe in the new year away from here.

EMAN: You are hurting yourself.

SUNMA: Tonight. Only tonight. We will come back tomorrow, as early as you like. But let us go away for this one night. Don't let another year break on me in this place . . . you don't know how important it is to me, but I will tell you, I will tell you on the way . . . but we must not be here today, Eman, do this one thing for me.

EMAN (*sadly*): I cannot.

SUNMA (*suddenly calm*): I was a fool to think it would be otherwise. The whole village may use you as they will but for me there is nothing. Sometimes I think you believe that doing anything for me makes you unfaithful to some part of your life. If it was a woman then I pity her for what she must have suffered.

(*Eman winces and hardens slowly. Sunma notices noth-ing.*)

Keeping faith with so much is slowly making you inhuman. (*Seeing the change in Eman.*) Eman. Eman. What is it?

(*As she goes toward him, Eman goes into the house.*)

SUNMA (*apprehensive, follows him*): What did I say? Eman, forgive me, forgive me please. (*Eman remains facing into the slow darkness of the room. Sunma, distressed, cannot decide what to do.*) I swear I didn't know . . . I would not have said it for all the world.

(*A lorry is heard taking off somewhere nearby. The sound comes up and slowly fades away into the dis-tance. Sunma starts visibly, goes slowly to the window.*)

SUNMA (*as the sound dies off, to herself*): What happens now?

EMAN (*joining her at the window*): What did you say?

SUNMA: Nothing.

EMAN: Was that not the lorry going off?

SUNMA: It was.

EMAN: I am sorry I couldn't help you.

(*Sunma, about to speak, changes her mind.*)

EMAN: I think you ought to go home now.

SUNMA: No, don't send me away. It's the least you can do for me. Let me stay here until all the noise is over.

EMAN: But are you not needed at home? You have a part in the festival.

SUNMA: I have renounced it; I am Jaguna's eldest daughter only in name.

EMAN: Renouncing one's self is not so easy—surely you know that.

SUNMA: I don't want to talk about it. Will you at least let us be together tonight?

EMAN: But...

SUNMA: Unless you are afraid my father will accuse you of harboring me.

EMAN: All right, we will go out together.

SUNMA: Go out? I want us to stay here.

EMAN: When there is so much going on outside?

SUNMA: Someday you will wish that you went away when I tried to make you.

EMAN: Are we going back to that?

SUNMA: No. I promise you I will not recall it again. But you must know that it was also for your sake that I tried to get us away.

EMAN: For me? How?

SUNMA: By yourself you can do nothing here. Have you not noticed how tightly we shut out strangers? Even if you lived here for a lifetime, you would remain a stranger.

EMAN: Perhaps that is what I like. There is peace in being a stranger.

SUNMA: For a while perhaps. But they would reject you in the end. I tell you it is only I who stand between you and contempt. And because of this you have earned their hatred. I don't know why I say this now, except that somehow, I feel that it no longer matters. It is only I who have stood between you and much humiliation.

EMAN: Think carefully before you say any more. I am incapable of feeling indebted to you. This will make no difference at all.

SUNMA: I ask for nothing. But you must know it all the same. It is true I hadn't the strength to go by myself. And I must confess this now, if you had come with me, I would have done everything to keep you from returning.

EMAN: I know that.

SUNMA: You see, I bare myself to you. For days I had thought it over, this was to be a new beginning for us. And I placed my fate wholly in your hands. Now the thought will not leave me, I have a feeling which will not be shaken off, that in some way, you have tonight totally destroyed my life.

EMAN: You are depressed, you don't know what you are saying.

SUNMA: Don't think I am accusing you. I say all this only because I cannot help it.

EMAN: We must not remain shut up here. Let us go and be part of the living.

SUNMA: No. Leave them alone.

EMAN: Surely you don't want to stay indoors when the whole town is alive with rejoicing.

SUNMA: Rejoicing! Is that what it seems to you? No, let us remain here. Whatever happens I must not go out until all this is over.

(*There is silence. It has grown much darker.*)

EMAN: I shall light the lamp.

SUNMA (*eager to do something*): No, let me do it.

(*She goes into the inner room.*)

(*Eman paces the room, stops by a shelf and toys with the seeds in an "ayo" board, takes down the whole board and places it on a table, playing by himself.*)

(*The Girl is now seen coming back, still dragging her "carrier." Ifada brings up the rear as before. As he comes round the corner of the house two men emerge from the shadows. A sack is thrown over Ifada's head, the rope is pulled tight rendering him instantly helpless. The Girl has reached the front of the house before she turns round at the sound of scuffle. She is in time to see Ifada thrown over the shoulders and borne away. Her face betraying no emotion at all, the Girl backs slowly away, turns and flees, leaving the "carrier" behind. Sunma enters, carrying two kerosene lamps. She hangs one up from the wall.*)

EMAN: One is enough.

SUNMA: I want to leave one outside.

(*She goes out, hangs the lamp from a nail just above the door. As she turns she sees the effigy and gasps. Eman rushes out.*)

EMAN: What is it? Oh, is that what frightened you?

SUNMA: I thought . . . I didn't really see it properly.

(*Eman goes towards the object, stoops to pick it up.*)

EMAN: It must belong to that sick girl.

SUNMA: Don't touch it.

EMAN: Let's keep it for her.

SUNMA: Leave it alone. Don't touch it, Eman.

EMAN (*shrugs and goes back*): You are very nervous.

SUNMA: Let's go in.

EMAN: Wait. (*He detains her by the door, under the lamp.*) I know there is something more than you've told me. What are you afraid of tonight?

SUNMA: I was only scared by that thing. There is nothing else.

EMAN: I am not blind, Sunma. It is true I would not run away when you wanted me to, but that doesn't mean I do not feel things. What does tonight really mean that it makes you so helpless?

SUNMA: It is only a mood. And your indifference to me . . . let's go in.

(*Eman moves aside and she enters; he remains there for a moment and then follows.*)

(*She fiddles with the lamp, looks vaguely round the room, then goes and shuts the door, bolting it. When she turns, it is to meet Eman's eyes, questioning.*)

SUNMA: There is a cold wind coming in.

(*Eman keeps his gaze on her.*)

SUNMA: It *was* getting cold.

(*She moves guiltily to the table and stands by the "ayo" board, rearranging the seeds. Eman remains where he is a few moments, then brings a stool and sits opposite her. She sits down also and they begin to play in silence.*)

SUNMA: What brought you here at all, Eman? And what makes you stay?

(*There is another silence.*)

SUNMA: I am not trying to share your life. I know you too well by now. But at least we have worked together since you came. Is there nothing at all I deserve to know?

EMAN: Let me continue a stranger—especially to you. Those who have much to give fulfill themselves only in total loneliness.

SUNMA: Then there is no love in what you do.

EMAN: There is. Love comes to me more easily with strangers.

SUNMA: That is unnatural.

EMAN: Not for me. I know I find consummation only when I have spent myself for a total stranger.

SUNMA: It seems unnatural to me. But then I am a woman. I have a woman's longings and weaknesses. And the ties of blood are very strong in me.

EMAN (*smiling*): You think I have cut loose from all these—ties of blood.

SUNMA: Sometimes you are so inhuman.

EMAN: I don't know what that means. But I am very much my father's son.

(*They play in silence. Suddenly Eman pauses, listening.*)

EMAN: Did you hear that?

SUNMA (*quickly*): I heard nothing . . . it's your turn.

EMAN: Perhaps some of the mummers are coming this way.

(*Eman, about to play, leaps up suddenly.*)

SUNMA: What is it? Don't you want to play anymore?

(*Eman moves to the door.*)

SUNMA: No. Don't go out, Eman.

EMAN: If it's the dancers, I want to ask them to stay. At least we won't have to miss everything.

SUNMA: No, no. Don't open the door. Let us keep out everyone tonight.

(*A terrified and disordered figure bursts suddenly round the corner, past the window, and begins hammering at the door. It is Ifada. Desperate with terror, he pounds madly at the door, dumb-moaning all the while.*)

EMAN: Isn't that Ifada?

SUNMA: They are only fooling about. Don't pay any attention.

EMAN (*looks round the window*): That is Ifada. (*Begins to unbolt the door.*)

SUNMA (*pulling at his hands*): It is only a trick they are playing on you. Don't take any notice, Eman.

EMAN: What are you saying? The boy is out of his senses with fear.

SUNMA: No, no. Don't interfere, Eman. For God's sake, don't interfere.

EMAN: Do you know something of this then?

SUNMA: You are a stranger here, Eman. Just leave us alone and go your own way. There is nothing you can do.

EMAN (*he tries to push her out of the way but she clings fiercely to him*): Have you gone mad? I tell you the boy must come in.

SUNMA: Why won't you listen to me, Eman? I tell you it's none of your business. For your own sake, do as I say.

(*Eman pushes her off, unbolts the door. Ifada rushes in, clasps Eman round the knees, dumb-moaning against his legs.*)

EMAN (*manages to rebolt the door*): What is it, Ifada? What is the matter?

(*Shouts and voices are heard coming nearer the house.*)

SUNMA: Before it's too late, let him go. For once, Eman, believe what I tell you. Don't harbor him or you will regret it all your life.

(*Eman tries to calm Ifada who becomes more and more abject as the outside voices get nearer.*)

EMAN: What have they done to him? At least tell me that. What is going on, Sunma?

SUNMA (*with sudden venom*): Monster! Could you not take yourself somewhere else?

EMAN: Stop talking like that.

SUNMA: He could have run into the bush couldn't he? Toad! Why must he follow us with his own disasters!

VOICES OUTSIDE: It's here . . . Round the back . . . Spread, spread . . . this way . . . no, head him off . . . use the bush path and head him off . . . get some more lights . . .

(*Eman listens. Lifts Ifada bodily and carries him into the inner room. Returns at once, shutting the door behind him.*)

SUNMA (*slumps into a chair, resigned*): You always follow your own way.

JAGUNA (*comes round the corner followed by Oroge and three men, one bearing a torch*): I knew he would come here.

OROGE: I hope our friend won't make trouble.

JAGUNA: He had better not. You, recall all the men and tell them to surround the house.

OROGE: But he may not be in the house after all.

JAGUNA: I know he is here . . . (*to the men*) . . . go on, do as I say. (*He bangs on the door.*) Teacher, open your door . . . you two, stay by the door. If I need you I will call you.

(*Eman opens the door.*)

JAGUNA (*speaks as he enters*): We know he is here.

EMAN: Who?

JAGUNA: Don't let us waste time. We are grown men, teacher. You understand me and I understand you. But we must take back the boy.

EMAN: This is my house.

JAGUNA: Daughter, you'd better tell your friend. I don't think he quite knows our ways. Tell him why he must give up the boy.

SUNMA: Father, I . . .

JAGUNA: Are you going to tell him or aren't you?

SUNMA: Father, I beg you, leave us alone tonight . . .

JAGUNA: I thought you might be a hindrance. Go home then if you will not use your sense.

SUNMA: But there are other ways . . .

JAGUNA (*turning to the men*): See that she gets home. I no longer trust her. If she gives trouble carry her. And see that the women stay with her until all this is over.

(*Sunma departs, accompanied by one of the men.*)

JAGUNA: Now, teacher . . .

OROGE (*restrains him*): You see, Mister Eman, it is like this. Right now, nobody knows that Ifada has taken refuge here. No one except us and our men—and they know how to keep their mouths shut. We don't want to have to burn down the house you see, but if the word gets around, we would have no choice.

JAGUNA: In fact, it may be too late already. A carrier should end up in the bush, not in a house. Anyone who doesn't guard his door when the carrier goes by has himself to blame. A contaminated house should be burnt down.

OROGE: But we are willing to let it pass. Only, you must bring him out quickly.

EMAN: All right. But at least you will let me ask you something.

JAGUNA: What is there to ask? Don't you understand what we have told you?

EMAN: Yes. But why did you pick on a helpless boy. Obviously he is not willing.

JAGUNA: What is the man talking about? Ifada is a godsend. Does he have to be willing?

EMAN: In my home, we believe that a man should be willing.

OROGE: Mister Eman, I don't think you quite understand. This is not a simple matter at all. I don't know what you do, but here, it is not a cheap task for anybody. No one in his senses would do such a job. Why do you think we give refuge to idiots like him? We don't know where he came from. One morning, he is simply there, just like that. From nowhere at all. You see, there is a purpose in that.

JAGUNA: We only waste time.

OROGE: Jaguna, be patient. After all, the man has been with us for some time now and deserves to know. The evil of the old year is no light thing to load on any man's head.

EMAN: I know something about that.

OROGE: You do? (*Turns to Jaguna who snorts impatiently.*) You see I told you so didn't I? From the moment you came I saw you were one of the knowing ones.

JAGUNA: Then let him behave like a man and give back the boy.

EMAN: It is you who are not behaving like men.

JAGUNA (*advances aggressively*): That is a quick mouth you have . . .

OROGE: Patience, Jaguna . . . if you want the new year to cushion the land there must be no deeds of anger. What did you mean, my friend?

EMAN: It is a simple thing. A village which cannot produce its own carrier contains no men.

JAGUNA: Enough. Let there be no more talk or this business will be ruined by some rashness. You . . . come inside. Bring the boy out, he must be in the room there.

EMAN: Wait.

(*The men hesitate.*)

JAGUNA (*hitting the nearer one and propelling him forward*): Go on. Have you changed masters now that you listen to what he says?

OROGE (*sadly*): I am sorry you would not understand, Mister Eman. But you ought to know that no carrier may return to the village. If he does, the people will stone him to death. It has happened before. Surely it is too much to ask a man to give up his own soil.

EMAN: I know others who have done more.

(*Ifada is brought out, abjectly dumb-moaning.*)

EMAN: You can see him with your own eyes. Does it really have meaning to use one as unwilling as that.

OROGE (*smiling*): He shall be willing. Not only willing but actually joyous. I am the one who prepares them all, and I have seen worse. This one escaped before I began to prepare him for the event. But you will see him later tonight, the most joyous creature in the festival. Then perhaps you will understand.

EMAN: Then it is only a deceit. Do you believe the spirit of a new year is so easily fooled?

JAGUNA: Take him out. (*The men carry out Ifada.*) You see, it is so easy to talk. You say there are no men in this village because they cannot provide a willing carrier. And yet I heard Oroge tell you we only use strangers. There is only one other stranger in the village, but I have not heard him offer himself (*spits*). It is so easy to talk is it not? (*He turns his back on him.*)

(*They go off, taking Ifada with them, limp and silent. The only sign of life is that he strains his neck to keep his eyes on Eman till the very moment that he disappears from sight. Eman remains where they left him, staring after the group.*)

(*A blackout lasting no more than a minute. The lights come up slowly and Ifada is seen returning to the house. He stops at the window and looks in. Seeing no one, he bangs on the sill. Appears surprised that there is no response. He slithers down on his favorite spot, then sees the effigy still lying where the Girl had dropped it in her flight. After some hesitation, he goes towards it, begins to strip it of the clothing. Just then the Girl comes in.*)

GIRL: Hey, leave that alone. You know it's mine.

(*Ifada pauses, then speeds up his action.*)

GIRL: I said it is mine. Leave it where you found it.

(*She rushes at him and begins to struggle for possession of the carrier.*)

GIRL: Thief! Thief! Let it go, it is mine. Let it go. You animal, just because I let you play with it. Idiot! Idiot!

(*The struggle becomes quite violent. The Girl is hanging on the effigy and Ifada lifts her with it, flinging her all about. The Girl hangs on grimly.*)

GIRL: You are spoiling it . . . why don't you get your own? Thief! Let it go, you thief!

(*Sunma comes in walking very fast, throwing apprehensive glances over her shoulder. Seeing the two children, she becomes immediately angry. Advances on them.*)

SUNMA: So you've made this place your playground. Get away, you untrained pigs. Get out of here.

(*Ifada flees at once, the Girl retreats also, retaining possession of the "carrier."*)

(*Sunma goes to the door. She has her hand on the door when the significance of Ifada's presence strikes her for the first time. She stands rooted to the spot, then turns slowly round.*)

SUNMA: Ifada! What are you doing here? (*Ifada is bewildered. Sunma turns suddenly and rushes into the house, flying into the inner room and out again.*) Eman! Eman! Eman! (*She rushes outside.*) Where did he go? Where did they take him? (*Ifada distressed, points. Sunma seizes him by the arm, drags him off.*) Take me there at once. God help you if we are too late. You loathsome thing, if you have let him suffer . . .

(*Her voice fades into other shouts, running footsteps, banged tins, bells, dogs, etc., rising in volume.*)

(*It is a narrow passageway between two mud houses. At the far end one man after another is seen running across the entry, the noise dying off gradually.*)

(*About halfway down the passage, Eman is crouching against the wall, tense with apprehension. As the noise dies off, he seems to relax, but the alert hunted look is still in his eyes, which are ringed in a reddish color. The rest of his body has been whitened with a floury substance. He is naked down to the waist, wears a baggy pair of trousers, calf-length, and around both feet are bangles.*)

EMAN: I will simply stay here till dawn. I have done enough.

(*A window is thrown open and a woman empties some slop from a pail. With a startled cry Eman leaps aside to avoid it and the woman puts out her head.*)

WOMAN: Oh, my head. What have I done! Forgive me, neighbor. . . . Eh, it's the carrier!

(*Very rapidly she clears her throat and spits on him, flings the pail at him, and runs off, shouting.*)

He's here. The carrier is hiding in the passage. Quickly, I have found the carrier!

(*The cry is taken up and Eman flees down the passage. Shortly afterwards his pursuers come pouring down the passage in full cry. After the last of them come Jaguna and Oroge.*)

OROGE: Wait, wait. I cannot go so fast.

JAGUNA: We will rest a little then. We can do nothing anyway.

OROGE: If only he had let me prepare him.

JAGUNA: They are the ones who break first, these fools who think they were born to carry suffering like a hat. What are we to do now?

OROGE: When they catch him I must prepare him.

JAGUNA: He? It will be impossible now. There can be no joy left in that one.

OROGE: Still, it took him by surprise. He was not expecting what he met.

JAGUNA: Why then did he refuse to listen? Did he think he was coming to sit down to a feast? He had not even gone through one compound before he bolted. Did he think he was taken round the people to be blessed? A woman, that is all he is.

OROGE: No, no. He took the beating well enough. I think he is the kind who would let himself be beaten from night till dawn and not utter a sound. He would let himself be stoned until he dropped dead.

JAGUNA: Then what made him run like a coward?

OROGE: I don't know. I don't really know. It is a night of curses, Jaguna. It is not many unprepared minds will remain unhinged under the load.

JAGUNA: We must find him. It is a poor beginning for a year when our own curses remain hovering over our homes because the carrier refused to take them.

(*They go. The scene changes. Eman is crouching beside some shrubs, torn and bleeding.*)

EMAN: They are even guarding my house . . . as if I would go there, but I need water . . . they could at least grant me that . . . I can be thirsty too . . . (*He pricks his ears.*) . . . there must be a stream nearby . . . (*As he looks round him, his eyes widen at a scene he encounters.*)

(*An Old Man, short and vigorous looking, is seated on a stool. He also is wearing calf-length baggy trousers, white. On his head, a white cap. An attendant is engaged in rubbing his body with oil. Round his eyes, two white rings have already been marked.*)

OLD MAN: Have they prepared the boat?
ATTENDANT: They are making the last sacrifice.
OLD MAN: Good. Did you send for my son?
ATTENDANT: He's on his way.
OLD MAN: I have never met the carrying of the boat with such a heavy heart. I hope nothing comes of it.
ATTENDANT: The gods will not desert us on that account.
OLD MAN: A man should be at his strongest when he takes the boat, my friend. To be weighed down inside and out is not a wise thing. I hope when the moment comes I shall have found my strength.

(*Enter Eman, a wrapper round his waist and a danski° over it.*)

OLD MAN: I meant to wait until after my journey to the river, but my mind is so burdened with my own grief and yours I could not delay it. You know I must have all my strength. But I sit here, feeling it all eaten slowly away by my unspoken grief. It helps to say it out. It even helps to cry sometimes.

(*He signals to the attendant to leave them.*)

Come nearer . . . we will never meet again, son. Not on this side of the flesh. What I do not know is whether you will return to take my place.
EMAN: I will never come back.
OLD MAN: Do you know what you are saying? Ours is a strong breed, my son. It is only a strong breed that can take this boat to the river year after year and wax stronger on it. I have taken down each year's evils for over twenty years. I hoped you would follow me.
EMAN: My life here died with Omae.
OLD MAN: Omae died giving birth to your child and you think the world is ended. Eman, my pain did not begin when Omae died. Since you sent her to stay with me, son, I lived with the burden of knowing that this child would die bearing your son.
EMAN: Father . . .
OLD MAN: Don't you know it was the same with you? And me? No woman survives the bearing of the strong ones. Son, it is not the mouth of the boaster that says he belongs to the strong breed. It is the tongue that is red with pain and black with sorrow. Twelve years you were away my son, and for those twelve years I knew the love of an old man for his daughter and the pain of a man helplessly awaiting his loss.

danski: A brief Yoruba garment.

EMAN: I wish I had stayed away. I wish I never came back to meet her.
OLD MAN: It had to be. But you know now what slowly ate away my strength. I awaited your return with love and fear. Forgive me then if I say that your grief is light. It will pass. This grief may drive you now from home. But you must return.
EMAN: You do not understand. It is not grief alone.
OLD MAN: What is it then? Tell me, I can still learn.
EMAN: I was away twelve years. I changed much in that time.
OLD MAN: I am listening.
EMAN: I am unfitted for your work, father. I wish to say no more. But I am totally unfitted for your call.
OLD MAN: It is only time you need, son. Stay longer and you will answer the urge of your blood.
EMAN: That I stayed at all was because of Omae. I did not expect to find her waiting. I would have taken her away, but hard as you claim to be, it would have killed you. And I was a tired man. I needed peace. Because Omae was peace, I stayed. Now nothing holds me here.
OLD MAN: Other men would rot and die doing this task year after year. It is strong medicine which only we can take. Our blood is strong like no other. Anything you do in life must be less than this, son.
EMAN: That is not true, father.
OLD MAN: I tell you it is true. Your own blood will betray you, son, because you cannot hold it back. If you make it do less than this, it will rush to your head and burst it open. I say what I know, my son.
EMAN: There are other tasks in life, father. This one is not for me. There are even greater things you know nothing of.
OLD MAN: I am very sad. You only go to give to others what rightly belongs to us. You will use your strength among thieves. They are thieves because they take what is ours, they have no claim of blood to it. They will even lack the knowledge to use it wisely. Truth is my companion at this moment, my son. I know everything I say will surely bring the sadness of truth.
EMAN: I am going, father.
OLD MAN: Call my attendant. And be with me in your strength for this last journey. A-ah, did you hear that? It came out without my knowing it; this is indeed my last journey. But I am not afraid.

(*Eman goes out. A few moments later, the attendant enters.*)

ATTENDANT: The boat is ready.
OLD MAN: So am I.

(*He sits perfectly still for several moments. Drumming begins somewhere in the distance, and the Old Man sways his head almost imperceptibly. Two men come in bearing a miniature boat, containing an indefinable mound. They rush it in and set it briskly down near the Old Man, and stand well back. The Old Man gets up slowly, the Attendant watching him keenly. He signs to the men, who lift the boat quickly onto the Old Man's head. As soon as it touches his head, he holds it down with both hands and runs off, the men give him a start, then follow at a trot.)*

(As the last man disappears Oroge limps in and comes face to face with Eman—as carrier—who is now seen still standing beside the shrubs, staring into the scene he has just witnessed. Oroge, struck by the look on Eman's face, looks anxiously behind him to see what has engaged Eman's attention. Eman notices him then, and the pair stare at each other. Jaguna enters, sees him and shouts, "Here he is," rushes at Eman who is whipped back to the immediate and flees, Jaguna in pursuit. Three or four others enter and follow them. Oroge remains where he is, thoughtful.)

JAGUNA *(reenters)*: They have closed in on him now, we'll get him this time.

OROGE: It is nearly midnight.

JAGUNA: You were standing there looking at him as if he was some strange spirit. Why didn't you shout?

OROGE: You shouted didn't you? Did that catch him?

JAGUNA: Don't worry. We have him now. But things have taken a bad turn. It is no longer enough to drive him past every house. There is too much contamination about already.

OROGE *(not listening)*: He saw something. Why may I not know what it was?

JAGUNA: What are you talking about?

OROGE: Hm. What is it?

JAGUNA: I said there is too much harm done already. The year will demand more from this carrier than we thought.

OROGE: What do you mean?

JAGUNA: Do we have to talk with the full mouth?

OROGE: S-sh . . . look!

(Jaguna turns just in time to see Sunma fly at him, clawing at his face like a crazed tigress.)

SUNMA: Murderer! What are you doing to him. Murderer! Murderer!

(Jaguna finds himself struggling really hard to keep off his daughter; he succeeds in pushing her off and striking her so hard on the face that she falls to her knees. He moves on her to hit her again.)

OROGE *(comes between)*: Think what you are doing, Jaguna, she is your daughter.

JAGUNA: My daughter! Does this one look like my daughter? Let me cripple the harlot for life.

OROGE: That is a wicked thought, Jaguna.

JAGUNA: Don't come between me and her.

OROGE: Nothing in anger—do you forget what tonight is?

JAGUNA: Can you blame me for forgetting?

(Draws his hand across his cheek—it is covered with blood.)

OROGE: This is an unhappy night for us all. I fear what is to come of it.

JAGUNA: Let's go. I cannot restrain myself in this creature's presence. My own daughter . . . and for a stranger . . .

(They go off, Ifada, who came in with Sunma and had stood apart, horror-stricken, comes shyly forward. He helps Sunma up. They go off, he holding Sunma bent and sobbing.)

(Enter Eman—as carrier. He is physically present in the bounds of this next scene, a side of a round thatched hut. A young girl, about fourteen, runs in, stops beside the hut. She looks carefully to see that she is not observed, puts her mouth to a little hole in the wall.)

OMAE: Eman . . . Eman . . .

(Eman—as carrier—responds, as he does throughout the scene, but they are unaware of him.)

EMAN *(from inside)*: Who is it?

OMAE: It is me, Omae.

EMAN: How dare you come here!

(Two hands appear at the hole and pushing outwards, create a much larger hole through which Eman puts out his head. It is Eman as a boy, the same age as the girl.)

Go away at once. Are you trying to get me into trouble!

OMAE: What is the matter?

EMAN: You. Go away.

OMAE: But I came to see you.

EMAN: Are you deaf? I say I don't want to see you. Now go before my tutor catches you.

OMAE: All right. Come out.

EMAN: Do what!

OMAE: Come out.

EMAN: You must be mad.

OMAE *(sits on the ground)*: All right, if you don't come out I shall simply stay here until your tutor arrives.

EMAN *(about to explode, thinks better of it and the head disappears. A moment later he emerges from behind the hut)*: What sort of a devil has got into you?

OMAE: None. I just wanted to see you.

EMAN *(his mimicry is nearly hysterical)*: "None. I just wanted to see you." Do you think this place is the stream where you can go and molest innocent people?

OMAE *(coyly)*: Aren't you glad to see me?

EMAN: I am not.

OMAE: Why?

EMAN: Why? Do you really ask me why? Because you are a woman and a most troublesome woman. Don't you know anything about this at all. We are not meant to see any woman. So go away before more harm's done.

OMAE *(flirtatious)*: What is so secret about it anyway? What do they teach you?

EMAN: Nothing any woman can understand.

OMAE: Ha ha. You think we don't know eh? You've all come to be circumcised.

EMAN: Shut up. You don't know anything.

OMAE: Just think, all this time you haven't been circumcised, and you dared make eyes at us women.

EMAN: Thank you—woman. Now go.

OMAE: Do they give you enough to eat?

EMAN (*testily*): No. We are so hungry that when silly girls like you turn up, we eat them.

OMAE (*feigning tears*): Oh, oh, oh, he's abusing me. He's abusing me.

EMAN (*alarmed*): Don't try that here. Go quickly if you are going to cry.

OMAE: All right, I won't cry.

EMAN: Cry or no cry, go away and leave me alone. What do you think will happen if my tutor turns up now?

OMAE: He won't.

EMAN (*mimicking*): "He won't." I suppose you are his wife and he tells you where he goes. In fact this is just the time he comes round to our huts. He could be at the next hut this very moment.

OMAE: Ha-ha. You're lying. I left him by the stream, pinching the girls' bottoms. Is that the sort of thing he teaches you?

EMAN: Don't say anything against him or I shall beat you. Isn't it you loose girls who tease him, wiggling your bottoms under his nose?

OMAE (*going tearful again*): A-ah, so I am one of the loose girls eh?

EMAN: Now don't start accusing me of things I didn't say.

OMAE: But you said it. You said it.

EMAN: I didn't. Look, Omae, someone will hear you and I'll be in disgrace. Why don't you go before anything happens?

OMAE: It's all right. My friends have promised to hold your old rascal tutor till I get back.

EMAN: Then you go back right now. I have work to do. (*Going in.*)

OMAE (*runs after and tries to hold him. Eman leaps back, genuinely scared*): What is the matter? I was not going to bite you.

EMAN: Do you know what you nearly did? You almost touched me!

OMAE: Well?

EMAN: Well! Isn't it enough that you let me set my eyes on you? Must you now totally pollute me with your touch? Don't you understand anything?

OMAE: Oh, that.

EMAN (*nearly screaming*): It is not "oh that." Do you think this is only a joke or a little visit like spending the night with your grandmother? This is an important period of my life. Look, these huts, we built them with our own hands. Every boy builds his own. We learn things, do you understand? And we spend much time just thinking. At least, I do. It is the first time I have had nothing to do except think. Don't you see, I am becoming a man. For the first time, I understand that I have a life to fulfill. Has that thought ever worried you?

OMAE: You are frightening me.

EMAN: There. That is all you can say. And what use will that be when a man finds himself alone—like that? (*Points to the hut.*) A man must go on his own, go where no one can help him, and test his strength. Because he may find himself one day sitting alone in a wall as round as that. In there, my mind could hold no other thought. I may never have such moments again to myself. Don't dare to come and steal any more of it.

OMAE (*this time, genuinely tearful*): Oh, I know you hate me. You only want to drive me away.

EMAN (*impatiently*): Yes, yes, I know I hate you—but go.

OMAE (*going, all tears. Wipes her eyes, suddenly all mischief*): Eman.

EMAN: What now?

OMAE: I only want to ask one thing . . . do you promise to tell me?

EMAN: Well, what is it?

OMAE (*gleefully*): Does it hurt?

(*She turns instantly and flees, landing straight into the arms of the returning tutor.*)

TUTOR: Te-he-he . . . what have we here? What little mouse leaps straight into the beak of the wise old owl eh?

(*Omae struggles to free herself, flies to the opposite side, grimacing with distaste.*)

TUTOR: I suppose you merely came to pick some fruits eh? You did not sneak here to see any of my children.

OMAE: Yes, I came to steal your fruits.

TUTOR: Te-he-he . . . I thought so. And that dutiful son of mine over there. He saw you and came to chase you off my fruit trees didn't he? Te-he-he . . . I'm sure he did, isn't that so, my young Eman?

EMAN: I was talking to her.

TUTOR: Indeed you were. Now be good enough to go into your hut until I decide your punishment. (*Eman withdraws.*) Te-he-he . . . now now, my little daughter, you need not be afraid of me.

OMAE (*spiritedly*): I am not.

TUTOR: Good. Very good. We ought to be friendly. (*His voice becomes leering.*) Now this is nothing to worry you, my daughter . . . a very small thing indeed. Although of course if I were to let it slip that your young Eman had broken a strong taboo, it might go hard on him you know. I am sure you would not like that to happen, would you?

OMAE: No.

TUTOR: Good. You are sensible, my girl. Can you wash clothes?

OMAE: Yes.

TUTOR: Good. If you will come with me now to my hut, I shall give you some clothes to wash, and then we will forget all about this matter eh? Well, come on.

OMAE: I shall wait here. You go and bring the clothes.

TUTOR: Eh? What is that? Now now, don't make me angry. You should know better than to talk back at your elders. Come now.

(*He takes her by the arm and tries to drag her off.*)

OMAE: No no, I won't come to your hut. Leave me. Leave me alone, you shameless old man.
TUTOR: If you don't come I shall disgrace the whole family of Eman, and yours too.

(*Eman reenters with a small bundle.*)

EMAN: Leave her alone. Let us go, Omae.
TUTOR: And where do you think you are going?
EMAN: Home.
TUTOR: Te-he-he . . . As easy as that eh? You think you can leave here any time you please? Get right back inside that hut!

(*Eman takes Omae by the arm and begins to walk off.*)

TUTOR: Come back at once.

(*He goes after him and raises his stick. Eman catches it, wrenches it from him, and throws it away.*)

OMAE (*hopping delightedly*): Kill him. Beat him to death.
TUTOR: Help! Help! He is killing me! Help!

(*Alarmed, Eman clamps his hand over his mouth.*)

EMAN: Old tutor, I don't mean you any harm, but you mustn't try to harm me either. (*He removes his hand.*)
TUTOR: You think you can get away with your crime. My report shall reach the elders before you ever get into town.
EMAN: You are afraid of what I will say about you? Don't worry. Only if you try to shame me, then I will speak. I am not going back to the village anyway. Just tell them I have gone, no more. If you say one word more than that I shall hear of it the same day and I shall come back.
TUTOR: You are telling me what to do? But don't think to come back next year because I will drive you away. Don't think to come back here even ten years from now. And don't send your children.

(*Goes off with threatening gestures.*)

EMAN: I won't come back.
OMAE: Smoked vulture! But Eman, he says you cannot return next year. What will you do?
EMAN: It is a small thing one can do in the big towns.
OMAE: I thought you were going to beat him that time. Why didn't you crack his dirty hide?
EMAN: Listen carefully, Omae . . . I am going on a journey.
OMAE: Come on. Tell me about it on the way.
EMAN: No, I go that way. I cannot return to the village.
OMAE: Because of that wretched man? Anyway you will first talk to your father.
EMAN: Go and see him for me. Tell him I have gone away for some time. I think he will know.
OMAE: But, Eman . . .
EMAN: I haven't finished. You will go and live with him till I get back. I have spoken to him about you. Look after him!

OMAE: But what is this journey? When will you come back?
EMAN: I don't know. But this is a good moment to go. Nothing ties me down.
OMAE: But, Eman, you want to leave me.
EMAN: Don't forget all I said. I don't know how long I will be. Stay in my father's house as long as you remember me. When you become tired of waiting, you must do as you please. You understand? You must do as you please.
OMAE: I cannot understand anything, Eman. I don't know where you are going or why. Suppose you never came back! Don't go, Eman. Don't leave me by myself.
EMAN: I must go. Now let me see you on your way.
OMAE: I shall come with you.
EMAN: Come with me! And who will look after you? Me? You will only be in my way, you know that! You will hold me back and I shall desert you in a strange place. Go home and do as I say. Take care of my father and let him take care of you.

(*He starts going but Omae clings to him.*)

OMAE: But, Eman, stay the night at least. You will only lose your way. Your father, Eman, what will he say? I won't remember what you said . . . come back to the village . . . I cannot return alone, Eman . . . come with me as far as the crossroads.

(*His face set, Eman strides off and Omae loses balance as he increases his pace. Falling, she quickly wraps her arms around his ankle, but Eman continues unchecked, dragging her along.*)

OMAE: Don't go, Eman . . . Eman, don't leave me, don't leave me . . . don't leave your Omae . . . don't go, Eman . . . don't leave your Omae . . .

(*Eman—as carrier—makes a nervous move as if he intends to go after the vanished pair. He stops but continues to stare at the point where he last saw them. There is stillness for a while. Then the Girl enters from the same place and remains looking at Eman. Startled, Eman looks apprehensively round him. The Girl goes nearer but keeps beyond arm's length.*)

GIRL: Are you the carrier?
EMAN: Yes. I am Eman.
GIRL: Why are you hiding?
EMAN: I really came for a drink of water . . . er . . . is there anyone in front of the house?
GIRL: No.
EMAN: But there might be people in the house. Did you hear voices?
GIRL: There is no one here.
EMAN: Good. Thank you. (*He is about to go, stops suddenly.*) Er . . . would you . . . you will find a cup on the table. Could you bring me the water out here? The water pot is in a corner.

(*The Girl goes. She enters the house, then, watching Eman carefully, slips out and runs off.*)

EMAN (*sitting*): Perhaps they have all gone home. It will be good to rest. (*He hears voices and listens hard.*) Too late. (*Moves cautiously nearer the house.*) Quickly, girl, I can hear people coming. Hurry up. (*Looks through the window.*) Where are you? Where is she? (*The truth dawns on him suddenly and he moves off, sadly.*)

(*Enter Jaguna and Oroge, led by the Girl.*)

GIRL (*pointing*): He was there.

JAGUNA: Ay, he's gone now. He is a sly one is your friend. But it won't save him forever.

OROGE: What was he doing when you saw him?

GIRL: He asked me for a drink of water.

JAGUNA: ⎱
OROGE: ⎰ Ah! (*They look at each other.*)

OROGE: We should have thought of that.

JAGUNA: He is surely finished now. If only we had thought of it earlier.

OROGE: It is not too late. There is still an hour before midnight.

JAGUNA: We must call back all the men. Now we need only wait for him—in the right place.

OROGE: Everyone must be told. We don't want anyone heading him off again.

JAGUNA: And it works so well. This is surely the help of the gods themselves, Oroge. Don't you know at once what is on the path to the stream?

OROGE: The sacred trees.

JAGUNA: I tell you it is the very hand of the gods. Let us go.

(*An overgrown part of the village. Eman wanders in, aimlessly, seemingly uncaring of discovery. Beyond him, an area lights up, revealing a group of people clustered round a spot, all the heads are bowed. One figure stands away and separate from them. Even as Eman looks, the group breaks up and the people disperse, coming down and past him. Only three people are left, a man [Eman] whose back is turned, the village priest, and the isolated one. They stand on opposite sides of the grave, the man on the mound of earth. The Priest walks round to the man's side and lays a hand on his shoulder.*)

PRIEST: Come.

EMAN: I will. Give me a few moments here alone.

PRIEST: Be comforted.

(*They fall silent.*)

EMAN: I was gone twelve years but she waited. She whom I thought had too much of the laughing child in her. Twelve years I was a pilgrim, seeking the vain shrine of secret strength. And all the time, strange knowledge, this silent strength of my child-woman.

PRIEST: We all saw it. It was a lesson to us; we did not know that such goodness could be found among us.

EMAN: Then why? Why the wasted years if she had to perish giving birth to my child? (*They are both silent.*) I do not really know for what great meaning I

searched. When I returned, I could not be certain I had found it. Until I reached my home and I found her a full-grown woman, still a child at heart. When I grew to believe it, I thought, this, after all, is what I sought. It was here all the time. And I threw away my new-gained knowledge. I buried the part of me that was formed in strange places. I made a home in my birthplace.

PRIEST: That was as it should be.

EMAN: Any truth of that was killed in the cruelty of her brief happiness.

PRIEST (*looks up and sees the figure standing away from them, the child in his arms. He is totally still*): Your father—he is over there.

EMAN: I knew he would come. Has he my son with him?

PRIEST: Yes.

EMAN: He will let no one take the child. Go and comfort him, priest. He loved Omae like a daughter, and you all know how well she looked after him. You see how strong we really are. In his heart of hearts the old man's love really awaited a daughter. Go and comfort him. His grief is more than mine.

(*The Priest goes. The Old Man has stood well away from the burial group. His face is hard and his gaze unswerving from the grave. The Priest goes to him, pauses, but sees that he can make no dent in the man's grief. Bowed, he goes on his way.*)

(*Eman, as carrier, walking towards the graveside, the other Eman having gone. His feet sink into the mound and he breaks slowly onto his knees, scooping up the sand in his hands and pouring it on his head. The scene blacks out slowly.*)

(*Enter Jaguna and Oroge.*)

OROGE: We have only a little time.

JAGUNA: He will come. All the wells are guarded. There is only the stream left him. The animal must come to drink.

OROGE: You are sure it will not fail—the trap, I mean.

JAGUNA: When Jaguna sets the trap, even elephants pay homage—their trunks downwards and one leg up in the sky. When the carrier steps on the fallen twigs, it is up in the sacred trees with him.

OROGE: I shall breathe again when this long night is over.

(*They go out.*)

(*Enter Eman—as carrier—from the same direction as the last two entered. In front of him is a still figure, the Old Man as he was, carrying the dwarf boat.*)

EMAN (*joyfully*): Father.

(*The figure does not turn round.*)

EMAN: It is your son, Eman. (*He moves nearer.*) Don't you want to look at me? It is I, Eman. (*He moves nearer still.*)

OLD MAN: You are coming too close. Don't you know what I carry on my head?

EMAN: But, Father, I am your son.

OLD MAN: Then go back. We cannot give the two of us.

EMAN: Tell me first where you are going.

OLD MAN: Do *you* ask that? Where else but to the river?

EMAN (*visibly relieved*): I only wanted to be sure. My throat is burning. I have been looking for the stream all night.

OLD MAN: It is the other way.

EMAN: But you said . . .

OLD MAN: I take the longer way, you know how I must do this. It is quicker if you take the other way. Go now.

EMAN: No, I will only get lost again. I shall go with you.

OLD MAN: Go back, my son. Go back.

EMAN: Why? Won't you even look at me?

OLD MAN: Listen to your father. Go back.

EMAN: But, father!

(*He makes to hold him. Instantly the old man breaks into a rapid trot. Eman hesitates, then follows, his strength nearly gone.*)

EMAN: Wait, father. I am coming with you . . . wait . . . wait for me, father . . .

(*There is a sound of twigs breaking, of a sudden trembling in the branches. Then silence.*)

(*The front of Eman's house. The effigy is hanging from the sheaves. Enter Sunma, still supported by Ifada, she stands transfixed as she sees the hanging figure. Ifada appears to go mad, rushes at the object, and tears it down. Sunma, her last bit of will gone, crumbles against the wall. Some distance away from them, partly hidden, stands the Girl, impassively watching. Ifada hugs the effigy to him, stands above Sunma. The Girl remains where she is, observing.*)

(*Almost at once, the villagers begin to return, subdued and guilty.*)

(*They walk across the front, skirting the house as widely as they can. No word is exchanged. Jaguna and Oroge eventually appear. Jaguna, who is leading, sees Sunma as soon as he comes in view. He stops at once, retreating slightly.*)

OROGE (*almost whispering*): What is it?

JAGUNA: The viper.

(*Oroge looks cautiously at the woman.*)

OROGE: I don't think she will even see you.

JAGUNA: Are you sure? I am in no frame of mind for another meeting with her.

OROGE: Let's go home.

JAGUNA: I am sick to the heart of the cowardice I have seen tonight.

OROGE: That is the nature of men.

JAGUNA: Then it is a sorry world to live in. We did it for them. It was all for their own common good. What did it benefit me whether the man lived or died. But did you see them? One and all they looked up at the man and words died in their throats.

OROGE: It was no common sight.

JAGUNA: Women could not have behaved so shamefully. One by one they crept off like sick dogs. Not one could raise a curse.

OROGE: It was not only him they fled. Do you see how unattended we are?

JAGUNA: There are those who will pay for this night's work!

OROGE: Ay, let us go home.

(*They go off. Sunma, Ifada, and the Girl remain as they are, the light fading slowly on them.*)

COMMENTARY

Lewis Nkosi (*b. 1935*)

INTERVIEW WITH WOLE SOYINKA   *1962*

This early interview with Soyinka was taped in Lagos, Nigeria, in August 1962, while The Strong Breed *was very fresh in his mind. In fact, it had not yet had its first publication, which in Nigeria was in 1963. Nkosi in the interview highlights the impact of Bertolt Brecht's theater on Soyinka's writing.*

Nkosi: Well, Wole Soyinka, could you tell us what set you off on this road to writing?

Soyinka: I suppose that requires really going back a bit. I would say I began writing seriously, or rather taking myself seriously, taking my *writing* seriously about three, four years ago, but I can only presume that I have always been interested in writing. In school I wrote the usual little sketches for production, the occasional verse, you know, the short story, etc., and I think about 1951 I had the great excitement of having a short story of mine broadcast on the Nigerian Broadcasting Service and that was sort of my first public performance.

Nkosi: What schools did you attend?

Soyinka: I went to Government School, Ibadan; after that I spent a couple of years in the University College, Ibadan.

Nkosi: You have now published drama or rather you've had some plays produced?

Soyinka: Yes, "produced" is the correct word. I haven't had any plays published although some are in print right now and will come out shortly.

Nkosi: Could you tell us what those plays are?

Soyinka: There is *The Lion and the Jewel* which was the first play I wrote.

Nkosi: No, the second.

Soyinka: The first one I sent up, I suppose like most people do, is the *A Dance of Forests* which I wrote in 1960 and timed it for the Independence Celebrations; there is the *House of Banigeji* which has never been performed. And I have written about four one-acts including *The Trials of Brother Jero* which was done quite recently in Nigeria.

Nkosi: The *A Dance of the Forests* won you a prize, didn't it?

Soyinka: Yes, Nigerian Independence competition prize 1960.

Nkosi: Have you got any particular authors that have influenced you most?

Soyinka: This is a very difficult question for me because I am not aware of any conscious influence on my work, but I can say that if I wanted to aim at any particular kind of theater, I think, however subconsciously, I might aim at Brecht's kind of theater, which I admire tremendously, just his complete freedom with the medium of the theater.

Nkosi: In your last play, *A Dance of the Forests*, which caused a lot of people a tremendous amount of agony trying to figure out just exactly what it was trying to do — they felt that there were some hidden meanings contained in lots of symbolism which they couldn't gather. Now as you're the author, we are lucky to have you here, and we think that you probably might enlighten us about just what you were trying to say in that work of yours.

Soyinka: Well, let me say first of all that I think that my prime duty as a playwright is to provide excellent theater; in other words, I think that I have only one commitment to the public, and that is to my audience and that is to make sure they do not leave the theater bored. I don't believe that I have any obligation to enlighten, to instruct, to teach: I don't possess that sense of duty or didacticism — very much unlike Brecht for instance, for, you see, what I like in Brecht is his sort of theater, its liveliness and freedom, not so much his purpose or intentions. I believe my primary duty is just to see that I provide excellent theater for the audience. But inevitably, it is just common sense to say that one just cannot write about just nothing. In *A Dance of the Forests*, I was very much conscious of all the potentialities of existing theatrical idioms in Nigeria and I only know that there was one thing which motivated, maybe, guided the form and the shape of the play or the eventual fate of the characters. I use this word "motivated" quite cautiously because I do not think I consciously tried to preach or bring out, you know, a series of symbolisms at all, but the main thing was the realization that human beings are just destructive all over the world. I think this is it—I have thought about this again and again but during the production—I produced it myself—and in trying to see the play take shape on the stage, I find that the main thing is my own personal conviction or observation that human beings are simply cannibals all over the world so that their main preoccupation seems to be eating up one another. This I think is the main thing I would say was in the back of my mind when I wrote it.

Nkosi: Yes, that sounds very much like Tennessee Williams's idea of the world conscious of the evil.

Soyinka: Well, I don't sort of regard it so much as . . .

Nkosi: The ferocity of human beings.

Soyinka: Yes, the carnivorous nature of. . . .

Nkosi: Yes, I wonder whether now—have you pursued this theme in the other plays or are the other plays different?

Soyinka: . . . Fundamentally, I think they're different. I think that sort of semiconsciously the moment I realize I'm pursuing a theme again, it seems to ring a bell warning that I have preceded myself somewhere; I have such a feeling about this that I shirk from it but I would say there are traces of it in my other plays—in, for instance, my favorite one-act play which is *The Strong Breed*. I think this one is also very much mixed up with the whole element of sacrifice, so contrasting the idea of selfishness with willing self-sacrifice as opposed to the other general cannibalism of human beings.

Contemporary Drama

Experimentation

The experimentation in drama that flourished in the first half of the twentieth century has continued in contemporary drama. In fact, the achievements of Tennessee Williams, Arthur Miller, Samuel Beckett, and other midcentury playwrights encouraged later playwrights to experiment more daringly with mixing media such as film, video, opera, rock, and other music with live actors. Mixed-media approaches are still options for playwrights in the twenty-first century, but most contemporary plays celebrated by critics and audiences have been relatively traditional. They build on the achievement of nineteenth-century realism and twentieth-century expressionism.

Harold Pinter's distinctive style, developed in the late 1950s and early 1960s, is connected with some of the absurdist experiments in drama. His dialogue is acerbic, repetitive, sometimes apparently aimless. However, he is able to produce intense emotional situations, such as that in *The Dumb Waiter* (1957), in which two "hit men" wait for instructions in a basement room. *The Caretaker* (1960) and *The Homecoming* (1965), his first commercial successes, established him as a major figure in modern theater. He has also been a screenwriter for such films as *The Quiller Memorandum* (1966), *The French Lieutenant's Woman* (1981), and *The Handmaid's Tale* (1990). His experiments with time and sequence in his full-length play *Betrayal* (1978), for which he also wrote the screenplay, have inspired other playwrights, such as Paula Vogel, to experiment with the backward movement of action.

Most of the interesting late-twentieth-century experimental theater was done in groups such as Richard Schechner's Performance Group, which created what Schechner called ENVIRONMENTAL THEATER in New York City in the late 1960s, and Jerzy Grotowski's Polish Laboratory Theatre in Wroclaw, Poland, during the same period. Ensembles like the Bread and Puppet Theatre, the San Francisco Mime Troupe, and Luis Valdez's El Teatro Campesino on the West Coast combined a radical political message with theatrical experimentation. The work of these groups is effective primarily at the performance level; their texts are not representative of their impact on audiences.

Theater of Cruelty

The ensembles of the 1960s and 1970s were strongly influenced by the work of Antonin Artaud (1896–1948), French actor, director, and a theorist of theater. In creating what came to be known as the THEATER OF CRUELTY, he insisted on removing the comforting distance between actors and audience. Thus the audience was involved in a direct, virtually physical fashion with the dramatic action. Artaud designed theater to be a total experience—a sensational spectacle that did not depend on coherent plot or development. He concentrated on what he called a total theater that emphasized movement, gesture, music, sound, light, and other nonverbal elements to intensify the experience.

Artaud's manifestos, collected in a work called *The Theater and Its Double* (1938), inspired some of the most important twentieth-century theater practitioners, including Peter Brook and Robert Wilson. Artaud's notion of a "serious" theater is at the root of his influence:

> Our long habit of seeking diversion has made us forget the idea of a serious theater, which, overturning all our preconceptions, inspires us with the fiery magnetism of its images and acts upon us like a spiritual therapeutics whose touch can never be forgotten.
> Everything that acts is a cruelty. It is upon this idea of extreme action, pushed beyond all limits, that theater must be rebuilt.

Artaud compared the theater artist he envisioned to a victim "burnt at the stake, signaling through the flames."

Environmental Theater

Richard Schechner's most famous production, based on Euripides' *The Bacchae*, was *Dionysus in 69* (1968), in which Pentheus is torn to pieces in an impassioned frenzy. Part of the point of Schechner's production was to inspire the audience so much that they would take to the stage, becoming indistinguishable from the actors. *Dionysus in 69* was an effort to draw on the same spiritual energies tapped by Greek drama by connecting with the feasts of Dionysus, god of wine and ecstasy. The play was a spontaneous and partly improvised performance piece rather than a text meant to be read. At one point the audience and actors disrobed in a simulation of a Greek religious orgy, and Schechner's goal of involving audience and actors in a pagan ritual was realized night after night during the run.

In a similar way Julian Beck and Judith Malina's Living Theatre maintained a special relationship with the audience. Beck's plays were designed to break down the absolutes of dramatic space and audience space by having the actors roam through the audience and interact apparently at random with audience members. *Paradise Now* (1968) is his best-known play. Like Schechner's *Dionysus in 69,* it was essentially a performance piece. Certain segments were improvised; therefore, as a reading text, it has relatively little power.

"Poor Theater"

Jerzy Grotowski called his work "poor theater" because it was meant to contrast with the "rich theater" of the commercial stage, with its expensive lighting, decorated stages, rich costumes, numerous props, and elaborate settings. Grotowski's Laboratory Theatre, begun in 1959, relied on preexisting texts but interpreted them broadly through a total reconception of their meaning. For example, Grotowski's *Akropolis* (1962; revised frequently from 1963 to 1975) adapted an older Polish drama by Stanislaw Wyspiański (1904) and reset it in modern times in Auschwitz with the actors, dressed in ragged sackcloth prison uniforms, looking wretched and starving. At the end of the play the prisoners follow a headless puppet-corpse, Christ, into an afterlife. They march in an eerie ritual procession offstage into the waiting prison camp ovens.

Grotowski's theater has been influential worldwide. When the Polish government clamped down on the Solidarity° movement in the late 1970s, Grotowski left Poland. After 1970 Grotowski shifted his focus from public performances to small, intense group workshops and to the ritual performances of cultures from all over the world. The first phase of his work with the Laboratory Theatre has remained the most influential. One of his actors, Richard Cieslak, traveled widely training people in Grotowski's methods.

Theater of Images

Robert Wilson experimented in the 1970s, 1980s, and 1990s with repetitive narratives that sometimes take eight hours to perform. His multimedia dramas involve huge casts and ordinarily cover an immense historical range (Figure 30). One of his most extraordinary successes was *Einstein on the Beach* (1976), an opera written in collaboration with composer Philip Glass. Eight hours long, it was originally produced in a conventional theater, but it uses dramatic techniques that involve extensive patterns of repetition, the creation of enigmatic and evocative images, and characters who are cartoonlike caricatures of historical people. The overall effect is hypnotic; one of the points of Wilson's work seems to be to induce a trancelike state in his audience. One of his multimedia productions, *CIVIL warS* (1983), continued to develop this concept of massive theater that transcends conventional dramatic boundaries. In 1994 Wilson produced a monologue version of *Hamlet* that received some acclaim.

Gay and Lesbian Theater and Other New Ensembles

Some of the most energetic theater of the late twentieth century came from groups that were excluded for long periods from representation in mainstream theater. Gay, lesbian, African American, Hispanic American, and Native American groups have been virtually ignored by commercial theater and as a result have formed their own collectives and groups.

One reason for the development of gay theater in the United States and Great Britain in the 1960s was the decriminalization of homosexuality beginning in 1967 in Boston. Depiction of homosexual love onstage waited even longer, until the Gay Workshop's plays in London beginning in 1976. The first openly gay play was Mart Crowley's *The Boys in the Band* (1968), a popular success produced just after the repeal of a New York law prohibiting homosexuality from being represented on stage.

The Ridiculous Theatrical Company, founded by Charles Ludlam (1940–1987) in 1969, produced a formidable body of work rooted in the experiences of the homosexual community of New York. Its influence spread to many parts of the world. One of Ludlam's catchphrases was "plays without the stink of art." His plays were often ridiculously funny. *Bluebeard* (1970), for example, focused on creating a third gender by inventing a third genital. *Camille* (1973), starring Ludlam himself in the title role, hilariously spoofed not only Dumas's play but most of the "Hallmark card" conventions about romantic love. A gifted female impersonator, Ludlam played Hedda Gabler at the American Ibsen Theatre in Pittsburgh. Under the direction of Ludlam's partner, Everett Quinton, the Ridiculous Theatrical Company continues to produce Ludlam's plays as well as new plays in his tradition.

Solidarity: A labor-organizing movement in Communist Poland led by Lech Walesa.

FIGURE 30. Multimedia
effects in Robert Wilson's
CIVIL warS.

Some of the most highly praised plays of the 1980s and 1990s addressed the
issues of AIDS and its ravaging of the gay community. Harvey Fierstein's *Torch
Song Trilogy* (1982) was named best play of the year and appeared several
years later on television. *As Is* by William M. Hoffman (1985) has been
described by Don Shewey as the "best gay play anyone has written on AIDS
yet." Tony Kushner dazzled New York with *Angels in America Part One: Millennium Approaches* (1992) and *Part Two: Perestroika* (1992). This two-part
drama approached the problems of gay life in America on both a personal and
a public, political level. The plays are called a "fantasia" and use a free-form,
nonrealistic style of presentation. In late 2003, HBO produced an award-
winning version for television starring Al Pacino and Meryl Streep.

Lesbian theatrical groups have sprung up in the United States and Great
Britain. They often merge with women's theater groups and address issues such
as male violence, societal restrictions on women, and women's opportunities.
A number of important collectives, such as the Rhode Island Women's Theater
and At the Foot of the Mountain in Minneapolis, treated general women's
issues in the 1970s. Groups such as Medusa's Revenge (founded 1976) and

Atlanta's Red Dyke Theater (1974) centered more on lesbian experience. These last two groups disbanded after a few years of successful productions. Megan Terry's Omaha Magic Theater, founded with Joanne Schmidman, has been a long-lasting theater focusing on women's issues. Other groups such as Spider-woman, consisting of three Native American sisters, and the highly successful Split Britches consider Cafe WOW in New York's East Village to be the home of lesbian theater. Gay and lesbian theater groups have often been concerned with erasing stereotypes while also celebrating gay and lesbian lifestyles. Plays that once played only to gay and lesbian audiences — such as Martin Sherman's (b. 1939) *Bent* (1977) and Larry Kramer's (b. 1935) *The Normal Heart* (1985) — are now performed in theaters worldwide.

Other important women playwrights have made their mark in contemporary theater, with plays such as María Irene Fornés's *Fefu and Her Friends* (1977), a sprawling play featuring women in roles traditionally reserved for men. It has become a cult classic, with many productions in regional theaters. Her *The Conduct of Life* (1985) is a cruel parody of macho values in a Latin American dictatorship. It won an Obie Award for best play of the year. Caryl Churchill has been a dominant figure in British drama since the first production of *Cloud Nine* (1979), a drama that critiques colonialism and gender stereotyping. *Top Girls* (1982) is one of her most successful plays. It centers on an employment agency for women but has as its premise the introduction of famous women from the past of several cultures. It is a powerful feminist statement. *Fen* (1983), *Serious Money* (1987), and *The Skriker* (1994) have solidified her reputation as an experimental, powerful dramatist. Marsha Norman's *Getting Out* (1977), *'night Mother* (1982), and *The Secret Garden* (1991) have been produced to considerable acclaim. Norman has become an important presence in American drama. Emily Mann's *Execution of Justice* (1983) centers on the trial of Dan White, who murdered Harvey Milk, an openly gay San Francisco city councilman. Anne Devlin's *Ourselves Alone* (1986); Lynn Siefert's *Coyote Ugly* (1986); Tina Howe's *Painting Churches* (1982); Anna Deavere Smith's *Fires in the Mirror: Crown Heights, Brooklyn and Other Identities* (1991) and *Twilight: Los Angeles 1992* (1992); Suzan-Lori Parks's *The Death of the Last Black Man in the Whole Entire World* (1990), *The America Play* (1993), *Venus* (1996), *In the Blood* (1999), and *Topdog/Underdog* (2001), which won the Pulitzer Prize for Drama, the first for a black woman; Dael Orlandersmith's *Yellowman* (2000); Lynn Nottage's *Crumbs from the Table of Joy* (1995) and *Intimate Apparel* (2004); and Sarah Ruhl's *The Clean House* (2004) and *Eurydice* (2006) have all enhanced the stature of women in contemporary theater.

Through the 1970s, 1980s, and 1990s numerous black theatrical groups developed in many parts of the world. An important Afro-Caribbean theater group was formed in the Keskidee Center in North London, with Edgar White (b. 1947) as one of its directors. White's plays are often centered in Caribbean mystical experiences, including Rastafarianism. *The Nine Night* (1983), produced in London, focuses on a Jamaican funeral tradition designed to help the deceased enter the gates of heaven.

Experiments with Theater Space

Drama around the world has developed alternatives to the proscenium theater. Theater in the round, which seats audiences on all sides of the actors, has been exceptionally powerful for certain plays. Peter Weiss's *The Persecution and*

Assassination of Jean-Paul Marat as Performed by the Inmates of the Asylum of Charenton under the Direction of the Marquis de Sade (1964) was especially effective in this format. Other theatrical experiments explored the power of spaces one would not have thought appropriate for drama. For example, Wladimir Pereira Cardoso designed an elaborate welded-steel set for a production of Jean Genet's *The Balcony* in the Ruth Escobar Theater in São Paulo, Brazil. The set was a huge suspended cone in which people sat looking inward while the actors were suspended in the spherical space before them. The production was first staged in 1969 and was seen through 1971 and most of 1972 by many thousands of people. The set was constructed of eighty tons of iron assembled like a trellis and requiring 500,000 welds. The entire insides of the theater were torn out to accommodate the new set. The audience of 250 was seated on circular platforms and the actors moved through the space on ramps, on suspended cables, and on moving platforms. The same theater produced *The Voyage,* an adaptation of an epic poem, *The Lusiads,* about the origin of Portuguese people. That set used open welded platforms suggesting ships' decks. In Dubrovnik, Yugoslavia, a replica of Columbus's *Santa Maria*—built much larger than the original—was used to stage Miroslav Krleza's expressionist play *Christopher Columbus,* written in 1917. The ship was docked in Dubrovnik Harbor for the performances.

Richard Foreman's Ontological-Hysteric Theatre performs in a loft in New York City with all audience members facing in the same direction. This is not fundamentally different from the traditional proscenium theater, but the open loft space and the visible movements of actors offstage create a new relationship to the action. Foreman's work, such as *Sophia = (Wisdom)* (1970 and later), which has been performed in many parts, has none of the usually accepted narrative clues to its action. However, it aims to explore hitherto hidden aspects of experience, such as sexual taboos and unorthodox relationships. The relationship of the author to the performance is also experimental in his theater, since he directs his actors, often using a loud buzzer, as if they were extensions of his will. His work, begun in the 1960s, has continued to this day. He collaborated in the staging of Suzan-Lori Parks's *Venus* (1996).

Experimentation within the Tradition

Much of the powerful and lasting drama of the 1980s and 1990s through the early years of the twenty-first century has been achieved in a proscenium theater, using traditional methods of DRAMATURGY, the craft or techniques of dramatic composition. Contemporary dramatists are by no means shy of experimentation, but they are also sensitive to the continuing resources of the traditional stage as it was conceived by Chekhov and Ibsen and Miller. Marsha Norman, who wrote *'night, Mother,* has said that her plays are "wildly traditional. I'm a purist about structure. Plays are like plane rides. You [the audience] buy the ticket and you have to get where the ticket takes you. Or else you've been had."

Sam Shepard, one of the most prolific modern playwrights, experiments with his material, much of which premiered in small theaters in Greenwich Village, such as the La Mama Experimental Theater Club. But his most widely known plays, among them *Buried Child* (1978), are produced easily on conventional stages. Shepard's work is wide-ranging and challenging. His language is coarse, a representation of the way he has heard people speak, and the violence he portrays onstage is strong enough to alienate many in the audience. Shepard, important as he is, has not found a popular commercial audience for his plays. At root, his work is always experimental.

Brian Friel (b. 1929) began his career as an experimentalist in *Philadelphia, Here I Come!* (1964), in which Gar O'Donnell, the main character, appears both as his public self, represented by one actor, and as his private self, represented by another actor. This experimental drama ran for 326 performances on Broadway. Friel's political drama *Freedom of the City* (1974) addressed the "troubles" in Northern Ireland at a time of bombings and threats. *Translations* (1980) experiments with language—having Irish-speaking characters speak Irish to one another to baffle the British characters, while we "listen in" as if the Irish were being translated for us. *Faith Healer* (1979) presents characters onstage one at a time—with no interaction—telling us their stories in a powerful way. Throughout his career, Friel has been on the edge of experiment.

Athol Fugard, a South African, writes powerful plays that also work well on conventional proscenium stages. Like Shepard's, his subject matter is not the kind that permits an audience to sit back relaxed and appreciate the drama with a sense of detachment. Instead, the plays usually disturb audiences. His primary subject matter is the devastation—for blacks and whites—caused by apartheid in South Africa. Fugard's work with black actors in South Africa produced a vital experimental theater out of which his best early work grew.

Fugard's *The Blood Knot* (1961) and *Boesman and Lena* (1969), part of a trilogy on South Africa, are based on the theme of racial discrimination. But other plays, such as *A Lesson from Aloes* (1978) and *My Children! My Africa!* (1989), are involved with problems of individuals in relation to their political world. Fugard is in many ways a traditional playwright, except for his subject matter. His characters are thoroughly developed, but with great economy. In *"MASTER HAROLD"* . . . *and the boys,* for example, we are given a deep understanding of Hally and Sam, whose relationship, past, present, and future, is the center of the play. Fugard is not writing the well-made play, any more than the other contemporary playwrights in this collection are. There is nothing "mechanical" in Fugard's work but rather a sense of organic growth, of actions arising from perceptible conditions and historical circumstances. These contribute to the sense of integrity that his plays communicate.

Some of Caryl Churchill's plays, emphasizing themes of socialism, colonialism, and feminism, were developed in workshops and collaborations with actors and directors. When writing a play, she experiments early in the first stages by spending time in the environments her plays depict. When she worked on *Top Girls* (1982), she came up with the idea of setting the action in an employment agency after she had talked with many people whose lives are wrapped up in business. For *Serious Money* (1987), she and the group developing the play spent time at the London Stock Exchange, absorbing the atmosphere of frenetic buying and selling.

Although she claims to be a traditionalist, Marsha Norman has written experimental plays. Her first success, *Getting Out* (1977), portrays the same character at two periods in her life—as an adolescent and as an adult—on separate parts of the stage at the same time. Norman's *'night, Mother* is another traditionally structured play. It respects the Aristotelian unities of time, place, and action, and it is confrontational. Thelma and her daughter,

Jessie, are in a power struggle over Jessie's right to commit suicide. The technique is naturalistic, and the play's subject matter, as in the plays of Strindberg and Ibsen, is discomforting to its contemporary audiences.

August Wilson's series of ten plays treats the subject of black life in modern America. He completed the Pittsburgh Cycle just before he died in 2005, and each of the first four won the New York Drama Critics' Circle Award for best play of the year. All of Wilson's plays have explored the way the heritage of blacks enables them to live intelligently in the present, with understanding and dignity. People in his plays have lost touch with the past and, for that reason, risk a loss of self-understanding. Wilson's plays also show the pain endured by blacks in an America that is supposed to be the land of opportunity. Like Arthur Miller in *Death of a Salesman* and Lorraine Hansberry in *A Raisin in the Sun,* Wilson explores the nature and consequences of the American dream, especially for those effectively excluded from this dream. Blacks' frustration, exploitation, and suffering are presented in Wilson's powerful characters, such as Troy Maxson in *Fences* (1985). Troy is a garbage collector who was a star baseball player at a time when blacks could play only in their own leagues. (The major leagues were exclusively white until 1947, when Jackie Robinson joined the Brooklyn Dodgers and the game began to be integrated.) The play centers on Maxson's anger, his pride in his family, and his concerns for his son, who is growing up into a world in which he must empower himself to achieve what he most wants for himself. Cory, Troy's son, does not see the same kind of discrimination and has not felt the unfairness that was Troy's primary experience in growing up. Showing the world as Troy Maxson sees it is one of the functions of the play.

Wilson's plays have a naturalistic surface, but they also allude to the supernatural, as in *The Piano Lesson* (1990). Some of the roots of this tradition are in the black church and some in African religion, a source shared by Soyinka and Wilson, among others.

Among current playwrights, David Henry Hwang has been active in writing for both stage and film. His work has often centered on Chinese Americans and the problems they encounter in their experiences in the United States. Hwang has sensitized audiences to subjects about which playwrights had hitherto been silent. His first success, *FOB* (1980), focused on how new immigrants were viewed by Chinese Americans who had already assimilated. The play's title is an acronym for "fresh off the boat." Hwang's most successful play, *M. Butterfly* (1987), is about a romance between a French diplomat and a transvestite Chinese opera singer.

Since his short but intense *The Zoo Story* (1958), Edward Albee has been a powerful force in American theater. He has won three Pulitzer Prizes for drama: for *A Delicate Balance* (1966), *Seascape* (1974), and *Three Tall Women* (1991). He is better known for *Who's Afraid of Virginia Woolf?* (1961), however, a portrait of a violent, alcohol-filled academic marriage between George and Martha, portrayed memorably by Richard Burton and Elizabeth Taylor in Mike Nichols's 1966 film version. Not all his plays have been successful, but throughout his career he has maintained a reputation as an important experimentalist. His Tony Award–winning play *The Goat, or Who Is Sylvia?* (2002) is a complex portrait of a prize-winning architect who falls in love with a goat. Albee thus pushes beyond the questions of hetero- or homosexuality into the taboo of bestiality. Beneath the surface, however, he presses the issues of tragedy as it is expressed in a modern situation.

David Mamet responds to a social situation in *Oleanna* (1992). The characters, a male college professor and a female student, at first adopt an ordinary teacher-student relationship; eventually, though, that relationship alters. Mamet explores questions of power and issues of sexual harassment. As the lines he draws shift back and forth, the audience never knows exactly how clear the lines are meant to be. The issues in the play are thus subject to a number of different interpretations. Widely considered Mamet's best play, *Glengarry Glen Ross* (1983) offers a savage portrait of the masculine world of salesmanship. Deception, competition, and outright theft dominate the play, demonstrating a failure of values of the main characters, all of whom feel justified in their willingness to push property on those who do not want or need it. Mamet's language carries the weight of a philosophy that scorns the get-ahead attitude of the salesman.

China's most distinguished modern playwright, Gao Xingjian, now lives and writes in Paris, after having lived through the Cultural Revolution of the 1960s, when all his plays and manuscripts were destroyed and he was forced to work as a laborer for several years. His work has been banned in China because it is seen as critical of the communist system in place in that country. Having lived in France since 1987, he has been influenced by playwrights such as Samuel Beckett and Bertolt Brecht. One of his plays, *Bus Stop* (1983), resembles Beckett's *Waiting for Godot* in that his characters wait patiently for the bus to come—a symbol of a positive change in their lives—but it never arrives. *The Other Shore* (1986) explores the religious aspirations of his characters from a perspective of Pure Land Buddhism, the other shore being the land of the dead, a world with ambiguous virtues. Gao is also a novelist and wrote *Soul Mountain* (1989), a best-seller in its English translation (1999). Gao won the Nobel Prize for literature in 2000.

Tony Kushner's two-part drama *Angels in America: Millennium Approaches* (1992) and *Perestroika* (1992) explores issues in modern American history, with an emphasis on religion, politics, and a variety of hysterias. The plays explore homophobia, red-baiting politics, and the impact of AIDS on contemporary society. The open, dynamic structure of the play is enormously powerful. The entire drama lasts six and a half hours and has been seen not only in San Francisco, where it opened, but also in New York, London, other European cities, and regional theaters throughout the United States. The Golden Globe award-winning 2003 HBO production made the play available to many millions of viewers and expanded some of Kushner's vision for the drama. His *Homebody/Kabul* (2001), which examines the political circumstances in Afghanistan in 1998 after American bombing raids, reflects his continuing interest in exploring contemporary historical events; his chamber opera *Caroline, or Change* (2003) considers racial issues in Louisiana in 1963.

In the late 1990s, young men and women made important contributions to theater. José Rivera (b. 1955) presented two plays that drew on the tradition of magic realism that is prominent in Latin American fiction. *Marisol* (1992) and *Cloud Tectonics* (1995) are visually and emotionally impressive pieces that work counter to the Ibsenist tradition of realism. As especially theatrical pieces, they give the director a considerable degree of freedom in staging.

Rivera's *Boleros for the Disenchanted*, staged at the Yale Repertory Theatre in May 2008, treats the subjects of love, aging, and marriage. Yasmina Reza (b. 1959) had great success in France, England, the United States, and many other nations with her award-winning comedy *"Art,"* which raises unexpected questions about taste and friendship. Martin McDonagh (b. 1970) startled the London theater scene with his Leenane trilogy: *The Beauty Queen of Leenane* (1996), *A Skull in Connemara* (1997), and *The Lonesome West* (1997). These three plays and his *The Cripple of Inishmaan* (1996) were produced at the same time in London, a record for a twenty-seven-year-old playwright. His *The Lieutenant of Inishmore* (2003) is a brutal farce centering on IRA terrorism. In 2003 his *The Pillowman* had pedophilia as its subject. McDonagh is one of the most productive modern playwrights. Paula Vogel (b. 1951) created a portrait of an adolescent girl, Li'l Bit, involved with an incestuous Uncle Peck in *How I Learned to Drive* (1997). The play won the 1998 Pulitzer Prize and established Vogel as one of the most important American playwrights. Her play *The Long Christmas Ride Home* (November 2003) continues her experimentation into the realm of puppet theater. The effect recalls techniques of Japanese Bunraku theater.

Nilo Cruz (b. 1961) won the Pulitzer Prize in 2003 for *Anna in the Tropics*. He was the first Hispanic Pulitzer winner in drama. Among his many plays is *Lorca in a Green Dress* (2003), an experiment in literary allusion. The energy of twenty-first-century drama continues to astound audiences. Moisés Kaufman's Tectonic Theater Project began *The Laramie Project* in 1998 after Matthew Shepherd, a homosexual young man, was brutally beaten, tied to a fence, and left to die in Laramie, Wyoming. The group conducted interviews of townspeople for a year and a half and presented the play, which is in some ways a portrait of the community, in Laramie in 2000. It has been televised and seen across the country. Doug Wright created a play, *I Am My Own Wife*, about Charlotte von Mahlsdorf, a transvestite who survived the Nazis and the Russians in Berlin. Directed by Moisés Kaufman, *I Am My Own Wife* won every major award in 2004, including the Pulitzer. The single actor on stage, Jefferson Mays, played dozens of characters, all convincingly. Neil LaBute makes films as well as writing plays. His *The Shape of Things* (2001) uses a highly experimental approach to language in which silences play a profound role as he explores the dark side of femininity and the complexities of art. John Patrick Shanley won the Pulitzer Prize in 2005 for *Doubt,* a play about a Catholic nun's suspicions of the behavior of a priest who befriends a young boy. The staging of the play was traditional, but the subject matter struck a painful note for some audiences. Rolin Jones's experimental and enormously entertaining *The Intelligent Design of Jenny Chow* (2006) resembles a video game, with Jenny creating a robotic other who crosses continents. Suzan-Lori Park's extraordinary experiment, *365 Days / 365 Plays,* involved her writing a play every day for a year. She has permitted groups to stage the plays without royalty, and projects have been established to produce the plays across the country. These, and many more excellent playwrights, are making contemporary drama a powerful force all over the globe.

The Contemporary Theater

Most theaters in the major cities of the world that compare with those on Broadway and London's West End are generally compatible with the needs of the nineteenth-century realist plays, many of which still entertain a wide range of

FIGURE 31.   The Questors
Theatre, Ealing, London,
1964.

audiences. However, modern theaters are not limited to large urban centers, and
those that have been built since the 1950s recognize the needs of experimental
drama as well as traditional drama. For this reason, many contemporary theaters
attempt to accommodate the needs of theater in the round, the thrust theater
(which is virtually in the round), and the proscenium theater, all in one place.
Such a theater is illustrated in Figure 31, The Questors Theatre in Ealing,
London, built in 1964. The illustration shows half of the stage as proscenium and
half as thrust, demonstrating its versatility. Like many regional theaters, this one
does not have a large seating capacity, although it has an unusually large facility
for workshops, rehearsal spaces, and costume construction. The Tyrone Guthrie
Theater in Minneapolis (Figure 32), designed in 1963, has respected the needs of
modern drama for almost fifty years, producing a number of important playwrights who have become significant on the international stage. Its flexible plan
has influenced a number of newer theaters.

The black box theater seems not to have become the widely used space that
writers in the 1960s thought might be the theater of the future. Yet there are a
number of theaters around the world in which the audience essentially sits in a
black box environment with only a minimal setting, and in immediate contact
with the actors, who, in some cases, work around them. Plain spaces such as
lofts and barns and spacious multipurpose rooms still provide venues for new

FIGURE 32. The Tyrone
Guthrie Theater, Minneapolis,
Minnesota, 1963.

and old plays. Small, flexible theaters, such as London's popular Cottesloe, seat three hundred at most, yet their intimacy intensifies the effect of the drama.

Proscenium theaters probably make up the largest number of dramatic spaces even today because of the large number of restored theaters whose designs generally date to the era of the Drury Lane Theatre renovations in the late eighteenth and early nineteenth centuries. Many forms of technical innovations, such as portable microphones, elaborate methods of flying actors, and stage effects such as fog and stage flooding, have made it possible for audiences in larger theaters to feel closely connected with the dramatic action. Techniques that simulate heavy rainfall on stage, as in Sarah Ruhl's *Eurydice,* in which Orpheus, when descending to the underworld, arrives in a stunning downpour in an elevator (Figure 33), create a most striking effect and would have been difficult, if not impossible, in earlier centuries. Music and dance are central to some contemporary dramas that are not considered musicals, such as Wole Soyinka's *The Lion and the Jewel.* Sound systems in modern theaters accommodate the most difficult audio challenges. Video is common in the theater, whether in the

FIGURE 33. Orpheus (played by Joseph Parks) descending into the underworld in a rainy elevator in the Yale Repertory Theatre's 2006 performance of Sarah Ruhl's *Eurydice*.

form of projections on scrims or of working television sets in living rooms or bedrooms on stage. Complex lighting and shifting scene changes can be made convincingly realistic. What Aristotle called "spectacle" has been available in most ages in the theater, but the technology of the electronic age provides resources never before possible. Yet even so, a great many successful dramatists insist on the simplest of dramatic effect and the simplest of theatrical spaces.

The Contemporary Actor

For the most part, the ambition of eighteenth-century British actor David Garrick to create a style of acting that is as natural as everyday life has been the goal for most contemporary actors. Marlon Brando in Tennessee Williams's *A Streetcar Named Desire* put Stanislavsky's theories of acting to work and became celebrated as a Method actor. He studied at the Actors Studio, which was founded by Elia Kazan and others but later run and developed by Lee Strasberg with other important teachers such as Sanford Meisner. The modern Method involved relaxation techniques, memory exercises, and a great deal of self-analysis. The point, as Stanislavsky said, was to recreate in oneself the life of the character on stage.

Marlon Brando became the first widely celebrated Method actor, and his particular style, of mumbling lines or moodily half-articulating them, became

FIGURE 34.   Al Pacino as salesman Erie Smith in Eugene O'Neill's *Hughie* (1996) at Circle in the Square Theater.

associated unfairly with Method acting. James Dean, who was a film star rather than a stage star, emulated him and made it seem all the more certain that Brando's style was that of the Method actor. But other Method actors, such as Al Pacino (Figure 34), who has done some important stage work, particularly in his performance in Eugene O'Neill's *Hughie* in 1996, also studied with Lee Strasberg. Pacino can be seen online in a video on YouTube reading and discussing the play.

Among the great actors to have worked in the Actors Studio, Lee J. Cobb seems to have influenced a number of later actors, such as George C. Scott in the 1960s. Robert de Niro, Ellen Burstyn, Jane Fonda, Paul Newman, Joanne Woodward, Maureen Stapleton, Rod Steiger, Christopher Walken, Mickey Rourke, Julia Roberts, Harvey Keitel, Sidney Poitier, Jack Nicholson, Steve McQueen, and Marilyn Monroe were all products of the Actors Studio. The influence of the Method is still present in contemporary drama.

In England, however, the traditional training of actors continues. Whereas Method acting concentrates on the inner potential of the actor's psyche, the Royal Academy of Dramatic Arts in London and the London Academy of Music and Dramatic Arts train actors in the traditional basics, such as dance and movement, voice and projection, analysis of texts, and the study of the techniques of the best historical actors. John Gielgud, Laurence Olivier, Jeremy Irons, and Judi Dench (Figure 35) are products of such training. Sometimes their techniques are described as being external—they are "applied" outwardly as a means of creating the character on stage—as opposed to the internal process of the Method

FIGURE 35.   Judi Dench
as Viola with Gordon Reid
as Sebastian in the 1969
production of *Twelfth Night*
at the Royal Shakespeare
Theatre.

actor. Both techniques work well on the modern stage, and some actors (such as
Johnny Depp and Julianne Moore) use them both.

The purpose of the actor is to create character and to hope that we will
believe the character rather than the actor. And in the dramas that disregard
psychological realism, the purpose of the actor is to stimulate the audience into
recognition of the power of the drama itself, to interpret the action in an
authentic and honest fashion.

Contemporary Drama Timeline

DATE	THEATER	POLITICAL	SOCIAL/CULTURAL
1950–present	**1951:** Anna Deavere Smith, African American playwright and actress, born. Among her works are *Fires in the Mirror* (1991) and *Twilight: Los Angeles, 1992* (1992).	**1950:** U.S. Senator Joseph McCarthy begins his war on Communism by investigating the alleged "un-American activities" of hundreds of U.S. citizens.	**1950:** Simone de Beauvoir (1908–1986), French author, publishes *The Second Sex*.
	1951: Lee Strasberg becomes artistic director of the Actors Studio in New York.	**1951:** The USSR explodes its first atomic bomb.	**1952:** Ralph Ellison (1914–1994), African American novelist, publishes *Invisible Man*.
	1954: Joseph Papp founds the New York Shakespeare festival.	**1953:** Joseph Stalin dies. **1954:** *Brown v. Board of Education* finds school segregation unconstitutional.	**1954:** Elvis Presley (1935–1977) makes his first recording at Sun Studios.
	1956: John Osborne's *Look Back in Anger* is produced in London.	**1954:** Senator Joseph McCarthy's witch hunt for Communist infiltration in the United States ends.	
	1956: Tony Kushner, American playwright, born. He is best known for the plays *Angels in America, Parts 1 and 2* (1992).	**1955:** Communist Eastern European allies sign the Warsaw Pact. **1955:** Montgomery, Alabama, bus boycott	**1957:** Jack Kerouac (1922–1969) publishes *On the Road*.
	1959: Jerzy Grotowski establishes the Laboratory Theatre in Poland. In 1968 he publishes *Towards a Poor Theatre*.	**1958:** Fidel Castro begins total war against Batista in Cuba; in 1959 he becomes premier.	
	1960s: Off-Off-Broadway flourishes with the formation of such groups as Café Cino (1958), La Mama ETC (1962), the Open Theatre (1963), and the Performance Group (1967).	**1958–1969:** Charles de Gaulle is president of France. **1960:** The Belgian Congo is granted independence.	
	1962: Peter Schumann founds the Bread and Puppet Theatre, an influential political ensemble, in New York City.	**1961:** The Berlin Wall blocks movement to and from East and West Germany.	
	1963: The National Theatre is established in London under the direction of Laurence Olivier.	**1962:** The cold war reaches one of its tensest moments when the United States confronts the USSR over Soviet nuclear missile bases in Cuba.	**1962:** James Watson and Francis Crick share the Nobel Prize for defining the 3-D molecular structure of DNA. **1962:** César Chávez (1927–1993) organizes California migrant farm workers.
	1964: Ariane Mnouchkine forms the Théâtre du Soleil in Paris.	**1962:** The first U.S. combat troops are sent to fight in South Vietnam.	**1962:** Alexander Solzhenitsyn's *One Day in the Life of Ivan Denisovich* describes life in the Soviet gulag.
	1964: Peter Brook's production of Peter Weiss's *Marat/Sade* opens at the Royal Shakespeare Company.	**1963:** President John F. Kennedy is assassinated in Dallas. **1965:** Malcolm X is assassinated in New York.	**1964:** The Beatles appear on *The Ed Sullivan Show*. **1965:** The National Endowment for the Arts is established by the U.S. government.

Contemporary Drama Timeline (continued)

DATE	THEATER	POLITICAL	SOCIAL/CULTURAL
1950–present (continued)	**1968:** The Negro Ensemble Company is established in the United States under the direction of Douglas Turner Ward.	**1967:** In the Six-Day War, Israel responds to Arab provocation by capturing territory from Egypt, Syria, and Jordan.	**1966:** The National Organization for Women (NOW) is established to end discrimination against women.
	1968: The Living Theatre produces its highly influential experimental work *Paradise Now*.	**1967:** Thurgood Marshall (1908–1993) is the first African American appointed to the U.S. Supreme Court.	**1967:** Dr. Christiaan N. Barnard performs the world's first human heart transplant operation in South Africa.
	1968: Theatrical censorship, in place since the Licensing Act of 1737, is finally abolished in England.	**1968:** The American civil rights leader Martin Luther King Jr. is assassinated.	
	1968: *Hair!*, the first rock musical, hits Broadway; it is followed by *Jesus Christ Superstar* in 1971.	**1968:** Students demonstrate throughout France.	**1969:** U.S. astronaut Neil Armstrong walks on the moon.
	1968: The Performance Group produces *Dionysus in 69* under the direction of Richard Schechner.	**1970–1975:** Civil war is fought in Cambodia; Communist leader Pol Pot takes power in 1975 and begins genocidal campaign.	**1969:** New York City police raid the Stonewall Inn, and the resulting three-day protest becomes a symbol for the emerging gay rights movement.
	1970: Peter Brook's acclaimed production of *A Midsummer Night's Dream* opens at the Royal Shakespeare Company.	**1972:** U.S. President Richard Nixon and Soviet leader Leonid Brezhnev sign the Strategic Arms Limitation Treaty (SALT).	
		1972: Philippine President Ferdinand Marcos declares martial law and assumes dictatorial powers.	
		1973: In *Roe v. Wade*, the U.S. Supreme Court legalizes abortion.	
		1973: U.S. troops are withdrawn from Vietnam.	
		1974: President Nixon resigns from office as a result of the Watergate scandal.	
	1975: Michael Bennett's musical *A Chorus Line* opens on Broadway and runs until 1990.	**1975:** The Spanish dictator Francisco Franco dies.	**1976:** The Episcopal Church approves the ordination of women to be priests and bishops.
		1976: The Chinese Communist leader Mao Zedong dies. Deng Xiaoping emerges as the new Chinese leader in 1978.	
	1978: Harold Pinter's *Betrayal* premieres at the National Theatre in London.	**1976:** Waves of violence against apartheid in Cape Town, Soweto, and Johannesburg, South Africa	

Contemporary Drama Timeline (continued)

DATE	THEATER	POLITICAL	SOCIAL/CULTURAL
1950–present (continued)	**1979:** Caryl Churchill's *Cloud Nine* premieres. **1979:** Stephen Sondheim's *Sweeney Todd* opens on Broadway. Other musicals by the prolific composer include *Sunday in the Park with George* (1984), *Into the Woods* (1987), and *Passion* (1995). **1980:** Sam Shepard's *True West* premieres.	**1979:** After the overthrow of Shah Mohammad Reza Pahlavi, the Ayatollah Khomeini establishes the Islamic Republic of Iran. **1980:** The Iran-Iraq War begins when Iraq invades Iran; the war lasts for eight years.	
	1982: Athol Fugard's *"MASTER HAROLD"... and the boys* premieres at the Yale Repertory Theatre. **1983:** Marsha Norman's *'night, Mother* opens at New York's Golden Theater and wins the Pulitzer Prize. **1985:** August Wilson's *Fences* premieres at the Yale Repertory Theatre and wins the Pulitzer Prize in 1987. **1987:** The immensely popular Broadway adaptation of Victor Hugo's *Les Misérables* opens, ultimately closing in March 2003.	**1981:** General Idi Amin begins his eight-year reign of terror in Uganda. **1981:** Egyptian leader Anwar Sadat is assassinated by Muslim extremists. **1985:** Mikhail Gorbachev becomes the leader of the Soviet Union and institutes a policy of *glasnost* (openness). **1989:** A student demonstration in Beijing's Tiananmen Square results in bloodshed. **1989:** Communism crumbles in Eastern Europe, and the Berlin Wall is torn down.	**1981:** Sandra Day O'Connor becomes the first woman appointed to the U.S. Supreme Court. **1981:** IBM markets its first personal computer. **1982:** Wisconsin becomes the first state to protect gays and lesbians under civil rights legislation. **1986:** In *Bowers v. Hardwick,* the U.S. Supreme Court upholds the constitutionality of the Georgia state law against sodomy. **1986:** The U.S. space shuttle *Challenger* explodes seconds after liftoff, killing all seven on board.
	1990s: In a proliferation of Shakespeare on film, new versions of *Hamlet, Henry V, Much Ado about Nothing, Othello,* and *Richard III* are released.	**1990:** Iraq invades Kuwait, which leads to the Gulf War in 1991. **1990:** East and West Germany reunite after 45 years of separation. **1990:** The South African nationalist leader Nelson Mandela is released from prison. **1990–1991:** South Africa repeals its apartheid laws. **1991:** The Soviet Union collapses. U.S. President George H. W. Bush officially recognizes the twelve new countries created as a result.	**1990:** Octavio Paz, Mexican poet, receives the Nobel Prize for literature. **1990:** The National Endowment for the Arts is attacked when controversial awards are publicized.

Contemporary Drama Timeline (continued)

DATE	THEATER	POLITICAL	SOCIAL/CULTURAL
1950–present (continued)	**1992:** David Mamet's *Oleanna* premiers off-Broadway and runs for over 250 performances.	**1991:** Yugoslavia dissolves. Croatia, Slovenia, Bosnia-Herzegovina, and Macedonia declare independence, and bitter fighting ensues for several years.	**1993:** Toni Morrison (b. 1931), African American novelist, is awarded the Nobel Prize for literature.
	1996: Jonathan Larson's *Rent,* a musical based on Puccini's *La Bohème,* wins the Pulitzer Prize.	**1994:** Nelson Mandela (b. 1918) is elected the first black president of South Africa after that nation's first multiracial elections.	**mid-1990s:** *Internet* and *World Wide Web* become household words.
	1997: Martin McDonagh, at age 27, has four plays running simultaneously in London.	**1994:** Chechnya declares independence from Russia; Russian troops invade the republic in 1994 and again in 1999.	
	1998: Paula Vogel's play *How I Learned to Drive* wins the Pulitzer Prize.	**1995:** The Israeli leader Yitzhak Rabin is assassinated.	**1995:** Shannon Faulkner is the first woman to be admitted to the Citadel military academy.
	1998: Yasmina Reza's *"Art"* wins a Tony Award for best play.	**1997:** Hong Kong is returned to China after 156 years as a British colony.	**1995:** The National Endowment for the Arts budget is slashed by the newly elected Republican Congress. The Public Broadcasting Corporation and the National Endowment for the Humanities also come under fire.
	2000: Lee Blessing's *Cobb* makes a political statement about baseball.	**1998:** Asian nations face dramatic recession after economic booms of the 1980s and early 1990s.	
	2000: Gao Xingjian wins Nobel Prize for literature.	**1999:** Congress impeaches President Clinton for his improper conduct in the White House, but the president remains in office.	**1996:** In *Rome v. Evans,* the U.S. Supreme Court rules that the equal protection clause of the Constitution applies to lesbians and gay men.
	2002: Suzan-Lori Parks's *Topdog/Underdog* wins the Pulitzer Prize.	**1999:** U.N. troops keep a tentative peace between ethnic Albanians and Serbian Albanians in Kosovo.	**1997:** Scottish scientist Ian Wilmot clones a sheep.
	2002: Edward Albee's *The Goat, or Who Is Sylvia?* wins Drama Desk Award for best play.	**1999:** The United States transfers the Panama Canal to Panama.	**2001:** The human genome is decoded.
	2003: Nilo Cruz's *Anna in the Tropics* wins the Pulitzer Prize.	**2000:** Boris Yeltsin resigns as president of Russia.	**2003:** A law barring partial-birth abortions comes under fire with legal challenges.
	2004: Doug Wright's *I Am My Own Wife* wins the Pulitzer Prize.	**2001:** On September 11, Al Qaeda terrorists destroy the World Trade Center with two airliners. A third plane damages the Pentagon.	**2004:** Spirit and Rover explore the surface of Mars, sending back 3-D images.
	2007: David Lindsay-Abaire's *Rabbit Hole* wins the Pulitzer Prize.	**2002:** U.S. attacks Taliban forces in Afghanistan.	**2007:** China launches its first lunar orbiter in preparation to put a man on the moon in 2020.
	2008: Conor McPherson's *The Seafarer* produced on Broadway.	**2003:** U.S. attacks Saddam Hussein in Iraq, bringing down his government.	
		2008: Iraqi insurgency continues to destabilize the government.	

Luis Valdez

Luis Valdez, one of ten children, was born in 1940 in Delano, California, to *campesinos,* or farm workers. When he was six years old, he watched a teacher use part of a paper bag to make papier-mâché masks for a theater production. This experience transformed his world view and eventually led him to the theater. His experiences in the fields, however, lasted until he was eighteen, when he went to San Jose State College. Although he began college as a math and physics major, in deference to his parents, after less than a year at San Jose State he joined the theater and declared a major in English. He wrote and acted in plays at San Jose State, where his first full-length play, *The Shrunken Head of Pancho Villa* (1964), was produced.

After college he joined the famous San Francisco Mime Troupe. In 1965, still a member of César Chávez's United Farm Workers Union, he founded El Teatro Campesino, or the Farm Workers Theater, for which he became artistic director and playwright. The theater, which has won a number of awards and is now part of the Mexican American Centro Campesino Cultural in Fresno, began as a theater for striking farm workers and their union, earning money for the union and spreading news about its activities. Eventually, Valdez began writing plays on a number of related subjects, such as the Vietnam War in *Dark Root of a Scream* (1967). He wrote several plays in a form he called *mito,* or myth. One of them, *Bernabé* (1970), introduced a figure who was a zoot suiter and focused on historical issues concerning Chicanos. Another of his important plays, *Los Vendidos (The Sellouts),* was written in 1967 and continues to be performed.

In 1978, Valdez produced *Zoot Suit,* his first major success; he went on to write *Bandido!* (1982), which he calls "an antimelodrama," about a Mexican bandit named Tiburcio Vásquez, who holds the unpleasant distinction of having been, in 1875, the last man publicly executed by the law in San Jose, California. *I Don't Have to Show You No Stinking Badges!* (1986), set in California during Ronald Reagan's presidency, concerns Buddy Villa and his wife Connie, who have spent their working lives as extras in TV and films. Videotaped inserts and music make this play a multimedia experience.

In addition to his activities as a playwright, Luis Valdez also directs films and plays. He directed the film *Zoot Suit* (1981) and the film *La Bamba* (1987), the biography of the Mexican American rock 'n' roll singer Richie Valens, who died in a plane crash with Buddy Holly in 1959. Valdez also wrote the script for that film. In 1987, he produced a television version of his 1983 play *Corridos! Tales of Passion and Revolution.* Performances of *Corridos!* filled a relatively large house in San Francisco for six months before moving to Los Angeles. Its subject is Mexican history, something many in his audience knew little about. Valdez is currently working on a film on the life of César Chávez.

ZOOT SUIT

In some sense *Zoot Suit* is a musical drama, although it can be read as a straight drama as well. A zoot suit had baggy pleated trousers with narrow, pegged ankles and a jacket with wide lapels and long tails (drape), usually to the back of the knees. With it, a zoot suiter usually wore a gold watch chain that came down almost to the ankles and a hat with a long feather. In 1942 it was the epitome of "cool" in jazz circles and was a style favored by some Chicano youths in Los Angeles. Wartime rationing effectively banned the production of the suit, although demand continued to flout the regulations. El Pachuco in this play is the "spirit" of the zoot suiter, and Henry Reyna is the leader of the zoot suiters, a loosely formed gang.

The language of the play is a dialect that mixes English, Spanish, and Los Angeles Spanish slang. It is called Caló (for California/Los Angeles) or *pachuco*. Valdez makes no effort to translate for English-only speakers, but the sense of the language is generally clear to most audiences.

The play is partially based on the zoot-suit riots in Los Angeles in 1942 in which military personnel stripped the suits from zoot suiters, whom they felt were unpatriotic, and during which a murder was committed. In the play, Henry Reyna is falsely accused and convicted of the murder and is imprisoned until an appeal can demonstrate that he was not involved in the crime. The play itself investigates the hopes and yearnings of Henry Reyna and his friends and family. The structure of the play takes us from a dance hall in Los Angeles to a court for the trial, and then to San Quentin prison where Henry becomes close friends with Alice, a member of the press who buoys his hopes for justice.

Justice, however, seems less and less likely to be accorded to Henry, partly because the "system" needs a scapegoat, and Henry is available. But Henry has to make choices for himself, and in the process he changes some of his thinking. Although Henry eventually wins his appeal, the play ends without an ending. Instead of one ending, Valdez provides several possibilities, depending on who you think Henry Reyna is: a leader, victim, warrior, friend, or someone else. The audience decides.

Zoot Suit in Performance

Zoot Suit opened on July 30, 1978, in Los Angeles and played to full houses for almost a year. It then moved to a Broadway production in New York, where it ran for a month. It remains the first and only Chicano play to have been performed on Broadway. Luis Valdez directed the film version of the play in 1981 with Daniel Valdez, his brother, in the role of Henry Reyna. Daniel Valdez also composed the music for the film. Despite the obvious challenges in producing *Zoot Suit,* the play continues to be staged. El Teatro Campesino produced the play in San Juan Bautista, California, in late 2002. Illinois State University staged the play in November 2003 as part of its "new vision of multiculturalism."

Luis Valdez (b. 1940)

ZOOT SUIT

Characters

EL PACHUCO°
HENRY REYNA

His Family:
ENRIQUE REYNA
DOLORES REYNA
LUPE REYNA
RUDY REYNA

His Friends:
GEORGE SHEARER
ALICE BLOOMFIELD

His Gang:
DELLA BARRIOS
SMILEY TORRES
JOEY CASTRO
TOMMY ROBERTS
ELENA TORRES
BERTHA VILLARREAL

The Downey Gang:
RAFAS
RAGMAN
HOBO
CHOLO
ZOOTER
GÜERA
HOBA
BLONDIE
LITTLE BLUE

Detectives:
LIEUTENANT EDWARDS
SERGEANT SMITH

The Press:
PRESS
CUB REPORTER
NEWSBOY

The Court:
JUDGE F. W. CHARLES
BAILIFF

The Prison:
GUARD

The Military:
BOSUN'S MATE
SAILORS
MARINE
SWABBIE
MANCHUKA
SHORE PATROLMAN

Others:
GIRLS
PIMP
CHOLO

Setting: *The giant facsimile of a newspaper front page serves as a drop curtain.*

The huge masthead reads: LOS ANGELES HER-ALD EXPRESS Thursday, June 3, 1943.

A headline cries out: ZOOT-SUITER HORDES IN-VADE LOS ANGELES. U.S. NAVY AND MARINES ARE CALLED IN.

Behind this are black drapes creating a place of haunting shadows larger than life. The somber shapes and outlines of pachuco images hang subtly, black on black, against a background of heavy fabric evoking memories and feelings like an old suit hanging forgotten in the depths of a closet somewhere, sometime. . . . Below this is a sweeping, curving place of levels and rounded corners with the hard, ingrained brilliance of countless spit shines, like the memory of a dance hall.

ACT 1 • Prologue

(A switchblade plunges through the newspaper. It slowly cuts a rip to the bottom of the drop. To the sounds of "Perdido" by Duke Ellington, El Pachuco

El Pachuco: For some people the word *pachuco* indicates someone from El Paso. However, it also refers to a specific form of Chicano subculture that was prevalent in the 1940s in the Southwest. Considered gangsters by some, pachucos were characterized by their distinctive clothing, appearance, and language. Though not the only youth group to wear the zoot suit (an oversized suit), this was one of their cultural practices. They also developed particular versions of Spanish dialect. Some scholars call it Caló and trace it back to the language of gypsies in Spain; others see this language practice as innovation based on the encounter between two cultures, Mexican and American. In this account it is seen as a form of code switching and language adaptation. Regardless of their particular mannerisms, pachucos shared a general distrust of assimilation and insisted on forming their own identity outside of the U.S. mainstream, something that made them suspicious to both the U.S. legal system and Mexicans and Mexican Americans who were trying to assimilate.

*emerges from the slit. He adjusts his clothing, meticu-
lously fussing with his collar, suspenders, cuffs. He tends
to his hair, combing back every strand into a long luxurious ducktail, with infinite loving pains. Then he
reaches into the slit and pulls out his coat and hat. He
dons them. His fantastic costume is complete. It is a
zoot suit. He is transformed into the very image of the
pachuco myth, from his pork-pie hat to the tip of his
four-foot watch chain. Now he turns to the audience.
His three-soled shoes with metal taps click-clack as he
proudly, slovenly, defiantly makes his way downstage.
He stops and assumes a pachuco stance.)*

PACHUCO: ¿Que le watcha a mis trapos, ese?
   ¿Sabe qué, carnal?
   Estas garras me las planté porque
   Vamos a dejarnos caer un play, ¿sabe?

(He crosses to center stage, models his clothes.)

5   Watcha mi tacuche, ese. Aliviánese con mis calcos,
          tando,
       lisa, tramos, y carlango, ese.

(Pause.)

       Nel, sabe qué, usted está muy verdolaga. Como se
          me hace
       que es puro square.°

*(El Pachuco breaks character and addresses the audi-
ence in perfect English.)*

       Ladies and gentlemen
10   the play you are about to see
       is a construct of fact and fantasy.
       The Pachuco Style was an act in Life
       and his language a new creation.
       His will to be was an awesome force
15   eluding all documentation . . .
       A mythical, quizzical, frightening being
       precursor of revolution
       Or a piteous, hideous heroic joke
       deserving of absolution?
20   I speak as an actor on the stage.
       The Pachuco was existential
       for he was an Actor in the streets
       both profane and reverential.
       It was the secret fantasy of every bato
25   in or out of the Chicanada°
       to put on a Zoot Suit and play the Myth
       más chucote que la chingada.°

1, Prologue. 1–8. **¿Que le watcha . . . que es puro square:**
You're looking at my clothes, man? / You know what, brother
(sense of soul brotherhood)? / I dressed up in these duds
because / We are going to drop by a play, you know? Look at
my suit, man. It goes well with my shoes, hat, / shirt, pants, and
coat, dude. No, you know what, you are very inexperienced. It
seems to me / that you're a pure square.   **25. Chicanada:** Chicano world or community.   **27. más chucote que la chingada:**
More pachuco-like than hell.

(Puts hat back on and turns.)

   ¡Pos órale!°

*(Music. The newspaper drop flies. El Pachuco begins his
chuco stroll upstage, swinging his watch chain.)*

Scene 1. Zoot Suit

*(The scene is a barrio dance in the forties. Pachucos and
Pachucas in zoot suits and pompadours.*
   *They are members of the 38th Street Gang, led by
Henry Reyna, 21, dark, Indian-looking, older than his
years, and Della Barrios, 20, his girlfriend in miniskirt
and fingertip coat. A sailor called Swabbie dances with
his girlfriend Manchuka among the Couples. Movement. Animation. El Pachuco sings.)*

PACHUCO: PUT ON A ZOOT SUIT, MAKES YOU
          FEEL REAL ROOT
       LOOK LIKE A DIAMOND, SPARKLING,
          SHINING
       READY FOR DANCING
       READY FOR THE BOOGIE TONIGHT!

*(The Couples, dancing, join the Pachuco in exclaiming
the last term of each line in the next verse.)*

       THE HEPCATS UP IN HARLEM WEAR THAT
          DRAPE SHAPE   5
       COMO LOS PACHUCONES° DOWN IN L.A.
       WHERE HUISAS° IN THEIR POMPADOURS
          LOOK REAL KEEN
       ON THE DANCE FLOOR OF THE
          BALLROOMS
       DONDE BAILAN° SWING.

       YOU BETTER GET HEP TONIGHT   10
       AND PUT ON THAT ZOOT SUIT!

*(The Downey Gang, a rival group of pachucos enters
upstage left. Their quick dance step becomes a challenge
to 38th Street.)*

DOWNEY GANG: Downey . . . ¡Rifa!°
HENRY *(gesturing back)*: ¡Toma!°

*(The music is hot. El Pachuco slides across the floor and
momentarily breaks the tension. Henry warns Rafas, the
leader of the Downey Gang, when he sees him push his
brother Rudy.)*

       ¡Rafas!
PACHUCO *(sings)*: TRUCHA, ESE LOCO, VAMOS AL
          BORLO°   15
       WEAR THAT CARLANGO, TRAMOS Y TANDO

---

28. **¡Pos órale!:** Well listen!   1, 1. 6. **COMO LOS PACHU-
CONES:** Like the pachucos.   7. **HUISAS:** Girls.   9. **DONDE
BAILAN:** Where they dance.   12. **¡Rifa!:** The best. An equivalent expression might be "Rules!"   13. **¡Toma!:** Take that (ref-
erencing the gesture).   15. **TRUCHA . . . AL BORLO:** Hey,
crazy man, we are going to party (dance).

DANCE WITH YOUR HUISA
DANCE TO THE BOOGIE TONIGHT!

'CAUSE THE ZOOT SUIT IS THE STYLE IN
CALIFORNIA
20   TAMBIÉN EN COLORADO Y ARIZONA°
THEY'RE WEARING THAT TACUCHE EN EL
PASO
Y EN TODOS LOS SALONES DE CHICAGO°

YOU BETTER GET HEP TONIGHT
AND PUT ON THAT ZOOT SUIT!

Scene 2. *The Mass Arrests*

(*We hear a siren, then another, and another. It sounds like gangbusters. The dance is interrupted. Couples pause on the dance floor.*)

PACHUCO: Trucha, la jura. ¡Pélenle!°

(*Pachucos start to run out, but Detectives leap onstage with drawn guns. A Cub Reporter takes flash pictures.*)

SGT. SMITH: Hold it right there, kids!
LT. EDWARDS: Everybody get your hands up!
RUDY: Watcha! This way! (*Rudy escapes with some others.*)
5   LT. EDWARDS: Stop or I'll shoot!

(*Edwards fires his revolver into the air. A number of pachucos and their girlfriends freeze. The cops round them up. Swabbie, an American sailor, and Manchuka, a Japanese-American dancer, are among them.*)

SGT. SMITH: ¡Ándale!° (*Sees Swabbie.*) You! Get out of here.
SWABBIE: What about my girl?
SGT. SMITH: Take her with you.

(*Swabbie and Manchuka exit.*)

10   HENRY: What about my girl?
LT. EDWARDS: No dice, Henry. Not this time. Back in line.
SGT. SMITH: Close it up!
LT. EDWARDS: Spread!

(*The Pachucos turn upstage in a line with their hands up. The sirens fade and give way to the sound of a teletype. The Pachucos turn and form a lineup, and the Press starts shooting pictures as he speaks.*)

15   PRESS: The City of the Angels, Monday, August 2, 1942. The *Los Angeles Examiner* Headline:
THE LINEUP (*in chorus*): Death Awakens Sleepy Lagoon (*Breath.*) L.A. Shaken by Lurid "Kid" Murder.

PRESS: The City of the Angels, Monday, August 2, 1942. The *Los Angeles Times* Headline: 20
THE LINEUP: One Killed, Ten Hurt in Boy Wars: (*Breath.*) Mexican Boy Gangs Operating Within City.
PRESS: The City of the Angels, August 2, 1942. *Los Angeles Herald Express* Headline: 25
THE LINEUP: Police Arrest Mexican Youths. Black Widow Girls° in Boy Gangs.
PRESS: The City of the Angels . . .
PACHUCO (*sharply*): El Pueblo de Nuestra Señora la Reina de los Ángeles de Porciúncula, pendejo.°   30
PRESS (*eyeing the Pachuco cautiously*): The *Los Angeles Daily News* Headline:
BOYS IN THE LINEUP: Police Nab 300 in Roundup.
GIRLS IN THE LINEUP: Mexican Girls Picked Up in Arrests.   35
LT. EDWARDS: Press Release, Los Angeles Police Department: A huge showup of nearly 300 boys and girls rounded up by the police and sheriff's deputies will be held tonight at eight o'clock in Central Jail at First and Hill Street. Victims of assault, robbery, purse   40
snatching, and similar crimes are asked to be present for the identification of suspects.
PRESS: Lieutenant . . . ?

(*Edwards poses as the Press snaps a picture.*)

LT. EDWARDS: Thank you.
PRESS: Thank you.   45

(*Smith gives a signal, and the lineup moves back, forming a straight line in the rear, leaving Henry up front by himself.*)

LT. EDWARDS: Move! Turn! Out!

(*As the rear line moves off to the left following Edwards, Smith takes Henry by the arm and pulls him downstage, shoving him to the floor.*)

Scene 3. *Pachuco Yo*

SGT. SMITH: Okay, kid you wait here till I get back. Think you can do that? Sure you can. You pachucos are regular tough guys.

(*Smith exits. Henry sits up on the floor. El Pachuco comes forward.*)

HENRY: Bastards. (*He gets up and paces nervously. Pause.*) ¿Ese? ¿Ese?°   5
PACHUCO (*behind him*): ¿Qué pues, nuez?°

---

20. TAMBIÉN . . . ARIZONA: Also in Colorado and Arizona. 21–22. TACUCHE . . . CHICAGO: Zoot suit in El Paso and in all of the dance halls of Chicago. 1, 2. 1. Trucha . . . ¡Pélenle!: Watch out, the police. Get out of here (beat it)! 6. ¡Ándale!: Move it!

26–27. Black Widow Girls: Female gang whose members' distinctive dress included zoot jackets, short black skirts, and black fishnet stockings. 29–30. El Pueblo de . . . pendejo: The city of Our Lady Queen of the Angels Portiuncula, idiot (the original Spanish name for Los Angeles). 1, 3. 5. ¿Ese? ¿Ese?: Man? (Also dude or homeboy.) 6. ¿Qué pues, nuez?: Well what, nut?

HENRY (*turning*): Where the hell you been, ese?

PACHUCO: Checking out the barrio. Qué desmadre, ¿no?°

HENRY: What's going on, ese? This thing is big.

10   PACHUCO: The city's cracking down on pachucos, carnal.° Don't you read the newspapers? They're
screaming for blood.

HENRY: All I know is they got nothing on me. I didn't do
anything.

15   PACHUCO: You're Henry Reyna, ese—Hank Reyna!
The snarling juvenile delinquent. The zootsuiter. The
bitter young pachuco gang leader of 38th Street.
That's what they got on you.

HENRY: I don't like this, ese. (*Suddenly intense.*)
20   I DON'T LIKE BEING LOCKED UP!

PACHUCO: Calmantes montes, chicas patas.° Haven't
I taught you to survive? Play it cool.

HENRY: They're going to do it again, ese! They're going
to charge me with some phony rap and keep me until
25   they make something stick.

PACHUCO: So what's new?

HENRY (*pause*): I'm supposed to report for the Navy
tomorrow. (*The Pachuco looks at him with silent disdain.*) You don't want me to go, do you?

30   PACHUCO: Stupid move, carnal.

HENRY (*hurt and angered by Pachuco's disapproval*):
I've got to do something.

PACHUCO: Then hang tough. Nobody's forcing you to
do shit.

HENRY: I'm forcing me, ese—ME, you understand?

35   PACHUCO: Muy patriotic, eh?

HENRY: Yeah.

PACHUCO: Off to fight for your country.

HENRY: Why not?

PACHUCO: Because this ain't your country. Look what's
40   happening all around you. The Japs have sewed up
the Pacific. Rommel is kicking ass in Egypt but the
Mayor of L.A. has declared all-out war on Chicanos.
On you! ¿Te curas?°

HENRY: Órale.°

45   PACHUCO: Qué mamada, ¿no?° Is that what you want to
go out and die for? Wise up. These bastard paddy
cops have it in for you. You're a marked man. They
think you're the enemy.

HENRY (*refusing to accept it*): Screw them bastard cops!

50   PACHUCO: And as soon as the Navy finds out you're in
jail again, ya estuvo, carnal.° Unfit for military duty
because of your record. Think about it.

HENRY (*pause*): You got a frajo?

PACHUCO: Simón. (*He pulls out a cigarette, hands it to
Henry, lights it for him. Henry is pensive.*)

55   HENRY (*smokes, laughs ironically*): I was all set to come
back a hero, see? Me la rayo.° For the first time in my

life I really thought Hank Reyna was going someplace.

PACHUCO: Forget the war overseas, carnal. Your war is
on the homefront.   60

HENRY (*with new resolve*): What do you mean?

PACHUCO: The barrio needs you, carnal. Fight back!
Stand up to them with some style. Show the world a
Chicano has balls. Hang tough. You can take it.
Remember, Pachuco Yo!   65

HENRY (*assuming the style*): Con safos, carnal.°

Scene 4. The Interrogation

(*The Press enters, followed by Edwards and Smith.*)

PRESS (*to the audience*): Final Edition, the *Los Angeles
Daily News*. The police have arrested twenty-two
members of the 38th Street Gang, pending further
investigation of various charges.

LT. EDWARDS: Well, son, I was hoping I wouldn't see   5
you in here again.

HENRY: Then why did you arrest me?

LT. EDWARDS: Come on, Hank, you know why you're
here.

HENRY: Yeah. I'm a Mexican.   10

LT. EDWARDS: Don't give me that. How long have I
known you? Since '39?

HENRY: Yeah, when you got me for stealing a car,
remember?

LT. EDWARDS: All right. That was a mistake. I didn't   15
know it was your father's car. I tried to make it up to
you. Didn't I help you set up the youth club?

SGT. SMITH: They turned it into a gang, Lieutenant.
Everything they touch turns to shit.

LT. EDWARDS: I remember a kid just a couple of years   20
back. Head boy at the Catholic Youth Center. His
idea of fun was going to the movies. What happened
to that nice kid, Henry?

PRESS: He's "Gone with the Wind," trying to look like
Clark Gable.   25

SGT. SMITH: Now he thinks he's Humphrey Bogart.

PACHUCO: So who are you, puto? Pat O'Brien?

LT. EDWARDS: This is the wrong time to be antisocial,
son. This country's at war, and we're under strict
orders to crack down on all malcontents.   30

SGT. SMITH: Starting with all pachucos and draft
dodgers.

HENRY: I ain't no draft dodger.

LT. EDWARDS: I know you're not. I heard you got
accepted by the Navy. Congratulations. When do you   35
report?

HENRY: Tomorrow?

SGT. SMITH: Tough break!

LT. EDWARDS: It's still not too late, you know. I could
still release you in time to get sworn in.   40

---

8. **Qué desmadre, ¿no?**: What a mess.   **10–11. carnal**: Brother.
21. Calmantes . . . patas: Take it easy, Chicano.   **43. ¿Te
curas?**: Are you charged (excited)?   **44. Órale**: O.K.   **45. Qué
mamada, ¿no?**: What stupidity, right?   **51. ya estuvo, carnal**:
That's enough, brother.   **56. Me la rayo**: I would be in good
circumstances.

66. **Con safos, carnal**: Be safe, brother.

HENRY: If I do what?

LT. EDWARDS: Tell me, Henry, what do you know about a big gang fight last Saturday night, out at Sleepy Lagoon?

45 PACHUCO: Don't tell 'em shit.

HENRY: Which Sleepy Lagoon?

LT. EDWARDS: You mean there's more than one? Come on, Hank, I know you were out there. I've got a statement from your friends that says you were beaten up.

50 Is that true? Were you and your girl attacked?

HENRY: I don't know anything about it. Nobody's ever beat me up.

SGT. SMITH: That's a lie and you know it. Thanks to your squealer friends, we've got enough dope on you

55 to indict for murder right now.

HENRY: Murder?

SGT. SMITH: Yeah, murder. Another greaser named José Williams.

HENRY: I never heard of the bato.

60 SGT. SMITH: Yeah, sure.

LT. EDWARDS: I've been looking at your record, Hank. Petty theft, assault, burglary, and now murder. Is that what you want? The gas chamber? Play square with me. Give me a statement as to what happened at the

65 Lagoon, and I'll go to bat for you with the Navy. I promise you.

PACHUCO: If that ain't a line of gabacho bullshit, I don't know what is.

LT. EDWARDS: Well?

70 PACHUCO: Spit in his pinche face.

SGT. SMITH: Forget it, Lieutenant. You can't treat these animals like people.

LT. EDWARDS: Shut up! I'm thinking of your family, Hank. Your old man would be proud to see you in

75 the Navy. One last chance, son. What do you say?

HENRY: I ain't your son, cop.

LT. EDWARDS: All right, Reyna, have it your way.

(*Edwards and Press exit.*)

PACHUCO: You don't deserve it, ese, but you're going to get it anyway.

80 SGT. SMITH: All right, muchacho, it's just me and you now. I hear tell you pachucos wear these monkey suits as a kind of armor. Is that right? How's it work? This is what you zooters need—a little old-fashioned discipline.

85 HENRY: Screw you, flatfoot.

SGT. SMITH: You greasy son of a bitch. What happened at the Sleepy Lagoon? Talk! Talk! Talk!

(*Smith beats Henry with a rubber sap. Henry passes out and falls to the floor, with his hands still handcuffed behind his back. Dolores his mother appears in a spot upstage, as he falls.*)

DOLORES: Henry!

(*Lights change. Four Pachuco Couples enter, dancing a 40s pasodoble (two-step) around Henry on the floor, as they swing in a clothesline of newspaper sheets. Music.*)

PACHUCO: Get up and escape, Henry . . .

90 leave reality behind
with your buenas garras
muy chamberlain°
escape through the barrio streets of your mind
through a neighborhood of memories

95 all chuckhole lined
and the love
and the pain
as fine as wine . . .

(*Henry sits up, seeing his mother Dolores folding newspaper sheets like clothes on a clothesline.*)

DOLORES: Henry?

PACHUCO: It's a lifetime ago, last Saturday night . . . 100
before Sleepy Lagoon and the big bad fight.

DOLORES: Henry!

PACHUCO: Tu mamá, carnal.°

(*He recedes into the background.*)

DOLORES (*at the clothesline*): Henry, ¿hijo? Ven a cenar.° 105

HENRY (*gets up off the floor*): Sorry, jefita,° I'm not hungry. Besides, I got to pick up Della. We're late for the dance.

DOLORES: Dance? In this heat? Don't you muchachos ever think of anything else? God knows I suffer la 110 pena negra° seeing you go out every night.

HENRY: This isn't just any night, jefa.° It's my last chance to use my tacuche.

DOLORES: Tacuche? Pero tu padre . . .°

HENRY (*revealing a stubborn streak*): I know what mi 115 'apá° said, 'amá. I'm going to wear it anyway.

DOLORES (*sighs, resigns herself*): Mira, hijo.° I know you work hard for your clothes. And I know how much they mean to you. Pero por diosito santo,° I just don't know what you see en esa cochinada de 120 "soot zoot."°

HENRY (*smiling*): Drapes, 'amá, we call them drapes.

DOLORES (*scolding playfully*): Ay sí, drapes, muy funny, ¿verdad?° And what do the police call them, eh? They've put you in jail so many times. ¿Sabes qué?° 125 I'm going to send them all your clothes!

HENRY: A qué mi 'amá.° Don't worry. By this time next week, I'll be wearing my Navy blues. Okay?

1, 4. 91–92. buenas . . . chamberlain: Good threads, very high class (literally, good rags). **103. Tu mamá, carnal:** Your mother, brother. **105. Henry . . . cenar:** Henry, son? Come to dinner. **106. jefita:** Mom (literally, little boss, an affectionate term for a parent). **110–111. la pena negra:** Through hell (literally, the black pain). **112. jefa:** Mom. **113. tacuche:** Zoot suit. **114. Pero tu padre:** But your father. **115–116. mi 'apá:** My dad. **117. Mira, hijo:** Look, son. **119. Pero . . . santo:** But for God's sake. **120–121. en esa . . . "soot zoot":** In that filthy thing, that "soot zoot" (mispronunciation indicating her generational distance from pachuco culture). **124. ¿verdad?:** Truthfully. **125. ¿Sabes qué?:** You know what? **127. A qué mi 'amá:** That's my mom.

DOLORES: Bendito sea Dios.° I still can't believe you're
130   going off to war. I almost wish you were going back
       to jail.
HENRY: ¡Órale!°

(*Lupe Reyna, 16, enters dressed in a short skirt and
baggy coat. She is followed by Della Barrios, 17,
dressed more modestly. Lupe hides behind a newspaper
sheet on the line.*)

LUPE: Hank! Let's go, carnal. Della's here.
HENRY: Della . . . Órale, esa.° What are you doing here?
135   I told you I was going to pick you up at your house.
DELLA: You know how my father gets.
HENRY: What happened?
DELLA: I'll tell you later.
DOLORES: Della, hija, buenas noches.° How pretty you
140   look.
DELLA: Buenas noches.

(*Dolores hugs Della, then spots Lupe hiding behind the
clothesline.*)

DOLORES (*to Lupe*): ¿Oye y tú?° What's wrong with
       you? What are you doing back there.
LUPE: Nothing, 'amá.
145 DOLORES: Well, come out then.
LUPE: We're late, 'amá.
DOLORES: Come out, te digo.°

(*Lupe comes out exposing her extremely short skirt.
Dolores gasps.*)

       ¡Válgame Dios!° Guadalupe, are you crazy? Why
       bother to wear anything?
150 LUPE: Ay, 'amá, it's the style. Short skirt and fingertip
       coat. Huh, Hank?
HENRY: Uh, yeah, 'amá.
DOLORES: ¿Oh sí? And how come Della doesn't get to
       wear the same style?
155 HENRY: No . . . that's different. No, chale.°
ENRIQUE (*off*): ¡VIEJA!°
DOLORES: Ándale.° Go change before your father sees
       you.
ENRIQUE: I'm home. (*Coming into the scene.*) Buenas
160   noches, everybody. (*All respond. Enrique sees Lupe.*)
       ¡Ay, jijo!° Where's the skirt?!
LUPE: It's here.
ENRIQUE: Where's the rest of it?
DOLORES: She's going to the dance.
165 ENRIQUE: ¿Y a mí qué me importa?° Go and change
       those clothes. Ándale.
LUPE: Please, 'apá?

ENRIQUE: No, señorita.
LUPE: Chihuahua,° I don't want to look like a square.
ENRIQUE: ¡Te digo que no!° I will not have my daughter   170
       looking like a . . .
DOLORES: Like a puta° . . . I mean, a pachuca.
LUPE (*pleading for help*): Hank . . .
HENRY: Do what they say, sis.
LUPE: But you let Henry wear his drapes.   175
ENRIQUE: That's different. He's a man. Es hombre.
DOLORES: Sí, that's different. You men are all alike.
       From such a stick, such a splinter: De tal palo, tal
       astillota.
ENRIQUE: Natural, muy natural, and look how he came   180
       out. ¡Bien macho! Like his father. ¿Verdad, m'ijo?°
HENRY: If you say so, jefito.°
ENRIQUE (*to Della*): Buenas noches.
DELLA: Buenas noches.
HENRY: 'Apá, this is Della Barrios.   185
ENRIQUE: Mira, mira° . . . So this is your new girlfriend,
       eh? Muy bonita.° Quite a change from the last one.
DOLORES: Ay, señor.
ENRIQUE: It's true. What was her name?
DELLA: Bertha?   190
ENRIQUE: That's the one. The one with the tattoo.
DOLORES: Este hombre.° We have company.
ENRIQUE: That reminds me. I invited the compadres to
       the house mañana.°
DOLORES: ¿Que qué?°   195
ENRIQUE: I'm buying a big keg of cerveza° to go along
       with the menudo.°
DOLORES: Oye, ¿cuál menudo?°
ENRIQUE (*cutting her off*): ¡Qué caray, mujer!° It isn't
       every day a man's son goes off to fight for his   200
       country. I should know. Della, m'ija, when I was in
       the Mexican Revolution, I was not even as old as my
       son is.
DOLORES: N'ombre,° don't start with your revolution.
       We'll be here all night.   205
HENRY: Yeah, jefe, we've got to go.
LUPE (*comes forward. She has rolled down her skirt*):
       'Apá, is this better?
ENRIQUE: Bueno. And you leave it that way.
HENRY: Órale, pues.° It's getting late. Where's Rudy?
LUPE: He's still getting ready. Rudy!   210

(*Rudy Reyna, 19, comes downstage in an old suit made
into a tacuche.*)°

RUDY: Let's go everybody. I'm ready.

---

129. **Bendito sea Dios:** Blessed be God.   132. **¡Órale!:** Come
on!   134. **Órale, esa:** Hey, girl.   139. **hija, buenas noches:**
Honey (literally, daughter), good evening.   142. **¿Oye y
tú?:** Listen and you?   147. **te digo:** I told you.   148. **¡Vál-
game Dios!:** Goodness, gracious!   155. **No, chale:** No, no.
156. **¡VIEJA!:** Old woman (wife).   157. **Ándale:** That's it.
161. **¡Ay, jijo!:** My goodness!   165. **¿Y . . . importa?:** What
difference does that make to me?

169. **Chihuahua:** Expression of frustration.   170. **¡Te digo que
no!:** I told you no!   172. **puta:** Whore.   181. **¿Verdad, m'ijo?:**
Right, son?   182. **jefito:** Dad.   186. **Mira, mira:** Look, look.
187. **Muy bonita:** Very pretty.   192. **Este hombre:** This man.
194. **mañana:** Tomorrow.   195. **¿Que qué?:** What's that?
196. **cerveza:** Beer.   197. **menudo:** Tripe soup, a dish eaten
at special occasions.   198. **Oye, ¿cuál menudo?:** Hey, what
menudo?   199. **¡Qué caray, mujer!:** Damn it, woman!
204. **N'ombre:** No, man.   209. **Órale, pues:** Come on, then.
210. **tacuche:** Zoot suit.

ENRIQUE: Oye, oye, ¿y tú?° What are you doing with my coat?

RUDY: It's my tacuche, 'apá.

215   ENRIQUE: ¡Me lleva la chingada!°

DOLORES: Enrique . . . ¡por el amor de Dios!°

ENRIQUE (*to Henry*): You see what you're doing? First that one and now this one. (*To Rudy.*) Hijo,° don't go out like that. Por favor. You look like an idiot,

220   pendejo.°

RUDY: Órale, Hank. Don't I look all right?

HENRY: Nel, ese,° you look fine. Watcha. Once I leave for the service, you can have my tacuche. Then you can really be in style. ¿Cómo la ves?°

225   RUDY: Chale.° Thanks, carnal, but if I don't join the service myself, I'm gonna get my own tacuche.

HENRY: You sure? I'm not going to need it where I'm going. ¿Tú sabes?°

RUDY: Are you serious?

230   HENRY: Simón.°

RUDY: I'll think about it.

HENRY: Pos, no hay pedo, ese.°

ENRIQUE: ¿Cómo que pedo? Nel, ¿Simón?° Since when did we stop speaking Spanish in this house? Have

235   you no respect?

DOLORES: Muchachos, muchachos, go to your dance.

(*Henry starts upstage.*)

HENRY: Buenas noches . . .

(*Enrique holds out his hand. Henry stops, looks, and then returns to kiss his father's hand. Then he moves to kiss his mother and Rudy in turn kisses Enrique's hand. Enrique says "Buenas Noches" to each of his sons.*)

HENRY: Órale, we'd better get going . . .

(*General "goodbyes" from everybody.*)

ENRIQUE (*as Rudy goes past him*): Henry! Don't let your

240   brother drink beer.

RUDY: Ay, 'apá. I can take care of myself.

DOLORES: I'll believe that when I see it. (*She kisses him on the nose.*)

LUPE: Ahí te watcho, 'amá.°

ENRIQUE: ¿Que qué?°

245   LUPE: I mean, I'll see you later.

(*Henry, Della, Lupe, and Rudy turn upstage. Music starts.*)

ENRIQUE: Mujer, why didn't you let me talk?

DOLORES (*sighing*): Talk, señor, talk all you want. I'm listening.

(*Enrique and Dolores exit up right. Rudy and Lupe exit up left. Lights change. We hear hot dance music. Henry and Della dance at center stage. El Pachuco sings.*)

PACHUCO: CADA SÁBADO EN LA NOCHE
YO ME VOY A BORLOTEAR   250
CON MI LINDA PACHUCONA
LAS CADERAS A MENEAR°

ELLA LE HACE MUY DE AQUELLAS
CUANDO EMPIEZA A GUARACHAR
AL COMPÁS DE LOS TIMBALES   255
YO ME SIENTO PETATEAR°

(*From upstage right, three pachucos now enter in a line, moving to the beat. They are Joey Castro, 17; Smiley Torres, 23; and Tommy Roberts, 19, Anglo. They all come downstage left in a diagonal.*)

LOS CHUCOS SUAVES BAILAN RUMBA
BAILAN LA RUMBA Y LE ZUMBAN
BAILAN GUARACHA SABROSÓN
EL BOTECITO Y EL DANZÓN!°   260

(*Chorus repeats, the music fades. Henry laughs and happily embraces Della.*)

Scene 5. *The Press*

(*Lights change. El Pachuco escorts Della off right. The Press appears at upstage center.*)

PRESS: *Los Angeles Times*: August 8, 1942.

(*A Newsboy enters, lugging in two more bundles of newspapers, hawking them as he goes. People of various walks of life enter at intervals and buy newspapers. They arrange themselves in the background reading.*)

NEWSBOY: EXTRA! EXTRAAA! READ ALL ABOUT IT. SPECIAL SESSION OF L.A. COUNTY GRAND JURY CONVENES. D.A. CHARGES CONSPIR-ACY IN SLEEPY LAGOON MURDER. EXTRAAA!   5

(*A Cub Reporter emerges and goes to the Press, as Lieutenant Edwards enters.*)

CUB REPORTER: Hey, here comes Edwards!

(*Edwards is besieged by the Press, joined by Alice Bloomfield, 26, a woman reporter.*)

---

212. **Oye, oye, ¿y tú?**: Listen, listen, and you? 215. **¡Me lleva la chingada!**: I'm (vulgar term)! 216. **¡por el amor de Dios!**: For the love of God! 218. **Hijo**: Son. 220. **pendejo**: Idiot. 222. **Nel, ese**: No, man. 224. **¿Cómo la ves?**: How does that seem to you? 225. **Chale**: No. 228. **¿Tú sabes?**: You know? 230. **Simón**: Yes. 232. **Pos . . . ese**: Well, that's no lie, man. 233. **¿Cómo . . . Simón?**: What's this nonsense? No, Yes? (He is upset because his sons are speaking Chicano slang.) 243. **Ahí . . . 'amá**: See you later, mom. 244. **¿Que qué?**: What's that?

249–252. **CADA . . . MENEAR**: Every Saturday night / I go to party (dance) / With my beautiful pachuca / Shaking her hips. 253–256. **ELLA . . . PETATEAR**: She seems very fine / When she begins to dance / To the rhythm of the drums / I feel like I'm dying. 257–260. **LOS CHUCOS . . . DANZÓN!**: The fine pachucos dance the rumba / Dance the rumba and they get high / They dance the dance (similar to the flamenco) deliciously / The botecito (literally little jail or little boat; the name of a dance) / And the danzón (a Cuban dance)!

PRESS: How about it, Lieutenant? What's the real scoop on the Sleepy Lagoon? Sex, violence . . .

CUB REPORTER: Marijuana?

10 NEWSBOY: Read all about it! Mexican Crime Wave Engulfs L.A.

LT. EDWARDS: Slums breed crime, fellas. That's your story.

ALICE: Lieutenant. What exactly is the Sleepy Lagoon?

15 CUB REPORTER: A great tune by Harry James, doll. Wanna dance?

(*Alice ignores the Cub.*)

LT. EDWARDS: It's a reservoir. An old abandoned gravel pit, really. It's on a ranch between here and Long Beach. Serves as a swimming hole for the younger

20 Mexican kids.

ALICE: Because they're not allowed to swim in the public plunges?

PRESS: What paper are you with, lady? The *Daily Worker*?

25 LT. EDWARDS: It also doubles as a sort of lovers' lane at night—which is why the gangs fight over it. Now they've finally murdered somebody.

NEWSBOY: EXTRA! EXTRA! ZOOT-SUITED GOONS OF SLEEPY LAGOON!

30 LT. EDWARDS: But we're not going to mollycoddle these youngsters any more. And you can quote me on that.

PRESS: One final question, Lieutenant. What about the 38th Street Gang—weren't you the first to arrest Henry Reyna?

35 LT. EDWARDS: I was. And I noticed right away the kid had great leadership potential. However . . .

PRESS: Yes?

LT. EDWARDS: You can't change the spots on a leopard.

PRESS: Thank you, sir.

(*People with newspapers crush them and throw them down as they exit. Edwards turns and exits. Alice turns toward Henry for a moment.*)

40 NEWSBOY: EXTRA, EXTRA. READ ALL ABOUT THE MEXICAN BABY GANGSTERS. EXTRA, EXTRA.

(*The Press and Cub Reporter rush out happily to file their stories. The Newsboy leaves, hawking his papers. Alice*

45 *exits, with determination. Far upstage, Enrique enters with a rolling garbage can. He is a street sweeper. During the next scene he silently sweeps up the newspapers, pausing at the last to read one of the news stories.*)

Scene 6. *The People's Lawyer*

JOEY: ¡Chale, ese, chale! Qué pinche agüite.°

SMILEY: Mexican Baby Gangsters?!

TOMMY: Zoot-suited goons! I knew it was coming. Every time the D.A. farts, they throw us in the can.

1, 6. 1. **¡Chale . . . agüite:** No, man, no! What a damned nuisance.

SMILEY: Pos, qué chingados,° Hank. I can't believe this. 5 Are they really going to pin us with a murder rap? I've got a wife and kid, man!

JOEY: Well, there's one good thing anyway. I bet you know that we've made the headlines. Everybody knows we got the toughest gang in town. 10

TOMMY: Listen to this pip-squeak. The biggest heist he ever pulled was a Tootsie Roll.

JOEY (*grabbing his privates*): Here's your Tootsie Roll, ese.

TOMMY: What, that? Get my microscope, Smiley. 15

JOEY: Why don't you come here and take a little bite, joto.

TOMMY: Joto? Who you calling a joto, maricón?°

JOEY: You, white boy. Did I ever tell you, you got the finest little duck ass in the world. 20

TOMMY: No, you didn't tell me that, culero.°

(*Joey and Tommy start sparring.*)

SMILEY (*furious*): Why don't you batos knock it off?

HENRY (*cool*): Cálmenla.°

SMILEY: ¡Pinches chavalos!° (*The batos stop.*)

JOEY: We're just cabuliando, ese. 25

TOMMY: Simón, ese. Horsing around. (*He gives Joey a final punch.*)

SMILEY (*with deep self-pity*): I'm getting too old for this pedo,° Hank. All this farting around con esos chavalillos.°

HENRY: Relax, carnal. No te agüites.° 30

SMILEY: You and me have been through a lot, Hank. Parties, chingazos,° jail. When you said let's join the pachucada,° I joined the pachucada. You and me started the 38th, bato. I followed you even after my kid was born, but what now, carnal? This pinche 35 pedo° is serious.

TOMMY: He's right, Hank. They indicted the whole gang.

JOEY: Yeah, you know the only one who ain't here is Rudy.

(*Henry turns sharply.*)

He was at the Sleepy Lagoon too, ese. Throwing 40 chingazos.°

HENRY: Yeah, but the cops don't know that, do they? Unless one of us turned stoolie.

JOEY: Hey, ese, don't look at me. They beat the shit out of me, but that's all they got. Shit. 45

TOMMY: That's all you got to give. (*Laughs.*)

HENRY: Okay! Let's keep it that way. I don't want my carnalillo° pulled into this. And if anybody asks

---

5. **Pos, qué chingados:** Anyhow, what (vulgar term). 18. **joto, maricón:** Homosexual (derogatory). 21. **culero:** (Vulgar term), son-of-a-bitch. 23. **Cálmenla:** Cool it. 24. **¡Pinches chavalos!:** Damned inexperienced boys. 28. **pedo:** Nonsense. 28–29. **con esos chavalillos:** With these little neophytes. 30. **No te agüites:** Don't let it get to you. 32. **chingazos:** Fights. 33. **pachucada:** World of the pachucos; pachuco population. 35–36. **pinche pedo:** Damned nonsense. 41. **chingazos:** Punches. 48. **carnalillo:** Little brother.

about him, you batos don't know nothing. You get
50   me?
SMILEY: Simón.
TOMMY: Crazy.
JOEY (*throwing his palms out*): Say, Jackson, I'm cool.
        You know that.
55   HENRY: There's not a single paddy we can trust.
TOMMY: Hey, ese, what about me?
HENRY: You know what I mean.
TOMMY: No, I don't know what you mean. I'm here
        with the rest of yous.
60   JOEY: Yeah, but you'll be the first one out, cabrón.°
TOMMY: Gimme a break, maníaco. ¡Yo soy pachuco!°
HENRY: Relax, ese. Nobody's getting personal with you.
        Don't I let you take out my carnala?° Well, don't I?
TOMMY: Simón.
65   HENRY: That's because you respect my family. The rest
        of them paddies are after our ass.
PACHUCO: Talk about paddies, ese, you got company.

(*George Shearer enters upstage right and comes down.
He is a middle-aged lawyer, strong and athletic, but with
the slightly frazzled look of a people's lawyer.*)

GEORGE: Hi, boys.
HENRY: Trucha!°
70   GEORGE: My name is George Shearer. I've been retained
        by your parents to handle your case. Can we sit and
        talk for a little bit?

(*Pause. The Boys eye George suspiciously. He slides a
newspaper bundle a few feet upstage.*)

PACHUCO: Better check him out, ese. He looks like
        a cop.
75   HENRY (*to the Guys, sotto voce*): Pónganse al alba. Este
        me huele a chota.°
GEORGE: What was that? Did you say I could sit down?
        Thank you. (*He pulls a bundle upstage. He sits.*)
        Okay, let me get your names straight first. Who's José
80   Castro?
JOEY: Right here, ese. What do you want to know?
GEORGE: We'll get to that. Ismael Torres?
SMILEY (*deadpan*): That's me. But they call me Smiley.
GEORGE (*a wide grin*): Smiley? I see. You must be Thomas
85   Roberts.
TOMMY: I ain't Zoot Suit Yokum.
GEORGE: Which means you must be Henry Reyna.
HENRY: What if I am. Who are you?
GEORGE: I already told you, my name's George Shearer.
90   Your parents asked me to come.
HENRY: Oh yeah? Where did they get the money for
        a lawyer?
GEORGE: I'm a people's lawyer, Henry.
SMILEY: People's lawyer?
95   JOEY: Simón, we're people.

TOMMY: At least they didn't send no animal's lawyer.
HENRY: So what does that mean? You doing this for free
        or what?
GEORGE (*surprise turning to amusement*): I try not to
        work for free, if I can help it, but I do sometimes. In   100
        this case, I expect to be paid for my services.
HENRY: So who's paying you? For what? And how
        much?
GEORGE: Hey, hey, hold on there. I'm supposed to ask
        the questions. You're the one going on trial, not me.   105
PACHUCO: Don't let him throw you, ese.
GEORGE: I sat in on part of the Grand Jury. It was quite
        a farce, wasn't it? Murder one indictment and all.
SMILEY: You think we stand a chance?
GEORGE: There's always a chance, Smiley. That's what   110
        trials are for.
PACHUCO: He didn't answer your question, ese.
HENRY: You still didn't answer my question, mister.
        Who's paying you? And how much?
GEORGE (*getting slightly peeved*): Well, Henry, it's really   115
        none of your damned business.

(*The Boys react.*)

But for whatever it's worth, I'll tell you a little story.
The first murder case I ever tried, and won inciden-
tally, was for a Filipino. I was paid exactly three dol-
lars and fifty cents plus a pack of Lucky Strike   120
cigarettes, and a note for a thousand dollars—never
redeemed. Does that answer your question?
HENRY: How do we know you're really a lawyer?
GEORGE: How do I know you're Henry Reyna? What
        do you really mean, son? Do you think I'm a cop?   125
HENRY: Maybe.
GEORGE: What are you trying to hide from the cops?
        Murder?

(*The Boys react.*)

All right! Aside from your parents, I've been called
into this case by a citizens' committee that's forming   130
in your behalf, Henry. In spite of evidence to the con-
trary, there are some people out there who don't
want to see you get the shaft.
HENRY: ¿Sabes qué, mister?° Don't do us any favors.
GEORGE (*starting to leave*): All right, you want another   135
        lawyer? I'll talk to the Public Defender's office.
JOEY (*grabbing his briefcase*): Hey, wait a minute, ese.
        Where are you going?
TOMMY: De cincho se le va a volar la tapa.°
JOEY: Nel, este bolillo no sabe nada.°   140
GEORGE (*exploding*): All right, kids, cut the crap!
SMILEY (*grabs his briefcase and crosses to Henry*): Let's
        give him a break, Hank. (*Smiley hands the briefcase
        to George.*)

---

60. cabrón: Son-of-a-bitch. **61. maníaco . . . pachuco!:**
Maniac. I'm a pachuco! **63. carnala:** Sister. **69. Trucha!:**
Heads up! (Watch out!) **75–76. Pónganse . . . chota:** Put
yourselves on alert. I will uncover this cop. **134. ¿Sabes qué, mister?:** You know what, mister? **139. De
cincho . . . tapa:** It's a cinch he's going to blow his top.
140. Nel . . . nada: No, this Anglo (derogatory) doesn't know a
thing.

GEORGE: Thank you. (*He starts to exit. Stops.*) You
145   know, you're making a big mistake. I wonder if you
      know who your friends are? You boys are about to
      get a mass trial. You know what that is? Well, it's
      a new one on me too. The Grand Jury has indicted
      you all on the same identical crime. Not just you
150   four. The whole so-called 38th Street Gang. And you
      know who the main target is? You, Henry, because
      they're saying you're the ringleader. (*Looks around
      at the Guys.*) And I suppose you are. But you're lead-
      ing your buddies here down a dead-end street. The
155   D.A.'s coming after you, son, and he's going to put
      you and your whole gang right into the gas chamber.

(*George turns to leave. Smiley panics. Joey and Tommy
react with him.*)

SMILEY/JOEY/TOMMY (*all together*): Gas chamber! But
      we didn't do nothing! We're innocent!
HENRY: ¡Cálmenla!°

(*The batos stop in their tracks.*)

160   Okay. Say we believe you're a lawyer, what does that
      prove? The press has already tried and convicted us.
      Think you can change that?
GEORGE: Probably not. But then, public opinion comes
      and goes, Henry. What matters is our system of jus-
165   tice. I believe it works, however slowly the wheels
      may grind. It could be a long uphill fight, fellas, but
      we can make it. I know we can. I've promised your
      parents the best defense I'm capable of. The question
      is, Henry, will you trust me?
170   HENRY: Why should I? You're a gringo.
GEORGE (*calmly, deliberately*): ¿Cómo sabes?°
TOMMY (*shocked*): Hey, you speak Spanish?
GEORGE: Más o menos.°
JOEY: You mean you understood us a while ago?
175   GEORGE: More or less.
JOEY (*embarrassed*): ¡Híjole, qué gacho, ese!°
GEORGE: Don't worry. I'm not much on your pachuco
      slang. The problem seems to be that I look like an
      Anglo to you. What if I were to tell you that I had
180   Spanish blood in my veins? That my roots go back to
      Spain, just like yours? What if I'm an Arab? What if
      I'm a Jew? What difference does it make? The ques-
      tion is, will you let me help you?

(*Pause. Henry glances at the Pachuco.*)

PACHUCO: ¡Chale!
185   HENRY (*pause*): Okay!
SMILEY: Me too!
JOEY: Same here!
TOMMY: ¡Órale!
GEORGE (*eagerly*): Okay! Let's go to work. I want to
190   know exactly what happened right from the begin-
      ning. (*George sits down and opens his briefcase.*)

---

159. ¡Cálmenla!: Cool it.   **171.** ¿Cómo sabes?: How do you
know?   **173.** Más o menos: More or less.   **176.** ¡Híjole . . . ese!:
Heavens, how bad is that!

HENRY: Well, I think the pedo° really started at the
      dance last Saturday night . . .

(*El Pachuco snaps his fingers and we hear dance music.
Lights change. George exits.*)

Scene 7. *The Saturday Night Dance*

(*Swabbie and Manchuka come running onstage as the
barrio dance begins to take shape. Henry and the batos
move upstage to join other Pachucos and Pachucas
coming in. Henry joins Della Barrios; Joey teams up
with Bertha Villarreal, Tommy picks up Lupe Reyna;
and Smiley escorts his wife Elena Torres. They represent
the 38th Street neighborhood. Also entering the dance
comes the Downey Gang, looking mean. Rudy stands
upstage, in the background, drinking a bottle of beer.
El Pachuco sings.*)

PACHUCO: CUANDO SALGO YO A BAILAR
      YO ME PONGO MUY CATRÍN
      LAS HUISITAS TODAS GRITAN, DADDY
      VAMOS A BAILAR EL SWING!°

(*The Couples dance. A lively swing number. The music
comes to a natural break and shifts into a slow number.
Bertha approaches Henry and Della downstage on the
dance floor.*)

BERTHA: Ese, ¡surote!° How about a dance for old time's   5
      sake? No te hagas gacho.°
HENRY (*slow dancing with Della*): Sorry, Bertha.
BERTHA: Is this your new huisa? This little fly chick?
DELLA: Listen, Bertha . . .
HENRY (*stops her*): Chale. She's just jealous. Beat it,   10
      Bertha.
BERTHA: Beat it yourself. Mira. You got no hold on me,
      cabrón. Not any more. I'm as free as a bird.
SMILEY (*coming up*): Ese, Hank, that's the Downey Gang
      in the corner. You think they're looking for trouble?   15
HENRY: There's only a couple of them.
BERTHA: That's all we need.
SMILEY: Want me to alert the batos?
HENRY: Nel, be cool.
BERTHA: Be cool? Huy, yu, yui. Forget it, Smiley. Since   20
      he joined the Navy, this bato forgot the difference
      between being cool and being cool-O.

(*She laughs and turns but Henry grabs her angrily by the
arm. Bertha pulls free and walks away cool and tough.
The music changes and the beat picks up. El Pachuco
sings as the Couples dance.*)

PACHUCO: CUANDO VOY AL VACILÓN
      Y ME METO YO A UN SALÓN

---

192. pedo: Nonsense.   **1, 7. 1–4. CUANDO . . . EL SWING!:**
When I go out dancing / I get dressed up very stylishly / The
girls all yell, Daddy / We're going to dance that swing!   **5. Ese,
¡surote!:** Hey dude, two-timer!   **6. No te hagas gacho:** Don't
become a bad man.

25   LAS CHAVALAS GRITAN, PAPI VENTE
    VAMOS A BAILAR DANSÓN!°

(*The dance turns Latin. The music comes to another natural break and holds. Lupe approaches Henry on the dance floor.*)

LUPE: Hank. Rudy's at it again. He's been drinking since we got here.

HENRY (*glancing over at Rudy*): He's okay, sis, let the
30   carnal enjoy himself.

RUDY (*staggering over*): ¡Ese, carnal!

HENRY: What you say, brother?

RUDY: I'm flying high, Jackson. Feeling good.

LUPE: Rudy, if you go home drunk again, mi 'apá's going
35   to use you for a punching bag.

(*Rudy kisses her on the cheek and moves on.*)

DELLA: How are you feeling?

HENRY: Okay.

DELLA: Still thinking about Bertha?

HENRY: Chale, ¿qué traes?° Listen, you want to go out
40   to the Sleepy Lagoon? I've got something to tell you.

DELLA: What?

HENRY: Later, later.

LUPE: You better tell Rudy to stop drinking.

HENRY: Relax, sis. If he gets too drunk, I'll carry him
45   home. (*Music picks up again. El Pachuco sings a third verse.*)

PACHUCO: TOCAN MAMBO SABROSÓN
    SE ALBOROTA EL CORAZÓN
    Y CON UNA CHAVALONA VAMOS
    VAMOS A BAILAR EL MAMBO°

(*The Couples do the mambo. In the background, Rudy gets into an argument with Rafas, the leader of the Downey Gang. A fight breaks out as the music comes to a natural break. Rafas pushes Rudy, half drunk, onto the floor.*)

50 RAFAS: ¡Y a ti qué te importa, puto!°

RUDY (*he falls*): ¡Cabrón!

HENRY (*reacting immediately*): Hey!

(*The whole dance crowd tenses up immediately, splitting into separate camps. Batos from 38th clearly outnumber the Guys from Downey.*)

RAFAS: He started it, ese. El comenzó a chingar conmigo.°

RUDY: You chicken shit, ese! Tú me haces la puñeta,
55   ¡pirujo!°

RAFAS: Come over here and say that, puto!

HENRY (*pulling Rudy behind him*): ¡Agüítala, carnal!°
(*Faces Rafas.*) You're a little out of your territory, ¿que no Rafas?

RAFAS: It's a barrio dance, ese. We're from the barrio. 60

HENRY: You're from Downey.

RAFAS: Vale madre.° ¡Downey Rifa!

DOWNEY GANG: ¡SIMÓN!

RAFAS: What are you going to do about it?

HENRY: I'm going to kick your ass. 65

(*The Two Sides start to attack each other.*)

    ¡Cálmenla!

(*All stop.*)

RAFAS (*pulls out a switchblade*): You and how many batos?

HENRY: Just me and you, cabrón. That's my carnalillo
you started pushing around, see? And nobody chinga 70
con mi familia° without answering to me, ese! Hank
Reyna! (*He pulls out another switchblade.*)

BERTHA: ALL-RIGHT!

HENRY: Let's see if you can push me around like you did
my little brother, ese. Come on . . . COME ON! 75

(*They knife fight. Henry moves in fast. Recoiling, Rafas falls to the floor. Henry's blade is at his throat. El Pachuco snaps his fingers. Everyone freezes.*)

PACHUCO: Qué mamada,° Hank. That's exactly what
the play needs right now. Two more Mexicans killing
each other. Watcha . . . Everybody's looking at you.

HENRY (*looks out at the audience*): Don't give me that
bullshit. Either I kill him or he kills me. 80

PACHUCO: That's exactly what they paid to see. Think
about it.

(*El Pachuco snaps again. Everybody unfreezes.*)

HENRY (*kicks Rafas*): Get out of here. ¡Píntate!°

BERTHA: What?

GÜERA (*Rafas's girlfriend runs forward*): Rafas. 85
¡Vámonos!° (*She is stopped by other Downey batos.*)

RAFAS: Está suave.° I'll see you later.

HENRY: Whenever you want, cabrón.

(*The Downey Gang retreats, as the 38th razzes them all the way out. Insults are exchanged. Bertha shouts "¡Chinga tu madre!" and they are gone. The 38th whoops in victory.*)

SMILEY: Órale, you did it, ese! ¡Se escamaron todos!°

TOMMY: We sure chased those jotos out of here. 90

BERTHA: I could have beat the shit out of those two
rucas.°

23–26. CUANDO . . . DANSÓN!: When I go to the fiesta / And I get to the dancehall / The girls yell, Daddy come / We are going to dance the dansón!   **39. Chale, ¿qué traes?:** No, what's bothering you?   **46–49. TOCAN . . . MAMBO:** They play mambo deliciously / The heart falls in love (gets excited) / With a sweetheart we go / We go to dance the mambo.   **50. ¡Y . . . puto!:** And what does it matter to you, male prostitute?   **53. El comenzó . . . conmigo:** He started to fight with me.   **54–55. Tú me . . . ¡pirujo!:** I'm better than you are, homosexual (derogatory)!

57. ¡Agüítala, carnal!: Calm down, brother!   **62. Vale madre:** That doesn't mean anything.   **70–71. chinga con mi familia:** (Vulgar term) with my family.   **76. Qué mamada:** What stupidity.   **83. ¡Píntate!:** Scram!   **86. ¡Vámonos!:** Let's go!   **87. Está suave:** That's cool.   **89. ¡Se escamaron todos!:** They all got scared!   **92. rucas:** Homegirls.

JOEY: That pinche° Rafas is yellow without his gang, ese.

95 LUPE: So why didn't you jump out there?

JOEY: Chale, Rudy ain't my baby brother.

RUDY (*drunk*): Who you calling a baby, pendejo? I'll show you who's a baby!

JOEY: Be cool, ese.

100 TOMMY: Man, you're lucky your brother was here.

BERTHA: Why? He didn't do nothing. The old Hank would have slit Rafas' belly like a fat pig.

HENRY: Shut your mouth, Bertha!

RUDY: ¿Por qué, carnal?° You backed down, ese. I could
105 have taken that sucker on by myself.

HENRY: That's enough, Rudy. You're drunk.

DELLA: Hank, what if Rafas comes back with all his gang?

HENRY (*reclaiming his leadership*): We'll kill the sons of
110 bitches.

JOEY: ¡Órale! ¡La 38th rifa!°

(*Music. Everybody gets back with furious energy. El Pachuco sings.*)

PACHUCO: DE LOS BAILES QUE MENTÉ
    Y EL BOLERO Y EL BEGUÍN
    DE TODOS LOS BAILES JUNTOS
115 ME GUSTA BAILAR EL SWING! HEY!°

(*The dance ends with a group exclamation: HEY!*)

Scene 8. El Día de la Raza

(*The Press enters upstage level, pushing a small hand truck piled high with newspaper bundles. The batos and rucas on the dance floor freeze in their final dance positions. El Pachuco is the only one who relaxes and moves.*)

PRESS: October 12, 1942: Columbus Day. Four Hundred and Fiftieth Anniversary of the Discovery of America. Headlines!

(*In their places, the Couples now stand straight and recite a headline before exiting. As they do so, the Press moves the bundles of newspapers on the floor to outline the four corners of a jail cell.*)

SMILEY/ELENA: President Roosevelt Salutes Good
5 Neighbors In Latin America.

(*Smiley and Elena exit.*)

TOMMY/LUPE: British Begin Drive to Oust Rommel From North Africa.

(*Tommy and Lupe exit.*)

---

93. **pinche**: Damned   104. **¿Por qué, carnal?**: Why, brother?
111. **¡Órale! ¡La 38th rifa!**: Right on! The 38th (street gang) rules!   **112–15. DE LOS . . . HEY!**: Of the dances that I mentioned / And the bolero and the beguine / Of all the dances joined together / I like to dance swing! Hey!

RUDY/CHOLO: Japs In Death Grip On Pacific Isles.

(*Rudy and Cholo exit. Press tosses another bundle.*)

ZOOTER/LITTLE BLUE: Web Of Zoot Crime Spreads.

(*Zooter and Little Blue exit.*)

MANCHUKA/SWABBIE: U.S. Marines Land Bridgehead   10
On Guadalcanal.

(*Manchuka and Swabbie exit.*)

JOEY/BERTHA: First Mexican Braceros Arrive in U.S.A.

(*Joey and Bertha exit.*)

DELLA: Sleepy Lagoon Murder Trial Opens Tomorrow.

(*Della and the Press exit. As they exit, George and Alice enter upstage left. Henry is center, in a "cell" outlined by four newspaper bundles left by the Press.*)

GEORGE: Henry? How you doing, son? Listen, I've brought somebody with me that wants very much to   15
meet you. I thought you wouldn't mind.

(*Alice crosses to Henry.*)

ALICE: Hello! My name is Alice Bloomfield and I'm a reporter from the *Daily People's World*.

GEORGE: And . . . And I might add, a red hot member of the ad hoc committee that's fighting for you guys.   20

ALICE: Oh, George! I'd hardly call it fighting, for Pete's sake. This struggle has just barely begun. But we're sure going to win it, aren't we, Henry?

HENRY: I doubt it.

GEORGE: Oh come on, Henry. How about it, son? You   25
all set for tomorrow? Anything you need, anything I can get for you?

HENRY: Yeah. What about the clean clothes you promised me? I can't go to court looking like this.

GEORGE: You mean they didn't give them to you?   30

HENRY: What?

GEORGE: Your mother dropped them off two days ago. Clean pants, shirt, socks, underwear, the works. I cleared it with the Sheriff last week.

HENRY: They haven't given me nothing.   35

GEORGE: I'm beginning to smell something around here.

HENRY: Look, George, I don't like being like this. I ain't dirty. Go do something, man!

GEORGE: Calm down. Take it easy, son. I'll check on it right now. Oh! Uh, Alice?   40

ALICE: I'll be okay, George.

GEORGE: I'll be right back.   (*He exits.*)

ALICE (*pulling out a pad and pencil*): Now that I have you all to myself, mind if I ask you a couple of questions?   45

HENRY: I got nothing to say.

ALICE: How do you know? I haven't asked you anything yet. Relax. I'm from the progressive press. Okay?

(*Henry stares at her, not knowing quite how to react. Alice sits on a bundle and crosses her goodlooking legs. Henry concentrates on that.*)

50 Now. The regular press is saying the Pachuco Crime Wave is fascist inspired—any thoughts about that?

HENRY (*bluntly*): No.

ALICE: What about the American Japanese? Is it true they are directing the subversive activities of the pachucos from inside the relocation camps?

(*Henry turns to The Pachuco with a questioning look.*)

55 PACHUCO: This one's all yours, ese.

HENRY: Look, lady, I don't know what the hell you're talking about.

ALICE: I'm talking about you, Henry Reyna. And what the regular press has been saying. Are you aware

60 you're in here just because some bigshot up in San Simeon wants to sell more papers? It's true.

HENRY: So?

ALICE: So, he's the man who started this Mexican Crime Wave stuff. Then the police got into the act. Get the

65 picture? Somebody is using you as a patsy.

HENRY (*his machismo insulted*): Who you calling a patsy?

ALICE: I'm sorry, but it's true.

HENRY (*backing her up*): What makes you so god-damned smart?

70 ALICE (*starting to get scared and trying not to show it*): I'm a reporter. It's my business to know.

PACHUCO: Puro pedo. She's just a dumb broad only good for you know what.

HENRY: Look, Miss Bloomfield, just leave me alone, all right?

(*Henry moves away. Alice takes a deep breath.*)

75 ALICE: Look, let's back up and start all over, okay? Hello. My name is Alice Bloomfield, and I'm not a reporter. I'm just somebody that wants very much to be your friend. (*Pause. With sincere feeling.*) Can you believe that?

80 HENRY: Why should I?

ALICE: Because I'm with you.

HENRY: Oh, yeah? Then how come you ain't in jail with me?

ALICE (*holding her head up*): We are all in jail, Henry.

85 Some of us just don't know it.

PACHUCO: Mmm, pues. No comment.

(*Pause. Henry stares at her, trying to figure her out. Alice tries a softer approach.*)

ALICE: Believe it or not, I was born in Los Angeles just like you. But for some strange reason I grew up here, not knowing very much about Mexicans at all. I'm

90 just trying to learn.

HENRY (*intrigued, but cynical*): What?

ALICE: Little details. Like that tattooed cross on your hand. Is that the sign of the pachuco?

(*Henry covers his right hand with an automatic reflex, then he realizes what he has done.*)

HENRY (*smiles to himself, embarrassed*): Órale.

95 ALICE: Did I embarrass you? I'm sorry. Your mother happened to mention it.

HENRY (*surprised*): My mother? You talked to my jefita?

ALICE (*with enthusiasm*): Yes! And your father and Lupe and Rudy. The whole family gave me a helluva interview. But your mother was sensational. I espe-

100 cially liked her story about the midnight raid. How the police rushed into your house with drawn guns, looking for you on some trumped up charge, and how your father told them you were already in jail . . . God, I would have paid to have seen the

105 cops' faces.

HENRY (*hiding his sentiment*): Don't believe anything my jefa tells you. (*Then quickly.*) There's a lot she doesn't know. I'm no angel.

ALICE: I'll just bet you're not. But you have been taken

110 in for suspicion a dozen times, kept in jail for a few days, then released for lack of evidence. And it's all stayed on your juvenile record.

HENRY: Yeah, well I ain't no punk, see.

ALICE: I know. You're an excellent mechanic. And you

115 fix all the guys' cars. Well, at least you're not one of the lumpen proletariat.

HENRY: The lumpen what?

ALICE: Skip it. Let's just say you're a classic social victim.

HENRY: Bullshit.

120 ALICE (*pause. A serious question*): Are you saying you're guilty?

HENRY: Of what?

ALICE: The Sleepy Lagoon Murder.

HENRY: What if I am?

125 ALICE: Are you?

HENRY (*pause, a serious answer*): Chale. I've pulled a lot of shit in my time, but I didn't do that.

(*George re-enters flushed and angry, trying to conceal his frustration.*)

GEORGE: Henry, I'm sorry, but dammit, something's coming off here, and the clothes have been withheld.

130 I'll have to bring it up in court.

HENRY: In court?

GEORGE: They've left me no choice.

ALICE: What's going on?

HENRY: It's a set up, George. Another lousy set up!

135 GEORGE: It's just the beginning, son. Nobody said this was going to be a fair fight. Well, if they're going to fight dirty, so am I. Legally, but dirty. Trust me.

ALICE (*passionately*): Henry, no matter what happens in the trial, I want you to know I believe you're inno-

140 cent. Remember that when you look out, and it looks like some sort of lynch mob. Some of us . . . a lot of us . . . are right there with you.

GEORGE: Okay, Alice, let's scram. I've got a million things to do. Henry, see you tomorrow under the big

145 top, son. Good luck, son.

ALICE: Thumbs up, Henry, we're going to beat this rap!

(*Alice and George exit. El Pachuco watches them go, then turns to Henry.*)

PACHUCO: "Thumbs up, Henry, we're going to beat this rap." You really think you're going to beat this one,

150 ese?

HENRY: I don't want to think about it.

PACHUCO: You've got to think about it, Hank. Everybody's playing you for a sucker. Wake up, carnal!

155 HENRY: Look, bato, what the hell do you expect me to do?

PACHUCO: Hang tough. (*Grabs his scrotum.*) Stop going soft.

HENRY: Who's going soft?

PACHUCO (*incisively*): You're hoping for something that
160 isn't going to happen, ese. These paddies are leading you by the nose. Do you really believe you stand a chance?

HENRY (*stubborn all the more*): Yeah. I think I got a chance.

165 PACHUCO: Just because that white broad says so?

HENRY: Nel, ese, just because Hank Reyna says so.

PACHUCO: The classic social victim, eh?

HENRY (*furious but keeping his cool*): Mira, ese. Hank Reyna's no loser. I'm coming out of this on top. ¿Me
170 entiendes,° Mendez? (*He walks away with a pachuco gait.*)

PACHUCO (*forcefully*): Don't try to out-pachuco ME, ese! We'll see who comes out on top. (*He picks up a bundle of newspapers and throws it upstage center. It
175 lands with a thud.*) Let's go to court!

Scene 9. *Opening of the Trial*

(*Music. The Judge's bench, made up of more newspaper bundles piled squarely on a four-wheeled hand truck is pushed in by the batos. The Press rides it in, holding the State and Federal Flags. A Bailiff puts in place a hand cart: the Judge's throne. From the sides, spectators enter, including Henry's family and friends: Alice, Della, Bertha, Elena.*)

PRESS: The largest mass trial in the history of Los Angeles County opens this morning in the Superior Court at ten A.M. The infamous Sleepy Lagoon Murder case involves sixty-six charges against twenty-two defen-
5 dants with seven lawyers pleading for the defense, two for the prosecution. The District Attorney estimates that over a hundred witnesses will be called and has sworn—I quote—"to put an end to Mexican baby gangsterism." End quote.

10 BAILIFF (*bangs a gavel on the bench*): The Superior Court of the State of California. In and For the County of Los Angeles. Department forty-three. The honorable F. W. Charles, presiding. All rise!

(*Judge Charles enters. All rise. El Pachuco squats. The Judge is played by the same actor that portrays Edwards.*)

JUDGE: Please be seated.

169–170. ¿**Me entiendes:** You understand me?

(*All sit. Pachuco stands.*)

Call this case, Bailiff.   15

BAILIFF (*reading from a sheet*): The people of the State of California Versus Henry Reyna, Ismael Torres, Thomas Roberts, Jose Castro and eighteen other . . . (*slight hesitation*) . . . pa-coo-cos.

JUDGE: Is Counsel for the Defense present?   20

GEORGE (*rises*): Yes, Your Honor.

JUDGE: Please proceed. (*Signals the Press.*)

PRESS: Your Honor . . .

GEORGE (*moving in immediately*): If the Court please, it was reported to me on Friday that the District Attor-   25
ney has absolutely forbidden the Sheriff's Office to permit these boys to have clean clothes or haircuts. Now, it's been three months since the boys were arrested . . .

PRESS (*jumping in*): Your Honor, there is testimony we   30
expect to develop that the 38th Street Gang are characterized by their style of haircuts . . .

GEORGE: Three months, Your Honor.

PRESS: . . . the thick heavy heads of hair, the ducktail comb, the pachuco pants . . .   35

GEORGE: Your Honor, I can only infer that the Prosecution . . . is trying to make these boys look disreputable, like mobsters.

PRESS: Their appearance is distinctive, Your Honor. Essential to the case.   40

GEORGE: You are trying to exploit the fact that these boys look foreign in appearance! Yet clothes like these are being worn by kids all over America.

PRESS: Your Honor . . .

JUDGE (*bangs the gavel*): I don't believe we will have any   45
difficulty if their clothing becomes dirty.

GEORGE: What about the haircuts, Your Honor?

JUDGE (*ruling*): The zoot haircuts will be retained throughout the trial for purposes of identification of defendants by witnesses.   50

PACHUCO: You hear that one, ese? Listen to it again.

(*Snaps. Judge repeats automatically.*)

JUDGE: The zoot haircuts will be retained throughout the trial for purposes of identification of defendants by witnesses.

PACHUCO: He wants to be sure we know who you are.   55

JUDGE: It has been brought to my attention the Jury is having trouble telling one boy from another, so I am going to rule the defendants stand each time their names are mentioned.

GEORGE: I object. If the Prosecution makes an accusa-   60
tion, it will mean self-incrimination.

JUDGE (*pause*): Not necessarily. (*To Press.*) Please proceed.

GEORGE (*still trying to set the stage*): Then if the Court please, might I request that my clients be allowed to   65
sit with me during the trial so that I might consult with them?

JUDGE: Request denied.

GEORGE: May I inquire of Your Honor, if the defendant Thomas Robert might rise from his seat and walk over to counsel table so as to consult with me during the trial?

JUDGE: I certainly will not permit it.

GEORGE: You will not?

JUDGE: No. This is a small courtroom, Mr. Shearer. We can't have twenty-two defendants all over the place.

GEORGE: Then I object. On the grounds that that is a denial of the rights guaranteed all defendants by both the federal and state constitutions.

JUDGE: Well, that is your opinion. (*Gavel.*) Call your first witness.

PRESS: The prosecution calls Lieutenant Sam Edwards of the Los Angeles Police Department.

PACHUCO (*snaps, does double take on Judge*): You know what. We've already heard from that bato. Let's get on with the defense.

(*Snaps. Press sits. George stands.*)

GEORGE: The defense calls Adela Barrios.

BAILIFF (*calling out*): Adeela Barreeos to the stand.

(*Della Barrios comes forth out of the spectators. Bertha leans forward.*)

BERTHA (*among the spectators*): Don't tell 'em nothing.

(*The Bailiff swears in Della silently.*)

PACHUCO: Look at your gang. They do look like mobsters. Se watchan bien gachos.°

(*Henry looks at the batos, who are sprawled out in their places.*)

HENRY (*under his breath*): Come on, Batos, sit up.

SMILEY: We're tired, Hank.

JOEY: My butt is sore.

TOMMY: Yeah, look at the soft chairs the jury's got.

HENRY: What did you expect? They're trying to make us look bad. Come on! Straighten up.

SMILEY: Simón, batos, Hank is right.

JOEY: ¡Más alba nalga!°

TOMMY: Put some class on your ass.

HENRY: Sit up! (*They all sit up.*)

GEORGE: State your name please.

DELLA: Adela Barrios. (*She sits.*)

GEORGE: Miss Barrios, were you with Henry Reyna on the night of August 1, 1942?

DELLA: Yes.

JUDGE (*to Henry*): Please stand.

(*Henry stands.*)

GEORGE: Please tell the court what transpired that night.

DELLA (*pause, takes a breath*): Well, after the dance that Saturday night, Henry and I drove out to the Sleepy Lagoon about eleven-thirty.

1, 9. 91. Se watchan bien gachos: They look like real bad guys.
99. ¡Más alba nalga!: Sit up (literally, more alert rump)!

Scene 10. Sleepy Lagoon

(*Music: THE HARRY JAMES THEME. El Pachuco creates the scene. The light changes. We see a shimmering pattern of light on the floor growing to the music. It becomes the image of the Lagoon. As the music soars to a trumpet solo, Henry reaches out to Della, and she glides to her feet.*)

DELLA: There was a full moon that night, and as we drove up to the Lagoon we noticed right away the place was empty . . .

(*A pair of headlights silently pulls in from the black background upstage center.*)

Henry parked the car on the bank of the reservoir and we relaxed.

(*Headlights go off.*)

It was such a warm, beautiful night, and the sky was so full of stars, we couldn't just sit in the car. So we got out, and Henry took my hand . . .

(*Henry stands and takes Della's hand.*)

We went for a walk around the Lagoon. Neither of us said anything at first, so the only sounds we could hear were the crickets and the frogs . . .

(*Sounds of crickets and frogs, then music faintly in the background.*)

When we got to the other side of the reservoir, we began to hear music, so I asked Henry, what's that?

HENRY: Sounds like they're having a party.

DELLA: Where?

HENRY: Over at the Williams' Ranch. See the house lights.

DELLA: Who lives there?

HENRY: A couple of families. Mexicanos. I think they work on the ranch. You know, their name used to be Gonzales, but they changed it to Williams.

DELLA: Why?

HENRY: I don't know. Maybe they think it gives 'em more class.

(*We hear Mexican music.*)

Ay, jijo.° They're probably celebrating a wedding or something.

DELLA: As soon as he said wedding, he stopped talking and we both knew why. He had something on his mind, something he was trying to tell me without sounding like a square.

HENRY: Della . . . what are you going to do if I don't come back from the war?

DELLA: That wasn't the question I was expecting, so I answered something dumb, like I don't know, what's going to keep you from coming back?

1, 10. 25. Ay, jijo: Heavens.

HENRY: Maybe wanting too much out of life, see? Ever since I was a kid, I've had this feeling like there's a big party going on someplace, and I'm invited, but I don't know how to get there. And I want to get there so bad, I'll even risk my life to make it. Sounds crazy, huh?

(*Della and Henry kiss. They embrace and then Henry speaks haltingly.*)

If I get back from the war . . . will you marry me?

DELLA: Yes! (*She embraces him and almost causes them to topple over.*)

HENRY: ¡Órale! You'll knock us into the Lagoon. Listen, what about your old man? He ain't going to like you marrying me.

DELLA: I know. But I don't care. I'll go to hell with you if you want me to.

HENRY: ¿Sabes qué?° I'm going to give you the biggest pachuco wedding L.A. has ever seen.

(*Another pair of headlights comes in from the left. Della goes back to her narration.*)

DELLA: Just then another car pulled up to the Lagoon. It was Rafas and some drunk guys in a gang from Downey. They got out and started to bust the windows on Henry's car. Henry yelled at them, and they started cussing at us. I told Henry not to say anything, but he cussed them back!

HENRY: You stay here, Della.

DELLA: Henry, no! Don't go down there! Please don't go down there!

HENRY: Can't you hear what they're doing to my car?

DELLA: There's too many of them. They'll kill you!

HENRY: ¡Chale!

(*Henry turns and runs upstage, where he stops in a freeze.*)

DELLA: Henry! Henry ran down the back of the Lagoon and attacked the gang by himself. Rafas had about ten guys with him and they jumped on Henry like a pack of dogs. He fought them off as long as he could, then they threw him on the ground hard and kicked him until he passed out . . .

(*Headlights pull off.*)

After they left, I ran down to Henry and held him in my arms until he came to. And I could tell he was hurt, but the first thing he said was . . .

PACHUCO: Let's go into town and get the guys.

(*Music: Glen Miller's "In the Mood." Henry turns to the batos and they stand. Smiley, Joey, and Tommy are joined by Rudy, Bertha, Lupe, and Elena, who enter from the side. They turn downstage in a body and freeze.*)

DELLA: It took us about an hour to go into town and come back. We got to the Lagoon with about eight cars, but the Downey gang wasn't there.

JOEY: Órale, ¿pos qué pasó?° Nobody here.

SMILEY: Then let's go to Downey.

THE BOYS (*ad lib*): Let's go!

HENRY: ¡Chale! ¡Chale!

(*Pause. They all stop.*)

Ya estuvo.° Everybody go home.

(*A collective groan from The Boys.*)

Go home!

DELLA: That's when we heard music coming from the Williams' Ranch again. We didn't know Rafas and his gang had been there too, causing trouble. So when Joey said . . .

JOEY: Hey, there's a party! Bertha, let's crash it.

DELLA: We all went there yelling and laughing.

(*The group of batos turns upstage in a mimetic freeze.*)

At the Williams' Ranch they saw us coming and thought we were the Downey Gang coming back again . . . They attacked us.

(*The group now mimes a series of tableaus showing the fight.*)

An old man ran out of the house with a kitchen knife and Henry had to hit him. Then a girl grabbed me by the hair and in a second everybody was fighting! People were grabbing sticks from the fence, bottles, anything! It all happened so fast, we didn't know what hit us, but Henry said let's go!

HENRY: ¡Vámonos!° Let's get out of here.

DELLA: And we started to back off . . . Before we got to the cars, I saw something out of the corner of my eye . . . It was a guy. He was hitting a man on the ground with a big stick.

(*El Pachuco mimes this action.*)

Henry called to him, but he wouldn't stop. He wouldn't stop . . . He wouldn't stop . . . He wouldn't stop . . .

(*Della in tears, holds Henry in her arms. The batos and rucas start moving back to their places, quietly.*)

Driving back in the car, everybody was quiet, like nothing had happened. We didn't know José Williams had died at the party that night and that the guys would be arrested the next day for murder.

(*Henry separates from her and goes back to stand in his place. Della resumes the witness stand.*)

---

49. **¿Sabes qué?:** You know what?

76. **Órale, ¿pos qué pasó?:** Hey man, well what happened?
80. **Ya estuvo:** That's enough.　97. **¡Vámonos!:** Let's go!

Scene 11. The Conclusion of the Trial

(*Lights change back to courtroom, as Judge Charles bangs his gavel. Everyone is seated back in place.*)

GEORGE: Your witness.

PRESS (*springing to the attack*): You say Henry Reyna hit the man with his fist. (*Indicates Henry standing.*) Is this the Henry Reyna?

DELLA: Yes. I mean, no. He's Henry, but he didn't . . .

PRESS: Please be seated.

(*Henry sits.*)

Now, after Henry Reyna hit the old man with his closed fist, is that when he pulled the knife?

DELLA: The old man had the knife.

PRESS: So Henry pulled one out, too?

GEORGE (*rises*): Your Honor, I object to counsel leading the witness.

PRESS: I am not leading the witness.

GEORGE: You are.

PRESS: I certainly am not.

GEORGE: Yes, you are.

JUDGE: I would suggest, Mr. Shearer, that you look up during the noon hour just what a leading question is.

GEORGE: If the Court please, I am going to assign that remark of Your Honor as misconduct.

JUDGE (*to Press*): Proceed.

(*George crosses back to his chair.*)

PRESS: Where was Smiley Torres during all this? Is it not true that Smiley Torres grabbed a woman by the hair and kicked her to the ground? Will Smiley Torres please stand? (*Smiley stands.*) Is this the man?

DELLA: Yes, it's Smiley, but he . . .

PRESS: Please be seated.

(*Smiley sits. Press picks up a two-by-four.*)

Wasn't José Castro carrying a club of some kind?

GEORGE (*on his feet again*): Your Honor, I object! No such club was ever found. The Prosecution is implying that this two-by-four is associated with my client in some way.

PRESS: I'm not implying anything, Your Honor, I'm merely using this stick as an illustration.

JUDGE: Objection overruled.

PRESS: Will José Castro please stand?

(*Joey stands.*)

Is this the man who was carrying a club?

(*Della refuses to answer.*)

Answer the question please.

DELLA: I refuse.

PRESS: You are under oath. You can't refuse.

JUDGE: Answer the question, young lady.

DELLA: I refuse.

PRESS: Is this the man you saw hitting another man with a two-by-four? Your Honor . . .

JUDGE: I order you to answer the question.

GEORGE: Your Honor, I object. The witness is obviously afraid her testimony will be manipulated by the Prosecution.

PRESS: May I remind the court that we have a signed confession from one José Castro taken while in jail . . .

GEORGE: I object. Those were not confessions! Those are statements. They are false and untrue, Your Honor, obtained through beatings and coercion of the defendants by the police!

JUDGE: I believe the technical term is admissions, Mr. Prosecutor. Objection sustained.

(*Applause from spectators.*)

At the next outburst, I will clear this courtroom. Go on, Mr. Prosecutor.

PRESS: Sit down please.

(*Joey sits. George goes back to his seat.*)

Is Henry Reyna the leader of the 38th Street Gang?

(*Henry stands.*)

DELLA: Not in the sense that you mean.

PRESS: Did Henry Reyna, pachuco ringleader of the 38th Street Gang, willfully murder José Williams?

DELLA: No. They attacked us first.

PRESS: I didn't ask for your comment.

DELLA: But they did, they thought we were the Downey gang.

PRESS: Just answer my questions.

DELLA: We were just defending ourselves so we could get out of there.

PRESS: Your Honor, will you instruct the witness to be cooperative.

JUDGE: I must caution you, young lady, answer the questions or I'll hold you in contempt.

PRESS: Was this the Henry Reyna who was carrying a three-foot lead pipe?

GEORGE: I object!

JUDGE: Overruled.

DELLA: No.

PRESS: Was it a two-foot lead pipe?

GEORGE: Objection!

JUDGE: Overruled.

DELLA: No!

PRESS: Did he kick a woman to the ground?

DELLA: No, he was hurt from the beating.

PRESS: Sit down.

(*Henry sits.*)

Did Tommy Roberts rip stakes from a fence and hit a man on the ground?

GEORGE: Objection!

JUDGE: Overruled.

DELLA: I never saw him do anything.

PRESS: Did Joey Castro have a gun?

GEORGE: Objection!

JUDGE: Overruled.

(*Joey stands.*)

95   PRESS: Sit down.

(*Joey sits.*)

Did Henry Reyna have a blackjack in his hand?

(*Henry stands.*)

DELLA: No.
PRESS: A switchblade knife?
DELLA: No.
100 PRESS: A two-by-four?
DELLA: No.
PRESS: Did he run over to José Williams, hit him on the head, and kill him?
DELLA: He could barely walk, how could he run to any
105   place?
PRESS (*moving in for the kill*): Did Smiley Torres?

(*The batos stand and sit as their names are mentioned.*)

Did Joey Castro? Did Tommy Roberts? Did Henry Reyna? Did Smiley Torres? Did Henry Reyna? Did Henry Reyna? Did Henry Reyna kill José Williams?!
110 DELLA: No, no, no!
GEORGE (*on his feet again*): Your Honor, I object! The Prosecution is pulling out objects from all over the place, none of which were found at Sleepy Lagoon, and none of which have been proven to be associated
115   with my clients in any way.
JUDGE: Overruled.
GEORGE: If Your Honor please, I wish to make an assignment of misconduct!
JUDGE: We have only had one this morning. We might as
120   well have another now.
GEORGE: You have it, Your Honor.
JUDGE: One more remark like that and I'll hold you in contempt. Quite frankly, Mr. Shearer, I am getting rather tired of your repeated useless objections.
125 GEORGE: I have not made useless objections.
JUDGE: I am sorry. Somebody is using ventriloquism. We have a Charlie McCarthy using Mr. Shearer's voice.
GEORGE: I am going to assign that remark of Your Honor as misconduct.
130 JUDGE: Fine. I would feel rather bad if you did not make an assignment of misconduct at least three times every session. (*Gavel.*) Witness is excused.

(*Della stands.*)

However, I am going to remand her to the custody of the Ventura State School for Girls for a period of one
135   year . . .
HENRY: What?
JUDGE: . . . to be held there as a juvenile ward of the State. Bailiff!
GEORGE: If the court please . . . If the court please . . .

(*Bailiff crosses to Della and takes her off left.*)

140 JUDGE: Court is in recess until tomorrow morning.

(*Judge retires. Press exits. Henry meets George halfway across center stage. The rest of the batos stand and stretch in the background.*)

GEORGE: Now, Henry, I want you to listen to me, please. You've got to remember he's the judge, Hank. And this is his courtroom.
HENRY: But he's making jokes, George, and we're get-   145
ting screwed!
GEORGE: I know. I can't blame you for being bitter, but believe me, we'll get him.
HENRY: I thought you said we had a chance.
GEORGE (*passionately*): We do! This case is going to be   150
won on appeal.
HENRY: Appeal? You mean you already know we're going to lose?
PACHUCO: So what's new?
GEORGE: Don't you see, Henry, Judge Charles is hang-   155
ing himself as we go. I've cited over a hundred sepa-
rate cases of misconduct by the bench, and it's all gone into the record. Prejudicial error, denial of due process, inadmissible evidence, hearsay . . .
HENRY: ¿Sabes qué, George? Don't tell me any more.

(*Henry turns. Alice and Enrique approach him.*)

ALICE: Henry . . . ?   160
HENRY (*turns furiously*): I don't want to hear it, Alice!

(*Henry sees Enrique, but neither father nor son can think of anything to say. Henry goes back upstage.*)

ALICE: George, is there anything we can do?
GEORGE: No. He's bitter, and he has a right to be.

(*Judge Charles pounds his gavel. All go back to their places and sit.*)

JUDGE: We'll now hear the Prosecution's concluding statement.   165
PRESS: Your Honor, ladies and gentlemen of the jury. What you have before you is a dilemma of our times. The City of Los Angeles is caught in the midst of the biggest, most terrifying crime wave in its history. A crime wave that threatens to engulf the very founda-   170
tions of our civic well-being. We are not only dealing with the violent death of one José Williams in a drunken barrio brawl. We are dealing with a threat and danger to our children, our families, our homes. Set these pachucos free, and you shall unleash the   175
forces of anarchy and destruction in our society. Set these pachucos free and you will turn them into heroes. Others just like them must be watching us at this very moment. What nefarious schemes can they be hatching in their twisted minds? Rape, drugs,   180
assault, more violence? Who shall be their next inno-
cent victim in some dark alley way, on some lonely street? You? You? Your loved ones? No! Henry Reyna and his Latin juvenile cohorts are not heroes. They are criminals, and they must be stopped. The   185
specific details of this murder are irrelevant before the overwhelming danger of the pachuco in our

midst. I ask you to find these zoot-suited gangsters guilty of murder and to put them in the gas chamber where they belong.

190

(*The Press sits down. George rises and takes center stage.*)

GEORGE: Ladies and gentlemen of the jury, you have heard me object to the conduct of this trial. I have tried my best to defend what is most precious in our American society—a society now at war against the forces of racial intolerance and totalitarian injustice. The prosecution has not provided one witness that actually saw, with his own eyes, who actually murdered José Williams. These boys are not the Downey gang, yet the evidence suggests that they were attacked because the people at the ranch thought they were. Henry Reyna and Della Barrios were victims of the same bunch. Yes, they might have been spoiling for a revenge—who wouldn't under the circumstances—but not with the intent to conspire to commit murder. So how did José Williams die? Was it an accident? Was it manslaughter? Was it murder? Perhaps we may never know. All the prosecution has been able to prove is that these boys wear long hair and zoot suits. And all the rest has been circumstantial evidence, hearsay, and war hysteria. The prosecution has tried to lead you to believe that they are some kind of inhuman gangsters. Yet they are Americans. Find them guilty of anything more serious than a juvenile bout of fisticuffs, and you will condemn all American youth. Find them guilty of murder, and you will murder the spirit of racial justice in America. (*George sits down.*)

195

200

205

210

215

JUDGE: The jury will retire to consider its verdict.

(*The Press stands and starts to exit with the Bailiff. El Pachuco snaps. All freeze.*)

PACHUCO: Chale. Let's have it.

(*Snaps again. The Press turns and comes back again.*)

220   JUDGE: Has the jury reached a verdict?
PRESS: We have, Your Honor.
JUDGE: How say you?
PRESS: We find the defendants guilty of murder in the first and second degrees.

225   JUDGE: The defendants will rise.

(*The batos come to their feet.*)

Henry Reyna, José Castro, Thomas Roberts, Ismael Torres, and so forth. You have been tried by a jury of your peers and found guilty of murder in the first and second degrees. The Law prescribes the capital punishment for this offense. However, in view of your youth and in consideration of your families, it is hereby the judgment of this court that you be sentenced to life imprisonment . . .

230

RUDY: No!

235   JUDGE: . . . and sent to the State Penitentiary at San Quentin. Court adjourned.

(*Gavel. Judge exits. Dolores, Enrique, and family go to Henry. Bertha crosses to Joey; Lupe goes to Tommy. Elena crosses to Smiley. George and Alice talk.*)

DOLORES: ¡Hijo mío! ¡Hijo de mi alma!°

(*Bailiff comes down with a pair of handcuffs.*)

BAILIFF: Okay, boys.

(*He puts the cuffs on Henry. Rudy comes up.*)

RUDY: ¿Carnal?

(*Henry looks at the Bailiff, who gives him a nod of permission to spend a moment with Rudy. Henry embraces him with the cuffs on. George and Alice approach.*)

GEORGE: Henry? I can't pretend to know how you feel, son. I just want you to know that our fight has just begun.

240

ALICE: We may have lost this decision, but we're going to appeal immediately. We're going to stand behind you until your name is absolutely clear. I swear it!

245

PACHUCO: What the hell are they going to do, ese? They just sent you to prison for life. Once a Mexican goes in, he never comes out.

BAILIFF: Boys?

(*The Boys exit with the Bailiff. As they go Enrique calls after them.*)

ENRIQUE (*holding back tears*): Hijo. Be a man, hijo. (*Then to his family.*) Vámonos . . . ¡Vámonos!

250

(*The family leaves and El Pachuco slowly walks to center stage.*)

PACHUCO: We're going to take a short break right now, so you can all go out and take a leak, smoke a frajo. Ahí los watcho.

(*He exits up center and the newspaper backdrop comes down.*)

ACT 2 • *Prologue*

(*Lights up and El Pachuco emerges from the shadows. The newspaper drop is still down. Music.*)

PACHUCO: Watchamos pachucos
    los batos°
    the dudes
    street-corner warriors who fought and moved
    like unknown soldiers in wars of their own
    El Pueblo de Los was the battle zone
    from Sleepy Lagoon to the Zoot Suit wars
    when Marines and Sailors made their scores
    stomping like Nazis on East L.A. . . .

5

---

237. **¡Hijo mío! ¡Hijo de mi alma!:** My son! Son of my soul!
2, Prologue. 1–2. Watchamos . . . batos: We are watching pachucos, the dudes.

10   pero ¿saben qué?°
        That's later in the play. Let's pick it up in prison.
        We'll begin this scene
        inside the walls of San Quintín.

Scene 1. San Quentin

(*A bell rings as the drop rises. Henry, Joey, Smiley, and Tommy enter accompanied by a Guard.*)

GUARD: All right, people, lock up.

(*Boys move downstage in four directions. They step into "cells" simply marked by shadows of bars on the floor in their separate places. Newspaper handcarts rest on the floor as cots. Sound of cell doors closing. The Guard paces back and forth upstage level.*)

HENRY: San Quentin, California
        March 3, 1943
        Dear Family:
5   Coming in from the yard in the evening, we are
        quickly locked up in our cells. Then the clank and
        locking of the doors leaves one with a rather empty
        feeling. You are standing up to the iron door, waiting
        for the guard to come along and take the count, lis-
10   tening as his footsteps fade away in the distance. By
        this time there is a tense stillness that seems to crawl
        over the cellblock. You realize you are alone, so all
        alone.
PACHUCO: This all sounds rather tragic, doesn't it?
15 HENRY: But here comes the guard again, and he calls out
        your number in a loud voice . . .
GUARD (*calls numbers; Boys call name*): 24-545
HENRY: Reyna!
GUARD: 24-546
20 JOEY: Castro!
GUARD: 24-547
TOMMY: Roberts!
GUARD: 24-548
SMILEY: Torres!

(*Guard passes through dropping letters and exits up left.*)

25 HENRY: You jump to your feet, stooping to pick up the
        letter . . .
JOEY (*excited*): Or perhaps several letters . . .
TOMMY: You are really excited as you take the letters
        from the envelope.
30 SMILEY: The censor has already broken the seal when he
        reads it.
HENRY: You make a mental observation to see if you
        recognize the handwriting on the envelope.
SMILEY (*anxious*): It's always nice to hear from home . . .
35 JOEY: Or a close comrade . . .
TOMMY: Friends that you know on the outside . . .
HENRY: Or perhaps it's from a stranger.

2, Prologue. 10. pero ¿saben qué?: But what did they know?

(*Pause. Spotlight at upstage center. Alice walks in with casual clothes on. Her hair is in pigtails, and she wears a pair of drapes. She is cheerful.*)

Scene 2. The Letters

Dear Boys,
Announcing the publication (mimeograph) of the Appeal News, your very own newsletter, to be sent to you twice a month for the purpose of keeping you reli-
ably informed of everything—the progress of the Sleep-   5
ing Lagoon Defense Committee (we have a name now) and, of course, the matter of your appeal.
Signed,
Your editor
Alice Bloomfield.   10

(*Music. "Perdido" by Duke Ellington. Alice steps down and sits on the lip of the upstage level. The Boys start swinging the bat, dribbling the basketball, shadow-boxing, and exercising. Alice mimes typing movements and we hear the sounds of a typewriter. Music fades. Alice rises.*)

ALICE: The Appeal News Volume I, Number I, April 7,
        1943.
        Boys,
        You can, you must, and you will help us on the out-
        side by what you do on the inside. Don't forget, what   15
        you do affects others. You have no control over that.
        When the time comes, let us be proud to show the
        record.
        Signed,
        Your editor.   20

(*Music up again. The Boys go through their activities. Alice moves downstage center and the music fades.*)

SMILEY (*stepping toward her*): April 10, 1943
        Dear Miss Bloomfield,
        I have discovered from my wife that you are con-
        ducting door-to-door fund-raising campaigns in Los
        Angeles. She doesn't want to tell you, but she feels   25
        bad about doing such a thing. It's not our custom to
        go around the neighborhoods asking for money.
ALICE (*turning toward Smiley*): Dear Smiley,
        Of course, I understand your feelings . . .
SMILEY (*adamant*): I don't want my wife going around   30
        begging.
ALICE: It isn't begging—it's fund-raising.
SMILEY: I don't care what you call it. If that's what it's
        going to take, count me out.
ALICE: All right. I won't bother your wife if she really   35
        doesn't want me to. Okay?

(*Smiley looks at her and turns back to his upstage posi-tion. Music. The batos move again. Tommy crosses to Alice. Another fade.*)

TOMMY: April 18, 1943
        Dear Alice,

Trying to find the words and expression to thank you
40   for your efforts in behalf of myself and the rest of the
batos makes me realize what a meager vocabulary I
possess . . .
ALICE: Dear Tommy,
Your vocabulary is just fine. Better than most.
45   TOMMY: Most what?
ALICE: People.
TOMMY (glances at Henry): Uh, listen, Alice. I don't
want to be treated any different than the rest of the
batos, see? And don't expect me to talk to you like
50   some square Anglo, some pinche gabacho.° You just
better find out what it means to be Chicano, and it
better be pretty damn quick.
ALICE: Look, Tommy, I didn't . . .
TOMMY: I know what you're trying to do for us and
55   that's reet, see? Shit. Most paddies would probably
like to see us locked up for good. I been in jail a
couple of times before, but never nothing this deep.
Strange, ain't it, the trial in Los? I don't really know
what happened or why. I don't give a shit what the
60   papers said. We didn't do half the things I read
about. I also know that I'm in here just because I
hung around with Mexicans . . . or pachucos. Well,
just remember this, Alicia . . . I grew up right alongside most of these batos, and I'm pachuco too.
65   Simón, esa, you better believe it!

(Music up. Movement. Tommy returns to his position.
Henry stands. Alice turns toward him, but he walks over
to The Pachuco, giving her his back.)

JOEY (stepping forward anxiously): May 1, 1943
Dear Alice . . . Darling!
I can't help but spend my time thinking about you.
How about sending us your retra—that is, your
70   photograph? Even though Tommy would like one
of Rita Hayworth—he's always chasing Mexican
skirts (Ha! Ha!)—I'd prefer to see your sweet face
any day.
ALICE (directly to him): Dear Joey,
75   Thank you so much. I really appreciated receiving
your letter.
JOEY: That's all reet, Grandma! You mind if I call you
Grandma?
ALICE: Oh, no.
80   JOEY: Eres una ruca de aquellas.°
ALICE: I'm a what?
JOEY: Ruca. A fine chick.
ALICE (pronounces the word): Ruca?
JOEY: De aquellas. (Makes a cool gesture, palms out at
hip level.)
85   ALICE (imitating him): De aquellas.
JOEY: All reet! You got it. (Pause.) P.S. Did you forget
the photograph?
ALICE (she hands it to him): Dearest Joey,

Of course not. Here it is, attached to a copy of the
Appeal News. I'm afraid it's not exactly a pin-up.   90
JOEY (kissing the photo): Alice, honey, you're a doll!

(Joey shows the photo to Tommy, then Smiley, who is
curious enough to come into the circle. Alice looks at
Henry, but he continues to ignore her.)

ALICE (back at center): The Appeal News, Volume I,
Number 3, May 5, 1943.
Dear Boys,
Feeling that el Cinco de Mayo is a very appropriate   95
day—the CIO radio program, "Our Daily Bread," is
devoting the entire time this evening to a discussion
of discrimination against Mexicans in general and
against you guys in particular.

(Music up. The repartee between Alice and the batos is
now friendly and warm. Even Smiley is smiling with
Alice. They check out her "drapes.")

Scene 3. The Incorrigible Pachuco

(Henry stands at downstage left, looks at the group,
then decides to speak.)

HENRY: May 17, 1943
Dear Miss Bloomfield,
I understand you're coming up to Q this weekend,
and I would like to talk to you—in private. Can you
arrange it?   5

(The batos turn away, taking a hint.)

ALICE (eagerly): Yes, yes, I can. What can I do for you,
Henry?

(Henry and Alice step forward toward each other. El
Pachuco moves in.)

HENRY: For me? ¡Ni madre!°
ALICE (puzzled): I don't understand.
HENRY: I wanted you to be the first to know, Alice. I'm   10
dropping out of the appeal.
ALICE (unbelieving): You're what?
HENRY: I'm bailing out, esa. Dropping out of the case,
see?
ALICE: Henry, you can't!   15
HENRY: Why can't I?
ALICE: Because you'll destroy our whole case! If we
don't present a united front, how can we ask the pub-
lic to support us?
HENRY: That's your problem. I never asked for their   20
support. Just count me out.
ALICE (getting nervous, anxious): Henry, please, think
about what you're saying. If you drop out, the rest of
the boys will probably go with you. How can you
even think of dropping out of the appeal? What about   25
George and all the people that have contributed their

2, 2. 50. **pinche gabacho:** Damned Anglo (derogatory).
80. **Eres . . . aquellas:** You are a fine chick.

2, 3. 8. **¡Ni madre!:** It doesn't matter, or, it's not worth a damn.

time and money in the past few months? You just
can't quit on them!

HENRY: Oh no? Just watch me.

30 ALICE: If you felt this way, why didn't you tell me before?

HENRY: Why didn't you ask me? You think you can just
move in and defend anybody you feel like? When did
I ever ask you to start a defense committee for me?
Or a newspaper? Or a fund-raising drive and all that
35 other shit? I don't need defending, esa. I can take care
of myself.

ALICE: But what about the trial, the sentence. They gave
you life imprisonment?

HENRY: It's my life!

40 ALICE: Henry, honestly—are you kidding me?

HENRY: You think so?

ALICE: But you've seen me coming and going. Writing to
you, speaking for you, traveling up and down the
state. You must have known I was doing it for you.
45 Nothing has come before my involvement, my attachment, my passion for this case. My boys have been
everything to me.

HENRY: My boys? My boys! What the hell are we—
your personal property? Well, let me set you straight,
50 lady, I ain't your boy.

ALICE: You know I never meant it that way.

HENRY: You think I haven't seen through your bullshit?
Always so concerned. Come on, boys. Speak out,
boys. Stand up for your people. Well, you leave my
55 people out of this! Can't you understand that?

ALICE: No, I can't understand that.

HENRY: You're just using Mexicans to play politics.

ALICE: Henry, that's the worst thing anyone has ever
said to me.

60 HENRY: Who are you going to help next—the Colored
People?

ALICE: No, as a matter of fact, I've already helped the
Colored People. What are you going to do next—go
to the gas chamber?

65 HENRY: What the hell do you care?

ALICE: I don't!

HENRY: Then get the hell out of here!

ALICE (furiously): You think you're the only one who
doesn't want to be bothered? You ought to try work-
70 ing in the Sleepy Lagoon defense office for a few
months. All the haggling, the petty arguments, the
lack of cooperation. I've wanted to quit a thousand
times. What the hell am I doing here? They're coming
at me from all sides. You're too sentimental and emo-
75 tional about this, Alice. You're too cold hearted,
Alice. You're collecting money and turning it over to
the lawyers, while the families are going hungry.
They're saying you can't be trusted because you're a
Communist, because you're a Jew. Okay! If that's the
80 way they feel about me, then to hell with them! I hate
them too. I hate their language, I hate their enchi-
ladas, and I hate their goddamned mariachi music!

(Pause. They look at each other. Henry smiles, then Alice—
feeling foolish—and they both break out laughing.)

HENRY: All right! Now you sound like you mean it.

ALICE: I do.

HENRY: Okay! Now we're talking straight.   85

ALICE: I guess I have been sounding like some square
paddy chick. But, you haven't exactly been Mister
Cool yourself . . . ese.

HENRY: So, let's say we're even Steven.

ALICE: Fair enough. What now?   90

HENRY: Why don't we bury the hatchet, you know what
I mean?

ALICE: Can I tell George you'll go on with the appeal?

HENRY: Yeah. I know there's a lot of people out there
who are willing and trying to help us. People who   95
feel that our conviction was an injustice. People like
George . . . and you. Well, the next time you see
them, tell them Hank Reyna sends his thanks.

ALICE: Why don't you tell them?

HENRY: You getting wise with me again?   100

ALICE: If you write an article—and I know you can—
we'll publish it in the *People's World*. What do you
say?

PACHUCO: Article! Pos who told you, you could write,
ese?   105

HENRY (laughs): Chale.

ALICE: I'm serious. Why don't you give it a try?

HENRY: I'll think about it. (Pause.) Listen, you think you
and I could write each other . . . outside the news-
letter?   110

ALICE: Sure.

HENRY: Then it's a deal. (They shake hands.)

ALICE: I'm glad we're going to be communicating. I
think we're going to be very good friends.

(Alice lifts her hands to Henry's shoulder in a gesture of
comradeship. Henry follows her hand, putting his on
top of hers.)

HENRY: You think so?   115

ALICE: I know so.

GUARD: Time, miss.

ALICE: I gotta go. Think about the article, okay? (She
turns to the Boys.) I gotta go, boys.

JOEY: Goodbye, Grandma! Say hello to Bertha.   120

SMILEY: And to my wife!

TOMMY: Give my love to Lupe!

GUARD: Time!

ALICE: I've got to go. Goodbye, goodbye.

(Alice exits, escorted by the Guard upstage left. As she
goes, Joey calls after her.)

JOEY: See you, Grandma.   125

TOMMY (turning to Joey and Smiley): She loves me.

PACHUCO: Have you forgotten what happened at the
trial? You think the Appeals Court is any different?
Some paddy judge sitting in the same fat-ass judg-
ment of your fate.   130

HENRY: Come on, ese, give me a break!

PACHUCO: One break, coming up!

(He snaps his fingers. The Guard blows his whistle.)

GUARD: Rec time!

Jorge Galvan as El Pachuco in
Zoot Suit at the
San Diego Repertory Theatre,
1997.

Alice Bloomfield (Carla
Harting) and Henry
Reyna (David Barrear)
talking in prison in *Zoot
Suit* at the San Diego
Repertory Theatre, 1997.
El Pachuco stands in the
background.

(*The batos move upstage to the upper level. Music. The Boys mime a game of handball against the backdrop. During the game, George enters at stage right and comes downstage carrying his briefcase. The Guard blows a whistle and stops the game.*)

GUARD: Reyna, Castro, Roberts, Torres!—You got a visitor.

135

Scene 4. Major George

(*The Boys turn and see George. They come down enthusiastically.*)

JOEY: ¡Óra-leh! ¡Ese, Cheer!°
SMILEY: George!
GEORGE: Hi, guys!

(*The Boys shake his hand, pat him on the back. Henry comes to him last.*)

How are you all doing? You boys staying in shape?

5 JOEY: Ese, you're looking at the hero of the San Quentin athletic program. Right, batos? (*He shadowboxes a little.*)
TOMMY: Ten rounds with a busted ankle.
JOEY: ¡Simón! And I won the bout, too. I'm the terror of the flyweights, ese. The killer fly!
10 TOMMY: They got us doing everything, Cheer. Baseball, basketball.
SMILEY: Watch repairing.
GEORGE (*impressed*): Watch repairing?
SMILEY: I'm also learning to improve my English and
15 arithmetic.
GEORGE: Warden Duffy has quite a program. I hear he's a good man?
JOEY: Simón, he's a good man. We've learned our lesson . . . Well, anyway, I've learned my lesson, boy.
20 No more pachuquismo for me. Too many people depending on us to help out. The raza° here in Los. The whole Southwest. Mexico, South America! Like you and Grandma say, this is the people's world. If you get us out of here, I figure the only thing I could
25 do is become a union organizer. Or go into major league baseball.
GEORGE: Baseball?
JOEY: Simón, ese. You're looking at the first Mexican Babe Ruth. Or maybe, "Babe Root." Root! You get it?
30 TOMMY: How about "Baby Zoot"?
JOEY: Solid, Jackson.
GEORGE: Babe Zooter!
JOEY: Solid tudee, that's all reet, ese.
GEORGE: What about you, Henry? What have you been
35 doing?
HENRY: Time, George, I've been doing time.
TOMMY: Ain't it the truth?

2, 4. 1. ¡Ese, Cheer!: Hey it's Cheer! (nickname for George).
21. raza: The race, the people, Chicanos.

SMILEY: Yeah, George! When you going to spring us out of here, ese?
HENRY: How's the appeal coming?   40
GEORGE (*getting serious*): Not bad. There's been a development I have to talk to you about. But other than that . . .
HENRY: Other than what?
SMILEY (*pause*): Bad news?   45
GEORGE (*hedging*): It all depends on how you look at it, Smiley. It really doesn't change anything. Work on the brief is going on practically day and night. The thing is, even with several lawyers on the case now, it'll still be several months before we file. I want to be   50
honest about that.
HENRY (*suspiciously*): Is that the bad news?
GEORGE: Not exactly. Sit down, boys. (*Pause. He laughs to himself.*) I really don't mean to make such a big deal out of this thing. Fact is I'm still not quite used   55
to the idea myself. (*Pause.*) You see . . . I've been drafted.
JOEY: Drafted?
TOMMY: Into the Army?
SMILEY: You?   60
GEORGE: That's right. I'm off to war.
JOEY: But . . . you're old, Cheer.
HENRY (*a bitter edge*): Why you, George? Why did they pick on you?
GEORGE: Well, Henry, I wouldn't say they "picked" on   65
me. There's lots of men my age overseas. After all, it is war time and . . .
HENRY: And you're handling our appeal.
GEORGE (*pause*): We have other lawyers.
HENRY: But you're the one who knows the case!   70
GEORGE (*pause*): I knew you were going to take this hard. Believe me, Henry, my being drafted has nothing to do with your case. It's just a coincidence.
HENRY: Like our being in here for life is a coincidence?
GEORGE: No, that's another . . .   75
HENRY: Like our being hounded every goddam day of our life is a coincidence?
GEORGE: Henry . . .

(*Henry turns away furiously. There is a pause.*)

It's useless anger, son, believe me. Actually, I'm quite flattered by your concern, but I'm hardly   80
indispensable.
HENRY (*deeply disturbed*): What the hell are you talking about, George?
GEORGE: I'm talking about all the people trying to get you out. Hundreds, perhaps thousands. Alice and I   85
aren't the only ones. We've got a heck of a fine team of lawyers working on the brief. With or without me, the appeal will be won. I promise you that.
HENRY: It's no use, George.
GEORGE: I realize all that sounds pretty unconvincing   90
under the circumstances, but it's true.
HENRY: Those bastard cops are never going to let us out of here. We're here for life and that's it.
GEORGE: You really believe that?

95 HENRY: What do you expect me to believe?
GEORGE: I wish I could answer that, son, but that's really for you to say.
GUARD: Time, Counselor.
GEORGE: Coming. (*Turns to the other Boys.*) Listen,
100 boys, I don't know where in the world I'll be the day your appeal is won—and it will be won—whether it's in the Pacific somewhere or in Europe or in a hole in the ground . . . Take care of yourselves.
TOMMY: See you around, George.
105 SMILEY: So long, George.
JOEY: 'Bye, Cheer.
GEORGE: Yeah. See you around. (*Pause.*) Goodbye, Henry. Good luck and God bless you.
HENRY: God bless you, too, George. Take care of your-
110 self.
TOMMY: Say, George, when you come back from the war, we're going to take you outa town and blast some weed.
JOEY: We'll get you a pair of buns you can hold in your
115 hands!
GEORGE: I may just take you up on that.

(*The Guard escorts George out, then turns back to the Boys.*)

GUARD: All right, new work assignments. Everybody report to the jute mill. Let's go.

(*Smiley, Joey, and Tommy start to exit. Henry hangs back.*)

What's the matter with you, Reyna? You got lead in
120 your pants? I said let's go.
HENRY: We're supposed to work in the mess hall.
GUARD: You got a new assignment.
HENRY: Since when?
GUARD: Since right now. Get going!
125 HENRY (*hanging back*): The warden know about this?
GUARD: What the hell do you care? You think you're something special? Come on, greaseball. Move!
HENRY: Make me, you bastard!
GUARD: Oh yeah.

(*The Guard pushes Henry. Henry pushes back. The batos react, as the Guard traps Henry with his club around the chest. The Boys move to Henry's defense.*)

130 Back!
HENRY (*to the batos*): Back off! BACK OFF! Don't be stupid.
GUARD: Okay, Reyna, you got solitary! Bastard, huh? Into the hole!

(*He pushes Henry onto center stage. Lights down. A single spot.*)

135 Line, greaseballs. Move out!

(*As they march.*)

Quickly, quickly. You're too slow. Move, move, move.

(*The Boys exit with the Guard.*)

Scene 5. Solitary

(*A lone saxophone sets the mood.*)

PACHUCO: Too bad, ese. He set you up again.
HENRY (*long pause. He looks around*): Solitary, ese . . . they gave me solitary. (*He sits down on the floor, a forlorn figure.*)
PACHUCO: Better get used to it, carnal. That's what this stretch is going to be about, see? You're in here for   5
life, bato.
HENRY: I can't accept it, ese.
PACHUCO: You've got to, Hank . . .
only this reality is real now,
only this place is real,   10
sitting in the lonely cell of your will . . .
HENRY: I can't see my hands.
PACHUCO: Then tell your eyes to forget the light, ese
Only the hard floor is there, carnal
Only the cold hard edge of this reality   15
and there is no time . . .
Each second is a raw drop of blood from your brain
that you must swallow
drop by drop
and don't even start counting   20
or you'll lose your mind . . .
HENRY: I've got to know why I'm here, ese! I've got to have a reason for being here.
PACHUCO: You're here, Hank, because you chose to be—
because you protected your brother and your family.   25
And nobody knows the worth of that effort better than you, ese.
HENRY: I miss them, ese . . . my jefitos, my carnalillo, my sis . . . I miss Della.
PACHUCO (*a spot illuminates Henry's family standing upstage; El Pachuco snaps it off*): Forget them!   30
Forget them all.
Forget your family and the barrio
beyond the wall.
HENRY: There's still a chance I'll get out.
PACHUCO: Fat chance.   35
HENRY: I'm talking about the appeal!
PACHUCO: And I'm talking about what's real! ¿Qué traes, Hank?° Haven't you learned yet?
HENRY: Learned what?
PACHUCO: Not to expect justice when it isn't there.   40
No court in the land's going to set you free.
Learn to protect your loves by binding them
in hate, ese! Stop hanging on to false hopes.
The moment those hopes come crashing down,
you'll find yourself on the ground foaming at   45
the mouth. ¡Como loco!°
HENRY (*turning on him furiously*): ¿Sabes qué? Don't tell me any more. I don't need you to tell me what to do. Fuck off! FUCK OFF!

2, 5. 37–38. **¿Qué traes, Hank?:** What's wrong, Hank?
46. **¡Como loco!:** Like a lunatic!

(*Henry turns away from El Pachuco. Long pause. An anxious, intense moment. El Pachuco shifts gears and breaks the tension with a satirical twist. He throws his arms out and laughs.*)

50 PACHUCO: ¡Órale pues!°
    Don't take the pinche play so seriously, Jesús!
    Es puro vacilón!°
    Watcha.

(*He snaps his fingers. Lights change. We hear the sounds of the city.*)

    This is Los, carnal.
55 You want to see some justice for pachucos?
    Check out what's happening back home today.
    The Navy has landed, ese—
    on leave with full pay
    and war's breaking out in the streets of L.A.!

Scene 6. Zoot Suit Riots

(*We hear music: the bugle call from "Bugle Call Rag." Suddenly the stage is awash in colored lights. The city of Los Angeles appears in the background in a panoramic vista of lights tapering into the night horizon. Sailors and Girls jitterbug on the dance floor. It is the Avalon Ballroom. The music is hot, the dancing hotter. El Pachuco and Henry stand to the side.*

The scene is in dance and mostly pantomime. Occasionally words are heard over the music which is quite loud. On the floor are two Sailors [Swabbie is one] and a Marine dancing with the Girls. A Shore Patrolman speaks to the Cigarette Girl. A Pimp comes on and watches the action. Little Blue and Zooter are also on the floor. Rudy enters wearing Henry's zoot suit with Bertha and Lupe. Lupe takes their picture, then all three move up center to the rear of the ballroom. Cholo comes in down center, sees them and moves up stage. All four make an entrance onto the dance floor.

The Marine takes his girl aside after paying her. She passes the money to the Pimp. The Sailors try to pick up on Lupe and Bertha, and Cholo pushes one back. The Sailors complain to the Shore Patrol, who throws Cholo out the door down center. There is an argument that Rudy joins. The Sailors go back to Bertha and Lupe who resist. Cholo and Rudy go to their defense and a fight develops. Zooter and Little Blue split. Cholo takes the Girls out and Rudy pulls a knife. He is facing the three Sailors and the Marine, when The Pachuco freezes the action.)

PACHUCO (*forcefully*): Órale, that's enough!

(*El Pachuco takes Rudy's knife and with a tap sends him off-stage. Rudy exits with the Girls. El Pachuco is now facing the angry Servicemen. He snaps his fingers. The Press enters quickly to the beeping sound of a radio broadcast.*)

PRESS: Good evening, Mr. and Mrs. North and South America and all the ships at sea. Let's go to press. FLASH. Los Angeles, California, June 3, 1943. Serious rioting broke out here today as flying squadrons of Marines and soldiers joined the Navy in a new assault on zooter-infested districts. A fleet of twenty taxicabs carrying some two hundred servicemen pulled out of the Naval Armory in Chavez Ravine tonight and assembled a task force that invaded the eastside barrio.

(*Unfreeze. The following speeches happen simultaneously.*)

MATE: You got any balls in them funny pants, boy?
SAILOR: He thinks he's tough . . .
SWABBIE: How about it, lardhead? You a tough guy or just a draft dodger?
PRESS: The Zoot Suiters, those gamin' dandies . . .
PACHUCO (*cutting them off*): Why don't you tell them what I really am, ese, or how you've been forbidden to use the very word . . .
PRESS: We are complying in the interest of the war.
PACHUCO: How have you complied?
PRESS: We're using other terms.
PACHUCO: Like *pachuco* and *zoot suiter*?
PRESS: What's wrong with that? The Zoot Suit Crime Wave is even beginning to push the war news off the front page.
PACHUCO: The Press distorted the very meaning of the word "zoot suit."
    All it is for you guys is another way to say
       Mexican.
    But the ideal of the original chuco°
    was to look like a diamond
    to look sharp
    hip
    bonaroo°
    finding a style of urban survival
    in the rural skirts and outskirts
    of the brown metropolis of Los, cabrón.
PRESS: It's an afront to good taste.
PACHUCO: Like the Mexicans, Filipinos, and blacks who wear them.
PRESS: Yes!
PACHUCO: Even the white kids and the Wops and the Jews are putting on the drape shape.
PRESS: You are trying to outdo the white man in exaggerated white man's clothes!
PACHUCO: Because everybody knows
    that Mexicans, Filipinos, and blacks
    belong to the huarache°
    the straw hat and the dirty overall.

---

50. **¡Órale pues!:** Listen then!   52. **Es puro vacilón!:** It's pure fantasy!

2, 6. 29. **chuco:** Pachuco.   33. **bonaroo:** Wonderful. 47. **huarache:** Mexican sandal.

PRESS: You savages weren't even wearing clothes when
50   the white man pulled you out of the jungle.
MARINE: My parents are going without collars and cuffs
    so you can wear that shit.
PRESS: That's going too far, too goddamned far, and it's
    got to be stopped!
55 PACHUCO: Why?
PRESS: Don't you know there's a war on? Don't you
    fucking well know you can't get away with that shit?
    What are we fighting for if not to annihilate the ene-
    mies of the American way of life?
60 MATE: Let's tear it off his back!
SAILORS/MARINE: Let's strip him! Get him! (Etc.)
PRESS: KILL THE PACHUCO BASTARD!!

(*Music: "American Patrol" by Glenn Miller. The Press
gets a searchlight from upstage center while the Four
Servicemen stalk El Pachuco.*)

SAILOR: Heh, zooter. Come on, zooter!
SWABBIE: You think you're more important than the
65   war, zooter?
MATE: Let's see if you got any balls in them funny pants,
    boy.
SWABBIE: Watch out for the knife.
SAILOR: That's a real chango monkey suit he's got on.
70 MATE: I bet he's half monkey—just like the Filipinos
    and niggers that wear them.
SWABBIE: You trying to outdo the white man in them
    glad rags, Mex?

(*They fight now to the finish. El Pachuco is overpow-
ered and stripped as Henry watches helplessly from his
position. The Press and Servicemen exit with pieces of
El Pachuco's zoot suit. El Pachuco stands. The only item
of clothing on his body is a small loincloth. He turns
and looks at Henry, with mystic intensity. He opens his
arms as an Aztec conch blows, and he slowly exits backward with powerful calm into the shadows. Silence.
Henry comes downstage. He absorbs the impact of what
he has seen and falls to his knees at center stage, spent
and exhausted. Lights down.*)

Scene 7. Alice

(*The Guard and Alice enter from opposite sides of the
stage. The Guard carries a handful of letters and is reading one of them.*)

GUARD: July 2, 1943.
ALICE: Dear Henry,
    I hope this letter finds you in good health and good
    spirits—but I have to assume you've heard about
5   the riots in Los Angeles. It was a nightmare, and it
    lasted for a week. The city is still in a state of shock.
GUARD (*folds letter back into envelope, then opens
    another*): August 5, 1943.
ALICE: Dear Henry,
    The riots here in L.A. have touched off race riots
10   all over the country—Chicago, Detroit, even little

Beaumont, Texas, for Christ's sake. But the one in
Harlem was the worst. Millions of dollars worth of
property damage. 500 people were hospitalized, and
five Negroes were killed.
GUARD: Things are rough all over.   15
ALICE: Please write to me and tell me how you feel.
GUARD (*the Guard folds up the second letter, stuffs it
    back into its envelope and opens a third*): August 20,
    1943.
ALICE: Dear Henry,
    Although I am disappointed not to have heard from   20
    you, I thought I would send you some good news for
    a change. Did you know we had a gala fund-raiser at
    the Mocambo?
GUARD: The Mocambo . . . Hotcha!°
ALICE: . . . and Rita Hayworth lent your sister Lupe a   25
    ball gown for the occasion. She got dressed at Cecil B.
    DeMille's house, and she looked terrific. Her escort
    was Anthony Quinn, and Orson Welles said . . .
GUARD: Orson Welles! Well! Sounds like Louella Par-
    sons. (*He folds up the letter.*) September 1, 1943.   30
ALICE: Henry, why aren't you answering my letters?
GUARD: He's busy. (*He continues to stuff the envelope.*)
ALICE: Henry, if there's something I've said or done . . . ?

(*The Guard shuffles the envelopes.*)

Henry . . .

(*Lights change. Guard crosses to center stage, where
Henry is still doubled up on the floor.*)

GUARD: Welcome back to the living, Reyna. It's been a   35
    long hot summer. Here's your mail.

(*The Guard tosses the letters to the floor directly in front
of Henry's head. Henry looks up slowly and grabs one
of the letters. He opens it, trying to focus. The Guard
exits.*)

ALICE: Henry, I just found out you did ninety days in
    solitary. I'm furious at the rest of the guys for keeping
    it from me. I talked to Warden Duffy, and he said you
    struck a guard. Did something happen I should know   40
    about? I wouldn't ask if it wasn't so important, but a
    clean record . . .

(*Henry rips up the letter he has been reading and scatters the others. Alarmed.*)

Henry?

(*Henry pauses, his instant fury spent and under control.
He sounds almost weary, but the anger is still there.*)

HENRY: You still don't understand, Alice.
ALICE (*softly, compassionate*): But I do! I'm not accusing   45
    you of anything. I don't care what happened or why
    they sent you there. I'm sure you had your reasons.
    But you know the public is watching you.
HENRY (*frustrated, a deep question*): Why do you do
    this, Alice?   50

2, 7. 24. **Hotcha!:** Expression used as a song lyric or title.

ALICE: What?

HENRY: The appeal, the case, all the shit you do. You think the public gives a goddamn?

ALICE (*with conviction*): Yes! We are going to get you
55   out of here, Henry Reyna. We are going to win!

HENRY (*probing*): What if we lose?

ALICE (*surprised but moving on*): We're not going to lose.

HENRY (*forcefully, insistent, meaning more than he is saying*): What if we do? What if we get another
60   crooked judge, and he nixes the appeal?

ALICE: Then we'll appeal again. We'll take it to the Supreme Court. (*A forced laugh.*) Hell, we'll take it all the way to President Roosevelt!

HENRY (*backing her up—emotionally*): What if we still
65   lose?

ALICE (*bracing herself against his aggression*): We can't.

HENRY: Why can't we?

ALICE (*giving a political response in spite of herself*): Because we've got too much support. You should see the kinds of people responding to us. Unions, Mexi-
70   cans, Negroes, Oakies. It's fantastic.

HENRY (*driving harder*): Why can't we lose, Alice?

ALICE: I'm telling you.

HENRY: No, you're not.

ALICE (*starting to feel vulnerable*): I don't know what to
75   tell you.

HENRY: Yes, you do!

ALICE (*frightened*): Henry . . . ?

HENRY: Tell me why we can't lose, Alice!

ALICE (*forced to fight back, with characteristic passion*): Stop it, Henry! Please stop it! I won't have you treat
80   me this way. I never have been able to accept one person pushing another around . . . pushing me around! Can't you see that's why I'm here? Because I can't stand it happening to you. Because I'm a Jew, god-dammit! I have been there . . . I have been there! If
85   you lose, I lose.

(*Pause. The emotional tension is immense. Alice fights to hold back tears. She turns away.*)

HENRY: I'm sorry . . .

ALICE (*pause*): It's stupid for us to fight like this. I look forward to coming here for weeks. Just to talk to you, to be with you, to see your eyes.

90 HENRY (*pause*): I thought a lot about you when I was in the hole. Sometimes . . . sometimes I'd even see you walk in, in the dark, and talk to me. Just like you are right now. Same look, same smile, same perfume . . . (*He pauses.*) Only the other one never gave
95   me so much lip. She just listened. She did say one thing. She said . . .

ALICE (*trying to make light of it, then more gently*): I can't say that to you, Henry. Not the way you want it.

HENRY: Why not?

100 ALICE (*she means it*): Because I can't allow myself to be used to fill in for all the love you've always felt and always received from all your women.

HENRY (*with no self-pity*): Give it a chance, Alice.

ALICE (*beside herself*): Give it a chance? You crazy idiot.
105   If I thought making love to you would solve all your problems, I'd do it in a second. Don't you know that? But it won't. It'll only complicate things. I'm trying to help you, goddammit. And to do that, I have to be your friend, not your white woman.

110 HENRY (*getting angry*): What makes you think I want to go to bed with you. Because you're white? I've had more white pieces of ass than you can count, ¿sabes? Who do you think you are? God's gift to us brown animals.

ALICE (*slaps him and stops, horrified, a whirlpool of
115   emotions*): Oh, Hank. All the love and hate it's taken to get us together in this lousy prison room. Do you realize only Hitler and the Second World War could have accomplished that? I don't know whether to laugh or cry.

(*Alice folds into her emotional spin, her body shaking. Suddenly she turns, whipping herself out of it with a cry, both laughing and weeping. They come to each other and embrace. Then they kiss—passionately. The Guard enters. He frowns.*)

120 GUARD: Time, Miss.

ALICE (*turning*): Already? Oh, my God, Henry, there's so many messages I was going to give you. Your mother and father send their love, of course. And Lupe and . . . Della. And . . . oh, yes. They want you
125   to know Rudy's in the Marines.

HENRY: The Marines?

ALICE: I'll write you all about it. Will you write me?

HENRY (*a glance at the Guard*): Yes.

GUARD (*his tone getting harsher*): Let's go, lady.

130 HENRY: Goodbye, Licha.

ALICE: I'll see you on the outside . . . Hank.

(*Alice gives Henry a thumb up gesture, and the Guard escorts her out. Henry turns downstage, full of thoughts. He addresses El Pachuco, who is nowhere to be seen.*)

HENRY: You were wrong, ese . . . There is something to hope for. I know now we're going to win the appeal. Do you hear me, ese? Ese! (*Pause.*) Are you even
135   there any more?

(*The Guard re-enters at a clip.*)

GUARD: Okay, Reyna, come on.

HENRY: Where to?

GUARD: We're letting you go . . .

(*Henry looks at him incredulously. The Guard smiles.*)

. . . to Folsom Prison with all the rest of the hardcore
140   cons. You really didn't expect to walk out of here a free man, did you? Listen, kid, your appeal stands about as much chance as the Japs and Krauts of winning the war. Personally, I don't see what that broad sees in you. I wouldn't give you the sweat off my
145   balls. Come on!

(*Henry and the Guard turn upstage to leave. Lights change. El Pachuco appears halfway up the backdrop, fully dressed again and clearly visible. Henry stops with a jolt as he sees him. El Pachuco lifts his arms. Lights go down as we hear the high sound of a bomb falling to earth.*)

Scene 8. *The Winning of the War*

(*The aerial bomb explodes with a reverberating sound and a white flash that illuminates the form of pachuco images in the black backdrop. Other bombs fall and all hell breaks loose. Red flashes, artillery, gunfire, ack-ack. Henry and the Guard exit. The Four Servicemen enter as an honor guard. Music: Glen Miller's "Saint Louis Blues March." As the Servicemen march on we see Rudy down left in his marine uniform, belt undone. Enrique, Dolores, and Lupe join him. Dolores has his hat, Lupe her camera. Enrique fastens two buttons on the uniform as Rudy does up his belt. Dolores inspects his collar and gives him his hat. Rudy puts on his hat and all pose for Lupe. She snaps the picture and Rudy kisses them all and is off. He picks up the giant switchblade from behind a newspaper bundle and joins the Servicemen as they march down in drill formation. The family marches off, looking back sadly. The drill ends and Rudy and the Shore Patrol move to one side. As Rudy's interrogation goes on, People in the barrio come on with newspapers to mime daily tasks. The Press enters.*)

PRESS: The *Los Angeles Examiner*, July 1, 1943. Headline: WORLD WAR II REACHES TURNING POINT. If the late summer of 1942 was the low point, a year later the war for the Allies is pounding
5   its way to certain victory.
SHORE PATROL: July 10!
RUDY: U.S., British, and Canadian troops invade Sicily, Sir!
SHORE PATROL: August 6!
10   RUDY: U.S. troops occupy Solomon Island, Sir!
SHORE PATROL: September 5!
RUDY: MacArthur's forces land on New Guinea, Sir!
SHORE PATROL: October 1!
RUDY: U.S. Fifth Army enters Naples, Sir!
15   PRESS: On and on it goes. From Corsica to Kiev, from Tarawa to Anzio. The relentless advance of the Allied armies cannot be checked.

(*One by one, Henry's family and friends enter, carrying newspapers. They tear the papers into small pieces.*)

The *Los Angeles Times*, June 6, 1944. Headline: Allied forces under General Eisenhower land in
20   Normandy.
SHORE PATROL: August 19!
RUDY: American First Army reaches Germany, Sir!
SHORE PATROL: October 17!
RUDY: MacArthur returns to the Philippines, Sir!
25   PRESS: On the homefront, Americans go on with their

daily lives with growing confidence and relief, as the war pushes on toward inevitable triumph. (*Pause.*) The *Los Angeles Daily News*, Wednesday, November 8, 1944. Headline: District Court of Appeals decides in Sleepy Lagoon murder case . . . boys in pachuco   30
murder given . . .
PEOPLE: FREEDOM!!!

(*Music bursts forth as the joyous crowd tosses the shredded newspaper into the air like confetti. The Boys enter upstage center, and the crowd rushes to them, weeping and cheering. There are kisses and hugs and tears of joy. Henry is swept forward by the triumphal procession.*)

Scene 9. *Return to the Barrio*

(*The music builds and people start dancing. Others just embrace. The tune is "Soldado Razo" played to a lively corrido beat. It ends with joyous applause, laughter, and tears.*)

RUDY: ¡Ese carnal!
HENRY: Rudy!!
DOLORES: ¡Bendito sea Dios! Who would believe this day would ever come? Look at you—you're all home!   5
LUPE: I still can't believe it. We won! We won the appeal!

(*Cheers.*)

ENRIQUE: I haven't felt like this since Villa took Zacatecas. (*Laughter, cheers.*) ¡Pero mira!° Look who's here. Mis hijos. (*Puts his arm around Henry and   10
Rudy.*) It isn't every day a man has two grown sons come home from so far away—one from the war, the other from . . . bueno, who cares? The Sleepy Lagoon is history, hombre. For a change, los Mexicanos have won!   15

(*Cheers.*)

GEORGE: Well, Henry. I don't want to say I told you so, but we sure taught Judge Charles a lesson in misconduct, didn't we? (*More cheers.*) Do you realize this is the greatest victory the Mexican-American community has ever had in the history of this whole blasted   20
country?
DOLORES: Yes, but if it wasn't for the unselfish thoughtfulness of people like you and this beautiful lady—and all the people who helped out, Mexicanos, Negros, all Americanos—our boys would not be   25
home today.
GEORGE: I only hope you boys realize how important you are now.
JOEY: Pos, I realize it, ese.

(*Laughter.*)

2, 9. 9. **¡Pero mira!:** But look!

30 RUDY: I came all the way from Hawaii just to get here,
      carnal. I only got a few days, but I'm going to get you
      drunk.
    HENRY: Pos, we'll see who gets who drunk, ese.

*(Laughter and hoots. Henry spots El Pachuco entering
from stage right.)*

    DOLORES: Jorge, Licha, todos.° Let's go into the house,
35   eh? I've made a big pot of menudo, and it's for
      everybody.
    ENRIQUE: There's ice-cold beer too. Vénganse, vamos
      todos.°
    GEORGE *(to Alice)*: Alice . . . Menudo, that's Mexican
40   chicken soup?

*(Everybody exits, leaving Henry behind with El
Pachuco.)*

    HENRY: It's good to see you again, ese. I thought I'd lost
      you.
    PACHUCO: H'm pues, it'd take more than the U.S. Navy
      to wipe me out.
45 HENRY: Where you been?
    PACHUCO: Pos, here in the barrio. Welcome back.
    HENRY: It's good to be home.
    PACHUCO: No hard feelings?
    HENRY: Chale—we won, didn't we?
50 PACHUCO: Simón.
    HENRY: Me and the batos have been in a lot of fights
      together, ese. But we won this one, because we
      learned to fight in a new way.
    PACHUCO: And that's the perfect way to end this play—
55   happy ending y todo. *(Pachuco makes a sweeping
      gesture. Lights come down. He looks up at the lights,
      realizing something is wrong. He flicks his wrist, and
      the lights go back up again.)*

      But life ain't that way, Hank.
      The barrio's still out there, waiting and wanting.
      The cops are still tracking us down like dogs.
      The gangs are still killing each other,
60   Families are barely surviving,
      And there in your own backyard . . . life goes on.

(Soft music. Della enters.)

    DELLA: Hank?

(Henry goes to her and they embrace.)

    HENRY: Where were you? Why didn't you come to the
      Hall of Justice to see us get out?
65 DELLA: I guess I was a little afraid things had changed.
      So much has happened to both of us.
    PACHUCO: Simón. She's living in your house.
    DELLA: After I got back from Ventura, my parents gave
      me a choice. Forget about you or get out.
70 HENRY: Why didn't you write to me?

    DELLA: You had your own problems. Your jefitos took
      care of me. Hey, you know what, Hank, I think they
      expect us to get married.
    PACHUCO: How about it, ese? You still going to give her
      that big pachuco wedding you promised?   75
    HENRY: I have to think about it.
    ALICE *(off-stage)*: Henry?
    PACHUCO *(snaps fingers)*: Wish you had the time. But
      here comes Licha.
    ALICE *(entering)*: Henry, I've just come to say good night.   80

(Della freezes and Henry turns to Alice.)

    HENRY: Good night? Why are you leaving so soon?
    ALICE: Soon? I've been here all afternoon. There'll be
      other times, Henry. You're home now, with your
      family, that's what matters.   85
    HENRY: Don't patronize me, Alice.
    ALICE *(surprised)*: Patronize you?
    HENRY: Yeah. I learned a few words in the joint.
    ALICE: Yo también,° Hank. Te quiero.°

(Pachuco snaps. Alice freezes, and Rudy enters.)

    RUDY: Ese, carnal, congratulations, the jefita just told
      me about you and Della. That's great, ese. But if you   90
      want me to be best man, you better do it in the next
      three days.
    HENRY: Wait a minute, Rudy, don't push me.
    RUDY: Qué pues,° getting cold feet already?

*(Henry is beginning to be surrounded by separate con-
versations.)*

    DELLA: If you don't want me here, I can move out.   95
    RUDY: Watcha. I'll let you and Della have our room
      tonight, bato. I'll sleep on the couch.
    ALICE: You aren't expecting me to sleep here, are you?
    HENRY: I'm not asking you to.
    PACHUCO/ALICE/RUDY/DELLA: Why not?   100
    RUDY: The jefitos will never know, ese.
    ALICE: Be honest, Henry.
    DELLA: What do you want me to do?
    HENRY: Give me a chance to think about it. Give me a
      second!   105
    PACHUCO: One second!

(Pachuco snaps. Enrique enters.)

    ENRIQUE: Bueno, bueno, pues,° what are you doing out
      here, hijo? Aren't you coming in for menudo?
    HENRY: I'm just thinking, jefito.
    ENRIQUE: ¿De qué, hombre?° Didn't you do enough of   110
      that in prison? Andale, this is your house. Come in
      and live again.
    HENRY: 'Apá, did you tell Della I was going to marry her?
    ENRIQUE: Yes, but only after you did.

---

34. Jorge, Licha, todos: George, Alice, everyone.   **37–38. Vén-
ganse, vamos todos:** Come back, let's go everyone.

88. Yo también: Me too.   **Te quiero:** I love you.   **94. Qué
pues:** Well what.   **107. Bueno, bueno, pues:** Good, good,
certainly.   **110. ¿De qué, hombre?:** About what, man?

115 RUDY: ¿Qué traes, carnal?° Don't you care about Della anymore?

ALICE: If it was just me and you, Henry, it might be different. But you have to think of your family.

HENRY: I don't need you to tell me my responsibilities.

120 ALICE: I'm sorry.

RUDY: Sorry, carnal.

DELLA: I don't need anybody to feel sorry for me. I did what I did because I wanted to. All I want to know is what's going to happen now. If you still want me, órale, suave. If you don't, that's okay, too. But I'm not going to hang around like a pendeja all my life.

RUDY: Your huisa's looking finer than ever, carnal.

ALICE: You're acting as if nothing has happened.

ENRIQUE: You have your whole life ahead of you.

130 ALICE: You belong here, Henry. I'm the one that's out of place.

RUDY: If you don't pick up on her, I'm going to have to step in.

HENRY: That's bullshit. What about what we shared in prison? I've never been that close to anybody.

ALICE: That was in prison.

HENRY: What the hell do you think the barrio is?

RUDY: It's not bullshit!

HENRY: Shut up, carnalillo!

140 RUDY: Carnalillo? How can you still call me that? I'm not your pinche little brother no more.

GEORGE (entering): You guys have got to stop fighting, Henry, or the barrio will never change. Don't you realize you men represent the hope of your people?

145 ALICE: Della was in prison too. You know you had thousands of people clamoring for your release, but you were Della's only hope.

HENRY: Look, esa, I know you did a year in Ventura. I know you stood up for me when it counted. I wish I could make it up to you.

150 DELLA: Don't give me your bullshit, Henry. Give it to Alice.

ALICE: I think it's time for Alice Bloomfield to go home.

HENRY: Don't be jealous, esa.

155 DELLA: Jealous? Mira, cabrón, I know I'm not the only one you ever took to the Sleepy Lagoon.

RUDY: The Sleepy Lagoon ain't shit. I saw real lagoons in those islands, ese—killing Japs! I saw some pachucos go out there that are never coming back.

160 DELLA: But I was always there when you came back, wasn't I?

DOLORES (entering): Henry? Come back inside, hijo. Everybody's waiting for you.

RUDY: Why didn't you tell them I was there, carnal? I was at the Sleepy Lagoon. Throwing chingazos with everybody!

HENRY: Don't you understand, Rudy? I was trying to keep you from getting a record. Those bastard cops are never going to leave us alone.

GEORGE: You've got to forget what happened, Henry.   170

HENRY: What can I give you, Della? I'm an ex-con.

DELLA: So am I!

SMILEY (entering): Let's face it, Hank. There's no future for us in this town. I'm taking my wife and kid and moving to Arizona.   175

DOLORES (simultaneously): I know what you are feeling, hijo, it's home again. I know inside you are afraid that nothing has changed. That the police will never leave you in peace. Pero no le hace.° Everything is going to be fine now. Marry Della and fill this house with children. Just do one thing for me— forget the zoot suit clothes.

ENRIQUE: If there's one thing that will keep a man off the streets it's his own familia.

GEORGE: Don't let this thing eat your heart out for the rest of your . . .   180

ALICE: Sometimes the best thing you can do for someone you love is walk away.   185

DELLA: What do you want, Hank?

RUDY: It cost me more than it did you.   190

SMILEY: We started the 38th and I'll never forget you, carnal. But I got to think about my family.   195

HENRY: Wait a minute! I don't know if I'll be back in prison tomorrow or not! I have nothing to give you, Della. Not even a piece of myself.

DELLA: I have my life to live, too, Hank. I love you. I would even die for you. Pero me chingan la madre° if I'm going to throw away my life for nothing.   200

HENRY: But I love you . . .

(Both Girls turn. Henry looks at Alice, then to the whole group upstage of him. Still turning, he looks at Della and goes to embrace her. The freeze ends and other people enter.)

LUPE: ¡Órale, Hank! Watcha Joey. The crazy bato went all the way to his house and put on his drapes.

JOEY: ¡Esos, batooooooosss! ¡Esas, huisaaaaaaass!°   205

TOMMY: Look at this cat! He looks all reet.

LUPE: Yeah, like a parakeet!

HENRY: ¿Y tú, ese?° How come you put on your tacuche? Where's the party?

JOEY: Pos, ain't the party here?   210

RUDY: Yeah, ese, but this ain't the Avalon Ballroom. The zoot suit died under fire here in Los. Don't you know that, cabrón?

ENRIQUE: Rudolfo!

LUPE: And he was supposed to get Henry drunk.   215

RUDY: Shut up, esa!

ENRIQUE: ¡Ya pues!° Didn't you have any menudo?

---

115. ¿Qué traes, carnal?: What's wrong, brother?

184. Pero no le hace: But it doesn't happen.   200. Pero me chingan la madre: But I'll be damned.   205. ¡Esos . . . huisaaaaaaass!: Hey dudes! Hey girls!   208. ¿Y tú, ese?: And you man?   217. ¡Ya pues!: Enough already!

Vieja,° fix him a great big bowl of menudo and put
plenty of chile in it. We're going to sweat it out of
him.

220 RUDY: I don't need no pinche menudo.

HENRY: Watch your language, carnal.

RUDY: And I don't need you! I'm a man. I can take care
of myself!

JOEY: Muy marine el bato° . . .

225 ENRIQUE: Rudy, hijo. Are you going to walk into the
kitchen or do I have to drag you?

RUDY: Whatever you say, jefito.

GEORGE: Well, Alice. This looks like the place where we
came in. I think it's about time we left.

230 ALICE: Say the word, George, just say the word.

DOLORES: No, no. You can't leave so soon.

JOEY: Chale, chale, chale. You can't take our Grandma.
¿Qué se trae, carnal? Póngase más abusado, ese. No
se haga tan square.°

235 GEORGE: Okay, square I got. What was the rest of it?

JOEY: Pos, le estoy hablando en chicas patas, ese. Es
puro chicano.°

RUDY: ¿Qué chicano? Ni que madre, cabrón.° Why
don't you grow up?

240 JOEY: Grow up, ese?

RUDY: Try walking downtown looking like that. See if
the sailors don't skin your ass alive.

JOEY: So what? It's no skin off your ass. Come on,
Bertha.

245 RUDY: She's staying with me.

JOEY: She's mine.

RUDY: Prove it, punk.

(*Rudy attacks Joey and they fight. The Batos and Rucas
take out Joey. Henry pacifies Rudy, who bursts out crying. Enrique, Della, Dolores, Alice, Lupe, and George
are the only ones left. Rudy in a flush of emotion.*)

Cabrones, se amontonaron.° They ganged up on me,
carnal. You left me and they ganged up on me. You
250 shouldn't have done it, carnal. Why didn't you take me
with you. For the jefitos? The jefitos lost me anyway.

HENRY: Come on in the house, Rudy . . .

RUDY: No! I joined the Marines. I didn't have to join,
255 but I went. ¿Sabes por qué? Because they got me, carnal. Me chingaron, ese.° (*Sobs.*) I went to the pinche
show with Bertha, all chingón in your tacuche, ese. I
was wearing your zoot suit, and they got me. Twenty
sailors, Marines. We were up in the balcony. They
260 came down from behind. They grabbed me by the
neck and dragged me down the stairs, kicking and

punching and pulling my greña.° They dragged me
out into the streets . . . and all the people watched
while they stripped me. (*Sobs.*) They stripped me,
carnal. Bertha saw them strip me. Hijos de la chin-   265
gada,° they stripped me.

(*Henry goes to Rudy and embraces him with fierce love
and desperation. Pause. Tommy comes running in.*)

TOMMY: ¡Órale! There's cops outside. They're trying to
arrest Joey.

(*George crosses to Tommy.*)

GEORGE (*bursting out*): Joey?

TOMMY: They got him up against your car. They're try-   270
ing to say he stole it!

GEORGE: Oh, God. I'll take care of this.

ALICE: I'll go with you.

(*George, Tommy, and Alice exit.*)

HENRY: Those fucking bastards! (*He starts to exit.*)

DELLA: Henry, no!   275

HENRY: What the hell do you mean no? Don't you see
what's going on outside?

DELLA: They'll get you again! That's what they want.

HENRY: Get out of my way! (*He pushes her out of the
way, toward Dolores.*)

ENRIQUE (*stands up before Henry*): ¡Hijo!   280

HENRY: Get out of my way, jefe!°

ENRIQUE: You will stay here!

HENRY: Get out of my way!

(*Enrique powerfully pushes him back and throws Henry
to the floor and holds.*)

ENRIQUE: ¡TE DIGO QUE NO!

(*Silent moment. Henry stands up and offers to strike
Enrique. But something stops him. The realization that
if he strikes back or even if he walks out the door, the
family bond is irreparably broken. Henry tenses for a
moment, then relaxes and embraces his father. Della
goes to them and joins the embrace. Then Dolores, then
Lupe, then Rudy. All embrace in a tight little group.
Press enters right and comes down.*)

PRESS: Henry Reyna went back to prison in 1947 for   285
robbery and assault with a deadly weapon. While
incarcerated, he killed another inmate and he wasn't
released until 1955, when he got into hard drugs. He
died of the trauma of his life in 1972.

PACHUCO: That's the way you see it, ese. But there's   290
other ways to end this story.

RUDY: Henry Reyna went to Korea in 1950. He was
shipped across in a destroyer and defended the 38th
Parallel until he was killed at Inchon in 1952, being
posthumously awarded the Congressional Medal of   295
Honor.

---

218. **Vieja:** Old woman (wife).   224. **Muy marine el bato:** The
dude's acting like a marine.   233–234. **¿Qué . . . square:**
What's wrong, brother? Smarten up, man. That doesn't seem
very square.   236–237. **Pos . . . chicano:** Anyhow, I was speaking in Chicano, man. It's pure Chicano.   238. **¿Qué . . . cabrón:**
What Chicano? Nothing that matters (vulgar term).
248. **Cabrones, se amontonaron:** (Vulgar term) they ganged
up on me.   256. **Me chingaron, ese:** They (vulgar term) me
up, man.

262. **greña:** Hair.   265–266. **Hijos de la chingada:** (Vulgar
term).   281. **jefe:** Dad.

ALICE: Henry Reyna married Della in 1948 and they have five kids, three of them now going to the University, speaking calo and calling themselves
300   Chicanos.
GEORGE: Henry Reyna, the born leader . . .
JUDGE: Henry Reyna, the social victim . . .
BERTHA: Henry Reyna, the street corner warrior . . .
SMILEY: Henry Reyna, el carnal de aquellas° . . .

304. **el carnal de aquellas:** The outstanding brother.

JOEY: Henry Reyna, the zoot suiter . . .   305
TOMMY: Henry Reyna, my friend . . .
LUPE: Henry Reyna, my brother . . .
ENRIQUE: Henry Reyna . . .
DOLORES: Our son . . .
DELLA: Henry Reyna, my love . . .   310
PACHUCO: Henry Reyna . . . El Pachuco . . . The man . . . the myth . . . still lives. (*Lights down and fade out.*)

Harold Pinter

Harold Pinter (b. 1930) has written plays for the commercial stage, radio, and television as well as film scripts produced by some of the best directors of his time. Pinter was born into relatively humble circumstances in East London, but his early schooling distinguished him, and he eventually enrolled in London's prestigious Royal Academy of Dramatic Arts to study acting. When he finished his studies, he joined a company, toured for several years, and began to write for the stage. His previous writing efforts had been in prose: short stories and a long novel, *The Dwarfs* (1956), purportedly autobiographical, but never finished and not published until 1990. Produced as a radio play in 1960, it expresses some of the themes of his best work: the disintegration of a mind and the cruelty of people to their fellow beings.

In 1957 Pinter wrote three important plays, the one-act *The Room* and *The Dumb Waiter* and the full-length *The Birthday Party* (finished in 1958). All were well received. They established his method in dialogue and to a large extent the style that has dominated his work. The critic Martin Esslin, who coined the term "theater of the absurd," saw in Pinter's work an absurdist strain, especially in the nihilism—the belief in nothing—that sometimes shows up in his work. Pinter's characters usually reveal no spiritual awareness and no longing for spiritual values.

Pinter's dialogue sometimes has qualities of aimlessness, at least on the surface. But always the dialogue penetrates the unconsciousness of the audience and reveals the nature of the characters and their situation. Even the repetitious dialogue makes the audience more aware of the limitations and the pain of the circumstances in which Pinter's people find themselves.

Early reaction to the plays sometimes saw the aimless dialogue and the absurdist qualities as shortcomings rather than as indictments of the social order from which the plays arose. Yet the brutality of his characters to one another, their lack of sympathy for one another, and their demands for dominance have all become hallmarks of late-twentieth-century life.

The first of Pinter's plays to catch the attention of the general theater public was the commercially produced *The Caretaker* (1960), a play about two brothers, one of whom, Aston, invites a bewildered and all but mentally destroyed tramp, Davies, to become a caretaker in his room. Davies hardly knows who he is. His identity is essentially reduced to nothing by his soul-destroying life, and he speaks in broken language, especially when he is trying to explain that he left his identity papers in his beloved Sidcup—some fifteen years before—and that if they could find those papers, he would know where he was born and who he was. At the end of the play the younger brother, Mick, torments Davies, demanding that he leave, twisting his arm, verbally abusing him, but then relenting. The play ends with the shards of a life, as Davies says: "Listen . . . if I . . . go down . . . if I was to . . . get my papers . . . would you . . . would you let . . . would you . . . if I got down . . . and got my . . . (*Long silence.*)"

Pinter's *The Homecoming* (1965) has a brutal, shocking quality. A professor returns to England from America with his wife, and it becomes clear that he plans to return to America but that his wife will stay on as a mistress to his father and his brothers. The matter-of-factness with which the situation is treated and the way the relationships are portrayed contribute to the play's shock value. *The Homecoming* established Pinter as a major playwright.

In 1968 his play *Landscape* was censored for the use of obscenities, but eventually it and another short play, *Silence,* were produced in London in 1969 and in New York in 1970. *Old Times* was produced in London and in New York in 1971. Throughout the 1970s Pinter directed many plays by other playwrights and acted in films and on stage. *The Hothouse,* which was revived in 1995, was first produced in Hampstead in 1980. He later directed it himself in Providence, Rhode Island. He wrote the screenplay for *Betrayal* in 1982, and he also wrote the screenplay for *The French Lieutenant's Woman* (1981), which received an Academy Award nomination for best film. In 1992 he adapted Kazuo Ishiguro's novel *Remains of the Day* for the screen and also wrote the screenplay for Franz Kafka's *The Trial.*

Recent plays include the full-length *Moonlight* (1993) and the short play *Ashes to Ashes* (1996). *Celebrations* (2000) is a short play and was paired at the Almeida Theatre in London with *The Room* (1957), his first play. Ordinarily, Pinter does not let his short plays be paired with other pieces. Even *Mountain Language* (1988), which lasted only twenty minutes, was produced alone by the Royal National Theatre in its Lyttelton Theatre. Pinter's most recent play, *War* (2003), includes a speech and eight poems on the theme of conflict. In addition to his playwriting, Pinter has also continued acting and appears in a major role as Sir Thomas Bertram in Patricia Rozema's film of Jane Austen's novel *Mansfield Park* (1999).

In 2005 Pinter won the Nobel Prize for literature. In 2006 he played Krapp in Beckett's *Krapp's Last Tape.*

THE HOMECOMING

The shock value of *The Homecoming* was much more pronounced in 1965 than it is today, partly because the idea of the dysfunctional family was less common then than it is now. Playwrights such as Sam Shepard in the United States and Edward Bond in England—among many other writers exploring the inner workings of the family—have made the themes in *The Homecoming* more intelligible today than they were in 1965. Moreover, the impact of absurdist drama has been absorbed over the years, and audience expectations are less rigid now than in 1965. However, Pinter's play still sets the bar for portraying not only dysfunctional but also brutal, irrational, and ironic forces at work in a family of men.

The very title is ironic. Ordinarily, a homecoming involves a warm and loving family filled with delight at receiving back into its bosom a wandering child. Homecomings are reasons for celebrations, for joyous gatherings. Norman Rockwell images of homecomings graced magazine covers for years and helped to establish our understanding of the expression. Pinter destroys that image with his own portrait, one that tears away any veneer of social acceptability. He forces us to look at a picture of hostility, anger, envy, and lust.

Beginning with the father Max's intimidation of his son Lenny, and then moving to Max's brother Sam, the limousine driver who gets no respect, we see from the beginning of the play that there is no pretense of geniality or even reasonable manners in this family. The characters sound pathological, even deep within their tangled language. Soon we learn that Max is a butcher, concerned with flesh and dead animals. Indeed, he cuts through everything, including the basics of family civility.

Pinter's use of silences, pauses, and a variety of rhythms within the dialogue helps us parse the emotional lives of the characters—at least insofar as they understand their own situations. We are not necessarily meant to see these characters as "realistic" in the nineteenth-century sense of the term. Rather, they are fields of force that are brought to bear against one another; thus they have abstract power in the drama without actually being symbols. They are themselves, unique—and horrifying. This is not the comfortable theater of the popular stage.

The very act of coming home takes place at night. Teddy and Ruth have been married for six years, yet people at "home" know nothing about the marriage or about the fact that there are three grandchildren. Teddy has not called ahead to let his father get ready for a celebration. He and Ruth essentially sneak into the house after everyone has gone to bed. Teddy finds that his room upstairs is still as he left it, but Ruth does not wish to sleep just yet. They have come from a vacation in Venice, usually a romantic place to visit. Because of Ruth's restlessness, the family members are slowly roused and, one by one, come to see who has entered the house.

Immediately, the men living here with no woman begin to initiate a sexual dynamic. Accusing Ruth of being a whore and a slut, Max demands that she leave. After a few moments of brutality, in which Max punches another son, Joey, a demolition worker, in the stomach, and spouts abuse at everyone present, he turns and offers to embrace Teddy, the philosophy professor who has come home. Tellingly, no embrace occurs as the first act ends.

Some commentators have interpreted Ruth's decision to stay with Max and his sons and brother as being a metaphor for marriage as a form of prostitution. Teddy explains what a pleasant life he has in the United States teaching at the university and entertaining intelligent friends. But Ruth never comments on her life with Teddy. Instead, she listens to the plans that Max and his sons have worked out, which include Ruth occupying her own apartment, making her own money through prostitution, and then looking after the men. Her terms are exorbitant, yet the men give in quickly. She establishes her needs, her limits, and her demands. Critics have seen this as an instance in which the woman turns the tables on the men and dominates them with her sexual power so that the play ends with her in the ascendant position.

The Homecoming in Performance

The first performance was directed by Peter Hall and produced by the Royal Shakespeare Company at the Aldwych in London's West End in 1965. The play had toured extensively before coming to London, but it was still a powerful shocker for most of the audience. Even Peter Hall, in an interview with Irving Wardle, said, "It's not a pleasant play. It's a play that's uncomfortable." He went on to compare the family with a human jungle. Paul Rogers played Max as a total bully, and Vivian Merchant played a seductive Ruth. Pinter wrote the play for the Aldwych, where his earlier work had been performed. His instructions to the set designer were to put nothing on the stage except what was absolutely required. The large stage with very little furniture was itself a powerful image of brutality. The New York performance followed in 1967, and Walter Kerr, the *Times* critic, complained that Pinter was holding too much back for too long. His review was anything but positive. By the 1990 Cambridge, Massachusetts, production at the American Repertory Theatre, the play had been performed often in the United States and abroad. The reviews of the ART performance not only praised the play but also read numerous subtleties into it and even considered it to have theological implications. One reviewer said, it "is perfect, simply, devastatingly perfect." Ian Holm, who had played Lenny in the premiere, returned to play Max in the 2001 Dublin Gate Theatre production that eventually toured and played at the Lincoln Center Festival in New York City. In early 2007, Pinter himself played Max on a radio production in London. The 2007 production at the Cort Theater in New York City starred Ian McShane as Max. McShane, fresh from his performances as a foul-mouthed brute on HBO's *Deadwood*, seemed ideally suited to the part. Ben Brantley, in the *New York Times*, said of the production that on its fortieth anniversary, the play is universal and "lives up to its reputation."

Harold Pinter (b. 1930)

THE HOMECOMING   *1965*

Characters

MAX, *a man of seventy*
LENNY, *a man in his early thirties*
SAM, *a man of sixty-three*
JOEY, *a man in his middle twenties*
TEDDY, *a man in his middle thirties*
RUTH, *a woman in her early thirties*

Summer

An old house in North London.
  A large room, extending the width of the stage.
  The back wall, which contained the door, has been removed.
  A square arch shape remains. Beyond it, the hall. In the hall a staircase, ascending U.L., well in view. The front door U.R.

A coatstand, hooks, etc.
  In the room a window, R. Odd tables, chairs. Two large armchairs. A large sofa, L. Against R. wall a large sideboard, the upper half of which contains a mirror. U.L., a radiogram.

ACT 1

Evening.

Lenny is sitting on the sofa with a newspaper, a pencil in his hand. He wears a dark suit. He makes occasional marks on the back page.
  Max comes in, from the direction of the kitchen. He goes to sideboard, opens top drawer, rummages in it, closes it.

He wears an old cardigan and a cap, and carries a stick.

He walks downstage, stands, looks about the room.

MAX: What have you done with the scissors?

(*Pause.*)

I said I'm looking for the scissors. What have you done with them?

(*Pause.*)

Did you hear me? I want to cut something out of the paper.

LENNY: I'm reading the paper.

MAX: Not that paper. I haven't even read that paper. I'm talking about last Sunday's paper. I was just having a look at it in the kitchen.

(*Pause.*)

Do you hear what I'm saying? I'm talking to you! Where's the scissors?

LENNY (*looking up, quietly*): Why don't you shut up, you daft prat?

(*Max lifts his stick and points it at him.*)

MAX: Don't you talk to me like that. I'm warning you.

(*He sits in large armchair.*)

There's an advertisement in the paper about flannel vests. Cut price. Navy surplus. I could do with a few of them.

(*Pause.*)

I think I'll have a fag. Give me a fag.

(*Pause.*)

I just asked you to give me a cigarette.

(*Pause.*)

Look what I'm lumbered with.

(*He takes a crumpled cigarette from his pocket.*)

I'm getting old, my word of honor.

(*He lights it.*)

You think I wasn't a tearaway? I could have taken care of you, twice over. I'm still strong. You ask your Uncle Sam what I was. But at the same time I always had a kind heart. Always.

(*Pause.*)

I used to knock about with a man called MacGregor. I called him Mac. You remember Mac? Eh?

(*Pause.*)

Huhh! We were two of the worst hated men in the West End of London. I tell you, I still got the scars. We'd walk into a place, the whole room'd stand up, they'd make way to let us pass. You never heard such silence. Mind you, he was a big man, he was over six foot tall. His family were all MacGregors, they came all the way from Aberdeen, but he was the only one they called Mac.

(*Pause.*)

He was very fond of your mother, Mac was. Very fond. He always had a good word for her.

(*Pause.*)

Mind you, she wasn't such a bad woman. Even though it made me sick just to look at her rotten stinking face, she wasn't such a bad bitch. I gave her the best bleeding years of my life, anyway.

LENNY: Plug it, will you, you stupid sod, I'm trying to read the paper.

MAX: Listen! I'll chop your spine off, you talk to me like that! You understand? Talking to your lousy filthy father like that!

LENNY: You know what, you're getting demented.

(*Pause.*)

What do you think of Second Wind for the three-thirty?

MAX: Where?

LENNY: Sandown Park.

MAX: Don't stand a chance.

LENNY: Sure he does.

MAX: Not a chance.

LENNY: He's the winner.

(*Lenny ticks the paper.*)

MAX: He talks to me about horses.

(*Pause.*)

I used to live on the course. One of the loves of my life. Epsom? I knew it like the back of my hand. I was one of the best-known faces down at the paddock. What a marvelous open-air life.

(*Pause.*)

He talks to me about horses. You only read their names in the papers. But I've stroked their manes, I've held them, I've calmed them down before a big race. I was the one they used to call for. Max, they'd say, there's a horse here, he's highly strung, you're the only man on the course who can calm him. It was true. I had a . . . I had an instinctive understanding of animals. I should have been a trainer. Many times I was offered the job—you know, a proper post, by the Duke of . . . I forget his name . . . one of the Dukes. But I had family obligations, my family needed me at home.

(*Pause.*)

The times I've watched those animals thundering past the post. What an experience. Mind you, I didn't lose, I made a few bob out of it, and you know why? Because I always had the smell of a good horse.

I could smell him. And not only the colts but the fillies. Because the fillies are more highly strung than the colts, they're more unreliable, did you know that? No, what do you know? Nothing. But I was always able to tell a good filly by one particular trick. I'd look her in the eye. You see? I'd stand in front of her and look her straight in the eye, it was a kind of hypnotism, and by the look deep down in her eye I could tell whether she was a stayer or not. It was a gift. I had a gift.

(*Pause.*)

And he talks to me about horses.
LENNY: Dad, do you mind if I change the subject?

(*Pause.*)

I want to ask you something. That dinner we had before, what was the name of it? What do you call it?

(*Pause.*)

Why don't you buy a dog? You're a dog cook. Honest. You think you're cooking for a lot of dogs.
MAX: If you don't like it get out.
LENNY: I am going out. I'm going out to buy myself a proper dinner.
MAX: Well, get out! What are you waiting for?

(*Lenny looks at him.*)

LENNY: What did you say?
MAX: I said shove off out of it, that's what I said.
LENNY: You'll go before me, Dad, if you talk to me in that tone of voice.
MAX: Will I, you bitch?

(*Max grips his stick.*)

LENNY: Oh, Daddy, you're not going to use your stick on me, are you? Eh? Don't use your stick on me, Daddy. No, please. It wasn't my fault, it was one of the others. I haven't done anything wrong, Dad, honest. Don't clout me with that stick, Dad.

(*Silence.*)
(*Max sits hunched. Lenny reads the paper.*)
(*Sam comes in the front door. He wears a chauffeur's uniform.*)
(*He hangs his hat on a hook in the hall and comes into the room. He goes to a chair, sits in it and sighs.*)

Hullo, Uncle Sam.
SAM: Hullo.
LENNY: How are you, Uncle?
SAM: Not bad. A bit tired.
LENNY: Tired? I bet you're tired. Where you been?
SAM: I've been to London Airport.
LENNY: All the way up to London Airport? What, right up the M4?
SAM: Yes, all the way up there.
LENNY: Tch, tch, tch. Well, I think you're entitled to be tired, Uncle.
SAM: Well, it's the drivers.

LENNY: I know. That's what I'm talking about. I'm talking about the drivers.
SAM: Knocks you out.

(*Pause.*)

MAX: I'm here, too, you know.

(*Sam looks at him.*)

I said I'm here, too. I'm sitting here.
SAM: I know you're here.

(*Pause.*)

SAM: I took a Yankee out there today . . . to the Airport.
LENNY: Oh, a Yankee, was it?
SAM: Yes, I been with him all day. Picked him up at the Savoy at half past twelve, took him to the Caprice for his lunch. After lunch I picked him up again, took him down to a house in Eaton Square—he had to pay a visit to a friend there—and then round about tea-time I took him right the way out to the Airport.
LENNY: Had to catch a plane there, did he?
SAM: Yes. Look what he gave me. He gave me a box of cigars.

(*Sam takes a box of cigars from his pocket.*)

MAX: Come here. Let's have a look at them.

(*Sam shows Max the cigars. Max takes one from the box, pinches it and sniffs it.*)

It's a fair cigar.
SAM: Want to try one?

(*Max and Sam light cigars.*)

You know what he said to me? He told me I was the best chauffeur he'd ever had. The best one.
MAX: From what point of view?
SAM: Eh?
MAX: From what point of view?
LENNY: From the point of view of his driving, Dad, and his general sense of courtesy, I should say.
MAX: Thought you were a good driver, did he, Sam? Well, he gave you a first-class cigar.
SAM: Yes, he thought I was the best he'd ever had. They all say that, you know. They won't have anyone else, they only ask for me. They say I'm the best chauffeur in the firm.
LENNY: I bet the other drivers tend to get jealous, don't they, Uncle?
SAM: They do get jealous. They get very jealous.
MAX: Why?

(*Pause.*)

SAM: I just told you.
MAX: No, I just can't get it clear, Sam. Why do the other drivers get jealous?
SAM: Because (a) I'm the best driver, and because . . . (b) I don't take liberties.

(*Pause.*)

I don't press myself on people, you see. These big businessmen, men of affairs, they don't want the driver jawing all the time, they like to sit in the back, have a bit of peace and quiet. After all, they're sitting in a Humber° Super Snipe, they can afford to relax. At the same time, though, this is what really makes me special . . . I do know how to pass the time of day when required.

(*Pause.*)

For instance, I told this man today I was in the second world war. Not the first. I told him I was too young for the first. But I told him I fought in the second.

(*Pause.*)

So did he, it turned out.

(*Lenny stands, goes to the mirror and straightens his tie.*)

LENNY: He was probably a colonel, or something, in the American Air Force.
SAM: Yes.
LENNY: Probably a navigator, or something like that, in a Flying Fortress. Now he's most likely a high executive in a worldwide group of aeronautical engineers.
SAM: Yes.
LENNY: Yes, I know the kind of man you're talking about.

(*Lenny goes out, turning to his right.*)

SAM: After all, I'm experienced. I was driving a dust cart at the age of nineteen. Then I was in long-distance haulage. I had ten years as a taxi-driver and I've had five as a private chauffeur.
MAX: It's funny you never got married, isn't it? A man with all your gifts.

(*Pause.*)

Isn't it? A man like you?
SAM: There's still time.
MAX: Is there?

(*Pause.*)

SAM: You'd be surprised.
MAX: What you been doing, banging away at your lady customers, have you?
SAM: Not me.
MAX: In the back of the Snipe? Been having a few crafty reefs in a layby, have you?
SAM: Not me.
MAX: On the back seat? What about the armrest, was it up or down?
SAM: I've never done that kind of thing in my car.
MAX: Above all that kind of thing, are you, Sam?

Humber: An elegant British automobile.

SAM: Too true.
MAX: Above having a good bang on the back seat, are you?
SAM: Yes, I leave that to others.
MAX: You leave it to others? What others? You paralyzed prat!
SAM: I don't mess up my car! Or my . . . my boss's car! Like other people.
MAX: Other people? What other people?

(*Pause.*)

What other people?

(*Pause.*)

SAM: Other people.

(*Pause.*)

MAX: When you find the right girl, Sam, let your family know, don't forget, we'll give you a number one send-off, I promise you. You can bring her to live here, she can keep us all happy. We'd take it in turns to give her a walk round the park.
SAM: I wouldn't bring her here.
MAX: Sam, it's your decision. You're welcome to bring your bride here, to the place where you live, or on the other hand you can take a suite at the Dorchester. It's entirely up to you.
SAM: I haven't got a bride.

(*Sam stands, goes to the sideboard, takes an apple from the bowl, bites into it.*)

Getting a bit peckish.

(*He looks out of the window.*)

Never get a bride like you had, anyway. Nothing like your bride . . . going about these days. Like Jessie.

(*Pause.*)

After all, I escorted her once or twice, didn't I? Drove her round once or twice in my cab. She was a charming woman.

(*Pause.*)

All the same, she was your wife. But still . . . they were some of the most delightful evenings I've ever had. Used to just drive her about. It was my pleasure.
MAX (*softly, closing his eyes*): Christ.
SAM: I used to pull up at a stall and buy her a cup of coffee. She was a very nice companion to be with.

(*Silence.*)
(*Joey comes in the front door. He walks into the room, takes his jacket off, throws it on a chair and stands.*)
(*Silence.*)

JOEY: Feel a bit hungry.
SAM: Me, too.

MAX: Who do you think I am, your mother? Eh? Honest. They walk in here every time of the day and night like bloody animals. Go and find yourself a mother.

(*Lenny walks into the room, stands.*)

JOEY: I've been training down at the gym.

SAM: Yes, the boy's been working all day and training all night.

MAX: What do you want, you bitch? You spend all the day sitting on your arse at London Airport, buy yourself a jamroll. You expect me to sit here waiting to rush into the kitchen the moment you step in the door? You've been living sixty-three years, why don't you learn to cook?

SAM: I can cook.

MAX: Well, go and cook!

(*Pause.*)

LENNY: What the boys want, Dad, is your own special brand of cooking, Dad. That's what the boys look forward to. The special understanding of food, you know, that you've got.

MAX: Stop calling me Dad. Just stop all that calling me Dad, do you understand?

LENNY: But I'm your son. You used to tuck me up in bed every night. He tucked you up, too, didn't he, Joey?

(*Pause.*)

He used to like tucking up his sons.

(*Lenny turns and goes towards the front door.*)

MAX: Lenny.

LENNY (*turning*): What?

MAX: I'll give you a proper tuck up one of these nights, son. You mark my word.

(*They look at each other.*)
(*Lenny opens the front door and goes out.*)
(*Silence.*)

JOEY: I've been training with Bobby Dodd.

(*Pause.*)

And I had a good go at the bag as well.

(*Pause.*)

I wasn't in bad trim.

MAX: Boxing's a gentleman's game.

(*Pause.*)

I'll tell you what you've got to do. What you've got to do is you've got to learn how to defend yourself, and you've got to learn how to attack. That's your only trouble as a boxer. You don't know how to defend yourself, and you don't know how to attack.

(*Pause.*)

Once you've mastered those arts you can go straight to the top.

(*Pause.*)

JOEY: I've got a pretty good idea . . . of how to do that.

(*Joey looks round for his jacket, picks it up, goes out of the room and up the stairs.*)
(*Pause.*)

MAX: Sam . . . why don't you go, too, eh? Why don't you just go upstairs? Leave me quiet. Leave me alone.

SAM: I want to make something clear about Jessie, Max. I want to. I do. When I took her out in the cab, round the town, I was taking care of her, for you. I was looking after her for you, when you were busy, wasn't I? I was showing her the West End.

(*Pause.*)

You wouldn't have trusted any of your other brothers. You wouldn't have trusted Mac, would you? But you trusted me. I want to remind you.

(*Pause.*)

Old Mac died a few years ago, didn't he? Isn't he dead?

(*Pause.*)

He was a lousy stinking rotten loudmouth. A bastard uncouth sodding runt. Mind you, he was a good friend of yours.

(*Pause.*)

MAX: Eh, Sam . . .

SAM: What?

MAX: Why do I keep you here? You're just an old grub.

SAM: Am I?

MAX: You're a maggot.

SAM: Oh yes?

MAX: As soon as you stop paying your way here, I mean when you're too old to pay your way, you know what I'm going to do? I'm going to give you the boot.

SAM: You are, eh?

MAX: Sure. I mean, bring in the money and I'll put up with you. But when the firm gets rid of you—you can flake off.

SAM: This is my house as well, you know. This was our mother's house.

MAX: One lot after the other. One mess after the other.

SAM: Our father's house.

MAX: Look what I'm lumbered with. One cast-iron bunch of crap after another. One flow of stinking pus after another.

(*Pause.*)

Our father? I remember him. Don't worry. You kid yourself. He used to come over to me and look down at me. My old man did. He'd bend right over me, then he'd pick me up. I was only that big. Then he'd dandle me. Give me the bottle. Wipe me clean. Give me a smile. Pat me on the bum. Pass me around, pass me from hand to hand. Toss me up in the air. Catch me coming down. I remember my father.

(*Blackout.*
Lights up.
Night.
Teddy and Ruth stand at the threshold of the room.
They are both well dressed in light summer suits and
light raincoats.
Two suitcases are by their side.
They look at the room. Teddy tosses the key in his hand,
smiles.)

TEDDY: Well, the key worked.

(*Pause.*)

 They haven't changed the lock.

(*Pause.*)

RUTH: No one's here.
TEDDY (*looking up*): They're asleep.

(*Pause.*)

RUTH: Can I sit down?
TEDDY: Of course.
RUTH: I'm tired.

(*Pause.*)

TEDDY: Then sit down.

(*She does not move.*)

 That's my father's chair.
RUTH: That one?
TEDDY (*smiling*): Yes, that's it. Shall I go up and see if
 my room's still there?
RUTH: It can't have moved.
TEDDY: No, I mean if my bed's still there.
RUTH: Someone might be in it.
TEDDY: No. They've got their own beds.

(*Pause.*)

RUTH: Shouldn't you wake someone up? Tell them you're
 here?
TEDDY: Not at this time of night. It's too late.

(*Pause.*)

 Shall I go up?

(*He goes into the hall, looks up the stairs, comes back.*)

 Why don't you sit down?

(*Pause.*)

 I'll just go up . . . have a look.

(*He goes up the stairs, stealthily.*)
(*Ruth stands, then slowly walks across the room.*)
(*Teddy returns.*)

 It's still there. My room. Empty. The bed's there.
 What are you doing?

(*She looks at him.*)

Blankets, no sheets. I'll find some sheets. I could hear
snores. Really. They're all still here, I think. They're
all snoring up there. Are you cold?
RUTH: No.
TEDDY: I'll make something to drink, if you like. Something hot.
RUTH: No, I don't want anything.

(*Teddy walks about.*)

TEDDY: What do you think of the room? Big, isn't it? It's
 a big house. I mean, it's a fine room, don't you think?
 Actually there was a wall, across there . . . with a
 door. We knocked it down . . . years ago . . . to make
 an open living area. The structure wasn't affected,
 you see. My mother was dead.

(*Ruth sits.*)

 Tired?
RUTH: Just a little.
TEDDY: We can go to bed if you like. No point in waking
 anyone up now. Just go to bed. See them all in the
 morning . . . see my father in the morning. . . .

(*Pause.*)

RUTH: Do you want to stay?
TEDDY: Stay?

(*Pause.*)

 We've come to stay. We're bound to stay . . . for a
 few days.
RUTH: I think . . . the children . . . might be missing us.
TEDDY: Don't be silly.
RUTH: They might.
TEDDY: Look, we'll be back in a few days, won't we?

(*He walks about the room.*)

 Nothing's changed. Still the same.

(*Pause.*)

 Still, he'll get a surprise in the morning, won't he? The
 old man. I think you'll like him very much. Honestly.
 He's a . . . well, he's old, of course. Getting on.

(*Pause.*)

 I was born here, do you realize that?
RUTH: I know.

(*Pause.*)

TEDDY: Why don't you go to bed? I'll find some sheets. I
 feel . . . wide awake, isn't it odd? I think I'll stay up
 for a bit. Are you tired?
RUTH: No.
TEDDY: Go to bed. I'll show you the room.
RUTH: No, I don't want to.
TEDDY: You'll be perfectly all right up there without me.
 Really you will. I mean, I won't be long. Look, it's
 just up there. It's the first door on the landing. The

bathroom's right next door. You . . . need some rest, you know.

(*Pause.*)

I just want to . . . walk about for a few minutes. Do you mind?
RUTH: Of course I don't.
TEDDY: Well . . . Shall I show you the room?
RUTH: No, I'm happy at the moment.
TEDDY: You don't have to go to bed. I'm not saying you have to. I mean, you can stay up with me. Perhaps I'll make a cup of tea or something. The only thing is we don't want to make too much noise, we don't want to wake anyone up.
RUTH: I'm not making any noise.
TEDDY: I know you're not.

(*He goes to her.*)

(*Gently.*) Look, it's all right, really. I'm here. I mean . . . I'm with you. There's no need to be nervous. Are you nervous?
RUTH: No.
TEDDY: There's no need to be.

(*Pause.*)

They're very warm people, really. Very warm. They're my family. They're not ogres.

(*Pause.*)

Well, perhaps we should go to bed. After all, we have to be up early, see Dad. Wouldn't be quite right if he found us in bed, I think. (*He chuckles.*) Have to be up before six, come down, say hullo.

(*Pause.*)

RUTH: I think I'll have a breath of air.
TEDDY: Air?

(*Pause.*)

What do you mean?
RUTH (*standing*): Just a stroll.
TEDDY: At this time of night? But we've . . . only just got here. We've got to go to bed.
RUTH: I just feel like some air.
TEDDY: But I'm going to bed.
RUTH: That's all right.
TEDDY: But what am I going to do?

(*Pause.*)

The last thing I want is a breath of air. Why do you want a breath of air?
RUTH: I just do.
TEDDY: But it's late.
RUTH: I won't go far. I'll come back.

(*Pause.*)

TEDDY: I'll wait up for you.
RUTH: Why?
TEDDY: I'm not going to bed without you.

RUTH: Can I have the key?

(*He gives it to her.*)

Why don't you go to bed?

(*He puts his arms on her shoulders and kisses her.*)
(*They look at each other, briefly. She smiles.*)

I won't be long.

(*She goes out of the front door.*)
(*Teddy goes to the window, peers out after her, half turns from the window, stands, suddenly chews his knuckles.*)
(*Lenny walks into the room from U.L. He stands. He wears pajamas and dressing-gown. He watches Teddy.*)
(*Teddy turns and sees him.*)
(*Silence.*)

TEDDY: Hullo, Lenny.
LENNY: Hullo, Teddy.

(*Pause.*)

TEDDY: I didn't hear you come down the stairs.
LENNY: I didn't.

(*Pause.*)

I sleep down here now. Next door. I've got a kind of study, workroom cum bedroom next door now, you see.
TEDDY: Oh. Did I . . . wake you up?
LENNY: No. I just had an early night tonight. You know how it is. Can't sleep. Keep waking up.

(*Pause.*)

TEDDY: How are you?
LENNY: Well, just sleeping a bit restlessly, that's all. Tonight, anyway.
TEDDY: Bad dreams?
LENNY: No, I wouldn't say I was dreaming. It's not exactly a dream. It's just that something keeps waking me up. Some kind of tick.
TEDDY: A tick?
LENNY: Yes.
TEDDY: Well, what is it?
LENNY: I don't know.

(*Pause.*)

TEDDY: Have you got a clock in your room?
LENNY: Yes.
TEDDY: Well, maybe it's the clock.
LENNY: Yes, could be, I suppose.

(*Pause.*)

Well, if it's the clock I'd better do something about it. Stifle it in some way, or something.

(*Pause.*)

TEDDY: I've . . . just come back for a few days.
LENNY: Oh yes? Have you?

(*Pause.*)

TEDDY: How's the old man?
LENNY: He's in the pink.

(*Pause.*)

TEDDY: I've been keeping well.
LENNY: Oh, have you?

(*Pause.*)

Staying the night then, are you?
TEDDY: Yes.
LENNY: Well, you can sleep in your old room.
TEDDY: Yes, I've been up.
LENNY: Yes, you can sleep there.

(*Lenny yawns.*)

Oh well.
TEDDY: I'm going to bed.
LENNY: Are you?
TEDDY: Yes, I'll get some sleep.
LENNY: Yes, I'm going to bed, too.

(*Teddy picks up the cases.*)

I'll give you a hand.
TEDDY: No, they're not heavy.

(*Teddy goes into the hall with the cases.*)
(*Lenny turns out the light in the room.*)
(*The light in the hall remains on.*)
(*Lenny follows into the hall.*)

LENNY: Nothing you want?
TEDDY: Mmmm?
LENNY: Nothing you might want, for the night? Glass of water, anything like that?
TEDDY: Any sheets anywhere?
LENNY: In the sideboard in your room.
TEDDY: Oh, good.
LENNY: Friends of mine occasionally stay there, you know, in your room, when they're passing through this part of the world.

(*Lenny turns out the hall light and turns on the first landing light.*)
(*Teddy begins to walk up the stairs.*)

TEDDY: Well, I'll see you at breakfast, then.
LENNY: Yes, that's it. Ta-ta.

(*Teddy goes upstairs.*)
(*Lenny goes off L.*)
(*Silence.*)
(*The landing light goes out.*)
(*Slight night light in the hall and room.*)
(*Lenny comes back into the room, goes to the window and looks out.*)
(*He leaves the window and turns on a lamp.*)
(*He is holding a small clock.*)
(*He sits, places the clock in front of him, lights a cigarette and sits.*)
(*Ruth comes in the front door.*)

(*She stands still. Lenny turns his head, smiles. She walks slowly into the room.*)

LENNY: Good evening.
RUTH: Morning, I think.
LENNY: You're right there.

(*Pause.*)

My name's Lenny. What's yours?
RUTH: Ruth.

(*She sits, puts her coat collar around her.*)

LENNY: Cold?
RUTH: No.
LENNY: It's been a wonderful summer, hasn't it? Remarkable.

(*Pause.*)

Would you like something? Refreshment of some kind? An aperitif, anything like that?
RUTH: No, thanks.
LENNY: I'm glad you said that. We haven't got a drink in the house. Mind you, I'd soon get some in, if we had a party or something like that. Some kind of celebration . . . you know.

(*Pause.*)

You must be connected with my brother in some way. The one who's been abroad.
RUTH: I'm his wife.
LENNY: Eh listen, I wonder if you can advise me. I've been having a bit of a rough time with this clock. The tick's been keeping me up. The trouble is I'm not all that convinced it was the clock. I mean there are lots of things which tick in the night, don't you find that? All sorts of objects, which, in the day, you wouldn't call anything else but commonplace. They give you no trouble. But in the night any given one of a number of them is liable to start letting out a bit of a tick. Whereas you look at these objects in the day and they're just commonplace. They're as quiet as mice during the daytime. So . . . all things being equal . . . this question of me saying it was the clock that woke me up, well, that could very easily prove something of a false hypothesis.

(*He goes to the sideboard, pours from a jug into a glass, takes the glass to Ruth.*)

Here you are. I bet you could do with this.
RUTH: What is it?
LENNY: Water.

(*She takes it, sips, places the glass on a small table by her chair.*)
(*Lenny watches her.*)

Isn't it funny? I've got my pajamas on and you're fully dressed?

(*He goes to the sideboard and pours another glass of water.*)

Mind if I have one? Yes, it's funny seeing my old brother again after all these years. It's just the sort of tonic my Dad needs, you know. He'll be chuffed to his bollocks in the morning, when he sees his eldest son. I was surprised myself when I saw Teddy, you know. Old Ted. I thought he was in America.

RUTH: We're on a visit to Europe.

LENNY: What, both of you?

RUTH: Yes.

LENNY: What, you sort of live with him over there, do you?

RUTH: We're married.

LENNY: On a visit to Europe, eh? Seen much of it?

RUTH: We've just come from Italy.

LENNY: Oh, you went to Italy first, did you? And then he brought you over here to meet the family, did he? Well, the old man'll be pleased to see you, I can tell you.

RUTH: Good.

LENNY: What did you say?

RUTH: Good.

(*Pause.*)

LENNY: Where'd you go to in Italy?

RUTH: Venice.

LENNY: Not dear old Venice? Eh? That's funny. You know, I've always had a feeling that if I'd been a soldier in the last war—say in the Italian campaign—I'd probably have found myself in Venice. I've always had that feeling. The trouble was I was too young to serve, you see. I was only a child, I was too small, otherwise I've got a pretty shrewd idea I'd probably have gone through Venice. Yes, I'd almost certainly have gone through it with my battalion. Do you mind if I hold your hand?

RUTH: Why?

LENNY: Just a touch.

(*He stands and goes to her.*)

Just a tickle.

RUTH: Why?

(*He looks down at her.*)

LENNY: I'll tell you why.

(*Slight pause.*)

One night, not too long ago, one night down by the docks, I was standing alone under an arch, watching all the men jibbing the boom, out in the harbor, and playing about with the yardarm, when a certain lady came up to me and made me a certain proposal. This lady had been searching for me for days. She'd lost track of my whereabouts. However, the fact was she eventually caught up with me, and when she caught up with me she made me this certain proposal. Well, this proposal wasn't entirely out of order and normally I would have subscribed to it. I mean I would have subscribed to it in the normal course of events. The only trouble was she was falling apart with the pox. So I turned it down. Well, this lady was very

insistent and started taking liberties with me down under this arch, liberties which by any criterion I couldn't be expected to tolerate, the facts being what they were, so I clumped her one. It was on my mind at the time to do away with her, you know, to kill her, and the fact is, that as killings go, it would have been a simple matter, nothing to it. Her chauffeur, who had located me for her, he'd popped round the corner to have a drink, which just left this lady and myself, you see, alone, standing underneath this arch, watching all the steamers steaming up, no one about, all quiet on the Western Front, and there she was up against this wall—well, just sliding down the wall, following the blow I'd given her. Well, to sum up, everything was in my favor, for a killing. Don't worry about the chauffeur. The chauffeur would never have spoken. He was an old friend of the family. But . . . in the end I thought . . . Aaah, why go to all the bother . . . you know, getting rid of the corpse and all that, getting yourself into a state of tension. So I just gave her another belt in the nose and a couple of turns of the boot and sort of left it at that.

RUTH: How did you know she was diseased?

LENNY: How did I know?

(*Pause.*)

I decided she was.

(*Silence.*)

You and my brother are newly-weds, are you?

RUTH: We've been married six years.

LENNY: He's always been my favorite brother, old Teddy. Do you know that? And my goodness we are proud of him here, I can tell you. Doctor of Philosophy and all that . . . leaves quite an impression. Of course, he's a very sensitive man, isn't he? Ted. Very. I've often wished I was as sensitive as he is.

RUTH: Have you?

LENNY: Oh yes. Oh yes, very much so. I mean, I'm not saying I'm not sensitive. I am. I could just be a bit more so, that's all.

RUTH: Could you?

LENNY: Yes, just a bit more so, that's all.

(*Pause.*)

I mean, I am very sensitive to atmosphere, but I tend to get desensitized, if you know what I mean, when people make unreasonable demands on me. For instance, last Christmas I decided to do a bit of snow-clearing for the Borough Council, because we had a heavy snow over here that year in Europe. I didn't have to do this snow-clearing—I mean I wasn't financially embarrassed in any way—it just appealed to me, it appealed to something inside me. What I anticipated with a good deal of pleasure was the brisk cold bite in the air in the early morning. And I was right. I had to get my snowboots on and I had to stand on a corner, at about five-thirty in the morning, to wait for the lorry to pick me up, to take me to the allotted area. Bloody freezing. Well, the lorry came, I jumped on the tailboard, headlights on, dipped, and off we went. Got there, shovels up, fags on, and off we went, deep into the December snow, hours before cockcrow. Well, that morning, while I was having my midmorning cup of tea in a neighboring cafe, the shovel standing by my chair, an old lady approached me and asked me if I would give her a hand with her iron mangle. Her brother-in-law, she said, had left it for her, but he'd left it in the wrong room, he'd left it in the front room. Well, naturally, she wanted it in the back room. It was a present he'd given her, you see, a mangle, to iron out the washing. But he'd left it in the wrong room, he'd left it in the front room, well that was a silly place to leave it, it couldn't stay there. So I took time off to give her a hand. She only lived up the road. Well, the only trouble was when I got there I couldn't move this mangle. It must have weighed about half a ton. How this brother-in-law got it up there in the first place I can't even begin to envisage. So there I was, doing a bit of shoulders on with the mangle, risking a rupture, and this old lady just standing there, waving me on, not even lifting a little finger to give me a helping hand. So after a few minutes I said to her, now look, why don't you stuff this iron mangle up your arse? Anyway, I said, they're out of date, you want to get a spin drier. I had a good mind to give her a workover there and then, but as I was feeling jubilant with the snow-clearing I just gave her a short-arm jab to the belly and jumped on a bus outside. Excuse me, shall I take this ashtray out of your way?

RUTH: It's not in my way.

LENNY: It seems to be in the way of your glass. The glass was about to fall. Or the ashtray. I'm rather worried about the carpet. It's not me, it's my father. He's obsessed with order and clarity. He doesn't like mess. So, as I don't believe you're smoking at the moment, I'm sure you won't object if I move the ashtray.

(*He does so.*)

And now perhaps I'll relieve you of your glass.

RUTH: I haven't quite finished.

LENNY: You've consumed quite enough, in my opinion.

RUTH: No, I haven't.

LENNY: Quite sufficient, in my own opinion.

RUTH: Not in mine, Leonard.

(*Pause.*)

LENNY: Don't call me that, please.

RUTH: Why not?

LENNY: That's the name my mother gave me.

(*Pause.*)

Just give me the glass.

RUTH: No.

(*Pause.*)

LENNY: I'll take it, then.

RUTH: If you take the glass . . . I'll take you.

(*Pause.*)

LENNY: How about me taking the glass without you taking me?

RUTH: Why don't I just take you?

(*Pause.*)

LENNY: You're joking.

(*Pause.*)

You're in love, anyway, with another man. You've had a secret liaison with another man. His family didn't even know. Then you come here without a word of warning and start to make trouble.

(*She picks up the glass and lifts it towards him.*)

RUTH: Have a sip. Go on. Have a sip from my glass.

(*He is still.*)

Sit on my lap. Take a long cool sip.

(*She pats her lap. Pause.*)
(*She stands, moves to him with the glass.*)

Put your head back and open your mouth.

LENNY: Take that glass away from me.

RUTH: Lie on the floor. Go on. I'll pour it down your throat.

LENNY: What are you doing, making me some kind of proposal?

(*She laughs shortly, drains the glass.*)

RUTH: Oh, I was thirsty.

(*She smiles at him, puts the glass down, goes into the hall and up the stairs.*)
(*He follows into the hall and shouts up the stairs.*)

LENNY: What was that supposed to be? Some kind of proposal?

(*Silence.*)
(*He comes back into the room, goes to his own glass, drains it.*)
(*A door slams upstairs.*)
(*The landing light goes on.*)
(*Max comes down the stairs, in pajamas and cap. He comes into the room.*)

MAX: What's going on here? You drunk?

(*He stares at Lenny.*)

What are you shouting about? You gone mad?

(*Lenny pours another glass of water.*)

Prancing about in the middle of the night shouting your head off. What are you, a raving lunatic?

LENNY: I was thinking aloud.

MAX: Is Joey down here? You been shouting at Joey?

LENNY: Didn't you hear what I said, Dad? I said I was thinking aloud.

MAX: You were thinking so loud you got me out of bed.

LENNY: Look, why don't you just . . . pop off, eh?

MAX: Pop off? He wakes me up in the middle of the night, I think we got burglars here, I think he's got a knife stuck in him, I come down here, he tells me to pop off.

(*Lenny sits down.*)

He was talking to someone. Who could he have been talking to? They're all asleep. He was having a conversation with someone. He won't tell me who it was. He pretends he was thinking aloud. What are you doing, hiding someone here?

LENNY: I was sleepwalking. Get out of it, leave me alone, will you?

MAX: I want an explanation, you understand? I asked you who you got hiding here.

(*Pause.*)

LENNY: I'll tell you what, Dad, since you're in the mood for a bit of a . . . chat, I'll ask you a question. It's a question I've been meaning to ask you for some time. That night . . . you know . . . the night you got me . . . that night with Mum, what was it like? Eh? When I was just a glint in your eye. What was it like? What was the background to it? I mean, I want to know the real facts about my background. I mean, for instance, is it a fact that you had me in mind all the time, or is it a fact that I was the last thing you had in mind?

(*Pause.*)

I'm only asking this in a spirit of inquiry, you understand that, don't you? I'm curious. And there's lots of people of my age share that curiosity, you know that, Dad? They often ruminate, sometimes singly, sometimes in groups, about the true facts of that particular night — the night they were made in the image of those two people *at it*. It's a question long overdue, from my point of view, but as we happen to be passing the time of day here tonight I thought I'd pop it to you.

(*Pause.*)

MAX: You'll drown in your own blood.

LENNY: If you prefer to answer the question in writing I've got no objection.

(*Max stands.*)

I should have asked my dear mother. Why didn't I ask my dear mother? Now it's too late. She's passed over to the other side.

(*Max spits at him.*)

(*Lenny looks down at the carpet.*)

Now look what you've done. I'll have to Hoover that in the morning, you know.

(*Max turns and walks up the stairs.*)

(*Lenny sits still.*)

(*Blackout.*)

(*Lights up.*)

(*Morning.*)

(*Joey in front of the mirror. He is doing some slow limbering-up exercises. He stops, combs his hair, carefully. He then shadowboxes, heavily, watching himself in the mirror.*)

(*Max comes in from U.L.*)

(*Both Max and Joey are dressed. Max watches Joey in silence. Joey stops shadowboxing, picks up a newspaper and sits.*)

(*Silence.*)

MAX: I hate this room.

(*Pause.*)

It's the kitchen I like. It's nice in there. It's cosy.

(*Pause.*)

But I can't stay in there. You know why? Because he's always washing up in there, scraping the plates, driving me out of the kitchen, that's why.

JOEY: Why don't you bring your tea in here?

MAX: I don't want to bring my tea in here. I hate it here. I want to drink my tea in there.

(*He goes into the hall and looks towards the kitchen.*)

What's he doing in there?

(*He returns.*)

What's the time?

JOEY: Half past six.

MAX: Half past six.

(*Pause.*)

I'm going to see a game of football this afternoon. You want to come?

(*Pause.*)

I'm talking to you.

JOEY: I'm training this afternoon. I'm doing six rounds with Blackie.

MAX: That's not till five o'clock. You've got time to see a game of football before five o'clock. It's the first game of the season.

JOEY: No, I'm not going.

MAX: Why not?

(*Pause.*)

(*Max goes into the hall.*)

Sam! Come here!

(*Max comes back into the room.*)

(*Sam enters with a cloth.*)

SAM: What?

MAX: What are you doing in there?

SAM: Washing up.

MAX: What else?

SAM: Getting rid of your leavings.

MAX: Putting them in the bin, eh?

SAM: Right in.

MAX: What point you trying to prove?

SAM: No point.

MAX: Oh yes, you are. You resent making my breakfast, that's what it is, isn't it? That's why you bang round the kitchen like that, scraping the frying-pan, scraping all the leavings into the bin, scraping all the plates, scraping all the tea out of the teapot . . . that's why you do that, every single stinking morning. I know. Listen, Sam. I want to say something to you. From my heart.

(*He moves closer.*)

I want you to get rid of these feelings of resentment you've got towards me. I wish I could understand them. Honestly, have I ever given you cause? Never. When Dad died he said to me, Max, look after your brothers. That's exactly what he said to me.

SAM: How could he say that when he was dead?

MAX: What?

SAM: How could he speak if he was dead?

(*Pause.*)

MAX: Before he died, Sam. Just before. They were his last words. His last sacred words, Sammy. A split second after he said those words . . . he was a dead man. You think I'm joking? You think when my father spoke—on his death-bed—I wouldn't obey his words to the last letter? You hear that, Joey? He'll stop at nothing. He's even prepared to spit on the memory of our Dad. What kind of a son were you, you wet wick? You spent half your time doing crossword puzzles! We took you into the butcher's shop, you couldn't even sweep the dust off the floor. We took MacGregor into the shop, he could run the place by the end of a week. Well, I'll tell you one thing. I respected my father not only as a man but as a number one butcher! And to prove it I followed him into the shop. I learned to carve a carcass at his knee. I commemorated his name in blood. I gave birth to three grown men! All on my own bat. What have you done?

(*Pause.*)

What have you done? You tit!

SAM: Do you want to finish the washing up? Look, here's the cloth.

MAX: So try to get rid of these feelings of resentment, Sam. After all, we are brothers.

SAM: Do you want the cloth? Here you are. Take it.

(*Teddy and Ruth come down the stairs. They walk across the hall and stop just inside the room.*)
(*The others turn and look at them. Joey stands.*)
(*Teddy and Ruth are wearing dressing-gowns.*)
(*Silence.*)
(*Teddy smiles.*)

TEDDY: Hullo . . . Dad . . . We overslept.

(*Pause.*)

What's for breakfast?

(*Silence.*)
(*Teddy chuckles.*)

Huh. We overslept.

(*Max turns to Sam.*)

MAX: Did you know he was here?

SAM: No.

(*Max turns to Joey.*)

MAX: Did you know he was here?

(*Pause.*)

I asked you if you knew he was here.

JOEY: No.

MAX: Then who knew?

(*Pause.*)

Who knew?

(*Pause.*)

I didn't know.

TEDDY: I was going to come down, Dad, I was going to . . . be here, when you came down.

(*Pause.*)

How are you?

(*Pause.*)

Uh . . . look, I'd . . . like you to meet . . .

MAX: How long you been in this house?

TEDDY: All night.

MAX: All night? I'm a laughing-stock. How did you get in?

TEDDY: I had my key.

(*Max whistles and laughs.*)

MAX: Who's this?

TEDDY: I was just going to introduce you.

MAX: Who asked you to bring tarts in here?

TEDDY: Tarts?

MAX: Who asked you to bring dirty tarts into this house?

TEDDY: Listen, don't be silly —

MAX: You been here all night?

TEDDY: Yes, we arrived from Venice —

MAX: We've had a smelly scrubber in my house all night. We've had a stinking pox-ridden slut in my house all night.

TEDDY: Stop it! What are you talking about?

MAX: I haven't seen the bitch for six years, he comes home without a word, he brings a filthy scrubber off the street, he shacks up in my house!

TEDDY: She's my wife! We're married!

(*Pause.*)

MAX: I've never had a whore under this roof before. Ever since your mother died. My word of honor. (*To*

Joey.) Have you ever had a whore here? Has Lenny ever had a whore here? They come back from America, they bring the slopbucket with them. They bring the bedpan with them. (*To Teddy.*) Take that disease away from me. Get her away from me.

TEDDY: She's my wife.

MAX (*to Joey*): Chuck them out.

(*Pause.*)

A Doctor of Philosophy. Sam, you want to meet a Doctor of Philosophy? (*To Joey.*) I said chuck them out.

(*Pause.*)

What's the matter? You deaf?

JOEY: You're an old man. (*To Teddy.*) He's an old man.

(*Lenny walks into the room, in a dressing-gown.*)
(*He stops*).
(*They all look round*).
(*Max turns back, hits Joey in the stomach with all his might.*)
(*Joey contorts, staggers across the stage. Max, with the exertion of the blow, begins to collapse. His knees buckle*).
(*He clutches his stick.*)
(*Sam moves forward to help him.*)
(*Max hits him across the head with his stick. Sam sits, head in hands.*)
(*Joey, hands pressed to his stomach, sinks down at the feet of Ruth.*)
(*She looks down at him.*)
(*Lenny and Teddy are still.*)
(*Joey slowly stands. He is close to Ruth. He turns from Ruth, looks round at Max.*)
(*Sam clutches his head.*)
(*Max breathes heavily, very slowly gets to his feet.*)
(*Joey moves to him.*)
(*They look at each other.*)
(*Silence.*)
(*Max moves past Joey, walks towards Ruth. He gestures with his stick.*)

MAX: Miss.

(*Ruth walks towards him.*)

RUTH: Yes?

(*He looks at her.*)

MAX: You a mother?

RUTH: Yes.

MAX: How many you got?

RUTH: Three.

(*He turns to Teddy.*)

MAX: All yours, Ted?

(*Pause.*)

Teddy, why don't we have a nice cuddle and kiss, eh? Like the old days? What about a nice cuddle and kiss, eh?

TEDDY: Come on, then.

(*Pause.*)

MAX: You want to kiss your old father? Want a cuddle with your old father?

TEDDY: Come on, then.

(*Teddy moves a step towards him.*)

Come on.

(*Pause.*)

MAX: You still love your old Dad, eh?

(*They face each other.*)

TEDDY: Come on, Dad. I'm ready for the cuddle.

(*Max begins to chuckle, gurgling.*)
(*He turns to the family and addresses them.*)

MAX: He still loves his father!

Curtain

ACT 2

Afternoon.
  Max, Teddy, Lenny, and Sam are about the stage, lighting cigars.
  Joey comes in from U.L. with a coffee tray, followed by Ruth. He puts the tray down. Ruth hands coffee to all the men. She sits with her cup. Max smiles at her.

RUTH: That was a very good lunch.

MAX: I'm glad you liked it. (*To the others.*) Did you hear that? (*To Ruth.*) Well, I put my heart and soul into it, I can tell you. (*He sips.*) And this is a lovely cup of coffee.

RUTH: I'm glad.

(*Pause.*)

MAX: I've got the feeling you're a first-rate cook.

RUTH: I'm not bad.

MAX: No, I've got the feeling you're a number one cook. Am I right, Teddy?

TEDDY: Yes, she's a very good cook.

(*Pause.*)

MAX: Well, it's a long time since the whole family was together, eh? If only your mother was alive. Eh, what do you say, Sam? What would Jessie say if she was alive? Sitting here with her three sons. Three fine grown-up lads. And a lovely daughter-in-law. The only shame is her grandchildren aren't here. She'd have petted them and cooed over them, wouldn't she, Sam? She'd have fussed over them and played with them, told them stories, tickled them— I tell you she'd have been hysterical. (*To Ruth.*) Mind you, she taught those boys everything they know. She taught them all the morality they know.

I'm telling you. Every single bit of the moral code they live by—was taught to them by their mother. And she had a heart to go with it. What a heart. Eh, Sam? Listen, what's the use of beating round the bush? That woman was the backbone to this family. I mean, I was busy working twenty-four hours a day in the shop, I was going all over the country to find meat, I was making my way in the world, but I left a woman at home with a will of iron, a heart of gold and a mind. Right, Sam?

(*Pause.*)

What a mind.

(*Pause.*)

Mind you, I was a generous man to her. I never left her short of a few bob. I remember one year I entered into negotiations with a top-class group of butchers with continental connections. I was going into association with them. I remember the night I came home, I kept quiet. First of all I gave Lenny a bath, then Teddy a bath, then Joey a bath. What fun we used to have in the bath, eh, boys? Then I came downstairs and I made Jessie put her feet up on a pouffe—what happened to that pouffe, I haven't seen it for years—she put her feet up on the pouffe and I said to her, Jessie, I think our ship is going to come home, I'm going to treat you to a couple of items, I'm going to buy you a dress in pale corded blue silk, heavily encrusted in pearls, and for casual wear, a pair of pantaloons in lilac flowered taffeta. Then I gave her a drop of cherry brandy. I remember the boys came down, in their pajamas, all their hair shining, their faces pink, it was before they started shaving, and they knelt down at our feet, Jessie's and mine. I tell you, it was like Christmas.

(*Pause.*)

RUTH: What happened to the group of butchers?
MAX: The group? They turned out to be a bunch of criminals like everyone else.

(*Pause.*)

This is a lousy cigar.

(*He stubs it out.*)
(*He turns to Sam.*)

What time you going to work?
SAM: Soon.
MAX: You've got a job on this afternoon, haven't you?
SAM: Yes, I know.
MAX: What do you mean, you know? You'll be late. You'll lose your job? What are you trying to do, humiliate me?
SAM: Don't worry about me.
MAX: It makes the bile come up in my mouth. The bile—you understand? (*To Ruth.*) I worked as a butcher all my life, using the chopper and the slab, the slab, you know what I mean, the chopper and the slab! To keep my family in luxury. Two families! My mother was bedridden, my brothers were all invalids. I had to earn the money for the leading psychiatrists. I had to read books! I had to study the disease, so that I could cope with an emergency at every stage. A crippled family, three bastard sons, a slutbitch of a wife—don't talk to me about the pain of childbirth—I suffered the pain, I've still got the pangs—when I give a little cough my back collapses—and here I've got a lazy idle bugger of a brother won't even get to work on time. The best chauffeur in the world. All his life he's sat in the front seat giving lovely hand signals. You call that work? This man doesn't know his gearbox from his arse!
SAM: You go and ask my customers! I'm the only one they ever ask for.
MAX: What do the other drivers do, sleep all day?
SAM: I can only drive one car. They can't all have me at the same time.
MAX: Anyone could have you at the same time. You'd bend over for half a dollar on Blackfriars Bridge.
SAM: Me!
MAX: For two bob and a toffee apple.
SAM: He's insulting me. He's insulting his brother. I'm driving a man to Hampton Court at four forty-five.
MAX: Do you want to know who could drive? Mac-Gregor! MacGregor was a driver.
SAM: Don't you believe it.

(*Max points his stick at Sam.*)

MAX: He didn't even fight in the war. This man didn't even fight in the bloody war!
SAM: I did!
MAX: Who did you kill?

(*Silence.*)
(*Sam gets up, goes to Ruth, shakes her hand and goes out of the front door.*)
(*Max turns to Teddy.*)

Well, how you been keeping, son?
TEDDY: I've been keeping very well, Dad.
MAX: It's nice to have you with us, son.
TEDDY: It's nice to be back, Dad.

(*Pause.*)

MAX: You should have told me you were married, Teddy. I'd have sent you a present. Where was the wedding, in America?
TEDDY: No. Here. The day before we left.
MAX: Did you have a big function?
TEDDY: No, there was no one there.
MAX: You're mad. I'd have given you a white wedding. We'd have had the cream of the cream here. I'd have been only too glad to bear the expense, my word of honor.

(*Pause.*)

TEDDY: You were busy at the time. I didn't want to bother you.

MAX: But you're my own flesh and blood. You're my first born. I'd have dropped everything. Sam would have driven you to the reception in the Snipe, Lenny would have been your best man, and then we'd have all seen you off on the boat. I mean, you don't think I disapprove of marriage, do you? Don't be daft. (*To Ruth.*) I've been begging my two youngsters for years to find a nice feminine girl with proper credentials— it makes life worth living. (*To Teddy.*) Anyway, what's the difference, you did it, you made a wonderful choice, you've got a wonderful family, a marvelous career . . . so why don't we let bygones be bygones?

(*Pause.*)

You know what I'm saying? I want you both to know that you have my blessing.

TEDDY: Thank you.

MAX: Don't mention it. How many other houses in the district have got a Doctor of Philosophy sitting down drinking a cup of coffee?

(*Pause.*)

RUTH: I'm sure Teddy's very happy . . . to know that you're pleased with me.

(*Pause.*)

I think he wondered whether you would be pleased with me.

MAX: But you're a charming woman.

(*Pause.*)

RUTH: I was . . .

MAX: What?

(*Pause.*)

What she say?

(*They all look at her.*)

RUTH: I was . . . different . . . when I met Teddy . . . first.

TEDDY: No you weren't. You were the same.

RUTH: I wasn't.

MAX: Who cares? Listen, live in the present, what are you worrying about? I mean, don't forget the earth's about five thousand million years old, at least. Who can afford to live in the past?

(*Pause.*)

TEDDY: She's a great help to me over there. She's a wonderful wife and mother. She's a very popular woman. She's got lots of friends. It's a great life, at the University . . . you know . . . it's a very good life. We've got a lovely house . . . we've got all . . . we've got everything we want. It's a very stimulating environment.

(*Pause.*)

My department . . . is highly successful.

(*Pause.*)

We've got three boys, you know.

MAX: All boys? Isn't that funny, eh? You've got three, I've got three. You've got three nephews, Joey. Joey! You're an uncle, do you hear? You could teach them how to box.

(*Pause.*)

JOEY (*to Ruth*): I'm a boxer. In the evenings, after work. I'm in demolition in the daytime.

RUTH: Oh?

JOEY: Yes. I hope to be full time, when I get more bouts.

MAX (*to Lenny*): He speaks so easily to his sister-in-law, do you notice? That's because she's an intelligent and sympathetic woman.

(*He leans to her.*)

Eh, tell me, do you think the children are missing their mother?

(*She looks at him.*)

TEDDY: Of course they are. They love her. We'll be seeing them soon.

(*Pause.*)

LENNY (*to Teddy*): Your cigar's gone out.

TEDDY: Oh, yes.

LENNY: Want a light?

TEDDY: No. No.

(*Pause.*)

So has yours.

LENNY: Oh, yes.

(*Pause.*)

Eh, Teddy, you haven't told us much about your Doctorship of Philosophy. What do you teach?

TEDDY: Philosophy.

LENNY: Well, I want to ask you something. Do you detect a certain logical incoherence in the central affirmations of Christian theism?

TEDDY: That question doesn't fall within my province.

LENNY: Well, look at it this way . . . you don't mind my asking you some questions, do you?

TEDDY: If they're within my province.

LENNY: Well, look at it this way. How can the unknown merit reverence? In other words, how can you revere that of which you're ignorant? At the same time, it would be ridiculous to propose that what we *know* merits reverence. What we know merits any one of a number of things, but it stands to reason reverence isn't one of them. In other words, apart from the known and the unknown, what else is there?

(*Pause.*)

TEDDY: I'm afraid I'm the wrong person to ask.

LENNY: But you're a philosopher. Come on, be frank.

What do you make of all this business of being and not-being?

TEDDY: What do you make of it?

LENNY: Well, for instance, take a table. Philosophically speaking. What is it?

TEDDY: A table.

LENNY: Ah. You mean it's nothing else but a table. Well, some people would envy your certainty, wouldn't they, Joey? For instance, I've got a couple of friends of mine, we often sit round the Ritz Bar having a few liqueurs, and they're always saying things like that, you know, things like: Take a table, take it. All right, I say, *take* it, *take* a table, but once you've taken it, what you going to do with it? Once you've got hold of it, where you going to take it?

MAX: You'd probably sell it.

LENNY: You wouldn't get much for it.

JOEY: Chop it up for firewood.

(*Lenny looks at him and laughs.*)

RUTH: Don't be too sure though. You've forgotten something. Look at me. I . . . move my leg. That's all it is. But I wear . . . underwear . . . which moves with me . . . it . . . captures your attention. Perhaps you misinterpret. The action is simple. It's a leg . . . moving. My lips move. Why don't you restrict . . . your observations to that? Perhaps the fact that they move is more significant . . . than the words which come through them. You must bear that . . . possibility . . . in mind.

(*Silence.*)
(*Teddy stands.*)

I was born quite near here.

(*Pause.*)

Then . . . six years ago, I went to America.

(*Pause.*)

It's all rock. And sand. It stretches . . . so far . . . everywhere you look. And there's lots of insects there.

(*Pause.*)

And there's lots of insects there.

(*Silence.*)
(*She is still.*)
(*Max stands.*)

MAX: Well, it's time to go to the gym. Time for your workout, Joey.

LENNY (*standing*): I'll come with you.

(*Joey sits looking at Ruth.*)

MAX: Joe.

(*Joey stands. The three go out.*)
(*Teddy sits by Ruth, holds her hand.*)
(*She smiles at him.*)
(*Pause.*)

TEDDY: I think we'll go back. Mmnn?

(*Pause.*)

Shall we go home?

RUTH: Why?

TEDDY: Well, we were only here for a few days, weren't we? We might as well . . . cut it short, I think.

RUTH: Why? Don't you like it here?

TEDDY: Of course I do. But I'd like to go back and see the boys now.

(*Pause.*)

RUTH: Don't you like your family?

TEDDY: Which family?

RUTH: Your family here.

TEDDY: Of course I like them. What are you talking about?

(*Pause.*)

RUTH: You don't like them as much as you thought you did?

TEDDY: Of course I do. Of course I . . . like them. I don't know what you're talking about.

(*Pause.*)

Listen. You know what time of the day it is there now, do you?

RUTH: What?

TEDDY: It's morning. It's about eleven o'clock.

RUTH: Is it?

TEDDY: Yes, they're about six hours behind us . . . I mean . . . behind the time here. The boys'll be at the pool . . . now . . . swimming. Think of it. Morning over there. Sun. We'll go anyway, mmnn? It's so clean there.

RUTH: Clean.

TEDDY: Yes.

RUTH: Is it dirty here?

TEDDY: No, of course not. But it's cleaner there.

(*Pause.*)

Look, I just brought you back to meet the family, didn't I? You've met them, we can go. The fall semester will be starting soon.

RUTH: You find it dirty here?

TEDDY: I didn't say I found it dirty here.

(*Pause.*)

I didn't say that.

(*Pause.*)

Look. I'll go and pack. You rest for a while. Will you? They won't be back for at least an hour. You can sleep. Rest. Please.

(*She looks at him.*)

You can help me with my lectures when we get back. I'd love that. I'd be so grateful for it, really. We can bathe till October. You know that. Here, there's nowhere to bathe, except the swimming bath down

the road. You know what it's like? It's like a urinal. A
filthy urinal!

(*Pause.*)

You liked Venice, didn't you? It was lovely, wasn't it?
You had a good week. I mean . . . I took you there. I
can speak Italian.

RUTH: But if I'd been a nurse in the Italian campaign I
would have been there before.

(*Pause.*)

TEDDY: You just rest. I'll go and pack.

(*Teddy goes out and up the stairs.*)
(*She closes her eyes.*)
(*Lenny appears from U.L.*)
(*He walks into the room and sits near her.*)
(*She opens her eyes.*)
(*Silence.*)

LENNY: Well, the evenings are drawing in.
RUTH: Yes, it's getting dark.

(*Pause.*)

LENNY: Winter'll soon be upon us. Time to renew one's
wardrobe.

(*Pause.*)

RUTH: That's a good thing to do.
LENNY: What?

(*Pause.*)

RUTH: I always . . .

(*Pause.*)

Do you like clothes?
LENNY: Oh, yes. Very fond of clothes.

(*Pause.*)

RUTH: I'm fond . . .

(*Pause.*)

What do you think of my shoes?
LENNY: They're very nice.
RUTH: No, I can't get the ones I want over there.
LENNY: Can't get them over there, eh?
RUTH: No . . . you don't get them there.

(*Pause.*)

I was a model before I went away.
LENNY: Hats?

(*Pause.*)

I bought a girl a hat once. We saw it in a glass case, in
a shop. I tell you what it had. It had a bunch of daffodils on it, tied with a black satin bow, and then it
was covered with a cloche of black veiling. A cloche.
I'm telling you. She was made for it.
RUTH: No . . . I was a model for the body. A photographic model for the body.

LENNY: Indoor work?
RUTH: That was before I had . . . all my children.

(*Pause.*)

No, not always indoors.

(*Pause.*)

Once or twice we went to a place in the country, by
train. Oh, six or seven times. We used to pass a . . . a
large white water tower. This place . . . this
house . . . was very big . . . the trees . . . there was a
lake, you see . . . we used to change and walk down
towards the lake . . . we went down a
path . . . on stones . . . there were . . . on this path.
Oh, just . . . wait . . . yes . . . when we changed in
the house we had a drink. There was a cold buffet.

(*Pause.*)

Sometimes we stayed in the house but . . . most
often . . . we walked down to the lake . . . and did
our modeling there.

(*Pause.*)

Just before we went to America I went down there. I
walked from the station to the gate and then I walked
up the drive. There were lights on . . . I stood in the
drive . . . the house was very light.

(*Teddy comes down the stairs with the cases. He puts
them down, looks at Lenny.*)

TEDDY: What have you been saying to her?

(*He goes to Ruth.*)

Here's your coat.

(*Lenny goes to the radiogram and puts on a record of
slow jazz.*)

Ruth. Come on. Put it on.
LENNY (*to Ruth*): What about one dance before you go?
TEDDY: We're going.
LENNY: Just one.
TEDDY: No. We're going.
LENNY: Just one dance, with her brother-in-law, before
she goes.

(*Lenny bends to her.*)

Madam?

(*Ruth stands. They dance, slowly.*)
(*Teddy stands, with Ruth's coat.*)
(*Max and Joey come in the front door and into the
room.*)
(*They stand.*)
(*Lenny kisses Ruth. They stand, kissing.*)

JOEY: Christ, she's wide open. Dad, look at that.

(*Pause.*)

She's a tart.

(*Pause.*)

Old Lenny's got a tart in here.

(*Joey goes to them. He takes Ruth's arm. He smiles at Lenny. He sits with Ruth on the sofa, embraces and kisses her.*)
(*He looks up at Lenny.*)

Just up my street.

(*He leans her back until she lies beneath him. He kisses her.*)
(*He looks up at Teddy and Max.*)

It's better than a rubdown, this.

(*Lenny sits on the arm of the sofa. He caresses Ruth's hair as Joey embraces her.*)
(*Max comes forward, looks at the cases.*)

MAX: You going, Teddy? Already?

(*Pause.*)

Well, when you coming over again, eh? Look, next time you come over, don't forget to let us know beforehand whether you're married or not. I'll always be glad to meet the wife. Honest. I'm telling you.

(*Joey lies heavily on Ruth.*)
(*They are almost still.*)
(*Lenny caresses her hair.*)

Listen, you think I don't know why you didn't tell me you were married? I know why. You were ashamed. You thought I'd be annoyed because you married a woman beneath you. You should have known me better. I'm broadminded. I'm a broadminded man.

(*He peers to see Ruth's face under Joey, turns back to Teddy.*)

Mind you, she's a lovely girl. A beautiful woman. And a mother too. A mother of three. You've made a happy woman out of her. It's something to be proud of. I mean, we're talking about a woman of quality. We're talking about a woman of feeling.

(*Joey and Ruth roll off the sofa onto the floor.*)
(*Joey clasps her. Lenny moves to stand above them. He looks down on them. He touches Ruth gently with his foot.*)
(*Ruth suddenly pushes Joey away.*)
(*She stands up.*)
(*Joey gets to his feet, stares at her.*)

RUTH: I'd like something to eat. (*To Lenny.*) I'd like a drink. Did you get any drink?
LENNY: We've got drink.
RUTH: I'd like one, please.
LENNY: What drink?
RUTH: Whisky.
LENNY: I've got it.

(*Pause.*)

RUTH: Well, get it.

(*Lenny goes to the sideboard, takes out bottle and glasses.*)
(*Joey moves towards her.*)

Put the record off.

(*He looks at her, turns, puts the record off.*)

I want something to eat.

(*Pause.*)

JOEY: I can't cook. (*Pointing to Max.*) He's the cook.

(*Lenny brings her a glass of whisky.*)

LENNY: Soda on the side?
RUTH: What's this glass? I can't drink out of this. Haven't you got a tumbler?
LENNY: Yes.
RUTH: Well, put it in a tumbler.

(*He takes the glass back, pours whisky into a tumbler, brings it to her.*)

LENNY: On the rocks? Or as it comes?
RUTH: Rocks? What do you know about rocks?
LENNY: We've got rocks. But they're frozen stiff in the fridge.

(*Ruth drinks.*)
(*Lenny looks round at the others.*)

Drinks all round?

(*He goes to the sideboard and pours drinks.*)
(*Joey moves closer to Ruth.*)

JOEY: What food do you want?

(*Ruth walks round the room.*)

RUTH (*to Teddy*): Have your family read your critical works?
MAX: That's one thing I've never done. I've never read one of his critical works.
TEDDY: You wouldn't understand them.

(*Lenny hands drinks all round.*)

JOEY: What sort of food do you want? I'm not the cook, anyway.
LENNY: Soda, Ted? Or as it comes?
TEDDY: You wouldn't understand my works. You wouldn't have the faintest idea of what they were about. You wouldn't appreciate the points of reference. You're way behind. All of you. There's no point in my sending you my works. You'd be lost. It's nothing to do with the question of intelligence. It's a way of being able to look at the world. It's a question of how far you can operate on things and not in things. I mean it's a question of your capacity to ally the two, to relate the two, to balance the two. To see, to be able to *see*! I'm the one who can see. That's why I can write my critical works. Might do you good . . . have

a look at them . . . see how certain people can view . . . things . . . how certain people can maintain . . . intellectual equilibrium. Intellectual equilibrium. You're just objects. You just . . . move about. I can observe it. I can see what you do. It's the same as I do. But you're lost in it. You won't get me being . . . I won't be lost in it.

(*Blackout.*)
(*Lights up.*)
(*Evening.*)
(*Teddy sitting, in his coat, the cases by him. Sam.*)
(*Pause.*)

SAM: Do you remember MacGregor, Teddy?
TEDDY: Mac?
SAM: Yes.
TEDDY: Of course I do.
SAM: What did you think of him? Did you take to him?
TEDDY: Yes. I liked him. Why?

(*Pause.*)

SAM: You know, you were always my favorite, of the lads. Always.

(*Pause.*)

When you wrote to me from America I was very touched, you know. I mean you'd written to your father a few times but you'd never written to me. But then, when I got that letter from you . . . well, I was very touched. I never told him. I never told him I'd heard from you.

(*Pause.*)

(*Whispering.*) Teddy, shall I tell you something? You were always your mother's favorite. She told me. It's true. You were always the . . . you were always the main object of her love.

(*Pause.*)

Why don't you stay for a couple more weeks, eh? We could have a few laughs.

(*Lenny comes in the front door and into the room.*)

LENNY: Still here, Ted? You'll be late for your first seminar.

(*He goes to the sideboard, opens it, peers in it, to the right and the left, stands.*)

Where's my cheese-roll?

(*Pause.*)

Someone's taken my cheese-roll. I left it there. (*To Sam.*) You been thieving?
TEDDY: I took your cheese-roll, Lenny.

(*Silence.*)
(*Sam looks at them, picks up his hat and goes out of the front door.*)
(*Silence.*)

LENNY: You took my cheese-roll?

TEDDY: Yes.
LENNY: I made that roll myself. I cut it and put the butter on. I sliced a piece of cheese and put it in between. I put it on a plate and I put it in the sideboard. I did all that before I went out. Now I come back and you've eaten it.
TEDDY: Well, what are you going to do about it?
LENNY: I'm waiting for you to apologize.
TEDDY: But I took it deliberately, Lenny.
LENNY: You mean you didn't stumble on it by mistake?
TEDDY: No, I saw you put it there. I was hungry, so I ate it.

(*Pause.*)

LENNY: Barefaced audacity.

(*Pause.*)

What led you to be so . . . vindictive against your own brother? I'm bowled over.

(*Pause.*)

Well, Ted, I would say this is something approaching the naked truth, isn't it? It's a real cards on the table stunt. I mean, we're in the land of no holds barred now. Well, how else can you interpret it? To pinch your younger brother's specially made cheese-roll when he's out doing a spot of work, that's not equivocal, it's unequivocal.

(*Pause.*)

Mind you, I will say you do seem to have grown a bit sulky during the last six years. A bit sulky. A bit inner. A bit less forthcoming. It's funny, because I'd have thought that in the United States of America, I mean with the sun and all that, the open spaces, on the old campus, in your position, lecturing, in the center of all the intellectual life out there, on the old campus, all the social whirl, all the stimulation of it all, all your kids and all that, to have fun with, down by the pool, the Greyhound buses and all that, tons of iced water, all the comfort of those Bermuda shorts and all that, on the old campus, no time of the day or night you can't get a cup of coffee or a Dutch gin, I'd have thought you'd have grown more forthcoming, not less. Because I want you to know that you set a standard for us, Teddy. Your family looks up to you, boy, and you know what it does? It does its best to follow the example you set. Because you're a great source of pride to us. That's why we were so glad to see you come back, to welcome you back to your birthplace. That's why.

(*Pause.*)

No, listen, Ted, there's no question that we live a less rich life here than you do over there. We live a closer life. We're busy, of course. Joey's busy with his boxing, I'm busy with my occupation, Dad still plays a good game of poker, and he does the cooking as well, well up to his old standard, and Uncle Sam's the best chauffeur in the firm. But nevertheless we do make up a unit, Teddy, and you're an integral part of it. When we all sit round the backyard having a quiet gander at the night sky, there's always an empty chair standing in the circle, which is in fact yours. And so when you at length return to us, we do expect a bit of grace, a bit of je ne sais quoi,° a bit of generosity of mind, a bit of liberality of spirit, to reassure us. We do expect that. But do we get it? Have we got it? Is that what you've given us?

(*Pause.*)

TEDDY: Yes.

(*Joey comes down the stairs and into the room, with a newspaper.*)

LENNY (*to Joey*): How'd you get on?
JOEY: Er . . . not bad.
LENNY: What do you mean?

(*Pause.*)

   What do you mean?
JOEY: Not bad.
LENNY: I want to know what you *mean* — by not bad.
JOEY: What's it got to do with you?
LENNY: Joey, you tell your brother everything.

(*Pause.*)

JOEY: I didn't get all the way.
LENNY: You didn't get all the way?

(*Pause.*)

   (*With emphasis.*) You didn't get all the way?
   But you've had her up there for two hours.
JOEY: Well?
LENNY: You didn't get all the way and you've had her up there for two hours!
JOEY: What about it?

(*Lenny moves closer to him.*)

LENNY: What are you telling me?
JOEY: What do you mean?
LENNY: Are you telling me she's a tease?

(*Pause.*)

   She's a tease!

(*Pause.*)

   What do you think of that, Ted? Your wife turns out to be a tease. He's had her up there for two hours and he didn't go the whole hog.
JOEY: I didn't say she was a tease.
LENNY: Are you joking? It sounds like a tease to me, don't it to you, Ted?
TEDDY: Perhaps he hasn't got the right touch.
LENNY: Joey? Not the right touch? Don't be ridiculous.

je ne sais quoi: (French) I don't know what.

He's had more dolly than you've had cream cakes. He's irresistible. He's one of the few and far between. Tell him about the last bird you had, Joey.

(*Pause.*)

JOEY: What bird?
LENNY: The last bird! When we stopped the car . . .
JOEY: Oh, that . . . yes . . . well, we were in Lenny's car one night last week . . .
LENNY: The Alfa.
JOEY: And er . . . bowling down the road . . .
LENNY: Up near the Scrubs.
JOEY: Yes, up over by the Scrubs . . .
LENNY: We were doing a little survey of North Paddington.
JOEY: And er . . . it was pretty late, wasn't it?
LENNY: Yes, it was late. Well?

(*Pause.*)

JOEY: And then we . . . well, by the curb, we saw this parked car . . . with a couple of girls in it.
LENNY: And their escorts.
JOEY: Yes, there were two geezers in it. Anyway . . .

(*Pause.*)

   What we do then?
LENNY: We stopped the car and got out!
JOEY: Yes . . . we got out . . . and we told the . . . two escorts . . . to go away . . . which they did . . . and then we . . . got the girls out of the car . . .
LENNY: We didn't take them over the Scrubs.
JOEY: Oh, no. Not over the Scrubs. Well, the police would have noticed us there . . . you see. We took them over a bombed site.
LENNY: Rubble. In the rubble.
JOEY: Yes, plenty of rubble.

(*Pause.*)

   Well . . . you know . . . then we had them.
LENNY: You've missed out the best bit. He's missed out the best bit!
JOEY: What bit?
LENNY (*to Teddy*): His bird says to him, I don't mind, she says, but I've got to have some protection. I've got to have some contraceptive protection. I haven't got any contraceptive protection, old Joey says to her. In that case I won't do it, she says. Yes you will, says Joey, never mind about the contraceptive protection.

(*Lenny laughs.*)

   Even my bird laughed when she heard that. Yes, even she gave out a bit of a laugh. So you can't say old Joey isn't a bit of a knockout when he gets going, can you? And here he is upstairs with your wife for two hours and he hasn't even been the whole hog. Well, your wife sounds like a bit of a tease to me, Ted. What do you make of it, Joey? You satisfied? Don't tell me you're satisfied without going the whole hog?

(*Pause.*)

JOEY: I've been the whole hog plenty of times. Sometimes . . . you can be happy . . . and not go the whole hog. Now and again . . . you can be happy . . . without going any hog.

(*Lenny stares at him.*)
(*Max and Sam come in the front door and into the room.*)

MAX: Where's the whore? Still in bed? She'll make us all animals.
LENNY: The girl's a tease.
MAX: What?
LENNY: She's had Joey on a string.
MAX: What do you mean?
TEDDY: He had her up there for two hours and he didn't go the whole hog.

(*Pause.*)

MAX: My Joey? She did that to my boy?

(*Pause.*)

To my youngest son? Tch, tch, tch, tch. How you feeling, son? Are you all right?
JOEY: Sure I'm all right.
MAX (*to Teddy*): Does she do that to you, too?
TEDDY: No.
LENNY: He gets the gravy.
MAX: You think so?
JOEY: No he don't.

(*Pause.*)

SAM: He's her lawful husband. She's his lawful wife.
JOEY: No he don't! He don't get no gravy! I'm telling you. I'm telling all of you. I'll kill the next man who says he gets the gravy.
MAX: Joey . . . what are you getting so excited about? (*To Lenny.*) It's because he's frustrated. You see what happens?
JOEY: Who is?
MAX: Joey. No one's saying you're wrong. In fact everyone's saying you're right.

(*Pause.*)
(*Max turns to the others.*)

You know something? Perhaps it's not a bad idea to have a woman in the house. Perhaps it's a good thing. Who knows? Maybe we should keep her.

(*Pause.*)

Maybe we'll ask her if she wants to stay.

(*Pause.*)

TEDDY: I'm afraid not, Dad. She's not well, and we've got to get home to the children.
MAX: Not well? I told you, I'm used to looking after people who are not so well. Don't worry about that. Perhaps we'll keep her here.

(*Pause.*)

SAM: Don't be silly.
MAX: What's silly?
SAM: You're talking rubbish.
MAX: Me?
SAM: She's got three children.
MAX: She can have more! Here. If she's so keen.
TEDDY: She doesn't want any more.
MAX: What do you know about what she wants, eh, Ted?
TEDDY (*smiling*): The best thing for her is to come home with me, Dad. Really. We're married, you know.

(*Max walks about the room, clicks his fingers.*)

MAX: We'd have to pay her, of course. You realize that? We can't leave her walking about without any pocket money. She'll have to have a little allowance.
JOEY: Of course we'll pay her. She's got to have some money in her pocket.
MAX: That's what I'm saying. You can't expect a woman to walk about without a few bob to spend on a pair of stockings.

(*Pause.*)

LENNY: Where's the money going to come from?
MAX: Well, how much is she worth? What we talking about, three figures?
LENNY: I asked you where the money's going to come from. It'll be an extra mouth to feed. It'll be an extra body to clothe. You realize that?
JOEY: I'll buy her clothes.
LENNY: What with?
JOEY: I'll put in a certain amount out of my wages.
MAX: That's it. We'll pass the hat round. We'll make a donation. We're all grown-up people, we've got a sense of responsibility. We'll all put a little in the hat. It's democratic.
LENNY: It'll come to a few quid, Dad.

(*Pause.*)

I mean, she's not a woman who likes walking around in second-hand goods. She's up to the latest fashion. You wouldn't want her walking about in clothes which don't show her off at her best, would you?
MAX: Lenny, do you mind if I make a little comment? It's not meant to be critical. But I think you're concentrating too much on the economic considerations. There are other considerations. There are the human considerations. You understand what I mean? There are the human considerations. Don't forget them.
LENNY: I won't.
MAX: Well don't.

(*Pause.*)

Listen, we're bound to treat her in something approximating, at least, to the manner in which she's accustomed. After all, she's not someone off the street, she's my daughter-in-law!
JOEY: That's right.

MAX: There you are, you see. Joey'll donate, Sam'll donate. . . .

(*Sam looks at him.*)

I'll put in a few bob out of my pension, Lenny'll cough up. We're laughing. What about you, Ted? How much you going to put in the kitty?

TEDDY: I'm not putting anything in the kitty.

MAX: What? You won't even help to support your own wife? I thought he was a son of mine. You lousy stinkpig. Your mother would drop dead if she heard you take that attitude.

LENNY: Eh, Dad.

(*Lenny walks forward.*)

I've got a better idea.

MAX: What?

LENNY: There's no need for us to go to all this expense. I know these women. Once they get started they ruin your budget. I've got a better idea. Why don't I take her up with me to Greek Street?

(*Pause.*)

MAX: You mean put her on the game?

(*Pause.*)

We'll put her on the game. That's a stroke of genius, that's a marvelous idea. You mean she can earn the money herself — on her back?

LENNY: Yes.

MAX: Wonderful. The only thing is, it'll have to be short hours. We don't want her out of the house all night.

LENNY: I can limit the hours.

MAX: How many?

LENNY: Four hours a night.

MAX (*dubiously*): Is that enough?

LENNY: She'll bring in a good sum for four hours a night.

MAX: Well, you should know. After all, it's true, the last thing we want to do is wear the girl out. She's going to have her obligations this end as well. Where you going to put her in Greek Street?

LENNY: It doesn't have to be right in Greek Street, Dad. I've got a number of flats all around that area.

MAX: You have? Well, what about me? Why don't you give me one?

LENNY: You're sexless.

JOEY: Eh, wait a minute, what's all this?

MAX: I know what Lenny's saying. Lenny's saying she can pay her own way. What do you think, Teddy? That'll solve all our problems.

JOEY: Eh, wait a minute. I don't want to share her.

MAX: What did you say?

JOEY: I don't want to share her with a lot of yobs!

MAX: Yobs! You arrogant git! What arrogance. (*To Lenny.*) Will you be supplying her with yobs?

LENNY: I've got a very distinguished clientele, Joey. They're more distinguished than you'll ever be.

MAX: So you can count yourself lucky we're including you in.

JOEY: I didn't think I was going to have to share her!

MAX: Well, you *are* going to have to share her! Otherwise she goes straight back to America. You understand?

(*Pause.*)

It's tricky enough as it is, without you shoving your oar in. But there's something worrying me. Perhaps she's not so up to the mark. Eh? Teddy, you're the best judge. Do you think she'd be up to the mark?

(*Pause.*)

I mean what about all this teasing? Is she going to make a habit of it? That'll get us nowhere.

(*Pause.*)

TEDDY: It was just love play . . . I suppose . . . that's all I suppose it was.

MAX: Love play? Two bleeding hours? That's a bloody long time for love play!

LENNY: I don't think we've got anything to worry about on that score, Dad.

MAX: How do you know?

LENNY: I'm giving you a professional opinion.

(*Lenny goes to Teddy.*)

LENNY: Listen, Teddy, you could help us, actually. If I were to send you some cards, over to America . . . you know, very nice ones, with a name on, and a telephone number, very discreet, well, you could distribute them . . . to various parties, who might be making a trip over here. Of course, you'd get a little percentage out of it.

MAX: I mean, you needn't tell them she's your wife.

LENNY: No, we'd call her something else. Dolores, or something.

MAX: Or Spanish Jacky.

LENNY: No, you've got to be reserved about it, Dad. We could call her something nice . . . like Cynthia . . . or Gillian.

(*Pause.*)

JOEY: Gillian.

(*Pause.*)

LENNY: No, what I mean, Teddy, you must know lots of professors, heads of departments, men like that. They pop over here for a week at the Savoy, they need somewhere they can go to have a nice quiet poke. And of course you'd be in a position to give them inside information.

MAX: Sure. You can give them proper data. You know, the kind of thing she's willing to do. How far she'd be prepared to go with their little whims and fancies. Eh, Lenny? To what extent she's various. I mean if you don't know who does?

(*Pause.*)

I bet you before two months we'd have a waiting list.

LENNY: You could be our representative in the States.

MAX: Of course. We're talking in international terms! By the time we've finished Pan American'll give us a discount.

(*Pause.*)

TEDDY: She'd get old . . . very quickly.

MAX: No . . . not in this day and age! With the health service? Old! How could she get old? She'll have the time of her life.

(*Ruth comes down the stairs, dressed.*)
(*She comes into the room.*)
(*She smiles at the gathering, and sits.*)
(*Silence.*)

TEDDY: Ruth . . . the family have invited you to stay, for a little while longer. As a . . . as a kind of guest. If you like the idea I don't mind. We can manage very easily at home . . . until you come back.

RUTH: How very nice of them.

(*Pause.*)

MAX: It's an offer from our heart.

RUTH: It's very sweet of you.

MAX: Listen . . . it would be our pleasure.

(*Pause.*)

RUTH: I think I'd be too much trouble.

MAX: Trouble? What are you talking about? What trouble? Listen, I'll tell you something. Since poor Jessie died, eh, Sam? we haven't had a woman in the house. Not one. Inside this house. And I'll tell you why. Because their mother's image was so dear any other woman would have . . . tarnished it. But

you . . . Ruth . . . you're not only lovely and beautiful, but you're kin. You're kith. You belong here.

(*Pause.*)

RUTH: I'm very touched.

MAX: Of course you're touched. I'm touched.

(*Pause.*)

TEDDY: But Ruth, I should tell you . . . that you'll have to pull your weight a little, if you stay. Financially. My father isn't very well off.

RUTH (*to Max*): Oh, I'm sorry.

MAX: No, you'd just have to bring in a little, that's all. A few pennies. Nothing much. It's just that we're waiting for Joey to hit the top as a boxer. When Joey hits the top . . . well . . .

(*Pause.*)

TEDDY: Or you can come home with me.

LENNY: We'd get you a flat.

(*Pause.*)

RUTH: A flat?

LENNY: Yes.

RUTH: Where?

LENNY: In town.

(*Pause.*)

But you'd live here, with us.

MAX: Of course you would. This would be your home. In the bosom of the family.

LENNY: You'd just pop up to the flat a couple of hours a night, that's all.

Ian Hart as Lenny, Lia Williams as Ruth, and Ian Holm as Max in the Dublin's Gate Theatre's 2001 production of *The Homecoming*.

Ian McShane as Max, Raul
Esparza as Lenny, Eve Best
as Ruth, and Gareth Saxe as
Joey in the 2007 Cort Theatre
production, New York.

MAX: Just a couple of hours, that's all. That's all.
LENNY: And you make enough money to keep you going
here.

(*Pause.*)

RUTH: How many rooms would this flat have?
LENNY: Not many.
RUTH: I would want at least three rooms and a bath-
room.
LENNY: You wouldn't need three rooms and a bathroom.
MAX: She'd need a bathroom.
LENNY: But not three rooms.

(*Pause.*)

RUTH: Oh, I would. Really.
LENNY: Two would do.
RUTH: No. Two wouldn't be enough.

(*Pause.*)

I'd want a dressing-room, a rest-room, and a bedroom.

(*Pause.*)

LENNY: All right, we'll get you a flat with three rooms
and a bathroom.
RUTH: With what kind of conveniences?
LENNY: All conveniences.
RUTH: A personal maid?
LENNY: Of course.

(*Pause.*)

We'd finance you, to begin with, and then, when you
were established, you could pay us back, in installments.

RUTH: Oh, no, I wouldn't agree to that.
LENNY: Oh, why not?
RUTH: You would have to regard your original outlay
simply as a capital investment.

(*Pause.*)

LENNY: I see. All right.
RUTH: You'd supply my wardrobe, of course?
LENNY: We'd supply everything. Everything you need.
RUTH: I'd need an awful lot. Otherwise I wouldn't be
content.
LENNY: You'd have everything.
RUTH: I would naturally want to draw up an inventory
of everything I would need, which would require
your signatures in the presence of witnesses.
LENNY: Naturally.
RUTH: All aspects of the agreement and conditions of
employment would have to be clarified to our mutual
satisfaction before we finalized the contract.
LENNY: Of course.

(*Pause.*)

RUTH: Well, it might prove a workable arrangement.
LENNY: I think so.
MAX: And you'd have the whole of your daytime free,
of course. You could do a bit of cooking here if you
wanted to.
LENNY: Make the beds.
MAX: Scrub the place out a bit.
TEDDY: Keep everyone company.

(*Sam comes forward.*)

SAM (*in one breath*): MacGregor had Jessie in the back of my cab as I drove them along.

(*He croaks and collapses.*)
(*He lies still.*)
(*They look at him.*)

MAX: What's he done? Dropped dead?
LENNY: Yes.
MAX: A corpse? A corpse on my floor? Get him out of here! Clear him out of here!

(*Joey bends over Sam.*)

JOEY: He's not dead.
LENNY: He probably was dead, for about thirty seconds.
MAX: He's not even dead!

(*Lenny looks down at Sam.*)

LENNY: Yes, there's still some breath there.
MAX (*pointing at Sam*): You know what that man had?
LENNY: Has.
MAX: Has! A diseased imagination.

(*Pause.*)

RUTH: Yes, it sounds a very attractive idea.
MAX: Do you want to shake on it now, or do you want to leave it till later?
RUTH: Oh, we'll leave it till later.

(*Teddy stands.*)
(*He looks down at Sam.*)

TEDDY: I was going to ask him to drive me to London Airport.

(*He goes to the cases, picks one up.*)

Well, I'll leave your case, Ruth. I'll just go up the road to the Underground.
MAX: Listen, if you go the other way, first left, first right, you remember, you might find a cab passing there.
TEDDY: Yes, I might do that.
MAX: Or you can take the tube to Piccadilly Circus, won't take you ten minutes, and pick up a cab from there out to the Airport.
TEDDY: Yes, I'll probably do that.
MAX: Mind you, they'll charge you double fare. They'll charge you for the return trip. It's over the six-mile limit.
TEDDY: Yes. Well, bye-bye, Dad. Look after yourself.

(*They shake hands.*)

MAX: Thanks, son. Listen. I want to tell you something. It's been wonderful to see you.

(*Pause.*)

TEDDY: It's been wonderful to see you.
MAX: Do your boys know about me? Eh? Would they like to see a photo, do you think, of their grandfather?
TEDDY: I know they would.

(*Max brings out his wallet.*)

MAX: I've got one on me. I've got one here. Just a minute. Here you are. Will they like that one?
TEDDY (*taking it*): They'll be thrilled.

(*He turns to Lenny.*)

Good-bye, Lenny.

(*They shake hands.*)

LENNY: Ta-ta, Ted. Good to see you. Have a good trip.
TEDDY: Bye-bye, Joey.

(*Joey does not move.*)

JOEY: Ta-ta.

(*Teddy goes to the front door.*)

RUTH: Eddie.

(*Teddy turns.*)
(*Pause.*)

Don't become a stranger.

(*Teddy goes, shuts the front door.*)
(*Silence.*)
(*The three men stand.*)
(*Ruth sits relaxed in her chair.*)
(*Sam lies still.*)
(*Joey walks slowly across the room.*)
(*He kneels at her chair.*)
(*She touches his head, lightly.*)
(*He puts his head in her lap.*)
(*Max begins to move above them, backwards and forwards.*)
(*Lenny stands still.*)
(*Max turns to Lenny.*)

MAX: I'm too old, I suppose. She thinks I'm an old man.

(*Pause.*)

I'm not such an old man.

(*Pause.*)

(*To Ruth.*) You think I'm too old for you?

(*Pause.*)

Listen. You think you're just going to get that big slag all the time? You think you're just going to have him . . . you're going to just have him all the time? You're going to have to work! You'll have to take them on, you understand?

(*Pause.*)

Does she realize that?

(*Pause.*)

Lenny, do you think she understands . . .

(*He begins to stammer.*)

What . . . what . . . what . . . we're getting at?

What . . . we've got in mind? Do you think she's got it clear?

(*Pause.*)

I don't think she's got it clear.

(*Pause.*)

You understand what I mean? Listen, I've got a funny idea she'll do the dirty on us, you want to bet? She'll use us, she'll make use of us, I can tell you! I can smell it! You want to bet?

(*Pause.*)

She won't . . . be adaptable!

(*He falls to his knees, whimpers, begins to moan and sob.*)
(*He stops sobbing, crawls past Sam's body round her chair, to the other side of her.*)

I'm not an old man.

(*He looks up at her.*)

Do you hear me?

(*He raises his face to her.*)

Kiss me.

(*She continues to touch Joey's head, lightly.*)
(*Lenny stands, watching.*)

Curtain

COMMENTARY

Ronald Knowles
THE HOMECOMING   *1995*

In an excerpt from a longer essay, Ronald Knowles discusses some of the complexities of The Homecoming, *beginning with Pinter's approach to sentimentalism, one of the common ingredients of nineteenth-century drama. Knowles also addresses the question of reality and points to a confounding aspect of Pinter that seems to admit conflicting realities that almost demand a Freudian analysis.*

One day Pinter was told the story of someone from his kind of background who left home for the United States, did well, married and had children, and suddenly returned with his wife without telling anyone. The anecdote sunk into the unconscious, and then, in due course, a play was engendered. Many would regard *The Homecoming* as Pinter's greatest achievement. Indeed, some would regard it as among the greatest plays of the twentieth century. Without doubt it may be grouped with Pinter's most famous plays, yet in its day *The Homecoming* was regarded by some critics as cynical, obscene, and degrading.

Teddy, a lecturer in philosophy, returns with Ruth to the all-male household of his brothers Lenny, a pimp, and Joey, a demolition worker; Uncle Sam, a chauffeur; and Max, his father, a retired butcher. The unexpected return provokes a mixed reaction, but it is far from the sentimental coziness of welcome implied by the title. In very broad terms it can be said that Pinter's play, along with various other art forms of the twentieth century, is written out of a strong sense of distaste for the culture of sentimentality which colored much nineteenth-century art and subsequently became a potent factor of popular twentieth-century culture, particularly in the cinema and the musical theater—above all in periods conducive to escapist entertainment, such as the postwar years of 1920–30 and 1945–60. Sentimentality is, indeed, an element of *The Homecoming,* but it is subjected to the most extreme of reversals, such as the close, when Ruth is invited by the family to remain as a prostitute domestically and publicly.

The Homecoming has a radical greatness in the way it confronts assumptions about the idea of the nuclear family, and thus of twentieth-century Western society, and reexamines what is found. The ideal facade consists of love, care, and kindness, responsibility, dignity, and commitment, but the reality may be considerably less than this. The small detail of Joey, the younger brother, as a laborer in the demolition business is very important for Pinter's conception of the play as a whole. The experience of *The Homecoming* is like knocking down an old building, clearing the rubble, and examining just what the foundations are made of. Certainly scarifying in places, the play is not finally cynical. Although humanity can undergo deprivation and distortion, in the midst of seeming perversity, at the close an ineradicable human need survives. There is ugliness and dismay but not just that: there is the need for love, though dumb and crippled, but hardly of the Dickensian kind.

The following analysis of *The Homecoming* will develop from three different standpoints. First, some ground needs to be cleared concerning the question of "realistic," "realism," and "reality." Once it is grasped that a work of art can represent different kinds of reality at the same time, then it is possible to move on to the issue of structure, style, and formalization. A first impression of the play may seem to be overwhelmingly naturalistic, but a further more penetrating overview will show how the play is entirely structured, from one line to the work as a whole, by a principle of binary opposition in which drama derives from the interaction of a series of polar opposites. This concept from the theory of structuralism will be seen to be immensely fruitful not only in the play but also as a constituent element of Pinter's creative imagination. It is worth noting Pinter's remark of 1966: "The only play which gets remotely near to a structural entity which satisfies me is *The Homecoming.*"[1] Third, this structuralist position will be reexamined in the light of Freud's theories on male sexuality, particularly his focus on the male impulse to degrade the female.

One of the vexed problems of literature, theory, and criticism is that it isn't really possible to get along without the word *reality,* yet, ironically, as soon as it is introduced, it seems to raise more questions than it answers. Whenever the word is used as a singular noun, it implies a unilateral view of the subject. From certain positions of an extreme kind—for example, those of a priest or physicist—this might well be insisted on: Reality as God, or Energy. But it is necessary to consider the idea of reality more pluralistically, as consisting of several realities. Few people would take exception to discussion of such concepts as political or economic reality. Considering realities and the individual, it would not be difficult to find some agreement. To deny a reality to environment, the reality of material surroundings, hardly seems sane. As a corollary of this, there is social being, the objective actuality of the self and interrelationships at work, at home, and in the community. To complement these external realities there is the subjective inner reality of selfhood—of such things as beliefs, hopes, dreams, and feelings.

[1]"Harold Pinter: An Interview" (with Lawrence Bensky), in *Pinter: A Collection of Critical Essays,* edited by Arthur Ganz (Englewood Cliffs, N.J.: Prentice-Hall, 1972), 26.

Here lies the problem. To juggle with Orwellian[2] phraseology: all things are real, but some things are more real than others. In different situations the claim of one kind of reality might seem greater than another. There is not necessarily a fixed hierarchy of realities, though many might insist that the psychological reality of the individual is paramount. Conversely, part of the heritage of romanticism is that the experience of the artist, transmuted into art, offers the greatest reality since, by virtue of genius, reality is thereby made manifest, often by symbolism, the vehicle of a transcendental reality. Where the greater reality of one thing is granted, then, the lesser reality of another is implied, hence the hierarchy previously mentioned. And then this whole stable positivist approach can be shaken by the admission that what seems real can become unreal, particularly within the ineluctable dimension of time. This is a major aspect of Pinter's memory plays.

The selection and representation of any particular kind, or kinds, of reality in drama will depend on the relationship of convention and style to the cultural moment, within a spectrum of relative influences and values, not least of which is censorship. In short, what might seem very realistic in one decade can, in retrospect, seem relatively formalized, or even unreal, in another. Thus, the realism of the 1950s kitchen-sink dramatists seems almost stagy by later standards. Applying these considerations to *The Homecoming*, certain discriminations can be made without which, as in some early audiences, the ending might seem objectionably bizarre, unreal, and thus unacceptable.

At the outset the play appears to be grounded in the domestic realism of an urban sitting room, which is seemingly corroborated by the colloquial London speech:

MAX: . . . Do you hear what I'm saying? I'm talking to you! Where's the scissors?
LENNY: (*looking up, quietly*) Why don't you shut up, you daft prat?

As the action proceeds with the entries of the other members of the family, Joey and Sam, an all-male household is presented, in which aggravation, sarcasm, and provocation have become entirely habitual. After a blackout, without any expository anticipation, Teddy and Ruth appear. Within a page or so of dialogue Teddy directs Ruth's and the audience's attention to something of an oddity of the room's structure—the rear wall is missing: "Actually there was a wall, across there . . . with a door. We knocked it down . . . years ago . . . to make an open living area. The structure wasn't affected, you see. My mother was dead." This correlation of the physical and emotional is emphatically and overtly symbolic—so much so that in the original production the set designer, John Bury, with Pinter's approval, left the load-supporting beam exposed.[3] This huge gap in all their lives was further symbolized in the original production by an almost colorless set, which was recreated by the same director, Peter Hall, for the 1991 London production in honor of Pinter's sixtieth birthday. What is dimly latent in this sterile set is hinted at in Teddy's nervous speech, and the audience response is accordingly deepened by apprehension and confirmed by the defamatory attacks, directly and indirectly, on Ruth, the lone woman surrounded by womenless men. At this point, however, the

---

[2] A reference to George Orwell (pseudonym for Eric Blair, 1903–1950), whose analysis of political terminology revealed its duplicity and contradictory nature.

[3] John Lahr, ed., *A Casebook on Harold Pinter's "The Homecoming"* (New York: Grove Press, 1971), 28.

movement combining the realistic with the symbolic is hardly unusual but, rather, is quite typical of much twentieth-century drama. What audiences found too outrageous to accept was the final action of the second half.

Act 2 starts solidly with after-dinner coffee being distributed and cozy sentimental recall—but not for long. Shortly, the antagonism and sarcasm return in language, but, as Teddy and Ruth are preparing for departure, the action also becomes bizarre. As Teddy "*stands, with* RUTH'S *coat,*" looking on, Lenny dances with Ruth and kisses her. Joey thus encouraged takes Ruth to the sofa, "*embraces and kisses her.*" Lenny then caresses her at the same time. As the erotic action continues, the stage direction is crucial: "JOEY *lies heavily on* RUTH. *They are almost still.* LENNY *caresses her hair.*" Thus, the arrested movement of Joey and Ruth presents a formalized, nonnaturalistic pose. Immediately, the following sequence of stage directions occurs:

> JOEY *and* RUTH *roll off the sofa onto the floor.*
> JOEY *clasps her.* LENNY *moves to stand above them. He looks down on them. He touches* RUTH *gently with his foot.* RUTH *suddenly pushes* JOEY *away. She stands up.*
> JOEY *gets to his feet, stares at her.*

The erotic is almost compromised by farce here because, while this is happening, Max is talking to Teddy paternally as if nothing untoward were happening and it was the most normal situation in the world. This aspect of the bizarre is then dramatically furthered by Ruth virtually taking charge and beginning to order the men around. While the men talk, Ruth disappears upstairs for two hours with Joey, yet Teddy is seemingly undisturbed. Upon returning, she is propositioned by the family to stay on as a prostitute and communal concubine. The play closes with an all-important tableau, like that of Joey over Ruth, which must be returned to with discussion of Freud.

Many have rejected all this as unreal. Others have lamely accommodated it with the label "surreal." If an earlier part of the discussion is returned to, it is possible to arrive at greater insight. *The Homecoming* at the outset largely depicts an external social reality of domestic relationships. Subjective reality, at this stage, is only hinted at—what did the death of Jessie, wife and mother, mean for them all? The entry of Ruth, another wife and mother, exacerbates this question and brings into conflict two planes of reality, the social and the psychological. Pinter's technique is to intercut and juxtapose each until one becomes a critique of the other. Psychological reality subverts the social reality in which Teddy in fact hides, refusing in his cold intellectuality to be drawn further. As in twentieth-century graphic art, one plane is superimposed on another. By the final tableau the innermost conflicting subjectivity of debasement and love is externalized, exposed, and objectified, creating one of the most powerful conclusions of modern drama. If the play is now reexamined in terms of style and structure, it will be shown how these planes of reality are highly formalized throughout by a thoroughgoing structuralist mode in the concept of binary opposition.

Edward Albee

Edward Albee (b. 1928) has won three Pulitzer Prizes for drama: *A Delicate Balance* (1966), *Seascape* (1974), and *Three Tall Women* (1991). However, some of his earlier plays are much better known and are considered much more powerful, such as his first, a one-act play called *The Zoo Story* (1958); *The Death of Bessie Smith* (1959); *The American Dream* (1960); and *Who's Afraid of Virginia Woolf?* (1961), which was made into a memorable film. Albee is known as an experimental writer, concerned with style and ideas in equal measure, but also concerned with jolting the audience into awareness.

Critics have dissected some of Albee's plays in terms of their homoerotic themes; Albee certainly does not limit himself to such issues, although certain plays, such as *Tiny Alice* (1964), sometimes rely on sexual slang for their effect. His portrait of the savage marital battle between George and Martha (echoing the names of our country's founding "father" and "mother") in *Who's Afraid of Virginia Woolf?* has sometimes been used as an example of Albee's distaste for conventional heterosexual marriage. In *Three Tall Women*, the main character is in bed, dying. She has turned her back on her gay son, and while her mind wanders she is visited by two women who help clarify the nature of her life. *The Goat, or Who Is Sylvia?* (2002) stimulated considerable controversy because of the perceived bestiality in Martin's confession that he had fallen in love with a goat. Clearly, the sexual quotient in Albee's plays takes on a special importance.

Albee is unusual in that his first plays made him a major figure in American drama. He was born in Washington, D.C., and adopted by Reed and Frances Albee. His father was part owner of a vaudeville circuit, so in one sense it may be said that Albee was born into a theatrical family. He grew up in Larchmont, New York, although his parents wintered in warm climates; eventually Edward had to go to boarding school. The one he liked most was Choate, in Connecticut, where he was encouraged to write. He attended Trinity College in Hartford for only two years. When he left school he knew he wanted to write, and to give himself the space to do so, he took a number of jobs that did not make serious intellectual demands on him. He also had a trust fund to supplement his income and thus had few financial worries. His first play was written in three weeks when he was thirty, but no New York producer would take it. *The Zoo Story*, in which a conservative gentleman and a young man from the counterculture have an emotional encounter, was first produced in 1959 in Berlin, Germany. Later that year it was produced at the Provincetown Playhouse in Greenwich Village on the same bill with Samuel Beckett's *Krapp's Last Tape*.

After his early successes, Albee had a number of plays produced that brought him no acclaim. Some were panned outright, and all tended to dilute his impact as a major playwright. The period from the late 1970s through the 1980s was especially problematic, with a string of failures: *The Lady from*

Dubuque (1977), *Another Part of the Zoo* (1981), *The Man Who Had Three Arms* (1981), *Finding the Sun* (1982), and *The Marriage Play* (1987). Then Albee came roaring back with *Three Tall Women* in 1991, despite the fact that it opened off-Broadway. Today Albee is regarded as one of America's most important living playwrights. His plays are produced regularly in the United States and abroad, and theaters such as the Goodman in Chicago have staged Albee festivals to honor his lifelong achievement.

THE ZOO STORY

After the first production of the play in the United States in 1960, reviewers soon compared Albee with both Pinter and Ionesco. They saw in Albee's dialogue the influence of the distinctive Pinter language, and in Albee's dramatic concept the influence of the absurdist Ionesco. *The Zoo Story* is an uncomfortable play, like many of its era, but it is not an absurdist experiment. If anything, it is almost a naturalistic portrait of two very different men inhabiting the same city, meeting in a park where it is natural for strangers to start up a conversation. But the conversation of Peter and Jerry is anything but ordinary. Peter, the essentially middle-class citizen with a good job, a wife, two children, two parakeets, and an uptown apartment, sits peacefully reading on the park bench when he is interrupted.

Peter's initial reluctance is palpable. He tries to take refuge behind his book, he tries to light his pipe—but Jerry insists on talking. At first he is cautious, questioning, not too aggressive, but eventually his tone changes and he begins to sound unbalanced. Early performances portrayed Jerry as pathological, although the text does not necessarily support such an extreme interpretation. But Jerry is totally unlike Peter. Jerry is essentially homeless. He lives in a minuscule room at a brownstone boarding house. He has no wife, no children, no animals—at least none that he owns. He claims to have been homosexual, even though he complains about a "colored queen" who lives on the other side of the beaverboard "wall" that separates their rooms. As he reminds Peter that he has everything, Jerry clearly has nothing. He enumerates all his possessions in one speech, listing such things as plates, toilet articles, a hot plate, a can opener, and two empty picture frames. He has no photographs to put in the frames because he has no family or friends.

The only genuine relationship Jerry seems to have is with a dog that is enraged whenever they see one another. The most intense moments of the dialogue occur when Jerry relates the story of himself and the dog. This is such a brilliant piece of dialogue that it is frequently used by actors as an audition piece. Jerry said he tried to befriend the dog by feeding it hamburgers, and although the dog paused long enough to eat the hamburger, it soon growled and threatened him again. Because he was smart and quick, Jerry was never bitten, but he also never had a reasonable relationship with the dog.

The reason Jerry leaves the West Side and goes all the way down to the Village, which is miles from where he begins, and then walks back to the zoo is to make contact with one animal or another. The zoo story that Jerry promises to tell is about establishing relationships between animals: Jerry and whatever the zoo offers. But Jerry finds himself in Central Park north of the zoo and decides to talk with Peter. Peter's general discomfort engaging in this conversation grows steadily throughout the play, just as Jerry's intensity grows by the minute until it becomes uncontrollable. Eventually their status shifts and a tragedy occurs. However, in the action that ends the play, Jerry, who thanks Peter, has finally made genuine, if horrid, contact with another being.

The Zoo Story **in Performance**

The first production was in German translation in Berlin on a double bill with *Krapp's Last Tape* in 1959. The pair then went on to tour twelve German cities. People had a difficult time interpreting the drama, but they could see that the theme of loneliness pervaded both plays. The first New York production was off Broadway at the Provincetown Playhouse in 1960, with George Maharis as Jerry and William Daniels as Peter. The run lasted for 582 performances and was a great success. The *Times* critic, a baffled Harold Clurman, said what he got from the play was that one should not strike up conversations with strangers in Central Park. A London production in 1960 played for 40 performances. Numerous performances, usually with another short play, took place in New York and London throughout the 1960s. There were so many college and amateur productions of the play that Edward Albee took the play, along with several other of his "one acts," to the Kennedy Center in Washington, D.C., in 1979 and directed them himself. He wanted to establish an authentic production to stand as a model for others. An outdoor production during the Edinburgh Festival in 1999 performed the play on a different park bench every day. In 2004 at the Hartford Stage, Albee produced a prequel called *Homelife* that was performed with *The Zoo Story* under the title of *Peter and Jerry*. Albee said he thought that not enough was known about Peter and that he wanted to present him in greater depth. The success of this experiment was limited. Critics generally felt it did not add to the original (one critic said it was like adding moisturizer to perfectly good soap).

Edward Albee (*b.* 1928)
THE ZOO STORY

1958

The Players

PETER: A man in his early forties, neither fat nor gaunt, neither handsome nor homely. He wears tweeds, smokes a pipe, carries horn-rimmed glasses. Although he is moving into middle age, his dress and his manner would suggest a man younger.

JERRY: A man in his late thirties, not poorly dressed, but carelessly. What was once a trim and lightly muscled body has begun to go to fat; and while he is no longer handsome, it is evident that he once was. His fall from physical grace should not suggest debauchery; he has, to come closest to it, a great weariness.

The Scene: *It is Central Park; a Sunday afternoon in summer; the present. There are two park benches, one toward either side of the stage; they both face the audience. Behind them: foliage, trees, sky. At the beginning, Peter is seated on one of the benches.*

(Stage Directions: As the curtain rises, Peter is seated on the bench stage-right. He is reading a book. He stops reading, cleans his glasses, goes back to reading. Jerry enters.)

JERRY: I've been to the zoo. (*Peter doesn't notice*) I said, I've been to the zoo. MISTER, I'VE BEEN TO THE ZOO!

PETER: Hm? . . . What? . . . I'm sorry, were you talking to me?

JERRY: I went to the zoo, and then I walked until I came here. Have I been walking north?

PETER (*Puzzled*): North? Why . . . I . . . I think so. Let me see.

JERRY (*Pointing past the audience*): Is that Fifth Avenue?

PETER: Why yes; yes, it is.

JERRY: And what is that cross street there; that one, to the right?

PETER: That? Oh, that's Seventy-fourth Street.

JERRY: And the zoo is around Sixty-fifth Street; so, I've been walking north.

PETER (*Anxious to get back to his reading*): Yes; it would seem so.

JERRY: Good old north.

PETER (*Lightly, by reflex*): Ha, ha.

JERRY (*After a slight pause*): But not due north.

PETER: I . . . well, no, not due north; but, we . . . call it north. It's northerly.

JERRY (*Watches as Peter, anxious to dismiss him, prepares his pipe*): Well, boy; *you're* not going to get lung cancer, are you?

PETER (*Looks up, a little annoyed, then smiles*): No, sir. Not from this.

JERRY: No, sir. What you'll probably get is cancer of the mouth, and then you'll have to wear one of those things Freud wore after they took one whole side of his jaw away. What do they call those things?

PETER (*Uncomfortable*): A prosthesis?

JERRY: The very thing! A prosthesis. You're an educated man, aren't you? Are you a doctor?

PETER: Oh, no; no. I read about it somewhere; *Time* magazine, I think. (*He turns to his book*)

JERRY: Well, *Time* magazine isn't for blockheads.

PETER: No, I suppose not.

JERRY (*After a pause*): Boy, I'm glad that's Fifth Avenue there.

PETER (*Vaguely*): Yes.

JERRY: I don't like the west side of the park much.

PETER: Oh? (*Then, slightly wary, but interested*) Why?

JERRY (*Offhand*): I don't know.

PETER: Oh. (*He returns to his book*)

JERRY (*He stands for a few seconds, looking at Peter, who finally looks up again, puzzled*): Do you mind if we talk?

PETER (*Obviously minding*): Why . . . no, no.

JERRY: Yes you do; you do.

PETER (*Puts his book down, his pipe out and away, smiling*): No, really; I don't mind.

JERRY: Yes you do.

PETER (*Finally decided*): No; I don't mind at all, really.

JERRY: It's . . . it's a nice day.

PETER (*Stares unnecessarily at the sky*): Yes. Yes, it is; lovely.

JERRY: I've been to the zoo.

PETER: Yes, I think you said so . . . didn't you?

JERRY: You'll read about it in the papers tomorrow, if you don't see it on your TV tonight. You have TV, haven't you?

PETER: Why yes, we have two; one for the children.

JERRY: You're married!

PETER (*With pleased emphasis*): Why, certainly.

JERRY: It isn't a law, for God's sake.

PETER: No . . . no, of course not.

JERRY: And you have a wife.

PETER (*Bewildered by the seeming lack of communication*): Yes!

JERRY: And you have children.

PETER: Yes; two.

JERRY: Boys?

PETER: No, girls . . . both girls.

JERRY: But you wanted boys.

Mark Richman as Jerry and William Daniels as Peter in the 1960 Provincetown Playhouse production of *The Zoo Story.*

PETER: Well . . . naturally, every man wants a son, but . . .

JERRY (*Lightly mocking*): But that's the way the cookie crumbles?

PETER (*Annoyed*): I wasn't going to say that.

JERRY: And you're not going to have any more kids, are you?

PETER (*A bit distantly*): No. No more. (*Then back, and irksome*) Why did you say that? How would you know about that?

JERRY: The way you cross your legs, perhaps; something in the voice. Or maybe I'm just guessing. Is it your wife?

PETER (*Furious*): That's none of your business! (*A silence*) Do you understand? (*Jerry nods. Peter is quiet now*) Well, you're right. We'll have no more children.

JERRY (*Softly*): That *is* the way the cookie crumbles.

PETER (*Forgiving*): Yes . . . I guess so.

JERRY: Well, now; what else?

PETER: What were you saying about the zoo . . . that I'd read about it, or see . . . ?

JERRY: I'll tell you about it, soon. Do you mind if I ask you questions?

PETER: Oh, not really.

JERRY: I'll tell you why I do it; I don't talk to many people—except to say like: give me a beer, or where's the john, or what time does the feature go on, or keep your hands to yourself, buddy. You know—things like that.

PETER: I must say I don't . . .

JERRY: But every once in a while I like to talk to somebody, really *talk*; like to get to know somebody, know all about him.

PETER (*Lightly laughing, still a little uncomfortable*): And am I the guinea pig for today?

JERRY: On a sun-drenched Sunday afternoon like this? Who better than a nice married man with two daughters and . . . uh . . . a dog? (*Peter shakes his head*) No? Two dogs. (*Peter shakes his head again*) Hm. No dogs? (*Peter shakes his head, sadly*) Oh, that's a shame. But you look like an animal man. CATS? (*Peter nods his head, ruefully*) Cats! But, that can't be your idea. No, sir. Your wife and daughters? (*Peter nods his head*) Is there anything else I should know?

PETER (*He has to clear his throat*): There are . . . there are two parakeets. One . . . uh . . . one for each of my daughters.

JERRY: Birds.

PETER: My daughters keep them in a cage in their bedroom.

JERRY: Do they carry disease? The birds.

PETER: I don't believe so.

JERRY: That's too bad. If they did you could set them loose in the house and the cats could eat them and die, maybe. (*Peter looks blank for a moment, then laughs*) And what else? What do you do to support your enormous household?

PETER: I . . . uh . . . I have an executive position with a . . . a small publishing house. We . . . uh . . . we publish textbooks.

JERRY: That sounds nice; very nice. What do you make?

PETER (*Still cheerful*): Now look here!

JERRY: Oh, come on.

PETER: Well, I make around eighteen thousand a year, but I don't carry more than forty dollars at any one time . . . in case you're a . . . a holdup man . . . ha, ha, ha.

JERRY (*Ignoring the above*): Where do you live? (*Peter is reluctant*) Oh, look; I'm not going to rob you, and I'm not going to kidnap your parakeets, your cats, or your daughters.

PETER (*Too loud*): I live between Lexington and Third Avenue, on Seventy-fourth Street.

JERRY: That wasn't so hard, was it?

PETER: I didn't mean to seem . . . ah . . . it's that you don't really carry on a conversation; you just ask questions and I'm . . . I'm normally . . . . uh . . . reticent. Why do you just stand there?

JERRY: I'll start walking around in a little while, and eventually I'll sit down. (*Recalling*) Wait until you see the expression on his face.

PETER: What? Whose face? Look here; is this something about the zoo?

JERRY (*Distantly*): The what?

PETER: The zoo; the zoo. Something about the zoo.

JERRY: The zoo?

PETER: You've mentioned it several times.

JERRY (*Still distant, but returning abruptly*): The zoo? Oh, yes; the zoo. I was there before I came here. I told you that. Say, what's the dividing line between upper-middle-middle-class and lower-upper-middle-class?

PETER: My dear fellow, I . . .

JERRY: Don't my dear fellow me.

PETER (*Unhappily*): Was I patronizing? I believe I was; I'm sorry. But, you see, your question about the classes bewildered me.

JERRY: And when you're bewildered you become patronizing?

PETER: I . . . I don't express myself too well, sometimes. (*He attempts a joke on himself*) I'm in publishing, not writing.

JERRY (*Amused, but not at the humor*): So be it. The truth *is*: I was being patronizing.

PETER: Oh, now; you needn't say that.

(*It is at this point that Jerry may begin to move about the stage with slowly increasing determination and authority, but pacing himself, so that the long speech about the dog comes at the high point of the arc*)

JERRY: All right. Who are your favorite writers? Baudelaire and J. P. Marquand?

PETER (*Wary*): Well, I like a great many writers; I have a considerable . . . catholicity of taste, if I may say so. Those two men are fine, each in his way. (*Warming up*) Baudelaire, of course . . . uh . . . is by far the finer of the two, but Marquand has a place . . . in our . . . uh . . . national . . .

JERRY: Skip it.

PETER: I . . . sorry.

JERRY: Do you know what I did before I went to the zoo today? I walked all the way up Fifth Avenue from Washington Square; all the way.

PETER: Oh; you live in the Village! (*This seems to enlighten Peter*)

JERRY: No, I don't. I took the subway down to the Village so I could walk all the way up Fifth Avenue to the zoo. It's one of those things a person has to do; sometimes a person has to go a very long distance out of his way to come back a short distance correctly.

PETER (*Almost pouting*): Oh, I thought you lived in the Village.

JERRY: What were you trying to do? Make sense out of things? Bring order? The old pigeonhole bit? Well, that's easy; I'll tell you. I live in a four-story brownstone roominghouse on the upper West Side between Columbus Avenue and Central Park West. I live on the top floor; rear; west. It's a laughably small room, and one of my walls is made of beaverboard; this beaverboard separates my room from another laughably small room, so I assume that the two rooms were once one room, a small room, but not necessarily laughable. The room beyond my beaverboard wall is occupied by a colored queen who always keeps his door open; well, not always, but *always* when he's plucking his eyebrows, which he does with Buddhist concentration. This colored queen has rotten teeth, which is rare, and he has a Japanese kimono, which is also pretty rare; and he wears this kimono to and from the john in the hall, which is pretty frequent. I mean, he goes to the john a lot. He never bothers me, and he never brings anyone up to his room. All he does is pluck his eyebrows, wear his kimono and go to the john. Now, the two front rooms on my floor are a little larger, I guess; but they're pretty small, too. There's a Puerto Rican family in one of them, a husband, a wife, and some kids; I don't know how many. These people entertain a lot. And in the other front room, there's somebody living there, but I don't know who it is. I've never seen who it is. Never. Never ever.

PETER (*Embarrassed*): Why . . . why do you live there?

JERRY (*From a distance again*): I don't know.

PETER: It doesn't sound like a very nice place . . . where you live.

JERRY: Well, no; it isn't an apartment in the East Seventies. But, then again, I don't have one wife, two daughters, two cats and two parakeets. What I do have, I have toilet articles, a few clothes, a hot plate that I'm not supposed to have, a can opener, one that works with a key, you know, a knife, two forks, and two spoons, one small, one large; three plates, a cup, a saucer, a drinking glass, two picture frames, both empty, eight or nine books, a pack of pornographic playing cards, regular deck, an old Western Union typewriter that prints nothing but capital letters, and a small strongbox without a lock which has in

it . . . what? Rocks! Some rocks . . . sea-rounded rocks I picked up on the beach when I was a kid. Under which . . . weighed down . . . are some letters . . . please letters . . . please why don't you do this, and please when will you do that letters. And when letters, too. When will you write? When will you come? When? These letters are from more recent years.

PETER (*Stares glumly at his shoes, then*): About those two empty picture frames . . . ?

JERRY: I don't see why they need any explanation at all. Isn't it clear? I don't have pictures of anyone to put in them.

PETER: Your parents . . . perhaps . . . a girl friend . . .

JERRY: You're a very sweet man, and you're possessed of a truly enviable innocence. But good old Mom and good old Pop are dead . . . you know? . . . I'm broken up about it, too . . . I mean really. BUT. That particular vaudeville act is playing the cloud circuit now, so I don't see how I can look at them, all neat and framed. Besides, or, rather, to be pointed about it, good old Mom walked out on good old Pop when I was ten and a half years old; she embarked on an adulterous turn of our southern states . . . a journey of a year's duration . . . and her most constant companion . . . among others, among many others . . . was a Mr. Barleycorn.° At least, that's what good old Pop told me after he went down . . . came back . . . brought her body north. We'd received the news between Christmas and New Year's, you see, that good old Mom had parted with the ghost in some dump in Alabama. And, without the ghost . . . she was less welcome. I mean, what was she? A stiff . . . a northern stiff. At any rate, good old Pop celebrated the New Year for an even two weeks and then slapped into the front of a somewhat moving city omnibus, which sort of cleaned things out family-wise. Well no; then there was Mom's sister, who was given neither to sin nor the consolations of the bottle. I moved in on her, and my memory of her is slight excepting I remember still that she did all things dourly: sleeping, eating, working, praying. She dropped dead on the stairs to her apartment, my apartment then, too, on the afternoon of my high school graduation. A terribly middle-European joke, if you ask me.

PETER: Oh, my; oh, my.

JERRY: Oh, your what? But that was a long time ago, and I have no feeling about any of it that I care to admit to myself. Perhaps you can see, though, why good old Mom and good old Pop are frameless. What's your name? Your first name?

PETER: I'm Peter.

JERRY: I'd forgotten to ask you. I'm Jerry.

PETER (*With a slight, nervous laugh*): Hello, Jerry.

JERRY (*Nods his hello*): And let's see now; what's the point of having a girl's picture, especially in two

---

Mr. Barleycorn: Whiskey.

frames? I have two picture frames, you remember. I never see the pretty little ladies more than once, and most of them wouldn't be caught in the same room with a camera. It's odd, and I wonder if it's sad.

PETER: The girls?

JERRY: No. I wonder if it's sad that I never see the little ladies more than once. I've never been able to have sex with, or, how is it put? . . . make love to anybody more than once. Once; that's it. . . . Oh, wait; for a week and a half, when I was fifteen . . . and I hang my head in shame that puberty was late . . . I was a h-o-m-o-s-e-x-u-a-l. I mean, I was queer . . . (*Very fast*) . . . queer, queer, queer . . . with bells ringing, banners snapping in the wind. And for those eleven days, I met at least twice a day with the park superintendent's son . . . a Greek boy, whose birthday was the same as mine, except he was a year older. I think I was very much in love . . . maybe just with sex. But that was the jazz of a very special hotel, wasn't it? And now; oh, do I love the little ladies; really, I love them. For about an hour.

PETER: Well, it seems perfectly simple to me. . . .

JERRY (*Angry*): Look! Are you going to tell me to get married and have parakeets?

PETER (*Angry himself*): Forget the parakeets! And stay single if you want to. It's no business of mine. I didn't start this conversation in the . . .

JERRY: All right, all right. I'm sorry. All right? You're not angry?

PETER (*Laughing*): No, I'm not angry.

JERRY (*Relieved*): Good. (*Now back to his previous tone*) Interesting that you asked me about the picture frames. I would have thought that you would have asked me about the pornographic playing cards.

PETER (*With a knowing smile*): Oh, I've seen those cards.

JERRY: That's not the point. (*Laughs*) I suppose when you were a kid you and your pals passed them around, or you had a pack of your own.

PETER: Well, I guess a lot of us did.

JERRY: And you threw them away just before you got married.

PETER: Oh, now; look here. I didn't *need* anything like that when I got older.

JERRY: No?

PETER (*Embarrassed*): I'd rather not talk about these things.

JERRY: So? Don't. Besides, I wasn't trying to plumb your post-adolescent sexual life and hard times; what I wanted to get at is the value difference between pornographic playing cards when you're a kid, and pornographic playing cards when you're older. It's that when you're a kid you use the cards as a substitute for a real experience, and when you're older you use real experience as a substitute for the fantasy. But I imagine you'd rather hear about what happened at the zoo.

PETER (*Enthusiastic*): Oh, yes; the zoo. (*Then, awkward*) That is . . . if you. . . .

JERRY: Let me tell you about why I went . . . well, let me tell you some things. I've told you about the fourth floor of the roominghouse where I live. I think the rooms are better as you go down, floor by floor. I guess they are; I don't know. I don't know any of the people on the third and second floors. Oh, wait! I do know that there's a lady living on the third floor, in the front. I know because she cries all the time. Whenever I go out or come back in, whenever I pass her door, I always hear her crying, muffled, but . . . very determined. Very determined indeed. But the one I'm getting to, and all about the dog, is the landlady. I don't like to use words that are too harsh in describing people. I don't like to. But the landlady is a fat, ugly, mean, stupid, unwashed, misanthropic, cheap, drunken bag of garbage. And you may have noticed that I very seldom use profanity, so I can't describe her as well as I might.

PETER: You describe her . . . vividly.

JERRY: Well, thanks. Anyway, she has a dog, and I will tell you about the dog, and she and her dog are the gatekeepers of my dwelling. The woman is bad enough; she leans around in the entrance hall, spying to see that I don't bring in things or people, and when she's had her mid-afternoon pint of lemon-flavored gin she always stops me in the hall, and grabs ahold of my coat or my arm, and she presses her disgusting body up against me to keep me in a corner so she can talk to me. The smell of her body and her breath . . . you can't imagine it . . . and somewhere, somewhere in the back of that pea-sized brain of hers, an organ developed just enough to let her eat, drink, and emit, she has some foul parody of sexual desire. And I, Peter, I am the object of her sweaty lust.

PETER: That's disgusting. That's . . . horrible.

JERRY: But I have found a way to keep her off. When she talks to me, when she presses herself to my body and mumbles about her room and how I should come there, I merely say: but, Love; wasn't yesterday enough for you, and the day before? Then she puzzles, she makes slits of her tiny eyes, she sways a little, and then, Peter . . . and it is at this moment that I think I might be doing some good in that tormented house . . . a simple-minded smile begins to form on her unthinkable face, and she giggles and groans as she thinks about yesterday and the day before; as she believes and relives what never happened. Then, she motions to that black monster of a dog she has, and she goes back to her room. And I am safe until our next meeting.

PETER: It's so . . . unthinkable. I find it hard to believe that people such as that really *are*.

JERRY (*Lightly mocking*): It's for reading about, isn't it?

PETER (*Seriously*): Yes.

JERRY: And fact is better left to fiction. You're right, Peter. Well, what I have been meaning to tell you about is the dog; I shall, now.

PETER (*Nervously*): Oh, yes; the dog.

JERRY: Don't go. You're not thinking of going, are you?

PETER: Well . . . no, I don't think so.

JERRY (*As if to a child*): Because after I tell you about the dog, do you know what then? Then . . . then I'll tell you about what happened at the zoo.

PETER (*Laughing faintly*): You're . . . you're full of stories, aren't you?

JERRY: You don't *have* to listen. Nobody is holding you here; remember that. Keep that in your mind.

PETER (*Irritably*): I know that.

JERRY: You do? Good.

(*The following long speech, it seems to me, should be done with a great deal of action, to achieve a hypnotic effect on Peter, and on the audience, too. Some specific actions have been suggested, but the director and the actor playing Jerry might best work it out for themselves*)

ALL RIGHT. (*As if reading from a huge billboard*) THE STORY OF JERRY AND THE DOG! (*Natural again*) What I am going to tell you has something to do with how sometimes it's necessary to go a long distance out of the way in order to come back a short distance correctly; or, maybe I only think that it has something to do with that. But, it's why I went to the zoo today, and why I walked north . . . northerly, rather . . . until I came here. All right. The dog, I think I told you, is a black monster of a beast: an oversized head, tiny, tiny ears, and eyes . . . bloodshot, infected, maybe; and a body you can see the ribs through the skin. The dog is black, all black; all black except for the bloodshot eyes, and . . . yes . . . and an open sore on its . . . *right* forepaw; that is red, too. And, oh yes; the poor monster, and I do believe it's an old dog . . . it's certainly a misused one . . . almost always has an erection . . . of sorts. That's red, too. And . . . what else? . . . oh, yes; there's a gray-yellow-white color, too, when he bares his fangs. Like this: Grrrrrr! Which is what he did when he saw me for the first time . . . the day I moved in. I worried about that animal the very first minute I met him. Now, animals don't take to me like Saint Francis had birds hanging off him all the time. What I mean is: animals are indifferent to me . . . like people (*He smiles slightly*) . . . most of the time. But this dog wasn't indifferent. From the very beginning he'd snarl and then go for me, to get one of my legs. Not like he was rabid, you know; he was sort of a stumbly dog, but he wasn't half-assed, either. It was a good, stumbly run; but I always got away. He got a piece of my trouser leg, look, you can see right here, where it's mended; he got that the second day I lived there; but, I kicked free and got upstairs fast, so that was that. (*Puzzles*) I still don't know to this day how the other roomers manage it, but you know what I *think*: I think it had to do only with me. Cozy. So. Anyway, this went on for over a week, whenever I came in; but never when I went out. That's funny. Or, it *was* funny. I could pack up and live in the street for all the dog cared. Well, I thought about it up in my room one day, one of the times after I'd bolted upstairs, and I made up my mind. I decided: First, I'll kill the dog with kindness, and if that doesn't work . . . I'll just kill him. (*Peter winces*) Don't react, Peter; just listen. So, the next day I went out and bought a bag of hamburgers, medium rare, no catsup, no onion; and on the way home I threw away all the rolls and kept just the meat.

(*Action for the following, perhaps*)

When I got back to the roominghouse the dog was waiting for me. I half opened the door that led into the entrance hall, and there he was; waiting for me. It figured. I went in, very cautiously, and I had the hamburgers, you remember; I opened the bag, and I set the meat down about twelve feet from where the dog was snarling at me. Like so! He snarled; stopped snarling; sniffed; moved slowly; then faster; then faster toward the meat. Well, when he got to it he stopped, and he looked at me. I smiled; but tentatively, you understand. He turned his face back to the hamburgers, smelled, sniffed some more, and then . . . RRRAAAAGGGGGHHHH, like that . . . he tore into them. It was as if he had never eaten anything in his life before, except like garbage. Which might very well have been the truth. I don't think the landlady ever eats anything but garbage. But. He ate all the hamburgers, almost all at once, making sounds in his throat like a woman. *Then*, when he'd finished the meat, the hamburger, and tried to eat the paper, too, he sat down and smiled. I think he smiled; I know cats do. It was a very gratifying few moments. Then, BAM, he snarled and made for me again. He didn't get me this time, either. So, I got upstairs, and I lay down on my bed and started to think about the dog again. To be truthful, I was offended, and I was damn mad, too. It was six perfectly good hamburgers with not enough pork in them to make it disgusting. I was offended. But, after a while, I decided to try it for a few more days. If you think about it, this dog had what amounted to an antipathy toward me; really. And, I wondered if I mightn't overcome this antipathy. So, I tried it for five more days, but it was always the same: snarl, sniff; move; faster; stare; gobble; RAAGGGHHH; smile; snarl; BAM. Well, now; by this time Columbus Avenue was strewn with hamburger rolls and I was less offended than disgusted. So, I decided to kill the dog.

(*Peter raises a hand in protest*)

Oh, don't be so alarmed, Peter; I didn't succeed. The day I tried to kill the dog I bought only one hamburger and what I thought was a murderous portion of rat poison. When I bought the hamburger I asked the man not to bother with the roll, all I wanted was the meat. I expected some reaction from him, like: we don't sell no hamburgers without rolls; or, wha' d'ya wanna do, eat it out'a ya han's? But no; he smiled benignly, wrapped up the hamburger in waxed paper, and said: A bite for ya pussy-cat? I wanted to say: No, not really; it's part of a plan to poison a dog I know. But, you can't say "a dog I know" without sounding funny; so I said, a little too loud, I'm afraid, and too formally: YES, A BITE FOR MY PUSSY-CAT. People looked up. It always happens when I try to simplify things; people look up. But that's neither hither nor thither. So. On my way back to the roominghouse, I kneaded the hamburger and the rat poison together between my hands, at that point feeling as much sadness as disgust. I opened the door to the entrance hall, and there the monster was, waiting to take the offering and then jump me. Poor bastard; he never learned that the moment he took to smile before he went for me gave me time enough to get out of range. BUT, there he was; malevolence with an erection, waiting. I put the poison patty down, moved toward the stairs and watched. The poor animal gobbled the food down as usual, smiled, which made me almost sick, and then, BAM. But, I sprinted up the stairs, as usual, and the dog didn't get me, as usual. AND IT CAME TO PASS THAT THE BEAST WAS DEATHLY ILL. I knew this because he no longer attended me, and because the landlady sobered up. She stopped me in the hall the same evening of the attempted murder and confided the information that God had struck her puppy-dog a surely fatal blow. She had forgotten her bewildered lust, and her eyes were wide open for the first time. They looked like the dog's eyes. She sniveled and implored me to pray for the animal. I wanted to say to her: Madam, I have myself to pray for, the colored queen, the Puerto Rican family, the person in the front room whom I've never seen, the woman who cries deliberately behind her closed door, and the rest of the people in all roominghouses, everywhere; besides, Madam, I don't understand how to pray. But . . . to simplify things . . . I told her I would pray. She looked up. She said that I was a liar, and that I probably wanted the dog to die. I told her, and there was so much truth here, that I didn't want the dog to die. I didn't, and not just because I'd poisoned him. I'm afraid that I must tell you I wanted the dog to live so that I could see what our new relationship might come to.

(*Peter indicates his increasing displeasure and slowly growing antagonism*)

Please understand, Peter; that sort of thing is important. You must believe me; it *is* important. We have to know the effect of our actions. (*Another deep sigh*) Well, anyway; the dog recovered. I have no idea why, unless he was a descendant of the puppy that guarded the gates of hell or some such resort. I'm not up on my mythology. (*He pronounces the word myth-o-logy*) Are you?

(*Peter sets to thinking, but Jerry goes on*)

At any rate, and you've missed the eight-thousand-dollar question, Peter; at any rate, the dog recovered

his health and the landlady recovered her thirst, in no way altered by the bow-wow's deliverance. When I came home from a movie that was playing on Forty-second Street, a movie I'd seen, or one that was very much like one or several I'd seen, after the landlady told me puppykins was better, I was so hoping for the dog to be waiting for me. I was . . . well, how would you put it . . . enticed? . . . fascinated? . . . no, I don't think so . . . heart-shatteringly anxious, that's it; I was heart-shatteringly anxious to confront my friend again.

(*Peter reacts scoffingly*)

Yes, Peter; friend. That's the only word for it. I was heart-shatteringly et cetera to confront my doggy friend again. I came in the door and advanced, unafraid, to the center of the entrance hall. The beast was there . . . looking at me. And, you know, he looked better for his scrape with the nevermind. I stopped; I looked at him; he looked at me. I think . . . I think we stayed a long time that way . . . still, stone-statue . . . just looking at one another. I looked more into his face than he looked into mine. I mean, I can concentrate longer at looking into a dog's face than a dog can concentrate at looking into mine, or into anybody else's face, for that matter. But during that twenty seconds or two hours that we looked into each other's face, we made contact. Now, here is what I had wanted to happen: I loved the dog now, and I wanted him to love me. I had tried to love, and I had tried to kill, and both had been unsuccessful by themselves. I hoped . . . and I don't really know why I expected the dog to understand anything, much less my motivations . . . I hoped that the dog would understand.

(*Peter seems to be hypnotized*)

It's just . . . it's just that . . . (*Jerry is abnormally tense, now*) . . . it's just that if you can't deal with people, you have to make a start somewhere. WITH ANIMALS! (*Much faster now, and like a conspirator*) Don't you see? A person has to have some way of dealing with SOMETHING. If not with people . . . if not with people . . . SOMETHING. With a bed, with a cockroach, with a mirror . . . no, that's too hard, that's one of the last steps. With a cockroach, with a . . . with a . . . with a carpet, a roll of toilet paper . . . no, not that, either . . . that's a mirror, too; always check bleeding. You see how hard it is to find things? With a street corner, and too many lights, all colors reflecting on the oily-wet streets . . . with a wisp of smoke, a wisp . . . of smoke . . . with . . . with pornographic playing cards, with a strongbox . . . WITHOUT A LOCK . . . with love, with vomiting, with crying, with fury because the pretty little ladies aren't pretty little ladies, with making money with your body which is an act of love and I could prove it, with howling because you're alive; with God. How about that?

WITH GOD WHO IS A COLORED QUEEN WHO WEARS A KIMONO AND PLUCKS HIS EYEBROWS, WHO IS A WOMAN WHO CRIES WITH DETERMINATION BEHIND HER CLOSED DOOR . . . with God who, I'm told, turned his back on the whole thing some time ago . . . with . . . some day, with people. (*Jerry sighs the next word heavily*) People. With an idea; a concept. And where better, where ever better in this humiliating excuse for a jail, where better to communicate one single, simpleminded idea than in an entrance hall? Where? It would be A START! Where better to make a beginning . . . to understand and just possibly be understood . . . a beginning of an understanding, than with . . .

(*Here Jerry seems to fall into almost grotesque fatigue*)

. . . than with A DOG. Just that; a dog.

(*Here there is a silence that might be prolonged for a moment or so; then Jerry wearily finishes his story*)

A dog. It seemed like a perfectly sensible idea. Man is a dog's best friend, remember. So: the dog and I looked at each other. I longer than the dog. And what I saw then has been the same ever since. Whenever the dog and I see each other we both stop where we are. We regard each other with a mixture of sadness and suspicion, and then we feign indifference. We walk past each other safely; we have an understanding. It's very sad, but you'll have to admit that it is an understanding. We had made many attempts at contact, and we had failed. The dog has returned to garbage, and I to solitary but free passage. I have not returned. I mean to say, I have *gained* solitary free passage, if that much further loss can be said to be gain. I have learned that neither kindness nor cruelty by themselves, independent of each other, creates any effect beyond themselves; and I have learned that the two combined, together, at the same time, are the teaching emotion. And what is gained is loss. And what has been the result: the dog and I have attained a compromise; more of a bargain, really. We neither love nor hurt because we do not try to reach each other. And, *was* trying to feed the dog an act of love? And, perhaps, was the dog's attempt to bite me *not* an act of love? If we can so misunderstand, well then, why have we invented the word love in the first place?

(*There is silence. Jerry moves to Peter's bench and sits down beside him. This is the first time Jerry has sat down during the play*)

The Story of Jerry and the Dog: the end.

(*Peter is silent*)

Well, Peter? (*Jerry is suddenly cheerful*) Well, Peter? Do you think I could sell that story to the *Reader's Digest* and make a couple of hundred bucks for *The Most Unforgettable Character I've Ever Met?* Huh?

(*Jerry is animated, but Peter is disturbed*)

Oh, come on now, Peter; tell me what you think.

PETER (*Numb*): I . . . I don't understand what . . . I don't think I . . . (*Now, almost tearfully*) Why did you tell me all of this?

JERRY: Why not?

PETER: I DON'T UNDERSTAND!

JERRY (*Furious, but whispering*): That's a lie.

PETER: No. No, it's not.

JERRY (*Quietly*): I tried to explain it to you as I went along. I went slowly; it all has to do with . . .

PETER: I DON'T WANT TO HEAR ANY MORE. I don't understand you, or your landlady, or her dog. . . .

JERRY: *Her* dog! I thought it was my . . . No. No, you're right. It *is* her dog. (*Looks at Peter intently, shaking his head*) I don't know what I was thinking about; of course you don't understand. (*In a monotone, wearily*) I don't live in your block; I'm not married to two parakeets, or whatever your setup is. I am a *permanent transient*, and my home is the sickening roominghouses on the West Side of New York City, which is the greatest city in the world. Amen.

PETER: I'm . . . I'm sorry; I didn't mean to . . .

JERRY: Forget it. I suppose you don't quite know what to make of me, eh?

PETER (*A joke*): We get all kinds in publishing. (*Chuckles*)

JERRY: You're a funny man. (*He forces a laugh*) You know that? You're a very . . . a richly comic person.

PETER (*Modestly, but amused*): Oh, now, not really. (*Still chuckling*)

JERRY: Peter, do I annoy you, or confuse you?

PETER (*Lightly*): Well, I must confess that this wasn't the kind of afternoon I'd anticipated.

JERRY: You mean, I'm not the gentleman you were expecting.

PETER: I wasn't expecting anybody.

JERRY: No, I don't imagine you were. But I'm here, and I'm not leaving.

PETER (*Consulting his watch*): Well, you may not be, but I must be getting home soon.

JERRY: Oh, come on; stay a while longer.

PETER: I really should get home; you see . . .

JERRY (*Tickles Peter's ribs with his fingers*): Oh, come on.

PETER (*He is very ticklish; as Jerry continues to tickle him his voice becomes falsetto*): No, I . . . OHHHHH! Don't do that. Stop, Stop. Ohhh, no, no.

JERRY: Oh, come on.

PETER (*As Jerry tickles*): Oh, hee, hee, hee. I must go. I . . . hee, hee, hee. After all, stop, stop, hee, hee, hee, after all, the parakeets will be getting dinner ready soon. Hee, hee. And the cats are setting the table. Stop, stop, and, and . . . (*Peter is beside himself now*) . . . and we're having . . . hee, hee . . . uh . . . ho, ho, ho.

(*Jerry stops tickling Peter, but the combination of the tickling and his own mad whimsy has Peter laughing almost hysterically. As his laughter continues, then subsides, Jerry watches him, with a curious fixed smile*)

JERRY: Peter?

PETER: Oh, ha, ha, ha, ha, ha. What? What?

JERRY: Listen, now.

PETER: Oh, ho, ho. What . . . what is it, Jerry? Oh, my.

JERRY (*Mysteriously*): Peter, do you want to know what happened at the zoo?

PETER: Ah, ha, ha. The what? Oh, yes; the zoo. Oh, ho, ho. Well, I had my own zoo there for a moment with . . . hee, hee, the parakeets getting dinner ready, and the . . . ha, ha, whatever it was, the . . .

JERRY (*Calmly*): Yes, that was very funny, Peter. I wouldn't have expected it. But do you want to hear about what happened at the zoo, or not?

PETER: Yes. Yes, by all means; tell me what happened at the zoo. Oh, my. I don't know what happened to me.

JERRY: Now I'll let you in on what happened at the zoo; but first, I should tell you why I went to the zoo. I went to the zoo to find out more about the way people exist with animals, and the way animals exist with each other, and with people too. It probably wasn't a fair test, what with everyone separated by bars from everyone else, the animals for the most part from each other, and always the people from the animals. But, if it's a zoo, that's the way it is. (*He pokes Peter on the arm*) Move over.

PETER (*Friendly*): I'm sorry, haven't you enough room? (*He shifts a little*)

JERRY (*Smiling slightly*): Well, all the animals are there, and all the people are there, and it's Sunday and all the children are there. (*He pokes Peter again*) Move over.

PETER (*Patiently, still friendly*): All right.

(*He moves some more, and Jerry has all the room he might need*)

JERRY: And it's a hot day, so all the stench is there, too, and all the balloon sellers, and all the ice cream sellers, and all the seals are barking, and all the birds are screaming. (*Pokes Peter harder*) Move over!

PETER (*Beginning to be annoyed*): Look here, you have more than enough room! (*But he moves more, and is now fairly cramped at one end of the bench*)

JERRY: And I am there, and it's feeding time at the lions' house, and the lion keeper comes into the lion cage, one of the lion cages, to feed one of the lions. (*Punches Peter on the arm, hard*) MOVE OVER!

PETER (*Very annoyed*): I can't move over any more, and stop hitting me. What's the matter with you?

JERRY: Do you want to hear the story? (*Punches Peter's arm again*)

PETER (*Flabbergasted*): I'm not so sure! I certainly don't want to be punched in the arm.

JERRY (*Punches Peter's arm again*): Like that?

PETER: Stop it! What's the matter with you?

JERRY: I'm crazy, you bastard.

PETER: That isn't funny.

JERRY: Listen to me, Peter. I want this bench. You go sit on the bench over there, and if you're good I'll tell you the rest of the story.

PETER (*Flustered*): But . . . whatever for? What is the matter with you? Besides, I see no reason why I should give up this bench. I sit on this bench almost every Sunday afternoon, in good weather. It's secluded here; there's never anyone sitting here, so I have it all to myself.

JERRY (*Softly*): Get off this bench, Peter; I want it.

PETER (*Almost whining*): No.

JERRY: I said I want this bench, and I'm going to have it. Now get over there.

PETER: People can't have everything they want. You should know that; it's a rule; people can have some of the things they want, but they can't have everything.

JERRY (*Laughs*): Imbecile! You're slow-witted!

PETER: Stop that!

JERRY: You're a vegetable! Go lie down on the ground.

PETER (*Intense*): Now *you* listen to me. I've put up with you all afternoon.

JERRY: Not really.

PETER: LONG ENOUGH. I've put up with you long enough. I've listened to you because you seemed . . . well, because I thought you wanted to talk to somebody.

JERRY: You put things well; economically, and, yet . . . oh, what is the word I want to put justice to your . . . JESUS, you make me sick . . . get off here and give me my bench.

PETER: MY BENCH!

JERRY (*Pushes Peter almost, but not quite, off the bench*): Get out of my sight.

PETER (*Regaining his position*): God da . . . mn you. That's enough! I've had enough of you. I will not give up this bench; you can't have it, and that's that. Now, go away.

(*Jerry snorts but does not move*)

Go away, I said.

(*Jerry does not move*)

Get away from here. If you don't move on . . . you're a bum . . . that's what you are. . . . If you don't move on, I'll get a policeman here and make you go.

(*Jerry laughs, stays*)

I warn you, I'll call a policeman.

JERRY (*Softly*): You won't find a policeman around here; they're all over on the west side of the park chasing fairies down from trees or out of the bushes. That's all they do. That's their function. So scream your head off; it won't do you any good.

PETER: POLICE! I warn you, I'll have you arrested. POLICE! (*Pause*) I said POLICE! (*Pause*) I feel ridiculous.

JERRY: You look ridiculous: a grown man screaming for the police on a bright Sunday afternoon in the park with nobody harming you. If a policeman *did* fill his quota and come sludging over this way he'd probably take you in as a nut.

PETER (*With disgust and impotence*): Great God, I just came here to read, and now you want me to give up the bench. You're mad.

JERRY: Hey, I got news for you, as they say. I'm on your precious bench, and you're never going to have it for yourself again.

PETER (*Furious*): Look, you; get off my bench. I don't care if it makes any sense or not. I want this bench to myself; I want you OFF IT!

JERRY (*Mocking*): Aw . . . look who's mad.

PETER: GET OUT!

JERRY: No.

PETER: I WARN YOU!

JERRY: Do you know how ridiculous you look *now*?

PETER (*His fury and self-consciousness have possessed him*): It doesn't matter. (*He is almost crying*) GET AWAY FROM MY BENCH!

JERRY: Why? You have everything in the world you want; you've told me about your home, and your family, and *your own* little zoo. You have everything, and now you want this bench. Are these the things men fight for? Tell me, Peter, is this bench, this iron and this wood, is this your honor? Is this the thing in the world you'd fight for? Can you think of anything more absurd?

PETER: Absurd? Look, I'm not going to talk to you about honor, or even try to explain it to you. Besides, it isn't a question of honor; but even if it were, you wouldn't understand.

JERRY (*Contemptuously*): You don't even know what you're saying, do you? This is probably the first time in your life you've had anything more trying to face than changing your cats' toilet box. Stupid! Don't you have any idea, not even the slightest what other people *need*?

PETER: Oh, boy, listen to you; well, you don't need this bench. That's for sure.

JERRY: Yes; yes, I do.

PETER (*Quivering*): I've come here for years; I have hours of great pleasure, great satisfaction, right here. And that's important to a man. I'm a responsible person, and I'm a GROWNUP. This is my bench, and you have no right to take it away from me.

JERRY: Fight for it, then. Defend yourself; defend your bench.

PETER: You've *pushed* me to it. Get up and fight.

JERRY: Like a man?

PETER (*Still angry*): Yes, like a man, if you insist on mocking me even further.

JERRY: I'll have to give you credit for one thing: you *are* a vegetable, and a slightly nearsighted one, I think . . .

PETER: THAT'S ENOUGH. . . .

JERRY: . . . but, you know, as they say on TV all the time — you know — and I mean this, Peter, you have a certain dignity; it surprises me. . . .

PETER: STOP!

JERRY (*Rises lazily*): Very well, Peter, we'll battle for the bench, but we're not evenly matched.

(*He takes out and clicks open an ugly-looking knife*)

PETER (*Suddenly awakening to the reality of the situation*): You *are* mad! You're stark raving mad! YOU'RE GOING TO KILL ME!

(*But before Peter has time to think what to do, Jerry tosses the knife at Peter's feet*)

JERRY: There you go. Pick it up. You have the knife and we'll be more evenly matched.

PETER (*Horrified*): No!

JERRY (*Rushes over to Peter, grabs him by the collar; Peter rises; their faces almost touch*): Now you pick up that knife and you fight with me. You fight for your self-respect; you fight for that goddamned bench.

PETER (*Struggling*): No! Let . . . let go of me! He . . . Help!

JERRY (*Slaps Peter on each "fight"*): You fight, you miserable bastard; fight for that bench; fight for your parakeets; fight for your cats, fight for your two daughters; fight for your wife; fight for your manhood, you pathetic little vegetable. (*Spits in Peter's face*) You couldn't even get your wife with a male child.

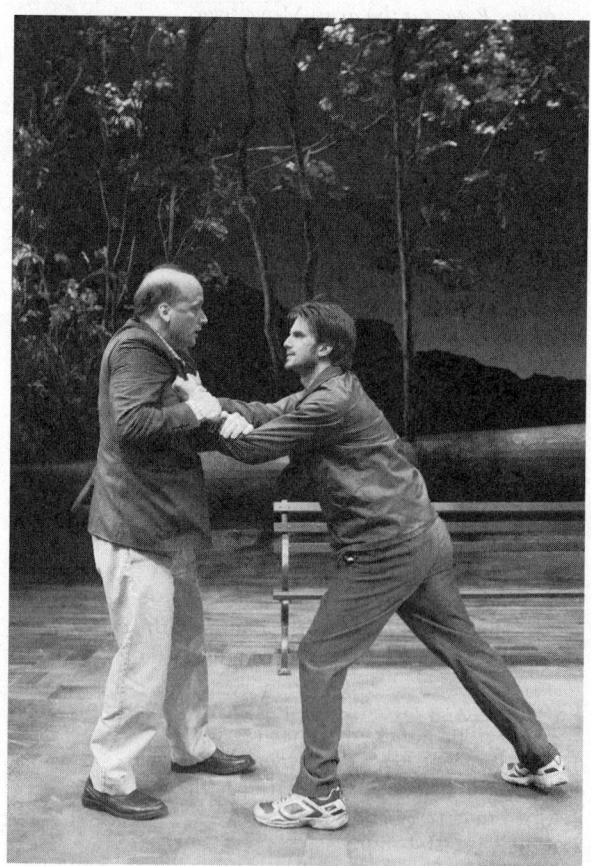

Frank Wood as Peter and Frederick Weller as Jerry in the 2004 performance at the Hartford Stage Company.

PETER (*Breaks away, enraged*): It's a matter of genetics, not manhood, you . . . you monster.

(*He darts down, picks up the knife and backs off a little; he is breathing heavily*)

I'll give you one last chance; get out of here and leave me alone!

(*He holds the knife with a firm arm, but far in front of him, not to attack, but to defend*)

JERRY (*Sighs heavily*): So be it!

(*With a rush he charges Peter and impales himself on the knife. Tableau: For just a moment, complete silence, Jerry impaled on the knife at the end of Peter's still firm arm. Then Peter screams, pulls away, leaving the knife in Jerry. Jerry is motionless, on point. Then he, too, screams, and it must be the sound of an infuriated and fatally wounded animal. With the knife in him, he stumbles back to the bench that Peter had vacated. He crumbles there, sitting, facing Peter, his eyes wide in agony, his mouth open*)

PETER (*Whispering*): Oh my God, oh my God, oh my God. . . .

(*He repeats these words many times, very rapidly*)

JERRY: (*Jerry is dying; but now his expression seems to change. His features relax, and while his voice varies, sometimes wrenched with pain, for the most part he seems removed from his dying. He smiles*)
Thank you, Peter. I mean that, now; thank you very much. (*Peter's mouth drops open. He cannot move; he is transfixed*)
Oh, Peter, I was so afraid I'd drive you away. (*He laughs as best he can*) You don't know how afraid I was you'd go away and leave me. And now I'll tell you what happened at the zoo. I think . . . I think this is what happened at the zoo . . . I think. I think that while I was at the zoo I decided that I would walk north . . . northerly, rather . . . until I found you . . . or somebody . . . and I decided that I would talk to you . . . I would tell you things . . . and things that I would tell you would . . . Well, here we are. You see? Here we *are*. But . . . I don't know . . . could I have planned all this? No . . . no, I couldn't have. But I think I did. And now I've told you what you wanted to know, haven't I? And now you know all about what happened at the zoo. And now you know what you'll see in your TV, and the face I told

you about . . . you remember . . . the face I told you about . . . my face, the face you see right now. Peter . . . Peter? . . . Peter . . . thank you. I came unto you (*He laughs, so faintly*) and you have comforted me. Dear Peter.

PETER (*Almost fainting*): Oh my God!

JERRY: You'd better go now. Somebody might come by, and you don't want to be here when anyone comes.

PETER (*Does not move, but begins to weep*): Oh my God, oh my God.

JERRY (*Most faintly, now; he is very near death*): You won't be coming back here any more, Peter; you've been dispossessed. You've lost your bench, but you've defended your honor. And Peter, I'll tell you something now; you're not really a vegetable; it's all right, you're an animal. You're an animal, too. But you'd better hurry now, Peter. Hurry, you'd better go . . . see?

(*Jerry takes a handkerchief and with great effort and pain wipes the knife handle clean of fingerprints*)

Hurry away, Peter.

(*Peter begins to stagger away*)

Wait . . . wait, Peter. Take your book . . . book. Right here . . . beside me . . . on your bench . . . my bench, rather. Come . . . take your book.

(*Peter starts for the book, but retreats*)

Hurry . . . Peter.

(*Peter rushes to the bench, grabs the book, retreats*)

Very good, Peter . . . very good. Now . . . hurry away.

(*Peter hesitates for a moment, then flees, stage-left*)

Hurry away. . . . (*His eyes are closed now*) Hurry away, your parakeets are making the dinner . . . the cats . . . are setting the table . . .

PETER (*Off stage*): (*A pitiful howl*)
OH MY GOD!

JERRY: (*His eyes still closed, he shakes his head and speaks; a combination of scornful mimicry and supplication*)
Oh . . . my . . . God.

(*He is dead*)

Curtain

COMMENTARY

Robert B. Bennett

TRAGIC VISION IN THE ZOO STORY
1977

In this excerpt from a study of Albee, Robert B. Bennett considers the play as a tragedy, comparing, at particular points, Jerry with Hamlet and Hamlet's inquiry into the spiritual nature of man. The animal qualities of man are expressed in terms of cruelty, whereas the human qualities are expressed in terms of kindness. The indifference Bennett proposes is generally assigned to Peter, but Bennett points out that all three qualities are in Jerry. The conflict between the animal and the human provides a basis for understanding the play.

While the conclusion to *The Zoo Story* has met with the approval of some readers and the disapproval of others, the meaning of the protagonist's death has not been disputed. The consensus has been that Albee intends us to understand Jerry's death as a Christ-like sacrifice. Rose Zimbardo and George Wellwarth praise the symbolism. Martin Esslin and Brian Way complain that the play's ending loses absurdist rigor and degenerates into sentimentality.[1] Similarly Lee Baxandall argues that when Albee resorts to aesthetic solutions, which are symbolically instead of historically meaningful, he does not offer a solution viable in drama, "the most socially rooted of the arts."[2]

Apparently unheeded by all these viewpoints are Albee's stage directions. These, it seems to me, are included in order to prevent us and the actor who plays Jerry from either sentimentalizing his death scene or regarding it purely as a Christ-like sacrifice. Albee writes:

> Oh, Peter, I was so afraid I'd drive you away. (*He laughs as best he can*) You don't know how afraid I was you'd go away and leave me. . . . Peter . . . thank you. I came unto you (*He laughs, so faintly*) and you have comforted me. Dear Peter.[3]

The biblical phrasing and the expression of thanks and affection would, by themselves, be sentimental. Laughter, however, is an expression not of compassion, but of psychic distance. Moreover, Jerry's going on to praise Peter for being an animal like the rest of us ("You're an animal, too") may be laughable and depressing, but it is not melodramatic; and his scornfully mimicking Peter in his dying breath should discourage us from accusing Jerry of emotional over-indulgence. At the

[1]Zimbardo, "Symbolism and Naturalism in Edward Albee's *The Zoo Story*," *Twentieth Century Literature* 8 (April 1962), 15; Wellwarth, *The Theater of Protest and Paradox*, 2nd ed. (New York, 1971), p. 322; Esslin, *The Theatre of the Absurd*, 2nd ed. (Garden City, New York, 1969), p. 267; Way, "Albee and the Absurd," in *American Theatre*, ed. J. R. Brown and Bernard Harris (New York, 1967), p. 204.

[2]"The Theater of Edward Albee," in *The Modern American Theater*, ed. Alvin Kernan (Englewood Cliffs, New Jersey, 1967), p. 98.

[3]Edward Albee, *The American Dream* and *The Zoo Story* (New York, 1959), p. 48.

same time, however, Jerry clearly wants to believe that a God exists and that love is possible; and he has witnessed what seem to be similar longings in the other persons in his rooming-house. Indeed, Jerry is not a hardened absurdist;[4] and if Albee's stage directions are followed, there will be supplication along with mimicry in his ambivalent last words. Jerry hopes that his death is possibly sacrificial and that he has created by his act an effect beyond itself; but he is not so spiritually entranced as to fail to realize that his Christ-like self-sacrifice for Peter's regeneration — what Baxandall means presumably by his "aestheticism of symbolic transcendence" ("Theater of Edward Albee") — may possibly be no more than a glorified front to a suicide. In other words Jerry, and Albee, are as conscious of the frailty of the symbolic solution as Baxandall is.

To regard the dramatic experience of *The Zoo Story* as embodying a doctrinally absolute statement underestimates the play's complexity. Albee does not here presume the absurdist's certainty that all is meaningless nor the social protester's certainty that he knows what is wrong and how to correct it.[5] Rather, in the manner of tragedy, this play tests and questions, by the experience it presents, the propositions of religion and philosophy. Through Jerry, Albee asks how we can tell whether spiritual love is a genuine human faculty or an illusion. Jerry hopes that man is a spiritual creature, expects that he is no more than an animal with illusory and frustrated spiritual longings, and fears that man may have lost even his animal instincts as a result of social conditioning. At the time of the play Jerry is consumed by a need to resolve these doubts; and, to borrow Arthur Miller's description of the tragic hero, he "is ready to lay down his life, if need be, to secure . . . his personal dignity."[6]

Jerry's concern about his personal dignity is more cosmic than social and is centered in the question, "If we can so misunderstand, well then, why have we invented the word love in the first place?" Jerry realizes that if man is incapable of loving, he cannot be blamed for not loving. On this level of perception, Jerry sees Peter as man (*Homo sapiens*) to be understood by comparison with animal and vegetable nature. Jerry does not pigeonhole Peter as the affluent-New-York-businessman; this label is merely the superficial and illusory identity that he sees standing in the way of Peter's self-knowledge. Whereas Michael Rutenberg sees Jerry as a social critic like Vance Packard,[7] I find him less obviously but more importantly a philosopher like Hamlet. Just as Hamlet questions why the Creator has given us "godlike reason/To fust in us unus'd" (IV.iv.33–39), so Jerry wonders why man possesses the urge for spiritual communion if there is no worldly way to express and fulfill it. If love can only "fust in us unus'd," he seems to say, then man is "a beast, no more."

---

[4]Spokesmen for *The Zoo Story* as absurdist theater include Esslin, *Theatre of the Absurd,* p. 267; Charles R. Lyons, "Two Projections of the Isolation of the Human Soul: Brecht and Albee," *Drama Survey* 4 (Summer 1965), 121. Way sees the play as a confusion of absurdist and social protest drama ("Albee and the Absurd," p. 204). Spokesmen against the absurdist designation include Michael Rutenberg, *Edward Albee: Playwright in Protest* (New York, 1969), p. 11; and Thomas B. Morgan, "Angry Playwright in a Soft Spell," *Life,* 26 May 1967, p. 97.

[5]The majority of critics, including Rutenberg, Baxandall, and Morgan, read *The Zoo Story* as a social tract.

[6]From "Tragedy and the Common Man," *New York Times,* 27 Feb. 1949, II, pp. 1, 3; rpt. in *Death of a Salesman: Text and Criticism,* ed. Gerald Weales (New York, 1967), pp. 143–47.

[7]*Edward Albee,* pp. 16 and 20.

The dramatic power of tragedy usually depends heavily upon the playwright's giving expression to a full complex of feelings and perceptions within the protagonist toward himself and his world. These will have been generated by an experience that has jarred him from a conventional pattern of existence. In *The Zoo Story* the three attitudes of love, hate, and indifference provide the general frames of reference for the conflicting forces within Jerry himself and between Jerry and Peter. Kindness proceeds from spiritual nature; cruelty from animal nature; and indifference from social conditioning which reduces one's personality, Jerry suggests, to the level of a vegetable. Jerry, as author of the incident, tries to shape his actions according to the hypothesis that kindness (love) and cruelty (hate) in combination form the teaching emotion, an emotion which can harmonize the elements of spirit and body in man, and resolve the tensions that divide his amphibian nature. The seeming antithesis between the separate emotions of love and hate dissolves, Jerry has learned, when both are understood to be expressions of passionate commitment that together vie against the inclination toward apathy in the effort to define what man is or what he can become. Although one probably first thinks of the play as a conflict between the loving-hating Jerry and the indifferent Peter, I shall try to show that indifference has not been foreign to Jerry's nature, either in his past or in the present, and that the play is also importantly a conflict of all three attitudes within Jerry himself. As is true of most tragedies, there is no clear resolution in this play's conclusion. Death ends the struggle but does not definitively answer the questions, although the final projection is admittedly bleak.

In order fully to understand *The Zoo Story* as tragedy, we must first reassess some of the common assumptions that, if accepted, undermine the play's basic dynamics and reduce the play from a dramatic experience to a philosophical lesson. Frequently Jerry is spoken of as a symbol "meaning" something instead of a human being who is doing and feeling something. "The old pigeonhole bit" of calling Jerry a Christ figure or "a universal symbol of alienated modern man"[8] automatically sets a critical distance between us and Jerry and makes genuine sympathy for him impossible. We have already seen the inadequacy of a strict reading of Jerry as Christ-like. This is an image to which he consciously aspires but not one that he uncritically accepts as achieved or even as valid. The symbol, thus, remains subordinate to and less than the experience. Those who suggest that Jerry is "alienated modern man" incapable of love not only limit the play's vision but seriously misrepresent it. While their argument rightly observes that Jerry in the past has not been able to love "the little ladies" or his lonely compeers in the rooming-house, it must assume, in order to sustain its point, that Jerry, contrary to his claim, has learned nothing from his experience with the dog, and that he shows no love in his relationship with Peter. It must interpret Jerry's sharing with Peter his most personal feelings, thoughts, and experiences as insincere or as yielding to an irresistible impulse rather than, in the way Albee's stage directions urge, as an honest and difficult giving of himself. In general, studies have discussed Jerry as if his nature were frozen, not vital and developing. Jerry's comment, "every once in a while I like to talk to somebody, really *talk*," has encouraged critical inferences such as, "Jerry, weary of the indecisive encounters with the Peters..." (Baxandall, "Theater of Edward Albee"), which see his present action as part of an habitual effort to make

[8]Mary M. Nilan, "Albee's *The Zoo Story:* Alienated Man and the Nature of Love," *Modern Drama* 16 (1973), 58.

contact. But Jerry's own account of his past indicates that what he is doing with Peter is as new to him as it is to Peter. When Jerry describes the colored queen who leaves his door open and the woman who cries behind her closed door, we realize that he observed and did not respond to their passive invitations for a relief from loneliness. Similarly Jerry never saw the prostitutes more than once. Jerry's intense assault on Peter is in striking contrast to his former aloofness. The intervening event between his past and present that causes this change is his collective encounter with the landlady and the dog. This is an experience of tragic awakening which shapes his vision of man and possesses his spirit.

Jerry differs from Peter and from us not in his complex human nature but in his particular tragic experience; and his plight sets in bold relief a universal human problem. Two experiences, his lifelong poverty and the recent rooming-house episode, separate Jerry from Peter. Jerry's poverty has made him more aware than Peter of a spiritual side to his nature that needs fulfillment. Preoccupation with the paraphernalia of society, says *The Zoo Story* (in a manner that reminds us of *Everyman*), encourages man to ignore the existential loneliness of his human condition and, hence, stifles his initiative to seek spiritual fulfillment. The traditional tragic situation in which alienation from society brings suffering and spiritual awareness is present here in the colored queen, the weeping woman, and the little ladies, as well as in Jerry. It is because these characters manifest in their actions an intense spiritual longing, a sensitivity not evident in Peter, that Jerry holds the existence of God and love possible ("with making money with your body which is an act of love . . . WITH GOD WHO IS A COLORED QUEEN . . . WHO IS A WOMAN WHO CRIES WITH DETERMINATION BEHIND HER CLOSED DOOR." But whereas poverty has simply stimulated an awareness of spiritual privation, the encounter with the landlady and the dog has gone farther by jolting Jerry with the suggestion that the fault for his loneliness lies not with God, the stars, or society, but with himself. The actions of his two assailants not only force Jerry to recognize his own resistance to involvement, but also suggest to him a possible method for overcoming such resistance in others. The landlady made advances of love to Jerry, so far as her level of being could approach it, and Jerry responded with the same wish to be rid of her that Peter has toward him. The dog made advances that Jerry describes as antipathy and, on reflection, possibly love; and it received a similar resistance from Jerry. Jerry fed and poisoned the dog to get it to leave him *alone*. Critics impose a conventional symbolism on the dog's behavior, ignoring Jerry's unconventional perception; and they miss the point of the encounter. Rutenberg writes:

> The symbolism, unmistakably, is that the dog represents that vicious aspect of society which attacks whenever Jerry tries to gain entrance. The dog never attacks when Jerry leaves the premises, only when he enters. Later in the play Peter "will respond to the invasion of his 'property' with the same ferocity the dog has shown," clearly illustrating this animalistic reaction to an invasion of one's private thoughts. (*Edward Albee*)

Perhaps the dog was protecting his domain (which is an animal trait people possess, not a feature of society which dogs have picked up), but Jerry believes and tries to explain to Peter that the dog's attempt to bite him was probably an act of love. The parallels between the dog and Peter that Rutenberg, quoting Zimbardo, draws are misleading (*Edward Albee*). The dog attacks Jerry of its own initiative.

Peter, left to his own initiative, would have walked home. His defense of the bench comes only after Jerry's calculated efforts to provoke at least an animal response in Peter. There is nothing in the play's final action which relates to an invasion of Peter's private thoughts, about which Jerry has ceased to concern himself since Peter's reaction to Jerry's long monologue. The parallels that do exist are between the dog's attack on Jerry and Jerry's assault on Peter, and between Jerry's attempts to keep the dog away and Peter's efforts to avoid involvement with Jerry. For Rutenberg's symbolic formula to work, Peter would have to knock Jerry off the bench the moment Jerry sits down. Albee's point is that Jerry has worked Peter out of his social mold as a vegetable into an animal state that is at least Peter's own self. The importance to Jerry of the assaults of the landlady and the dog is that together they have had effects outside of themselves. They have aroused in Jerry strong feelings, a violent antipathy toward the landlady and a love for the dog, curiously counterbalancing the feelings they have shown him. They have possessed Jerry with an idea of communication that he must test. And apparently they have dispossessed him of the rooming-house, just as he will dispossess Peter of the bench. Quickly, as if embarrassed to admit it, Jerry tells Peter toward the end of his narrative, "I have not returned". Their invasion of Jerry's private space has made it impossible for him to remain spiritually isolated, aware only of his own loneliness and his own needs.

Sam Shepard

Samuel Shepard Rogers VII was born in Illinois in 1943, but his father was a career man in the army, and like most "army brats," Shepard found himself repeatedly uprooted, moving from base to base around the country. If he has roots as a writer, they are clearly in the American West, but not necessarily the West created by writers of westerns, comic books, and second-rate movies. Shepard's plays often have a surreal quality, as though they are set in a world of the imagination rather than in a real place like Paris, Texas.

Shepard has won numerous awards, including ten Obie Awards (given to off-Broadway plays) between 1966 and 1979, an Obie Award for sustained achievement in 1980, the New York Drama Critics' Circle Award for *A Lie of the Mind* in 1985, and a Pulitzer Prize for *Buried Child* in 1979. His work has been produced primarily in the experimental theater of downtown New York in places such as La Mama and in regional theaters throughout the United States known for artistic integrity but not for reaching a broad spectrum of theatergoers. In his way, Shepard has been an underground playwright who has won the respect of most theater people, including the best playwrights.

Shepard's love for, and frustrations with, music have found their way into a major theme of his work. He plays drums and guitar and has never realized an early desire for a career in rock music. But the subversive qualities of rock and jazz—their implicit critique of middle-class life—appear in his plays in his analyses of the middle-class family. His primary themes center on the family and its complications, the nature of the person alone, and the myth of the Old West. In each theme Shepard expresses a deep sense of longing and of loss, emotions that his audiences have found significant.

Because his father began to drink and family life became intolerable, Shepard left home after a year at college and toured with the Bishops Company Repertory Players. At nineteen he wound up in New York working in one of the best jazz clubs of the day, the Village Gate. During this time in Greenwich Village he began to write one-act plays with extraordinary energy. Like Jack Kerouac, he almost never revised his work. He wrote it in a burst of energy and then had it performed to audiences whose admiration grew.

In the 1970s Shepard began acting in major motion pictures. One of the ironies of his life is that he became a matinee idol after appearing in movies such as *The Right Stuff, Fool for Love, Country,* and *Crimes of the Heart.* The critic Harry Haun said of him, "He is the Recluse as Superstar, the man who has arrived on his own terms, carefully sculpting a special myth for himself."

His output for the stage has been prodigious. It includes dozens of one-act plays, and he has a central body of work that has gained him an enviable reputation. *Operation Sidewinder* (1970) was performed at the Vivian Beaumont Theater—a public theater at Lincoln Center in New York City—to mixed reviews. The play, set in the West, involves a giant mechanical snake designed to make contact with travelers from outer space and also features Hopi snake dances and military scenes.

The Tooth of Crime (1972) is about turf wars between an aging rock star and an up-and-coming young star. Its brutality and directness make it intense, exciting, and revealing of the California rock 'n' roll scene in the early 1970s.

Curse of the Starving Class (1977) and *Buried Child* (1978) both helped solidify Shepard's reputation. *Suicide in B-Flat* (1976) and *True West* (1980) only made it clearer that his work was developing a consistent vein of black humor and dark criticism of the sanctity of family life. *A Lie of the Mind* (1985), like *Buried Child,* is about disturbed family life. It is filled with secrets: incest, murder, and sin. *New York Times* critic Mel Gussow said that it explores "the damage that one does to filial, fraternal, and marital bonds." Incest—or potential incest—is also a theme in *Fool for Love* (1983), in which Shepard starred on film. The play is set in the West and contains all the themes for which his work is known.

Shepard continued to write plays even while directing and acting in films. His late plays have not had quite the impact of his earlier work, but they have been produced in the United States and abroad. *States of Shock* (1991), *Simpatico* (1994), *When the World Was Green* (1996), *Eyes for Consuela* (1998), and *The Late Henry Moss* (2000) all preceded *The God of Hell* (2004), which introduced midwestern characters from Wisconsin. The political content of Shepard's late plays is evident here when a dairy farmer and his wife take in Greg Haynes, a radioactive man on the run who worked in a plutonium-producing plant. Then Welch, a salesman pursuing Haynes, shows up selling patriotic pins and mementos and ends up terrorizing the family. Randy Quaid played the farmer and Tim Roth played Welch for the production in Westbeth, New York.

The Abbey Theatre in Dublin produced Shepard's *Kicking a Dead Horse* (2007), which he wrote for the actor Stephen Rae. The set included a dead horse that the character Hobart Struther, a New York art dealer who has given up the city to live in the West, kicks now and then while he is digging what seems to be the horse's grave. The play is one man's search for "authenticity" in his life, while at the same time deromanticizing the life of the cowboy. One critic saw a connection with "the U.S. kicking a dead horse" in Iraq. *Kicking a Dead Horse* was produced at the Public Theatre of New York at the end of the 2007–2008 season.

Shepard began his work with a sense of the West drawn from popular literature, reshaped it, and produced it in a new form. If the American West has a reality that survived its mythicization in the dime novel and John Wayne's movies, then Shepard is partly responsible for the way we now see it.

BURIED CHILD

Buried Child won the Pulitzer Prize for drama in 1979. The play was developed in an intense collaborative effort with cast, crew, director, and playwright using a process of give-and-take that has generally pleased Sam Shepard. In some cases he has turned down offers of major commercial productions of his plays because they would preclude that kind of collaborative atmosphere.

Critics have seen this play as loosely related to *Curse of the Starving Class* (1977) and *True West* (1980), forming a "family" trilogy. The three plays are very different in style, but they all offer a view of the American family that is painfully distant from the sentimental idealism of popular magazines of the 1940s and 1950s. Shepard emphasizes the rootlessness of the family, its emotional chill, and its capacity for violence.

Buried Child is beguilingly ordinary at first glance. The simple interior is dominated by a television set and an old sofa. Vince's girlfriend Shelly, who is visiting for the first time, had imagined that the house would resemble a Norman Rockwell painting—that is, a stereotypical American home. It falls short of that, but the living room is nonetheless a recognizable, low-key, ordinary room that might be found anywhere in middle America. However, beginning with the ordinariness of the setting, the ordinariness of Tilden's walking in with an armful of corn, and Dodge's wracking cough, Shepard builds a portrait of an extraordinary family.

Dodge's one-track alcoholic mind seems a minor aberration at first. And Halie's nagging seems relatively normal. Even Tilden's distant relationship with his father seems close to ordinary. But when Vince and Shelly walk in and Vince identifies himself first to his grandfather and then to his father—whom he does not expect to find here—we begin to see that something is odd and that the situation is anything but ordinary. Neither grandfather nor father recognizes him. Eventually, as we watch Shepard explore the family relationships, we begin to sense that the surface ordinariness hides a deeper structure, one that is built on myth.

The play draws on agricultural myth similar to that in *Oedipus Rex,* which begins with a curse on the land. The crops have failed and there has been no rain. Yet Tilden walks in with an armful of corn, which Halie thinks he must have stolen. Critics have compared Tilden with the corn god, a symbol of renewal. Shepard adds to that the sense of doom visited upon the family as if its genes carried destruction. As in Wole Soyinka's *The Strong Breed,* responsibility is transmitted from father to son. Those who are of the strong breed do not escape their fate. It is not clear how responsibility is transmitted in Shepard's family until we begin to see that Vince assumes the role of Tilden and Halie's offspring, the child of incest who is buried on the arid land. In the terms of *The Strong Breed,* Vince can be thought of as a "carrier," willing or unwilling. When Dodge bequeaths the house to Vince, he seals Vince's fate.

Certainly during the course of the play, we begin to see that a change is at hand. The rains have come. Halie, who doubted the existence of the corn, calls down at the end of the play: "It's like a paradise out there, Dodge. You oughta' take a look. A miracle." But the "old king," Dodge, is dead. Vince has come to take his place.

Buried Child in Performance

Buried Child was first produced at the Magic Theatre in San Francisco in June 1978. Later that year it was transferred to the Theater for the New City in Greenwich Village. In May 1979 it was awarded the Pulitzer Prize.

About the Yale Repertory Theatre production of 1979, *New York Times* critic Mel Gussow said, "The tone of the play is almost surrealistic. Like a figure out of Ionesco, the father brings in armloads of fresh vegetables from a garden that has been barren for years." In commenting on the New York and Yale productions of the play, he said they ended with "a dirge for the decline of traditional values, a wake for the American dream."

In 1980 the Trinity Repertory Company in Providence produced the play, directed by Adrian Hall, the director of the Yale production. It contrasted with the New York production in that the sets and lighting were "slicker," more detailed, and more subtle. One critic labeled the first production of *Buried Child* a "Gothic comedy," and that description has affected subsequent productions. For example, the MIT student production in 1985 aimed at Gothic effects: dark colors, suspense, and other staple ingredients of horror films. *Buried Child* finally made it to Broadway in 1996 when it was performed at the Brooks Atkinson Theater. Gary Sinise directed the play in a production that was originally mounted in Chicago at the Steppenwolf Theatre Company, in which Ethan Hawke played Vince. Ben Brantley said that the play "has the intangible spookiness of nightmares." A 2006 production at the American Theatre of Actors in New York was cited as introducing an ironic touch of the Norman Rockwell image of an American family, echoing Shelly's line when she first sees the family home: "It's like a Norman Rockwell cover or something." Productions of that sort remind us that on one level, at least, the play is about a haunted house.

Sam Shepard (b. 1943)

BURIED CHILD
1978

While the rain of your fingertips falls,
while the rain of your bones falls,
and your laughter and marrow fall down,
you come flying.   — PABLO NERUDA

Characters

DODGE, *in his seventies*
HALIE, *his wife, mid-sixties*
TILDEN, *their oldest son*
BRADLEY, *their next oldest son, an amputee*
VINCE, *Tilden's son*
SHELLY, *Vince's girlfriend*
FATHER DEWIS, *a Protestant minister*

ACT 1

Scene: *Day. Old wooden staircase down left with pale, frayed carpet laid down on the steps. The stairs lead offstage left up into the wings with no landing. Up right is an old, dark green sofa with the stuffing coming out in spots. Stage right of the sofa is an upright lamp with a faded yellow shade and a small night table with several small bottles of pills on it. Down right of the sofa, with the screen facing the sofa, is a large, old-fashioned brown TV. A flickering blue light comes from the screen, but no image, no sound. In the dark, the light of the lamp and the TV slowly brighten in the black space. The space*

behind the sofa, upstage, is a large, screened-in porch with a board floor. A solid interior door to stage right of the sofa, leading into the room onstage; and another screen door up left, leading from the porch to the outside. Beyond that are the shapes of dark elm trees.

Gradually the form of Dodge is made out, sitting on the couch, facing the TV, the blue light flickering on his face. He wears a well-worn T-shirt, suspenders, khaki work pants, and brown slippers. He's covered himself in an old brown blanket. He's very thin and sickly looking, in his late seventies. He just stares at the TV. More light fills the stage softly. The sound of light rain. Dodge slowly tilts his head back and stares at the ceiling for a while, listening to the rain. He lowers his head again and stares at the TV. He turns his head slowly to the left and stares at the cushion of the sofa next to the one he's sitting on. He pulls his left arm out from under the blanket, slides his hand under the cushion, and pulls out a bottle of whiskey. He looks down left toward the staircase, listens, then uncaps the bottle, takes a long swig, and caps it again. He puts the bottle back under the cushion and stares at the TV. He starts to cough slowly and softly. The coughing gradually builds. He holds one hand to his mouth and tries to stifle it. The coughing gets louder, then suddenly stops when he hears the sound of his wife's voice coming from the top of the staircase.

HALIE'S VOICE: Dodge?

(*Dodge just stares at the TV. Long pause. He stifles two short coughs.*)

HALIE'S VOICE: Dodge! You want a pill, Dodge?

(*He doesn't answer. Takes the bottle out again and takes another long swig. Puts the bottle back, stares at TV, pulls blanket up around his neck.*)

HALIE'S VOICE: You know what it is, don't you? It's the rain! Weather. That's it. Every time. Every time you get like this, it's the rain. No sooner does the rain start then you start. (*Pause.*) Dodge?

(*He makes no reply. Pulls a pack of cigarettes out from his sweater and lights one. Stares at TV. Pause.*)

HALIE'S VOICE: You should see it coming down up here. Just coming down in sheets. Blue sheets. The bridge is pretty near flooded. What's it like down there? Dodge?

(*Dodge turns his head back over his left shoulder and takes a look out through the porch. He turns back to the TV.*)

DODGE (*to himself*): Catastrophic.
HALIE'S VOICE: What? What'd you say, Dodge?
DODGE (*louder*): It looks like rain to me! Plain old rain!
HALIE'S VOICE: Rain? Of course it's rain! Are you having a seizure or something! Dodge? (*Pause.*) I'm coming down there in about five minutes if you don't answer me!
DODGE: Don't come down.
HALIE'S VOICE: What!
DODGE (*louder*): Don't come down!

(*He has another coughing attack. Stops.*)

HALIE'S VOICE: You should take a pill for that! I don't see why you just don't take a pill. Be done with it once and for all. Put a stop to it.

(*He takes bottle out again. Another swig. Returns bottle.*)

HALIE'S VOICE: It's not Christian, but it works. It's not necessarily Christian, that is. We don't know. There's some things the ministers can't even answer. I, personally, can't see anything wrong with it. Pain is pain. Pure and simple. Suffering is a different matter. That's entirely different. A pill seems as good an answer as any. Dodge? (*Pause.*) Dodge, are you watching baseball?
DODGE: No.
HALIE'S VOICE: What?
DODGE (*louder*): No!
HALIE'S VOICE: What're you watching? You shouldn't be watching anything that'll get you excited! No horse racing!

DODGE: They don't race on Sundays.
HALIE'S VOICE: What?
DODGE (*louder*): They don't race on Sundays!
HALIE'S VOICE: Well they shouldn't race on Sundays.
DODGE: Well they don't!
HALIE'S VOICE: Good. I'm amazed they still have that kind of legislation. That's amazing.
DODGE: Yeah, it's amazing.
HALIE'S VOICE: What?
DODGE (*louder*): It is amazing!
HALIE'S VOICE: It is. It truly is. I would've thought these days they'd be racing on Christmas even. A big flashing Christmas tree right down at the finish line.
DODGE (*shakes his head*): No.
HALIE'S VOICE: They used to race on New Year's! I remember that.
DODGE: They never raced on New Year's!
HALIE'S VOICE: Sometimes they did.
DODGE: They never did!
HALIE'S VOICE: Before we were married they did!

(*Dodge waves his hand in disgust at the staircase. Leans back in sofa. Stares at TV.*)

HALIE'S VOICE: I went once. With a man.
DODGE (*mimicking her*): Oh, a "man."
HALIE'S VOICE: What?
DODGE: Nothing!
HALIE'S VOICE: A wonderful man. A breeder.
DODGE: A what?
HALIE'S VOICE: A breeder! A horse breeder! Thoroughbreds.
DODGE: Oh, thoroughbreds. Wonderful.
HALIE'S VOICE: That's right. He knew everything there was to know.
DODGE: I bet he taught you a thing or two, huh? Gave you a good turn around the old stable!
HALIE'S VOICE: Knew everything there was to know about horses. We won bookoos of money that day.
DODGE: What?
HALIE'S VOICE: Money! We won every race I think.
DODGE: Bookoos?
HALIE'S VOICE: Every single race.
DODGE: Bookoos of money?
HALIE'S VOICE: It was one of those kind of days.
DODGE: New Year's!
HALIE'S VOICE: Yes! It might've been Florida. Or California! One of those two.
DODGE: Can I take my pick?
HALIE'S VOICE: It was Florida!
DODGE: Aha!
HALIE'S VOICE: Wonderful! Absolutely wonderful! The sun was just gleaming. Flamingos. Bougainvilleas. Palm trees.
DODGE (*to himself, mimicking her*): Bougainvilleas. Palm trees.
HALIE'S VOICE: Everything was dancing with life! There were all kinds of people from everywhere. Everyone was dressed to the nines. Not like today. Not like they dress today.

DODGE: When was this anyway?

HALIE'S VOICE: This was long before I knew you.

DODGE: Must've been.

HALIE'S VOICE: Long before. I was escorted.

DODGE: To Florida?

HALIE'S VOICE: Yes. Or it might've been California. I'm not sure which.

DODGE: All that way you were escorted?

HALIE'S VOICE: Yes.

DODGE: And he never laid a finger on you, I suppose? (*Long silence.*) Halie?

(*No answer. Long pause.*)

HALIE'S VOICE: Are you going out today?

DODGE (*gesturing toward rain*): In this?

HALIE'S VOICE: I'm just asking a simple question.

DODGE: I rarely go out in the bright sunshine, why would I go out in this?

HALIE'S VOICE: I'm just asking because I'm not doing any shopping today. And if you need anything you should ask Tilden.

DODGE: Tilden's not here!

HALIE'S VOICE: He's in the kitchen.

(*Dodge looks toward stage left, then back toward TV.*)

DODGE: All right.

HALIE'S VOICE: What?

DODGE (*louder*): All right!

HALIE'S VOICE: Don't scream. It'll only get your coughing started.

DODGE: All right.

HALIE'S VOICE: Just tell Tilden what you want and he'll get it. (*Pause.*) Bradley should be over later.

DODGE: Bradley?

HALIE'S VOICE: Yes. To cut your hair.

DODGE: My hair? I don't need my hair cut!

HALIE'S VOICE: It won't hurt!

DODGE: I don't need it!

HALIE'S VOICE: It's been more than two weeks, Dodge.

DODGE: I don't need it!

HALIE'S VOICE: I have to meet Father Dewis for lunch.

DODGE: You tell Bradley that if he shows up here with those clippers, I'll kill him!

HALIE'S VOICE: I won't be very late. No later than four at the very latest.

DODGE: You tell him! Last time he left me almost bald! And I wasn't even awake! I was sleeping! I woke up and he'd already left!

HALIE'S VOICE: That's not my fault!

DODGE: You put him up to it!

HALIE'S VOICE: I never did!

DODGE: You did too! You had some fancy, stupid meeting planned! Time to dress up the corpse for company! Lower the ears a little! Put up a little front! Surprised you didn't tape a pipe to my mouth while you were at it! That woulda' looked nice! Huh? A pipe? Maybe a bowler hat! Maybe a copy of the *Wall Street Journal* casually placed on my lap!

HALIE'S VOICE: You always imagine the worst things of people!

DODGE: That's not the worst! That's the least of the worst!

HALIE'S VOICE: I don't need to hear it! All day long I hear things like that and I don't need to hear more.

DODGE: You better tell him!

HALIE'S VOICE: You tell him yourself! He's your own son. You should be able to talk to your own son.

DODGE: Not while I'm sleeping! He cut my hair while I was sleeping!

HALIE'S VOICE: Well, he won't do it again.

DODGE: There's no guarantee.

HALIE'S VOICE: I promise he won't do it without your consent.

DODGE (*after pause*): There's no reason for him to even come over here.

HALIE'S VOICE: He feels responsible.

DODGE: For my hair?

HALIE'S VOICE: For your appearance.

DODGE: My appearance is out of his domain! It's even out of mine! In fact, it's disappeared! I'm an invisible man!

HALIE'S VOICE: Don't be ridiculous.

DODGE: He better not try it. That's all I've got to say.

HALIE'S VOICE: Tilden will watch out for you.

DODGE: Tilden won't protect me from Bradley!

HALIE'S VOICE: Tilden's the oldest. He'll protect you.

DODGE: Tilden can't even protect himself!

HALIE'S VOICE: Not so loud! He'll hear you. He's right in the kitchen.

DODGE (*yelling off left*): Tilden!

HALIE'S VOICE: Dodge, what are you trying to do?

DODGE (*yelling off left*): Tilden, get in here!

HALIE'S VOICE: Why do you enjoy stirring things up?

DODGE: I don't enjoy anything!

HALIE'S VOICE: That's a terrible thing to say.

DODGE: Tilden!

HALIE'S VOICE: That's the kind of statement that leads people right to the end of their rope.

DODGE: Tilden!

HALIE'S VOICE: It's no wonder people turn to Christ!

DODGE: TILDEN!!

HALIE'S VOICE: It's no wonder the messengers of God's word are shouted down in public places!

DODGE: TILDEN!!!!

(*Dodge goes into a violent, spasmodic coughing attack as Tilden enters from stage left, his arms loaded with fresh ears of corn. Tilden is Dodge's oldest son, late forties, wears heavy construction boots, covered with mud, dark green work pants, a plaid shirt, and a faded brown windbreaker. He has a butch haircut, wet from the rain. Something about him is profoundly burned out and displaced. He stops center stage with the ears of corn in his arms and just stares at Dodge until he slowly finishes his coughing attack. Dodge looks up at him slowly. He stares at the corn. Long pause as they watch each other.*)

HALIE'S VOICE: Dodge, if you don't take that pill nobody's going to force you.

(The two men ignore the voice.)

DODGE (*to Tilden*): Where'd you get that?

TILDEN: Picked it.

DODGE: You picked all that?

(Tilden nods.)

DODGE: You expecting company?

TILDEN: No.

DODGE: Where'd you pick it from?

TILDEN: Right out back.

DODGE: Out back where!

TILDEN: Right out in back.

DODGE: There's nothing out there!

TILDEN: There's corn.

DODGE: There hasn't been corn out there since about nineteen thirty-five! That's the last time I planted corn out there!

TILDEN: It's out there now.

DODGE (*yelling at stairs*): Halie!

HALIE'S VOICE: Yes dear!

DODGE: Tilden's brought a whole bunch of corn in here! There's no corn out in back is there?

TILDEN (*to himself*): There's tons of corn.

HALIE'S VOICE: Not that I know of!

DODGE: That's what I thought.

HALIE'S VOICE: Not since about nineteen thirty-five!

DODGE (*to Tilden*): That's right. Nineteen thirty-five.

TILDEN: It's out there now.

DODGE: You go and take that corn back to wherever you got it from!

TILDEN (*after pause, staring at Dodge*): It's picked. I picked it all in the rain. Once it's picked you can't put it back.

DODGE: I haven't had trouble with neighbors here for fifty-seven years. I don't even know who the neighbors are! And I don't wanna know! Now go put that corn back where it came from!

(Tilden stares at Dodge, then walks slowly over to him and dumps all the corn on Dodge's lap and steps back. Dodge stares at the corn, then back to Tilden. Long pause.)

DODGE: Are you having trouble here, Tilden? Are you in some kind of trouble?

TILDEN: I'm not in any trouble.

DODGE: You can tell me if you are. I'm still your father.

TILDEN: I know you're still my father.

DODGE: I know you had a little trouble back in New Mexico. That's why you came out here.

TILDEN: I never had any trouble.

DODGE: Tilden, your mother told me all about it.

TILDEN: What'd she tell you?

(Tilden pulls some chewing tobacco out of his jacket and bites off a plug.)

DODGE: I don't have to repeat what she told me! She told me all about it!

TILDEN: Can I bring my chair in from the kitchen?

DODGE: What?

TILDEN: Can I bring in my chair from the kitchen?

DODGE: Sure. Bring your chair in.

(Tilden exits left. Dodge pushes all the corn off his lap onto the floor. He pulls the blanket off angrily and tosses it at one end of the sofa, pulls out the bottle and takes another swig. Tilden enters again from left with a milking stool and a pail. Dodge hides the bottle quickly under the cushion before Tilden sees it. Tilden sets the stool down by the sofa, sits on it, puts the pail in front of him on the floor. Tilden starts picking up the ears of corn one at a time and husking them. He throws the husks and silk in the center of the stage and drops the ears into the pail each time he cleans one. He repeats this process as they talk.)

DODGE (*after pause*): Sure is nice looking corn.

TILDEN: It's the best.

DODGE: Hybrid?

TILDEN: What?

DODGE: Some kinda fancy hybrid?

TILDEN: You planted it. I don't know what it is.

DODGE (*pause*): Tilden, look, you can't stay here forever. You know that, don't you?

TILDEN (*spits in spittoon*): I'm not.

DODGE: I know you're not. I'm not worried about that. That's not the reason I brought it up.

TILDEN: What's the reason?

DODGE: The reason is I'm wondering what you're gonna do.

TILDEN: You're not worried about me, are you?

DODGE: I'm not worried about you.

TILDEN: You weren't worried about me when I wasn't here. When I was in New Mexico.

DODGE: No, I wasn't worried about you then either.

TILDEN: You shoulda worried about me then.

DODGE: Why's that? You didn't do anything down there, did you?

TILDEN: I didn't do anything.

DODGE: Then why should I have worried about you?

TILDEN: Because I was lonely.

DODGE: Because you were lonely?

TILDEN: Yeah. I was more lonely than I've ever been before.

DODGE: Why was that?

TILDEN (*pause*): Could I have some of that whiskey you've got?

DODGE: What whiskey? I haven't got any whiskey.

TILDEN: You've got some under the sofa.

DODGE: I haven't got anything under the sofa! Now mind your own damn business! Jesus God, you come into the house outa the middle of nowhere, haven't heard or seen you in twenty years and suddenly you're making accusations.

TILDEN: I'm not making accusations.

DODGE: You're accusing me of hoarding whiskey under the sofa!

TILDEN: I'm not accusing you.

DODGE: You just got through telling me I had whiskey under the sofa!

HALIE'S VOICE: Dodge?

DODGE (*to Tilden*): Now she knows about it!

TILDEN: She doesn't know about it.

HALIE'S VOICE: Dodge, are you talking to yourself down there?

DODGE: I'm talking to Tilden!

HALIE'S VOICE: Tilden's down there?

DODGE: He's right here!

HALIE'S VOICE: What?

DODGE (*louder*): He's right here!

HALIE'S VOICE: What's he doing?

DODGE (*to Tilden*): Don't answer her.

TILDEN (*to Dodge*): I'm not doing anything wrong.

DODGE: I know you're not.

HALIE'S VOICE: What's he doing down there!

DODGE (*to Tilden*): Don't answer.

TILDEN: I'm not.

HALIE'S VOICE: Dodge!

(*The men sit in silence. Dodge lights a cigarette. Tilden keeps husking corn, spits tobacco now and then in spittoon.*)

HALIE'S VOICE: Dodge! He's not drinking anything, is he? You see to it that he doesn't drink anything! You've gotta watch out for him. It's our responsibility. He can't look after himself anymore, so we have to do it. Nobody else will do it. We can't just send him away somewhere. If we had lots of money we could sent him away. But we don't. We never will. That's why we have to stay healthy. You and me. Nobody's going to look after us. Bradley can't look after us. Bradley can hardly look after himself. I was always hoping that Tilden would look out for Bradley when they got older. After Bradley lost his leg. Tilden's the oldest. I always thought he'd be the one to take responsibility. I had no idea in the world that Tilden would be so much trouble. Who would've dreamed. Tilden was an All-American, don't forget. Don't forget that. Fullback. Or quarterback. I forget which.

TILDEN (*to himself*): Fullback. (*Still husking.*)

HALIE'S VOICE: Then when Tilden turned out to be so much trouble, I put all my hopes on Ansel. Of course Ansel wasn't as handsome, but he was smart. He was the smartest probably. I think he probably was. Smarter than Bradley, that's for sure. Didn't go and chop his leg off with a chain saw. Smart enough not to go and do that. I think he was smarter than Tilden too. Especially after Tilden got in all that trouble. Doesn't take brains to go to jail. Anybody knows that. Course then when Ansel died that left us all alone. Same as being alone. No different. Same as if they'd all died. He was the smartest. He could've earned lots of money. Lots and lots of money.

(*Halie enters slowly from the top of the staircase as she continues talking. Just her feet are seen at first as she makes her way down the stairs, a step at a time. She appears dressed completely in black, as though in mourning. Black handbag, hat with a veil, and pulling on elbow-length black gloves. She is about sixty-five with pure white hair. She remains absorbed in what she's saying as she descends the stairs and doesn't really notice the two men who continue sitting there as they were before she came down, smoking and husking.*)

HALIE: He would've took care of us, too. He would've seen to it that we were repaid. He was like that. He was a hero. Don't forget that. A genuine hero. Brave. Strong. And very intelligent. Ansel could've been a great man. One of the greatest. I only regret that he didn't die in action. It's not fitting for a man like that to die in a motel room. A soldier. He could've won a medal. He could've been decorated for valor. I've talked to Father Dewis about putting up a plaque for Ansel. He thinks it's a good idea. He agrees. He knew Ansel when he used to play basketball. Went to every game. Ansel was his favorite player. He even recommended to the City Council that they put up a statue of Ansel. A big, tall statue with a basketball in one hand and a rifle in the other. That's how much he thinks of Ansel.

(*Halie reaches the stage and begins to wander around, still absorbed in pulling on her gloves, brushing lint off her dress, and continuously talking to herself as the men just sit.*)

HALIE: Of course, he'd still be alive today if he hadn't married into the Catholics. The Mob. How in the world he never opened his eyes to that is beyond me. Just beyond me. Everyone around him could see the truth. Even Tilden. Tilden told him time and again. Catholic women are the Devil incarnate. He wouldn't listen. He was blind with love. Blind. I knew. Everyone knew. The wedding was more like a funeral. You remember? All those Italians. All that horrible black, greasy hair. The smell of cheap cologne. I think even the priest was wearing a pistol. When he gave her the ring I knew he was a dead man. I knew it. As soon as he gave her the ring. But then it was the honeymoon that killed him. The honeymoon. I knew he'd never come back from the honeymoon. I kissed him and he felt like a corpse. All white. Cold. Icy blue lips. He never used to kiss like that. Never before. I knew then that she'd cursed him. Taken his soul. I saw it in her eyes. She smiled at me with that Catholic sneer of hers. She told me with her eyes that she'd murder him in his bed. Murder my son. She told me. And there was nothing I could do. Absolutely nothing. He was going with her, thinking he was free. Thinking it was love. What could I do? I couldn't tell him she was a witch. I couldn't tell him that. He'd have turned on me. Hated me. I couldn't stand him hating me and then dying before he ever saw me again. Hating me in his death bed. Hating me and loving her! How could I do that? I had to let him go. I had to. I watched him leave. I watched him throw gardenias as he helped her into the limousine. I watched his face disappear behind the glass.

(*She stops abruptly and stares at the corn husks. She looks around the space as though just waking up. She turns and looks hard at Tilden and Dodge who continue sitting calmly. She looks again at the corn husks.*)

HALIE (*pointing to the husks*): What's this in my house! (*Kicks husks.*) What's all this!

(*Tilden stops husking and stares at her.*)

HALIE (*to Dodge*): And you encourage him!

(*Dodge pulls blanket over him again.*)

DODGE: You're going out in the rain?
HALIE: It's not raining.

(*Tilden starts husking again.*)

DODGE: Not in Florida it's not.
HALIE: We're not in Florida!
DODGE: It's not raining at the race track.
HALIE: Have you been taking those pills? Those pills always make you talk crazy. Tilden, has he been taking those pills?
TILDEN: He hasn't took anything.
HALIE (*to Dodge*): What've you been taking?
DODGE: It's not raining in California or Florida or the race track. Only in Illinois. This is the only place it's raining. All over the rest of the world it's bright golden sunshine.

(*Halie goes to the night table next to the sofa and checks the bottle of pills.*)

HALIE: Which ones did you take? Tilden, you must've seen him take something.
TILDEN: He never took a thing.
HALIE: Then why's he talking crazy?
TILDEN: I've been here the whole time.
HALIE: Then you've both been taking something!
TILDEN: I've just been husking the corn.
HALIE: Where'd you get that corn anyway? Why is the house suddenly full of corn?
DODGE: Bumper crop!
HALIE (*moving center*): We haven't had corn here for over thirty years.
TILDEN: The whole back lot's full of corn. Far as the eye can see.
DODGE (*to Halie*): Things keep happening while you're upstairs, ya know. The world doesn't stop just because you're upstairs. Corn keeps growing. Rain keeps raining.
HALIE: I'm not unaware of the world around me! Thank you very much. It so happens that I have an overall view from the upstairs. The back yard's in plain view of my window. And there's no corn to speak of. Absolutely none!
DODGE: Tilden wouldn't lie. If he says there's corn, there's corn.
HALIE: What's the meaning of this corn, Tilden!

TILDEN: It's a mystery to me. I was out in back there. And the rain was coming down. And I didn't feel like coming back inside. I didn't feel the cold so much. I didn't mind the wet. So I was just walking. I was muddy but I didn't mind the mud so much. And I looked up. And I saw this stand of corn. In fact I was standing in it. So, I was standing in it.
HALIE: There isn't any corn outside, Tilden! There's no corn! Now, you must've either stolen this corn or you bought it.
DODGE: He doesn't have any money.
HALIE (*to Tilden*): So you stole it!
TILDEN: I didn't steal it. I don't want to get kicked out of Illinois. I was kicked out of New Mexico and I don't want to get kicked out of Illinois.
HALIE: You're going to get kicked out of this house, Tilden, if you don't tell me where you got that corn!

(*Tilden starts crying softly to himself but keeps husking corn. Pause.*)

DODGE (*to Halie*): Why'd you have to tell him that? Who cares where he got the corn? Why'd you have to go and tell him that?
HALIE (*to Dodge*): It's your fault you know! You're the one that's behind all this! I suppose you thought it'd be funny! Some joke! Cover the house with corn husks. You better get this cleaned up before Bradley sees it.
DODGE: Bradley's not getting in the front door!
HALIE (*kicking husks, striding back and forth*): Bradley's going to be very upset when he sees this. He doesn't like to see the house in disarray. He can't stand it when one thing is out of place. The slightest thing. You know how he gets.
DODGE: Bradley doesn't even live here!
HALIE: It's his home as much as ours. He was born in this house!
DODGE: He was born in a hog wallow.
HALIE: Don't you say that! Don't you ever say that!
DODGE: He was born in a goddamn hog wallow! That's where he was born and that's where he belongs! He doesn't belong in this house!
HALIE (*she stops*): I don't know what's come over you, Dodge. I don't know what in the world's come over you. You've become an evil man. You used to be a good man.
DODGE: Six of one, a half dozen of another.
HALIE: You sit here day and night, festering away! Decomposing! Smelling up the house with your putrid body! Hacking your head off till all hours of the morning! Thinking up mean, evil, stupid things to say about your own flesh and blood!
DODGE: He's not my flesh and blood! My flesh and blood's buried in the back yard!

(*They freeze. Long pause. The men stare at her.*)

HALIE (*quietly*): That's enough, Dodge. That's quite enough. I'm going out now. I'm going to have lunch with Father Dewis. I'm going to ask him about a monument. A statue. At least a plaque.

(She crosses to the door up right. She stops.)

HALIE: If you need anything, ask Tilden. He's the oldest. I've left some money on the kitchen table.

DODGE: I don't need anything.

HALIE: No, I suppose not. *(She opens the door and looks out through porch.)* Still raining. I love the smell just after it stops. The ground. I won't be too late.

(She goes out door and closes it. She's still visible on the porch as she crosses toward stage left screen door. She stops in the middle of the porch, speaks to Dodge but doesn't turn to him.)

HALIE: Dodge, tell Tilden not to go out in the back lot anymore. I don't want him back there in the rain.

DODGE: You tell him. He's sitting right here.

HALIE: He never listens to me, Dodge. He's never listened to me in the past.

DODGE: I'll tell him.

HALIE: We have to watch him just like we used to now. Just like we always have. He's still a child.

DODGE: I'll watch him.

HALIE: Good.

(She crosses to screen door, left, takes an umbrella off a hook, and goes out the door. The door slams behind her. Long pause. Tilden husks corn, stares at pail. Dodge lights a cigarette, stares at TV.)

TILDEN *(still husking)*: You shouldn't a told her that.

DODGE *(staring at TV)*: What?

TILDEN: What you told her. You know.

DODGE: What do you know about it?

TILDEN: I know. I know all about it. We all know.

DODGE: So what difference does it make? Everybody knows, everybody's forgot.

TILDEN: She hasn't forgot.

DODGE: She should've forgot.

TILDEN: It's different for a woman. She couldn't forget that. How could she forget that?

DODGE: I don't want to talk about it!

TILDEN: What do you want to talk about?

DODGE: I don't want to talk about anything! I don't want to talk about troubles or what happened fifty years ago or thirty years ago or the race track or Florida or the last time I seeded the corn! I don't want to talk!

TILDEN: You don't wanna die, do you?

DODGE: No, I don't wanna die either.

TILDEN: Well, you gotta talk or you'll die.

DODGE: Who told you that?

TILDEN: That's what I know. I found that out in New Mexico. I thought I was dying but I just lost my voice.

DODGE: Were you with somebody?

TILDEN: I was alone. I thought I was dead.

DODGE: Might as well have been. What'd you come back here for?

TILDEN: I didn't know where to go.

DODGE: You're a grown man. You shouldn't he needing

your parents at your age. It's unnatural. There's nothing we can do for you now anyway. Couldn't you make a living down there? Couldn't you find some way to make a living? Support yourself? What'd ya come back here for? You expect us to feed you forever?

TILDEN: I didn't know where else to go.

DODGE: I never went back to my parents. Never. Never even had the urge. I was independent. Always independent. Always found a way.

TILDEN: I didn't know what to do. I couldn't figure anything out.

DODGE: There's nothing to figure out. You just forge ahead. What's there to figure out?

(Tilden stands.)

TILDEN: I don't know.

DODGE: Where are you going?

TILDEN: Out back.

DODGE: You're not supposed to go out there. You heard what she said. Don't play deaf with me!

TILDEN: I like it out there.

DODGE: In the rain?

TILDEN: Especially in the rain. I like the feeling of it. Feels like it always did.

DODGE: You're supposed to watch out for me. Get me things when I need them.

TILDEN: What do you need?

DODGE: I don't need anything! But I might. I might need something any second. Any second now. I can't be left alone for a minute!

(Dodge starts to cough.)

TILDEN: I'll be right outside. You can just yell.

DODGE *(between coughs)*: No! It's too far! You can't go out there! It's too far! You might not ever hear me!

TILDEN *(moving to pills)*: Why don't you take a pill? You want a pill?

(Dodge coughs more violently, throws himself back against sofa, clutches his throat. Tilden stands by helplessly.)

DODGE: Water! Get me some water!

(Tilden rushes off left. Dodge reaches out for the pills, knocking some bottles to the floor, coughing in spasms. He grabs a small bottle, takes out pills, and swallows them. Tilden rushes back on with a glass of water. Dodge takes it and drinks, his coughing subsides.)

TILDEN: You all right now?

(Dodge nods. Drinks more water. Tilden moves in closer to him. Dodge sets glass of water on the night table. His coughing is almost gone.)

TILDEN: Why don't you lay down for a while? Just rest a little.

(Tilden helps Dodge lay down on the sofa. Covers him with blanket.)

DODGE: You're not going outside, are you?

TILDEN: No.

DODGE: I don't want to wake up and find you not here.

TILDEN: I'll be here.

(*Tilden tucks blanket around Dodge.*)

DODGE: You'll stay right here?

TILDEN: I'll stay in my chair.

DODGE: That's not a chair. That's my old milking stool.

TILDEN: I know.

DODGE: Don't call it a chair.

TILDEN: I won't.

(*Tilden tries to take Dodge's baseball cap off.*)

DODGE: What're you doing! Leave that on me! Don't take that offa me! That's my cap!

(*Tilden leaves the cap on Dodge.*)

TILDEN: I know.

DODGE: Bradley'll shave my head if I don't have that on. That's my cap.

TILDEN: I know it is.

DODGE: Don't take my cap off.

TILDEN: I won't.

DODGE: You stay right here now.

TILDEN (*sits on stool*): I will.

DODGE: Don't go outside. There's nothing out there.

TILDEN: I won't.

DODGE: Everything's in here. Everything you need. Money's on the table. TV. Is the TV on?

TILDEN: Yeah.

DODGE: Turn it off! Turn the damn thing off! What's it doing on?

TILDEN (*shuts off TV, light goes out*): You left it on.

DODGE: Well, turn it off.

TILDEN (*sits on stool again*): It's off.

DODGE: Leave it off.

TILDEN: I will.

DODGE: When I fall asleep you can turn it on.

TILDEN: Okay.

DODGE: You can watch the ball game. Red Sox. You like the Red Sox don't you?

TILDEN: Yeah.

DODGE: You can watch the Red Sox. Pee Wee Reese. Pee Wee Reese. You remember Pee Wee Reese?

TILDEN: No.

DODGE: Was he with the Red Sox?

TILDEN: I don't know.

DODGE: Pee Wee Reese. (*Falling asleep.*) You can watch the Cardinals. You remember Stan Musial.

TILDEN: No.

DODGE: Stan Musial. (*Falling into sleep.*) Bases loaded. Top a' the sixth. Bases loaded. Runner on first and third. Big fat knuckle ball. Floater. Big as a blimp. Cracko! Ball just took off like a rocket. Just pulverized. I marked it. Marked it with my eyes. Straight between the clock and the Burma Shave ad. I was the first kid out there. First kid. I had to fight hard for that ball. I wouldn't give it up. They almost tore the ears right off me. But I wouldn't give it up.

(*Dodge falls into deep sleep. Tilden just sits staring at him for a while. Slowly he leans toward the sofa, checking to see if Dodge is well asleep. He reaches slowly under the cushion and pulls out the bottle of booze. Dodge sleeps soundly. Tilden stands quietly, staring at Dodge as he uncaps the bottle and takes a long drink. He caps the bottle and sticks it in his hip pocket. He looks around at the husks on the floor and then back to Dodge. He moves center stage and gathers an armload of corn husks then crosses back to the sofa. He stands holding the husks over Dodge and looking down at him he gently spreads the corn husks over the whole length of Dodge's body. He stands back and looks at Dodge. Pulls out bottle, takes another drink, returns bottle to his hip pocket. He gathers more husks and repeats the procedure until the floor is clean of corn husks and Dodge is completely covered in them except for his head. Tilden takes another long drink, stares at Dodge sleeping, then quietly exits stage left. Long pause as the sound of rain continues. Dodge sleeps on. The figure of Bradley appears up left, outside the screen porch door. He holds a wet newspaper over his head as a protection from the rain. He seems to be struggling with the door, then slips and almost falls to the ground. Dodge sleeps on, undisturbed.*)

BRADLEY: Sonuvabitch! Sonuvagoddamnbitch!

(*Bradley recovers his footing and makes it through the screen door onto the porch. He throws the newspaper down, shakes the water out of his hair, and brushes the rain off of his shoulders. He is a big man dressed in a gray sweatshirt, black suspenders, baggy dark blue pants, and black janitor's shoes. His left leg is wooden, having been amputated above the knee. He moves with an exaggerated, almost mechanical limp. The squeaking sounds of leather and metal accompany his walk coming from the harness and hinges of the false leg. His arms and shoulders are extremely powerful and muscular due to a lifetime dependency on the upper torso doing all the work for the legs. He is about five years younger than Tilden. He moves laboriously to the stage right door and enters, closing the door behind him. He doesn't notice Dodge at first. He moves toward the staircase.*)

BRADLEY (*calling to upstairs*): Mom!

(*He stops and listens. Turns upstage and sees Dodge sleeping. Notices corn husks. He moves slowly toward sofa. Stops next to pail and looks into it. Looks at husks. Dodge stays asleep. Talks to himself.*)

BRADLEY: What in the hell is this?

(*He looks at Dodge's sleeping face and shakes his head in disgust. He pulls out a pair of black electric hair clippers from his pocket. Unwinds the cord and crosses to the lamp. He jabs his wooden leg behind the knee, causing it to bend at the joint and awkwardly kneels to plug the cord into a floor outlet. He pulls himself to his feet again by using the sofa as leverage. He moves to Dodge's head and again jabs his false leg. Goes down on*) *one knee. He violently knocks away some of the corn husks, and then jerks off Dodge's baseball cap and throws it down center stage. Dodge stays asleep. Bradley switches on the clippers. Lights start dimming. Bradley cuts Dodge's hair while he sleeps. Lights dim slowly to black with the sound of clippers and rain.)*

ACT 2

Scene: *Same set as act 1. Night. Sound of rain. Dodge still asleep on sofa. His hair is cut extremely short and in places the scalp is cut and bleeding. His cap is still center stage. All the corn and husks, pail and milking stool have been cleared away. The lights come up to the sound of a young girl laughing offstage left. Dodge remains asleep. Shelly and Vince appear up left outside the screen porch door sharing the shelter of Vince's overcoat above their heads. Shelly is about nineteen, black hair, very beautiful. She wears tight jeans, high heels, purple T-shirt, and a short rabbit fur coat. Her makeup is exaggerated and her hair has been curled. Vince is Tilden's son, about twenty-two, wears a plaid shirt, jeans, dark glasses, cowboy boots and carries a black saxophone case. They shake the rain off themselves as they enter the porch through the screen door.*

SHELLY *(laughing, gesturing to house)*: This is it? I don't believe this is it!
VINCE: This is it.
SHELLY: This is the house?
VINCE: This is the house.
SHELLY: I don't believe it!
VINCE: How come?
SHELLY: It's like a Norman Rockwell cover or something.
VINCE: What's a' matter with that? It's American.
SHELLY: Where's the milkman and the little dog? What's the little dog's name? Spot. Spot and Jane. Dick and Jane and Spot.
VINCE: Knock it off.
SHELLY: Dick and Jane and Spot and Mom and Dad and Junior and Sissy!

(She laughs. Slaps her knee.)

VINCE: Come on! It's my heritage. What dya' expect?

(She laughs more hysterically, out of control.)

SHELLY: "And Tuffy and Toto and Dooda and Bonzo all went down one day to the corner grocery store to buy a big bag of licorice for Mr. Marshall's pussy cat!"

(She laughs so hard she falls to her knees holding her stomach. Vince stands there looking at her.)

VINCE: Shelly, will you get up!

(She keeps laughing. Staggers to her feet. Turning in circles holding her stomach.)

SHELLY *(continuing her story in kid's voice)*: "Mr. Marshall was on vacation. He had no idea that the four

little boys had taken such a liking to his little kitty cat."
VINCE: Have some respect, would ya'!
SHELLY *(trying to control herself)*: I'm sorry.
VINCE: Pull yourself together.
SHELLY *(salutes him)*: Yes, sir.

(She giggles.)

VINCE: Jesus Christ, Shelly.
SHELLY *(pause, smiling)*: And Mr. Marshall—
VINCE: Cut it out.

(She stops. Stands there staring at him. Stifles a giggle.)

VINCE *(after pause)*: Are you finished?
SHELLY: Oh brother!
VINCE: I don't wanna go in there with you acting like an idiot.
SHELLY: Thanks.
VINCE: Well, I don't.
SHELLY: I won't embarrass you. Don't worry.
VINCE: I'm not worried.
SHELLY: You are too.
VINCE: Shelly, look, I just don't wanna go in there with you giggling your head off. They might think something's wrong with you.
SHELLY: There is.
VINCE: There is not!
SHELLY: Something's definitely wrong with me.
VINCE: There is not!
SHELLY: There's something wrong with you too.
VINCE: There's nothing wrong with me either!
SHELLY: You wanna know what's wrong with you?
VINCE: What?

(Shelly laughs.)

VINCE *(crosses back left toward screen door)*: I'm leaving!
SHELLY *(stops laughing)*: Wait! Stop. Stop! *(Vince stops.)* What's wrong with you is that you take the situation too seriously.
VINCE: I just don't want to have them think that I've suddenly arrived out of the middle of nowhere completely deranged.
SHELLY: What do you want them to think then?
VINCE *(pause)*: Nothing. Let's go in.

(He crosses porch toward stage right interior door. Shelly follows him. The stage right door opens slowly. Vince sticks his head in, doesn't notice Dodge sleeping. Calls out toward staircase.)

VINCE: Grandma!

(Shelly breaks into laughter, unseen behind Vince. Vince pulls his head back outside and pulls door shut. We hear their voices again without seeing them.)

SHELLY'S VOICE *(stops laughing)*: I'm sorry. I'm sorry, Vince. I really am. I really am sorry. I won't do it again. I couldn't help it.
VINCE'S VOICE: It's not all that funny.

SHELLY'S VOICE: I know it's not. I'm sorry.

VINCE'S VOICE: I mean this is a tense situation for me! I haven't seen them for over six years. I don't know what to expect.

SHELLY'S VOICE: I know. I won't do it again.

VINCE'S VOICE: Can't you bite your tongue or something?

SHELLY'S VOICE: Just don't say "Grandma," okay? (*She giggles, stops.*) I mean if you say "Grandma," I don't know if I can stop myself.

VINCE'S VOICE: Well try!

SHELLY'S VOICE: Okay. Sorry.

(*Door opens again. Vince sticks his head in then enters. Shelly follows behind him. Vince crosses to staircase, sets down saxophone case and overcoat, looks up staircase. Shelly notices Dodge's baseball cap. Crosses to it. Picks it up and puts it on her head. Vince goes up the stairs and disappears at the top. Shelly watches him, then turns and sees Dodge on the sofa. She takes off the baseball cap.*)

VINCE'S VOICE (*from above stairs*): Grandma!

(*Shelly crosses over to Dodge slowly and stands next to him. She stands at his head, reaches out slowly, and touches one of the cuts. The second she touches his head, Dodge jerks up to a sitting position on the sofa, eyes open. Shelly gasps. Dodge looks at her, sees his cap in her hands, quickly puts his hand to his bare head. He glares at Shelly, then whips the cap out of her hands and puts it on. Shelly backs away from him. Dodge stares at her.*)

SHELLY: I'm uh — with Vince.

(*Dodge just glares at her.*)

SHELLY: He's upstairs.

(*Dodge looks at the staircase, then back to Shelly.*)

SHELLY (*calling upstairs*): Vince!

VINCE'S VOICE: Just a second!

SHELLY: You better get down here!

VINCE'S VOICE: Just a minute! I'm looking at the pictures.

(*Dodge keeps staring at her.*)

SHELLY (*to Dodge*): We just got here. Pouring rain on the freeway so we thought we'd stop by. I mean Vince was planning on stopping anyway. He wanted to see you. He said he hadn't seen you in a long time.

(*Pause. Dodge just keeps staring at her.*)

SHELLY: We were going all the way through to New Mexico. To see his father. I guess his father lives out there. We thought we'd stop by and see you on the way. Kill two birds with one stone, you know? (*She laughs, Dodge stares, she stops laughing.*) I mean Vince has this thing about his family now. I guess it's a new thing with him. I kind of find it hard to relate to. But he feels it's important. You know. I mean he feels he wants to get to know you all again. After all this time.

(*Pause, Dodge just stares at her. She moves nervously to staircase and yells up to Vince.*)

SHELLY: Vince, will you come down here please!

(*Vince comes halfway down the stairs.*)

VINCE: I guess they went out for a while.

(*Shelly points to sofa and Dodge. Vince turns and sees Dodge. He comes all the way down staircase and crosses to Dodge. Shelly stays behind near staircase, keeping her distance.*)

VINCE: Grandpa?

(*Dodge looks up at him, not recognizing him.*)

DODGE: Did you bring the whiskey?

(*Vince looks back at Shelly, then back to Dodge.*)

VINCE: Grandpa, it's Vince. I'm Vince. Tilden's son. You remember?

(*Dodge stares at him.*)

DODGE: You didn't do what you told me. You didn't stay here with me.

VINCE: Grandpa, I haven't been here until just now. I just got here.

DODGE: You left. You went outside like we told you not to do. You went out there in back. In the rain.

(*Vince looks back at Shelly. She moves slowly toward sofa.*)

SHELLY: Is he okay?

VINCE: I don't know. (*Takes off his shades.*) Look, Grandpa, don't you remember me? Vince. Your Grandson.

(*Dodge stares at him, then takes off his baseball cap.*)

DODGE (*points to his head*): See what happens when you leave me alone? See that? That's what happens.

(*Vince looks at his head. Vince reaches out to touch his head. Dodge slaps his hand away with the cap and puts it back on his head.*)

VINCE: What's going on, Grandpa? Where's Halie?

DODGE: Don't worry about her. She won't be back for days. She says she'll be back but she won't be. (*He starts laughing.*) There's life in the old girl yet! (*Stops laughing.*)

VINCE: How did you do that to your head?

DODGE: I didn't do it! Don't be ridiculous!

VINCE: Well, who did then?

(*Pause. Dodge stares at Vince.*)

DODGE: Who do you think did it? Who do you think?

(*Shelly moves toward Vince.*)

SHELLY: Vince, maybe we oughta' go. I don't like this. I mean this isn't my idea of a good time.

VINCE (*to Shelly*): Just a second. (*To Dodge.*) Grandpa, look, I just got here. I just now got here. I haven't been here for six years. I don't know anything that's happened.

(*Pause. Dodge stares at him.*)

DODGE: You don't know anything?
VINCE: No.
DODGE: Well, that's good. That's good. It's much better not to know anything. Much, much better.
VINCE: Isn't there anybody here with you?

(*Dodge turns slowly and looks off to stage left.*)

DODGE: Tilden's here.
VINCE: No, Grandpa, Tilden's in New Mexico. That's where I was going. I'm going out there to see him.

(*Dodge turns slowly back to Vince.*)

DODGE: Tilden's here.

(*Vince backs away and joins Shelly. Dodge stares at them.*)

SHELLY: Vince, why don't we spend the night in a motel and come back in the morning? We could have breakfast. Maybe everything would be different.
VINCE: Don't be scared. There's nothing to be scared of. He's just old.
SHELLY: I'm not scared!
DODGE: You two are not my idea of the perfect couple!
SHELLY (*after pause*): Oh really? Why's that?
VINCE: Shh! Don't aggravate him.
DODGE: There's something wrong between the two of you. Something not compatible.
VINCE: Grandpa, where did Halie go? Maybe we should call her.
DODGE: What are you talking about? Do you know what you're talking about? Are you just talking for the sake of talking? Lubricating the gums?
VINCE: I'm trying to figure out what's going on here!
DODGE: Is that it?
VINCE: Yes. I mean I expected everything to be different.
DODGE: Who are you to expect anything? Who are you supposed to be?
VINCE: I'm Vince! Your Grandson!
DODGE: Vince. My Grandson.
VINCE: Tilden's son.
DODGE: Tilden's son, Vince.
VINCE: You haven't seen me for a long time.
DODGE: When was the last time?
VINCE: I don't remember.
DODGE: You don't remember?
VINCE: No.
DODGE: You don't remember. How am I supposed to remember if you don't remember?
SHELLY: Vince, come on. This isn't going to work out.
VINCE (*to Shelly*): Just take it easy.
SHELLY: I'm taking it easy! He doesn't even know who you are!
VINCE (*crossing toward Dodge*): Grandpa, look—
DODGE: Stay where you are! Keep your distance!

(*Vince stops. Looks back at Shelly, then to Dodge.*)

SHELLY: Vince, this is really making me nervous. I mean he doesn't even want us here. He doesn't even like us.
DODGE: She's a beautiful girl.
VINCE: Thanks.
DODGE: Very Beautiful Girl.
SHELLY: Oh my God.
DODGE (*to Shelly*): What's your name?
SHELLY: Shelly.
DODGE: Shelly. That's a man's name isn't it?
SHELLY: Not in this case.
DODGE (*to Vince*): She's a smart-ass too.
SHELLY: Vince! Can we go?
DODGE: She wants to go. She just got here and she wants to go.
VINCE: This is kind of strange for her.
DODGE: She'll get used to it. (*To Shelly.*) What part of the country do you come from?
SHELLY: Originally?
DODGE: That's right. Originally. At the very start.
SHELLY: L.A.
DODGE: L.A. Stupid country.
SHELLY: I can't stand this, Vince! This is really unbelievable!
DODGE: It's stupid! L.A. is stupid! So is Florida! All those Sunshine States. They're all stupid! Do you know why they're stupid?
SHELLY: Illuminate me.
DODGE: I'll tell you why. Because they're full of smart-asses! That's why!

(*Shelly turns her back to Dodge, crosses to staircase, and sits on bottom step.*)

DODGE (*to Vince*): Now she's insulted.
VINCE: Well, you weren't very polite.
DODGE: She's insulted! Look at her! In my house she's insulted! She's over there sulking because I insulted her!
SHELLY (*to Vince*): This is really terrific. This is wonderful. And you were worried about me making the right first impression!
DODGE (*to Vince*): She's a fireball, isn't she? Regular fireball. I had some a' them in my day. Temporary stuff. Never lasted more than a week.
VINCE: Grandpa—
DODGE: Stop calling me Grandpa will ya'! It's sickening. "Grandpa." I'm nobody's Grandpa!

(*Dodge starts feeling around under the cushion for the bottle of whiskey. Shelly gets up from the staircase.*)

SHELLY (*to Vince*): Maybe you've got the wrong house. Did you ever think of that? Maybe this is the wrong address!
VINCE: It's not the wrong address! I recognize the yard.
SHELLY: Yeah, but do you recognize the people? He says he's not your Grandfather.
DODGE (*digging for bottle*): Where's that bottle!
VINCE: He's just sick of something. I don't know what's happened to him.
DODGE: Where's my goddamn bottle!

(*Dodge gets up from sofa and starts tearing the cushions off it and throwing them downstage, looking for the whiskey.*)

SHELLY: Can't we just drive on to New Mexico? This is terrible, Vince! I don't want to stay here. In this house. I thought it was going to be turkey dinners and apple pie and all that kinda stuff.

VINCE: Well, I hate to disappoint you!

SHELLY: I'm not disappointed! I'm fuckin' terrified! I wanna' go!

(*Dodge yells toward stage left.*)

DODGE: Tilden! Tilden!

(*Dodge keeps ripping away at the sofa looking for his bottle, he knocks over the night stand with the bottles. Vince and Shelly watch as he starts ripping the stuffing out of the sofa.*)

VINCE (*to Shelly*): He's lost his mind or something. I've got to try to help him.

SHELLY: You help him! I'm leaving!

(*Shelly starts to leave. Vince grabs her. They struggle as Dodge keeps ripping away at the sofa and yelling.*)

DODGE: Tilden! Tilden, get your ass in here! Tilden!

SHELLY: Let go of me!

VINCE: You're not going anywhere! You're going to stay right here!

SHELLY: Let go of me, you sonuvabitch! I'm not your property!

(*Suddenly Tilden walks on from stage left just as he did before. This time his arms are full of carrots. Dodge, Vince, and Shelly stop suddenly when they see him. They all stare at Tilden as he crosses slowly center stage with the carrots and stops. Dodge sits on sofa, exhausted.*)

DODGE (*panting, to Tilden*): Where in the hell have you been?

TILDEN: Out back.

DODGE: Where's my bottle?

TILDEN: Gone.

(*Tilden and Vince stare at each other. Shelly backs away.*)

DODGE (*to Tilden*): You stole my bottle!

VINCE (*to Tilden*): Dad?

(*Tilden just stares at Vince.*)

DODGE: You had no right to steal my bottle! No right at all!

VINCE (*to Tilden*): It's Vince. I'm Vince.

(*Tilden stares at Vince, then looks at Dodge, then turns to Shelly.*)

TILDEN (*after pause*): I picked these carrots. If anybody wants any carrots, I picked 'em.

SHELLY (*to Vince*): This is your father?

VINCE (*to Tilden*): Dad, what're you doing here?

(*Tilden just stares at Vince, holding carrots, Dodge pulls the blanket back over himself.*)

DODGE (*to Tilden*): You're going to have to get me another bottle! You gotta get me a bottle before Halie comes back! There's money on the table. (*Points to stage left kitchen.*)

TILDEN (*shaking his head*): I'm not going down there. Into town.

(*Shelly crosses to Tilden. Tilden stares at her.*)

SHELLY (*to Tilden*): Are you Vince's father?

TILDEN (*to Shelly*): Vince?

SHELLY (*pointing to Vince*): This is supposed to be your son! Is he your son? Do you recognize him? I'm just along for the ride here. I thought everybody knew each other!

(*Tilden stares at Vince. Dodge wraps himself up in the blanket and sits on sofa staring at the floor.*)

TILDEN: I had a son once but we buried him.

(*Dodge quickly looks at Tilden. Shelly looks to Vince.*)

DODGE: You shut up about that! You don't know anything about that!

VINCE: Dad, I thought you were in New Mexico. We were going to drive down there and see you.

TILDEN: Long way to drive.

DODGE (*to Tilden*): You don't know anything about that! That happened before you were born! Long before!

VINCE: What's happened, Dad? What's going on here? I thought everything was all right. What's happened to Halie?

TILDEN: She left.

SHELLY (*to Tilden*): Do you want me to take those carrots for you?

(*Tilden stares at her. She moves in close to him. Holds out her arms. Tilden stares at her arms then slowly dumps the carrots into her arms. Shelly stands there holding the carrots.*)

TILDEN (*to Shelly*): You like carrots?

SHELLY: Sure. I like all kinds of vegetables.

DODGE (*to Tilden*): You gotta get me a bottle before Halie comes back!

(*Dodge hits sofa with his fist. Vince crosses up to Dodge and tries to console him. Shelly and Tilden stay facing each other.*)

TILDEN (*to Shelly*): Back yard's full of carrots. Corn. Potatoes.

SHELLY: You're Vince's father, right?

TILDEN: All kinds of vegetables. You like vegetables?

SHELLY (*laughs*): Yeah. I love vegetables.

TILDEN: We could cook these carrots, ya' know. You could cut 'em up and we could cook 'em.

SHELLY: All right.

TILDEN: I'll get you a pail and a knife.

SHELLY: Okay.

TILDEN: I'll be right back. Don't go.

(*Tilden exits offstage left. Shelly stands center, arms full of carrots. Vince stands next to Dodge. Shelly looks toward Vince, then down at the carrots.*)

DODGE (*to Vince*): You could get me a bottle. (*Pointing off left.*) There's money on the table.

VINCE: Grandpa, why don't you lay down for a while?

DODGE: I don't wanna lay down for a while! Every time I lay down something happens! (*Whips off his cap, points at his head.*) Look what happens! That's what happens! (*Pulls his cap back on.*) You go lie down and see what happens to you! See how you like it! They'll steal your bottle! They'll cut your hair! They'll murder your children! That's what'll happen.

VINCE: Just relax for a while.

DODGE (*pause*): You could get me a bottle, ya' know. There's nothing stopping you from getting me a bottle.

SHELLY: Why don't you get him a bottle, Vince? Maybe it would help everybody identify each other.

DODGE (*pointing to Shelly*): There, see? She thinks you should get me a bottle.

(*Vince crosses to Shelly.*)

VINCE: What're you doing with those carrots?

SHELLY: I'm waiting for your father.

DODGE: She thinks you should get me a bottle!

VINCE: Shelly, put the carrots down, will ya'! We gotta deal with the situation here! I'm gonna need your help.

SHELLY: I'm helping.

VINCE: You're only adding to the problem! You're making things worse! Put the carrots down!

(*Vince tries to knock the carrots out of her arms. She turns away from him, protecting the carrots.*)

SHELLY: Get away from me! Stop it!

(*Vince stands back from her. She turns to him still holding the carrots.*)

VINCE (*to Shelly*): Why are you doing this! Are you trying to make fun of me? This is my family, you know!

SHELLY: You coulda' fooled me! I'd just as soon not be here myself. I'd just as soon be a thousand miles from here. I'd rather be anywhere but here. You're the one who wants to stay. So I'll stay. I'll stay and I'll cut the carrots. And I'll cook the carrots. And I'll do whatever I have to do to survive. Just to make it through this.

VINCE: Put the carrots down, Shelly.

(*Tilden enters from left with pail, milking stool, and a knife. He sets the stool and pail center stage for Shelly. Shelly looks at Vince, then sits down on stool, sets the carrots on the floor, and takes the knife from Tilden. She looks at Vince again, then picks up a carrot, cuts the ends off, scrapes it, and drops it in pail. She repeats this; Vince glares at her. She smiles.*)

DODGE: She could get me a bottle. She's the type a' girl that could get me a bottle. Easy. She'd go down there.

Slink up to the counter. They'd probably give her two bottles for the price of one. She could do that.

(*Shelly laughs. Keeps cutting carrots. Vince crosses up to Dodge, looks at him. Tilden watches Shelly's hands. Long pause.*)

VINCE (*to Dodge*): I haven't changed that much. I mean physically. Physically I'm just about the same. Same size. Same weight. Everything's the same.

(*Dodge keeps staring at Shelly while Vince talks to him.*)

DODGE: She's a beautiful girl. Exceptional.

(*Vince moves in front of Dodge to block his view of Shelly. Dodge keeps craning his head around to see her as Vince demonstrates tricks from his past.*)

VINCE: Look. Look at this. Do you remember this? I used to bend my thumb behind my knuckles. You remember? I used to do it at the dinner table.

(*Vince bends a thumb behind his knuckles for Dodge and holds it out to him. Dodge takes a short glance then looks back at Shelly. Vince shifts position and shows him something else.*)

VINCE: What about this?

(*Vince curls his lips back and starts drumming on his teeth with his fingernails making little tapping sounds. Dodge watches awhile. Tilden turns toward the sound. Vince keeps it up. He sees Tilden taking notice and crosses to Tilden as he drums on his teeth. Dodge turns TV on, watches it.*)

VINCE: You remember this, Dad?

(*Vince keeps on drumming for Tilden. Tilden watches awhile, fascinated, then turns back to Shelly. Vince keeps up the drumming on his teeth, crosses back to Dodge doing it. Shelly keeps working on carrots, talking to Tilden.*)

SHELLY (*to Tilden*): He drives me crazy with that sometimes.

VINCE (*to Dodge*): I know! Here's one you'll remember. You used to kick me out of the house for this one.

(*Vince pulls his shirt out of his belt and holds it tucked under his chin with his stomach exposed. He grabs the flesh on either side of his belly button and pushes it in and out to make it look like a mouth talking. He watches his belly button and makes a deep sounding cartoon voice to synchronize with the movement. He demonstrates it to Dodge, then crosses down to Tilden doing it. Both Dodge and Tilden take short, uninterested glances then ignore him.*)

VINCE (*deep cartoon voice*): "Hello. How are you? I'm fine. Thank you very much. It's so good to see you looking well this fine Sunday morning. I was going down to the hardware store to fetch a pail of water."

SHELLY: Vince, don't be pathetic, will ya!

Ethan Hawke as Vince and
James Gammon as Dodge in
the Steppenwolf Theatre
Company's 1995 production
of *Buried Child*.

(*Vince stops. Tucks his shirt back in.*)

SHELLY: Jesus Christ. They're not gonna play. Can't you
see that?

(*Shelly keeps cutting carrots. Vince slowly moves toward
Tilden. Tilden keeps watching Shelly. Dodge watches TV.*)

VINCE (*to Shelly*): I don't get it. I really don't get it.
Maybe it's me. Maybe I forgot something.

DODGE (*from sofa*): You forgot to get me a bottle!
That's what you forgot. Anybody in this house could
get me a bottle. Anybody! But nobody will. Nobody
understands the urgency! Peelin carrots is more
important. Playin piano on your teeth! Well I hope
you all remember this when you get up in years.
When you find yourself immobilized. Dependent on
the whims of others.

(*Vince moves up toward Dodge. Pause as he looks at him.*)

VINCE: I'll get you a bottle.
DODGE: You will?
VINCE: Sure.

(*Shelly stands holding knife and carrot.*)

SHELLY: You're not going to leave me here, are you?
VINCE (*moving to her*): You suggested it! You said,
"Why don't I go get him a bottle?" So I'll go get him
a bottle!
SHELLY: But I can't stay here.
VINCE: What is going on! A minute ago you were ready
to cut carrots all night!
SHELLY: That was only if you stayed. Something to keep
me busy, so I wouldn't be so nervous. I don't want to
stay here alone.

DODGE: Don't let her talk you out of it! She's a bad
influence. I could see it the minute she stepped in
here.
SHELLY (*to Dodge*): You were asleep!
TILDEN (*to Shelly*): Don't you want to cut carrots
anymore?
SHELLY: Sure. Sure I do.

(*Shelly sits back down on stool and continues cutting
carrots. Pause. Vince moves around, stroking his hair,
staring at Dodge and Tilden. Vince and Shelly exchange
glances. Dodge watches TV.*)

VINCE: Boy! This is amazing. This is truly amazing.
(*Keeps moving around.*) What is this anyway? Am I
in a time warp or something? Have I committed an
unpardonable offense? It's true, I'm not married.
(*Shelly looks at him, then back to carrots.*) But I'm
also not divorced. I have been known to plunge into
sinful infatuation with the Alto Saxophone. Sucking
on number 5 reeds deep into the wee wee hours.
SHELLY: Vince, what are you doing that for? They don't
care about any of that. They just don't recognize you,
that's all.
VINCE: How could they not recognize me! How in the
hell could they not recognize me! I'm their son!
DODGE (*watching TV*): You're no son of mine. I've had
sons in my time and you're not one of 'em.

(*Long pause. Vince stares at Dodge, then looks at
Tilden. He turns to Shelly.*)

VINCE: Shelly, I gotta go out for a while. I just gotta go
out. I'll get a bottle and I'll come right back. You'll be
okay here. Really.

SHELLY: I don't know if I can handle this, Vince.

VINCE: I just gotta think or something. I don't know. I gotta put this all together.

SHELLY: Can't we just go?

VINCE: No! I gotta find out what's going on.

SHELLY: Look, you think you're bad off, what about me? Not only don't they recognize me but I've never seen them before in my life. I don't know who these guys are. They could be anybody!

VINCE: They're not anybody!

SHELLY: That's what you say.

VINCE: They're my family for Christ's sake! I should know who my own family is! Now give me a break. It won't take that long. I'll just go out and I'll come right back. Nothing'll happen. I promise.

(*Shelly stares at him. Pause.*)

SHELLY: All right.

VINCE: Thanks. (*He crosses up to Dodge.*) I'm gonna go out now, Grandpa, and I'll pick you up a bottle. Okay?

DODGE: Change of heart huh? (*Pointing off left.*) Money's on the table. In the kitchen.

(*Vince moves toward Shelly.*)

VINCE (*to Shelly*): You be all right?

SHELLY (*cutting carrots*): Sure. I'm fine. I'll just keep real busy while you're gone.

(*Vince looks at Tilden who keeps staring down at Shelly's hands.*)

DODGE: Persistence, see? That's what it takes. Persistence. Persistence, fortitude, and determination. Those are the three virtues. You stick with those three and you can't go wrong.

VINCE (*to Tilden*): You want anything, Dad?

TILDEN (*looks up at Vince*): Me?

VINCE: From the store? I'm gonna get Grandpa a bottle.

TILDEN: He's not supposed to drink. Halie wouldn't like it.

VINCE: He wants a bottle.

TILDEN: He's not supposed to drink.

DODGE (*to Vince*): Don't negotiate with him! Don't make any transactions until you've spoken to me first! He'll steal you blind!

VINCE (*to Dodge*): Tilden says you're not supposed to drink.

DODGE: Tilden's lost his marbles! Look at him! He's around the bend. Take a look at him.

(*Vince stares at Tilden. Tilden watches Shelly's hands as she keeps cutting carrots.*)

DODGE: Now look at me. Look here at me!

(*Vince looks back to Dodge.*)

DODGE: Now, between the two of us, who do you think is more trustworthy? Him or me? Can you trust a man who keeps bringing in vegetables from out of nowhere? Take a look at him.

(*Vince looks back at Tilden.*)

SHELLY: Go get the bottle, Vince.

VINCE (*to Shelly*): You sure you'll be all right?

SHELLY: I'll be fine. I feel right at home now.

VINCE: You do?

SHELLY: I'm fine. Now that I've got the carrots everything is all right.

VINCE: I'll be right back.

(*Vince crosses stage left.*)

DODGE: Where are you going?

VINCE: I'm going to get the money.

DODGE: Then where are you going?

VINCE: Liquor store.

DODGE: Don't go anyplace else. Don't go off some place and drink. Come right back here.

VINCE: I will.

(*Vince exits stage left.*)

DODGE (*calling after Vince*): You've got responsibility now! And don't go out the back way either! Come out through this way! I wanna' see you when you leave! Don't go out the back!

VINCE'S VOICE (*off left*): I won't!

(*Dodge turns and looks at Tilden and Shelly.*)

DODGE: Untrustworthy. Probably drown himself if he went out the back. Fall right in a hole. I'd never get my bottle.

SHELLY: I wouldn't worry about Vince. He can take care of himself.

DODGE: Oh he can, huh? Independent.

(*Vince comes on again from stage left with two dollars in his hand. He crosses stage right past Dodge.*)

DODGE (*to Vince*): You got the money?

VINCE: Yeah. Two bucks.

DODGE: Two bucks. Two bucks is two bucks. Don't sneer.

VINCE: What kind do you want?

DODGE: Whiskey! Gold Star Sour Mash. Use your own discretion.

VINCE: Okay.

(*Vince crosses to stage right door. Opens it. Stops when he hears Tilden.*)

TILDEN (*to Vince*): You drove all the way from New Mexico?

(*Vince turns and looks at Tilden. They stare at each other. Vince shakes his head, goes out the door, crosses porch, and exits out screen door. Tilden watches him go. Pause.*)

SHELLY: You really don't recognize him? Either one of you?

(*Tilden turns again and stares at Shelly's hands as she cuts carrots.*)

DODGE (*watching TV*): Recognize who?

SHELLY: Vince.

DODGE: What's to recognize?

(*Dodge lights a cigarette, coughs slightly, and stares at TV.*)

SHELLY: It'd be cruel if you recognized him and didn't tell him. Wouldn't be fair.

(*Dodge just stares at TV, smoking.*)

TILDEN: I thought I recognized him. I thought I recognized something about him.

SHELLY: You did?

TILDEN: I thought I saw a face inside his face.

SHELLY: Well, it was probably that you saw what he used to look like. You haven't seen him for six years.

TILDEN: I haven't?

SHELLY: That's what he says.

(*Tilden moves around in front of her as she continues with carrots.*)

TILDEN: Where was it I saw him last?

SHELLY: I don't know. I've only known him for a few months. He doesn't tell me everything.

TILDEN: He doesn't?

SHELLY: Not stuff like that.

TILDEN: What does he tell you?

SHELLY: You mean in general?

TILDEN: Yeah.

(*Tilden moves around behind her.*)

SHELLY: Well, he tells me all kinds of things.

TILDEN: Like what?

SHELLY: I don't know! I mean I can't just come right out and tell you how he feels.

TILDEN: How come?

(*Tilden keeps moving around her slowly in a circle.*)

SHELLY: Because it's stuff he told me privately!

TILDEN: And you can't tell me?

SHELLY: I don't even know you!

DODGE: Tilden, go out in the kitchen and make me some coffee! Leave the girl alone.

SHELLY (*to Dodge*): He's all right.

(*Tilden ignores Dodge, keeps moving around Shelly. He stares at her hair and coat. Dodge stares at TV.*)

TILDEN: You mean you can't tell me anything?

SHELLY: I can tell you some things. I mean we can have a conversation.

TILDEN: We can?

SHELLY: Sure. We're having a conversation right now.

TILDEN: We are?

SHELLY: Yes. That's what we're doing.

TILDEN: But there's certain things you can't tell me, right?

SHELLY: Right.

TILDEN: There's certain things I can't tell you either.

SHELLY: How come?

TILDEN: I don't know. Nobody's supposed to hear it.

SHELLY: Well, you can tell me anything you want to.

TILDEN: I can?

SHELLY: Sure.

TILDEN: It might not be very nice.

SHELLY: That's all right. I've been around.

TILDEN: It might be awful.

SHELLY: Well, can't you tell me anything nice?

(*Tilden stops in front of her and stares at her coat. Shelly looks back at him. Long pause.*)

TILDEN (*after pause*): Can I touch your coat?

SHELLY: My coat? (*She looks at her coat then back to Tilden.*) Sure.

TILDEN: You don't mind?

SHELLY: No. Go ahead.

(*Shelly holds her arm out for Tilden to touch. Dodge stays fixed on TV. Tilden moves in slowly toward Shelly, staring at her arm. He reaches out very slowly and touches her arm, feels the fur gently, then draws his hand back. Shelly keeps her arm out.*)

SHELLY: It's rabbit.

TILDEN: Rabbit.

(*He reaches out again very slowly and touches the fur on her arm then pulls back his hand again. Shelly drops her arm.*)

SHELLY: My arm was getting tired.

TILDEN: Can I hold it?

SHELLY (*pause*): The coat? Sure.

(*Shelly takes off her coat and hands it to Tilden. Tilden takes it slowly, feels the fur, then puts it on. Shelly watches as Tilden strokes the fur slowly. He smiles at her. She goes back to cutting carrots.*)

SHELLY: You can have it if you want.

TILDEN: I can?

SHELLY: Yeah. I've got a raincoat in the car. That's all I need.

TILDEN: You've got a car?

SHELLY: Vince does.

(*Tilden walks around stroking the fur and smiling at the coat. Shelly watches him when he's not looking. Dodge sticks with TV, stretches out on sofa wrapped in blanket.*)

TILDEN (*as he walks around*): I had a car once! I had a white car! I drove. I went everywhere. I went to the mountains. I drove in the snow.

SHELLY: That must've been fun.

TILDEN (*still moving, feeling coat*): I drove all day long sometimes. Across the desert. Way out across the desert. I drove past towns. Anywhere. Past palm trees. Lightning. Anything. I would drive through it. I would drive through it and I would stop and I would look around and I would drive on. I would get back in and drive! I loved to drive. There was nothing I loved more. Nothing I dreamed of was better than driving.

DODGE (*eyes on TV*): Pipe down, would ya'!

(*Tilden stops. Stares at Shelly.*)

SHELLY: Do you do much driving now?
TILDEN: Now? Now? I don't drive now.
SHELLY: How come?
TILDEN: I'm grown up now.
SHELLY: Grown up?
TILDEN: I'm not a kid.
SHELLY: You don't have to be a kid to drive.
TILDEN: It wasn't driving then.
SHELLY: What was it?
TILDEN: Adventure. I went everywhere.
SHELLY: Well, you can still do that.
TILDEN: Not now.
SHELLY: Why not?
TILDEN: I just told you. You don't understand anything. If I told you something you wouldn't understand it.
SHELLY: Told me what?
TILDEN: Told you something that's true.
SHELLY: Like what?
TILDEN: Like a baby. Like a little tiny baby.
SHELLY: Like when you were little?
TILDEN: If I told you you'd make me give your coat back.
SHELLY: I won't. I promise. Tell me.
TILDEN: I can't. Dodge won't let me.
SHELLY: He won't hear you. It's okay.

(*Pause. Tilden stares at her. Moves slightly toward her.*)

TILDEN: We had a baby. (*Motioning to Dodge.*) He did. Dodge did. Could pick it up with one hand. Put it in the other. Little baby. Dodge killed it.

(*Shelly stands.*)

TILDEN: Don't stand up. Don't stand up!

(*Shelly sits again. Dodge sits up on sofa and looks at them.*)

TILDEN: Dodge drowned it.
SHELLY: Don't tell me anymore! Okay?

(*Tilden moves closer to her. Dodge takes more interest.*)

DODGE: Tilden? You leave that girl alone!
TILDEN (*pays no attention*): Never told Halie. Never told anybody. Just drowned it.
DODGE (*shuts off TV*): Tilden!
TILDEN: Nobody could find it. Just disappeared. Cops looked for it. Neighbors. Nobody could find it.

(*Dodge struggles to get up from sofa.*)

DODGE: Tilden, what're you telling her! Tilden!

(*Dodge keeps struggling until he's standing.*)

TILDEN: Finally everybody just gave up. Just stopped looking. Everybody had a different answer. Kidnap. Murder. Accident. Some kind of accident.

(*Dodge struggles to walk toward Tilden and falls. Tilden ignores him.*)

DODGE: Tilden, you shut up! You shut up about it!

(*Dodge starts coughing on the floor. Shelly watches him from the stool.*)

TILDEN: Little tiny baby just disappeared. It's not hard. It's so small. Almost invisible.

(*Shelly makes a move to help Dodge. Tilden firmly pushes her back down on the stool. Dodge keeps coughing.*)

TILDEN: He said he had his reasons. Said it went a long way back. But he wouldn't tell anybody.
DODGE: Tilden! Don't tell her anything! Don't tell her!
TILDEN: He's the only one who knows where it's buried. The only one. Like a secret buried treasure. Won't tell any of us. Won't tell me or mother or even Bradley. Especially Bradley. Bradley tried to force it out of him but he wouldn't tell. Wouldn't even tell why he did it. One night he just did it.

(*Dodge's coughing subsides. Shelly stays on stool staring at Dodge. Tilden slowly takes Shelly's coat off and holds it out to her. Long pause. Shelly sits there trembling.*)

TILDEN: You probably want your coat back now.

(*Shelly stares at coat but doesn't move to take it. The sound of Bradley's leg squeaking is heard off left. The others on stage remain still. Bradley appears up left outside the screen door wearing a yellow rain slicker. He enters through screen door, crosses porch to stage right door and enters stage. Closes door. Takes off rain slicker and shakes it out. He sees all the others and stops. Tilden turns to him. Bradley stares at Shelly. Dodge remains on floor.*)

BRADLEY: What's going on here? (*Motioning to Shelly.*) Who's that?

(*Shelly stands, moves back away from Bradley as he crosses toward her. He stops next to Tilden. He sees coat in Tilden's hand and grabs it away from him.*)

BRADLEY: Who's she supposed to be?
TILDEN: She's driving to New Mexico.

(*Bradley stares at her. Shelly is frozen. Bradley limps over to her with the coat in his fist. He stops in front of her.*)

BRADLEY (*to Shelly, after pause*): Vacation?

(*Shelly shakes her head "no," trembling.*)

BRADLEY (*to Shelly, motioning to Tilden*): You taking him with you?

(*Shelly shakes her head "no." Bradley crosses back to Tilden.*)

BRADLEY: You oughta'. No use leaving him here. Doesn't do a lick a' work. Doesn't raise a finger. (*Stopping, to Tilden.*) Do ya'. (*To Shelly.*) 'Course he used to be an All-American. Quarterback or fullback or somethin'. He tell you that?

(*Shelly shakes her head "no."*)

BRADLEY: Yeah, he used to be a big deal. Wore letter-men's sweaters. Had medals hanging all around his neck. Real purty. Big deal. (*He laughs to himself, notices Dodge on floor, crosses to him, stops.*) This one too. (*To Shelly.*) You'd never think it to look at him, would ya'? All bony and wasted away.

(*Shelly shakes her head again. Bradley stares at her, crosses back to her, clenching the coat in his fist. He stops in front of Shelly.*)

BRADLEY: Women like that kinda' thing, don't they?
SHELLY: What?
BRADLEY: Importance. Importance in a man?
SHELLY: I don't know.
BRADLEY: Yeah. You know, you know. Don't give me that. (*Moves closer to Shelly.*) You're with Tilden?
SHELLY: No.
BRADLEY (*turning to Tilden*): Tilden! She with you?

(*Tilden doesn't answer. Stares at floor.*)

BRADLEY: Tilden!

(*Tilden suddenly bolts and runs off up stage left. Bradley laughs. Talks to Shelly. Dodge starts moving his lips silently as though talking to someone invisible on the floor.*)

BRADLEY (*laughing*): Scared to death! He was always scared!

(*Bradley stops laughing. Stares at Shelly.*)

BRADLEY: You're scared too, right? (*Laughs again.*) You're scared and you don't even know me. (*Stops laughing.*) You don't gotta be scared.

(*Shelly looks at Dodge on the floor.*)

SHELLY: Can't we do something for him?
BRADLEY (*looking at Dodge*): We could shoot him. (*Laughs.*) We could drown him! What about drowning him?
SHELLY: Shut up!

(*Bradley stops laughing. Moves in closer to Shelly. She freezes. Bradley speaks slowly and deliberately.*)

BRADLEY: Hey! Missus. Don't talk to me like that. Don't talk to me in that tone a' voice. There was a time when I had to take that tone a' voice from pretty near everyone. (*Motioning to Dodge.*) Him, for one! Him and that half brain that just ran outa' here. They don't talk to me like that now. Not anymore. Everything's turned around now. Full circle. Isn't that funny?
SHELLY: I'm sorry.
BRADLEY: Open your mouth.
SHELLY: What?
BRADLEY (*motioning for her to open her mouth*): Open up.

(*She opens her mouth slightly.*)

BRADLEY: Wider.

(*She opens her mouth wider.*)

BRADLEY: Keep it like that.

(*She does. Stares at Bradley. With his free hand he puts his fingers into her mouth. She tries to pull away.*)

BRADLEY: Just stay put!

(*She freezes. He keeps his fingers in her mouth. Stares at her. Pause. He pulls his hand out. She closes her mouth, keeps her eyes on him. Bradley smiles. He looks at Dodge on the floor and crosses over to him. Shelly watches him closely. Bradley stands over Dodge and smiles at Shelly. He holds her coat up in both hands over Dodge, keeps smiling at Shelly. He looks down at Dodge, then drops the coat so that it lands on Dodge and covers his head. Bradley keeps his hands up in the position of holding the coat, looks over at Shelly, and smiles. The lights black out.*)

ACT 3

Scene: *Same set. Morning. Bright sun. No sound of rain. Everything has been cleared up again. No sign of carrots. No pail. No stool. Vince's saxophone case and overcoat are still at the foot of the staircase. Bradley is asleep on the sofa under Dodge's blanket. His head toward stage left. Bradley's wooden leg is leaning against the sofa right by his head. The shoe is left on it. The harness hangs down. Dodge is sitting on the floor, propped up against the TV set facing stage left wearing his baseball cap. Shelly's rabbit fur coat covers his chest and shoulders. He stares off toward stage left. He seems weaker and more disoriented. The lights rise slowly to the sound of birds and remain for a while in silence on the two men. Bradley sleeps very soundly. Dodge hardly moves. Shelly appears from stage left with a big smile, slowly crossing toward Dodge balancing a steaming cup of broth in a saucer. Dodge just stares at her as she gets close to him.*

SHELLY (*as she crosses*): This is going to make all the difference in the world, Grandpa. You don't mind me calling you Grandpa, do you? I mean I know you minded when Vince called you that but you don't even know him.
DODGE: He skipped town with my money, ya' know. I'm gonna hold you as collateral.
SHELLY: He'll be back. Don't you worry.

(*She kneels down next to Dodge and puts the cup and saucer in his lap.*)

DODGE: It's morning already! Not only didn't I get my bottle but he's got my two bucks!
SHELLY: Try to drink this, okay? Don't spill it.
DODGE: What is it?
SHELLY: Beef bouillon. It'll warm you up.

DODGE: Bouillon! I don't want any goddamn bouillon! Get that stuff away from me!

SHELLY: I just got through making it.

DODGE: I don't care if you just spent all week making it! I ain't drinking it!

SHELLY: Well, what am I supposed to do with it then? I'm trying to help you out. Besides, it's good for you.

DODGE: Get it away from me!

(*Shelly stands up with cup and saucer.*)

DODGE: What do you know what's good for me anyway?

(*She looks at Dodge, then turns away from him, crossing to staircase, sits on bottom step, and drinks the bouillon. Dodge stares at her.*)

DODGE: You know what'd be good for me?

SHELLY: What?

DODGE: A little massage. A little contact.

SHELLY: Oh no. I've had enough contact for a while. Thanks anyway.

(*She keeps sipping bouillon, stays sitting. Pause as Dodge stares at her.*)

DODGE: Why not? You got nothing better to do. That fella's not gonna be back here. You're not expecting him to show up again, are you?

SHELLY: Sure. He'll show up. He left his horn here.

DODGE: His horn? (*Laughs.*) You're his horn?

SHELLY: Very funny.

DODGE: He's run off with my money! He's not coming back here.

SHELLY: He'll be back.

DODGE: You're a funny chicken, you know that?

SHELLY: Thanks.

DODGE: Full of faith. Hope. Faith and hope. You're all alike, you hopers. If it's not God then it's a man. If it's not a man then it's a woman. If it's not a woman then it's the land or the future of some kind. Some kind of future.

(*Pause.*)

SHELLY (*looking toward porch*): I'm glad it stopped raining.

DODGE (*looks toward porch then back to her*): That's what I mean. See, you're glad it stopped raining. Now you think everything's gonna be different. Just 'cause the sun comes out.

SHELLY: It's already different. Last night I was scared.

DODGE: Scared a' what?

SHELLY: Just scared.

DODGE: Bradley? (*Looks at Bradley.*) He's a pushover. 'Specially now. All ya' gotta do is take his leg and throw it out the back door. Helpless. Totally helpless.

(*Shelly turns and stares at Bradley's wooden leg, then looks at Dodge. She sips bouillon.*)

SHELLY: You'd do that?

DODGE: Me? I've hardly got the strength to breathe.

SHELLY: But you'd actually do it if you could?

DODGE: Don't be so easily shocked, girlie. There's nothing a man can't do. You dream it up and he can do it. Anything.

SHELLY: You've tried I guess.

DODGE: Don't sit there sippin' your bouillon and judging me! This is my house!

SHELLY: I forgot.

DODGE: You forgot? Whose house did you think it was?

SHELLY: Mine.

(*Dodge just stares at her. Long pause. She sips from cup.*)

SHELLY: I know it's not mine but I had that feeling.

DODGE: What feeling?

SHELLY: The feeling that nobody lives here but me. I mean everybody's gone. You're here, but it doesn't seem like you're supposed to be. (*Pointing to Bradley.*) Doesn't seem like he's supposed to be here either. I don't know what it is. It's the house or something. Something familiar. Like I know my way around here. Did you ever get that feeling?

(*Dodge stares at her in silence. Pause.*)

DODGE: No. No, I never did.

(*Shelly gets up. Moves around space holding cup.*)

SHELLY: Last night I went to sleep up there in that room.

DODGE: What room?

SHELLY: That room up there with all the pictures. All the crosses on the wall.

DODGE: Halie's room?

SHELLY: Yeah. Whoever "Halie" is.

DODGE: She's my wife.

SHELLY: So you remember her?

DODGE: Whad'ya mean! 'Course I remember her! She's only been gone for a day—half a day. However long it's been.

SHELLY: Do you remember her when her hair was bright red? Standing in front of an apple tree?

DODGE: What is this, the third degree or something! Who're you to be askin' me personal questions about my wife!

SHELLY: You never look at those pictures up there?

DODGE: What pictures!

SHELLY: Your whole life's up there hanging on the wall. Somebody who looks just like you. Somebody who looks just like you used to look.

DODGE: That isn't me! That never was me! This is me. Right here. This is it. The whole shootin' match, sittin' right in front of you.

SHELLY: So the past never happened as far as you're concerned?

DODGE: The past? Jesus Christ. The past. What do you know about the past?

SHELLY: Not much. I know there was a farm.

(*Pause.*)

DODGE: A farm?

SHELLY: There's a picture of a farm. A big farm. A bull. Wheat. Corn.

DODGE: Corn?

SHELLY: All the kids are standing out in the corn. They're all waving these big straw hats. One of them doesn't have a hat.

DODGE: Which one was that?

SHELLY: There's a baby. A baby in a woman's arms. The same woman with the red hair. She looks lost standing out there. Like she doesn't know how she got there.

DODGE: She knows! I told her a hundred times it wasn't gonna' be the city! I gave her plenty a' warning.

SHELLY: She's looking down at the baby like it was somebody else's. Like it didn't even belong to her.

DODGE: That's about enough outa' you! You got some funny ideas. Some damn funny ideas. You think just because people propagate they have to love their offspring? You never seen a bitch eat her puppies? Where are you from anyway?

SHELLY: L.A. We already went through that.

DODGE: That's right, L.A. I remember.

SHELLY: Stupid country.

DODGE: That's right! No wonder.

(*Pause.*)

SHELLY: What's happened to this family anyway?

DODGE: You're in no position to ask! What do you care? You some kinda' Social Worker?

SHELLY: I'm Vince's friend.

DODGE: Vince's friend! That's rich. That's really rich. "Vince"! "Mr. Vince"! "Mr. Thief" is more like it! His name doesn't mean a hoot in hell to me. Not a tinkle in the well. You know how many kids I've spawned? Not to mention Grand kids and Great Grand kids and Great Great Grand kids after them?

SHELLY: And you don't remember any of them?

DODGE: What's to remember? Halie's the one with the family album. She's the one you should talk to. She'll set you straight on the heritage if that's what you're interested in. She's traced it all the way back to the grave.

SHELLY: What do you mean?

DODGE: What do you think I mean? How far back can you go? A long line of corpses! There's not a living soul behind me. Not a one. Who's holding me in their memory? Who gives a damn about bones in the ground?

SHELLY: Was Tilden telling the truth?

(*Dodge stops short. Stares at Shelly. Shakes his head. He looks off stage left.*)

SHELLY: Was he?

(*Dodge's tone changes drastically.*)

DODGE: Tilden? (*Turns to Shelly, calmly.*) Where is Tilden?

SHELLY: Last night. Was he telling the truth about the baby?

(*Pause.*)

DODGE (*turns toward stage left*): What's happened to Tilden? Why isn't Tilden here?

SHELLY: Bradley chased him out.

DODGE (*looking at Bradley asleep*): Bradley? Why is he on my sofa? (*Turns back to Shelly.*) Have I been here all night? On the floor?

SHELLY: He wouldn't leave. I hid outside until he fell asleep.

DODGE: Outside? Is Tilden outside? He shouldn't be out there in the rain. He'll get himself into trouble. He doesn't know his way around here anymore. Not like he used to. He went out West and got himself into trouble. Got himself into bad trouble. We don't want any of that around here.

SHELLY: What did he do?

(*Pause.*)

DODGE (*quietly stares at Shelly*): Tilden? He got mixed up. That's what he did. We can't afford to leave him alone. Not now.

(*Sound of Halie laughing comes from off left. Shelly stands, looking in direction of voice, holding cup and saucer, doesn't know whether to stay or run.*)

DODGE (*motioning to Shelly*): Sit down! Sit back down!

(*Shelly sits. Sound of Halie's laughter again.*)

DODGE (*to Shelly in a heavy whisper, pulling coat up around him*): Don't leave me alone now! Promise me? Don't go off and leave me alone. I need somebody here with me. Tilden's gone now and I need someone. Don't leave me! Promise!

SHELLY (*sitting*): I won't.

(*Halie appears outside the screen porch door, up left with Father Dewis. She is wearing a bright yellow dress, no hat, white gloves and her arms are full of yellow roses. Father Dewis is dressed in traditional black suit, white clerical collar, and shirt. He is a very distinguished gray-haired man in his sixties. They are both slightly drunk and feeling giddy. As they enter the porch through the screen door, Dodge pulls the rabbit fur coat over his head and hides. Shelly stands again. Dodge drops the coat and whispers intensely to Shelly. Neither Halie nor Father Dewis are aware of the people inside the house.*)

DODGE (*to Shelly in a strong whisper*): You promised!

(*Shelly sits on stairs again. Dodge pulls coat back over his head. Halie and Father Dewis talk on the porch as they cross toward stage right interior door.*)

HALIE: Oh, Father! That's terrible! That's absolutely terrible. Aren't you afraid of being punished?

(*She giggles.*)

DEWIS: Not by the Italians. They're too busy punishing each other.

(*They both break out in giggles.*)

HALIE: What about God?

DEWIS: Well, prayerfully, God only hears what he wants to. That's just between you and me of course. In our heart of hearts we know we're every bit as wicked as the Catholics.

(*They giggle again and reach the stage right door.*)

HALIE: Father, I never heard you talk like this in Sunday sermon.

DEWIS: Well, I save all my best jokes for private company. Pearls before swine, you know.

(*They enter the room laughing and stop when they see Shelly. Shelly stands. Halie closes the door behind Father Dewis. Dodge's voice is heard under the coat, talking to Shelly.*)

DODGE (*under coat, to Shelly*): Sit down, sit down! Don't let 'em buffalo you!

(*Shelly sits on stair again. Halie looks at Dodge on the floor, then looks at Bradley asleep on sofa and sees his wooden leg. She lets out a shriek of embarrassment for Father Dewis.*)

HALIE: Oh my gracious! What in the name of Judas Priest is going on in this house!

(*She hands over the roses to Father Dewis.*)

HALIE: Excuse me, Father.

(*Halie crosses to Dodge, whips the coat off him, and covers the wooden leg with it. Bradley stays asleep.*)

HALIE: You can't leave this house for a second without the Devil blowing in through the front door!

DODGE: Gimme back that coat! Gimme back that goddamn coat before I freeze to death!

HALIE: You're not going to freeze! The sun's out in case you hadn't noticed!

DODGE: Gimme back that coat! That coat's for live flesh not dead wood!

(*Halie whips the blanket off Bradley and throws it on Dodge. Dodge covers his head again with blanket. Bradley's amputated leg can be faked by having half of it under a cushion of the sofa. He's fully clothed. Bradley sits up with a jerk when the blanket comes off him.*)

HALIE (*as she tosses blanket*): Here! Use this! It's yours anyway! Can't you take care of yourself for once!

BRADLEY (*yelling at Halie*): Gimme that blanket! Gimme back that blanket! That's my blanket!

(*Halie crosses back toward Father Dewis who just stands there with the roses. Bradley thrashes helplessly on the sofa trying to reach blanket. Dodge hides himself deeper in blanket. Shelly looks on from staircase, still holding cup and saucer.*)

HALIE: Believe me, Father, this is not what I had in mind when I invited you in.

DEWIS: Oh, no apologies please. I wouldn't be in the ministry if I couldn't face real life.

(*He laughs self-consciously. Halie notices Shelly again and crosses over to her. Shelly stays sitting. Halie stops and stares at her.*)

BRADLEY: I want my blanket back! Gimme my blanket!

(*Halie turns toward Bradley and silences him.*)

HALIE: Shut up, Bradley! Right this minute! I've had enough!

(*Bradley slowly recoils, lies back down on sofa, turns his back toward Halie and whimpers softly. Halie directs her attention to Shelly again. Pause.*)

HALIE (*to Shelly*): What're you doing with my cup and saucer?

SHELLY (*looking at cup, back to Halie*): I made some bouillon for Dodge.

HALIE: For Dodge?

SHELLY: Yeah.

HALIE: Well, did he drink it?

SHELLY: No.

HALIE: Did you drink it?

SHELLY: Yes.

(*Halie stares at her. Long pause. She turns abruptly away from Shelly and crosses back to Father Dewis.*)

HALIE: Father, there's a stranger in my house. What would you advise? What would be the Christian thing?

DEWIS (*squirming*): Oh, well. . . . I . . . . I really—

HALIE: We still have some whiskey, don't we?

(*Dodge slowly pulls the blanket down off his head and looks toward Father Dewis. Shelly stands.*)

SHELLY: Listen, I don't drink or anything. I just—

(*Halie turns toward Shelly viciously.*)

HALIE: You sit back down!

(*Shelly sits again on stair. Halie turns again to Dewis.*)

HALIE: I think we have plenty of whiskey left! Don't we, Father?

DEWIS: Well, yes. I think so. You'll have to get it. My hands are full.

(*Halie giggles. Reaches into Dewis's pockets, searching for bottle. She smells the roses as she searches. Dewis stands stiffly. Dodge watches Halie closely as she looks for bottle.*)

HALIE: The most incredible things, roses! Aren't they incredible, Father?

DEWIS: Yes. Yes, they are.

HALIE: They almost cover the stench of sin in this house. Just magnificent! The smell. We'll have to put some at the foot of Ansel's statue. On the day of the unveiling.

(*Halie finds a silver flask of whiskey in Dewis's vest pocket. She pulls it out. Dodge looks on eagerly. Halie crosses to Dodge, opens the flask, and takes a sip.*)

HALIE (*to Dodge*): Ansel's getting a statue, Dodge. Did you know that? Not a plaque but a real live statue. A full bronze. Tip to toe. A basketball in one hand and a rifle in the other.

BRADLEY (*his back to Halie*): He never played basketball!

HALIE: You shut up, Bradley! You shut up about Ansel! Ansel played basketball better than anyone! And you know it! He was an All-American! There's no reason to take the glory away from others.

(*Halie turns away from Bradley, crosses back toward Dewis, sipping on the flask and smiling.*)

HALIE (*to Dewis*): Ansel was a great basketball player. One of the greatest.

DEWIS: I remember Ansel.

HALIE: Of course! You remember. You remember how he could play. (*She turns toward Shelly.*) Of course, nowadays they play a different brand of basketball. More vicious. Isn't that right, dear?

SHELLY: I don't know.

(*Halie crosses to Shelly, sipping on flask. She stops in front of Shelly.*)

HALIE: Much, much more vicious. They smash into each other. They knock each other's teeth out. There's blood all over the court. Savages.

(*Halie takes the cup from Shelly and pours whiskey into it.*)

HALIE: They don't train like they used to. Not at all. They allow themselves to run amuck. Drugs and women. Women mostly.

(*Halie hands the cup of whiskey back to Shelly slowly. Shelly takes it.*)

HALIE: Mostly women. Girls. Sad, pathetic little girls. (*She crosses back to Father Dewis.*) It's just a reflection of the times, don't you think, Father? An indication of where we stand?

DEWIS: I suppose so, yes.

HALIE: Yes. A sort of bad omen. Our youth becoming monsters.

DEWIS: Well, I uh —

HALIE: Oh you can disagree with me if you want to, Father. I'm open to debate. I think argument only enriches both sides of the question don't you? (*She moves toward Dodge.*) I suppose, in the long run, it doesn't matter. When you see the way things deteriorate before your very eyes. Everything running downhill. It's kind of silly to even think about youth.

DEWIS: No, I don't think so. I think it's important to believe in certain things.

HALIE: Yes. Yes, I know what you mean. I think that's right. I think that's true. (*She looks at Dodge.*) Certain basic things. We can't shake certain basic things. We might end up crazy. Like my husband. You can see it in his eyes. You can see how mad he is.

(*Dodge covers his head with the blanket again. Halie takes a single rose from Dewis and moves slowly over to Dodge.*)

HALIE: We can't not believe in something. We can't stop believing. We just end up dying if we stop. Just end up dead.

(*Halie throws the rose gently onto Dodge's blanket. It lands between his knees and stays there! Long pause as Halie stares at the rose. Shelly stands suddenly. Halie doesn't turn to her but keeps staring at rose.*)

SHELLY (*to Halie*): Don't you wanna' know who I am! Don't you wanna know what I'm doing here! I'm not dead!

(*Shelly crosses toward Halie. Halie turns slowly toward her.*)

HALIE: Did you drink your whiskey?

SHELLY: No! And I'm not going to either!

HALIE: Well, that's a firm stand. It's good to have a firm stand.

SHELLY: I don't have any stand at all. I'm just trying to put all this together.

(*Halie laughs and crosses back to Dewis.*)

HALIE (*to Dewis*): Surprises, surprises! Did you have any idea we'd be returning to this?

SHELLY: I came here with your grandson for a little visit! A little innocent friendly visit.

HALIE: My grandson?

SHELLY: Yes! That's right. The one no one remembers.

HALIE (*to Dewis*): This is getting a little far-fetched.

SHELLY: I told him it was stupid to come back here. To try to pick up from where he left off.

HALIE: Where was that?

SHELLY: Wherever he was when he left here! Six years ago! Ten years ago! Whenever it was. I told him nobody cares.

HALIE: Didn't he listen?

SHELLY: No! No, he didn't. We had to stop off at every tiny little meatball town that he remembered from his boyhood! Every stupid little donut shop he ever kissed a girl in. Every drive-in. Every drag strip. Every football field he ever broke a bone on.

HALIE (*suddenly alarmed, to Dodge*): Where's Tilden?

SHELLY: Don't ignore me!

HALIE: Dodge! Where's Tilden gone?

(*Shelly moves violently toward Halie.*)

SHELLY (*to Halie*): I'm talking to you!

(*Bradley sits up fast on the sofa, Shelly backs away.*)

BRADLEY (*to Shelly*): Don't you yell at my mother!

HALIE: Dodge! (*She kicks Dodge.*) I told you not to let Tilden out of your sight! Where's he gone to?

DODGE: Gimme a drink and I'll tell ya'.

DEWIS: Halie, maybe this isn't the right time for a visit.

(*Halie crosses back to Dewis.*)

HALIE (*to Dewis*): I never should've left. I never, never should've left! Tilden could be anywhere by now! Anywhere! He's not in control of his faculties. Dodge knew that. I told him when I left here. I told him specifically to watch out for Tilden.

(*Bradley reaches down, grabs Dodge's blanket, and yanks it off him. He lays down on sofa and pulls the blanket over his head.*)

DODGE: He's got my blanket again! He's got my blanket!

HALIE (*turning to Bradley*): Bradley! Bradley, put that blanket back!

(*Halie moves toward Bradley. Shelly suddenly throws the cup and saucer against the stage right door. Dewis ducks. The cup and saucer smash into pieces. Halie stops, turns toward Shelly. Everyone freezes. Bradley slowly pulls his head out from under blanket, looks toward stage right door, then to Shelly. Shelly stares at Halie. Dewis cowers with roses. Shelly moves slowly toward Halie. Long pause. Shelly speaks softly.*)

SHELLY (*to Halie*): I don't like being ignored. I don't like being treated like I'm not here. I didn't like it when I was a kid and I still don't like it.

BRADLEY (*sitting up on sofa*): We don't have to tell you anything, girl. Not a thing. You're not the police, are you? You're not the government. You're just some prostitute that Tilden brought in here.

HALIE: Language! I won't have that language in my house!

SHELLY (*to Bradley*): You stuck your hand in my mouth and you call me a prostitute!

HALIE: Bradley! Did you put your hand in her mouth? I'm ashamed of you. I can't leave you alone for a minute.

BRADLEY: I never did. She's lying!

DEWIS: Halie, I think I'll be running along now. I'll just put the roses in the kitchen.

(*Dewis moves toward stage left. Halie stops him.*)

HALIE: Don't go now, Father! Not now.

BRADLEY: I never did anything, Mom! I never touched her! She propositioned me! And I turned her down. I turned her down flat!

(*Shelly suddenly grabs her coat off the wooden leg and takes both the leg and coat downstage, away from Bradley.*)

BRADLEY: Mom! Mom! She's got my leg! She's taken my leg! I never did anything to her! She's stolen my leg!

(*Bradley reaches pathetically in the air for his leg. Shelly sets it down for a second, puts on her coat fast, and picks the leg up again. Dodge starts coughing softly.*)

HALIE (*to Shelly*): I think we've had about enough of you, young lady. Just about enough. I don't know where you came from or what you're doing here but you're no longer welcome in this house.

SHELLY (*laughs, holds leg*): No longer welcome!

BRADLEY: Mom! That's my leg! Get my leg back! I can't do anything without my leg.

(*Bradley keeps making whimpering sounds and reaching for his leg.*)

HALIE: Give my son back his leg. Right this very minute!

(*Dodge starts laughing softly to himself in between coughs.*)

HALIE (*to Dewis*): Father, do something about this, would you! I'm not about to be terrorized in my own house!

BRADLEY: Gimme back my leg!

HALIE: Oh, shut up, Bradley! Just shut up! You don't need your leg now! Just lay down and shut up!

(*Bradley whimpers. Lays down and pulls blanket around him. He keeps one arm outside blanket, reaching out toward his wooden leg. Dewis cautiously approaches Shelly with the roses in his arms. Shelly clutches the wooden leg to her chest as though she's kidnapped it.*)

DEWIS (*to Shelly*): Now, honestly dear, wouldn't it be better to try to talk things out? Try to use some reason?

SHELLY: There isn't any reason here! I can't find a reason for anything.

DEWIS: There's nothing to be afraid of. These are all good people. All righteous people.

SHELLY: I'm not afraid!

DEWIS: But this isn't your house. You have to have some respect.

SHELLY: You're the strangers here, not me.

HALIE: This has gone far enough!

DEWIS: Halie, please. Let me handle this.

SHELLY: Don't come near me! Don't anyone come near me. I don't need any words from you. I'm not threatening anybody. I don't even know what I'm doing here. You all say you don't remember Vince, okay, maybe you don't. Maybe it's Vince that's crazy. Maybe he's made this whole family thing up. I don't even care anymore. I was just coming along for the ride. I thought it'd be a nice gesture. Besides, I was curious. He made all of you sound familiar to me. Every one of you. For every name, I had an image. Every time he'd tell me a name, I'd see the person. In fact, each of you was so clear in my mind that I actually believed it was you. I really believed when I walked through that door that the people who lived here would turn out to be the same people in my imagination. But I don't recognize any of you. Not one. Not even the slightest resemblance.

DEWIS: Well, you can hardly blame others for not fulfilling your hallucination.

SHELLY: It was no hallucination! It was more like a prophecy. You believe in prophecy, don't you?

HALIE: Father, there's no point in talking to her any further. We're just going to have to call the police.

BRADLEY: No! Don't get the police in here. We don't want the police in here. This is our home.

SHELLY: That's right. Bradley's right. Don't you usually settle your affairs in private? Don't you usually take them out in the dark? Out in the back?

BRADLEY: You stay out of our lives! You have no business interfering!

SHELLY: I don't have any business period. I got nothing to lose.

(*She moves around, staring at each of them.*)

BRADLEY: You don't know what we've been through. You don't know anything!

SHELLY: I know you've got a secret. You've all got a secret. It's so secret in fact, you're all convinced it never happened.

(*Halie moves to Dewis.*)

HALIE: Oh, my God, Father!

DODGE (*laughing to himself*): She thinks she's going to get it out of us. She thinks she's going to uncover the truth of the matter. Like a detective or something.

BRADLEY: I'm not telling her anything! Nothing's wrong here! Nothin's ever been wrong! Everything's the way it's supposed to be! Nothing ever happened that's bad! Everything is all right here! We're all good people!

DODGE: She thinks she's gonna suddenly bring everything out into the open after all these years.

DEWIS (*to Shelly*): Can't you see that these people want to be left in peace? Don't you have any mercy? They haven't done anything to you.

DODGE: She wants to get to the bottom of it. (*To Shelly.*) That's it, isn't it? You'd like to get right down to bedrock? You want me to tell ya'? You want me to tell ya' what happened? I'll tell ya'. I might as well.

BRADLEY: No! Don't listen to him. He doesn't remember anything!

DODGE: I remember the whole thing from start to finish. I remember the day he was born.

(*Pause.*)

HALIE: Dodge, if you tell this thing—if you tell this, you'll be dead to me. You'll be just as good as dead.

DODGE: That won't be such a big change, Halie. See this girl, this girl here, she wants to know. She wants to know something more. And I got this feeling that it doesn't make a bit a' difference. I'd sooner tell it to a stranger than anybody else.

BRADLEY (*to Dodge*): We made a pact! We made a pact between us! You can't break that now!

DODGE: I don't remember any pact.

BRADLEY (*to Shelly*): See, he doesn't remember anything. I'm the only one in the family who remembers. The only one. And I'll never tell you!

SHELLY: I'm not so sure I want to find out now.

DODGE (*laughing to himself*): Listen to her! Now she's runnin' scared!

SHELLY: I'm not scared!

(*Dodge stops laughing, long pause. Dodge stares at her.*)

DODGE: You're not, huh? Well, that's good. Because I'm not either. See, we were a well-established family

once. Well-established. All the boys were grown. The farm was producing enough milk to fill Lake Michigan twice over. Me and Halie here were pointed toward what looked like the middle part of our life. Everything was settled with us. All we had to do was ride it out. Then Halie got pregnant again. Outa' the middle a' nowhere, she got pregnant. We weren't planning on havin' any more boys. We had enough boys already. In fact, we hadn't been sleepin' in the same bed for about six years.

HALIE (*moving toward stairs*): I'm not listening to this! I don't have to listen to this!

DODGE (*stops Halie*): Where are you going! Upstairs! You'll just be listenin' to it upstairs! You go outside, you'll be listenin' to it outside. Might as well stay here and listen to it.

(*Halie stays by stairs.*)

BRADLEY: If I had my leg you wouldn't be saying this. You'd never get away with it if I had my leg.

DODGE (*pointing to Shelly*): She's got your leg. (*Laughs.*) She's gonna keep your leg too. (*To Shelly.*) She wants to hear this. Don't you?

SHELLY: I don't know.

DODGE: Well even if ya' don't I'm gonna' tell ya'. (*Pause.*) Halie had this kid. This baby boy. She had it. I let her have it on her own. All the other boys I had had the best doctors, best nurses, everything. This one I let her have by herself. This one hurt real bad. Almost killed her, but she had it anyway. It lived, see. It lived. It wanted to grow up in this family. It wanted to be just like us. It wanted to be a part of us. It wanted to pretend that I was its father. She wanted me to believe in it. Even when everyone around us knew. Everyone. All our boys knew. Tilden knew.

HALIE: You shut up! Bradley, make him shut up!

BRADLEY: I can't.

DODGE: Tilden was the one who knew. Better than any of us. He'd walk for miles with that kid in his arms. Halie let him take it. All night sometimes. He'd walk all night out there in the pasture with it. Talkin' to it. Singin' to it. Used to hear him singing to it. He'd make up stories. He'd tell that kid all kinds a' stories. Even when he knew it couldn't understand him. Couldn't understand a word he was sayin'. Never would understand him. We couldn't let a thing like that continue. We couldn't allow that to grow up right in the middle of our lives. It made everything we'd accomplished look like it was nothin'. Everything was canceled out by this one mistake. This one weakness.

SHELLY: So you killed him?

DODGE: I killed it. I drowned it. Just like the runt of a litter. Just drowned it.

(*Halie moves toward Bradley.*)

HALIE (*to Bradley*): Ansel would've stopped him! Ansel would've stopped him from telling these lies! He was a hero! A man! A whole man! What's happened to the men in this family! Where are the men!

(*Suddenly Vince comes crashing through the screen porch door up left, tearing it off its hinges. Everyone but Dodge and Bradley back away from the porch and stare at Vince who has landed on his stomach on the porch in a drunken stupor. He is singing loudly to himself and hauls himself slowly to his feet. He has a paper shopping bag full of empty booze bottles. He takes them out one at a time as he sings and smashes them at the opposite end of the porch, behind the solid interior door, stage right. Shelly moves slowly toward stage right, holding wooden leg and watching Vince.*)

VINCE (*singing loudly as he hurls bottles*): "From the Halls of Montezuma to the Shores of Tripoli. We will fight our country's battles on the land and on the sea."

(*He punctuates the words "Montezuma," "Tripoli," "battles," and "sea" with a smashed bottle each. He stops throwing for a second, stares toward stage right of the porch, shades his eyes with his hand as though looking across to a battlefield, then cups his hands around his mouth and yells across the space of the porch to an imaginary army. The others watch in terror and expectation.*)

VINCE (*to imagined army*): Have you had enough over there! 'Cause there's a lot more here where that came from! (*Pointing to paper bag full of bottles.*) A helluva lot more! We got enough over here to blow ya' from here to Kingdomcome!

(*He takes another bottle, makes high whistling sound of a bomb, and throws it toward stage right porch. Sound of bottle smashing against wall. This should be the actual smashing of bottles and not tape sound. He keeps yelling and heaving bottles one after another.*)

(*Vince stops for a while, breathing heavily from exhaustion. Long silence as the others watch him. Shelly approaches tentatively in Vince's direction, still holding Bradley's wooden leg.*)

SHELLY (*after silence*): Vince?

(*Vince turns toward her. Peers through screen.*)

VINCE: Who? What? Vince who? Who's that in there?

(*Vince pushes his face against the screen from the porch and stares in at everyone.*)

DODGE: Where's my goddamn bottle!
VINCE (*looking in at Dodge*): What? Who is that?
DODGE: It's me! Your Grandfather! Don't play stupid with me! Where's my two bucks!
VINCE: Your two bucks?

(*Halie moves away from Dewis, upstage, peers out at Vince, trying to recognize him.*)

HALIE: Vincent? Is that you, Vincent?

(*Shelly stares at Halie, then looks out at Vince.*)

VINCE (*from porch*): Vincent who? What is this! Who are you people?
SHELLY (*to Halie*): Hey, wait a minute. Wait a minute! What's going on?

HALIE (*moving closer to porch screen*): We thought you were a murderer or something. Barging in through the door like that.
VINCE: I am a murderer! Don't underestimate me for a minute! I'm the Midnight Strangler! I devour whole families in a single gulp!

(*Vince grabs another bottle and smashes it on the porch. Halie backs away.*)

SHELLY (*approaching Halie*): You mean you know who he is?
HALIE: Of course I know who he is! That's more than I can say for you.
BRADLEY (*sitting up on sofa*): You get off our front porch, you creep! What're you doing out there breaking bottles? Who are these foreigners anyway! Where did they come from?
VINCE: Maybe I should come in there and break them!
HALIE (*moving toward porch*): Don't you dare! Vincent, what's got into you! Why are you acting like this?
VINCE: Maybe I should come in there and usurp your territory!

(*Halie turns back toward Dewis and crosses to him.*)

HALIE (*to Dewis*): Father, why are you just standing around here when everything's falling apart? Can't you rectify this situation?

(*Dodge laughs, coughs.*)

DEWIS: I'm just a guest here, Halie. I don't know what my position is exactly. This is outside my parish anyway.

(*Vince starts throwing more bottles as things continue.*)

BRADLEY: If I had my leg I'd rectify it! I'd rectify him all over the goddamn highway! I'd pull his ears out if I could reach him!

(*Bradley sticks his fist through the screening of the porch and reaches out for Vince, grabbing at him and missing. Vince jumps away from Bradley's hand.*)

VINCE: Aaaah! Our lines have been penetrated! Tentacles animals! Beasts from the deep!

(*Vince strikes out at Bradley's hand with a bottle. Bradley pulls his hand back inside.*)

SHELLY: Vince! Knock it off, will ya'! I want to get out of here!

(*Vince pushes his face against screen, looks in at Shelly.*)

VINCE (*to Shelly*): Have they got you prisoner in there, dear? Such a sweet young thing too. All her life in front of her. Nipped in the bud.
SHELLY: I'm coming out there, Vince! I'm coming out there and I want us to get in the car and drive away from here. Anywhere. Just away from here.

(*Shelly moves toward Vince's saxophone case and overcoat. She sets down the wooden leg, downstage left, and picks up the saxophone case and overcoat. Vince watches her through the screen.*)

VINCE (*to Shelly*): We'll have to negotiate. Make some kind of a deal. Prisoner exchange or something. A few of theirs for one of ours. Small price to pay if you ask me.

(*Shelly crosses toward stage right door with overcoat and case.*)

SHELLY: Just go and get the car! I'm coming out there now. We're going to leave.

VINCE: Don't come out here! Don't you dare come out here!

(*Shelly stops short of the door, stage right.*)

SHELLY: How come?

VINCE: Off limits! Verboten! This is taboo territory. No man or woman has ever crossed the line and lived to tell the tale!

SHELLY: I'll take my chances.

(*Shelly moves to stage right door and opens it. Vince pulls out a big folding hunting knife and pulls open the blade. He jabs the blade into the screen and starts cutting a hole big enough to climb through. Bradley cowers in a corner of the sofa as Vince rips at the screen.*)

VINCE (*as he cuts screen*): Don't come out here! I'm warning you! You'll disintegrate!

(*Dewis takes Halie by the arm and pulls her toward staircase.*)

DEWIS: Halie, maybe we should go upstairs until this blows over.

HALIE: I don't understand it. I just don't understand it. He was the sweetest little boy!

(*Dewis drops the roses beside the wooden leg at the foot of the staircase, then escorts Halie quickly up the stairs. Halie keeps looking back at Vince as they climb the stairs.*)

HALIE: There wasn't a mean bone in his body. Everyone loved Vincent. Everyone. He was the perfect baby.

DEWIS: He'll be all right after a while. He's just had a few too many that's all.

HALIE: He used to sing in his sleep. He'd sing. In the middle of the night. The sweetest voice. Like an angel. (*She stops for a moment.*) I used to lie awake listening to it. I used to lie awake thinking it was all right if I died. Because Vincent was an angel. A guardian angel. He'd watch over us. He'd watch over all of us.

(*Dewis takes her all the way up the stairs. They disappear above. Vince is now climbing through the porch screen onto the sofa. Bradley crashes off the sofa, holding tight to his blanket, keeping it wrapped around him. Shelly is outside on the porch. Vince holds the knife in his teeth once he gets the hole wide enough to climb through. Bradley starts crawling slowly toward his wooden leg, reaching out for it.*)

DODGE (*to Vince*): Go ahead! Take over the house! Take over the whole goddamn house! You can have it! It's

yours. It's been a pain in the neck ever since the very first mortgage. I'm gonna die any second now. Any second. You won't even notice. So I'll settle my affairs once and for all.

(*As Dodge proclaims his last will and testament, Vince climbs into the room, knife in mouth, and strides slowly around the space, inspecting his inheritance. He casually notices Bradley as he crawls toward his leg. Vince moves to the leg and keeps pushing it with his foot so that it's out of Bradley's reach, then goes on with his inspection. He picks up the roses and carries them around smelling them. Shelly can be seen outside on the porch, moving slowly center and staring in at Vince. Vince ignores her.*)

DODGE: The house goes to my Grandson, Vincent. All the furnishings, accoutrements, and paraphernalia therein. Everything tacked to the walls or otherwise resting under this roof. My tools—namely my band saw, my skill saw, my drill press, my chain saw, my lathe, my electric sander, all go to my eldest son, Tilden. That is, if he ever shows up again. My shed and gasoline powered equipment, namely my tractor, my dozer, my hand tiller plus all the attachments and riggings for the above mentioned machinery, namely my spring tooth harrow, my deep plows, my disk plows, my automatic fertilizing equipment, my reaper, my swathe, my seeder, my John Deere Harvester, my post hole digger, my jackhammer, my lathe—(*to himself*) Did I mention my lathe? I already mentioned my lathe—my Bennie Goodman records, my harnesses, my bits, my halters, my brace, my rough rasp, my forge, my welding equipment, my shoeing nails, my levels and bevels, my milking stool—no, not my milking stool—my hammers and chisels, my hinges, my cattle gates, my barbed wire, self-tapping augers, my horse hair ropes, and all related materials are to be pushed into a gigantic heap and set ablaze in the very center of my fields. When the blaze is at its highest, preferably on a cold, windless night, my body is to be pitched into the middle of it and burned till nothing remains but ash.

(*Pause. Vince takes the knife out of his mouth and smells the roses. He's facing toward audience and doesn't turn around to Shelly. He folds up knife and pockets it.*)

SHELLY (*from porch*): I'm leaving, Vince. Whether you come or not, I'm leaving.

VINCE (*smelling roses*): Just put my horn on the couch there before you take off.

SHELLY (*moving toward hole in screen*): You're not coming?

(*Vince stays downstage, turns, and looks at her.*)

VINCE: I just inherited a house.

SHELLY (*through hole, from porch*): You want to stay here?

VINCE (*as he pushes Bradley's leg out of reach*): I've gotta carry on the line. I've gotta see to it that things keep rolling.

(*Bradley looks up at him from floor, keeps pulling himself toward his leg. Vince keeps moving it.*)

SHELLY: What happened to you, Vince? You just disappeared.

VINCE (*pause, delivers speech front*): I was gonna run last night. I was gonna run and keep right on running. I drove all night. Clear to the Iowa border. The old man's two bucks sitting right on the seat beside me. It never stopped raining the whole time. Never stopped once. I could see myself in the windshield. My face. My eyes. I studied my face. Studied everything about it. As though I was looking at another man. As though I could see his whole race behind him. Like a mummy's face. I saw him dead and alive at the same time. In the same breath. In the windshield, I watched him breathe as though he was frozen in time. And every breath marked him. Marked him forever without him knowing. And then his face changed. His face became his father's face. Same bones. Same eyes. Same nose. Same breath. And his father's face changed to his grandfather's face. And it went on like that. Changing. Clear on back to faces I'd never seen before but still recognized. Still recognized the bones underneath. The eyes. The breath. The mouth. I followed my family clear into Iowa. Every last one. Straight into the Corn Belt and further. Straight back as far as they'd take me. Then it all dissolved. Everything dissolved.

(*Shelly stares at him for a while then reaches through the hole in the screen and sets the saxophone case and Vince's overcoat on the sofa. She looks at Vince again.*)

SHELLY: Bye, Vince.

(*She exits left off the porch. Vince watches her go. Bradley tries to make a lunge for his wooden leg. Vince quickly picks it up and dangles it over Bradley's head like a carrot. Bradley keeps making desperate grabs at the leg. Dewis comes down the staircase and stops halfway, staring at Vince and Bradley. Vince looks up at Dewis and smiles. He keeps moving backwards with the leg toward upstage left as Bradley crawls after him.*)

VINCE (*to Dewis as he continues torturing Bradley*): Oh, excuse me, Father. Just getting rid of some of the vermin in the house. This is my house now, ya' know? All mine. Everything. Except for the power tools and stuff. I'm gonna get all new equipment anyway. New plows, new tractor, everything. All brand new. (*Vince teases Bradley closer to the up left corner of the stage.*) Start right off on the ground floor.

(*Vince throws Bradley's wooden leg far offstage left. Bradley follows his leg offstage, pulling himself along on the ground, whimpering. As Bradley exits, Vince pulls the blanket off him and throws it over his own shoulder. He crosses toward Dewis with the blanket and smells the roses. Dewis comes to the bottom of the stairs.*)

DEWIS: You'd better go up and see your Grandmother.

VINCE (*looking up stairs, back to Dewis*): My Grandmother? There's nobody else in this house. Except for you. And you're leaving, aren't you?

(*Dewis crosses toward stage right door. He turns back to Vince.*)

DEWIS: She's going to need someone. I can't help her. I don't know what to do. I don't know what my position is. I just came in for some tea. I had no idea there was any trouble. No idea at all.

(*Vince just stares at him. Dewis goes out the door, crosses porch, and exits left. Vince listens to him leaving. He smells roses, looks up the staircase, then smells roses again. He turns and looks upstage at Dodge. He crosses up to him and bends over looking at Dodge's open eyes. Dodge is dead. His death should have come completely unnoticed by the audience. Vince covers Dodge's body with the blanket, then covers his head. He sits on the sofa, smelling roses and staring at Dodge's body. Long pause. Vince places the roses on Dodge's chest, then lays down on the sofa, arms folded behind his head, staring at the ceiling. His body is in the same relationship to Dodge's. After a while Halie's voice is heard coming from above the staircase. The lights start to dim almost imperceptively as Halie speaks. Vince keeps staring at the ceiling.*)

HALIE'S VOICE: Dodge? Is that you, Dodge? Tilden was right about the corn, you know. I've never seen such corn. Have you taken a look at it lately? Tall as a man already. This early in the year. Carrots too. Potatoes. Peas. It's like a paradise out there, Dodge. You oughta' take a look. A miracle. I've never seen it like this. Maybe the rain did something. Maybe it was the rain.

(*As Halie keeps talking offstage, Tilden appears from stage left, dripping with mud from the knees down. His arms and hands are covered with mud. In his hands he carries the corpse of a small child at chest level, staring down at it. The corpse mainly consists of bones wrapped in muddy, rotten cloth. He moves slowly downstage toward the staircase, ignoring Vince on the sofa. Vince keeps staring at the ceiling as though Tilden wasn't there. As Halie's voice continues, Tilden slowly makes his way up the stairs. His eyes never leave the corpse of the child. The lights keep fading.*)

HALIE'S VOICE: Good hard rain. Takes everything straight down deep to the roots. The rest takes care of itself. You can't force a thing to grow. You can't interfere with it. It's all hidden. It's all unseen. You just gotta wait till it pops up out of the ground. Tiny little shoot. Tiny little white shoot. All hairy and fragile. Strong though. Strong enough to break the earth even. It's a miracle, Dodge. I've never seen a crop like this in my whole life. Maybe it's the sun. Maybe that's it. Maybe it's the sun.

(*Tilden disappears above. Silence. Lights go to black.*)

Brian Friel

Born in County Tyrone, Northern Ireland, in 1929, Brian Friel has become Ireland's major playwright. His distinction has grown in recent years with dramatic successes in Ireland, London, and New York. From 1950 to 1960 he was a schoolteacher, but since 1960 he has been a full-time writer. His first well-received play was *Philadelphia, Here I Come!* (1964), which tells the story of Gar O'Donnell, who is about to emigrate to the United States from his tiny hamlet of Ballybeg, County Donegal, the village Friel generally uses for his settings. Ballybeg is tiny, depressed, unable to offer work or dignity to its young men, and those with spirit find that their choices are circumscribed by the limitations of the economy. America offers the most hope, and that is where Gar decides to go. The play captured the imagination of many Irish Americans because of their response to the theme of emigration, but it transcends ethnic concerns. In many ways it has a universal theme—the story of all young men who grow up and realize they must break with their home and set out on their own.

The Loves of Cass McGuire (1966) was first broadcast as a radio play and then produced in New York, Belfast, and London. It tells the story of an old woman whose hopes in life have been dashed by circumstances, none of which improve during the play. After demonstrating an interest in the pathos of individual lives such as those of Gar O'Donnell and Cass McGuire, Friel explored in several different directions. He showed a satirical streak in the political play *The Mundy Scheme* (1969), which focuses on a crazy plan of Irish politicians to capitalize on the Irish tradition of holding wakes for the dead. Mundy's proposal is to convert Ireland into the graveyard of all Europe, thus turning much unarable land to good account. *Freedom of the City* was produced in Dublin, London, and Chicago in 1973 and in New York the following year. It tells the story of three very different people—Michael, twenty-two, and Skinner, twenty-one, both with differing social attitudes, and Lily, forty-three, mother of eleven—who occupy the mayor's office in the Guildhall (town hall) of Derry City during a student protest march. Eventually the three discover common political ground and, through a series of unexpected incidents, find themselves facing death at the hands of surrounding soldiers.

Faith Healer (1979) ostensibly portrays a wandering man who heals people in a miraculous way. But the deep structure of the play is about art and the price that artists pay for their talent. It played in New York and London to considerable acclaim. One of the most highly regarded of Friel's plays is *Translations* (1980). Produced in Derry, London, and New York to appreciative crowds, it is set in 1833 in Baile Beg (Ballybeg) and follows the efforts of English surveyors to rename Irish places while making survey maps. These maps translate Irish place names in high-handed, arbitrary fashion. For example, the surveyors choose Burnfoot for Bun na hAbhann, which in Irish means "mouth of the river," because Burnfoot is the closest they can get to the

Irish word in English. Throughout the play Irish characters speak Irish—or at least we are to understand that they do—while the English speak English.

Much of Friel's work has concerned Irish political issues, but plays such as *Translations* are easy for non-Irish audiences to understand and appreciate. Despite its portrayal of the English as unconscious oppressors, audiences in London's National Theatre were wildly enthusiastic about it during its extensive 1981 run. *Making History* (1989), set in Elizabethan Ireland, also concerns English oppression and is part of a historical cycle of plays. Friel's *Dancing at Lughnasa* (1990) is a personal examination of a childhood in Ballybeg in the 1930s.

Brian Friel has never been an actor, but he brings to the stage a keen ear for language in the Irish tradition of William Congreve, Bernard Shaw, Oscar Wilde, Lady Gregory, John Millington Synge, Sean O'Casey, and Samuel Beckett. His characters' speeches are rich with the rhythms of everyday Irish country life and the color and metaphor of people whose joy in language is intense and satisfying. He is a member—along with critic Seamus Deane, poets Seamus Heaney and Tom Paulin, and actor Stephen Rea—of an Irish literary group called Field Day, which has its own press; publishes poetry, fiction, and drama; and has produced an ambitious three-volume anthology of Irish literature. Friel has published *Selected Stories* (1979) and *The Diviner* (1983), a book of short stories. In addition to all this, he has also translated Chekhov's *Three Sisters* (1981) and adapted Turgenev's *Fathers and Sons* (1987) for the stage. He is a towering figure in contemporary literature.

FAITH HEALER

First produced in 1979 and performed many times since, *Faith Healer* is an experimental play that explores the entire question of talent and the life of the artist. Its structure is particularly interesting because Friel places only one of his three characters on stage at a time, rather than having them interact with each other. They each face the audience with an apparent understanding and awareness that the audience is there, which is quite unlike the traditional soliloquy of Shakespeare. In Hamlet's case, he is speaking to himself alone, apparently unaware of the audience. This is one reason why we tend to accept what a Shakespearian character says in soliloquy as the absolute truth. The dramatic monologue, which Friel uses, may also be the absolute truth, but it is not an instance of a character speaking to himself. Instead, it is that age-old device of the storyteller telling us a story we will not forget. In 1979, however, the dramatic monologue was a considerable innovation.

One-person plays were common enough at the time, but they were usually bio-dramas: the story of a famous person, with the audience familiar with the events described. The technique of presenting each character in turn to tell a story that overlaps in some places but moves in different directions in other places was uncommon. Frank Hardy, the faith healer, begins the play and ends it. His wife Grace tells their story, and Teddy, the agent, describes his own experiences with Frank and Grace in a way that helps us understand the significance of their touring lives.

The play begins with a litany of strange place names—towns in Wales that, we are told, are dying away. All the names are obscure, but one repeats itself throughout the play, until it takes on a special meaning: Kinlochbervie. We learn that it was there, in a valley, with a broken-down car, that Grace gave birth to a stillborn son who is buried in a simple grave with a homemade wooden cross marker. With that child died some of Grace's hopes, and even some of Frank's. He later says he would like to have had a child and to have seen whether he or she would have had the "gift" that Frank had.

The gift at first seems to refer specifically to Frank's ability to heal the lame, the blind, and the infirm in the countryside and remote villages where people still might have enough faith in the wandering "mountebank" who promises to make the sick well simply by his glance or his touch. Grace's father, a lawyer, complains that Frank is a fraud—that his daughter is beguiled and too easily led by a cheat who will amount to nothing. Grace simply loves him, despite the brawls that she and Frank have as they travel, and despite her leaving him for a while and then returning. She tells us her story and gives us an understanding of what it is like to be with Frank as he works. She tells us how one night under a tent, ten people came, all with incurable problems, and with an act of extraordinary power, Frank Hardy healed them all. Even the polio victim got up and walked away.

However, it is Teddy, the manager, who tells us what the real gift is. Teddy begins to explain it, even though he is almost unaware of himself as he does so. He says, "Did you ever look back over all the great artists—Old Freddy [Astaire] here, Lillie Langtry, Sir Laurence Olivier, Houdini, Charlie Chaplin, Gracie Fields—and did you ever ask yourself what makes them all top-liners, what have they all got in common?" Teddy tell us that it is ambition, talent, and that they "haven't the brains to analyze it." All these figures are show people who acted on stage, and we begin to see that Friel is not just writing a play about an obscure fraud who preys on the gullible and stupid, but is writing a play about artists who involve themselves in the world of the imagination. Even Grace at one point thinks of herself as "one of his fictions," inviting us to recall Pirandello's *Six Characters in Search of an Author*. The last lines of the play consider the corporeal world that Frank seems about to leave as nothing more than "mere imaginings," but they are the imaginings of an artist who, like Frank, has a talent that sometimes produces extraordinary successes, virtual miracles.

Friel, an Irish playwright, has the Irish Frank Hardy and the Irish Grace Hardy act as the talent and the nurturer of talent, whereas Teddy the businessman is English. At one point Teddy complains that in court he is the only authentic Englishman, and he resents the fact that he has to repeat his words slowly so that the Irish court can understand him. This play is not a political play—one of the few of Friel's plays that are not. But his English/Irish sensibilities are still apparent.

The one thing that Teddy tells us is that talent is ruined by brains. A quality that all artists have is that "not one of them has two brains to rub together." By this he does not mean that they are ignorant, but rather that they do not think about their talent; they neither analyze it nor try to understand it. They simply express it. And the life of the artist, as we can see from Frank's experience, is painful because one's talent is not always evident, and especially in the theater, one's talent may not be enough for success. The talented artist can suffer terrible losses, as we learn from Grace's experience at Kinlochbervie.

Faith Healer in Performance

The premier in New York's Longacre Theatre with James Mason as Frank was essentially a failure. José Quintero directed, and the production closed after twenty performances. Most reviewers were puzzled by the fact that the play was composed of four monologues that did not seem to support each other's stories. They felt that James Mason, who had not acted on stage in thirty-two years, was wrong for the part. The London Royal Court Theatre production in 1981 starred Patrick Magee as Frank and Helen Mirren as Grace. One reviewer praised Magee, saying, "the result is a performance that combines all Magee's baleful black Irish authority." But critics did not feel Mirren's performance was adequate. In 1983 in the intimate Vineyard Theater, an off-Broadway house in New York, with J. T. Walsh as Frank, the play began to impress reviewers as something important. Donal McCann and Sinead Cusack played in the 1992 Royal Court production using a stage that was bare and simple — like most earlier productions, almost emulating the "poor theater" aesthetic. By this time, reviewers began to see that the play was not about religion or politics but about "the tortured process of creativity itself." Joe Dowling directed the 1994 production at the Long Wharf Theatre in New Haven with Donal McCann, Judy Geeson, and Ron Cook. The production was riveting, with the audience mesmerized by the brilliance of Friel's language and by the complexity of the story being told. A 2006 production in Dublin at the Gate Theatre starred Ralph Fiennes as Frank and Cherry Jones as Grace. Fiennes brought the play to Broadway's Booth Theatre, where it ran for 136 performances. It seems to have taken twenty-five years or so for critics to catch up to Brian Friel.

Brian Friel *(b. 1929)*

FAITH HEALER   *1979*

Characters

FRANK
GRACE
TEDDY

Note: Stage directions have been kept to a minimum. In all four parts the director will decide when and where the monologist sits, walks, stands, etc.

Part One • Frank

The stage is in darkness. Brief pause.
    Then out of this darkness comes Frank's incantation, "Aberarder, Aberayron. . . ." At the end of the second line bring up lights very slowly, first around him and then gradually on the whole set. Throughout this opening incantation he is standing downstage left, feet

together, his face tilted upwards, his eyes shut tight, his hands in his overcoat pockets, his shoulders hunched.

He is middle-aged; gray or graying; pale, lined face. The overcoat is unbuttoned, the collar up at the back; either navy or black, and of heavy-nap material; a good coat once but now shabby, stained, slept-in. Underneath he is wearing a dark suit that is polished with use; narrow across the shoulders; sleeves and legs too short. A soiled white shirt. A creased tie. Vivid green socks.

Three rows of chairs—not more than fifteen seats in all—occupy one-third of the acting area stage left. These seats are at right angles to the audience.

On the backdrop is a large poster:

THE FANTASTIC FRANCIS HARDY
FAITH HEALER
ONE NIGHT ONLY

This poster is made of some fabric, linen perhaps, and is soiled and abused.

FRANK (*eyes closed*):

Aberarder, Aberayron,
Llangranog, Llangurig,
Abergorlech, Abergynolwyn,
Llandefeilog, Llanerchymedd,
Aberhosan, Aberporth . . .

All those dying Welsh villages. (*Eyes open.*) I'd get so tense before a performance, d'you know what I used to do? As we drove along those narrow, winding roads I'd recite the names to myself just for the mesmerism, the sedation, of the incantation—

Kinlochbervie, Inverbervie,
Inverdruie, Invergordon,
Badachroo, Kinlochewe,
Ballantrae, Inverkeithing,
Cawdor, Kirkconnel,
Plaidy, Kirkinner . . .

Welsh—Scottish—over the years they became indistinguishable. The kirks or meeting-houses or schools—all identical, all derelict. Maybe in a corner a withered sheaf of wheat from a harvest thanksgiving of years ago or a fragment of a Christmas decoration across a window—relics of abandoned rituals. Because the people we moved among were beyond that kind of celebration.

Hardly ever cities or towns because the halls were far too dear for us. Seldom England because Teddy and Gracie were English and they believed, God help them, that the Celtic temperament was more receptive to us. And never Ireland because of me—

I beg your pardon—The *Fantastic Francis Hardy, Faith Healer, One Night Only.* (*A slight bow.*) The man on the tatty banner.

(*He takes off his overcoat, selects an end chair from one of the rows, and throws the coat across it. This chair and coat will be in the same position at the opening of Part Four.*)

When we started out—oh, years and years ago—we used to have *Francis Hardy, Seventh Son of a Seventh Son* across the top. But it made the poster too expensive and Teddy persuaded me to settle for the modest "fantastic." It was a favorite word of his and maybe in this case he employed it with accuracy. As for the Seventh Son—that was a lie. I was in fact the only child of elderly parents, Jack and Mary Hardy, born in the village of Kilmeedy in County Limerick where my father was sergeant of the guards. But that's another story . . .

The initials were convenient, weren't they? FH—Faith Healer. Or if you were a believer in fate, you might say my life was determined the day I was christened. Perhaps if my name had been Charles Potter I would have been . . . Cardinal Primate; or Patsy Muldoon, the Fantastic Prime Minister. No, I don't mock those things. By no means. I'm not respectful but I don't mock.

Faith healer—faith healing. A craft without an apprenticeship, a ministry without responsibility, a vocation without a ministry. How did I get involved? As a young man I chanced to flirt with it and it possessed me. No, no, no, no, no—that's rhetoric. No; let's say I did it . . . because I could do it. That's accurate enough. And occasionally it worked—oh, yes, occasionally it *did* work. Oh, yes. And when it did, when I stood before a man and placed my hands on him and watched him become whole in my presence, those were nights of exultation, of consummation—no, not that I was doing good, giving relief, spreading joy—good God, no, nothing at all to do with that; but because the questions that undermined my life then became meaningless and because I knew that for those few hours I had become whole in myself, and perfect in myself, and in a manner of speaking, an aristocrat, if the term doesn't offend you.

But the questionings, the questionings . . . They began modestly enough with the pompous struttings of a young man: *Am I endowed with a unique and awesome gift?*—my God, yes, I'm afraid so. And I suppose the other extreme was *Am I a con man?*—which of course was nonsense, I think. And between those absurd exaggerations the possibilities were legion. Was it all chance?—or skill?—or illusion?—or delusion? Precisely what power did I possess? Could I summon it? When and how? Was I its servant? Did it reside in my ability to invest someone with faith in me or did I evoke from him a healing faith in himself? Could my healing be effected without faith? But faith in what?—in me?—in the possibility?—faith in faith? And is the power diminishing? You're beginning to masquerade, aren't you? You're becoming a husk, aren't you? And so it went on and on and on. Silly, wasn't it? Considering that nine times out of ten nothing at all happened. But they persisted right to the end, those nagging, tormenting, maddening questions that rotted my life. When I refused to confront them, they ambushed me. And when they threatened to submerge me, I silenced them with whiskey. That was efficient for a while. It got me through the job night after night. And when nothing happened or when something did happen, it helped me to accept that. But I can tell you this: there was one thing I did know, one thing I always knew right from the beginning—I always knew, drunk or sober, I always knew when nothing was going to happen.

Teddy. Yes, let me tell you about Teddy, my manager. Cockney. Buoyant. Cheerful. Tiny nimble feet. Dressed in cord jacket, bow-tie, greasy velour hat. I never knew much about his background except that he had been born into show business. And I never understood why he stayed with me because we barely scraped a living. But he had a devotion to me and I think he had a vague sense of being associated with something . . . spiritual and that gave him satisfaction. If you met him in a bar he'd hold you with those brown eyes of his. "I've 'andled some of *the* most sensational properties in my day, dear 'eart, believe me. But I've threw 'em all up for Mr 'ardy 'ere, 'cos 'e is just the most fantastic fing you've ever seen." And listening to him I'd almost forget what indeed he had given up to tour with us—a Miss Mulatto and Her Three Pigeons, and a languid whippet called Rob Roy who took sounds from a set of bagpipes. Humbling precedents, if I were given to pride. And he believed all along and right up to the end that somewhere one day something "fantastic" was going to happen to us. "Believe me, dear 'eart," perhaps when we had barely enough petrol to take us to the next village, "believe me, we are on the point of making a killing." He was a romantic man. And when he talked about this killing, I had a fairy-tale image of us being summoned to some royal bedroom and learned doctors being pushed aside and I'd raise the sleeping princess to life and we'd be wined and dined for seven days and seven nights and sent on our way with bags of sovereigns. But he was a man of many disguises. Perhaps he wasn't romantic. Perhaps he knew that's what I'd think. Perhaps he was a much more perceptive man than I knew.

And there was Grace, my mistress. A Yorkshire woman. Controlled, correct, methodical, orderly. Who fed me, washed and ironed for me, nursed me, humored me. Saved me, I'm sure, from drinking myself to death. Would have attempted to reform me because that was her nature, but didn't because her instincts were wiser than her impulses. Grace Dodsmith from Scarborough—or was it Knaresborough? I don't remember, they all sound so alike it doesn't matter. She never asked for marriage and for all her tidiness I don't think she wanted marriage—her loyalty was adequate for her. And it was never a heady relationship, not even in the early days. But it lasted. A surviving relationship. And yet as we grew older together I thought it wouldn't. Because that very virtue of hers—that mulish, unquestioning, indefatigable loyalty—settled on us like a heavy dust. And nothing I did, neither my bitterness nor my deliberate neglect nor my blatant unfaithfulness, could disturb it.

We'd arrive in the van usually in the early evening. Pin up the poster. Arrange the chairs and benches. Place a table inside the door for the collection. Maybe sweep the place out. Gracie'd make tea on the primus stove. Teddy'd try out his amplifying system. I'd fortify myself with some drink. Then we'd wait. And wait. And as soon as darkness fell, a few would begin to sidle in—

Penllech, Pencader,
Dunvegan, Dunblane,
Ben Lawers, Ben Rinnes,
Kirkliston, Bennane . . .

Teddy and his amplifying system: I fought with him about it dozens of times and finally gave in to him. Our row was over what he called "atmospheric background music." When the people would have gathered Teddy would ask them—he held the microphone up to his lips and assumed a special, reverential tone—he'd ask them to stay in their seats while I moved among them. "Everybody'll be attended to, dear 'eart. Relax. Take it easy. And when Mr 'ardy gets to you, no need to tell 'im wot's bovvering you—Mr 'ardy knows. Just trust 'im. Put yourself in 'is 'ands. And God bless you all. And

Ralph Fiennes as Frank Hardy, the faith healer, in the 2006 production at the Gate Theatre, Dublin.

now, dear 'eart—Mr 'ardy, Faif 'ealer!" At which point I'd emerge—and at the same moment Teddy'd put on his record.

And as I'd move from seat to seat, among the crippled and the blind and the disfigured and the deaf and the barren, a voice in the style of the thirties crooned Jerome Kern's song:

> Lovely, never, never change,
> Keep that breathless charm,
> Won't you please arrange it,
> 'Cause I love you
> Just the way you look tonight.

Yes; we were always balanced somewhere between the absurd and the momentous.

(*Moving through seats*) And the people who came—what is there to say about them? They were a despairing people. That they came to me, a mountebank, was a measure of their despair. They seldom spoke. Sometimes didn't even raise their eyes. They just sat there, very still, assuming that I divined their complaints. Abject. Abased. Tight. Longing to open themselves and at the same time fearfully herding the anguish they contained against disturbance. And they hated me—oh, yes, yes, yes, they hated me. Because by coming to me they exposed, publicly acknowledged, their desperation. And even though they told themselves they were here because of the remote possibility of a cure, they knew in their hearts they had come not to be cured but for confirmation that they were incurable; not in hope but for the elimination of hope; for the removal of that final, impossible chance—that's why they came—to seal their anguish, for the content of a finality.

And they knew that I knew. And so they defied me to endow them with hopelessness. But I couldn't do even that for them. And they knew I couldn't. A peculiar situation, wasn't it? No, not peculiar—eerie. Because occasionally, just occasionally, the miracle would happen. And then—panic—panic—panic! Their ripping apart! The explosion of their careful calculations! The sudden flooding of dreadful, hopeless hope! I often thought it would have been a kindness to them not to go near them.

And there was another thing about them. When Teddy was introducing me, I would look at them and sometimes I got a strange sense that they weren't there on their own behalf at all but as delegates, *legati*,° chosen because of their audacity; and that outside, poised, mute, waiting in the half-light, were hundreds of people who held their breath while we were in the locality. And I sometimes got the impression, too, that if we hadn't come to them, they would have sought us out.

We were in the north of Scotland when I got word that my mother had had a heart attack. In a village called Kinlochbervie, in Sutherland, about as far

---

legati: Roman ambassadors sent to foreign countries.

north as you can go in Scotland. A picturesque little place, very quiet, very beautiful, looking across to the Isle of Lewis in the Outer Hebrides; and we were enjoying a few days rest there. Anyhow, when the news came, Teddy drove me down to Glasgow. Gracie wanted to come with me and couldn't understand when I wouldn't take her. But she used her incomprehension as fuel for her loyalty and sent me off with a patient smile.

It was my first time home in twenty years. My father had retired and was living in a housing estate outside Dublin. When he opened the door he didn't recognize me—I had to tell him who I was. Then he shook my hand as if I were an acquaintance and led me up to the bedroom.

She was exactly as I remembered her—illness hadn't ravaged her. Sleeping silently. Her skin smooth and girlish, her chin raised as if in expectation. Jesus, I thought, O my Jesus, what am I going to do?

"She looks nice," he said.

"Yes," I said. "She looks great."

He cleared his throat.

"She passed away quietly. You missed her by approximately one hour and ten minutes," as if he were giving evidence. And then he cried.

And I felt such overwhelming relief that when he cried, I cried easily with him.

Twelve years later I was back in Ireland again; with Teddy and Gracie. Things had been lean for a long time. Or as Teddy put it, "If we want to eat, we've got to open up new territory, dear 'eart. You've cured 'em all 'ere. Come on—let's go to the lush pickings of Ireland." And I agreed because I was as heartsick of Wales and Scotland as they were. And the whiskey wasn't as efficient with the questions as it had been. And my father had died in the meantime. And I suppose because I always knew we would end up there. So on the last day of August we crossed from Stranraer to Larne and drove through the night to County Donegal. And there we got lodgings in a pub, a lounge bar, really, outside a village called Ballybeg, not far from Donegal Town.

There was no sense of home-coming. I tried to simulate it but nothing stirred. Only a few memories, wan and neutral. One of my father watching me through the bars of the dayroom window as I left for school—we lived in a rented house across the street. One of playing with handcuffs, slipping my hands in and out through the rings. One of my mother making bread and singing a hymn to herself. "Yes, heaven, yes, heaven, yes, heaven is the prize." And one of a group of men being shown over the barracks—I think they were inspectors from Dublin—and my father saying, "Certainly, gentlemen, by all means, gentlemen, anything you say, gentlemen." Maybe one or two other memories. They evoked nothing.

When we came downstairs to the lounge in the pub we got caught up in the remnants of a wedding party—four young men, locals, small farmers, whose friend had just gone off on his honeymoon a few hours earlier. Good suits. White carnations. Dark, angular faces. Thick fingers and black nails. For a while they pretended to ignore us. Then Ned, the biggest of them, asked bluntly who we were and what we were. Teddy told them. "Dear 'eart . . . the . . . most . . . sensational . . . fantastic." And either at the extravagance of the introduction or because of an unease they suddenly exploded with laughter and we were embraced. We formed a big circle and drank and chatted. Gracie sang—"Ilkley Moor"?—something like that. Teddy entertained them with tales of our tours ranging from the outrageous to the maudlin and ended with his brown eyes moist with tears: "Dear 'earts, the insights it 'as given me into tortured 'umanity." And I told myself that I was indeed experiencing a home-coming. All irony was suspended.

Then suddenly a man called Donal who had scarcely spoken up to this thrust a bent finger in front of my face and challenged, "Straighten that, Mr Hardy." And the bar went still.

I caught the finger between the palms of my hands and held it there and looked into his face. Already he was uneasy—he wanted to withdraw the challenge. He began to stammer how the accident happened— something about a tractor, a gearbox, a faulty setting. And as he spoke I massaged the finger. And when he stopped talking I opened my hands and released him. The finger was whole . . .

> Badrallach, Kilmore,
> Llanfaethlu, Llanfechell,
> Kincardine, Kinross,
> Loughcarron, Lougligelly . . .

We caroused right through the night. Toasts to the landlord who claimed he met my father once and as the night went on that they were close friends. Toasts to Teddy and Gracie. Toasts to my return. To Donal's finger. Toasts to the departed groom and his prowess. To the bride and her fertility. To the rich harvest— the corn, the wheat, the barley. Toasts to all Septembers and all harvests and to all things ripe and eager for the reaper. A Dionysian night. A Bacchanalian° night. A frenzied, excessive Irish night when ritual was consciously and relentlessly debauched.

Then sometime before dawn McGarvey was remembered. Their greatest, their closest friend McGarvey who in his time had danced with them and drunk with them and built roads with them and cut turf with them. McGarvey who ought to have been best man that day—my God, who else?—and who wasn't even at the wedding reception. And as they created him I saw McGarvey in my mind, saw his strained face and his mauve hands and his burning eyes, crouched in his wheelchair and sick with bitterness. Saw him and knew him before Teddy in

---

Dionysian . . . Bacchanalian: Dionysus and Bacchus are names for the god of wine.

his English innocence asked why he wasn't there; before Ned told us of the fall from the scaffolding and the paralysis. Saw him and recognized our meeting: an open place, a walled yard, trees, orange skies, warm wind. And knew, knew with cold certainty that nothing was going to happen. Nothing at all.

I stood at the window and watched them set off to fetch McGarvey. Four of them getting into a battered car; now serious and busy with good deeds; now being polite to one another, holding doors open, you sit in front, no you, no you. Then they were gone, the car sluggish under their weight.

Teddy lay slumped in a stupor in a corner. Gracie went round the tables, emptying ashtrays, gathering glasses and leaving them on the counter, straightening chairs. No intimation whatever of danger. I suggested she should go to bed and she went off. Why wouldn't she?—the housework was finished.

(He comes right down, walking very slowly, until he is as close as he can be to the audience. Pause.)

The first Irish tour! The great home-coming! The new beginning! It was all going to be so fantastic! And there I am, pretending to subscribe to the charade. *(He laughs.)* Yes; the restoration of Francis Hardy. *(Laughs again.)*

But we'll come to that presently. Or as Teddy would have put it: Why don't we leave that until later, dear 'eart? Why don't we do that? Why not? Indeed.

(He looks at the audience for about three seconds. Then quick black.)

Part Two • Grace

We discover Grace Hardy on stage, the same set as Part One, with the rows of seats removed. She is sitting on a wooden chair beside a small table on which are ashtrays, packets of cigarettes, the remains of a bottle of whiskey, a glass.

She is in early middle age. Indifferent to her appearance and barely concealing her distraught mental state. Smoking a lot—sometimes lighting one cigarette from the other.

GRACE *(eyes closed)*:
> Aberarder, Aberayron,
> Llangranog, Llangurig,
> Abergorlech, Abergynolwyn,
> Penllech, Pencader,
> Llandefeilog, Llanerchymedd . . .

That most persistent of all the memories, *(Eyes open.)* that most persistent and most agonizing—

But I *am* getting stronger, I *am* becoming more controlled—I'm sure I am. I measure my progress— a silly index, I know, and he would certainly have scoffed at it—but I can almost measure my progress by the number of hours I sleep and the amount I drink and the number of cigarettes I smoke. And, as they say, I've a lot to be thankful for; I know I have. And I like living in London. And the bedsitter's small but it's warm and comfortable. And it's a pleasant walk to the library in Paddington where I work four hours every morning. And on my way home, if the day's fine, I usually go through the park. And at night I listen to the radio or I read—oh, I read a lot—fiction, romance, history, biography, whatever I take home with me, whatever's handy; and I've begun to make a rug for the hearth—I'll do a bit at that or maybe I'll try a new recipe or read the paper or knit or—or—And on Thursday afternoons I go to the doctor to get my pills renewed. He said to me last week, he said to me, "Of course you've had a traumatic experience, Mrs Hardy; absolutely horrific. But it's over—finished with. And you've really got to be stern with yourself. You were a solicitor once, weren't you? Well, what you must do now is bring the same mental rigour, the same discipline to your recovery that you once brought to a legal case." And he looked so pleased with his analogy and so clean and so pleasant and so efficient and, yes, so innocent, sitting there behind his desk with his grey suit and his college tie and his clear eyes and his gold pen poised, and he meant so well and he was so patient and it was all so simple for him; and I found myself nodding yes, yes, yes to him, yes, yes; and I thought: That's how you used to nod to Frank, too, especially in that last year—yes, yes, yes, Frank, you know you can, Frank, I swear you can—but he's watching me warily—nothing was simple for him—he's watching me and testing me with his sly questions and making his own devious deductions, probing my affirmations for the hair-crack, tuned for the least hint of excess or uncertainty, but all the same, all the same drawing sustenance from me—oh, yes, I'm sure of that—finding some kind of sustenance in me—I'm absolutely sure of that, because finally he drained me, finally I was exhausted.

But I *am* making progress. And I suppose what I really mean by that is that there are certain restricted memories that I can invite now, that I can open myself fully to, like a patient going back to solids. I can think about the night the old farmer outside Cardiff gave him £200 for curing his limp—just handed him his wallet—and we booked into the Royal Abercorn and for four nights we lived like kings. And the weekend we spent one Easter walking in the Grampian mountains. I can think about that; yes, memories like that I can receive and respond to them. Because they *were* part of our lives together. But then as soon as I begin to open under them, just as soon as it seems that I'm beginning to come together again—

(*Eyes closed tight.*)

Abergorlech, Abergynolwyn,
Llandefeilog, Llanerchymedd,
Aberhosan, Aberporth . . .

It's winter, it's night, it's raining, the Welsh roads are narrow, we're on our way to a performance. (*Eyes open.*) He always called it a performance, teasing the word with that mocking voice of his—"Where do I perform tonight?" "Do you expect a performance in a place like this?"—as if it were a game he might take part in only if he felt like it, maybe because that was the only way he could talk about it. Anyhow Teddy's driving as usual, and I'm in the passenger seat, and he's immediately behind us, the Fantastic Francis Hardy, Faith Healer, with his back to us and the whiskey bottle between his legs, and he's squatting on the floor of the van—no, not squatting—crouched, wound up, concentrated, and happy—no, not happy, certainly not happy, I don't think he ever knew what happiness was—but always before a performance he'd be . . . in complete mastery—yes, that's close to it—in such complete mastery that everything is harmonized for him, in such mastery that anything is possible. And when you speak to him he turns his head and looks beyond you with those damn benign eyes of his, looking past you out of his completion, out of that private power, out of that certainty that was accessible only to him. God, how I resented that privacy! And he's reciting the names of all those dying Welsh villages—Aberarder, Aberayron, Llangranog, Llangurig—releasing them from his mouth in that special voice he used only then, as if he were blessing them or consecrating himself. And then, for him, I didn't exist. Many, many, many times I didn't exist for him. But before a performance this exclusion—no, it wasn't an exclusion, it was an erasion—this erasion was absolute: he obliterated me. Me who tended him, humored him, nursed him, sustained him—who debauched myself for him. Yes. That's the most persistent memory. Yes. And when I remember him like that in the back of the van, God how I hate him again—

Kinlochbervie, Inverbervie,
Inverdruie, Invergordon,
Badachroo, Kinlochewe,
Ballantrae, Inverkeithing,
Cawdor, Kirkconnel,
Plaidy, Kirkinner . . .

(*Quietly, almost dreamily*) Kinlochbervie's where the baby's buried, two miles south of the village, in a field on the left-hand side of the road as you go north. Funny, isn't it, but I've never met anybody who's been to Kinlochbervie, not even Scottish people. But it *is* a very small village and very remote, right away up in the north of Sutherland, about as far north as you can go in Scotland. And the people there told me that in good weather it is very beautiful and that you can see right across the sea to the Isle of Lewis in the Outer Hebrides. We just happened to be there and we were never back there again and the week that we were there it rained all the time, not really rained but a heavy wet mist so that you could scarcely see across the road. But I'm sure it is a beautiful place in good weather. Anyhow, that's where the baby's buried, in Kinlochbervie, in Sutherland, in the north of Scotland. Frank made a wooden cross to mark the grave and painted it white and wrote across it *Infant Child of Francis and Grace Hardy*—no name, of course, because it was still-born—just *Infant Child*. And I'm sure that cross is gone by now because it was a fragile thing and there were cows in the field and it wasn't a real cemetery anyway. And I had the baby in the back of the van and there was no nurse or doctor so no one knew anything about it except Frank and Teddy and me. And there was no clergyman at the graveside—Frank just said a few prayers that he made up. So there is no record of any kind. And he never talked about it afterwards; never once mentioned it again; and because he didn't, neither did I. So that was it. Over and done with. A finished thing. Yes. But I think it's a nice name, Kinlochbervie—a complete sound—a name you wouldn't forget easily . . . (*Tense again.*) God, he was such a twisted man! With such a talent for hurting. One of his mean tricks was to humiliate me by always changing my surname. It became Dodsmith or Elliot or O'Connell or McPherson—whatever came into his head; and I came from Yorkshire or Kerry or London or Scarborough or Belfast; and he had cured me of a blood disease; and we weren't married—I was his mistress—always that—that was the one constant: "You haven't met Gracie McClure, have you? She's my mistress," knowing so well that that would wound me and it always did; it shouldn't have; I should have become so used to it; but it always did. And Teddy—Teddy wasn't just a fit-up man who was always in trouble with the police for pilfering but a devoted servant, dedicated acolyte to the holy man. It wasn't that he was simply a liar— I never understood it—yes, I knew that he wanted to hurt me, but it was much more complex than that; it was some compulsion he had to adjust, to refashion, to re-create everything around him. Even the people who came to him—they weren't just sick people who were confused and frightened and wanted to be cured; no, no; to him they were . . . yes, they were real enough, but not real as persons, real as fictions, his fictions, extensions of himself that came into being only because of him. And if he cured a man, that man became for him a successful fiction and therefore actually real, and he'd say to me afterwards, "Quite an interesting character that, wasn't he? I knew that would work." But if he didn't cure him, the man was forgotten immediately, allowed to dissolve and vanish as if he had never existed. Even his father, and if he loved anyone he loved his father, even he was constantly re-created, even after his death. He was in fact a storeman in a factory in Limerick—I met him once, a nice old man; but Frank wasn't content with that—he made him a stonemason and a gardener and a bus-driver and a guard and a musician. It was as if—and I'm groping

Cherry Jones as Grace in the 2006 production of *Faith Healer* at the Booth Theatre, New York.

at this—but it seemed to me that he kept remaking people according to some private standard of excellence of his own, and as his standards changed, so did the person. But I'm sure it was always an excellence, a perfection, that was the cause of his restlessness and the focus of it.

We were in Wales when he got word of his father's death. He went home alone. And when he came back he spoke of the death as if it had been his mother's. "She passed away quietly," he said. "I don't know how father'll manage without her." And the point was his mother had been dead for years when I first met him. Oh, he was a convoluted man.

The first day I went to the doctor, he was taking down all the particulars and he said to me, "And what was your late husband's occupation, Mrs Hardy?" "He was an artist," I said—quickly— casually—but with complete conviction—just the way he might have said it. Wasn't that curious? Because the thought had never occurred to me before. And then because I said it and the doctor wrote it down, I knew it was true . . .

I left him once. Yes; I left *him*! Up and left. God,

when I think of it! We'd been married seven years at the time, and within that twelve months I'd had a pleurisy and then two miscarriages in quick succession and I suppose I was feeling very sorry for myself. And we'd been living that winter in a derelict cottage in Norfolk miles from anyone—it was really a converted byre.° I remember kneeling before a tiny grate and crying because the timber was so wet the fire wouldn't light, and trying to get to sleep on a damp mattress on the floor. Anyway we'd had a fight about something silly; and I must have been very depressed or suddenly worked myself up into a stupid panic because on some mad impulse I tore a page off an old calendar and wrote on the back of it, "Dear Frank I'm leaving you because I cannot endure the depravity of our lives any longer do not follow me I love you deeply Grace." Wasn't it awful! "I love you deeply"—to a man like that. And "Do not follow me"—do not follow me!—God, I had some kind of innocence then!

Anyhow I went home. For the first time and the last time. I got the night-crossing from Glasgow and then the bus to Omagh and walked the three miles out to Knockmoyle. I remember I stood at the gates for a while and looked up the long straight avenue flanked with tall straight poplars, across the lawn, beyond the formal Japanese garden and into the chaotic vegetable plot where my mother messed about and devoted her disturbed life to. It was Bridie, the housekeeper, who reared me; and mother in her headscarf and wellingtons was a strange woman who went in and out of the mental hospital.

Father was in the breakfast-room, in a wicker chair beside a huge fire, with a rug around his knees and his head slightly forward and staring straight in front of him just as he did when he was on the bench and hectoring a defendant. The stroke had spared his features and he looked so distinguished with his patrician face and his white hair perfectly groomed and his immaculate grey suit.

And I knocked on the table so that I wouldn't startle him and I said, "It's me, Father. It's Grace."

"What's that? Speak up!"

And I could hear old Bridie moving about the kitchen and I was afraid she'd hear me and come up and throw her arms around me before I'd have a chance to kiss him over and over again and say sorry and tell him how often I thought about him.

I moved round so that I was directly in front of him.

"It's Grace, Father."

"Yes? Yes?"

"Grace—Gracie."

"Raise your voice. You're mumbling."

"Timmikins," I said—that's what he used to call me when I was a child.

"Who?"

"Timmikins," I said again.

byre: A cow barn.

"I know who it is," he said.

"I came home to see you," I said.

He gazed at me for a long, long time. And his mouth opened and shut but no sound came. And then finally and suddenly the words and the remembrance came together for him.

"You ran off with the mountebank." And he wasn't accusing—all he wanted was corroboration.

"Frank and I got married," I said.

"Yes, you ran off with the mountebank just after you qualified. And you killed your mother—you know that. But I told her you'd be back. Six months, I said; give her six months and she'll come crawling back."

I was crouching in front of him and holding his cold hands and our faces so close that I could smell his breath.

"Father," I said, "Father, listen—"

But words were now spilling out of him, not angry words but the tired formula words of the judge sentencing me to nine months in jail but suspending the sentence because he understood I came from a professional family with a long and worthy record of public service and hoping that I would soon regret and atone for the blemish I had brought on that family and on my own profession and threatening that if I ever appeared before him again he would have no option but to send me to jail and impose the maximum penalty et cetera, et cetera, et cetera.

And as I watched him and listened to him and felt the darts of his spittle on my face, I had an impulse—and I thank God I resisted it—a calm, momentary impulse to do an ugly, shameful thing: I wanted to curse him—no, not curse him—assault and defile him with obscenities and to articulate them slowly and distinctly and brutally into his patrician face; words he never used; a language he didn't speak; a language never heard in that house. But even in his confusion he'd understand it and recognize it as the final rejection of his tall straight poplars and the family profession and his formal Japanese gardens. But more important, much, much more important, recognize it as my proud testament to my mountebank and the van and the wet timber and the primus stove and the dirty halls and everything he'd call squalor. But thank God I didn't do that. Instead—and he was still sentencing me—I just walked away. And I never saw him again. And he died before the year was over. And the next night I was back in the Norfolk byre, back on the damp mattress and kissing Frank's face and shoulders and chest and telling him how sorry I was; and he's drunk and giving me his sly smile and saying little. And then I was pregnant again and this time I held on to it for the full time. And that was the black-faced, macerated baby that's buried in a field in Kinlochbervie in Sutherland in the north of Scotland—

Badrallach, Kilmore,
Llanfaethlu, Llanfechell,
Kincardine, Kinross,
Loughcarron, Lougligelly . . .

(*At banner*) Faith healer—faith healing—I never understood it, never. I tried to. In the beginning I tried diligently—as the doctor might say I brought all my mental rigor to bear on it. But I couldn't even begin to apprehend it—this gift, this craft, this talent, this art, this magic—whatever it was he possessed, that defined him, that was, I suppose, essentially him. And because it was his essence and because it eluded me I suppose I *was* wary of it. Yes, of course I was. And he knew it. Indeed, if by some miracle Frank could have been the same Frank without it, I would happily have robbed him of it. And he knew that, too—how well he knew that; and in his twisted way read into it the ultimate treachery on my part. So what I did was, I schooled myself—I tried to school myself—to leave it to him and him with it and be content to be outside them. And for a time that seemed to work for both of us: we observed the neutrality of the ground between us. But as time went on and particularly in the last few years when he became more frantic and more truculent, he began to interpret my remove as resentment, even as hostility, or he pretended he did—you could never be sure with him—and he insisted on dragging me into feud between himself and his talent. And then we would snarl and lunge and grapple at one another and things were said that should never have been said and that lay afterwards on our lives like slow poison. When his talent was working for him, the aggression wasn't quite so bitter—after he'd cured someone he'd be satisfied just to flaunt himself, to taunt me: "And what does the legal mind make of all that? Just a con, isn't it? Just an illusion, isn't it?" And I'd busy myself putting away the chairs or taking down the banner. But when he couldn't perform—and in those last two years that became more and more frequent, the more desperate he became—then he'd go for me with bared teeth as if I were responsible and he'd scream at me, "You were at your very best tonight, Miss O'Dwyer, weren't you? A great night for the law, wasn't it? You vengeful, spiteful bitch." And I'd defend myself. And we'd tear one another apart.

As soon as we'd open the doors, that's where I'd take my seat, at a table if there was one, or if there wasn't, with a tray on my knee; because sometimes they'd pay on their way in, now and again far more than they could afford, I suppose in the hope that somehow it would sweeten Frank to them. And that's where I'd sit all through the performance and collect whatever they'd leave on the way out.

And when they'd all be seated—"all"! Many a time we were lucky to have half a dozen—then Teddy'd put on the record, a worn-out hissing, version of a song called "The Way You Look Tonight." I begged Frank to get something else, anything else. But he wouldn't. It had to be that. "I like it," he'd say, "and it confuses them."

Then Teddy'd come out and make his announcement.

And then Frank would appear.

I wish you could have seen him. It wasn't that he was a handsome man. He wasn't really. But when he came out before those people and moved among them and touched them—even though he was often half drunk—he had a special . . . magnificence. And I'd sit there and watch him and I'd often find myself saying to myself, "Oh you lucky woman." Oh, yes, oh, indeed, yes.

(*She sits and pours a drink.*)

I didn't want to come back to Ireland. Neither did Teddy. But he insisted. He had been in bad shape for months and although he didn't say it—he would never have said it—I knew he had some sense that Ireland might somehow recharge him, maybe even restore him. Because in that last year he seemed to have lost touch with his gift. And of course he was drinking too much and missing performances and picking fights with strangers—cornering someone in a pub and boasting that he could perform miracles and having people laugh at him; or else lying in the back of the van—we lived in it most of the time now—lying in the van and not speaking or eating for days.

But the real trouble was the faith healing. It wasn't that he didn't try—I suppose trying hadn't much to do with it anyway—but he tried too hard, he tried desperately, and usually nothing happened, nothing at all. I remember, just a few weeks before we came back, he met an old woman in an off-licence in Kilmarnock and he told her he could cure her arthritis. And he tried. And he failed. In the old days he wouldn't have given her another thought; but he became obsessed with that old woman, found out where she lived, went to her house again and again until finally her son-in-law threw him out and threatened to get the police for him.

So on the last day of August we crossed from Stranraer to Larne and drove through the night to County Donegal. And there we got lodgings in a pub, a lounge bar, really, outside a village called Ballybeg, not far from Donegal Town. (*She moves again.*) And the strange thing was that night began so well. I remember watching him and thinking: Yes, his sense was true, he is going to be restored here—he was so easy and so relaxed and so charming, and there was nobody more charming than him when he wanted to be. I could tell even by the way he was drinking—not gulping down the first three or four drinks as if they were only preliminaries. And he chatted to the landlord and they talked about the harvest and about fishing and about the tourist trade. He even introduced me as his wife—God, I suppose that ought to have alerted me.

And there was a group of young men in the lounge, five of them, local men on their way home from their friend's wedding; and one of them, the youngest of them, was in a wheelchair. And they were sitting in a corner by themselves and you could tell they wanted to be left alone. And when I saw him go over to them I had a second of unease. But whatever it was he said to them, they smiled and shook hands with him and moved into the center of the lounge and he called me over and we all sat round in a big circle and one of them ordered a drink and the landlord joined us and we just sat there and chatted and laughed and told stories and sang songs. Where was Teddy? (*remembering*) Yes, he was there, too, just outside the circle, slightly drunk and looking a bit bewildered. And it began as such a happy night—yes, happy, happy, happy! The young men were happy. I was happy. And Frank—yes, yes, I know he was happy too. And then out of the blue—we were talking about gambling—Frank suddenly leaned across to one of the wedding guests, a young man called Donal, and said, "I can cure that finger of yours." And it was dropped as lightly, as casually, as naturally into the conversation as if he had said, "This is my round." So naturally that the others didn't even hear it and went on talking. And he caught the twisted finger between his palms and massaged it gently and then released it and the finger was straight and he turned immediately to me and gave me an icy, exultant, theatrical smile and said, "That's the curtain-raiser."

And I knew at once—I knew it instinctively—that before the night was out he was going to measure himself against the cripple in the wheelchair.

And he did. Yes. Outside in the yard. I watched from an upstairs window. But that was hours later, just after daybreak. And throughout the night the others had become crazed with drink and he had gone very still and sat with his eyes half-closed but never for a second taking them off the invalid.

Before they all went out to the yard—it was almost dawn then—I gripped him by the elbow. "For Christ's sake, Frank, please, for my sake," and he looked at me, no, not at me, not at me, past me, beyond me, out of those damn benign eyes of his; and I wasn't there for him . . .

Aberarder, Kinlochbervie,
Aberayron, Kinlochbervie,
Invergordon, Kinlochbervie . . . in Sutherland, in the north of Scotland . . .

(*by rote*) But I *am* getting stronger. I *am* becoming more controlled. I can measure my progress by the number of hours I sleep and the amount I drink and—and—

O my God I'm in such a mess—I'm really in such a mess—how I want that door to open—how I want that man to come across that floor and put his white hands on my face and still this tumult inside me—O my God I'm one of his fictions too, but I need him to sustain me in that existence—O my God I don't know if I can go on without his sustenance.

(*Fade to black.*)

Part Three • Teddy

We discover Teddy on stage. He is probably in his fifties but it would be difficult to pinpoint his age accurately

because he has a showman's verve and perkiness that make him appear younger than that.

He is wearing a bow-tie, checked shirt, smoking jacket/dressing gown (short), house slippers.

We discover him sitting beside the table—the same small table as in Part Two; but Teddy's chair is more comfortable than Grace's. He is listening to a recording of Fred Astaire singing "The Way You Look Tonight"— an old record-player and a very abused record.

Occasionally during his monologue he goes to a small locker—like a hospital locker—where he keeps his bottles of beer. Beside this locker is an empty dog-basket.

The poster is in the same position as in Part One and Part Two.

(No attempt has been made to write this monologue in the phonetic equivalent of Cockney/London English. But the piece must be played in that dialect.)

Teddy is sitting with his eyes closed, his head back, listening to the music.

Some day when I'm awf'ly low
When the world is cold,
I will feel a glow
Just thinking of you
And the way you look tonight . . .

(At the end of the first verse he opens his eyes, sees that his glass is empty, goes to the locker, gets a bottle of beer and comes back to his seat. Omit all the middle verses—go from the first verse to the last. As Teddy gets his drink he sings odd lines with the record.)

Lovely, never, never change,
Keep that breathless charm,
Won't you please arrange it
'Cause I love you
Just the way you look tonight.
Mm, mm, mm, mm,
Just the way you look tonight.

TEDDY: What about that then, eh? Fred Astaire. Fantastic, isn't it? One of the greats, Freddy. Just fantastic. I could listen to that all day—(*Sings.*) "Just the way you look . . . " It was Gracie insisted on that for our theme music. And do you know why, dear heart? She wouldn't admit it to him but she told me. Because that was the big hit the year she and Frank were married. Can you imagine! But of course as time goes by she forgets that. And of course he never knows why it's our theme—probably thinks I've got some sort of a twisted mind. So that the two of them end up blaming *me* for picking it! But by that time I really like the tune, you know; and anyway it's the only record we have. So I keep it. And old Teddy, he's the only one of the three of us that knows its romantic significance. I'll tell you something, dear heart: spend your life in show-business and you become a philosopher.

But it is a fantastic tune, isn't it? Did you ever look back over all the great artists—old Freddy here,

Lillie Langtry, Sir Laurence Olivier, Houdini, Charlie Chaplin, Gracie Fields—and did you ever ask yourself what makes them all top-liners, what have they all got in common? Okay, I'll tell you. Three things. Number one: they've got ambition this size. Okay? Number two: they've got a talent that is sensational and unique—there's only one Sir Laurence—right? Number three: not one of them has two brains to rub together. You think I'm joking? I promise you. They know they have something fantastic, sure, they're not that stupid. But what it is they have, how they do it, how it works, what that sensational talent is, what it all means—believe me, they don't know and they don't care and even if they did care they haven't the brains to analyze it.

Let me tell you about two dogs I had once. Okay? One was a white poodle and she was so brilliant—I mean, that dog, she knew what you were thinking—about before you even thought about it yourself. Before I'd come home at night, d'you know what that dog would do? She'd switch on the electric fire, pull the curtains, and leave my slippers and a bottle of beer sitting there beside my chair. But put her in front of an audience—fell apart—couldn't do nothing. Right. Now the other dog he was a whippet. Maybe you remember him, Rob Roy, the Piping Dog?

(*Brief pause.*)

Well, it was quite a few years ago. Anyway, you see that whippet, he was fantastic. I mean to say, just tell me how many times in your life has it been your privilege to hear a three-year-old male whippet dog play "Come into the Garden, Maud" on the bagpipes *and* follow for his encore with "Plaisir d'Amour." Okay? Agreed. Sensational talent. Ambition? I couldn't stop him rehearsing. Morning, noon and night he'd sit there blowing the bloody thing and working them bellows with his back leg—all night long if I'd let him. That's all he lived for, being on top of the heap. And brains? Had he brains, that whippet? Let me tell you. I had that dog four and a half years, until he expired from pulmonary exhaustion. And in all that time that whippet couldn't even learn his name! I mean it. I mean apart from his musical genius that whippet in human terms was educationally subnormal. A retarded whippet, in fact. I'd stub my toe against something, and I'd say "God!", and who'd come running to me, wagging his tail? I tell you: a philosopher—that's what you become.

I'll give you another example. One of the best acts I ever handled—Miss Mulatto and Her Pigeons. You see that kid? D'you know what that kid could do? I swear to God this is no lie, that kid talked pigeon! I swear. Fluent. That kid could plant her pigeons all over the house—some here, some there, some down there; and then she'd stand in the center of the stage and she'd speak to them in a great flood of pigeon, you know—I can't do it, I can't even speak English—but this flood of pigeon would come out of her. And suddenly all those birds—a hundred and twenty of them, I should know, six to a box, twenty boxes, that's when I had to buy the van—all those birds would rise up from all over the house and come flying in like a bloody massive snowstorm and smother her on the stage. Fantastic. Can you imagine it? Her being able to talk to every one of them hundred and twenty birds and for all I know maybe them all speaking different languages! I said to her once, "Mary Brigid," I said, that was her name, Mary Brigid O'Donnell, I said, "What do you say to them?" And she tossed her head and she said, "Say to them? How would I know what I say to them, Teddy? I just make sounds at them." See?

(*He touches his head.*)

Nothing. Empty. But what a talent! What an artist! And another thing, when those birds all died that winter of '47—all of them, just like that, within twenty-four hours, we were in Crewe at the time, the vet said it was galloping shingles—after those birds died, Mary Brigid never worked again. I suppose it'd be like as if . . . as if someone sat on Yehudi Menuhin's fiddle and smashed it. God! Bloody artists!

(*Teddy disposes of the empty bottle and sings as he does.*)

Oh, but you're lovely
With your smile so warm,
And your cheek so soft
There is nothing for me but to love you—

I'll tell you something: if you're thinking of going into the promotion business, let me tell you something—I'll give you this for nothing—it's the best advice you'll ever get—and it has been the one ruling principle in all my years as a professional man: if you're going to handle great artists, you must handle them—believe me, I know what I'm talking about—you must handle them on the basis of a relationship that is strictly business only. Personally, in the privacy of your heart, you may love them or you may hate them. But that has nothing to do with it. Your client he has his job to do. You have your job to do. On that basis you complement each other. But let that relationship between you spill over into friendship or affection and believe me, dear heart, the coupon's torn. The one rule I've always lived by: friends is friends and work is work, and as the poet says, never the twain shall meet. Okay? Okay. (*indicating poster*) Him? No, he was no great artist. Course he was no great artist. Never anything more than a mediocre artist. At best. Believe me. I should know, shouldn't I? Sure he had talent. Talent? He had more talent—listen to me—he had more talent than—and brains?—brains!—that's all the stupid bastard had was brains! For Christ's sake, brains! And what did they do for him, I ask you, all those bloody brains? They bloody castrated him—that's what they done for him—bloody knackered him! So what do you end up handling? A bloody fantastic talent that hasn't one ounce of ambition because his bloody brains has him bloody castrated! Tell me—go ahead—you tell me—you tell me—I genuinely want to know—what sort of act is that to work with, to spend your life with? How do you handle an act like that? You tell *me*. I never knew! I never learned! Oh, for God's sake, no wonder I have ulcers!

(*Pause. Then softly:*)

But when his brain left him alone. When he was in form.

There was one night in particular. Wales it was. Village called Llanblethian. An old Methodist church that I get for ten bob. A week before Christmas.

And we're flat broke. And Frank, he's on two bottles of whiskey a day at this stage. And Gracie and him they've been fighting something terrible and she's disappeared off somewhere. And I've a pocketful of bills to pay.

Okay. Eight o'clock. I open the doors. I'm not exactly knocked down in the stampede. As a matter of fact, dear heart—nobody. God. And now it's snowing. I close the doors. Frank, he's looking like he's about to die, and his hands and his shoulders they're shaking like this. "Get me a drink," he says. I pretend I don't hear him. The door's flung open. The stampede? (*He shakes his head.*) Gracie. "Where's the genius?" she shouts. "I came to see the great Irish genius. Where is he?" And he hears her and he screams, "Get that bitch out! Get rid of that bitch!" "Oh, he's here, is he?" she says. "Physician, heal thyself!" she says with this great, mad, mocking voice. "Out! Out!" he shouts. "The genius!" she screams. "Out! Out!" "Genius!" And their voices they're echoing up through those dirty big oak rafters of the church so that it goes on and on and on . . . Oh, God, I mean to say, dear heart . . .

Finally—it must be near nine o'clock now—we're about to pack up and the door opens and in come ten people. I don't remember all the details now. There's two kids, I know; one of them has this great big lump on his cheek. And there's a woman with crutches. And there's another young woman with a crying baby in her arms. And there's a young man with dark glasses and one of those white sticks for blind people. Five or six others—I can't remember—I mean I didn't know then the kind of night it was going to be, did I? Oh, yes, and an old man, a farmer—he's lame—he's helped in by his daughter. And they all sit down. And I goes through my paces: Ladies and gentlemen and etcetera and so on. And then I goes to Frank and I says, "Okay, Frank?" And very slowly he straightens up and when I see his face I'm sure he's going to be sick and he doesn't answer me at all but sort of—you know—drifts past me and down to them and among them.

(*He slowly pours the remains of a bottle into his glass. Then takes a drink.*)

All I can say now is that it was . . . I mean I don't ask you to believe what happened. Quite honestly—and I don't say this with no belligerence—it makes no difference to me whether you believe me or not. But what happened that night in that old Methodist hall in the village of Llanbethian in Glamorganshire in Wales is that every single person in that church was cured. Ten people. All made right again. I'd seen him do fantastic things before but I'd never seen him do anything on that scale. Never. And I'll tell you a funny thing: there was no shouting or cheering or dancing with joy, nothing at all like that. Hardly a word was spoken. It was like as if not only had he taken away whatever it was was wrong with them, but like he had given them some great content in themselves as well. That sounds silly, doesn't it? But that's the way it seemed.

And when he had finished, they all got to their feet and shook his hand, one after the other, very formal like. And the old farmer, the one who'd been lame and had been helped in by his daughter, he made a little speech. He said, in that lilting Welsh accent—I can't do that neither—he said, "Mr Hardy, as long as men live in Glamorganshire, you'll be remembered here." And whatever way he said it, you knew it was true; and whatever way he said Glamorganshire, it sounded like the whole world. And then he took out his wallet and placed it on the table and he said, "I hope I'm not insulting you, sir." And they all went out.

(*Short pause.*)

That was one of the big nights, that was. I mean we were stunned—Gracie—me—Frank himself; we just stood looking at one another. I mean to say—ten people—all in a few minutes. And then he suddenly went crazy with delight. And he threw his arms around me and kissed me on both cheeks. And then he ran down to Gracie and caught her in his arms and lifted her up into the air and danced her up and down the aisle of that old church and the two of them sang at the top of their voices, "Lovely, never never change," trying to sing and dance and at the same time breaking their sides laughing. And then he flung the doors open and they ran outside and sang and danced in the snow. What a pair! Oh my dear, what a pair! Like kids they were. Just like kids. Then I heard the van starting up. But by the time I got out they were gone. Just like that. Didn't see them again for four days—what happened was they went off to some posh hotel in Cardiff and lived it up until the wallet was empty. Just like kids, you know. Thoughtless; no thought for tomorrow. And no cruelty intended—oh no, no cruelty. But at a time like that a bit thoughtless. And that's understandable, too, after a night like that, isn't it? just a little bit thoughtless—that's all.

(He goes to the locker for another bottle. As he goes:)

What a funny couple they were, though. Oh dear, what a funny couple. I mean to spend the greater part of their lives together, fighting as they did; and when I say fighting, I mean really sticking the old knife in and turning it as hard as they could. I never understood it—job for the head-shrink, isn't it?—why two people should burn themselves out in that way. Sure they could have split. Why didn't they then? Don't ask me. For God's sake why didn't I leave them and get myself something nice and simple and easy like—like—like a whistling dolphin? And what was the fighting all about in the end? All right you could say it was because the only thing that finally mattered to him was his work—and that would be true. Or you could say it was because the only thing that finally mattered to her was him—and I suppose that would be true, too. But when you put the two propositions together like that—I don't know—somehow they both become only half-truths, you know.

Or maybe you could say that no artist should ever be married. I've heard that theory, too; and after a lifetime in the profession I would incline to the conclusion that that theory has quite a bit of validity in it. I mean look at Rob Roy, the Piping Dog, just consider for one minute the fortune I could have made in stud fees when that dog was a household name. Queuing up with their bitches they were; queuing bloody up. Twenty nicker a throw they were offering me. I thought I was sitting on a gold-mine. Do you know what I did in anticipation of the fortune that was going to come pouring in? I got a fifteen-foot black Carrara marble headstone with gold lettering put up over my mother's grave. Set me back £214, that did. Okay—and what happened?—what happened every single time? I'll tell you. I come into the room here with a very beautiful and very sexy whippet bitch. He's just been rehearsing and he's lying there in that basket, gasping for breath. I say to him, "Look at this then, old Rob. Who's good to you then, eh?" But he's temperamental—he won't look up. And the bitch, she's rolling her eyes and waggling all over and laughing like a bloody gypsy. "Come on, boy," I say, "come on, come on. You've got a nice friend here." And what does he do every time, every single time? He gets to his feet. He gives this great yawn. And then suddenly—just like that—goes for her throat! For her bloody *throat* for God's sake! Tries to tear her limb from bloody limb! Course he's stupid but he's not that stupid! I mean he knows what it's all about! My God he knows! My God, there's days he's so randy, that whippet, there's days I daren't strap the bloody bagpipes to him! And yet look what he does when it's bloody handed to him on a plate—some of the most beautiful whippet bitches in the country and every one of them crying out for it! Goes for her throat and tries to desecrate my mother's memory at the same time! Oh my God—artists! I ask you!

(He gathers the empty bottles on the table and drops them into a waste-paper basket. As he does:)

Ups and downs—losses and gains—roundabouts and swings—isn't that it?

And if that night in Llanbethian was one of the high spots, I suppose the week we spent in that village in Sutherland was about as bad a patch as we ever struck. For Gracie it was. Certainly for Gracie. And for me, too, I think. Oh, that's going back a fair few years. About the time he really began to lose control of the drinking. Anyway, there we were away up in Sutherland—what *was* the name of that village? Inverbuie? Inverbervie? Kinlochbervie?—that's it!— Kinlochbervie!—very small, very remote, right away up in the north of Sutherland, about as far north as you can go in Scotland, and looking across at the Isle of Lewis in the Outer Hebrides.

I'll always remember our first sight of that village. We climb up this long steep hill through this misty fog and when we get to the top we stop; and away down below us in the valley—there's Kinlochbervie; and it is just bathed in sunshine. First time we've seen the sun in about a month. And now here's this fantastic little village sitting on the edge of the sea, all blue and white and golden, and all lit up and all sparkling and all just heavenly. And Gracie she turns to me and she says, "Teddy," she says, "this is where my baby'll be born." Even though she wasn't due for three more weeks. But she was right. That's where the baby was born.

Okay. We head down into the valley and just about two miles out of the village the front axle goes thrackk! Terrific. Frank, he's out cold in the back. So I leave Gracie sunbathing herself on a stone wall and I hikes it into Kinlochbervie to get help.

That was a Tuesday morning. The following Friday we're still there, still waiting for a local fisherman called Campbell who's out in his trawler to come back 'cause he's the only local who owns a tractor and we're depending on his mother who happens to be deaf as a post to persuade him when he comes back to tow us the thirty-five miles to the nearest village where there's a blacksmith but there's a chance, too, that this blacksmith might not be at home when we get there because his sister, Annie, she's getting married to a postman in Glasgow and the blacksmith may be the best man. One of those situations—you know. *(Shouts.)* "Are you sure this blacksmith can fix axles, dear heart?" "Och, Annie, she's a beautiful big strong girl with brown eyes."

Right. We hang about. And since funds are low— as usual—Gracie and Frank they sleep in the van and I'm kipping in a nearby field. I don't mind; the weather's beautiful. Saturday passes—no Campbell. Sunday passes—no Campbell. And then on Sunday evening . . . the baby's born.

(Very slowly he goes for another beer, opens it, pours it. As he does this he whistles a few lines of "The Way You

Look Tonight" through his teeth. Then with sudden anger:)

Christ, you've got to admit he really was a bastard in many ways! I know he was drinking heavy—I know—I know all that! But for Christ's sake to walk away deliberately when your wife's going to have your baby in the middle of bloody nowhere—I mean to say, to do that deliberately, that's some kind of bloody-mindedness, isn't it? And make no mistake, dear heart: it was deliberate, it was bloody-minded. 'Cause as soon as she starts having the pains, I go looking for him, and there he is heading up the hill, and I call after him, and I know he hears me, but he doesn't answer me. Oh, Christ, there really was a killer instinct deep down in that man!

(Pause. He takes a drink, puts the glass down on the table and looks at it.)

I don't know . . . I don't know how we managed. God, when I think of it. Her lying on my old raincoat in the back of the van . . . shouting for him, screaming for him . . . all that blood . . . her bare feet pushing, kicking against my shoulders . . . "Frank!" she's screaming, "Frank! Frank!" and I'm saying, "My darling, he's coming—he's coming, my darling—he's on his way—he'll be here any minute" . . . and then that—that little wet thing with the black face and the black body, a tiny little thing, no size at all . . . a boy it was . . .

(Pause.)

And afterwards she was so fantastic—I mean she was so bloody fantastic. She held it in her arms, just sitting there on the roadside with her back leaning against the stone wall and her legs stretched out in front of her, just sitting there in the sun and looking down at it in her arms. And then after about half an hour she said, "It's time to bury it now, Teddy." And we went into a nearby field and I had to chase the cows away 'cause they kept following us and I dug the hole and I put it in the hole and I covered it up again. And then she asked me was I not going to say no prayers over it and I said sure, why not, my darling, I said; but not being much of a praying man I didn't know right what to say; so I just said this was the infant child of Francis Hardy, Faith Healer, and his wife, Grace Hardy, both citizens of Ireland, and this was where their infant child lies, in Kinlochbervie, in Sutherland; and God have mercy on all of us, I said.

And all the time she was very quiet and calm. And when the little ceremony was concluded, she put her two white hands on my face and brought me to her and kissed me on the forehead. Just once. On the forehead.

And later that evening I made a cross and painted it white and placed it on top of the grave. Maybe it's still there. You never know. About two miles south of the village of Kinlochbervie. In a field on the left-hand side of the road as you go north. Maybe it's still there. Could well still be. Why not? Who's to say?

(Pause.)

Oh, he came back all right; just before it was dark. Oh, sure. Sober as a judge, all spruced up, healthy-looking, sunburned, altogether very cocky; and full of old chat to me about should we have a go in the Outer Hebrides or maybe we should cross over to the east coast or should we plan a journey even further north now that the weather was so good—you know, all business, things he never gave a damn about. And he seemed so—you know—so on top of things, I thought for a while, I thought: My God, he doesn't know! He genuinely doesn't know! But then suddenly in the middle of all this great burst of interest I see him glancing into the van with the corner of the eye—not that there was anything to see; I had it all washed out by then—but it was the way he done it and the way he kept on talking at the same time that I *knew* that *he* knew; and not only that he knew but that he knew it all right down to the last detail. And even though the old chatter never faltered for a minute, whatever way he kept talking straight into my face, I knew too that—oh, I don't know how to put it—but I got this feeling that in a kind of way—being the kind of man he was—well somehow I got the feeling, I *knew* that he *had* to keep talking because he had suffered all that she had suffered and that now he was . . . about to collapse. Yeah. Funny, wasn't it? And many a time since then I get a picture of him going up that hill that Sunday afternoon, like there's some very important appointment he's got to keep, walking fast with his head down and pretending he doesn't hear me calling him. And I've thought maybe—course it was bloody minded of him! I'm not denying that!—but maybe being the kind of man he was, you know, with that strange gift he had, I've thought maybe—well, maybe he had to have his own way of facing things . . .

Oh, I don't know. None of my business, was it? None of my concern, thank the Lord, except in so far as it might affect the performance of my client. Listen to me, dear heart, I'll give you this for nothing, the best advice you'll ever get—the *one* rule I've always lived by: friends is friends and work is work and never the twain shall meet as the poet says. Okay? Okay.

(With a glass in his hand he goes slowly upstage until he is standing beneath the poster. As he goes he hums the lines "Some day when I'm awf'ly low, When the world is cold." He reads:)

The Fantastic Francis Hardy, Faith Healer: One Night Only. Nice poster though, isn't it? A lifetime in the business and that's the only memento I've kept. That's a fact. See some people in our profession?—they hoard everything: press-clippings, posters, notices, photographs, interviews—they keep them all. Never believed in that, though. I mean the way I look at it, you've got to be a realist, you know, live in the present. Look at Sir Laurence—you think he spends his days poring over old albums? No, we don't have time for that. And believe me I've had my share of triumphs and my share of glory over the years; and I'm grateful for that. But I mean it doesn't butter no parsnips for me today, does it?

And do you know, dear heart, it was almost thrown out! Well, I mean it *was* thrown out—I just happened to spot it in this pile of stuff that Gracie's landlord had dumped outside for the dustmen. I'd come straight from the morgue in Paddington, and the copper there, he'd given me her address; and there I was, walking along the street, looking for Number 27; and there it is, lying on the footpath where her landlord had dumped it. I mean, if it had been raining, it would have been destroyed, wouldn't it? But there it was, neat as you like. And just as I was picking it up, this city gent, he's walking past and he says, "How dare you steal private property, sir!" (*in a fury*) And I caught him by the neck and I put my fist up to his face and I said to him, I said to him, "You open your fucking mouth once more, mate, just once fucking more, and I'll fucking well make fucking sausage meat of you!"

(*Pause while he controls himself again.*)

If you'll pardon the language, dear heart. But I just went berserk. I mean half an hour before, this copper he'd brought me to Paddington and I'm still in a state of shock after that. And besides it's only—what?—twelve months since the whole County Donegal thing: that night in the Ballybeg pub and then hanging about waiting for the trial of those bloody Irish Apaches and nobody in the courtroom understands a word I'm saying—they had to get an interpreter to explain to the judge in English what the only proper Englishman in the place was saying! God!

And I'm still only getting over all that when this copper comes up here one morning while I'm shaving and I opens the door and he asks me my name and I tell him and then he says I'm to go to Paddington with him right away to . . .

(*He stops suddenly and stares for a long time at the audience. Then:*)

Tell you what—why don't I go back twelve months and tell you first about that night in Ballybeg? Why don't I do that? Why not?

(*He gets another bottle, opens it, pours it.*)

It was the last day of August and we crossed from Stranraer to Larne and drove through the night to County Donegal. And there we got lodgings in a pub, a lounge bar, really, outside a village called Ballybeg, not far from Donegal Town.

(*He takes a drink and leaves the glass down. Pause.*)

You see that night in that pub in Ballybeg? You know how I spent that night? I spent the whole of that night just watching them. Mr and Mrs Frank Hardy. Side by side. Together in Ireland. At home in Ireland. Easy; relaxed; chatting; laughing. And it was like as if I was seeing them for the first time in years and years—no! not seeing them but *remembering them*. Funny thing that, wasn't it? I'm not saying they were strangers to *me*—strangers! I mean, Frank and Gracie, how could they be strangers to *me!*—but it was like as if I was seeing them as they were once, as they might have been all the time—like if there was never none of the bitterness and the fighting and the wettings and the bloody van and the smell of the primus stove and the bills and the booze and the dirty halls and that hassle that we never seemed to be able to rise above. Like away from all that, all that stuff cut out, this is what they could be.

And there they were, the center of that big circle round that big lounge, everybody wanting to talk to them, them talking to everybody, now and then exchanging an odd private word between themselves, now and then even touching each other very easy and very casual.

And she was sitting forward in this armchair. And she was all animation and having a word with everybody and laughing all the time. And she was wearing this red dress. And her hair it was tied back with a black ribbon. And how can I tell you how fantastic she looked?

And then sometime around midnight someone said, "Why don't you sing us a song, Gracie?" And as natural as you like, as if she done it every day of the week, she stood up and she sang an Irish song called "Believe me if all those endearing young charms/ Which I gaze on so fondly today." Christ, I don't mean that's the title; that's the whole first verse for Christ's sake. And it wasn't that she was a sensational singer—no, no, she wasn't. I mean she had this kind of very light, wavery kind of voice—you know, like the voice of a kid of ten or eleven. But she stands up there in that Irish pub, in that red dress and with her hair all back from her face; and she's looking at him as she's singing; and we're all looking at her; and the song—it sort of comes out of her very simple and very sweet, like in a way not as if she's performing but as if the song's just sort of rising out of her by itself. And I'm sitting there just outside the circle, sitting there very quiet, very still. And I'm saying to myself, "O Jesus, Teddy boy . . . Oh my Jesus . . . What are you going to do?"

And then I looks over at Frank—I mean I just happen to look over, you know the way you do—and there he is, gazing across at me. And the way he's gazing at me and the look he has on his face is exactly the way he looks into somebody he knows he's going to cure. I don't know—it's a hard thing to explain if you've never seen it. It's a very serious look and it's a very compassionate look. It's a look that says two things. It says: No need to speak—I know exactly what the trouble is. And at the same time it says: I am now going to cure you of that trouble. That's the look he gave me. He held me in that look for—what?—thirty seconds. And then he turned away from me and looked at her—sort of directed his look towards her so that I had to look at her too. And suddenly she is this terrific woman that of course I love very much, married to this man that I love very much—love maybe even more. But that's all. Nothing more. That's all. And that's enough.

And for the first time in twenty years I was so content—so content, dear heart, do you know what I done? I got drunk in celebration—slowly, deliberately, happily slewed! And someone must have carried me upstairs to bed because the next thing I know Gracie's hammering on my chest and shouting and sobbing, "Get up, Teddy! Get up! Something terrible has happened! Something horrible!"

(*Long pause as he goes and gets another beer.*)

But I was telling you about the poster and how it's lying on the street outside Gracie's digs. That's it. How I've just come from Paddington and how the copper he's given me her address. That's right—I've told you all that. Or to go back to the morning of that same day—twelve months exactly after that night in Ballybeg.

Okay. I'm shaving. Knock at the door. This copper. Asks me my name. I tell him. Asks me to come with him to the morgue in Paddington to identify a body. What body? Body of a lady. And I say what lady? And he says a Mrs Grace Hardy. And I say come off it, she's in Ireland, that's where I left her. And he says you must be mistaken, she's been in London for the past four months, living in digs in Number 27, Limewood Avenue. Limewood Avenue! I mean this here is Limewood Grove! Limewood Avenue's just four streets away. And I say she's there now, is she? And he says no, she's dead, she's in the morgue. And I say you must be wrong, copper. And he says no mistake, she's dead, from an overdose of sleeping tablets, and would I come with him please and make a formal identification.

So the copper he brought me in a van to Paddington—you know, just like our van; only his van I'm sure it's taxed and insured. But it's the same inside: two seats in the front, me driving, her beside me, and Frank in the back all hunched up with the bottle between his legs. And there she was. Gracie all right. Looking very beautiful. Oh my dear I can't tell you how beautiful she looked.

And the copper he said, "Is that Grace Hardy?" "It is," I said. "Did you know her well?" "Oh, yes," I said, "a professional relationship going back twenty-odd years." 'Cause that's what it was, wasn't it, a professional relationship? Well it certainly wasn't nothing more than that, I mean, was it?

(*He stands for some seconds just looking at the audience. Then he does not see them any more. He sits on his chair and puts on the record. After the first few lines fade rapidly to black.*)

Part Four • Frank

The poster is gone. The set is empty except for the single chair across which lies Frank's coat exactly as he left it in Part One.

We discover Frank standing downstage left, where we left him.

In this final section Frank is slightly less aloof, not quite as detached as in Part One. To describe him now as agitated would be a gross exaggeration. But there should be tenuous evidence of a slightly heightened pulse-rate, of something approximating to excitement in him, perhaps in the way his mind leaps without apparent connection from thought to thought; and his physical movements are just a shade sharper.

FRANK (*eyes shut*):
Aberarder, Kinlochbervie,
Aberayron, Kinlochbervie,
Invergordon, Kinlochbervie . . . in Sutherland, in the north of Scotland . . .

(*He opens his eyes. A very brief pause. Then, recovering quickly:*)

But I've told you all that, haven't I?—how we were holidaying in Kinlochbervie when I got word that my mother had died? Yes, of course I have. I've told you all that. (*Begins moving.*) A picturesque little place, very quiet, very beautiful, looking across to the Isle of Lewis . . . about as far north as you can go in . . . in Scotland . . .

(*He keeps moving. As he does he searches his pockets. Produces a newspaper clipping, very tattered, very faded.*)

I carried this around with me for years. A clipping from the *West Glamorgan Chronicle*. "A truly remarkable event took place in the old Methodist church in Llanblethian on the night of December 21st last when an itinerant Irish faith healer called Francis Harding . . ." For some reason they never seemed to—(*He shrugs in dismissal.*) ". . . cured ten local people of a variety of complaints ranging from blindness to polio. Whether these very astonishing cures were effected by autosuggestion or whether Mr Harding is indeed the possessor of some extra-terrestrial power . . ." Nice word that. ". . . we are not as yet in a position to adjudicate. But our preliminary investigations would indicate that something of highly unusual proportions took place that night in Llanblethian."

"Unusual proportions" . . . (*Short laugh.*)

Never knew why I kept it for so long. Its testimony? I don't think so. Its reassurance? No, not that. Maybe, I think . . . maybe just as an identification. Yes, I think that's why I kept it. It identified me—even though it got my name wrong.

Yes, that *was* a strange night. One of those rare nights when I could—when I could have moved mountains. Ten people—one after the other. And only one of them came back to thank me—an old farmer who was lame. I remember saying to Gracie the next day, "Where are the other nine?"—in fun, of course; of course in fun. But she chose to misunderstand me and that led to another row.

Yes; carried it for years; until we came back to Ireland. And that night in that pub in Ballybeg I crumpled it up (*He does this now.*) and threw it away.

I never met her father, the judge. Shortly after Gracie and I ran off together, he wrote me a letter; but I never met him. He said in it—the only part I remember—he used the phrase "implicating my only child in your career of chicanery." And I remember being angry and throwing the letter to her; and I remember her reading that line aloud and collapsing on the bed with laughing and kicking her heels in the air and repeating the phrase over and over again—I suppose to demonstrate her absolute loyalty to me. And I remember thinking how young she *did* look and how cruel her laughter at him was. Because by then my anger against him had died and I had some envy of the man who could use the word "chicanery" with such confidence.

I would have liked to have had a child. But she was barren. And anyhow the life we led wouldn't have been suitable. And he might have had the gift. And he might have handled it better than I did. I wouldn't have asked for anything from him—love, affection, respect—nothing like that. But I would have got pleasure just in looking at him. Yes. A child would have been something. What is a piece of paper? Or those odd moments of awe, of gratitude, of adoration? Nothing, nothing, nothing . . .

(*Looking around*) It was always like this—shabby, shabby, bleak, derelict. We never got that summons to Teddy's royal palace; not even to a suburban drawing-room. And it would have been interesting to have been just once—not for the pretensions, no, no, but to discover was it possible in conditions other than these, just for the confirmation that this despair, this surrender wasn't its own healing. Yes, that would have been interesting.

And yet . . . and yet . . .

(*Suddenly, rapidly*) Not for a second, not for a single second was I disarmed by the warmth and the camaraderie and the deference and the joviality and the joy and the effusion of that home-coming welcome that night in that pub in Ballybeg. No, not for a second. Of course I responded to it. Naturally I responded to it. And yes, the thought did cross my mind that at long last is there going to be—what?—a fulfilment, an integration, a full blossoming? Yes, that thought occurred to me. But the moment that boy Donal threatened me with his damned twisted finger, that illusion quickly vanished. And I knew, I knew instinctively why I was being hosted.

Aberarder, Kinlochbervie,
Aberayron, Kinlochbervie,
Invergordon, Kinlochbervie . . .

Where had we got to? Ah, yes—Teddy had been put to bed and Gracie had finished her housekeeping—I could hear her moving about upstairs; and the wedding guests had gone to get McGarvey. Only the landlord and myself in that huge, garish lounge.

I walked around it for a time.

I thought of Teddy asleep upstairs, at peace and reconciled at last. And I wondered had I held on to him out of selfishness, should I have attempted to release him years ago. But I thought—no; his passion was a sustaining one. And maybe, indeed, maybe I had impoverished him now.

And I thought of Gracie's mother and the one time we met, in Dublin, on her way back to hospital. We were in a restaurant together, the three of us, Gracie and she and I; and she never spoke until Gracie had gone off to pay the bill and then she said, "I suffer from nerves, you know," her face slightly averted from me but looking directly at me at the same time and smiling at me. I said I knew. I was afraid she was going to ask me for help. "What do you make of that?" I said I was sure she would get better this time. "You know, there are worse things," she said. I said I knew that. "Much, much worse," she went on and she was almost happy-looking now. "Look at her father—he is obsessed with order. That's worse." I suppose so, I said. "And Grace—she wants devotion, and that's worse still." "Is it?" I asked. "And what do you want?" And before I could answer, Gracie came back, and the smile vanished, and the head dropped. And that was all. No request for help. And I never heard her voice again.

And I remembered—suddenly, for no reason at all—the day my father took me with him to the horse fair in Ballinasloe. And the only incident I remembered was that afternoon, in a pub. And a friend of my father's, Eamon Boyle, was with us; and the two men were slightly drunk. And Boyle put his hand on my head and said to my father, "And what's this young man going to be, Frank?" And my father opened his mouth and laughed and said, "Be Jaysus, Boyle, it'll be hard for him to beat his aul fella!" And for the first time I saw his mouth was filled with rotten teeth. And I remember being ashamed in case Boyle had seen them, too. Just a haphazard memory. Silly. Nothing to it. But for some reason it came back to me that night.

And I thought of the first big row Grace and I had. I don't know what it was about. But I know we were in Norfolk at the time, living in a converted byre. And she was kneeling in front of the grate, trying to kindle some wet timber; and I can't remember what I said but I remembered her reply; and what she said was: "If you leave me, Frank, I'll kill myself." And it wasn't that she was demented—in fact she was almost calm, and smiling. But whatever way she looked straight at me, without fully facing me, I recognized then for the first time that there was more of her mother than her father in her; and I realized that I would have to be with her until the very end.

(*He walks upstage. Pause.*)

I must have walked that floor for a couple of hours. And all the time the landlord never moved from behind the bar. He hadn't spoken since the wedding guests left. He wouldn't even look at me. I think he hated me. I know he did. I asked him for a last drink. Then he spoke in a rush: "Get to hell out of here before they come back, mister! I know them fellas — savage bloody men. And there's nothing you can do for McGarvey — nothing nobody can do for McGarvey. You know that. "I know that," I said. "But if you do nothing for him, mister, they'll kill you. I know them. They'll kill you." "I know that, too," I said. But he rushed into a back room.

I poured a drink for myself. A small Irish with an equal amount of water. The thought occurred to me to get drunk but I dismissed it as . . . inappropriate. Then I heard the car return and stop outside. A silence. Then Donal's head round the door.

"McGarvey's here. But he's shy about coming in. Come you out. They're waiting for you out there in the yard."

"Coming," I said.

(*He puts on the hat and overcoat and buttons it slowly. When that is done he goes on.*)

There were two yards in fact. The first one I went into — it was immediately behind the lounge — it was a tiny area, partially covered, dark, cluttered with barrels and boxes of empties and smelling of stale beer and toilets. I knew that wasn't it.

Then I found a wooden door. I passed through that and there was the other, the large yard. And I knew it at once.

I would like to describe that yard to you.

It was a September morning, just after dawn. The sky was orange and everything glowed with a soft radiance — as if each detail of the scene had its own self-awareness and was satisfied with itself.

The yard was a perfect square enclosed by the back of the building and three high walls. And the wall facing me as I walked out was breached by an arched entrance.

Almost in the center of the square but a little to my left was a tractor and a trailer. In the back of the trailer were four implements: there was an axe and there was a crowbar and there was a mallet and there

was a hayfork. They were resting against the side of the trailer.

In the corners facing me and within the walls were two mature birch trees and the wind was sufficient to move them.

The ground was cobbled but pleasant to walk on because the cobbles were smooth with use.

And I walked across that yard, over those worn cobbles, towards the arched entrance, because framed in it, you would think posed symmetrically, were the four wedding guests; and in front of them, in his wheelchair, McGarvey.

The four looked . . . diminished in that dawn light; their faces whiter; their carnations chaste against the black suits. Ned was on the left of the line, Donal on the right, and the other two, whose names I never knew, between them.

And McGarvey. Of course, McGarvey. More shrunken than I had thought. And younger. His hands folded patiently on his knees; his feet turned in, his head slightly to the side. A figure of infinite patience, of profound resignation, you would imagine. Not a hint of savagery. And Ned's left hand protectively on his shoulder.

And although I knew that nothing was going to happen, nothing at all, I walked across the yard towards them. And as I walked I became possessed of a strange and trembling intimation: that the whole corporeal world — the cobbles, the trees, the sky, those four malign implements — somehow they had shed their physical reality and had become mere imaginings, and that in all existence there was only myself and the wedding guests. And that intimation in turn gave way to a stronger sense: that even we had ceased to be physical and existed only in spirit, only in the need we had for each other.

(*He takes off his hat as if he were entering a church and holds it at his chest. He is both awed and elated. As he speaks the remaining lines he moves very slowly down stage.*)

And as I moved across that yard towards them and offered myself to them, then for the first time I had a simple and genuine sense of home-coming. Then for the first time there was no atrophying terror; and the maddening questions were silent.

At long last I was renouncing chance.

(*Pause for about four seconds. Then quick black.*)

Athol Fugard

Athol Fugard (b. 1932) was an actor before becoming a playwright. Fugard's wife, the actress Sheila Meiring, stimulated his interest in theater, and in 1956 he began working with a theater group called the Serpent Company in Cape Town, South Africa. The group included both black and white actors at a time when racial mixing was illegal, and it went on to make a notable contribution to world drama.

Fugard, who is white, met Zakes Mokae, a black musician and actor, in the early days of the Serpent players, and the two collaborated on several works. Mokae has said that the tradition in Africa was not so much for a solitary playwright to compose a work that others would act out as it was for people to develop a communal approach to drama, crafting a dramatic piece through their interaction. To some extent, Fugard in his early efforts did just that. He worked with actors, watched the developments among them, and then shaped the drama accordingly.

In 1960 he began to write a two-person play called *The Blood Knot* while he was in England trying to establish a theater group there. This play was part of a trilogy called *The Family,* with *Hello and Goodbye* (1965) and *Boesman and Lena* (1969). *The Blood Knot* was given its first performance in Dorkay House in Johannesburg, South Africa, late in 1961. As Fugard has said, the entire production, which starred Fugard and Mokae, was put together so quickly that the government never had time to stop it. The play is about two brothers, one black, the other light-skinned enough to pass for white. It is exceptionally powerful, and in the play's first performances in Johannesburg, it was a sensation. It toured South Africa and had a revival in New Haven and in New York in 1984 and 1985.

While they toured South Africa, Fugard and Mokae were victims of the country's apartheid policies. They could not travel in the same train car: Fugard went first class, and Mokae had to go in special cars for blacks. After *The Blood Knot*'s success the government passed laws making it all but impossible for black and white actors to work together on the stage, but that policy has now changed.

Fugard has had a considerable number of plays produced in New York and London over the years. *Sizwe Banzi Is Dead* (1972), written with black actors John Kani and Winston Ntshona, is about a man who exchanges identity with a corpse as a way of avoiding the racial laws of South Africa; it was well received. *The Island* (1975), also written with Kani and Ntshona, starred the latter two, who have become associated with Fugard and his work. They portray prisoners who, while putting on *Antigone,* become immersed in the political themes of the play, seeing it as an example of the political repression they experience in their own lives. A revival in New York in April 2003, with Kani and Ntshona in a mildly revised version, received excellent reviews.

Fugard's plays *A Lesson from Aloes* (1978) and *The Road to Mecca* (1984) were successful in their first American productions at the Yale Repertory Theatre and on Broadway. Fugard's works are not always concerned with racial problems, but they usually center on political issues and the stress that individuals feel in trying to be themselves in an intolerant society.

The situation in South Africa has improved since *"MASTER HAROLD"...
and the boys* was first produced in 1982. Apartheid has been abolished, and the government is in the hands of the African National Congress. The shift has been more successful than white South Africans expected, although political tensions still exist. Fugard's attachment and commitment to South Africa remain deep and lifelong. He has been criticized by black writers for dealing with themes they feel belong to them, while also being criticized by whites for his sympathies toward blacks. In the new South Africa some of these problems have begun to sort themselves out. *Valley Song* (1996), produced at London's Royal Court Theatre, explores the problems and the promise of the new South Africa. Fugard's recent plays have premiered at the McCarter Theatre in Princeton, New Jersey. In May 1998 *The Captain's Tiger* was directed by Fugard, who also acted in the role of Tiger, a character on board a ship. Fugard himself had left university to work on ships around Africa. In May 2001, Fugard directed *Sorrows and Rejoicing*, a play about a man who dies and whose white wife and colored mistress meet at his funeral. Fugard's *Exits and Entrances* (2004) was written for the Fountain Theater in Los Angeles. It is a one-act meditation on Fugard's life in the theater. Another play, *The Abbess,* is under development. It is based on the life of Saint Hildegard of Bingen (1098–1179)—a Benedictine abbess known for her correspondence; her work in medicine; and her music, poems, writing, and drama.

"MASTER HAROLD" . . . AND THE BOYS

Athol Fugard has said that *"MASTER HAROLD"... and the boys* (1982) is a very personal play in which he exorcises personal guilt (Fugard's entire name is Harold Athol Lannigan Fugard). As a white South African he has written numerous plays that represent the racial circumstances of life in that troubled nation. This play has won international distinction and has made a reputation for its stars, especially Zakes Mokae, with whom Fugard has worked for more than thirty years.

Hally, the teenage son of the restaurant's owners, reveals throughout the play (which is set in 1950) that he is more attached emotionally to Sam, the black waiter who has befriended him, than he is even to his own parents, owners of the restaurant where Sam works. His attitude toward his father is complicated by his father's alcoholism and confinement. At that time in South Africa, even such an alcoholic was considered superior to a black man such as Sam, even though he is intelligent, quick, thoughtful, and generous. When Hally reveals his anxiety about his father, Sam warns him that it is dishonorable to treat one's father the way he does, but Sam's presumption in admonishing Hally triggers Hally's meanspirited outburst toward him.

Zakes Mokae, who created the role of Sam in the first performance of the play at the Yale Repertory Theatre, has commented extensively about his role and the character of Sam. He has observed that some black audience members called out during a performance that he should beat up Hally the minute Hally demands that Sam call him Master Harold. But other black audience members spoke with him after the performance and agreed that, because Sam had never taken that kind of stand against Harold or his father, he was getting what he deserved. Mokae himself has pointed out that Sam is probably not living in Port Elizabeth legally and that to have taken action, even if he had wanted to, would have ended with his ejection from the town into exile.

Zakes Mokae understands the character from his perspective as a black South African, and he realizes Sam's limits. But he has said that in his version of the play, Sam would give Hally a beating and "suffer the consequences." He points out, however, that he is an urban South African, unlike Sam, and his attitude is quite different from anything that Sam would have understood. As an urban black, Mokae could not have been sent into exile, although he could certainly have been punished, for beating a white boy.

On the question of whether the play made a positive contribution to white-black relations in South Africa, Mokae feels that a play cannot change people's minds. Audiences were not likely to seek to change the government of South Africa simply because they had seen a play. At the same time, however, he feels that it was productive to talk about the apartheid and racial distrust in South Africa.

Unfortunately, the government of South Africa decided the play was too inflammatory for performance in that country, and it was banned briefly from performance in Johannesburg and other theatrical centers in South Africa. This suggests that although Zakes Mokae did not believe one play would have much impact on injustices in South Africa, it is likely that the government feared otherwise.

In an important way, *"MASTER HAROLD" . . . and the boys* is a personal statement by Fugard that establishes the extent to which apartheid damages even a person sympathetic to black rights. It is astonishing in retrospect to think, as his interviewer, Heinrich von Staden, once said, that Hally could grow up to be Athol himself. If this is true, then it is also true that the play is hopeful.

One sign of hope is that the violence in the play is restrained. Sam does not beat Hally for humiliating him, although he probably would like to. And no one in the play makes a move to be physically threatening to Sam. However faint, these are signs of hope. And as Zakes Mokae has said about the situation in his homeland, "One is always optimistic. It can't go on forever." He was right. On June 5, 1991, Parliament abandoned apartheid, and South Africa had a new beginning.

"MASTER HAROLD" . . . and the boys in Performance

The world premiere of *"MASTER HAROLD" . . . and the boys* was at the Yale Repertory Theatre in March 1982. Fugard himself directed the play, with Zakes Mokae as Sam, Danny Glover as Willie, and Željko Ivanek as Hally. It was the first of his plays to premiere outside South Africa. Fugard chose New Haven, Connecticut, in part because the play's setting was so personal that he feared it might disturb his brother and sister if it were produced first in South Africa. The setting was a bright tea room—a restaurant that serves light meals—interpreted to look like the tea room Fugard's mother actually ran in Port Elizabeth when he was a child. The space was open, the walls a whitish hue, everything simple and plain in decoration.

New York Times critic Frank Rich reviewed the premiere, saying, "'MASTER HAROLD' . . . and the boys* is only an anecdote, really, and it's often as warm and musical as the men's dance. But somewhere along the way it rises up and breaks over the audience like a storm." Alan Stern of the *Boston Phoenix* linked the play with Greek tragedy:

> One reason for the play's potency is that, as in Greek tragedy, the events seem preordained—they're the by-product of social forces and human nature. Even as he spits in Sam's face, Hally realizes the magnitude of his action, that he is the one who will be harmed by it. And yet he can't help himself. Power corrupts, and in a society that sanctions the domination of one man—or set of men—over another, all relationships, even the promising ones, are poisoned.

Zakes Mokae and Danny Glover starred in the Broadway production in May 1982. After a brief period in which it was banned, the play was produced in Johannesburg, South Africa, in March 1983 with a South African cast. Joseph Lelyveld, in the *New York Times*, said of that production, "Athol Fugard's confessional drama about a white adolescent's initiation in the uses of racial power has come home to South Africa, and it left its multiracial audience . . . visibly shaken and stunned. . . . Many, blacks and whites, were crying."

The play was televised in 1984 with Matthew Broderick as Hally. It has had revivals in 1985 by the Trinity Repertory Company in Providence, in 1986 by the Boston Shakespeare Company in Boston, and in 1987 at the American Stage Festival in Milford, New Hampshire. These productions, although without Fugard's direction and without a "star" cast, had the same effect on their audiences as the major productions in New York and Johannesburg. Clifford Gallo in the *Boston Globe* called the American Stage Festival production "a devastating look at the loss of racial innocence in a nation where political and social inequality are the norm." Danny Glover revived the play in June 2003 in New York's Royale Theatre. This time he played Sam, whereas twenty years before he had played Willie.

Athol Fugard (b. 1932)
"MASTER HAROLD" . . . AND THE BOYS

Characters

WILLIE
SAM
HALLY

The St. George's Park Tea Room on a wet and windy Port Elizabeth afternoon.

Tables and chairs have been cleared and are stacked on one side except for one which stands apart with a single chair. On this table a knife, fork, spoon and side plate in anticipation of a simple meal, together with a pile of comic books.

Other elements: a serving counter with a few stale cakes under glass and a not very impressive display of sweets, cigarettes and cool drinks, etc.; a few cardboard advertising handouts—Cadbury's Chocolate, Coca-Cola—and a blackboard on which an untrained hand has chalked up the prices of Tea, Coffee, Scones, Milkshakes—all flavors—and Cool Drinks; a few sad ferns in pots; a telephone; an old-style jukebox.

There is an entrance on one side and an exit into a kitchen on the other.

Leaning on the solitary table, his head cupped in one hand as he pages through one of the comic books, is Sam. A black man in his mid-forties. He wears the white coat of a waiter. Behind him on his knees, mopping down the floor with a bucket of water and a rag, is Willie. Also black and about the same age as Sam. He has his sleeves and trousers rolled up.

The year: 1950.

WILLIE (*singing as he works*): "She was scandalizin'
    my name,
  She took my money
  She called me honey
  But she was scandalizin' my name.
  Called it love but was playin' a game. . . ."

(He gets up and moves the bucket. Stands thinking for a moment, then, raising his arms to hold an imaginary partner, he launches into an intricate ballroom dance step. Although a mildly comic figure, he reveals a reasonable degree of accomplishment.)

Hey, Sam.

(Sam, absorbed in the comic book, does not respond.)

Hey, Boet° Sam!

(Sam looks up.)

Boet: Brother.

I'm getting it. The quickstep. Look now and tell me. (*He repeats the step.*) Well?
SAM (*encouragingly*): Show me again.
WILLIE: Okay, count for me.
SAM: Ready?
WILLIE: Ready.
SAM: Five, six, seven, eight. . . . (*Willie starts to dance.*) A-n-d one two three four . . . and one two three four. . . . (*Ad libbing as Willie dances.*) Your shoulders, Willie . . . your shoulders! Don't look down! Look happy, Willie! Relax, Willie!
WILLIE (*desperate but still dancing*): I am relax.
SAM: No, you're not.
WILLIE (*he falters*): Ag no man, Sam! Mustn't talk. You make me make mistakes.
SAM: But you're stiff.
WILLIE: Yesterday I'm not straight . . . today I'm too stiff!
SAM: Well, you are. You asked me and I'm telling you.
WILLIE: Where?
SAM: Everywhere. Try to glide through it.
WILLIE: Glide?
SAM: Ja, make it smooth. And give it more style. It must look like you're enjoying yourself.
WILLIE (*emphatically*): I wasn't.
SAM: Exactly.
WILLIE: How can I enjoy myself? Not straight, too stiff and now it's also glide, give it more style, make it smooth. . . . Haai! Is hard to remember all those things, Boet Sam.
SAM: That's your trouble. You're trying too hard.
WILLIE: I try hard because it *is* hard.
SAM: But don't let me see it. The secret is to make it look easy. Ballroom must look happy, Willie, not like hard work. It must. . . . Ja! . . . it must look like romance.
WILLIE: Now another one! What's romance?
SAM: Love story with happy ending. A handsome man in tails, and in his arms, smiling at him, a beautiful lady in evening dress!
WILLIE: Fred Astaire, Ginger Rogers.
SAM: You got it. Tapdance or ballroom, it's the same. Romance. In two weeks' time when the judges look at you and Hilda, they must see a man and a woman who are dancing their way to a happy ending. What I saw was you holding her like you were frightened she was going to run away.
WILLIE: Ja! Because that is what she wants to do! I got no romance left for Hilda anymore, Boet Sam.
SAM: Then pretend. When you put your arms around Hilda, imagine she is Ginger Rogers.
WILLIE: With no teeth? You try.

SAM: Well, just remember, there's only two weeks left.

WILLIE: I know, I know! (*To the jukebox.*) I do it better with music. You got sixpence for Sarah Vaughan?

SAM: That's a slow foxtrot. You're practicing the quick-step.

WILLIE: I'll practice slow foxtrot.

SAM (*shaking his head*): It's your turn to put money in the jukebox.

WILLIE: I only got bus fare to go home. (*He returns disconsolately to his work.*) Love story and happy ending! She's doing it all right, Boet Sam, but is not me she's giving happy endings. Fuckin' whore! Three nights now she doesn't come practice. I wind up gramophone, I get record ready and I sit and wait. What happens? Nothing. Ten o'clock I start dancing with my pillow. You try and practice romance by yourself, Boet Sam. Struesgod, she doesn't come tonight I take back my dress and ballroom shoes and I find me new partner. Size twenty-six. Shoes size seven. And now she's also making trouble for me with the baby again. Reports me to Child Wellfed, that I'm not giving her money. She lies! Every week I am giving her money for milk. And how do I know is my baby? Only his hair looks like me. She's fucking around all the time I turn my back. Hilda Samuels is a bitch! (*Pause.*) Hey, Sam!

SAM: Ja.

WILLIE: You listening?

SAM: Ja.

WILLIE: So what you say?

SAM: About Hilda?

WILLIE: Ja.

SAM: When did you last give her a hiding?

WILLIE (*reluctantly*): Sunday night.

SAM: And today is Thursday.

WILLIE (*he knows what's coming*): Okay.

SAM: Hiding on Sunday night, then Monday, Tuesday, and Wednesday she doesn't come to practice . . . and you are asking me why?

WILLIE: I said okay, Boet Sam!

SAM: You hit her too much. One day she's going to leave you for good.

WILLIE: So? She makes me the hell-in too much.

SAM (*emphasizing his point*): *Too* much and *too* hard. You had the same trouble with Eunice.

WILLIE: Because she also make the hell-in, Boet Sam. She never got the steps right. Even the waltz.

SAM: Beating her up every time she makes a mistake in the waltz? (*Shaking his head.*) No, Willie! That takes the pleasure out of ballroom dancing.

WILLIE: Hilda is not too bad with the waltz, Boet Sam. Is the quickstep where the trouble starts.

SAM (*teasing him gently*): How's your pillow with the quickstep?

WILLIE (*ignoring the tease*): Good! And why? Because it got no legs. That's her trouble. She can't move them quick enough, Boet Sam. I start the record and before halfway Count Basie is already winning. Only time we catch up with him is when gramophone runs down. (*Sam laughs.*) Haaikona, Boet Sam, is not funny.

SAM (*snapping his fingers*): I got it! Give her a handicap.

WILLIE: What's that?

SAM: Give her a ten-second start and then let Count Basie go. Then I put my money on her. Hot favorite in the Ballroom Stakes: Hilda Samuels ridden by Willie Malopo.

WILLIE (*turning away*): I'm not talking to you no more.

SAM (*relenting*): Sorry, Willie. . . .

WILLIE: It's finish between us.

SAM: Okay, okay . . . I'll stop.

WILLIE: You can also fuck off.

SAM: Willie, listen! I want to help you!

WILLIE: No more jokes?

SAM: I promise.

WILLIE: Okay. Help me.

SAM (*his turn to hold an imaginary partner*): Look and learn. Feet together. Back straight. Body relaxed. Right hand placed gently in the small of her back and wait for the music. Don't start worrying about making mistakes or the judges or the other competitors. It's just you, Hilda and the music, and you're going to have a good time. What Count Basie do you play?

WILLIE: "You the cream in my coffee, you the salt in my stew."

SAM: Right. Give it to me in strict tempo.

WILLIE: Ready?

SAM: Ready.

WILLIE: A-n-d . . . (*Singing.*)
  "You the cream in my coffee.
  You the salt in my stew.
  You will always be my necessity.
  I'd be lost without you. . . ." (*etc.*)

(*Sam launches into the quickstep. He is obviously a much more accomplished dancer than Willie. Hally enters. A seventeen-year-old white boy. Wet raincoat and school case. He stops and watches Sam. The demonstration comes to an end with a flourish. Applause from Hally and Willie.*)

HALLY: Bravo! No question about it. First place goes to Mr. Sam Semela.

WILLIE (*in total agreement*): You was gliding with style, Boet Sam.

HALLY (*cheerfully*): How's it, chaps?

SAM: Okay, Hally.

WILLIE (*springing to attention like a soldier and saluting*): At your service, Master Harold!

HALLY: Not long to the big event, hey!

SAM: Two weeks.

HALLY: You nervous?

SAM: No.

HALLY: Think you stand a chance?

SAM: Let's just say I'm ready to go out there and dance.

HALLY: It looked like it. What about you, Willie?

(*Willie groans.*)

What's the matter?

SAM: He's got leg trouble.

HALLY (*innocently*): Oh, sorry to hear that, Willie.

WILLIE: Boet Sam! You promised. (*Willie returns to his work.*)

(*Hally deposits his school case and takes off his raincoat. His clothes are a little neglected and untidy: black blazer with school badge, gray flannel trousers in need of an ironing, khaki shirt and tie, black shoes. Sam has fetched a towel for Hally to dry his hair.*)

HALLY: God, what a lousy bloody day. It's coming down cats and dogs out there. Bad for business, chaps. . . . (*Conspiratorial whisper.*) . . . but it also means we're in for a nice quiet afternoon.

SAM: You can speak loud. Your Mom's not here.

HALLY: Out shopping?

SAM: No. The hospital.

HALLY: But it's Thursday. There's no visiting on Thursday afternoons. Is my Dad okay?

SAM: Sounds like it. In fact, I think he's going home.

HALLY (*stopped short by Sam's remark*): What do you mean?

SAM: The hospital phoned.

HALLY: To say what?

SAM: I don't know. I just heard your Mom talking.

HALLY: So what makes you say he's going home?

SAM: It sounded as if they were telling her to come and fetch him.

(*Hally thinks about what Sam has said for a few seconds.*)

HALLY: When did she leave?

SAM: About an hour ago. She said she would phone you. Want to eat?

(*Hally doesn't respond.*)

Hally, want your lunch?

HALLY: I suppose so. (*His mood has changed.*) What's on the menu? . . . as if I don't know.

SAM: Soup, followed by meat pie and gravy.

HALLY: Today's?

SAM: No.

HALLY: And the soup?

SAM: Nourishing pea soup.

HALLY: Just the soup. (*The pile of comic books on the table.*) And these?

National Theatre of London's 1983 production of *"MASTER HAROLD" . . . and the boys* with (from left to right) Ramolao Makene as Willie, Duart Sylwain as Hally, and John Kani as Sam.

SAM: For your Dad. Mr. Kempston brought them.
HALLY: You haven't been reading them, have you?
SAM: Just looking.
HALLY (*examining the comics*): *Jungle Jim . . . Batman and Robin . . . Tarzan . . .* God, what rubbish! Mental pollution. Take them away.

(*Sam exits waltzing into the kitchen. Hally turns to Willie.*)

HALLY: Did you hear my Mom talking on the telephone, Willie?
WILLIE: No, Master Hally. I was at the back.
HALLY: And she didn't say anything to you before she left?
WILLIE: She said I must clean the floors.
HALLY: I mean about my Dad.
WILLIE: She didn't say nothing to me about him, Master Hally.
HALLY (*with conviction*): No! It can't be. They said he needed at least another three weeks of treatment. Sam's definitely made a mistake. (*Rummages through his school case, finds a book and settles down at the table to read.*) So, Willie!
WILLIE: Yes, Master Hally! Schooling okay today?
HALLY: Yes, okay. . . . (*He thinks about it.*) . . . No, not really. Ag, what's the difference? I don't care. And Sam says you've got problems.
WILLIE: Big problems.
HALLY: Which leg is sore?

(*Willie groans.*)

   Both legs.
WILLIE: There is nothing wrong with my legs. Sam is just making jokes.
HALLY: So then you *will* be in the competition.
WILLIE: Only if I can find a partner.
HALLY: But what about Hilda?
SAM (*returning with a bowl of soup*): She's the one who's got trouble with her legs.
HALLY: What sort of trouble, Willie?
SAM: From the way he describes it, I think the lady has gone a bit lame.
HALLY: Good God! Have you taken her to see a doctor?
SAM: I think a vet would be better.
HALLY: What do you mean?
SAM: What do you call it again when a racehorse goes very fast?
HALLY: Gallop?
SAM: That's it!
WILLIE: Boet Sam!
HALLY: "A gallop down the homestretch to the winning post." But what's that got to do with Hilda?
SAM: Count Basie always gets there first.

(*Willie lets fly with his slop rag. It misses Sam and hits Hally.*)

HALLY (*furious*): For Christ's sake, Willie! What the hell do you think you're doing?
WILLIE: Sorry, Master Hally, but it's him. . . .

HALLY: Act your bloody age! (*Hurls the rag back at Willie.*) Cut out the nonsense now and get on with your work. And you too, Sam. Stop fooling around.

(*Sam moves away.*)

   No. Hang on. I haven't finished! Tell me exactly what my Mom said.
SAM: I have. "When Hally comes, tell him I've gone to the hospital and I'll phone him."
HALLY: She didn't say anything about taking my Dad home?
SAM: No. It's just that when she was talking on the phone. . . .
HALLY (*interrupting him*): No, Sam. They can't be discharging him. She would have said so if they were. In any case, we saw him last night and he wasn't in good shape at all. Staff nurse even said there was talk about taking more X-rays. And now suddenly today he's better? If anything, it sounds more like a bad turn to me . . . which I sincerely hope it isn't. Hang on . . . how long ago did you say she left?
SAM: Just before two . . . (*His wrist watch.*) . . . hour and a half.
HALLY: I know how to settle it. (*Behind the counter to the telephone. Talking as he dials.*) Let's give her ten minutes to get to the hospital, ten minutes to load him up, another ten, at the most, to get home, and another ten to get him inside. Forty minutes. They should have been home for at least half an hour already. (*Pause—he waits with the receiver to his ear.*) No reply, chaps. And you know why? Because she's at his bedside in hospital helping him pull through a bad turn. You definitely heard wrong.
SAM: Okay.

(*As far as Hally is concerned, the matter is settled. He returns to his table, sits down, and divides his attention between the book and his soup. Sam is at his school case and picks up a textbook.*)

   Modern Graded Mathematics for Standards Nine and Ten. (*Opens it at random and laughs at something he sees.*) Who is this supposed to be?
HALLY: Old fart-face Prentice.
SAM: Teacher?
HALLY: Thinks he is. And believe me, that is not a bad likeness.
SAM: Has he seen it?
HALLY: Yes.
SAM: What did he say?
HALLY: Tried to be clever, as usual. Said I was no Leonardo da Vinci and that bad art had to be punished. So, six of the best, and his are bloody good.
SAM: On your bum?
HALLY: Where else? The days when I got them on my hands are gone forever, Sam.
SAM: With your trousers down!
HALLY: No. He's not quite that barbaric.
SAM: That's the way they do it in jail.
HALLY (*flicker of morbid interest*): Really?

SAM: Ja. When the magistrate sentences you to "strokes with a light cane."

HALLY: Go on.

SAM: They make you lie down on a bench. One policeman pulls down your trousers and holds your ankles, another one pulls your shirt over your head and holds your arms. . . .

HALLY: Thank you! That's enough.

SAM: . . . and the one that gives you the strokes talks to you gently and for a long time between each one. (*He laughs.*)

HALLY: I've heard enough, Sam! Jesus! It's a bloody awful world when you come to think of it. People can be real bastards.

SAM: That's the way it is, Hally.

HALLY: It doesn't *have* to be that way. There is something called progress, you know. We don't exactly burn people at the stake anymore.

SAM: Like Joan of Arc.

HALLY: Correct. If she was captured today, she'd be given a fair trial.

SAM: And then the death sentence.

HALLY (*a world-weary sigh*): I know, I know! I oscillate between hope and despair for this world as well, Sam. But things will change, you wait and see. One day somebody is going to get up and give history a kick up the backside and get it going again.

SAM: Like who?

HALLY (*after thought*): They're called social reformers. Every age, Sam, has got its social reformer. My history book is full of them.

SAM: So where's ours?

HALLY: Good question. And I hate to say it, but the answer is: I don't know. Maybe he hasn't even been born yet. Or is still only a babe in arms at his mother's breast. God, what a thought.

SAM: So we just go on waiting.

HALLY: Ja, looks like it. (*Back to his soup and the book.*)

SAM (*reading from the textbook*): "Introduction: In some mathematical problems only the magnitude. . . ." (*He mispronounces the word "magnitude."*)

HALLY (*correcting him without looking up*): Magnitude.

SAM: What's it mean?

HALLY: How big it is. The size of the thing.

SAM (*reading*): ". . . magnitude of the quantities is of importance. In other problems we need to know whether these quantities are negative or positive. For example, whether there is a debit or credit bank balance . . ."

HALLY: Whether you're broke or not.

SAM: ". . . whether the temperature is above or below Zero. . . ."

HALLY: Naught degrees. Cheerful state of affairs! No cash and you're freezing to death. Mathematics won't get you out of that one.

SAM: "All these quantities are called . . ." (*spelling the word*) . . . s-c-a-l. . . .

HALLY: Scalars.

SAM: Scalars! (*Shaking his head with a laugh.*) You understand all that?

HALLY (*turning a page*): No. And I don't intend to try.

SAM: So what happens when the exams come?

HALLY: Failing a maths exam isn't the end of the world, Sam. How many times have I told you that examination results don't measure intelligence?

SAM: I would say about as many times as you've failed one of them.

HALLY (*mirthlessly*): Ha, ha, ha.

SAM (*simultaneously*): Ha, ha, ha.

HALLY: Just remember Winston Churchill didn't do particularly well at school.

SAM: You've also told me that one many times.

HALLY: Well, it just so happens to be the truth.

SAM (*enjoying the word*): Magnitude! Magnitude! Show me how to use it.

HALLY (*after thought*): An intrepid social reformer will not be daunted by the magnitude of the task he has undertaken.

SAM (*impressed*): Couple of jaw-breakers in there!

HALLY: I gave you three for the price of one. Intrepid, daunted, and magnitude. I did that once in an exam. Put five of the words I had to explain in one sentence. It was half a page long.

SAM: Well, I'll put my money on you in the English exam.

HALLY: Piece of cake. Eighty percent without even trying.

SAM (*another textbook from Hally's case*): And history?

HALLY: So-so. I'll scrape through. In the fifties if I'm lucky.

SAM: You didn't do too badly last year.

HALLY: Because we had World War One. That at least has some action. You try to find that in the South African Parliamentary system.

SAM (*reading from the history textbook*): "Napoleon and the principle of equality." Hey! This sounds interesting. "After concluding peace with Britain in 1802, Napoleon used a brief period of calm to insti-tute . . ."

HALLY: Introduce.

SAM: ". . . many reforms. Napoleon regarded all people as equal before the law and wanted them to have equal opportunities for advancement. All ves-ti-ges of the feu-dal sys-tem with its oppression of the poor were abol-ished." Vestiges, feudal system, and abol-ished. I'm all right on oppression.

HALLY: I'm thinking. He swept away . . . abol-ished . . . the last remains . . . vestiges . . . of the bad old days . . . feudal system.

SAM: Ha! There's the social reformer we're waiting for. He sounds like a man of some magnitude.

HALLY: I'm not so sure about that. It's a damn good title for a book, though. A man of magnitude!

SAM: He sounds pretty big to me, Hally.

HALLY: Don't confuse historical significance with greatness. But maybe I'm being a bit prejudiced. Have a look in there and you'll see he's two chapters long. And hell! . . . has he only got dates, Sam, all of which you've got to remember! This campaign and that campaign, and then, because of all the fighting, the next thing is we get Peace Treaties all over the place. And what's the end of the story? Battle of Waterloo, which he loses. Wasn't worth it. No, I don't know about him as a man of magnitude.

SAM: Then who would you say was?

HALLY: To answer that, we need a definition of greatness, and I suppose that would be somebody who . . . somebody who benefited all mankind.

SAM: Right. But like who?

HALLY (*he speaks with total conviction*): Charles Darwin. Remember him? That big book from the library. *The Origin of the Species.*

SAM: Him?

HALLY: Yes. For his Theory of Evolution.

SAM: You didn't finish it.

HALLY: I ran out of time. I didn't finish it because my two weeks was up. But I'm going to take it out again after I've digested what I read. It's safe. I've hidden it away in the Theology section. Nobody ever goes in there. And anyway who are you to talk? You hardly even looked at it.

SAM: I tried. I looked at the chapters in the beginning and I saw one called "The Struggle for an Existence." Ah ha, I thought. At last! But what did I get? Something called the mistiltoe which needs the apple tree and there's too many seeds and all are going to die except one . . . ! No, Hally.

HALLY (*intellectually outraged*): What do you mean, No! The poor man had to start somewhere. For God's sake, Sam, he revolutionized science. Now we know.

SAM: What?

HALLY: Where we come from and what it all means.

SAM: And that's a benefit to mankind? Anyway, I still don't believe it.

HALLY: God, you're impossible. I showed it to you in black and white.

SAM: Doesn't mean I got to believe it.

HALLY: It's the likes of you that kept the Inquisition in business. It's called bigotry. Anyway, that's my man of magnitude. Charles Darwin! Who's yours?

SAM (*without hesitation*): Abraham Lincoln.

HALLY: I might have guessed as much. Don't get sentimental, Sam. You've never been a slave, you know. And anyway we freed your ancestors here in South Africa long before the Americans. But if you want to thank somebody on their behalf, do it to Mr. William Wilberforce.° Come on. Try again. I want a real genius.

(*Now enjoying himself, and so is Sam. Hally goes behind the counter and helps himself to a chocolate.*)

SAM: William Shakespeare.

HALLY (*no enthusiasm*): Oh. So you're also one of them, are you? You're basing that opinion on only one play,

---

Mr. William Wilberforce: (1759–1833), British statesman who supported a bill outlawing the slave trade and suppressing slavery in the British Empire.

you know. You've only read my *Julius Caesar* and even I don't understand half of what they're talking about. They should do what they did with the old Bible: bring the language up to date.

SAM: That's all you've got. It's also the only one *you've* read.

HALLY: I know. I admit it. That's why I suggest we reserve our judgment until we've checked up on a few others. I've got a feeling, though, that by the end of this year one is going to be enough for me, and I can give you the names of twenty-nine other chaps in the Standard Nine class of the Port Elizabeth Technical College who feel the same. But if you want him, you can have him. My turn now. (*Pacing.*) This is a damned good exercise, you know! It started off looking like a simple question and here it's got us really probing into the intellectual heritage of our civilization.

SAM: So who is it going to be?

HALLY: My next man . . . and he gets the title on two scores: social reform and literary genius . . . is Leo Nikolaevich Tolstoy.

SAM: That Russian.

HALLY: Correct. Remember the picture of him I showed you?

SAM: With the long beard.

HALLY (*trying to look like Tolstoy*): And those burning, visionary eyes. My God, the face of a social prophet if ever I saw one! And remember my words when I showed it to you? Here's a *man*, Sam!

SAM: Those were words, Hally.

HALLY: Not many intellectuals are prepared to shovel manure with the peasants and then go home and write a "little book" called *War and Peace*. Incidentally, Sam, he was somebody else who, to quote, ". . . did not distinguish himself scholastically."

SAM: Meaning?

HALLY: He was also no good at school.

SAM: Like you and Winston Churchill.

HALLY (*mirthlessly*): Ha, ha, ha.

SAM (*simultaneously*): Ha, ha, ha.

HALLY: Don't get clever, Sam. That man freed his serfs of his own free will.

SAM: No argument. He was a somebody, all right. I accept him.

HALLY: I'm sure Count Tolstoy will be very pleased to hear that. Your turn. Shoot. (*Another chocolate from behind the counter.*) I'm waiting, Sam.

SAM: I've got him.

HALLY: Good. Submit your candidate for examination.

SAM: Jesus.

HALLY (*stopped dead in his tracks*): Who?

SAM: Jesus Christ.

HALLY: Oh, come on, Sam!

SAM: The Messiah.

HALLY: Ja, but still . . . No, Sam. Don't let's get started on religion. We'll just spend the whole afternoon arguing again. Suppose I turn around and say Mohammed?

SAM: All right.

HALLY: You can't have them both on the same list!

SAM: Why not? You like Mohammed, I like Jesus.

HALLY: I *don't* like Mohammed. I never have. I was merely being hypothetical. As far as I'm concerned, the Koran is as bad as the Bible. No. Religion is out! I'm not going to waste my time again arguing with you about the existence of God. You know perfectly well I'm an atheist . . . and I've got homework to do.

SAM: Okay, I take him back.

HALLY: You've got time for one more name.

SAM (*after thought*): I've got one I know we'll agree on. A simple straightforward great Man of Magnitude . . . and no arguments. And *he* really *did* benefit all mankind.

HALLY: I wonder. After your last contribution I'm beginning to doubt whether anything in the way of an intellectual agreement is possible between the two of us. Who is he?

SAM: Guess.

HALLY: Socrates? Alexandre Dumas? Karl Marx? Dostoevsky? Nietzsche?

(*Sam shakes his head after each name.*)

Give me a clue.

SAM: The letter *P* is important. . . .

HALLY: Plato!

SAM: . . . and his name begins with an *F*.

HALLY: I've got it. Freud and Psychology.

SAM: No. I didn't understand him.

HALLY: That makes two of us.

SAM: Think of moldy apricot jam.

HALLY (*after a delighted laugh*): Penicillin and Sir Alexander Fleming! And the title of the book: *The Microbe Hunters*. (*Delighted.*) Splendid, Sam! Splendid. For once we are in total agreement. The major breakthrough in medical science in the Twentieth Century. If it wasn't for him, we might have lost the Second World War. It's deeply gratifying, Sam, to know that I haven't been wasting my time in talking to you. (*Strutting around proudly.*) Tolstoy may have educated his peasants, but I've educated you.

SAM: Standard Four to Standard Nine.

HALLY: Have we been at it as long as that?

SAM: Yep. And my first lesson was geography.

HALLY (*intrigued*): Really? I don't remember.

SAM: My room there at the back of the old Jubilee Boarding House. I had just started working for your Mom. Little boy in short trousers walks in one afternoon and asks me seriously: "Sam, do you want to see South Africa?" Hey man! Sure I wanted to see South Africa!

HALLY: Was that me?

SAM: . . . So the next thing I'm looking at a map you had just done for homework. It was your first one and you were very proud of yourself.

HALLY: Go on.

SAM: Then came my first lesson. "Repeat after me, Sam: Gold in the Transvaal, mealies in the Free State,

sugar in Natal, and grapes in the Cape." I still know it!

HALLY: Well, I'll be buggered. So that's how it all started.

SAM: And your next map was one with all the rivers and the mountains they came from. The Orange, the Vaal, the Limpopo, the Zambezi. . . .

HALLY: You've got a phenomenal memory!

SAM: You should be grateful. That is why you started passing your exams. You tried to be better than me.

(*They laugh together. Willie is attracted by the laughter and joins them.*)

HALLY: The old Jubilee Boarding House. Sixteen rooms with board and lodging, rent in advance and one week's notice. I haven't thought about it for donkey's years . . . and I don't think that's an accident. God, was I glad when we sold it and moved out. Those years are not remembered as the happiest ones of an unhappy childhood.

WILLIE (*knocking on the table and trying to imitate a woman's voice*): "Hally, are you there?"

HALLY: Who's that supposed to be?

WILLIE: "What you doing in there, Hally? Come out at once!"

HALLY (*to Sam*): What's he talking about?

SAM: Don't you remember?

WILLIE: "Sam, Willie . . . is he in there with you boys?"

SAM: Hiding away in our room when your mother was looking for you.

HALLY (*another good laugh*): Of course! I used to crawl and hide under your bed! But finish the story, Willie. Then what used to happen? You chaps would give the game away by telling her I was in there with you. So much for friendship.

SAM: We couldn't lie to her. She knew.

HALLY: Which meant I got another rowing for hanging around the "servants' quarters." I think I spent more time in there with you chaps than anywhere else in that dump. And do you blame me? Nothing but bloody misery wherever you went. Somebody was always complaining about the food, or my mother was having a fight with Micky Nash because she'd caught her with a petty officer in her room. Maud Meiring was another one. Remember those two? They were prostitutes, you know. Soldiers and sailors from the troopships. Bottom fell out of the business when the war ended. God, the flotsam and jetsam that life washed up on our shores! No joking, if it wasn't for your room, I would have been the first certified ten-year-old in medical history. Ja, the memories are coming back now. Walking home from school and thinking: "What can I do this afternoon?" Try out a few ideas, but sooner or later I'd end up in there with you fellows. I bet you I could still find my way to your room with my eyes closed. (*He does exactly that.*) Down the corridor . . . telephone on the right, which my Mom keeps locked because somebody is using it on the sly and not paying . . . past the kitchen and unappetizing cooking smells . . . around the corner into the backyard, hold my breath again because there are more smells coming when I pass your lavatory, then into that little passageway, first door on the right and into your room. How's that?

SAM: Good. But, as usual, you forgot to knock.

HALLY: Like that time I barged in and caught you and Cynthia . . . at it. Remember? God, was I embarrassed! I didn't know what was going on at first.

SAM: Ja, that taught you a lesson.

HALLY: And about a lot more than knocking on doors, I'll have you know, and I don't mean geography either. Hell, Sam, couldn't you have waited until it was dark?

SAM: No.

HALLY: Was it that urgent?

SAM: Yes, and if you don't believe me, wait until your time comes.

HALLY: No, thank you. I am not interested in girls. (*Back to his memories. . . . Using a few chairs he recreates the room as he lists the items.*) A gray little room with a cold cement floor. Your bed against that wall . . . and I now know why the mattress sags so much! . . . Willie's bed . . . it's propped up on bricks because one leg is broken . . . that wobbly little table with the washbasin and jug of water . . . Yes! . . . stuck to the wall above it are some pin-up pictures from magazines. Joe Louis. . . .

WILLIE: Brown Bomber. World Title. (*Boxing pose.*) Three rounds and knockout.

HALLY: Against who?

SAM: Max Schmeling.

HALLY: Correct. I can also remember Fred Astaire and Ginger Rogers, and Rita Hayworth in a bathing costume which always made me hot and bothered when I looked at it. Under Willie's bed is an old suitcase with all his clothes in a mess, which is why I never hide there. Your things are neat and tidy in a trunk next to your bed, and on it there is a picture of you and Cynthia in your ballroom clothes, your first silver cup for third place in a competition and an old radio which doesn't work anymore. Have I left out anything?

SAM: No.

HALLY: Right, so much for the stage directions. Now the characters. (*Sam and Willie move to their appropriate positions in the bedroom.*) Willie is in bed, under his blankets with his clothes on, complaining nonstop about something, but we can't make out a word of what he's saying because he's got his head under the blankets as well. You're on your bed trimming your toenails with a knife—not a very edifying sight—and as for me. . . . What am I doing?

SAM: You're sitting on the floor giving Willie a lecture about being a good loser while you get the checkerboard and pieces ready for a game. Then you go to Willie's bed, pull off the blankets and make him play with you first because you know you're going to win, and that gives you the second game with me.

HALLY: And you certainly were a bad loser, Willie!

WILLIE: Haai!

HALLY: Wasn't he, Sam? And so slow! A game with you almost took the whole afternoon. Thank God I gave up trying to teach you how to play chess.

WILLIE: You and Sam cheated.

HALLY: I never saw Sam cheat, and mine were mostly the mistakes of youth.

WILLIE: Then how is it you two was always winning?

HALLY: Have you ever considered the possibility, Willie, that it was because we were better than you?

WILLIE: Every time better?

HALLY: Not every time. There were occasions when we deliberately let you win a game so that you would stop sulking and go on playing with us. Sam used to wink at me when you weren't looking to show me it was time to let you win.

WILLIE: So then you two didn't play fair.

HALLY: It was for your benefit, Mr. Malopo, which is more than being fair. It was an act of self-sacrifice. (*To Sam.*) But you know what my best memory is, don't you?

SAM: No.

HALLY: Come on, guess. If your memory is so good, you must remember it as well.

SAM: We got up to a lot of tricks in there, Hally.

HALLY: This one was special, Sam.

SAM: I'm listening.

HALLY: It started off looking like another of those useless nothing-to-do afternoons. I'd already been down to Main Street looking for adventure, but nothing had happened. I didn't feel like climbing trees in the Donkin Park or pretending I was a private eye and following a stranger . . . so as usual: See what's cooking in Sam's room. This time it was you on the floor. You had two thin pieces of wood and you were smoothing them down with a knife. It didn't look particularly interesting, but when I asked you what you were doing, you just said, "Wait and see, Hally. Wait . . . and see" . . . in that secret sort of way of yours, so I knew there was a surprise coming. You teased me, you bugger, by being deliberately slow and not answering my questions!

(*Sam laughs.*)

And whistling while you worked away! God, it was infuriating! I could have brained you! It was only when you tied them together in a cross and put that down on the brown paper that I realized what you were doing. "Sam is making a kite?" And when I asked you and you said, "Yes" . . . ! (*Shaking his head with disbelief.*) The sheer audacity of it took my breath away. I mean, seriously, what the hell does a black man know about flying a kite? I'll be honest with you, Sam, I had no hopes for it. If you think I was excited and happy, you got another guess coming. In fact, I was shit-scared that we were going to make fools of ourselves. When we left the boarding house to go up onto the hill, I was praying quietly that there wouldn't be any other kids around to laugh at us.

SAM (*enjoying the memory as much as Hally*): Ja, I could see that.

HALLY: I made it obvious, did I?

SAM: Ja. You refused to carry it.

HALLY: Do you blame me? Can you remember what the poor thing looked like? Tomato-box wood and brown paper! Flour and water for glue! Two of my mother's old stockings for a tail, and then all those bits and pieces of string you made me tie together so that we could fly it! Hell, no, that was now only asking for a miracle to happen.

SAM: Then the big argument when I told you to hold the string and run with it when I let go.

HALLY: I was prepared to run, all right, but straight back to the boarding house.

SAM (*knowing what's coming*): So what happened?

HALLY: Come on, Sam, you remember as well as I do.

SAM: I want to hear it from you.

(*Hally pauses. He wants to be as accurate as possible.*)

HALLY: You went a little distance from me down the hill, you held it up ready to let it go. . . . "This is it," I thought. "Like everything else in my life, here comes another fiasco." Then you shouted, "Go, Hally!" and I started to run. (*Another pause.*) I don't know how to describe it, Sam. Ja! The miracle happened! I was running, waiting for it to crash to the ground, but instead suddenly there was something alive behind me at the end of the string, tugging at it as if it wanted to be free. I looked back . . . (*Shakes his head.*) . . . I still can't believe my eyes. It was flying! Looping around and trying to climb even higher into the sky. You shouted to me to let it have more string. I did, until there was none left and I was just holding that piece of wood we had tied it to. You came up and joined me. You were laughing.

SAM: So were you. And shouting, "It works, Sam! We've done it!"

HALLY: And we had! I was so proud of us! It was the most splendid thing I had ever seen. I wished there were hundreds of kids around to watch us. The part that scared me, though, was when you showed me how to make it dive down to the ground and then just when it was on the point of crashing, swoop up again!

SAM: You didn't want to try yourself.

HALLY: Of course not! I would have been suicidal if anything had happened to it. Watching you do it made me nervous enough. I was quite happy just to see it up there with its tail fluttering behind it. You left me after that, didn't you? You explained how to get it down, we tied it to the bench so that I could sit and watch it, and you went away. I wanted you to stay, you know. I was a little scared of having to look after it by myself.

SAM (*quietly*): I had work to do, Hally.

HALLY: It was sort of sad bringing it down, Sam. And it looked sad again when it was lying there on the ground. Like something that had lost its soul. Just tomato-box wood, brown paper and two of my mother's old stockings! But, hell, I'll never forget that first moment when I saw it up there. I had a stiff neck the next day from looking up so much.

(*Sam laughs. Hally turns to him with a question he never thought of asking before.*)

Why did you make that kite, Sam?

SAM (*evenly*): I can't remember.

HALLY: Truly?

SAM: Too long ago, Hally.

HALLY: Ja, I suppose it was. It's time for another one, you know.

SAM: Why do you say that?

HALLY: Because it feels like that. Wouldn't be a good day to fly it, though.

SAM: No. You can't fly kites on rainy days.

HALLY (*He studies Sam. Their memories have made him conscious of the man's presence in his life.*): How old are you, Sam?

SAM: Two score and five.

HALLY: Strange, isn't it?

SAM: What?

HALLY: Me and you.

SAM: What's strange about it?

HALLY: Little white boy in short trousers and a black man old enough to be his father flying a kite. It's not every day you see that.

SAM: But why strange? Because the one is white and the other black?

HALLY: I don't know. Would have been just as strange, I suppose, if it had been me and my Dad . . . cripple man and a little boy! Nope! There's no chance of me flying a kite without it being strange. (*Simple statement of fact—no self-pity.*) There's a nice little short story there. "The Kite-Flyers." But we'd have to find a twist in the ending.

SAM: Twist?

HALLY: Yes. Something unexpected. The way it ended with us was too straightforward . . . me on the bench and you going back to work. There's no drama in that.

WILLIE: And me?

HALLY: You?

WILLIE: Yes me.

HALLY: You want to get into the story as well, do you? I got it! Change the title: "Afternoons in Sam's Room" . . . expand it and tell all the stories. It's on its way to being a novel. Our days in the old Jubilee. Sad in a way that they're over. I almost wish we were still in that little room.

SAM: We're still together.

HALLY: That's true. It's just that life felt the right size in there . . . not too big and not too small. Wasn't so hard to work up a bit of courage. It's got so bloody complicated since then.

(The telephone rings. Sam answers it.)

SAM: St. George's Park Tea Room . . . Hello, Madam . . . Yes, Madam, he's here. . . . Hally, it's your mother.

HALLY: Where is she phoning from?

SAM: Sounds like the hospital. It's a public telephone.

HALLY *(relieved)*: You see! I told you. *(The telephone.)* Hello, Mom . . . Yes . . . Yes no fine. Everything's under control here. How's things with poor old Dad? . . . Has he had a bad turn? . . . What? . . . Oh, God! . . . Yes, Sam told me, but I was sure he'd made a mistake. But what's this all about, Mom? He didn't look at all good last night. How can he get better so quickly? . . . Then very obviously you must say no. Be firm with him. You're the boss. . . . You know what it's going to be like if he comes home. . . . Well then, don't blame me when I fail my exams at the end of the year. . . . Yes! How am I expected to be fresh for school when I spend half the night massaging his gammy leg? . . . So am I! . . . So tell him a white lie. Say Dr. Colley wants more X-rays of his stump. Or bribe him. We'll sneak in double tots of brandy in future. . . . What? . . . Order him to get back into bed at once! If he's going to behave like a child, treat him like one. . . . All right, Mom! I was just trying to . . . I'm sorry. . . . I said I'm sorry. . . . Quick, give me your number. I'll phone you back. *(He hangs up and waits a few seconds.)* Here we go again! *(He dials.)* I'm sorry, Mom. . . . Okay. . . . But now listen to me carefully. All it needs is for you to put your foot down. Don't take no for an answer. . . . Did you hear me? And whatever you do, don't discuss it with him. . . . Because I'm frightened you'll give in to him. . . . Yes, Sam gave me lunch. . . . I ate all of it! . . . No, Mom not a soul. It's still raining here. . . . Right, I'll tell them. I'll just do some homework and then lock up. . . . But remember now, Mom. Don't listen to anything he says. And phone me back and let me know what happens. . . . Okay. Bye, Mom. *(He hangs up. The men are staring at him.)* My Mom says that when you're finished with the floors you must do the windows. *(Pause.)* Don't misunderstand me, chaps. All I want is for him to get better. And if he was, I'd be the first person to say: "Bring him home." But he's not, and we can't give him the medical care and attention he needs at home. That's what hospitals are there for. *(Brusquely.)* So don't just stand there! Get on with it!

(Sam clears Hally's table.)

You heard right. My Dad wants to go home.

SAM: Is he better?

HALLY *(sharply)*: No! How the hell can he be better when last night he was groaning with pain? This is not an age of miracles!

SAM: Then he should stay in hospital.

HALLY *(seething with irritation and frustration)*: Tell me something I don't know, Sam. What the hell do you think I was saying to my Mom? All I can say is fuck-it-all.

SAM: I'm sure he'll listen to your Mom.

HALLY: You don't know what she's up against. He's already packed his shaving kit and pajamas and is sitting on his bed with his crutches, dressed and ready to go. I know him when he gets in that mood. If she tries to reason with him, we've had it. She's no match for him when it comes to a battle of words. He'll tie her up in knots. *(Trying to hide his true feelings.)*

SAM: I suppose it gets lonely for him in there.

HALLY: With all the patients and nurses around? Regular visits from the Salvation Army? Balls! It's ten times worse for him at home. I'm at school and my mother is here in the business all day.

SAM: He's at least got you at night.

HALLY *(before he can stop himself)*: And we've got him! Please! I don't want to talk about it anymore. *(Unpacks his school case, slamming down books on the table.)* Life is just a plain bloody mess, that's all. And people are fools.

SAM: Come on, Hally.

HALLY: Yes, they are! They bloody well deserve what they get.

SAM: Then don't complain.

HALLY: Don't try to be clever, Sam. It doesn't suit you. Anybody who thinks there's nothing wrong with this world needs to have his head examined. Just when things are going along all right, without fail someone or something will come along and spoil everything. Somebody should write that down as a fundamental law of the Universe. The principle of perpetual disappointment. If there is a God who created this world, he should scrap it and try again.

SAM: All right, Hally, all right. What you got for homework?

HALLY: Bullshit, as usual. *(Opens an exercise book and reads.)* "Write five hundred words describing an annual event of cultural or historical significance."

SAM: That should be easy enough for you.

HALLY: And also plain bloody boring. You know what he wants, don't you? One of their useless old ceremonies. The commemoration of the landing of the 1820 Settlers, or if it's going to be culture, Carols by Candlelight every Christmas.

SAM: It's an impressive sight. Make a good description, Hally. All those candles glowing in the dark and the people singing hymns.

HALLY: And it's called religious hysteria. *(Intense irritation.)* Please, Sam! Just leave me alone and let me get on with it. I'm not in the mood for games this afternoon. And remember my Mom's orders . . . you're to help Willie with the windows. Come on now, I don't want any more nonsense in here.

SAM: Okay, Hally, okay.

(Hally settles down to his homework; determined preparations . . . pen, ruler, exercise book, dictionary, another cake . . . all of which will lead to nothing.)

(Sam waltzes over to Willie and starts to replace tables and chairs. He practices a ballroom step while doing so. Willie watches. When Sam is finished, Willie tries.)

Good! But just a little bit quicker on the turn and only move in to her after she's crossed over. What about this one?

(Another step. When Sam is finished, Willie again has a go.)

Much better. See what happens when you just relax and enjoy yourself? Remember that in two weeks' time and you'll be all right.

WILLIE: But I haven't got partner, Boet Sam.

SAM: Maybe Hilda will turn up tonight.

WILLIE: No, Boet Sam. *(Reluctantly.)* I gave her a good hiding.

SAM: You mean a bad one.

WILLIE: Good bad one.

SAM: Then you mustn't complain either. Now you pay the price for losing your temper.

WILLIE: I also pay two pounds ten shilling entrance fee.

SAM: They'll refund you if you withdraw now.

WILLIE *(appalled)*: You mean, don't dance?

SAM: Yes.

WILLIE: No! I wait too long and I practice too hard. If I find me new partner, you think I can be ready in two weeks? I ask Madam for my leave now and we practice every day.

SAM: Quickstep nonstop for two weeks. World record, Willie, but you'll be mad at the end.

WILLIE: No jokes, Boet Sam.

SAM: I'm not joking.

WILLIE: So then what?

SAM: Find Hilda. Say you're sorry and promise you won't beat her again.

WILLIE: No.

SAM: Then withdraw. Try again next year.

WILLIE: No.

SAM: Then I give up.

WILLIE: Haaikona, Boet Sam, you can't.

SAM: What do you mean, I can't? I'm telling you: I give up.

WILLIE *(adamant)*: No! *(Accusingly.)* It was you who start me ballroom dancing.

SAM: So?

WILLIE: Before that I use to be happy. And is you and Miriam who bring me to Hilda and say here's partner for you.

SAM: What are you saying, Willie?

WILLIE: You!

SAM: But me what? To blame?

WILLIE: Yes.

SAM: Willie . . . ? *(Bursts into laughter.)*

WILLIE: And now all you do is make jokes at me. You wait. When Miriam leaves you is my turn to laugh. Ha! Ha! Ha!

SAM *(he can't take Willie seriously any longer)*: She can leave me tonight! I know what to do. *(Bowing before*

an imaginary partner.) May I have the pleasure? *(He dances and sings.)*
"Just a fellow with his pillow . . .
Dancin' like a willow . . .
In an autumn breeze. . . ."

WILLIE: There you go again!

(Sam goes on dancing and singing.)

Boet Sam!

SAM: There's the answer to your problem! Judges' announcement in two weeks' time: "Ladies and gentlemen, the winner in the open section . . . Mr. Willie Malopo and his pillow!"

(This is too much for a now really angry Willie. He goes for Sam, but the latter is too quick for him and puts Hally's table between the two of them.)

HALLY *(exploding)*: For Christ's sake, you two!

WILLIE *(still trying to get at Sam)*: I donner you, Sam! Struesgod!

SAM *(still laughing)*: Sorry, Willie . . . Sorry. . . .

HALLY: Sam! Willie! *(Grabs his ruler and gives Willie a vicious whack on the bum.)* How the hell am I supposed to concentrate with the two of you behaving like bloody children!

WILLIE: Hit him too!

HALLY: Shut up, Willie.

WILLIE: He started jokes again.

HALLY: Get back to your work. You too, Sam. *(His ruler.)* Do you want another one, Willie?

(Sam and Willie return to their work. Hally uses the opportunity to escape from his unsuccessful attempt at homework. He struts around like a little despot, ruler in hand, giving vent to his anger and frustration.)

Suppose a customer had walked in then? Or the Park Superintendent. And seen the two of you behaving like a pair of hooligans. That would have been the end of my mother's license, you know. And your jobs? Well, this is the end of it. From now on there will be no more of your ballroom nonsense in here. This is a business establishment, not a bloody New Brighton dancing school. I've been far too lenient with the two of you. *(Behind the counter for a green cool drink and a dollop of ice cream. He keeps up his tirade as he prepares it.)* But what really makes me bitter is that I allow you chaps a little freedom in here when business is bad and what do you do with it? The foxtrot! Specially you, Sam. There's more to life than trotting around a dance floor and I thought at least you knew it.

SAM: It's a harmless pleasure, Hally. It doesn't hurt anybody.

HALLY: It's also a rather simple one, you know.

SAM: You reckon so? Have you ever tried?

HALLY: Of course not.

SAM: Why don't you? Now.

HALLY: What do you mean? Me dance?

SAM: Yes. I'll show you a simple step—the waltz—then you try it.

HALLY: What will that prove?

SAM: That it might not be as easy as you think.

HALLY: I didn't say it was easy. I said it was simple—like in simple-minded, meaning mentally retarded. You can't exactly say it challenges the intellect.

SAM: It does other things.

HALLY: Such as?

SAM: Make people happy.

HALLY (*the glass in his hand*): So do American cream sodas with ice cream. For God's sake, Sam, you're not asking me to take ballroom dancing serious, are you?

SAM: Yes.

HALLY (*sigh of defeat*): Oh, well, so much for trying to give you a decent education. I've obviously achieved nothing.

SAM: You still haven't told me what's wrong with admiring something that's beautiful and then trying to do it yourself.

HALLY: Nothing. But we happen to be talking about a foxtrot, not a thing of beauty.

SAM: But that is just what I'm saying. If you were to see two champions doing, two masters of the art . . . !

HALLY: Oh God, I give up. So now it's also art!

SAM: Ja.

HALLY: There's a limit, Sam. Don't confuse art and entertainment.

SAM: So then what is art?

HALLY: You want a definition?

SAM: Ja.

HALLY (*He realizes he has got to be careful. He gives the matter a lot of thought before answering.*): Philosophers have been trying to do that for centuries. What is Art? What is Life? But basically I suppose it's . . . the giving of meaning to matter.

SAM: Nothing to do with beautiful?

HALLY: It goes beyond that. It's the giving of form to the formless.

SAM: Ja, well, maybe it's not art, then. But I still say it's beautiful.

HALLY: I'm sure the word you mean to use is entertaining.

SAM (*adamant*): No. Beautiful. And if you want proof come along to the Centenary Hall in New Brighton in two weeks' time.

(*The mention of the Centenary Hall draws Willie over to them.*)

HALLY: What for? I've seen the two of you prancing around in here often enough.

SAM (*he laughs*): This isn't the real thing, Hally. We're just playing around in here.

HALLY: So? I can use my imagination.

SAM: And what do you get?

HALLY: A lot of people dancing around and having a so-called good time.

SAM: That all?

HALLY: Well, basically it is that, surely.

SAM: No, it isn't. Your imagination hasn't helped you at all. There's a lot more to it than that. We're getting ready for the championships, Hally, not just another dance. There's going to be a lot of people, all right, and they're going to have a good time, but they'll only be spectators, sitting around and watching. It's just the competitors out there on the dance floor. Party decorations and fancy lights all around the walls! The ladies in beautiful evening dresses!

HALLY: My mother's got one of those, Sam, and, quite frankly, it's an embarrassment every time she wears it.

SAM (*undeterred*): Your imagination left out the excitement.

(*Hally scoffs.*)

Oh, yes. The finalists are not going to be out there just to have a good time. One of those couples will be the 1950 Eastern Province Champions. And your imagination left out the music.

WILLIE: Mr. Elijah Gladman Guzana and his Orchestral Jazzonions.

SAM: The sound of the big band, Hally. Trombone, trumpet, tenor and alto sax. And then, finally, your imagination also left out the climax of the evening when the dancing is finished, the judges have stopped whispering among themselves and the Master of Ceremonies collects their scorecards and goes up onto the stage to announce the winners.

HALLY: All right. So you make it sound like a bit of a do. It's an occasion. Satisfied?

SAM (*victory*): So you admit that!

HALLY: Emotionally yes, intellectually no.

SAM: Well, I don't know what you mean by that, all I'm telling you is that it is going to be *the* event of the year in New Brighton. It's been sold out for two weeks already. There's only standing room left. We've got competitors coming from Kingwilliamstown, East London, Port Alfred.

(*Hally starts pacing thoughtfully.*)

HALLY: Tell me a bit more.

SAM: I thought you weren't interested . . . intellectually.

HALLY (*mysteriously*): I've got my reasons.

SAM: What do you want to know?

HALLY: It takes place every year?

SAM: Yes. But only every third year in New Brighton. It's East London's turn to have the championships next year.

HALLY: Which, I suppose, makes it an even more significant event.

SAM: Ah ha! We're getting somewhere. Our "occasion" is now a "significant event."

HALLY: I wonder.

SAM: What?

HALLY: I wonder if I would get away with it.

SAM: But what?

HALLY (*to the table and his exercise book*): "Write five hundred words describing an annual event of cultural or historical significance." Would I be stretching poetic license a little too far if I called your ballroom championships a cultural event?

SAM: You mean . . . ?

HALLY: You think we could get five hundred words out of it, Sam?

SAM: Victor Sylvester has written a whole book on ballroom dancing.

WILLIE: You going to write about it, Master Hally?

HALLY: Yes, gentlemen, that is precisely what I am considering doing. Old Doc Bromely—he's my English teacher—is going to argue with me, of course. He doesn't like natives. But I'll point out to him that in strict anthropological terms the culture of a primitive black society includes its dancing and singing. To put my thesis in a nutshell: The war-dance has been replaced by the waltz. But it still amounts to the same thing: the release of primitive emotions through movement. Shall we give it a go?

SAM: I'm ready.

WILLIE: Me also.

HALLY: Ha! This will teach the old bugger a lesson. (*Decision taken.*) Right. Let's get ourselves organized. (*This means another cake on the table. He sits.*) I think you've given me enough general atmosphere, Sam, but to build the tension and suspense I need facts. (*Pencil poised.*)

WILLIE: Give him facts, Boet Sam.

HALLY: What you called the climax . . . how many finalists?

SAM: Six couples.

HALLY (*making notes*): Go on. Give me the picture.

SAM: Spectators seated right around the hall. (*Willie becomes a spectator.*)

HALLY: . . . and it's a full house.

SAM: At one end, on the stage, Gladman and his Orchestral Jazzonions. At the other end is a long table with the three judges. The six finalists go onto the dance floor and take up their positions. When they are ready and the spectators have settled down, the Master of Ceremonies goes to the microphone. To start with, he makes some jokes to get people laughing. . . .

HALLY: Good touch. (*As he writes.*) " . . . creating a relaxed atmosphere which will change to one of tension and drama as the climax is approached."

SAM (*onto a chair to act out the M.C.*): "Ladies and gentlemen, we come now to the great moment you have all been waiting for this evening. . . . The finals of the 1950 Eastern Province Open Ballroom Dancing Championships. But first let me introduce the finalists! Mr. and Mrs. Welcome Tchabalala from Kingwilliamstown . . ."

WILLIE (*he applauds after every name*): Is when the people clap their hands and whistle and make a lot of noise, Master Hally.

SAM: "Mr. Mulligan Njikelane and Miss Nomhle Nkonyeni of Grahamstown; Mr. and Mrs. Norman Nchinga from Port Alfred; Mr. Fats Bokolane and Miss Dina Plaatjies from East London; Mr. Sipho

Danny Glover, who played Willie in the 1982 Broadway production, played the older waiter, Sam, in the 2003 New York revival of *"MASTER HAROLD" . . . and the boys*, directed by Lonny Price.

Dugu and Mrs. Mable Magada from Peddie; and from New Brighton our very own Mr. Willie Malopo and Miss Hilda Samuels."

(*Willie can't believe his ears. He abandons his role as spectator and scrambles into position as a finalist.*)

WILLIE: Relaxed and ready to romance!

SAM: The applause dies down. When everybody is silent, Gladman lifts up his sax, nods at the Orchestral Jazzonions. . . .

WILLIE: Play the jukebox please, Boet Sam!

SAM: I also only got bus fare, Willie.

HALLY: Hold it, everybody. (*Heads for the cash register behind the counter.*) How much is in the till, Sam?

SAM: Three shillings. Hally . . . Your Mom counted it before she left.

(*Hally hesitates.*)

HALLY: Sorry, Willie. You know how she carried on the last time I did it. We'll just have to pool our combined imaginations and hope for the best. (*Returns to the table.*) Back to work. How are the points scored, Sam?

SAM: Maximum of ten points each for individual style, deportment, rhythm, and general appearance.

WILLIE: Must I start?

HALLY: Hold it for a second, Willie. And penalties?

SAM: For what?

HALLY: For doing something wrong. Say you stumble or bump into somebody . . . do they take off any points?

SAM (*aghast*): Hally . . . !

HALLY: When you're dancing. If you and your partner collide into another couple.

(*Hally can get no further. Sam has collapsed with laughter. He explains to Willie.*)

SAM: If me and Miriam bump into you and Hilda. . . .

(*Willie joins him in another good laugh.*)

Hally, Hally . . . !

HALLY (*perplexed*): Why? What did I say?

SAM: There's no collisions out there, Hally. Nobody trips or stumbles or bumps into anybody else. That's what that moment is all about. To be one of those finalists on that dance floor is like . . . like being in a dream about a world in which accidents don't happen.

HALLY (*genuinely moved by Sam's image*): Jesus, Sam! That's beautiful!

WILLIE (*can endure waiting no longer*): I'm starting!

(*Willie dances while Sam talks.*)

SAM: Of course it is. That's what I've been trying to say to you all afternoon. And it's beautiful because that is what we want life to be like. But instead, like you said, Hally, we're bumping into each other all the time. Look at the three of us this afternoon: I've bumped into Willie, the two of us have bumped into you, you've bumped into your mother, she bumping into your Dad. . . . None of us knows the steps and there's no music playing. And it doesn't stop with us. The whole world is doing it all the time. Open a newspaper and what do you read? America has bumped into Russia, England is bumping into India, rich man bumps into poor man. Those are big collisions, Hally. They make for a lot of bruises. People get hurt in all that bumping, and we're sick and tired of it now. It's been going on for too long. Are we never going to get it right? . . . Learn to dance life like champions instead of always being just a bunch of beginners at it?

HALLY (*deep and sincere admiration of the man*): You've got a vision, Sam!

SAM: Not just me. What I'm saying to you is that everybody's got it. That's why there's only standing room left for the Centenary Hall in two weeks' time. For as long as the music lasts, we are going to see six couples get it right, the way we want life to be.

HALLY: But is that the best we can do, Sam . . . watch six finalists dreaming about the way it should be?

SAM: I don't know. But it starts with that. Without the dream we won't know what we're going for. And anyway I reckon there are a few people who have got past just dreaming about it and are trying for something real. Remember that thing we read once in the paper about the Mahatma Gandhi? Going without food to stop those riots in India?

HALLY: You're right. He certainly was trying to teach people to get the steps right.

SAM: And the Pope.

HALLY: Yes, he's another one. Our old General Smuts° as well, you know. He's also out there dancing. You know, Sam, when you come to think of it, that's what the United Nations boils down to . . . a dancing school for politicians!

SAM: And let's hope they learn.

HALLY (*a little surge of hope*): You're right. We mustn't despair. Maybe there's some hope for mankind after all. Keep it up, Willie. (*Back to his table with determination.*) This is a lot bigger than I thought. So what have we got? Yes, our title: "A World Without Collisions."

SAM: That sounds good! "A World Without Collisions."

HALLY: Subtitle: "Global Politics on the Dance Floor." No. A bit too heavy, hey? What about "Ballroom Dancing as a Political Vision"?

(*The telephone rings. Sam answers it.*)

SAM: St. George's Park Tea Room . . . Yes, Madam . . . Hally, it's your Mom.

HALLY (*back to reality*): Oh, God, yes! I'd forgotten all about that. Shit! Remember my words, Sam? Just when you're enjoying yourself, someone or something will come along and wreck everything.

SAM: You haven't heard what she's got to say yet.

HALLY: Public telephone?

SAM: No.

HALLY: Does she sound happy or unhappy?

SAM: I couldn't tell. (*Pause.*) She's waiting, Hally.

HALLY (*to the telephone*): Hello, Mom . . . No, everything is okay here. Just doing my homework. . . . What's your news? . . . You've what? . . . (*Pause. He takes the receiver away from his ear for a few seconds. In the course of Hally's telephone conversation, Sam and Willie discreetly position the stacked tables and chairs. Hally places the receiver back to his ear.*) Yes, I'm still here. Oh, well, I give up now. Why did you do it, Mom? . . . Well, I just hope you know what you've let us in for. . . . (*Loudly.*) I said I hope you know what you've let us in for! It's the end of the peace and quiet we've been having. (*Softly.*) Where is he? (*Normal voice.*) He can't hear us from

---

General Smuts: (1870–1950), South African statesman who fought the British in the Boer War in 1899, was instrumental in forming the Union of South Africa in 1910, and was active in the creation of the United Nations.

in there. But for God's sake, Mom, what happened? I told you to be firm with him. . . . Then you and the nurses should have held him down, taken his crutches away. . . . I know only too well he's my father! . . . I'm not being disrespectful, but I'm sick and tired of emptying stinking chamber pots full of phlegm and piss. . . . Yes, I do! When you're not there, he asks *me* to do it. . . . If you really want to know the truth, that's why I've got no appetite for my food. . . . Yes! There's a lot of things you don't know about. For your information, I still haven't got that science textbook I need. And you know why? He borrowed the money you gave me for it. . . . Because I didn't want to start another fight between you two. . . . He says that every time. . . . All right, Mom! (*Viciously.*) Then just remember to start hiding your bag away again, because he'll be at your purse before long for money for booze. And when he's well enough to come down here, you better keep an eye on the till as well, because that is also going to develop a leak. . . . Then don't complain to me when he starts his old tricks. . . . Yes, you do. I get it from you on one side and from him on the other, and it makes life hell for me. I'm not going to be the peacemaker anymore. I'm warning you now: when the two of you start fighting again, I'm leaving home. . . . Mom, if you start crying, I'm going to put down the receiver. . . . Okay. . . . (*Lowering his voice to a vicious whisper.*) Okay, Mom. I heard you. (*Desperate.*) No. . . . Because I don't want to. I'll see him when I get home! Mom! . . . (*Pause. When he speaks again, his tone changes completely. It is not simply pretense. We sense a genuine emotional conflict.*) Welcome home, chum! . . . What's that? . . . Don't be silly, Dad. You being home is just about the best news in the world. . . . I bet you are. Bloody depressing there with everybody going on about their ailments, hey! . . . How you feeling? . . . Good. . . . Here as well, pal. Coming down cats and dogs. . . . That's right. Just the day for a kip° and a toss in your old Uncle Ned. . . . Everything's just hunky-dory on my side, Dad. . . . Well, to start with, there's a nice pile of comics for you on the counter. . . . Yes, old Kemple brought them in. *Batman and Robin, Submariner* . . . just your cup of tea. . . . I will. . . . Yes, we'll spin a few yarns tonight. . . . Okay, chum, see you in a little while. . . . No, I promise. I'll come straight home. . . . (*Pause—his mother comes back on the phone.*) Mom? Okay. I'll lock up now. . . . What? . . . Oh, the brandy . . . Yes, I'll remember! . . . I'll put it in my suitcase now, for God's sake. I know well enough what will happen if he doesn't get it. . . . (*Places a bottle of brandy on the counter.*) I *was* kind to him, Mom. I didn't say anything nasty! . . . All right. Bye. (*End of telephone conversation. A desolate Hally doesn't move. A strained silence.*)

kip: Nap.

SAM (*quietly*): That sounded like a bad bump, Hally.

HALLY (*Having a hard time controlling his emotions. He speaks carefully.*): Mind your own business, Sam.

SAM: Sorry. I wasn't trying to interfere. Shall we carry on? Hally? (*He indicates the exercise book. No response from Hally.*)

WILLIE (*also trying*): Tell him about when they give out the cups, Boet Sam.

SAM: Ja! That's another big moment. The presentation of the cups after the winners have been announced. You've got to put that in.

(*Still no response from Hally.*)

WILLIE: A big silver one, Master Hally, called floating trophy for the champions.

SAM: We always invite some big-shot personality to hand them over. Guest of honor this year is going to be His Holiness Bishop Jabulani of the All African Free Zionist Church.

(*Hally gets up abruptly, goes to his table, and tears up the page he was writing on.*)

HALLY: So much for a bloody world without collisions.

SAM: Too bad. It was on its way to being a good composition.

HALLY: Let's stop bullshitting ourselves, Sam.

SAM: Have we been doing that?

HALLY: Yes! That's what all our talk about a decent world has been . . . just so much bullshit.

SAM: We did say it was still only a dream.

HALLY: And a bloody useless one at that. Life's a fuckup and it's never going to change.

SAM: Ja, maybe that's true.

HALLY: There's no maybe about it. It's a blunt and brutal fact. All we've done this afternoon is waste our time.

SAM: Not if we'd got your homework done.

HALLY: I don't give a shit about my homework, so, for Christ's sake, just shut up about it. (*Slamming books viciously into his school case.*) Hurry up now and finish your work. I want to lock up and get out of here. (*Pause.*) And then go where? Home-sweet-fucking-home. Jesus, I hate that word.

(*Hally goes to the counter to put the brandy bottle and comics in his school case. After a moment's hesitation, he smashes the bottle of brandy. He abandons all further attempts to hide his feelings. Sam and Willie work away as unobtrusively as possible.*)

Do you want to know what is really wrong with your lovely little dream, Sam? It's not just that we are all bad dancers. That does happen to be perfectly true, but there's more to it than just that. You left out the cripples.

SAM: Hally!

HALLY (*now totally reckless*): Ja! Can't leave them out, Sam. That's why we always end up on our backsides on the dance floor. They're also out there dancing . . . like a bunch of broken spiders trying to do the quickstep! (*An ugly attempt at laughter.*) When you come to think of it, it's a bloody comical sight. I mean, it's bad enough on two legs . . . but one and a pair of crutches! Hell, no, Sam. That's guaranteed to turn that dance floor into a shambles. Why you shaking your head? Picture it, man. For once this afternoon let's use our imaginations sensibly.

SAM: Be careful, Hally.

HALLY: Of what? The truth? I seem to be the only one around here who is prepared to face it. We've had the pretty dream, it's time now to wake up and have a good long look at the way things really are. Nobody knows the steps, there's no music, the cripples are also out there tripping up everybody and trying to get into the act, and it's all called the All-Comers-How-to-Make-a-Fuckup-of-Life Championships. (*Another ugly laugh.*) Hang on, Sam! The best bit is still coming. Do you know what the winner's trophy is? A beautiful big chamber pot with roses on the side, and it's full to the brim with piss. And guess who I think is going to be this year's winner.

SAM (*almost shouting*): Stop now!

HALLY (*suddenly appalled by how far he has gone*): Why?

SAM: Hally? It's your father you're talking about.

HALLY: So?

SAM: Do you know what you've been saying?

(*Hally can't answer. He is rigid with shame. Sam speaks to him sternly.*)

No, Hally, you mustn't do it. Take back those words and ask for forgiveness! It's a terrible sin for a son to mock his father with jokes like that. You'll be punished if you carry on. Your father is your father, even if he is a . . . cripple man.

WILLIE: Yes, Master Hally. Is true what Sam say.

SAM: I understand how you are feeling, Hally, but even so. . . .

HALLY: No, you don't!

SAM: I think I do.

HALLY: And I'm telling you you don't. Nobody does. (*Speaking carefully as his shame turns to rage at Sam.*) It's your turn to be careful, Sam. Very careful! You're treading on dangerous ground. Leave me and my father alone.

SAM: I'm not the one who's been saying things about him.

HALLY: What goes on between me and my Dad is none of your business!

SAM: Then don't tell me about it. If that's all you've got to say about him, I don't want to hear.

(*For a moment Hally is at loss for a response.*)

HALLY: Just get on with your bloody work and shut up.

SAM: Swearing at me won't help you.

HALLY: Yes, it does! Mind your own fucking business and shut up!

SAM: Okay. If that's the way you want it, I'll stop trying.

(*He turns away. This infuriates Hally even more.*)

HALLY: Good. Because what you've been trying to do is meddle in something you know nothing about. All that concerns you in here, Sam, is to try and do what you get paid for—keep the place clean and serve the customers. In plain words, just get on with your job. My mother is right. She's always warning me about allowing you to get too familiar. Well, this time you've gone too far. It's going to stop right now.

(*No response from Sam.*)

You're only a servant in here, and don't forget it.

(*Still no response. Hally is trying hard to get one.*)

And as far as my father is concerned, all you need to remember is that he is your boss.

SAM (*needled at last*): No, he isn't. I get paid by your mother.

HALLY: Don't argue with me, Sam!

SAM: Then don't say he's my boss.

HALLY: He's a white man and that's good enough for you.

SAM: I'll try to forget you said that.

HALLY: Don't! Because you won't be doing me a favor if you do. I'm telling you to remember it.

(*A pause. Sam pulls himself together and makes one last effort.*)

SAM: Hally, Hally . . . ! Come on now. Let's stop before it's too late. You're right. We *are* on dangerous ground. If we're not careful, somebody is going to get hurt.

HALLY: It won't be me.

SAM: Don't be so sure.

HALLY: I don't know what you're talking about, Sam.

SAM: Yes, you do.

HALLY (*furious*): Jesus, I wish you would stop trying to tell me what I do and what I don't know.

(*Sam gives up. He turns to Willie.*)

SAM: Let's finish up.

HALLY: Don't turn your back on me! I haven't finished talking.

(*He grabs Sam by the arm and tries to make him turn around. Sam reacts with a flash of anger.*)

SAM: Don't do that, Hally! (*Facing the boy.*) All right, I'm listening. Well? What do you want to say to me?

HALLY (*pause as Hally looks for something to say*): To begin with, why don't you also start calling me Master Harold, like Willie.

SAM: Do you mean that?

HALLY: Why the hell do you think I said it?

SAM: And if I don't?

HALLY: You might just lose your job.

SAM (*quietly and very carefully*): If you make me say it once, I'll never call you anything else again.

HALLY: So? (*The boy confronts the man.*) Is that meant to be a threat?

SAM: Just telling you what will happen if you make me do that. You must decide what it means to you.

HALLY: Well, I have. It's good news. Because that is exactly what Master Harold wants from now on.

Think of it as a little lesson in respect, Sam, that's long overdue, and I hope you remember it as well as you do your geography. I can tell you now that somebody who will be glad to hear I've finally given it to you will be my Dad. Yes! He agrees with my Mom. He's always going on about it as well. "You must teach the boys to show you more respect, my son."

SAM: So now you can stop complaining about going home. Everybody is going to be happy tonight.

HALLY: That's perfectly correct. You see, you mustn't get the wrong idea about me and my Dad, Sam. We also have our good times together. Some bloody good laughs. He's got a marvelous sense of humor. Want to know what our favorite joke is? He gives out a big groan, you see, and says: "It's not fair, is it, Hally?" Then I have to ask: "What, chum?" And then he says: "A nigger's arse" . . . and we both have a good laugh.

(*The men stare at him with disbelief.*)

What's the matter, Willie? Don't you catch the joke? You always were a bit slow on the uptake. It's what is called a pun. You see, fair means both light in color and to be just and decent. (*He turns to Sam.*) I thought *you* would catch it, Sam.

SAM: Oh ja, I catch it all right.

HALLY: But it doesn't appeal to your sense of humor.

SAM: Do you really laugh?

HALLY: Of course.

SAM: To please him? Make him feel good?

HALLY: No, for heavens sake! I laugh because I think it's a bloody good joke.

SAM: You're really trying hard to be ugly, aren't you? And why drag poor old Willie into it? He's done nothing to you except show you the respect you want so badly. That's also not being fair, you know . . . and *I* mean just or decent.

WILLIE: It's all right, Sam. Leave it now.

SAM: It's me you're after. You should just have said "Sam's arse" . . . because that's the one you're trying to kick. Anyway, how do you know it's not fair? You've never seen it. Do you want to? (*He drops his trousers and underpants and presents his backside for Hally's inspection.*) Have a good look. A real Basuto arse . . . which is about as nigger as they can come. Satisfied? (*Trousers up.*) Now you can make your Dad even happier when you go home tonight. Tell him I showed you my arse and he is quite right. It's not fair. And if it will give him an even better laugh next time, I'll also let *him* have a look. Come, Willie, let's finish up and go.

(*Sam and Willie start to tidy up the tea room. Hally doesn't move. He waits for a moment when Sam passes him.*)

HALLY (*quietly*): Sam . . .

(*Sam stops and looks expectantly at the boy. Hally spits in his face. A long and heartfelt groan from Willie. For a few seconds Sam doesn't move.*)

SAM (*taking out a handkerchief and wiping his face*): It's all right, Willie.

(*To Hally.*)

Ja, well, you've done it . . . Master Harold. Yes, I'll start calling you that from now on. It won't be difficult anymore. You've hurt yourself, Master Harold. I saw it coming. I warned you, but you wouldn't listen. You've just hurt yourself *bad*. And you're a coward, Master Harold. The face you should be spitting in is your father's . . . but you used mine, because you think you're safe inside your fair skin . . . and this time I don't mean just or decent. (*Pause, then moving violently toward Hally.*) Should I hit him, Willie?

WILLIE (*stopping Sam*): No, Boet Sam.

SAM (*violently*): Why not?

WILLIE: It won't help, Boet Sam.

SAM: I don't want to help! I want to hurt him.

WILLIE: You also hurt yourself.

SAM: And if he had done it to you, Willie?

WILLIE: Me? Spit at me like I was a dog? (*A thought that had not occurred to him before. He looks at Hally.*) Ja. Then I want to hit him. I want to hit him hard!

(*A dangerous few seconds as the men stand staring at the boy. Willie turns away, shaking his head.*)

But maybe all I do is go cry at the back. He's little boy, Boet Sam. Little *white* boy. Long trousers now, but he's still little boy.

SAM (*his violence ebbing away into defeat as quickly as it flooded*): You're right. So go on, then: groan again, Willie. You do it better than me. (*To Hally.*) You don't know all of what you've just done . . . Master Harold. It's not just that you've made me feel dirtier than I've ever been in my life . . . I mean, how do I wash off yours and your father's filth? . . . I've also failed. A long time ago I promised myself I was going to try and do something, but you've just shown me . . . Master Harold . . . that I've failed. (*Pause.*) I've also got a memory of a little white boy when he was still wearing short trousers and a black man, but they're not flying a kite. It was the old Jubilee days, after dinner one night. I was in my room. You came in and just stood against the wall, looking down at the ground, and only after I'd asked you what you wanted, what was wrong, I don't know how many times, did you speak and even then so softly I almost didn't hear you. "Sam, please help me to go and fetch my Dad." Remember? He was dead drunk on the floor of the Central Hotel Bar. They'd phoned for your Mom, but you were the only one at home. And do you remember how we did it? You went in first by yourself to ask permission for me to go into the bar. Then I loaded him onto my back like a baby and carried him back to the boarding house with you following behind carrying his crutches. (*Shaking his head as he remembers.*) A crowded Main Street with all the people watching a little white boy following his drunk father on a nigger's back! I felt for that little boy . . . Master Harold. I felt for him. After that we still had to clean him up, remember? He'd messed in his trousers, so we had to clean him up and get him into bed.

HALLY (*great pain*): I love him, Sam.

SAM: I know you do. That's why I tried to stop you from saying these things about him. It would have been so simple if you could have just despised him for being a weak man. But he's your father. You love him and you're ashamed of him. You're ashamed of so much! . . . And now that's going to include yourself. That was the promise I made to myself: to try and stop that happening. (*Pause.*) After we got him to bed you came back with me to my room and sat in a corner and carried on just looking down at the ground. And for days after that! You hadn't done anything wrong, but you went around as if you owed the world an apology for being alive. I didn't like seeing that! That's not the way a boy grows up to be a man! . . . But the one person who should have been teaching you what that means was the cause of your shame. If you really want to know, that's why I made you that kite. I wanted you to look up, be proud of something, of yourself . . . (*bitter smile at the memory*) . . . and you certainly were that when I left you with it up there on the hill. Oh, ja . . . something else! . . . If you ever do write it as a short story, there *was* a twist in our ending. I couldn't sit down there and stay with you. It was a "Whites Only" bench. You were too young, too excited to notice then. But not anymore. If you're not careful . . . Master Harold . . . you're going to be sitting up there by yourself for a long time to come, and there won't be a kite in the sky. (*Sam has got nothing more to say. He exits into the kitchen, taking off his waiter's jacket.*)

WILLIE: Is bad. Is all bad in here now.

HALLY (*books into his school case, raincoat on*): Willie . . . (*It is difficult to speak.*) Will you lock up for me and look after the keys?

WILLIE: Okay.

(*Sam returns. Hally goes behind the counter and collects the few coins in the cash register. As he starts to leave. . . .*)

SAM: Don't forget the comic books.

(*Hally returns to the counter and puts them in his case. He starts to leave again.*)

SAM (*to the retreating back of the boy*): Stop . . . Hally. . . .

(*Hally stops, but doesn't turn to face him.*)

Hally . . . I've got no right to tell you what being a man means if I don't behave like one myself, and I'm not doing so well at that this afternoon. Should we try again, Hally?

HALLY: Try what?

SAM: Fly another kite, I suppose. It worked once, and this time I need it as much as you do.

HALLY: It's still raining, Sam. You can't fly kites on rainy days, remember.

SAM: So what do we do? Hope for better weather tomorrow?

HALLY (*helpless gesture*): I don't know. I don't know anything anymore.

SAM: You sure of that, Hally? Because it would be pretty hopeless if that was true. It would mean nothing has been learnt in here this afternoon, and there was a hell of a lot of teaching going on . . . one way or the other. But anyway, I don't believe you. I reckon there's one thing you know. You don't *have* to sit up there by yourself. You know what that bench means now, and you can leave it any time you choose. All you've got to do is stand up and walk away from it.

(*Hally leaves. Willie goes up quietly to Sam.*)

WILLIE: Is okay, Boet Sam. You see. Is . . . (*he can't find any better words*) . . . is going to be okay tomorrow. (*Changing his tone.*) Hey, Boet Sam! (*He is trying hard.*) You right. I think about it and you right. Tonight I find Hilda and say sorry. And make promise I won't beat her no more. You hear me, Boet Sam?

SAM: I hear you, Willie.

WILLIE: And when we practice I relax and romance with her from beginning to end. Nonstop! You watch! Two weeks' time: "First prize for promising newcomers: Mr. Willie Malopo and Miss Hilda Samuels." (*Sudden impulse.*) To hell with it! I walk home. (*He goes to the jukebox, puts in a coin and selects a record. The machine comes to life in the gray twilight, blushing its way through a spectrum of soft, romantic colors.*) How did you say it, Boet Sam? Let's dream. (*Willie sways with the music and gestures for Sam to dance.*)

(*Sarah Vaughan sings.*)

"Little man you're crying,
I know why you're blue,
Someone took your kiddy car away;
Better go to sleep now,
Little man you've had a busy day." (*etc., etc.*)
You lead. I follow.

(*The men dance together.*)

"Johnny won your marbles,
Tell you what we'll do;
Dad will get you new ones right away;
Better go to sleep now,
Little man you've had a busy day."

COMMENTARIES

Heinrich von Staden (*b.* 1939)
INTERVIEW WITH ATHOL FUGARD   1982

When "MASTER HAROLD" . . . *and the boys was first produced at the Yale Repertory Theatre, Athol Fugard had the chance to respond to some questions about its significance to him. He revealed that the play was deeply personal and that through it he had been able to exorcise a demon that had haunted him for some time. In this interview Fugard details his involvement with South African drama and black actors in South Africa. He also comments on the extent to which censorship and other political pressures in South Africa made it difficult for his work to be produced in his own country.*

von Staden: The bombs of fiction — Athol, aren't they more explosive than TNT?

Fugard: I'd like to believe that. You understand I've got to be careful about that one. I've got to be careful about flattering myself about the potency of the one area of activity which I've got, which is theater and being a writer.

von Staden: How often have there been productions of your plays for nonsegregated audiences in South Africa?

Fugard: I've had to change my tactics in terms of that over the years. At a period when the policy on segregated audiences in South Africa was rigid and very strictly enforced, I had to make a decision whether to take on an act of silence, just be silent because I couldn't go into a theater that was decent in my terms, or whether to take on the compromising circumstances of segregated audiences simply because I felt that if a play has got something to say, at least say it. And there were years when I decided to do the latter. I did perform before segregated audiences. In a sense I regret that decision now. I think I might possibly have looked after myself — and maybe the situation — better by not accepting that compromise. But I did.

von Staden: But do you think you had a genuine choice at that time?

Fugard: I had a choice between silence or being heard.

von Staden: Let me ask you along similar lines, when you are writing a play or a novel like *Tsotsi,* do you sense constraints on the way you are writing in view of the fact that certain things are anathema to the government, also in fiction?

Fugard: I would like to believe that I have operated at the table at which I sit and write, that I have operated totally without self-censorship. Maybe some awareness of what is possible and is not possible has operated subconsciously and is deciding choices I make in terms of what I favor. I think it may be pertinent to the conversation we are having, that *"MASTER HAROLD"* . . . *and the boys* is the first play of mine in twenty-four years of writing that will have its premiere outside of South Africa. And one of the reasons why I'm doing that this time is that there are elements in *"MASTER HAROLD"* . . . *and the boys* that might have run into censorship problems. [. . .]

1412

von Staden: Here you are, a person who, critics say, has achieved exceptional insight into human nature, and you never obtained a university degree. What institutions, what processes do you think contributed most to the insights you have?

Fugard: Well, I think to be a South African is in a way to be at a university that teaches you about that. The South African experience is certainly one in which, if you're prepared to keep your eyes open and look, you're going to see a lot of suffering. But then, in terms of personal specifics, I suppose for me there was a very, very important relationship, a friendship, with a black man in what I suppose is any person's most formative and definitive years, the age between eleven, ten up until the age of twenty-one. It was a black man in Port Elizabeth, and my play *"MASTER HAROLD" . . . and the boys* reflects something of that friendship, tries to talk about it, look at it. I left South Africa, hitchhiked through the African continent, ended up as a sailor on a ship which, apart from the officers and engineers, had a totally nonwhite, had a totally black crew, and I was a sailor in a totally black crew. There was that, I think I can't nail down any one specific traumatic incident as being totally decisive. But I could be certain that *"MASTER HAROLD" . . . and the boys* deals with one specific moment which I'm trying to exorcise out of my soul.

von Staden: In all of your plays and in the novel you always have a South African setting. Yet your plays and your novels, though so rooted in the specifics of the South African situation, seem to have a tremendous appeal to audiences that are largely ignorant of the situation there. To what do you ascribe that?

Fugard: You take a chance. As a storyteller one year ago, I took a chance [. . .] I realized that it was finally time to deal with the story of a seventeen-year-old boy and his friendship with two black men. And it's a gamble. There's no formula. There is no way that you can make or decide or guarantee before the event that that story is going to resonate outside of its specific context. You just take a bloody chance.

Athol Fugard (*b. 1932*)
FROM NOTEBOOKS 1960–1977   *1983*

Like most playwrights, Athol Fugard is a journal writer. In his notebooks he has written scraps of memory that have special meaning to him. In one entry for March 1961, long before he began to write "MASTER HAROLD" . . . and the boys (1982), he describes one of his childhood memories. It concerns the real-life Sam, and it recounts — very painfully — the personal crime that Fugard's play deals with. His gesture of contempt for the man who was like a grandfather to him became a demon that had to be exorcised.

Sam Semela — Basuto — with the family fifteen years. Meeting him again when he visited Mom set off string of memories.

The kite which he produced for me one day during those early years when Mom ran the Jubilee Hotel and he was a waiter there. He had made it himself: brown paper, its ribs fashioned from thin strips of tomato-box plank which he had smoothed down, a paste of flour and water for glue. I was surprised and bewildered that he had made it for me.

I vaguely recall shyly "haunting" the servants' quarters in the well of the hotel — cold, cement-gray world — the pungent mystery of the dark little rooms — a world

I didn't understand. Frightened to enter any of the rooms. Sam, broad-faced, broader based—he smelled of woodsmoke. The "kaffir smell" of South Africa is the smell of poverty—woodsmoke and sweat.

Later, when he worked for her at the Park café, Mom gave him the sack: ". . . he became careless. He came late for work. His work went to hell. He didn't seem to care no more." I was about thirteen and served behind the counter while he waited on table.

Realize now he was the most significant—the only—friend of my boyhood years. On terrible windy days when no one came to swim or walk in the park, we would sit together and talk. Or I was reading—Introductions to Eastern Philosophy or Plato and Socrates—and when I had finished he would take the book back to New Brighton.

Can't remember now what precipitated it, but one day there was a rare quarrel between Sam and myself. In a truculent silence we closed the café, Sam set off home to New Brighton on foot and I followed a few minutes later on my bike. I saw him walking ahead of me and, coming out of a spasm of acute loneliness, as I rode up behind him I called his name, he turned in mid-stride to look back and, as I cycled past, I spat in his face. Don't suppose I will ever deal with the shame that overwhelmed me the second after I had done that.

Now he is thin. We had a long talk. He told about the old woman ("Ma") whom he and his wife have taken in to look after their house while he goes to work—he teaches ballroom dancing. "Ma" insists on behaving like a domestic—making Sam feel guilty and embarrassed. She brings him an early morning cup of coffee. Sam: "No, Ma, you mustn't, man." Ma: "I must." Sam: "Look, Ma, if I want it, I can make it." Ma: "No, I must."

Occasionally, when she is doing something, Sam feels like a cup of tea but is too embarrassed to ask her, and daren't make one for himself. Similarly, with his washing. After three days or a week away in other towns, giving dancing lessons, he comes back with underclothes that are very dirty. He is too shy to give them out to be washed so washes them himself. When Ma sees this she goes and complains to Sam's wife that he doesn't trust her, that it's all wrong for him to do the washing.

Of tsotsis,° he said: "They grab a old man, stick him with a knife, and ransack him. And so he must go to hospital and his kids is starving with hungry." Of others: "He's got some little moneys. So he is facing starvation for the weekend."

Of township snobs, he says there are the educational ones: "If you haven't been to the big school, like Fort Hare, what you say isn't true." And the money ones: "If you aren't selling shops or got a business or a big car, man, you're nothing."

Sam's incredible theory about the likeness of those "with the true seed of love." Starts with Plato and Socrates—they were round. "Man is being shrinking all the time. An Abe Lincoln, him too, taller, but that's because man is shrinking." Basically, those with the true seed of love look the same—"It's in the eyes."

He spoke admiringly of one man, a black lawyer in East London, an educated man—university background—who was utterly without snobbery, looking down on no one—any man, educated or ignorant, rich or poor, was another *man* to him, another human being, to be respected, taken seriously, to be talked to, listened to.

"They" won't allow Sam any longer to earn a living as a dancing teacher. "You must get a job!" One of his fellow teachers was forced to work at Fraser's Quarries.

tsotsis: Gang members.

David Mamet

The title of one of David Mamet's plays, *A Life in the Theatre* (1977), may have been autobiographically inspired. Mamet has spent his life—from high school onward—in the theater, as actor, director, playwright, and screenwriter. Born in Chicago in 1947, he graduated with an English major from Goddard College in Vermont, where he wrote several plays, including his undergraduate thesis, *Camel* (1968). *Sexual Perversity in Chicago* (1975), Mamet's first resounding commercial success, was first drafted when he was at Goddard. In the same year, *American Buffalo* premiered in the Goodman Theatre in Chicago, launching a series of productions around the country. The Broadway production was not especially well received, but it was the first American play produced at London's new National Theatre in 1978. After a 1980 revival in New Haven's Long Wharf Theater with Al Pacino as Teach, it moved to Circle in the Square in New York in 1981 and then to Broadway in 1983. A study of petty thieves living a darkly comic underground life, *American Buffalo* has become one of Mamet's most highly regarded plays.

His much-acclaimed *Glengarry Glen Ross* (1983) premiered in London at the National Theatre, then moved to Broadway the following year, where it won the Pulitzer Prize and many other awards. This tale of scheming real estate salesmen derives in part from Mamet's experience working in a real estate office as a young man. The portrait of avarice and deceit is an indictment of one aspect of American business. *Glengarry Glen Ross* was eventually revised for film.

In the 1980s and 1990s Mamet wrote many stage plays, radio plays, and film scripts. He adapted Chekhov's *The Cherry Orchard* (1985), wrote *Goldberg Street* for radio performance, and wrote the screenplays for *The Untouchables* (1987), *House of Games* (1987, nominated for a Golden Globe Award), *Things Change* (1988), and *Homicide* (1991). *Speed the Plow* (1988) opened on Broadway with Madonna playing a secretary from a temp agency. It draws on Mamet's experience in the film industry and explores the insecurities and double-dealing of those who make decisions about producing movies. *The Cryptogram* (1994) was produced first in London in June 1994, then in February 1995 at the American Repertory Theatre in Boston; the New York production was at the Westside Arts Theater in March 1995. *Boston Marriage* (1999) examines a lesbian relationship between Victorian blue-bloods, a novel subject for Mamet, who is sometimes criticized as being misogynistic. His courtroom farce *Romance* (2005) opened at the Atlantic Theater in New York to disappointing reviews. To an extent, it was a study in ethnic slurs.

In the early 1970s Mamet was involved in Chicago's St. Nicholas Theatre Company, a group that gathered to produce a variety of plays, including some of his own. William H. Macy, Steven Schacter, and Patricia Cox were the principal actors, and others joined with them. Soon, however, Mamet's responsibilities as a writer and his occasional stints as a university professor at Goddard and elsewhere led him to leave Chicago and settle in New York.

GLENGARRY GLEN ROSS

Mamet's examination of the world of sleazy real estate salesmen is at once both comic and savage. The level of deceit that pervades the play is so deep that one almost begins to accept the views of Shelly "the Machine" Levene, who, as he ages, loses his credibility as a sales "closer" but continues to deceive himself and anyone who will listen into thinking he can still "do the job" and sell the way he once did. Of course, with Shelly it is difficult to know what to believe. Perhaps he once was a top-notch salesman, but then again, his ability to fabricate stories about himself is so advanced that it is possible he was never actually "on top." In the opening scene in the Chinese restaurant, he reveals himself to Williamson, the office manager who seems to be the "nephew of somebody," as a man willing to exaggerate his achievements and explain away his defeats as things beyond his control.

Whether or not Shelly Levene is a sympathetic character may depend on the point of view of the individual reader or audience member. Although he does not project the image of a man who was once useful and is now being cast aside because of age, he may be seen as a remote likeness of Willy Loman in *Death of a Salesman*. On the other hand, like Willy, he seems to have consistently chosen values that would ultimately doom him as a man. The language of the play constantly reminds us that these salesmen are men. MEN in capital letters, men who seem to be comparable to yesterday's warriors. In act 2, Roma tells us that only men can do this job because it takes a man, by which he suggests that there is something noble, something daring about going out and selling property to people who may not even want it. Roma, almost aware of Mamet's judgment, says, "it's not a world of men, Machine . . . it's a world of clock watchers, bureaucrats, officeholders . . . what it is, it's a fucked-up world . . . there's no adventure *to* it." Mamet's imagery constantly defaults back to a revelation of male homosocial behavior, implying a brutal world built of conflict and survival, a world of predatory behavior resembling that of primitive hunters. Yet in actuality, these men are more like con men than like hunters.

In act 2, Roma sets up a con when Mr. Lingk comes into the office to ask for his money back. Lingk knows that he has three days in which to make up his mind to get a refund, and Roma tries to con him into thinking that he can wait four days. One important detail is that the "deal" they make occurs casually between Roma and Lingk in a restaurant in scene 3 of act 1. They begin their casual conversation when they are sitting in different booths from one another. They are just guys having a conversation. However, because one of the guys, Roma, is a skilled salesman, he is able to take the relatively untutored Lingk into his confidence and sell him property. In a marvelous twist, Lingk comes back in act 2 in the middle of a robbery investigation at the insistence of his wife. He reveals that it is not his decision to ask for his money back, but his wife's. She demands that he get their check back or she will go to the attorney general. She is the force behind his request, and it is she who undoes all the macho posturing of Roma, who tries everything he can think of, including having Levene masquerade as a very important customer who has "purchased" a great deal of property. In a sense, Roma is trying to "rob" Lingk of both his money and his will to resist. Simultaneously, the actual robbery of the real estate office is under investigation, further bewildering Lingk. Shelly Levene has let himself be drawn into a ridiculous scheme to steal leads—the names and addresses of people with enough resources to be potential buyers—and sell them to a competing firm. The entire scheme is self-defeating in the long run, but it produces immediate cash. Levene is so unsuccessful as a salesman that he has no money and sees this scheme as a temporary way out. In the process, as if displaying his lack of awareness, Levene seems to have skimmed off one of the leads and then had a "sit" with Bruce and Harriett Nyborg and "sold" them $82,000 worth of property. Near the end of the play, Williamson is astonished at Levene's naïveté: "They're nuts . . . they used to call in every week." The Nyborgs just like to talk to people—they are not legitimate customers, and Levene allows himself to be conned by them.

Levene is delusional when he tells Williamson that although he's committed a crime, it has taught him something: "What it taught me, that you've got to get *out* there. Big deal. So I wasn't cut out to be a thief. I was cut out to be a salesman." In Mamet's play, there is not much of a distinction.

Glengarry Glen Ross in Performance

The play premiered at the 300-seat Cottesloe Theatre, London, part of the South Bank group of National Theatres, on September 21, 1983. Derek Newark played Levene and Jack Shepherd played Roma. The American premiere followed on February 6, 1984, in Chicago at the Goodman Theatre, with Robert Prosky as Levene, Joe Mantegna as Roma, and Mike Nussbaum as Aaronow. J. T. Walsh played Williamson. Both productions were well received by reviewers and audiences alike, and the play won the Pulitzer Prize for 1984. Numerous productions have followed both regionally and abroad. The film version (1992), with Jack Lemmon as Levene and Al Pacino as Roma, was not a box-office success but has since become a cult classic. The first major theatrical revival was at the McCarter Theatre in Princeton, New Jersey, on February 18, 2000, with Scott Zigler directing. Charles Durning played Levene, Daniel Benzali played Moss, and Ruben Santiago-Hudson played Roma. Daniel L. Lewis in *Variety* said, "David Mamet's scorching 1984 drama *Glengarry Glen Ross* has lost none of its bite or blistering dramatic thrust in director Scott Zigler's McCarter Theatre production." Amy Morton directed the play at Steppenwolf Theatre in Chicago in November 2001–January 2002. In her production Mike Nussbaum, who had played Aaronow in 1984, now played Shelly Levene. The reviews noted that, even without any recognizable "stars" in the performance, the play still had power and verve. The 2005 revival had plenty of stars. Alan Alda, Liev Schreiber, Jeffrey Tambor, and Gordon Clapp in Joe Mantello's production at the Royale Theatre in New York garnered excellent reviews. Schreiber was cited for his powerful portrayal of Roma, and Santo Loquasto's stage design was especially effective.

David Mamet *(b. 1947)*

GLENGARRY GLEN ROSS

Always be closing. —PRACTICAL SALES MAXIM

The Characters

WILLIAMSON
BAYLEN
ROMA — Men in their early forties.
LINGK

LEVENE
MOSS — Men in their fifties.
AARONOW

THE SCENE

The three scenes of ACT ONE *take place in a Chinese restaurant.*

ACT TWO *takes place in a real estate office.*

ACT ONE • *Scene One*

A booth at a Chinese restaurant, Williamson and Levene are seated at the booth.

LEVENE: John . . . John . . . John. Okay. John. John. Look (*Pause.*) The Glengarry Highland's leads, you're sending Roma out. Fine. He's a good man. We know what he is. He's fine. All I'm saying, you look at the *board,* he's throwing . . . wait, wait, wait, he's throwing them *away,* he's throwing the leads away. All that I'm saying, that you're wasting leads. I don't want to tell you your *job.* All that I'm saying, things get *set,* I know they do, you get a certain *mindset.* . . . guy gets a reputation. We know how this . . . all I'm saying, put a *closer* on the job. There's more than one man for the . . . Put a . . . wait a second, put a *proven man out* . . . and you watch, now *wait* a second— and you watch your *dollar* volumes. . . . You start closing them for *fifty* 'stead of *twenty-five* . . . you put a *closer* on the . . .

WILLIAMSON: Shelly, you blew the last . . .

LEVENE: No. John. No. Let's wait, let's back up here, I did . . . will you please? Wait a second. Please. I didn't "blow" them. No. I didn't "blow" them. No. One kicked *out,* one I closed . . .

WILLIAMSON: . . . you didn't close . . .

LEVENE: . . . I, if you'd *listen* to me. Please. I *closed* the cocksucker. His *ex,* John, his *ex,* I didn't know he was married . . . he, the *judge* invalidated the . . .

WILLIAMSON: Shelly . . .

LEVENE: . . . and what is that, John? What? Bad *luck.* That's all it is. I pray in your *life* you will never find it runs in streaks. That's what it does, that's all it's doing. Streaks. I pray it misses you. That's all I want to say.

WILLIAMSON (*Pause*): What about the other two?

LEVENE: What two?

WILLIAMSON: Four. You had four leads. One kicked out, one the *judge,* you say . . .

LEVENE: . . . you want to see the court records? John? Eh? You want to go down . . .

WILLIAMSON: . . . no . . .

LEVENE: . . . do you want to go down*town* . . . ?

WILLIAMSON: . . . no . . .

LEVENE: . . . then . . .

WILLIAMSON: . . . I only . . .

LEVENE: . . . then what is this "you *say*" shit, what is that? (*Pause.*) What is that . . . ?

WILLIAMSON: All that I'm saying . . .

LEVENE: What is this "you *say*"? A deal kicks out . . . I got to *eat.* Shit, Williamson, *shit.* You . . . Moss . . . Roma . . . look at the *sheets* . . . look at the *sheets.* Nineteen *eighty,* eighty-one . . . eighty-*two* . . . six months of eighty-two . . . who's there? Who's up there?

WILLIAMSON: Roma.

LEVENE: Under him?

WILLIAMSON: Moss.

LEVENE: Bull*shit.* John. Bull*shit.* April, September 1981. It's *me.* It isn't *fucking* Moss. Due respect, he's an *order* taker, John. He *talks,* he talks a good game, look at the *board,* and it's *me,* John, it's me . . .

WILLIAMSON: Not lately it isn't.

LEVENE: Lately kiss my ass lately. That isn't how you build an org . . . talk, talk to Murray. Talk to Mitch. When we were on Peterson, who paid for his fucking *car*? You talk to him. The *Seville* . . . ? He came in, "You bought that for me Shelly." Out of *what*? Cold *calling. Nothing.* Sixty-*five,* when we were there, with Glen *Ross* Farms? You call 'em downtown. What was that? *Luck*? That was "luck"? *Bull*shit, John. You're burning my ass, I can't get a fucking *lead* . . . you think that was luck. My stats for those years? Bull*shit* . . . over that period of time. . . ? Bull*shit.* It wasn't luck. It was *skill.* You want to throw that away, John. . . ? You want to throw that away?

WILLIAMSON: It isn't me . . .

LEVENE: . . . it isn't you. . . ? Who *is* it? Who is this I'm talking to? I need the *leads* . . .

WILLIAMSON: . . . after the thirtieth . . .

LEVENE: Bull*shit* the thirtieth, I don't get on the board the thirtieth, they're going to can my ass. I need the leads. I need them now. Or I'm gone, and you're going to miss me, John, I swear to you.

WILLIAMSON: Murray . . .

LEVENE: . . . you *talk* to Murray . . .

WILLIAMSON: I have. And my job is to marshal those leads . . .

LEVENE: Marshal the leads . . . marshal the leads? What the fuck, what bus did *you* get off of, we're here to fucking *sell*. *Fuck* marshaling the leads. What the fuck talk is that? What the fuck talk is that? Where did you learn that? In school? (*Pause.*) That's "talk," my friend, that's "talk." Our job is to *sell*. I'm the *man* to sell. I'm getting garbage. (*Pause.*) You're giving it to me, and what I'm saying is it's *fucked*.

WILLIAMSON: You're saying that I'm fucked.

LEVENE: Yes. (*Pause.*) I am. I'm sorry to antagonize you.

WILLIAMSON: Let me . . .

LEVENE: . . . and I'm going to get bounced and you're . . .

WILLIAMSON: . . . let me . . . are you listening to me . . . ?

LEVENE: Yes.

WILLIAMSON: Let me tell you something, Shelly. I do what I'm hired to do. I'm . . . wait a second. I'm *hired* to watch the leads. I'm given . . . hold on, I'm given a *policy*. My job is to *do that*. What I'm *told*. That's it. You, wait a second, *anybody* falls below a certain mark I'm not *permitted* to give them the premium leads.

LEVENE: Then how do they come up above that mark? With *dreck*. . . ? That's *nonsense*. Explain this to me. 'Cause it's a waste, and it's a stupid waste. I want to tell you something . . .

WILLIAMSON: You know what those leads cost?

LEVENE: The premium leads. Yes. I know what they cost. John. Because I, *I* generated the dollar revenue sufficient to *buy* them. Nineteen senny-*nine*, you know what I made? Senny-*nine*? Ninety-six thousand dollars. John? For *Murray* . . . For *Mitch* . . . look at the sheets . . .

WILLIAMSON: Murray said . . .

LEVENE: *Fuck* him. *Fuck* Murray. John? You know? You tell him I said so. What does *he* fucking know? He's going to have a "sales" contest . . . you know what our sales contest used to be? *Money*. A *fortune*. Money lying on the ground. Murray? When was the last time *he* went out on a sit? Sales contest? It's *laughable*. It's cold out there now, John. It's tight. Money is *tight*. This ain't sixty-five. It ain't. It just ain't. See? See? Now, I'm a good *man*—but I need a . . .

WILLIAMSON: Murray said . . .

LEVENE: John. John . . .

WILLIAMSON: Will you please wait a second. Shelly. Please. Murray told me: the hot leads . . .

LEVENE: . . . ah, *fuck* this . . .

WILLIAMSON: The . . . Shelly? (*Pause.*) The hot leads are assigned according to the board. During the contest. *Period*. Anyone who beats fifty per . . .

LEVENE: That's fucked. That's fucked. You don't look at the fucking *percentage*. You look at the *gross*.

WILLIAMSON: Either way. You're out.

LEVENE: I'm out.

WILLIAMSON: Yes.

LEVENE: I'll tell you why I'm out. I'm *out*, you're giving me toilet paper. John. I've *seen* those leads. I saw them when I was at Homestead, we pitched those cock-suckers Rio Rancho nineteen sixty-*nine* they wouldn't buy. They couldn't buy a fucking *toaster*. They're *broke,* John. They're cold. They're deadbeats, you can't judge on that. Even so. Even so. Alright. Fine. Fine. Even so. I go in, FOUR FUCKING LEADS they got their money in a *sock*. They're fucking *Polacks,* John. Four leads. I close two. *Two*. Fifty per . . .

WILLIAMSON: . . . they kicked out.

LEVENE: They *all* kick out. You run in *streaks*, pal. *Streaks*. I'm . . . I'm . . . don't look at the *board*, look at *me*. Shelly Levene. *Anyone*. *Ask* them on Western. Ask Getz at Homestead. Go ask Jerry Graff. You know who I am . . . I NEED A SHOT. I got to get on the fucking board. Ask them. *Ask* them. Ask them who ever picked up a check I was flush. Moss, Jerry Graff, Mitch himself . . . Those guys *lived* on the business I brought in. They *lived* on it . . . and so did Murray, John. You were here you'd of benefited from it too. And now I'm saying this. Do I want charity? Do I want *pity*? I want *sits*. I want leads don't come right out of a *phone book*. Give me a lead hotter than that, I'll go in and close it. Give me a chance. That's all I want. I'm going to *get* up on that fucking board and all I want is a chance. It's a *streak* and I'm going to turn it around. (*Pause.*) I need your help. (*Pause.*)

WILLIAMSON: I can't do it, Shelly. (*Pause.*)

LEVENE: Why?

WILLIAMSON: The leads are assigned randomly . . .

LEVENE: *Bullshit, bullshit,* you assign them. . . . What are you *telling* me?

WILLIAMSON: . . . apart from the top men on the contest board.

LEVENE: Then put me on the board.

WILLIAMSON: You start closing again, you'll *be* on the board.

LEVENE: I can't close these leads, John. No one can. It's a joke. John, look, just give me a hot lead. Just give me two of the premium leads. As a "test," alright? As a "test" and I promise you . . .

WILLIAMSON: I can't do it, Shel. (*Pause.*)

LEVENE: I'll give you ten percent. (*Pause.*)

WILLIAMSON: Of what?

LEVENE: Of my end what I close.

WILLIAMSON: And what if you don't close.

LEVENE: I *will* close.

WILLIAMSON: What if you *don't* close. . . ?

LEVENE: I *will* close.

WILLIAMSON: What if you *don't*? Then I'm *fucked*. You see. . . ? Then it's *my* job. That's what I'm *telling* you.

LEVENE: I *will* close. John, John, ten percent. I can get hot. You *know* that . . .

WILLIAMSON: Not lately you can't . . .

LEVENE: Fuck that. That's defeatist. Fuck that. Fuck it. . . . Get on my side. *Go* with me. Let's *do* something. You want to run this office, *run* it.

WILLIAMSON: Twenty percent. (*Pause.*)

LEVENE: Alright.

WILLIAMSON: And fifty bucks a lead.

LEVENE: John. (*Pause.*) Listen. I want to talk to you. Permit me to do this a second. I'm older than you. A man acquires a reputation. On the street. What he does when he's *up*, what he does otherwise. . . . I said "ten," you said "no." You said "twenty." I said "fine," I'm not going to fuck with you, how can I beat that, you tell me? . . . Okay. Okay. We'll . . . Okay. Fine. We'll . . . Alright, twenty percent, and fifty bucks a lead. That's fine. For now. That's fine. A month or two we'll talk. A month from now. Next month. After the thirtieth. (*Pause.*) We'll talk.

WILLIAMSON: What are we going to say?

LEVENE: No. You're right. That's for later. We'll talk in a month. What have you got? I want two sits. Tonight.

WILLIAMSON: I'm not sure I have two.

LEVENE: I saw the board. You've got *four* . . .

WILLIAMSON (*Snaps*): I've got *Roma*. Then I've got Moss . . .

LEVENE: *Bullshit.* They ain't been in the office yet. Give 'em some stiff. We have a deal or not? Eh? Two sits. The Des Plaines. Both of 'em, six and ten, you can do it . . . six and ten . . . eight and eleven, I don't give a shit, you set 'em up? Alright? The two sits in Des Plaines.

WILLIAMSON: Alright.

LEVENE: Good. Now we're talking. (*Pause.*)

WILLIAMSON: A hundred bucks. (*Pause.*)

LEVENE: Now? (*Pause.*) Now?

WILLIAMSON: Now. (*Pause.*) Yes . . . When?

LEVENE: Ah, *shit*, John. (*Pause.*)

WILLIAMSON: I wish I could.

LEVENE: You fucking asshole. (*Pause.*) I haven't got it. (*Pause.*) I haven't got it, John. (*Pause.*) I'll pay you tomorrow. (*Pause.*) I'm coming in here with the sales, I'll pay you *tomorrow*. (*Pause.*) I haven't *got* it, when I pay, the *gas* . . . I get back the hotel, I'll bring it in tomorrow.

WILLIAMSON: Can't do it.

LEVENE: I'll give you thirty on them now, I'll bring the rest tomorrow. I've got it at the hotel. (*Pause.*) John? (*Pause.*) We do that, for chrissake?

WILLIAMSON: No.

LEVENE: I'm asking you. As a favor to me? (*Pause.*) John. (*Long pause.*) John: my *daughter* . . .

WILLIAMSON: I can't do it, Shelly.

LEVENE: Well, I want to tell you something, fella, wasn't long I could pick up the phone, call *Murray* and I'd have your job. You know that? Not too *long* ago. For what? For *nothing*. "Mur, this new kid burns my ass." "Shelly, he's out." You're gone before I'm back from lunch. I bought him a trip to Bermuda once . . .

WILLIAMSON: I have to go . . . (*Gets up.*)

LEVENE: Wait. Alright. Fine. (*Starts going in pocket for money.*) The one. Give me the lead. Give me the one lead. The best one you have.

WILLIAMSON: I can't split them. (*Pause.*)

LEVENE: Why?

WILLIAMSON: Because I say so.

LEVENE (*Pause*): Is that it? Is that *it*? You want to do business that way. . . ?

Williamson gets up, leaves money on the table.

LEVENE: You want to do business that way. . . ? Alright. Alright. Alright. Alright. What is there on the other list. . . ?

WILLIAMSON: You want something off the B list?

LEVENE: *Yeah.* Yeah.

WILLIAMSON: Is that what you're saying?

LEVENE: That's what I'm saying. Yeah. (*Pause.*) I'd like something off the other list. Which, very least, that I'm entitled to. If I'm still *working* here, which for the moment I guess that I am. (*Pause.*) What? I'm sorry I spoke harshly to you.

WILLIAMSON: That's alright.

LEVENE: The deal still stands, our other thing.

Williamson shrugs. Starts out of the booth.

LEVENE: Good. Mmm. I, you know, I left my wallet back at the hotel.

Scene Two

A booth at the restaurant. Moss and Aaronow seated. After the meal.

MOSS: Polacks and deadbeats.

AARONOW: . . . Polacks . . .

MOSS: Deadbeats *all.*

AARONOW: . . . they hold on to their money . . .

MOSS: All of 'em. They, *hey*: it happens to us all.

AARONOW: Where am I going to work?

MOSS: You have to cheer up, George, you aren't out yet.

AARONOW: I'm not?

MOSS: You missed a fucking sale. Big deal. A deadbeat Polack. Big deal. How you going to sell 'em in the *first* place. . . ? Your mistake, you shoun'a took the lead.

AARONOW: I had to.

MOSS: You had to, yeah. Why?

AARONOW: To get on the . . .

MOSS: To get on the board. Yeah. How you goan'a get on the board sell'n a Polack? And I'll tell you, I'll tell you what *else*. You listening? I'll tell you what else: don't ever try to sell an Indian.

AARONOW: I'd never try to sell an Indian.

MOSS: You get those names come up, you ever get 'em, "Patel"?

AARONOW: Mmm . . .

MOSS: You ever get 'em?

AARONOW: Well, I think I had one once.

MOSS: You did?

AARONOW: I . . . I don't know.

MOSS: You had one you'd know it. *Patel.* They keep coming up. I don't know. They like to talk to salesmen. (*Pause.*) They're *lonely,* something. (*Pause.*) They like to feel *superior,* I don't know. Never bought a fucking thing. You're sitting down "The Rio Rancho *this,* the blah blah blah," "The Mountain View —" "Oh yes. My brother told me that. . . ." They got a grapevine. Fuckin' Indians, George. Not my cup of tea. Speaking of which I want to tell you something: (*Pause*) I never got a cup of tea with them. You see them in the restaurants. A supercilious race. What is this *look* on their face all the time? I don't know. (*Pause.*) I don't know. Their broads all look like they just got fucked with a dead *cat, I* don't know. (*Pause.*) I don't know. I don't like it. Christ . . .

AARONOW: What?

MOSS: The whole fuckin' thing . . . The pressure's just too great. You're ab . . . you're absolu . . . they're too important. All of them. You go in the door. I . . . "I got to *close* this fucker, or I don't eat lunch," "or I don't win the *Cadillac.* . . ." We fuckin' work too hard. You work too hard. We all, I remember when we were at Platt . . . huh? Glen Ross Farms . . . *didn't* we sell a bunch of that. . . ?

AARONOW: They came in and they, you know . . .

MOSS: Well, they fucked it up.

AARONOW: They did.

MOSS: They killed the goose.

AARONOW: They did.

MOSS: And now . . .

AARONOW: We're stuck with *this* . . .

MOSS: We're stuck with *this* fucking shit . . .

AARONOW: . . . *this* shit . . .

MOSS: It's too . . .

AARONOW: It is.

MOSS: Eh?

AARONOW: It's too . . .

MOSS: You get a bad month, all of a . . .

AARONOW: You're on this . . .

MOSS: All of, they got you on this "board . . ."

AARONOW: I, I . . . I . . .

MOSS: Some *contest* board . . .

AARONOW: I . . .

MOSS: It's not right.

AARONOW: It's not.

MOSS: No. (*Pause.*)

AARONOW: And it's not right to the *customers.*

MOSS: I know it's not. I'll tell you, you got, you know, you got . . . what did I learn as a kid on Western? Don't sell a guy one car. Sell him *five* cars over fifteen years.

AARONOW: That's right?

MOSS: Eh. . . ?

AARONOW: That's right?

MOSS: Goddamn right, that's right. Guys come on: "Oh, the blah blah blah, *I* know what I'll do: I'll go in and rob everyone blind and go to Argentina cause nobody ever *thought* of this before."

AARONOW: . . . that's right . . .

MOSS: Eh?

AARONOW: No. That's absolutely right.

MOSS: And so they kill the goose. I, I, I'll . . . and a fuckin' *man,* worked all his *life* has got to . . .

AARONOW: . . . that's right . . .

MOSS: . . . cower in his boots . . .

AARONOW (*simultaneously with "boots"*): Shoes, boots, yes . . .

MOSS: For some fuckin' "Sell ten thousand and you win the steak knives . . ."

AARONOW: For some *sales* pro . . .

MOSS: . . . sales promotion, "You *lose,* then we fire your . . ." No. It's *medieval* . . . it's wrong. "Or we're going to fire your ass." It's wrong.

AARONOW: Yes.

MOSS: Yes, it is. And you know who's responsible?

AARONOW: Who?

MOSS: You know who it is. It's Mitch. And Murray. 'Cause it doesn't have to be this way.

AARONOW: No.

MOSS: Look at Jerry Graff. He's *clean,* he's doing business for *himself,* he's got his, that *list* of his with the *nurses* . . . see? You see? That's *thinking.* Why take ten percent? A ten percent comm . . . why are we giving the rest away? What are we giving ninety per . . . for *nothing.* For some jerk sit in the office tell you "Get out there and close." "Go win the Cadillac." Graff. He goes out and *buys.* He pays top dollar for the . . . you see?

AARONOW: Yes.

MOSS: That's *thinking.* Now, he's got the leads, he goes in business for *himself.* He's . . . that's what I . . . that's *thinking!* "Who? Who's got a steady *job,* a couple bucks nobody's touched, who?"

AARONOW: Nurses.

MOSS: So Graff buys a fucking list of nurses, one grand — if he paid two I'll eat my hat — four, five thousand nurses, and he's going *wild* . . .

AARONOW: He is?

MOSS: He's doing *very* well.

AARONOW: I heard that they were running cold.

MOSS: The nurses?

AARONOW: Yes.

MOSS: You hear a *lot* of things. . . . He's doing very well. He's doing *very* well.

AARONOW: With River Oaks?

MOSS: River Oaks, Brook Farms. *All* of that shit. Somebody told me, you know what he's clearing *himself*? Fourteen, fifteen grand a *week.*

AARONOW: Himself?

MOSS: That's what I'm *saying.* Why? The *leads.* He's got the good leads . . . what are we, we're sitting in the shit here. Why? We have to go to *them* to *get* them. Huh. Ninety percent our sale, we're *paying* to the *office* for the *leads.*

AARONOW: The leads, the overhead, the telephones, there's *lots* of things.

MOSS: What do you need? A *telephone,* some broad to say "Good morning," nothing . . . nothing . . .

AARONOW: No, it's not that simple, Dave . . .

MOSS: *Yes*. It *is*. It *is* simple, and you know what the hard part is?

AARONOW: What?

MOSS: Starting up.

AARONOW: What hard part?

MOSS: Of doing the thing. The dif . . . the difference. Between me and Jerry Graff. Going to business for yourself. The hard part is . . . you know what it is?

AARONOW: What?

MOSS: Just the *act*.

AARONOW: What act?

MOSS: To say "I'm going on my own." 'Cause what you do, George, let me tell you what you do: you find yourself in *thrall* to someone else. And we *enslave* ourselves. To *please*. To win some fucking *toaster* . . . to . . . to . . . and the guy who got there first made *up* those . . .

AARONOW: That's right . . .

MOSS: He made *up* those rules, and we're working for *him*.

AARONOW: That's the truth . . .

MOSS: That's the *God's* truth. And it gets me depressed. I *swear* that it does. At MY AGE. To see a goddamn: "Somebody wins the Cadillac this month. P.S. Two guys get fucked."

AARONOW: *Huh*.

MOSS: You don't *ax* your sales force.

AARONOW: No.

MOSS: You . . .

AARONOW: You . . .

MOSS: You *build* it!

AARONOW: That's what I . . .

MOSS: You fucking *build* it! Men come . . .

AARONOW: Men come *work* for you . . .

MOSS: . . . you're absolutely right.

AARONOW: They . . .

MOSS: They have . . .

AARONOW: When they . . .

MOSS: Look look look look, when they *build* your business, then you can't fucking turn around, *enslave* them, treat them like *children*, fuck them up the ass, leave them to fend for themselves . . . no. (*Pause*.) No. (*Pause*.) You're absolutely right, and I want to tell you something.

AARONOW: What?

MOSS: I want to tell you what somebody should do.

AARONOW: What?

MOSS: Someone should stand up and strike *back*.

AARONOW: What do you mean?

MOSS: *Somebody* . . .

AARONOW: Yes. . . ?

MOSS: Should do something to *them*.

AARONOW: What?

MOSS: Something. To pay them back. (*Pause*.) Someone, someone should hurt them. Murray and Mitch.

AARONOW: Someone should hurt them.

MOSS: Yes.

AARONOW (*Pause*.): How?

MOSS: How? Do something to hurt them. Where they live.

AARONOW: What? (*Pause*.)

MOSS: Someone should rob the office.

AARONOW: Huh.

MOSS: That's what I'm *saying*. We were, if we were that kind of guys, to knock it off, and *trash* the joint, it looks like robbery, and *take* the fuckin' leads out of the files . . . go to Jerry Graff. (*Long pause*.)

AARONOW: What could somebody get for them?

MOSS: What could we *get* for them? I don't know. Buck a *throw* . . . buck-a-half a throw . . . I don't know. . . . Hey, who knows what they're worth, what do they *pay* for them? All told . . . must be, I'd . . . three bucks a throw . . . I don't know.

AARONOW: How many leads have we got?

MOSS: The *Glengarry* . . . the premium leads. . . ? I'd say we got five thousand. Five. Five thousand leads.

AARONOW: And you're saying a fella could take and sell these leads to Jerry Graff.

MOSS: Yes.

AARONOW: How do you know he'd buy them?

MOSS: Graff? Because I worked for him.

AARONOW: You haven't talked to him.

MOSS: No. What do you mean? Have I talked to him about *this*? (*Pause*.)

AARONOW: Yes. I mean are you actually *talking* about this, or are we just . . .

MOSS: No, we're just . . .

AARONOW: We're just *"talking"* about it.

MOSS: We're just *speaking* about it. (*Pause*.) As an *idea*.

AARONOW: As an idea.

MOSS: Yes.

AARONOW: We're not actually *talking* about it.

MOSS: No.

AARONOW: Talking about it as a . . .

MOSS: *No*.

AARONOW: As a *robbery*.

MOSS: As a "robbery"?! No.

AARONOW: *Well*. Well . . .

MOSS: *Hey*. (*Pause*.)

AARONOW: So all this, um, you didn't, actually, you didn't actually go talk to Graff.

MOSS: Not actually, no. (*Pause*.)

AARONOW: You didn't?

MOSS: No. Not actually.

AARONOW: Did you?

MOSS: What did I say?

AARONOW: What did you say?

MOSS: Yes. (*Pause*.) I said, "Not actually." The fuck *you* care, George? We're just *talking* . . .

AARONOW: We are?

MOSS: Yes. (*Pause*.)

AARONOW: Because, because, you know, it's a *crime*.

MOSS: That's right. It's a crime. It is a crime. It's also very safe.

AARONOW: You're actually *talking* about this?

MOSS: That's right. (*Pause*.)

AARONOW: You're going to steal the leads?

MOSS: Have I said that? (*Pause.*)

AARONOW: Are you? (*Pause.*)

MOSS: Did I say that?

AARONOW: Did you talk to Graff?

MOSS: Is that what I said?

AARONOW: What did he say?

MOSS: What did he say? He'd *buy* them. (*Pause.*)

AARONOW: You're going to steal the leads and sell the leads to him? (*Pause.*)

MOSS: Yes.

AARONOW: What will he pay?

MOSS: A buck a shot.

AARONOW: For five thousand?

MOSS: However they are, that's the deal. A buck a throw. Five thousand dollars. Split it half and half.

AARONOW: You're saying "me."

MOSS: Yes. (*Pause.*) Twenty-five hundred apiece. One night's work, and the job with Graff. Working the premium leads. (*Pause.*)

AARONOW: A job with Graff.

MOSS: Is that what I said?

AARONOW: He'd give me a job.

MOSS: He would take you on. Yes. (*Pause.*)

AARONOW: Is that the truth?

MOSS: Yes. It is, George. (*Pause.*) Yes. It's a big decision. (*Pause.*) And it's a big reward. (*Pause.*) It's a big reward. For one night's work. (*Pause.*) But it's got to be tonight.

AARONOW: What?

MOSS: What? What? The *leads*.

AARONOW: You have to steal the leads tonight?

MOSS: That's *right*, the guys are moving them downtown. After the thirtieth. Murray and Mitch. After the contest.

AARONOW: You're, you're saying so you have to go in there tonight and . . .

MOSS: *You* . . .

AARONOW: I'm sorry?

MOSS: *You*. (*Pause.*)

AARONOW: Me?

MOSS: *You* have to go in. (*Pause.*) *You* have to get the leads. (*Pause.*)

AARONOW: I do?

MOSS: Yes.

AARONOW: I . . .

MOSS: It's not something for nothing, George, I took you in on this, you have to go. That's your thing. I've made the deal with Graff. I can't go. I can't go in, I've spoken on this too much. I've got a big mouth. (*Pause.*) "The fucking leads" et cetera, blah blah blah ". . . the fucking tight ass company . . ."

AARONOW: They'll know when you go over to Graff . . .

MOSS: What will they know? That I stole the leads? I *didn't* steal the leads, I'm going to the *movies* tonight with a friend, and then I'm going to the Como Inn. Why did I go to Graff? I got a better deal. *Period*. Let 'em prove something. They can't prove anything that's not the case. (*Pause.*)

AARONOW: *Dave*.

MOSS: Yes.

AARONOW: You want me to break into the office tonight and steal the leads?

MOSS: Yes. (*Pause.*)

AARONOW: No.

MOSS: Oh, yes, George.

AARONOW: What does that mean?

MOSS: Listen to this. I have an alibi, I'm going to the Como Inn, why? Why? The place gets robbed, they're going to come looking for *me*. Why? Because I probably did it. Are you going to turn me in? (*Pause.*) George? Are you going to turn me in?

AARONOW: What if you don't get caught?

MOSS: They come to you, you going to turn me in?

AARONOW: Why would they come to me?

MOSS: They're going to come to *everyone*.

AARONOW: Why would I *do* it?

MOSS: You wouldn't, George, that's why I'm talking to you. Answer me. They come to you. You going to turn me in?

AARONOW: No.

MOSS: Are you sure?

AARONOW: Yes. I'm sure.

MOSS: Then listen to this: I have to get those leads tonight. That's something I have to do. If I'm not at the *movies* . . . if I'm not eating over at the inn . . . If you don't do this, then *I* have to come in here . . .

AARONOW: . . . you don't have to come in . . .

MOSS: . . . and *rob* the place . . .

AARONOW: . . . I thought that we were only talking . . .

MOSS: . . . they *take* me, then. They're going to ask me who were my accomplices.

AARONOW: *Me?*

MOSS: Absolutely.

AARONOW: That's ridiculous.

MOSS: Well, to the law, you're an accessory. Before the fact.

AARONOW: I didn't ask to be.

MOSS: Then tough luck, George, because you are.

AARONOW: Why? *Why*, because you only *told* me about it?

MOSS: That's right.

AARONOW: Why are you doing this to me, Dave. Why are you talking this way to me? I don't understand. Why are you doing this at *all* . . . ?

MOSS: That's none of your fucking business . . .

AARONOW: Well, well, well, *talk* to me, we sat down to eat *dinner*, and here I'm a *criminal* . . .

MOSS: You *went* for it.

AARONOW: In the abstract . . .

MOSS: So I'm making it concrete.

AARONOW: Why?

MOSS: Why? Why *you* going to give me five grand?

AARONOW: Do you need five grand?

MOSS: Is that what I just said?

AARONOW: You need money? Is that the . . .

MOSS: Hey, hey, let's just keep it simple, what I need is not the . . . what do *you* need. . . ?

AARONOW: What is the five grand? (*Pause.*) What is the, you said that we were going to *split* five . . .

MOSS: I lied. (*Pause.*) Alright? My end is *my* business. Your end's twenty-five. In or out. You tell me, you're out you take the consequences.

AARONOW: I do?

MOSS: Yes. (*Pause.*)

AARONOW: And why is that?

MOSS: Because you listened.

Scene Three

The restaurant. Roma is seated alone at the booth. Lingk is at the booth next to him. Roma is talking to him.

ROMA: . . . all train compartments smell vaguely of shit. It gets so you don't mind it. That's the worst thing that I can confess. You know how long it took me to get there? A long time. When you *die* you're going to regret the things you don't do. You think you're *queer*. . . ? I'm going to tell you something: we're *all* queer. You think that you're a *thief*? So *what*? You get befuddled by a middle-class morality. . . ? Get *shut* of it. Shut it out. You cheated on your wife. . . ? You *did* it, *live* with it. (*Pause.*) You fuck little girls, so *be* it. There's an absolute morality? May *be*. And *then* what? If you *think* there is, then *be* that thing. Bad people go to hell? I don't *think* so. If you think that, act that way. A hell exists on earth? Yes. I won't live in it. That's *me*. You ever take a dump made you feel you'd just slept for twelve hours. . . ?

LINGK: Did I. . . ?

ROMA: Yes.

LINGK: I don't know.

ROMA: Or a *piss*. . . ? A great meal fades in reflection. Everything else gains. You know why? 'Cause it's only food. This shit we eat, it keeps us going. But it's only food. The great fucks that you may have had. What do you remember about them?

LINGK: What do I. . . ?

ROMA: Yes.

LINGK: Mmmm . . .

ROMA: I don't know. For *me*, I'm saying, what it is, it's probably not the orgasm. Some broads, forearms on your neck, something her *eyes* did. There was a *sound* she made . . . or, me, lying in the, I'll tell you: me lying in bed; the next day she brought me café au lait. She gives me a cigarette, my balls feel like concrete. Eh? What I'm saying, what is our life? (*Pause.*) It's looking forward or it's looking back. And that's our life. That's *it*. Where is the *moment*? (*Pause.*) And what is it that we're afraid of? Loss. What else? (*Pause.*) The *bank* closes. We get *sick*, my wife died on a plane, the stock market collapsed . . . the house burnt down . . . what of these happen. . . ? None of 'em. We worry anyway. What does this mean? I'm not *secure*. How can I be secure? (*Pause.*) Through amassing wealth beyond all measure? No. And what's beyond all measure? That's a sickness. That's a trap. There is no measure. Only greed. How can we act? The right way, we would say, to deal with

this: "There is a one-in-a-million chance that so and so will happen. . . . *Fuck* it, it won't happen to *me*. . . ." No. We know that's not the right way I think. (*Pause.*) We say the *correct* way to deal with this is "There is a one-in-so-and-so chance this will happen . . . God *protect* me. I am powerless, let it not happen to me. . . ." But no to *that*. I say. There's something else. What is it? "If it happens, AS IT MAY for that is not within our powers, I will *deal* with it, just as I do *today* with what draws my concern today." I say *this* is how we must act. I do those things which seem correct to me *today*. I trust myself. And if security concerns me, I do that which *today* I think will make me secure. And every day I *do* that, when that day *arrives* that I need a reserve, (a) odds are that I have it, and (b) the *true* reserve that I have is the strength that I have of *acting each day* without fear. (*Pause.*) According to the dictates of my mind. (*Pause.*) Stocks, bonds, objects of art, real estate. Now: what are they? (*Pause.*) An opportunity. To what? To make money? Perhaps. To *lose* money? Perhaps. To "indulge" and to "learn" about ourselves? Perhaps. *So fucking what?* What *isn't*? They're an *opportunity*. That's all. They're an *event*. A guy comes up to you, you make a call, you send in a brochure, it doesn't matter, "There're these *properties* I'd like for you to see." What does it mean? What you *want* it to mean. (*Pause.*) Money? (*Pause.*) If that's what it signifies to you. Security? (*Pause.*) Comfort? (*Pause.*) All it is is THINGS THAT HAPPEN TO YOU. (*Pause.*) That's all it is. How are they different? (*Pause.*) Some poor newly married guy gets run down by a cab. Some *busboy* wins the lottery. (*Pause.*) All it is, it's a carnival. What's special . . . what *draws* us? (*Pause.*) We're all different. (*Pause.*) We're not the same. (*Pause.*) We are not the same. (*Pause.*) Hmmm. (*Pause. Sighs.*) It's been a long day. (*Pause.*) What are you drinking?

LINGK: Gimlet.

ROMA: Well, let's have a couple more. My name is Richard Roma, what's yours?

LINGK: Lingk. James Lingk.

ROMA: James. I'm glad to meet you. (*They shake hands.*) I'm glad to meet you, James. (*Pause.*) I want to show you something. (*Pause.*) It might mean *nothing* to you . . . and it might not. I don't know. I don't know anymore. (*Pause. He takes out a small map and spreads it on a table.*) What is that? Florida. Glengarry Highlands. Florida. "Florida. *Bullshit*." And maybe that's true; and that's what *I* said: but look *here*: what is this? This is a piece of land. Listen to what I'm going to tell you now:

ACT TWO

The real estate office. Ransacked. A broken plate-glass window boarded up, glass all over the floor. Aaronow and Williamson standing around, smoking.

Pause.

AARONOW: People used to say that there are numbers of such magnitude that multiplying them by two made no difference. (*Pause.*)
WILLIAMSON: Who used to say that?
AARONOW: In school. (*Pause.*)

Baylen, a detective, comes out of the inner office.

BAYLEN: Alright. . . ?

Roma enters from the street.

ROMA: *Williamson . . . Williamson,* they stole the *contracts. . . ?*
BAYLEN: Excuse me, sir . . .
ROMA: Did they get my contracts?
WILLIAMSON: They got . . .
BAYLEN: Excuse me, fella.
ROMA: . . . did they . . .
BAYLEN: Would you excuse us, please. . . ?
ROMA: Don't *fuck* with me, fella. I'm talking about a fuckin' Cadillac car that you owe me . . .
WILLIAMSON: They didn't get your contract. I filed it before I left.
ROMA: They didn't get my contracts?
WILLIAMSON: They—excuse me . . . (*He goes back into inner room with the Detective.*)
ROMA: Oh, *fuck. Fuck.* (*He starts kicking the desk.*) FUCK FUCK FUCK! WILLIAMSON!!! WILLIAMSON!!! (*Goes to the door Williamson went into, tries the door; it's locked.*) OPEN THE FUCKING . . . WILLIAMSON . . .
BAYLEN (*coming out*): Who are you?

Williamson comes out.

WILLIAMSON: They didn't get the contracts.
ROMA: Did they . . .
WILLIAMSON: They got, listen to me . . .
ROMA: Th . . .
WILLIAMSON: Listen to me: They got *some* of them.
ROMA: Some of them . . .
BAYLEN: Who told you. . . ?
ROMA: Who told me wh. . . ? You've got a fuckin', you've . . . a . . . who is this. . . ? You've got a board-up on the window. . . . *Moss* told me.
BAYLEN (*Looking back toward the inner office.*): Moss . . . Who told him?
ROMA: How the fuck do *I* know? (*To Williamson:*) *What . . . talk* to me.
WILLIAMSON: They took *some* of the con . . .
ROMA: . . . some of the contracts . . . Lingk. James Lingk. I closed . . .
WILLIAMSON: You closed him yesterday.
ROMA: *Yes.*
WILLIAMSON: It went down. I filed it.
ROMA: You did?
WILLIAMSON: Yes.
ROMA: Then I'm over the fucking top and you owe me a Cadillac.

WILLIAMSON: I . . .
ROMA: And I don't want any fucking shit and I don't give a shit, Lingk puts me over the top, you filed it, that's fine, any other shit kicks out *you* go back. You . . . *you* reclose it, 'cause I *closed* it and you . . . you owe me the car.
BAYLEN: Would you excuse us, please.
AARONOW: I, um, and may . . . maybe they're in . . . they're in . . . you should, John, if we're ins . . .
WILLIAMSON: I'm sure that we're insured, George . . . (*Going back inside.*)
ROMA: Fuck insured. You owe me a car.
BAYLEN (*Stepping back into the inner room*): Please don't leave. I'm going to talk to you. What's your name?
ROMA: Are you talking to me? (*Pause.*)
BAYLEN: Yes. (*Pause.*)
ROMA: My name is Richard Roma.

Baylen goes back into the inner room.

AARONOW: I, you know, they should be insured.
ROMA: What do *you* care. . . ?
AARONOW: Then, you know, they wouldn't be so ups . . .
ROMA: Yeah. That's swell. Yes. You're right. (*Pause.*) How are you?
AARONOW: I'm fine. You mean the *board?* You mean the *board. . . ?*
ROMA: I don't . . . yes. Okay, the board.
AARONOW: I'm, I'm, I'm, I'm fucked on the board. *You.* You see how . . . I . . . (*Pause.*) I can't . . . my mind must be in other places. 'Cause I can't do any . . .
ROMA: *What?* You can't do any *what?* (*Pause.*)
AARONOW: I can't close 'em.
ROMA: Well, they're old. I saw the shit that they were giving you.
AARONOW: Yes.
ROMA: Huh?
AARONOW: Yes. They are old.
ROMA: They're ancient.
AARONOW: Clear . . .
ROMA: Clear Meadows. That shit's dead. (*Pause.*)
AARONOW: It *is* dead.
ROMA: It's a waste of time.
AARONOW: Yes. (*Long pause.*) I'm no fucking good.
ROMA: That's . . .
AARONOW: Everything I . . . *you* know . . .
ROMA: That's not . . . Fuck that shit, George. You're a, *hey,* you had a bad month. You're a good man, George.
AARONOW: I am?
ROMA: You hit a bad streak. We've all . . . look at this: fifteen units Mountain View, the fucking things get stole.
AARONOW: He said he filed . . .
ROMA: He filed half of them, he filed the *big* one. All the little ones, I have, I have to go back and . . . ah, *fuck,* I got to go out like a fucking schmuck hat in my hand and reclose the . . . (*Pause.*) I mean, talk about a bad streak. That would sap *anyone's* self confi . . . I got to go out and reclose all my . . . Where's the phones?

AARONOW: They stole . . .

ROMA: They stole the . . .

AARONOW: What. What kind of outfit are we running where . . . where anyone . . .

ROMA (*To himself*): They stole the phones.

AARONOW: Where criminals can come in here . . . they take the . . .

ROMA: They stole the phones. They stole the leads. They're . . . *Christ.* (*Pause.*) What am I going to do this month? Oh, *shit* . . . (*Starts for the door.*)

AARONOW: You think they're going to catch . . . where are you going?

ROMA: Down the street.

WILLIAMSON (*Sticking his head out of the door*): Where are you going?

ROMA: To the restaura . . . what do you fucking. . . ?

WILLIAMSON: Aren't you going out today?

ROMA: With what? (*Pause.*) With what, John, they took the leads . . .

WILLIAMSON: I have the stuff from last year's . . .

ROMA: Oh. Oh. Oh, your "nostalgia" file, that's fine. No. Swell. 'Cause I don't have to . . .

WILLIAMSON: . . . you want to go out today. . . ?

ROMA: 'Cause I don't have to *eat* this month. No. Okay. Give 'em to me . . . (*To himself:*) Fucking Mitch and Murray going to shit a br . . . what am I going to do all . . .

Williamson starts back into the office. He is accosted by Aaronow.

AARONOW: Were the leads . . .

ROMA: . . . what am I going to *do* all month. . . ?

AARONOW: Were the leads insured?

WILLIAMSON: I don't know, George, why?

AARONOW: 'Cause, you know, 'cause they weren't, I know that Mitch and Murray uh . . . (*Pause.*)

WILLIAMSON: What?

AARONOW: That they're going to be upset.

WILLIAMSON: That's right. (*Going back into his office. Pause. To Roma:*) You want to go out today. . . ?

Pause. Williamson returns to his office.

AARONOW: He said we're all going to have to go talk to the guy.

ROMA: What?

AARONOW: He said we . . .

ROMA: To the cop?

AARONOW: Yeah.

ROMA: Yeah. That's swell. *Another* waste of time.

AARONOW: A waste of time? Why?

ROMA: *Why?* 'Cause they aren't going to find the guy.

AARONOW: The cops?

ROMA: Yes. The cops. No.

AARONOW: They aren't?

ROMA: No.

AARONOW: Why don't you think so?

ROMA: Why? Because they're *stupid.* "Where were you last night . . ."

AARONOW: Where were you?

ROMA: Where was *I*?

AARONOW: Yes.

ROMA: I was at home, where were *you*?

AARONOW: At home.

ROMA: *See.* . . ? Were you the guy who broke in?

AARONOW: Was I?

ROMA: Yes.

AARONOW: No.

ROMA: Then don't sweat it, George, you know why?

AARONOW: No.

ROMA: You have nothing to hide.

AARONOW (*Pause*): When I talk to the police, I get nervous.

ROMA: Yeah. You know who doesn't?

AARONOW: No, who?

ROMA: Thieves.

AARONOW: Why?

ROMA: They're inured to it.

AARONOW: You think so?

ROMA: Yes. (*Pause.*)

AARONOW: But what should I *tell* them?

ROMA: The truth, George. Always tell the truth. It's the easiest thing to remember.

Williamson comes out of the office with leads. Roma takes one, reads it.

ROMA: *Patel?* Ravidam *Patel?* How am I going to make a living on these deadbeat *wogs?* Where did you get this, from the *morgue?*

WILLIAMSON: If you don't want it, give it back.

ROMA: I don't "want" it, if you catch my drift.

WILLIAMSON: I'm giving you *three* leads. You . . .

ROMA: What's the fucking point in *any* case. . . ? What's the *point.* I got to argue with *you,* I got to knock heads with the *cops,* I'm busting my *balls,* sell you *dirt* to fucking *deadbeats* money in the *mattress,* I come back you can't even manage to keep the contracts safe, I have to go back and close them *again.* . . . What the fuck am I wasting my time, fuck this shit. I'm going out and reclose last week's . . .

WILLIAMSON: The word from Murray is: leave them alone. If we need a new signature he'll go out himself, he'll be the *president,* just come *in,* from out of *town* . . .

ROMA: Okay, okay, okay, gimme this shit. Fine. (*Takes the leads.*)

WILLIAMSON: Now, I'm giving you three . . .

ROMA: Three? I count *two.*

WILLIAMSON: Three.

ROMA: Patel? Fuck *you.* Fuckin' *Shiva* handed him a million dollars, told him "sign the deal," he wouldn't sign. And Vishnu, too. Into the bargain. Fuck *that,* John. You know your business, I know mine. Your business is being an *asshole,* and I find out whose fucking *cousin* you are, I'm going to go to him and figure out a way to have your *ass* . . . fuck you—I'll wait for the new leads.

Shelly Levene enters.

Alan Alda as Shelly Levene,
Tom Wopat as James Lingk,
and Liev Schreiber as Richard
Roma in the 2005 revival
at the Royale Theatre,
New York.

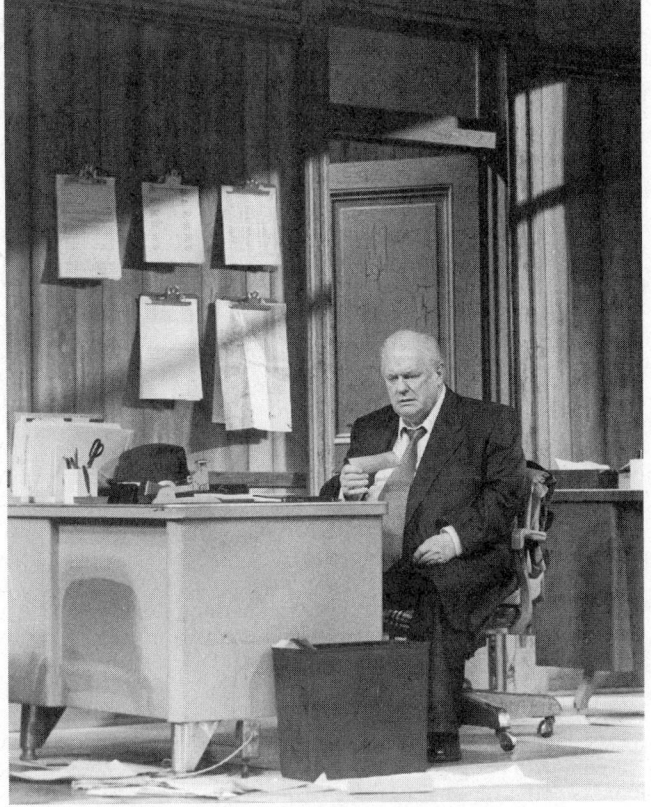

Charles Durning as Shelly
Levene in director Scott
Zigler's 2000 production of
Glengarry Glen Ross at the
McCarter Theatre in
Princeton, New Jersey.

LEVENE: Get the *chalk*. Get the *chalk* . . . get the *chalk*! I closed 'em! I *closed* the cocksucker. Get the chalk and put me on the *board*. I'm going to Hawaii! Put me on the Cadillac board, Williamson! Pick up the fuckin' chalk. Eight units. Mountain View . . .

ROMA: You sold eight Mountain View?

LEVENE: You bet your ass. Who wants to go to lunch? Who wants to go to lunch? I'm buying. (*Slaps contract down on Williamson's desk.*) Eighty-two fucking grand. And twelve grand in commission. John. (*Pause.*) On fucking deadbeat magazine subscription leads.

WILLIAMSON: Who?

LEVENE (*Pointing to contract*): *Read* it. Bruce and Harriett Nyborg. (*Looking around.*) What happened here?

AARONOW: Fuck. I had them on River Glen.

Levene looks around.

LEVENE: What happened?

WILLIAMSON: Somebody broke in.

ROMA: Eight units?

LEVENE: That's right.

ROMA: *Shelly* . . . !

LEVENE: Hey, big fucking deal. Broke a bad streak . . .

AARONOW: Shelly, the Machine, Levene.

LEVENE: You . . .

AARONOW: That's great.

LEVENE: Thank you, George.

Baylen sticks his head out of the room; calls in, "Aaronow." Aaronow goes into the side room.

LEVENE: Williamson, get on the phone, call Mitch . . .

ROMA: They took the phones . . .

LEVENE: They . . .

BAYLEN: *Aaronow* . . .

ROMA: They took the typewriters, they took the leads, they took the cash, they took the *contracts* . . .

LEVENE: Wh . . . wh . . . Wha . . . ?

AARONOW: We had a robbery. (*Goes into the inner room.*)

LEVENE (*Pause.*): When?

ROMA: Last night, this morning. (*Pause.*)

LEVENE: They took the leads?

ROMA: Mmm.

Moss comes out of the interrogation.

MOSS: Fuckin' asshole.

ROMA: What, they beat you with a rubber bat?

MOSS: Cop couldn't find his dick two hands and a map. Anyone talks to this guy's an *asshole* . . .

ROMA: You going to turn State's?

MOSS: Fuck you, Ricky. I ain't going out today. I'm going home. I'm going home because nothing's *accomplished* here. . . . Anyone *talks* to this guy is . . .

ROMA: Guess what the Machine did?

MOSS: Fuck the Machine.

ROMA: Mountain View. Eight units.

MOSS: Fuckin' cop's got no right talk to me that way. I didn't rob the place . . .

ROMA: You hear what I said?

MOSS: Yeah. He closed a deal.

ROMA: Eight units. Mountain View.

MOSS (*To Levene*): You did that?

LEVENE: Yeah. (*Pause.*)

MOSS: Fuck you.

ROMA: Guess who?

MOSS: When . . .

LEVENE: Just now.

ROMA: Guess who?

MOSS: You just this morning . . .

ROMA: Harriett and blah blah Nyborg.

MOSS: You did that?

LEVENE: Eighty-two thousand dollars. (*Pause.*)

MOSS: Those fuckin' *deadbeats* . . .

LEVENE: My ass. I told 'em. (*To Roma:*) Listen to this: I said . . .

MOSS: Hey, I don't want to hear your fucking war stories . . .

ROMA: Fuck *you*, Dave . . .

LEVENE: "You have to believe in your*self* . . . you"— look—"alright. . . ?"

MOSS (*To Williamson*): Give me some leads. I'm going out . . . I'm getting out of . . .

LEVENE: ". . . you have to believe in your*self* . . ."

MOSS: Na, fuck the leads, I'm going home.

LEVENE: "Bruce, Harriett . . . Fuck *me,* believe in your*self* . . ."

ROMA: We haven't got a lead . . .

MOSS: Why not?

ROMA: They took 'em . . .

MOSS: Hey, they're fuckin' garbage any case. . . . This whole goddamn . . .

LEVENE: ". . . You look around, you say, 'This one has so-and-so, and I have nothing . . .'"

MOSS: *Shit.*

LEVENE: "' *Why?* Why don't I get the opportunities. . . ?'"

MOSS: And did they steal the contracts. . . ?

ROMA: Fuck *you* care. . . ?

LEVENE: "I want to tell you something, Harriett . . ."

MOSS: . . . the fuck is *that* supposed to mean. . . ?

LEVENE: Will you shut up, I'm telling you this . . .

Aaronow sticks his head out.

AARONOW: Can we get some coffee. . . ?

MOSS: How ya doing? (*Pause.*)

AARONOW: Fine.

MOSS: Uh-huh.

AARONOW: If anyone's going, I could use some coffee.

LEVENE: "You *do* get the . . ." (*To Roma:*) Huh? Huh?

MOSS: *Fuck* is that supposed to mean?

LEVENE: "You *do* get the opportunity. . . . You *get* them. As *I* do, as *anyone* does . . ."

MOSS: Ricky? . . . That I don't care they stole the contracts? (*Pause.*)

LEVENE: I got 'em in the kitchen. I'm eating her crumb cake.

MOSS: What does that mean?

ROMA: It *means*, Dave, you haven't closed a good one in a month, none of my business, you want to push me to answer you. (*Pause.*) And so you haven't got a contract to get stolen or so forth.

MOSS: You have a mean streak in you, Ricky, you know that . . . ?

LEVENE: Rick. Let me tell you. Wait, we're in the . . .

MOSS: Shut the fuck up. (*Pause.*) Ricky. You have a mean streak in you. . . . (*To Levene:*) And what the fuck are *you* babbling about. . . ? (*To Roma:*) Bring that shit up. Of my volume. You were on a bad one and I brought it up to *you* you'd harbor it. (*Pause.*) You'd harbor it a long long while. And you'd be right.

ROMA: Who said "Fuck the Machine"?

MOSS: "*Fuck the Machine*"? "*Fuck the Machine*"? What is this. *Courtesy* class. . . ? You're *fucked,* Rick—are you fucking *nuts*? You're hot, so you think you're the *ruler* of this place . . . ?! You want to . . .

LEVENE: Dave . . .

MOSS: . . . Shut up. Decide who should be dealt with how? Is that the thing? I come into the fuckin' office today, I get humiliated by some jagoff cop. I get accused of . . . I get this *shit* thrown in my face by you, you genuine shit, because you're top name on the board . . .

ROMA: Is that what I did? Dave? I humiliated you? My *God* . . . I'm *sorry* . . .

MOSS: Sittin' on top of the *world,* sittin' on top of the *world,* everything's fucking *peach*fuzz . . .

ROMA: Oh, and I don't get a moment to spare for a bust-out *humanitarian* down on his luck lately. Fuck *you,* Dave, you know you got a big *mouth,* and *you* make a close the whole *place* stinks with your *farts* for a week. "How much you just ingested," what a big *man* you are, "Hey, let me buy you a pack of gum. I'll show you how to *chew* it." Your *pal* closes, all that comes out of your mouth is *bile,* how fucked *up* you are . . .

MOSS: *Who's* my pal. . . ? And what are you, Ricky, huh, what are you, Bishop *Sheean*? Who the fuck are *you,* Mr. Slick. . . ? What are you, friend to the *working*man? Big deal. Fuck *you,* you got the memory a fuckin' *fly.* I never liked you.

ROMA: What is this, your farewell speech?

MOSS: I'm going home.

ROMA: Your farewell to the troops?

MOSS: I'm not going home. I'm going to Wis*con*sin.

ROMA: Have a good trip.

MOSS (*Simultaneously with "trip"*): And fuck *you.* Fuck the *lot* of you. Fuck you *all.*

Moss exits. Pause.

ROMA (*To Levene*): You were saying? (*Pause.*) Come on. Come on, you got them in the kitchen, you got the stats spread out, you're in your shirt-sleeves, you can *smell* it. Huh? Snap out of it, you're eating her *crumb* cake. (*Pause.*)

LEVENE: I'm eating her *crumb* cake . . .

ROMA: How was it. . . ?

LEVENE: From the store.

ROMA: Fuck *her* . . .

LEVENE: "What we have to do is *admit* to ourself that we see that opportunity . . . and *take* it. (*Pause.*) And that's it." And we *sit* there. (*Pause.*) I got the pen out . . .

ROMA: "Always be closing . . ."

LEVENE: That's what I'm *saying.* The *old* ways. The *old* ways . . . convert the motherfucker . . . *sell* him . . . *sell* him . . . *make him sign the check.* (*Pause.*) The . . . Bruce, Harriett . . . the kitchen, blah: they got their money in *government* bonds. . . . I say *fuck* it, we're going to go the whole route. I plat it out eight units. Eighty-two grand. I tell them. "This is now. This is that *thing* that you've been dreaming of, you're going to find that suitcase on the train, the guy comes in the door, the bag that's full of money. This is it, *Harriett* . . ."

ROMA (*Reflectively*): Harriett . . .

LEVENE: *Bruce* . . . "I don't want to fuck *around* with you. I don't want to go *round* this, and *pussyfoot* around the thing, you have to look back on this. I do, too. I came here to do good for you and me. For *both* of us. Why take an interim position? *The only arrangement I'll accept* is full investment. Period. The whole eight units. I know that you're saying 'be safe,' I know what you're saying. I know if I left you to yourselves, you'd say 'come back tomorrow,' and when I walked out that door, you'd make a cup of *coffee* . . . you'd sit *down* . . . and you'd think 'let's be safe . . .' and not to disappoint me you'd go *one* unit or maybe two, because you'd become scared because you'd met possi*bil*ity. But this won't do, and that's not the subject. . . ." Listen to this, I actually said this. "That's not the subject of our *evening* together." Now I handed them the pen. I held it in my hand. I turned the contract, eight units eighty-two grand. "Now I want you to sign." (*Pause.*) I sat there. Five minutes. Then, I sat there, Ricky, *twenty-two minutes* by the kitchen clock. (*Pause.*) Twenty-two minutes by the kitchen clock. Not a *word,* not a *motion.* What am I thinking? "My arm's getting tired?" *No.* I did it. I *did* it. Like in the *old* days, Ricky. Like I was taught . . . Like, like, like I *used* to do . . . I did it.

ROMA: Like you taught me . . .

LEVENE: Bullshit, you're . . . No. That's raw . . . well, if I *did,* then I'm *glad* I did. I, *well.* I locked on them. All on them, nothing on me. All my thoughts are on them. I'm holding the last thought that I spoke: "Now is the time." (*Pause.*) They signed, Ricky. It was *great.* It was fucking great. It was like they wilted all at once. No *gesture* . . . nothing. Like together. They, I swear to God, they both kind of *imperceptibly slumped.* And he reaches and takes the pen and signs, he passes it to her, she signs. It was so fucking solemn. I just let it sit. I nod like this. I nod again. I grasp his hands. I shake his hands. I grasp *her* hands. I nod at her like this. "Bruce . . . Harriett . . ." I'm beaming at them. I'm nodding like this. I point back in the living room, back to the sideboard. (*Pause.*) *I didn't fucking know there was a sideboard there!!* He goes back, he brings us a drink. Little shot glasses. A pattern in 'em. And we toast. In silence. (*Pause.*)

ROMA: That was a great sale, Shelly. (*Pause.*)

LEVENE: Ah, fuck. Leads! Leads! Williamson! (*Williamson sticks his head out of the office.*) Send me *out*! Send me *out*!

WILLIAMSON: The leads are coming.

LEVENE: *Get* 'em to me!

WILLIAMSON: I talked to Murray and Mitch an hour ago. They're coming in, you understand they're a bit *upset* over this morning's . . .

LEVENE: Did you tell 'em my sale?

WILLIAMSON: How could I tell 'em your sale? Eh? I don't have a tel . . . I'll tell 'em your sale when they bring in the leads. Alright? Shelly. Alright? We had a little . . . You closed a deal. You made a good sale. Fine.

LEVENE: It's better than a good sale. It's a . . .

WILLIAMSON: Look: I have a lot of things on my mind, they're coming in, alright, they're very upset, I'm trying to make some *sense* . . .

LEVENE: All that I'm *telling* you: that one thing you can tell them it's a remarkable sale.

WILLIAMSON: The only thing remarkable is who you made it to.

LEVENE: What does *that* fucking mean?

WILLIAMSON: That if the sale sticks, it will be a miracle.

LEVENE: Why should the sale not stick? Hey, *fuck* you. That's what I'm saying. You have no idea of your job. A man's his job and you're *fucked* at yours. You hear what I'm saying to you? Your "end of month board . . ." You can't run an office. I don't care. You don't know what it *is,* you don't have the *sense,* you don't have the *balls.* You ever been on a sit? *Ever?* Has this cocksucker ever been . . . you ever sit down with a cust . . .

WILLIAMSON: I were you, I'd calm down, Shelly.

LEVENE: *Would* you? *Would* you. . . ? Or you're gonna *what,* fire me?

WILLIAMSON: It's not impossible.

LEVENE: On an eighty-thousand dollar *day?* And it ain't even *noon.*

ROMA: You closed 'em today?

LEVENE: Yes. I did. This *morning.* (*To Williamson:*) What I'm *saying* to you: things can *change.* You *see?* This is where you fuck *up,* because this is something you don't *know.* You can't look down the *road.* And see what's *coming.* Might be someone *else,* John. It might be someone *new,* eh? Someone *new.* And you can't look *back.* 'Cause you don't know *history.* You ask them. When we were at Rio Rancho, who was top man? A month. . . ? Two months. . . ? Eight months in twelve for three years in a row. You know what that means? You know what that means? Is that *luck?* Is that some, some, some purloined leads? That's *skill.* That's *talent,* that's, that's . . .

ROMA: . . . *yes* . . .

LEVENE: . . . and you don't *remember.* 'Cause you weren't *around.* That's cold *calling.* Walk up to the door. I don't even know their *name.* I'm selling something they don't even *want.* You talk about soft sell . . . before we had a name for it . . . before we called it anything, we did it.

ROMA: That's right, Shel.

LEVENE: And, and, and, I *did* it. And I put a kid through *school.* She . . . and . . . Cold *calling,* fella. Door to door. But you don't know. You don't know. You never heard of a *streak.* You never heard of "marshaling your sales force. . . ." What are you, you're a *secretary,* John. Fuck *you.* That's my message to you. Fuck you and kiss my ass. You don't like it, I'll go talk to Jerry Graff. Period. Fuck you. Put me on the board. And I want three worthwhile leads today and I don't want any bullshit about them and I want 'em close together 'cause I'm going to hit them all today. That's all I have to say to you.

ROMA: He's right, Williamson.

Williamson goes into a side office. Pause.

LEVENE: It's not right. I'm sorry, and I'll tell you who's to blame is Mitch and Murray.

Roma sees something outside the window.

ROMA (*Sotto*): Oh, Christ.

LEVENE: The hell with him. We'll go to lunch, the leads won't be up for . . .

ROMA: You're a client. I just sold you five waterfront Glengarry Farms. I rub my head, throw me the cue "Kenilworth."

LEVENE: What is it?

ROMA: Kenilw . . .

Lingk enters the office.

ROMA (*To Levene*): I own the property, my *mother* owns the property, I put her *into* it. I'm going to show you on the plats. You look when you get home A–3 through A–14 and 26 through 30. You take your time and if you still feel.

LEVENE: No, Mr. Roma. I don't need the time, I've made a lot of *investments* in the last . . .

LINGK: I've got to talk to you.

ROMA (*Looking up*): Jim! What are you doing here? Jim Lingk, D. Ray Morton . . .

LEVENE: Glad to meet you.

ROMA: I just put Jim into Black Creek . . . are you acquainted with . . .

LEVENE: No . . . Black *Creek.* Yes. In *Florida?*

ROMA: Yes.

LEVENE: I wanted to *speak* with you about . . .

ROMA: Well, we'll do that this weekend.

LEVENE: My *wife* told me to look into . . .

ROMA: *Beautiful.* Beautiful rolling land. I was telling Jim and Jinny, Ray, I want to tell you something. (*To Levene:*) You, Ray, you eat in a lot of restaurants. I know you do. . . . (*To Lingk:*) Mr. Morton's with American

Express . . . he's . . . (*To Levene:*) I can tell Jim what you do. . . ?

LEVENE: Sure.

ROMA: Ray is director of all European sales and services for American Ex . . . (*To Levene:*) But I'm saying you haven't had a *meal* until you've tasted . . . I was at the Lingks' last . . . as a matter of fact, what was that service feature you were talking about. . . ?

LEVENE: Which . . .

ROMA: "Home Cooking" . . . what did you call it, you said it . . . it was a tag phrase that you had . . .

LEVENE: Uh . . .

ROMA: Home . . .

LEVENE: Home cooking . . .

ROMA: The monthly interview. . . ?

LEVENE: Oh! For the *magazine* . . .

ROMA: Yes. Is this something that I can talk ab . . .

LEVENE: Well, it isn't coming *out* until the February iss . . . *sure*. Sure, go ahead, Ricky.

ROMA: You're sure?

LEVENE (*nods*): Go ahead.

ROMA: Well, Ray was eating at one of his company's men's home in France . . . the man's French, isn't he?

LEVENE: No, his *wife* is.

ROMA: Ah. Ah, his wife is. Ray: what *time* do you have. . . ?

LEVENE: Twelve-fifteen.

ROMA: Oh! My God . . . I've got to get you on the *plane*!

LEVENE: Didn't I say I was taking the two o' . . .

ROMA: No. You said the one. That's why you said we couldn't talk till Kenilworth.

LEVENE: Oh, my God, you're right! I'm on the one. . . . (*Getting up.*) Well, let's *scoot* . . .

LINGK: I've got to talk to you . . .

ROMA: I've got to get Ray to O'Hare . . . (*To Levene:*) Come on, let's hustle. . . . (*Over his shoulder:*) John! Call American Express in *Pittsburgh* for Mr. Morton, will you, tell them he's on the one o'clock. (*To Lingk:*) I'll see you. . . . Christ, I'm sorry you came all the way in. . . . I'm running Ray over to O'Hare. . . . You wait here, I'll . . . no. (*To Levene:*) I'm meeting your man at the bank. . . . (*To Lingk:*) I wish you'd phoned. . . . I'll tell you, wait: are you and Jinny going to be home tonight? (*Rubs forehead.*)

LINGK: I . . .

LEVENE: Rick.

ROMA: What?

LEVENE: *Kenilworth.* . . ?

ROMA: I'm sorry. . . ?

LEVENE: *Kenilworth.*

ROMA: Oh, God . . . Oh, God . . . (*Roma takes Lingk aside, sotto*) Jim, excuse me. . . . Ray, I told you, who he is is *the* senior vice-president American Express. His family owns 32 per. . . . Over the past years I've sold him . . . I can't tell you the dollar amount, but *quite* a lot of land. I promised five *weeks* ago that I'd go to the wife's birthday party in Kenilworth tonight. (*Sighs.*) I *have* to go. You understand. They treat me

like a member of the family, so I have to go. It's funny, you know, you get a picture of the Corporation-Type Company Man, all business . . . this man, *no*. We'll go out to his home sometime. Let's see. (*He checks his datebook.*) Tomorrow. No. Tomorrow, I'm in L.A. . . . *Monday* . . . I'll take you to lunch, where would you like to go?

LINGK: My wife . . . (*Roma rubs his head.*)

LEVENE (*Standing in the door*): Rick. . . ?

ROMA: I'm sorry, Jim. I can't talk now. I'll call you tonight . . . I'm sorry. I'm coming, Ray. (*Starts for the door.*)

LINGK: My wife said I have to cancel the deal.

ROMA: It's a common reaction, Jim. I'll tell you what it is, and I know that that's why you married her. One of the reasons is *prudence*. It's a sizable investment. One thinks *twice* . . . it's also something *women* have. It's just a reaction to the size of the investment. *Monday,* if you'd invite me for dinner again . . . (*To Levene:*) This woman can *cook* . . .

LEVENE (*Simultaneously*): I'm sure she can . . .

ROMA (*To Lingk*): We're going to talk. I'm going to *tell* you something. Because (*Sotto:*) there's something about your acreage I want you to know. I can't talk about it now. I really shouldn't. And, in fact, by *law,* I . . . (*Shrugs, resigned.*) The man next to you, he bought his lot at forty-*two*, he phoned to say that he'd *already* had an offer . . . (*Roma rubs his head.*)

LEVENE: Rick. . . ?

ROMA: I'm coming, Ray . . . what a day! I'll call you this evening, Jim. I'm sorry you had to come in . . . Monday, lunch.

LINGK: My wife . . .

LEVENE: Rick, we really have to go.

LINGK: My wife . . .

ROMA: Monday.

LINGK: She called the consumer . . . the attorney, I don't know. The attorney gen . . . they said we have three days . . .

ROMA: *Who* did she call?

LINGK: I don't know, the attorney gen . . . the . . . some consumer office, umm . . .

ROMA: Why did she do *that*, Jim?

LINGK: I don't know. (*Pause.*) They said we have three days. (*Pause.*) They said we have three days.

ROMA: Three days.

LINGK: To . . . you know. (*Pause.*)

ROMA: No, I don't know. *Tell* me.

LINGK: To change our minds.

ROMA: Of *course* you have three days. (*Pause.*)

LINGK: So we can't talk *Monday*. (*Pause.*)

ROMA: Jim, Jim, you saw my book . . . I *can't*, you saw my book . . .

LINGK: But we have to *before* Monday. To get our money ba . . .

ROMA: Three *business* days. They mean three *business* days.

LINGK: Wednesday, Thursday, Friday.

ROMA: I don't understand.

Kevin Spacey as Williamson (left) and Jack Lemmon as Levene (right) in the 1992 film version of *Glengarry Glen Ross* (New Line Cinema), directed by James Foley.

The premiere production of *Glengarry Glen Ross* in 1983 at the Cottesloe Theatre in London, directed by Bill Bryden, with Jack Shepherd as Roma (left) and Tony Haygarth as Lingk (right).

LINGK: That's what they are. Three business . . . if I wait till Monday, my time limit runs out.

ROMA: You don't count Saturday.

LINGK: I'm not.

ROMA: No, I'm saying you don't include Saturday . . . in your three days. It's not a *business* day.

LINGK: But I'm not *counting* it. (*Pause.*) Wednesday. Thursday. Friday. So it would have elapsed.

ROMA: What would have elapsed?

LINGK: If we wait till Mon . . .

ROMA: When did you write the check?

LINGK: Yest . . .

ROMA: What was yesterday?

LINGK: Tuesday.

ROMA: And when was that check cashed?

LINGK: I don't know.

ROMA: What was the *earliest* it could have been cashed? (*Pause.*)

LINGK: I don't know.

ROMA: *Today.* (*Pause.*) *Today.* Which, in any case, it was not, as there were a couple of points on the agreement I wanted to go over with you in any case.

LINGK: The check wasn't cashed?

ROMA: I just called downtown, and it's on their desk.

LEVENE: Rick . . .

ROMA: One moment, I'll be right with you. (*To Lingk:*) In fact, a . . . *one* point, which I spoke to you of which (*Looks around.*) I can't talk to you about here.

Detective puts his head out of the doorway.

BAYLEN: Levene!!!

LINGK: I, I . . .

ROMA: Listen to me, the *statute,* it's for your protection. I have no complaints with that, in fact, I was a member of the board when we *drafted* it, so quite the *opposite.* It *says* that you can change your mind three working days from the time the deal is closed.

BAYLEN: Levene!

ROMA: Which, wait a second, which is not until the check is cashed.

BAYLEN: Levene!!

Aaronow comes out of the Detective's office.

AARONOW: I'm *through,* with *this* fucking meshugaas. No one should talk to a man that way. How are you *talking* to me that. . . ?

BAYLEN: Levene! (*Williamson puts his head out of the office.*)

AARONOW: . . . how can you *talk* to me that . . . that . . .

LEVENE (*To Roma*): Rick, I'm going to flag a cab.

AARONOW: *I* didn't rob . . .

Williamson sees Levene.

WILLIAMSON: Shelly: get in the office.

AARONOW: *I* didn't . . . why should *I* . . . "Where were you last . . ." Is anybody listening to me. . . ? Where's Moss. . . ? Where. . . ?

BAYLEN: Levene? (*To Williamson:*) Is this Lev . . . (*Baylen accosts Lingk.*)

LEVENE (*Taking Baylen into the office*): Ah. Ah. Perhaps I can advise you on that. . . . (*To Roma and Lingk, as he exits:*) Excuse us, will you. . . ?

AARONOW (*Simultaneous with Levene's speech above*): . . . Come in here . . . I *work* here, I don't come in here to be *mistreated* . . .

WILLIAMSON: Go to *lunch,* will you . . .

AARONOW: I want to *work* today, that's why I came . . .

WILLIAMSON: The leads come in, I'll let . . .

AARONOW: . . . that's why I came in. I thought I . . .

WILLIAMSON: Just go to lunch.

AARONOW: I don't *want* to go to lunch.

WILLIAMSON: Go to lunch, George.

AARONOW: Where does he get off to talk that way to a working man? It's not . . .

WILLIAMSON (*Buttonholes him*): Will you take it outside, we have people trying to do *business* here . . .

AARONOW: That's what, that's what, that's what *I* was trying to do. (*Pause.*) That's why I came *in* . . . I meet *gestapo* tac . . .

WILLIAMSON (*Going back into his office*): Excuse me . . .

AARONOW: I meet *gestapo* tactics . . . I meet *gestapo* tactics. . . . That's not right. . . . No man has the right to . . . "Call an attorney," that means you're guilt . . . you're under sus . . . "Co. . . ," he says, "cooperate" or we'll go downtown. *That's* not . . . as long as I've . . .

WILLIAMSON (*Bursting out of his office*): Will you get out of here. Will you get *out* of here. Will you. I'm trying to run an *office* here. Will you go to lunch? Go to lunch. Will you go to lunch? (*Retreats into office.*)

ROMA (*To Aaronow*): Will you excuse . . .

AARONOW: Where did Moss. . . ? I . . .

ROMA: Will you excuse us please?

AARONOW: Uh, uh, did he go to the restaurant? (*Pause.*) I . . . I . . . (*Exits.*)

ROMA: I'm *very* sorry, Jimmy. I apologize to you.

LINGK: It's not me, it's my wife.

ROMA (*Pause.*): What is?

LINGK: I told you.

ROMA: Tell me again.

LINGK: What's going on here?

ROMA: Tell me again. Your wife.

LINGK: I told you.

ROMA: You tell me again.

LINGK: She wants her money back.

ROMA: We're going to speak to her.

LINGK: No. She told me "right now."

ROMA: We'll speak to her, Jim . . .

LINGK: She won't listen.

Detective sticks his head out.

BAYLEN: *Roma.*

LINGK: She told me if not, I have to call the State's attorney.

ROMA: No, no. That's just something she "said." We don't have to do that.

LINGK: She told me I *have* to.

ROMA: No, Jim.

LINGK: I *do*. If I don't get my *money* back . . .

(*Williamson points out Roma to Baylen.*)

BAYLEN: Roma! (*To Roma:*) I'm talking to you . . .

ROMA: I've . . . look. (*Generally:*) Will someone get this guy off my back.

BAYLEN: You have a problem?

ROMA: Yes, I have a problem. Yes, I *do*, my fr . . . It's not me that ripped the joint off, I'm doing *business*. I'll be with you in a *while*. You got it . . . ? (*Looks back. Lingk is heading for the door.*) Where are you going?

LINGK: I'm . . .

ROMA: Where are you going. . . ? This is *me*. . . . This is Ricky, Jim. Jim, anything you *want*, you *want* it, you *have* it. You understand? This is *me*. Something *upset* you. Sit down, now sit down. You tell me what it is. (*Pause.*) Am I going to help you fix it? You're god-damned right I am. Sit down. Tell you something. . . ? *Sometimes* we need someone from *outside*. It's . . . no, sit down. . . . Now *talk* to me.

LINGK: I can't negotiate.

ROMA: What does that mean?

LINGK: That . . .

ROMA: . . . what, what, *say* it. Say it to me . . .

LINGK: I . . .

ROMA: What. . . ?

LINGK: I . . .

ROMA: What. . . ? Say the words.

LINGK: I don't have the *power*. (*Pause.*) I said it.

ROMA: What power?

LINGK: The power to negotiate.

ROMA: To negotiate what? (*Pause.*) To negotiate what?

LINGK: *This*.

ROMA: What, "this"? (*Pause.*)

LINGK: The deal.

ROMA: The "deal," *forget* the deal. *Forget* the deal, you've got something on your mind, Jim, what is it?

LINGK (*rising*): I can't talk to you, *you* met my wife, I . . . (*Pause.*)

ROMA: What? (*Pause.*) What? (*Pause.*) What, Jim: I tell you what, let's get out of here . . . let's go get a drink.

LINGK: She told me not to talk to you.

ROMA: Let's . . . no one's going to know, let's go around the *corner* and we'll get a drink.

LINGK: She told me I had to get back the check or call the State's att . . .

ROMA: *Forget* the deal, Jimmy. (*Pause.*) *Forget* the deal . . . you know me. The deal's *dead*. Am I talking about the *deal*? That's *over*. Please. Let's talk about *you*. Come on. (*Pause. Roma rises and starts walking toward the front door.*) Come on. (*Pause.*) Come on, Jim. (*Pause.*) I want to tell you something. Your life is your own. You have a contract with your wife. You have certain things you do *jointly*, you have a *bond* there . . . and there are *other* things. Those things are yours. You needn't feel *ashamed*, you needn't feel that you're being *untrue* . . . or that she would abandon you if she knew. This is your life. (*Pause.*) Yes.

Now I want to *talk* to you because you're obviously upset and that *concerns* me. Now let's go. Right now.

Lingk gets up and they start for the door.

BAYLEN (*Sticks his head out of the door*): Roma . . .

LINGK: . . . and . . . and . . . (*Pause.*)

ROMA: What?

LINGK: And the check is . . .

ROMA: What did I *tell* you? (*Pause.*) What did I say about the three days. . . ?

BAYLEN: Roma, would you, I'd like to get some lunch . . .

ROMA: I'm talking with Mr. Lingk. If you please, I'll be back in. (*Checks watch.*) I'll be back in a while. . . . I told you, check with Mr. Williamson.

BAYLEN: The people downtown said . . .

ROMA: You call them again. Mr. Williamson . . . !

WILLIAMSON: Yes.

ROMA: Mr. Lingk and I are going to . . .

WILLIAMSON: Yes. Please. Please. (*To Lingk:*) The police (*Shrugs.*) can be . . .

LINGK: What are the police doing?

ROMA: It's nothing.

LINGK: What are the *police* doing here . . . ?

WILLIAMSON: We had a slight burglary last night.

ROMA: It was nothing . . . I was assuring Mr. Lingk . . .

WILLIAMSON: Mr. Lingk. James Lingk. Your contract went out. Nothing to . . .

ROMA: John . . .

WILLIAMSON: Your contract went out to the bank.

LINGK: You cashed the check?

WILLIAMSON: We . . .

ROMA: . . . Mr. Williamson . . .

WILLIAMSON: Your check was cashed yesterday afternoon. And we're completely insured, as you know, in *any* case. (*Pause.*)

LINGK (*To Roma*): You cashed the check?

ROMA: Not to my knowledge, no . . .

WILLIAMSON: I'm sure we can . . .

LINGK: Oh, Christ . . . (*Starts out the door.*) Don't follow me. . . . Oh, Christ. (*Pause. To Roma:*) I know I've let you down. I'm sorry. For . . . Forgive . . . for . . . I don't know anymore. (*Pause.*) Forgive me. (*Lingk exits. Pause.*)

ROMA (*To Williamson*): You stupid fucking cunt. *You*, Williamson . . . I'm talking to *you*, shithead. . . . You just cost me *six thousand dollars*. (*Pause.*) Six thousand dollars. And one Cadillac. That's right. What are you going to do about it? What are you going to do about it, asshole. You fucking *shit*. Where did you learn your *trade*. You stupid fucking *cunt*. You *idiot*. Whoever told you you could work with *men*?

BAYLEN: Could I . . .

ROMA: I'm going to have your *job*, shithead. I'm going *downtown* and talk to Mitch and Murray, and I'm going to Lemkin. I don't care *whose* nephew you are, who you know, whose dick you're sucking on. You're going *out*, I swear to you, you're going . . .

BAYLEN: Hey, fella, let's get this done . . .

ROMA: Anyone in this office lives on their *wits*. . . . (*To Baylen:*) I'm going to be with you in a second. (*To Williamson:*) What you're hired for is to *help* us— does that seem clear to you? To *help* us. *Not* to fuck us up . . . to help *men* who are going *out* there to try to earn a *living*. You *fairy*. You company man . . . I'll tell you something else. I hope you knocked the joint off, I can tell our friend here something might help him catch you. (*Starts into the room.*) You want to learn the first rule you'd know if you ever spent a day in your life . . . you never open your mouth till you know what the shot is. (*Pause.*) You fucking *child* . . . (*Roma goes to the inner room.*)

LEVENE: You *are* a shithead, Williamson . . . (*Pause.*)

WILLIAMSON: Mmm.

LEVENE: You can't think on your feet you should keep your mouth closed. (*Pause.*) You hear me? I'm *talk-ing* to you. Do you hear me. . . ?

WILLIAMSON: Yes. (*Pause.*) I hear you.

LEVENE: You can't learn that in an office. Eh? He's right. You have to learn it on the streets. You can't *buy* that. You have to *live* it.

WILLIAMSON: Mmm.

LEVENE: *Yes.* Mmm. *Yes. Precisely. Precisely.* 'Cause your partner *depends* on it. (*Pause.*) I'm *talking* to you, I'm trying to tell you something.

WILLIAMSON: You are?

LEVENE: Yes, I am.

WILLIAMSON: What are you trying to tell me?

LEVENE: What Roma's trying to tell you. What I told you yesterday. Why you don't belong in this business.

WILLIAMSON: Why I don't . . .

LEVENE: You listen to me, someday you might say, "Hey . . ." No, fuck that, you just listen what I'm going to say: your partner *depends* on you. Your partner . . . a man who's your "partner" *depends* on you . . . you have to go *with* him and *for* him . . . or you're shit, you're *shit*, you can't exist alone . . .

WILLIAMSON (*Brushing past him*): Excuse me . . .

LEVENE: . . . excuse you, *nothing*, you be as cold as you want, but you just fucked a good man out of six thousand dollars and his goddamn bonus 'cause you didn't know the *shot*, if you can do that and you aren't man enough that it gets you, then I don't know what, if you can't take *some thing* from that . . . (*Blocking his way.*) you're *scum*, you're fucking white-bread. You be as cold as you want. A *child* would know it, he's right. (*Pause.*) You're going to make something up, be sure it will *help* or keep your mouth closed. (*Pause.*)

WILLIAMSON: Mmm. (*Levene lifts up his arm.*)

LEVENE: Now I'm done with you. (*Pause.*)

WILLIAMSON: How do you know I made it up?

LEVENE (*Pause*): What?

WILLIAMSON: How do you know I made it up?

LEVENE: What are you talking about?

WILLIAMSON: You said, "You don't make something up unless it's sure to help." (*Pause.*) How did you know that I made it up?

LEVENE: What are you talking about?

WILLIAMSON: I told the customer that his contracts had gone to the bank.

LEVENE: Well, hadn't it?

WILLIAMSON: No. (*Pause.*) It hadn't.

LEVENE: Don't *fuck* with me, John, don't *fuck* with me . . . what are you saying?

WILLIAMSON: Well, I'm saying this, Shel: usually I take the contracts to the bank. Last night I didn't. How did you know that? One night in a year I left a con-tract on my desk. Nobody knew that but *you*. Now how did you know that? (*Pause.*) You want to talk to me, you want to talk to someone *else* . . . because this is *my* job. This is my job on the line, and you are going to *talk* to me. Now how did you know that contract was on my desk?

LEVENE: You're so full of shit.

WILLIAMSON: You robbed the office.

LEVENE (*Laughs*): Sure! I robbed the office. Sure.

WILLIAMSON: What'd you do with the leads? (*Pause. Points to the Detective's room.*) You want to go in there? I tell him what I know, he's going to dig up *something*. . . . You got an alibi last night? You bet-ter have one. What did you do with the leads? If you tell me what you did with the leads, we can talk.

LEVENE: I don't know what you are saying.

WILLIAMSON: If you tell me where the leads are, I won't turn you in. If you *don't*, I am going to tell the cop you stole them, Mitch and Murray will see that you go to jail. Believe me they will. Now, what did you do with the leads? I'm walking in that door—you have five seconds to tell me: or you are going to jail.

LEVENE: I . . .

WILLIAMSON: I don't care. You understand? *Where are the leads?* (*Pause.*) Alright. (*Williamson goes to open the office door.*)

LEVENE: I sold them to Jerry Graff.

WILLIAMSON: How much did you get for them? (*Pause.*) How much did you get for them?

LEVENE: Five thousand. I kept half.

WILLIAMSON: Who kept the other half? (*Pause.*)

LEVENE: Do I have to tell you? (*Pause. Williamson starts to open the door.*) Moss.

WILLIAMSON: *That* was easy, *wasn't* it? (*Pause.*)

LEVENE: It was his idea.

WILLIAMSON: *Was* it?

LEVENE: I . . . I'm sure he got more than the five, actually.

WILLIAMSON: Uh-huh?

LEVENE: He told me my share was twenty-five.

WILLIAMSON: Mmm.

LEVENE: Okay: I . . . look: I'm going to make it worth your while. I am. I turned this thing around. I closed the *old* stuff, I can do it again. *I'm* the one's going to close 'em. I am! *I* am! 'Cause I turned this thing a . . . I can do *that*, I can do *anyth* . . . last night. I'm going to tell you, I was ready to Do the Dutch. Moss gets me, "Do this, we'll get well. . . ." Why not. Big fuckin' deal. I'm halfway hoping to get caught. To put me out of my . . . (*Pause.*) But it *taught* me something. What it taught me, that you've got to get *out* there. Big deal. So I wasn't cut out to be a thief. I was cut out to be a salesman. And now I'm back, and I got my *balls* back . . . and, you know, John, you have the *advantage* on me now. Whatever it takes to make it right, we'll make it right. We're going to make it right.

WILLIAMSON: I want to tell you something, Shelly. You have a big mouth. (*Pause.*)

LEVENE: What?

WILLIAMSON: You've got a big mouth, and now I'm going to show you an even bigger one. (*Starts toward the Detective's door.*)

LEVENE: Where are you going, John? . . . you can't do that, you don't want to do that . . . hold, hold on . . . hold on . . . wait . . . wait . . . wait . . . (*Pulls money out of his pockets.*) Wait . . . uh, look . . . (*Starts splitting money.*) Look, twelve, twenty, two, twen . . . twenty-five hundred, it's . . . take it. (*Pause.*) Take it all. . . . (*Pause.*) Take it!

WILLIAMSON: No, I don't think so, Shel.

LEVENE: I . . .

WILLIAMSON: No, I think I don't want your money. I think you fucked up my office. And I think you're going away.

LEVENE: I . . . what? Are you, are you, that's why. . . ? Are you nuts? I'm . . . I'm going to *close* for you, I'm going to . . . (*Thrusting money at him.*) Here, here, I'm going to *make* this office . . . I'm going to be back there Number One. . . . Hey, hey, hey! This is only the beginning. . . . List . . . list . . . listen. Listen. Just one moment. List . . . here's what . . . here's what we're going to do. Twenty percent. I'm going to give you twenty percent of my sales. . . . (*Pause.*) Twenty percent. (*Pause.*) For as long as I am with the firm. (*Pause.*) Fifty percent. (*Pause.*) You're going to be my partner. (*Pause.*) Fifty percent. Of all my sales.

WILLIAMSON: What sales?

LEVENE: What sales. . . ? I just *closed* eighty-two *grand*. . . . Are you fuckin' . . . I'm *back* . . . I'm *back*, this is only the beginning.

WILLIAMSON: Only the beginning . . .

LEVENE: Abso . . .

WILLIAMSON: Where have you been, Shelly? Bruce and Harriett Nyborg. Do you want to see the *memos* . . . ? They're nuts . . . they used to call in every week. When I was with Webb. And we were selling Arizona . . . they're nuts . . . did you see how they were *living*? How can you delude yours . . .

LEVENE: I've got the check . . .

WILLIAMSON: Forget it. Frame it. It's worthless. (*Pause.*)

LEVENE: The check's no good?

WILLIAMSON: You stick around I'll pull the memo for you. (*Starts for the door.*) I'm busy now . . .

LEVENE: Their check's no good? They're nuts . . . ?

WILLIAMSON: Call up the bank. *I* called them.

LEVENE: You did?

WILLIAMSON: I called them when we had the lead . . . four months ago. (*Pause.*) The people are insane. They just like talking to salesmen. (*Williamson starts for door.*)

LEVENE: Don't.

WILLIAMSON: I'm sorry.

LEVENE: *Why?*

WILLIAMSON: Because I don't like you.

LEVENE: John: John: . . . my *daughter* . . .

WILLIAMSON: Fuck you. (*Roma comes out of the Detective's door. Williamson goes in.*)

ROMA (*To Baylen*): Asshole . . . (*To Levene:*) Guy couldn't find his fuckin' couch the *living room* . . . Ah, Christ . . . what a day, what a day . . . I haven't even had a cup of *coffee*. . . . Jagoff John opens his mouth he blows my Cadillac. . . . (*Sighs.*) I swear . . . it's not a world of men . . . it's not a world of men, Machine . . . it's a world of clock watchers, bureaucrats, officeholders . . . what it is, it's a fucked-up world . . . there's no adventure *to* it. (*Pause.*) Dying breed. Yes it is. (*Pause.*) We are the members of a dying breed. That's . . . that's . . . that's why we have to stick together. Shel: I want to talk to you. I've wanted to talk to you for some time. For a long time, actually. I said, "The Machine, there's a man I would work with. There's a man. . . ." You know? I never said a thing. I should have, don't know why I didn't. And that shit you were slinging on my guy today was *so* good . . . it . . . it was, and, excuse me, 'cause it isn't even my place to say it. It was admirable . . . it was the old stuff. Hey, I've been on a hot streak, so *what*? There's things that I could learn from you. You eat today?

LEVENE: Me.

ROMA: Yeah.

LEVENE: Mm.

ROMA: Well, you want to swing by the Chinks, watch me eat, we'll talk?

LEVENE: I think I'd better stay here for a while.

Baylen sticks his head out of the room:

BAYLEN: Mr. *Levene*. . . ?

ROMA: You're done, come down and let's . . .

BAYLEN: Would you come in here, please?

ROMA: And let's put this together. Okay? Shel? Say okay. (*Pause.*)

LEVENE (*Softly, to himself*): Huh.

BAYLEN: Mr. Levene, I think we have to talk.

ROMA: I'm going to the Chinks. You're done, come down, we're going to smoke a cigarette.

LEVENE: I . . .

BAYLEN (*Comes over*): . . . Get in the room.

ROMA: Hey, hey, hey, *easy* friend, that's the "Machine." That is Shelly "The Machine" Lev . . .

BAYLEN: Get in the goddamn room. (*Baylen starts manhandling Shelly into the room.*)

LEVENE: Ricky, I . . .

ROMA: Okay, okay, I'll be at the resta . . .

LEVENE: Ricky . . .

BAYLEN: "Ricky" can't help you, pal.

LEVENE: . . . I only want to . . .

BAYLEN: Yeah. What do you want? You want to *what*? (*He pushes Levene into the room, closes the door behind him. Pause.*)

ROMA: WILLIAMSON: listen to me: when the *leads* come in . . . listen to me: when the *leads* come in I want my top two off the list. For *me.* My usual two. Anything you give *Levene* . . .

WILLIAMSON: . . . I wouldn't worry about it.

ROMA: Well I'm *going* to worry about it, and so are you, so shut up and *listen.* (*Pause.*) I GET HIS ACTION. My stuff is *mine,* whatever *he* gets for himself, I'm talking half. You put me in with him.

Aaronow enters.

AARONOW: Did they. . . ?

ROMA: You understand?

AARONOW: Did they catch. . . ?

ROMA: Do you understand? My stuff is mine, his stuff is ours. I'm taking half of his commissions—now, *you* work it out.

WILLIAMSON: Mmm.

AARONOW: Did they find the guy who broke into the office yet?

ROMA: No. *I* don't know. (*Pause.*)

AARONOW: Did the leads come in yet?

ROMA: No.

AARONOW (*Settling into a desk chair*): Oh, God, I hate this job.

ROMA (*Simultaneous with "job," exiting the office*): I'll be at the restaurant.

COMMENTARY

Anne Dean

GLENGARRY GLEN ROSS   *1990*

In her discussion, Anne Dean focuses on the economic issues in Mamet's play— the central question of capitalism and the competition that makes it such an efficient economic system. In the play, the salesmen compete for the prize, a Cadillac, the symbol of success in America. Those who fail, however, face the possibility of being let go entirely. Dean compares the salesmen in Glengarry Glen Ross *with Willy Loman in Arthur Miller's* Death of a Salesman. *Driving both is the quest for success.*

At the end of Arthur Miller's Death of Salesman, Charley offers a valediction on Willy Loman:

> for a salesman, there is no rock bottom to the life. . . . He's a man way out there in the blue, riding on a smile and a shoe shine. . . . A salesman is got to dream, boy. It comes with the territory.[1]

Like Willy, the salesmen in Mamet's *Glengarry Glen Ross* all have their dreams. They dream of the rich customer who will enable them to stop working for those who exploit them and they dream, continually, of success. For several generations of writers who have criticized the American Dream, the salesman has symbolized its shortcomings. It is true that such a profession can be the route to great wealth,

---

[1] Arthur Miller, "Requiem," *Death of a Salesman* (London: Penguin, 1980), p. 111.

the means for an ordinary man to make good by sheer hard work, but this is not the aspect that such writers choose to emphasize. To them, a society that advocates this kind of "self-improvement" is a consumer society based on materialism and has, at its heart, an emptiness that cannot be assuaged by yet more money in the bank. Just as the salesmen's lives are fueled by the promise of happiness and contentment in return for material success, so too are the lives of their clients; the clients are as much a part of the capitalist hegemony as the men from whom they purchase their symbols of material success. Their purchases are invested by the salesmen with amazing, life-enhancing properties that somehow hold the promise of a better future. The truth is, however, usually rather different. In the same way as the salesmen's endless quest for spurious success is essentially a chimera, so the goods they sell are probably quite worthless. The salesmen are, therefore, exploiting those who, like them, need to dream and to believe in a brighter future. It is a vicious circle.

Probably the most famous literary salesman is Miller's Willy Loman, whose frustrated dreams eventually split his family and destroy him. His relentless quest for success, together with an unrealistic view of the world, results, as Eleanor Clark puts it, in his being "done . . . in" largely due to "the capitalist system."[2] Similarly, G. F. Babbitt in Sinclair Lewis's satirical novel, *Babbitt,* neglects his emotional life in the belief that "the one purpose of the real-estate business was to make money for George F. Babbitt,"[3] although he finds that success does not bring him the happiness he seeks. Hickey, that hypocritical shatterer of illusions in Eugene O'Neill's *The Iceman Cometh,* is undone not directly through capitalism—although there is certainly a suggestion that the need for professional kudos is at least partly to blame for his tragedy—but through his need to hang onto the "pipe dreams" he exhorts his friends to eschew. Hickey is the archetypal salesman in literature, a peculiar mixture of both victim and oppressor whose downfall is brought about by self-delusion and societal pressure.

Mamet has commented on the theme of capitalism that runs through both *Glengarry Glen Ross* and *American Buffalo* (which was written about nine years earlier). Both plays are, he says, "set deeply in the milieu of capitalism [which is] obviously an idea whose time has come and gone."[4]

He goes on to explain how

> in America we're still suffering from loving a frontier ethic—that is to say, take the land from the Indians and give it to the railroad. Take the money from the blacks and give it to the rich. The ethic was always something for nothing. It never really existed when the American frontier was open . . . it never was anything more transcendent than something for nothing . . . The idea of go West and make your fortune, there's gold lying in the ground, was an idea promulgated by the storekeepers in the gold rush and the railroads in the westward expansion as a way of enslaving the common man and woman . . . playing on their greed. As W. C. Fields said, you can't cheat an honest man. So, because we've been rather dishonest about our basic desire to get something for nothing in this country we've

---

[2]Eleanor Clark cited in Dennis Welland, *Miller the Playwright* (London and New York: Eyre Methuen, 1983), p. 39.

[3]Sinclair Lewis, *Babbitt* (New York: Harcourt, Brace & Co., 1922), p. 49.

[4]Christopher Bigsby, *Contemporary Writers: David Mamet* (London: Methuen, 1985), p. 111.

always been enslaved by the myth of the happy capitalist. Familiar American pieties are always linked to criminality. That's why they're familiar American pieties.[5]

Elsewhere he notes that "American capitalism comes down to one thing. . . . The operative axiom is 'Hurrah for me and fuck you.' Anything else is a lie."[6] Thus, Mamet lays the blame for modern-day greed and corruption on the ethics that have existed since the early days of the American Republic. From the outset, people have been urged to live falsely, to seek financial success by any means open to them, including cheating and stealing. Mamet believes that this has led to the diminishment of important emotional bonds whose value is then viewed only as a means of achieving pecuniary gain. His plays are frequently concerned with the fact that ordinary human relationships have been corrupted and subverted by social fiats, and *Glengarry Glen Ross* is perhaps the most frightening example of this tendency. The archaic—although still powerful—New World ethos of seizing rapaciously what is denied by right is exposed as both immoral and callous and, in these plays, Mamet draws attention to the deforming effect upon individual morality. His characters are, therefore, essentially very unhappy; on the surface they may be tough and smiling, but underneath this brittle veneer, they are aware of a terrible void in their lives. Mamet has noted how

> the American ethic of business, of boosterism, never made anybody happy. It has made a lot of people rich, but it never made anybody happy. So we live in a very, very unhappy country here. I have always considered it to be part of my job to talk about the things that I see, and certainly the most pervasive aspect of America is that we are so damned unhappy over here, but we are smiling all the time.[7]

Glengarry Glen Ross is, he says, an attempt to write about "those guys you see on planes. They all sit together, and you can never understand what they're talking about, and they all have these papers filled with columns and figures. They're all named Bob. And when they laugh, it's 'Ha-*ha*!'—this imitation laugh."[8] During an interview with Mel Gussow, Mamet recalled a conversation he had had with his wife's stepfather about the cruelty and ruthlessness of the world of salesmanship. He had been told how "as an effect of the recession, how 'vicious the competition was for jobs and sales, especially among older men.' He described one incident in which an older salesman was so terrified about making a presentation that he had a heart attack on the spot, 'and the new president of the company stepped over his body to leave the room.'"[9]

Mamet's characters must convince themselves that material gain is the ultimate achievement—there is simply nothing else. In this world, business has become an end in itself; people frantically pursue their individual goals for success and happiness and find it to be an endless pursuit. Once they reach one pinnacle, they must move on to another. Mamet demonstrates how inextricably people can become

[5]Ibid.
[6]Program notes for *Glengarry Glen Ross*.
[7]*Kaleidoscope*, Radio 4 (B.B.C. Radio) 19 April 1985.
[8]Jennifer Allen, "David Mamet's Hard Sell," *New York,* 9 April 1984, p. 40.
[9]Mel Gussow, "Real Estate World a Model for Mamet," *New York Times,* 28, March 1984, p. C19.

enmeshed in their jobs, almost losing their identity behind a job title. Certainly his salesmen seem to have little life outside the office. One of them actually says, "A man's his job" (act 2), which suggests that he has become a mere extension of his livelihood. There are very few moments in the play when the characters use any language that is not expressly concerned with business and even when they do it quickly becomes apparent that it is a ploy designed to coerce a colleague or cheat a client. When Roma talks to a customer about his wife, he uses the vocabulary of the boardroom to make his point:

> *Roma:* . . . You have a contract with your wife. You have certain things you do *jointly,* you have a *bond* there . . . (act 2)

It is as if the world has ceased to exist outside of the office; Roma and his cronies have distorted speech so much through cunning and artifice—and downright professional obsession—that it seems they no longer have a need for language that does not immediately relate to their business interests. Mamet is not, however, out to condemn such characters, but merely to expose a system that has created them. He insists that it was not his intention to offer an indictment or a commentary: "My job is to create a closed moral universe,"[10] he says, and to leave evaluation to the audience. To Mamet, the "play is about a society based on business . . . a society with only one bottom line: How much money you make."[11]

The premise upon which *Glengarry Glen Ross* is based is, in a way, a paradigm of capitalism. The company's bosses have organized a sales competition in which the salesman with the highest "grosses"—financial profit—wins a Cadillac and is automatically guaranteed the best "leads" (addresses of prospective land buyers), the runners-up win a set of steak knives, and the losers are sacked. That the successful salesman is given the best leads while the runners-up are forced to accept inferior leads from the "B" list or are even dismissed, underlines the unfairness of a system that penalizes those who are weak and needy but rewards those who least need such support. With no other choice but to capitulate to the demands of their employers, it is not surprising that the salesmen should rail against the iniquities of an unfair system. Their jobs may be their lives, but they should be *better* jobs; despite their refusal to look beneath the shallowness of their lives, there remains a level at which they are conscious of a serious deficiency.

Corrupted by the constant need to beat their colleagues at any cost, these men have become expert manipulators. Their ability to cajole and confuse with superbly calculated verbal onslaughts is quite mesmerizing. Jack Shepherd, who played Richard Roma in the National Theatre production remarks that they are "vicious existentialists, experts in deception, superb liars. . . . persuasive, ruthless, competitive, disloyal."[12] These men think nothing of trampling over anyone who stands in their way. Theirs is a world in which loyalty and trust have almost no place and where language can no longer be trusted as a means of straightforward communication. Merely listening to the wrong words can mean dire consequences, as Aaronow finds to his cost. A major theme in this play is the corruption of the function of language, and Robert Cushman has observed how Mamet drives home his point about

[10]Ibid.
[11]Ibid.
[12]Jack Shepherd, National Theatre Study Notes for *Glengarry Glen Ross*, p. 7.

the unreliability of language through his characters' "intoxicating mixture of evasions, pleadings, browbeatings, stonewalling and spiel."[13] The language in *Glengarry Glen Ross* is quite stunning in its versatility, and Mamet's command over dialogue reaches its most dazzling pitch. What is perhaps most striking is the almost operatic quality of some of the verbal set pieces. The terse, sometimes stichomythic quality of his earlier dialogue still exists here, but Mamet now seems to be experimenting with new and more lengthy forms of linguistic control. There are in this work a number of bravura monologues and brilliantly sustained "duets" that the salesmen utilize to bewilder and impress their audience. In *Sexual Perversity in Chicago,* some of Bernie Litko's absurdly inflated fantasies take a similar form, but even they are a pale prelude to the heights achieved here. Mamet demonstrates with consummate skill his ability to condense and expand salient aspects of the American language into what truly become the "tainted arias"[14] of which Christopher Bigsby has spoken. Roma's mesmerizing monologue in the company of the inarticulate Lingk, Levene's poetic and almost orgasmic evocation of a great sale, and the brilliant entrapment of Aaronow into criminal culpability by his colleague, Moss, surpass even Mamet's own dizzying standards of linguistic invention.

The world of sales and salesmanship offers myriad opportunities for those who enjoy spinning a yarn and acting a part. In the brutally competitive world in which he moves, the salesman must become expert in linguistic technique; so long as he can keep his narrative flowing and uninterrupted he is able to feel, at least momentarily, safe. Through the pattern of his words, he can manipulate and persuade and thus his fantasies of success and those of his client can become a temporary reality. As Barbara Hardy observes, storytellers of any kind must be "fluent and vivid . . . artists who keep an eye on the subject, on the listeners, and on the occasion. They are sincerely involved and engrossed in their stories but are self-consciously practised in that manipulation of effect which belongs to all oratory and is essential to the art of narrative improvisation."[15] In *Glengarry Glen Ross,* Mamet's salesmen spill out their endless, brilliant chatter to anyone who is prepared to listen but at the heart of their manipulation lies aridity and emptiness. Behind the foul-mouthed, incessantly "macho" bravado lies a desperate bluster, a braggadocio show of power by men who are only too aware of their own powerlessness. They may live by victimizing their colleagues and clients, but the most abject victims of their trade are themselves.

This play is Mamet's most successful to date. It was premiered at the National Theatre in London in 1983, winning two British drama awards before opening on Broadway where it won the Pulitzer Prize in 1984. Despite the fact that it is by far the most abrasive and scatological that Mamet has yet written, it has been much praised for its poetic qualities. Benedict Nightingale comments upon the "gaudy, swaggering poetry [Mamet] has fashioned out of the street-wise idiom of Chicago [which] sucks us in, carries us along, bouncing us over minor implausibilities like a stream over rusty cans."[16] Connie Booth describes the work as one of "poetic brilliance . . . It is caustic, sharp, and tragic. The language isn't easy or melodic but it is

[13]Robert Cushman, *The Observer,* 11 September 1983, p. 31.
[14]Bigsby, *Contemporary Writers,* p. 126.
[15]Barbara Hardy, *Tellers and Listeners: The Narrative Imagination* (London: The Athlone Press, 1975), p. 135.
[16]Bernard Nightingale, "Bard of Modern Immorality," p. 5.

certainly true poetry in every sense of the word."[17] Mamet was worried about the play when he read it through for the first time. The mixture of an episodic first act with a conventionally structured second act prompted him to send a copy to Harold Pinter for his comments. Pinter told him that, in his opinion, the only thing wrong with the play was that it was not currently in production. Mamet now believes that its structure gives the work an extra dimension, and adds to its appeal. He has noted, "people love my new play . . . Because I finally had the will to write a second act. I wrote a million episodic plays. I can write them with my left hand. So what? Who cares? Fortunately, I got sick of it before [the audience] did."[18]

[17]Connie Booth, interview with author, 2 December 1986, Hampstead, London.
[18]Allen, "Mamet's Hard Sell," p. 41.

August Wilson

August Wilson (1945–2005) was born in Pittsburgh, the son of a white father who abandoned his family and a black mother who had come from North Carolina to a Pittsburgh slum, where she worked to keep her family together. Wilson's early childhood was spent in an environment very similar to that of his play *Fences*, and Troy Maxson seems to be patterned somewhat on Wilson's stepfather.

Wilson's writing is rooted to a large extent in music, specifically the blues. As a poet, writing over several years, Wilson found himself interested in the speech patterns and rhythms that were familiar to him from black neighborhoods, but the value of those patterns became clearer to him when he grew older and moved from Pittsburgh to Minneapolis. From a distance, he was able to see more clearly what had attracted him to the language and begin to use it more fully in his work.

In the 1960s and 1970s Wilson became involved in the civil rights movement and began to describe himself as a black nationalist, a term he has said he feels comfortable with. He began writing plays in the 1960s in Pittsburgh and

August Wilson in a portrait by David Cooper made in 2004, just one year before his untimely death.

then took a job in St. Paul writing dramatic skits for the Science Museum of Minnesota. He founded the Playwrights Center in Minneapolis and wrote a play, *Jitney,* about a gypsy cab station. *Jitney* was first produced in 1982 and was staged in New York in April 2000 in a revised version at the Second Stage Theater. *Fullerton Street,* about Pittsburgh, was another play written in this early period. Wilson's first commercial success, *Ma Rainey's Black Bottom,* eventually premiered at the Yale Repertory Theatre in 1984 and then went to Broadway, where it enjoyed 275 performances and won the New York Drama Critics' Circle Award.

Ma Rainey's Black Bottom was the first of a planned sequence of ten plays based on the black American experience. As Wilson said, "I think the black Americans have the most dramatic story of all mankind to tell." The concept of such a vast project echoes Eugene O'Neill's projected group of eleven plays based on the Irish American experience. (Unfortunately, O'Neill destroyed all but *A Touch of the Poet, More Stately Mansions,* and part of *Calms of Capricorn* in his series.) Wilson's project, however, was completed and produced some of the most successful plays in the recent American theater.

Ma Rainey is about the legendary black blues singer who preceded Bessie Smith and Billie Holiday. The play is about the ways in which she was exploited by white managers and recording executives and the way she dealt with her exploitation. In the cast of the play are several black musicians in the backup band. Levee, the trumpet player, has a dream of leading his own band and establishing himself as an important jazz musician. But he is haunted by memories of seeing his mother raped by a gang of white men when he was a boy. He wants to "improve" the session he's playing by making the old jazz tune "Black Bottom" swing in the new jazz style, but Ma Rainey keeps him in tow and demands that they play the tune in the old way. Levee finally cracks under the pressure, and the play ends painfully.

Fences opened at the Yale Repertory Theatre in 1985 and in New York in early 1987, where it won the Pulitzer Prize as well as the New York Drama Critics' Circle Award. This long-running success established Wilson firmly as an important writer. *Joe Turner's Come and Gone* opened at the Yale Repertory Theatre in late 1986 and moved to New York in early 1988, where it too was hailed as an important play, winning its author another New York Drama Critics' Circle Award. Set in a rooming house in Pittsburgh in 1911, *Joe Turner* is a study of the children of former slaves. They have come north to find work, and some of them have been found by the legendary bounty hunter Joe Turner. As a study of a people in transition, the play is a quiet masterpiece. It incorporates a number of important African traditions, especially religious rituals of healing as performed by Bynum, the "bone man," a seer and a medicine man. In this play and others, Wilson makes a special effort to highlight the elements of African heritage that white society strips away from blacks.

The next play in Wilson's projected series, *The Piano Lesson,* which premiered at the Yale Repertory Theatre in 1987, also portrays the complexity of black attitudes toward the past and black heritage. The piano represents two kinds of culture: the white culture that produced the musical instrument and the black culture, in the form of Papa Boy Willie, who carved into it images from black Africa. The central question in the play is whether Boy Willie should sell the piano and use the money for a down payment on land and therefore on the future. Or should he follow his sister Berniece's advice and keep it because it is too precious to sell? The conflict is deep, and the play ultimately focuses on a profound moment of spiritual exorcism. How one exorcises the past—how one lives with it or without it—is a central theme in Wilson's work.

His next play, *Two Trains Running,* is set in 1969, in the decade that saw the Vietnam War, racial and political riots, and the assassinations of John and Robert Kennedy, Malcolm X, and Martin Luther King Jr. The play premiered at the Yale Repertory Theatre in 1990 and opened on Broadway at the Walter Kerr Theater in April 1992, directed by Lloyd Richards. The characters remain in Memphis Lee's diner—scheduled for demolition—throughout the play. The two trains in the title are heading to Africa and to the old South, but the characters are immobile and seem indifferent to both of them. Wilson moved away from the careful structure of the well-made play in this work and produced an open-ended conclusion, leaving the racial and philosophical tensions unresolved.

Seven Guitars (1996) takes place in a backyard in Pittsburgh in 1948 on the eve of the landmark boxing match between Joe Louis and "Jersey" Joe Walcott. The play focuses on a blues musician, Floyd Barton, who hopes to regain his lost love, put his band back together, and move to Chicago to make his second recording. *Seven Guitars* emphasizes the blues, especially in its long first act, with Barton's friends gathered in his backyard to mourn his death and the loss of his talent. People did much the same when Joe Louis, the "Brown Bomber," lost his fight, a loss that punctuated the end of an era. The second act focuses on Hedley, a West Indian boarder, whom critic Margo Jefferson describes as "half madman and half prophet." Hedley recites a litany of racial injustices and gives voice to a torrent of wrongs. Hedley's voice is a counterpoint to the blues; he gives us a powerful range of responses to the condition of being black in Pittsburgh in the late 1940s.

King Hedley II (2001), set in 1985, picks up some of the characters of *Seven Guitars,* including the character Hedley, and develops further the experience of living in the Hill District of Pittsburgh. Wilson describes *King Hedley II* as focusing on "the breakdown of the black community's extended-family structure." At this point, the sequence of the plays detailing the African American experience for each decade of the twentieth century needed only the first and last decades' plays. *Gem of the Ocean,* set in 1904, introduced Aunt Ester, who had been alluded to in earlier plays. Her birthday, more than 280 years before, coincides with the introduction of African slaves into the United States. She has a healing power that helps cleanse some of the characters of their sense of guilt. The production, directed by Marion McClinton, featured Phylicia Rashad as Aunt Ester and won the Tony award for best play of 2005. It ran for 72 performances. The final play in the cycle is *Radio Golf,* which premiered at Yale Repertory Theatre and then moved to the Cort Theatre on Broadway in April 2007. It too won the Tony for best play of 2007, but it ran for only 64 performances. The play is set in 1997 and focuses on the Bedford Hills Redevelopment company, a storefront on Centre Street in Pittsburgh. This company's project involves the total demolition and reconstruction of the Hill District, including the destruction of Aunt Ester's home, the setting of *Gem of the Ocean*. The struggle between doing what is right and doing what is profitable and practicable is central to the drama. Wilson, then living in Seattle, returned to his hometown for the December 1999 premiere of *King Hedley II,* the first play produced in the new O'Reilly Theater by the Pittsburgh Public Theater. It moved in March 2000 to the Seattle Repertory Theater. Wilson died of liver cancer knowing his project was complete.

MA RAINEY'S BLACK BOTTOM

According to comments August Wilson made years later, he experienced a moment of enlightenment in 1965 when he listened to an old 78 rpm record of the blues artist Ma Rainey singing "Nobody in Town Can Bake a Sweet Jelly-roll Like Mine" and quickly found himself immersed in the blues. Ma Rainey, singing in the 1920s, was giving voice to the pain and suffering of black Americans dating all the way back to slavery. Wilson had discovered a rich vein in American history, and he began to see the blues as revealing the world of African Americans.

His play was not quick to develop and went through many drafts and revisions, but it eventually became the first of his remarkable series of plays written for each decade of the twentieth century. *Ma Rainey's Black Bottom,* set in Chicago in 1927 several years before the singer retired, is also the most musical of Wilson's plays, although it is not a musical as such. The stage design of the play, described carefully in Wilson's stage directions, confounded some critics. One area of the stage was the recording studio, where Ma Rainey, her agent Irvin, and the owner of the studio, Sturdyvant, conduct most of their interaction. The second area is the band room in which Levee, Toledo, Cutler, and Slow Drag spend their time waiting for Ma Rainey and talking about their experiences with the indifference or cruelty of white society. One of Wilson's strongest devices in the play is having Toledo and Levee give long speeches that are riveting narratives in themselves. The first act ends with a powerful story of Levee's mother and father facing violence and dispossession by white farmers who coveted the family farm. Levee's father, however, struck back, which is why Levee tells the story. It is a way of offering his credentials in knowing how to deal with the white man.

Levee is the trumpet player, and he longs to play music other than the kind that Ma Rainey demands he play. He sees an opportunity to break away from tradition and produce a music that the people want, not what he calls the "jug band" music of Ma Rainey. Levee thinks he knows how to handle Sturdyvant because he thinks Sturdyvant likes his music and will back him up. At the end of the play he learns the truth about Sturdyvant and, to an extent, about himself. Through the many drafts of Wilson's play, Levee develops into the strongest character, apart from Ma Rainey herself. He argues with band members, and boasts that he can read and write music when they cannot. He sees himself as someone moving ahead on his own and feels tied down by Ma Rainey.

Ma Rainey knows just how important she is to the white men who make the records for her, and she is under no illusion that they like her or value her only insofar as she can make money for them. Thus she deliberately makes it hard for them to take her for granted. When she arrives, she expects her Coca-Cola and will not budge until someone goes out and gets it for her. She will not sing without her Coca-Cola. She has determined that she will not use Levee's arrangement of her song, no matter who thinks it is an improvement. She wants her nephew Sylvester to introduce the record even though he stutters, and after a few false starts she gets her wish. Ma Rainey is the ranking artist, and she knows her worth and will not submit to the demands of anyone else. Near the end of the play, she even holds out from signing the releases that will permit Sturdyvant to sell the records she has made. She understands the ways in which her artistry is being exploited, but she will not sell herself short.

The conflict with Levee is complex. On the one hand, this play takes place in Chicago in the decade in which Chicago-style jazz was developed. Ma Rainey and Bessie Smith toured together from 1912 to 1915, and both Rainey and Smith were still singing their style of the blues in the late 1920s, but a new style had begun to emerge, beginning in 1918, with bands like Freddy Keppard's, Joe King Oliver's, and Jelly Roll Morton's. This may be the style Levee refers to when he says the people want something else. But then, when he talks about sweet music, he may simply mean that he wants to abandon the blues and what it stands for, which for Wilson would be a form of heresy. As Ma Rainey says, "White folks don't understand about the blues. They hear it come out, but they don't know how it got there. They don't understand that's life's way of talking." It may be that Levee also doesn't understand.

The violence at the end of the play is the result of frustration on the part of Levee, who has spent the entire play trying to push his own ideas forward, only to have them disregarded by Toledo, by Cutler, and especially by Ma Rainey. He is criticized by the band for having spent too much money on his Florsheim shoes and for not following Ma Rainey's orders to play the song the way she wants it played. Then, at the end of the play, Sturdyvant tells Levee he does not think Levee's new songs are going to sell and he offers him only $5 a song. This is not just an insult but a rebuke. It brings Levee to the breaking point, and he strikes out at the first person who accidentally steps on his shoes: Toledo, who is not just stepping on his shoes but also, symbolically, stomping on his dream.

Ma Rainey's Black Bottom in Performance

The play was developed in the summer of 1982 at the Eugene O'Neill Theater Center in Waterford, Connecticut. Lloyd Richards, director of the center, brought the play to New Haven, where it premiered in 1984 at the Yale Repertory Theatre. It took the audience by surprise with its energy, intensity, and convincing performances. Charles S. Dutton played Levee and Theresa Merritt played Ma Rainey. Both were later nominated for acting awards when the play went to the Cort Theatre on Broadway in 1984, where it was named best play of the year by the New York Drama Critics' Circle. Frank Rich at the *New York Times* said, "the writer August Wilson sends the entire history of black America crashing down upon our heads. This play is a searing inside account of what white racism does to its victims—and it floats on the same authentic artistry as the blues music it celebrates." The National Theatre in London produced the play in 1991 to positive reviews. The play has been revived many times in regional theaters in the United States and abroad. One of the most widely anticipated productions opened in 2003, when Marion McClinton directed the play at the Royale Theatre in New York, with Charles S. Dutton as Levee and Whoopi Goldberg as Ma Rainey. Unfortunately, this lackluster production was impaired by constant disagreements about how the play should be staged. In contrast, the City Theatre's production in Sacramento in 2005 played to sold-out houses and strong reviews. *Ma Rainey's Black Bottom* is currently produced in university theaters and public theaters around the world.

August Wilson (1945–2005)

MA RAINEY'S BLACK BOTTOM   *1989*

They tore the railroad down
so the Sunshine Special can't run
I'm going away baby
build me a railroad of my own   — BLIND LEMON JEFFERSON

Characters

STURDYVANT	LEVEE
IRVIN	MA RAINEY
CUTLER	POLICEMAN
TOLEDO	DUSSIE MAE
SLOW DRAG	SYLVESTER

Setting: *There are two playing areas: what is called the "band room," and the recording studio. The band room is at stage left and is in the basement of the building. It is entered through a door up left. There are benches and chairs scattered about, a piano, a row of lockers, and miscellaneous paraphernalia stacked in a corner and long since forgotten. A mirror hangs on a wall with various posters.*

The studio is upstairs at stage right, and resembles a recording studio of the late 1920s. The entrance is from a hall on the right wall. A small control booth is at the rear and its access is gained by means of a spiral staircase. Against one wall there is a line of chairs, and a horn through which the control room communicates with the performers. A door in the rear wall allows access to the band room.

The Play: *It is early March in Chicago, 1927. There is a bit of a chill in the air. Winter has broken but the wind coming off the lake does not carry the promise of spring. The people of the city are bundled and brisk in their defense against such misfortunes as the weather, and the business of the city proceeds largely undisturbed.*

Chicago in 1927 is a rough city, a bruising city, a city of millionaires and derelicts, gangsters and roughhouse dandies, whores and Irish grandmothers who move through its streets fingering long black rosaries.

Somewhere a man is wrestling with the taste of a woman in his cheek. Somewhere a dog is barking. Somewhere the moon has fallen through a window and broken into thirty pieces of silver.

It is one o'clock in the afternoon. Secretaries are returning from their lunch, the noon Mass at St. Anthony's is over, and the priest is mumbling over his vestments while the altar boys practice their Latin. The procession of cattle cars through the stockyards continues unabated. The busboys in Mac's Place are cleaning away the last of the corned beef and cabbage, and on the city's Southside, sleepy-eyed negroes move lazily toward their small cold-water flats and rented rooms to await the onslaught of night, which will find them crowded in the bars and juke joints both dazed and dazzling in their rapport with life. It is with these negroes that our concern lies most heavily: their values, their attitudes, and particularly their music.

It is hard to define this music. Suffice it to say that it is music that breathes and touches. That connects. That is in itself a way of being, separate and distinct from any other. This music is called blues. Whether this music came from Alabama or Mississippi or other parts of the South doesn't matter anymore. The men and women who make this music have learned it from the narrow crooked streets of East St. Louis, or the streets of the city's Southside, and the Alabama or Mississippi roots have been strangled by the northern manners and customs of free men of definite and sincere worth, men for whom this music often lies at the forefront of their conscience and concerns. Thus they are laid open to be consumed by it; its warmth and redress, its braggadocio and roughly poignant comments, its vision and prayer, which would instruct and allow them to reconnect, to reassemble and gird up for the next battle in which they would be both victim and the ten thousand slain.

ACT 1

(The lights come up in the studio. Irvin enters, carrying a microphone. He is a tall, fleshy man who prides himself on his knowledge of blacks and his ability to deal with them. He hooks up the microphone, blows into it, taps it, etc. He crosses over to the piano, opens it, and fingers a few keys. Sturdyvant is visible in the control booth. Preoccupied with money, he is insensitive to black performers and prefers to deal with them at arm's length. He puts on a pair of earphones.)

STURDYVANT: *(Over speaker.)* Irv . . . let's crack that mike, huh? Let's do a check on it.

IRVIN: *(Crosses to mike, speaks into it.)* Testing . . . one . . . two . . . three . . .

(There is a loud feedback. Sturdyvant fiddles with the dials.) Testing . . . one . . . two . . . three . . . testing. How's that, Mel?

(Sturdyvant doesn't respond.)

Testing . . . one . . . two . . .

STURDYVANT: *(Taking off earphones.)* Okay . . . that checks: We got a good reading.

(Pause.)

You got that list, Irv?

IRVIN: Yeah . . . yeah, I got it. Don't worry about nothing.

STURDYVANT: Listen, Irv . . . you keep her in line, okay? I'm holding you responsible for her . . . If she starts any of her . . .

IRVIN: Mel, what's with the goddamn horn? You wanna talk to me . . . okay! I can't talk to you over the goddamn horn . . . Christ!

STURDYVANT: I'm not putting up with any shenanigans. You hear, Irv?

(Irvin crosses over to the piano and mindlessly runs his fingers over the keys.)

I'm just not gonna stand for it. I want you to keep her in line. Irv?

(Sturdyvant enters from the control booth.)

Listen, Irv . . . you're her manager . . . she's your responsibility . . .

IRVIN: Okay, okay, Mel . . . let me handle it.

STURDYVANT: She's your responsibility. I'm not putting up with any Royal Highness . . . Queen of the Blues bullshit!

IRVIN: Mother of the Blues, Mel. Mother of the Blues.

STURDYVANT: I don't care what she calls herself. I'm not putting up with it. I just want to get her in here . . . record those songs on that list . . . and get her out. Just like clockwork, huh?

IRVIN: Like clockwork, Mel. You just stay out of the way and let me handle it.

STURDYVANT: Yeah . . . yeah . . . you handled it last time. Remember? She marches in here like she owns the damn place . . . doesn't like the songs we picked out . . . says her throat is sore . . . doesn't want to do more than one take . . .

IRVIN: Okay . . . okay . . . I was here! I know all about it.

STURDYVANT: Complains about the building being cold . . . and then . . . trips over the mike wire and threatens to sue me. That's taking care of it?

IRVIN: I've got it all worked out this time. I talked with her last night. Her throat is fine . . . We went over the songs together . . . I got everything straight, Mel.

STURDYVANT: Irv, that horn player . . . the one who gave me those songs . . . is he gonna be here today? Good. I want to hear more of that sound. Times are changing. This is a tricky business now. We've got to jazz it up . . . put in something different. You know, something wild . . . with a lot of rhythm. *(Pause.)* You know what we put out last time, Irv? We put out garbage last time. It was garbage. I don't even know why I bother with this anymore.

IRVIN: You did all right last time, Mel. Not as good as you did before, but you did all right.

STURDYVANT: You know how many records we sold in New York? You wanna see the sheet? And you know what's in New York, Irv? Harlem. Harlem's in New York, Irv.

IRVIN: Okay, so they didn't sell in New York. But look at Memphis . . . Birmingham . . . Atlanta. Christ, you made a bundle.

STURDYVANT: It's not the money, Irv. You know I couldn't sleep last night? This business is bad for my nerves. My wife is after me to slow down and take a vacation. Two more years and I'm gonna get out . . . get into someting respectable. Textiles. That's a respectable business. You know what you could do with a shipload of textiles from Ireland?

(*A buzzer is heard offstage.*)

IRVIN: Why don't you go upstairs and let me handle it, Mel?

STURDYVANT: Remember . . . you're responsible for her.

(*Sturdyvant exits to the control booth. Irvin crosses to get the door. Cutler, Slow Drag, and Toledo enter. Cutler is in his mid-fifties, as are most of the others. He plays guitar and trombone and is the leader of the group, possibly because he is the most sensible. His playing is solid and almost totally unembellished. His understanding of his music is limited to the chord he is playing at the time he is playing it. He has all the qualities of a loner except the introspection. Slow Drag, the bass player, is perhaps the one most bored by life. He resembles Cutler, but lacks Cutler's energy. He is deceptively intelligent, though, as his name implies, he appears to be slow. He is a rather large man with a wicked smile. Innate African rhythms underlie everything he plays, and he plays with an ease that is at times startling. Toledo is the piano player. In control of his instrument, he understands and recognizes that its limitations are an extension of himself. He is the only one in the group who can read. He is self-taught but misunderstands and misapplies his knowledge, though he is quick to penetrate to the core of a situation and his insights are thought-provoking. All of the men are dressed in a style of clothing befitting the members of a successful band of the era.*)

IRVIN: How you boys doing, Cutler? Come on in.

(*Pause.*)

Where's Ma? Is she with you?

CUTLER: I don't know, Mr. Irvin. She told us to be here at one o'clock. That's all I know.

IRVIN: Where's . . . huh . . . the horn player? Is he coming with Ma?

CUTLER: Levee's supposed to be here same as we is, I reckon he'll be here in a minute. I can't rightly say.

IRVIN: Well, come on . . . I'll show you to the band room, let you get set up and rehearsed. You boys hungry? I'll call over to the deli and get some sandwiches. Get you fed and ready to make some music. Cutler . . . here's the list of songs we're gonna record.

STURDYVANT: (*Over speaker.*) Irvin, what's happening? Where's Ma?

IRVIN: Everything under control, Mel. I got it under control.

STURDYVANT: Where's Ma? How come she isn't with the band?

IRVIN: She'll be here in a minute, Mel. Let me get these fellows down to the band room, huh?

(*They exit the studio. The lights go down in the studio and up in the band room. Irvin opens the door and allows them to pass as they enter.*)

You boys go ahead and rehearse. I'll let you know when Ma comes.

(*Irvin exits. Cutler hands Toledo the list of songs.*)

CUTLER: What we got here, Toledo?

TOLEDO: (*Reading.*) We got . . . "Prove It on Me" . . . "Hear Me Talking to You . . . "Ma Rainey's Black Bottom" . . . and "Moonshine Blues."

CUTLER: Where Mr. Irvin go? Them ain't the songs Ma told me.

SLOW DRAG: I wouldn't worry about it if I were you, Cutler. They'll get it straightened out. Ma will get it straightened out.

CUTLER: I just don't want no trouble about these songs, that's all. Ma ain't told me them songs. She told me something else.

SLOW DRAG: What she tell you?

CUTLER: This "Moonshine Blues" wasn't in it. That's one of Bessie's° songs.

TOLEDO: Slow Drag's right . . . I wouldn't worry about it. Let them straighten it up.

CUTLER: Levee know what time he supposed to be here?

SLOW DRAG: Levee gone out to spend your four dollars. He left the hotel this morning talking about he was gonna go buy some shoes, Say it's the first time he ever beat you shooting craps.

CUTLER: Do he know what time he supposed to be here? That's what I wanna know. I ain't thinking about no four dollars.

SLOW DRAG: Levee sure was thinking about it. That four dollars liked to burn a hole in his pocket.

CUTLER: Well, he's supposed to be here at one o'clock. That's what time Ma said. That nigger get out in the streets with that four dollars and ain't no telling when he's liable to show. You ought to have seen him at the club last night, Toledo. Trying to talk to some gal Ma had with her.

TOLEDO: You ain't got to tell me, I know how Levee do.

(*Buzzer is heard offstage.*)

Bessie: Bessie Smith (1895–1937), a blues singer who toured with Ma Rainey from 1912 to 1915.

SLOW DRAG: Levee tried to talk to that gal and got his feelings hurt. She didn't want no part of him. She told Levee he'd have to turn his money green before he could talk with her.

CUTLER: She out for what she can get. Anybody could see that.

SLOW DRAG: That's why Levee run out to buy some shoes. He's looking to make an impression on that gal.

CUTLER: What the hell she gonna do with his shoes? She can't do nothing with the nigger's shoes.

(*Slow Drag takes out a pint bottle and drinks.*)

TOLEDO: Let me hit that, Slow Drag.

SLOW DRAG: (*Handing him the bottle.*) This some of that good Chicago bourbon!

(*The door opens and Levee enters, carrying a shoe box. In his early thirties, Levee is younger than the other men. His flamboyance is sometimes subtle and sneaks up on you. His temper is rakish and bright. He lacks fuel for himself and is somewhat of a buffoon. But it is an intelligent buffoonery, clearly calculated to shift control of the situation to where he can grasp it. He plays trumpet. His voice is strident and totally dependent on his manipulation of breath. He plays wrong notes frequently. He often gets his skill and talent confused with each other.*)

CUTLER: Levee . . . where Mr. Irvin go?

LEVEE: Hell, I don't know. I ain't none of his keeper.

SLOW DRAG: What you got there, Levee?

LEVEE: Look here, Cutler . . . I got me some shoes!

CUTLER: Nigger, I ain't studying you.

(*Levee takes the shoes out of the box and starts to put them on.*)

TOLEDO: How much you pay for something like that, Levee?

LEVEE: Eleven dollars. Four dollars of it belong to Cutler.

SLOW DRAG: Levee say if it wasn't for Cutler . . . he wouldn't have no new shoes.

CUTLER: I ain't thinking about Levee or his shoes. Come on . . . let's get ready to rehearse.

SLOW DRAG: I'm with you on that score, Cutler. I wanna get out of here. I don't want to be around here all night. When it comes time to go up there and record them songs . . . I just wanna go up there and do it. Last time it took us all day and half the night.

TOLEDO: Ain't but four songs on the list. Last time we recorded six songs.

SLOW DRAG: It felt like it was sixteen!

LEVEE: (*Finishes with his shoes.*) Yeah! Now I'm ready! I can play some good music now!

(*He goes to put up his old shoes and looks around the room.*)

Charles S. Dutton as Levee, Leonard Jackson as Slow Drag, and Robert Judd as Toledo in the Yale Repertory Theatre's original 1984 production of *Ma Rainey's Black Bottom.*

Damn! They done changed things around. Don't never leave well enough alone.

TOLEDO: Everything changing all the time. Even the air you breathing change. You got, monoxide, hydrogen . . . changing all the time. Skin changing . . . different molecules and everything.

LEVEE: Nigger, what is you talking about? I'm talking about the room. I ain't talking about no skin and air. I'm talking about something I can see! Last time the band room was upstairs. This time it's downstairs. Next time it be over there. I'm talking about what I can see. I ain't talking about no molecules or nothing.

TOLEDO: Hell, I know what you talking about. I just said everything changin'. I know what you talking about, but you don't know what I'm talking about.

LEVEE: That door! Nigger, you see that door? That's what I'm talking about. That door wasn't there before.

CUTLER: Levee, you wouldn't know your right from your left. This is where they used to keep the recording horns and things . . . and damn if that door wasn't there. How in hell else you gonna get in here? Now, if you talking about they done switched rooms, you right. But don't go telling me that damn door wasn't there!

SLOW DRAG: Damn the door and let's get set up. I wanna get out of here.

LEVEE: Toledo started all that about the door. I'm just saying that things change.

TOLEDO: What the hell you think I was saying? Things change. The air and everything. Now you gonna say you was saying it. You gonna fit two propositions on the same track . . . run them into each other, and because they crash, you gonna say it's the same train.

LEVEE: Now this nigger talking about trains! We done went from the air to the skin to the door . . . and now trains. Toledo, I'd just like to be inside your head for five minutes. Just to see how you think. You done got more shit piled up and mixed up in there than the devil got sinners. You been reading too many goddamn books.

TOLEDO: What you care about how much I read? I'm gonna ignore you 'cause you ignorant.

(*Levee takes off his coat and hangs it in the locker.*)

SLOW DRAG: Come on, let's rehearse the music.

LEVEE: You ain't gotta rehearse that . . . ain't nothing but old jug-band music. They need one of them jug bands for this.

SLOW DRAG: Don't make me no difference. Long as we get paid.

LEVEE: That ain't what I'm talking about, nigger. I'm talking about art!

SLOW DRAG: What's drawing got to do with it?

LEVEE: Where you get this nigger from, Cutler? He sound like one of them Alabama niggers.

CUTLER: Slow Drag's all right. It's you talking all that weird shit about art. Just play the piece, nigger. You wanna be one of them . . . what you call . . . virtuoso or something, you in the wrong place. You ain't no Buddy Bolden° or King Oliver° . . . you just an old trumpet player come a dime a dozen. Talking about art.

LEVEE: What is you? I don't see your name in lights.

CUTLER: I just play the piece. Whatever they want. I don't go talking about art and criticizing other people's music.

LEVEE: I ain't like you, Cutler. I got talent! Me and this horn . . . we's tight. If my daddy knowed I was gonna turn out like this, he would've named me Gabriel. I'm gonna get me a band and make me some records. I done give Mr. Sturdyvant some of my songs I wrote and he say he's gonna let me record them when I get my band together.

(*Takes some papers out of his pocket.*)

I just gotta finish the last part of this song. And Mr. Sturdyvant want me to write another part to this song.

SLOW DRAG: How you learn to write music, Levee?

LEVEE: I just picked it up . . . like you pick up anything. Miss Eula used to play the piano . . . she learned me a lot. I knows how to play *real* music . . . not this old jug-band shit. I got style!

TOLEDO: Everybody got style. Style ain't nothing but keeping the same idea from beginning to end. Everybody got it.

LEVEE: But everybody can't play like I do. Everybody can't have their own band.

CUTLER: Well, until you get your own band where you can play what you want, you just play the piece and stop complaining. I told you when you came on here, this ain't none of them hot bands. This is an accompaniment band. You play Ma's music when you here.

LEVEE: I got sense enough to know that. Hell, I can look at you all and see what kind of band it is. I can look at Toledo and see what kind of band it is.

TOLEDO: Toledo ain't said nothing to you now. Don't let Toledo get started. You can't even spell music, much less play it.

LEVEE: What you talking about? I can spell music. I got a dollar say I can spell it! Put your dollar up. Where your dollar?

(*Toledo waves him away.*)

Now come on. Put your dollar up. Talking about I can't spell music.

(*Levee peels a dollar off his roll and slams it down on the bench beside Toledo.*)

TOLEDO: All right, I'm gonna show you. Cutler. Slow Drag. You hear this? The nigger betting me a dollar he can spell music. I don't want no shit now!

Buddy Bolden (1877–1931) and **Joe King Oliver** (1885–1938): Great early jazz trumpeters.

(Toledo lays a dollar down beside Levee's.)

All right. Go ahead. Spell it.

LEVEE: It's a bet then. Talking about I can't spell music.

TOLEDO: Go ahead, then. Spell it. Music. Spell it.

LEVEE: I can spell it, nigger! M-U-S-I-K. There!

(He reaches for the money.)

TOLEDO: Naw! Naw! Leave that money alone! You ain't spelled it.

LEVEE: What you mean I ain't spelled it? I said M-U-S-I-K!

TOLEDO: That ain't how you spell it! That ain't how you spell it! It's M-U-S-I-C! C, nigger. Not K! C! M-U-S-I-C!

LEVEE: What you mean, C? Who say it's C?

TOLEDO: Cutler. Slow Drag. Tell this fool.

(They look at each other and then away.)

Well, I'll be a monkey's uncle!

(Toledo picks up the money and hands Levee his dollar back.)

Here's your dollar back, Levee. I done won it, you understand. I done won the dollar. But if don't nobody know but me, how am I gonna prove it to you?

LEVEE: You just mad 'cause I spelled it.

TOLEDO: Spelled what! M-U-S-I-K don't spell nothing. I just wish there was some way I could show you the right and wrong of it. How you gonna know something if the other fellow don't know if you're right or not? Now I can't even be sure that I'm spelling it right.

LEVEE: That's what I'm talking about. You don't know it. Talking about C. You ought to give me that dollar I won from you.

TOLEDO: All right, All right. I'm gonna show you how ridiculous you sound. You know the Lord's Prayer?

LEVEE: Why? You wanna bet a dollar on that?

TOLEDO: Just answer the question. Do you know the Lord's Prayer or don't you?

LEVEE: Yeah, I know it. What of it?

TOLEDO: Cutler?

CUTLER: What you Cutlering me for? I ain't got nothing to do with it.

TOLEDO: I just want to show the man how ridiculous he is.

CUTLER: Both of you all sound like damn fools. Arguing about something silly. Yeah, I know the Lord's Prayer. My daddy was a deacon in the church. Come asking me if I know the Lord's Prayer. Yeah, I know it.

TOLEDO: Slow Drag?

SLOW DRAG: Yeah.

TOLEDO: All right. Now I'm gonna tell you a story to show just how ridiculous he sound. There was these two fellows, see. So, the one of them go up to this church and commence to taking up the church learning. The other fellow see him out on the road and he say, "I done heard you taking up the church learning," say, "Is you learning anything up there?" The other

one say, "Yeah, I done take up the church learning and I's learning all kinds of things about the Bible and what it say and all. Why you be asking?" The other one say, "Well, do you know the Lord's Prayer?" And he say, "Why, sure I know the Lord's Prayer, I'm taking up learning at the church ain't I? I know the Lord's Prayer backwards and forwards." And the other fellow says, "I bet you five dollars you don't know the Lord's Prayer, 'cause I don't think you knows it. I think you be going up to the church 'cause the Widow Jenkins be going up there and you just wanna be sitting in the same room with her when she cross them big, fine, pretty legs she got." And the other one say, "Well, I'm gonna prove you wrong and I'm gonna bet you that five dollars." So he say, "Well, go on and say it then." So he commenced to saying the Lord's Prayer. He say, "Now I lay me down to sleep, I pray the Lord my soul to keep." The other one say, "Here's your five dollars. I didn't think you knew it."

(They all laugh.)

Now, that's just how ridiculous Levee sound. Only 'cause I knowed how to spell music, I still got my dollar.

LEVEE: That don't prove nothing. What's that supposed to prove?

(Toledo takes a newspaper out of his back pocket and begins to read.)

TOLEDO: I'm through with it.

SLOW DRAG: Is you all gonna rehearse this music or ain't you?

(Cutler takes out some papers and starts to roll a reefer.)

LEVEE: How many times you done played them songs? What you gotta rehearse for?

SLOW DRAG: This a recording session. I wanna get it right the first time and get on out of here.

CUTLER: Slow Drag's right. Let's go on and rehearse and get it over with.

LEVEE: You all go and rehearse, then. I got to finish this song for Mr. Sturdyvant.

CUTLER: Come on, Levee . . . I don't want no shit now. You rehearse like everybody else. You in the band like everybody else. Mr. Sturdyvant just gonna have to wait. You got to do that on your own time. This is the band's time.

LEVEE: Well, what is you doing? You sitting there rolling a reefer talking about let's rehearse. Toledo reading a newspaper. Hell, I'm ready if you wanna rehearse. I just say there ain't no point in it. Ma ain't here. What's the point in it?

CUTLER: Nigger, why you gotta complain all the time?

TOLEDO: Levee would complain if a gal ain't laid across his bed just right.

CUTLER: That's what I know. That's why I try to tell him just play the music and forget about it. It ain't no big thing.

TOLEDO: Levee ain't got an eye for that. He wants to tie on to some abstract component and sit down on the elemental.

LEVEE: This is get-on-Levee time, huh? Levee ain't said nothing except this some old jug-band music.

TOLEDO: Under the right circumstances you'd play anything. If you know music, then you play it. Straight on or off to the side. Ain't nothing abstract about it.

LEVEE: Toledo, you sound like you got a mouth full of marbles. You the only cracker-talking nigger I know.

TOLEDO: You ought to have learned yourself to read . . . then you'd understand the basic understanding of everything.

SLOW DRAG: Both of you all gonna drive me crazy with that philosophy bullshit. Cutler, give me a reefer.

CUTLER: Ain't you got some reefer? Where's your reefer? Why you all the time asking me?

SLOW DRAG: Cutler, how long I done known you? How long we been together? Twenty-two years. We been doing this together for twenty-two years. All up and down the back roads, the side roads, the front roads . . . We done played the juke joints, the whore-houses, the barn dances, and city sit-downs . . . I done lied for you and lied with you . . . We done laughed together, fought together, slept in the same bed together, done sucked on the same titty . . . and now you don't wanna give me no reefer.

CUTLER: You see this nigger trying to talk me out of my reefer, Toledo? Running all that about how long he done knowed me and how we done sucked on the same titty. Nigger, you *still* ain't getting none of my reefer!

TOLEDO: That's African.

SLOW DRAG: What? What you talking about? What's African?

LEVEE: I know he ain't talking about me. You don't see me running around in no jungle with no bone between my nose.

TOLEDO: Levee, you worse than ignorant. You ignorant without a premise.

(*Pauses.*)

Now, what I was saying is what Slow Drag was doing is African. That's what you call an African conceptualization. That's when you name the gods or call on the ancestors to achieve whatever your desires are.

SLOW DRAG: Nigger, I ain't no African! I ain't doing no African nothing!

TOLEDO: Naming all those things you and Cutler done together is like trying to solicit some reefer based on a bond of kinship. That's African. An ancestral retention. Only you forgot the name of the gods.

SLOW DRAG: I ain't forgot nothing. I was telling the nigger how cheap he is. Don't come talking that African nonsense to me.

TOLEDO: You just like Levee. No eye for taking an abstract and fixing it to a specific. There's so much that goes on around you and you can't even see it.

CUTLER: Wait a minute . . . wait a minute. Toledo, now when this nigger . . . when an African do all them things you say and name all the gods and what-not . . . then what happens?

TOLEDO: Depends on if the gods is sympathetic with his cause for which he is calling them with the right names. Then his success comes with the right proportion of his naming. That's the way that go.

CUTLER: (*Taking out a reefer.*) Here, Slow Drag. Here's a reefer. You done talked yourself up on that one.

SLOW DRAG: Thank you. You ought to have done that in the first place and saved me all the aggravation.

CUTLER: What I wants to know is . . . what's the same titty we done sucked on. That's what I want to know.

SLOW DRAG: Oh, I just threw that in there to make it sound good.

(*They all laugh.*)

CUTLER: Nigger, you ain't right.

SLOW DRAG: I knows it.

CUTLER: Well, come on . . . let's get it rehearsed. Time's wasting.

(*The musicians pick up their instruments.*)

Let's do it. "Ma Rainey's Black Bottom." One . . . two . . . You know what to do.

(*They begin to play. Levee is playing something different. He stops.*)

LEVEE: Naw! Naw! We ain't doing it that way.

(*Toledo stops playing, then Slow Drag.*)

We doing my version. It say so right there on that piece of paper you got. Ask Toledo. That's what Mr. Irvin told me . . . say it's on the list he gave you.

CUTLER: Let me worry about what's on the list and what ain't on the list. How you gonna tell me what's on the list?

LEVEE: 'Cause I know what Mr. Irvin told me! Ask Toledo!

CUTLER: Let me worry about what's on the list. You just play the song I say.

LEVEE: What kind of sense it make to rehearse the wrong version of the song? That's what I wanna know. Why you wanna rehearse that version.

SLOW DRAG: You supposed to rehearse what you gonna play. That's the way they taught me. Now, *whatever* version we gonna play . . . let's go on and rehearse it.

LEVEE: That's what I'm trying to tell the man.

CUTLER: You trying to tell me what we is and ain't gonna play. And that ain't none of your business. Your business is to play what I say.

LEVEE: Oh, I see now. You done got jealous cause Mr Irvin using my version. You done got jealous cause I proved I know something about music.

CUTLER: What the hell . . . nigger, you talk like a fool! What the hell I got to be jealous of you about? The day I get jealous of you I may as well lay down and die.

TOLEDO: Levee started all that 'cause he too lazy to rehearse.

(*To Levee.*)

You ought to just go on and play the song . . . What difference does it make?

LEVEE: Where's the paper? Look at the paper! Get the paper and look at it! See what it say. Gonna tell me I'm too lazy to rehearse.

CUTLER: We ain't talking about the paper. We talking about you understanding where you fit in when you around here. You just play what I say.

LEVEE: Look . . . I don't care what you play! All right? It don't matter to me. Mr. Irvin gonna straighten it up! I don't care what you play.

CUTLER: Thank you.

(*Pauses.*)

Let's play this "Hear Me Talking to You" till we find out what's happening with the "Black Bottom." Slow Drag, you sing Ma's part.

(*Pauses.*)

"Hear Me Talking to You." Let's do it. One . . . Two . . . You know what to do.

(*They play.*)

SLOW DRAG: (*Singing*)
Rambling man makes no change in me
I'm gonna ramble back to my used-to-be
Ah, you hear me talking to you
I don't bite my tongue
You wants to be my man
You got to fetch it with you when you come.

Eve and Adam in the garden taking a chance
Adam didn't take time to get his pants
Ah, you hear me talking to you
I don't bite my tongue
You wants to be my man
You got to fetch it with you when you come.

Our old cat swallowed a ball of yarn
When the kittens were born they had sweaters on
Ah, you hear me talking to you
I don't bite my tongue
You wants to be my man
You got to fetch it with you when you come.

(*Irvin enters. The musicians stop playing.*)

IRVIN: Any of you boys know what's keeping Ma?

CUTLER: Can't say, Mr. Irvin. She'll be along directly, I reckon. I talked to her this morning, she say she'll be here in time to rehearse.

IRVIN: Well, you boys go ahead.

(*He starts to exit.*)

CUTLER: Mr. Irvin, about these songs . . . Levee say . . .

IRVIN: Whatever's on the list, Cutler. You got that list I gave you?

CUTLER: Yessir, I got it right here.

IRVIN: Whatever's on there. Whatever that says.

CUTLER: I'm asking about this "Black Bottom" piece . . . Levee say . . .

IRVIN: Oh, it's on the list. "Ma Rainey's Black Bottom" on the list.

CUTLER: I know it's on the list. I wanna know what version. We got two versions of that song.

IRVIN: Oh. Levee's arrangement. We're using Levee's arrangement.

CUTLER: Ok. I got that straight. Now, this "Moonshine Blues" . . .

IRVIN: We'll work it out with Ma, Cutler. Just rehearse whatever's on the list and use Levee's arrangement on that "Black Bottom" piece.

(*He exits.*)

LEVEE: See, I told you! It don't mean nothing when I say it. You got to wait for Mr. Irvin to say it. Well, I told you the way it is.

CUTLER: Levee, the sooner you understand it ain't what you say, or what Mr. Irvin say . . . it's what Ma say that counts.

SLOW DRAG: Don't nobody say when it come to Ma. She's gonna do what she wants to do. Ma says what happens with her.

LEVEE: Hell, the man's the one putting out the record! He's gonna put out what he wanna put out!

SLOW DRAG: He's gonna put out what Ma want him to put out.

LEVEE: You heard what the man told you . . . "Ma Rainey's Black Bottom," Levee's arrangement. There you go! That's what he told you.

SLOW DRAG: What you gonna do, Cutler?

CUTLER: Ma ain't told me what version. Let's go on and play it Levee's way.

TOLEDO: See, now . . . I'll tell you something. As long as the colored man look to white folks to put the crown on what he say . . . as long as he looks to white folks for approval . . . then he ain't never gonna find out who he is and what he's about. He's just gonna be about what white folks want him to be about. That's one sure thing.

LEVEE: I'm just trying to show Cutler where he's wrong.

CUTLER: Cutler don't need you to show him nothing.

SLOW DRAG: (*Irritated.*) Come on, let's get this shit rehearsed! You all can bicker afterward!

CUTLER: Levee's confused about who the boss is. He don't know Ma's the boss.

LEVEE: Ma's the boss on the road! We at a recording session. Mr. Sturdyvant and Mr. Irvin say what's gonna be here! We's in Chicago, we ain't in Memphis! I don't know why you all wanna pick me about it, shit! I'm with Slow Drag . . . Let's go on and get it rehearsed.

CUTLER: All right. All right. I know how to solve this. "Ma Rainey's Black Bottom." Levee's version. Let's do it. Come on.

TOLEDO: How that first part go again, Levee?

LEVEE: It go like this.

(*He plays.*)

That's to get the people's attention to the song. That's when you and Slow Drag come in with the rhythm part. Me and Cutler play on the breaks.

(*Becoming animated.*)

Now we gonna dance it . . . but we ain't gonna coun-
trify it. This ain't no barn dance. We gonna play it
like . . .

CUTLER: The man ask you how the first part go. He
don't wanna hear all that. Just tell him how the piece
go.

TOLEDO: I got it. I got it. Let's go. I know how to do it.

CUTLER: "Ma Rainey's Black Bottom." One . . .
two . . . You know what to do.

(*They begin to play. Levee stops.*)

LEVEE: You all got to keep up now. You playing in the
wrong time. Ma come in over the top. She got to find
her own way in.

CUTLER: Nigger, will you let us play this song? When
you get your own band . . . then you tell them that
nonsense. We know how to play the piece. I was
playing music before you was born. Gonna tell me
how to play . . . All right. Let's try it again.

SLOW DRAG: Cutler, wait till I fix this. This string
started to unravel.

(*Playfully.*)

And you know I want to play Levee's music right.

LEVEE: If you was any kind of musician, you'd take care
of your instrument. Keep it in tip-top order. If you
was any kind of musician, I'd let you be in my band.

SLOW DRAG: Shhheeeeet!

(*He crosses to get his string and steps on Levee's shoes.*)

LEVEE: Damn, Slow Drag! Watch them big-ass shoes
you got.

SLOW DRAG: Boy, ain't nobody done nothing to you.

LEVEE: You done stepped on my shoes.

SLOW DRAG: Move them the hell out the way, then. You
was in my way . . . I wasn't in your way.

(*Cutler lights up another reefer. Slow Drag rummages
around in his belongings for a string. Levee takes out a
rag and begins to shine his shoes.*)

You can shine these when you get done, Levee.

CUTLER: If I had them shoes Levee got, I could buy me a
whole suit of clothes.

LEVEE: What kind of difference it make what kind of
shoes I got? Ain't nothing wrong with having nice
shoes. I ain't said nothing about your shoes. Why
you wanna talk about me and my Florsheims?

CUTLER: Any man who takes a whole week's pay and
puts it on some shoes—you understand what I
mean, what you walk around on the ground with—
is a fool! And I don't mind telling you.

LEVEE: (*Irritated.*) What difference it make to you,
Cutler?

SLOW DRAG: The man ain't said nothing about your
shoes. Ain't nothing wrong with having nice shoes.
Look at Toledo.

TOLEDO: What about Toledo?

SLOW DRAG: I said ain't nothing wrong with having nice
shoes.

LEVEE: Nigger got them clodhoppers! Old brogans! He
ain't nothing but a sharecropper.

TOLEDO: You can make all the fun you want. It don't
mean nothing. I'm satisfied with them and that's
what counts.

LEVEE: Nigger, why don't you get some decent shoes?
Got nerve to put on a suit and tie with them farming
boots.

CUTLER: What you just tell me? It don't make no difference about the man's shoes. That's what you told me.

LEVEE: Aw, hell, I don't care what the nigger wear. I'll be
honest with you. I don't care if he went barefoot.

(*Slow Drag has put his string on the bass and is tuning it.*)

Play something for me, Slow Drag.

(*Slow Drag plays.*)

A man got to have some shoes to dance like this! You
can't dance like this with them clodhoppers Toledo
got.

(*Levee sings.*)

Hello Central give me Doctor Jazz
He's got just what I need I'll say he has
When the world goes wrong and I have got the
    blues
He's the man who makes me get on my dancing
    shoes.

TOLEDO: That's the trouble with colored folks . . .
always wanna have a good time. Good times done
got more niggers killed than God got ways to count.
What the hell having a good time mean? That's what
I wanna know.

LEVEE: Hell, nigger . . . it don't need explaining. Ain't
you never had no good time before?

TOLEDO: The more niggers get killed having a good
time, the more good times niggers wanna have.

(*Slow Drag stops playing.*)

There's more to life than having a good time. If there
ain't, then this is a piss-poor life we're having . . . if
that's all there is to be got out of it.

SLOW DRAG: Toledo, just 'cause you like to read them
books and study and whatnot . . . that's your good
time. People get other things they likes to do to have
a good time. Ain't no need you picking them about it.

CUTLER: Niggers been having a good time before you
was born, and they gonna keep having a good time
after you gone.

TOLEDO: Yeah, but what else they gonna do? Ain't
nobody talking about making the lot of the colored
man better for him here in America.

LEVEE: Now you gonna be Booker T. Washington.°

Booker T. Washington (1856–1915): Born into slavery, a major
figure fighting for the rights of African Americans.

TOLEDO: Everybody worried about having a good time. Ain't nobody thinking about what kind of world they gonna leave their youngens. "Just give me the good time, that's all I want." It just makes me sick.

SLOW DRAG: Well, the colored man's gonna be all right. He got through slavery, and he'll get through whatever else the white man put on him. I ain't worried about that. Good times is what makes life worth living. Now, you take the white man . . . The white man don't know how to have a good time. That's why he's troubled all the time. He don't know how to have a good time. He don't know how to laugh at life.

LEVEE: That's what the problem is with Toledo . . . reading all them books and things. He done got to the point where he forgot how to laugh and have a good time. Just like the white man.

TOLEDO: I know how to have a good time as well as the next man. I said, there's got to be more to life than having a good time. I said the colored man ought to be doing more than just trying to have a good time all the time.

LEVEE: Well, what is you doing, nigger? Talking all them highfalutin ideas about making a better world for the colored man. What is you doing to make it better? You playing the music and looking for your next piece of pussy same as we is. What is you doing? That's what I wanna know. Tell him, Cutler.

CUTLER: You all leave Cutler out of this, Cutler ain't got nothing to do with it.

TOLEDO: Levee, you just about the most ignorant nigger I know. Sometimes I wonder why I ever bother to try and talk with you.

LEVEE: Well, what is you doing? Talking that shit to me about I'm ignorant! What is you doing? You just a whole lot of mouth. A great big windbag. Thinking you smarter than everybody else. What is you doing, huh?

TOLEDO: It ain't just me, fool! It's everybody! What you think . . . I'm gonna solve the colored man's problems by myself? I said, we. You understand that? We. That's every living colored man in the world got to do his share. Got to do his part. I ain't talking about what I'm gonna do . . . or what you or Cutler or Slow Drag or anybody else. I'm talking about all of us together. What all of us is gonna do. That's what I'm talking about, nigger!

LEVEE: Well, why didn't you say that, then?

CUTLER: Toledo, I don't know why you waste your time on this fool.

TOLEDO: That's what I'm trying to figure out.

LEVEE: Now there go Cutler with his shit. Calling me a fool. You wasn't even in the conversation. Now you gonna take sides and call me a fool.

CUTLER: Hell, I was listening to the man. I got sense enough to know what he was saying. I could tell it straight back to you.

LEVEE: Well, you go on with it. But I'll tell you this . . . I ain't gonna be too many more of your fools. I'll

tell you that. Now you put that in your pipe and smoke it.

CUTLER: Boy, ain't nobody studying you. Telling me what to put in my pipe. Who's you to tell me what to do?

LEVEE: All right, I ain't nobody. Don't pay me no mind. I ain't nobody.

TOLEDO: Levee, you ain't nothing but the devil.

LEVEE: There you go! That's who I am. I'm the devil. I ain't nothing but the devil.

CUTLER: I can see that. That's something you know about. You know all about the devil.

LEVEE: I ain't saying what I know. I know plenty. What you know about the devil? Telling me what I know. What you know?

SLOW DRAG: I know a man sold his soul to the devil.

LEVEE: There you go! That's the only thing I ask about the devil . . . to see him coming so I can sell him this one I got. 'Cause if there's a god up there, he done went to sleep.

SLOW DRAG: Sold his soul to the devil himself. Name of Eliza Cottor. Lived in Tuscaloosa County, Alabama. The devil came by and he done upped and sold him his soul.

CUTLER: How you know the man done sold his soul to the devil, nigger? You talking that old-woman foolishness.

SLOW DRAG: Everybody know. It wasn't no secret. He went around working for the devil and everybody knowed it. Carried him a bag . . . one of them carpet-bags. Folks say he carried the devil's papers and whatnot where he put your fingerprint on the paper with blood.

LEVEE: Where he at now? That's what I want to know. He can put my whole handprint if he want to!

CUTLER: That's the damnedest thing I ever heard! Folks kill me with that talk.

TOLEDO: Oh, that's real enough, all right. Some folks go arm in arm with the devil, shoulder to shoulder, and talk to him all the time. That's real, ain't nothing wrong in believing that.

SLOW DRAG: That's what I'm saying. Eliza Cotter is one of them. All right. The man living up in an old shack on Ben Foster's place, shoeing mules and horses, making them charms and things in secret. He done hooked up with the devil, showed up one day fancied out with just the finest clothes you ever seen on a colored man . . . dressed just like one of them crackers . . . and carrying this bag with them papers and things. All right. Had a pocketful of money, just living the life of a rich man. Ain't done no more work or nothing. Just had him a string of women he run around with and throw his money away on. Bought him a big fine house . . . Well, it wasn't all that big, but it did have one of them white picket fences around it. Used to hire a man once a week just to paint that fence. Messed around there and one of the fellows of them gals he was messing with got fixed on him wrong and Eliza killed him. And he laughed about it. Sheriff come and arrest him, and then let him go. And he went around in that town laughing about killing this fellow. Trial come up, and the judge cut him loose. He must have been in converse with the devil too . . . 'cause he cut him loose and give him a bottle of whiskey! Folks ask what done happened to make him change, and he'd tell them straight out he done sold his soul to the devil and ask them if they wanted to sell theirs 'cause he could arrange it for them. Preacher see him coming, used to cross on the other side of the road. He'd just stand there and laugh at the preacher and call him a fool to his face.

CUTLER: Well, whatever happened to this fellow? What come of him? A man who, as you say, done sold his soul to the devil is bound to come to a bad end.

TOLEDO: I don't know about that. The devil's strong. The devil ain't no pushover.

SLOW DRAG: Oh, the devil had him under his wing, all right. Took good care of him. He ain't wanted for nothing.

CUTLER: What happened to him? That's what I want to know.

SLOW DRAG: Last I heard, he headed north with that bag of his, handing out hundred-dollar bills on the spot to whoever wanted to sign on with the devil. That's what I hear tell of him.

CUTLER: That's a bunch of fool talk. I don't know how you fix your mouth to tell that story. I don't believe that.

SLOW DRAG: I ain't asking you to believe it. I'm just telling you the facts of it.

LEVEE: I sure wish I knew where he went. He wouldn't have to convince me long. Hell, I'd even help him sign people up.

CUTLER: Nigger, God's gonna strike you down with that blasphemy you talking.

LEVEE: Oh, shit! God don't mean nothing to me. Let him strike me! Here I am, standing right here. What you talking about he's gonna strike me? Here I am! Let him strike me! I ain't scared of him. Talking that stuff to me.

CUTLER: All right. You gonna be sorry. You gonna fix yourself to have bad luck. Ain't nothing gonna work for you.

(*Buzzer sounds offstage.*)

LEVEE: Bad luck? What I care about some bad luck? You talking simple. I ain't knowed nothing but bad luck all my life. Couldn't get no worse. What the hell I care about some bad luck? Hell, I eat it everyday for breakfast! You dumber than I thought you was . . . talking about bad luck.

CUTLER: All right, nigger, you'll see! Can't tell a fool nothing. You'll see!

IRVIN: (*Irvin enters the studio, checks his watch, and calls down the stairs.*) Cutler . . . you boys' sandwiches are up here . . . Cutler?

CUTLER: Yessir, Mr. Irvin . . . be right there.

TOLEDO: I'll walk up there and get them.

(*Toledo exits. The lights go down in the band room and up in the studio. Irvin paces back and forth in an agitated manner. Sturdyvant enters.*)

STURDYVANT: Irv, what's happening? Is she here yet? Was that her?

IRVIN: It's the sandwiches, Mel. I told you . . . I'll let you know when she comes, huh?

STURDYVANT: What's keeping her? Do you know what time it is? Have you looked at the clock? You told me she'd be here. You told me you'd take care of it.

IRVIN: Mel, for Chrissakes! What do you want from me? What do you want me to do?

STURDYVANT: Look what time it is, Irv. You told me she'd be here.

IRVIN: She'll be here, okay? I don't know what's keeping her. You know they're always late, Mel.

STURDYVANT: You should have went by the hotel and made sure she was on time. You should have taken care of this. That's what you told me, huh? "I'll take care of it."

IRVIN: Okay! Okay! I didn't go by the hotel! What do you want me to do? She'll be here, okay? The band's here . . . she'll be here.

STURDYVANT: Okay, Irv. I'll take your word. But if she doesn't come . . . if she doesn't come . . .

(*Sturdyvant exits to the control booth as Toledo enters.*)

TOLEDO: Mr. Irvin . . . I come up to get the sandwiches.

IRVIN: Say . . . uh . . . look . . . one o'clock, right? She said one o'clock.

TOLEDO: That's what time she told us. Say be here at one o'clock.

IRVIN: Do you know what's keeping her? Do you know why she ain't here?

TOLEDO: I can't say, Mr. Irvin. Told us one o'clock.

(*The buzzer sounds. Irvin goes to the door. There is a flurry of commotion as Ma Rainey enters, followed closely by the Policeman, Dussie Mae, and Sylvester. Ma Rainey is a short, heavy woman. She is dressed in a full-length fur coat with matching hat, an emerald-green dress, and several strands of pearls of varying lengths. Her hair is secured by a headband that matches her dress. Her manner is simple and direct, and she carries herself in a royal fashion. Dussie Mae is a young, dark-skinned woman whose greatest asset is the sensual energy which seems to flow from her. She is dressed in a fur jacket and a tight-fitting canary-yellow dress. Sylvester is an Arkansas country boy, the size of a fullback. He wears a new suit and coat, in which he is obviously uncomfortable. Most of the time, he stutters when he speaks.*)

MA RAINEY: Irvin . . . you better tell this man who I am! You better get him straight!

IRVIN: Ma, do you know what time it is? Do you have any idea? We've been waiting . . .

DUSSIE MAE: (*To Sylvester.*) If you was watching where you was going . . .

SYLVESTER: I was watching . . . What you mean?

IRVIN: (*notices Policeman.*) What's going on here? Officer, what's the matter?

MA RAINEY: Tell the men who he's messing with!

POLICEMAN: Do you know this lady?

MA RAINEY: Just tell the man who I am! That's all you gotta do.

POLICEMAN: Lady, will you let me talk, huh?

MA RAINEY: Tell the man who I am!

IRVIN: Wait a minute . . . wait a minute! Let me handle it. Ma, will you let me handle it?

MA RAINEY: Tell him who he's messing with!

IRVIN: Okay! Okay! Give me a chance! Officer, this is one of our recording artists . . . Ma Rainey.

MA RAINEY: Madame Rainey! Get it straight! Madame Rainey! Talking about taking me to jail!

IRVIN: Look, Ma . . . give me a chance, okay? Here . . . sit down. I'll take care of it. Officer, what's the problem?

DUSSIE MAE: (*To Sylvester.*) It's all your fault.

SYLVESTER: I ain't done nothing . . . Ask Ma.

POLICEMAN: Well . . . when I walked up on the incident . . .

DUSSIE MAE: Sylvester wrecked Ma's car.

SYLVESTER: I d-d-did not! The m-m-man ran into me!

POLICEMAN: (*To Irvin.*) Look, buddy . . . if you want it in a nutshell, we got her charged with assault and battery.

MA RAINEY: Assault and what for what!

DUSSIE MAE: See . . . we was trying to get a cab . . . and so Ma . . .

MA RAINEY: Wait a minute! I'll tell you if you wanna know what happened. (*She points to Sylvester.*) Now, that's Sylvester. That's my nephew. He was driving my car . . .

POLICEMAN: Lady, we don't know whose car he was driving.

MA RAINEY: That's my car!

DUSSIE MAE and SYLVESTER: That's Ma's car!

MA RAINEY: What you mean you don't know whose car it is? I bought and paid for that car.

POLICEMAN: That's what you say, lady . . . We still gotta check.

(*To Irvin.*)

They hit a car on Market Street. The guy said the kid ran a stoplight.

SYLVESTER: What you mean? The man c-c-come around the corner and hit m-m-me!

POLICEMAN: While I was calling a paddy wagon to haul them to the station, they try to hop into a parked cab. The cabbie said he was waiting on a fare . . .

MA RAINEY: The man was just sitting there. Wasn't waiting for nobody. I don't know why he wanna tell that lie.

POLICEMAN: Look, lady . . . will you let me tell the story?

MA RAINEY: Go ahead and tell it then. But tell it right!

POLICEMAN: Like I say . . . she tries to get in this cab. The cabbie's waiting on a fare. She starts creating a

disturbance. The cabbie gets out to try and explain the situation to her . . . and she knocks him down.

DUSSIE MAE: She ain't hit him! He just fell!

SYLVESTER: He just s-s-s-slipped!

POLICEMAN: He claims she knocked him down. We got her charged with assault and battery.

MA RAINEY: If that don't beat all to hell. I ain't touched the man! The man was trying to reach around me to keep his car door closed. I opened the door and it hit him and he fell down. I ain't touched the man!

IRVIN: Okay. Okay . . . I got it straight now, Ma. You didn't touch him. All right? Officer, can I see you for a minute?

DUSSIE MAE: Ma was just trying to open the door.

SYLVESTER: He j-j-just got in t-t-the way!

MA RAINEY: Said he wasn't gonna haul no colored folks . . . if you want to know the truth of it.

IRVIN: Okay, Ma . . . I got it straight now. Officer?

(*Irvin pulls the Policeman off to the side.*)

MA RAINEY: (*Noticing Toledo.*) Toledo, Cutler and everybody here?

TOLEDO: Yeah, they down in the band room. What happened to your car?

STURDYVANT: (*Entering*) Irv, what's the problem? What's going on? Officer . . .

IRVIN: Mel, let me take care of it. I can handle it.

STURDYVANT: What's happening? What the hell's going on?

IRVIN: Let me handle it, Mel, huh?

(*Sturdyvant crosses over to Ma Rainey.*)

STURDYVANT: What's going on, Ma. What'd you do?

MA RAINEY: Sturdyvant, get on away from me! That's the last thing I need . . . to go through some of your shit!

IRVIN: Mel, I'll take care of it. I'll explain it all to you. Let me handle it, huh?

(*Sturdyvant reluctantly returns to the control booth.*)

POLICEMAN: Look, buddy, like I say . . . we got her charged with assault and battery . . . and the kid with threatening the cabbie.

SYLVESTER: I ain't done n-n-nothing!

MA RAINEY: You leave the boy out of it. He ain't done nothing. What's he supposed to have done?

POLICEMAN: He threatened the cabbie, lady! You just can't go around threatening people.

SYLVESTER: I ain't done nothing to him! He's the one talking about he g-g-gonna get a b-b-baseball bat on me! I just told him what I'd do with it. But I ain't done nothing 'cause he didn't get the b-b-bat!

IRVIN: (*Pulling the Policeman aside.*) Officer . . . look here . . .

POLICEMAN: We was on our way down to the precinct . . . but I figured I'd do you a favor and bring her by here. I mean, if she's as important as she says she is . . .

IRVIN: (*Slides a bill from his pocket.*) Look, Officer . . . I'm Madame Rainey's manager . . . It's good to meet you.

(*He shakes the Policeman's hand and passes him the bill.*)

As soon as we're finished with the recording session, I'll personally stop by the precinct house and straighten up this misunderstanding.

POLICEMAN: Well . . . I guess that's all right. As long as someone is responsible for them.

(*He pockets the bill and winks at Irvin.*)

No need to come down . . . I'll take care of it myself. Of course, we wouldn't want nothing like this to happen again.

IRVIN: Don't worry, Officer . . . I'll take care of everything. Thanks for your help.

(*Irvin escorts the Policeman to the door and returns. He crosses over to Ma Rainey.*)

Here, Ma . . . let me take your coat.

(*To Sylvester.*)

I don't believe I know you.

MA RAINEY: That's my nephew, Sylvester.

IRVIN: I'm very pleased to meet you. Here . . . you can give me your coat.

MA RAINEY: That there is Dussie Mae.

IRVIN: Hello . . .

(*Dussie Mae hands Irvin her coat.*)

Listen, Ma, just sit there and relax. The boys are in the band room rehearsing. You just sit and relax a minute.

MA RAINEY: I ain't for no sitting. I ain't never heard of such. Talking about taking me to jail. Irvin, call down there and see about my car.

IRVIN: Okay, Ma . . . I'll take care of it. You just relax.

(*Irvin exits with the coats.*)

MA RAINEY: Why you all keep it so cold in here? Sturdyvant try and pinch every penny he can. You all wanna make some records, you better put some heat on in here or give me back my coat.

IRVIN: (*Entering*) We got the heat turned up, Ma. It's warming up. It'll be warm in a minute.

DUSSIE MAE: (*Whispering to Ma Rainey.*) Where's the bathroom?

MA RAINEY: It's in the back. Down the hall next to Sturdyvant's office. Come on, I'll show you where it is. Irvin, call down there and see about my car. I want my car fixed today.

IRVIN: I'll take care of everything, Ma.

(*He notices Toledo.*)

Say . . . uh . . . uh . . .

TOLEDO: Toledo.

IRVIN: Yeah . . . Toledo. I got the sandwiches, you can take down to the rest of the boys. We'll be ready to

go in a minute. Give you boys a chance to eat and then we'll be ready to go.

(*Irvin and Toledo exit. The lights go down in the studio and come up in the band room.*)

LEVEE: Slow Drag, you ever been to New Orleans?

SLOW DRAG: What's in New Orleans that I want?

LEVEE: How you call yourself a musician and ain't never been to New Orleans.

SLOW DRAG: You ever been to Fat Back, Arkansas?

(*Pauses.*)

All right, then. Ain't never been nothing in New Orleans that I couldn't get in Fat Back.

LEVEE: That's why you backwards. You just an old country boy talking about Fat Back, Arkansas, and New Orleans in the same breath.

CUTLER: I been to New Orleans. What about it?

LEVEE: You ever been to Lula White's?

CUTLER: Lula White's? I ain't never heard of it.

LEVEE: Man, they got some gals in there just won't wait! I seen a man get killed in there once. Got drunk and grabbed one of the gals wrong . . . I don't know what the matter of it was. But he grabbed her and she stuck a knife in him all the way up to the hilt. He ain't even fell. He just stood there and choked on his own blood. I was just asking Slow Drag 'cause I was gonna take him to Lula White's when we get down to New Orleans and show him a good time. Introduce him to one of them gals I know down there.

CUTLER: Slow Drag don't need you to find him no pussy. He can take care of his own self. Fact is . . . you better watch your gal when Slow Drag's around. They don't call him Slow Drag for nothing.

(*He laughs.*)

Tell him how you got your name Slow Drag.

SLOW DRAG: I ain't thinking about Levee.

CUTLER: Slow Drag break a woman's back when he dance. They had this contest one time in this little town called Bolingbroke about a hundred miles outside of Macon. We was playing for this dance and they was giving twenty dollars to the best slow draggers. Slow Drag looked over the competition, got down off the bandstand, grabbed hold of one of them gals, and stuck to her like a fly to jelly. Like wood to glue. Man had that gal whooping and hollering so . . . everybody stopped to watch. This fellow come in . . . this gal's fellow . . . and pulled a knife a foot long on Slow Drag. 'Member that, Slow Drag?

SLOW DRAG: Boy that mama was hot! The front of her dress was wet as a dishrag!

LEVEE: So what happened? What the man do?

CUTLER: Slow Drag ain't missed a stroke. The gal, she just look at her man with that sweet dizzy look in her eye. She ain't about to stop! Folks was clearing out, ducking and hiding under tables, figuring there's gonna be a fight. Slow Drag just looked over the gal's shoulder at the man and said, "Mister, if you'd quit hollering and wait a minute . . . you'll see I'm doing you a favor. I'm helping this gal win ten dollars so she can buy you a gold watch." The man just stood there and looked at him, all the while stroking that knife. Told Slow Drag, say, "All right, then, nigger. You just better make damn sure you win." That's when folks started calling him Slow Drag. The women got to hanging around him so bad after that, them fellows in that town ran us out of there.

(*Toledo enters, carrying a small cardboard box with the sandwiches.*)

LEVEE: Yeah . . . well, them gals in Lula White's will put a harness on his ass.

TOLEDO: Ma's up there. Some kind of commotion with the police.

CUTLER: Police? What the police up there for?

TOLEDO: I couldn't get it straight. Something about her car. They gone now . . . she's all right. Mr. Irvin sent some sandwiches.

(*Levee springs across the room.*)

LEVEE: Yeah, all right. What we got here?

(*He takes two sandwiches out of the box.*)

TOLEDO: What you doing grabbing two? There ain't but five in there . . . How you figure you get two?

LEVEE: 'Cause I grabbed them first. There's enough for everybody . . . What you talking about? It ain't like I'm taking food out of nobody's mouth.

CUTLER: That's all right. He can have mine too. I don't want none.

(*Levee starts toward the box to get another sandwich.*)

TOLEDO: Nigger, you better get out of here. Slow Drag, you want this?

SLOW DRAG: Naw, you can have it.

TOLEDO: With Levee around, you don't have to worry about no leftovers. I can see that.

LEVEE: What's the matter with you? Ain't you eating two sandwiches? Then why you wanna talk about me? Talking about there won't be no leftovers with Levee around. Look at your own self before you look at me.

TOLEDO: That's what you is. That's what we all is. A leftover from history. You see now, I'll show you.

LEVEE: Aw, shit . . . I done got the nigger started now.

TOLEDO: Now, I'm gonna show you how this goes . . . where you just a leftover from history. Everybody come from different places in Africa, right? Come from different tribes and things. Soonawhile they began to make one big stew. You had the carrots, the peas, and potatoes and whatnot over here. And over there you had the meat, the nuts, the okra, corn . . . and then you mix it up and let it cook right through to get the flavors flowing together . . . then you got one thing. You got a stew.

Now you take and eat the stew. You take and make your history with that stew. All right. Now it's over. Your history's over and you done ate the stew. But you look around and you see some carrots over here, some potaotes over there. That stew's still there. You done made your history and it's still there. You can't eat it all. So what you got? You got some leftovers. That's what it is. You got leftovers and you can't do nothing with it. You already making you another history . . . cooking you another meal, and you don't need them leftovers no more. What to do?

See, we's the leftovers. The colored man is the leftovers. Now, what's the colored man gonna do with himself? That's what we waiting to find out. But first we gotta know we the leftovers. Now, who knows that? You find me a nigger that knows that and I'll turn any whichaway you want me to. I'll bend over for you. You ain't gonna find that. And that's what the problem is. The problem ain't with the white man. The white man knows you just a leftover. 'Cause he the one who done the eating and he know what he done ate. But we don't know that we been took and made history out of. Done went and filled the white man's belly and now he's full and tired and wants you to get out the way and let him be by himself. Now, I know what I'm talking about. And if you wanna find out, you just ask Mr. Irvin what he had for supper yesterday. And if he's an honest white man . . . which is asking for a whole heap of a lot . . . he'll tell you he done ate your black ass and if you please I'm full up with you . . . so go on and get off the plate and let me eat something else.

SLOW DRAG: What that mean? What's eating got to do with how the white man treat you? He don't treat you no different according to what he ate.

TOLEDO: I ain't said it had nothing to do with how he treat you.

CUTLER: The man's trying to tell you something, fool!

SLOW DRAG: What he trying to tell me? Ain't you here. Why you say he was trying to tell *me* something? Wasn't he trying to tell you too?

LEVEE: He was trying all right. He was trying a whole heap. I'll say that for him. But trying ain't worth a damn. I got lost right there trying to figure out who puts nuts in their stew.

SLOW DRAG: I knowed that before. My grandpappy used to put nuts in his stew. He and my grandmama both. That ain't nothing new.

TOLEDO: They put nuts in their stew all over Africa. But the stew they eat, and the stew your grandpappy made, and all the stew that you and me eat, and the stew Mr. Irvin eats . . . ain't in no way the same stew. That's the way that go. I'm through with it. That's the last you know me to ever try and explain something to you.

CUTLER: (*After a pause.*) Well, time's getting along . . . Come on, let's finish rehearsing.

LEVEE: (*Stretching out on a bench.*) I don't feel like rehearsing. I ain't nothing but a leftover. You go and rehearse with Toledo . . . He's gonna teach you how to make a stew.

SLOW DRAG: Cutler, what you gonna do? I don't want to be around here all day.

LEVEE: I know my part. You all go on and rehearse your part. You all need some rehearsal.

CUTLER: Come on, Levee, get up off your ass and rehearse the songs.

LEVEE: I already know them songs . . . What I wanna rehearse them for?

SLOW DRAG: You in the band, ain't you? You supposed to rehearse when the band rehearse.

TOLEDO: Levee think he the king of the barnyard. He thinks he's the only rooster know how to crow.

LEVEE: All right! All right! Come on, I'm gonna show you I know them songs. Come on, let's rehearse. I bet you the first one mess be Toledo. Come on . . . I wanna see if he know how to crow.

CUTLER: "Ma Rainey's Black Bottom," Levee's version. Let's do it.

(*They begin to rehearse. The lights go down in the band room and up in the studio. Ma Rainey sits and takes off her shoe, rubs her feet. Dussie Mae wanders about looking at the studio. Sylvester is over by the piano.*)

MA RAINEY: (*Singing to herself.*)
Oh, Lord, these dogs of mine
They sure do worry me all the time
The reason why I don't know
Lord, I beg to be excused
I can't wear me no sharp-toed shoes.
I went for a walk
I stopped to talk
Oh, how my corns did bark.

DUSSIE MAE: It feels kinda spooky in here. I ain't never been in no recording studio before. Where's the band at?

MA RAINEY: They off somewhere rehearsing. I don't know where Irvin went to. All this hurry up and he goes off back there with Sturdyvant. I know he better come on 'cause Ma ain't gonna be waiting. Come here . . . let me see that dress.

(*Dussie Mae crosses over. Ma Rainey tugs at the dress around the waist, appraising the fit.*)

That dress looks nice. I'm gonna take you tomorrow and get you some more things before I take you down to Memphis. They got clothes up here you can't get in Memphis. I want you to look nice for me. If you gonna travel with the show you got to look nice.

DUSSIE MAE: I need me some more shoes. These hurt my feet.

MA RAINEY: You get you some shoes that fit your feet. Don't you be messing around with no shoes that pinch your feet. Ma know something about bad feet. Hand me my slippers out my bag over yonder.

(*Dussie Mae brings the slippers.*)

DUSSIE MAE: I just want to get a pair of them yellow ones. About a half-size bigger.

MA RAINEY: We'll get you whatever you need. Sylvester, too . . . I'm gonna get him some more clothes. Sylvester, tuck your clothes in. Straighten them up and look nice. Look like a gentleman.

DUSSIE MAE: Look at Sylvester with that hat on.

MA RAINEY: Sylvester, take your hat off inside. Act like your mama taught you something. I know she taught you better than that.

(*Sylvester bangs on the piano.*)

Come on over here and leave that piano alone.

SYLVESTER: I ain't d-d-doing nothing to the p-p-piano. I'm just l-l-looking at it.

MA RAINEY: Well. Come on over here and sit down. As soon as Mr. Irvin comes back, I'll have him take you down and introduce you to the band.

(*Sylvester comes over.*)

He's gonna take you down there and introduce you in a minute . . . have Cutler show you how your part go. And when you get your money, you gonna send some of it home to your mama. Let her know you doing all right. Make her feel good to know you doing all right in the world.

(*Dussie Mae wanders about the studio and opens the door leading to the band room. The strains of Levee's version of "Ma Rainey's Black Bottom" can be heard. Irvin enters.*)

IRVIN: Ma, I called down to the garage and checked on your car. It's just a scratch. They'll have it ready for you this afternoon. They're gonna send it over with one of their fellows.

MA RAINEY: They better have my car fixed right too. I ain't going for that. Brand-new car . . . they better fix it like new.

IRVIN: It was just a scratch on the fender, Ma . . . They'll take care of it . . . don't worry . . . they'll have it like new.

MA RAINEY: Irvin, what is that I hear? What is that the band's rehearsing? I know they ain't rehearsing Levee's "Black Bottom." I know I ain't hearing that?

IRVIN: Ma, listen . . . that's what I wanted to talk to you about. Levee's version of that song . . . it's got a nice arrangement . . . a nice horn intro . . . It really picks it up . . .

MA RAINEY: I ain't studying Levee nothing. I know what he done to that song and I don't like to sing it that way. I'm doing it the old way. That's why I brought my nephew to do the voice intro.

IRVIN: Ma, that's what the people want now. They want something they can dance to. Times are changing. Levee's arrangement gives the people what they want. It gets them excited . . . makes them forget about their troubles.

MA RAINEY: I don't care what you say, Irvin. Levee ain't messing up my song. If he got what the people want, let him take it somewhere else. I'm singing Ma Rainey's song. I ain't singing Levee's song. Now that's all there is to it. Carry my nephew on down there and introduce him to the band. I promised my sister I'd look out for him and he's gonna do the voice intro on the song my way.

IRVIN: Ma, we just figured that . . .

MA RAINEY: Who's this "we"? What you mean "we"? I ain't studying Levee nothing. Come talking this "we" stuff. Who's "we"?

IRVIN: Me and Sturdyvant. We decided that it would . . .

MA RAINEY: You decided, huh? I'm just a bump on the log. I'm gonna go which ever way the river drift. Is that it? You and Sturdyvant decided.

IRVIN: Ma, it was just that we thought it would be better.

MA RAINEY: I ain't got good sense. I don't know nothing about music. I don't know what's a good song and what ain't. You know more about my fans than I do.

IRVIN: It's not that, Ma. It would just be easier to do. It's more what the people want.

MA RAINEY: I'm gonna tell you something, Irvin . . . and you go on up there and tell Sturdyvant. What you all say don't count with me. You understand? Ma listens to her heart. Ma listens to the voice inside her. That's what counts with Ma. Now, you carry my nephew on down there . . . tell Cutler he's gonna do the voice intro on that "Black Bottom" song and that Levee ain't messing up my song with none of his music shit. Now, if that don't set right with you and Sturdyvant . . . then I can carry my black bottom on back down South to my tour, 'cause I don't like it up here no ways.

IRVIN: Okay, Ma . . . I don't care. I just thought . . .

MA RAINEY: Damn what you thought! What you look like telling me how to sing my song? This Levee and Sturdyvant nonsense . . . I ain't going for it! Sylvester, go on down there and introduce yourself. I'm through playing with Irvin.

SYLVESTER: Which way you go? Where they at?

MA RAINEY: Here . . . I'll carry you down there myself.

DUSSIE MAE: Can I go? I wanna see the band.

MA RAINEY: You stay your behind up here. Ain't no cause in you being down there. Come on, Sylvester.

IRVIN: Okay, Ma. Have it your way. We'll be ready to go in fifteen minutes.

MA RAINEY: We'll be ready to go when Madame says we're ready. That's the way it goes around here.

(*Ma Rainey and Sylvester exit. The lights go down in the studio and up in the band room. Ma Rainey enters with Sylvester.*)

Cutler, this here is my nephew Sylvester. He's gonna do that voice intro on the "Black Bottom" song using the old version.

LEVEE: What you talking about? Mr. Irvin say he's using my version. What you talking about?

MA RAINEY: Levee, I ain't studying you or Mr. Irvin. Cutler, get him straightened out on how to do his part. I ain't thinking about Levee. These folks done messed with the wrong person this day. Sylvester,

Cutler gonna teach you your part. You go ahead and get it straight. Don't worry about what nobody else say.

(*Ma Rainey exits.*)

CUTLER: Well, come on in, boy. I'm Cutler. You got Slow Drag . . . Levee . . . and that's Toledo over there. Sylvester, huh?

SYLVESTER: Sylvester Brown.

LEVEE: I done wrote a version of that song what picks it up and sets it down in the people's lap! Now she come talking this! You don't need that old circus bullshit! I know what I'm talking about. You gonna mess up the song Cutler and you know it.

CUTLER: I ain't gonna mess up nothing. Ma say . . .

LEVEE: I don't care what Ma say! I'm talking about what the intro gonna do to the song. The peoples in the North ain't gonna buy all that tent-show nonsense. They wanna hear some music!

CUTLER: Nigger, I done told you time and again . . . you just in the band. You plays the piece . . . whatever they want! Ma says what to play! Not you! You ain't here to be doing no creating, Your job is to play whatever Ma says!

LEVEE: I might not play nothing! I might quit!

CUTLER: Nigger, don't nobody care if you quit. Whose heart you gonna break?

TOLEDO: Levee ain't gonna quit. He got to make some money to keep him in shoe polish.

LEVEE: I done told you all . . . you all don't know me. You don't know what I'll do.

CUTLER: I don't think nobody too much give a damn! Sylvester, here's the way your part go. The band plays the intro . . . I'll tell you where to come in. The band plays the intro and then you say, "All right, boys, you done seen the rest . . . Now I'm gonna show you the best. Ma Rainey's gonna show you her black bottom." You got that?

(*Sylvester nods.*)

Let me hear you say it one time.

SYLVESTER: "All right, boys, you done s-s-seen the rest n-n-now I'm gonna show you the best. M-m-m-m-m-m-ma Rainey's gonna s-s-show you her black b-b-bottom."

LEVEE: What kind of . . . All right, Cutler! Let me see you fix that! You straighten that out! You hear that shit, Slow Drag? How in the hell the boy gonna do the part and he can't even talk!

SYLVESTER: W-w-w-who's you to tell me what to do, nigger! This ain't your band! Ma tell me to d-d-d-do it and I'm gonna do it. You can go to hell, n-n-n-nigger!

LEVEE: B-b-b-boy, ain't nobody studying you. You go on and fix that one, Cutler. You fix that one and I'll . . . I'll shine your shoes for you. You go on and fix that one!

TOLEDO: You say you Ma's nephew, huh?

SYLVESTER: Yeah. So w-w-what that mean?

TOLEDO: Oh, I ain't meant nothing . . . I was just asking.

SLOW DRAG: Well, come on and let's rehearse so the boy can get it right.

LEVEE: I ain't rehearsing nothing! You just wait till I get my band. I'm gonna record that song and show you how it supposed to go!

CUTLER: We can do it without Levee. Let him sit on over there. Sylvester, you remember your part?

SYLVESTER: I remember it pretty g-g-g-good.

CUTLER: Well, come on, let's do it, then.

(*The band begins to play. Levee sits and pouts. Sturdyvant enters the band room.*)

STURDYVANT: Good . . . you boys are rehearsing, I see.

LEVEE: (*Jumping up.*) Yessir! We rehearsing, We know them songs real good.

STURDYVANT: Good! Say, Levee, did you finish that song?

LEVEE: Yessir, Mr. Sturdyvant. I got it right here. I wrote that other part just like you say. It go like:

You can shake it, you can break it
You can dance at any hall
You can slide across the floor
You'll never have to stall
My jelly, my roll,
Sweet Mama, don't you let it fall.

Then I put that part in there for the people to dance, like you say, for them to forget about their troubles.

STURDYVANT: Good! Good! I'll just take this. I wanna see you about your songs as soon as I get the chance.

LEVEE: Yessir! As soon as you get the chance, Mr. Sturdyvant.

(*Sturdyvant exits.*)

CUTLER: You hear, Levee? You hear this nigger? "Yessuh, we's rehearsing, boss."

SLOW DRAG: I heard him. Seen him too. Shuffling them feet.

TOLEDO: Aw, Levee can't help it none. He's like all of us. Spooked up with the white men.

LEVEE: I'm spooked up with him, all right. You let one of them crackers fix on me wrong. I'll show you how spooked up I am with him.

TOLEDO: That's the trouble of it. You wouldn't know if he was fixed on you wrong or not. You so spooked up by him you ain't had the time to study him.

LEVEE: I studies the white man. I got him studied good. The first time one fixes on me wrong, I'm gonna let him know just how much I studied. Come telling me I'm spooked up with the white man. You let one of them mess with me, I'll show you how spooked up I am.

CUTLER: You talking out your hat. The man come in here, call you a boy, tell you to get up off your ass and rehearse, and you ain't had nothing to say to him, except "Yessir!"

LEVEE: I can say "yessir" to whoever I please. What you got to do with it? I know how to handle white folks. I

been handling them for thirty-two years, and now you gonna tell me how to do it. Just 'cause I say "yessir" don't mean I'm spooked up with him. I know what I'm doing. Let me handle him my way.

CUTLER: Well, go on and handle it, then.

LEVEE: Toledo, you always messing with somebody! Always agitating somebody with that old philosophy bullshit you be talking. You stay out of my way about what I do and say. I'm my own person. Just let me alone.

TOLEDO: You right, Levee. I apologize. It ain't none of my business that you spooked up by the white man.

LEVEE: All right! See! That's the shit I'm talking about. You all back up and leave Levee alone.

SLOW DRAG: Aw, Levee, we was all just having fun. Toledo ain't said nothing about you he ain't said about me. You just taking it all wrong.

TOLEDO: I ain't meant nothing by it Levee.

(*Pauses.*)

Cutler, you ready to rehearse?

LEVEE: Levee got to be Levee! And he don't need nobody messing with him about the white man—cause you don't know nothing about me. You don't know Levee. You don't know nothing about what kind of blood I got! What kind of heart I got beating here!

(*He pounds his chest.*)

I was eight years old when I watched a gang of white mens come into my daddy's house and have to do with my mama any way they wanted.

(*Pauses.*)

We was living in Jefferson County, about eighty miles outside of Natchez. My daddy's name was Memphis . . . Memphis Lee Green . . . had him near fifty acres of good farming land. I'm talking about good land! Grow anything you want! He done gone off of shares and bought this land from Mr. Hallie's widow woman after he done passed on. Folks called him an uppity nigger 'cause he done saved and borrowed to where he could buy this land and be independent.

(*Pauses.*)

It was coming on planting time and my daddy went into Natchez to get him some seed and fertilizer. Called me, say, "Levee you the man of the house now. Take care of your mama while I'm gone." I wasn't but a little boy, eight years old.

(*Pauses.*)

My mama was frying up some chicken when them mens come in that house. Must have been eight or nine of them. She standing there frying that chicken and them mens come and took hold of her just like you take hold of a mule and make him do what you want.

(*Pauses.*)

There was my mama with a gang of white mens. She tried to fight them off, but I could see where it wasn't gonna do her any good, I didn't know what they were doing to her . . . but I figured whatever it was they may as well do to me too. My daddy had a knife that he kept around there for hunting and working and whatnot. I knew where he kept it and I went and got it.

I'm gonna show you how spooked up I was by the white man. I tried my damndest to cut one of them's throat! I hit him on the shoulder with it. He reached back and grabbed hold of that knife and whacked me across the chest with it.

(*Levee raises his shirt to show a long ugly scar.*)

That's what made them stop. They was scared I was gonna bleed to death. My mama wrapped a sheet around me and carried me two miles down to the Furlow place and they drove me up to Doc Albans. He was waiting on a calf to be born, and say he ain't had time to see me. They carried me up to Miss Etta, the midwife, and she fixed me up.

My daddy came back and acted like he done accepted the facts of what happened. But he got the names of them mens from mama. He found out who they was and then we announced we was moving out of that county. Said good-bye to everybody . . . all the neighbors. My daddy went and smiled in the face of one of them crackers who had been with my mama. Smiled in his face and sold him our land. We moved over with relations in Caldwell. He got us settled in and then he took off one day. I ain't never seen him since. He sneaked back, hiding up in the woods, laying to get them eight or nine men.

(*Pauses.*)

He got four of them before they got him. They tracked him down in the woods. Caught up with him and hung him and set him afire.

(*Pauses.*)

My daddy wasn't spooked up by the white man. Nosir! And that taught me how to handle them. I seen my daddy go up and grin in this cracker's face . . . smile in his face and sell him his land. All the while he's planning how he's gonna get him and what he's gonna do to him. That taught me how to handle them. So you all just back up and leave Levee alone about the white man. I can smile and say yessir to whoever I please. I got time coming to me. You all just leave Levee alone about the white man.

(*There is a long pause. Slow Drag begins playing on the bass and sings.*)

SLOW DRAG: (*Singing.*)
If I had my way
If I had my way
If I had my way
I would tear this old building down.

ACT 2

(*The lights come up in the studio. The musicians are setting up their instruments. Ma Rainey walks about shoeless, singing softly to herself. Levee stands near Dussie Mae, who hikes up her dress and crosses her leg. Cutler speaks to Irvin off to the side.*)

CUTLER: Mr. Irvin, I don't know what you gonna do. I ain't got nothing to do with it, but the boy can't do the part. He stutters. He can't get it right. He stutters right through it every time.

IRVIN: Christ! Okay, We'll . . . Shit! We'll just do it like we planned. We'll do Levee's version. I'll handle it, Cutler. Come on, let's go. I'll think of something.

(*He exits to the control booth.*)

MA RAINEY: (*Calling Cutler over.*) Levee's got his eyes in the wrong place. You better school him, Cutler.

CUTLER: Come on, Levee . . . let's get ready to play! Get your mind on your work!

IRVIN: (*Over speaker.*) Okay, boys, we're gonna do "Moonshine Blues" first. "Moonshine Blues," Ma.

MA RAINEY: I ain't doing no "Moonshine" nothing. I'm doing the "Black Bottom" first. Come on, Sylvester.

(*To Irvin.*)

Where's Sylvester's mike? You need a mike for Sylvester. Irvin . . . get him a mike.

IRVIN: Uh . . . Ma, the boys say he can't do it. We'll have to do Levee's version.

MA RAINEY: What you mean he can't do it? Who say he can't do it? What boys say he can't do it?

IRVIN: The band, Ma . . . the boys in the band.

MA RAINEY: What band? The band work for me! I say what goes! Cutler, what's he talking about? Levee, this some of your shit?

IRVIN: He stutters, Ma. They say he stutters.

MA RAINEY: I don't care if he do. I promised the boy he could do the part . . . and he's gonna do it! That's all there is to it. He don't stutter all the time. Get a microphone down here for him.

IRVIN: Ma, we don't have time. We can't . . .

MA RAINEY: If you wanna make a record, you gonna find time. I ain't playing with you, Irvin. I can walk out of here and go back to my tour. I got plenty fans. I don't need to go through all of this. Just go and get the boy a microphone.

(*Irvin and Sturdyvant consult in the booth, Irvin exits.*)

STURDYVANT: All right, Ma . . . we'll get him a microphone. But if he messes up . . . He's only getting one chance The cost . . .

MA RAINEY: Damn the cost. You always talking about the cost. I make more money for this outfit than anybody else you got put together. If he messes up he'll just do it till he gets it right. Levee, I know you had something to do with this. You better watch yourself.

LEVEE: It was Cutler!

SYLVESTER: It was you! You the only one m-m-mad about it.

LEVEE: The boy stutter. He can't do the part. Everybody see that. I don't know why you want the boy to do the part no ways.

MA RAINEY: Well, can or can't . . . he's gonna do it! You ain't got nothing to do with it!

LEVEE: I don't care what you do! He can sing the whole goddamned song for all I care!

MA RAINEY: Well, all right. Thank you.

(*Irvin enters with a microphone and hooks it up. He exits to the control booth.*)

MA RAINEY: Come on, Sylvester. You just stand here and hold your hands like I told you. Just remember the words and say them . . . That's all there is to it. Don't worry about messing up. If you mess up, we'll do it again. Now, let me hear you say it. Play for him, Cutler.

CUTLER: One . . . two . . . you know what to do.

(*The band begins to play and Sylvester curls his fingers and clasps his hands together in front of his chest, pulling in opposite directions as he says his, lines.*)

SYLVESTER: "All right, boys, you d-d-done s-s-seen the best . . .

(*Levee stops playing.*)

Now I'm g-g-g-gonna show you the rest . . . Ma R-r-rainey's gonna show you her b-b-b-black b-b-b-bottom."

(*The rest of the band stops playing.*)

MA RAINEY: That's all right. That's real good. You take your time, you'll get it right.

STURDYVANT: (*Over speaker.*) Listen, Ma . . . now, when you come in, don't wait so long to come in. Don't take so long on the intro, huh?

MA RAINEY: Sturdyvant, don't you go trying to tell me how to sing, You just take care of that up there and let me take care of this down here. Where's my Coke?

IRVIN: Okay, Ma. We're all set up to go up here. "Ma Rainey's Black Bottom," boys.

MA RAINEY: Where's my Coke? I need a Coke. You ain't got no Coke down here? Where's my Coke?

IRVIN: What's the matter, Ma? What's . . .

MA RAINEY: Where's my Coke? I need a Coca-Cola.

IRVIN: Uh . . . Ma, look, I forgot the Coke, huh? Let's do it without it, huh? Just this one song. What say, boys?

MA RAINEY: Damn what the band say! You know I don't sing nothing without my Coca-Cola!

STURDYVANT: We don't have any, Ma. There's no Coca-Cola here. We're all set up and we'll just go ahead and . . .

MA RAINEY: You supposed to have Coca-Cola. Irvin knew that. I ain't singing nothing without my Coca-Cola!

(*She walks away from the mike, singing to herself. Sturdyvant enters from the control booth.*)

STURDYVANT: Now, just a minute here, Ma. You come in an hour late . . . we're way behind schedule as it is . . . the band is set up and ready to go . . . I'm burning my lights . . . I've turned up the heat . . . We're ready to make a record and what? You decide you want a Coca-Cola?

MA RAINEY: Sturdyvant, get out of my face.

(*Irvin enters.*)

Irvin . . . I told you keep him away from me.

IRVIN: Mel, I'll handle it.

STURDYVANT: I'm tired of her nonsense, Irv. I'm not gonna put up with this!

IRVIN: Let me handle it, Mel. I know how to handle her.

(*Irvin to Ma Rainey.*)

Look, Ma . . . I'll call down to the deli and get you a Coke. But let's get started, huh? Sylvester's standing there ready to go . . . the band's set up . . . let's do this one song, huh?

MA RAINEY: If you too cheap to buy me a Coke, I'll buy my own. Slow Drag! Sylvester, go with Slow Drag and get me a Coca-Cola.

(*Slow Drag comes over.*)

Slow Drag, walk down to that store on the corner and get me three bottles of Coca-Cola. Get out my face, Irvin. You all just wait until I get my Coke. It ain't gonna kill you.

IRVIN: Okay, Ma. Get your Coke, for Chrissakes! Get your Coke!

(*Irvin and Sturdyvant exit into the hallway followed by Slow Drag and Sylvester. Toledo, Cutler and Levee head for the band room.*)

MA RAINEY: Cutler, come here a minute. I want to talk to you.

(*Cutler crosses over somewhat reluctantly.*)

What's all this about "the boys in the band say"? I tells you what to do. I says what the matter is with the band. I say who can and can't do what.

CUTLER: We just say 'cause the boy stutter . . .

MA RAINEY: I know he stutters. Don't you think I know he stutters. This is what's gonna help him.

CUTLER: Well, how can he do the part if he stutters? You want him to stutter through it? We just thought it be easier to go on and let Levee do it like we planned.

MA RAINEY: I don't care if he stutters or not! He's doing the part and I don't wanna hear any more of this shit about what the band says. And I want you to find somebody to replace Levee when we get to Memphis. Levee ain't nothing but trouble.

CUTLER: Levee's all right. He plays good music when he puts his mind to it. He knows how to write music too.

MA RAINEY: I don't care what he know. He ain't nothing but bad news. Find somebody else. I know it was his idea about who to say who can do what.

(*Dussie Mae wanders over to where they are sitting.*)

Dussie Mae, go sit your behind down somewhere and quit flaunting yourself around.

DUSSIE MAE: I ain't doing nothing.

MA RAINEY: Well, just go on somewhere and stay out of the way.

CUTLER: I been meaning to ask you, Ma . . . about these songs. This "Moonshine Blues" . . . that's one of them songs Bessie Smith sang, I believes.

MA RAINEY: Bessie what? Ain't nobody thinking about Bessie. I taught Bessie. She ain't doing nothing but imitating me. What I care about Bessie? I don't care if she sell a million records. She got her people and I got mine. I don't care what nobody else do. Ma was the *first* and don't you forget it!

CUTLER: Ain't nobody said nothing about that. I just said that's the same song she sang.

MA RAINEY: I been doing this a long time. Ever since I was a little girl. I don't care what nobody else do. That's what gets me so mad with Irvin. White folks try to be put out with you all the time. Too cheap to buy me a Coca-Cola. I lets them know it, though. Ma don't stand for no shit. Wanna take my voice and trap it in them fancy boxes with all them buttons and dials . . . and then too cheap to buy me a Coca-Cola. And it don't cost but a nickel a bottle.

CUTLER: I knows what you mean about that.

MA RAINEY: They don't care nothing about me. All they want is my voice. Well, I done learned that, and they gonna treat me like I want to be treated no matter how much it hurt them. They back there now calling me all kinds of names . . . calling me everything but a child of god. But they can't do nothing else. They ain't got what they wanted yet. As soon as they get my voice down on them recording machines, then it's just like if I'd be some whore and they roll over and put their pants on. Ain't got no use for me then. I know what I'm talking about. You watch. Irvin right there with the rest of them. He don't care nothing about me either. He's been my manager for six years, always talking about sticking together, and the only time he had me in his house was to sing for some of his friends.

CUTLER: I know how they do.

MA RAINEY: If you colored and can make them some money, then you all right with them. Otherwise, you just a dog in the alley. I done made this company more money from my records than all the other recording artists they got put together. And they wanna balk about how much this session is costing them.

CUTLER: I don't see where it's costing them all what they say.

MA RAINEY: It ain't! I don't pay that kind of talk no mind.

(*The lights go down on the studio and come up on the band room. Toledo sits reading a newspaper. Levee sings and hums his song.*)

LEVEE: (*Singing.*)
You can shake it, you can break it
You can dance at any hall
You can slide across the floor
You'll never have to stall
My jelly, my roll,
Sweet Mama, don't you let it fall.

Wait till Sturdyvant hear me play that! I'm talking about some real music, Toledo! I'm talking about *real* music!

(*The door opens and Dussie Mae enters.*)

Hey, mama! Come on in.

DUSSIE MAE: Oh, hi! I just wanted to see what it looks like down here.

LEVEE: Well, come on in . . . I don't bite.

DUSSIE MAE: I didn't know you could really write music. I thought you was just jiving me at the club last night.

LEVEE: Naw, baby . . . I knows how to write music. I done give Mr. Sturdyvant some of my songs and he says he's gonna let me record them. Ask Toledo. I'm gonna have my own band! Toledo, ain't I give Mr. Sturdyvant some of my songs I wrote?

TOLEDO: Don't get Toledo mixed up in nothing.

(*He exits.*)

DUSSIE MAE: You gonna get your own band sure enough?

LEVEE: That's right! Levee Green and his Footstompers.

DUSSIE MAE: That's real nice.

LEVEE: That's what I was trying to tell you last night. A man what's gonna get his own band need to have a woman like you.

DUSSIE MAE: A woman like me wants somebody to bring it and put it in my hand. I don't need nobody wanna get something for nothing and leave me standing in my door.

LEVEE: That ain't Levee's style, sugar. I got more style than that. I knows how to treat a woman. Buy her presents and things . . . treat her like she wants to be treated.

DUSSIE MAE: That's what they all say . . . till it come time to be buying the presents.

LEVEE: When we get down to Memphis, I'm gonna show you what I'm talking about. I'm gonna take you out and show you a good time. Show you Levee knows how to treat a woman.

DUSSIE MAE: When you getting your own band?

LEVEE: (*Moves closer to slip his arm around her.*) Soon as Mr. Sturdyvant say. I done got my fellows already picked out. Getting me some good fellows know how to play real sweet music.

DUSSIE MAE: (*Moves away.*) Go on now, I don't go for all that pawing and stuff. When you get your own band, maybe we can see about this stuff you talking.

LEVEE: (*Moving toward her.*) I just wanna show you I know what the women like. They don't call me Sweet Lemonade for nothing.

(*Levee takes her in his arms and attempts to kiss her.*)

DUSSIE MAE: Stop it now. Somebody's gonna come in here.

LEVEE: Naw they ain't. Look here, sugar . . . what I wanna know is . . . can I introduce my red rooster to your brown hen?

DUSSIE MAE: You get your band, then we'll see if that rooster know how to crow.

(*He grinds up against her and feels her buttocks.*)

LEVEE: Now I know why my grandpappy sat on the back porch with his straight razor when grandma hung out the wash.

DUSSIE MAE: Nigger, you crazy!

LEVEE: I bet you sound like the midnight train from Alabama when it crosses the Mason-Dixon line.

DUSSIE MAE: How's you get so crazy?

LEVEE: It's women like you . . . drives me that way.

(*He moves to kiss her as the lights go down in the band room and up in the studio. Ma Rainey sits with Cutler and Toledo.*)

MA RAINEY: It sure done got quiet in here. I never could stand no silence. I always got to have some music going on in my head somewhere. It keeps things balanced. Music will do that. It fills things up. The more music you got in the world, the fuller it is.

CUTLER: I can agree with that. I got to have my music too.

MA RAINEY: White folks don't understand about the blues. They hear it come out, but they don't know how it got there. They don't understand that's life's way of talking. You don't sing to feel better. You sing 'cause that's a way of understanding life.

CUTLER: That's right. You get that understanding and you done got a grip on life to where you can hold your head up and go on to see what else life got to offer.

MA RAINEY: The blues help you get out of bed in the morning. You get up knowing you ain't alone. There's something else in the world. Something's been added by that song. This be an empty world without the blues. I take that emptiness and try to fill it up with something.

TOLEDO: You fill it up with something the people can't be without, Ma. That's why they call you the Mother of the Blues. You fill up that emptiness in a way ain't nobody ever thought of doing before. And now they can't be without it.

MA RAINEY: I ain't started the blues way of singing. The blues always been here.

CUTLER: In the church sometimes you find that way of singing. They got blues in the church.

MA RAINEY: They say I started it . . . but I didn't. I just helped it out. Filled up that empty space a little bit. That's all. But if they wanna call me the Mother of the Blues, that's all right with me. It don't hurt none.

(*Slow Drag and Sylvester enter with the Cokes.*)

It sure took you long enough. That store ain't but on the corner.

SLOW DRAG: That one was closed. We had to find another one.

MA RAINEY: Sylvester, go and find Mr. Irvin and tell him we ready to go.

(*Sylvester exits. The lights in the band room come up while the lights in the studio stay on. Levee and Dussie Mae are kissing. Slow Drag enters. They break their embrace. Dussie Mae straightens up her clothes.*)

SLOW DRAG: Cold out. I just wanted to warm up with a little sip.

(*He goes to his locker, takes out his bottle and drinks.*)

Ma got her Coke, Levee. We about ready to start.

(*Slow Drag exits. Levee attempts to kiss Dussie Mae again.*)

DUSSIE MAE: No . . . Come on! I got to go. You gonna get me in trouble.

(*She pulls away and exits up the stairs. Levee watches after her.*)

LEVEE: Good God! Happy birthday to the lady with the cakes!

(*The lights go down in the band room and come up in the studio. Ma Rainey drinks her Coke. Levee enters from the band room. The musicians take their places. Sylvester stands by his mike. Irvin and Sturdyvant look on from the control booth.*)

IRVIN: We're all set up here, Ma. We're all set to go. You ready down there?

MA RAINEY: Sylvester you just remember your part and say it. That's all there is to it.

(*To Irvin.*)

Yeah, we ready.

IRVIN: Okay, boys. "Ma Rainey's Black Bottom." Take one.

CUTLER: One . . . two . . . You know what to do.

(*The band plays.*)

SYLVESTER: All right boys, you d-d-d-done s-s-seen the rest. . . .

IRVIN: Hold it!

(*The band stops. Sturdyvant changes the recording disk and nods to Irvin.*)

Okay. Take two.

CUTLER: One . . . two . . . You know what to do.

(*The band plays.*)

SYLVESTER: All right, boys, you done seen the rest . . . now I'm gonna show you the best. Ma Rainey's g-g-g-gonna s-s-show you her b-b-black bottom.

IRVIN: Hold it! Hold it!

(*The band stops. Sturdyvant changes the recording disk.*)

Okay. Take Three. Ma, let's do it without the intro, huh? No voice intro . . . you just come in singing.

MA RAINEY: Irvin, I done told you . . . the boy's gonna do the part. He don't stutter all the time. Just give him a chance. Sylvester, hold your hands like I told you and just relax. Just relax and concentrate.

IRVIN: All right. Take three.

CUTLER: One . . . Two . . . You know what to do.

(*The band plays.*)

SYLVESTER: All right, boys, you done seen the rest . . . now, I'm gonna show you the best. Ma Rainey's gonna show you her black bottom."

MA RAINEY: (*Singing.*)

Way down south in Alabamy
I got a friend they call dancing Sammy
Who's crazy about all the latest dances
Black Bottom stomping, two babies prancing

The other night at a swell affair
As soon as the boys found out that I was there
They said, come on, Ma, let's go to the cabaret.
When I got there, you ought to hear them say,

I want to see the dance you call the black bottom
I want to learn that dance
I want to see the dance you call your big black
    bottom
It'll put you in a trance.

All the boys in the neighborhood
They say your black bottom is really good
Come on and show me your black bottom
I want to learn that dance

I want to see the dance you call the black bottom
I want to learn that dance
Come on and show the dance you call your big
    black bottom
It puts you in a trance.

Early last morning about the break of day
Grandpa told my grandma, I heard him say,
Get up and show your old man your black bottom
I want to learn that dance

(*Instrumental break.*)

I done showed you all my black bottom
You ought to learn that dance.

IRVIN: Okay, that's good, Ma. That sounded great! Good job, boys!

MA RAINEY: (*To Sylvester.*) See! I told you. I knew you could do it. You just have to put your mind to it. Didn't he do good, Cutler? Sound real good. I told him he could do it.

CUTLER: He sure did. He did better than I thought he was gonna do.

IRVIN: (*Entering to remove Sylvester's mike.*) Okay,

boys . . . Ma . . . let's do "Moonshine Blues" next, huh? "Moonshine Blues," boys.

STURDYVANT: (*over speaker.*) Irv! Something's wrong down there. We don't have it right.

IRVIN: What? What's the matter Mel . . .

STURDYVANT: We don't have it right. Something happened. We don't have the goddamn song recorded!

IRVIN: What's the matter? Mel, what happened? You sure you don't have nothing?

STURDYVANT: Check that mike, huh, Irv. It's the kid's mike. Something's wrong with the mike. We've got everything all screwed up here.

IRVIN: Christ almighty! Ma, we got to do it again. We don't have it. We didn't record the song.

MA RAINEY: What you mean you didn't record it? What was you and Sturdyvant doing up there?

IRVIN: (*Following the mike wire.*) Here . . . Levee must have kicked the plug out.

LEVEE: I ain't done nothing: I ain't kicked nothing!

SLOW DRAG: If Levee had his mind on what he's doing . . .

MA RAINEY: Levee, if it ain't one thing, it's another. You better straighten yourself up!

LEVEE: Hell . . . it ain't my fault. I ain't done nothing!

STURDYVANT: What's the matter with that mike, Irv? What's the problem?

IRVIN: It's the cord, Mel. The cord's all chewed up. We need another cord.

MA RAINEY: This is the most disorganized . . . Irvin, I'm going home! Come on. Come on, Dussie.

(*Ma Rainey walks past Sturdyvant as he enters from the control booth. She exits offstage to get her coat.*)

STURDYVANT: (*To Irvin.*) Where's she going?

IRVIN: She said she's going home.

STURDYVANT: Irvin, you get her! If she walks out of here . . .

(*Ma Rainey enters carrying her and Dussie Mae's coat.*)

MA RAINEY: Come on, Sylvester.

IRVIN: (*Helping her with her coat.*) Ma . . . Ma . . . listen. Fifteen minutes! All I ask is fifteen minutes!

MA RAINEY: Come on, Sylvester, get your coat.

STURDYVANT: Ma, if you walk out of this studio . . .

IRVIN: Fifteen minutes, Ma!

STURDYVANT: You'll be through . . . washed up! If you walk out on me . . .

IRVIN: Mel, for Chrissakes, shut up and let me handle it!

(*He goes after Ma Rainey, who has started for the door.*)

Ma, listen. These records are gonna be hits! They're gonna sell like crazy! Hell, even Sylvester will be a star. Fifteen minutes. That's all, I'm asking! Fifteen minutes.

MA RAINEY: (*Crosses to a chair and sits with her coat on.*) Fifteen minutes! You hear me, Irvin? Fifteen minutes . . . and then I'm gonna take my black bottom on back down to Georgia. Fifteen minutes. Then Madame Rainey is leaving!

IRVIN: (*Kisses her.*) All right, Ma . . . fifteen minutes. I

Top: Theresa Merritt as Ma Rainey in the original 1984 Yale Repertory Theatre production.
Bottom: The 2003 Broadway production with Whoopi Goldberg as Ma Rainey.

promise. (*To the band.*) You boys go ahead and take a break. Fifteen minutes and we'll be ready to go.

CUTLER: Slow Drag, you got any of that bourbon left?

SLOW DRAG: Yeah, there's some down there.

CUTLER: I could use a little nip.

(*Cutler and Slow Drag exit to the band room, followed by Levee and Toledo. The lights go down in the studio and up in the band room.*)

SLOW DRAG: Don't make me no difference if she leave or not. I was kinda hoping she would leave.

CUTLER: I'm like Mr. Irvin . . . After all this time we done put in here, it's best to go ahead and get something out of it.

TOLEDO: Ma gonna do what she wanna do, that's for sure. If I was Mr. Irvin, I'd best go on and get them cords and things hooked up right. And I wouldn't take no longer than fifteen minutes doing it.

CUTLER: If Levee had his mind on his work, we wouldn't be in this fix. We'd be up there finishing up. Now we got to go back and see if that boy get that part right. Ain't no telling if he ever get that right again in his life.

LEVEE: Hey, Levee ain't done nothing!

SLOW DRAG: Levee up there got one eye on the gal and the other on his trumpet.

CUTLER: Nigger, don't you know that's Ma's gal?

LEVEE: I don't care whose gal it is. I ain't done nothing to her. I just talk to her like I talk to anybody else.

CUTLER: Well, that being Ma's gal, and that being that boy's gal, is one and two different things. The boy is liable to kill you . . . but you' ass gonna be out there scraping the concrete looking for a job if you messing with Ma's gal.

LEVEE: How am I messing with her? I ain't done nothing to the gal. I just asked her her name. Now, if you telling me I can't do that, then Ma will just have to go to hell.

CUTLER: All I can do is warn you.

SLOW DRAG: Let him hang himself, Cutler. Let him string his neck out.

LEVEE: I ain't done nothing to the gal! You all talk like I done went and done something to her. Leave me go with my business. . . .

CUTLER: I'm through with it. Try and talk to a fool . . .

TOLEDO: Some mens got it worse than others . . . this foolishness I'm talking about. Some mens is excited to be fools. That excitement is something else. I know about it. I done experienced it. It makes you feel good to be a fool. But it don't last long. It's over in a minute. Then you got to tend with the consequences. You got to tend with what comes after. That's when you wish you had learned something about it.

LEVEE: That's the best sense you made all day. Talking about being a fool. That's the only sensible thing you said today. Admitting you was a fool.

TOLEDO: I admits it, all right. Ain't nothing wrong with it. I done been a little bit of everything.

LEVEE: Now you're talking. You's as big a fool as they make.

TOLEDO: Gonna be a bit more things before I'm finished with it. Gonna be foolish again. But I ain't never been the same fool twice. I might be a different kind of fool, but I ain't gonna be the same fool twice. That's where we parts ways.

SLOW DRAG: Toledo, you done been a fool about a woman?

TOLEDO: Sure, Sure I have. Same as everybody.

SLOW DRAG: Hell, I ain't never seen you mess with no woman. I thought them books was your woman.

TOLEDO: Sure I messed with them. Done messed with a whole heap of them. And gonna mess with some more. But I ain't gonna be no fool about them. What you think? I done come in the world full-grown, with my head in a book? I done been young. Married. Got kids. I done been around and I done loved women to where you shake in your shoes just at the sight of them. Feel it all up and down your spine.

SLOW DRAG: I didn't know you was married.

TOLEDO: Sure. Legally. I been married legally. Got the papers and all. I done been through life. Made my marks. Followed some signs on the road. Ignored some others. I done been all through it. I touched and been touched by it. But I ain't never been the same fool twice. That's what I can say.

LEVEE: But you been a fool. That's what counts. Talking about I'm a fool for asking the gal her name and here you is one yourself.

TOLEDO: Now, I married a woman. A good woman. To this day I can't say she wasn't a good woman. I can't say nothing bad about her. I married that woman with all the good graces and intentions of being hooked up and bound to her for the rest of my life. I was looking for her to put me in my grave. But, you see . . . it ain't all the time what you' intentions and wishes are. She went out and joined the church. All right. There ain't nothing wrong with that. A good Christian woman going to church and wanna do right by her god. There ain't nothing wrong with that. But she got up there, got to seeing them good Christian mens and wondering why I ain't like that. Soon she figure she got a heathen on her hands. She figured she couldn't live like that. The church was more important than I was. So she left. Packed up one day and moved out. To this day I ain't never said another word to her. Come home one day and my house was empty! And I sat down and figured out that I was a fool not to see that she needed something that I wasn't giving her. Else she wouldn't have been up there at the church in the first place. I ain't blaming her. I just said it wasn't gonna happen to me again. So, yeah, Toledo been a fool about a woman. That's part of making life.

CUTLER: Well, yeah, I been a fool too. Everybody done been a fool once or twice. But, you see, Toledo, what you call a fool and what I call a fool is two different things. I can't see where you was being a fool for that.

You ain't done nothing foolish. You can't help what happened, and I wouldn't call you a fool for it. A fool is responsible for what happens to him. A fool cause it to happen. Like Levee . . . if he keeps messing with Ma's gal and his feet be out there scraping the ground. That's a fool.

LEVEE: Ain't nothing gonna happen to Levee. Levee ain't gonna let nothing happen to him. Now, I'm gonna say it again. I asked the gal her name. That's all I done. And if that's being a fool, then you looking at the biggest fool in the world . . . 'cause I sure as hell asked her.

SLOW DRAG: You just better not let Ma see you ask her. That's what the man's trying to tell you.

LEVEE: I don't need nobody to tell me nothing.

CUTLER: Well, Toledo, all I gots to say is that from the looks of it . . . from your story . . . I don't think life did you fair.

TOLEDO: Oh, life is fair. It's just in the taking what it gives you.

LEVEE: Life ain't shit. You can put it in a paper bag and carry it around with you. It ain't got no balls. Now, death . . . death got some style! Death will kick your ass and make you wish you never been born! That's how bad death is! But you can rule over life. Life ain't nothing.

TOLEDO: Cutler, how's your brother doing?

CUTLER: Who, Nevada? Oh, he's doing all right. Staying in St. Louis. Got a bunch of kids, last I heard.

TOLEDO: Me and him was all right with each other. Done a lot of farming together down in Plattsville.

CUTLER: Yeah, I know you all was tight. He in St. Louis now. Running an elevator, last I hear about it.

SLOW DRAG: That's better than stepping in muleshit.

TOLEDO: Oh, I don't know now. I liked farming. Get out there in the sun . . . smell that dirt. Be out there by yourself . . . nice and peaceful. Yeah, farming was all right by me. Some times I think I'd like to get me a little old place . . . but I done got too old to be following behind one of them balky mules now.

LEVEE: Nigger talking about life is fair. And ain't got a pot to piss in.

TOLEDO: See, now, I'm gonna tell you something. A nigger gonna be dissatisfed no matter what. Give a nigger some bread and butter . . . and he'll cry 'cause he ain't got no jelly. Give him some jelly, and he'll cry 'cause he ain't got no knife to put it on with. If there's one thing I done learned in this life, it's that you can't satisfy a nigger no matter what you do. A nigger's gonna make his own dissatisfaction.

LEVEE: Niggers got a right to be dissatisfed. Is you gonna be satisfied with a bone somebody done throwed you when you see them eating the whole hog?

TOLEDO: You lucky they let you be an entertainer. They ain't got to accept your way of entertaining. You lucky and don't even know it. You's entertaining and the rest of the people is hauling wood. That's the only kind of job for the colored man.

SLOW DRAG: Ain't nothing wrong with hauling wood. I done hauled plenty wood. My daddy used to haul wood. Ain't nothing wrong with that. That's honest work.

LEVEE: That ain't what I'm talking about. I ain't talking about hauling no wood. I'm talking about being satisfied with a bone somebody done throwed you. That's what's the matter with you all. You satisfied sitting in one place. You got to move on down the road from where you sitting . . . and all the time you got to keep an eye out for that devil who's looking to buy up souls. And hope you get lucky and find him!

CUTLER: I done told you about that blasphemy. Taking about selling your soul to the devil.

TOLEDO: We done the same thing, Cutler. There ain't no difference. We done sold Africa for the price of tomatoes. We done sold ourselves to the white man in order to be like him. Look at the way you dressed . . . That ain't African. That's the white man. We trying to be just like him. We done sold who we are in order to become someone else. We's imitation white men.

CUTLER: What else we gonna be, living over here?

LEVEE: I'm Levee. Just me. I ain't no imitation nothing!

SLOW DRAG: You can't change who you are by how you dress. That's what I got to say.

TOLEDO: It ain't all how you dress, It's how you act, how you see the world. It's how you follow life.

LEVEE: It don't matter what you talking about. I ain't no imitation white man. And I don't want to be no white man. As soon as I get my band together and make them records like Mr. Sturdyvant done told me I can make, I'm gonna be like Ma and tell the white man just what he can do. Ma tell Mr. Irvin she gonna leave . . . and Mr. Irvin get down on his knees and beg her to stay! That's the way I'm gonna be! Make the white man respect me!

CUTLER: The white man don't care nothing about Ma. The colored folks made Ma a star. White folks don't care nothing about who she is . . . what kind of music she make.

SLOW DRAG: That's the truth about that. You let her go down to one of them white-folks hotels and see how big she is.

CUTLER: Hell, she ain't got to do that. She can't even get a cab up here in the North. I'm gonna tell you something. Reverend Gates . . . you know Reverend Gates? . . . Slow Drag know who I'm talking about. Reverend Gates . . . now I'm gonna show you how this go where the white man don't care a thing about who you is. Reverend Gates was coming from Tallahassee to Atlanta, going to see his sister, who was sick at that time with the consumption. The train come up through Thomasville, then past Moultrie, and stopped in this little town called Sigsbee . . .

LEVEE: You can stop telling that right there! That train don't stop in Sigsbee. I know what train you talking about. That train got four stops before it reach

Macon to go on to Atlanta. One in Thomasville, one in Moultrie, one in Cordele . . . and it stop in Centerville.

CUTLER: Nigger, I know what I'm talking about. You gonna tell me where the train stop?

LEVEE: Hell, yeah, if you talking about it stop in Sigsbee. I'm gonna tell you the truth.

CUTLER: I'm talking about *this* train! I don't know what train you been riding. I'm talking about *this* train!

LEVEE: Ain't but one train. Ain't but one train come out of Tallahassee heading north to Atlanta, and it don't stop at Sigsbee. Tell him, Toledo . . . that train don't stop at Sigsbee. The only train that stops at Sigsbee is the Yazoo Delta, and you have to transfer at Moultrie to get it!

CUTLER: Well, hell, maybe that what he done! I don't know. I'm just telling you the man got off the train at Sigsbee . . .

LEVEE: All right . . . you telling it. Tell it your way. Just make up anything.

SLOW DRAG: Levee, leave the man alone and let him finish.

CUTLER: I ain't paying Levee no never mind.

LEVEE: Go on and tell it your way.

CUTLER: Anyway . . . Reverend Gates got off this train in Sigsbee. The train done stopped there and he figured he'd get off and check the schedule to be sure he arrive in time for somebody to pick him up. All right. While he's there checking the schedule, it come upon him that he had to go to the bathroom. Now, they ain't had no colored rest rooms at the station. The only colored rest room is an outhouse they got sitting way back two hundred yards or so from the station. All right. He in the outhouse and the train go off and leave him there. He don't know nothing about this town. Ain't never been there before—in fact, ain't never even heard of it before.

LEVEE: I heard of it! I know just where it's at . . . and he ain't got off no train coming out of Tallahassee in Sigsbee!

CUTLER: The man standing there, trying to figure out what he's gonna do . . . where this train done left him in this strange town. It started getting dark. He see where the sun's getting low in the sky and he's trying to figure out what he's gonna do, when he noticed a couple of white fellows standing across the street from this station. Just standing there, watching him. And then two or three more come up and joined the other one. He look around, ain't seen no colored folks nowhere. He didn't know what was getting in these here fellows' minds, so he commence to walking. He ain't knowed where he was going. He just walking down the railroad tracks when he hear them call him. "Hey, nigger!" See, just like that. "Hey, nigger!" He kept on walking. They called him some more and he just keep walking. Just going down the tracks. And then he heard a gunshot where somebody done fired a gun in the air. He stopped then, you know.

TOLEDO: You don't even have to tell me no more. I know the facts of it. I done heard the same story a hundred times. It happened to me too. Same thing.

CUTLER: Naw, I'm gonna show you how the white folks don't care nothing about who or what you is. They crowded around him. These gang of mens made a circle around him. Now, he's standing there, you understand . . . got his cross around his neck like them preachers wear. Had his little Bible with him what he carry all the time. So they crowd on around him and one of them ask who he is. He told them he was Reverend Gates and that he was going to see his sister who was sick and the train left without him. And they said, "Yeah, nigger . . . but can you dance?" He looked at them and commenced to dancing. One of them reached up and tore his cross off his neck. Said he was committing a heresy by dancing with a cross and Bible. Took his Bible and tore it up and had him dancing till they got tired of watching him.

SLOW DRAG: White folks ain't never had no respect for the colored minister.

CUTLER: That's the only way he got out of there alive . . . was to dance. Ain't even had no respect for a man of God! Wanna make him into a clown. Reverend Gates sat right in my house and told me that story from his own mouth. So . . . the white folks don't care nothing about Ma Rainey. She's just another nigger who they can use to make some money.

LEVEE: What I wants to know is . . . if he's a man of God, then where the hell was God when all of this was going on? Why wasn't God looking out for him. Why didn't God strike down them crackers with some of this lightning you talk about to me?

CUTLER: Levee, you gonna burn in hell.

LEVEE: What I care about burning in hell? You talk like a fool . . . burning in hell. Why didn't God strike some of them crackers down? Tell me that! That's the question! Don't come telling me this burning-in-hell shit! He a man of God . . . why didn't God strike some of them crackers down? I'll tell you why! I'll tell you the truth! It's sitting out there as plain as day! 'Cause he a white man's God. That's why! God ain't never listened to no nigger's prayers. God take a nigger's prayers and throw them in the garbage. God don't pay niggers no mind. In fact . . . God hate niggers! Hate them with all the fury in his heart. Jesus don't love you, nigger! Jesus hate your black ass! Come talking that shit to me. Talking about burning in hell! God can kiss my ass.

(*Cutler can stand no more. He jumps up and punches Levee in the mouth. The force of the blow knocks Levee down and Cutler jumps on him.*)

CUTLER: You worthless . . . That's my God! That's my God! That's my God! You wanna blaspheme my God!

(*Toledo and Slow Drag grab Cutler and try to pull him off Levee.*)

SLOW DRAG: Come on, Cutler . . . let it go! It don't mean nothing!

(*Cutler has Levee down on the floor and pounds on him with a fury.*)

CUTLER: Wanna blaspheme my God! You worthless . . . talking about my God!

(*Toledo and Slow Drag succeed in pulling Cutler off Levee, who is bleeding at the nose and mouth.*)

LEVEE: Naw, let him go! Let him go!

(*He pulls out a knife.*)

That's your God, huh? That's your God, huh? Is that right? Your God, huh? All right. I'm gonna give your God a chance. I'm gonna give your God a chance. I'm gonna give him a chance to save your black ass.

(*Levee circles Cutler with the knife. Cutler picks up a chair to protect himself.*)

TOLEDO: Come on, Levee . . . put the knife up!
LEVEE: Stay out of this, Toledo!
TOLEDO: That ain't no way to solve nothing.

(*Levee alternately swipes at Cutler during the following.*)

LEVEE: I'm calling Cutler's God! I'm talking to Cutler's God! You hear me? Cutler's God! I'm calling Cutler's God. Come on and save this nigger! Strike me down before I cut his throat!
SLOW DRAG: Watch him, Cutler! Put that knife up, Levee!
LEVEE: (*To Cutler.*) I'm calling your God! I'm gonna give him a chance to save you! I'm calling your God! We gonna find out whose God he is!
CUTLER: You gonna burn in hell, nigger!
LEVEE: Cutler's God! Come on and save this nigger! Come on and save him like you did my mama! Save him like you did my mama! I heard her when she called you! I heard her when she said, "Lord, have mercy! Jesus, help me! Please, God, have mercy on me, Lord Jesus, help me!" And did you turn your back? Did you turn your back, motherfucker? Did you turn your back?

(*Levee becomes so caught up in his dialogue with God that he forgets about Cutler and begins to stab upward in the air, trying to reach God.*)

Come on! Come on and turn your back on me! Turn your back on me! Come on! Where is you? Come on and turn your back on me! Turn your back on me, motherfucker! I'll cut your heart out! Come on, turn your back on me! Come on! What's the matter? Where is you? Come on and turn your back on me! Come on, what you scared of? Turn your back on me! Come on! Coward, motherfucker!

(*Levee folds his knife and stands triumphantly.*)

Your God ain't shit, Cutler.

(*The lights fade to black.*)

MA RAINEY: (*Singing.*)
Ah, you hear me talking to you
I don't bite my tongue
You wants to be my man
You got to fetch it with you when you come.

(*Lights come up in the studio. The last bars of the last song of the session are dying out.*)

IRVIN: (*Over speaker.*) Good! Wonderful! We have that, boys. Good session. That's great, Ma, We've got ourselves some winners.
TOLEDO: Well, I'm glad that's over.
MA RAINEY: Slow Drag, where you learn to play the bass at? You had it singing! I heard you! Had that bass jumping all over the place.
SLOW DRAG: I was following Toledo. Nigger got them long fingers striding all over the piano. I was trying to keep up with him.
TOLEDO: That's what you supposed to do, ain't it? Play the music. Ain't nothing abstract about it.
MA RAINEY: Cutler, you hear Slow Drag on that bass? He make it do what he want it to do! Spank it just like you spank a baby.
CUTLER: Don't be telling him that. Nigger's head get so big his hat won't fit him.
SLOW DRAG: If Cutler tune that guitar up, we would really have something.
CUTLER: You wouldn't know what a tuned-up guitar sounded like if you heard one.
TOLEDO: Cutler was talking. I heard him moaning. He was all up in it.
MA RAINEY: Levee . . . what is that you doing? Why you playing all them notes? You play ten notes for every one you supposed to play. It don't call for that.
LEVEE: You supposed to improvise on the theme. That's what I was doing.
MA RAINEY: You supposed to play the song the way I sing it. The way everybody else play it. You ain't supposed to go off by yourself and play what you want.
LEVEE: I was playing the song. I was playing it the way I felt it.
MA RAINEY: I couldn't keep up with what was going on. I'm trying to sing the song and you up there messing up my ear. That's what you was doing. Call yourself playing music.
LEVEE: Hey . . . I know what I'm doing. I know what I'm doing, all right. I know how to play music. You all back up and leave me alone about my music.
CUTLER: I done told you . . . it ain't about *your* music. It's about *Ma's* music.
MA RAINEY: That's all right, Cutler. I done told you what to do.
LEVEE: I don't care what you do. You supposed to improvise on the theme. Not play note for note the same thing over and over again.
MA RAINEY: You just better watch yourself. You hear me?

LEVEE: What I care what you or Cutler do? Come telling me to watch myself. What's that supposed to mean?

MA RAINEY: All right . . . you gonna find out what it means.

LEVEE: Go ahead and fire me. I don't care. I'm gonna get my own band anyway.

MA RAINEY: You keep messing with me.

LEVEE: Ain't nobody studying you. You ain't gonna do nothing to me. Ain't nobody gonna do nothing to Levee.

MA RAINEY: All right, nigger . . . you fired!

LEVEE: You think I care about being fired? I don't care nothing about that. You doing me a favor.

MA RAINEY: Cutler, Levee's out! He don't play in my band no more.

LEVEE: I'm fired . . . Good! Best thing that ever happened to me. I don't need this shit!

(*Levee exits to the band room. Irvin enters from the control booth.*)

MA RAINEY: Cutler, I'll see you back at the hotel.

IRVIN: Okay, boys . . . you can pack up. I'll get your money for you.

CUTLER: That's cash money, Mr. Irvin. I don't want no check.

IRVIN: I'll see what I can do. I can't promise you nothing.

CUTLER: As long as it ain't no check. I ain't got no use for a check.

IRVIN: I'll see what I can do, Cutler.

(*Cutler, Toledo, and Slow Drag exit to the band room.*)

Oh, Ma, listen . . . I talked to Sturdyvant, and he said . . . Now, I tried to talk him out of it . . . He said the best he can do is to take your twenty-five dollars of your money and give it to Sylvester.

MA RAINEY: Take what and do what? If I wanted the boy to have twenty-five dollars of my money, I'd give it to him. He supposed to get his own money. He supposed to get paid like everybody else.

IRVIN: Ma, I talked to him . . . He said . . .

MA RAINEY: Go talk to him again! Tell him if he don't pay that boy, he'll never make another record of mine again. Tell him that. You supposed to be my manager. All this talk about sticking together. Start sticking! Go on up there and get that boy his money!

IRVIN: Okay, Ma . . . I'll talk to him again. I'll see what I can do.

MA RAINEY: Ain't no see about it! You bring that boy's money back here!

(*Irvin exits. The lights stay on in the studio and come up in the band room. The men have their instruments packed and sit waiting for Irvin to come and pay them. Slow Drag has a pack of cards.*)

SLOW DRAG: Come on, Levee, let me show you a card trick.

LEVEE: I don't want to see no card trick. What you wanna show me for? Why you wanna bother me with that?

SLOW DRAG: I was just trying to be nice.

LEVEE: I don't need you to be nice to me. What I need you to be nice to me for? I ain't gonna be nice to you. I ain't even gonna let you be in my band no more.

SLOW DRAG: Toledo, let me show you a card trick.

CUTLER: I just hope Mr. Irvin don't bring no check down here. What the hell I'm gonna do with a check?

SLOW DRAG: All right now . . . pick a card. Any card . . . go on . . . take any of them. I'm gonna show you something.

TOLEDO: I agrees with you, Cutler. I don't want no check either.

CUTLER: It don't make no sense to give a nigger a check.

SLOW DRAG: Okay, now. Remember your card. Remember which one you got. Now . . . put it back in the deck. Anywhere you want. I'm gonna show you something.

(*Toledo puts the card in the deck.*)

You remember your card? All right. Now I'm gonna shuffle the deck. Now . . . I'm gonna show you what card you picked. Don't say nothing now. I'm gonna tell you what card you picked.

CUTLER: Slow Drag, that trick is as old as my mama.

SLOW DRAG: Naw, naw . . . wait a minute! I'm gonna show him his card . . . There it go! The six of diamonds. Ain't that your card? Ain't that it?

TOLEDO: Yeah, that's it . . . the six of diamonds.

SLOW DRAG: Told you! Told you I'd show him what it was!

(*The lights fade in the band room and come up full on the studio. Sturdyvant enters with Irvin.*)

STURDYVANT: Ma, is there something wrong? Is there a problem?

MA RAINEY: Sturdyvant, I want you to pay that boy his money.

STURDYVANT: Sure, Ma. I got it right here. Two hundred for you and twenty-five for the kid, right?

(*Sturdyvant hands the money to Irvin, who hands it to Ma Rainey and Sylvester.*)

Irvin misunderstood me. It was all a mistake. Irv made a mistake.

MA RAINEY: A mistake, huh?

IRVIN: Sure, Ma. I made a mistake. He's paid, right? I straightened it out.

MA RAINEY: The only mistake was when you found out I hadn't signed the release forms. That was the mistake. Come on, Sylvester.

(*She starts to exit.*)

STURDYVANT: Hey, Ma . . . come on, sign the forms, huh?

IRVIN: Ma . . . come on now.

MA RAINEY: Get your coat, Sylvester. Irvin, where's my car?

IRVIN: It's right out front, Ma, Here . . . I got the keys right here. Come on, sign the forms, huh?

MA RAINEY: Irvin, give me my car keys!

IRVIN: Sure, Ma . . . just sign the forms, huh?

(*He gives her the keys, expecting a trade-off.*)

MA RAINEY: Send them to my address and I'll get around to them.

IRVIN: Come on, Ma . . . I took care of everything, right? I straightened everything out.

MA RAINEY: Give me the pen, Irvin.

(*She signs the forms.*)

You tell Sturdyvant . . . one more mistake like that and I can make my records someplace else.

(*She turns to exit.*)

Sylvester, straighten up your clothes. Come on, Dussie Mae.

(*She exits, followed by Dussie Mae and Sylvester. The lights go down in the studio and come up on the band room.*)

CUTLER: I know what's keeping him so long. He up there writing out checks. You watch. I ain't gonna stand for it. He ain't gonna bring me no check down here. If he do, he's gonna take it right back upstairs and get some cash.

TOLEDO: Don't get yourself all worked up about it. Wait and see. Think positive.

CUTLER: I am thinking positive. He positively gonna give me some cash. Man give me a check last time . . . you remember . . . we went all over Chicago trying to get it cashed. See a nigger with a check, the first thing they think is he done stole it someplace.

LEVEE: I ain't had no trouble cashing mine.

CUTLER: I don't visit no whorehouses.

LEVEE: You don't know about my business. So don't start nothing. I'm tired of you as it is. I ain't but two seconds off your ass no way.

TOLEDO: Don't you all start nothing now.

CUTLER: What the hell I care what you tired of. I wasn't even talking to you. I was talking to this man right here.

(*Irvin and Sturdyvant enter.*)

IRVIN: Okay boys. Mr. Sturdyvant has your pay.

CUTLER: As long as it's cash money, Mr. Sturdyvant. 'Cause I have too much trouble trying to cash a check.

STURDYVANT: Oh, yes . . . I'm aware of that. Mr. Irvin told me you boys prefer cash, and that's what I have for you.

(*He starts handing out the money.*)

That was a good session you boys put in . . . That's twenty-five for you. Yessir, you boys really know your business and we are going to . . . Twenty-five for you . . . We are going to get you back in here real

soon . . . twenty-five . . . and have another session so you can make some more money . . . and twenty-five for you. Okay, thank you, boys. You can get your things together and Mr. Irvin will make sure you find your way out.

IRVIN: I'll be out front when you get your things together, Cutler.

(*Irvin exits. Sturdyvant starts to follow.*)

LEVEE: Mr. Sturdyvant, sir. About them songs I give you? . . .

STURDYVANT: Oh, yes, . . . uh . . . Levee. About them songs you gave me. I've thought about it and I just don't think the people will buy them. They're not the type of songs we're looking for.

LEVEE: Mr. Sturdyvant, sir . . . I done got my band picked out and they's real good fellows. They knows how to play real good. I know if the peoples hear the music, they'll buy it.

STURDYVANT: Well, Levee, I'll be fair with you . . . but they're just not the right songs.

LEVEE: Mr. Sturdyvant, you got to understand about that music. That music is what the people is looking for. They's tired of jug-band music. They wants something that excites them. Something with some fire to it.

STURDYVANT: Okay, Levee. I'll tell you what I'll do, I'll give you five dollars a piece for them. Now that's the best I can do.

LEVEE: I don't want no five dollars, Mr. Sturdyvant. I wants to record them songs, like you say.

STURDYVANT: Well, Levee, like I say . . . they just aren't the kind of songs we're looking for.

LEVEE: Mr. Sturdyvant, you asked me to write them songs. Now, why didn't you tell me that before when I first give them to you? You told me you was gonna let me record them. What's the difference between then and now?

STURDYVANT: Well, look . . . I'll pay you for your trouble . . .

LEVEE: What's the difference, Mr. Sturdyvant? That's what I wanna know.

STURDYVANT: I had my fellows play your songs, and when I heard them, they just didn't sound like the kind of songs I'm looking for right now.

LEVEE: You got to hear *me* play them, Mr. Sturdyvant! You ain't heard *me* play them. That's what's gonna make them sound right.

STURDYVANT: Well, Levee, I don't doubt that really. It's just that . . . well, I don't think they'd sell like Ma's records. But I'll take them off your hands for you.

LEVEE: The people's tired of jug-band music, Mr. Sturdyvant. They wants something that's gonna excite them! They wants something with some fire! I don't know what fellows you had playing them songs . . . but if I could play them! I'd set them down in the people's lap! Now you told me I could record them songs!

STURDYVANT: Well, there's nothing I can do about that. Like I say, it's five dollars a piece. That's what I'll give you. I'm doing you a favor. Now, if you write any more, I'll help you out and take them off your hands. The price is five dollars apiece. Just like now.

(*He attempts to hand Levee the money, finally shoves it in Levee's coat pocket and is gone in a flash. Levee follows him to the door and it slams in his face. He takes the money from his pocket, balls it up and throws it on the floor. The other musicians silently gather up their belongings. Toledo walks past Levee and steps on his shoe.*)

LEVEE: Hey! Watch it . . . Shit Toledo! You stepped on my shoe!

TOLEDO: Excuse me there, Levee.

LEVEE: Look at that! Look at that! Nigger, you stepped on my shoe. What you do that for?

TOLEDO: I said I'm sorry.

LEVEE: Nigger gonna step on my goddamn shoe! You done fucked up my shoe! Look at that! Look at what you done to my shoe, nigger! I ain't stepped on your shoe! What you wanna step on my shoe for?

CUTLER: The man said he's sorry.

LEVEE: Sorry! How the hell he gonna be sorry after he gone ruint my shoe? Come talking about sorry!

(*Turns his attention back to Toledo.*)

Nigger, you stepped on my shoe! You know that!

(*Levee snatches his shoe off his foot and holds it up for Toledo to see.*)

See what you done done?

TOLEDO: What you want me to do about it? It's done now. I said excuse me.

LEVEE: Wanna go and fuck up my shoe like that. I ain't done nothing to your shoe. Look at this!

(*Toledo turns and continues to gather up his things. Levee spins him around by his shoulder.*)

LEVEE: Naw . . . naw . . . look what you done!

(*He shoves the shoe in Toledo's face.*)

Look at that! That's my shoe! Look at that! You did it! You did it! You fucked up my shoe! You stepped on my shoe with them raggedy-ass clodhoppers!

TOLEDO: Nigger, ain't nobody studying you and your

shoe! I said excuse me. If you can't accept that, then the hell with it. What you want me to do?

(*Levee is in a near rage, breathing hard. He is trying to get a grip on himself, as even he senses, or perhaps only he senses, he is about to lose control. He looks around, uncertain of what to do. Toledo has gone back to packing, as have Cutler and Slow Drag. They purposefully avoid looking at Levee in hopes he'll calm down if he doesn't have an audience. All the weight in the world suddenly falls on Levee and he rushes at Toledo with his knife in his hand.*)

LEVEE: Nigger, you stepped on my shoe!

(*He plunges the knife into Toledo's back up to the hilt. Toledo lets out a sound of surprise and agony. Cutler and Slow Drag freeze. Toledo falls backward with Levee, his hand still on the knife, holding him up. Levee is suddenly faced with the realization of what he has done. He shoves Toledo forward and takes a step back. Toledo slumps to the floor.*)

He . . . he stepped on my shoe. He did. Honest, Cutler, he stepped on my shoe. What he do that for? Toledo, what you do that for? Cutler, help me. He stepped on my shoe, Cutler.

(*He turns his attention to Toledo.*)

Toledo! Toledo, get up.

(*He crosses to Toledo and tries to pick him up.*)

It's okay, Toledo. Come on . . . I'll help you. Come on, stand up now. Levee'll help you.

(*Toledo is limp and heavy and awkward. He slumps back to the floor. Levee gets mad at him.*)

Don't look at me like that! Toledo! Nigger, don't look at me like that! I'm warning you, nigger! Close your eyes! Don't you look at me like that! (*He turns to Cutler*) Tell him to close his eyes. Cutler. Tell him don't look at me like that.

CUTLER: Slow Drag, get Mr. Irvin down here.

(*The sound of a trumpet is heard, Levee's trumpet, a muted trumpet struggling for the highest of possibilities and blowing pain and warning.*)

(*Black out.*)

COMMENTARY

Joan Herrington
The Development of *Ma Rainey's Black Bottom*   1998

Joan Herrington, professor at Western Michigan University, has published exten-
sively on August Wilson and other modern playwrights and directors. Her study of
the development of the script of Ma Rainey's Black Bottom *reminds us that play-*
writing is not just a matter of sitting down and writing dialogue. The process of
revision, which in the case of Wilson's play also involved the process of rethinking
the drama, can be complex and lengthy. In this play, Wilson's commitment to the
members of the band, who were hardly considered in the first draft, became the
center of the drama.

Ma Rainey was developed at the O'Neill Playwrights Conference in 1982. Then, in
April 1984, Lloyd Richards° directed a production of the play at the Yale Repertory Theatre. Six months later, *Ma Rainey's Black Bottom* opened on Broadway at
the Cort Theater. The play won the New York Drama Critics Circle Award for Best
American Play and was nominated for Drama Desk and Tony Awards. Critical
acclaim and audience enthusiasm rewarded Wilson for the painstaking revisions he
had made on his script during the course of its development.

    Ma Rainey's Black Bottom examines racism and the African American search
for identity within the context of the American music world of the 1920s. The
action of the play centers on a recording session by Ma Rainey and her band in a
Chicago studio. The characters are revealed in a series of scenes: Ma Rainey, Ma's
girl friend, Dussie Mae, and Ma's nephew Sylvester; the four band members,
Cutler, Slow Drag, Toledo, and Levee, around whom the play centers; Ma's manager, Irvin, and the recording studio owner, Sturdyvant. All afternoon the characters wait to lay down the music. Ultimately, the record is cut, but the exploitative
conditions in which the recording takes place lead to a violent confrontation.

    When Wilson returned to *Ma Rainey's Black Bottom* in 1981, with the realiza-
tion that the relationships of the band members were central to his story, he found
that Levee, the newest member of the band, emerged as the play's central character.
Ambitious and volatile, Levee has seen the destruction caused by racial oppression
but turns a blind eye to it now, knowing that the prize he covets — the opportunity
to write and record his songs with his own band — can only be awarded by the
white man. Levee is writing music in a new style and he wants Sturdyvant to produce it. So, Levee plays by the white man's rules and he loses.

    Ultimately, Levee realizes that he has accepted a society that refuses to recognize
his worth or allow him to contribute. His existence denied, he explodes as Wilson

---

Lloyd Richards: Dean of the Yale School of Drama and a prominent director on Broadway.

exposes the cost of Levee's compromise. With no other outlet for his anger, Levee stabs and kills his fellow band member, Toledo, for stepping on his shoe.

With his plot laid out and his characters created, Wilson proceeded from his first draft. And in his play of the blues, Wilson echoed Baraka's° dramatic warnings of the dangers of assimilation as he clarified Levee's story through five more extensively rewritten drafts of the script. To begin, Wilson revisited Ma Rainey and her place in the play, as he realized that to tell the story of Levee he needed a clearer vision of Ma. The final drama contrasts the aspirations and actions of the two. Levee believes that music can afford him the opportunity to fulfill his potential and participate in the American dream. He sees Ma Rainey's success without understanding the compromises she has made to achieve it, witnesses Ma's modest control over her own career without acknowledging the accompanying abuse and humiliation.

Thus, the play pits Levee against Ma, but it also pits Levee against the producers, and, ultimately, Levee against his fellow band members. But in the early drafts, Levee was not a moving or compelling figure; he was reckless, personally and musically, and largely responsible for his own downfall. So Wilson's job was to subtly strengthen the character so that his failure is more Aristotelian. In the rewrite, he became a grander man undone by his tragic flaw — a misunderstanding of the balance of power which makes success on his terms impossible. Through his revisions, Wilson created a character of greater dignity by showing the audience Levee's genuine musical ability, by more clearly establishing the actively destructive role Sturdyvant plays in Levee's story, and by revealing the charged emotional state of an isolated man.

Wilson began with the structure, incorporating Ma Rainey more fully into the play's action, melding the two sides of his collage, in order to successfully contrast the two central characters. Title notwithstanding, in the first three drafts which followed Wilson's return to the play in 1981, Ma did not enter until the second act. In these versions, the entire first act was set in the band room and involved only the band members.

The move toward a more integrated structure had been encouraged by Lloyd Richards. Thus, while working on the play in preparation for production at the Yale Rep, Wilson rearranged a number of scenes so that Ma enters earlier. The result is action that alternates between the upstairs recording studio, where Levee wants to be, and the downstairs band room he longs to escape. In establishing the two theatrical playing areas, and the status accruing to them, Wilson strengthens the contrast between Ma, who exists primarily in the studio, and Levee, who exists primarily in the band room. Indeed, it is Levee's longing to move up to and beyond Ma, which fuels his ultimate downfall.

Levee believes he can achieve greater success than Ma because he has a vision for a different sound; he has written a new version of Ma's standard song, "Ma Rainey's Black Bottom." At the center of Levee's conflict with Ma is the interpretation of the music. Ma understands the value of the blues she sings, how they're rooted in her people, her culture, her very soul. Levee wants to update the sound to please the white producer looking for better sales.

Levee's rejection of traditional blues is a denial of a cultural connection — a denial he makes in an effort to assimilate and cash in, but a denial which is

Imamu Amiri Baraka: American poet and playwright.

ultimately self-destructive. In order to illustrate Levee's mistake, Wilson added a passage in which Ma defines the cultural function of the blues.

> White folks don't understand about the blues. They hear it come out but they don't understand how it got there. They don't understand that's life's way of talking. You don't sing to feel better. You sing cause that's a way of understanding life.

The meaning of the music was also revealed through added dialogue for another band member, Cutler: "You get the understanding and you done got a grip on life to where you can hold your head up and go on to see what else life got to offer."

To further illustrate his point, Wilson made music a more integral part of the characters' lives. In the revisions he did for the Yale Rep, Wilson had Ma sing to herself as she waits for the recording session to begin. The music seems to cure her aching feet and ease her unrest. In the final draft of the script, Cutler, the band leader, has a new line. Each time the band begins rehearsing, Cutler leads them in: "One, two, you know what to do." It becomes a ritual revealing the comforting quality of familiar music and pointing up the uncertainty generated by Levee's desire for change. This fuller appreciation of the blues by the other characters makes clearer what is being lost with Levee's desire to move away from what he terms "jug band" music.

If Levee's pursuits, a new sound and a band of his own, were completely without merit, however, there would be little dramatic tension. Thus Wilson needed to reveal that Levee's dreams, while ill-considered, are fueled by true talent, and he made a number of additions in order to acknowledge Levee's musical ability.

Wilson had the musicians show more respect for Levee's music. At one point in the play, Sturdyvant decides that the band will record Levee's version of "Black Bottom." In the early drafts, the other members of the band are contemptuous of Levee's interpretation and break off rehearsing to indulge in a petty but protracted argument about how to play the music. In the final script, the band takes Levee's version more seriously during the rehearsal.

In the successive drafts, many of the exchanges that undercut Levee's general credibility were deleted. For example, while at the O'Neill Conference, Wilson removed a line by Slow Drag indicating that Levee just wants to be troublesome. In fact, Levee wants to be successful.

Levee knows that life has dealt him a poor hand but he believes in possibility, and Wilson needed to encourage the audience to root for the young artist despite his shortsightedness. So he revealed Levee's own passion for his new music by adding a small but revealing moment to the play. Toledo and Levee are alone in the band room and Levee is working on a new song, humming and singing to himself. "Wait till Mr. Sturdyvant hear me play that! I'm talking about some real music here, Toledo! I'm talking about real music." Levee's enthusiasm is contagious.

Wilson also took time to clarify Levee's dream of forming his band and recording music. He did so through changes made in Levee's encounter with Ma's girl-friend. In early drafts, Levee merely sweet-talks Dussie Mae. "You the kind of woman make a man forget to butter his grits. You just like one of them old balky mules you like to ride out to pasture."

In a revised version of the script, Levee tries to win the woman by offering plans for his band and his career. What Wilson gains from this is twofold: first, the opportunity to show Levee describing the vision he has of his musical future;

second, the chance to show even more of what is at stake for Levee—musical success will provide not only artistic and financial gains, but may provide the key to companionship as well.

Levee wants to have everything Ma has, including Ma's girlfriend. But in the later versions of the play, it becomes clear—to all but the shortsighted Levee—that the relationship between the women is insignificant. What seemed a special prize for Levee is, in fact, expendable as far as Ma is concerned. In the final version, when Ma is leaving, she invites Dussie Mae to join her, but only as an afterthought.

Levee's miscalculations result from his failure to understand the deal Ma has struck with the white world, and his inability to see the place to which the music industry has relegated her. Dialogue added in later versions makes it clear how Levee views that place.

> As soon as I get my band together and make them records like Mr. Sturdyvant done told me I can make, I'm gonna be like Ma and tell the white man just what he can do. . . . That's the way I'm gonna be! Make the white man respect me.

But Wilson is very careful in the play to reveal how grossly inaccurate Levee's perception is. In all the drafts of the play, Ma painfully acknowledges her position while declaring her determination to fight back: "They don't care nothing about me. All they want is my voice. Well, I done learned that, and they gonna treat me like I want to be treated no matter how much it hurt them." And Wilson kept refining his portrayal of Ma's conflict with Irvin and Sturdyvant to show her constant battle to be granted even the most minimal of amenities—a Coca-Cola while recording, heat in the studio. Near the end of the play, Sturdyvant tries to cheat Ma's nephew Sylvester out of his pay for reciting the introduction on the recording of "Black Bottom." Irvin tells Ma that Sylvester's money is to come out of her salary. Through a progressive series of additions to the script, Wilson clarified the circumstances to reveal how limited her ability is to fight back; she does get the money for Sylvester, but only because Sturdyvant realizes that she has not yet signed the release forms for the new record.

An arrogant Levee believes in his music, but he also believes that he will be cleverer than Ma at pleasing his white bosses. He hopes to convince Sturdyvant to hire the band he has put together to record his new songs.

Through successive drafts, Wilson refined his portrait of Sturdyvant's role in Levee's downfall to further establish the destructive nature of exploitation and the cost paid for tolerating it. In the early drafts, Levee approaches Sturdyvant when the company owner first comes to the band room. Levee wants to discuss the status of the songs he has submitted. In these drafts. Levee pursues a recording opportunity without encouragement and with a hat-in-hand tone; his colleagues accuse him of "shuffling his feet" when Sturdyvant is in the room.

In all the drafts, Sturdyvant refuses at the end of the play to allow Levee to record his songs and patronizingly pays Levee five dollars for each song he has written. But Wilson decided that Sturdyvant's final action would be more obviously exploitative if throughout the play he was seen to be more actively encouraging Levee to write the songs.

In a series of additions made for the Yale Rep production, Wilson moved Sturdyvant into this stance. In a rewritten first scene, Levee is working to finish a song in response to a direct request by Sturdyvant for more music. This addition also provides the opportunity to see Levee at work on his music. Here he is at the moment of creation, glimpsing a whole world of possibility, one that supports his miscalculation about the opportunities available to him.

When Sturdyvant enters the band room, he begins the discussion by asking Levee if he has finished the song, and, in this rewritten version, Levee actually plays a section of the new song. Again, Wilson presents an energetic and hopeful Levee, and an enthusiastic and encouraging Sturdyvant. In the final version of the opening scene of the play, Sturdyvant checks eagerly with Irvin to be sure that Levee will be attending the recording session. Demonstrating the fervor of his interest increases the audience's awareness of his subsequent betrayal

In the first three drafts, in his final scene, when Sturdyvant tells Levee that he will not record his songs, Levee responds, "I wanna hold you to what you told me." In the final version, this line was cut. He just keeps trying to sell his music on its merits and its potential for Sturdyvant: "That music is what people is looking for. They's tired of jug-band music." Levee wants to be appreciated for his artistry. Only when Levee realizes that this approach is going nowhere does he resort to trying to win on ethical grounds:

> STURDYVANT: Well, Levee, like I say . . . they just aren't the kind of songs we're looking for.
> LEVEE: Now, why didn't you tell me that before when I first give them to you? You told me you was gonna let me record them. . . . What's the difference between then and now? [. . .]

Wilson drafted and redrafted the play, carefully balancing false opportunity against veiled oppression, examining the tragic combination of forces which drive a man toward destruction. Wilson's first version of the full-length play contained two hastily-joined sections—the drama in the band room, the domain of the African American men, and the drama in the recording studio, the domain of the white men. In working to create a cohesive whole, Wilson wove the two parts together.

Critics maintained that the play never overcame its bifurcated focus, but audiences seem to have found the bifurcation an apt and powerful metaphor for the inequities of the segregated world Wilson was portraying. *Ma Rainey's Black Bottom* ran for 275 performances on Broadway, introducing its playwright to a welcoming world.

FENCES

Fences (1985), like most of August Wilson's plays, was directed by Lloyd Richards, who also directed the first production of Lorraine Hansberry's *A Raisin in the Sun*. Richards was, until 1991, the dean of the School of Drama at Yale University and ran the Yale Repertory Theatre, where he directed the first several of the plays Wilson wrote in his projected ten-play cycle about black American life.

Fences presents a slice of life in a black tenement in Pittsburgh in the 1950s. Its main character, Troy Maxson, is a garbage collector who has taken great pride in keeping his family together and providing for them. When the play opens, he and his friend Bono are talking about Troy's challenge to the company and the union about blacks' ability to do the same "easy" work that whites do. Troy's rebellion and frustration set the tone of the entire play: he is looking for his rights, and, at age fifty-three, he has missed many opportunities to get what he deserves.

Troy's struggle for fairness becomes virtually mythic as he describes his wrestling with death during a bout of pneumonia in 1941. He describes a three-day struggle in which he eventually overcame his foe. Troy—a good baseball player who was relegated to the Negro leagues—sees death as nothing but a fastball, and he could always deal with a fastball. Both Bono and Troy's wife, Rose, show an intense admiration for him as he describes his ordeal.

The father-son relationship that begins to take a central role in the drama is complicated by strong feelings of pride and independence on both sides. Troy's son Cory wants to play football, and Troy wants him to work on the fence he's mending. Cory's youthful enthusiasm probably echoes Troy's own youthful innocence, but Troy resents it in Cory, seeing it as partly responsible for his own predicament. Cory cannot see his father's point of view and feels that he is exempt from the kind of prejudice his father suffered.

The agony of the father-son relationship, their misperceptions of each other, persist through the play. Rose's capacity to cope with the deepest of Troy's anxieties—his fear of death—is one of her most important achievements in the play. At the end of the play Rose demands that Cory give Troy the respect he deserves, although Cory's anger and inexperience make it all but impossible for him to see his father as anything other than an oppressor. Cory feels that he must say no to his father once, but Rose will not let him deny his father. When the play ends with Gabriel's fantastic ritualistic dance, the audience feels a sense of closure, of spiritual finish.

Fences in Performance

Like many of America's best plays, *Fences* began in a workshop production. Its first version was performed in a reading without full production—no sets, no full lighting, actors working "on book" instead of fully memorizing the play—in the summer of 1983 at the Eugene O'Neill Center in Waterford, Connecticut. This early version was four hours long.

Once Wilson found the focus of his play, it premiered in 1985 at the Yale Repertory Theatre in New Haven. Lloyd Richards, then dean of Yale Drama School, directed this as well as the New York production. The New York opening on March 27, 1987, starred Mary Alice, James Earl Jones, and Ray Aranha, the cast from New Haven. Frank Rich at the *New York Times* praised James Earl Jones, congratulating him on finding "what may be the best role of his career." Rich also said, "*Fences* leaves no doubt that Mr. Wilson is a major writer, combining a poet's ear for vernacular with a robust sense of humor (political and sexual), a sure instinct for crackling dramatic incident and a passionate commitment to a great subject." The play ran for 575 performances.

From the first, *Fences* was recognized as an important play. It won four Tony Awards: best play, best actor, best actress in a supporting role, and best director. It also won the New York Drama Critics' Circle Award for best play and the Pulitzer Prize. Before the New York production, it had traveled to Chicago, San Francisco, and Seattle. It has been performed numerous times since.

August Wilson (1945–2005)

FENCES

1987

Characters

TROY MAXSON
JIM BONO, *Troy's friend*
ROSE, *Troy's wife*
LYONS, *Troy's oldest son by previous marriage*
GABRIEL, *Troy's brother*
CORY, *Troy and Rose's son*
RAYNELL, *Troy's daughter*

Setting: *The setting is the yard which fronts the only entrance to the Maxson household, an ancient two-story brick house set back off a small alley in a big-city neighborhood. The entrance to the house is gained by two or three steps leading to a wooden porch badly in need of paint.*

A relatively recent addition to the house and running its full width, the porch lacks congruence. It is a sturdy porch with a flat roof. One or two chairs of dubious value sit at one end where the kitchen window opens onto the porch. An old-fashioned icebox stands silent guard at the opposite end.

The yard is a small dirt yard, partially fenced, except for the last scene, with a wooden sawhorse, a pile of lumber, and other fence-building equipment set off to the side. Opposite is a tree from which hangs a ball made of rags. A baseball bat leans against the tree. Two oil drums serve as garbage receptacles and sit near the house at right to complete the setting.

The Play: *Near the turn of the century, the destitute of Europe sprang on the city with tenacious claws and an honest and solid dream. The city devoured them. They swelled its belly until it burst into a thousand furnaces and sewing machines, a thousand butcher shops and bakers' ovens, a thousand churches and hospitals and funeral parlors and money-lenders. The city grew. It nourished itself and offered each man a partnership limited only by his talent, his guile, and his willingness and capacity for hard work. For the immigrants of Europe, a dream dared and won true.*

The descendants of African slaves were offered no such welcome or participation. They came from places called the Carolinas and the Virginias, Georgia, Alabama, Mississippi, and Tennessee. They came strong, eager, searching. The city rejected them and they fled and settled along the riverbanks and under bridges in shallow, ramshackle houses made of sticks and tarpaper. They collected rags and wood. They sold the use of their muscles and their bodies. They cleaned houses and washed clothes, they shined shoes, and in quiet desperation and vengeful pride, they stole, and lived in pursuit of their own dream. That they could breathe free, finally, and stand to meet life with the force of dignity and whatever eloquence the heart could call upon.

By 1957, the hard-won victories of the European immigrants had solidified the industrial might of America. War had been confronted and won with new energies that used loyalty and patriotism as its fuel. Life was rich, full, and flourishing. The Milwaukee Braves won the World Series, and the hot winds of change that would make the sixties a turbulent, racing, dangerous, and provocative decade had not yet begun to blow full.

ACT I • Scene I

(It is 1957. Troy and Bono enter the yard, engaged in conversation. Troy is fifty-three years old, a large man with thick, heavy hands; it is this largeness that he strives to fill out and make an accommodation with. Together with his blackness, his largeness informs his sensibilities and the choices he has made in his life.)

(Of the two men, Bono is obviously the follower. His commitment to their friendship of thirty-odd years is rooted in his admiration of Troy's honesty, capacity for hard work, and his strength, which Bono seeks to emulate.)

(It is Friday night, payday, and the one night of the week the two men engage in a ritual of talk and drink. Troy is usually the most talkative and at times he can be crude and almost vulgar, though he is capable of rising to profound heights of expression. The men carry lunch buckets and wear or carry burlap aprons and are dressed in clothes suitable to their jobs as garbage collectors.)

BONO: Troy, you ought to stop that lying!

TROY: I ain't lying! The nigger had a watermelon this big.

(He indicates with his hands.)

Talking about . . . "What watermelon, Mr. Rand?" I liked to fell out! "What watermelon, Mr. Rand?" . . . And it sitting there big as life.

BONO: What did Mr. Rand say?

TROY: Ain't said nothing. Figure if the nigger too dumb to know he carrying a watermelon, he wasn't gonna get much sense out of him. Trying to hide that great big old watermelon under his coat. Afraid to let the white man see him carry it home.

BONO: I'm like you . . . I ain't got no time for them kind of people.

TROY: Now what he look like getting mad cause he see the man from the union talking to Mr. Rand?

BONO: He come to me talking about . . . "Maxson gonna get us fired." I told him to get away from me with that. He walked away from me calling you a troublemaker. What Mr. Rand say?

TROY: Ain't said nothing. He told me to go down the Commissioner's office next Friday. They called me down there to see them.

BONO: Well, as long as you got your complaint filed, they can't fire you. That's what one of them white fellows tell me.

TROY: I ain't worried about them firing me. They gonna fire me cause I asked a question? That's all I did. I went to Mr. Rand and asked him, "Why? Why you got the white mens driving and the colored lifting?" Told him "what's the matter, don't I count? You think only white fellows got sense enough to drive a truck. That ain't no paper job! Hell, anybody can drive a truck. How come you got all whites driving and the colored lifting?" He told me "take it to the union." Well, hell, that's what I done! Now they wanna come up with this pack of lies.

BONO: I told Brownie if the man come and ask him any questions . . . just tell the truth! It ain't nothing but something they done trumped up on you cause you filed a complaint on them.

TROY: Brownie don't understand nothing. All I want them to do is change the job description. Give everybody a chance to drive the truck. Brownie can't see that. He ain't got that much sense.

BONO: How you figure he be making out with that gal be up at Taylors' all the time . . . that Alberta gal?

TROY: Same as you and me. Getting just as much as we is. Which is to say nothing.

BONO: It is, huh? I figure you doing a little better than me . . . and I ain't saying what I'm doing.

TROY: Aw, nigger, look here . . . I know you. If you had got anywhere near that gal, twenty minutes later you be looking to tell somebody. And the first one you gonna tell . . . that you gonna want to brag to . . . is gonna be me.

BONO: I ain't saying that. I see where you be eyeing her.

TROY: I eye all the women. I don't miss nothing. Don't never let nobody tell you Troy Maxson don't eye the women.

BONO: You been doing more than eyeing her. You done bought her a drink or two.

TROY: Hell yeah, I bought her a drink! What that mean? I bought you one, too. What that mean cause I buy her a drink? I'm just being polite.

BONO: It's all right to buy her one drink. That's what you call being polite. But when you wanna be buying two or three . . . that's what you call eyeing her.

TROY: Look here, as long as you known me . . . you ever known me to chase after women?

BONO: Hell yeah! Long as I done known you. You forgetting I knew you when.

TROY: Naw, I'm talking about since I been married to Rose?

BONO: Oh, not since you been married to Rose. Now, that's the truth, there. I can say that.

TROY: All right then! Case closed.

BONO: I see you be walking up around Alberta's house. You supposed to be at Taylors' and you be walking up around there.

TROY: What you watching where I'm walking for? I ain't watching after you.

BONO: I seen you walking around there more than once.

TROY: Hell, you liable to see me walking anywhere! That don't mean nothing cause you see me walking around there.

BONO: Where she come from anyway? She just kinda showed up one day.

TROY: Tallahassee. You can look at her and tell she one of them Florida gals. They got some big healthy women down there. Grow them right up out the ground. Got a little bit of Indian in her. Most of them niggers down in Florida got some Indian in them.

BONO: I don't know about that Indian part. But she damn sure big and healthy. Woman wear some big stockings. Got them great big old legs and hips as wide as the Mississippi River.

TROY: Legs don't mean nothing. You don't do nothing but push them out of the way. But them hips cushion the ride!

BONO: Troy, you ain't got no sense.

TROY: It's the truth! Like you riding on Goodyears!

(Rose enters from the house. She is ten years younger than Troy, her devotion to him stems from her recognition of the possibilities of her life without him: a succession of abusive men and their babies, a life of partying and running the streets, the Church, or aloneness with its attendant pain and frustration. She recognizes Troy's spirit as a fine and illuminating one and she either ignores or forgives his faults, only some of which she recognizes. Though she doesn't drink, her presence is an integral part of the Friday night rituals. She alternates between the porch and the kitchen, where supper preparations are under way.)

ROSE: What you all out here getting into?

TROY: What you worried about what we getting into for? This is men talk, woman.

ROSE: What I care what you all talking about? Bono, you gonna stay for supper?

BONO: No, I thank you, Rose. But Lucille say she cooking up a pot of pigfeet.

TROY: Pigfeet! Hell, I'm going home with you! Might even stay the night if you got some pigfeet. You got something in there to top them pigfeet, Rose?

ROSE: I'm cooking up some chicken. I got some chicken and collard greens.

TROY: Well, go on back in the house and let me and Bono finish what we was talking about. This is men talk. I got some talk for you later. You know what kind of talk I mean. You go on and powder it up.

ROSE: Troy Maxson, don't you start that now!

TROY *(puts his arm around her)*: Aw, woman . . . come here. Look here, Bono . . . when I met this woman . . . I got out that place, say, "Hitch up my pony, saddle up my mare . . . there's a woman out there for me somewhere. I looked here. Looked there. Saw Rose and latched on to her." I latched on to her and told her—I'm gonna tell you the truth—I told her, "Baby, I don't wanna marry, I just wanna be your man." Rose told me . . . tell him what you told me, Rose.

ROSE: I told him if he wasn't the marrying kind, then move out the way so the marrying kind could find me.

TROY: That's what she told me. "Nigger, you in my way. You blocking the view! Move out the way so I can find me a husband." I thought it over two or three days. Come back—

ROSE: Ain't no two or three days nothing. You was back the same night.

TROY: Come back, told her . . . "Okay, baby . . . but I'm gonna buy me a banty rooster and put him out there in the backyard . . . and when he see a stranger come, he'll flap his wings and crow . . ." Look here, Bono, I could watch the front door by myself . . . it was that back door I was worried about.

ROSE: Troy, you ought not talk like that. Troy ain't doing nothing but telling a lie.

TROY: Only thing is . . . when we first got married . . . forget the rooster . . . we ain't had no yard!

BONO: I hear you tell it. Me and Lucille was staying down there on Logan Street. Had two rooms with the outhouse in the back. I ain't mind the outhouse none. But when that goddamn wind blow through there in the winter . . . that's what I'm talking about! To this day I wonder why in the hell I ever stayed down there for six long years. But see, I didn't know I could do no better. I thought only white folks had inside toilets and things.

ROSE: There's a lot of people don't know they can do no better than they doing now. That's just something you got to learn. A lot of folks still shop at Bella's.

TROY: Ain't nothing wrong with shopping at Bella's. She got fresh food.

ROSE: I ain't said nothing about if she got fresh food. I'm talking about what she charge. She charge ten cents more than the A&P.

TROY: The A&P ain't never done nothing for me. I spends my money where I'm treated right. I go down to Bella, say, "I need a loaf of bread, I'll pay you Friday." She give it to me. What sense that make when I got money to go and spend it somewhere else and ignore the person who done right by me? That ain't in the Bible.

ROSE: We ain't talking about what's in the Bible. What sense it make to shop there when she overcharge?

TROY: You shop where you want to. I'll do my shopping where the people been good to me.

ROSE: Well, I don't think it's right for her to overcharge. That's all I was saying.

BONO: Look here . . . I got to get on. Lucille going be raising all kind of hell.

TROY: Where you going, nigger? We ain't finished this pint. Come here, finish this pint.

BONO: Well, hell, I am . . . if you ever turn the bottle loose.

TROY *(hands him the bottle)*: The only thing I say about the A&P is I'm glad Cory got that job down there. Help him take care of his school clothes and things. Gabe done moved out and things getting tight around here. He got that job. . . . He can start to look out for himself.

ROSE: Cory done went and got recruited by a college football team.

TROY: I told that boy about that football stuff. The white man ain't gonna let him get nowhere with that football. I told him when he first come to me with it. Now you come telling me he done went and got more tied up in it. He ought to go and get recruited in how to fix cars or something where he can make a living.

ROSE: He ain't talking about making no living playing football. It's just something the boys in school do. They gonna send a recruiter by to talk to you. He'll tell you he ain't talking about making no living playing football. It's a honor to be recruited.

TROY: It ain't gonna get him nowhere. Bono'll tell you that.

BONO: If he be like you in the sports . . . he's gonna be all right. Ain't but two men ever played baseball as good as you. That's Babe Ruth and Josh Gibson.° Them's the only two men ever hit more home runs than you.

TROY: What it ever get me? Ain't got a pot to piss in or a window to throw it out of.

ROSE: Times have changed since you was playing baseball, Troy. That was before the war. Times have changed a lot since then.

TROY: How in hell they done changed?

ROSE: They got lots of colored boys playing ball now. Baseball and football.

BONO: You right about that, Rose. Times have changed, Troy. You just come along too early.

TROY: There ought not never have been no time called too early! Now you take that fellow . . . what's that fellow they had playing right field for the Yankees back then? You know who I'm talking about, Bono. Used to play right field for the Yankees.

ROSE: Selkirk?

TROY: Selkirk! That's it! Man batting .269, understand? .269. What kind of sense that make? I was hitting .432 with thirty-seven home runs! Man batting .269 and playing right field for the Yankees! I saw Josh Gibson's daughter yesterday. She walking around with raggedy shoes on her feet. Now I bet you Selkirk's daughter ain't walking around with raggedy shoes on her feet! I bet you that!

ROSE: They got a lot of colored baseball players now. Jackie Robinson was the first. Folks had to wait for Jackie Robinson.

TROY: I done seen a hundred niggers play baseball better than Jackie Robinson. Hell, I know some teams Jackie Robinson couldn't even make! What you talking about Jackie Robinson. Jackie Robinson wasn't nobody. I'm talking about if you could play ball then they ought to have let you play. Don't care what color you were. Come telling me I come along too early. If you could play . . . then they ought to have let you play.

(*Troy takes a long drink from the bottle.*)

ROSE: You gonna drink yourself to death. You don't need to be drinking like that.

Josh Gibson: (1911–1947), powerful black baseball player known in the 1930s as the Babe Ruth of the Negro leagues.

TROY: Death ain't nothing. I done seen him. Done wrassled with him. You can't tell me nothing about death. Death ain't nothing but a fastball on the outside corner. And you know what I'll do to that! Lookee here, Bono . . . am I lying? You get one of them fastballs, about waist high, over the outside corner of the plate where you can get the meat of the bat on it . . . and good god! You can kiss it goodbye. Now, am I lying?

BONO: Naw, you telling the truth there. I seen you do it.

TROY: If I'm lying . . . that 450 feet worth of lying!

(*Pause.*)

That's all death is to me. A fastball on the outside corner.

ROSE: I don't know why you want to get on talking about death.

TROY: Ain't nothing wrong with talking about death. That's part of life. Everybody gonna die. You gonna die, I'm gonna die. Bono's gonna die. Hell, we all gonna die.

ROSE: But you ain't got to talk about it. I don't like to talk about it.

TROY: You the one brought it up. Me and Bono was talking about baseball . . . you tell me I'm gonna drink myself to death. Ain't that right, Bono? You know I don't drink this but one night out of the week. That's Friday night. I'm gonna drink just enough to where I can handle it. Then I cuts it loose. I leave it alone. So don't you worry about me drinking myself to death. 'Cause I ain't worried about Death. I done seen him. I done wrestled with him.

Look here, Bono . . . I looked up one day and Death was marching straight at me. Like Soldiers on Parade! The Army of Death was marching straight at me. The middle of July, 1941. It got real cold just like it be winter. It seem like Death himself reached out and touched me on the shoulder. He touch me just like I touch you. I got cold as ice and Death standing there grinning at me.

ROSE: Troy, why don't you hush that talk.

TROY: I say . . . What you want, Mr. Death? You be wanting me? You done brought your army to be getting me? I looked him dead in the eye. I wasn't fearing nothing. I was ready to tangle. Just like I'm ready to tangle now. The Bible say be ever vigilant. That's why I don't get but so drunk. I got to keep watch.

ROSE: Troy was right down there in Mercy Hospital. You remember he had pneumonia? Laying there with a fever talking plumb out of his head.

TROY: Death standing there staring at me . . . carrying that sickle in his hand. Finally he say, "You want bound over for another year?" See, just like that . . . "You want bound over for another year?" I told him, "Bound over hell! Let's settle this now!"

It seem like he kinda fell back when I said that, and all the cold went out of me. I reached down and grabbed that sickle and threw it just as far as I could throw it . . . and me and him commenced to wrestling.

We wrestled for three days and three nights. I can't say where I found the strength from. Every time it seemed like he was gonna get the best of me, I'd reach way down deep inside myself and find the strength to do him one better.

ROSE: Every time Troy tell that story he find different ways to tell it. Different things to make up about it.

TROY: I ain't making up nothing. I'm telling you the facts of what happened. I wrestled with Death for three days and three nights and I'm standing here to tell you about it.

(*Pause.*)

All right. At the end of the third night we done weakened each other to where we can't hardly move. Death stood up, throwed on his robe . . . had him a white robe with a hood on it. He throwed on that robe and went off to look for his sickle. Say, "I'll be back." Just like that. "I'll be back." I told him, say, "Yeah, but . . . you gonna have to find me!" I wasn't no fool. I wan't going looking for him. Death ain't nothing to play with. And I know he's gonna get me. I know I got to join his army . . . his camp followers. But as long as I keep my strength and see him coming . . . as long as I keep up my vigilance . . . he's gonna have to fight to get me. I ain't going easy.

BONO: Well, look here, since you got to keep up your vigilance . . . let me have the bottle.

TROY: Aw hell, I shouldn't have told you that part. I should have left out that part.

ROSE: Troy be talking that stuff and half the time don't even know what he be talking about.

TROY: Bono know me better than that.

BONO: That's right. I know you. I know you got some Uncle Remus° in your blood. You got more stories than the devil got sinners.

TROY: Aw hell, I done seen him too! Done talked with the devil.

ROSE: Troy, don't nobody wanna be hearing all that stuff.

(*Lyons enters the yard from the street. Thirty-four years old, Troy's son by a previous marriage, he sports a neatly trimmed goatee, sport coat, white shirt, tieless and buttoned at the collar. Though he fancies himself a musician, he is more caught up in the rituals and "idea" of being a musician than in the actual practice of the music. He has come to borrow money from Troy, and while he knows he will be successful, he is uncertain as to what extent his lifestyle will be held up to scrutiny and ridicule.*)

LYONS: Hey, Pop.

TROY: What you come "Hey, Popping" me for?

LYONS: How you doing, Rose?

(*He kisses her.*)

Mr. Bono. How you doing?

Uncle Remus: Black storyteller who recounts traditional African American tales in the book by Joel Chandler Harris.

BONO: Hey, Lyons . . . how you been?

TROY: He must have been doing all right. I ain't seen him around here last week.

ROSE: Troy, leave your boy alone. He come by to see you and you wanna start all that nonsense.

TROY: I ain't bothering Lyons.

(*Offers him the bottle.*)

Here . . . get you a drink. We got an understanding. I know why he come by to see me and he know I know.

LYONS: Come on, Pop . . . I just stopped by to say hi . . . see how you was doing.

TROY: You ain't stopped by yesterday.

ROSE: You gonna stay for supper, Lyons? I got some chicken cooking in the oven.

LYONS: No, Rose . . . thanks. I was just in the neighborhood and thought I'd stop by for a minute.

TROY: You was in the neighborhood all right, nigger. You telling the truth there. You was in the neighborhood cause it's my payday.

LYONS: Well, hell, since you mentioned it . . . let me have ten dollars.

TROY: I'll be damned! I'll die and go to hell and play blackjack with the devil before I give you ten dollars.

BONO: That's what I wanna know about . . . that devil you done seen.

LYONS: What . . . Pop done seen the devil? You too much, Pops.

TROY: Yeah, I done seen him. Talked to him too!

ROSE: You ain't seen no devil. I done told you that man ain't had nothing to do with the devil. Anything you can't understand, you want to call it the devil.

TROY: Look here, Bono . . . I went down to see Hertzberger about some furniture. Got three rooms for two-ninety-eight. That what it say on the radio. "Three rooms . . . two-ninety-eight." Even made up a little song about it. Go down there . . . man tell me I can't get no credit. I'm working every day and can't get no credit. What to do? I got an empty house with some raggedy furniture in it. Cory ain't got no bed. He's sleeping on a pile of rags on the floor. Working every day and can't get no credit. Come back here—Rose'll tell you—madder than hell. Sit down . . . try to figure what I'm gonna do. Come a knock on the door. Ain't been living here but three days. Who know I'm here? Open the door . . . devil standing there bigger than life. White fellow . . . got on good clothes and everything. Standing there with a clipboard in his hand. I ain't had to say nothing. First words come out of his mouth was . . . "I understand you need some furniture and can't get no credit." I liked to fell over. He say, "I'll give you all the credit you want, but you got to pay the interest on it." I told him, "Give me three rooms worth and charge whatever you want." Next day a truck pulled up here and two men unloaded them three rooms. Man what drove the truck give me a book. Say send ten dollars, first of every month to the address in the book and everything will be all right. Say if I miss a payment the devil was coming back and it'll be hell to pay. That was fifteen years ago. To this day . . . the first of the month I send my ten dollars, Rose'll tell you.

ROSE: Troy lying.

TROY: I ain't never seen that man since. Now you tell me who else that could have been but the devil? I ain't sold my soul or nothing like that, you understand. Naw, I wouldn't have truck with the devil about nothing like that. I got my furniture and pays my ten dollars the first of the month just like clockwork.

BONO: How long you say you been paying this ten dollars a month?

TROY: Fifteen years!

BONO: Hell, ain't you finished paying for it yet? How much the man done charged you.

TROY: Ah hell, I done paid for it. I done paid for it ten times over! The fact is I'm scared to stop paying it.

ROSE: Troy lying. We got that furniture from Mr. Glickman. He ain't paying no ten dollars a month to nobody.

TROY: Aw hell, woman. Bono know I ain't that big a fool.

LYONS: I was just getting ready to say . . . I know where there's a bridge for sale.

TROY: Look here, I'll tell you this . . . it don't matter to me if he was the devil. It don't matter if the devil give credit. Somebody has got to give it.

ROSE: It ought to matter. You going around talking about having truck with the devil . . . God's the one you gonna have to answer to. He's the one gonna be at the Judgment.

LYONS: Yeah, well, look here, Pop . . . let me have that ten dollars. I'll give it back to you. Bonnie got a job working at the hospital.

TROY: What I tell you, Bono? The only time I see this nigger is when he wants something. That's the only time I see him.

LYONS: Come on, Pop, Mr. Bono don't want to hear all that. Let me have the ten dollars. I told you Bonnie working.

TROY: What that mean to me? "Bonnie working." I don't care if she working. Go ask her for the ten dollars if she working. Talking about "Bonnie working." Why ain't you working?

LYONS: Aw, Pop, you know I can't find no decent job. Where am I gonna get a job at? You know I can't get no job.

TROY: I told you I know some people down there. I can get you on the rubbish if you want to work. I told you that the last time you came by here asking me for something.

LYONS: Naw, Pop . . . thanks. That ain't for me. I don't wanna be carrying nobody's rubbish. I don't wanna be punching nobody's time clock.

TROY: What's the matter, you too good to carry people's rubbish? Where you think that ten dollars you talking about come from? I'm just supposed to haul people's rubbish and give my money to you cause you too lazy to work. You too lazy to work and wanna know why you ain't got what I got.

ROSE: What hospital Bonnie working at? Mercy?

LYONS: She's down at Passavant working in the laundry.

TROY: I ain't got nothing as it is. I give you that ten dollars and I got to eat beans the rest of the week. Naw . . . you ain't getting no ten dollars here.

LYONS: You ain't got to be eating no beans. I don't know why you wanna say that.

TROY: I ain't got no extra money. Gabe done moved over to Miss Pearl's paying her the rent and things done got tight around here. I can't afford to be giving you every payday.

LYONS: I ain't asked you to give me nothing. I asked you to loan me ten dollars. I know you got ten dollars.

TROY: Yeah, I got it. You know why I got it? Cause I don't throw my money away out there in the streets. You living the fast life . . . wanna be a musician . . . running around in them clubs and things . . . then, you learn to take care of yourself. You ain't gonna find me going and asking nobody for nothing. I done spent too many years without.

LYONS: You and me is two different people, Pop.

TROY: I done learned my mistake and learned to do what's right by it. You still trying to get something for nothing. Life don't owe you nothing. You owe it to yourself. Ask Bono. He'll tell you I'm right.

LYONS: You got your way of dealing with the world . . . I got mine. The only thing that matters to me is the music.

TROY: Yeah, I can see that! It don't matter how you gonna eat . . . where your next dollar is coming from. You telling the truth there.

LYONS: I know I got to eat. But I got to live too. I need something that gonna help me to get out of the bed in the morning. Make me feel like I belong in the world. I don't bother nobody. I just stay with my music cause that's the only way I can find to live in the world. Otherwise there ain't no telling what I might do. Now I don't come criticizing you and how you live. I just come by to ask you for ten dollars. I don't wanna hear all that about how I live.

TROY: Boy, your mamma did a hell of a job raising you.

LYONS: You can't change me, Pop. I'm thirty-four years old. If you wanted to change me, you should have been there when I was growing up. I come by to see you . . . ask for ten dollars and you want to talk about how I was raised. You don't know nothing about how I was raised.

ROSE: Let the boy have ten dollars, Troy.

TROY (to Lyons): What the hell you looking at me for? I ain't got no ten dollars. You know what I do with my money.

(To Rose.)

Give him ten dollars if you want him to have it.

ROSE: I will. Just as soon as you turn it loose.

TROY (*handing Rose the money*): There it is. Seventy-six dollars and forty-two cents. You see this, Bono? Now, I ain't gonna get but six of that back.

ROSE: You ought to stop telling that lie. Here, Lyons.

(*She hands him the money.*)

LYONS: Thanks, Rose. Look . . . I got to run . . . I'll see you later.

TROY: Wait a minute. You gonna say, "thanks, Rose" and ain't gonna look to see where she got that ten dollars from? See how they do me, Bono?

LYONS: I know she got it from you, Pop. Thanks. I'll give it back to you.

TROY: There he go telling another lie. Time I see that ten dollars . . . he'll be owing me thirty more.

LYONS: See you, Mr. Bono.

BONO: Take care, Lyons!

LYONS: Thanks, Pop. I'll see you again.

(*Lyons exits the yard.*)

TROY: I don't know why he don't go and get him a decent job and take care of that woman he got.

BONO: He'll be all right, Troy. The boy is still young.

TROY: The *boy* is thirty-four years old.

ROSE: Let's not get off into all that.

BONO: Look here . . . I got to be going. I got to be getting on. Lucille gonna be waiting.

TROY (*puts his arm around Rose*): See this woman, Bono? I love this woman. I love this woman so much it hurts. I love her so much . . . I done run out of ways of loving her. So I got to go back to basics. Don't you come by my house Monday morning talking about time to go to work . . . 'cause I'm still gonna be stroking!

ROSE: Troy! Stop it now!

BONO: I ain't paying him no mind, Rose. That ain't nothing but gin-talk. Go on, Troy. I'll see you Monday.

TROY: Don't you come by my house, nigger! I done told you what I'm gonna be doing.

(*The lights go down to black.*)

Scene II

(*The lights come up on Rose hanging up clothes. She hums and sings softly to herself. It is the following morning.*)

ROSE (*sings*): Jesus, be a fence all around me every day
Jesus, I want you to protect me as I travel on my way.
Jesus, be a fence all around me every day.

(*Troy enters from the house.*)

Jesus, I want you to protect me
As I travel on my way.

(*To Troy.*) 'Morning. You ready for breakfast? I can fix it soon as I finish hanging up these clothes.

TROY: I got the coffee on. That'll be all right. I'll just drink some of that this morning.

ROSE: That 651 hit yesterday. That's the second time this month. Miss Pearl hit for a dollar . . . seem like those that need the least always get lucky. Poor folks can't get nothing.

TROY: Them numbers don't know nobody. I don't know why you fool with them. You and Lyons both.

ROSE: It's something to do.

TROY: You ain't doing nothing but throwing your money away.

ROSE: Troy, you know I don't play foolishly. I just play a nickel here and a nickel there.

TROY: That's two nickels you done thrown away.

ROSE: Now I hit sometimes . . . that makes up for it. It always comes in handy when I do hit. I don't hear you complaining then.

TROY: I ain't complaining now. I just say it's foolish. Trying to guess out of six hundred ways which way the number gonna come. If I had all the money niggers, these Negroes, throw away on numbers for one week — just one week — I'd be a rich man.

ROSE: Well, you wishing and calling it foolish ain't gonna stop folks from playing numbers. That's one thing for sure. Besides . . . some good things come from playing numbers. Look where Pope done bought him that restaurant off of numbers.

TROY: I can't stand niggers like that. Man ain't had two dimes to rub together. He walking around with his shoes all run over bumming money for cigarettes. All right. Got lucky there and hit the numbers . . .

ROSE: Troy, I know all about it.

TROY: Had good sense, I'll say that for him. He ain't throwed his money away. I seen niggers hit the numbers and go through two thousand dollars in four days. Man bought him that restaurant down there . . . fixed it up real nice . . . and then didn't want nobody to come in it! A Negro go in there and can't get no kind of service. I seen a white fellow come in there and order a bowl of stew. Pope picked all the meat out the pot for him. Man ain't had nothing but a bowl of meat! Negro come behind him and ain't got nothing but the potatoes and carrots. Talking about what numbers do for people, you picked a wrong example. Ain't done nothing but make a worser fool out of him than he was before.

ROSE: Troy, you ought to stop worrying about what happened at work yesterday.

TROY: I ain't worried. Just told me to be down there at the Commissioner's office on Friday. Everybody think they gonna fire me. I ain't worried about them firing me. You ain't got to worry about that.

(*Pause.*)

Where's Cory? Cory in the house? (*Calls.*) Cory?

ROSE: He gone out.

TROY: Out, huh? He gone out 'cause he know I want him to help me with this fence. I know how he is. That boy scared of work.

(*Gabriel enters. He comes halfway down the alley and, hearing Troy's voice, stops.*)

TROY (*continues*): He ain't done a lick of work in his life.

ROSE: He had to go to football practice. Coach wanted them to get in a little extra practice before the season start.

TROY: I got his practice . . . running out of here before he get his chores done.

ROSE: Troy, what is wrong with you this morning? Don't nothing set right with you. Go on back in there and go to bed . . . get up on the other side.

TROY: Why something got to be wrong with me? I ain't said nothing wrong with me.

ROSE: You got something to say about everything. First it's the numbers . . . then it's the way the man runs his restaurant . . . then you done got on Cory. What's it gonna be next? Take a look up there and see if the weather suits you . . . or is it gonna be how you gonna put up the fence with the clothes hanging in the yard.

TROY: You hit the nail on the head then.

ROSE: I know you like I know the back of my hand. Go on in there and get you some coffee . . . see if that straighten you up. 'Cause you ain't right this morning.

(*Troy starts into the house and sees Gabriel. Gabriel starts singing. Troy's brother, he is seven years younger than Troy. Injured in World War II, he has a metal plate in his head. He carries an old trumpet tied around his waist and believes with every fiber of his being that he is the Archangel Gabriel. He carries a chipped basket with an assortment of discarded fruits and vegetables he has picked up in the strip district and which he attempts to sell.*)

GABRIEL (*singing*): Yes, ma'am, I got plums
    You ask me how I sell them
    Oh ten cents apiece
    Three for a quarter
    Come and buy now
    'Cause I'm here today
    And tomorrow I'll be gone

(*Gabriel enters.*)

    Hey, Rose!

ROSE: How you doing, Gabe?

GABRIEL: There's Troy . . . Hey, Troy!

TROY: Hey, Gabe.

(*Exit into kitchen.*)

ROSE (*to Gabriel*): What you got there?

GABRIEL: You know what I got, Rose. I got fruits and vegetables.

ROSE (*looking in basket*): Where's all these plums you talking about?

GABRIEL: I ain't got no plums today, Rose. I was just singing that. Have some tomorrow. Put me in a big order for plums. Have enough plums tomorrow for St. Peter and everybody.

(*Troy reenters from kitchen, crosses to steps.*)
(*To Rose.*)

    Troy's mad at me.

TROY: I ain't mad at you. What I got to be mad at you about? You ain't done nothing to me.

GABRIEL: I just moved over to Miss Pearl's to keep out from in your way. I ain't mean no harm by it.

TROY: Who said anything about that? I ain't said anything about that.

GABRIEL: You ain't mad at me, is you?

TROY: Naw . . . I ain't mad at you, Gabe. If I was mad at you I'd tell you about it.

GABRIEL: Got me two rooms. In the basement. Got my own door too. Wanna see my key?

(*He holds up a key.*)

    That's my own key! Ain't nobody else got a key like that. That's my key! My two rooms!

TROY: Well, that's good, Gabe. You got your own key . . . that's good.

ROSE: You hungry, Gabe? I was just fixing to cook Troy his breakfast.

GABRIEL: I'll take some biscuits. You got some biscuits? Did you know when I was in heaven . . . every morning me and St. Peter would sit down by the gate and eat some big fat biscuits? Oh, yeah! We had us a good time. We'd sit there and eat us them biscuits and then St. Peter would go off to sleep and tell me to wake him up when it's time to open the gates for the judgment.

ROSE: Well, come on . . . I'll make up a batch of biscuits.

(*Rose exits into the house.*)

GABRIEL: Troy . . . St. Peter got your name in the book. I seen it. It say . . . Troy Maxson. I say . . . I know him! He got the same name like what I got. That's my brother!

TROY: How many times you gonna tell me that, Gabe?

GABRIEL: Ain't got my name in the book. Don't have to have my name. I done died and went to heaven. He got your name though. One morning St. Peter was looking at his book . . . marking it up for the judgment . . . and he let me see your name. Got it in there under M. Got Rose's name . . . I ain't seen it like I seen yours . . . but I know it's in there. He got a great big book. Got everybody's name what was ever been born. That's what he told me. But I seen your name. Seen it with my own eyes.

TROY: Go on in the house there. Rose going to fix you something to eat.

GABRIEL: Oh, I ain't hungry. I done had breakfast with Aunt Jemimah. She come by and cooked me up a whole mess of flapjacks. Remember how we used to eat them flapjacks?

TROY: Go on in the house and get you something to eat now.

GABRIEL: I got to go sell my plums. I done sold some tomatoes. Got me two quarters. Wanna see?

(*He shows Troy his quarters.*)

I'm gonna save them and buy me a new horn so St. Peter can hear me when it's time to open the gates.

(*Gabriel stops suddenly. Listens.*)

Hear that? That's the hellhounds. I got to chase them out of here. Go on get out of here! Get out!

(*Gabriel exits singing.*)

Better get ready for the judgment
Better get ready for the judgment
My Lord is coming down

(*Rose enters from the house.*)

TROY: He gone off somewhere.
GABRIEL (*offstage*): Better get ready for the judgment
Better get ready for the judgment morning
Better get ready for the judgment
My God is coming down
ROSE: He ain't eating right. Miss Pearl say she can't get him to eat nothing.
TROY: What you want me to do about it, Rose? I done did everything I can for the man. I can't make him get well. Man got half his head blown away . . . what you expect?
ROSE: Seem like something ought to be done to help him.
TROY: Man don't bother nobody. He just mixed up from that metal plate he got in his head. Ain't no sense for him to go back into the hospital.
ROSE: Least he be eating right. They can help him take care of himself.
TROY: Don't nobody wanna be locked up, Rose. What you wanna lock him up for? Man go over there and fight the war . . . messin' around with them Japs, get half his head blown off . . . and they give him a lousy three thousand dollars. And I had to swoop down on that.
ROSE: Is you fixing to go into that again?
TROY: That's the only way I got a roof over my head . . . cause of that metal plate.
ROSE: Ain't no sense you blaming yourself for nothing. Gabe wasn't in no condition to manage that money. You done what was right by him. Can't nobody say you ain't done what was right by him. Look how long you took care of him . . . till he wanted to have his own place and moved over there with Miss Pearl.
TROY: That ain't what I'm saying, woman! I'm just stating the facts. If my brother didn't have that metal plate in his head . . . I wouldn't have a pot to piss in or a window to throw it out of. And I'm fifty-three years old. Now see if you can understand that!

(*Troy gets up from the porch and starts to exit the yard.*)

ROSE: Where you going off to? You been running out of here every Saturday for weeks. I thought you was gonna work on this fence?
TROY: I'm gonna walk down to Taylors'. Listen to the ball game. I'll be back in a bit. I'll work on it when I get back.

(*He exits the yard. The lights go to black.*)

Scene III

(*The lights come up on the yard. It is four hours later. Rose is taking down the clothes from the line. Cory enters carrying his football equipment.*)

ROSE: Your daddy like to had a fit with you running out of here this morning without doing your chores.
CORY: I told you I had to go to practice.
ROSE: He say you were supposed to help him with this fence.
CORY: He been saying that the last four or five Saturdays, and then he don't never do nothing but go down to Taylors'. Did you tell him about the recruiter?
ROSE: Yeah, I told him.
CORY: What he say?
ROSE: He ain't said nothing too much. You get in there and get started on your chores before he gets back. Go on and scrub down them steps before he gets back here hollering and carrying on.
CORY: I'm hungry. What you got to eat, Mama?
ROSE: Go on and get started on your chores. I got some meat loaf in there. Go on and make you a sandwich . . . and don't leave no mess in there.

(*Cory exits into the house. Rose continues to take down the clothes. Troy enters the yard and sneaks up and grabs her from behind.*)

Troy! Go on, now. You liked to scared me to death. What was the score of the game? Lucille had me on the phone and I couldn't keep up with it.
TROY: What I care about the game? Come here, woman. (*He tries to kiss her.*)
ROSE: I thought you went down Taylors' to listen to the game. Go on, Troy! You supposed to be putting up this fence.
TROY (*attempting to kiss her again*): I'll put it up when I finish with what is at hand.
ROSE: Go on, Troy. I ain't studying you.
TROY (*chasing after her*): I'm studying you . . . fixing to do my homework!
ROSE: Troy, you better leave me alone.
TROY: Where's Cory? That boy brought his butt home yet?
ROSE: He's in the house doing his chores.
TROY (*calling*): Cory! Get your butt out here, boy!

(*Rose exits into the house with the laundry. Troy goes over to the pile of wood, picks up a board, and starts sawing. Cory enters from the house.*)

TROY: You just now coming in here from leaving this morning?
CORY: Yeah, I had to go to football practice.
TROY: Yeah, what?
CORY: Yessir.
TROY: I ain't but two seconds off you noway. The garbage sitting in there overflowing . . . you ain't done none of your chores . . . and you come in here talking about "Yeah."

CORY: I was just getting ready to do my chores now, Pop . . .

TROY: Your first chore is to help me with this fence on Saturday. Everything else come after that. Now get that saw and cut them boards.

(*Cory takes the saw and begins cutting the boards. Troy continues working. There is a long pause.*)

CORY: Hey, Pop . . . why don't you buy a TV?

TROY: What I want with a TV? What I want one of them for?

CORY: Everybody got one. Earl, Ba Bra . . . Jesse!

TROY: I ain't asked you who had one. I say what I want with one?

CORY: So you can watch it. They got lots of things on TV. Baseball games and everything. We could watch the World Series.

TROY: Yeah . . . and how much this TV cost?

CORY: I don't know. They got them on sale for around two hundred dollars.

TROY: Two hundred dollars, huh?

CORY: That ain't that much, Pop.

TROY: Naw, it's just two hundred dollars. See that roof you got over your head at night? Let me tell you something about that roof. It's been over ten years since that roof was last tarred. See now . . . the snow come this winter and sit up there on that roof like it is . . . and it's gonna seep inside. It's just gonna be a little bit . . . ain't gonna hardly notice it. Then the next thing you know, it's gonna be leaking all over the house. Then the wood rot from all that water and you gonna need a whole new roof. Now, how much you think it cost to get that roof tarred?

CORY: I don't know.

TROY: Two hundred and sixty-four dollars . . . cash money. While you thinking about a TV, I got to be thinking about the roof . . . and whatever else go wrong around here. Now if you had two hundred dollars, what would you do . . . fix the roof or buy a TV?

CORY: I'd buy a TV. Then when the roof started to leak . . . when it needed fixing . . . I'd fix it.

TROY: Where you gonna get the money from? You done spent it for a TV. You gonna sit up and watch the water run all over your brand new TV.

CORY: Aw, Pop. You got money. I know you do.

TROY: Where I got it at, huh?

CORY: You got it in the bank.

TROY: You wanna see my bankbook? You wanna see that seventy-three dollars and twenty-two cents I got sitting up in there?

CORY: You ain't got to pay for it all at one time. You can put a down payment on it and carry it on home with you.

TROY: Not me. I ain't gonna owe nobody nothing if I can help it. Miss a payment and they come and snatch it right out your house. Then what you got? Now, soon as I get two hundred dollars clear, then I'll buy a TV. Right now, as soon as I get two hundred and sixty-four dollars, I'm gonna have this roof tarred.

CORY: Aw . . . Pop!

TROY: You go on and get you two hundred dollars and buy one if ya want it. I got better things to do with my money.

CORY: I can't get no two hundred dollars. I ain't never seen two hundred dollars.

TROY: I'll tell you what . . . you get you a hundred dollars and I'll put the other hundred with it.

CORY: All right, I'm gonna show you.

TROY: You gonna show me how you can cut them boards right now.

(*Cory begins to cut the boards. There is a long pause.*)

CORY: The Pirates won today. That makes five in a row.

TROY: I ain't thinking about the Pirates. Got an all-white team. Got that boy . . . that Puerto Rican boy . . . Clemente. Don't even half-play him. That boy could be something if they give him a chance. Play him one day and sit him on the bench the next.

CORY: He gets a lot of chances to play.

TROY: I'm talking about playing regular. Playing every day so you can get your timing. That's what I'm talking about.

CORY: They got some white guys on the team that don't play every day. You can't play everybody at the same time.

TROY: If they got a white fellow sitting on the bench . . . you can bet your last dollar he can't play! The colored guy got to be twice as good before he get on the team. That's why I don't want you to get all tied up in them sports. Man on the team and what it get him? They got colored on the team and don't use them. Same as not having them. All them teams the same.

CORY: The Braves got Hank Aaron and Wes Covington. Hank Aaron hit two home runs today. That makes forty-three.

TROY: Hank Aaron ain't nobody. That's what you supposed to do. That's how you supposed to play the game. Ain't nothing to it. It's just a matter of timing . . . getting the right follow-through. Hell, I can hit forty-three home runs right now!

CORY: Not off no major-league pitching, you couldn't.

TROY: We had better pitching in the Negro leagues. I hit seven home runs off of Satchel Paige.° You can't get no better than that!

CORY: Sandy Koufax. He's leading the league in strike-outs.

TROY: I ain't thinking of no Sandy Koufax.

CORY: You got Warren Spahn and Lew Burdette. I bet you couldn't hit no home runs off of Warren Spahn.

TROY: I'm through with it now. You go on and cut them boards.

(*Pause.*)

Satchel Paige: (1906–1982), legendary black pitcher in the Negro leagues.

Your mama tell me you done got recruited by a college football team? Is that right?

CORY: Yeah. Coach Zellman say the recruiter gonna be coming by to talk to you. Get you to sign the permission papers.

TROY: I thought you supposed to be working down there at the A&P. Ain't you suppose to be working down there after school?

CORY: Mr. Stawicki say he gonna hold my job for me until after the football season. Say starting next week I can work weekends.

TROY: I thought we had an understanding about this football stuff? You suppose to keep up with your chores and hold that job down at the A&P. Ain't been around here all day on a Saturday. Ain't none of your chores done . . . and now you telling me you done quit your job.

CORY: I'm gonna be working weekends.

TROY: You damn right you are! And ain't no need for nobody coming around here to talk to me about signing nothing.

CORY: Hey, Pop . . . you can't do that. He's coming all the way from North Carolina.

TROY: I don't care where he coming from. The white man ain't gonna let you get nowhere with that football noway. You go on and get your book-learning so you can work yourself up in that A&P or learn how to fix cars or build houses or something, get you a trade. That way you have something can't nobody take away from you. You go on and learn how to put your hands to some good use. Besides hauling people's garbage.

CORY: I get good grades, Pop. That's why the recruiter wants to talk with you. You got to keep up your grades to get recruited. This way I'll be going to college. I'll get a chance . . .

TROY: First you gonna get your butt down there to the A&P and get your job back.

CORY: Mr. Stawicki done already hired somebody else 'cause I told him I was playing football.

TROY: You a bigger fool than I thought . . . to let somebody take away your job so you can play some football. Where you gonna get your money to take out your girlfriend and whatnot? What kind of foolishness is that to let somebody take away your job?

CORY: I'm still gonna be working weekends.

TROY: Naw . . . naw. You getting your butt out of here and finding you another job.

CORY: Come on, Pop! I got to practice. I can't work after school and play football too. The team needs me. That's what Coach Zellman say . . .

TROY: I don't care what nobody else say. I'm the boss . . . you understand? I'm the boss around here. I do the only saying what counts.

CORY: Come on, Pop!

TROY: I asked you . . . did you understand?

CORY: Yeah . . .

TROY: What?!

CORY: Yessir.

TROY: You go on down there to that A&P and see if you can get your job back. If you can't do both . . . then you quit the football team. You've got to take the crookeds with the straights.

CORY: Yessir.

(*Pause.*)

Can I ask you a question?

TROY: What the hell you wanna ask me? Mr. Stawicki the one you got the questions for.

CORY: How come you ain't never liked me?

TROY: Liked you? Who the hell say I got to like you? What law is there say I got to like you? Wanna stand up in my face and ask a damn fool-ass question like that. Talking about liking somebody. Come here, boy, when I talk to you.

(*Cory comes over to where Troy is working. He stands slouched over and Troy shoves him on his shoulder.*)

Straighten up, goddammit! I asked you a question . . . what is there say I got to like you?

CORY: None.

TROY: Well, all right then! Don't you eat every day?

(*Pause.*)

    Answer me when I talk to you! Don't you eat every day?

CORY: Yeah.

TROY: Nigger, as long as you in my house, you put that sir on the end of it when you talk to me!

CORY: Yes . . . sir.

TROY: You eat every day.

CORY: Yessir!

TROY: Got a roof over your head.

CORY: Yessir!

TROY: Got clothes on your back.

CORY: Yessir.

TROY: Why you think that is?

CORY: Cause of you.

TROY: Ah, hell I know it's 'cause of me . . . but why do you think that is?

CORY (*hesitant*): Cause you like me.

TROY: Like you? I go out of here every morning . . . bust my butt . . . putting up with them crackers° every day . . . cause I like you? You about the biggest fool I ever saw.

(*Pause.*)

    It's my job. It's my responsibility! You understand that? A man got to take care of his family. You live

crackers: White people (derogatory).

ABOVE LEFT: Lynn Thigpen and James Earl Jones in the 1987 production of *Fences.* ABOVE: James Earl Jones as Troy Maxson in *Fences.* RIGHT: Jones and Courtney Vance as his son Cory.

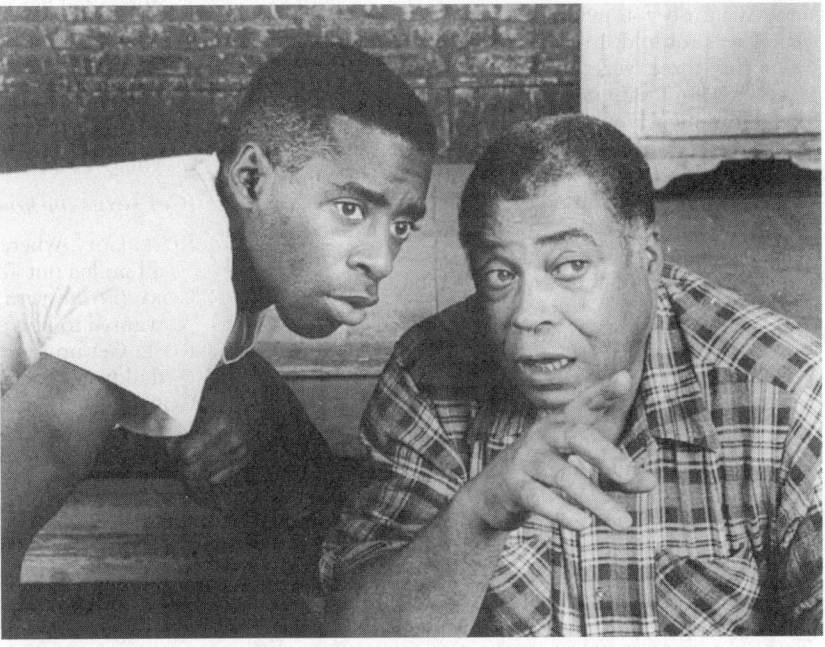

in my house . . . sleep you behind on my bed-clothes . . . fill you belly up with my food . . . cause you my son. You my flesh and blood. Not 'cause I like you! Cause it's my duty to take care of you. I owe a responsibility to you! Let's get this straight right here . . . before it go along any further . . . I ain't got to like you. Mr. Rand don't give me my money come pay-day cause he likes me. He gives me cause he owe me. I done give you everything I had to give you. I gave you your life! Me and your mama worked that out between us. And liking your black ass wasn't part of the bargain. Don't you try and go through life worrying about if somebody like you or not. You best be making sure they doing right by you. You understand what I'm saying, boy?

CORY: Yessir.

TROY: Then get the hell out of my face, and get on down to that A&P.

(*Rose has been standing behind the screen door for much of the scene. She enters as Cory exits.*)

ROSE: Why don't you let the boy go ahead and play football, Troy? Ain't no harm in that. He's just trying to be like you with the sports.

TROY: I don't want him to be like me! I want him to move as far away from my life as he can get. You the only decent thing that ever happened to me. I wish him that. But I don't wish him a thing else from my life. I decided seventeen years ago that boy wasn't getting involved in no sports. Not after what they did to me in the sports.

ROSE: Troy, why don't you admit you was too old to play in the major leagues? For once . . . why don't you admit that?

TROY: What do you mean too old? Don't come telling me I was too old. I just wasn't the right color. Hell, I'm fifty-three years old and can do better than Selkirk's .269 right now!

ROSE: How's was you gonna play ball when you were over forty? Sometimes I can't get no sense out of you.

TROY: I got good sense, woman. I got sense enough not to let my boy get hurt over playing no sports. You been mothering that boy too much. Worried about if people like him.

ROSE: Everything that boy do . . . he do for you. He wants you to say "Good job, son." That's all.

TROY: Rose, I ain't got time for that. He's alive. He's healthy. He's got to make his own way. I made mine. Ain't nobody gonna hold his hand when he get out there in that world.

ROSE: Times have changed from when you was young, Troy. People change. The world's changing around you and you can't even see it.

TROY (*slow, methodical*): Woman . . . I do the best I can do. I come in here every Friday. I carry a sack of potatoes and a bucket of lard. You all line up at the door with your hands out. I give you the lint from my pockets. I give you my sweat and my blood. I ain't

got no tears. I done spent them. We go upstairs in that room at night . . . and I fall down on you and try to blast a hole into forever. I get up Monday morning . . . find my lunch on the table. I go out. Make my way. Find my strength to carry me through to the next Friday.

(*Pause.*)

That's all I got, Rose. That's all I got to give. I can't give nothing else.

(*Troy exits into the house. The lights go down to black.*)

Scene IV

(*It is Friday. Two weeks later. Cory starts out of the house with his football equipment. The phone rings.*)

CORY (*calling*): I got it!

(*He answers the phone and stands in the screen door talking.*)

Hello? Hey, Jesse. Naw . . . I was just getting ready to leave now.

ROSE (*calling*): Cory!

CORY: I told you, man, them spikes is all tore up. You can use them if you want, but they ain't no good. Earl got some spikes.

ROSE (*calling*): Cory!

CORY (*calling to Rose*): Mam? I'm talking to Jesse.

(*Into phone.*)

When she say that? (*Pause.*) Aw, you lying, man. I'm gonna tell her you said that.

ROSE (*calling*): Cory, don't you go nowhere!

CORY: I got to go to the game, Ma!

(*Into the phone.*)

Yeah, hey, look, I'll talk to you later. Yeah, I'll meet you over Earl's house. Later. Bye, Ma.

(*Cory exits the house and starts out the yard.*)

ROSE: Cory, where you going off to? You got that stuff all pulled out and thrown all over your room.

CORY (*in the yard*): I was looking for my spikes. Jesse wanted to borrow my spikes.

ROSE: Get up there and get that cleaned up before your daddy get back in here.

CORY: I got to go to the game! I'll clean it up *when I get back*.

(*Cory exits.*)

ROSE: That's all he need to do is see that room all messed up.

(*Rose exits into the house. Troy and Bono enter the yard. Troy is dressed in clothes other than his work clothes.*)

BONO: He told him the same thing he told you. Take it to the union.

TROY: Brownie ain't got that much sense. Man wasn't thinking about nothing. He wait until I confront them on it . . . then he wanna come crying seniority.

(*Calls.*)

Hey, Rose!

BONO: I wish I could have seen Mr. Rand's face when he told you.

TROY: He couldn't get it out of his mouth! Liked to bit his tongue! When they called me down there to the Commissioner's office . . . he thought they was gonna fire me. Like everybody else.

BONO: I didn't think they was gonna fire you. I thought they was gonna put you on the warning paper.

TROY: Hey, Rose!

(*To Bono.*)

Yeah, Mr. Rand like to bit his tongue.

(*Troy breaks the seal on the bottle, takes a drink, and hands it to Bono.*)

BONO: I see you run right down to Taylors' and told that Alberta gal.

TROY (*calling*): Hey, Rose! (*To Bono.*) I told everybody. Hey, Rose! I went down there to cash my check.

ROSE (*entering from the house*): Hush all that hollering, man! I know you out here. What they say down there at the Commissioner's office?

TROY: You supposed to come when I call you, woman. Bono'll tell you that.

(*To Bono.*)

Don't Lucille come when you call her?

ROSE: Man, hush your mouth. I ain't no dog . . . talk about "come when you call me."

TROY (*puts his arm around Rose*): You hear this Bono? I had me an old dog used to get uppity like that. You say, "C'mere, Blue!" . . . and he just lay there and look at you. End up getting a stick and chasing him away trying to make him come.

ROSE: I ain't studying you and your dog. I remember you used to sing that old song.

TROY (*he sings*): Hear it ring! Hear it ring! I had a dog his name was Blue.

ROSE: Don't nobody wanna hear you sing that old song.

TROY (*sings*): You know Blue was mighty true.

ROSE: Used to have Cory running around here singing that song.

BONO: Hell, I remember that song myself.

TROY (*sings*): You know Blue was a good old dog.
Blue treed a possum in a hollow log.

That was my daddy's song. My daddy made up that song.

ROSE: I don't care who made it up. Don't nobody wanna hear you sing it.

TROY (*makes a song like calling a dog*): Come here, woman.

ROSE: You come in here carrying on, I reckon they ain't fired you. What they say down there at the Commissioner's office?

TROY: Look here, Rose . . . Mr. Rand called me into his office today when I got back from talking to them people down there . . . it come from up top . . . he called me in and told me they was making me a driver.

ROSE: Troy, you kidding!

TROY: No I ain't. Ask Bono.

ROSE: Well, that's great, Troy. Now you don't have to hassle them people no more.

(*Lyons enters from the street.*)

TROY: Aw hell, I wasn't looking to see you today. I thought you was in jail. Got it all over the front page of the *Courier* about them raiding Sefus' place . . . where you be hanging out with all them thugs.

LYONS: Hey, Pop . . . that ain't got nothing to do with me. I don't go down there gambling. I go down there to sit in with the band. I ain't got nothing to do with the gambling part. They got some good music down there.

TROY: They got some rogues . . . is what they got.

LYONS: How you been, Mr. Bono? Hi, Rose.

BONO: I see where you playing down at the Crawford Grill tonight.

ROSE: How come you ain't brought Bonnie like I told you. You should have brought Bonnie with you, she ain't been over in a month of Sundays.

LYONS: I was just in the neighborhood . . . thought I'd stop by.

TROY: Here he come . . .

BONO: Your daddy got a promotion on the rubbish. He's gonna be the first colored driver. Ain't got to do nothing but sit up there and read the paper like them white fellows.

LYONS: Hey, Pop . . . if you knew how to read you'd be all right.

BONO: Naw . . . naw . . . you mean if the nigger knew how to *drive* he'd be all right. Been fighting with them people about driving and ain't even got a license. Mr. Rand know you ain't got no driver's license?

TROY: Driving ain't nothing. All you do is point the truck where you want it to go. Driving ain't nothing.

BONO: Do Mr. Rand know you ain't got no driver's license? That's what I'm talking about. I ain't asked if driving was easy. I asked if Mr. Rand know you ain't got no driver's license.

TROY: He ain't got to know. The man ain't got to know my business. Time he find out, I have two or three driver's licenses.

LYONS (*going into his pocket*): Say, look here, Pop . . .

TROY: I knew it was coming. Didn't I tell you, Bono? I

know what kind of "Look here, Pop" that was. The nigger fixing to ask me for some money. It's Friday night. It's my payday. All them rogues down there on the avenue . . . the ones that ain't in jail . . . and Lyons is hopping in his shoes to get down there with them.

LYONS: See, Pop . . . if you give somebody else a chance to talk sometime, you'd see that I was fixing to pay you back your ten dollars like I told you. Here . . . I told you I'd pay you when Bonnie got paid.

TROY: Naw . . . you go ahead and keep that ten dollars. Put it in the bank. The next time you feel like you wanna come by here and ask me for something . . . you go on down there and get that.

LYONS: Here's your ten dollars, Pop. I told you I don't want you to give me nothing. I just wanted to borrow ten dollars.

TROY: Naw . . . you go on and keep that for the next time you want to ask me.

LYONS: Come on, Pop . . . here go your ten dollars.

ROSE: Why don't you go on and let the boy pay you back, Troy?

LYONS: Here you go, Rose. If you don't take it I'm gonna have to hear about it for the next six months.

(*He hands her the money.*)

ROSE: You can hand yours over here too, Troy.

TROY: You see this, Bono. You see how they do me.

BONO: Yeah, Lucille do me the same way.

(*Gabriel is heard singing offstage. He enters.*)

GABRIEL: Better get ready for the Judgment! Better get ready for . . . Hey! . . . Hey! . . . There's Troy's boy!

LYONS: How are you doing, Uncle Gabe?

GABRIEL: Lyons . . . The King of the Jungle! Rose . . . hey, Rose. Got a flower for you.

(*He takes a rose from his pocket.*)

Picked it myself. That's the same rose like you is!

ROSE: That's right nice of you, Gabe.

LYONS: What you been doing, Uncle Gabe?

GABRIEL: Oh, I been chasing hellhounds and waiting on the time to tell St. Peter to open the gates.

LYONS: You been chasing hellhounds, huh? Well . . . you doing the right thing, Uncle Gabe. Somebody got to chase them.

GABRIEL: Oh, yeah . . . I know it. The devil's strong. The devil ain't no pushover. Hellhounds snipping at everybody's heels. But I got my trumpet waiting on the judgment time.

LYONS: Waiting on the Battle of Armageddon, huh?

GABRIEL: Ain't gonna be too much of a battle when God get to waving that Judgment sword. But the people's gonna have a hell of a time trying to get into heaven if them gates ain't open.

LYONS (*putting his arm around Gabriel*): You hear this, Pop. Uncle Gabe, you all right!

GABRIEL (*laughing with Lyons*): Lyons! King of the Jungle.

ROSE: You gonna stay for supper, Gabe. Want me to fix you a plate?

GABRIEL: I'll take a sandwich, Rose. Don't want no plate. Just wanna eat with my hands. I'll take a sandwich.

ROSE: How about you, Lyons? You staying? Got some short ribs cooking.

LYONS: Naw, I won't eat nothing till after we finished playing.

(*Pause.*)

You ought to come down and listen to me play, Pop.

TROY: I don't like that Chinese music. All that noise.

ROSE: Go on in the house and wash up, Gabe . . . I'll fix you a sandwich.

GABRIEL (*to Lyons, as he exits*): Troy's mad at me.

LYONS: What you mad at Uncle Gabe for, Pop.

ROSE: He thinks Troy's mad at him cause he moved over to Miss Pearl's.

TROY: I ain't mad at the man. He can live where he want to live at.

LYONS: What he move over there for? Miss Pearl don't like nobody.

ROSE: She don't mind him none. She treats him real nice. She just don't allow all that singing.

TROY: She don't mind that rent he be paying . . . that's what she don't mind.

ROSE: Troy, I ain't going through that with you no more. He's over there cause he want to have his own place. He can come and go as he please.

TROY: Hell, he could come and go as he please here. I wasn't stopping him. I ain't put no rules on him.

ROSE: It ain't the same thing, Troy. And you know it.

(*Gabriel comes to the door.*)

Now, that's the last I wanna hear about that. I don't wanna hear nothing else about Gabe and Miss Pearl. And next week . . .

GABRIEL: I'm ready for my sandwich, Rose.

ROSE: And next week . . . when that recruiter come from that school . . . I want you to sign that paper and go on and let Cory play football. Then that'll be the last I have to hear about that.

TROY (*to Rose as she exits into the house*): I ain't thinking about Cory nothing.

LYONS: What . . . Cory got recruited? What school he going to?

TROY: That boy walking around here smelling his piss . . . thinking he's grown. Thinking he's gonna do what he want, irrespective of what I say. Look here, Bono . . . I left the Commissioner's office and went down to the A&P . . . that boy ain't working down there. He lying to me. Telling me he got his job back . . . telling me he working weekends . . . telling me he working after school . . . Mr. Stawicki tell me he ain't working down there at all!

LYONS: Cory just growing up. He's just busting at the seams trying to fill out your shoes.

TROY: I don't care what he's doing. When he get to the point where he wanna disobey me . . . then it's time for him to move on. Bono'll tell you that. I bet he ain't never disobeyed his daddy without paying the consequences.

BONO: I ain't never had a chance. My daddy came on through . . . but I ain't never knew him to see him . . . or what he had on his mind or where he went. Just moving on through. Searching out the New Land. That's what the old folks used to call it. See a fellow moving around from place to place . . . woman to woman . . . called it searching out the New Land. I can't say if he ever found it. I come along, didn't want no kids. Didn't know if I was gonna be in one place long enough to fix on them right as their daddy. I figured I was going searching too. As it turned out I been hooked up with Lucille near about as long as your daddy been with Rose. Going on sixteen years.

TROY: Sometimes I wish I hadn't known my daddy. He ain't cared nothing about no kids. A kid to him wasn't nothing. All he wanted was for you to learn how to walk so he could start you to working. When it come time for eating . . . he ate first. If there was anything left over, that's what you got. Man would sit down and eat two chickens and give you the wing.

LYONS: You ought to stop that, Pop. Everybody feed their kids. No matter how hard times is . . . everybody care about their kids. Make sure they have something to eat.

TROY: The only thing my daddy cared about was getting them bales of cotton in to Mr. Lubin. That's the only thing that mattered to him. Sometimes I used to wonder why he was living. Wonder why the devil hadn't come and got him. "Get them bales of cotton in to Mr. Lubin" and find out he owe him money . . .

LYONS: He should have just went on and left when he saw he couldn't get nowhere. That's what I would have done.

TROY: How he gonna leave with eleven kids? And where he gonna go? He ain't knew how to do nothing but farm. No, he was trapped and I think he knew it. But I'll say this for him . . . he felt a responsibility toward us. Maybe he ain't treated us the way I felt he should have . . . but without that responsibility he could have walked off and left us . . . made his own way.

BONO: A lot of them did. Back in those days what you talking about . . . they walk out their front door and just take on down one road or another and keep on walking.

LYONS: There you go! That's what I'm talking about.

BONO: Just keep on walking till you come to something else. Ain't you never heard of nobody having the walking blues? Well, that's what you call it when you just take off like that.

TROY: My daddy ain't had them walking blues! What you talking about? He stayed right there with his family. But he was just as evil as he could be. My mama couldn't stand him. Couldn't stand that evilness. She run off when I was about eight. She sneaked off one night after he had gone to sleep. Told me she was coming back for me. I ain't never seen her no more. All his women run off and left him. He wasn't good for nobody.

When my turn come to head out, I was fourteen and got to sniffing around Joe Canewell's daughter. Had us an old mule we called Greyboy. My daddy sent me out to do some plowing and I tied up Greyboy and went to fooling around with Joe Canewell's daughter. We done found us a nice little spot, got real cozy with each other. She about thirteen and we done figured we was grown anyway . . . so we down there enjoying ourselves . . . ain't thinking about nothing. We didn't know Greyboy had got loose and wandered back to the house and my daddy was looking for me. We down there by the creek enjoying ourselves when my daddy come up on us. Surprised us. He had them leather straps off the mule and commenced to whupping me like there was no tomorrow. I jumped up, mad and embarrassed. I was scared of my daddy. When he commenced to whupping on me . . . quite naturally I run to get out of the way.

(*Pause.*)

Now I thought he was mad cause I ain't done my work. But I see where he was chasing me off so he could have the gal for himself. When I see what the matter of it was, I lost all fear of my daddy. Right there is where I become a man . . . at fourteen years of age.

(*Pause.*)

Now it was my turn to run him off. I picked up them same reins that he had used on me. I picked up them reins and commenced to whupping on him. The gal jumped up and run off . . . and when my daddy turned to face me, I could see why the devil had never come to get him . . . cause he was the devil himself. I don't know what happened. When I woke up, I was laying right there by the creek, and Blue . . . this old dog we had . . . was licking my face. I thought I was blind. I couldn't see nothing. Both my eyes were swollen shut. I layed there and cried. I didn't know what I was gonna do. The only thing I knew was the time had come for me to leave my daddy's house. And right there the world suddenly got big. And it was a long time before I could cut it down to where I could handle it.

Part of that cutting down was when I got to the place where I could feel him kicking in my blood and knew that the only thing that separated us was the matter of a few years.

(*Gabriel enters from the house with a sandwich.*)

LYONS: What you got there, Uncle Gabe?

GABRIEL: Got me a ham sandwich. Rose gave me a ham sandwich.

TROY: I don't know what happened to him. I done lost touch with everybody except Gabriel. But I hope he's dead. I hope he found some peace.

LYONS: That's a heavy story, Pop. I didn't know you left home when you was fourteen.

TROY: And didn't know nothing. The only part of the world I knew was the forty-two acres of Mr. Lubin's land. That's all I knew about life.

LYONS: Fourteen's kinda young to be out on your own. (*Phone rings.*) I don't even think I was ready to be out on my own at fourteen. I don't know what I would have done.

TROY: I got up from the creek and walked on down to Mobile. I was through with farming. Figured I could do better in the city. So I walked the two hundred miles to Mobile.

LYONS: Wait a minute . . . you ain't walked no two hundred miles, Pop. Ain't nobody gonna walk no two hundred miles. You talking about some walking there.

BONO: That's the only way you got anywhere back in them days.

LYONS: Shhh. Damn if I wouldn't have hitched a ride with somebody!

TROY: Who you gonna hitch it with? They ain't had no cars and things like they got now. We talking about 1918.

ROSE (*entering*): What you all out here getting into?

TROY (*to Rose*): I'm telling Lyons how good he got it. He don't know nothing about this I'm talking.

ROSE: Lyons, that was Bonnie on the phone. She say you supposed to pick her up.

LYONS: Yeah, okay, Rose.

TROY: I walked on down to Mobile and hitched up with some of them fellows that was heading this way. Got up here and found out . . . not only couldn't you get a job . . . you couldn't find no place to live. I thought I was in freedom. Shhh. Colored folks living down there on the riverbanks in whatever kind of shelter they could find for themselves. Right down there under the Brady Street Bridge. Living in shacks made of sticks and tarpaper. Messed around there and went from bad to worse. Started stealing. First it was food. Then I figured, hell, if I steal money I can buy me some food. Buy me some shoes too! One thing led to another. Met your mama. I was young and anxious to be a man. Met your mama and had you. What I do that for? Now I got to worry about feeding you and her. Got to steal three times as much. Went out one day looking for somebody to rob . . . that's what I was, a robber. I'll tell you the truth. I'm ashamed of it today. But it's the truth. Went to rob this fellow . . . pulled out my knife . . . and he pulled out a gun. Shot me in the chest. It felt just like somebody had taken a hot branding iron and laid it on me. When he shot me I jumped at him with my knife. They told me I killed him and they put me in the penitentiary and locked me up for fifteen years. That's where I met Bono. That's where I learned how to play baseball. Got out that place and your mama had taken you and went on to make life without me. Fifteen years was a long time for her to wait. But that fifteen years cured me of that robbing stuff. Rose'll tell you. She asked me when I met her if

I had gotten all that foolishness out of my system. And I told her, "Baby, it's you and baseball all what count with me." You hear me, Bono? I meant it too. She say "Which one comes first?" I told her, "Baby, ain't no doubt it's baseball . . . but you stick and get old with me and we'll both outlive this baseball." Am I right, Rose? And it's true.

ROSE: Man, hush your mouth. You ain't said no such thing. Talking about, "Baby, you know you'll always be number one with me." That's what you was talking.

TROY: You hear that, Bono. That's why I love her.

BONO: Rose'll keep you straight. You get off the track, she'll straighten you up.

ROSE: Lyons, you better get on up and get Bonnie. She waiting on you.

LYONS (*gets up to go*): Hey, Pop, why don't you come on down to the Grill and hear me play?

TROY: I ain't going down there. I'm too old to be sitting around in them clubs.

BONO: You got to be good to play down at the Grill.

LYONS: Come on, Pop . . .

TROY: I got to get up in the morning.

LYONS: You ain't got to stay long.

TROY: Naw, I'm gonna get my supper and go on to bed.

LYONS: Well, I got to go. I'll see you again.

TROY: Don't you come around my house on my payday.

ROSE: Pick up the phone and let somebody know you coming. And bring Bonnie with you. You know I'm always glad to see her.

LYONS: Yeah, I'll do that, Rose. You take care now. See you, Pop. See you, Mr. Bono. See you, Uncle Gabe.

GABRIEL: Lyons! King of the Jungle!

(*Lyons exits.*)

TROY: Is supper ready, woman? Me and you got some business to take care of. I'm gonna tear it up too.

ROSE: Troy, I done told you now!

TROY (*puts his arm around Bono*): Aw hell, woman . . . this is Bono. Bono like family. I done known this nigger since . . . how long I done know you?

BONO: It's been a long time.

TROY: I done known this nigger since Skippy was a pup. Me and him done been through some times.

BONO: You sure right about that.

TROY: Hell, I done know him longer than I known you. And we still standing shoulder to shoulder. Hey, look here, Bono . . . a man can't ask for no more than that.

(*Drinks to him.*)

I love you, nigger.

BONO: Hell, I love you too . . . but I got to get home see my woman. You got yours in hand. I got to go get mine.

(*Bono starts to exit as Cory enters the yard, dressed in his football uniform. He gives Troy a hard, uncompromising look.*)

CORY: What you do that for, Pop?

(*He throws his helmet down in the direction of Troy.*)

ROSE: What's the matter? Cory . . . what's the matter?
CORY: Papa done went up to the school and told Coach Zellman I can't play football no more. Wouldn't even let me play the game. Told him to tell the recruiter not to come.
ROSE: Troy . . .
TROY: What you Troying me for. Yeah, I did it. And the boy know why I did it.
CORY: Why you wanna do that to me? That was the one chance I had.
ROSE: Ain't nothing wrong with Cory playing football, Troy.
TROY: The boy lied to me. I told the nigger if he wanna play football . . . to keep up his chores and hold down that job at the A&P. That was the conditions. Stopped down there to see Mr. Stawicki . . .
CORY: I can't work after school during the football season, Pop! I tried to tell you that Mr. Stawicki's holding my job for me. You don't never want to listen to nobody. And then you wanna go and do this to me!
TROY: I ain't done nothing to you. You done it to yourself.
CORY: Just cause you didn't have a chance! You just scared I'm gonna be better than you, that's all.
TROY: Come here.
ROSE: Troy . . .

(*Cory reluctantly crosses over to Troy.*)

TROY: All right! See. You done made a mistake.
CORY: I didn't even do nothing!
TROY: I'm gonna tell you what your mistake was. See . . . you swung at the ball and didn't hit it. That's strike one. See, you in the batter's box now. You swung and you missed. That's strike one. Don't you strike out!

(*Lights fade to black.*)

ACT II • *Scene I*

(*The following morning. Cory is at the tree hitting the ball with the bat. He tries to mimic Troy, but his swing is awkward, less sure. Rose enters from the house.*)

ROSE: Cory, I want you to help me with this cupboard.
CORY: I ain't quitting the team. I don't care what Poppa say.
ROSE: I'll talk to him when he gets back. He had to go see about your Uncle Gabe. The police done arrested him. Say he was disturbing the peace. He'll be back directly. Come on in here and help me clean out the top of this cupboard.

(*Cory exits into the house. Rose sees Troy and Bono coming down the alley.*)

Troy . . . what they say down there?

TROY: Ain't said nothing. I give them fifty dollars and they let him go. I'll talk to you about it. Where's Cory?
ROSE: He's in there helping me clean out these cupboards.
TROY: Tell him to get his butt out here.

(*Troy and Bono go over to the pile of wood. Bono picks up the saw and begins sawing.*)

TROY (*to Bono*): All they want is the money. That makes six or seven times I done went down there and got him. See me coming they stick out their *hands.*
BONO: Yeah. I know what you mean. That's all they care about . . . that money. They don't care about what's right.

(*Pause.*)

Nigger, why you got to go and get some hard wood? You ain't doing nothing but building a little old fence. Get you some soft pine wood. That's all you need.
TROY: I know what I'm doing. This is outside wood. You put pine wood inside the house. Pine wood is inside wood. This here is outside wood. Now you tell me where the fence is gonna be?
BONO: You don't need this wood. You can put it up with pine wood and it'll stand as long as you gonna be here looking at it.
TROY: How you know how long I'm gonna be here, nigger? Hell, I might just live forever. Live longer than old man Horsely.
BONO: That's what Magee used to say.
TROY: Magee's a damn fool. Now you tell me who you ever heard of gonna pull their own teeth with a pair of rusty pliers.
BONO: The old folks . . . my granddaddy used to pull his teeth with pliers. They ain't had no dentists for the colored folks back then.
TROY: Get clean pliers! You understand? Clean pliers! Sterilize them! Besides we ain't living back then. All Magee had to do was walk over to Doc Goldblum's.
BONO: I see where you and that Tallahassee gal . . . that Alberta . . . I see where you all done got tight.
TROY: What you mean "got tight"?
BONO: I see where you be laughing and joking with her all the time.
TROY: I laughs and jokes with all of them, Bono. You know me.
BONO: That ain't the kind of laughing and joking I'm talking about.

(*Cory enters from the house.*)

CORY: How you doing, Mr. Bono?
TROY: Cory? Get that saw from Bono and cut some wood. He talking about the wood's too hard to cut. Stand back there, Jim, and let that young boy show you how it's done.
BONO: He's sure welcome to it.

(*Cory takes the saw and begins to cut the wood.*)

Whew-e-e! Look at that. Big old strong boy. Look like Joe Louis. Hell, must be getting old the way I'm watching that boy whip through that wood.

CORY: I don't see why Mama want a fence around the yard noways.

TROY: Damn if I know either. What the hell she keeping out with it? She ain't got nothing nobody want.

BONO: Some people build fences to keep people out . . . and other people build fences to keep people in. Rose wants to hold on to you all. She loves you.

TROY: Hell, nigger, I don't need nobody to tell me my wife loves me, Cory . . . go on in the house and see if you can find that other saw.

CORY: Where's it at?

TROY: I said find it! Look for it till you find it!

(*Cory exits into the house.*)

What's that supposed to mean? Wanna keep us in?

BONO: Troy . . . I done known you seem like damn near my whole life. You and Rose both. I done know both of you all for a long time. I remember when you met Rose. When you was hitting them baseball out the park. A lot of them old gals was after you then. You had the pick of the litter. When you picked Rose, I was happy for you. That was the first time I knew you had any sense. I said . . . My man Troy knows what he's doing . . . I'm gonna follow this nigger . . . he might take me somewhere. I been following you too. I done learned a whole heap of things about life watching you. I done learned how to tell where the shit lies. How to tell it from the alfalfa. You done learned me a lot of things. You showed me how to not make the same mistakes . . . to take life as it comes along and keep putting one foot in front of the other.

(*Pause.*)

Rose a good woman, Troy.

TROY: Hell, nigger, I know she a good woman. I been married to her for eighteen years. What you got on your mind, Bono?

BONO: I just say she a good woman. Just like I say anything. I ain't got to have nothing on my mind.

TROY: You just gonna say she a good woman and leave it hanging out there like that? Why you telling me she a good woman?

BONO: She loves you, Troy. Rose loves you.

TROY: You saying I don't measure up. That's what you trying to say. I don't measure up cause I'm seeing this other gal. I know what you trying to say.

BONO: I know what Rose means to you, Troy. I'm just trying to say I don't want to see you mess up.

TROY: Yeah, I appreciate that, Bono. If you was messing around on Lucille I'd be telling you the same thing.

BONO: Well, that's all I got to say. I just say that because I love you both.

TROY: Hell, you know me . . . I wasn't out there looking for nothing. You can't find a better woman than Rose. I know that. But seems like this woman just stuck onto me where I can't shake her loose. I done wrestled with it, tried to throw her off me . . . but she just stuck on tighter. Now she's stuck on for good.

BONO: You's in control . . . that's what you tell me all the time. You responsible for what you do.

TROY: I ain't ducking the responsibility of it. As long as it sets right in my heart . . . then I'm okay. Cause that's all I listen to. It'll tell me right from wrong every time. And I ain't talking about doing Rose no bad turn. I love Rose. She done carried me a long ways and I love and respect her for that.

BONO: I know you do. That's why I don't want to see you hurt her. But what you gonna do when she find out? What you got then? If you try and juggle both of them . . . sooner or later you gonna drop one of them. That's common sense.

TROY: Yeah, I hear what you saying, Bono. I been trying to figure a way to work it out.

BONO: Work it out right, Troy. I don't want to be getting all up between you and Rose's business . . . but work it so it come out right.

TROY: Ah hell, I get all up between you and Lucille's business. When you gonna get that woman that refrigerator she been wanting? Don't tell me you ain't got no money now. I know who your banker is. Mellon don't need that money bad as Lucille want that refrigerator. I'll tell you that.

BONO: Tell you what I'll do . . . when you finish building this fence for Rose . . . I'll buy Lucille that refrigerator.

TROY: You done stuck your foot in your mouth now!

(*Troy grabs up a board and begins to saw. Bono starts to walk out the yard.*)

Hey, nigger . . . where you going?

BONO: I'm going home. I know you don't expect me to help you now. I'm protecting my money. I wanna see you put that fence up by yourself. That's what I want to see. You'll be here another six months without me.

TROY: Nigger, you ain't right.

BONO: When it comes to my money . . . I'm right as fireworks on the Fourth of July.

TROY: All right, we gonna see now. You better get out your bankbook.

(*Bono exits, and Troy continues to work. Rose enters from the house.*)

ROSE: What they say down there? What's happening with Gabe?

TROY: I went down there and got him out. Cost me fifty dollars. Say he was disturbing the peace. Judge set up a hearing for him in three weeks. Say to show cause why he shouldn't be recommitted.

ROSE: What was he doing that cause them to arrest him?

TROY: Some kids was teasing him and he run them off home. Say he was howling and carrying on. Some folks seen him and called the police. That's all it was.

ROSE: Well, what's you say? What'd you tell the judge?

TROY: Told him I'd look after him. It didn't make no sense to recommit the man. He stuck out his big greasy palm and told me to give him fifty dollars and take him on home.

ROSE: Where's he at now? Where'd he go off to?

TROY: He's gone on about his business. He don't need nobody to hold his hand.

ROSE: Well, I don't know. Seem like that would be the best place for him if they did put him into the hospital. I know what you're gonna say. But that's what I think would be best.

TROY: The man done had his life ruined fighting for what? And they wanna take and lock him up. Let him be free. He don't bother nobody.

ROSE: Well, everybody got their own way of looking at it I guess. Come on and get your lunch. I got a bowl of lima beans and some cornbread in the oven. Come on get something to eat. Ain't no sense you fretting over Gabe.

(*Rose turns to go into the house.*)

TROY: Rose . . . got something to tell you.

ROSE: Well, come on . . . wait till I get this food on the table.

TROY: Rose!

(*She stops and turns around.*)

I don't know how to say this.

(*Pause.*)

I can't explain it none. It just sort of grows on you till it gets out of hand. It starts out like a little bush . . . and the next thing you know it's a whole forest.

ROSE: Troy . . . what is you talking about?

TROY: I'm talking, woman, let me talk. I'm trying to find a way to tell you . . . I'm gonna be a daddy. I'm gonna be somebody's daddy.

ROSE: Troy . . . you're not telling me this? You're gonna be . . . what?

TROY: Rose . . . now . . . see . . .

ROSE: You telling me you gonna be somebody's daddy? You telling your *wife* this?

(*Gabriel enters from the street. He carries a rose in his hand.*)

GABRIEL: Hey, Troy! Hey, Rose!

ROSE: I have to wait eighteen years to hear something like this.

GABRIEL: Hey, Rose . . . I got a flower for you.

(*He hands it to her.*)

That's a rose. Same rose like you is.

ROSE: Thanks, Gabe.

GABRIEL: Troy, you ain't mad at me is you? Them bad mens come and put me away. You ain't mad at me is you?

TROY: Naw, Gabe, I ain't mad at you.

ROSE: Eighteen years and you wanna come with this.

GABRIEL (*takes a quarter out of his pocket*): See what I got? Got a brand new quarter.

TROY: Rose . . . it's just . . .

ROSE: Ain't nothing you can say, Troy. Ain't no way of explaining that.

GABRIEL: Fellow that give me this quarter had a whole mess of them. I'm gonna keep this quarter till it stop shining.

ROSE: Gabe, go on in the house there. I got some watermelon in the frigidaire. Go on and get you a piece.

GABRIEL: Say, Rose . . . you know I was chasing hell-hounds and them bad mens come and get me and take me away. Troy helped me. He come down there and told them they better let me go before he beat them up. Yeah, he did!

ROSE: You go on and get you a piece of watermelon, Gabe. Them bad mens is gone now.

GABRIEL: Okay, Rose . . . gonna get me some watermelon. The kind with the stripes on it.

(*Gabriel exits into the house.*)

ROSE: Why, Troy? Why? After all these years to come dragging this in to me now. It don't make no sense at your age. I could have expected this ten or fifteen years ago, but not now.

TROY: Age ain't got nothing to do with it, Rose.

ROSE: I done tried to be everything a wife should be. Everything a wife could be. Been married eighteen years and I got to live to see the day you tell me you been seeing another woman and done fathered a child by her. And you know I ain't never wanted no half nothing in my family. My whole family is half. Everybody got different fathers and mothers . . . my two sisters and my brother. Can't hardly tell who's who. Can't never sit down and talk about Papa and Mama. It's your papa and your mama and my papa and my mama . . .

TROY: Rose . . . stop it now.

ROSE: I ain't never wanted that for none of my children. And now you wanna drag your behind in here and tell me something like this.

TROY: You ought to know. It's time for you to know.

ROSE: Well, I don't want to know, goddamn it!

TROY: I can't just make it go away. It's done now. I can't wish the circumstance of the thing away.

ROSE: And you don't want to either. Maybe you want to wish me and my boy away. Maybe that's what you want? Well, you can't wish us away. I've got eighteen years of my life invested in you. You ought to have stayed upstairs in my bed where you belong.

TROY: Rose . . . now listen to me . . . we can get a handle on this thing. We can talk this out . . . come to an understanding.

ROSE: All of a sudden it's "we." Where was "we" at when you was down there rolling around with some godforsaken woman? "We" should have come to an understanding before you started making a damn fool of yourself. You're a day late and a dollar short when it comes to an understanding with me.

TROY: It's just . . . She gives me a different idea . . . a different understanding about myself. I can step out of this house and get away from the pressures and problems . . . be a different man. I ain't got to wonder how

I'm gonna pay the bills or get the roof fixed. I can just be a part of myself that I ain't never been.

ROSE: What I want to know . . . is do you plan to continue seeing her. That's all you can say to me.

TROY: I can sit up in her house and laugh. Do you understand what I'm saying. I can laugh out loud . . . and it feels good. It reaches all the way down to the bottom of my shoes.

(*Pause.*)

Rose, I can't give that up.

ROSE: Maybe you ought to go on and stay down there with her . . . if she's a better woman than me.

TROY: It ain't about nobody being a better woman or nothing. Rose, you ain't the blame. A man couldn't ask for no woman to be a better wife than you've been. I'm responsible for it. I done locked myself into a pattern trying to take care of you all that I forgot about myself.

ROSE: What the hell was I there for? That was my job, not somebody else's.

TROY: Rose, I done tried all my life to live decent . . . to live a clean . . . hard . . . useful life. I tried to be a good husband to you. In every way I knew how. Maybe I come into the world backwards, I don't know. But . . . you born with two strikes on you before you come to the plate. You got to guard it closely . . . always looking for the curve ball on the inside corner. You can't afford to let none get past you. You can't afford a call strike. If you going down . . . you going down swinging. Everything lined up against you. What you gonna do. I fooled them, Rose. I bunted. When I found you and Cory and a halfway decent job . . . I was safe. Couldn't nothing touch me. I wasn't gonna strike out no more. I wasn't going back to the penitentiary. I wasn't gonna lay in the streets with a bottle of wine. I was safe. I had me a family. A job. I wasn't gonna get that last strike. I was on first looking for one of them boys to knock me in. To get me home.

ROSE: You should have stayed in my bed, Troy.

TROY: Then when I saw that gal . . . she firmed up my backbone. And I got to thinking that if I tried . . . I just might be able to steal second. Do you understand after eighteen years I wanted to steal second.

ROSE: You should have held me tight. You should have grabbed me and held on.

TROY: I stood on first base for eighteen years and I thought . . . well, goddamn it . . . go on for it!

ROSE: We're not talking about baseball! We're talking about you going off to lay in bed with another woman . . . and then bring it home to me. That's what we're talking about. We ain't talking about no baseball.

TROY: Rose, you're not listening to me. I'm trying the best I can to explain it to you. It's not easy for me to admit that I been standing in the same place for eighteen years.

ROSE: I been standing with you! I been right here with you, Troy. I got a life too. I gave eighteen years of my life to stand in the same spot with you. Don't you think I ever wanted other things? Don't you think I had dreams and hopes? What about my life? What about me. Don't you think it ever crossed my mind to want to know other men? That I wanted to lay up somewhere and forget about my responsibilities? That I wanted someone to make me laugh so I could feel good? You not the only one who's got wants and needs. But I held on to you, Troy. I took all my feelings, my wants and needs, my dreams . . . and I buried them inside you. I planted a seed and watched and prayed over it. I planted myself inside you and waited to bloom. And it didn't take me no eighteen years to find out the soil was hard and rocky and it wasn't never gonna bloom.

But I held on to you, Troy. I held you tighter. You was my husband. I owed you everything I had. Every part of me I could find to give you. And upstairs in that room . . . with the darkness falling in on me . . . I gave everything I had to try and erase the doubt that you wasn't the finest man in the world. And wherever you was going . . . I wanted to be there with you. Cause you was my husband. Cause that's the only way I was gonna survive as your wife. You always talking about what you give . . . and what you don't have to give. But you take too. You take . . . and don't even know nobody's giving!

(*Rose turns to exit into the house; Troy grabs her arm.*)

TROY: You say I take and don't give!

ROSE: Troy! You're hurting me!

TROY: You say I take and don't give.

ROSE: Troy . . . you're hurting my arm! Let go!

TROY: I done give you everything I got. Don't you tell that lie on me.

ROSE: Troy!

TROY: Don't you tell that lie on me!

(*Cory enters from the house.*)

CORY: Mama!

ROSE: Troy. You're hurting me.

TROY: Don't you tell me about no taking and giving.

(*Cory comes up behind Troy and grabs him. Troy, surprised, is thrown off balance just as Cory throws a glancing blow that catches him on the chest and knocks him down. Troy is stunned, as is Cory.*)

ROSE: Troy. Troy. No!

(*Troy gets to his feet and starts at Cory.*)

Troy . . . no. Please! Troy!

(*Rose pulls on Troy to hold him back. Troy stops himself.*)

TROY (*to Cory*): All right. That's strike two. You stay away from around me, boy. Don't you strike out. You living with a full count. Don't you strike out.

(*Troy exits out the yard as the lights go down.*)

Scene II

(*It is six months later, early afternoon. Troy enters from the house and starts to exit the yard. Rose enters from the house.*)

ROSE: Troy, I want to talk to you.

TROY: All of a sudden, after all this time, you want to talk to me, huh? You ain't wanted to talk to me for months. You ain't wanted to talk to me last night. You ain't wanted no part of me then. What you wanna talk to me about now?

ROSE: Tomorrow's Friday.

TROY: I know what day tomorrow is. You think I don't know tomorrow's Friday? My whole life I ain't done nothing but look to see Friday coming and you got to tell me it's Friday.

ROSE: I want to know if you're coming home.

TROY: I always come home, Rose. You know that. There ain't never been a night I ain't come home.

ROSE: That ain't what I mean . . . and you know it. I want to know if you're coming straight home after work.

TROY: I figure I'd cash my check . . . hang out at Taylors' with the boys . . . maybe play a game of checkers . . .

ROSE: Troy, I can't live like this. I won't live like this. You livin' on borrowed time with me. It's been going on six months now you ain't been coming home.

TROY: I be here every night. Every night of the year. That's 365 days.

ROSE: I want you to come home tomorrow after work.

TROY: Rose . . . I don't mess up my pay. You know that now. I take my pay and I give it to you. I don't have no money but what you give me back. I just want to have a little time to myself . . . a little time to enjoy life.

ROSE: What about me? When's my time to enjoy life?

TROY: I don't know what to tell you, Rose. I'm doing the best I can.

ROSE: You ain't been home from work but time enough to change your clothes and run out . . . and you wanna call that the best you can do?

TROY: I'm going over to the hospital to see Alberta. She went into the hospital this afternoon. Look like she might have the baby early. I won't be gone long.

ROSE: Well, you ought to know. They went over to Miss Pearl's and got Gabe today. She said you told them to go ahead and lock him up.

TROY: I ain't said no such thing. Whoever told you that is telling a lie. Pearl ain't doing nothing but telling a big fat lie.

ROSE: She ain't had to tell me. I read it on the papers.

TROY: I ain't told them nothing of the kind.

ROSE: I saw it right there on the papers.

TROY: What it say, huh?

ROSE: It said you told them to take him.

TROY: Then they screwed that up, just the way they screw up everything. I ain't worried about what they got on the paper.

ROSE: Say the government send part of his check to the hospital and the other part to you.

TROY: I ain't got nothing to do with that if that's the way it works. I ain't made up the rules about how it work.

ROSE: You did Gabe just like you did Cory. You wouldn't sign the paper for Cory . . . but you signed for Gabe. You signed that paper.

(*The telephone is heard ringing inside the house.*)

TROY: I told you I ain't signed nothing, woman! The only thing I signed was the release form. Hell, I can't read, I don't know what they had on that paper! I ain't signed nothing about sending Gabe away.

ROSE: I said send him to the hospital . . . you said let him be free . . . now you done went down there and signed him to the hospital for half his money. You went back on yourself, Troy. You gonna have to answer for that.

TROY: See now . . . you been over there talking to Miss Pearl. She done got mad cause she ain't getting Gabe's rent money. That's all it is. She's liable to say anything.

ROSE: Troy, I seen where you signed the paper.

TROY: You ain't seen nothing I signed. What she doing got papers on my brother anyway? Miss Pearl telling a big fat lie. And I'm gonna tell her about it too! You ain't seen nothing I signed. Say . . . you ain't seen nothing I signed.

(*Rose exits into the house to answer the telephone. Presently she returns.*)

ROSE: Troy . . . that was the hospital. Alberta had the baby.

TROY: What she have? What is it?

ROSE: It's a girl.

TROY: I better get on down to the hospital to see her.

ROSE: Troy . . .

TROY: Rose . . . I got to go see her now. That's only right . . . what's the matter . . . the baby's all right, ain't it?

ROSE: Alberta died having the baby.

TROY: Died . . . you say she's dead? Alberta's dead?

ROSE: They said they done all they could. They couldn't do nothing for her.

TROY: The baby? How's the baby?

ROSE: They say it's healthy. I wonder who's gonna bury her.

TROY: She had family, Rose. She wasn't living in the world by herself.

ROSE: I know she wasn't living in the world by herself.

TROY: Next thing you gonna want to know if she had any insurance.

ROSE: Troy, you ain't got to talk like that.

TROY: That's the first thing that jumped out your mouth. "Who's gonna bury her?" Like I'm fixing to take on that task for myself.

ROSE: I am your wife. Don't push me away.

TROY: I ain't pushing nobody away. Just give me some space. That's all. Just give me some room to breathe.

(*Rose exits into the house. Troy walks about the yard.*)

TROY (*with a quiet rage that threatens to consume him*): All right . . . Mr. Death. See now . . . I'm gonna tell you what I'm gonna do. I'm gonna take and build me a fence around this yard. See? I'm gonna build me a fence around what belongs to me. And then I want you to stay on the other side. See? You stay over there until you're ready for me. Then you come on. Bring your army. Bring your sickle. Bring your wrestling clothes. I ain't gonna fall down on my vigilance this time. You ain't gonna sneak up on me no more. When you ready for me . . . when the top of your list say Troy Maxson . . . that's when you come around here. You come up and knock on the front door. Ain't nobody else got nothing to do with this. This is between you and me. Man to man. You stay on the other side of that fence until you ready for me. Then you come up and knock on the front door. Anytime you want. I'll be ready for you.

(*The lights go down to black.*)

Scene III

(*The lights come up on the porch. It is late evening three days later. Rose sits listening to the ball game waiting for Troy. The final out of the game is made and Rose switches off the radio. Troy enters the yard carrying an infant wrapped in blankets. He stands back from the house and calls.*)

(*Rose enters and stands on the porch. There is a long, awkward silence, the weight of which grows heavier with each passing second.*)

TROY: Rose . . . I'm standing here with my daughter in my arms. She ain't but a wee bittie little old thing. She don't know nothing about grownups' business. She innocent . . . and she ain't got no mama.

ROSE: What you telling me for, Troy?

(*She turns and exits into the house.*)

TROY: Well . . . I guess we'll just sit out here on the porch.

(*He sits down on the porch. There is an awkward indelicateness about the way he handles the baby. His largeness engulfs and seems to swallow it. He speaks loud enough for Rose to hear.*)

A man's got to do what's right for him. I ain't sorry for nothing I done. It felt right in my heart.

(*To the baby.*)

What you smiling at? Your daddy's a big man. Got these great big old hands. But sometimes he's scared. And right now your daddy's scared cause we sitting out here and ain't got no home. Oh, I been homeless before. I ain't had no little baby with me. But I been homeless. You just be out on the road by your lonesome and you see one of them trains coming and you just kinda go like this . . .

(*He sings as a lullaby.*)

Please, Mr. Engineer let a man ride the line
Please, Mr. Engineer let a man ride the line
I ain't got no ticket please let me ride the blinds

(*Rose enters from the house. Troy hearing her steps behind him, stands and faces her.*)

She's my daughter, Rose. My own flesh and blood. I can't deny her no more than I can deny them boys.

(*Pause.*)

You and them boys is my family. You and them and this child is all I got in the world. So I guess what I'm saying is . . . I'd appreciate it if you'd help me take care of her.

ROSE: Okay, Troy . . . you're right. I'll take care of your baby for you . . . cause . . . like you say . . . she's innocent . . . and you can't visit the sins of the father upon the child. A motherless child has got a hard time.

(*She takes the baby from him.*)

From right now . . . this child got a mother. But you a womanless man.

(*Rose turns and exits into the house with the baby. Lights go down to black.*)

Scene IV

(*It is two months later. Lyons enters from the street. He knocks on the door and calls.*)

LYONS: Hey, Rose! (*Pause.*) Rose!

ROSE (*from inside the house*): Stop that yelling. You gonna wake up Raynell. I just got her to sleep.

LYONS: I just stopped by to pay Papa this twenty dollars I owe him. Where's Papa at?

ROSE: He should be here in a minute. I'm getting ready to go down to the church. Sit down and wait on him.

LYONS: I got to go pick up Bonnie over her mother's house.

ROSE: Well, sit it down there on the table. He'll get it.

LYONS (*enters the house and sets the money on the table*): Tell Papa I said thanks. I'll see you again.

ROSE: All right, Lyons. We'll see you.

(*Lyons starts to exit as Cory enters.*)

CORY: Hey, Lyons.

LYONS: What's happening, Cory. Say man, I'm sorry I missed your graduation. You know I had a gig and couldn't get away. Otherwise, I would have been there, man. So what you doing?

CORY: I'm trying to find a job.

LYONS: Yeah I know how that go, man. It's rough out here. Jobs are scarce.

CORY: Yeah, I know.

LYONS: Look here, I got to run. Talk to Papa . . . he know some people. He'll be able to help get you a job. Talk to him . . . see what he say.

CORY: Yeah . . . all right, Lyons.

LYONS: You take care. I'll talk to you soon. We'll find some time to talk.

(*Lyons exits the yard. Cory wanders over to the tree, picks up the bat, and assumes a batting stance. He studies an imaginary pitcher and swings. Dissatisfied with the result, he tries again. Troy enters. They eye each other for a beat. Cory puts the bat down and exits the yard. Troy starts into the house as Rose exits with Raynell. She is carrying a cake.*)*

TROY: I'm coming in and everybody's going out.

ROSE: I'm taking this cake down to the church for the bake sale. Lyons was by to see you. He stopped by to pay you your twenty dollars. It's laying in there on the table.

TROY (*going into his pocket*): Well . . . here go this money.

ROSE: Put it in there on the table, Troy. I'll get it.

TROY: What time you coming back?

ROSE: Ain't no use in you studying me. It don't matter what time I come back.

TROY: I just asked you a question, woman. What's the matter . . . can't I ask you a question?

ROSE: Troy, I don't want to go into it. Your dinner's in there on the stove. All you got to do is heat it up. And don't you be eating the rest of them cakes in there. I'm coming back for them. We having a bake sale at the church tomorrow.

(*Rose exits the yard. Troy sits down on the steps, takes a pint bottle from his pocket, opens it, and drinks. He begins to sing.*)

TROY: Hear it ring! Hear it ring!
  Had an old dog his name was Blue
  You know Blue was mighty true
  You know Blue as a good old dog
  Blue trees a possum in a hollow log
  You know from that he was a good old dog

(*Bono enters the yard.*)

BONO: Hey, Troy.

TROY: Hey, what's happening, Bono?

BONO: I just thought I'd stop by to see you.

TROY: What you stop by and see me for? You ain't stopped by in a month of Sundays. Hell, I must owe you money or something.

BONO: Since you got your promotion I can't keep up with you. Used to see you every day. Now I don't even know what route you working.

TROY: They keep switching me around. Got me out in Greentree now . . . hauling white folks' garbage.

BONO: Greentree, huh? You lucky, at least you ain't got to be lifting them barrels. Damn if they ain't getting heavier. I'm gonna put in my two years and call it quits.

TROY: I'm thinking about retiring myself.

BONO: You got it easy. You can *drive* for another five years.

TROY: It ain't the same, Bono. It ain't like working the back of the truck. Ain't got nobody to talk to . . . feel like you working by yourself. Naw, I'm thinking about retiring. How's Lucille?

BONO: She all right. Her arthritis get to acting up on her sometime. Saw Rose on my way in. She going down to the church, huh?

TROY: Yeah, she took up going down there. All them preachers looking for somebody to fatten their pockets.

(*Pause.*)

  Got some gin here.

BONO: Naw, thanks. I just stopped by to say hello.

TROY: Hell, nigger . . . you can take a drink. I ain't never known you to say no to a drink. You ain't got to work tomorrow.

BONO: I just stopped by. I'm fixing to go over to Skinner's. We got us a domino game going over his house every Friday.

TROY: Nigger, you can't play no dominoes. I used to whup you four games out of five.

BONO: Well, that learned me. I'm getting better.

TROY: Yeah? Well, that's all right.

BONO: Look here . . . I got to be getting on. Stop by sometime, huh?

TROY: Yeah, I'll do that, Bono. Lucille told Rose you bought her a new refrigerator.

BONO: Yeah, Rose told Lucille you had finally built your fence . . . so I figured we'd call it even.

TROY: I knew you would.

BONO: Yeah . . . okay. I'll be talking to you.

TROY: Yeah, take care, Bono. Good to see you. I'm gonna stop over.

BONO: Yeah. Okay, Troy.

(*Bono exits. Troy drinks from the bottle.*)

TROY: Old Blue died and I dig his grave
  Let him down with a golden chain
  Every night when I hear old Blue bark
  I know Blue treed a possum in Noah's Ark.
  Hear it ring! Hear it ring!

(*Cory enters the yard. They eye each other for a beat. Troy is sitting in the middle of the steps. Cory walks over.*)

CORY: I got to get by.

TROY: Say what? What's you say?

CORY: You in my way. I got to get by.

TROY: You got to get by where? This is my house. Bought and paid for. In full. Took me fifteen years. And if you wanna go in my house and I'm sitting on the steps . . . you say excuse me. Like your mama taught you.

CORY: Come on, Pop . . . I got to get by.

(*Cory starts to maneuver his way past Troy. Troy grabs his leg and shoves him back.*)

TROY: You just gonna walk over top of me?

CORY: I live here too!

TROY (*advancing toward him*): You just gonna walk over top of me in my own house?

CORY: I ain't scared of you.

TROY: I ain't asked if you was scared of me. I asked you if you was fixing to walk over top of me in my own house? That's the question. You ain't gonna say excuse me? You just gonna walk over top of me?

CORY: If you wanna put it like that.

TROY: How else am I gonna put it?

CORY: I was walking by you to go into the house cause you sitting on the steps drunk, singing to yourself. You can put it like that.

TROY: Without saying excuse me???

(*Cory doesn't respond.*)

I asked you a question. Without saying excuse me???

CORY: I ain't got to say excuse me to you. You don't count around here no more.

TROY: Oh, I see . . . I don't count around here no more. You ain't got to say excuse me to your daddy. All of a sudden you done got so grown that your daddy don't count around here no more . . . Around here in his own house and yard that he done paid for with the sweat of his brow. You done got so grown to where you gonna take over. You gonna take over my house. Is that right? You gonna wear my pants. You gonna go in there and stretch out on my bed. You ain't got to say excuse me cause I don't count around here no more. Is that right?

CORY: That's right. You always talking this dumb stuff. Now, why don't you just get out my way.

TROY: I guess you got someplace to sleep and something to put in your belly. You got that, huh? You got that? That's what you need. You got that, huh?

CORY: You don't know what I got. You ain't got to worry about what I got.

TROY: You right! You one hundred percent right! I done spent the last seventeen years worrying about what you got. Now it's your turn, see? I'll tell you what to do. You grown . . . we done established that. You a man. Now, let's see you act like one. Turn your behind around and walk out this yard. And when you get out there in the alley . . . you can forget about this house. See? 'Cause this is my house. You go on and be a man and get your own house. You can forget about this. 'Cause this is mine. You go on and get yours 'cause I'm through with doing for you.

CORY: You talking about what you did for me . . . what'd you ever give me?

TROY: Them feet and bones! That pumping heart, nigger! I give you more than anybody else is ever gonna give you.

CORY: You ain't never gave me nothing! You ain't never done nothing but hold me back. Afraid I was gonna be better than you. All you ever did was try and make me scared of you. I used to tremble every time you called my name. Every time I heard your footsteps in the house. Wondering all the time . . . what's Papa gonna say if I do this? . . . What's he gonna say if I do that? . . . What's Papa gonna say if I turn on the radio? And Mama, too . . . she tries . . . but she's scared of you.

TROY: You leave your mama out of this. She ain't got nothing to do with this.

CORY: I don't know how she stand you . . . after what you did to her.

TROY: I told you to leave your mama out of this!

(*He advances toward Cory.*)

CORY: What you gonna do . . . give me a whupping? You can't whup me no more. You're too old. You just an old man.

TROY (*shoves him on his shoulder*): Nigger! That's what you are. You just another nigger on the street to me!

CORY: You crazy! You know that?

TROY: Go on now! You got the devil in you. Get on away from me!

CORY: You just a crazy old man . . . talking about I got the devil in me.

TROY: Yeah, I'm crazy! If you don't get on the other side of that yard . . . I'm gonna show you how crazy I am! Go on . . . get the hell out of my yard.

CORY: It ain't your yard. You took Uncle Gabe's money he got from the army to buy this house and then you put him out.

TROY (*Troy advances on Cory*): Get your black ass out of my yard!

(*Troy's advance backs Cory up against the tree. Cory grabs up the bat.*)

CORY: I ain't going nowhere! Come on . . . put me out! I ain't scared of you.

TROY: That's my bat!

CORY: Come on!

TROY: Put my bat down!

CORY: Come on, put me out.

(*Cory swings at Troy, who backs across the yard.*)

What's the matter? You so bad . . . put me out!

(*Troy advances toward Cory.*)

CORY (*backing up*): Come on! Come on!

TROY: You're gonna have to use it! You wanna draw that bat back on me . . . you're gonna have to use it.

CORY: Come on! . . . Come on!

(*Cory swings the bat at Troy a second time. He misses. Troy continues to advance toward him.*)

TROY: You're gonna have to kill me! You wanna draw that bat back on me. You're gonna have to kill me.

(*Cory, backed up against the tree, can go no farther. Troy taunts him. He sticks out his head and offers him a target.*)

Come on! Come on!

(*Cory is unable to swing the bat. Troy grabs it.*)

TROY: Then I'll show you.

(*Cory and Troy struggle over the bat. The struggle is fierce and fully engaged. Troy ultimately is the stronger and takes the bat from Cory and stands over him ready to swing. He stops himself.*)

Go on and get away from around my house.

(*Cory, stung by his defeat, picks himself up, walks slowly out of the yard and up the alley.*)

CORY: Tell Mama I'll be back for my things.
TROY: They'll be on the other side of that fence.

(*Cory exits.*)

TROY: I can't taste nothing. Helluljah! I can't taste nothing no more. (*Troy assumes a batting posture and begins to taunt Death, the fastball on the outside corner.*) Come on! It's between you and me now! Come on! Anytime you want! Come on! I be ready for you . . . but I ain't gonna be easy.

(*The lights go down on the scene.*)

Scene V

(*The time is 1965. The lights come up in the yard. It is the morning of Troy's funeral. A funeral plaque with a light hangs beside the door. There is a small garden plot off to the side. There is noise and activity in the house as Rose, Gabriel, and Bono have gathered. The door opens and Raynell, seven years old, enters dressed in a flannel nightgown. She crosses to the garden and pokes around with a stick. Rose calls from the house.*)

ROSE: Raynell!
RAYNELL: Mam?
ROSE: What you doing out there?
RAYNELL: Nothing.

(*Rose comes to the door.*)

ROSE: Girl, get in here and get dressed. What you doing?
RAYNELL: Seeing if my garden growed.
ROSE: I told you it ain't gonna grow overnight. You got to wait.
RAYNELL: It don't look like it never gonna grow. Dag!
ROSE: I told you a watched pot never boils. Get in here and get dressed.
RAYNELL: This ain't even no pot, Mama.
ROSE: You just have to give it a chance. It'll grow. Now you come on and do what I told you. We got to be getting ready. This ain't no morning to be playing around. You hear me?
RAYNELL: Yes, mam.

(*Rose exits into the house. Raynell continues to poke at her garden with a stick. Cory enters. He is dressed in a Marine corporal's uniform, and carries a duffel bag. His posture is that of a military man, and his speech has a clipped sternness.*)

CORY (*to Raynell*): Hi.

(*Pause.*)

I bet your name is Raynell.
RAYNELL: Uh huh.
CORY: Is your mama home?

(*Raynell runs up on the porch and calls through the screen door.*)

RAYNELL: Mama . . . there's some man out here. Mama?

(*Rose comes to the door.*)

ROSE: Cory? Lord have mercy! Look here, you all!

(*Rose and Cory embrace in a tearful reunion as Bono and Lyons enter from the house dressed in funeral clothes.*)

BONO: Aw, looka here . . .
ROSE: Done got all grown up!
CORY: Don't cry, Mama. What you crying about?
ROSE: I'm just so glad you made it.
CORY: Hey Lyons. How you doing, Mr. Bono.

(*Lyons goes to embrace Cory.*)

LYONS: Look at you, man. Look at you. Don't he look good, Rose. Got them Corporal stripes.
ROSE: What took you so long.
CORY: You know how the Marines are, Mama. They got to get all their paperwork straight before they let you do anything.
ROSE: Well, I'm sure glad you made it. They let Lyons come. Your Uncle Gabe's still in the hospital. They don't know if they gonna let him out or not. I just talked to them a little while ago.
LYONS: A Corporal in the United States Marines.
BONO: Your daddy knew you had it in you. He used to tell me all the time.
LYONS: Don't he look good, Mr. Bono?
BONO: Yeah, he remind me of Troy when I first met him.

(*Pause.*)

Say, Rose, Lucille's down at the church with the choir. I'm gonna go down and get the pallbearers lined up. I'll be back to get you all.
ROSE: Thanks, Jim.
CORY: See you, Mr. Bono.
LYONS (*with his arm around Raynell*): Cory . . . look at Raynell. Ain't she precious? She gonna break a whole lot of hearts.
ROSE: Raynell, come and say hello to your brother. This is your brother, Cory. You remember Cory.
RAYNELL: No, Mam.
CORY: She don't remember me, Mama.
ROSE: Well, we talk about you. She heard us talk about you. (*To Raynell.*) This is your brother, Cory. Come on and say hello.
RAYNELL: Hi.
CORY: Hi. So you're Raynell. Mama told me a lot about you.
ROSE: You all come on into the house and let me fix you some breakfast. Keep up your strength.

CORY: I ain't hungry, Mama.

LYONS: You can fix me something, Rose. I'll be in there in a minute.

ROSE: Cory, you sure you don't want nothing. I know they ain't feeding you right.

CORY: No, Mama . . . thanks. I don't feel like eating. I'll get something later.

ROSE: Raynell . . . get on upstairs and get that dress on like I told you.

(*Rose and Raynell exit into the house.*)

LYONS: So . . . I hear you thinking about getting married.

CORY: Yeah, I done found the right one, Lyons. It's about time.

LYONS: Me and Bonnie been split up about four years now. About the time Papa retired. I guess she just got tired of all them changes I was putting her through.

(*Pause.*)

I always knew you was gonna make something out yourself. Your head was always in the right direction. So . . . you gonna stay in . . . make it a career . . . put in your twenty years?

CORY: I don't know. I got six already, I think that's enough.

LYONS: Stick with Uncle Sam and retire early. Ain't nothing out here. I guess Rose told you what happened with me. They got me down the workhouse. I thought I was being slick cashing other people's checks.

CORY: How much time you doing?

LYONS: They give me three years. I got that beat now. I ain't got but nine more months. It ain't so bad. You learn to deal with it like anything else. You got to take the crookeds with the straights. That's what Papa used to say. He used to say that when he struck out. I seen him strike out three times in a row . . . and the next time up he hit the ball over the grandstand. Right out there in Homestead Field. He wasn't satisfied hitting in the seats . . . he want to hit it over everything! After the game he had two hundred people standing around waiting to shake his hand. You got to take the crookeds with the straights. Yeah, Papa was something else.

CORY: You still playing?

LYONS: Cory . . . you know I'm gonna do that. There's some fellows down there we got us a band . . . we gonna try and stay together when we get out . . . but yeah, I'm still playing. It still helps me to get out of bed in the morning. As long as it do that I'm gonna be right there playing and trying to make some sense out of it.

ROSE (*calling*): Lyons, I got these eggs in the pan.

LYONS: Let me go on and get these eggs, man. Get ready to go bury Papa.

(*Pause.*)

How you doing? You doing all right?

(*Cory nods. Lyons touches him on the shoulder and they share a moment of silent grief. Lyons exits into the house. Cory wanders about the yard. Raynell enters.*)

RAYNELL: Hi.

CORY: Hi.

RAYNELL: Did you used to sleep in my room?

CORY: Yeah . . . that used to be my room.

RAYNELL: That's what Papa call it. "Cory's room." It got your football in the closet.

(*Rose comes to the door.*)

ROSE: Raynell, get in there and get them good shoes on.

RAYNELL: Mama, can't I wear these. Them other one hurt my feet.

ROSE: Well, they just gonna have to hurt your feet for a while. You ain't said they hurt your feet when you went down to the store and got them.

RAYNELL: They didn't hurt then. My feet done got bigger.

ROSE: Don't you give me no backtalk now. You get in there and get them shoes on.

(*Raynell exits into the house.*)

Ain't too much changed. He still got that piece of rag tied to that tree. He was out here swinging that bat. I was just ready to go back in the house. He swung that bat and then he just fell over. Seem like he swung it and stood there with this grin on his face . . . and then he just fell over. They carried him on down to the hospital, but I knew there wasn't no need . . . why don't you come on in the house?

CORY: Mama . . . I got something to tell you. I don't know how to tell you this . . . but I've got to tell you . . . I'm not going to Papa's funeral.

ROSE: Boy, hush your mouth. That's your daddy you talking about. I don't want hear that kind of talk this morning. I done raised you to come to this? You standing there all healthy and grown talking about you ain't going to your daddy's funeral?

CORY: Mama . . . listen . . .

ROSE: I don't want to hear it, Cory. You just get that thought out of your head.

CORY: I can't drag Papa with me everywhere I go. I've got to say no to him. One time in my life I've got to say no.

ROSE: Don't nobody have to listen to nothing like that. I know you and your daddy ain't seen eye to eye, but I ain't got to listen to that kind of talk this morning. Whatever was between you and your daddy . . . the time has come to put it aside. Just take it and set it over there on the shelf and forget about it. Disrespecting your daddy ain't gonna make you a man, Cory. You got to find a way to come to that on your own. Not going to your daddy's funeral ain't gonna make you a man.

CORY: The whole time I was growing up . . . living in his house . . . Papa was like a shadow that followed you everywhere. It weighed on you and sunk into your flesh. It would wrap around you and lay there until you couldn't tell which one was you anymore. That shadow digging in your flesh. Trying to crawl in. Trying to live through you. Everywhere I looked, Troy Maxson was staring back at me . . . hiding under the bed . . . in the closet. I'm just saying I've got to find a way to get rid of that shadow, Mama.

ROSE: You just like him. You got him in you good.

CORY: Don't tell me that, Mama.

ROSE: You Troy Maxson all over again.

CORY: I don't want to be Troy Maxson. I want to be me.

ROSE: You can't be nobody but who you are, Cory. That shadow wasn't nothing but you growing into yourself. You either got to grow into it or cut it down to fit you. But that's all you got to make life with. That's all you got to measure yourself against that world out there. Your daddy wanted you to be everything he wasn't . . . and at the same time he tried to make you into everything he was. I don't know if he was right or wrong . . . but I do know he meant to do more good than he meant to do harm. He wasn't always right. Sometimes when he touched he bruised. And sometimes when he took me in his arms he cut.

When I first met your daddy I thought . . . Here is a man I can lay down with and make a baby. That's the first thing I thought when I seen him. I was thirty years old and had done seen my share of men. But when he walked up to me and said "I can dance a waltz that'll make you dizzy," I thought, Rose Lee, here is a man that you can open yourself up to and be filled to bursting. Here is a man that can fill all them empty spaces you been tipping around the edges of. One of them empty spaces was being somebody's mother.

I married your daddy and settled down to cooking his supper and keeping clean sheets on the bed. When your daddy walked through the house he was so big he filled it up. That was my first mistake. Not to make him leave some room for me. For my part in the matter. But at that time I wanted that. I wanted a house that I could sing in. And that's what your daddy gave me. I didn't know to keep up his strength I had to give up little pieces of mine. I did that. I took on his life as mine and mixed up the pieces so that you couldn't hardly tell which was which anymore. It was my choice. It was my life and I didn't have to live it like that. But that's what life offered me in the way of being a woman and I took it. I grabbed hold of it with both hands.

By the time Raynell came into the house, me and your daddy had done lost touch with one another. I didn't want to make my blessing off of nobody's misfortune . . . but I took on to Raynell like she was all them babies I had wanted and never had.

(*The phone rings.*)

Like I'd been blessed to relive a part of my life. And if the Lord see fit to keep up my strength . . . I'm gonna do her just like your daddy did you . . . I'm gonna give her the best of what's in me.

RAYNELL (*entering, still with her old shoes*): Mama . . . Reverend Tollivier on the phone.

(*Rose exits into the house.*)

RAYNELL: Hi.

CORY: Hi.

RAYNELL: You in the Army or the Marines?

CORY: Marines.

RAYNELL: Papa said it was the Army. Did you know Blue?

CORY: Blue? Who's Blue?

RAYNELL: Papa's dog what he sing about all the time.

CORY (*singing*): Hear it ring! Hear it ring!
    I had a dog his name was Blue
    You know Blue was mighty true
    You know Blue was a good old dog
    Blue treed a possum in a hollow log
    You know from that he was a good old dog.
    Hear it ring! Hear it ring!

(*Raynell joins in singing.*)

CORY AND RAYNELL: Blue treed a possum out on a limb
    Blue looked at me and I looked at him
    Grabbed that possum and put him in a sack
    Blue stayed there till I came back
    Old Blue's feets was big and round
    Never allowed a possum to touch the ground.

    Old Blue died and I dug his grave
    I dug his grave with a silver spade
    Let him down with a golden chain
    And every night I call his name
    Go on Blue, you good dog you
    Go on Blue, you good dog you

RAYNELL: Blue laid down and died like a man
    Blue laid down and died . . .

BOTH: Blue laid down and died like a man
    Now he's treeing possums in the Promised Land
    I'm gonna tell you this to let you know
    Blue's gone where the good dogs go
    When I hear old Blue bark
    When I hear old Blue bark
    Blue treed a possum in Noah's Ark
    Blue treed a possum in Noah's Ark.

(*Rose comes to the screen door.*)

ROSE: Cory, we gonna be ready to go in a minute.

CORY (*to Raynell*): You go on in the house and change them shoes like Mama told you so we can go to Papa's funeral.

RAYNELL: Okay, I'll be back.

(*Raynell exits into the house. Cory gets up and crosses over to the tree. Rose stands in the screen door watching him. Gabriel enters from the alley.*)

GABRIEL (*calling*): Hey, Rose!

ROSE: Gabe?

GABRIEL: I'm here, Rose. Hey Rose, I'm here!

(*Rose enters from the house.*)

ROSE: Lord . . . Look here, Lyons!

LYONS: See, I told you, Rose . . . I told you they'd let him come.

CORY: How you doing, Uncle Gabe?

LYONS: How you doing, Uncle Gabe?

GABRIEL: Hey, Rose. It's time. It's time to tell St. Peter to open the gates. Troy, you ready? You ready, Troy. I'm gonna tell St. Peter to open the gates. You get ready now.

(Gabriel, with great fanfare, braces himself to blow. The trumpet is without a mouthpiece. He puts the end of it into his mouth and blows with great force, like a man who has been waiting some twenty-odd years for this single moment. No sound comes out of the trumpet. He braces himself and blows again with the same result. A third time he blows. There is a weight of impossible description that falls away and leaves him bare and exposed to a frightful realization. It is a trauma that a sane and normal mind would be unable to withstand. He begins to dance. A slow, strange dance, eerie and life-giving. A dance of atavistic signature and ritual. Lyons attempts to embrace him. Gabriel pushes Lyons away. He begins to howl in what is an attempt at song, or perhaps a song turning back into itself in an attempt at speech. He finishes his dance and the gates of heaven stand open as wide as God's closet.)

That's the way that go!

COMMENTARY

Joan Herrington
THE DEVELOPMENT OF *FENCES* 1998

Among the interesting things we know about Wilson's decision to write Fences *is the fact that he was struck by some of the criticism of* Ma Rainey's Black Bottom *because of its unusual structure. With* Fences *Wilson decided to write a play that respected the unities of time, place, and action. He also wanted to write a play about family, and in the process he chose baseball and its attendant mythologies as the all-American game. Wilson struggled with clarifying the relationship of Troy Maxon with his sons and their differing needs. He also struggled with Troy's relationship with his wife through many stages of revision. Herrington gives us a good view of what was involved in the writing of the play.*

Troy's relationship with his second son, Cory, is a vital part of the play as Wilson examines Troy's attempt to guide the boy into a responsible life. A high school senior, Cory has been recruited to play college football. But Troy will not sign the papers to permit this.

Although Wilson presents Cory's position sympathetically, he supports Troy's decision. "Blacks who received sports scholarships to go to school were exploited. Very few got an education. Troy makes the right choice when he tells his son that football won't lead anywhere. He's telling his son to get a job so he won't have to carry garbage."

Despite Wilson's implicit endorsement of Troy's decision, he fully understands its negative impact on his son. And as Wilson worked on *Fences,* he continually labored over his portrayal of their relationship. In the first version of the play, there is an extended scene between Cory and Troy in which they discuss the purchase of a new television set. Cory doesn't understand why they cannot buy a TV, and Troy tries to explain the financial management of a household. The scene concludes with Troy offering to pay half if Cory can come up with the other half. Here we have an opportunity to see father and son interact in a nonconfrontational manner, and also to see Troy exercising a fatherly concern for his son beyond feeding and clothing him. During work at the O'Neill Conference, this section was effectively moved from the second to the first half of the play, where it serves as groundwork to inform the later conflicts between Troy and Cory.

At the Yale Rep, however, the entire section was dropped in an effort to shorten the work. But the omission of the exchange between Troy and Cory left too large a gap in the portrayal of Troy's exercise of familial responsibility. At the conclusion of the play, in all the drafts, Cory complains of a lack of understanding and emotional support from Troy, and he provokes Troy by asking him what he ever gave to his son. Troy responds: "Them feet and bones. That pumping heart. I give you more than anybody else is ever gonna give you."

Troy is angry with Cory's implication that he has somehow failed the boy, for he believes that he has fulfilled his obligation to his son. With the long scene about the television having been cut, however, we can see only that Troy has provided Cory the bare bones. But Wilson wanted the audience to know that Troy has, in fact, provided more—more guidance, more support, more sympathy—and he restored the television scene in the final version.

While doing so, Wilson also gave Troy the opportunity to explain more fully his attitude toward Cory's college recruitment. In earlier drafts, Troy had challenged Cory, in anger, to give up football: "You go on and get your book learning where you can learn to do something besides carry people's garbage." In Wilson's final revision, Troy is more patient, more loving and concerned, and his speech has a more inspirational quality. Wilson moved Troy from an expression of bitterness over his own life to an expression of a positive dream for his son.

> You go on and get your book learning so you can work yourself up in that A&P or learn how to fix cars or build houses or something, get you a trade. That way you have something can't nobody take away from you. You go on and learn how to put your hands to some good use. Besides hauling people's garbage.

It is important to see that Troy has good intentions even as the play reveals his failings. As a younger man, Troy pursued his personal destiny in baseball at the cost of his family. Now, later in life, he professes to have made responsibility to others his priority. But Troy's efforts are neither wholehearted nor entirely successful, and Wilson uses Cory to make this point. As he revised the play, Wilson gave Cory a more mature understanding of the workings and failings of his family, particularly his father.

In early drafts, Cory was angry at his father and revealed his emotions in naive, sophomoric outbursts: "I hate your blood in me." As the drafts progressed, Cory challenges Troy on substantive issues. At the play's close, in the final draft, Cory upbraids Troy for his mistreatment of Rose, "I don't know how [Rose] stand you . . . after what you did to her." Although Cory's understanding of the issue is not complete, it goes straight to the core of Troy's view of himself as a responsible man, forcing him to come to terms with the fact that he put himself, his own fulfillment, before his responsibility to his wife.

The structure of the play leads to a dramatic confrontation, both physical and emotional, between Troy and Cory. Recognizing the flaws in his father and needing to make his own choices, Cory has become a man. There isn't room in the house for two men, and a simple argument about Troy moving over on the steps so that Cory can pass into the house blows up into the final exchange between them.

In early drafts, this final scene was potentially more violent. In the first versions, at the height of the confrontation, when Cory picks up Troy's baseball bat, Troy brings out a gun, points it at his son, and the stage directions read that he cocks the trigger. Wilson dropped this detail before the Yale Rep production when he read that Marvin Gaye° had been shot by his father. In the later drafts, the only weapon in the scene is the baseball bat, symbolically more powerful in its meaning to Troy, and dramatically more powerful, too, since it can be used as a weapon only when two people are in close physical proximity to each other.

The conflict between father and son continued to change in other ways, too. In the production at the Yale Rep, Cory swings the bat once and then retreats into the alley as Troy continues to approach. The conflict is interrupted by the arrival of Rose, prompting Cory to leave the yard.

Wilson realized that the interruption left the conflict unresolved. Thus, in the final version, Rose does not enter, and the climax of the play is more meaningful as the complex relationship between father and son is more intricately explored. Cory swings the bat once and misses. Then he swings again and misses. Troy offers him the chance to swing a third time, having positioned himself as a target impossible to miss. Now, Cory cannot swing. The two men struggle for the bat, and Troy takes it away. Troy prepares to swing, but he stops himself. Defeated, Cory leaves the yard and does not return until after Troy's death, years later. In this final version the anger between Cory and Troy is the most visceral. And yet it is in this version where we clearly see that neither one can intentionally injure the other.

Whether Cory becomes like his father or learns to be different is explored by Wilson in the final "interaction" between the two. The play concludes after a passage of eight years and the death of Troy. The issue of Cory's sense of responsibility is explored one last time through his indecision about whether to attend Troy's funeral. Wilson, like his character, changed his mind many times about whether Cory would go.

In the first draft, Cory does not attend his father's funeral. He expresses his continued bitterness to Lyons in an extensive exchange. Then, as a casualty of Wilson's feeling that the exchange between the half-brothers did not ring true, as well as his concern for the running time of the show, this long discussion was cut before the first performance at the O'Neill Conference. Cory merely wanders away during a discussion between Lyons and Rose and does not return. Dissatisfied with Cory's disrespectful choice, the audience responded negatively. For the second O'Neill performance, Cory's discussion with Lyons and his subsequent departure were dropped, leaving the implication that Cory does attend the funeral.

Both of these versions were unsatisfactory to Wilson. So, in the Yale Rep version, Cory tells Rose that he is not going to the funeral and Rose, playing the role Wilson had previously assigned to Lyons, urges Cory to attend. Wilson also rearranged the scene so that the entire family surrounds the young man at the moment of his decision. Cory knows he must go to the funeral, and in this final draft, Wilson provides Cory a subtle acknowledgment of his choice as he says to

Marvin Gaye: Popular American songwriter killed April 1, 1984.

his half-sister Raynell, "You go on in the house and change them shoes like Mama told you so we can go to Papa's funeral."

Rose, having survived the most damaging kind of betrayal from Troy, is a powerful spokesperson for remaining true to one's commitments even without the expectation of reciprocity. In progressive drafts, Wilson carefully refined her character so that as she moved toward greater forgiveness and understanding, Troy's betrayal appeared all the more dramatic.

The most significant change in Rose was in her day-to-day relationship with Troy and how this, in turn, affects his relationship with Alberta. In the early version of the play, Rose is much more a nagging wife. She bothers Troy constantly about his drinking (which is considerably greater in the early drafts). She reprimands Troy for his neglect of Cory, and when she is tired of Troy's shouting, she tells him to go shout somewhere else. Although certainly none of these faults warrants Troy's infidelity, they perhaps provide him an excuse. As the versions progress, this side of Rose almost completely disappears, and Troy's affair seems less excusable, more stark a violation of his marital responsibility.

But Rose is tolerant—more and more so as the drafts of the play progressed. In the early versions of the play, Troy's announcement that he will be a father comes as a complete surprise to Rose. In later versions of the play, Rose suspects that he is having an affair as she catches inconsistencies in his explanations of his whereabouts, but she says nothing.

When Troy finally tells his wife about Alberta, Rose preaches the bible of familial responsibility.

> I gave eighteen years of my life to stand in the same spot with you. Don't you think I ever wanted things? Don't you think I had dreams and hopes? . . . Don't you think it ever crossed my mind to want to know other men? That I wanted to lay up somewhere and forget about my responsibilities? . . . But I held on to you, Troy . . . I took all my feelings, my wants and needs, my dreams . . . and I buried them inside you . . . I held on to you, Troy.

In the second, third, and fourth drafts of the script, there is no further mention of the affair until Troy brings home the baby. But in the final version, Wilson chose to extend the duration of Rose's tolerance by reinserting an original scene which had been cut to shorten the script. Here, six months after Rose learns of Troy's infidelity, she confronts him about his continuing attention to Alberta, telling him he's living on "borrowed time" with her. Rose retains her composure and her emotional charge as she points out the fallacy in Troy's theory that his physical presence in bed at the end of every night fulfills his obligation to his household regardless of where he has been up to that time.

As Rose grows more philosophical, even under the burden of a betrayal that she understands to be ongoing, our sympathy for her becomes stronger. And Rose's eventual decision to accept Troy's bastard child but to sexually renounce its father—the same in all drafts of the play—makes more sense as the action of a woman who, over time, has come to recognize the impossibility of change in her husband.

Rose stands in the center of the play as a model of responsibility but also as an example of the cost of responsibility to others at the expense of self. In response to Troy's explanation of his affair, Rose responds that she also has needs and wants not satisfied at home. But ultimately she sees no options for herself simply because, as she explains to Troy, "You my husband."

Rose's selflessness moves toward an ultimate commitment outside of herself—that is, to the church. In successive versions of the play, Rose becomes more involved with the church, participates more in its events, sings more of its hymns, and ends the final version of the play completely engrossed in the institution.

Troy remains independent, somehow able to reconcile to his own satisfaction a complex range of conflicting needs and desires. Wilson performed a complicated balancing act of his own to get the audience to be sympathetic to the choices Troy makes, even to support them. He accomplished this through careful selection of the details, choosing those that would highlight Troy's concern with personal autonomy, dignity, self-realization.

A CASEBOOK ON

August Wilson

When August Wilson died in October 2005, America lost its ranking playwright, a man whose work on his astounding project of writing a separate play about African Americans for each decade of the twentieth century was only just completed. But people were already talking with him about what projects he might undertake next, and it seemed clear to everyone that he, at age sixty, was in the prime of his artistic life. His death shocked the world of drama and the world of dramatic literature. He left us a legacy that compares with that of Eugene O'Neill, a writer whose own long-range project was equally ambitious but incomplete.

O'Neill's influence in spirit was revealed by Wilson's decision, after many years of involvement in local dramatic groups and years of writing plays that were produced in Pittsburgh and Minneapolis, to submit a play to the Eugene O'Neill Theater Center in Waterford, Connecticut, on the grounds of O'Neill's family home. Wilson's play *Jitney* had been rejected the year before, but he had a new play under way that he thought might be accepted. That was *Ma Rainey's Black Bottom*. After some anxiety and rewriting, he submitted the play by the deadline and was delighted to learn that the O'Neill accepted it. He spent most of the summer at the O'Neill Center with actors and other playwrights working on their scripts. The development process at the O'Neill is collaborative, and Wilson soon learned to profit from the collaboration of dramaturge, director, and actors in shaping the play to make it the strongest it could be.

Lloyd Richards, who had directed the Broadway premier of Lorraine Hansberry's *A Raisin in the Sun*, was director of the O'Neill Center and also dean of the Yale School of Drama. When he felt the play was ready, he asked Wilson to premier it at the Yale Repertory Theatre before taking it to Broadway. Thus the process of development continued even after Wilson's experiences at the O'Neill, and the production under the direction of Richards was a great success.

The premier run in New Haven in 1984 was remarkable for many reasons. One was that the play itself was tight and riveting. Another was that actors on stage, with Charles S. Dutton as Levee and Theresa Merritt as Ma, were later nominated for awards for their performances. A third factor was the singing of Ma Rainey and the music of the band, which was strong and dynamic. The actors learned to play their instruments in the process of rehearsing the play, something the audience did not know at the time. But everyone at the theater knew that an important event in American drama was unfolding. Wilson himself sat in the audience several times to see exactly what he had done. Later that year, the New York production won the Drama Critics' Circle Award.

The collaboration with Lloyd Richards continued for some time. *Fences* was produced in 1985 at the Yale Repertory Theater, where a number of technical problems were overcome before the play went to Broadway that same year. With James Earl Jones as Troy Maxson and Mary Alice as Rose, the play won the 1985 Pulitzer Prize for drama. Its success in New York was stunning in terms of both critical acclaim and financial reward. The play made Wilson an independent, full-time playwright.

As years passed, Wilson added to his series of plays examining the lives of African Americans in each decade. After *Ma Rainey's Black Bottom*, which is set in Chicago, Wilson set the rest of his plays in the Hill District of Pittsburgh, where he grew up. The plays that address each decade are

1900s	*Gem of the Ocean* (produced 2004)
1910s	*Joe Turner's Come and Gone* (produced 1986)
1920s	*Ma Rainey's Black Bottom* (produced 1984)
1930s	*The Piano Lesson* (produced 1987)
1940s	*Seven Guitars* (produced 1996)
1950s	*Fences* (produced 1985)
1960s	*Two Trains Running* (produced 1990)
1970s	*Jitney* (produced 1982)
1980s	*King Hedley II* (produced 2001)
1990s	*Radio Golf* (produced 2005)

No other major modern playwright has completed such an ambitious project as Wilson's, which won him numerous Drama Critics' Circle Awards and two Pulitzer Prizes, for *Fences* and *The Piano Lesson*. A character named Aunt Ester never appears in his plays, but she is referred to in *The Piano Lesson*, and it is in her house that *Gem of the Ocean* takes place—when she is 287 years old. Wilson began to see that she was the conscience of the entire sequence of plays and that she reached into the collective memory of African Americans and was their touchstone.

Apart from the influence of history, which permeates the sequence, Wilson was deeply influenced by a number of sources that he himself named. The distinguished African American painter Romare Bearden gave him images of black culture that inspired his plays. The blues—as sung by Ma Rainey and others and as played by great musicians—was a major influence on his work. Amiri Baraka, an African American poet and dramatist, was also an important influence on Wilson, especially in Baraka's stand against the oppression of white America and against assimilation into it. Baraka's plays *Dutchman* and *The Slave* convinced Wilson that he could put on stage material that confronted the pain of African Americans *and* succeeded as literature and drama.

The last of the influences whom Wilson cited is the Argentinian writer Jorge Luis Borges, who, although blind, created fantasy visions and fantasy worlds that were highly intellectual and challenging. Borges's ability to be serious and profound while also introducing a form of magic realism inspired Wilson, some of whose plays involve spiritual experiences that cannot be explained through ordinary logic.

In the selections that follow, Wilson's achievement is assessed briefly by writers who followed his career closely and with enormous respect. Clearly, it will take many years for us to fully appreciate what August Wilson has given to American drama.

Mark William Rocha
AUGUST WILSON AND THE FOUR B'S: INFLUENCES   *1994*

In this extensive essay, Mark Rocha examines the influences that August Wilson said were most important to him in his dramatic writing. Rocha demonstrates the range of influence of all four of the B's: Bearden, Baraka, Borges, and the Blues, showing us that the art of Romare Bearden and the blues of Ma Rainey were probably the most influential of all.

In terms of influence on my work, I have what I call my four B's: Romare Bearden; Imamu Amiri Baraka, the writer; Jorge Luis Borges, the Argentine short-story writer; and the biggest B of all: the blues.   —AUGUST WILSON, "HOW TO WRITE A PLAY"

Few American playwrights have been as explicit in naming influences as August Wilson. In the dozens of interviews Wilson has granted in the eight years since *Ma Rainey's Black Bottom* appeared on Broadway in 1984, Wilson has been unusually forthcoming not only in citing his influences but in explaining specifically how the four B's can be found in his plays. And indeed when I interviewed Wilson on January 24, 1992, I found him to be so eager to discuss the four B's that at one point he enthusiastically took up a book of Romare Bearden's works, turned to the work entitled *Mill Hand's Lunch Bucket,* and reviewed in animated detail how it served as the source for *Joe Turner's Come and Gone.*

To be sure, a good deal of Wilson's citation of the four B's may be ascribed to a generous and magnanimous soul who is sincerely grateful to those who have nourished his art. There is also behind Wilson's acknowledgment of indebtedness a sense of homage and respect that characterizes an African sensibility, for as Wilson notes, "In Africa a man is judged not by what he has but by what is owed to him."[1] But I also want to argue here that Wilson's consistent invocation of his four B's goes beyond the expression of gratitude and respect, and is part of a conscious, deliberate, programmatic effort to turn every interview he gives, and certainly the one he gave me, into a scene of instruction. Wilson doesn't just talk about his four B's, he *teaches* them, not merely as discrete influences, but as constituent elements of an African American cosmology. In offering his four B's—Bearden, Baraka, Borges,° and the Blues—Wilson not only inscribes a theory of African American literature but also names the creators of the sign system he inhabits. To read or see a Wilson play without learning about the four B's is, in the vernacular, "not to see where he's coming from."

Bearden, Baraka, Borges: Romare Bearden (1911–1988), prominent African American painter. Amiri Baraka (b. 1934), African American poet and playwright. Jorge Luis Borges (1899–1986), Argentinian short story writer with an international reputation.

[1]Mark William Rocha, "A Conversation with August Wilson." *Diversity: A Journal of Multicultural Issues* 1 (Fall 1992): 29.

But before we see where Wilson is coming from, it is worth a moment to clarify where Wilson is *not* coming from, because Wilson has also been unusually explicit in stating who has *not* influenced him, which I take as further evidence of Wilson's instructional agenda with regard to the four B's. Despite the fact that in 1987 he told the *Los Angeles Times* that he is "sitting in the same chair as Shakespeare, confronting the same problems as Arthur Miller and Eugene O'Neill,"[2] Wilson has insisted many times that he has never read any of the canonical Western playwrights. In 1988 he commented, "I haven't read Ibsen, Shaw, Shakespeare. . . . I'm not familiar with *Death of a Salesman.* I haven't read Tennessee Williams. I very purposefully didn't read them."[3] And when I spoke with Wilson and referred to Aristotle and the Western theory of tragedy, Wilson made a point of saying he had never read the *Poetics* even though in 1990 he told *The Boston Globe,* "As far as playwriting goes, it's Aristotle."[4]

I do not raise this to reveal a discrepancy in Wilson's testimony. Rather I wish to call attention to *why* Wilson goes so far out of his way to disconnect himself from the Western tradition of drama, even though his plays reside comfortably within that tradition. I do of course hold it as improbable that Wilson, a playwright who has collaborated for eight years with Lloyd Richards° and the Yale Repertory Theater, has never read O'Neill or Miller. Consider, for one example, that it is nearly impossible to avoid one reading of *Fences* as a deliberate point-to-point signifyin(g) parody of *Death of a Salesman.* It is thus all the more significant that Wilson argues so vociferously for himself as liberated from Western influence. I therefore interpret Wilson to be "facing" the Western tradition, to use a vernacular term from the vocabulary of Signifyin(g) compiled by Henry Louis Gates.° Gates explains, ". . . 'In your face' is a standard Signifyin(g) retort, meaning that by which you intended to confine (or define) me I shall return to you squarely in your face."[5] Gates offers Signifyin(g) as the basis for an intertextual theory of literary history in which an African American writer like Wilson would both repeat and revise the work of literary antecedents, which in Wilson's case means "getting in the face" of the American triumvirate of O'Neill, Miller, and Williams. While Wilson's facing, especially of O'Neill, may also be usefully read under the paradigm of Harold Bloom's° psycho-drama of the strong poet displacing his ancestor, Wilson's response to the anxiety of influence extends beyond the text of his plays to include his aggressive public act—an act of black signifyin(g)—of "calling O'Neill out" by publicly refusing his influence. When informed he had won his second Pulitzer Prize in 1990 for *The Piano Lesson,* Wilson's first comment was, "Well, O'Neill won four, so I guess I better get going."[6]

Wilson's obvious desire to "get over on" the Western tradition is first and foremost what bonds him so strongly to his brother-poet Baraka, who in his quest for a post-white, post-American, post-Western form is the discoverer of the African American literary landscape in which Wilson has found a place. Baraka has spent his entire career "facing" the Western tradition, no clearer instance of which comes from his autobiographical novel, *The System of Dante's Hell* (1965), when the

Lloyd Richards: (1919–2006), African American director and dean of the Yale Drama School.
Louis Gates: Henry Louis Gates (b. 1950), professor at Harvard University and chair of the African and African American Studies Program, who has written on Wilson.
Harold Bloom: (b. 1930), professor and literary theorist at Yale University.

[2]Janice Arkatov, "August Wilson: His Way." *Los Angles Times* 7 June 1987, Calendar: 35
[3]David Savran, *In Their Own Words.* New York: Theater Communication Group, 1988: 292.
[4]Kevin Kelly, "August Wilson's True Stories." *The Boston Globe* 29 April 1990: B29.
[5]Henry Louis Gates, Jr., *The Signifying Monkey* (Oxford: Oxford University Press, 1988), p. 66.
[6]Maureen Fitzgerald, "The Heat of August." *Philadelphia Inquirer Magazine* 15 July 1990: 33.

Prodigal asks, "Who is T. S. Eliot? So what?"[7] Without Baraka posing this question, August Wilson would not be possible.

Baraka is Wilson's brother-poet for several reasons. First, the two are closer together in age than one might think, Baraka born in 1934 and Wilson in 1945. But more importantly, both poets experienced an almost ritual exorcism of Western poetic influence that was enacted in the year 1965 — the year that Malcolm X° was killed. Kimberly Benston has called 1965 Baraka's "year of crossroads," during which he divorced his wife and moved uptown to Harlem, whereupon he set himself to realizing the dead prophet Malcolm X's dream of a black nation.[8] Wilson, in characteristically mythic fashion, designates April 1, 1965, only a few weeks after Malcolm X's death, as the birth of his life as a poet:

> That was the day I made a commitment to being a writer. I spent $20 for a typewriter . . . I didn't even have enough left over to take the bus home, so I carried it up the street, plopped it down on the kitchen table in my basement apartment, sat down and plunked out my name. I didn't know how to type. I just wanted to see what AUGUST WILSON looked like. I saw it there, standin' up on the paper, and said, "That's alright, man, all right."[9]

This is an unmistakable answer to Baraka's call in "Poem for Black Hearts," to "quit stuttering and shuffling, look up" in the name of the "Great Malcolm."[10] Moreover, the central image of the black poet alone with his typewriter in his underground cell, in addition to recalling of course Ellison's *Invisible Man*,° recalls precisely the same image in Baraka's play, *A Recent Killing*, the story of a black soldier who is jailed for aiding a rebellion and who graduates to a new resolution for action symbolized by the tableau of a gun leaning against the typewriter by his bed. It is crucial to see that Wilson met Baraka through Malcolm X. Wilson wrote one of his early plays on Malcolm X (the play is yet unpublished but has been performed in Minnesota and elsewhere by Minneapolis's Playwright's Center). More recently, *Two Trains Running* refers explicitly to Malcolm X and his problematic relationship within the black community.[11] Wilson must therefore be identified, as he so forthrightly identifies himself, as a Black Nationalist. The overtly political agenda of Black Nationalism is every bit as much at the heart of Wilson's plays as Baraka's, and when we grant Baraka as one of Wilson's four B's, we put the claws back on the tiger, something that is quite necessary in light of the surprisingly benign, almost cuddly August Wilson we are given in the press. If by comparison to Baraka's, Wilson's plays seem less political, it is because our sense of the term political is too much caught up with confrontation, with the "facing of the Man" which so concerns Baraka. Yet a closer look within Wilson's plays will show that he continues and deepens the motif of facing the white man which Baraka developed so fully.

Benston has recently proposed the scenario of "facing" as an organizing metaphor for African American literary history. Benston's "facing tradition" perfectly

---

Malcolm X (born Malcolm Little): (1925–1965), black activist and American Black Muslim minister.

Invisible Man: Novel by Ralph Ellison (1914–1994), African American writer and teacher.

[7]Amiri Baraka, *The System of Dante's Hell* (New York: Grove Press), 1965, p. 134.

[8]Kimberly Benston, *Baraka: The Renegade and the Mask* (New Haven: Yale University Press, 1976), p. 43.

[9]Kevin Kelly, "August Wilson's True Stories." *The Boston Globe* 29 April 1990: B29.

[10]Amiri Baraka, *Selected Poetry of Amiri Baraka/Leroi Jones* (New York: William Morrow, 1969), p. 104.

[11]August Wilson, *Two Trains Running* (New York: Plume, 1993), I.2.40–41.

comprehends the intertextual relationship of Wilson and Baraka, especially with respect to "the face-to-face encounter that constitutes a primal scene in African American literature: confrontation with the face of mastery."[12] It is no exaggeration to say that Baraka's plays are about little else but this black-white confrontation: Clay's confrontation with Lula in *Dutchman* and Walker's confrontation with Easley in *The Slave* are two of the best-known of such scenes, but the examples in Baraka's plays are legion and achieve an apotheosis in *Slave Ship*, Baraka's "historical pageant" which predicts a final triumphant confrontation over the white man. One might then say that Baraka taught Wilson how to *do* the facing of the white man, a lesson Wilson applies to every one of his five major plays that currently constitute his historical cycle: in *Ma Rainey* we have Levee's confrontation with the record producer Sturdyvant, in *Joe Turner* it's Herald Loomis's facing of the prison warden Joe Turner, in *Fences* it's Troy Maxson's facing of his boss Mr. Rand, in *The Piano Lesson* it's Boy Willie's facing of his family's slavemaster Sutter, and in *Two Trains Running* it's Hambone's facing of the grocery store owner Lutz. Like Baraka's, Wilson's plays are organized around these facings with the signal difference that in Wilson's plays the confrontation occurs offstage so that emphasis is placed not so much on the confrontation itself but upon how the black community invests itself in that face-to-face encounter.

Wilson has noted that the Baraka plays that he liked most were the ones published in the volume *Four Black Revolutionary Plays* (1969), which served as the main fare of the Black Horizons Theater of Pittsburgh, which Wilson founded with Rob Penny in 1968 and operated until 1972. Wilson thus not only subscribed to but lived the well-known Barakan manifesto, "The Revolutionary Theater," directing many of Baraka's plays. The experience had a profound effect, for Wilson transported three quintessentially Barakan elements to his own plays: the motion of history as the emergence of the African "Geist"° out of the bones of the Middle Passage, the enactment of the ritual dance in which personal experience and racial history converge, and, most importantly, the quest for one's song that is ultimately realized in the blues.

Clay's epiphanic speech in *Dutchman* aptly expresses the significance of the blues in Baraka and serves as a stepping-off point for considering Wilson's biggest B of all. Clay has finally been stirred to speak the truth of his experience to Lula which his appearance belies. He rages at whites who misinterpret black culture and experience:

> They [the ofays] say, "I love Bessie Smith." And don't even understand that Bessie Smith is saying, "Kiss my ass, kiss my black unruly ass." Before love, suffering, desire, anything you can explain, she's saying, and very plainly, "Kiss my black ass." And if you don't know that, it's you that's doing the kissing.[13]

"Kiss my black ass" would be a suitable subtitle for Wilson's *Ma Rainey's Black Bottom*, the first of his "blues plays." The twenty-year gestation period of *Ma Rainey* dates back to the day in 1965 when August Wilson was transfixed and transformed by his discovery of Bessie Smith and came to an understanding of her coded message, which Baraka revealed not only through Clay but through such

---

Geist: Spirit, usually the spirit of the age or culture.

[12]Kimberly Benston, "Facing Tradition: Revisionary Scenes in African American Literature." *PMLA* 105 (January 1990): 100.

[13]Leroi Jones, *Dutchman. Two Plays by Leroi Jones* (New York: William Morrow, 1964), sc. 2, 34–35.

books as *Blues People* (1963). Wilson has often recounted how he bought a record player and a pile of old 78's for a few dollars and then found Bessie Smith's "Nobody in Town Can Bake a Jelly Roll Like Mine." He played the record twenty-two times in a row:

> I was stunned . . . It was one of the most beautiful songs I'd ever heard. I thought, "This person is talking to me. This is mine."
>
> I began to look at people in the rooming house [where I lived] differently. I had seen them as beaten. I was twenty, and these were old people. I didn't see the value to their lives. You could never have told me there was a richness and fullness to their lives. I began to see it.[14]

If Baraka is Wilson's brother, then Bessie Smith may well be figured as Wilson's mother, for she gave birth to Wilson as what Houston Baker° would call a "blues detective" who is able to decipher black forms by looking to "the limitless freedom of myth and fictive discourse."[15] It took Wilson nearly twenty years to decipher fully in *Ma Rainey's Black Bottom* (1984) what Bessie Smith first brought into Wilson's view. In this first play of the current cycle, Ma Rainey becomes the embodiment of an African American cultural history which she pronounces with full authority:

> White folks don't understand about the blues. They hear it come out, but they don't know how it got there. They don't understand that's life's way of talking. You don't sing to feel better. You sing cause that's a way of understanding life.[16]

Wilson best elaborates the monumental importance of the blues to his plays:

> I think that what's contained in the blues is the African American's response to the world. We are not a people with a long history of writing things out; it's been an oral tradition . . .
>
> The thing with the blues is that there's an entire philosophical system at work. And I've found that whatever you want to know about the black experience in America is contained in the blues . . .
>
> So it [the blues] is the Book. It is our sacred book. Every other people has a sacred book, so I claim it as that. Anything I want to know, I go there and find it out.[17]

Wilson's plays are replete with knowledge from his sacred book of the blues. The title of *Joe Turner* comes from a W.C. Handy° song, *Ma Rainey* is of course about the real-life "Mother of the Blues," and *Fences, The Piano Lesson*, and *Two Trains Running* each contain numerous epigrams, allusions, and lyrics drawn from specific blues songs. In Wilson's plays, the blues are what Baker identifies as "the expressive site where American experience is named"[18] and constitute an ontology that is the very

---

Houston Baker: (b. 1943), distinguished University Professor at Vanderbilt University and prominent literary critic of African American literature.
  W. C. Handy: (1873–1958) was known as "The Father of the Blues." He wrote "St. Louis Blues," "Beale Street Blues," and "Yellow Dog Blues," among others.
  [14]Chip Brown, "Light in August." *Esquire* April 1989: 122.
  [15]*Ibid.*
  [16]August Wilson, *Ma Rainey's Black Bottom. Three Plays* (Pittsburgh: University of Pittsburgh Press, 1991), II. 67.
  [17]Dinah Livingston, "Cool August." *Minnesota Monthly* October 1987: 32.
  [18]Houston Baker, *Blues, Ideology, and Afro-American Literature* (Chicago: University of Chicago Press, 1984), p. 64.

idea of America itself: that the sign "America" signifies the broken promise of presence. All blues songs begin from the ontological awareness of the American condition as the sign of an absence, a broken promise—usually the specific premise is "my lover's gone"—and the blues is the form blacks invented to mediate this absence. So when August Wilson discovered the blues, he in effect discovered America.

In Wilson, the blues is *the* American language for telling and confronting the tragic reality of an America that is always already absent. Any American history is as much about our future as about our past, and Wilson's American history in the current cycle asserts that the sign of "America" itself can only be read into the future as a tragedy, as an experiment that *must* fail because it was committed to the impossible from the beginning. As James Baldwin° first pointed out thirty years ago, Americans do not wish to face the reality expressed in the blues that life is tragic and the only fact we have is the final absence of death. Wilson's "blues plays" may be taken together as an enactment of Baldwin's prescription that, "one ought to rejoice in the *fact* of death—ought to decide, indeed, to *earn* one's death by confronting with passion the conundrum of life."[19]

One black way of confronting the conundrum of life with passion is through ritual, and it is on this ground that Wilson met Romare Bearden (1912–1988), the African American artist best known for his collages of black life created during the 1960s and 1970s. Wilson holds Bearden in reverential esteem, for Bearden has not only served as the explicit inspiration for at least two of Wilson's plays—*Joe Turner* and *The Piano Lesson*—Bearden also serves Wilson as a kind of father-figure (both grew up in Pittsburgh), a personification of the ideal for a black artist. Indeed, Wilson has adopted Bearden's credo as his own: "I try to explore, in terms of the life I know best, those things which are common to all cultures."[20]

The life Bearden knew best was characterized by *The Prevalence of Ritual*, the title of a series of collages that were collected in a volume in 1971, a volume which had a catalyzing effect on Wilson. Wilson describes the moment as a young struggling poet when he first encountered Bearden:

[*The Prevalence of Ritual*] lay open on the table . . . I looked. What for me had been so difficult, Bearden made seem so simple, so easy. What I saw was black life presented on its own terms, on a grand and epic scale, with all its richness and fullness, in a language that was vibrant and which, made attendant to everyday life, ennobled it, affirmed its value, and exalted its presence . . . I was looking at myself in ways I hadn't thought of before and have never ceased to think of since.[21]

Bearden offered Wilson a new visual language that created a world populated by conjure women, trains, guitar players, birds, masked figures, and the rituals of baptisms, funerals, dinners, parades. Wilson was of course impressed by the black experience Bearden represented, but he was equally interested in his mode of representation. Wilson volunteers the creation story of this new black form.

One day [in 1963] Bearden and some of his colleagues had arranged to work together on a collaborative work—it was supposed to be a collage of black life at that time—but

James Baldwin: (1924–1987), African American writer, author of *The Fire Next Time* (essays) and the plays *Blues for Mr. Charley* and *The Amen Corner*.

[19]James Baldwin, *The Fire Next Time* (New York: Dell, 1962), p. 124.
[20]August Wilson, "How to Write a Play Like August Wilson." *The New York Times* 10 March 1991, sec. 2: 5.
[21]Les Payne, "Jazz Came Alive on His Canvas." *Newsday* 9 December 1990, Currents: 6.

when it came time to actually do it, Bearden was the only one who showed up. So he went ahead and just started doing it on his own.[22]

Bearden "riffed" on the quintessentially twentieth-century language of collage, first introduced by Picasso in his Cubist experiments, to create a form capable of expressing what Ralph Ellison has called the "sharp breaks, leaps in consciousness, distortions, paradoxes, reversals, telescoping of time and Surreal blending of styles, values, hopes and dreams which characterize much of Negro American history."[23] Wilson describes the structure of his own plays as having this collagist form:

> In Bearden you've got all these pieces. There's an eye here, a head over there, a huge over-sized hand on a small body. It's like that with me. I've got all these images, and the point is how *I* put them together. The pieces are always there; it's how I put them together, the relationships between them that counts.[24]

The first Bearden work to compel a Wilson play was *Mill Hand's Lunch Bucket* (1978), part of Bearden's series called "Pittsburgh Memories." When I showed Wilson a detail from it in *Memory and Metaphor*, a retrospective volume on Bearden, he welcomed the chance to explain how it gave birth to *Joe Turner's Come and Gone*, pointing to each element of its tableau as he went along:

> It's Pittsburgh, so you can see the steel mill through the window there. Seth is coming down the steps on the left and Bertha is standing at the center. Between them you can see the figure of a man seated, and he's hunched over, looking down. I wanted to know more about that man. What burden was he shouldering? So I started writing down his story and he became Herald Loomis.[25]

Even the character names in *Joe Turner* were supplied by another Bearden painting in the same series, *Miss Bertha and Mr. Seth*. Wilson has called *Joe Turner* his favorite play, which may have something to do with its being the most Beardenesque of his five plays. *Joe Turner* was the third play Wilson wrote in the current cycle. The very next play he wrote, *The Piano Lesson*, was also inspired by a Bearden painting of the same title, so years hence critics may be speaking of the two plays as comprising Wilson's "Bearden period." But it would be a mistake to limit Bearden's influence on Wilson to these two plays because the Bearden sensibility suffuses each of the plays to some degree. In the playbill of the Yale Rep production of *Two Trains*, for example, Wilson includes a detail from Bearden's 1968 collage, *Family Dinner*, which could serve as a subtitle for this play that takes place entirely in Memphis' restaurant. And Wilson's affinity for Bearden has its common source in the blues. Bearden himself was explicit, saying: "I paint out of the tradition of the blues, of call and recall. You start a theme and you call and recall."[26] Wilson writes plays out of the same tradition; his is a drama of call and recall. Bearden helped to give Wilson a field of reference for the blues that made of the blues idiom

[22]Mark William Rocha, "A Conversation with August Wilson," *Diversity: A Journal of Multicultural Issues* 1 (Fall 1992): 31–32.

[23]Quoted in Romare Bearden, *Memory and Metaphor: The Art of Romare Bearden 1940–1987*. Oxford University Press: 1991, p. 9.

[24]Mark William Rocha, "A Conversation with August Wilson," *Diversity: A Journal of Multicultural Issues* 1 (Fall 1992): 32.

[25]*Ibid.*

[26]Quoted in Romare Bearden, *Memory and Metaphor: The Art of Romare Bearden 1940–1987*. Oxford University Press: 1991, p. 64.

a historical language. So Bearden is as indispensable to Wilson as Baraka and the blues. Extending the familial metaphor, with Baraka as his brother, Bessie and Bearden may be taken as Wilson's artistic mother and father.

Where does Jorge Luis Borges (1899–1986) fit into Wilson's family? Possibly as a learned Latin cousin from whom Wilson has taken lessons in aesthetics. Wilson's debt to the Argentinian fabulist has been the least explored of the four B's, but he was no less emphatic about the influence of Borges:

> It's the *way* Borges tells a story. In Borges, it's not what happens, but *how*. A lot of times, he'll tell you what's going to happen up front, as in ["The Dead Man"] in which we're told at the beginning that a nobody from the slums will be shot in the head as a leader of his people. All of the interest is in how the story is going to be told.[27]

Reading Borges has also taught Wilson the ethics of listening which are so important in the black communities in his plays:

> With Borges you've got all these wires carrying electrical impulses, but they don't all connect up. When you encounter one of those little breaks, I think he wants you to stop and say, "Now wait a second, how does *that* connect?" That's why so many of his stories are about writing stories, like ["Pierre Menard, Author of the *Quixote*"].[28]

Wilson's interest in storytelling is the basis of his strongest bond with Borges. Mary Lusky Friedman has recently identified a "Borgesean Paradigm" that may be usefully applied to Wilson:

> Reduced to its most schematic outline, the fantasy that informs each one of Borges' tales tells the following story: A mishap sets in motion a protagonist, who responds to the calamity by setting out on a journey. In the course of this journey Borges' hero travels through surroundings that are progressively more impoverished and irreal until at last he arrives at a structure that walls him in. Immured there, he is privy to a marvelous but blighting experience, an experience that blasts his selfhood and annihilates him.[29]

This also serves as an apt description of Wilson's protagonists, each of whom conducts a Borgesean quest to locate or lose a text. So Loomis in *Joe Turner* ultimately finds his "song of self-sufficiency" rooted in the blues; Levee in *Ma Rainey* unsuccessfully tries to transcend his father's revenge tragedy by selling Sturdyvant his own songs, which are not rooted in the blues; Berniece in *The Piano Lesson* exorcises the ghost of Sutter by locating herself in the song of her ancestors; Troy Maxson in *Fences* invests his legacy for his son in the song of Old Blue; Hambone in *Two Trains Running* demands a ham instead of a chicken, a quest which is inscribed in his last words, "Black is beautiful." As with Borges's protagonist-narrators, Wilson's characters experience an annihilation which paradoxically creates a narrated self. Like Borges, Wilson presents meta-drama after meta-drama in which the primary self-reflexive topic of the plays is the very creation of text itself.

In the Wilsonian quest, as in the Borgesean journey, "the very act of narrating may be seen as a verbal journey . . . [Borges's] fictional speakers advertise their narrations alternately as ways of retrieving a valued memory from oblivion or of exorcising an

[27]Mark William Rocha, "A Conversation with August Wilson." *Diversity: A Journal of Multicultural Issues* 1 (Fall 1992): 31.

[28]*Ibid.*

[29]Mary Lusky Friedman, *The Emperor's Kites: A Morphology of Borges' Tales* (Durham: Duke University Press, 1987), p. 6.

experience so unsettling that it undermines the narrator's mental integrity."[30] Seen in this light, Wilson's obsession with the past is less that of a historian than of a Borgesean trickster who both delights and despairs in the knowledge that the past is a life-long process of (re)invention.

Many other lines can be drawn from Borges to Wilson: the primacy of myth, the principle of irreality in which magic is viewed in anthropological terms as a complete system, the humor that equips one to face absurdity, and the postmodern stance that all significant human experience is textual. Friedman's Borgesean Paradigm, which views Borges's stories as repeated "attempts to resolve conflicts arising from his ambivalence for his father,"[31] further suggests a possible visceral identification by Wilson for Borges. Wilson's father, Frederick August Kittel, was white and abandoned his family when Wilson was a child. As an adult, Wilson legally adopted his mother's family name. These facts have heretofore gone unexamined. But a future biography of Wilson will benefit from a detailed assessment of the way Wilson's plays, like Borges's stories, enact an exorcism of the father and then a quest for a refigured father.

But perhaps most importantly, Borges may be viewed as the master signifier upon the Western literary tradition so fully represented by his father's library. Borges thus grants Wilson access to the Western tradition without the need for Wilson's deference to it. Through the mediation of Borges, Wilson is able to find a usable past in the Western tradition and identify himself as a writer not of America but of the intercultural Americas.

This adumbration of August Wilson's four B's is intended only to suggest the outline of these influences. It bears reiterating that the four B's are much more than discrete influences whose traces are to be sifted out of Wilson's plays, but together form the sign system from which Wilson's plays are written. Approached in this way, the four B's provide the growing numbers who read Wilson with an extraordinary opportunity to attain a truly interdisciplinary perspective. Reading Wilson requires that we learn about the blues and American music, about Bearden and modern art, about Baraka and Black Nationalism, and about Borges and the postmodern. Now that Wilson's plays are routinely anthologized, he has replaced Lorraine Hansberry as everyone's "obligatory" black playwright. This time let us be sensitive readers and learn that difference is *different* and take August Wilson with his four B's as he clearly asks us to do.

---

[30]Mary Lusky Friedman, *The Emperor's Kites: A Morphology of Borges' Tales* (Durham: Duke University Press, 1987), p. 6.
[31]*Ibid*, p. vii.

Harry J. Elam, Jr.
AUGUST WILSON

2005

Harry J. Elam, Jr., is the Olive H. Palmer Professor in the Humanities at Stanford University. He is the Senior Associate Vice Provost for Undergraduate Education in Drama as well as Director of the Institute for Diversity in the Arts. His works include Taking It to the Streets: The Social Protest Theater of Luis Valdez and Amiri Baraka *(1997; 2001) and* The Past as Present in the Drama of August Wilson *(2004). In this selection, Elam gives us a clear perspective on Wilson's strongest influence—the blues.*

Despite the impact of Bearden, Borges, and Baraka on Wilson and his work, the most significant and most transformative of the four influences (referred to as the "4Bs" because all begin with the letter "B") is the blues. Twelve years prior to encountering Bearden in 1965, Wilson discovered the blues while listening to an old recording of Bessie Smith's "Nobody in Town Can Bake a Sweet Jellyroll Like Mine." This recording transformed his life and his cultural ideology. The blues become not only a guiding force in his writing, but also the foundation he discovers for African American expressive culture and for what Wilson believes is a distinctly African American way of "being."[1] According to Wilson, the cultural, social, political, and spiritual all interact within the blues. Forged in and from the economics of slavery as a method of mediating the pains and dehumanization of that experience, the blues are purposefully duplicitous, containing a matrix of meanings. The blues for Wilson continue to offer a methodology for negotiating the difficult spaces of African American existence and achieving African American survival.

Structurally, Wilson's "bluesology" acts as an aesthetic and cultural intervention disrupting the conventional frame of realism. Rather than plot or action, character and the lyrical music of the dialogue drive the plays. Wilson, a poet before he became a playwright, celebrates the poetic power contained in the speech of poor and uneducated peoples. Wilson allows his characters to voice their history in the verbal equivalent of musical solos. For instance, Troy Maxson—an illiterate garbage man and central figure in *Fences*—fashions his identity and self-awareness through bold expressive tales. Like the ancient city of Troy, he is an epic force, impregnable and larger than life. Troy's stories, which serve to describe the African American experiences as well as his individual life, expand the realistic canvas of the play, reaching beyond the conventional temporal and spatial limits to reveal the inner presence of history impacting on an individual.

Ralph Ellison calls the blues a unique combination of the "tragic and the comic," of poetry and ritual.[2] Wilson's plays embody this blues formula on a multitude of occasions. In each of the plays, Wilson's characters engage in a series of vernacular games, the dozens, and signifyin'. All these cultural activities are extensions of the blues or variations on a blues theme. Wilson sets his works in sites that enable such communal engagement, verbal jousting, and oral transmission of culture. For

[1]August Wilson, *Three Plays by August Wilson* (Pittsburgh: University of Pittsburgh Press, 1991), pp. ix–x.
[2]Ralph Ellison, *The Shadow and the Act* (New York: Random House, 1964), p. 256.

instance, he places the band interaction in *Ma Rainey* in the band room downstairs (in another area onstage), separated from the recording studio above (a separate stage area). The band room represents what Houston A. Baker terms a "blues matrix." Baker envisions the blues matrix as a "point of ceaseless input and output, a web of intersecting, crisscrossing impulses always in productive transit."[3] For Baker the prototypical site of the blues matrix is a railroad crossing, "the juncture of multidirectionality," and a place "betwixt and between."[4] Situated at the blues matrix, the blues singer transcends spatial and sociohistorical limitations. The band room as blues matrix is equally a site of power and potential. The band room is a space of unfinished business, where the band must rehearse its songs and await the arrival of Ma Rainey. It is a metaphorical space where the band members enact rituals and tales of survival that replicate the patterns of black experiences in America. [...]

Bolstered by the blues and other influences, Wilson set out to become a playwright. At his friend Claude Purdy's instigation, he moved to St. Paul, Minnesota, in 1978 and wrote plays, including *Black Bart and the Sacred Hills,* for Purdy to direct with his company. In order to subsidize his income, Wilson also worked as a scriptwriter for the Science Museum of Minnesota. His career and his destiny changed forever in 1982, when he submitted an early draft of his play, *Ma Rainey's Black Bottom,* to the Eugene O'Neill Playwrights Workshop in Waterford, Connecticut. It was accepted (he had tried the previous year with *Fullerton Street,* but it was turned down). At the O'Neill, he met Lloyd Richards, the Director of the O'Neill Playwrights Workshop as well as the Artistic Director of the Yale Drama School. Richards was also the first black director ever on Broadway, directing the production of Lorraine Hansberry's *A Raisin in the Sun* in 1959. Richards and Wilson began a friendship and collaboration that would lead to the production of six of Wilson's cycle plays at regional theatres across the country and on Broadway.

Ma Rainey's Black Bottom (1984), Wilson's first critically acclaimed play, and arguably the most musical of his plays to date, establishes a foundation for Wilson's blues theology that he examines with his later plays. In *Ma Rainey,* the significance of finding one's cultural and spiritual regeneration through the blues song plays out principally through the conflicting views of the title character, Ma Rainey, and the spirited young trumpet player, Levee. Levee fails to understand his relationship to the music, and never realizes his blues song. Ma Rainey, in contrast, recognizes that the blues can become both a self-accentuating song and a declaration of the collective, cultural memory of African Americans.

In *Ma Rainey,* as in Wilson's subsequent works, the dominant culture seeks to suppress, to control, and to commodify the black blues song. *Ma Rainey* opens with two white characters, Ma Rainey's manager, Irvin, and Sturdyvant, the recording studio owner and a producer of "race records," onstage. Together Irvin and Sturdyvant concoct their plan for the recording session and for capturing Ma Rainey's blues voice with a less than generous contract. Wilson juxtaposes Irvin and Sturdyvant's plan to commercialize Ma Rainey's blues song with Ma's own resolve to protect the integrity of herself and her music. Ma testifies to Wilson's contention that the blues are a uniquely black voice that whites' desire but cannot

---

[3]Houston A. Baker, *Blues, Ideology, and Afro-American Literature: A Vernacular Theory* (Chicago: University of Chicago Press, 1984), p. 3.

[4]*Ibid.,* p. 7.

understand: "White folks don't understand about the blues. They hear it come out, but they don't know how it got there."[5] [...]

Wilson's blues theology privileges the blues musician. He posits the blues musician as a potentially powerful site of black resistive agency. Too often, however, the musicians fail to realize the power they possess. As with any gift or power, the power of the blues musician exacts certain costs and expectations from the ones to whom it is given. Lyons in *Fences,* Jeremy in *Joe Turner's Come and Gone,* and Wining Boy in *The Piano Lesson,* for instance, all represent blues musicians who have misunderstood the spiritual force of the blues song and the cultural responsibility inherent in their ability to play the blues. As a result, they are exploited for their music and fall victim to those who wish to control their spirit and song. The band members in *Ma Rainey,* similarly, fail to realize fully the power and privilege of their music, their blues voice. Toledo, the piano player, chastises his fellow band members, "You lucky they [white people] let you be an entertainer. They ain't got to accept your way of entertaining. You lucky and don't even know it."[6] Still, it is on and through these musicians that Wilson positions himself as blues musician improvising on a theme. Toledo's declarations of the need for African Americans to recognize their connections to Africa represent an important element of Wilson's blues theology. Wilson believes that in order for African Americans to be able to sing their own song, to feel truly liberated in the American context, they must rediscover their "African-ness." Wilson puts it this way: "One of the things I'm trying to say in my writing is that we can never begin to make a contribution to the society except as Africans."[7] Toledo, accordingly, reprimands the band and himself for not being African and for being imitation white men.

Ma Rainey, the title character based on the legendary blues singer Gertrude "Ma Rainey" Pridgett, recognizes the power of the music to move through her. "You don't sing to feel better. . . . You sing 'cause it's a way of understanding life."[8] Ma explains that singing the blues is not simply therapy but rather an engagement with a complex and enabling force that acts to understand and even to transform and to transcend life. Ma remains a fiercely independent woman throughout the action of the play. Recognizing that the purpose of the recording session is to record her voice and her music, Ma will not be objectified; instead, she uses her position as a desired musical commodity to legitimize her authority. She vociferously maintains that the band works for her, not the other way around. After the recording session, Ma exercises her blues voice in one final act of defiance. She delays signing the release forms that legally grant Irvin and Sturdyvant control over her recorded music. Through this act, she asserts the power of the blues singer to overcome material limitations. She retains her artistic autonomy and rebuts others who wish to claim her song.

Still, the play does not end with Ma's defiant exit from the recording studio, but escalates into tragedy in the band room below. The ending of *Ma Rainey,* in which one of the band members murders another, is a complex and confounding blues moment. It stands in stark contrast to endings of Wilson's later dramas such as

[5]August Wilson, *Three Plays by August Wilson* (Pittsburgh: University of Pittsburgh Press, 1991), p. 499.
[6]*Ibid.,* p. 507.
[7]David Savran, *In Their Own Words.* New York: Theatre Communications Group, 1988, p. 296.
[8]August Wilson, *Three Plays by August Wilson* (Pittsburgh: University of Pittsburgh Press, 1991), p. 499.

Fences, Joe Turner, and *Piano Lesson,* in which characters reach moments of spiritual fulfillment, acknowledge their relationships to the African American past, and perform actions of self-actualization, self-determination, and collective communion. Present in the final scene of *Ma Rainey,* in contrast, is the ironic anguish of the blues wail. After being exploited by the white studio owner Sturdyvant, Levee transfers his anger and stabs Toledo, who unfortunately steps on his shoes. Levee's stabbing of Toledo, like all acts of black-on-black violence, strikes out against African American collectivity and cultural unity. The murder of Toledo represents a performance of tragic, unfulfilled promise, a loss of the black self that must be reclaimed through the triumph of the blues voice. The death of Toledo stands as a lesson that African Americans must learn from and that Wilson builds upon in his later plays.

Wilson claims that he started *Fences* (1986), his first Pulitzer Prize–winning play, with "the image of a man standing in his yard with a baby in his arms."[9] Beginning with this image, Wilson sought to subvert the dominant culture's representations of African American men as irresponsible, absentee fathers. Wilson creates Troy Maxson, a larger-than-life figure, who feels an overwhelming sense of duty and responsibility to his family. With an impenetrable resolve, he perceives familial values only from his perspective. Troy's self-involved concept of familial duty and responsibility prevents him from seeing the harm he causes, the pain his decisions inflict on other family members.

Through a series of retrospective stories performed by Troy, Wilson reveals Troy's victimization by and resentment of the forces of social and economic oppression. Wilson also uses these moments to disclose the influence that Troy's prior relationship with his father now exacts on his relationship with his own son Cory. Physically beaten by his father, Troy was forced to strike out on his own. During the course of the play, Cory must undergo a similar rite of passage. Repeating the family history, Cory physically confronts his father, is beaten by Troy, and forced to leave his father's house. The repetition of behavior patterns by father and son underscores Wilson's conviction that history plays an important role in determining contemporary identity. Only by literally confronting the embodiment of the past, one's father or "forefathers," can one gain entrance into the future or ascendancy into adulthood.

In the play's second act, Troy's adultery provides the catalyst that propels his wife, Rose, to reassess her position, to gain a greater self-awareness and to change. Rose blooms. Although Rose spiritually distances herself from Troy, she does not leave the marriage. Her final assessment of their marriage, delivered to her son Cory in the last scene, functions to reconcile father and son and emphasizes Rose's own resignation to "what life offered me in terms of being a woman."[10] At the close of *Fences,* Cory is able to accept the continued "presence" of his father in his life. This acceptance comes after Cory has returned home from the Marines and announces to Rose his intent to boycott his father's funeral. Wilson juxtaposes Cory's return with the entrance of a new character, Troy's seven-year-old daughter from his affair, Raynell (Cory's half-sister). Wilson uses Raynell as a critical element

[9]Quoted in Hillary DeVries, "A Song in Search of Itself," *American Theater* (January 1987), p. 25.

[10]August Wilson, *Three Plays by August Wilson* (Pittsburgh: University of Pittsburgh Press, 1991), p. 190.

in his redemptive strategy. Raynell visually represents the inextricable connection between past and present. Not only is she the manifestation of Troy's past infidelities but the signifier of his redemption. Her appearance enables both the audience and Cory to understand better the importance of inheritance, the perpetuation and veneration of history. In addition, here as in other Wilson works the child, Raynell, symbolizes the hope for the family's future. Significantly, her entrance into the action occurs not just on the day of Troy's funeral, but in the year 1965, in the midst of the civil rights era, a period of intense struggle and new opportunity for African Americans.

Romare Bearden
MILL HAND'S LUNCH BUCKET (1978)
AND PIANO LESSON (1983)

Bearden (1911–1988) was born in North Carolina but lived most of his life in New York City. He studied at several universities, earning a degree in education from New York University. He had a career as a social worker from the 1930s through the 1960s, but all the while he was also pursuing his career as an artist. Eventually he became self-sufficient as an artist working in a wide variety of media: oils, watercolor, and especially collage. His collages draw on his research into European and African art and have been inspiration for numerous musicians and writers, such as August Wilson. Bearden's interests were wide-ranging, from art history to music and ethnography. His works have a distinctive quality that makes them almost instantly recognizable as Beardens.

Romare Bearden, *Mill Hand's Lunch Bucket* (1978). Part of Bearden's series of collages called "Pittsburgh Memories," *Mill Hand's Lunch Bucket* inspired Wilson to write his play *Joe Turner's Come and Gone*—in which the seated, hunched figure in Bearden's work becomes the character Herald Loomis. (Romare Bearden, *Mill Hand's Lunch Bucket*, 1978 (Pittsburgh Memory series) collage on board 13¾" × 18⅛". Art © Romare Bearden Foundation/Licensed by VAGA, NY, NY.)

Romare Bearden, *Piano Lesson* (1983). Wilson acknowledged that Bearden's collage—featuring jazz pianist Mary Lou Williams, who was, like Wilson, a native of Pittsburgh—served as the inspiration for his play of the same title. (Romare Bearden, *Piano Lesson*, 1983: © Romare Bearden Foundation/ Licensed by VAGA, NY, NY.)

Amiri Baraka (b. 1934)
KA'BA

Baraka (Everett LeRoi Jones) was born in Newark, New Jersey, in a working-class home. He studied for two years at Rutgers University and then took a degree in English from Howard University in 1954. After he got out of the Air Force, he became associated with major poets and writers in New York's Greenwich Village in 1958, during the period of the Beat writers. That year he established Totem Press and published writers such as Jack Kerouac. His major break with white society came with the death of Malcolm X in 1965, after which he left his marriage to a white woman and moved to Harlem. Dutchman (1964) made him a recognized playwright and clarified his social views. After the riots following the death of Martin Luther King, Jr., Baraka became a Muslim and took a Muslim name. He then became a major controversial voice of protest and has remained passionately outspoken to this day. Ka'Ba is the most sacred site of Islam, and it is in the direction of Ka'Ba that Muslims pray.

A closed window looks down
on a dirty courtyard, and Black people

Poet, playwright, and activist LeRoi Jones in 1964, just three years before he converted to Islam and changed his name to Imamu Ameer Baraka and eventually to Amiri Baraka.

call across or scream across or walk across
defying physics in the stream of their will.

Our world is full of sound
Our world is more lovely than anyone's
tho we suffer, and kill each other
and sometimes fail to walk the air.

We are beautiful people
With African imaginations
full of masks and dances and swelling chants
with African eyes, and noses, and arms
tho we sprawl in gray chains in a place
full of winters, when what we want is sun.

We have been captured,
and we labor to make our getaway, into
the ancient image; into a new

Correspondence with ourselves
and our Black family. We need magic
now we need the spells, to raise up
return, destroy, and create. What will be

the sacred word?

Ma Rainey *(1886–1939)*

Gertrude Pridgett (1886–1939) was born into show business. Her parents toured in minstrel shows, and when she married William "Pa" Rainey, she became "Ma" Rainey. She had a solo singing career and recorded for Paramount from 1923 to 1928. Some of her songs, including "Don't Fish in My Sea," can be heard online at http://www.redhotjazz.com/rainey.html. Ma Rainey styled herself as the mother of the blues, which may be a fair claim. The next great blues singer, Bessie Smith, was befriended by Rainey, who assisted her in her career. Rainey left show business in 1935 with enough money to live comfortably. She was a strong influence on August Wilson.

BAD LUCK BLUES   *1923*

WRITTEN BY LOVIE AUSTIN, RECORDED BY MA RAINEY

> Hey people, listen while I spread my news
> Hey people, listen while I spread my news
> I wanna tell you people all about my bad luck blues
> Did you ever wake up just at the break of day
> Did you ever break up just at the wake of day
> With your arms around the pillow where your daddy used to lay
> Lord, look where the chump's°
> done gone

chump: Fool, one that is easily deceived or cheated.

Lord, Lord, look where the time's done gone
Hey Lord, there's something going all wrong
What's the use of living if you can't get the man you love
The use of living if you can't get the man you love
You might as well go die, give your soul to the Maker above

DON'T FISH IN MY SEA   *1926*

RECORDED BY MA RAINEY

My daddy come home this mornin', drunk as he could be
My daddy come home this mornin', drunk as he could be
I know that he's done got bad on me
He used to stay out late, now he don't come home at all
He used to stay out late, now he don't come home at all
I know there's another mule°
been kicking in my stable
If you don't like my ocean, don't fish in my sea
If you don't like my ocean, don't fish in my sea
Stay out of my valley, let my mountain be
I ain't had no loving since God knows when
I ain't had no loving since God knows when
That's the reason I'm through with these no-good, trifling° men
You'll never miss the sunshine till the rain begin to fall
You'll never miss the sunshine till the rain begin to fall
You'll never miss your ham till another mule be in your stall

mule: A hybrid between a horse and a donkey; especially the offspring of a male donkey and a mare.   **trifling:** Talking in a mocking manner or with the intent to delude or mislead, treating someone or something as unimportant.

Elisabeth J. Heard
AN INTERVIEW WITH
AUGUST WILSON ON PLAYWRITING   *2001*

Elisabeth J. Heard, professor at Saint Louis University, was a Ph.D. candidate at the Pennsylvania State University when she interviewed Wilson and gave him an opportunity to talk about his methods of writing. Heard's questions tease out some important responses from Wilson and give us a good understanding of the way he worked.

HEARD: How do you begin writing a play? Where do you start—with the situation, characters, settings, etc.?
WILSON: Well, I generally start with a line of dialogue. Someone says something and they're talking to someone else. I don't all the time know who's talking or who they are talking to, but you take the line of dialogue and it starts from there. The next thing you know you've got four pages of dialogue, and after a while you say, "Well, let me name this guy; let's give him a name. Who's talking?" And in the process of him talking you find out things about him. So the more the characters talk the more you know about them. It generally starts there. And then I say, "Okay, so where are they?" and then I'll come up with a setting or something. Once you get the set and

one or two characters, then it begins to take on a life of its own. Other characters walk in, and I'm not sure how it happens from there, but it's a process. I don't, for instance, start at the beginning of the play and say, "Here's what's going to happen," and go from beginning to end. Very often I don't know what the ending is or what the events of the play are going to be, but I trust that these characters will tell me or that the story will develop naturally out of the dialogue of the characters.

HEARD: Do you even start with the decade?

WILSON: Oh yeah, I start with the decade. I know some things when I start. I know, let's say, that the play is going to be a 1970s or a 1930s play, and it's going to be about a piano, but that's it. I slowly discover who the characters are as I go along. In *The Piano Lesson*, for instance, the question I had was, "Can you acquire a sense of self-worth by denying your past?" So I said, "Okay, let me invent this situation and place characters on stage who ask that question. They don't necessarily have to answer it, but let's pose the question." So I know I want to do that, but *how* I'm going to do that I very often don't know. I do know some things before I start.

HEARD: How do you choose the themes you're going to investigate for each decade? There are so many different things that can be chosen for each individual decade.

WILSON: I consider what I know about a particular decade and sort of go from there. I think if I knew other things then I'd write other things. The old adage is, "You write what you know," and even though you're writing about the 1930s, that's not what you're *really* writing about. You're only writing about love, honor, duty, betrayal. Those are the things which the play is made out of, and you're using 1936 Pittsburgh and that milieu to tell the story and to address those themes.

HEARD: It's interesting that you chose the subject of *Jitney* for your '70s play. If you had to do it over again, would you still choose this subject?

WILSON: It is not so much *Jitney*, it's the period of urban renewal that was part of the early '70s and the late '70s. It is just a setting, if you will, an opportunity to use this group of men to expose the culture, to get at some of the ways that this particular community of people solved its problems, abused itself, and all those kinds of things. If I were to do it today I might come up with a different setting, but it would be the same community and concern their struggles to remain whole in the face of all these things that threaten to tear them apart.

HEARD: What contributed early in your career to your sense of what worked on stage and what didn't? Was it through your own success or failure? Through reading other playwrights or seeing other plays?

WILSON: I still don't know what works until it works, until I see it working. It wasn't through seeing other playwrights or reading other plays because I haven't done much of either of those. Again, you have an intuitive sense that this is dramatic or a nice shape to a scene; you intuitively know how to tell a good story (because all a play is is a story), where the highlights are, what information to withhold, and how to reveal things. This comes from an innate sense of storytelling. Here again you don't always know what works, but if you have an opportunity to workshop a play, see a production of a play, and sit with the audience in a play, you certainly can tell the parts that don't work. And then you say, "Show me the parts that do and I'll make the parts that don't . . . I'll make them like that." This is the general idea.

HEARD: What level of internal development of a character do you believe is necessary to bring a character to life for your audience?

WILSON: I think that things like that [i.e., a few, simple lines], all of those kinds of things contribute to the life of the characters; they don't have to be big things, they can be little things, moments, like Doub in *Jitney* saying, "Well, I won't worry, I got my railroad pension." That tells you an immeasurable amount about the guy. He used to work at the railroad, and he worked long enough that he has a pension from the railroad. The line used to read, "I got my pension, and I'm not worried about it." Well, that doesn't tell you as much. It tells you he has a pension, he worked somewhere. But once you say "railroad," then you as the audience are able to connect him to every railroad worker you know, and that makes him come alive more because now it is a specific kind of thing. The man worked twenty-seven years on the railroad. And he has two sons "like I tell my boys" (well, we don't know how many he has), but that line didn't used to be in there. And by simply having him say, "like I tell my boys," we immediately connect him to a family, connect him to the railroad. He says, "I don't have nobody but myself," which implies that his wife is dead, his kids are out of the house, and he worked twenty-seven years on the railroad, and he's driving jitneys. So with just three or four lines of dialogue we know a tremendous amount about this character. He has the tendency to come more to life.

HEARD: Was the absence of those lines a result of your being a beginning playwright?

WILSON: I'm not sure that it was because it was my first play. I do the same thing in the play I'm writing now. I think that it's part of the process and the discovery that the playwright makes, and it doesn't have anything to do with whether it's your first play or you're now more mature and you don't make those mistakes. It would be nice, of course, if you hit it the first time as you wrote. You may write the railroad pension the first time and you may not, but if I look at the work I did yesterday, I would still see that there are ways to improve it. Somewhere down the line in some rehearsal I may say, "Oh, I see, why don't I just say the railroad there?" Those are not necessarily things that were missing because I was a beginning playwright. It's just a part of the process of developing a play. [...]

HEARD: I read that you experimented with a new revision strategy for this play. Will you continue to use this strategy with future plays?

WILSON: You are talking about writing in the moment?

HEARD: Yes, getting feedback from the actors and directors, writing new parts, and bringing them the next day.

WILSON: That's a good way to work. I don't know if it is necessarily a new way to work because generally I'd do the whole rewrite, come to rehearsal, and continue to work on it. But one time when I did *Seven Guitars*, I didn't do a rewrite. I did the rewrite during the rehearsal process, and it seemed to work as well if not better than the other way. I guess I'm not consciously aware that I made a change, but I'll certainly continue doing what I'm doing, working the way I'm working, and I enjoy the rehearsal process and working through there. So I will continue that.

In the past I would rewrite the whole thing and bring it in, and, of course, there were certain revisions that were made in the rehearsal process. But the bulk of the work had been done, so I would sort of lay back off of it (if that's a way of saying it) because I already did the rewrite, and now I was just patching up various things. With *Seven Guitars* I didn't do the rewrite prior to rehearsal. I came into rehearsal knowing that the play had to be rewritten. And I did my rewrite there in rehearsal, which didn't allow me to lay back off the material and do patchwork. I had to get in there and do the actual work, which seemed to work better in the sense that I wasn't writing in a vacuum. I had the actors there, so you could press and then you could see a response, or you could do something and see an immediate response. If you're at home doing the rewrite, you can't get that response — you're sort of working in a vacuum, so to speak.

HEARD: Were there other benefits from writing in the moment and getting the immediate feedback?

WILSON: I think so. It is a different kind of work, so you write different things. I think that if I'm at home sitting doing the rewrite, I'm going to write something different than if I'm there in the rehearsal room doing it. It's kind of hard to explain, but if you're tossed into the fire at any particular moment, then you are going to write something different than you will in another particular moment. And that is from day to day. Here at this moment on Tuesday at this rehearsal I'll come up with this, and I'm going to rewrite that; I'm going to rewrite it tonight. If I rewrite it next week I'm going to write something different. So you have to choose what is the right moment to do it because you sort of only get to do it once. I found more immediacy in the rehearsal process. I certainly wrote different things — I don't know if I wrote better things — and I enjoyed it.

HEARD: Does choosing your actors give you confidence in what the actor says, or in the suggestions that he or she may have in order to help mold and craft the play to its final production?

WILSON: Not necessarily. Sometimes you can choose wrong. Sometimes you can get into rehearsal and say, "Wow, this isn't what I thought it was going to be." Some actors work well in rehearsal, show you different things; other actors will do the same thing all the way through. They're looking to you for something. You have actors and you watch them search, and then their search gives you ideas about the characters because they show you different aspects of them. And you say, "Oh, yeah, I see how he's playing that. He's playing this character this way, so I'll help him by writing for the character which he is portraying," while another actor will give you something different. So here again it is crucially important who those particular actors are and what they show you from day to day in the rehearsal room. They can help you develop the character that way. So you don't always choose right. Then again, you don't always get who you want, either. So it is six-in-one, half-a-dozen-in-the-other. I've been fortunate to get some good actors, and we've had a good rehearsal process, and they enjoy the work also. And if you have actors who don't mind if you bring in a new monologue from day to day, etc., they just roll with the punches. That's good when you have actors who are willing to do more and work harder.

HEARD: I know that you play an important part in choosing the directors for your plays. Do you choose directors because you want them to carry out your vision, or do you choose those who will add something and go beyond the text?

WILSON: The director works as an interpretive artist, but he's still an artist, so you also have to give him room to create and to put his vision of the play or his translation or interpretation of the material on the stage. So you look for a director who has an overall sense of a play, and if you have a body of work, then an overall sense of your work, so that he or she knows what your requirements are. For instance, there are some lines that can be played rather broadly, but if you know my work, you know that all my characters maintain their dignity, and there should be no buffoonery on stage; so I look for directors who keep the actors reined in, and make a clear interpretation where all the actors maintain their dignity. Basically you look for someone who understands your work and who's part of it, whose sensibilities are similar to yours, whose feelings about the material are similar to yours.

HEARD: Your plays are staged using only one set, which you describe in detail in the printed versions of the scripts. How important is it to you that set designers adhere to your vision of the set?

WILSON: I welcome designers who create the environment with a minimum of guidance. There are certain things that I require; they are relatively simple. I mean, for instance, if the play is set in a jitney station, I don't want the designer to put it in a backyard. But within the confines of that, I think that the designer is free to create his or her vision of the concept of what that space is like. These people have gone to school and have studied this, and they create the environment. I think that as a playwright, if I detail that environment, then I'm taking away something from them. I'm taking away their creativity and their ability to have input themselves, not just to follow what the playwright has written. So I do a minimum set description and let the designers create within that. [...]

HEARD: So you don't write for any particular audience?

WILSON: No, I write for the play, if you will. I write to create a work of art that exists on its own terms and is true to itself. I don't have any particular audience in mind, other than the fact that the play is an artwork which is written with the audience factor sort of built in so that, craft-wise, when you do your exposition, the exposition is for the purpose of the audience knowing certain aspects of the play at certain times, and knowing what happened prior to the events of the play and things of that sort, but I don't write for a particular audience.

Peter Wolfe
August Wilson: Conclusion

Peter Wolfe, professor at the University of Missouri-St. Louis, ended his book on August Wilson with this conclusion. In it he sums up Wilson's achievement as the major American playwright of his time. Wolfe focuses on Wilson's views of black Americans and their struggle against prejudice and the limitations imposed by a society that has difficulties with their Africanness. Wolfe considers all the plays that Wilson had written up to his time of Wolfe's writing, exploring some of the more difficult issues that challenged Wilson's audiences.

August Wilson is patently American in the doggedness of his search for the meaning of life. As an artist, though, he inscribes his polemic into his art.[1] There's nothing misty or wet eyed in his compassion. It's cool, fierce, hard, and gentle. In its restraint, it's also just and equal. He has framed his vision against a backdrop of an American ideal that has failed blacks, giving them poverty and humiliation rather than neat suburban homes enclosed by well-trimmed lawns. Exploding stereotypes of the ghetto poor, his juxtapositions of the ordinary and the African-American surreal evoke anger, affection, and, sometimes, a little hope. Rather than debating social issues, he concerns himself with the salvation of black Americans. His people defy both liberal pieties and the reductive conservative arguments about the poor. Young men like Cory Maxson of *Fences,* Boy Willie Charles of *The Piano Lesson,* and Sterling Johnson of *Two Trains Running* lack a trade, a formal education, and the mind-set to build happy, productive futures. The cartoonish names they often have, like Levee or Poochie, defy white audiences to sympathize with them or take them seriously. But these victims deserve everyone's serious attention. In naming them, Wilson has issued two challenges—an artistic one to himself to gain that attention and a moral one to us to heed the issues he's dramatizing.

This regard may not come easily. Black-white relationships in the plays sound a note of stalemate and resignation. As Wilson told Bill Moyers in 1989, blacks have been thwarted in their wish to be part of something important in America: "The social contract that White America has given blacks is that if you want to participate in society, you have to deny who you are. You cannot participate in this society as Africans."[2] An empiricist, Wilson doesn't subject black Pittsburgh to cubist fragmentation or dislocation in his treatment of black exclusion. The same culture that's haunted by white racism also suffers from self-division. Both the members of Memphis Lee's set in *Trains* and Ma Rainey's musicians fret each others' nerves. The violence that explodes at the end of *Ma Rainey, Trains,* and *Guitars* also refers to the emergence in urban America of street gangs, drug traffickers, and police violence. Yet the interplay of constants and variables in Wilson's work rules out pessimism. Muddles, evasions, and deceptions abound in the plays together with violence. But *Joe Turner,* the Wilson script with the earliest time setting, 1911, shows, in Seth Bynum and Rutherford Selig, a productive, smooth-running black-

[1]Bigsby, C. W. E. *Modern American Drama, 1945–1990.* Cambridge: Cambridge University Press, 1992, pp. 291–92.

[2]Moyers, Bill. "August Wilson: Playwright." In *A World of Ideas,* 167–80. New York: Doubleday, 1989, p. 177.

white business partnership grounded in mutual respect. *Trains,* the Broadway-produced script set most recently in time, 1969, shows in Memphis a black man defeating city hall despite working within a system concocted to favor whites.

Then there's that side of Wilson that gives blacks no chance to attain justice and equality. This Wilson scorns the perversities of twentieth-century capitalism—the greed, squalor, and escalating inequities that have widened the gap between rich and poor. Particularly loathsome to him is the truth that many of his fellow blacks have bought into this system of competition and striving. Better for them, he believes, to return to the rural South and a way of life that bypasses the cynicism, sterility, and disillusionment of the industrial North.[3] Like the feudal baronies of yore, the rural South can offer security and identity in exchange for a willingness to build one's life around an ethos of limited expectations. But how limited and for how long? one wonders. The collective willingness to settle for less that Wilson alludes to has helped sustain the larger mysteries of black life by cheating and exploiting blacks. The "attitude of brutal reductionism"[4] that Gates finds in Wilson's work is politically naive. It may also be rearguard. The urbanization of the South has softened the demarcation lines that governed attitudes about North and South before World War II. This softening, or blurring, has created new opportunities, some of which have removed those barriers that blocked Levee's stardom as a jazz artist or Troy's career as a major leaguer.

But black enterprise can transcend the urges of time. A development like the $35,000 the city council of Pittsburgh gives Memphis for his condemned building forecasts a future in which black families will dine on ham. Wilson offers no agenda for this boon, though, at least in his plays. His distinctive voice and vision blend the strange and the commonplace, the straight-faced and the playful. Building his plays in layers, he'll use a comic plot to develop a period piece and then refract the finished product through a prism of racial prejudice. The light emitted by this prism depends on its source. Which can change; rather than providing formulas, Wilson dramatizes his reading of the human condition in ways that make it accessible, plausible, and exciting. The black and white keys of the piano in *Piano Lesson* symbolize a direction for racial harmony.[5] The song that brings about this harmony may still be both unwritten and unsung. But Wilson has been teaching us how to recognize it when we hear it. His beam of refracted light stops here. Taking care not to overexpose his poetic conceits, he builds provocative encounters around ordinary, yet high-tension, ingredients and then invites us into the force field they have created. It's our choice to view the Charles family piano as a product of wood and wires or as a font of pride, hope, and courage. [. . .]

Family is a caution in the plays of Wilson, who is an expert in the rhythms and nuances of black households. Taking up from Chekhov and Terence Rattigan, he writes about family members who either put up with each other or destroy each other out of motives of love or loneliness. The clash of desires and aims moves quickly to the fore of the family-based *Fences* and *Piano Lesson.* What follows the clash

[3]Pettengill, Richard. "The Historical Perspective." In *August Wilson: A Casebook,* ed. Marilyn Elkins, Garland Reference Library of the Humanities, vol. 1626, 207–26. New York: Garland, 1994, pp. 215–18.

[4]Gates, Henry Louis Jr. "Department of Disputation: The Chitlin' Circuit." *New Yorker,* 3 February 1997, 44–55, p. 46.

[5]Feingold, Michael. "August Wilson's Bottomless Blackness." *Village Voice,* 27 November 1984, 117–18, p. 118.

exhibits healthy artistic vital signs. It would be hard to know what to add to a Wilson play and, after seeing or reading it again, still harder to know what to take out. His women seem less fully imagined than his men because he sometimes seems more interested in the effect a Martha Pentecost (of *Joe Turner*) will have on her man than in her individuality. (In Alberta of *Fences* and Aunt Ester of *Trains*, he conceived two important female characters who never appear onstage.) Yet these women have a complexity and an ambiguity that raises them above the level of caricature.

What's more, they exercise the power of choice. Martha disclaimed her marriage to Loomis after his disappearance from home went into its third year. After learning of Troy's infidelity, Rose rears his child by another woman but banishes him from her bed. Ma fires Levee. The decisiveness displayed by these three women often stems from a richness of heart knowledge and an intuitive wisdom lacking in the warrior spirit. Wilson celebrated these gifts as far back as 1971 in the poems "Bessie" and "Morning Song," both of which focus on long-dead women whom posterity has unjustly forgotten. Wilson's appreciation of the female sensibility can express itself technically. Berniece Charles is the only female role of any size in *Piano Lesson,* and *Trains* includes but one female role, period. But these roles are among the choicest in the last 20 years of American drama, and the actresses playing them on Broadway all won acclaim that has helped their stage careers. *Joe Turner* and *Guitars* include several women whom Wilson leaves on the stage for extended periods without feeling compelled to intrude a man in their midst.

Often, one of these women will drive the plot. But in what direction? Because Wilson portrays life as a multifaceted mystery, his plot dynamics include shocks. One of his most striking features is the artistic control that makes these shocks memorable. He refuses to heat up his scripts with special effects, mawkishness, or a knowing irony that's sometimes called "attitude." The scripts are precise, elegant, and economical. Telling incidentals like Levee's new Florsheims, Seth Holly's tin sheets, and the sugar dispenser in Memphis Lee's diner help steer us through a complex of feelings. This sharpness and economy also improve the plays, Wilson's fastidiousness with detail shearing away the fat that could pad both the obsessiveness of his themes and the intensity informing his vision.

Sometimes, this vision discloses the larger truth. A family historian and a social chronicler both, Wilson can also rise to tragedy, the spiritual grace and incandescent beauty of his prose lifting a script to sudden heights. Recalling Plato's cave allegory (from *The Republic*), which confuses shadow with substance, Wilson's familiarity with both the sinister and the seriously strange convolutes surface and interior. Exteriors can count a great deal in a world that disavows a clean split between mind and body, a world, moreover, in which a person is judged by his or her skin color. The emergence of Sutter's ghost in the Charles home in *Piano Lesson* posits a reality behind language that keeps eluding us but that can be sensed through an ancestral retention. Wilson is a religious writer. He portrays the designs of the black people's God in both man and nature. He writes of the afterlife, of sin and redemption, of faith, forgiveness, and retribution. He's also sure that his people have souls, convincing us of their soul's existence by grounding an important event, like the advent of Loomis's wife in *Joe Turner,* in the supernatural (Martha is discovered in a church).

The issues rising from the event enact themselves as blood and sinew. No sooner does Wilson raise the knout of polemic than he goes straight for the guts. He'll look at the grossest aspects of his people's lives with such discrimination that the people attain rather than lose stature as they try to span the breach between what's right and what they're afraid they're going to do. Nearly every Wilson playscript turns on this paradox—that the more we learn about a character, the more mysterious the character becomes. Wilson's deviation from both the American norm of practicality and the American democratic manner creates much of his charisma. An internal mechanism buried so deeply inside his people that all they can say about it is that it's there imbues the everyday life of the plays with the possibility of the miraculous. This possibility stems from the collective unconscious, and it can be intuited through an awareness of motifs beating up from African-based myth and folklore, particularly the blues. The blues links Wilson to the great fund of wisdom and connection seated in his African origins.

All this makes up the theoretical background. The foreground consists of fragmentation, decay, and violence, with the violence often referring to the blues, a tradition and a value system Wilson ironically posits as a source of wholeness and joy. That his only two onstage murder victims are both blues musicians marks the distance between the actual and the ideal. Slow Drag and Floyd Barton also convey Wilson's commitment to the complexities nourishing his art. Fantastic but rooted in solid emotional reality, his plays evoke rather than argue or cast blame. He trusts his own private way of looking at things. Capable of being irreverent and traditional at the same time, he knows how to trade on the direct, the vivid, and the raw without forgetting how they're nuanced by subtlety and ambiguity. Through it all, the precision of his prose and his slanting shafts of humor keep sentimentality and despair at bay. He writes with deceptive fluency; Gates calls his "great gift" an "unruly luxuriance of language—an ability to ease between trash talk and near-choral transport."[6] An extraordinarily gifted stylist Wilson is, conveying, again and again, in sharp, often funny dialogue the exact words for his characters' half-formulated thoughts.

Full of peopled space, his plays stand their own ground. He's an authentic black American artist whose dedication precludes any ambitions to play the virtuoso, the cosmopolite, or the scourge. Nor has this creator of stunning linguistic effects and delicately shaded roles melted into his public image. The plays keep coming. For this, we should feel both exhilarated and grateful. August Wilson is a remarkable playwright who merits the superlatives that have been lavished on him. He has also bequeathed to his successors, regardless of race, an awful lot to live up to.

---

[6]Gates, Henry Louis Jr. "Department of Disputation: The Chitlin' Circuit." *New Yorker*, 3 February 1997, 44–55, p. 47.

Tony Kushner

Tony Kushner was born in 1956 in New York City, but his family soon moved to Louisiana, where his father ran the family lumberyard. His parents were classical musicians, and their home was filled with art. Kushner dates his interest in theater to early memories of seeing his mother onstage. He also recollects from childhood "fairly clear memories of being gay since I was six." He did not, however, "come out" until after he had tried psychotherapy to change his sexual orientation.

After finishing his undergraduate education at Columbia University, Kushner studied directing in graduate school at New York University, partly because he was not confident of his chances to become a playwright. Among his early plays are *Yes, Yes, No, No* (1985), a children's play produced in St. Louis; *Stella* (1987), an adaptation from Goethe produced in New York; *A Bright Room Called Day* (1987), produced in San Francisco; and *The Illusion* (1988), adapted from Corneille, produced in New York, then in Hartford in 1990. He worked with Argentinian playwright Ariel Dorfman to adapt Dorfman's *Widows,* produced in Los Angeles in 1991. *A Bright Room Called Day,* about left-wing politics in Nazi Germany, was not well reviewed after its New York production in 1991. Frank Rich, for example, said that it was "an early front-runner for the most infuriating play of 1991." But some people saw in it the power that was to show up later in his work. The Eureka Theater in San Francisco commissioned him to write a play that ultimately turned out to be *Angels in America: A Gay Fantasia on National Themes* (1992), the play that catapulted him to international prominence.

Among Kushner's projects is a series of three plays that he describes as having money as its subject—meaning, in part, the effects of economics, in the forms of both poverty and wealth, on individuals. The first of these plays, titled *Henry Box Brown* (1997), centers on the true story of a black American who escaped slavery by being smuggled out of the South in a crate. Brown eventually made his way to England, where he joined with a number of other former slaves in producing dramatic "panoramas" intended to discourage the English from buying slave-picked cotton, on which their textile industry largely relied. Kushner has said, "I've always been drawn to writing historical characters. . . . The best stories are the ones you find in history."

Kushner's play *Homebody/Kabul* (2001) seems connected with history, too. It is set in London and Afghanistan in 1998, after a U.S. bombing raid. Some of the dialogue is in Pashto. It was described by Paul Taylor, a London critic, as "a deeply felt expansively ruminative drama."

Among his many projects was a chamber opera about a black maid working for a Jewish family in Louisiana, *Caroline, or Change* (2003), written in collaboration with Jeanine Tesori and performed at the Joseph Papp Public Theater in New York.

In June 2006, Opera Unlimited produced *Angels in America* at the Calderwood Pavilion in the Boston Center for the Arts. The music was written by Peter Eotvos and the libretto was by Mari Mezei. In another interesting development, Kushner newly translated Brecht's *Mother Courage* for an August 2006 production at the Public Theater at the Delacorte Theater Central Park, New York. Meryl Streep was an extraordinarily energetic Mother Courage, Kevin Kline was the cook, and Austin Pendleton was the chaplain. Kushner's activism and energy have helped fuel anticipation of his next contribution to contemporary drama.

ANGELS IN AMERICA: MILLENNIUM APPROACHES

Kushner began work on this play shortly after Oskar Eustis of the Eureka Theater commissioned a two-and-a-half hour play with songs. Once Kushner got a presentable version, he showed it to Eustis and realized that, even incomplete, it was already longer than a one-evening play. Eventually, *Millennium Approaches* and *Perestroika*, the second part of *Angels* (not included here), grew to be more than seven hours long. Although the two parts are thematically linked and contain many of the same characters, both parts of *Angels* stand on their own as complete plays. Kushner said that he never expected to see his play produced anywhere but in a small theater in San Francisco; certainly he never expected it to be a smash hit on Broadway. It won the 1993 Pulitzer Prize for drama, another surprise.

Angels in America has epic, Brechtian proportions. Kushner has said that he set out to write a play on "AIDS, Mormons, and Roy Cohn." He chose AIDS because it is a scourge that has destroyed large numbers of the gay community. He chose Mormons because he saw in them a group that valued goodness and godliness but that could not tolerate gays. He chose Roy Cohn because, when Cohn was an aid to Senator Joseph McCarthy during the anti-Communist hysteria of the 1950s, he persecuted gays even though he was himself a closet homosexual. His homosexuality did not become public until he contracted AIDS and died in 1986. In Cohn, Kushner had found a villain whose rapacious individualism and unquenchable thirst for power helped symbolize the selfishness of the 1980s. In its New York production Ron Liebman was an overbearingly powerful Cohn, shouting orders, raising hypocrisy to an art form, with depths of contempt matching a profound love of power.

Kushner indicated that his play was a "fantasia on national themes," and it certainly lives up to its title. Kushner set his play in 1985, during the second presidential term of Ronald Reagan. He critiques the values of the Reagan years and politics in general. Jews, WASPs, and Mormons all suffer under his scrutiny. Moreover, he goes beyond national themes and introduces cosmological themes, notably with the introduction of an angel descending through the ceiling at the end of *Millennium Approaches*.

The play also focuses on problems of individuals. Cohn's friend and protégé Joe Pitt works for the Reagan administration and struggles with his growing awareness that he is gay. A conservative Mormon, Joe faces these complex, threatening feelings honestly and painfully. Harper, Joe's wife, relies on pills, listens all day to talk shows, and has no job but thinks of herself as part of a traditional marriage and fights to hold on to it. Louis Ironson, a liberal but not profoundly political homosexual, is partnered with Prior Walter, who is dying from AIDS. Louis has hidden his sexuality from his family and finds it impossible to stay with Prior as his lover's illness worsens. Kushner makes sure that we see all these sets of people interrelated throughout the play, despite their distinctness and the unlikeliness of their ever knowing one another.

Though the scope of the play is enormous, its focus is essentially on politics. Kushner's own views contrast sharply with Cohn's conservative politics, and he is surprised that both conservatives and liberals found the play rewarding, because he felt it to be a pointed attack on conservative values.

Angels in America: Millennium Approaches in Performance

The 1991 premiere of the play was in a workshop version in the Eureka Theater in San Francisco. Its first full-scale production came in July 1992 at London's Royal National Theatre, where it was a sensation. Some reviewers speculated that in London the political theater of Caryl Churchill and other playwrights such as David Hare and David Edgar prepared the way for this play. The audiences were enormously enthusiastic, and the positive reviews the play received attracted attention in the United States. Despite Kushner's relatively unknown status, the two parts of the drama (over seven hours long) were staged in the Mark Taper Forum in Los Angeles in 1992, directed by Oskar Eustis and Tony Taccone. *Millennium Approaches* appeared on Broadway in April 1993 at the Walter Kerr Theater, directed by George C. Wolfe. Frank Rich gave it a strong, positive review in the *New York Times* and said, "When first seen a year or so ago, the play seemed defined by its anger at the reigning political establishment, which tended to reward the Roy Cohns and ignore the Prior Walters. Mr. Kushner has not revised the text since — a crony of Cohn's still boasts of a Republican lock on the White House until the year 2000 — but the shift in Washington has had the subliminal effect of making *Angels in America* seem more focused on what happens next than on the past."

The second part of the work, *Perestroika*, arrived on Broadway in November 1993. Frank Rich in the *New York Times* said it was "also a true millennial work of art, uplifting, hugely comic and pantheistically religious in a very American style." After its Broadway run, the play moved to regional theaters, touring throughout the United States. The staging of the drama includes moments that may be described as magic realism, featuring ghosts, hallucinations, and other illusions. But Kushner has said, "The play benefits from a pared-down style of presentation, with minimal scenery and scene shifts done rapidly (no blackouts!), employing the cast as well as stagehands — which makes for an actor-driven event, as this must be." He said that it was not a problem if "wires showed," "but the magic should at the same time be thoroughly amazing."

One of Kushner's signal successes in 2003 was seeing *Angels in America* air in a six-part production over two evenings on Home Box Office (HBO) cable television, directed by Mike Nichols and starring Al Pacino in the role of Roy Cohn, Meryl Streep as both Hannah Pitt and Ethel Rosenberg, and Emma Thompson as the Angel. The production was beautifully done and won a Golden Globe award. Kushner made more inroads into television with the 2004 HBO production of *Homebody/Kabul* (2001).

Tony Kushner *(b. 1956)*

ANGELS IN AMERICA: MILLENNIUM APPROACHES   *1992*

A GAY FANTASIA ON NATIONAL THEMES

Characters

ROY M. COHN, *a successful New York lawyer and unofficial power broker*

JOSEPH PORTER PITT, *chief clerk for Justice Theodore Wilson of the Federal Court of Appeals, Second Circuit*

HARPER AMATY PITT, *Joe's wife, an agoraphobic with a mild Valium addiction*

LOUIS IRONSON, *a word processor working for the Second Circuit Court of Appeals*

PRIOR WALTER, *Louis's boyfriend. Occasionally works as a club designer or caterer, otherwise lives very modestly but with great style off a small trust fund.*

HANNAH PORTER PITT, *Joe's mother, currently residing in Salt Lake City, living off her deceased husband's army pension*

BELIZE, *a former drag queen and former lover of Prior's. A registered nurse. Belize's name was originally Norman Arriaga; Belize is a drag name that stuck.*

THE ANGEL, *four divine emanations, Fluor, Phosphor, Lumen and Candle; manifest in One: the Continental Principality of America. She has magnificent steel-gray wings.*

Other Characters in Part One

RABBI ISIDOR CHEMELWITZ, *an orthodox Jewish rabbi, played by the actor playing Hannah*

MR. LIES, *Harper's imaginary friend, a travel agent, who in style of dress and speech suggests a jazz musician; he always wears a large lapel badge emblazoned "IOTA" (The International Order of Travel Agents). He is played by the actor playing Belize.*

THE MAN IN THE PARK, *played by the actor playing Prior*

THE VOICE, *the voice of The Angel*

HENRY, *Roy's doctor, played by the actor playing Hannah*

EMILY, *a nurse, played by the actor playing The Angel*

MARTIN HELLER, *a Reagan Administration Justice Department flackman, played by the actor playing Harper*

SISTER ELLA CHAPTER, *a Salt Lake City real-estate saleswoman, played by the actor playing The Angel*

PRIOR 1, *the ghost of a dead Prior Walter from the 13th century, played by the actor playing Joe. He is a blunt, gloomy medieval farmer with a guttural Yorkshire accent.*

PRIOR 2, *the ghost of a dead Prior Walter from the 17th century, played by the actor playing Roy. He is a Londoner, sophisticated, with a High British accent.*

THE ESKIMO, *played by the actor playing Joe*

THE WOMAN IN THE SOUTH BRONX, *played by the actor playing The Angel*

ETHEL ROSENBERG, *played by the actor playing Hannah*

Playwright's Notes

A Disclaimer: Roy M. Cohn, the character, is based on the late Roy M. Cohn (1927–1986), who was all too real; for the most part the acts attributed to the character Roy, such as his illegal conferences with Judge Kaufmann during the trial of Ethel Rosenberg, are to be found in the historical record. But this Roy is a work of dramatic fiction; his words are my invention, and liberties have been taken.

A Note about the Staging: The play benefits from a pared-down style of presentation, with minimal scenery and scene shifts done rapidly (no blackouts!), employing the cast as well as stagehands—which makes for an actor-driven event, as this must be. The moments of magic—the appearance and disappearance of Mr. Lies and the ghosts, the Book hallucination, and the ending—are to be fully realized, as bits of wonderful theatrical illusion—which means it's OK if the wires show, and maybe it's good that they do, but the magic should at the same time be thoroughly amazing.

> *In a murderous time*
> *the heart breaks and breaks*
> *and lives by breaking.*
> —STANLEY KUNITZ
> "THE TESTING-TREE"

ACT 1
BAD NEWS • *October–November 1985*

Scene 1

(The last days of October. Rabbi Isidor Chemelwitz alone onstage with a small coffin. It is a rough pine box with two wooden pegs, one at the foot and one at the head, holding the lid in place. A prayer shawl embroidered with a Star of David is draped over the lid, and by the head a yarzheit candle is burning.)

RABBI ISIDOR CHEMELWITZ (*he speaks sonorously, with a heavy Eastern European accent, unapologetically consulting a sheet of notes for the family names*): Hello and good morning. I am Rabbi Isidor Chemelwitz of the Bronx Home for Aged Hebrews. We are here this morning to pay respects at the passing of Sarah Ironson, devoted wife of Benjamin Ironson, also deceased, loving and caring mother of her sons Morris, Abraham, and Samuel, and her daughters Esther and Rachel; beloved grandmother of Max, Mark, Louis, Lisa, Maria . . . uh . . . Lesley, Angela, Doris, Luke and Eric. (*Looks more closely at paper.*) Eric? This is a Jewish name? (*Shrugs.*) Eric. A large and loving family. We assemble that we may mourn collectively this good and righteous woman.

(He looks at the coffin.)

This woman. I did not know this woman. I cannot accurately describe her attributes, nor do justice to her dimensions. She was. . . . Well, in the Bronx Home of Aged Hebrews are many like this, the old, and to many I speak but not to be frank with this one. She preferred silence. So I do not know her and yet I know her. She was . . .

(he touches the coffin)

. . . not a person but a whole kind of person, the ones who crossed the ocean, who brought with us to America the villages of Russia and Lithuania—and how we struggled, and how we fought, for the family, for the Jewish home, so that you would not grow up *here*, in this strange place, in the melting pot where nothing melted. Descendants of this immigrant woman, you do not grow up in America, you

and your children and their children with the goyische names. You do not live in America. No such place exists. Your clay is the clay of some Litvak shtetl, your air the air of the steppes—because she carried the old world on her back across the ocean, in a boat, and she put it down on Grand Concourse Avenue, or in Flatbush, and she worked that earth into your bones, and you pass it to your children, this ancient, ancient culture and home.

(Little pause.)

You can never make that crossing that she made, for such Great Voyages in this world do not any more exist. But every day of your lives the miles that voyage between that place and this one you cross. Every day. You understand me? In you that journey is.

So . . .

She was the last of the Mohicans, this one was. Pretty soon . . . all the old will be dead.

Scene 2

(Same day. Roy and Joe in Roy's office. Roy at an impressive desk, bare except for a very elaborate phone system, rows and rows of flashing buttons which bleep and beep and whistle incessantly, making chaotic music underneath Roy's conversations. Joe is sitting, waiting. Roy conducts business with great energy, impatience and sensual abandon: gesticulating, shouting, cajoling, crooning, playing the phone, receiver and hold button with virtuosity and love.)

ROY (*hitting a button*): Hold. (*To Joe.*) I wish I was an octopus, a fucking octopus. Eight loving arms and all those suckers. Know what I mean?

JOE: No, I . . .

ROY (*gesturing to a deli platter of little sandwiches on his desk*): You want lunch?

JOE: No, that's OK really I just . . .

ROY (*hitting a button*): Ailene? Roy Cohn. Now what kind of a greeting is. . . . I thought we were friends, Ai. . . . Look Mrs. Soffer you don't have to get. . . . You're upset. You're yelling. You'll aggravate your condition, you shouldn't yell, you'll pop little blood vessels in your face if you yell. . . . No that was a joke, Mrs. Soffer, I was joking. . . . I already apologized sixteen times for that, Mrs. Soffer, you . . . (*While she's fulminating, Roy covers the mouthpiece with his hand and talks to Joe.*) This'll take a minute, *eat* already, what is this tasty sandwich here it's— (*He takes a bite of a sandwich.*) Mmmmm, liver or some. . . . Here.

(He pitches the sandwich to Joe, who catches it and returns it to the platter.)

ROY (*back to Mrs. Soffer*): Uh huh, uh huh. . . . No, I already told you, it wasn't a vacation, it was business, Mrs. Soffer, I have clients in Haiti, Mrs. Soffer, I. . . . Listen, Ailene, YOU THINK I'M THE ONLY

GODDAM LAWYER IN HISTORY EVER MISSED A COURT DATE? Don't make such a big fucking. . . . Hold. (*He hits the hold button.*) You HAG!

JOE: If this is a bad time . . .

ROY: *Bad* time? This is a *good* time! (*Button.*) Baby doll, get me. . . . Oh fuck, wait . . . (*Button, button.*) Hello? Yah. Sorry to keep you holding, Judge Hollins, I. . . . Oh *Mrs.* Hollins, sorry dear deep voice you got. Enjoying your visit? (*Hand over mouthpiece again, to Joe.*) She sounds like a truck-driver and he sounds like Kate Smith, very confusing. Nixon appointed him, all the geeks are Nixon appointees . . . (*To Mrs. Hollins.*) Yeah yeah right good so how many tickets dear? Seven. For what, *Cats, 42nd Street*, what? No you wouldn't like *La Cage*, trust me, I know. Oh for godsake. . . . Hold. (*Button, button.*) Baby doll, seven for *Cats* or something, anything hard to get, I don't give a fuck what and neither will they. (*Button; to Joe.*) You see *La Cage*?

JOE: No, I . . .

ROY: Fabulous. Best thing on Broadway. Maybe ever. (*Button.*) Who? Aw, Jesus H. Christ, Harry, *no*, Harry, Judge John Francis Grimes, Manhattan Family Court. Do I have to do every goddam thing myself? *Touch* the bastard, Harry, and don't call me on this line again, I told you not to . . .

JOE (*starting to get up*): Roy, uh, should I wait outside or . . .

ROY (*to Joe*): Oh sit. (*To Harry.*) You hold. I pay you to hold fuck you Harry you jerk. (*Button.*) Half-wit dick-brain. (*Instantly philosophical.*) I see the universe, Joe, as a kind of sandstorm in outer space with winds of mega-hurricane velocity, but instead of grains of sand it's shards and splinters of glass. You ever feel that way? Ever have one of those days?

JOE: I'm not sure I . . .

ROY: So how's life in Appeals? How's the Judge?

JOE: He sends his best.

ROY: He's a good man. Loyal. Not the brightest man on the bench, but he has manners. And a nice head of silver hair.

JOE: He gives me a lot of responsibility.

ROY: Yeah, like writing his decisions and signing his name.

JOE: Well . . .

ROY: He's a nice guy. And you cover admirably.

JOE: Well, thanks, Roy, I . . .

ROY (*button*): Yah? Who is *this*? Well who the fuck are *you*? Hold—(*button*) Harry? Eighty-seven grand, something like that. Fuck him. Eat me. New Jersey, chain of porno film stores in, uh, Weehawken. That's—Harry, that's the beauty of the law. (*Button.*) So, baby doll, what? *Cats*? Bleah. (*Button.*) *Cats!* It's about cats. Singing cats, you'll love it. Eight o'clock, the theatre's always at eight. (*Button.*) Fucking tourists. (*Button, then to Joe.*) Oh live a little, Joe, *eat* something for Christ sake—

JOE: Um, Roy, could you . . .

ROY: What? (*To Harry.*) Hold a minute. (*Button.*) Mrs. Soffer? Mrs. . . . (*Button.*) God-fucking-dammit to hell, where is . . .

JOE (*overlapping*): Roy, I'd really appreciate it if . . .

ROY (*overlapping*): Well she was here a minute ago, baby doll, see if . . .

(*The phone starts making three different beeping sounds, all at once.*)

ROY (*smashing buttons*): Jesus fuck this goddam thing . . .

JOE (*overlapping*): I really wish you wouldn't . . .

ROY (*overlapping*): Baby doll? Ring the *Post* get me Suzy see if . . .

(*The phone starts whistling loudly.*)

ROY: CHRIST!

JOE: *Roy.*

ROY (*into receiver*): Hold. (*Button; to Joe.*) *What?*

JOE: Could you please not take the Lord's name in vain (*Pause.*)
I'm sorry. But please. At least while I'm . . .

ROY (*laughs, then*): Right. Sorry. Fuck. Only in America. (*Punches a button.*) Baby doll, tell 'em all to fuck off. Tell'em I died. You handle Mrs. Soffer. Tell her it's on the way. Tell her I'm schtupping the judge. I'll call her back. I *will* call her. I *know* how much I borrowed. She's got four hundred times that stuffed up her. . . . Yeah, tell her I said that. (*Button. The phone is silent.*) So, Joe.

JOE: I'm sorry Roy, I just . . .

ROY: No no no no, principles count, I respect principles, I'm not religious but I like God and God likes me. Baptist, Catholic?

JOE: Mormon.

ROY: Mormon. Delectable. Absolutely. Only in America. So, Joe. Whattya think?

JOE: It's . . . well . . .

ROY: Crazy life.

JOE: Chaotic.

ROY: Well but God bless chaos. Right?

JOE: Ummm . . .

ROY: Huh. Mormons. I knew Mormons, in, um, Nevada.

JOE: Utah, mostly.

ROY: No, these Mormons were in Vegas.
So. So, how'd you like to go to Washington and work for the Justice Department?

JOE: Sorry?

ROY: How'd you like to go to Washington and work for the Justice Department? All I gotta do is pick up the phone, talk to Ed, and you're in.

JOE: In . . . what, exactly?

ROY: Associate Assistant Something Big. Internal Affairs, heart of the woods, something nice with clout.

JOE: Ed . . . ?

ROY: Meese. The Attorney General.

JOE: Oh.

ROY: I just have to pick up the phone . . .
JOE: I have to think.
ROY: Of course.
> (*Pause.*)
> It's a great time to be in Washington, Joe.
JOE: Roy, it's incredibly exciting . . .
ROY: And it would mean something to me. You understand?

(*Little pause.*)

JOE: I . . . can't say how much I appreciate this Roy, I'm sort of . . . well, stunned, I mean. . . . Thanks, Roy. But I have to give it some thought. I have to ask my wife.
ROY: Your wife. Of course.
JOE: But I really appreciate . . .
ROY: Of course. Talk to your wife.

Scene 3

(*Later that day. Harper at home, alone. She is listening to the radio and talking to herself, as she often does. She speaks to the audience.*)

HARPER: People who are lonely, people left alone, sit talking nonsense to the air, imagining . . . beautiful systems dying, old fixed orders spiraling apart . . .
    When you look at the ozone layer, from outside, from a spaceship, it looks like a pale blue halo, a gentle, shimmering aureole encircling the atmosphere encircling the earth. Thirty miles above our heads, a thin layer of three-atom oxygen molecules, product of photosynthesis, which explains the fussy vegetable preference for visible light, its rejection of darker rays and emanations. Danger from without. It's a kind of gift, from God, the crowning touch to the creation of the world: guardian angels, hands linked, make a spherical net, a blue-green nesting orb, a shell of safety for life itself. But everywhere, things are collapsing, lies surfacing, systems of defense giving way. . . . This is why, Joe, this is why I shouldn't be left alone.
    (*Little pause.*)
    I'd like to go traveling. Leave you behind to worry. I'll send postcards with strange stamps and tantalizing messages on the back. "Later maybe." "Nevermore . . ."

(*Mr. Lies, a travel agent, appears.*)

HARPER Oh! You startled me!
MR. LIES: Cash, check or credit card?
HARPER: I remember you. You're from Salt Lake. You sold us the plane tickets when we flew here. What are you doing in Brooklyn?
MR. LIES: You said you wanted to travel . . .
HARPER: And here you are. How thoughtful.
MR. LIES: Mr. Lies. Of the International Order of Travel Agents. We mobilize the globe, we set people adrift, we stir the populace and send nomads eddying across the planet. We are adepts of motion, acolytes of the flux. Cash, check or credit card. Name your destination.
HARPER: Antarctica, maybe. I want to see the hole in the ozone. I heard on the radio . . .
MR. LIES (*he has a computer terminal in his briefcase*): I can arrange a guided tour. Now?
HARPER: Soon. Maybe soon. I'm not safe here you see. Things aren't right with me. Weird stuff happens . . .
MR. LIES: Like?
HARPER: Well, like you, for instance. Just appearing. Or last week . . . well never mind.
    People are like planets, you need a thick skin. Things get to me, Joe stays away and now. . . . Well look. My dreams are talking back to me.
MR. LIES: It's the price of rootlessness. Motion sickness. The only cure: to keep moving.
HARPER: I'm undecided. I feel . . . that something's going to give. It's 1985. Fifteen years till the third millennium. Maybe Christ will come again. Maybe seeds will be planted, maybe there'll be harvests then, maybe early figs to eat, maybe new life, maybe fresh blood, maybe companionship and love and protection, safety from what's outside, maybe the door will hold, or maybe . . . maybe the troubles will come, and the end will come, and the sky will collapse and there will be terrible rains and showers of poison light, or maybe my life is really fine, maybe Joe loves me and I'm only crazy thinking otherwise, or maybe not, maybe it's even worse than I know, maybe . . . I want to know, maybe I don't. The suspense, Mr. Lies, it's killing me.
MR. LIES: I suggest a vacation.
HARPER (*hearing something*): That was the elevator. Oh God, I should fix myself up, I. . . . You have to go, you shouldn't be here . . . you aren't even real.
MR. LIES: Call me when you decide . . .
HARPER: Go!

(*The Travel Agent vanishes as Joe enters.*)

JOE: Buddy?
    Buddy? Sorry I'm late. I was just . . . out. Walking. Are you mad?
HARPER: I got a little anxious.
JOE: Buddy kiss.

(*They kiss.*)

JOE: Nothing to get anxious about.
    So. So how'd you like to move to Washington?

Scene 4

(*Same day. Louis and Prior outside the funeral home, sitting on a bench, both dressed in funereal finery, talking. The funeral service for Sarah Ironson has just concluded and Louis is about to leave for the cemetery.*)

LOUIS: My grandmother actually saw Emma Goldman speak. In Yiddish. But all Grandma could remember was that she spoke well and wore a hat.

What a weird service. That rabbi . . .

PRIOR: A definite find. Get his number when you go to the graveyard. I want him to bury me.

LOUIS: Better head out there. Everyone gets to put dirt on the coffin once it's lowered in.

PRIOR: Oooh. Cemetery fun. Don't want to miss that.

LOUIS: It's an old Jewish custom to express love. Here, Grandma, have a shovelful. Latecomers run the risk of finding the grave completely filled.

She was pretty crazy. She was up there in that home for ten years, talking to herself. I never visited. She looked too much like my mother.

PRIOR (*hugs him*): Poor Louis. I'm sorry your grandma is dead.

LOUIS: Tiny little coffin, huh?

Sorry I didn't introduce you to. . . . I always get so closety at these family things.

PRIOR: Butch. You get butch. (*Imitating.*) "Hi Cousin Doris, you don't remember me I'm Lou, Rachel's boy." Lou, not Louis, because if you say Louis they'll hear the sibilant S.

LOUIS: I don't have a . . .

PRIOR: I don't blame you, hiding. Bloodlines. Jewish curses are the worst. I personally would dissolve if anyone ever looked me in the eye and said "Feh." Fortunately WASPs don't say "Feh." Oh and by the way, darling, cousin Doris is a dyke.

LOUIS: No.

Really?

PRIOR: You don't notice anything. If I hadn't spent the last four years fellating you I'd swear you were straight.

LOUIS: You're in a pissy mood. Cat still missing?

(*Little pause.*)

PRIOR: Not a furball in sight. It's your fault.

LOUIS: It is?

PRIOR: I warned you, Louis. Names are important. Call an animal "Little Sheba" and you can't expect it to stick around. Besides, it's a dog's name.

LOUIS: I wanted a dog in the first place, not a cat. He sprayed my books.

PRIOR: He was a female cat.

LOUIS: Cats are stupid, high-strung predators. Babylonians sealed them up in bricks. Dogs have brains.

PRIOR: Cats have intuition.

LOUIS: A sharp dog is as smart as a really dull two-year-old child.

PRIOR: Cats know when something's wrong.

LOUIS: Only if you stop feeding them.

PRIOR: They know. That's why Sheba left, because she knew.

LOUIS: Knew what?

(*Pause.*)

PRIOR: I did my best Shirley Booth this morning, floppy slippers, housecoat, curlers, can of Little Friskies; "Come back, Little Sheba, come back. . . ." To no avail. Le chat, elle ne reviendra jamais, jamais . . .°

(*He removes his jacket, rolls up his sleeve, shows Louis a dark-purple spot on the underside of his arm near the shoulder.*)

See.

LOUIS: That's just a burst blood vessel.

PRIOR: Not according to the best medical authorities.

LOUIS: What?

(*Pause.*)

Tell me.

PRIOR: K.S., baby. Lesion number one. Lookit. The wine-dark kiss of the angel of death.

LOUIS (*very softly, holding Prior's arm*): Oh please . . .

PRIOR: I'm a lesionnaire. The Foreign Lesion. The American Lesion. Lesionnaire's disease.

LOUIS: Stop.

PRIOR: My troubles are lesion.

LOUIS: Will you *stop*.

PRIOR: Don't you think I'm handling this well?

I'm going to die.

LOUIS: Bullshit.

PRIOR: Let go of my arm.

LOUIS: No.

PRIOR: Let go.

LOUIS (*grabbing Prior, embracing him ferociously*): No.

PRIOR: I can't find a way to spare you baby. No wall like the wall of hard scientific fact. K.S. Wham. Bang your head on that.

LOUIS: Fuck you. (*Letting go.*) Fuck you fuck you fuck you.

PRIOR: Now that's what I like to hear. A mature reaction.

Let's go see if the cat's come home.

Louis?

LOUIS: When did you find this?

PRIOR: I couldn't tell you.

LOUIS: Why?

PRIOR: I was scared, Lou.

LOUIS: Of what?

PRIOR: That you'll leave me.

LOUIS: Oh.

(*Little pause.*)

PRIOR: Bad timing, funeral and all, but I figured as long as we're on the subject of death . . .

LOUIS: I have to go bury my grandma.

PRIOR: Lou?

(*Pause.*)

Then you'll come home?

LOUIS: Then I'll come home.

Le chat . . . jamais: The cat will never ever return.

Scene 5

(*Same day, later on. Split scene: Joe and Harper at home; Louis at the cemetery with Rabbi Isidor Chemelwitz and the little coffin.*)

HARPER: Washington?

JOE: It's an incredible honor, buddy, and . . .

HARPER: I have to think.

JOE: Of course.

HARPER: Say no.

JOE: You said you were going to think about it.

HARPER: I don't want to move to Washington.

JOE: Well I do.

HARPER: It's a giant cemetery, huge white graves and mausoleums everywhere.

JOE: We could live in Maryland. Or Georgetown.

HARPER: We're happy here.

JOE: That's not really true, buddy, we . . .

HARPER: Well happy enough! Pretend-happy. That's better than nothing.

JOE: It's time to make some changes, Harper.

HARPER: No changes. Why?

JOE: I've been chief clerk for four years. I make twenty-nine thousand dollars a year. That's ridiculous. I graduated fourth in my class and I make less than anyone I know. And I'm . . . I'm tired of being a clerk, I want to go where something good is happening.

HARPER: Nothing good happens in Washington. We'll forget church teachings and buy furniture at . . . at *Conran's* and become yuppies. I have too much to do here.

JOE: Like what?

HARPER: I *do* have things . . .

JOE: What things?

HARPER: I have to finish painting the bedroom.

JOE: You've been painting in there for over a year.

HARPER: I know, I. . . . It just isn't done because I never get time to finish it.

JOE: Oh that's . . . that doesn't make sense. You have all the time in the world. You could finish it when I'm at work.

HARPER: I'm afraid to go in there alone.

JOE: Afraid of what?

HARPER: I heard someone in there. Metal scraping on the wall. A man with a knife, maybe.

JOE: There's no one in the bedroom, Harper.

HARPER: Not now.

JOE: Not this morning either.

HARPER: How do you know? You were at work this morning. There's something creepy about this place. Remember *Rosemary's Baby*?

JOE: *Rosemary's Baby*?

HARPER: Our apartment looks like that one. Wasn't that apartment in Brooklyn?

JOE: No, it was . . .

HARPER: Well, it looked like this. It did.

JOE: Then let's move.

HARPER: Georgetown's worse. *The Exorcist* was in Georgetown.

JOE: The devil, everywhere you turn, huh, buddy?

HARPER: Yeah. Everywhere.

JOE: How many pills today, buddy?

HARPER: None. One. Three. Only three.

LOUIS (*pointing at the coffin*): Why are there just two little wooden pegs holding the lid down?

RABBI ISIDOR CHEMELWITZ: So she can get out easier if she wants to.

LOUIS: I hope she stays put.
    I pretended for years that she was already dead. When they called to say she had died it was a surprise. I abandoned her.

RABBI ISIDOR CHEMELWITZ: "Sharfer vi di tson fun a shlang iz an umdankbar kind!"

LOUIS: I don't speak Yiddish.

RABBI ISIDOR CHEMELWITZ: Sharper than the serpent's tooth is the ingratitude of children. Shakespeare. *King Lear.*

LOUIS: Rabbi, what does the Holy Writ say about someone who abandons someone he loves at a time of great need?

RABBI ISIDOR CHEMELWITZ: Why would a person do such a thing?

LOUIS: Because he has to. Maybe because this person's sense of the world, that it will change for the better with struggle, maybe a person who has this neo-Hegelian positivist sense of constant historical progress towards happiness or perfection or something, who feels very powerful because he feels connected to these forces, moving uphill all the time . . . maybe that person can't, um, incorporate sickness into his sense of how things are supposed to go. Maybe vomit . . . and sores and disease . . . really frighten him, maybe . . . he isn't so good with death.

RABBI ISIDOR CHEMELWITZ: The Holy Scriptures have nothing to say about such a person.

LOUIS: Rabbi, I'm afraid of the crimes I may commit.

RABBI ISIDOR CHEMELWITZ: Please, mister. I'm a sick old rabbi facing a long drive home to the Bronx. You want to confess, better you should find a priest.

LOUIS: But I'm not a Catholic, I'm a Jew.

RABBI ISIDOR CHEMELWITZ: Worse luck for you, bubbulah. Catholics believe in forgiveness. Jews believe in Guilt. (*He pats the coffin tenderly.*)

LOUIS: You just make sure those pegs are in good and tight.

RABBI ISIDOR CHEMELWITZ: Don't worry, mister. The life she had, she'll stay put. She's better off.

JOE: Look, I know this is scary for you. But try to understand what it means to me. Will you try?

HARPER: Yes.

JOE: Good. Really try.
    I think things are starting to change in the world.

HARPER: But I don't want . . .

JOE: Wait. For the good. Change for the good. America has rediscovered itself. Its sacred position among nations. And people aren't ashamed of that like they used to be. This is a great thing. The truth restored. Law restored. That's what President Reagan's done, Harper. He says "Truth exists and can be spoken proudly." And the country responds to him. We become better. More good. I need to be a part of that, I need something big to lift me up. I mean, six years ago the world seemed in decline, horrible, hopeless, full of unsolvable problems and crime and confusion and hunger and . . .

HARPER: But it still seems that way. More now than before. They say the ozone layer is . . .

JOE: Harper . . .

HARPER: And today out the window on Atlantic Avenue there was a schizophrenic traffic cop who was making these . . .

JOE: Stop it! I'm trying to make a point.

HARPER: So am I.

JOE: You aren't even making sense, you . . .

HARPER: My point is the world seems just as . . .

JOE: It only seems that way to you because you never go out in the world, Harper, and you have emotional problems.

HARPER: I do so get out in the world.

JOE: You don't. You stay in all day, fretting about imaginary . . .

HARPER: I get out. I do. You don't know what I do.

JOE: You don't stay in all day.

HARPER: No.

JOE: Well. . . . Yes you do.

HARPER: That's what you think.

JOE: Where do you go?

HARPER: Where do you go? When you walk.
(*Pause, then angrily.*) And I DO NOT have emotional problems.

JOE: I'm sorry.

HARPER: And if I do have emotional problems it's from living with you. Or . . .

JOE: I'm sorry buddy, I didn't mean to . . .

HARPER: Or if you do think I do then you should never have married me. You have all these secrets and lies.

JOE: I want to be married to you, Harper.

HARPER: You shouldn't. You never should.
(*Pause.*)
Hey buddy. Hey buddy.

JOE: Buddy kiss . . .

(*They kiss.*)

HARPER: I heard on the radio how to give a blowjob.

JOE: What?

HARPER: You want to try?

JOE: You really shouldn't listen to stuff like that.

HARPER: Mormons can give blowjobs.

JOE: *Harper.*

HARPER (*imitating his tone*): Joe.
It was a little Jewish lady with a German accent. This is a good time. For me to make a baby.

(*Little pause. Joe turns away.*)

HARPER: Then they went on to a program about holes in the ozone layer. Over Antarctica. Skin burns, birds go blind, icebergs melt. The world's coming to an end.

Scene 6

(*First week of November. In the men's room of the offices of the Brooklyn Federal Court of Appeals; Louis is crying over the sink; Joe enters.*)

JOE: Oh, um. . . . Morning.

LOUIS: Good morning, counselor.

JOE (*he watches Louis cry*): Sorry, I . . . I don't know your name.

LOUIS: Don't bother. Word processor. The lowest of the low.

JOE (*holding out hand*): Joe Pitt. I'm with Justice Wilson . . .

LOUIS: Oh, I know that. Counselor Pitt. Chief Clerk.

JOE: Were you . . . are you OK?

LOUIS: Oh, yeah. Thanks. What a nice man.

JOE: Not so nice.

LOUIS: What?

JOE: Not so nice. Nothing. You sure you're . . .

LOUIS: Life sucks shit. Life . . . just sucks shit.

JOE: What's wrong?

LOUIS: Run in my nylons.

JOE: Sorry . . . ?

LOUIS: Forget it. Look, thanks for asking.

JOE: Well . . .

LOUIS: I mean it really is nice of you.
(*He starts crying again.*)
Sorry, sorry, sick friend . . .

JOE: Oh, I'm sorry.

LOUIS: Yeah, yeah, well, that's sweet.
Three of your colleagues have preceded you to this baleful sight and you're the first one to ask. The others just opened the door, saw me, and fled. I hope they had to pee real bad.

JOE (*handing him a wad of toilet paper*): They just didn't want to intrude.

LOUIS: Hah. Reaganite heartless macho asshole lawyers.

JOE: Oh, that's unfair.

LOUIS: What is? Heartless? Macho? Reaganite? Lawyer?

JOE: I voted for Reagan.

LOUIS: You did?

JOE: Twice.

LOUIS: Twice? Well, oh boy. A Gay Republican.

JOE: Excuse me?

LOUIS: Nothing.

JOE: I'm not . . .
Forget it.

LOUIS: Republican? Not Republican? Or . . .

JOE: What?

LOUIS: What?

JOE: Not gay. I'm not gay.

LOUIS: Oh. Sorry.
(*Blows his nose loudly.*) It's just . . .
JOE: Yes?
LOUIS: Well, sometimes you can tell from the way a person sounds that . . . I mean you *sound* like a . . .
JOE: No I don't. Like what?
LOUIS: Like a Republican.

(*Little pause. Joe knows he's being teased; Louis knows he knows. Joe decides to be a little brave.*)

JOE (*making sure no one else is around*): Do I? Sound like a . . . ?
LOUIS: What? Like a . . . ? Republican, or . . . ? Do I?
JOE: Do you what?
LOUIS: Sound like a . . . ?
JOE: Like a . . . ?
I'm . . . confused.
LOUIS: Yes.
My name is Louis. But all my friends call me Louise. I work in Word Processing. Thanks for the toilet paper.

(*Louis offers Joe his hand, Joe reaches, Louis feints and pecks Joe on the cheek, then exits.*)

Scene 7

(*A week later. Mutual dream scene. Prior is at a fantastic makeup table, having a dream, applying the face. Harper is having a pill-induced hallucination. She has these from time to time. For some reason, Prior has appeared in this one. Or Harper has appeared in Prior's dream. It is bewildering.*)

PRIOR (*alone, putting on makeup, then examining the results in the mirror; to the audience*): "I'm ready for my closeup, Mr. DeMille."
One wants to move through life with elegance and grace, blossoming infrequently but with exquisite taste, and perfect timing, like a rare bloom, a zebra orchid. . . . One wants. . . . But one so seldom gets what one wants, does one? No. One does not. One gets fucked. Over. One . . . dies at thirty, robbed of . . . decades of majesty.
Fuck this shit. Fuck this shit.
(*He almost crumbles; he pulls himself together; he studies his handiwork in the mirror.*)
I look like a corpse. A corpsette. Oh my queen; you know you've hit rock-bottom when even drag is a drag.

(*Harper appears.*)

HARPER: Are you. . . . Who are you?
PRIOR: Who are you?
HARPER: What are you doing in my hallucination?
PRIOR: I'm not in your hallucination. You're in my dream.
HARPER: You're wearing makeup.
PRIOR: So are you.

HARPER: But you're a man.
PRIOR (*feigning dismay, shock, he mimes slashing his throat with his lipstick and dies, fabulously tragic. Then*): The hands and feet give it away.
HARPER: There must be some mistake here. I don't recognize you. You're not. . . . Are you my . . . some sort of imaginary friend?
PRIOR: No. Aren't you too old to have imaginary friends?
HARPER: I have emotional problems. I took too many pills. Why are you wearing makeup?
PRIOR: I was in the process of applying the face, trying to make myself feel better—I swiped the new fall colors at the Clinique counter at Macy's. (*Showing her.*)
HARPER: You stole these?
PRIOR: I was out of cash; it was an emotional emergency!
HARPER: Joe will be so angry. I promised him. No more pills.
PRIOR: These pills you keep alluding to?
HARPER: Valium. I take Valium. Lots of Valium.
PRIOR: And you're dancing as fast as you can.
HARPER: I'm not *addicted*. I don't believe in addiction, and I never . . . well, I never drink. And I *never* take drugs.
PRIOR: Well, smell *you*, Nancy Drew.
HARPER: Except Valium.
PRIOR: Except Valium; in wee fistfuls.
HARPER: It's terrible. Mormons are not supposed to be addicted to anything. I'm a Mormon.
PRIOR: I'm a homosexual.
HARPER: Oh! In my church we don't believe in homosexuals.
PRIOR: In my church we don't believe in Mormons.
HARPER: What church do . . . oh! (*She laughs.*) I get it.
I don't understand this. If I didn't ever see you before and I don't think I did then I don't think you should be here, in this hallucination, because in my experience the mind, which is where hallucinations come from, shouldn't be able to make up anything that wasn't there to start with, that didn't enter it from experience, from the real world. Imagination can't create anything new, can it? It only recycles bits and pieces from the world and reassembles them into visions. . . . Am I making sense right now?
PRIOR: Given the circumstances, yes.
HARPER: So when we think we've escaped the unbearable ordinariness and, well, untruthfulness of our lives, it's really only the same old ordinariness and falseness rearranged into the appearance of novelty and truth. Nothing unknown is knowable. Don't you think it's depressing?
PRIOR: The limitations of the imagination?
HARPER: Yes.
PRIOR: It's something you learn after your second theme party: It's All Been Done Before.
HARPER: The world. Finite. Terribly, terribly. . . . Well . . .

This is the most depressing hallucination I've ever had.

PRIOR: Apologies. I do try to be amusing.

HARPER: Oh, well, don't apologize, you. . . . I can't expect someone who's really sick to entertain me.

PRIOR: How on earth did you know . . .

HARPER: Oh that happens. This is the very threshhold of revelation sometimes. You can see things . . . how sick you are. Do you see anything about me?

PRIOR: Yes.

HARPER: What?

PRIOR: You are amazingly unhappy.

HARPER: Oh big deal. You meet a Valium addict and you figure out she's unhappy. That doesn't count. Of course I. . . . Something else. Something surprising.

PRIOR: Something surprising.

HARPER: Yes.

PRIOR: Your husband's a homo.

(*Pause.*)

HARPER: Oh, ridiculous.
   (*Pause, then very quietly.*)
   Really?

PRIOR (*shrugs*): Threshhold of revelation.

HARPER: Well I don't like your revelations. I don't think you intuit well at all. Joe's a very normal man, he . . .
   Oh God. Oh God. He. . . . Do homos take, like, lots of long walks?

PRIOR: Yes. We do. In stretch pants with lavender coifs. I just looked at you, and there was . . .

HARPER: A sort of blue streak of recognition.

PRIOR: Yes.

HARPER: Like you knew me incredibly well.

PRIOR: Yes.

HARPER: Yes.
   I have to go now, get back, something just . . . fell apart.
   Oh God, I feel so sad . . .

PRIOR: I . . . I'm sorry. I usually say, "Fuck the truth," but mostly, the truth fucks you.

HARPER: I see something else about you . . .

PRIOR: Oh?

HARPER: Deep inside you, there's a part of you, the most inner part, entirely free of disease. I can see that.

PRIOR: Is that. . . . That isn't true.

HARPER: Threshold of revelation.
   Home . . .

(*She vanishes.*)

PRIOR: People come and go so quickly here . . .
   (*To himself in the mirror.*) I don't think there's any uninfected part of me. My heart is pumping polluted blood. I feel dirty.

(*He begins to wipe makeup off with his hands, smearing it around. A large gray feather falls from up above. Prior stops smearing the makeup and looks at the feather. He goes to it and picks it up.*)

A VOICE (*it is an incredibly beautiful voice*): Look up!

PRIOR (*looking up, not seeing anyone*): Hello?

A VOICE: Look up!

PRIOR: Who is that?

A VOICE: Prepare the way!

PRIOR: I don't see any . . .

(*There is a dramatic change in lighting, from above.*)

A VOICE: Look up, look up,
   prepare the way
   the infinite descent
   A breath in air
   floating down
   Glory to . . .

(*Silence.*)

PRIOR: Hello? Is that it? Helloooo!
   What the fuck . . . ? (*He holds himself.*)
   Poor me. Poor poor me. Why me? Why poor poor me? Oh I don't feel good right now. I really don't.

Scene 8

(*That night. Split scene: Harper and Joe at home; Prior and Louis in bed.*)

HARPER: Where were you?

JOE: Out.

HARPER: Where?

JOE: Just out. Thinking.

HARPER: It's late.

JOE: I had a lot to think about.

HARPER: I burned dinner.

JOE: Sorry.

HARPER: Not my dinner. My dinner was fine. Your dinner. I put it back in the oven and turned everything up as high as it could go and I watched till it burned black. It's still hot. Very hot. Want it?

JOE: You didn't have to do that.

HARPER: I know. It just seemed like the kind of thing a mentally deranged sex-starved pill-popping housewife would do.

JOE: Uh huh.

HARPER: So I did it. Who knows anymore what I have to do?

JOE: How many pills?

HARPER: A bunch. Don't change the subject.

JOE: I won't talk to you when you . . .

HARPER: No. No. Don't do that! I'm . . . I'm fine, pills are not the problem, not our problem, I WANT TO KNOW WHERE YOU'VE BEEN! I WANT TO KNOW WHAT'S GOING ON!

JOE: Going on with what? The job?

HARPER: Not the job.

JOE: I said I need more time.

HARPER: Not the job!

JOE: Mr. Cohn, I talked to him on the phone, he said I had to hurry . . .

HARPER: Not the . . .

JOE: But I can't get you to talk sensibly about anything so . . .

HARPER: SHUT UP!

JOE: Then what?

HARPER: Stick to the subject.

JOE: I don't know what that is. You have something you want to ask me? Ask me. Go.

HARPER: I . . . can't. I'm scared of you.

JOE: I'm tired, I'm going to bed.

HARPER: Tell me without making me ask. Please.

JOE: This is crazy, I'm not . . .

HARPER: When you come through the door at night your face is never exactly the way I remembered it. I get surprised by something . . . mean and hard about the way you look. Even the weight of you in the bed at night, the way you breathe in your sleep seems unfamiliar.

You terrify me.

JOE (cold): I know who you are.

HARPER: Yes. I'm the enemy. That's easy. That doesn't change.

You think you're the only one who hates sex; I do; I hate it with you; I do. I dream that you batter away at me till all my joints come apart, like wax, and I fall into pieces. It's like a punishment. It was wrong of me to marry you. I knew you . . . (She stops herself.) It's a sin, and it's killing us both.

JOE: I can always tell when you've taken pills because it makes you red-faced and sweaty and frankly that's very often why I don't want to . . .

HARPER: Because . . .

JOE: Well, you aren't pretty. Not like this.

HARPER: I have something to ask you.

JOE: Then ASK! ASK! What in hell are you . . .

HARPER: Are you a homo?

(Pause.)

Are you? If you try to walk out right now I'll put your dinner back in the oven and turn it up so high the whole building will fill with smoke and everyone in it will asphyxiate. So help me God I will.

Now answer the question.

JOE: What if I . . .

(Small pause.)

HARPER: Then tell me, please. And we'll see.

JOE: No. I'm not.

I don't see what difference it makes.

LOUIS: Jews don't have any clear textual guide to the afterlife; even that it exists. I don't think much about it. I see it as a perpetual rainy Thursday afternoon in March. Dead leaves.

PRIOR: Eeeugh. Very Greco-Roman.

LOUIS: Well for us it's not the verdict that counts, it's the act of judgment. That's why I could never be a lawyer. In court all that matters is the verdict.

PRIOR: You could never be a lawyer because you are oversexed. You're too distracted.

LOUIS: Not distracted; abstracted. I'm trying to make a point:

PRIOR: Namely:

LOUIS: It's the judge in his or her chambers, weighing, books open, pondering the evidence, ranging freely over categories: good, evil, innocent, guilty; the judge in the chamber of circumspection, not the judge on the bench with the gavel. The shaping of the law, not its execution.

PRIOR: The point, dear, the point . . .

LOUIS: That it should be the questions and shape of a life, its total complexity gathered, arranged and considered, which matters in the end, not some stamp of salvation or damnation which disperses all the complexity in some unsatisfying little decision—the balancing of the scales . . .

PRIOR: I like this; very zen; it's . . . reassuringly incomprehensible and useless. We who are about to die thank you.

LOUIS: You are not about to die.

PRIOR: It's not going well, really . . . two new lesions. My leg hurts. There's protein in my urine, the doctor says, but who knows what the fuck that portends. Anyway it shouldn't be there, the protein. My butt is chapped from diarrhea and yesterday I shat blood.

LOUIS: I really hate this. You don't tell me . . .

PRIOR: You get too upset, I wind up comforting you. It's easier . . .

LOUIS: Oh thanks.

PRIOR: If it's bad I'll tell you.

LOUIS: Shitting blood sounds bad to me.

PRIOR: And I'm telling you.

LOUIS: And I'm handling it.

PRIOR: Tell me some more about justice.

LOUIS: I am handling it.

PRIOR: Well Louis you win Trooper of the Month.

(Louis starts to cry.)

PRIOR: I take it back. You aren't Trooper of the Month. This isn't working . . .

Tell me some more about justice.

LOUIS: You are not about to die.

PRIOR: Justice . . .

LOUIS: . . . is an immensity, a confusing vastness. Justice is God.

Prior?

PRIOR: Hmmm?

LOUIS: You love me.

PRIOR: Yes.

LOUIS: What if I walked out on this? Would you hate me forever?

(Prior kisses Louis on the forehead.)

PRIOR: Yes.

JOE: I think we ought to pray. Ask God for help. Ask him together . . .

HARPER: God won't talk to me. I have to make up people to talk to me.

JOE: You have to keep asking.

HARPER: I forgot the question.

Oh yeah. God, is my husband a . . .

JOE (*scary*): Stop it. Stop it. I'm warning you.

> Does it make any difference? That I might be one thing deep within, no matter how wrong or ugly that thing is, so long as I have fought, with everything I have, to kill it. What do you want from me? What do you want from me, Harper? More than that? For God's sake, there's nothing left, I'm a shell. There's nothing left to kill.

> As long as my behavior is what I know it has to be. Decent. Correct. That alone in the eyes of God.

HARPER: No, no, not that, that's Utah talk, Mormon talk, I hate it, Joe, tell me, say it . . .

JOE: All I will say is that I am a very good man who has worked very hard to become good and you want to destroy that. You want to destroy me, but I am not going to let you do that.

(*Pause.*)

HARPER: I'm going to have a baby.

JOE: Liar.

HARPER: You liar.

> A baby born addicted to pills. A baby who does not dream but who hallucinates, who stares up at us with big mirror eyes and who does not know who we are.

(*Pause.*)

JOE: Are you really . . .

HARPER: No. Yes. No. Yes. Get away from me.

> Now we both have a secret.

PRIOR: One of my ancestors was a ship's captain who made money bringing whale oil to Europe and returning with immigrants—Irish mostly, packed in tight, so many dollars per head. The last ship he captained foundered off the coast of Nova Scotia in a winter tempest and sank to the bottom. He went down with the ship—la Grande Geste—but his crew took seventy women and kids in the ship's only longboat, this big, open rowboat, and when the weather got too rough, and they thought the boat was overcrowded, the crew started lifting people up and hurling them into the sea. Until they got the ballast right. They walked up and down the longboat, eyes to the waterline, and when the boat rode low in the water they'd grab the nearest passenger and throw them into the sea. The boat was leaky, see; seventy people; they arrived in Halifax with nine people on board.

LOUIS: Jesus.

PRIOR: I think about that story a lot now. People in a boat, waiting, terrified, while implacable, unsmiling men, irresistibly strong, seize . . . maybe the person next to you, maybe you, and with no warning at all, with time only for a quick intake of air you are pitched into freezing, turbulent water and salt and darkness to drown.

> I like your cosmology, baby. While time is running out I find myself drawn to anything that's suspended, that lacks an ending—but it seems to me that it lets you off scot-free.

LOUIS: What do you mean?

PRIOR: No judgment, no guilt or responsibility.

LOUIS: For me.

PRIOR: For anyone. It was an editorial "you."

LOUIS: Please get better. Please.

> Please don't get any sicker.

Scene 9

(*Third week in November. Roy and Henry, his doctor, in Henry's office.*)

HENRY: Nobody knows what causes it. And nobody knows how to cure it. The best theory is that we blame a retrovirus, the Human Immunodeficiency Virus. Its presence is made known to us by the useless antibodies which appear in reaction to its entrance into the bloodstream through a cut, or an orifice. The antibodies are powerless to protect the body against it. Why, we don't know. The body's immune system ceases to function. Sometimes the body even attacks itself. At any rate it's left open to a whole horror house of infections from microbes which it usually defends against.

> Like Kaposi's sarcomas. These lesions. Or your throat problem. Or the glands.

> We think it may also be able to slip past the blood-brain barrier into the brain. Which is of course very bad news.

> And it's fatal in we don't know what percent of people with suppressed immune responses.

(*Pause.*)

ROY: This is very interesting, Mr. Wizard, but why the fuck are you telling me this?

(*Pause.*)

HENRY: Well, I have just removed one of three lesions which biopsy results will probably tell us is a Kaposi's sarcoma lesion. And you have a pronounced swelling of glands in your neck, groin, and armpits—lymphadenopathy is another sign. And you have oral candidiasis and maybe a little more fungus under the fingernails of two digits on your right hand. So that's why . . .

ROY: This disease . . .

HENRY: Syndrome.

ROY: Whatever. It afflicts mostly homosexuals and drug addicts.

HENRY: Mostly. Hemophiliacs are also at risk.

ROY: Homosexuals and drug addicts. So why are you implying that I . . .

> (*Pause.*)

> What are you implying, Henry?

HENRY: I don't . . .

ROY: I'm not a drug addict.

HENRY: Oh come on Roy.

ROY: What, what, come on Roy what? Do you think I'm a junkie, Henry, do you see tracks?

HENRY: This is absurd.

ROY: Say it.

HENRY: Say what?

ROY: Say, "Roy Cohn, you are a . . ."

HENRY: Roy.

ROY: "You are a. . . ." Go on. Not "Roy Cohn you are a drug fiend." "Roy Marcus Cohn, you are a . . ." Go on, Henry, it starts with an "H."

HENRY: Oh I'm not going to . . .

ROY: *With an "H,"* Henry, and it isn't "Hemophiliac." Come on . . .

HENRY: What are you doing, Roy?

ROY: No, say it. I mean it. Say: "Roy Cohn, you are a homosexual."

(*Pause.*)

And I will proceed, systematically, to destroy your reputation and your practice and your career in New York State, Henry. Which you know I can do.

(*Pause.*)

HENRY: Roy, you have been seeing me since 1958. Apart from the facelifts I have treated you for everything from syphilis . . .

ROY: From a whore in Dallas.

HENRY: From syphilis to venereal warts. In your rectum. Which you may have gotten from a whore in Dallas, but it wasn't a female whore.

(*Pause.*)

ROY: So say it.

HENRY: Roy Cohn, you are . . .

You have had sex with men, many many times, Roy, and one of them, or any number of them, has made you very sick. You have AIDS.

ROY: AIDS.

Your problem, Henry, is that you are hung up on words, on labels, that you believe they mean what they seem to mean. AIDS. Homosexual. Gay. Lesbian. You think these are names that tell you who someone sleeps with, but they don't tell you that.

HENRY: No?

ROY: No. Like all labels they tell you one thing and one thing only: where does an individual so identified fit in the food chain, in the pecking order? Not ideology, or sexual taste, but something much simpler: clout. Not who I fuck or who fucks me, but who will pick up the phone when I call, who owes me favors. This is what a label refers to. Now to someone who does not understand this, homosexual is what I am because I have sex with men. But really this is wrong. Homosexuals are not men who sleep with other men. Homosexuals are men who in fifteen years of trying cannot get a pissant antidiscrimination bill through City Council. Homosexuals are men who know nobody and who nobody knows. Who have zero clout. Does this sound like me, Henry?

HENRY: No.

ROY: No. I have clout. A lot. I can pick up this phone, punch fifteen numbers, and you know who will be on the other end in under five minutes, Henry?

HENRY: The President.

ROY: Even better, Henry. His wife.

HENRY: I'm impressed.

ROY: I don't want you to be impressed. I want you to understand. This is not sophistry. And this is not hypocrisy. This is reality. I have sex with men. But unlike nearly every other man of whom this is true, I bring the guy I'm screwing to the White House and President Reagan smiles at us and shakes his hand. Because *what* I am is defined entirely by *who* I am. Roy Cohn is not a homosexual. Roy Cohn is a heterosexual man, Henry, who fucks around with guys.

HENRY: OK, Roy.

ROY: And what is my diagnosis, Henry?

HENRY: You have AIDS, Roy.

ROY: No, Henry, no. AIDS is what homosexuals have. I have liver cancer.

(*Pause.*)

HENRY: Well, whatever the fuck you have, Roy, it's very serious, and I haven't got a damn thing for you. The NIH in Bethesda has a new drug called AZT with a two-year waiting list that not even I can get you onto. So get on the phone, Roy, and dial the fifteen numbers, and tell the First Lady you need in on an experimental treatment for liver cancer, because you can call it any damn thing you want, Roy, but what it boils down to is very bad news.

ACT 2
IN VITRO • December 1985–January 1986

Scene 1

(*Night, the third week in December. Prior alone on the floor of his bedroom; he is much worse.*)

PRIOR: Louis, Louis, please wake up, oh God.

(*Louis runs in.*)

PRIOR: I think something horrible is wrong with me I can't breathe . . .

LOUIS (*starting to exit*): I'm calling the ambulance.

PRIOR: No, wait, I . . .

LOUIS: *Wait?* Are you fucking crazy? Oh God you're on fire, your head is on fire.

PRIOR: It hurts, it hurts . . .

LOUIS: I'm calling the ambulance.

PRIOR: I don't want to go to the hospital, I don't want to go to the hospital please let me lie here, just . . .

LOUIS: No, no, God, Prior, stand up . . .

PRIOR: DON'T TOUCH MY LEG!

LOUIS: We have to . . . oh God this is so crazy.

PRIOR: I'll be OK if I just lie here Lou, really, if I can only sleep a little . . .

(*Louis exits.*)

PRIOR: Louis?
　　NO! NO! Don't call, you'll send me there and I won't come back, please, please Louis I'm begging, baby, please . . .
　　(*Screams.*) LOUIS!!
LOUIS (*from off; hysterical*): WILL YOU SHUT THE FUCK UP!
PRIOR (*trying to stand*): Aaaah. I have . . . to go to the bathroom. Wait. Wait, just . . . oh. Oh God. (*He shits himself.*)
LOUIS (*entering*): Prior? They'll be here in . . .
　　Oh my God.
PRIOR: I'm sorry, I'm sorry.
LOUIS: What did . . . ? What?
PRIOR: I had an accident.

(*Louis goes to him.*)

LOUIS: This is blood.
PRIOR: Maybe you shouldn't touch it . . . me. . . . I . . .
　　(*He faints.*)
LOUIS (*quietly*): Oh help. Oh help. Oh God oh God oh God help me I can't I can't I can't.

Scene 2

(*Same night. Harper is sitting at home, all alone, with no lights on. We can barely see her. Joe enters, but he doesn't turn on the lights.*)

JOE: Why are you sitting in the dark? Turn on the light.
HARPER: No. I heard the sounds in the bedroom again. I know someone was in there.
JOE: No one was.
HARPER: Maybe actually in the bed, under the covers with a knife.
　　Oh, boy. Joe. I, um, I'm thinking of going away. By which I mean: I think I'm going off again. You . . . you know what I mean?
JOE: Please don't. Stay. We can fix it. I pray for that. This is my fault, but I can correct it. You have to try too . . .

(*He turns on the light. She turns it off again.*)

HARPER: When you pray, what do you pray for?
JOE: I pray for God to crush me, break me up into little pieces and start all over again.
HARPER: Oh. Please. Don't pray for that.
JOE: I had a book of Bible stories when I was a kid. There was a picture I'd look at twenty times every day: Jacob wrestles with the angel. I don't really remember the story, or why the wrestling—just the picture. Jacob is young and very strong. The angel is . . . a beautiful man, with golden hair and wings, of course. I still dream about it. Many nights. I'm. . . . It's me. In that struggle. Fierce, and unfair. The angel is not human, and it holds nothing back, so how could anyone human win, what kind of a

fight is that? It's not just. Losing means your soul thrown down in the dust, your heart torn out from God's. But you can't not lose.
HARPER: In the whole entire world, you are the only person, the only person I love or have ever loved. And I love you terribly. Terribly. That's what's so awfully, irreducibly real. I can make up anything but I can't dream that away.
JOE: Are you . . . are you really going to have a baby?
HARPER: It's my time, and there's no blood. I don't really know. I suppose it wouldn't be a great thing. Maybe I'm just not bleeding because I take too many pills. Maybe I'll give birth to a pill. That would give a new meaning to pill-popping, huh?
　　I think you should go to Washington. Alone. Change, like you said.
JOE: I'm not going to leave you, Harper.
HARPER: Well maybe not. But I'm going to leave you.

Scene 3

(*One AM, the next morning. Louis and a nurse, Emily, are sitting in Prior's room in the hospital.*)

EMILY: He'll be all right now.
LOUIS: No he won't.
EMILY: No. I guess not. I gave him something that makes him sleep.
LOUIS: Deep asleep?
EMILY: Orbiting the moons of Jupiter.
LOUIS: A good place to be.
EMILY: Anyplace better than here. You his . . . uh?
LOUIS: Yes. I'm his uh.
EMILY: This must be hell for you.
LOUIS: It is. Hell. The After Life. Which is not at all like a rainy afternoon in March, by the way, Prior. A lot more vivid than I'd expected. Dead leaves, but the crunchy kind. Sharp, dry air. The kind of long, luxurious dying feeling that breaks your heart.
EMILY: Yeah, well we all get to break our hearts on this one.
　　He seems like a nice guy. Cute.
LOUIS: Not like this.
　　Yes, he is. Was. Whatever.
EMILY: Weird name. Prior Walter. Like, "The Walter before this one."
LOUIS: Lots of Walters before this one. Prior is an old old family name in an old old family. The Walters go back to the Mayflower and beyond. Back to the Norman Conquest. He says there's a Prior Walter stitched into the Bayeux tapestry.
EMILY: Is that impressive?
LOUIS: Well, it's old. Very old. Which in some circles equals impressive.
EMILY: Not in my circle. What's the name of the tapestry?
LOUIS: The Bayeux tapestry. Embroidered by La Reine Mathilde.

EMILY: I'll tell my mother. She embroiders. Drives me nuts.

LOUIS: Manual therapy for anxious hands.

EMILY: Maybe you should try it.

LOUIS: Mathilde stitched while William the Conqueror was off to war. She was capable of . . . more than loyalty. Devotion.

She waited for him, she stitched for years. And if he had come back broken and defeated from war, she would have loved him even more. And if he had returned mutilated, ugly, full of infection and horror, she would still have loved him; fed by pity, by a sharing of pain, she would love him even more, and even more, and she would never, never have prayed to God, please let him die if he can't return to me whole and healthy and able to live a normal life. . . . If he had died, she would have buried her heart with him.

So what the fuck is the matter with me?

(*Little pause.*)

Will he sleep through the night?

EMILY: At least.

LOUIS: I'm going.

EMILY: Its one A.M. Where do you have to go at . . .

LOUIS: I know what time it is. A walk. Night air, good for the. . . . The park.

EMILY: Be careful.

LOUIS: Yeah. Danger.

Tell him, if he wakes up and you're still on, tell him goodbye, tell him I had to go.

Scene 4

(*An hour later. Split scene. Joe and Roy in a fancy [straight] bar; Louis and a Man in the Rambles in Central Park. Joe and Roy are sitting at the bar; the place is brightly lit. Joe has a plate of food in front of him but he isn't eating. Roy occasionally reaches over the table and forks small bites off Joe's plate. Roy is drinking heavily, Joe not at all. Louis and the Man are eyeing each other, each alternating interest and indifference.*)

JOE: The pills were something she started when she miscarried or . . . no, she took some before that. She had a really bad time at home, when she was a kid, her home was really bad. I think a lot of drinking and physical stuff. She doesn't talk about that, instead she talks about . . . the sky falling down, people with knives hiding under sofas. Monsters. Mormons. Everyone thinks Mormons don't come from homes like that, we aren't supposed to behave that way, but we do. It's not lying, or being two-faced. Everyone tries very hard to live up to God's strictures, which are very . . . um . . .

ROY: Strict.

JOE: I shouldn't be bothering you with this.

ROY: No, please. Heart to heart. Want another. . . . What is that, seltzer?

JOE: The failure to measure up hits people very hard. From such a strong desire to be good they feel very far from goodness when they fail.

What scares me is that maybe what I really love in her is the part of her that's farthest from the light, from God's love; maybe I was drawn to that in the first place. And I'm keeping it alive because I need it.

ROY: Why would you need it?

JOE: There are things. . . . I don't know how well we know ourselves. I mean, what if? I know I married her because she . . . because I loved it that she was always wrong, always doing something wrong, like one step out of step. In Salt Lake City that stands out. I never stood out, on the outside, but inside, it was hard for me. To pass.

ROY: Pass?

JOE: Yeah.

ROY: Pass as what?

JOE: Oh. Well. . . . As someone cheerful and strong. Those who love God with an open heart unclouded by secrets and struggles are cheerful; God's easy simple love for them shows in how strong and happy they are. The saints.

ROY: But you had secrets? Secret struggles . . .

JOE: I wanted to be one of the elect, one of the Blessed. You feel you ought to be, that the blemishes are yours by choice, which of course they aren't. Harper's sorrow, that really deep sorrow, she didn't choose that. But it's there.

ROY: You didn't put it there.

JOE: No.

ROY: You sound like you think you did.

JOE: I am responsible for her.

ROY: Because she's your wife.

JOE: That. And I do love her.

ROY: Whatever. She's your wife. And so there are obligations. To her. But also to yourself.

JOE: She'd fall apart in Washington.

ROY: Then let her stay here.

JOE: She'll fall apart if I leave her.

ROY: Then bring her to Washington.

JOE: I just can't, Roy. She needs me.

ROY: Listen, Joe. I'm the best divorce lawyer in the business.

(*Little pause.*)

JOE: Can't Washington wait?

ROY: You do what you need to do, Joe. What *you* need. *You.* Let her life go where it wants to go. You'll both be better for that. *Somebody* should get what they want.

MAN: What do you want?

LOUIS: I want you to fuck me, hurt me, make me bleed.

MAN: I want to.

LOUIS: Yeah?

MAN: I want to hurt you.

LOUIS: Fuck me.

MAN: Yeah?

LOUIS: Hard.

MAN: Yeah? You been a bad boy?

(*Pause. Louis laughs, softly.*)

LOUIS: Very bad. Very bad.

MAN: You need to be punished, boy?

LOUIS: Yes. I do.

MAN: Yes what?

(*Little pause.*)

LOUIS: Um, I . . .

MAN: Yes *what*, boy?

LOUIS: Oh. Yes sir.

MAN: I want you to take me to your place, boy.

LOUIS: No, I can't do that.

MAN: No *what*?

LOUIS: No sir, I can't, I . . .
    I don't live alone, sir.

MAN: Your lover know you're out with a man tonight, boy?

LOUIS: No sir, he . . .
    My lover doesn't know.

MAN: Your lover know you . . .

LOUIS: Let's change the subject, OK? Can we go to your place?

MAN: I live with my parents.

LOUIS: Oh.

ROY: Everyone who makes it in this world makes it because somebody older and more powerful takes an interest. The most precious asset in life, I think, is the ability to be a good son. You have that, Joe. Somebody who can be a good son to a father who pushes them farther than they would otherwise go. I've had many fathers, I owe my life to them, powerful, powerful men. Walter Winchell, Edgar Hoover. Joe McCarthy most of all. He valued me because I am a good lawyer, but he loved me because I was and am a good son. He was a very difficult man, very guarded and cagey; I brought out something tender in him. He would have died for me. And me for him. Does this embarrass you?

JOE: I had a hard time with my father.

ROY: Well sometimes that's the way. Then you have to find other fathers, substitutes, I don't know. The father-son relationship is central to life. Women are for birth, beginning, but the father is continuance. The son offers the father his life as a vessel for carrying forth his father's dream. Your father's living?

JOE: Um, dead.

ROY: He was . . . what? A difficult man?

JOE: He was in the military. He could be very unfair. And cold.

ROY: But he loved you.

JOE: I don't know.

ROY: No, no, Joe, he did, I know this. Sometimes a father's love has to be very, very hard, unfair even, cold to make his son grow strong in a world like this. This isn't a good world.

MAN: Here, then.

LOUIS: I . . . Do you have a rubber?

MAN: I don't use rubbers.

LOUIS: You should. (*He takes one from his coat pocket.*) Here.

MAN: I don't use them.

LOUIS: Forget it, then. (*He starts to leave.*)

MAN: No, wait.
    Put it on me. Boy.

LOUIS: Forget it, I have to get back. Home. I must be going crazy.

MAN: Oh come on please he won't find out.

LOUIS: It's cold. Too cold.

MAN: It's never too cold, let me warm you up. Please?

(*They begin to fuck.*)

MAN: Relax.

LOUIS (*a small laugh*): Not a chance.

MAN: It . . .

LOUIS: What?

MAN: I think it broke. The rubber. You want me to keep going? (*Little pause.*) Pull out? Should I . . .

LOUIS: Keep going.
    Infect me.
    I don't care. I don't care.

(*Pause. The Man pulls out.*)

MAN: I . . . um, look, I'm sorry, but I think I want to go.

LOUIS: Yeah.
    Give my best to mom and dad.

(*The Man slaps him.*)

LOUIS: Ow!

(*They stare at each other.*)

LOUIS: It was a joke.

(*The Man leaves.*)

ROY: How long have we known each other?

JOE: Since 1980.

ROY: Right. A long time. I feel close to you, Joe. Do I advise you well?

JOE: You've been an incredible friend, Roy, I . . .

ROY: I want to be family. Familia, as my Italian friends call it. La Familia. A lovely word. It's important for me to help you, like I was helped.

JOE: I owe practically everything to you, Roy.

ROY: I'm dying, Joe. Cancer.

JOE: Oh my God.

ROY: Please. Let me finish.
    Few people know this and I'm telling you this only because. . . . I'm not afraid of death. What can death bring that I haven't faced? I've lived; life is the worst. (*Gently mocking himself.*) Listen to me, I'm a philosopher.
    Joe. You must do this. You must must must. Love; that's a trap. Responsibility; that's a trap too. Like a father to a son I tell you this: Life is full of horror; nobody escapes, nobody; save yourself. Whatever

pulls on you, whatever needs from you, threatens you. Don't be afraid; people are so afraid; don't be afraid to live in the raw wind, naked, alone. . . . Learn at least this: What you are capable of. Let nothing stand in your way.

Scene 5

(*Three days later. Prior and Belize in Prior's hospital room. Prior is very sick but improving. Belize has just arrived.*)

PRIOR: Miss Thing.

BELIZE: Ma cherie bichette.

PRIOR: Stella.

BELIZE: Stella for star. Let me see. (*Scrutinizing Prior.*) You look like shit, why yes indeed you do, comme la merde!°

PRIOR: Merci.

BELIZE (*taking little plastic bottles from his bag, handing them to Prior*): Not to despair, Belle Reeve. Lookie! Magic goop!

PRIOR (*opening a bottle, sniffing*): Pooh! What kinda crap is that?

BELIZE: Beats me. Let's rub it on your poor blistered body and see what it does.

PRIOR: This is not Western medicine, these bottles . . .

BELIZE: Voodoo cream. From the botanica° 'round the block.

PRIOR: And you a registered nurse.

BELIZE (*sniffing it*): Beeswax and cheap perfume. Cut with Jergen's Lotion. Full of good vibes and love from some little black Cubana witch in Miami.

PRIOR: Get that trash away from me, I am immune-suppressed.

BELIZE: I *am* a health professional. I *know* what I'm doing.

PRIOR: It stinks. Any word from Louis?

(*Pause. Belize starts giving Prior a gentle massage.*)

PRIOR: Gone.

BELIZE: He'll be back. I know the type. Likes to keep a girl on edge.

PRIOR: It's been . . .

(*Pause.*)

BELIZE (*trying to jog his memory*): How long?

PRIOR: I don't remember.

BELIZE: How long have you been here?

PRIOR (*getting suddenly upset*): I don't remember, I don't give a fuck. I want Louis. I want my fucking boyfriend, where the fuck is he? I'm dying, I'm dying, where's Louis?

BELIZE: Shhhh, shhh . . .

PRIOR: This is a very strange drug, this drug. Emotional lability, for starters.

BELIZE: Save a tab or two for me.

PRIOR: Oh no, not this drug, ce n'est pas pour la joyeux noël et la bonne année, this drug she is serious poisonous chemistry, ma pauvre bichette.°
    And not just disorienting. I hear things. Voices.

BELIZE: Voices.

PRIOR: A voice.

BELIZE: Saying what?

(*Pause.*)

PRIOR: I'm not supposed to tell.

BELIZE: You better tell the doctor. Or I will.

PRIOR: No no don't. Please. I want the voice; it's wonderful. It's all that's keeping me alive. I don't want to talk to some intern about it.
    You know what happens? When I hear it, I get hard.

BELIZE: Oh my.

PRIOR: Comme ça. (*He uses his arm to demonstrate.*) And you know I am slow to rise.

BELIZE: My jaw aches at the memory.

PRIOR: And would you deny me this little solace—betray my concupiscence to Florence Nightingale's storm troopers?

BELIZE: Perish the thought, ma bébé.°

PRIOR: They'd change the drug just to spoil the fun.

BELIZE: You and your boner can depend on me.

PRIOR: Je t'adore, ma belle nègre.°

BELIZE: All this girl-talk shit is politically incorrect, you know. We should have dropped it back when we gave up drag.

PRIOR: I'm sick, I get to be politically incorrect if it makes me feel better. You sound like Lou.
    (*Little pause.*)
    Well, at least I have the satisfaction of knowing he's in anguish somewhere. I loved his anguish. Watching him stick his head up his asshole and eat his guts out over some relatively minor moral conundrum—it was the best show in town. But Mother warned me: if they get overwhelmed by the little things . . .

BELIZE: They'll be belly-up bustville when something big comes along.

PRIOR: Mother warned me.

BELIZE: And they do come along.

PRIOR: But I didn't listen.

BELIZE: No. (*Doing Hepburn.*) Men are beasts.

PRIOR (*also Hepburn*): The absolute lowest.

BELIZE: I have to go. If I want to spend my whole lonely life looking after white people I can get underpaid to do it.

PRIOR: You're just a Christian martyr.

BELIZE: Whatever happens, baby, I will be here for you.

PRIOR: Je t'aime.°

---

comme la merde: Like shit.   **botanica:** Shop that sells magic charms and herbs.

ce n'est pas . . . bichette: This drug isn't for a merry Christmas or a happy New Year . . . my poor little bitch.   **ma bébé:** My baby.   **Je t'adore . . . nègre:** I adore you, my beautiful negro.   **Je t'aime:** I love you.

BELIZE: Je t'aime. Don't go crazy on me, girlfriend, I already got enough crazy queens for one lifetime. For two. I can't be bothering with dementia.

PRIOR: I promise.

BELIZE (*touching him; softly*): Ouch.

PRIOR: Ouch. Indeed.

BELIZE: Why'd they have to pick on you?

And eat more, girlfriend, you really do look like shit.

(*Belize leaves.*)

PRIOR (*after waiting a beat*): He's gone.

Are you still . . .

VOICE: I can't stay. I will return.

PRIOR: Are you one of those "Follow me to the other side" voices?

VOICE: No. I am no nightbird. I am a messenger . . .

PRIOR: You have a beautiful voice, it sounds . . . like a viola, like a perfectly tuned, tight string, balanced, the truth. . . . Stay with me.

VOICE: Not now. Soon I will return, I will reveal myself to you; I am glorious, glorious; my heart, my countenance and my message. You must prepare.

PRIOR: For what? I don't want to . . .

VOICE: No death, no:

A marvelous work and a wonder we undertake, an edifice awry we sink plumb and straighten, a great Lie we abolish, a great error correct, with the rule, sword and broom of Truth!

PRIOR: What are you talking about, I . . .

VOICE: I am on my way; when I am manifest, our Work begins:

Prepare for the parting of the air,

The breath, the ascent,

Glory to . . .

Scene 6

(*The second week of January. Martin, Roy and Joe in a fancy Manhattan restaurant.*)

MARTIN: It's a revolution in Washington, Joe. We have a new agenda and finally a real leader. They got back the Senate but we have the courts. By the nineties the Supreme Court will be block-solid Republican appointees, and the Federal bench—Republican judges like land mines, everywhere, everywhere they turn. Affirmative action? Take it to court. Boom! Land mine. And we'll get our way on just about everything: abortion, defense, Central America, family values, a live investment climate. We have the White House locked till the year 2000. And beyond. A permanent fix on the Oval Office? It's possible. By '92 we'll get the Senate back, and in ten years the South is going to give us the House. It's really the end of Liberalism. The end of New Deal Socialism. The end of ipso facto secular humanism. The dawning of a genuinely American political personality. Modeled on Ronald Wilson Reagan.

JOE: It sounds great, Mr. Heller.

MARTIN: Martin. And Justice is the hub. Especially since Ed Meese took over. He doesn't specialize in Fine Points of the Law. He's a flatfoot, a cop. He reminds me of Teddy Roosevelt.

JOE: I can't wait to meet him.

MARTIN: Too bad, Joe, he's been dead for sixty years!

(*There is a little awkwardness. Joe doesn't respond.*)

MARTIN: Teddy Roosevelt. You said you wanted to. . . . Little joke. It reminds me of the story about the . . .

ROY (*smiling, but nasty*): Aw shut the fuck up Martin.

(*To Joe.*) You see that? Mr. Heller here is one of the mighty, Joseph, in D.C. he sitteth on the right hand of the man who sitteth on the right hand of The Man. And yet I can say "shut the fuck up" and he will take no offense. Loyalty. He . . .

Martin?

MARTIN: Yes, Roy?

ROY: Rub my back.

MARTIN: Roy . . .

ROY: No no really, a sore spot, I get them all the time now, these. . . . Rub it for me darling, would you do that for me?

(*Martin rubs Roy's back. They both look at Joe.*)

ROY (*to Joe*): How do you think a handful of Bolsheviks turned St. Petersburg into Leningrad in one afternoon? *Comrades.* Who do for each other. Marx and Engels. Lenin and Trotsky. Josef Stalin and Franklin Delano Roosevelt.

(*Martin laughs.*)

ROY: *Comrades*, right Martin?

MARTIN: This man, Joe, is a Saint of the Right.

JOE: I know, Mr. Heller, I . . .

ROY: And you see what I mean, Martin? He's special, right?

MARTIN: Don't embarrass him, Roy.

ROY: Gravity, decency, smarts! His strength is as the strength of ten because his heart is pure! And he's a Royboy, one hundred percent.

MARTIN: We're on the move, Joe. On the move.

JOE: Mr. Heller, I . . .

MARTIN (*ending backrub*): We can't wait any longer for an answer.

(*Little pause.*)

JOE: Oh. Um, I . . .

ROY: Joe's a married man, Martin.

MARTIN: Aha.

ROY: With a wife. She doesn't care to go to D.C., and so Joe cannot go. And keeps us dangling. We've seen that kind of thing before, haven't we? These men and their wives.

MARTIN: Oh yes. Beware.

JOE: I really can't discuss this under . . .

MARTIN: Then *don't* discuss. Say yes, Joe.

ROY: Now.

MARTIN: Say yes I will.

ROY: Now.

Now. I'll hold my breath till you do, I'm turning blue waiting. . . . *Now*, goddammit!

MARTIN: Roy, calm down, it's not . . .

ROY: Aw, fuck it. (*He takes a letter from his jacket pocket, hands it to Joe.*)
Read. Came today.

(*Joe reads the first paragraph, then looks up.*)

JOE: Roy. This is . . . Roy, this is terrible.

ROY: You're telling me.
A letter from the New York State Bar Association, Martin.
They're gonna try and disbar me.

MARTIN: Oh my.

JOE: Why?

ROY: Why, Martin?

MARTIN: Revenge.

ROY: The whole Establishment. Their little rules. Because I know no rules. Because I don't see the Law as a dead and arbitrary collection of antiquated dictums, thou shall, thou shalt not, because, because I know the Law's a pliable, breathing, sweating . . . *organ*, because, because . . .

MARTIN: Because he borrowed half a million from one of his clients.

ROY: Yeah, well, there's that.

MARTIN: *And* he forgot to *return* it.

JOE: Roy, that's. . . . You borrowed money from a client?

ROY: I'm deeply ashamed.

(*Little pause.*)

JOE (*very sympathetic*): Roy, you know how much I admire you. Well I mean I know you have unorthodox ways, but I'm sure you only did what you thought at the time you needed to do. And I have faith that . . .

ROY: Not so damp, please. I'll deny it was a loan. She's got no paperwork. Can't prove a fucking thing.

(*Little pause. Martin studies the menu.*)

JOE (*handing back the letter, more official in tone*): Roy I really appreciate your telling me this, and I'll do whatever I can to help.

ROY (*holding up a hand, then, carefully*): I'll tell you what you can do.
I'm about to be tried, Joe, by a jury that is not a jury of my peers. The disbarment committee: genteel gentleman Brahmin lawyers, country-club men. I offend them, to these men . . . I'm what, Martin, some sort of filthy little Jewish troll?

MARTIN: Oh well, I wouldn't go so far as . . .

ROY: Oh well I would.
Very fancy lawyers, these disbarment committee lawyers, fancy lawyers with fancy corporate clients and complicated cases. Antitrust suits. Deregulation.

Environmental control. Complex cases like these need Justice Department cooperation like flowers need the sun. Wouldn't you say that's an accurate assessment, Martin?

MARTIN: I'm not here, Roy. I'm not hearing any of this.

ROY: No. Of course not.
Without the light of the sun, Joe, these cases, and the fancy lawyers who represent them, will wither and die.
A well-placed friend, someone in the Justice Department, say, can turn off the sun. Cast a deep shadow on my behalf. Make them shiver in the cold. If they overstep. They would fear that.

(*Pause.*)

JOE: Roy. I don't understand.

ROY: You do.

(*Pause.*)

JOE: You're not asking me to . . .

ROY: Sssshhhh. Careful.

JOE (*a beat, then*): Even if I said yes to the job, it would be illegal to interfere. With the hearings. It's unethical. No. I can't.

ROY: Un-ethical.
Would you excuse us, Martin?

MARTIN: Excuse you?

ROY: Take a walk, Martin. For real.

(*Martin leaves.*)

ROY: Un-ethical. Are you trying to embarrass me in front of my friend?

JOE: Well it is unethical, I can't . . .

ROY: Boy, you are really something. What the fuck do you think this is, Sunday School?

JOE: No, but Roy this is . . .

ROY: This is . . . this is gastric juices churning, this is enzymes and acids, this is intestinal is what this is, bowel movement and blood-red meat—this stinks, this is *politics*, Joe, the game of being alive. And you think you're. . . . What? Above that? Above alive is what? Dead! In the clouds! You're on earth, goddammit! Plant a foot, stay a while.
I'm sick. They smell I'm weak. They want blood this time. I must have eyes in Justice. In Justice you will protect me.

JOE: Why can't Mr. Heller . . .

ROY: Grow up, Joe. The administration can't get involved.

JOE: But I'd be part of the administration. The same as him.

ROY: Not the same. Martin's Ed's man. And Ed's Reagan's man. So Martin's Reagan's man.
And you're mine.
(*Little pause. He holds up the letter.*)
This will never be. Understand me?
(*He tears the letter up.*)
I'm gonna be a lawyer, Joe, I'm gonna be a lawyer, Joe, I'm gonna be a goddam motherfucking legally

licensed member of the bar lawyer, just like my
daddy was, till my last bitter day on earth, Joseph,
until the day I die.

(*Martin returns.*)

ROY: Ah, Martin's back.
MARTIN: So are we agreed?
ROY: Joe?

(*Little pause.*)

JOE: I will think about it.
    (*To Roy.*) I will.
ROY: Huh.
MARTIN: It's the fear of what comes after the doing that
    makes the doing hard to do.
ROY: Amen.
MARTIN: But you can almost always live with the conse-
    quences.

Scene 7

(*That afternoon. On the granite steps outside the Hall of
Justice, Brooklyn. It is cold and sunny. A Sabrett wagon
is selling hot dogs. Louis, in a shabby overcoat, is sitting
on the steps contemplatively eating one. Joe enters with
three hot dogs and a can of Coke.*)

JOE: Can I . . . ?
LOUIS: Oh sure. Sure. Crazy cold sun.
JOE (*sitting*): Have to make the best of it.
    How's your friend?
LOUIS: My . . . ? Oh. He's worse. My friend is worse.
JOE: I'm sorry.
LOUIS: Yeah, well. Thanks for asking. It's nice. You're
    nice. I can't believe you voted for Reagan.
JOE: I hope he gets better.
LOUIS: Reagan?
JOE: Your friend.
LOUIS: He won't. Neither will Reagan.
JOE: Let's not talk politics, OK?
LOUIS (*pointing to Joe's lunch*): You're eating *three* of
    those?
JOE: Well . . . I'm . . . hungry.
LOUIS: They're really terrible for you. Full of rat-poo
    and beetle legs and wood shavings 'n' shit.
JOE: Huh.
LOUIS: And . . . um . . . irridium, I think. Something toxic.
JOE: You're eating one.
LOUIS: Yeah, well, the shape, I can't help myself, plus
    I'm *trying* to commit suicide, what's your excuse?
JOE: I don't have an excuse. I just have Pepto-Bismol.

(*Joe takes a bottle of Pepto-Bismol and chugs it. Louis
shudders audibly.*)

JOE: Yeah I know but then I wash it down with Coke.

(*He does this. Louis mimes barfing in Joe's lap. Joe
pushes Louis's head away.*)

JOE: Are you *always* like this?
LOUIS: I've been worrying a lot about his kids.
JOE: Whose?
LOUIS: Reagan's. Maureen and Mike and little orphan
    Patti and Miss Ron Reagan Jr., the you-should-
    pardon-the-expression heterosexual.
JOE: Ron Reagan Jr. is *not*. . . . You shouldn't just make
    these assumptions about people. How do you know?
    About him? What he is? You don't know.
LOUIS (*doing Tallulah*): Well darling he never sucked *my*
    cock but . . .
JOE: Look, if you're going to get vulgar . . .
LOUIS: No no really I mean. . . . What's it like to be the
    child of the Zeitgeist? To have the American Animus
    as your dad? It's not really a *family*, the Reagans, I
    read *People*, there aren't any connections there, no
    love, they don't ever even speak to each other except
    through their agents. So what's it like to be Reagan's
    kid? Enquiring minds want to know.
JOE: You can't believe everything you . . .
LOUIS (*looking away*): But . . . I think we all know what
    that's like. Nowadays. No connections. No respon-
    sibilities. All of us . . . falling through the cracks that
    separate what we owe to our selves and . . . and what
    we owe to love.
JOE: You just. . . . Whatever you feel like saying or
    doing, you don't care, you just . . . do it.
LOUIS: Do what?
JOE: It. Whatever. Whatever it is you want to do.
LOUIS: Are you trying to tell me something?

(*Little pause, sexual. They stare at each other. Joe looks
away.*)

JOE: No, I'm just observing that you . . .
LOUIS: Impulsive.
JOE: Yes, I mean it must be scary, you . . .
LOUIS (*shrugs*): Land of the free. Home of the brave.
    Call me irresponsible.
JOE: It's kind of terrifying.
LOUIS: Yeah, well, freedom is. Heartless, too.
JOE: Oh you're not heartless.
LOUIS: You don't know.
    Finish your weenie.

(*He pats Joe on the knee, starts to leave.*)

JOE: Um . . .

(*Louis turns, looks at him. Joe searches for something to
say.*)

JOE: Yesterday was Sunday but I've been a little unfo-
    cused recently and I thought it was Monday. So I
    came here like I was going to work. And the whole
    place was empty. And at first I couldn't figure out
    why, and I had this moment of incredible . . . fear
    and also. . . . It just flashed through my mind: The
    whole Hall of Justice, it's empty, it's deserted, it's
    gone out of business. Forever. The people that make
    it run have up and abandoned it.
LOUIS (*looking at the building*): Creepy.

JOE: Well yes but. I felt that I was going to scream. Not because it was creepy, but because the emptiness felt so *fast*.

And . . . well, good. A . . . happy scream.

I just wondered what a thing it would be . . . if overnight everything you owe anything to, justice, or love, had really gone away. Free.

It would be . . . heartless terror. Yes. Terrible, and . . .

Very great. To shed your skin, every old skin, one by one and then walk away, unencumbered, into the morning.

(*Little pause. He looks at the building.*)

I can't go in there today.

LOUIS: Then don't.

JOE (*not really hearing Louis*): I can't go in, I need . . .

(*He looks for what he needs. He takes a swig of Pepto-Bismol.*)

I can't *be* this anymore. I need . . . a change, I should just . . .

LOUIS (*not a come-on, necessarily; he doesn't want to be alone*): Want some company? For whatever?

(*Pause. Joe looks at Louis and looks away, afraid. Louis shrugs.*)

LOUIS: Sometimes, even if it scares you to death, you have to be willing to break the law. Know what I mean?

(*Another little pause.*)

JOE: Yes.

(*Another little pause.*)

LOUIS: I moved out. I moved out on my . . .

I haven't been sleeping well.

JOE: Me neither.

(*Louis goes up to Joe, licks his napkin and dabs at Joes mouth.*)

LOUIS: Antacid moustache.

(*Points to the building.*) Maybe the court won't convene. Ever again. Maybe we are free. To do whatever.

Children of the new morning, criminal minds. Selfish and greedy and loveless and blind. Reagan's children.

You're scared. So am I. Everybody is in the land of the free. God help us all.

Scene 8

(*Late that night. Joe at a payphone phoning Hannah at home in Salt Lake City.*)

JOE: Mom?

HANNAH: Joe?

JOE: Hi.

HANNAH: You're calling from the street. It's . . . it must be four in the morning. What's happened?

JOE: Nothing, nothing, I . . .

HANNAH: It's Harper. Is Harper. . . . Joe? Joe?

JOE: Yeah, hi. No, Harper's fine. Well, no, she's . . . not fine. How are you, Mom?

HANNAH: What's happened?

JOE: I just wanted to talk to you. I, uh, wanted to try something out on you.

HANNAH: Joe, you haven't . . . have you been drinking, Joe?

JOE: Yes ma'am. I'm drunk.

HANNAH: That isn't like you.

JOE: No. I mean, who's to say?

HANNAH: Why are you out on the street at four A.M.? In that crazy city. It's dangerous.

JOE: Actually, Mom, I'm not on the street. I'm near the boathouse in the park.

HANNAH: What park?

JOE: Central Park.

HANNAH: CENTRAL PARK! Oh my Lord. What on earth are you doing in Central Park at this time of night? Are you . . .

Joe, I think you ought to go home right now. Call me from home.

(*Little pause.*)

Joe?

JOE: I come here to watch, Mom. Sometimes. Just to watch.

HANNAH: Watch what? What's there to watch at four in the . . .

JOE: Mom, did Dad love me?

HANNAH: What?

JOE: Did he?

HANNAH: You ought to go home and call from there.

JOE: Answer.

HANNAH: Oh now really. This is maudlin. I don't like this conversation.

JOE: Yeah, well, it gets worse from here on.

(*Pause.*)

HANNAH: Joe?

JOE: Mom. Momma. I'm a homosexual, Momma.

Boy, did that come out awkward.

(*Pause.*)

Hello? Hello?

I'm a homosexual.

(*Pause.*)

Please, Momma. Say something.

HANNAH: You're old enough to understand that your father didn't love you without being ridiculous about it.

JOE: What?

HANNAH: You're ridiculous. You're being ridiculous.

JOE: I'm . . .

What?

HANNAH: You really ought to go home now to your wife. I need to go to bed. This phone call. . . . We will just forget this phone call.

JOE: Mom.

HANNAH: No more talk. Tonight. This . . .

(*Suddenly very angry.*) Drinking is a sin! A sin! I raised you better than that. (*She hangs up.*)

Scene 9

(*The following morning, early. Split scene: Harper and Joe at home; Louis and Prior in Prior's hospital room. Joe and Louis have just entered. This should be fast and obviously furious; overlapping is fine; the proceedings may be a little confusing but not the final results.*)

HARPER: Oh God. Home. The moment of truth has arrived.

JOE: Harper.

LOUIS: I'm going to move out.

PRIOR: The fuck you are.

JOE: Harper. Please listen. I still love you very much. You're still my best buddy; I'm not going to leave you.

HARPER: No, I don't like the sound of this. I'm leaving.

LOUIS: I'm leaving.
    I already have.

JOE: Please listen. Stay. This is really hard. We have to talk.

HARPER: We are talking. Aren't we. Now please shut up. OK?

PRIOR: Bastard. Sneaking off while I'm flat out here, that's low. If I could get up now I'd beat the holy shit out of you.

JOE: Did you take pills? How many?

HARPER: No pills. Bad for the . . . (*Pats stomach.*)

JOE: You aren't pregnant. I called your gynecologist.

HARPER: I'm seeing a new gynecologist.

PRIOR: You have no right to do this.

LOUIS: Oh, that's ridiculous.

PRIOR: No right. It's criminal.

JOE: Forget about that. Just listen. You want the truth. This is the truth.
    I knew this when I married you. I've known this I guess for as long as I've known anything, but . . . I don't know, I thought maybe that with enough effort and will I could change myself . . . but I can't . . .

PRIOR: Criminal.

LOUIS: There oughta be a law.

PRIOR: There is a law. You'll see.

JOE: I'm losing ground here, I go walking, you want to know where I walk, I . . . go to the park, or up and down 53rd Street, or places where. . . . And I keep swearing I won't go walking again, but I just can't.

LOUIS: I need some privacy.

PRIOR: That's new.

LOUIS: Everything's new, Prior.

JOE: I try to tighten my heart into a knot, a snarl, I try to learn to live dead, just numb, but then I see someone I want, and it's like a nail, like a hot spike right through my chest, and I know I'm losing.

PRIOR: Apartment too small for three? Louis and Prior comfy but not Louis and Prior and Prior's disease?

LOUIS: Something like that.
    I won't be judged by you. This isn't a crime, just — the inevitable consequence of people who run out of — whose limitations. . . .

PRIOR: Bang bang bang. The court will come to order.

LOUIS: I mean let's talk practicalities, schedules; I'll come over if you want, spend nights with you when I can, I can . . .

PRIOR: Has the jury reached a verdict?

LOUIS: I'm doing the best I can.

PRIOR: Pathetic. Who cares?

JOE: My whole life has conspired to bring me to this place, and I can't despise my whole life. I think I believed when I met you I could save you, you at least if not myself, but . . .
    I don't have any sexual feelings for you, Harper. And I don't think I ever did.

(*Little pause.*)

HARPER: I think you should go.

JOE: Where?

HARPER: Washington. Doesn't matter.

JOE: What are you talking about?

HARPER: Without me.
    Without me, Joe. Isn't that what you want to hear?

(*Little pause.*)

JOE: Yes.

LOUIS: You can love someone and fail them. You can love someone and not be able to . . .

PRIOR: You *can*, theoretically, yes. A person can, maybe an editorial "you" can love, Louis, but not *you*, specifically you, I don't know, I think you are excluded from that general category.

HARPER: You were going to save me, but the whole time you were spinning a lie. I just don't understand that.

PRIOR: A person could theoretically love and maybe many do but we both know now you can't.

LOUIS: I do.

PRIOR: You can't even say it.

LOUIS: I love you, Prior.

PRIOR: I repeat. Who cares?

HARPER: This is so scary, I want this to stop, to go back . . .

PRIOR: We have reached a verdict, your honor. This man's heart is deficient. He loves, but his love is worth nothing.

JOE: Harper . . .

HARPER: Mr. Lies, I want to get away from here. Far away. Right now. Before he starts talking again. Please, please . . .

JOE: As long as I've known you Harper you've been afraid of . . . Of men hiding under the bed, men hiding under the sofa, men with knives.

PRIOR (*shattered; almost pleading; trying to reach him*): I'm dying! You stupid fuck! Do you know what that is! Love! Do you know what love means? We lived together four-and-a-half years, you animal, you idiot.

LOUIS: I have to find some way to save myself.

JOE: Who are these men? I never understood it. Now I know.

HARPER: What?

JOE: It's me.

HARPER: It is?

PRIOR: GET OUT OF MY ROOM!

JOE: I'm the man with the knives.

HARPER: You are?

PRIOR: If I could get up now I'd kill you. I would. Go away. Go away or I'll scream.

HARPER: Oh God . . .

JOE: I'm sorry . . .

HARPER: It is you.

LOUIS: Please don't scream.

PRIOR: Go.

HARPER: I recognize you now.

LOUIS: Please . . .

JOE: Oh. Wait, I. . . . Oh!
    (*He covers his mouth with his hand, gags, and removes his hand, red with blood.*)
    I'm bleeding.

(*Prior screams.*)

HARPER: Mr. Lies.

MR. LIES (*appearing, dressed in antarctic explorer's apparel*): Right here.

HARPER: I want to go away. I can't see him anymore.

MR. LIES: Where?

HARPER: Anywhere. Far away.

MR. LIES: Absolutamento.

(*Harper and Mr. Lies vanish. Joe looks up, sees that she's gone.*)

PRIOR (*closing his eyes*): When I open my eyes you'll be gone.

(*Louis leaves.*)

JOE: Harper?

PRIOR (*opening his eyes*): Huh. It worked.

JOE (*calling*): Harper?

PRIOR: I hurt all over. I wish I was dead.

Scene 10

(*The same day, sunset. Hannah and Sister Ella Chapter, a real-estate saleswoman, Hannah Pitt's closest friend, in front of Hannah's house in Salt Lake City.*)

SISTER ELLA CHAPTER: Look at that view! A view of heaven. Like the living city of heaven, isn't it, it just fairly glimmers in the sun.

HANNAH: Glimmers.

SISTER ELLA CHAPTER: Even the stone and brick it just glimmers and glitters like heaven in the sunshine. Such a nice view you get, perched up on a canyon rim. Some kind of beautiful place.

HANNAH: It's just Salt Lake, and you're selling the house *for* me, not *to* me.

SISTER ELLA CHAPTER: I like to work up an enthusiasm for my properties.

HANNAH: Just get me a good price.

SISTER ELLA CHAPTER: Well, the market's off.

HANNAH: At least fifty.

SISTER ELLA CHAPTER: Forty'd be more like it.

HANNAH: Fifty.

SISTER ELLA CHAPTER: Wish you'd wait a bit.

HANNAH: Well I can't.

SISTER ELLA CHAPTER: Wish you would. You're about the only friend I got.

HANNAH: Oh well now.

SISTER ELLA CHAPTER: Know why I decided to like you? I decided to like you 'cause you're the only unfriendly Mormon I ever met.

HANNAH: Your wig is crooked.

SISTER ELLA CHAPTER: Fix it.

(*Hannah straightens Sister Ella's wig.*)

SISTER ELLA CHAPTER: New York City. All they got there is tiny rooms.
    I always thought: People ought to stay put. That's why I got my license to sell real estate. It's a way of saying: Have a house! Stay put! It's a way of saying traveling's no good. Plus I needed the cash. (*She takes a pack of cigarettes out of her purse, lights one, offers pack to Hannah.*)

HANNAH: Not out here, anyone could come by.
    There's been days I've stood at this ledge and thought about stepping over.
    It's a hard place, Salt Lake: baked dry. Abundant energy; not much intelligence. That's a combination that can wear a body out. No harm looking someplace else. I don't need much room.
    My sister-in-law Libby thinks there's radon gas in the basement.

SISTER ELLA CHAPTER: Is there gas in the . . .

HANNAH: Of course not. Libby's a fool.

SISTER ELLA CHAPTER: 'Cause I'd have to include that in the description.

HANNAH: There's no gas, Ella. (*Little pause.*) Give a puff. (*She takes a furtive drag of Ella's cigarette.*) Put it away now.

SISTER ELLA CHAPTER: So I guess it's goodbye.

HANNAH: You'll be all right, Ella, I wasn't ever much of a friend.

SISTER ELLA CHAPTER: I'll say something but don't laugh, OK?
    This is the home of saints, the godliest place on earth, they say, and I think they're right. That mean there's no evil here? No. Evil's everywhere. Sin's everywhere. But this . . . is the spring of sweet water in the desert, the desert flower. Every step a Believer takes away from here is a step fraught with peril. I fear for you, Hannah Pitt, because you are my friend. Stay put. This is the right home of saints.

HANNAH: Latter-day saints.

SISTER ELLA CHAPTER: Only kind left.

HANNAH: But still. Late in the day . . . for saints and everyone. That's all. That's all.

Fifty thousand dollars for the house, Sister Ella Chapter; don't undersell. It's an impressive view.

ACT 3
NOT-YET-CONSCIOUS,
FORWARD DAWNING • *January 1986*

Scene 1

(*Late night, three days after the end of act 2. The stage is completely dark. Prior is in bed in his apartment, having a nightmare. He wakes up, sits up and switches on a nightlight. He looks at his clock. Seated by the table near the bed is a man dressed in the clothing of a 13th-century British squire.*)

PRIOR (*terrified*): Who are you?
PRIOR 1: My name is Prior Walter.

(*Pause.*)

PRIOR: My name is Prior Walter.
PRIOR 1: I know that.
PRIOR: Explain.
PRIOR 1: You're alive. I'm not. We have the same name. What do you want me to explain?
PRIOR: A ghost?
PRIOR 1: An ancestor.
PRIOR: Not *the* Prior Walter? The Bayeux tapestry Prior Walter?
PRIOR 1: His great-great grandson. The fifth of the name.
PRIOR: I'm the thirty-fourth, I think.
PRIOR 1: Actually the thirty-second.
PRIOR: Not according to Mother.
PRIOR 1: She's including the two bastards, then; I say leave them out. I say no room for bastards. The little things you swallow . . .
PRIOR: Pills.
PRIOR 1: Pills. For the pestilence. I too . . .
PRIOR: Pestilence. . . . You too what?
PRIOR 1: The pestilence in my time was much worse than now. Whole villages of empty houses. You could look outdoors and see Death walking in the morning, dew dampening the ragged hem of his black robe. Plain as I see you now.
PRIOR: You died of the plague.
PRIOR 1: The spotty monster. Like you, alone.
PRIOR: I'm not alone.
PRIOR 1: You have no wife, no children.
PRIOR: I'm gay.
PRIOR 1: So? Be gay, dance in your altogether for all I care, what's that to do with not having children?
PRIOR: Gay homosexual, not bonny, blithe and . . . never mind.
PRIOR 1: I had twelve. When I died.

(*The second ghost appears, this one dressed in the clothing of an elegant 17th-century Londoner.*)

PRIOR 1 (*pointing to Prior 2*): And I was three years younger than him.

(*Prior sees the new ghost, screams.*)

PRIOR: Oh God another one.
PRIOR 2: Prior Walter. Prior to you by some seventeen others.
PRIOR 1: He's counting the bastards.
PRIOR: Are we having a convention?
PRIOR 2: We've been sent to declare her fabulous incipience. They love a well-paved entrance with lots of heralds, and . . .
PRIOR 1: The messenger come. Prepare the way. The infinite descent, a breath in air . . .
PRIOR 2: They chose us, I suspect, because of the mortal affinities. In a family as long-descended as the Walters there are bound to be a few carried off by plague.
PRIOR 1: The spotty monster.
PRIOR 2: Black Jack. Came from a water pump, half the city of London, can you imagine? His came from fleas. Yours, I understand, is the lamentable consequence of venery . . .
PRIOR 1: Fleas on rats, but who knew that?
PRIOR: Am I going to die?
PRIOR 2: We aren't allowed to discuss . . .
PRIOR 1: When you do, you don't get ancestors to help you through it. You may be surrounded by children but you die alone.
PRIOR: I'm afraid.
PRIOR 1: You should be. There aren't even torches, and the path's rocky, dark and steep.
PRIOR 2: Don't alarm him. There's good news before there's bad.

We two come to strew rose petal and palm leaf before the triumphal procession. Prophet. Seer. Revelator. It's a great honor for the family.
PRIOR 1: He hasn't got a family.
PRIOR 2: I meant for the Walters, for the family in the larger sense.
PRIOR (*singing*): All I want is a room somewhere, Far away from the cold night air . . .
PRIOR 2 (*putting a hand on Prior's forehead*): Calm, calm, this is no brain fever . . .

(*Prior calms down, but keeps his eyes closed. The lights begin to change. Distant Glorious Music.*)

PRIOR 1 (*low chant*): Adonai, Adonai,
Olam ha-yichud,
Zefirot, Zazahot,
Ha-adam, ha-gadol
Daughter of Light,
Daughter of Splendors,
Fluor! Phosphor!
Lumen! Candle!
PRIOR 2 (*simultaneously*): Even now,
From the mirror-bright halls of heaven,

Across the cold and lifeless infinity of space,
The Messenger comes
Trailing orbs of light,
Fabulous, incipient,
Oh Prophet,
To you . . .
PRIOR 1 AND PRIOR 2: Prepare, prepare,
The Infinite Descent,
A breath, a feather,
Glory to . . .

(*They vanish.*)

Scene 2

(*The next day. Split scene. Louis and Belize in a coffee shop. Prior is at the outpatient clinic at the hospital with Emily, the nurse; she has him on a pentamidine IV drip.*)

LOUIS: Why has democracy succeeded in America? Of course by succeeded I mean comparatively, not literally, not in the present, but what makes for the prospect of some sort of radical democracy spreading outward and growing up? Why does the power that was once so carefully preserved at the top of the pyramid by the original framers of the Constitution seem drawn inexorably downward and outward in spite of the best effort of the Right to stop this? I mean it's the really hard thing about being Left in this country, the American Left can't help but trip over all these petrified little fetishes: freedom, that's the worst; you know, *Jeane Kirkpatrick*° for God's sake will go on and on about freedom and so what does that mean, the word freedom, when she talks about it, or human rights; you have Bush talking about human rights, and so what are these people talking about, they might as well be talking about the mating habits of Venusians, these people don't begin to know what, ontologically, freedom is or human rights, like they see these bourgeois property-based Rights-of-Man-type rights but that's not enfranchisement, not democracy, not what's implicit, what's potential within the idea, not the idea with blood in it. That's just liberalism, the worst kind of liberalism, really, bourgeois tolerance, and what I think is that what AIDS shows us is the limits of tolerance, that it's not enough to be tolerated, because when the shit hits the fan you find out how much tolerance is worth. Nothing. And underneath all the tolerance is intense, passionate hatred.
BELIZE: Uh huh.
LOUIS: Well don't you think that's true?
BELIZE: Uh huh. It is.

Jeane Kirkpatrick: (1920–2006), former U.S. ambassador to the United Nations.

LOUIS: *Power* is the object, not being tolerated. Fuck assimilation. But I mean in spite of all this the thing about America, I think, is that ultimately we're different from every other nation on earth, in that, with people here of every race, we can't. . . . Ultimately what defines us isn't race, but politics. Not like any European country where there's an insurmountable fact of a kind of racial, or ethnic, monopoly, or monolith, like all Dutchmen, I mean Dutch people, are well, Dutch, and the Jews of Europe were never Europeans, just a small problem. Facing the monolith. But here there are so many small problems, it's really just a collection of small problems, the monolith is missing. Oh, I mean, of course I suppose there's the monolith of White America. White Straight Male America.
BELIZE: Which is not unimpressive, even among monoliths.
LOUIS: Well, no, but when the race thing gets taken care of, and I don't mean to minimalize how major it is, I mean I know it is, this is a really, really incredibly racist country but it's like, well, the British. I mean, all these blue-eyed pink people. And it's just weird, you know, I mean I'm not all that Jewish-looking, or . . . well, maybe I am but, you know, in New York, everyone is . . . well, not everyone, but so many are but so but in England, in London I walk into bars and I feel like Sid the Yid, you know I mean like Woody Allen in *Annie Hall*, with the payess and the gabardine coat, like never, never anywhere so much — I mean, not actively despised, not like they're Germans, who I think are still terribly anti-Semitic, and racist too, I mean black-racist, they pretend otherwise but, anyway, in London, there's just . . . and at one point I met this black gay guy from Jamaica who talked with a lilt but he said his family'd been living in London since before the Civil War — the American one — and how the English never let him forget for a minute that he wasn't blue-eyed and pink and I said yeah, me too, these people are anti-Semites and he said yeah but the British Jews have the clothing business all sewed up and blacks there can't get a foothold. And it was an incredibly awkward moment of just. . . . I mean there we were, in this bar that was gay but it was a *pub*, you know, the beams and the plaster and those horrible little, like, two-day-old fish and egg sandwiches — and just so British, so *old*, and I felt, well, there's no way out of this because both of us are, right now, too much immersed in this history, hope is dissolved in the sheer age of this place, where race is what counts and there's no real hope of change — it's the racial destiny of the Brits that matters to them, not their political destiny, whereas in America . . .
BELIZE: Here in America race doesn't count.
LOUIS: No, no, that's not. . . . I mean you *can't* be hearing that . . .
BELIZE: I . . .
LOUIS: It's — look, race, yes, but ultimately race here is a political question, right? Racists just try to use race

here as a tool in a political struggle. It's not really about race. Like the spiritualists try to use that stuff, are you enlightened, are you centered, channeled, whatever, this reaching out for a spiritual past in a country where no indigenous spirits exist—only the Indians, I mean Native American spirits and we killed them off so now, there are no gods here, no ghosts and spirits in America, there are no angels in America, no spiritual past, no racial past, there's only the political, and the decoys and the ploys to maneuver around the inescapable battle of politics, the shifting downwards and outwards of political power to the people . . .

BELIZE: POWER to the People! AMEN! (*Looking at his watch.*) *OH MY GOODNESS!* Will you look at the time, I gotta . . .

LOUIS: Do you. . . . You think this is, what, racist or naive or something?

BELIZE: Well it's certainly *something*. Look, I just remembered I have an appointment . . .

LOUIS: What? I mean I really don't want to, like, speak from some position of privilege and . . .

BELIZE: I'm sitting here, thinking, eventually he's *got* to run out of steam, so I let you rattle on and on saying about maybe seven or eight things I find really offensive.

LOUIS: What?

BELIZE: But I know you, Louis, and I know the guilt fueling this peculiar tirade is obviously already swollen bigger than your hemorrhoids.

LOUIS: I don't have hemorrhoids.

BELIZE: I hear different. May I finish?

LOUIS: Yes, but I don't have hemorrhoids.

BELIZE: So finally, when I . . .

LOUIS: Prior told you, he's an asshole, he shouldn't have . . .

BELIZE: You promised, Louis. Prior is not a subject.

LOUIS: You brought him up.

BELIZE: I brought up hemorrhoids.

LOUIS: So it's indirect. Passive-aggressive.

BELIZE: Unlike, I suppose, banging me over the head with your theory that America doesn't have a race problem.

LOUIS: Oh be fair I never said that.

BELIZE: Not exactly, but . . .

LOUIS: I said . . .

BELIZE: . . . but it was close enough, because if it'd been that blunt I'd've just walked out and . . .

LOUIS: You deliberately misinterpreted! I . . .

BELIZE: Stop interrupting! I haven't been able to . . .

LOUIS: Just let me . . .

BELIZE: NO! What, *talk*? You've been running your mouth nonstop since I got here, yaddadda yaddadda blah blah blah, up the hill, down the hill, playing with your MONOLITH . . .

LOUIS (*overlapping*): Well, you could have joined in at any time instead of . . .

BELIZE (*continuing over Louis*): . . . and girlfriend it is truly an *awesome* spectacle but I got better things to

do with my time than sit here listening to this racist bullshit just because I feel sorry for you that . . .

LOUIS: I am not a racist!

BELIZE: Oh come on . . .

LOUIS: So maybe I am a racist but . . .

BELIZE: Oh I really hate that! It's no fun picking on you Louis; you're so guilty, it's like throwing darts at a glob of jello, there's no satisfying hits, just quivering, the darts just blop in and vanish.

LOUIS: I just think when you are discussing lines of oppression it gets very complicated and . . .

BELIZE: Oh is that a fact? You know, we black drag queens have a rather intimate knowledge of the complexity of the lines of . . .

LOUIS: *Ex*-black drag queen.

BELIZE: Actually ex-ex.

LOUIS: You're doing drag again?

BELIZE: I don't. . . . Maybe. I don't have to tell you. Maybe.

LOUIS: I think it's sexist.

BELIZE: I didn't ask you.

LOUIS: Well it is. The gay community, I think, has to adopt the same attitude towards drag as black women have to take towards black women blues singers.

BELIZE: Oh my we *are* walking dangerous tonight.

LOUIS: Well, it's all internalized oppression, right, I mean the masochism, the stereotypes, the . . .

BELIZE: Louis, are you deliberately trying to make me hate you?

LOUIS: No, I . . .

BELIZE: I mean, are you deliberately transforming yourself into an arrogant, sexual-political Stalinist-slash-racist flag-waving thug for my benefit?

(*Pause.*)

LOUIS: You know what I think?

BELIZE: What?

LOUIS: You hate me because I'm a Jew.

BELIZE: I'm leaving.

LOUIS: It's true.

BELIZE: You have no basis except your . . .

Louis, it's good to know you haven't changed; you are still an honorary citizen of the Twilight Zone, and after your pale, pale white polemics on behalf of racial insensitivity you have a flaming *fuck* of a lot of nerve calling me an anti-Semite. Now I really gotta go.

LOUIS: You called me Lou the Jew.

BELIZE: That was a joke.

LOUIS: I didn't think it was funny. It was hostile.

BELIZE: It was three years ago.

LOUIS: So?

BELIZE: You just called yourself Sid the Yid.

LOUIS: That's not the same thing.

BELIZE: Sid the Yid is different from Lou the Jew.

LOUIS: Yes.

BELIZE: Someday you'll have to explain that to me, but right now . . .

You hate me because you hate black people.

LOUIS: I do not. But I do think most black people are anti-Semitic.

BELIZE: "Most black people." *That's* racist, Louis, and *I* think most Jews . . .

LOUIS: Louis Farrakhan.

BELIZE: Ed Koch.

LOUIS: Jesse Jackson.

BELIZE: Jackson. Oh really, Louis, this is . . .

LOUIS: Hymietown! Hymietown!

BELIZE: Louis, you voted for Jesse Jackson. You send checks to the Rainbow Coalition.

LOUIS: I'm ambivalent. The checks bounced.

BELIZE: All your checks bounce, Louis; you're ambivalent about everything.

LOUIS: What's that supposed to mean?

BELIZE: You may be dumber than shit but I refuse to believe you can't figure it out. Try.

LOUIS: I was never ambivalent about Prior. I love him. I do. I really do.

BELIZE: Nobody said different.

LOUIS: Love and ambivalence are. . . . Real love isn't ambivalent.

BELIZE: "Real love isn't ambivalent." I'd swear that's a line from my favorite bestselling paperback novel, *In Love with the Night Mysterious*, except I don't think you ever read it.

(*Pause.*)

LOUIS: I never read it, no.

BELIZE: You ought to. Instead of spending the rest of your life trying to get through *Democracy in America*. It's about this white woman whose Daddy owns a plantation in the Deep South in the years before the Civil War—the American one—and her name is Margaret, and she's in love with her Daddy's number-one slave, and his name is Thaddeus, and she's married but her white slave-owner husband has AIDS: Antebellum Insufficiently Developed Sex-organs. And there's a lot of hot stuff going down when Margaret and Thaddeus can catch a spare torrid ten under the cotton-picking moon, and then of course the Yankees come, and they set the slaves free, and the slaves string up old Daddy, and so on. Historical fiction. Somewhere in there I recall Margaret and Thaddeus find the time to discuss the nature of love; her face is reflecting the flames of the burning plantation—you know, the way white people do—and his black face is dark in the night and she says to him, "Thaddeus, real love isn't ever ambivalent."

(*Little pause. Emily enters and turns off IV drip.*)

BELIZE: Thaddeus looks at her; he's contemplating her thesis; and he isn't sure he agrees.

EMILY (*removing IV drip from Prior's arm*): Treatment number . . . (*consulting chart*) four.

PRIOR: Pharmaceutical miracle. Lazarus breathes again.

LOUIS: Is he. . . . How bad is he?

BELIZE: You want the laundry list?

EMILY: Shirt off, let's check the . . .

(*Prior takes his shirt off. She examines his lesions.*)

BELIZE: There's the weight problem and the shit problem and the morale problem.

EMILY: Only six. That's good. Pants.

(*He drops his pants. He's naked. She examines.*)

BELIZE: And. He thinks he's going crazy.

EMILY: Looking good. What else?

PRIOR: Ankles sore and swollen, but the leg's better. The nausea's mostly gone with the little orange pills. BM's pure liquid but not bloody anymore, for now, my eye doctor says everything's OK, for now, my dentist says "Yuck!" when he sees my fuzzy tongue, and now he wears little condoms on his thumb and forefinger. And a mask. So what? My dermatologist is in Hawaii and my mother . . . well leave my mother out of it. Which is usually where my mother is, out of it. My glands are like walnuts, my weight's holding steady for week two, and a friend died two days ago of bird tuberculosis; bird tuberculosis; that scared me and I didn't go to the funeral today because he was an Irish Catholic and it's probably open casket and I'm afraid of . . . something, the bird TB or seeing him or. . . . So I guess I'm doing OK. Except for of course I'm going nuts.

EMILY: We ran the toxoplasmosis series and there's no indication . . .

PRIOR: I know, I know, but I feel like something terrifying is on its way, you know, like a missile from outer space, and it's plummeting down towards the earth, and I'm ground zero, and . . . I am generally known where I am known as one cool, collected queen. And I am ruffled.

EMILY: There's really nothing to worry about. I think that shochen bamromim hamtzeh menucho nechono al kanfey haschino.

PRIOR: What?

EMILY: Everything's fine. Bemaalos k'doshim ut'horim kezohar horokeea mazhirim . . .

PRIOR: Oh I don't understand what you're . . .

EMILY: Es nishmas Prior sheholoch leolomoh, baavur shenodvoo z'dokoh b'ad hazkoras nishmosoh.

PRIOR: Why are you doing that?! Stop it! Stop it!

EMILY: Stop what?

PRIOR: You were just . . . weren't you just speaking in Hebrew or something.

EMILY: *Hebrew?* (*Laughs.*) I'm basically Italian-American. No. I didn't speak in Hebrew.

PRIOR: Oh no, oh God please I really think I . . .

EMILY: Look, I'm sorry, I have a waiting room full of. . . . I think you're one of the lucky ones, you'll live for years, probably—you're pretty healthy for someone with no immune system. Are you seeing someone? Loneliness is a danger. A therapist?

PRIOR: No, I don't need to see anyone, I just . . .

EMILY: Well think about it. You aren't going crazy. You're just under a lot of stress. No wonder . . . (*She starts to write in his chart.*)

(*Suddenly there is an astonishing blaze of light, a huge chord sounded by a gigantic choir, and a great book with steel pages mounted atop a molten-red pillar pops up from the stage floor. The book opens; there is a large Aleph inscribed on its pages, which bursts into flames. Immediately the book slams shut and disappears instantly under the floor as the lights become normal again. Emily notices none of this, writing. Prior is agog.*)

EMILY (*laughing, exiting*): Hebrew . . .

(*Prior flees.*)

LOUIS: Help me.

BELIZE: I beg your pardon?

LOUIS: You're a nurse, give me something, I . . . don't know what to do anymore, I. . . . Last week at work I screwed up the Xerox machine like permanently and so I . . . then I tripped on the subway steps and my glasses broke and I cut my forehead, here, see, and now I can't see much and my forehead . . . it's like the Mark of Cain,° stupid, right, but it won't heal and every morning I see it and I think, Biblical things, Mark of Cain, Judas Iscariot° and his silver and his noose, people who . . . in betraying what they love betray what's truest in themselves, I feel . . . nothing but cold for myself, just cold, and every night I miss him, I miss him so much but then . . . those sores, and the smell and . . . where I thought it was going. . . . I could be . . . I could be . . . sick too, maybe I'm sick too. I don't know.
    Belize. Tell him I love him. Can you do that?

BELIZE: I've thought about it for a very long time, and I still don't understand what love is. Justice is simple. Democracy is simple. Those things are unambivalent. But love is very hard. And it goes bad for you if you violate the hard law of love.

LOUIS: I'm dying.

BELIZE: He's dying. You just wish you were.
    Oh cheer up, Louis. Look at that heavy sky out there.

LOUIS: Purple.

BELIZE: *Purple?* Boy, what kind of a homosexual are you, anyway? That's not purple, Mary, that color up there is (*very grand*) mauve.
    All day today it's felt like Thanksgiving. Soon, this . . . ruination will be blanketed white. You can smell it—can you smell it?

LOUIS: Smell what?

BELIZE: Softness, compliance, forgiveness, grace.

LOUIS: No . . .

BELIZE: I can't help you learn that. I can't help you, Louis. You're not my business. (*He exits.*)

(*Louis puts his head in his hands, inadvertently touching his cut forehead.*)

Mark of Cain: In Genesis Cain murdered his brother Abel and subsequently was marked on his forehead by God.   **Judas Iscariot:** An apostle who betrayed Jesus for thirty pieces of silver.

LOUIS: Ow FUCK! (*He stands slowly, looks towards where Belize exited.*) Smell what?
    (*He looks both ways to be sure no one is watching, then inhales deeply, and is surprised.*) Huh. Snow.

Scene 3

(*Same day. Harper in a very white, cold place, with a brilliant blue sky above; a delicate snowfall. She is dressed in a beautiful snowsuit. The sound of the sea, faint.*)

HARPER: Snow! Ice! Mountains of ice! Where am I? I . . .
    I feel better, I do, I . . . feel better. There are ice crystals in my lungs, wonderful and sharp. And the snow smells like cold, crushed peaches. And there's something . . . some current of blood in the wind, how strange, it has that iron taste.

MR. LIES: Ozone.

HARPER: Ozone! Wow! Where am I?

MR. LIES: The Kingdom of Ice, the bottommost part of the world.

HARPER (*looking around, then realizing*): Antarctica. This is Antarctica!

MR. LIES: Cold shelter for the shattered. No sorrow here, tears freeze.

HARPER: Antarctica, Antarctica, oh boy oh boy, LOOK at this, I. . . . Wow, I must've really snapped the tether, huh?

MR. LIES: Apparently

HARPER: That's great. I want to stay here forever. Set up camp. Build things. Build a city, an enormous city made up of frontier forts, dark wood and green roofs and high gates made of pointed logs and bonfires burning on every street corner. I should build by a river. Where are the forests?

MR. LIES: No timber here. Too cold. Ice, no trees.

HARPER: Oh details! I'm sick of details! I'll plant them and grow them. I'll live off caribou fat, I'll melt it over the bonfires and drink it from long, curved goat-horn cups. It'll be great. I want to make a new world here. So that I never have to go home again.

MR. LIES: As long as it lasts. Ice has a way of melting . . .

HARPER: No. Forever. I can have anything I want here — maybe even companionship, someone who has . . . desire for me. You, maybe.

MR. LIES: It's against the by-laws of the International Order of Travel Agents to get involved with clients. Rules are rules. Anyway, I'm not the one you really want.

HARPER: There isn't anyone . . . maybe an Eskimo. Who could ice-fish for food. And help me build a nest for when the baby comes.

MR. LIES: There are no Eskimo in Antarctica. And you're not really pregnant. You made that up.

HARPER: Well all of this is made up. So if the snow feels cold I'm pregnant. Right? Here, I can be pregnant. And I can have any kind of a baby I want.

MR. LIES: This is a retreat, a vacuum, its virtue is that it lacks everything; deep-freeze for feelings. You can be numb and safe here, that's what you came for. Respect the delicate ecology of your delusions.

HARPER: You mean like no Eskimo in Antarctica.

MR. LIES: Correcto. Ice and snow, no Eskimo. Even hallucinations have laws.

HARPER: Well then who's that?

(*The Eskimo appears.*)

MR. LIES: An Eskimo.

HARPER: An antarctic Eskimo. A fisher of the polar deep.

MR. LIES: There's something wrong with this picture.

(*The Eskimo beckons.*)

HARPER: I'm going to like this place. It's my own National Geographic Special! Oh! Oh! (*She holds her stomach.*) I think . . . I think I felt her kicking. Maybe I'll give birth to a baby covered with thick white fur, and that way she won't be cold. My breasts will be full of hot cocoa so she doesn't get chilly. And if it gets really cold, she'll have a pouch I can crawl into. Like a marsupial. We'll mend together. That's what we'll do; we'll mend.

Scene 4

(*Same day. An abandoned lot in the South Bronx. A homeless Woman is standing near an oil drum in which a fire is burning. Snowfall. Trash around. Hannah enters dragging two heavy suitcases.*)

HANNAH: Excuse me? I said excuse me? Can you tell me where I am? Is this Brooklyn? Do you know a Pineapple Street? Is there some sort of bus or train or . . . ?

I'm lost, I just arrived from Salt Lake. City. Utah? I took the bus that I was told to take and I got off—well it was the very last stop, so I had to get off, and I *asked* the driver was this Brooklyn, and he nodded yes but he was from one of those foreign countries where they think it's good manners to nod at everything even if you have no idea what it is you're nodding at, and in truth I think he spoke no English at all, which I think would make him ineligible for employment on public transportation. The public being English-speaking, mostly. Do you speak English?

(*The Woman nods.*)

HANNAH: I was supposed to be met at the airport by my son. He didn't show and I don't wait more than three and three-quarters hours for *anyone*. I should have been patient, I guess, I. . . . Is this . . .

WOMAN: Bronx.

HANNAH: Is that. . . . The *Bronx?* Well how in the name of Heaven did I get to the Bronx when the bus driver said . . .

WOMAN (*talking to herself*): Slurp slurp slurp will you STOP that disgusting slurping! YOU DISGUSTING SLURPING FEEDING ANIMAL! Feeding yourself, just feeding yourself, what would it matter, to you or to ANYONE, if you just stopped. Feeding. And DIED?

(*Pause.*)

HANNAH: Can you just tell me where I . . .

WOMAN: Why was the Kosciusko Bridge named after a Polack?

HANNAH: I don't know what you're . . .

WOMAN: That was a joke.

HANNAH: Well what's the punchline?

WOMAN: I don't know.

HANNAH (*looking around desperately*): Oh for pete's sake, is there anyone else who . . .

WOMAN (*again, to herself*): Stand further off you fat loathsome whore, you can't have any more of this soup, slurp slurp slurp you animal, and the—I know you'll just go pee it all away and where will you do that? Behind what bush? It's FUCKING COLD out here and I . . .

Oh that's right, because it was supposed to have been a tunnel!

That's not very funny.

Have you read the prophecies of Nostradamus?

HANNAH: Who?

WOMAN: Some guy I went out with once somewhere, Nostradamus. Prophet, outcast, eyes like. . . . Scary shit, he . . .

HANNAH: Shut up. Please. Now I want you to stop jabbering for a minute and pull your wits together and tell me how to get to Brooklyn. Because you know! And you are going to tell me! Because there is no one else around to tell me and I am wet and cold and I am very angry! So I am sorry you're psychotic but just make the effort—take a deep breath—DO IT!

(*Hannah and the Woman breathe together.*)

HANNAH: That's good. Now exhale.

(*They do.*)

HANNAH: Good. Now how do I get to Brooklyn?

WOMAN: Don't know. Never been. Sorry. Want some soup?

HANNAH: Manhattan? Maybe you know . . . I don't suppose you know the location of the Mormon Visitor's . . .

WOMAN: 65th and Broadway.

HANNAH: How do you . . .

WOMAN: Go there all the time. Free movies. Boring, but you can stay all day.

HANNAH: Well. . . . So how do I.

WOMAN: Take the D Train. Next block make a right.

HANNAH: Thank you.

WOMAN: Oh yeah. In the new century I think we will all be insane.

Scene 5

(*Same day. Joe and Roy in the study of Roy's brownstone. Roy is wearing an elegant bathrobe. He has made a considerable effort to look well. He isn't well, and he hasn't succeeded much in looking it.*)

JOE: I can't. The answer's no. I'm sorry.

ROY: Oh, well, apologies . . .

> I can't see that there's anyone asking for apologies.

(*Pause.*)

JOE: I'm sorry, Roy.

ROY: Oh, well, apologies.

JOE: My wife is missing, Roy. My mother's coming from Salt Lake to . . . to help look, I guess. I'm supposed to be at the airport now, picking her up but. . . . I just spent two days in a hospital, Roy, with a bleeding ulcer, I was spitting up blood.

ROY: Blood, huh? Look, I'm very busy here and . . .

JOE: It's just a job.

ROY: A *job*? A *job*? *Washington*! Dumb Utah Mormon hick shit!

JOE: Roy . . .

ROY: *WASHINGTON!* When Washington called me I was younger than you, you think I said "Aw fuck no I can't go I got two fingers up my asshole and a little moral nosebleed to boot!" When Washington calls you my pretty young punk friend you go or you can go fuck yourself sideways 'cause the train has pulled out of the station, and you are *out*, nowhere, out in the cold. Fuck you, Mary Jane, get outta here.

JOE: Just let me . . .

ROY: Explain? Ephemera. You broke my heart. Explain that. Explain that.

JOE: I love you. Roy.

> There's so much that I want, to be . . . what you see in me, I want to be a participant in the world, in your world, Roy, I want to be capable of that, I've tried, really I have but . . . I can't do this. Not because I don't believe in you, but because I believe in you so much, in what you stand for, at heart, the order, the decency. I would give anything to protect you, but. . . . There are laws I can't break. It's too ingrained. It's not me. There's enough damage I've already done.
>
> Maybe you were right, maybe I'm dead.

ROY: You're not dead, boy, you're a sissy.

> You love me; that's moving, I'm moved. It's nice to be loved. I warned you about her, didn't I, Joe? But you don't listen to me, why, because you say Roy is smart and Roy's a friend but Roy . . . well, he isn't nice, and you wanna be nice. Right? A nice, nice man!
>
> (*Little pause.*)
>
> You know what my greatest accomplishment was, Joe, in my life, what I am able to look back on and be proudest of? And I have helped make Presidents and unmake them and mayors and more goddam judges than anyone in NYC ever—AND several million

dollars, tax-free—and what do you think means the most to me?

> You ever hear of Ethel Rosenberg? Huh, Joe, huh?

JOE: Well, yeah, I guess I. . . . Yes.

ROY: Yes. Yes. You have heard of Ethel Rosenberg. Yes. Maybe you even read about her in the history books.

> If it wasn't for me, Joe, Ethel Rosenberg would be alive today, writing some personal-advice column for *Ms.* magazine. She isn't. Because during the trial, Joe, I was on the phone every day, talking with the judge . . .

JOE: Roy . . .

ROY: Every day, doing what I do best, talking on the telephone, making sure that timid Yid nebbish on the bench did his duty to America, to history. That sweet unprepossessing woman, two kids, boo-hoo-hoo, reminded us all of our little Jewish mamas—she came this close to getting life; I pleaded till I wept to put her in the chair. Me. I did that. I would have fucking pulled the switch if they'd have let me. Why? Because I fucking hate traitors. Because I fucking hate communists. Was it legal? Fuck legal. Am I a nice man? Fuck nice. They say terrible things about me in the *Nation*. Fuck the *Nation*. You want to be Nice, or you want to be Effective? Make the law, or subject to it. Choose. Your wife chose. A week from today, she'll be back. SHE knows how to get what SHE wants. Maybe I ought to send *her* to Washington.

JOE: I don't believe you.

ROY: Gospel.

JOE: You can't possibly mean what you're saying.

> Roy, you were the Assistant United States Attorney on the Rosenberg case, ex-parte communication with the judge during the trial would be . . . censurable, at least, probably conspiracy and . . . in a case that resulted in execution, it's . . .

ROY: What? Murder?

JOE: You're not well is all.

ROY: What do you mean, not well? Who's not well?

(*Pause.*)

JOE: You said . . .

ROY: No I didn't. I said what?

JOE: Roy, you have cancer.

ROY: No I don't.

(*Pause.*)

JOE: You told me you were dying.

ROY: What the fuck are you talking about, Joe? I never said that. I'm in perfect health. There's not a goddam thing wrong with me.

> (*He smiles.*)
>
> Shake?

(*Joe hesitates. He holds out his hand to Roy. Roy pulls Joe into a close, strong clinch.*)

ROY (*more to himself than to Joe*): It's OK that you hurt me because I love you, baby Joe. That's why I'm so rough on you.

(*Roy releases Joe. Joe backs away a step or two.*)

ROY: Prodigal son. The world will wipe its dirty hands all over you.
JOE: It already has, Roy.
ROY: Now go.

(*Roy shoves Joe, hard. Joe turns to leave. Roy stops him, turns him around.*)

ROY (*smoothing Joe's lapels, tenderly*): I'll always be here, waiting for you . . .
    (*Then again, with sudden violence, he pulls Joe close, violently.*)
    What did you want from me, what was all this, what do you want, treacherous ungrateful little . . .

(*Joe, very close to belting Roy, grabs him by the front of his robe, and propels him across the length of the room. He holds Roy at arm's length, the other arm ready to hit.*)

ROY (*laughing softly, almost pleading to be hit*): Transgress a little, Joseph.

(*Joe releases Roy.*)

ROY: There are so many laws; find one you can break.

(*Joe hesitates, then leaves, backing out. When Joe has gone, Roy doubles over in great pain, which he's been hiding throughout the scene with Joe.*)

ROY: Ah, Christ . . .
    Andy! Andy! Get in here! Andy!

(*The door opens, but it isn't Andy. A small Jewish Woman dressed modestly in a fifties hat and coat stands in the doorway. The room darkens.*)

ROY: Who the fuck are you? The new nurse?

(*The figure in the doorway says nothing. She stares at Roy. A pause. Roy looks at her carefully, gets up, crosses to her. He crosses back to the chair, sits heavily.*)

ROY: Aw, fuck. Ethel.
ETHEL ROSENBERG (*her manner is friendly, her voice is ice-cold*): You don't look good, Roy.
ROY: Well, Ethel. I don't feel good.
ETHEL ROSENBERG: But you lost a lot of weight. That suits you. You were heavy back then. Zaftig, mit hips.
ROY: I haven't been that heavy since 1960. We were all heavier back then, before the body thing started. Now I look like a skeleton. They stare.
ETHEL ROSENBERG: The shit's really hit the fan, huh, Roy?

(*Little pause. Roy nods.*)

ETHEL ROSENBERG: Well the fun's just started.
ROY: What is this, Ethel, Halloween? You trying to scare me?

(*Ethel says nothing.*)

ROY: Well you're wasting your time! I'm scarier than you any day of the week! So beat it, Ethel! BOOO! BETTER DEAD THAN RED! Somebody trying to shake me up? HAH HAH! From the throne of God in heaven to the belly of hell, you can all fuck yourselves and then go jump in the lake because I'M NOT AFRAID OF YOU OR DEATH OR HELL OR ANYTHING!
ETHEL ROSENBERG: Be seeing you soon, Roy. Julius sends his regards.
ROY: Yeah, well send this to Julius!

(*He flips the bird in her direction, stands and moves towards her. Halfway across the room he slumps to the floor, breathing laboriously, in pain.*)

ETHEL ROSENBERG: You're a very sick man, Roy.
ROY: Oh God . . . ANDY!

ETHEL ROSENBERG: Hmmm. He doesn't hear you, I guess. We should call the ambulance.
(*She goes to the phone.*)
Hah! Buttons! Such things they got now.
What do I dial, Roy?

(*Pause. Roy looks at her, then:*)

ROY: 911.
ETHEL ROSENBERG (*dials the phone*): It sings!
(*Imitating dial tones.*) La la la . . .
Huh.
Yes, you should please send an ambulance to the home of Mister Roy Cohn, the famous lawyer.
What's the address, Roy?
ROY (*a beat, then*): 244 East 87th.
ETHEL ROSENBERG: 244 East 87th Street. No apartment number, he's got the whole building.
My name? (*A beat.*) Ethel Greenglass Rosenberg.

(*Small smile.*) Me? No I'm not related to Mr. Cohn. An old friend.
(*She hangs up.*)
They said a minute.
ROY: I have all the time in the world.
ETHEL ROSENBERG: You're immortal.
ROY: I'm immortal. Ethel. (*He forces himself to stand.*)
I have *forced* my way into history. I ain't never gonna die.
ETHEL ROSENBERG (*a little laugh, then*): History is about to crack wide open. Millennium approaches.

Scene 6

(*Late that night. Prior's bedroom. Prior 1 watching Prior in bed, who is staring back at him, terrified. Tonight Prior 1 is dressed in weird alchemical robes and*

FAR LEFT: Ron Liebman as Roy Cohn in the Broadway production of *Angels in America: Millennium Approaches*. LEFT: Scene from the end of *Angels in America: Millennium Approaches*.

hat over his historical clothing and he carries a long palm-leaf bundle.)

PRIOR 1: Tonight's the night! Aren't you excited? Tonight she arrives! Right through the roof! Ha-adam, Ha-gadol . . .

PRIOR 2 (appearing, similarly attired): Lumen! Phosphor! Fluor! Candle! An unending billowing of scarlet and . . .

PRIOR: Look. Garlic. A mirror. Holy water. A crucifix. FUCK OFF! Get the fuck out of my room! GO!

PRIOR 1 (to Prior 2): Hard as a hickory knob, I'll bet.

PRIOR 2: We all tumesce when they approach. We wax full, like moons.

PRIOR 1: Dance.

PRIOR: Dance?

PRIOR 1: Stand up, dammit, give us your hands, dance!

PRIOR 2: Listen . . .

(A lone oboe begins to play a little dance tune.)

PRIOR 2: Delightful sound. Care to dance?

PRIOR: Please leave me alone, please just let me sleep . . .

PRIOR 2: Ah, he wants someone familiar. A partner who knows his steps. (To Prior.) Close your eyes. Imagine . . .

PRIOR: I don't . . .

PRIOR 2: Hush. Close your eyes.

(Prior does.)

PRIOR 2: Now open them.

(Prior does. Louis appears. He looks gorgeous. The music builds gradually into a full-blooded, romantic dance tune.)

PRIOR: Lou.

LOUIS: Dance with me.

PRIOR: I can't, my leg, it hurts at night . . .
Are you . . . a ghost, Lou?

LOUIS: No. Just spectral. Lost to myself. Sitting all day on cold park benches. Wishing I could be with you. Dance with me, babe . . .

(Prior stands up. The leg stops hurting. They begin to dance. The music is beautiful.)

PRIOR 1 (to Prior 2): Hah. Now I see why he's got no children. He's a sodomite.

PRIOR 2: Oh be quiet, you medieval gnome, and let them dance.

PRIOR 1: I'm not interfering, I've done my bit. Hooray, hooray, the messenger's come, now I'm blowing off. I don't like it here.

(Prior 1 vanishes.)

PRIOR 2: The twentieth century. Oh dear, the world has gotten so terribly, terribly old.

(Prior 2 vanishes. Louis and Prior waltz happily. Lights fade back to normal. Louis vanishes.
Prior dances alone.
Then suddenly, the sound of wings fills the room.)

Scene 7

(Split scene. Prior alone in his apartment; Louis alone in the park.
Again, a sound of beating wings.)

PRIOR: Oh don't come in here don't come in . . . LOUIS!!
No. My name is Prior Walter, I am . . . the scion of an ancient line, I am . . . abandoned I . . . no, my name is . . . is . . . Prior and I live . . . here and now, and . . . in the dark, in the dark, the Recording Angel opens its hundred eyes and snaps the spine of the Book of Life and . . . hush! Hush!
I'm talking nonsense, I . . .
No more mad scene, hush, hush.

(Louis in the park on a bench. Joe approaches, stands at a distance. They stare at each other, then Louis turns away.)

LOUIS: Do you know the story of Lazarus?

JOE: Lazarus?

LOUIS: Lazarus. I can't remember what happens, exactly.

JOE: I don't. . . . Well, he was dead, Lazarus, and Jesus breathed life into him. He brought him back from death.

LOUIS: Come here often?

JOE: No. Yes. Yes.

LOUIS: Back from the dead. You believe that really happened?

JOE: I don't know anymore what I believe.

LOUIS: This is quite a coincidence. Us meeting.

JOE: I followed you.
From work. I . . . followed you here.

(Pause.)

LOUIS: You followed me.
You probably saw me that day in the washroom and thought: there's a sweet guy, sensitive, cries for friends in trouble.

JOE: Yes.

LOUIS: You thought maybe I'll cry for you.

JOE: Yes.

LOUIS: Well I fooled you. Crocodile tears. Nothing . . .
(He touches his heart, shrugs.)

(Joe reaches tentatively to touch Louis's face.)

LOUIS (pulling back): What are you doing? Don't do that.

JOE (withdrawing his hand): Sorry. I'm sorry.

LOUIS: I'm . . . just not . . . I think, if you touch me, your hand might fall off or something. Worse things have happened to people who have touched me.

JOE: Please.
Oh, boy . . .
Can I . . .
I . . . want . . . to touch you. Can I please just touch you . . . um, here?
(He puts his hand on one side of Louis's face. He holds it there.)
I'm going to hell for doing this.

LOUIS: Big deal. You think it could be any worse than New York City?

(*He puts his hand on Joe's hand. He takes Joe's hand away from his face, holds it for a moment, then:*) Come on.

JOE: Where?

LOUIS: Home. With me.

JOE: This makes no sense. I mean I don't know you.

LOUIS: Likewise.

JOE: And what you do know about me you don't like.

LOUIS: The Republican stuff?

JOE: Yeah, well for starters.

LOUIS: I don't not like that. I *hate* that.

JOE: So why on earth should we . . .

(*Louis goes to Joe and kisses him.*)

LOUIS: Strange bedfellows. I don't know. I never made it with one of the damned before.

I would really rather not have to spend tonight alone.

JOE: I'm a pretty terrible person, Louis.

LOUIS: Lou.

JOE: No, I really really am. I don't think I deserve being loved.

LOUIS: There? See? We already have a lot in common.

(*Louis stands, begins to walk away. He turns, looks back at Joe. Joe follows. They exit.*)

(*Prior listens. At first no sound, then once again, the sound of beating wings, frighteningly near.*)

PRIOR: That sound, that sound, it. . . . What is that, like birds or something, like a *really* big bird, I'm frightened, I . . . no, no fear, find the anger, find the . . . anger, my blood is clean, my brain is fine, I can handle pressure, I am a gay man and I am used to pressure, to trouble, I am tough and strong and. . . . Oh. Oh my goodness. I . . . (*He is washed over by an intense sexual feeling.*) Ooohhhh. . . . I'm hot, I'm . . . so . . . aw Jeez what is going on here I . . . must have a fever I . . .

(*The bedside lamp flickers wildly as the bed begins to roll forward and back. There is a deep bass creaking and groaning from the bedroom ceiling, like the timbers of a ship under immense stress, and from above a fine rain of plaster dust.*)

PRIOR: OH!

PLEASE, OH PLEASE! Something's coming in here, I'm scared, I don't like this at all, something's approaching and I. . . . OH!

(*There is a great blaze of triumphal music, heralding. The light turns an extraordinary harsh, cold, pale blue, then a rich, brilliant warm golden color, then a hot, bilious green, and then finally a spectacular royal purple. Then silence.*)

PRIOR (*an awestruck whisper*): God almighty . . .

Very Steven Spielberg.

(*A sound, like a plummeting meteor, tears down from very, very far above the earth, hurtling at an incredible velocity towards the bedroom; the light seems to be sucked out of the room as the projectile approaches; as the room reaches darkness, we hear a terrifying CRASH as something immense strikes earth; the whole building shudders and a part of the bedroom ceiling, lots of plaster and lathe and wiring, crashes to the floor. And then in a shower of unearthly white light, spreading great opalescent gray-silver wings, the Angel descends into the room and floats above the bed.*)

ANGEL: Greetings, Prophet;

The Great Work begins:

The Messenger has arrived.

(*Blackout.*)

COMMENTARY

Andrea Bernstein

INTERVIEW WITH TONY KUSHNER   *1995*

Andrea Bernstein, a freelance cultural critic, engaged Tony Kushner in a discussion of the politics in his plays. Kushner's responses to her questions establish his credentials as a left-thinking critic of contemporary political life. His discussion of his work is centered much more in political reality than it is in dramatic technique or concern for theater. Yet Kushner is able to zero in on the dramatic moment and present contemporary politics as a dialectical struggle.

Tony Kushner, a gay Jewish socialist who was raised in Louisiana, won a Pulitzer Prize and two Tony Awards for his two-part, seven-hour Broadway production of *Angels in America: A Gay Fantasia on National Themes*. Other plays, *A Bright Room Called Day* (1985) and *Slavs!* (1994), are also concerned with the moral responsibilities of people in politically repressive times. Such concerns may be especially relevant in America today, where, as he observes: "What used to be called liberal is now called radical, what used to be called radical is now called insane, what used to be called reactionary is now called moderate, and what used to be called insane is now called solid conservative thinking."

Q: Angels in America opened on Broadway just months after the Clinton inauguration. It ends with a very hopeful speech about healing. Do you still feel that hope?

A: You have to have hope. It's irresponsible to give *false* hope, which I think a lot of playwrights are guilty of. But I also think it's irresponsible to simply be a nihilist, which quite a lot of playwrights, especially playwrights younger than me, have become guilty of. I don't believe you would bother to write a play if you really had no hope. That passage was one of the very first things I ever wrote when I was working on *Angels*. I read it to the woman who I was originally writing the part of the angel for, who died of breast cancer before the play was finished. In one of my last conversations with her, she told me that she thought about that image a lot and that she hoped I would include it in the play. I think I wouldn't have included it otherwise, but I'm glad I did now.

Q: Angels in America was a political play—and that's something Americans and critics frequently resist. How did you overcome that resistance?

A: What I found in the audience response is a huge hunger for political issues and political discussion. So I always wonder: Is it that Americans don't like politics, or is it that so much theater that is political isn't well done? One of the things I learned in *Slavs!* is that it's much easier to talk about being gay than it is to talk about being a socialist. People are afraid of socialism, and plays that deal with economics are scarier to them. I'll learn more about that—my next three plays are all about money.

Also, *Angels* is very entertaining. It does things formally that are new, and people were excited by the size and the scope. It's a good play and that makes all the difference.

Thelma and Louise, for instance, is a really terrific movie, and genuinely left in its political sensibilities. It's well-made, so the fact that it is unquestionably coming from a feminist perspective didn't make it absolutely marginal the way you would expect such a film to be. It had guns—that probably helped.

Q: People loved *Forrest Gump,* too.

A: People shouldn't trust artists and they shouldn't trust art. Part of the fun of art is that it invites you to interpret it.

There's a very complicated relationship between form and content and between aesthetics and politics. Good politics will produce good aesthetics, really good politics will produce really good aesthetics, and really good aesthetics, if somebody's really asking the hard questions and answering them honestly, they'll probably produce truth, which is to say progressive politics.

Q: Is it hard to write characters that are not caricatures and to overcome the barrier that people have about listening to politics from a character on stage?

A: I think that a character's politics have to live in the same sort of relationship to the character's psyche that people's politics live in relationship to their own psyches. People are never consistent. People will always do surprising things, both good and bad, and the way that people surprise themselves and their audience are the most interesting moments of human behavior. The space between what we'd like to be and what we actually are is where you find out the most interesting things.

Q: Do you see your plays as part of a political movement?

A: I do. I would hate to write anything that wasn't. I would like my plays to be of use to progressive people. I think preaching to the converted is exactly what art ought to do.

I am happiest when people who are politically engaged in the world say, "Your play meant a lot to me; it helped me think about something, or made me feel like I wasn't the only person who felt this way."

It's the way you feel when you go to a demo, which is the only way to keep sane a lot of the time. You need to remind yourself there are many bodies who are as angry about something as you are.

When I teach writing, I always tell my students you should assume that the audience you're writing for is smarter than you. You can't write if you don't think they're on your side, because then you start to yell at them or preach down to them.

Q: The character Prelapsarianov—the "world's oldest living Bolshevik"—gives the same speech in both *Angels* and *Slavs!:* "How are we to proceed without theory? Is it enough to reject the past, is it wise to move forward in this blind fashion, without the cold brilliant light of theory to guide the way? . . . You who live in this sour little age cannot imagine the sheer grandeur of the prospect we gazed upon."

A: In both *Perestroika* [part two of *Angels*] and *Slavs!*, the whole play proceeds from the question: If you don't know where you're going, can you move? And do you even have a choice, or do you just dive in and work it out as you're going?

That speech came out of a fight I had with my friend Oskar Eustis about Gorbachev. Oskar's point, which became the basis of Prelapsarianov's speech, is that if you don't have a theory to start with—Gorbachev pretended to be about democratic socialism but actually sort of was and sort of wasn't; he was also sort of about preserving the Communist Party power elite—what do you do? It's one of those big conundrums.

Q: So what *do* you do?

A: You can't stay back. The fundamental question is: Are we made by history or do we make history—and the answer is yes. I was rereading Marx's *Eighteenth Brumaire of Louis Bonaparte* recently. The whole tradition in socialist struggle is looking to the past for an antecedent form upon which the present revolutionary response is to be modeled. We may need to stop doing that.

Q: Why does the play *Slavs!* end with the question: "What is to be done?"

A: I wanted someone to ask the question: What if this really is the end of history? What if there really is literally nothing to be done, and we're simply stuck with capitalism—although I don't really think it is a possibility.

I still believe in a dialectical ordering of the universe. There is a dynamic principle at work—it isn't always mechanically moving things toward the good, but there's always either some sort of progress or decay. And there's too much misery in the world. That is not something that can hold.

Q: What do you think is to be done?

A: I'm 38 now. One of the painful rites of passage that everyone on the left goes through is to realize it's a lifelong struggle. What we're dealing with from Nixon on as a counter-reaction to the '60s is a very widespread, long-term historical trend. It's going to take many years and probably a few decades to reverse. People need to be willing to take an issue that they feel passionately about, address themselves to it as extensively as they are capable of and build common cause between issue groups.

Everybody on the left needs to start talking about how to create, first on local levels and eventually on a national level, a third party or at least a party that could establish some kind of position in Congress. That's the eternal dream of the left.

Q: You think there's no hope for revitalizing the Democratic Party?

A: It's a waste of time at this point. There's a famous story about Paul Wellstone refusing to shake Jesse Helms' hand and being chastised by everyone in the Senate because he wouldn't do it—he was told this is a gentlemen's club where we're all colleagues. That's what's wrong.

Q: One of the characters in *A Bright Room Called Day* keeps saying—as Nazism progressively snatches power and the Weimar Republic falls—that each turn for the worse would be the essential spur for people to rise up and oppose fascism. That didn't happen. Do you see parallels today?

A: You don't want to be opportunistic about it and say, "Oh, goody, millions of people are going to be thrown out of their homes—now we'll really get things cooking." It's like people saying the AIDS epidemic helped organize the gay and lesbian community.

Q: Speaking of which, there's a lot of discussion now about the second wave of the AIDS epidemic, and about gay men not practicing safer sex. Where do you weigh in?

A: It's very difficult to ask people to abstain from pleasure indefinitely, especially sexual erotic pleasure, which is so incredibly important to human beings and the enjoyment of which among homosexuals is so much of a political battlefield. There is absolutely no question that safer sex is not as gratifying and that given all the despair and the unbelievably imponderable weight of loss that the community has had to deal with, self-destructive behaviors are going to be engaged in.

Q: Do you think the gay community should be discussing this publicly?

A: Of course it's going to be discussed publicly. But you have to be smart. When you make a public utterance you are responsible for being responsible. We're still an embattled community, and if you're stupid about it you'll give aid to the enemy.

Q: Do you have that conundrum as a playwright?

A: You have to say: What am I feeding into? I think you should ask yourself that question and then make the decision based on the answers you come up with. I regret having made the only black person in *Angels* a nurse; that was an inept thing to do.

I was very scared about writing a play where there's a couple, one has AIDS and the other walks out. I thought, this is transgressive and scary and am I going to become public enemy number one in the gay community for having written a character like Louis?

On the other hand, you have to be willing to scare the horses. You have to be interesting and you have to be daring and you have to be willing to write things that shock. Shock is part of art. Art that's polite is not much fun.

Paula Vogel

"My play dramatizes the gifts we receive from the people who hurt us."

— PAULA VOGEL

Paula Vogel (b. 1951) came from a Washington, D.C., working-class family and knew she would have to make it on her own if she made it at all. For her, that knowledge was essentially the best inheritance she could have had. Her early years were marred by her parents' divorce and the loss of a father whom she came to know only in later years when her closest sibling, Carl, was dying of AIDS. Her earliest efforts in playwriting also met with rejection. After losing her scholarship to Bryn Mawr College, she devoted herself to dramatic literature and graduated from Catholic University in Washington but then was turned down by the Yale School of Drama. Her earliest plays were also turned down by the Eugene O'Neill National Playwright's Conference. In retrospect, she feels that these were good things because they made her learn her craft in a difficult—and original—way, which led eventually to her winning the Pulitzer Prize for *How I Learned to Drive*.

Vogel's earliest exposure to theater was in Washington, D.C. She talks about having "stumbled into drama class" when she was a sophomore in high school and beginning to find her way in theater. Her high school drama teacher was gay, and she feels he must have realized that she was herself a lesbian. She resisted taking acting roles—although she coached other students—and spent her years in high school as a stage manager. As a young playwright she found other friends who were trying to write, and they gathered together to read each other's work. They occasionally did exercises, some of which became useful teaching tools for Vogel at Brown University. For example, they wrote complete plays in forty-eight hours as a way of getting the essentials down as quickly as possible. Some of her earliest work had its origin in these experiments, including a version of *How I Learned to Drive*.

Some of her plays have startling images, such as a bizarre Groucho Marx–like doctor treating a dying AIDS patient in *The Baltimore Waltz* (which won an Obie Award for best play in 1992), a play about the death of her beloved brother Carl, who had begun a professional career as an English professor but switched to being a librarian. He was gay, and according to Vogel, homophobia hurt him more than the disease that killed him. Her plays are famous for scatological humor, jokes about the body, and extremely plain talk.

Among her early plays is one about lesbians who parent several little boys: *And Baby Makes Seven* (1984)—a daring excursion into territory that few playwrights have explored. Another early play, *The Oldest Profession* (1988), treats older prostitutes. *Hot 'n' Throbbing* (1994) examines the effect of theater on its characters. *The Mineola Twins* (1996) was written before *How I Learned to Drive* but was produced later, in 1999. Vogel thinks of this play as a comedy and something of a contrast to *How I Learned to Drive*, which is, if not a tragedy, certainly serious in nature. Yet it too has moments of genuine comedy.

Paula Vogel's most recent play is *The Long Chrismas Ride Home*, which opened in June 2003 at Providence's Trinity Repertory Company. It moved into the Vineyard Theatre in New York in December 2003 to good reviews. *New York Times* critic Ben Brantley said of the June production that "*The Long Christmas Ride Home* is partly a latter-day answer to the works of Thornton Wilder, including *Our Town*, and the short pieces *The Long Christmas Dinner* and *The Happy Journey to Trenton and Camden*."[1] The play employs half-size puppets, borrowing from the Japanese Bunraku-style theater. Using puppets to help portray a dysfunctional family has been widely praised for producing appropriate and subtle emotional nuances. The 2004 production at Long Wharf Theatre was enormously effective and powerful theater.

How I Learned to Drive

How I Learned to Drive was first produced in New York off-Broadway in 1997. It won not only the Pulitzer Prize but also the New York Drama Critics' Circle, Drama Desk, and Obie awards for best play of the year. It is published in a volume with *The Mineola Twins* called *The Mammary Plays*. Vogel explains that large-busted women remained an emblem for her in the construction of both plays. As a feminist, Vogel is interested in our fetishization of women's bodies, and both these plays move toward revealing the way the culture, both men and women, regard women's bodies, even while praising their minds.

All the characters in Li'l Bit's family are named in an unusual way. Li'l Bit explains, "In my family, if we call someone 'Big Papa,' it's not because he's tall. In my family, folks tend to get nicknamed for their genitalia. Uncle Peck, for example. My mamma's adage was 'the titless wonder.' Even Li'l Bit was named after she was physically examined at birth. Uncle Peck, married to Li'l Bit's mother's sister Mary, is not a blood relation—a fact he constantly stresses to Li'l Bit—and he tells her he has loved her since she was small enough to hold in his hand. Even Big Papa chases Grandma around the house: it's an unusual and curious family.

The play is about sexual molestation—but about many other things, too. It is about families, about growing up, about becoming independent, and most of all about being a survivor. In an interview with Arthur Holmberg, literary director of American Repertory Theatre, Vogel has said, "My play dramatizes the gifts we receive from the people who hurt us." When asked what gift Li'l Bit received, Vogel responded, "She received the gift of how to survive." Vogel uses learning to drive as a complex metaphor for sexual initiation. At the same time, the metaphor examines what a man expects from a close relationship with a woman and what a woman expects from a close relationship with a man. Uncle Peck is

[1]*New York Times*, June 10, 2003, p. E6.

careful never to hurt Li'l Bit and always reminds her that he doesn't want her to do anything she doesn't wish to do. But at the same time, Uncle Peck "has a way" with adolescent girls, as his wife tells us. He listens to Li'l Bit and becomes her confidante, patiently waiting for her to accept him on his own terms.

Although he is a predator, Uncle Peck is not necessarily a villain in the play. He takes advantage of Li'l Bit starting at age eleven and continues until she is eighteen and in college. For Vogel, part of the learning process for Li'l Bit is, as Vogel has said, becoming "an adult looking at and understanding her complicity." Then the next step is self-forgiveness. This step is essential to moving forward in her life.

How I Learned to Drive in Performance

The Vineyard Theatre in New York produced the play in February 1997 and moved it to the large Century Theater in April. It was reviewed warmly and received positively by audiences, eventually winning Vogel the Pulitzer Prize for drama for 1997. The play relies on an interesting device, the Greek Chorus, a character who speaks in the voice of characters alluded to but not present, such as Li'l Bit's mother, grandmother, grandfather, and aunt. Vogel also wanted to have slides shown at critical moments, such as the scene in which Uncle Peck is taking photographs of Li'l Bit and the scene in which Uncle Peck rhapsodizes over 1950s automobiles. Not all directors use the slides. For example, they were not used in the original New York production. Vogel's method of writing, like that of many playwrights, is to respond to the actors' interpretation of lines during rehearsal and rewriting. *How I Learned to Drive* benefited from that method.

In 1998 *How I Learned to Drive* had twenty-six regional productions and was the most produced play in the United States. Many more regional and international productions have followed, with numerous university productions virtually every year since.

Paula Vogel (b. 1951)
HOW I LEARNED TO DRIVE

1997

Characters

LI'L BIT, *A woman who ages forty-something to eleven years old.*

PECK, *Attractive man in his forties. Despite a few problems, he should be played by an actor one might cast in the role of Atticus in* To Kill a Mockingbird.

THE GREEK CHORUS, *If possible, these three members should be able to sing three-part harmony.*

> MALE GREEK CHORUS, *Plays Grandfather, Waiter, High School Boys. Thirties–forties.*

FEMALE GREEK CHORUS, *Plays Mother, Aunt Mary, High School Girls. Thirty–fifty.*
TEENAGE GREEK CHORUS, *Plays Grandmother, High School Girls, and the voice of eleven-year-old Li'l Bit. Note on the casting of this actor: I would strongly recommend casting a young woman who is "of legal age," that is, twenty-one to twenty-five years old, who can look as close to eleven as possible. The contrast with the other cast members will help. If the actor is too young, the audience may feel uncomfortable.*

(*As the house lights dim, a Voice announces:*)

Safety First — You and Driver Education.

(*Then the sound of a key turning the ignition of a car. Li'l Bit steps into a spotlight on the stage; "well-endowed," she is a softer-looking woman in the present time than she was at seventeen.*)

LI'L BIT: Sometimes to tell a secret, you first have to teach a lesson. We're going to start our lesson tonight on an early, warm summer evening.

In a parking lot overlooking the Beltsville Agricultural Farms in suburban Maryland.

Less than a mile away, the crumbling concrete of U.S. One wends its way past one-room revival churches, the porno drive-in, and boarded up motels with For Sale signs tumbling down.

Like I said, it's a warm summer evening.

Here on the land the Department of Agriculture owns, the smell of sleeping farm animals is thick on the air. The smells of clover and hay mix in with the smells of the leather dashboard. You can still imagine how Maryland used to be, before the malls took over. This countryside was once dotted with farmhouses—from their porches you could have witnessed the Civil War raging in the front fields.

Oh yes. There's a moon over Maryland tonight, that spills into the car where I sit beside a man old enough to be—did I mention how still the night is? Damp soil and tranquil air. It's the kind of night that makes a middle-aged man with a mortgage feel like a country boy again.

It's 1969. And I am very old, very cynical of the world, and I know it all. In short, I am seventeen years old, parking off a dark lane with a married man on an early summer night.

(*Lights up on two chairs facing front—or a Buick Riviera, if you will. Waiting patiently, with a smile on his face, Peck sits sniffing the night air. Li'l Bit climbs in beside him, seventeen years old and tense. Throughout the following, the two sit facing directly front. They do not touch. Their bodies remain passive. Only their facial expressions emote.*)

PECK: Ummm. I love the smell of your hair.

LI'L BIT: Uh-huh.

PECK: Oh, Lord. Ummmm. (*Beat.*) A man could die happy like this.

LI'L BIT: Well, *don't.*

PECK: What shampoo is this?

LI'L BIT: Herbal Essence.

PECK: Herbal Essence. I'm gonna buy me some. Herbal Essence. And when I'm all alone in the house, I'm going to get into the bathtub, and uncap the bottle and—

LI'L BIT: —Be good.

PECK: What?

LI'L BIT: Stop being . . . bad.

PECK: What did you think I was going to say? What do you think I'm going to do with the shampoo?

LI'L BIT: I don't want to know. I don't want to hear it.

PECK: I'm going to wash my hair. That's all.

LI'L BIT: Oh.

PECK: What did you think I was going to do?

LI'L BIT: Nothing . . . I don't know. Something . . . nasty.

PECK: With shampoo? Lord, gal—your mind!

LI'L BIT: And whose fault is it?

PECK: Not mine. I've got the mind of a boy scout.

LI'L BIT: Right. A horny boy scout.

PECK: Boy scouts are always horny. What do you think the first Merit Badge is for?

LI'L BIT: There. You're going to be nasty again.

PECK: Oh, no. I'm good. Very good.

LI'L BIT: It's getting late.

PECK: Don't change the subject. I was talking about how good I am. (*Beat.*) Are you ever gonna let me show you how good I am?

LI'L BIT: Don't go over the line now.

PECK: I won't. I'm not gonna do anything you don't want me to do.

LI'L BIT: That's right.

PECK: And I've been good all week.

LI'L BIT: You have?

PECK: Yes. All week. Not a single drink.

LI'L BIT: Good boy.

PECK: Do I get a reward? For not drinking?

LI'L BIT: A small one. It's getting late.

PECK: Just let me undo you. I'll do you back up.

LI'L BIT: All right. But be quick about it.

(*Peck pantomimes undoing Li'l Bit's brassiere with one hand.*)

You know, that's amazing. The way you can undo the hooks through my blouse with one hand.

PECK: Years of practice.

LI'L BIT: You would make an incredible brain surgeon with that dexterity.

PECK: I'll bet Clyde—what's the name of the boy taking you to the prom?

LI'L BIT: Claude Souders.

PECK: Claude Souders. I'll bet it takes him two hands, lights on, and you helping him on to get to first base.

LI'L BIT: Maybe.

(*Beat.*)

PECK: Can I . . . kiss them? Please?

LI'L BIT: I don't know.

PECK: Don't make a grown man beg.

LI'L BIT: Just one kiss.

PECK: I'm going to lift your blouse.

LI'L BIT: It's a little cold.

(*Peck laughs gently.*)

PECK: That's not why you're shivering.

(*They sit, perfectly still, for a long moment of silence. Peck makes gentle, concentric circles with his thumbs in the air in front of him.*)

How does that feel?

(*Li'l Bit closes her eyes, carefully keeps her voice calm:*)

LI'L BIT: It's . . . okay.

(*Sacred music, organ music or a boy's choir swells beneath the following.*)

PECK: I tell you, you can keep all the cathedrals of Europe. Just give me a second with these—these celestial orbs—

(*Peck bows his head as if praying. But he is kissing her nipple. Li'l Bit, eyes still closed, rears back her head on the leather Buick car seat.*)

LI'L BIT: Uncle Peck—we've got to go. I've got graduation rehearsal at school tomorrow morning. And you should get on home to Aunt Mary—
PECK:—All right, Li'l Bit.
LI'L BIT:—*Don't* call me that no more. (*Calmer.*) Any more. I'm a big girl now, Uncle Peck. As you know.

(*Li'l Bit pantomimes refastening her bra behind her back.*)

PECK: That you are. Going on eighteen. Kittens will turn into cats. (*Sighs.*) I live all week long for these few minutes with you—you know that?
LI'L BIT: I'll drive.

(*A Voice cuts in with:*)

Idling in the Neutral Gear.

(*Sound of car revving cuts off the sacred music; Li'l Bit, now an adult, rises out of the car and comes to us.*)

LI'L BIT: In most families, relatives get names like "Junior," or "Brother," or "Bubba." In my family, if we call someone "Big Papa," it's not because he's tall. In my family, folks tend to get nicknamed for their genitalia. Uncle Peck, for example. My mama's adage was "the titless wonder," and my cousin Bobby got branded for life as "B.B."

(*In unison with Greek Chorus:*)

LI'L BIT: For blue balls.   GREEK CHORUS: For blue balls.
FEMALE GREEK CHORUS (*as Mother*): And of course, we were so excited to have a baby girl that when the nurse brought you in and said, "It's a girl! It's a baby girl!" I just had to see for myself. So we whipped your diapers down and parted your chubby little legs—and right between your legs there was—

(*Peck has come over during the above and chimes along:*)

PECK: Just a little bit.   GREEK CHORUS: Just a little bit.
FEMALE GREEK CHORUS (*as Mother*): And when you were born, you were so tiny that you fit in Uncle Peck's outstretched hand.

(*Peck stretches his hand out.*)

PECK: Now that's a fact. I held you, one day old, right in this hand.

(*A traffic signal is projected of a bicycle in a circle with a diagonal red slash.*)

LI'L BIT: Even with my family background, I was sixteen or so before I realized that pedophilia did not mean people who loved to bicycle . . . .

(*A Voice intrudes:*)

Driving in First Gear.

LI'L BIT: 1969. A typical family dinner.
FEMALE GREEK CHORUS (*as Mother*): Look, Grandma. Li'l Bit's getting to be as big in the bust as you are.
LI'L BIT: Mother! Could we please change the subject?
TEENAGE GREEK CHORUS (*as Grandmother*): Well, I hope you are buying her some decent bras. I never had a decent bra, growing up in the Depression, and now my shoulders are just crippled—crippled from the weight hanging on my shoulders—the dents from my bra straps are big enough to put your finger in.—Here, let me show you—

(*As Grandmother starts to open her blouse:*)

LI'L BIT: Grandma! Please don't undress at the dinner table.
PECK: I thought the entertainment came *after* the dinner.
LI'L BIT (*to the audience*): This is how it always starts. My grandfather, Big Papa, will chime in next with—
MALE GREEK CHORUS (*as Grandfather*): Yup. If Li'l Bit gets any bigger, we're gonna haveta buy her a wheelbarrow to carry in front of her—
LI'L BIT:—Damn it—
PECK:—How about those Redskins on Sunday, Big Papa?
LI'L BIT (*to the audience*): The only sport Big Papa followed was chasing Grandma around the house—
MALE GREEK CHORUS (*as Grandfather*):—Or we could write to Kate Smith. Ask her for somma her used brassieres she don't want anymore—she could maybe give to Li'l Bit here—
LI'L BIT:—I can't stand it. I can't.
PECK: Now, honey, that's just their way—
FEMALE GREEK CHORUS (*as Mother*): I tell you, Grandma, Li'l Bit's at that age. She's so sensitive, you can't say boo—
LI'L BIT: I'd like some privacy, that's all. Okay? Some goddamn privacy—
PECK:—Well, at least she didn't use the savior's name—
LI'L BIT (*to the audience*): And Big Papa wouldn't let a dead dog lie. No sirree.
MALE GREEK CHORUS (*as Grandfather*): Well, she'd better stop being so sensitive. 'Cause five minutes before Li'l Bit turns the corner, her tits turn first—

LI'L BIT (*starting to rise from the table*):—That's it. That's it.

PECK: Li'l Bit, you can't let him get to you. Then he wins.

LI'L BIT: I hate him. *Hate* him.

PECK: That's fine. But hate him and eat a good dinner at the same time.

(*Li'l Bit calms down and sits with perfect dignity.*)

LI'L BIT: The gumbo is really good, Grandma.

MALE GREEK CHORUS (*as Grandfather*): A'course, Li'l Bit's got a big surprise coming for her when she goes to that fancy college this fall—

PECK: Big Papa—let it go.

MALE GREEK CHORUS (*as Grandfather*): What does she need a college degree for? She's got all the credentials she'll need on her chest—

LI'L BIT:—Maybe I want to learn things. Read. Rise above my cracker° background—

PECK:—Whoa, now, Li'l Bit—

MALE GREEK CHORUS (*as Grandfather*): What kind of things do you want to read?

LI'L BIT: There's a whole semester course, for example, on Shakespeare—

(*Greek Chorus, as Grandfather, laughs until he weeps.*)

MALE GREEK CHORUS (*as Grandfather*): Shakespeare. That's a good one. Shakespeare is really going to help you in life.

PECK: I think it's wonderful. And on scholarship!

MALE GREEK CHORUS (*as Grandfather*): How is Shakespeare going to help her lie on her back in the dark?

(*Li'l Bit is on her feet.*)

LI'L BIT: You're getting old, Big Papa. You are going to die—very very soon. Maybe even *tonight*. And when you get to heaven, God's going to be a beautiful black woman in a long white robe. She's gonna look at your chart and say: Uh-oh. Fornication. Dog-ugly mean with blood relatives. Oh. Uh-oh. Voted for George Wallace. Well, one last chance: If you can name the play, all will be forgiven. And then she'll quote: "The quality of mercy is not strained." Your answer? Oh, too bad—*Merchant of Venice*: Act IV, Scene iii. And then she'll send your ass to fry in hell with all the other crackers. Excuse me, please.
   (*To the audience.*) And as I left the house, I would always hear Big Papa say:

MALE GREEK CHORUS (*as Grandfather*): Lucy, your daughter's got a mouth on her. Well, no sense in wasting good gumbo. Pass me her plate, Mama.

LI'L BIT: And Aunt Mary would come up to Uncle Peck:

FEMALE GREEK CHORUS (*as Aunt Mary*): Peck, go after her, will you? You're the only one she'll listen to when she gets like this.

PECK: She just needs to cool off.

---

cracker: A derogatory term for a poor, southern, white person.

FEMALE GREEK CHORUS (*as Aunt Mary*): Please, honey— Grandma's been on her feet cooking all day.

PECK: All right.

LI'L BIT: And as he left the room, Aunt Mary would say:

FEMALE GREEK CHORUS (*as Aunt Mary*): Peck's so good with them when they get to be this age.

(*Li'l Bit has stormed to another part of the stage, her back turned, weeping with a teenage fury. Peck, cautiously, as if stalking a deer, comes to her. She turns away even more. He waits a bit.*)

PECK: I don't suppose you're talking to family. (*No response.*) Does it help that I'm in-law?

LI'L BIT: Don't you dare make fun of this.

PECK: I'm not. There's nothing funny about this. (*Beat.*) Although I'll bet when Big Papa is about to meet his maker, he'll remember *The Merchant of Venice*.

LI'L BIT: I've got to get away from here.

PECK: You're going away. Soon. Here, take this.

(*Peck hands her his folded handkerchief. Li'l Bit uses it, noisily. Hands it back. Without her seeing, he reverently puts it back.*)

LI'L BIT: I hate this family.

PECK: Your grandfather's ignorant. And you're right— he's going to die soon. But he's family. Family is . . . family.

LI'L BIT: Grown-ups are always saying that. Family.

PECK: Well, when you get a little older, you'll see what we're saying.

LI'L BIT: Uh-huh. So family is another acquired taste, like French kissing?

PECK: Come again?

LI'L BIT: You know, at first it really grosses you out, but in time you grow to like it?

PECK: Girl, you are . . . a handful.

LI'L BIT: Uncle Peck—you have the keys to your car?

PECK: Where do you want to go?

LI'L BIT: Just up the road.

PECK: I'll come with you.

LI'L BIT: No—please? I just need to . . . to drive for a little bit. Alone.

(*Peck tosses her the keys.*)

PECK: When can I see you alone again?

LI'L BIT: Tonight.

(*Li'l Bit crosses to center stage while the lights dim around her. A Voice directs:*)

Shifting Forward from First to Second Gear.

LI'L BIT: There were a lot of rumors about why I got kicked out of that fancy school in 1970. Some say I got caught with a man in my room. Some say as a kid on scholarship I fooled around with a rich man's daughter.
   (*Li'l Bit smiles innocently at the audience.*) I'm not talking.

But the real truth was I had a constant companion in my dorm room—who was less than discreet. Canadian V.O. A fifth a day.

1970. A Nixon recession. I slept on the floors of friends who were out of work themselves. Took factory work when I could find it. A string of dead-end jobs that didn't last very long.

What I did, most nights, was cruise the Beltway and the back roads of Maryland, where there was still country, past the battlefields and farm houses. Racing in a 1965 Mustang—and as long as I had gasoline for my car and whiskey for me, the nights would pass. Full tanked, I would speed past the churches and the trees on the bend, thinking just one notch of the steering wheel would be all it would take, and yet some . . . reflex took over. My hands on the wheel in the nine and three o'clock position—I never so much as got a ticket. He taught me well.

(*A Voice announces:*)

You and the Reverse Gear.

LI'L BIT: Back up. 1968. On the Eastern Shore. A celebration dinner.

(*Li'l Bit joins Peck at a table in a restaurant.*)

PECK: Feeling better, missy?

LI'L BIT: The bathroom's really amazing here, Uncle Peck! They have these little soaps—instead of borax or something—and they're in the shape of shells.

PECK: I'll have to take a trip to the gentleman's room just to see.

LI'L BIT: How did you know about this place?

PECK: This inn is famous on the Eastern Shore—it's been open since the seventeenth century. And I know how you like history. . . .

(*Li'l Bit is shy and pleased.*)

LI'L BIT: It's great.

PECK: And you've just done your first, legal, long-distance drive. You must be hungry.

LI'L BIT: I'm starved.

PECK: I would suggest a dozen oysters to start, and the crab imperial. . . . (*Li'l Bit is genuinely agog.*) You might be interested to know the town history. When the British sailed up this very river in the dead of night—see outside where I'm pointing?—they were going to bombard the heck out of this town. But the town fathers were ready for them. They crept up all the trees with lanterns so that the British would think they saw the town lights and they aimed their cannons too high. And that's why the inn is still here for business today.

LI'L BIT: That's a great story.

PECK (*casually*): Would you like to start with a cocktail?

LI'L BIT: You're not . . . you're not going to start drinking, are you, Uncle Peck?

PECK: Not me. I told you, as long as you're with me, I'll never drink. I asked you if *you'd* like a cocktail

before dinner. It's nice to have a little something with the oysters.

LI'L BIT: But . . . I'm not . . . legal. We could get arrested. Uncle Peck, they'll never believe I'm twenty-one!

PECK: So? Today we celebrate your driver's license—on the first try. This establishment reminds me a lot of places back home.

LI'L BIT: What does that mean?

PECK: In South Carolina, like here on the Eastern Shore, they're . . . (*Searches for the right euphemism.*) . . . "European." Not so puritanical. And very understanding if gentlemen wish to escort very attractive young ladies who might want a before-dinner cocktail. If you want one, I'll order one.

LI'L BIT: Well—sure. Just . . . one.

(*The Female Greek Chorus appears in a spot.*)

FEMALE GREEK CHORUS (*as Mother*): A Mother's Guide to Social Drinking:

A lady never gets sloppy—she may, however, get tipsy and a little gay.

Never drink on an empty stomach. Avail yourself of the bread basket and generous portions of butter. *Slather* the butter on your bread.

Sip your drink, slowly, let the beverage linger in your mouth—interspersed with interesting, fascinating conversation. Sip, never . . . slurp or gulp. Your glass should always be three-quarters full when his glass is empty.

Stay away from *ladies'* drinks: drinks like pink ladies, slow gin fizzes, piña coladas, mai tais, planter's punch, white Russians, black Russians, red Russians, melon balls, blue balls, hummingbirds, hemorrhages, and hurricanes. In short, avoid anything with sugar, or anything with an umbrella. Get your vitamin C from *fruit*. Don't order anything with Voodoo or Vixen in the title or sexual positions in the name like Dead Man Screw or the Missionary. (*She sort of titters.*)

Believe me, they are lethal. . . . I think you were conceived after one of those.

Drink, instead, like a man: straight up or on the rocks, with plenty of water in between.

Oh, yes. And never mix your drinks. Stay with one all night long, like the man you came in with: bourbon, gin, or tequila till dawn, damn the torpedoes, full speed ahead!

(*As the Female Greek Chorus retreats, the Male Greek Chorus approaches the table as a Waiter.*)

MALE GREEK CHORUS (*as Waiter*): I hope you all are having a pleasant evening. Is there something I can bring you, sir, before you order?

(*Li'l Bit waits in anxious fear. Carefully, Uncle Peck says with command:*)

PECK: I'll have a plain iced tea. The lady would like a drink, I believe.

(The Male Greek Chorus does a double take; there is a moment when Uncle Peck and he are in silent communication.)

MALE GREEK CHORUS (*as Waiter*): Very good. What would the . . . lady like?

LI'L BIT (*a bit flushed*): Is there . . . is there any sugar in a martini?

PECK: None that I know of.

LI'L BIT: That's what I'd like then — a dry martini. And could we maybe have some bread?

PECK: A drink fit for a woman of the world. — Please bring the lady a dry martini, be generous with the olives, straight up.

(The Male Greek Chorus anticipates a large tip.)

MALE GREEK CHORUS (*as Waiter*): Right away. Very good, sir.

(The Male Greek Chorus returns with an empty martini glass which he puts in front of Li'l Bit.)

PECK: Your glass is empty. Another martini, madam?

LI'L BIT: Yes, thank you.

(Peck signals the Male Greek Chorus, who nods.)

So why did you leave South Carolina, Uncle Peck?

PECK: I was stationed in D.C. after the war, and decided to stay. Go North, Young Man, someone might have said.

LI'L BIT: What did you do in the service anyway?

PECK (*suddenly taciturn*): I . . . I did just this and that. Nothing heroic or spectacular.

LI'L BIT: But did you see fighting? Or go to Europe?

PECK: I served in the Pacific Theater. It's really nothing interesting to talk about.

LI'L BIT: It is to me. (*The Waiter has brought another empty glass.*) Oh, goody. I love the color of the swizzle sticks. What were we talking about?

PECK: Swizzle sticks.

LI'L BIT: Do you ever think of going back?

PECK: To the Marines?

LI'L BIT: No — to South Carolina.

PECK: Well, we do go back. To visit.

LI'L BIT: No, I mean to live.

PECK: Not very likely. I think it's better if my mother doesn't have a daily reminder of her disappointment.

LI'L BIT: Are these floorboards slanted?

PECK: Yes, the floor is very slanted. I think this is the original floor.

LI'L BIT: Oh, good.

(The Female Greek Chorus as Mother enters swaying a little, a little past tipsy.)

FEMALE GREEK CHORUS (*as Mother*): Don't leave your drink unattended when you visit the ladies' room. There is such a thing as white slavery; the modus operandi is to spike an unsuspecting young girl's drink with a "mickey" when she's left the room to powder her nose.

But if you feel you have had more than your sufficiency in liquor, do go to the ladies' room — often. Pop your head out of doors for a refreshing breath of the night air. If you must, wet your face and head with tap water. Don't be afraid to dunk your head if necessary. A wet woman is still less conspicuous than a drunk woman.

(The Female Greek Chorus stumbles a little; conspiratorially.) When in the course of human events it becomes necessary, go to a corner stall and insert the index and middle finger down the throat almost to the epiglottis. Divulge your stomach contents by such persuasion, and then wait a few moments before rejoining your beau waiting for you at your table.

Oh, no. Don't be shy or embarrassed. In the very best of establishments, there's always one or two debutantes crouched in the corner stalls, their beaded purses tossed willy-nilly, sounding like cats in heat, heaving up the contents of their stomachs.

(The Female Greek Chorus begins to wander off.)

I wonder what is it they do in the men's rooms. . . .

LI'L BIT: So why is your mother disappointed in you, Uncle Peck?

LI'L BIT: Every mother in Horry County has Great Expectations.

LI'L BIT: — Could I have another mar-ti-ni, please?

PECK: I think this is your last one.

(Peck signals the Waiter. The Waiter looks at Li'l Bit and shakes his head no. Peck raises his eyebrow, raises his finger to indicate one more, and then rubs his fingers together. It looks like a secret code. The Waiter sighs, shakes his head sadly, and brings over another empty martini glass. He glares at Peck.)

LI'L BIT: The name of the county where you grew up is "Horry"? (*Li'l Bit, plastered, begins to laugh. Then she stops.*) I think your mother should be proud of you.

(Peck signals for the check.)

PECK: Well, missy, she wanted me to do — to *be* everything my father was not. She wanted me to amount to something.

LI'L BIT: But you have! You've amounted a lot. . . .

PECK: I'm just a very ordinary man.

(The Waiter has brought the check and waits. Peck draws out a large bill and hands it to the Waiter. Li'l Bit is in the soppy stage.)

LI'L BIT: I'll bet your mother loves you, Uncle Peck.

(Peck freezes a bit. To Male Greek Chorus as Waiter:)

PECK: Thank you. The service was exceptional. Please keep the change.

MALE GREEK CHORUS (*as Waiter, in a tone that could freeze*): Thank you, sir. Will you be needing any help?

PECK: I think we can manage, thank you.

(*Just then, the Female Greek Chorus as Mother lurches on stage; the Male Greek Chorus as Waiter escorts her off as she delivers:*)

FEMALE GREEK CHORUS (*as Mother*): Thanks to judicious planning and several trips to the ladies' loo, your mother once out-drank an entire regiment of British officers on a good-will visit to Washington! Every last man of them! Milquetoasts! How'd they ever kick Hitler's cahones, huh? No match for an American lady — I could drink every man in here under the table.
    (*She delivers one last crucial hint before she is gently "bounced."*)
    As a last resort, when going out for an evening on the town, be sure to wear a skin-tight girdle — so tight that only a surgical knife or acetylene torch can get it off you — so that if you do pass out in the arms of your escort, he'll end up with rubber burns on his fingers before he can steal your virtue —

(*A Voice punctures the interlude with:*)

Vehicle Failure.
Even with careful maintenance and preventive operation of your automobile, it is all too common for us to experience an unexpected breakdown. If you are driving at any speed when a breakdown occurs, you must slow down and guide the automobile to the side of the road.

(*Peck is slowly propping up Li'l Bit as they work their way to his car in the parking lot of the inn.*)

PECK: How are you doing, missy?
LI'L BIT: It's so far to the car, Uncle Peck. Like the lanterns in the trees the British fired on. . . .

(*Li'l Bit stumbles. Peck swoops her up in his arms.*)

PECK: Okay, I think we're going to take a more direct route.

(*Li'l Bit closes her eyes.*)

    Dizzy?

(*She nods her head.*)

    Don't look at the ground. Almost there — do you feel sick to your stomach?

(*Li'l Bit nods. They reach the "car." Peck gently deposits her on the front seat.*)

    Just settle here a little while until things stop spinning.

(*Li'l Bit opens her eyes.*)

LI'L BIT: What are we doing?
PECK: We're just going to sit here until your tummy settles down.
LI'L BIT: It's such nice upholst'ry —
PECK: Think you can go for a ride, now?

LI'L BIT: Where are you taking me?
PECK: Home.
LI'L BIT: You're not taking me — upstairs? There's no room at the inn? (*Li'l Bit giggles.*)
PECK: Do you want to go upstairs?

(*Li'l Bit doesn't answer.*)

    Or home?
LI'L BIT: — This isn't right, Uncle Peck.
PECK: What isn't right?
LI'L BIT: What we're doing. It's wrong. It's very wrong.
PECK: What are we doing?

(*Li'l Bit does not answer.*)

    We're just going out to dinner.
LI'L BIT: You know. It's not nice to Aunt Mary.
PECK: You let me be the judge of what's nice and not nice to my wife.

(*Beat.*)

LI'L BIT: Now you're mad.
PECK: I'm not mad. It's just that I thought you . . . understood me, Li'l Bit. I think you're the only one who does.
LI'L BIT: Someone will get hurt.
PECK: Have I forced you to do anything?

(*There is a long pause as Li'l Bit tries to get sober enough to think this through.*)

LI'L BIT: . . . I guess not.
PECK: We are just enjoying each other's company. I've told you, nothing is going to happen between us until you want it to. Do you know that?
LI'L BIT: Yes.
PECK: Nothing is going to happen until you want it. (*A second more, with Peck staring ahead at the river while seated at the wheel of his car. Then, softly:*) Do you want something to happen?

(*Peck reaches over and strokes her face, very gently. Li'l Bit softens, reaches for him, and buries her head in his neck. Then she kisses him. Then she moves away, dizzy again.*)

LI'L BIT: . . . I don't know.

(*Peck smiles; this has been good news for him — it hasn't been a "no."*)

PECK: Then I'll wait. I'm a very patient man. I've been waiting for a long time. I don't mind waiting.
LI'L BIT: Someone is going to get hurt.
PECK: No one is going to get hurt. (*Li'l Bit closes her eyes.*) Are you feeling sick?
LI'L BIT: Sleepy.

(*Carefully, Peck props Li'l Bit up on the seat.*)

PECK: Stay here a second.
LI'L BIT: Where're you going?
PECK: I'm getting something from the back seat.

LI'L BIT (*scared; too loud*): What? What are you going to do?

(*Peck reappears in the front seat with a lap rug.*)

PECK: Shhh. (*Peck covers Li'l Bit. She calms down.*) There. Think you can sleep?

(*Li'l Bit nods. She slides over to rest on his shoulder. With a look of happiness, Peck turns the ignition key. Beat. Peck leaves Li'l Bit sleeping in the car and strolls down to the audience. Wagner's Flying Dutchman comes up faintly.*) (*A Voice interjects:*)

Idling in the Neutral Gear.

TEENAGE GREEK CHORUS: Uncle Peck Teaches Cousin Bobby How to Fish.

PECK: I get back once or twice a year—supposedly to visit Mama and the family, but the real truth is to fish. I miss this the most of all. There's a smell in the Low Country—where the swamp and fresh inlet join the saltwater—a scent of sand and cypress, that I haven't found anywhere yet.

I don't say this very often up North because it will just play into the stereotype everyone has, but I will tell you: I didn't wear shoes in the summertime until I was sixteen. It's unnatural down here to pen up your feet in leather. Go ahead—take 'em off. Let yourself breathe—it really will make you feel better.

We're going to aim for some pompano today— and I have to tell you, they're a very shy, mercurial fish. Takes patience, and psychology. You have to believe it doesn't matter if you catch one or not.

Sky's pretty spectacular—there's some beer in the cooler next to the crab salad I packed, so help yourself if you get hungry. Are you hungry? Thirsty? Holler if you are.

Okay. You don't want to lean over the bridge like that—pompano feed in shallow water, and you don't want to get too close—they're frisky and shy little things—wait, check your line. Yep, something's been munching while we were talking.

Okay, look: We take the sand flea and you take the hook like this—right through his little sand flea rump. Sand fleas should always keep their backs to the wall. Okay. Cast it in, like I showed you. That's great! I can taste that pompano now, sautéed with some pecans and butter, a little bourbon—now—let it lie on the bottom—now, reel, jerk, reel, jerk—

Look—look at your line. There's something calling, all right. Okay, tip the rod up—not too sharp— hook it—all right, now easy, reel and then rest—let it play. And reel—play it out, that's right—really good! I can't believe it! It's a pompano.—Good work! Way to go! You are an official fisherman now. Pompano are hard to catch. We are going to have a delicious little—

What? Well, I don't know how much pain a fish feels—you can't think of that. Oh, no, don't cry, come on now, it's just a fish—the other guys are going to see you.—No, no, you're just real sensitive, and I think that's wonderful at your age—look, do you want me to cut it free? You do?

Okay, hand me those pliers—look—I'm cutting the hook—okay? And we're just going to drop it in— no I'm not mad. It's just for fun, okay? There—it's going to swim back to its lady friend and tell her what a terrible day it had and she's going to stroke him with her fins until he feels better, and then they'll do something alone together that will make them both feel good and sleepy. . . .

(*Peck bends down, very earnest.*) I don't want you to feel ashamed about crying. I'm not going to tell anyone, okay? I can keep secrets. You know, men cry all the time. They just don't tell anybody, and they don't let anybody catch them. There's nothing you could do that would make me feel ashamed of you. Do you know that? Okay. (*Peck straightens up, smiles.*)

Do you want to pack up and call it a day? I tell you what—I think I can still remember—there's a really neat tree house where I used to stay for days. I think it's still here—it was the last time I looked. But it's a secret place—you can't tell anybody we've gone there—least of all your mom or your sisters.—This is something special just between you and me. Sound good? We'll climb up there and have a beer and some crab salad—okay, B.B.? Bobby? Robert. . . .

(*Li'l Bit sits at a kitchen table with the two Female Greek Chorus members.*)

LI'L BIT (*to the audience*): Three women, three generations, sit at the kitchen table.
    On Men, Sex, and Women: Part I:

FEMALE GREEK CHORUS (*as Mother*): Men only want one thing.

LI'L BIT (*wide-eyed*): But what? What is it they want?

FEMALE GREEK CHORUS (*as Mother*): And once they have it, they lose all interest. So Don't Give It to Them.

TEENAGE GREEK CHORUS (*as Grandmother*): I never had the luxury of the rhythm method. Your grandfather is just a big bull. A big bull. Every morning, every evening.

FEMALE GREEK CHORUS (*as Mother, whispers to Li'l Bit*): And he used to come home for lunch every day.

LI'L BIT: My god, Grandma!

TEENAGE GREEK CHORUS (*as Grandmother*): Your grandfather only cares that I do two things: have the table set and the bed turned down.

FEMALE GREEK CHORUS (*as Mother*): And in all that time, Mother, you never have experienced—?

LI'L BIT (*to the audience*):—Now my grandmother believed in all the sacraments of the church, to the day she died. She believed in Santa Claus and the Easter Bunny until she was fifteen. But she didn't believe in—

TEENAGE GREEK CHORUS (*as Grandmother*):— Orgasm! That's just something you and Mary have made up! I don't believe you.

FEMALE GREEK CHORUS (*as Mother*): Mother, it happens to women all the time—

TEENAGE GREEK CHORUS (*as Grandmother*):—Oh, now you're going to tell me about the G force!

LI'L BIT: No, Grandma, I think that's astronauts—

FEMALE GREEK CHORUS (*as Mother*): Well, Mama, after all, you were a child bride when Big Papa came and got you—you were a married woman and you still believed in Santa Claus.

TEENAGE GREEK CHORUS (*as Grandmother*): It was legal, what Daddy and I did! I was fourteen and in those days, fourteen was a grown-up woman—

(*Big Papa shuffles in the kitchen for a cookie.*)

MALE GREEK CHORUS (*as Grandfather*):—Oh, now we're off on Grandma and the Rape of the Sa-bean Women!

TEENAGE GREEK CHORUS (*as Grandmother*): Well, you were the one in such a big hurry—

MALE GREEK CHORUS (*as Grandfather to Li'l Bit*):— I picked your grandmother out of that herd of sisters just like a lion chooses the gazelle—the plump, slow, flaky gazelle dawdling at the edge of the herd—your sisters were too smart and too fast and too scrawny—

LI'L BIT (*to the audience*):—The family story is that when Big Papa came for Grandma, my Aunt Lily was waiting for him with a broom—and she beat him over the head all the way down the stairs as he was carrying out Grandma's hope chest—

MALE GREEK CHORUS (*as Grandfather*):—And they were *mean*. 'Specially Lily.

FEMALE GREEK CHORUS (*as Mother*): Well, you were robbing the baby of the family!

TEENAGE GREEK CHORUS (*as Grandmother*): I still keep a broom handy in the kitchen! And I know how to use it! So get your hand out of the cookie jar and don't you spoil your appetite for dinner—out of the kitchen!

(*Male Greek Chorus as Grandfather leaves chuckling with a cookie.*)

FEMALE GREEK CHORUS (*as Mother*): Just one thing a married woman needs to know how to use—the rolling pin or the broom. I prefer a heavy, cast-iron fry pan—they're great on a man's head, no matter how thick the skull is.

TEENAGE GREEK CHORUS (*as Grandmother*): Yes, sir, your father is ruled by only two bosses! Mr. Gut and Mr. Peter! And sometimes, first thing in the morning, Mr. Sphincter Muscle!

FEMALE GREEK CHORUS (*as Mother*): It's true. Men are like children. Just like little boys.

TEENAGE GREEK CHORUS (*as Grandmother*): Men are bulls! Big bulls!

(*The Greek Chorus is getting aroused.*)

FEMALE GREEK CHORUS (*as Mother*): They'd still be crouched on their haunches over a fire in a cave if we hadn't cleaned them up!

TEENAGE GREEK CHORUS (*as Grandmother, flushed*): Coming in smelling of sweat—

FEMALE GREEK CHORUS (*as Mother*):—Looking at those naughty pictures like boys in a dime store with a dollar in their pockets!

TEENAGE GREEK CHORUS (*as Grandmother; raucous*): No matter to them what they smell like! They've got to have it, right then, on the spot, right there! Nasty!—

FEMALE GREEK CHORUS (*as Mother*):—Vulgar!

TEENAGE GREEK CHORUS (*as Grandmother*): Primitive!—

FEMALE GREEK CHORUS (*as Mother*):—Hot!—

LI'L BIT: And just about then, Big Papa would shuffle in with—

MALE GREEK CHORUS (*as Grandfather*):—What are you all cackling about in here?

TEENAGE GREEK CHORUS (*as Grandmother*): Stay out of the kitchen! This is just for girls!

(*As Grandfather leaves:*)

MALE GREEK CHORUS (*as Grandfather*): Lucy, you'd better not be filling Mama's head with sex! Every time you and Mary come over and start in about sex, when I ask a simple question like, "What time is dinner going to be ready?," Mama snaps my head off!

TEENAGE GREEK CHORUS (*as Grandmother*): Dinner will be ready when I'm good and ready! Stay out of this kitchen!

(*Li'l Bit steps out.*)

(*A Voice directs:*)

When Making a Left Turn, You Must Downshift While Going Forward.

LI'L BIT: 1979. A long bus trip to Upstate New York. I settled in to read, when a young man sat beside me.

MALE GREEK CHORUS (*as Young Man; voice cracking*): "What are you reading?"

LI'L BIT: He asked. His voice broke into that miserable equivalent of vocal acne, not quite falsetto and not tenor, either. I glanced a side view. He was appealing in an odd way, huge ears at a defiant angle springing forward at ninety degrees. He must have been shaving, because his face, with a peach sheen, was speckled with nicks and styptic. "I have a class tomorrow," I told him.

MALE GREEK CHORUS (*as Young Man*): "You're taking a class?"

LI'L BIT: "I'm teaching a class." He concentrated on lowering his voice.

MALE GREEK CHORUS (*as Young Man*): "I'm a senior. Walt Whitman High."

LI'L BIT: The light was fading outside, so perhaps he was—with a very high voice.

I felt his "interest" quicken. Five steps ahead of the hopes in his head, I slowed down, waited, pretended surprise, acted at listening, all the while knowing we would get off the bus, he would just then seem to think to ask me to dinner, he would chivalrously insist on walking me home, he would continue to converse in the street until I would casually invite him up to my room—and—I was only into the second moment of conversation and I could see the whole evening before me.

And dramaturgically speaking, after the faltering and slightly comical "first act," there was the very briefest of intermissions, and an extremely capable and forceful and *sustained* second act. And after the second act climax and a gentle denouement—before the post-play discussion—I lay on my back in the dark and I thought about you, Uncle Peck. Oh. Oh—this is the allure. Being older. Being the first. Being the translator, the teacher, the epicure, the already jaded. This is how the giver gets taken.

(*Li'l Bit changes her tone.*) On Men, Sex, and Women: Part II:

(*Li'l Bit steps back into the scene as a fifteen-year-old, gawky and quiet, as the gazelle at the edge of the herd.*)

TEENAGE GREEK CHORUS (*as Grandmother, to Li'l Bit*): You're being mighty quiet, missy. Cat Got Your Tongue?

LI'L BIT: I'm just listening. Just thinking.

TEENAGE GREEK CHORUS (*as Grandmother*): Oh, yes, Little Miss Radar Ears? Soaking it all in? Little Miss Sponge? Penny for your thoughts?

(*Li'l Bit hesitates to ask but she really wants to know.*)

LI'L BIT: Does it—when you do it—you know, theoretically when I do it and I haven't done it before—I mean—does it hurt?

FEMALE GREEK CHORUS (*as Mother*): Does what hurt, honey?

LI'L BIT: When a . . . when a girl does it for the first time—with a man—does it hurt?

TEENAGE GREEK CHORUS (*as Grandmother; horrified*): *That's* what you're thinking about?

FEMALE GREEK CHORUS (*as Mother, calm*): Well, just a little bit. Like a pinch. And there's a little blood.

TEENAGE GREEK CHORUS (*as Grandmother*): Don't tell her that! She's too young to be thinking those things!

FEMALE GREEK CHORUS (*as Mother*): Well, if she doesn't find out from me, where is she going to find out? In the street?

TEENAGE GREEK CHORUS (*as Grandmother*): Tell her it hurts! It's agony! You think you're going to die! Especially if you do it before marriage!

FEMALE GREEK CHORUS (*as Mother*): Mama! I'm going to tell her the truth! Unlike you, you left me and Mary completely in the dark with fairy tales and told us to go to the priest! What does an eighty-year-old priest know about lovemaking with girls!

LI'L BIT (*getting upset*): It's not fair!

FEMALE GREEK CHORUS (*as Mother*): Now, see, she's getting upset—you're scaring her.

TEENAGE GREEK CHORUS (*as Grandmother*): Good! Let her be good and scared! It hurts! You bleed like a

Tim Crowe as Uncle Peck and Annie Sullivan as Li'l Bit in the Trinity Repertory Theater's production of *How I Learned to Drive.*

stuck pig! And you lay there and say, "Why, O Lord, have you forsaken me?!"

LI'L BIT: It's not fair! Why does everything have to hurt for girls? Why is there always blood?

FEMALE GREEK CHORUS (*as Mother*): It's not a lot of blood—and it feels wonderful after the pain subsides. . . .

TEENAGE GREEK CHORUS (*as Grandmother*): You're encouraging her to just go out and find out with the first drugstore joe who buys her a milkshake!

FEMALE GREEK CHORUS (*as Mother*): Don't be scared. It won't hurt you—if the man you go to bed with really loves you. It's important that he loves you.

TEENAGE GREEK CHORUS (*as Grandmother*):—Why don't you just go out and rent a motel room for her, Lucy?

FEMALE GREEK CHORUS (*as Mother*): I believe in telling my daughter the truth! We have a very close relationship! I want her to be able to ask me anything—I'm not scaring her with stories about Eve's sin and snakes crawling on their bellies for eternity and women bearing children in mortal pain—

TEENAGE GREEK CHORUS (*as Grandmother*):—If she stops and thinks before she takes her knickers off, maybe someone in this family will finish high school!

(*Li'l Bit knows what is about to happen and starts to retreat from the scene at this point.*)

FEMALE GREEK CHORUS (*as Mother*): Mother! If you and Daddy had helped me—I wouldn't have had to marry that—that no-good-son-of-a—

TEENAGE GREEK CHORUS (*as Grandmother*):—He was good enough for you on a full moon! I hold you responsible!

FEMALE GREEK CHORUS (*as Mother*):—You could have helped me! You could have told me something about the facts of life!

TEENAGE GREEK CHORUS (*as Grandmother*):—I told you what my mother told me! A girl with her skirt up can outrun a man with his pants down!

(*The Male Greek Chorus enters the fray; Li'l Bit edges farther downstage.*)

FEMALE GREEK CHORUS (*as Mother*): And when I turned to you for a little help, all I got afterwards was—

MALE GREEK CHORUS (*as Grandfather*): You Made Your Bed; Now Lie On It!

(*The Greek Chorus freezes, mouths open, argumentatively.*)

LI'L BIT (*to the audience*): Oh, please! I still can't bear to listen to it, after all these years—

(*The Male Greek Chorus "unfreezes," but out of his open mouth, as if to his surprise, comes a bass refrain from a Motown song.*)

MALE GREEK CHORUS: "Do-Bee-Do-Wah!"

(*The Female Greek Chorus member is also surprised; but she, too, unfreezes.*)

FEMALE GREEK CHORUS: "Shoo-doo-be-doo-be-doo; shoo-doo-be-doo-be-doo."

(*The Male and Female Greek Chorus members continue with their harmony, until the Teenage member of the Chorus starts in with Motown lyrics such as "Dedicated to the One I Love," or "In the Still of the Night," or "Hold Me"—any Sam Cooke will do. The three modulate down into three-part harmony, softly, until they are submerged by the actual recording playing over the radio in the car in which Uncle Peck sits in the driver's seat, waiting. Li'l Bit sits in the passenger's seat.*)

LI'L BIT: Ahh. That's better.

(*Uncle Peck reaches over and turns the volume down; to Li'l Bit:*)

PECK: How can you hear yourself think?

(*Li'l Bit does not answer.*)

(*A Voice insinuates itself in the pause:*)

Before You Drive.
Always check under your car for obstructions—broken bottles, fallen tree branches, and the bodies of small children. Each year hundreds of children are crushed beneath the wheels of unwary drivers in their own driveways. Children depend on you to watch them.

(*Pause.*)

(*The Voice continues:*)

You and the Reverse Gear.

(*In the following section, it would be nice to have slides of erotic photographs of women and cars: women posed over the hood; women draped along the sideboards; women with water hoses spraying the car; and the actress playing Li'l Bit with a Bel Air or any 1950s car one can find for the finale.*)

LI'L BIT: 1967. In a parking lot of the Beltsville Agricultural Farms. The Initiation into a Boy's First Love.

PECK (*with a soft look on his face*): Of course, my favorite car will always be the '56 Bel Air Sports Coupe. Chevy sold more '55s, but the '56!—a V-8 with Corvette option, 225 horsepower; went from zero to sixty miles per hour in 8.9 seconds.

LI'L BIT (*to the audience*): Long after a mother's tits, but before a woman's breasts:

PECK: Super-Turbo-Fire! What a Power Pack—mechanical lifters, twin four-barrel carbs, lightweight valves, dual exhausts—

LI'L BIT (*to the audience*): After the milk but before the beer:

PECK: A specific intake manifold, higher-lift camshaft, and the tightest squeeze Chevy had ever made—

LI'L BIT (*to the audience*): Long after he's squeezed down the birth canal but before he's pushed his way back in: The boy falls in love with the thing that bears his weight with speed.

PECK: I want you to know your automobile inside and out. — Are you there? Li'l Bit?

(*Slides end here.*)

LI'L BIT: — What?

PECK: You're drifting. I need you to concentrate.

LI'L BIT: Sorry.

PECK: Okay. Get into the driver's seat. (*Li'l Bit does.*) Okay. Now. Show me what you're going to do before you start the car.

(*Li'l Bit sits, with her hands in her lap. She starts to giggle.*)

LI'L BIT: I don't know, Uncle Peck.

PECK: Now, come on. What's the first thing you're going to adjust?

LI'L BIT: My bra strap? —

PECK: — Li'l Bit. What's the most important thing to have control of on the inside of the car?

LI'L BIT: That's easy. The radio. I tune the radio from Mama's old fart tunes to —

(*Li'l Bit turns the radio up so we can hear a 1960s tune. With surprising firmness, Peck commands:*)

PECK: — Radio off. Right now. (*Li'l Bit turns the radio off.*) When you are driving your car, with your license, you can fiddle with the stations all you want. But when you are driving with a learner's permit in my car, I want all your attention to be on the road.

LI'L BIT: Yes, sir.

PECK: Okay. Now the seat — forward and up. (*Li'l Bit pushes it forward.*) Do you want a cushion?

LI'L BIT: No — I'm good.

PECK: You should be able to reach all the switches and controls. Your feet should be able to push the accelerator, brake and clutch all the way down. Can you do that?

LI'L BIT: Yes.

PECK: Okay, the side mirrors. You want to be able to see just a bit of the right side of the car in the right mirror — can you?

LI'L BIT: Turn it out more.

PECK: Okay. How's that?

LI'L BIT: A little more. . . . Okay, that's good.

PECK: Now the left — again, you want to be able to see behind you — but the left lane — adjust it until you feel comfortable. (*Li'l Bit does so.*) Next. I want you to check the rearview mirror. Angle it so you have a clear vision of the back. (*Li'l Bit does so.*) Okay. Lock your door. Make sure all the doors are locked.

LI'L BIT (*making a joke of it*): But then I'm locked in with you.

PECK: Don't fool.

LI'L BIT: All right. We're locked in.

PECK: We'll deal with the air vents and defroster later. I'm teaching you on a manual — once you learn manual, you can drive anything. I want you to be able to drive any car, any machine. Manual gives you *control*. In ice, if your brakes fail, if you need more power — okay? It's a little harder at first, but then it becomes like breathing. Now. Put your hands on the wheel. I never want to see you driving with one hand. Always two hands. (*Li'l Bit hesitates.*) What? What is it now?

LI'L BIT: If I put my hands on the wheel — how do I defend myself?

PECK (*softly*): Now listen. Listen up close. We're not going to fool around with this. This is serious business. I will never touch you when you are driving a car. Understand?

LI'L BIT: Okay.

PECK: Hands on the nine o'clock and three o'clock position gives you maximum control and turn.

(*Peck goes silent for a while. Li'l Bit waits for more instruction.*)

Okay. Just relax and listen to me, Li'l Bit, okay? I want you to lift your hands for a second and look at them.

(*Li'l Bit feels a bit silly, but does it.*)

Those are your two hands. When you are driving, your life is in your own two hands. Understand?

(*Li'l Bit nods.*)

I don't have any sons. You're the nearest to a son I'll ever have — and I want to give you something. Something that really matters to me.

There's something about driving — when you're in control of the car, just you and the machine and the road — that nobody can take from you. A power. I feel more myself in my car than anywhere else. And that's what I want to give to you.

There's a lot of assholes out there. Crazy men, arrogant idiots, drunks, angry kids, geezers who are blind — and you have to be ready for them. I want to teach you to drive like a man.

LI'L BIT: What does that mean?

PECK: Men are taught to drive with confidence — with aggression. The road belongs to them. They drive defensively — always looking out for the other guy. Women tend to be polite — to hesitate. And that can be fatal.

You're going to learn to think what the other guy is going to do before he does it. If there's an accident, and ten cars pile up, and people get killed, you're the one who's gonna steer through it, put your foot on the gas if you have to, and be the only one to walk away. I don't know how long you or I are going to live, but we're for damned sure not going to die in a car.

So if you're going to drive with me, I want you to take this very seriously.

LI'L BIT: I will, Uncle Peck. I want you to teach me to drive.

PECK: Good. You're going to pass your test on the first try. Perfect score. Before the next four weeks are over, you're going to know this baby inside and out. Treat her with respect.

LI'L BIT: Why is it a "she"?

PECK: Good question. It doesn't have to be a "she"—but when you close your eyes and think of someone who responds to your touch—someone who performs just for you and gives you what you ask for—I guess I always see a "she." You can call her what you like.

LI'L BIT (*to the audience*): I closed my eyes—and decided not to change the gender.

(*A Voice:*)

Defensive driving involves defending yourself from hazardous and sudden changes in your automotive environment. By thinking ahead, the defensive driver can adjust to weather, road conditions, and road kill. Good defensive driving involves mental and physical preparation. Are you prepared?

(*Another Voice chimes in:*)

You and the Reverse Gear.

LI'L BIT: 1966. The Anthropology of the Female Body in Ninth Grade—Or A Walk Down Mammary Lane.

(*Throughout the following, there is occasional rhythmic beeping, like a transmitter signaling. Li'l Bit is aware of it, but can't figure out where it is coming from. No one else seems to hear it.*)

MALE GREEK CHORUS: In the hallway of Francis Scott Key Middle School.

(*A bell rings; the Greek Chorus is changing classes and meets in the hall, conspiratorially.*)

TEENAGE GREEK CHORUS: She's coming!

(*Li'l Bit enters the scene; the Male Greek Chorus member has a sudden, violent sneezing and lethal allergy attack.*)

FEMALE GREEK CHORUS: Jerome? Jerome? Are you all right?

MALE GREEK CHORUS: I—don't—know. I can't breathe—get Li'l Bit—

TEENAGE GREEK CHORUS: —He needs oxygen!—

FEMALE GREEK CHORUS: —Can you help us here?

LI'L BIT: What's wrong? Do you want me to get the school nurse—

(*The Male Greek Chorus member wheezes, grabs his throat and sniffs at Li'l Bit's chest, which is beeping away.*)

MALE GREEK CHORUS: No—it's okay—I only get this way when I'm around an allergy trigger—

LI'L BIT: Golly. What are you allergic to?

MALE GREEK CHORUS (*with a sudden grab of her breast*): Foam rubber.

(*The Greek Chorus members break up with hilarity; Jerome leaps away from Li'l Bit's kicking rage with agility; as he retreats:*)

LI'L BIT: Jerome! Creep! Cretin! Cro-Magnon!

TEENAGE GREEK CHORUS: Rage is not attractive in a girl.

FEMALE GREEK CHORUS: Really. Get a Sense of Humor.

(*A Voice echoes:*)

Good defensive driving involves mental and physical preparation. Were You Prepared?

FEMALE GREEK CHORUS: Gym Class: In the showers.

(*The sudden sound of water; the Female Greek Chorus members and Li'l Bit, while fully clothed, drape towels across their fronts, miming nudity. They stand, hesitate, at an imaginary shower's edge.*)

LI'L BIT: Water looks hot.

FEMALE GREEK CHORUS: Yesss. . . .

(*Female Greek Chorus members are not going to make the first move. One dips a tentative toe under the water, clutching the towel around her.*)

LI'L BIT: Well, I guess we'd better shower and get out of here.

FEMALE GREEK CHORUS: Yep. You go ahead. I'm still cooling off.

LI'L BIT: Okay.—Sally? Are you gonna shower?

TEENAGE GREEK CHORUS: After you—

(*Li'l Bit takes a deep breath for courage, drops the towel and plunges in: The two Female Greek Chorus members look at Li'l Bit in the all together, laugh, gasp and high-five each other.*)

TEENAGE GREEK CHORUS: Oh my god! Can you believe—

FEMALE GREEK CHORUS: Told you! It's not foam rubber! I win! Jerome owes me fifty cents!

(*A Voice editorializes:*)

Were You Prepared?

(*Li'l Bit tries to cover up; she is exposed, as suddenly 1960s Motown fills the room and we segue into:*)

FEMALE GREEK CHORUS: The Sock Hop.

(*Li'l Bit stands up against the wall with her female classmates. Teenage Greek Chorus is mesmerized by the music and just sways alone, lip-synching the lyrics.*)

LI'L BIT: I don't know. Maybe it's just me—but—do you ever feel like you're just a walking Mary Jane joke?

FEMALE GREEK CHORUS: I don't know what you mean.

LI'L BIT: You haven't heard the Mary Jane jokes? (*Female Greek Chorus member shakes her head no.*) Okay. "Little Mary Jane is walking through the woods, when all of a sudden this man who was hiding behind a tree *jumps* out, *rips* open Mary Jane's blouse, and *plunges* his hands on her breasts. And Little Mary Jane just laughed and laughed because she knew her money was in her shoes."

(*Li'l Bit laughs; the Female Greek Chorus does not.*)

FEMALE GREEK CHORUS: You're weird.

(*In another space, in a strange light, Uncle Peck stands and stares at Li'l Bit's body. He is setting up a tripod, but he just stands, appreciative, watching her.*)

LI'L BIT: Well, don't you ever feel . . . self-conscious? Like you're being looked at all the time?

FEMALE GREEK CHORUS: That's not a problem for me.—Oh—look—Greg's coming over to ask you to dance.

(*Teenage Creek Chorus becomes attentive, flustered. Male Greek Chorus member, as Greg, bends slightly as a very short young man, whose head is at Li'l Bit's chest level. Ardent, sincere, and socially inept, Greg will become a successful gynecologist.*)

TEENAGE GREEK CHORUS (*softly*): Hi, Greg.

(*Greg does not hear. He is intent on only one thing.*)

MALE GREEK CHORUS (*as Greg, to Li'l Bit*): Good evening. Would you care to dance?

LI'L BIT (*gently*): Thank you very much, Greg—but I'm going to sit this one out.

MALE GREEK CHORUS (*as Greg*): Oh. Okay. I'll try my luck later.

(*He disappears.*)

TEENAGE GREEK CHORUS: Oohhh.

(*Li'l Bit relaxes. Then she tenses, aware of Peck's gaze.*)

FEMALE GREEK CHORUS: Take pity on him. Someone should.

LI'L BIT: But he's so short.

TEENAGE GREEK CHORUS: He can't help it.

LI'L BIT: But his head comes up to (*Li'l Bit gestures*) here. And I think he asks me on the fast dances so he can watch me—you know—jiggle.

FEMALE GREEK CHORUS: I wish I had your problems.

(*The tune changes; Greg is across the room in a flash.*)

MALE GREEK CHORUS (*as Greg*): Evening again. May I ask you for the honor of a spin on the floor?

LI'L BIT: I'm . . . very complimented, Greg. But I . . . I just don't do fast dances.

MALE GREEK CHORUS (*as Greg*): Oh. No problem. That's okay.

(*He disappears. Teenage Greek Chorus watches him go.*)

TEENAGE GREEK CHORUS: That is just so—sad.

(*Li'l Bit becomes aware of Peck waiting.*)

FEMALE GREEK CHORUS: You know, you should take it as a compliment that the guys want to watch you

jiggle. They're guys. That's what they're supposed to do.

LI'L BIT: I guess you're right. But sometimes I feel like these alien life forces, these two mounds of flesh have grafted themselves onto my chest, and they're using me until they can "propagate" and take over the world and they'll just keep growing, with a mind of their own until I collapse under their weight and they suck all the nourishment out of my body and I finally just waste away while they get bigger and bigger and—(*Li'l Bit's classmates are just staring at her in disbelief.*)

FEMALE GREEK CHORUS:—You are the strangest girl I have ever met.

(*Li'l Bit's trying to joke but feels on the verge of tears.*)

LI'L BIT: Or maybe someone's implanted radio transmitters in my chest at a frequency I can't hear, that girls can't detect, but they're sending out these signals to men who get mesmerized, like sirens, calling them to dash themselves on these "rocks"—

(*Just then, the music segues into a slow dance, perhaps a Beach Boys tune like "Little Surfer," but over the music there's a rhythmic, hypnotic beeping transmitted, which both Greg and Peck hear. Li'l Bit hears it too, and in horror she stares at her chest. She, too, is almost hypnotized. In a trance, Greg responds to the signals and is called to her side—actually, her front. Like a zombie, he stands in front of her, his eyes planted on her two orbs.*)

MALE GREEK CHORUS (*as Greg*): This one's a slow dance. I hope your dance card isn't . . . filled?

(*Li'l Bit is aware of Peck; but the signals are calling her to him. The signals are no longer transmitters, but an electromagnetic force, pulling Li'l Bit to his side, where he again waits for her to join him. She must get away from the dance floor.*)

LI'L BIT: Greg—you really are a nice boy. But I don't like to dance.

MALE GREEK CHORUS (*as Greg*): That's okay. We don't have to move or anything. I could just hold you and we could just *sway* a little—

LI'L BIT:—No! I'm sorry—but I think I have to leave; I hear someone calling me—

(*Li'l Bit starts across the dance floor, leaving Greg behind. The beeping stops. The lights change, although the music does not. As Li'l Bit talks to the audience, she continues to change and prepare for the coming session. She should be wearing a tight tank top or a sheer blouse and very tight pants. To the audience:*)

In every man's home some small room, some zone in his house, is set aside. It might be the attic, or the study, or a den. And there's an invisible sign as if from the old treehouse: Girls Keep Out. Here, away from female eyes, lace doilies and crochet, he keeps his manly toys: the Vargas pinups, the tackle. A scent of tobacco and WD-40. (*She inhales deeply.*) A dash of his Bay Rum. Ahhh . . . (*Li'l Bit savors it for just a moment more.*) Here he keeps his secrets: a violin or saxophone, drum set or darkroom, and the stacks of *Playboy.* (*In a whisper.*) Here, in my aunt's home, it was the basement. Uncle Peck's turf.

(*A Voice commands:*)

You and the Reverse Gear.

LI'L BIT: 1965. The Photo Shoot.

(*Li'l Bit steps into the scene as a nervous but curious thirteen-year-old. Music, from the previous scene, continues to play, changing into something like Roy Orbison later—something seductive with a beat. Peck fiddles, all business, with his camera. As in the driving lesson, he is all competency and concentration. Li'l Bit stands awkwardly. He looks through the Leica camera on the tripod, adjusts the back lighting, etc.*)

PECK: Are you cold? The lights should heat up some in a few minutes—
LI'L BIT: —Aunt Mary is?
PECK: At the National Theatre matinee. With your mother. We have time.
LI'L BIT: But—what if—
PECK: —And so what if they return? I told them you and I were going to be working with my camera. They won't come down.

(*Li'l Bit is quiet, apprehensive.*)

Look, are you sure you want to do this?
LI'L BIT: I said I'd do it. But—
PECK: —I know. You've drawn the line.
LI'L BIT (*reassured*): That's right. No frontal nudity.
PECK: Good heavens, girl, where did you pick that up?
LI'L BIT (*defensive*): I read.

(*Peck tries not to laugh.*)

PECK: And I read *Playboy* for the interviews. Okay. Let's try some different music.

(*Peck goes to an expensive reel-to-reel and forwards. Something like "Sweet Dreams" begins to play.*)

LI'L BIT: I didn't know you listened to this.
PECK: I'm not dead, you know, I try to keep up. Do you like this song?

(*Li'l Bit nods with pleasure.*)

Good. Now listen—at professional photo shoots, they always play music for the models. Okay? I want you to just enjoy the music. Listen to it with your body, and just—respond.
LI'L BIT: Respond to the music with my . . . body?
PECK: Right. Almost like dancing. Here—let's get you on the stool, first. (*Peck comes over and helps her up.*)
LI'L BIT: But nothing showing—

(*Peck firmly, with his large capable hands, brushes back her hair, angles her face. Li'l Bit turns to him like a plant to the sun.*)

PECK: Nothing showing. Just a peek.

(*He holds her by the shoulders, looking at her critically. Then he unbuttons her blouse to the midpoint, and runs his hands over the flesh of her exposed sternum, arranging the fabric, just touching her. Deliberately, calmly. Asexually. Li'l Bit quiets, sits perfectly still, and closes her eyes.*)

Okay?
LI'L BIT: Yes.

(*Peck goes back to his camera.*)

PECK: I'm going to keep talking to you. Listen without responding to what I'm saying; you want to *listen* to the music. Sway, move just your torso or your head—I've got to check the light meter.
LI'L BIT: But—you'll be watching.
PECK: No—I'm not here—just my voice. Pretend you're in your room all alone on a Friday night with your mirror—and the music feels good—just move for me, Li'l Bit—

(*Li'l Bit closes her eyes. At first self-conscious; then she gets more into the music and begins to sway. We hear the camera start to whir. Throughout the shoot, there can be a slide montage of actual shots of the actor playing Li'l Bit—interspersed with other models à la Playboy, Calvin Klein, and Victoriana/Lewis Carroll's Alice Liddell.*)

That's it. That looks great. Okay. Just keep doing that. Lift your head up a bit more, good, good, just keep moving, that a girl—you're a very beautiful young woman. Do you know that?

(*Li'l Bit looks up, blushes. Peck shoots the camera. The audience should see this shot on the screen.*)

LI'L BIT: No. I don't know that.
PECK: Listen to the music.

(*Li'l Bit closes her eyes again.*)

Well you are. For a thirteen-year-old, you have a body a twenty-year-old woman would die for.
LI'L BIT: The boys in school don't think so.
PECK: The boys in school are little Neanderthals in short pants. You're ten years ahead of them in maturity; it's gonna take a while for them to catch up.

(*Peck clicks another shot; we see a faint smile on Li'l Bit on the screen.*)

Girls turn into women long before boys turn into men.
LI'L BIT: Why is that?
PECK: I don't know, Li'l Bit. But it's a blessing for men.

(*Li'l Bit turns silent.*)

Keep moving. Try arching your back on the stool, hands behind you, and throw your head back.

(*The slide shows a Playboy model in this pose.*)

Oohh, great. That one was great. Turn your head away, same position. (*Whir.*) Beautiful.

(*Li'l Bit looks at him a bit defiantly.*)

LI'L BIT: I think Aunt Mary is beautiful.

(*Peck stands still.*)

PECK: My wife is a very beautiful woman. Her beauty doesn't cancel yours out. (*More casually; he returns to the camera.*) All the women in your family are beautiful. In fact, I think all women are. You're not listening to the music. (*Peck shoots some more film in silence.*) All right, turn your head to the left. Good. Now take the back of your right hand and put it on your right cheek—your elbow angled up—now slowly, slowly, stroke your cheek, draw back your hair with the back of your hand. (*Another classic Playboy or Vargas.*) Good. One hand above and behind your head; stretch your body; smile. (*Another pose.*) Li'l Bit. I want you to think of something that makes you laugh—

LI'L BIT: I can't think of anything.

PECK: Okay. Think of Big Papa chasing Grandma around the living room.

(*Li'l Bit lifts her head and laughs. Click. We should see this shot.*)

Good. Both hands behind your head. Great! Hold that. (*From behind his camera.*) You're doing great work. If we keep this up, in five years we'll have a really professional portfolio.

(*Li'l Bit stops.*)

LI'L BIT: What do you mean in five years?

PECK: You can't submit work to *Playboy* until you're eighteen. —

(*Peck continues to shoot; he knows he's made a mistake.*)

LI'L BIT: —Wait a minute. You're joking, aren't you, Uncle Peck?

PECK: Heck, no. You can't get into *Playboy* unless you're the very best. And you are the very best.

LI'L BIT: I would never do that!

(*Peck stops shooting. He turns off the music.*)

PECK: Why? There's nothing wrong with *Playboy*—it's a very classy maga—

LI'L BIT (*more upset*): But I thought you said I should go to college!

PECK: Wait—Li'l Bit—it's nothing like that. Very respectable women model for *Playboy*—actresses with major careers—women in college—there's an Ivy League issue every—

LI'L BIT: —I'm never doing anything like that! You'd show other people these—other *men*—what I'm doing.—Why would you do that?! Any *boy* around

here could just pick up, just go into The Stop & Go and *buy*—Why would you ever want to—to share—

PECK: —Whoa, whoa. Just stop a second and listen to me. Li'l Bit. Listen. There's nothing wrong in what we're doing. I'm very proud of you. I think you have a wonderful body and an even more wonderful mind. And of course I want other people to *appreciate* it. It's not anything shameful.

LI'L BIT (*hurt*): But this is something—that I'm only doing for you. This is something—that you said was just between us.

PECK: It is. And if that's how you feel, five years from now, it will remain that way. Okay? I know you're not going to do anything you don't feel like doing. (*He walks back to the camera.*) Do you want to stop now? I've got just a few more shots on this roll—

LI'L BIT: I don't want anyone seeing this.

PECK: I swear to you. No one will. I'll treasure this— that you're doing this only for me.

(*Li'l Bit, still shaken, sits on the stool. She closes her eyes.*)

Li'l Bit? Open your eyes and look at me.

(*Li'l Bit shakes her head no.*)

Come on. Just open your eyes, honey.

LI'L BIT: If I look at you—if I look at the camera: You're gonna know what I'm thinking. You'll see right through me—

PECK: —No, I won't. I want you to look at me. All right, then. I just want you to listen. Li'l Bit.

(*She waits.*)

I love you.

(*Li'l Bit opens her eyes; she is startled. Peck captures the shot. On the screen we see right through her. Peck says softly.*)

Do you know that?

(*Li'l Bit nods her head yes.*)

I have loved you every day since the day you were born.

LI'L BIT: Yes.

(*Li'l Bit and Peck just look at each other. Beat. Beneath the shot of herself on the screen, Li'l Bit, still looking at her uncle, begins to unbutton her blouse.*
A neutral Voice cuts off the above scene with:)

Implied Consent.
As an individual operating a motor vehicle in the state of Maryland, you must abide by "Implied Consent." If you do not consent to take the blood alcohol content test, there may be severe penalties: a suspension of license, a fine, community service, and a possible jail sentence.

(*The Voice shifts tone:*)

Idling in the Neutral Gear.

MALE GREEK CHORUS (*announcing*): Aunt Mary on behalf of her husband.

(*Female Greek Chorus checks her appearance, and with dignity comes to the front of the stage and sits down to talk to the audience.*)

FEMALE GREEK CHORUS (*as Aunt Mary*): My husband was such a good man—is. Is such a good man. Every night, he does the dishes. The second he comes home, he's taking out the garbage, or doing yard work, lifting the heavy things I can't. Everyone in the neighborhood borrows Peck—it's true—women with husbands of their own, men who just don't have Peck's abilities—there's always a knock on our door for a jump start on cold mornings, when anyone needs a ride, or help shoveling the sidewalk—I look out, and there Peck is, without a coat, pitching in.

I know I'm lucky. The man works from dawn to dusk. And the overtime he does every year—my poor sister. She sits every Christmas when I come to dinner with a new stole, or diamonds, or with the tickets to Bermuda.

I know he has troubles. And we don't talk about them. I wonder, sometimes, what happened to him during the war. The men who fought World War II didn't have "rap sessions" to talk about their feelings. Men in his generation were expected to be quiet about it and get on with their lives. And sometimes I can feel him just fighting the trouble—whatever has burrowed deeper than the scar tissue—and we don't talk about it. I know he's having a bad spell because he comes looking for me in the house, and just hangs around me until it passes. And I keep my banter light—I discuss a new recipe, or sales, or gossip—because I think domesticity can be a balm for men when they're lost. We sit in the house and listen to the peace of the clock ticking in his well-ordered living room, until it passes.

(*Sharply.*) I'm not a fool. I know what's going on. I wish you could feel how hard Peck fights against it—he's swimming against the tide, and what he needs is to see me on the shore, believing in him, knowing he won't go under, he won't give up—

And I want to say this about my niece. She's a sly one, that one is. She knows exactly what she's doing; she's twisted Peck around her little finger and thinks it's all a big secret. Yet another one who's borrowing my husband until it doesn't suit her anymore.

Well. I'm counting the days until she goes away to school. And she manipulates someone else. And then he'll come back again, and sit in the kitchen while I bake, or beside me on the sofa when I sew in the evenings. I'm a very patient woman. But I'd like my husband back.

I am counting the days.

(*A Voice repeats:*)

You and the Reverse Gear.

MALE GREEK CHORUS: Li'l Bit's Thirteenth Christmas. Uncle Peck Does the Dishes. Christmas 1964.

(*Peck stands in a dress shirt and tie, nice pants, with an apron. He is washing dishes. He's in a mood we haven't seen. Quiet, brooding. Li'l Bit watches him a moment before seeking him out.*)

LI'L BIT: Uncle Peck?

(*He does not answer. He continues to work on the pots.*)

I didn't know where you'd gone to.

(*He nods. She takes this as a sign to come in.*)

Don't you want to sit with us for a while?

PECK: No. I'd rather do the dishes.

(*Pause. Li'l Bit watches him.*)

LI'L BIT: You're the only man I know who does dishes.

(*Peck says nothing.*)

I think it's really nice.

PECK: My wife has been on her feet all day. So's your grandmother and your mother.

LI'L BIT: I know. (*Beat.*) Do you want some help?

PECK: No. (*He softens a bit towards her.*) You can help by just talking to me.

LI'L BIT: Big Papa never does the dishes. I think it's nice.

PECK: I think men should be nice to women. Women are always working for us. There's nothing particularly manly in wolfing down food and then sitting around in a stupor while the women clean up.

LI'L BIT: That looks like a really neat camera that Aunt Mary got you.

PECK: It is. It's a very nice one.

(*Pause, as Peck works on the dishes and some demon that Li'l Bit intuits.*)

LI'L BIT: Did Big Papa hurt your feelings?

PECK (*tired*): What? Oh, no—it doesn't hurt me. Family is family. I'd rather have him picking on me than—I don't pay him any mind, Li'l Bit.

LI'L BIT: Are you angry with us?

PECK: No, Li'l Bit. I'm not angry.

(*Another pause.*)

LI'L BIT: We missed you at Thanksgiving. . . . I did. I missed you.

PECK: Well, there were . . . "things" going on. I didn't want to spoil anyone's Thanksgiving.

LI'L BIT: Uncle Peck? (*Very carefully.*) Please don't drink anymore tonight.

PECK: I'm not . . . overdoing it.

LI'L BIT: I know. (*Beat.*) Why do you drink so much?

(*Peck stops and thinks, carefully.*)

PECK: Well, Li'l Bit—let me explain it this way. There are some people who have a . . . a "fire" in the belly. I think they go to work on Wall Street or they run for office. And then there are people who have a "fire" in their heads—and they become writers or scientists or historians. (*He smiles a little at her.*) You. You've got a "fire" in the head. And then there are people like me.

LI'L BIT: Where do you have . . . a fire?

PECK: I have a fire in my heart. And sometimes the drinking helps.

LI'L BIT: There's got to be other things that can help.

PECK: I suppose there are.

LI'L BIT: Does it help—to talk to me?

PECK: Yes. It does. (*Quiet.*) I don't get to see you very much.

LI'L BIT: I know. (*Li'l Bit thinks.*) You could talk to me more.

PECK: Oh?

LI'L BIT: I could make a deal with you, Uncle Peck.

PECK: I'm listening.

LI'L BIT: We could meet and talk—once a week. You could just store up whatever's bothering you during the week—and then we could talk.

PECK: Would you like that?

LI'L BIT: As long as you don't drink. I'd meet you somewhere for lunch or for a walk—on the weekends—as long as you stop drinking. And we could talk about whatever you want.

PECK: You could do that for me?

LI'L BIT: I don't think I'd want Mom to know. Or Aunt Mary. I wouldn't want them to think—

PECK: —No. It would just be us talking.

LI'L BIT: I'll tell Mom I'm going to a girlfriend's. To study. Mom doesn't get home until six, so you can call me after school and tell me where to meet you.

PECK: You get home at four?

LI'L BIT: We can meet once a week. But only in public. You've got to let me—draw the line. And once it's drawn, you mustn't cross it.

PECK: Understood.

LI'L BIT: Would that help?

(*Peck is very moved.*)

PECK: Yes. Very much.

LI'L BIT: I'm going to join the others in the living room now. (*Li'l Bit turns to go.*)

PECK: Merry Christmas, Li'l Bit.

(*Li'l Bit bestows a very warm smile on him.*)

LI'L BIT: Merry Christmas, Uncle Peck.

(*A Voice dictates:*)

Shifting Forward from Second to Third Gear.

(*The Male and Female Greek Chorus members come forward.*)

MALE GREEK CHORUS: 1969. Days and Gifts: A Countdown:

FEMALE GREEK CHORUS: A note. "September 3, 1969. Li'l Bit: You've only been away two days and it feels

like months. Hope your dorm room is cozy. I'm sending you this tape cassette—it's a new model—so you'll have some music in your room. Also that music you're reading about for class—*Carmina Burana.* Hope you enjoy. Only ninety days to go!—Peck."

MALE GREEK CHORUS: September 22. A bouquet of roses. A note: "Miss you like crazy. Sixty-nine days . . ."

TEENAGE GREEK CHORUS: September 25. A box of chocolates. A card: "Don't worry about the weight gain. You still look great. Got a post office box—write to me there. Sixty-six days.—Love, your candy man."

MALE GREEK CHORUS: October 16. A note: "Am trying to get through the Jane Austen you're reading—*Emma*—here's a book in return: *Liaisons Dangereuses.* Hope you're saving time for me." Scrawled in the margin the number: "47."

FEMALE GREEK CHORUS: November 16. "Sixteen days to go!—Hope you like the perfume.—Having a hard time reaching you on the dorm phone. You must be in the library a lot. Won't you think about me getting you your own phone so we can talk?"

TEENAGE GREEK CHORUS: November 18. "Li'l Bit—got a package returned to the P.O. Box. Have you changed dorms? Call me at work or write to the P.O. Am still on the wagon. Waiting to see you. Only two weeks more!"

MALE GREEK CHORUS: November 23. A letter. "Li'l Bit. So disappointed you couldn't come home for the turkey. Sending you some money for a nice dinner out—nine days and counting!"

GREEK CHORUS (*in unison*): November 25th. A letter:

LI'L BIT: "Dear Uncle Peck: I am sending this to you at work. Don't come up next weekend for my birthday. I will not be here—"

(*A Voice directs:*)

Shifting Forward from Third to Fourth Gear.

MALE GREEK CHORUS: December 10, 1969. A hotel room. Philadelphia. There is no moon tonight.

(*Peck sits on the side of the bed while Li'l Bit paces. He can't believe she's in his room, but there's a desperate edge to his happiness. Li'l Bit is furious, edgy. There is a bottle of champagne in an ice bucket in a very nice hotel room.*)

PECK: Why don't you sit?

LI'L BIT: I don't want to.—What's the champagne for?

PECK: I thought we might toast your birthday—

LI'L BIT: —I am so pissed off at you, Uncle Peck.

PECK: Why?

LI'L BIT: I mean, are you crazy?

PECK: What did I do?

LI'L BIT: You scared the holy crap out of me—sending me that stuff in the mail—

PECK: — They were gifts! I just wanted to give you some little perks your first semester —

LI'L BIT: — Well, what the hell were those numbers all about! Forty-four days to go — only two more weeks. — And then just numbers — 69 — 68 — 67 — like some serial killer!

PECK: Li'l Bit! Whoa! This is me you're talking to — I was just trying to pick up your spirits, trying to celebrate your birthday.

LI'L BIT: My *eighteenth* birthday. I'm not a child, Uncle Peck. You were counting down to my eighteenth birthday.

PECK: So?

LI'L BIT: So? So statutory rape is not in effect when a young woman turns eighteen. And you and I both know it.

(*Peck is walking on ice.*)

PECK: I think you misunderstand.

LI'L BIT: I think I understand all too well. I know what you want to do five steps ahead of you doing it. Defensive Driving 101.

PECK: Then why did you suggest we meet here instead of the restaurant?

LI'L BIT: I don't want to have this conversation in public.

PECK: Fine. Fine. We have a lot to talk about.

LI'L BIT: Yeah. We do.

(*Li'l Bit doesn't want to do what she has to do.*) Could I . . . have some of that champagne?

PECK: Of course, madam! (*Peck makes a big show of it.*) Let me do the honors. I wasn't sure which you might prefer — Taittingers or Veuve Clicquot — so I thought we'd start out with an old standard — Perrier Jouet. (*The bottle is popped.*)

Quick — Li'l Bit — your glass! (*Uncle Peck fills Li'l Bit's glass. He puts the bottle back in the ice and goes for a can of ginger ale.*) Let me get some of this ginger ale — my bubbly — and toast you.

(*He turns and sees that Li'l Bit has not waited for him.*)

LI'L BIT: Oh — sorry, Uncle Peck. Let me have another.

(*Peck fills her glass and reaches for his ginger ale; she stops him.*)

Uncle Peck — maybe you should join me in the champagne.

PECK: You want me — to drink?

LI'L BIT: It's not polite to let a lady drink alone.

PECK: Well, missy, if you insist. . . . (*Peck hesitates.*) — Just one. It's been a while. (*Peck fills another flute for himself.*) There. I'd like to propose a toast to you and your birthday! (*Peck sips it tentatively.*) I'm not used to this anymore.

LI'L BIT: You don't have anywhere to go tonight, do you?

(*Peck hopes this is a good sign.*)

PECK: I'm all yours. — God, it's good to see you! I've gotten so used to . . . to . . . talking to you in my head. I'm used to seeing you every week — there's so

much — I don't quite know where to begin. How's school, Li'l Bit?

LI'L BIT: I — it's hard. Uncle Peck. Harder than I thought it would be. I'm in the middle of exams and papers and — I don't know.

PECK: You'll pull through. You always do.

LI'L BIT: Maybe. I . . . might be flunking out.

PECK: You always think the worst, Li'l Bit, but when the going gets tough —

(*Li'l Bit shrugs and pours herself another glass.*)

— Hey, honey, go easy on that stuff, okay?

LI'L BIT: Is it very expensive?

PECK: Only the best for you. But the cost doesn't matter — champagne should be "sipped."

(*Li'l Bit is quiet.*)

Look — if you're in trouble in school — you can always come back home for a while.

LI'L BIT: *No* — (*Li'l Bit tries not to be so harsh.*) — Thanks, Uncle Peck, but I'll figure some way out of this.

PECK: You're supposed to get in scrapes, your first year away from home.

LI'L BIT: Right. How's Aunt Mary?

PECK: She's fine. (*Pause.*) Well — how about the new car?

LI'L BIT: It's real nice. What is it, again?

PECK: It's a Cadillac El Dorado.

LI'L BIT: Oh. Well, I'm real happy for you, Uncle Peck.

PECK: I got it for you.

LI'L BIT: What?

PECK: I always wanted to get a Cadillac — but I thought, Peck, wait until Li'l Bit's old enough — and thought maybe you'd like to drive it, too.

LI'L BIT (*confused*): Why would I want to drive your car?

PECK: Just because it's the best — I want you to have the best.

(*They are running out of "gas"; small talk.*)

LI'L BIT: Listen, Uncle Peck, I don't know how to begin this, but —	PECK: I have been thinking of how to say this in my head, over and over —

PECK: Sorry.

LI'L BIT: You first.

PECK: Well, your going away — has just made me realize how much I miss you. Talking to you and being alone with you. I've really come to depend on you, Li'l Bit. And it's been so hard to get in touch with you lately — the distance and — and you're never in when I call — I guess you've been living in the library —

LI'L BIT: — No — the problem is, I haven't been in the library —

PECK: — Well, it doesn't matter — I hope you've been missing me as much.

LI'L BIT: Uncle Peck — I've been thinking a lot about this — and I came here tonight to tell you that — I'm not doing very well. I'm getting very confused — I can't concentrate on my work—and now that I'm away—I've been going over and over it in my mind—and I don't want us to "see" each other anymore. Other than with the rest of the family.

PECK (*quiet*): Are you seeing other men?

LI'L BIT (*getting agitated*): I—no, that's not the reason—I—well, yes, I am seeing other—listen, it's not really anybody's business!

PECK: Are you in love with anyone else?

LI'L BIT: That's not what this is about.

PECK: Li'l Bit—you're scared. Your mother and your grandparents have filled your head with all kinds of nonsense about men—I hear them working on you all the time—and you're scared. It won't hurt you—if the man you go to bed with really loves you. (*Li'l Bit is scared. She starts to tremble.*) And I have loved you since the day I held you in my hand. And I think everyone's just gotten you frightened to death about something that is just like breathing—

LI'L BIT: Oh, my god—(*She takes a breath.*) I can't see you anymore, Uncle Peck.

(*Peck downs the rest of his champagne.*)

PECK: Li'l Bit. Listen. Listen. Open your eyes and look at me. Come on. Just open your eyes, honey. (*Li'l Bit, eyes*

squeezed shut, refuses.) All right then. I just want you to listen. Li'l Bit—I'm going to ask you just this once. Of your own free will. Just lie down on the bed with me—our clothes on—just lie down with me, a man and a woman . . . and let's . . . hold one another. Nothing else. Before you say anything else. I want the chance to . . . hold you. Because sometimes the body knows things that the mind isn't listening to . . . and after I've held you, then I want you to tell me what you feel.

LI'L BIT: You'll just . . . hold me?

PECK: Yes. And then you can tell me what you're feeling.

(*Li'l Bit—half wanting to run, half wanting to get it over with, half wanting to be held by him:*)

LI'L BIT: Yes. All right. Just hold. Nothing else.

(*Peck lies down on the bed and holds his arms out to her. Li'l Bit lies beside him, putting her head on his chest. He looks as if he's trying to soak her into his pores by osmosis. He strokes her hair, and she lies very still. The Male Greek Chorus member and the Female Greek Chorus member as Aunt Mary come into the room.*)

MALE GREEK CHORUS: Recipe for a Southern Boy:

FEMALE GREEK CHORUS (*as Aunt Mary*): A drawl of molasses in the way he speaks.

Mary Louise Parker as Li'l Bit and David Morse as Uncle Peck in *How I Learned to Drive* in 1997 at the Vineyard Theatre, New York City.

MALE GREEK CHORUS: A gumbo of red and brown mixed in the cream of his skin.

(*While Peck lies, his eyes closed, Li'l Bit rises in the bed and responds to her aunt.*)

LI'L BIT: Warm brown eyes—

FEMALE GREEK CHORUS (*as Aunt Mary*): Bedroom eyes—

MALE GREEK CHORUS: A dash of Southern Baptist Fire and Brimstone—

LI'L BIT: A curl of Elvis on his forehead—

FEMALE GREEK CHORUS (*as Aunt Mary*): A splash of Bay Rum—

MALE GREEK CHORUS: A closely shaven beard that he razors just for you—

FEMALE GREEK CHORUS (*as Aunt Mary*): Large hands— rough hands—

LI'L BIT: Warm hands—

MALE GREEK CHORUS: The steel of the military in his walk—

LI'L BIT: The slouch of the fishing skiff in his walk—

MALE GREEK CHORUS: Neatly pressed khakis—

FEMALE GREEK CHORUS (*as Aunt Mary*): And under the wide leather of the belt—

LI'L BIT: Sweat of cypress and sand—

MALE GREEK CHORUS: Neatly pressed khakis—

LI'L BIT: His heart beating Dixie—

FEMALE GREEK CHORUS (*as Aunt Mary*): The whisper of the zipper—you could reach out with your hand and—

LI'L BIT: His mouth—

FEMALE GREEK CHORUS (*as Aunt Mary*): You could just reach out and—

LI'L BIT: Hold him in your hand—

FEMALE GREEK CHORUS (*as Aunt Mary*): And his mouth—

(*Li'l Bit rises above her uncle and looks at his mouth; she starts to lower herself to kiss him—and wrenches herself free. She gets up from the bed.*)

LI'L BIT: —I've got to get back.

PECK: Wait—Li'l Bit. Did you . . . feel nothing?

LI'L BIT (*lying*): No. Nothing.

PECK: Do you—do you think of me?

(*The Greek Chorus whispers:*)

FEMALE GREEK CHORUS: Khakis—

MALE GREEK CHORUS: Bay Rum—

FEMALE GREEK CHORUS: The whisper of the—

LI'L BIT: —No.

(*Peck, in a rush, trembling, gets something out of his pocket.*)

PECK: I'm forty-five. That's not old for a man. And I haven't been able to do anything else but think of you. I can't concentrate on my work—Li'l Bit. You've got to—I want you to think about what I am about to ask you.

LI'L BIT: I'm listening.

(*Peck opens a small ring box.*)

PECK: I want you to be my wife.

LI'L BIT: This isn't happening.

PECK: I'll tell Mary I want a divorce. We're not blood-related. It would be legal—

LI'L BIT: —What have you been thinking! You are married to my aunt, Uncle Peck. She's my family. You have—you have gone way over the line. Family is family.
      (*Quickly, Li'l Bit flies through the room, gets her coat.*) I'm leaving. Now. I am not seeing you. Again.

(*Peck lies down on the bed for a moment, trying to absorb the terrible news. For a moment, he almost curls into a fetal position.*)

I'm not coming home for Christmas. You should go home to Aunt Mary. Go home now, Uncle Peck.

(*Peck gets control, and sits, rigid.*)

Uncle Peck?—I'm sorry but I have to go.

(*Pause.*)

Are you all right?

(*With a discipline that comes from being told that boys don't cry, Peck stands upright.*)

PECK: I'm fine. I just think—I need a real drink.

(*The Male Greek Chorus has become a bartender. At a small counter, he is lining up shots for Peck. As Li'l Bit narrates, we see Peck sitting, carefully and calmly downing shot glasses.*)

LI'L BIT (*to the audience*): I never saw him again. I stayed away from Christmas and Thanksgiving for years after.
      It took my uncle seven years to drink himself to death. First he lost his job, then his wife, and finally his driver's license. He retreated to his house, and had his bottles delivered.

(*Peck stands, and puts his hands in front of him— almost like Superman flying.*)

One night he tried to go downstairs to the basement— and he flew down the steep basement stairs. My aunt came by weekly to put food on the porch, and she noticed the mail and the papers stacked up, uncollected.
      They found him at the bottom of the stairs. Just steps away from his dark room.
      Now that I'm old enough, there are some questions I would have liked to have asked him. Who did it to you, Uncle Peck? How old were you? Were you eleven?

(*Peck moves to the driver's seat of the car and waits.*)

Sometimes I think of my uncle as a kind of Flying Dutchman. In the opera, the Dutchman is doomed to wander the sea; but every seven years he can come ashore, and if he finds a maiden who will love him of her own free will—he will be released.

And I see Uncle Peck in my mind, in his Chevy '56, a spirit driving up and down the back roads of Carolina—looking for a young girl who, of her own free will, will love him. Release him.

(*A Voice states:*)

You and the Reverse Gear.

LI'L BIT: The summer of 1962. On Men, Sex, and Women: Part III:

(*Li'l Bit steps, as an eleven-year-old, into:*)

FEMALE GREEK CHORUS (*as Mother*): It is out of the question. End of Discussion.
LI'L BIT: But why?
FEMALE GREEK CHORUS (*as Mother*): Li'l Bit—we are not discussing this. I said no.
LI'L BIT: But I could spend an extra week at the beach! You're not telling me why!
FEMALE GREEK CHORUS (*as Mother*): Your uncle pays entirely too much attention to you.
LI'L BIT: He listens to me when I talk. And—and he talks to me. He teaches me about things. Mama—he knows an awful lot.
FEMALE GREEK CHORUS (*as Mother*): He's a small town hick who's learned how to mix drinks from Hugh Hefner.
LI'L BIT: Who's Hugh Hefner?

(*Beat.*)

FEMALE GREEK CHORUS (*as Mother*): I am not letting an eleven-year-old girl spend seven hours alone in the car with a man. . . . I don't like the way your uncle looks at you.
LI'L BIT: For god's sake, mother! Just because you've gone through a bad time with my father—you think every man is evil!
FEMALE GREEK CHORUS (*as Mother*): Oh no, Li'l Bit— not all men. . . . We . . . we just haven't been very lucky with the men in our family.
LI'L BIT: Just because you lost your husband—I still deserve a chance at having a father! Someone! A man who will look out for me! Don't I get a chance?
FEMALE GREEK CHORUS (*as Mother*): I will feel terrible if something happens.
LI'L BIT: Mother! It's in your head! Nothing will happen! I can take care of myself. And I can certainly handle Uncle Peck.
FEMALE GREEK CHORUS (*as Mother*): All right. But I'm warning you—if anything happens, I hold you responsible.

(*Li'l Bit moves out of this scene and toward the car.*)

LI'L BIT: 1962. On the Back Roads of Carolina: The First Driving Lesson.

(*The Teenage Greek Chorus member stands apart on stage. She will speak all of Li'l Bit's lines. Li'l Bit sits beside Peck in the front seat. She looks at him closely, remembering.*)

PECK: Li'l Bit? Are you getting tired?
TEENAGE GREEK CHORUS: A little.
PECK: It's a long drive. But we're making really good time. We can take the back road from here and see . . . a little scenery. Say—I've got an idea—(*Peck checks his rearview mirror.*)
TEENAGE GREEK CHORUS: Are we stopping, Uncle Peck?
PECK: There's no traffic here. Do you want to drive?
TEENAGE GREEK CHORUS: I can't drive.
PECK: It's easy. I'll show you how. I started driving when I was your age. Don't you want to?—
TEENAGE GREEK CHORUS:—But it's against the law at my age!
PECK: And that's why you can't tell anyone I'm letting you do this—
TEENAGE GREEK CHORUS:—But—I can't reach the pedals.
PECK: You can sit in my lap and steer. I'll push the pedals for you. Did your father ever let you drive his car?
TEENAGE GREEK CHORUS: No way.
PECK: Want to try?
TEENAGE GREEK CHORUS: Okay. (*Li'l Bit moves into Peck's lap. She leans against him, closing her eyes.*)
PECK: You're just a little thing, aren't you? Okay—now think of the wheel as a big clock—I want you to put your right hand on the clock where three o'clock would be; and your left hand on the nine—

(*Li'l Bit puts one hand to Peck's face, to stroke him. Then, she takes the wheel.*)

TEENAGE GREEK CHORUS: Am I doing it right?
PECK: That's right. Now, whatever you do, don't let go of the wheel. You tell me whether to go faster or slower—
TEENAGE GREEK CHORUS: Not so fast, Uncle Peck!
PECK: Li'l Bit—I need you to watch the road—

(*Peck puts his hands on Li'l Bit's breasts. She relaxes against him, silent, accepting his touch.*)

TEENAGE GREEK CHORUS: Uncle Peck—what are you doing?
PECK: Keep driving. (*He slips his hands under her blouse.*)
TEENAGE GREEK CHORUS: Uncle Peck—please don't do this—
PECK:—Just a moment longer . . . (*Peck tenses against Li'l Bit.*)
TEENAGE GREEK CHORUS (*trying not to cry*): This isn't happening.

(*Peck tenses more, sharply. He buries his face in Li'l Bit's neck, and moans softly. The Teenage Greek Chorus exits, and Li'l Bit steps out of the car. Peck, too, disappears.*)
  (*A Voice reflects:*)

Driving in Today's World.

LI'L BIT: That day was the last day I lived in my body. I retreated above the neck, and I've lived inside the "fire" in my head ever since.

And now that seems like a long, long time ago. When we were both very young.

And before you know it, I'll be thirty-five. That's getting up there for a woman. And I find myself believing in things that a younger self vowed never to believe in. Things like family and forgiveness.

I know I'm lucky. Although I still have never known what it feels like to jog or dance. Any thing that . . . "jiggles." I do like to watch people on the dance floor, or out on the running paths, just jiggling away. And I say—good for them. (*Li'l Bit moves to the car with pleasure.*)

The nearest sensation I feel—of flight in the body—I guess I feel when I'm driving. On a day like today. It's five A.M. The radio says it's going to be clear and crisp. I've got five hundred miles of highway ahead of me—and some back roads too. I filled the tank last night, and had the oil checked. Checked the tires, too. You've got to treat her . . . with respect.

First thing I do is: Check under the car. To see if any two year olds or household cats have crawled beneath, and strategically placed their skulls behind my back tires. (*Li'l Bit crouches.*)

Nope. Then I get in the car. (*Li'l Bit does so.*)

I lock the doors. And turn the key. Then I adjust the most important control on the dashboard—the radio—(*Li'l Bit turns the radio on: We hear all of the Greek Chorus overlapping, and static:*)

FEMALE GREEK CHORUS (*overlapping*):— "You were so tiny you fit in his hand—"

MALE GREEK CHORUS (*overlapping*):— "How is Shakespeare gonna help her lie on her back in the—"

TEENAGE GREEK CHORUS (*overlapping*):— "Am I doing it right?"

(*Li'l Bit fine-tunes the radio station. A song like "Dedicated to the One I Love" or Orbison's "Sweet Dreams" comes on, and cuts off the Greek Chorus.*)

LI'L BIT: Ahh . . . (*Beat.*) I adjust my seat. Fasten my seat belt. Then I check the right side mirror—check the left side. (*She does.*) Finally, I adjust the rearview mirror.

(*As Li'l Bit adjusts the rearview mirror, a faint light strikes the spirit of Uncle Peck, who is sitting in the back seat of the car. She sees him in the mirror. She smiles at him, and he nods at her. They are happy to be going for a long ride together. Li'l Bit slips the car into first gear; to the audience:*)

And then—I floor it.

(*Sound of a car taking off. Blackout.*)

COMMENTARIES

Christopher Bigsby
PAULA VOGEL   *1999*

In this excerpt from his discussion of Paula Vogel, English theater scholar Christopher Bigsby examines some of the complexities of How I Learned to Drive. *He comments on the attractive qualities of Peck and the seductive qualities of Li'l Bit, while also examining the subtleties of the metaphors of driving embedded in the play. He also reminds us that for Vogel, the attraction for pedophiles is not the gender of the prey, but the age. Bigsby sees the play as a complex structure that avoids psychological cliché.*

[. . .] Peck is an attractive man in his forties. He should, Vogel instructs, and despite what she calls "a few problems," be played by an actor one might cast in the role of Atticus in *To Kill a Mockingbird*, hence his name (Gregory Peck [played Atticus] in the movie). Li'l Bit is by turns a woman in her thirties or forties and a prematurely developed young girl seen at various moments from the age of eleven through her twenties. The action takes place in suburban Maryland, described by the older Li'l Bit as near the crumbling concrete of U.S. One, which "winds its way past one-room revival churches, the porno drive-in, and boarded up motels with For Sale signs tumbling down." Once there had been another Maryland, "before the Malls took over," but even then innocence had been tainted: "This countryside was once dotted with farmhouses—from their porches you could have witnessed the Civil War raging in the front fields." This is a moralized landscape, invested with the qualities of a country whose own insistent innocence had itself never been entirely plausible, never quite realized. *How I Learned to Drive,* indeed, is surely in part about an America which struggles to sustain notions of innocence, spiritual concern, and family values while flooding its consciousness with sexual titillation: a cheerleader culture of prepubescent beauty pageants, eroticized movies and advertisements, as though sex were a language in which it is necessary to become fluent as soon as possible. In such a context, moral affront at Lolita-like affairs becomes more difficult to sustain or at least more profoundly ambiguous. [. . .]

The audience's attitude to Peck, and to his relationship with Li'l Bit, is in part shaped by the fact of the play's broken chronology. The first scene finds the young girl at seventeen, "going on eighteen," allowing what Blanche DuBois (who herself conducts affairs with teenage boys) would have called "little familiarities" at the hands of a man who is, admittedly, more than twice her age. Despite the disproportion between their ages, however, this seems a relationship which if disturbing is relaxed and not overtly exploitative. Though hardly an innocent encounter it is presented as little more than a parodic teenage tryst. If the genders were reversed we would have *Tea and Sympathy.* Peck partly undresses and fondles Li'l Bit but Vogel instructs that this is to be performed in mime while the mock solemnity with which it is enacted—"Sacred music, organ music or a boys' choir" swells as she permits the intimacies—defuses its potential for affront. If anything, power seems to reside with the young woman and not the man whose behavior makes him seem younger than he is, and more dependent.

In *How I Learned to Drive* we see the effect before we understand the cause, detect the trauma before being told its root. We learn early that at eighteen Li'l Bit leaves college for a string of dead-end jobs because of her fondness for alcohol, spending the nights driving through the countryside "thinking just one notch of the steering wheel would be all it would take" to end it all. However, it takes much of the play to understand what lies behind this suicidal impulse.

Meanwhile, though Peck damages Li'l Bit, she is his lifeline, all that stops him free-falling towards death, and despite his calculated seduction of a vulnerable girl he still offers her an understanding that no one else in her family cares to do, and, ultimately, warns her against himself, thus surrendering the one thing that holds him back from despair, an action that has led Vogel to call him "heroic." As Vogel observed, "I see him as teaching her ego formation, as giving her the tools to grow up and reject him and destroy him."

Peck never forces himself on Li'l Bit, though he plots his campaign with the skill of a practiced seducer and there are suggestions that she has not been his only victim. When she storms out of the family home in a teenage fury Peck's wife, Aunt Mary, observes that "Peck's so good with them when they get to be this age," while his approach to the weeping girl is described in a stage note to be "like stalking a deer."

His method is obliquely exposed in what is one of the most disturbing scenes in the play, when he describes a fishing trip back in South Carolina with a young male cousin. His strategy with fish mirrors that which he adopts with the young woman he desires: "they're very shy, mercurial, fish. Takes patience and psychology. You have to believe it doesn't matter if you catch one or not . . . you don't want to get close — they're frisky and shy little things . . . easy, reel and then net — let it play." And when the fish is landed his comments to his young cousin are a displaced version of his relationship with the young Li'l Bit: "I don't want you to feel ashamed about crying. I'm not going to tell anyone, okay? I can keep secrets . . . There's nothing you could do that would make me feel ashamed of you . . . you can't tell anybody . . . least of all your mom or your sisters. This is something special between you and me." It is Peck's apparently genuine gentleness combined with his patient cunning that is the source of his seductive power. He is driven by his sexual need but that very need gives him an insight into the vulnerabilities of others.

For Vogel, it is clear that Peck does molest his young cousin. Indeed she saw his equal attraction to young girls and boys as a necessary counterbalance to assumptions that pedophiles are gay: "it is the age that is the attraction, not the gender." When she was invited to delete the scene she insisted on retaining it, not least because she felt she owed a debt to her gay brother to clarify what she saw as a slur on gay men. At the same time the scene had not featured in her own outline for the play. It was a product of the process of writing, but it gave her and the audience what she came to feel was a crucial sense of distance, and became a vital element in the drama.

Vogel reminds her audience of the arbitrariness of the lines drawn by society. What is legitimate at eighteen is statutory rape at the age of seventeen. As Li'l Bit's grandmother reminds her daughter, "It was legal, what Daddy and I did! I was fourteen and in those days, fourteen was a grown-up woman." As a gay writer Vogel knows all too well the capricious nature of sexual prohibitions. But, as the play progresses so she raises the stakes and the audience is forced to revise its reaction to the early scene, forced to question its liberal or sentimental response as Li'l Bit becomes first seventeen, then sixteen, then fifteen and, finally, eleven. If the line was not crossed in the opening scene then it is later and we are led, little by little, into the heart of that darkness, a darkness which Li'l Bit herself, however, eventually begins to understand or at least to find echoed in her own experience.

At the age of twenty-seven she experiences the same thrill that she imagines, in retrospect, Peck must have felt as she meets a teenage boy on a bus and seduces him, staging a drama in which she is author, director and principal actor: "dramatically speaking," she explains,

> after the faltering and slightly comical "first act," there was the very briefest of intermissions, and an extremely capable and forceful and sustained [. . .] discussion — I lay on my back in the dark and I thought about you, Uncle Peck. Oh. Oh — this is the allure. Being older. Being the first. Being the translator, the teacher, the epicure, the already jaded. This is how the giver gets taken.

In one sense this could be seen as an account of how abused becomes abuser but it is equally an attempt to understand the seductiveness of seduction, the allure of innocence, the compelling nature of power, the fascination that lies in devising a plot that will enfold another's life. And the fact that Vogel chooses a theatrical metaphor is, perhaps, not without its significance in that the playwright, too, deals in the manipulation of emotions, the seduction of others. She, too, takes her audience to places they have not been, exposes them to experiences which threaten their composure, moral assurance and, ultimately, therefore, innocence. She, too, works by stealth. The description of Peck's fishing technique could, indeed, be seen as an account of her own dramatic strategy in *How I Learned to Drive:* "reel and then rest—let it play."

As the play's title suggests, the principal metaphor is that of the driving lesson. On a literal level it is this that enables Peck to secure time alone with Li'l Bit. But beyond this it charts their developing relationship and Li'l Bit's increasing autonomy. When Peck insists that "when you are driving, your life is in your own two hands," he is offering her a lesson in responsibility for her own life. When he speaks of the power it conveys, he is explaining the necessity for her to realize her own strength. Most significantly, when he instructs her in the need to "think what the other guy is going to do before he does it," this is something more than a piece of roadcraft advice. It is, we later realize, a genuine warning against his own planned action, a moment of honesty, a proffered grace. To think ahead, he insists, is to be the only one to survive an impending disaster. Indeed it is tempting to think that perhaps Peck has summoned Li'l Bit into being, or at least forged her into a weapon against himself, precisely to be his nemesis, to punish himself for past, present and future sins. Certainly he trains her to survive without him while simultaneously struggling to hold on to her.

Throughout the play, a Voice, of "the type . . . that driver education films employ" [. . .], offers a commentary on driver skills which likewise comments, often ironically, on Li'l Bit's unfolding relationship with Peck. Thus, at this moment, it remarks that "Good defensive driving involves mental and physical preparation" and asks *"Are you prepared?"* Another Voice immediately adds: "You and the Reverse Gear." Li'l Bit does not go into reverse any more than does Peck and the drive (automotive and sexual) continues, as does the journey on which they are, apparently mutually, engaged. The question *"Are you prepared?"* however, echoes throughout the text.

The references to driving thus apply as much to Li'l Bit's relationship with Peck as to road safety awareness, and that fact is underlined by phrases which implicitly comment on the unfolding action: Idling in Neutral Gear, Shifting Forward from First Gear to Second Gear, You and the Reverse Gear (the last displayed as the action moves back into the past), *Vehicle failure* (displayed as Li'l Bit is incapacitated by drink), *Implied consent, Children depend on you to watch them.* These comments, in turn, are accompanied by projected signs with equally evident ambiguities: Slow Children, Dangerous Curves, One Way. Indeed, this parallel even infiltrates the stage directions, Vogel referring to Li'l Bit and Peck as "running out of gas," a phrase glossed as meaning "running out of small talk."

Where does responsibility lie in this relationship? Clearly with Peck, but there is a level at which Li'l Bit colludes. There is, in the words of the Voice, an "Implied consent," and this is where the play treads dangerous ground. Plainly in *Lolita* the young girl is a knowing collaborator in her own seduction. In Vogel's play she is led to such implied consent by Peck's seductive skills, but also by their shared sense of exclusion. She responds to his evident need as he in turn offers her understanding. He exploits her youth and innocence, damages her, but also, in his own terms, seeks her consent and will not transgress the terms of that consent. He indulges his own needs, subordinating hers to his, rationalizing his behavior, and yet, finally, hands her back her life at ultimate cost to himself. Nothing he does justifies his actions but his own vulnerabilities are real. There is a kind of innocence even at the center of his corrupting power, for there is no reason to doubt that at the heart of his obsession there is love, as at the heart of his love there is obsession. [. . .]

Meanwhile, beneath his practical competency, his air of quiet assurance, Peck is plainly lonely and disturbed, driven by demons he can neither name nor defeat. His wife can do nothing to address his needs. Aware of his relationship with their niece, she sees it as a temporary infatuation inspired by a manipulative girl. Yet whatever pain lies at the heart of Peck's life all she can offer is domesticity, routine and what she imagines to be a restorative banality, as if this man could settle for something as prosaic as that. She lives with a stranger and seems to understand nothing beyond the fact of his suffering. The plight of her niece, meanwhile, matters not at all. She offers less love than a baffled and frustrated attempt at understanding.

Li'l Bit, by contrast, does care for Peck. On their last encounter in a hotel we are told that she is "half wanting to run, half wanting to get it over with, half wanting to be held by him." She comes close to kissing him but tears herself away. He is destroyed. The lifeline cut, he is, finally, lost. As Li'l Bit explains: "It took my uncle seven years to drink himself to death. First he lost his job, then his wife, and finally his driver's license. He retreated to his house, and had his bottles delivered." The loss of his driver's license is simultaneously a fact and a symbol as he loses that power over his direction, that command of his life, which he had once tried to teach the young girl he both abused and loved as they sat side by side and he taught her the ambiguous lessons of life.

Nor is Li'l Bit shown as ultimately damaged. This is not an accusatory play. Indeed, it ends on a note of reconciliation. As Li'l Bit drives off in her car, in the final scene, she looks in her rearview mirror and smiles at the spirit of Peck who sits behind her. She is now in charge of the car. She did, in the end, accept his advice and anticipated the problems coming towards her. She is, as he had urged her to be, the only one to survive the accident. [. . .]

Vogel has talked of her alarm at the growth of a victim culture in the United States—the desire to shuffle off responsibility for one's life by locating some external cause for failure. "I hate the word victim," she has said. "It's a buzz word people use these days. We're all victims just by virtue of being alive."[1] Li'l Bit's education is thus not only in the occasional cruelties and disabling selfishness of others, but the knowledge and acceptance of her ultimate responsibility for her own life. She comes to recognize in herself a desire for power as well as that unfocused need which had characterized Peck, until he chose to focus it on a girl whose very innocence made her a *tabula rasa,* a place to inscribe his own desperation. [. . .] And if Li'l Bit learns from Peck how cruelly exploitative some people are she also learns their potential for something which perhaps could only be called love.

She learns that her own life consists of everything that has happened to her and that a life of blame or regret is no life at all. Ironically, she never accuses him of the crime which in truth he committed. Indeed, in some ways she devises the rules of the deeply suspect games they play. Even as a woman in her thirties (who, after all, narrates this play much as did Tom in *The Glass Menagerie*) revisiting her own past, she does so not to lay blame or make accusations but to understand her life so that she may live it without regret. As a result, the audience does not reject Peck but grants him his own pain, his own bruised dignity, his own curious courage in the face of feelings he struggles to contain. But they do so not because of the man

---

[1]Steven Druckman, "A Playwright on the Edge," *New York Times* (March 16, 1997), H6.

himself—manipulative, exploitative, dangerous but also compassionate, understanding, self-sacrificing—but because Li'l Bit accepts him in all his confusions and moral equivocations. The man we see is the man she reconstitutes in her memory. She declines the opportunity retrospectively to invent him as pure villain and herself as simple victim, and as a result can take her life in her hands and not, finally, cede it to another, not entomb herself in a myth that can only leave her the helpless product of circumstance, the residue of process and the result of abuse. As Vogel has said, "I had no interest in a movie-of-the-week drama about child-molesting." She wished, rather, "to see if audiences will *allow* themselves to find this erotic; otherwise, they only see victimization without empowerment."[2] To her, the essence of the play lay not simply in the fact of the relationship but its consequence. As she explained, "it seems to me that one thing that gets left out when we're talking about trauma is the victim's responsibility to look the experience squarely in the eye and then to move on. That's the journey I wanted to craft here" (*Playbill*, Century Theatre).

How I Learned to Drive plays against our expectations. It seeks to go beyond the labels, the categories which do little to explain ourselves to ourselves. It is about a love affair which, if not mutual, nevertheless, and not entirely paradoxically, does have love on each side. It is about a man whose loneliness is too deep to be filled, who looks for consolation in the wrong place but loves enough eventually to release the object of that love, a man who inhabits a society that is itself deeply confused as to the role of sexuality. The music to which Vogel wrote the play and which she suggests should accompany the action, is, as she has said, "rife with pedophilia," a word she seldom uses in interviews: "Dream Baby," "You're Sixteen," "Little Surfer Girl," "This Girl Is a Woman Now," "Come Back When You Grow Up." Peck, in other words, is not some aberration, someone to be labeled and filed away. He inhabits an ambiguity that reaches out beyond the parameters of his own special need.

David Savran (b. 1950)
PAULA VOGEL   *1999*

David Savran, Paula Vogel's colleague in the English Department at Brown University, is well known for his series of interviews with contemporary playwrights. His interview with Paula Vogel appears in his book The Playwright's Voice (1999), *but this excerpt is his review of Vogel's career and precedes the interview itself. His observations describe in an economical fashion the special features of her work.*

In her playwriting classes, Paula Vogel always asks her students to write the impossible: a play with a dog as protagonist, a play that cannot be staged, a play that dramatizes the end of the world in five pages. And while these provocative exercises stretch students' imaginations in remarkable ways, they also inadvertently reveal much about Vogel's own playwriting. For all her plays endeavor to stage the impossible. They defy traditional theater logic, subtly calling conventions into

---

[2]Steven Druckman, "A Playwright on the Edge," *New York Times* (March 16, 1997), H6.

question or, in some cases, pushing them well past their limits. What other play-wright would dare memorialize her brother in a play filled with fart jokes and riotous sex, whose medical authority, a cross between Dr. Strangelove and Grou-cho Marx, ends up drinking his own piss? What other feminist would dare write so many jokes about tits?

For a Vogel play is never simply a politely dramatized fiction, it is always a med-itation on the theater itself—on role-playing, on the socially sanctioned scripts from which characters diverge at their peril, and on a theatrical tradition that has punished women who don't remain quiet, passive and demure. Take, for example, *The Mineola Twins* (1996), which plays deliriously and chillingly with the age-old farcical convention of using one virtuosic actor (and a battery of wigs) to play two startlingly dissimilar identical twins. Or *Hot 'n' Throbbing* (1994), which trans-forms a theater into a living room and a living room into a theater in order to dramatize the fatal consequences of stage directions gone out of control. Or her Pulitzer Prize–winning *How I Learned to Drive* (1997), which does far more than explain the effects of sexual predation on a young girl; it literally splits her into two—a body and a voice—in order to represent the radical alienation from Self that results from having been molested.

In *How I Learned to Drive*, Vogel turns the theater itself into a vehicle for mem-ory, using first gear to move forward in time and reverse to move backwards. By reenacting the driving lessons given her by her Uncle Peck, Li'l Bit remembers her strangely—and literally—intoxicating sexual initiation. For there is no question but that her uncle's seduction has caused her to retreat "above the neck." At the same time, Peck, that most charming of pedophiles and himself a victim of abuse, is the only member of her family who makes a real effort to understand, nurture, and help her grow up. For *How I Learned to Drive* is the story not only of Li'l Bit's molestation. It is also a slyly subversive dramatization of how a girl—perhaps any girl—becomes an adult.

At the beginning of the play, Li'l Bit remembers the suburban Maryland of her youth, completely absorbed in the touch, smell, and taste of a "warm summer evening." These sensory perceptions connect her to the past, to the land and to her own body as she renders herself miraculously whole again through the power of memory. But as Li'l Bit knows all too well—and any adult will tell you—this pri-mordial wholeness cannot last, and the remainder of the play shows her being taken for a drive that will lead her into another realm, one dominated by the senses of sight and hearing. For if touch, smell, and taste are the tokens of intimacy and wholeness, then sight and hearing are undeniably the most objectifying of the senses; they introduce a radical separation between subject and object. This is per-haps why the very center of the play is a photo shoot, for it is in this scene that Li'l Bit most graphically becomes an object for Uncle Peck and, more ominously, for herself as well. Yet this sequence is so effective theatrically because it tacitly recog-nizes that sight and hearing are also the senses, by no mere coincidence, upon which theater depends. It demonstrates that the theater, like the photo shoot, will always produce figures who are subjected to the scrutiny of voyeuristic spectators (or lascivious uncles). Li'l Bit, in other words, suddenly discovers that she has become an actor in a drama that has been scripted for her by an exploitative, if well-meaning spectator who is, in turn, the product of a society that values women for their allure. Yet *How I Learned to Drive* is no more an indictment of theater than it is of eroticism. For it is precisely the theater that gives Li'l Bit the time and the place to remember, that is, to reconstruct herself, to put herself back together. In learning to drive, the play shows us, Li'l Bit learns how to desire, how to use the theater, and the act of self-presentation, to put herself quite literally in the driver's seat.

In *How I Learned to Drive,* Li'l Bit is literally haunted by the unquiet spirit of her Uncle Peck in the same way that Anna in *The Baltimore Waltz* (1992)—and Vogel herself—is haunted by the spirit of her dead brother, Carl. For in attempting to remember, Vogel's theater calls up ghosts, figures lighter than air yet heavy with the past. It is obsessed with commemorating what has been lost, while understanding that loss always pays a kind of dividend that is experienced both on a personal and cultural level. For Vogel's ghosts always materialize at the place where memory turns into history, the particular into the universal. Thus, *Baltimore Waltz* becomes an exhilarating tribute and love letter not only to Carl, but to everyone who has died of AIDS, in the same way that *Drive,* by staging Li'l Bit's singular journey, dramatizes the relentless process by which we are each being produced as the subjects and objects of our own dramas.

For all their precision in documenting the act of remembering, Vogel's plays are perhaps unique in the way that they locate memory in the body. For it is far more than her punning sensibility that inspires her to title her most recent collection *The Mammary Plays* (TCG, 1998). Summoning up the "full-figured gal" of TV-commercial fame, both *Drive* and *The Mineola Twins* simultaneously exploit and critique the cliché of this "stacked" femme fatale. Both tacitly acknowledge that female bodies are steeped in history, that "sometimes the body," as Uncle Peck puts it, "knows things that the mind isn't listening to." And like her other plays, they are intent on listening to and reclaiming that lost, forgotten history. For as a feminist writer, Vogel not only attends to the deeply contradictory representations of women in our culture, but also delineates female characters who are prepared to use their physical charms (if need be) to wrest control of their lives. From the sprightly geriatric prostitutes of *The Oldest Profession* (1988) who have seized the means of production; to Myra, Mineola's answer to Patricia Hearst and Patricia Ireland; to the lesbian parents of three imaginary little boys in *And Baby Makes Seven* (1984); Vogel's women are themselves playwrights who attempt to write their way out of difficult situations and script more creative, bountiful lives. Like Vogel herself, they are committed to redressing a history of oppression by rewriting the scenes they have been handed. By so turning her female characters (and her students!) into playwrights of no mean accomplishments, she suggests that although a triumphal feminist theater seems an impossibility in our time, one may nonetheless endeavor to stage that impossibility, along with the glittering promises it holds.

Caryl Churchill

Caryl Churchill (b. 1938) is in many ways a conventional middle-class woman. She was born in London to a comfortable family: her father was a political cartoonist and her mother a model. During World War II, her family emigrated to Canada, and much of her growing up was done in Montreal. She returned to England for college, receiving her degree in English literature at Oxford.

Churchill says that through all these years she did all the right things. She was a proper intellectual, a proper student, a proper person. She began writing plays in Oxford, where they were produced by students. After college, she married David Harter, also from Oxford, who became a lawyer in London. She raised three sons and at the same time tried to keep alive her dream of being a writer. Most of her early work was written for radio, and many of the plays were short. With so many children in the house, she says, it was difficult to sustain a long project.

Churchill's social conscience has been a significant part of her playwriting and her life. She found herself sometimes depressed by the dullness of the middle-class life demanded of the wife of a lawyer, and much of her early drama is satire directed at what many people thought was an enviable lifestyle.

In the early 1970s her husband left a very lucrative practice and has since devoted himself to helping the poor at a nearby legal aid center. She has become involved in theater groups, among them a group of women called Monstrous Regiment. She is closely aligned with the Royal Court Theatre in London, noted for producing satiric, biting, experimental drama with a punch.

Her first play staged at the Royal Court Theatre was a farcical but serious play called *Owners* (1972). It attacks the way that the concept of ownership destroys potential relationships. Churchill's basic socialist views are very apparent in the play, which is a critique of the values that most capitalists take for granted: being aggressive, getting ahead, doing well. Although this play is not explicitly feminist, Churchill combines socialism and feminism in most of her plays, thus often producing an unusual approach to her subject matter. *Owners* has been criticized for its Brechtian use of disconnected scenes and its loose plot, but when it was produced off Broadway in 1973, it marked Churchill as a serious playwright.

After a year as a playwright in residence at the Royal Court Theatre, Churchill produced *Objections to Sex and Violence* (1975). The play was not immensely successful, but it introduced themes of feminism into her work. Among other themes, the play examines in depth the domination of women by men and the relationship of violence to sex roles.

In 1976 Churchill produced *Vinegar Tom*, a play about witch hunts set in the seventeenth century. After researching witch trials, Churchill concluded that women were convenient scapegoats for men when times became difficult. A companion play also set in the seventeenth century is *Light Shining in*

Buckinghamshire, which studies revolutions. The play was developed by the Joint Stock Theatre Group and produced at the Royal Court Theatre to uniformly positive reviews.

Her first play to receive wide notice was *Cloud Nine* (1979). It treats several themes simultaneously, among them colonization. The first act is set in the Victorian era in a British colony of Africa. The play is broadly satirical, involving farcical moments in the relationships of colonialist and native, master and servant, and man and woman. Churchill cast certain parts of the play in a cross-gender fashion: a woman plays a sensitive schoolboy, and a man plays an unfulfilled wife. The effect is both comic and instructive, since one of her most important purposes is to cast some light on gender distinctions. She said that she saw "parallels between the way colonizers treat the colonized and the way men tended to treat women in our own society." *Cloud Nine* was produced in the Lucille Lortel Theatre, where it ran for two years off Broadway and won an Obie award.

Top Girls (1982) played at the Royal Court Theatre in London and at the Public Theater in New York, where the reviews were mixed. The play, essentially feminist in theme, was praised in England for being "the best British play ever from a woman dramatist." *Fen* (1983) was warmly praised by critics and audiences alike. A study of the effects of poverty on women, the play was developed with the Joint Stock Theatre Group and set in the area of England called the Fens, a flat country prone to flooding, where women work the fields and most of the people are poor.

Churchill's *Serious Money* (1987) is a verse play (like her first Oxford play) about the London stock market. It ran on Broadway to exceptional acclaim, partly because it played just after the stock market crash of October 1987. The play is a satiric study of those for whom only greed and getting ahead matter.

Churchill has written a number of plays for radio and television, such as *Lovesick, Abortive, Not Not Not Not Not Enough Oxygen, Schreber's Nervous Illness, The Hospital at the Time of the Revolution,* and *The Judge's Wife.* These are gathered in a volume called *Shorts* (1990). *The Skriker* (1994) is an experiment in fantasy, with a spirit world that parallels the real world. *Blue Heart* (1999) consists of two one-act plays: *Heart's Desire* and *Blue Kettle.* These are relatively realistic domestic dramas. *Heart's Desire* is a satire set in a sparkling kitchen where Alice and Brian wait, with Brian's sister Maisie, for the return of their daughter from Australia. Their peaceful setting is invaded by alcoholics and terrorists, among others, and yet the play has been described as "achingly, aggressively funny." *Blue Kettle* features a young man who searches for women who have given up children for adoption and then claims to be their lost son. It is a somber play that deals with the failure of language.

Among Churchill's latest plays, *Far Away* (2000) is a dark piece on the subject of modern life and modern politics as seen in the context of the millennium. *A Number* (2002) treats the relationship of fathers and sons in a remarkably unusual way. A man has his son cloned twenty-one times and, in this play, interacts with two of those clones. *A Dream Play* (2005) is an adaptation of a Strindberg play with the addition of Freudian implications. *Drunk Enough to Say I Love You?* (2006) focuses on world domination, torture, and war, but from the perspective of a computer game. Jack (Union Jack), a British man, goes to America to live with Sam (Uncle Sam), and the two plot the control of the world. One review said simply that it was the best value in London theater during its run. Churchill is one of the most prolific of modern playwrights and continues to stir audiences all over the world.

FAR AWAY

One of the early reviews of *Far Away* describes it as a "brief nightmare of a play." That is an apt description, given the way Joan's innocence at the beginning of the play contrasts with her experience of killing at the end of the play. Churchill wrote the play at the beginning of the millennium, after the war in Bosnia and the Persian Gulf War ended but the threat of more turmoil lay ahead. We see this play in the light of ongoing genocides in several parts of the world in the twenty-first century, and we quickly become as involved as the characters on stage.

The title, *Far Away*, evokes the opening of a fairy tale: "Far away, and long ago . . . ," but in this play Churchill looks not backward but into the future. The fairy tale quality of the title persists in the opening of the play, in which Harper tells little Joan, who cannot sleep because of what she has seen, that everything is all right—that what she has seen is not quite what she thinks she has seen. Harper is like every parent who tries to calm a disturbed child and who, in the process, tells what seem like innocent lies in order to restore confidence in the child. The references to nighttime animals, such as the owl and other birds, fail to calm Joan. She has seen violent images that she does not understand: children being beaten and men being clubbed and imprisoned— all by her own uncle. Harper's reassurance never truly comforts Joan and never truly explains what is happening. Later, we realize that the visions Joan has are merely a preparation for what is to come.

The scenes that follow, several years later, show Joan and Todd in a factory making hats. Clearly the hats are metaphors. As Todd himself says, "The hats are ephemeral. It's like a metaphor for something or other." And Joan answers, "Well, life." Todd agrees, but we are not sure this explanation is the end of it. The hats they make are fantastic and become more fantastic as they go on making them. In scene 5, which has no dialogue, just a procession of men wearing all these hats, we see that the destination of the hats is not life but the execution of all the men who wear them. In a stage direction for that scene, Churchill says that five men are too few and that twenty are better than ten. She also suggests a hundred because there really is no end to the ritual killings of the modern age.

The third part of the play brings Harper, Todd, and Joan together, although when the scene begins, Joan, who was an insomniac in scene 1, is now in a deep sleep. Harper and Todd talk about the current situation, a war greater than any total war in history. There is no safe place and no safe side to be on. In this war, the animals, who continue to care for their offspring, have taken sides in this global conflict. The very elements—the winds, gravity, the weather, even light—

are taking sides in the fight. In Joan's remarkable final speech, she reveals that the world has become her nightmare from the opening scene.

Far Away in Performance

Stephen Daldry's production at the Royal Court Theatre, Upstairs, in December 2000, was praised for its vitality, daring, and the moods established by the sets and lighting. One reviewer noted that the clothing and furniture of the opening scene suggested the 1930s, which might then connect to the rise of fascism, whereas another reviewer saw the drama as pointing to a time (the present) when more tyrannical governments were exterminating large numbers of their citizens. The distinguished director Peter Brook brought the play, in French, to Paris at the Theatre des Bouffes du Nord in 2002, also to very positive reviews. As in England, the play was considered apocalyptic in its darkness. The New York Theatre Workshop production in 2002, with Frances McDormand as Harper, garnered extremely positive reviews. The play's message resonated powerfully in New York, especially in light of the destruction of the World Trade towers on September 11, 2001. McDormand's excellent sense of timing—particularly her hesitations in scene 1—were noted in the reviews. The Zeitgeist Theater produced the play in Boston in 2004 in a black box setting that, reviewers felt, was less powerful than the New York and London productions with their more lavish costumes and settings. Joy Zinoman produced the play in 2004 at the Studio Theater in Washington, D.C., again to very positive reviews even in a stripped-down version. Peter Marks, in the *Washington Post,* said, "Her play, *Far Away,* is a quick jab at the brain and the solar plexus, an insinuating little work that melds terror and whimsy in a way you've never seen before." Genesis West's 2006 production in Santa Barbara lightened the mood a bit by auctioning off the hats at the end of the run. More productions have followed in Australia and Europe. As long as this play reflects the world we live in, or will live in, it will continue to be performed.

Caryl Churchill (b. 1938)
FAR AWAY

2000

Characters

JOAN, *a girl*
HARPER, *her aunt*
TODD, *a young man*

Playwright's Note: *The Parade (scene 2.5): five is too few and twenty better than ten. A hundred?*

1.

Harper's house. Night.

JOAN: I can't sleep.
HARPER: It's the strange bed.
JOAN: No, I like different places.
HARPER: Are you cold?
JOAN: No.
HARPER: Do you want a drink?
JOAN: I think I am cold.
HARPER: That's easy enough then. There's extra blankets in the cupboard.
JOAN: Is it late?
HARPER: Two.
JOAN: Are you going to bed?
HARPER: Do you want a hot drink?
JOAN: No thank you.
HARPER: I should go to bed then.
JOAN: Yes.

HARPER: It's always odd in a new place. When you've been here a week you'll look back at tonight and it won't seem the same at all.

JOAN: I've been to a lot of places. I've stayed with friends at their houses. I don't miss my parents if you think that.

HARPER: Do you miss your dog?

JOAN: I miss the cat I think.

HARPER: Does it sleep on your bed?

JOAN: No because I chase it off. But it gets in if the door's not properly shut. You think you've shut the door but it hasn't caught and she pushes it open in the night.

HARPER: Come here a minute. You're shivering. Are you hot?

JOAN: No, I'm all right.

HARPER: You're over-tired. Go to bed. I'm going to bed myself.

JOAN: I went out.

HARPER: When? just now?

JOAN: Just now.

HARPER: No wonder you're cold. It's hot in the daytime here but it's cold at night.

Frances McDormand as Harper and Alexa Eisenstein as Young Joan in the 2002 New York Theater Workshop production of *Far Away*.

JOAN: The stars are brighter here than at home.

HARPER: It's because there's no street lights.

JOAN: I couldn't see much.

HARPER: I don't expect you could. How did you get out? I didn't hear the door.

JOAN: I went out the window.

HARPER: I'm not sure I like that.

JOAN: No it's quite safe, there's a roof and a tree.

HARPER: When people go to bed they should stay in bed. Do you climb out of the window at home?

JOAN: I can't at home because—No I don't.

HARPER: I'm responsible for you.

JOAN: Yes, I'm sorry.

HARPER: Well that's enough adventures for one night. You'll sleep now. Off you go. Look at you, you're asleep on your feet.

JOAN: There was a reason.

HARPER: For going out?

JOAN: I heard a noise.

HARPER: An owl?

JOAN: A shriek.

HARPER: An owl then. There are all sorts of birds here, you might see a golden oriole. People come here specially to watch birds and we sometimes make tea or coffee or sell bottles of water because there's no café and people don't expect that and they get thirsty. You'll see in the morning what a beautiful place it is.

JOAN: It was more like a person screaming.

HARPER: It is like a person screaming when you hear an owl.

JOAN: It was a person screaming.

HARPER: Poor girl, what a fright you must have had imagining you heard somebody screaming. You should have come straight down here to me.

JOAN: I wanted to see.

HARPER: It was dark.

JOAN: Yes but I did see.

HARPER: Now what did you imagine you saw in the dark?

JOAN: I saw my uncle.

HARPER: Yes I expect you did. He likes a breath of air. He wasn't screaming I hope?

JOAN: No.

HARPER: That's all right then. Did you talk to him? I expect you were frightened he'd say what are you doing out of your bed so late.

JOAN: I stayed in the tree.

HARPER: He didn't see you?

JOAN: No.

HARPER: He'll be surprised won't he, he'll laugh when he hears you were up in the tree. He'll be cross but he doesn't mean it, he'll think it's a good joke, it's the sort of thing he did when he was a boy. So bed now. I'll go up too.

JOAN: He was pushing someone. He was bundling someone into a shed.

HARPER: He must have been putting a big sack in the shed. He works too late.

JOAN: I'm not sure if it was a woman. It could have been a young man.

HARPER: Well I have to tell you, when you've been married as long as I have. There are things people get up to, it's natural, it's nothing bad, that's just friends of his your uncle was having a little party with.

JOAN: Was it a party?

HARPER: Just a little party.

JOAN: Yes because there wasn't just that one person.

HARPER: No, there'd be a few of his friends.

JOAN: There was a lorry.°

HARPER: Yes, I expect there was.

JOAN: When I put my ear against the side of the lorry I heard crying inside.

HARPER: How could you do that from up in the tree?

JOAN: I got down from the tree. I went to the lorry after I looked in the window of the shed.

HARPER: There might be things that are not your business when you're a visitor in someone else's house.

JOAN: Yes, I'd rather not have seen. I'm sorry.

HARPER: Nobody saw you?

JOAN: They were thinking about themselves.

HARPER: I think it's lucky nobody saw you.

JOAN: If it's a party, why was there so much blood?

HARPER: There isn't any blood.

JOAN: Yes.

HARPER: Where?

JOAN: On the ground.

HARPER: In the dark? how would you see that in the dark?

JOAN: I slipped in it.

(*She holds up her bare foot.*)

I mostly wiped it off.

HARPER: That's where the dog got run over this afternoon.

JOAN: Wouldn't it have dried up?

HARPER: Not if the ground was muddy.

JOAN: What sort of dog?

HARPER: A big dog, a big mongrel.

JOAN: That's awful, you must be very sad, had you had him long?

HARPER: No, he was young, he ran out, he was never very obedient, a lorry was backing up.

JOAN: What was his name?

HARPER: Flash.

JOAN: What color was he?

HARPER: Black with a bit of white.

JOAN: Why were the children in the shed?

HARPER: What children?

JOAN: Don't you know what children?

HARPER: How could you see there were children?

JOAN: There was a light on. That's how I could see the blood inside the shed. I could see the faces and which ones had blood on.

HARPER: You've found out something secret. You know that don't you?

JOAN: Yes.

HARPER: Something you shouldn't know.

lorry: A truck.

JOAN: Yes I'm sorry.

HARPER: Something you must never talk about. Because if you do you could put people's lives in danger.

JOAN: Why? who from? from my uncle?

HARPER: Of course not from your uncle.

JOAN: From you?

HARPER: Of course not from me, are you mad? I'm going to tell you what's going on. Your uncle is helping these people. He's helping them escape. He's giving them shelter. Some of them were still in the lorry, that's why they were crying. Your uncle's going to take them all into the shed and then they'll be all right.

JOAN: They had blood on their faces.

HARPER: That's from before. That's because they were attacked by the people your uncle's saving them from.

JOAN: There was blood on the ground.

HARPER: One of them was injured very badly but your uncle bandaged him up.

JOAN: He's helping them.

HARPER: That's right.

JOAN: There wasn't a dog. There wasn't a party.

HARPER: No, I'm trusting you with the truth now. You must never talk about it or you'll put your uncle's life in danger and mine and even your own. You won't even say anything to your parents.

JOAN: Why did you have me to stay if you've got this secret going on?

HARPER: The lorry should have come yesterday. It won't happen again while you're here.

JOAN: It can now because I know. You don't have to stop for me. I could help uncle in the shed and look after them.

HARPER: No, he has to do it himself. But thank you for offering, that's very kind. So after all that excitement do you think you could go back to bed?

JOAN: Why was uncle hitting them?

HARPER: Hitting who?

JOAN: He was hitting a man with a stick. I think the stick was metal. He hit one of the children.

HARPER: One of the people in the lorry was a traitor. He wasn't really one of them, he was pretending, he was going to betray them, they found out and told your uncle. Then he attacked your uncle, he attacked the other people, your uncle had to fight him.

JOAN: That's why there was so much blood.

HARPER: Yes, it had to be done to save the others.

JOAN: He hit one of the children.

HARPER: That would have been the child of the traitor. Or sometimes you get bad children who even betray their parents.

JOAN: What's going to happen?

HARPER: They'll go off in the lorry very early in the morning.

JOAN: Where to?

HARPER: Where they're escaping to. You don't want to have to keep any more secrets.

JOAN: He only hit the traitors.

HARPER: Of course. I'm not surprised you can't sleep, what an upsetting thing to see. But now you understand, it's not so bad. You're part of a big movement now to make things better. You can be proud of that. You can look at the stars and think here we are in our little bit of space, and I'm on the side of the people who are putting things right, and your soul will expand right into the sky.

JOAN: Can't I help?

HARPER: You can help me clean up in the morning. Will you do that?

JOAN: Yes.

HARPER: So you'd better get some sleep.

2.

Several years later. A hat makers.

1.

(*Joan and Todd are sitting at a workbench. They have each just started making a hat.*)

TODD: There's plenty of blue.

JOAN: I think I'm starting with black.

TODD: Color always wins.

JOAN: I will have color, I'm starting with black to set the color off.

TODD: I did one last week that was an abstract picture of the street, blue for the buses, yellow for the flats, red for the leaves, grey for the sky. Nobody got it but I knew what it was. There's little satisfactions to be had.

JOAN: Don't you enjoy it?

TODD: You're new aren't you?

JOAN: This is my first hat. My first professional hat.

TODD: Did you do hat at college?

JOAN: My degree hat was a giraffe six feet tall.

TODD: You won't have time to do something like that in the week.

JOAN: I know.

TODD: We used to get two weeks before a parade and then they took it down to one and now they're talking about cutting a day.

JOAN: So we'd get an extra day off?

TODD: We'd get a day's less money. We wouldn't make such good hats.

JOAN: Can they do that?

TODD: You'd oppose it would you?

JOAN: I've only just started.

TODD: You'll find there's a lot wrong with this place.

JOAN: I thought it was one of the best jobs.

TODD: It is. Do you know where to go for lunch?

JOAN: I think there's a canteen isn't there?

TODD: Yes but we don't go there. I'll show you where to go.

2.

(*Next day. They are working on the hats, which are by now far more brightly decorated. [That is,] the ones they were working on have been replaced by ones nearer completion.*)

JOAN: Your turn.

TODD: I go for a swim in the river before work.

JOAN: Isn't it dangerous?

TODD: Your turn.

JOAN: I've got a pilot's licence.

TODD: I stay up till four every morning watching the trials.

JOAN: I'm getting a room in a subway.

TODD: I've got my own place.

JOAN: Have you?

TODD: Do you want to see it? That's coming on.

JOAN: I don't understand yours but I like the feather.

TODD: I'm not trying. I've been here too long.

JOAN: Will you leave?

TODD: My turn. There's something wrong with how we get the contracts.

JOAN: But we want the contracts.

TODD: What if we don't deserve them? What if our work isn't really the best?

JOAN: So what's going on?

TODD: I'll just say a certain person's brother-in-law. Where does he work do you think?

JOAN: Where does he work?

TODD: I'm not talking about it in here. Tell me something else.

JOAN: I don't like staying in in the evenings and watching trials.

TODD: I watch them at night after I come back.

JOAN: Back from where?

TODD: Where do you like?

3.

(*Next day. They're working on the hats, which are getting very big and extravagant.*)

TODD: I don't enjoy animal hats myself.

JOAN: I was a student.

TODD: Abstract hats are back in a big way.

JOAN: I've always liked abstract hats.

TODD: You must have not noticed when everyone hated them.

JOAN: It was probably before my time.

Silence. They go on working.

JOAN: It's just if you're going on about it all the time I don't know why you don't do something about it.

TODD: This is your third day.

JOAN: The management's corrupt—you've told me. We're too low paid—you've told me.

Silence. They go on working.

TODD: Too much green.

JOAN: It's meant to be too much.

Silence. They go on working.

TODD: I noticed you looking at that fair boy's hat. I hope you told him it was derivative.

Silence. They go on working.

TODD: I'm the only person in this place who's got any

principles, don't tell me I should do something, I spend my days wondering what to do.

JOAN: So you'll probably come up with something.

Silence. They go on working.

4.

(*Next day. They are working on the hats, which are now enormous and preposterous.*)

TODD: That's beautiful.

JOAN: You like it?

TODD: I do.

JOAN: I like yours too.

TODD: You don't have to say that. It's not one of my best.

JOAN: No it's got—I don't know, it's a confident hat.

TODD: I have been doing parades for six years. So I'm a valued old hand. So when I go and speak to a certain person he might pay attention.

JOAN: You're going to speak to him?

TODD: I've an appointment after work.

JOAN: You might lose your job.

TODD: I might.

JOAN: I'm impressed.

TODD: That was the idea.

JOAN: Will you mention the brother-in-law?

TODD: First I'll talk about the money. Then I'll just touch in the brother-in-law. I've a friend who's a journalist.

JOAN: Will you touch in the journalist?

TODD: I might imply something without giving the journalist away. It might be better if he can't trace the journalist back to me.

JOAN: Though he will suspect.

TODD: However much he suspects. One thing if I lost my job.

JOAN: What's that?

TODD: I'd miss you.

JOAN: Already?

5.

(*Next day. A procession of ragged, beaten, chained prisoners, each wearing a hat, on their way to execution. The finished hats are even more enormous and preposterous than in the previous scene.*)

6.

(*A new week. Joan and Todd are starting work on new hats.*)

JOAN: I still can't believe it.

TODD: No one's ever won in their first week before.

JOAN: It's all going to be downhill from now on.

TODD: You can't win every week.

JOAN: That's what I mean.

TODD: No but you'll do a fantastic body of work while you're here.

The parade scene from the Royal Court Theatre's 2000 production of *Far Away*.

JOAN: Sometimes I think it's a pity that more aren't kept.

TODD: There'd be too many, what would they do with them?

JOAN: They could reuse them.

TODD: Exactly and then we'd be out of work.

JOAN: It seems so sad to burn them with the bodies.

TODD: No I think that's the joy of it. The hats are ephemeral. It's like a metaphor for something or other.

JOAN: Well, life.

TODD: Well, life, there you are. Out of nearly three hundred hats I've made here I've only had three win and go in the museum. But that's never bothered me. You make beauty and it disappears, I love that.

JOAN: You're so . . .

TODD: What?

JOAN: You make me think in different ways. Like I'd never have thought about how this place is run and now I see how important it is.

TODD: I think it did impress a certain person that I was speaking from the high moral ground.

JOAN: So tell me again exactly what he said at the end.

TODD: "These things must be thought about."

JOAN: I think that's encouraging.

TODD: It could mean he'll think how to get rid of me.

JOAN: That's a fantastic shape to start from.

TODD: It's a new one for me. I'm getting inspired by you.

JOAN: There's still the journalist. If he looks into it a bit more we could expose the corrupt financial basis of how the whole hat industry is run, not just this place, I bet the whole industry is dodgy.

TODD: Do you think so?

JOAN: I think we should find out.

TODD: You've changed my life, do you know that?

JOAN: If you lose your job I'll resign.

TODD: We might not get jobs in hats again.

JOAN: There's other parades.

TODD: But I think you're a hat genius.

JOAN: Unless all the parades are corrupt.

TODD: I love these beads. Use these beads.

JOAN: No, you have them.

TODD: No, you.

3.

(*Several years later. Harper's house, daytime.*)

HARPER: You were right to poison the wasps.

TODD: Yes, I think all the wasps have got to go.

HARPER: I was outside yesterday on the edge of the wood when a shadow came over and it was a cloud of butterflies, and they came down just beyond me and the trees and bushes were red with them. Two of them clung to my arm, I was terrified, one of them got in my hair, I managed to squash them.

TODD: I haven't had a problem with butterflies.

HARPER: They can cover your face. The Romans used to commit suicide with gold leaf, just flip it down their throat and it covered their windpipe, I think of that with butterflies.

TODD: I was passing an orchard, there were horses standing under the trees, and suddenly wasps attacked them out of the plums. There were the horses galloping by screaming with their heads made of wasp. I wish she'd wake up.

HARPER: We don't know how long she'd been walking.

TODD: She was right to come.

HARPER: You don't go walking off in the middle of a war.

TODD: You do if you're escaping.

HARPER: We don't know that she was escaping.

TODD: She was getting to a place of safety to regroup.

HARPER: Is this a place of safety?

TODD: Relatively, yes of course it is. Everyone thinks it's just a house.

HARPER: The cats have come in on the side of the French.

TODD: I never liked cats, they smell, they scratch, they only like you because you feed them, they bite, I used to have a cat that would suddenly just take some bit of you in its mouth.

HARPER: Did you know they've been killing babies?

TODD: Where's that?

HARPER: In China. They jump in the cots when nobody's looking.

TODD: But some cats are still ok.

HARPER: I don't think so.

TODD: I know a cat up the road.

HARPER: No, you must be careful of that.

TODD: But we're not exactly on the other side from the French. It's not as if they're the Moroccans and the ants.

HARPER: It's not as if they're the Canadians, the Venezuelans and the mosquitoes.

TODD: It's not as if they're the engineers, the chefs, the children under five, the musicians.

HARPER: The car salesmen.

TODD: Portuguese car salesmen.

HARPER: Russian swimmers.

TODD: Thai butchers.

HARPER: Latvian dentists.

TODD: No, the Latvian dentists have been doing good work in Cuba. They've a house outside Havana.

HARPER: But Latvia has been sending pigs to Sweden. The dentists are linked to international dentistry and that's where their loyalty lies, with dentists in Dar-es-Salaam.

TODD: We don't argue about Dar-es-Salaam.

HARPER: You would attempt to justify the massacre in Dar-es-Salaam?

   She's come here because you're here on leave and if anyone finds out I'll be held responsible.

TODD: It's only till tomorrow. I'll wake her up. I'll give her a few more minutes.

HARPER: Did you see the program about crocodiles?

TODD: Yes but crocodiles, the way they look after the baby crocodiles and carry them down to the water in their mouths.

HARPER: Don't you think everyone helps their own children?

TODD: I'm just saying I wouldn't be sorry if the crocodiles were on one of the sides we have alliances with. They're unstoppable, come on.

HARPER: Crocodiles are evil and it is always right to be opposed to crocodiles. Their skin, their teeth, the foul smell of their mouths from the dead meat. Crocodiles wait till zebras are crossing the river and bite the weak ones with those jaws and pull them down. Crocodiles invade villages at night and take children out of their beds. A crocodile will carry a dozen heads back to the river, tenderly like it carries its young, and put them in the water where they bob about as trophies till they rot.

TODD: I'm just saying we could use that.

HARPER: And the fluffy little darling waterbirds, the smallest one left behind squeaking wait for me, wait for me. And their mother who would give her life to save them.

TODD: Do we include mallards in this?

HARPER: Mallards are not a good waterbird. They commit rape, and they're on the side of the elephants and the Koreans. But crocodiles are always in the wrong.

TODD: Do you think I should wake her up or let her sleep? We won't get any time together.

HARPER: You agree with me about the crocodiles?

TODD: What's the matter? you don't know whose side I'm on?

HARPER: I don't know what you think.

TODD: I think what we all think.

HARPER: Take deer.

TODD: You mean sweet little bambis?

HARPER: You mean that ironically?

TODD: I mean it sarcastically.

HARPER: Because they burst out of parks and storm down from mountains and terrorize shopping malls. If the does run away when you shoot they run into somebody else and trample them with their vicious little shining hooves, the fawns get under the feet of shoppers and send them crashing down escalators, the young bucks charge the plate glass windows—

TODD: I know to hate deer.

HARPER: and the old ones, do you know how heavy their antlers are or how sharp the prongs are when they twist into teenagers running down the street?

TODD: Yes I do know that.

He lifts his shirt and shows a scar.

HARPER: Was that a deer?

TODD: In fact it was a bear. I don't like being doubted.

HARPER: It was when the elephants went over to the Dutch, I'd always trusted elephants.

TODD: I've shot cattle and children in Ethiopia. I've gassed mixed troops of Spanish, computer programmers and dogs. I've torn starlings apart with my bare hands. And I liked doing it with my bare hands. So don't suggest I'm not reliable.

HARPER: I'm not saying you can't kill.

TODD: And I know it's not all about excitement. I've done boring jobs. I've worked in abattoirs stunning pigs and musicians and by the end of the day your back aches and all you can see when you shut your eyes is people hanging upside down by their feet.

HARPER: So you'd say the deer are vicious?

TODD: We've been over that.

HARPER: If a hungry deer came into the yard you wouldn't feed it?

TODD: Of course not.

HARPER: I don't understand that because the deer are with us. They have been for three weeks.

TODD: I didn't know. You said yourself.

HARPER: Their natural goodness has come through. You can see it in their soft brown eyes.

TODD: That's good news.

HARPER: You hate the deer. You admire the crocodiles.

TODD: I've lost touch because I'm tired.

HARPER: You must leave.

TODD: I'm your family.

HARPER: Do you think I sleep?

(*Joan comes in and walks into Todd's arms.*)

HARPER: You can't stay here, they'll be after you. What are you going to say when you go back, you ran off to spend a day with your husband? Everyone has people they love they'd like to see or anyway people they'd rather see than lie in a hollow waiting to be bitten by ants. Are you not going back at all because if you're not you might as well shoot me now. Did anyone see you leave? which way did you come? were you followed? There are ospreys here who will have seen you arrive. And you're risking your life for you don't know what because he says things that aren't right. Don't you care? Maybe you don't know right from wrong yourself, what do I know about you after two years, I'd like to be glad to see you but how can I?

JOAN: Of course birds saw me, everyone saw me walking along but nobody knew why, I could have been on a mission, everyone's moving about and no one knows why, and in fact I killed two cats and a child under five so it wasn't that different from a mission, and I don't see why I can't have one day and then go back, I'll go on to the end after this. It wasn't so much the birds I was frightened of, it was the weather, the weather here's on the side of the Japanese. There were thunderstorms all through the mountains, I went through towns I hadn't been before. The rats are bleeding out of their mouths and ears, which is good, and so were the girls by the side of the road. It was tiring there because everything's been recruited, there were piles of bodies and if you stopped to find out there was one killed by coffee or one killed by pins, they were killed by heroin, petrol, chainsaws, hairspray, bleach, foxgloves, the smell of smoke was where we were burning the grass that wouldn't serve. The Bolivians are working with gravity, that's a secret so as not to spread alarm. But we're getting further with noise and there's thousands dead of light in Madagascar. Who's going to mobilize darkness and silence? that's what I wondered in the night. By the third day I could hardly walk but I got down to the river. There was a camp of Chilean soldiers upstream but they hadn't seen me and fourteen black and white cows downstream having a drink so I knew I'd have to go straight across. But I didn't know whose side the river was on, it might help me swim or it might drown me. In the middle the current was running much faster, the water was brown, I didn't know if that meant anything. I stood on the bank a long time. But I knew it was my only way of getting here so at last I put one foot in the river. It was very cold but so far that was all. When you've just stepped in you can't tell what's going to happen. The water laps round your ankles in any case.

Moisés Kaufman and the Tectonic Theater Project

Moisés Kaufman was born in 1963 in Caracas, Venezuela, and came to the United States in 1987. His parents were Romanian and Ukrainian Jews who had left Eastern Europe. He studied at a major university where most of the students studied business. After he came to New York, he said, "Being Jewish in a Catholic country, gay in an Orthodox Jewish school, an artist in a business school, and coming to the United States and becoming a Latino has given me an outsider's perspective." He was part of the noncommercial theater community of New York for many years.

Along with Jeffrey LaHoste, Kaufman founded the Tectonic Theater Project, a collaborative group of theatrical artists who were the driving force behind *The Laramie Project* from its inception in 1998 to the play's production in 2000. The Tectonic Theater Project's first play was *Women in Beckett* (1991), an adaptation of Samuel Beckett's short plays for women: *Footfalls, Not I, Rockaby,* and *Come and Go.* The casting included women between the ages of sixty and eighty. The group went on to produce a number of experimental plays, including *Machinal,* by Sophie Treadwell, and *Marlowe's Eyes*, by Naomi Iizuka, as well as other theatrical projects. In 1994 the Tectonic Theater Project produced Franz Xaver Kroetz's *The Nest,* which won several awards in its New York production and was named one of the ten best plays of the year by the *Village Voice.* Kaufman, in addition to being a writer, also directed a number of important theater projects, such as Beckett's *Endgame* and *In the Winter of Cities* by Tennessee Williams, both in the Frederick Loewe Theater at New York University.

The Tectonic Theater Project uses the word *tectonic* for its association with *architectonic,* which refers to principles of structure. Its projects often exhibit unusual structures, differing from conventional plays in several ways. For one thing, these projects employ many more characters than one expects from a contemporary play; *The Laramie Project* has more than sixty speaking parts. At the other extreme, the Tectonic Theater Project was instrumental in developing Doug Wright's *I Am My Own Wife,* a play with only one actor who assumes the roles of dozens of characters. In 1994, because the Tectonic Theater Project had made a decision to emphasize the text to a greater extent than before, Moisés Kaufman developed a play that relied on transcripts from trials and brought the company international recognition. This play was called *Gross Indecency: The Three Trials of Oscar Wilde.*

The budget for *Gross Indecency* was a mere $15,000, and the production began in Greenwich House, a small Greenwich Village theater. By word of mouth its reputation grew steadily until it moved into a larger space, the Minetta Lane Theatre, also in Greenwich Village. Once the press was lured downtown to write reviews, the play became a sensation. The play relied almost entirely on transcripts of the trials of Wilde, and on other documents from the period of 1895, when Wilde sued the Marquess of Queensbury for libel, for having accused him of being a sodomite. At the time, the Irish Oscar Wilde was 41, and the most distinguished playwright in England, with two plays—*The Importance of Being Ernest* and *An Ideal Husband*—being performed simultaneously in London's West End. As a result of the trials, Wilde was imprisoned and put to hard labor, his reputation destroyed, and his plays withdrawn. The point Kaufman was making is that a great writer was utterly destroyed by a society that could not tolerate his sexual orientation. The play itself was intense, focused, and (even with a minimum set and simple courtroom lighting) enormously involving. It ran for six hundred performances in New York and then went on to many cities in the United States and abroad.

Moisés Kaufman directed Doug Wright's Pulitzer Prize–winning *I Am My Own Wife* in December 2003, enlisting some of the techniques of the Tectonic Theater Project. In September 2007, at the Arena Theatre in Washington, D.C., the Project launched Kaufman's *33 Variations,* a play based on Beethoven's decision to write the *Diabelli Variations,* a piece that may be the most extensive theme-and-variation composition for piano. The play involves an actress who, in a section devoted to Beethoven's process of composition, plays some of the variations in the order in which they were composed. The modern section of the play focuses on Katherine Brandt, a musicologist who is suffering from amyotrophic lateral sclerosis (ALS), or "Lou Gehrig's disease." The two stories are told almost simultaneously as Brandt goes to Berlin to research the composition of the *Diabelli* and as she has to rely more and more on her reluctant daughter.

Moisés Kaufman and the Tectonic Theater Project continue to develop new projects, and Kaufman has won a Guggenheim Award to help sustain him in his work.

The Laramie Project

This play was begun after the murder of Matthew Shepard, an openly gay, twenty-one-year-old university student who was beaten so severely by two equally young men from Laramie, Wyoming, that the medical examiner almost refused to believe the damage done to him had been perpetrated by another human being. After he was beaten, Shepard was tied to a fence on a remote road, as if crucified, and left to die. When he was discovered by a bicyclist, he was first thought to be a Hallowe'en decoration or a battered scarecrow. The beating of Shepard was so savage that Laramie, a bulwark of the Western ethic of live and let live, and of the conservative values of independence and hard work, was shocked, not least to think how their town would be forever remembered by the rest of the nation.

The Tectonic Theater Project, consisting of artistic director Moisés Kaufman; managing director Jeffrey LaHoste, head writer and assistant director Leigh Fondakowski; associate writers Stephen Belber, Greg Pierotti, and Stephen Wangh; dramaturges Amanda Gronich, Sarah Lambert, John McAdams, Maude Mitchell, Andy Paris, Barbara Pitts, and Kelli Simpkins, set out in 1998 to make six visits to Laramie to talk with residents about what happened and what their reactions and feelings about the killing were and had become. The people they spoke with urged them to respect the feelings of the town and not to exaggerate or falsify the information they gathered. The members of the company were in Laramie so frequently over a period of two years that they became well known and — ultimately — trusted.

The play, drawn from some two hundred interviews, lasts two and a half hours on stage, and, as acknowledged by most of the people represented from Laramie, as well as by the critics who first saw the play, the project treats Laramie with considerable sensitivity. The play naturally reveals some antigay sentiment, even among those in the clergy. But it also reveals a considerable amount of soul-searching on the part of those who had believed that nothing like this killing could have happened in Laramie. Even the two young men who committed the crime — men who had been known for violence and for robbing unsuspecting young men they met in bars — were treated with a sense of compassion. Matthew Shepard's father came forth to offer forgiveness to those who had killed his son, and that went a long way toward helping the town begin the process of healing and coming to terms with what had happened.

The subject of the play is similar in some ways to Thornton Wilder's *Our Town* in that it portrays small-town America at a critical time in its history. The persons speaking are the inhabitants of that town, addressing their own neighbors and reflecting on the lives they live. A narrator helps to keep the material focused, and the dialogue seems spontaneous and unrehearsed. Another playwright who has approached similar material is Anna Deavere Smith, whose best-known play *Fires in the Mirror: Crown Heights, Brooklyn and Other Identities* (1992) is part of an ongoing series of theatrical pieces called *On the Road: A Search for American Character*. Smith transcribes interviews and impersonates all the speakers in a one-woman tour de force. By contrast, *The Laramie Project* used eight actors to deliver the lines of more than sixty characters, nearly all identified by their real names and their real positions in the town. (A few who speak are not identified simply because the original interviewee did not want his or her name revealed.)

In many ways, what the play achieves is a portrait of a single town in the West, but it also signals a warning to the larger community concerning the question of tolerance and the willingness to live true to the values of honesty and justice that are supposed to inform our society.

The Laramie Project in Performance

The Laramie Project premiered on February 27, 2000, at the Ricketson Theatre; it was produced by the Denver Theatre Centre, with help from Donovan Marley, the theater's artistic director. The stage setting, by Robert Brill, was bare: a brick back wall, a few chairs, a desk, one light, and some videos and film clips. The actors were the members of the Tectonic Theater Project who had worked on the interviews and helped in organizing and writing the material. In May of 2000, the play moved to the Union Square Theatre in New York with the same cast. The run continued until September with "packed houses," but then it ended so that the entire group could produce the film that HBO had scheduled for production in November. The HBO production used the original eight members of the Tectonic Theater Project and added a number of well-known actors, such as Steve Buscemi, Laura Linney, Kathleen Chalfant, and Peter Fonda. In 2001 the Tectonic Theater Project went to Sydney, Australia, to perform the play at the Belvoir Street Theatre, after which it played in Tokyo and then returned to the La Jolla Playhouse in California. Rob Ruggiero produced the play at TheaterWorks in Hartford, Connecticut, from August 1 to October 7, just before the HBO television production. In 2003 the play was presented at the Artwood Theatre, Toronto, and at the Cochrane Theatre, London, and in 2005 at London's Sound Theatre. With or without the original members of the Tectonic Theater Project, the play reaches out to audiences in the United States and abroad.

Moisés Kaufman (b. 1963) and The Tectonic Theater Project
THE LARAMIE PROJECT   2000

Characters

SHERRY AANENSON, *Russell Henderson's landlord, in her forties*

ANONYMOUS, *Friend of Aaron McKinney, in his twenties; works for the railroad*

BAILIFF

BAPTIST MINISTER, *Originally from Texas, in his fifties*

BAPTIST MINISTER'S WIFE, *In her late forties*

STEPHEN BELBER, *Member of Tectonic Theater Project*

DR. CANTWAY, *Emergency room doctor at Ivinson Memorial Hospital in Laramie, in his fifties*

CATHERINE CONNOLLY, *Out lesbian professor at the university, in her forties*

MURDOCK COOPER, *Rancher, in his fifties; resident of Centennial, a nearby town*

ROB DeBREE, *Detective sergeant for the Albany County Sheriff's Department, in his forties; chief investigator of Matthew's murder*

KERRY DRAKE, *Reporter with the* Casper Star-Tribune, *in his forties*

PHILIP DUBOIS, *President of the University of Wyoming, in his forties*

TIFFANY EDWARDS, *Local reporter, in her twenties*

E-MAIL WRITER

GIL AND EILEEN ENGEN, *Ranchers; he is in his sixties; she is in her fifties*

REGGIE FLUTY, *The policewoman who responded to the 911 call and discovered Matthew at the fence, in her late thirties*

LEIGH FONDAKOWSKI, *Member of Tectonic Theater Project*

MATT GALLOWAY, *Bartender at the Fireside, in his twenties; student at the University of Wyoming*

GOVERNOR JIM GERINGER, *Republican governor of Wyoming, forty-five years old*

ANDREW GOMEZ, *Latino from Laramie, in his twenties*

AMANDA GRONICH, *Member of Tectonic Theater Project*

RUSSELL HENDERSON, *One of the perpetrators, twenty-one years old*

REBECCA HILLIKER, *Head of the theater department at the University of Wyoming, in her forties; midwestern accent*

SERGEANT HING, *Detective at the Laramie Police Department, in his forties*

JEN, *A friend of Aaron McKinney, in her early twenties*

SHERRY JOHNSON, *Administrative assistant at the university, in her forties*

STEPHEN MEAD JOHNSON, *Unitarian minister, in his fifties*

TWO JUDGES

JURORS AND FOREPERSON

MOISÉS KAUFMAN, *Member of Tectonic Theater Project*

AARON KREIFELS, *University student, nineteen years old*

PHIL LABRIE, *Friend of Matthew Shepard, in his late twenties; eastern European accent*

DOUG LAWS, *Stake Ecclesiastical leader for the Mormon Church in Laramie, in his fifties*

JEFFREY LOCKWOOD, *Laramie resident, in his forties*

AARON McKINNEY, *One of the perpetrators, twenty-one years old*

BILL McKINNEY, *Father of Aaron McKinney, in his forties; truck driver*

ALISON MEARS, *Volunteer for a social service agency in town, in her fifties; very good friend of Marge Murray*
MEDIA/NEWSPAPER PEOPLE
MATT MICKELSON, *Owner of the Fireside, in his thirties*
CONRAD MILLER, *Car mechanic, in his thirties*
MORMON HOME TEACHER TO RUSSELL HENDERSON, *In his sixties*
MARGE MURRAY, *Reggie Fluty's mother, in her seventies; has emphysema but continues to smoke*
DOC O'CONNOR, *Limousine driver and local entrepreneur, in his fifties*
ANDY PARIS, *Member of Tectonic Theater Project*
ROMAINE PATTERSON, *Lesbian, twenty-one years old*
JON PEACOCK, *Matthew Shepard's academic adviser, in his thirties; political science professor*
REVEREND FRED PHELPS, *Minister from Kansas, in his sixties*
GREG PIEROTTI, *Member of Tectonic Theater Project*
BARBARA PITTS, *Member of Tectonic Theater Project*
KRISTIN PRICE, *Girlfriend of Aaron McKinney, in her twenties; has a son with Aaron; Tennessee accent*
PRIEST AT THE FUNERAL
CAL RERUCHA, *Prosecuting attorney, in his fifties*
ZACKIE SALMON, *Administrator at the University of Wyoming, in her forties; lesbian; Texas accent*
FATHER ROGER SCHMIT, *Catholic priest, in his forties; very outspoken*
JEDADIAH SCHULTZ, *University student, nineteen years old*
SHADOW, *DJ at the Fireside; African American man, in his thirties*
SHANNON, *A friend of Aaron McKinney, in his early twenties*
DENNIS SHEPARD, *Father of Matthew Shepard, in his forties; Wyoming native*
APRIL SILVA, *Bisexual university student, nineteen years old*
JONAS SLONAKER, *Gay man, in his forties*
RULON STACEY, *CEO Poudre Valley Hospital in Fort Collins, Colorado, in his forties; a Mormon*
TRISH STEGER, *Romaine Patterson's sister, in her forties; owner of a shop in town*
LUCY THOMPSON, *Grandmother of Russell Henderson, in her sixties; working-class woman who provided a popular day-care service for the town*
ZUBAIDA ULA, *Muslim woman, in her twenties*
WAITRESS (DEBBIE REYNOLDS)
HARRY WOODS, *Gay Laramie resident, fifty-two years old*
NOTE: *When a character is not named (for example, friend of Aaron McKinney, "Baptist minister"), it is at the person's request.*

Place: Laramie, Wyoming, U.S.A.

Time: 1998–99

About the Staging: The set is a performance space. There are a few tables and chairs. Costumes and props are always visible. The basic costumes are the ones worn by the company of actors. Costumes to portray the people of Laramie should be simple: a shirt, a pair of glasses, a hat. The desire is to suggest, not re-create. Along the same lines, this should be an actor-driven event. Costume changes, set changes, and anything else that happens on the stage should be done by the company of actors.

About the Text: When writing this play, we used a technique I developed called moment work. It is a method to create and analyze theater from a structuralist (or tectonic) perspective. For that reason, there are no scenes in this play, only moments. A moment does not mean a change of locale or an entrance or exit of actors or characters. It is simply a unit of theatrical time that is then juxtaposed with other units to convey meaning.

ACT I • *Moment: A Definition*

NARRATOR: On November 14, 1998, the members of Tectonic Theater Project traveled to Laramie, Wyoming, and conducted interviews with the people of the town. During the next year, we would return to Laramie several times and conduct over two hundred interviews. The play you are about to see is edited from those interviews, as well as from journal entries by members of the company and other found texts. Company member Greg Pierotti:

GREG PIEROTTI: My first interview was with Detective Sergeant Hing of the Laramie Police Department. At the start of the interview he was sitting behind his desk, sitting something like this (*he transforms into Sergeant Hing*):
I was born and raised here.
My family is, uh, third generation.
My grandparents moved here in the early nineteen hundreds.
We've had basically three, well, my daughter makes it fourth generation.
Quite a while. . . . It's a good place to live. Good people — lots of space.

Now, all the towns in southern Wyoming are laid out and spaced because of the railroad came through.
It was how far they could go before having to refuel and rewater.
And, uh, Laramie was a major stopping point.
That's why the towns are spaced so far apart.
We're one of the largest states in the country, and the least populated.
REBECCA HILLIKER: There's so much space between people and towns here, so much time for reflection.
NARRATOR: Rebecca Hilliker, head of the theater department at the University of Wyoming:
REBECCA HILLIKER: You have an opportunity to be happy in your life here. I found that people here were nicer than in the Midwest, where I used to teach, because they were happy. They were glad the sun was shining. And it shines a lot here.

SERGEANT HING: What you have is, you have your old-time traditional-type ranchers, they've been here forever—Laramie's been the hub of where they come for their supplies and stuff like that.

EILEEN ENGEN: Stewardship is one thing all our ancestors taught us.

NARRATOR: Eileen Engen, rancher:

EILEEN ENGEN: If you don't take care of the land, then you ruin it and you lose your living. So you first of all have to take care of your land and do everything you can to improve it.

DOC O'CONNOR: I love it here.

NARRATOR: Doc O'Connor, limousine driver:

DOC O'CONNOR: You couldn't put me back in that mess out there back east. Best thing about it is the climate. The cold, the wind. They say the Wyoming wind'll drive a man insane. But you know what? It don't bother me. Well, some of the times it bothers me. But most of the time it don't.

SERGEANT HING: And then you got, uh, the university population.

PHILIP DUBOIS: I moved here after living in a couple of big cities.

NARRATOR: Philip Dubois, president of the University of Wyoming:

PHILIP DUBOIS: I loved it there. But you'd have to be out of your mind to let your kids out after dark. And here, in the summertime, my kids play out at night till eleven and I don't think twice about it.

SERGEANT HING: And then you have the people who live in Laramie, basically.

ZACKIE SALMON: I moved here from rural Texas.

NARRATOR: Zackie Salmon, Laramie resident:

ZACKIE SALMON: Now, in Laramie, if you don't know a person, you will definitely know someone they know. So it can only be one degree removed at most. And for me—I love it! I mean, I love to go to the grocery store 'cause I get to visit with four or five or six people every time I go. And I don't really mind people knowing my business—'cause what's my business? I mean, my business is basically good.

DOC O'CONNOR: I like the trains, too. They don't bother me. Well, some of the times they bother me, but most times they don't. Even though one goes by every thirteen minutes out where I live. . . .

NARRATOR: Doc actually lives up in Bossier. But everybody in Laramie knows him. He's also not really a doctor.

DOC O'CONNOR: They used to carry cattle . . . them trains. Now all they carry is diapers and cars.

APRIL SILVA: I grew up in Cody, Wyoming.

NARRATOR: April Silva, university student:

APRIL SILVA: Laramie is better than where I grew up. I'll give it that.

SERGEANT HING: It's a good place to live. Good people, lots of space. Now, when the incident happened with that boy, a lot of press people came here. And one time some of them followed me out to the crime scene. And uh, well, it was a beautiful day, absolutely gorgeous day, real clear and crisp and the sky was that blue that, uh . . . you know, you'll never be able to paint, it's just sky blue—it's just gorgeous. And the mountains in the background and a little snow on 'em, and this one reporter, uh, lady . . . person, that was out there, she said . . .

REPORTER: Well, who found the boy, who was out here anyway?

SERGEANT HING: And I said, "Well, this is a really popular area for people to run, and mountain biking's really big out here, horseback riding, it's just, well, it's close to town." And she looked at me and she said:

REPORTER: Who in the hell would want to run out here?

SERGEANT HING: And I'm thinking, "Lady, you're just missing the point." You know, all you got to do is turn around, see the mountains, smell the air, listen to the birds, just take in what's around you. And they were just—nothing but the story. I didn't feel judged, I felt that they were stupid. They're, they're missing the point—they're just missing the whole point.

JEDADIAH SCHULTZ: It's hard to talk about Laramie now, to tell you what Laramie is, for us.

NARRATOR: Jedadiah Schultz:

JEDADIAH SCHULTZ: If you would have asked me before, I would have told you Laramie is a beautiful town, secluded enough that you can have your own identity. . . . A town with a strong sense of community—everyone knows everyone. . . . A town with a personality that most larger cities are stripped of. Now, after Matthew, I would say that Laramie is a town defined by an accident, a crime. We've become Waco, we've become Jasper. We're a noun, a definition, a sign. We may be able to get rid of that . . . but it will sure take a while.

Moment: Journal Entries

NARRATOR: Journal entries—members of the company. Andy Paris:

ANDY PARIS: Moisés called saying he had an idea for his next theater project. But there was a somberness to his voice, so I asked what it was all about and he told me he wanted to do a piece about what's happening in Wyoming.

NARRATOR: Stephen Belber:

STEPHEN BELBER: Leigh told me the company was thinking of going out to Laramie to conduct interviews and that they wanted me to come. But I'm hesitant. I have no real interest in prying into a town's unraveling.

NARRATOR: Amanda Gronich:

AMANDA GRONICH: I've never done anything like this in my life. How do you get people to talk to you? What do you ask?

NARRATOR: Moisés Kaufman:

MOISÉS KAUFMAN: The company has agreed that we should go to Laramie for a week and interview people.

Am a bit afraid about taking ten people in a trip of this nature. Must make some safety rules. No one works alone. Everyone carries cell phones. Have made some preliminary contacts with Rebecca Hilliker, head of the theater department at the University of Wyoming. She is hosting a party for us our first night in Laramie and has promised to introduce us to possible interviewees.

Moment: *Rebecca Hilliker*

REBECCA HILLIKER: I must tell you that when I first heard that you were thinking of coming here, when you first called me, I wanted to say, You've just kicked me in the stomach. Why are you doing this to me?

But then I thought, That's stupid, you're not doing this to me. And, more important, I thought about it and decided that we've had so much negative closure on this whole thing. And the students really need to talk. When this happened they started talking about it, and then the media descended and all dialogue stopped.

You know, I really love my students because they are free thinkers. And you may not like what they have to say, and you may not like their opinions, because they can be very redneck, but they are honest and they're truthful—so there's an excitement here, there's a dynamic here with my students that I never had when I was in the Midwest or in North Dakota, because there, there was so much Puritanism that dictated how people looked at the world that a lot of times they didn't have an opinion, you couldn't get them to express an opinion. And, quite honestly, I'd rather have opinions that I don't like—and have that dynamic in education.

There's a student I think you should talk to. His name is Jedadiah Schultz.

Moment: Angels in America

JEDADIAH SCHULTZ: I've lived in Wyoming my whole life. The family has been in Wyoming, well . . . for generations. Now when it came time to go to college, my parents can't—couldn't afford to send me to college. I wanted to study theater. And I knew that if I was going to go to college I was going to have to get on a scholarship—and so, uh, they have this competition each year, this Wyoming state high school competition. And I knew that if I didn't take first place in, uh, duets that I wasn't gonna get a scholarship. So I went to the theater department of the university looking for good scenes, and I asked one of the professors—I was like, "I need—I need a killer scene," and he was like, "Here you go, this is it." And it was from *Angels in America*.

So I read it and I knew that I could win best scene if I did a good enough job.

And when the time came I told my mom and dad so that they would come to the competition. Now you have to understand, my parents go to everything—every ball game, every hockey game—everything I've ever done.

And they brought me into their room and told me that if I did that scene, that they would not come to see me in the competition. Because they believed that it is wrong—that homosexuality is wrong—they felt that strongly about it that they didn't want to come see their son do probably the most important thing he'd done to that point in his life. And I didn't know what to do.

I had never, ever gone against my parents' wishes. So I was kind of worried about it. But I decided to do it.

And all I can remember about the competition is that when we were done, me and my scene partner, we came up to each other and we shook hands and there was a standing ovation.

Oh, man, it was amazing! And we took first place and we won. And that's how come I can afford to be here at the university, because of that scene. It was one of the best moments of my life. And my parents weren't there. And to this day, that was the one thing that my parents didn't see me do.

And thinking back on it, I think, why did I do it? Why did I oppose my parents? 'Cause I'm not gay. So why did I do it? And I guess the only honest answer I can give is that, well (*he chuckles*) I wanted to win. It was such a good scene; it was like the best scene!

Do you know Mr. Kushner? Maybe you can tell him.

Moment: *Journal Entries*

NARRATOR: Company member Greg Pierotti:

GREG PIEROTTI: We arrived today in the Denver Airport and drove to Laramie. The moment we crossed the Wyoming border I swear I saw a herd of buffalo. Also, I thought it was strange that the Wyoming sign said: WYOMING—LIKE NO PLACE ON EARTH instead of WYOMING—LIKE NO PLACE ELSE ON EARTH.

NARRATOR: Company member Leigh Fondakowski:

LEIGH FONDAKOWSKI: I stopped at a local inn for a bite to eat. And my waitress said to me:

WAITRESS: Hi, my name is Debbie. I was born in nineteen fifty-four and Debbie Reynolds was big then, so, yes, there are a lot of us around, but I promise that I won't slap you if you leave your elbows on the table.

MOISÉS KAUFMAN: Today Leigh tried to explain to me to no avail what chicken fried steak was.

WAITRESS: Now, are you from Wyoming? Or are you just passing through?

LEIGH FONDAKOWSKI: We're just passing through.

NARRATOR: Company member Barbara Pitts:

BARBARA PITTS: We arrived in Laramie tonight. Just past the WELCOME TO LARAMIE sign—POPULATION 26,687—the first thing to greet us was Wal-Mart. In the dark, we could be on any main drag in America—fast-food chains, gas stations. But as we drove into the downtown area by the railroad tracks, the buildings still look like a turn-of-the-century western town. Oh, and as we passed the University Inn, on the sign where amenities such as heated pool or cable TV are usually touted, it said: HATE IS NOT A LARAMIE VALUE.

NARRATOR: Greg Pierotti:

Moment: Alison and Marge

GREG PIEROTTI: I met today with two longtime Laramie residents, Alison Mears and Marge Murray, two social service workers who taught me a thing or two.

ALISON MEARS: Well, what Laramie used to be like when Marge was growing up, well, it was mostly rural.

MARGE MURRAY: Yeah, it was. I enjoyed it, you know. My kids all had horses.

ALISON MEARS: Well, there was more land, I mean, you could keep your pet cow. Your horse. Your little chickens. You know, just have your little bit of acreage.

MARGE MURRAY: Yeah, I could run around the house in my all togethers, do the housework while the kids were in school. And nobody could see me. And if they got that close . . .

ALISON MEARS: Well, then that's their problem.

MARGE MURRAY: Yeah.

GREG PIEROTTI: I just want to make sure I got the expression right: in your all togethers?

MARGE MURRAY: Well, yeah, honey, why wear clothes?

ALISON MEARS: Now, how's he gonna use that in his play?

GREG PIEROTTI: So this was a big ranching town?

ALISON MEARS: Oh, not just ranching, this was a big railroad town at one time. Before they moved everything to Cheyenne and Green River and Omaha. So now, well, it's just a drive-through spot for the railroad—because even, what was it, in the fifties? Well, they had one big roundhouse, and they had such a shop they could build a complete engine.

MARGE MURRAY: They did, my mom worked there.

GREG PIEROTTI: Your mom worked in a roundhouse?

MARGE MURRAY: Yep. She washed engines. Her name was Minnie. We used to, you know, sing that song for her, you know that song.

GREG PIEROTTI: What song?

MARGE MURRAY: "Run for the roundhouse, Minnie, they can't corner you there."

(*They crack up.*)

ALISON MEARS: But I'll tell you, Wyoming is bad in terms of jobs. I mean, the university has the big high whoop-de-do jobs. But Wyoming, unless you're a professional, well, the bulk of the people are working minimum-wage jobs.

MARGE MURRAY: Yeah, I've been either in the service industry or bartending most of my life. Now I know everybody in town.

ALISON MEARS: And she does.

MARGE MURRAY: And I do. Now that I'll tell ya, here in Laramie there is a difference and there always has been. What it is is a class distinction. It's about the well-educated and the ones that are not. And the educated don't understand why the ones that are not don't get educated. That's why I told you before my kids had to fight because their mother was a bartender. Never mind I was the best damn bartender in town.

ALISON MEARS: And she was.

MARGE MURRAY: That's not bragging, that's fact.

ALISON MEARS: But here in Laramie, if it weren't for the university, we'd just be S.O.L.

GREG PIEROTTI: What's S.O.L.?

ALISON MEARS: Well, do I have to say it? Well, it's shit outta luck. (*She cracks up.*) Oh Lordy, you've got that on your tape. Boy, you are getting an education today.

GREG PIEROTTI: Yeah, I guess I am. So, let me just ask you—what was your response when this happened to Matthew Shepard?

MARGE MURRAY: Well, I've been close enough to the case to know many of the people. I have a daughter that's on the Sheriff's Department.

As far as the gay issue, I don't give a damn one way or the other as long as they don't bother me. And even if they did, I'd just say no thank you. And that's the attitude of most of the Laramie population. They might poke one, if they were in a bar situation, you know, they had been drinking, they might actually smack one in the mouth, but then they'd just walk away. Most of 'em, they would just say, "I don't swing that way," and whistle on about their business. Laramie is live and let live.

ALISON MEARS: I'd say that Marge probably knows a lot more except she's even willing to say, and we have to respect her for that.

MARGE MURRAY: Well, uh, where are you going with this story?

GREG PIEROTTI: Oh, well, we still haven't decided. When we've finished, we are going to try to bring it around to Laramie.

MARGE MURRAY: Okay, then, there are parts I won't tell you.

Moment: Matthew

NARRATOR: Company member Andy Paris:

ANDY PARIS: Today, for the first time, we met someone who actually knew Matthew Shepard. Trish Steger, owner of a shop in town, referred to him as Matt.

TRISH STEGER: Matt used to come into my shop—that's how I knew him.

ANDY PARIS: It was the first time I heard him referred to as Matt instead of Matthew. Did he go by Matt to everyone?

DOC O'CONNOR: Well, on the second of October, I get a phone call about, uh, ten after seven.

NARRATOR: Doc O'Connor:

DOC O'CONNOR: It was Matthew Shepard. And he said, "Can you pick me up at the corner of Third and Grand?" So, anyhow, I pull up to the corner, to see who Matthew Shepard, you know. It's a little guy, about five-two, soakin' wet, I betcha ninety-seven pounds tops. They say he weighed a hundred and ten, but I wouldn't believe it. They also said he was five-five in the newspapers, but this man, he was really only about five-two, maybe five-one. So he walks up the window—I'm gonna try and go in steps so you can better understand the principle of this man. So he walks up to the window, and I say, "Are you Matthew Shepard?" And he says, "Yeah, I'm Matthew Shepard. But I don't want you to call me Matthew, or Mr. Shepard. I don't want you to call me anything. My name is Matt. And I want you to know, I am gay and we're going to go to a gay bar. Do you have a problem with that?" And I said, "How're you payin'?"

The fact is . . . Laramie doesn't have any gay bars . . . and for that matter neither does Wyoming . . . so he was hiring me to take him to Fort Collins, Colorado, about an hour away.

Matt was a blunt little shit, you know what I'm sayin'? But I liked him 'cause he was straightforward, you see what I'm saying? Maybe gay but straightforward, you see what I'm saying?

TRISH STEGER: I don't know, you know, how does any one person ever tell about another? You really should talk to my sister Romaine. She was a very close friend of Matthew's.

ROMAINE PATTERSON: We never called him Matthew, actually, most of the time we called him Choo-choo. You know, because we used to call him Mattchew, and then we just called him Choo-choo.

And whenever I think of Matthew, I always think of his incredible beaming smile. I mean, he'd walk in and he'd be like (*demonstrates*) you know, and he'd smile at everyone . . . he just made you feel great. . . . And he—would like stare people down in the coffee shop . . . 'cause he always wanted to sit on the end seat so that he could talk to me while I was working. And if someone was sitting in that seat, he would just sit there and stare at them. Until they left. And then he would claim his spot.

But Matthew definitely had a political side to him. . . . I mean, he really wanted to get into political affairs . . . that's all his big interest was, was watching CNN and MSNBC, I mean, that's the only TV station I ever saw his TV tuned in to. He was just really smart in political affairs, but not too smart on like commonsense things . . .

So, he moves to Laramie to go to school.

JON PEACOCK: Matthew was very shy when he first came in.

NARRATOR: Jon Peacock, Matthew Shepard's academic adviser:

JON PEACOCK: To the point of being somewhat mousy I'd almost say. He was having some difficulties adjusting, but this was home for him and he made that quite clear. And so his mousiness, his shyness gave way to a person who was excited about this track that he was going to embark on. He was just figuring out wanting to work on human rights, how he was going to do that. And when that happens this person begins to bloom a little bit. He was starting to say, "Wow, there are opportunities here. There are things I can do in this world. I can be important."

ROMAINE PATTERSON: I did hear from Matthew about forty-eight hours before his attack. And he told me that he had joined the gay and lesbian group on campus, and he said he was enjoying it, you know, he was getting ready for Pride Week and whatnot. I mean, he was totally stoked about school—yeah, he was really happy about being there.

JON PEACOCK: And in retrospect—and I can only say this in retrospect of course—I think that's where he was heading, towards human rights. Which only adds to the irony and tragedy of this.

Moment: Who's Getting What?

DOC O'CONNOR: Let me tell you something else here. There's more gay people in Wyoming than meets the eye. I know, I know for a fact. They're not particularly, ah, the whattayou call them, the queens, the gay people, queens, you know, runaround faggot-type people. No, they're the ones that throw bails of hay, jump on horses, brand 'em, and kick ass, you see what I'm saying? As I always say, Don't fuck with a Wyoming queer, 'cause they will kick you in your fucking ass, but that's not the point of what I'm trying to say. 'Cause I know a lot of gay people in Wyoming, I know a lot of people period. I've been lived up here some forty-odd years, you see what I'm saying?

And I don't think Wyoming people give a damn one way or another if you're gay or straight, that's just what I just said, doesn't matter. If there's eight men and one woman in a Wyoming bar, which is often the case, now you stop and think—who's getting what? You see what I'm saying? Now jeez, it don't take a big intelligent mind to figure that one out.

Moment: Easier Said Than Done

CATHERINE CONNOLLY: My understanding when I first came here . . .

NARRATOR: Catherine Connolly:

CATHERINE CONNOLLY: . . . is that I was the first "out" lesbian or gay faculty member on campus. And that was in nineteen ninety-two. So, that wasn't that long ago. Um, I was asked at my interview what my husband did, um, and so I came out then. . . . Do you want a funny story?

When you first get here as a new faculty member, there's all these things you have to do. And so, I was in my office and I noticed that this woman called. . . . I was expecting, you know, it was a health insurance phone call, something like that, and so I called her back. And I could hear her, she's working on her keyboard, clicking away. I said, you know, "This is Cathy Connolly returning your phone call." And she said, "Oh. It's you." And I thought, "This is bizarre." And she said, "I hear—I hear—I hear you're gay. I hear you are." I was like, "Uh huh." And she said, "I hear you came as a couple. I'm one too. Not a couple, just a person." And so—she was—a kind of lesbian who knew I was coming and she wanted to come over and meet me immediately. And she later told me that there were other lesbians that she knew who wouldn't be seen with me. That I would irreparably taint them, that just to be seen with me could be a problem.

JONAS SLONAKER: When I came here I knew it was going to be hard as a gay man.

NARRATOR: Jonas Slonaker:

JONAS SLONAKER: But I kept telling myself: People should live where they want to live. And there would be times I would go down to Denver and I would go to gay bars and, um, people would ask where I was from and I'd say, "Laramie, Wyoming." And I met so many men down there from Wyoming. So many gay men who grew up here, and they're like: "This is not a place where I can live, how can you live there, I had to get out, grrr, grrr, grrr." But every once in a while there would be a guy, "Oh gosh, I miss Laramie. I mean I really love it there, that's where I want to live." And they get this starry-eyed look and I'm like: If that's where you want to live, do it. I mean, imagine if more gay people stayed in small towns. But it's easier said than done of course.

Moment: *Journal Entries*

MOISÉS KAUFMAN: Today we are moving from our motel and heading for the Best Western.

NARRATOR: Moisés Kaufman:

MOISÉS KAUFMAN: My hope is that it is a better Western.

NARRATOR: Amanda Gronich:

AMANDA GRONICH: Today we divided up to go to different churches in the community. Moisés and I were given a Baptist church. We were welcomed into the services by the reverend himself standing at the entrance to the chapel. This is what I remember of his sermon that morning.

Moment: *The Word*

BAPTIST MINISTER: My dear brothers and sisters: I am here today to bring you the Word of the Lord. Now, I have a simple truth that I tell to my colleagues and I'm gonna tell it to you today: The word is either sufficient or it is not.

Scientists tell me that human history, that the world is five billion or six billion years old—after all, what's a billion years give or take? The Bible tells me that human history is six thousand years old.

The word is either sufficient or it is not.

STEPHEN MEAD JOHNSON: Ah, the sociology of religion in the West . . .

NARRATOR: Stephen Mead Johnson, Unitarian minister:

STEPHEN MEAD JOHNSON: Dominant religious traditions in this town: Baptist, Mormon—they're everywhere, it's not just Salt Lake, you know, they're all over—they're like jam on toast down here.

DOUG LAWS: The Mormon Church has a little different thing going that irritates some folks.

NARRATOR: Doug Laws, Stake Ecclesiastical leader for the Mormon Church:

DOUG LAWS: And that is that we absolutely believe that God still speaks to man. We don't think that it happened and some folks wrote it in the Bible. God speaks to us today, and we believe that. We believe that the prophet of the church has the authority to receive inspiration and revelation from God.

STEPHEN MEAD JOHNSON: So, the spectrum would be—uh, on the left side of that panel: So far left that I am probably sitting by myself, is me—and the Unitarian Church. Unitarians are by and large humanists, many of whom are atheists. I mean—we're, you know, we're not even sure we're a religion. And to my right on the spectrum, to his credit, Father Roger, Catholic priest, who is well-established here, and God bless him—he did not equivocate at all when this happened—he hosted the vigil for Matthew that night.

FATHER ROGER SCHMIT: I was really jolted because, you know, when we did the vigil—we wanted to get other ministers involved and we called some of them, and they were not going to get involved. And it was like, "We are gonna stand back and wait and see which way the wind is blowing." And that angered me immensely. We are supposed to stand out as leaders. I thought, "Wow, what's going on here?"

DOUG LAWS: God has set boundaries. And one of our responsibilities is to learn: What is it that God wants? So you study Scripture, you look to your leaders. Then you know what the bounds are. Now once you kinda know what the bounds are, then you sorta get a feel for what's out-of-bounds.

There is a proclamation that came out on the family. A family is defined as one woman and one man and children. That's a family. That's about as clear as you can state it. There's no sexual deviation in the Mormon Church. No—no leniency. We just think it's out-of-bounds.

BAPTIST MINISTER: I warn you: You will be mocked! You will be ridiculed for the singularity of your faith! But you let the Bible be your guide. It's in there. It's all in there.

STEPHEN MEAD JOHNSON: The Christian pastors, many of the conservative ones, were silent on this. Conservative Christians use the Bible to show the rest of the world, It says here in the Bible. And most Americans believe, and they do, that the Bible is the word of God, and how you gonna fight that?

BAPTIST MINISTER: I am a Biblicist. Which means: The Bible doesn't need me to be true. The Bible is true whether I believe it or not. The word is either sufficient or it is not.

STEPHEN MEAD JOHNSON: I arrived in Laramie on September fifteenth. I looked around—tumbleweed, cement factory—and said, "What in the hell am I doing in Wyoming?" Three weeks later, I found out what the hell I'm doing in Wyoming.

Moment: A Scarf

STEPHEN BELBER: I had breakfast this morning with a university student named Zubaida Ula. She is an Islamic feminist who likes to do things her own way.

ZUBAIDA ULA: I've lived in Laramie since I was four. Yeah. My parents are from Bangladesh. Two years ago, because I'm Muslim, I decided to start wearing a scarf. That's really changed my life in Laramie. Yeah.

Like people say things to me like, "Why do you have to wear that thing on your head?" Like when I go to the grocery store, I'm not looking to give people Islam 101, you know what I mean? So I'll be like, "Well, it's part of my religion," and they'll be—this is the worst part cuz they'll be like, "I know it's part of your religion, but why?" And it's—how am I supposed to go into the whole doctrine of physical modesty and my own spiritual relationship with the Lord, standing there with my pop and chips? You know what I mean?

STEPHEN BELBER: Yeah.

ZUBAIDA ULA: You know, it's so unreal to me that, yeah, that a group from New York would be writing a play about Laramie. And then I was picturing like you're gonna be in a play about my town. You're gonna be onstage in New York and you're gonna be acting like you're us. That's so weird.

Moment: Lifestyle 1

BAPTIST MINISTER'S WIFE: Hello?

AMANDA GRONICH: Yes, hello. My name is Amanda Gronich and I am here in Laramie working with a theater company. I went to the reverend's, your husband's church on Sunday, and I was extremely interested in talking with the reverend about some of his thoughts about recent events.

BAPTIST MINISTER'S WIFE: Well, I don't think he'll want to talk to you. He has very biblical views about homosexuality—he doesn't condone that kind of violence. But he doesn't condone that kind of lifestyle, you know what I mean? And he was just bombarded with press after this happened and the media has been just terrible about this whole thing.

AMANDA GRONICH: Oh, I know, I really understand, it must have just been terrible.

BAPTIST MINISTER'S WIFE: Oh, yes, I think we are all hoping this just goes away.

AMANDA GRONICH: Well, um, do you think maybe I could call back and speak with your husband just briefly?

BAPTIST MINISTER'S WIFE: Well, all right, you can call him back tonight at nine.

AMANDA GRONICH: Oh, thank you so much. I'll do that.

Moment: The Fireside

STEPHEN BELBER: Today Barbara and I went to the Fireside Bar, which is the last place Matthew was seen in public.

BARBARA PITTS: The Fireside—definitely feels like a college bar, with a couple of pool tables and a stage area for karaoke. Still, the few regulars in the late afternoon were hardly the college crowd.

STEPHEN BELBER: First person we talked to was Matt Mickelson, the owner.

MATT MICKELSON: My great-great-grandfather moved here in eighteen sixty-two, he owned Laramie's first opera house, it was called Old Blue Front, and in eighteen seventy Louisa Grandma Swain cast the first woman's ballot in any free election in the world, and that's why Wyoming is the Equality State, so what I want to do is reestablish my bar business as the Old Blue Front Opera House and Good Time Emporium, you know, I want to have a restaurant, I want to have a gift shop, I want to have a pool hall, and do all this shit, you know . . . every night's ladies' night . . .

So the Fireside is the first step towards the Old Blue Front Opera House and Good Time Emporium.

BARBARA PITTS: So, what about the night Matthew Shepard was here?

MATT MICKELSON: We had karaoke that night, twenty or thirty people here—Matthew Shepard came in, sitting right—right where you're sitting, just hanging out. . . . I mean, if you wanna talk to somebody, you should talk to Matt Galloway, he was the kid that was bartending that night. You'd have to meet him, his character stands for itself.

(*Calling*) Hey, is Galloway bartending tonight?

MATT GALLOWAY: Okay. I'm gonna make this brief, quick, get it over with, but it will be everything—factual. Just the facts. Here we go. Ten o'clock. I clock in, usual time, Tuesday nights. Ten-thirty—Matthew Shepard shows up—alone—sits down, orders a Heineken.

NARRATOR: Phil Labrie, friend of Matthew Shepard:

PHIL LABRIE: Matt liked to drink Heineken and nothing else. Heineken even though you have to pay nine-fifty for a six-pack. He'd always buy the same beer.

MATT GALLOWAY: So what can I tell you about Matt?

If you had a hundred customers like him it'd be the—the most perfect bar I've ever been in. Okay? And nothing to do with sexual orientation. Um, absolute mannerisms. Manners. Politeness, intelligence.

Taking care of me, as in tips. Everything—conversation, uh, dressed nice, clean-cut. Some people you just know, sits down, "Please," "Thank you"—offers intellect, you know, within—within—within their vocabulary.

Um, so, he kicks it there. Didn't seem to have any worries, or like he was looking for anyone. Just enjoy his drink and the company around.

Now approximately eleven forty-five, eleven-thirty–eleven forty-five, Aaron McKinney and Russell Henderson come in—I didn't know their names then, but they're the accused, they're the perps, they're the accused. They walked in, just very stone-faced, you know. Dirty. Grungy. Rude. "Gimme." That type of thing. They walked up to the bar, uh, and, as you know, paid for a pitcher with dimes and quarters, uh, which is something that I mean you don't forget. You don't forget that. Five-fifty in dimes and quarters. That's a freakin' nightmare.

Now Henderson and McKinney, they didn't seem intoxificated at all. They came in—they just ordered a beer, took the pitcher with them back there into the pool room, and kept to themselves. Next thing I knew, probably a half hour later, they were kind of walking around—no beer. And I remember thinking to myself that I'm not gonna ask them if they want another one, because obviously they just paid for a pitcher with dimes and quarters, I have a real good feeling they don't have any more money.

NARRATOR: Romaine Patterson:

ROMAINE PATTERSON: Money meant nothing to Matthew, because he came from a lot of it. And he would like hand over his wallet in two seconds—because money meant nothing. His—shoes—might have meant something. They can say it was robbery . . . I don't buy it. For even an iota of a second.

MATT GALLOWAY: Then a few moments later I looked over and Aaron and Russell had been talking to Matthew Shepard.

KRISTIN PRICE: Aaron said that a guy walked up to him and said that he was gay, and wanted to get with Aaron and Russ.

NARRATOR: Kristin Price, girlfriend of Aaron McKinney:

KRISTIN PRICE: And Aaron got aggravated with it and told him that he was straight and didn't want anything to do with him and walked off. He said that is when he and Russell went to the bathroom and decided to pretend they were gay and get him in the truck and rob him. They wanted to teach him a lesson not to come on to straight people.

MATT GALLOWAY: Okay, no. They stated that Matt approached them, that he came on to them. I absolutely, positively disbelieve and refute the statement one hundred percent. Refute it. I'm gonna give you two reasons why.

One. Character reference.

Why would he approach them? Why them? He wasn't approaching anybody else in the bar. They say he's gay, he was a flaming gay, he's gonna come on to people like that. Bullshit. He never came on to me. Hello?!? He came on to them? I don't believe it.

Two. Territorialism is—is—is the word I will use for this. And that's the fact that Matt was sitting there. Russell and Aaron were in the pool area. Upon their first interaction, they were in Matt's area, in the area that Matt had been seen all night. So who approached who by that?

ROMAINE PATTERSON: But Matthew was the kind of person . . . like, he would never not talk to someone for any reason. If someone started talking to him, he'd just be like, "Oh, blah, blah, blah." He never had any problem just striking up a conversation with anybody.

PHIL LABRIE: Matt did feel lonely a lot of times. Me knowing that—and knowing how gullible Matt

could be . . . he would have walked right into it. The fact that he was at the bar alone without any friends made him that much more vulnerable.

MATT GALLOWAY: So the only thing is—and this is what I'm testifying to—'cause, you know, I'm also, basically, the key eyewitness in this case, uh (pause) basically what I'm testifying is that I saw Matthew leave. I saw two individuals leave with Matthew. I didn't see their faces, but I saw the back of their heads. At the same time, McKinney and Henderson were no longer around. You do the math.

MATT MICKELSON: Actually, I think the DJ was the last one to talk to him on his way out that night . . . gave him a cigarette or something. His name is Shadow.

SHADOW: I was the last person that Matt talked to before he left the Fireside. . . . I was just bullshittin' around with my shit, and he stopped me, I stopped him actually, and he's like, "Hey, Shadow, da da da," and I was like, "What, man, you gettin' ready to leave?" he's like, "Yeah, man, and this an' that." But then I noticed them two guys and they stood outside, you could see, you could see it, they were standing there, you know, and he was looking over to them, and they were lookin' back at him. And I stood and talked to Matt for like a good ten minutes and you seen the guys with him, you seen 'em getting like, you seen 'em like worried, like, you know, anxious to leave and shit. . . . So when they took off, I seen it, when they took off, it was in a black truck, it was a small truck, and the three of them sat in the front seat and Matt sat in the middle.

And I didn't think nothin' of it, you know. I didn't figure them guys was gonna be like that.

Moment: McKinney and Henderson

NARRATOR: A friend of Aaron McKinney:

ANONYMOUS: Oh, I've known Aaron a long time. Aaron was a good kid, I liked Aaron a lot, that's why I was shocked when I heard this, I'm like . . . I know he was, he was living out far . . . at his trailer house is what he told me, with his girl . . . they just started dating last summer . . . they musta gotten pregnant as soon as they started dating, you know, 'cause they had a kid. He was only twenty-one years old, but he was running around with a kid. . . . You see, that's the kinda person Aaron was, just like he always dressed in like big clothes, you know like, in like Tommy "Hile-figer," Polo, Gucci . . .

At the time I knew him, he was just, he was just a young kid trying to, you know, he just wanted to fit in, you know, acting tough, acting cool, but, you know, you could get in his face about it and he would back down, like he was some kinda scared kid.

NARRATOR: Sherry Aanenson:

SHERRY AANENSON: Russell was just so sweet. He was the one who was the Eagle Scout. I mean, his whole presence was just quiet and sweet. So of course it doesn't make sense to me and I know people snap and whatever and like it wasn't a real intimate relationship, I was just his landlord. I did work with him at the Chuck Wagon too. And I remember like at the Christmas party he was just totally drunk out of his mind, like we all were pretty much just party-party time.... And he wasn't belligerent, he didn't change, his personality didn't change. He was still the same little meek Russell, I remember him coming up to me and saying, "When you get a chance, Sherry, can I have a dance?" Which we never did get around to doing that but . . . Now I just want to shake him, you know—What were you thinking? What in the hell were you thinking?

Moment: The Fence

STEPHEN MEAD JOHNSON: The fence—I've been out there four times, I've taken visitors. That place has become a pilgrimage site. Clearly that's a very powerful personal experience to go out there. It is so stark and so empty and you can't help but think of Matthew out there for eighteen hours in nearly freezing temperatures, with that view up there isolated, and, the "God, my God, why have you forsaken me" comes to mind.

NARRATOR: Company member Greg Pierotti:

GREG PIEROTTI: Phil Labrie, a friend of Matthew's, took us to the fence this morning. I broke down the minute I touched it. I feel such a strong kinship with this young man. On the way back, I made sure that no one saw me crying.

NARRATOR: Leigh Fondakowski:

LEIGH FONDAKOWSKI: Greg was crying on the way back. I couldn't bring myself to tears, but I felt the same way. I have an interview this afternoon with Aaron Kreifels. He's the boy who found Matthew out there at the fence. I don't think I'm up for it right now. I'll see if someone else can do it.

Moment: Finding Matthew Shepard

AARON KREIFELS: Well I, uh, I took off on my bicycle about five P.M. on Wednesday from my dorm. I just kinda felt like going for a ride. So I—I went up to the top of Cactus Canyon, and I'm not superfamiliar with that area, so on my way back down, I didn't know where I was going, I was just sort of picking the way to go, which now . . . it just makes me think that God wanted me to find him because there's no way that I was going to go that way.

So I was in some deep-ass sand, and I wanted to turn around—but for some reason, I kept going. And, uh, I went along. And there was this rock, on the—on the ground—and I just drilled it. I went—over the handlebars and ended up on the ground.

So, uh, I got up, and I was just kind of dusting myself off, and I was looking around and I noticed something—which ended up to be Matt, and he was just lying there by a fence, and I—I just thought it was a scarecrow. I was like, Halloween's coming up, thought it was a Halloween gag, so I didn't think much of it, so I got my bike, walked it around the fence that was there, it was a buck-type fence. And, uh, got closer to him, and I noticed his hair—and that was a major key to me noticing it was a human being—was his hair. 'Cause I just thought it was a dummy, seriously, I noticed—I even noticed the chest going up and down, I still thought it was a dummy, you know. I thought it was just like some kind of mechanism.

But when I saw hair, well, I knew it was a human being.

So . . . I ran to the nearest house and—I just ran as fast as I could . . . and called the police.

REGGIE FLUTY: I responded to the call.

NARRATOR: Officer Reggie Fluty:

REGGIE FLUTY: When I got there, the first—at first the only thing I could see was partially somebody's feet, and I got out of my vehicle and raced over—I seen what appeared to be a young man, thirteen, fourteen years old because he was so tiny laying on his back and he was tied to the bottom end of a pole.

I did the best I could. The gentleman that was laying on the ground, Matthew Shepard, he was covered in dry blood all over his head, there was dry blood underneath him and he was barely breathing . . . he was doing the best he could.

I was going to breathe for him and I couldn't get his mouth open—his mouth wouldn't open for me.

He was covered in, like I said, partially dry blood and blood all over his head—the only place that he did not have any blood on him, on his face, was what appeared to be where he had been crying down his face.

His head was distorted—you know, it did not look normal—he looked as if he had a real harsh head wound.

DR. CANTWAY: I was working the emergency room the night Matthew Shepard was brought in. I don't think that any of us, ah, can remember seeing a patient in that condition for a long time—those of us who've worked in big city hospitals have seen this. Ah, but we have some people here who've not worked in a big city hospital. And, ah, it's not something you expect here.

Ah, you expect it, you expect this kind of injuries to come from a car going down a hill at eighty miles an hour. You expect to see gross injuries from something like that—this horrendous, terrible thing. Ah, but you don't expect to see that from someone doing this to another person.

The ambulance report said it was a beating, so we knew.

AARON KREIFELS: There was nothing I could do. I mean, if there was anything that I could of done to help him I would've done it but there was nothing.

And I, I was yelling at the top of my lungs at him, trying to get something outta him.

Like: "Hey, wake up," "HELLO!"

But he didn't move, he didn't flinch, he didn't anything . . .

REGGIE FLUTY: He was tied to the fence—his hands were thumbs out in what we call a cuffing position—the way we handcuff people. He was bound with a real thin white rope, it went around the bottom of the pole, about four inches up off the ground.

His shoes were missing.

He was tied extremely tight—so I used my boot knife and tried to slip it between the rope and his wrist—I had to be extremely careful not to harm Matthew any further.

DR. CANTWAY: Your first thought is . . . well, certainly you'd like to think that it's somebody from out of town, that comes through and beats somebody. I mean, things like this happen, you know, shit happens, and it happens in Laramie. But if there's been somebody who has been beaten repeatedly, ah, certainly this is something that offends us. I think that's a good word. It offends us!

REGGIE FLUTY: He was bound so tight—I finally got the knife through there—I'm sorry—we rolled him over to his left side—when we did that he quit breathing. Immediately, I put him back on his back—and that was just enough of an adjustment—it gave me enough room to cut him free there—

I seen the EMS unit trying to get to the location, once the ambulance got there we put a neck collar on him, placed him on a back board, and scooted him from underneath the fence—then Rob drove the ambulance to Ivinson Hospital's emergency room . . .

DR. CANTWAY: Now, the strange thing is, twenty minutes before Matthew came in, Aaron McKinney was brought in by his girlfriend. Now I guess he had gotten into a fight later on that night back in town, so I am workin' on Aaron and the ambulance comes in with Matthew. Now at this point I don't know that there's a connection—at all. So I tell Aaron to wait and I go and treat Matthew. So there's Aaron in one room of the ER and Matthew in another room two doors down.

Now as soon as we saw Matthew . . . It was very obvious that his care was beyond our capabilities. Called the neurosurgeon at Poudre Valley, and he was on the road in an hour and fifteen minutes, I think.

REGGIE FLUTY: They showed me a picture . . . days later I saw a picture of Matthew . . . I would have never recognized him.

DR. CANTWAY: Then two days later I found out the connection and I was . . . very . . . struck!!! They were two kids!!!!! They were both my patients and they were two kids. I took care of both of them. . . . Of both their bodies. And . . . for a brief moment I wondered if this is how God feels when he looks down at us. How we are all his kids. . . . Our bodies. . . . Our souls. . . . And I felt a great deal of compassion. . . . For both of them. . . .

End of Act One

ACT II • *Moment: A Laramie Man*

NARRATOR: This is Jon Peacock, Matthew's academic adviser.

JON PEACOCK: Well, the news reports started trickling out on Thursday, but no names were mentioned, the brutality of the crime was not mentioned. All that was mentioned was that there was a man, Laramie man, found beaten, out on the prairie basically. Later on in the evening they mentioned his name. It was like, That can't, that's not the Matthew Shepard I know, that's not my student, that's not this person who I've been meeting with.

ROMAINE PATTERSON: I was in the coffee shop.

NARRATOR: Romaine Patterson:

ROMAINE PATTERSON: And someone pulled me aside and said: "I don't know much, but they say that there's been a young man who's been beaten in Laramie. And they said his name was Matthew Shepard." And he said, "Do you think this could be our Matthew?"

And I said, "Well, yeah, it sounds like it could be our Matthew."

So I called up my sister Trish and I said, "Tell me what you know." I'm just like, "I need to know anything you know because I don't know anything."

TRISH STEGER: So I'm talking to my sister on the phone and that's when the whole story came up on Channel 5 news and it was just like *baboom*.

JON PEACOCK: And the news reports kept rolling in, young University of Wyoming student, his age, his description, it's like, "Oh my God."

TRISH STEGER: And, uh (*pause*) I—I felt sick to my stomach . . . it's just instantly sick to my stomach. And I had to tell Romaine, "Yes, it was Matthew. It was your friend."

MATT GALLOWAY: Well, I'll tell you—I'll tell you what is overwhelming.

NARRATOR: Matt Galloway:

MATT GALLOWAY: Friday morning I first find out about it. I go to class, walk out, boom there it is—in the *Branding Iron*. So immediately I drive to the nearest newsstand, buy a *Laramie Boomerang* 'cause I want more details, buy that—go home . . . before I can even open the paper, my boss calls me, he says:

MATT MICKELSON: Did you hear about what happened?

MATT GALLOWAY: I'm like, "Yeah."

MATT MICKELSON: Was he in the bar Tuesday night?

MATT GALLOWAY: I go, "Yes, yes he was."

MATT MICKELSON: You've got to get down to the bar right now, we've got to talk about this, we've got to discuss what's going to go on.

JON PEACOCK: By this time, I was starting to get upset, but still the severity wasn't out yet.

RULON STACEY: It was Thursday afternoon.

NARRATOR: Rulon Stacey at Poudre Valley Hospital:

RULON STACEY: I got a call: "We just got a kid in from Wyoming and it looks like he may be the victim of a hate crime. We have a couple of newspaper reporters here asking questions." And so, we agreed that we needed one spokesperson: As CEO, I'll do that and we'll try and gather all the information that we can.

ROMAINE PATTERSON: And then I watched the ten o'clock news that night, where they started speaking about the nature and the seriousness of it . . .

MATT GALLOWAY: So I'm on the phone with Mickelson and he's like:

MATT MICKELSON: We need to go to the arraignment so we can identify these guys, and make sure these guys were in the bar.

MATT GALLOWAY: So we go to the arraignment.

Moment: The Essential Facts

NEWSPERSON: Our focus today turns to Laramie, Wyoming, and the Albany County Courthouse, where Aaron James McKinney and Russell Arthur Henderson are being charged with the brutal beating of Matthew Shepard, a gay University of Wyoming student.

NARRATOR: Catherine Connolly:

CATHERINE CONNOLLY: The arraignment was on Friday. Right around lunchtime. And I said, "I'm just going." I just took off—it's just down the street. So I walked a few blocks and I went. Has anybody told you about the arraignment?

There were probably about a hundred people from town and probably as many news media. By that point, a lot more of the details had come out. The fact that the perpetrators were kids themselves, local kids, that everyone who's from around here has some relationship to. And what—Everyone was really I think waiting on pins and needles for what would happen when the perpetrators walked in. And what happened—there's two hundred people in the room at this point . . . they walked in in their complete orange jumpsuits and their shackles, and, you could have heard a pin drop.

It was incredibly solemn.

I mean, lots of people were teary at that point. Then the judge came in and did a reading—there was a reading of the evidence that the prosecution has and—it's just a—it's a statement of facts, and the reading of the facts was . . .

JUDGE: The essential facts are that the defendants, Aaron James McKinney and Russell Arthur Henderson, met Matthew Shepard at the Fireside Bar, and after Mr. Shepard confided he was gay, the subjects deceived Mr. Shepard into leaving with them in their vehicle to a remote area. Upon arrival at said area, both subjects tied their victim to a buck fence, robbed him, tortured him, and beat him. . . . Both defendants were later contacted by officers of the Laramie Police Department, who observed inside the cab of their pickup a credit card and a pair of black patent leather shoes belonging to the victim, Matthew Shepard.

(*The Judge goes sotto voce here while Catherine Connolly speaks.*)

The subjects took the victim's credit card, wallet containing twenty dollars in cash, his shoes, and other items, and obtained the victim's address in order to later burglarize his home.

CATHERINE CONNOLLY: I don't think there was any person who was left in that courtroom who wasn't crying at the end of it. I mean it lasted—five minutes, but it kept on getting more and more horrific, ending with:

JUDGE: Said defendants left the victim begging for his life.

Moment: Live and Let Live

NARRATOR: Sergeant Hing:

SERGEANT HING: How could this happen? I—I think a lot of people just don't understand, and even I don't really understand, how someone can do something like that. We have one of the most vocal populations of gay people in the state. . . . And it's pretty much: Live and let live.

NARRATOR: Laramie resident Jeffrey Lockwood:

JEFFREY LOCKWOOD: My secret hope was that they were from somewhere else, that then of course you can create that distance: We don't grow children like that here. Well, it's pretty clear that we do grow children like that here . . .

CATHERINE CONNOLLY: So that was the arraignment, and my response—was pretty catatonic—not sleeping, not eating. Don't—you know, don't leave me alone right now.

JON PEACOCK: More and more details came in about the sheer brutality, um, motivations, how this happened. And then quite frankly the media descended and there was no time to reflect on it anymore.

Moment: The Gem City of the Plains

(*Many reporters enter the stage, followed by media crews carrying cameras, microphones, and lights. They start speaking into the cameras. Simultaneously, television monitors enter the space—in our production they flew in from above the light grid. In the monitors, one can see in live feed the reporters speaking as well as other media images. The texts overlap to create a kind of media cacophony. This moment should feel like an invasion and should be so perceived by the other actors onstage.*)

NEWSPERSON 1: Laramie, Wyoming—often called the Gem City of the Plains—is now at the eye of the storm.

(*Enter Newsperson 2. Newsperson 1 goes sotto voce.*)

The cowboy state has its rednecks and yahoos for sure, but there are no more bigots per capita in

Wyoming than there are in New York, Florida, or California. The difference is that in Wyoming there are fewer places to blend in if you're anything other than prairie stock.

NEWSPERSON 2: Aaron McKinney and his friend Russell Henderson came from the poor side of town.

(*Enter Newsperson 3. Newsperson 2 goes sotto voce.*)

Both were from broken homes and as teenagers had had run-ins with the law. They lived in trailer parks and scratched out a living working at fast-food restaurants and fixing roofs.

NEWSPERSON 3: As a gay college student lay hospitalized in critical condition after a severe beating . . . this small city, which bills itself as Wyoming's Hometown, wrestled with its attitudes toward gay men.

(*Enter Newsperson 4. Newsperson 3 goes sotto voce.*)

NEWSPERSON 4: People would like to think that what happened to Matthew was an exception to the rule, but it was an extreme version of what happens in our schools on a daily basis.

(*The voices and sounds have escalated to a high pitch. And the last text we hear is:*)

NEWSPERSON 1: It's a tough business, as Matt Shepard knew, and as his friends all know, to be gay in cowboy country.

(*These reporters continue speaking into the cameras sotto voce over the next texts.*)

JON PEACOCK: It was huge. Yeah. It was herds and— and we're talking hundreds of reporters, which makes a huge dent in this town's population. There's reporters everywhere, news trucks everywhere on campus, everywhere in the town. And we're not used to that type of attention to begin with, we're not used to that type of exposure.

NARRATOR: Tiffany Edwards, local reporter:

TIFFANY EDWARDS: These people are predators. Like this one journalist actually caught one of the judges in the bathroom at the urinal and was like asking him questions. And the judge was like, "Excuse me, can I please have some privacy?" And the journalist was like *OFFENDED* that he asked for privacy. I mean, this is not how journalism started, like the Gutenberg press, you know.

DOC O'CONNOR: I'll tell you what, when *Hard Copy* came and taped me, I taped them at the exact same time. I have every word I ever said on tape so if they ever do anything funny they better watch their fuckin' ass.

NEWSPERSON: Wyoming governor Jim Geringer, a first-term Republican up for reelection:

GOVERNOR GERINGER: I am outraged and sickened by the heinous crime committed on Matthew Shepard. I extend my most heartfelt sympathies to the family.

NEWSPERSON: Governor, you haven't pushed hate crime legislation in the past.

GOVERNOR GERINGER: I would like to urge the people of Wyoming against overreacting in a way that gives one group "special rights over others."

The 2000 Denver production of *The Laramie Project*, starring Andy Paris (forefront), John McAdams (background), and Stephen Belber (background).

James Patterson (center) and cast in the 2003 production of *The Laramie Project* at the Cochrane Theatre, London.

We will wait and see if the vicious beating and torture of Matthew Shepard was motivated by hate.

SERGEANT HING: You've got the beginning of the news story where they have the graphics in the background, and they've got: "Murder in Wyoming," and Wyoming's dripping red like it's got blood on it or something, and it's like, what's the—what is this, this is sensationalism. And . . . we're here going, "Wait a minute. We had the guys in jail in less than a day. I think that's pretty damn good."

EILEEN ENGEN: And for us to be more or less maligned.

NARRATOR: Eileen and Gil Engen:

EILEEN ENGEN: That we're not a good community and we are—The majority of people here are good people.

GIL ENGEN: You git bad apples once in a while. And I think that the gay community took this as an advantage, said this is a good time for us to exploit this.

NEWSPERSON: Bill McKinney, father of one of the accused:

BILL MCKINNEY: Had this been a heterosexual these two boys decided to take out and rob, this never would have made the national news. Now my son is guilty before he's even had a trial.

TIFFANY EDWARDS: Look, I do think that, um, the media actually made people accountable. Because they made people think. Because people were sitting in their homes, like watching TV and listening to CNN and watching Dan Rather and going, "Jesus Christ, well that's not how it is here." Well how is it here?

Moment: Medical Update

NARRATOR: Matthew Shepard update at three P.M., Saturday, October tenth.

RULON STACEY: By this point, I looked out there and where there had been two or three reporters . . . it must have been ten or fifteen still photographers, another twenty or thirty reporters, and ten video cameras. The parents had just arrived. I had barely introduced myself to them. I looked out there and I thought, "My gosh. What am I going to do?"

(*He crosses to the area where the reporters are gathered with their cameras. As he arrives, several camera flashes go off. He speaks straight into the camera. We see his image on the monitors around the stage.*)

Matthew Shepard was admitted in critical condition approximately nine-fifteen P.M., October seventh. When he arrived, he was unresponsive, and breathing support was being provided.

Matthew's major injuries upon arrival consisted of hypothermia and a fracture from behind his head to just in front of the right ear. This has caused bleeding in the brain, as well as pressure on the brain. There were also several lacerations on his head, face, and neck.

Matthew's temperature has fluctuated over the last twenty-four hours, ranging from ninety-eight to one hundred and six degrees. We have had difficulty controlling his temperature.

Matthew's parents arrived at seven P.M., October ninth, and are now at his bedside. The following is a statement from them:

First of all, we want to thank the American public for their kind thoughts about Matthew and their fond wishes for his speedy recovery. We appreciate your prayers and goodwill, and we know that they are something Matthew would appreciate, too.

We also have a special request for the members of the media. Matthew is very much in need of his family at this time, and we ask that you respect our privacy, as well as Matthew's, so we can concentrate all of our efforts, thoughts, and love on our son.

Thank you very much.

Moment: Seeing Matthew

NARRATOR: Both Aaron McKinney and Russell Henderson pled not guilty to charges. Their girlfriends, Chasity Pasley and Kristin Price, also pled not guilty after being charged as accessories after the fact. On our next trip, we spoke to the chief investigating officer on the case, Detective Rob DeBree of the Albany County Sheriff's Department.

ROB DEBREE: I guess the thing that bothered me the most was when I went down to Poudre Valley, where Matthew was, and the thing that bothered me the most is seeing him, touching him. As a homicide detective, you look at bodies. . . . This poor boy is sitting here, fighting all his life, trying to make it. I wanted it so by the book you know.

AARON KREIFELS: I keep seeing that picture in my head when I found him . . .

NARRATOR: Aaron Kreifels:

AARON KREIFELS: . . . and it's not pleasant whatsoever. I don't want it to be there. I wanna like get it out. That's the biggest part for me is seeing that picture in my head. And it's kind of unbelievable to me, you know, that—I happened to be the person who found him—because the big question with me, like with my religion, is like, Why did God want ME to find him?

CATHERINE CONNOLLY: I know how to take care of myself, and I was irrationally terrified.

NARRATOR: Catherine Connolly:

CATHERINE CONNOLLY: So what that means is, not letting my twelve-year-old son walk the streets, seeing a truck do a U-turn and thinking it's coming after me. Having to stop because I'm shaking so bad. And, in fact, the pickup truck did not come after me, but my reaction was to have my heart in my mouth.

MATT GALLOWAY: Ultimately, no matter how you dice it, I did have an opportunity.

NARRATOR: Matt Galloway:

MATT GALLOWAY: If I had—amazing hindsight of 20/20—to have stopped—what occurred . . . and I keep thinkin', "I shoulda noticed. These guys

shouldn'ta been talking to this guy. I shoulda not had my head down when I was washing dishes for those twenty seconds. Things I coulda done. What the hell was I thinking?"

ROB DEBREE: So you do a lot of studying, you spend hours and hours and hours. You study and study and study . . . talking to the officers, making sure they understand, talk to your witnesses again, and then always coming back to I get this flash of seeing Matthew. . . . I wanted it so tight that there was no way that they were gonna get out of this.

REGGIE FLUTY: One of the things that happened when I got to the fence . . .

NARRATOR: Reggie Fluty:

REGGIE FLUTY: . . . It was just such an overwhelming amount of blood . . . and we try to wear protective gloves, but we had a really cheap sheriff at the time, and he bought us shit gloves, you know, you put 'em on, you put 'em on, and they kept breaking, so finally you just ran out of gloves, you know. So, you figure, well, you know, "Don't hesitate," you know, that's what your mind tells you all the time—Don't hesitate—and so you just keep moving and you try to help Matthew and find an airway and, you know, that's what you do, you know.

MARGE MURRAY: The thing I wasn't telling you before is that Reggie is my daughter.

NARRATOR: Marge Murray:

MARGE MURRAY: And when she first told me she wanted to be a police officer, well, I thought there was not a better choice for her. She could handle whatever came her way. . . .

REGGIE FLUTY: Probably a day and a half later, the hospital called me and told me Matthew had HIV. And the doctor said, "You've been exposed, and you've had a bad exposure," because, you see, I'd been—been building—building a, uh, lean-to for my llamas, and my hands had a bunch of open cuts on 'em, so I was kinda screwed (*she laughs*) you know, and you think, "Oh, shoot," you know.

MARGE MURRAY: Would you like to talk about losing sleep?

REGGIE FLUTY: So I said to the doctor, "Okay, what do I do?" And they said, "Get up here." So, I got up there and we started the ATZ (*sic*) drugs. Immediately.

MARGE MURRAY: Now they told me that's a medication that if it's administered thirty-six hours after you've been exposed . . . it can maybe stop your getting the disease . . .

REGGIE FLUTY: That is a mean nasty medicine. Mean. I've lost ten pounds and a lot of my hair. Yeah . . .

MARGE MURRAY: And quite frankly I wanted to lash out at somebody. Not at Matthew, please understand that, not one of us was mad at Matthew. But we maybe wanted to squeeze McKinney's head off. And I think about Henderson. And, you know, two absolutely human beings cause so much grief for so many people. . . . It has been terrible for my whole family, but mostly for her and her kids.

REGGIE FLUTY: I think it brought home to my girls what their mom does for a living.

MARGE MURRAY: Well, Reggie, you know what I'm gonna tell you now.

REGGIE FLUTY: And my parents told me, you know, they both said the same damn thing.

MARGE MURRAY: You're quitting this damn job!

REGGIE FLUTY: And it's just a parent thing, you know, and they're terribly proud of you, 'cause you do a good job whether it's handling a drunk or handling a case like this, but you're, you know, they don't want you getting hurt—

MARGE MURRAY: Like I said, there's a right way, a wrong way, and then there's Reggie's way.

REGGIE FLUTY: So finally I said, "Oh, for God's sakes, lighten up, Francis!"

MARGE MURRAY: You are so stubborn!

REGGIE FLUTY: They say I'm stubborn, and I don't believe them, but I just think, you know, okay, I've heard your opinion and now here's mine. I'm thirty-nine years old, you know, what are they gonna do, spank me?

MARGE MURRAY: Reggie, don't give me any ideas.

REGGIE FLUTY: It'd look pretty funny. You know, what can they say?

MARGE MURRAY: I just hope she doesn't go before me. I just couldn't handle that.

Moment: E-Mail

NARRATOR: University of Wyoming president Philip Dubois:

PHILIP DUBOIS: Well, this is a young person—who read my statement on the *Denver Post* story, and sent me an e-mail, to me directly, and said:

E-MAIL WRITER: You and the straight people of Laramie and Wyoming are guilty of the beating of Matthew Shepard just as the Germans who looked the other way are guilty of the deaths of the Jews, the Gypsies, and the homosexuals. You have taught your straight children to hate their gay and lesbian brothers and sisters. Unless and until you acknowledge that Matt Shepard's beating is not just a random occurrence, not just the work of a couple of random crazies, you have Matthew's blood on your hands.

PHILIP DUBOIS: And uh, well, I just can't begin to tell you what that does to you. And it's like, you can't possibly know what I'm thinking, you can't possibly know what this has done to me and my family and my community.

Moment: Vigils

(*We see images of the vigils taking place around the country in the monitors as:*)

NARRATOR: That first week alone, vigils were held in Laramie, Denver, Fort Collins, and Colorado Springs. Soon after in Detroit, Chicago, San Francisco, Washington, D.C., Atlanta, Nashville, Minneapolis, and Portland, Maine, among others. In Los Angeles, five thousand people gathered, and in New York City a political rally ended in civil disobedience and hundreds of arrests. And the Poudre Valley Hospital Web site received close to a million visitors from across the country and around the world, all expressing hope for Matthew's recovery.

Moment: Medical Update

NARRATOR: Matthew Shepard medical update at nine A.M., Sunday, October eleventh.

(*Rulon Stacey is in front of the cameras. We see him on the monitors.*)

RULON STACEY: As of nine A.M. today, Matthew Shepard remains in critical condition. The family continues to emphasize that the media respect their privacy. The family also wants to thank the American public for their kind thoughts and concern for Matthew.

Moment: Live and Let Live

JEDADIAH SCHULTZ: There are certain things when I sit in church.

NARRATOR: Jedadiah Schultz:

JEDADIAH SCHULTZ: And the reverend will tell you flat out he doesn't agree with homosexuality—and I don't know—I think right now, I'm going through changes, I'm still learning about myself and—you know I don't feel like I know enough about certain things to make a decision that says, "Homosexuality is right." When you've been raised your whole life that it's wrong—and right now, I would say that I don't agree with it—yeah, that I don't agree with it but—maybe that's just because I couldn't do it—and speaking in religious terms—I don't think that's how God intended it to happen. But I don't hate homosexuals and, I mean—I'm not going to persecute them or anything like that. At all—I mean, that's not gonna be getting in the way between me and the other person at all.

CONRAD MILLER: Well, it's preached in schools that being gay is okay.

NARRATOR: Conrad Miller:

CONRAD MILLER: And if my kids asked me, I'd set them down and I'd say, "Well, this is what gay people do. This is what animals do. Okay?" And I'd tell 'em, "This is the life, this is the lifestyle, this is what they do." And I'd say, "This is why I believe it's wrong."

MURDOCK COOPER: There's more gay people around than what you think.

NARRATOR: Murdock Cooper:

MURDOCK COOPER: It doesn't bother anybody because most of 'em that are gay or lesbian they know damn well who to talk to. If you step out of line you're asking for it. Some people are saying he made a pass at them. You don't pick up regular people. I'm not excusing their actions, but it made me feel better because it was partially Matthew Shepard's fault and partially the guys who did it . . . you know, maybe it's fifty-fifty.

ZACKIE SALMON: Yes, as a lesbian I was more concerned for my safety.

NARRATOR: Zackie Salmon:

ZACKIE SALMON: I think we all were. And I think it's because somewhere inside we know it could happen to us anytime, you know. I mean, I would be afraid to walk down the street and display any sort of physical affection for my partner. You don't do that here in Laramie.

JONAS SLONAKER: Well, there's this whole idea: You leave me alone, I leave you alone.

NARRATOR: Jonas Slonaker:

JONAS SLONAKER: And it's even in some of the western literature, you know, live and let live. That is such crap. I tell my friends that—even my gay friends bring it up sometimes. I'm like, "That is crap, you know?" I mean, basically what it boils down to: If I don't tell you I'm a fag, you won't beat the crap out of me. I mean, what's so great about that? That's a great philosophy?

Moment: It Happened Here

ZUBAIDA ULA: We went to the candle vigil.

NARRATOR: Zubaida Ula:

ZUBAIDA ULA: And it was so good to be with people who felt like shit. I kept feeling like I don't deserve to feel this bad, you know? And someone got up there and said, "C'mon, guys, let's show the world that Laramie is not this kind of a town." But it is that kind of a town. If it wasn't this kind of a town, why did this happen here? I mean, you know what I mean, like— that's a lie. Because it happened here. So how could it not be a town where this kind of thing happens? Like, that's just totally—like, looking at an Escher painting and getting all confused, like, it's just totally like circular logic like how can you even say that? And we have to mourn this and we have to be sad that we live in a town, a state, a country where shit like this happens. And I'm not going to step away from that and say, "We need to show the world this didn't happen." I mean, these are people trying to distance themselves from this crime. And we need to own this crime. I feel. Everyone needs to own it. We are like this. We ARE like this. WE are LIKE this.

Moment: Shannon and Jen

STEPHEN BELBER: I was in the Fireside one afternoon and I ran into two friends of Aaron McKinney, Shannon and Jen. (*To Shannon and Jen*) You knew Aaron well, right?

SHANNON: Yeah, we both did. When I first found out about this, I thought it was really really awful. I don't know whether Aaron was fucked up or whether he was coming down or what, but Matthew had money.

Shit, he had better clothes than I did. Matthew was a little rich bitch.

JEN: You shouldn't call him a rich bitch though, that's not right.

SHANNON: Well, I'm not saying he's a bad guy either, because he was just in the wrong place at the wrong time, said the wrong things. And I don't know, I won't lie to you. There was times that I was all messed up on meth and I thought about going out and robbing. I mean, I never did. But yeah, it was there. It's easy money.

JEN: Aaron's done that thing before. They've both done it. I know one night they went to Cheyenne to go do it and they came back with probably three hundred dollars. I don't know if they ever chose like gay people as their particular targets before, but anyone that looked like they had a lot of money and that was you know, they could outnumber, or overpower, was fair game.

STEPHEN BELBER: But do you think there was any homophobia involved in this that contributed to some of it?

JEN: Probably. It probably would've pissed him off that Matthew was gay 'cause he didn't like—the gay people that I've seen him interact with, he was fine as long as, you know, they didn't hit on him. As long as it didn't come up.

SHANNON: Yeah, as long as they weren't doing it in front of him.

STEPHEN BELBER: Do you get the impression that Aaron knew other gay people?

SHANNON: I'm sure that he knew people that are gay. I mean, he worked up at KFC and there was a couple people up there that—yeah (*he laughs*)—and I'm not saying it's bad or anything 'cause I don't know, half the people I know in Laramie are gay.

STEPHEN BELBER: What would you guys say to Aaron if you saw him right now?

SHANNON: First of all, I'd ask him if he'd ever do anymore tweak.

JEN: He wouldn't I bet. If I saw Aaron now, I'd be like, "Man, why'd you fuck up like that?" But, I'd want to make sure he's doing good in there. But, I'm sure he is though. I'd probably just want to like hang out with him.

SHANNON: Smoke a bowl with him.

JEN: I bet he wants one so bad.

STEPHEN BELBER: So, you guys both went to Laramie High?

SHANNON: Yeah. Can't you tell? We're a product of our society.

Moment: Homecoming

NEWSPERSON: On a day that is traditionally given over to nothing more profound than collegiate exuberance and the fortunes of the University of Wyoming football team, this community on the high plains had a different kind of homecoming Saturday, as many searched their souls in the wake of a vicious, apparent antigay hate crime.

NARRATOR: University president Philip Dubois:

PHILIP DUBOIS: This was homecoming weekend. There were a lot of people in town, and there's a homecoming parade that was scheduled, and then the students organized to tag onto the back of it—you know, behind the banner supporting Matt, and everybody wearing the armbands that the students had created . . .

HARRY WOODS: I live in the center of town.

NARRATOR: Harry Woods:

HARRY WOODS: And my apartment has windows on two opposite streets. One goes north and one goes south. And that is exactly the homecoming parade route. Now, on the day of the parade, I had a cast on my leg because of a fall. So I was very disappointed because I really wanted to walk with the people that were marching for Matthew. But I couldn't. So I watched from my window. And it was . . . it was just . . . I'm fifty-two years old and I'm gay. I have lived here for many years and I've seen a lot. And I was very moved when I saw the tag on the end of the homecoming parade. About a hundred people walking behind a banner for Matthew Shepard.

So then the parade went down to the end of the block to make a U-turn, and I went to the other side of my apartment to wait for it to come south down the other street.

MATT GALLOWAY: I was right up in front there where they were holding the banner for Matthew, and let me tell you . . . I've never had goose bumps so long in my life. It was incredible. A mass of people. Families—mothers holding their six-year-old kids, tying these armbands around these six-year-old kids and trying to explain to them why they should wear an armband. Just amazing. I mean it was absolutely one of the most—beautiful things I've ever done in my life.

HARRY WOODS: Well, about ten minutes went by, and sure enough the parade started coming down the street. And then I noticed the most incredible thing . . . as the parade came down the street . . . the number of people walking for Matthew Shepard had grown five times. There were at least five hundred people marching for Matthew. Five hundred people. Can you imagine? The tag at the end was larger than the entire parade. And people kept joining in. And you know what? I started to cry. Tears were streaming down my face. And I thought, "Thank God that I got to see this in my lifetime." And my second thought was, "Thank you, Matthew."

Moment: One of Ours

SHERRY JOHNSON: I really haven't been all that involved, per se. My husband's a highway patrolman, so that's really the only way that I've known about it.

Now when I first found out I just thought it was horrible. I just, I can't . . . Nobody deserves that! I don't care who ya are.

But, the other thing that was not brought out—at the same time this happened that patrolman was killed. And there was nothing. Nothing. They didn't say anything about the old man that killed him. He was driving down the road and he shouldn't have been driving and killed him. It was just a little piece in the paper. And we lost one of our guys.

You know, my husband worked with him. This man was brand-new on the force. But, I mean, here's one of ours, and it was just a little piece in the paper.

And a lot of it is my feeling that the media is portraying Matthew Shepard as a saint. And making him as a martyr. And I don't think he was. I don't think he was that pure.

Now, I didn't know him, but . . . there's just so many things about him that I found out that I just, it's scary. You know about his character and spreading AIDS and a few other things, you know, being the kind of person that he was. He was, he was just a barfly, you know. And I think he pushed himself around. I think he flaunted it.

Everybody's got problems. But why they exemplified him I don't know. What's the difference if you're gay? A hate crime is a hate crime. If you murder somebody you hate 'em. It has nothing to do with if you're gay or a prostitute or whatever.

I don't understand. I don't understand.

Moment: Two Queers and a Catholic Priest

NARRATOR: Company member Leigh Fondakowski:

LEIGH FONDAKOWSKI: This is one of the last days on our second trip to Laramie. Greg and I have been conducting interviews nonstop and we are exhausted.

GREG PIEROTTI: We are to meet Father Roger at seven-thirty in the morning. I was wishing we could skip it all together, but we have to follow through to the end. So here we go: seven-thirty A.M., two queers and a Catholic priest.

FATHER ROGER SCHMIT: Matthew Shepard has served us well. You realize that? He has served us well. And I do not mean to condemn Matthew to perfection, but I cannot mention anyone who has done more for this community than Matthew Shepard.

And I'm not gonna sit here and say, "I was just this bold guy—no fear." I was scared. I was very vocal in this community when this happened—and I thought, "You know, should we, uh, should we call the bishop and ask him permission to do the vigil?" And I was like, "Hell, no, I'm not going to do that." His permission doesn't make it correct, you realize that? And I'm not knocking bishops, but what is correct is correct.

You people are just out here on a search, though. I will do this. I will trust you people that if you write a play of this, that you (*pause*) say it right, say it correct. I think you have a responsibility to do that.

Don't—don't—don't, um (*pause*) don't make matters worse. . . . You think violence is what they did to Matthew—they did do violence to Matthew—but you know, every time that you are called a fag, or you are called a you know, a lez or whatever . . .

LEIGH FONDAKOWSKI: Or a dyke.

FATHER ROGER SCHMIT: Dyke, yeah, dyke. Do you realize that is violence? That is the seed of violence. And I would resent it immensely if you use anything I said, uh, you know, to—to somehow cultivate that kind of violence, even in its smallest form. I would resent it immensely. You need to know that.

LEIGH FONDAKOWSKI: Thank you, Father, for saying that.

FATHER ROGER SCHMIT: Just deal with what is true. You know what is true. You need to do your best to say it correct.

Moment: *Christmas*

NARRATOR: Andrew Gomez:

ANDREW GOMEZ: I was in there, I was in jail with Aaron in December. I got thrown in over Christmas. Assault and battery, two counts. I don't wanna talk about it. But we were sittin' there eatin' our Christmas dinner, tryin' to eat my stuffing, my motherfucking bread, my little roll and whatnot, and I asked him, I was like, "Hey, homey, tell me something, tell me something please, why did you—" Okay, I'm thinking how I worded this, I was like, "Why did you kill a faggot if you're gonna be destined to BE a faggot later?" You know? I mean, think about it, he's either gonna get humped a lot or he's gonna die. So why would you do that, think about that. I don't understand that.

And you know what he told me? Honest to God, this is what he said, he goes: "He tried to grab my dick." That's what he said, man! He's dumb, dog, he don't even act like it was nothin'.

Now I heard they was auctioning those boys off. Up there in the max ward, you know, where the killers go, I heard that when they found out Aaron was coming to prison, they were auctioning those boys off. "I want him. I'll put aside five, six, seven cartons of cigarettes." Auction his ass off. I'd be scared to go to prison if I was those two boys.

Moment: *Lifestyle 2*

BAPTIST MINISTER: Hello.

AMANDA GRONICH: Reverend?

BAPTIST MINISTER: Yes, hello.

AMANDA GRONICH: I believe your wife told you a bit about why I'm contacting you.

BAPTIST MINISTER: Yes, she did. And let me tell you—uh—I don't know that I really want to talk to anyone about any of this incident—uh—I am somewhat involved and I just don't think—

AMANDA GRONICH: Yes, I completely understand and I don't blame you. You know, I went to your service on Sunday.

BAPTIST MINISTER: You went to the services on Sunday?

AMANDA GRONICH: Yes, I did.

BAPTIST MINISTER: On Sunday?

AMANDA GRONICH: Yes, this past Sunday.

BAPTIST MINISTER: Did I meet you?

AMANDA GRONICH: Yes, you welcomed me at the beginning, I believe.

BAPTIST MINISTER: I see, Well, let me tell you. I am not afraid to be controversial or to speak my mind, and that is not necessarily the views of my congregation per se. Now as I said, I am somewhat involved—that half the people in the case—well, the girlfriend of the accused is a member of our congregation, and one of the accused has visited.

AMANDA GRONICH: Mmmmmm.

BAPTIST MINISTER: Now, those two people, the accused, have forfeited their lives. We've been after the two I mentioned for ages, trying to get them to live right, to do right. Now, one boy is on suicide watch and I am working with him—until they put him in the chair and turn on the juice I will work for his salvation. Now I think they deserve the death penalty—I will try to deal with them spiritually.

AMANDA GRONICH: Right, I understand.

BAPTIST MINISTER: Now, as for the victim, I know that that lifestyle is legal, but I will tell you one thing: I hope that Matthew Shepard as he was tied to that fence, that he had time to reflect on a moment when someone had spoken the word of the Lord to him—and that before he slipped into a coma he had a chance to reflect on his lifestyle.

AMANDA GRONICH: Thank you, Reverend, I appreciate your speaking with me.

(*Rain begins to fall on the stage.*)

Moment: *That Night*

RULON STACEY: About eleven-thirty that night, I had just barely gone to bed, and Margo, our chief operating officer, called and said, "His blood pressure has started to drop." "Well, let's wait and see." She called me about ten after—he just died. So I quick got dressed and came in, and uh went into the ICU where the family was, and Judy came up and she put her arms around me and I put my arms around her and we just stood there—honestly, for about ten minutes just—'cause what else do you do?

And then we had to sit and talk about things that you just—"Dennis, it's now public knowledge. . . . And I'm gonna go out there now and tell the whole world that this has happened."

'Cause by this point it was clear to us that it was the world—it was the whole world.

And so Judy told me what she wanted me to say. And I went out at four A.M.

(*He crosses to the camera.*)

Moment: *Medical Update*

NARRATOR: Matthew Shepard medical update for four-thirty A.M., Monday, October twelfth.

RULON STACEY: At twelve midnight on Monday, October twelfth, Matthew Shepard's blood pressure began to drop. We immediately notified his family, who were already at the hospital.

At twelve fifty-three A.M. Matthew Shepard died. His family was at his bedside.

The family did release the following statement,

The family again asked me to express their sincerest gratitude to the entire world for the overwhelming response for their son.

The family was grateful that they did not have to make a decision regarding whether or not to continue life support for their son. Like a good son, he was caring to the end and removed guilt or stress from the family.

He came into the world premature and left the world premature.

Matthew's mother said:

Go home, give your kids a hug, and don't let a day go by without telling them that you love them.

Moment: Magnitude

RULON STACEY: And—I don't know *how* I let that happen—I lost it on national television, but, you now, we had been up for like seventy-two hours straight and gone home and gone to sleep for half an hour and had to get up and come in—and maybe I was just way—I don't know—but (*pause*) in a moment of complete brain-deadness, while I was out there reading that statement I thought about my own four daughters—and go home, hug your kids (*he begins to cry*) and, oh, she doesn't have her kid anymore.

And there I am and I'm thinking, "This is so lame."

Um, and then we started to get people sending us e-mails and letters. And most of them were just generally very kind. But I did get this one. This guy wrote me and said, "Do you cry like a baby on TV for all of your patients or just the faggots?" And as I told you before, homosexuality is not a lifestyle with which I agree. Um, but having been thrown into this (*pause*) I guess I didn't understand the magnitude with which some people hate. And of all the letters that we got, there were maybe two or three that were like that, most of them were, Thank you for your caring and compassion, and Matthew had caring and compassion from the moment he got here.

Moment: H-O-P-E

STEPHEN BELBER: I spoke with Doc today and told him we would soon be coming back out for the upcoming trials of Russell Henderson and Aaron McKinney, and this is what he had to say.

DOC O'CONNOR: I'll tell you what, if they put those two boys to death, that would defeat everything Matt would be thinking about on them. Because Matt

would not want those two to die. He'd want to leave them with hope. (*Spelling*) H-O-P-E. Just like the whole world hoped that Matt would survive. The whole thing, you see, the whole thing, ropes around hope, H-O-P-E.

End of Act II

ACT III

(*The stage is now empty except for several chairs stage right. They occupy that half of the stage. They are all facing the audience and arranged in rows as if to suggest a church or a courthouse. As the lights come up, several actors are sitting there dressed in black. Some of them have umbrellas. A few beats with just this image in silence. Then Matt Galloway enters stage left. Looks at them and says:*)

Moment: Snow

MATT GALLOWAY: The day of the funeral, it was snowing so bad, big huge wet snowflakes. And when I got there, there were thousands of people in just black, with umbrellas everywhere. And there were two churches—one for the immediate family, uh, invited guests, people of that nature, and then one church for everybody else who wanted to be there. And then, still, hundreds of people outside that couldn't fit into either of the churches. And there was a big park by the church, and that's where these people were. And this park was full.

PRIEST: The liturgy today is an Easter liturgy. It finds its meaning in the Resurrection. The service invites your full participation.

PRIEST: The Lord be with you.

PEOPLE: And also with you.

PRIEST: Let us pray.

TIFFANY EDWARDS: And I guess it was like the worst storm that they have had.

NARRATOR: Tiffany Edwards:

TIFFANY EDWARDS: Like that anybody could ever tell, like trees fell down and the power went out for a couple of days because of it and I just thought, "It's like the forces of the universe at work, you know." Whatever higher spirit, you know, is like that blows storms, was blowin' this storm.

PRIEST: For our brother, Matthew, let us pray to our Lord Jesus Christ, who said, "I am the Resurrection and the Life." We pray to the Lord.

PEOPLE: HEAR US, LORD.

(*The Priest begins and goes into sotto voce.*)

PRIEST: Lord, you who consoled Martha and Mary in their distress: draw near to us who mourn for Matthew, and dry the tears of those who weep. We pray to the Lord.

PEOPLE: HEAR US, LORD.

PRIEST: You wept at the grave of Lazarus, your friend: comfort us in our sorrow. We pray to the Lord.

PEOPLE: HEAR US, LORD.

PRIEST: You raised the dead to life: give to our brother eternal life. We pray to the Lord.

PEOPLE: HEAR US, LORD.

PRIEST: You promised paradise to the thief who repented: bring our brother the joys of heaven. We pray to the Lord.

PEOPLE: HEAR US, LORD.

PRIEST: He was nourished with your Body and Blood; grant him a place at the table in your heavenly kingdom. We pray to the Lord.

PEOPLE: HEAR US, LORD.

PRIEST: Comfort us in our sorrows at the death of our brother; let our faith be our consolation, and eternal life our hope. We pray to the Lord.

KERRY DRAKE: My most striking memory from the funeral . . .

NARRATOR: Kerry Drake, *Casper Star-Tribune*:

KERRY DRAKE: . . . is seeing the Reverend Fred Phelps from Kansas . . . that scene go up in the park.

REVEREND FRED PHELPS: Do you believe the Bible? Do you believe you're supposed to separate the precious from the vile? You don't believe that part of the Bible? You stand over there ignorant of the fact that the Bible — two times for every verse it talks about God's love it talks about God's hate.

(*Reverend Fred Phelps continues sotto voce.*)

KERRY DRAKE: A bunch of high school kids who got out early came over and started yelling at some of these people in the protest — the Fred Phelps people — and across the street you had people lining up for the funeral . . . Well, I remember a guy, this skinhead coming over, and he was dressed in leather and spikes everywhere, and he came over from across the street where the protest was and he came into the crowd and I just thought, "Oh, this is gonna be a really ugly confrontation" BUT instead he came over and he started leading them in "Amazing Grace."

(*The people sing "Amazing Grace."*)

REVEREND FRED PHELPS: We wouldn't be here if this was just another murder the state was gonna deal with. The state deals with hundreds of murders every single day. But this murder is different, because the fags are bringing us out here trying to make Matthew Shepard into a poster boy for the gay lifestyle. And we're going to answer it. It's just that simple.

(*Reverend Fred Phelps continues sotto voce.*)

NARRATOR: Six months later, the company returned to Laramie for the trial of Russell Henderson, the first of the two perpetrators. It was to be a capital murder trial. When we got to the Albany County Courthouse, Fred Phelps was already there.

REVEREND FRED PHELPS: You don't like that attribute of God.

NARRATOR: But so was Romaine Patterson.

REVEREND FRED PHELPS: That perfect attribute of God. Well, WE love that attribute of God, and we're going to preach it. Because God's hatred is pure. It's a determination — it's a determination that he's gonna send some people to hell. That's God's hatred . . .

(*Continues sotto voce.*)

We're standing here with God's message. We're standing here with God's message. Is homosexuality — is being a fag okay? What do you mean it's not for you to judge? If God doesn't hate fags, why does he put 'em in hell? . . . You see the barrenness and sterility of your silly arguments when set over against some solid gospel truth? Barren and sterile. Like your lifestyle. Your silly arguments.

ROMAINE PATTERSON: After seeing Fred Phelps protesting at Matthew's funeral and finding out that he was coming to Laramie for the trial of Russell Henderson, I decided that someone needed to stand toe-to-toe with this guy and show the differences. And I think at times like this, when we're talking about hatred as much as the nation is right now, that someone needs to show that there is a better way of dealing with that kind of hatred.

So our idea is to dress up like angels. And so we have designed an angel outfit — for our wings are huge — they're like big-ass wings — and there'll be ten to twenty of us that are angels — and what we're gonna do is we're gonna encircle Phelps . . . and because of our big wings — we are gonna comple-tely block him.

So this big-ass band of angels comes in, we don't say a fuckin' word, we just turn our backs to him and we stand there. . . . And we are a group of people bringing forth a message of peace and love and compassion. And we're calling it "Angel Action."

Yeah, this twenty-one-year-old little lesbian is ready to walk the line with him.

REVEREND FRED PHELPS: When those old preachers laid their hands on me it's called an ordination. Mine was from Isaiah fifty-eight: one — "Cry aloud. Spare not. Lift up thy voice like a trumpet and show my people their transgressions."

ROMAINE PATTERSON: And I knew that my angels were gonna be taking the brunt of everything he had to yell and say. I mean, we were gonna be blocking his view and he was gonna be liked pissed off to all hell. . . . So I went out and bought all my angels earplugs.

(*"Amazing Grace" ends.*)

Moment: Jury Selection

BAILIFF: The court is in session.

(*All stand.*)

NARRATOR: Romaine Patterson's sister, Trish Steger:

TRISH STEGER: As soon as they started jury selection,

you know, everybody was coming into my shop with "I don't want to be on this trial. I hope they don't call me." Or, "Oh my God, I've been called. How do I get off?" Just wanting to get as far away from it as they could . . . very fearful that they were going to have to be part of that jury.

And then I heard . . . Henderson had to sit in the courtroom while they question the prospective jurors. And one of the questions that they ask is: Would you be willing to put this person to death?

And I understand that a lot of the comments were: "Yes, I would."

JUROR: Yes, I would, Your Honor.

JUROR: Yes, sir.

JUROR: Absolutely.

JUROR: Yes, sir!

(*Jurors continue underneath.*)

JUROR: No problem.

JUROR: Yep.

TRISH STEGER: Well, can you imagine hearing that? You know, juror after juror after juror . . .

Moment: Russell Henderson

(*"Amazing Grace" begins again.*)

JUDGE: You entered a not guilty plea earlier, Mr. Henderson. But I understand you wish to change your plea today. Is that correct?

RUSSELL HENDERSON: Yes, sir.

JUDGE: You understand, Mr. Henderson, that the recommended sentence here is two life sentences?

RUSSELL HENDERSON: Yes, sir.

JUDGE: Do you understand that those may run concurrently or they may run consecutively?

RUSSELL HENDERSON: Yes, sir.

JUDGE: Mr. Henderson, I will now ask you how you wish to plead. Guilty or not guilty?

RUSSELL HENDERSON: Guilty.

JUDGE: Before the Court decides whether the sentences will be concurrent or consecutive, I understand that there are statements to be made by at least one individual.

NARRATOR: This is an excerpt from a statement made to the court by Lucy Thompson.

MS. THOMPSON: As the grandmother and the person who raised Russell, along with my family, we have written the following statement: Our hearts ache for the pain and suffering that the Shepards have went through. We have prayed for your family since the very beginning. Many times throughout the day I have thought about Matt. And you will continue to be in our thoughts and prayers, as we know that your pain will never go away. You have showed such mercy in allowing us to have this plea, and we are so grateful that you are giving us all the opportunity to live. Your Honor, we, as a family, hope that as you sentence Russell, that you will do it concurrently two life terms. For the Russell we know and love, we

humbly plead, Your Honor, to not take Russell completely out of our lives forever.

JUDGE: Thank you. Mr. Henderson, you have a constitutional right to make a statement if you would like to do so. Do you have anything you would like to say?

RUSSELL HENDERSON: Yes, I would, Your Honor. Mr. and Mrs. Shepard, there is not a moment that goes by that I don't see what happened that night. I know what I did was very wrong, and I regret greatly what I did. You have my greatest sympathy for what happened. I hope that one day you will be able to find it in your hearts to forgive me. Your Honor, I know what I did was wrong. I'm very sorry for what I did, and I'm ready to pay my debt for what I did.

JUDGE: Mr. Henderson, you drove the vehicle that took Matthew Shepard to his death. You bound him to that fence in order that he might be more savagely beaten and in order that he might not escape to tell his tale. You left him out there for eighteen hours, knowing full well that he was there, perhaps having an opportunity to save his life, and you did nothing. Mr. Henderson, this Court does not believe that you really feel any true remorse for your part in this matter. And I wonder, Mr. Henderson, whether you fully realize the gravity of what you've done.

The Court finds it appropriate, therefore, that sentence be ordered as follows: As to Count Three, that being felony murder with robbery, you are to serve a period of imprisonment for the term of your natural life. On Count One, kidnapping, that you serve a period of imprisonment for the term of your natural life. Sentencing for Count One to run consecutive to sentencing for Count Three.

NARRATOR: After the hearing, we spoke with Russell Henderson's Mormon home teacher.

MORMON HOME TEACHER: I've known Russell's family for thirty-eight years. Russell's only twenty-one, so I've known him his entire life. I ordained Russell a priest of the Mormon Church, so when this happened, you can imagine—disbelief. . . . After the sentencing . . . the church held a disciplinary council, and the result of that meeting was to excommunicate Russell from the Mormon Church. And what that means is that your name is taken off the records of the church, so you just disappear.

Russell's reaction to that was not positive, it hurt him, it hurt him to realize how serious a transgression he had committed.

But I will not desert Russell. That's a matter of my religion and my friendship with the family.

(*All exit. Lights fade on Russell, his grandmother, and his home teacher.*)

Moment: Angels in America

NARRATOR: Before we left Laramie, we met again with Rebecca Hilliker at the theater department. She is producing *Angels in America* this year at the university.

REBECCA HILLIKER: I think that's the focus the university has taken—is that we have a lot of work to do. That we have an obligation to find ways to reach our students. . . . And the question is, How do we move—how do we reach a whole state where there is some really deep-seated hostility toward gays? How do you reach them?

This is the beginning . . . and guess who's auditioning for the lead?

JEDADIAH SCHULTZ: MY PARENTS!

NARRATOR: Jedadiah Schultz:

JEDADIAH SCHULTZ: My parents were like, "So what plays are you doing this year at school?" And I was like, "*Angels in America,*" and I told them the whole list of plays. And they're like, "*Angels in America*? Is that . . . that play you did in high school? That scene you did in high school?" And I was like, "Yeah." And she goes: "Huh. So are you gonna audition for it?" And I was like, "Yeah." And we got in this huge argument . . . and my best, the best thing that I knew I had them on is it was just after they had seen me in a performance of *Macbeth,* and onstage like I murdered like a little kid, and Lady Macduff and these two other guys and like and she goes, "Well, you know homosexuality is a sin"—she kept saying that—and I go, "Mom, I just played a murderer tonight. And you didn't seem to have a problem with that . . ."

I tell you. I've never prepared myself this much for an audition in my life. Never ever. Not even close.

ROB DEBREE: Not having to deal that much with the gay society here in Laramie.

NARRATOR: Detective Sergeant Rob DeBree:

ROB DEBREE: Well, once we started working into the case, and actually speaking to the people that were gay and finding out what their underlying fears were, well, then it sort of hit home. This is America. You don't have the right to feel that fear.

And we're still going to have people who hold with the old ideals, and I was probably one of them fourteen months ago. I'm not gonna put up with it, and I'm not going to listen to it. And if they don't like my views on it, fine. The door goes both ways. I already lost a couple of buddies. I don't care. I feel more comfortable and I can sleep at night.

REGGIE FLUTY: Well, you're tested every three months.

NARRATOR: Reggie Fluty:

REGGIE FLUTY: And I was able to have the DNA test done. And so they got me to Fort Collins, they drew the blood there, flew it to Michigan, and did all the DNA work there and—which was—a week later . . . I knew I was negative for good.

MARGE MURRAY: I'll tell ya, we were all on our knees saying Hail Marys.

REGGIE FLUTY: You were just elated, you know, and you think, "Thank God!"

MARGE MURRAY: So what's the first thing she does?

REGGIE FLUTY: I stuck my tongue right in my husband's mouth. I was just happy, you know, you're just so happy. You think, "Yeah, I hope I did this service well," you know, I hope I did it with some kind of integrity. So, you're just really happy . . . and my daughters just bawled.

MARGE MURRAY: They were so happy.

REGGIE FLUTY: And the force . . .

MARGE MURRAY: Oh boy . . .

REGGIE FLUTY: We went out and got shitfaced.

MARGE MURRAY: (*Simultaneous*) Shitfaced.

REGGIE FLUTY: They all bought me drinks too, it was great . . . and everybody hugged and cried, and, you know, I kissed everybody who walked through the door . . .

MARGE MURRAY: Reggie, they don't need to know that.

REGGIE FLUTY: I didn't care if they were male or female, they each got a kiss on the lips.

(*Reggie and Marge exit together, arguing as they go.*)

MARGE MURRAY: Now what part of what I just said didn't you understand?

REGGIE FLUTY: Oh, get over it, Maw!

Moment: A Death Penalty Case

NARRATOR: Almost a year to the day that Matthew Shepard died, the trial for Aaron James McKinney was set to begin.

CAL RERUCHA: Probably the question that most of you have in your mind is ah, ah, how the McKinney case will proceed.

NARRATOR: Cal Rerucha, prosecuting attorney:

CAL RERUCHA: And it's the decision of the county attorney's office that that will definitely be a death penalty case.

MARGE MURRAY: Part of me wants McKinney to get it. But I'm not very proud of that. I was on and off, off and on. I can't say what I would do . . . I'm too personally involved.

ZACKIE SALMON: Oh, I believe in the death penalty one hundred percent. You know, because I want to make sure that guy's ass dies. This is one instance where I truly believe with all my heart an eye for an eye, a tooth for a tooth.

MATT MICKELSON: I don't know about the death penalty. But I don't ever want to see them ever walk out of Rawlins Penitentiary. I'll pay my nickel, or whatever, my little percentage of tax, nickel a day to make sure that his ass stays in there and never sees society again and definitely never comes into my bar again.

MATT GALLOWAY: I don't believe in the death penalty. It's too much for me. I don't believe that one person should be killed as redemption for his having killed another. Two wrongs don't make a right.

ZUBAIDA ULA: How can I protest, if the Shepards want McKinney dead? I just can't interfere in that. But on a personal level, I knew Aaron in grade school. We never called him Aaron, he was called A.J. . . . How can we put A.J. McKinney—how can we put A.J. McKinney to death?

FATHER ROGER SCHMIT: I think right now our most important teachers must be Russell Henderson and

Aaron McKinney. They have to be our teachers. How did you learn? What did we as a society do to teach you that? See, I don't know if many people will let them be their teachers. I think it would be wonderful if the judge said: "In addition to your sentence, you must tell your story, you must tell your story."

BAILIFF: All rise. State of Wyoming versus Aaron James McKinney, docket number 6381. The Honorable Barton R. Voigt presiding. The Court is in session.

Moment: Aaron McKinney

NARRATOR: During the trial of Aaron McKinney, the prosecution played a tape recording of his confession.

ROB DEBREE: My name is Rob DeBree, sergeant for the Sheriff's Office. You have the right to remain silent. Anything you say can and may be used against you in a court of law.

NARRATOR: The following is an excerpt of that confession.

ROB DEBREE: Okay, so you guys, you and Russ go to the Fireside. So you're at the Fireside by yourselves, right?

AARON MCKINNEY: Yeah.

ROB DEBREE: Okay, where do you go after you leave the Fireside?

AARON MCKINNEY: Some kid wanted a ride home.

ROB DEBREE: What's he look like?

AARON MCKINNEY: Mmm, like a queer. Such a queer dude.

ROB DEBREE: He looks like a queer?

AARON MCKINNEY: Yeah, like a fag, you know?

ROB DEBREE: Okay. How did you meet him?

AARON MCKINNEY: He wanted a ride home and I just thought, well, the dude's drunk, let's just take him home.

ROB DEBREE: When did you and Russ talk about jacking him up?

AARON MCKINNEY: We kinda talked about it at the bar.

ROB DEBREE: Okay, what happened next?

AARON MCKINNEY: We drove him out past Wal-Mart. We got over there, and he starts grabbing my leg and grabbing my genitals. I was like, "Look, I'm not a fuckin' faggot. If you touch me again you're gonna get it." I don't know what the hell he was trying to do but I beat him up pretty bad. Think I killed him.

ROB DEBREE: What'd you beat him with?

AARON MCKINNEY: Blacked out. My fist. My pistol. The butt of the gun. Wondering what happened to me. I had a few beers and, I don't know. It's like I could see what was going on, but I don't know, but I don't know, it was like somebody else was doing it.

ROB DEBREE: What was the first thing that he said or that he did in the truck that made you hit him?

AARON MCKINNEY: Well, he put his hand on my leg, slid his hand like as if he was going to grab my balls.

Moment: Gay Panic

ZACKIE SALMON: When that defense team argued that McKinney did what he did because Matthew made a pass at him . . . I just wanted to vomit, because that's like saying that it's okay. It's like the "Twinkie Defense," when the guy killed Harvey Milk and Moscone. It's the same thing.

REBECCA HILLIKER: As much as, uh, part of me didn't want the defense of them saying that it was a gay bashing or that it was gay panic, part of me is really grateful. Because I was really scared that in the trial they were going to try and say that it was a robbery, or it was about drugs. So when they used "gay panic" as their defense, I felt, this is good, if nothing else the truth is going to be told . . . the truth is coming out.

Moment: Aaron McKinney (continued)

ROB DEBREE: Did he ever try to defend himself against you or hit you back?

AARON MCKINNEY: Yeah, sort of. He tried his little swings or whatever but he wasn't very effective.

ROB DEBREE: Okay. How many times did you hit him inside the truck before you guys stopped where you left him?

AARON MCKINNEY: I'd say I hit him two or three times, probably three times with my fists and about six times with the pistol.

ROB DEBREE: Did he ask you to stop?

AARON MCKINNEY: Well, yeah. He was getting the shit kicked out of him.

ROB DEBREE: What did he say?

AARON MCKINNEY: After he asked me to stop most all he was doing was screaming.

ROB DEBREE: So Russ kinda dragged him over to the fence, I'm assuming, and tied him up?

AARON MCKINNEY: Something like that. I just remember Russ was laughing at first but then he got pretty scared.

ROB DEBREE: Was Matthew conscious when Russ tied him up?

AARON MCKINNEY: Yeah. I told him to turn around and don't look at my license plate number 'cause I was scared he would tell the police. And then I asked him what my license plate said. He read it and that's why I hit him a few more times.

ROB DEBREE: Just to be sure? (Pause) So obviously you don't like gay people?

AARON MCKINNEY: No, I don't.

ROB DEBREE: Would you say you hate them?

AARON MCKINNEY: Uh, I really don't hate them but, you know, when they start coming on to me and stuff like that I get pretty aggravated.

ROB DEBREE: Did he threaten you?

AARON MCKINNEY: This gay dude?

ROB DEBREE: Yeah.

AARON MCKINNEY: Not really.

ROB DEBREE: Can you answer me one thing? Why'd you guys take his shoes?

AARON MCKINNEY: I don't know. (Pause) Now I'm never going to see my son again.

ROB DEBREE: I don't know. You'll probably go to court sometime today.

AARON MCKINNEY: Today? So I'm gonna go in there and just plead guilty or not guilty today?

ROB DEBREE: No, no, you're just going to be arraigned today.

AARON MCKINNEY: He is gonna die for sure?

ROB DEBREE: There is no doubt that Mr. Shepard is going to die.

AARON MCKINNEY: So what are they going to give me, twenty-five to life or just the death penalty and get it over with?

ROB DEBREE: That's not our job. That's the judge's job and the jury.

Moment: *The Verdict*

NARRATOR: Has the jury reached a verdict?

FOREPERSON: We have, Your Honor.

> We the jury, impaneled and sworn to try the above entitled case, after having well and truly tried the matter, unanimously find as follows:
>
> As to the charge of kidnapping, we find the defendant, Aaron James McKinney, guilty.
>
> As to the charge of aggravated robbery, we find the defendant, Aaron James McKinney, guilty.
>
> As to the charge of first-degree felony murder (kidnapping), we find the defendant, Aaron James McKinney, guilty.

(*Verdict goes sotto voce. Narration begins.*)

> As to the charge of first-degree felony murder (robbery), we find the defendant, Aaron James McKinney, guilty.
>
> As to the charge of premeditated first-degree murder, we find the defendant, Aaron James McKinney, not guilty.
>
> As to the lesser-included offense of second-degree murder, we find the defendant, Aaron James McKinney, guilty.

Moment: *Dennis Shepard's Statement*

NARRATOR: Aaron McKinney was found guilty of felony murder, which meant the jury could give him the death penalty. That evening, Judy and Dennis Shepard were approached by McKinney's defense team, who pled for their client's life. The following morning, Dennis Shepard made a statement to the Court. Here is some of what he said.

DENNIS SHEPARD: My son Matthew did not look like a winner. He was rather uncoordinated and wore braces from the age of thirteen until the day he died. However, in his all too brief life he proved that he was a winner. On October 6, 1998, my son tried to show the world that he could win again. On October 12, 1998, my firstborn son and my hero lost. On October 12, 1998, my firstborn son and my hero died, fifty days before his twenty-second birthday.

I keep wondering the same thing that I did when I first saw him in the hospital. What would he have become? How could he have changed his piece of the world to make it better?

Matt officially died in a hospital in Fort Collins, Colorado. He actually died on the outskirts of Laramie, tied to a fence. You, Mr. McKinney, with your friend Mr. Henderson left him out there by himself, but he wasn't alone. There were his lifelong friends with him, friends that he had grown up with. You're probably wondering who these friends were. First he had the beautiful night sky and the same stars and moon that we used to see through a telescope. Then he had the daylight and the sun to shine on him. And through it all he was breathing in the scent of pine trees from the snowy range. He heard the wind, the ever-present Wyoming wind, for the last time. He had one more friend with him, he had God. And I feel better knowing he wasn't alone.

Matt's beating, hospitalization, and funeral focused worldwide attention on hate. Good is coming out of evil. People have said enough is enough. I miss my son, but I am proud to be able to say that he is my son.

Judy has been quoted as being against the death penalty. It has been stated that Matt was against the death penalty. Both of these statements are wrong. Matt believed that there were crimes and incidents that justified the death penalty. I too believe in the death penalty. I would like nothing better than to see you die, Mr. McKinney. However, this is the time to begin the healing process. To show mercy to someone who refused to show any mercy. Mr. McKinney, I am going to grant you life, as hard as it is for me to do so, because of Matthew. Every time you celebrate Christmas, a birthday, the Fourth of July, remember that Matt isn't. Every time you wake up in your prison cell, remember that you had the opportunity and the ability to stop your actions that night. You robbed me of something very precious, and I will never forgive you for that. Mr. McKinney, I give you life in the memory of one who no longer lives. May you have a long life, and may you thank Matthew every day for it.

Moment: *Aftermath*

REGGIE FLUTY: Me and DeBree hugged and cried. . . . And, you know, everybody had tears in their eyes, and you're just so thankful, you know, and Mr. Shepard was cryin', and then that got me bawlin' and everybody just—

ROB DEBREE: This is all we've lived and breathed for a year. Daily. This has been my case daily. And now it's over.

REGGIE FLUTY: Maybe now we can go on and we can quit being stuck, you know?

AARON KREIFELS: It just hit me today, the minute that I got out of the courthouse. That the reason that God wanted me to find him is, for he didn't have to die out there alone, you know. And if I wouldn't of came along, they wouldn't of found him for a couple of weeks at least. So it makes me feel really good that he didn't have to die out there alone.

MATT GALLOWAY: I'm just glad it's over. I really am. Testifying in that trial was one of the hardest things I've ever done. And don't get me wrong, I love the stage, I really do, I love it. But it's tricky, because basically what you have is lawyers questioning you from this angle but the answers need to be funneling this way, to the jury. So what you have to do is establish a funneling system. And that's hard for me because I'm a natural conversationalist, so it's just natural instinct that when someone asks you a question, you look at that person to make eye contact. But it's kind of tough when you literally have to scoot over—change your position, in effect, funnel over to where the jury is. But I was able to do that several times over the course of my testimony.

(*Everyone is amused and baffled by this last text.*)

REGGIE FLUTY: It's time to move on. And I think for even the citizens are having the town painted red so to speak. They're gonna just be glad to maybe get moved on.

Moment: Epilogue

ANDY PARIS: On our last trip, I had the good fortune of seeing Jedadiah Schultz play the role of Prior in *Angels in America*. After a performance, we spoke.

JEDADIAH SCHULTZ: I didn't for the longest time let myself become personally involved in the Matthew Shepard thing. It didn't seem real, it just seemed way blown out of proportion. Matthew Shepard was just a name instead of an individual. . . .

I don't know, it's weird. It's so weird, man. I just— I just feel bad. Just for all that stuff I told you, for the person I used to be. That's why I want to hear those interviews from last year when I said all that stuff. I don't know. I just can't believe I ever said that stuff about homosexuals, you know. How did I ever let that stuff make me think that you were different from me?

NARRATOR: This is Romaine Patterson.

ROMAINE PATTERSON: Well, a year ago, I wanted to be a rock star. That was my goal. And now, um, well, now it's obviously changed in the fact that, um, throughout the last year I—I've really realized my role in, um, in taking my part. And, um, so now instead of going to school to be in music, I'm gonna go to school for communications and political science. Um, because I have a career in political activism.

Actually, I just recently found out I was gonna be honored in Washington, D.C, from the Anti-Defamation League. And whenever I think about the angels or any of the speaking that I've done, you know . . . Matthew gave me—Matthew's like guiding this little path with his light for me to walk down. And he just—every time we get to like a door, he opens it. And he just says, "Okay, next step."

And if I get to be a rock star on the side, okay.

NARRATOR: This is Jonas Slonaker.

JONAS SLONAKER: Change is not an easy thing, and I don't think people were up to it here. They got what they wanted. Those two boys got what they deserve, and we look good now. Justice has been served. The OK Corral. We shot down the villains. We sent the prostitutes on the train. The town's cleaned up, and we don't need to talk about it anymore.

You know, it's been a year since Matthew Shepard died, and they haven't passed shit in Wyoming . . . at a state level, any town, nobody anywhere, has passed any kind of laws, antidiscrimination laws or hate crime legislation, nobody has passed anything anywhere. What's come out of it? What's come out of this that's concrete or lasting?

NARRATOR: We all said we would meet again—one last time at the fence.

DOC O'CONNOR: I been up to that site in my limousine, okay? And I remembered to myself the night he and I drove around together, he said to me, "Laramie sparkles, doesn't it?" And where he was up there, if you sit exactly where he was, up there, Laramie sparkles from there, with a low-lying cloud, . . . it's the blue lights that's bouncing off the clouds from the airport, and it goes *tst tst tst tst* . . . right over the whole city. I mean, it blows you away. . . . Matt was right there in that spot, and I can just picture in his eyes, I can just picture what he was seeing. The last thing he saw on this earth was the sparkling lights.

Moment: Departure

MOISÉS KAUFMAN: We've spent the last two days packing a year's worth of materials and saying our good-byes. We've been here six times and conducted over two hundred interviews. Jedadiah cried when he said good-bye.

LEIGH FONDAKOWSKI: Marge wished us luck, and when we asked her how Laramie would feel seeing a play about itself, she said:

MARGE MURRAY: I think we'd enjoy it. To show it's not the hellhole of the earth would be nice, but that is up to how you portray us. And that in turn is up to how Laramie behaves.

GREG PIEROTTI: As we were getting off the phone she said to me:

MARGE MURRAY: Now, you take care. I love you, honey.

STEPHEN BELBER: Doc asked me if I wanted to ghostwrite a book about the whole event. Galloway offered me or anyone else a place to stay if and when we come back to Laramie. He also seemed interested as to whether there'd be any open auditions for this play.

ANDY PARIS: We left Laramie at about seven in the evening. On the way to Denver, I looked in my rearview mirror to take one last look at the town.

FATHER ROGER SCHMIT: And I will speak with you, I will trust that if you write a play of this, that you say it right. You need to do your best to say it correct.

ANDY PARIS: And in the distance I could see the sparkling lights of Laramie, Wyoming.

End of Play

Lynn Nottage

Lynn Nottage, born in 1965 in Brooklyn, New York, has written a number of award-winning plays in the last ten years. She was educated at Brown University and then at Yale School of Drama, where she was recently visiting lecturer in playwriting. After leaving Yale with her degree, she spent four years working for Amnesty International, learning firsthand about international injustice. She has been especially fascinated by Africa, where she spent time with director Kate Whoriskey and then later with family members. She left Amnesty International during the period of the Rwandan genocide, during which the Hutu and Tutsi people slaughtered each other. Her pain over this tragedy was intensified because she realized that the outside world was not going to attempt to stop the genocide. Nothing was being done, while people were dying by the hundreds of thousands throughout the country.

Nottage's purpose in returning to Africa in 2004, after the opening of her play *Fabulation: Or, the Education of Undine*, was to search for material for a drama on the subject of the refugee women and girls who had fled the Sudan and the Democratic Republic of the Congo—women who had been raped and sometimes mutilated and who had lost virtually everything. What she found in Uganda was a theatrical group working on local pieces in the communal fashion typical of African theater. A performance by orphan children moved her deeply.

Nottage's interest in Africa predates her visits. *Mud, River, Stone* (1996) was produced in New York in 1997 at Playwrights Horizons and directed by Roger Rees. It is set in both New York and southeast Africa and concerns a hostage situation in which a white neo-colonialist, an African aid worker, an African American couple, and a United Nations worker—all people who did not know one another—discuss the situation in Africa as they understand it. An earlier play, *Por'knockers* (1995), is also a political play, although a satire. The pork knockers of the title are people of mixed ethnicities who have subsisted by panning for gold in remote South American regions and who are now disappearing. The play, which was written prior to the Oklahoma City bombing, focuses on the plans and rationale of a group called the People's Diasporatic Party, who blow up a federal building that they mistakenly think is empty.

One of her most unusual works is *Poof!* (1993) a ten-minute play produced at the Humana Festival at the Actors Theatre of Louisville. In it an abusive husband experiences spontaneous human combustion. In this satire, Loureen begins the play by damning her husband Samuel, who then suddenly explodes and leaves a pile of ash. Loureen and her friend Florence discuss what she should do, a conversation that ultimately leads her to put off calling the police. The play is vigorous and comic but with a serious undertone.

The play that brought Nottage to the attention of major critics is *Crumbs from the Table of Joy* (1995), a memory play featuring an adolescent girl,

Ernestine, whose conventional African American family lives in Brooklyn in the 1950s. Ernestine's mother has died and her aunt, Lily, has come to visit the family. Ermina, Ernestine's younger sister, and their father, Godfrey, take her in without understanding Lily's agenda. Lily feels that because she is the sister of Ernestine's dead mother, she has a claim on Godfrey. Lily, however, is a fast, boisterous woman who frightens Godfrey, a devotee of Father Divine, the black evangelist who was among the most popular religious figures of his day. The play moves in a new direction when Godfrey brings home a white woman, a German émigré, whom he decides to marry, thus rejecting Lily entirely. The portrait of a mixed-race marriage in this period is handled with delicacy and understanding. And although the play is not a bright and cheerful portrait of any of the characters, it is touching and significant.

In an interesting departure, one of Nottage's more recent plays is *Las Meninas,* a historical comedy that focuses on an illegitimate daughter of Marie Therese, the wife of Louis XIV, who had an affair with an African dwarf named Nabo. The daughter was sent off to a convent and became a nun, while Nabo was sent away. The play was produced in 2002 at the San Jose Repertory Theater in California.

Nottage won the Drama Critics' Circle Award for best play in 2004 with *Intimate Apparel.* She also won the Obie Award for Playwriting for *Fabulation* in 2005 and received a Guggenheim Award for playwriting that same year. She has won a number of other awards for her plays.

INTIMATE APPAREL

Probably the most subtle of her plays, *Intimate Apparel* (2004) is set in Lower Manhattan in 1905, during the building of the Panama Canal and after the Spanish-American War (1898). The play was inspired partly by experiences in her family, but more immediately by a drawing of a particularly interesting undergarment in a public library book detailing the history of lingerie.

Nottage's 1905 New York is a city of immigrants. Esther, age 35 and a shy, virginal seamstress who makes beautiful intimate garments, moved to Mrs. Dickson's rooming house from the South eighteen years ago. Mr. Marks, a Jewish fabric merchant, has come from Romania, and George Armstrong, a Barbadian, has come from working on the Panama Canal. One of the primary thrusts of the play is the search for intimacy among the characters, whose scenes, ironically, often take place in boudoirs in their undergarments.

Esther, who is plain and shy and has not been among the twenty-one girls who have left Mrs. Dickson's to marry, has virtually given up hope of marriage. She is both saddened and envious as she sews an undergarment for the twenty-second of Mrs. Dickson's girls to leave. As she tells Mrs. Dickson, "Each time I think why ain't it me. Silly Corinna Mae ain't got no brain at all, and just as plain as flour." Her disappointment is relieved only when Mrs. Dickson remembers the letter she has from George Armstrong, who heard of Esther through a member of her church. Scene one ends with Armstrong, "in a musical Barbadian accent," reading his letter aloud.

Apart from her hopes for a suitor, Esther's dream is to save enough money to open her own beauty parlor. Sewn in her quilt is half the money she has earned since arriving in New York. It is almost enough, but not quite. Her customer Mrs. Van Buren, who lives on Fifth Avenue and loves Esther's work, complains about her indifferent husband. She wants Esther to make her intimate apparel that is the same as that worn by the working girls in the Tenderloin (the red-light district) so that she can get her husband's attention. Another client, a piano-playing Tenderloin girl called Mayme, complains that she gets too much attention from men and that *she* would like to have the same intimate apparel that the fine ladies on Fifth Avenue have. In an ironic moment, Esther tells Mayme that "What she got you wants, and what you got she want."

Esther buys the fabric she needs from Mr. Marks. In the process of working with Mr. Marks, Esther finds herself taken by his tenderness and attention, but because he is an Orthodox Jew, he cannot so much as touch her. He has been committed by his parents to marry a woman he has never seen who is still in Romania. Thus, even though they might want to become more intimate, their cultures keep them apart.

Things change for Esther when she gets a letter from George Armstrong, a laborer on the Panama Canal. Esther cannot read or write, so Mrs. Van Buren eagerly writes her letters for her and reads George's letters to her. Slowly, Esther sees her opportunity for a truly intimate relationship. The focus of the play is on the search for intimacy and love on the part of all the characters and on the impediments that make those goals so difficult to find. Act 2 opens with Esther and George married in their boudoir, with Esther in her beautiful wedding dress and George in a shabby suit. The disparity in the clothes matches the disjunction in their characters, and the scene foreshadows the outcome of the play.

Intimate Apparel in Performance

Baltimore's Center Stage premiered the play in February and March 2003, after which the play was staged in April 2003 by the South Coast Repertory Theatre, which had commissioned its writing. Kate Whoriskey directed, Shané Williams played Esther, and Kevin Jackson played George. The critical reception was unanimously positive. When the play moved to the Laura Pels Theatre in New York in April 2004, Viola Davis played Esther and Russell Hornsby played George. The play won the Drama Critics' Circle Award for best play of the year. That year the play moved west to the Mark Taper Forum in Los Angeles, with essentially the same cast. Phil Gallo in *Daily Variety* called it "a note perfect play." The reviews credited the excellent acting, staging, and particularly the costuming. For all these productions, reviewers commented on the conventional and realistic staging of the play (set in 1905), reflecting the style of the late nineteenth and early twentieth centuries. Later productions of the play have been numerous. *Intimate Apparel* was the most produced play (apart from Shakespeare and Dickens) of the 2005–2006 season and had nine productions across the United States from 2006 to 2007.

Lynn Nottage *(b. 1965)*

INTIMATE APPAREL

2004

Characters

ESTHER, 35, *African American*
MRS. DICKSON, 50s, *African American*
MRS. VAN BUREN, 30s, *White American*
MR. MARKS, 30s, *Romanian Jewish immigrant*
MAYME, 30s, *African American*
GEORGE, 30s, *Barbadian immigrant*

Place: *Lower Manhattan.*

Time: *1905.*

Production Note: *The set should be spare to allow for fluid movement between the various bedrooms. The action should flow seamlessly from scene to scene. The act endings mark the only true blackouts in the play.*

ACT ONE

Scene 1: Wedding Corset — White Satin with Pink Roses

(*Lower Manhattan, 1905. A bedroom. It is simple, unadorned with the exception of beautifully embroidered curtains and a colorful crazy quilt. A clumsy ragtime melody bleeds in from the parlor. In the distance the sound of laughter and general merriment. Esther, a rather plain African American woman (35), sits at a sewing machine table diligently trimming a camisole with lace. She is all focus and determination.*)

MRS. DICKSON: (*O.S.*)° Don't be fresh, Lionel. I know your mama since before the war. (*Mrs. Dickson, fifty, a handsome, impeccably groomed African American woman, enters laughing.*) There you are. Mr. Charles was admiring the bread pudding and I told him that our Esther made it. It seems he has a sweet tooth.

ESTHER: Mr. Charles is overly generous, come, the pudding ain't nothing special.

MRS. DICKSON: And did I mention that our most available Mr. Charles was promoted to head Bellman at just about the finest hotel in New York? Yes.

ESTHER: But he still fetching luggage.

MRS. DICKSON: Not just any luggage, high-class luggage.

ESTHER: And is high-class luggage easier to carry?

MRS. DICKSON: I reckon it is easier to haul silk than cotton, if you know what I'm saying. (*Mrs. Dickson*

O.S.: Off stage.

laughs.) And he sporting a right smart suit this evening.

ESTHER: Yes, it cashmere.

MRS. DICKSON: You can tell more about a man by where he shops, than his practiced conversation. 'Cause any man who's had enough tonic can talk smooth, but not every man has the good sense to shop at—

ESTHER and MRS. DICKSON: Saperstein's. (*Esther laughs. Mrs. Dickson examines the embroidery.*)

MRS. DICKSON: Lovely.

ESTHER: It's for Corinna Mae's wedding night.

MRS. DICKSON: Don't tell me you've been in here all evening? Corinna Mae is getting ready to leave with her fiancé.

ESTHER: I wish I could find my party face. It really is a lovely affair. You done a fine job.

MRS. DICKSON: Come now, it ain't over yet. Put aside your sewing and straighten yourself up. There. You'll have a dance before this evening's out.

ESTHER: Please, Mrs. Dickson, I can't, really. I'll just stand there like a wallflower.

MRS. DICKSON: Nonsense, I've danced a half a dozen times, and my feet are just about worn out.

ESTHER: If I had your good looks I'd raise a bit of dust myself. Ain't nobody down there interested in me.

MRS. DICKSON: Esther, you're being silly. You've been moping around here for days. What's the matter?

ESTHER: If you must know, I turned thirty-five Thursday past. (*A moment.*)

MRS. DICKSON: Oh Lord, I forgot, child. I sure did. Look at that. With Corinna Mae carrying on and all these people, it slipped my mind. Happy birthday, my sweet Esther. (*Mrs. Dickson gives her a big hug.*)

ESTHER: It's fine. You had all this to prepare for. And I been living in this rooming house for so long, I reckon I'm just another piece of furniture.

MRS. DICKSON: Never. You were a godsend when you come to me at seventeen. Yes. I remember thinking how sweet and young you was with a sack full of overripe fruit smelling like a Carolina orchard.

ESTHER: And now? Twenty-two girls later, if you count Lerleen. That's how many of these parties I have had to go to and play merry. I should be happy for them, I know, but each time I think why ain't it me. Silly Corinna Mae, ain't got no brain at all, and just as plain as flour.

MRS. DICKSON: Your time will come, child.

ESTHER: What if it don't? Listen to her laughing. God forgive me, but I hate her laughter, I hate her happiness and I feel simply awful for saying so. And I'm

Shané Williams as Esther and Brenda Pressley as Mrs. Dickson in the 2003 production of *Intimate Apparel* at the South Coast Repertory Theatre.

afraid if I go back in there, she'll see it all over my face, and it's her day.

MRS. DICKSON: There are a number of young men open to your smile. A sour face don't buy nothing but contempt. Why our Mr. Charles has had three servings of your bread pudding.

ESTHER: And he shouldn't have had any. (*Esther laughs.*) He weighs nearly as much as your horse.

MRS. DICKSON: Nonsense, he weighs more than poor Jessup. Shhh. He is a good man, poised for success. Yes.

ESTHER: But he's been coming to these parties for near two years and if he ain't met a woman, I'd bet it ain't a woman he after. I've been warned about men in refined suits. But still, Esther would be lucky for his attention, that's what you thinking. Well, I ain't giving up so easy.

MRS. DICKSON: Good for you. But there are many a cautionary tale bred of overconfidence. When I met the late Mr. Dickson he was near sixty and I forgave his infatuation with the opiates, for he come with this rooming house and look how many good years it's given me. Sure I cussed that damn pipe, and I cussed him for making me a widow, but sometimes we get to a point where we can't be so particular.

ESTHER: (*Snaps.*) Well, I ain't going down there to be paraded like some featherless bird. (*A moment.*) I'm sorry, would you kindly take this down to Corinna Mae?

MRS. DICKSON: I'll do no such thing. You can bring it down yourself. (*Mrs. Dickson starts for the door, but abruptly stops.*) It tough Esther for a colored woman in this city. I ain't got to tell you that. You nimble with your fingers, but all Corinna Mae got be her honey-colored skin. And you good and smart and deserve all the attention in that room, but today's her day and all I ask is that you come toast her as I know she'd toast you. Put aside your feelings and don't say nothing about Sally's piano playing, the girl trying. For God's sake, this a party not a wake.

ESTHER: Let me fix my hair. (*Mrs. Dickson suddenly remembers the letter tucked in her dress pocket and extends it to Esther.*)

MRS. DICKSON: And I thought you might want this letter. It come this morning, I didn't want to forget.

ESTHER: Who'd be writing me?

MRS. DICKSON: (*Reading.*) Mr. George Armstrong.

ESTHER: It ain't someone I know. Armstrong? There was an Armstrong that attended my church, but he dead a long time now. Will you read the letter to me? (*Esther takes the letter.*)

MRS. DICKSON: I got a house full of people. You best remind me tomorrow. And I will see you downstairs, shortly. Plenty of punch left and it better than New Year's, so best hurry. I made certain everybody be leaving this party happy. (*Mrs. Dickson exits. Esther examines the letter, then places it on the sewing table unopened. Lights crossfade, allowing Esther to linger in half-light during George's letter. A Panama bunk. George, a muscular handsome African-Caribbean man, rises from his cot. He wipes mud from his face and bare arms, as he speaks with a musical Barbadian accent.*)

GEORGE: Dear Miss Mills,

My name is George Armstrong. I work in Panama alongside Carson Wynn, your deacon's son. We digging a big hole across the land, they say one day ships will pass from one ocean to the next. It is important work, we told. If importance be measured by how many men die, then this be real important work. One man drops for every twenty feet of canal dug, like so many flies. Carson say if we eat a can of sardines, they'll protect us against the mosquitoes and fever. I say, not as long as we be digging. Lord knows our minds deserve a bit of shade. But ain't such a thing to be had, not here at least. Don't think me too forward, but I thought it would be nice to have someone to think about, someone not covered from head to toe in mud, someone to ward off this awful boredom. Carson speaks so highly of his church that I find comfort in his recollections. I ask if I may write you? And if you so please, I'd welcome your words.

    Sincerely,
    George Armstrong

Scene 2: *Gardenia Ball Corset — Pink Silk and Crepe de Chine*

(*An elegant boudoir. The silhouette of a naked woman moves gracefully behind a translucent screen. She slides her torso into the fitted lingerie. Esther sits at the dressing table exploring the carefully arranged silver grooming set. She jumps to attention at the sound of Mrs. Van Buren's voice, which betrays the slightest hint of a Southern accent.*)

MRS. VAN BUREN: I feel exposed. I think the straps need to be tightened, Esther.

ESTHER: No ma'am, that's the way it's meant to be, but I'll add a little more fabric to—

MRS. VAN BUREN: No, no, if this is what you made for that singer, it is what I want. All right. I'm coming out. (*Mrs. Van Buren emerges from behind the dressing screen wearing a very low corset embossed with lavender flowers. She's an attractive white woman in her early thirties and attempts to carry herself with great poise and confidence.*) Oh God, I look ridiculous, and I'm behaving absolutely foolishly, but I'm not sure what else to do. Look at me. I've spent a fortune on feathers and every manner of accouterment. (*Esther begins to tighten the lacing of the corset.*) They've written positively splendid things about me in the columns this season.

ESTHER: I'm sure they did.

MRS. VAN BUREN: But does it matter? Has he spent an evening at home? Or even noticed that I've painted the damn boudoir vermilion red?

ESTHER: You look lovely, Mrs. Van Buren.

MRS. VAN BUREN: Ha! I feel like a tart from the Tenderloin. Granted I've never been, but I'm told. Are you sure this is what you made for that . . . singer?

ESTHER: It is identical to the stitching. (*Mrs. Van Buren examines herself in the mirror, at first with disgust, which gradually gives way to curiosity.*)

MRS. VAN BUREN: And you say the French women are wearing these?

ESTHER: So I'm told.

MRS. VAN BUREN: I don't believe it. It hardly seems decent. But I suppose the French aren't known for their modesty. (*She strikes a provocative, though slightly self-conscious pose.*)

ESTHER: Well, it the rage. Some ladies ain't even wearing corsets in private.

MRS. VAN BUREN: Is that true?

ESTHER: Most gals don't like 'em, even fine ladies like yourself. Truth is I ain't known a man to court pain for a woman's glance.

MRS. VAN BUREN: You're not one of those suffragettes, are you?

ESTHER: Oh God no, Mrs. Van Buren.

MRS. VAN BUREN: Indeed. I'd just as soon not tamper in men's business. (*Mrs. Van Buren pours a snifter of brandy.*)

ESTHER: Talk and a nickel will buy you five cents worth of trouble. (*Mrs. Van Buren gulps back the brandy.*)

MRS. VAN BUREN: It's come to this. If Mother dear could see what has become of her peach in the big city. (*Mrs. Van Buren clumsily tugs at the bodice. Esther runs her fingers gracefully along the seam, down the curve of Mrs. Van Buren's waist. Mrs. Van Buren tenses slightly at the sensation of being touched. Distracted, she touches the beading along the corset, in doing so . . .*) Do we really need all of these dangling things?

ESTHER: Oh, I hope you ain't mind, I added a touch of beading along the trim.

MRS. VAN BUREN: It is different.

ESTHER: Do you like it?

MRS. VAN BUREN: I confess, I almost do. It's a bit naughty. (*Giggles.*) Yes, I might even wear it beneath my gown tonight. Do you think anyone will notice? It is the annual Gardenia Ball, quite the event of the season.

ESTHER: So I hear.

MRS. VAN BUREN: And do you know what that means? (*A moment.*) They'll all be there, parading their good fortune. I'll have to smile, be polite, because I'm known for that, but I will dread every last minute, every bit of forced conversation with the Livingstons and the Babcocks. They want to know. All of them do. "When are you going to have a child, Evangeline?" And my answer is always the same, "Why we're working on it, dear, speak to Harold." And dear Harry will be in a sour mood for a week. You probably don't even know what I'm talking about. Have you children?

ESTHER: No, Mrs. Van Buren. I ain't been married.

MRS. VAN BUREN: Never? May I tell you something?

ESTHER: Yes. If you like.

MRS. VAN BUREN: I've given him no children. (*Whispered.*) I'm afraid I can't. It's not for the lack of trying. One takes these things for granted, you assume when it comes time that it will happen, and when it doesn't who is to blame? They think it's vanity that's kept me childless, I've heard the women whispering. If only I were that vain. But it's like he's given up.

ESTHER: But, you're so beautiful.

MRS. VAN BUREN: You think so?

ESTHER: Yes. I can't imagine he'd ever lose interest.

MRS. VAN BUREN: But he has turned to other interests. Trust me. This will stay between us? I'm told you're discreet.

ESTHER: I just sew, missus. I don't hear anything that I ain't supposed to.

MRS. VAN BUREN: You understand why. I'd rather not be a divorcée, at my age it would prove disastrous.

ESTHER: Do you think there's something wrong with a woman alone?

MRS. VAN BUREN: What I think is of little consequence. If I were (*Whispered.*) brave I'd collect my things right now and find a small clean room someplace on the other side of the park. No, further in fact. And I'd . . . But it isn't a possibility, is it? (*A moment. Suddenly . . .*)

ESTHER: I don't know that I'll marry.

MRS. VAN BUREN: Of course you will, it's just a matter of finding the right gentleman.

ESTHER: Ma'am, I don't want to speak out of turn. But, I been working since I was nine years old with barely a day's rest. In fact, the other evening I was at my sewing machine and I stopped work and all this time had passed, gone. Years really. And I known right there that some things ain't meant to be. And that's all right, ain't it? And I wouldn't have thought no more about it, but then I got this . . . (*Esther stops mid-thought and busies herself with her sewing basket.*)

MRS. VAN BUREN: Yes?

ESTHER: I'm almost ashamed to say it. At my age it foolish, I know.

MRS. VAN BUREN: What is it?

ESTHER: A gentleman . . . A gentleman has taken interest in me.

MRS. VAN BUREN: Really? How wonderful! Is he respectable?

ESTHER: I don't know, I mean, I don't know him actually. I got me this letter from Panama. A man in Panama. He wrote about two weeks back. I been carrying it around since. But, I ain't so sure I should answer.

MRS. VAN BUREN: And why not?

ESTHER: I ain't much of a writer.

MRS. VAN BUREN: Oh—

ESTHER: No, I ain't a writer at all. The fact is I can't read.

MRS. VAN BUREN: Do you have the letter? May I see it? (*Esther hesitates, then pulls the letter from her smock and hands it to Mrs. Van Buren, who quickly peruses it and smiles.*) Panama. He has lovely penmanship, that's important. He isn't careless with his stroke, that's the mark of a thoughtful man. It's a good thing, I believe.

ESTHER: I won't respond, of course, if it ain't appropriate.

MRS. VAN BUREN: Nonsense. He's halfway across the world. I'm sure he's perfectly harmless. A bit lonesome perhaps, that's all.

ESTHER: But, if I have Mrs. Dickson over at the rooming house help me, she'll get all up in my business. And she's got an opinion about everything and I'd rather not be lectured or questioned or bothered. She's just about the busiest . . . in any event, she said to rip it up promptly, a decent woman wouldn't resort to such a dalliance. But as you can see he has taken interest in me.

MRS. VAN BUREN: Would you like me to help you write to him, Esther?

ESTHER: I couldn't ask.

MRS. VAN BUREN: You needn't, I insist.

ESTHER: I never done this before.

MRS. VAN BUREN: Nor have I.

ESTHER: Maybe it ain't such a good idea, Mrs. Van Buren. I ain't really got much to say.

MRS. VAN BUREN: Goodness, of course you do—

ESTHER: (*With conviction.*) No, I don't! I live in a rooming house with seven unattached women and sew intimate apparel for ladies, but that ain't for a gentleman's eyes. Sure I can tell him anything there is to know about fabric, but that hardly seems a life worthy of words.

MRS. VAN BUREN: It is a beginning. Come Esther, don't be shy. (*Mrs. Van Buren sits at her dressing table and retrieves a sheet of stationery.*) Now, how shall we start?

ESTHER: I don't know.

MRS. VAN BUREN: What sort of things do you like to do?

ESTHER: I . . . I go to church every Sunday, well practically, but I don't really listen to the sermons, I just like the company and the singing of course . . . And on Tuesdays . . . I take the trolley downtown to Orchard Street, and I climb five flights, in darkness, to this tiny apartment. And, when I open the door my eyes are met . . . (*Mr. Marks, a handsome Orthodox Jewish man, enters with a bolt of gorgeous flowing fabric which he proudly displays. Lost in the sweet recollection, Esther resumes speaking.*) He keeps a wealth of fabric in that apartment. He got everything you need, even things you don't know you need—

MRS. VAN BUREN: Esther, you're jumping a bit ahead of yourself. (*Lights fade around Mr. Marks.*) Shall we begin with "Dear Mr. Armstrong—"

ESTHER: Yes. That's good. "Dear Mr. Armstrong—"

MRS. VAN BUREN: "I received your letter—" (*Lights crossfade. George enters in his work clothing. The crossfade should allow time for Esther and George to dwell on the stage together, but only for several moments.*)

GEORGE: Dear Miss Mills,

   I received your letter. It two months in the coming, so please forgive me, I've already written you twice since. I am most happy to make your acquaintance, and I'm anxious to hear all about you. As for me, I'd like to report on our good progress, but it isn't the case. This canal seem a near-impossible mission, but here we be, digging until day end bathed in mud up to our necks. They say a mad Frenchmen dreamed up this Panama project, and convinced the devil to give him an army of workers. The price, this great fissure across the land that reach right into the earth's belly. Indeed, chaos is a jackhammer away, that's what be said here anyway. But when the great oceans meet and the gentlemen celebrate, will we colored men be given glasses to raise? Today we severed the roots of a giant flamboyant, and watched it tumble to the ground. I stood thigh deep in crimson blossoms, swathed in the sweet aroma of death and wondered how a place so beautiful could become a morgue. But the days aren't all bad. If you take a moment to listen to the forest around us there is so much life just out of sight. And there be men from every corner of the Caribbean, sharing tales around fires, heads light on rum and laughter. But now, I read your letter. I see you sitting at your sewing machine. I hear the sound of the wheel turning, the tiny stitches drawing together the pieces of satin. They got machines here that take six men to operate, and slice through stone like butter. All this wonder and waste, but your letter be the most splendid thing and shall ride in me pocket, until the next.

Yours Considerately,
George Armstrong

Scene 3: Imperial Silk, Embroidered with Blue Thread

(*Another bedroom in a cramped tenement flat. It is small and cluttered with bolts of fabric. Mr. Marks, a handsome Orthodox Jewish man, scrambles to put on his suit jacket as a knock sounds on the door. His worn black suit is missing the top button. With haste, he folds up his bed roll and opens the door breathless. Esther stands in the doorway. She notices the bed roll but chooses to ignore it.*)

ESTHER: Mr. Marks? Am I too early?

MARKS: No, not at all. Come in. Come in. I've a number of new things to show you.

ESTHER: Good —

MARKS: Ah. Let me get. (*He unrolls an extraordinary length of silk.*) Feel this one. Japanese silk, your special order for the lady on Fifth Avenue. It took me nearly one month to find this very piece. I had to go everywhere. Lovely. Yes?

ESTHER: Lovely. Look at how finely embroidered. Beautiful. I never —

MARKS: I have two extra yards left, I give to you for next to nothing. If you'd like.

ESTHER: Next to nothing is too much for me. You know my answer. What will I do with it?

MARKS: Make something lovely for yourself.

ESTHER: It will be wasted on me.

MARKS: You'll never see this again. I guarantee. I'll let our Fifth Avenue lady cover the difference. How about that? I see how much you like. I promise it is the very best quality. She don't know what she has, she don't come down here to feel the fabric herself, to feel the difference, the texture, she don't know how remarkable a weave.

ESTHER: I could make a shawl.

MARKS: (*Fishing.*) Or a smoking jacket for your gentleman, perhaps.

ESTHER: (*Bashfully.*) My gentleman? Oh no. (*Esther self-consciously runs the fabric across her face, then releases it.*) You've distracted me, Mr. Marks. You always get me to buy something I don't need.

MARKS: When I see something of quality, I like to share with my favorite customers. Everybody want the same thing. But you want different. I like that.

ESTHER: Thank you. (*Mr. Marks warmly smiles at Esther. She averts her gaze, allowing her eyes to fall on the spot where he's — missing a button. Mr. Marks self-consciously touches the spot.*)

MARKS: Ah, look at that. I have lost a button. (*He returns his attention to the silk.*) I buy at the docks yesterday morning, it come right off a ship from the Orient, I see it and think Esther Mills will like. Of course. Everybody else gabardine, wool, nainsook. (*Flirtatiously.*) But it isn't often that something so fine and delicate enters the store. Look at the way the gold thread is interwoven; a hand took the time to gently wind it through each and every stitch like a magician. It is magnificent, yes. You'll make something exquisite. I can see from your hands that you are blessed with the needle and the thread, which means you'll never be without warmth.

ESTHER: I'm afraid it was either learn to sew or turn back sheets for fifty cents a day.

MARKS: You make it sound too simple. My father sew, my brother sew, yes, for the finest families. But I don't have the discipline, the fingers. Look at the size of these hands. Like Cirnati, Romanian sausage. I wish for your hands. (*Esther laughs and returns to examining the fabric, reveling in the tactile pleasure of the texture. There is a sensual way Esther regards the fabric. Mr. Marks can't help but notice this. She brings the fabric to her nose and sniffs. Marks watches her with genuine delight.*)

ESTHER: It's fruit dye. Am I right? It smells like —

MARKS: — an imperial palace, it is signed by the artist right there. I wouldn't be surprised if it was created for an empress.

ESTHER: You really want me to buy this, don't you? All right, it means I'll go without sugar for a week, will that make you happy?

MARKS: It makes you happy, it makes me happy.

ESTHER: Oh Lord, I do want it. (*Esther affectionately grasps Mr. Marks' hand, he abruptly pulls it away. Esther is taken aback.*) The color won't rub off on you.

MARKS: No, no. I'm sorry. It's not that. Please. My religious belief doesn't permit me to touch a woman who isn't my wife or my relative.

ESTHER: Oh, I see.

MARKS: It is the rabbinical law, not mine.

ESTHER: Your wife must be a happy woman.

MARKS: I am not married. Not yet. My fiancée is in Romania. Um, my family made the arrangement years ago.

ESTHER: Oh? I bet you miss her something awful. (*Marks rubs his hand where Esther touched him. He laughs, a bit self-consciously.*)

MARKS: I haven't ever met her, actually. (*Lights cross-fade.*)

Scene 4: Heliotrope Handkerchief

(*Another bedroom. A canopy bed dominates. Mayme, a strikingly beautiful African-American woman (30) sits at an upright piano. She plays a frenzied upbeat rag. Her silk robe is torn, and her face trembles with outrage. Esther bangs on the door, then finally enters carrying a carpetbag.*)

ESTHER: I been knocking for ages. Didn't you hear me? . . . What's going on? (*A moment.*)

MAYME: They really do make me sick. Always stinking of booze. And look what he done. It's the only pretty thing I own and look what he done. (*Mayme pulls her torn silk robe tight around her body.*)

ESTHER: That ain't nothing, I can fix it for you.

MAYME: All the pawing and pulling. For a dollar they think they own you. (*Mayme quickly washes her face and privates in a basin.*) You don't approve of me, Esther. I don't mind. Sit. I'm awfully glad to see ya, 'am. When you knocked on the door, I thought Christ almighty, not another one. I'm so damn tired, I don't know what to do. (*Mayme sits down at the upright piano and gracefully plays a slow well-considered rag.*)

ESTHER: Oh, pretty. Did you write that, Mayme?

MAYME: Yeah . . . (*Continuing to play.*) My daddy gave me twelve lashes with a switch for playing this piece in our parlor. One for each year I studied the piano. He was too proper to like anything colored, and a syncopated beat was about the worst crime you could commit in his household. (*Mayme stops playing.*) I woke up with the sudden urge to play it.

ESTHER: You must have gotten a lot of licks in your time.

MAYME: Yeah, baby, I wasn't born this black and blue. (*Mayme picks up a bottle of moonshine and takes a belt.*)

ESTHER: That there the reason you tired, that ignorant oil is unforgiving. Best let it lie.

MAYME: Oh bother, stop playing mother hen and come show me what you got.

ESTHER: Anything else, Mistress?

MAYME: Hush your mouth, you're far too sweet for sarcasm. (*Esther pulls a corset from her bag, it's pale blue with lines of royal blue glass beads ornamenting the bodice, like Mrs. Van Buren's. Touched:*) Is that for me? (*Mayme leaps up from the piano and holds the corset up to her body.*)

ESTHER: I made one just like it for a lady on Fifth Avenue.

MAYME: It's so pretty. This is really for me? No kidding? Can I try it on?

ESTHER: Of course you can.

MAYME: Feel it. It feels like Fifth Avenue, does. You outdone yourself this time, honey.

Viola Davis and Lauren Velez in the Roundabout Theatre Company's 2002 production of *Intimate Apparel.*

ESTHER: Stop talking and put it on. (*Mayme gives Esther a kiss on the cheek.*) And look at the flowers, ain't they sweet? It took me a whole day just to sew them on. (*Mayme takes off her robe and puts on the corset.*)

MAYME: For shame. This the prettiest thing anybody ever made for me. Truly.

ESTHER: You know that white lady I talk about sometime, hold on . . . (*Mayme grabs the bed post, as Esther pulls the corset tight.*) She keep asking me what they be wearing up in the Tenderloin. All that money and high breeding and she want what you wearing.

MAYME: No kidding?

ESTHER: What she got, you want, what you got, she want.

MAYME: Onliest, I ain't got the money to pay for it. (*Mayme models the corset.*) Whatcha think? Do I look like a Fifth Avenue bird?

ESTHER: Grand. You look grand. Mr. Marks say, that satin foulard was made for the finest ladies in Paris.

MAYME: No kidding.

ESTHER: I wasn't going to buy it. But, oh Lord, if he didn't talk me into it.

MAYME: Mr. Marks? (*A moment.*) Who is this Mr. Marks?

ESTHER: He just a salesman. That's all.

MAYME: It sound to me like you bit sweet on him.

ESTHER: Me? Oh no, he a Jew. (*Mayme looks into Esther's eyes.*)

MAYME: And? I been with a Jew, with a Turk even. And let me tell ya, a gentle touch is gold in any country.

ESTHER: I see the bodice is bit snug—

MAYME: Is he handsome?

ESTHER: I ain't noticed.

MAYME: Good patient, Esther. Come, he wouldn't be your first, would he?

ESTHER: I ain't listenin'.

MAYME: (*Softening her tone.*) You dear thing. (*Mayme laughs long and hard. Esther doesn't respond.*) No kidding. I can't even remember what it was like. Ain't that something.

ESTHER: Let's not talk about this.

MAYME: Mercy, what you must think of me. (*Mayme, suddenly self-conscious, touches the beading on the corset.*)

ESTHER: And if you must know, I'm being courted by a gentleman.

MAYME: Courted by a gentleman. Beg my pardon. Not that Panama man? Oh come on, don't tell me you still writing him.

ESTHER: He writing me.

MAYME: You'd rather a man all the way across the ocean then down Broadway. Are you expecting him to arrive in the mail like some tonic from a catalogue?

ESTHER: Please don't make sport, Mayme.

MAYME: I'm just playing with you.

ESTHER: (*Wounded.*) I ain't expectin' nothing. (*A moment. Mayme acknowledges Esther's hurt. She caresses her friend's face.*)

MAYME: Sure you are. Sure you are, honey. Who ain't? (*Mayme sits on bed, beside Esther.*) I am a concert pianist playing recitals for audiences in Prague and I have my own means, not bad for a colored girl from Memphis . . . (*Mayme plays a few bars of classical music, perhaps allowing it to become a rag.*) And Madame always takes tea twice a week with her dear friend Miss Esther Mills, who's known in circles for . . . for what? I forget. (*Esther is reluctant to share her dream.*) Come on, Miss Esther, don't be proud.

ESTHER: I own a quaint beauty parlor for colored ladies.

MAYME: Of course.

ESTHER: The smart set. Someplace east of Amsterdam, fancy, where you get pampered and treated real nice. 'Cause no one does it for us. We just as soon wash our heads in a bucket and be treated like mules. But what I'm talking about is someplace elegant.

MAYME: Go on, missie, you too fancy for me.

ESTHER: When you come in Miss Mayme, I'll take your coat and ask, "Would you like a cup of tea?"

MAYME: Why, thank you.

ESTHER: And I'll open a book of illustrations, and show you the latest styles.

MAYME: I can pick anything in the book?

ESTHER: Yes.

MAYME: How about if I let you choose?

ESTHER: Very well. Make yourself comfortable, put your feet up, I know they're tired.

MAYME: Shucks, you don't know the half of it.

ESTHER: And in no time flat for the cost a ride uptown and back, you got a whole new look.

MAYME: Just like that? I reckon I'd pay someone good money to be treated like a lady. It would be worth two, three days on my back. Yes, it would.

ESTHER: You think so?

MAYME: I know so.

ESTHER: And if I told you I got a little something saved? I keep it sewed up in the lining of a crazy quilt.

MAYME: On a cold lonely night wouldn't that quilt be a poor woman's dream.

ESTHER: I been saving it slowly since I come North. It for that beauty parlor. I ain't told nobody that. Honest, for true.

MAYME: Where'd you get such a damn serious face?

ESTHER: Why not?

MAYME: Because, we just fooling that's all. I ain't been to Prague, ain't never gonna go to Prague.

ESTHER: But come, is this what you want to be doing ten years from now, twenty?

MAYME: You think I ain't tried to make a go of it. You think I just laid down and opened my legs 'cause it was easy. It don't look like nothing, but this saloon is better then a lot of them places, ask anybody. Only last night one of Bert Williams'° musicians sat up front, and he stayed through the entire show. You think some of those gals in the big revues didn't start right where I am.

ESTHER: You got this beautiful piano that you play better than anyone I know. There are a dozen church choirs—

MAYME: Let me tell you, so many wonderful ideas been conjured in this room. They just get left right in that bed there, or on this piano bench. They are scattered all over this room. Esther, I ain't waiting for anybody to rescue me. My Panama man come and gone long time now. It sweet that he write you but, my dear, it ain't real.

ESTHER: Yes, he here in my pocket in a cambric walking suit, he has a heliotrope handkerchief stuffed in his pocket and a sweet way about him. He so far away, I can carry him in my pocket like a feather. (*Esther laughs and produces a letter from her apron.*)

MAYME: You're funny. You and your silly letter.

ESTHER: Ain't a week go by without one. It got so I know the postman by name. (*Esther holds out the letter.*)

Bert Williams: (1875–1922) Very successful black vaudeville entertainer, comedian, and recording artist.

MAYME: I ain't interested. Put it away.

ESTHER: C'mon Miss Mayme . . . don't be proud, you know you want to read it. (*Esther dangles the letter, threatening to put it away at any moment.*)

MAYME: Hell, give it here. (*Mayme snatches the letter and quickly peruses it, allowing herself a smile.*) Ooo.

ESTHER: What it say?

MAYME: Your man got himself a new pair of socks. Wait . . . uh-oh, he askin' what you look like. Ain't you told him?

ESTHER: No. I'm afraid, I ain't known what to say.

MAYME: Tell him the truth.

ESTHER: That I don't look like much.

MAYME: You tell him that you're about as lovely a person as there is.

ESTHER: You know that ain't so.

MAYME: Of course, it is. And what does it matter? You think half the men that come in here bother looking at my face. No ma'am. He don't care about this. (*Mayme grabs Esther's face and gives her a kiss on the forehead. She playfully shows off her physical attributes which are accentuated by the formfitting lingerie.*) He interested in this, my dear. This is what he's asking about. (*Mayme laughs.*)

ESTHER: I wouldn't dare write about something like that. He Christian!

MAYME: And it's in his weakness that he'll find his strength. Hallelujah! C'mon, I'm just playing with you.

ESTHER: I'm being serious and you got your mind in the gutter.

MAYME: Oh for God's sake, the man just asking what you look like 'cause he want something pretty to think about come sundown.

ESTHER: You reckon? Then will you help me write something? (*Mayme hands back the letter to Esther.*)

MAYME: No, what about your white lady? Why not have her do it? (*A moment. Esther opens her carpetbag.*)

ESTHER: 'Cause I'm asking you, my friend.

MAYME: No, my writing ain't perfect.

ESTHER: Don't bother about the handwriting, we'll tell him I pricked my finger while sewing. He'll understand. Please.

MAYME: Oh. (*Mayme fetches a sheet of paper and a pen and sits on the bed. Esther sits next to her.*) I ain't romantic, I find this silly, really I do. Only 'cause it's you. So, how do I begin?

ESTHER: "Dear George." (*Mayme concentrates, then slowly writes.*)

MAYME: (*Savoring the notion.*) A love letter to a gentleman. Yes, I know. "Dear George, I write you wearing a lavender silk robe with—" (*Esther giggles. Lights crossfade. George enters carrying a lantern, he is soaked through by the rain.*)

GEORGE: Dear Esther,

Thank you for your sweet words. Your pricked finger delivered the most unexpected lift. It quiet now. The only motion is the rain. The only sound is the rain. It is the white season, and the work all but stop. The rum shop be the onliest business that do prosper. I seen months of hard work lost in an evening and good men befriend the devil overnight. And if I told you it's been months since I've seen a decent a woman it wouldn't be a lie. There are caravans of sweet-faced Indian girls offering up their childhood for a half-day's wage. Yes, many men leave here with less than they come. I shan't be one. It isn't appropriate, but I will say it. I crave a gentlewoman's touch, even if only be to turn down my collar or brush away the dirt in the evenings. Indeed, I'd like to meet you as a gentleman. I think much about the suit I will wear, and the colors that your eyes find pleasing. I imagine your cobble stone roads and the splendid carriages on the avenues, and a dry place to sit. I think of you running silk thread between your fingers and find a bit of holy relief, for your letters arrive just in time to ward off temptation.

Yours Affectionately,

George

(*Lights crossfade to:*)

Scene 5: Hand-Dyed Silk

(*Esther's boudoir. Esther sits at the sewing machine, working on a silk camisole. Mrs. Dickson enters carrying a letter, which she hands to Esther.*)

MRS. DICKSON: I don't trust him, not one bit. He writes too often.

ESTHER: It's open.

MRS. DICKSON: I'm sorry, I opened it by mistake. I didn't mean to, but I'm glad I did.

ESTHER: 'Cause you the landlady don't give you the right to tamper with my things.

MRS. DICKSON: What are your intentions?

ESTHER: We corresponding. That's all.

MRS. DICKSON: I know these kind of men. Sugared words, but let them stick to the page and go no further. He'll steal your common sense, he will and walk away. It just don't seem like you, Esther, you're too practical a girl for this.

ESTHER: Don't set your clock by my habits.

MRS. DICKSON: His tone is very familiar. And I don't approve.

ESTHER: I'm sorry, but I needn't your approval.

MRS. DICKSON: My goodness. I hope you ain't expecting anything to come of this.

ESTHER: And if I am?

MRS. DICKSON: Our Mr. Charles has asked me twice about you this week. I told him he was most welcome to call.

ESTHER: Mr. Charles is a fool and a glutton. And I'm sure he don't even know who I am.

MRS. DICKSON: You are a stubborn little country girl. And very particular. And it wouldn't hurt you to be more receptive.

ESTHER: To who? Mr. Charles? Remember it's me you're talking to, not Doreen or Erma, or one of those other silly open-hearted little gals. And yes, I'm writing letters to a man. And it may come to nothing. But I am his sweetheart twice a month, and I can fill that envelope with anything that I want.

MRS. DICKSON: Yes. It's an innocent enough flirtation, and I had my share in my youth. And believe me when I say I was romanced by many bright and willing young men. (*Mrs. Dickson takes Esther's hand.*) It's potent, I know, but I ain't ashamed to admit that my pride ultimately led to compromise. And if you're not careful, Esther—

ESTHER: DON'T! This quilt is filled with my hard work, one hundred dollars for every year I been seated at that sewing machine. It's my beauty parlor. So you see I don't need Mr. Charles for his good job and position. (*Mrs. Dickson pulls the quilt off of the bed.*)

MRS. DICKSON: You think this is enough? Do you? You think this gonna make you happy when another half dozen girls waltz away in camisoles of your making. When the Bellman's Ball come around another year and you here fluffing ruffles for some girl from Kentucky, who just happy to be wearing shoes.

ESTHER: No, I don't think that. And I'd give this quilt and everything in it to be with someone I care for, I would.

MRS. DICKSON: This man in Panama, he's paper and I'll show how easily he goes away. (*Mrs. Dickson rips up the letter.*)

ESTHER: Mrs. Dickson!

MRS. DICKSON: You'll thank me. (*Mrs. Dickson exits. Esther picks up the pieces of the letter. Lights crossfade to George in Panama, as he picks up pieces of fabric.*)

GEORGE: Dear Esther, I opened the letter and these tiny bits of fabric tumbled out onto the ground. Imagine my surprise, gray wool, pink silk and the blue flannel, which I tucked in the back of my shirt this morning— (*Lights crossfade to Marks' boudoir. Marks unrolls a cobalt blue roll of silk. Esther touches the various fabrics—muslin, taffeta, satin, tulle. Marks unfurls a vibrant roll of magenta cloth.*)

MARKS: It is hand-dyed silk, I washed it yesterday and look.

ESTHER: Yes, beautiful.

MARKS: Have you ever seen anything like that?

ESTHER: No.

MARKS: It looks fragile, but feel. (*Esther runs her hand across the blue material and smiles.*) Ah, it will feel even better against your back.

ESTHER: The ladies will like this indeed. You shouldn't have shown me this . . . (*She pulls the fabric around her shoulders. He then wraps a strip of magenta cloth around his shoulders.*)

MARKS: Look at this color.

ESTHER: It look very good on you, Mr. Marks.

MARKS: Does it? (*Esther laughs. Mr. Marks laughs. An awkward moment, fraught with the unspoken attraction that lies between them.*)

ESTHER: Your button?

MARKS: I forget.

ESTHER: If you take off your jacket, I'll sew it on for you.

MARKS: Don't worry. It is fine. (*Mr. Marks buttons the remaining buttons on the coat.*)

ESTHER: It'll take me no time.

MARKS: No. Thank you. Truly. It is fine. (*A moment.*)

ESTHER: Why do you always wear black? You sell all of these magnificent colors, and yet every time I see you, you're wearing black.

MARKS: You ask a very complicated question. It's an act of faith, that is the simplest way I know how to explain. It is one of the many ways that I show my devotion to God. (*A moment.*)

ESTHER: Is marrying someone you don't know another?

MARKS: It is a thousand years of history and struggle behind the answer to that question.

ESTHER: And yet it seems as simple as taking off a jacket. (*A moment.*) I'm sorry, I didn't mean to upset you.

MARKS: You haven't upset me.

ESTHER: If you wrap the magenta, I'll pay you next week.

MARKS: To answer your question, it has always been that way in my family.

ESTHER: But this a new country.

MARKS: But we come with our pockets stuffed, yes. We don't throw away nothing for fear we might need it later . . . I wear my father's suit. It is old, I know, but this simple black fabric is my most favorite. Why? Because when I wear it, it reminds me that I live every day with a relationship to my ancestors and God. (*As Marks turns to wrap the fabric, Esther ever so gently touches the back of his collar. He doesn't register the gesture. Or does he? Lights fade around Mr. Marks' boudoir as they rise in Mrs. Van Buren's boudoir. Mrs. Van Buren wears a lacy kimono and corset made of hand-dyed magenta silk.*)

MRS. VAN BUREN: Hand-dyed silk? Is it popular?

ESTHER: It will be by fall.

MRS. VAN BUREN: Really? I'll have to weave that tidbit into conversation this evening. My in-laws are coming. The frog and the wart. Oh, and did I tell you? I saw Mr. Max Fiedler of Germany conduct selections from *Don Juan*.° I had to endure an encore from the soprano, what was her name? Something Russian, no doubt. I'd rather have gone to the electric show at Madison Square Garden, but you see Harry isn't impressed with electricity. "Miracle upon miracle, but there remain things science will never be able to give us," he says, so he refrains from enthusiasm. By the way, I bled this morning, and when I delivered the news to Harry, he spat at me. This civilized creature of society. We all bleed, Esther. And yet I actually

Don Juan: A "tone poem" by composer Richard Strauss. It was performed in 1905 for New York audiences by the Philharmonic Society, conducted by Max Fiedler.

felt guilt, as though a young girl again apologizing for becoming a woman. (*Mrs. Van Buren sheds her kimono, revealing a low-cut magenta corset with a pale pink camisole beneath.*) Maybe I'll be a bohemian, a bohemian needn't a husband, she's not bound by convention.

ESTHER: I don't see why you let him do you this way, missus. If you don't mind me saying. (*A moment.*)

MRS. VAN BUREN: Have you been to the opera? (*Esther, aware that she overstepped, nervously adjusts the bodice.*)

ESTHER: Never.

MRS. VAN BUREN: Oh God, you're lucky. It's one of those things required of me. I'm certain you've found a more engaging means of entertainment.

ESTHER: I actually only been to the theatre once.

MRS. VAN BUREN: Really? What did you see?

ESTHER: Nothing special. A blind gal from Alabama sang spirituals. I need you to lift your arms.

MRS. VAN BUREN: Like this? (*Mrs. Van Buren seductively lifts her arms.*) It's pinching me right here. (*Esther stands behind Mrs. Van Buren and wraps her arms around her torso. She runs her fingers along the top of the corset, then reaches in to adjust her breast. Esther tightens the bodice as Mrs. Van Buren continues to speak.*) I've never been to a colored show, I'm told they're quite good.

ESTHER: I suppose.

MRS. VAN BUREN: I should like to see one for myself. You must take me to one of your shows.

ESTHER: And will you take me to the opera next time you go?

MRS. VAN BUREN: I would, if I could. It would be marvelously scandalous, just the sort of thing to perk up this humdrum season. (*Mrs. Van Buren touches Esther's hand with an unexpected tenderness. Esther politely withdraws her fingers.*) It is so easy to be with you. (*Whispered.*) Your visits are just about the only thing I look forward to these days. You, and our letters to George, of course. Shall we write something dazzling to him? Something delicious. (*A moment. Esther seems hesitant.*)

ESTHER: But, if—

MRS. VAN BUREN: What? Why not?

ESTHER: Perhaps something simple this time, I believe there real affection growing.

MRS. VAN BUREN: Yes, one would hope. He seems quite taken.

ESTHER: I don't want him to be disappointed.

MRS. VAN BUREN: And he needn't be. We'll send him your warmth and he'll find you irresistible.

ESTHER: Do you think we could describe this silk? (*Esther runs her fingers down the front of Mrs. Van Buren's silk corset.*) Will you tell him what it feel like against your skin? How it soft and supple to the touch. I ain't got the words, but I want him to know this color, magenta red. What it make you feel right now. It—

MRS. VAN BUREN: The silk? Are you sure?

ESTHER: Yes.

MRS. VAN BUREN: Mercy, if my friends knew I spend the day writing love letters to a colored laborer, they'd laugh me out of Manhattan.

ESTHER: People do a lot of things that they don't ever speak of.

MRS. VAN BUREN: I smoked opium once, with the most proper of women. She dared me and I did it. And you? What have you done? (*A moment.*)

ESTHER: I touched someone, who I knew I wasn't supposed to touch. I touched them because I wanted to, it was wrong, but I couldn't help myself. (*Mrs. Van Buren takes in Esther's words. The lights rise on George sitting on his bunk illuminated by a kerosene lantern. Esther remains on stage in half-light, as if listening to George speaking directly to her.*)

GEORGE: Dearest Esther,

It dawn. No work has begun, the morning is still holding the ocean, not yet blue. But I can see past everything green to the horizon. And it is here in half-light that I imagine you. Six months have passed since our first correspondence, and much has changed. A water boy from my parish died, taken by fever two nights past. All their magic machinery and there's nothing could be done for this boy. It got me thinking about his family behind and the wife he'd never meet. He die so easy. Why he? His young life end, and not more than a word from the Yankee chief, 'cept regret that the new boy ain't so quick. This morn I try to remember his small blackened face and cannot even recall his smile, though his hand give me water each and every day since I be here. Why this boy go out my mind, I ask? Tomorrow I too could be sucked into the ground without tears and ride the death train that pass through here five times a day. When I first come, a solid ox was the dream of this man. But I watch the splendid way the American gentlemen touch their fine machines and laugh away the jungle, and I know what great and terrible things their sleep brings. And yet, your America sounds like a wondrous place, a man such as myself would be willing to surrender much for a taste of the modern world. Yes, I see beyond the tilting palms, through the mangroves and across the Caribbean sea to where you sit. I kneel beside you at this moment and I tell you, I am a good strong man. What I've come to feel for you can best be described as love. I love you. There is no other way to say it, will you marry me?

Most Adoringly,
George

(*Lights crossfade to:*)

Scene 6: White Cotton Bed Linen

(*Mayme's boudoir. Mayme hangs a pair of wet stockings on the bed post.*)

MAYME: Why ya smiling so big? Close your mouth 'fore your teeth dry out.

ESTHER: He's asked me to marry him.

MAYME: What? No kiddin'.

ESTHER: It in writin'.

MAYME: Show me. (*Esther hands Mayme the letter.*) Our own Miss Esther.

ESTHER: He say he loves me.

MAYME: And do you love him?

ESTHER: As much as you can love a man you ain't seen. I'm thirty-five, Mayme, and he wants to marry me. And there ain't gonna be no more opportunities I'm afraid. I've told him yes.

MAYME: Well, goddamn. I'm sure he's a fine man.

ESTHER: Yes, I suppose. Any man go through this much trouble to court a woman must have his virtues.

MAYME: I reckon.

ESTHER: He write that he arriving next month.

MAYME: That soon . . . you hardly ready.

ESTHER: I know. I'm getting married! Oh God, will you come to witness the ceremony?

MAYME: Me? You want to bring me around your new husband?

ESTHER: It would be nice to have a friend witness.

MAYME: No, I ain't been to church since I was seventeen. It ain't about you, it's just a promise I made to myself years ago. I ain't got nothing to say to God, and it don't seem right to go up into somebody's home and you ain't on speaking terms.

ESTHER: It just a building.

MAYME: Just the same, I'd rather not be reminded. But thank you, my dear, it's a long time since I been invited anyplace proper.

ESTHER: Me too. (*Mayme laughs and grabs a bottle of liquor.*)

MAYME: Hell, we ought to celebrate. Somebody give me this gin. It look expensive. Whatcha think? Should I open it?

ESTHER: Sure. Why not. (*While speaking, Mayme pours them each a glass of gin.*)

MAYME: We gonna toast to one less spinster in New York.

ESTHER: Oh God, I hope I ain't making a mistake.

MAYME: You'll be fine. You're about the most sensible gal I know. Enjoy this, honey. It's a splendid feeling. Yes, indeed. I was engaged once. You won't tell nobody. A mortician's apprentice who hated music. Need I say more.

ESTHER: Do you regret not marrying him?

MAYME: Some days. No, some evenings, honey. (*Mayme thrusts her glass into the air.*) But here's to Esther, you will be a beautiful bride, and may happiness follow. (*They toast and drink. Mayme sits at the piano.*) My dear, you're gonna go to socials and other ridiculous functions that married folk attend. Drink lots of lemonade, God forbid, and become an awful gossip. And you know, it won't be appropriate to visit a place like this.

ESTHER: Who say?

MAYME: (*Snaps.*) I say. (*A moment.*)

ESTHER: We friends, ain't no Panama man gonna change that.

MAYME: Well, I hope he is wonderful. (*Mayme starts to play piano.*)

GIVE ME A MAN THAT'LL COME AND BAKE ME A CAKE. PUT IN SOME SUGAR AND SPICE.

YES, HE CAN PUT IT IN MY OVEN ANY OL' TIME AND WATCH IT RISE ON UP.

GIVE ME A MAN THAT'LL COME AND MOW MY LAWN FROM THE FRONT TO THE BACK.

(*Esther joins in.*)

YES, HE CAN TEND MY GARDEN ANY OL' TIME AND WATCH IT RISE ON UP.

A WOMAN NEEDS A HANDYMAN TO TAKE CARE OF HER HOME.

A WOMAN NEEDS A CANDYMAN WHO'LL FIGHT THE BEES FOR THE COMB.

(*Esther stops singing, she silently contemplates her decision, uncertain.*)

GIVE ME A MAN THAT'LL COME AND BAKE ME A CAKE.

LOAD IT WITH SOME SUGAR AND SPICE.

YES, HE CAN PUT IT IN MY OVEN ANY OL' TIME AND WATCH IT RISE ON UP.

(*Lights crossfade. Esther's boudoir. Mrs. Dickson is packing Esther's suitcase. Esther crosses into her boudoir.*)

MRS. DICKSON: Who is going to sit next to me at the table? There is Bertha, but she has no conversation. Oh, I could move Erma down closer, but she and Bertha don't speak. It'll be an absolute mess at the dinner table without you. That's for certain. Oh, it's gonna be a shame to let this room to anybody else. It has so many of your sweet touches. Yes.

ESTHER: You wasn't always pleased with my conversation if I recall.

MRS. DICKSON: Who told you that? Well, they lie. (*Mrs. Dickson holds up a dress.*) Oh no. Not this little frumpy thing, really Esther. My grandmother wouldn't even wear a collar like so and she was a right proud Christian soldier. Yes.

ESTHER: Well, I like it. It's the most refined thing I own. I paid five whole dollars for it.

MRS. DICKSON: You'll scare off your gentleman, and it ain't worth five dollars of misery. You needn't be a prude. Trust me, your man'll have needs, and it's your duty to keep his member firmly at home. Yes.

ESTHER: Excuse me?

MRS. DICKSON: I shan't repeat it. But there ain't no greater disappointment than a husband without much . . . vigor. Believe me, I know. And sometime he gotta be pleasured to ensure your own satisfaction. You understand. I ain't an expert, but I do have some experience. And I'll tell you, give and take make for the best of partnerships. Never mind what the minister tells you about decency, what go on between a man and wife be their own business. He will test you and he will try you, but don't let him beat on you, don't take no shit from him, understand.

ESTHER: Mrs. Dickson.

MRS. DICKSON: Excuse me for saying, but if he raises his hand once, he'll do it again. I thought we should have this conversation before you go off. I don't mean to scare you, but I know you come as an innocent and we're friends so I feel I can speak plainly.

ESTHER: Thank you, but I do believe I'm old enough to handle things for myself.

MRS. DICKSON: Just the same, I thought I'd say it. Now whatcha want me to do with this dress?

ESTHER: It that bad?

MRS. DICKSON: Let's just say we'll give it to Deacon Wynn and let the church ladies fight over it. Yes. (*Mrs. Dickson sits on the bed.*) You really going to do this, ain't you?

ESTHER: You didn't expect me to be here for the rest of my life?

MRS. DICKSON: I guess I sort of did. I'm so used to hearing your sewing machine and foot tapping up here. Yes, I reckon I'm going to miss it.

ESTHER: Another gal will move into this room, and by supper you'll be fussing about something new.

MRS. DICKSON: You say that with such certainty. You hurt my feelings, Miss Esther Mills. (*Mrs. Dickson dabs her eyes with a handkerchief.*) Eighteen years is a long time. Yes. I don't reckon I've known anyone else that long. It'll be lonely.

ESTHER: You have plenty of suitors to keep you busy.

MRS. DICKSON: But ain't a working man amongst them. (*A moment.*) You know you don't have to do this.

ESTHER: Yes I do. I stay on here, I'll turn to dust one day, get swept up and released into the garden without notice. I've finally found someone. Just as you found Mr. Dickson.

MRS. DICKSON: I married him, because I was thirty-seven years old, I had no profession and there wasn't a decent colored fella in New York City that would have me.

ESTHER: But you come to love each other.

MRS. DICKSON: I suppose. He give me some laughs. But you see, my mother wanted me to marry up. She was a washerwoman, and my father was the very married minister of our mission. He couldn't even look out at her there in the church pews, but she'd sit there proudly every Sunday, determined to gain God's favor. Marry good. She didn't ever want me to be embarrassed of my fingers the way she was of hers. I'd watch her put witch hazel and hot oil on her delicate hands, but they remained raw and chapped and she kept them hidden inside gray wool gloves. In the winter they'd bleed so bad sometimes, but she'd plunge her hands into the hot water without flinching, knead and scrub the clothing clean. Fold and press for hours and hours, the linen, the bedding, the stockings and the britches, sometimes wearing the frayed gloves so as not to leave bloodstains on her precious laundry. She wouldn't even let me help her,

she didn't want my hands to show the markings of labor. I was going to marry up. Love was an entirely impractical thing for a woman in her position. "Look what love done to me," Mama used to say. "Look what love done to me." (*A moment.*) So I did what was necessary to gain favor. I allowed myself to be flattered by gentlemen. You understand? Yes, this "pretty" gal done things, un-pretty things, for this marble mantle, gaslights in every room, a player piano and an indoor toilet.

ESTHER: But Mr. Dickson was a good man.

MRS. DICKSON: Bless his broken-down soul. He had fine suits and perfect diction, and was too high on opium to notice that he was married. But I would not be a washerwoman if it killed me. And I have absolutely marvelous hands to prove it. (*Mrs. Dickson laughs, displaying her hands.*) But you have godly fingers and a means, and you deserve a gentleman. Why gamble it all away for a common laborer?

ESTHER: . . . Love.

MRS. DICKSON: Don't you let a man have no part of your heart without getting a piece of his. (*Lights crossfade to George.*)

GEORGE: Dear Esther, I held in the port of Havana, Cuba awaiting passage to New York City. A passenger come down with cholera. So here I wait, fighting patience. We sail tomorrow—(*Crossfade to Mr. Marks' boudoir, where Mr. Marks has just finished preparing a cup of tea. Esther hesitantly enters.*)

MARKS: Miss Mills, where have you been? I thought I'd lost you to a competitor. (*A moment.*) I keep looking out the window at Mr. Friedlander's shop, he's giving away thread with each purchase. Yesterday, stress tonic. Tomorrow, who knows? I saw this morning Mrs. Simons, Mrs. Simons my cousin's wife, go into Mr. Friedlander's. His fabric is inferior, I tell her this. But she wants the stress tonic . . . then go to the pharmacy I say. Where have you been? I've been going crazy. I couldn't bear to lose you to Friedlander.

ESTHER: I'm sorry, I—

MARKS: No, I'm sorry. You've been busy, of course. I thought something might have happened to you.

ESTHER: Don't tell me you were worried about me.

MARKS: Well, yes. I didn't have your address, otherwise I would have inquired about your health.

ESTHER: I'm very well, thank you. (*A moment. Esther smiles. Mr. Marks shyly looks away.*)

MARKS: I found something I think you'll love. (*Excited.*) Do you have a moment?

ESTHER: Yes.

MARKS: I'll get it. (*He fingers through the bolts of fabric, but suddenly stops himself. He struggles for a moment with whether to broach a question.*) I just made tea, would you have a cup of tea with me?

ESTHER: Thank you, that would be nice. (*Mr. Marks clears a chair for Esther. She sits, a bit disarmed by the invitation. Mr. Marks pours her a cup of tea, then one for himself. He sits down on a chair across from her. A moment. He touches the spot where the button is missing.*)

MARKS: Is the tea hot enough? Milk? Would you like sugar, of course?

ESTHER: No, thank you, it's fine. (*Esther smiles.*)

MARKS: You have a lovely smile. (*Esther stops smiling. Mr. Marks stands up, embarrassed by his candor.*) Let me show you the fabric.

ESTHER: Actually, I have a special request. I'll need fabric for a wedding gown, something simple, Mr. Marks. The bride don't got a lot of money to throw away.

MARKS: Satin? Chiffon? Cotton? Silk? Yes. Tulle?

ESTHER: Satin, I think.

MARKS: She hasn't told you?

ESTHER: Silk. (*Mr. Marks pulls down several bolts of fabric. Esther examines each one, her excitement muted.*)

MARKS: That one you're touching is very popular. And the price will please you. Thirty cents a yard.

ESTHER: Twenty?

MARKS: Twenty-five cents. The bride will like.

ESTHER: It's too much. Something less expensive, I'll dress it up with lace and ribbons. (*Esther points to a faded old roll.*) How about this one?

MARKS: It's a wedding. This is for an older woman—

ESTHER: I ain't so young.

MARKS: —the bride's mother perhaps. (*A moment.*) You are getting married?

ESTHER: (*A moment.*) Yes. You seem surprised.

MARKS: (*He is.*) No, no. Not at all. My congratulations. (*Mr. Marks pulls out his finest wedding fabric.*) Please. I'm sure the rich lady who ordered this didn't appreciate the delicacy of the fabric. She gave no thought to who crafted this perfection, the labor that went into making it. How many hands touched it. Look. Beautiful. You deserve to wear it on your wedding day.

ESTHER: It's so beautiful, it looks like little fairy hands made it. It's too fine for me.

MARKS: Come, touch it and then refuse. Please. Touch. (*Marks watches Esther run her fingers across the fabric. He also touches it, sensually. She closes her eyes. He continues to watch her, savoring the moment.*) It is exquisite. Miss Mills, many fine ladies have worn it against their skin, but it was made for you. I know this . . . (*Esther holds the fabric to her face and begins to weep.*) . . . May it be your first gift. (*He wants to offer comfort, but he cannot touch her.*)

ESTHER: I won't let you.

MARKS: It would be my pleasure. (*Esther accepts the length of fabric. They gaze at each other, neither able to articulate the depth of their feelings. A moment. Esther and Marks exit the stage, as the lights rise on Mayme seated at the piano. She plays a rag. Mrs. Van Buren enters smoking a cigarette and nursing a glass of brandy. She studies her image in the vanity mirror. Marks reenters fiddling with the buttons on his jacket. He takes out a needle and thread and contemplates whether to sew on a new button. Mrs. Dickson*

enters carrying a wedding veil, she toys with the delicate fabric. George enters in an ill-fitted suit, his best. He moves downstage with the uncertainty of a new arrival. Esther, dressed in a wedding gown, nervously enters. Mrs. Dickson places the veil on Esther's head. Everyone but George and Esther exit. Esther joins George downstage, each of them in a separate pool of light. George and Esther look at each other, for the first time, then look out into the world. There is a flash—as from an old-fashioned flash camera. The sepia tone image is captured. A projected title card appears above their heads: "Unidentified Negro Couple ca. 1905." Blackout.)

End of Act One

ACT TWO

Scene 1: The Wedding Corset—White Satin Embroidered with Orange Blossoms

(*Esther stands in a pool of light, she wears a spectacular white wedding gown. Another pool of light engulfs George, he wears a worn gray dress suit frayed around the sleeves, certainly his best. Lights rise. A spare studio flat, an iron bed dominates the room. George and Esther stand on either side of the bed, which is covered with the crazy quilt. A silence divides them. Finally Esther speaks.*)

ESTHER: Don't really feel much different. I guess I expected somethin' to be different. It was a nice ceremony. Didn't you think? I wish my family coulda witnessed it all. My mother in particular. When the minister said man and wife I nearly fainted, I did. I been waiting to hear those words, since . . . they nearly took my breath away. Man and wife, and the truth is we barely know each other. I've written you near everything there is to know about me, and here we is and I fear I ain't got no more to say. (*Note: George's accent is a touch heavier and more distinctly Barbadian than in the first act.*)

GEORGE: We ain't need to say nothin' now. We got plenty of time for that. It late. (*George takes off his jacket and tosses it across the bed. He loosens his top button. Esther picks up the jacket, quickly surveys the label, then neatly folds it, placing it at the bottom of the bed.*)

ESTHER: Do you wish to bathe? I'll fetch the basin. (*George kneels on the bed and extends his hand to Esther.*)

GEORGE: Why don't yuh come sit by me. Let me see yuh. (*Esther sinks on the bed with her back to George. He gently strokes her cheek. Esther trembles.*) Are yuh afraid of me? Yuh shaking.

ESTHER: Am I? None of this be familiar.

GEORGE: Give yuh hand 'ere. (*Esther gingerly passes her hand to George. He sits next to her, kissing each of her fingers, then places her hand on his crotch.*) See. It ain't scary at all. (*Esther leaves her hand resting on his crotch, uncomfortable. A moment.*) I expected yuh to be—

ESTHER: Prettier.

GEORGE: No, I was gonna say—

ESTHER: It's okay, I lived with this face all my life, ain't no surprises. We should say what we think now and get it out of the way.

GEORGE: I suppose from yuh letters—

ESTHER: I described my character. And I think you'll find me truthful. (*George begins to unbutton Esther's dress. She stiffens at his touch.*) You're very handsome. More than I thought and I must say it do make me a little uncomfortable. (*Esther withdraws her hand from his crotch.*) And the other thing I think you must know, I ain't been with a man before. I been kissed and done some kissing, but you know what I'm saying. And it might be awkward on this first night, even if we man and wife—

GEORGE: Then we'll make it less awkward. (*George slips Esther's dress off of her shoulders and plants a kiss on her bare back. She's wearing a stunning wedding corset of white satin embroidered with orange blossoms.*) Real nice. Pretty. I like it. (*He runs his fingers across the delicate lace covering her breasts.*)

ESTHER: Wait. I made something for you. (*Esther stands up and quickly fetches the smoking jacket.*) Here.

GEORGE: What it?

ESTHER: It's Japanese silk. Put it on. (*George clumsily pulls the smoking jacket around his muscular body. He clearly isn't comfortable with the delicacy of the garment.*) Careful. (*George explores the jacket with his weather-worn fingers.*) It ain't too small?

GEORGE: Nah. But I afraid, I soil it. (*George removes the jacket and tosses it on the bed. He pulls Esther into his arms.*)

ESTHER: Not yet.

GEORGE: Yuh got somethin' in mind?

ESTHER: Couldn't we wait a bit?

GEORGE: Minister say man and wife.

ESTHER: Please, I'd like to know about your mother or about your birthplace, Bar-ba-dos. Something I don't know. That wasn't in the letters. Something for us, right now. (*A moment.*)

GEORGE: Like what? (*Esther pulls away and picks up the smoking jacket.*)

ESTHER: I come here from North Carolina at seventeen after my mother died of influenza, God bless her loving spirit. My father died two years later, he was a slave you see and didn't take to life as a freeman. He'd lost his tongue during a nasty fight over a chicken when I was a baby, so I never heard him speak, no complaints, no praise, no gentle words, no goodbye. He was . . . silent. Broken really. I come to this city by myself, worked my way North little by little, picking berries in every state until I get here. An old woman in the rooming house teach me to sew intimate apparel, saying folks'll pay you good money

for your discretion. It was just about the best gift anybody give me. It was as though God kissed my hands when I first pulled the fabric through the sewing machine and held up a finished garment. I discovered all I need in these fingers. (*A moment.*) I wanted you to know that about me.

GEORGE: My parents were chattel . . . born to children of chattel. (*George takes off his shirt.*) We cut sugar cane and die and that our tale for as long as anybody could say. Nothin' worthy of a retelling, really. I come here so the story'll be different, that I hopin'. Now if yuh don' mind, I spent many nights on a hard wood floor, a bed be long overdue. (*Esther gives him her hand.*) We married. I ain' gonna commit no crime 'ere, a man and wife don't 'ave no quarrel in the bedroom. (*George gently pulls her onto the bed. The lights slowly fade as Esther succumbs to his embrace. Ragtime piano. Mayme and Mrs. Van Buren enter, dressed in their twin corsets. They stand over the wedding bed.*)

MAYME: What is he like? (*George climbs out of bed, he stands in a pool of light and slowly goes through the ritual of dressing. Esther kneels on her bed wrapped in the crazy quilt.*)

ESTHER: He handsome enough.

MRS. VAN BUREN: Come, what did he say when he saw you? (*Esther climbs out of bed. As they speak, if necessary, Mayme and Mrs. Van Buren may help Esther dress.*)

ESTHER: He ain't say much of nothing. He just stood there for a moment regarding me with his eyes. Yellow, cotton and cane eyes. I didn't have no tongue.

MRS. VAN BUREN: He must be something of a romantic. He traveled halfway across the world because of some promise on a paper.

ESTHER: And he still smell of salt and ground nuts. It make me sick and it make me excited.

MRS. VAN BUREN: I was tipsy on my wedding night. I recall being in love with the notion of love, and everything took on a rosy glow. Harry was foolish and confident and I was frightened to death.

MAYME: Is he as we imagined?

ESTHER: Yes, he is sturdy enough and quite a pleasure to behold. His hands thick, stained dark from work. North Carolina field hands. But he got a melodious voice, each word a song unto itself. (*Mayme and Mrs. Van Buren reluctantly retreat into the darkness. Esther and George button their shirts.*) And when he finally fell asleep I placed my head on his chest, and listened for the song of cicadas at dusk, and imagined the sweet aroma of the mango trees and the giant flamboyant with its crimson tears. (*Esther and George stand on either side of the bed, dressed.*)

Scene 2: Valenciennes Lace

(*George/Esther's boudoir. A rag plays. George smoothes down his overgrown hair, pleased with himself. His clothing is worn but that doesn't seem to trouble him. Esther takes in George from the corner of her eye, quickly averting her gaze when he glances over. He smiles to himself.*)

ESTHER: Do you want me to fix you something?

GEORGE: I ain't really hungry, you know.

ESTHER: Where are you going? It Sunday. I promised Mrs. Dickson we'd dine with her this afternoon after the church social.

GEORGE: That woman ask too many questions for me liking.

ESTHER: That's what ladies do. She's just being attentive. (*George grabs his hat and toys with it for a moment. He ventures to speak, but stops himself. Finally:*)

GEORGE: Say Mrs. Armstrong, you got two dollars?

ESTHER: What for?

GEORGE: I need a proper hat if yuh want me to look for real work. It near three months now, and this a farmer's hat I tol'. The rag man wouldn' even give me a penny for it.

ESTHER: Two dollars. That's a lot of money. I tol' you I'd make you a worsted suit. Right smart. (*George gently touches Esther's hand.*)

GEORGE: C'mon, Mrs. Armstrong. Just two dollars.

ESTHER: But this is the last time. Hear? (*Esther, reluctant, goes over to the quilt and opens the seam with her scissors. She digs in and pulls out two dollars.*) There.

GEORGE: That all you got?

ESTHER: Yes. Why do you need to go out?

GEORGE: I tell some fellas I stop off for a quick ale, be back 'fore yuh know.

ESTHER: But it Sunday. I'll put on some tea, and sit, let me mend your shirt. You can't go out with a hole in your shirt. (*Esther touches the hole in his shirt.*) What will they say about your wife? I won't hear the end of it from Mrs. Dickson.

GEORGE: She a real madam. "Yuh working, George?" "Oh, nuh?" (*Chupses.*) I ain' been this idle since a boy in St. Lucy. But that busylickum ain' 'ear nothing. (*Chupses again.*) I got me pats on the back from white engineers, and a letter of recommendation from the Yankee crew chief heself. But 'ere, I got to watch buildings going up left and right, steel girders as thick as tamarind trees, ten, twelve stories high. Thursday last I stood all day, it cold too, waitin' for the chief, waiting to interview. Do yuh have tools, boy? Yes! Do yuh know how to operate a machine, boy? Yes. But 'e point just so to the Irishmen, the German and the tall Norwegian who's at least fifty years plus five. And I got more experience than the lot. I tell 'e so. Next time, 'e say. Next time, George. Can you believe? And when everyone gone, 'e pass me this damn note like it money. (*George takes a letter from his pocket and unfolds it.*) Look. (*He hands the note to Esther. She examines it, pretending to read.*) What do you t'ink? (*George watches her ever so carefully . . .*)

ESTHER: I don't know what to say. I suppose he mean what he say. (*She anxiously places the letter on the bed.*)

GEORGE: But what do you t'ink? You t'ink what he say true?

ESTHER: Why wouldn't he be truthful? (*Frustrated, George takes off his shirt and tosses it to Esther. He then throws himself across the bed and lights a cigarette. Esther goes about mending George's shirt by hand.*) Did you try over at that butcher's? Like I asked. I know they could use an extra man 'cause it's always crowded in there. Especially on Friday.

GEORGE: I don' know. We'll see.

ESTHER: There are worse things you could do. And I thought maybe we could go to the church social before Mrs. Dickson's.

GEORGE: I ain' a church man, really. (*Esther stops sewing.*)

ESTHER: You do believe, don't you? Why in letters you said—

GEORGE: I say a lot of t'ings. (*A moment. Esther returns to sewing. George feels the quilt.*)

ESTHER: Please, I ain't been to a social. I sat up in Saint Martin's for years, and didn't none of them church ladies bother with me until I walked in on your arm, and suddenly they want Mrs. Armstrong over for tea.

GEORGE: Yuh and yuh monkey chaser yuh mean?

ESTHER: Oh that ain't so. Most of them folks ain't been nowhere to speak of. But they are fine people, and who knows where help will come from?

GEORGE: I want to build t'ings, not polish silver or port luggage. Them fine jobs for yuh Yankee gentlemen, but not me. I ain' come 'ere for that! They'll have me a bootblack 'fore long, let the damn Italians blacken their hands, I say. Mine been black long enough. A man at the saloon, smart looking fella, say the onliest way for a colored man in this country is for 'e to be 'e own man. Have 'e own business, otherwise 'e always be shining the white man nickel. You understand, no? And really, how it look to people. Me, sitting 'ere, waitin' on fortune, you out there courtin' it.

ESTHER: I am your wife, and whatever I got, yours. And George mind your smoking on the bed. The Chinaman two floors down burn up that way. (*George puts out the cigarette.*)

GEORGE: Listen, this fella at the saloon talk about a man sellin' a stable with a dozen strong draft horses. 'E in a bit of debt, and need money quick quick. A dozen horses for nothin'. Did you 'ear what I say?

ESTHER: That saloon talk. That man'll take your money to Shanghai. It just a dream, it ain't gonna feed you today.

GEORGE: You t'ink I stupid?

ESTHER: No. But supposin' he honest, where would you get the money for twelve horses?

GEORGE: Where, Mrs. Armstrong? (*George gently strokes the quilt.*) Am I wrong?

ESTHER: My quilt? Never mind with that money. It just there and it gonna stay there.

GEORGE: Yuh a squirrel, for true. That's what yuh call them city rats, no?

ESTHER: A squirrel ain't a rat. That money for my beauty parlor, I told you that.

GEORGE: (*George laughs.*) That funny.

ESTHER: Why's that funny to you?

GEORGE: You ownin' a beauty parlor.

ESTHER: Yes. (*George studies Esther. She self-consciously returns to sewing.*)

GEORGE: Look at yuh. How yuh know pretty from the lookin' glass? (*A moment.*)

ESTHER: (*Wounded.*) I make pretty things. (*George pops up off the bed and takes Esther in his arms.*)

GEORGE: I sorry, Mrs. Armstrong, I ain' know what I say. Yuh be real sweet, if you done up yuh hair, nice. Put a little paint on yuh lips. (*George runs his hand across Esther's mouth. He grabs her and tries to do a quick dance.*)

ESTHER: I ain't that kind of woman.

GEORGE: No, yuh ain'. (*George lets go of Esther's arm. Gently.*) Please, Esther.

ESTHER: No. That eighteen years there.

GEORGE: (*Chupses.*) Yuh vex me so. Where's me shirt?

ESTHER: It ain't finished. (*George grabs the shirt from Esther and puts it on.*) Be careful, you'll tear —

GEORGE: I going o'er to the Empty Cup for an ale. I see yuh later.

ESTHER: That a notorious place.

GEORGE: How yuh know?

ESTHER: I know. (*George chupses dismissively.*) Why are you so cross with me? You got your ale money and enough for God knows what else. Ain't that so?

GEORGE: Yes, it yuh nickel. How do t'ink that make me feel?

ESTHER: I come here with nothing.

GEORGE: Don't look at me so.

ESTHER: I slept in a cold church for nine days, and picked up breadcrumbs thrown to pigeons.

GEORGE: Yes. Yuh done good, but five hundred days digging don' amount to nothing 'ere. It always gray, why it so gray? Work on the Isthmus, it hard, but at least the sun shine.

ESTHER: I know you here 'cause of me, and I want you to be happy. We stood in that church, and promised before God to take care of each other. That means something, even if it gray. You listenin'?

GEORGE: I listenin'.

ESTHER: You got a good arm George Armstrong, and I'd be proud to walk in on it whether it shining shoes or picking cotton.

GEORGE: I just tired of comin' home to put me hand in yuh pocket. (*George grabs his hat and coat. Esther attempts to turn down his collar. He brushes her hand away.*) I off.

ESTHER: What about Mrs. Dickson and the social?

GEORGE: I be back for supper. (*George grabs his coat and exits. Esther picks up George's work letter and crumples it up. Crossfade to Mr. Marks' boudoir.*

Mr. Marks hums a rag as he searches through the piles of fabric. Esther enters.)

MARKS: Here it is. Scottish wool, it isn't as expensive as one would think. It is very good.

ESTHER: Are you humming a rag, Mr. Marks?

MARKS: No, it's a Romanian song. I can't remember the words. It is driving me mad.

ESTHER: (*Esther smiles.*) I'm very happy to see that you replaced the button on your suit.

MARKS: (*Proudly.*) You noticed. It was time, don't you think? (*Mr. Marks displays the fabric.*) You wanted Scottish wool, yes?

ESTHER: Scottish wool. Yes. (*Esther feels the fabric.*) It's so heavy. Would you wear a suit made of this?

MARKS: Well, yes. You see how soft it is. I bought it from a gentlemen who said it came from his village. He had a wonderful story about his mother caring for the sheep like small children. He said every night she'd tell them a fairy tale, and each morning give the creatures a kiss and a sprinkle of salt. The neighbors would watch and laugh. Watch and laugh. But come time to shear the animals, what wonderful wool they produced for his mother. Like no other. (*Esther feels the fabric, lovingly. Mr. Marks revels in her delight.*) He could have been a thief for all I know, but the color is a lovely coffee, very subtle. Don't you think? So I pay too much, but not enough for the quality. Ah! Yes. I have something else to show you. It's here. Where is it? Where are you? Here we are. (*Mr. Marks unfurls a roll of lace.*) I almost let it go last week, but I was waiting for you. I wanted you to see it.

ESTHER: Oh, yes.

MARKS: I knew you'd like it. (*Elated.*) The wait was worth seeing your smile again. (*Marks playfully drapes the lace around Esther's neck. They find themselves standing dangerously close to each other. They are so close that they can inhale each other's words. A moment.*) Miss Mills, if I may say —

ESTHER: Armstrong. (*Esther removes the lace.*)

MARKS: I apologize. I forget. I forget. (*A moment. Mr. Marks takes the lace and places it on the cutting board.*)

ESTHER: It is pretty, thank you, but today I've come for fabric for a gentleman's suit. Next time.

MARKS: Yes. Just a minute, I have some other wools, gabardine, if you'd like to see? I have no story for them, but they are sturdy and reliable, will give you no problems. (*As Mr. Marks turns to search for another bolt of fabric, Esther gently runs her fingers across the lace. Mr. Marks turns with the dark drab suit fabrics. Mr. Marks slowly rolls the lace, his disappointment palpable.*) Next time.

ESTHER: Mr. Marks?

MARKS: Yes? (*Esther wants to say something, but she can't quite find the words.*) Is there — ?

ESTHER: No. No . . . I'm sorry . . . I can't do this. (*Distraught.*) I thought I'd be able to, but I can't. I can't come here anymore. I—

MARKS: Why do you say this? Did I do something to offend, tell me, did I—

ESTHER: No.

MARKS: Then—

ESTHER: Please, I think you know why. (*A moment.*)

MARKS: How many yards will you need for the gentleman's suit?

ESTHER: Four yards. The Scottish wool . . . and if you would, please wrap the Valenciennes lace. (*Crossfade to Mrs. Van Buren's boudoir. Light pours into her room.*)

Scene 3: Rose Chemise

(*Mrs. Van Buren's boudoir. Mrs. Van Buren sits on the bed cradling a snifter of brandy. She's upbeat, almost cheerful. However, Esther is distracted, consumed by her own thoughts.*)

MRS. VAN BUREN: He's gone to Europe.

ESTHER: I'm sorry to hear that.

MRS. VAN BUREN: You needn't be. It's a relief actually. Some business obligation, I don't expect to see him for months. He'll find ways of prolonging his stay, no doubt. Anyway, I'm considering a visit with friends in Lenox this summer. It'll be good to escape the city. Don't you think? You could come, of course, I'll recommend your services to several women.

ESTHER: I thank you, but I can't. (*Esther drapes the Valenciennes lace over the bed post.*) Here. I found a strand of lace for your rose chemise. I know it ain't exactly what you wanted, but—

MRS. VAN BUREN: I had all but forgotten. I ordered it over four weeks ago. Four whole weeks. It's not like you to—

ESTHER: I been busy.

MRS. VAN BUREN: Oh? Indeed. How is our Mr. Armstrong?

ESTHER: Good. Well, he . . . good. Work scarce, and he so particular. He wanting, but his pride make him idle. And I try, I do, but he ain't really take to this city.

MRS. VAN BUREN: But he will. I am certain. Oh Esther, it must be wonderful to be in love.

ESTHER: I suppose. (*A moment. Mrs. Van Buren quickly examines the lace, indifferent, she tosses it onto the bed. Esther bristles at her employer's lack of interest.*)

MRS. VAN BUREN: Is everything all right?

ESTHER: Yes.

MRS. VAN BUREN: Such a long face so early in the day. I won't allow it. (*Esther doesn't smile.*) Come.

ESTHER: I'd like to settle matters. Please. You ain't paid me in two months and I need the money.

MRS. VAN BUREN: Of course, I hadn't realized. (*Mrs. Van Buren sits at her dressing table. Smiling to herself.*) You know what? I miss writing our letters. I do! I've been absolutely without purpose for months.

ESTHER: (*Snaps.*) Let's not talk about the letters!

MRS. VAN BUREN: (*Surprised.*) Fine, we won't.

ESTHER: I'm sorry, Mrs. Van Buren.

MRS. VAN BUREN: Something is wrong.

ESTHER: No. Nothing. (*Esther sits on the edge of Mrs. Van Buren's bed. She carefully refolds the lace, attempting to hold back tears, but they come anyway.*)

MRS. VAN BUREN: Esther, what is it?

ESTHER: The other day George asked me to read a letter. I took it in my hand and I lied. I lie every day. And I'm a Christian woman. (*Mrs. Van Buren takes Esther's hand and sits down on the bed next to her.*)

MRS. VAN BUREN: We do what we must, no? We are ridiculous creatures sometimes. (*A moment.*)

ESTHER: Do you love Mr. Van Buren?

MRS. VAN BUREN: I am a married women, such a question is romantic.

ESTHER: But I fear my love belongs someplace else.

MRS. VAN BUREN: And why is that?

ESTHER: I shouldn't say. No, I can't. Perhaps I'm wrong.

MRS. VAN BUREN: Perhaps not. (*Mrs. Van Buren pulls Esther close and plants a kiss on Esther's lips. Esther for a moment gives in to the sensation of being touched, then abruptly pulls away. Shocked.*) I'm sorry. I didn't mean to do that. I'm sorry. Please don't go. I just wanted to show you what it's like to be treated lovingly.

ESTHER: Don't say that. You don't love me.

MRS. VAN BUREN: How do you know? Please. We will forget this and continue to be friends.

ESTHER: Friends? How we friends? When I ain't never been through your front door. You love me? What of me do you love?

MRS. VAN BUREN: Esther, you are the only one who's been in my boudoir in all these months. And honestly, it's only in here with you, that I feel . . . happy. Please, I want us to be friends?

ESTHER: I'm sorry. I can't.

MRS. VAN BUREN: (*Screams.*) Coward! (*A moment.*) I'm sorry. (*Mrs. Van Buren digs into her dressing table drawer and produces a wad of money. She tosses the money on the bed.*) There.

ESTHER: I'm not the coward. (*Esther picks up the money. Crossfade to Mayme's boudoir. Mayme plays a slow seductive rag. George enters, he watches Mayme gracefully regard the instrument. He places money on top of the piano, then straddles the piano bench behind Mayme. He kisses her neck and cups her breasts in his hands. Crossfade to Esther's boudoir. Esther sits alone, waiting. Crossfade to Mayme's boudoir.*)

Scene 4: Gentlemen's Suit

(*Mayme's boudoir. Esther enters. Mayme is dressed in a red flowing dressing gown and bubbles over with excitement.*)

MAYME: I've saved up every penny I have. It's been two months and I want something new, Esther. Simple, this time, without all the pronouncement. Something a young gal might wear on her wedding night.

ESTHER: Wedding night? What ain't I heard? I don't believe those words got any place in your mouth.

MAYME: Seriously.

ESTHER: What's going on? C'mon, are you gonna tell me?

MAYME: It ain't nothing really. A fella, perhaps.

ESTHER: I thought you didn't feel nothing for these fools.

MAYME: Nothing ain't never felt so good.

ESTHER: Who is he?

MAYME: He ain't nobody really, but he real sweet. Like a schoolboy almost. We call him Songbird, 'cause he sing to speak. He come in like all them others. Hands crude and calloused, a week's wage in his pocket. But when we done I didn't want him to leave and I asked him to have a drink. Fool drunk up all my liquor, but it ain't bother me. In fact I was fixin' to run out and git some more, but he placed his hands around my waist, real gentle and pulled me close. I actually wanted him to kiss me, I didn't even mind his sour tongue in my mouth, I wanted him there, inside me. He ain't like a lot of the colored men who pass through here with anger about their touch. He a gentleman. Comes three times a week on schedule like the iceman. He was here last night until midnight, but he don't ever stay later. He just leaves his scent, which lingers until two A.M. or three, and I lie awake until it disappears.

ESTHER: He sounds wonderful.

MAYME: Yeah, I reckon.

ESTHER: What?

MAYME: Whatcha think? He got a wife. Yeah. A rich wife. But she troubles him, he say. Troubles him to no end. You should hear him go on about this poor gal. Made me feel bad for her.

ESTHER: She terrible, I'm sure. But just the same, you on uneasy ground.

MAYME: You find it shocking?

ESTHER: Yes, I find it shocking.

MAYME: Hush your mouth, you wouldn't understand. You want to see what my songbird give me? (*Mayme pulls George's Japanese smoking jacket from beneath her pillow. She displays it proudly.*) And you know me, I don't usually take gifts from men, but when he give me this, it took my breath away. It's so pretty. Look Esther. Feel it.

ESTHER: He give you this?

MAYME: Yup.

ESTHER: He must like you a bunch to give you something so fine.

MAYME: What can I tell you, the man got taste, honey.

ESTHER: I've only seen fabric like this just once before. It's Japanese silk.

MAYME: How'd you know?

ESTHER: It's expensive fabric. Very hard to find. You see the pictures were embroidered by an imperial artist, he signed it there. He give you this?

MAYME: He say I his gal. But this time a little part of me is hoping he telling the truth.

ESTHER: And what about his wife?

MAYME: What about her? I'm sure she just a sorry gal.

ESTHER: How you know she ain't a good person? And he just saying what you want to hear. That his words are a smooth tonic to make you give out what ain't free. How you know his wife ain't good?

MAYME: I don't know. But do it matter?

ESTHER: Yeah it do. You ever think about where they go after they leave here? Who washes their britches after they been soiled in your bed?

MAYME: No, I don't actually. Why would I?

ESTHER: 'Cause there's some poor woman out there waiting, getting up every five minutes, each time a carriage pass the window or a dog bark. Who thinks a great deal of her husband, thinks so much of him that she don't bother to ask questions, she just know that there are places that he go that gentlewomen don't belong.

MAYME: I don't want to hear it.

ESTHER: She thinks he's playing cards or simply restless. But still when the door opens and he lies down next to her, that poor stupid woman don't feel angry, because his body is warm and she ain't alone.

MAYME: What?! You troubled because he married? They all married. You ain't completely clean of this business. Truth. No, I don't care to think about those women. I don't care to think about the kind of lives that keep them sitting in their windows, worrying while their husbands—

ESTHER: I pity your heart. You are the worst sort of scavenger. (*Lights rise on George and Esther's boudoir. George stands in a brand-new suit.*)

MAYME: What's the matter with you?

ESTHER: I don't feel so good. That's all.

MAYME: I thought you'd be happy for me.

ESTHER: I think I'm gonna go home, if you don't mind. (*Lights crossfade. Esther and George's boudoir. George stands in a new wool suit.*)

GEORGE: Yuh t'ink I'd be taken for a Yankee gentleman? I do t'ink so, no? I'd like one them tall hats, whatcha call 'em? Like that fella across the way, yuh know, the one always be talkin' about 'e rich brother in Chicago. (*Affecting an American accent.*) Yes, sir my name George Armstrong and I from New York, yes sir, born here. (*George laughs.*) It fit real nice. But, it seem to me that the fellas be wearin' shorter jackets with a touch of color. (*Esther pins George's pants.*)

ESTHER: Sporting fellas, they ain't gentlemen. This Scottish wool. It white folk quality and it'll keep you warm through the winter. There is a lovely story—

GEORGE: Yeah? I'm sure it excitin'. (*Esther runs her hands down George's legs, then adjusts the hem. He does not respond to her touch.*)

ESTHER: Be that way, I won't tell it then. There. You look good, George. Really. Now take off the pants so I can hem them proper.

GEORGE: Nah, don't bother. I need them for this evenin'.

ESTHER: This evening? Why? Don't go out. I bought fresh pork chops from Mrs. Franklin's son. I was gonna smother them in onions, the way you like. But it ain't worth the trouble if you ain't gonna eat. And . . . and I have something for you, I was going to save it for later . . . but . . . (*A moment.*) Do you want to see?

GEORGE: (*Excited.*) Sure.

ESTHER: Close your eyes. C'mon. And don't smile. (*George closes his eyes. Esther puts a rose in her hair and a touch of color on her lips. She nervously slips off her dress, revealing an elaborate corset similar to Mayme's.*) You can open your eyes. (*Esther awkwardly poses, awaiting George's reaction. His disappointment is palpable. He clearly was expecting something else. George chuckles to himself with a mixture of amusement and disgust.*)

GEORGE: What yuh doing?

ESTHER: Don't you like it?

GEORGE: Come, put yuh clothin' on.

ESTHER: What's the matter? Ain't this to your liking? Ain't this what you want? (*Esther places George's hands around her waist.*) Feel it. It satin. See.

GEORGE: No, don't do this Esther. C'mon, this ain' yuh. 'Ear.

ESTHER: (*Timidly.*) If I ain't mistaken, a man has certain obligations. (*A moment.*) Why won't you touch me? (*A moment.*)

GEORGE: You want me to touch yuh?

ESTHER: Yes. (*George grabs Esther around the waist. He plants a heavy hard kiss on her mouth. She nevertheless succumbs to his touch.*)

GEORGE: Like so? You want me to touch you. That all you want of George? You want me to bend and please, so you can feel mighty. No. (*George pushes Esther away.*) 'Least in Panama a man know where 'e stand. 'E know 'e chattel. That as long as 'e have a goat 'e happy. 'E know when 'e drunk, 'e drunk and there ain' no judgment if so. But then 'e drink in words of this woman. She tell 'e about the pretty avenues, she tell 'e plentiful. She fill up 'e head so it 'ave no taste for goat milk. She offer 'e the city stroke by stroke. She tantalize 'e with Yankee words. But 'e not find she. Only this woman 'ere, that say touch me, George. And ask 'e to lie down on what she promise, lie down on 'e stable with a dozen strong horses for the work sites, ask 'e to lie down as they haul lumber and steel. Strong sturdy beasts. They are. 'E lie down, but what 'e get? No, he ain't gonna lie down no more.

ESTHER: Stop it. Why you talking this way?

GEORGE: I t'ink yuh know. (*A moment. George eyes the quilt.*)

ESTHER: No. Please don't ask me again.

GEORGE: But it there dreamin' a fine fine house wit it own yard. It taunt 'e so, 'e can't even show what kind of man 'e be. What 'e hands can do.

ESTHER: No. That half my life. Thousands of tiny stitches and yards of fabric passed through that old machine.

GEORGE: And for what, huh? For it sit?

ESTHER: No.

GEORGE: Stop sayin' no! Ain't you see. If 'e own wife ain't willin' to believe in 'e, who will? 'E stand in work lines that wind around city blocks. But 'e don't have to no more, 'cause 'e know a fella got twelve draft horses and want to sell them quick quick. And 'e buy them and in two years, they'll have enough money for a beauty parlor even. They'll have the finest stable in New York City. People'll tip their hats and pay tribute. They'll call them Mr. and Mrs. Armstrong. The Armstrongs. Them church ladies will clear the front row just for them. And 'e will—

ESTHER: (*Esther wants to believe him.*) He will what?

GEORGE: 'E will sit with she and nod graciously to the ladies. 'E will come home for supper every evenin'. (*Seductively.*) 'E will lie with she.

ESTHER: Only she? (*George strokes Esther's back tenderly, she savors his touch. He kisses her neck, her back, her shoulders, her breasts. He embraces her, almost too much so. Esther nevertheless surrenders to the unexpected affection.*) Are you telling me the truth? Is this the truth?

GEORGE: Yes.

ESTHER: Please, you're not just saying that. You're not laughing at me are you?

GEORGE: No, I ain' laughin'. (*Finally, Esther breaks the embrace. She hesitates, then tears into the quilt, wrenching it apart with her bare hands. She pulls the money out and examines it, before placing it in George's outstretched hands.*)

ESTHER: There. There. There. (*She's almost relieved to be shedding the money. Surprised, George smiles and gathers the money into a pile.*)

GEORGE: So much 'ere. Sweet mercy, look at it all. Good lord, that fella ain' gonna believe it. I gonna place the money square in 'e hand, wipe that silly Yankee grin off 'e lips. I show 'e.

ESTHER: George, it's late, you ain't gotta do this now . . . put it back. It'll still be there in the morning.

GEORGE: Woman, how yuh get so much?

ESTHER: Leave it. Come. George, I said put it back, it'll be there in the morning! . . . (*Esther beckons him to the bed. He looks at her pleading outstretched hand, but instead chooses to fetch a worn bag for the wrinkled money. Esther, humiliated, studies her husband with growing horror. Aghast, she slowly lowers her hand and pulls on her dress.*) George? (*George continues to take unbridled delight in the money.*) George?

GEORGE: (*Snaps.*) What?

ESTHER: (*Whispered.*) Do you love me?

GEORGE: What the matter wit' you? You look as though you seen a duppy.

ESTHER: Do I?

GEORGE: Why yuh look at me strange?

ESTHER: I asked you something.

GEORGE: Yuh my wife, ain't yuh?

ESTHER: Am I? (*Whispered.*) I didn't write them letters.

GEORGE: I didn' hear what yuh said.

ESTHER: (*Louder, almost too much so.*) I said I didn't write them letters. (*George studies Esther with disbelief.*) All this time I was afraid that you'd find me out. This good noble man from Panama. (*Esther retrieves a pile of letters tied with a satin ribbon.*) I have all of your letters here. I look at them every day. I have one that looks as though it's weeping, because the words fade away into nothing, and another that looks as if it's been through a hard day, because there's a smudge of dirt at each corner, and it smells of kerosene and burnt sugar. But I can't tell you what it say, because I don't read. I can't tell whether there are any truths, but I keep them, 'cause George give me his heart, though it covered in mud and filthy, but he give it to me in one of these letters. And I believed him. I believed him! (*A moment.*) But you ain't the man in these letters, because that gentleman would have thanked me. Who wrote them letters, George? Tell me! (*George considers.*) YOU TELL ME!

GEORGE: An old mulatto man. I paid him ten cents for each letter, ten cents extra for the fancy writing.

ESTHER: I ain't really Mrs. Armstrong, am I? I been holding on to that, and that woman ain't real. We more strangers now, than on the eve of our wedding. At least I knew who I was back then. But I ain't gonna let you hurt that woman. No! She's a good decent woman and worthy. Worthy!

GEORGE: Esther! (*George reaches out to Esther.*)

ESTHER: No, don't touch me! (*Esther backs away from George.*)

GEORGE: Please. I ain' a thief. No. They warn't my words, but that don't mean I ain't feel them t'ings. I go now, and I gonna bring yuh back them horses.

ESTHER: I hope they real strong horses.

GEORGE: You'll see. And, we'll begin here. (*Lights crossfade. Mayme's boudoir. Ragtime music plays, fast and furious.*)

Scene 5: Smoking Jacket

(*Mayme's boudoir. Mayme is lying on the bed wrapped in the Japanese smoking jacket. She sits up, pours herself a shot of moonshine and slams it back. A knock sounds on the door.*)

MAYME: Hold on, hold on. (*Mayme opens the door. Esther, calm, enters. Mayme's unable to disguise her surprise.*) Esther. What . . . I got someone coming shortly. You can't stay. (*Mayme nervously wraps the robe around her body*.) I can't put him off. You understand. Come back later and we'll catch up. (*Esther grabs Mayme's arm.*) What's wrong? (*Esther gathers her strength.*)

ESTHER: He gone.

MAYME: Who gone?

ESTHER: George.

MAYME: You ain't serious.

ESTHER: He has another woman.

MAYME: How do you know?

ESTHER: She told me so.

MAYME: She did? Well, she must be a cruel heartless heifer.

ESTHER: You think so?

MAYME: Yes.

ESTHER: But, she ain't. When I left home this morning I intended to do harm to his whore. I was going to march into her room and scratch her face with my scissors. I was going to scar her. Make her ugly. Make her feel what I'm feeling. But, she gonna know soon enough.

MAYME: You gotta go now.

ESTHER: No.

MAYME: Please, we'll talk about it later. I got someone coming.

ESTHER: Do you know what I done? I tore a hole in my quilt and give him my beauty parlor. Half my life bent at the machine, and I give it to him, just like that.

MAYME: Oh, Esther. Why?

ESTHER: I wanted to be held. (*Distracted.*) I thought if . . . He ain't come home last night. I sat at the sewing machine all night, trying to make something, I just kept sewing together anything I could find until I had a strip a mile long, so long it fill up the apartment. (*A moment. Mayme runs her fingers along the fabric of the jacket.*) Do you know where he is, Mayme?

MAYME: Why would I know?

ESTHER: Because you're wearing the jacket I give him on our wedding night.

MAYME: How come you ain't say nothing before? (*Mayme, horrified, rips off the jacket.*)

ESTHER: What am I gonna say?

MAYME: Yeah, yeah. Last night Songbird come around the saloon in a new suit with bottomless pockets, throwing dice all night, and boasting of easy money. I ask him where he got the money and he say his luck turn and he was gonna ride it out. If you can imagine that. He was gonna buy himself draft horses. The world changing and he wants big strong horses. He made me laugh. He promised to take me out someplace special, but I didn't have nothing nice to wear. And honestly it made me think about how long it been since I done something for myself. Gone someplace like you said, where a colored woman could go to put up her feet and get treated good for a change. And I see the dice rolling, and I think Lord, God, wouldn't a place like that be wonderful. But every time the dice roll, that place is a little further away. Until it all gone. And then I put my arms around this man, and I know who he is. He George. And maybe I known all along.

ESTHER: Why didn't you stop him?

MAYME: Because, he belong to me as well. (*Mayme places it in Esther's hands.*) But this yours.

ESTHER: Foolish country gal.

MAYME: No, you are grand, Esther. And I ain't worthy of your forgiveness, nor will forget what you done for me. You ain't never treat me like a whore. Ever. (*George knocks on door.*)

ESTHER: Please don't answer that door. (*George rattles door and knocks.*) Please don't, please don't answer.

MAYME: He's going to leave.

GEORGE: (*Knocks and rattles door more urgently, shouts.*) Mayme!

(*He rattles door again.*)

ESTHER: LET HIM GO! (*Mayme moves toward the door, Esther grabs her arm.*) Let him go. He ain't real, he a duppy, a spirit. We be chasing him forever. (*George knocks and rattles door even more persistently. Eventually he stops. Silence. Mayme sits on her bed. Esther exits with the smoking jacket. Crossfade to Mr. Marks' Boudoir, as Esther moves into Mr. Marks' Boudoir.*)

Scene 6: *Japanese Silk*

(*Marks' boudoir. Mr. Marks unfurls a roll of ocean-blue fabric. As he turns, he finds himself facing Esther.*)

ESTHER: Hello, Mr. Marks.

MARKS: (*Surprised.*) Miss Mills, I'm sorry, Mrs. Armstrong. How have you been?

ESTHER: I seen worse days. And you?

MARKS: I've seen better days. (*He laughs.*)

ESTHER: I've been meaning to stop in. I walked past here a half dozen times trying to get up the courage to come in. You remember you sold me a rather special length of fabric some time ago.

MARKS: Please, remind me.

ESTHER: Japanese silk, with—

MARKS: Of course, I remember it.

ESTHER: Well, I made it into a man's smoking jacket, at your suggestion. (*She holds it up.*)

MARKS: It is very nice, it will please your husband, I'm sure.

ESTHER: I want you to have it.

MARKS: Me? I can't—

ESTHER: Yes, you will. (*Marks accepts the jacket, genuinely touched by the gesture.*)

MARKS: Thank you.

ESTHER: I can't stay. (*Esther begins to leave.*)

MARKS: Wait, one moment. (*He removes his outer jacket, revealing the fringes of his Tallit Katen. He carefully puts on the silk jacket.*) What do you think?

ESTHER: It fits wonderfully. (*Esther takes a step toward Marks, hesitates, then takes another step forward. She raises her hands.*) May I? (*He nervously holds his breath and nods yes. Esther reaches toward Marks, expecting him to move away. She smoothes the shoulders of the garment, then expertly runs her hands down the jacket's lapels, straightening the wrinkled material. Marks does not move. Silence. Their eyes are fixed upon one another, then Esther reluctantly walks away, exiting the boudoir without*

a word. Marks is left alone onstage to contemplate the moment. A gentle rag plays. Lights crossfade; we're in Esther's original boudoir.*)

Scene 7: *Patchwork Quilt*

(*Esther's boudoir. Mrs. Dickson's rooming house. Mrs. Dickson folds laundry, humming a ragtime tune. Esther enters.*)

ESTHER: The girl downstairs told me I could find you up here.

MRS. DICKSON: My Lord, Mrs. Armstrong. I been telling everyone how you forgot us.

ESTHER: It ain't been that long.

MRS. DICKSON: Feel so. (*The women hug.*) Look at you. I was about to take some tea, come on into the kitchen, I'm glad for the company. These new girls are always out and about. They trouble me so these days, but whatcha gonna do? And I want to hear about everything.

ESTHER: Have you rented this room?

MRS. DICKSON: Why do you ask?

ESTHER: I don't much feel like saying why. If you please, just a yes or no would suit me fine.

MRS. DICKSON: No.

ESTHER: Well then, you won't mind another person at supper this evening. It's Friday and you don't know how I been missing your carrot salad.

MRS. DICKSON: Of course. Esther—

ESTHER: I'm fine. (*Esther takes Mrs. Dickson's hand.*) And I'd love that cup of tea.

MRS. DICKSON: Come on downstairs and we'll catch up. I'll tell you about Corinna Mae, girl's as big as a house, I swear to God. (*Esther barely listening takes in the room.*) She didn't waste any time getting pregnant and already talking nonsense about her man. When they first was married he was good enough for her, but to hear it now you'd think the man didn't have no kind of sense.

ESTHER: I don't care to hear about Corinna Mae.

MRS. DICKSON: Oh, I just thought—

ESTHER: I'd like to sit here for a moment.

MRS. DICKSON: Oh, yes. I gotta bring a few more things in off the line before the sunset, I'll see you downstairs shortly.

ESTHER: Of course. Mrs. Dickson, thank you for not asking.

(*Mrs. Dickson lovingly takes Esther's hand, giving it a supportive squeeze. Mrs. Dickson picks up the laundry basket and exits. Esther lightly touches her belly. A moment. She walks over to the old sewing machine and begins to sew together pieces of fabric, the beginnings of a new quilt. Lights shift: sepia tone, the quality of an old photograph. A slow gentle rag plays in the distance. As the lights fade, projected title card: "Unidentified Negro Seamstress. Ca. 1905." Blackout.*)

End of Play

Doug Wright

Douglas Wright (b. 1964), born in Dallas, Texas, took his undergraduate degree at Yale University in 1985 and then earned his master's degree in playwriting at New York University in 1987. He has been a prolific screen writer as well as a playwright. His screenplays for *Memoirs of a Geisha* (2005) and *Quills* (2000) are the best known of his produced films. *Quills* was adapted by him from his own play about the notorious Marquis de Sade (1740–1814), who was imprisoned for thirty years of his life in the Bastille and the Charenton Insane Asylum. (The term *sadism* is derived from his name because his works, most of which he wrote while imprisoned, include some brutal pornographic novels.) Wright came to work on the material for his play after a friend gave him a biography of Sade that described how his papers and quill pens were taken from him in order to keep him from writing more pornography. The resulting play, *Quills* (1996), won an Obie Award for Outstanding Achievement in Playwriting, as well as the Kesselring Award for best new American play of the year. The film version of *Quills* was nominated for three Academy Awards, and the screenplay was nominated for a Golden Globe Award and won an award from the Writers Guild of America.

Some of Wright's earlier plays have been produced off-Broadway. *The Stonewater Rapture* (1987), written while he was at New York University, tells the story of two Texas teenagers and their sexual awakening. *Watbanaland* (1994) was produced at the WPA Theater off-Broadway in New York. Ben Brantley at the *New York Times* described it as "a feverish meditation on fertility and sterility." The play's title refers to the visitation of an African tribal chieftain who compared the natural tribal ways of his land with the hectic civilization that seemed about to engulf the characters in the play. Brantley offered a much warmer assessment of *Unwrap Your Candy* (2001), which played at the Vineyard Theater in New York. A series of four short plays, *Unwrap Your Candy* is an experiment in which the opening play consists of a group of actors who take theater seats in front of the house facing the audience. They are a mirror of the audience, and the point of the play is to integrate the audience more fully into the evening of theater. The *New York Times* review described the play as witty and entertaining.

Wright gained international recognition in 2003 with *I Am My Own Wife*, which won the Pulitzer Prize, the Tony Award for Best Play, the Drama Desk Award, and an Outer Critics' Circle Award. This one-person play was a tour de force in terms of both its staging and the script, which included dialogue from more than thirty characters. This play has gone on to tour internationally and has established Wright's reputation as a major figure in American playwriting.

The book *Grey Gardens* (2006), also a musical on Broadway, was written by Wright, who adapted the material from Albert and David Maysles's 1976 documentary film about "Big" Edie Beale and "Little" Edie Beale, a formerly high-society mother and daughter living in rustic squalor in East Hampton, New York. Their fall from wealth and celebrity was meticulously detailed in the film and brought to life somewhat more cheerfully in the musical. The film has long been a cult classic, and the musical played to enthusiastic reviews and was nominated for a number of awards.

Wright serves on the board of the New York Theater Workshop and has been given an award by the American Academy of Arts and Letters.

I Am My Own Wife

Moisés Kaufman, who worked with Doug Wright in the early stages of developing *I Am My Own Wife,* directed the first production on Broadway. The strategy of using interviews to provide the matter of the play resembles Kaufman's *The Laramie Project*. In researching the life of Lothar Berfelde, better known as Charlotte von Mahlsdorf, Wright's goal was to uncover the facts in the life of a transvestite homosexual man who somehow survived Nazi Germany living as a woman and *then* survived the modern era's repressive Communist government in East Germany without being imprisoned, shot, or pilloried. All the while, Charlotte was the owner of the Gründerzeit Museum, a museum celebrating Germany's 1890s, and the proprietor of an underground pub for homosexuals.

Wright, himself homosexual, found Charlotte's story almost unbelievable, but as he got to know her — through the good graces of a friend — he found her so remarkable, and so irresistible a personality, that he determined to write a play about her. She agreed to his interviews with her and over a period of years told him her story. After the reunification of the country, Charlotte won an important medal from the German government honoring her heroism and her ability to survive under such circumstances.

She told Wright stories of what life was like during the war, during the period after the war when the Russians occupied her portion of Berlin, and under the East German government's Communist regime. Throughout most of the interviews, Wright regarded her as a hero, but eventually, when the German Secret Police (the Stasi) disbanded and made its files available to researchers, Wright slowly began to realize that Charlotte had been a regular informer for the Stasi and had provided reliable information for a long time. This revelation complicated his entire attitude toward Charlotte and made it very difficult for him to continue work on the project as he had come to conceive it. He found it troubling to discover that Charlotte had informed on one of her closest, most trusted friends, who was then imprisoned. As a result of these conflicts, the play becomes a search for the true Charlotte von Mahlsdorf, a remarkably challenging project.

I Am My Own Wife in Performance

The most striking thing about the performance of this play is that only one actor plays all thirty-five roles, changing accents, vocal style, and physical mannerisms! At first glimpse, that feat seems almost impossible, and then it seems that it might just be a virtuoso performance without substance. But soon after the play begins, the audience realizes that it is possible for this one actor to bring the entire play to life. In this sense, the technique of this play harks back to Thespis, the first Greek actor, who stepped out of the chorus to become a unique player. At first, Greek drama needed only one actor, and after seeing *I Am My Own Wife,* playgoers can see what Thespis was able to accomplish.

The very first performance, starring Jefferson Mays (who worked on the development of the play along with Kaufman and Wright), took place as a one-night showcase at the Sundance Theater Laboratory in Park City, Utah, in January 2001. The play was then workshopped again that year in La Jolla, California, and in 2003 in Chicago. The premier in New York took place in Playwrights Horizons in May 2003, where it ran throughout the summer. In early December 2003, it moved to the Lyceum Theater on Broadway to begin an extensive run. The stage was filled with antique furniture and with numerous gramophones and so many exotic old record players that it resembled the Gründerzeit Museum. Mays appeared in a black dress with a white lace collar, with pearls around his neck and a black scarf on his head, looking for all the world like an innocent sixty-five-year-old grandmother. Bruce Weber at the *New York Times* said that the play "was the most stirring new work to appear on Broadway this fall." In 2005 *I Am My Own Wife* toured with other actors to Washington, D.C., Chicago, La Jolla, Boston, San Francisco, and Los Angeles. The production in Krakow, Poland, in 2005 faced the Polish taboo against cross-dressing, so Wright planned a party for transvestites to open a dialogue. He had a difficult time finding enough transvestites in Krakow and had to send for some from Warsaw. Jefferson Mays played Charlotte von Mahlsdorf again at Dublin's Gaiety Theatre in 2005 and again in 2006 at the Duke of York's Theatre in London's West End. In 2006 and 2007, *I Am My Own Wife* toured throughout the United States and in several countries abroad. The play won the Pulitzer Prize for drama in 2004.

Doug Wright (b. 1964)
I AM MY OWN WIFE

2003

Characters

CHARLOTTE VON MAHLSDORF
JOHN MARKS
DOUG WRIGHT
TANTE LUISE
SS OFFICER

SS COMMANDER
YOUNG LOTHAR BERFELDE
HERR BERFELDE
PRISON GUARD
MINNA MAHLICH

CULTURAL MINISTER
STASI OFFICIAL
ALFRED KIRSCHNER
YOUNG HOMOSEXUAL MAN
AMERICAN SOLDIER AND HIS BUDDY
CUSTOMS OFFICIAL
STASI AGENT
PRISON OFFICIAL
NURSE
GERMAN NEWS ANCHOR
POLITICIAN MARKUS KAUFMANN
ULRIKE LIPTSCH
JOSEF RÜDIGER
ZIGGY FLUSS
FIRST NEO-NAZI
SECOND NEO-NAZI
BRIGITTE KLENSCH
KARL HENNING
FRANÇOIS GARNIER
SHIRLEY BLACKER
DAISUKE YAMAGISHI
MARK FINLEY
PRADEEP GUPTA
CLIVE TWIMBLEY
DIETER JORGENSEN

ACT ONE

(*The French doors at the rear of the room open, and standing before us is Charlotte von Mahlsdorf.*

She is, in fact, a man, roughly sixty-five years old. Charlotte wears a simple black housedress with peasant stitching, a kerchief on her head, and an elegant strand of pearls.

She gazes at the audience for a moment; the tiniest flicker of a smile dances on her lips. Then, surprisingly, she closes the doors as quickly as she appeared, and is gone.

A pause. The stage is empty again.

In a moment, the doors reopen. Charlotte reappears. Cradled in her arms is a huge antique Edison phonograph, complete with an enormous horn in the shape of a flower. She grins, satisfied, and sets the phonograph on a small plinth.

She steps back for a moment to admire the music machine. When she speaks, it's in broken English, but the cadences of her voice are delicate; there's a musical lilt to her inflection. She has a German accent.)

A Lecture on the Phonograph

CHARLOTTE: Thomas Alva Edison was the inventor of the first talking machine of the world, in July of 1877. And, you see, the record is not *ein Plattenspieler; nein.*° It is a cylinder made of wax. And this record is working with a hundred and sixty revolutions per minute, and is playing four minutes long. And the record is made by the National Phonograph Company in Orange, New Jersey. At one time, I had over *fünfzehntausend* cylinders.

(*Charlotte indicates a painting of the Edison phonograph with an attendant dog, its ears cocked to listen.*)

And you see on the wall a painting: the dog Nipper, *His Master's Voice.* The most famous trademark in all the world. Next month, this phonograph will be half a century old.

(*She begins to turn the handle on the phonograph, readying it for play.*)

For fifty years, I've been turning its crank.
The loudness depends on a big or a small horn. Metal horns are better for bands and the voices of men. And the wooden horns, they are better for the strings and the voices of the female. *Die Sopranistin.*° And Edison's phonograph has in the needle a little sapphire.

(*She plucks a tiny disposable needle from a drawer concealed in the phonograph. She holds it up to the light, and says emphatically*):

Nicht Diamant, nur Saphir.° And when it grazes the record it sounds so nice.

(*She installs the needle on the arm, then delicately places the arm on the wax cylinder. The machine begins to play—an old German waltz, scratchy and exquisite.*)

In the Second World War, when the airplanes flew over Mahlsdorf, and the bombs were coming down, I played British and American records. And I thought, They can hear in the airplanes that I am playing Edison records. I thought, If they hear me they will know I'm their friend.

(*A pause as Charlotte revels in the music.*

Then—abruptly—the music stops. Charlotte is supplanted by someone else, a thirty-something newsman named John Marks.

John has the intrepid spirit of a Saturday serial matinee hero. His voice has a Texas twang. His masculine edge stands in sharp contrast to Charlotte's demure nature.)

Plattenspieler: Flat record (literally, not a record player). **Sopranistin:** The sopranos. **Nicht . . . Saphir:** Not a diamond, only a sapphire.

The World Flips Upside Down

JOHN:
From the desk of John Marks
Bureau Chief, Berlin
U.S. News & World Report
September, 1990.

Dear Doug,
It's a funhouse over here. You can't imagine. The Berlin Wall falls and the world flips upside down.
All the great and powerful leaders are turning out to be clowns. Erich Honecker, one of the most feared and respected dictators in the world, has in one year become a fugitive. He wanders around the grounds of a Soviet military hospital in his pajamas. Secret police files kept on East Germans for four decades are being released, and it turns out husbands spied on their wives, children on their parents, dissidents on each other.

(*He steps forward, and adopts a more confidential tone.*)

Now, in the midst of all this craziness, I've found a true character; she's way up your alley. (And, believe me, I use the term "she" loosely.) I'd love to interview her—make her my first official article for *U.S. News & World Report*. But I'm afraid my editor will say her story's too extreme. Still, I think she may well be the most singular, eccentric individual the Cold War ever birthed.
Have I piqued your interest?

Love,
John

(*Another abrupt shift. Doug is a playwright, in his mid-thirties, with an eager-to-please manner and a somewhat mellifluous voice.*)

DOUG: "Piqued" indeed.
August 8, 1992. I've been in Berlin for two days now. I'm sleeping on John's floor. Today we went to the Reichstag. There were demonstrations, because Christo° wants to cover it in pink tulle. Now we're in John's car, headed toward the east.

(*Doug glances out an invisible window, as though he were riding in a car with John.*)

Through the windshield, I can see fragments of the infamous wall still standing. Slapped onto one in bold paint are the words "Art Survives."
A sign whizzes past: "Mahlsdorf." It's a grim place; vast apartment complexes rise like cement gulags. Then we turn a corner, and it's like we've turned back the clock two hundred years or more. Standing before us is a huge, weather-beaten mansion

made entirely of stone. About a hundred tourists are gathered at the front door. Suddenly, with a creak, it opens.

(*Doug morphs into Charlotte. She fingers her pearls. Music from an Edison Amberol wafts through the air.*)

Das Gründerzeit Museum

CHARLOTTE: *Wilkommen in meinem Gründerzeit-Museum.* Welcome to my Gründerzeit Museum.
Here, people can always come to see my collection. Everything from *die Gründerzeit*; this was the period in Germany between 1890 and 1900. *Wie soll ich sagen . . .* ° "the Gay Nineties." Petroleum lamps and vases, gramophones, records, matchboxes, telephones, ink wells, Polyphones, pictures, credenzas, bureaus, and, of course, clocks.
No matter what people want to see or hear, I'll show or play it. Some people, they come to see me. *Ich bin Transvestit.*° But soon they look at the furniture.
Folgen Sie mir bitte, ja?°

(*Charlotte pulls the doors of the museum open.*)

CHARLOTTE: This old door? It is not original, *nein*. I saved it from a house on Prenzlauer Street. Before the Russians blew up the houses, I took such things.

(*As Charlotte enters the museum, Doug addresses the audience directly, recounting the adventurous step into the unknown.*)

DOUG: She ushers us into the foyer of the museum. The ceilings are high, at least fifteen feet. We're huddled together like schoolchildren. For the next two hours—room by room, object by object—she guides us through the house.

(*Charlotte seats herself at a small, ornately carved wooden table. From beneath it she pulls a velvet jewelry box. She places it squarely in the center of the table. With great ceremony, she opens it.*)

CHARLOTTE: Come in, please. There is room for everyone, yes?

(*Charlotte pulls a small, lovingly carved, elegantly furnished doll dresser from the box. She holds it sweetly in her palm and approaches the audience, holding it out for inspection.*)

CHARLOTTE: Here we have *eine alte Anrichte.*° A cupboard, yes? *Und dieses Möbelstück*° is made of oak, in the style of neo-Renaissance. But this was not handmade; this was factory-made. So-called mass

---

Christo: Christo Javacheff (b. 1935), an environmental artist who wrapped the Reichstag (Parliament) in 1995.

Wie . . . sagen: How shall I say?   **Ich bin Transvestit:** I am a transvestite.   **Folgen . . . ja?:** Will you follow me, please?   **Eine . . . Anrichte:** An old dresser.   **Und . . . Möbelstück:** And this furniture.

production. And the trim? People would tear it off; they would burn it. They did not like the scalloped wood, the tiny turrets, the ornamental molding. "Too old-fashioned! Too difficult to dust!" But me . . . I had a feeling for such things. And so I saved it.

(*She removes a tiny lacquer cabinet of lighter wood.*)

Und hier haben wir ein Vertiko. An old sideboard, *ja*? It was designed and built by *ein Tischlermeister*, Otto Vertiko, in *achtzehnhundertfünfundneunzig*.°

(*She pulls out a tiny bust on a pedestal.*)

And this is a bust of Wilhelm II, the last German emperor. During the Second World War, they wanted to melt it down for munitions. And so — with my school friend Christian — I pulled it from the bonfire, yes? It looks like a bronze bust, but it is only zinc. Galvanized. Not so expensive.

(*Next, a miniature clock with an open, suspended pendulum.*)

In French, this clock is called "*regulatour.*" Because it is regulating the time. And *auf Deutsch* we say "*Wanduhr,*" *oder* "*Freischwinger.*" Because the pendulum isn't encased in a glass box; it's freely suspended. Of course, American soldiers thought they were nice. They didn't have them in the USA. It made a nice gift to bring to the little wife at home, *ja*?

To wind such a clock, you need a key. And I collected, when I was a child, many keys. Keys for desks. Keys for doors. Keys with no locks; castaways. These I still carry in my apron, *ja*?

(*She extracts a tiny gramophone.*)

And here we have an old gramophone. *Nicht* phonograph, *Sondern*° gramophone. Instead of cylinders, round plates, flat, *mit* grooves. At one time I had many such records — Mendelssohn and Offenbach. But during the time of Hitler it was very dangerous to possess music from Jewish composers. And so I thought, I must save these records. And so I took old paper — brown grocery paper — and I cut it in the shape of labels. And I wrote with ink false titles: Aryan polkas and waltzes, yes? And I glued them onto the records, for safety. And when the war was over I took a sponge and with water I took the labels back off. And then the Hebrew titles with the dog Nipper were visible again.

(*A dainty little kitchen contraption, affixed to the edge of a tiny cutting table.*)

The kitchen is as it was for a housewife of 1890 in Berlin. This machine is for pitting the stones of cherries.

Und . . . achtzehnhundertfünfundneunzig: And here we have a . . . eighteen ninety-five.   **Sondern:** But.

(*She regards the tiny room — now spread out before her on the table, like the parlor in a dollhouse — for a moment.*)

When families died, I became this furniture. When the Jews were deported in the Second World War, I became it. When citizens were burned out of their homes by the Communists, I became it. After the coming of the wall, when the old mansion houses were destroyed to create the people's architecture, I became it.

(*A pause, and then*):

I am like a maidservant in this house; you must clean and clean, because the dust is growing! And the dust is looking like the dust of 1890! And you must put it away! I worked thirteen years with two hands to repair this old house. Each tile on the roof, I know. Each plank of the floor, like an old lover. In August 1993, the collection exists at the museum in this house for thirty-three years.

(*She holds up a small collection box.*)

And now you may make *eine Spende*. A small contribution. We have a cash box. Each person, what he or she thinks.

(*She curtsies, then transforms into Doug.*)

Popping the Question

DOUG:
From the desk of Doug Wright
New York City

Dear Charlotte von Mahlsdorf,
Recently, while in Berlin, I visited your museum. My childhood friend John Marks and I were awestruck by your furniture collection and your astounding array of Edison phonographs.

But I must confess, I was no less impressed by the mere fact of your survival. I grew up gay in the Bible Belt; I can only begin to imagine what it must have been like during the Third Reich.

The Nazis, and then the Communists? It seems to me you're an impossibility. You shouldn't even exist. So here's the presumptuous portion of my letter. I would love the opportunity to continue to study your life in order to write a play about you. With your support, I can apply for funding, fly back to Berlin, and begin to write in earnest. As far as grant applications go — forgive me — but from where I sit, you're a slam dunk.

Even if you reject my proposal, please know that the morning you shared with us was one of the most memorable of my life. Thank you for your kind attention, and I look forward to hearing from you.

Sincerely,
Doug Wright

(*Charlotte puts the letter down; she pauses, considering the request.*)

CHARLOTTE:
Dear Mr. Wright,
Yes. Perhaps it is possible for you to make a play. Maybe you will visit Berlin after Christmas.

Sincerely,
Charlotte von Mahlsdorf

(*Doug, ecstatic, springs into action, giving the thumbs-up sign; they're in business now! He circles the stage, reciting into his mini recorder.*)

DOUG: Testing. Testing one-two-three. Testing.
Tape One. It's January 20, 1993. I'm headed to the Gründerzeit Museum in Mahlsdorf for my first official interview with Charlotte von Mahlsdorf. With me, John Marks.

(*He sits. On one side, presumably, is John Marks. On the other, Charlotte.*)

Translating Tante Luise

DOUG: John—if you could, please—would you ask Charlotte about her given name? Her legal name?
JOHN: (*his Texas twang evident*) *Was war Ihr Geburtsname?*°
CHARLOTTE: *Mein Geburtsname war Lothar. Lothar Berfelde.*
JOHN: It was Lothar—
DOUG: Yeah, yeah. I got that. And next, could you ask her when she knew . . . the precise time . . . that her name ought to be Charlotte?
JOHN: (*even sharper on the ear this time*) *Und wann wussten Sie, dass Ihr Name Charlotte hätte sein sollen?*°

(*Charlotte decides to put an end to this auditory torture.*)

CHARLOTTE: I can tell it in English, yes?

(*John and Doug exchange a look. Charlotte takes over the telling of the tale.*)

CHARLOTTE: *Meine* Tante Luise was working on an estate in East Prussia, and she raised horses. On a large farm. And since she was fifteen years old she never wore ladies' clothes.
No.
Only boots. And jodhpurs. The clothes of a land inspector, and not a fine lady.

(*She gives a long, knowing look to punctuate that thought. Then she continues.*)

Was . . . Geburtsname: What was your birth name? **Und . . . sollen?:** And when did you know your name should be Charlotte?

And so I was coming in August in 1943 to East Prussia and I found in her closet clothes. Girl's clothes. And . . .

(*She whispers with an almost erotic intensity.*)

. . . I . . . put . . . them . . . on.

(*Charlotte steps before an imaginary mirror. She gazes into it as if she were looking at herself—truly examining herself—for the first time. And she's delighted by her image in the glass. She turns, raising her skirt as if it were an exotic fan.*

Suddenly she's stricken with a look of terror. She sees another reflection, looming behind her.)

And my aunt was coming into the room, and I was standing there, and she looked at us in the mirror, and then she said:

(*Charlotte becomes Tante Luise, with a stirring alto voice.*)

TANTE LUISE: *Weisst du, mit uns beiden hat die Natur sich einen Scherz erlaubt. Du hättest ein Mädchen werden müssen und ich ein Mann!*

(*She repeats the phrase—eloquently—in English.*)

Did you know that nature has dared to play a joke on us? You should've been born a girl, and I should've been a man!

(*Tante Luise morphs back into Charlotte.*)

CHARLOTTE: And there was—on the bookshelf—a book. And *meine* Tante took this book down and handed it to me. The binding, it was blue. And I opened it. And on its *Titelbild*—"frontispiece"—"*Die Transvestiten, by Magnus Hirschfeld.*" *Und ich spürte eine Gänsehaut . . . über meinen Rücken kriechen.* I felt a shiver down my spine. And *meine* Tante Luise said, "Read."

(*Charlotte begins to read.*)

In each person, there is a delicate balance of male and female substances. Just as we can't find two matching leaves from the same tree, it is scientifically impossible to find two human beings whose male and female characteristics match in kind and number.

(*She passes the book to Doug.*)

CHARLOTTE: (*to Doug*) Read.

(*Now he reads from the text.*)

DOUG: *And so we must treat sexual intermediaries—those individuals who defy the ready classification of "man" or "woman"—as a common . . . utterly natural . . . phenomenon?*

(*He looks to Charlotte for approval; she nods and says*):

CHARLOTTE: Yes. And *meine* Tante said:
TANTE LUISE: This book is not just any book. This book, it will be your Bible.

CHARLOTTE: (*to Doug, lightheartedly*) *Möchten Sie ein paar Spritzekuchen?*°

(*Doug ducks aside, his invisible tape recorder primed, and makes a few private observations.*)

The Giveaway

DOUG: Charlotte's just slipped into the kitchen, to bring us some *Kaffee und Kuchen.* I brought a camera, but I'm too shy to ask her to pose . . . I'm afraid she'll think I've only come to gawk. So I wanted to record a quick . . . visual . . . an impression.

She's about five eight, maybe a hundred and seventy pounds. Sixty-five years old. Doesn't look like a drag queen *at all.* No makeup. I asked her about that; she says she "doesn't need it." She's got piercing eyes— really smart eyes—and a sly little crooked smile. She still wears her own hair, which is white, goose-feather white, cut in—I guess you'd call it a pageboy. She's got on a black peasant dress, a string of pearls, and heavy black shoes. Orthopedic shoes.

She doesn't have breasts—not really—but just enough paunch to sort of enhance the impression.

But her hands are big, and thick. The hands of a woodworker. A craftsman. Definitely a man's hands.

(*Doug raises his own hands as if they belonged to Charlotte. As he does so, he transforms back into her.*

Charlotte puts another Edison Amberol on the phonograph, and the room fills with the sound of nostalgia.)

Are You a Boy or a Girl?

CHARLOTTE: And the last days of the world war were the most dangerous time for me because I refused to carry a weapon or to wear a uniform. Instead, I had my hair long and blond and my mother's coat, and the shoes of a girl. And so I was—in Germany we say "*Freiwild.*" Like the Jews, we were wild game.

Berlin was destroyed. I was walking about—the houses were all broken—and the street was full of rubble. Yes. And I would turn a street, and there was coming Russian airplanes with the splatter bombs— so close you could see the pilot with the helmet and the goggles. And this was very dangerous, because wherever you were standing the splatter bombs exploded into the earth. Pieces went everywhere. There was no escape.

And there was—on the corner—standing an air-raid shelter. And so I went inside. And I was sitting there maybe half an hour.

And I could hear the bombs, and the old building was shaking. And suddenly the door opened, and in came four SS officers. Infantry police. *Die Ketten-hunde.*°

And they were looking for boys and men and old men which were hiding, without weapons. And so they dragged me up to the police station. And I had to stand outside against the wall.

The SS men were standing four, maybe five meters away.

(*She becomes the SS Officer, and plays out the scene in real time.*)

SS OFFICER: (*doctrinaire*) All deserters shall be shot.
CHARLOTTE: And they wanted to shoot me. I looked down—I didn't want to see them shoot. I thought, I'll wait until I feel it. But when I looked to the ground I saw the boots of a commander.

(*Her gaze rises as she sizes up the Commander with both awe and dread.*)

And he looked at me.
SS COMMANDER: Are you a boy or a girl?
CHARLOTTE: And I thought, If they shoot me, what's the difference between a boy and a girl, because dead is dead!

(*She becomes a child and answers.*)

YOUNG LOTHAR: I am a boy.
SS COMMANDER: How old are you, then?
YOUNG LOTHAR: Sixteen.
CHARLOTTE: And he turned around to face the execution squad commander.
SS COMMANDER: (*with some measure of self-contempt*) We are not so far gone that we have to shoot school-children.
CHARLOTTE: And this was my salvation.

(*Charlotte lifts the needle off the wax roll and becomes Doug.*)

Listening

DOUG:
My dear Charlotte,
Enclosed please find two antique cylinders. Your favorite: John Philip Sousa. *El Capitan* and *Semper Fidelis.* They're Blue Amberols, so you should be able to play them on your Edison Standard.

I, meanwhile, am listening to our interview tapes every chance I get. On the treadmill. In the car. I've also started reading the works of Magnus Hirschfeld,° and studying German history since the time of Wilhelm II. Still, all I can think about is the story of your life.

Möchten Sie ein paar Spritzekuchen?: Would you like a little coffee cake?

Kettenhunde: Watchdogs. **Magnus Hirschfeld:** (1868–1935) German physician and sexologist.

(Then, with feeling):

> You are teaching me a history I never knew I had. Thank you.

(a pause)

Tape Seven. January 26, 1993.
CHARLOTTE: *Heute habe ich einen Spitznamen für dich.°*
DOUG: A nickname? For me?
CHARLOTTE: "Thomas Alva Edison."

(Charlotte smiles inscrutably, then sits.)

> You have a talking machine, too, yes? Only his was made of tinfoil with a tiny stylus, and yours . . . yours is a . . .

(She leans in to read the inscription on Doug's tape recorder.)

> . . . "Sony Microcassette Recorder with voice activation and automatic playback." Hmm.
DOUG: *(grinning)* Charlotte's boyhood. Continued from previous tape.

(Charlotte begins to speak.)

Vaterland°

CHARLOTTE: When I was a baby and then a little child—
DOUG: Can I interrupt you for a moment, and play that back? I'm not sure—the batteries—
CHARLOTTE: Hmm. Yes, of course.

(Doug futzes with the tape recorder.)

TAPE RECORDING: *(the voice of Charlotte)* "When I was a baby and then a little child—"
DOUG: We're good. Go ahead.
CHARLOTTE: My father was a Nazi.

(Doug reacts.)

> And he was brutal. And he was for militarism. And the years of marriage for my mother were a moratorium. My mother, she wanted to *sich scheiden lassen.* Get a divorce. And my aunt said one day to me:
TANTE LUISE: If your father beats your mother once more, she could die.
CHARLOTTE: And it was luck for us that in 1943 in Berlin the government decreed the evacuation of mothers with children, because of the air raids. And so my mother took the children to East Prussia, to the house of my aunt. And at that time we became good friends. Because my aunt was a lesbian, and I was the same.
> And one day I was cleaning the furniture, and I looked through the window and it was snowing, and there was coming in the snow a man with a hat and a

bag and I became horribly scared because I realized this was my father.
> And my aunt and my father had a very heart discussion. And my aunt said:
TANTE LUISE: Your wife really wants a divorce from you.
CHARLOTTE: And suddenly my father pulled out a revolver, and pointed it at my aunt. And he said:
HERR BERFELDE: One more word and I'll shoot you.
CHARLOTTE: But my aunt took her revolver from the desk and said:
TANTE LUISE: I'll count to three, and then you better be out the door! Otherwise, *I'll* shoot.
CHARLOTTE: And she said:
TANTE LUISE: . . . *three!*
CHARLOTTE: *Und die Kugel durchschlug das Holz und blieb in der gegenüberliegenden Tür stecken*—the bullet went through one door and into the next, where it lodged, and my father returned to Berlin. And then I asked my aunt, and she said:
TANTE LUISE: Yes, of course. It's a shame I didn't kill him.
CHARLOTTE: Then, on the twenty-sixth of January 1945, my mother got a letter saying the government was taking over our house for Berliners who had lost their homes in the bombing. And so I went with the train to Berlin because I had to rearrange the furniture. To make room for the refugees.

(Charlotte seats herself at the table of antique models; it now suggests the house of her childhood, rendered in miniature. The scene seems to play out—doll-sized—in front of her.)

> And so I was coming into our house, and my father was living there, of course. And one evening, maybe it was the second or third day. No. I think it was a week—it was in the first week of February 1945—and one evening my father said to me:
HERR BERFELDE: This is the hour I ask you, Are you for me or your mother? Do you stand beside her or me?
CHARLOTTE: I was fifteen years old. And I asked him, "Aren't you ashamed of the way you've treated my mother?" And he said:
HERR BERFELDE: I'll shoot you down like a dog, and then I'll go to East Prussia and shoot your mother and your sister and your brother.
CHARLOTTE: And I thought of the words of my aunt. And I knew that my father would do this.
> He locked me in the bedroom by turning the key. Because it was war, I could hear the Allied bombs coming in the night. And then under the bed I saw a large wooden utensil used to mix cake—*wie sagt man°*—a rolling pin. And I thought, I can take this as a weapon.
> I wanted to sneak out the door, but it was tightly locked. But even then I had in my pocket . . . keys. So I very carefully opened the door, and I was going in the next room.

Heute habe ich einen Spitznamen für dich: Today I have a nickname for you.   **Vaterland:** Fatherland.

wie sagt man: How do you say.

It was very dark, except for a little moonlight which was shining. And I saw my father. He was lying on the sofa in the dining room, and his gun lay on the chair next to him. And I saw the chair. I saw the pistol. And, in that moment, the clock—we had a Westminster clock—and the clock was chiming, and I saw my father's hand; he was reaching for his weapon. And in this moment I began beating him.

(*She says with sudden ferocity*):

Eins! Zwei! Drei! Vier! Fünf!°

(*A pause. She dissociates herself for a moment, becoming oddly contemplative.*)

Hmm. *Yes.*

And the next day the Criminal Police came. And they asked me for the motive. And I told them. And when I was arrested they brought me before the Youth Justice. And I was sentenced to the Youth Prison in Tegel. Four years' detention. And when they took me to the jail my mother was there. And we looked at each other in the eyes, and we knew that we were finally free from the monster.

(*Charlotte bolts up from the table and becomes Doug, frantically scribing a letter.*)

Auf Deutsch

DOUG: Oh, John!
I'm in way over my head. To kill: "*töten, tötete, hat getötet.*" Christ, this language doesn't make any sense.
I'm still winding my way through *Die Transvestiten.* Sigh. In some sentences I can barely discern the verb. And the vocabulary I'm learning is…well…so *specific.* Yesterday in German class I made an ass of myself. The teacher told us to make "small talk." I froze, couldn't remember a single phrase. So I blurted out a few new words I'd translated the night before: "*Hi, ich bin Doug, und ich trage schwarze spitzenunterwäsche.*" "Hi, my name's Doug, and I'm wearing black lace panties!"
The whole class just stared at me. Except for this one guy named Morris, who offered to take me shopping. Maybe I should try reading something else?
Love,
Doug

(*Once again, Doug readies an interview tape for Charlotte.*)

Durch Die Luft

DOUG: Tape Nine. March 5, 1993.

(*Doug practices a few innocuous lines of German.*)

Eins! . . . Fünf!: One, two, three, four, five.

"*Guten Abend*, Charlotte. *Und wie geht es* Dir *heute? Wie geht es* Ihnen *heute?*"°

(*He appears at Charlotte's door. He greets Charlotte in her native tongue.*)

Guten Abend, Charlotte.
CHARLOTTE: *Guten Abend.*
DOUG: *Ich habe Deutsch gelernt, um Dein phantastisches Leben besser zu verstehen.*°
CHARLOTTE: Excuse me?
DOUG: *Jetzt sollen wir Deutsch sprechen, ja?*°
CHARLOTTE: You are learning to speak German?
DOUG: *Ein bisschen, ja. Ich habe mit Berlitz studiert.*°
CHARLOTTE: You speak German. Me, English. I wear your clothes, and you wear mine.
DOUG: *Als das Ende des Kriegs kam, waren Sie noch im Gefängnis?*°
CHARLOTTE: The Youth Penitentiary at Tegel? *Nein.* A miracle allowed me to escape, yes? I was serving my sentence, sitting on a cot brushing my hair with an old ivory comb from *meine* Tante. And I heard a guard cry in the hallway:
PRISON GUARD: The Russians! They're flying over our roof!
CHARLOTTE: And it was true! Soon the bombs began to fall! The walls, they toppled down like sand castles in the tide. And the guard cried, "Run!" And so I picked up my blanket and my alarm clock, and I ran. I ran. I ran. Through the iron gates. Past the ruins of the old Jewish synagogue. And I saw on the street the large Russian tanks. And behind the tanks were coming horses with painted wagons. The Allies were coming to Berlin. And then there came a coach with the officers! Decorated. Yes, yes. Russian soldiers, and they were giving loaves of bread to the people!
And it was spring! And the birds were singing in the trees! And it was an awful war.

Eine Spende

(*A telephone rings: short, European tones. It rings again. And again.*)

ANSWERING MACHINE: (*the voice of John*) "*Sie haben die Wohnung von John Marks erreicht. Bitte hinterlassen Sie eine Nachricht nach dem Pfeifton.*"°
DOUG: Are you there? Hello? Anybody home?

(*a protracted beep*)

DOUG: …Christ, pick up, pick up, pick up…

(*John picks up.*)

Guten . . . heute?: Good evening. How are you today? **Ich…verstehen:** I am learning German so as to better understand your fantastic life. **Jetzt . . . ja?:** Now we can speak German. **Ein . . . studiert:** A little, yes. I studied with Berlitz. **Als . . . Gefängnis:** When the war ended were you in prison? **Sie . . . Pfeifton:** You have reached John Marks. Please leave a message after the beep.

JOHN: (*groggy*) Huh?

DOUG: John?

JOHN: Doug?

DOUG: Listen, I've run out of grant money, so I'm canceling my May trip. But all is not lost—I've decided to sell my car.

JOHN: You ever heard of time zones? It's four fucking a.m.

DOUG: It's an '86 Honda Civic, and I think I can get about three thousand dollars for it. That should finance at least a month overseas, maybe more—

JOHN: Whoa, whoa, whoa. You're gonna *sell your car?* Don't you think you're going a little loopy?

DOUG: (*a burst of frustration*) John!...(*impassioned*) Don't you see? She doesn't run a museum, she is one! The rarest artifact she has isn't a grandfather clock or a Biedermeier tallboy. It's her. (*in slow, measured tones*) So, please. If I come in June, can I still crash on your floor?

(*A pause, and then Doug speaks into his recorder, triumphant.*)

Tape Fifteen. June 20, 1993.

(*Charlotte smiles enigmatically, and gestures for Doug to follow.*)

CHARLOTTE: Careful—you must watch the stairs. Today you follow me at your own risk. I show you *das Geheimnis*—the secret—of *meinem Gründerzeit Museum.*

(*Doug obliges.*)

DOUG: (*into tape*) Charlotte's disappearing down a series of steps; I guess I'm supposed to go down after her. Christ, it's steep. Now we're in the basement, I think, of the house. It's dark. She's lighting a gas lamp.

(*Doug looks about the room in wonder.*)

Holy shit. It's huge. Old-fashioned, rough-hewn tables on wrought-iron stands. Cane-back chairs. There's an enormous bar, made of oak, stocked high with glasses, liquors, and—it's porcelain, I can't quite tell, but it might be an ancient beer pump.

Mulack-Ritze

CHARLOTTE: Welcome to *die Mulack-Ritze.* An old tavern from the yesterday.

DOUG: The walls are mottled and old. Signs everywhere. There's one, written in thin script on yellowed paper:

CHARLOTTE: "Prostitution Is Strictly Forbidden! At Least, According to the Police."

DOUG: On a placard in bold type:

CHARLOTTE: "*Tanzen ist Verboten.*" Dancing is forbidden. But we had this old phonograph—*mit einem Blumentrichter*°—and we would dance in the back, *ja?*

---

mit einem Blumentrichter: With a flower horn.

A long time ago, this old bar was sitting in the barn district of Berlin on Mulackstrasse, number fifteen. From the time of the Emperor Wilhelm II, it was a restaurant for gays and lesbians. The owners wanted homosexuals because they didn't get drunk, they didn't fight, and they always had money to pay for the bill.

At this very table *haben* Bertolt Brecht, Marlene Dietrich, the sexologist Magnus Hirschfeld, *und* the actress Henny Porten *alle gesessen, ja?*° This table, he is over one hundred years old. If I could, I would take an old gramophone needle and run it along the surface of the wood. To hear the music of the voices. All that was said.

Minna Mahlich, she was the barmaid, *ja?* And in 1963 she came to me and she said:

MINNA MAHLICH: The *Kommunisten,* they want to close us down. *Unsere Geschichte ist dekadent, ja?*° Our history is decadent. We have only one day. And then the bulldozers.

CHARLOTTE: And I thought, That is not good.

So I bought this furniture—I paid a little bit of money—and I bought it for this museum here. Everything—every glass—is original, *ja?* I took it all with me here for safety and I hid it in *meinem Keller.* And the next day the Russians came, and the old bar on Mulackstrasse, they broke it down.

And then came the wall. And for us here in Eastern Berlin it was finished, gay life. The bars, closed. Personal advertisements in the newspaper, canceled. No place to meet but the tramway stations and the public toilets. We were not supposed to exist. *Persona non grata.*

So I thought to give homosexual women and men community in this house. Yes. It was a museum for all people, but I thought, Why not for homosexuals?

So we met here—in *die Mulack-Ritze*—on the Sunday afternoons. And sometimes in front of the crowd Minna would run a finger along the bar, and when it came up black with dust, she'd cry:

MINNA MAHLICH: Charlotte, you pig! You haven't cleaned!

CHARLOTTE: And I'd tell the visitors, "This is a historic moment! This is Minna Mahlich, the last owner of the Mulack-Ritze." And the people would all clap and laugh.

And there was over the bar an attic. When a boy or girl met a man, and wanted to go upstairs, they could. Two men, two girls, a boy and a girl—it didn't matter. And they'd go into this room. A divan, a sofa, a chaise longue, a bed. A screen separated each space. Every piece of furniture was always in use. A pair in every free seat!

And anyone with an interest in sadomasochism, whether it was two or four or six, could have the room to themselves for a few hours. Whips and things to beat on the behind.

---

alle gesessen, ja?: All had sat (at the table).   **Unsere . . . ja?:** Our history is decadent, right?

And the Stasi—the Communist secret police, the most feared government spies of all the world—was coming, and they were looking in the windows, and they were saying, What's this?" So what could I do? I painted all the windows black.

(*Doug speaks reverently—in hushed tones—into his own recorder.*)

DOUG: When the wall falls, Charlotte tells me—she had the only surviving Weimar cabaret in all of Eastern Germany. Hidden in the basement of her house in Mahlsdorf. Which she ran—under the watchful eye of the Stasi—for almost thirty years.

(*Suddenly, a blast of pompous music. The Minister of Cultural Affairs approaches the podium to make a speech.*)

Bundesverdienstkreuz°

CULTURAL MINISTER: On behalf of the Cultural Ministry of the *Bundesrepublik Deutschland*, it gives me great joy and honor, in recognition of your astonishing efforts at conservation, your steadfast preservation of a noted period in German industrial design—

(*Charlotte intercedes, to ensure that he says it correctly.*)

CHARLOTTE: *Die Gründerzeit.*
CULTURAL MINISTER: (*utterly charmed by Charlotte*)— *die Gründerzeit*, and your timely rescue of the Mulack-Ritze, to offer you membership in the high order of the *Bundesrepublik Deutschland* and deliver unto you the Medal of Honor—a cross upon a ribbon.

(*The music amps, followed by thunderous applause and cheers. Charlotte curtsies. The sound fades.*)

CHARLOTTE: The day I received the medal was for me recognition of my work, and I thought—*wie soll ich sagen*—° I thought, It's good, because other people see that a transvestite can work. A transvestite becomes such a medal!
    If other people—heterosexual people—they look at the television, and they read the newspapers and they say, "Ah! He or she is able to work, *ja.*"
JOHN: They presented the award on national German television. Aw, Doug, I wish you could've been there. Picture of an elderly man, in a skirt and a string of pearls. Nobody laughed. No catcalls. And, at the end of the ceremony, the Cultural Minister himself even leaned down to kiss her hand.

Berlin From Behind

DOUG: (*to Charlotte*) Charlotte, what was it like? To visit the West after the wall came down?

Bundesverdienstkreuz: Federal distinguished service medal. **wie soll ich sagen:** How shall I say.

(*A sudden blast of music; it's cheesy German disco, a song called "Super Paradise."*

Charlotte smooths the creases in her skirt and plucks a small guidebook called Berlin von Hinten° from the table. A few well-placed steps across the stage, and she has crossed the border into Western Berlin.

She reaches a particular address, and admires the facade of an imagined building. She consults her guidebook, and reads aloud.*)

CHARLOTTE: "Café Anal. The crowd is gay and lesbian, leftist punks and muesli freaks. Sunday night is two-for-one beer blast. Other events include gay slide shows about South America, karaoke, and drag-queen bingo!"

(*Charlotte raises an eyebrow, then moves on, dancing ever so slightly to the throbbing beat.*)

    "Buddy's Bar. The dignified ambience of black leather is enhanced with hot music and stimulating porn videos, and a young boy can usually be persuaded to give a little show."

(*Charlotte folds down the corner of the page; this pub is definitely worth remembering.*

A final stop on her whirlwind tour.*)

    "Prinz Eisenherz Buchladen. This gay bookstore stocks everything ever written by homophiles, nancies, pansies, sissies, trannies, sodomites, Sapphists, fruitcakes, homos, faggots, lezzies, dykes, queens, queers, gender-benders, and friends of Dorothy."

(*Charlotte balks.*)

CHARLOTTE: (*muttering to herself*) I don't know what that means . . .

(*The music stops. Doug asks, in measured tones*):

DOUG: Now, Charlotte, I heard in the seventies the Stasi came to you, and offered to treat you very well if you would give the names and addresses of the people who frequented your museum. I heard they actually promised you a car. Is that right?

I, Lothar Berfelde

(*Charlotte's demeanor changes; she speaks cautiously.*)

CHARLOTTE: Yes. And one day they came, and one of the two men said to me:
STASI OFFICIAL: You have to sit down. Take a paper and a pencil, and I will dictate to you the following . . .
CHARLOTTE: (*suspiciously*) And I thought, What's that?
DOUG: (*with certainty*) So you didn't do it?

Berlin von Hinten: Berlin from Behind.

The award-winning set designed by Derek McLane for the 2003–2004 Broadway production of *I Am My Own Wife*.

Jefferson Mays in the 2003–2004 Broadway production of *I Am My Own Wife*, directed by Moisés Kaufman.

Bradley Greenwald in the 2006 Jungle Theatre production of *I Am My Own Wife*, directed by Joel Sass.

CHARLOTTE: (*indignant*) He wanted me to write exactly what he said!

DOUG: (*with apprehension*) And what was the text you were expected to write?

(*Charlotte picks up a slip of paper from the table; she reads haltingly.*)

CHARLOTTE: "I, Lothar Berfelde, commit myself willingly and freely to working together with the Ministry for State Security. I will report all information which may have the character of an action inimical to the state."

(*She pauses. It's difficult to continue, but she manages.*)

"I will be known by the code name Park. I pledge to keep this secret even from my nearest friends and relatives."

(*Another pause. She thinks of her mother. Of her siblings. Then—staunchly—to Doug, the end of the pledge.*)

"I have been informed that if I break this oath I will be prosecuted according to the laws of the GDR."

DOUG: (*hoping against hope*) And you had to sign it?

CHARLOTTE: (*quietly, definitively*) I signed it.

(*Tension fills the room.*)

And I said to myself, "I'll still do whatever I want." *Ich mache doch was ich will.*

DOUG: And then they left.

CHARLOTTE: *Ja, ja.*

(*Another pause. Charlotte turns cagey.*)

Meine Tante Luise always said, "Be as smart as the snakes; it's in the Bible." She said, "Never forget that you are living in the lion's den. Sometimes, you must howl with the wolves."

(*John bounds out of Charlotte's chair.*)

Bated Breath

JOHN: Doug. Listen up. (*beat*) The German press got its hands on Charlotte's Stasi file. She was an informant, all right. For four years, in the mid-seventies. It says she was "willing." Even "enthusiastic." And that museum of hers? It was a drop-off point for secret packages and documents of interest to the Stasi. Charlotte reported on illegal antiques dealings. It even says she was responsible for an arrest. A fellow collector. A friend.

The tabloids are having a field day. I've enclosed a few clippings.

(*Doug sifts through them, finding each new headline more incredible than the last.*)

DOUG: "Charlotte von Mahlsdorf, Sexual Outlaw and Soviet Spy?" (*beat*) "Mata Hari Was a Man: The Real

Story of Berlin's Most Notorious Transvestite." (*beat*) "Comrade Charlotte: Is the Disguise She's Wearing More Than Just a Dress?" (*beat*) John? I'll get back to Berlin just as soon as I can.

(*Once again — from the phonograph — the mesmerizing lilt of a German waltz. Charlotte dances — a quiet little reverie — all to herself.*)

Horns

CHARLOTTE: Even when I was a little child, no one wanted phonographs. Everyone said to me, "It's so old-fashioned!" They all wanted radios. But what did I want with a radio? To hear Hitler babble? No, thank you! That is the reason that, even today, I don't have a radio or a television.

For me, gramophones, Polyphones, Pianolas — I must truly say — these machines gave me so much pleasure in my childhood. If I hadn't had them, I'm not sure I would've survived. Things were so ghastly with my father — everything my mother and I went through.

But the music would pour through the horn and make things better.

(*And it carries her away, into some distant corner of her own mind.*)

ACT TWO

(*In the darkness, the rollicking sound of an old Pianola. Unexpectedly, it ends with the loud slam of a prison door.*

Lights rise on Alfred Kirschner, lying on the floor of his prison cell, striated by light. He looks a bit like a cockroach that's been flipped on its back, helplessly.

Alfred's prison uniform hangs on his thin bones like sails on a mast. His glasses are thick, distorting his eyes. His cap is woolen and patched. He has a caustic wit. Slowly, he rises to a sitting position and addresses Charlotte as if she were the audience.)

A Letter from Prison

ALFRED:
The 17th of April, 1972.

Dear Charlotte,
I was dining at lunch, a scrumptious vegetable stew with mashed potatoes —

(*He bellows down the prison corridor to some unseen cook*):

Truly exquisite!

(*Then he turns back to Charlotte and resumes.*)

— when your note arrived. Today's the day I put aside to answer letters, and I thought, Well, if I don't get any mail today I'll just stop writing altogether. Then I'll die, lost and forgotten by the world. So it came in the nick of time. You urged me, "Don't give up! You're not forgotten! You never had hordes of friends, but so what? You always gave a little joy to people, and that's enough." What sweet sentiments, Charlotte. For your sake, I won't give up, and I'll live patiently for the day I'll be set free.

At night, I wrap myself in blankets. I still have headaches and dizzy spells, but I don't think it's the fault of prison conditions. I think it's just age. I've gone so blind I can barely read. I just wander from one doctor to the next. They zap you with electricity, record it on paper and — voilà — an electrocardiogram. The dentist here is a real dictator. He plans to pull another one of my teeth. By the time you get this letter, I'll probably be nothing but gums. Alfred sans teeth is not a pretty sight!

(*Alfred curls his lips over his gums to appear toothless, and grimaces to illustrate his point.*)

Please give your family my warm regards. Tell them I'm still the same old Alfred —

(*To a prison guard, somewhere in the darkness*):

— and I won't be beaten down!

(*Again, back to Charlotte.*)

When I'm released, I know exactly what I'll do. I'll play my favorite old waltz on the piano. Strauss, probably. Then I'll put "Frühlingskinder"° on the Polyphone and play that, too.
With a calliopic and symphonic farewell,
Your Alfred

(*Alfred removes his glasses and becomes Doug. Doug stares at the glasses, considering them for a moment.*)

Erasure

DOUG:
Charlotte,
I'm afraid — for me — your Stasi file is an exercise in frustration.

(*Doug rests the glasses upside down on a nearby sideboard. As he speaks, he pulls off Alfred's beret. Beneath it is Charlotte's black kerchief.*)

I've noticed repeated references to a fellow antiques collector; sometimes they use the word *Kunsthändler*. Other times, *Sammler*.° But whenever his actual name appears, it's been blacked out. I turn the pages over, I hold them up to the light, and still I can't make it out.

Frühlingskinder: "Children of Spring Waltz," by Richard Strauss.
Kunsthändler . . . Sammler: Art dealer, collector.

(*Doug unbuttons Alfred's shirt to reveal Charlotte's blouse and pearls. He lowers Alfred's trousers, and under them is Charlotte's pleated black skirt.*)

> "Today, the informant Park had tea with BLANK. Park received a birthday card from BLANK. At 2:30 p.m. in the afternoon, Park telephoned BLANK."

(*Doug now stands in Charlotte's signature garb. He puts Alfred's clothes in the sideboard.*)

> I suspect BLANK was important to you. Otherwise, why would he merit inclusion in your file? Please. Shed light, if you can.

(*Delicately, Charlotte turns Alfred's old glasses upright; he seems to stare out at her from a shelf on the sideboard. She considers him for a moment, fondly.*)

Mythology

CHARLOTTE: I still have his birth certificate. Alfred Kirschner, born on the first of September, 1911.

> We became friends because it was a rainy day. I was walking through the streets of Berlin, and I saw an antiquity shop. I had no money to buy old things, I only wanted to stay dry. As I strolled through the stock, I glanced around the corner, and I saw Alfred. He was looking at a Polyphone.

(*She turns to Alfred, adopting both roles.*)

> Do you own such a machine?

ALFRED: Of course. I'm a collector. I've been a collector since my childhood.

CHARLOTTE: I am a collector since my childhood, too!

ALFRED: Back at my house . . . just two or three blocks from here . . . I have about fifteen thousand records.

CHARLOTTE: (*flirtatiously*) Touché! I only have twelve thousand.

ALFRED: And where do you live?

CHARLOTTE: (*flouncing her skirts ever so slightly*) In Mahlsdorf. Across from the pig farm. Near the paper factory.

(*She turns to us.*)

> With that, Alfred bought a few music boxes.

ALFRED: The weather is so awful today; why not pay me a visit in Mulackstrasse? Mahlsdorf's a long way in this maelstrom.

CHARLOTTE: (*with recognition and delight*) Mulackstrasse? That's where you live?

ALFRED: What about it?

CHARLOTTE: Remember the old pub, the Mulack-Ritze? Now it's in my museum!

ALFRED: (*with a hint of seduction*) I've heard of your museum, and of you — but now I'm meeting you in the flesh . . .

CHARLOTTE: And so off we went to his apartment. He made some *Kaffee mit Schlag und Kuchen*.° And we

Kaffee . . . Kuchen: Coffee with heavy cream and cakes.

played a large Polyphone. And it wasn't long before he said:

ALFRED: Look in my private room.

CHARLOTTE: And I did. And there were records everywhere. Whole shelves. He had Caruso records. Comedians, dance orchestras, jazz, opera. Polyphones, gramophones, phonographs, juke boxes, symphonions, Pianolas, Spieldosen, orchestrions, Echophones, calliopes, Victrolas, Edison Standards, Amberols, paper rolls, hurdy-gurdies, organettes. Clocks, too. Wall clocks, mantel clocks, grandfather clocks, regulators by Lenzkirch and Gustav Becker, cuckoo clocks, alarm clocks, chronometers, and pocket watches. A breastplate from the Middle Ages. Of course, everybody knew that Alfred was homosexual. Later, I'd visit his house. Sometimes homosexual men were standing before his door, like prostitutes.

(*A young man idles at Alfred's stoop, insolently smoking a rolled cigarette.*)

YOUNG HOMOSEXUAL MAN: You can't ring Alfred now. He has one man or two men with him. Just wait till he's ready, when he's done with his sexuality.

CHARLOTTE: No! I just came to swap gramophone records.

YOUNG HOMOSEXUAL MAN: Oh, you're a transvestite!

CHARLOTTE: And how they cackled until Alfred opened the door to let me in.

(*Charlotte steps into a focused pool of light, adopting the role of narrator in the upcoming tale.*)

> One day Alfred bought a clock from a local antiques dealer. He was headed home down Mulackstrasse, and he noticed that a motor car was following him. And in this motor car there were two army soldiers from the American base. One of the soldiers rolled down the car window:

(*The American Soldier has a decidedly Midwestern accent.*)

AMERICAN SOLDIER: Hey, can we buy that clock off you?

ALFRED: Not this one; it's mine.

AMERICAN SOLDIER: My mom said I couldn't come home without a clock. One of those Black Forest jobs. Man, that'd look sweet back in Terre Haute.

ALFRED: I do have other clocks I'm willing to sell.

AMERICAN SOLDIER: Oh, yeah?

CHARLOTTE: And the soldiers trooped into Mulackstrasse, into his apartment, where he had nine or ten regulators for sale.

ALFRED: (*to the two soldiers*) Take your pick.

AMERICAN SOLDIER: Beautiful. We'll take two.

CHARLOTTE: At that time — in the seventies — people thought gaudy old standing clocks were just old-fashioned junk. Kitsch. In Berlin, you could pick up a grandfather clock for, maybe, fifty marks. Very cheap!

AMERICAN SOLDIER: Shit, Sergeant Matheson paid twice that on the Ku'Damm.

(*Charlotte does a double take at the Soldier, a bit taken aback at his interruption. He cowers apologetically. She continues with her tale.*)

CHARLOTTE: Anyway. Not long after that, Alfred came to me with a proposition.

ALFRED: (*the wheeler-dealer*) People are always giving you clocks as gifts. Half the time, you don't want them. They're early twentieth century, and that's too modern for your museum—

CHARLOTTE: Alfred... what are you suggesting?...

ALFRED: I've got a friend named Edward. He's got an automobile. We can drive to Pankow, to the woods near Weissensee, with the clocks in tow.

CHARLOTTE: (*intrigued in spite of herself*) Yes?

ALFRED: We'll sell a bundle, right out of the back of the car.

CHARLOTTE: Sure enough, the American soldiers came, and they looked into the back of Edward's car.

AMERICAN SOLDIER: These are damn nice.

ALFRED: Why not buy them all, as souvenirs? To send back home. How many have I got here? Nine, ten, eleven...

AMERICAN SOLDIER: Hell, our car isn't big enough. (*the glorious dawning of an idea*) We'll come next week with a little bus.

CHARLOTTE: So we met them again the following week.

AMERICAN SOLDIER: Hey. We're back. (*sotto voce, to his buddy*) See, I told you—*one of these dudes wears a dress.*

CHARLOTTE: Into the bus they put one, two, three, four clocks. And they're prepared to drive across the border, back into Western Berlin.

CUSTOMS OFFICIAL: *Halten Sie, bitte.*

AMERICAN SOLDIER: They can't stop us... we're Americans, man.

CUSTOMS OFFICIAL: *Wir müssen diesen Autobus inspizieren.*°

AMERICAN SOLDIER: (*to the Customs Official*) Sure, no prob. (*to his fellow soldier*) Hey, Dave. It's friggin' Customs. They want to, like, case our bus... You crazy? You tell 'em no. I'm not telling 'em no. Just... holy shit... *just get out of the goddamn bus.* Come on, man, it's not worth it. They're fuckin' *cuckoo clocks*, for chrissakes.

(*Charlotte takes over the narrative again.*)

CHARLOTTE: And they detained the soldiers for six, seven hours. And the border agents wrote down the number of their bus. And the Stasi started keeping a list of all our little sales. And the next time the bus came to meet us they followed it with an automobile of their own. Some months later, Alfred heard a knock on his door.

STASI AGENT: We have reason to believe that you're engaging in illegal sales, with foreign military personnel. We hope—for your sake—we have made a grave error in judgment.

CHARLOTTE: Alfred came back to me. Naturally, I expected him to mend his ways.

ALFRED: (*incorrigible as ever*) Lottchen, I've an idea. Why don't we sell the clocks out of your basement instead of the car?

CHARLOTTE: But Alfred—

ALFRED: There's no other place in all of Eastern Berlin quite so secret.

CHARLOTTE: So Alfred brought the clocks around to my place, and we stashed them here. Right here, in this basement corridor, there were five, six, seven clocks. Standing in the darkness, like sentinels, *ja?*

(*The stage is plunged into near-darkness, except for a small light illuminating Charlotte. We hear the ticking of an enormous clock.*)

And then at midnight:

ALFRED: Lottchen! Open the door! We're in terrible danger.

CHARLOTTE: What now?

ALFRED: They followed us. The Stasi came to my apartment. They tore through my desk, they found Western currency. Tomorrow they're coming to see you!

CHARLOTTE: What can I do, hmm? I'll bolt the door.

ALFRED: Save yourself, Lottchen. Renounce me.

CHARLOTTE: Don't be ridiculous.

ALFRED: Tell them the clocks are mine.

CHARLOTTE: I could never!

ALFRED: Why should we both go to prison?

CHARLOTTE: I won't say such a thing—I *can't!*

ALFRED: They'll force their way into your house. They'll go traipsing into the basement, into the bar. They'll confiscate your Polyphones and your Pianolas—they'll take your sideboard and your *Vertiko*...

CHARLOTTE: *Quatsch! Du bist zu dramatisch!*°

ALFRED: Listen to me! They'll auction off your entire collection, and all to fill their own fat coffers.

CHARLOTTE: *Das ist nicht möglich. Das können sie nicht tun.*°

ALFRED: Your museum will be finished. Through.

(*The ear-piercing gong of a clock striking midnight. Charlotte stands, framed by the accusatory white glow of Stasi searchlights.*)

CHARLOTTE: So when the Stasi came...

(*She sits. A light shines on her from above, like an interrogation. Her voice cracks and her eyes well with tears.*)

"Yes, I have a colleague. Sometimes he sells clocks to American soldiers. For a little extra money, ja? No. I will not write down his name. His address?

Wir ... inspizieren: We need to search this bus.

Quatsch ... dramatisch: Nonsense! You're overdramatizing.
Das ... tun: That's not possible. They can't do that.

Certainly not. You must not ask me to take up paper and pen. That I will not do."

(*A pause. Charlotte relents.*)

"I will say it. I will whisper it only."

(*The light softens, and Charlotte resumes the tale.*)

And they arrested him.

(*The brutal slam of a prison door. Again, the harsh lines of prison light. Alfred pens another note behind bars.*)

ALFRED:
My dear Charlotte,
    I've been in jail for one week now. When the Stasi discovered that I was a homosexual, they feared I might be labeled a mental defective, and exempt from a trial. But at the institution Herr Doktor Kreinholz...may God damn him forever...he said I was perfectly sane. And so I was thrown to the dogs.
    You know they perform a strip search when you're being admitted to prison. Needless to say with me, they got a big surprise.

CHARLOTTE: (*reading the letter*) Mein Gott!

(*She's amused in spite of herself, and imparts the contents to us with a tiny grin.*)

    They found a cock ring around Alfred's penis and his nuts. They couldn't get it off, because he had such big private parts. So they sent him to the hospital in the prison to see if they could remove it, but even they couldn't get it off. And finally a metal specialist came, and he slid a piece of metal between Alfred's ring and his sex organs, and then he sawed it off.

ALFRED: What a sad parting, I told the doctor. I've been wearing that sweet little band of steel for over ten years!

CHARLOTTE: I visited Alfred Kirschner in jail. I had on my red coat with the flared skirt, and my hair was quite long.

(*She rises to enter the visitation area and is stopped by an Official.*)

PRISON OFFICIAL: Who are you, and who do you intend to visit today?

CHARLOTTE: I am the wife of Alfred Kirschner, of course.

(*He admits her, and she sits before Alfred. She smiles at him fondly, pressing her hand against the glass that separates them, hoping to impart some small measure of hope.*

Alfred slinks back in his chair, dejected.)

ALFRED: My cell is too damn cold...my rheumatism. My knees are brittle, like porcelain.

CHARLOTTE: I've brought you some warm clothes.

ALFRED: Have you heard from Edward? Or Minna Mahlich?

CHARLOTTE: They're all afraid. "Guilt by association." They don't want the Stasi investigating their lives, too.

(*Charlotte returns to us to finish the story.*)

    Originally, I intended to burn all of Alfred's letters. I was always afraid if the Stasi searched my house they would find them and ask, "Why do you keep the correspondence of a criminal?" See, the first letter is crinkled. But I rescued it from the wastepaper basket. Because one day I felt I'd be able to tell the truth. And today is that time.
    Here...written in his own hand, on the back of *eine Speisekarte*...a menu from an old restaurant...

ALFRED: (*as though it were a love letter*) This is my last will and testament. In the case of my death, I give my entire collection of clocks, records, cylinders, and everything else in my possession to Lothar Berfelde, also known as Charlotte von Mahlsdorf. Affectionately, Alfred Kirschner.

CHARLOTTE: While he was incarcerated, his home was broken into and the Stasi impounded everything that he owned. Just like the Nazis during the deportation of Jewish people, they took all his things.

(*She turns in a slow circle, as if gazing upon the ravaged apartment for the first time.*)

    He was left with only his bed. It was awful. After his release from jail, I went to the church in Weissensee and I found Alfred a place in their nursing home.

(*Once again, she tries to appear optimistic.*)

    One day, Alfred, you'll have your own flat again.

ALFRED: (*bitterly, with contempt*) No. Never again. I don't want to collect anything anymore.

CHARLOTTE: One night the telephone rang. It was *eine Krankenschwester*. A nurse on the line.

NURSE: You must come at once. Alfred died tonight.

CHARLOTTE: It's true, he left me everything. All in this small folder. Here's an old bill from the electric company, one he couldn't pay. Here's a picture of Alfred with an Electrola gramophone. Ah! Yes! An old postage stamp, from East Prussia.

(*She picks Alfred's glasses up off the sideboard and contemplates them a final time.*)

    Alfred was more intelligent than I.

(*She slides open a drawer and—delicately—places the glasses inside, shutting it gently. A burial.*)

    Still, that's all he had left—scraps of paper, yes?

Aktenvermerk°

(*John strides forward, commandeering the scene from Charlotte.*)

JOHN: Now, Doug, that's one helluva story. That midnight visit? Alfred's heroic offer to take the fall on her

---

Aktenvermerk: A note of respect.

behalf? *He begs her to sing like a bird?* It's like some Cold War thriller written by Armistead Maupin.° Trouble is, it doesn't scan with the facts in her file. Charlotte was already in deep with the Stasi and had been for at least a year. You think Alfred knew that? Just listen to this:

(*A Stasi Agent appears in a pool of light. He boasts about Charlotte to his superior officer.*)

STASI AGENT: We asked the informant — code name "Park" — if he could gather evidence about the suspect Alfred Kirschner. He assured us that he had Herr Kirschner's absolute trust, and could elicit information without arousing his suspicion.

For the past five months, Park has duly recounted conversations with Herr Kirschner directly to us. He has reported Herr Kirschner's illegal transactions with American soldiers. He has confirmed that Herr Kirschner was routinely offered Western currency in exchange for illicit goods.

Customs officials successfully arrested Alfred Kirschner in the first week of August 1971. We have, of course, granted Park full immunity. He may even merit a promotion.

(*The Agent disappears. Doug turns to John in protest.*)

DOUG: John! We can't go looking to the Stasi file for facts. Those agents had quotas to fill, supervisors to impress. Reports were doctored all the time! One entry contradicts the next.

(*The same Stasi Agent reappears. This time he makes profuse apologies to the same superior officer.*)

STASI AGENT: Unfortunately, the informant Park is poorly suited for covert operations. He is too easily distracted by old furniture. His manner of dress is willfully bizarre. His penmanship is so slow, so painstaking — so full of curlicues and frippery — that it's futile to ask for written reports. We are reduced to taking dictation. After forty-eight months of service, mountains of paperwork, and numerous visits to the Gründerzeit Museum, he has yielded nothing useful. And so we have decided to terminate our association.

A Convenient Lapse

DOUG: I went back to Mahlsdorf, file in hand.

(*Doug musters the courage to confront Charlotte.*)

Charlotte, I know this is difficult. And I know I'm an American, from thousands of miles away... I didn't even really know what the Cold War *was* until it ended... so I've no right to sit in judgment. But about Alfred Kirschner... his arrest...

Armistead Maupin: (b. 1944) Gay writer best known for *Tales of the City*, set in San Francisco.

(*Charlotte delicately straightens her pearls.*)

CHARLOTTE: Hmm. Yes. Of course.

(*Wafting through the air, the sound of Alfred's old music boxes.*)

Here is an old sweater I made for Alfred when he was in prison. And the buttons — the brass buttons — are from the coat of my granduncle, when he served under the Kaiser himself.

DOUG: That's not... my question was —

CHARLOTTE: These hands have laid mortar and brick; they have carved walnut. But for Alfred they learned to knit.

DOUG: But, Charlotte, I —

CHARLOTTE: (*beat*) It is beautiful, yes?

(*Charlotte seems lost in her own private, hermetically sealed world of denial.*

Suddenly, the driving beat of broadcast news music. A square of light — like a television screen — appears, and the German News Anchor steps into it. He double-checks the feed in his ear, then launches into the evening telecast.)

The Cross

GERMAN NEWS ANCHOR: Should Charlotte von Mahlsdorf be required to relinquish the Medal of Honor? That question is on the minds of Germans everywhere today as news of Charlotte's Stasi involvement continues to dominate headlines. Conservative politician Markus Kaufmann:

(*Markus Kaufmann leans forward toward an invisible microphone.*)

MARKUS KAUFMANN: It's terrible. It's a tragedy. If anyone suffered because of her cooperation... if a human price was paid... then of course she should be stripped of the medal. It's a civic honor, not a badge of shame.

GERMAN NEWS ANCHOR: Humboldt University student Ulrike Liptsch:

(*Ulrike plays with the tips of her long blond hair, then tosses it back over her shoulder. Although she's a serious student of political science, she will one day become a supermodel.*)

ULRIKE LIPTSCH: My friends and I, we think it's stupid. To take away the medal. We shouldn't even look at Charlotte's Stasi files; we should just burn them. One out of every three citizens was working as an informant. Finger-pointing is pointless; it doesn't unify, it only tears people apart.

GERMAN NEWS ANCHOR: Outspoken former political dissident Josef Rüdiger:

(*Josef is a bitter man, with the deep-seated anger that comes from unspeakable suffering.*)

JOSEF RÜDIGER: I spent two years at the Stasi prison in Bautzen. They dislocated my shoulders from my sockets; they forced a catheter up my urinary tract and filled it with alcohol. And still I uttered no one's name but my own. (*beat*) Complicity in this country should always be treated as a criminal act. Hasn't the twentieth century taught us that much?

GERMAN NEWS ANCHOR: The President's office said the prestigious medal had been revoked only once before, when a previous recipient revealed he'd formerly been a member of the SS.

The Three M's

(*Charlotte turns to face her Accusers and says with severity*):

CHARLOTTE: (*to Marcus Kaufman*) Museum. (*to Ulrike Liptsch*) Möbel. (*to Josef Rüdiger*) Männer.

(*She turns to the audience—all smiles again—to translate.*)

Museum. Furniture. Men.

(*Then back to the unseen chorus of critics in a spirited, vehement defense.*)

This is the order in which I have lived my life.

(*Charlotte again enlists the audience as her confidant and friend, telling it another of her many tales.*)

One day I had an appointment to visit a clockmaker in Kopenick. And on the way I saw a man. And he said, "*Fräulein, nicht so stolz!*" Lady, not so proud! So I smiled. And I was wearing my leather shorts, and he said to me, "You have such a nice backside. A nice ass for whipping."

And I thought, Yes. And he asked me to go inside the public tramway station, to the toilets. But only a few shops away there was . . . waiting for me . . . *eine alte Standuhr* . . . a standing clock . . . made of oak, with a perfect mechanism from the last century. And to be late for a clockmaker is *unhöflich*. Too impolite.

(*Finally, she turns back to her detractors, emphatic once more.*)

For me, there was no choice.

(*A blast of Euro-pop, and sensationalist, hip talk-show host Ziggy Fluss seizes the stage.*)

Celebrity

ZIGGY FLUSS: Good evening, Deutschland, and welcome to the Ziggy Fluss show. I'm Ziggy Fluss. Among tonight's special guests . . . the tiny *Grossmutter°* with the great big secret . . . Germany's most controversial

Grossmutter: Grandmother.

transvestite . . . Berlin's own Trannie Granny, Charlotte von Mahlsdorf!

(*Applause. Charlotte enters, caught like a doe in headlights. Hesitantly, she approaches her assigned seat, next to Ziggy.*)

Good evening, Charlotte!

CHARLOTTE: *Guten Abend.*

ZIGGY FLUSS: You're used to the red-hot glare of studio lights, aren't you, Charlotte? You've been on the news, you've done the talk-show circuit.

CHARLOTTE: Yes.

ZIGGY FLUSS: But you still don't own a television, correct?

CHARLOTTE: *Nein.* If I want to look at myself, I look in the mirror, *ja?*

ZIGGY FLUSS: *Wunderschön, wunderschön. Eine gute Antwort!°*

(*laughter and applause*)

Tell me, are the rumors true? Have you really decided to move to Sweden?

CHARLOTTE: I was in Stockholm on a tour for my book—*meine Selbstbiographie°*—and the people, they have been very kind to me.

ZIGGY FLUSS: What about your furniture, eh? All those Gründerzeit goodies. Any plans to open a new museum in Scandinavia?

CHARLOTTE: Yes, of course. An old friend of mine heard I was leaving town. She said to me, "You can't transplant an old tree." I told her, "I am not a tree. I am a flower. And I always carry my flowerpot with me."

(*The studio audience loves it; she's so damned enchanting.*)

ZIGGY FLUSS: But Berlin's the city that made you a star! How can you leave her behind?

CHARLOTTE: I'm afraid that there is too much violence here.

ZIGGY FLUSS: And not just on television, am I right?

CHARLOTTE: A short time after I became the *Bundesverdienstkreuz,* we had a garden party in my museum. Almost *achthundert* people, *ja?* We played Donna Summer on the hi-fi, and everyone was dancing and singing under paper lanterns. And I heard a window smash in my basement. A rock. The Brown plague had come back again. *Kristallnacht°* once more.

ZIGGY FLUSS: Sure, I read about it. Front page of *Die Morgenpost.* Your museum was vandalized, correct?

CHARLOTTE: The neo-Nazis knew I was a homosexual. They came over the wall—thirty of them—with flare guns and gas pistols. The gays were all cowards, running inside, but the lesbians stayed to fight. And my friend Sylvia, she was in the cellar, trying to shut

Wunderschön . . . Antwort: Wonderful, wonderful, a good answer. **meine Selbstbiographie:** My autobiography. **Kristallnacht:** The night of broken glass, November 9 and 10, 1938, when the Nazi Brownshirts smashed Jewish storefronts and beat Jews throughout Germany and parts of Austria.

the door, and she got a gas pistol in the eye. Her retina was damaged. A young girl from Frankfurt an der Oder almost died. They cracked open her cranium with an iron stick.

(*Ziggy Fluss swallows. His lightweight show has taken a very sudden, very grave turn.*)

ZIGGY FLUSS: Holy Christ.

(*Charlotte—deep in the story now—rises from her chair, reliving the attack.*)

CHARLOTTE: And I was coming from the cellar with an old pickax, and a skinhead met me on the stair. He had a swastika tattooed on his arm, yes?

FIRST NEO-NAZI: Hitler forgot to shove you in an oven in Sachsenhausen!

CHARLOTTE: And I swung and hit the blade in the old banister, splitting it open like a sapling, *ja*? And from behind me, another *laut* voice.

SECOND NEO-NAZI: We should drown you in the Ostsee!

CHARLOTTE: And there was a second, *mit einem Schlagholz*; a club. And I said, "I have met you before! When I was sixteen years old!"

And then *die Polizei* came. And the young men scattered. Like *die Asche*, after a fire. No one was arrested. No one went to jail.

(*A pause. Charlotte takes her seat again.*

Even the pathologically upbeat Ziggy is momentarily wiped out by the raw power of her story.)

ZIGGY FLUSS: (*under his breath*) Wow. *Autsch! Die Brutalität. Solche Brutalität.*

CHARLOTTE: My old Victrola, it was smashed. Broken bottles. Electric wires on the ground.

ZIGGY FLUSS: Young people today. It's bad, isn't it? They're hurting, they're disillusioned. They've been promised so much, especially in the East. Reunification. Now they feel they've been had.

CHARLOTTE: It's no excuse.

ZIGGY FLUSS: (*chastened*) No, you can't make excuses, can you?

CHARLOTTE: *Nein. Niemals.*

In Solingen, Turkish women getting burned out of their homes. Asylum seekers from Yugoslavia being beaten on the streets. Anti-Semitism has come back. So has homophobia. Every day, new threats.

ZIGGY FLUSS: Keep talking, Charlotte, and I'll move, too! Ibiza, or maybe Mykonos, right?

(*A quick spasm of laughter from the studio; Ziggy silences it with a look. He has a hard-hitting question to ask now.*)

Now, Charlotte . . . you know Ziggy has to ask. Your flight from Berlin happens to coincide with recent, widely published news reports about your Stasi involvement. Some of your critics suggest that you'd rather skip town than face the prospect of a tarnished reputation here at home.

CHARLOTTE: Hmm. Yes. Of course.

(*Charlotte smiles sweetly and answers in careful, deliberate tones.*)

In Mahlsdorf, my museum had twenty-three rooms. In Porla-Brunn, I will have only eight. But that is good for a woman my age, yes? Not so much furniture to dust.

(*She looks searchingly at the audience for the same warm smiles—the same compassion—her wonderful anecdotes always engender. It's hard to tell . . . has she won her listeners over yet again? Or is she being met by stony silence?*

Quietly, compassionately—almost apologetically— Ziggy places a hand on her knee.)

ZIGGY FLUSS: *Fantastisch*, Charlotte, *wirklich Fantastisch*. You'll come back and visit us again, won't you?

CHARLOTTE: *Danke schön.*

ZIGGY FLUSS: We'll be back after a short break, with American singing sensation David Hasselhoff.

Editorials: A Phantasmagoria

(*As Charlotte makes a beeline for her waiting limousine, she's beset by reporters.*)

BRIGITTE KLENSCH: (*chasing after Charlotte*) Excuse me, Frau von Mahlsdorf. Brigitte Klensch, journalist, Berlin. You say you murdered your father. Has anyone inquired after his death certificate? Court records from your trial?

CHARLOTTE: Pardon me, please. *Mein Auto*—the driver, he is waiting.

BRIGITTE KLENSCH: To date, I've found nothing to confirm your claims.

CHARLOTTE: (*evasively*) In the war, such records, they were lost, yes? Flying through the air like burning leaves . . .

KARL HENNING: Charlotte! Karl Henning, from Munich. Isn't it true that the Stasi hired you to appraise furniture?

CHARLOTTE: I remember 1945 like it was only yesterday, but if you ask me, "What did you have for breakfast?" I don't know!

KARL HENNING: According to records we've obtained, you valued furnishings torn from the homes of dissidents, of political prisoners, of the wronged and the oppressed.

CHARLOTTE: You are from the West, yes? Did the Stasi ever come to your door? Tell me, I ask you!

FRANÇOIS GARNIER: François Garnier, Paris. Did the Stasi really pay you in contraband?

CHARLOTTE: I took nothing!

FRANÇOIS GARNIER: Not even an inkwell, a cigarette box for your museum?

CHARLOTTE: (*vehemently*) As a mother would take an orphan child, yes?

SHIRLEY BLACKER: (*very Brooklyn*) Shirley Blacker, New York City. Why do you suppose the public accepted your story with so little scrutiny?

CHARLOTTE: Please! I am old—so old—*I am tired*...

DAISUKE YAMAGISHI: Daisuke Yamagishi, Tokyo. Is it true your family considers you a public embarrassment? That even your own brother refutes your claims?

MARK FINLEY: (*gay activist*) Mark Finley, San Francisco. We—as homosexuals—have been systematically denied our own history. Our own past. Perhaps that's why we're so eager to embrace a martyr, even when she's made of glass?

PRADEEP GUPTA: Pradeep Gupta, Bombay. Is it true that you're really a woman after all?

CLIVE TWIMBLEY: (*a heated East Ender*) Clive Twimbley, London. Did you know that the very man responsible for your medal recently told this newspaper—and I quote—"Whenever Charlotte von Mahlsdorf opens her mouth to yawn, she's already begun to lie."

(*Charlotte pauses, stunned, more accustomed to adoration than to such vicious censure. She turns to the throng, and says with quiet intensity, as a balm to soothe herself*):

CHARLOTTE: When I was almost forty years old, my mother was doing the laundry, yes? Hanging my stockings and my garters on the line. And she turned to me, and she said, "Lottchen, it's all very well to play dress-up. But now you've grown into a man. When will you marry?"

(*She raises her eyes to look at them, each in turn.*)

And I said to her, "Never, my dear Mutti. *Ich bin meine eigene Frau.* I am my own wife."

(*A Psychiatrist steps forward to "settle" the matter with science.*)

Diagnosis

DIETER JORGENSEN: Dieter Jorgensen, psychiatrist, Bonn. Berlin's most notorious transvestite is neither a raconteur nor Machiavellian; she is, in fact, mentally ill. Charlotte von Mahlsdorf suffers from autism. Listen to the manner in which she recounts her stories: in a highly ritualized, cadenced way, less to communicate content than to provide a kind of rhythmic reassurance to the chaos in her psyche. This is true of autistic adults; repetition is a palliative. Her stories aren't lies per se; they're self-medication.

Abdication

(*We join Doug in the middle of an impassioned, climactic argument with John Marks.*)

DOUG: So, at the end of the day, what have I got? A shoebox full of scratchy audiotapes. A used copy of *Die Transvestiten*. Enormous personal bias. Not to mention, my German *sucks*.

JOHN: I say, you go with what's in plain, old-fashioned black and white. The press reports, the file—

DOUG: But I need to believe in her stories as much as she does! I need to believe that—a long time ago, in an attic—a generous aunt handed her confused nephew a book and a blessing. That a little boy—*in his mother's housecoat*—survived *storm troopers*. That Lothar Berfelde navigated a path between the two most repressive regimes the Western world has ever known—the *Nazis* and the *Communists*—in a pair of heels. I need to believe that things like that are true. That they can happen in the world.

JOHN: So, what're you gonna do?

DOUG: I don't have a clue. I'm curating her now, and I don't have the faintest idea what to edit and what to preserve.

(*Suddenly, from the recesses of the past, an idea. A memory of something said.*)

Tape Eight. March 4, 1993.

(*Doug turns to Charlotte to proffer a query.*)

Charlotte, what do you do when a piece loses its luster? Are you ever tempted to strip the wood or replace the veneer?

On Curating

CHARLOTTE: I did not refinish the pieces. No. *Diese alte Anrichte?*° The polish is as old as the object itself. It is antique, too.

(*Charlotte approaches the miniature museum; she takes out the large, velvet-lined box. She picks up the tiny Vertiko.*)

Nicks and cuts. Stains. Cracks.

(*She places it tenderly in the box. Next, a tiny sideboard.*)

A missing balustrade, a broken spindle. These things, they are proof of its history. And so you must leave it.

(*She places it snugly in the box, too. Then the small sofa; the doll-size chair.*)

The furniture in my museum is more than one century old. People sat on it, slept on it, wrote letters on it, ate from it.

(*She tucks away the kitchen contraption.*)

People tried to burn it. In Nazi times. In Stasi times.

(*The bust of Kaiser Wilhelm II. The regulator.*)

And still, it is standing. It was not only decoration. It was used.

(*Doug passes a diminutive phonograph to her.*)

Diese alte Anrichte: This old sideboard.

DOUG: Does a piece ever get so old—so damaged—that you throw it away?

(*She takes it from him and places it in the box, too.*)

CHARLOTTE: *Nein*. You must save everything. And you must show it—*auf Englisch*, we say—"as is."

(*She closes the lid with finality.*)

It is a record, yes? Of living. Of lives.

(*Charlotte removes her kerchief and becomes Doug. As he speaks, Doug unclasps Charlotte's pearls from around his neck.*

He places them gently on top of the furniture box.)

DOUG: Charlotte von Mahlsdorf did, in fact, move to Sweden, where she lived for almost seven years. But in April of 2002 she decided to take a holiday, to fly back to Berlin—a homecoming of sorts. While visiting her beloved Gründerzeit Museum, she suffered a heart attack. Alone in a garden of gramophone horns, she died. A few days after her funeral, an envelope arrived in my mailbox; I recognized her familiar script. But no letter. Instead, she'd enclosed a single photograph, sepia with age. In it she's a child. A boy. Lothar Berfelde, at ten years old.

Between Two Lions

(*Doug crosses to the center of the room, entering a pool of light.*)

He's at the zoo in Berlin. He's wearing a sailor suit, with a blue collar and matching cuffs. His ears are sticking out at an angle; he's got a very adorable smile. He's on a bench.

Sitting on either side of him, two lions. Cubs, sure, but they're still as big as he is. And they're not fond of posing, either. Their eyes are dangerously alert. At any moment, they might revolt; they might scratch or bite.

(*He says with awe*):

But Lothar has one arm around each lion, and they're resting their forepaws on his knees.

(*Doug walks over to the phonograph and places the needle on the wax cylinder.*

Through its horn, the sound of an original, taped interview with Charlotte Von Mahlsdorf, made in 1993 on a scratchy microcassette.

The sound quality is poor, but the words are intelligible.)

TAPE RECORDING: (*the voice of Doug*) Tape Four with Charlotte von Mahlsdorf, February 2nd, 1993. I'm on the way to Mahlsdorf to meet with her now.

(*A soft click as the tape recorder is turned off, then on again.*)

TAPE RECORDING: (*the voice of Charlotte*) Now this is the first room of the museum. And this here is a little phonograph, and on this record you see a picture of Thomas Alva Edison. And he was the inventor of the first talking machine of the world, in July of 1877. And the record is made by the National Phonograph Company in Orange, New Jersey.

(*On the recording, we hear Charlotte place the needle on the Edison wax roll. The needle idles a moment, then we hear the tinny, glorious sound of an old-fashioned waltz.*

Doug stands, listening.

Fade out.)

COMMENTARY

Doug Wright (b. 1964)
PORTRAIT OF AN ENIGMA   2003

Doug Wright details the steps he took from his first hearing about Charlotte von Mahlsdorf to his anticipation of the play opening on Broadway. He gives us a full picture of the stages of composition and collaboration with Moisés Kaufman and Jefferson Mays, beginning with Sundance and moving on to the Playwrights Horizons opening. Rarely do we get such a clear sense of the development of a play as we have here.

October, 1994. I have scoured my bathtub to a pristine white; my pencils have all been sharpened to lethal points. I have ground the coffee for the coming week, alphabetized my CD collection, and ironed my underwear. My loose change has been sorted and wrapped. I have sifted the cat litter, and answered phone calls dating back six months or more. I have no more excuses. It is time to write.

To ensure the speedy arrival of the Muse, I've erected a small shrine atop my desk. A toy Trabant, the notorious East German automobile, squats in front of me like a paperweight. A scrappy ceramic terrier, his ear cocked in perpetual alert, crouches next to my telephone. On the boom box near my computer, the great cabaret singer Hildegard Knef is belting out "*In Dieser Stadt.*" My German dictionary lies at my side. Lining my bookshelves are pocket guides to Berlin, the short stories of Christopher Isherwood, dog-eared catalogs from a place called the *Gründerzeit* Museum, and encyclopedic volumes dedicated to antique furniture and daily life in the Third Reich. Yellowed postcards are tacked to the wall, and at my feet a tattered clump of paper; it's a Xerox copy of a Secret Police file. A framed portrait of my subject peers down from the wall, ready to bless and curse me as I mold her life into a play. With these artfully arranged knickknacks, I'm desperately trying to will inspiration into the room.

Still, no words come. My fingers hover, unmoving, over the keys.

Hours pass. Then years.

Back in the summer of 1992, my dear childhood friend John Marks alerted me to an astonishing subject for a play. At the time, he was bureau chief for *U.S. News and World Report* in Berlin, and—in the media's thirst for human interest stories following the fall of the wall—he had stumbled across a true eccentric in the local news: an elderly East German transvestite who lived in a rural suburb called Mahlsdorf about forty minutes outside the city.

Charlotte von Mahlsdorf, John told me, had lived openly as a cross-dresser under the twentieth century's two most conformist regimes—the Nazis and the Communists—for almost her entire life. Born Lothar Berfelde in 1928, she had long considered herself a member of the "third sex": a female spirit trapped in a male body. Hence her preference for female pronouns even before it became the politically correct mode of address for the transgendered. In addition to her sartorial quirks, Charlotte was a compulsive collector, a hoarder of history. In her mammoth stone mansion she housed a one-of-a-kind museum of curios, antiques, and bric-a-brac from the late nineteenth century. Perhaps most astonishingly, hidden in her basement, Charlotte had preserved the only surviving Weimar cabaret in all of Eastern Germany—an old tavern from the *Scheunenviertel°* known as *The Mulack-Ritze.* For this effort she received the *Bundesverdienstkreuz,* or Order of Merit, from the Cultural Ministry following reunification.

As John recounted her story, I was mesmerized. I'd long held a casual interest in gay history, and Charlotte seemed like a veritable treasure trove. There are only a handful of books about gay life in Germany during the Second World War, and even fewer about the plight of the homosexual under Communism. Charlotte's story, I reasoned, might help to fill in the considerable blanks. Furthermore, her quiet heroism—maintaining an unwavering sense of herself during such repressive times—could be a boon to gay men and women everywhere. In an age where politicians still routinely decry homosexuality on the evening news and "fag" remains the most stinging of all playground epithets, Charlotte's dogged insistence on her own sexuality could prove downright curative; an antidote for a community too often besieged by public condemnation and internalized self-loathing. She was a bona fide gay hero. If her life didn't merit two hours on a New York stage, I reasoned, whose would?

In a spasm of bravery I wrote Charlotte, asking her permission to visit. She granted it in a letter penned in baroque script on parchment paper. My first official trip was in January of 1993. Soon I was flying in and out of Tegel regularly. I'd take the rickety U-bahn ride out to Mahlsdorf with my cassette recorder in hand, my translator Jeffrey Schneider at my side, and a list of questions scrawled on a yellow legal pad. Each time I showed up at Charlotte's door, it would creak open, and she'd whisk us inside, down into the dusky basement where we'd sit in cane-backed chairs and talk into the wee hours of the morning. (Charlotte was a night owl and rarely wanted to conduct our interviews before at least 10 p.m.) With a jar of yogurt in her hand, she would spill anecdotes and memories into my squawk box in her cadenced, almost singsong voice.

Meanwhile, Charlotte's fame throughout Germany was skyrocketing. She was profiled in magazines, and a frequent guest on talk shows. (Once, she appeared on a tabloid program with a dwarf, in a show dedicated to "celebrating difference"!) She appeared in a documentary about her life by the maverick gay filmmaker Rosa von Praunheim and even wrote her autobiography. As her trust in me grew, Charlotte let me accompany her on lecture tours. We would travel to tiny East German hamlets like Luckenwalde, and I would sit with the recorder running as the most unlikely fans imaginable—pig farmers and rubber tire magnates, bourgeois housewives and children—treated her with the respect of a visiting dignitary, fawning over her appearance and complimenting her signature pearls. Charlotte was so sweetly self-effacing, so coyly feminine, and so full of modest charm that even the hardcore locals forgave the fact that she was hiding a man's body beneath her pleats. Back in the United States, I'd transcribe my audiotapes dutifully into my computer. Over a two-year period, I had amassed over five hundred pages of transcript. In my giddy naïveté, I presumed the play would pour forth with relative ease.

Scheunenviertel: Slums.

But then something happened. Something so deeply unsettling it would cause my writerly imagination to freeze and prevent me from jotting a single word.

Like so many citizens of the East German state, Charlotte had a Stasi file, the confidential and incendiary report kept by the East German Secret Police. The document sat locked in a filing cabinet at the vast gray complex of offices known as the Ministry for State Security. After the collapse of Communism, Charlotte was allowed to apply for a copy, but it often took months, even years, to receive it because of the enormous backlog of requests. Foreign researchers with academic or press credentials could obtain the files with comparative speed. In a heart-stopping gesture, Charlotte cut a deal with me. If I would petition for her file and obtain it quickly, then I could keep a copy of my own. Together, ours would be the first civilian eyes to peruse its contents. (Later, the German press would discover it and cause a firestorm.)

To this day, I'm not sure why she gave the papers to me so willingly; perhaps she was simply overeager and wanted them too hastily. Perhaps she mistrusted my translation skills and presumed I'd never be able to actually read the file, or maybe she doubted my ability to piece together its dense, bureaucratic content. Another possibility was that she was seeking some kind of absolution and I was her chosen confessor.

The document was incriminating. Reputedly, in order to preserve her museum and maintain her idiosyncratic lifestyle, Charlotte had been more complicit with the Communist authorities than I ever dreamed. My gay hero had been a Soviet-sponsored spy.

I wanted my play to be a paean to Charlotte, but she was proving to be a much more complicated figure than I had ever imagined. Worse still, she had become a cherished friend; I loved her like a grandmother and I worried that the very act of writing a play about her might be tantamount to betrayal. The file claimed that she had willingly served as an informant, but—if I included that revelation in my play—was I merely informing on her?

I was further inhibited by the prospect of writing because—in order to capture the full measure of Charlotte's life—the script would have to span the entire twentieth century. I was daunted, too, by the challenge of accurately depicting realms of oppression that were firmly outside my experience. Nazis! Communists! As a privileged, white, gay man from the ranch-style suburbs of Dallas, Texas, I couldn't claim any authority on subjects that enormous, that brutal. I'd barely made it through William L. Shirer's epic tome *The Rise and Fall of the Third Reich,* and I knew next to nothing about life at the Kremlin at the height of the Cold War. In the face of history so vast, I was an ill-informed pipsqueak, an intellectual rube.

And so I became paralyzed; unable to write a word, staring dumbly at my blank computer screen for six long years, souvenir curios strewn across my desk like so many impotent talismans. I'd complete other projects during that time—a play about the Marquis de Sade called *Quills* and its subsequent screenplay—but Charlotte was relegated to the bottom drawer.

Finally—in the spring of 2000—the dam burst. I was at a writer's retreat in Ucross, Wyoming; nothing but vast sky, cattle, and time to scribe. The retreat's artistic director, Robert Blacker, and I were engrossed in conversation over chocolate chip cookies and milk. I was feebly defending my writer's block. "I just can't do it, Robert," I moaned. "I can't write this play. My subject exceeds me."

Robert exploded. "You're right!" he cried. "You have absolutely no authority—moral or academic—to write about twentieth-century Europe! No credibility whatsoever!" He sat back in his chair, his eyes penetrating mine. "You're an authority on one subject, and one subject alone: *your ongoing obsession with a remarkable character.*"

I felt a chill along my spine.

"Your passion for her, your disillusionment—it has all the makings of a romance," he continued. "Whatever you do, don't write a play about history. Write a play about your love affair with Charlotte von Mahlsdorf. If you're lucky, the requisite history will take care of itself."

It was the most liberating gift a fellow artist could give: permission to write my own story. For the first time, the play's structure dawned on me. It wouldn't be a straightforward biographical drama; it would chart my own relationship with my heroine. I would even appear as a character, a kind of detective searching for Charlotte's true self.

At first, the notion appalled me: depicting myself onstage? It felt like the most flagrant act of narcissism a writer could commit. Furthermore, I was a playwright, not a memoirist; I hid my true self behind invented characters far more colorful and articulate than I. Nevertheless, the thematic possibilities seemed rich; if Charlotte were a curator of nineteenth-century antiquities, I would present myself in the play as a curator of her. The whole piece could be a rumination on the preservation of history: Who records it and why? What drives its documentation? Is it objective truth, or the personal motive of the historian? When past events are ambiguous, should the historian strive to posit definitive answers or leave uncertainty intact? The only way to pose these questions was through my own inclusion as a character. And if I were going to be presumptuous enough to parlay Charlotte's life as drama, how could I be bashful about my own? It would be hypocrisy of the most cowardly sort.

Enthused for the first time in years, I began to flip through my notes, and certain leitmotifs popped off the paper: Edison Amberols, my ever-growing stack of microcassettes, Charlotte's sepia photographs and aged diaries. Wasn't the whole play—at its core—about the process of recording?

I went back to my taped interviews with Charlotte and listened to them with renewed vigor. To my refreshed ear, her broken English suddenly constituted a remarkable kind of poetry. For example, a word in German for "to receive" is *bekommen*. In the past tense, Charlotte would say, "*Ich bekam diese Möbel*" or "I received this furniture." But when she translated that from German to English, she would say, "I became this furniture." How beautiful and true! I realized her own malaprop-ridden syntax was far better than any language I could invent on her behalf. I decided to compose the play largely from the interviews themselves.

Immediately, I felt a surge of guilt. I'd be hijacking a technique that the renowned director Moisés Kaufman had perfected with his play *The Laramie Project*. I'd known Moisés for years; we'd spent time together at countless theater festivals across the country. How dare I appropriate his methodology! Then I thought, "My God, he's one of your dearest friends. Just ask the master to join you in the process."

That summer I was invited to work on the piece at the Sundance Theater Lab in Utah and I called Moisés, proposing that he direct. The story appealed to him immediately, because it possessed the two traits I think he relishes most: (1) a wildly compelling narrative, and (2) true sociological import. "Darling!" he exclaimed in his lilting Venezuelan accent, "a play about a transvestite; how theatrical!"

At the Lab—with my newfound director in tow to advise me—I could finally start fashioning a script. In addition, Sundance was willing to provide me with a cast of actors who could perform scenes as soon as the pages slid forth from the laser printer.

This induced another massive attack of guilt. Actors are expensive, especially for the workshop of an unwritten play. They have to be transported, housed, and fed, and they're a notoriously hungry lot. And the characters who populated Charlotte's life were legion; how many people would I need? The cast was potentially huge! "Just one actor to start," I told myself. "Someone to play Charlotte herself. Until the play truly locates its shape, it seems presumptuous to ask for more."

Instinctively, I rang up Jefferson Mays. He had appeared in the original production of my play *Quills* at the New York Theatre Workshop in the role of the priest, and gave a fearless, shockingly inventive performance. He was only too happy to leave a sweltering New York in July for the cool mountains of the Wild West, and soon the three of us—Moisés, Jefferson, and I—were on an airplane, headed for a month of immersion in all things Charlotte, my transcripts wedged in the overhead bin, and her Stasi file safely stowed under the seat in front of me.

A tiny cabin by a gurgling stream was our rehearsal hall. On the first day we convened, Moisés decided to employ some techniques he'd evolved with the Tectonic Theater Company. He asked me to pick out a few highlights from my voluminous notebooks—a favorite anecdote or a particularly telling interview exchange. I dutifully did so—a story about Charlotte's first dress, and another about her favorite gramophone—and I passed the pages to Jefferson. He started to read aloud.

At first, it was unnerving. With his startling gift for mimicry, he was transporting me back to Mahlsdorf, all the way to that notorious basement bar. Charlotte was thousands of miles away, but it felt as if she were truly in the room with us. In addition to Charlotte, Jefferson began to imitate other voices on the tape: my translator, even me.

I suddenly realized that I didn't need a bigger cast. In a play about a character that has to adopt a variety of guises in order to survive, it made sense to let one actor play all the roles. Furthermore, I loved the idea that Jefferson would inevitably be costumed in Charlotte's customary black dress and pearls, so every other character he played would, by default, also be wearing a little black dress. In our production, transvestism would be the norm, not the exception. Everyone from the callow playwright (me) to the fiercest Nazi officer would wear a skirt. How very democratic! Now I knew conclusively that *I Am My Own Wife* would be a one-woman show, performed by a man.

After a few days of scouring transcripts, I became dispirited again. A play is, after all, more than a series of interview exchanges: question, answer, question, answer, question, answer. Our work was feeling stagnant. Moisés knew he had to do something to break down the incapacitating wall I'd built between myself and my chosen subject. So he decided some lighthearted theatrical game-playing might do just the trick. He gave us all homework: that evening, we had to create small, two-minute sketches inspired by the transcripts we'd read.

The next day, like school children at show-and-tell, we performed our pieces for each other. Moisés went first. He draped a dress over a metal folding chair, and then, without uttering a word, very slowly—with the titillating deliberation of a striptease artist—he doffed his clothes. He stood in the breezy mountain air in nothing but boxer shorts and a mischievous gleam in his eye. Then, with incalculable grace, he slid one arm into the gown, then the next. In full, feminine glory, he smoothed his skirt, and smiled a smile of sheer transcendence. In some nether region between masculinity and femininity, he seemed to locate his true self. That was his presentation.

Next, I stood up and announced the title of my performance piece: "Charlotte Goes West." I cracked open a popular gay German guidebook called *Berlin von Hinten* (*Berlin from Behind*) and read descriptions of the various clubs and bars Charlotte had visited in those fateful weeks after the wall crumbled: a dive called Café Anal, with a papier-mâché waterfall and late-night drag shows; a bordello called Kumpelnest, boasting a clientele ranging from "post-punk to love-hungry gays!" Even a sauna called the Steam Club, famous for the adjustable air-jet nozzles in its Jacuzzi. With a satisfied blush, I sat down.

Jefferson performed last. With deceptive simplicity, he placed a shoe box on the table in the center of the room. Then, with an impish grin, he opened it, and plucked out a stunning homemade gramophone rendered in perfect miniature. He set it on the table. Next, he pulled out a tiny couch with felt cushions, then a grandfather clock. He'd stayed up into the wee hours, and crafted paper reproductions of Charlotte's beloved museum furniture, using shirt cardboard and a razor from his toiletry kit. Soon an entire room was arrayed before us like a dollhouse. My sense of theatrical possibility exploded, and I suddenly saw countless new ways of dramatizing my existing text. For the first time, the play started unspooling gloriously in my head.

I left Sundance with the show's first act, which dealt primarily with Charlotte's life during World War II. I'd been able to successfully avoid grappling with all the troubling information in her Stasi file. With palpable foreboding, I knew that material would have to figure prominently in the second act.

The following summer, Jefferson and I traveled to the La Jolla Playhouse near San Diego to further workshop the play; Moisés, who was directing a movie for HBO, was unable to join us.

As I sat under palm fronds in Southern California, poring over my smudged Xerox of Charlotte's file, I began to fret. When press reports had finally surfaced in Germany in 1997 about Charlotte's Stasi cooperation, they'd caused a furor. At the time, readers of her autobiography felt betrayed; why hadn't she disclosed the information in her own book? Gay men and women who had placed her on a pedestal were outraged; perhaps she wasn't such an effective poster girl, after all. And the general citizenry certainly didn't look too kindly on complicity. I feared that—if I included the detailed information contained in her file—my play might stoke the fires of outrage against her. Did I want to bear culpability for that?

Yet in my heart I knew that, despite my intentions to enshrine Charlotte, the Stasi file was a dramatist's goldmine. It made for a better play. To omit its content would render my central character benign: precious Trannie Granny, rescuing wartime artifacts, running her covert museum, and providing a role model for homosexuals everywhere. That's a character more suited to public relations than the rigors of drama. Dramatic heroines require dimension, the requisite character flaw that renders them human. I urgently needed to include Charlotte's duplicity; it was the price she paid for living the unequivocal, unapologetic life of a transvestite. To suggest she accomplished something so bold without compromise was to minimize the achievement itself. True iconoclasm always comes at a price.

I renewed my research, scouring German periodicals and Web sites. Much to my relief, I soon learned that many of my dramaturgical fears had been outpaced by history and popular opinion. During the reunification process, the press learned that countless citizens had functioned as informants; it was almost commonplace.

In the effort to reunify, the German people had no choice; they had to collectively forgive minor collaborators. The stigma, while still present, was markedly lessened. Animosity toward Charlotte had waned in the four years following those stinging newspaper reports, and—at long last—I felt permission to freely examine her own Stasi past. I could present Charlotte with all her haunting, vexing complexities intact and not damn her in the process.

Jefferson and I worked feverishly, and by the end of July 2001, I'd roughly shaped the entire play. Moisés took two days off filming to come and see a performance of our work so far. "Why, Douglas," he beamed, "I think you're onto something."

The three of us continued to travel across the country from theater to theater, honing the text in a series of workshops. At the Wilma Theater in Philadelphia, Jefferson performed the whole play with nothing but a music stand. At the About Face Theater Company in Chicago, we built an entire set, only to impulsively tear down three of its walls in a frenzy of inspiration. At the New York Theatre Workshop in Manhattan's East Village, the first act flew by, but the second sagged. Performance after performance, I would add new scenes and characters. (Some nights, Jefferson would have to fold three or four new accents into the show with nary a rehearsal.) Eventually—at our off-Broadway premiere at Playwrights Horizons—audiences confirmed our hunch; Charlotte von Mahlsdorf's life merited attention.

Unfortunately, Charlotte herself would never see a production. I had kept her apprised of the play's progress over the years, but regrettably she passed away in April of 2002. (When I got the news, I was thunderstruck. I had recently finalized plans to visit her at her new home in Sweden; the plane tickets were sitting in my bureau drawer. Instead, I'd find myself flying to Berlin for her memorial service.)

Further, though I was heartsick, there was a part of me that was also relieved. I'm often asked, "If she were still alive, what would she think of your script?" I can't answer for her. Nevertheless, I fervently hope—beneath the pages of transcript, the Stasi files, the old letters, and the newspaper articles that constitute the work—she'd see a love letter, peering out through all that paper.

As I write this, my slightly fictionalized Charlotte is preparing to make her Broadway debut. I have no idea how she'll fare in a venue that seems to favor Phantoms, smart-aleck puppets, and—lately—Mel Brooks. She doesn't have a chorus line or a knock-'em-dead eleven o'clock number—just a cunning smile and a few tantalizing secrets to share. I only pray she can cast the same enthralling spell over audiences at the Lyceum Theater as she did over me.

And that that spell will inspire others to continue excavating Charlotte's life. For although I dutifully set out to evoke the life of a real person, I have nevertheless taken the customary liberties of the dramatist. I have edited Charlotte's anecdotes for clarity; I have condensed several characters into one when it best served the drama of her story; I have created certain archetypal figures in the play, such as newspaper reporters, bureaucrats, and specialists; I have imagined certain scenes while wholly inventing others for narrative clarity and in pursuit of my own thematic purpose. While I hope the text does justice to the fundamental truths of Charlotte's singular life, it is not intended as definitive biography.

Hopefully, some day my play will be outdistanced by new revelations from scholars and critics far more expert than I, as it is my ardent wish that she move beyond the confines of the stage and into the pages of accredited history books.

Even at this late date, I'm still reluctant to call the play "finished." At the end of my long journey with Charlotte, I found she remained—at heart—an enigma. And how can you conclusively paint a portrait of that?

Conor McPherson

Conor McPherson, born in 1970, went through school without much success until he reached University College Dublin, where his interest in playwriting began to show in a number of plays, such as *Taking Stock* (1989), *Michelle Pfeiffer* (1990), and *Scenes Federal* (1991), which were produced locally. Because these were not developed into professional plays, McPherson got his master's degree in English and philosophy, and he worked as a university tutor in ethics and moral philosophy for some two years.

Still feeling the attraction of the stage, McPherson established a theater company with some friends in Dublin. The Fly by Night Theatre Company produced many of his plays in The International Bar in Dublin, a site that had hosted a number of other developing theater groups since 1980. In 1994 his plays *Rum and Vodka* and *The Good Thief* were performed at the City Arts Center in Dublin and attracted the attention of a larger audience. The alcoholism that suffuses *Rum and Vodka* also attracted the attention of critics, who interpreted the drinking and drunkenness that were central to many of his plays as a kind of trademark. These two plays exhibited another trademark quality of McPherson's work: the reliance on the monologue. McPherson's early plays were largely monologues, and even his very successful later plays were often a succession of monologues told by a succession of characters. McPherson has said that he is fascinated by people who can sit down and tell a story that completely entrances him. He has said, "I love it when somebody sits back and tells me story after story. . . . That's my favorite kind of relationship." As in the work of Brian Friel and some other Irish playwrights, the monologue has taken on a distinctive modern Irish tone that has sometimes irritated critics.

The Good Thief (1994), *This Lime Tree Bower* (1995), and *St. Nicholas* (1997) were performed not only in Dublin but also in New York, and all three are essentially monologues or sequences of monologues. The first of these plays involves a thug who ruminates on his chosen profession and begins to think he might shift gears despite the fact that he's got an assignment to rough up a fellow he hardly knows. *This Lime Tree Bower* is a succession of three monologues that includes an academic who has fallen far from grace. *St. Nicholas* is a sly dig at drama critics of the sort that everybody hates. The critic in this play falls into a den of vampires—also a sly bit of wit because *Dracula,* the epitome of vampire novels, is only one of many early Irish vampire tales.

The Weir (1997) was the play that brought McPherson great international recognition. It won the Olivier Prize for best play in London that year, although, despite a long run and excellent reviews, it did not win a Tony Award in New York. The play involves four men drinking at their favorite country pub, exchanging stories about the local scene. They are interrupted when a woman who has bought a local house enters, and they begin to tell her some ghost stories, as if hoping to scare her a bit. But the tables turn when she tells them a ghost story that trumps theirs! This play established McPherson's repu-tation and has been performed widely since its premier.

Interestingly, McPherson not only wrote about alcoholism but was himself a formidable drinker even while he was working on his early plays. In 2001 he collapsed on the opening night of a new play, *Port Authority,* suffering an attack of pancreatitis, a potentially fatal disorder. He came very close to dying at the age of 29, and that experience changed him entirely. He joined Alco-holics Anonymous and stopped drinking. He began to see the world in a differ-ent light and achieved the insights he needed to begin work on his next play, *Shining City* (2004), which also reads something like a ghost story. In it a busi-nessman, John, comes to see Ian, a psychotherapist who has just begun his practice, because John has been seeing the ghost of his wife, who died in an accident. In this play, McPherson abandons the monologue and develops a highly original type of dialogue marked by striking pauses that give a peculiar emphasis to everything that is said. The dialogue is ordinary in every way, except that it accretes significance and begins to build meaning out of what, on the surface, sounds almost commonplace. Other playwrights, such as Pinter, Mamet, and Albee, have also been complimented on their oblique dialogue, and McPherson is certainly comparable to them in this play.

McPherson's penchant for the supernatural continues in his most recent play, *The Seafarer* (2006), in which four men sit down to play poker and a Mr. Lockhart joins them, only to slowly reveal that he is none other than the devil. Mr. Lockhart is asked about heaven and hell, and he describes them in extraordinary detail in an extensive monologue that echoes some of the style of McPherson's earlier plays. McPherson is one of the most prolific of mod-ern playwrights—an international figure whose work is always eagerly an-ticipated by audiences in the United States and abroad.

SHINING CITY

Although there are never more than two people talking in any of the scenes of this play, one has the feeling that other "spirits" somewhere off stage are involved tangentially in the action. McPherson's dialogue, often oblique and sometimes repetitive—with his use of long pauses and silent, "understood" words indicated in the stage directions—sometimes resembles ordinary con-versation. Other times, it seems stylized and calculated to annoy the audience or alert it to pay attention. One needs to read the dialogue aloud to get an experience approaching that of attending a performance on stage. The fact that people talk around things, rarely coming out and saying what they mean, is made much more apparent by McPherson's unusual use of silence in the midst of emotionally loaded conversation.

The first scene with Ian (a priest who has recently lost his faith, left his order, and set himself up as a psychological counselor in Dublin) and John (a man whose wife has died in an automobile accident but continues to haunt him) begins innocently enough. But soon it develops into a complex expression of emotion on John's part that begins to reveal his sense of guilt. Meanwhile, Ian, the former priest, is faced with interpreting the appearance of a ghost, while being himself convinced that John's vision of Mari in her red coat has been a hallucination. Ian, once committed to the supernatural, now doubts. John himself knows only that he has seen his dead wife and cannot continue living in his house. His reaction is so strong and so definite that the audience begins to understand that his relationship with his wife was marked by loss and confusion, just as Ian's life is now.

When Neasa appears in scene 2, several things become clearer about Ian and his own emotional life. He tells Neasa that they need to separate, but he gives her no reasons. They have a child together, and slowly we realize that Neasa was instrumental in helping Ian work through the spiritual crisis that resulted in his leaving the church. Even though there is no absolute parallel between Ian's Neasa and John's wife, it is obvious that we are overhearing a conversation in scene 2 that is loaded with similar anxieties. Almost irrational forces are at work on each man, moving him to a position that even he does not fully understand. The entire question of human commitment becomes a central issue by the end of this scene.

When John returns in scene 3, his revelation of his infidelity comes slowly but helps us understand the level of anxiety he showed earlier in the play. In his long speech—almost a typical McPherson monologue—John talks about his feelings about his wife and about his life. He talks about what he expected life would be like when he was young and just starting out. His expectations were neither entirely clear nor in any way special, but he finds now that he had "been slightly left behind, a little bit, you know?" Things were dull and ordinary, and compared with friends who had children, as he and his wife Mari could not, John felt left behind. What he experienced was a general malaise until he met Vivien, a woman who excited him and sent him provocative text messages. When John and Vivien went to a hotel room, however, they could not make love: "It was just a huge mistake." Out of a sense of guilt, John bought Mari the red coat that she is wearing when he sees her ghost. The experience in the hotel room so unsettles him that he cannot go to work; he isolates himself, certain that something bad will happen "because there was some kind of evil in me." Searching for a connection with someone, he heads to a brothel and, after having second thoughts and getting a beating, returns home to Mari and explodes in anger against her. After that she takes the car and crashes, and John says, "I probably did it to her, Ian." His guilt is overwhelming.

Scene 4 explores Ian's issues, as he picks up Laurence, a "rent boy," to have gay sex, something Ian has never done. Ian's commitments both to the church and to Neasa seem somehow wrong, and in this scene he tries to find what he thinks he needs in a relationship. Laurence is married with a child, but his life, too, is disordered. When Ian explains that he has never been with a man, Laurence simply says, "What difference does it make?"

The final scene reveals that Ian is moving to Limerick to be with his fiancée and their daughter, while John explains that his life has turned around. But the dramatic ending of the play may call their generally positive views of their current lives into question.

Shining City in Performance

McPherson himself directed the first London production at the Royal Court Theatre in May 2004, with Michael McElhatton as Ian. The reviews were uniformly positive, and Nick Curtis for the *Evening Standard* said that the play contained a scene "that literally lifted the hairs on my scalp." The play moved to Dublin's Gaiety Theatre in September 2004 with the same cast, but the Dublin reviews were not as enthusiastic as those in London and New York. In the *Irish Times*, Fintan O'Toole said that if it weren't for the fact that McPherson directed the play himself, he would have thought that "a flawed but sensitive, intelligent and often beautifully written play had been vandalized by a fool who had lost his nerve." The 2006 New York production at the Biltmore Theatre played for 101 performances, with Brian F. O'Byrne as Ian, Oliver Platt as John, Martha Plimpton as Neasa, and Peter Scanavino as Laurence. Ben Brantley at the *New York Times* said it was "a quiet, haunting, and absolutely glorious new play." Additional productions took place at Australia's Hoy Polloy Theatre in June 2007, in New Zealand and the United Kingdom in 2007, and at Boston's Huntington Theatre in March 2008.

Conor McPherson *(b. 1970)*

SHINING CITY

Characters

IAN, *forties*
JOHN, *fifties*
NEASA, *thirties*
LAURENCE, *twenties*

Setting: *The play is set in Ian's office in Dublin, around Phibsboro maybe, or Berkeley Road, an old part of the city which, while it retains a sense of history, is not a salubrious area. It has a Victorian feel, lots of redbrick terraced houses dominated by the Mater Hospital, Mountjoy Prison, and the church spires of Phibsboro Church and the church at Berkeley Road. It doesn't feel like a suburb, if anything it feels like a less commercial part of the city center, which is only a short walk away.*

Ian's office is perhaps in an older, larger building than most in the area, up on the third floor. From his elevated position, at the back of the building, one or two church spires loom outside.

There is a big sash window at the back. There are some shelves with books on them. A stereo and some CDs. There are more books on the floor, as though they have been unpacked but have yet to be put away. Ian has a desk, stage left-ish, with a chair behind it. There is also a chair in front of the desk which Ian uses for sitting with clients. Clients sit on a little two-seater sofa near the middle of the room, a little more stage right. There's

a coffee table near the sofa with a box of tissues and a jug of water.

At the back, stage right, is a door to a little bathroom. Stage right is a cabinet of some kind, a filing cabinet maybe, or a bookcase.

The door is stage right, and when it is open we can see out to the banister and the top of the stairs. Beside the door is a hand-set for an intercom to the main door to the street on the ground floor.

The play has five scenes and about two months elapse between each scene.

The time is the present.

SCENE ONE

(As the lights come up there is no one onstage, It is daytime. We hear distant church bells. Music is playing softly on the stereo. We hear the toilet flush, and Ian, a man in his forties, comes out of the bathroom. He takes a tissue from the box and goes to the window, blowing his nose. He is a man who has struggled with many personal fears in his life and has had some victories, some defeats. The resulting struggle has made him very sharp. He is essentially a gentle man, but sometimes his desire to get to the lifeboats, to feel safe, drives him in ways that even he himself doesn't fully understand. A loud,

ugly buzzer goes off. Ian turns off the stereo and goes to the intercom, picking up the handset.)

IAN: Hello? (*Pushing a button on the intercom*) Okay, come in.

(*Pause.*)

Are you in? Okay. (*Pushing the button*) Push the door. Are you in?

(*Pause.*)

Hello? No? Okay, okay, hold on.

(*He hangs up the handset and goes out, leaving the door open. He goes down the stairs.*)

(*Off*) Now.

JOHN (*Off*): Sorry.

IAN (*Off*): No, I'm sorry. Come on up. Yeah. It was fixed. I don't know if all this rain . . . We're all the way up, I'm afraid.

JOHN (*Off*): Straight on?

IAN (*Off*): Eh, the next one. Yeah. And that's it there. The door is open.

(*John comes in. He is in his fifties and dressed quite respectably. He has an air of confusion when we first see him, not just because of his recent experiences but also because he has yet to accept that the world is not as orderly and predictable as he thought. He has always found problems to arise from what he regards as other people's ignorance. He almost regards himself as a benchmark for normality. He carries an anorak. He seems very tired. Ian follows him in and indicates for him to have a seat on the sofa.*)

Now, right.

JOHN (*Sits*): Thanks.

IAN (*Sits*): I'm sorry about that.

JOHN: No, sure I wasn't sure I had the right . . . I was in a bit of a flap, God, the parking around here is horrendous, isn't it?

IAN: I know.

JOHN: I left myself a bit of time but I was almost like a curbcrawler out there looking for a spot.

IAN: I know, I tell you I'm only here, I've only been here two weeks, and I'm not sure . . . between ourselves . . . that I'm going to . . . (*He nods*) because there's . . . many disadvantages . . .

JOHN: Ah, no, I parked up in the hospital in the end, which is what I should have done in the first place. I'll know the next time. It's my own fault.

IAN: No, I know, I should have probably . . . But like I say, I'm still sort of only getting myself sorted out here but I should have . . .

JOHN: Ah sure no, it's grand, sure I'm here now.

IAN: Yes! Well good.

JOHN: Yeah, well that's the main thing . . . Can I eh . . . (*Indicates water*)

IAN (*Indicates affirmatively*): Please.

(*John pours himself some water and drinks a few mouthfuls. Ian reaches around behind him and takes a letter from his desk.*)

So . . . (*Glancing at letter*) John . . . (*Pause*) How are you?

JOHN: Not too bad. A bit . . . Eh . . . heh . . . eh . . . I've never . . . ehm . . . been to see . . . someone before . . .

IAN: All right. Well that's okay.

JOHN: Em . . . (*He doesn't seem to know where to begin*)

IAN: I got a, I have a letter . . .

JOHN: Right.

IAN: From Dr. Casey . . .

JOHN: That's right. Yeah, he was . . . there was some guy he wanted me to see and . . . we couldn't get an appointment, for four months or something!

IAN: Okay.

JOHN: Yeah, so . . .

IAN: And you haven't been sleeping so well. Is that right?

JOHN: Well, yeah . . .

(*Pause.*)

IAN: Which can be very debilitating, I know.

JOHN: Yeah . . . and ehm . . . (*He holds his hand up to the bridge of his nose as though he is about to sneeze and there is silence. He is silently crying*) Can I . . . ? (*He indicates tissues*)

IAN: Of course. Please.

JOHN (*Composes himself*): Sorry.

IAN (*Reassuringly*): That's fine. That's fine.

JOHN: You have the tissues ready and everything.

(*They smile.*)

I'm em. I'm recently bereaved. I don't know if Dr. Casey . . .

IAN (*Affirmative*): Mm-hm.

JOHN: My wife passed away a few months ago. And em . . .

(*Pause.*)

She . . . she, she died in em, horrible circumstances, really, you know?

IAN: Okay.

JOHN: She was in a taxi. And a . . . stolen car crashed into them. And she was . . . trapped, in, the car. It was a, a horrific crash, and she . . . didn't, she couldn't survive. And I was on my . . . I was too late getting to the hospital. And the eh . . . reality of . . . the reality of it. It's been absolutely . . . It really, now . . . It's . . . (*He nods*) You know . . .

(*Pause.*)

IAN: I can em . . . I can only imagine what . . .

JOHN: We have no children. And eh . . . (*Pause*) And I've eh . . . been on my own an awful lot, you know? Like, I've really been on my own an awful lot of the time, really, you know?

IAN: Okay.

JOHN: And I don't . . . I mean I don't even know where she was that night, you know? Or where she was coming from. Do you know what I mean, you know? Like we weren't even . . . communicating. At the time, do you understand me?

IAN: Okay.

JOHN: And no one else was injured. And I've no . . . idea . . . wh . . . (*Long pause*) But, em, I've . . . em . . . I've seen her. (*Short pause*) I've em . . .

IAN: Sorry. You've seen her?

JOHN: I've seen her in the house. She's been in the house.

IAN: You've . . .

JOHN: Yeah.

IAN: This is . . .

JOHN: Yeah.

IAN: Since . . .

JOHN: Yeah, since . . .

IAN: Since she . . .

JOHN: Yeah since she . . .

IAN: Sorry, go on . . .

JOHN: Yeah, no, she em . . . about eh, about two months ago. I . . . met up with my brother, I have a brother, Jim, and we met one evening, for a pint in Clontarf Castle. We're just, are we just going into this? You just . . .

IAN: Well, no, just whatever you want, you just tell me . . . in your own, we don't have to, you can . . . You're telling me so, I'd like to . . .

JOHN: No I just, I wasn't sure if, but, you know, we . . . my brother, you know, we don't, we haven't . . . eh . . . I don't see him. You know, to a certain degree, we've been out of contact. He only lives in Clontarf. But for . . . you know . . . he . . . but since the . . . funeral . . . He, you know, we've had contact again. And it's fine, you know. But for a long time . . . he's been very supportive, but you know we don't get on, basically, you know? And I don't . . . there's no need for me . . . to infringe on his privacy and his family. And you know, so we've drifted again. But em, the . . . the last time that I saw him, this night that I'm talking about a couple of months ago. I mean, I could feel . . . that . . . it was a sympathy vote, like . . . we'd . . . very little to . . . to say to each other. And I mean, he's very quiet anyway, you know? And I . . . didn't feel . . . right, myself that evening, anyway and . . . And I mean, there was no . . . problem, as such. But I . . . just wanted to leave, you know? And I kind of just got a bit annoyed and I kind of . . . fucking . . . just went home, you know?

(*He checks with Ian, to see if this is all all right to continue with. Ian nods gently.*)

And eh . . .

And I didn't really . . . when I got home, there was nothing untoward when I got in the door. Only that I remember now, because I heard it again, there was the sound, the tune of an ice-cream van. The music, you know? But there couldn't have been because they don't go round at night. But, I heard it when I got in the door. And I . . . didn't think about it or . . . But eh . . . I was, I was just going into the living room and I put the lights on, and . . . when I turned around I could see that she was standing there behind the door looking at me.

(*Pause.*)

IAN: Your wife?

JOHN: Yeah. She . . . I could only see half of her, behind the door, looking out at me. Eh . . . but I could see that . . . her hair was soaking wet, and all plastered to her face. And I, I fucking jumped, you know? And I fucking just stood there, I froze, it was terrifying. And I mean she was as real as . . . you know if you've ever seen a dead body? How strange it is, but . . . it's . . . real! That feeling . . .

IAN: And what happened then?

JOHN: I just, I don't know how long we were standing there looking at each other. I mean it might have been only a few seconds. But it was like if you're a kid and you get a fright, it's only for a second, you know, if you have a bad dream or you think you see something, but then, you wake up or there's nothing there or whatever, but this just didn't stop, I mean she was just there, and it was real. The feeling is like . . . I mean, I mean it's unbelievable, you know? It's . . . it's . . . I can't describe it.

IAN: And did she . . . did you . . .

JOHN: Well finally, I don't know how, but I just got my legs going and I just had no choice and I just went straight out the door, straight by her, I mean the door was open, she was behind it, and I just went straight out and right out of the house. (*Pause*) And then, of course, I was just standing in the garden with no coat on, with really no fucking idea what I was doing, you know? So I just got in the car. (*Pause*) And I kind of just sat there. Where I live is just a quiet cul-de-sac. There wasn't anyone around even that I could . . . even the neighbors, I've never, you know, those people . . . I just sat there, looking at the house, just so . . . frightened, you know? And . . . there was just nothing I could do. So I just drove away. (*Short pause*) Just down to this B and B. Bec . . . because I . . . I just didn't want to be on my own like. (*Short pause*) The woman there, I'd say she knew there was something weird going on all right. I had no luggage and it was so late. She probably thought I'd had a row, you know?

IAN: You didn't go to your brother?

JOHN: No. (*Pause*) He's . . . we'd, we'd had a . . . I mean I'd walked out on him, earlier, you know? . . . No.

IAN: Did you tell anyone? Is there anyone that you . . . who you . . .

JOHN: No, I . . . I . . . I just . . . I just went back the next day, you know? I . . . I just, I suppose, I made myself, I refused to . . . the next morning it was like, "What the fuck am I doing?" You know? I mean you

Oliver Platt as John and Brian
F. O'Byrne as Ian in the 2006
Biltmore Theatre production,
New York.

just don't know what to do. I rang them in work and said I wouldn't be in, because I sort of knew if I didn't go back . . . I mean when it gets bright you just . . . For some reason I was, I was just able to go back.

IAN: But you didn't talk to anybody about what had happened?

JOHN: No. I suppose I should have but . . .

(*Silence.*)

IAN: And did you see . . . her again? Or . . .

JOHN: Yeah, no, well the next time I didn't . . . see anything, I was in the bath, and . . .

IAN: When, how long was this, after . . .

JOHN: Two . . . days later, you know, not long . . .

IAN: Okay.

JOHN: I figured, you know, I, I rationalized it, that maybe . . . I hadn't . . . seen her or . . . Like there was nothing there! And I thought maybe it . . . that . . . just the fucking grief I suppose . . . you know . . .

IAN: Of course.

JOHN: You might say it's mad, but what choice did I have?

IAN: No.

JOHN: I mean, I have to get on with my life!

IAN: I know.

JOHN: So yeah, there I was, having a bath. It was fairly late. And I was just trying to relax. I had the radio on. I was listening to Vincent Browne. And the door was closed. I had . . . I had locked it. It's stupid 'cause there was . . . I was there on my own, but, I

don't know. It's just a habit or it made me feel a bit better, you know, more safe. And I was lying there and I thought I, I thought I heard something, you know? Like . . . someone in the house. Just not even a noise, just a feeling. You can just feel, you know, don't you? When someone is there. But I, I just turned off the radio, just to see if . . . and then I heard her, she was knocking on the door and going . . . (*He bangs his fist urgently on the wooden arm of the sofa*) "John! John!"

IAN: Oh my God.

JOHN: Yeah! So I, I leapt up out of the bath, and I slipped, and I took an awful . . . I went right over and really bruised my hip and my shoulder, and by the time I had sorted myself out, I got a grip and I . . . eventually, opened the door, but of course, and I know you're going to think I was dreaming or whatever, there was nothing there. But it was absolutely terrifying. And at the same time I was completely frantic, do you understand me?

IAN: Well, of course you were. What, what did you . . .

JOHN: Back down to the B and B! What could I do?! (*Pause*) I'm still there!

IAN: You're still . . .

JOHN: I'm living there! What can I do?

IAN: I know.

JOHN: I mean I have to sell the house! That's where I'm at, you know? I'm not working. I'm completely on my own. I mean the woman in the B and B doesn't know what to make of me. I mean she's very nice and everything, but what can I say to her? I told her I'm getting work done. And her husband is a builder, and he was asking me all these questions one morning. And I know nothing about it, you know? I think they think I'm a nutcase!

(*Silence.*)

IAN: Okay. (*Pause*) Well . . .

JOHN: Do you believe me?

IAN (*Taking up a writing pad*): Well, let's, let me get some details, is that all right?

(*John nods.*)

How old are you, John?

JOHN: Fifty-four.

IAN: And what do you do?

JOHN: I'm a . . . I'm a rep for a catering suppliers . . . on an independent basis . . .

IAN: And have you . . .

JOHN (*Interrupting Ian*): Wait. Do you believe me?

IAN: . . . had any . . . sorry?

JOHN: Do you believe what I'm saying to you? That this is happening to me?

(*Pause.*)

IAN: I believe you . . . that . . . I believe something is . . . I believe you, in that I don't think you're making it up.

JOHN: I'm not making it up.

IAN: Yes but . . . I believe you're telling me you saw something, but if you're asking me if I believe in ghosts, I . . .

JOHN: Yeah but can you help me with this? Because . . . (*His voice suddenly cracks*) I really don't know what the fuck I'm going to do here . . . (*He puts his hand to his mouth*)

(*Pause.*)

IAN: I know. I know. Don't worry. You're not on your own now, okay? We'll sort it out.

(*Pause.*)

Don't worry.

(*Short pause.*)

Don't worry.

(*Lights down.*)

SCENE TWO

(*It is night. Ian and Neasa are in the office. Perhaps she sits on the clients' couch. Maybe at the beginning it looks like a therapy session. She is in her thirties and is more working class than Ian. She is rooted in a harder; less forgiving reality. She has always had a stubbornness which has kept her focused, but has also sometimes blinded her so that, while she is a strong person, often it is others who have used her strength.*)

NEASA: Are you fucking joking me, Ian?

IAN: No, I'm . . .

NEASA: No, no no no no no no . . .

IAN: Look, I know, but . . .

NEASA: No no no—(*As though it's so obvious*)—you come home now.

IAN: Neasa, I'm . . . I'm just not going to do that. (*He goes to the desk and takes a cigarette from a pack.*)

NEASA: No. Because people have fights, Ian, and everybody hates it—but you know you have to do it sometimes, you know? That's . . . Please don't smoke, Ian, 'cause it'll make me want to smoke.

IAN: Okay! What's that smell?

NEASA: It's new . . . stuff for the . . . thing . . . on my leg.

IAN (*Beat*): And this is not because we had a fight! What do you think I am?! I know that people have fights—this is not because . . . It's not because I'm "hurt" or something—it's, it's because . . .

NEASA: Oh, it's not because you're hurt, no? It's not because you're sulking and you've been letting me stew in my own juice for four days, no?

IAN: No I haven't actually—I've been trying to just fucking think about what I need to figure out what I need to do, you know?

NEASA: But you couldn't phone me, to tell me that, no? You just let . . . me just . . .

IAN (*Shouts*): Anytime I thought about phoning you I knew that it would just turn into this! We said, both of us said that we should give it a bit of time to . . . but oh no . . .

NEASA (*Shouts*): I didn't know you were going to leave me on my own for a whole week, and I didn't even know where you were!

IAN: It's not a week, it's a couple of days, Jesus!

NEASA: It's not just a couple of days when you're on your own with a baby—it's completely fucking exhausting not knowing where you are—and I can't fucking do it!

What am I supposed to say to your brother? He hasn't even asked me where you are! No one knows what to say.—Of course she's delighted—she hates me—they think I've ruined your life. She's delighted with herself that I'm sitting up there on my own—she's so fucking smug now!

IAN (*Annoyed, embarrassed, dismissive*): It doesn't matter what they think.

NEASA: That's easy for you to say! I have nowhere to fucking go! It's their house! What right do I have to stay there if you're not there?

IAN: It's none of their business!

NEASA: What do you mean it's none of their business? You don't know what it's like! I'm sitting up there on my own in the boxroom with the baby, they don't even come near me. And I can't go downstairs! You should have seen the face on her when I asked her to mind Aisling tonight! (*Shouts*) You don't know what it's like!

IAN: Look! This is all . . . getting sorted out! I nearly have a thousand euros in the bank—if you just let me get on with my work, if you just let me do it my way, you'll have your own place, there'll be no more of this and we can get on with it, but if you're going to . . . (*Unsaid: "harass me"*) I can't . . . (*Unsaid: "work"*)

NEASA: What do you mean, my own place?

IAN: Can you not see that this is happening?! I don't . . . want . . . I can't . . . I can't . . . I can't . . . I don't . . . I don't want this relationship anymore!

NEASA: What the fuck are you talking about? What the *fuck* are you talking about?

IAN: God! Can you not hear me?! Can you not listen to what I'm saying?

NEASA: I don't know if I can! Because have you completely lost touch with reality? Have you completely fucking lost touch with fucking reality?

IAN: This is reality!!

NEASA: What are you talking about? What about the baby?!

IAN: But this is not about the baby!

NEASA: What are you talk— How can it not be about the baby?!

IAN (*Shouts*): Because it's not about that! Because it's about that *I* can't continue with *you*! With you and me!

NEASA: But what do you mean? What have I done? What have I done?

IAN: It's not what you've *done* or what I've *done*. It's . . . It's . . .

NEASA: What . . . What, Ian . . .

IAN: IT'S BECAUSE I CAN'T DO IT!

(*Pause.*)

NEASA: I knew this. I knew this was going to happen. I knew it. I knew it.

IAN: Look, if you'd just listen to me for once, and hear something that goes in, we're going to get you out of my brother's house. It's all going to be sorted out and I'm earning some money now and everything.

NEASA: Yeah, now that it's all . . . Now you're on your feet. My father fucking said this to me, you know? He fucking said it to me. A priest . . . ?

IAN: I'm not a . . . !!

NEASA: An ex-priest? Forget it—he said anyone who goes next or near the priests is a fucking headcase to begin with. But I wouldn't listen to him!

IAN: Oh yeah, and your dad is a real one to know.

NEASA: Yeah, he's a drunk. But he's a human being, you know? He has feelings—he knows things, you know?

IAN: Yeah, well, is your father going to find you somewhere to live?

NEASA: Oh yeah, like you really found us somewhere to live, Ian. Squashed into your brother's house with that fucking bitch always fucking looking at me like I'm going to rob something, like she has anything . . .

IAN: Wait, now, don't fucking . . . What did you think was going to fucking happen?! I said it to you, I have to start all over again and it's gonna be tough!

(*Sarcastic*) Of course you didn't know that—you didn't know any of that!

NEASA: Yeah but I didn't think that at the end of it all you were . . . (*Despair, bewilderment.*) Are you breaking it off with me?! (*Pause*) I was just thinking about it. Do you remember the week you left the order—about . . . a day later, you were so worried about money, I'd say like a *day* later—I *immediately* started working all the extra shifts I could get. I kept having to lick up to that sleazy bollocks Darren, just to keep working in that fucking *kip* of a pub . . .

IAN: Look, I know, I know that.

NEASA: Just so you wouldn't have to worry about anything! No one could understand how I put up with the things that he said to me in front of people. But I did it so you could have the money for your course!

IAN: I know. I know. And . . . look . . . I'm . . . going to do everything that I can. And, I promise, I'm going to look after you, you know?

NEASA (*Shouts*): But I don't want for you to "look after" me! I never wanted for anyone to have to look after me! I even said—when I got pregnant—I even said then we should leave it and we should wait until we have some more money. I said, "This is too soon." YOU SAID, "NO," YOU SAID, "NO,

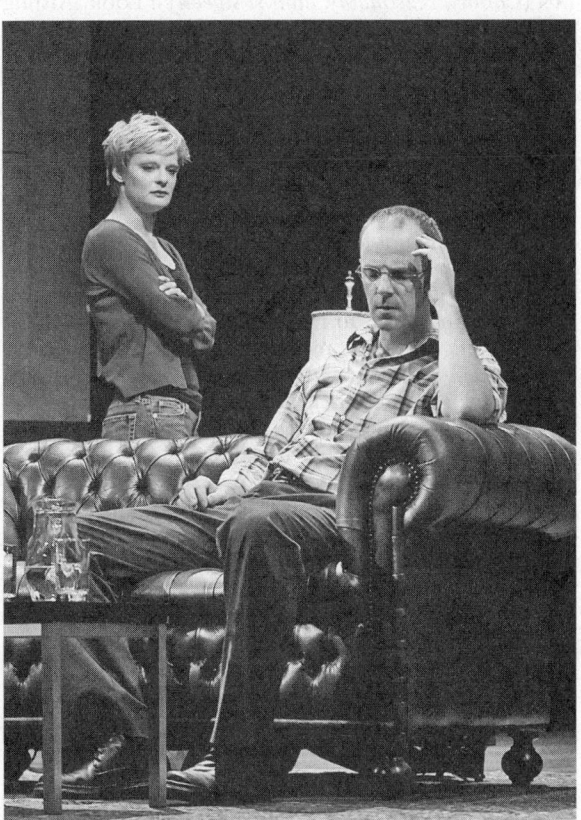

Martha Plimpton as Neasa and Brian F. O'Byrne as Ian in the 2006 Biltmore Theatre production, New York.

NOT TO DO THAT!" Because you thought it was "wrong"! Now look! (*Short pause*) What am I going to do? How can I go back there on my own again tonight? What am I going to say to your brother?

IAN: Don't say anything to him. I'll talk to him.

(*She stands there. She is ruined.*)

NEASA: What am I going to do?

IAN: Can you not go back around to your granny, even for a few . . . ?

NEASA: My dad is back there!

(*Ian throws his eyes to heaven, as if this is an endless saga.*)

IAN (*Beat*): Look, I know. I know that this . . . seems . . . like . . . but . . . this is the worst point, you know? And I've . . . I know I've made some huge mistakes, and I'm the first person who'll say that, you know? But I've got to put it right, and I'm going to put it right. But we can't continue like this and . . .

NEASA: Ian, I don't think I can do this on my own. I didn't think that this was going to happen.

IAN: I know but . . . you're not on your own. I'm with you in this, you know?

NEASA: But what are you saying to me?

IAN (*Calmly, reasonably, almost sweetly*): Look. Aisling is our daughter. And I'm her father and you're her mother. And I fully . . . you know? I want to be her father and . . . be, you know . . . but you and I . . . are breaking up. And that's all, you know? That's all that's happening here. That's all it is.

NEASA: How can you say that? How can you say that that's all it is? Can you see what this is doing to me?

IAN: I know. But we can't . . . I . . . can't . . .

NEASA: Do you not love me anymore?

IAN: I . . . I'll always . . . I mean, you have been . . . you were the only . . . when . . . when it was all so hard for me . . . And I had to make that big decision—and it was a *huge* thing for me— (*As though he has accomplished something completely unthinkable*) —to turn my back on the Church?!—that was a *huge* thing for me. You were there for me, and I couldn't have come through it without you. I just couldn't have done it, I just couldn't have, you know? But . . . the fucking huge mistake I made was thinking that that was the end of the journey for me—and it wasn't.

(*Pause.*)

NEASA: Have you met somebody else?

IAN: No, no I haven't. I promise you. It's not that . . . (*Pause*) I can't stay with you, with us, I can't do it. But I'm going to make sure that you want for nothing.

NEASA: But I just don't understand any of this. I just can't believe that it's happening even, you know?

(*She takes a bottle of wine from her bag.*)

I bought this this afternoon because I thought we were going to make up, and then you were going to come home with me.

(*She is shaking with fear and dread.*)

IAN: I'm sorry. I'm sorry. I'm sorry.

(*Silence.*)

NEASA: Is this . . . Is this because of me and Mark Whelan?

IAN: What?

(*Pause.*)

NEASA: Is it because . . .

IAN: Because what? (*Pause*) Because what? (*Pause*) What do you, what are you . . . ?

NEASA: Look, it doesn't matter, okay? Forget I asked.

IAN: No, wait, hold on. What do you mean is this because of you and Mark Whelan? What about you and Mark Whelan?

NEASA: Please, Ian, just . . . Please . . .

IAN: What do you mean it doesn't matter? What doesn't matter?

NEASA: Nothing, just . . . because I wanted just to ask you . . . if that was why.

IAN: But why are you asking me that? Did you . . .

NEASA: Ian, please, I'm asking you not to ask me about this now, please!

IAN: Not to ask you about what though?

(*Pause.*)

Not to ask you about what?

(*Pause.*)

I'm not . . . (*Unsaid: "surprised"*) Because, do you remember, I asked you about him before.

NEASA: And I told you.

IAN: You said there was nothing going on!

NEASA: There wasn't . . . then, when . . .

IAN: So what? Have you something you want to tell me?

NEASA: It doesn't make any difference, Ian, please, believe me. I just wanted to know if it was because . . .

IAN: Yeah, but, like I mean, what?

NEASA: Please, Ian. Please, I'm asking you, okay?

IAN: Yeah, but . . . I mean . . . wait a minute . . . What about you and Mark Whelan, you know? (*Pause*) Have you had sex with him?

(*Pause. She doesn't know what to say—all she knows is that it feels like her world is ending.*)

That's a "yes" then, I suppose then, yeah?

(*Pause.*)

NEASA: Can you not see what this is doing to me, Ian? Can you not see what this is doing to me? You're doing it anyway, Ian, you're leaving me anyway. Please don't leave me, please don't do it.

(*Ian knows that he shouldn't continue with this, but he can't help it. He feels angry, frightened, powerless, but also adrenalized.*)

IAN: Yeah, but you know what? This is fucking . . .
You're throwing the baby in my face . . . and you're
screwing around!

NEASA: I'm not!

IAN: But it's like I'm the one who, you know, that I . . .

NEASA: It was before the baby, Ian, I wasn't screwing
around!

IAN: When before the baby? Just before?

NEASA: No, she's our baby Ian, no!

IAN: Is she? I mean, wh . . . because I don't *know* . . .
anything, here.

(*Pause.*)

Because I was shocked when you got pregnant, we
both were. I thought we both were.

NEASA: No, no no no, she's your baby, she's your baby,
she's yours and mine—this is crazy! Just, you have to
believe me. Don't even . . .

IAN: Look, wait, hold on, hold on. This is . . . What are
we talking about here?

(*Pause.*)

NEASA: Nothing. Really. Nothing. There was just . . . no
one to talk to and—

IAN (*Interrupting*): When?

NEASA: Just in, all around that time. When you came
out and you were freaked-out all the time, and you
were starting your course. And I was working all the
time. I just couldn't . . . keep going back up to your
brother's house on my break, with her always there,
Ian, it was horrible.

IAN: You know they've been so good to us really when
you think about it, you know that?

NEASA: I know but, I was just always on my own!

IAN: But you weren't! When?

NEASA: I just . . . I didn't have anyone even that I could
just have a normal talk to.

(*Pause.*)

I just feel like it's all my fault now, you know? And
I was . . . I was worried all the time about everything, even then, you know? Mark just, would always ask me if I was all right, and how I was getting
on . . .

IAN: Oh, I never asked you how you were? I'm just a
fucking animal, yeah?

NEASA: I just believed him, when he asked.

(*Pause.*)

IAN (*Dismissive*): Yeah, well.

NEASA: I didn't know what was going on. It was just like
things were supposed to get better and they just kept
getting worse and worse. I couldn't go back up there
on my break. She always was saying something
about the smell of smoke off me. I was working in
a pub! You know? What did she want me to do?
And . . . I started going around to Mark's flat—I
told you, I told you I was doing that.

IAN: Yeah but . . .

NEASA: Yeah, well, I didn't . . . I didn't know that . . .
anything . . . was . . . going to happen. I didn't think
that there was even anything like that with him . . .
But one day he was . . . he didn't say anything to
me . . . We just got in the door and I just knew
that . . . what he was . . . I didn't know what to do. I
just, I only kind of realized when we got in the door
that . . . he was . . . It was just really, I didn't . . . it
was just really quick and it was, I didn't even want to
do it. We both felt terrible after it. I'm sorry Ian. I'm
sorry. It was only once. It was only one time. It wasn't
anything, really, And I've never gone there after.
I'm sorry, Ian.
I don't love him, Ian. I never loved him. I only
ever wanted to be with you. Really. Really.
And I don't know what happened.
Say something. Say something to me, will you?

(*Long pause.*)

IAN: I'm sorry.

(*Silence.*
Neasa starts to get her stuff together. She leaves the
bottle of wine.)

NEASA: I better go. 'Cause I'm gonna miss the last bus.

IAN: Look. I'll . . . I'll call you tomorrow, and . . .

NEASA (*Almost silently*): Yeah.

(*She goes to the door.*)

IAN: Neasa.

(*She pauses.*)

Look, I'm . . .

(*Pause.*)

NEASA: It's not your fault.

(*She leaves. He stands there.*
Lights down.)

SCENE THREE

(*Lights up on the office. It is the afternoon. The door is*
open and there is no one in the office. There is a bit more
furniture around the place, maybe a plant or two. John
comes in and stands there. He looks a bit better than he
did in Scene One, and there is something more focused
about him, he means business. Ian follows him in.)

IAN (*Slightly exasperated*): Well, I don't know . . .

JOHN: I'm sorry, God. I can never . . .

IAN: No! You know I've asked them every single week,
and they say they have a caretaker who keeps missing
me. I think it's a total spoof.

JOHN: Don't give them the rent.

IAN: You think?

JOHN: They'll he round in a flash. That's the language
they speak, you know. Money talks in this town. It
rules really, you know?

IAN: God, tell me about it! Keeps me fit anyway, going up and down the stairs.
JOHN: Yeah! Well . . .

(*John really has his bearings in the office now. He throws his jacket over a chair and sits, unbidden, on the sofa, pouring himself a glass of water. Ian sits.*)

IAN: So . . . how are you?
JOHN: Yeah, well I'm . . . this helps, you know . . .
IAN: Good, good . . .
JOHN: I, you know, I focus around it. It's been a good week em . . . They're, you know still very good about everything at work, there's no pressure to go in . . . em . . . the time is . . . good . . . it's . . .

(*Pause.*)

IAN: Are you sleeping or . . .
JOHN: Well, the same really. You know, I do . . . get a few hours. But, it's like there's something in me's determined to keep me up all night, you know? I never go off till around five, six, even. Then, of course, nine o'clock, the woman knocks on the door so I won't "miss breakfast." God forbid! You know?

(*They smile.*)

So . . . of course I'm in bits but, I get up, go down. I'm always the last. She usually has a few staying there, but, they're on business or whatever, they're . . . they're gone out, you know? So, I sit there, watching the traffic outside, and . . . I have an egg, cup of coffee . . . Get myself going then . . . you know . . .
IAN: You're still getting your walk in . . .
JOHN: Rain or shine. I get out, go down the coast. Down as far as the Bull Wall. The B and B is more the Fairview end so, you know, it's a good walk . . . Get the paper, throw any stuff into the laundry there. There's a little café next door, there near the Dollymount House. So, you know . . . that's . . . been the little routine, but I've em . . . I've bitten the bullet and done what you suggested. Couple of mornings I got in the car, dropped into the house, you know?
IAN: Okay. So, how is that?
JOHN: It's okay, you know, it's okay. (*Pause*) So quiet, obviously . . . but I . . . did, I do what you say, and I focus on eh, a small, objective. I stay . . . (*Unsaid: "centered on it"*) There were a couple of bills there, or whatever, there on the mat. Okay. Down to the post office, paid that . . . Em . . .

(*Pause.*)

IAN: And how does it feel in the house? When you're there.
JOHN: In the house, itself? Like I say. I'm aware, I'm wary . . . but in a funny way I . . . I can't . . . I can . . . hardly accept what I saw . . . you know . . . But, I know that I did, and so, obviously . . .
IAN: You're a little . . .
JOHN: I'm a little uneasy.

IAN (*Nods*): Okay.
JOHN: But that's . . . that's also to do with . . . Like, when Mari was alive, you know, we had . . . stopped communicating. But now . . . she's gone, I really feel like there was a lot of communication. Even though, it wasn't . . . verbal . . . I suppose. I mean, she was there. And I was there. And in that, there's obviously, the presence of . . . you know, a living person, I'm not saying this very well. But I think, you know, I believe that . . . we had a huge importance in each other's lives. You know?
IAN: I don't doubt it for a second.
JOHN (*Very affirmative*): Yeah. (*Beat*) Yeah. I know.

(*Pause.*)

You know, when you're young. And you're told about . . . what to expect I suppose. It is kind of happy ever after. But it's . . . you know, it's weird to accept what happiness really is, you know, or what it is . . . nothing is ever like anyone expects, is it, you know? Like, it's not a fairy tale . . . I mean, it has to be just kind of ordinary, you know? A bit boring even, otherwise it's probably not real, you know?
IAN: Yeah . . . ?
JOHN: No, it's, it's just that . . . we probably had it, you know? I mean when I think of it, really, we . . . we had it all, you know? But it's, it's hard to . . . accept . . . that this is it. You . . . you go . . . searching, not *searching*, I wasn't going anywhere searching for anything, but, I think I was always slightly . . . waiting . . . you know?

This is something I probably wouldn't even have admitted before, you know? But maybe I felt that when we were married, and all settled in and eh . . . maybe even before we found out that we couldn't, that Mari couldn't, have children, I think that maybe even before that . . . I felt that I had kind of settled for second best, you know? I mean I mean I look at it now, and man, these are old feelings. Just fucking there all the time, for . . . all the way along.

(*Silence.*)

That's terrible, isn't it?
IAN: You felt what you felt . . .
JOHN (*Slight self-disgust*): Yeah but, what . . . who the fuck did I think I was? You know?

(*Pause.*)

You see, we'd, I think, we'd been slightly left behind, a little bit, you know? All our . . . all our friends, they, you know, they had families. And, that . . . that . . . bound them together, you know? And, you see, I think that that . . . that we were . . . we were slightly left behind a little bit maybe. And that we felt that there was something kind of wrong with us, not anything serious or really wrong, but that there was a whole . . . you know, a whole experience, a whole way, maybe, of . . . of relating to everything, that wasn't . . . it wasn't available to us. (*Suddenly*) It was a pain in the fucking hole to tell you the truth!

You know. I don't know if you have children, and I don't mean anything, because this is nothing about those people, but you know, I found, we found, that, okay, of course we were invited to places, you know, to parties and everything. But that's what there was to talk about, you know? "Oh my sons are ten and eleven." "Oh my son is eleven!" You know?

And of course! Look, that's what people talk about. Of course they do. It's perfectly normal to want to talk about the things that are happening in your life. But, you know, that was what we were always sort of on the edge of. You know, those conversations. You know, you'd be trying to, waiting for the subject to change and then of course, some stupid fucker would turn around and go, "Do you have any kids, yourself, John?" And I'd be, and I know that this happened to Mari too, I'd be like, "Eh, no, no actually, I don't." Which'd be then . . . "Oh! Right! Okay!" You know?

I mean, I don't know if it felt like a big thing at the time, in a funny way, but it must have been, because I always felt . . . that it . . . wasn't . . . addressed because in a way, maybe I felt that the whole thing should be different — not just that we should adopt some kid or something — but that I should change the whole . . . the whole fucking thing, you know? Start again, somewhere else. Which then, of course, just feels mad and you want to let yourself believe that all these things aren't that important but . . . it was there and . . . what can I say? There was all this shit going on and I . . . our life just carried on and we grew up basically and our childbearing years were over and we got on with it, and that's, but then, out the fucking blue, about three years ago . . .

(*Pause.*)

I met someone, you know?

(*Pause.*)

I mean . . . I didn't meet her, we'd already met her, we both had met her, up at a . . . party up there in Howth up there, you know? House of a guy I was doing some business with.

(*Suddenly*) This is fucking mad fucking shit, now, you know?

IAN: I know. I know. It's okay . . .

JOHN: Yeah, well, like I say it was someone we'd both seen around a little bit for years. She's wealthy, you know? The husband is loaded, you know? And I suppose just the ordinary feelings of that . . . surface . . . glamour . . . I mean you'd see this woman, there was no doubt about it, she was, you know, the most beautiful woman in the room or whatever, or even wherever you'd go she'd be one of the top five best-looking women there, you know? I mean, that's what we're talking about here, you know? And obviously that's . . . that's very attractive, you know?

But about three years ago we were invited up to this guy, O'Leary, big hotel guy, up to his mansion up there on Howth Head. And both of us were excited about it and looking forward to it, you know, Mari liked dressing up. She had a good figure and she could, she could definitely hold her own, and this would have been a big deal and we were in good form going up there beforehand. And it was, you know, there were people up there parking the cars for you and all this, you know what I mean? Up these steps like, and butlers standing there with champagne and hot ports and all this, serious stuff now, you know?

And in we go, into this place, serious mansion now, you know? And as usual, you know, we're fucking standing there on our own — fucking, you know, trying to talk to each other, but of course we both wanted to get stuck in and meet some other people and I was dying for a slash and Mari doesn't want to let me go and leave her on her own there, and all that, yeah?

But eventually we get talking to another couple, and a business guy I know comes in and it's warming up and I leg it down to the jacks and kind of — the way it goes, you know, I don't see Mari until everyone sits down later on for something to eat, 'cause when I'm coming out of the toilet and I'm going through the kitchen I meet a few other people who are there, and then I meet this . . . this woman that I'm talking about . . .

Her name is Vivien . . .

And I stop and say hello and, you know, we're standing there at the . . . you know, in the middle of a kitchen, sometimes in those big houses . . .

IAN: An island.

JOHN: Yeah, and there were these stools and it was like we were sitting at a bar somewhere, you know? The champagne keeps coming round, and it's great, you know? Because not only is this woman so beautiful to look at but we're having a brilliant chat, you know? 'Cause I had been in hospital for a few days having this thing done on my sinuses and it was weird because she was asking me about it and no one had asked me anything really, you know, not even Mari, although she had been great and everything and she came to see me every day — but I'd felt just this . . . just this real lonely feeling when I was in there, you know? I don't know why, or what happened but when I was in there, I just felt a bit scared and . . . and em . . .

But I'd had these feelings and anyway, for some reason I mentioned this to . . . to Vivien, and you know, God it just felt like I was being taken seriously. You know, and the champagne is coming round and it turns out that Vivien was in hospital at nearly the same time, you know? And she starts telling me that . . . she'd had . . . a miscarriage, you know? And she's telling me all this and she already has four kids who are teenagers and this pregnancy was out of the blue, and there'd been all this going on, and it hadn't worked out, and all this had . . . you know brought up, a lot of things for her about many things in her life and it's all this and, so like we're having this big talk, and then, you know, it's an hour and a half later, and we're all being called in to sit down at this huge dinner . . . and on the way in, she . . . she takes my mobile number and puts it in her phone. And although in one way it just seemed like a normal thing to do, in another it was . . . you know . . . and I didn't really . . . let on to Mari that I'd only been talking to Vivien all that time when I got back, you know, I played up the other people that I'd only seen or just said hello to.

So we're there and we don't have a great time, because Mari is pissed off that I'd left her talking to these fuckers she didn't really know, and of course, about twelve o'clock, she says she doesn't feel so good, so great! We're the first ones to leave and we're not talking in the car and it's basically just one of those, and I'm kind of used to it, you know?

But Christmas, you know, we go over to her folks' house and do the whole bit, and when I get home, bit tipsy, I'm upstairs getting changed and I see on my phone, I have a text. And it's from Vivien and it's, "Great to see you the other night. Happy Christmas."

So I'm like standing up there in the bedroom, in my socks, you know, and I'm like some youngfella, and I text her back, "It was great to see you too," you know, "Happy Christmas."

And some part of me knew, you know? That I was sort of going into something . . . you know? And . . .

(*Pause.*)

But, you know there were no more texts and . . . but, something had . . . I mean whatever it triggered off . . . you know . . . here I was all of a sudden, just really thinking about this woman. Who . . . in many ways was different to what I knew, you know? And probably the big one was . . . you know . . . that . . . She was a mother.

Whatever that . . . means, you know? But anyway, Christmas was gone, and the new year and all that bollocks, which is a very depressing time of the year as far as I'm concerned and there were no more texts . . . and . . . I don't know what I was expecting to happen but I just got more and more into a filthy mood, over those days. And Mari was asking me what was wrong with me, and I was bulling because I'd erased Vivien's text, and I wanted to look at it again as something to hang on to, which was you know, whatever.

But as usual, Mari dragged me into the Christmas sales because I needed new clothes and we were in fucking . . . Roches Stores or somewhere and . . . I got a text . . . from Vivien, and it was just like, "How are you?" You know? And man, it was like someone had thrown me a rope, you know? I was like, "Thank God!" You know? There's someone in the world who actually cares about how I'm getting on,

you know? Like, this was what that meant to me. Crazy fucking shit, you know?

So I slipped off and said I wanted to have a look at some shoes or something, and I texted her back, quickly just saying, "Post-Xmas blues," or something and bang! She texted me right back like, "Hang in there," or something and that's, it's so fucking stupid, but that's how it continued then all day really.

IAN: Your wife didn't hear all these texts going off?
JOHN (*Shakes his head*): No, I had the phone on silent, vibrate, in my pocket, you know? I mean, you know? I was already . . . you know . . . ?
IAN: Mm. Yeah I know.
JOHN: And of course, suddenly I'm all chipper then, and I take Mari for her lunch in the Westbury! You know, I'm all cheered up. That morning she'd seen this bright red coat in one of the designer shops in Brown Thomas or somewhere. Reduced from like three grand to two grand or something, and of course it was still too dear and all that, but after lunch I took her down and bought it for her, you know? The fucking guilt, you know?

I mean, this is the terrible side of it. That coat was then, like her good coat from then on, you know?

(*Pause.*)

She was wearing it, you know, the night she was . . . the night she died, you know?

(*Pause.*)

She had it on when I saw her, you know? Behind the door there.

(*He exhales deeply.*)

So, but, you know, we went home, life continues. Back to work, which I was glad about, because, you know, it gave me more time to myself. You know? Texting Vivien? You know?
IAN: Mmm.
JOHN: And then of course . . .
IAN: What were the texts?
JOHN: Ah, it was just normal stuff, you know? Nothing. "How are you doing?" "Back to work today." "Ah well, keep your chin up!" You know? Nothing— except that it shouldn't have been happening . . . you know, so . . . so then, of course, as time goes on, that's, that's not enough for me . . . ? So . . . I, I text her and say, "Let's have a coffee sometime." And that's opened it up, because, at first I hear nothing, and I think, "Whoa, I've gone too far . . ." But then bang! Like a day later . . . She fucking rings me! Right in the middle of a meeting with these two business guys down in Longford, in the Longford Arms Hotel. And I see her name come up on the phone—so I'm like, "I have to take this." So I go outside and it's like, "God it's great to hear you," you know? It was just . . . it just felt like such a fucking relief, you know?

And she's on for like a big chat on the phone, but I'm like . . . I can't do it, so I kind of cut to the chase, and I say, "Let's meet up!" you know? And she's, you know, suddenly I sense a kind of reluctance, like she's not saying no, but . . . I can just . . . (*Unsaid: "sense it"*) But I drive it on and I say, "Let's meet on Friday, get some lunch, just get a quick sandwich somewhere," or something, and she's like, "Where?" And so like, without either of us acknowledging it, I say, "The Killiney Court Hotel," because it's really miles out of the way for both of us, and no one would see us, you know, but of course I don't say that, but I figure she gets it, and I say I'm going to be out that way and so on. All very innocent, like—(*Sarcastic*) "Yeah, right!" But my heart was pounding while I'm talking to her, you know? And I could . . . like the stakes were really going up!

IAN (*Affirmative*): Well, yeah . . .

JOHN: And . . . I mean, I don't know if you know what it's like, but . . . Having a secret like that from your wife . . . Nothing is as strong as a secret like that, I mean for binding two people. In my *mind* anyway! As far as I was concerned, we were already like two fugitives or something, you know? So, but, we made this arrangement. And of course, the next few days was kind of mad, like, "What am I doing? This is crazy." I was . . . I was just like an actor, or something, in my own life, just playing this part in something that just didn't seem real, you know, or as real as . . . I mean, crazy, you know? Like I felt I could just look behind everything because it was only scenery, everywhere I went. Because, I suppose in a mad way I believed that *something else* was my reality! And that all this other shit—my life!—was . . .

Like I found myself looking at Mari while she was prattling on and thinking, "Who the fuck is this fucking woman?" What's happened? That we live in the same house? There's been some fucking . . . mistake, you know?

IAN (*Affirmative*): Mmm.

JOHN: So a few days later, Friday, you know, I had cleared the decks, I had nothing else to do so I was over there in Killiney at like twelve o'clock, you know? And it was a horrible day, you know? It never really got bright—didn't rain, but it was . . . almost like GOD KNOWS WHAT YOU'RE DOING . . . you know?

(*They both laugh a little.*)

And eh . . . we met, you know? (*Suddenly without any defense or guile*) I couldn't believe it when I saw her coming through the door. I just could not fucking believe it, you know? I was like, thank God, you know? Like how can this beautiful woman be coming in here to be with me? You know? This is *real*, you know? God. And she just came in there and she sat down where I was sitting. And she was really nervous too, you know? And she just starts talking, talking, talking. Her kid is in this new school and all this, and her husband is going through this huge deal at work and he's in Japan all the time and she's getting

this work done by these builders, and basically all this bollocks that I realize I have no interest in at all! And there was this horrible feeling that all this going on and on was just really a bit annoying, you know? This just wasn't . . . I was selfish basically, and I . . . I wanted this to be more about me, you know?!

(*They smile.*)

So we got a few hot whiskeys and after I feel like I've been politely listening to all this shite for long enough, I started to move it around more to . . . us being there, and . . . and I knew I was rushing it but . . . I was really just, trying to move it on to the next stage. Because I didn't want the whole . . . illusion of it . . . wrecked. I mean, I was putting everything into this—the whole lot—all the eggs in the one basket, I mean, insane, you know?

And I mean, madly, I just said to her, "Look, I need to . . . be with you, you know? And hold you and . . ." Crazy.

And she just went so quiet then that I thought, okay, I've fucked it, you know, she's . . . you know, she thought this was something else . . . like we were going to be just friends in some . . . bizarre way I don't fucking . . . relate to, you know? And it was three o'clock now and I'd have to start heading soon now anyway, but then she goes, "Yeah, okay, let's . . ." But then I'm like slightly, like, "Don't just do this for me!" You know, like, don't kill yourself . . . But sure, I didn't even know what I was doing, you know?

I was like a robot. But everything I was doing was wrong so nothing made sense, like I got the key, and I was convinced your woman behind the desk was going to call the fucking guards, you know?! And this was before that place closed down, it was between when they had sold it and when they closed it down, there was hardly anyone around. Going up to the room, you know? And we didn't say anything. It was just, it was just . . . frightening really. And we go in and the room was like . . . it was like walking into one of the rooms in *Fawlty Towers*° or something, like it was straight out of the 1970s. All brown and pink flowery patterns everywhere. And it was freezing. It was . . . it was horrible.

But. We sat on the bed. And we . . . started . . . sort of . . . kissing, but, I wasn't . . . it was just so obvious that this wasn't what she wanted. And to tell you the truth I was completely out of practice and I . . . tried to put my hand up her skirt and . . . you know, but she just stopped me. And neither of us were . . . it was just a huge mistake. I had fucked the whole thing to hell, really, you know? And I wanted to just go back to before, when we were just going to meet, you know?

Fawlty Towers: A British television comedy set in a dowdy hotel.

But I didn't . . . I wasn't able to . . . quite express that, so . . . I was just sort of apologizing, and really, we both had to go then and . . .

It was just fucking awful to tell you the truth, and there didn't seem to even be time to . . . make it . . . like, to have a drink and work it out or make it okay again. It was just over and we just, said good-bye in the car park, you know? Brilliant.

And of course when I got home, just the distance that I felt between me and Mari, I realized that whatever about the way we might have been before, it was nothing compared to this. This was like the Grand Canyon opening up, you know? I knew that I'd driven an unbelievable wedge . . . between us.

And of course, Mari can tell there's something wrong and she's . . . asking me, is there anything she can . . . She came and started stroking my back saying, "God, those are big heavy sighs, John." You know? So I just said, "Ah it's a thing at work, don't worry about it." Whatever, you know?

But seriously, you know, as the days went on, I mean I wasn't getting any sleep, and I was getting up in the middle of the night and just sitting in the kitchen, and then, not able to go into work.

(*Pause.*)

It was just so . . . I just felt like a piece of shit, you know?

I mean, I had gone from sharing this—I suppose it was a dream—of a . . . special communication or a secret . . . relationship that . . . and now it was, I mean I just felt like some sort of criminal. And I really felt so isolated and cut off and like there was nothing in my life to look forward to. And I just felt like, I knew then that something bad was going to happen, because I deserved it, because there was like some kind of evil in me, that I did.

IAN: Mari didn't . . . you didn't . . .

JOHN: Well, she just didn't know what to do, because I was just only, barely communicating with her. Because I fucking hate myself by this stage, you know?

And when I think about what I must have done to her. With all the silence and . . .

(*Pause.*)

I started pretending I had to stay down the country, for work, you know, overnight, but I was really just staying in places just so that I didn't have to deal with the terrible *pressure* of going home, you know? And facing that, and facing myself, and, you know? I'd just be sitting there in some hotel bar in the midlands, you know? Just smoking cigarettes and looking at football or Man United or whatever—just unable to deal with anything, really. And I just, I had been staying in this place in Kildare and I had to leave and come back to Dublin, because I could only ever justify staying away for a night or possibly two at a push, and I was having a cup of coffee before I

hit the road and I picked up this magazine, in a whole rack of old magazines, and I saw an ad for like, an escort service, a brothel. I knew what it was. And . . . I just needed to . . . connect with something, or someone, you know? When you're so alone like that . . . and when you feel . . . you know . . . I just . . . I just dialed the number and this woman answered and she sounded so nice, and you know, she told me where to go. To this place on the South Circular Road. And I fucking drove there, you know? I just . . .

(*Long pause.*)

IAN: Are you okay?
JOHN: Yeah, it's just, this is terrible.
IAN: No.
JOHN: I just find it so fucking hard . . .
IAN: You're doing so well, John. This is such important work, you know?

(*Pause.*)

Do you want to leave it there? We can just sit for a while . . . ?
JOHN: How's the time, are we finished?
IAN: No we have time, but maybe you'd just prefer to . . .
JOHN: Well . . . No, I'll, I'll finish what I . . . I came . . . today to . . . you know . . .
IAN: Okay.
JOHN: Yeah, so I eh . . . anyway, I went to this place. Which was something I had never done. And this woman answered the door, and I was hoping the minute I saw her that she wasn't, I mean, she was a bit older now . . . And she brought me into this room. And there was just a couch there, and a shower over in one corner and some towels on a chair, and she says that this girl, Jeanette, was going to come in in a minute. And she says it's thirty euros to be there and then whatever I work out with Jeanette is between ourselves. And I mean, I'm already like, God this is, I haven't even met this girl, you know, but I give this woman thirty euros and she tells me to relax and take a shower and Jeanette will be in in ten minutes.

So I'm there in this room. And I can hear people in the house, talking or moving around or whatever, and it's a bit, you know . . . but I was hoping that whatever was going to happen was going to give me some relief, you know? Not a sexual thing, I don't . . . (*Unsaid: "think"*) Just some . . . I mean, I know it sounds . . . "Oh that's what everybody says . . ." but you know . . .
IAN: No, I know.
JOHN: So I just, fuck it, I took a shower in there . . . in the corner. And I dried myself and . . . then I put my clothes back on!

(*They smile briefly.*)

And I'm in there maybe fifteen minutes and nothing is happening, you know, so I stick my head out the door, but I don't see anyone, and I decide to wait. And the doorbell goes and I hear the woman bringing in some other guy and she takes him off somewhere. And by this stage . . . I'm like . . . this is just freaking me out, really, but at the same time, like I say, I'm hoping for some . . . you know, I'm hanging in there. So I wait and I hear a bit of movement, and I hear someone leaving so I think maybe it's going to happen now, but then twenty minutes go by so I just, I'm like, forget it.

So I put on my coat and I open the door to go and the woman who let me in is coming down the hall going like, (*Strong Dublin accent*) "What are you doing? Go in and have a shower!" And she comes right up to me and the smell of drink off her, you know? And I'm like, "Look, I'm going to leave it."

And then this guy appears, you know? Like a total skanger. Just with these really dead eyes, you know? And he's like, "What's going on?" And they're much louder than they have to be, if you know what I mean.

And for some reason I . . . just . . . decide. That . . . I'm not gonna take this fucking shit anymore, I've just had enough so although I'm probably definitely on a hiding to nothing, I say, "Give me my thirty euros back . . ." which of course, is madness, you know? But of course this *is* fucking madness, you know?

So she shouts, "We don't owe you any money— we provide the amenities and that's what you were charged for. We don't owe you a fucking penny!" And your man is like, "Come on now, you're either going to have to go in and have a shower or you're going to have to go." But by this stage I suppose these two people represent everything that's wrong with the world to me and it's like I'm . . . I just refuse to accept this, you know? And I'm . . . *demanding* my money back! I just want to have a transaction where some normal rules apply again, you know? And look where I was trying to fucking achieve that! You know?

(*They smile.*)

And then, I just, before I know it, your man just hits me right in the stomach! And I mean, I'm not fit, and I haven't been in a fight since I was maybe ten or something! But that feeling of being completely winded, of not being able to breathe and being completely paralyzed—it just . . . I just bent over slowly and I could hear this awful groan coming out and it was me making it—you know—completely out of my control. And I just went down and down until I was on my knees on the floor. And I hear your man going, "Now you brought that on yourself." And he was so fucking right, you know?

And then they sat me on the stairs, you know? They were getting a bit worried, because I just could not breathe. She's going like, "What did you hit him for?" And he's saying to me, "You'll be all right,

you'll be all right . . ." And I felt fucking grateful! It was so stupid but in a mad way, that's what I wanted! I wanted someone to tell me that things were going to be okay. I mean I was really clinging to the fucking wreckage here now, you know?

(*He sighs deeply.*)

And . . . I went home. Still completely able to . . . I went in and Mari had my dinner there on the table, you know, chops and peas and potatoes. And the pain in my stomach was . . . I could barely fucking walk, you know? And, of course she . . . the minute she sees me she just . . . she was like, "Oh my God, John, what's happened? Are you all right?"

And I . . . (*He almost starts crying but keeps it together*) I just turned on her, Ian, you know? I just . . . exploded. And I ate the head off her. I was like an animal. And it was just so . . . sudden. She looked so frightened, I had never seen that look, of real fear, and I was doing it! You know?

(*He starts crying.*)

And, I pushed her up against the wall and I told her, "You're fucking killing me."

And I . . . grabbed her by the shoulders and I shook her. I shook her so hard. I could feel how small and helpless she was. It was a terrible feeling. And I said to her, "Don't fucking speak to me anymore. Don't you dare fucking speak to me." And she just cowered down on the floor—nothing like this had ever happened between us before, you know? And she curled herself up into a little ball there down beside the bin. And the sobs just came out of her, you know? Just the total . . . bewilderment, you know?

(*Pause. John is in the deep pit of his self-loathing.*)

And after that, like from then on, I couldn't . . . And I just don't understand. How, why I just couldn't have talked to her? She only wanted to help me. But it was like . . . (*Short pause*) I was in a kind of a storm, you know? You're only just barely hanging on, just hanging in there. And I was frightened that she'd, or anyone would . . . see how weak I was. And how . . . disgusting I was. And she'd hate me, you know? Everything just developed into a kind of paralysis. That's the only way I can describe it. You just can't fucking move, you know?

Because, I think I killed her that day, you know? I mean, I didn't kill her. But I might as well have.

I mean, I don't even know where she was going the night that . . . or where she had been. We didn't even speak to each other before she died, she was on her own, you know? I just feel like I just fucking left her alone in the world, you know? If I could have even slept in the bed beside her, maybe that might have even been enough! You know, I . . . I probably didn't even have to say anything . . . And now I can't go back!

(*Long pause.*)

I just . . . I believe in a way that I probably did it to her, Ian, you know?

IAN: No.

JOHN: And that's probably why I've seen her, you know?

IAN: No. I don't . . .

JOHN: Like she only wanted to fucking help me, you know?

IAN: But it was an accident. She was in an accident.

JOHN: But I . . . I mean I think about it. Where would she have been going? She wouldn't have been out on her own in town if . . . you know . . . And she was so kind, you know? I . . . I mean, is it . . . ? Is it that, in some way, she . . . Is she trying to . . .

IAN: I really don't think that . . .

JOHN: Is she trying to hurt me? Or I mean . . .

IAN: Well you see I'm not convinced that . . .

JOHN: Or maybe I've got it wrong. You know? Maybe I've got the whole thing arseways.

(*Pause.*)

Maybe she's . . . Maybe she's just trying to save me, you know?

(*Lights down.*)

SCENE FOUR

(*A church bell strikes twice in the distance. It is night. The office is in darkness except for what light spills in from the street. We hear someone coming up the stairs. The door opens and Ian comes in and switches on a lamp or two. Laurence comes in and hovers near the door. He is skinny and wears sports gear and sneakers. It is hard to tell if he is thirty and looks much younger or twenty and looks much older. He has a nervous, twitchy energy and seems like he lives from minute to minute. He has a dirty bandage on his right hand.*)

IAN: Come in. Come in. It's okay. There's no one else. There's no one in the whole building. This is . . . where I work.

(*Laurence shuts the door. They stand there. Ian doesn't seem to know what to do.*)

Let me eh . . . I think I have eh . . . would you . . . drink a glass of wine?

LAURENCE (*Shrugs*): . . . Yeah.

IAN: Okay . . . Let me, eh . . . Let me . . .

(*He bustles about and finds the bottle Neasa brought. He finds two mugs.*)

I say "glass" . . . but . . . I'll just . . . Eh . . .

(*He motions to Laurence that he wants to get past him, and he goes into the bathroom to wash the mugs. We hear him in there while Laurence stands alone in the* room. *He comes back out with the mugs and stops abruptly.*)

Corkscrew. Didn't think of that. Didn't think of it. Em.

LAURENCE: You can push it in.

IAN: The . . .

LAURENCE: You can push the cork down. If you have something to . . .

IAN: Like eh . . .

LAURENCE: Just a knife.

IAN: I have a knife. (*He goes to a box which has a few kitchen things*) Just a cutlery knife . . .

LAURENCE: Yeah, just anything . . .

(*Ian holds up an ordinary "knife and fork" knife.*)

Yeah, you . . .

(*He goes to Ian, who takes the bottle up, and they awkwardly jockey for position.*)

IAN: Will I . . . or . . . (*He hands the bottle to Laurence*)

LAURENCE: Yeah, you just . . . you push it down. My . . . (*He gestures with his bandaged hand*)

IAN: Oh yes, you just . . . (*He takes the bottle and attempts to push the cork in*)

LAURENCE: If you, just . . . if you take that, tear off the . . .

IAN: Oh yeah, yeah. (*He uses the knife to cut the seal away from around the cork*) Actually I'm going to put it on the . . . Just . . . (*He puts the bottle on the floor and pushes the cork down with the knife*) It's going down.

LAURENCE (*Indicating the bathroom*): Is that the jacks?

IAN: Oh yeah, go ahead.

(*Laurence goes into the bathroom. Ian struggles on the floor. Finally the cork goes in.*)

(*Calls out*) I've done it, it's gone in!

(*He pours two mugs of wine. He stands there, waiting. He seems disconnected for a moment, almost not part of his own life. The toilet flushes. Laurence emerges. Ian hands him a drink.*)

Now. God, the things we do, ha? Well, cheers.

(*They drink.*)

God, it's all right. Here. (*He gives Laurence another drink*) Is your hand all right?

LAURENCE: Ah yeah. It's wrecked.

IAN: What happened to it?

LAURENCE: Ah, a banger. I was eh . . . I was letting off a banger, with my son, on Halloween. Sometimes my eyes aren't that good. And the fucking thing nearly blew my fucking hand off.

IAN: Oh my God. Is it all right?

LAURENCE: Ah it's wrecked. I can only move these two fingers.

IAN: Oh no.

LAURENCE: Yeah, it's a fucking killer, you know? I can't work, you know?

IAN: Oh no. What, what do you, what, what are you working at or . . .

LAURENCE: Ah, I was lined up to get a job driving a van, but . . .

IAN: Oh no.

LAURENCE: Yeah.

(*Pause.*)

IAN: Is it . . . is it healing or are you getting treatment for it or . . .

LAURENCE: Ah, I'm supposed to keep . . . to go in for physiotherapy but it's, it's tricky 'cause I'm trying to keep a few things organized at the moment and I, sometimes . . . the appointments don't suit me, then, you know?

IAN: Right . . .

LAURENCE: Because of the times. But this fucking thing is filthy, I need to . . . but they keep you waiting for so long in there, though, you know?

IAN: God, well . . . God, well you . . . you don't want to let it get infected.

LAURENCE: I know. I know. But, yeah, you know, I have to do it. You know?

(*Pause.*)

IAN: Are you cold? Do you want me to turn that, turn that on?

LAURENCE: Yeah, I'm freezing. Are you not cold?

IAN: Oh sure, I'll . . . (*He goes and turns on an electric heater*) This heats up real fast.

(*Pause.*)

I'd say it gets pretty cold when you're . . . up there just . . .

LAURENCE: Yeah, it's . . . you know . . . but sometimes you just fucking have to, 'cause . . .

IAN: Yeah . . . Yeah . . . (*Pause*) I've never eh . . . I've never gone up there, before, you know? I've never . . . this is the . . . I mean . . . Do you, do . . . I, do you, do I pay you now, or do I . . . ?

LAURENCE: Yeah, well, whatever. If you want to get it out of the way, you don't have to think about it then, anymore, you know?

IAN: Yeah, yeah, that's . . . okay, let's . . . okay. (*He counts out some money from his pocket*) Em. (*He hands it to Laurence*) That's . . .

LAURENCE: Yeah. You don't have to be so nervous.

IAN: Yeah. I know. I'm sorry. I just, em . . . I've never . . .

LAURENCE: Because you're making me nervous.

IAN: Oh no, I don't want to, I'm sorry.

LAURENCE: Yeah, no, it's just, I get, like I just . . .

IAN: I know, I know, it's contagious. I know. I've never . . .

LAURENCE (*Indicating sound system*): Do you want to turn on some music or something?

IAN: Yeah! Yeah, I'll . . . (*Goes over to the stereo and starts looking through some CDs*) God, what'll I put on?

LAURENCE: Just whatever you want.

IAN: Yeah, but em . . . Do you like the Eagles?

LAURENCE: Don't know them.

IAN: No. Hold on, someone burned this for me . . . (*He puts on a CD. It is slow, mellow country rock*) This is, you know, it's quite laid-back.

(*Laurence makes a slight move as though he may be coming toward Ian. Ian halts him with his voice.*)

You have a son?

LAURENCE: Yeah.

IAN: Is he . . . How old is he?

LAURENCE (*Without much enthusiasm*): He's six.

IAN: Wow, is he . . .

LAURENCE: He's with his ma. She's nuts, you know, her mother looks after him more.

IAN: Right.

LAURENCE: Yeah, but look, I don't really wanna . . .

IAN: Yeah, of course, I'm sorry.

(*Pause.*)

Are you a bit warmer?

LAURENCE: Yeah, yeah.

IAN: God . . . I'd say it's cold up there, though, when you're waiting around, is it?

LAURENCE: Yeah it's weird, you know? I mean, it's a bit . . .

IAN: Mmm.

LAURENCE: Yeah, I got the shit kicked out of me one time up there, you know?

IAN: Oh no . . .

LAURENCE: Yeah, ah it was my own fault. I wouldn't even be out there tonight only, I've been staying with my cousin in this flat in town. But this young one came to stay there, and she said there was some money gone out of her bag, and . . . it wasn't me, like, but . . . now . . . I have to try to . . .

IAN: Yeah . . .

LAURENCE: Get a few quid together.

IAN: I know.

LAURENCE: So I can go back and . . .

IAN: Yeah . . .

LAURENCE: I don't even want to go back, though, but I need an address.

IAN: Yeah.

LAURENCE: This is where you work, yeah?

IAN: Yeah, well, yeah . . . I've been here for a few months, you know?

LAURENCE: What do you work at?

IAN: Well, I'm a therapist, you know?

LAURENCE: A therapist?

IAN: Yeah, you know . . .

LAURENCE: What, do you . . .

IAN: Well, you know, people can come, and . . . talk to me, or . . .

LAURENCE: What, like mad people?

IAN: No, not mad . . . Just maybe . . . people who might just feel a little bit . . . stuck, you know? And maybe they . . . just need a . . . just another point of view on what's going on, if they're carrying, you know, a big burden, you know? Of some guilt maybe. You know? Or where they might feel it's hard to go on because they've got themselves just in a bit of a corner, because they're worried about other people, or maybe it's just that they have some old feeling . . . Maybe even from years ago, just even sometimes things can happen to us when we're children, and that, you know, maybe that sets the tone for how people get on later. Where maybe they get a bit stuck. And maybe I can just invite them to consider something that maybe they didn't think was that important before, but, you know, maybe it was . . . and . . .

LAURENCE: Do you ever hypnotize people?

IAN: No, no I don't. We . . . no, it's, it's all fully conscious. It's . . . about perceiving reality, I suppose.

(*Pause. Laurence puts his drink down as if to move toward Ian.*)

I have a daughter. That I haven't seen . . . either . . . you know, much . . . She's with her mother . . . I mean, I know what you . . . when you say . . .

(*Laurence moves toward Ian. Ian stands very still. Laurence puts his hand on Ian's arm and gently moves him closer.*)

LAURENCE: It's all right. Don't be frightened.

(*Laurence takes Ian's drink and puts it down. Ian is shaking. Laurence pulls Ian toward him and holds him, swaying to the music. Ian tentatively puts his arms around Laurence. Suddenly the music breaks into faster, wholly inappropriate hillbilly fiddle/banjo music.*)

IAN: Sorry!

(*He goes to the stereo and turns it off.*)

God, that's, look, em . . . when I say that I haven't, you know, done this, or gone up to the park before, I don't mean that I haven't just gone up to the park at night, you know . . . I mean. (*Pause*) I mean I've never been with a man. (*Pause*) Do you understand me?

LAURENCE (*Shrugs*): That's all right. The men who go up there are all fucking married, you know? Loads of them are! That's why . . . they . . . (*Pause*) What difference does it make? (*Pause*) You should just do what you want to do, you know? (*Pause*) Put on the other music. Put on the music that was on before. (*Reassuringly*) I have nowhere else to go.

(*Ian puts on the other music. He goes to the bottle and pours them both another drink. He hands a mug to Laurence, avoiding eye contact. Laurence takes his hand. Ian looks into Laurence's eyes. Laurence returns his gaze. They move closer together.*

Lights down.)

SCENE FIVE

(*It is daytime. Bright sunlight streams into the room. As the scene progresses, the room should become more dusky. There are dust sheets on the desk and most of the furniture and books are gone. There are boxes all around the office. Ian is on the floor, gift-wrapping a child's teddy bear with great difficulty. There is a little transistor radio on the floor and indistinct daytime radio is playing while Ian packs. The intercom buzzer goes off and Ian goes to answer it, maybe a bit pissed off; he doesn't expect anyone.*)

IAN: Yeah? Hello? Hello? Yeah, hold on. (*He presses the buzzer to release the door*) Hello? Are you in? Hello? What? Hello? (*He presses the button again*) Hello? Are you there? What?

(*There is a knock on his door. Ian opens it to reveal John, carrying a present.*)

Oh, hello!

JOHN: Sorry, I'm barging in on you.

IAN: No! No! I just I couldn't hear . . . come in, come in!

JOHN (*Coming in*): No, I just . . . I've had this, fucking . . . I've had it in the car and I, 'cause I wanted to get you something.

IAN: Oh no!

JOHN: And then, of course, I've been driving around with it in the boot for the last six weeks, you know what I mean?

IAN: Oh no . . .

JOHN: It's nothing.

IAN: Oh no . . .

JOHN: It's a lamp, it's nothing.

IAN: Oh but still, thanks, you . . . come in, sit down, there's nowhere to sit.

JOHN: And I was going by, and I thought . . . God, I should just call in, and I thought, well, it's lunchtime, he probably won't have anyone there, and . . .

IAN: No, no, I'm . . .

JOHN: Janey Mack, you're . . .

IAN: Well, no, it's lucky you . . . I'm moving! I'm going, you know?

JOHN: You're moving your office?

IAN: I'm, well, no, I'm moving. I'm, I'm going down to Limerick, believe it or not.

JOHN: Limerick?

IAN: Yeah, my fiancée is there and . . . (*As though these are tedious little details that are too boring to go into*) With our . . . baby, and some . . . friends of hers have lent her a house there, so . . .

JOHN: Yeah.

IAN: I'm going down . . . and I've, you know, I'm applying for a . . . I've an interview down there. For a post so . . .

JOHN: Yeah.

IAN: Mmm. You know, so . . . it's time, and . . .

JOHN: Yeah, well great! That sounds good. Dublin's . . . you know . . .

IAN: Yeah.

JOHN: It's a tough town.

(*Pause.*)

IAN: Yeah, well, look, let me, move some of this stuff. Sit down!

(*He bustles around*)

JOHN: Ah, I'm not gonna stay, really.

IAN: No, no! Look, the kettle is still . . . on the go, we're still . . . Let me . . . (*Disappears into the bathroom with the kettle. Off*) So, how are you keeping?

JOHN: Yeah. You know, I'm good! You know, I have to say, I'm good. Thank God, you know? I'm getting there, you know, definitely, and I really, you know . . .

(*Ian reemerges and plugs the kettle in.*)

I just wanted to say thanks, because, you know . . .

IAN: No, no. You did the work, you know?

JOHN: Yeah, no, but, you know, I mean . . . I wanted to, you know . . .

IAN: God, well, you didn't have to. And you shouldn't have. Really, you know?

JOHN: Yeah, well . . .

IAN: No, well, thank you, I mean . . . will I open it?

JOHN: Yeah, yeah! Go ahead, open it, it's nothing, you know? It's really, it's not . . .

(*Ian starts to open the gift.*)

I mean, I have no eye for these things. The girl in the shop, you know, I—it was her really. I mean, I said it was a present and she said, who is it for, and then of course I realized, "God, I know nothing about this man!" You know? (*They laugh*) Because I don't! I mean, it's weird, isn't it?

IAN: Well, it's, you know, it's . . . (*Unsaid: "normal"*)

JOHN: So I said, it was just a thank-you present really.

IAN: Tch, God, no . . .

JOHN: And she . . .

(Ian produces a stunning antique lamp from the box.)

IAN: Oh my God!

JOHN: Ah, no, sure . . .

IAN: This is too much.

JOHN: No, it's nothing.

IAN: Is it, it's . . . an antique, or . . .?

JOHN: It's, ah, it's from the thirties or fucking something, I don't know.

IAN: No, well that's, it's too much . . .

JOHN: Please, no. Do you like it?

IAN: It's beautiful, really . . .

JOHN: Well, you know, thank you, you know, that's . . . (*Unsaid: "why I'm here"*) I . . .

IAN: Thank you, really, thanks, God . . .

JOHN (*Producing a card from his pocket*): And this is just a little card. You know, to go . . .

IAN: Oh, God . . . God, thanks, thanks John, really. (*Reads the card*)

JOHN (*Interrupting Ian reading it*): Ah, read it later.

IAN: Tch. God, no, well. I don't know what to say now.

JOHN: Ah there's . . . (*Unsaid: "nothing to say"*)

IAN: God, well let me make you a cup of tea. Here, sit down, take off your coat.

JOHN: I'm grand, really.

IAN (*Producing an old stool from somewhere*): No, sit down there, here.

(*John sits a bit awkwardly.*)

So, God, how are you keeping?

JOHN: I'm good, you know? I'm good. I'm . . . I've just bought an apartment.

IAN: Oh wow, so we're both . . .

JOHN: We're both moving. Yeah . . . nearly finished the, the legal . . . which can be a nightmare . . . but it's . . . it's . . .

IAN: If it's what you've got to do, that's right, I know . . .

JOHN: Yeah, it's lovely. It's down there on the seafront, just there near St. Anne's Park.

IAN: Oh very nice, yeah, I know there.

JOHN: Yeah, it's those ones there . . .

IAN: They're nice, yeah.

JOHN: Yeah, so whole new . . .

(*Ian finds teabags and cups.*)

IAN: And you're . . . You're good . . . in yourself, and . . .

JOHN: I'm . . . really good, Ian, you know? I have to say. I'm looking forward to the move. And I've . . . actually been in the house again, this last month, you know?

IAN: Oh right! God, that's . . . do you take sugar?

JOHN: No, no, it's fine.

IAN: Good, because I don't . . . eh . . .

(*They laugh a little.*)

JOHN: No I don't, anyway, so . . . and eh, yeah, I've been there, in the house. And I mean, there was a time, as you know, I couldn't even have envisaged myself spending even one night there, so, no I'm . . .

IAN: But you're going to move on and . . .

JOHN: I'm moving on . . . It's, it's just . . . It just feels right. It just feels like that's, that's what . . . I . . . what I . . . that's just what I want to do! I mean, I don't want to be some old guy on his own in there. You know? That house is all to do with me and Mari, and it's even too big for two people—it was too big when we moved in. I mean, if there had been kids, okay, but, you know, that didn't happen and . . . I mean, I just feel like my life isn't over, you know? Like why should I stay in the house out of some kind of mad fucking duty to fucking . . . you know . . . I mean . . .

IAN: I know, you're right, I know. I mean it's so . . .

JOHN: I mean we create these fucking . . .

IAN: I know, I know.

JOHN: These mad . . .

IAN: I know. I know. But that's, you know, that's great, you're . . .

JOHN: Yeah . . . I'm . . . you know, I'm getting on with it, and I really see it now like a . . . like a new chapter is opening up, and like *you* know, there was a time I could never have thought that that was even possible! You know, I mean . . .

IAN: Well, that's great, I mean, that's . . .

JOHN: And that's why, I mean, I want to thank you really, because . . .

IAN: Yeah, well, like I say, you did the work.

JOHN: . . . I don't know what I . . . would've . . .

IAN: Well, look I'm . . . I'm glad. I'm happy for you, I mean that. And, you know, I hope, you know you . . .

JOHN: My fucking brother introduced me to a woman, there, you know?

IAN: Oh . . . ?

JOHN: Yeah, I mean, he's a prick. He can be a bit of an arsehole. But he's, you know . . . he's all right, you know, really.

IAN: Yeah, I know what you mean.

JOHN: Yeah, him and his missus were killed asking me over for some dinner there four or five weeks ago. I was like . . . (*Sarcastic*) "Yeah, right . . ." you know. Because I can sometimes do without that, you know what I mean? But I . . . went over. There were a few people there. This girl was there. I knew her, though, slightly, from before, she used to work where I—she used to work there, coincidentally, and she's . . . she's a bit younger than me now, you know, but . . .

IAN (*Shrugs*): Well . . .

JOHN: Yeah, sure, what fucking difference does it make? I agree. Although . . . if she was a good bit *older* than me now, the shoe might well be very much on the other fucking foot now, you know what I mean?

(*They laugh.*)

No, but, she's a nice girl, you know? Sure, I'm not . . . we just went to the pictures and had a drink, you know, just . . . (*Short pause*) We're going to the theatre tomorrow night.

IAN: Oh!

JOHN: I know! (*As though the theatre is rubbish*) "Good luck!" Ah, but, sure . . .

IAN: Yeah, well, that's . . . (*Short pause*) Don't feel that you have to rush into anything, John, you know?

JOHN: No, no, no, no, I'm not, no. I'm, it just feels like it's just a part of . . . just a new . . . it's all just a new . . . it's good, you know? Don't worry.

IAN: Yeah, yeah, no, I'm . . .

JOHN: But Jesus! Do you know who I saw?

IAN: Yeah?

JOHN: Vivien.

IAN: Yeah?

JOHN: Vivien, the . . .

IAN: Yeah.

JOHN: The object of my . . . my downfall. The big . . .

IAN: Yeah.

JOHN: Yeah, saw her there at a do. God, it was weird, you know? I mean she had great sympathy for me and everything, but it was really like nothing had ever happened? Between us? Weird, you know? And do you know what was really weird? I realized we had *nothing* in common. What about that, you know?

(*Ian nods.*)

Serious. Serious fucking shit. I came away thinking, "I don't even like this woman," you know? Bizarre. When I . . . (*Short pause*) Mad.

(*Pause.*)

IAN: God, John. Well, you know, it sounds like you're doing really well though, you know?

JOHN: Well, I'm, you know . . .

IAN: But you're getting out, you're meeting people . . . and . . .

JOHN: Ah, I'm just, I'm just taking it handy. And . . . it was a great help, you were a great help, Ian, to me, you know? I mean it and . . . I wish you all the best, you know?

IAN: Well, look, I wish you all the best too, John. I really do, you know, and . . . you know, it makes me feel good to see you . . . that you're, you know . . .

JOHN: Well, thanks. Thank you. You know? (*Short pause*) And I'll . . . I only came to . . . I better let you . . .

IAN: Well, I'm, yeah . . . I said I'd drop the keys back this afternoon and . . . I'm . . .

JOHN: Do you want a hand with anything?

IAN: No, no, no . . .

JOHN: Are you sure?

IAN: Really, don't . . . I'm, I'm nearly there now.

(*They are standing. John picks up his coat.*)

JOHN: Okay.

IAN: So, no ghosts.

JOHN: No, No ghosts. (*He exhales*) But, I'll tell you, you know, even if I saw one, Ian, it's not . . . I mean, seeing something is one thing but . . . it's how it makes you *feel*, isn't it? It's how that makes you feel. That's what's important. Someone could see something and it doesn't really matter. Someone else'll see it and . . . it's the end of the world, you know?

IAN (*Affirmative*): Mmm.

JOHN: That's the reality, you know? What it *does* to you is the reality.

IAN: I know.

JOHN: But you don't believe in ghosts anyway, Ian. You've got it sussed.

(*They are moving toward the door.*)

IAN: John, there was a time I would've given anything to see one. Just to know that there was . . . something else. Do you know what I mean?

JOHN: Sure.

IAN: Just something else, besides all the . . . you know . . . the pain and the confusion. Just something that gave everything . . . *some* meaning, you know? I'm talking about God, really, you know?

JOHN: I know. Where is He?

IAN: I know. But don't get me wrong. I think you had a real experience. I think you really experienced something—but I think it happened because you needed to experience it.

JOHN: Yeah, I know . . .

IAN: You were pulling all this . . . you felt maybe you couldn't move on without being . . . punished somehow and . . .

JOHN: I know.

IAN: It happened! But . . . I don't believe you saw a ghost. Does that make sense?

JOHN: Well, yeah, it makes sense to me now, but there was a time it really wouldn't have, you know? (*Pause*) But that was a different time.

IAN: Yeah, it was.

JOHN (*Opening the door*): I'll tell you, the mind, it's mad isn't it?

IAN: John, we know nothing. We just know nothing really.

JOHN: We're just barely fucking hanging in there, really, aren't we?

IAN: Well, some better than others. But you're doing good, John, you know? Considering, I mean, you know?

JOHN: I know. I know that. But I had to fucking go there to find that out. Do you know what I mean?

IAN: I do. I know.

(*Pause.*)

JOHN: Look, I'll love you and leave you. Good luck with everything, all right?

IAN: Well you too, and thanks, for the present. It really is so thoughtful—

JOHN (*Interrupting*): Ah, it's nothing, good luck.

(*They shake hands.*)

I'll see you.

IAN: Well . . . Actually, I'll wait here till you get out down there. And I can buzz it if . . . 'cause it's still . . .

JOHN: Oh, nothing changes! I'll see you Ian, good luck.

IAN: I'll see you, John, bye now.

(*Ian hovers near the open door while John goes down. He picks up a flyer off the floor at the threshold and crumples it up. He picks up two books off the floor and looks at the back of one of them. We hear the outer door slam shut. In the distance we hear the faint sound of an ice-cream van's music.*)

(*Calls out*) Did you get out?

(*There is no answer.*

Ian throws one of the two books in a box near the door. He shuts the door and crosses the room to throw the other book in a different box.

In the darkening gloom of the afternoon, we see that Mari's ghost has appeared behind the door. She is looking at Ian, just as John described her; she wears her red coat, which is filthy, her hair is wet. She looks beaten up. She looks terrifying.

Ian has his back to her at his desk, going through some old mail. But he seems to sense something and turns.

Lights down.)

End of Play

Sarah Ruhl

Although she is from Chicago, Sarah Ruhl (b. 1974) now lives in New York City and is married to a physician at New York University. She studied with Paula Vogel at Brown University and, in 2006, won a MacArthur Fellowship, which provides her with $100,000 a year for five years—freeing her to write without financial concerns. Since the production of *The Clean House* (2004), which won the Susan Smith Blackburn Award for the best play of the year by a woman and was a finalist for the 2005 Pulitzer Prize, her plays are eagerly anticipated. In almost record time, she has become a powerful force in modern theater. Paula Vogel said that her work takes us "back to the importance of theatre as myth, the importance of theatre as community."

Some of her earlier plays, such as *Melancholy Play* (2002), deal with psychological issues. Ruhl explores melancholy and sadness in this play, with a special perspective on the medication that often masks such emotions. Not all sadness is depression, she argues, and using Prozac and other such drugs to treat sadness is not necessarily valid. One need not always be "up," and moments of sadness are normal human feelings, not medical emergencies.

Late: A Cowboy Song was given a reading in 2002 in Dallas, Texas, but the full production was not presented until 2005 in Houston at Stages Repertory Theatre. Set in Pittsburgh, it examines questions of identity and focuses on a man and woman who change their lives after a chance meeting with a cowgirl. Unfortunately, the reviews were not kind to this play.

By contrast, *The Clean House* not only was successful in its premier at Yale Repertory Theatre, and in its later production in New York, but also has gone on to become one of the most produced plays of the past few years. Another recent Ruhl play is *Eurydice* (2006), an adaptation of the myth of Orpheus and Eurydice, in which the poet Orpheus sings so beautifully that the very rocks feel emotion. After Orpheus loses his wife Eurydice to the underworld, he goes down to Hades himself to bring her back, but on the way up the path to sunlight, he breaks Pluto's rule and turns to look at his wife. For this, he loses her forever. The reviews for *Eurydice* have been overwhelmingly positive, and the staging, like that in *The Clean House*, has been praised as highly original. For example, when Orpheus arrives in the underworld, he is in a slightly tilted elevator, a device that Offenbach used in his opera *Orpheus in the Underworld* (1874). In Ruhl's play, however, the elevator contains a wild rainstorm, and when the door opens, water runs out on stage. The dramatic effect is extraordinary.

Ruhl's next work, *Passion Play* (2007), developed over a period of ten years. It began when, as a student in Providence, R.I., she saw a performance of the passion play and began writing an undergraduate thesis. A traditional play that has been performed for centuries in one form or another, the passion play tells the story of the crucifixion of Jesus Christ. The production in Oberammergau, Germany, has been put on regularly since the Middle Ages, and because it has changed little in all that time, it is often discussed as contributing to European anti-Semitism. What Ruhl did with the play, which was produced by the Goodman Theatre in Chicago in September 2007, was to explore it in different contexts, both historically and geographically. The play is told in three parts. The first is set in England in 1571 under the reign of Queen Elizabeth, in the period during which there was a very severe crackdown on Roman Catholics, who were thought to be a threat to the English Crown. The second part is set in Germany in 1934, when Hitler especially approved of the passion play at Oberammergau because it fueled his hatred of the Jews, helped spread anti-Semitism, and made it politically easier for him to begin murdering Europe's Jews. The third part is set in Spearfish, South Dakota, in the 1980s during Ronald Reagan's presidency, at the Black Hills passion play. This event is a huge outdoor undertaking that reenacts the last days of Jesus's life using period costumes, dozens of players, and a great deal of sophisticated technology in a pageant described as the most impressive of its kind.

Ruhl's play merges religion and politics to demonstrate the ways in which the religious material of the passion play can be molded into a political message appropriate for its time. She comments on both religion and politics at a time when they have once again merged as a force in the modern world. *Dead Man's Cell Phone* (2008), commissioned by and performed at Playwrights Horizons in New York, starred Mary-Louise Parker, Kathleen Chalfant, and Anne Bogart. This play deals with moral issues and the way people connect with one another. It centers on a woman who answers a cell phone, only to discover that the owner is dead and that the man's life was strange and challenging in ways that she could never have imagined.

THE CLEAN HOUSE

The stimulus for writing this play came from a comment made by one of Sarah Ruhl's friends, who was having difficulty finding someone to clean a house. Soon, Ruhl began to think through and map out some of the extraordinary intersections that make this play compelling. Lane is a doctor whose house is being cleaned by Matilde, a Portuguese woman who was born laughing and who is not fully committed to cleaning Lane's house. Lane's husband Charles, a surgeon, is uninvolved in Matilde's concerns. He is not aware that Matilde, searching for the perfect joke, feels she has a calling to create jokes, as did her parents. Lane's sister Virginia visits and discovers Matilde's secret, and then she creates a secret of her own by cleaning her sister's house herself without Lane's knowledge. Virginia, unlike Lane, enjoys cleaning house. Cleaning together, Matilde and Virginia discover that Charles is having an affair.

The play introduces Ana, an Argentine woman dying of cancer. Charles not only has fallen in love with his patient but believes that she is his *bashert,* a Yiddish word for "soulmate." Under Jewish law, one is obligated to leave a marriage if one meets one's bashert. Charles and Ana leave to live together. Lane, who finds all this improbable—her husband is not Jewish, although Ana is—tries to work things out despite her confusion. Meanwhile Charles, even more improbably, treks to Alaska in search of a special yew tree the bark of which may contain a medication that will save Ana, who does not want to go to the hospital or accept chemotherapy.

The complications that arise from these circumstances are deftly woven together in such a way as to involve every character and to produce changes that surprise everyone. This play is not naturalistic, nor is it necessarily expressionist or symbolic. Yet it creates emotional tension and emotional responses in the audience that are similar to those expected in an Aristotelian mimetic drama. In terms of staging, when Charles and Ana live in their house by the sea, their balcony is raised to the upper half of the stage and overlooks Lane's living room. The staging is daring and powerful in part because of the stark white furniture and the brilliance of the very white lighting. The lights and interior decoration seem to spell out "clean house" while the complexities of the drama unfold.

The Clean House in Performance

Although the first act of *The Clean House* was commissioned in 2000 by the McCarter Theatre Center in Princeton, N. J., the world premier of the full play was at Yale Repertory Theatre in September 2004. In December the play opened in Philadelphia at the Wilma Theater, then in 2005 it went to the South Coast Repertory Theatre and to the Wooly Mammoth Theatre in Washington, D. C. About the Washington production, Jayne Blanchard said, "It will change how you view dusting and Windex forever." London and Melbourne productions followed in 2006, as did the Chicago production in the Goodman Theatre and the New York production at the Mitzi Newhouse Theatre in Lincoln Center. That production, which starred Jill Clayburgh as Virginia, Blair Brown as Lane, and Vanessa Aspilaga as Matilde, garnered extraordinary reviews celebrating a distinct new talent. Bill Rauch directed, as he had in the world premier production. The reviews echoed each other in claiming *The Clean House* was "the finest and funniest" play to be seen that season. Productions have followed in Vancouver, Providence, Houston, and enough other venues that the play was among the most frequently produced of the 2006 and 2007 seasons.

Sarah Ruhl (b. 1974)

THE CLEAN HOUSE

2004

Characters

LANE, *A doctor, a woman in her early fifties. She wears white.*

MATILDE, *Lane's cleaning lady, a woman in her late twenties. She wears black. She is Brazilian. She has a refined sense of deadpan.*

VIRGINIA, *Lane's sister, a woman in her late fifties.*

CHARLES, *Lane's husband, a man in his fifties. A compassionate surgeon. He is childlike underneath*

his white coat. In Act I, Charles plays Matilde's father.

ANA, *An Argentinean woman. She is impossibly charismatic. In Act I, she plays Matilde's mother. She is older than Lane.*

Note: Everyone in this play should be able to tell a really good joke.

Place: *A metaphysical Connecticut. Or, a house that is not far from the sea and not far from the city.*

Set: *A white living room. White couch, white vase, white lamp, white rug. A balcony.*

Note: *The living room needn't be full of living room detail, though it should feel human. The space should transform and surprise. The balcony should feel high but also intimate—a close-up shot.*

A Note on Pronunciation: *"Matilde" is pronounced by the Americans in the play as "Matilda." It is pronounced by Ana as "Mathilda" at first, until Ana realizes that Matilde is Brazilian. And it is pronounced by Matilde, and the more observant characters in the play, as "Ma-chil-gee," which is the correct Brazilian pronunciation.*

A Note on Double Casting: *It is important that Ana and Charles play Matilde's mother and father in Act I. How much can they create, without speaking, a sense of memory and longing, through silence, gesture and dance? Ana's transformation at the very end of the play should create a full circle for Matilde, from the dead to the living and back again.*

ACT 1 • 1. *Matilde*

(*Matilde tells a long joke in Portuguese to the audience. We can tell she is telling a joke even though we might not understand the language.*
She finishes the joke.
She exits.)

2. *Lane*

LANE (*to the audience*): It has been such a hard month.
My cleaning lady—from Brazil—decided that she was depressed one day and stopped cleaning my house.
I was like: clean my house!
And she wouldn't!
We took her to the hospital and I had her medicated and she Still Wouldn't Clean.
And—in the meantime—*I've* been cleaning my house!
I'm sorry, but I did not go to medical school to clean my own house.

3. *Virginia*

VIRGINIA (*to the audience*): People who give up the *privilege* of cleaning their own houses—they're insane people.
If you do not clean: how do you know if you've made any progress in life? I love dust. The dust always makes progress. Then I remove the dust. That is progress.

If it were not for dust I think I would die. If there were no dust to clean then there would be so much leisure time and so much thinking time and I would have to do something besides thinking and that thing might be to slit my wrists.
Ha ha ha ha ha ha just kidding.
I'm not a morbid person. That just popped out!
My sister is a wonderful person. She's a doctor. At an important hospital. I've always wondered how one hospital can be more important than another hospital. They are places for human waste. Places to put dead bodies.
I'm sorry. I'm being morbid again.
My sister has given up the privilege of cleaning her own house. Something deeply personal—she has given up. She does not know how long it takes the dust to accumulate under her bed. She does not know if her husband is sleeping with a prostitute because she does not smell his dirty underwear. All of these things, she fails to know.
I know when there is dust on the mirror. Don't misunderstand me—I'm an educated woman. But if I were to die at any moment during the day, no one would have to clean my kitchen.

4. *Matilde*

MATILDE (*to the audience*): The story of my parents is this. It was said that my father was the funniest man in his village. He did not marry until he was sixty-three because he did not want to marry a woman who was not funny. He said he would wait until he met his match in wit.
And then one day he met my mother. He used to say: your mother—and he would take a long pause—(*Matilde takes a long pause*)—is funnier than I am. We have never been apart since the day we met, because I always wanted to know the next joke.
My mother and father did not look into each other's eyes. They laughed like hyenas. Even when they made love they laughed like hyenas. My mother was old for a mother. She refused many proposals. It would kill her, she said, to have to spend her days laughing at jokes that were not funny.

(*Pause.*)

I wear black because I am in mourning. My mother died last year. Have you ever heard the expression: "I almost died laughing"? Well that's what she did. The doctors couldn't explain it. They argued. They said she choked on her own spit, but they don't really know. She was laughing at one of my father's jokes. A joke he took one year to make up, for the anniversary of their marriage. When my mother died laughing, my father shot himself. And so I came here, to clean this house.

5. *Lane and Matilde*

(*Lane enters.*
Matilde is looking out the window.)

LANE: Are you all right?
MATILDE: Yes.
LANE: Would you please clean the bathroom when you get a chance?
MATILDE: Yes.
LANE: Soon?
MATILDE: Yes.

(*Matilde looks at Lane.*)

LANE: The house is very dirty.

(*Matilde is silent.*)

This is difficult for me. I don't like to order people around. I've never had a live-in maid.

(*Matilde is silent.*)

Matilde—what did you do in your country before you came to the United States?
MATILDE: I was a student. I studied humor. You know—jokes.
LANE: I'm being serious.
MATILDE: I'm being serious too. My parents were the funniest people in Brazil. And then they died.
LANE: I'm sorry.
That must be very difficult.
MATILDE: I was the third funniest person in my family. Then my parents died, making me the first funniest. There was no one left to laugh at my jokes, so I left.
LANE: That's very interesting. I don't—always—understand the arts. Listen. Matilde. I understand that you have a life, an emotional life—and that you are also my cleaning lady. If I met you at—say—a party—and you said, I am from a small village in Brazil, and my parents were comedians, I would say, that's very interesting. You sound like a very interesting woman.
  But life is about context.
  And I have met you in the context of my house, where I have hired you to clean. And I don't want an interesting person to clean my house. I just want my house—cleaned.

(*Lane is on the verge of tears.*)

MATILDE (*with compassion*): Is something wrong?
LANE: No, it's just that—I don't like giving orders in my own home. It makes me—uncomfortable. I want you to do all the things I want you to do without my having to tell you.
MATILDE: Do you tell the nurses at the hospital what to do?
LANE: Yes.
MATILDE: Then pretend I am your nurse.
LANE: Okay.
  Nurse—would you polish the silver, please?
MATILDE: A doctor does not say: Nurse—would you polish the silver, please?

A doctor says: Nurse—polish the silver!
LANE: You're right. Nurse—polish the silver!
MATILDE: Yes, Doctor.

(*Matilde gets out silver polish and begins polishing.*)

(*Lane watches her for a moment, then exits.*)

6. *Matilde*

(*Matilde stops cleaning.*)

MATILDE: This is how I imagine my parents.

(*Music.*)

(*A dashing couple appears.*)

They are dancing.
They are not the best dancers in the world.
They laugh until laughing makes them kiss.
They kiss until kissing makes them laugh.

(*They dance.*
They laugh until laughing makes them kiss.
They kiss until kissing makes them laugh.
Matilde watches.
Matilde longs for them.)

7. *Virginia and Matilde*

(*The doorbell rings.*
The music stops.
Matilde's parents exit.
They blow kisses to Matilde.
Matilde waves back.
The doorbell rings again.
Matilde answers the door.
Virginia is there.)

MATILDE: Hello.
VIRGINIA: Hello. You are the maid?
MATILDE: Yes.
  You are the sister?
VIRGINIA: Yes.
  How did you know?
MATILDE: I dusted your photograph.
  My boss said: this is my sister. We don't look alike.
  I thought: you don't look like my boss. You must be her sister.
  My name is Matilde. (*Brazilian pronunciation of Matilde: Ma-chil-gee*)
VIRGINIA: I thought your name was Matilde. (*American pronunciation of Matilde: Matilda*)
MATILDE: Kind of.
VIRGINIA: Nice to meet you.
MATILDE: Nice to meet you. I don't know your name.
VIRGINIA: Oh! My name is Virginia.
MATILDE: Like the state?

VIRGINIA: Yes.

MATILDE: I've never been to Virginia.

VIRGINIA: Maybe I should go.

MATILDE: To Virginia?

VIRGINIA: No. I mean, am I interrupting you?

MATILDE: No. I was just—cleaning. Your sister is at work.

VIRGINIA: She's always at work.

MATILDE: Would you like to come in?

VIRGINIA: Yes. Actually—I came to see you.

(*They enter the living room.*)

Lane tells me that you've been feeling a little blue.

MATILDE: Blue?

VIRGINIA: Sad.

MATILDE: Oh. She told you that?

VIRGINIA: Come, sit on the couch with me.

MATILDE: Okay.

(*Virginia goes to sit on the couch.*
She pats the couch.
Matilde sits down next to her.)

VIRGINIA: Do you miss home?

MATILDE: Of course I do. Doesn't everyone?

VIRGINIA: Is that why you've been sad?

MATILDE: No, I don't think so. It's just that—I don't like to clean houses. I think it makes me sad.

VIRGINIA: You don't like to clean houses.

MATILDE: No.

VIRGINIA: But that's so simple!

MATILDE: Yes.

VIRGINIA: Why don't you like to clean?

MATILDE: I've never liked to clean. When I was a child I thought: if the floor is dirty, look at the ceiling. It is always clean.

VIRGINIA: I like cleaning.

MATILDE: You do? Why?

VIRGINIA: It clears my head.

MATILDE: So it is, for you, a religious practice?

VIRGINIA: No. It's just that: cleaning my house—makes me feel clean.

MATILDE: But you don't clean other people's houses. For money.

VIRGINIA: No—I clean my own house.

MATILDE: I think that is different.

VIRGINIA: Do you feel sad *while* you are cleaning? Or before? Or after?

MATILDE: I am sad when I think about cleaning. But I try not to think about cleaning while I am cleaning. I try to think of jokes. But sometimes the cleaning makes me mad. And then I'm not in a funny mood. And *that* makes me sad. Would you like a coffee?

VIRGINIA: I would *love* some coffee.

(*Matilde goes to get a cup of coffee from the kitchen.*
Virginia takes stock of her sister's dust.
Virginia puts her finger on the tabletops to test the dust.
Then she wipes her dirty finger on her skirt.

Then she tries to clean her skirt but she has nothing to clean it with.
Matilde comes back and gives her the coffee.)

Thank you.

MATILDE: You're welcome.

(*Virginia drinks the coffee.*)

VIRGINIA: This is good coffee.

MATILDE: We make good coffee in Brazil.

VIRGINIA: Oh—that's right. You do!

MATILDE: Does that help you to place me in my cultural context?

VIRGINIA: Lane didn't describe you accurately. How old are you?

MATILDE: Young enough that my skin is still good. Old enough that I am starting to think: is my skin still good? Does that answer your question?

VIRGINIA: Yes. You're twenty-seven.

MATILDE: You're good.

VIRGINIA: Thank you. Listen. Matilde. (*American pronunciation*)

MATILDE: Matilde. (*Brazilian pronunciation*)

VIRGINIA: Yes. I have a proposition for you.

MATILDE: A proposition?

VIRGINIA: A deal. I like to clean. You do not like to clean. Why don't I clean for you?

MATILDE: You're joking.

VIRGINIA: No.

MATILDE: I don't get it. What do you want from me?

VIRGINIA: Nothing.

MATILDE: Then—why?

VIRGINIA: I have my house cleaned by approximately 3:12 every afternoon. I have folded the corner of every sheet. The house is quiet. The gold draperies are singing a little lullaby to the ottoman. The silverware is gently sleeping in its box. I tuck in the forks, the spoons, the knives. I do not have children.

MATILDE: I'm sorry.

VIRGINIA (*with increasing velocity*): Don't be sorry. My husband is barren. Is that the right word for a man? I never thought that the world was quite good enough for children anyway. I didn't trust myself to cope with how sick and ugly the world is and how beautiful children are, and the idea of watching them grow into the dirt and mess of the world—someone might kidnap them or rape them or otherwise trample on their innocence, leaving them in the middle of the road, naked, in some perverse sexual position, to die, while strangers rode past on bicycles and tried not to look. I've thought about doing some volunteer work, but I don't know who to volunteer for.

(*A pause. She looks at Matilde.*)

Since I was twenty-two, my life has gone downhill, and not only have I not done what I wanted to do, but I have lost the qualities and temperament that would help me reverse the downward spiral—and now I am a completely different person.

I don't know why I am telling you all of this, Mathalina.

(*Matilde thinks about correcting Virginia. She doesn't.*)

MATILDE: Go on.
VIRGINIA: I used to study Greek literature. One summer my husband and I went to Europe. It was supposed to be relaxing but I have trouble relaxing on vacations. We were going to see ruins and I was going to write about ruins but I found that I had nothing to say about them. I thought: why doesn't someone just sweep them up! Get a very large broom!

I'm sorry. I was trying to say . . .
MATILDE: You were telling me how your life has gone downhill since you were twenty-two.
VIRGINIA: Yes. The point is: every day my house is cleaned by three o'clock. I have a lot of—time.

I'd be very happy to come here and clean Lane's house before Lane gets home from work. That is what I'm telling you. Only don't tell her. She wouldn't like it.
MATILDE: I will let you clean the house if it will make you feel better.
VIRGINIA: Let's start in the bathroom. I love cleaning the toilet. It's so dirty, and then it's so clean!

8. Lane and Matilde

(*Matilde is reading the funny papers.*
Lane enters.)

LANE: It's so clean!
MATILDE: Yes.
LANE: The medication is helping?
MATILDE: I'm feeling much better.
LANE: Well—that's terrific.

(*Lane exits.*
Matilde takes out her medication.
She undoes the bottle,
takes one pill out,
looks at it,
and throws it in the garbage can.)

9. Matilde

MATILDE (*Matilde to the audience*): The perfect joke makes you forget about your life. The perfect joke makes you remember about your life. The perfect joke is stupid when you write it down. The perfect joke was not made up by one person. It passed through the air and you caught it. A perfect joke is somewhere between an angel and a fart.

This is how I imagine my parents:

(*Music.*
Matilde's mother and father appear.
They sit at a café.)

My mother and father are at a café.
My mother is telling my father a joke.
It is a dirty joke.
My father is laughing so hard that he is banging his knee on the underside of the table.
My mother is laughing so hard that she spits out her coffee.
I am with them at the café. I am eight years old.
I say: what's so funny?
(I *hate* not understanding a joke.)
My mother says: ask me again when you're thirty.
Now I'm almost thirty. And I'll never know the joke.

(*Matilde's mother and father look at her.*)

(*They exit.*)

10. Virginia and Matilde

(*The next day.*
Virginia folds laundry.
Matilde watches.
Virginia is happy to be cleaning.)

MATILDE: You're good at that.
VIRGINIA: Thank you.
MATILDE: You want to hear a joke?
VIRGINIA: Not really.
MATILDE: Why?
VIRGINIA: I don't like to laugh out loud.
MATILDE: Why?
VIRGINIA: I don't like my laugh. It's like a wheeze. Someone once told me that. Who was it—my husband? Do you have a husband?
MATILDE: No.
VIRGINIA: That's good.
MATILDE: Do you like your husband?
VIRGINIA: My husband is like a well-placed couch. He takes up the right amount of space. A man should not be too beautiful. Or too good in bed. A man should be—functional. And well chosen. Otherwise you're in trouble.
MATILDE: Does he make you laugh?
VIRGINIA: Oh no. Something uncontrollable would come out of my mouth when he wanted it to. I wouldn't like that.
MATILDE: A good joke cleans your insides out. If I don't laugh for a week, I feel dirty. I feel dirty now, like my insides are rotting.
VIRGINIA: Someone should make you laugh. I'm not the person to do it.
MATILDE: Virginia. My mother once said to me: Matilde, in order to tell a good joke, you have to believe that your problems are very small, and that

the world is very big. She said: if more women knew more jokes, there would be more justice in this world.

(*Virginia thinks about that.*
Virginia comes across a white pair of women's under-
wear.
Matilde watches.)

VIRGINIA: I've never seen my sister's underwear before.
MATILDE: Her underwear is practical. And white.

(*Virginia continues to fold underwear.*)

VIRGINIA: I wonder if Lane has gone through meno-pause yet. Her underwear *is* very white. Some women throw out underwear when they get a bloodstain. Other women keep washing the stain.
MATILDE: I can't afford to throw away underwear. If I could, believe me, I would. I would buy new under-wear every day: purple, red, gold, orange, silver . . .

(*Virginia folds a pair of men's underwear.*)

VIRGINIA: It's a little weird to be touching my brother-in-law's underwear.
　　He's a very handsome man.
　　When he and Lane first met, I thought: Lane gets the best of everything. A surgeon. With a specialty. He's—charismatic.

(*Virginia touches her brother-in-law's underwear as she folds.*)

　　Then I thought: it's better to have a husband who is not *too* handsome. Then you don't worry about him.

(*Virginia comes across a pair of women's black under-wear.*)

　　These don't look like Lane.
MATILDE: No.
VIRGINIA: Too shiny.
MATILDE: Too sexy.

(*Matilde and Virginia look at each other.*)

11. Lane and Virginia Have Coffee

(*Lane and Virginia have coffee in the living room.*)

VIRGINIA: The house is so clean!
LANE: Thanks.
VIRGINIA: It's working out—with your maid? What's her name?
LANE (*American pronunciation*): Matilde.
VIRGINIA: That's right: Matilde. (*American pronuncia-tion*)
　　Don't they say Matilde (*Brazilian pronunciation*) in Brazil?
LANE: I don't know.
VIRGINIA: I think they do.
LANE: How would you know?

(*Virginia shrugs.*)

VIRGINIA: Mmm . . .
LANE: Well, I'm sure she would tell me if I were saying her name wrong. Anyway. She seems much better. How are you?
VIRGINIA: Oh, fine.
　　How's Charles?
LANE: Why do you ask?
VIRGINIA: No reason.
LANE: He's fine.
VIRGINIA: That's good. The last time I saw Charles was Christmas. You both work so hard.
LANE: He's been doing nine surgeries a day—we hardly see each other. I mean, of course we see each other, but, you know how it is. More coffee?
VIRGINIA: No, thanks.
LANE: Matilde! Could you clear these, please?

(*Matilde enters.*)

MATILDE (*To Virginia*): Your cup, miss?
VIRGINIA: Oh, I'll get it—

(*Matilde winks at Virginia.*)
(*Matilde clears the plates.*)

　　Thanks.
MATILDE: Did everyone like their coffee?
LANE and VIRGINIA: Yes.
MATILDE: Good.

(*Matilde exits.*)

LANE: Oh. That's Matilde. Sorry. That was rude. I should have introduced you. Or is it rude? Do you introduce the maid to the company?
VIRGINIA: I'm not the company. I'm your sister.
LANE: You're right.
　　I should have introduced you. I can't get used to having another person in the house.
VIRGINIA: Mmm. Yes. It must make you uncomfortable to—I don't know—read a magazine while someone cleans up after you.
LANE: I don't read magazines, Virginia. I go to work exhausted and I come home exhausted. That is how most of the people in this country function. At least people who have jobs.

(*A pause.*
For a moment,
Lane and Virginia experience
a primal moment during which they
are seven and nine years old,
inside the mind, respectively.
They are mad.
Then they return quite naturally
to language, as adults do.)

　　Sorry—I didn't mean—
VIRGINIA: I know.

(*At the same time:*)

VIRGINIA: Are you—?　　　　LANE: I keep meaning to—

VIRGINIA: What?
LANE: Oh—it's just—I keep meaning to have you two over for dinner. It's ridiculous—living so close and never seeing each other.
VIRGINIA: You're right. Maybe next week?
LANE: Next week is crazy. But soon.

(*Virginia nods.*)

12. *Lane and Matilde*

(*Night.*
Matilde tries to think up the perfect joke.
Matilde looks straight ahead,
in the dark, in the living room.
She thinks.
Lane comes home from work.
She turns a light on.)

LANE: Oh! You startled me.
MATILDE: You startled me, too.
LANE: What are you doing in the dark?
MATILDE: I was trying to think up a joke.
     Almost had one.
     Now it's gone.
LANE: Oh—well—can you get it back again?
MATILDE: I doubt it.
LANE: Oh.
     Is Charles home?
MATILDE: No.
LANE: Did he call?
MATILDE (*with compassion*): No.
LANE: Oh, well, he's probably just sleeping at the hospital.

(*Matilde is silent.*)

> Sometimes there's no time to call home from the hospital. You're going from patient to patient, and it's—you know—crazy. When we were younger—Charles and I—we would page each other, we had this signal—two for good night—and three for—well, I don't know why I'm thinking about this right now. The point is—when you get older, you just *know* that a person is thinking of you, and working hard, and thinking of you, and you don't need them to call anymore. Since Charles and I are both doctors we both—understand—how it is.

MATILDE: Mmm.
LANE: Well, good night.
MATILDE: Good night.
LANE: Are you going to—just—sit here in the dark?
MATILDE: I might stay up a little longer to—what's the word?—tidy up.
LANE: Oh. Great. Just shut the light off when you—

(*Matilde turns the light off.*)

     Oh. Good night.
MATILDE: Good night.

(*Lane exits.*
Matilde tries to think up the perfect joke.

She closes her eyes.
The lights around her go from night to day
as she composes.)

13. *Virginia and Matilde. Then Lane.*

(*Virginia enters.*
Matilde opens her eyes.
Virginia irons.
Matilde watches.)

MATILDE: I have a really good joke coming.
VIRGINIA: That's good.
MATILDE: You know how most jokes go in threes? Like this: Da da DA. I'm making up one that goes in sixes: Da da Da, da da DA.
VIRGINIA: I didn't know jokes had time signatures.
MATILDE: Oh, they do. Ask me what my profession is then ask me what my greatest problem is.
VIRGINIA: What's your profession?
MATILDE: I'm a comedian.
VIRGINIA: What's your—
MATILDE: Timing.
VIRGINIA: That's good.
MATILDE: But you're not laughing.
VIRGINIA: I'm laughing on the inside.
MATILDE: Oh. I like it better when people laugh on the outside.
     I'm looking for the perfect joke, but I'm afraid if I found it, it would kill me.

(*Virginia comes upon a pair of women's red underwear.*)

VIRGINIA: My God!
MATILDE: Oh . . .
     No—(*As in—he wouldn't dare*)
VIRGINIA: No.
MATILDE: But—(*As in—he might dare*)
VIRGINIA: Do you think—here—in the house?
MATILDE: Maybe a park. I bet he puts them in his pocket, afterwards, and forgets, because he's so happy. And then she's walking around for the day, with no underwear, and you know what? She probably likes it.
VIRGINIA: I hope it's not a nurse. It's such a cliché.
MATILDE: If she's a nurse, they would pass each other in the hospital, and she would say: hello, Doctor. And she knows, and he knows: no underwear.
VIRGINIA: No underwear in a *hospital*? It's unsanitary.
MATILDE: Or—maybe he just *likes* women's underwear. He might *try* them on.
VIRGINIA: Charles? No!
MATILDE: It's possible. You don't like to think about it, because he's your brother-in-law, but these things happen, Virginia. They do.

(*Lane enters.*
Virginia quickly puts down the iron and sits.
Matilde stands and begins to iron badly.
Virginia hides the red underwear.)

LANE (*to Virginia*): What are you doing here?
VIRGINIA: Nothing.
     How was work?

(*Lane moves to the kitchen.*)

     Where are you going?
LANE: I'm going in the other room to shoot myself.
VIRGINIA: You're joking, right?
LANE (*from the kitchen*): Right.

(*Matilde and Virginia look at each other.*
Matilde folds underwear.
Virginia sits.
Virginia stands.
Virginia sits.
Virginia stands.
Virginia has a deep impulse to order the universe.
Virginia arranges objects on the coffee table.
Lane enters.
Her left hand is bleeding.
She holds it with a dish towel.)

VIRGINIA: Lane—what—are you—?
LANE: I'm disguising myself as a patient.
VIRGINIA: That's not funny.
LANE: I cut myself.

(*They look at her, alarmed.*)

     Don't worry. Even my wounds are superficial.
VIRGINIA: Lane?
LANE: Can opener. I was making a martini.
VIRGINIA: Why do you need a can opener to make a martini?
LANE: I didn't have the right kind of fucking olives, okay? I only have black olives! In a fucking can.
VIRGINIA: Lane?
LANE: He's gone off with a patient.
VIRGINIA: What?
LANE: His patient.
MATILDE: Oh . . .
LANE: Yes.

(*Virginia and Matilde glance toward the red underwear and look away.*)

VIRGINIA: Was it a—?
LANE: Mastectomy. Yes.
VIRGINIA: Wow. That's very—
LANE: Generous of him?
MATILDE (*to Virginia*): A mastectomy?

(*Virginia gestures toward her breast.*
Matilde nods.)

VIRGINIA: How old is she?
LANE: Sixty-seven.
VIRGINIA AND MATILDE: Oh!
LANE: What?
VIRGINIA: Not what I expected.
LANE: A young nurse? The maid? No. He's in love.
VIRGINIA: But—with an older woman?
LANE: Yes.

VIRGINIA: I'm almost—impressed. She must have substance.
LANE: She's not a doctor.
VIRGINIA: Well, most men in his position . . . he's still—so—good-looking . . .
LANE: Virginia!
VIRGINIA: Sorry.
LANE: I've never been jealous, I've never been suspicious. I've never thought any other woman was my equal. I'm the best doctor. I'm the smartest, the most well-loved by my patients. I'm athletic. I have poise. I've aged well. I can talk to *anyone* and be on equal footing. How, I thought, could he even *look* at anyone else. It would be absurd.
VIRGINIA: Wow. You really are—confident.
LANE: I was blind. He didn't want a doctor. He wanted a housewife.

(*A pause.*
Lane looks around the house.
She sees the objects on the coffee table—
a vase, some magazines, forcefully arranged.
She sees Matilde folding laundry, badly.)

(*To Virginia*) Have you been cleaning my house?

(*Virginia and Matilde look at each other.*
Matilde stops folding laundry.)

VIRGINIA: No, I haven't been cleaning your house.
LANE: Those objects on the coffee table—that is how you arrange objects.

(*Virginia looks at the coffee table.*)

VIRGINIA: I don't know what you mean.
LANE: Matilde—has Virginia been cleaning the house?
VIRGINIA: I said no.
LANE: I asked Matilde.
     Has Virginia been cleaning the house?
MATILDE: Yes.
LANE: For how long?
MATILDE: Two weeks.
LANE: You're fired.

(*A pause.*)

     You're both fired.
VIRGINIA: You can't do that.
     This is my fault.
LANE: I'm *paying* her to clean my house!
VIRGINIA: And your house is clean!
LANE: This has nothing to do with you, Virginia.
VIRGINIA: This has *everything* to do with me.
LANE: Matilde—do you have enough money saved for a plane ticket back home?
MATILDE: No.
LANE: You can stay one more week. I will buy you a plane ticket.
VIRGINIA: Lane. Your husband left you today.
LANE: I'm aware of that.
VIRGINIA: You're not capable of making a rational decision.
LANE: I'm always capable of making a rational decision!

MATILDE: You don't need to buy me a plane ticket. I'm moving to New York to become a comedian. I only need a bus ticket.

VIRGINIA (*to Lane*): You can't do this!

LANE: I will not have you cleaning my house, just because the maid is depressed—

VIRGINIA: She's not depressed. She doesn't like to clean! It makes her sad.

(*Lane looks at Matilde.*)

LANE: Is that true?

MATILDE: Yes.

LANE: So—
then—
(*To Virginia*) why?

VIRGINIA: I don't know.

LANE: You looked through my things.

VIRGINIA: Not really.

LANE: I find this—incomprehensible.

VIRGINIA: Can't I do a nice thing for you without having a *motive*?

LANE: No.

VIRGINIA: That's—

LANE: You have better things to do than clean my house.

VIRGINIA: Like what?

LANE: I—

VIRGINIA: Like what?

LANE: I don't know.

VIRGINIA: No, you don't know.
I wake up in the morning, and I wish that I could sleep through the whole day, but there I am, I'm awake.
So I get out of bed. I make eggs for my husband. I throw the eggshells in the disposal. I listen to the sound of delicate eggshells being ground by an indelicate machine. I clean the sink. I sweep the floor. I wipe coffee grounds from the counter.
I might have done something different with my life. I might have been a scholar. I might have described one particular ruin with the cold-blooded poetry of which only a first-rate scholar is capable. Why didn't I?

LANE: I don't know.

VIRGINIA: I wanted something—big. I didn't know how to ask for it. Don't blame Matilde. Blame me. I wanted—a task.

LANE: I'm sorry.
I don't know what to say.
Except:
(*To Matilde*) you're fired.

VIRGINIA: It's not her fault! You can't do this.

LANE (*to Virginia*): What would you like me to do?

VIRGINIA: Let me . . . take care of you.

LANE: I don't need to be taken care of.

VIRGINIA: Everybody needs to be taken care of.

LANE: Virginia. I'm all grown-up.
I DO NOT WANT TO BE TAKEN CARE OF.

VIRGINIA: WHY NOT?

LANE: I don't want my sister to clean my house. I want a stranger to clean my house.

(*Virginia and Lane look at Matilde.*)

MATILDE: It's all right. I'll go.
I'll pack my things.
Good-bye, Virginia.
Good luck finding a task.

(*She embraces Virginia.*)

Good-bye, Doctor.
Good luck finding your husband.

(*She exits.
Lane and Virginia look at each other.*)

14. *Lane. Then Matilde. Then Virginia.*

(*Lane, to the audience:*)

LANE: This is how I imagine my ex-husband and his new wife.

(*Charles and Ana appear.
He undoes her gown.
Is it a hospital gown or a ball gown?*)

My husband undoes her gown.
He is very gentle.
He kisses her right breast.

(*Charles kisses Ana's right breast.*)

He kisses the side of it.
He kisses the shadow.
He kisses her left torso.

(*He kisses her left torso.*)

He kisses the scar,

(*He kisses the scar.*)

the one he made.
It's a good scar.
He's a good surgeon.
He kisses her mouth.
He kisses her forehead.
It's a sacred ritual, and
I hate him.

(*Matilde enters with her suitcase.
The lovers remain.
They continue to kiss one another
on different body parts, a ritual.*)

MATILDE: Is there anything else before I go?

LANE: No. Thank you.

MATILDE: Who are they?

LANE: My husband and the woman he loves. Don't worry. It's only my imagination.

MATILDE: They look happy.

LANE: Yes.

MATILDE: People imagine that people who are in love are happy.

LANE: Yes.

John Dossett as Charles and Concetta Tomei as Ana on the balcony, with Vanessa Aspillaga (Matilde) and Blair Brown (Lane) in the 2006 New York production of *The Clean House*.

MATILDE: That is why, in your country, people kill themselves on Valentine's Day.

LANE: Yes.

MATILDE: Love isn't clean like that. It's dirty. Like a good joke. Do you want to hear a joke?

LANE: Sure.

(*Matilde tells a joke in Portuguese.*)

Is that the end?

MATILDE: Yes.

LANE: Was it funny?

MATILDE: Yes. It's not funny in translation.

LANE: I suppose I should laugh then.

MATILDE: Yes.

(*Lane tries to laugh.*
She cries.)

You're crying.

LANE: No, I'm not.

MATILDE: I think that you're crying.

LANE: Well—yes. I think I am.

(*Lane cries.*
She laughs.
She cries.
She laughs.
And this goes on for some time.
Virginia enters.)

VIRGINIA: Charles is at the door.

LANE: What?

VIRGINIA: Charles. In the hall.

MATILDE: Oh . . .

LANE: You let him in?

VIRGINIA: What could I do?
    And—there's a woman with him.

LANE: In the *house*?

VIRGINIA: Yes.

LANE: What does she look like?
    Is she pretty?

VIRGINIA: No.

(*With a sense of apology*) She's beautiful.

LANE: Oh.

(*From offstage:*)

CHARLES: Lane?

(*The women look at each other.*
Blackout.
Intermission.)

ACT 2

(*The white living room has become a hospital.*
Or the idea of a hospital.
There is a balcony above the white living room.)

1. Charles Performs Surgery on the Woman He Loves

(*Ana lies under a sheet.*
Beautiful music.
A subtitle projects: Charles Performs Surgery on the Woman He Loves.
Charles takes out surgical equipment.
He does surgery on Ana.
It is an act of love.
If the actor who plays Charles is a good singer,
it would be nice if he could sing
an ethereal medieval love song in Latin
about being medically cured by love
as he does the surgery.
If the actress who plays Ana is a good singer,
it would be nice if she recovered from the surgery
and slowly sat up and sang a contrapuntal melody.
When the surgery is over,
Charles takes off Ana's sheet.
Underneath the sheet,
she is dressed in a lovely dress.
They kiss.)

2. Ana

ANA (*to the audience*): I have avoided doctors my whole
life.
    I don't like how they smell. I don't like how they
talk. I don't admire their emotional lives. I don't like
how they walk. They walk very fast to get somewhere—tac tac tac—I am walking somewhere important. I don't like that. I like a man who saunters.
Like this.

(*Ana saunters across the stage like a man.*)

But with Charles, it was like—BLAM!
    My mind was going: you're a doctor, I hate you.
    But the rest of me was gone, walking out the door,
with him.
    When he performed surgery on me,
we were already in love.
    I was under general anesthetic but I could sense
him there.
    I think he put something extra in—during the
surgery.
    Into the missing place.
    There are stories of surgeons who leave things
inside the body by mistake:
    rubber gloves, sponges, clamps—
    But—you know—I think Charles left his soul
inside me.
    Into the missing place.

(*She touches her left breast.*)

3. Charles

CHARLES (*to the audience*): There are jokes about breast
surgeons.
    You know—something like—I've seen more
breasts in this city than—
    I don't know the punch line.
    There must be a punch line.

I'm not a man who falls in love easily. I've been faithful to my wife. We fell in love when we were twenty-
two. We had plans. There was justice in the world.
There was justice in love. If a person was good
enough, an equally good person would fall in love
with that person. And then I met—Ana. Justice had
nothing to do with it.

There once was a very great American surgeon
named Halsted. He was married to a nurse. He loved
her—immeasurably. One day Halsted noticed that
his wife's hands were chapped and red when she
came back from surgery. And so he invented rubber
gloves. For her. It is one of the great love stories in
medicine. The difference between inspired medicine
and uninspired medicine is love.

When I met Ana, I knew:
I loved her to the point of invention.

4. Charles and Ana

CHARLES: I'm afraid that you have breast cancer.
ANA: If you think I'm going to cry, I'm not going to cry.
CHARLES: It's normal to cry—
ANA: I don't cry when I'm supposed to cry.
    Are you going to cut it off?
CHARLES: You must need some time—to digest—
ANA: No. I don't need time. Tell me everything.
CHARLES: You have a variety of options. Many women
    don't opt for a mastectomy. A lumpectomy and radi-
    ation can be just as effective as—
ANA: I want you to cut it off.
CHARLES: You might want to talk with family members—
    with a husband—are you married?—or with—
ANA: Tomorrow.
CHARLES: Tomorrow?
ANA: Tomorrow.
CHARLES: I'm not sure I have any appointments open
    tomorrow—
ANA: I'd like you to do it tomorrow.
CHARLES: Then we'll do it tomorrow.

(*They look at each other.*
They fall in love.)

ANA: Then I'll see you tomorrow, at the surgery.
CHARLES: Good-bye, Ana.
ANA: Good-bye.

(*They look at each other.*
They fall in love some more.)

    Am I going to die?
CHARLES: No. You're not going to die.
    I won't let you die.

(*They fall in love completely.*
They kiss wildly.)

    What's happening?
ANA: I don't know.
CHARLES: This doesn't happen to me.
ANA: Me neither.
CHARLES: Ana, Ana, Ana, Ana . . . your name goes
    backwards and forwards . . . I love you . . .
ANA: And I love you.
    Take off your white coat.

(*They kiss.*)

5. Lane, Virginia, Matilde, Charles, and Ana

(*We are back in the white living room.*
We are deposited at the end of the last scene of the first act.
Charles is at the door, with Ana.)

CHARLES: Lane?
LANE: Charles.
CHARLES: Lane. I want us all to know each other. I want
    to do things right, from the beginning. Lane: this is
    Ana. Ana: this is my wife, Lane.

ANA: Nice to meet you. I've heard wonderful things about you. I've heard that you are a wonderful doctor.

LANE: Thank you.

(*Ana holds out her hand to Lane.*
Lane looks around in disbelief.
Then Lane shakes Ana's hand.)

CHARLES: This is my sister-in-law, Virginia.

ANA: Hello.

VIRGINIA: How do you do.

MATILDE (*To Ana*): You look like my mother.

ANA: Ah!

LANE (*To Ana*): This is the maid, Matilde.
(*To Charles*) I fired her this morning.

ANA: Encantada, Matilde.

(*Nice to meet you, Matilde.*)

MATILDE: Encantada. Sou do Brasil.

(*Nice to meet you. I'm from Brazil.*)

ANA: Ah! Eu falo um pouco de portugues, mas falo mal.

(*I know a little bit of Portuguese, but it's bad.*)

MATILDE: Eh! boa tentativa! 'ta chegando la! Es usted de Argentina?

(*Ah! Good try! Not bad!*
You're from Argentina?)

ANA (*in Spanish*): ¿Cómo lo sabe?

(*How did you know?*)

MATILDE (*imitating Ana's accent*): ¿Cómo lo sabe?
(*How did you know?*)

(*They laugh.*)

LANE: We've all met. You can leave now, Charles.

CHARLES: What happened to your wrist?

LANE: Can opener.

CHARLES: Oh.

(*Charles examines the bandage on Lane's wrist.*
She pulls her hand away.)

MATILDE: ¿Ha usted estado alguna vez en Brasil?

(*Have you ever been to Brazil?*)

ANA: Una vez, para estudiar rocas.

(*Once to study rocks.*)

MATILDE: (*For a moment not understanding the Spanish pronunciation*) Rocas?
Ah, *rochas*!

(*Ah, rocks! In Brazil it is pronounced "hochas."*)

ANA: Si! *rochas*! (*Pronounces it "hochas."*)

(*They laugh.*)

VIRGINIA: Should we sit down?

LANE: Virginia!

(*They all sit down.*)

(*To Virginia*) Could you get us something to drink.

VIRGINIA: What would you like?

MATILDE: I would like a coffee.

ANA: That sounds nice. I'll have coffee, too.

VIRGINIA: Charles?

CHARLES: Nothing for me, thanks.

VIRGINIA: Lane?

LANE: I would like some hard alcohol in a glass with ice. Thank you.

(*Virginia exits.*)

So.

CHARLES: Lane. I know this is unorthodox. But I want us to know each other.

ANA: You are very generous to have me in your home.

LANE: Not at all.

ANA: Yes, you are very generous. I wanted to meet you. I am not a home-wrecker. The last time I fell in love it was with my husband, a long time ago. He was a geologist and a very wild man, an alcoholic. But so fun! So crazy! He peed on lawns and did everything bad and I loved it. But I did not want to have children with him because he was too wild, too crazy. I said you have to stop drinking and then he did stop drinking and then he died of cancer when he was thirty-one.

(*Matilde murmurs with sympathy.*)

My heart was broken and I said to myself: I will never love again. And I didn't. I thought I was going to meet my husband in some kind of afterlife with fabulous rocks. Blue and green rocks. And then I met Charles. When Charles said he was married I said Charles we should stop but then Charles referred to Jewish law and I had to say that I agreed and that was that. I wanted you to understand.

LANE: Well, I don't understand. What about Jewish law.

CHARLES: In Jewish law you are legally obligated to break off relations with your wife or husband if you find what is called your *bashert*.

ANA: Your soul mate.

CHARLES: You are *obligated* to do this. Legally bound. There's something—metaphysically—objective about it.

LANE: You're not Jewish.

CHARLES: I know. But I heard about the *bashert*—on a radio program. And it always stuck with me. When I saw Ana I knew that was it. I knew she was my *bashert*.

ANA: There is a *midrash* that says when a baby is forty days old, inside the mother's stomach, God picks out its soul mate, and people have to spend the rest of their lives running around to find each other.

LANE: So you are Jewish?

ANA: Yes.

LANE: And your husband was a geologist.

ANA: Yes.

LANE: And you're from Argentina.

ANA: Yes.

LANE: Well. It's all making sense.

CHARLES: Lane. Something very objective happened to me. It's as though I suddenly tested positive for a genetic disease that I've had all along. *Ana has been in my genetic code.*

ANA: Yes. It is strange. We didn't feel guilty because it was so *objective.*

CHARLES: Lane. Something very objective happened to me. It's as though I suddenly tested positive for a genetic disease that I've had all along. *Ana has been in my genetic code.*

ANA: Yes. It is strange. We didn't feel guilty because it was so *objective.* And yet both of us are moral people. I don't know Charles very well but I think he is moral but to tell you the truth even if he were immoral I would love him because the love I feel for your husband is so overpowering.

LANE: And this is what you've come to tell me. That you're both innocent according to Jewish law.

ANA and CHARLES: Yes.

(*Virginia enters with the drinks.*)

MATILDE: Thank you.

ANA: Thank you.

(*Lane takes a glass from Virginia.*)

LANE (*to Virginia*): Charles has come to tell me that according to Jewish law, he has found his soul mate, and so our marriage is dissolved. He doesn't even need to feel guilty. How about that.

VIRGINIA: You have found your *bashert.*

LANE: How the hell do you know about a *bashert?*

VIRGINIA: I heard it on public radio.

CHARLES: I'm sorry that it happened to you, Lane. It could just as well have happened the other way. You might have met your *bashert,* and I would have been forced to make way. There are things—big invisible things—that come unannounced—they walk in, and we have to give way. I would even congratulate you. Because I have always loved you.

LANE: Well. Congratulations.

(*A silence. A cold one.*)

MATILDE: Would anyone like to hear a joke?

ANA: I would.

(*Matilde tells a short joke in Portuguese. Ana laughs. No one else laughs.*)

¡Qué bueno! ¡Qué chiste más bueno!

(*What a good joke!*)
(*To Lane*) You are firing Matilde?

LANE: Yes.

ANA: Then we'll hire her to clean our house. I hate to clean. And Charles likes things to be clean. At least I think he does. Charles? Do you like things to be clean?

CHARLES: Sure. I like things to be clean.

ANA: Matilde? Would you like to work for us?

MATILDE: There is something you should know. I don't like to clean so much.

ANA: Of course you don't. Do you have any other skills?

MATILDE: I can tell jokes.

ANA: Perfect. She's coming to live with us.

LANE: My God! You can't just walk into my home and take everything away from me.

ANA: I thought you fired this young woman.

LANE: Yes. I did.

ANA: Have you changed your mind?

LANE: I don't know. Maybe.

ANA: Matilde, do you have a place to live?

MATILDE: No.

ANA: So she'll come live with us.

VIRGINIA: Matilde is like family.

MATILDE: What?

VIRGINIA: Matilde is like a sister to me.

ANA: Is this true?

MATILDE: I don't know. I never had a sister.

VIRGINIA: We clean together. We talk, and fold laundry, as women used to do. They would gather at the public fountains and wash their clothes and tell stories. Now we are alone in our separate houses and it is terrible.

ANA: So it is Virginia who wants you to stay. Not Lane.

LANE: We both want her to stay. We love (*An attempt at the Brazilian pronunciation*) Matilde.

ANA: Matilde?

MATILDE: I am confused.

LANE: I depend on Matilde. I couldn't stand to replace her. Matilde—are you unhappy here with us?

MATILDE: I—

LANE: Is it the money? You could have a raise.

ANA: Matilde—you should do as you wish. My house is easy to clean. I own hardly anything. I own one table, two chairs, a bed, one painting and I have a little fish whose water needs to be changed. I don't have rugs so there is no vacuuming. But you would have to do Charles' laundry. I will not be his washerwoman.

VIRGINIA: Excuse me. But I think that people who are in love—really in love—would like to clean up after each other. If I were in love with Charles I would enjoy folding his laundry.

(*Virginia looks at Charles.
Lane looks at Virginia.
Virginia looks at Lane.*)

ANA: Matilde—what do you think? If you stay with us, there is only one condition: you will have to tell one joke a day. I like to laugh.

VIRGINIA: Please don't leave us, Matilde.

MATILDE: I will split my time. Half with Lane and Virginia, half with Ana and Charles. How is that?

ANA: Lane?

LANE: Matilde is a free agent.

ANA: Of course she is.

CHARLES: Well.
That's settled.

LANE: Are you leaving now?

CHARLES: Do you want me to leave?

LANE: Yes.

CHARLES: Okay. Then we'll leave.

Ana and I are going apple picking this afternoon.
She's never been apple picking.
Would anyone like to join us?

MATILDE: I've never been apple picking

CHARLES: So Matilde will come. Virginia?

VIRGINIA: I love apple picking.

LANE: Virginia!

CHARLES: Lane?

LANE: You must be insane! Apple picking! My god! I'M SORRY! But—apple picking? This is not a foreign film! We don't have an *arrangement*! You don't even *like* foreign films! Maybe you'll pretend to like foreign films, for *Ana*, but I can tell you now, Ana, he doesn't like them! He doesn't like reading the subtitles! It gives him a headache!

CHARLES: Lane. I don't expect you to—understand this—immediately. But since this thing—has happened to me—I want to live life to the fullest. I know—what it must sound like. But it's different. I want to go apple picking. I want to go to Machu Picchu. You can be part of that. I want to share my happiness with you.

LANE: I don't want your happiness.

MATILDE (*to Ana*): Es cómo una telenovela.

(*It's like a soap opera.*)

CHARLES: Lane—I—

LANE: What.

CHARLES: I hope that you'll forgive me one day.

LANE: Go pick some apples.
Good-bye.

CHARLES: Good-bye.

ANA: Good-bye.

MATILDE: Good-bye.

VIRGINIA: I'll stay.

(*Ana, Matilde and Charles exit.*)

LANE: I want to be alone.

VIRGINIA: No, you don't.

LANE: Yes, I do.

VIRGINIA: No, you don't.
Do you want—I don't know—a hot water bottle?

LANE: No, I don't want a hot water bottle, Virginia.

VIRGINIA: I just thought—

LANE: —That I'm nine years old with a cold?

VIRGINIA: I don't know what else to do.

(*A pause.*)

LANE: You know, actually, I think I'd like one. It sounds nice.

6. Ana's Balcony

(*Ana and Matilde are up on Ana's balcony.
It is high above the white living room.
It is a small perch, overlooking the sea,
with two chairs, and a fish bowl.
Through French doors,*

one can enter or exit the balcony.
A room leading to the balcony is suggested but unseen.
Ana and Matilde are surrounded by apples.
The following dialogue may be spoken
in a combination of Portuguese and Spanish
and subtitled in English.
Underneath the balcony,
Lane is in her living room.
She lies down with a hot water bottle.
Ana polishes an apple.
Ana and Matilde look around at all of the apples.*)

ANA: We're never going to eat all of these damn apples.

MATILDE: But it's nice to have so many.
So many that it's *crazy* to have so many.
Because you can never eat them all.

ANA: Yes.

(*Ana picks out an apple and eats it.*)

MATILDE: I like the green ones.
Which ones do you like?

ANA: The yellow ones. They're sweeter.

MATILDE: We could take one bite of each, and if it's not a really, really good apple we can throw it into the sea.

ANA: Now you're talking like a North American.

MATILDE: It will be fun.

ANA: Okay.

(*They start taking bites of each apple
and if they don't think it's a perfect apple they throw it
into the sea.
The sea is also Lane's living room.
Lane sees the apples fall into her living room.
She looks at them.*)

MATILDE: I made up eighty-four new jokes since I started working for you. I only made up one at the other house. It was a good one though. Sometimes you have to *suffer* for the really good ones.

ANA: Why don't you tell jokes for a job?

MATILDE: Someday.

(*Matilde throws an apple core into the living room.*)

ANA: Why someday? Why not now?

MATILDE: I'm looking for the perfect joke. But I am afraid if I found it, it would kill me.

ANA: Why?

MATILDE: My mother died laughing.

ANA: I'm sorry.

MATILDE: Thank you.
She was laughing at one of my father's jokes.

ANA: What was the joke?

MATILDE: I'll never know.
Let's not talk about sad things.

CHARLES: (*From offstage*) Ana!

ANA: We're on the balcony!

(*Matilde bites an apple.*)

MATILDE: Try this one.

ANA: Mmmm. Perfecta.

(*Charles rushes in wearing scrubs.*
He goes to Ana and kisses her all over
and continues to kiss her all over.)

   We were just eating apples.
CHARLES: Aren't they delicious?
ANA: Here is the very best one.

(*Charles takes a bite of the best apple.*)

CHARLES: Divine!
   Excuse me, Matilde.
   I need to borrow this woman.

(*He kisses Ana.*)
(*He picks up Ana and carries her off into the bedroom.*)

MATILDE: Have fun.
ANA and CHARLES: Thank you! We will!

(*They exit.*
Matilde, to the audience:)

MATILDE: The perfect joke happens by accident. Like a
   boil on your backside that you pop. The perfect joke
   is the perfect music. You want to hear it only once in
   your life, and then, never again.

(*A subtitle projects: Matilde Tries to Think Up the Per-*
fect Joke.
She looks out at the sea.
She thinks.)

7. *Matilde, Virginia, and Lane*

(*Virginia is cleaning. She is happy.*
Lane, in pajamas, shuffles cards.
Lane shouts to Matilde who is on the balcony:)

LANE: Matilde! Your deal.

(*Matilde leaves the balcony.*)

VIRGINIA: Lane—your couch is filthy. Wouldn't it be nice
   to have a fresh, clean slip-cover? I could sew you one.
LANE: That would be nice. It would give you a project.

(*Matilde enters.*)

   Your deal.

(*Matilde sits.*
Above them, on the balcony,
Ana and Charles dance a slow dance.)

   So.
   Are you happy there? At the other house?
MATILDE: Yes.
LANE: What's her house like?
MATILDE: It's little. She has a balcony that overlooks the
   sea.
LANE: What's her furniture like?
MATILDE: A table from one place—a chair from
   another place. It doesn't go together. But it's nice.
LANE: What does she cook?
MATILDE: I'm not a spy!

LANE: I'm sorry.

(*They play cards.*
On the balcony,
Charles and Ana finish their dance.
They exit, into the bedroom.
Lane puts down a card.)

   Do they seem like they are very much in love?
MATILDE: Yes.
LANE: How can you tell?
MATILDE: They stay in bed half the day. Charles doesn't
   go to work. He cancels half his patients. He wants to
   spend all his time with Ana.
LANE: Oh.

(*A pause.*)

MATILDE: Because Ana is dying again.
VIRGINIA: What?
MATILDE: Her disease came back.
   She says she won't take any medicine.
   She says it's poison.
   He says: you have to go to the hospital!
   And she says: I won't go to the hospital!
   Then they really fight.
   It's like a soap opera.
   Charles yells and throws things at the wall.
LANE: Charles never yells.
MATILDE: Oh, he yells.
   They broke all the condiments and spices yesterday.
   There was this one yellow spice—
   it got in their hair and on their faces
   until they were all yellow.

(*A spice jar goes flying from the balcony.*
A cloud of yellow spice lands in Lane's living room.)

LANE: She won't go to the hospital?
MATILDE: No.
   I might have to spend more time at the other house.
   To help.
VIRGINIA: Poor Charles.
LANE: Poor Charles?
   Poor Ana.
   Poor me!
   Poor sounds funny if you say it lots of times in a row:
   poor, poor, poor, poor, poor, poor, poor. Poor. Poor.
   Poor. Doesn't it sound funny?
VIRGINIA: Lane? Are you all right?
LANE: Oh, me? I'm fine.

8. *Ana and Charles Try to Read*
One Another's Mind

(*Ana and Charles on the balcony.*
Ana is dressed in a bathrobe.)

CHARLES: Eight.
ANA: No, seven. You were very close.
CHARLES: I'll go again.
ANA: Okay.
CHARLES: Four.

ANA: Yes!

CHARLES: I knew it! I could see four apples. Now: colors.

ANA: Okay.

CHARLES: I'll start.

ANA: Red.

CHARLES: No.

ANA: Blue.

CHARLES: No.

ANA: I give up.

CHARLES: Purple. We have to concentrate harder. Like this. Ready? You go.

ANA: I'm tired.

CHARLES: Sorry. I'll stop.

ANA: Why all these guessing games?

CHARLES: You know Houdini?

ANA: The magician?

CHARLES: Yes. Houdini and his wife practiced reading each other's minds. So that—if one of them died— they'd be able to talk to each other—you know, after.

ANA: Did it work?

CHARLES: No.

ANA: Oh.

CHARLES: But I love you more than Houdini loved his wife. He was distracted—by his magic. I'm not distracted. Ana. Let's go to the hospital.

ANA: I told you.
   No hospitals!

(*Charles is sad.*)

ANA: Charles, don't be sad.

CHARLES: Don't be sad! My God!

ANA: I can't take this.
   I'm going for a swim.
   Matilde!
   Come look after Charles.
   I'm going swimming.

(*Ana exits.*
Charles looks out over the balcony.
watching Ana run out to the water.)

CHARLES: Ana! Think of a country under the water! I'll guess it from the balcony!

MATILDE: She can't hear you.

(*Charles disrobes to his underwear.*
He throws his clothes off the balcony.
They land in Lane's living room.)

CHARLES: Excuse me, Matilde. I'm going for a swim.

MATILDE: I thought you can't swim.

CHARLES: I'll learn to swim.

(*Underneath the balcony, in Lane's living room,*
Lane comes across Charles's sweater.
She breathes it in.
Charles leans over the balcony.)

CHARLES: Ana! What's the country? I think it's a very small country! Is it Luxembourg? Ana!

(*He, runs off.*
Matilde looks out over the water.
A pause.)

Matilde is startled.
Suddenly, with great clarity.
Matilde thinks up the perfect joke.)

MATILDE: My God.
   Oh no.
   My God.
   It's the perfect joke.
   Am I dead?
   No.

9. *Lane and Virginia. Then Matilde.*

(*Lane sits with Charles's sweater in her hands.*
Virginia enters, vacuuming.)

LANE: Stop it!

VIRGINIA: What?

LANE: Stop cleaning!

VIRGINIA: Why?

LANE: I DON'T WANT ANYTHING IN MY HOUSE TO BE CLEAN EVER AGAIN! I WANT THERE TO BE DIRT AND PIGS IN THE CORNER. MAYBE SOME COW MANURE SOME BIG DIRTY SHITTY COWS AND SOME SHITTY COW SHIT LOTS OF IT AND LOTS OF DIRTY FUCKING SOCKS—AND NONE OF THEM MATCH— NONE OF THEM—BECAUSE YOU KNOW WHAT—THAT IS HOW I FEEL.

(*Lane unplugs the vacuum.*)

VIRGINIA: Wow. I'm sorry.

LANE: And you know what? I will not let my house be a breeding ground for your weird obsessive dirt fetish. I will not permit you to feel like a better person just because you push dirt around all day on my behalf.

VIRGINIA: I was just trying to help.

LANE: Well, it's not helping.

VIRGINIA: I wonder—when it was—that you became— such a bitch? Oh, yes, I remember. Since the day you were born, you thought that anyone with a *problem* had a defect of the will. You're wrong about that. Some people have problems, real problems—

LANE: Yes. I see people with *real problems* all day long. At the hospital.

VIRGINIA: I think—there's a small part of me that's enjoyed watching your life fall apart. To see you lose your composure—for once! I thought: we can be real sisters who tell each other real things. But I was wrong. Well, fine. I'm not picking up your dry cleaning anymore. I'm going to get a job.

LANE: What job?

VIRGINIA: Any job!

LANE: What are you qualified to do at this point?

VIRGINIA: No wonder Charles left. You have no compassion.

LANE: I do so have compassion. I do so have compassion!	VIRGINIA: Ana is a woman with compassion.

VIRGINIA: Really. How so.

LANE: I traded my whole life to help people who are sick! What do you do?

(*Virginia and Lane breathe.*
Virginia and Lane are in a state of silent animal warfare,
a brand of warfare particular to sisters.)

   I'm going to splash some water on my face.

VIRGINIA: Good.

(*Lane exits.*
Virginia, alone.
On the balcony, Ana puts on a record—
an aria, most likely Italian.
Ana listens to opera on the balcony, looking out over the sea.
Virginia dumps a plant on the ground and the dirt spills onto the floor.
She realizes with some surprise that she enjoys this.
Virginia makes a giant operatic mess in the living room.
Matilde enters.)

MATILDE: What are you doing?
   Virginia?

VIRGINIA: I'M MAKING A MESS!

(*Virginia finishes making her operatic mess.*
The aria ends.
Ana leaves the balcony.)

MATILDE: You are okay?

VIRGINIA: Actually. I feel fabulous.

(*Matilde sits down.*
Matilde puts her head in her arms.
Lane enters.)

LANE: What the hell happened here?

VIRGINIA: I was mad. Sorry.

(*Virginia flicks a speck of dirt.*
Lane looks at Matilde.)

LANE (*to Virginia*): What's wrong with her?

(*Virginia shrugs.*)

MATILDE: It's a mess.

VIRGINIA: I'll clean it up.

MATILDE: Not this—Ana, Charles—it's a mess.

LANE: Have they—fallen out of love?

MATILDE: No.

VIRGINIA: Is she very sick?

MATILDE: Yes.

LANE: Oh.

VIRGINIA: How terrible.

MATILDE: Yes.
   And now Charles has gone away.

LANE: What?

MATILDE (*to Lane*): To Alaska.

VIRGINIA: What?

MATILDE (*to Virginia*): To Alaska.

LANE: But—why?

MATILDE: He says he's going to chop down a tree for Ana.

VIRGINIA: What?

MATILDE: A "you" tree.
   He called it a you tree.

(*Matilde points: you.*)

VIRGINIA: A you tree?

MATILDE: A you tree. He says he's going to invent a new "you medicine."

VIRGINIA: My God. He's gone crazy with love!

LANE: He's not crazy. It's a yew tree. (*Spelling it out*) Y-E-W. A Pacific yew tree. The bark was made into Taxol in 1967. It makes cancer cells clog up with microtubules so they're slower to grow and divide.

MATILDE: He said it was a special tree.

LANE: Yes. It is a special tree.

MATILDE: He wants to plant the tree in Ana's courtyard so she can smell the tree from her balcony.
   She won't go to the hospital. So he said he would bring the hospital to her.

VIRGINIA: That's beautiful.

LANE: It's not beautiful, Virginia. There is a woman dying, alone, while Charles chops down a fucking tree.
   How heroic.

VIRGINIA: Does she need a doctor?

MATILDE: Yes. But she won't go to the hospital.
   So I thought I would ask.
   Do you know any doctors who go to the house?

VIRGINIA: You mean house calls?

MATILDE: Yes, house calls.

(*Virginia and Matilde look at Lane.*)

LANE: Why are you looking at me?

(*They continue to look at Lane.*)

LANE: You want me to take care of my husband's soul mate.

VIRGINIA: Look at her as a patient. Not a person.
   You can do that.

LANE: If she wanted to see a doctor, she'd go to the hospital. I am *not* going to her house. It would be totally inappropriate.

(*They look at Lane.*
In the distance, Charles walks slowly across the stage dressed in a parka,
looking for his tree.
A great freezing wind.)

10. *Lane Makes a House Call to Her Husband's Soul Mate*

(*On Ana's balcony.*
Lane listens to Ana's heart with a stethoscope.)

LANE: Breathe in.
   Breathe in again.

(Lane takes off her stethoscope.)

Are you having any trouble breathing?
ANA: No. But sometimes it hurts when I breathe.
LANE: Where?
ANA: Here.
LANE: Do you have pain when you're at rest?
ANA: Yes.
LANE: Where?
ANA: In my spine.
LANE: Is the pain sharp, or dull?
ANA: Sharp.
LANE: Does it radiate?
ANA: Like light?
LANE: I mean—does it move from one place to another?
ANA: Yes. From here to there.
LANE: How's your appetite?
ANA: Not great.
  You must hate me.
LANE: Look—I'm being a doctor right now. That's all.

(Lane palpates Ana's spine.)

Does that hurt?
ANA: It hurts already.
LANE: I can't know anything without doing tests.
ANA: I know.
LANE: And you won't go to the hospital.
ANA: No.
LANE: All right.
ANA: Do you think I'm crazy?
LANE: No.

(A small pause.)

ANA: Well. Can I get you anything to drink? I have some iced tea.
LANE: Sure. Thank you.

*(Ana exits.
Lane looks out over the balcony at the water.
Lane starts to weep.
Ana enters with iced tea.)*

ANA: Lane?
LANE: Oh God! I'm not going to cry in front of you.
ANA: It's okay. You can cry. You must hate me.
LANE: I don't hate you.
ANA: Why are you crying?
LANE: Okay! I hate you!
  You—glow—with some kind of—thing—I can't *acquire* that—this—thing—sort of—glows off you—like a veil—in reverse—you're like *anyone's* soul mate—because you have that—thing—you have a balcony—I don't have a balcony—Charles looks at you—he glows, too—you're like two glowworms—he never looked at me like that.
ANA: Lane.
LANE: I looked at our wedding pictures to see—maybe—he looked at me that way—back then—and no—he didn't—he looked at me with *admiration*—I didn't know there was another way to be looked at—how

could I know—I didn't know his face was capable of *doing that*—the way he looked at you—in my living room.
ANA: I'm sorry.
LANE: No you're not. If you were really sorry, you wouldn't have done it. We do as we please, and then we say we're sorry. But we're not sorry. We're just—uncomfortable—watching other people in pain.

(Ana hands Lane an iced tea.)

LANE: Thank you.

*(Lane drinks her iced tea.
They both look at the fish in the bowl.)*

LANE: What kind of fish is that?
ANA: A fighting fish.
LANE: How old is it?
ANA: Twelve.
LANE: That's old for a fish.
ANA: I keep expecting it to die. But it doesn't.

*(Lane taps on the bowl.
The fish wriggles.)*

ANA: How did you and Charles fall in love?
LANE: He didn't tell you?
ANA: No.
LANE: Oh. Well, we were in medical school together. We were anatomy partners. We fell in love over a dead body.

*(They look at each other.
Lane forgives Ana.)*

ANA: Want an apple?
LANE: Sure.

*(Ana gives Lane an apple.
Lane takes a bite and stops.)*

LANE: Did Charles pick this apple?
ANA: I don't know who picked it.

(Lane eats the apple.)

LANE: It's good.

*(In the distance,
Charles walks across the stage in a heavy parka.
He carries a pick axe.
On the balcony, it is snowing.)*

11. *Lane Calls Virginia*

(Lane and Virginia on the telephone.)

LANE: I saw Ana.
VIRGINIA: And?
LANE: She's coming to live with me.
VIRGINIA: What?
LANE: She can't be alone. She's too sick. I invited her.
VIRGINIA: That's generous. I'm impressed.

LANE: So will you be around—during the day—to help
  Matilde look after her?
VIRGINIA: Oh, me? No. I got a job.
LANE: What?
VIRGINIA: I got a job.
LANE: Doing what?
VIRGINIA: I'm a checkout girl. At the grocery store.
LANE: You're not.
VIRGINIA: I am. I had my first day. I liked it. I liked using
  the cash register. I liked watching the vegetables go
  by on the conveyer belt. Purple, orange, red, green,
  yellow. My colleagues were nice. They helped me if
  my receipts got stuck in the machine. There was fel-
  low feeling among the workers. Solidarity. And I
  liked it.
LANE: Wow.
VIRGINIA: So, I'm sorry. But I'll be too busy to help you.

(*Pause.*)

LANE: You made that story up.
VIRGINIA: Fine.
LANE: So you'll help me.
VIRGINIA: You want my help?
LANE: Yes.
VIRGINIA: Are you sure?
LANE: Yes.
VIRGINIA: Say: I want your help.

(*A small pause.*)

LANE: I want your help.
VIRGINIA: Then I'll help you.

12. Ana and Virginia. Then Matilde. Then Lane.

(*All of Ana's possessions have been moved into Lane's
living room.*
Ana's fish is in a bowl on the coffee table.
There are bags of apples on the carpet.
And luggage. With clothes spilling out of a bag.
Virginia is preparing a special tray of food for Ana.
Virginia listens to Ana.)

ANA: People talk about *cancer* like it's this special thing
  you have a *relationship* with. And it becomes blood
  count, biopsy, chemotherapy, radiation, bone marrow, blah blah blah blah blah. As long as I live I want
  to retain my own language.
      Mientras tengo vida, quiero procurar mantener
  mi proprio idioma.
      No extra hospital words. I don't want a relation-
  ship with a disease. I want to have a relationship with
  death. That's important. But to have, a relationship
  with a *disease*—that's some kind of bourgeois invention. And I hate it.

(*Virginia gives Ana the tray.*)

  Thank you.

(*Ana eats a bite.*)

VIRGINIA: Do you like it?
ANA: It's delicious. What is it?
VIRGINIA: A casserole. No one makes casserole any-
  more. I thought it might be comforting.
ANA: What's in it?
VIRGINIA: Things you wouldn't want to know about.
ANA: Well, it's good.
      Thank you for taking care of me, Virginia.

(*Virginia is moved.*)

      What's wrong?
VIRGINIA: I'm not used to people thanking me.

(*Matilde enters, holding a telegram.*
She hands it to Ana.)

MATILDE: There is a telegram. From Charles.

(*In the distance, Charles appears
wearing a heavy parka.*
Inside the living room, it snows.)

CHARLES: Dear Ana. Stop.
  Have cut down tree. Stop.
  Cannot get on plane with tree. Stop.
  Must learn to fly plane. Stop.
  Wait for me. Stop.
  Your beloved, Charles.
ANA: I want him to be a nurse and he wants to be an
  explorer.
  Asi es la vida.
  (*That's life.*)

(*Charles exits.*
Lane enters.)

LANE: Hi.
ANA: Hello!

(*An awkward moment.*)

VIRGINIA: Would anyone like ice cream? I made some
  ice cream.
MATILDE: You *made* it?
VIRGINIA: It was no trouble.
ANA: I love ice cream.
VIRGINIA: Do you like chocolate?
ANA: Who doesn't like chocolate. Crazy people.
VIRGINIA: I'll get spoons.
MATILDE: I'll help you.

(*Matilde and Virginia exit.*
Lane sees Ana's fish.)

LANE: He made it all right.
ANA: He's a strong fish.

(*Lane taps the fish bowl.*
The fish wriggles.
*Matilde and Virginia come back with spoons and ice
cream.*
*After a moment of hesitation, Lane takes a spoon from
Virginia.*)

They all eat ice cream out of the same container.)

Mmmm! Amazing!
MATILDE: It must be what God eats when he is tired.
ANA: So soft!
MATILDE: Sometimes ice cream in this country is so hard.
ANA: Sí.
LANE: I like ice cream.

(*They all eat ice cream.*)

ANA: Can you imagine a time before ice cream? When they couldn't keep things frozen? There was once a ship filled with ice—it sailed from Europe to South America. The ice melted by the time it got to South America. And the captain of the ship was bankrupt. All he had to sell when he got there was water.
VIRGINIA: A ship full of water.
MATILDE: A ship full of water.

(*They finish the ice cream.
No one cleans up.*)

VIRGINIA: (*To Ana*) You look feverish, Are you warm?
ANA: I'm cold.
VIRGINIA: I'll get a thermometer.
ANA: No thermometers!
LANE: How about a blanket?
ANA: Okay, I'd like a blanket.
LANE (*to Virginia*): Where do I keep blankets?

VIRGINIA: I'll show you.

(*Lane and Virginia exit.*)

ANA: Matilde. My bones hurt.
MATILDE: I know they do.
ANA: Do you know what it feels like when your bones hurt?
MATILDE: No.
ANA: I hope you never know.
    Matilde. You once told me that your father killed your mother with a joke.
MATILDE: Yes.
ANA: I would like you to kill me with a joke.
MATILDE: I don't want to kill you.
    I like you.
ANA: If you like me, help me.
MATILDE: What about Charles? Will you wait for him?
ANA: No.
MATILDE: Why?
ANA: I'd lose all my bravery.
MATILDE: I understand.
ANA: You'll do it then?

(*A pause.*)

MATILDE: Okay.
ANA: When?
MATILDE: When you want me to.
ANA: You don't need time to make up a joke?
MATILDE: I made it up on your balcony.

Vanessa Aspillaga as Matilde the housekeeper, with Jill Clayburgh as Virginia, Blair Brown as Lane, and Concetta Tomei as Ana in the 2006 New York production of *The Clean House*.

ANA: Tomorrow, then.
MATILDE: Tomorrow.

(*Lane enters with a blanket.*
She hands it to Ana.)

LANE: I hope it's warm enough.
ANA: Thank you.
    (*To Matilde*) Good night.
MATILDE: (*To Ana*) Good night.

(*Ana puts her head on the pillow, closing her eyes.*)

    (*Whispering to Lane*) Are you coming?
LANE: In a minute.

(*Matilde exits.*
Lane sits on the floor and watches Ana sleep.
She guards her the way a dog would guard a rival dog,
if her rival were sick.)

13. *Matilde Tells Ana a Joke*

(*The light turns from night to day.*
The next day.
Lane, Virginia and Matilde are gathered around Ana.)

ANA: I want to say good-bye to everyone before Matilde
    tells me a joke.
LANE: Can't I give you anything for the pain?
ANA: No.
LANE: You're sure?
ANA: Yes. Good-bye, Lane.
LANE: Good-bye, Ana.

(*They embrace.*)

ANA: Take care of Charles.
LANE: You think I'll be taking care of him?
ANA: Of course.
LANE: Why?
ANA: You love him.
    Good-bye Virginia.

(*Virginia weeps.*)

    Don't cry. Thank you for taking care of me.

(*Virginia weeps.*)

    Oh—see? That makes it worse. Oh, Virginia. I can't
    take it. Matilde. Let's have the joke.
MATILDE: Are you ready?
ANA: Yes.
    Everyone's always dying lying down.
    I want to die standing up.

(*Ana stands.*)

(*To Lane and Virginia*) The two of you had better leave
    the room.
    I don't want you dying before your time.

(*They nod.*
They leave.)

    Matilde.
    Deseo el chiste ahora.
(*I want the joke now.*)

(*The lights change.*
Music.
Matilde whispers a joke in Ana's ear.
We don't hear it.
We hear sublime music instead.
A subtitle projects: The Funniest Joke in the World.
Ana laughs and laughs.
Ana collapses.
Matilde kneels beside her.
Matilde wails.)

MATILDE: Ohhh . . .

(*Lane and Virginia rush in.*
Lane checks Ana's pulse.
The women look at one another.)

VIRGINIA: What do we do?
LANE: I don't know.
VIRGINIA: You're the doctor!
LANE: I've never seen someone die in a house before.
    Only in a hospital.
    Where they clean everything up.
VIRGINIA: What do the nurses do?
MATILDE: They close the eyes.
LANE: That's right.

(*Matilde closes Ana's eyes.*)

MATILDE: And they wash the body.
LANE: I'll wash her.

(*Lane goes to get a towel and a bowl of water.*)

VIRGINIA: Should we say a prayer?
MATILDE: You say a prayer, Virginia.
    A prayer cleans the air the way water cleans the dirt.
VIRGINIA: Ana. I hope you are apple picking.

(*Lane enters with a bowl of water.*
She washes Ana's body.
Time slows down.)

CHARLES: (*From offstage*) Ana!

(*Charles pounds on the door.*)

    Ana! Ana!

(*The women look at one another.*
Lane goes to Charles.
Charles walks in carrying an enormous tree.
He is sweating and breathing heavily.
He has carried his tree great distances.)

    I brought back this tree.
    The bark—
LANE: I know.

CHARLES: It won't help?
LANE: No.
CHARLES: Why?
LANE: Charles.
CHARLES: You were here?
LANE: Yes.
CHARLES: Can I see her?

(*Lane nods.*)

LANE: Charles?

(*Lane kisses Charles on the forehead.*)

CHARLES: Thank you. Will you hold my tree?

(*Lane nods.*
Lane holds the tree.
Charles moves toward Ana's body.
He collapses over her body
as the lights come up on Matilde.)

14. Matilde

(*Matilde, to the audience:*)

MATILDE: This is how I imagine my parents.

(*Ana and Charles transform into Matilde's mother and father.*
Under Charles's parka he is dressed as Matilde's father.
Under Ana's bathrobe, she is dressed as Matilde's mother.)

My mother is about to give birth to me.
The hospital is too far away.
My mother runs up a hill in December and says: now!
My mother is lying down under a tree.
My father is telling her a joke to try and keep her calm.

(*Matilde's father whispers a joke in Portuguese to Matilde's mother.*)

My mother laughed.
She laughed so hard that I popped out.
My mother said I was the only baby who laughed when I came into the world.
She said I was laughing at my father's joke.
I laughed to take in the air.
I took in some air, and then I cried.

(*Matilde looks at her parents.*
A moment of completion between them.
Matilde looks at the audience.)

I think maybe heaven is a sea of untranslatable jokes.
Only everyone is laughing.

The End

A Note on Jokes

Thanks is due to all the people who helped me with jokes and translations in The Clean House: *Caridad Svich, Fernando Oliveira, Anna Fluck, Giovanna Sardelli, Claudine Barros.*

I want the choice of jokes to be somewhat open, allowing for the possibility that different productions may come up with different and more perfect Brazilian jokes. So please use these jokes as you will.

(Joke #1, to be told in Act 1, Scene 1:) *Um homem tava a ponto de casar e ele tava muito nervosa ao prepararse pra noite de nupias porque ele nunca tuvo sexo en la vida de ele. Enton ele vai pra médico e pergunta: "O que que eu devo fazor?" O médico fala: "Não se preocupa. Voce coloca uma nota de dez dolares na bolso direito y voce practica: '10, 10, 10, 10.'"*

Enton el homen vai pra casa y practica todo semana: "10, 10, 10." Aí ele volta pra médico y lhe fala: "Muito bem! Agora você coloca uma nota de, 10 no bolso direito e uma nota do 20 (vinte) no bolso esquerdo e practica: '10, 20; 10, 20; 10, 20; 10 20'"

Ele foi pra casa praticou toda semana: "10, 20; 10, 20; 10, 20." Ele volta pra medico y ele falou: "É isso aí! Agora você coloca uma nota de 10 no bolso direito, uma de 20 no bolso esquerdo e uma de 100 (cem) na frente. Aí você practica: '10, 20, 100; 10, 20, 100; 10, 20, 100.'"

Aí ele casou. A noite de núpcias chegou. Ele tava con sua mulher todo bonita e gustosa e ele comencou a fazer amor: "10, 20, 100; 10, 20, 100; 10, 20, 100. Ai, que se foda o trocado: 100, 100, 100!!!"

Translation: *A man is getting married. He's never had sex and he's very nervous about his wedding night. So, he goes to a doctor and he says, "I'm really nervous, what should I do?" The doctor says, "Don't worry about it. Go home and put a ten-dollar bill in your right pocket and you practice: '10! 10! 10!,' moving your hips to the left."*

So, he goes home and after a week of practice, he returns to the doctor who says, "Very good. Now, go back home and put a ten-dollar bill in your right-hand pocket, a twenty-dollar bill in your left-hand pocket and go: '10! 20! 10! 20!'" (The joke teller moves hips from side to side)

So, he practices, does very well, returns to the doctor who says, "Perfect! Now you're going to put a ten-dollar bill in your left-hand pocket, a twenty-dollar bill in your right-hand pocket and a hundred-dollar dollar bill in front, where you will go like this, '10! 20! 100!, 10! 20!, 100!'"

The man practices as he is told, goes back to the doctor who says, "Perfect! You're ready to go!"

The big day arrives and the man is very excited about his night with his wife. The time comes and he is in bed and he starts with his wife: "10! 20! 100!, 10! 20! 100!, 10! 20! 100! Oh, fuck the change: 100! 100! 100!"

(Joke #2, to be told in Act 1, Scene 14:) *Por que os homens na cama são como comida de microondas. Estão prontos em trinta segundos.*

Translation: *Why are men in bed like microwave food?*

They're done in thirty seconds.

(Joke #3, to be told in Act 2, Scene 5:) *O melhor investimento que existe é comprar um argentino pelo valor que ele vale e depois vendê-lo pelo valor que ele acha que vale.*

Translation: *The best investment ever is to buy an Argentinean for what he is really worth and later sell him for what he thinks he is worth.*

Suzan-Lori Parks

"She is an utterly astounding and beautiful creature who may become one of the most valuable artists of our time."

— JAMES BALDWIN

Suzan-Lori Parks (b. 1964) was named by Mel Gussow in the *New York Times* as the "year's most promising playwright" in 1989. She lives in Venice, California, with her husband, Paul Oscher, a blues musician who has played with Muddy Waters. Currently, Parks teaches drama and playwriting at the California Institute of the Arts in Valencia and is head of the A. S. K. (Audrey Skirball-Kenis) Theatre project, searching for new plays in the Los Angeles area. Parks's work has been supported by grants from numerous agencies, including the Rockefeller and Ford Foundations and the National Endowment for the Arts, from which she has twice received a playwriting fellowship. She also received a MacArthur Award in 2001. Her work has been seen primarily in off-Broadway theaters in New York as well as in important regional theaters.

Parks was the child of an army officer and grew up in several different locations. She says, "I've heard horrible stories about twelve-step groups for army people. But I had a great childhood. My parents were really into experiencing the places we lived." She lived, for example, in a small town in Germany and attended German schools, studying in German. She went to Mt. Holyoke College and took courses at nearby Hampshire College, where she studied writing with James Baldwin. After that experience she went to London for a year to study acting. "It really made a difference in my writing. It dawned on me that a lot of people write with ideas in mind. . . . But I never really have ideas, per se. I have these movements, these gestures. Then I figure out how to put those gestures into words."

She is aware of being influenced by a number of important literary figures, among them Gertrude Stein, James Joyce, William Faulkner, and Samuel Beckett, but echoes of other writers such as Shakespeare and Richard Wright can be heard in *The Death of the Last Black Man in the Whole Entire World* (1990). Parks's approach to language is partly vernacular as she attempts to reproduce speech both as it is spoken and as her audience assumes it may be spoken. But she is interested in the hypnotic and musical value of words, which accounts for much of the patterning of repetition that marks her work.

Her plays have been performed in the BACA (Brooklyn Arts Council Association) Downtown Theater, the Manhattan Theater Club, and the Joseph Papp Public Theater in Manhattan. Her early short plays are *Betting on the Dust Commander, Fishes, The Sinners' Place*, and *The America Play*. Her full-length play *Imperceptible Mutabilities in the Third Kingdom*, directed by her long-time collaborator Liz Diamond, won the Obie Award for the best off-Broadway play of 1990. One section of *Mutabilities* takes place on Emancipation Day in 1865 and is played in whiteface by African American actors. Another section, "Greeks," makes reference to her own family, with a character called Mr. Sergeant Smith. Parts of the play have been described as "like a choral poem."

Parks has produced a film, *Anemone Me* (1990), that has been shown in New York. Her *Devotees in the Garden of Love* (1992) premiered at the Actors Theatre of Louisville, Kentucky. Her next play, *Venus* (1996), was a coproduction of the Joseph Papp Public Theater and Yale Repertory Theatre. It was directed by Richard Foreman, the founder of the Ontological-Hysteric Theater. The play focuses on the life of a black woman brought to England as the Venus Hottentot, a sideshow freak displaying "an intensely ugly figure, distorted beyond all European notions of beauty." The authorities put an end to the sideshow, and Parks explores this mysterious woman's life. Parks has also written *Girl 6* (1996), a film directed by Spike Lee.

Parks's *In the Blood* (1999) focuses on Hester, a welfare mother of five. She faces poverty, the welfare system's workfare, and sterilization. The play examines our attitudes toward poverty and responsibility.

Topdog/Underdog (2001) won the Pulitzer Prize for drama, the first awarded to a black woman playwright. She followed this with *Fucking A* (2003), with the A standing for abortion rather than adultery, as it does in Nathaniel Hawthorne's novel *The Scarlet Letter*. Parks's protagonist, like Hawthorne's, is Hester, a carryover from *In the Blood*. Parks has said that characters stay with her, as in the case also of the black Lincoln impersonator who is central to *The America Play*, and she feels free to follow up with new plays on old themes. In 2003 Parks published her first novel, *Getting Mother's Body*, which was inspired by a novel by William Faulkner. Parks is an energetic and carefully focused playwright with a special interest in the language of speech and the language of gesture—in almost equal measure.

365 DAYS/365 PLAYS

Suzan-Lori Parks began, with the encouragement of a friend, to write a play every day for a year, beginning on November 13 and continuing until the next year on November 12. It was a daring idea by a writer who was known for being daring in her work. The completed project inspired more than 600 theater companies and arts organizations to produce the plays every day from November 13, 2006, to November 12, 2007. This phenomenon became the 365 National Festival. The entire project's development can be viewed on www.365days365plays.com.

Several patterns began to develop in the short plays, and a few of them are illustrated in the selections that follow. Some plays concern a single idea, such as *Father Comes Home from the War*, variations of which consist of 11 plays. A play about a father coming home from the war is appropriate in years in which some fathers are actually returning from war, but it is especially appropriate for Parks, whose father was a soldier. Another group of plays concerns Abraham Lincoln, who has been either alluded to or present in several of her earlier plays. *Topdog/Underdog* featured a character who impersonated

Lincoln in a sideshow. Parks's plays here underscore ironic moments in Lincoln's life, both before and after his death.

Her approach to the idea of tragedy is worked out in another group of these plays. Oedipus, from *Oedipus Rex* (the play that Aristotle used as a basis for his theories on tragedy), appears in Parks's plays dealing with specific moments of his life. Some of the plays are meta-theatrical, concerned with the very act of imagining dramatic action while creating dramatic action. Another group of plays employs a red carpet, which evokes the red carpet that Clytemnestra rolled out for her husband Agamemnon, a prelude to murder. References to Hindu deities such as Ganesha, Krishna, and Arjuna also show up in these plays, extending their reach beyond the limits of European literature. Some of the plays contain social commentary, and some comment on art in general.

Some of the plays are styled as "tribute plays"; that is, they are designed as a memorial to individuals who are important to Parks. Plays that refer to the English playwright Sarah Kane, the American dancer and actor Gregory Hines, and the singer Barry White, are joined by *A Prayer for Johnny Cash*. All of these public figures died, though not necessarily during the year Parks wrote about them. Parks also introduces inanimate objects, such as the "madeleine" (a small pastry cake) that inspired the remembrances of Marcel Proust's protagonist in his novel *In Search of Lost Time*. Ants and bees also figure in some plays, as does a bear. Even kings make an appearance in the collection. The range is remarkable, and the energy of each play is striking.

365 Days/365 Plays in Performance

The 365 National Festival in 2006 and 2007 began in August 2006 with a reading of the first five months of the project at the Public Theater in New York, with Bonnie Metzgar directing. In September the second half of the plays was read, also at the Public Theater. After that, in November, the project continued as plays were performed and read throughout the United States. Certain theater companies were designated as hub theaters to facilitate productions by theaters of all kinds, school venues, and large and small theaters, both commercial and community. Atlanta, Austin, Texas, Chicago, Colorado, Los Angeles, Minneapolis, New York City, New Haven, San Francisco, Seattle, and Washington, D.C. all had hub theaters that reached out to several hundred regional theaters to provide wide exposure for these plays.

Suzan-Lori Parks *(b. 1964)*

365 DAYS/365 PLAYS
THE 3 CONSTANTS

2006

For 365 Days/365 Plays, I'm inviting everybody to perform these 3 Constants along with your selected plays — sprinkle them where you like. — XOXOXOX S-L P

The 1st Constant (Remember Who You Are)

(2 benches or 2 chairs. Someone on the bench (or chair). Someone Else comes in.)

SOMEONE ELSE: This seat taken?
SOMEONE: Nope.
SOMEONE ELSE: You sleep?
SOMEONE: Yep.
SOMEONE ELSE: Oh. Sorry.

(Someone Else goes through an elaborate before-sleep ritual. Feel free, do whatever you want. Brush yr teeth, floss maybe, pray maybe. You could stretch or gargle. Take out yr contacts, oil yr feet and hands, cold-creme yr face, roll up yr hair in curlers or wrap it in a doo-rag. Lock up yr belongings. Kiss yr beloved's image. Thank God. Do whatcha gotta do.)

SOMEONE ELSE:°
SOMEONE ELSE:

(Rest)

SOMEONE ELSE: Yr sleeping with one eye open.
SOMEONE: Yes.
SOMEONE ELSE: How come?
SOMEONE: To watch over you.
SOMEONE ELSE: But—. But you dont even know me!!!!
SOMEONE: I am That, you are That, all this is That, and Thats all there is.
SOMEONE:
SOMEONE ELSE:

(Rest)
(They sleep.)

The 2nd Constant (Action in Inaction)

(Someone standing still. They could be dressed in mourning. The sound of wind or whales forever.)

The 3rd Constant (Inaction in Action)

(Onstage are 365 things to do, that is, 365 tasks. What are the tasks? Yr choice. Lights up. Dart around trying to

This indicates a long pause.

do all the tasks. Make it clear that you desire to complete all the tasks. Dart around as fast as possible. Do yr best. Dont be shy about going all out. There isnt anything to hold out for. This is it. Hurry hurry hurry. Lights go out long before yr done.)

November
13 START HERE

KRISHNA:° We start here. Come on.
ARJUNA: Where to?
KRISHNA: Does it matter?
ARJUNA: Yeah. Because I have a choice in the matter and if we're going somewhere I dont like, I may choose not to go. Because I have a choice.
KRISHNA: You have a choice?
ARJUNA: Yeah.
KRISHNA: Are you sure?
ARJUNA: This is a free country.
KRISHNA: Is it?
KRISHNA:
ARJUNA:
KRISHNA: Yr sitting down.
ARJUNA: No Im not.
KRISHNA: Yr legs are folded underneath you and yr bottom is resting. On the ground. Where I come from we call that sitting.
ARJUNA: All I know is that my legs folded and my mind stopped. And now I have a great need to cry.
KRISHNA: Cry? Who for?
ARJUNA: Myself. My country.
KRISHNA: Yr *free* country.
ARJUNA: Yrs too.

(Rest)

It was such a great idea. In the beginning. When they were all starting out. They had no idea that— that—. That it would end up like this.
KRISHNA: It hasnt ended up like this. It *is* like this. This isnt the end, its—
ARJUNA: The beginning?

Krishna: A deity, an avatar of the Lord God Vishnu in the Hindu religion. He appeared to Arjuna, a hero of the Indian epic *Mahabarata*.

KRISHNA: Thats right. Come on.

ARJUNA: Mmmm.

KRISHNA: Dont hold back.

ARJUNA: Eeeeeee.

KRISHNA: Lets go.

ARJUNA: Ooooooo.

KRISHNA: Yr having 2nd thoughts. I understand. Everything you own, everything you are, everything you know is back there, right? Yr not prepared, you think. You forgot to pack yr toothbrush. You forgot to lock the front door. You forgot to turn on the machine. You forgot to turn off the stove. You may have left the bathwater running. You dont speak the language of—wherever it is we're headed.

ARJUNA: Right.

KRISHNA: Hear that sound?

ARJUNA: Sounds like leaves moving in the wind.

KRISHNA: Its the sound of writing. Theyre writing yr name in the Book.

ARJUNA: *My* name?

KRISHNA: Why not yr name?

(*Rest*)

ARJUNA: Im afraid. A little.

KRISHNA: Good.

(*Rest*)

At the start theres always energy. Sometimes joy. Sometimes fear. By the end, youll be so deep into the habit of continuing on, youll pray that youll never stop. Happens all the time. But dont take my word for it. Lets go and youll see for yrself.

(*Rest*)

Get up. There you go. Breathe. Ok. Come on.

ARJUNA: Where to?

KRISHNA: For me to know and for you to find out.

KRISHNA & ARJUNA: Hahahahahahah.

KRISHNA: Come on. Not to worry. Walk with me. Keep the feet moving. And, with any luck, we'll get there.

(*They start out.*)

November

14 FATHER COMES HOME FROM THE WARS (PART 1)

FATHER: Hi honey, Im home.

MOTHER: Yr home.

FATHER: Yes.

MOTHER: I wasnt expecting you. Ever.

FATHER: Should I go back out and come back in again?

MOTHER: Please.

(*He goes back out and comes back in again.*)

MOTHER: Once more.

FATHER: Yr kidding.

MOTHER: Please.

(*He goes back out and comes back in again.*)

MOTHER: Yr home.

FATHER: Yes.

MOTHER: Let me get a good look at you.

FATHER: I'll just turn around.

MOTHER: Please.

(*He turns around once. Counterclockwise.*)

MOTHER: They should of sent a letter. A letter saying you were coming home. Or at least a telephone call. That is the least they could do. Give a woman and her family and her friends and neighbors a chance to get ready. A chance to spruce things up. Put new ribbons in the hair of the dog. Get the oil changed. Have everything running. Smoothly. And bake a cake of course. Hang streamers. Tell the yard man to—tidy up his act. Oh God. Long story. Oh God. Long story. I woulda invited the neighbors over. Had everyone on the block jump out from their hiding places from behind the brand-new furniture with the plastic still on it and say— WHAT? Say: "Welcome Home" of course. And then after a few slices of cake and a few drinks theyd all get the nerve to say what theyre really thinking. For now itll stay unthought and unsaid. Well. You came home. All in one piece looks like. We're lucky. I guess. We're lucky, right? Hhhhh.

FATHER: They sent a letter saying I was coming or at least they telephoned. Maybe you didnt open the letter. I dont blame you. It could have been bad news. I see yr unopened envelopes piled up. I dont blame you. I dont blame you at all. They called several times. Maybe you were out. Maybe you were screwing the yard man. If you had known I was coming you woulda put new ribbons in the hair of the dog, got the oil changed, baked a cake and invited all the neighbors over so they could jump out of their various hiding places behind the brand-new furniture purchased with the blood of some people I used to know—and some blood of some people I used to kill. Oh God. Long story. Oh God. Long story. And theyd shout at me—WHAT? "Welcome Home" of course. And then after a few slices of cake and a few drinks theyd get the nerve to tell me what they really think: "Murderer, baby killer, racist, government pawn, ultimate patsy, stooge, fall guy, camp follower, dumbass, dope fiend, loser." Hhhhh.

MOTHER:

FATHER:

(*Rest*)

MOTHER: I cant understand a word yr saying.

FATHER: I dont speak English anymore.

MOTHER: I dont blame you. SIT DOWN, I'LL FIX YOU SOMETHING.

Didi O'Connell and Reg E. Cathey in a "Father Comes Home from the Wars" scene from the 2006 Public Theater production of *365 Days/365 Plays*.

(*He sits. She takes a heavy frying pan and holds it over his head. Almost murder. She lowers the pan.*)

MOTHER:
FATHER:

(*Rest*)

(*He sits. Again she raises the frying pan and holds it over his head. Almost murder. She lowers the pan.*)

FATHER: Where are the children?
MOTHER: What children?

(*Sound of the wind and the rain.*)

November
3 SWEET (FATHER COMES HOME FROM THE WARS PART 10)

(*A Man eats slowly, but like an animal. A Woman watches.*)

WOMAN: Yr home.
MAN: I know.

(*His plate is empty. The Woman piles more food onto his plate.*)

MAN: Im home but I still got the taste for killing, you know?

WOMAN: Lemmie put some sugar on. It tastes like shit without sugar.

(*She pours a lot of sugar on his food. He continues eating. At last his plate is empty. He puts his knife in its sheath.*)

MAN: Im gonna go out for awhile.
WOMAN: Where to?
MAN: Nowhere special. I'll just, you know—
WOMAN: Walk around.
MAN: Yeah.

(*Rest*)

WOMAN: Just smell them before you cut them, ok?
MAN: Have I ever killed one of our own?
WOMAN: No, but—
MAN: Yr talking to me like I killed one of our own.
WOMAN: You never done nothing like that—its just—I worry.
MAN: If you kept them in the house you wouldnt have no worries.
WOMAN: Theyre grown. And the house is small.
MAN: So I'll get us a bigger house. WHEN I GET A BIGGER JOB!

(*Rest*)

In the meantime, I gotta go out.
WOMAN:
MAN:

(*Rest*)

MAN: Itll wear off in awhile. The taste for it.
WOMAN: Lets hope.

(*He goes. She frets, then cleans up the dishes.
A Young Man enters.*)

JUNIOR: Hey Mom. Wheres Pop?—
WOMAN: Out bowling—with his bowling buddies,
Junior.
JUNIOR: Sweet. Im history, K?
WOMAN: Oh no yr not.
JUNIOR: Come on, I did my homework. And my chores.
WOMAN: One step out there and yr grounded, mister.
JUNIOR: You cant ground me, Ive served my country.

(*Rest*)

Later. K, Mom?

(*He kisses her and goes.
As soon as he has cleared the stage, Sister comes on.*)

SISTER: Wheres Junior and Pop?
WOMAN: Out and about.
SISTER: Im—
WOMAN: Dont—
SISTER: Hey—
WOMAN: Sure. Yr history. I know. Whatever. Sweet.
SISTER:
WOMAN:

(*Sister goes.*)

(*The Woman very meticulously cleans up the dishes and
sits. Then she quickly gets up, puts on a coat and hat
and hurries out the door. The house is empty. No foul
play will happen to any of them, although, of course,
they may cause foul play to others, and, of course, none
of them will ever ever return.*)

November
4 FATHER COMES HOME FROM THE
WARS (*Part 11: His Eternal Return—A Play
for My Father*)

(*During this play we hear a war news-in-brief
soundtrack, laced with military band music thats
played at a slower than normal speed. The action is
as follows:
A never-ending loop of action—5 Servicemen walk
downstage together. All wear military uniforms from the
same side of the same war, but not necessarily the same
branch of Service. They stand upstage and walk very
vibrantly and heroically downstage. Theyre returning
home as heroes.
As they reach centerstage, 5 women, their Servicewives, stand up from the audience, and run toward
the men. Just as the Servicemen reach the downstage
edge, the Servicewives meet them. The Servicemen pick
up their Servicewives, twirling them around very joyfully.*)

(*Before each Wife returns to the ground a Child
comes onstage and, racing toward its respective Mother
and Father, jumps for joy.
This action repeats. New Servicemen walk downstage, new Wives leap up from the audience and rush
into their arms, new Children run in to cheer.
The action repeats eternally. Long after the audience
has emptied of Women; long after the Men have grown
out of the desire to be hugged and kissed and welcomed;
long after the Children have become less cheerful and
more sensible and have taken up trades, like accounting
or teaching or real estate or politics; long after the Children's Children have outgrown joy and have all grown
up and moved away. Forever.*)

November
26 MRS. KECKLEY & MRS. LINCOLN

(*1865. Mrs. Lincoln, wife of the 16th President, and
Mrs. Keckley, her Negro dressmaker and handmaid.
Lots of dresses spread about. Mrs. Lincoln studies each
dress in turn.*)

MRS. LINCOLN: I'll wear my red.
MRS. KECKLEY: Yr red?
MRS. LINCOLN: Yes?
MRS. KECKLEY: Yr red is very—red.
MRS. LINCOLN: You think?
MRS. KECKLEY: Mmm.
MRS. LINCOLN: Theyll all be looking at me, though. The
redll shut them up.
MRS. KECKLEY: Theyve got things to shut them up
already. Not to disagree with you, maam, but the
war is preying heavy on their minds.
MRS. LINCOLN: "Preying heavy on their minds." I like
that.
MRS. KECKLEY: Thank you, maam.
MRS. LINCOLN: I hate when you call me that. "Maam."
I want to feel young. I want to feel like I have my
whole life ahead of me. I had 26 suitors. In one season. But you look down at the floor. Youve heard me
tell that story already. Is that the difference between a
young girl of 15 and a married woman, do you
think? The young girl does not repeat herself, while
the old married woman—. 26 suitors. In one season.
A young girl would repeat that. Because it is worth
repeating. It bears repeating. And the things I bear.
And the children I have born.

(*Rest*)

Call me Mary.
MRS. KECKLEY: What about yr blue?
MRS. LINCOLN: Are you hard-of-hearing, Mrs. Keckley?
Should we call in Doctor Wilke and have you fitted
for an ear trumpet?
MRS. KECKLEY: Yr yellow would suit the occasion,
maam.
MRS. LINCOLN: "Mary." I won't consider another dress

or another thing, I wont move a muscle or take another breath until you call me Mary.

MRS. LINCOLN:

MRS. KECKLEY:

(*Rest*)

MRS. KECKLEY: Yr yellow would suit the occasion, Mary.

MRS. LINCOLN: Ah, it feels good to breathe again, Elizabeth. You are blushing. Ha. I can see the color coming up. It makes you look purple. It makes you look purple, Elizabeth.

MRS. KECKLEY: You need to get dressed. Mary.

MRS. LINCOLN: We both live in this country. We both inhabit the White House. You know what its like, living here. In the joyless gloom, while the war continues. Sunshine, rain, snow, spring and still, the war continues. An admirable thing. Like a woman. War is female, wouldnt you say? Because it is so tenacious.

(*Rest*)

Just a little longer. Its only for fun. I'll call you Elizabeth and you call me Mary. For just a little longer. Just for fun.

MRS. KECKLEY: The white, I think, Mary.

MRS. LINCOLN: Why didnt we think of that before? The white with the red roses, and cut so low that the president will look at me and his eyes will travel from my eyes down to my mouth and, then, fall into the chasm of my bosom. 26 suitors, Elizabeth, and he was the—tallest.

MRS. KECKLEY:

MRS. LINCOLN:

(*Rest*)

MRS. KECKLEY & MRS. LINCOLN: Hahahahahahahahhaha!

MRS. LINCOLN: Of course I didnt know that at the time, I was only a girl.

MRS. KECKLEY: You didnt know that all tall drinks of water are—(well equipped)?

MRS. LINCOLN: I'll swear an oath on my marriage bed, I'll swear that I had no idea. But on my marriage bed, Elizabeth, I tell you, Mary did discover.

MRS. KECKLEY: He's a fine man, Mary.

MRS. LINCOLN: I'll give him that.

MRS. KECKLEY: Lets get you dressed. We wouldnt want to keep yr president waiting.

MRS. LINCOLN: He's yr president too.

MRS. KECKLEY:

MRS. KECKLEY:

(*Rest*)

MRS. KECKLEY: Step into yr dress. There, that's it. Pretty as a picture.

(*Mrs. Lincoln steps into her white dress. Mrs. Keckley continues helping her get dressed, lacing up the back, etc. There is a sound of a gunshot.*)

MRS. LINCOLN: What in God's name was that?!

MRS. KECKLEY: Just the sound of a car backfiring.

MRS. LINCOLN: The sound of a what-whating?

MRS. KECKLEY: Just the sound of the War, maam, getting closer.

MRS. LINCOLN: I thought you said—something else.

MRS. KECKLEY: Take a look in the mirror, maam. See how pretty you look.

MRS. LINCOLN: We're going to see *Our American Cousin* tonight. I wonder if its any good.

MRS. KECKLEY: Its a comedy.

MRS. LINCOLN: A comedy! We are the lucky ones, Mrs. Keckley! We are the lucky ones!

(*Mrs. Keckley takes a headdress of roses from a box. Mrs. Lincoln claps her hands in delight as Mrs. Keckley puts it on her head.*)

December
2 ABRAHAM LINCOLN AT 89

(*Abraham Lincoln, former 16th President of the United States; the former 1st Lady, Mary Todd Lincoln; Elizabeth Keckley, her dressmaker and handmaid; and other foreign and domestic Dignitaries, in addition to a respectable representation of the Local Population, all gathered to celebrate the Former President's birthday.*)

THE WEALTHIEST MAN IN THE WORLD: Happy birthday, Mr. Former President! Greetings from my considerable corner of the world. You must be over a 100 by now! Happy birthday!

LINCOLN: Im not over 100! Im 89!

MARY TODD LINCOLN: He's funny about his age. I am too. And today's not even his birthday, either.

MRS. KECKLEY: ((Dont spoil it.))

THE WEALTHIEST MAN IN THE WORLD: 89! 89! Of course! Of course! Happy 89th birthday!

1ST FOREIGN DIGNITARY: Thats very novel, sir, to celebrate the 89th year. In my country we would celebrate the 80th or the 90th.

LINCOLN: I might not be alive that long.

MARY TODD LINCOLN: Yr not alive now!

LINCOLN: Mary, we have guests. My wife is not at her best. She takes the war very hard.

MRS. KECKLEY: Mrs. Lincoln, I'd like you to try on the rose headdress.

MARY TODD LINCOLN: I dont want to try on the rose headdress. It reminds me of a funeral wreath. It reminds me of what I was wearing. When. He. Left.

LINCOLN: Mary, dont you worry about a thing. I'll handle the guests. I'll tell them the joke about how I won the presidency. Go along with Mrs. Keckley, dear, dont you worry about a thing. (*Aside*) She thinks that folks dont like my jokes. She says my jokes aren't "cultured."

3RD FOREIGN DIGNITARY: Cultured? I'll show you cultured.

(*He performs a very beautiful and complicated dance*

telling the story of his national heroine and hero, how they met, wooed, were wed and then, owing to the evil deeds of the lesser of 2 evils, were torn from each other's arms. Her tears made the world's first oceans, his search for her made the world's first land masses; their separation created night and their ultimate and glorious reunion created day. It all took eons to happen and it all happened in an instant. An instant which ends with the birthday party of a Former American President: great beauty and tableau.)

THE ASSEMBLED GUESTS:
THE ASSEMBLED GUESTS:

(*Rest*)

(*Lincoln applauds. The others follow suit. Lincoln dabs his eyes. The others follow suit. He bursts into tears. The others as well.*)

LINCOLN: Moving. Very moving. Well well well. Too bad Mary missed it.
3RD FOREIGN DIGNITARY: I'll perform it again at her request.
LINCOLN: How bout we get some of these candles lit?
CANDLE LIGHTER: My pleasure, Mr. Former President.
LINCOLN: And count em as you light em. I like to hear the numbers go by.
CANDLE LIGHTER: My pleasure, Mr. Former President.

(*The Candle Lighter lights each candle on the cake. As he lights, he says the number out loud (the counting should continue softly underneath the remaining dialogue). The Assembled Guests watch the Candle Lighter for a bit and then, all except for Lincoln, grow bored.*)

2ND FOREIGN DIGNITARY: Nothing like a good war, I always say.
LINCOLN: Only when we cease to fight do we truly conquer.
1ST LOCAL: Thats ridiculous, Mr. Former President.
THE WEALTHIEST MAN IN THE WORLD: In my corner of the world youd be executed for yr insolence.
2ND FOREIGN DIGNITARY: Where I come from we do not invite locals to view the Former Head of State lying in state.
THE ASSEMBLED GUESTS:
THE ASSEMBLED GUESTS:
LINCOLN: What did you say?
1ST LOCAL: You said, "Only when we cease to fight do we truly conquer," and I said, "Thats ridiculous."
2ND FOREIGN DIGNITARY: Im not going to repeat myself.
THE WEALTHIEST MAN IN THE WORLD: Just as well.
1ST LOCAL: This is ridiculous.
LINCOLN: Yep, I suppose it is. Did you ever hear how I won over my constituents? I won by a majority, because of the possum and the squirrels, and the bears and the bobcat and whatnot. It was the critters who put me in office.

(*Rest*)

Ha ha ha ha ha ha.

(*Rest*)

THE ASSEMBLED GUESTS: Hahahahahahahahha.

(*Mary Todd Lincoln reenters, in a completely different dress. Mrs. Keckley wears the dress that Mrs. Lincoln was wearing and Mrs. Lincoln wears—well, perhaps she wears Mrs. Keckley's dress.*)

MARY TODD LINCOLN: You like it?
LINCOLN: Very much. Gentlemen, my wife. Greet her in the manner of yr country, culture or social class.

(*One by one each guest performs the male-female curtsy-greeting of their country, custom, culture or class. Then, all in unison, they repeat their individual curtsies, revolving around the triumphant Mary Todd Lincoln as if she were on a brilliant pedestal, or they, devotees of the maypole. As they devote themselves to her, Mary performs rhythmic breathing and various mudras. Perhaps it is all accompanied by music. This display is not at all tacky or excessive, but very devotional and a little sad.*)

LINCOLN: This is the best birthday Ive ever had.
MARY TODD LINCOLN: But you didnt live to be a 100.
THE WEALTHIEST MAN IN THE WORLD: He's 89!
MARY TODD LINCOLN: Its an act of self-flattery having a one-hundredth birthday party when you didnt live to be 100. He didnt live to 89, either, truth be told.
2ND FOREIGN DIGNITARY: Truth be told!!!
LINCOLN: Mary, please, darling. We have guests.
LINCOLN
MARY TODD

(*Rest*)

(*The Narrator, from one of the earlier plays, enters from the wings.*)

NARRATOR: To be continued.
LINCOLN: Really?
NARRATOR: You heard me.
MARY TODD LINCOLN: We must be good.
NARRATOR: Good enough.
THE ASSEMBLED GUESTS: All right, then!
LINCOLN: We are the lucky ones!

(*All are very happy. The Candle Lighter continues lighting and counting the candles as the lights fade.*)

April
18 PROJECT ULYSSES

(*A Chorus of Young Men apparently lounging around on a basketball court. Spy comes in. He's got news but isnt ready to spill it. The Young Men act like they could care less. Then their enthusiasm betrays their cool.*)

Scene from the 2006 Public Theater production of *365 Days/365 Plays*.

CHORUS: Spy!
SPY: Thats my name.
From when my mother
first looked me in the face.
CHORUS: Spy!
Spill it.
SPY: Spill what?
CHORUS: Like we all gathered here together
and sit for nothing.
Theres news.
SPY: Says who?
CHORUS: Says, says you, thats who says.
SPY: I aint said nothing—
CHORUS: Yet!
SPY: If you know theres news
why dont you spill it, then?
If yr so sure and shit,
if yr so knowledgeable,
so know-it-all, so big-head,
they call you Spy?
NOT!
CHORUS: Why does he go through this every time?
I drive a cab for a living and
if I took the long way around,
Lord knows folks wouldnt like it.
Theyd take away my license.
Theyd lock me up
under the jail.
Shit.
But, Spy. He takes the long way around every time.

Making us wait to hear what we wanna know.
SPY: Tell you what.
Ima tell you.
CHORUS: At last.
So tell.
Go on.
He back?
SPY: Ulysses?
CHORUS: Ulysses.
SPY: Not yet.
CHORUS: Then we still got a chance
to get with Penny, his girl.
SPY: But Im the only one with her number.
CHORUS: We know.
SPY: Slide me some paper
I'll call her for you.
Maybe she'll talk.
CHORUS: For true?
SPY: Somebody's gotta get with her
maybe that somebody will be you.

(*Members of the Chorus give Spy money, then exit.*)

SPY: Penelope is hot.
And Ulysses is out at the war.
I got Penny's number.
And, even though she's true like Truth,
those fools keep paying me to hook them up.
Im making some cash.
Theyre playing the Lotto.
Spoils of war, folks, spoils of war.

February
9 THE ORIGINAL MOTHERFUCKER

(*A Man comes in—he's being led by a Child. His arm is outstretched and his hand is on the Child's narrow shoulder. The Man is blind.*)

CHILD: This looks like the place.
MAN: You think?
CHILD: From what you told me.
MAN: A clearing?
CHILD: Yeah.
MAN: And people—people out there and watching me—us?
CHILD: Yeah.
MAN: You sure?
CHILD:
MAN:
CHILD:
MAN: Its just that, last time—
CHILD: I aint had as much experience in the world as you. Some trees look like people, and "clearings"—how was I supposed to know what that was?
MAN: You could have asked.
CHILD: If I had asked I wouldnt be much of a man, would I?
MAN: Yr a child.
CHILD: Word coulda gotten out. You coulda let news of my uncertainty slip. Say you was in a bar, drinking. And say you got drunk. You coulda blabbed my business. Patrollers come looking for me, patrollers find me. Take away my chance for manhood. So I made a mistake about the "clearing" and the "audience" yesterday, so what. We're here now. Lots of space with nothing. And some folks out there.
MAN: How many?
CHILD: You didnt ask for a guide who could count. If you wanted a guide who could count it woulda cost you more.
MAN: I didnt think counting was—anything special.
CHILD: You aint from around here.
MAN: No. No Im not.
CHILD: Where you from?
MAN: —. Set up the campstool, please. Ive gotta do my talk then we can go back, ok?
CHILD: Yeah, sure.

(*The Child sets up a measly campstool. The Man sits.*)

CHILD: You want the sign hung on you?
MAN: Please.

(*The Child hangs a sign around the Man's neck. The words face the Man's chest so we cant read them.*)

MAN: Are the words facing out?
CHILD: Words?
MAN: The black squiggles.
CHILD: What about the squiggles?
MAN: —. Can you see them.
CHILD: Nope.

MAN: Please turn the sign around so that you can see the squiggles.

(*The Child turns the sign so that the squiggles are visible. The sign reads: "Oedipus, Former King."*)

CHILD: I can see the squiggles now.
MAN: Good. Thank you.
CHILD: Now what.
MAN: I wont be long.
CHILD: You want me to wait.
MAN: I wont be long.
CHILD: Waiting costs.
MAN: I'll pay it.
CHILD: Where you want me to wait.
MAN: Just a stone's throw—a short stone's throw away.
CHILD: Ok.

(*But the Child doesnt move. He stands there.*)

MAN: I can hear you breathing.
CHILD: Good thing you *can* hear, right?

(*The Child walks a short distance away. Fishes in his pockets, finds cigarettes, smokes as he waits.*)

OEDIPUS, FORMER KING:
OEDIPUS, FORMER KING:
OEDIPUS, FORMER KING:

(*Rest*)

OEDIPUS: Im Oedipus Rex. Oedipus the King. Also known as Oedipus the *Former* King. Also know as the original motherfucker. Im supposed to talk about it here. Its part of the sentence that Ive imposed on myself. A caution. But the more I caution, the less I have to say about it all.

(*Rest*)

I shouldnt of married *anybody*. Or killed *anybody*. That would have been smart. But no one told me about the oracle.
  Although—Im not saying Im innocent. Just ignorant.

(*Rest*)

Mother knew. I mean she knew of the oracle. So she shouldnt of married anybody, especially after her husband had been killed—but think about it—he had been killed by "3 men." Thats what the reports had said. Not "1 man" but "3." So she's thinking that, after all her loss, the oracle was bullshit, not bullshit, but incorrectly read. And there she was, she'd already given her dear son away and now her husband was dead and—she was queen, but not for long, not if she didnt remarry, and this handsome stranger comes to town. And its been years since she's seen me and I dont have any memory of her at all, and so we didnt recognize each other, I mean, what mother can really imagine the man her son will become?

(*Rest*)

My first time with her was my first time. And it was—really something. We would sneak around before the wedding. I'd saved the whole city. I coulda had anybody I wanted, but I only wanted her. And she was the queen and she coulda had anybody or anything she wanted. And since she'd given me away, things between her and the king hadnt been the same. They hadnt had any more children, and they hadnt gotten together much. It was as if, when they gave me away, it was as if the wind stopped blowing. Although they gave me away for their own safety. Go figure. I got her pregnant and we hurried up the wedding. We were going to get married anyway, but we rushed it. She didnt want tongues wagging. And everything was great. No wars. Plenty of everything. Everybody who wanted a job had a job, everybody who didnt was taken care of too. It was all good. And then the wind started blowing again. It was the strangest thing.

(*Rest*)

You know and on our wedding night she was looking at my ankles. I had a woody like Texas and she's looking at my ankles and Im like, come on, little mamma, lets get busy. Funny. I called her "little mamma" even then—before I knew she was my mother. But men call their wives "mother" dont they? Whether or not they have kids. Its a term of endearment. Im just here to fill in some gaps about the play: like what the writer didnt get around to writing, or what was cut, or what the censors cut.

(*Rest*)

Our children were slow. I mean, they were actually mentally challenged. Because she was my mom. And—she was looking at my ankles. I shoulda let her. Instead I just took her. We were a perfect fit. And something in me knew, I knew—that fitting that good was not good. And then, the next morning. I think she knew too but. It was like she had already gotten lost. And she knew there was no way out but deeper in.

(*Rest*)

I knew this sailor once. He had been shipwrecked and had, for 8 whole days, been floating around in the middle of the sea with nothing to hold on to but a plank of wood. For 8 whole days. Then he was rescued. "For my whole life, I've always been a little at sea," he said. "Circumstances just took their time catching up to me." Like Mom, always a little lost— and then lost for real and in my arms that morning. No way out but deeper in.

OEDIPUS, FORMER KING:
OEDIPUS, FORMER KING:
OEDIPUS, FORMER KING:

(*Rest*)

CHILD: You done?
OEDIPUS: Yeah.

(*The Child folds up the campstool and removes the sign. He stands in front of Oedipus.*)

OEDIPUS: Howd I do?
CHILD: I didnt listen. Did you want me to listen?
OEDIPUS: No.
CHILD: I could listen next time, if you want.

(*Oedipus makes a vague gesture of: "Dont sweat it, kid." He puts his hand on the Child's shoulder and they exit.*)

April
2 GREEK TRAGEDY & JERRY SPRINGER

HOST: Today we're talking with some of the "heroes" if you will of Greek Tragedy.

(*Applause.*)

HOST: Introduce yrselves.
OEDIPUS: King Oedipus. I killed my father and married my mother.
TANTALUS: King Tantalus. Dont blame yrself, Ed. I ate my own sons.
OEDIPUS: I blame myself.
TANTALUS: I blame fate.
CASSANDRA: Fate. What did fate ever do that we didnt see coming?
CLYTEMNESTRA: My husband, Agamemnon, was a pig and so I cut him down like I would a rabid hog.
HOST: Yr children have a different take on that.
CLYTEMNESTRA: Youve spoken with my children?!
HOST: Come on in, kids. Folks meet—Clytemnestra's kids.

(*The Kids rush at Clytemnestra and fight with their mama.*)

Writing about Drama

Why Write about Drama?

The act of writing involves making a commitment to ideas, and that commitment helps clarify your thinking. Your writing forces you to examine the details, the elements of a play that might otherwise pass unnoticed, and it helps you develop creative interpretations that enrich your appreciation of the plays you read. Besides deepening your own understanding, your writing can contribute to that of your peers and readers, as the commentaries in this book are meant to do.

Because every reader of plays has a unique experience and background, every reader can contribute something to the experience and awareness of others. You will see things that others do not. You will interpret things in a way that others will not. Naturally, every reader's aim is to respect the text, but it is not reasonable to think that there is only one way to interpret a text. Nor is it reasonable to think that only a few people can give "correct" interpretations. One of the most interesting aspects of writing about drama is that it is usually preceded by discussion, through which a range of possible interpretations begins to appear. When you start to write, you commit yourself to working with certain ideas, and you begin to deepen your thinking about those ideas as you write.

Conventions in Writing Criticism about Drama

Ordinarily, when you are asked to write about a play, you are expected to produce a critical and analytical study. A critical essay will go beyond any subjective experience and include a discussion of what the play achieves and how it does so. If you have a choice, you should choose a play that you admire and enjoy. If you have special background material on that play, such as a playbill or newspaper article, or if you have seen a production, these aids will be especially useful in writing.

For a critical study you will need to go far beyond retelling the events of the play. You may have to describe what you feel happens in a given scene or moment in a play, but simply rewriting the plot of the play in your own words does not constitute an interpretation. A critical reading of the play demands that you isolate evidence and comment on it. For example, you may want to quote passages of dialogue or stage direction to point out an idea that plays a key role in the drama. When you do so, quote in moderation. A critical essay that is merely a string of quotations linked together with a small amount of your commentary will not suffice. Further, make sure that the quotations you use are illustrations of your point; explain clearly their importance to your discussion.

Approaches to Criticism

Many critical approaches are available to the reader of drama. One approach might emphasize the response of audience members or readers, recognizing that the audience brings a great deal to the play even before the action begins. The audience's or reader's previous experience with drama influences expectations about what will happen on stage and about how the central characters will behave. Personal and cultural biases also influence how an audience member reacts to the unfolding drama. Reader response criticism pays close attention to these responses and to what causes them.

Another critical approach might treat the play as the coherent work of a playwright who intends the audience to perceive certain meanings in the play. This approach assumes that a careful analysis, or close reading, of the play will reveal the author's meanings.

Either approach can lead to engaging essays on drama. In the pages that follow, you will find directions on how to pay attention to your responses as an audience member or reader and advice about how to read a play with close attention to dialogue, images, and patterns of action.

Reader Response Criticism

Response criticism depends on a full experience of the text—a good understanding of its meaning as well as of its conventions of staging and performance.

Your responses to various elements of the drama, whether to the characters, the setting, the theme, or the dialogue, may change and grow as you see a play or read it through. You might have a very different reaction to a play during a second reading or viewing of it. Keeping a careful record of your responses as you read is a first step in response criticism.

There is, however, a big difference between recording your responses and examining them. Douglas Atkins of the University of Kansas speaks not only of reader response in criticism but also of reader responsibility, by which he means that readers have the responsibility to respond on more than a superficial level when they read drama. This book helps you reach deeper critical levels because you can read each play in light of the history of drama. This book also gives you important background material and commentary from the playwrights and from professional critics. Reading such criticism helps you understand what the critic's role is and what a critic can say about drama.

Reading drama in a historical perspective is important because it can highlight similarities between plays of different eras. Anyone who has read *Oedipus Rex* and *Antigone* will be better prepared to respond to *Hamlet*. In addition to the history and criticism of drama presented in this book, the variety of style, subject matter, and scope of the plays gives you the opportunity to read and respond to a broad range of drama. The more plays you read carefully, the better you will become at responding to drama and writing about it.

When you write response criticism, keep these guidelines in mind:

1. As you read, make note of the important effects the text has on you. Annotate in the margins moments that are especially effective. Do you find yourself alarmed, disturbed, sympathetic, or unsympathetic to a character? Do

you sense suspense, or are you confused about what is happening? Do you feel personally involved with the action, or is it very distant? Do you find the situation funny? What overall response do you find yourself experiencing?

2. By analyzing the following two elements of your response, establish why the play had the effects you experienced. Do you think it would have those effects on others? Have you observed that it does?

First, determine what it is about the play that causes you to have the response you do. Is it the structure of the play, the way the characters behave, their talk? Is it an unusual use of language, allusions to literature you know (or don't know)? Is the society portrayed especially familiar (or especially unfamiliar) to you? What does the author seem to expect the audience to know before the play begins?

Second, determine what it is about you, the reader, that causes you to respond as you do. Were you prepared for the dramatic conventions of the play, in terms of its genre as tragedy, comedy, or tragicomedy, or in terms of its place in the history of drama? How does your preparation affect your response? Did you have difficulty interpreting the language of the play because of unfamiliarity? Are you especially responsive to certain kinds of plays because of familiarity?

3. What do your responses to the play tell you about your own limitations, your own expertise, your own values, and your own attitudes toward social behavior, uses of language, and your sense of what is "normal"? Be sure to be willing to face your limitations as well as your strengths.[1]

Reader response criticism is flexible and useful in the way it allows you to explore possible interpretations of a text. Everyone is capable of responding to drama, and everyone's response will differ depending on his or her preparation and background.

Close Reading

Analyzing a play by close reading means examining the text in detail, looking for patterns that might not be evident with a less attentive approach to the text. Annotation is the key to close reading, since the critic's job is to keep track of elements in the play that, incidental though they may seem alone, imply a greater significance when seen together.

Close reading implies rereading, because the first time through a text, you do not know just what will be meaningful as the play unfolds, and you will want to read it again to confirm and deepen your impressions. You will usually make only a few discoveries the first time through. However, it is important to annotate the text even the first time you read it.

In annotating a play, try following these guidelines:

1. Underline all the speeches and images you think are important. Look for dialogue that you think reveals the play's themes, the true nature of the characters, and the position of the playwright.

2. Watch for repetition of imagery (such as the garden and weed imagery in *Hamlet*) and keep track of it through annotation. Do the same for repeated

---

[1]Adapted from Kathleen McCormick, "Theory in the Reader: Bleich, Holland, and Beyond," *College English* 47 (1985): 838.

ideas in the dialogue and for repeated comments on government or religion or psychology. Such repetitions will reveal their importance to the playwright.

3. Color-code or number-code various patterns in the text; then gather them either in photocopies or in lists for examination before you begin to plan your essay.

Criticism that uses the techniques of close reading pays very careful attention to the elements of drama—plot, characterization, setting, dialogue (use of language), movement, and theme—that were discussed earlier in relation to Lady Gregory's *The Rising of the Moon.* As you read a play, keep track of its chief elements; often, they will give you useful ideas for your paper. You may find it helpful to refer to the earlier discussion of the elements in *The Rising of the Moon,* because a short critical essay about that play is presented here (pp. 1774–76).

Annotating the special use of any of the primary elements will help you decide how important they are and whether a close study of them can contribute to an interesting interpretation of the play. You may not want to discuss all the elements in an essay, or if you do, only one may be truly dominant, but you should be aware of them in any play you write about.

From Prewriting to Final Draft: A Sample Essay on *The Rising of the Moon*

Most good writing results from good planning. When you write criticism about drama, consider these important stages:

1. When possible, choose a play that you enjoy.
2. Annotate the play very carefully.
3. Spend time prewriting.
4. Write a good first draft, then revise for content, organization, style, and mechanics.

The essay on Lady Gregory's *The Rising of the Moon* at the end of this section involved several stages of writing. First, the writer read and annotated the play. In the process of doing so, she noticed the unusual stage direction beginning the play, *Moonlight,* and noticed also that when the two policemen leave the Sergeant, they take the lantern, but the Sergeant reminds them that it is very lonely waiting there "with nothing but the moon." Second, she used the stage directions regarding moonlight to guide her in several important techniques of prewriting, including brainstorming, clustering, freewriting, drafting a trial thesis, and outlining.

The first stage, brainstorming, involved listing ideas, words, or phrases suggested by reading the play. The idea of moonlight and the moon recurred often. Then the writer practiced clustering: beginning with *moon,* a key term developed from brainstorming, then radiating from it all the associations that naturally suggested themselves. (See the cluster diagram on p. 1773)

Next the student chose the term romance because it had generated a number of responses, and she performed a freewriting exercise around that term. Freewriting is a technique in which a writer takes four or five minutes to write whatever comes to mind. The technique is designed to be done quickly, so the conscious censor has to be turned off. Anything you write in freewriting may be useful because you may produce ideas you did not know you had.

The following passage is part of the freewriting exercise the student wrote using *romance* as a key term. The passage is also an example of invisible writing, because the writing was done on a computer and the writer turned off the monitor so that she could not censor or erase what she was writing. The writer could only go forward, as fast as possible!

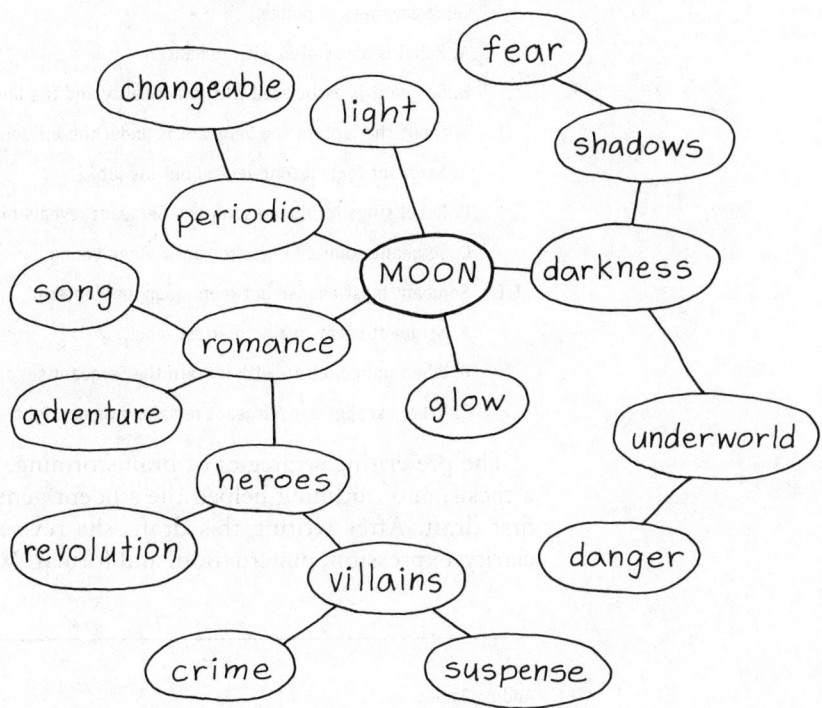

The setting of the play is completely romantic. In a lot of ways the play wouldn't work in a different setting. When you think about it the moon in the title is what makes all the action possible. Moon associated with darkness, underworld, world of fairies, so the moon is what makes all the action possible. Moon makes Sergeant look at things differently. The moon is the rebel moon — that's what title means. Rebel moon is rising, always rising. So the world the policeman lives in — sun lights up everything in practical and nonromantic way — is like lantern that second policeman brings to dockside. It shows things in a harsh light. Moon shows things in soft light. Without the moon there would be a different play.

The freewriting gave the writer a new direction — discussing the setting of the play, especially the role of light. The clustering began with the moon, veered off to the concept of the romantic elements in the play, and then came back to the way the moon and the lantern function in the play. The writer was now ready to work up a trial thesis:

Lady Gregory uses light to create a romantic setting that helps us understand the relationship between the rebel and the Sergeant and the values that they each stand for.

Because the thesis is drafted before the essay is written, the thesis is like a trial balloon. It may work or it may not. At this point it gives the writer direction.

Next the student outlined the essay. Because the writer did not know the outcome of the essay yet, her outline was necessarily sketchy:

I. Moonlight is associated with romance and rebellion; harsh light of lantern is associated with repressiveness of police.

   A. Rebel is associated with romance.

   B. Sergeant is associated with practicality and the law.

II. Without the lantern the Sergeant is under the influence of the romantic moon and the rebel.

   A. Sergeant feels resentment about his job.

   B. Rebel sings forbidden song and Sergeant reveals his former sympathies.

   C. Sergeant admits he was romantic when young.

III. Sergeant must choose between moon and lantern.

   A. Sergeant seems ready to arrest rebel.

   B. When police return with lantern the Sergeant sends them away.

   C. Rebel escapes and Sergeant remains in moonlight.

The prewriting strategies of brainstorming, clustering, freewriting, drafting a thesis, and outlining helped the student generate ideas and material for her first draft. After writing this draft, she revised it carefully for organization, clarity, expression, punctuation, and format. What follows is her final draft.

Andrea James

Professor Jacobus

English 233

19 October

The Use of Light in The Rising of the Moon

Lady Gregory uses light imagery in The Rising of the Moon to contrast rebellion and repressiveness. Her initial stage direction is basic: Moonlight. She suggests some of the values associated with moonlight, such as rebellion and romance, caution and secrecy, daring exploits, and even the underworld. All these are set against the policemen, who are governed not by the moon, which casts shadows and makes the world look magical, but by the lantern, which casts a harsh light that even the Sergeant eventually rejects.

The ballad singer, the rebel, is associated with romance from the start: "Dark hair — dark eyes, smooth face. . . . There isn't another man in Ireland would have broken jail the way he did" (27–28). He is dark, handsome, and recklessly brave. The Sergeant, by contrast, is a practical man, no romantic. He sees that he might have a chance to arrest the rebel and gain the reward for his capture if he stays right on the quay, a likely place for the rebel to escape from. But he unknowingly spoils his chances by refusing to keep the lantern the policemen offer. He tells the policemen, "You can take the lantern. Don't be too long now. It's very lonesome here with nothing but the moon" (28). What he does not realize is that with the lantern as his guiding light, he will behave like a proper Sergeant. But with the moon to guide him, he will side with the rebel.

It takes only a few minutes for the rebel to show up on the scene. At first, the Sergeant is very tough and abrupt with the rebel, who is disguised as "Jimmy Walsh, a ballad singer." The rebel tells the Sergeant that he is a traveler, that he is from Ennis, and that he has been to Cork. Unlike the Sergeant, who has stayed in one place and is a family man, the ballad singer appears to be a romantic figure, in the sense that he follows his mind to go where he wants to, sings what he wants to, and does what he wants to.

When the ballad singer begins singing, the Sergeant reacts badly, telling the singer, "Stop that noise" (28). Maybe he is envious of the ballad singer's freedom. When the Sergeant tries to make the rebel leave, the rebel instead begins telling stories about the man the Sergeant is looking for. He reminds the Sergeant of deeds done that would frighten anyone. "It was after the time of the attack on the police barrack at Kilmallock. . . . Moonlight . . . just like this" (29). The moonlight of the tale and the moonlight of the setting combine to add mystery and suspense to the situation.

The effect of the rebel's talk — and of the moonlight — is to make the Sergeant feel sorry for himself in a thankless job. "It's little we get but abuse from the people, and no choice but to obey our orders," he says bitterly while sitting on the barrel sharing a pipe with the singer (29). When the rebel sings an illegal song, the Sergeant corrects a few words, revealing his former sympathies with the people. The rebel realizes this, telling the Sergeant, "It was with the people you were, and not with the law you were, when you were a young man" (30). The Sergeant admits that when he was young he too was a romantic, but now that he is older he is practical and law-abiding: "Well, if I was foolish then, that time's gone. . . . I have my duties and I know them" (30).

Pulled by his past and his present, the Sergeant is suddenly forced to choose when the ballad singer's signal to his friend reveals the singer's identity to the Sergeant. He must decide whether his heart is with the world of moonlight or the world of the lantern. He seizes the rebel's hat and wig and seems about to arrest him when the policemen, with their lantern, come back. The Sergeant orders the policemen back to the station, and they offer to leave the lantern with him. But the Sergeant refuses. We know that he will not turn the rebel in. He has chosen the world of moonlight, of the rebel.

Before they leave the policemen try to make the world of the lantern seem the right choice. Policeman B says:

> Well, I thought it might be a comfort to you. I often think when I have it in my hand and can be flashing it about into every dark corner (<u>doing so</u>) that it's the same as being beside the fire at home, and the bits of bogwood blazing up now and again. (<u>Flashes it about, now on the barrel, now on Sergeant.</u>) (31)

The Sergeant reacts furiously and tells them to get out — "yourselves and your lantern!"

The play ends with the Sergeant giving the hat and wig back to the rebel, obviously having chosen the side of the people. When the rebel leaves, the Sergeant wonders if he himself was crazy for losing his chance at the reward. But as the curtain goes down, the Sergeant is still in the moonlight.

How to Write a Review

What Is the Purpose of a Review?

A review is more than a critical essay because it covers the actual performance of a play. As a reviewer you write after digesting an evening's entertainment and observing how actors and a director present a production for your enjoyment. Your responsibility is to respond both to the production and to the text of the play; thus, you will discuss the quality of the acting, the effectiveness of the setting, the interpretation of the text, and the power of the direction.

Reviews of plays ordinarily appear in daily newspapers or in weekly or semi-weekly publications timely enough to help a prospective playgoer decide whether to see the play. Considering the cost of tickets in contemporary theater, the best reviewers can perform a valuable service by letting readers know what they feel is most worth seeing. Regular reviewers, such as Ben Brantley and Margo Jefferson in the *New York Times*, Daniel Mendelsohn of *The New York Review of Books*, and Michael Billington of *The Guardian*, develop their own following because playgoers know from experience whether they can rely on these reviewers' judgments.

Another purpose of theater reviews is to set a standard to which producers aspire. Criticism can promote excellence because experienced and demanding critics force producers of drama to maintain high standards. The power of theater critics in major cities is legendary: more than a few plays have closed prematurely after savage reviews in London, New York, Chicago, and elsewhere. Knowing that they will undergo scrutiny by knowledgeable reviewers convinces writers, directors, actors, and producers to do their best.

What You Need to Write a Good Review

The best reviewers ordinarily bring three qualifications to their work: experience in the theater, a knowledge of theatrical history, and a sensitivity to dramatic production. Some reviewers have had experience onstage as actors or as production assistants. They are familiar with the process of preparing a play for the stage and in some cases may actually have written for the stage. Other reviewers who have not had such experience have, instead, spent hours in the theater watching plays; their rich experience of seeing a variety of plays enables them to make useful comparisons.

Knowledge of the basics of theater history is fundamental equipment for a good reviewer. New plays that borrow from the traditions of the Greek chorus, or plays that emulate medieval pageants or nineteenth-century melodrama, need reviewers who understand their sources. Suzan-Lori Parks, for example, admits responding to the influence of Bertolt Brecht and Samuel Beckett. She expects her audience to recognize some of that influence, but she knows that her reviewers will spot most or all of it. This book is structured around the history of drama so that readers will better understand drama's roots and evolution. In that sense this book is an aid in helping a theater enthusiast to become a competent reviewer.

Besides knowing the history of drama, the reviewer needs also to be extremely well read. Some reviewers, for example, have not had the opportunity to see all of Shakespeare's plays, but a good reviewer will have read most of them and can refer to them as necessary. The same will be true of the plays of Bernard Shaw; many have not been produced in the last dozen years or so. In the case of contemporary playwrights, it is common for a reviewer to refer to the playwright's earlier work to put the current production in a useful context. A knowledgeable reviewer knows not only the history of theater but also the work of other playwrights that may be relevant to the play under review.

Most students of theater have enough sensitivity to dramatic productions to write adequate reviews. The most sensitive reviewers will pay close attention to the suitability of the acting almost as a matter of first importance, especially if the play is well known. Most contemporary reviews single out actors and comment on their performance in some detail. Reviewers usually know the work of the most busy actors, and in some cases they will make comparisons with earlier roles. They will also indicate whether the actor has developed further as an artist or has perhaps walked mechanically through the part. The reviewer's sensitivity to individual actors is developed in part from past experience and therefore from having a benchmark against which to match a performance. Curiosity about an actor's performance sometimes drives a review, as in Ben Brantley's examination of Fiona Shaw's acting in *Medea* (p. 161), which was the main focus of his essay on the play.

Obviously, neither Ben Brantley nor any other reviewer is going to review *Medea* with an eye toward telling us that it is a good or bad play; the history of criticism has already done that. The reviewer of *Medea*, like the reviewer of any of Euripides' great plays, will aim to tell us about the quality of the acting or the effectiveness of the setting. Being sensitive to the effective use of lighting, props, costumes, and stage design is essential for any reviewer, but it is probably even more crucial for a reviewer of classic theater.

Preparing to Review a Classic Play

If you have the opportunity to review a play that is well established—like most of the plays in this collection—you need special preparation. Besides having read the text before seeing the play, you need to imagine how the play should be staged. Once you understand what the play is about and what its implications may be, you then need to consult reviews or descriptions of early productions. You may do so by referring to the index of any major newspaper or to *New York Theatre Critics' Reviews*, which includes multiple reviews of important productions over the years. The point is simply to come to the experience of the drama as a fully informed viewer. Knowing how the play has been staged in the past will help you see the innovations and special interpretation of the current production.

Preparing to Review a New Play

Sometime you may have the opportunity to review a new play—one that playgoers, including the reviewers, have not had the chance to read in advance. In that case you need to pay special attention to the text, taking notes when necessary, to follow the development of the drama's ideas and issues. You are still responsible for commenting on the acting and the production, but in the case of a new play, your responsibility shifts to preparing the prospective audience to understand and respond to the play. They will need to know what the play is about, how it presents the primary issues in the drama, and what is at stake. You may need to tell something of the plot, but always with an eye toward not giving too much away, especially if the play involves suspense. Ask yourself how much the reader needs to know to decide whether to see the play.

Reviewers of new plays usually include a special commentary on a new or relatively unknown playwright. The most important information here would be any previous work of the playwright. The best reviewers will have seen that work and are prepared to relate it to the new play at hand. Reviewers of August Wilson, for example, spent time in the late 1980s establishing his credentials as a playwright. Later, when a new play of his was produced, reviewers usually attempted to describe how the new play fit into the growing body of his work. Because Wilson was in the process of writing a series of plays on African American life centering on specific decades of the twentieth century, the reviewer did the reader a service by explaining how each new play fit into his overall scheme.

Guidelines for Writing Reviews

Good reviewers approach the job of writing reviews from many different angles. Some of the reviews in this book begin with a generalization on the play's theme. Some begin with a personal observation about the play at hand or a personal experience in the theater. Others begin with a note on the background of the playwright, the actors, or the director. There are many ways to write a review. The following suggestions can help you structure your reaction.

1. If you are reviewing a professionally produced play, request a press kit from the theater. These kits usually include a great deal of information that could interest readers.

2. In your review, provide any necessary background on a playwright who is contemporary or relatively unknown. The press kit should contain some information; if not, the program may do so. Check with the press representative or with the box office manager to see whether the playwright is in the house. If so, then before the play begins, ask to arrange an interview.

Sample Review

Mel Gussow, in reviewing the Yale Repertory Theatre's production of Molière's *Tartuffe* in 1991, centers not only on the set design but also on the actor playing the title role (p. 537). Gussow begins by complimenting the director by name, Walton Jones, then goes on to call attention to the "large mahoganylike doors" that expedite the quick entrances and exits that keep the dynamic of the play moving. Gussow is interested in them because they function in special ways that make them unique and effective for this play. The man responsible for the "jack-in-the-box" set is given credit as well, Kevin Rupnick.

In terms of the rhythm of the play, Gussow reminds more than once that there is a "breathlessness" to the production because of the speed with which things happen. In a classic play like *Tartuffe* there can be a tendency for some directors to be so respectful of the text that they can let the play drag — but not this production. Gussow does imply a negative criticism in calling it a "tricked-up approach to Molière," but he quickly explains that it "is enlivened by several performances" and then credits the star playing Tartuffe.

Several paragraphs of the review are about Austin Pendleton himself because of his creditable performance. He is a short actor and Gussow seems amused when he tells us that Pendleton used his stature to good effect, "playing one scene on his knees behind a portable pulpit that is the height of a go-cart." When Gussow tells us that Pendleton's success is that he plays the part as a fanatic, he also tells us that this must be "regarded as a Pendleton specialty" and then cites his role in another drama. A good reviewer will have seen many plays and, when appropriate, can call our attention to the achievement of a major figure like Pendleton by which we can compare the current performance.

Again, because *Tartuffe* is such a well-known play among theatergoers, Gussow tells us almost nothing about what happens. If this play were being performed for the first time, however, he would need to tell us something of what the play is about, describing the action in sufficient detail without giving away the entire plot.

When you write your own review, be sure to set up a checklist based on this one so that you include the important information:

Author and title of play	Description of the action
What the play is about	Who the director is
The play's main issues	Theater and dates of performance
The actors, with comments	The setting and its effectiveness
Your final recommendation to your readers	

Take the list to the theater with you and keep your notes on it. When you begin writing your review, look at the reviews in this book or in your local newspaper. Your review aims at providing your readers a valuable service by telling them whether you recommend that they attend the theater or not.

Glossary of Dramatic Terms

Act. A major division in the action of a play. Most plays from the Elizabethan era until the nineteenth century were divided into five acts by the playwrights or by later editors. In the nineteenth century many writers began to write four-act plays. Today one-, two-, and three-act plays are most common.

Action. What happens in a play; the events that make up the **plot.**

Agon. The Greek word for "contest." In Greek tragedy the *agon* was often a formal debate in which the **chorus** divided and took the sides of the disputants.

Alienation effect. In his **epic theater,** Bertolt Brecht (1898–1956) tried to make the familiar unfamiliar (or to alienate it) to show the audience that familiar, seemingly "natural," and therefore unalterable social conditions could be changed. Different devices achieved the alienation effect by calling attention to the theater as theater—stage lights brought in front of the curtain, musicians put onstage instead of hidden in an orchestra pit, placards indicating scene changes and interrupting the linear flow of the action, actors distancing themselves from their characters to invite the audience to analyze and criticize the characters instead of empathizing with them. These alienating devices prevented the audience from losing itself in the illusion of reality. (See **epic theater.**)

Allegory. A literary work that is coherent on at least two levels simultaneously: a literal level consisting of recognizable characters and events and an allegorical level in which the literal characters and events represent moral, political, religious, or other ideas and meanings.

Anagnorisis. Greek term for a character's discovery or recognition of someone or something previously unknown. *Anagnorisis* often paves the way for a reversal of fortune (see *peripeteia*). An example in *Oedipus Rex* is Oedipus's discovery of his true identity.

Antagonist. A character or force in conflict with the **protagonist.** The antagonist is often another character but may also be an intangible force such as nature or society. The dramatic conflict can even take the form of a struggle with the protagonist's own character.

Anticlimax. See **plot.**

Antimasque. See **masque.**

Antistrophe. The second of the three parts of the verse ode sung by the **chorus** in Greek drama. While singing the **strophe,** the chorus moves in a dance rhythm from right to left; during the antistrophe, it moves from left to right back to its original position. The third part, the **epode,** was sung standing still.

Apron stage. The apron is the part of the stage extending in front of the **proscenium arch.** A stage is an apron stage if all or most of it is in front of any framing structures. The Elizabethan stage, which the audience surrounded on three sides, is an example of an apron stage.

Arena stage. A stage surrounded on all sides by the audience, actors make exits and entrances through the aisles. Usually used in **theater in the round.**

Arras. A curtain hung at the back of the Elizabethan playhouse to partition off an alcove or booth. The curtain could be pulled back to reveal a room or a cave.

Aside. A short speech made by a character to the audience which, by **convention,** the other characters onstage cannot hear.

Atellan farce. Broad and sometimes coarse popular humor indigenous to the town of Atella in Italy. By the third century BCE, the Romans had imported the Atellan farce, which they continued to modify and develop.

Blank verse. An unrhymed verse form often used in writing drama. Blank verse is composed of ten-syllable lines accented on the second, fourth, sixth, eighth, and tenth syllables (**iambic pentameter**).

Bombast. A loud, pompous speech whose inflated diction is disproportionate to the subject matter it expresses.

Bourgeois drama. Drama that treats middle-class subject matter or characters rather than the lives of the rich and powerful.

Braggart soldier. A **stock character** in comedy who is usually cowardly, parasitical, pompous, and easily victimized by practical jokers. Sir John Falstaff in Shakespeare's *Henry IV* (parts 1, 2) is an example of this type.

Burla (plural, *burle*). Jests or practical jokes that were part of the comic **stage business** in the **commedia dell'arte.**

Buskin. A thick-soled boot possibly worn by Greek tragedians to increase their stature. Later called a *cothurnus.*

Catastrophe. See **plot.**

Catharsis. The feeling of emotional purgation or release that, according to Aristotle, an audience should feel after watching a tragedy.

Ceremonial drama. Egyptian passion play about the god Osiris.

Character. Any person appearing in a drama or narrative.

Stock character. A stereotypical character type whose behavior, qualities, or beliefs conform to familiar dramatic **conventions,** such as the clever servant or the **braggart soldier.** (Also called *type character.*)

Chiton. Greek tunic worn by Roman actors.

Choregos. An influential citizen chosen to pay for the training and costuming of the **chorus** in Greek drama competitions. He probably also paid for the musicians and met other financial production demands not paid for by the state.

Chorus. A masked group that sang and danced in Greek tragedy. The chorus usually chanted in unison, offering advice and commentary on the action but rarely participating. See also **strophe, antistrophe,** and **epode.**

City Dionysia. See **Dionysus.**

Claptrap. A dramatic device designed to get the audience clapping; it is not usually connected to the core of the drama.

Climax. See **plot.**

Closet drama. A drama, usually in verse, meant for reading rather than for performance. Hrosvitha's *Dulcitius,* Percy Bysshe Shelley's *Prometheus Unbound,* and John Milton's *Samson Agonistes* are examples.

Comedy. A type of drama intended to interest and amuse rather than to concern the audience deeply. Although characters experience various discomfitures, the audience feels confident that they will overcome their ill fortune and find happiness at the end.

Comedy of humors. Form of comedy developed by Ben Jonson in the seventeenth century in which characters' actions are determined by the preponderance in their systems of one of the four bodily fluids, or humors—blood, phlegm, choler (yellow bile), and melancholy (black bile). Characters' dispositions are exaggerated and stereotyped; common types are the melancholic and the belligerent bully.

Comedy of manners. Realistic, often satiric comedy concerned with the manners and conventions of high society. Usually refers to the Restoration comedies of late seventeenth-century England, which feature witty dialogue, or **repartee.** An example is William Congreve's *The Way of the World.*

Drawing room comedy. A type of comedy of manners concerned with life in polite society. The action generally takes place in a drawing room.

Farce. A short dramatic work that depends on exaggerated, improbable situations, incongruities, coarse wit, and horseplay for its comic effect.

High comedy. Comedy that appeals to the intellect, often focusing on the pretensions, foolishness, and incongruity of human behavior. **Comedy of manners** with its witty dialogue is a type of high comedy.

Low comedy. Comedy that lacks the intellectual appeal of **high comedy,** depending instead on boisterous buffoonery, "gags," and jokes for its comic effect.

Middle Comedy. This transitional Greek style of comedy extended from 375 to about 330 BCE. It marks a change, especially in language, which grew less formal and closer to the way people spoke. Little evidence of Middle Comedy exists, but from surviving statuettes we can surmise that costumes on stage resembled what Athenians actually wore on the street.

New Comedy. Emerging between the fourth and third centuries BCE in ancient Greece, New Comedy replaced the farcical **Old Comedy.** New Comedy, usually associated with Menander, is witty and intellectually engaging; it is often thought of as the first **high comedy.**

Old Comedy. Greek comedy of the fifth century BCE that uses bawdy farce to attack social, religious, and political institutions satirically. Old Comedy is usually associated with Aristophanes.

Sentimental comedy. Comedy populated by stereotypical virtuous **protagonists** and villainous **antagonists** that resolves the domestic trials of middle-class people in a pat, happy ending.

Slapstick. Low comedy that involves little plot or character development but rather consists of physical horseplay or practical jokes.

Comic relief. The use of humorous characters, speeches, or scenes in an otherwise serious or tragic drama.

Commedia dell'arte. Italian **low comedy** dating from around the mid-sixteenth century in which professional actors playing **stock characters** improvised dialogue to fit a given **scenario.**

Complication. See **plot.**

Conflict. See **plot.**

Convention. Any feature of a literary work that has become standardized over time, such as the **aside** or the **stock character.** Often refers to an unrealistic device (such as Danish characters speaking English in *Hamlet*) that the audience tacitly agrees to accept.

Coryphaeus. See *koryphaios.*

Cosmic irony. See **irony.**

Cothurnus. See **buskin.**

Craft play. Medieval sacred drama based on Old and New Testament stories. Craft plays were performed outside the church by members of a particular trade guild, and their subject matter often reflected the guild's trade. The fisherman's guild, for example, might present the story of Noah and the flood.

Crisis. Same as **climax.** See **plot.**

Cycle. A group of medieval **mystery plays** written in the vernacular (the language in common use rather than Latin) for performance outside the church. Cycles, each of which treated biblical stories from creation through the last judgment, are named after the town in which they were produced. Most extant mystery plays are from the York, Chester, Wakefield (Towneley), and N-Town cycles.

Cyclorama. A large painted backdrop, usually curved and covering all of the stage with a complex scene against which the action takes place.

Dadaism. A post–World War I art movement that was in part anti-art; a revolt against pretension in the arts.

Decorum. A quality that exists when the style of a work is appropriate to the speaker, the occasion, and the subject matter. Kings should speak in a "high style" and clowns in a "low style," according to many Renaissance authors. Decorum was a guiding critical principle in **neoclassicism.**

Defamiliarization effect (*Verfremdungseffekt*). See **alienation effect.**

Denouement. See **plot.**

Deus ex machina. Latin for "a god out of a machine." In Greek drama, a mechanical device called a *mekane* could lower "gods" onto the stage to solve the seemingly unsolvable problems of mortal characters. Also used to describe a playwright's use of a forced or improbable solution to plot complications—for example, the discovery of a lost will or inheritance that will pay off the evil landlord.

Dialogue. Spoken interchange or conversation between two or more characters. Also see **soliloquy.**

Diction. A playwright's choice of words or the match between language and subject matter. Also refers collectively to an actor's phrasing, enunciation, and manner of speaking.

Dionysus. Greek nature god of wine, mystic revelry, and irrational impulse. Greek tragedy probably sprang from dramatized ritual choral celebrations in his honor.

City Dionysia. (Also called Great or Greater Dionysia.) The most important of the four Athenian festivals in honor of Dionysus. This spring festival sponsored the first tragedy competitions; comedy was associated with the winter festival, the Lenaea.

Director. The person responsible for a play's interpretation and staging and for the guidance of the actors.

Disguising. Medieval entertainment featuring a masked procession of actors performing short plays in pantomime; probably the origin of the court **masque.**

Dithyramb. Ancient Greek choral hymn sung and danced to honor **Dionysus;** originally divided into an improvised story sung by a choral leader and a traditional refrain sung by the **chorus.** Believed by some to be the origin of Greek tragedy.

Domestic tragedy. A serious play usually focusing on the family and depicting the fall of a middle-class **protagonist** rather than of a powerful or noble hero. Also called *bourgeois tragedy.* An example is Arthur Miller's *Death of a Salesman,* which traces the emotional collapse and eventual suicide of Willy Loman, a traveling salesman.

Double plot. See **plot.**

Drama. A play written in prose or verse that tells a story through **dialogue** and actions performed by actors impersonating the characters of the story.

Dramatic illusion. The illusion of reality created by drama and accepted by the audience for the duration of the play.

Dramatic irony. See **irony.**

Dramatist. The author of a play; playwright.

Dramaturge. One who represents the playwright and guides the production. In some cases, the dramaturge researches different aspects of the production or earlier productions of the play.

Dramaturgy. The art of writing plays.

Drawing room comedy. See **comedy.**

Empathy. The sense of feeling *with* a character. (Distinct from sympathy, which is feeling *for* a character.)

Ensemble acting. Performance by a group of actors, usually members of a **repertory** company, in which the integrated acting of all members is emphasized over individual star performances. The famous nineteenth-century director Konstantin Stanislavsky promoted this type of acting in the Moscow Art Theatre.

Environmental theater. A term used by Richard Schechner, director of the Performance Group in the late 1960s and early 1970s, to describe his work and the work of other theater companies, including the Bread and Puppet Theatre, Open Theatre, and Living Theatre. He also used the term to describe the indigenous theater of Africa and Asia. Environmental theater occupies the whole of a performance space; it is not confined to a stage separated from the audience. Action can take place in and around the audience, and audience members are often encouraged to participate in the theater event.

Epic drama. A type of theater first associated with German director Erwin Piscator (1893–1966). Bertolt Brecht (1898–1956) used the term to distinguish his own theater from the "dramatic" theater that created the illusion of reality and invited the audience to identify and empathize with the characters. Brecht criticized the dramatic theater for encouraging the audience to believe that social conditions were "natural" and therefore unalterable. According to Brecht, the theater should show human beings as dependent on certain political and economic factors and at the same time as capable of altering them. "The spectator is given the chance to criticize human behavior from a social point of view, and the scene is played as a piece of history," he wrote. Epic theater calls attention to itself as theater, bringing the stage lights in front of the curtain and interrupting the linear flow of the action to help the audience analyze the action and characters onstage. (See **alienation effect**.)

Epilogue. A final speech added to the end of a play. An example is Puck's "If we shadows have offended . . ." speech that ends Shakespeare's *A Midsummer Night's Dream*.

Epitasis. Ancient term for the **rising action** of a **plot**. (See also **plot**.)

Epode. The third of three parts of the verse ode sung by the **chorus** in a Greek drama. The epode follows the **strophe** and **antistrophe**.

Existentialism. A post–World War II philosophy that insisted humans had to give their lives value and significance because nothing outside themselves could do so.

Exodos. The concluding scene, which includes the exit of all characters and the **chorus**, of a Greek drama.

Exposition. See **plot**.

Expressionism. Early twentieth-century literary movement in Germany that posited that art should represent powerful emotional states and moods. Expressionists abandon **realism** and **verisimilitude**, producing distorted, nightmarish images of the individual unconscious.

Falling action. See **plot**.

Farce. See **comedy**.

First Folio. The first collected edition of thirty-six of Shakespeare's plays, collected by two of his fellow actors and published posthumously in 1623.

Foil. A character who, through difference or similarity, brings out a particular aspect of another character. Laertes, reacting to the death of his father, acts as a foil for Hamlet.

Foreshadowing. Ominous hints of events to come that help to create an air of suspense in a drama.

Frons scaena. The elaborately decorated façade of the **scaena** or stage house used in presenting Roman drama. (Also called *scaena frons*.)

Hamartia. An error or wrong act through which the fortunes of the **protagonist** are reversed in a tragedy.

High comedy. See **comedy**.

History play. A drama set in a time other than that in which it was written. The term usually refers to Elizabethan drama, such as Shakespeare's Henry plays, that draws its plots from English historical materials such as Holinshed's *Chronicles*.

Hubris (or *hybris*). Excessive pride or ambition. In ancient Greek tragedy hubris often causes the **protagonist**'s fall.

Humor character. A stereotyped character in the **comedy of humors** (see **comedy**). Clever plots often play on the character's personality distortions (caused by an imbalance of humors), revealing his or her absurdity.

Iambic pentameter. A poetic meter that divides a line into five parts (or feet), each part containing an unaccented syllable followed by an accented syllable. The line "When I consider everything that grows" is an example of iambic pentameter verse.

Imitation. See *mimesis*.

Impressionism. A highly personal style of writing in which the author presents characters, scenes, or moods as they appear to him or her at a particular moment rather than striving for an objectively realistic description.

Interlude. A short play, usually either farcical or moralistic, performed between the courses of a feast or between the acts of a longer play. The interlude thrived during the late fifteenth and early sixteenth centuries in England.

Irony. The use of words to suggest a meaning that is the opposite of the literal meaning, as in "I can't wait to take the exam." Irony is present in a literary work that gives expression to contradictory attitudes or impulses to entertain ambiguity or to maintain detachment.

Cosmic irony. Irony present when destiny or the gods seem to be in favor of the **protagonist** but are actually engineering his or her downfall. (Same as *irony of fate*.)

Dramatic irony. Irony present when the outcome of an event or situation is the opposite of what a character expects.

Tragic irony. Irony that exists when a character's lack of complete knowledge or understanding (which the audience possesses) results in his or her fall or has tragic consequences for loved ones. An example from *Oedipus Rex* is Oedipus's declaration that he will stop at nothing to banish King Laios's murderer, whom the audience knows to be Oedipus himself.

Jongleur. Early medieval French musical entertainer who recited lyrics, ballads, and stories. Forerunner of the minstrel.

Koryphaios. The leader of the **chorus** in Greek drama.

Kothornos. See **buskin.**

Lazzo (plural, *lazzi*). Comic routines or **stage business** associated with the stock situations and characters of the Italian **commedia dell'arte.** A scenario might, for example, call for the *lazzo* of fear.

Liturgical drama. Short dramatized sections of the medieval church service. Some scholars believe that these playlets evolved into the vernacular **mystery plays,** which were performed outside the church by lay people.

Low comedy. See **comedy.**

Mansion. Scenic structure used in medieval drama to indicate the locale or scene of the action. Mansions were areas inside the church used for performing liturgical drama; later more elaborate structures were built on pageant wagons to present **mystery plays** outside the church.

Mask. A covering used to disguise or ornament the face; used by actors in Greek drama and revived in the later **commedia dell'arte** and court **masque** to heighten dramatic effect.

Masque (also *mask*). A short but elaborately staged court drama, often mythological and allegorical, principally acted and danced by masked courtiers. (Professional actors often performed the major speaking and singing roles.) Popular in England during the late sixteenth and early seventeenth centuries, masques were often commissioned to honor a particular person or occasion. Ben Jonson was the most important masque writer; the genre's most elaborate sets and costumes were designed by Jonson's occasional partner Inigo Jones.

Antimasque. A parody of the court **masque** developed by Ben Jonson featuring broad humor, grotesque characters, and ludicrous actions.

Mekane. See *deus ex machina.*

Melodrama. A suspenseful play filled with situations that appeal to the audience's emotions. Justice triumphs in a happy ending: the good characters (completely virtuous) are rewarded, and the bad characters (thoroughly villainous) are punished.

Method acting. A naturalistic technique of acting developed by the Russian director Konstantin Stanislavsky and adapted for American actors by Lee Strasberg, among others. The Method actor identifies with the **character** he or she portrays and experiences the emotions called for by the play in an effort to render the character with emotional **verisimilitude.**

Middle Comedy. See **comedy.**

Mimesis. The Greek word for "imitation." Aristotle used the term to define the role of art as an imitation of an action.

Miracle play. A type of medieval sacred drama that depicts the lives of saints, focusing especially on the miracles performed by saints.

Mise-en-scène. The stage setting of a play, including the use of scenery, props, and stage movement.

Moira. Greek word for "fate."

Morality play. Didactic late medieval drama (flourishing in England c. 1400–1550) that uses **allegory** to dramatize some aspects of the Christian moral life. Abstract qualities or entities such as Virtue, Vice, Good Deeds, Knowledge, and Death are cast as characters who discuss with the **protagonist** issues related to salvation and the afterlife. *Everyman* is an example.

Motivation. The reasons for a character's actions in a drama. For drama to be effective, the audience must believe that a character's actions are justified and plausible given what they know about him or her.

Mouth of hell. A stage prop in medieval drama suggesting the entrance to hell. Often in the shape of an open-mouthed monster's head, the mouth of hell was positioned over a smoke-and-fire-belching pit in the stage that appeared to swallow up sinners.

Mystery play. A sacred medieval play dramatizing biblical events such as the creation, the fall of Adam and Eve, and Christ's birth and resurrection. The genre probably evolved from **liturgical drama;** mystery plays were often incorporated into larger **cycles** of plays.

Naturalism. Literary philosophy popularized during the nineteenth century that casts art's role as the scientifically accurate reflection of a "slice of life." Naturalism is aligned with the belief that each person is a product of heredity and environment driven by internal and external forces beyond his or her control. August Strindberg's *Miss Julie*, with its focus on reality's sordidness and humankind's powerlessness, draws on naturalism.

Neoclassicism. A movement in sixteenth-century Italy and seventeenth-century France to revive and emulate classical attitudes toward art based on principles of order, harmony, unity, restrained wit, and **decorum.** The neoclassical movement in France gave rise to a corresponding movement in England during the late seventeenth and eighteenth centuries.

Nero. Roman emperor who was noted for extreme sadism and cruelty.

New Comedy. See **comedy.**

Ode. A dignified Greek three-part song sung by the **chorus** in Greek drama. The parts are the **strophe,** the **antistrophe,** and the **epode.**

Old Comedy. See **comedy.**

Orchestra. Literally the "dancing place"; the circular stage where the Greek **chorus** performed.

Pageant cart. A movable stage or wagon (often called a pageant wagon) on which a set was built for the performance of medieval drama. The term **pageant** can also refer to the spectacle itself.

Pallium. Long white cloak or mantle worn by Greek actors or Romans in Greek-based plays.

Pantomime. Silent acting using facial expression, body movement, and gesture to convey the plot and the characters' feelings.

Parodos. The often stately entrance song of the **chorus** in Greek drama. The term also refers to the aisles (plural, *paradoi*) on either side of the orchestra by which the chorus entered the Greek theater.

Pastoral drama. A dramatic form glorifying shepherds and rural life in an idealized natural setting; usually implies a negative comparison to urban life.

Pathos. The quality of evoking pity.

Performance art. A mid-twentieth-century form that often mixes media: music, video, film, opera, dance, and spoken text. It was originally defined in terms of artists using a live production for dramatic effect; Anna Deavere Smith's work is a good example. However, it has widened to include performances that cross defined dramatic "boundaries." Dancers Martha Clarke and Pina Bausch, musicians such as Laurie Anderson, and experimental directors such as Richard Foreman have been identified as performance artists.

Peripeteia. A reversal of fortune, for better or worse, for the **protagonist.** Used especially to describe the main character's fall in Greek tragedy.

Phallus. An appendage meant to suggest the penis added to the front of blatantly comic male characters' costumes in some Greek comedy; associated chiefly with the Greek **satyr play.**

Play. A literary genre whose plot is usually presented dramatically by actors portraying characters before an audience.

Play-within-the-play. A brief secondary drama presented to or by the characters of a play that reflects or comments on the larger work. An example is the Pyramus and Thisbe episode in Shakespeare's *A Midsummer Night's Dream.*

Plot. The events of a play or narrative. The sequence and relative importance a **dramatist** assigns to these events.

Anticlimax. An unexpectedly trivial or significant conclusion to a series of significant events; an unsatisfying resolution that often occurs in place of a conventional **climax.**

Catastrophe. The outcome or conclusion of a play; usually applied specifically to tragedy. (Denouement is a parallel term applied to both comedy and tragedy.)

Climax. The turning point in a drama's action, preceded by the **rising action** and followed by the **falling action.** Same as **crisis.**

Complication. The part of the plot preceding the **climax** that establishes the entanglements to be untangled in the **denouement.** Part of the **rising action.**

Conflict. The struggle between the **protagonist** and the **antagonist** that propels the **rising action** of the plot and is resolved in the **denouement.**

Denouement. The "unknotting" of the plot's **complication;** the resolution of a drama's action. See **catastrophe.**

Double plot. A dramatic structure in which two related plots function simultaneously.

Exposition. The presentation of essential information, especially about events that have occurred prior to the first scene of a play. The exposition appears early in the play and initiates the **rising action.**

Falling action. The events of the plot following the **climax** and ending in the **catastrophe** or resolution.

Rising action. The events of the plot leading up to the **climax.**

Subplot. A secondary plot intertwined with the main plot, often reflecting or commenting on the main plot.

Underplot. Same as **subplot.**

Problem play. A drama that argues a point or presents a problem (usually a social problem). Ibsen is a notable writer of problem plays.

Prologos. In Greek drama, an introductory scene for actor or actors that precedes the entrance of the **chorus.** This **convention** has evolved into the modern dramatic introductory monologue or **prologue.**

Prologue. A preface or introduction preceding the play proper.

Proscaena. The space in front of the *scaena* in a Roman theater.

Proscenium arch. An arched structure over the front of the stage from which a curtain often hangs. The arch frames the action onstage and separates the audience from the action.

Proskenion. The playing space in front of the *skene* or scene house in Greek drama.

Protagonist. The main character in a drama. This character is usually the most interesting and sympathetic and is the person involved in the **conflict** driving the **plot.**

Protasis. Classical term for the introductory act or **exposition** of a drama.

Psychomachia. Psychological struggle; a war of souls.

Quem Quaeritis trope. A brief dramatized section of the medieval church's Easter liturgy. The oldest extant **trope** and the probable origin of liturgical drama, it enacts the visit of the three Marys to Christ's empty tomb (*quem quaeritis* means "Whom do you seek?" in Latin).

Realism. The literary philosophy holding that art should accurately reproduce an image of life. Avoiding the use of dramatic **conventions** such as asides and soliloquies, it depicts ordinary people in ordinary situations. Ibsen's *A Doll House* is an example of realism in drama.

Recognition. See *anagnorisis*.

Repartee. Witty and pointed verbal exchanges usually found in the **comedy of manners.**

Repertory. A theater company or group of actors that presents a set of plays alternately throughout a season. The term also refers to the set of plays itself.

Restoration comedy. A type of **comedy of manners** that developed in England in the late seventeenth century. Often features **repartee** in the service of complex romantic plots. Oliver Goldsmith's *She Stoops to Conquer* is an example.

Revenge tragedy. Sensational tragedy popularized during the Elizabethan age that is notable for bloody plots involving such elements as murder, ghosts, insanity, and crimes of lust.

Reversal. See *peripeteia*.

Riposte. A quick or sharp reply; similar to **repartee.**

Rising action. See **plot.**

Ritual. Repeated formalized or ceremonial practices, many of which have their roots in primitive cultures. Certain theorists hold that primitive ritual evolved into drama.

Satire. A work that makes fun of a social institution or human foible, often in an intellectually sophisticated way, to persuade the audience to share the author's views. Molière's *The Misanthrope* contains social satire.

Satyr play. A comic play performed after the tragic trilogy in Greek tragedy competitions. The satyr play provided **comic relief** and was usually a farcical, boisterous treatment of mythological material.

Scaena. The stage house in Roman drama; the façade of the *scaena* (called the *frons scaena*) was often elaborately ornamented.

Scenario. The plot outline around which professional actors of the **commedia dell'arte** improvised their plays. Most scenarios specified the action's sequence and the entrances of the main characters.

Scene. Division of an **act** in a drama. By traditional definition a scene has no major shift in place or time frame, and it is performed by a static group of actors onstage (in French drama, if an actor enters or exits, the group is altered, and the scene, technically, should change). The term also refers to the physical surroundings or locale in which a play's action is set.

Scenery. The backdrop and set (furniture and so on) onstage that suggest to the audience the surroundings in which a play's **action** takes place.

Scenography. Painting of backdrops and hangings.

Senecan tragedy. Tragic drama modeled on plays written by Seneca. The genre usually has five acts and features a **chorus;** it is notable for its thematic concern with bloodshed, revenge, and unnatural crimes. (See also **revenge tragedy.**)

Sentimental. Refers to tender emotions in excess of what the situation calls for.

Sentimental comedy. See **comedy.**

Setting. All details of time, location, and environment relating to a play.

Skene. The building or scene house in the Greek theater that probably began as a dressing room and eventually was incorporated into the action as part of the scenery.

Slapstick. See **comedy.**

Slice of life. See **naturalism.**

Social problem play. Same as **problem play.**

Social realism. Drama that reflects the difficulties of modern life; drama with a political content aimed at reforming society.

Sock. Derived from the Latin *soccus*, the term refers to a light slipper or sock worn by Roman comic actors.

Soliloquy. A speech in which an actor, usually alone onstage, utters his or her thoughts aloud, revealing personal feelings. Hamlet's "To be, or not to be" speech is an example.

Spectacle. In Aristotle's terms, the costumes and scenery in a drama—the elements that appeal to the eye.

Stage business. Minor physical action, including an actor's posture and facial expression, and the use of props, all of which make up a particular interpretation of a character.

Stasimon. In a Greek tragedy, a song sung by the chorus after it has taken its position. The chorus stands still and is not interrupted by dialogue during stasima (plural).

Stichomythia. Dialogue in which two speakers engage in a verbal duel in alternating lines.

Stock character. See **character.**

Strophe. The first of three parts of the verse **ode** sung by the Greek **chorus.** While singing the strophe, the chorus moves in a dancelike pattern from right to left. See also **antistrophe** and **epode.**

Subplot. See **plot.**

Subtext. A level of meaning implicit in or underlying the surface meaning of a text.

Surrealism. A literary movement flourishing in France during the early twentieth century that valued the unwilled expression of the unconscious (usually as revealed in dreams) over a rendering of "reality" structured by the conscious mind.

Suspense. The sense of tension aroused by an audience's uncertainty about the resolution of dramatic conflicts.

Suspension of disbelief. An audience's willingness to accept the world of the drama as reality during the course of a play.

Symbolism. A literary device in which an object, event, or action is used to suggest a meaning beyond its literal meaning. The lantern in *The Rising of the Moon* has a symbolic function.

Theater. The building in which a play is performed. Also used to refer to drama as an art form.

Theater in the round. The presentation of a play on an **arena stage** surrounded by the audience.

Theater of the absurd. A type of twentieth-century drama presenting the human condition as meaningless, absurd, and illogical. An example of the genre is Samuel Beckett's *Happy Days.*

Theater of cruelty. A type of drama created by Antonin Artaud in the 1930s that uses shock techniques to expose the audience's primitive obsessions with cruelty and sexuality. The purpose was to overwhelm spectators' rational minds, leading them to understand and even participate in the cycle of cruelty and ritual purgation dramatized in the performance.

Theme. Main idea or general topic of a play, not always easy to determine. Some plays have several topics that develop simultaneously.

Three unities. Aristotle noted that a play's action usually occurs in one day or a little more and that the plot should reveal clearly ordered actions and incidents moving toward the plot's resolution. Later scholars and critics, especially those in the neoclassical tradition, interpreted Aristotle's ideas as rules (unity of time and unity of action) and added a third, unity of place (a play's action should occur in a single locale).

Thrust stage. A stage extending beyond the **proscenium arch**, usually surrounded on three sides by the audience.

Tiring house. From "attiring house," the backstage space in Elizabethan public theaters used for storage and as a dressing room. The term also refers to the changing space beneath the medieval pageant wagon.

Total theater. A concept of the theater as an experience synthesizing all the expressive arts, including music, dance, lighting, and so on.

Tragedy. Serious drama in which a **protagonist**, traditionally of noble position, suffers a series of unhappy events culminating in a **catastrophe** such as death or spiritual breakdown. Shakespeare's *Hamlet*, which ends with the prince's death, is an example of Elizabethan tragedy.

Tragicomedy. A play that combines elements of tragedy and comedy. Chekhov's *The Cherry Orchard* is an example. Tragicomedies often include a serious plot in which the expected tragic **catastrophe** is replaced by a happy ending.

Trope. Interpolation into or expansion of an existing medieval liturgical text. These expansions, such as the *Quem Quaeritis* trope, gave rise to **liturgical drama.**

Type character. See **character.**

Underplot. See **plot.**

Unity. The sense that the events of a play and the actions of the characters follow one another naturally to form one complete action. Unity is present when characters' behavior seems **motivated** and the work is perceived to be a connected artistic whole. See also **three unities.**

Verfremdungseffekt. German term coined by Bertolt Brecht to mean "alienation." See also **alienation effect.**

Verisimilitude. The degree to which a dramatic representation approximates an appearance of reality.

Well-made play. Drama that relies for effect on the suspense generated by its logical, cleverly constructed plot rather than on characterization. Plots often involve a withheld secret, a battle of wits between hero and villain, and a resolution in which the secret is revealed and the **protagonist** saved. The plays of Eugène Scribe (1791–1861) have defined the type.

Acknowledgments
(continued from p. iv)

Text Credits

Greek Drama

Agamemnon from *The Oresteia by Aeschylus: A New Translation for the State,* by David Greene and Wendy Doniger O'Flaherty. Copyright © 1989 by The University of Chicago. Reprinted by permission of The University of Chicago Press.

"*Oresteia:* Trilogy Preserved" from *Aeschylus* by Lois S. Spatz. Copyright © 1982, a part of Cengage Learning, Inc. Reproduced by permission.

The Oedipus Rex of Sophocles: An English Version by Dudley Fitts and Robert Fitzgerald, copyright 1949 by Harcourt, Inc., and renewed 1977 by Cornelia Fitts and Robert Fitzgerald. Reprinted by permission of the publisher. CAUTION: All rights, including professional, amateur, motion picture, recitation, lecturing, performance, public reading, radio broadcasting, and television are strictly reserved. Inquiries on all rights should be addressed to Harcourt, Inc., Permissions Department, Orlando, FL 32887-67777.

"Poetics: Comedy and Epic and Tragedy" by Aristotle, from *Poetics,* translated by Gerald F. Else. Copyright © 1967. Reprinted by permission of The University of Michigan Press.

Excerpt from "The Structural Study of Myth" by Claude Lévi-Strauss. Reprinted from *The Bibliographical and Special Series* of the American Folklore Society, Vol. 5 (1955). Copyright © 1955 by Indiana University Press.

The Antigone of Sophocles: An English Version by Dudley Fitts and Robert Fitzgerald, copyright 1939 by Harcourt, Inc., and renewed 1967 by Dudley Fitts and Robert Fitzgerald. Reprinted by permission of the publisher. CAUTION: All rights, including professional, amateur, motion picture, recitation, lecturing, performance, public reading, radio broadcasting, and television are strictly reserved. Inquiries on all rights should be addressed to Harcourt, Inc., Permissions Department, Orlando, FL 32887-67777.

"Emotion and Meaning in Greek Tragedy," excerpt from *Greek Tragedy in Action* by Oliver Taplin (Routledge). Reprinted by permission of International Thompson Publishing Services.

Excerpt from *Antigone* by Jean Anouilh, adapted and translated by Lewis Galantière. Copyright 1946 by Random House, Inc., and renewed 1974 by Lewis Galantière. Reprinted by permission of Random House, Inc.

Medea by Euripedes, translated by Paul Roche. Copyright © 1974 by Paul Roche from *Three Plays of Euripides: Alcestis, Medea, The Bacchae,* translated by Paul Roche. Used by permission of W. W. Norton & Company, Inc.

"A '*Medea*' for the World Today." Review of *Medea* by Ben Brantley. From *The New York Times,* October 4, 2002. Copyright © 2002 by The New York Times Company. Used by permission and protected by the Copyright Laws of the United States. The printing, copying, redistribution, or retransmission of the Material without express written permission is prohibited.

Lysistrata: An English Version from *Aristophanes: Four Comedies* by Dudley Fitts, copyright 1954 by Harcourt, Inc. and renewed 1982 by Cornelia Fitts, Daniel H. Fitts and Deborah W. Fitts. Reprinted by permission of the publisher. CAUTION: Professionals and amateurs are hereby warned that all titles included in this volume, being fully protected under the copyright laws of the United States of America, Canada, the British Empire and all other countries which are signatories to the Universal Copyright Convention and the International Copyright Union, are subject to royalty. All rights, including professional, amateur, motion picture, recitation, lecturing, public reading, radio broadcasting, and television and the rights of translation into foreign languages are strictly reserved. Inquiries on professional rights should be addressed to Lucy Kroll Agency, 390 West End Avenue, New York, NY 10024. Inquiries on all other rights should be addressed to Harcourt Brace and Company, Orlando, Permissions Department, Florida 32887-6777.

Roman Drama

Excerpt from *The Twin Menaechmi* (Act III) from *Six Plays of Plautus* by Plautus, translated by Lionel Casson. Translation copyright © 1963 by Lionel Casson. Reprinted by permission of Doubleday, a division of Random House, Inc.

Excerpt from *The Brothers* from *The Mother-In-Law* by Terence from *Comedies of Terence,* translated by Robert Graves. Reprinted by permission of Carcanet Press Limited on behalf of The Trustees of the Robert Graves Copyright Trust.

Excerpt from *Thyestes* by Seneca from *The Complete Roman Drama* by George E. Duckworth. Translated by Ella Isabel Harris. Copyright 1942 and renewed 1970 by Random House, Inc. Reprinted by permission of Random House, Inc.

Medieval Drama

Dulcitius by Hrotsvitha. From "Dulcitius: The Martyrdom of the Holy Virgins Agape, Chionia, and Hirena." In *The Plays of Hrosvit of Gandersheim,* Vol. 51, Series B, translated by Kathrina M. Wilson. Copyright © 1989. Reprinted by permission of the translator.

"Re-viewing Hrotsvit" excerpted from "Re-viewing Hrotsvit" by Sue Ellen Case. *Theatre Journal* 35 (December 1983). © The Johns Hopkins University Press. Reprinted by permission of The Johns Hopkins University Press.

Everyman and *The Second Shepherd's Pageant* from *Everyman and Medieval Miracle Plays* edited by A. C. Cawley, originally published by J. M. Dent, London in *Everyman and Medieval Miracle Plays,* 1956, reprinted by permission of Everyman's Library, an imprint of Alfred A. Knopf.

Renaissance Drama

Doctor Faustus by Christopher Marlowe from *Doctor Faustus, Text and Major Criticism,* edited with notes by Irving Ribner. Copyright © 1985 by Irving Ribner. Reprinted by permission of Clifford N. Ribner and Jonathan P. Ribner.

Notes to *A Midsummer Night's Dream,* and *Hamlet,* by William Shakespeare from *The Complete Works of Shakespeare,* 4th edition, by David Bevington. Copyright © 1997 by Addision-Wesley Educational Publishers, Inc. Reprinted by permission of Pearson Education, Inc.

"On A Midsummer Night's Dream" by Linda Bamber. Reprinted from *Comic Women, Tragic Men: A Study of Gender and Genre in Shakespeare* by Linda Bamber with the permission of the publishers, Stanford University Press. Copyright © 1982 by the Board of Trustees of the Leland Stanford Junior University.

"The Play Is the Message . . ." by Peter Brook from *The Shifting Point: Theatre, Film, Opera* by Peter Brook. Copyright © 1987 by Peter Brook. Reprinted by permission of HarperCollins Publishers, Inc.

Review of *A Midsummer Night's Dream* by Clive Barnes. "A Magical 'Midsummer Night's Dream'" from *The New York Times,* August 28, 1970. Copyright © 1970 by The New York Times Company. Reprinted by permission.

"Hamlet and His Problems" from "Hamlet" in *Selected Essays* by T. S. Eliot, copyright 1950 by Harcourt Brace and Company, renewed © 1978 by Esme Valerie Eliot. Reprinted by permission of Harcourt, Inc., and Faber and Faber Ltd.

"Notes & Commentary" from *Othello,* by William Shakespeare, edited by Gerald Eades Bentley, copyright © 1958, 1970 by Penguin Books, © 2000 Penguin Putnam Inc. Used by permission of Penguin, a division of Penguin Group (USA) Inc.

"Macready's Othello" from *Othello: A Contextual History* by Virginia Mason Vaughan. Copyright © 1994. Reprinted by permission of Cambridge University Press.

The Masque of Blackness by Ben Jonson from *Ben Jonson: The Complete Masques,* edited by Stephen Orgel. Copyright © 1969 by Yale University. Reprinted by permission of Yale University Press.

"Africa in English Masque and Pageantry" by Eldred Jones from *Othello's Countrymen* by Eldred Jones. Copyright © 1965. Reprinted by permission of the author.

Life Is a Dream by Pedro Calderón de la Barca. Copyright © 2008 by University Press of Colorado. Reproduced by permission of University Press of Colorado in the format Textbook via Copyright Clearance Center.

Review of José Rivera's Production of *Sueño* by Ed Morales from *American Theatre* 15:5 (May/June 1998). Reprinted by permission of Theatre Communications Group.

Late Seventeenth- and Eighteenth-Century Drama

Nineteenth-Century Drama through the Turn of the Twentieth Century

Drama in the Early and Mid-Twentieth Century

"Laurette Taylor in *The Glass Menagerie*," excerpt from *The Kindness of Strangers: The Life of Tennessee Williams* by Donald Spoto. Copyright © 1985 by Donald Spoto. Reprinted by permission of the Elaine Markson Literary Agency.

"Problems in *The Glass Menagerie*," by Benjamin Nelson. From *Tennessee Williams: The Man and His Work* by Benjamin Nelson. Copyright © 1961. Reprinted by permission of the author.

Death of a Salesman by Arthur Miller. Copyright 1949, renewed © 1977 by Arthur Miller. All rights reserved. Used by permission of Viking Penguin, a division of Penguin Group (USA), Inc.

"In Memoriam" by Arthur Miller from *The New Yorker*, December 25, 1995 and January 1, 1996. Copyright © 1995, 1996 by Arthur Miller. Reprinted with permission of The Wylie Agency, Inc.

"Tragedy and the Common Man," excerpt from *The Theatre Essays of Arthur Miller*, edited by Robert A. Martin. Copyright 1949, renewed 1977 by Arthur Miller. Reprinted by permission of Viking Penguin, a division of Penguin Group (USA) Inc.

"Designing of a Play: *Death of a Salesman*." Excerpts from *Designing for the Theatre: A Memoir and a Portfolio* by Jo Mielziner. All rights reserved, reprinted by permission of Scribner, an imprint of Simon and Schuster Adult Publishing Group. Copyright © 1965 by Jo Mielziner.

Excerpts from *Death of a Salesman: The Design Process*. "The Design Process" and "Racial Consciousness in Casting *Death of a Salesman*" by Brenda Murphy. Copyright © 1995. Reprinted by permission of Cambridge University Press.

"The American Theater" copyright 1954 by Arthur Miller from *The Theater Essays of Arthur Miller* by Arthur Miller, edited by Robert A. Martin. Used by permission of Viking Penguin, a division of Penguin Group (USA) Inc.

"Directing *Death of a Salesman*." Excerpt from *Elia Kazan: A Life* by Elia Kazan. Copyright ©1988 by Elia Kazan. Reprinted with the permission of Alfred A. Knopf, a division of Random House, Inc.

"Memorable Willy" from *Arthur Miller* by June Schlueter and James K. Flanagan. Copyright © 1987 by June Schlueter and James K. Flanagan. Reprinted by permission.

Death of a Salesman in Taipei by Catherine Diamond from *Theatre Review* 45 (1993). Copyright © 1993 by Catherine Diamond.

The Bald Soprano by Eugene Ionesco from *The Bald Soprano and Other Plays* by Eugene Ionesco, translated by Donald M. Allen. Copyright © 1958 by Grove Press Inc. Used by permission of Grove/Atlantic, Inc.

"The Tragedy of Language: How an English Primer Became My First Play," by Eugene Ionesco, translated by Jack Undanle from *The Tulane Drama Review*, Volume 4, Number 3 (March 1960). Reprinted by permission of the MIT Press.

Krapp's Last Tape by Samuel Beckett from *Krapp's Last Tape and Other Dramatic Pieces* by Samuel Beckett. Copyright © 1957 by Samuel Beckett. Copyright © 1958, 1959, 1960 by Grove Press Inc. Used by permission of Grove/Atlantic, Inc.

Excerpt from "The Theatre of the Absurd" by Martin Esslin. Reprinted by permission of the author.

Excerpt from *Just Play: Beckett's Theater* by Ruby Cohn. Copyright © 1980 by Princeton University Press. Reprinted by permission of Princeton University Press.

A Raisin in the Sun by Lorraine Hansberry. Copyright © 1958 by Robert Nemiroff, as an unpublished work. Copyright © 1959, 1966, 1984 by Robert Nemiroff. Reprinted by permission of Random House, Inc.

"Dream Deferred" ("Harlem") by Langston Hughes from *The Panther and the Lash* by Langston Hughes. Copyright 1951 by Langston Hughes. Reprinted by permission of Alfred A. Knopf, a division of Random House, Inc.

The Strong Breed by Wole Soyinka. From *Wole Soyinka: Collected Plays I*. Copyright © 1973 by Oxford University Press. Reprinted by permission of Oxford University Press.

"Interview with Wole Soyinka," excerpt from *African Writers Talking: A Collection of Radio Interviews*, edited by Cosmo Pieterse and Dennis Duerden (New York: Holmes & Meier, 1972). Copyright © 1972 by Cosmo Pieterse and Dennis Duerden. Reprinted by permission of the publisher.

Contemporary Drama

Zoot Suit is reprinted by permission from the publisher of *Zoot Suit and Other Plays*. Copyright © 1992 by Arte Público Press — University of Houston.

The Homecoming by Harold Pinter. Copyright © 1965, 1966 by H. Pinter Ltd. Used by permission of Grove/Atlantic, Inc.

"*The Homecoming*" from *Understanding Harold Pinter* by Ronald Knowles. Copyright © 1995. Reprinted by permission of the University of South Carolina Press.

The Zoo Story by Edward Albee. Copyright © 1959, renewed 1987 by Edward Albee. Reprinted by permission of William Morris Agency on behalf of the Author. "The Zoo Story" Copyright © 1959, renewed 1987 by Edward Albee. Reprinted by permission of William Morris Agency, LLC on behalf of the Author. CAUTION: Professionals and amateurs are hereby warned that "The Zoo Story" is subject to royalty. It is fully protected under the copyright laws of the United States of America and of all countries covered by the International Copyright Union (including the Dominion of Canada and the rest of the British Commonwealth), the Berne Convention, the Pan American Copyright Convention and the Universal Copyright Convention as well as all countries with which the United States has reciprocal copyright relations. All rights, including professional/amateur stage rights, motion picture, recitation, lecturing, public reading, radio broadcasting, television, video or sound recording, all other forms of mechanical or electronic reproduction, such as CD-ROM, CD-I, information storage and retrieval systems and photocopying, and the rights of translation into foreign languages, are strictly reserved. Particular emphasis is laid upon the matter of readings, permission for which must be secured from the Author's agent in writing. Inquiries concerning rights should be addressed to: William Morris Agency, LLC, 1325 Avenue of the Americas, New York, NY 10019, Attn: Eric Lupfer.

"Tragic Vision in *The Zoo Story*" by Robert B. Bennett from *Modern Drama* 20.1 (March 1977), the Graduate Centre for the Study of Drama at the University of Toronto. Copyright © 1977. Reprinted by permission of the publisher, The University of Toronto Press.

Buried Child copyright © 1979 by Sam Shepard from *Seven Plays* by Sam Shepard. Used by permission of Bantam Books, a division of Random House, Inc.

Faith Healer by Brian Friel from *Selected Plays* by Brian Friel. Copyright © 1986. Reprinted by permission of The Catholic University of America Press.

"*MASTER HAROLD*" . . . *and the boys* by Athol Fugard. Copyright © 1982 by Athol Fugard. Reprinted by permission of Alfred A. Knopf, a division of Random House, Inc.

"Interview with Athol Fugard" by Heinrich von Staden from *Theater* (Yale) Vol. 14, No. 1, Winter 1982. Reprinted by permission of the author.

Excerpt from *Notebooks 1960–1977* by Athol Fugard. Copyright © 1983 by Athol Fugard. Reprinted by permission of Alfred A. Knopf, a division of Random House, Inc.

Glengarry Glen Ross by David Mamet. Copyright © 1982, 1983 by David Mamet. Used by permission of Grove/Atlantic, Inc.

"Glengarry Glen Ross" excerpt from *David Mamet: Language as Dramatic Action*. Copyright © 1990 by Anna Dean. Reprinted with the permission of Fairleigh Dickinson University Press/Associated University Presses.

Ma Rainey's Black Bottom by August Wilson, copyright © 1985 by August Wilson. Used by permission of Dutton Signet, a division of Penguin Group (USA) Inc.

"The Development of *Ma Rainey's Black Bottom*" from *I Ain't Sorry for Nothin' I Done* by Joan Herrington. Copyright © 1998. Reprinted by permission of Applause Theatre & Cinema Books, LLC, and Joan Herrington.

Fences by August Wilson. Copyright © 1986 August Wilson. Used by permission of Dutton Signet, a division of Penguin Group (USA) Inc.

"The Development of *Fences*" from *I Ain't Sorry for Nothin' I Done* by Joan Herrington. Copyright © 1998. Reprinted by permission of Applause Theatre & Cinema Books, LLC, and Joan Herrington.

"August Wilson" by Harry J. Elam, Jr. from *A Companion to Twentieth Century Drama*, edited by David Krasner. Copyright © 2005. Reprinted by permission of Harry J. Elam, Jr.

"August Wilson and the Four B's: Influences" by Mark William Rocha, from *August Wilson: A Casebook*, edited by Marilyn Elkins. © 1994. Garland Publishing. Reprinted by permission.

"Ka'Ba" by Amiri Baraka from *The Amiri Baraka Reader*. Copyright © 1999. Thunder's Mouth Press. Reprinted by permission of Perseus Book Group.

"An Interview with August Wilson on Playwriting" by Elisabeth J. Heard from *African American Review*, Volume 35, Number 1. Copyright © 2001 Elisabeth J. Heard. Reprinted by permission of Elisabeth J. Heard.

"August Wilson: Conclusions" from Wolfe, Peter. *United States Authors Series—August Wilson*. © 1999 Gale, a part of Cengage Learning, Inc. Reproduced by permission. www.cengage.com/permissions.

From *Angels in America, Part I: Millennium Approaches* by Tony Kushner. Copyright © 1992–1993 by Tony Kushner. Published by Theatre Communications Group. Used by permission of Theatre Communications Group.

"Interview with Tony Kushner" by Andrea Bernstein reprinted with permission from *Mother Jones* magazine, © 1995, Foundation for National Progress.

How I Learned to Drive by Paula Vogel from *The Mammary Plays*. Copyright © 1998 by Paula Vogel. Used by permission of Theatre Communications Group.

"Paula Vogel" by Christopher Bigsby from *Contemporary American Playwrights* by Christopher Bigsby. Copyright © 1999 by Christopher Bigsby. Reprinted by permission of Cambridge University Press.

"Paula Vogel" by David Savran from *The Playwright's Voice: American Dramatists on Memory, Writing and the Politics of Culture* by David Savran. Copyright © 1999 by David Savran. Used by permission of Theatre Communications Group.

Far Away by Caryl Churchill. Copyright © 2000 Caryl Churchill Ltd. Reprinted by permission of Nick Hern Books: www.nickhernbooks. co.uk; published in the USA by Theatre Communications Group: www.tcg.org.

The Laramie Project by Moisés Kaufman and The Members of Tectonic Theater Project, copyright © 2001 by Moisés Kaufman. Used by permission of Vintage Books, a division of Random House, Inc.

Intimate Apparel by Lynn Nottage. Copyright © 2003, 2006 by Lynn Nottage. Published by Theatre Communications Group. Used by permission of Theatre Communications Group.

I Am My Own Wife by Doug Wright. Copyright © 2004 by Doug Wright. Reprinted by permission of Faber and Faber, Inc., an affiliate of Farrar, Straus and Giroux, LLC.

"Portrait of an Enigma" *Introduction* to *I Am My Own Wife* by Doug Wright. Copyright © 2004 by Doug Wright. Reprinted by permission of Faber and Faber, Inc., an affiliate of Farrar, Straus and Giroux, LLC.

Shining City by Conor McPherson. Copyright © 2004 Conor McPherson. Reprinted by permission of Nick Hern Books; www.nickhernbooks.co.uk; published in the USA by Theatre Communications Group: www.tcg.org.

The Clean House by Sarah Ruhl from *The Clean House and Other Plays* by Sarah Ruhl. Copyright © 2003, 2006 by Sarah Ruhl. Published by Theatre Communications Group. Used by permission of Theatre Communications Group.

Selections from *365 Days/365 Plays* by Suzan-Lori Parks. *365 Days/365 Plays* by Suzan-Lori Parks. Copyright © 2006 by Suzan-Lori Parks. Published by Theatre Communications Group. Used by permission of Theatre Communications Group.

Image Credits

Greek Drama

Page 32, Figure 1: Theater at Epidaurus. © Michael Nicholson/Corbis. Page 33, Figure 2: Hellenistic theatre at Eretria. Richard and Helen Leacroft, *Theatre and Playhouse*, Methuen Publishing Ltd. Page 34, Figure 3: Roman rendering of Greek masks. Scala/Art Resource NY. Page 56: © Donald Cooper/PhotoStage. Page 57: © Richard Feldman. Page 70: © Gianni Dagli Orti/CORBIS. Page 77: © Henry S. Kranzler. Page 78 (top): © Henry S. Kranzler. Page 78 (bottom): Museum fur Gestaltung, Zurich. Page 81: © Dr. Jaromir Svobodao. Page 89: Michael Paul/Act One, Too Ltd. Page 111: © Martha Swope. Page 113: © Martha Swope. Page 117 (top): © Martha Swope. Page 117 (bottom): © Martha Swope. Page 118: Photo by Ron Howard/SCR. Page 152: © Donald Cooper/PhotoStage. Page 159: © 2003 Stephanie Berger. All Rights Reserved. Page 180 (top): © Richard Feldman. Page 180 (bottom): © Donald Cooper/PhotoStage. Page 181: Photo by Guy Delahave.

Roman Drama

Page 190, Figure 4: Roman theater at Sabratha, Libya. © Roger Wood/CORBIS. Page 191, Figure 5: Theater of Marcellus. Bieber, Margarete; *History of the Greek and Roman Theatre* © 1939 Princeton University Press, 1961 edition, 1989 renewed PUP. Reprinted by permission of Princeton University Press. Page 192, Figure 6: Roman bas relief. Scala/Art Resource, NY.

Medieval Drama

Page 210, Figure 7: Pageant wagon. From *Early English Stages 1300 to 1660* by Glylnne William Gladstone Wickam. Copyright © 2008 Columbia University Press. Reprinted with permission of the publisher. Page 211, Figure 8: *Procession of the Ommeganck at Brussels in 1615* (oil), by Denis Van Alsloot. Copyright © V&A Images/Victoria and Albert Museum—All rights reserved. Page 228 (top): Photograph Joe Cocks Studio. Courtesy of the Shakespearean Birthplace Trust. Page 228 (bottom): Photograph Joe Cocks Studio. Courtesy of the Shakespearean Birthplace Trust. Page 249: Act One, Too Ltd/Michael Paul.

Renaissance Drama

Page 254, Figure 9: Teatro Olimpico, Vicenza, Italy. Alinari/Art Resource. Page 255, Figure 10: Perspective setting by Puruzzi. Scala/Art Resource. Page 258, Figure 11: Conjectural reconstruction of Globe Theatre. By Permission of the Folger Shakespeare Library. Page 259, Figure 12: William Kempe as one of Shakespeare's Clowns. Public Domain. Page 278: © Donald Cooper/PhotoStage. Page 287: Photofest. Page 296: By Permission of the Folger Shakespeare Library. Page 308 (top): © Richard Feldman. Page 308 (bottom): Photofest. Page 309 (left): © Richard Feldman. Page 309 (right): © Richard Feldman. Page 318 © Martha Swope. Page 319: © Martha Swope. Page 324: © Osterreichisches Theatermuseum. Page 356: © Richard Feldman. Page 357: © Richard Feldman. Page 370 (top left): © Donald Cooper/PhotoStage. Page 370 (top right): © Donald Cooper/PhotoStage. Page 370 (bottom): Photofest. Page 371 (top): © Donald Cooper/PhotoStage. Page 371 (bottom): © Donald Cooper/PhotoStage. Page 375: Photofest. Page 415 (top): Angus McBean Photograph, Copyright © Harvard Theatre Collection. Page 415 (bottom): © T. Charles Erickson. Page 425: Photofest. Page 434 (top): Special Collections and University Archives, Rutgers University Libraries. Page 434 (bottom): Reproduced from the Collections of the Library of Congress. Page 451: © Carol Rosegg. Page 455: © Devonshire Collection, Chatsworth. Reproduced by the permission of the Trustees of the Chatsworth Settlement. Photo: Photographic Survey Courtauld Institute of Art. Page 470: © T. Charles Erickson. Page 471 (top): © T. Charles Erickson. Page 471 (bottom): Douglas Robertson.

Late Seventeenth- and Eighteenth-Century Drama

Page 499, Figure 13: Richard and Helen Leacroft, *Theatre and Playhouse*, Methuen Publishing Ltd. Page 502, Figure 14: The National Trust/The Bridgeman Art Library. Page 503, Figure 15: Walker Art Gallery/The Bridgeman Art Library. Page 524: Elliott Franks/Arena PAL. Page 532: AFP/Getty Images. Page 536: Sara Krulwich/The New York Times/Redux. Page 552: © Jonathan Slaff. Page 555: © Shakespeare Birthplace Trust. Page 599 (top): © Burstein Collection/CORBIS. Page 599 (bottom): © Reunion des Musses Nationaux/Art Resource, NY. Page 611: © Richard Feldman. Page 632: Photo by Tom Bloom. Courtesy of The Pearl Theatre. Page 641: Courtesy of The Guthrie Theater, Photo by Marty Nordstrum.

Nineteenth-Century Drama through the Turn of the Twentieth Century

Page 645, Figure 16: Photograph of Proscenium arch, Auditorium, Chicago, 1889. Chicago Historical Society, HB-31105C, photograph by Hedrich Blessing. Page 646, Figure 17: Diagram of the Theatre Royal, Drury Lane, 1812. Richard and Helen Leacroft, *Theatre and Playhouse*, Methuen Publishing Ltd. Page 647, Figure 18: Mr. Edward Forrest as Macbeth. Courtesy of the Folger Library. Page 647, Figure 19: Mr.